CHILTON'S
Auto Repair Manual

1972

DISCARD

Managing Editor
John Milton

Assistant Managing Editor
John Kelly

Senior Technical Editors
Peter Meyer
John Weise

Technical Editors

John Baxter	Frank Foster	Howard Kenig
Zane Binder	Kerry Freeman	Leo Mealey
Arthur Birney	Jon Jay	Carl Mogerman
Stephen Davis	James Johnson	Svante Mossberg
Joseph DeNuccio		William Wartman

CHILTON BOOK COMPANY

PHILADELPHIA   NEW YORK   LONDON

Copyright © Chilton Book Company 1972
Published in Philadelphia by Chilton Book Company and simultaneously in Ontario, Canada, by Thomas Nelson & Sons, Ltd.
ISBN: 0-8019-5646-3   Library of Congress Catalog Card No. 54-17274   Manufactured in the United States of America

Contents

Car Section

Unit Repair Section

Troubleshooting, Tune-up and Engine Rebuilding Section

Index

Buick

YEAR IDENTIFICATION

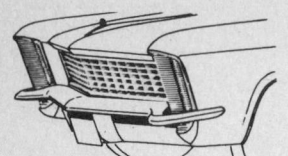

1965 Riviera

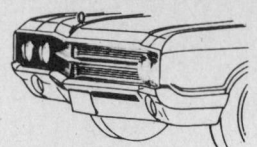

1965 Electra-Le Sabre

1965 Wildcat

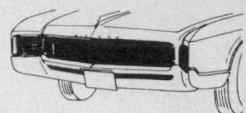

1966 Riviera

1966 Electra-Le Sabre

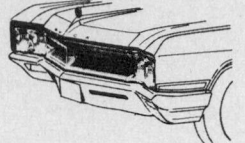

1966 Wildcat

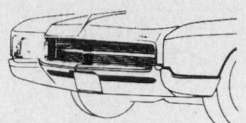

1967 Riviera

1967 Electra-Le Sabre

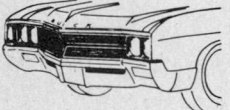

1967 Wildcat

1968-69 Riviera

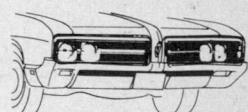

1968 Le Sabre

1968 Electra

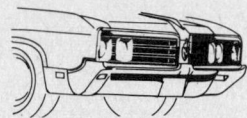

1968 Wildcat

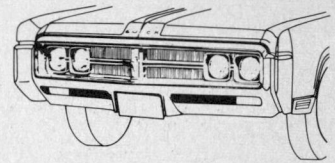

1969 Wildcat

1969 Le Sabre

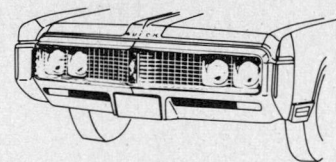

1969 Electra

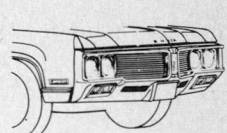

1970 Le Sabre

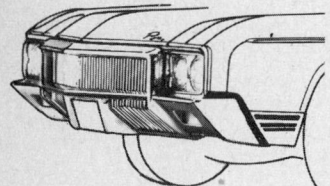

1970 Riviera

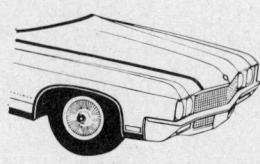

1971 Electra

1971 Riviera

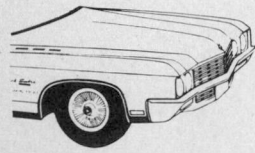

1971 Le Sabre

1971 Centurion

1972 Riviera

1972 Electra

FIRING ORDER

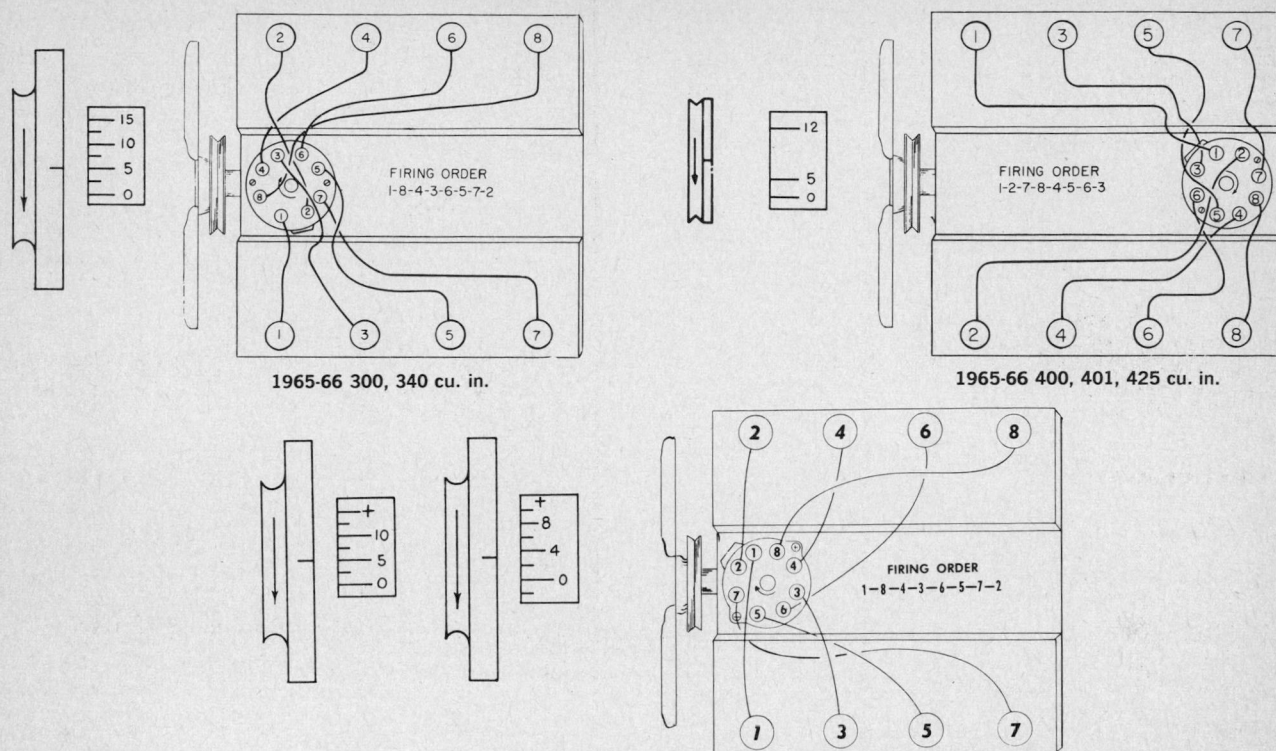

1965-66 300, 340 cu. in.

FIRING ORDER 1-8-4-3-6-5-7-2

1965-66 400, 401, 425 cu. in.

FIRING ORDER 1-2-7-8-4-5-6-3

1967-72 350, 400, 430, 455 cu. in. (Left timing mark 1967-69)

FIRING ORDER 1—8—4—3—6—5—7—2

CAR SERIAL NUMBER LOCATION AND ENGINE IDENTIFICATION

The car serial number is used for registration and other legal records. This number is unique to the individual car. The production code number identifies the type of engine and its production date. The Engine Identification Code chart can be used to determine the type of engine in the particular vehicle. The engine number also appears on the vehicle identification plate following model and series identification.

1965

The serial number identification plate is attached to the left front body hinge pillar.

The engine serial and production code numbers on the 401 and 425 cu. in. engines are on the top surface of the engine crankcase, just forward of the valve lifter cover. The production code number is on the left and the serial number is on the right.

On the 300 cu. in. engine, the serial number is on the left front face of the engine crankcase to the side of the distributor cap. The production code number is between the two middle branches of the right exhaust manifold.

1966

The serial number identification plate is attached to the left front body hinge pillar.

The engine serial and production code numbers on the 401 and 425 cu. in. engines are on the top surface of the crankcase, just forward of the valve lifter cover. The production code number is on the left and the serial number is on the right.

On the 300 and 340 cu. in. engines, the serial number is on the left front face of the engine crankcase to the side of the distributor cap. The production code number is between the two middle branches of the right exhaust manifold.

1967

The car serial number identification plate is attached to the left front body hinge pillar.

On the 300 and 340 cu. in. engines,

the serial number is on the left front face of the crankcase to the side of the distributor cap. The production code number is between the two middle branches of the right exhaust manifold.

On the 400 and 430 cu. in. engines, the production code number is between the two front branches of the right exhaust manifold, while the engine serial number is between the two rear branches.

1968

The serial number identification plate is attached to the left front body hinge pillar.

On the 350 cu. in. engine, the serial number is on the front of the left cylinder bank just below the cylinder

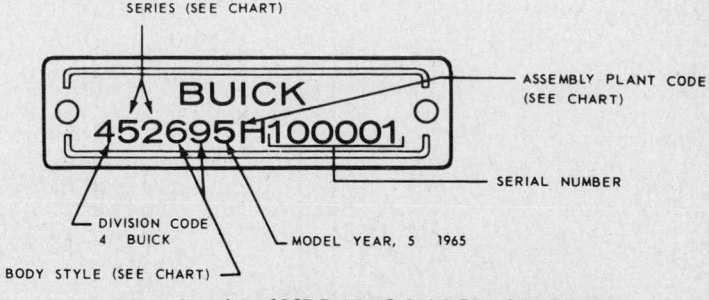

SERIES (SEE CHART)

BUICK
452695H100001

ASSEMBLY PLANT CODE (SEE CHART)

SERIAL NUMBER

DIVISION CODE 4 BUICK

MODEL YEAR, 5 1965

BODY STYLE (SEE CHART)

Serial number plate, 1965 Buick (© Buick Div., G.M. Corp.)

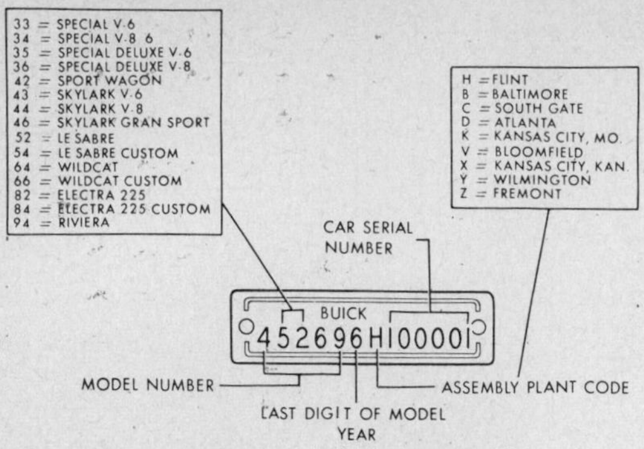

33 = SPECIAL V-6
34 = SPECIAL V-8 6
35 = SPECIAL DELUXE V-6
36 = SPECIAL DELUXE V-8
42 = SPORT WAGON
43 = SKYLARK V-6
44 = SKYLARK V-8
46 = SKYLARK GRAN SPORT
52 = LE SABRE
54 = LE SABRE CUSTOM
64 = WILDCAT
66 = WILDCAT CUSTOM
82 = ELECTRA 225
84 = ELECTRA 225 CUSTOM
94 = RIVIERA
H = FLINT
B = BALTIMORE
C = SOUTH GATE
D = ATLANTA
K = KANSAS CITY, MO.
V = BLOOMFIELD
X = KANSAS CITY, KAN.
Y = WILMINGTON
Z = FREMONT
CAR SERIAL NUMBER
BUICK
452696H100001
MODEL NUMBER
ASSEMBLY PLANT CODE
LAST DIGIT OF MODEL YEAR

Serial number plate, 1966 Buick
(© Buick Div., G.M. Corp.)

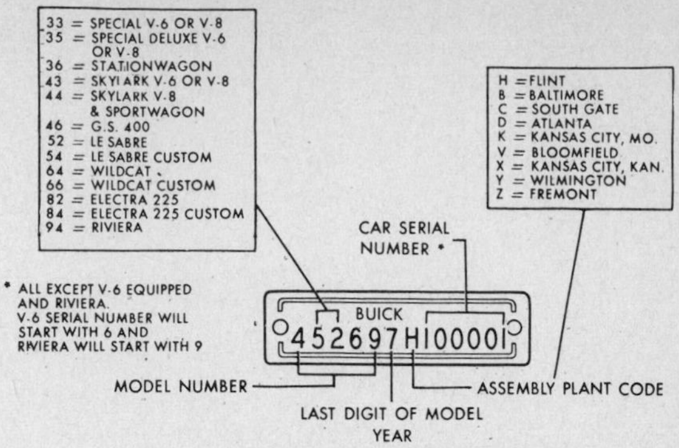

33 = SPECIAL V-6 OR V-8
35 = SPECIAL DELUXE V-6 OR V-8
36 = STATIONWAGON
43 = SKYLARK V-6 OR V-8
44 = SKYLARK V-8 & SPORTWAGON
46 = G.S. 400
52 = LE SABRE
54 = LE SABRE CUSTOM
64 = WILDCAT
66 = WILDCAT CUSTOM
82 = ELECTRA 225
84 = ELECTRA 225 CUSTOM
94 = RIVIERA
H = FLINT
B = BALTIMORE
C = SOUTH GATE
D = ATLANTA
K = KANSAS CITY, MO.
V = BLOOMFIELD
X = KANSAS CITY, KAN.
Y = WILMINGTON
Z = FREMONT
CAR SERIAL NUMBER *
* ALL EXCEPT V-6 EQUIPPED AND RIVIERA. V-6 SERIAL NUMBER WILL START WITH 6 AND RIVIERA WILL START WITH 9
BUICK
452697H100001
MODEL NUMBER
ASSEMBLY PLANT CODE
LAST DIGIT OF MODEL YEAR

Serial number plate, 1967 Buick
(© Buick Div., G.M. Corp.)

33 = SPECIAL DELUXE L-6
34 = SPECIAL DELUXE V-8 & G.S. 350 V-8
35 = SKYLARK L-6
44 = SKYLARK CUSTOM V-8
46 = G.S. 400
48 = SPORTWAGON WOOD GRAIN
52 = LE SABRE
54 = LE SABRE CUSTOM
64 = WILDCAT
66 = WILDCAT CUSTOM
82 = ELECTRA 225
84 = ELECTRA 225 CUSTOM
94 = RIVIERA
H = FLINT
B = BALTIMORE
C = SOUTH GATE
D = ATLANTA
K = KANSAS CITY, MO.
V = BLOOMFIELD
X = KANSAS CITY, KAN.
Y = WILMINGTON
Z = FREMONT
I = OSHAWA, CANADA
CAR SERIAL NUMBER *
* ALL EXCEPT L-6 EQUIPPED AND RIVIERA. L-6 SERIAL NUMBER WILL START WITH 6 AND RIVIERA WILL START WITH 9
BUICK
452698H100001
MODEL NUMBER
ASSEMBLY PLANT CODE
LAST DIGIT OF MODEL YEAR

Serial number plate, 1968 Buick
(© Buick Div., G.M. Corp.)

33 = SPECIAL DELUXE L-6
34 = SPECIAL DELUXE V-8 & G.S-350 V-8
35 = SKYLARK L-6
44 = SKYLARK CUSTOM SPORTWAGON V 8
46 = G.S. 400
52 = LE SABRE
54 = LE SABRE CUSTOM
64 = WILDCAT
66 = WILDCAT CUSTOM
82 = ELECTRA 225
84 = ELECTRA 225 CUSTOM
94 = RIVIERA
H = FLINT
B = BALTIMORE
C = SOUTH GATE
D = ATLANTA
K = KANSAS CITY, MO
V = BLOOMFIELD
X = KANSAS CITY, KAN
Y = WILMINGTON
Z = FREMONT
I = OSHAWA, CANADA
CAR SERIAL NUMBER *
* ALL EXCEPT L-6 EQUIPPED AND RIVIERA. L-6 SERIAL NUMBER WILL START WITH 6 AND RIVIERA WILL START WITH 9
BUICK
452699H100001
MODEL NUMBER
ASSEMBLY PLANT CODE
LAST DIGIT OF MODEL YEAR

Serial number plate, 1969 Buick
(© Buick Div., G.M. Corp.)

33 = SKYLARK L6
34 = SPORTWAGON V-8 & GS V-8
35 = SKYLARK 350
44 = SKYLARK CUSTOM
46 = GS 455
52 = LESABRE
54 = LESABRE CUSTOM
64 = LESABRE 455
60 = ESTATE WAGON
66 = WILDCAT CUSTOM
82 = ELECTRA 225
84 = ELECTRA 225 CUSTOM
94 = RIVIERA
C = SOUTHGATE
D = DORA VILLE
G = FRAMINGHAM
H = FLINT
K = LEEDS, MO.
X = FAIRFAX, KAN.
Y = WILMINGTON
Z = FREMONT
CAR SERIAL NUMBER *
* ALL EXCEPT L-6 EQUIPPED AND RIVIERA. L-6 SERIAL NUMBER WILL START WITH 6 AND RIVIERA WILL START WITH 9
BUICK
452690H100001
MODEL NUMBER
ASSEMBLY PLANT CODE
LAST DIGIT OF MODEL YEAR

Serial number plate, 1970 Buick
(© Buick Div., G.M. Corp.)

33 - SKYLARK L6
34 - SPORTWAGON V-8 & GS V-8
44 - SKYLARK CUSTOM
52 - LESABRE
54 - LESABRE CUSTOM
60 - ESTATE WAGON
66 - CENTURION
82 - ELECTRA 225
84 - ELECTRA 225 CUSTOM
94 - RIVIERA
C - SOUTHGATE
G - FRAMINGHAM
H - FLINT
X - FAIRFAX, KAN.
Y - WILMINGTON
Z - FREMONT
CAR SERIAL NUMBER*
*ALL EXCEPT L-6 EQUIPPED LE SABRE, CENTURION AND RIVIERA.
L-6 SERIAL NUMBER WILL START WITH 6, FLINT-BUILT LE SABRES AND CENTURIONS WILL START WITH 4, AND RIVIERA WILL START WITH 9
BUICK
452691H100001
MODEL NUMBER
ASSEMBLY PLANT CODE
LAST DIGIT OF MODEL YEAR

Serial number plate, 1971 Buick
(© Buick Div., G.M. Corp.)

head. The production code number is between the left exhaust manifold and the two front spark plugs on the left bank.

On the 400 and 430 cu. in. engines, the serial number is between the two front spark plugs and the exhaust manifold on the left side. The production code number is between the two rear spark plugs and the exhaust manifold, also on the left side.

1969

The serial number identification plate is attached to the top of the instrument panel on the left side.

On the 350 cu. in. engine, the serial number is on the front of the left cylinder bank just below the cylinder head. The production code number is between the left exhaust manifold and the two front spark plugs on the left bank.

On the 400 and 430 cu. in. engines, the serial number is between the two front spark plugs and the exhaust manifold on the left side. The production code number is between the two rear spark plugs and the exhaust manifold, also on the left side.

1970-72

The serial number identification plate is attached to the top of the

RIGHT SIDE
ENGINE SERIAL NUMBER
F 12 07 2A
9H600001
ENGINE UNIT NUMBER
F 12 07 SA
TRANSMISSION OR OPTION USAGE
DAY
MONTH
PLANT

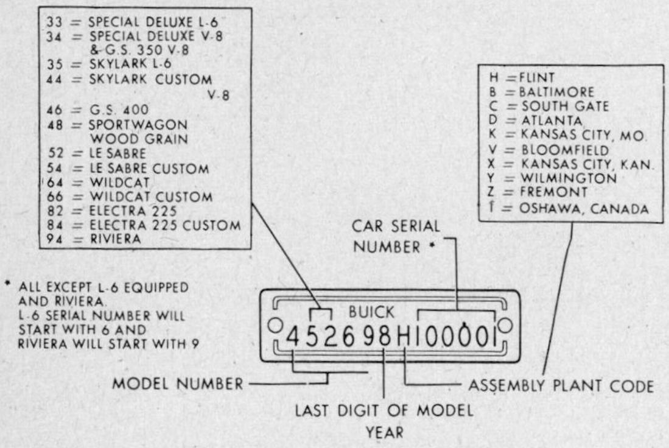

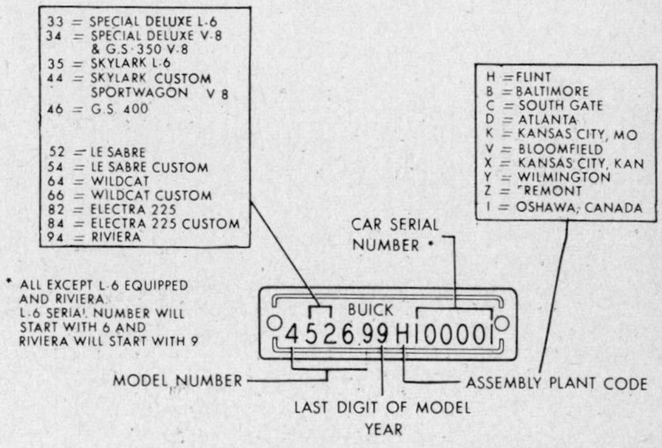

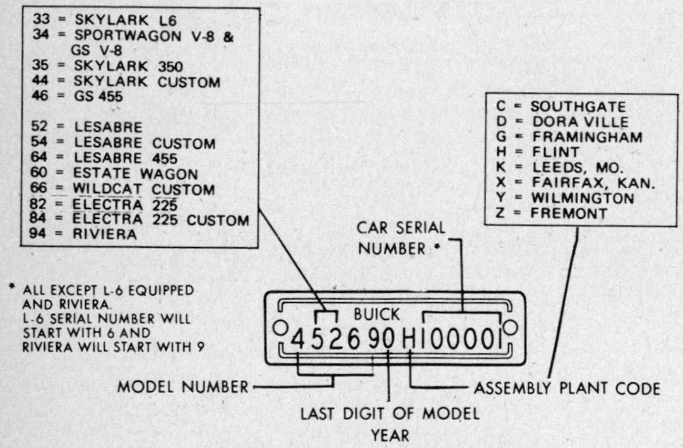

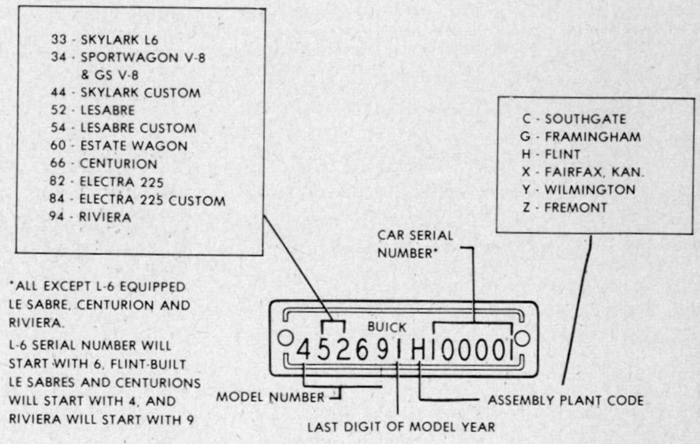

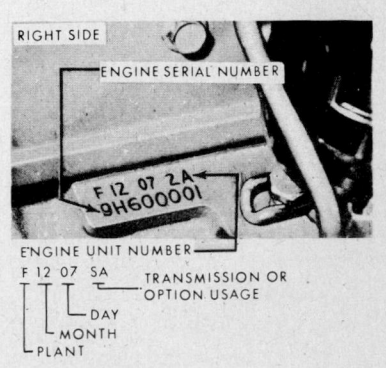

Production code number, typical
(© Buick Div., G.M. Corp.)

instrument panel on the left side.

On the 350 cu. in. engine, the serial number is on the front of the left cylinder bank just below the cylinder head. The production code number is between the left exhaust manifold and the two front spark plugs on the left bank.

On the 455 cu. in. engine, the serial number is between the two front spark plugs and the exhaust manifold on the left side. The production code number is between the two rear spark plugs and the exhaust manifold, also on the left side.

Engine numbers, 1968-72 350 cu. in. (© Buick Div., G.M. Corp.)

Engine numbers, 1967-72 400, 430, and 455 cu. in. (© Buick Div., G.M. Corp.)

Engine numbers, 1965-66 401 and 425 cu. in. (© Buick Div., G.M. Corp.)

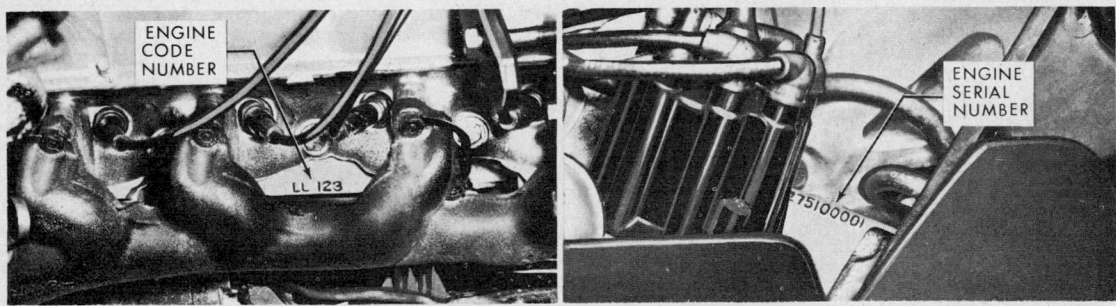

Engine numbers, 1965-67 300 and 340 cu. in. (© Buick Div., G.M. Corp.)

ENGINE IDENTIFICATION CODE

No. Cyls.	Cu. In. Displ.	Type	YEAR AND CODE						
			1965	1966	1967	1968	1969	1970	1971
8	300	Std. Eng.	LI	ML	NL				
8	300	4 Bbl.	LP						
8	401	4 Bbl.	LT						
8	401	Riviera	LW						
8	425	2-4 Bbl.	LX						
8	340	2 Bbl.		MA	NA				
8	340	4 Bbl.		MB	NB				
8	425	4 Bbl.		MW					
8	401	4 Bbl.		MR, MT					
8	430	4 Bbl.			ND, MD	PD	RD		
8	350	2 Bbl.				PO	RO	SO	TC
8	350	4 Bbl.				PP	RP	SB, SP	TD
8	400	4 Bbl.			NR	PR	RR		
8	455	4 Bbl.						SP, SS, SF	TA, TR

CAPACITIES

YEAR	MODEL	ENGINE CRANKCASE ADD 1 Qt. FOR NEW FILTER	TRANSMISSIONS Pts. TO REFILL AFTER DRAINING			DRIVE AXLE (Pts.)	GASOLINE TANK (Gals.)	COOLING SYSTEM (Qts.) WITH HEATER
			Manual		Automatic			
			3-Speed	4-Speed				
1965	45000	4	2	None	19	$4\frac{1}{2}$	25	$18\frac{1}{2}$
	46000	4	$3\frac{1}{2}$	$2\frac{1}{2}$	22	$4\frac{1}{2}$	25	$18\frac{1}{2}$
	48000	4	None	None	22	$4\frac{1}{2}$	25	$18\frac{1}{2}$
	49000	4	None	None	22	$4\frac{1}{2}$	20	$18\frac{1}{2}$
1966	45000	4	$3\frac{1}{3}$	None	19	$2\frac{1}{2}$	25	$14\frac{1}{2}$
	46000	4	$3\frac{1}{2}$	None	22	2	25	18
	48000	4	None	None	22	2	25	18
	49000	4	None	None	22	2	21	18
1967	45000	4	$3\frac{1}{3}$	None	19	$2\frac{3}{4}$	25	13
	46000, 48000, 49000	4	None	None	22	$4\frac{1}{4}$	25 ①	18
1968-69	45000	4	$3\frac{1}{2}$	$3\frac{1}{2}$	19	$4\frac{1}{4}$	25	$13\frac{1}{4}$
	46000, 48000, 49000	4	None	$3\frac{1}{2}$	22	$4\frac{1}{2}$	25 ①	$16\frac{3}{4}$
1970	45000	4	$3\frac{1}{2}$	None	20	3	25	$16\frac{1}{4}$
	46000	4	$3\frac{1}{2}$	None	20 ②	$4\frac{1}{4}$	25 ③	$19\frac{3}{4}$
	48000	4	None	None	20	$4\frac{1}{4}$	25	$16\frac{1}{2}$
	49000	4	None	None	23	$4\frac{1}{4}$	21	$19\frac{3}{4}$
1971-72	45000	4	$3\frac{1}{2}$	None	20 ⑤	$4\frac{1}{4}$ ④	25	$16\frac{1}{2}$
	46000	4	$3\frac{1}{2}$	None	23	$5\frac{1}{2}$	25 ③	$18\frac{3}{4}$
	48000, 49000	4	None	None	23	$5\frac{1}{2}$	25	$18\frac{3}{4}$

① —Riviera (49000), 21 gals
② —Estate Wagon (46000), 23 pts.
③ —Estate Wagon (46000), 23 gals.
④ —LeSabre (45000), with 455 V8, $5\frac{1}{2}$ pts.
⑤ —LeSabre (45000), with 455 V8, 23 pts.

WHEEL ALIGNMENT

YEAR	MODEL	CASTER		CAMBER		TOE-IN (In.)	KING-PIN INCLINATION (Deg.)	WHEEL PIVOT RATIO	
		Range (Deg.)	Pref. Setting (Deg.)	Range (Deg.)	Pref. Setting (Deg.)			Inner Wheel	Outer Wheel
1965-66	All Series	$\frac{1}{2}$P to $1\frac{1}{2}$P	1P	$\frac{1}{4}$P to $\frac{3}{4}$P	$\frac{1}{2}$P	$\frac{7}{32}$ to $\frac{5}{16}$	10	$22\frac{1}{4}$	20
1967	All Series	$\frac{1}{2}$P to $1\frac{1}{2}$P	1P	$\frac{1}{4}$P to $\frac{3}{4}$P	$\frac{1}{2}$P	$\frac{7}{32}$ to $\frac{5}{16}$	10	20	18
1968	All Series	$\frac{1}{2}$P to $1\frac{1}{2}$P	1P	$\frac{1}{4}$N to $\frac{3}{4}$P	$\frac{1}{4}$P	$\frac{7}{32}$ to $\frac{5}{16}$	10	20	18
1969	LeSabre, Wildcat, Electra	$\frac{1}{4}$P to $1\frac{1}{4}$P	$\frac{3}{4}$P	$\frac{1}{2}$N to $\frac{1}{2}$P	0	$\frac{7}{32}$ to $\frac{5}{16}$	$10\frac{3}{4}$	20	$19\frac{1}{2}$
	Riviera	$\frac{1}{2}$P to $1\frac{1}{2}$P	1P	$\frac{1}{4}$N to $\frac{3}{4}$P	$\frac{1}{4}$P	$\frac{5}{32}$ to $\frac{1}{4}$	$10\frac{3}{4}$	20	$16\frac{3}{4}$
1970	LeSabre, Wildcat, Electra	$\frac{1}{4}$P to $1\frac{1}{4}$P	$\frac{3}{4}$P	$\frac{1}{2}$N to $\frac{1}{2}$P	0	$\frac{7}{32}$ to $\frac{5}{16}$	$10\frac{1}{2}$	20	$19\frac{1}{2}$
	Riviera	$\frac{1}{2}$P to $1\frac{1}{2}$P	1P	$\frac{1}{4}$N to $\frac{3}{4}$P	$\frac{1}{4}$P	$\frac{5}{32}$ to $\frac{1}{4}$	$10\frac{1}{2}$	20	$16\frac{3}{4}$
1971-72	All Series	$\frac{1}{2}$P to $1\frac{1}{2}$P	1P	$\frac{1}{4}$N to $\frac{3}{4}$P	$\frac{1}{4}$P	$\frac{5}{32}$ to $\frac{1}{4}$	$10\frac{1}{2}$	$35\frac{1}{4}$	$32\frac{1}{4}$

N—Negative   P—Positive   ★—Estate Wagon inner wheel: $34\frac{3}{4}$, outer wheel: $31\frac{1}{2}$.

GENERAL ENGINE SPECIFICATIONS

YEAR	CU. IN. DISPLACEMENT	CARBURETOR	ADVERTIZED HORSEPOWER @ RPM	ADVERTIZED TORQUE @ RPM (FT. LBS.)	A.M.A. HORSEPOWER	BORE & STROKE (IN.)	ADVERTIZED COMPRESSION RATIO	VALVE LIFTER TYPE	NORMAL OIL PRESSURE (PSI)
1965	V8—300	2-BBL.	210 @ 4600	310 @ 2400	45.0	3.7500 x 3.40	9.0:1	Hyd.	33
	V8—300	4-BBL.	250 @ 4800	335 @ 3000	45.0	3.7500 x 3.40	11.0:1	Hyd.	33
	V8—401	4-BBL.	325 @ 4400	445 @ 2800	56.1	4.1875 x 3.64	10.25:1	Hyd.	40
	V8—425	4-BBL.	340 @ 4400	465 @ 2800	59.5	4.3125 x 3.64	10.25:1	Hyd.	40
	V8—425	2 x 4-BBL.	360 @ 4400	465 @ 2800	59.5	4.3125 x 3.64	10.25:1	Hyd.	40
1966	V8—340	2-BBL.	220 @ 4000	340 @ 2400	45.0	3.7500 x 3.850	9.0:1	Hyd.	33
	V8—340	4-BBL.	260 @ 4000	365 @ 2800	45.0	3.7500 x 3.850	10.25:1	Hyd.	33
	V8—401	4-BBL.	325 @ 4400	445 @ 2800	56.1	4.1875 x 3.640	10.25:1	Hyd.	40
	V8—425	4-BBL.	340 @ 4400	465 @ 2800	59.5	4.3125 x 3.640	10.25:1	Hyd.	40
	V8—425	2 x 4-BBL.	360 @ 4400	465 @ 2800	59.5	4.3125 x 3.640	10.25:1	Hyd.	40
1967	V8—340	2-BBL.	220 @ 4200	340 @ 2400	45.0	3.7500 x 3.850	9.0:1	Hyd.	33
	V8—340	4-BBL.	260 @ 4200	365 @ 2800	45.0	3.7500 x 3.850	10.25:1	Hyd.	33
	V8—430	4-BBL.	360 @ 5000	475 @ 3200	56.1	4.1875 x 3.900	10.25:1	Hyd.	40
1968–69	V8—350	2-BBL.	230 @ 4400	350 @ 2400	46.2	3.8000 x 3.850	9.0:1	Hyd.	37
	V8—350	4-BBL.	280 @ 4600	375 @ 3200	46.2	3.8000 x 3.850	10.25:1	Hyd.	37
	V8—430	4-BBL.	360 @ 5000	475 @ 3200	56.1	4.1875 x 3.900	10.25:1	Hyd.	40
1970	V8—350	2-BBL.	260 @ 4600	360 @ 2600	46.2	3.8000 x 3.850	9.0:1	Hyd.	37
	V8—350	4-BBL.	285 @ 4600	375 @ 3000	46.2	3.8000 x 3.850	9.0:1	Hyd.	37
	V8—350	4-BBL.	315 @ 4800	410 @ 3200	46.2	3.8000 x 3.850	10.25:1	Hyd.	37
	V8—455	4-BBL.	370 @ 4600	510 @ 2800	59.5	4.3125 x 3.900	10.0:1	Hyd.	40
1971	V8—350	2-BBL.	230 @ 4400	350 @ 2400	46.2	3.8000 x 3.850	8.5:1	Hyd.	37
	V8—350	4-BBL.	260 @ 4600	360 @ 3000	46.2	3.8000 x 3.850	8.5:1	Hyd.	37
	V8—455	4-BBL.	315 @ 4400	450 @ 2800	59.5	4.3125 x 3.900	8.5:1	Hyd.	40
	V8—455	4-BBL.	330 @ 4600	455 @ 2800	59.5	4.3125 x 3.900	8.5:1	Hyd.	40
1972	V8—350	2-BBL.	155 @ 3800 ①	270 @ 2400 ②	46.2	3.8000 x 3.850	8.5:1	Hyd.	37
	V8—350(A)	4-BBL.	180 @ 3800 ③	275 @ 2400 ④	46.2	3.8000 x 3.850	8.5:1	Hyd.	37
	V8—350(B)	4-BBL.	195 @ 4000 ⑤	290 @ 2800 ⑥	46.2	3.8000 x 3.950	8.5:1	Hyd.	37
	V8—455(A)	4-BBL.	225 @ 4000	360 @ 2600	59.5	4.3125 x 3.900	8.5:1	Hyd.	40
	V8—455(B)	4-BBL.	250 @ 4000	375 @ 2800	59.5	4.3125 x 3.900	8.5:1	Hyd.	40
	V8—455GS	4-BBL.	260 @ 4400	380 @ 2800	59.5	4.3125 x 3.900	8.5:1	Hyd.	40
	V8—455 Stage 1	4-BBL.	270 @ 4400	390 @ 3000	59.5	4.3125 x 3.900	8.5:1	Hyd.	40

① —Cal. 150 @ 3800   ③ —Cal. 175 @ 3800   ⑤ —Cal. 190 @ 4000   (A)—Single exhaust
② —Cal. 265 @ 2400   ④ —Cal. 275 @ 2400   ⑥ —Cal. 285 @ 2800   (B)—Dual exhaust

TORQUE SPECIFICATIONS

YEAR	CYLINDER HEAD BOLTS (FT. LBS.)	ROD BEARING BOLTS (FT. LBS.)	MAIN BEARING BOLTS (FT. LBS.)	CRANKSHAFT BALANCER BOLT (FT. LBS.)	FLYWHEEL TO CRANKSHAFT BOLTS (FT. LBS.)	MANIFOLD (FT. LBS.) Intake	MANIFOLD (FT. LBS.) Exhaust
1965–72	65–75 ①	40–45	100–110	200–220 ②	60	55 ③	20 ④

① —1967 400, 430 cu. in.—100–120 ft. lbs.
  1968–72 400, 430, 455 cu. in.—100 ft. lbs.
② —All V8 except 455 cu. in.—120–140 ft. lbs. minimum.   455 V8—200 ft. lbs. minimum.

③ —1965—30 ft. lbs.
  455 V8—65 ft. lbs.
④ —1965–67—15 ft. lbs.

CYLINDER HEAD BOLT TIGHTENING SEQUENCE

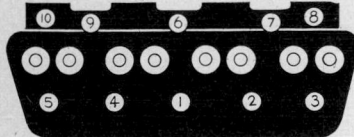

1965-67 300 cu. in.
1966-67 340 cu. in.
1967-69 400, 430 cu. in.
1968-69 350 cu. in.

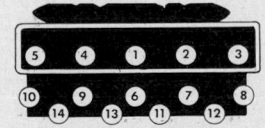

1965-66 400, 401, 425 cu. in.

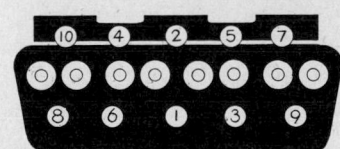

1970-71 350, 455 cu. in.

TUNE-UP SPECIFICATIONS

YEAR	MODEL	SPARK PLUGS		DISTRIBUTOR		IGNITION TIMING (Deg.) ▲	CRANKING COMP. PRESSURE (Psi)	VALVES		Intake Opens (Deg.)	FUEL PUMP PRESSURE (Psi)	IDLE SPEED (Rpm) ★
		Type	Gap (In.)	Point Dwell (Deg.)	Point Gap (In.)			Tappet (Hot) Clearance (In.)				
								Intake	Exhaust			
1965	V8—300 Cu. In.; 2-BBL.	44FFS	.032	30°	.016	2½B	160	Zero	Zero	26B	6	550
	V8—300, 401 Cu. In.; 4-BBL.	44S	.032	30°	.016	2½B	170	Zero	Zero	28B	6	500
	V8—425 Cu. In.; 4-BBL.	44S	.032	30°	.016	2½B	170	Zero	Zero	29B	6	525
	V8—425 Cu. In.; 2-4-BBL. M.T.	44S	.032	30°	.016	2½B	170	Zero	Zero	28B	6	525
	V8—425 Cu. In.; 2-4-BBL. A.T.	44S	.032	30°	.016	12B	170	Zero	Zero	28B	6	525
1966	V8—340 Cu. In.	44TS	.032	30°	.016	2½B	160	Zero	Zero	32B	6	550
	V8—401 Cu. In.	44S	.032	30°	.016	2½B	170	Zero	Zero	28B	6	500
	V8—425 Cu. In.	44S	.032	30°	.016	2½B	170	Zero	Zero	29B	6	525
	V8—425 (2-4-BBL.)	44S	.032	30°	.016	12B	170	Zero	Zero	28B	6	525
1967	V8—340 Cu. In.	44S	.032	30°	.016	2½B	160	Zero	Zero	32B	5	550
	V8—430 Cu. In.	44TS	.032	30°	.016	2½B	170	Zero	Zero	14B	6	550
1968	V8—350 Cu. In.	44TS	.030	30°	.016	2½B	165	Zero	Zero	24B	5	550
	V8—430 Cu. In.; 4-BBL.	44TS	.030	30°	.016	2½B	170	Zero	Zero	14B	6¼	550
1969	V8—350 Cu. In.	R45TS	.030	30°	.016	TDC	165	Zero	Zero	24B②	5	550
	V8—430 Cu. In.	R44TS	.030	30°	.016	TDC	170	Zero	Zero	14B	6¼①	550
1970	V8—350 Cu. In.	R45TS	.030	30°	.016	6B	165	Zero	Zero	24B	5-8	700
	V8—455 Cu. In.	R44TS	.030	30°	.016	6B	180	Zero	Zero	18B	5-8①	700
1971-72	V8—350 Cu. In.	R45TS	.030	30°	.016	**6B	165	Zero	Zero	24B②	5-8	***
	V8—455 Cu. In.	R44TS	.030	30°	.016	**6B	165	Zero	Zero	12B	5-8	***

★—With synchromesh transmission in N and automatic in D. Add 50 rpm if air conditioned.

▲—With vacuum advance disconnected. NOTE: These settings are only approximate. Engine design, altitude, temperature, fuel octane rating and the condition of the individual engine are all factors which can influence timing. The limiting advance factor must, therefore, be the "knock point" of the individual engine.

①—Pump is in fuel tank—Riviera only.
②—28B with 4 Bbl.
B—Before top dead center.
TDC—Top dead center.
**—350 V8 and 455 V8; automatic transmission—4B.
***—350 V8 and 455 V8: automatic transmission—600 in drive.
Manual transmission—800 (350 V8); 700 (455 V8).

Caution

General adoption of anti-pollution laws has changed the design of almost all car engine production to effectively reduce crankcase emission and terminal exhaust products. It has been necessary to adopt stricter tune-up rules, especially timing and idle speed procedures. Both of these values are peculiar to the engine and to its application, rather than to the engine alone. With this in mind, car manufacturers supply idle speed data for the engine and application involved. This information is clearly displayed in the engine compartment of each vehicle.

CRANKSHAFT BEARING JOURNAL SPECIFICATIONS

YEAR AND MODEL		MAIN BEARING JOURNALS (IN.)				CONNECTING ROD BEARING JOURNALS (IN.)		
		Journal Diameter	Oil Clearance	Shaft End-Play	Thrust On No.	Journal Diameter	Oil Clearance	End-Play
1965-66	401 Cu. In.	2.4985	.0015	.006	3	2.2495	.0012	.009
	425 Cu. In.	2.4985	.0015	.006	3	2.2495	.0012	.009
	300 Cu. In.	2.2992	.0013	.006	3	2.0000	.0012	.009
	340 Cu. In.	2.9995	.0015	.006	3	2.0000	.0012	.010
1967	340 Cu. In.	2.9995	.0015	.006	3	2.0000	.0012	.010
	430 Cu. In.	3.2500	.0012	.006	3	2.2495	.0012	.010
1968-69	350 Cu. In.	2.9995	.0010	.006	3	2.0000	.0012	.008
	430 Cu. In.	3.2500	.0012	.006	3	2.2500	.0012	.008
1970-72	350 Cu. In.	2.9995	.0004-.0015	.002-.006	3	2.0000	.0002-.0023	.006-.014
	455 Cu. In.	3.2500	.0007-.0018	.003-.009	3	2.2500	.0002-.0023	.005-.012

GENERAL CHASSIS AND BRAKE SPECIFICATIONS

YEAR AND MODEL		CHASSIS		BRAKE CYLINDER BORE				BRAKE DRUM	
		Overall Length (In.)	Tire Size	Master Cylinder (In.)		Wheel Cylinder Diameter (In.)		Diameter (In.)	
				Std.	Power	Front	Rear	Front	Rear
1965	V8, 45000, LeSabre	216.9	8.15 x 15	1.0	1.0	1.125	1.0	12.002	12.002
	V8, 46000, Wildcat	219.9	8.45 x 15	1.0	1.0	1.125	1.0	12.002	12.002
	V8, 48000, Electra	222.9	8.75 x 15	1.0	1.0	1.125	1.0	12.002	12.002
	V8, 49000, Riviera	208.9	8.45 x 15	1.0	1.0	1.125	1.0	12.002	12.002
1966	V8, 45000, LeSabre	217.0	8.15 x 15	1.0	1.0	1.125	1.0	12.002	12.002
	V8, 46000, Wildcat	220.1	8.45 x 15	1.0	1.0	1.125	1.0	12.002	12.002
	V8, 48000, Electra	223.5	8.85 x 15	1.0	1.0	1.125	1.0	12.002	12.002
	V8, 49000, Riviera	211.2	8.45 x 15	1.0	1.0	1.125	1.0	12.002	12.002
1967	V8, 45000, LeSabre	217.5	8.45 x 15	1.0①	1.0	1.188	1.0	12.002	12.002
	V8, 46000, Wildcat	220.5	8.45 x 15	1.0①	1.0	1.188	1.0	12.002	12.002
	V8, 48000, Electra	223.9	8.85 x 15	1.0①	1.0	1.188	1.0	12.002	12.002
	V8, 49000, Riviera	211.3	8.45 x 15	1.0①	1.0	1.188	.938	12.002	12.002
1968-69	V8, 4500, LeSabre	217.5	8.45 x 15	1.0①	1.0	1.188	1.0	12.002	12.002
	V8, 4600, Wildcat	220.5	8.45 x 15	1.0①	1.0	1.188	1.0	12.002	12.002
	V8, 4800, Electra	224.9	8.85 x 15	1.0①	1.0	1.188	1.0	12.002	12.002
	V8, 4900, Riviera	215.2	8.45 x 15	1.0①	1.0	1.188	.938	12.002	12.002
1970	V8, 4500, LeSabre	219.4	H78	1.0①	1.0	1.188	1.0	12.00	12.00
	V8, 4600, Wildcat	219.4	H78	1.0①	1.0	1.188	1.0	12.00	12.00
	V8, 4600, Sta. Wag.	223.3	L78 x 15	1.0①	1.0	1.188	1.0	12.00	12.00
	V8, 4800, Electra	225.4	J78	1.0①	1.0	1.188	1.0	12.00	12.00
	V8, 4900, Riviera	215.5	H78	1.0①	1.0	1.188	.938	12.00	12.00
1971-72	V8, 45000, LeSabre	220.7	H78 x 15	1.125	1.125	*	.9375	*	11.00
	V8, 46000, Centurion	220.7	H78 x 15	1.125	1.125	*	.9375	*	11.00
	V8, 46000, Sta. Wag.	226.8	L78 x 15	1.125	1.125	*	.9375	*	12.00
	V8, 48000, Electra	226.2	J78 x 15	1.125	1.125	*	.9375	*	11.00
	V8, 49000, Riviera	217.4	H78 x 15	1.125	1.125	*	.9375	*	11.00

*—Front disc brakes standard.
①—Optional front disc brakes 1.125 in.

AC GENERATOR AND REGULATOR SPECIFICATIONS

YEAR AND MODEL		ALTERNATOR				REGULATOR					
		Field Current Draw @ 12V.	Output @ Generator RPM		Model	Field Relay			Regulator		
			1100	6500		Air Gap (In.)	Point Gap (In.)	Volts to Close	Air Gap (In.)	Point Gap (In.)	Volts at 125°
1965-66	1100691	2.2-2.6	10A	42A	1119515	.015	.030	2.3-3.7	.060	.014	13.5-14.3
	1100705	2.2-2.6	10A	37A	1119515	.015	.030	2.3-3.7	.060	.014	13.5-14.3
	1100708	2.2-2.6	10A	42A	1119515	.015	.030	2.3-3.7	.060	.014	13.5-14.3
	1100709	2.2-2.6	10A	55A	1119515	.015	.030	2.3-3.7	.060	.014	13.5-14.3
	1100710	2.2-2.6	10A	55A	1119515	.015	.030	2.3-3.7	.060	.014	13.5-14.3
1967-69	1100691	2.2-2.6	10A	42A	1119515	.015	.030	2.3-3.7	.060	.014	13.6-14.4
	1100691	2.2-2.6	10A	42A	1119515	.015	.030	2.3-3.7	.060	.014	13.6-14.4
	1100774	2.2-2.6	10A	55A	1119515	.015	.030	2.3-3.7	.060	.014	13.6-14.4
1970	1100691	2.2-2.6	10A	42A	1119515	.015	.030	2.3-3.7	.060	.014	13.6-14.4
	1100691	2.2-2.6	10A	42A	1119515	.015	.030	2.3-3.7	.060	.014	13.6-14.4
	1100774	2.2-2.6	10A	55A	1119515	.015	.030	2.3-3.7	.060	.014	13.6-14.4
1971-72	1100926	4.0-4.5	15A	42A	1116384	——Transistor type—no adjustment——					13.6-14.3
	1100943	2.2-2.6	15A	42A	1119515	.015	.030	1.5-3.2	.067	.014	13.5-14.5
	1100924	4.0-4.5	20A	55A	1116384	——Transistor type—no adjustment——					13.6-14.3
	1100931	2.2-2.6	20A	55A	1119515	.015	.030	1.5-3.2	.067	.014	13.5-14.5
	1100932	2.2-2.6	20A	61A	1119515	.015	.030	1.5-3.2	.067	.014	13.5-14.5
	1100933	2.8-3.2	20A	63A	1119519	.015	.030	1.5-3.2	.067	.014	13.5-14.5

BATTERY AND STARTER SPECIFICATIONS

YEAR AND MODEL		BATTERY				STARTERS					
		Ampere Hour Capacity	Volts	Group Number	Terminal Grounded	Lock Test		No-Load Test			Brush Spring Tension (Oz.)
						Amps.	Volts	Amps.	Volts	RPM	
1965-66	4500	61	12	28M	Neg.	330	3.0	85	10.6	4,350	35
	Exc. 4500	70	12	3SM	Neg.	330	2.0	110	10.6	4,450	35
1967	4500	61	12	2SMD	Neg.	Not Recommended		85	10.6	3,600	35
	Exc. 4500	70	12	2STA	Neg.	Not Recommended		120	10.6	4,700	35
1968	4500	61	12	9MJ3F	Neg.	Not Recommended		85	10.6	4,350	35
	Exc. 4500	70	12	9MJ6A	Neg.	Not Recommended		88	10.6	5,000	35
1969	4500	61	12	9MJ3F	Neg.	Not Recommended		70	9.0	4,000	35
	Exc. 4500	70	12	9MJ6A	Neg.	Not Recommended		61	9.0	5,200	35
1970-72	4500	61	12	R89	Neg.	Not Recommended		80	9.0	3,500-6,000	35
	4600 (455)	70	12	Y91	Neg.	Not Recommended		45-80	9.0	4,000-6,500	35
	46, 48, 49	70	12	Y91	Neg.	Not Recommended		45-80	9.0	4,000-6,500	35

VALVE SPECIFICATIONS

YEAR AND MODEL	SEAT ANGLE (DEG.)	FACE ANGLE (DEG.)	VALVE LIFT INTAKE (IN.)	VALVE LIFT EXHAUST (IN.)	VALVE SPRING PRESSURE (VALVE OPEN) LBS. @ IN.	VALVE SPRING INSTALLED HEIGHT (IN.)	STEM TO GUIDE CLEARANCE (IN.)		STEM DIAMETER (IN.)	
							INTAKE	EXHAUST	INTAKE	EXHAUST
1965 300 Cu. In.	45	45	.401	.401	168 @ 1.26	1.64	.0020-.0025①	.0025-.0030①	.3407-.3412②	.3402-.3407②
401, 425 Cu. In.	45	45	.431★	.431★	101 @ 1.16	1.60	.0020-.0030①	.0025-.0035①	.3720-.3730②	.3715-.3725②
1966 340 Cu. In.	45	45	.401	.401	164 @ 1.34	1.72	.0012-.0032	.0025-.0030①	.3405-.3415②	.3402-.3407②
401 Cu. In.	45	45	.431	.431	101 @ 1.16	1.60	.0020-.0030①	.0025-.0035①	.3720-.3730②	.3715-.3720②
425 Cu. In.	45	45	.439	.441	101 @ 1.16	1.60	.0020-.0030①	.0025-.0035①	.3720-.3730②	.3715-.3720②
1967 340 Cu. In.	45	45	.399	.399	164 @ 1.34	1.72	.0012-.0032	.0015-.0035①	.3405-.3415	.3402-.3407②
430 Cu. In.	45	45	.421	.450	177 @ 1.45	1.89	.0015-.0035	.0015-.0035①	.3720-.3730	.3720-.3730②
1968-69 350 Cu. In.	45	45	.371	.384	180 @ 1.34	1.72	.0015-.0035	.0015-.0035①	.3720-.3730	.3720-.3730②
430 Cu. In.	45	45	.418	.448	177 @ 1.45	1.89	.0015-.0035	.0015-.0035①	.3720-.3730	.3720-.3730②
1970-72 350 Cu. In.	45	45	.382	.398	180 @ 1.34⑤	1.72	.0015-.0035③	.0015-.0032	.3720-.3730③	.3723-.3730④
455 Cu. In.	45	45	.387	.456	198 @ 1.45	1.89	.0015-.0035③	.0015-.0032	.3720-.3730③	.3723-.3730④

★—425 Cu. In.—intake .439, exhaust .441.
① —±.001 in. Guide Tapers with larger diameter at bottom.
② —±.0005 in. Guide Tapers with larger diameter at top.
③—.0003 in. maximum taper.
④—.0002 in. maximum taper.
⑤—exhaust valve spring pressure: 197 @ 1.34.

FUSES AND CIRCUIT BREAKERS

1965
Back-up lights........................ 10 AMP. 1¼ in.
Clock .... 2 AMP. ⅝ in.
Directional signal & stop lights.......... 10 AMP. 1¼ in.
Dome & trunk light .... 20 AMP. 1¼ in.
Heater, defroster, air conditioner .... 30 AMP. 1¼ in.
Instrument lights .... 5 AMP. 1¼ in.
Radio .... 7.5 AMP. ⅞ in.
Tail, license & instrument rheostat....... 10 AMP. 1¼ in.
W/S washer & wiper .... 25 AMP. 1¼ in.
Antenna motor .... 15 AMP 1¼ in.
Head & front parking lights on H. L. switch . 15 AMP. CB

1966
Back-up lights........................ 10 AGC
Blowers .... 30 AGC
Clock, radio .... 7.5 AGC
Directional sig. & stop .... 10 AGC
Dome, lighter........................ 20 SFE
License, tail, cornering .... 15 AGC
Instrument lamps.................... 4 AGC
High beam indicator .... 15 AMP. CB
Headlamps, parking .... 15 AMP. CB
Trans. selector; wipers................ 25 AGC

1967-72
Back-up lights-directional sig. .... 20 SAE
Blowers .... 25 AGC
Clock .... 20 AGC
Dome light, lighter, trunk .... 20 SAE
Hazard flasher & stop lamp .... 20 SAE
License, tail, cornering...................... 20 SAE
Instrument lamps........................... 10 AGC
Radio.................................... 10 AMP
Wipers................................... 25 AGC

LIGHT BULBS

1965

Ash tray	1445; .5 CP
Ash tray (4700)	53; 1 CP
Auto. trans. control dial (console)	1816; 3 CP
Auto. trans. control dial (instrument panel)	194; 2 CP
Back-up	1156; 32 CP
Clock dial	1893; 2 CP
Cornering	1195; 50 CP
Courtesy, console, rear seat side rail or arm rest	90; 6 CP
Cruise control dial	53; 1 CP
Dome, center roof	1004; 15 CP
Glove box	1893; 2 CP
Headlight high beam indicator	194; 2 CP
Headlight, $5\frac{3}{4}$ in. dia., type 1 (inner)	4001; 37.5 W
Headlight, $5\frac{3}{4}$ in. dia., type 2 (outer)	4002-L; 37.5–55 W
Heater-air conditioner control dial	1893; 2 CP
Ignition switch	1445; .5 CP
Indicator lights (hot, cold, oil and amp.)	194; 2 CP
Instrument cluster dials	161; 1 CP
License	1155; 4 CP
Parking brake warning	1816; 3 CP
Parking, lower (4700)	1155; 4 CP
Radio dial	1881; 1 CP
Turn signal and parking, front	1157A; 32–4 CP
Turn signal, tail and stop, rear	1157; 32–4 CP
Turn signal indicator	194; 2 CP
Trunk	89; 6 CP

1967–69

Ash tray	1445; .5 CP
Ash tray (4900)	53; 1 CP
Auto. trans. control dial	1816; 2 CP
Auto. trans. control dial (4900)	1893; 2 CP
A/C control	1893; 2 CP
Back-up	1157; 32–4 CP
Cornering	1195; 50 CP
Courtesy, console, rear seat side rail or arm rest	90; 6 CP
Cruise control dial	161; 1 CP
Dome, center roof	1004; 15 CP
Glove box	1893; 2 CP
Headlight high beam indicator	161; 1 CP
Headlight high beam indicator (4900)	194; 2 CP
Headlight, $5\frac{3}{4}$ in. dia., type 1 (inner)	4001; 375 CP
Headlight $5\frac{3}{4}$ in. dia., type 2 (outer)	4002L; 37.5–55 CP
Heater air cond. control dial	1893; 2 CP
Ignition switch	53; 1 CP
Indicator lights (hot, cold, oil & amp.)	194; 2 CP
Instrument cluster dials	194; 2 CP
License	97; 4 CP
Parking brake warning	194; 2 CP
Radio dial	1892; 1 CP
Turn signal and parking, front	1157A; 32–4 CP
Turn signal, tail & stop, rear	1157; 32–4 CP
Turn signal indicator	161; 1 CP
Trunk	89; 6 CP

1970

Ash tray (4900)	1445; .5CP
Ash tray (exc. 4900)	1455; 5CP
Auto. trans. control dial	1816; 2CP
Auto. trans. control dial (4900)	1893; 2CP
A/C control	1893; 2CP
Back-up	1157; 32–4CP
Cornering (exc. 4900)	1195; 50CP
Courtesy, console, rear seat (4900)	1295; 50CP
Courtesy, console, rear seat	212; 6CP
Courtesy lights under dash	89; 6CP
Cruise control dial	181; 3CP
Dome, center roof	211; 12CP
Glove compartment	1893; 2CP
Headlight high beam indicator	194; 2CP
Headlight, $5\frac{3}{4}$ in. type 1 inner	4001; 375CP
Headlight, $5\frac{3}{4}$ in. type 2 outer	4002L; 37.5–55CP
Heater, A/C control dial	53; 1CP
Ignition switch	53; 1CP
Indicator lights (hot, cold, oil, amps.)	194; 2CP
Instrument cluster	194; 2CP
License	97; 4CP
Parking brake warning	194; 2CP
Radio dial	1893; 2CP
Turn and parking (front)	1157A; 32–4CP
Turn, tail, stop (rear)	1157; 32–3CP
Turn indicator	194; 2CP
Trunk	89; 6CP
Water temperature indicator	194; 2CP

1971–72

Ash tray	1445; .5 CP	Cylinder head temp	257; 2 CP
Auto. trans quadrant	1816; 2 CP	Glove compartment	1893; 2 CP
Auto. trans quadrant	1893; 2 CP	Headlamp, type 1	4001; 37.5 W
A/C control	1893; 2 CP	Headlamp, type 2	4002-L; 37.5 W
Back-up	1157; 32 CP	Heater control	1893; 2 CP
Back-up (wagon)	1156; 32 CP	Ignition switch	168; 3 CP
Clock	1893; 2 CP	Indicator lights	194; 2 CP
Cornering	1295; 50 CP	Instrument cluster	194; 2 CP
Courtesy, dash lights	89; 6 CP	License	97; 4 CP
Courtesy, glove compartment	1893; 2 CP	License (Riviera)	197; 3 CP
Courtesy, rear console	181; 3 CP	Radio dial	564; 2 CP
Courtesy, roof	211; 12 CP	Side marker	194; 2 CP
Courtesy, sail panel	212; 6 CP	Trouble light	1004; 15 CP
Courtesy, side panel (conv.)	90; 6 CP	Trunk	89; 6 CP
Courtesy, tail gate (wagon)	212; 6 CP	Turn and parking (front)	1157 NA; 33 CP
Cruise control dial	194; 2 CP	Turn, tail, stop (rear)	1157; 33 CP

Distributor

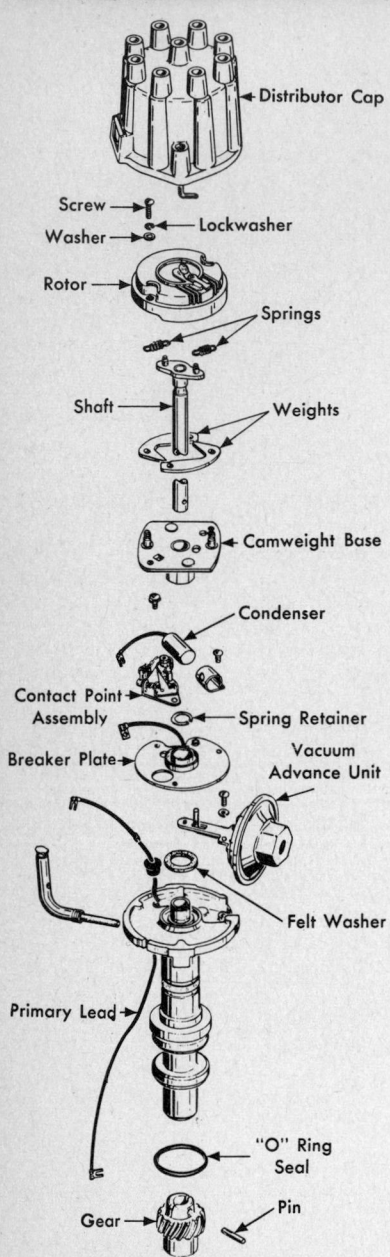

Distributor Cap

Screw — Lockwasher
Washer
Rotor
Springs
Shaft — Weights
Camweight Base
Condenser
Contact Point Assembly — Spring Retainer
Breaker Plate — Vacuum Advance Unit
Felt Washer
Primary Lead
"O" Ring Seal
Gear — Pin

Distributor—exploded view
(© Buick Div. G.M. Corp.)

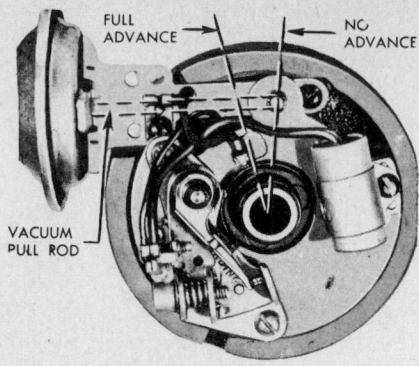

FULL ADVANCE — NO ADVANCE

VACUUM PULL ROD

**Vacuum advance mechanism
401 and 425 cu. in. engine**
(© Buick Div. G.M. Corp.)

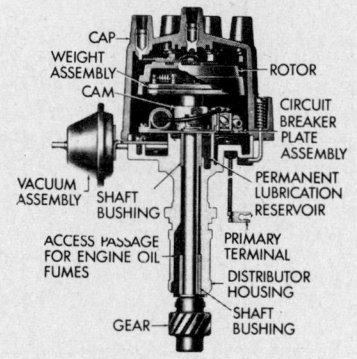

CAP
WEIGHT ASSEMBLY
CAM — ROTOR
CIRCUIT BREAKER PLATE ASSEMBLY
VACUUM ASSEMBLY
SHAFT BUSHING
PERMANENT LUBRICATION RESERVOIR
ACCESS PASSAGE FOR ENGINE OIL FUMES
PRIMARY TERMINAL
DISTRIBUTOR HOUSING
GEAR — SHAFT BUSHING

Distributor and cap assembly
(© Buick Div. G.M. Corp.)

a radio interference shield over the contact points. Only snap-lock point sets can be used because screw-type connectors will hit this shield and short ignition.

Distributor Installation

If engine was inadvertently turned over while distributor was out, proceed as follows:

Remove right rocker arm cover. Using a wrench on the crankshaft pulley bolt, turn the engine over until both valves for No. 1 cylinder are closed. The timing mark on the harmonic balancer behind the crankshaft pulley should be aligned with the correct degree mark. No. 1 cylinder is now at firing point.

Install distributor in engine with rotor in position to fire No. 1 cylinder. The vacuum unit should align with the match-mark made when distributor was removed. Press down lightly on distributor if it does not seat correctly. Use starter to turn engine until the tang on the distributor shaft slips into the slot in the oil pump shaft. This will not disturb the relationship between the distributor and the camshaft because the drive gear engages before the tang. However, it will be necessary to return the engine to the No. 1 firing point and check that rotor is also at No. 1 firing point. Reconnect vacuum tube and primary wire. Rotate the distributor body slightly until contacts just start to open. Install and tighten distributor clamp. Install distributor cap. Start engine and adjust point dwell.

If the engine has not been disturbed since the distributor was removed proceed as follows:

Insert distributor into the block so that the rotor is pointing to the mark made on distributor housing and the vacuum advance unit is aligned with the match-mark made on the engine. Connect the vacuum tube, primary wire, and install the distributor cap. Install distributor clamp. Check that spark plug wires are correctly routed. Start engine and adjust point dwell and then adjust ignition timing. Rotate distributor body counterclockwise to advance the timing.

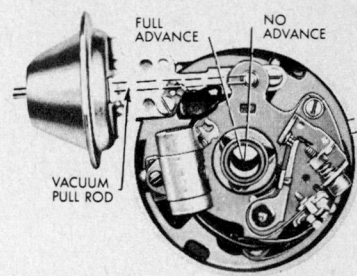

FULL ADVANCE — NO ADVANCE

VACUUM PULL ROD

**Vacuum advance mechanism—
all except 401 and 425 cu. in.**
(© Buick Div. G.M. Corp.)

Distributor Removal

Disconnect the distributor primary wire from the coil and the tube from the vacuum unit. Remove distributor cap by inserting a screwdriver into upper slotted end of cap latches, pressing down and turning 90° counterclockwise.

Make a mark on the distributor body in line with the rotor. Match-mark position of vacuum unit to the engine.

Remove clamp to release distributor and remove from crankcase.

NOTE: 1970-72 distributors have

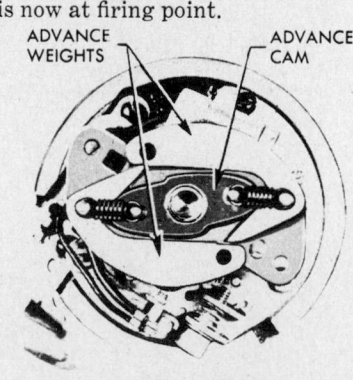

ADVANCE WEIGHTS — ADVANCE CAM

A—NO ADVANCE

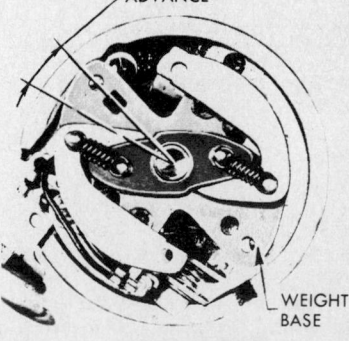

ADVANCE

WEIGHT BASE

B—FULL ADVANCE

Centrifugal advance mechanism, all except 401 and 425 cu. in.   (© Buick Div. G.M. Corp.)

Generator, Regulator

Alternator Removal and Installation

Unfasten bolt holding tension bar to generator. On some models, it may be necessary to loosen and rotate fan shroud to get at pivot bolt. Push generator in toward engine to release drive belt. Unfasten generator mounting bolt to release generator from engine.

When reinstalling, adjust generator drive belt to allow 1/2 in. play on the longest run between pulleys.

NOTE: on A/C models, remove brace.

AC Generator (Delcotron)

Delcotron, the AC generator by Delco-Remy, is used on Buick passenger cars. These units are furnished with a voltage regulator to suit the application. See Unit Repair Section for service details.

Battery, Starter

Detailed information on the battery and starter will be found in the Battery and Starter Specifications table.

A more general discussion of starters and their troubles can be found in the Unit Repair Section.

Starter Removal

1965-72

1. Disconnect battery.
2. Jack up car and remove the four flywheel inspection cover screws (3/8 in.).
3. Disconnect wires from solenoid.
4. Remove bolt from starter bracket (1/2 in.), then remove two 9/16 in. starter bolts.
5. Remove starter.

NOTE: On some models, it may be necessary to move exhaust pipe to gain clearance.

Instruments

Instrument Panel R & R

1965

The instrument panel contains three separate assemblies which may be removed individually. These assemblies contain the speedometer, clock and warning lights, and gas gauge. On some models, the clock or gas gauge is mounted separately.

Each of the three assemblies can be removed by removing one or two screws and pulling the assembly out of the panel housing. The speedometer cable may be disconnected after the speedometer assembly has been removed from the panel housing. The battery ground strap should be disconnected before removing any of the instrument assemblies.

1966-67 Except Riviera

Before performing any instrument panel services, disconnect the battery ground cable.

1. Remove two windshield side garnish moldings.
2. Remove screws and pull instrument panel upper cover rearward. Disconnect radio speaker wire and remove cover.
3. Remove ash tray.
4. Remove one 3/8 in. hex nut through hole in glove compartment.
5. Remove either radio bracket screw.
6. Remove two 3/8 in. hex head bolts from the outer ends of the instrument panel housing.
7. Remove air conditioner hose from center distribution duct and push out of way.
8. Remove light switch from instrument panel housing. Do not unplug connector.
9. Protect steering column against scratches, then tilt instrument panel back and position a 7/8 in. spacer block under each end of housing at attaching points.
10. Disconnect the following from instrument cluster:
    A. Shift indicator link.
    B. Printed circuit connector.
    C. Clock connector.
    D. Cruise switch connector.
    E. Cruise speedometer connector, and speedometer cable.
11. From below, remove 1/4 in. hex screws from bottom edge of instrument cluster.
12. From above, remove 1/4 in. hex screws from upper edge of cluster. Be careful not to lose two spacers.
13. Disconnect ground wire from upper edge of cluster.
14. Shift instrument cluster to the right and lift out.
15. Install by reversing removal procedure.

1968 Except Riviera

Caution If equipped with cruise control, upper speedometer cable must be disconnected from transducer before cluster housing is pulled back.

1. Disconnect battery ground cable.
2. Remove eight screws from instrument panel compartment body assembly and remove assembly.
3. Remove three 3/8 in. hex nuts at top underside of dash assembly and four screws at instrument panel housing assembly. Pull instrument panel upper cover rearward to remove.
4. Remove two screws from steering column filler and remove filler. Disconnect shift quadrant link wire at steering column. Remove two 3/8 in. hex nuts from steering column mounting bracket and one 3/8 in. hex bolt from column wedge. Lower steering column.
5. Remove two nuts from lower edge of instrument panel housing at steering column.
6. Remove four screws across upper edge of instrument panel housing.
7. Remove two screws at heater control installation and separate from instrument panel housing.
8. Remove four screws at ash tray assembly and remove assembly.
9. Remove one 3/8 in. hex nut at lower right side of instrument housing.
10. Remove headlight switch from instrument panel housing. Do not unplug connector.
11. Remove one 3/8 in. hex nut at lower left side of instrument housing.
12. Protect steering column so that instrument panel housing will not mar column when housing is tilted back.
13. Remove two screws at center air conditioning distribution duct (lower) and remove duct.
14. Disconnect from instrument cluster:
    A. Speedometer cable from below
    B. Printed circuit connector from above
    C. Wiring harness clip from below
    D. Clock connector and two clock bulbs from above.
    E. Cruise switch connector from above
    F. Courtesy light connector from above
    G. Windshield wiper or washer switch connector from above
    H. Antenna and accessory switch connectors from above
    I. Cluster ground wire from above.
15. Remove complete instrument panel housing assembly to work bench.
16. Remove six 1/4 in. hex screws and remove instrument panel cluster from instrument panel housing.
17. Install instrument cluster by reversing above steps.

1969-70 Except Riviera

Caution If equipped with cruise control, upper speedometer cable must be disconnected from transducer before cluster housing is pulled back.

1. Disconnect battery ground cable.
2. Remove lower instrument panel filler by removing four screws, then sliding filler forward and down.
3. Remove glove compartment, leaving glove compartment door.
4. Remove instrument panel cover by removing two nuts above the glove compartment opening, removing three screws through the cluster housing, and removing all screws across the bottom edge of the cover. Remove both courtesy lights.
5. Remove two nuts at steering column. Disconnect shift indicator link. Lower steering column.
6. Protect steering column to avoid marring paint.
7. Remove eight screws from instrument cluster housing. Pull housing back on steering column and rotate so that back of housing is visible.
8. Disconnect from instrument cluster:
   A. Speedometer cable.
   B. Heater-air conditioner control panel.
   C. Cluster wiring connector.
   D. Buzzer connector.
9. Remove six cluster to housing screws. Remove instrument panel cluster from instrument panel housing.
10. Install instrument cluster by reversing above steps.

Left-Side Trim Panel—1971-72 incl. Riviera

1. Disconnect battery ground cable.
2. Pull out headlight knob to last detent, press spring-loaded latch button and remove headlight knob and shaft. Remove escutcheon.
3. Remove panel by prying at lower right corner with screwdriver.
4. Disconnect "seelight" wires.

Right-Side Trim Panel—1971-72 incl. Riviera

1. Disconnect battery ground cable.
2. Remove radio knobs and escutcheons.
3. Remove cone-shaped knobs if equipped with speed-alert and trip-set devices.
4. Remove trim panel, as previously described above.

Speedometer—1971-72 incl. Riviera

1. Disconnect battery ground cable.
2. Remove lower instrument panel filler (eight screws hold plate).
3. Place shift lever in Low; disconnect indicator cable on column.
4. Remove the two upper screws that hold speedometer glass.
5. Pull out speedometer glass, top first.
6. Remove the three hex-head screws that hold speedometer; remove speedometer.

Printed Circuit—1971-72 incl. Riviera

1. Disconnect battery ground cable.
2. Remove lower instrument panel filler plate.
3. Place shift lever in Low; disconnect indicator cable on column.
4. Remove speedometer, as described above.
5. Disconnect speedometer cable under dash by unsnapping "Quick Disconnect" connection.
6. Using pliers, bend back clips that hold speed-alert and trip-set cables, then push cables out of panel.
7. Remove four hex-head nuts that hold circuit board (from behind); disconnect wiring harness plug.
8. Remove printed circuit board.

1966 Riviera

1. Disconnect battery ground cable.
2. Remove ash tray assembly, center air outlet and duct.
3. Remove radio.
4. Remove three Phillips screws at cluster housing and two 3/8 hex nuts at glove compartment opening. Remove upper cover assembly.
5. Pry off instrument panel molding.
6. Remove steering column lower cover.
7. Remove two 11/16 hex nuts and lower steering column.
8. Remove five 1/4 hex screws across bottom and six Phillips screws across top of panel lower housing. Unplug Electro-Cruise amplifier connector if installed. Remove panel lower housing.
9. Pad steering column for protection. Remove two 3/8 hex nuts from below upper housing assembly (one at each end). Remove four 1/4 hex screws across top of housing. Pull upper housing assembly out to rest on steering column and knees.
10. Rotate upper housing assembly so that cluster retaining screws can be seen. Disconnect speedometer cable, unplug cluster connector, cruise connector, courtesy light connector and clock connector. Remove two 1/4 hex wiring harness clamp screws.
11. Remove five 1/4 hex screws across bottom and five 3/8 hex nuts across top of cluster. Remove instrument cluster assembly.
12. Install instrument cluster by reversing above steps.

1967 Riviera

This procedure is identical to that outlined above for the 1966 Riviera, with the substitution of the following steps:

6. Remove instrument panel lower housing filler.
7. Remove instrument panel lower housing (right and left).
8. Lower steering column.

1968 Riviera

Caution If equipped with cruise control, upper speedometer cable must be disconnected from transducer before cluster housing is pulled back.

1. Remove eight screws from instrument panel compartment body assembly and remove assembly.
2. Remove four 3/8 in. hex nuts at right underside of dash assembly and four Phillips screws at housing assembly. Pull instrument panel upper cover rearward to remove.
3. Remove two screws from steering column filler and remove filler. If column shift, disconnect shift quadrant link at steering column. Remove two 9/16 in. hex nuts from steering column mounting bracket and one 9/16 in. hex nut from column wedge. Lower steering column.
4. Remove two nuts from lower edge of instrument panel housing at steering column.
5. Remove four screws across upper edge of instrument panel housing.
6. Remove one 3/8 in. hex nut at lower left side of instrument housing.
7. Remove four screws at ash tray assembly and remove assembly.
8. Remove one 3/8 in. hex nut at lower right side of instrument housing.
9. Remove two screws at heater control installation and separate from instrument panel housing.
10. Protect steering column so that instrument panel housing will not mar column when housing is tilted back.
11. Disconnect from instrument cluster:
    A. Speedometer cable from above
    B. Two wiring harness clips from above
    C. Printed circuit connector from above.
12. Disconnect from instrument housing assembly:
    A. Clock connector and two clock

bulbs from above
B. Cruise control connector from above
C. Courtesy light connector from above
D. Windshield wiper or washer switch connector from above
E. Antenna and accessory switch connectors from above
F. Cluster ground wire from above
G. Air conditioner hose from above
H. Headlight connector from above.
13. Remove instrument panel housing assembly.
14. Remove six ¼ in. hex screws and remove instrument panel cluster from instrument panel housing.
15. Install instrument cluster by reversing the above steps.

1969-70 Riviera

This procedure is identical to that outlined above for the 1968 Riviera, with the substitution of the following step:
1. Remove eight screws holding glove compartment. Remove glove compartment.

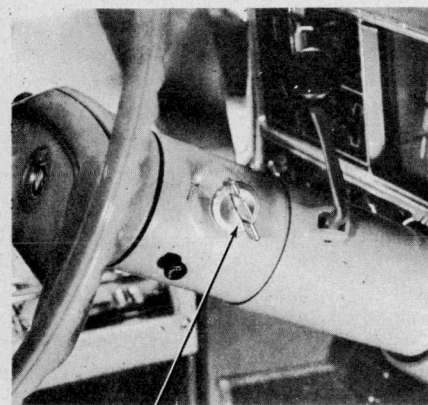

1969-72 ignition switch location
(© Buick Div., G.M. Corp.)

Speedminder

1965-67

These models have the buzzer unit mounted under the dash, to the right of steering column. The buzzer circuit contains a 7.5 amp. fuse that has a dual purpose with the parking brake warning light. It is marked Bk and Bz on the fuse block.

1968-69

Speedminders for these models are fused at the clock fuse on the fuse block.

1970-72

This unit is not fused, but is connected at the starter solenoid and protected by the fusible links at the starter motor.

Fuel Gauge—Dash Unit

On 1965 models access to the gas gauge is by removing the gauge unit mounting screws and pulling the assembly out of the panel housing. On 1966 and 1967 models the instrument panel upper cover must be removed. On 1968 models the center air-conditioning duct must be removed. 1969 and 1970 models have an access hole with a cover plate to the right of the gauge unit. On 1971 models, the speedometer must be removed.

Information covering operation and troubles of the fuel gauge will be found in the Unit Repair Section.

Temperature Gauge

1965 All Models, 1966-68 Except Riviera

A temperature switch located in the right cylinder head controls the operation of a cold indicator with a green lens and a hot indicator with a red lens. Le Sabre models have only the cold indicator.

1966-68 Riviera

A sending unit in the cylinder head controls the operation of a temperature gauge. When the engine is cold, the resistance of the sending unit is high, resulting in a cold reading on the gauge. As the engine approaches normal operating temperature, the resistance of the sending unit will become lower, resulting in a higher reading on the temperature gauge.

1969-72 All Models

A water temperature switch in the intake manifold controls the operation of a hot indicator with a red lens. A 265° F. metal temperature switch in the left cylinder head controls operation of a stop engine indicator. Le Sabre models have only the hot indicator.

Ignition Switch

Lock Cylinder Replacement —to 1968

1. Insert key and turn to Acc position.
2. With stiff wire (paper clip) in hole in face of switch depress lock pin and rotate cylinder counterclockwise and pull out.

Switch Replacement—to 1968

1. Disconnect battery.
2. Remove cylinder (as above).
3. Remove ignition switch nut.
4. Install in reverse of above.

Switch Replacement—1969-72

The ignition switch has been relocated. It is no longer in its familiar place on the instrument panel, but it occupies a position on the steering column, just above the gear selector lever. This lock also prevents shifting the transmission and locks the steering. The ignition lock cylinder cannot be removed until the steering column is partially disassembled to gain access to the internal lock cylinder retainer. The steering wheel, lock plate, and turn signal switch assembly must be removed first.

Standard Column

1. Remove steering wheel using proper puller.
2. Remove three cover screws and cover; remove cardboard retainers.
3. Depress lock plate, then remove wire snap-ring and lock plate.
4. Slide upper bearing preload spring and cancelling cam off shaft.
NOTE: steering shaft is now unsupported and could slide out the bottom of the column.
5. Slide thrust washer off shaft, then remove turn signal lever screw and lever.
6. Push in four-way flasher switch; remove knob.
7. Remove three turn signal switch mounting screws, pull connector out of its bracket on the column and tape the upper part of connector and wires together.
8. Pull turn signal switch out of column jacket.
9. Insert a small screwdriver into the slot next to the turn signal switch mounting screw boss (right-hand slot), depress spring latch and remove key lock.
10. Pull buzzer switch straight out, depressing switch clip with pliers.
11. Place ignition switch in accessory position by pulling up on connecting rod until there is a definite stop or detent felt.
12. Remove two attaching screws and ignition switch.

Tilt Column

1. Remove column mounting bracket from column.
NOTE: be careful not to damage the "breakaway" capsules.
2. Remove steering wheel using proper puller.
3. Remove turn signal wire protector (lower column).
4. Remove three column cover screws and cover.
5. Remove tilt release lever, turn signal switch lever, push four-way flasher knob in and remove knob, and remove upper shift lever.
6. Depress lock plate and remove the snap-ring; remove lock plate.
7. Remove cancelling cam and spring.

8. Remove three turn signal switch screws, tape wires to wire connector at upper end and place shift bowl in Low. Pull switch straight up and out.

9. Insert a small screwdriver into the slot next to the turn signal switch mounting screw boss (right-hand slot), depress spring latch and remove key lock.

10. Remove buzzer switch straight out, depressing switch clip with pliers.

11. Remove three housing cover screws and cover.

12. Install tilt release lever and place column in full UP position.

13. Place screwdriver in slot of tilt spring retainer, press in about 3/16 in. and turn counterclockwise. Remove spring and guide.

NOTE: spring is very strong—be careful.

14. Place column in neutral position, push in on upper steering shaft, remove inner race seat and race.

15. Remove upper flange pinch bolt, place ignition switch in accessory position, remove two switch mounting screws and switch.

NOTE: neutral start switch can be removed at this time, if necessary.

Lighting Switch

Replacement

1. Disconnect battery.

2. Remove screws that retain vent control plate or access door to instrument panel. (N.A.—1971-72).

3. Pull switch knob to last notch and depress spring loaded latch button on top of switch, while pulling knob and rod out of switch.

4. Remove escutcheon. Remove switch from cluster.

NOTE: remove left trim panel on 1971-72 models.

5. Disconnect multiple connector.

6. Install in reverse of above.

Brakes

Specific information on brake cylinder sizes can be found in the General Chassis and Brake Specifications table of this section.

Since 1967 a dual master cylinder is used on all models. Information on the dual type system and brake adjustments, lining replacement, bleeding procedure, master and wheel cylinder overhaul can be found in the Unit Repair Section.

Information on troubleshooting and overhauling power brakes can be found in the Unit Repair Section.

Information on the grease seals which may need replacement can be found in the Unit Repair Section.

Since 1967, some models are equipped with front wheel disc brakes. Beginning 1969 these disc brakes operate with single cylinder per wheel design. However, some 1969 models have the earlier four piston disc brakes. For details, consult the Unit Repair Section.

Self-adjusting brakes are standard equipment. Information on repairs and adjustments can be found in Unit Repair Section.

Master Cylinder Removal

1965-72

1. Disconnect brake pipe or pipes from master cylinder and tape end of pipe or pipes to prevent entrance of dirt.

2. Disconnect brake pedal from master cylinder at the pushrod.

3. Remove master cylinder-to-dash retaining bolts. Remove the master cylinder.

Power Brake Unit Removal

1965-72

1. Disconnect brake pipe or pipes from hydraulic master cylinder and tape pipe ends to exclude dirt.

2. Disconnect vacuum hose from power brake unit.

3. Remove four nuts holding power brake unit to dash.

4. Remove retainer and washer from brake pedal pin and disengage pushrod clevis.

5. Remove power brake unit from car.

Parking Brake Lever

The parking brake lever on all models is a foot-operated treadle.

To remove the treadle first disconnect the cable and then unbolt the treadle frame from its mounting under the dash.

Parking Brake Cable Replacement—1965-72

Front Cable

1. Raise car.

2. Remove jam nut and adjusting nut from equalizer. Remove retainer clip from rear portion of front cable at frame. The retainer clip is not used on the Riviera.

3. At front of cable, bend snap-in retainer fingers in, so that retainer can be removed.

4. Disconnect cable from pedal assembly and remove cable.

NOTE: installation of a new cable can be eased by tying a cord to either end of the cable being removed and then pulling the new cable through the proper routing by use of the same cord. This is necessary since the cable is not long enough to follow a new path.

5. Install cable by reversing removal procedure.

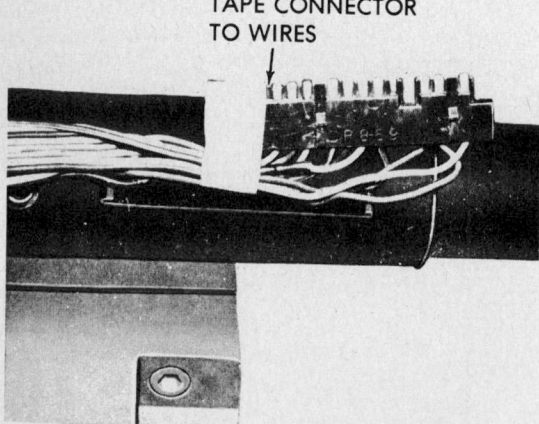

TAPE CONNECTOR TO WIRES

Tape connector wires to connector before removing turn signal switch
(© Buick Div. G.M. Corp.)

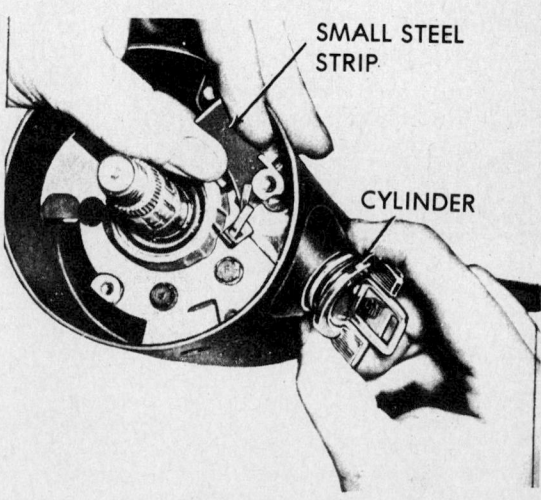

SMALL STEEL STRIP

CYLINDER

Removing ignition lock cylinder—1969-72
(© Buick Div. G.M. Corp.)

Center Cable

1. Raise car.
2. Remove jam nut and adjusting nut from equalizer.
3. Unhook connector at each end and disengage hooks and guides.
4. Install new cable by reversing removal procedure.

Rear Cable

1. Raise car.
2. Remove rear wheel and brake drum.
3. Loosen jam nut and adjusting nut at equalizer.
4. Disengage rear cable at connector.
5. Remove two bolts attaching cable assembly to backing plate. Disengage cable at brake shoe operating lever.
6. Install new cable by reversing removal procedure.

Parking Brake Adjustment— 1965-72

Adjustment of the parking brake is necessary whenever the rear brake cables have been disconnected or the parking brake pedal can be depressed more than sixteen rachet clicks under have foot pressure. The car should first be raised on a lift.

1. Make sure that service brakes are properly adjusted.
2. Depress parking brake pedal three rachet clicks.
3. Loosen jam nut on equalizer adjusting nut. Tighten adjusting nut until rear wheels can just be turned rearward by hand but not forward.
4. Release rachet one click; the rear wheels should rotate rearward freely and forward with a slight drag.
5. Release rachet one more click; rear wheels should turn freely in either direction.

NOTE: be sure that the parking brake does not drag. An overtightened, dragging parking brake on a car with automatic brake adjusters will result in an extremely short life for rear brake linings.

Fuel System

Data on capacity of the gas tank will be found in the Capacities Table. Data on correct engine idle speed and fuel pump pressure will be found in the Tune-Up Specifications Table.

Fuel Pump

1965-72

These models use a single action fuel pump mounted on the lower side of the engine front cover. Flexible type gas lines are used.

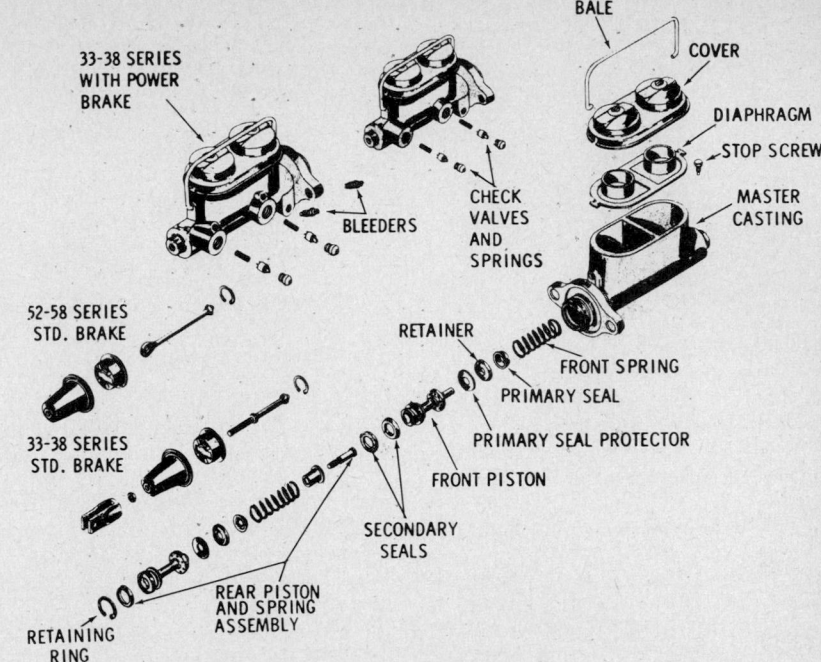

Master cylinder (Moraine) (© Buick Div. G.M. Corp.)

Beginning 1966, the repairable fuel pump was discontinued. If the fuel pump is unsatisfactory, renew the unit.

1969-70 Riviera Only

These models have a turbine type electric fuel pump mounted at the bottom of the fuel tank. This pump maintains a steady pressure whenever the engine is running. The electrical circuit to the pump is completed by an oil pressure switch switch is bypassed for starting. If oil pressure fails, the fuel pump will not operate.

1967-70 All Engines with Air Conditioners, All 400, 430, 455 Cu. In.

All air-conditioner equipped cars have a special fuel pump with a metering outlet for a vapor return system. Hot fuel and fuel vapor is returned to the fuel tank. The fuel pump is continuously cooled by circulating fuel from the tank, thus greatly reducing the possibility of vapor lock.

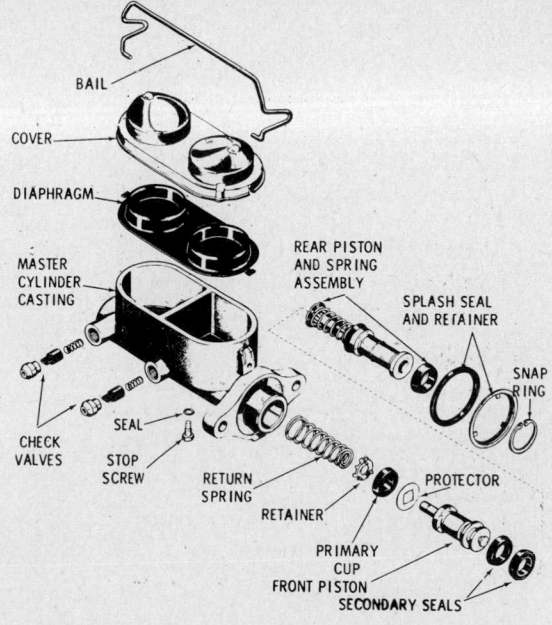

Dual-type master cylinder—Bendix (© Buick Div. G.M. Corp.)

Idle Speed and Mixture Adjustments

1965-66

On these models, the air cleaner must be removed.

1. Check that the PCV system is operative (not plugged).
2. Remove air cleaner; connect tachometer.
3. Start engine and allow to come to normal operating temperature.
4. Place manual transmission in N, automatic in D (wheels blocked).
5. Adjust throttle stop screw to obtain specified idle speed.
6. Adjust mixture needles alternately to obtain highest tachometer reading. Readjust idle stop screw to obtain specified idle again.
7. Make sure the transmission idle stator switch on the linkage is closed by disconnecting its wire. If idle speed doesn't decrease, the switch is not closed and should be adjusted.
8. Press down on the hot idle compensator valve, if so equipped. If idle drops, valve is open and should be unstuck and idle reset.

1967

Adjust with air cleaner removed.

1. If equipped with Automatic Level Control, disconnect vacuum line from compressor at the storage tank and plug it with a pencil.
2. The procedure is identical to that for 1965-66 models, with the exception of Step 6. Turn in the mixture needles, alternately, to obtain a 20 rpm drop from specified idle, then open them ¼ turn each. If this does not restore idle speed to specifications, turn them out ⅛ turn at a time until lean best idle is obtained.

1968-70

In 1968, the stator switch for the transmission was eliminated. The changing stator blade angle featured previously was discontinued that year. *Air cleaner must be in place to get proper idle, starting in 1968.*

1. Check PCV system for proper operation.
2. Connect tachometer; warm engine to normal operating temperature.
3. Place manual transmission in N, automatic in D (wheels blocked).
4. To make sure the Thermo Vacuum switch does not switch distributor vacuum over to full manifold vacuum due to overheated coolant, remove the hose from the distributor and plug.

NOTE: check that the compressor for the Automatic Level Control, if so equipped, is not running. The compressor now has a regulating valve to shut off vacuum at idle speed. If the compressor is running, this valve is faulty and must be replaced before a good idle can be obtained.

5. Adjust throttle stop screw to obtain an idle speed 20 rpm faster than specified.
6. Turn in each mixture needle, alternately, to obtain an idle speed 10 rpm less *per needle* than the basic idle setting of Step 5 (for a total of 20 rpm less).
7. Press down on the hot idle compensator, if so equipped. If idle drops, valve is open and should be unstuck and idle reset.

1971

Air cleaner must be in place to get proper, emission-free, idle speed.

1. Check PCV system for proper operation.
2. Connect tachometer; warm engine to normal operating temperature.
3. Place manual transmission in N, automatic in D (wheels blocked).
4. Remove distributor hose and plug.

NOTE: check that the compressor for the Automatic Level Control, if so equipped, is not runinng. The compressor has a regulating valve to shut off vacuum at idle speed. If the compressor is running, this valve is faulty and must be replaced before a good idle can be obtained.

5. Adjust throttle stop screw to obtain specified idle speed.
6. Adjust idle mixture needles, alternately, to obtain highest tachometer reading.
7. Readjust throttle stop and mixture screws as required to obtain an idle speed 50 rpm faster than specified, then turn in each screw (leaner) to reduce idle speed 25 rpm *per needle* (for a total reduction of 50 rpm).
8. Adjust fast idle speed.
9. If equipped with manual transmission, check throttle control solenoid adjustment as follows:

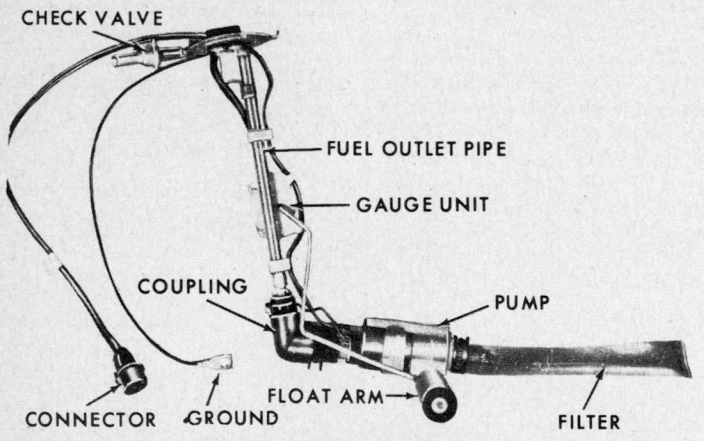

1969-70 electric fuel pump—Riviera

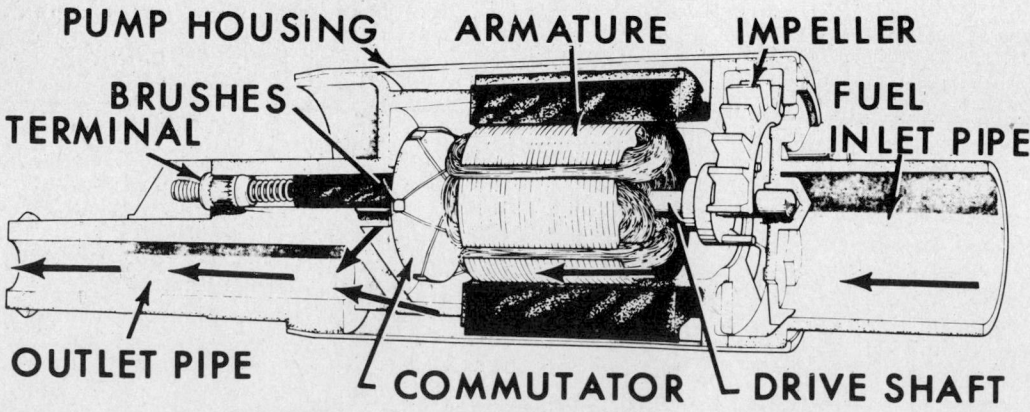

1969-70 electric pump—Riviera

Throttle control solenoid connections—
1971 V8 manual transmission
(© Buick Div. G.M. Corp.)

NOTE: this switch gives a higher idle speed in third and fourth gears to reduce misfiring and exhaust gas dilution on closed throttle deceleration.

   a. Place shift lever in N.
   b. Start engine; disconnect solenoid wire.
   c. Disconnect single relay connector and plug into the just vacated solenoid connector.
   d. Place throttle in hot (curb) idle position.
   e. Adjust solenoid plunger bolt to obtain 1,100 rpm idle.

NOTE: it may be necessary to move bracket to obtain this figure.

   f. Shut off engine.
10. Reconnect distributor vacuum line.
11. Reinstall idle limiter caps (if removed).

Exhaust System

All Buick models, except Riviera, have a standard single exhaust system. The Riviera has a standard dual exhaust system. For 1965-66 models, a dual exhaust system is optional on all models except the Estate Wagon. For 1967-72, a dual exhaust system is optional on all models except the Le Sabre and the Estate Wagon. The dual exhaust system is also optional for 1970-72 Le Sabre models equipped with the 455 cu. in. engine.

Most exhaust system connections are of the ball joint type to allow easy alignment. The rest are slip joint connections. No gaskets are used in the entire system.

NOTE: on 1971-72 Estate Wagons, the exhaust pipe is routed underneath the axle tube. For this reason, care must be exercised when jacking up the car so as not to crush this pipe.

Muffler

Removal and Installation

1. Remove U-bolts and clamps from muffler inlet and outlet. Split muffler inlet and outlet nipples on opposite sides so that they are loose on inner pipes. Be careful not to damage inner pipes.
2. Disconnect front or intermediate exhaust pipe at forward end ball joint.
3. Pull exhaust pipe forward and twist to disengage from muffler. Lay exhaust pipe on floor. Remove old muffler by pulling forward and twisting.
4. Subassemble exhaust pipe and new muffler on floor, tightening U-bolt and nuts snug but not firm enough to prevent movement.
5. Raise exhaust pipe-muffler subassembly into position, install bolts or nuts at forward ball joint just snug, install U-bolt and nuts at rear of muffler just snug.
6. Align muffler and exhaust pipe, tighten all fasteners.

Resonator

Removal and Installation

1. Remove tail pipe clamp bolt and spread clamp to allow resonator and tail pipe to pass through clamp.
2. Split resonator inlet nipple on opposite sides, being careful not to damage exhaust pipe.
3. Slide old resonator to rear and then forward out of tail pipe clamp.
4. Install new resonator and tail-pipe assembly, tighten all fasteners.

Front or Intermediate Exhaust Pipe

Removal and Installation

1. Cut off defective exhaust pipe just forward of muffler nipple.
2. Remove U-bolt and clamp from forward muffler nipple. Disconnect exhaust pipe at forward end ball joint.
3. Split stub end of exhaust pipe in muffler, collapse stub and remove.
4. Raise new exhaust pipe into position, install bolts at forward end ball joint, install new U-bolt and clamp.
5. Align exhaust pipe and tighten all fasteners.

Tail Pipe

Removal and Installation

1. Raise car so that rear axle and frame are separated as far as possible.
2. Cut off defective tail pipe behind muffler nipple.
3. Remove tail pipe clamp bolt and spread clamp. Remove old tail pipe.
4. Split stub end of tail pipe in muffler, collapse stub and remove.
5. Position new tail pipe over rear axle, install new U-bolt and clamp, install tail pipe hanger clamp bolt. Align tail pipe and tighten all fasteners.

Cooling System

Radiator Core Removal

1965-72

Remove the capscrews that hold the fan blades to the fan hub and take off the blades, spacer and pump pulley. Remove the top and bottom radiator hoses and the two hoses which connect the oil cooler to the radiator. Remove the bolts that hold the radiator core to the cradle and lift the core straight up.

Water Pump Removal

It is possible to remove and replace the water pump on all Buicks without disturbing the radiator core. This is accomplished by removing the fan belt, fan blades, and pulley, disconnecting the hoses and removing the water pump attaching bolts.

Water Manifolds

1965 All Engines, 1966 401 and 425 Cu. In.

To remove the water manifold, detach the upper radiator hose and remove the two attaching bolts which hold the manifold to the front of each cylinder head. Lift the manifold straight up to free the neoprene seal in the water pump housing.

Caution On assembly use a new seal. Mounting gaskets may be coated with compound.

Thermostat Removal

1965 All Engines, 1966 401 and 425 Cu. In.

The thermostat is contained in the water outlet elbow mounted on the front of the water manifold.

To replace the thermostat, disconnect the upper radiator hose, remove the water outlet attaching bolts, lift off the outlet and take out the thermostat.

1966 300 and 340 Cu. In., 1967-72 All Engines

The thermostat is contained in the water outlet elbow mounted on the front of the intake manifold.

To replace the thermostat, disconnect the upper radiator hose, remove the water outlet attaching bolts, lift off the outlet and take out the thermostat.

Caution In replacing a thermostat, avoid installing the unit backwards.

Engine

Exhaust Emission Control

1966-68 California

The Air Injection Reactor (A.I.R.) system of emission control, using an ancilliary air pump with external ducting, is incorporated into all cars manufactured for sale in California (and some non-California cars with special high-performance engines).

1968-71 Nationwide

The Combustion Control System (C.C.S.), a system of inter-related engine modifications, is used to meet federal anti-pollution standards.

1972 Nationwide

All 455 cu. in. engines for 1972 are equipped with a new Air Injector Reactor system. A redesigned air pump injects air into the exhaust manifold via ducts routed internally through the intake manifold. 350 cu. in. engines continue to use the C.C.S. engine modifications.

1972 California

All Buicks sold in California utilize a new system called Exhaust Gas Recirculation, along with the redesigned A.I.R. system described above. Exhaust Gas Recirculation effectively lowers combustion temperatures by diluting the fuel/air mixture with exhaust gases. The gases pass through a metering valve that opens only under acceleration or high engine speed

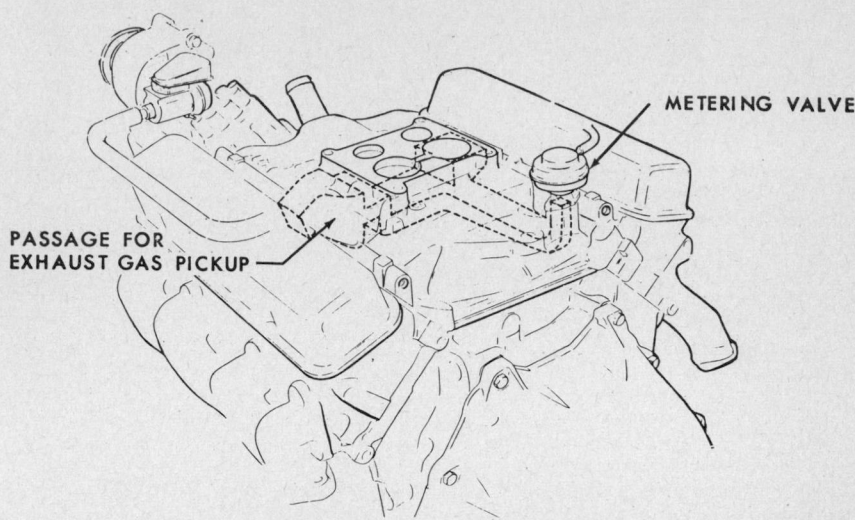

1972 Buick Exhaust Gas Recirculation system

before being ducted through passages in the intake manifold area below the carburetor.

Since 1968, all car manufacturers ost idle speeds and other pertinent lata relative to the specific engine-ar application, in a conspicuous lace in the engine compartment.

For details, consult the Unit Repair Section.

Engine Removal and Replacement

All Models—1965-72

The reason for removal, degree of disassembly, and extent and type of shop equipment may all influence the following procedure.

1. Drain cooling system.
2. Scribe hinge outline on underside of hood. Remove hood attaching bolts and remove hood.
3. Disconnect battery cables.
4. Remove radiator and heater hoses.
5. Disconnect transmission oil cooler lines. Remove fan shroud.
6. Remove attaching bolts and lift out radiator.
7. Disconnect exhaust pipe or pipes at the exhaust manifold/s.
8. Disconnect vacuum line to power brake unit.
9. Disconnect accelerator to carburetor linkage.
10. Disconnect all engine component wiring that would interfere with engine removal, such as generator wires, gauge sending unit wires, primary ignition wires, etc.
11. Disconnect gas line at fuel pump.
12. Detach power steering pump and position to the left.
13. Detach air conditioner compressor at bracket and position to the right. Do not disconnect hoses.
14. Disconnect transmission control linkage.
15. Disconnect vapor emission lines on 1970-72 models.
16. Attach lifting device to the engine and raise enough to support the engine weight.
17. Remove flywheel cover pan.
18. Separate engine from transmission at bell housing.
19. Remove engine attachment at engine mounts.
20. Lift engine forward and upward to clear engine compartment.
21. Install by reversing above procedure.

When installing an engine, the front mounting pad to frame bolts should be the last mounting bolts to be tightened

Engine Manifolds

All Models—1965-72

The intake manifold may be removed from the center of the engine block without removing any other part of the engine.

Take off the air cleaner and disconnect the vacuum and gas lines and accelerator linkage from the carburetor. Remove the air conditioning mounting bracket bolt, loosen the bracket to compressor bolts, and slide the bracket outboard. Drain the coolant. (This is unnecessary on engines with a water manifold mounted sep-

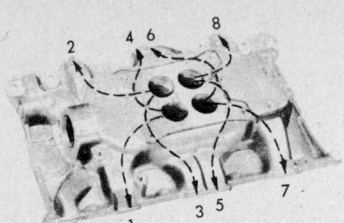

Intake manifold—300, 340 engine
(© Buick Div. G.M. Corp.)

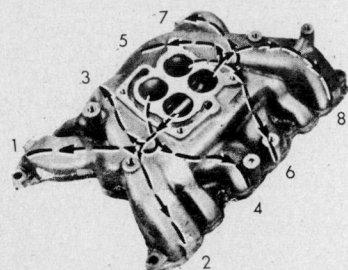

Intake manifold, 401-425 engines
(© Buick Div. G.M. Corp.)

Intake manifold—350, 400, 430 engines
(© Buick Div. G.M. Corp.)

arately ahead of the intake manifold.)

The exhaust manifolds on each side may be removed, with some slight difficulty, without removing any other part of the engine. If the car is equipped with power steering it will be necessary to remove the power steering gear box or to take off the cylinder head on the left bank in order to get at the manifold.

On 1971-72 left side exhaust manifolds (46—48—49000 series), pitman arm must be removed from pitman shaft and steering linkage relocated. Also, manual transmission clutch equalizer shaft must be removed.

In either case, whether or not the model is equipped with power steering, the right exhaust manifold may be removed without removing any other part of the engine.

Cylinder Head

Removal—1965-72

Remove the intake manifold as above.

Remove the rocker cover, then detach the exhaust manifold at the flange connection rather than at the head.

NOTE: the exhaust manifold can

be disconnected from the head but this procedure takes somewhat longer than detaching it at the exhaust flange connection. Remove the Delcotron and the air conditioning compressor to remove the right head. Remove the dipstick and power steering pump to remove the left head.

Remove the rocker cover and the rocker assemblies. Mark them carefully for reassembly. Remove pushrods.

NOTE: there are no oil line connec-

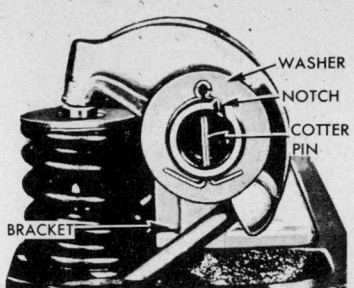

Rocker arm and shaft—401 and 425
(© Buick Div. G.M. Corp.)

**Intake manifold tightening sequence—
1971 up 350 and 455 V8**
(© Buick Div. G.M. Corp.)

tions to the rocker assemblies, since oil is fed through the rocker front bracket.

Detach the front water manifold, if applicable, from both cylinder heads, unbolt and lift off the head. It is important to prevent dirt from entering the engine. The hydraulic lifters, in particular, are very susceptible to dirt.

Valve System

Rocker Shaft and Pushrod Removal

To remove the rocker shafts, first remove the air cleaner, then the rocker cover. Then, take out the bolts which hold the rocker shaft brackets to the cylinder head.

Carefully mark the rocker shaft so that it will be returned to the same cylinder head from which it was removed.

NOTE: Nylon rocker arm retainers are removed by breaking them off with a chisel. New retainers must be installed using a 1/2 in. diameter drift.

If it is placed on the wrong head, the counter-bored bracket will not pass oil to the rocker shafts and they will very shortly wear out from lack of lubrication.

After the rocker shafts have been taken off, the pushrods can be removed from their bores without removing the cylinder head. Keep the pushrods in order, so that each can

be returned to its original location.

Rocker Shaft Lubrication

Oil is fed through the front rocker shaft bracket on both cylinder heads. The front bracket has an oversize bore which permits oil to pass around the outside of the bolt up to the hollowed out rocker shaft.

Valve Guide Replacement

Remove the cylinder head and the valves and valve spring assemblies. On engines equipped with removable

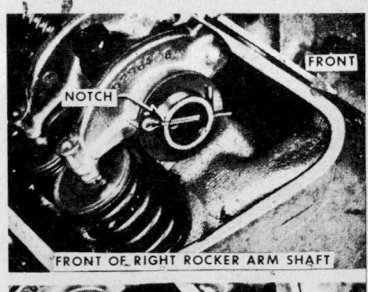

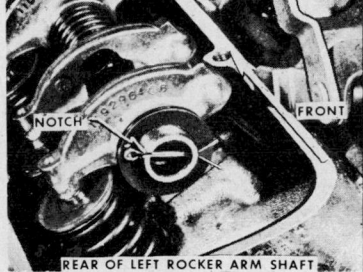

Rocker arm and shaft—300, 340, 1965-67
(© Buick Div., G.M. Corp.)

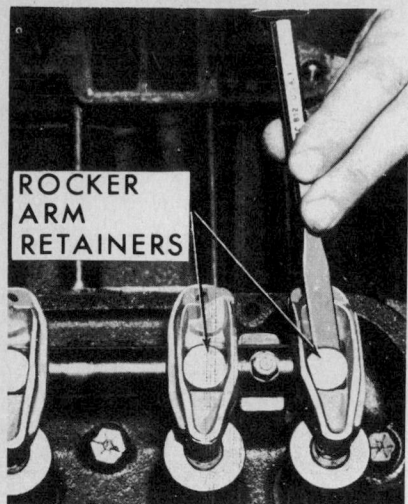

**Removing Nylon rocker arm retainers—
1971 up 350 and 455 V8**
(© Buick Div. G.M. Corp.)

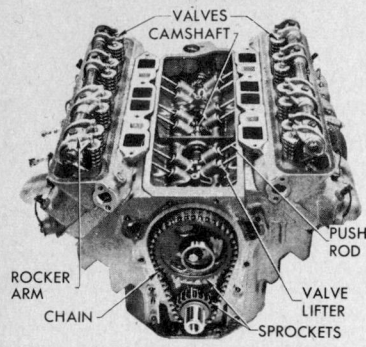

**Valve component locations—
1965-66 401 and 425 cu. in. engines**
(© Buick Div., G.M. Corp.)

guides carefully measure the amount the valve guide protrudes from the cylinder head before driving it out so that the new guide can be driven down exactly that amount. Make a stack of washers equivalent to the protrusion of the guide before removing the guide from the head.

When driving out the valve guides, support the cylinder head as near to the valve guide as is practical.

A pilot type driver should be used and the guide should be driven out from the bottom, or, it may be pressed out if an arbor press is available.

Place the new guide in the top of the head and tap it gently to insure that it is starting straight. Once started straight, it can be driven into position.

When the new valve guide has been driven in the correct distance, insert a new valve into the guide to make sure that the valve will operate freely up and down. The slightest sign of binding in the new valve guide means that the guide itself has become riveted over or slightly warped in the driving process and will have to be reamed.

Buick removable valve guides should be finish-reamed to size, after installation. Use a reamer that will give the valve stem to guide clearance listed in the Valve Specifications table.

NOTE: beginning 1965 the 300 cu. in. and the 340 cu. in. engines have valve guides that are cast integrally with the cylinder head. Since 1967, all guides are integral with the cylinder head.

In cases of excessive guide-to-valve stem clearance, the guides can be reamed and oversize valves installed. .004 in. oversize valves can be installed in the 300 and 340 cu. in. engines and .010 in. oversize valves can be installed in the 350, 400, 430, and 455 cu. in. engines.

Always reface the valve seat when new guides have been installed to be absolutely certain that the valve seat is in alignment with the new guide.

Valve Springs

To check the condition of the valve springs, line up the intake valve springs on a flat surface and, using a straightedge, compare the height of the springs. If all of the springs are the same height, as determined by the straightedge, it may be assumed that the springs are in good condition, since it is very unlikely that all of the springs would collapse the same amount.

If one or more of the springs are lower than the rest it is advisable to procure at least one new spring and then compare the other springs with the new one for free length.

Replace all springs that do not come up to the standard established

by the new one.

Repeat the operation on the exhaust valve springs.

Valve Removal

Remove the air cleaner, the rocker cover, the rockers and the intake manifold. Disconnect the exhaust manifolds at their flanges, leaving the manifold attached to the heads.

From the right bank, remove the generator mounting bracket, and from the left, the power steering pump. Disconnect the heat indicator, remove fuel and vacuum lines. Remove the bolts that hold the water manifolds, if applicable, to the cylinder heads, unbolt and remove the cylinder heads. Take the heads to a bench and, using a C-type or lever type valve spring compressor, compress the valve springs, remove the keepers, release the valve springs, and push the valves to the combustion chamber side of the head.

Hydraulic Lifters, Removal

To remove the lifters, remove the rocker cover and take off the rocker shaft assemblies and lift out the push-rods. Then remove the intake manifold.

The valve chamber cover plate can then be removed giving access to the lifters.

The lifters are barrel type which come right up out of their bores requiring no other tools than the fingers.

If more effort is required than can be given by the fingers, it indicates gum or sticky substances present in the oil which probably caused the failure.

NOTE: V8 lifters have a spherical shaped base to ensure lifter rotation. Do not grind these lifters to remove score marks.

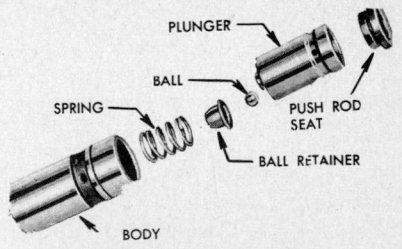

Hydraulic valve lifter parts
(© Buick Div. G.M. Corp.)

Timing Case Cover
Timing Chain

Vibration Damper Removal

Remove the radiator core and take out the cap screws that hold the fan pulley to the vibration damper. Remove the large bolt from the center of the crankshaft and insert a bolt type puller into the holes which held the fan pulley. Pull off the vibration damper.

Removing and installing valve guides
(© Buick Div. G.M. Corp.)

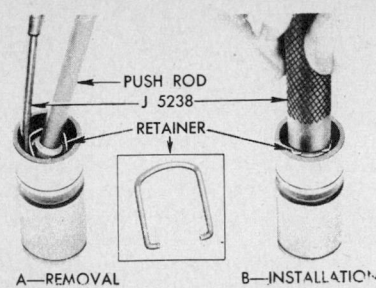

PUSH ROD
J 5238
RETAINER

A—REMOVAL   B—INSTALLATION

Removing and installing plunger retainer
(© Buick Div. G.M. Corp.)

Timing Chain and Front Oil Seal Replacement

1965-66 401 and 425 Cu. In.

Drain cooling system and remove radiator core, shroud, fan belt, fan and pulley and vibration damper.

Remove all bolts holding timing gear cover and the water manifold to the engine block and cylinder heads. Do not remove the five small bolts holding the water pump to the chain cover.

Remove water-manifold-timing-chain-cover assembly, being careful not to tear the oil pan gasket.

Remove oil slinger from crankshaft and remove the bolt, lockwasher and plain washer holding fuel-pump-drive eccentric and camshaft sprocket to camshaft.

If there has been doubt about the valve timing, turn the crankshaft so that the camshaft sprocket keyway points down. The "O" marks on the sprockets should be set to be nearest each other inline with the shaft centers.

Remove camshaft sprocket and timing chain.

End thrust of the camshaft is taken up by a thrust plate fastened to the block behind the sprocket. End-play of the camshaft is controlled by a spacer ring just behind the thrust plate and in front of the camshaft front bearing journal. The spacing ring provides end-play of the cam-

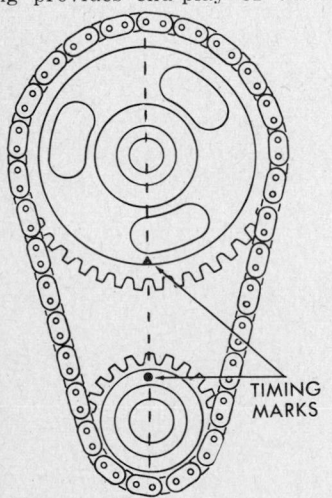

TIMING MARKS

Timing chain and sprocket marks

shaft of .004 to .008 in. when the camshaft sprocket is tightened into place.

Clean up the cover assembly, and, if the oil seal seems worn, replace it as follows:

Remove the braided fabric packing with a screwdriver and then tap the pressed steel retainer out of the cover. Work new packing into the retainer and drive the retainer into the recess. The packing should expand slightly as it seats. Install so that joint between ends of packing is toward top of engine. Smear the seal with vaseline.

When ready to install the chain turn the crankshaft, if it has been turned since chain was removed, so that pistons No. 1 and No. 4 are on top dead center. Turn camshaft so that sprocket keyway points down.

Place chain and sprocket back in place with the "O" marks on the sprockets set nearest each other in-line with the shaft centers.

Install fuel pump drive eccentric so that keyway fits over key in camshaft. Fasten all in place.

Install oil slinger on end of crankshaft with hollow side outward.

Reverse procedure to complete installation. Keep engine speed low for a short while after installation of oil seal.

1965-70 300, 340, 350 Cu. In.

1. Drain cooling system and remove radiator, shroud, fan, pulleys, and belts.
2. Remove crankshaft pulley, fuel pump and distributor.
3. Remove Delcotron and power steering pump, if necessary.
4. Loosen and slide rearward front clamp on thermostat by-pass hose. Remove harmonic balancer.
5. Remove bolts attaching timing chain cover to cylinder block and oil pan to timing chain cover bolts. Remove timing chain cover

assembly and gasket. Clean cover thoroughly, being careful not to damage the gasket surface.

6. Turn the crankshaft so that the timing marks on the sprockets are adjacent to each other on a line with the shaft centers.
7. Remove crankshaft oil slinger.
8. Remove bolt, special washer, distributor drive gear, and fuel pump eccentric from camshaft.
9. Pry camshaft and crankshaft sprockets forward until camshaft sprocket is free. Then remove both sprockets and chain.

If oil seal appears worn or has been leaking, replace as follows:

10. Use a punch to drive out the old seal and retainer. Drive from front to rear of the timing chain cover.
11. Coil new packing around opening so that ends are at top. Drive in retainer. Stake the retainer in at least three places. Size the packing by rotating a hammer handle, etc. around the packing until the balancer hub fits through the packing.

If engine has been disturbed since chain and sprockets were removed:

12. Turn crankshaft until No. 1 piston is at top dead center.

Engine lubrication—401 and 425 cu. in. engine
(© Buick Div. G.M. Corp.)

OVERSIZED BOLT HOLE

VALVE LIFTER OIL GALLERIES

MAIN OIL GALLERY

OIL FILTER

13. Mount sprocket temporarily and turn camshaft so that timing mark is straight down.
14. Assemble chain and sprockets and mount on shafts with their timing marks closest to each other.
15. Mount slinger on sprocket with the concave side to the front.
16. Reinstall fuel pump eccentric, distributor drive gear, special washer, and bolt on camshaft. Reinstall Woodruff key with oil groove forward.
17. Remove oil pump cover and pack the space around the oil pump gears full of petroleum jelly,

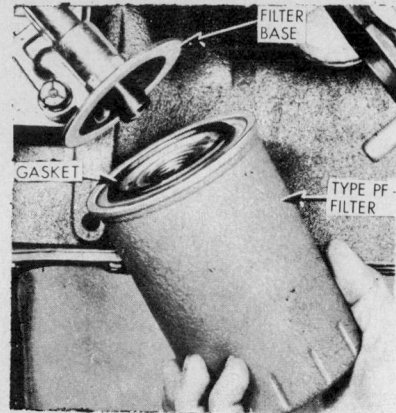

Oil filter installation (© Buick Div. G.M. Corp.)

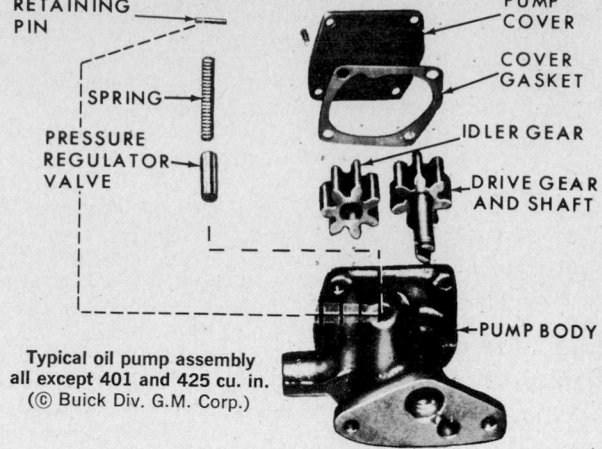

Typical oil pump assembly
all except 401 and 425 cu. in.
(© Buick Div. G.M. Corp.)

leaving no air spaces. Reinstall oil pump cover with new gasket. This step is very important. If it is not done the oil pump will not begin to pump oil as soon as the engine is started.

18. Reinstall timing chain cover with new gasket.

Keep engine speed low for a short time after installation of a new oil seal.

1967-72 400, 430, 455 Cu. In.

This procedure is identical to that outlined above for 300, 340, and 350 cu. in. engines with the substitution of the following steps:

8. Remove oil pan. Remove camshaft sprocket bolts.
16. Reinstall oil pan. Reinstall camshaft sprocket bolts.

Engine Lubrication

Oil Pan Removal—1965-72

The following procedures apply in general to all models:

1. Disconnect battery ground strap.
2. Raise car and support on stands.
3. Drain oil.
4. Disconnect or loosen shift linkage.
5. On manual transmission equipped models, loosen clutch equalizer bracket to frame mounting bolts and disconnect exhaust crossover pipe at engine.

Depending on the individual car model, it may be necessary to do one or more of the following:

1. Remove lower flywheel housing.
2. Disconnect idler arm at frame and push steering linkage forward.
3. Remove fan shroud to radiator tie bar bolts.
4. Remove engine mounting bolts and raise engine by jacking under the crankshaft pulley mounting. When this is done on air conditioned cars, it will be necessary to support the right side of the engine-transmission assembly due to the off-center

weight of the compressor.
5. Rotate crankshaft slightly while lowering pan to clear counterbalances.

Oil Pump Removal

With the exception of the 1965-66 401 and 425 cu. in. engines, the oil pump is located in the timing chain cover on the right-hand side. It is connected by a drilled passage in the crankcase to an oil screen housing and pipe assembly. The screen is submerged in the oil supply in the oil pan.

The 401 and 425 cu. in. engines have the oil pump bolted to the crankcase and contained in the oil

pan. To gain access to the oil pump, the oil pan must be removed.

Oil Filter

1965-67

A screw-off, disposable element and can-type filter is used. The filter should be changed at 6,000 miles or six-month intervals, whichever comes first.

1968-72

The filter should be changed at every other oil change. Oil changes should be made every four months or 6,000 miles, whichever occurs first.

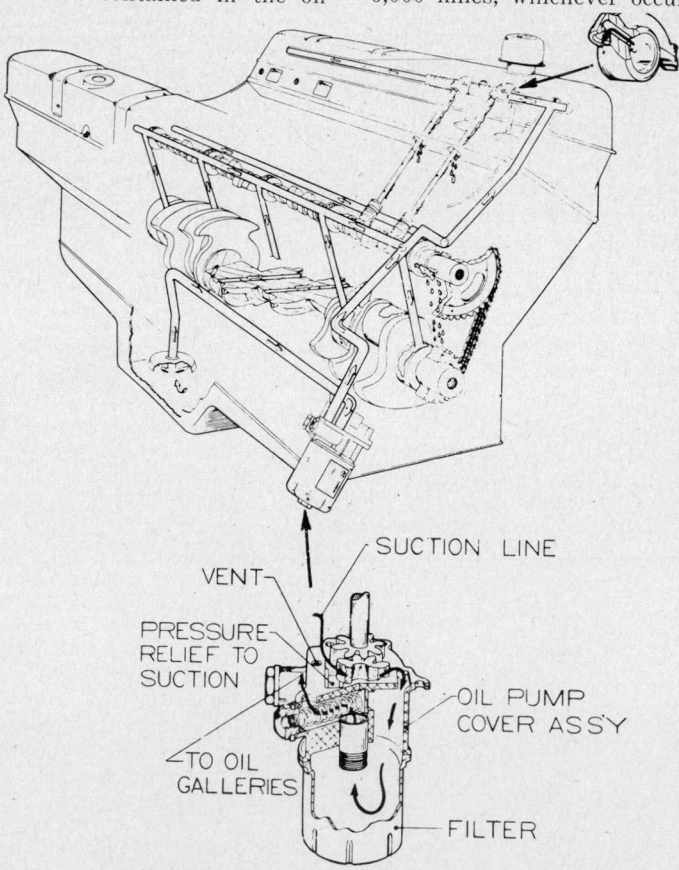

Oil flow—except 401 and 425 cu. in. engine (© Buick Div. G.M. Corp.)

A few cases of difficulty in oil filter replacement have come to our attention. The trouble starts with oil filter elements being turned on too tightly. The unit may be too tight to remove by hand and it may collapse in the grip of a tool that applies enough squeeze to grip the element hard enough to turn it.

1. Raise the car on a jack or hoist and place a drip pan under the filter.
2. With a 12 to 14 in. slender punch drive a hole in the element from one side to the other.

    NOTE: before punching the hole, consider the angle required for the punch to act as a lever, with the least interference.
3. With the drift all the way through the filter and acting as a lever, turn the unit counterclockwise far enough to break it loose.
4. Final loosening and removal can now be accomplished by hand.

Oil Filter Replacement

1. Coat the gasket on the new filter with oil.
2. Place the new filter in position on the block.
3. Hand tighten until contact is made between the filter gasket and the adapter face.
4. Tighten by further turning the filter two-thirds turn.
5. Run the engine at fast idle and check for oil leaks.
6. Check the oil and bring crankcase to level if necessary.

Rear Main Bearing Oil Seal Replacement

Buick uses an oil slinger and groove, a braided fabric seal and two neoprene strips to seal the rear main bearing. The braided fabric seal can be installed in the crankcase half (upper) only when crnkshaft is removed. However, the seal can be replaced in the lower half whenever the lower half (cap) has been removed. To renew the seals in the cap proceed as follows:

Remove the old seals and clean the cap. Place new braided seal in groove with both ends projecting above parting surface of cap. Force seal into groove by rubbing down with a hammer handle or other smooth tool until seal is seated in groove and ends project above the parting face of the cap not more than 1/16 in. Using

a razor blade, cut off ends flush with parting surface.

Just before installing the bearing cap, lightly lubricate the neoprene seals and install in bearing cap with the upper ends protruding about 1/16 in. The seals must not be cut to length. After installing the cap, force the seals up into the cap with a blunt instrument to insure a seal at the line between the cap and the case.

NOTE: the 1968-72 430 and 455 cu. in. engines use a rear bearing cap which does not have the neoprene seals. These engines are sealed at this point by a rear oil pan seal.

Caution
The engine must be operated at slow speed when first started after installation of new braided seals.

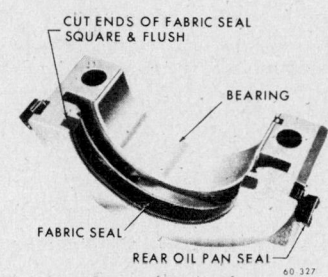

Rear main bearing cap—430 and 455 cu. in.
(© Buick Div. G.M. Corp.)

CUT ENDS OF FABRIC SEAL SQUARE AND FLUSH

SEAL
BEARING
SEAL - NEOPRENE COMPOSITION

Rear main bearing cap— except 430 and 455 cu. in.
(© Buick Div. G.M. Corp.)

Connecting Rods And Pistons

Fitting Pistons, Rings and Pins

When new rings are installed without reboring the cylinders, cylinder wall glaze should be broken. This can be done by using the finest grade stones in a cylinder hone.

New piston rings must be checked for clearance in cylinder bores and for gap.

When fitting new rings to new pistons the side clearance for compression rings should be .003 to .005 in.

Top Half, Rear Main Bearing Oil Seal Replacement

The following method has proven a distinct advantage in most cases and, if successful, saves many hours of labor.

1. Drain engine oil and remove oil pan.
2. Remove rear main bearing cap.
3. With a 6 in. length of 3/16 in. brazing rod, drive up on either exposed end of the top half oil seal. When the opposite end of the seal starts to protrude, have a helper grasp it with pliers and pull gently while the driven end is being tapped. It is surprising how easily most of these seals can be removed by this method.

   To replace the woven fabric-type seal:

   1. Obtain a 12 in. piece of copper wire (about the same gauge as that used in the strands of an insulated battery cable).
   2. Thread one strand of this wire through the new seal, about ½ in. from the end, bend back and make secure.
   3. Thoroughly saturate the new seal with engine oil.
   4. Push the copper wire up through the oil seal groove until it comes down on the opposite side of the bearing.
   5. Pull (with pliers) on the protruding copper wire while the crankshaft is being turned and the new seal is slowly fed into place.

      CAUTION: this snaking operation slightly reduces the diameter of the new seal and care will have to be used to keep the seal from slipping too far through the top half of the bearing.
   6. When an equal amount of seal is extending from each side, cut off the copper wire close to the seal and tamp both ends of the seal up into the groove (this will tend to expand the seal again).

      NOTE: don't worry about the copper wire left in the groove, it is too soft to cause damage.
   7. Replace the seal in the cap in the usual way and replace the oil pan.

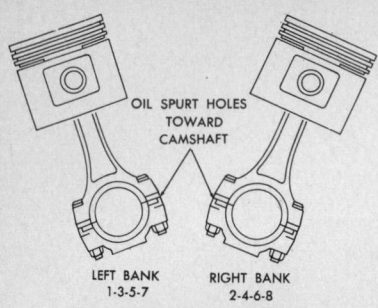

OIL SPURT HOLES
TOWARD
CAMSHAFT

LEFT BANK
1-3-5-7

RIGHT BANK
2-4-6-8

**Piston and rod assembly—
300-340, 400-430-455**

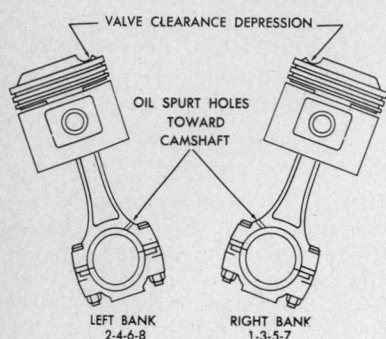

VALVE CLEARANCE DEPRESSION

OIL SPURT HOLES
TOWARD
CAMSHAFT

LEFT BANK
2-4-6-8

RIGHT BANK
1-3-5-7

Piston and rod assembly—401-425

Side clearance of the oil ring should be .0035 to .0095 in.

Check end gap of compression rings by placing them in the bore in which they will operate. Then, push them to the bottom of the bore with a piston. Now, measure the end-gap in each ring. The end-gap should be no less than .015 in. for all engines up to 1967. For 1968-70 models end gap should be no less than .010 in. for the 350 cu. in. engine and .013 in. for the 400, 430, and 455 cu. in. and all 1971-72 engines. End gap for oil rings for 1968-70 engines should be no less than .015 in. Oil ring end gap need not be measured on 1965-67 engines.

If piston pin bosses are worn out of round or oversize, the piston and pin should be replaced. Oversize pins are not practical because the pin is a press fit in the connecting rod. Piston pins must fit the piston with an easy finger push at 70° F.

In assembling the piston to the connecting rod, a press is ideal. However, substitutes are available that will serve the purpose.

When the rod assemblies are replaced in the engine, the connecting rod bearing oil spurt hole must point up toward the camshaft.

Piston to cylinder wall clearance should be .0008-.0020 for 350 cu. in. engines, .0010-.0016 for 455 cu. in. engines (measured at skirt top).

Front Suspension

Figures covering the caster, camber, toe-in, king pin inclination, and turning radius can be found in the Wheel Alignment table.

Tire size figures can be found in the General Chassis and Brake Specifications table.

Control Arms, and/or Ball Joint, Spring—R & R

Upper Control Arm

1. Raise car with jack under the frame. Remove wheel and tire.
2. Remove cotter pin from upper ball joint stud.
3. Loosen, but do not remove nut. Rap the knuckle sharply in the area of the tapered stud to free the stud from the knuckle.
4. With another jack, support the car weight under the outer edge of the lower control arm. Raise jack enough to free upper control arm from upper ball stud.
5. Wire brake and knuckle in place to prevent brake hose damage, then, lift upper arm from knuckle.

NOTE: if only ball joints are to be replaced, stop at this point. Center punch and drill out the four rivets, then chisel off their heads. Remove old ball joint—the new joint comes with four specially hardened bolts, which must be torqued to 8 ft. lbs. The nut goes on top.

6. Remove the upper control arm shaft-to-bracket nuts and lock washers. Carefully note the number, thickness, and location of the adjusting shims. Remove control arm assembly.
7. The upper control arm is serviced only as an assembly. Therefore, if the arm is bent, bushings worn,

or the control arm shaft bent, the entire assembly must be replaced.

Lower Control Arm, or Spring

1. Proceed as with upper control arm, Step 1.
2. Disconnect and remove shock absorber.
3. Remove front stabilizer rod link from lower control arm.
4. Disconnect brake reaction rod from lower control arm but leave it attached to the front frame crossmember up to 1970 models.
5. Remove control arm bumper up to 1970 models.
6. As a safety precaution and to gain maximum leverage, place a jack about ½ in. below the lower ball joint stud. Now, remove the ball stud cotter pin and loosen the nut about ⅛ in. Do not remove the nut.
7. Rap the steering knuckle in the area of the stud to separate the stud from the knuckle.
8. After the stud has broken loose from the knuckle, raise the jack against the control arm. Remove nut and separate the steering knuckle from the tapered stud.
9. Carefully lower jack under the control arm and release the spring. With the jack entirely lowered, it may be necessary to pry the spring off its seat on the lower control arm with a pry bar.
10. After the spring is removed, the lower control arm may be removed by removing the lock nut attaching the control arm to the frame.
11. Install by reversing removal procedure. Tighten castellated nut to 85 ft. lbs.

Front Wheel Bearing Adjustment

1965-72

Front wheels are now suspended upon tapered roller bearings. Adjust-

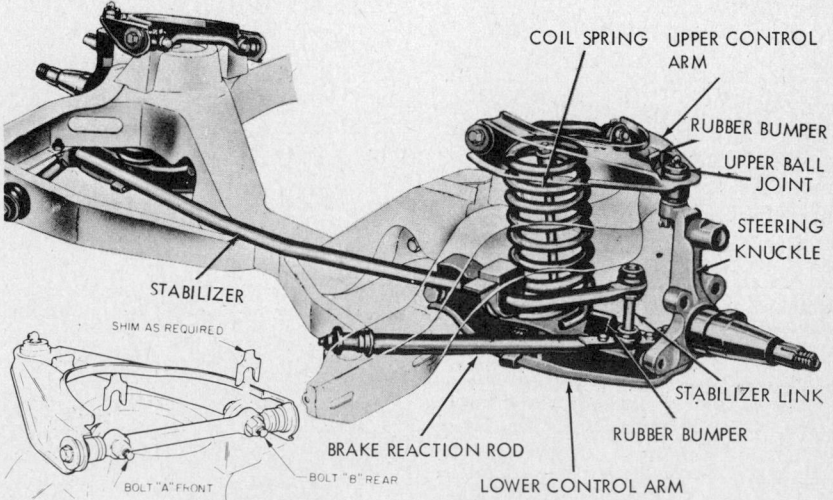

COIL SPRING   UPPER CONTROL ARM

RUBBER BUMPER

UPPER BALL JOINT

STEERING KNUCKLE

STABILIZER

SHIM AS REQUIRED

STABILIZER LINK

RUBBER BUMPER

BRAKE REACTION ROD

BOLT "A" FRONT

BOLT "B" REAR

LOWER CONTROL ARM

Typical front suspension—1965-70 (© Buick Div., G.M. Corp.)

ment of freshly cleaned and repacked roller bearings is as follows:

1. Torque spindle nut to 19 ft. lbs. while rotating the wheel.
2. Back off the nut until bearings are loose.
3. Retorque spindle nut to 11 ft. lbs. while rotating the wheel.
4. If either cotter pin hole in spindle lines up with nut castellations, back off the nut one-twelfth turn and install cotter pin. Otherwise, back off the nut to the first position that will accept an horizontal or vertical cotter pin.
5. Install cotter pin and lock spindle nut into position.

NOTE: .002-.006 in. end-play is normal.

Jacking and Hoisting

Jack car at front spring seat of lower control arm or center of crossmember.

Jack car at rear, at axle housing.

To lift at frame, use side rails in front of body floor pan and at rear side rail at lower control arm front pivot.

Steering Gear

Manual

Instructions covering the overhaul of the steering gear will be found in the Unit Repair Section. No manual steering is available on full-size Buicks starting in 1971.

Manual Steering Gear Removal

1965-70

The steering gear mechanism is in two pieces coupled together with a flexible coupling.

To remove the lower gear box, disconnect the coupling by removing the pinch bolt securing the flexible coupling flange to the steering gear stub shaft.

From under the car, disconnect the steering pitman arm from the pitman shaft and remove the bolts at outside of left frame side rail which hold the gear housing to the frame, and lower the gear assembly to the floor.

When reinstalling, tighten pitman arm nut to 140 ft. lbs.

Steering Idler Arm

The idler arm bracket is held to the right frame side rail by two cap screws. Remove the cap screws and lower the tie rods. Unscrew the bracket from the bushing and then take the bushing out of the idler arm.

Bracket and bushing are usually replaced in sets.

Power

Troubleshooting and repair instructions covering power steering gear are given in the Unit Repair Section.

Replacement of Pitman Shaft Seals with Power Steering Gear Still in Place

Disconnect pitman arm from pitman shaft. Clean end of pitman shaft and housing. Tape the splines of the pitman shaft to keep them from cutting the seal. Use only one layer of tape. Too much tape will prevent passage of the seal. Using lock-ring pliers remove the seal retaining ring.

CASTER AND CAMBER ADJUSTMENT

FOR CASTER AND CAMBER DIMENSIONS, SEE WHEEL ALIGNMENT AND SPEC CHART.

FOR INCREASED OR POSITIVE CASTER, DECREASE SHIMS AT BOLT "A" AND INCREASE SHIMS AT BOLT "B" BY TWICE THIS AMOUNT.

FOR DECREASED OR NEGATIVE CASTER, INCREASE SHIMS AT BOLT "A" AND DECREASE SHIMS AT BOLT "B" BY TWICE THIS AMOUNT.

FOR INCREASED CAMBER. DECREASE SHIMS AT BOTH "A" AND "B" BOLTS. SHIMMING GREATER THAN .750 NOT PERMISSIBLE.

SHIM THICKNESS AT "A" AND "B" LOCATION TO BE WITHIN .40 OF EACH OTHER

SHIM AS REQUIRED - AT LEAST ONE OF THESE SHIMS MUST BE USED AT EACH BOLT.
- .030 THICK
- .060 THICK
- .120 THICK

BOLT "B"-REAR
BOLT "A"-FRONT
VIEW A

INSTALL PIN HEAD TIGHT IN NUT SLOT & BEND APPROX AS SHOWN, AT BOTH UPPER & LOWER BALL STUDS.

AXIS OF COTTER PIN HOLES IN JOINT STUDS SHOULD BE LOCATED APPROX PARALLEL TO ℄ CAR WITH FRONT WHEELS STRAIGHT AHEAD.

VIEW B

NUT (2)
60-120 LB-IN
RETAINER (4)
GROMMET (4)
BOLT (4)
BUSHING (2)
BRACKET (2)

SCREW (4)
20-28 LB-FT
LINK (2)
BOLT (4)
(BOLT MUST BE INSTALLED IN DIRECTION SHOWN)

BAR-FRONT STABILIZER
TIGHTEN LOWER CONTROL ARM TO FRAME BUSHINGS WITH CONTROL ARM AT CURB POSITION.
TIGHTEN STABILIZER TO FRAME BRACKETS WITH STABILIZER IN CURB POSITION.

NUT (4)
90-115 LB-FT
BUMPER (2)
SPACER (2)
RETAINER (8)
GROMMET (8)
NUT (2)
14-20 LB-FT

NUT (2)
10-15 LB-FT

SCREW (4)
15-25 LB-FT

NUT (4)
65-85 LB-FT
ARM ASM-UPPER
INSULATOR (2)
BUMPER (2)
PERM ANTI-FREEZE MAY BE USED TO ASSIST INSTALLATION OF BUMPER

COTTER PIN (4)
STEERING KNUCKLE AND FT WHEEL HUB ASM
NUT (2)
40-60 LB-FT
WHEN CHECKING TORQUE, TIGHTEN TO NEXT COTTER PIN HOLE. THIS TORQUE NOT TO EXCEED 90 LB-FT.

NUT (2)
60-105 LB-FT
WHEN CHECKING TORQUE, TIGHTEN TO NEXT COTTER PIN HOLE. THIS TORQUE NOT TO EXCEED 125 LB-FT.

NUT (4)
ARM ASM-LOWER

WITH SUSPENSION ASSEMBLED, THE BOTTOM END OF COIL SPRING MUST SHOW IN FIRST HOLE AND NOT COVER SECOND HOLE.

VIEW C

Front suspension—starting 1971 (© Buick Div. G.M. Corp.)

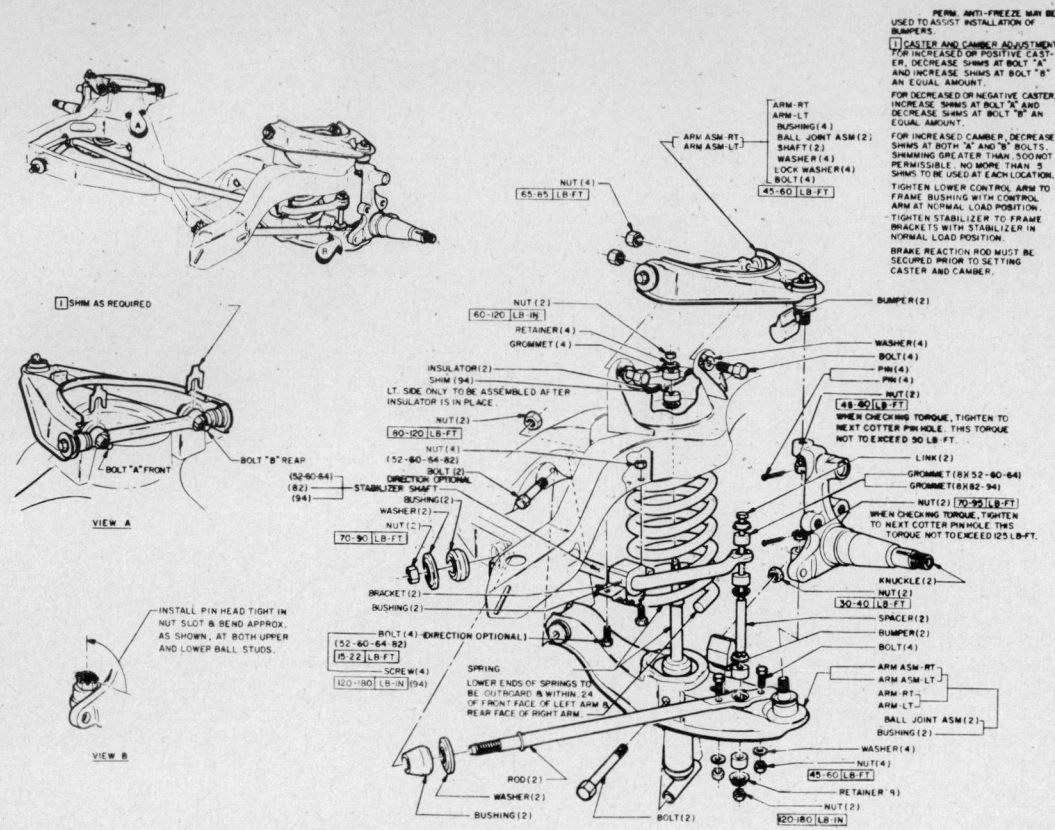

Front suspension—typical 1965-70 (© Buick Div. G.M. Corp.)

PERM. ANTI-FREEZE MAY BE USED TO ASSIST INSTALLATION OF BUMPERS.

1 CASTER AND CAMBER ADJUSTMENT FOR INCREASED OR POSITIVE CASTER, DECREASE SHIMS AT BOLT "A" AND INCREASE SHIMS AT BOLT "B" AN EQUAL AMOUNT.

FOR DECREASED OR NEGATIVE CASTER, INCREASE SHIMS AT BOLT "A" AND DECREASE SHIMS AT BOLT "B" AN EQUAL AMOUNT.

FOR INCREASED CAMBER, DECREASE SHIMS AT BOTH "A" AND "B" BOLTS. SHIMMING GREATER THAN .500 NOT PERMISSIBLE. NO MORE THAN 5 SHIMS TO BE USED AT EACH LOCATION.

TIGHTEN LOWER CONTROL ARM TO FRAME BUSHING WITH CONTROL ARM AT NORMAL LOAD POSITION.

TIGHTEN STABILIZER TO FRAME BRACKETS WITH STABILIZER IN NORMAL LOAD POSITION.

BRAKE REACTION ROD MUST BE SECURED PRIOR TO SETTING CASTER AND CAMBER.

1 SHIM AS REQUIRED

INSTALL PIN HEAD TIGHT IN NUT SLOT & BEND APPROX. AS SHOWN, AT BOTH UPPER AND LOWER BALL STUDS.

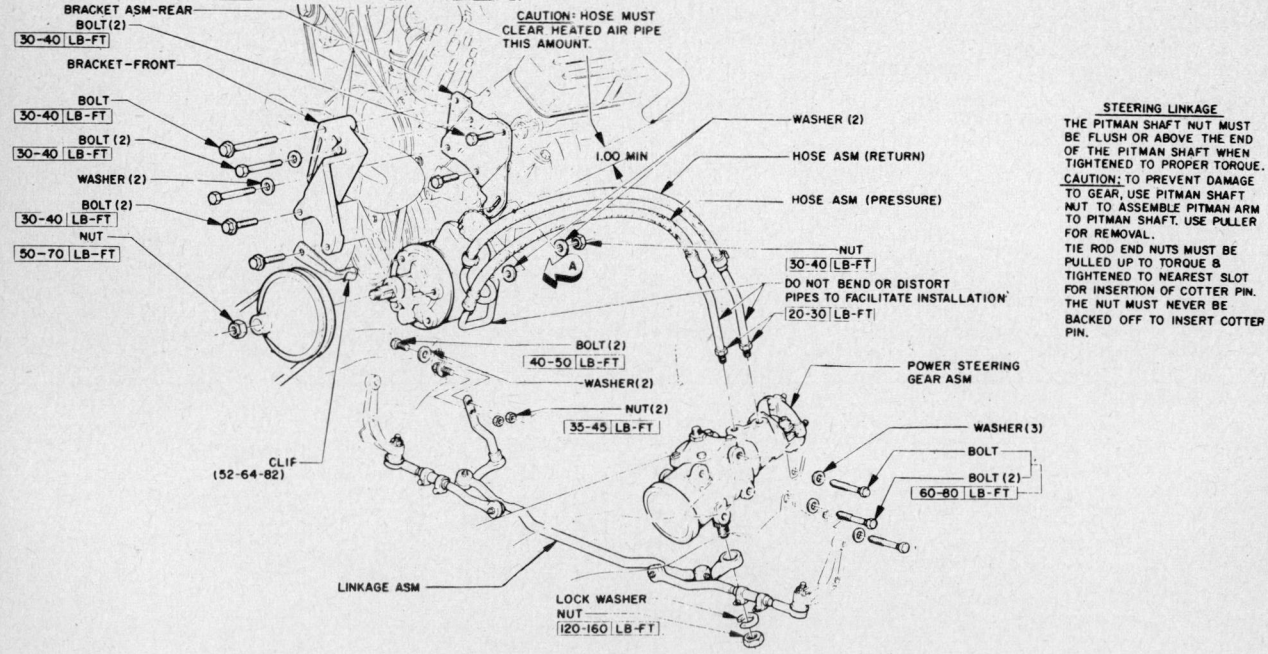

Power steering system (© Buick Div. G.M. Corp.)

CAUTION: HOSE MUST CLEAR HEATED AIR PIPE THIS AMOUNT.

STEERING LINKAGE
THE PITMAN SHAFT NUT MUST BE FLUSH OR ABOVE THE END OF THE PITMAN SHAFT WHEN TIGHTENED TO PROPER TORQUE.
CAUTION: TO PREVENT DAMAGE TO GEAR, USE PITMAN SHAFT NUT TO ASSEMBLE PITMAN ARM TO PITMAN SHAFT. USE PULLER FOR REMOVAL.
TIE ROD END NUTS MUST BE PULLED UP TO TORQUE & TIGHTENED TO NEAREST SLOT FOR INSERTION OF COTTER PIN. THE NUT MUST NEVER BE BACKED OFF TO INSERT COTTER PIN.

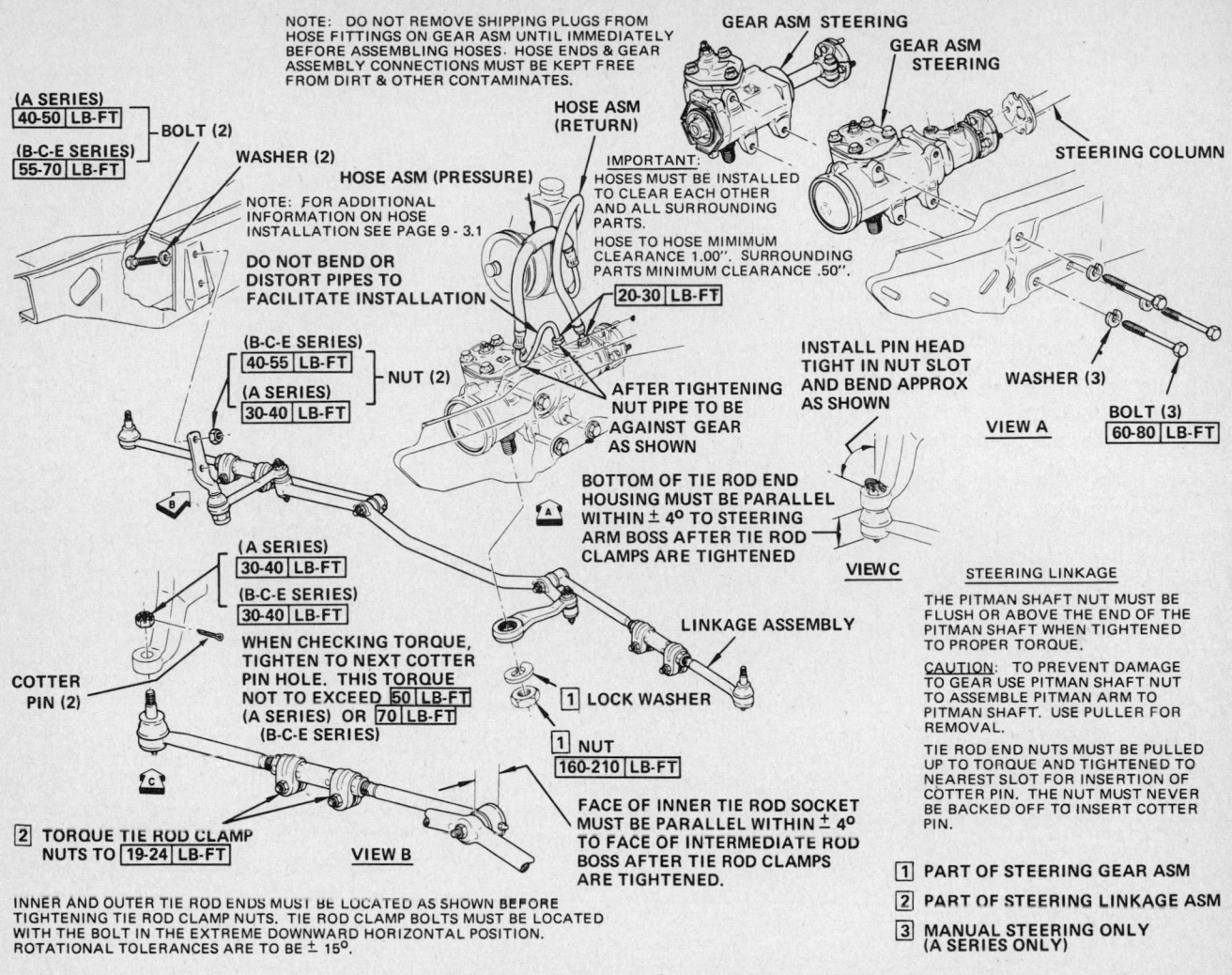

NOTE: DO NOT REMOVE SHIPPING PLUGS FROM HOSE FITTINGS ON GEAR ASM UNTIL IMMEDIATELY BEFORE ASSEMBLING HOSES. HOSE ENDS & GEAR ASSEMBLY CONNECTIONS MUST BE KEPT FREE FROM DIRT & OTHER CONTAMINATES.

GEAR ASM STEERING

GEAR ASM STEERING

(A SERIES) 40-50 LB-FT
(B-C-E SERIES) 55-70 LB-FT] BOLT (2)

WASHER (2)

HOSE ASM (PRESSURE)

HOSE ASM (RETURN)

IMPORTANT: HOSES MUST BE INSTALLED TO CLEAR EACH OTHER AND ALL SURROUNDING PARTS.

STEERING COLUMN

NOTE: FOR ADDITIONAL INFORMATION ON HOSE INSTALLATION SEE PAGE 9 - 3.1

DO NOT BEND OR DISTORT PIPES TO FACILITATE INSTALLATION

HOSE TO HOSE MIMIMUM CLEARANCE 1.00". SURROUNDING PARTS MINIMUM CLEARANCE .50".

20-30 LB-FT

(B-C-E SERIES) 40-55 LB-FT
(A SERIES) 30-40 LB-FT] NUT (2)

AFTER TIGHTENING NUT PIPE TO BE AGAINST GEAR AS SHOWN

INSTALL PIN HEAD TIGHT IN NUT SLOT AND BEND APPROX AS SHOWN

WASHER (3)

VIEW A

BOLT (3) 60-80 LB-FT

BOTTOM OF TIE ROD END HOUSING MUST BE PARALLEL WITHIN ± 4° TO STEERING ARM BOSS AFTER TIE ROD CLAMPS ARE TIGHTENED

(A SERIES) 30-40 LB-FT
(B-C-E SERIES) 30-40 LB-FT

WHEN CHECKING TORQUE, TIGHTEN TO NEXT COTTER PIN HOLE. THIS TORQUE NOT TO EXCEED 50 LB-FT (A SERIES) OR 70 LB-FT (B-C-E SERIES)

VIEW C

LINKAGE ASSEMBLY

STEERING LINKAGE

THE PITMAN SHAFT NUT MUST BE FLUSH OR ABOVE THE END OF THE PITMAN SHAFT WHEN TIGHTENED TO PROPER TORQUE.

CAUTION: TO PREVENT DAMAGE TO GEAR USE PITMAN SHAFT NUT TO ASSEMBLE PITMAN ARM TO PITMAN SHAFT. USE PULLER FOR REMOVAL.

COTTER PIN (2)

1 LOCK WASHER

1 NUT 160-210 LB-FT

TIE ROD END NUTS MUST BE PULLED UP TO TORQUE AND TIGHTENED TO NEAREST SLOT FOR INSERTION OF COTTER PIN. THE NUT MUST NEVER BE BACKED OFF TO INSERT COTTER PIN.

2 TORQUE TIE ROD CLAMP NUTS TO 19-24 LB-FT

VIEW B

FACE OF INNER TIE ROD SOCKET MUST BE PARALLEL WITHIN ± 4° TO FACE OF INTERMEDIATE ROD BOSS AFTER TIE ROD CLAMPS ARE TIGHTENED.

1 PART OF STEERING GEAR ASM
2 PART OF STEERING LINKAGE ASM
3 MANUAL STEERING ONLY (A SERIES ONLY)

INNER AND OUTER TIE ROD ENDS MUST BE LOCATED AS SHOWN BEFORE TIGHTENING TIE ROD CLAMP NUTS. TIE ROD CLAMP BOLTS MUST BE LOCATED WITH THE BOLT IN THE EXTREME DOWNWARD HORIZONTAL POSITION. ROTATIONAL TOLERANCES ARE TO BE ± 15°.

Power steering gear layout—starting 1971 © Buick Div. G.M. Corp.)

Start the engine and turn the steering wheel to the right so that the oil pressure in the housing will force the seals out. Catch the seal and the oil in a container. Turn off the engine when the two seals are out.

This method of seal removal eliminates the possible scoring of the seal seats while attempting to pry them out.

Inspect the two old seals for damage to the rubber covering on the outside diameter. If they seem scored or scratched, inspect the housing for burrs, etc., and remove them before installing the new seals.

Lubricate the two new seals with petroleum jelly. Put the one with a single lip in first, then insert a washer and drive seal in far enough to permit installation of double lip seal, washer and the seal retaining ring. The first seal is not supposed to bottom in its counterbore.

Fill reservoir to proper level, start engine, allow to idle for at least three minutes without turning steering wheel, turn wheel to right and check for leaks.

Remove the tape and reinstall the pitman arm. Tighten nut to 140 ft.

lbs. for constant ratio, 180 ft. lbs. for variable ratio units.

Power Steering Gear Removal

Disconnect the hoses at the steering gear and elevate their ends above the pump to prevent oil from draining out of the pump.

Remove pinch bolt securing flexible coupling to steering gear stub shaft. Working under the car, remove pitman shaft nut and remove the pitman arm. Remove sheet metal baffle. Remove the steering gear to frame bolts at outside of left frame rail. Remove steering gear.

Reverse procedure to install.

Power Steering Gear Pump Removal and Installation

Disconnect the drive belt and remove the pump pulley with a suitable puller. On some models, the pulley has bolt access holes which make pulley removal unnecessary. Disconnect the hoses from the pump and unbolt the pump from the bracket. Use caps or tape to cover the hose connectors, unions, and hose ends to keep out dirt.

Reinstall by reversing procedure. The drive belt should be adjusted to have about ½ in. play on the longest run between pulleys. After replacing pump, fill reservoir and bleed pump by idling engine for three minutes before moving the steering wheel. Then rotate steering wheel slowly throughout its entire range. Recheck oil level.

Variable Ratio Power Steering Gear and Pump 1969-72

This gear responds faster, requires less manual effort and retains feel-of-the-road steering. Parking effort is about one-half that of previous models.

Previous Buick constant ratio steering had approximately a 17.5 : 1 ratio. In other words, for each degree of turn the wheel had to be turned 17.5 degrees. With variable ratio steering, the ratio is between 15:1 and 16:1 in the straight-ahead position; about 13.1:1 at full lock for faster response.

Removal of variable ratio type power steering gear or pump involves the same procedure as for prior models.

More detailed information on maintenance and overhaul procedure is covered in the Unit Repair Section.

Clutch

1965-72

The only service adjustment that can be made on a Buick clutch is that of pedal clearance. If difficulty is experienced with the clutch and adjusting the clearance does not correct it, it will be necessary to remove the clutch from the car, since no practical in-car service is possible.

Clutch Removal and Installation

1965-66

1. Remove driveshaft from front flange.
2. Remove transmission.
3. Remove equalizer shaft and return spring.
4. Remove ball stud from release shaft.
5. Remove clutch release lever and seal and nylon bushing.

6. Remove socket head screw on clutch release shaft and second socket head screw with cone point from same hole.
7. Pull release shaft out approximately 3 in. and slide off yoke and throw-out bearing. Then remove shaft.
8. Mark clutch cover and flywheel to reinstall in same position.
9. Remove cover assembly by loosening bolts one turn at a time to hold spring pressure even. Spacers (¼ in. nuts) placed between release levers and cover edge will help and also simplify reinstalling.
10. To reinstall, reverse the above.

1967-72

1. Remove transmission.
2. Release equalizer assembly.
3. Remove pedal return spring from clutch fork. Disconnect rod assembly from clutch fork.
4. Remove flywheel housing.
5. Remove throwout bearing from clutch fork.
6. Disconnect clutch fork from ball

stud by moving toward center of flywheel housing.
7. Mark clutch cover and flywheel so that cover can be reinstalled in the same position. This is important to proper balance.
8. Loosen clutch cover to flywheel attaching bolts one turn at a time to maintain even spring pressure.
9. Support pressure plate and cover assembly while removing bolts. Remove pressure plate and driven plate. Caution should be used to keep the driven plate clean.
10. Reinstall by reversing procedure. Tighten presure plate to 30-40 ft. lbs.

Clutch Pedal Adjustment

1965-66, Except LeSabre

Clutch pedal clearance is adjusted under the dash at a turnbuckle on the rod between the clutch pedal and the equalizer. There should be 7/8-1 1/8 in. free-play of the clutch pedal before the throw out bearing strikes the diaphragm.

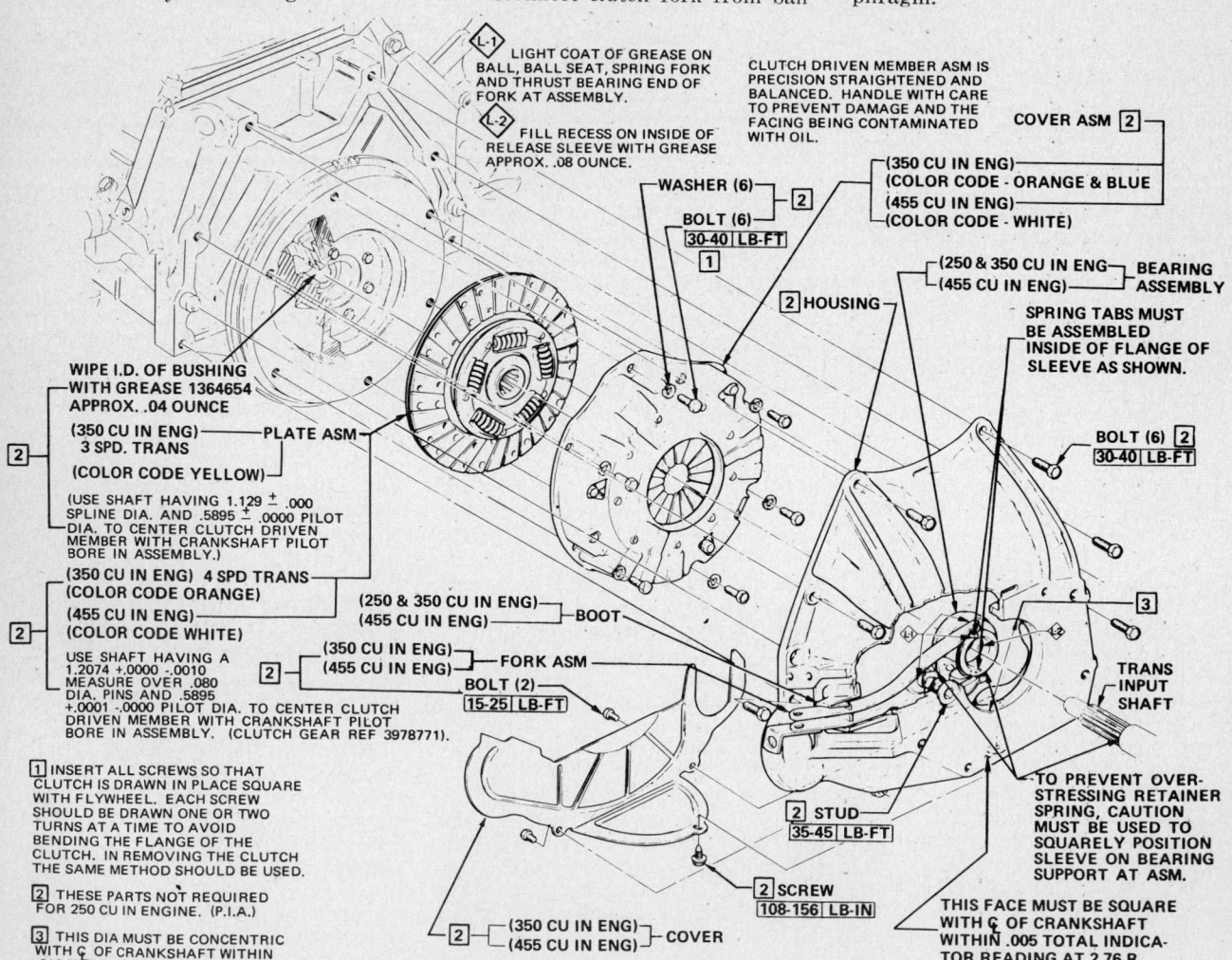

Typical clutch assembly sequence—1971 illustrated (© Buick Div. G.M. Corp.)

1965-66 LeSabre, 1967-72 All Models

Clutch pedal clearance is adjusted under the car at the link between the clutch throwout fork and the equalizer. There should be 5/8-7/8 in. freeplay of the clutch pedal before the throwout bearing strikes the fingers (or diaphragm).

Transmissions

Standard

Transmission refill capacities will be found in the Capacities table.

Shift Control Adjustment— Three-Speed Column Shift

1965-66

1. Place transmission levers in neutral.
2. Loosen shift rod adjusting clamp bolts.
3. Install a piece of 1/4 in. round stock (The unthreaded part of a 1/4 in. bolt is ideal.) into the bearing tab and first-reverse lever holes at the bottom of the steering column.
4. Push a large screwdriver blade between the selector plate and the second-third lever until the selector plate engages the tang on both shift levers.
5. Lift the column selector lever straight up toward the steering wheel several times to assure that the neutral positions in both the first-reverse and the second-third planes are aligned. If they are not aligned, shorten the first-reverse rod by pulling it through the swivel no more than 3/16 in.

1967-68

This procedure is identical to that described above for 1965-66 models with the substitutions of the following steps:
3. Install a 3/16 in. rod through the holes in the first-reverse lever, the selector plate, the second-third lever, and the alignment plate at the bottom of the steering column.
4. Eliminate this step.

1969-72

1. Place column selector lever in reverse position. Loosen first-reverse adjusting clamp bolts.
2. Shift first-reverse transmission lever into reverse. Tighten first-reverse adjusting clamp bolt to 17-23 ft. lbs.
3. Shift transmission levers into neutral positions. Loosen second-third adjusting clamp.
4. Install 3/16 in. rod into alignment holes. Tighten second-third adjusting clamp bolt to 17-23 ft. lbs.

1965 Four-Speed Floor Shift

The four-speed gearshift linkage uses three shift rods and levers. A simple gauge pin, a 1/4 in. dia. rod, will help in making the proper adjustments. An alternative method is to have an assistant hold the manual shift lever in neutral.

1. Loosen shift rod adjusting clamps.
2. Place transmission in neutral and install gauge pin through shift levers (or have assistant hold shifter lever in neutral).
3. Tighten shift rod adjusting clamps to 17-23 ft. lbs.
4. Remove gauge pin and check for complete and easy shifting.
5. Hold shift control lever in fourth gear, then turn stop bolt until it contacts shift lever. Repeat operation at forward stop bolt for third gear.

NOTE: console equipped cars have a gauge pin access hole under the carpet.

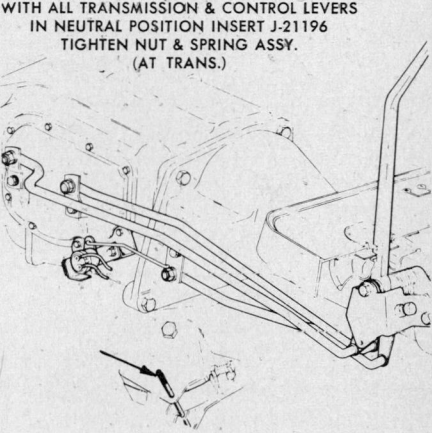

WITH ALL TRANSMISSION & CONTROL LEVERS IN NEUTRAL POSITION INSERT J-21196 TIGHTEN NUT & SPRING ASSY. (AT TRANS.)

Four-speed transmission controls with console—arrow points to 1/4-in. gauge pin (© Buick Div. G.M. Corp.)

Transmission Removal

NOTE: when removing any major part or assembly, always mark the parts so that the assemblies can be returned to the same position from which they were removed. This applies particularly to universal joint housings and covers, spring hangers, etc.

1964-72

1. Mark universal joint and transmission shaft companion flange for proper indexing at time of installation. Remove two U-bolts and disconnect driveshaft at the front joint. Slide the driveshaft rearward as far as possible and tie to one side.
2. Disconnect shift linkage from transmission.
3. Disconnect speedometer cable at transmission. Remove driven gear and sleeve.
4. Loosen all three exhaust pipe ball joints to permit transmission and rear of engine to be lowered.
5. Remove two bolts holding transmission mounting pad to transmission support. Leave mounting pad bolted to transmission.

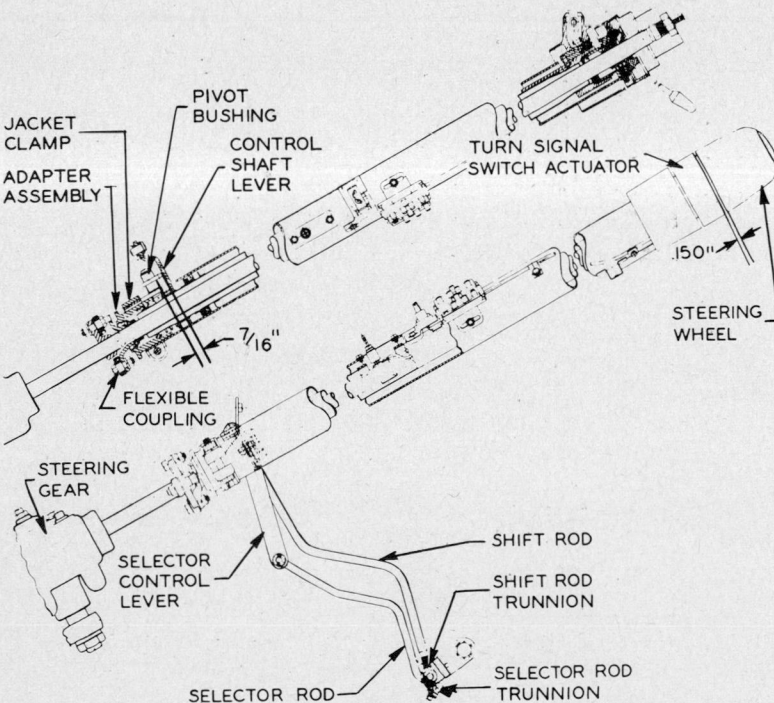

JACKET CLAMP

ADAPTER ASSEMBLY

PIVOT BUSHING

CONTROL SHAFT LEVER

TURN SIGNAL SWITCH ACTUATOR

.150"

STEERING WHEEL

7/16"

FLEXIBLE COUPLING

STEERING GEAR

SELECTOR CONTROL LEVER

SHIFT ROD

SHIFT ROD TRUNNION

SELECTOR ROD TRUNNION

SELECTOR ROD

Synchromesh transmission shift mechanism (© Buick Div. G.M. Corp.)

6. With a padded jack under the engine, raise the unit until the transmission mounting pad clears the transmission support.
7. Remove four bolts holding transmission support to body members. Remove support, then lower the jack to allow transmission to clear the underbody.
8. Remove upper left transmission to flywheel housing bolt and install a 7/16 14 x 4½ in. guidepin. Remove lower right bolt and pin.
9. Remove the other two transmission attaching bolts. Slide the transmission back until the drive gear shaft disengages the clutch disc and clears the flywheel housing. Lower the transmission.
10. Install transmission by reversing the above procedure.

Transmission Disassembly

Specific information on manual transmission overhaul can be found in the Unit Repair Section.

Automatic

When automatic transmission trouble is reported, a road test and careful diagnosis are in order. Transmission Removal and Replacement and Linkage Adjustments are covered here in the following paragraphs. For test procedures, transmission overhaul and other detailed information, see Unit Repair Section.

The Super Turbine 300 transmission is standard equipment on Le Sabre models with the smallest engine, 1965-69. The Euper Turbine 400 is optional on the small engine Le Sabres and standard on all other models, 1965-68. In 1969, the Super Turbine 400 is replaced by the virtually identical Turbo Hydra-Matic 400; it is optional on small engine Le Sabres and standard on all other models. In 1970, the Super Turbine 300 is eliminated; the Turbo Hydra-Matic 400 is the only automatic transmission used on 1970 to present Buicks.

Shift Control Adjustment

1965-66 Column Shift, 1965-68—Console Shift

1. Place manual control lever in Park position.
2. Loosen adjusting clamp bolt at transmission.
3. Place transmission lever in Park position.
4. Tighten adjusting clamp bolt to 17-23 ft. lbs. Overtightening will cause hard shifting.
5. Start engine. Check for proper shifting into all ranges.

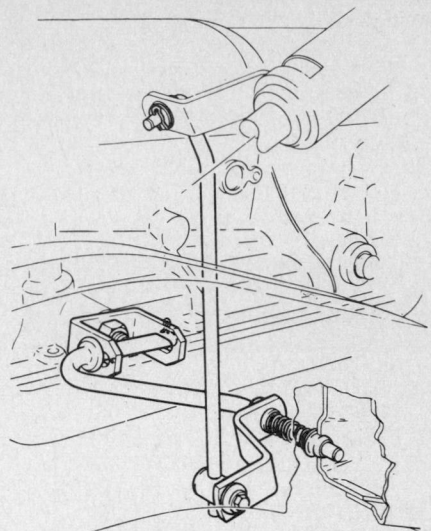

Typical column shift linkage—
Super Turbine transmissions
(© Buick Div. G.M. Corp.)

1967-70 Column Shift

This procedure is identical to that described above for 1965-66 column shift and 1965-68 console shift with the substitution of the following step:
1. Place manual control lever against Drive stop.

1969-72 Console Shift

These units are operated by a cable

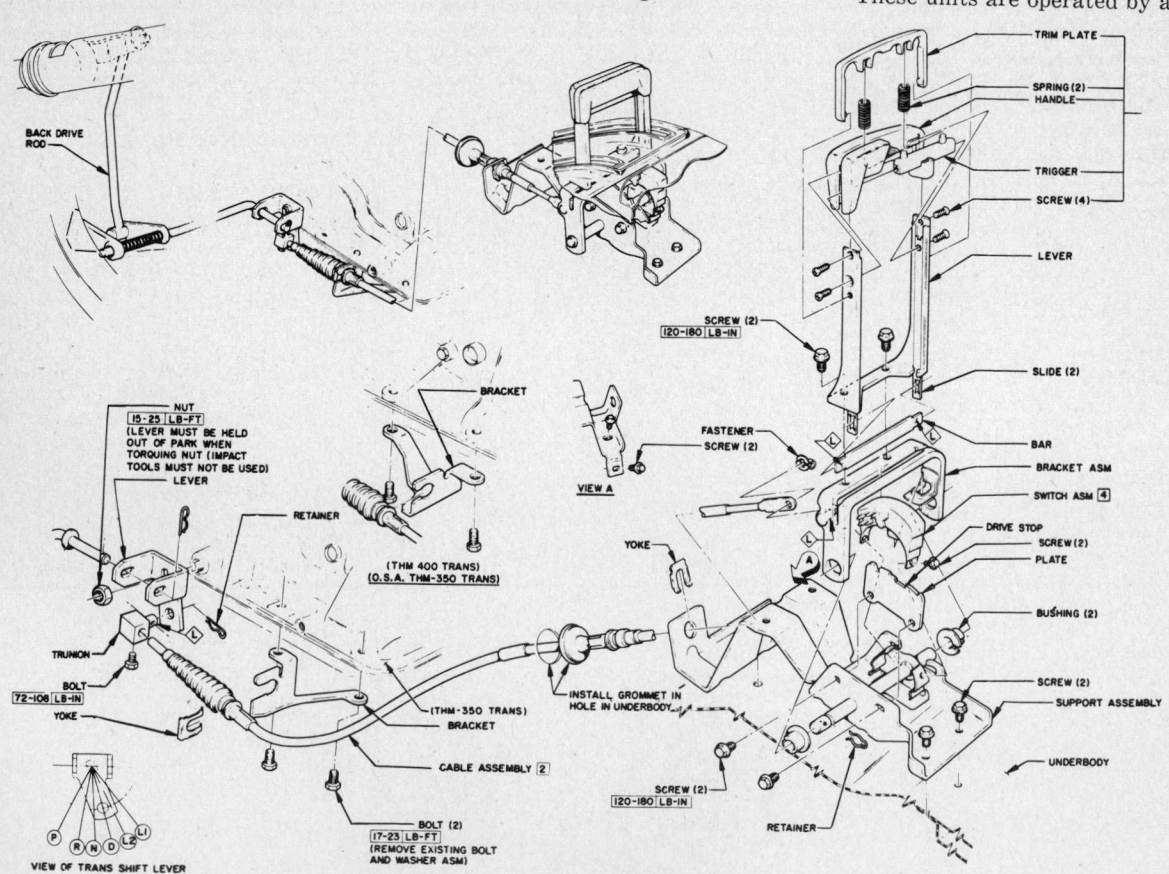

Cable type console shift linkage—starting 1969 Turbo-Hydramatic 400
(© Buick Div., G.M. Corp.)

linkage. Adjust as follows:

1. Loosen trunnion bolt at transmission end of cable.
2. Set manual control lever against Drive stop up to 1970, Neutral starting 1971.
3. Place transmission bar assembly in Drive position up to 1970, Neutral starting 1971.
4. Tighten trunnion bolt against cable end to 6-9 ft. lbs.
5. Place transmission bar assembly in Park position.
6. Loosen back drive rod clamp screw.
7. Push back drive rod (from linkage to steering column) up and hold lightly against stop.
8. Tighten screw in clamp at end of back drive rod to 17-23 ft. lbs.
9. Start engine. Check for proper shifting into all ranges.

1971-72 Column Shift

1. Loosen adjusting clamp bolt.
2. Place selector lever in Neutral.
3. Place transmission lever, at transmission, in Neutral.
4. Tighten adjusting clamp bolt to 17-23 ft. lbs.
5. Start engine. Check for proper shifting into all ranges.

Neutral Start Switch Adjustment—All Models

This safety switch prevents starting except in Neutral or Park positions. The switch combines function with the back-up light switch and is actuated by the transmission linkage. On column shift cars, the switch is under the instrument panel. On console shift cars, the switch is inside the console up to 1970, on the column thereafter. To check switch adjustment:

1. Turn on ignition switch.
2. Place shift control lever in Reverse, and make sure back-up lights are on.
3. Set parking brake. Hold foot brake. Place shift control in Neutral and make sure engine will start. Repeat in Park, Drive, and Reverse. Engine must start only in Neutral or Park.

4. To adjust switch, loosen mounting screws and move switch on slotted mounting holes.

Idle Stator and Detent Switch Adjustments

1965-67 Super Turbine 300, 400

Refer to the accompanying illustrations for these adjustment procedures.

Detent Switch Adjustment

1968-69 Super Turbine 300
1968-72 Super Turbine 400, Turbo Hydra-Matic 400

Refer to the accompanying illustrations for these adjustment procedures.

Transmission Removal— 1965-72

1. Raise car and provide support for front and rear of car.
2. Disconnect front exhaust pipe bolts at the exhaust manifold and at the connection of the intermediate exhaust pipe location (single exhaust only). On dual exhaust the exhaust pipes need not be removed.
3. Remove pinion flange U-bolts and slide propeller shaft toward transmission as far as possible to separate universal joint from pinion flange. Remove propeller shaft from car.
4. Place suitable jack under transmission and fasten transmission securely to jack.
5. Remove vacuum line to vacuum modulator hose from vacuum modulator.
6. Loosen cooler line bolts and separate cooler lines from transmission.
7. Remove transmission mounting pad to crossmember bolts.
8. Remove transmission cross member support to frame rail bolts. Remove crossmember.
9. Disconnect speedometer cable and electrical wiring.
10. Disconnect shift linkage from

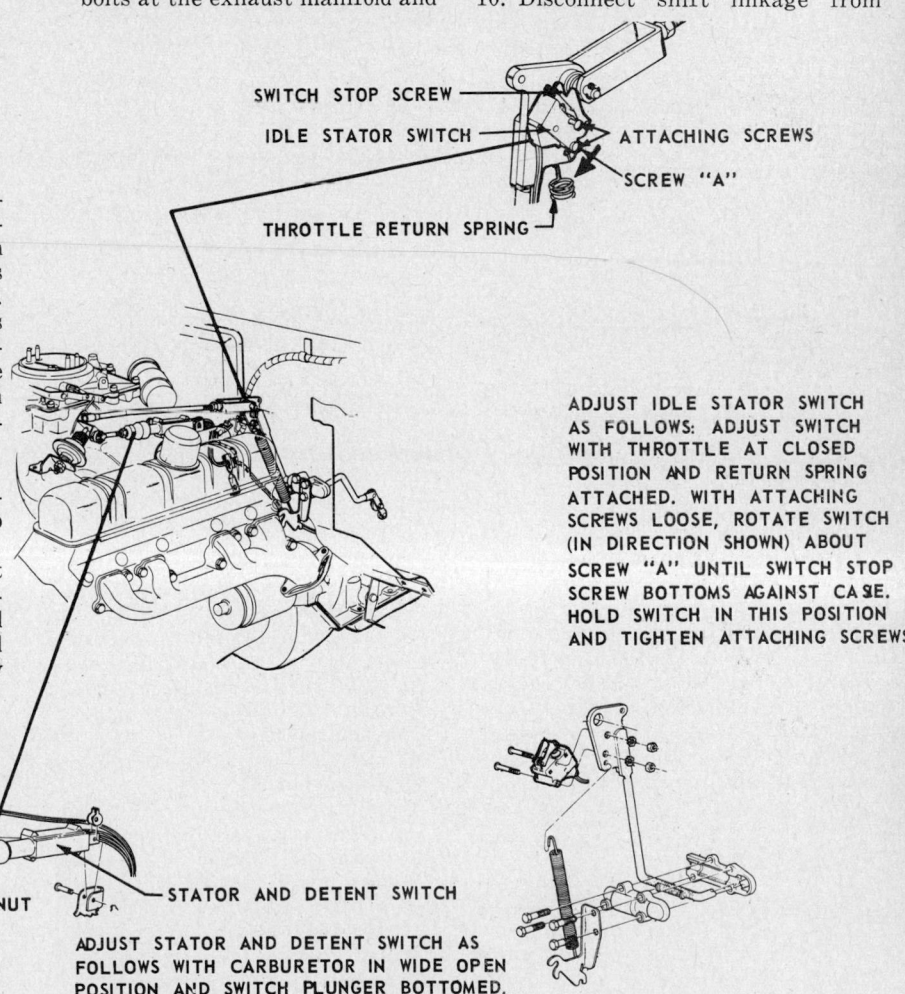

SWITCH STOP SCREW
IDLE STATOR SWITCH
ATTACHING SCREWS
SCREW "A"
THROTTLE RETURN SPRING

ADJUST IDLE STATOR SWITCH AS FOLLOWS: ADJUST SWITCH WITH THROTTLE AT CLOSED POSITION AND RETURN SPRING ATTACHED. WITH ATTACHING SCREWS LOOSE, ROTATE SWITCH (IN DIRECTION SHOWN) ABOUT SCREW "A" UNTIL SWITCH STOP SCREW BOTTOMS AGAINST CASE. HOLD SWITCH IN THIS POSITION AND TIGHTEN ATTACHING SCREWS.

THROTTLE ROD
CARBURETOR LEVER PIN
LINK
WASHER
NUT
RETAINER
STATOR AND DETENT SWITCH

ADJUST STATOR AND DETENT SWITCH AS FOLLOWS WITH CARBURETOR IN WIDE OPEN POSITION AND SWITCH PLUNGER BOTTOMED, ADJUST LINK UNTIL IT WILL SLIP OVER CARBURETOR LEVER PIN, THEN SCREW LINK INTO PLUNGER 1 1/2 TURNS. INSTALL WASHER AND RETAINER.

1965-67 Super Turbine 300 and 400 stator and detent switch adjustment
(© Buick Div., G.M. Corp.)

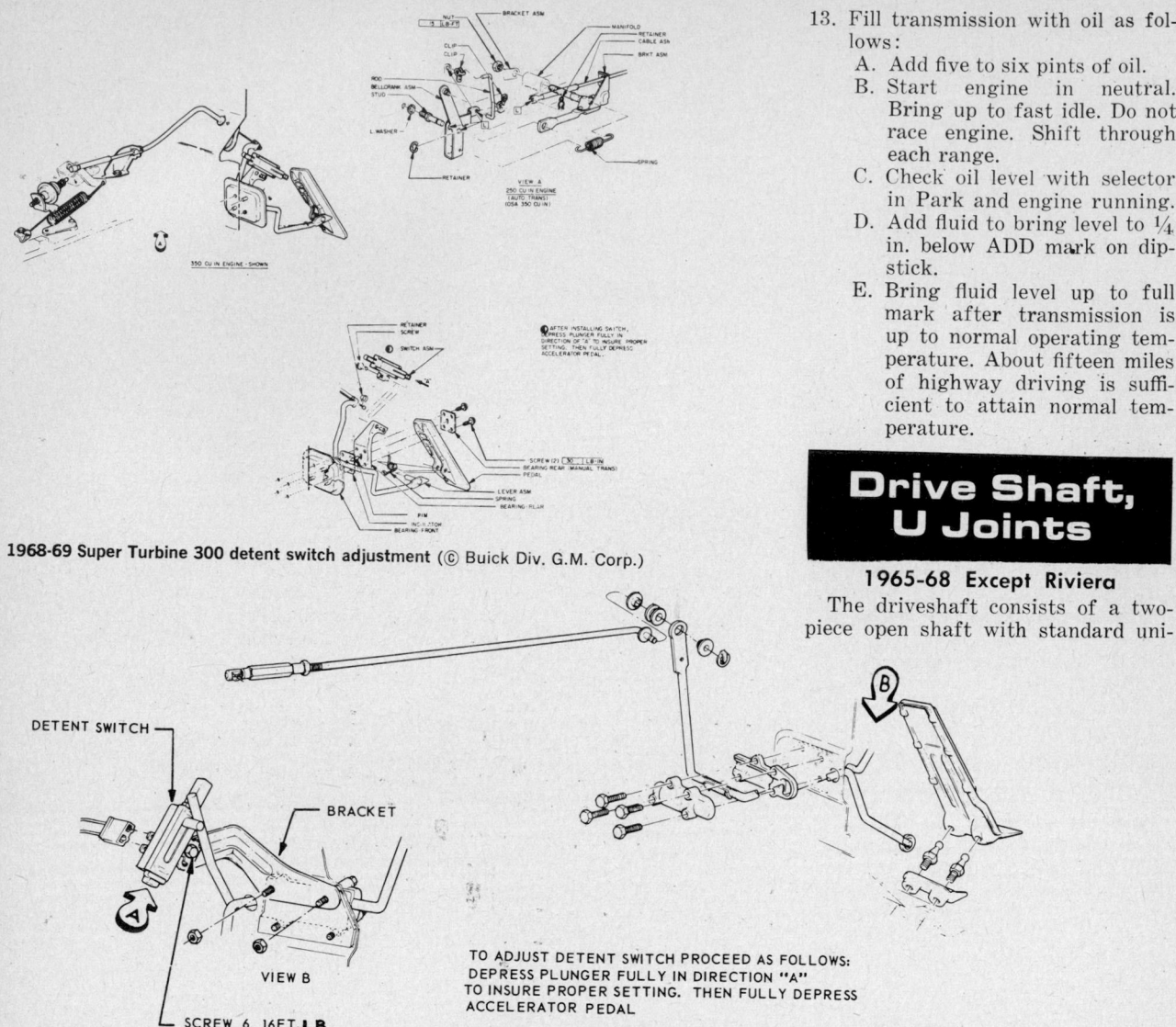

13. Fill transmission with oil as follows:
  A. Add five to six pints of oil.
  B. Start engine in neutral. Bring up to fast idle. Do not race engine. Shift through each range.
  C. Check oil level with selector in Park and engine running.
  D. Add fluid to bring level to ¼ in. below ADD mark on dipstick.
  E. Bring fluid level up to full mark after transmission is up to normal operating temperature. About fifteen miles of highway driving is sufficient to attain normal temperature.

Drive Shaft, U Joints

1965-68 Except Riviera

The driveshaft consists of a two-piece open shaft with standard uni-

1968-69 Super Turbine 300 detent switch adjustment (© Buick Div. G.M. Corp.)

DETENT SWITCH

BRACKET

VIEW B

SCREW 6 16FT. LB.

TO ADJUST DETENT SWITCH PROCEED AS FOLLOWS: DEPRESS PLUNGER FULLY IN DIRECTION "A" TO INSURE PROPER SETTING. THEN FULLY DEPRESS ACCELERATOR PEDAL

1968-70 Super Turbine 400 and Turbo-Hydramatic 400 detent switch adjustment (© Buick Div., G.M. Corp.)

transmission.
11. Disconnect transmission filler pipe at engine. Remove filler pipe from transmission.
12. Support engine at oil pan.
13. Remove transmission flywheel cover pan to case tapping screws. Remove flywheel cover pan.
14. Mark flywheel and converter pump for reassembly in same position, and remove three converter pump to flywheel bolts.
15. Remove transmission case to engine block bolts.
16. Move transmission rearward to provide clearance between converter pump and crankshaft. Lower transmission and move to bench.

Transmission Installation

1. Raise transmission into position using suitable jack. Rotate converter to permit coupling of flywheel and converter in original

relationship.
2. Install transmission case to engine block bolts. Torque to 30-40 ft. lbs. Do not overtighten.
3. Install flywheel to converter pump bolts. Torque to 25-35 ft. lbs.
4. Install transmission crossmember support. Install mounting pad to crossmember.
5. Remove transmission jack and engine support.
6. Install transmission flywheel cover pan with tapping screws.
7. Install transmission filler pipe using a new O-ring.
8. Reconnect speedometer cable and wiring.
9. Install propeller shaft. Connect propeller shaft to pinion flange.
10. Reinstall front exhaust crossover pipe.
11. Install oil cooler lines to transmission.
12. Install vacuum line to vacuum modulator.

versal joints front and rear. A double constant velocity joint is used between the shafts with a center support bearing at rear of front shaft and splined front yoke at front of rear shaft.

1969-70, Except Riviera

The driveshaft consists of a one-piece open shaft with universal joints front and rear. A splined slip yoke is located at the transmission end.

1965-70 Riviera

The driveshaft consists of a two-piece open shaft with a standard universal joint at the front. A double constant velocity (CV) joint is used between the shafts and at the rear. There is a center support bearing at the rear of the front shaft and a splined yoke at the front of the rear shaft.

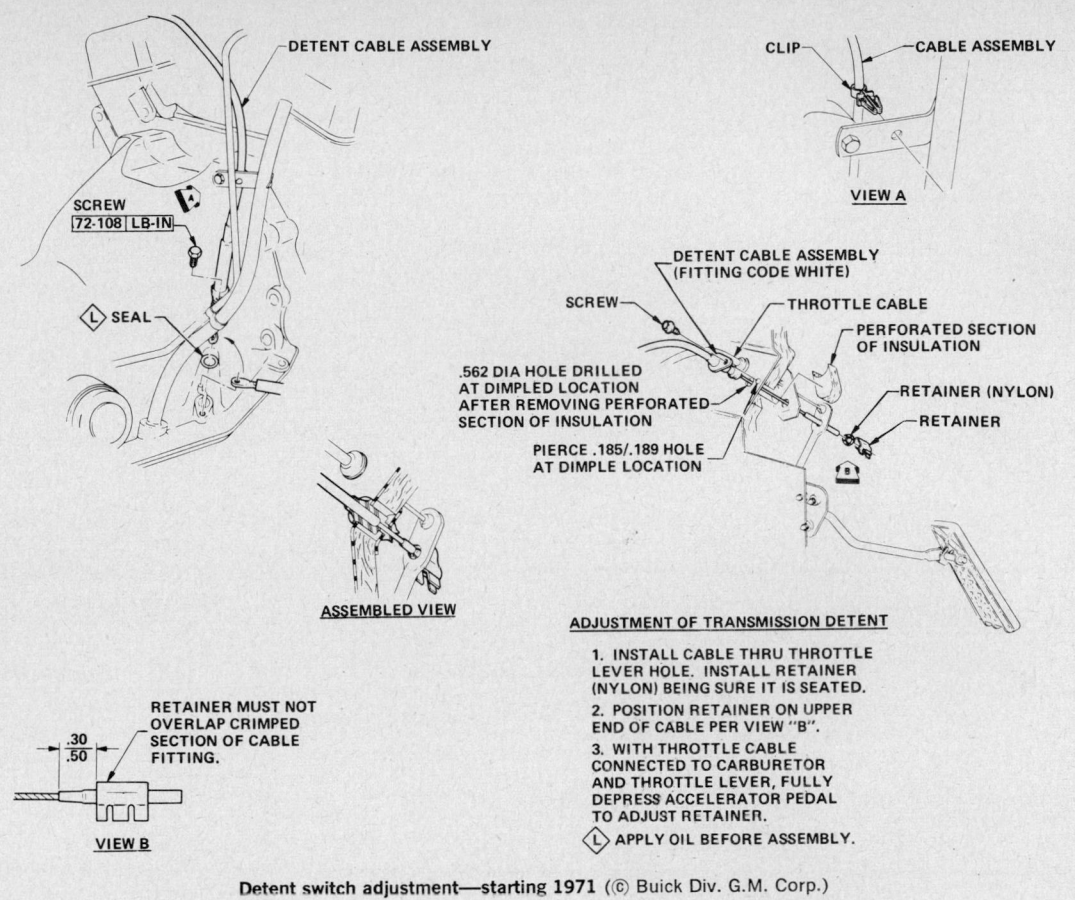

DETENT CABLE ASSEMBLY

SCREW 72-108 LB-IN

L SEAL

CLIP — CABLE ASSEMBLY

VIEW A

DETENT CABLE ASSEMBLY (FITTING CODE WHITE)

SCREW

THROTTLE CABLE

PERFORATED SECTION OF INSULATION

.562 DIA HOLE DRILLED AT DIMPLED LOCATION AFTER REMOVING PERFORATED SECTION OF INSULATION

RETAINER (NYLON)

RETAINER

PIERCE .185/.189 HOLE AT DIMPLE LOCATION

ASSEMBLED VIEW

ADJUSTMENT OF TRANSMISSION DETENT

1. INSTALL CABLE THRU THROTTLE LEVER HOLE. INSTALL RETAINER (NYLON) BEING SURE IT IS SEATED.
2. POSITION RETAINER ON UPPER END OF CABLE PER VIEW "B".
3. WITH THROTTLE CABLE CONNECTED TO CARBURETOR AND THROTTLE LEVER, FULLY DEPRESS ACCELERATOR PEDAL TO ADJUST RETAINER.

L APPLY OIL BEFORE ASSEMBLY.

RETAINER MUST NOT OVERLAP CRIMPED SECTION OF CABLE FITTING.

.30 / .50

VIEW B

Detent switch adjustment—starting 1971 (© Buick Div. G.M. Corp.)

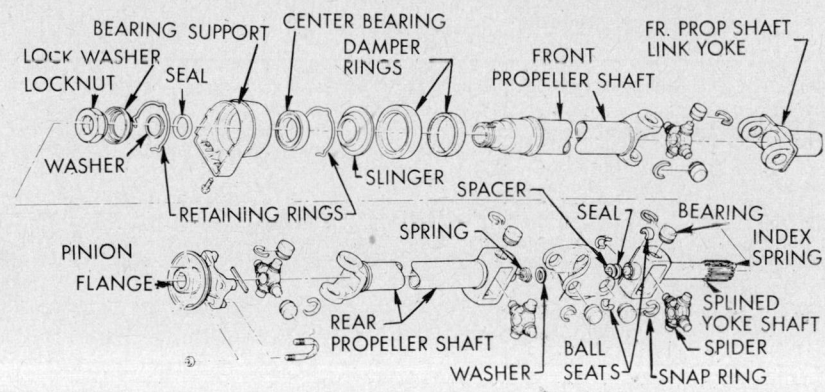

LOCK WASHER
LOCKNUT
WASHER
SEAL
BEARING SUPPORT
CENTER BEARING
DAMPER RINGS
FRONT PROPELLER SHAFT
FR. PROP SHAFT LINK YOKE
RETAINING RINGS
SLINGER

PINION FLANGE
SPRING
REAR PROPELLER SHAFT
SPACER
WASHER
BALL SEATS
SEAL
BEARING
INDEX SPRING
SPLINED YOKE SHAFT
SPIDER
SNAP RING

Typical constant velocity universal joint—44000, 46000 and 48000 ser., 1965-68
(© Buick Div., G.M. Corp.)

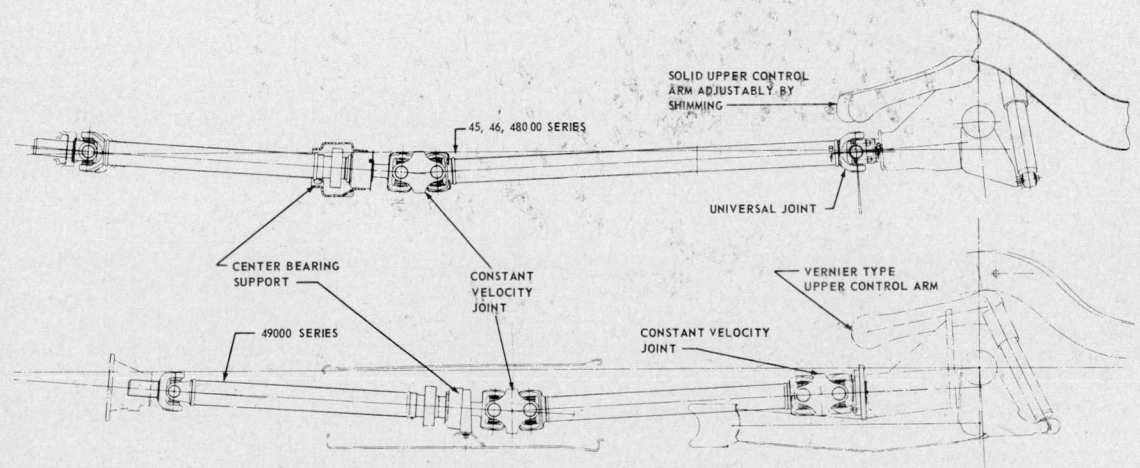

SOLID UPPER CONTROL ARM ADJUSTABLY BY SHIMMING

45, 46, 480 00 SERIES

UNIVERSAL JOINT

CENTER BEARING SUPPORT

CONSTANT VELOCITY JOINT

VERNIER TYPE UPPER CONTROL ARM

49000 SERIES

CONSTANT VELOCITY JOINT

Two-piece driveshaft assemblies up to 1970 (© Buick Div., G.M. Corp.)

1971-72 Except Estate Wagon

This driveshaft consists of a single tube having a single Carden U-joint at the front and a double Carden joint at the rear. A splined slip yoke at the front permits fore and aft movement of the driveshaft. This yoke is lubricated internally with transmission lube or grease. On cars with automatic transmission, the yoke has a vent hole in its end to prevent blowing the rear transmis-

Driveshaft Removal

1965-68 All Models, 1969-70 Riviera

1. Mark pinion flange and rear joint for reassembly. At rear pinion flange, remove U-bolt clamps from rear universal; on Riviera, remove four rear CV joint to pinion flange bolts. Use tape to secure bearings on the spider.

2. Remove four center bearing attaching bolts; two bolts on Riviera.

3. Support rear end of shaft. Slide assembly rearward until front yoke is free of transmission shaft splines. On Riviera, slide complete shaft assembly rearward through frame tunnel.

4. Protect the oil seal surface on the front yoke from dirt or marring.

NOTE: do not bend CV joint to its extreme angle at any time.

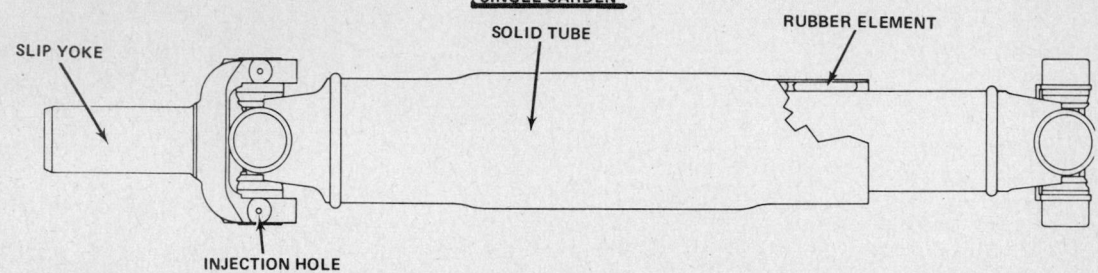

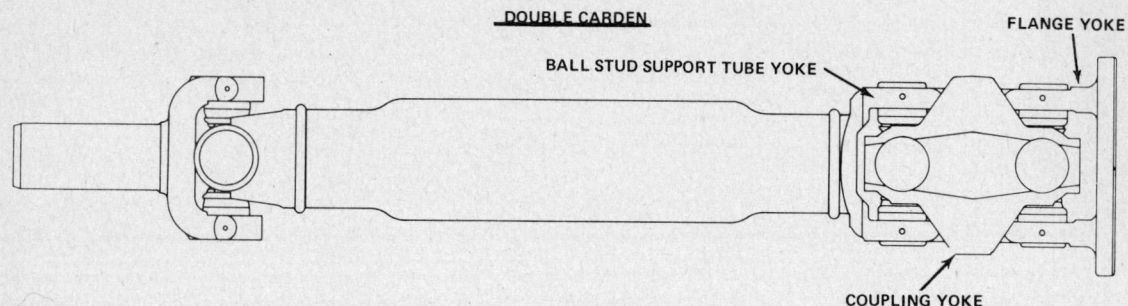

Driveshaft types—starting 1971 (© Buick Div. G.M. Corp.)

Slip yoke with vent hole
(© Buick Div. G.M. Corp.)

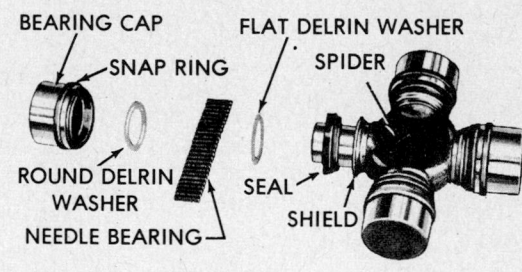

Typical U-joint
(© Buick Div. G.M. Corp.)

sion seal when installing the driveshaft—this hole must be free of dirt.

1971-72 Estate Wagon

This driveshaft consists of two tubes, one slipped inside the other and damped with rubber. Instead of the double rear Carden U-joint, as used on other full-size Buicks, this shaft utilizes a single Carden joint at each end. Lubrication of the front splined yoke is the same as for the double Carden joint shaft.

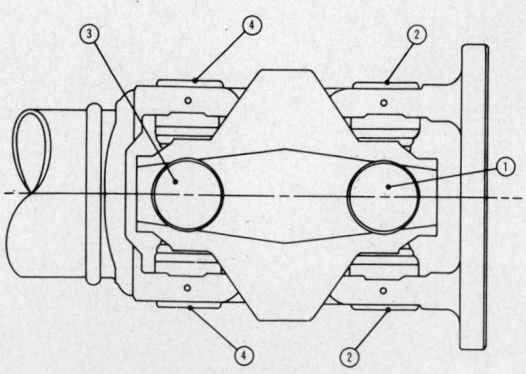

Bearing cap removal sequence—double Carden joint starting 1971
(© Buick Div. G.M. Corp.)

1969-70, Except Riviera, All 1971-72

1. Mark shaft and pinion flange for reassembly.
2. Remove U-bolts from rear pinion flange. Use tape to secure bearings on the spider.
3. Remove shaft assembly by sliding rearward to disengage splines on transmission shaft.

Driveshaft Disassembly

1965-68 All Models, 1969-70 Riviera

1. Loosen locknut and slide locknut and seal against the center CV joint. Slide the rear shaft from the front shaft.
2. Pull the center support and bearing assembly from the shaft by use of a suitable puller.
3. Remove retainers and drive center bearing from support.
4. Disassemble CV joints:

   A. Mark all yokes for reassembly.
   B. Remove universal joint bearings from link yoke.

C. Press two link yoke bearings out, one at a time.
D. Carefully work universal joint and ball stud yoke assembly out of link yoke.
E. Remove all remaining bearings from ball stud yoke. Slip out spider from yoke.
5. Pry out ball stud seat seal, spacer, ball seats, stop, spring, spring seat, and spring seat gasket.
6. Disassemble universal joints:
   A. Remove snap-rings, or push out nylon injection rings.
   B. Press out shaft bearings, one at a time.
7. Reverse procedure for reassembly. Always install complete universal joint repair sets when repairs or replacements are necessary.
NOTE: 1971 and up—production U-joints cannot be reused after injection rings are removed.

1969-70, Except Riviera, All 1971-72

This procedure is identical to that described above for 1965-68 all models, and 1969-70 Riviera, with the exclusion of Steps 1-5.

Lubrication of Slip Splines

1965-68 All Models, 1969-70 Riviera

Lubrication of driveshaft slip splines and constant velocity universal joint center ball is as follows:

The constant velocity universal joint center ball should be lubricated at 6,000 mile intervals.

1. Rotate driveshaft so fitting is visible through rear hole of frame tunnel.
2. Use special adapter held firmly against conical fitting to force grease into center ball socket.

The propeller shaft slip spline should be lubricated every 6,000 miles.

NOTE: due to the position of the slip spline when the car is raised on some types of modern hoists, it is necessary to fill the slip spline lubricant cavity by forcing lubricant through the spline into the cavity.

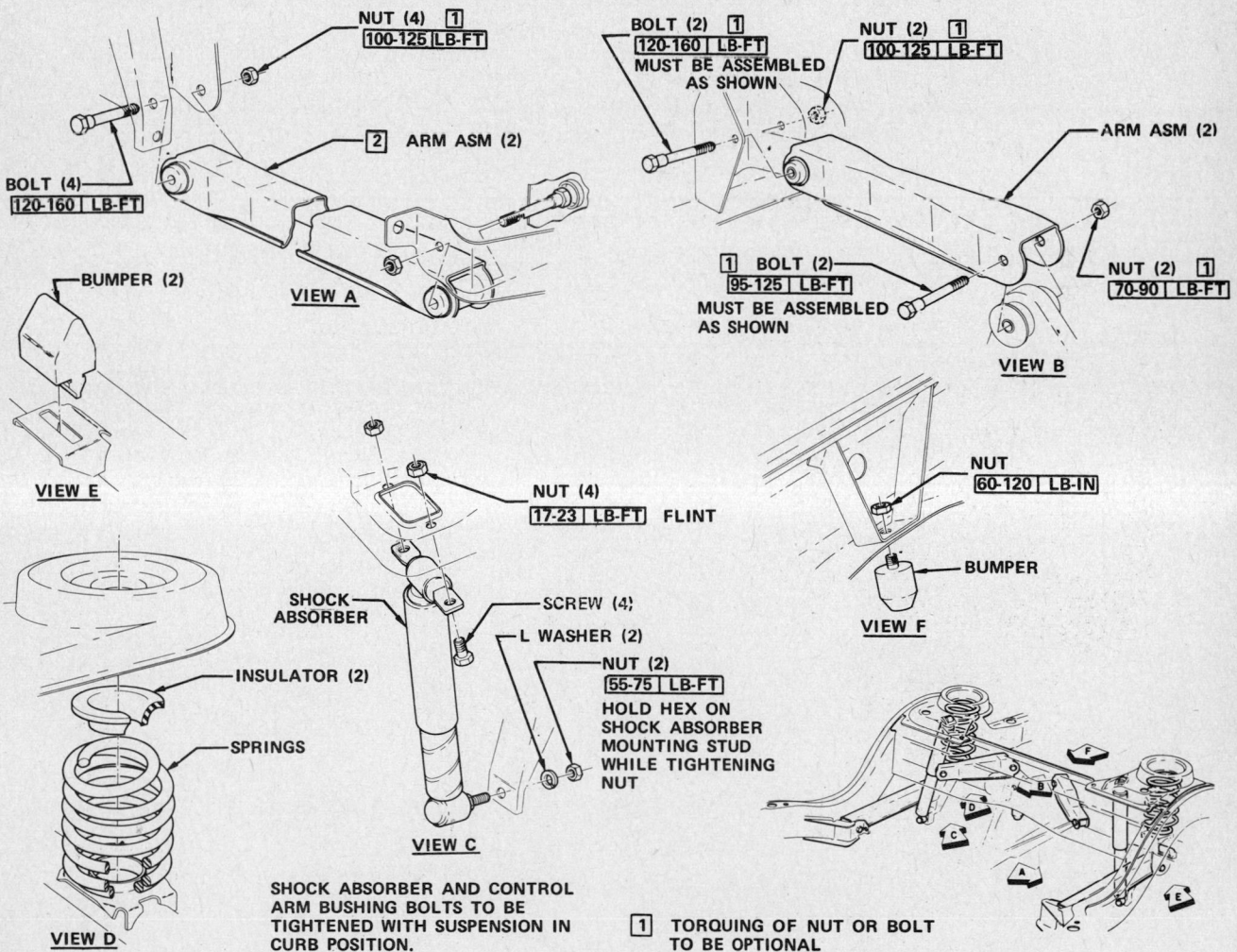

Rear suspension details—typical 1965-72 with coil springs
(© Buick Div. G.M. Corp.)

For this reason, either a fitting or an adapter is necessary in order to build up sufficient pressure to fill the slip spline cavity.

Drive Axle

Troubleshooting and Adjustment

General instructions covering the troubles of the drive axle and how to repair and adjust it, together with information on installation of drive axle bearings and grease seals, are given in the Unit Repair Section.

Capacities of the drive axles are given in the Capacities table.

Rear Axle Removal and Installation

1965-72

All repairs on the rear axle assembly can be made with the assembly mounted in the car. In the event of damage to the housing, remove as follows:

1. Raise rear of car with jack under differential and place jack stands under rear frame rails.
2. Mark rear universal and pinion flange for reassembly. Disconnect rear universal. On Riviera up to 1970, mark flanged ball stud yoke and rear pinion flange for reassembly, then disconnect rear CV joint.
3. Push driveshaft forward and support. Disconnect brake hose.
4. Detach parking brake cables. Remove, or disconnect lower mounts of, shock absorbers.
5. Lower jack under housing until rear coil springs, if so equipped, can be removed.
6. On 1971-72 Estate Wagons (leaf springs), support car at front spring hangers and at rear bumper, disconnect right exhaust system, remove spring plate nuts and spring plates, then remove front and rear bolts and entire leaf spring assemblies.
7. Disconnect sway bar, and upper control arms at axle housing on models with coil springs.
8. Disconnect lower control arms on models with coil springs.
9. Lower axle housing to floor.
10. To reinstall, reverse procedure.

Positive Traction Differential

No special attention is required in this area, except with the lubricant used.

Under no circumstances use anything but special positive traction lubricant.

Rear Coil Spring Removal— 1965-72 Except 1971-72 Estate Wagon

Disconnect the shock absorber link and the torsion bar. Place a jack at the frame in front of the rear spring and jack up the frame.

Remove the bolt that holds the spring to the lower perch.

NOTE: the left side of the car has a left-hand thread bolt holding the spring, and the right side of the car has a right-hand thread bolt hold-

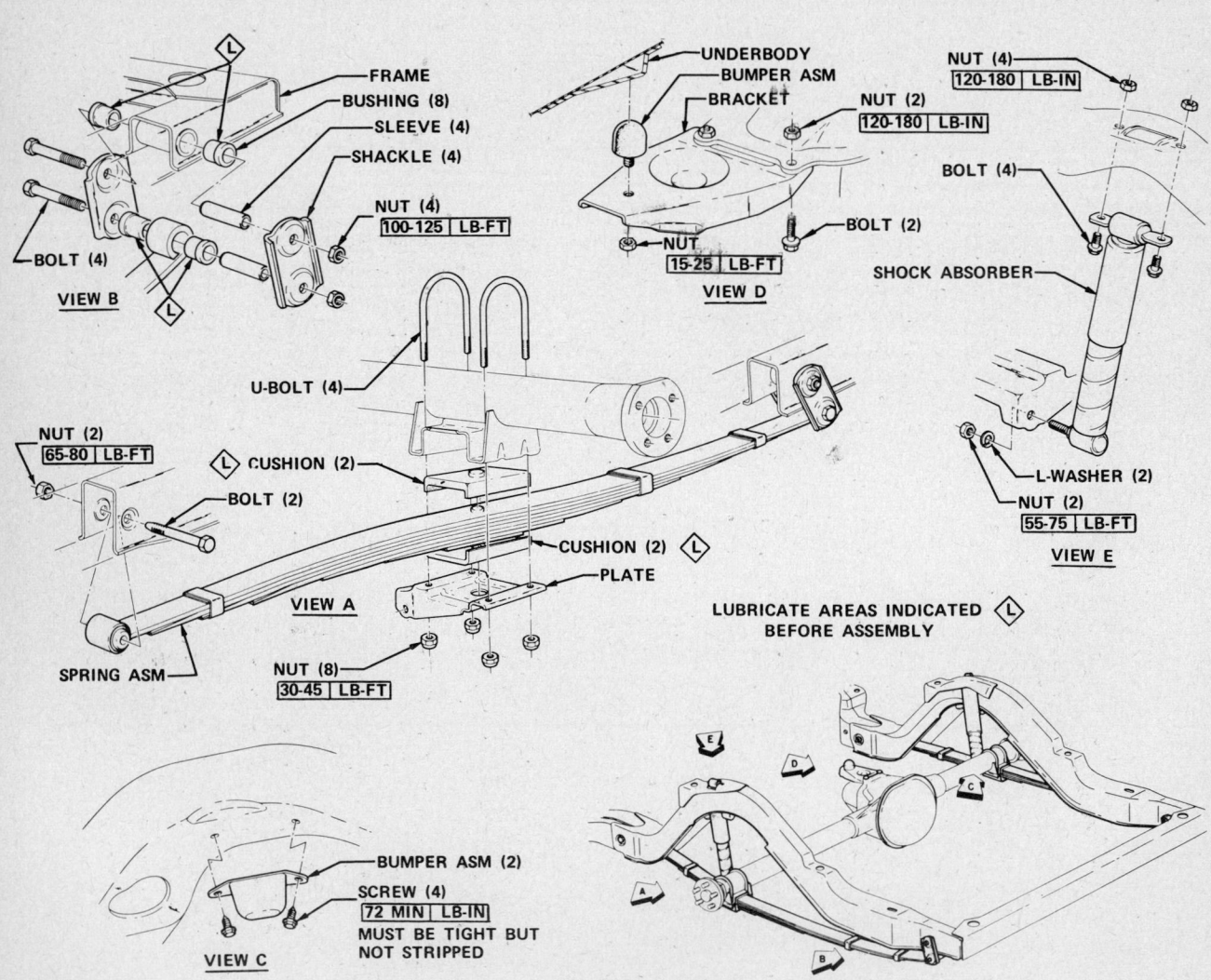

Rear suspension details—1971-72 Estate Wagon with leaf springs
(© Buick Div. G.M. Corp.)

ing the spring. Remove the upper and lower bolts and take out the coil spring. If necessary, jack the car up a sufficient amount so it will come out readily.

Automatic Level Control

The system consists of a 125 psi vacuum regulator valve, and a vacuum-operated air compressor, connected to height control valve mounted at rear suspension crossmember. The valve is then connected to Superlift rear shock absorbers.

The Superlift shock absorber is essentially a conventional shock absorber enclosed in an air chamber. A pliable nylon-reinforced neoprene boot seals the air dome to air piston. It will extend or retract under the pressure controlled by the valve.

As load is added to the vehicle, the control valve admits air under pressure to these shock absorbers, lifting vehicle to normal position. As load is reduced the valve releases air and lowers vehicle to the previous normal level.

The valve is connected by a link to the right rear upper control link except on 1971-72 Estate Wagon, which has the link connected directly to the axle housing. A deflection of at least ½ in. is required to make it operative.

A delay mechanism is built into the valve housing. This requires four to 22 seconds to cause valve to operate. It prevents operation during normal road motions.

Pressure at the shock absorber units is kept equal by the line connecting the two units, with only one unit connected directly to the control valve. This keeps approximately 8-15 psi on shock absorber units at all times. The pressure is released at the control valve and the equalizing pressure is maintained through a check valve at the release

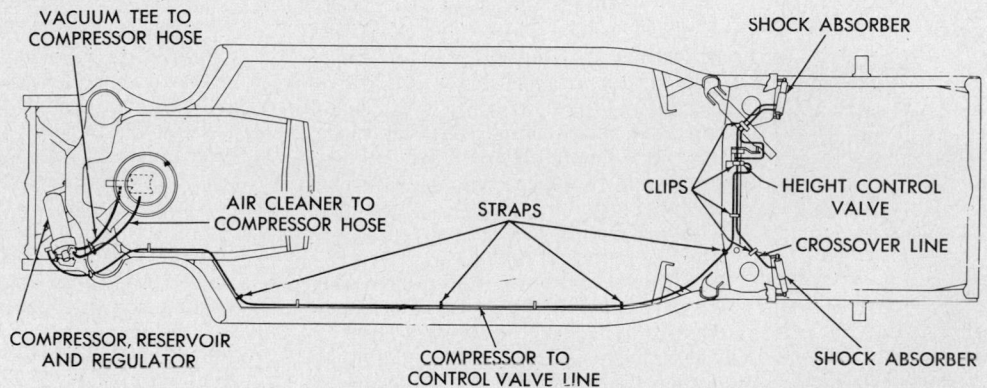

Automatic level control (© Buick Div. G.M. Corp.)

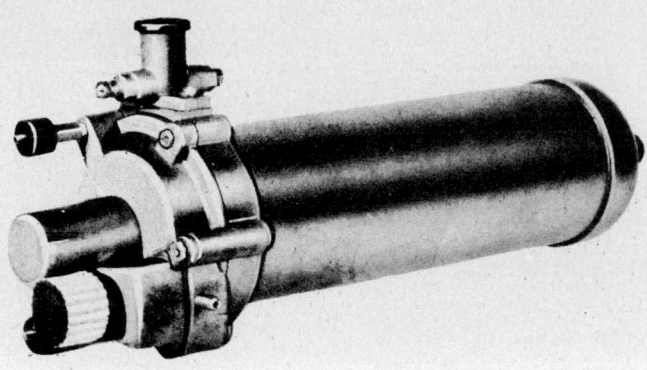

Compressor, reservoir tank and regulator valve assembly (© Buick Div. G.M. Corp.)

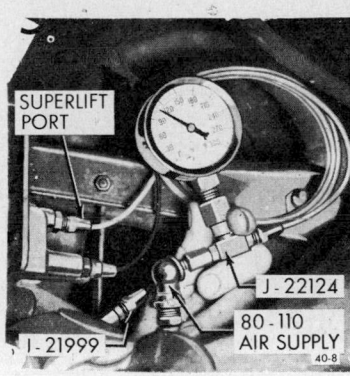

Connect test gauge to superlift port (© Buick Div. G.M. Corp.)

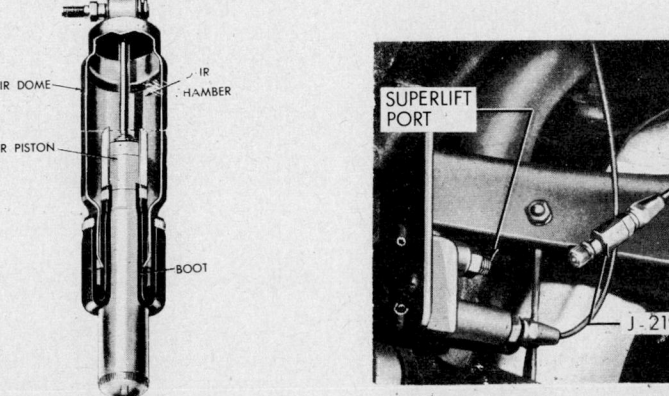

Superlift shock absorber (© Buick Div. G.M. Corp.)

Remove superlift air supply line (© Buick Div. G.M. Corp.)

Filling system through service valve (© Buick Div. G.M. Corp.)

Loosen height control valve lever nut
(© Buick Div. G.M. Corp.)

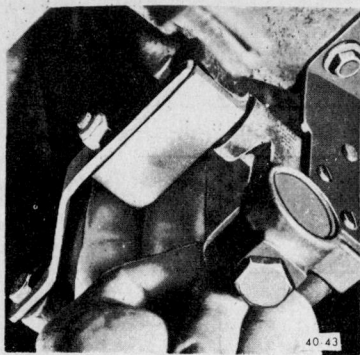

Hold overtravel body in exhaust position
(© Buick Div. G.M. Corp.)

fitting.

The compressor is located in the engine compartment. It is operated by vacuum surge through a line connected just forward of the carburetor insulator connection. Air at atmospheric pressure is taken into the compressor through a line connected to the air cleaner. The compressed air from the compressor is supplied to a reservoir and then to the control valve.

Any service work on this system or other parts of the vehicle that may deflate the system will require reinflation to approximately 140 psi.

All lines are 1/8 in. diameter flexible black tubing. When working on this system, use care not to kink the tubing. Keep tubing away from the exhaust system.

Testing and Adjustment
Trim Height
1. Record rear trim height. Measure from ground to lower edge of rear wheel cutout.
2. Place approximately 200 lbs. in trunk or on tailgate. Car should begin to level itself 4-22 seconds after loading and final position should be no lower than 1 in. below original measurement.
3. If measurement is more than 1 in. below original, bounce car to equalize rear suspension, then remeasure. If still not right, adjust *height control valve* (as de-

scribed later).

NOTE: with weight removed, car should return to originally measured height. If not, bounce car and remeasure; adjust height control valve if necessary.

Vacuum Regulator Valve
If compressor operates at curb idle speed, the problem can be caused by improperly connected vacuum connections, improperly adjusted deceleration valve, relay valve sticking or an intake manifold air leak.

To check relay valve, first disconnect and plug the yellow hose from the vacuum source, after first checking the lines for leaks. If compressor stops running, adjust the deceleration valve. The decel valve adjusting screw can be turned CCW to lessen spring tension and make the valve sensitive to a smaller vacuum. Turning the screw CW applies more spring tension and greater vacuum is required to open the valve. The proper adjustment is to turn the screw CW until the compressor stops, then 1/2 turn additional.

If, after adjusting decel valve, the compressor still operates, disconnect the white carburetor advance hose. If the compressor now stops running, either the carburetor is improperly adjusted or a manifold leak exists. If, on the other hand, the compressor does stop running at this point, the relay valve is defective and must be replaced.

With the engine running at fast idle (above 1,000 rpm), the compressor should operate unless balanced pressures exist in the system (150-275 psi). If system is balanced, deflate it by cracking open service valve until compressor operates. If the compressor does not operate, either the orifice in the spark advance port of the decel valve is plugged up, the PCV system has a leak, the relay valve is faulty, or the compressor hose has a leak. Remove the compressor and PCV hoses from the relay valve and connect them together. If the compressor begins to operate, the relay valve is not working and the entire vacuum regulator assembly must be replaced. If the compressor does not operate, remove the spark advance hose from the decel valve and clean the orifice with a piece of wire.

Trim Height Adjustment
1. Jack up car.
2. Remove Superlift air supply line at height control valve (as illustrated).
3. Connect a fill valve assembly (J-21999 or equivalent) to Superlift line.
4. Inflate Superlifts to 8-15 psi, using a tire gauge to check pressure.
5. Bounce car to neutralize suspen-

sion.
6. Connect a test gauge (0-300 psi) to the Superlift outlet on the height control valve and connect a compressed air source (80-110 psi) to the gauge through a T-fitting. (See illustration.)
7. Loosen the height control valve lever nut with a 7/16 in. box wrench.
8. Hold the overtravel body in the exhaust position until air escapes from the exhaust port. (See illustration.)
9. Slowly move the overtravel body toward the neutral position, which will be the point of minimum air bleed through the exhaust port. Tighten the nut to 75 *in. lbs.*, at which point only a slight air bleed should be coming out of the exhaust port.
10. Remove the test gauge, air pressure source, and fill valve.
11. Reconnect line to height control valve and tighten to 70 *in. lbs.*
12. Lower the car and inflate the system through the service valve on the compressor (see illustration). Load and unload the rear suspension by jumping on and off the rear bumper—this will inflate the Superlifts to their normal 8-15 psi.

Radio

Always disconnect the battery ground cable before working on any part of the instrument panel.

Removal and Installation
1965 Riviera
1. Remove two screws from center console front trim plate assembly and remove plate.
2. Remove two screws holding air conditioner center outlet assembly to radio trim plate and remove outlet ducts.
3. Remove four screws and lower air conditioner control assembly.
4. Remove two screws from lower corners of radio trim plate. Remove two screws securing underside of receiver to cross support. Partially withdraw radio and radio trim plate.
5. Disconnect antenna and wiring leads.
6. Remove radio and radio trim plate.
7. Install by reversing procedure.

1965 Except Riviera
1. Remove six screws from instrument panel cover and tilt cover upward.
2. Remove four nuts holding cove molding to instrument panel and remove radio and molding as an

assembly.

3. Install by reversing procedure.

1966-67 Riviera

1. Remove ash tray assembly.
2. Pry out chrome strip at center of instrument panel.
3. Remove two screws securing center outlet, lift off center outlet, and pull out plastic duct.
4. Remove knobs, two nuts, and escutcheon.
5. Disconnect antenna and wiring leads.
6. Remove radio support.
7. Lower radio through ash tray opening.
8. Install by reversing procedure.

1966-67 Except Riviera

1. Remove knobs and hex nuts.
2. Remove six screws and remove instrument panel cover.
3. Remove left and right mounting bracket screws.
4. Disconnect antenna and wiring leads.
5. Lift out radio.
6. Install by reversing procedure.

1968 All Models, 1969-70 Riviera

1. Remove ash tray assembly.
2. Remove knobs, escutcheons, and hex nuts.
3. Unplug antenna and wiring leads.
4. Remove radio downward.
5. Install by reversing procedure.

1969-70 Except Riviera

1. Remove center air-conditioning duct.
2. Remove right instrument trim panel and screw in bottom of radio.

3. Remove radio knobs, escutcheons, and two hex nuts.
4. Unplug antenna and wiring leads.
5. Remove radio downward.
6. Install by reversing procedure.

1971-72 All Models

1. Remove knobs and escutcheons from radio. If equipped with Trip-Set and/or Speed-Alert, remove cone-shaped knobs.
2. Remove face plate by pulling outward. *Disconnect Seelight before completely removing face plate, if equipped with Trip-Set/Speed-Alert.*
3. Remove the two hex nuts from the control shafts.
4. Remove ash tray and frame.
5. Disconnect the two connectors behind dash and unplug antenna.
6. Unscrew the support bracket nuts and remove radio to the rear and downwards.
7. Install by reversing removal procedure.

Windshield Wipers

Motor R & R

1965-72

1. Disconnect wire connectors from motor and pump.
2. Remove washer hoses from the pump.
3. Remove left side air intake grille.
4. Remove spring retainer clip from wiper motor shaft lever.

NOTE: on 1971-72 models, loosen two ⅜ in. adjusting nuts and slip drive link off crank arm.

5. Lift transmission drive links off motor shaft lever.
6. Remove motor attaching bolts, then lift out motor.
7. Install by reversing the above procedure.

Wiper Transmission

1965-72

1. Remove the wiper blade and arm, shaft and escutcheon retaining nuts and the escutcheon from the transmission shaft.
2. Remove air intake grille.
3. Remove spring retainer clip from wiper motor shaft. Lift drive links off motor shaft.

NOTE: on 1971-72 models, loosen adjusting nuts and slip drive link off crank arm.

4. Remove the transmission retaining screws.
5. Slide transmission and drive link toward opposite side of car. Lift transmission up at opening and remove.
6. Install by reversing the above procedure.

Heater System

1965-72

To remove heater core, it is necessary to take out heater assembly. This will be obvious upon inspection.

To remove heater blower and air inlet assembly it will be necessary to remove right front fender up to 1970. After 1970, the entire assembly can be removed easily after loosening hood hinge and removing plate.

Buick Special and Gran Sport

Index

YEAR IDENTIFICATION

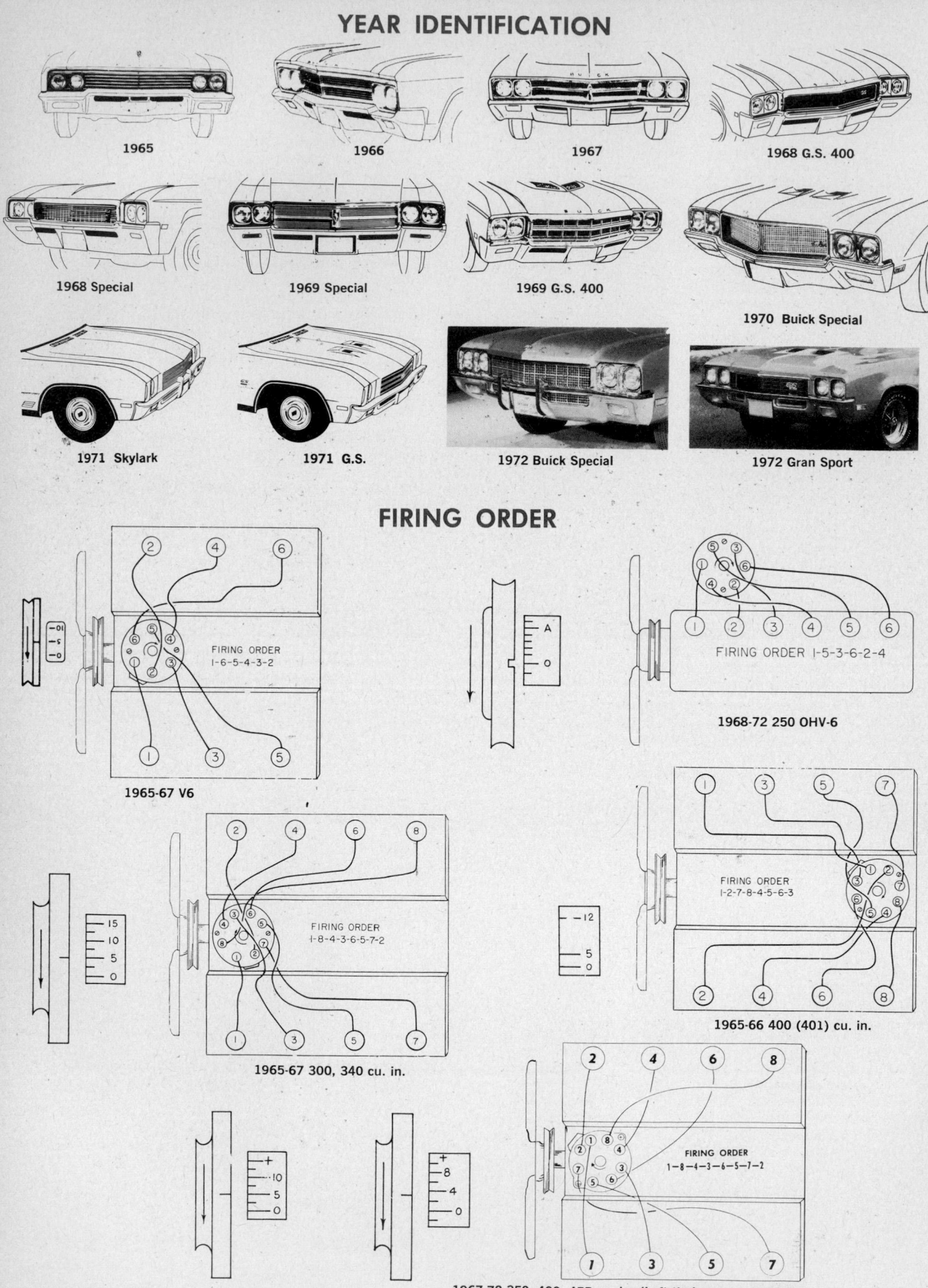

1965

1966

1967

1968 G.S. 400

1968 Special

1969 Special

1969 G.S. 400

1970 Buick Special

1971 Skylark

1971 G.S.

1972 Buick Special

1972 Gran Sport

FIRING ORDER

FIRING ORDER 1-6-5-4-3-2

1965-67 V6

FIRING ORDER 1-5-3-6-2-4

1968-72 250 OHV-6

FIRING ORDER 1-8-4-3-6-5-7-2

1965-67 300, 340 cu. in.

FIRING ORDER 1-2-7-8-4-5-6-3

1965-66 400 (401) cu. in.

FIRING ORDER 1-8-4-3-6-5-7-2

1967-72 350, 400, 455 cu. in. (Left timing mark 1967-69)

CAR SERIAL NUMBER LOCATION AND ENGINE IDENTIFICATION

The car serial number is used for registrations and other legal records. This number is unique to the individual car. The production code number identifies the type of engine and its production date. The Engine Identification Code chart can be used to determine the type of engine installed in the vehicle. The engine serial number also appears on the vehicle identification plate following model and series identification. The engine serial and car serial numbers are the same.

1965

The serial number identification plate is attached to the left front body hinge pillar.

On the 225 cu. in. V6 engine, the production code number is on the crankcase between the front and middle branches of the right exhaust manifold. The engine number is on the left front face of the crankcase, just below the cylinder head.

On the 300 cu. in. engine, the production code number is on the right of the crankcase between the middle branches of the right exhaust manifold. The engine number is on the left front face of the crankcase, just below the cylinder head.

On the 400 cu. in. engine, the production code number is on the right front edge of the crankcase, just below the valve lifter cover. The engine number is on the left front edge of the crankcase.

Serial number identification plate codes are as follows:

Assembly Plant Codes
Flint . . . . H
South Gate C
Fremont . . . . Z
Kansas City, Kansas X
Wilmington . . . . Y
Atlanta . . . . D
Baltimore . . . . B
Kansas City, Mo. . . . . K
Bloomfield V

Body Style Code No.
2-door coupe 27
4-door 2-seat station wag. 35
2-door hardtop coupe 37
4-door hardtop 39
2-door hardtop coupe 47
4-door 2-seat sportwagon 55
4-door 3-seat sportwagon 65
2-door convertible 67
4-door sedan 69

Series Identification	V6	V8
Special	33	34
Special Deluxe	35	36
Sportwagon		42
Skylark	43	44

Serial number and production code location—1965-66 400 cu. in.

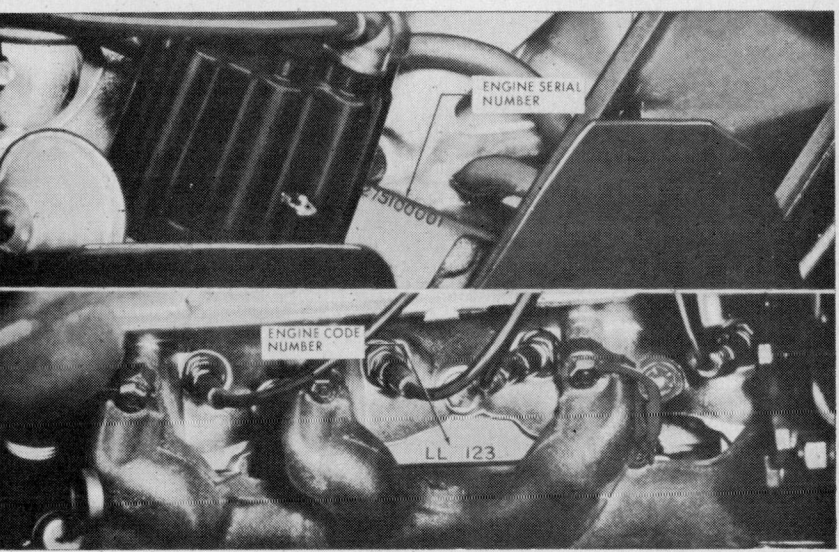

Serial number and production code location—1965-67 300 and 340 cu. in.

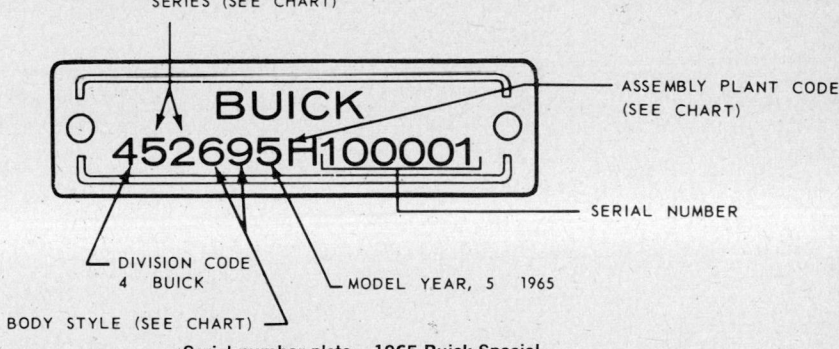

Serial number plate—1965 Buick Special

Serial number and production code location, 1967 400 cu. in.

1966

The car serial number identification plate is attached to the left front body hinge pillar. On the 225 cu. in. V6 engine, the production code number is between the front and middle branches of the right exhaust manifold. The engine number is on the left front face of the crankcase, just below the cylinder head.

On the 300 and 340 cu. in. engines, the production code number is between the middle branches of the right exhaust manifold. The engine number is just below the front of the left cylinder head.

On the 400 cu. in. engine, the production code number is on the right front edge of the crankcase, just below the valve lifter cover. The engine number is on the left front edge of the same surface.

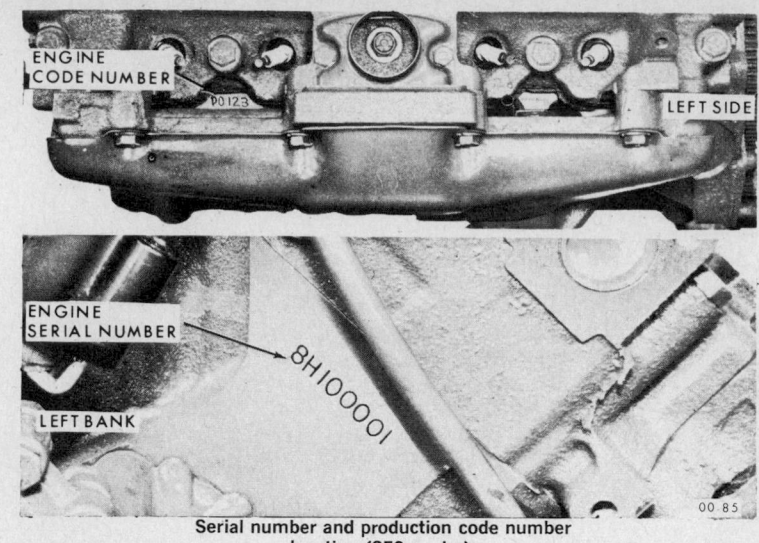

Serial number and production code number location (350 cu. in.), 1968-72 Buick Special

1967

The serial number identification plate is attached to the left front body hinge pillar.

On the 225 cu. in. V6 engine, the production code number is between the front and middle branches of the right exhaust manifold. The engine number is just below the front of the left cylinder head.

On the 300 and 340 cu. in. engines, the production code number is between the middle branches of the right exhaust manifold. The engine number is just below the front of the left cylinder head.

On the 400 cu. in. engine, the production code number is between the two forward branches of the right exhaust manifold and the engine number is between the rear branches.

1968

The serial number identification plate is attached to the left front body hinge pillar.

On the 250 cu. in. OHV6 engine, the engine number and the produc-

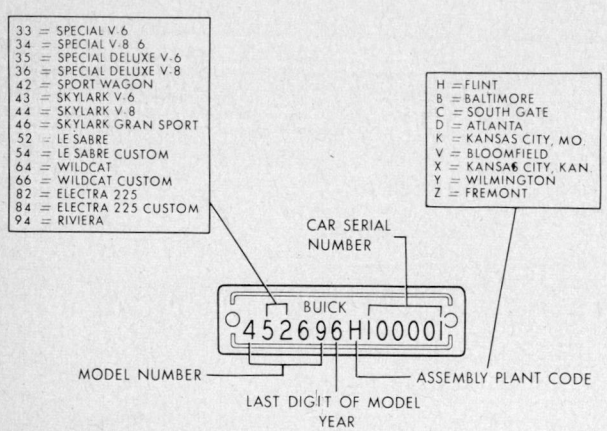

Serial number plate—1966 Buick Special

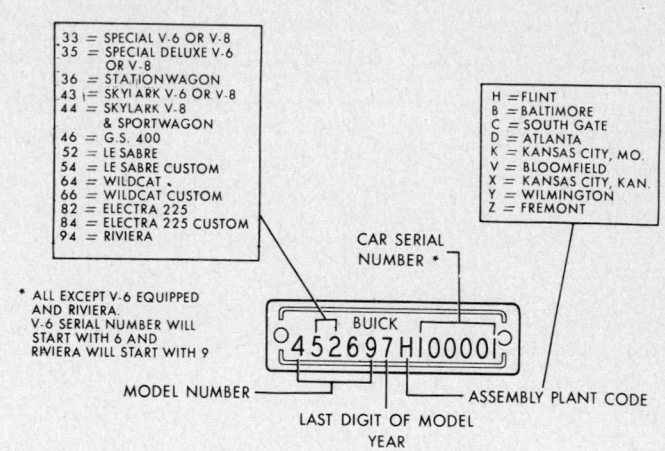

Serial number plate—1967 Buick Special

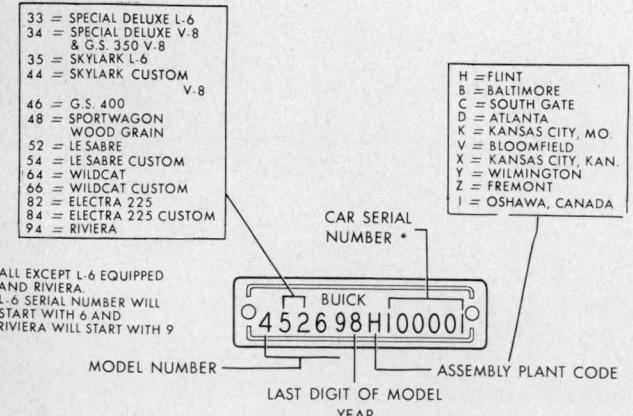

Serial number plate—1968 Buick Special

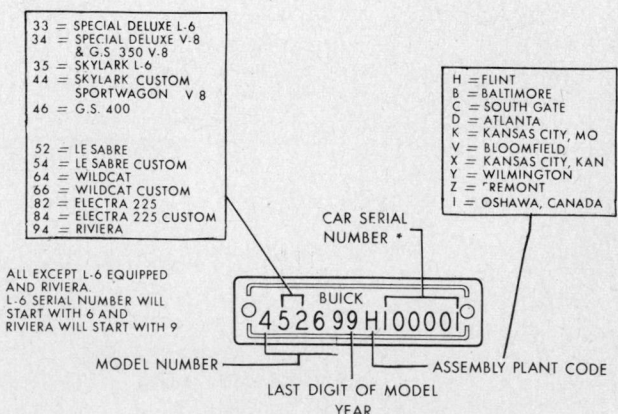

Serial number plate—1969 Buick Special

tion code number are on the right side of the engine, to the rear of the distributor.

On the 350 cu. in. V8 engine, the engine number is stamped on the front of the left cylinder bank. The production code number is between the left exhaust manifold and the two front spark plugs.

On the 400 cu. in. engine, the engine number is between the two front spark plugs and the left exhaust manifold, and the production code number is between the two rear plugs and the exhaust manifold, also on the left.

On the 250 cu. in. OHV6 engine, the engine number and the production code number are on the right side, rearward of the distributor.

On the 350 cu. in. V8 engine, the engine number is on the front of the left bank of cylinders. The production code number is between the left exhaust manifold and the two front spark plugs.

On the 400 cu. in. engine, the production code number is between the two rear spark plugs and the left exhaust manifold. The engine number is between the two front plugs and the left exhaust manifold.

On the 250 cu. in. OHV6 engine, the engine number and production code number are on the right side, to the rear of the distributor.

On the 350 cu. in. V8 engine, the engine number is on the front of the left bank of cylinders. The production code number is between the left exhaust manifold and the two front spark plugs.

On the 455 cu. in. engine, the production code number is between the two rear spark plugs and the left exhaust manifold. The engine number is between the two front spark plugs and the exhaust manifold.

1969

The serial number identification plate is attached to the top of the instrument panel on the left side and can be seen through the windshield.

1970-72

The serial number identification plate is attached to the top left of the instrument panel. It can be seen through the windshield.

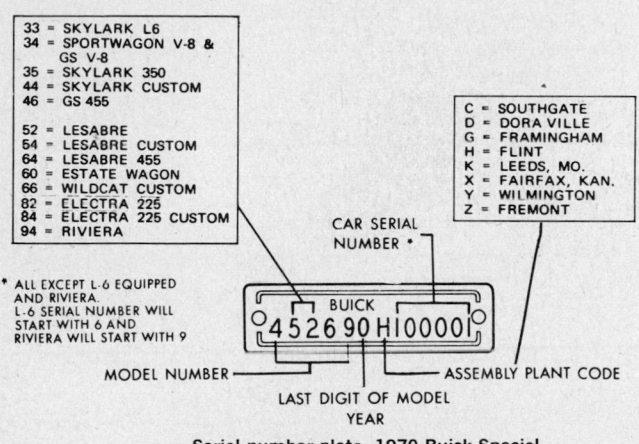

Serial number plate, 1970 Buick Special
(© Buick Div., G.M. Corp.)

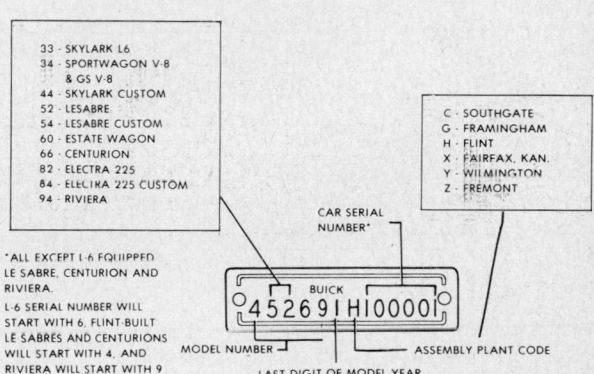

Serial number plate, 1971 Buick
(© Buick Div., G.M. Corp.)

Serial number and production code location (400 and 455 cu. in.)—1968-72 Buick Special

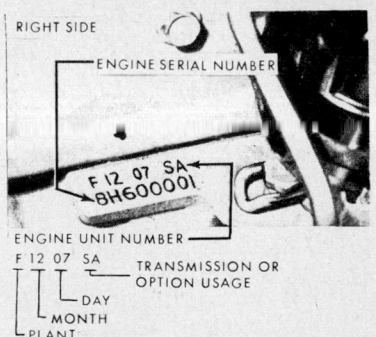

Serial number and production code location (OHV 6)—1968-71 Buick Special

ENGINE IDENTIFICATION CODE

No. Cyls.	Cu. In. Displ.	Type	YEAR AND CODE						
			1965	1966	1967	1968	1969	1970	1971
6	225	1 & 2 BBL.	LH	MH	NH				
8	300	Std. Eng.	LP	ML	NL				
8	300	HP	LL						
8	401	4-BBL.	LT						
8	340	2-BBL.		MA	NA				
8	340	4-BBL.		MB	NB				
8	455	4-BBL.						SR	TR
6	250	1-BBL.							
8	455	4-BBL. St. 1						SS	TS
8	350	2-BBL.				PO	RO	SO	TO
8	400	4-BBL.		MR, MT	NR	PR	RR		
8	350	4-BBL.				PP	RP	SB, SP	TB

2-BBL.—Two-barrel carburetor.
4-BBL.—Four-barrel carburetor.

HP—High Performance Engine.
St. 1—Stage 1.

GENERAL ENGINE SPECIFICATIONS

YEAR	CU. IN. DISPLACEMENT	CARBURETOR	ADVERTIZED HORSEPOWER @ RPM	ADVERTIZED TORQUE @ RPM (FT. LBS.)	A.M.A. HORSEPOWER	BORE & STROKE (IN.)	ADVERTIZED COMPRESSION RATIO	VALVE LIFTER TYPE	NORMAL OIL PRESSURE (PSI)
1965	V6—225	1-BBL.	155 @ 4400	225 @ 2400	33.8	3.750 x 3.400	9.0-1	Hyd.	33
	V8—300	2-BBL.	210 @ 4600	310 @ 2400	45.0	3.750 x 3.400	9.0-1	Hyd.	33
	V8—300	4-BBL.	250 @ 4800	335 @ 3000	45.0	3.750 x 3.400	11.0-1	Hyd.	33
	V8—400	4-BBL.	325 @ 4400	445 @ 2800	56.1	4.1875 x 3.640	10.25-1	Hyd.	40
1966	V6—225	1-BBL.	160 @ 4200	235 @ 2400	33.8	3.750 x 3.400	9.0-1	Hyd.	33
	V8—300	2-BBL.	210 @ 4600	310 @ 2400	45.0	3.750 x 3.400	9.0-1	Hyd.	33
	V8—340	2-BBL.	220 @ 4000	365 @ 2800	45.0	3.750 x 3.850	9.0-1	Hyd.	33
	V8—340	4-BBL.	260 @ 4000	365 @ 2800	45.0	3.750 x 3.850	10.25-1	Hyd.	33
	V8—400	4-BBL.	325 @ 4400	445 @ 2800	56.1	4.187 x 3.640	10.25-1	Hyd.	40
1967	V6—225	2-BBL.	160 @ 4200	235 @ 2400	33.8	3.750 x 3.400	9.0-1	Hyd.	33
	V8—300	2-BBL.	210 @ 4600	310 @ 2400	45.0	3.750 x 3.400	9.0-1	Hyd.	33
	V8—340	2-BBL.	220 @ 4200	340 @ 2400	45.0	3.750 x 3.850	9.0-1	Hyd.	33
	V8—340	4-BBL.	260 @ 4200	365 @ 2800	45.0	3.750 x 3.850	10.25-1	Hyd.	33
	V8—400	4-BBL.	340 @ 5000	440 @ 3200	52.2	4.040 x 3.900	10.25-1	Hyd.	37
1968-69	L6—250	1-BBL.	155 @ 4200	235 @ 1600	36.0	3.875 x 3.530	8.5-1	Hyd.	38
	V8—350	2-BBL.	230 @ 4400	350 @ 2400	46.2	3.800 x 3.850	9.0-1	Hyd.	37
	V8—350	4-BBL.	280 @ 4600	375 @ 3200	46.2	3.800 x 3.850	10.25-1	Hyd.	37
	V8—400	4-BBL.	340 @ 5000	440 @ 3200	52.2	4.040 x 3.900	10.25-1	Hyd.	37
1970	L6—250	1-BBL.	155 @ 4200	235 @ 1600	36.0	3.875 x 3.530	8.5-1	Hyd.	37
	V8—350	2-BBL.	260 @ 4600	360 @ 2600	46.2	3.800 x 3.850	9.0-1	Hyd.	37
	V8—350	4-BBL.	285 @ 4600	375 @ 3000	46.2	3.800 x 3.850	9.0-1	Hyd.	37
	V8—350	4-BBL.	315 @ 4800	410 @ 3200	46.2	3.800 x 3.850	10.25-1	Hyd.	40
	V8—455	4-BBL.	350 @ 4600	510 @ 2800	59.5	4.3125 x 3.900	10.0-1	Hyd.	40
	V8—455	4-BBL.	360 @ 4600	510 @ 2800	59.5	4.3125 x 3.900	10.0-1	Hyd.	40
1971	L6—250	1-BBL.	145 @ 4000	235 @ 2400	36.0	3.875 x 3.530	8.5-1	Hyd.	37
	V8—350	2-BBL.	230 @ 4400	350 @ 2400	46.2	3.800 x 3.850	8.5-1	Hyd.	37
	V8—350	4-BBL.	260 @ 4600	360 @ 3000	46.2	3.800 x 3.850	8.5-1	Hyd.	37
	V8—455	4-BBL.	315 @ 4400	450 @ 2800	59.5	4.3125 x 3.900	8.5-1	Hyd.	40
	V8—455	4-BBL.	345 @ 5000	460 @ 3000	59.5	4.3125 x 3.900	8.5-1	Hyd.	40
1972	350	2-BBL.	155 @ 3800 ①	270 @ 2400 ②	46.2	3.800 x 3.850	8.5-1	Hyd.	37
	350 (A)	4-BBL.	180 @ 3800 ③	275 @ 2400 ④	46.2	3.800 x 3.850	8.5-1	Hyd.	37
	350 (B)	4-BBL.	195 @ 4000 ⑤	290 @ 2800 ⑥	46.2	3.800 x 3.850	8.5-1	Hyd.	37
	455 (A)	4-BBL.	225 @ 4000	360 @ 2600	59.5	4.3125 x 3.900	8.5-1	Hyd.	40
	455 (B)	4-BBL.	250 @ 4000	375 @ 2800	59.5	4.3125 x 3.900	8.5-1	Hyd.	40
	455 GS	4-BBL.	260 @ 4400	380 @ 2800	59.5	4.3125 x 3.900	8.5-1	Hyd.	40
	455 Stage	4-BBL.	270 @ 4400	390 @ 300	59.5	4.3125 x 3.900	8.5-1	Hyd.	40

① —Cal. 150 @ 3800
② —Cal. 265 @ 2400
③ —Cal. 175 @ 3800
④ —Cal. 275 @ 2400

⑤ —Cal 190 @ 4000
⑥ —Cal 285 @ 2800

(A) —Single Exhaust
(B) —Dual Exhaust

TUNE-UP SPECIFICATIONS

YEAR	MODEL	SPARK PLUGS		DISTRIBUTOR		IGNITION TIMING (Deg.) ▲	CRANKING COMP. PRESSURE (Psi)	VALVES			FUEL PUMP PRESSURE (Psi)	IDLE SPEED (Rpm) ★
		Type	Gap (In.)	Point Dwell (Deg.)	Point Gap (In.)			Tappet (Hot) Clearance (In.) Intake	Tappet (Hot) Clearance (In.) Exhaust	Intake Opens (Deg.)		
1965	V6—225 Cu. In.	44S	.035	30°	.016	5B	160	Zero	Zero	24B	4¼-5¾	550
	V8—300 Cu. In.	44FFS	.035	30°	.016	2½B	160	Zero	Zero	26B	4¼-5¾	550
	V8—400 Cu. In.	44S	.035	30°	.016	2½B	160	Zero	Zero	28B	4¾-6½	500
1966	V6—225 Cu. In.	44TS	.035	30°	.016	5B	160	Zero	Zero	24B	4¼-5¾	550
	V8—300 Cu. In.	44S	.035	30°	.016	2½B	160	Zero	Zero	26B	4-5¼	550
	V8—340 Cu. In.	44TS	.035	30°	.016	2½B	160	Zero	Zero	32B	4¼-5¾	550
	V8—400 Cu. In.	44S	.035	30°	.016	2½B	160	Zero	Zero	38B	5½-7	500
1967	V6—225 Cu. In.	44TS	.035	30°	.016	5B	160	Zero	Zero	24B	4¼-5¾	550
	V8—300 Cu. In.	44S	.035	30°	.016	2½B	160	Zero	Zero	30B	4¼-5¾	550
	V8—340 Cu. In.	44S	.035	30°	.016	2½B	160	Zero	Zero	32B	4¼-5¾	550
1968	L6—250 Cu. In.; 1-BBL.	46N	.035	32.5°	.019	4B	130	Zero	Zero	16B	3½-4½	500
	V8—350 Cu. In.	44TS	.030	30°	.016	TDC	160	Zero	Zero	24B	4½-5½	550
	V8—400 Cu. In.; 4-BBL.	44TS	.030	30°	.016	TDC	170	Zero	Zero	14B	5½-7	600
1969	L6—250 Cu. In.; M.T.	46N	.035	32.5°	.019	TDC	130	Zero	Zero	16B	3½-4½	700
	L6—250 Cu. In.; A.T.	46N	.035	32.5°	.019	4B	130	Zero	Zero	16B	3½-4½	550
	V8—350 Cu. In.; A.T.	R45TS	.030	30°	.016	TDC	160	Zero	Zero	24B	4½-5½	550
	V8—350 Cu. In.; M.T., G.S.	R45TS	.030	30°	.016	TDC	160	Zero	Zero	24B	4½-5½	700
	V8—400 Cu. In.; M.T., G.S.	R44TS	.030	30°	.016	2½A	170	Zero	Zero	14B	4½-7	700
	V8—400 Cu. In.; A.T.	R44TS	.030	30°	.016	TDC	170	Zero	Zero	14B	4½-7	600
1970	L6—250 Cu. In.; M.T.	R46N	.035	32°	.019	TDC	130	Zero	Zero	16B	4-5	700
	L6—250 Cu. In.; A.T.	R46N	.035	32°	.019	4B	130	Zero	Zero	16B	4-5	550
	V8—350 Cu. In.; M.T.	R45TS	.030	30°	.016	6B	165	Zero	Zero	24B	4½-5½	700
	V8—455 Cu. In.	R44TS	.030	30°	.016	6B	180	Zero	Zero	18B •	4½ 5½	700
	V8—455 Cu. In., St. 1	R44TS	.030	30°	.016	10B	180	Zero	Zero	18B	4½-5½	700
1971-72	L6—250 Cu. In.	R46T	.035	32°	.019	4B	130	Zero	Zero	17½B	4-5	550
	V8—350 Cu. In.	R45TS	.030	30°	.016	6B③	165	Zero	Zero	24B①	4½-5½	800⑤
	V8—455 Cu. In.	R44TS	.030	30°	.016	6B④	165	Zero	Zero	12B②	4½-5½	700⑤

★—With synchromesh transmission in N and automatic in D. Add 50 rpm if air conditioned.
▲—With vacuum disconnected.
B—Before top dead center.
A—After top dead center.
TDC—Top dead center.
G.S.—Gran Sport.
M.T.—Manual transmission.
A.T.—Automatic transmission.

①—28B with 4 Bbl.
②—18B for Stage 1 engine.
③—Automatic trans., 2 Bbl., 10B. Automatic trans., 4 Bbl., 4B.
④—Automatic trans., 4B. Stage 1, auto. and man., 10B.
⑤—Automatic trans., 600 in drive.

Caution

General adoption of anti-pollution laws has changed the design of almost all car engine production to effectively reduce crankcase emission and terminal exhaust products. It has been necessary to adopt stricter tune-up rules, especially timing and idle speed procedures. Both of these values are peculiar to the engine and to its application, rather than to the engine alone. With this in mind, car manufacturers supply idle speed data for the engine and application involved. This information is clearly displayed in the engine compartment of each vehicle.

VALVE SPECIFICATIONS

YEAR AND MODEL		SEAT ANGLE (DEG.)	FACE ANGLE (DEG.)	VALVE LIFT INTAKE (IN.)	VALVE LIFT EXHAUST (IN.)	VALE SPRING PRESSURE (VALVE OPEN) LBS. @ IN.	VALVE SPRING INSTALLED HEIGHT (IN.)	STEM TO GUIDE CLEARANCE (IN.)		STEM DIAMETER (IN.)	
								Intake	Exhaust	Intake	Exhaust
1965	V6	45	45	.391	.401	168 @ 1.26	1.64	.0020–.0025①	.0025–.0030①	.3407–.3412②	.3402–.3407②
	V8—300	45	45	.391	.401	168 @ 1.26	1.64	.0020–.0025①	.0025–.0030①	.3407–.3412②	.3402–.3407②
	V8—400	45	45	.431	.431	101 @ 1.16	1.60	.0020–.0030①	.0025–.0035①	.3720–.3730①	.3715–.3725②
1966	V6	45	45	.401	.401	164 @ 1.34	1.72	.0020–.0025①	.0025–.0030①	.3407–.3412②	.3402–.3407②
	V8—300	45	45	.393	.401	164 @ 1.34	1.72	.0012–.0032	.0025–.0030①	.3405–.3415②	.3402–.3407②
	V8—340	45	45	.399	.399	164 @ 1.34	1.72	.0012–.0032	.0025–.0030①	.3405–.3415②	.3402–.3407②
	V8—400	45	45	.431	431	101 @ 1.16	1.60	.0020–.0030①	.0025–.0035①	.3720–.3730②	.3715–.3725②
1967	V6—225	45	45	.401	.401	168 @ 1.25	1.72	.0012–.0032	.0015–.0035①	.3405–.3415	.3402–.3407②
	V8—300	45	45	.393	.399	164 @ 1.34	1.72	.0012–.0032	.0015–.0035①	.3405–.3415	.3402–.3407②
	V8—340	45	45	.399	.399	164 @ 1.34	1.72	.0012–.0032	.0015–.0035①	.3405–.3415	.3402–.3407②
1968–69	L6—250	46	45	.388	.388	185 @ 1.27	1.66	.0010–.0027	.0010–.0027	.3410–.3417	.3410–.3417
	V8—350	45	45	.371	.384	180 @ 1.34	1.72	.0015–.0035	.0015–.0035①	.3720–3730	.3720–.3730②
	V8—400	45	45	.418	.448	177 @ 1.45	1.89	.0015–.0035	.0015–.0035①	.3720–.3730	.3720–.3730②
1970–72	L6—250	46	45	.388	.388	185 @ 1.27	1.66	.0010–.0027	.0010–.0027	.3410–.3417	.3410–.3417
	V8—350	45	45	.382	.398	180 @ 1.34⑤	1.72	.0015–.0035③	.0015–.0032①	.3720–.3730③	.3723–.3730④
	V8—455	45	45	.387	.456	198 @ 1.45	1.89	.0015–.0035③	.0015–.0032①	.3720–.3730③	.3723–.3730④

① —Plus or minus 0.001 in. Guide tapers with larger diameter at bottom.
② —Plus or minus 0.0005 in. Guide tapers with larger diameter at top.
③ —.0003 in. maximum taper.

④ —.0002 in. maximum taper.
⑤ —exhaust valve spring pressure: 197 @ 1.34.

CRANKSHAFT BEARING JOURNAL SPECIFICATIONS

YEAR	MODEL	MAIN BEARING JOURNALS (IN.)				CONNECTING ROD BEARING JOURNALS (IN.)		
		Journal Diameter	Oil Clearance	Shaft End-Play	Thrust On No.	Journal Diameter	Oil Clearance	End-Play
1965	V6	2.4995	.0005–.0021	.006	2	2.0000	.0020–.0023	.004–.008
	V8—300	2.4995	.0005–.0021	.006	3	2.0000	.0020–.0023	.004–.008
	V8—400	2.4985	.0005–.0019	.006	3	2.2495	.0020–.0023	.005–.012
1966	V6	2.4995	.0004–.0015	.006	2	2.0000	.0020–.0023	.006–.014
	V8—300	2.4995	.0004–.0015	.006	3	2.0000	.0020–.0023	.006–.014
	V8—340	2.9995	.0004–.0015	.006	3	2.0000	.0020–.0023	.006–.014
	V8—400	2.4985	.0004–.0015	.006	3	2.2495	.0020–.0023	.005–.012
1967	V6—225	2.4995	.0004–.0015	.006	2	2.0000	.0020–.0023	.006–.014
	V8—300	2.4995	.0004–.0015	.006	3	2.0000	.0020–.0023	.006–.014
	V8—340	2.9995	.0004–.0015	.006	3	2.0000	.0020–.0023	.006–.014
1968–69	L6—250	2.3004	.0003–.0029	.004	7	2.0000	.0007–.0027	.009–.013
	V8—350	2.9995	.0004–.0015	.006	3	2.0000	.0002–.0023	.006–.014
	V8—400	3.2500	.0007–.0018	.006	3	2.2500	.0002–.0023	.005–.012
1970–72	L6—250	2.3004	.0003–.0029	.002–.006	7	2.0000	.0007–.0027	.009–.013
	V8—350	2.9995	.0004–.0015	.002–.006	3	2.0000	.0002–.0023	.006–.014
	V8—455	3.2500	.0007–.0018	.003–.009	3	2.2500	.0002–.0023	.005–.012

WHEEL ALIGNMENT

YEAR	MODEL	CASTER		CAMBER		TOE-IN (In.)	KING-PIN INCLINATION (Deg.)	WHEEL PIVOT RATIO	
		Range (Deg.)	Pref. Setting (Deg.)	Range (Deg.)	Pref. Setting (Deg.)			Inner Wheel	Outer Wheel
1965–66	All	1N–0	½N	¼P–¾P	½P	⁷⁄₃₂–⁵⁄₁₆	8	21¼°	20°
1967–69	All	1N–0	½N	0–1P	½P	⅛–¼	8	20°	18½°
1970–72	All	1N–0	½N	0–1P	½P	⅛–¼	8	20°	18½°

N—Negative
P—Positive

AC GENERATOR AND REGULATOR SPECIFICATIONS

YEAR	MODEL	ALTERNATOR			REGULATOR						
		Field Current Draw @ 12V.	Output @ Generator RPM		Model	Field Relay			Regulator		
			1100	6500		Air Gap (In.)	Point Gap (In.)	Volts to Close	Air Gap (In.)	Point Gap (In.)	Volts at 125°
1965–66	1100705	2.2–2.6	10A	37A	1119515	.015	.030	2.3–3.7	.060	.014	13.6–14.4
	1100691	2.2–2.6	10A	42A	1119515	.015	.030	2.3–3.7	.060	.014	13.6–14.4
	1100708	2.2–2.6	10A	42A	1119515	.015	.030	2.3–3.7	.060	.014	13.6–14.4
	1100709	2.2–2.6	10A	55A	1119515	.015	.030	2.3–3.7	.060	.014	13.6–14.4
1967–69	1100761	2.2–2.6	10A	37A	1119515	.015	.030	2.3–3.7	.060	.014	13.6–14.4
	1100691	2.2–2.6	10A	42A	1119515	.015	.030	2.3–3.7	.060	.014	13.6–14.4
1970	1100761	2.2–2.6	10A	37A	1119515	.015	.030	2.3–3.7	.060	.014	13.6–14.4
	1100691	2.2–2.6	10A	42A	1119515	.015	.030	2.3–3.7	.060	.014	13.6–14.4
1971–72	1100905	2.2–2.6	15A	37A	1119515	.015	.030	1.5–3.2	.067	.014	13.5–14.5
	1100931	2.2–2.6	20A	55A	1119515	.015	.030	1.5–3.2	.067	.014	13.5–14.5

TORQUE SPECIFICATIONS

YEAR	MODEL	CYLINDER HEAD BOLTS (FT. LBS.)	ROD BEARING BOLTS (FT. LBS.)	MAIN BEARING BOLTS (FT. LBS.)	CRANKSHAFT BALANCER BOLT (FT. LBS.)	FLYWHEEL TO CRANKSHAFT BOLTS (FT. LBS.)	MANIFOLD (FT. LBS.)	
							Intake	Exhaust
1965–66	V6	65–70	30–35	100–125	140–160	50–60	25–30	10–15
	V8—300, V8—340	65–70	30–35	50–55▲	140–160	50–60	25–30	10–15
	V8—400	65–80	40–50	95–120	200–220	60–65	25–35	10–15
1967	V6	65–70	30–35	100–125	140–160	50–60	25–30	10–15
	V8	65–70①	30–35	50–55▲	140–160	50–60	25–30	10–15
1968–69	L6	90–95	35–45	60–70	Press Fit	55–65	25–35	■
	V8—350	65–70	30–35	50–55▲	140–160	50–60	25–30	10–15
	V8—400	100	45	110	200	50–60	55	18
1970–72	L6	95	35	60–70	Press Fit	55–65	25–35	■
	V8—350	75	35	95	120★	60	55	18
	V8—455	100	45	110	200★	58	55	18

① —V8—400 100-120 ft-lbs.
▲—Rear Main Bearing—65–75
■—Center Bolts 25–30; End Bolts 15–20.
★—Minimum

CYLINDER HEAD BOLT TIGHTENING SEQUENCE

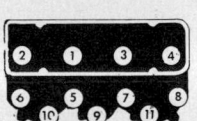

1967 V6

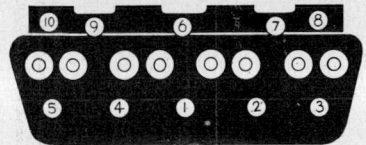

1965-67 300 cu. in.
1966-67 340 cu. in.
1967-69 400 cu. in.
1968-69 350 cu. in.

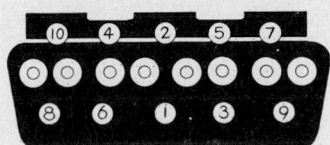

1970-72 350, 455 cu. in.

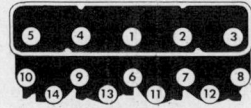

1965-66 400 (401)

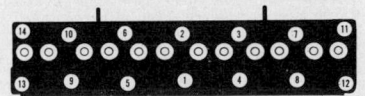

1968-71 L6

CAPACITIES

YEAR	MODEL	ENGINE CRANKCASE ADD 1 Qt. FOR NEW FILTER	TRANSMISSIONS Pts. TO REFILL AFTER DRAINING Manual 3-Speed	Manual 4-Speed	Automatic	DRIVE AXLE (Pts.)	GASOLINE TANK (Gals.)	COOLING SYSTEM (Qts.) WITH HEATER
1965	V6	4	2	$2\frac{1}{2}$	19.0	$2\frac{1}{2}$	20	$10\frac{3}{4}$
	V8—300	4	2	None	19.0	$2\frac{1}{2}$	20	$13\frac{3}{4}$
	V8—400	4	2	None	19.0	$2\frac{1}{2}$	20	$17\frac{3}{4}$
1966	V6	4	$3\frac{1}{3}$	None	19.0	$2\frac{1}{2}$	20	$11\frac{1}{4}$
	V8—300	4	$3\frac{1}{3}$	None	19.0	$2\frac{1}{2}$	20	$11\frac{1}{4}$
	V8—340	4	$3\frac{1}{3}$	None	19.0	$2\frac{1}{2}$	20	$12\frac{3}{4}$
	V8—400	4	$3\frac{1}{2}$	$2\frac{1}{2}$	19.0	$2\frac{1}{2}$	20	$18\frac{1}{2}$
1967	V6	4	$3\frac{3}{8}$	None	19.0	$2\frac{3}{4}$	20	$11\frac{1}{4}$
	V8—300, 340	4	$3\frac{3}{8}$	None	19.0	$2\frac{3}{4}$	20	$12\frac{3}{4}$
1968-69	L6—250	4	$3\frac{3}{8}$	None	20.0	$2\frac{3}{4}$	20	$11\frac{1}{4}$
	V8—350	4	$3\frac{3}{8}$	None	20.0	$2\frac{3}{4}$	20	$13\frac{1}{2}$
	V8—400	4	$3\frac{3}{8}$	$3\frac{1}{2}$	23.0	$2\frac{3}{4}$	20	$16\frac{1}{4}$
1970	L6—250	4	$3\frac{1}{2}$	None	20.0	3	20	$16\frac{1}{2}$
	V8—350	4	$3\frac{1}{2}$	None	20.0	3	20	$16\frac{1}{2}$
	V8—350 G.S.	4	$3\frac{1}{2}$	$3\frac{1}{2}$	20.0	3	20	$16\frac{1}{2}$
	V8—455 G.S.	4	$3\frac{1}{2}$	$3\frac{1}{2}$	23.0	3	20	19
1971-72	L6—250	4	$3\frac{1}{2}$	None	20.0	$4\frac{1}{4}$	20	16
	V8—350	4	$3\frac{1}{2}$	$3\frac{1}{2}$	20.0	$4\frac{1}{4}$	20	$16\frac{1}{2}$
	V8—455	4	$3\frac{1}{2}$	$3\frac{1}{2}$	23.0	$5\frac{1}{2}$	20	19

BATTERY AND STARTER SPECIFICATIONS

YEAR	MODEL	BATTERY Ampere Hour Capacity	Volts	Group Number	Terminal Grounded	STARTERS Lock Test Amps.	Lock Test Volts	No-Load Test Amps.	No-Load Test Volts	RPM	Brush Spring Tension (Oz.)
1965	V6	61	12	28M	Neg.	300	4.0	70	10.6	8,600	35
	V8	61	12	35M	Neg.	330	3.5	85	10.6	4,350	35
1966	V6—225	44	12	17M2	Neg.	300	3.5	62.5	10.6	6,700	35
	V8—300, 340	61	12	28M	Neg.	330	3.0	85	10.6	3,600	35
	V8—400	70	12	N.A.	Neg.	330	2.0	120	10.6	4,700	35
1967	V6—225	44	12	17M2	Neg.	Not Recommended		58	10.6	6,200	35
	V8—300, 340	66	12	2SMD	Neg.	Not Recommended		85	10.6	3,600	35
	V8—400	70	12	R69	Neg.	Not Recommended		85	10.6	6,200	35
1968	L6—250	45	12	17MJ1B	Neg.	Not Recommended		58	10.6	6,200	35
	V8—350	61	12	9MJ3F	Neg.	Not Recommended		85	10.6	3,600	35
	V8—400	70	12	9TJ3	Neg.	Not Recommended		85	10.6	3,600	35
1969	L6—250	44	12	Y54	Neg.	Not Recommended		68	10.6	6,700	35
	V8—350	61	12	9MJ3F	Neg.	Not Recommended		70	9.0	4,000	35
	V8—350 G.S.	61	12	9MJ3F	Neg.	Not Recommended		70	9.0	4,000	35
	V8—400 G.S.	70	12	9TJ3	Neg.	Not Recommended		61	9.0	5,200	35
1970-72	L6—250	44	12	Y55	Neg.	Not Recommended		49-87	9.0	6,200-10,700	35
	V8—350	61	12	R59	Neg.	Not Recommended		55-85	9.0	3,100-6,000	35
	V8—455	70	12	R69	Neg.	Not Recommended		48-80	9.0	4,100-6,500	35

G.S.—Gran Sport

GENERAL CHASSIS AND BRAKE SPECIFICATIONS

| | | CHASSIS | | | BRAKE CYLINDER BORE | | BRAKE DRUM | |
| | | Overall Length (In.) | Tire Size | Master Cylinder (In.) | Wheel Cylinder (In.) | | Diameter (In.) | |
YEAR	MODEL				Front	Rear	Front	Rear
1965	V6—4 dr. Sedans	203.4	6.95 x 14	1.00	1.0625	.938	9.5	9.5
	V6—Special, St. Wag.	203.4	7.35 x 14	1.00	1.0625	.938	9.5	9.5
	V8—Skylark	208.2	7.75 x 14	1.00	1.0625	.938	9.5	9.5
1966	Special Sdn.	204.0	6.95 x 14	1.00	1.0625	.938	9.5	9.5
	Special Wagon	204.0	7.75 x 14	1.00	1.0625	.938	9.5	9.5
	Sportswagon	209.0	8.25 x 14	1.00	1.0625	1.00	9.5	9.5
	Skylark	204.0	6.95 x 14	1.00	1.0625	.938	9.5	9.5
	Gran Sport	204.0	7.75 x 14	1.00	1.125	.938	9.5	9.5
1967	Sedan	205.0	7.75 x 14	1.00①	1.125	.938	9.5	9.5
	Special Wagon	209.3	7.75 x 14	1.00①	1.125	.938	9.5	9.5
	Sportswagon	214.0	8.25 x 14	1.00①	1.125	1.00	9.5	9.5
1968–69	All 2-Door (Exc. G.S.)	200.6	7.75 x 14★	1.00①	1.125	.875	9.5	9.5
	All 4-Door	204.6	7.75 x 14★	1.00①	1.125	.875	9.5	9.5
	Sta. Wagon (Deluxe)	209.0	7.75 x 14★	1.00①	1.125	.875	9.5	9.5
	Sta. Wagon (Spt. Wagon)	214.09	8.25 x.14	1.00①	1.125	1.00	9.5	9.5
	G.S. 350 & 400	200.6	7.75 x 14★★	1.00①	1.125	.875	9.5	9.5
1970–72	All 2-Door	†203.2	G78 x 14★★★	1.00①	1.125	.875	9.495–9.505	9.495–9.505
	All 4-Door	†207.2	G78 x 14	1.00①	1.125	.875	9.495–9.505	9.495–9.505
	Sport Wagon	212.7	H78 x 14	1.00①	1.125	.875	9.495–9.505	9.495–9.505
	Convertible	†203.2	G78 x 14	1.00①	1.125	.875	9.495–9.505	9.495–9.505

①—Optional disc brakes—1.125 in.
★—Optional—8.25 x 14
★★—Optional—On 350, 8.25 x 14; Standard on 400, F70 x 14

★★★—G60 x 15 optional on 1971-72 G.S. 400.
†—1970 is 1 in. shorter.
G.S.—Gran Sport

FUSES AND CIRCUIT BREAKERS

1965

Back-up, stop, turn signal .... 15 AMP. 1¼ in.
Heater, air conditioner .... 30 AMP. 1¼ in.
Dome, trunk, cigar lighter........... 15 AMP. 1¼ in.
Panel lights & rheostat .... 3 AMP. 1¼ in.
Radio .... 2.5 AMP ⅞ in
Tail, license, glove box, panel
   light & clock .... 10 AMP. 1¼ in.
Transmission shift solenoid, wiper
   & washer motor.................. 25 AMP. 1¼ in.
Headlamp and front parking .... 15 AMP. CB

1966

Same as 1965 except the following:
Instrument panel lights .... 4 AMP.
Radio.................................... 7.5 AMP.

1967–70

Radio, dir. signal .... 10 AMP. 1¼ in.
Stop lamps & hazard flasher .... 20 AMP. 1¼ in.
Heater & air conditioner .... 25 AMP. 1¼ in.

Instrument lights .... 4 AMP. 1¼ in.
Wiper, back-up & indicator lamps........ 20 AMP. 1¼ in.
Lighter & tail lamps.................... 20 AMP. 1¼ in.
Rear window defroster .... 5 AMP. ⅝ in.

1971–72

Same as 1967-70 except the following:
Rear window defroster...................... 20 AMP.
Windshield wiper .... 25 AMP.
Indicator lamps........................... 10 AMP.

LIGHT BULBS

1965

Automatic transmission control dial......... 1893; 2 CP
Back-up............................. 1156; 32 CP
Clock dial................................. 57; 2 CP
Courtesy light, instrument panel .... 89; 6 CP
Courtesy light, rear seat area................. 90; 6 CP
Dome, center roof .... 211; 15 CP
Glove box .... 1893; 2 CP

Headlight high beam indicator .... 158; 2 CP
Headlight, 5¾ in. dia., type 1 (inner)....... 4001; 37.5 W
Headlight, 5¾ in. dia., type 2 (outer).. 4002-L; 37.5-55 W
Heater-air conditioner control dial.......... 1893; 2 CP
Indicator lights (oil, temp. and gen.) .... 158; 2 CP
Instrument cluster dials..................... 158; 2 CP
License.................................... 97; 4 CP
Radio dial .... 1881; 2 CP
Trunk.................................... 89; 6 CP

Turn signal and parking, front .... 1157; 32-4 CP
Turn signal, tail and stop................ 1157; 32-4 CP
Turn signal indicator .... 158; 2 CP

1966–72

Same as 1965 except the following:
Indicator lights........................... 194; 2 CP
Instrument cluster........................ 194; 2 CP
Courtesy lights, rear seat .... 212; 2 CP

Distributor

Detailed information on direction of distributor rotation, cylinder numbering, firing order, point gap, point dwell, timing mark location, spark plugs, spark advance and idle speed, will be found in the Specifications tables of this section.

The distributor on the OHV 6 is located on the right side of the engine. On the V6, and most V8's, the distributor is located between the two cylinder banks, up front. On the early 400 cu. in. V8, the distributor is at the rear of the engine. The rotor turns clockwise, viewed from the top.

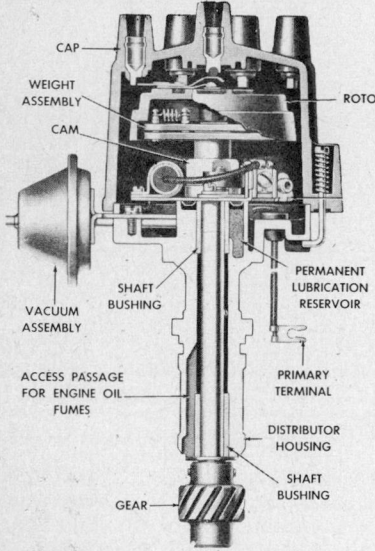

Distributor and cap assembly
(© Buick Div. G.M. Corp.)

Engine timing requirements are satisfied by centrifugal and vacuum advance mechanisms. Vacuum advance is controlled by the effort of a vacuum diaphragm working against spring tension. The diaphragm moves the breaker plate counterclockwise to advance the timing, and the springs move the plate clockwise to retard the timing. The degree of vacuum advance is determined by the amount of vacuum applied to the spring loaded diaphragm and breaker plate. Centrifugal advance is governed by engine speed. As speed increases, advance weights push against an advance cam which is integral with the distributor shaft. This causes the spark to be mechanically advanced. As speed decreases, the weights are returned by springs, returning the timing to the initial setting.

Caution Design of the V6-90° engine requires a special form of distributor cam. The distributor may be serviced in the regular way and should cause no more

problems than any other distributor, if the firing plan is thoroughly understood.

The distributor cam is not ground to standard six cylinder indexing intervals. This particular form requires that the original pattern of spark plug wiring be used. The engine will not run in balance if No. 1 spark plug wire is inserted into No. 6 distributor cap tower, even though each wire in firing sequence is advanced to the next distributor tower. There is a difference between the firing intervals of each succeeding cylinder through the 720° engine cycle.

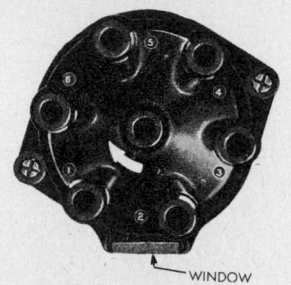

Spark plug wire installation in V6 engine
(© Buick Div. G.M. Corp.)

Distributor Removal

1. Remove distributor cap, primary wire and vacuum line at the distributor.
2. Scribe a mark on the distributor body, locating the position of the rotor and scribe another mark on the distributor body and engine block, showing the position of the body in the block.
3. Remove the hold-down screw and lift the distributor out of the block.

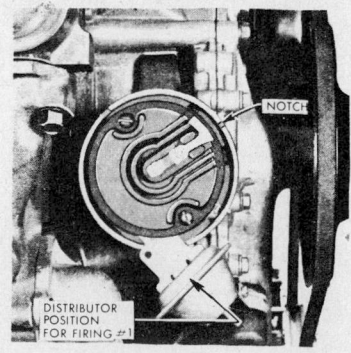

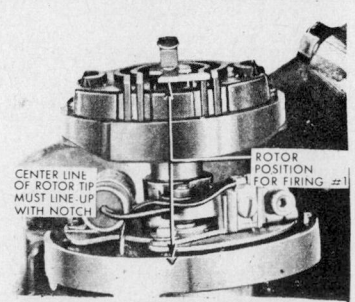

Installing distributor in V6 engine
(© Buick Div. G.M. Corp.)

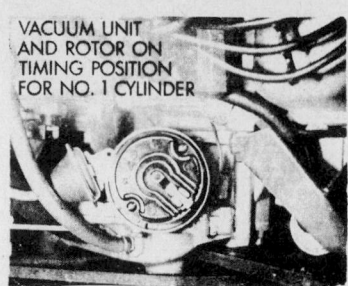

Installing distributor into V8 engine—except 1965-66 400 cu. in.
(© Buick Div. G.M. Corp.)

Distributor Installation

For firing order and cylinder numbering, see specifications.

1. If engine has been disturbed, rotate the crankshaft to bring the piston of No. 1 cylinder to the top of its compression stroke.
2. Position the distributor in the block with the rotor at No. 1 firing position. Make sure the oil pump intermediate drive shaft is properly seated in the oil pump.
3. Install the distributor lock but do not tighten.
4. Rotate the distributor body clockwise until the breaker points are just starting to open. Tighten the retaining screw.
5. Connect the primary wire and the vacuum line to the distributor, then install distributor cap.
6. Start the engine and check the timing with a timing light.

Generator, Regulator

Detailed facts on the generator and regulator can be found in the Specification tables.

General repair and troubleshooting can be found in the Unit Repair Section.

AC Generator (Delcotron)

An alternating current generator is used on Buick Special. This is to satisfy the increase in electrical loads imposed on the battery by conditions of traffic and driving patterns.

The Delcotron is covered in the Unit Repair Section.

Caution Since the Delcotron and regulator are designed for use on only one polarity system, the following precautions must be observed:

1. The polarity of the battery, generator and regulator must be matched and considered before making any electrical connections in the system.
2. When connecting a booster battery, be sure to connect the nega-

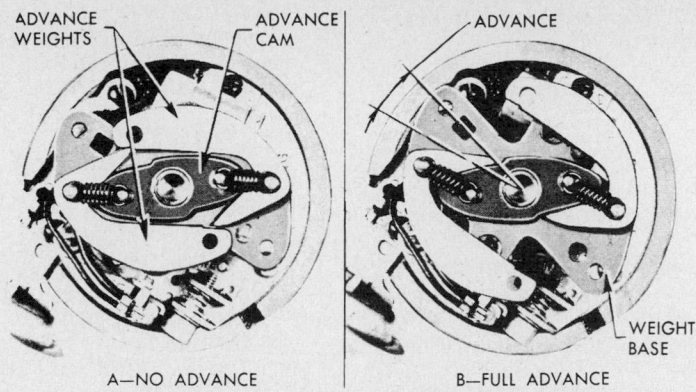

ADVANCE WEIGHTS   ADVANCE CAM   ADVANCE

WEIGHT BASE

A—NO ADVANCE   B—FULL ADVANCE

Centrifugal advance mechanism (© Buick Div. G.M. Corp.)

tive battery terminals together and the positive battery terminals together.

3. When connecting a charger to the battery, connect the charger positive lead to the battery positive terminal. Connect the charger negative lead to the battery negative terminal.

4. Never operate the Delcotron on open circuit. Be sure that all connections in the circuit are clean and tight.

5. Do not short across or ground any of the terminals on the Delcotron regulator.

6. Do not attempt to polarize the Delcotron.

7. Do not use test lamps of more than 12 volts for checking diode continuity.

8. Avoid long soldering times when replacing diodes or transistors. Prolonged heat is damaging to these units.

9. Disconnect the battery ground terminal when servicing any AC system. This will prevent the possibility of accidental reversing of polarity.

Delcotron R & R

Remove bolt holding tension bar to unit. Release drive belt. Unfasten mounting bolt to release Delcotron from engine. When reinstalling, adjust drive belt to allow ½ in. play on the longest run between pulleys.

NOTE: on some models, it may be necessary to loosen and rotate fan shroud. On all A/C models, remove compressor bracket.

Battery, Starter

Battery

A Delco 12 volt battery is used in all models. (See Battery and Starter Specifications.)

Starter

The starter circuit consists of the

battery, battery cables, starting motor, starter motor solenoid switch, ignition-starter switch and the neutral safety switch, (used on cars with automatic transmission).

The starting motor and solenoid assembly is mounted on the flywheel upper housing, left side, on the 1965-66 400 cu. in. engine. On all other models the starting motor and solenoid assembly is on the right side.

The solenoid switch closes the circuit between the battery and the starting motor. It also operates the shift lever that moves the drive pinion into mesh with the flywheel ring gear.

Starter R & R

L-6

1. Disconnect battery and solenoid wires.

2. Remove attaching bolts and lift out starter.

V8

1. Disconnect battery.

2. Jack up car.

3. Remove four screws (⅜ in.) that hold flywheel inspection cover.

4. Disconnect wires from solenoid.

5. Remove one bolt from starter bracket to engine block, then remove two rear starter bolts using a 9/16 in. socket. NOTE: the bracket bolt is hidden and must be removed using a short ½ in. open-end wrench. This bolt must be started by hand when installing.

6. Remove starter motor.

Instruments

1965-69

The instrument cluster includes the speedometer head, the generator charge indicator, the oil pressure indicator, the temperature indicator, the fuel gauge, light switch, wiper and washer switch, starter and ignition switch and the cigarette lighter. On 1969 models, the ignition switch

is on the right side of the steering column.

A printed circuit which is part of the speedometer housing is used to complete the circuit for the fuel gauge and the lights in the cluster.

1970-72

The instrument cluster assembly is comprised of three individual units. The left unit houses the fuel gauge, indicator lights and/or oil pressure gauge and ammeter. The center unit contains the speedometer. The right unit contains the optional clock or tachometer. Each unit contains its own printed circuit, fastened by three screws on the rear of the housing.

Cluster Removal and Installation

1965

1. Disconnect battery ground cable.

2. Remove cover extension assembly by removing four screws across bottom, then raising the entire extension to disengage four clips across top.

3. Remove heater control trim bezel by removing four corner screws.

4. Remove four screws from instrument cluster. Pull cluster out as far as connections allow.

5. Disconnect:
   a. Speedometer cable
   b. Printed circuit plug
   c. Shift indicator lamp
   d. Clock wire
   e. Light switch connector
   f. Wiper switch wires
   g. Lighter wire
   h. Accessory switch wires

6. Remove cluster

7. Reinstall by reversing procedure.

1966-67

1. Disconnect battery.

2. Remove five screws and pull instrument panel upper cover rearward to remove.

3. Lower steering column and remove one ¼ in. hex screw from lower edge of instrument panel housing.

4. Remove one ¼ in. hex screw from lower edge of instrument panel housing through glove compartment hole.

5. Remove four remaining ¼ in. hex screws from lower edge of instrument panel housing.

6. Remove six screws from across upper edge of instrument panel housing.

7. Disconnect speedometer cable.

8. Protect steering column from scratches, then pull instrument panel rearward and rotate it so back of cluster is accessible.

9. Disconnect from instrument clus-

ter:
A. Printed circuit connector.
B. Clock connector.
C. Shift quadrant light.
10. Remove four ¼ in. hex screws and remove instrument panel cluster.
11. Install by reversing removal procedure.

1968

1. Disconnect battery.
2. Remove six screws from instrument panel compartment body and remove assembly.
3. Remove radio knobs and escutcheons.
4. Remove two ⅝ in. hex nuts and two screws from radio filler plate and remove plate. Do not remove radio.
5. Remove four ⅜ in. hex nuts at top underside of dash assembly and two screws at housing assembly. Pull instrument panel upper cover rearward to remove.
6. Remove four screws from steering column filler and remove filler. If car is equipped with air conditioner, remove one screw at left air conditioner plenum chamber and remove plenum from instrument panel housing.
7. Remove four nuts from lower edge of instrument panel housing.
8. Remove four screws across upper edge of instrument panel housing.
9. Remove two nuts from steering column bracket and disconnect shift quadrant link wire at steering column. Lower steering column.
10. Protect steering column, then pull instrument panel rearward and rotate it so that back of cluster is visible.
11. Remove two nuts from heater control installation and separate from instrument panel housing.
12. Disconnect speedometer cable from below.
13. Disconnect from instrument cluster:
A. Wiring harness clip.
B. Printed circuit connector.
C. Clock connector.
14. Disconnect accessory switch and cruise control switch assembly wires from top side of instrument panel housing.
15. Disconnect headlight switch connector.
16. Disconnect windshield wiper/washer switch connector.
17. Disconnect cigarette lighter connector.
18. Remove instrument panel housing assembly.
19. Remove four ¼ in. hex screws and remove instrument panel cluster from instrument panel housing.

20. Install by reversing removal procedure.

1969-72

Caution If equipped with Cruise Control, upper speedometer cable must be disconnected from transducer before cluster housing is pulled back.
1. Disconnect battery ground cable.
2. Remove nine glove compartment screws and glove compartment.
3. Remove two screws through cluster housing. Remove two nuts above glove compartment opening. Pull instrument panel upper cover rearward to disengage three guide pins. Remove upper cover.
4. Remove steering column opening filler. Disconnect left air conditioning duct, if applicable.
5. Remove two nuts. Disconnect shift indicator link. Lower steering column.
6. Protect steering column.
7. Remove eight screws. Pull instrument cluster housing back. Rest housing on steering column and rotate so that back of cluster is visible.
8. Reinstall by reversing procedure.

Speedometer

To remove the speedometer head and printed circuit it is necessary to remove the instrument cluster. An external ground wire is used for the instrument panel gauges.

Wiper Switch Replacement

1965-66

This assembly can be removed by removing the set screw in knob and sliding knob from shaft. Then, unscrew bezel and lower switch so that wires can be disconnected.

1967

The assembly can be removed by simply pulling the knob from the shaft, and then unscrewing the bezel and lowering the switch so that the wires can be disconnected.

1968-72

1. Remove steering column opening filler by removing four screws.
2. Remove left air conditioning duct, if applicable.
3. Unplug switch connectors and remove two screws up to 1969; thereafter, three screws.
4. Remove wiper switch assembly.
5. Install by reversing removal procedure.

Ignition Switch Replacement

1965-68

1. Disconnect battery ground

strap.
2. Turn key to Accessory position.
3. Insert stiff wire into hole in face of lock cylinder to depress lock pin. Rotate cylinder counter-clockwise and pull out.
4. To remove ignition switch, remove retaining nut and lower switch.
To reinstall:
5. Install switch, tighten nut.
6. Insert key in cylinder, place cylinder in switch slightly counter-clockwise from Accessory position, press inward and turn cylinder clockwise.

1969-72

The ignition switch and lock is located, not in the instrument panel, but in the steering column. The ignition lock also locks the steering and the transmission.

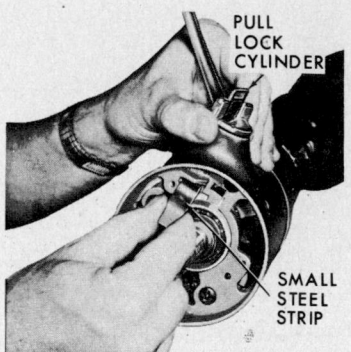

Removing ignition lock cylinder—1969-72
(© Buick Div., G.M. Corp.)

Standard Column—1969-72

1. Remove steering wheel using proper puller.
2. Remove three cover screws and cover; remove cardboard retainers.
3. Depress lock plate, then remove wire snap-ring and lock plate.
4. Slide upper bearing preload spring and cancelling cam off shaft.
NOTE: steering shaft is now unsupported and could slide out the bottom of the column.
5. Slide thrust washer off shaft, then remove turn signal lever screw and lever.
6. Push in four-way flasher switch; remove knob.
7. Remove three turn signal switch mounting screws, pull connector out of its bracket on the column and tape the upper part of connector and wires together.
8. Pull turn signal switch out of column jacket.
9. Insert a small screwdriver into the slot next to the turn signal switch mounting screw boss (right-hand slot), depress spring latch and remove key lock.
10. Pull buzzer switch straight out, depressing switch clip with

pliers.
11. Place ignition switch in accessory position by pulling up on connecting rod until there is a definite stop or detent felt.
12. Remove two attaching screws and ignition switch.

Tilt Column—1969-72

1. Remove column mounting bracket from column.
NOTE: be careful not to damage the "breakaway" capsules.
2. Remove steering wheel using proper puller.
3. Remove turn signal wire protector (lower column).
4. Remove three column cover screws and cover.
5. Remove tilt release lever, turn signal switch lever, push four-way flasher knob in and remove knob, and remove upper shift lever.
6. Depress lock plate and remove the snap-ring; remove lock plate.
7. Remove cancelling cam and spring.
8. Remove three turn signal switch screws, tape wires to wire connector at upper end and place shift bowl in Low. Pull switch straight up and out.
9. Insert a small screwdriver into the slot next to the turn signal switch mounting screw boss (right-hand slot), depress spring latch and remove key lock.
10. Remove buzzer switch straight out, depressing switch clip with pliers.
11. Remove three housing cover screws and cover.
12. Install tilt release lever and place column in full UP position.
13. Place screwdriver in slot of tilt spring retainer, pres in about 3/16 in. and turn counterclockwise. Remove spring and guide.
NOTE: spring is very strong—be careful.
14. Place column in neutral position, push in on upper steering shaft, remove inner race seat and race.
15. Remove upper flange pinch bolt, place ignition switch in accessory position, remove two switch mounting screws and switch.
NOTE: neutral start switch can be removed at this time, if necessary.

Lighting Switch Replacement

1. Disconnect battery.
2. Disconnect multiple connector from switch.
3. Pull switch knob to last notch and depress spring loaded latch button on top of switch while pulling knob and rod out of switch.
NOTE: on A/C cars, remove left duct if so equipped.
4. Remove escutcheon.
5. Install in reverse of above.

Brakes

Drum Brakes

The service brakes are of the conventional type, hydraulically operated. The lining is molded and attached to the shoes by tubular rivets. The primary shoe lining is shorter than the secondary lining and is of different composition.

Brake drum lining-contact-surfaces are cast iron, however, the drum proper is pressed steel or cast aluminum with integral cooling fins.

The parking brake on all models is operated by a foot pedal and actuates the rear brakes only.

1965-72

The brakes are self-adjusting. The system is designed to react and progressively tighten the star wheel adjuster, a notch at a time, as required. The self adjusters only operate when the brakes are applied while the car is moving rearward.

For detailed service brake information, see Unit Repair Section.

Pedal Travel Check

The distance the brake pedal moves from its rest position to its fully applied position is a good indication of brake condition. Because heat expands the brake drums and increases shoe-to-drum clearance, and pedal travel, this check should be made with the brakes *cold*.

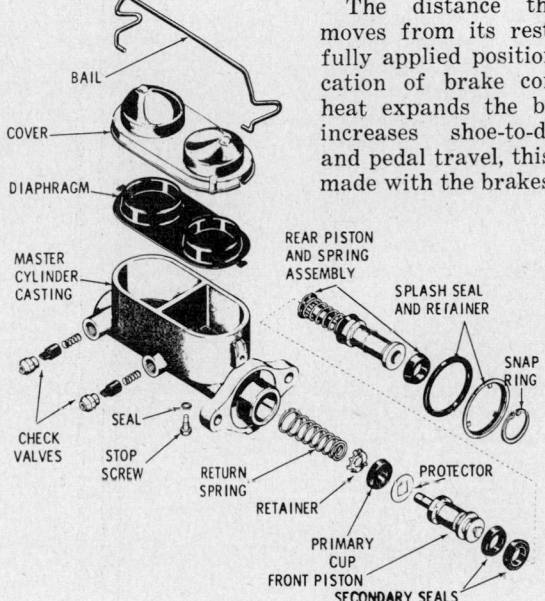

Dual master cylinder (Bendix)
(© Buick Div. G.M. Corp.)

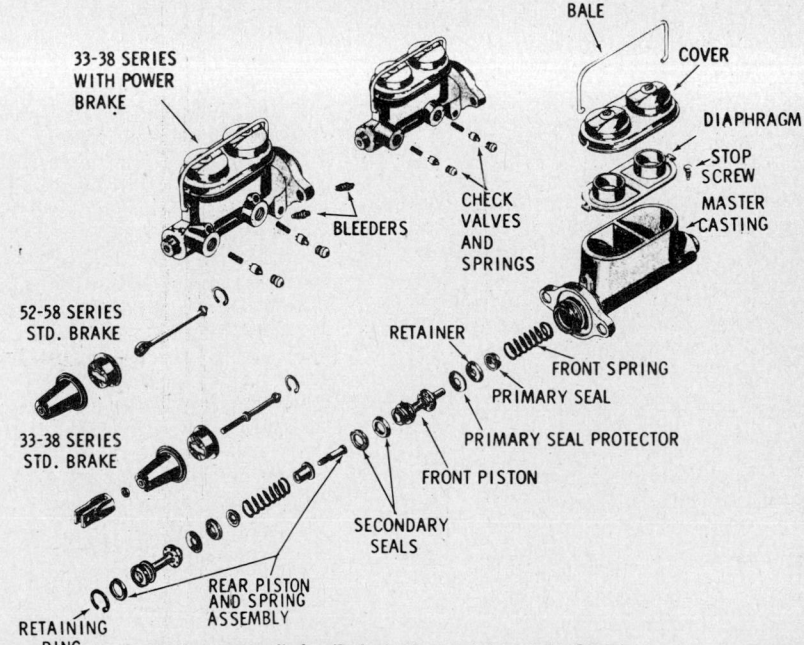

Dual master cylinder (Delco) (© Buick Div. G.M. Corp.)

NOTE: dimensions are the *maximum* pedal travel—not optimum Starred (*) dimensions are distance from floor.

Year	Manual Drum	Power Drum(+)
1965-70	*2¼"	*1½"
1971-72	4¾"	2⅜"

+Pump power brakes before checking.

Pedal Height and Stop Light Switch Adjustment

1965-66

1. Loosen the jam nut on the master cylinder pushrod clevis (under dash).
2. Clamp pushrod with vise-grip pliers and rotate rod clockwise to adjust outward, counterclockwise to adjust inward. Specified pedal height is 4½ in. from floor to center top of pedal pad for power brakes, 6½ in. for manual drum brakes.
3. Tighten jam nut, then disconnect stop light switch wires and turn switch in or out so that plunger is fully depressed against plate with pedal in released position.

1967-72

Brake pedal height is not adjustable because of solid design pushrod. In addition, no brake pedal return spring is used; the spring within the master cylinder returns the brake to rest position. Stop light switch is adjusted by turning switch in or out so that plunger is fully depressed against plate with pedal in released position.

Master Cylinder

A tandem master cylinder is standard equipment on all models. This type system is covered in the Unit Repair Section.

Disc Brakes

Disc brakes are optional on the front wheels of some models. For 1967-68 models, four-piston Delco-Moraine discs were optional. For 1969-72 models, a single-piston Delco-Moraine disc brake design is utilized. Information on disc brakes is in the Unit Repair Section.

Power Brakes

This installation is similar to that for full-size cars.

Repair methods are in Unit Repair Section. For master cylinder removal, power brake unit removal, and parking brake cable replacement procedures, refer to the Buick Section.

Fuel System

Throttle Linkage and Dashpot Adjustments

1965-67

The procedure for adjusting throttle linkage is identical on standard or automatic transmission cars. On automatic transmission cars, however, the linkage actuates other linkage connected to a valve in the transmission. Also, automatic transmission cars have a dashpot to prevent engine stalling from too quick release of the accelerator pedal.

1. To adjust throttle linkage, make sure the accelerator pedal is free.
2. On automatic transmission equipped cars, see Throttle Linkage Adjustment of Automatic Transmission.
3. Disconnect rear end of throttle rod from throttle operating lever.
4. While a helper presses the accelerator firmly against the floor, hold throttle in wide open position. Hold rear end of throttle rod at hole in throttle operating lever. The rod end must be 1/16 in. short of entering the hole in the lever. Adjust throttle rod length to obtain this condition.
5. Connect throttle rod to operating lever and attach cotter pin.
6. Now, press accelerator to the floor and recheck throttle for wide open position.
7. Hold choke valve closed and move throttle lever to wide open position to check adjustment of choke unloader.
8. Finally check that there is a full opening of the throttle valve as the accelerator pedal just strikes the floor.
9. Now adjust the dashpot by turning the plunger until it just touches the throttle lever.
10. With the gear selector in drive and the brakes firmly set, jab the accelerator and release it quickly. Note engine operation as the throttle closes.
11. If engine stalls due to too quick deceleration, move the dashpot plunger toward the throttle lever until the stalling is corrected. If too much time is required for throttle to close, move the plunger away from the throttle lever.
12. If correct control cannot be obtained, renew the dashpot.

1968-72

These models have a flexible cable type throttle linkage, which is not adjustable. Dashpot adjustment is the same as that shown above for

1965-66 models, Steps 9-12.

Idle Speed and Mixture Adjustment

1965-66

On V8 models, the air cleaner must be removed. On V6 models, better idle quality can be obtained with air cleaner installed.

1. Check that the PCV system is operative (not plugged).
2. Remove air cleaner; connect tachometer.
3. Start engine and allow to come to normal operating temperature.
4. Place manual transmission in N, automatic in D (wheels blocked).
5. Adjust throttle stop screw to obtain specified idle speed.
6. Adjust mixture needles alternately to obtain highest tachometer reading. Readjust idle stop screw to obtain specified idle again.
7. Make sure the transmission idle stator switch on the linkage is closed by disconnecting its wire. If idle speed doesn't decrease. the switch is not closed and should be adjusted.
8. Press down on the hot idle compensator valve, if so equipped. If idle drops, valve is open and should be unstuck and idle reset.

1967

1. If equipped with Automatic Level Control (Sportwagon), disconnect vacuum line from compressor at storage tank and plug it with a pencil.
2. The procedure is identical to that for 1965-66 models, with the exception of Step 6. Turn in the mixture needles, alternately, to obtain a 20 rpm drop from specified idle, then open them ¼ turn each. If this does not restore idle speed to specifications, turn them out ⅛ turn at a time until lean best idle is obtained.

1968-70

In 1968, the stator switch for the transmission was eliminated. The changing stator blade angle featured previously was discontinued that year. *Air cleaner must be in place to get proper idle, starting in 1968.*

1. Check PCV system for proper operation.
2. Connect tachometer; warm engine to normal operating temperature.
3. Place manual transmission in N, automatic in D (wheels blocked).
4. To make sure the Thermo Vacuum switch does not switch distributor vacuum over to full manifold vacuum due to over-

heated coolant, remove and plug line from distributor.

NOTE: check that the compressor for the Automatic Level Control, if so equipped, is not running. The compressor now has a regulating valve to shut off vacuum at idle speed. If the compressor is running, this valve is faulty and must be adjusted or replaced before a good idle can be obtained.

5. Adjust throttle stop screw to obtain specified idle speed. On L6 models to 1969, adjust solenoid plunger screw to obtain specified idle.

6. Adjust mixture needles to obtain highest tachometer reading. Readjust throttle stop or solenoid to obtain a speed 20 rpm faster than specified idle.

7. Turn in each mixture screw, alternately, to obtain an idle speed 10 rpm less *per needle* than the basic idle setting of Step 6. This results in a total idle drop of 20 rpm. On L6 models, the 20 rpm drop is achieved using the single mixture needle.

NOTE: on 1970 L6 models, stop engine after setting idle speed in Step 5. Turn mixture screw in until it seats gently, then unscrew exactly four turns. Disconnect and plug distributor vacuum, if not done already, start engine and set ignition timing. Readjust solenoid screw to 830 rpm (manual) or 630 rpm (automatic), then adjust mixture screw inward to obtain specified idle.

8. Press down on the hot idle compensator, if so equipped. If idle drops, valve is open and should be unstuck and idle reset.

1971 V8 Engines

Air cleaner must be in place to get proper, emission-free, idle speed.

1. Check PCV system for proper operation.
2. Connect tachometer; warm engine to normal operating temperature.
3. Place manual transmission in N, automatic in D (wheels blocked).
4. Remove distributor hose and plug.

NOTE: check that the compressor for the Automatic Level Control, if so equipped, is not running. The compressor has a regulating valve to shut off vacuum at idle speed. If the compressor is running, this valve is faulty and must be replaced before a good idle can be obtained.

5. Adjust throttle stop screw to obtain specified idle speed.
6. Adjust idle mixture needles, alternately, to obtain highest tachometer reading.
7. Readjust throttle stop and mixture screws as required to obtain an idle speed 50 rpm faster than

specified, then turn in each screw (leaner) to reduce idle speed 25 rpm *per needle* (for a total reduction of 50 rpm).

8. Adjust fast idle speed.
9. If equipped with manual transmission, check throttle control solenoid adjustment as follows:

NOTE: this switch gives a higher idle speed in third and fourth gears to reduce misfiring and exhaust gas dilution on closed throttle deceleration.

    a. Place shift lever in N.
    b. Start engine; disconnect solenoid wire.
    c. Disconnect single relay connector and plug into the just vacated solenoid connector.
    d. Place throttle in hot (curb) idle position.
    e. Adjust solenoid plunger bolt to obtain 1,100 rpm idle.

NOTE: it may be necessary to move bracket to obtain this figure.

    f. Shut off engine.
10. Reconnect distributor vacuum line.
11. Reinstall idle limiter caps (if removed).

1971 L6 Engine

1. Connect a tachometer, start engine and run until normal operating temperature is reached.
2. Disconnect and plug distributor vacuum line and set ignition timing.
3. Turn off engine, then turn mixture screw inward until it seats gently. Back out screw four full turns.
4. Start engine and adjust both idle mixture and idle speed screws to obtain best quality idle at 530 rpm (automatic in D) or 625 rpm (manual in N).
5. Adjust idle mixture screw *alone* to obtain 500 rpm (automatic in D) or 550 rpm (manual in N).
6. Check Combination Emission Control valve (C.E.C.) as follows:

NOTE: the idle stop solenoid is no longer used, having been replaced by the combination emission control valve. This valve is energized through the transmission to increase idle speed in high gear deceleration conditions and to provide full vacuum spark advance during high gear operation. The valve is de-energized at curb idle and in the lower gears to provide a retarded spark under these conditions, the result of which is lower hydrocarbon emission. The valve need not be adjusted unless the solenoid or throttle body is removed, or the carburetor overhauled.

    a. Disconnect the plug distributor vacuum line.
    b. Disconnect fuel tank line from vapor canister.
    c. Extend the C.E.C. valve

plunger to contact the throttle lever.
    d. Adjust plunger length to obtain specified idle speed.
    e. Reconnect fuel vapor line and distributor vacuum.
7. Install limiter cap on mixture screw, if removed.

Fuel Pump

An AC fuel pump is used. The pump lever works from the underside of a camshaft eccentric. It is of the single-action diaphragm type and is equipped with a pulsation dampening chamber for stabilizing fuel flow. Beginning 1966, fuel pumps are sealed units. They are not to be repaired.

Beginning 1966, all air conditioned cars with V8 engines and all cars with 400 and 455 cu. in. engines have a special fuel pump. This pump has a vapor return line which returns hot fuel and fuel vapor to the fuel tank. The possibility of vapor lock is thus greatly reduced by keeping cool fuel circulating through the pump.

Fuel Filter

V6 Engine

The V6 engine gas filter is located in the carburetor fuel inlet. The element is sintered bronze and placed with the cupped end outward. The element is so spring loaded as to permit fuel by-pass in the event of element clogging.

The element should be removed and cleaned in a good solvent at 12,000 mile or 12 month periods.

1965-66 V8 Engine

On these models, the fuel filter is of the disposable, in-line type, mounted between the fuel pump and the carburetor. Air conditioned models have a fuel filter with a vapor return outlet. The filter should be replaced every 12,000 miles.

1967-72 OHV 6 & V8 Engines

These engines have a pleated paper fuel filter located in the carburetor inlet. The filter should be replaced every 12,000 miles.

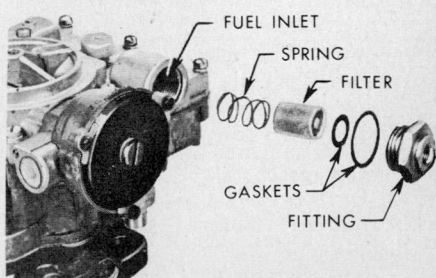

Fuel filter (© Buick Div. G.M. Corp.)

Manifolds

OHV 6 Models

This engine uses a combined intake

and exhaust manifold, equipped with thermostatic heat-riser valve.

To remove the manifold assembly, disconnect the exhaust pipe flange and remove all connections to the carburetor. Take off the vacuum lines at the manifold and also at the carburetor. Remove power steering pump and bracket.

Remove the carburetor. Unbolt the manifold from the side of the cylinder head.

Before reinstalling the manifold, thoroughly clean out the ports to prevent turbulence, particularly on the intake manifold.

Intake Manifold

V6 & V8 Engines

These engines have a low restriction, dual intake manifold. The manifold incorporates an exhaust heat passage to warm the carburetor throttle body. Engine coolant flows out of the engine through the water passages in the manifold and through the thermostat and water outlet elbow located at the front of the manifold. 1965-66 400 cu. in. engines do not have intake manifold water passages; they have a separate water manifold between the cylinder heads, forward of the intake manifold. The thermostat is contained in the water manifold.

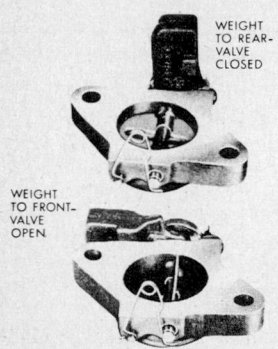

WEIGHT TO REAR-VALVE CLOSED

WEIGHT TO FRONT-VALVE OPEN

Manifold heat control valve

Intake Manifold Removal

This is a general procedure for all models.
1. Drain cooling system.
2. Remove carburetor air cleaner. Disconnect all tubes and hoses from the carburetor. Disconnect and remove the coil.
3. Disconnect temperature indicator wire from sending unit.
4. Disconnect accelerator and transmission linkage at carburetor. Disconnect throttle return spring.
5. Slide front thermostat by-pass hose clamp back on the hose. Disconnect upper radiator hose at outlet.
6. Disconnect heater hose at the temperature control valve inlet.

Force the end of the hose down to permit coolant to drain from intake manifold.
7. Remove manifold-to-head attaching bolts.
8. Remove intake manifold and carburetor as an assembly by sliding rearward to disengage the thermostat by-pass hose from the water pump. Remove intake manifold gasket.

Exhaust Manifold

V6 & V8 Engines

The controlling source of exhaust heat is a heat control valve in one of the exhaust manifolds. This valve has a thermostat spring which tends to hold the valve closed under cold operating conditions.

This tension causes pressure build-up in the exhaust manifold, which forces exhaust through the crossover passage under the carburetor to the opposite exhaust manifold and out the pipe and muffler.

Removal—1965-72 V6 and V8

1. Jack up car and support on axle stands.
2. Disconnect exhaust pipe from manifolds on both sides of engine and lower. If equipped with dual exhaust, disconnect and lower only on the side being worked on.
3. If equipped with manual transmission, remove equalizer shaft.
NOTE: on right side, it may be necessary to remove A/C, power steering, or alternator.
4. Remove exhaust manifold-to-cylinder head bolts.
5. Remove manifold from beneath car.
NOTE: on GS 400 models, it may be necessary to pull pitman arm from pitman shaft and to swing steering linkage forward to gain clearance.

Cooling System

The cooling system is pressurized to 15 psi. Coolant temperature is controlled by a thermostat housed in the forward (outlet) end of the intake manifold. In the 1965-66 400 cu. in. engine, the thermostat is housed in the water outlet manifold. In the OHV 6 engine, the thermostat is in the top front of the cylinder head. This thermostat controls circulation and temperature in the intake manifold as well as in the engine.

Caution Be sure the thermostat is not reversed in its installed position. The temperature-sensitive side should extend toward

the rear or down.

SPECIAL NOTE: it is advisable to use a highly inhibited ethylene-glycol antifreeze type coolant in the Buick Special, both winter and summer. The coolant should be changed every two years.

Water Pump

Removal—1965-72

1. Drain cooling system.
2. Loosen belt or belts, then remove fan blades and pulley or pulleys from hub on water pump shaft. Remove belt or belts.
3. Disconnect hose from water pump inlet and heater hose from nipple. Remove bolts, then remove pump and gasket from the timing case cover.
4. Check pump shaft bearings for end-play or roughness. If bearings are not serviceable, the assembly must be replaced.

Installation—1965-72

1. Install pump assembly with new gasket. Bolts and lock washers must be torqued evenly.
2. Connect radiator hose to pump inlet and heater hose to nipple. Fill cooling system and check all points of possible coolant leaks.
3. Install fan pulley or pulleys and fan blade. Install belt or belts and adjust for correct tension.

Engine Temperature and Oil Pressure Sending Unit

Temperature Gauge—1965-72

A temperature switch controls the operation of the temperature indicator light located in the instrument cluster. The temperature switch is located in the thermostat housing on the OHV 6; in the right cylinder head on the 1965-66 400 cu. in. V8; and in the right front of the intake manifold on the V6 and all other V8 engines.

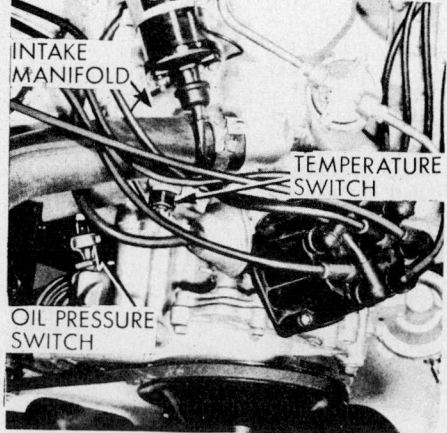

INTAKE MANIFOLD

TEMPERATURE SWITCH

OIL PRESSURE SWITCH

Oil pressure and temperature sending units— V8 except 1965-66 400 cu. in.
(© Buick Div. G.M. Corp.)

If the engine cooling system is not working properly and the coolant temperature reaches approximately 250°F, the temperature indicator light will burn in the instrument cluster.

Oil Pressure—1965-72

The oil pressure sending unit is located in the oil pump cover and operates an indicator light in the instrument cluster. On the 1965-66 400 cu. in. engine, the sending unit is on the right rear of the engine, in the main oil gallery.

If engine oil pressure drops below a safe level during operation, the circuit is completed through the sending unit to ground. This will cause the oil indicator light in the cluster to burn.

Engine

Buick Special models have used eight basic engines since 1965. From 1965 to 1967, the basic six-cylinder was a V6 of 225 cu. in. displacement, using a single-barrel carburetor in 1965 and a two-barrel unit in 1966-67. In 1968, the V6 was replaced by the standard 250 cu. in. OHV inline six used by Chevrolet. This engine is used up to and including the 1972 model year.

From 1965 to 1967, a 300 cu. in. V8 manufactured by Buick was used, in both two- and four-barrel versions. A similar V8, of 340 cu. in. displacement, was used in 1966 and 1967—it was basically a stroked version of the 300 engine.

The Buick Gran Sport used the old 401 Buick V8 in 1965 and 1966, although it was often termed the "400". The latest 400 V8, used in Gran Sport and some Sportwagons from 1967 to 1969, was a new engine completely unrelated to the old 400/401. This engine had a bore and stroke of 4.04 x 3.90 in., as opposed to the older engine's dimensions of 4.187 x 3.64 in.

In 1968, another new engine, the 350 cu. in., was introduced as the standard Skylark V8. This engine was also available in the G.S. 350, with slightly higher power, and is still the standard medium size Buick engine. In 1970, the 455 cu. in. V8 used in the larger Buick was added to the Skylark Gran Sport. This engine was available in both standard (350 horsepower) and Stage I (360 horsepower) tune.

Exhaust Emission Control

1966-68 California

The Air Injection Reactor (A.I.R.) system of emission control, using an ancilliary air pump with external ducting, is incorporated into all cars manufactured for sale in California (and some non-California cars with special high-performance engines).

1968-71 Nationwide

The Combustion Control System (C.C.S.), a system of inter-related engine modifications, is used to meet federal anti-pollution standards.

1972 Nationwide

All 455 cu. in. engines for 1972 are equipped with a new Air Injector Reactor system. A redesigned air pump injects air into the exhaust manifold via ducts routed internally through intake manifold. 350 cu. in. engines continue to use the C.C.S. engine modifications.

1972 California

All Buicks sold in California utilize a new system called Exhaust Gas Recirculation, along with the redesigned A.I.R. system described above. Exhaust Gas Recirculation effectively lowers combustion temperatures by diluting the fuel/air mixture with exhaust gases. The gases pass through a metering valve that opens only under acceleration or high engine speed before being ducted through passages in the intake manifold area below the carburetor.

Tuning specifications can be found on a plate in the engine compartment in all 1968 and later cars.

Engine R & R

This is a general procedure for all models.
1. Disconnect battery cables.
2. Drain cooling system and remove heater and radiator hoses.
3. Disconnect exhaust pipes at the manifolds.
4. Remove hood assembly.
5. Remove radiator.
6. On standard transmission models, disconnect the clutch control linkage. On automatic transmission equipped cars, disconnect the selector and throttle control linkage.
7. Disconnect the involved wiring such as generator, starter, sending units, etc.
8. Disconnect fuel line at fuel pump.
9. Disconnect accelerator linkage.
10. Disconnect vacuum lines to power brake unit, vacuum modulator and load leveler.
11. Remove the air conditioning compressor. Do not disconnect hoses.
12. Remove flywheel cover pan. Separate engine from transmission at bell housing.
13. Support transmission.
14. Disconnect both engine front mounts.
15. To afford clearance and prevent damage, it may be necessary to remove the oil filter unit.
16. Attach lifting device to engine.
17. Lift the engine out of the car.

Engine Installation

Install the engine in the reverse order of removal.

Cylinder Heads

Rocker Arm Removal
OHV 6

NOTE: these rocker arms are of the individual pedestal design and need not be removed to remove head.
1. Remove rocker arm cover.
2. Remove rocker arm nuts, rocker arm bolts, rocker arms, and pushrods. These should be reinstalled in their original locations.

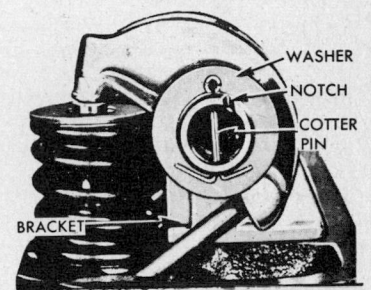

Rocker arm and shaft—1965-66 400 cu. in.
(© Buick Div. G.M. Corp.)

V6 and V8

1. Disconnect plug wires at the spark plugs and tie back out of the way.
2. Remove screws holding the rocker arm cover to the cylinder head. Remove rocker arm cover and gasket.
3. Remove rocker arm shaft bracket-to-cylinder head attaching bolts. Remove rocker arm and shaft assembly.
4. Remove the pushrods. These should be reinstalled in their original locations.
5. If lifters are to be serviced, re-

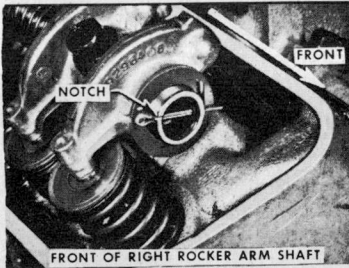

Rocker arm and shaft—
300 and 340 cu. in. 1965-67
(© Buick Div., G.M. Corp.)

move them. If not, protect them with clean cloth. It is extremely important to protect the hydraulic lifters from dirt.

Cylinder Head Removal

OHV 6

Refer to the Chevrolet Section for this procedure. This engine is virtually identical to the Chevrolet 6 for the same model year.

V6

1. Drain coolant and disconnect battery ground strap.
2. Remove intake manifold.
3. For right head only: Remove Delcotron and air conditioning compressor. Do not disconnect compressor hoses.
4. For left head only: Remove dipstick, power steering pump, and A.I.R. equipment. Do not disconnect steering unit hoses.
5. Disconnect exhaust pipe from manifold, remove manifold.
6. Remove rocker cover, rocker shaft assembly, and pushrods. The pushrods should be reinstalled in their original locations. It is important to protect the hydraulic lifters from dirt.
7. Loosen all head bolts, then remove all bolts and remove head and gasket.

1965-66 400 Cu. In.

1. Drain coolant and disconnect battery ground strap.
2. Remove intake manifold.
3. For right head only: Remove dipstick, automatic transmission filler pipe bracket, Delcotron mounting bracket, and air conditioning compressor. Do not disconnect compressor hoses.
4. For left head only: Remove power steering pump. Do not disconnect hoses.
5. Remove water manifold.
6. Disconnect exhaust pipe from manifold, remove manifold.
7. Remove rocker arm cover, rocker arm and shaft assembly, and push rods. The pushrods should be reinstalled in their original locations. It is extremely important to protect the hydraulic lifters from dirt.

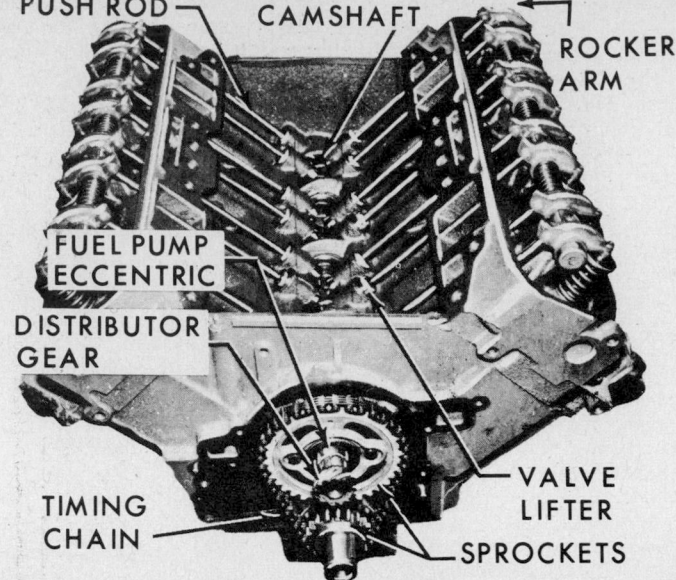

Engine valve mechanism—400 cu. in. 1967-70

NOTE: due to lack of space in certain engine compartments, some of the bolts and pushrods must be left in the head during removal. Tape these items to the head to prevent loss. These same parts must be in the head during installation.

8. Loosen all head bolts, remove all bolts, and remove head and gasket.

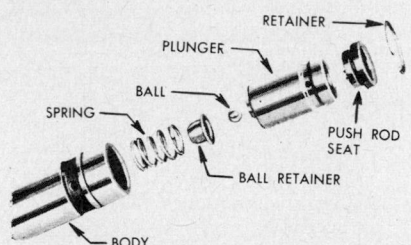

Valve lifter (© Buick Div. G.M. Corp.)

V8 Except 1965-66 400 Cu. In.

Head removal procedure for these engines is the same as that detailed above for the 1965-66 400 cu. in. with the substitution of the following steps.

3. For right head only: Remove Delcotron and air conditioning compressor. Do not disconnect compressor hoses.

4. For left head only: Remove dipstick and power steering pump. Do not disconnect hoses.
5. Delete Step 5.

For valve guide replacement procedure, refer to the Buick Section.

Timing Case

Timing Gear Replacement

OHV 6

The timing gears are arranged so that (unless deliberately disturbed) the valve timing will remain as set at the factory when the engine was assembled. Unless the gears are badly worn or seriously damaged the valve timing will remain constant within reasonable limits.

If it becomes necessary to replace the timing gears due to wear or damage, remove the radiator core, disconnect the front motor mounts and jack up the front of the engine. Remove the fan belt, fan pulley, oil pan and timing case cover.

NOTE: it is recommended that the camshaft be removed from the car in order to remove and replace the gear in an arbor press.

Many successful mechanics prefer removing the camshaft in order to avoid possible risk when attempting to press a gear onto the shaft in place on the car. Sometimes when the gear is being pressed on in place on the car, damage results to the thrust washer behind the cam gear. Unfortunately, this damage is not noticed until the engine is started.

To replace the gear by removing the camshaft, remove the rocker arm assemblies and the distributor, all of the pushrods and all of the lifters. The camshaft may then be pulled out toward the front of the engine. It will

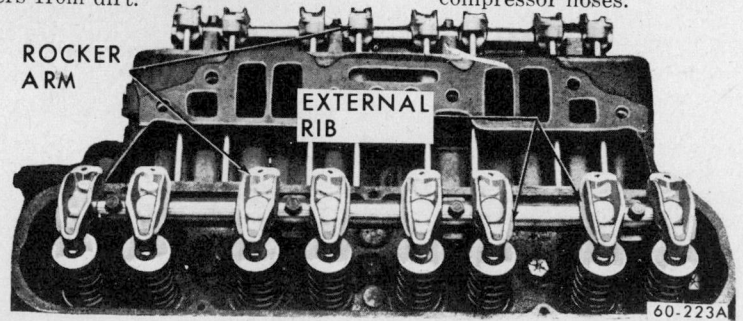

Rocker arms and shaft, 455 cu. in. (© Buick Div. G.M. Corp.)

be necessary to retime the ignition.

Runout of the camshaft timing gear should not exceed .004 in. Backlash between the two gears should not be less than .004 in. nor more than .006 in. End clearance of the thrust plate should be .001 to .005 in.

A different approach to this situation, and certainly a quicker one, is as follows:

1. Very carefully center punch and drill two ¼ in. holes in opposite sides of the camshaft gear hub.
2. Break the fiber part of the camshaft gear away from the steel hub.
3. Split the steel hub with a cold chisel at the two newly drilled holes.
4. Remove broken camshaft gear and clean entire timing case area.
5. Place the new gear on the camshaft to line up with the keyway and the gear timing marks.

NOTE: be sure to allow for the helical cut on the gear when aligning the marks for timing.

6. Have a reliable helper, with the aid of a pinch bar, buck up against one of the camshaft lobes from underneath. (The success of the job depends upon this man's care in holding forward thrust on the camshaft. Failure on his part will allow the camshaft to be forced back and dislodge the oil sealing expansion plug at the rear of the camshaft.)
7. With the aid of a 1¼ in. socket and a lead hammer, tap the new gear into place on the camshaft.

Caution The use of a dial indicator will reduce the possibility of driving the gear too far onto the camshaft. This would alter the desired camshaft thrust clearance of .001 to .005 in. Use care when approaching the final position of the gear on the shaft, because it is impossible to increase the thrust clearance without pulling the new gear. In the absence of a dial indicator, this end thrust can be measured with a feeler gauge. In this case the thrust clearance is to be measured between the camshaft gear hub and the thrust plate. A feeler gauge strip, inserted in either of the two large gear holes, will reach this point.

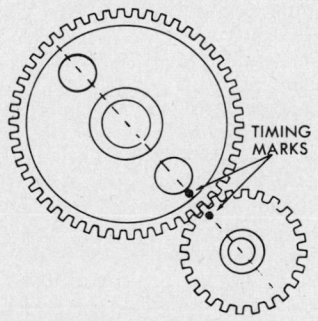

Timing marks—inline 6

Timing Chain Removal

V6

1. Drain cooling system.
2. Disconnect radiator and heater hoses at water pump and disconnect lower radiator hose at radiator. Remove attaching bolts and brackets and remove radiator.
3. Remove fan, fan pulleys and belt, or belts.
4. Remove crankshaft pulley.
5. Remove harmonic balancer from crankshaft.
6. If car has power steering, remove the pump bracket bolts and move the steering pump out of the way.
7. Disconnect lines and remove the fuel pump.
8. Remove generator.
9. Remove distributor cap and spark plug wire retainers from brackets on rocker arm cover. Swing distributor cap, with wires, out of the way. Disconnect distributor primary wire.
10. Remove distributor.
11. Loosen and slide front clamp on thermostat by-pass hose rearward.
12. Remove bolts attaching timing cover to cylinder block. Remove two oil pan to timing cover bolts.
13. Lift off the timing case cover.
14. Temporarily install harmonic balancer bolt and washer to the end of crankshaft. Rotate crankshaft so sprockets are positioned as for timing, (shafts and sprocket O-marks on a centerline). Now remove harmonic balancer bolt with a sharp rap on the wrench handle to prevent changing the position of the sprockets.

NOTE: some engines may have the timing mark on the cam gear stamped 180° from proper position. For this reason, carefully note positions of valve gear and timing marks before removing gears.

15. Remove front crankshaft oil slinger.
16. Remove bolt and special washer holding the camshaft distributor drive gear and fuel pump eccentric to the camshaft. Slide gear and eccentric off the shaft.
17. Use two large screwdrivers to alternately pry the camshaft sprocket then the crankshaft sprocket forward and off their respective shafts.
18. Thoroughly clean the sprockets, distributor drive gear, fuel pump eccentric and crankshaft oil slinger.

1965-66 400 Cu. In.

1. Drain cooling system.
2. Remove radiator core, fan belt, fan and pulley, and crankshaft balancer.
3. Remove all bolts attaching

timing chain cover and water manifold to crankcase and cylinder heads. Do not remove five bolts attaching water pump to chain cover.

4. Remove chain cover and water manifold. Be careful not to damage oil pan gasket.
5. Remove crankshaft oil slinger. Remove bolt, lockwasher, plain washer, and fuel pump operating eccentric.
6. Align timing marks on sprockets.
7. Use two large screwdrivers to alternately pry the camshaft sprocket, then the crankshaft sprocket, forward and off their respective shafts.
8. Thoroughly clean timing chain cover and crankcase surface. For timing chain cover oil seal replacement see Buick Section.

455 Cu. In.

1. Drain cooling system.
2. Remove radiator, fan, fan pulley and belt, and crankshaft pulley and pulley reinforcement.
3. Remove fuel pump and Delcotron.
4. Remove distributor.
5. Loosen clamp on thermostat bypass hose.
6. Remove harmonic balancer.
7. Remove timing chain cover to crankcase bolts. Remove oil pan to timing chain cover bolts. Thoroughly clean cover and crankcase surface. For timing chain cover oil seal replacement see Buick Section.
8. Align timing marks on sprockets.
9. Remove oil pan.
10. Remove crankshaft oil slinger. Remove camshaft sprocket bolts.
11. Use two large screwdrivers to alternately pry the camshaft sprocket, then the crankshaft sprocket, forward and off their respective shafts.

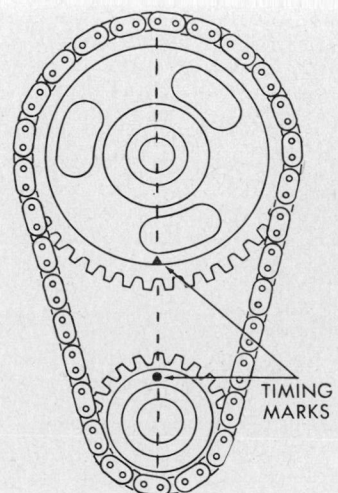

Valve timing mark V8

400 Cu. In. 1967-69, 300, 340, 350 Cu. In. 1965-72

This procedure is the same as that detailed above for the 455 cu. in. engine with the substitution of the following steps:

9. Delete Step 9.
10. Remove bolt, special washer, camshaft distributor drive gear, and fuel pump eccentric from camshaft. Remove crankshaft oil slinger.

Installation

V6 and V8, Except 1965-66 400 Cu. In. and 1970-72 455 Cu. In.

1. Make sure, with sprockets temporarily installed, that No. 1 piston is at top dead center and the camshaft sprocket O-mark straight down and on a centerline of both shafts.
2. Remove the camshaft sprocket and assemble the timing chain on both sprockets. Then slide the sprockets-and-chain assembly on the shafts with the O-marks in their closest together position and on a centerline with the sprocket hubs.
3. Assemble slinger on crankshaft with I.D. against the sprocket, (concave side toward front of engine).
4. Slide fuel pump eccentric on camshaft and Woodruff key with oil groove forward.
5. Install distributor drive gear.
6. Install drive gear and eccentric bolt and retaining washer. Torque to 40-55 ft. lbs.
7. Reinstall timing case cover by reversing removal procedure, paying particular attention to the following points.
   A. Remove oil pump cover and pack space around the oil pump gears completely full of petroleum jelly. There must be no air space left inside the pump. Reinstall the pump cover using new gasket.
   B. The gasket surface of the block and timing chain cover must be clean and smooth. Use a new gasket correctly positioned.
   C. Install chain cover being certain the dowel pins engage the dowel pin holes before starting the attaching bolts.
   D. Lube the bolt threads before installation and install them.
   E. If the car has power steering, the front pump bracket should be installed at this time.
   F. Lube the O.D. of the harmonic balancer hub before installation to prevent damage to the seal when starting the engine.

1965-66 400 Cu. In.

This procedure is similar to that outlined above for V6 and V8 except V8 1965-66 400 cu. in. and 1970-72 455 cu. in., with the substitution of the following steps:

7A. Delete this part of step 7. The oil pump on this engine is located in the oil pan and is thus not disturbed by this operation. Go on to parts B-F of Step 7.

455 Cu. In.

This procedure is similar to that above for V6 and V8, except V8 1965-66 400 cu. in. and 1970-72 455 cu. in., with the substitution of the following steps:

4. Delete Step 4.
5. Reinstall oil pan.
6. Install camshaft sprocket bolts. Torque to 22 ft. lbs.

Camshaft R & R
OHV 6—1968-72

1. Drain cooling system.
2. Remove radiator, fan, and water pump pulley.
3. Remove grille.
4. Remove valve cover and gasket, then loosen rocker arm nuts and pivot rockers out of the way.
5. Remove pushrods.
6. Remove distributor, fuel pump, and spark plugs.
7. Remove coil, pushrod (tappet gallery) covers and gasket; reach in and remove tappets, keeping them in order.
8. Remove harmonic balancer, then loosen oil pan bolts and allow pan to drop.
9. Remove timing gear cover.
10. Remove two camshaft thrust plate bolts by rotating cam gear holes to gain clearance.
11. Remove the camshaft by pulling it straight forward.

NOTE: do not wiggle the camshaft; cam bearings could be dislodged.

12. If cam gear is to be replaced, press it from the shaft using an arbor press.

NOTE: thrust plate must be positioned so that Woodruff key does not damage it during removal.

13. New cam gear must be pressed onto the shaft, with the shaft supported in back of the front bearing journal.

NOTE: the thrust plate end-play should be 0.001-0.005 in. If less than 0.001 in., replace spacer ring; if greater than 0.005 in., replace thrust plate.

14. Carefully install the camshaft into the engine, then turn crankshaft and camshaft so that timing marks coincide; tighten thrust plate bolts to 5-8 ft. lbs.
15. Check camshaft and crankshaft gear runout using a dial indicator. Cam gear runout should not

exceed 0.004 in., crank gear runout should not exceed 0.003 in.

NOTE: if runout is excessive, remove gear and clean burrs from shaft.

16. Check gear backlash using a dial indicator; it should not exceed 0.006 in. and should be not less than 0.004 in.
17. To complete installation, reverse Steps 1-9.

NOTE: install distributor with No. 1 piston at TDC on compression stroke so that vacuum diaphragm faces forward and rotor points to No. 1 spark plug wire cap tower. Make sure oil pump drive shaft is properly indexed with distributor drive shaft.

Engine Lubrication

The engine lubrication system is the force feed type, in which oil is supplied under pressure to the crankshaft, connecting rods, camshaft bearings and valve lifters. Oil is supplied under controlled volume to the rocker arm bearings and pushrods. All other moving engine parts are lubricated by gravity flow or splash.

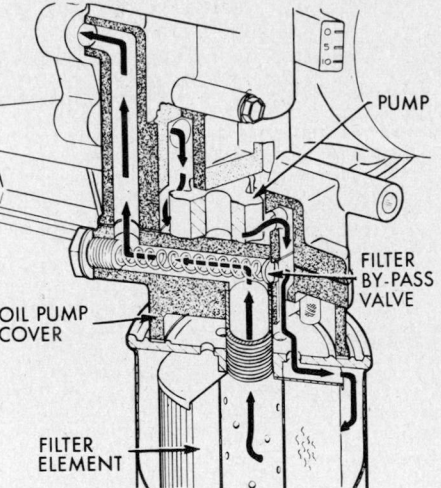

Oil flow through oil filter
(© Buick Div. G.M. Corp.)

Oil Pump

On the V6 and most V8s, the oil pump is located in the timing chain cover, where it is connected by a drilled passage in the cylinder crankcase to an oil screen housing and standpipe assembly.

Oil is drawn into the pump through the screen and pipe and is discharged to the oil pump cover assembly. The cover assembly consists of an oil pressure relief valve, an oil filter by-pass valve and a nipple for installation of an oil filter. The oil pressure relief valve limits oil pressure to a maximum of 30 psi for most 1965-66 engines; 33 psi for the 1965-66 400 cu. in. engine; 40 psi for all 1967-72 V8s; and 45 psi for the OHV 6 engine. The oil filter bypass valve

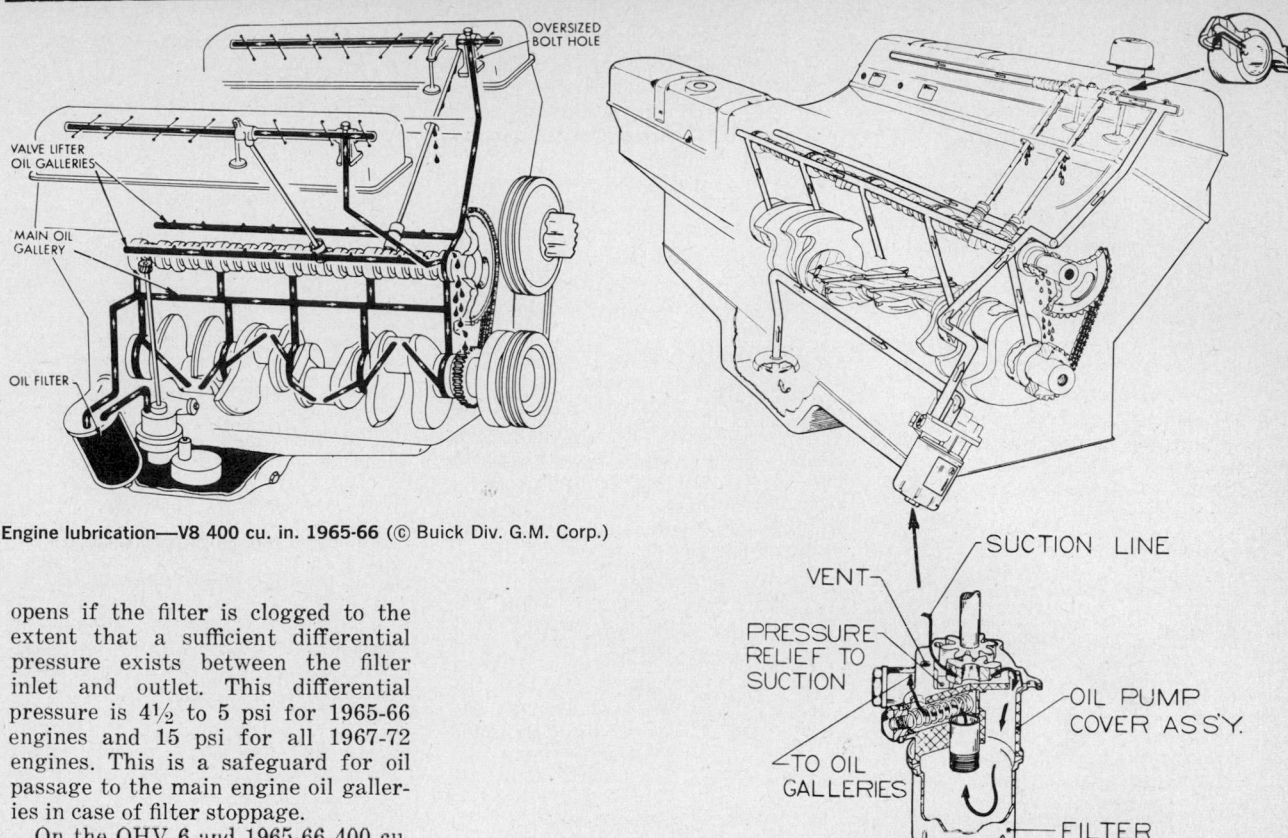

Engine lubrication—V8 400 cu. in. 1965-66 (© Buick Div. G.M. Corp.)

Engine lubrication—all V8 except 1965-66 400 cu. in. (© Buick Div. G.M. Corp.)

opens if the filter is clogged to the extent that a sufficient differential pressure exists between the filter inlet and outlet. This differential pressure is 4½ to 5 psi for 1965-66 engines and 15 psi for all 1967-72 engines. This is a safeguard for oil passage to the main engine oil galleries in case of filter stoppage.

On the OHV 6 and 1965-66 400 cu. in. V8 engine, the oil pump is located in the oil pan.

Oil Filter

An AC oil filter is mounted at the right front corner of the engine. On the 1965-66 400 cu. in. V8, the filter is mounted at the right rear. It requires no special tools and is completely disposable.

Oil Pan Removal and Installation

V6 and V8 Engines

1. Raise car and support on stands.
2. Drain engine oil.
3. Disconnect exhaust pipe at crossover.
4. If standard transmission equipped, loosen clutch equalizer-to-frame attaching bolts.
5. Remove steering idler arm bracket-to-suspension crossmember attaching bolts.
6. Support engine with a padded jack under the crankshaft pulley mounting.
7. Remove engine mounting bolts.
8. Raise engine.
9. Remove flywheel housing bolts. Then remove housing.
10. Remove oil pan bolts and lower the oil pan enough to remove oil pump pipe and screen-to-cylinder block attaching bolts.
11. Rotate crankshaft to provide maximum clearance at the front end of oil pan. Move the front of the pan to the right and lower the pan through opening between

crossmember and steering linkage intermediate shaft.
12. Install by reversing removal procedure.

OHV 6—1968-69

To remove the oil pan, it is necessary to remove the engine from the car. See Engine Removal.

OHV 6—1970-72

1. Disconnect battery, remove air cleaner and disconnect throttle linkage.
2. Remove fan shroud-to-radiator tie bar screws.
3. Jack up car and support on axle stands under lower A-frames.
4. Drain engine oil.
5. If equipped with automatic transmission:
   a. Remove flywheel housing inspection cover.
   b. Remove shift linkage bolt and swing linkage out of way.
   c. Disconnect exhaust pipe at manifold.
6. Remove front motor mount bolts.
7. Jack up engine as far as it will go, with padded jack under crank pully mounting.
8. Remove front motor mounts completely to gain clearance.
9. Remove oil pan bolts and oil pan.
10. To install, reverse removal procedure, tightening pan bolts to 10 ft. lbs.

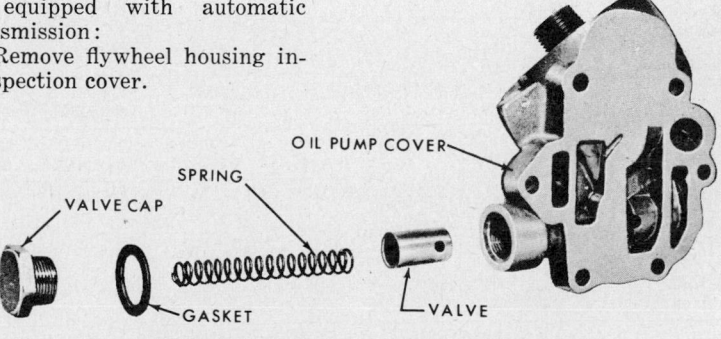

Pressure relief valve (© Buick Div. G.M. Corp.)

Connecting Rods and Pistons

Piston Assembly Removal

1. Remove cylinder heads.
2. Remove oil pan.
3. Examine cylinder bores for top ridge. If ridge exists, remove it before taking pistons out.
4. Number all the pistons, connecting rods and caps.

With the V6 engine the right bank is numbered 2-4-6. The left bank, 1-3-5, from the front. The 1965-66 400 cu. in. V8 is numbered 2-4-6-8, left; and 1-3-5-7, right. All other V8 engines are numbered 1-3-5-7, left; and 2-4-6-8, right. The OHV 6 engine is numbered 1-2-3-4-5-6, front to rear.

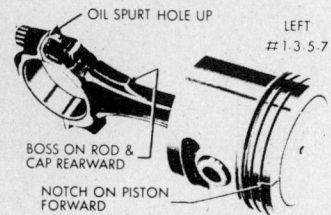

Piston and rod assembly, left bank—300, 340, 350, 455, starting 1967 400
(© Buick Div., G.M. Corp.)

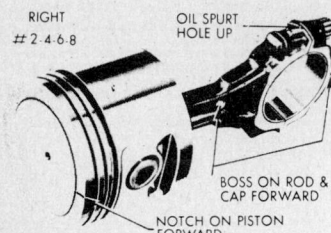

Piston and rod assembly, right bank—300, 340, 350, 455, starting 1967 400
(© Buick Div., G.M. Corp.)

5. With No. 1 crankpin straight down, remove cap and bearing shell from No. 1 connecting rod. Install connecting rod bolt guides to hold upper half of the bearing shell in place.
6. Push piston and rod assembly up out of the cylinder. Then remove bolt guides and reinstall cap and bearing shell on the rod.
7. Remove the remaining rod and piston assemblies in the same manner.
8. Carefully remove old rings with piston ring expander.
9. Carefully press out the old pin.
NOTE: check the cylinder bores for distortion, taper or other damage. Any cylinders requiring attention may be bored or honed the same as any other conventional cast iron cylinder block.

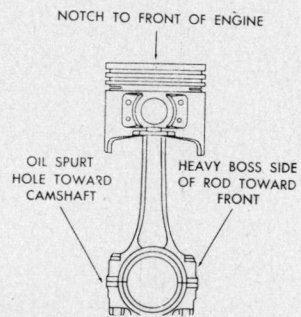

Piston and rod assembly—inline 6

Fitting Rings

For V6 and V8 engines, the rod assemblies are correctly installed when the oil spurt holes are toward the camshaft, the boss on the rod is on the same side as the boss on the rod cap, and these bosses are toward the other connecting rod on the same crankpin. OHV 6 rod assemblies are correctly installed when all the oil spurt holes are toward the camshaft.

Rear Main Bearing Oil Seal Replacement

For this procedure refer to the Buick Section. For the OHV 6 engine, refer to the Chevrolet Section.

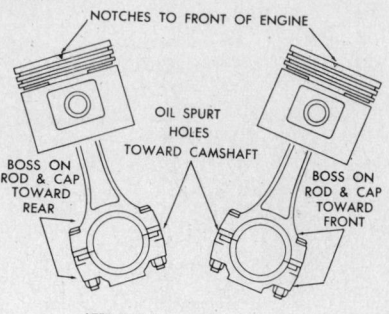

Piston and rod assembly—V6

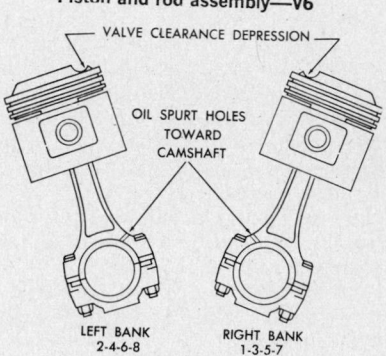

Piston and rod assembly—1965-66 400 cu. in.

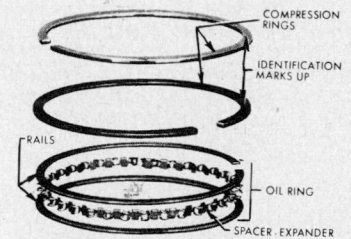

Piston rings—1965 300 cu. in.
(© Buick Div., G.M. Corp.)

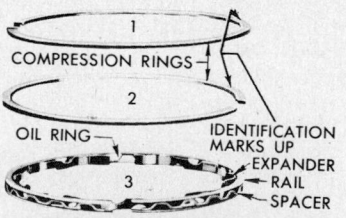

Piston rings—all V6, 1965-66 400, 1966-72 300-340-350
(© Buick Div., G.M. Corp.)

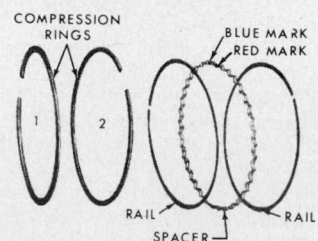

Piston rings—1967-72 400, 455 cu. in.
(© Buick Div., G.M. Corp.)

Piston Fitting Specifications

Engine	Ring Side Clearance (in.)		End Gap (in.)		Piston-to-Bore Clearance (in.)	
	Compression	Oil	Compression	Oil	Skirt Top	Skirt Bottom
V6—225	.003-.005	.0035-.0095	.010-.020	.015-.035	.0005-.0011 .0011-.0017*	.0005-.0021 .0011-.0027*
L6—250	.0012-.0027 .0012-.0032	.0000-.0050	.010-.020	.015-.025	.0005-.0011†	
V8—300	.003-.005	.0035-.0095	.010-.020	.015-.035	.0005-.0011 .0011-.0017*	.0005-.0021 .0011-.0017*
V8—340	.003-.005	.0035-.0095	.010-.020	.015-.035	.0005-.0011 .0011-.0017*	.0005-.0021 .0011-.0017*
V8—350	.003-.005	.0035-.0095	.010-.020	.015-.035	.0008-.0015	.0013-.0029
V8—400 1965-66	.003-.005	.0035-.0095	.015-.035	.015-.035	.0010-.0016	.0020-.0036
V8—400 1967-69	.003-.005	.0035-.0095	.013-.023	.015-.055	.0007-.0013	.0007-.0023
V8—455	.003-.005	.0035-.0095	.013-.023	.015-.035	.0010-.0016	.0030-.0042

*—1967
†—Measured 2.44 in. from piston top.

Front Suspension

The Unit Repair Section covers front suspension repair, adjustment, installation of front wheel bearings and grease seals, and troubleshooting.

Figures for caster, camber, toe-in, king pin inclination, and turning radius can be found in the Wheel Alignment table.

Tire size figures can be found in the General Chassis and Brake Specifications table.

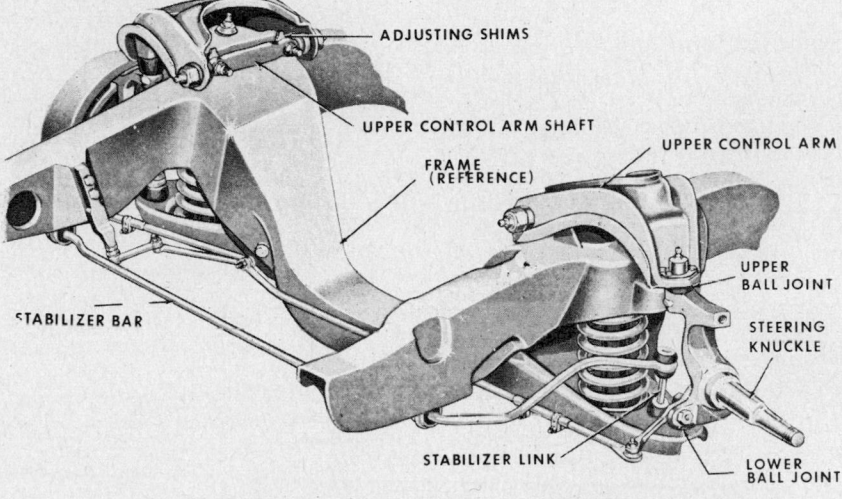

Front suspension (© Buick Div. G.M. Corp.)

Upper Ball Joint R & R— 1965-72

1. Jack up front of car and support on axle stands at frame (allow suspension to hang free).
2. Remove front tire and wheel assembly.
3. Remove upper ball stud cotter pin, then loosen (but do not remove) stud nut.
4. Strike steering knuckle near upper joint stud, or use a ball joint removing tool. This will separate the stud from the knuckle.
5. Place a jack under the lower control arm spring seat, then jack up lower arm to release tension from coil spring.
6. Remove upper stud nut and lift upper arm from knuckle.
7. Place a wood block between upper arm and frame, then centerpunch the four upper joint rivets, drill a 1/8 in. hole in each rivet, enlarge holes to 7/32 in. and chop off rivet heads with a chisel.
8. Punch out rivets and remove ball joint.
9. To install, reverse removal procedure.

NOTE: cotter pin hole in ball joint should be lined up front to rear. Install only hardened bolts from ball joint kit, with nuts on top and tightened to 8 ft. lbs. Never back off stud nut to align cotter pin holes; go to next tighter position that will allow pin to be installed.

Lower Ball Joint R & R— 1965-72

1. Jack up front of car and support on axle stands at frame (allow suspension to hang free).
2. Remove wheel, along with hub and brake drum.
3. Remove backing plate from

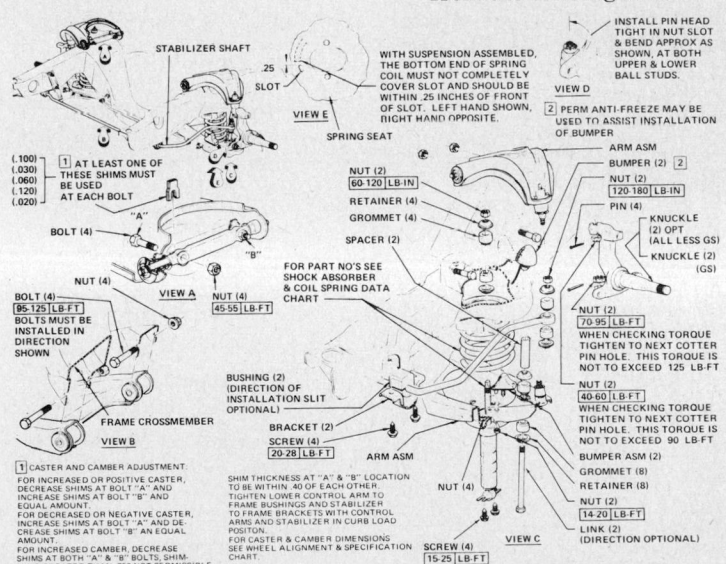

Typical front suspension and wheel alignment details—1965-72
(© Buick Div. G.M. Corp.)

steering knuckle and wire it out of the way.
4. Remove lower ball stud cotter pin, then loosen (but do not remove) stud nut.
5. Either drive old joint downward, or press it out of knuckle using a ball joint removing tool.

6. Place a jack under the lower control arm spring seat, then jack up lower arm to relieve tension from coil spring.
7. Drive or press lower joint out of control arm.
8. To install, reverse removal procedure. Lower joint must be pressed or pulled up into the control arm.

Coil Spring R&R—1965-72

1. Jack up front of car, then remove tire and wheel, along with drum.
2. Disconnect stabilizer bar link from lower control arm.
3. Disconnect and remove shock absorber.
4. Disconnect lower ball joint stud from steering knuckle, as outlined previously.
5. Install a spring compressor and compress coil spring.
6. Lower the jack under the control arm (placed there as part of Step 4), then carefully disengage spring compressor and remove coil spring.
7. To install, reverse removal procedure, noting correct position of spring.

Steering Wheel

Removal—1965-72

1. Unplug the horn wire connector from the steering column.
2. On cars with standard wheel or optional wood-rim wheel, pull off cap, remove three screws and bushing spacer, receiver cup, and Belleville spring. On cars with bar-type horn actuator, remove screws securing actuator from underside of steering

wheel, pull out lead connector plug, and remove actuator assembly.

3. Loosen steering wheel nut.
4. Apply steering wheel puller and pull wheel up to the nut. Now remove puller, nut and steering wheel.

Installation—1965-72

NOTE: location marks are provided on the steering wheel and shaft to simplify proper indexing at the time of installation.

1. Install wheel with the location mark aligned with that of the shaft.
2. Install the wheel nut and torque to 30 ft. lbs.
3. Reinstall horn button or actuator assembly.

Jacking, Hoisting

Jack car at front spring seat of lower control arm or center of cross member.

Jack car at rear at axle housing.

To lift at frame, use side rails in front of body floor pan and at rear side rail at lower control arm front pivot.

Steering Gear

Refer to the Unit Repair Section for adjustments and repairs to steering gear, both manual and power-assisted.

Manual

Removal and Installation

1. Raise and support front of car.
2. Remove pinch bolt securing flexible coupling flange to steering gear stub shaft.

3. Remove pitman arm retaining nut and pull off pitman arm.
CAUTION: do not hammer on puller. Hammering will damage the steering gear. If necessary, tapping on side of pitman arm may help in removal.
4. Remove steering gear to frame bolts and remove gear assembly.
5. Align mark on gear stub shaft with tab on coupling.
6. Install gear assembly to frame. Tighten bolts to 70 ft. lbs.
7. Install and tighten pinch bolt to 30 ft. lbs.
8. Reconnect pitman arm. Torque to 140 ft. lbs.

Power

Removal and Installation

This procedure is identical to that outlined above for the manual steering gear, with the substitution of the following step:

1. Raise and support front of car. Disconnect pressure and return hoses from steering gear. Elevate hose ends to prevent oil loss.

Clutch

A single plate, dry disc clutch is used in cars with manual transmissions. The unit is conventional in design with a diaphragm spring assembly. The clutch is not adjustable except for pedal clearance.

Clutch Removal

1965-72

1. Mark universal joint and transmission shaft companion flange for proper indexing at time of

installation. Remove two U-bolts and disconnect driveshaft at the front joint. Slide the driveshaft rearward as far as possible and

tie to one side.
2. Disconnect shift linkage from transmission.
3. Disconnect speedometer cable at transmission.
4. Loosen all three exhaust pipe ball joints to permit transmission and rear of engine to be lowered.
5. Remove two bolts holding transmission mounting pad to transmission support. Leave mounting pad bolted to transmission.
6. With a padded jack under the engine, raise the unit until the transmission mounting pad just clears the transmission support.
7. Remove four bolts holding transmission support to body members. Remove support, then lower the jack to allow transmission to clear the underbody.
8. Remove upper left transmission to flywheel housing bolt and install a guide pin. Remove lower right bolt and install a guide pin.
9. Remove the other two transmission attaching bolts. Slide the transmission back until the drive gear shaft disengages the clutch disc and clears the flywheel housing. Lower the transmission.
10. Remove pedal return spring from clutch fork.
11. Remove flywheel housing.
12. Remove throw-out bearing from clutch fork.
13. Disconnect clutch fork from ball stud.
14. Mark clutch cover and flywheel to assure proper balance on reassembly.
15. Loosen clutch cover to flywheel bolts one turn at a time until spring pressure is released.
16. Support pressure plate and cover assembly while removing last bolts, then remove cover assembly and driven plate.

1965-66 Skylark Gran Sport

This procedure is identical to that described above with the substitution of the following steps:

10. Disconnect lower clutch release rod assembly from equalizer. Remove equalizer.
11. Delete Step 11.
12. Delete Step 12.
13. Delete Step 13.

Clutch Installation

Install clutch by reversing removal procedure. Use a clutch aligning pilot or a spare main drive gear through the hub of driven plate and into the pilot bushing. Be sure to align the clutch cover-to-flywheel index marks.

Clutch Linkage Adjustment

Check pedal lash (free-play) by pushing down on the pedal by hand. Lash should be approximately ¾ in.

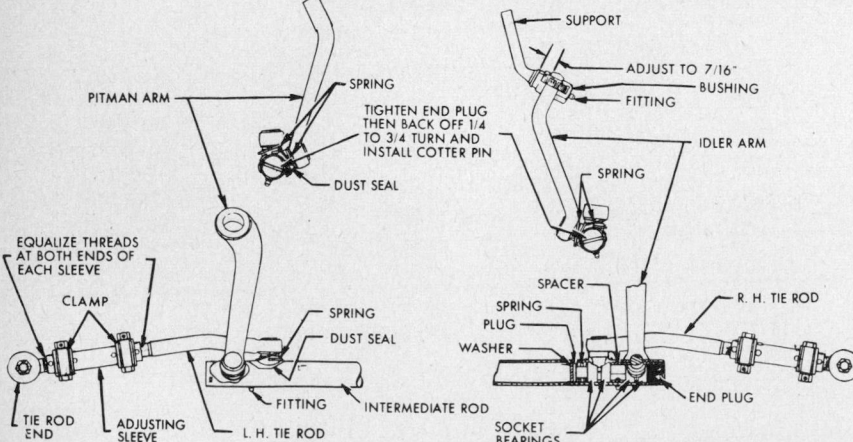

PITMAN ARM — SPRING — TIGHTEN END PLUG THEN BACK OFF 1/4 TO 3/4 TURN AND INSTALL COTTER PIN — DUST SEAL — EQUALIZE THREADS AT BOTH ENDS OF EACH SLEEVE — CLAMP — SPRING — DUST SEAL — TIE ROD END — ADJUSTING SLEEVE — FITTING — L. H. TIE ROD — INTERMEDIATE ROD

SUPPORT — ADJUST TO 7/16" — BUSHING — FITTING — IDLER ARM — SPRING — SPACER — SPRING — PLUG — WASHER — R. H. TIE ROD — END PLUG — SOCKET BEARINGS

Manual and power steering linkage (© Buick Div. G.M. Corp.)

measured at the pedal pad.

1. Make sure the pedal is at full release position, contacting the rubber bumper stop. Remove return spring.
2. Adjust clutch release rod underneath car to give zero lash at the clutch pedal.
3. Back off release rod adjustment 2-3 turns to give $3/4$ in. lash at pedal pad. (Equals 1/16-1/8 in. at pushrod.)
4. Tighten locknut on clutch release rod.

Standard Transmission

There are four basic types of standard transmissions used. First, the early three-speed unit with synchromesh on second and third gears only, which was discontinued at the end of the 1965 model year. This unit was used only with column shift linkage. The second, a three-speed unit having synchromesh on all forward gears, was introduced on some models in 1965 and became the basic three speed unit in 1966. This transmission was used with floorshift linkage only on 1965 Skylark Gran Sport models. The third is a heavy duty three-speed unit, available only with floorshift linkage. This unit is the same as that used on the larger series of Buicks. The fourth is a four-speed, all synchromesh unit, equipped only with floorshift linkage.

For repair procedures see Unit Repair Section.

Removal and Installation
See Clutch paragraphs.

Shift Linkage Adjustment

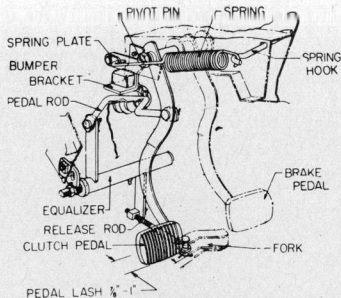

Clutch linkage

Adjustment Procedure —Three-Speed Column Shift
1965-66
1. Place column shift lever in Neutral.
2. Place transmission levers into neutral positions.

3. Loosen shift rod adjusting clamp bolts.
4. Install a 3/16 in. dia. rod through first-reverse lever and selector plate at bottom of steering column.
5. Push second-third shift rod through clamp until it sticks out from clamp 1/4 in.
6. Tighten shift rod adjusting clamps to 17-23 ft. lbs.
7. Lift column shift lever straight up toward steering wheel several times to assure a free neutral crossover. If neutral detents do not line up, loosen first-reverse rod clamp, pull first-reverse rod through clamp no more than 3/16 in., and tighten clamp.

1967
This procedure is similar to that outlined above for the 1965-66 models, with the substitution of the following steps:
4. Install a 3/16 in. dia. rod through first-reverse lever, selector plate, and second-third lever at bottom of steering column.
5. Push second-third shift rod through clamp until it sticks out from clamp 1/4-1/2 in.

1968
This procedure is similar to that for 1965-66 models, with the substitution of the following step:
4. Install a 3/16 in. dia. rod through second-third lever, selector plate, first-reverse lever, and alignment plate.

1969-72
1. Place column shift lever in Reverse.
2. Loosen first-reverse clamp bolt.
3. Place transmission first-reverse lever into reverse position. Tighten clamp bolt to 17-23 ft. lbs.
4. Shift transmission levers into neutral positions.
5. Loosen second-third clamp bolt.
6. Install a 3/16 in. dia. rod through second-third lever, selector plate, first-reverse lever, and alignment plate.
7. Tighten second-third clamp bolt to 17-23 ft. lbs.

Adjustment Procedure —Three-Speed Floorshift
1. Place transmission levers into neutral.
2. Loosen shift rod adjusting clamp bolts.
3. Place a 5/16 in. dia. rod in notch in rear portion of shift bracket assembly.
4. Move both shift levers back against rod.
5. Tighten shift rod adjusting bolts to 17-23 ft. lbs.

Adjustment Procedure —Four-Speed Floorshift
1. Place transmission levers in neutral positions.
2. Place a 5/16 in. dia. rod in rear lower portion of shift bracket assembly.
3. Adjust all three shift levers back against rod.
4. Tighten adjusting clamp bolts to 17-23 ft. lbs.

Hurst Shift Linkage Adjustment
1. Shift transmission into Reverse.
2. Push "back drive" (steering lock) rod up into reverse detent in steering column (if applicable).
3. Tighten clamp screw to 17-23 ft. lbs.
4. Place all transmission and control levers in Neutral.
5. Insert a 1/4 in. drill rod through adjustment hole in shifter and make sure all shift rods fit into their respective levers without tension. Adjust length of rods as necessary, then tighten swivel nuts.

Clutch Start Switch—1969-72
On all cars with manual transmission, a clutch start switch on the clutch pedal bracket prevents starting unless the clutch pedal is fully depressed. This switch is connected in series with the circuit from the ignition switch to the starter solenoid; therefore a no-start condition could be caused by its failure.

Automatic Transmission

Only the Turbo Hydra-Matic 350 is covered in this section. For removal, installation, and stator and detent switch adjustments for the Super Turbine 300, 400, and Turbo Hydra-Matic 100, see the Buick Section.

Shift linkage adjustment for all models is covered in this section.

The transmission model number is usually located on the right side of the transmission case. On the Turbo Hydra-Matic 350, the model designation and model year are stamped on the intermediate clutch accumulator cover on the middle right side.

Turbo Hydra-Matic 350
Removal
1. Raise and support car.
2. Disconnect exhaust pipe or pipes.
3. Remove driveshaft.
4. Place jack under transmission and fasten transmission to jack.
5. Remove vacuum line from vacuum modulator.
6. Disconnect oil cooler lines.

7. Remove detent cable from accelerator lever assembly and from detent valve link. Do not bend cable.
8. Remove transmission mounting pad to crossmember bolts. Remove crossmember.
9. Disconnect speedometer cable.
10. Disconnect shift linkage.
11. Remove transmission filler pipe.
12. Support engine at oil pan.
13. Remove flywheel cover pan. Mark flywheel and converter for reassembly. Remove converter to flywheel bolts.
14. Unbolt transmission and move rearward. Support converter and lower transmission.

Installation

1. Raise transmission into position.
2. Install transmission case to engine block bolts. Torque to 30-40 ft. lbs.
3. Install flywheel to converter pump bolts. Torque to 25-35 ft. lbs.
4. Install cross member support and mounting pad.
5. Remove transmission jack and engine support.
6. Install flywheel cover pan.
7. Install transmission filler pipe with new O-ring.
8. Reconnect speedometer cable.

9. Install driveshaft.
10. Reconnect exhaust pipe or pipes.
11. Install detent cable on detent valve link and on accelerator lever assembly. Do not bend cable.
12. Install oil cooler lines. Install vacuum line to vacuum modulator.
13. Add three pints of transmission fluid. With lever in Park, start engine. Do not race engine. Shift through each range. Check fluid level with lever in park, engine running, and vehicle on level surface. Add fluid to bring level to 1/4 in. below ADD mark. This allows for expansion caused by heat.

Detent Cable Adjustment

Refer to the accompanying illustration for this procedure.

Shift Linkage Adjustment

Column Shift All Models

1. Place selector lever in Drive (Neutral for 1971 up).
2. Loosen adjusting clamp bolt.
3. Place lever at transmission in drive (Neutral for 1971 up) position.
4. Tighten clamp bolt to 17-23 ft. lbs.

Console Shift 1965-66

1. Place selector lever in Park.
2. Loosen adjusting clamp bolt.
3. Place transmission in park position.
4. Tighten clamp bolt to 17-23 ft. lbs.

Console Shift 1967

1. Place selector lever in Drive.
2. Loosen adjusting clamp bolt.
3. Place transmission in drive position.
4. Tighten clamp bolt to 17-23 ft. lbs.

Console Shift 1968-72

This linkage uses a cable rather than a shifting rod.

1. Loosen trunnion bolt.
2. Set selector lever in Drive.
3. Place transmission in drive position.
4. Tighten trunnion bolt to 6-9 ft. lbs.
5. For 1969-72 models only: Place selector lever in Park. Place transmission in park position. Push back drive rod (to steering column) up to stop and hold lightly. Tighten back drive rod clamp screw.

Neutral Safety Switch

This switch prevents the engine

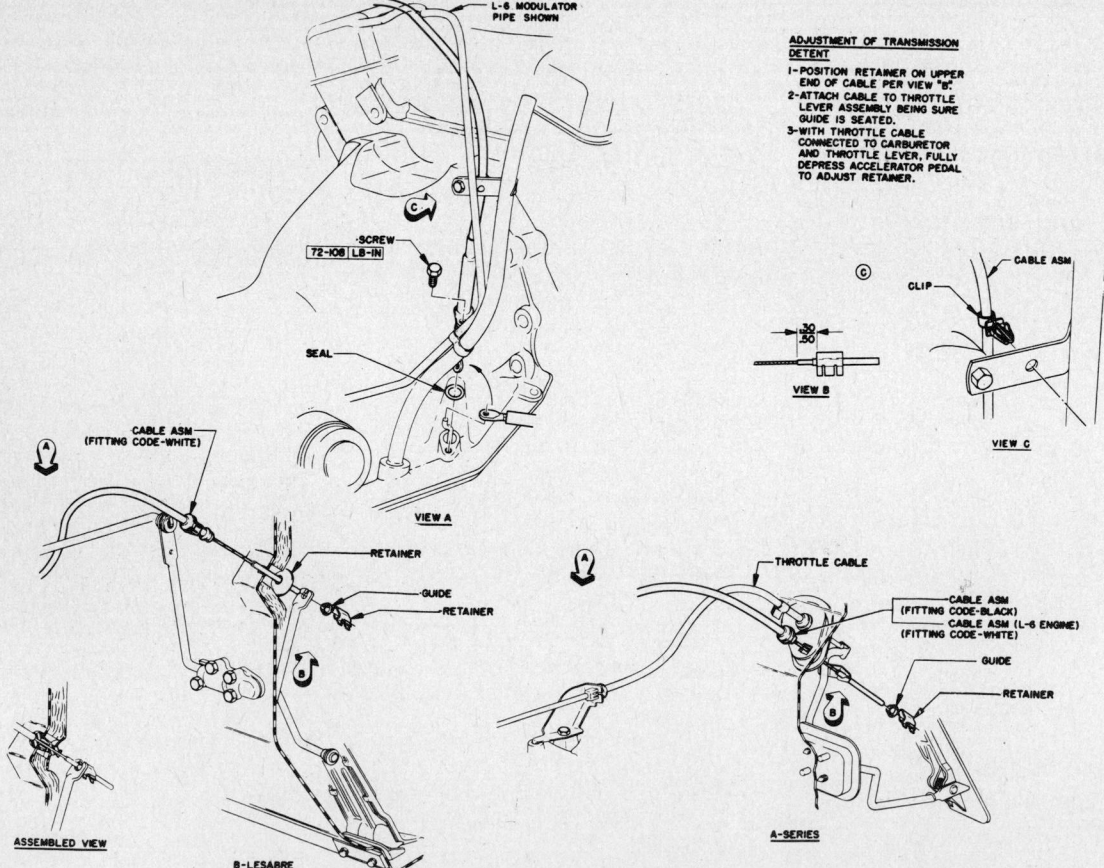

Transmission detent cable adjustment—Turbo-Hydramatic 350 (© Buick Div., G.M. Corp.)

from being started in any transmission position except Neutral or Park. The back-up light switch is combined with the neutral safety switch. On column shift cars and 1971-72 models with console shift, the switch is located on the steering column under the instrument panel. On console shift cars, the switch is located inside the console. When the neutral start portion of the switch is correctly adjusted, the back-up portion is adjusted automatically. Slotted mounting screw holes permit switch movement for adjustment.

Caution when checking to see if engine will start in transmission positions other than Drive or Park, always hold the service brake firmly.

U Joints, Drive Lines

The driveshaft is a one piece unit with a splined slip yoke and a universal joint at the transmission end, and a second universal joint at the differential end. The shaft, depending on application, can be a one-piece solid steel unit, or can be composed of two concentric tubes damped with rubber. For further information, consult the Buick Section.

Universal Joints—1969-72
Nylon-injected composite universal joints are used. To replace universal joints:
1. Mark driveshaft rear yoke and companion flange for correct alignment upon re-assembly.

2. Remove U-bolts from rear axle drive pinion companion flange.
3. If bearing tie wire has been removed, use band or tape to hold bearings onto the journals, to prevent loss of bearing rollers when joint is disconnected.
4. Slide assembly to the rear to clear splines at transmission output shaft.
5. By using a piece of pipe or similar tool, slightly larger than 1⅛ in. to encircle the bearing shell, apply force on the yoke until downward movement of the yoke and stationary position of journal force the bearing assembly almost out of the top of the yoke (the force applied on the yoke will shear nylon retainers which lock bearings in place).
6. Rotate propeller shaft 180° and repeat preceding step to partially remove the opposite bearing.
7. Complete removal of these bearings by tapping around the circumference of exposed portion of bearing.
8. Remove journal from driveshaft rear yoke.
9. Remove bearings and journal from splined yoke in the same way.
NOTE: new bearings and journal assembly kits must be used upon reassembly. The kit includes snap-rings and Delrin washers.
10. Install by inserting one bearing one-quarter way in one side of splined yoke, using brass hammer.
11. Insert journal into splined yoke (with dust shields installed).
12. Install opposite bearing, ensuring that the bearing rollers do not jam on journal. Check free ro-

tary movement of journal in bearing.
13. Now, press both bearings into place (just far enough to install snap rings).
14. Assemble opposite end universal in the same way.

Drive Axle, Suspension

The rear axle assembly is of the semi-floating type in which the car weight is carried on the axle shafts through bearings in the rear axle tubes. Car drive is transmitted from the axle housing to body members through two lower and two upper control arms. Large rubber bushings at either end of these arms are designed to absorb vibration and noise. The arms are angle mounted to control sidewise movement of the suspension.

Repair instructions are given in the Unit Repair Section.

Rear Axle Assembly Removal
It is not necessary to remove the rear axle assembly for normal repairs. However, if the housing is damaged, the rear axle assembly may be removed and installed using the following procedure.
1. Raise rear of car high enough to permit working under the car. Place a floor jack under center of axle housing so it just starts to raise rear axle assembly. Place car stands solidly under body members on both sides.
2. Mark rear universal joint and pinion flange for proper reassembly. Then disconnect rear universal joint at pinion flange.

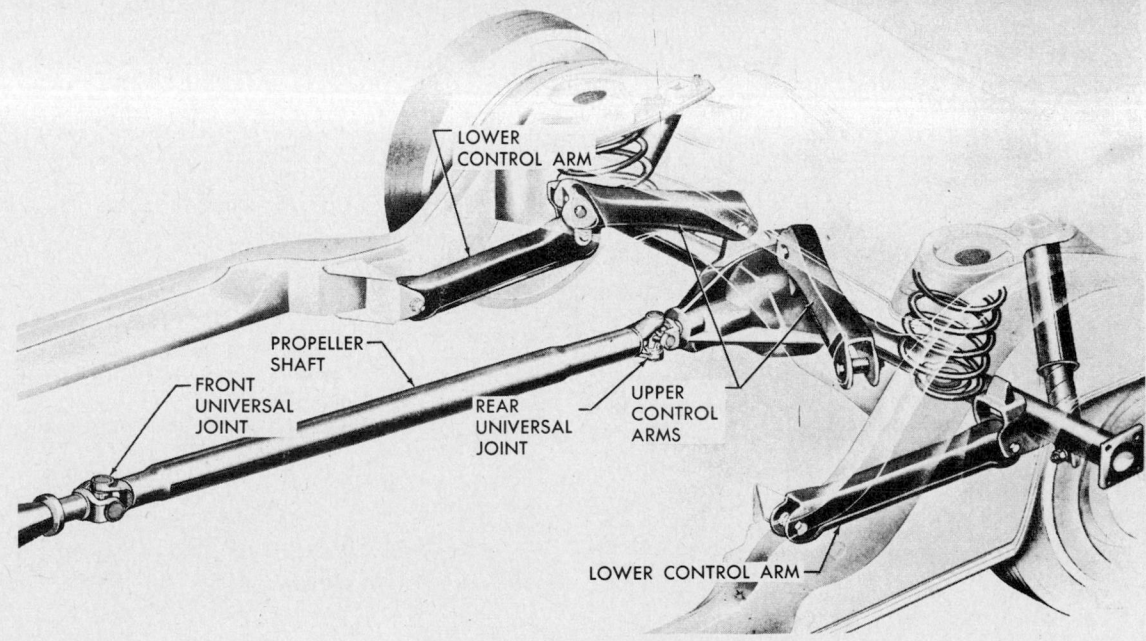

Rear suspension—1965-72 (© Buick Div., G.M. Corp.)

Wire the driveshaft back out of the way.

3. Disconnect parking brake cables. Slide cable back until free of body.
4. Disconnect rear brake hose at floor pan.
5. Disconnect shock absorbers at axle housing. Lower jack under housing until rear springs can be removed.
6. Disconnect upper control arms at axle.
7. Disconnect lower control arms at axle housing and roll rear axle assembly out from under the car.

Radio

Radio Removal and Installation

1965 Without Air Conditioning

1. Disconnect battery ground lead.
2. Pull off radio knobs and remove hex nuts.
3. Disconnect radio lead, speaker lead, and antenna lead connectors.
4. Remove screw holding support to radio. Withdraw radio from underside of instrument panel.
5. Install in reverse order of removal.

1965 With Air Conditioning

1. Disconnect battery ground lead.
2. Remove five screws and take out rim around instrument panel.
3. Remove four screws from heater and defroster control trim bezel. Remove bezel.
4. Remove four screws from radio and speaker insert panel. Partially remove insert. Disconnect wiring connectors and remove radio and panel assembly.
5. Install in reverse order of removal.

1966

1. Disconnect battery ground lead.
2. Pull off radio knobs and remove hex nuts.
3. If air conditioned: Remove clamps on outlet hoses to distribution duct, remove two screws securing duct to heater assembly, remove duct. Pry off spring clips holding center duct. Remove duct.
4. Disconnect wiring connectors.
5. Remove screw holding support to radio. Withdraw radio from underside of instrument panel.
6. Install in reverse order of removal.

1967

1. Disconnect battery ground lead.
2. Remove ashtray assembly.
3. Remove radio bracket to radio

screw. Remove radio knobs, escutcheons, and hex nuts. Disconnect wiring connectors.
4. Remove radio downward.
5. Install in reverse order of removal.

1968-72

NOTE: if equipped with stereo tape, remove tape player before starting Step 2.

1. Disconnect battery ground lead.
2. Remove radio knobs, escutcheons, and hex nuts.
3. Remove two screws from radio filler plate and remove plate.
4. Remove ashtray assembly.
5. Remove center air conditioning duct, if so equipped.
6. Remove radio bracket.
7. Remove two instrument panel attaching nuts at radio face.
8. Disconnect wiring and remove radio downward.
9. Install in reverse order of removal.

Windshield Wipers

All wiper motors are located on the engine side of the firewall. The transmission and linkage are located on the passenger compartment side of the dash, directly forward of the instrument panel. The cowl screen must be removed to allow the drive link to be disconnected from the crank arm.

The wiper-washer switch is included in the instrument cluster.

Heater System

Heater Core R & R

1965-67

1. Remove right front wheel.
2. Draw an arc on inside of skirt, 11 in. from upper bolt of wheel opening. Draw another arc 16¾ in. from lower bolt of wheel opening and punch dimple at intersection of two arcs.
3. Drill a ¾ in. hole through skirt at this dimple. Remove lower right attaching nut from heater assembly stud through this hole.
4. Disconnect air control cables from defroster door and outside air door levers.
5. Disconnect temperature control cable from lever of temperature door on heater assembly.
6. Drain radiator.
7. Disconnect inlet and outlet hoses.
8. Remove connector from blower resistor assembly.
9. Remove nuts and washers secur-

ing assembly to cowl, then lift out assembly
10. Install in reverse of above.
11. Use ¾ in. body plug to close hole in skirt.

1968-72

1. Remove right front fender skirt.
2. Drain radiator.
3. Disconnect control cables from defroster door and outside air inlet door. Disconnect temperature control cable from temperature door.
4. Remove nuts from heater assembly studs.
5. Disconnect inlet and outlet hoses.
6. Remove connector from blower motor resistor.
7. Remove screws securing defroster outlet assembly to top of heater assembly.
8. Work heater assembly rearward until studs clear dash. Remove heater assembly.
9. Install in reverse of above.

Heater Blower R & R

1965

1. Follow Steps 1 through 3 under 1965 heater core removal.
2. Remove lower right attaching nut from heater assembly through hole in skirt.
3. Remove remaining attaching nuts from heater assembly.
4. Remove screws holding blower and air inlet to cowl.
5. Disconnect blower wire and lift out blower and air inlet assembly.
6. Install in the reverse order and plug hole in fender skirt with ¾ in. body plug.

1966-67

1. Remove right front fender.
2. Remove nuts and screws securing blower and air inlet assembly to cowl.
3. Disconnect blower motor wire and remove assembly.
4. Install in reverse of above.

1968-72

Follow procedure above for 1966-67 models, substituting this step:

1. Remove right front fender skirt.

Cadillac

Index

YEAR IDENTIFICATION

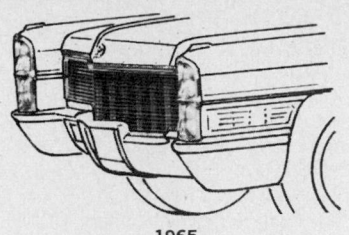

1965

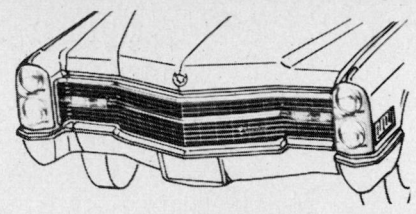

1966

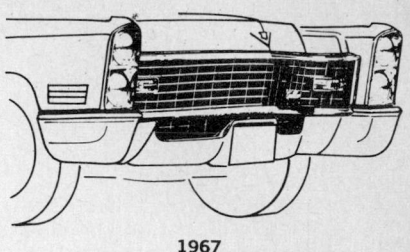

1967

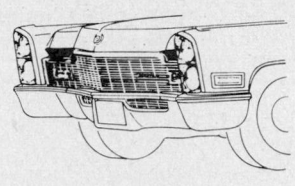

1968

1969-70

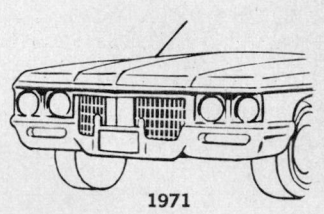

1971

1972

FIRING ORDER

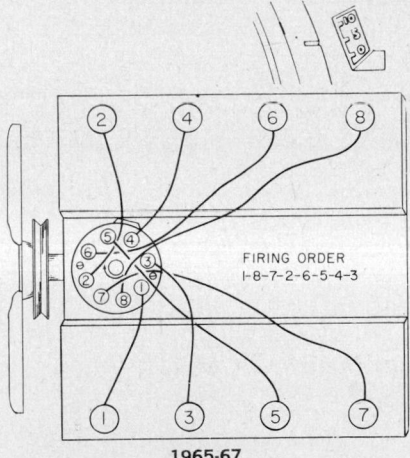

FIRING ORDER
1-8-7-2-6-5-4-3

1965-67

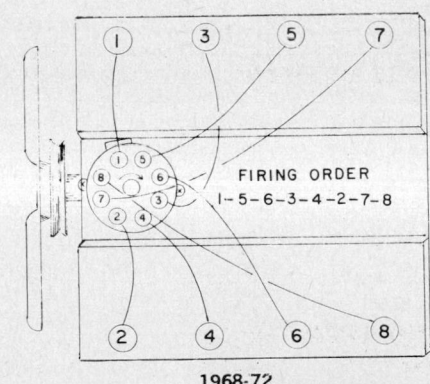

FIRING ORDER
1-5-6-3-4-2-7-8

1968-72

5° NOTCH ON TAB

NOTCH ON PULLEY
Timing marks—1968-70

8° ON TAB

NOTCH ON BALANCER
Timing marks—1971-72

CAR SERIAL NUMBER LOCATION AND ENGINE IDENTIFICATION

1965-67

Vehicle identification plates are located at the top rear of the engine block, adjacent to the transmission, and on the left front door lock pillar. The eight digit serial number consists of a sales code letter, the last digit of the model year (5, 6, or 7), and a six digit sequential serial number.

All models utilize a 429 cu. in. V8 engine. The engine serial number is stamped at the left rear of the cylinder block, just below the cylinder head.

1968-70

The vehicle identification plate is located on the top left side of the dashboard, and is visible through the windshield. The eight digit serial number consists of a sales code letter, the last digit of the model year (8, 9, or 0), and a six digit sequential serial number.

All models utilize a 472 cu. in. V8 engine. The vehicle identification number, less sales code, is stamped on the top rear of the engine block, adjacent to the transmission.

1971-72

The vehicle identification plate is located on the top left side of the dashboard, and is visible through the windshield. The thirteen digit serial number consists of the G.M. Division Code (6), a four digit series and model number, the last digit of the model year (1 or 2), plant designation, and a six digit sequential serial number.

All models utilize a 472 cu. in. V8 engine. A derivative of the vehicle identification number is stamped on the top rear of the engine block, adjacent to the transmission.

GENERAL ENGINE SPECIFICATIONS

YEAR	CU. IN. DISPLACEMENT	CARBURETOR	ADVERTIZED HORSEPOWER @ RPM	ADVERTIZED TORQUE @ RPM (FT. LBS.)	A.M.A. HORSEPOWER	BORE & STROKE (IN.)	ADVERTIZED COMPRESSION RATIO	VALVE LIFTER TYPE	NORMAL OIL PRESSURE (PSI)
1965-67	V8—429	4-BBL.	340 @ 4600	480 @ 3000	54.6	4.125 x 4.000	10.50-1	Hyd.	33
1968/69	V8—472	4-BBL.	375 @ 4400	525 @ 3000	59.2	4.300 x 4.060	10.50-1	Hyd.	33
1970	V8—472	4-BBL.	375 @ 4400	525 @ 3000	59.2	4.300 x 4.060	10.00-1	Hyd.	35-40
1971-72	V8—472	4-BBL.	345 @ 4400	500 @ 2800	59.2	4.300 x 4.060	8.5-1	Hyd.	35-40

TUNE-UP SPECIFICATIONS

YEAR	MODEL	SPARK PLUGS		DISTRIBUTOR		IGNITION TIMING (Deg.) ▲	CRANKING COMP. PRESSURE (Psi)	VALVES			FUEL PUMP PRESSURE (Psi)	IDLE SPEED (Rpm) ★
		Type	Gap (In.)	Point Dwell (Deg.)	Point Gap (In.)			Tappet (Hot) Clearance (In.) Intake	Exhaust	Intake Opens (Deg.)		
1965	V8—All	44	.035	30°	.016	5B	180	Zero	Zero	39B	5³/₄	480
1966-67	V8—429	44	.035	30°	.016	5B	180	Zero	Zero	39B	5³/₄	500
1968-69	V8—472	44N	.035	30°	.019	5B	180	Zero	Zero	18B	5³/₄	550
1970-72	V8—472	R46N	.035	28-32°	.016	7½B	165-185	Zero	Zero	18B	5¹/₄-6¹/₂	600

▲—With vacuum advance disconnected and hose plugged. NOTE: These settings are only approximate. Engine design, altitude, temperature, fuel octane rating and the condition of the individual engine are all factors which can influence timing. The limiting advance factor must, therefore, be the "knock point" of the individual engine.

B—Before top dead center.

★—See text for procedure.

Caution

General adoption of anti-pollution laws has changed the design of almost all car engine production to effectively reduce crankcase emission and terminal exhaust products. It has been necessary to adopt stricter tune-up rules, especially timing and idle speed procedures. Both of these values are peculiar to the engine and to its application, rather than to the engine alone. With this in mind, car manufacturers supply idle speed data for the engine and application involved. This information is clearly displayed in the engine compartment of each vehicle.

CRANKSHAFT BEARING JOURNAL SPECIFICATIONS

YEAR	MODEL	MAIN BEARING JOURNALS (IN.)				CONNECTING ROD BEARING JOURNALS (IN.)		
		Journal Diameter	Oil Clearance	Shaft End-Play	Thrust On No.	Journal Diameter	Oil Clearance	End-Play
1965-67	V8—429	3.000	.0003-.0026	.002-.012	3	2.2491	.0013	.008-.016
1968-69	V8—472	3.250	.0003-.0026	.002-.012	3	2.5000	.0005-.0028	.008-.016
1970-72	V8—472	3.250	.0003-.0026	.002-.012	3	2.5000	.0005-.0028	.008-.016

TORQUE SPECIFICATIONS

YEAR	MODEL	CYLINDER HEAD BOLTS (FT. LBS.)	ROD BEARING BOLTS (FT. LBS.)	MAIN BEARING BOLTS (FT. LBS.)	CRANKSHAFT BALANCER BOLTS (FT. LBS.)	FLYWHEEL TO CRANKSHAFT BOLTS (FT. LBS.)	MANIFOLD (FT. LBS.) Intake	MANIFOLD (FT. LBS.) Exhaust
1965-67	All V8—429	60	40-45	90-100	65-70	75-80	25-30	25-30
1968-72	All V8—472	115	40	90	Press-fit	75	30	35

NOTE—Some bolts and nuts are marked on the heads to indicate the grade of steel used. Do not use bolts of a lower grade than those originally installed. The marks consist of lines: SAE5—3 lines; SAE7—5 lines; SAE8—6 lines.

CYLINDER HEAD BOLT TIGHTENING SEQUENCE

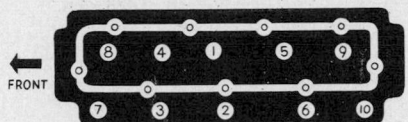

Cylinder head bolt tightening sequence—1968-72

Cylinder head bolt tightening sequence—1965-67

VALVE SPECIFICATIONS

YEAR AND MODEL	SEAT ANGLE (DEG.)	FACE ANGLE (DEG.)	VALVE LIFT INTAKE (IN.)	VALVE LIFT EXHAUST (IN.)	VALVE SPRING PRESSURE (VALVE OPEN) LBS. @ IN.	VALVE SPRING INSTALLED HEIGHT (IN.)	STEM TO GUIDE CLEARANCE (IN.) INTAKE	EXHAUST	STEM DIAMETER (IN.) INTAKE	EXHAUST
1965-67 V8—429	45	44	440	440	160 @ 1½	1 15/16	.0005-.0025	.0010-.0025	.3420	.3420
1968-70 V8—472	45	44	.440	.454	160 @ 1½	1 15/16	.0005-.0025	.0010-.0025	.3420	.3420
1971-72 V8 472	45	44	468	.468	160 @ 1½	1 15/16	.001-.0027	.001-.0025	.3415-.3425	.3415-.3420

GENERAL CHASSIS AND BRAKE SPECIFICATIONS

YEAR	MODEL	CHASSIS Overall Length (In.)	Tire Size	BRAKE CYLINDER BORE Master Cylinder (In.) Power	Wheel Cylinder Diameter (In.) Front	Rear	BRAKE DRUM Diameter (In.) Front	Rear
1965	Series—All Exc. 75	223.5	8.00 x 15	1	1 3/16	1.0	12	12
	Series 75	243.8	8.20 x 15	1	1 3/16	1.0	12	12
1966-67	Fleetwood Brougham & 60 Spd. Sdn.	227.5	9.00 x 15	1	1 3/16	1.0	12	12
	75 Sdn. & Limousine	244.5	8.20 x 15	1	1 3/16	1.0	12	12
	All others	224	9.00 x 15	1	1 3/16	1.0	12	12
1968	Fleetwood 60, Brougham	228.2	9.00 x 15	1	1 3/16	15/16	12	12
	Fleetwood 75	245.2	9.60 x 15	1	1 3/16	1.0	12	12
	All others	224.7	9.00 x 15	1	1 3/16	15/16	12	12
	w/Disc. Brakes	—	—	1	2 3/4 ①	13/16 ▲	12 (Disc.)	12
1969	Fleetwood 60, Brougham	228.2	9.00 x 15	1	2 3/4	7/8	12	12
	Fleetwood 75	245.2	9.00 x 15	1	2 3/4	7/8	12	12
	All others	224.7	9.00 x 15	1	2 3/4	13/16	12	12
1970	Calais, DeVille	225.8	L78 x 15	1	2 3/4 Disc	13/16	11.9 Disc	12
	Fleetwood 60, Brougham	228.8	L78 x 15	1	2 3/4 Disc	13/16	11.9 Disc	12
	Fleetwood 75	247.3	L78 x 15	1	2 3/4 Disc	7/8	11.9 Disc	12
1971-72	Calais, DeVille	225.8	L78 x 15	1 1/4	2 15/16 Disc	15/16	11.9 Disc	12
	Fleetwood 60, Brougham	228.8	L78 x 15	1 1/4	2 15/16 Disc	15/16	11.9 Disc	12
	Fleetwood 75	247.3	L78 x 15	1 1/4	2 15/16 Disc	15/16	11.9 Disc	12

▲—Fleetwood 75—7/8
①—1968—2 15/16 single cylinder disc.

AC GENERATOR AND REGULATOR SPECIFICATIONS

| YEAR | MODEL | ALTERNATOR | | | | REGULATOR | | | | | | |
| | | Field Current Draw @ 12V. | Output @ Generator RPM | | Model | Field Relay | | | Regulator | | |
			1100	6500		Air Gap (In.)	Point Gap (In.)	Volts to Close	Air Gap (In.)	Point Gap (In.)	Volts at 125°
1965	1100696	2.2–2.6	5A	42	1119515	.015	.030	2.3–3.7	.060	.014	13.5–14.4
	1100694	2.2–2.6	5A	55	1119515	.015	.030	2.3–3.7	.060	.014	13.5–14.4
1966–67	1100691	2.2–2.6	5A	42	1119515	.015	.030	2.3–3.7	.060	.014	13.5–14.4
	1100692	2.2–2.6	5A	55	1119515	.015	.030	2.3–3.7	.060	.014	13.5–14.4
1968–69	1100696	2.2–2.4	5A	42	1119515						13.5–14.4
	1100694	2.2–2.4	5A	55	1119515						13.5–14.4
	1100742	2.2–2.4	5A	63	1119519						13.5–14.4
1970	1100908	2.2–2.6	...	42	1119515						13.5–14.4
	1100694	2.2–2.4	...	55	1119515						13.5–14.4
	1100910	2.8–3.2	...	63	1119519						13.5–14.4
1971–72	1100558	2.2–2.6	...	42	1119515						13.5–14.4
	1100557	2.8–3.2	...	63	1119519						13.5–14.4
	1101015	4.0–4.5	...	80		Transistor Type—no adjustment					

CAPACITIES

| YEAR | MODEL | ENGINE CRANKCASE ADD 1 Qt. FOR NEW FILTER | TRANSMISSIONS Pts. TO REFILL AFTER DRAINING | | | DRIVE AXLE (Pts.) | GASOLINE TANK (Gals.) | COOLING SYSTEM (Qts.) WITH HEATER |
| | | | Manual | | Automatic | | | |
			3-Speed	4-Speed				
1965	All	4	None	None	18▲	5	26	17¹/₄■
1966–67	All	4	None	None	24	5	26	18■
1968–72	All	4	None	None	25	5	26	21.3●

▲—Turbo Hydramatic—24 Pts.
■—Series 67 & 75 use 1¹/₂ Qts. additional.
●—1968-72—75 Series—24.8 Qts.
*—1971-72—27.5 Gals.

BATTERY AND STARTER SPECIFICATIONS

| YEAR | MODEL | BATTERY | | | | STARTERS | | | | | | Brush Spring Tension (Oz.) |
| | | Ampere Hour Capacity | Volts | Group Number | Terminal Grounded | Lock Test | | | No-Load Test | | | |
						Amps.	Volts	Torque	Amps.	Volts	RPM	
1965–67	All Series	73	12	3KMB	Neg.	510	3.0	Locked	88	10.6	4,000	35
1968–72	All Series	74	12	—	Neg.	—	Not Recommended		70–99	10.6	7,800	35

WHEEL ALIGNMENT

| YEAR | MODEL | CASTER | | CAMBER | | TOE-IN (In.) | KING-PIN INCLINATION (Deg.) | WHEEL PIVOT RATIO | |
		Range (Deg.)	Pref. Setting (Deg.)	Range (Deg.)	Pref. Setting (Deg.)			Inner Wheel	Outer Wheel
1965–67	All Series	1¹/₂N–¹/₂N	1N	³/₈N–³/₈P	(2)	³/₁₆–¹/₄	6	22²/₃	20
1968	All Series	1¹/₂N–¹/₂N	1N	(1)	(1)	³/₁₆–¹/₄	6	20	18
1969–70	All Series	1¹/₂N–¹/₂N	1N	³/₈N–³/₈P	0	¹/₈–¹/₄	6	20	18
1971–72	All Series	1¹/₂N–¹/₂N	1N	(3)	(3)	¹/₈–¹/₄	6	20	18

(1)—Left ³/₈P–¹/₈N; zero preferred.
　　Right ¹/₈P–³/₈N; ¹/₄N preferred.
(2)—¹/₄–¹/₂, more on left than right.
(3)—Left ³/₈P–³/₈N; zero preferred.
　　Right ¹/₈P–⁵/₈N; ¹/₄N preferred
P—Positive.
N—Negative.

FUSES AND CIRCUIT BREAKERS

1965–69

Air conditioner and heater .... 25 AMP. FUSE
Antenna .... 14 AMP. FUSE
Body feed, cigar lighter, clock, map .... 25 AMP. FUSE
Cruise control......................... 6 AMP. FUSE
Guide-matic .... 4 AMP. FUSE
Head and parking lights .... 15 AMP. CB
Horns .... 25 or 40 AMP. CB
Instrument & back-up lights .... 10 AMP. FUSE
Radio .... 7½ AMP. FUSE
Seats and windows .... 40 AMP. CB
Tail and stop lights .... 25 AMP. FUSE
Cornering and courtesy lights .... 25 AMP. FUSE
Turn signal .... 15 AMP. FUSE
Windshield wipers .... 25 AMP. FUSE

1970

Body feed .... 25 AMP.
  Cigar lighters
  Clock
  Courtesy lights
  Glove box light
  Map light
  Trunk light

Cornering and Parking Lights .... 10 AMP.
  Ash tray light
  Cornering lights
  Front side marker lights
  Parking lights
Directional signal and back-up lights .... 20 AMP.
  Back-up lights
  Cruise control
  Rear window de-fogger
  Turn signals
Gages and transmission controls .... 10 AMP.
  Brake warning light
  CCS vacuum solenoid
  Downshift solenoid
  Fuel gauge
  Generator light
  Low oil pressure indicator
  Water temperature warning light
Headlights (integral with headlight switch).... 15 AMP. CB
Heater and accessories .... 25 AMP.
  Air conditioning amplifier
  Air conditioning blower relay
  Heater blower
  (On cars equipped with a heater only, the
  25 AMP fuse is replaced by a 15 AMP,
  fuse)

Horns... CB
  Convertible top
  Engine metal temperature light
  Horns
  Power seat
  Power windows
Instrument panel lights .... 4 AMP.
Low blower (air conditioning only) .... 10 AMP.
Radio and window control relay .... 7½ AMP.
Stop lights and hazard warning flasher .... 25 AMP.
Tail lights............................... 25 AMP.
  License light
  Rear side marker lights
  Tail lights
Twilight sentinel (integral with headlight
  switch) .... 15 AMP. CB
Windshield wipers.......................... 25 AMP.

1971–72

Same as 1970 except the following:
Turn signal.................................. 25 AMP.
Backup lights, Rear window de-fogger.......... 10 AMP.
Seat back lock (in-line, next to relay, under seat) 4 AMP.

LIGHT BULBS

1965–66

Ash tray, cruise control .... 1445; 1 CP
Back-up lamps .... 1156; 32 CP
Cornering lamps......................... 1195; 50 CP
Gen. & oil tell-tale, glove compartment,
  radio dial .... 1895; 2 CP
Headlamp (inner)....................... 4001; 37.5 CP
Headlamp (outer) .... 4002; 50/37.5 CP
License.............................. 67; 4 CP
Parking & turn signal
  stop, tail & turn .... 1157; 32/4 CP
Trunk lamp .... 89; 6 CP

1967–69

Same as 1965–66 except the following:
Gen. oil tell-tale .... 161; 1 CP
Radio dial .... 1816; 3 CP

1970

FUNCTION	BULB NO.	C/P
Ash tray lamp	1445	.7
Back-up lamp	1156	32
Back-up lamp	1295	50
Clock	1816	3
Console lamp	57	2
Cornering lamp	1295	50
Courtesy lamp—rear quarter	90	6

FUNCTION	BULB NO.	C/P
Courtesy lamp-console	212/212-1	6
Courtesy lamp-instrument panel	89	6
Courtesy lamp—rear door	212/212-1	6
Courtesy lamp—rear quarter armrest	212/212-1	6
Cruise control speed selector illum. auto. lock lamps	1445	.7
Engine temp. warning light	161	1
Generator telltale lamp	161	1
Glove compartment lamp	1816	3
Headlamp—inner	L4001	37.5 Watts
Headlamp—outer	L4002	37.5W/55.0W
Headlamp switch lamp	1895	2
Heater control or climate control lamp	1816	3
High beam indicator	161	1
License lamp	67	4
Low brake telltale lamp	161	1
Low oil pressure telltale lamp	168	3
Map lamp	89	6
Marker lamp-front side	97A	4
Marker lamp-rear side	194	2
Panel lamp	168	3
Park-signal lamp	1157 NA	32/3
Radio dial lamp	1816	3
*Radio AM-FM band indicators	2182D	.4

FUNCTION	BULB NO.	C/P
*Radio AM-FM stereo indicators	2182D	.4
*Radio-rear control indicator	250	1
Spot lamp-front compartment	90	6
Spot lamp-reading	1004	15
Stop, tail and signal	1157	32/3
Trunk compartment lamp	89	6
Trunk lid tell tale	161	1
Turn signal indicator	168	3
Warning lamp-front door (combined with courtesy light)	212/212-1	6
Warning lamp-rear door (combined with courtesy light)	212/212-1	6
Water temperature tell tale	168	3

*Serviceable only by Radio Technician.

1971–72

Same as 1970 except the following:

	BULB NO.	C/P
Low oil pressure telltale lamp	161	1
Map lamp	550	6
Marker lamp-rear	168	3
Panel lamp	194	2
Radio dial lamp	1895	2
Turn signal indicator	194	2
Water temperature	161	1

Distributor

Detailed information on direction of distributor rotation, cylinder numbering, firing order, point gap, cam dwell, timing mark location, spark plugs, spark advance, and idle speed will be found in the front portion of this section.

Distributor Point Replacement

1965-72

1. Remove distributor cap by depressing and turning the retaining screws.
2. Remove two screws securing rotor cap and remove cap.
3. Remove condenser and primary leads from nylon insulated connection.
4. Loosen two screws holding base of contact assembly in place and remove points.
5. Inspect weight assembly, replace or lubricate as required.
6. Place new points under the two screws and tighten screws.
7. Connect the condenser and primary leads at the nylon insulated connection.
NOTE: be sure leads do not interfere with cap, weight base, or breaker advance.
8. Install rotor cap. Square and round lugs must be properly aligned.
9. With ⅛ in. Allen wrench in-

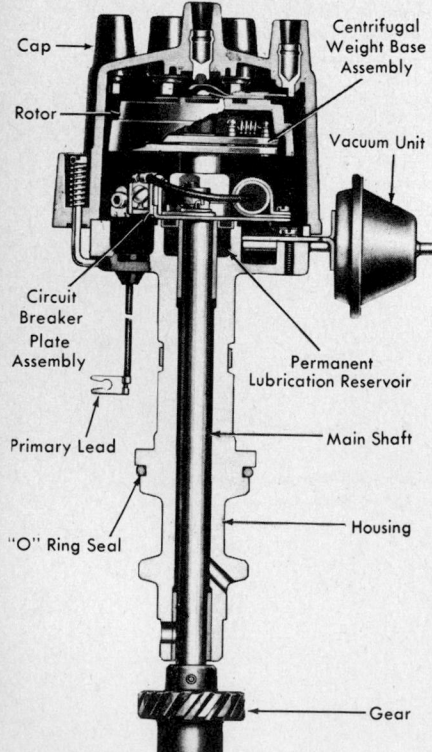

Distributor showing major components
(© Cadillac Div. G.M. Corp.)

Cap
Rotor
Circuit Breaker Plate Assembly
Primary Lead
"O" Ring Seal
Centrifugal Weight Base Assembly
Vacuum Unit
Permanent Lubrication Reservoir
Main Shaft
Housing
Gear

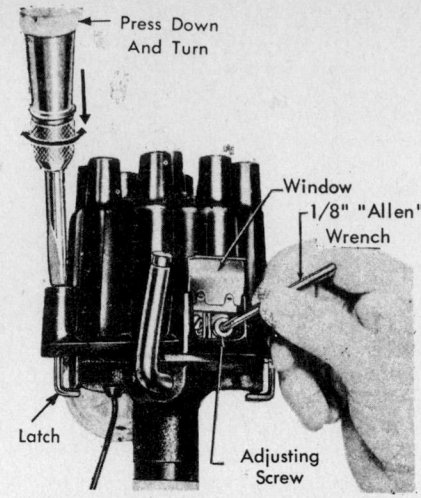

Press Down And Turn

Window 1/8" "Allen" Wrench

Latch

Adjusting Screw

Point adjustment with engine running

serted, turn until points close while rubbing block is on high point of lobe. Then turn screw counterclockwise one-half turn.
10. Replace distributor cap.
11. With engine warmed up and off fast idle, set points to get proper dwell angle.

Distributor Removal

All Models

Remove distributor cap. Disconnect vacuum line. Disconnect primary lead at distributor.

Turn the engine to top dead center for No. 1 cylinder so that the rotor points to the No. 1 cylinder tower in the distributor cap and the pointer on the timing case cover points to the O-mark on the crankshaft pulley.

Using a scribe mark, index the vacuum advance unit to the cylinder block so that the distributor body will be correctly replaced at reassembly. Remove clamp bolt and distributor.

Distributor Replacement

All Models

Install the distributor so that the vacuum advance unit aligns with the match-mark made at removal. Turn the rotor slightly left of center so that as the gear engages the camshaft it will revolve into the proper position, pointing to the No. 1 contact in the cap.

NOTE: if the engine has been cranked, remove the No. 1 spark plug. Crank the engine until the No. 1 piston is in firing position with the pointer and the O-mark on the crank-shaft pulley aligned. Then proceed as above.

Install the hold-down clamp. Connect the primary lead and install the cap.

Fill the distributor oiler tube with 10W oil or rotate lubricator.

Plug the distributor vacuum line to the carburetor.

Insert an adapter pin alongside the No. 1 wire in the distributor cap and connect a timing light.

Clean the crankshaft pulley markings and the pointer.

Set the timing to specifications.

Tighten clamp bolt to 18 ft. lbs.

Remove plug and adapter pin and reconnect the vacuum line to the advance unit.

Thermal Vacuum Switch

Starting 1968, a thermal vacuum switch was added to the distributor vacuum circuit to prevent engine overheating in heavy traffic. This switch is so designed to provide full vacuum advance in prolonged idling, or high temperature, situations. Under these conditions, the switch sends full manifold vacuum, instead of the normal carburetor vacuum, to the advance unit. Vacuum switch units having four ports, instead of the normal three, allow manifold vacuum to operate an idle speed-up device (the adjustment of which is found in *Fuel System*). The cut-off temperature of the switch is 220°F. An overheating condition may be due to a faulty switch.

To check the switch, proceed as follows:

1. Idle engine at 600 rpm and at normal operating temperature.
2. With an assistant in the car with his foot on the brake, and transmission in Reverse, disconnect the line from the distributor advance unit and check that vacuum is available (from port D). If vacuum is not available, the separate vacuum solenoid may be at fault.
3. Remove the line between the switch and the vacuum break T at carb. Vacuum still should be available at distributor line (from port D) and should not be available at the line just removed from port MT.
4. Block radiator with a piece of cardboard until "Engine Temp" light comes on.
5. Reconnect line removed in Step 3 and disconnect line between carburetor and switch port C. Vacuum now should be available at distributor line (from port D) and should not be available at line disconnected from port C.
6. If the previous checks indicate a faulty switch, replace the unit.

Generator, Regulator

Detailed facts on the generator and the regulator can be found in the Delcotron Specifications table.

General information on generator and regulator repair can be found in the Unit Repair Section.

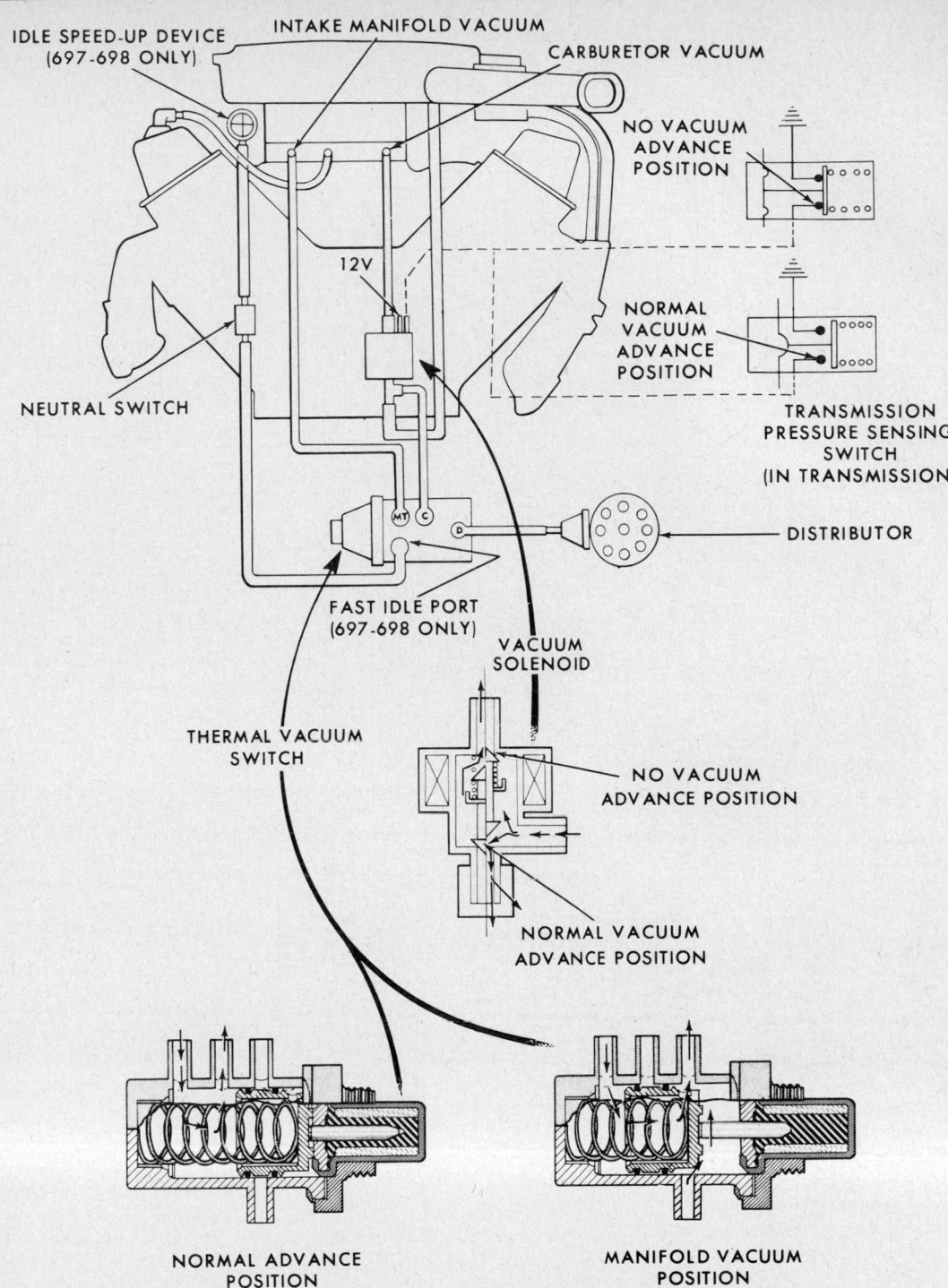

IDLE SPEED-UP DEVICE (697-698 ONLY)

INTAKE MANIFOLD VACUUM

CARBURETOR VACUUM

NO VACUUM ADVANCE POSITION

12V

NORMAL VACUUM ADVANCE POSITION

NEUTRAL SWITCH

TRANSMISSION PRESSURE SENSING SWITCH (IN TRANSMISSION)

DISTRIBUTOR

FAST IDLE PORT (697-698 ONLY)

VACUUM SOLENOID

THERMAL VACUUM SWITCH

NO VACUUM ADVANCE POSITION

NORMAL VACUUM ADVANCE POSITION

NORMAL ADVANCE POSITION

MANIFOLD VACUUM POSITION

Vacuum advance controls—1970 (© Cad. Div. G.M. Corp.)

NOTE: under no circumstances should the A.C. generator be polarized.

Generator Removal
All Models

Disconnect the battery. Disconnect the wire leads at the generator. Remove generator adjusting strap clamp screw, mounting bolts, and drive belt. Remove generator.

NOTE: heavy duty generator used on commercial chassis is slid backwards off its lower mounting bolts, after first loosening belt tensioner and removing fan belt and upper bolt.

Battery, Starter

Detailed information on the battery and starter will be found in the Battery and Starter Specifications table.

More information on starters can be found in the Unit Repair Section.

Starter R & R
All Models

1. Disconnect battery cable and jack up car.
2. Disconnect battery lead and two wires from solenoid.
3. Remove bolt that holds support bracket to starter.
4. Remove two starter-to-engine bolts.
5. Remove motor by pulling it forward and down, or toward right front wheel and over linkage.

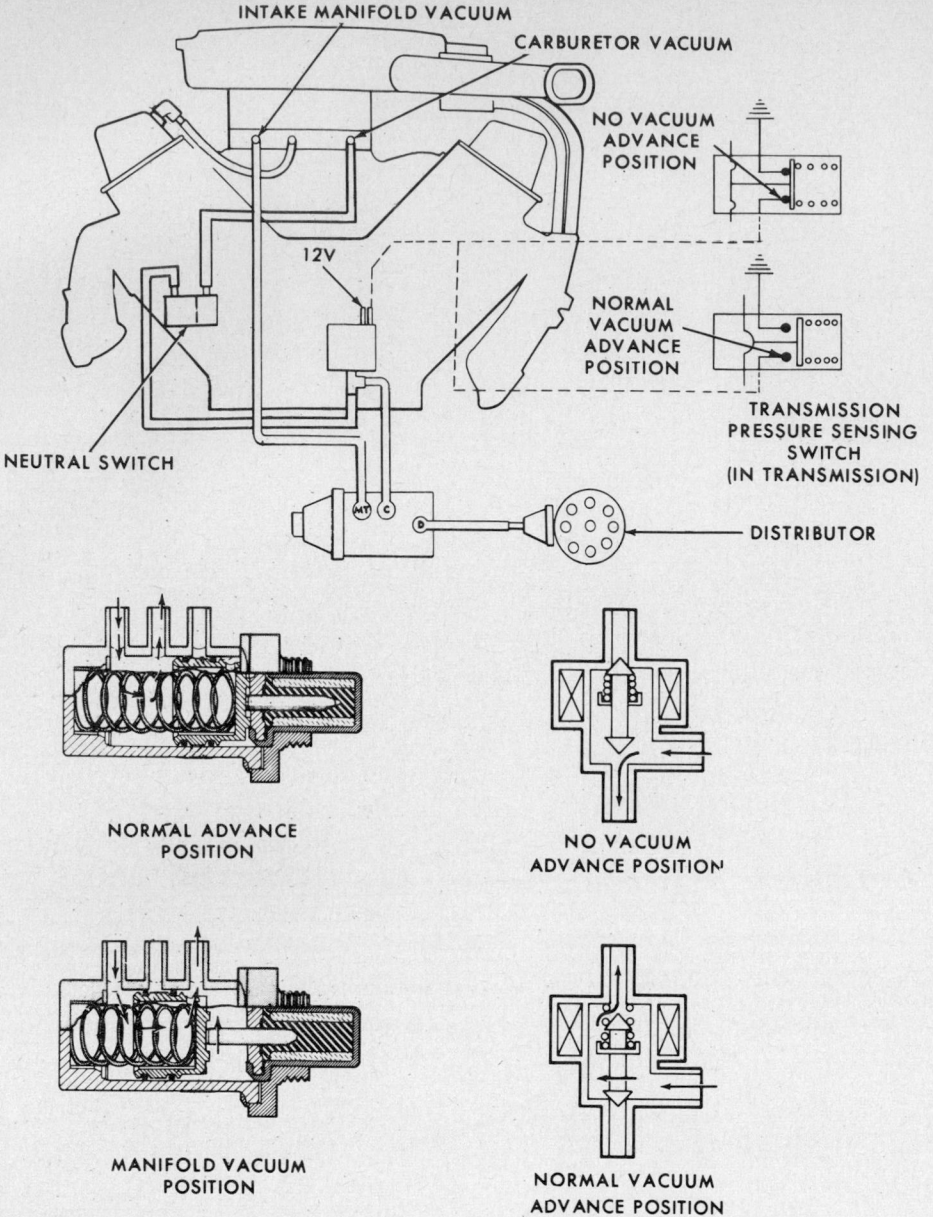

INTAKE MANIFOLD VACUUM

CARBURETOR VACUUM

NO VACUUM ADVANCE POSITION

12V

NORMAL VACUUM ADVANCE POSITION

TRANSMISSION PRESSURE SENSING SWITCH (IN TRANSMISSION)

NEUTRAL SWITCH

DISTRIBUTOR

NORMAL ADVANCE POSITION

NO VACUUM ADVANCE POSITION

MANIFOLD VACUUM POSITION

NORMAL VACUUM ADVANCE POSITION

Vacuum advance controls—1971-72 (© Cad. Div. G.M. Corp.)

6. To install, reverse removal procedure, tightening starter-to-engine bolts to 46 ft. lbs. and bracket bolt to 12 ft. lbs.

Instruments

Panel and Cluster R & R

1965-66

1. Disconnect battery.
2. Remove right and left windshield garnish moldings by removing four screws in each molding.
3. Remove six screws that hold upper panel cover to upper panel.
4. Raise upper panel high enough to gain access, and disconnect wire connectors for radio speaker/s, courtesy lights, and for Twilight Sentinel photocell and Automatic Climate Control sensor, if car is so equipped.
5. Pull upper panel cover rearward to disengage three hooks at front of cover from retainers on cowl, and remove cover.
6. Loosen set screw holding headlight switch housing to cluster bezel, using a 5/64 in. Allen wrench.
7. Carefully lift upward on bottom of headlight switch housing to disengage upper retainer clip from locating slot in cluster bezel opening. Pull headlight switch straight out to remove.
8. Disconnect headlight switch bulb socket from top of housing case.
9. Disconnect trunk warning lens

dial bulb socket from bottom of housing case.
10. On cars equipped with Guide-Matic and/or Twilight Sentinel, disconnect control switch lead connectors.
11. Disconnect multiple wire connector from top of headlight switch and remove the switch.
12. Loosen 5/64 in. Allen screw holding clock housing to cluster bezel. Lift up on clock housing to disengage upper retaining clip from locating slot in cluster bezel opening. Pull clock straight out to remove.
13. Disconnect clock feed wire, and two clock bulb sockets from housing case. Remove clock.
14. Disconnect steering shaft at flexible coupling.
15. Remove screw and lockwasher

holding lower shift lever to shift tube and separate lower shift lever from shift tube.

16. On cars with tilt and telescope steering wheel, position wheel in up position.

17. Remove four screws that hold lower end of steering column lower cover to lower instrument panel.

18. Remove one long screw holding upper end of steering column lower cover to clamp.

19. Disconnect front retainer flanges of steering column lower cover from front of lower instrument panel and lower steering column cover enough to gain access to cover.

20. Remove flasher unit from mounting clip and remove lower cover.

21. If car is a convertible, disconnect convertible top switch multiple connector from rear side of steering column lower cover.

22. On cars equipped with rear window defogger, disconnect blower switch single connector (light green wire and dark blue wire with white stripe) at accessory terminal on fuse panel. Disconnect blower switch T connector from wire assembly connector.

23. If the car has power windows or cruise control plus rear window defogger, disconnect override relay feed or cruise control wire from blower switch (6 in. long, dark blue wire with white stripe.)

24. If the car has a front seat warmer, detach connector leading from switch. Also remove two screws holding on-off switch to steering column lower cover. Remove the switch.

25. Remove transmission shift indicator pointer (use Allen wrench).

26. Disconnect horn wiring from chassis wiring harness. On tilt and telescope columns, disconnect connectors from turn signal and cornering switch on side of jacket. On standard column, disconnect multiple connectors.

27. Disconnect connectors and vacuum hoses from neutral safety and back-up light switch assembly.

28. Remove steering column lower cover clamp and remove two screws that hold clamp to instrument panel.

29. Remove two screws and washers that hold steering column upper clamp to support struts.

30. Slide rubber cover up on steering column and pull back carpet.

31. Remove steering column lower clamp screw, spacer and lockwasher, then loosen upper right support bolt at toe pan.

32. Pull steering column up and out of the car.

33. Disconnect seven cluster bulb sockets, fuel gauge connector, transmission stator switch and temperature gauge connectors.

34. Disconnect speedometer cable at speedometer head.

35. Working through headlight switch opening, remove screw that holds cluster bezel left lower mounting bracket to left mounting bracket on instrument panel center brace.

36. Working through clock opening, remove screw that holds cluster bezel right lower mounting bracket on instrument panel center brace.

37. Remove two screws that hold cluster bezel to upper instrument panel center molding. Remove bezel and cluster assembly from instrument panel.

38. Loosen set screw that holds trip odometer reset shaft knob to reset shaft. Remove knob.

39. Remove four screws that hold cluster panel to cluster bezel and remove cluster from bezel.

40. Install by reversing removal procedure.

1967

1. Disconnect negative battery cable, then remove three Phillips screws that secure cluster bezel to upper cover.

2. Open glove box and remove two upper screws.

3. Raise upper instrument panel cover high enough to disconnect radio speaker/s, Twilight Sentinel photocell and/or Automatic Climate Control sensor.

4. Pull upper cover to the rear to disengage three hooks from cowl retainers, then remove cover.

5. If equipped with Tilt Wheel, place wheel in full up position.

6. Remove two Phillips screws that hold lower end of column lower cover to instrument panel.

7. Remove one long special screw that secures upper end of lower cover to clamp.

8. Pull straight out on lower cover to disengage two upper pins.

9. Remove hazard warning flasher from clip and bulb socket from cover (if equipped with seat warmer). Remove lower cover.

10. Remove transmission shift indicator pointer, using an Allen wrench.

11. Disconnect multiple connector from cluster and disengage harness from clip.

12. Disconnect speedometer cable by pressing high points of wave washer.

13. Remove three upper screws that secure cluster to bezel.

14. Remove right and lower center (below clock) screws that secure cluster to bezel.

15. If equipped with A/C, remove center air outlet boot and center outlet.

16. If equipped with A/C, disengage left air outlet boot at inboard end.

17. Remove lower left cluster to bezel screw (from the back) using a flex driver.

18. If equipped with rear window defogger, seat warmer or convertible, disconnect wires.

19. Disconnect map light switch connector, then loosen upper left and right bezel to bracket screws.

20. Pry left corner of bezel forward and pull instrument panel cluster up to remove.

21. To install, reverse removal procedure.

1968

1. Follow Steps 1 through 12 of 1967 procedure.

2. If equipped with A/C, disengage left air outlet boot at outboard end.

3. Remove two upper screws that secure cluster to bezel.

4. Remove right and center (below clock) screws that secure cluster to bezel.

5. If equipped with A/C, remove center air outlet duct.

6. Remove radio knobs, using an Allen wrench.

7. Remove radio control shaft nuts and right bracket screw, then pull back and lower radio far enough to give clearance for cluster removal.

8. If equipped with rear window defogger, seat warmer or convertible, disconnect wires.

9. Loosen upper left and right bezel to bracket screws.

10. Pry left corner of bezel forward and pull instrument panel cluster up to remove.

11. To install, reverse removal procedure.

1969-70

1. Disconnect negative battery cable.

2. Disconnect radio speaker at radio.

3. Remove right and left windshield garnish moldings.

4. Open glove box and remove two upper screws.

5. Remove three Phillips screws that secure cluster bezel to upper cover.

6. Raise instrument panel cover high enough to disconnect Twilight Sentinel photocell and/or A/C sensor.

7. Pull upper cover to the rear to disengage three hooks from cowl retainers, then remove upper cover.

8. Remove two Phillips screws and

plate that holds top of clock to bezel.

9. Hold bottom of clock in while pushing up on top of clock. When clock snaps out, remove two bulbs and disconnect wires.
10. Remove clock from bezel.
11. Remove four Phillips screws that secure lower cover to bezel.
12. Remove two screws that secure lower cover to lower instrument panel.
13. Disengage lower cover by pulling up and out.
14. Disconnect ash tray wiring and Twilight Sentinel amplifier. Remove courtesy light bulb and socket.
15. Remove turn signal and hazard warning flashers from clips.
16. Remove lower cover.
17. Remove defroster hose behind radio.
18. Remove radio knobs.
19. Remove control shaft nuts.
20. Disconnect all wires going to radio.
21. Remove two screws and lower support bracket.
22. Pull radio back far enough to allow dial light to be removed, then remove radio.
23. Remove shift indicator pointer.
24. Remove odometer reset knob. Disconnect wiring and speedometer cable.
25. Remove four screws that secure cluster to bezel.
26. Remove cluster forward and to the right, while tipping right-hand corner downward.
27. To install, reverse removal procedure.

1971-72

1. Disconnect negative battery cable.
2. Disconnect radio speaker at radio.
3. Open glove box and remove two upper screws.
4. Remove four screws that secure cluster bezel to upper cover.
5. Raise instrument panel cover high enough to disconnect Twilight Sentinel photocell at left front speaker opening, clock wires and clock light.
6. Pull upper cover to the rear to disengage from cowl, then remove upper cover.
7. Disconnect ash tray wires.
8. Pull out ash tray and remove Phillips screws at bottom. Remove door cover and ash tray.
9. Remove four screws that secure lower cover to upper cover.
   NOTE: one screw is removed through ash tray opening.
10. Loosen two screws that secure lower cover to lower instrument panel.
11. Disengage lower cover by pulling straight out.

12. Disconnect Twilight Sentinel wiring; remove courtesy light, ash tray light and turn signal flasher.
13. Remove lower cover.
14. Disconnect speedometer cable, remove left-hand A/C outlet hose and disconnect cluster harness plug. Disengage harness from rear cluster clip.
15. Remove shift pointer.
16. Remove four screws (two upper and two lower) that secure cluster to bezel assembly.
17. Remove cluster forward and to the right, while tipping right-hand corner downward.
18. To install, reverse removal procedure.

Ignition Switch Replacement

1965-66

1. Disconnect battery.
2. Remove right and left windshield garnish mouldings.
3. Remove screws holding upper panel cover to upper panel.
4. Raise upper panel high enough to disconnect wire connectors from speaker, courtesy lights, Twilight Sentinel and Climate Control sensor if so equipped.
5. Pull upper panel cover rearward and disconnect three hooks at front of cover and remove cover.
6. Remove lock cylinder assembly.
7. Disconnect four-way connector at rear of ignition switch housing.
8. Remove switch nut.
9. Disconnect dial bulb socket at rear of housing and remove switch through rear.
10. Install in reverse of above.

1967-68

1. Disconnect battery.
2. Remove lock cylinder.
3. Remove steering column lower cover.
4. Remove switch nut that holds the switch assembly to the panel.
5. Disconnect dial bulb socket and wiring harness from back of switch assembly.
6. Pull switch rearward out of instrument panel.
7. Install by reversing removal procedure.

1969-72

1. Disconnect battery.
2. Position lock cylinder in "lock" position.
3. Remove steering column lower cover.
4. Loosen two nuts on upper steering column, allowing column to drop.

Caution Do not remove nuts, as column may bend under its own weight.

5. Disconnect ignition switch con-

nector at switch.
6. Remove two screws securing ignition switch to steering column. Remove switch.
7. To install, first assemble ignition switch on actuator rod and adjust to "lock" position, as follows:
   a. *Standard Column*—Hold switch actuating rod stationary with one hand while moving switch toward bottom of column until switch reaches end of travel (Acc. position). Back off one detent, then, with key also in "lock" position, tighten two switch mounting screws.
   b. *Tilt column*—Hold switch actuating rod stationary with one hand while moving switch toward upper end of column until switch reaches end of travel (Acc. position). Back off one detent, then, with key also in "lock" position, tighten two switch mounting screws.
8. Connct wires, tighten two steering column nuts, install lower cover and reconnect battery.

Lock Cylinder Replacement

Up to 1968

1. Insert key and turn to left of Acc. position.
2. With stiff wire in hole depress lock pin and rotate cylinder counterclockwise and pull out.

1969-72

The lock cylinder is removed as part of steering column disassembly. The Cadillac column is similar to the Buick unit; see the Buick car section for procedure.

NOTE: Cruise Control switch harness must be snaked out of column using piano wire.

Brakes

Specific information on brake cylinder sizes can be found in the General Chassis and Brake Specifications table.

Information on overhauling power brakes can be found in the Unit Repair Section. All Cadillac cars are equipped with power brakes, Fleetwood 75, Commercial and Eldorado models using a tandem diaphragm unit for more braking power.

Information on the grease seals which may need replacement can be found in the Unit Repair Section.

To gain access to the front wheel star wheel adjustment, it will be necessary to remove the wheel and tire (not the hub or drum).

The rear wheels also must be removed to adjust the rear star wheel.

Power Brake Unit R & R

1965-66

1. Disconnect output lines from master cylinder on power unit.
2. Disconnect vacuum hose from vacuum check valve on unit.
3. Remove clevis pin retaining power unit pushrod to brake pedal relay lever.
4. Remove four nuts to release power unit from cowl.

1967-72

1. Disconnect hydraulic lines from master cylinder.
2. Disconnect vacuum line from vacuum check valve on unit.
3. Remove steering column lower cover, as described under *Panel and Cluster R & R*.
4. Remove cotter pin, washer and spring spacer that secure power unit pushrod to brake pedal arm.
5. Remove the four nuts that secure power unit to firewall, then remove power unit.
6. To install, reverse removal procedure.

Description

The rear braking system of all models consists of power-assisted, hydraulic service brakes. The front braking system is same as rear for models 1965-68. Front disc brakes were optional on the 1968 model and standard on all 1969-72 cars. All models use a foot-operated parking brake, which is applied at rear wheels through mechanical linkage and is vacuum released when transmission is put in gear.

The service brake has a self-adjusting brake shoe mechanism consisting of a link, actuator, pawl, and pawl return spring. The actuator is held against the secondary shoe by means

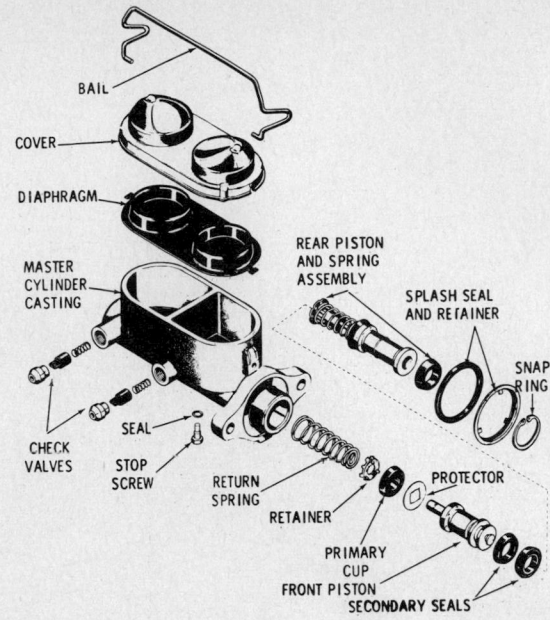

Master cylinder (Bendix) used with drum brakes (© Cadillac Div., G.M. Corp.)

of a hold-down cup and spring. The pawl is connected to the actuator and held in position by the pawl return spring.

The automatic adjustment takes place only when the brakes are applied when the car is moving rearward.

Over-adjustment is prevented by the shoe-to-drum clearance limiting secondary shoe travel to less than that required for the pawl to engage the next tooth of the star wheel.

Care must be used that the correct star wheel assembly is installed at the proper wheel, to insure that the self-adjuster work correctly.

Caution

Fixed anchors are used.

Periodic wheel removal and lining inspection becomes more important to insure against drum and shoe damage due to neglect.

Brake System Check

1. Start engine and allow to idle in Neutral. Depress brake pedal and hold—if pedal gradually falls away, a hydraulic system leak is indicated.
2. Check pedal travel from rest to full on position. Pedal travel should not exceed 1½ in. for 1965-67, 1¾ in. for 1968, 1⅞ in. for 1969-70, and 2-1/16 in. for 1971-72.
3. If pedal travel exceeds specifications, the system is probably contaminated by air bubbles and should be bled.

NOTE: disc brakes—tap calipers around piston area with plastic ham-

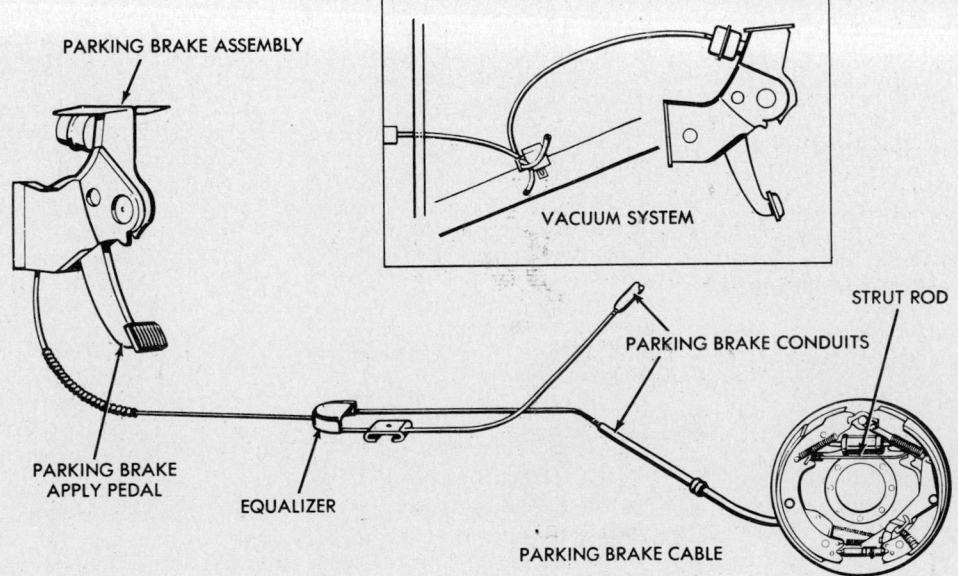

Parking brake layout—1965-72 (© Cad. Div. G.M. Corp.)

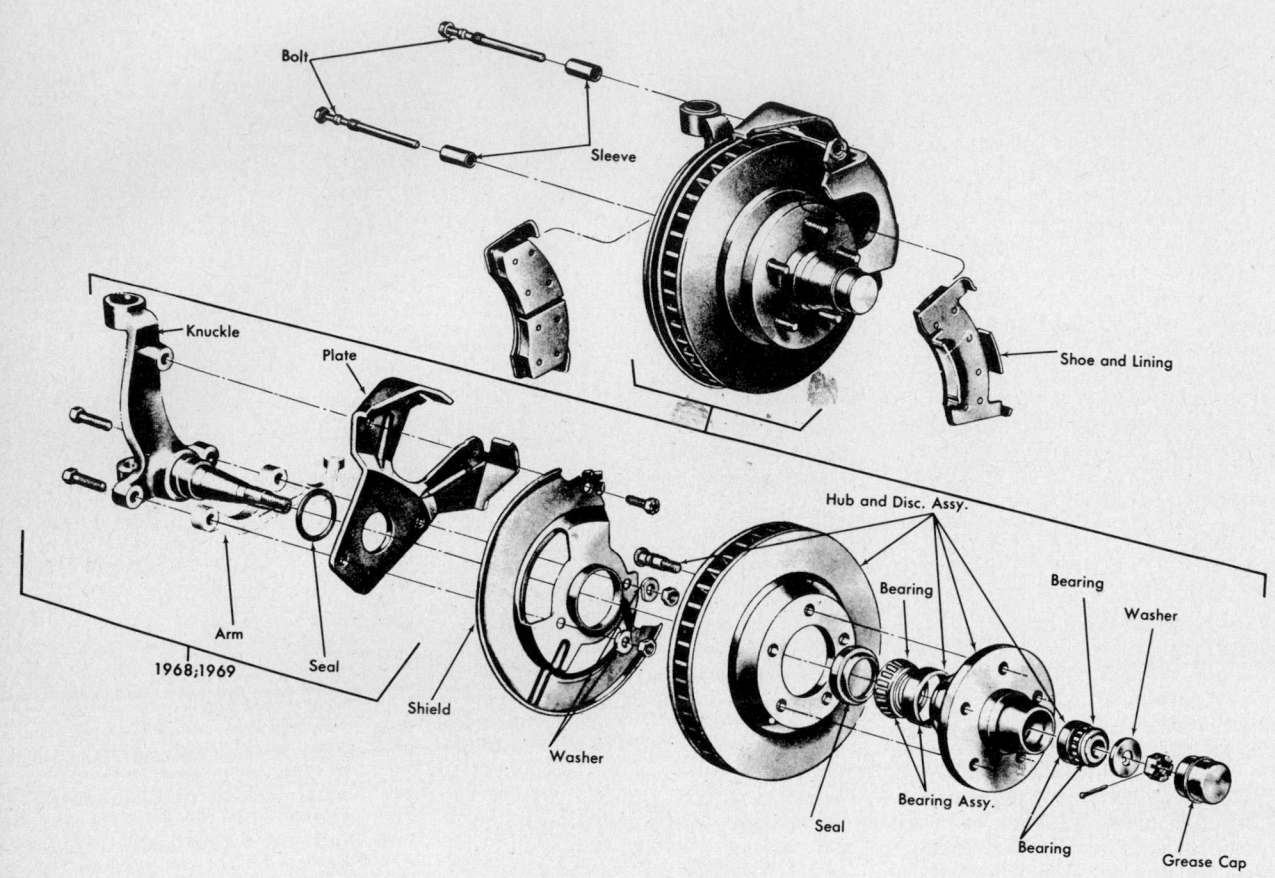

Front disc brake (© Cad. Div. G.M. Corp.)

mer to dislodge all air bubbles. Less common causes of excessive pedal travel include malfunctioning rear brake self-adjusters, tapered rear linings, worn out rear linings or complete loss of fluid from one brake circuit.

Vacuum Release Parking Brake

A vacuum release assists the foot-operated parking brake. With the engine running, the brake automatically releases when the car is put into gear. This device eliminates the possibility of driving the car with the parking brake engaged.

Preliminary Check

1. Check vacuum cylinder piston travel (on brake pedal support) by running engine at idle and shifting from Drive to Neutral. The manual release lever should move up and down as vacuum is applied and released.
2. If no movement is observed,

check for kinked or loose vacuum line connections all the way out to the intake manifold. Check neutral switch adjustment and vacuum release valve.
3. If movement is slow (greater than 2 seconds), vacuum diaphragm may be leaking or lines kinked partially closed.
4. If vacuum piston completes full stroke, but does not release brake, parking brake assembly is faulty and must be replaced as a unit.
5. If parking brake does not remain fully engaged in all gears with engine off, the assembly must be replaced.

Master Cylinder

1965-66

A dual master cylinder is used. The front reservoir supplying rear brakes and the rear one supplying the front brakes. This allows one pair of brakes to operate should there be a failure of

the opposite pair. If the lines have been disconnected, be sure to reinstall them in their proper place, i.e. front to rear cylinder and rear to front.

Two different brake units were used on these models—Bendix and Delco Moraine. For identification purposes, the Bendix unit is painted all black, while the Delco Moraine vacuum cylinder is zinc plated.

With a pressure bleeder, the Bendix system can be bled from front reservoir by covering rear reservoir with solid cap. The Moraine-type must be bled separately, front and rear.

Without a pressure bleeder, keep both reservoirs nearly full.

1967-72

The master cylinder design was revised. The master cylinder and reservoir responsible for front wheel brake application is now the front half of the cylinder instead of the rear, as in earlier models. Now, the

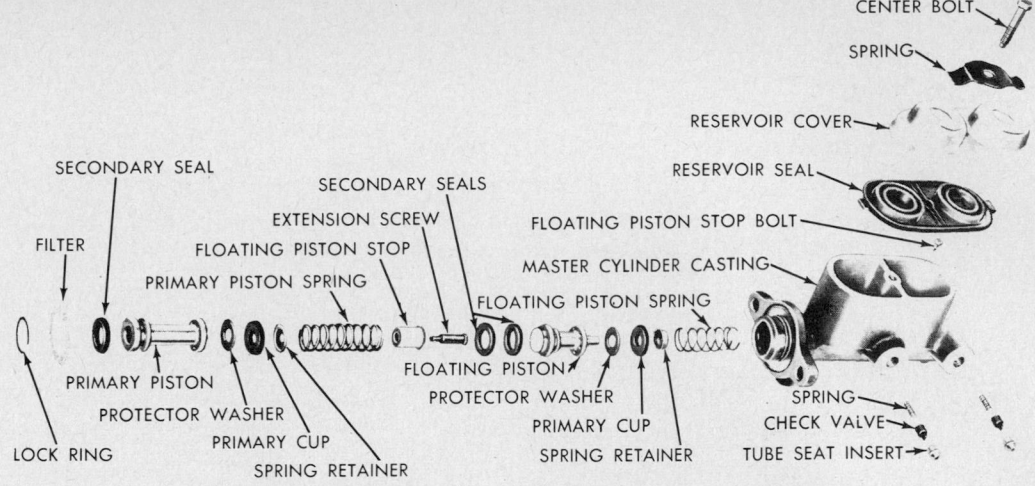

SECONDARY SEAL
FILTER
SECONDARY SEALS
EXTENSION SCREW
FLOATING PISTON STOP
PRIMARY PISTON SPRING
FLOATING PISTON STOP BOLT
MASTER CYLINDER CASTING
FLOATING PISTON SPRING
CENTER BOLT
SPRING
RESERVOIR COVER
RESERVOIR SEAL
PRIMARY PISTON
PROTECTOR WASHER
PRIMARY CUP
SPRING RETAINER
FLOATING PISTON
PROTECTOR WASHER
PRIMARY CUP
SPRING RETAINER
SPRING
CHECK VALVE
TUBE SEAT INSERT
LOCK RING

Delco-Moraine master cylinder—1965-66 (© Cad. Div. G.M. Corp.)

front portion of the master cylinder serves the front wheels and the rear portion of the cylinder serves the rear wheels.

Front Wheel Disc Brakes

Front disc brakes were optional for 1968 models, standard for all 1969-72 models. Illustrations and procedures can be found in the Unit Repair Section.

Eldorado brake rotors are larger than standard and are removable from the hub.

Fuel System

Data on capacity of the gas tank will be found in the Capacities table. Data on correct engine idle speed will be found in the Tune-Up Specifications table.

Information covering operation and troubles of the fuel gauge will be found in the Unit Repair Section.

Fuel Pump and Filter

The fuel pump is mounted on the engine front cover up to 1967, on the left-hand side of the engine from 1968 to 1972. The pump is driven by an eccentric machined as an integral part of the camshaft. There is a fuel filter between the fule pump and the carburetor. Up to 1967, the filter is mounted on the oil filler bracket. In

1968, the filter is an inline unit mounted near the fuel pump, and from 1969 onward the filter is an integral part of the fuel pump. The filter should be replaced every 12,000 miles. On air conditioned cars, the fuel filter has a passage and a connecting line to the fuel tank to return fuel vapors to the tank under high temperature conditions.

R & R Pump—1965-72

NOTE: on air conditioned cars, be sure to disconnect the flexible line connecting the fuel filter to the vapor return line from the tank.
1. If equipped with A.I.R. system, it may be necessary to remove air pump and bracket for clearance.
2. Remove center coil wire.

2A. For 1968-72 models, jack up front of car and support on axle stands so that pump can be removed from underneath.
3. Loosen two mounting bolts (or one bolt and one stud nut from 1968).
4. Turn over engine so that tension on mounting bolts is relieved.
5. Disconnect pump inlet line and pump outlet line. Plug inlet line.
6. Remove two mounting bolts and pump.
7. To install, reverse removal procedure. Make sure pump arm is properly positioned on cam eccentric; tighten bolts to 15 ft. lbs.

R & R Filter—1969-72

1. Jack up car and support on

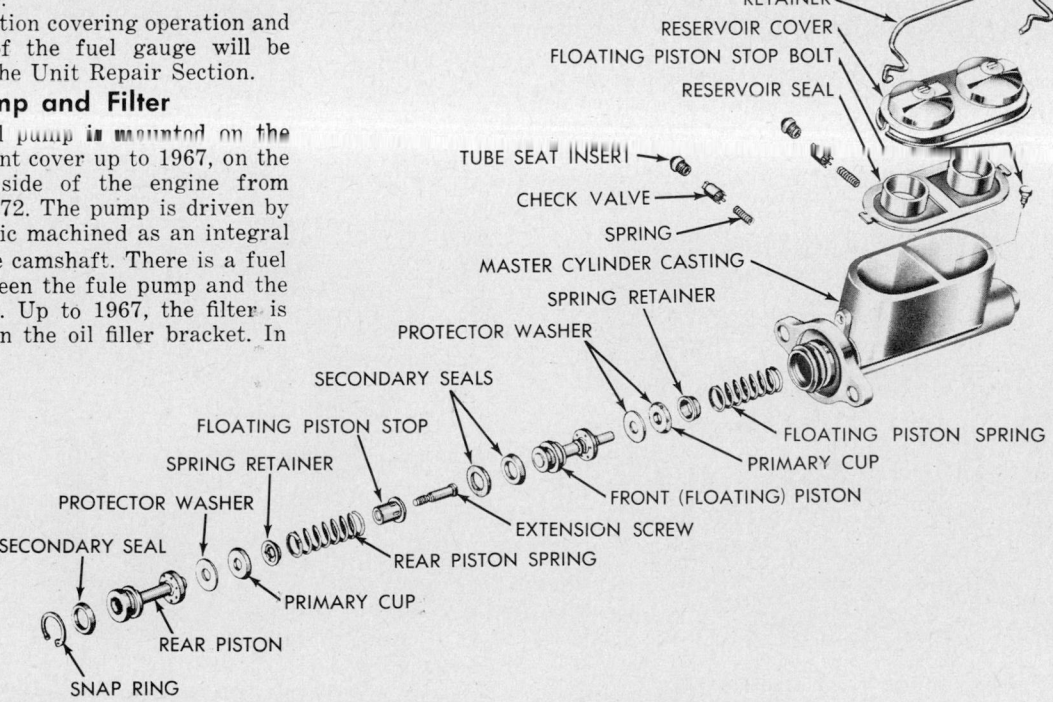

RETAINER
RESERVOIR COVER
FLOATING PISTON STOP BOLT
RESERVOIR SEAL
TUBE SEAT INSERT
CHECK VALVE
SPRING
MASTER CYLINDER CASTING
SPRING RETAINER
PROTECTOR WASHER
SECONDARY SEALS
FLOATING PISTON STOP
SPRING RETAINER
PROTECTOR WASHER
SECONDARY SEAL
REAR PISTON
SNAP RING
PRIMARY CUP
REAR PISTON SPRING
EXTENSION SCREW
FRONT (FLOATING) PISTON
PRIMARY CUP
FLOATING PISTON SPRING

Delco-Moraine master cylinder—1967-68 (© Cad. Div. G.M. Corp.)

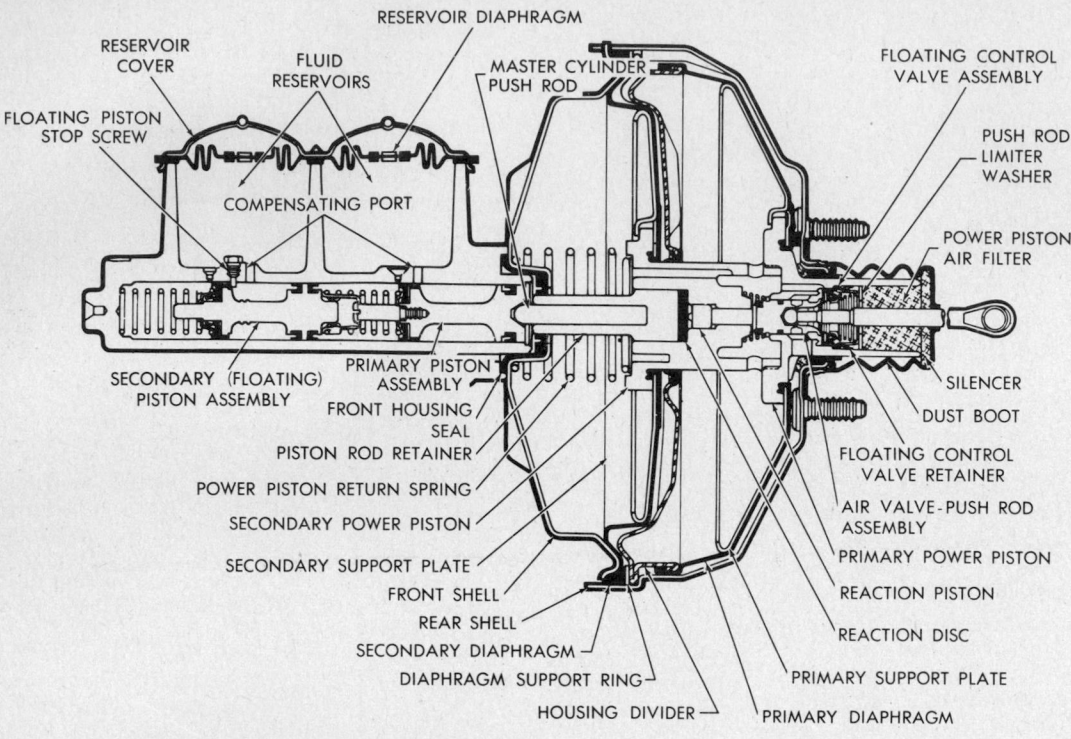

RESERVOIR COVER
RESERVOIR DIAPHRAGM
FLUID RESERVOIRS
MASTER CYLINDER PUSH ROD
FLOATING CONTROL VALVE ASSEMBLY
FLOATING PISTON STOP SCREW
PUSH ROD LIMITER WASHER
COMPENSATING PORT
POWER PISTON AIR FILTER
SECONDARY (FLOATING) PISTON ASSEMBLY
PRIMARY PISTON ASSEMBLY
SILENCER
FRONT HOUSING SEAL
DUST BOOT
PISTON ROD RETAINER
FLOATING CONTROL VALVE RETAINER
POWER PISTON RETURN SPRING
AIR VALVE-PUSH ROD ASSEMBLY
SECONDARY POWER PISTON
PRIMARY POWER PISTON
SECONDARY SUPPORT PLATE
REACTION PISTON
FRONT SHELL
REACTION DISC
REAR SHELL
SECONDARY DIAPHRAGM
PRIMARY SUPPORT PLATE
DIAPHRAGM SUPPORT RING
HOUSING DIVIDER
PRIMARY DIAPHRAGM

Tandem diaphragm power unit (© Cad. Div. G.M. Corp.)

stands.
2. Clamp or plug rubber section of inlet hose.
3. Disconnect fuel pump outlet line at fuel pump.
4. Remove fuel outlet nut and remove filter.
NOTE: use two wrenches to prevent loosening of nut welded to pump cover.
5. Install in reverse of above.

Throttle Check (Dashpot)

A vacuum-operated throttle check is used on some models. It operates by a combination of spring pressure and engine vacuum. Adjust length of plunger for correct operation: lengthen to prevent stalling; shorten to avoid racing.

Speed-Up Control Adjustment

Cars equipped with air conditioning have a vacuum-powered, solenoid-operated speed-up control attached to the carburetor.

This device increases the engine idle speed to 900 rpm when the transmission is in neutral and the air conditioner switch is on.

1965-66

1. Warm up engine.
2. Remove air cleaner.
3. Turn air conditioner on.
4. While in Neutral, adjust screw in speed-up unit plunger.
5. Shut off engine and replace air cleaner.

1967-68

1. In Park, warm up engine.
2. Remove air cleaner.
3. Remove and plug vacuum hose from Automatic Climate Control

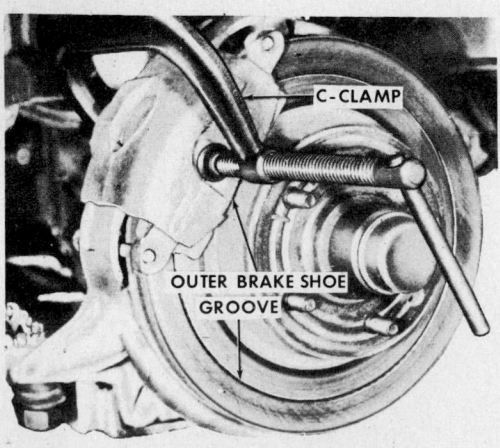

C-CLAMP
OUTER BRAKE SHOE GROOVE

Pushing disc brake caliper piston into bore (© Cad. Div. G.M. Corp.)

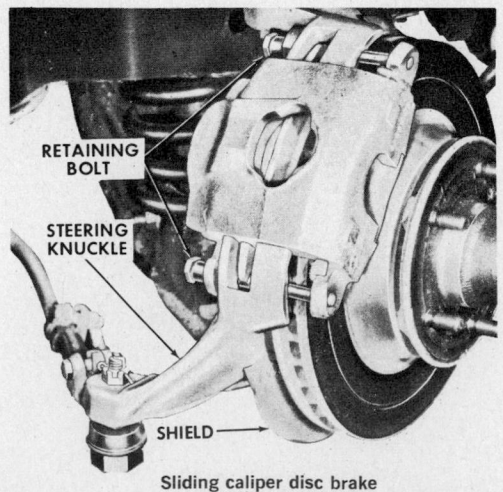

RETAINING BOLT
STEERING KNUCKLE
SHIELD

Sliding caliper disc brake (© Cad. Div. G.M. Corp.)

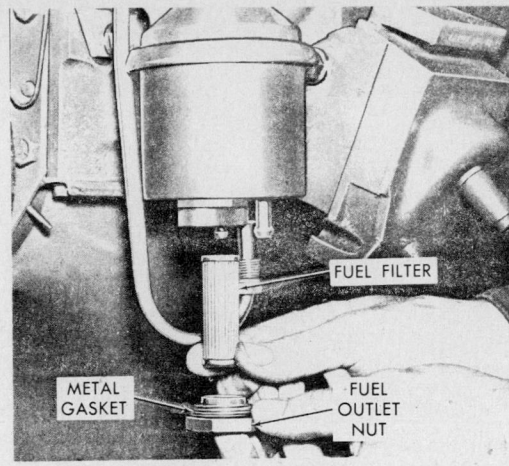

Fuel filter—1969-72
(© Cad. Div. G.M. Corp.)

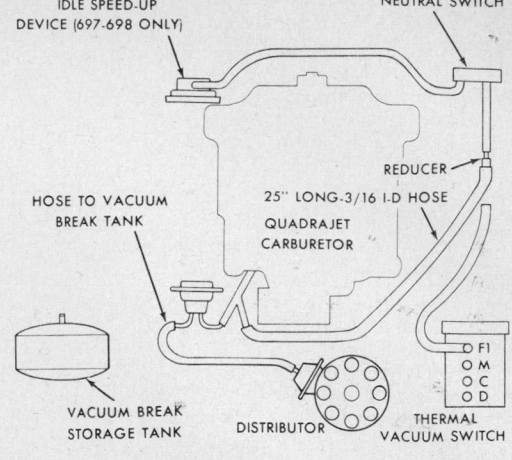

Idle speed-up adjustment—1970
(© Cad. Div. G.M. Corp.)

power servo vacuum actuator.

4. Set Automatic Climate Control selector on AUTO.

5. On 1967 model, adjust nuts on speed-up control rod to idle speed of 900. On 1968 model, the adjustment is made by turning the screw located on speed-up control arm.

6. Shut off engine, reconnect vacuum hose and install air cleaner.

1969

On these models, the speed-up control is actuated by water temperature, working only when radiator reaches 220°F. Air conditioner does not have to be on to have idle speed up. Curb and fast idle adjustments should be made before attempting the speed-up idle adjustment.

1. Warm up engine.

2. With engine off, remove air cleaner.

3. Disconnect vacuum hose leading from thermo vacuum switch to reducing nipple near dash, at reducing nipple.

4. Disconnect vacuum hose at diverter valve and connect to reducing nipple.

5. Disconnect and plug distributor vacuum hose at vacuum unit.

6. Disconnect manifold vacuum hose from thermo vacuum switch nipple at "MT" and connect to distributor vacuum unit. This is the nipple closest to the block.

7. Turn air conditioner to HIGH

and turn temperature dial to 65.

8. With transmission in Netural or Park, start engine and make adjustment at screw on idle speed-up control arm (900-950 rpm).

9. Turn engine off, reconnect hoses and install air cleaner.

1970 Fleetwood 75 and Commercial

Operation is similar to 1969. Different vacuum routing requires a slightly different procedure.

1. Set curb and fast idle.

2. Stop engine and remove air cleaner and heat duct.

3. Disconnect and plug distributor advance hose.

4. Disconnect vacuum hose at vacuum break tank and connect it to distributor advance unit.

5. Disconnect vacuum hose that goes from Thermo Vacuum switch to reducing nipple, at the reducing nipple.

6. Disconnect vacuum hose connector at carburetor vacuum break T.

7. Connect a 25 in. section of 3/16 in. vacuum hose between T and reducing nipple.

8. Turn A/C to HIGH and set dial to 65°F.

9. Start and warm up engine, then adjust idle speed-up in Neutral. Turn adjusting screw, as illustrated, to maintain 900-950 rpm.
NOTE: pull rod on idle speed-up

unit should move when selector lever is moved to Park or Neutral. If it does not, check neutral switch or for vacuum leaks.

10. Turn off engine, reconnect hoses and install air cleaner.

Idle Speed and Mixture Adjustments

1965

Adjust with air cleaner removed.

1. Make sure PCV valve is free and working properly.

2. Disconnect parking brake vacuum hose at vacuum cylinder and connect a vacuum gauge to this hose.

3. Connect a tachometer, set parking brake and allow engine to come up to normal operating temperature in Neutral.

4. Remove the air cleaner and make sure dashpot is disengaged.

5. With wheels chocked, place transmission in either Drive range.

6. Turn air adjustment screw to obtain 480-500 rpm with A/C on. Turning screw outward increases engine speed, but it also leans out the mixture. To compensate for this, adjust the idle mixture screw.

NOTE: press down on the brass hot idle compensator pin during adjustment. Be careful of the bimetallic strip, as it is easily damaged.

7. Turn one idle mixture screw to obtain highest tach and vacuum readings, then turn the other mixture screw to obtain highest readings.

8. Reset idle speed, as in Step 6.

9. Repeat Steps 6-8 until turning mixture screws does not cause an increase in speed and engine idles smoothly.

10. Install air cleaner and readjust idle if necessary.

11. Shut off engine, disconnect vacuum gauge and tach and recon-

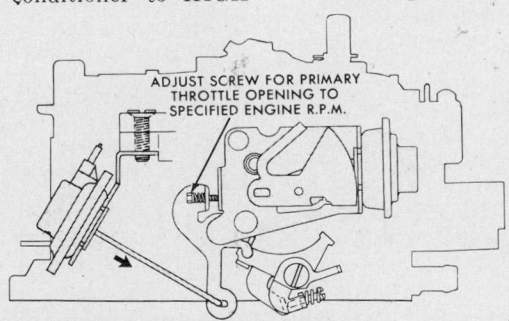

Speed up control adjustment. The adjustment is on the rod on earlier models.
(© Cadillac Div., G.M. Corp.)

nect vacuum hose.

NOTE: Carter AFB carburetor uses a stainless steel gasket between carburetor and manifold. If this is not installed, in addition to the composition gasket, the car will not idle properly.

1966-69

Adjust with air cleaner removed.

NOTE: on 1968-69 cars, disconnect and plug distributor vacuum advance hose.

1. Follow Steps 1-5 of 1965 procedure.

NOTE: plug parking brake vacuum hose instead of using a gauge.

2. To set transmission stator blades on 1966 cars, disconnect the pink wire from fitting on downshift switch and connect it to the white wire fitting with an alligator clip.
3. Adjust air adjusting screw to obtain an idle speed of 480-500 rpm for cars without A.I.R. system, 550 rpm for A.I.R. equipped cars. (A/C should be *off* for A.I.R. cars, *on* for all others.)

NOTE: press down on brass hot idle compensator pin while making adjustments. Be careful of the bimetallic strip, as it is easily damaged.

4. On 1967 cars with A/C, no A.I.R., disconnect and plug vacuum line from power servo on firewall.
5. Set idle speed screw 1½ turns in after contacting primary lever, both mixture screws out 4 turns from seated position.
6. Turn one idle mixture screw clockwise to obtain highest tach reading. Continue to turn screw until speed falls off 20 rpm—this is the lean idle fall-off point. Back off screw ¼ turn for non-A.I.R. cars, 1⅛ turns for 1966-67 A.I.R. cars, 1½ turns for 1968 A.I.R. cars, and 1 turn for 1969 A.I.R. cars.
7. Repeat Step 6, turning other mixture screw.
8. Reset idle speed as in Step 3, then repeat Steps 6 and 7 if speed exceeds 500 rpm for non-A.I.R. cars or 550 rpm for A.I.R. cars.
9. Install air cleaner and recheck idle speed.
10. Shut off engine, disconnect tach, reconnect pink wire on 1966 models, connect parking brake vacuum line and, on 1968-69 models, reconnect distributor vacuum advance.

1970

Adjust with air cleaner removed.

1. Disconnect and plug distributor vacuum advance line.
2. Disconnect and plug parking brake vacuum line at vacuum re-

lease cylinder.

3. Connect a tachometer, set parking brake and remove air cleaner.
4. Make sure dashpot is not touching linkage, then turn slow idle speed screw in approximately 1½ turns after it contacts primary throttle lever. Turn in both mixture screws until they seat gently, then unscrew them approximatley 6 turns.
5. Place car in Drive after warming up engine. Turn off A/C.

NOTE: press down on hot idle compensator pin while making adjustments.

6. Adjust slow idle screw to obtain 620 rpm.
7. Turn one mixture screw clockwise until speed falls off 10 rpm, then repeat Steps 6 and 7 for other mixture screw. Idle speed now should be 600 rpm, indicating a 10 rpm drop per mixture needle.
8. Install air cleaner, shut off engine and disconnect tach.
9. Connect parking brake vacuum line and distributor vacuum line.

1971

Adjust with air cleaner removed.

Idle speed is adjusted at a new anti-dieseling solenoid located where the dashpot was located in previous years. The throttle must be opened slightly to allow the plunger to move out all the way, then it must be closed against the now-extended solenoid plunger before making the idle speed adjustment. The solenoid plunger will retract when the ignition is shut off.

1. Disconnect and plug distributor vacuum advance hose and parking brake vacuum hose (at the release cylinder).
2. Connect a tachometer and set the parking brake with transmission in Neutral.
3. Remove the air cleaner and turn in mixture screws until they seat gently, then turn the screws out

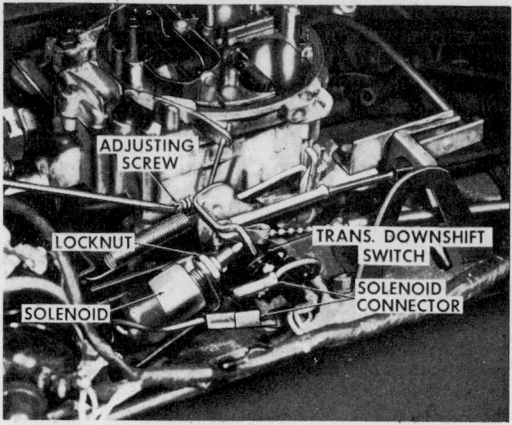

Adjusting anti-dieseling solenoid—1971-72
(© Cad. Div. G.M. Corp.)

approximately 6 turns.

4. Start engine and allow it to warm up.
5. Place car in Drive with A/C off.

NOTE: press down on hot idle compensator pin while making adjustments. This applies to Fleetwood 75 and Commercial models only.

6. Set idle speed to 620 rpm by adjusting anti-dieseling solenoid. Tighten jam nut.
7. Turn one mixture screw clockwise until idle speed falls off 10 rpm, then repeat for other screw. Idle speed now should be 600 rpm.
8. Install limiter caps, then disconnect wire that energizes solenoid. The plunger should retract to allow a slower idle speed of 350-400 rpm.
9. Shut off engine, disconnect tach, connect vacuum lines and solenoid wire and install air cleaner.

Exhaust System

Exhaust Pipe Removal
1965-67

1. Raise car.
2. Remove resonator.
3. Remove two nuts from both right and left exhaust manifold studs.
4. Lower exhaust pipe and remove heat control valve. Remove exhaust pipe.

1968-70

1. Raise car.
2. Loosen intermediate pipe hanger at transmission extension housing and remove lateral Y pipe.
3. Remove two nuts securing pipes to each exhaust manifold.
4. Allow exhaust pipe to drop and drive it forward out of intermediate pipe.

1971-72

1. Raise car.
2. Remove two nuts that secure pipes to each exhaust manifold.
3. Remove clamp that secures ex-

haust pipe to intermediate pipe.
4. Allow exhaust pipe to drop and drive it forward out of intermediate pipe.

Muffler Removal

1965-67

1. Raise car.
2. Remove clamp at rear of muffler.
3. Pry muffler outlet pipe rearward.
4. Support system with jack.
5. Remove clamp at front of muffler.
6. Remove muffler from intermediate pipe.

1968-72

1. Raise car.
2. Loosen resonator clamp and remove hanger blade.
3. Remove two nuts securing front clamp to muffler. Remove clamp.
4. Remove two nuts securing rear clamp to muffler. Remove clamp.
5. Slide rear portion of exhaust off intermediate pipe.
6. Remove muffler from muffler-to-resonator pipe.

Resonator Removal

1965-67

1. Raise car.
2. Remove clamp on rear of resonator.
3. Work intermediate pipe, muffler, and muffler outlet pipe rearward as a unit, until support blades slide from rubber slots in brackets.
4. Pry muffler and resonator outlet pipe rearward from resonator.
5. Loosen clamp at front of resonator.
6. Pry resonator rearward.
7. Slide hanger blade out of slot in support bracket. Remove resonator.

1968-72

1. Raise car.
2. Remove clamp at joint of resonator to muffler-to-resonator pipe.
3. Remove rear exhaust hanger at resonator outlet.
4. Separate resonator from muffler-to-resonator pipe.

Caution

do not use heat behind rear axle because of explosive fuel vapors. Support muffler to avoid damage.

Intermediate Pipe Removal

1965-67

1. Remove muffler.
2. Remove clamp at front end of intermediate pipe.
3. Remove intermediate pipe from resonator.

1968-70

1. Remove clamp securing muffler

to intermediate pipe and slide muffler off.
2. Remove clamp securing intermediate pipe to exhaust pipe.
3. Loosen lateral Y-pipe brace at transmission housing.
4. Slide intermediate pipe rearward, disengaging blade from hanger at transmission, and pipe from exhaust pipe.
5. Remove hanger blade from intermediate pipe.

1971-72

1. Raise car.
2. Remove muffler-to-intermediate pipe clamp.
3. Slide muffler off intermediate pipe.
4. Remove clamp securing intermediate pipe to exhaust pipe.

Tail Pipe Removal

On models from 1968 the tail pipe is part of the muffler assembly.

1965-67

1. Remove rearmost clamp and hanger blade.
2. Loosen or remove clamp securing tail pipe and muffler.
3. Remove clamp and hanger blade at support bracket located above rear axle.
4. Remove tail pipe from muffler.

Heat Control Valve Removal

Remove nuts securing right and left exhaust pipes to locating studs and remove heat control valve. Support muffler with jack stand.

NOTE: removal of resonator hanger at transmission may be necessary before removing valve.

Cooling System

Detailed information on cooling system capacity can be found in the Capacities table.

Information on the water temperature gauge can be found in the Unit Repair Section.

Radiator Core Removal

1965-72

1. Disconnect battery cable.
2. Drain cooling system.
3. Disconnect air conditioning compressor, if so equipped, and position out of the way without disconnecting hoses.
4. Remove clamp that holds A/C high pressure vapor line to cradle.
5. Loosen hose clamps and disconnect upper and lower radiator hoses.
6. Disconnect two transmission oil cooler lines and plug them.

NOTE: disconnect heater return hose, if so equipped.
7. Remove two top radiator cradle

clamps or straps and fan shroud. Disconnect reservoir hose from 1969.
8. Remove vacuum hoses, if so equipped. Mark for proper installation.
9. Pull radiator straight up and out of car.

Water Pump Removal

1965-67

1. Disconnect negative battery cable.
2. Drain coolant.
3. Unbolt compressor and swing out of way (A/C cars) without disconnecting hoses.
4. Remove four capscrews and fan shroud.
5. Remove two radiator cradle clamp screws and clamps. Push radiator forward far enough to gain access to fan.
6. Remove power steering pump bracket and position pump and hoses to one side.
7. Remove power steering belt and fan, pulley and fan belt.

NOTE: place A/C fans aside in installed position to prevent silicone fluid loss.
8. Remove generator - to - support bracket capscrew.
9. Disconnect water inlet and upper radiator hoses.
10. On A.I.R.-equipped cars, remove the three capscrews that hold the air pump bracket to the front engine cover. Loosen air pump adjusting bolt and bracket bolt, then remove belt.
11. Remove four capscrews that hold water outlet pipe to cylinder heads. Remove outlet pipe and discard gaskets.
12. Remove the nine remaining capscrews that hold water pump; remove pump.

1968-72

1. Disconnect negative battery cable.
2. Drain radiator and, on 1968 models, remove fan shroud.
3. Remove fan assembly. The screws cannot be removed entirely due to lack of clearance between fan and radiator. Slide loosened assembly near power steering pump to remove bolts and spacer.
4. Loosen generator mounting screws and remove generator belt.
5. Loosen power steering pump mounting screws and remove belts.
6. On 1968 models, remove A.I.R. belt.
7. Remove water pump pulley, disconnect water inlet and remove 11 screws and pump.

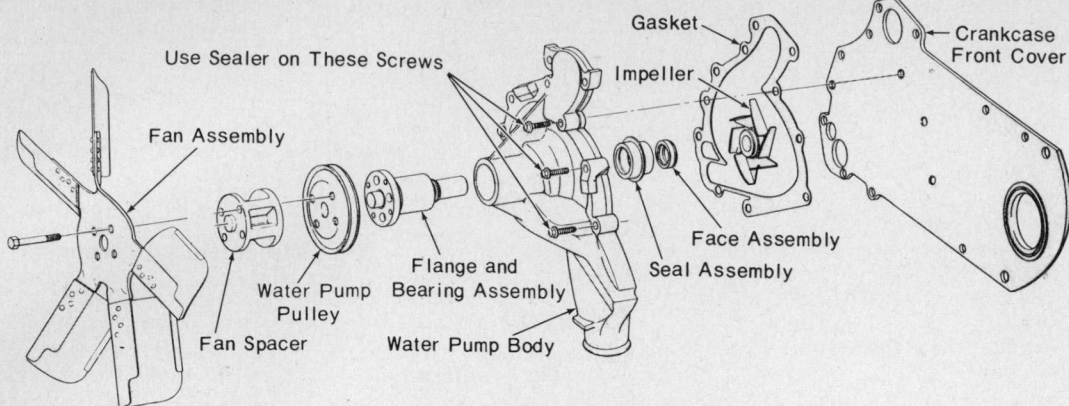

Use Sealer on These Screws　Gasket　Impeller　Crankcase Front Cover

Fan Assembly

Water Pump Pulley

Fan Spacer

Flange and Bearing Assembly

Water Pump Body

Face Assembly

Seal Assembly

Water pump—1968-72 (© Cad. Div. G.M. Corp.)

Engine

Exhaust Emission Control

In compliance with anti-pollution laws involving all of the continental United States, the Cadillac Division of General Motors has adopted as standard equipment; an integrated Air Injector Reactor emission control system. This method is designed and built into the engine castings and eliminates the need for some of the tubes and exterior air manifolding of previous plans. It does, however, use the same afterburner principle as that described in the Unit Repair Section.

The A.I.R. pump system was superceded in 1970 by the Controlled Combustion System (C.C.S), which depended on engine modifications to control exhaust emissions. This system was supplemented in 1971 by the A.I.R. system once again, due to the stricter emissions laws. An Evaporative Loss Control system was used on 1970 California cars, and all cars starting 1971, to reduce fuel vapor emission.

Any of the present methods of terminal exhaust emission control requires close and frequent attention to tune-up factors of engine maintenance.

Since 1968, all car manufacturers post idle speeds and other pertinent data relative to the specific engine-car application in a conspicuous place in the engine compartment.

Transmission Controlled Spark

On 1970 models, the T.C.S. system plays a major part in the operation of the Controlled Combustion System, which consists of a thermostatic air cleaner to regulate the temperature of incoming carburetor intake air, and the T.C.S. system. The T.C.S. system itself consists of a pressure sensitive switch in the transmission and a solenoid in the ported vacuum line between the carburetor and the thermal vacuum switch of the air cleaner. With the

transmission in first or second gear, the solenoid is energized. This eliminates vacuum advance to the distributor to reduce emissions. In third gear, the solenoid de-energizes and allows the vacuum advance to operate normally.

On the 1971-72 models, the system was modified slightly to bypass the T.C.S. solenoid in the Park and Neutral positions. The neutral switch senses when the transmission is shifted into Park or Neutral and allows distributor advance to be controlled through the Thermal Vacuum Switch, thus preventing overheating in traffic. The result is that there is spark advance at fast idle on 1971 models, no spark advance on 1970 models. See the Unit Repair Section for T.C.S. system tests.

Engine R & R

1965-67

The engine is removed together with the transmisison. Place the car on stand jacks and drain the cooling system, crankcase, and transmission. Disconnect the battery cables. Take a scribe and carefully mark the position of the hood hinges where they mount to the fender apron, and remove the hood complete with its hinge mechanism.

Disconnect the generator and remove the radiator core, fan and lower pulley. Unbolt and swing aside A/C compressor and power steering pump, without disconnecting hoses. Disconnect and remove the power brake vacuum line, the carburetor air cleaner, the carburetor and its linkage.

Remove the transmission gravel deflector and disconnect the levers and speedometer at the transmission, disconnect the fuel lines, take off the battery ground straps, the primary ignition wire, the oil pressure and cooling system temperature switch wires. Remove the ignition coil and take off the wires to the ignition resistor, disconnect the vacuum hoses to the manifold

and windshield wipers.

Split the rear universal joint and slide the driveshaft from the back of the transmission. Remove the frame intermediate support, disconnect the starter and disconnect the exhaust pipe at the exhaust manifolds. Remove the bolts that hold the front motor supports at the frame and then take off the idler arm support screws and lower the idler arm and steering connecting link. Attach a lifting device and take up the slack until the lifting device has a little load on it. Disconnect and remove the rear engine support bracket from the frame. Carefully lift the engine with its transmission out of the car.

It may be necessary to support the transmission on some sort of movable floor jack so that it can be kept in a downward position and yet guided out easily.

1968-72

1. Disconnect negative battery cable.
2. Remove hood, after scribing hood hinge outline for proper alignment.
3. Remove air cleaner and heat shroud.
4. Drain cooling system.
5. Remove radiator hose bracket, radiator cover and fan.
6. Remove upper radiator hose.
7. Disconnect throttle and Cruise Control linkage at carburetor.
8. Remove Cruise Control power unit on cars so equipped.
9. Disconnect power steering pump bracket and swing pump out of way with hoses still connected. Position power steering fluid cooler out of the way.
10. Remove A/C compressor bracket bolts and swing compressor out of way with hoses still connected.
11. Disconnect temperature sender wire, idle speed-up wire (if so equipped), ignition primary wire, downshift switch wire, T.C.S. solenoid and anti-dieseling solenoid wires, and all

12. Bend back clips and position wiring harness out of the way.
13. Disconnect all vacuum hoses, and purge hose from E.L.C. canister.
14. Disconnect alternator, heater switch and oil pressure sender wires.
15. Remove wiring harness from clips.
16. Remove water hose from fitting at rear of right-hand cylinder head.

NOTE: on A/C cars up to 1969, remove blower relay, power servo, and master switch from heater air selector.

17. Loosen and remove alternator and A.I.R. pumps and remove belts.
18. Disconnect tie struts and swing out of the way.
19. Remove upper two transmission-to-engine bolts. Remove two screws that secure right air deflector to lower radiator cradle.
20. Jack up car and support on axle stands.
21. Remove starter motor, then disconnect exhaust pipes from manifolds.
22. Remove front engine mount bolts, then disconnect and plug vapor return line at fuel pump (A/C cars only) and fuel inlet line. Remove oil filter, after draining engine oil.
23. Disconnect lower radiator hose and remove flywheel housing cover.
24. Remove the three screws that secure flex plate to converter. Engine must be rotated for access—a 1962 crankshaft balancer bolt works well.
25. Remove four transmission-to-engine bolts.
26. Lower the car to the ground.
27. Connect a lifting bracket to the engine.
28. Support transmission with a wood-padded floor jack.
29. Raise engine slightly and pull forward to disengage from transmission, then pull engine up and out.

Engine Manifolds

Exhaust Manifold Removal

To remove either of the exhaust manifolds, detach the manifold at the exhaust pipe flange and, in the case of the right manifold, remove the generator and then remove the bolts that hold the manifold to the cylinder head.

On some models, particularly those with heater ducts, access is easier from underneath the car.

However, they can be reached if the air intake ducts of the heater system are detached at both ends.

Intake Manifold Removal

Remove throttle linkage, gas and vacuum lines and the carburetor.

Take off the ignition wires, unbolt and lift off the manifold.

NOTE: on cars with air conditioning, partial removal of compressor is necessary. Do not disconnect compressor hoses.

Cylinder Head

Rocker Shaft Removal

1965-66

The rocker shafts can be removed and serviced without disturbing the cylinder head or manifolds.

Get the spark plug wires out of the way, remove whatever heater or throttle linkage passes over the rocker cover, and then unbolt and remove the rocker cover.

The rocker shafts are held on brackets; the bolts for these do not pass through the cylinder head. These bracket bolts hold the brackets to the head but do not hold the head on.

Unbolt and remove the rocker shafts, being careful to replace them on the head from which they were

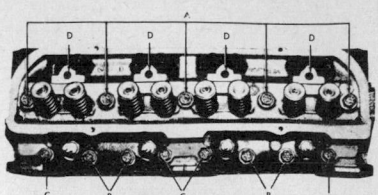

Cylinder head bolt location and length—1965-67
(© Cadillac Div., G.M. Corp.)

removed. If new rockers and/or shafts are to be installed, note the relative position the rocker occupies on the shaft. Then, if a new rocker is installed toward the center of the shaft, the balance of the rockers will be put on in the proper order, having the correct springs between the rockers.

Thoroughly, clean the rocker springs and shafts before reinstalling.

The push rods can be pulled directly up through the cylinder heads for examination to make sure that they are straight and not badly worn at either end.

Reinstall the rockers, reversing the removal procedure. The larger machined surface on the rocker bracket goes down. The little notch in the forward end of the rocker shaft points toward the camshaft.

1967-72

Valve rocker arms are no longer fitted to one common shaft per head; they are mounted in pairs (four pairs to each cylinder head). They are of the modified pedestal-mounted type.

Rocker arms may be removed in pairs and do not require cylinder-head removal.

Torque rocker arm mounting screws to 60 ft. lbs.

Cylinder Head Removal and Installation

Service Note

Care must be used when replacing cylinder-head bolts. They are of dif-

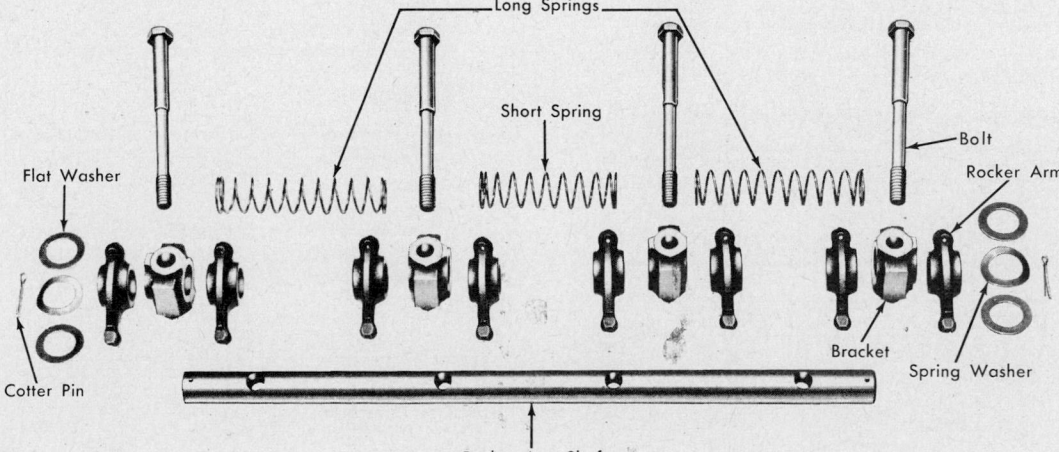

Long Springs

Short Spring

Flat Washer

Bolt

Rocker Arm

Cotter Pin

Bracket

Spring Washer

Rocker Arm Shaft

1967-72 rocker arm (© Cadillac Div., G.M. Corp.)

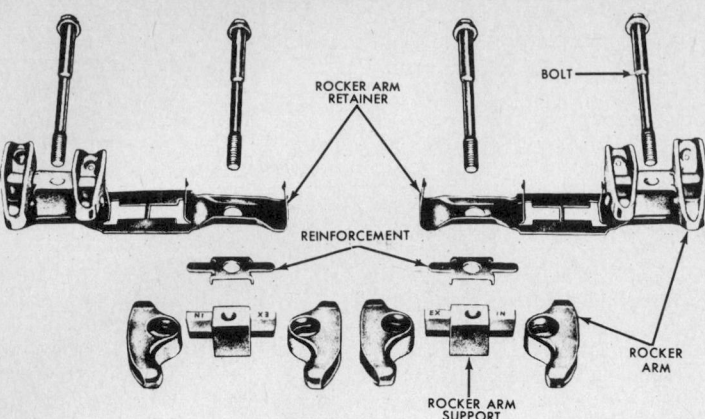

V8 472 cu. in. rocker arm (© Cadillac Div. G.M. Corp.)

ferent lengths.

1965-67

1. Disconnect the water manifold at the front of the cylinder head or heads. It is a good idea to remove the water pump and water manifold from the car. It is difficult to reinstall a cylinder head with the water pump in place on one head without damaging the water pump gasket.
2. Remove all vacuum lines and carburetor connections; disconnect all ignition, throttle and battery connections.
3. Take off the intake manifold with the carburetor in place or if desired remove the carburetor.
4. Remove the rocker covers.
NOTE: it is customary to remove the rocker covers together with the ignition wires and distributor cap as a unit unless service is to be done on the distributor.
5. Remove the generator if the right cylinder head is to be removed. The exhaust manifolds

may be disconnected either from the head or from the flange connection to the exhaust pipe. It is better to leave them connected to the head.
6. Remove the head bolts that hold the rocker assemblies to the cylinder head and lift off the rocker assemblies.
7. Remove the pushrods.
8. Remove the balance of the cylinder attaching bolts and lift the head off. It is very important that the head be handled carefully so as not to damage or mark the head gasket surface.
9. Installation is the reverse of the above.

1968-72

1. Remove intake manifold.
2. Drain engine coolant.
3. Disconnect ground strap at rear of cylinder heads from cowl. Disconnect wiring connector for high engine temperature warning system from sending unit at rear of left cylinder head.

4. Remove generator, if working on the right cylinder head, or partially remove the steering pump if working on the left head.
5. Disconnect A.I.R. injection pump tubes from cylinder heads.
6. Remove clamps holding the wire harness to the cylinder heads and tie harness back out of the way.
7. Remove screws holding exhaust manifolds to cylinder heads.
8. Remove screws holding the rocker arm cover to the heads.
9. Remove cover.
10. Remove screws holding each rocker arm support to cylinder head, then remove rocker arm assemblies. Store these assemblies so that they may be reinstalled in their correct locations.
11. Remove pushrods and store them with their respective rocker arm assemblies.
12. Install two 7/16 x 6 in. screws to be used as lifting handles in two of the rocker arm support screw holes.
13. Remove ten cylinder-head bolts.
14. Lift cylinder head off the block.
15. Remove all gasket material from the cylinder head and block mating surfaces.
16. Install by reversing removal procedures.

Pistons, Connecting Rods and Main Bearings

Piston and Rod Removal

Rod and piston assemblies on all models are removed through the top of the block.

It is possible to replace any and all of the rod or main bearings from un-

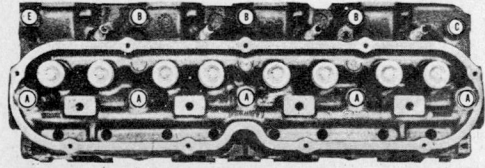

Bolt Location	Length
A (Bolt)	4.36''
B (Bolt)	4.77''
C (Bolt)	3.02''
D (Bolt/Stud)	3.02''
E (Bolt/Stud)	4.77''

Cylinder head bolt location and length—1968

FRONT OF ENGINE

Bolt Location	Length
A (Bolt)	4.36''
B (Bolt)	4.77''
C (Bolt)	3.02''

Cylinder head bolt location and length—1969

"B" on Eldorado Only

Cylinder head bolt location and length—
1970-72

Bolt Location	Length (in.)
A	4.36
B	4.77
C	3.02
D	4.77

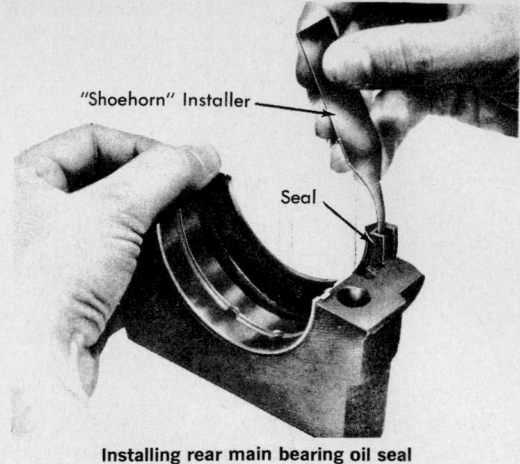

"Shoehorn" Installer

Seal

Installing rear main bearing oil seal
(© Cad. Div. G.M. Corp.)

derneath the car without removing the crankshaft.

Clean out carbon from top of cylinder bore and ream off the ridge at the top of the bore. This will prevent breakage of the piston ring lands. Push the piston and rod assemblies up and out of the tops of the cylinders. Be careful not to nick the lower edge of the bores.

Assembling Rod and Piston Assemblies to the Block

The numbers on the connecting rods face away from the camshaft; that is, the numbers on the left bank (odd numbers up to 1967, even from 1968) face to the left; the numbers on the right bank (even numbers up to 1967, odd from 1968) face to the right. As a double check, the word *rear*, (or "R"), stamped on the piston, faces the rear of the engine on both banks and an arrow on the piston top points to the front of the engine.

Rear Main Bearing Oil Seal Replacement

1. Remove the oil pan, after removing spark plug wires and plugs.
2. Remove the rear main bearing cap and loosen the bolts holding the other four bearings about three turns each. Remove the old rear main bearing seals.
3. Clean the groove in the cap and in the block. Lubricate seals with engine oil.

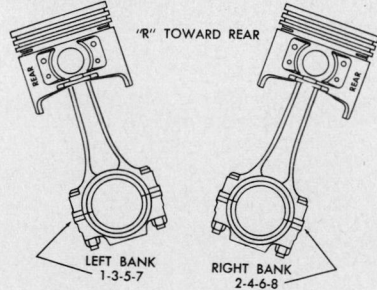

"R" TOWARD REAR

LEFT BANK
1-3-5-7

RIGHT BANK
2-4-6-8

Piston to connecting rod relationship

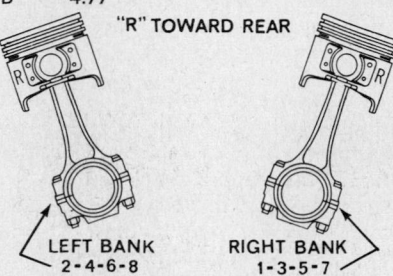

"R" TOWARD REAR

LEFT BANK
2-4-6-8

RIGHT BANK
1-3-5-7

**Piston to connecting rod relationship—
1965-67**

4. Make an installation tool, as illustrated.
5. Start the upper half into the groove in the block with the lip facing forward and rotate it into position, using the tool as a guide. Press firmly on both ends to be sure it is protruding uniformly on each side.
6. Install the lower half of the seal into the bearing cap with the lip facing forward and one end of the seal over the ridge and flush with the split line. Hold one finger over this end to prevent it from slipping, and push the seal into seated position by applying pressure to the other end. Be sure the seal is firmly seated and protrudes evenly on each side. Do not apply pressure to the lip. This may damage the effectiveness of the seal.
7. Apply rubber cement to the mating surfaces of the block and cap being careful not to get any cement on the bearing, the crankshaft or the seal. The cement coating should be about .010 in. thick.
8. Install the bearing cap, tightening the bolts with the fingers only.
9. Move the crankshaft forward and rearward by pounding on the counterweight with a plastic hammer to assure alignment of the rear main bearing thrust surfaces.
10. Tighten the bearing bolts to 90-100 ft. lbs. Be sure to tighten the bolts of the other four bearings

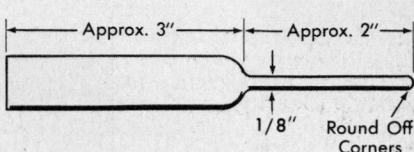

Approx. 3"   Approx. 2"

1/8"   Round Off Corners

Rear main bearing oil seal installation tool
(© Cad. Div. G.M. Corp.)

also.
11. Reinstall the oil pan.

Valve System

Checking Valve Guides

Check valve stem to guide clearance using a 1/16 in. wide strip of .005 in. shim stock. Bend the end of the shim and hang in the valve guide on the pushrod side. Shim should not extend more than ¼ in. into the guide. If the valve stem will enter the guide, the clearance is excessive.

Valve Guide Replacement

1965-67

Make a pile of washers equal to the projection of the valve guide, and set aside. Drive out valve guides from the bottom side of the cylinder head.

Using an installer or suitable driver, with the pile of washers, lubricate outer surface of the guide and start it into the head. Enter the longest taper first, pointing toward the rocker arm side.

Press guide into head until the installer contacts the plate or the piston end of the guide is flush with the pile of washers.

1968-72

The valve guides are cast integrally with the cylinder head. For excessive clearance between valve stem and guide, service valves are available with oversize stems (.003-.006-.013 in.). Guides must be reamed to compensate for these oversize stems.

Valve Lifter Removal

Lifters may be removed without taking off the cylinder head.

Remove throttle and gas lines from the carburetor, disconnect hoses, vacuum lines and wires that pass over the rocker covers. Remove the distributor cap and disconnect the wires at the spark plugs. Remove the bolts that hold the rocker covers to the cylinder head and lift off the rocker covers leaving the spark plug wires attached to them. Remove the bolts that hold the intake manifold to the cylinder block and lift off the intake manifold. If desired, the carburetor can be detached from the manifold first, but this is not necessary. Remove the valve chamber cover plate. Remove the bolts that hold the rocker shafts to the cylinder head and lift off the rocker shafts. Pull the pushrods up through the holes in the cylinder heads, and the lifters can be pulled up out of their bores.

Sometimes gum residue forms on the bottom of the lifter, making it very difficult to pull the lifter up out of its bore. If this condition is suspected before the job is started, put a good solvent in the engine oil and run the engine for the time specified by the manufacturer of the solvent in order to dissolve the gum.

However, even when gum is present on the bottom of the lifter body, the lifter can be pulled up out of its bore using special pliers. These pliers are designed to grip the lifter firmly, without scoring or scratching it.

If a special tool isn't available, a good substitute can be made by grinding the teeth out of an ordinary pair of pliers and grinding a circle almost the size of the valve lifter body. When the pliers are squeezed down on the lifter body, it will contact a large surface, thus preventing scoring.

Timing Case Cover—Chains and Sprockets

Timing Chain and Sprocket Removal

1965-67

1. Disconnect battery and remove carburetor air cleaner.
2. Drain coolant from engine cooling system.
3. Drain oil and remove engine oil pan.
4. Remove upper radiator hose.
5. Remove fan blade assembly, spacer and pulley.
   NOTE: where air conditioning is involved, partially remove the compressor. Remove the compressor belt, then, remove the radiator fan shroud.
6. Remove power steering pump belt, generator belt and pulley.
7. Remove lower radiator hose.
8. Without disconnecting the hoses, remove the power steering pump bracket from the cylinder block.

Position bracket out of the way.
9. Detach the generator support bracket from the cylinder-head water-outlet pipe and position the bracket out of the way.
10. Remove distributor assembly.
11. Remove fuel pump.
12. Remove four of the six cap screws that attach the crankshaft pulley to the harmonic balancer.
13. Remove cork plug from end of crankshaft, and install balancer puller pilot, J-21052-4 or equivalent in one bore in the end of the crankshaft.
14. Install puller base, J-21052-1 or

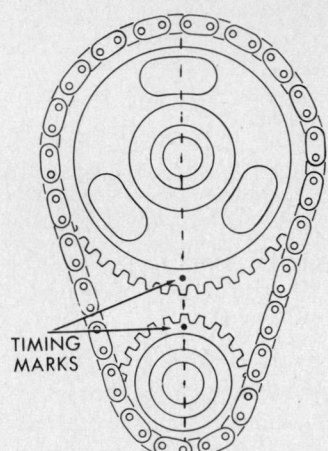

Timing location marks

equivalent on front of pulley, lining up index mark on puller base with key slot in harmonic balancer, and install attaching screws. Do not tighten screws.
15. Tighten puller screw to remove balancer. Remove pilot from end of crankshaft.
   NOTE: on engines equipped with an Air Injector Reactor System, remove the air pump and bracket assembly and swing it out of the way.
16. Remove oil filter from oil pump cover assembly.
17. Remove the four cap screws that hold the cylinder-head water-outlet pipe to cylinder heads and remove the outlet pipe.
18. Remove remaining cap screws that attach the front cover to the cylinder block and remove the cover with water pump attached.
19. Align the two sprocket timing marks, then, remove the two camshaft sprocket attaching screws.
20. Remove camshaft sprocket, with chain, from camshaft.
21. Remove crankshaft sprocket.
22. To assemble, reverse the above procedure.

1968-72

1. Disconnect negative battery cable and drain cooling system.
2. Detach upper radiator hose re-

WATER PUMP

DOWEL HOLES

WATER INLET PIPE

Key	No.	Size	Torque
A	(4)	1/4 -20 x 1-1/4	5 Foot-Pounds
B	(3)	3/8 -16 x 3-4/8	20 Foot-Pounds
C	(2)	5/16-18 x 3-1/4	10 Foot-Pounds
D	(1)	3/8 -16 x 5	20 Foot-Pounds
E	(1)	1/4 -20 x 2-1/4	5 Foot-Pounds

Front cover installation—1965-67
(© Cad. Div. G.M. Corp.)

tainer from cradle and position hose out of the way.

3. Remove fan, generator belt and power steering belts.

4. Remove four capscrews that secure crank pulley to harmonic balancer, then remove both pulley and balancer.

5. Remove plug from end of crankshaft, then install a puller as in Step 13 of earlier procedure and remove balancer hub from end of crank.

6. Drain engine oil and remove oil pan.

7. Disconnect lower radiator hose from water pump, then remove the ten screws that hold front cover to engine. Remove cover with water pump attached.

8. Remove distributor and fuel pump.

9. Remove oil slinger and fuel pump eccentric.

10. Remove two capscrews that secure camshaft sprocket.

11. Remove camshaft sprocket along with timing chain.

12. To install, reverse removal procedure.

Valve Timing Procedure

The chain and sprocket assembly used on all Cadillac models is such that, unless deliberately disturbed, the valve timing will remain as set by the factory, unless the chain and sprockets or both are badly worn or damaged.

Mount the timing chain over the camshaft and the crankshaft sprocket and start the camshaft sprocket over the shaft, being certain the aligning dowel is in a position where it will enter the hole in the camshaft freely. Make certain that the timing marks on the sprockets are in line between shaft centers.

Camshaft sprockets sometimes install a little stiffly. However, a comparatively easy way to install a tight-fitting sprocket is to draw it on carefully with two bolts somewhat longer than the regular mounting bolts. By drawing alternately against each bolt, and tapping gently with a plastic hammer, even a very tight camshaft gear sprocket can be installed.

When the camshaft is secured, turn the engine two full revolutions until the timing marks again assume the original position. Check to make certain that the punch marks, which are little round circles stamped into the front face of the sprockets, are in line between the shaft centers. See illustration.

Timing Case Cover Oil Seal

1965-72

These cars are equipped with a molded-type front cover crankshaft oil seal. The seal may be replaced

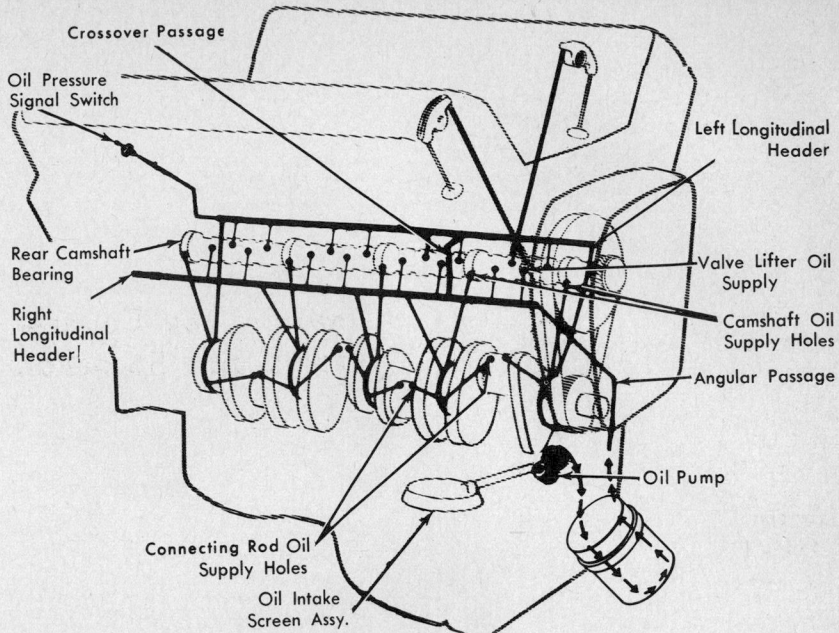

Engine oiling system—1969-72

without removing the engine front cover.

1. Disconnect the battery and remove carburetor air cleaner.

2. Remove power steering pump drive belt.

3. Remove generator drive belt.

4. On air conditioned cars, and cars equipped with the A.I.R. system, remove the pump drive belts.

5. Raise and support the front of the car stands. On 1968 to present cars, it will be necessary to remove the fan.

6. Remove pulley and harmonic bal-

ancer, as outlined in Timing Chain and Sprocket Removal.

7. With a thin blade screwdriver, pry out front cover oil seal.

8. Lubricate new dual-lip oil seal with wheel bearing grease. Position seal on end of crankshaft with garter spring side toward engine.

9. Using seal installer and adapter cover until it bottoms.

10. Assemble and install the remaining parts in reverse order of disassembly.

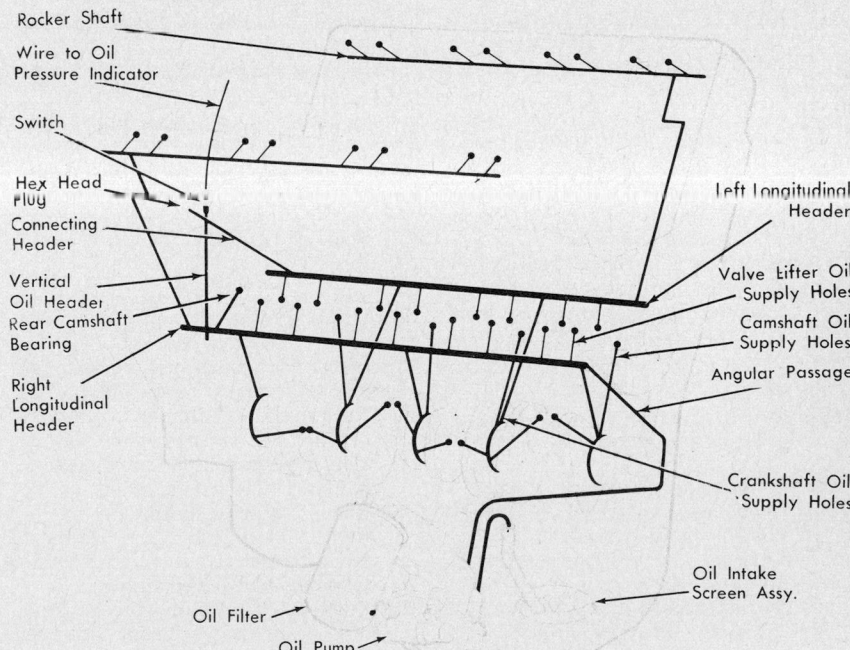

Engine oiling system—1965-68 (© Cadillac Div. G.M. Corp.)

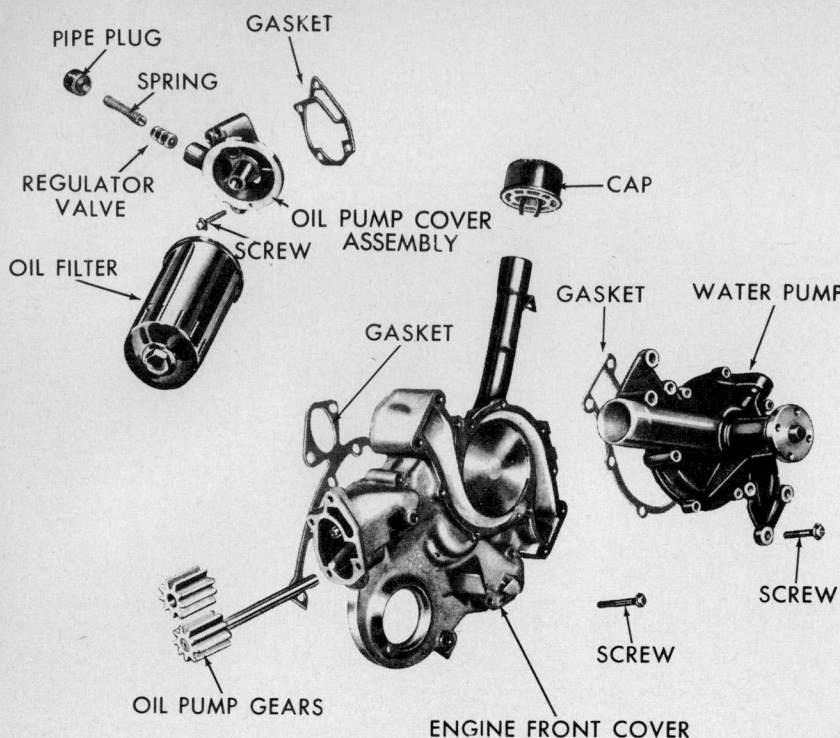

Engine front cover disassembled (© Cadillac Div. G.M. Corp.)

Engine Lubrication

Oil Pump Service

Removal, Inspection, Installation —1965-67

1. Remove engine front cover.
2. Remove four capscrews that secure pump cover plate to housing.
3. Remove cover plate, making sure pump gears do not fall out.
4. Slide drive shaft and gear out of housing.
5. Slide driven gear out of housing.
6. Remove hex plug from pump cover plate and remove pressure regulator spring and valve.
7. Inspect gears for burrs or scoring, as well as housing.
8. Check free length of regulator spring—it should be 2.77-2.89 in.
9. Check pump clearance limits.
10. Assembly and installation is the reverse of disassembly and removal.

Removal, Inspection, Installation —1968-72

1. Jack up car and remove oil filter.
2. Remove five capscrews that secure oil pump to engine.
 NOTE: remove screw nearest pressure regulator last.
3. Slide drive shaft, drive gear and driven gear out of housing.
4. Remove plug from housing cover, using 5/16 in. wrench. Remove pressure regulator valve and spring.

5. Check free length of regulator spring—it should be 2.77-2.89 in. for 1968 models, 2.57-2.69 in. from 1969 models.
6. Inspect gears and housing for burrs or scoring.
7. Check pump clearance limits.
8. Assembly, and installation is the reverse of disassembly and removal.

Oil Pump Specifications

Backlash between drive gears, 0.008-0.012 in.
Clearance between body and shaft not to exceed 0.005 in.
Clearance between body and gears not to exceed 0.005 in.
Gear end-play not to exceed 0.006 in.

Oil Pan Removal

1965-72

1. Drain engine oil and disconnect positive battery cable.
2. Disconnect exhaust crossover pipe at exhaust manifold.
3. Disconnect exhaust support bracket at transmission extension housing, and position exhaust system to one side.
4. Remove starter motor.
5. Remove two idler arm support mounting screws from frame side member, and lower support.
6. Disconnect pitman arm at drag link, and lower steering linkage.
7. Remove transmission lower cover.
8. Remove engine oil pan.
9. When reinstalling, reverse above

procedure and torque oil pan screws and nuts to 10 ft. lbs.

Jacking, Hoisting

1965-72

When jacking under front suspension arms, make sure lift is made from point outboard of the support plates on lower arms.

When lifting on frame area, make sure of solid contact at the corners of the perimeter frame offset close to the bend at front and rear areas.

Front Suspension

General instructions covering the front suspension, together with information on bearings and grease seals, are given in the Unit Repair Section.

Lower Control Arm and Coil Spring R & R

1. Disconnect front shock at its upper mount.
2. Raise car and support under front frame side rails.
3. Remove wheel and tire assembly.
4. Disconnect stabilizer link from lower arm or spring to be removed.
5. Disconnect tie-strut at lower arm.
6. Remove bolt holding shock to lower arm, and remove shock from car.
7. Remove nut from pivot bolt in lower arm at frame mount.
8. Position jack under outboard end of lower suspension arm so that jack is supporting the arm.
9. Remove locknut from lower ball joint stud. Install standard nut on joint stud and run nut to within two threads of knuckle.
10. Strike knuckle with a hammer in area of ball joint stud to loosen the joint. Raising the opposite rear corner of the car will help compress the spring and assist in removing the joint stud from the knuckle.
11. Use jack to lift spring load from nut and remove nut from joint stud.
12. Slowly lower jack and remove spring.
13. Remove pivot bolt from lower arm at frame mount and remove the arm.
14. Install by reversing the removal procedure.

Lower Ball Joint R & R

1. Follow Steps 1-12 of *Lower Con-*

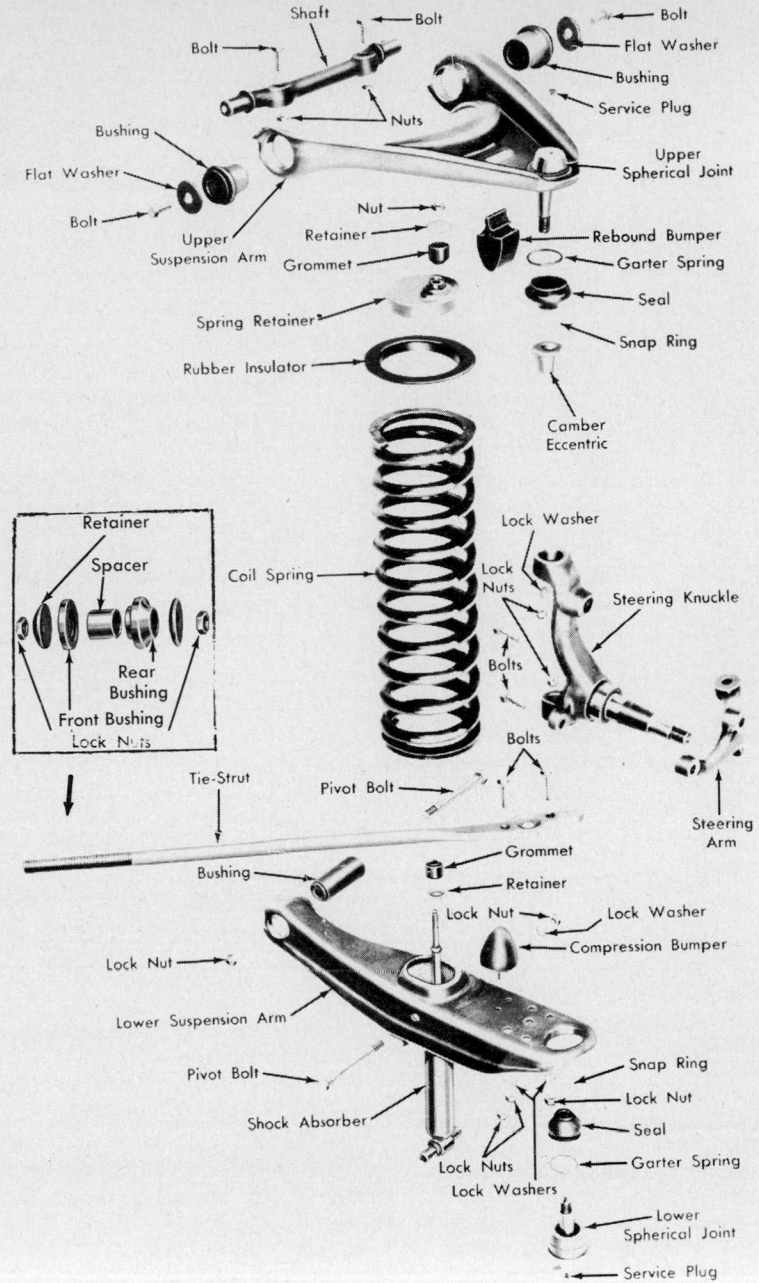

Typical front suspension—1965-70 © Cadillac Div., G.M. Corp.)

trol Arm and Coil Spring R&R.

2. Remove band and seal from ball joint.
3. If ball joint vertical movement exceeds 1/16 in. (.062 in.), press old ball joint out of lower control arm, using press tool.
4. Press new joint into arm until it bottoms on flange, using standard nut and flat washer to pull joint into position.
5. Reverse Steps 1-12 of *Lower Control Arm and Coil Spring* tightening stud nut to 85 ft. lbs.

Upper Ball Joint R & R

1. Jack up front of car and support on axle stands under coil springs.
2. Remove wheel and tire assembly.

3. Loosen upper ball joint locknut.
4. Matchmark camber eccentric and steering knuckle for proper alignment.
5. Strike steering knuckle near upper joint until joint taper is free.
6. Remove locknut, then remove camber eccentric using a puller.
7. Clean ball joint and install another nut on top of the reinstalled locknut. Turn the joint using a torque wrench. If torque exceeds or is less than 2-4 ft. lbs., the entire upper control arm with integral ball joint must replace as an assembly.
8. To install, reverse removal procedure. Tighten locknut on stud of ball joint to 60 ft. lbs.

NOTE: use a standard 1/2-20 nut and washer to pull camber eccentric into position.

Steering Gear

Power Steering Gear

Troubleshooting and repair instructions covering power steering gears are given in the Unit Repair Section. The 1965 Cadillac, and all 1965-72 Fleetwood 75 and Commercial models, uses a constant ratio power steering unit (17.5:1). All other models from 1966 use a variable ratio steering unit (16:1 on center, 11.5:1 at full lock for 1966-67 models; 16:1 on center, 12.2:1 at full lock from 1968).

NOTE: for power steering pump belt adjustment, loosen pump to mounting bracket screws, move pump upward until belt is tight. Tighten mounting bracket screws with car in neutral and engine running faster than idle speed, turn steering wheel full right or left. If belt squeals, it is too loose and should be tightened more.

Horn Ring and Steering Wheel Removal

Remove the screws on the underside of the steering wheel spokes near the center and remove the pad assembly.

Remove the nut holding the steering wheel to the steering shaft.

On tilt wheels, remove locking lever and flange and screw assembly. On all models, disconnect horn contact wire.

Use a puller to remove the steering wheel. Note the match-marking of the shaft and wheel.

When reinstalling, tighten nut to 30-35 ft. lbs. for 1965-70 models, 20 ft. lbs. for 1971-72 models.

Steering Linkage Removal and Disassembly

1. Remove cotter pins and nuts from outer tie-rod pivots.
2. Remove outer tie rod pivots from steering knuckles using tie-rod end puller.
3. Remove idler arm screws and lockwashers from side member.
4. Remove pitman arm cotter pin, nut and washer at steering linkage.
5. Remove steering linkage from pitman arm.
6. Remove drag link with tie-rods and idler arm attached.
7. Remove cotter pins and nuts from idler arm pivot and inner tie-rod pivots.
8. Remove tie-rod.
9. Remove idler arm from drag link.
10. Remove dust seals from pitman arm and idler arm pivot studs.

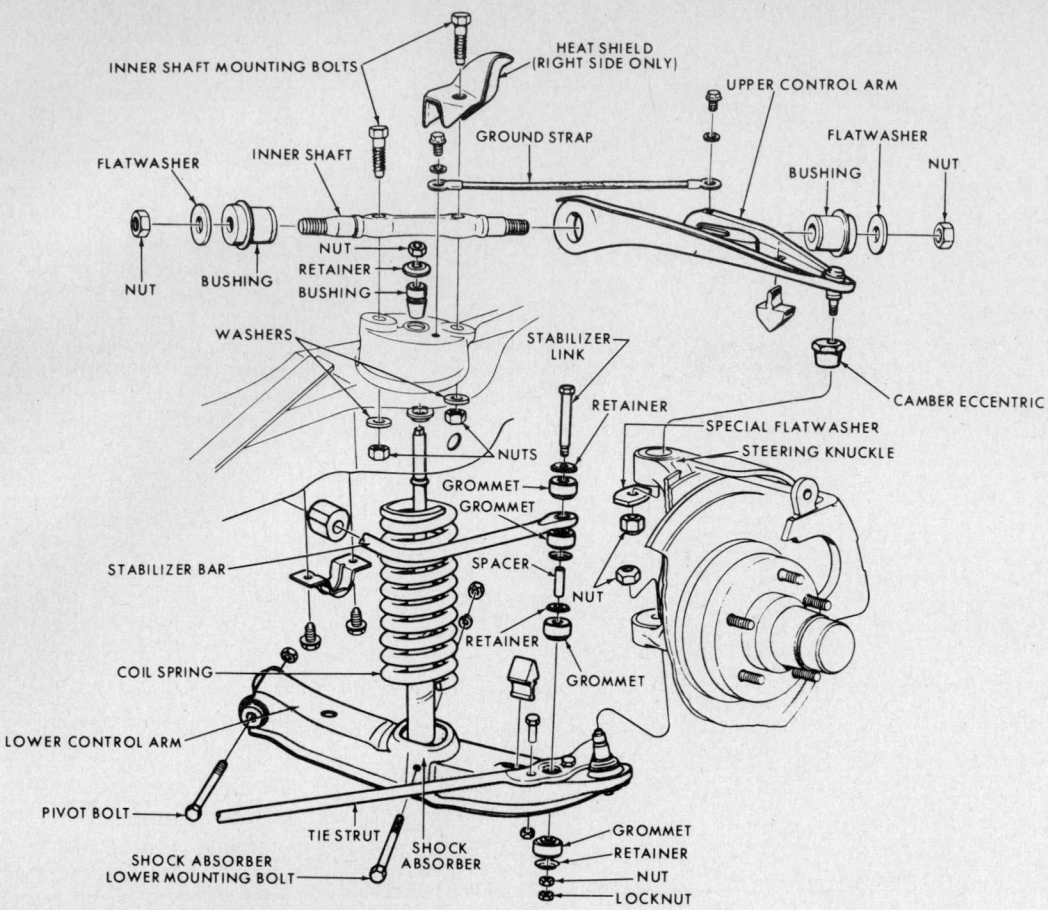

Front suspension—1971-72 (© Cad. Div. G.M. Corp.)

11. Remove outer tie-rod pivots by loosening nuts on outer clamp bolts and unscrewing the pivots from adjuster tubes.
12. To install, reverse removal procedure.

Steering Gear Assembly Removal and Installation

1. Remove pump reservoir cover and siphon out all fluid.
2. Disconnect the hoses at gear box and cap.
3. Support front end of car on stand jacks near outer end of lower suspension arms. (At frame side members if air suspended.)
4. Disconnect flexible coupling connecting gear to upper steering shaft.
5. Disconnect pitman arm from drag link.
6. Remove screws holding gear assembly to frame and so release gear assembly from car.
7. When reinstalling, tighten the flexible coupling bolts to 25-30 ft. lbs. Reconnect the pitman arm to the drag link and tighten to 60 ft. lbs.
8. Reconnect hoses. Bleed steering pump and check fluid level.

Pitman Shaft Seal Replacement (with Steering Gear in Place in Car)

NOTE: this procedure is recommended only for 1965 and 1971-72 models. Cadillac does not recommend this for 1966-70 due to clearance

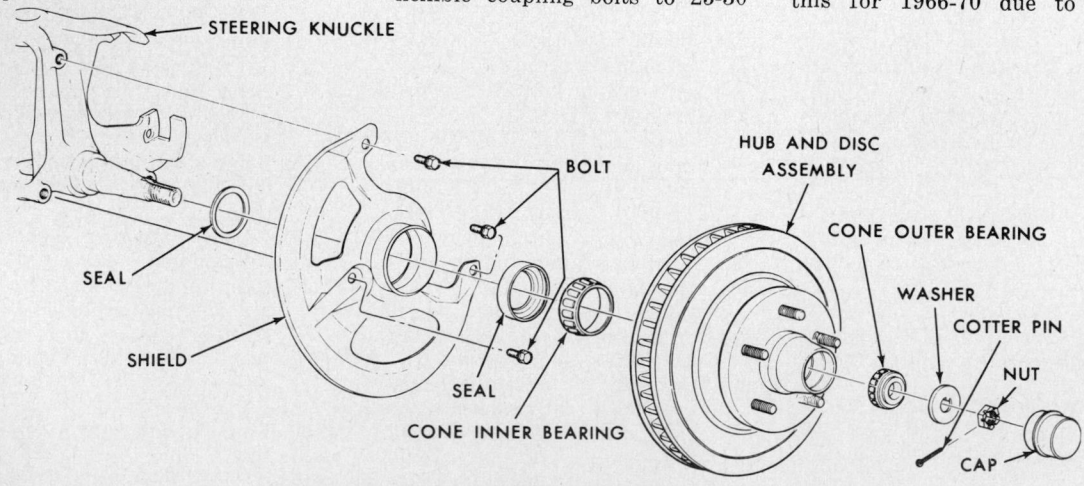

Hub and wheel bearing assembly—1971-72 (© Cad. Div. G.M. Corp.)

problems; remove steering gear from car and remove old seal with a screwdriver for these models.

1. Disconnect pitman arm from pitman shaft. Clean end of pitman shaft and housing. Tape the splines of the pitman shaft to keep them from cutting the seal. Use only one layer of tape. Too much tape will prevent passage of the seal. Using lock ring pliers remove the seal retaining ring.

2. Start the engine and turn the steering wheel to the left so that the oil pressure in the housing will force the seals out. Catch the seal and the oil in a container. Turn off the engine when the two seals are out. This method of seal removal eliminates the possible scoring of the seal seats while attempting to pry them out.

3. Inspect the two old seals for damage to the rubber covering on the outside diameter. If they are scored or scratched, inspect the housing for burrs, etc. and remove them before installing the new seals.

4. Lubricate the two new seals with petroleum jelly. Put the one with a single lip in first, then put in a washer. Drive seal in far enough to permit installation of double lip seal, washer and the seal retaining ring. The first seal is not supposed to bottom in its counterbore.

5. Fill reservoir to proper level, start engine, turn wheel to right and check for leaks.

6. Remove the tape and reinstall the pitman arm. Tighten nut to 115 ft. lbs. for 1965-66, 140 ft. lbs for 1967-69, and 185 ft. lbs. for 1970-72.

Automatic Transmission

When automatic transmission trouble is reported, a road test and careful diagnosis are in order. Transmission Removal and Replacement and Linkage Adjustments are covered here. For test procedures, transmission overhaul and other detailed information, see Unit Repair Section.

Neutral Safety Switch, All Models

NOTE: switch is on steering column under dash.

1. Check that the hand lever is correctly adjusted and that the neutral safety switch is properly positioned by this procedure.

2. Set the handbrake. Put the hand lever on the steering column in drive. Hold the ignition key on and slowly move the hand lever toward Neutral or Park until the starter cranks and the engine runs.

3. Without moving the lever farther, press the accelerator to determine whether the transmission is really in Neutral or Park.

4. If all is correct, the engine will have started when the hand lever got to the neutral position and the transmission will not be in gear. Also, back-up lights will go on with transmission in Reverse.

NOTE: a vacuum leak that can be corrected by moving shift lever is an indication that the switch only needs adjustment and is not defective.

5. Adjust the neutral safety switch by turning it and its mounting bracket until the above conditions are met.

Turbo Hydramatic

Removal and Installation—1965-72

1. Disconnect negative battery cable.

2. Jack up car and place on axle stands at front and rear.

NOTE: on 1965 Fleetwood 75 and Commercial, remove yaw bumpers and intermediate cross-member.

3. Disconnect relay rod from trunnion lever and wire relay rod out of the way.

4. Remove two screws and bearing assembly from frame side rail.

5. Disconnect trunnion from manual yoke on left side of transmission.

6. Disconnect speedometer cable and electrical wires or harness.

7. Remove transmission oil filler tube bracket screw.

8. Remove filler tube from transmission and plug hole.

9. Disconnect oil cooler lines at transmission, using a crowsfoot wrench and a long extension. Cap lines and plug holes to prevent entry of dirt.

10. Disconnect vacuum hose from modulator and wire it out of the way.

11. Remove resonator support bracket from extension housing.

12. Remove driveshaft, as described later in this section.

13. Remove starter motor, lower flywheel housing inspection cover and two engine-to-transmission struts.

14. Remove three converter-to-flex plate bolts. *Do not pry on ring gear to rotate engine.*

15. Place a wood-padded floor jack under rear of engine for support.

16. Place a transmission jack under transmission and raise slightly to unload rear engine mount.

17. Remove two bolts that secure rear mount to transmission.

18. Remove two bolts per side that secure rear mount to frame, then remove mount.

19. Remove six transmission-to-engine capscrews, lowering engine slightly to gain access to upper screws.

20. Disengage transmission from engine, being careful that the now unsupported converter does not fall out. Use of a piece of strap iron across converter face, bolted to bellhousing, is recommended.

21. To install, reverse removal procedure, using the following flex plate installation method to prevent transmission damage:

   a. Rotate converter until two of the three weld nuts line up with two bolt holes in flex plate, and so that weld nuts are flush with plate. Make sure converter is not cocked and that the converter pilot is properly seated in rear of crank.

   b. Install two attaching bolts through the accessible holes and tighten them to 28 ft. lbs. This is necessary to ensure proper converter alignment.

   c. Insert a screwdriver under converter weld nut and rotate converter and flex plate until third bolt can be installed. Tighten this bolt to 28 ft. lbs.

22. Transmission-to-engine bolts are torqued to 50 ft. lbs. for 1965 models, 30 ft. lbs. for 1966-72 models.

Manual Linkage Adjustment

1. Loosen nut on steering column manual lever.

2. Pull relay rod up, positioning transmission shift valve in Park, then push rod down to the third or Neutral step.

3. Position selector lever in Neutral.

4. Tighten nut on steering column manual lever.

5. Check that positions selected on selector lever correspond with appropriate detents on transmission.

U Joints, Drive Lines

Universal joints and drive lines can be divided into three groups: single-shaft models, two-piece shaft models (except Commercial after 1969), and two-piece shaft models (Commercial up to 1969).

Single-Piece Type

Two constant velocity universal

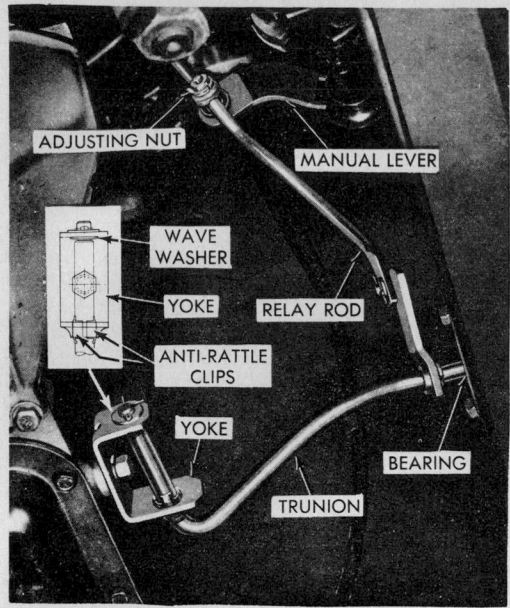

Manual linkage adjustment—1965-68
(© Cadillac Div. G.M. Corp.)

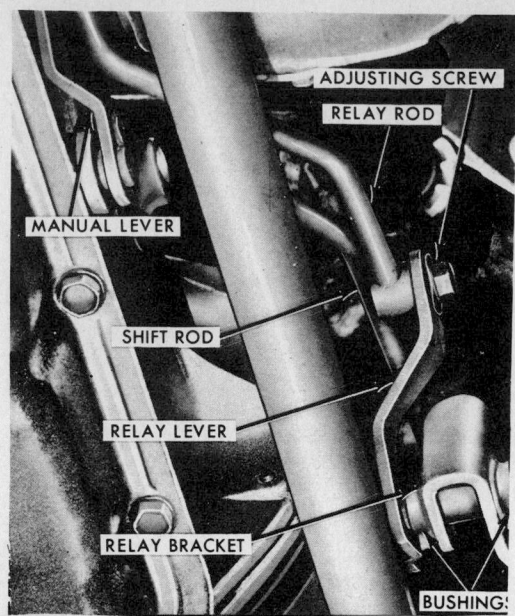

Manual linkage adjustment—1969
(© Cadillac Div. G.M. Corp.)

joints are used on the single-shaft type: one at the front, and one at the rear. This type propeller shaft is serviced as a complete assembly.

Two-Piece-Shaft Type— Except 1965-69 Commercial Models and 1965 Fleetwood 75

The two-piece propeller shaft uses three constant velocity universal joints are located at each end and at the approximate center of the shaft assembly. This shaft is used on 1970 up, Commercial models in addition to Fleetwood 75 models.

At the front end of the rear section of the propeller shaft is a splined male slip yoke that fits into a splined

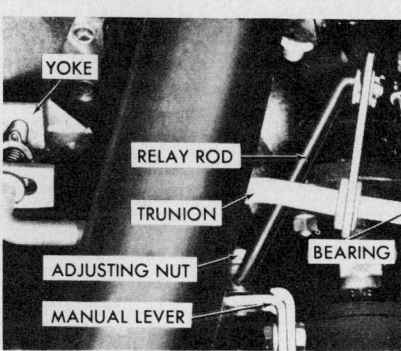

Manual linkage adjustment—1970-72
(© Cadillac Div., G.M. Corp.)

coupling in the rear end of the front section of the front shaft. This slip spline satisfies the normal lengthening and shortening of the propeller shaft due to road conditions and rear axle movement.

The propeller shaft assembly is attached to the transmission by means of a slip yoke, and to the differential drive pinion by a double flange connection. The propeller shaft assembly is supported midway by a bracket and bearing combination attached to a frame crossmember.

With the exception of the center bearing and support combination, the propeller shaft is serviced as an assembly.

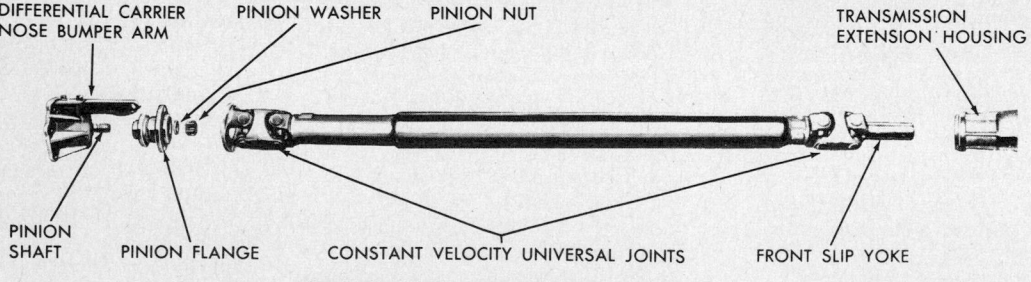

Single-piece driveshaft (© Cad. Div. G.M. Corp.)

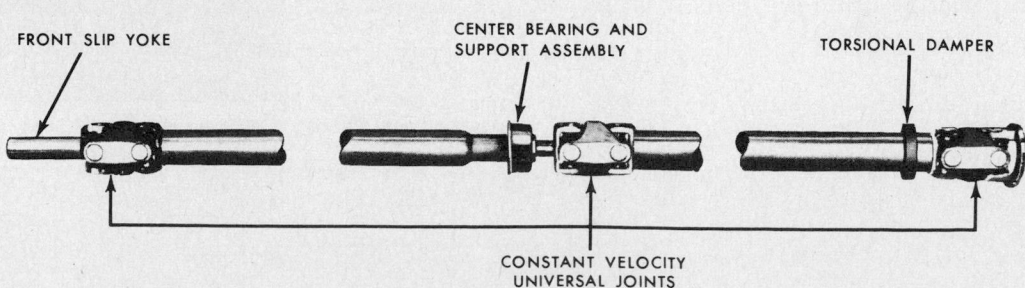

Two-piece driveshaft with C.V. joints (© Cad. Div. G.M. Corp.)

Press Bearings In with Vise

Guide Cross Into Bearings

Installing universal joint bearing

Two-Piece-Shaft Type— 1965-69 Commercial Models and 1965 Fleetwood 75

A two-piece propeller shaft assembly, using three standard universal joints, is used on commercial vehicles. Standard joints are used at each end of the shaft assembly and at the center support.

The universal joints are replaceable, but cannot be repacked. On original universal joints, the injected nylon ring that locks the bearing cup in the slip yoke will shear off when the bearing is removed. There are no provisions for replacing this nylon ring. When the joint becomes noisy or otherwise needs attention, renew the joint.

Front and rear sections of this shaft are splined together the same as in two-piece passenger car models.

The commercial vehicle two-piece-shaft type unit is attached to the transmission by means of a front slip yoke. The assembly is attached to the differential carrier by two U-bolts that hold the rear joint cross bearings to the differential carrier pinion yoke. The propeller shaft assembly is supported at the center by an adjustable center bearing support and bracket attached to a frame crossmember. The center bearing support is adjustable to compensate for various load influences.

Single-Piece Shaft R & R

1. Place transmission in Neutral

and jack up car; support on axle stands.
2. Remove the two accessible rear U-joint flange capscrews.
3. Rotate driveshaft and remove other two capscrews, after supporting rear of shaft on a chain. Never let the full weight of the driveshaft be supported only by the front constant velocity joint.
4. Push shaft forward to clear pinion flange, then pull rearward to disengage slip yoke from transmission. Plug transmission to prevent oil leak.
5. Lubricate slip yoke inside diameter with gear lube, outside of splines with A.T.F.
6. To install, reverse removal procedure, tightening rear U-joint fasteners to 70 ft. lbs. Place transmission in Park to hold shaft while tightening capscrews.

Two-Piece Shaft R & R

1. Follow Steps 1-6 of *Single-Piece Shaft R & R*, with the addition of the following step:
1A. Remove center bearing support after matchmarking it and crossmember. When installing, tighten the bolts to 16 ft. lbs.

Rear Suspension

Description

All Except Commercial

A four-link rear suspension system, consisting of upper and lower control arms, coil springs and shock absorbers is used. The coil springs are placed on brackets on the rear axle housing at their lower ends, the upper ends being seated in the frame crossmember. The upper and lower control arms are so placed to give the car good lateral stability. Cars can be equipped with Automatic Level Control, described later.

Commercial Chassis

The Commercial chassis uses semi-elliptic nine-leaf springs from 1965 to 1967, seven-leaf springs from 1968, approximately 2½ in. wide in a conventional Hotchkiss drive layout. The springs have zinc or full length polyethylene inner liners between first four leaves to provide correct interleaf friction and to prevent corrosion. Direct acting shock absorbers are provided, connected between the U-bolt spring plates and brackets welded to the frame crossmember. Automatic Level Control, with individual valving, is optional.

Coil Spring R & R

1965-70

1. Jack up rear of car and place axle stands under frame side rails.
2. Place a jack under the differential housing.
3. Remove tire and wheel assemblies.
4. If car has A.L.C., disconnect link at overtravel lever and position it in center position.
5. Remove shock absorber lower retaining nuts and washers.
6. Remove rear bolts from upper control arms, then free links from mountings.
   NOTE: it may be necessary to place another jack under differential pinion housing to facilitate bolt removal.
7. If removing right spring, disconnect brake hose at crossmember bracket and disconnect parking brake cable strap. Lower jacks under differential.
8. Place floor jack under control arm opposite of spring being removed. (If removing right spring, place jack under left control arm and vice-versa.)
9. Jack up on lower control arm until spring can be removed.
10. To install, reverse removal procedure. Tighten upper and lower control arm bolts to 75 ft. lbs.

1971-72

1. Follow Steps 1-5 of previous procedure.
2. Position container to catch brake fluid, then disconnect brake hose from steel line at frame.
3. Remove brake hose and clip from frame.
4. Disconnect rear U-joint and support driveshaft on a chain.
5. Remove nuts and bolts that secure both upper control arms to axle brackets.
6. Lower rear axle assembly slowly until springs are free.
7. To install, reverse removal procedure. Tighten upper and lower control arm bolts to 75 ft. lbs.

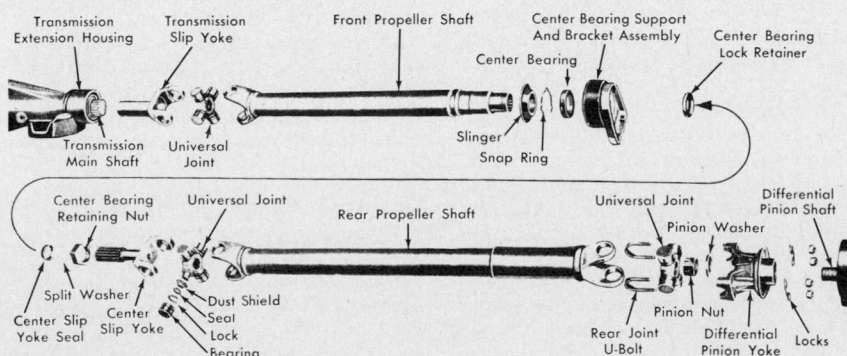

Transmission Extension Housing — Transmission Slip Yoke — Front Propeller Shaft — Center Bearing Support And Bracket Assembly — Center Bearing Lock Retainer — Center Bearing — Transmission Main Shaft — Universal Joint — Slinger — Snap Ring

Center Bearing Retaining Nut — Universal Joint — Rear Propeller Shaft — Universal Joint — Differential Pinion Shaft — Pinion Washer — Split Washer — Dust Shield — Seal — Lock — Bearing — Center Slip Yoke Seal — Center Slip Yoke — Pinion Nut — Rear Joint U-Bolt — Differential Pinion Yoke — Locks

Driveshaft—1965-69 Commercial and 1965 Fleetwood 75 © Cadillac Div., G.M. Corp.

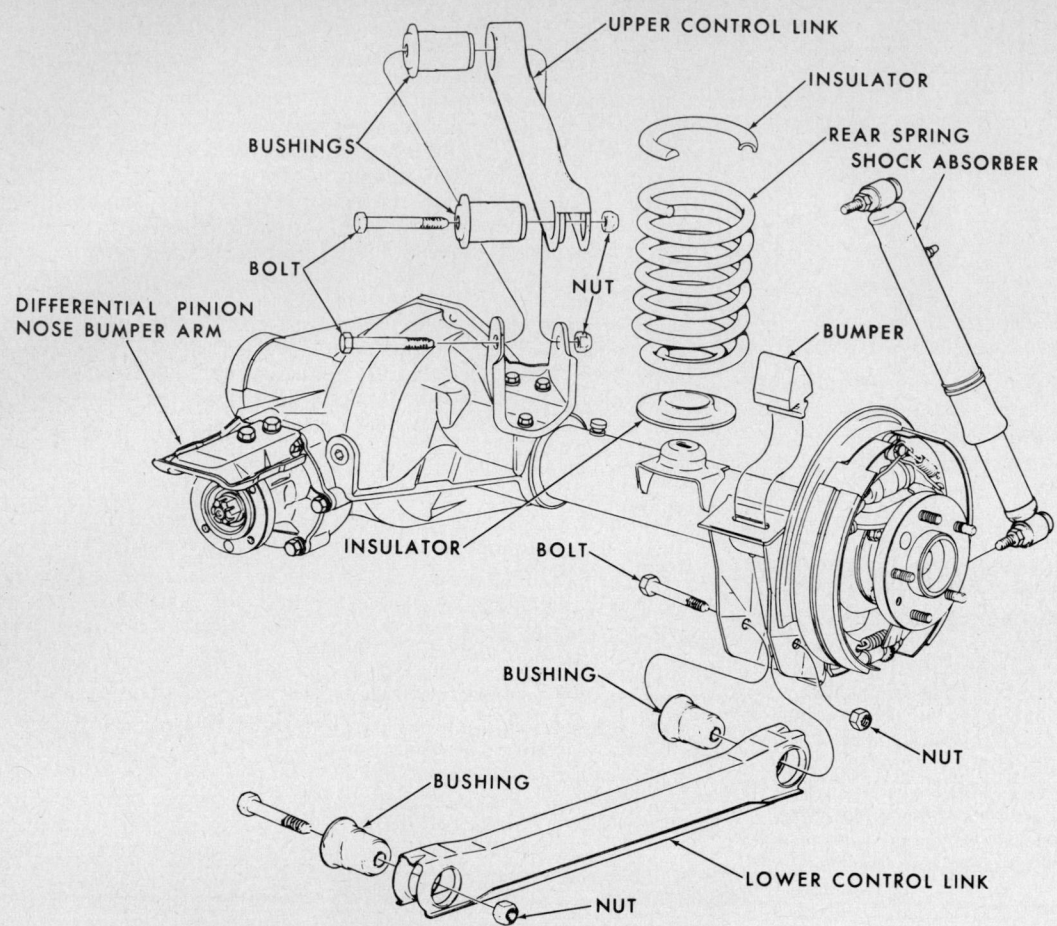

Rear suspension—1965-72 except Commercial models (© Cad. Div. G.M. Corp.)

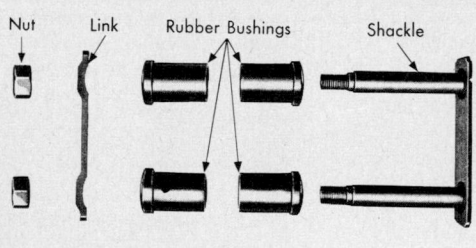

Spring shackle disassembled—1965-70
(© Cad. Div. G.M. Corp.)

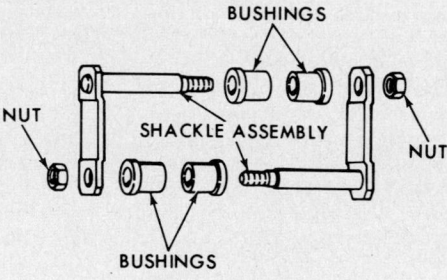

Spring shackle disassembled—1971-72
(© Cad. Div. G.M. Corp.)

Leaf Spring R & R

1. Jack up car and support on axle stands at frame side rails.
2. Place axle stands under axle housing, after jacking up housing.
3. Remove front eye bolt nut and drive out bolt.
4. Disconnect shock absorber from U-bolt plate.
5. Remove rear shackle nuts.
6. Remove U-bolt plate nuts, plate and insulators.
7. Disconnect rear shackle links and lower spring.
8. To install, reverse removal procedure. Tighten shackle nuts to 70 ft. lbs., U-bolt nuts to 45 ft. lbs., and lower shock nuts to 50 ft. lbs.

Automatic Level Control

The system consists of a vacuum-operated air compressor and a control valve mounted at rear suspension crossmember. The valve is then connected to Superlift rear shock absorbers.

The Superlift shock absorber is essentially a conventional shock absorber enclosed in an air chamber. A pliable nylon-reinforced neoprene boot seals the air dome to air piston. It will extend or retract under the pressure controlled by the valve.

As load is added to the vehicle, the control valve admits air under pressure to these shock absorbers, lifting vehicle to normal position. As load is reduced, the valve releases air and lowers vehicle to the previous normal level.

The valve is connected by a link to the right rear upper control link. A deflection of at least 1/2 in. is required to make it operative.

A delay mechanism is built into the valve housing. This requires that an attitude be assumed for four to 15 seconds in order for the valve to operate. It prevents operation during normal road motions.

Pressure at the shock absorber units is kept equal bp means of the line connecting the two units, with only one unit connected directly to the control valve. This keeps approximately 8-15 psi. on shock absorber units at all times. The pressure is released at the control velve and the equalizing pressure is maintained through a check valve at the release fitting.

The compressor is located in the engine compartment. It is operated by vacuum surge through a line connected just forward of the carburetor insulator connection. Air, at atmospheric pressure, is taken into the compressor through a line connected to the air cleaner. The compressed air from the compressor is supplied to a reservoir and then to the control valve.

Any service work on this system, or other parts of the vehicle, that may cause deflation will require system re-inflation to approximately 140 psi.

All lines are 1/8 in. diameter flexible black tubing. In working on this system, use care not to kink this tubing. Keep tubing away from the exhaust system. See the Buick Car Section for service.

Drive Axles

Troubleshooting and Adjustment

General instructions covering the troubles of the drive axle and how to repair and adjust it, together with information on installation of rear axle bearings and grease seals, are given in the Unit Repair Section.

Capacities of the drive axle are given in the Capacities table.

Rear Axle Shaft Removal

Raise car and remove wheels and brake drums. Remove retainer and backing plate to rear axle housing. Attach slide hammer to axle shaft puller and install on studs of rear axle shaft flange. Drive outward and remove axle shaft.

Windshield Wipers

Wiper and Washer Motor R & R

1965-70

1. Disconnect negative battery cable.
2. Disconnect three washer hoses from control valve. Matchmark hoses and valve nipples for proper assembly sequence.
3. Disconnect two-way connector at washer unit and three-way connector at wiper unit.
4. Remove rubber grommet or cover plate above wiper motor on firewall.
5. Loosen two locknuts that secure crank arm to ball socket. Disengage arm from socket, without removing the locknuts.
6. Remove three screws that secure wiper/washer to firewall and remove assembly.

7. To install, reverse removal procedure, making sure wiper crank is in Park position.

1971-72

1. Disconnect negative battery cable, after raising hood.
2. Remove cowl screen.
3. Reach through opening and disengage transmission drive link from wiper crank arm by loosening two nuts.
4. Disconnect wiring and washer hoses.
5. Remove three screws that secure wiper/washer unit to firewall.
6. Remove entire assembly.
7. To install, reverse removal procedure, making sure wiper crank arm is in Park position.

Wiper Transmission R & R

1965-67

1. Remove both wiper arms.
2. Remove escutcheons, spanner nuts and washers.
3. Raise hood and remove eight capscrews that secure front and side edges of ventilator frame to firewall, noting location of any shims.
NOTE: end screws are hidden and are reached by opening doors and removing door hinge pillar inspection plates.
4. Raise front edge of ventilator frame and disengage washer hoses.
5. Raise rear edge of ventilator frame and slide it forward to disengage from molding; remove molding.
6. Remove rubber grommet or cover plate above wiper motor on firewall.
7. Disengage motor crank arm from linkage by loosening two retaining nuts.
8. Remove three transmission hold-down screws at right- and left-hand sides.
9. Remove four hold-down screws at bellcranks, then remove transmission linkage as an assembly.
10. To install, reverse removal procedure, after lubricating ball sockets.
NOTE: rivets can be drilled out to replace only one side of transmission.

1968

1. Remove both wiper arms.
2. Remove six clips that secure rubber hood seal to cowl. Position seal out of the way.
3. Remove screws that secure cowl vent screen; remove screen.
4. Remove the three screws on each side that hold transmissions to cowl.
5. Remove the three screws that secure bellcrank assembly.
6. Remove cover plate on firewall

above wiper motor.
7. Loosen the two retaining locknuts and disengage motor crank arm.
8. Remove transmission through right-hand cowl opening.
9. To install, reverse removal procedure, after lubricating ball sockets.

1969-72

Same as 1968 procedure, except delete Step 5.

Radio

Removal

1965-66 & 1968

1. Remove upper instrument panel cover.
2. Remove radio knobs, springs and rings.
3. Disconnect dial bulb socket from radio.
4. Disconnect wire connector and antenna lead-in cable.
5. Disconnect foot control plug, if so equipped, from radio.
6. Using spanner nut wrench, remove spanner nuts that secure control shafts to upper panel, then remove escutcheons.
7. Remove locknut that holds radio front bracket to stud.
8. Loosen screw that holds rear bracket to radio and remove screw to upper panel.
9. Pull radio rearward, then remove through opening at top of panel.
NOTE: on AM-FM stereo radios, disconnect audio-amplifier unit connector after Step 1. On 1968 models, remove center A/C duct at same time.

1967

1. Remove upper instrument panel cover.
2. Remove ash tray housing assembly.
3. Remove screws that secure ash tray frame to retaining plate, disconnect ash tray frame connector, and remove frame.
4. Remove knobs, springs and rings.
5. Using spanner nut wrench, remove spanner nuts that hold control shafts to instrument panel.
6. Remove screw on right side that secures radio bracket to frame.
7. Pull radio rearward and lower to gain access to wire connectors.
8. On AM-FM stereo radio, disconnect audio-amplifier connector.
9. Disconnect wire connector and antenna lead-in cable.
10. Disconnect dial bulb socket from radio.
11. Disconnect foot control plug, if so equipped.

12. On stereo, remove tape securing speaker leads; two on instrument panel cluster and two at panel frame above glove compartment door.
13. Remove radio through ash tray housing hole.

1969-70

1. Remove steering column lower cover.
2. Remove defroster hose behind radio.
3. Remove radio knobs, washers and rings by pulling straight out.
4. Using spanner nut wrench, remove spanner nuts securing control shafts to instrument panel.
5. Disconnect wire connectors and antenna lead-in cable.
6. Remove screws securing support bracket to radio and panel center support and remove bracket.
7. Pull radio rearward and down.
8. Disconnect dial bulb socket and remove radio.

1971-72

This procedure is the same as 1969-70 procedure, except that Step 2 can be eliminated.

Heater System

Heater Blower—
Non-Air-Conditioned Cars

1965-68

1. Drain cooling system.
2. Disconnect electrical connection to blower motor.
3. Remove blower motor mounting screws and remove blower.
4. Remove heater hoses from fittings on assembly, leaving clamps on fittings.
5. Disconnect cable to temperature valve at pivot point on assembly. NOTE: disconnect vacuum manifold assembly and position out of the way, starting 1968.
6. Remove screws holding bottom of assembly to cowl.
7. Remove screws holding top of assembly to cowl, then remove assembly.
8. Install in reverse of above.

1969-70

1. Disconnect negative battery cable.
2. Drain cooling system.
3. Remove one screw that secures antenna bracket to wheelhousing.
4. Disconnect blower electrical connector.
5. Remove five screws that secure blower to case and remove blower motor by rotating it 180° while pulling out.

6. Remove heater hoses.
7. Disconnect green vacuum hose at vacuum power unit.
8. Disconnect temperature valve cable and remove cable clamp.
9. Remove screw that secures check valve and position valve out of the way.
10. Position power brake vacuum line out of the way.
11. Disconnect three-way connector at blower resistor.
12. Remove seat warmer relay, if so equipped.
13. Remove wiring harness from clip.
14. Remove seven screws that secure the bottom of the blower assembly to cowl.
15. Remove five screws and one nut that secure top of blower assembly to cowl.
16. Remove blower case assembly.
17. To install, reverse removal procedure.

1971-72

1. Disconnect negative battery cable.
2. Disconnect electrical connector.
3. Remove five blower-to-case screws and blower motor.

Heater Blower—
Air-Conditioned Cars

1965-68

1. Disconnect battery.
2. Disconnect motor feed wire.
3. Disconnect air hose at motor.
4. Disconnect ground wire and capacitor from 1968.
5. Remove screws holding motor to evaporator and remove motor.
6. Install in the reverse of above.

1969-72

1. Disconnect negative battery cable.
2. On 1969-70 models only, remove screw that secures antenna bracket to wheelhousing.
3. Remove rubber cooling hose from nipple and blower motor.
4. Disconnect electrical connector.
5. Remove five screws that secure motor to case, then twist motor 180° and pull out.

Heater Core—
Non-Air-Conditioned Cars

1965-70

1. Remove heater blower case assembly.
2. Remove screws from each side of heater core, securing wire retaining clamps to blower case, then remove clamps.
3. Pull core out of case and remove grommets from inlet and outlet fittings.
4. Install in reverse of above.

1971-72

1. Drain cooling system.
2. Remove heater hoses from core nipples.
3. Remove instrument panel top cover.
4. Remove screws and position center ventilator duct and sleeve out of the way.
5. Remove vacuum hoses from diverter door and defroster door vacuum actuators.
6. Unfasten the bowden cable from temperature door and case and move out of way.
7. Take out the screws, securing heater case to cowl.
8. Work heater case from position under instrument panel.
9. Remove the screws and clips securing the core to heater case, and lift out core.
10. To install, reverse removal procedure.

Heater Core—
Air-Conditioned Cars

1965-68

1. Drain cooling system.
2. Remove carburetor air cleaner.
3. Disconnect vacuum hose assembly connectors from servo vacuum valve and control vacuum valve on power servo unit.
4. Disconnect vacuum hose from power servo power unit.
5. Disconnect electrical connector from power servo unit.
6. Disconnect vacuum hoses and electrical connections from master switch.
7. Disconnect small diameter vacuum hose from center port of vacuum check valve.
8. Remove screw securing vacuum check valve mounting bracket to heater air-selector assembly, then position check valve and bracket out of way.
9. Disconnect vacuum hose from mode door vacuum power unit.
10. Disconnect cable from control valve on power servo unit.
11. Remove hoses from heater inlet and outlet fittings and disengage vacuum manifold from assembly, starting 1968.
12. Remove screws securing heater-air selector to cowl and remove assembly from engine compartment.
13. Remove screws securing heater core frame to heater-air selector case, then remove gasket from case.
14. Pull core frame, with core attached, away from heater-air selector case.
15. Remove grommets from inlet and outlet fittings.
16. Remove corner screws securing wire retaining clamps to core frame.

17. Remove clamps and core.
18. Install in reverse of above.

1969-70

1. Disconnect negative battery cable.
2. Remove air cleaner.
3. Drain coolant.
4. Disconnect two heater hoses at heater air selector.
5. Remove blower relay connector.
6. Remove connector from power servo.
7. Remove neutral switch, vacuum storage tank, and A.L.C. hoses from vacuum check valve.
8. Remove right and left tie struts.
NOTE: if equipped with Automatic Level Control, position left tie strut out of the way in the engine compartment.
9. Disconnect Thermal Vacuum Switch hose.
10. Disengage wiring harness from clips, then remove white vacuum hose at water valve.
11. Remove vacuum harness connector from cowl, then remove six air selector to cowl screws.
12. Remove one nut and blower relay ground wire from air selector stud.

13. Remove fuse block and position it out of the way.
14. Remove four mode selector screws.
15. Pull vacuum harness connector into passenger compartment and disconnect.
16. Guide heater and air modulator assembly from engine compartment.
17. Remove four screws that secure heater core frame to case.
18. Remove gasket, then pull heater core and frame away from case.
19. Remove rubber grommets from air inlet and outlet fittings.
20. Remove four screws, retaining clamps and heater core.
21. To install, reverse removal procedure.

1971-72

1. Drain cooling system.
2. Remove hoses from heater core nipples.
3. Remove instrument panel top cover.
4. Remove right and left A/C outlet hoses and center outlet connector.

5. Remove screws securing A/C distributor to heater case and lift off distributor.
6. Remove defroster nozzle.
7. Remove glove box.
8. Disconnect vacuum hoses at recirculator door, water valve, control head and supply hose.
9. Disconnect aspirator hose from in-car sensor.
10. Take off instrument panel braces.
11. On engine side of cowl remove the nuts securing heater case to cowl.
12. Work the heater case out from under dash.
13. Remove rubber seals from around core nipples.
14. Remove the screw and clip from beneath the seal.
15. Take out screws and clip from opposite end of core and remove core.
16. Reverse the above procedure for installation.

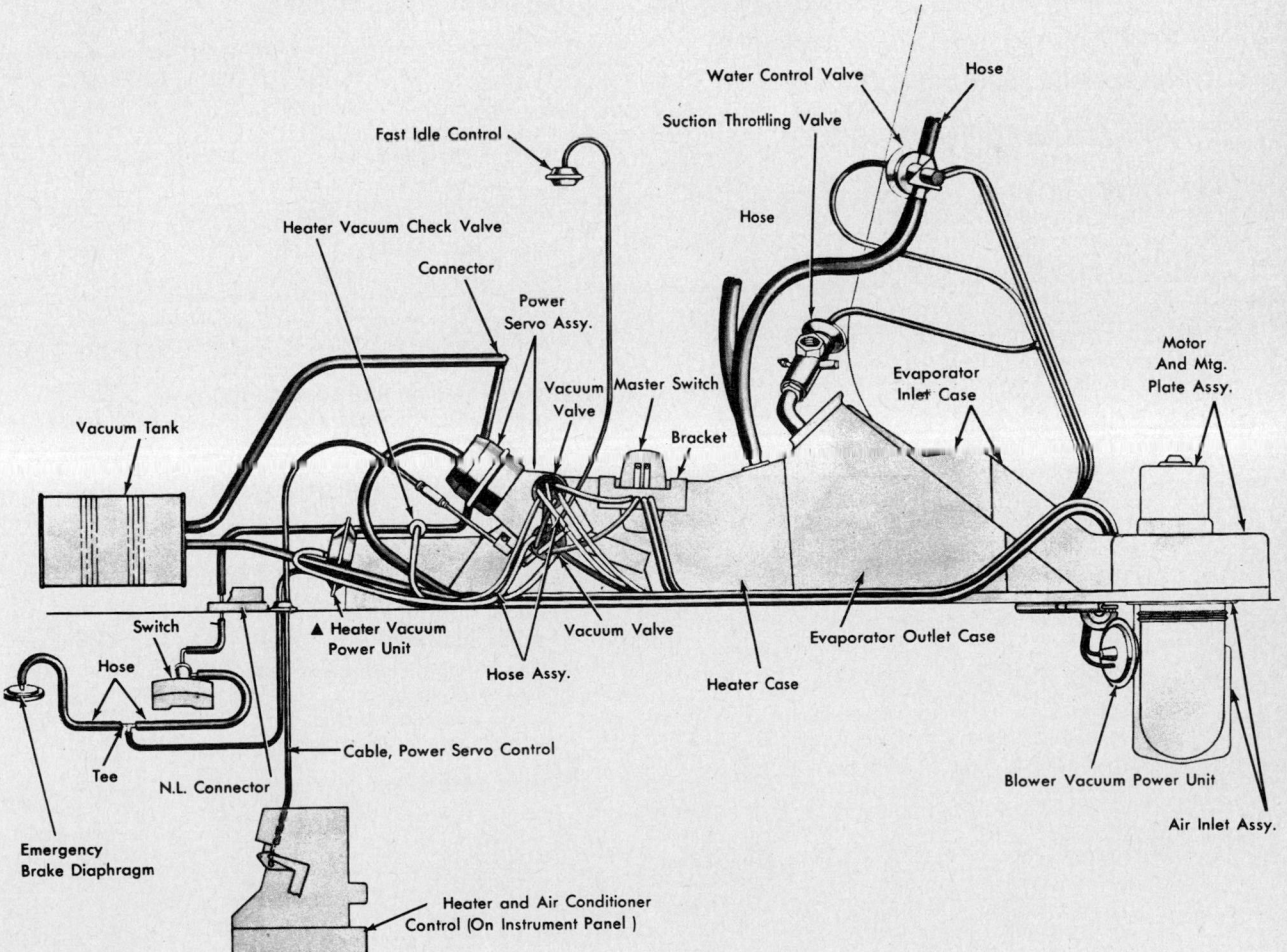

Heater and air conditioner (© Cad. Div. G.M. Corp.)

Cadillac Eldorado

Index

NOTE: For information not given in this section refer to same year model in Cadillac section.

YEAR IDENTIFICATION

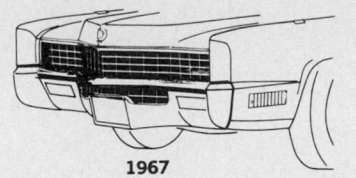

1967

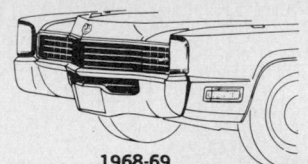

1968-69

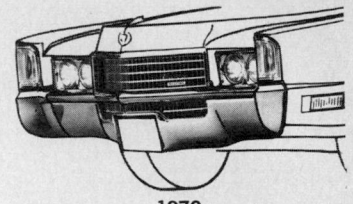

1970

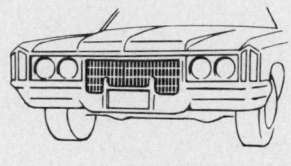

1971

1972

FIRING ORDER

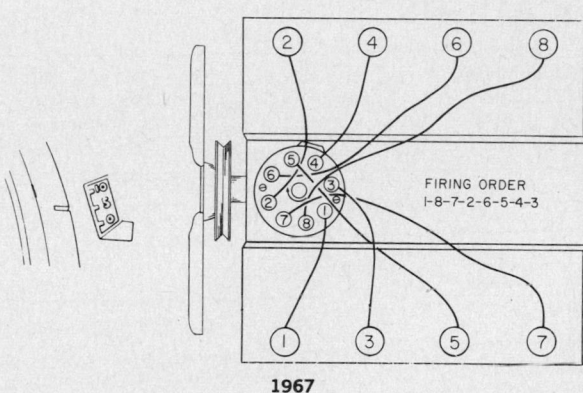

FIRING ORDER
1-8-7-2-6-5-4-3

1967

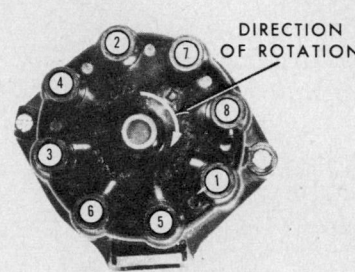

DIRECTION OF ROTATION

Distributor numbering— 1968 only

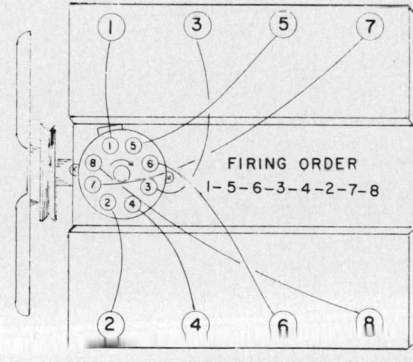

FIRING ORDER
1-5-6-3-4-2-7-8

1968-72

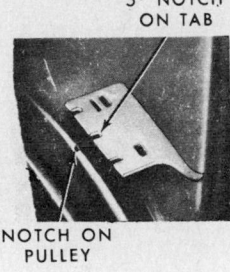

5° NOTCH ON TAB

NOTCH ON PULLEY

Timing marks—1968-70

8° ON TAB

NOTCH ON BALANCER

Timing marks 1971-72

CAR SERIAL NUMBER LOCATION AND ENGINE IDENTIFICATION

Vehicle identification plates are located at the top rear of the engine block, adjacent to the transmission, and on the left front door lock pillar. The eight digit serial number consists of a sales code letter, the last digit of the model year (7), and a six digit sequential serial number.

All models utilize a 429 cu. in. V8 engine. The engine serial number is stamped at the left rear of the cylinder block, just below the cylinder head.

1968-70

The vehicle identification plate is located on the top left side of the dashboard, and is visible through the windshield. The eight digit serial number consists of a sales code letter. The last digit of the model year (8, 9, or 0), and a six digit sequential number.

1968-69 models use a 472 cu. in. engine. A 500 cu. in. engine is used in 1970. The vehicle identification number, less sales code, is stamped on the top rear of the engine block, adjacent to the transmission.

1971-72

The vehicle identification plate is located on the top left side of the dashboard, and is visible through the windshield. The thirteen digit serial number consists of the G.M. Division Code (6), a four digit series and model number, the last digit of the model year (1 or 2), plant designation, and a six digit sequential serial number.

All models utilize a 500 cu. in. V8 engine. A derivative of the vehicle identification number is stamped on the top rear of the engine block, adjacent to the transmission.

GENERAL ENGINE SPECIFICATIONS

YEAR	CU. IN. DISPLACEMENT	CARBURETOR	ADVERTIZED HORSEPOWER @ RPM	ADVERTIZED TORQUE @ RPM (FT. LBS.)	A.M.A. HORSEPOWER	BORE & STROKE (IN.)	ADVERTISED COMPRESSION RATIO	VALVE LIFTER TYPE	NORMAL OIL PRESSURE (PSI)
1967	V8—429	4-BBL.	340 @ 4600	480 @ 3000	54.6	4.125 x 4.000	10.50–1	Hyd.	33
1968–69	V8—472	4-BBL.	375 @ 4400	525 @ 3000	59.2	4.300 x 4.060	10.50–1	Hyd.	33
1970	V8—500	4-BBL.	400 @ 4400	550 @ 3000	59.2	4.300 x 4.304	10.00–1	Hyd.	35–40
1971–72	V8—500	4-BBL.	365 @ 4400▲	535 @ 2800▲	59.2	4.300 x 4.304	8.5–1	Hyd.	35–40

▲—Horsepower and torque ratings for 1972 are SAE net ratings.

CRANKSHAFT BEARING JOURNAL SPECIFICATIONS

YEAR	MODEL	MAIN BEARING JOURNALS (IN.)				CONNECTING ROD BEARING JOURNALS (IN.)		
		Journal Diameter	Oil Clearance	Shaft End-Play	Thrust On No.	Journal Diameter	Oil Clearance	End-Play
1967	All	3.000	.0003–.0026	.003	3	2.2491	.0013	.011
1968–72	All	3.250	.0003–.0026	.002–.012	3	2.5000	.0005–.0028	.008–.016

TUNE-UP SPECIFICATIONS

YEAR	MODEL	SPARK PLUGS		DISTRIBUTOR		IGNITION TIMING (Deg.) ▲	CRANKING COMP. PRESSURE (Psi)	VALVES		Intake Opens (Deg.)	FUEL PUMP PRESSURE (Psi)	IDLE SPEED (Rpm) ★
		Type	Gap (In.)	Point Dwell (Deg.)	Point Gap (In.)			Tappet (Hot) Clearance (In.)				
								Intake	Exhaust			
1967	V8—429	44	.035	30°	.016	5B	180	Zero	Zero	39B	5³/₄	500
1968–69	V8—472	44N	.035	30°	.016	5B	180	Zero	Zero	18B	5³/₄	550
1970	V8—500	R46N	.035	28–32°	.016	7½B	165–185	Zero	Zero	18B	5¼–6½	600
1971–72	V8—500	R46N	.035	28–32°	.016	7½B	160–175	Zero	Zero	38B	6	600

▲—With vacuum advance disconnected and hose plugged. NOTE: These settings are only approximate. Engine design, altitude, temperature, fuel octane rating and the condition of the individual engine are all factors which can influence timing. The limiting advance factor must, therefore, be the "knock point" of the individual engine.

B—Before top dead center.

★—See text for procedure.

Caution

General adoption of anti-pollution laws has changed the design of almost all car engine production to effectively reduce crankcase emission and terminal exhaust products. It has been necessary to adopt stricter tune-up rules, especially timing and idle speed procedures. Both of these values are peculiar to the engine and to its application, rather than to the engine alone. With this in mind, car manufacturers supply idle speed data for the engine and application involved. This information is clearly displayed in the engine compartment of each vehicle.

AC GENERATOR AND REGULATOR SPECIFICATIONS

YEAR	MODEL	ALTERNATOR			REGULATOR						
		Field Current Draw @ 12V.	Output @ Generator RPM		Model	Field Relay			Regulator		
			1100	6500		Air Gap (In.)	Point Gap (In.)	Volts to Close	Air Gap (In.)	Point Gap (In.)	Volts at 125°
1967	1100760	2.2–2.6	5A	55	1119515	.015	.030	2.3–3.7	.060	.014	13.5–14.4
1968–69	1100696	2.2–2.4	5A	42	1119515	.015	.030	2.3–3.7	.060	.014	13.5–14.4
	1100694	2.2–2.6	5A	55	1119515	.015	.030	2.3–3.7	.060	.014	13.5–14.4
	1100742	2.2–2.4	5A	63	1119519	.015	.030	2.3–3.7	.060	.014	13.5–14.4
1970	1100909	2.2–2.6	—	42	1119515	.015	.030	1.5–3.2	.060	.014	13.5–14.4
	1100694	2.2–2.6	—	55	1119515	.015	.030	1.5–3.2	.060	.014	13.5–14.4
	1100910	2.8–3.2	—	63	1119519	.015	.030	1.5–3.2	.060	.014	13.5–14.4
1971–72	1100940	4.0–4.5	—	42	N.A.	Transistor type—no adjustment					
	1100937	4.0–4.5	—	63	N.A.	Transistor type—no adjustment					

VALVE SPECIFICATIONS

YEAR AND MODEL		SEAT ANGLE (DEG.)	FACE ANGLE (DEG.)	VALVE LIFT INTAKE (IN.)	VALVE LIFT EXHAUST (IN.)	VALVE SPRING PRESSURE (VALVE OPEN) LBS. @ IN.	VALVE SPRING INSTALLED HEIGHT (IN.)	STEM TO GUIDE CLEARANCE (IN.)		STEM DIAMETER (IN.)	
								INTAKE	EXHAUST	INTAKE	EXHAUST
1967	V8—429	45	44	.440	.440	160 @ 1½	1 15/16	.0005–.0025	.0010–.0025	.3415–.3425	.3415–.3420
1968–69	V8—472	45	44	.440	.454	160 @ 1½	1 15/16	.0005–.0025	.0010–.0025	.3415–.3425	.3415–.3420
1970	V8—500	45	44	.440	.454	160 @ 1½	1 15/16	.0005–.0025	.0010–.0025	.3415–.3425	.3415–.3420
1971–72	V8—500	45	44	.468	.468	160 @ 1½	1 15/16	.001–.0027	.001–.0025	.3415–.3425	.3415–.3420

TORQUE SPECIFICATIONS

YEAR	MODEL	CYLINDER HEAD BOLTS (FT. LBS.)	ROD BEARING BOLTS (FT. LBS.)	MAIN BEARING BOLTS (FT. LBS.)	CRANKSHAFT BALANCER BOLTS (FT. LBS.)	FLYWHEEL TO CRANKSHAFT BOLTS (FT. LBS.)	MANIFOLD (FT. LBS.)	
							Intake	Exhaust
1967	All	70–80	40–45	90–100	65–70	75–80	25–30	25–30
1968–72	All	115	40	90	Press-Fit	75	30	35

NOTE—Some bolts and nuts are marked on the heads to indicate the grade of steel used.
Do not use bolts of a lower grade than those originally installed. The marks consist
of lines: SAE5—3 lines; SAE7—5 lines; SAE8—6 lines.

CYLINDER HEAD BOLT TIGHTENING SEQUENCE

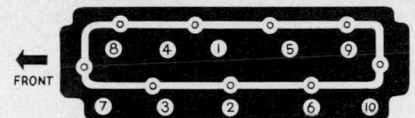

1968-72 cylinder head bolt tightening sequence

1967 cylinder head bolt tightening sequence

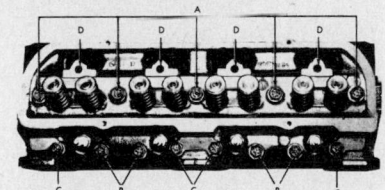

1967 Cylinder head cap screw location and length

Bolt Location	Length
A	4.06
B	2.75"
C	3.69"
D	5.94"

See text in Cadillac section for
1968-72 bolt location and length

BATTERY AND STARTER SPECIFICATIONS

YEAR	MODEL	BATTERY				STARTERS						
		Ampere Hour Capacity	Volts	Group Number	Terminal Grounded	Lock Test			No-Load Test			Brush Spring Tension (Oz.)
						Amps.	Volts	Torque	Amps.	Volts	RPM	
1967	V8—429	73	12	3KMB	Neg.	510	3.0	Locked	88	10.6	4,000	35
1968–70	V8—472,500	74	12	—	Neg.	Not Recommended			70–99	10.6	7,800	35
1971–72	V8—500	74	12	—	Neg.	Not Recommended			65–95	9	7,000	35

GENERAL CHASSIS AND BRAKE SPECIFICATIONS

YEAR	MODEL	CHASSIS		BRAKE CYLINDER BORE			BRAKE DRUM	
		Overall Length (In.)	Tire Size	Master Cylinder (In.) Power	Wheel Cylinder Diameter (In.)		Diameter (In.)	
					Front	Rear	Front	Rear
1967–69	V8—429,472	221.0	9.00 × 15	1	1 1/8 ①	7/8 ②	11	11 Drum
1970	V8—500	221.0	L78 × 15	1.125	2 15/16 Disc	7/8	11 Disc	11 Drum
1971–72	V8—500	221.6	L78 × 15	1.125	2 15/16 Disc	15/16	11 Disc	11 Drum

① Disc Brakes—1967-68—1 15/16—1969—2 15/16
② Disc Brakes—13/16

CAPACITIES

YEAR	MODEL	ENGINE CRANKCASE ADD 1 Qt. FOR NEW FILTER	TRANSMISSIONS Pts. TO REFILL AFTER DRAINING			DRIVE AXLE (Pts.)	GASOLINE TANK (Gals.)	COOLING SYSTEM (Qts.) WITH HEATER
			Manual		Automatic			
			3-Speed	4-Speed				
1967	V8—429	4	None	None	26	$4^1/_2$	24	17
1968-72	V8—472, 500	5	None	None	26	$4^1/_2$	24*	20①

NOTE— ① 1969-71—21.8 qts. & visual capacity tank
*—1971-72—27.5 Gals.

WHEEL ALIGNMENT

YEAR	MODEL	CASTER		CAMBER		TOE-IN (In.)	KING-PIN INCLINATION (Deg.)	WHEEL PIVOT RATIO	
		Range (Deg.)	Pref. Setting (Deg.)	Range (Deg.)	Pref. Setting (Deg.)			Inner Wheel	Outer Wheel
1967		$1^1/_2$N to $2^1/_2$N	2N	$^3/_8$N to $^3/_8$P	▲	0 to $^1/_8$	6	$22^2/_3$	20
1968-70		$1^1/_2$N to $2^1/_2$N	2N	$^3/_8$N to $^3/_8$P	0	0 to $^1/_8$	11	20	18
1971-72		$1^1/_2$N to $2^1/_2$N	1N	$^3/_8$N to $^3/_8$P	0	$1^1/_{16}$N–$^1/_{16}$P	11	20	18

▲—$^1/_4$° to $^1/_2$° more on left than right.
N—Negative
P—Positive

FUSES AND CIRCUIT BREAKERS

1967–69

Air conditioner and heater .... 25 AMP. FUSE
Antenna .... 14 AMP. FUSE
Body feed, cigar lighter, clock, map .... 25 AMP. FUSE
Cruise control.......................... 6 AMP. FUSE
Guide-matic .... 4 AMP. FUSE

Head and parking lights .... 25 AMP. CB
Horns .... 25 or 40 AMP. CB
Instrument and back-up lights .... 9 AMP. FUSE
Radio .... $7^1/_2$ AMP. FUSE
Seats and windows .... 40 AMP. CB

Tail and stop lights .... 25 AMP. FUSE
Cornering and courtesy lights .... 25 AMP. FUSE
Turn signal .... 14 AMP. FUSE
Windshield wipers .... 25 AMP. FUSE

1970

Body feed .... 25 AMP.
  Cigar lighters
  Clock
  Courtesy lights
  Glove box light
  Map light
  Trunk light
Cornering and parking lights................. 10 AMP.
  Ash tray light
  Cornering lights
  Front side marker lights
  Parking lights
Directional signal and back-up lights .... 20 AMP.
  Back-up lights
  Cruise control
  Rear window de-fogger
  Turn signals

Gages and transmission controls............... 10 AMP.
  Brake warning light
  CCS vacuum solenoid
  Downshift solenoid
  Fuel gage
  Generator light
  Low oil pressure indicator
  Water temperature warning light
Headlights (integral with headlight switch) .... 15 AMP.CB
Heater and accessories .... 25 AMP.
  Air conditioning amplifier
  Air conditioning blower relay
  Heater blower
  (On cars equipped with a heater only, the
   25 AMP fuse is replaced by a 15 AMP.
   fuse)

Horns.. CB
  Convertible top
  Engine metal temperature light
  Horns
  Power seat
  Power windows
Instrument panel lights .... 4 AMP.
Low blower (air conditioning only) .... 10 AMP.
Radio and window control relay .... $7^1/_2$ AMP.
Stop lights and hazard warning flasher .... 25 AMP.
Tail lights................................. 25 AMP.
  License light
  Rear side marker lights
  Tail lights
Twilight sentinel (integral with headlight
  switch)............................. 15 AMP. CB
Windshield wipers........................ 25 AMP.

1971–72

Same as 1970 except the following:

Turn signal................................. 25 AMP.
Back up lights .... 10 AMP.
  Rear window de-fogger
Seat back lock.............................. 4 AMP.
  (in-line, next to relay, under seat)

LIGHT BULBS

1967-69

Ash tray, rear radio, turn signal indicator..... 1445; 1 CP
Back-up lamp .... 1156; 32 CP
Clock, glove comp., fuel, temp., radio,
   speedometer, gen. & oil ind. .... 1895; 2 CP

Cornering .... 1195; 50 CP
Courtesy and door warning................. 212; 6 CP
Dome lamp .... 1004; 15 CP
Headlamp (inner) .... 4001; 37.5 W

Headlamp (outer)..................... 4002; 37.5-50 W
License lamp............................... 67; 4 CP
Stop, signal & turn..................... 1157; 32-4 CP

1970

FUNCTION	BULB NO.	C/P
Ash tray lamp	1445	.7
Back-up lamp	1156	32
Back-up lamp	1295	50
Clock	1816	3
Console lamp	57	2
Cornering lamp	1295	50
Courtesy lamp—rear quarter	90	6
Courtesy lamp-console	212/212-1	6
Courtesy lamp-instrument panel	89	6
Courtesy lamp—rear door	212/212-1	6
Courtesy lamp—rear quarter armrest	212/212-1	6
Cruise control speed selector illum. auto. lock lamps	1445	.7
Engine temp. warning light	161	1
Generator telltale lamp	161	1

FUNCTION	BULB NO.	C/P
Glove compartment lamp	1816	3
Headlamp—inner	L4001	37.5 Watts
Headlamp—outer	L4002	37.5W/55.0W
Headlamp switch lamp	1895	2
Heater control or climate control lamp	1816	3
High beam indicator	161	1
License lamp	67	4
Low brake telltale lamp	161	1
Low oil pressure telltale lamp	168	3
Map lamp	89	6
Marker lamp-front side	97A	4
Marker lamp-rear side	194	2
Panel lamp	168	3
Park-signal lamp	1157 NA	32/3
Radio dial lamp	1816	3
Radio AM-FM band indicators	2182D	.4

FUNCTION	BULB NO.	C/P
Radio AM-FM stereo indicators	2182D	.4
Radio-rear control indicator	250	1
Spot lamp-front compartment	90	6
Spot lamp-reading	1004	15
Stop, tail and signal	1157	32/3
Trunk compartment lamp	89	6
Trunk lid tell tale	161	1
Trunk signal indicator	168	3
Warning lamp-front door (combined with courtesy light)	212/212-1	6
Warning lamp-rear door (combined with courtesy light)	212/212-1	6
Water temperature tell tale	168	3

1971-72

Same as 1970 except the following:

Low oil pressure-telltale lamp	161	1
Map lamp	550	6
Marker lamp-rear	168	3
Panel lamp	194	2
Radio dial lamp	1895	2
Turn signal indicator	194	2
Water temperature	161	1

Distributor

Breaker Point Installation and/or Adjustment

1. Remove distributor cap by depressing and turning the retaining screws.
2. Remove two screws and rotor.
3. Remove condenser and primary leads from nylon insulated connection.
4. Loosen two screws holding base of contact assembly in place and remove points.
5. Inspect weight assembly, replace or lubricate as required.
6. Place new points under the two screws and tighten screws.

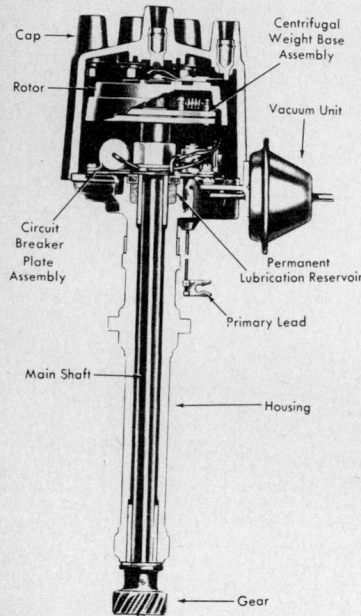

Distributor showing major components
(© Cadillac Div. G.M. Corp.)

7. Connect the condenser and primary leads at the nylon insulated connection.
NOTE: be sure leads do not interfere with cap, weight base, or breaker advance.

Adjusting distributor points
(© Cadillac Div. G.M. Corp.)

8. Install rotor. Square and round lugs must be properly aligned.
9. With 1/8 in. Allen wrench, turn until points close while rubbing block is on high point of lobe. Then turn screw counterclockwise one-half turn.
10. Replace distributor cap.
11. With engine warmed up and off fast idle, set points to get proper dwell angle.

Distributor Removal

1. Remove distributor cap. Disconnect vacuum hose. Disconnect primary lead at distributor.
2. Turn the engine to top dead center for No. 1 cylinder, see firing order illustrations. The pointer on the timing case cover will point to the O-mark on the crankshaft pulley.
3. Match-mark the vacuum advance unit to the cylinder block so that the distributor body will be correctly replaced at reassembly.
4. Remove hold-down clamp and distributor.

Distributor Replacement

1. Install rubber seal-ring below distributor housing mounting flange.
2. Install the distributor so that the vacuum advance unit aligns with the match-mark made at removal. Turn the rotor slightly left of center so that as the gear engages the camshaft it will revolve into the proper position, pointing to No. 1 contact in the cap.
NOTE: if the engine has been cranked, remove No. 1 spark plug. Crank the engine until No. 1 piston is in firing position with the pointer and the O-mark on the crankshaft pulley aligned.
3. Install the hold-down clamp. Connect the primary lead and install the cap.
4. Rotate cam lubricator.
5. Plug the distributor vacuum line to the carburetor.
6. Insert an adapter pin alongside No. 1 wire in the distributor cap and connect a timing light.
7. Clean· the crankshaft pulley markings and the pointer.
8. Start engine and rotate distributor until specified timing mark lines up with notch in pulley.
9. Tighten clamp bolt to 15-18 ft. lbs. and recheck timing.
10. Remove plug and reconnect the vacuum line to the advance unit.

Generator, Regulator

The Delco-Remy Delcotron alternator is used on all Eldorado models.

From 1967 to 1970, a 42 ampere unit was standard on cars without air conditioning and a 55 ampere unit standard on air conditioned models. In 1968, an optional 63 ampere alternator was made available for use in cars having radio equipment or other heavy electrical demands. The dual point (with field relay) regulators used with these alternators are mounted on the right-hand inner fender panel under the hood. The regulator used with the 63 ampere Delcotron is similar to the standard unit, with the addition of a field discharge diode in parallel with the voltage regulator contacts and the regulator "F" terminal to allow for the higher current.

In 1971, the standard alternator for non-air conditioned Eldorado models became a 42 ampere, integrated circuit Delcotron, and the standard alternator on air conditioned models a 63 ampere unit of similar design. These alternators are unlike their predecessors in that the regulator is now an integral part of of the alternator itself and is non-adjustable.

Both the conventional Delcotron and the new integrated circuit type are covered in the Unit Repair Section.

Removal and Installation

1967

1. Disconnect negative battery cable.
2. Disconnect wires and multiple connector from alternator.
3. Remove alternator bracket adjusting screw.
4. Remove front nut and washer from stud on exhaust manifold.
5. Remove V-belts.
6. Remove two screws that hold alternator support bracket to manifold.
7. Position alternator away from support brace and slide both alternator and bracket off locating stud.
8. To install, reverse removal procedure, tightening bracket-to-manifold screws to 18 ft. lbs.
NOTE: even if only one V-belt must be replaced, it is best to replace both so that tension is equally distributed between them.

1968-72

1. Disconnect negative battery cable.
2. Disconnect A.I.R. hose at check valve and remove heater hose clip from adjusting link.
3. For 1968-69 models, remove strut rod between adjusting link and cylinder head.
4. Remove cap, if installed, from "+" terminal.
5. Disconnect three wires from "+" terminal.

6. Unplug multiple connector.
7. Disconnect black wire from ground terminal.
8. Remove link adjusting screw and raise link, then loosen lower alternator mounting screw and remove V-belt.
9. Remove lower mounting screw, spacer and washer.

NOTE: it may be necessary to twist alternator towards fender to do this.

10. Remove alternator.
11. To install, reverse removal screws to 17 ft. lbs.

Battery, Starter

Detailed information on the battery and starter will be found in the Battery and Starter Specifications Table.

For starter diagnosis and repair procedures, see the Unit Repair Section.

Starter R & R—1967-72

1. Disconnect battery.
2. Raise front end of car.
3. Disconnect wires from starter solenoid.

4. Remove wire spring clip from solenoid housing. Remove support bracket.
5. Remove two starter mounting screws.
6. Remove starter motor by pulling it forward and lowering it.
7. Install by reversing removal procedure. Torque two starter screws to 46 ft. lbs.

Instruments

Upper Instrument Panel Cover Panel R & R

1967-68

1. Disconnect battery.
2. Remove three Phillips head screws holding the instrument panel cluster bezel to the upper cover.
3. From inside the glove compartment door, remove two upper screws holding the upper cover to the right panel.
4. Raise upper panel high enough for clearance, then disconnect the following wire connectors: radio speaker/or speakers, Twilight

Sentinel photocell and Automatic Climate Control sensor.
5. Pull upper cover rearward to disengage three hooks at the front of cover from retainers on cowl, and remove cover.
6. Install by reversing removal procedure.

1969-70

1. Disconnect battery.
2. Disconnect radio speaker connection near radio.
3. Remove three Phillips head screws that secure right and left garnish moldings and remove moldings.
4. Inside glove compartment, remove two screws that secure cover to instrument panel.
5. Remove screws that secure cover to bezel assembly.
6. Lift cover up and rearward to disengage from cowl.
7. Disconnect Twilight Sentinel photocell and clock wires. Remove cover.
8. Install in reverse of above.

1971-72

Procedure is the same as for 1969-70, except eliminate Step 3.

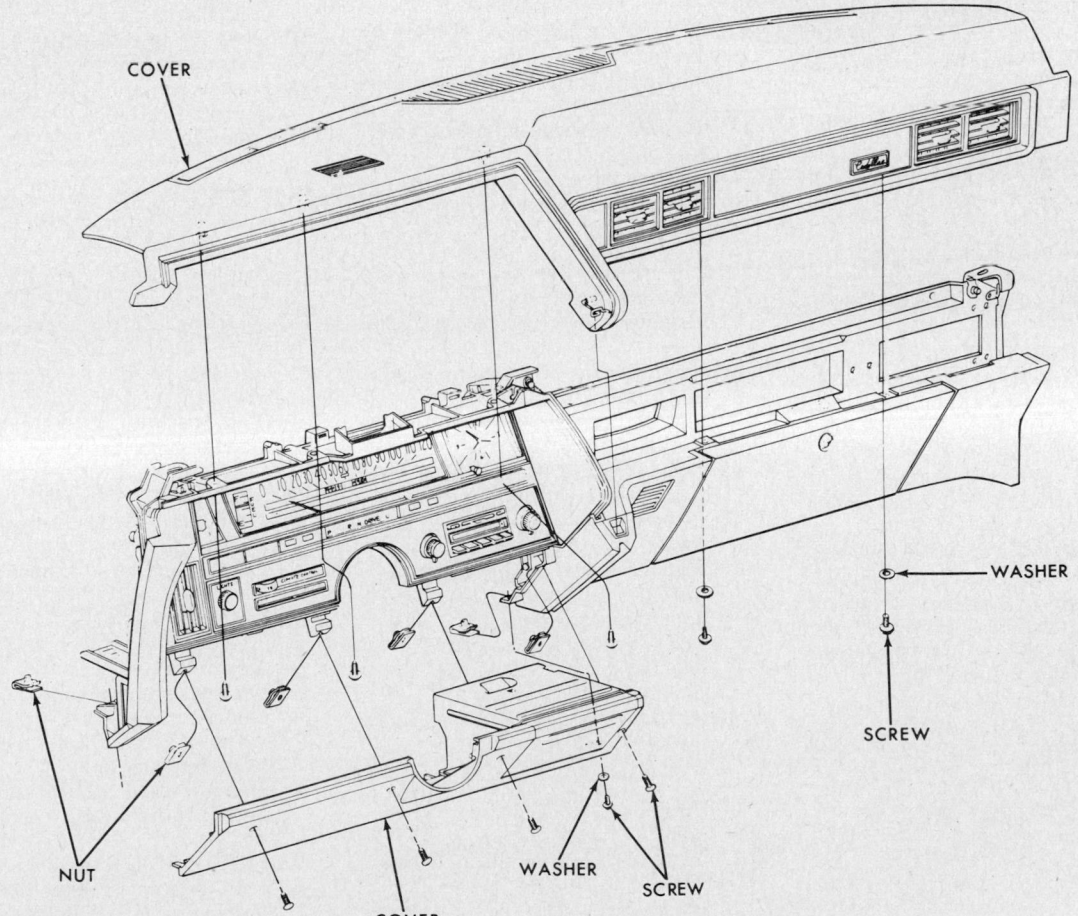

COVER

WASHER

SCREW

NUT   WASHER   SCREW

COVER

Typical instrument panel (© Cadillac Div. G.M. Corp.)

Steering Column Lower Cover R & R

1967-68

1. Disconnect battery.
2. On cars equipped with tilt and telescope steering wheel, put wheel in up position.
3. Remove two Phillips head screws holding the lower end of the steering column lower cover to the lower instrument panel.
4. Remove one long special screw holding upper end of steering column lower cover to clamp.
5. Disengage steering column lower cover by pulling straight out to disengage two upper pins from cover and gain access to flasher unit on rear side of lower cover.
6. Remove flasher unit from mounting clip.
7. Install by reversing removal procedure.

1969-70

1. Disconnect battery.
2. Remove screws that secure lower cover to bezel assembly and loosen two screws that secure lower cover to lower instrument panel.
3. Pull lower cover up and out to disengage.
4. Disconnect ash tray wiring and Twilight Sentinel, if so equipped. Remove courtesy light bulb and socket.
5. Remove flasher units from clips on rear sides of cover.
6. Remove cover.
7. Install in reverse of above.

1971-72

1. Disconnect negative battery cable.
2. Disconnect ash tray wires.
3. Pull out ash tray, remove two Phillips screws and ash tray door.
4. Remove ash tray.
5. Remove four screws that secure lower cover to upper cover. One is removed through ash tray opening.
6. Loosen two screws that secure lower cover to lower instrument panel.
7. Disengage lower cover by pulling straight out. Disconnect Twilight Sentinel wiring, remove courtesy lamp and turn signal flasher, then disconnect and remove ash tray light.
8. Remove lower cover.
9. To install, reverse removal procedure.

Instrument Cluster R & R

1967-68

1. Remove upper instrument panel cover as previously described.
2. Remove steering column lower cover as previously described.

3. Remove transmission shift indicator pointer with an Allen wrench.
4. Disconnect multiple connector at instrument panel cluster case and remove instrument panel harness from cluster attachment.
5. Disconnect speedometer cable at speedometer head by depressing rises on wave washer. These rises are 180° apart.
6. Remove three upper screws that hold instrument panel cluster to bezel.
7. Remove right and center screws that hold instrument panel cluster to bezel. Center screw is located below the clock.
8. On cars equipped with Automatic Climate Control, remove center air outlet boot at both ends and remove the boot.
9. Remove screws that hold the center air outlet and remove the outlet.
10. If car is equipped with Automatic Climate Control, remove left Climate Control air outlet boot at inlet end.
11. By using a flexible hex driver, remove left instrument panel cluster to bezel screw.
12. If car is equipped with rear window defogger, seat warmer or convertible top, disconnect connectors.
13. Disconnect map light switch connector.
14. Loosen upper left and right bezel to bracket screws.
15. Pry left corner of bezel forward and pull instrument panel cluster up to remove.
16. Install by reversing removal procedure.

1969-70

1. Disconnect battery.
2. Remove upper instrument panel cover.
3. Remove clock by removing screws and plate at top of clock, snapping clock out and removing bulbs and wires.
4. Remove radio as explained later in this section.
5. Remove steering column lower cover.
6. Remove screw that secures shift indicator pointer to steering column and remove pointer.
7. Pull off odometer reset knob.
8. Remove four screws that secure cluster to bezel assembly.
9. Move cluster forward and right, then downward to remove.

1971-72

1. Disconnect negative battery cable.
2. Remove instrument panel top cover.
3. Remove steering column lower cover.
4. Disconnect speedometer cable,

remove left-hand A/C outlet hose and disconnect cluster harness plug. Disengage harness from clip.
5. Remove shift indicator pointer.
6. Remove four screws (two upper and two lower) that secure cluster to bevel.
7. Remove cluster forward and to the right, while tipping right-hand corner downward.
8. To install, reverse removal procedure.

Speedometer Head R & R

1967-68

1. Remove cluster assembly as previously described.
2. Remove odometer reset knob retainer using a 1/16 in. Allen wrench.
3. Remove clock reset knob retainer using a 1/16 in. Allen wrench.
4. Remove lower clips that hold cluster lens to cluster case.
5. Remove self tapping screws that hold retainer to case.
6. With back of cluster case on the work bench, separate lens and retainer from cluster case.
7. Remove three screws and attached grommets that hold speedometer head to cluster case and place assembly with back of cluster case on the bench.
8. Remove speedometer head from cluster case.
9. Remove map light housing because it will have to be repositioned for assembly.
10. Install by reversing removal procedure.

1969-70

1. Remove cluster assembly.
2. Remove clips that secure cluster lens to case and remove lens.
3. Open staking along lower edges and remove sheet metal retainer and shift indicator dial.
4. Remove screws that secure speedometer head assembly to cluster case and remove assembly with back of cluster case.
5. Lift speedometer head assembly out of cluster case.
6. Install in reverse of above.

1971-72

1. Remove cluster assembly.
2. Remove seven screws that secure back case to dial assembly.
3. Remove three screws that secure printed circuit to fuel gauge; remove gauge.
4. Remove two nuts that secure speedometer head to dial assembly.
5. Slide speedometer head out of lens, making sure pointer is not damaged.
6. To install, reverse removal procedure.

Printed Circuit R & R

1967-68

1. Remove instrument panel cluster as previously described.
2. Remove one nut and wave washer holding printed circuit to clock.
3. Remove 12 wedge-base sockets and bulbs from cluster case.
4. Remove two screws from fuel gauge.
5. Remove two screws from temperature gauge.
6. Remove four screws that hold the printed circuit to cluster case and remove printed circuit.

NOTE: do not attempt to repair this printed circuit.

7. Install by reversing removal procedure.

1969-72

1. Remove instrument panel cluster.
2. Remove 14 sockets and bulbs from cluster case.
3. Snap off fuel gauge cover and remove screws that secure printed circuit flap to fuel gauge.
4. Remove screws that secure circuit to back of cluster case and remove circuit.
5. Install by reversing removal procedure.

Headlight Switch R & R

1967-68

1. Remove steering column lower cover as previously described.
2. Remove hoses at vacuum valve, which is integral with headlight switch.
3. Remove lower right screw holding headlight control switch housing to lower instrument panel.
4. On cars equipped with Automatic Climate Control, remove left outlet hose at inboard side to gain access to upper left screw.
5. Remove upper left screw that holds headlight control switch housing to lower instrument panel.
6. Pull headlight control switch assembly rearward, disconnect wiring harness connectors and two bulbs, then remove assembly.
7. Install by reversing removal procedure.

1969

1. Remove instrument panel upper cover.
2. Remove steering column lower cover.
3. Remove two screws that secure air conditioning duct to bezel assembly and remove duct.
4. Disconnect wiring harness that is below headlight switch assembly.
5. Depress spring loaded release button on top of headlight switch and remove switch, knob and rod assembly.
6. Remove screws that secure switch assembly to bezel.
7. Pull assembly rearward, disconnect wiring connectors, two bulbs and remove assembly.
8. Install in reverse of above.

1970-72

1. Remove steering column lower cover.
2. Disconnect wiring harness retainer below headlight switch assembly.
3. Depress spring loaded release button on top of headlight switch and remove switch, knob and rod assembly.
4. Remove screw with ground wire at bottom of switch housing.
5. Pull assembly down and rearward, disconnect wiring harness connectors, two bulbs and remove assembly.
6. Install in reverse of above.

Ignition Switch R & R

See *Cadillac Section* for same year Eldorado.

Brakes

Description

The brake system used in 1967 and 1968 consists of standard power drum brakes front and rear, with four-piston disc brakes by Delco-Moraine optional on the front. Two master cylinder types are used, depending on the type brake system. A Delco-Moraine master cylinder is used on drum brake models, and a Bendix master cylinder on models having disc front brakes. The Bendix master cylinder has no check valve in the front outlet because no residual brake pressure is required with disc brakes.

Starting in 1969, single-piston, sliding caliper Delco-Moraine disc brakes became standard equipment on the front wheels of all Eldorado models. The master cylinders used with these brakes are the same as for the same year Cadillac, even though the Eldorado uses tandem power booster units.

On all models from 1967, a foot-operated, vacuum parking brake working on the rear drums via mechanical linkage is used. This is virtually identical to the parking brake used on other Cadillac models with the exception of cable length and configuration.

For brake service, see the Unit Repair Section of this manual.

Power Brake Booster R & R

1967-72

1. Disconnect hydraulic lines from master cylinder.
2. Disconnect vacuum line from vacuum check valve on unit.
3. Remove steering column lower cover, as described previously.
4. Remove cotter pin, washer and spring spacer that secure power unit pushrod to brake pedal arm.
5. Remove the four nuts that secure power unit to firewall, then remove power unit.
6. To install, reverse removal procedure.

Brake System Check

1. Start engine and allow it to idle in Neutral. Depress brake pedal and hold—if pedal gradually falls away, a hydraulic system leak is indicated.
2. Check pedal travel from rest to full on position. Pedal travel should not exceed 1½ in. for 1967, 1¾ in. for 1968, 2 in. for 1967-70 with disc brakes, and 2 1/16 in. for 1971-72.
3. If pedal travel exceeds specifications, the system is probably contaminated by air bubbles and should be bled.

NOTE: disc brakes—tap calipers around piston area with plastic hammer to dislodge all air bubbles. Less common causes of excessive pedal travel include malfunctioning rear brake self-adjusters, tapered rear linings, worn out rear linings or complete loss of fluid from one brake circuit.

Parking Brake

Preliminary Check

1. Check vacuum cylinder piston travel (on brake pedal support) by running engine at idle and shifting from Drive to Neutral. The manual release lever should move up and down as vacuum is applied and released.
2. If no movement is observed, check for kinked or loose vacuum line connections all the way out to the intake manifold. Check neutral switch adjustment and vacuum release valve.
3. If movement is slow (greater than 2 seconds), vacuum diaphragm may be leaking or lines kinked partially closed.
4. If vacuum piston completes full stroke, but does not release brake, parking brake assembly is faulty and must be replaced as a unit.
5. If parking brake does not remain fully engaged in all gears with engine off, the assembly must be replaced.

Fuel System

Fuel Pump

The fuel pump is mounted on the left-front of the engine and is driven by an eccentric on the camshaft. The fuel filter is located on the engine oil filler tube on 1967 models, is an inline type on 1968 models, and is an integral part of the fuel pump on 1969-72 models. The pump is serviced only as an assembly.

All air conditoned cars have a provision to return excess fuel vapor to the gasoline tank to prevent vapor lock under high temperature conditions. On 1967-68 models, the bypass line runs from the fuel filter, and on 1969 and later cars, the line runs directly from the fuel pump.

The filters should be changed at least every 12,000 miles. On 1967-68 models, the replacement procedure is obvious; on 1969 and later models, see the Cadillac section for replacement procedure. Remove filter from underneath car starting 1968.

Pump R & R

1. If equipped with A.I.R. system, it may be necessary to remove air pump and bracket for clearance.
2. Remove center coil wire.
3. For 1968-72 models, jack up front of car and support on axle stands so that pump can be removed from underneath.
4. Loosen two mounting bolts, or one bolt and one nut.
5. Turn over engine to relieve tension on pump arm.
6. Disconnect pump inlet and outlet lines. Plug inlet line.
7. Disconnect vapor return line on 1969 and later models.
8. Remove mounting bolts and fuel pump.
9. To install, reverse removal procedure.

Thermal Vacuum Switch and Idle Speed-up Device

See Cadillac section.

Idle Speed and Mixture Adjustments

1967-69

Adjust with air cleaner removed.
1. Make sure PCV valve is free and working properly.
2. Disconnect parking brake vacuum hose at vacuum release cylinder and plug.
3. Connect a tachometer, set parking brake and allow engine to come up to normal operating temperature in Neutral.
4. Remove air cleaner and make

sure dashpot is disengaged.
5. With wheels chocked, place transmission in Drive.
6. On 1968-69 cars, disconnect and plug distributor vacuum line.
7. Adjust air adjusting screw to obtain an idle speed of 550 rpm with A/C *off.* for A.I.R. cars, 480-500 rpm with A/C *on* for non-A.I.R. cars.

NOTE: press down on brass hot idle compensator pin while making adjustments.
8. On 1967 cars having no A.I.R. but having A/C, disconnect and plug vacuum line from power servo on firewall.
9. Set idle speed screw 1½ turns in after contacting primary lever, both mixture screws out 4 turns from seated position.
10. Turn one mixture screw clockwise to obtain highest tach reading. Continue to turn screw until speed falls off 20 rpm—this is the lean idle fall off point. Back off screw ¼ turn for non-A.I.R. cars, 1⅛ turns for 1967 A.I.R. cars, 1½ turns for 1968 A.I.R. cars, and 1 turn for 1969 cars.
11. Repeat Step 10, turning other mixture screw.
12. Reset idle speed as in Step 7, then repeat Steps 10 and 11 if speed exceeds 500 rpm for non-A.I.R. cars or 550 rpm for A.I.R. cars.
13. Install air cleaner and recheck idle speed.
14. Shut off engine, disconnect tach, reconnect parking brake vacuum line and distributor vacuum line on 1968-69 models.

1970

Adjust with air cleaner removed.
1. Disconnect and plug distributor vacuum advance line.
2. Disconnect and plug parking brake vacuum line at vacuum release cylinder.
3. Connect a tachometer, set parking brake and remove air cleaner.
4. Make sure dashpot is not touching linkage, then turn slow idle speed screw in approximately 1½ turns after it contacts primary throttle lever. Turn in both mixture screws until they seat gently, then unscrew them approximately 6 turns.
5. Place car in Drive after warming up engine. Turn off A/C.

NOTE: press down on hot idle compensator pin while making adjustments.
6. Adjust slow idle screw to obtain 620 rpm.
7. Turn one mixture screw clockwise until speed falls off 10 rpm, then repeat Steps 6 and 7 for other mixture screw. Idle speed

now should be 600 rpm, indicating a 10 rpm drop per mixture needle.
8. Install air cleaner, shut off engine and disconnect tach.
9. Connect parking brake vacuum line and distributor vacuum line.

1971

Adjust with air cleaner removed.
Idle speed is adjusted at a new anti-dieseling solenoid located where the dashpot was located in previous years. The throttle must be opened slightly to allow the plunger to move out all the way, then it must be closed against the now-extended solenoid plunger before making the idle speed adjustment. The solenoid plunger will retract when the ignition is shut off.

1. Disconnect and plug distributor vacuum advance hose and parking brake vacuum hose (at the release cylinder).
2. Connect a tachometer and set the parking brake with transmission in Neutral.
3. Remove the air cleaner and turn in mixture screws until they seat gently, then turn the screws out approximately 6 turns.
4. Start engine and allow it to warm up.
5. Place car in Drive with A/C off.
6. Set idle speed to 620 rpm by adjusting anti-dieseling solenoid. Tighten jam nut.
7. Turn one mixture screw clockwise until idle speed falls off 10 rpm, then repeat for other screw. Idle speed now should be 600 rpm.
8. Install limiter caps, then disconnect wire that energizes solenoid. The plunger should retract to allow a slower idle speed of 350-400 rpm.
9. Shut off engine, disconnect tach, connect vacuum lines and solenoid wire and install air cleaner.

Exhaust System

Exhaust Pipe Removal

1967-70

1. Loosen clamp at muffler and drive exhaust pipe out of muffler.
2. Cut exhaust pipe at weld in pipe and remove rear portion.
3. Remove screws that secure left pipe flange to manifold or nuts that secure right pipe flange to manifold.
4. Remove forward portion of pipe.

NOTE: if right side is being removed, care must be exercised not to drop heat valve.

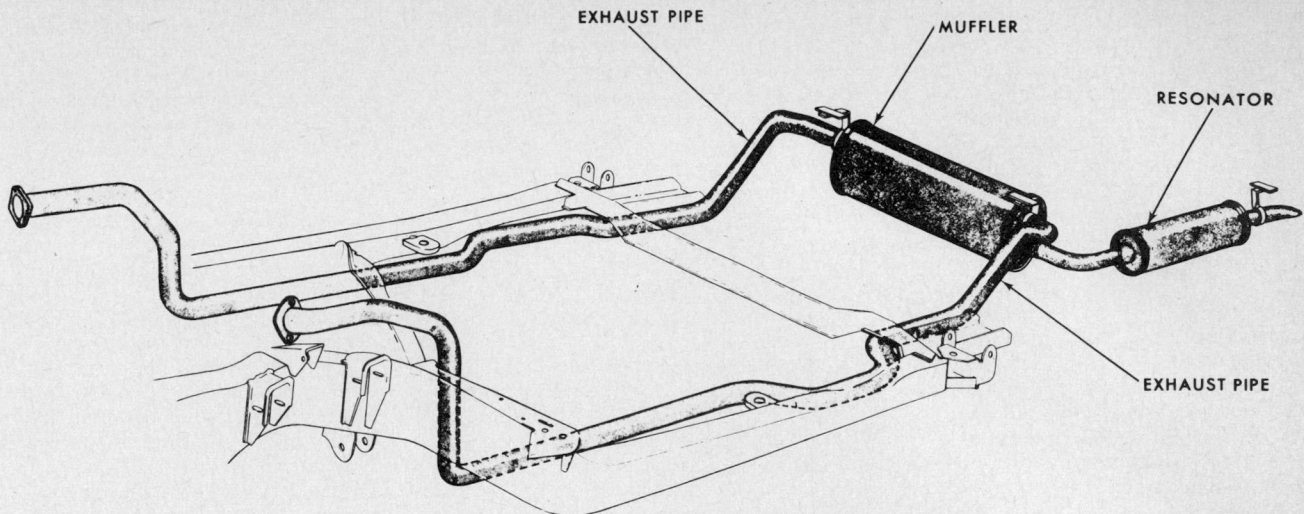

Eldorado exhaust system—1967-70 (© Cadillac Div., G.M. Corp.)

1971-72

1. Jack up car.
2. Remove clamp that holds exhaust pipe to Y pipe.
3. Remove nuts at manifold flange.
4. Disengage exhaust pipe from Y pipe and remove.

Muffler Removal

1967-70

1. Loosen clamp that secures resonator inlet at muffler.
2. Remove screws that secure resonator hanger to body, remove hanger, then resonator assembly.
3. Remove right and left exhaust pipes to muffler clamps and hangers and lower muffler until exhaust pipes rest on rear axle.
4. Tie right exhaust pipe securely to leaf spring.

Caution The spring should be padded for protection.

5. Drive muffler off right exhaust pipe.
6. Repeat Steps 4 and 5 for left side.

1971-72

1. Jack up car.
2. Remove clamps at front and rear of muffler.

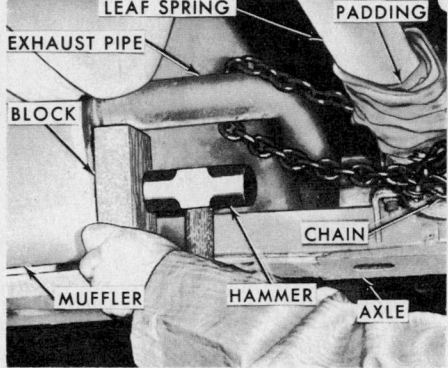

Muffler removal (© Cadillac Div. G.M. Corp.)

3. Disengage hanger and drive muffler off Y pipe.
4. Drive muffler off intermediate pipe.
NOTE: use heat as required.

Resonator Removal

1967-72

1. Remove clamp that secures resonator clamp at muffler.
2. Remove screws that secure resonator outlet hanger to body. Remove hanger.
3. Remove resonator assembly by driving inlet out of muffler.

4. Remove resonator hanger blade from resonator outlet pipe.

Cooling System

Detailed information on cooling system capacity can be found in the Capacities Table.

Information on the water temperature gauge can be found in the Unit Repair Section.

Other information pertaining to the cooling system may be found in the Cadillac section under the same year model.

Engine

Description

The engine in all Eldorado models is an overhead valve 90° V8 design. The 1967 model engine has a displacement of 429 cu. in. developing 340 horsepower at 4,000 rpm. The 1968-69 models have an engine of 472 cu. in. displacement developing 375

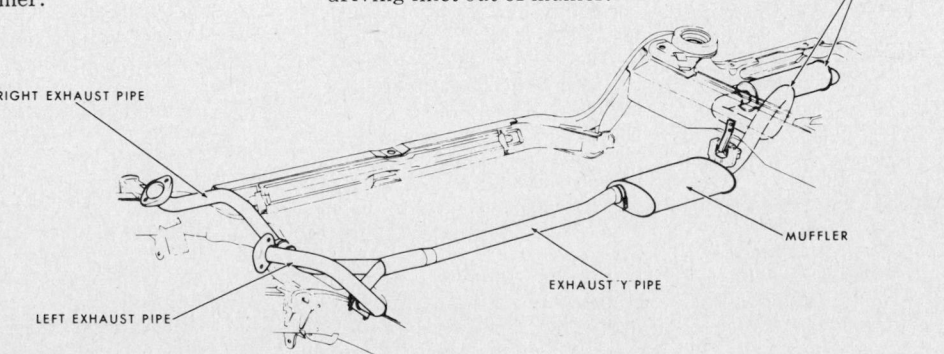

Exhaust system—1971-72 (© Cad. Div. G.M. Corp.)

horsepower at 4,400 rpm. The stroke on the 1970 engine has been increased, giving it 500 cu. in. displacement and developing 400 horsepower at 4,400 rpm. This engine is used on all 1970-72 Eldorado models.

Specifications tables are found at the beginning of this section. Other information may be found by referring to procedures given for the same year model in the Cadillac section.

Exhaust Emission Control

In compliance with anti-pollution laws involving all of the continental United States, the Cadillac Division of General Motors has adopted as standard equipment, an integrated Air Injector Reactor (A.I.R.) control system. This method is designed and built into the engine castings after 1967, and eliminates the need for some of the tubes and exterior air manifolding of previous plans. It does, however, use the same afterburner principle as that described in the Unit Repair Section. This method of control was not used on 1970 models, although it was revived for 1971 production. In 1970, a Controlled Combustion System (C.C.S.) was used, a major part of which is the T.C.S. Transmission Controlled Spark system.

Any of the present methods of terminal exhaust control require close and frequent attention to tune-up factors of engine maintenance.

Since 1968, all car manufacturers post idle speeds and other pertinent data relative to the specific engine-car application, in a conspicuous place in the engine compartment.

Transmission Controlled Spark

On 1970 models, the T.C.S. system plays a major part in the operation of the Controlled Combustion System, which consists of a thermostatic air cleaner to regulate the temperature of incoming carburetor intake air, and the T.C.S. system. The T.C.S. system itself consists of a pressure-sensitive switch in the transmission and a solenoid in the ported vacuum line between the carburetor and the thermal vacuum switch of the air cleaner. With the transmission in first or second gear, the solenoid is energized. This eliminates vacuum advance to the distributor to help reduce emissions. In third gear, the solenoid de-energizes and allows the vacuum advance to operate normally.

On the 1971 models, the system was modified slightly to bypass the T.C.S. solenoid in the Park and Neutral positions. The neutral switch senses when the transmission is shifted into Park or Neutral and allows distributor advance to be controlled through the Thermal Vacuum Switch, thus preventing overheating in traffic. The result is that there is spark advance at fast idle speed on 1971 models, whereas there was no spark advance at fast idle on 1970 models. See the Unit Repair Section of this manual for T.C.S. system tests.

Engine R & R

1967

1. Disconnect negative battery terminal.
2. Remove engine hood.
3. Remove two nuts holding the cowl rods at the wheel wells and pivot rods up from the cowl.
4. Remove the air cleaner.
5. Drain the cooling system.
6. Disconnect wires from generator.
7. On cars equipped with Automatic Climate Control, partially remove compressor.
8. Disconnect transmission cooler line at left front of final drive by removing the screw that holds attaching clip.
9. Remove heater hoses at engine and at water control valve.
10. Remove left and right shrouds by removing four screws that attach each shroud.
11. Remove four screws holding fan assembly to water pump pulley and remove as an assembly.

NOTE: fan clutches used on air-conditioned cars are always to be in an in-car position. When removed from car, support the assembly to keep clutch disc in a vertical plane to keep silicone fluid from leaking from clutch mechanism.

12. On cars equipped with Automatic Climate Control, disconnect vapor return line near fuel pump and remove clamp holding vacuum hoses to steel vapor return.
13. On cars equipped with exhaust emission control systems, remove the air pump.
14. Disconnect fuel line at the fuel pump and plug the end of the line.
15. Remove power steering pump bracket-to-cylinder block screws and position pump and bracket to one side. Remove pump belt. Do not disconnect power steering hoses.
16. Disconnect accelerator linkage at the carburetor.
17. Disconnect wiring connectors at transmission downshift switch.
18. Disconnect positive terminal wiring at coil and remove harness from two retaining clips on the left valve cover.
19. If car is equipped with Cruise Control, disconnect wiring connector at the power unit. Remove cotter pin securing accelerator linkage to exterior arm, remove washer and separate linkage from exterior arm. Also disconnect two cables at power unit.
20. Disconnect oil pressure switch connector at rear of engine.
21. Disconnect all vacuum hoses leading from intake manifold and carburetor.
22. Remove two nuts that hold left exhaust clamp to exhaust manifold and disconnect pipe.
23. Remove four upper transmission to adapter screws.
24. Remove right output shaft as described in later paragraph.
25. Disconnect starter motor retainer clamps by removing one screw at the bearing support and one screw at the engine mounting bracket.
26. Disconnect wiring at starter solenoid and remove two screws holding the starter motor to the engine and remove the starter.
27. Remove one screw at the brace at the final drive.
28. Remove two nuts holding the right exhaust pipe clamp at the exhaust manifold.
29. Remove four screws holding transmission front cover to transmission.

NOTE: the upper left screw is accessible with an extension and universal socket.

30. Remove three converter-to-flexplate attaching screws.

NOTE: this is done by removing the cork in the harmonic balancer and inserting a screw in the balancer. Rotate the screw to gain access to flexplate-to-converter screws. Do not pry on the flexplate ring gear to rotate the converter.

31. Remove vacuum modulator line at transmission and at engine.
32. Working through center crossmember, loosen, but do not remove, two transmission mounting nuts.
33. Remove two nuts and washers holding the engine mounting studs to front frame crossmember.

NOTE: there is one bolt left holding the final drive housing to the engine support bracket and two screws holding the transmission to the spacer to the engine. Do not proceed further until chain hoist is connected to the engine, because the engine may shift.

34. Attach chain hoist and take up slack.
35. Remove lower right and left transmission - to - adapter - to - cylinder-block screws.
36. Place small jack under final drive housing to support final drive and transmission.
37. Remove bolt and lockwasher holding final drive housing to engine support bracket.
38. Remove engine by pulling it slightly forward to disengage it

from transmission and up from engine compartment. Turn engine slightly clockwise while removing to assist in clearing engine compartment.

39. Secure converter holding strap J-21366 to transmission case using a 5/16—18 nut, because the converter is now free.
40. Install by reversing removal procedure.

1968-72

1. Follow Steps 1-16 of 1968-72 procedure in Cadillac Section.
2. Disconnect left exhaust pipe at manifold flange.
3. Remove screw that holds transmission cooler lines to motor mount.
4. Remove nut that secures dipstick tube to manifold.
5. Jack up car.
6. Remove starter motor.
7. Disconnect right exhaust pipe at manifold flange.
8. Remove transmission inspection cover.
9. Disconnect and plug vapor return line and fuel inlet at fuel pump.
10. Remove lower radiator hose at water pump.
11. Remove three screws that secure flex plate to converter.
12. Remove four screws that secure engine to transmission.
13. Remove front motor mount bolts and bolt that secures final drive to mount.
14. Remove right drive axle spindle nut and cotter pin.
15. Remove drive axle-to-output shaft screws and lockwashers. NOTE: discard screws and washers. Have an assistant hold brake pedal to prevent shaft from turning.
16. Remove shaft support-to-engine bolts, and one support-to-brace screw.
17. Rotate inboard end of drive axle rearward toward starter motor.
18. Pull output shaft straight out, then lower and remove from underside of car. Proceed with engine removal procedure.
19. Lower car, install lifting bracket and chain hoist and place a wood-padded jack under final drive.
20. Raise engine and pull forward to disengage transmission. Lift engine out of car.
21. To install, reverse removal procedure. See Cadillac Section for flex plate alignment.

Manifolds and Cylinder Head

See Cadillac Section.

Engine Lubrication

Oil Pan Removal

1967-72

1. Remove engine as previously described in Engine R & R.
2. Drain engine oil.
3. Remove two brackets-to-block bolts on each side of engine front mounting support.
4. Remove nuts and cap screws that hold oil pan to cylinder block and engine front cover, then remove the oil pan.
5. Remove side gaskets and rubber front and rear seals from oil pan. Discard the gaskets and seals.
6. Install by reversing the removal procedure. Torque to 10 ft. lbs.

Oil Pump Service

Removal, Inspection, Installation —1967

1. Remove engine front cover, as described later, or pull engine from car.
2. Remove four capscrews that secure pump cover plate to housing.
3. Remove cover plate, making sure pump gears do not fall out.
4. Slide drive shaft and gear out of housing.
5. Slide driven gear out of housing.
6. Remove hex plug from pump cover plate and remove pressure regulator spring and valve.
7. Inspect gears for burrs or scoring, as well as housing.
8. Check free length of regulator spring—it should be 2.77-2.89 in.
9. Check pump clearance limits.
10. Assembly and installation is the reverse of disassembly and removal.

Removal, Inspection, Installation —1968-72

1. Jack up car and remove oil filter.
2. Remove five capscrews that secure oil pump to engine. NOTE: remove screw nearest pressure regulator last.
3. Slide drive shaft, drive gear and driven gear out of housing.
4. Remove plug from housing cover, using 5/16 in. wrench. Remove pressure regulator valve and spring.
5. Check free length of regulator spring—it should be 2.77-2.89 in. for 1968 models, 2.57-2.69 in. from 1969 models.
6. Inspect gears and housing for burrs or scoring.
7. Check pump clearance limits.
8. Assembly, and installation is the reverse of disassembly and removal.

Oil Pump Specifications

Backlash between drive gears, 0.008-0.012 in.
Clearance between body and shaft not to exceed 0.005 in.
Clearance between body and gears not to exceed 0.005 in.
Gear end-play not to exceed 0.006 in.

Valve System

Checking Valve Guides

Check valve stem-to-guide clearance using a 1/16 in. wide strip of .005 in. shim stock. Bend the end of the shim and hang in the valve guide on the pushrod side. Shim should not extend more than 1/4 in. into the guide. If the valve stem will enter the guide the clearance is excessive. Guides are not replaceable and must be reamed oversize if worn.

Valve Lifter Removal

Lifters may be removed without taking off the cylinder head.

Remove throttle and gas lines from the carburetor, disconnect hoses, vacuum lines and wires that pass over the rocker covers. Remove the distributor cap and disconnect the wires at the spark plugs. Remove the bolts that hold the rocker covers to the cylinder head and lift off the rocker covers leaving the spark plug wires attached to them. Remove the bolts that hold the intake manifold to the cylinder block and lift off the intake manifold. If desired, the carburetor can be detached from the manifold first, but this is not necessary. Remove the valve chamber cover plate if applicable. Remove the bolts that hold the rockers or shafts to the cylinder head and lift off the rockers. Pull up the pushrods through the holes in the cylinder heads and the lifters can be pulled up out of their bores.

Sometimes gum residue forms on the bottom of the lifter, making it very difficult to pull the lifter up out of its bore. If this condition is suspected before the job is started, put a good solvent in the engine oil and run the engine for the time specified by the manufacturer of the solvent in order to dissolve this gum.

However, even when gum is present on the bottom of the lifter body, the lifter can be pulled up out of its bore using special pliers. These pliers are designed to grip the lifter body firmly without scoring or scratching it.

If a special tool isn't available, a good substitute can be made by grinding the teeth out of an ordinary pair of pliers and grinding a circle almost the size of the valve lifter body so that when the pliers are squeezed down on the lifter body it will contact a large surface of the lifter body, thus preventing scoring.

Pistons and Connecting Rods

Assembling Pistons to Connecting Rods

See Cadillac Section.

NOTE: fan clutches on air-conditioned cars are to be kept in an in-car position. When removed from car for any service procedure, support assembly to keep clutch disc in a vertical plane to prevent silicone fluid from leaking.

7. Remove power steering pump

21. On cars with exhaust emission control systems, remove three cap screws that hold air pump front mounting bracket to engine front cover. Loosen air pump drive belt adjusting bolt and remove the belt. Swing air pump and bracket to one side.

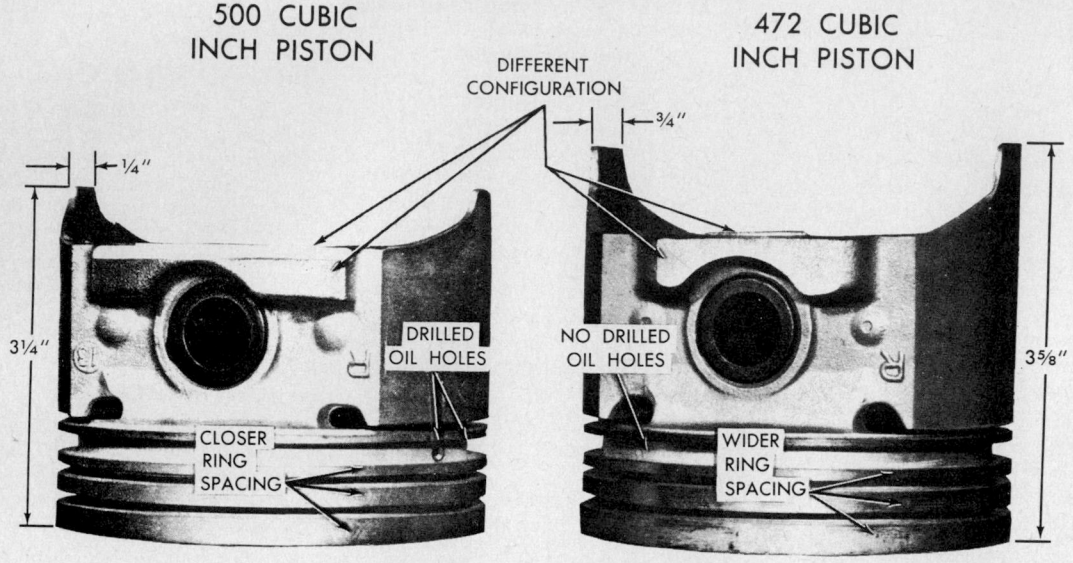

500 CUBIC INCH PISTON   472 CUBIC INCH PISTON

Piston identification (© Cadillac Div. G.M. Corp.)

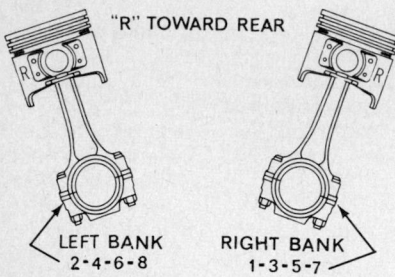

Piston to connecting rod relationship —1968-72

Assembling Rod and Piston Assemblies to the Block

See Cadillac Section.

Timing Cover, Chain and Sprockets

Timing Cover, Chain and Sprockets R & R

1967

1. Disconnect battery.
2. Remove carburetor air cleaner.
3. Drain coolant.
4. Remove oil-pan-to-front cover nuts and studs.
5. Remove upper radiator hose.
6. Remove the cap screws that hold the fan blade assembly to the water pump and remove fan blade assembly, or hub spacer and fan on non-air conditioned cars.

belt, generator belt and pulley.
8. Remove lower radiator hose.
9. Without disconnecting hoses, remove the power steering pump and bracket. Tie back out of way.
10. Disconnect generator support bracket at the cylinder head. Tie back out of way.
11. On air-conditioned cars, partially remove compressor. Also remove compressor lower mounting bracket attached to engine front cover.
12. Remove distributor assembly.
13. Remove fuel pump as previously described.
14. Remove four of the six cap screws that hold the crankshaft pulley to the harmonic balancer.
15. Remove cork plug from end of crankshaft.
16. Install harmonic balancer puller pilot, J-21052-4 or equivalent in bore end of crankshaft.
17. Install holding base, J-21052-1 or equivalent, on front of pulley, lining up the scribe mark on base with key slot in harmonic balancer, and install four holding screws with washers finger tight. Do not use a wrench to tighten screws.
18. Thread puller screw, J-21052-2, into base until screw contacts pilot.
19. With a wrench, remove balancer from crankshaft.
20. Remove pilot from end of crankshaft and remove the puller.

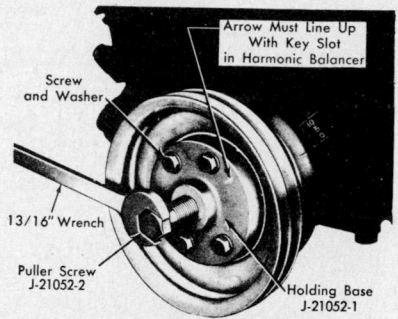

Balancer assembly removal (© Cadillac Div. G.M. Corp.)

22. Remove oil filter from oil pump cover assembly.
23. Remove four cap screws that hold the cylinder-head coolant-outlet pipe to the cylinder heads and remove outlet pipe.
24. Remove cap screw that holds fuel filter to bracket on oil filler tube.
25. Remove remaining nine cap screws that hold engine front cover to cylinder block and remove the cover with water pump attached.
26. Remove the cap screws that hold the camshaft sprocket to the camshaft.
27. Remove camshaft sprocket with chain, from camshaft.
28. Remove crankshaft sprocket from crankshaft.
29. Remove Woodruff key from crankshaft key slot.
30. Install chain and sprockets by, first seating Woodruff key in the

crankshaft key slot.

31. Install crankshaft sprocket on the crankshaft in line with the keyway.

32. Install camshaft sprocket in timing chain with timing mark toward the front.

33. Place chain over crankshaft sprocket.

34. Line up timing marks on both sprockets.

35. Hold camshaft sprocket in position against end of camshaft and press sprocket on camshaft by hand, being sure index hole in camshaft is lined up with index hole in sprocket.

36. Install two cap screws with lockwashers in camshaft sprocket and torque to 18 ft. lbs.

37. Install oil seal in front cover by prying out the old seal with a thin blade and, pressing a well greased new one into place. NOTE: it is not necessary to remove the engine front cover to replace an oil seal.

38. To install the cover, apply a small amount of gasket cement to the new front cover gasket and locate the gasket over locating dowels on cylinder block.

39. Install front cover with water pump attached, over end of crankshaft. Secure with 12 attaching screws. Refer to chart for screw locations and torque specifications.

40. Lubricate the new coolant outlet pipe to water pump O-ring seal with silicone, and install O-ring against shoulder in bore in pump body.

41. With cement on coolant outlet pipe flange surfaces, place new gaskets in position on coolant outlet pipe.

42. Install neck of coolant outlet pipe in bore in pump body, position flange surfaces against cylinder heads and install four attaching screws. Torque screws to 20 ft. lbs.

43. Install oil filter on oil pump cover assembly.

44. On cars with air-conditioning, install compressor lower mounting bracket to engine front cover. Also install compressor.

45. Install generator support bracket on coolant outlet pipe and secure with two attaching screws. Torque to 20 ft. lbs.

46. Secure fuel filter to bracket on oil filler tube with attaching screw and washer.

47. On cars with exhaust emission control system, position air pump and mounting bracket on engine front cover and secure with three attaching screws. See illustration for torque.

48. Install four pulley to harmonic balancer cap screws that were

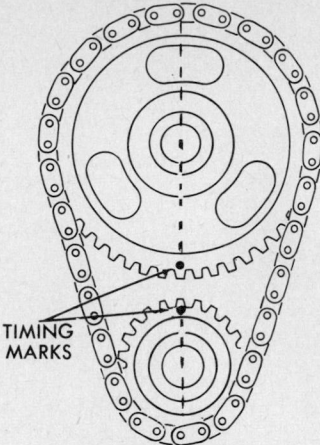

Timing gear location marks

previously removed. Torque all six screws to 18 ft. lbs.

49. Lubricate bore of balancer with E.P. lubricant to prevent seizure.

50. Position balancer on the crankshaft, with key and keyway lined up.

51. Place holding base, J-21052-1, against front face of pulley and thread installer screw, J-21052-5, into end of crankshaft. Position thrust bearing with inner race forward, washer next, and installer nut, J-21052-6, last.

52. With a wrench, press harmonic balancer onto the crankshaft.

53. When balancer is in place on the crankshaft, remove the installer tool. Finish positioning the balancer all the way on the crankshaft by, threading an appropriate bolt, (a 1962 Cadillac balancer-to-crankshaft screw will do) and washer in the end of the crankshaft. Tighten screw to 125 ft. lbs.

54. Remove this screw from the crankshaft, and install cork plug.

55. Install fuel pump.

56. Install power steering pump with bracket on the cylinder block and secure with two attaching screws.

57. Connect lower radiator hose at radiator outlet and water pump inlet pipe.

58. Install pulley and fan blade assembly on water pump and secure with four attaching screws. Torque screws to 18 ft. lbs.

59. On cars equipped with exhaust emission control system, install air pump drive belt and adjust.

60. Install generator belt and adjust.

61. Install upper radiator hose.

62. Install power steering pump belt and adjust.

63. On air-conditioned cars, install compressor, and adjust belt. Install fan shroud on radiator cradle and secure with eight cap screws. Torque screws to 12 ft. lbs.

64. Install two oil pan to engine

front cover studs and nuts.

65. Refill cooling system.

66. Reconnect battery.

67. Install distributor assembly and adjust timing to specifications.

68. Install carburetor air cleaner.

69. Run engine to check for coolant and oil leaks at all connections.

1968-72

The engine must be removed from the car before the front cover can be removed. The procedure is otherwise identical to that for the same year Cadillac as found in the Cadillac Section.

Front Suspension

Description

The front suspension consists of control arms, stabilizer bar, shock absorbers and a right and left torsion bar. Torsion bars are used in place of conventional coil springs. The front end of the torsion bar is attached to the lower control arm. The rear of torsion bar is mounted into an adjustable arm at the torsion bar crossmember. The carrying height of the car is controlled by this adjustment.

Wheel Hub (Front) R & R

1967-72

1. Remove hub cap, loosen wheel nuts, remove drive axle cotter pin and loosen drive axle nut.

2. Jack up car and place axle stands under lower control arms.

3. Remove axle nut and wheel and tire assembly.

4. Remove brake drum, or with disc brakes remove brake hose and caliper.
   NOTE: starting 1969, match-mark disc and hub, then remove disc.

5. Disconnect brake hose from steel line if equipped with drum brakes.

6. Remove upper ball joint cotter pin and loosen stud nut.

7. Strike steering knuckle near upper joint to separate it from taper.

8. Remove tie-rod end cotter pin and nut.

9. Separate tie-rod end from steering knuckle using a tie-rod splitter.

10. Remove lower ball joint cotter pin and stud nut.

11. Disconnect lower ball joint.

12. Remove hub, backing plate and steering knuckle as an assembly.

13. To install, reverse removal procedure. Tighten both ball joint stud nuts to 40 ft. lbs. up to 1969, 85 ft. lbs. starting 1970 and tie-rod nut to 30 ft. lbs. Drive axle nut must be tightened

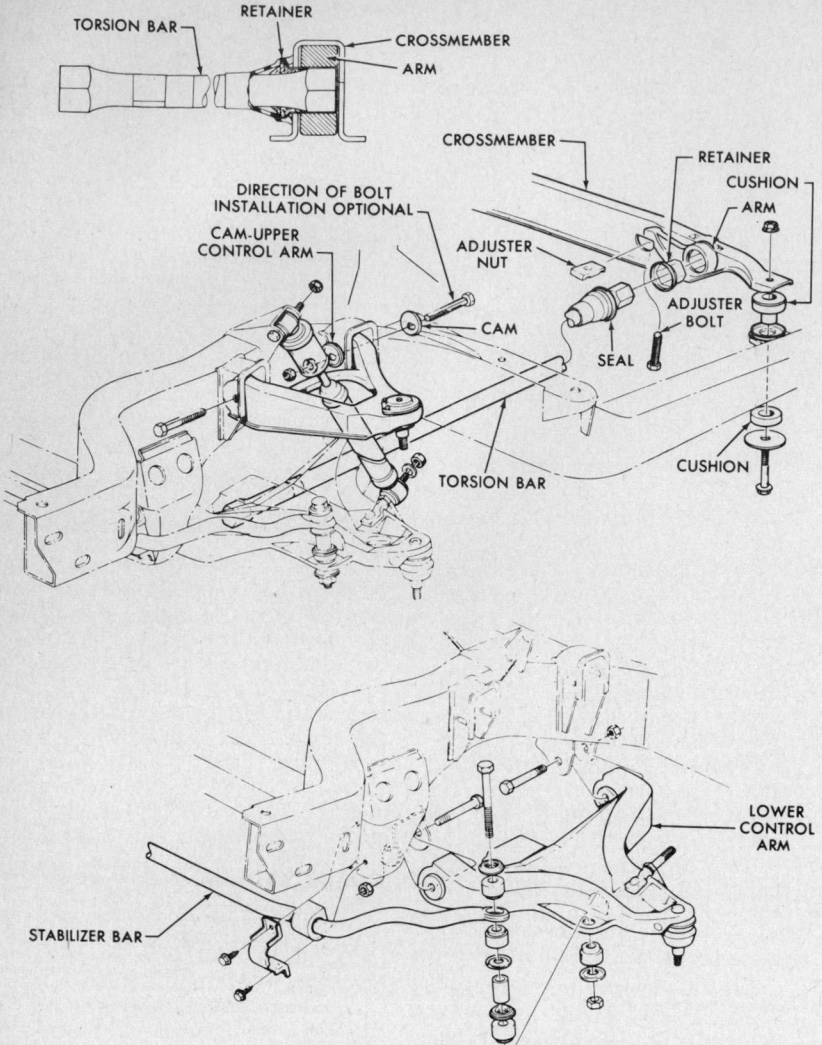

Front suspension disassembled. No retainer is used after 1969; crossmember mounts slightly different starting 1971.
(© Cadillac Div., G.M. Corp.)

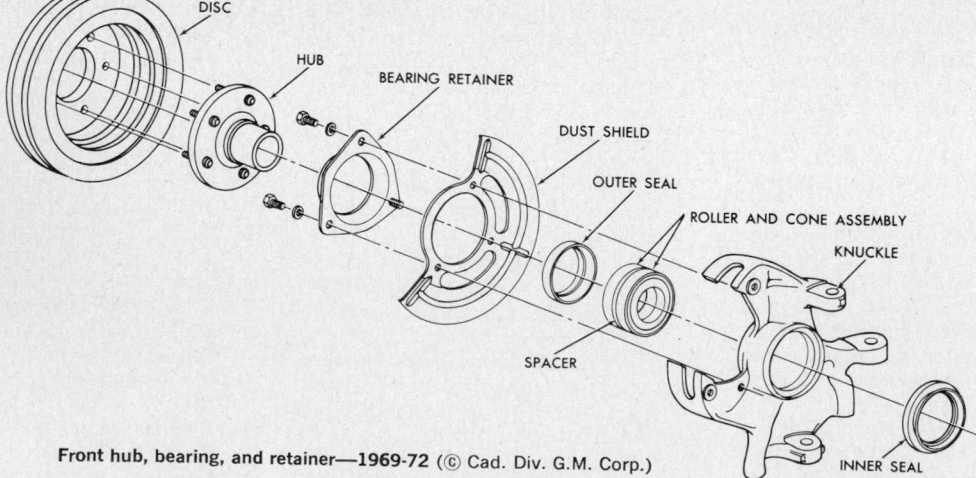

Front hub, bearing, and retainer—1969-72 (© Cad. Div. G.M. Corp.)

up and remove anchor bolt of cars with drum brakes.

5. Carefully lift brake backing plate outboard over end of axle shaft and support brake hose so that it is not damaged.

NOTE: it is not necessary to remove dust shield on cars with disc brakes. If only the O-ring seal is to be replaced, it can be done at this time without further disassembly.

6. Place rubber pad over lower control arm torsion bar connector to protect C.V. joint seal.
7. Using a brass drift and hammer loosen upper ball joint stud.
8. Remove cotter pin and nut from tie-rod end.
9. Using brass drift and hammer, remove tie-rod end from knuckle.
10. Remove cotter pin and nut from lower ball joint.
11. Carefully place ball joint puller adapter between ball joint seal and knuckle.
12. Remove lower ball joint from knuckle.
13. Remove knuckle.
14. Knuckle seal can be pried from the knuckle at this time.

Installation

1. Using seal installer, install seal into knuckle. Seal should be packed with chassis grease.
2. Install lower ball joint stud into knuckle and attach nut. Do not tighten nut at this time.
3. Install tie-rod and stud into knuckle and attach nut. Do not tighten nut at this time.
4. Install upper ball joint stud into knuckle and attach nut. Do not tighten nut at this time.

to 105-110 ft. lbs. to prevent loosening in service.

Steering Knuckle and Seal Replacement

Removal

1. Remove hub and drum or disc.

2. Remove upper ball joint cotter pin and nut. Remove caliper starting 1969.
3. Remove brake line hose clip from ball joint stud.

NOTE: do not loosen ball joint stud.

4. Bend lock plate on anchor bolt

5. Install backing plate onto knuckle with anchor bolt and lock plate. Do not tighten nut at this time.
6. Remove upper ball joint attaching nut and install brake line hose clip.
7. Torque ball joint nuts to a min-

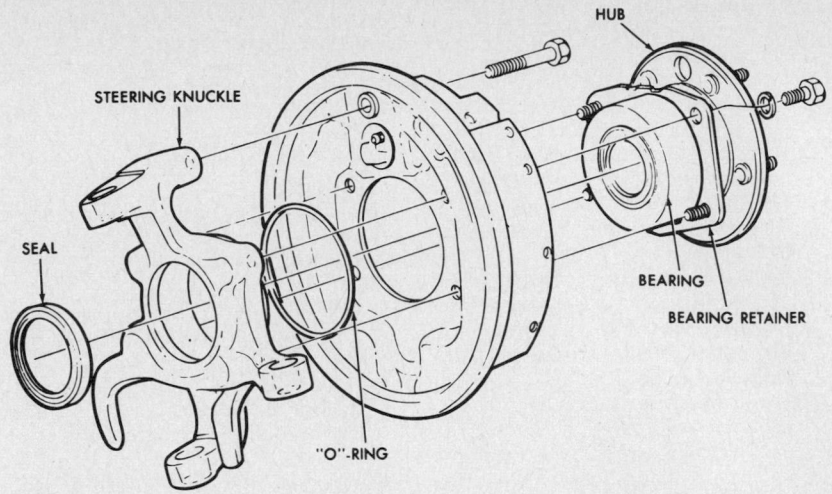

Front hub, bearing and retainer—1967-68 with drum brakes (© Cadillac Div. G.M. Corp.)

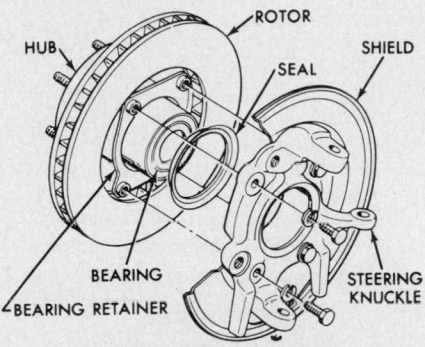

Front hub, bearing, and retainer
—1967-68 with disc brakes
(© Cad. Div. G.M. Corp.)

imum of 40 ft. lbs. up to 1969, 85 ft. lbs. starting 1970. Never back off to install cotter pins.

NOTE: cotter pin on upper ball joint must be bent up, only, to prevent interference with C. V. joint seal.

8. Torque tie-rod end to 30 ft. lbs. and install cotter pin.
9. Torque anchor bolt to 135 ft. lbs. on drum brake models, and bend lock plate onto flat of bolt head.
10. Install hub assembly.
11. Install drum or disc and wheel; install drive axle nut.
12. Remove floor stand and lower car.
13. Be sure to check camber, caster and toe-in, and adjust if necessary. Tighten drive axle and lug nuts to 105-110 ft. lbs.

Torsion Bar
Removal—1967

1. Loosen wheel lug nuts, jack up car and place on axle stands.
2. Remove wheel and tire assemblies.
3. Replace one nut per side on drum brake cars to prevent drum's falling off.
4. Remove hub cotter pin, nut and washer.

5. Remove brake line clip attached to frame.
6. Place a floor jack under the lower control arm of the side being worked on.
7. Using a hammer and brass drift, disconnect upper ball joint, remove nut and brake line clip.
8. Disconnect shock absorber at lower mount.
9. Disconnect tie-rod at steering knuckle.
10. Disconnect stabilizer bar; discard nut and bolt.
11. Disconnect lower ball joint.
12. Disengage backing plate (drum brakes) and hang it on a piece of wire.
13. Remove lower control arm-to-frame attaching *nuts*. *Do not remove bolts yet.*
14. Slowly lower the floor jack under the lower control arm.

The torsion bar is now unloaded.
15. Remove the torsion bar adjusting bolt at crossmember.
16. Pull down on lower control arm, while at the same time reaching back to remove torsion bar adjusting nut from crossmember.
17. Now, remove lower control arm-to-frame attaching *bolts*.
18. Disengage lower control arm from frame mounts.
19. Using extreme care, slide lower control arm off torsion bar. Slide torsion bar out of frame retainer and remove from car. *Any nicks on torsion bar can cause failure of the part.*

Installation—1967

1. Check rubber seal for damage and replace if necessary.
2. Lubricate about 3 in. of each end

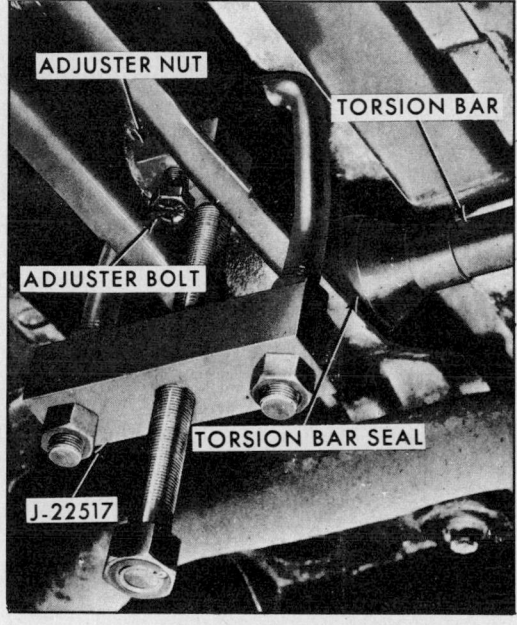

Torsion bar remover and installer
(© Cadillac Div. G.M. Corp.)

of bar with Lubriplate or Molykote.

NOTE: if retainers are used, they must be renewed each time bar is replaced.

3. Install torsion bar into lubricated retainer at crossmember.

NOTE: torsion bars are marked for proper installation.

4. Lubricate lower control arm bar connector and position lower arm on torsion bar. Make sure lower arm is level and that torsion bar is fully seated in crossmember.
5. Reverse Steps 1-18 of *Removal* procedure. Lower control arm-to-frame attaching bolts and nuts are tightened to 65 ft. lbs.

Removal—1968-70

1. Raise car and place jack under rear axle. Raise front of car and

place jacks under front lower control arms.

2. Install torsion bar remover and installer on torsion bar crossmember. Tighten center bolt on this tool until torsion bar adjusting arm is raised enough to permit removal of adjusting bolt and lock nut. Remove adjusting bolt and lock nut.

3. Remove torsion bar installer and remover and install on other end of torsion bar crossmember and repeat Step 2. Remove tool.

4. Remove torsion bar crossmember mounting bolts, bushings, retainers and parking brake cable clip.

5. Drive crossmember down, then rearward until both torsion bars are free. Adjusting arms will fall out.

6. Lift up on crossmember. Remove torsion bars by sliding them out of lower control arm connectors.

Installation—1968-70

1. Lubricate both ends of torsion bar for approximately 3 in. with extreme pressure chassis lubricant.

2. Place torsion bar in retainer at chassis crossmember.

3. Lubricate lower control arm torsion bar connector and slide torsion bar into connector.

4. Repeat procedure for other torsion bar.

5. Place torsion bar adjusting arm in crossmember, then slide torsion bar toward rear of car until seated in adjusting arm.

6. Repeat for other torsion bar.

7. Install bushings and retainers between crossmember and frame on both sides.

8. Raise front of car, positioning jacks under lower control arms.

9. Install crossmember mounting bolts and tighten to 40 ft. lbs.

10. Install torsion bar remover and installer on crossmember and tighten center bolt until torsion bar adjusting arm is high enough to permit installation of adjusting bolt and locknut. Install locknut and adjusting bolt.

11. Remove torsion bar remover and installer and install on other end of crossmember and repeat Step 10 for other torsion bar.

12. Remove torsion bar remover and installer.

13. Raise car, removing jacks, and lower car.

Removal—1971-72

1. Jack up car and support so that front suspension hangs at full rebound.

2. Remove adjusting bolt from both torsion bar locknuts.

3. Install torsion bar remover and installer tool on torsion bar crossmember.

4. Tighten center bolt of tool until adjusting arm is raised high enough to permit removal of locknut. Remove locknut.

5. Repeat Steps 3 and 4 on other side of crossmember.

6. Remove parking brake cable guide at right side of underbody.

7. Remove torsion bar crossmember bolts and retainers from both sides.

8. Move crossmember toward side opposite the torsion bar being removed. One side of crossmember should clear frame at this point.

9. Lower the free end on the crossmember and drive it rearward until torsion bar is free. It may be necessary to loosen parking brake adjuster nut to gain slack in cable.

NOTE: although both torsion bars can be removed at this point, it has been found much easier to do only one side at a time.

10. Remove torsion bar from lower control arm.

NOTE: nicks or scratches in torsion bar can cause its failure.

Installation—1971-72

1. Lubricate 3 in. of each end of torsion bar. Bars are marked L or R for left and right sides—do not interchange.

2. Slide torsion bar into lower control arm as far as it will go.

3. Position adjusting arm in crossmember. Holding arm in place, slide torsion bar rearward until it is seated in adjusting arm.

4. Position crossmember to frame and reverse Steps 1-7 of *Removal* procedure.

Upper Control Arm

Removal

NOTE: the upper control arm can be serviced as an assembly, although bushings and upper ball joint kits are available.

1. Hoist car and remove wheel.

2. Remove upper shock absorber attaching bolt.

3. Remove cotter pin and nut on upper ball joint.

4. Disconnect brake hose clamp from ball joint stud. Remove caliper.

5. Using hammer and a drift, drive on spindle until upper ball joint stud is disengaged.

6. Remove upper control arm cam assemblies and remove control arm from car.

Installation

1. Guide upper control arm over shock absorber and install bushing ends into frame horns.

2. Install cam assemblies.

NOTE: front cam is mounted up, rear cam is mounted down.

3. Install ball joint stud into knuckle. Install caliper.

4. Install brake hose clip on ball joint stud.

5. Install ball joint nut. Torque to 40 ft. lbs. up to 1969, 85 ft. lbs. thereafter, and insert cotter pin, crimp.

NOTE: cotter pin must be crimped toward upper control arm to prevent interference with outer C. V. joint seal.

6. Install upper shock attaching bolt and nut. Torque to 75 ft. lbs.

7. Install wheel.

8. Lower hoist.

9. Check camber, caster and toe-in, and adjust if necessary.

Upper Control Arm Bushing on the Car

The upper control arm bushings can be removed and installed on or off the car.

Removal

1. Hoist car and remove wheel.

2. Disconnect upper shock absorber attaching bolt.

3. Remove cam assemblies from control arms.

4. Move control arms out of frame horns and attach bushing removal tools.

Installation

1. Install tools and press bushings into control arm.

2. Move control arm into frame horns and install cam assemblies. Front cam is mounted up, rear cam is mounted down.

3. Connect upper shock absorber attaching bolt. Torque to 75 ft. lbs.

4. Replace wheel and lower car.

5. Align front wheels.

Lower Control Arm

Removal

1. Remove wheel disc and loosen wheel mounting nuts.

2. Remove hub cotter pin. Loosen nut.

3. Raise car and remove wheel and tire.

4. Remove torsion bar, as described previously.

5. Remove hub nut and washer, and brake line clips attached to frame.

6. Remove cotter pin, nut and brake line clip from upper ball joint and remove joint from steering knuckle with a hammer and drift.

7. Disconnect shock absorber and remove.

8. Disconnect tie-rod end at steering knuckle with tie-rod end puller.

9. Disconnect stablizer bar and nut and link bolt.

10. Disconnect lower ball joint with ball joint puller and adapter.
11. Disengage hub, knuckle and disc as an assembly and secure to upper control arm with wire.
12. Remove lower control arm to frame nuts and bolts and disengage arm from frame mounts.

Installation

1. Install hub, disc and knuckle assembly on drive axle.
2. Install lower control arms into mounts at chassis.
   NOTE: do not tighten nuts now.
3. Install lower control arm ball joint into steering knuckle. Tighten nut to 40 ft. lbs. to 1969, 85 ft. lbs. from 1970 and install cotter pin.
4. Tighten lower control arm bolts to 75 ft. lbs.
5. Install shock absorber and tighten nut to 75 ft. lbs.
6. Install upper control arm ball joint into steering knuckle and install brake line clip. Tighten nut to 40 ft. lbs. to 1969, 85 ft. lbs. from 1970 and install cotter pin.
7. Install brake line clip to chassis.
8. Install tie-rod end in steering knuckle, tightening nut to 30 ft. lbs.
9. Install stabilizer bar.
10. Install hub to drive axle washer and nut.
11. Install torsion bar.
12. Install wheel and tire.
13. Lower car.
14. Tighten hub to drive axle nut to 110 ft. lbs. and install cotter pin. Tighten wheel nuts to 105 ft. lbs.
15. Install wheel disc.

Lower Control Arm Bushings

Removal

Remove lower control arm and press bushings out of arm. To install, press bushings into arm and install arm. Check standing height and adjust if necessary.

Ball Joint Checks

Vertical Check

1. Raise the car and position floor stands under the left and right lower control arm, as near as possible to each lower ball joint. Car must be stable and should not rock on floor stands.
2. Position dial indicator to register vertical movement at wheel hub.
3. Place a pry bar between the lower control arm and the outer race, and pry down on the bar. Care must be used so that the drive axle seal is not damaged. The vertical reading must not exceed .125 in.

Horizontal Check

1. Place car on floor stands as outlined in Step 1 in the Vertical Check.
2. Position dial indicator at the rim of the wheel, to indicate side play.
3. Grasp wheel, top and bottom, and push in on the bottom of the tire while pulling out at the top. Read gauge, then reverse the push-pull procedure. Horizontal deflection on the gauge should not exceed .125 in. at the wheel rim.

Lower Control Arm Ball Joint

Removal

1. Remove knuckle.
2. Using chisel, cut the three rivet heads off.
3. By using a 7/32 in. drill bit, drill side rivets 3/16 in. deep.
4. Using hammer and punch, drive center rivet of joint, until joint is out of the control arm.

Installation

1. Install service ball joint into control arm and torque bolts and nut.
2. Reverse knuckle removal.

Lower Control Arm Ball Joint Seal

The lower ball joint seal can be installed with lower control arm either in or out of the car.

Removal

1. Remove steering knuckle.
2. Using hammer and chisel, drive seal from ball joint.
3. Wipe grease from ball joint and stud.

Installation

1. Position new seal over ball joint stud.
2. Lubricate jaws of camber adjusting wrench and carefully slide jaw between seal and retainer.
3. Tap lightly with hammer on center bolt of the wrench until retainer is fully seated.
4. Install knuckle.
5. Lubricate the ball joint fitting until grease is apparent in seal.

Stabilizer Bar

Removal

1. Remove link bolts, nuts, grommets, spacers and retainers from lower control arm. Discard bolts.
2. Remove two bolts attaching dust shield to frame, both sides.
3. Remove bracket to frame attaching bolts and remove stabilizer bar from front of car.

Installation

Reverse removal procedure.

NOTE: new link bolts are torqued to 14 ft. lbs., then cut off to leave 1/4 in. of bolt remaining.

Front Shock Absorber

Replacement

1. Remove wheel disc and loosen wheel mounting nuts.
2. Raise car, place on jacks, and remove wheel and tire.
3. Place a hydraulic jack under lower control arm and raise so that load is taken off shock absorber.
4. Disconnect shock absorber at upper and lower mount.
5. Compress shock absorber, working lower mount free from mount bolt.
6. Remove shock absorber.
7. Install by reversing procedure above, tightening shock absorber nuts to 75 ft. lbs. and wheel mounting nuts to 105 ft. lbs.

Standing Height—1967-70

The standing height is controlled by the adjustment setting of the torsion bar adjusting bolts. Clockwise rotation of the bolts increases the front height. It is very important that this height be considered and made correct before steering geometry is established.

For quick checks only, the locations at frame-to-ground points A and B, as illustrated, can be used up to 1970. However, locations C and D, are preferred and should always be used for proper measurements of standing heights up to 1970.

Quick Reference Locations —to 1970

Location A is at a point 2 in. behind the front edge of the door. This is 39 1/2 in. from the centerline of the front wheel.

Location B is at the middle of the spring bracket tab under the frame. This is 82 3/4 in. forward of the rear axle centerline.

Preferred Locations—to 1970

Location C is from center to center of the shock absorber upper and lower mounting bolts.

Location D is from the flat on the bottom of the stop bracket to the top of the axle. The rear view of D, as illustrated, shows this location more clearly.

Standing Height—1971-72

The procedure for checking standing height has been modified slightly starting with 1971 production. A quick check of height on these models can be made by measuring the distance between the lower edge of the front shock absorber dust cover and the lower shock bolt centerline (front) and the distance between the lower edge of the frame "kickover"

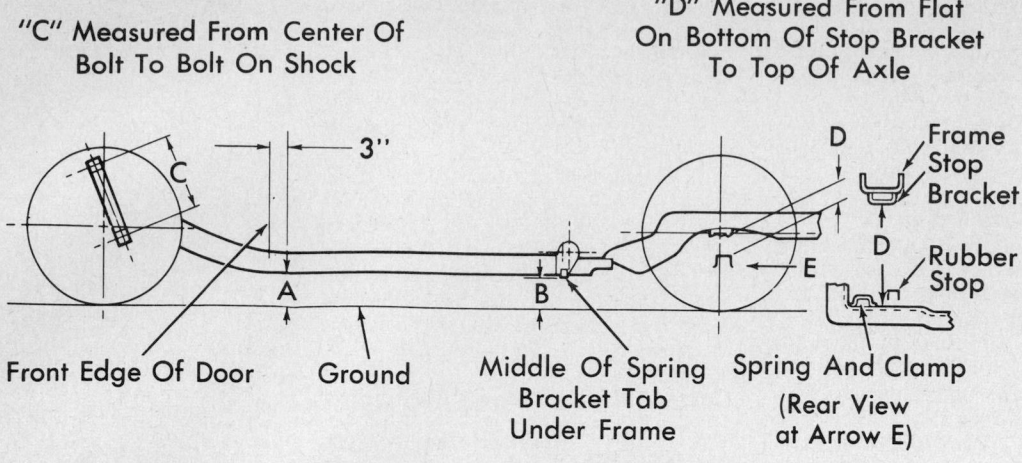

"C" Measured From Center Of Bolt To Bolt On Shock

"D" Measured From Flat On Bottom Of Stop Bracket To Top Of Axle

Front Edge Of Door   Ground   Middle Of Spring Bracket Tab Under Frame   Spring And Clamp (Rear View at Arrow E)

Reference Locations Frame To Ground		Preferred Locations	
"A" Front	"B" Rear	"C" Front True Shock Length	"D" Rear Standing Height
6¼" TO 6⁷⁄₁₆"	5¹⁵⁄₁₆" TO 6½"	14⅝" TO 14⅞"	4-23/32" To 5-15/32"

1969-70 Fleetwood Eldorado standing height chart (© Cadillac Div. G.M. Corp.)

and the top of the axle tube (rear) If equipped with Automatic Level Control, loosen the air lines at the rear shocks to bleed all air from the system.

Standing Height—1971-72

Model	Front	Rear
Coupe	8.0-8.25"	3.88-4.64"
Convertible	8.0-8.25"	3.88-4.64"

Caution Do not accidentally slip the measuring rule or device into the slot for the rubber bumper in the rear axle, because doing so would give a false reading.

Acceptable specifications are also given in illustration. Frame to ground dimensions must be within 1 in. from front to rear and within ⅝ in. from side to side.

If dimensions are not within tolerance, torsion bars must be adjusted.

Measuring Height—All Years

Before measuring standing height, check and correct the following items:
1. Car must be on a level surface.
2. Gas tank should be full or a compensating weight added. Estimate the amount of gasoline in the tank and add weights in the trunk in the space immediately above the float access hole area.
3. Front seat should be adjusted all the way to its rearmost position.
4. Front and rear tires should be inflated to 24 and 22 lbs. respec-

tively.
5. Both doors closed.
6. No passengers or additional weight should be in the car or trunk (except as indicated above).

Checking Rear Height with Automatic Level Control Disconnected

Though rear height readings can be taken without disconnecting the A.L.C., it is preferred that measurements be taken with the leveling system disconnected—to eliminate the possibility of the A.L.C. system affecting the reading.

The A.L.C. can be disconnected at the black line connection at the leveling valve.

After the measurement is taken and the black line is reconnected, the A.L.C. system should be refilled by

use of an air pressure hose to insure pressure reserve in the tank.

If rear of car raises when the automatic leveling system is reconnected, the leveling system should be checked and adjusted.

Alignment Procedures Setting Camber & Caster

1. Check camber. The preferred setting for camber is in the specifications. To adjust proceed as follows:
   A. Loosen nut on upper control arm front cam bolt.
   B. Note camber reading and rotate front bolt to correct for one-half of the incorrect reading or as near to that amount as possible. Tighten front nut.

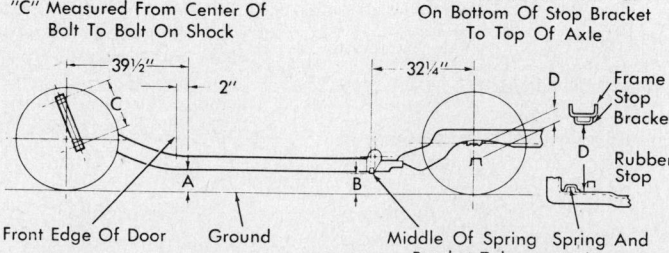

"C" Measured From Center Of Bolt To Bolt On Shock

"D" Measured From Flat On Bottom Of Stop Bracket To Top Of Axle

Front Edge Of Door   Ground   Middle Of Spring Bracket Tab Under Frame   Spring And Clamp

Reference Locations Frame To Ground		Preferred Locations	
"A" Front	"B" Rear	"C" Front True Shock Length	"D" Rear Standing Height
5-31/32" To 6-17/32"		14-15/32" To 14-23/32"	4-23/32" To 5-15/32"

1967-68 Fleetwood Eldorado standing height chart (© Cadillac Div. G.M. Corp.)

Caster, camber cam locations
(© Cadillac Div. G.M. Corp.)

C. Loosen nut on upper control arm rear cam bolt and rotate rear cam bolt to bring camber reading to 0°. Tighten rear nut.

D. Check caster. Preferred reading is in the specifications.

NOTE: if caster requires adjustment, proceed with Step E; if not, move to Step I.

E. Loosen front cam bolt nut.

F. Using camber scale on alignment equipment, rotate front bolt so that the camber changes an amount equal to one-quarter of the desired caster change.

NOTE: if adjusting to correct for excessive negative caster, rotate front bolt to increase positive camber. If adjusting to correct for excessive positive caster, rotate front bolt to increase negative camber.

G. Tighten front nut.

H. Loosen nut on rear cam bolt and rotate the rear bolt until

camber setting returns to 0°. This results in the correct caster setting.

I. Tighten upper control arm cam nuts to 75 ft. lbs. up to 1969, 95 ft. lbs. starting 1970. Hold head of bolt securely; any movement of the cam will affect final setting and will require a recheck of the camber and caster adjustments.

Relationship of Front and Rear Cams

When setting camber and caster, remember this relationship:

Front cams. If turned for more positive camber, then caster also becomes more positive.

In other words, when turning the front cams to obtain a more positive setting for camber, caster will follow to a more positive setting.

The same is true when turning for more positive caster: more positive camber will follow.

Rear cams. If turned for more positive camber, then caster becomes more negative.

When turning the rear cams to obtain a more positive setting for camber, caster will advance in the opposite direction toward a more negative setting.

Toe-in Adjustment

A. Center steering wheel, raise car and check wheel runout.

B. Loosen tie-rod adjuster nuts, and adjust to proper setting.

C. Tighten tie-rod adjuster nuts. Torque nuts 22 ft. lbs. Position tie-rod clamps so opening of clamps are facing UP. This is a very necessary setting. Interference and a possible tie up of front end linkage could occur, if clamps hit anything while turning.

Rear Suspension

1967-70

The rear suspension on the Cadillac Eldorado consists of two single leaf, semi-elliptical springs, two vertical and two horizontal shock absorbers.

1971-72

A new rear suspension system, introduced in 1971, has replaced the old leaf spring type used previously. This new system is a four-link, coil spring suspension having no components interchangeable with other Cadillac models. Instead of two vertical and two horizontal shock absorbers, as used on earlier models, Automatic Level Control Superlift shock absorbers are used exclusively.

Automatic Level Control

This system is basically the same as that used on other Cadillac models and functions identically. However, the on-car location of major components is different. Procedures will be found in the Cadillac section.

Rear Leaf Spring Removal —1967-70

1. Raise car.
2. Support rear axle at center with hydraulic jack.
3. Remove rear wheel from side being worked on.
4. Remove nut that secures Automatic Level Control link to axle bracket and remove link.
5. Remove nut that secures front of spring to frame bracket.
   NOTE: do not remove bolt now.
6. Remove two nuts at rear shackle

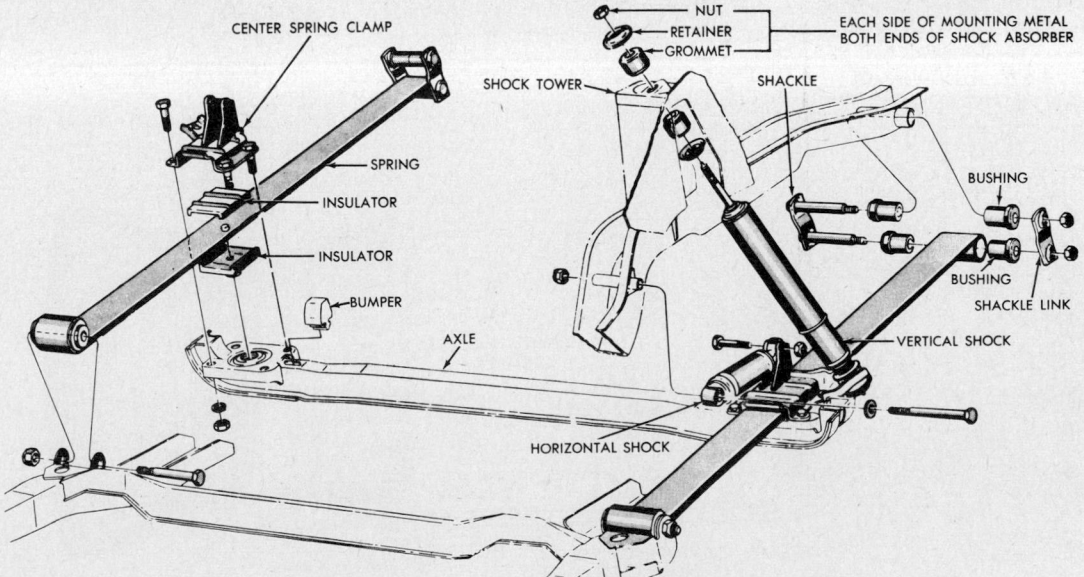

Rear suspension—1967-70 (© Cadillac Div., G.M. Corp.)

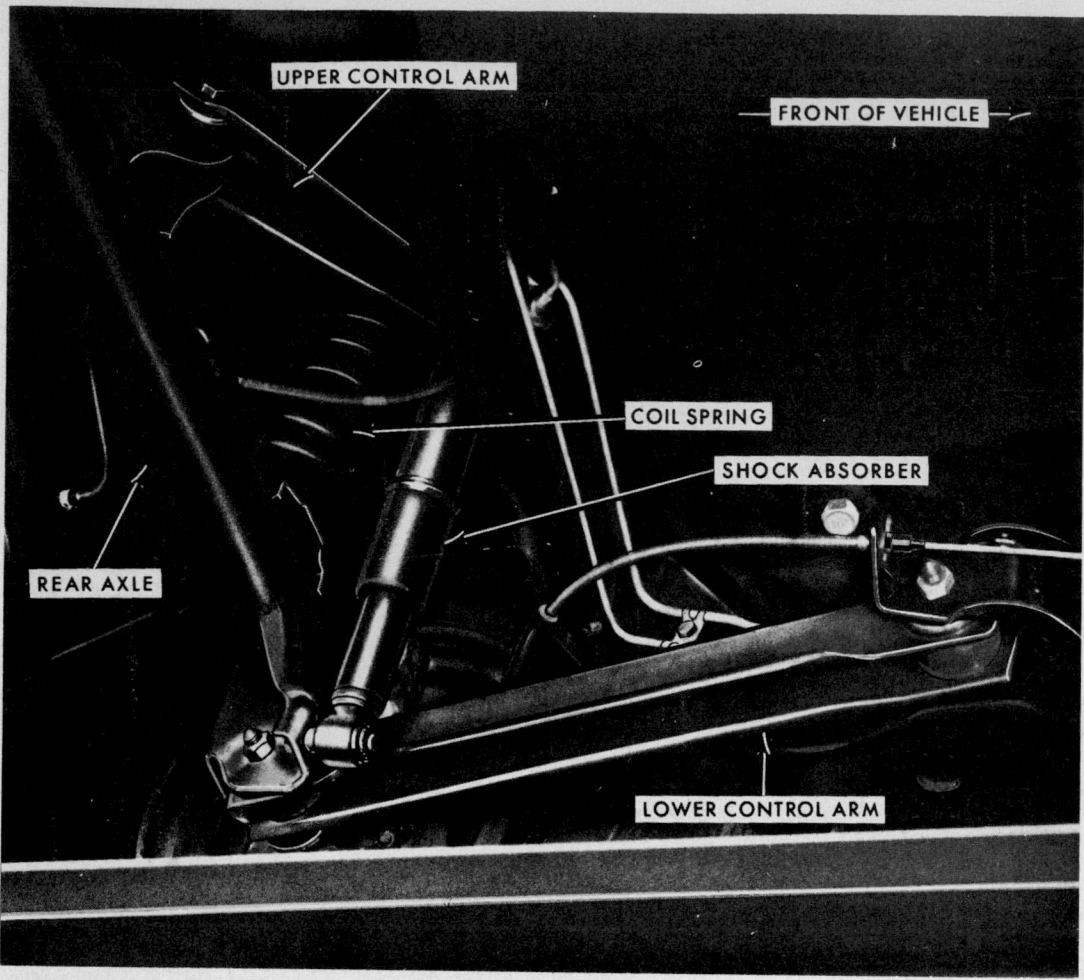

Coil spring rear suspension—1971-72 (© Cad. Div. G.M. Corp.)

outer link and remove link.

7. Remove four nuts and lockwashers that secure center spring clamp to rear axle and position out of the way.
8. Lower hydraulic jack until axle is free from spring.
9. Remove rear shackle assembly from spring and body.
10. Remove bolt from front of spring and remove spring.

Upper Control Arm R & R— 1971-72

1. Jack up car and support rear on axle stands under frame side members.
2. Disconnect A.L.C. system over-travel link at right upper control arm axle bracket, then position lever in 'center' position.
3. Disconnect lower shock bolt and

position shock out of the way.
4. Jack up under rear axle to unload upper control arm.
5. Remove bolt and nut that secures upper arm to axle bracket.
6. Remove bolt and nut that secures upper arm to crossmember; remove arm.

NOTE: bushings can be replaced at this point.

7. Install upper arm to brackets

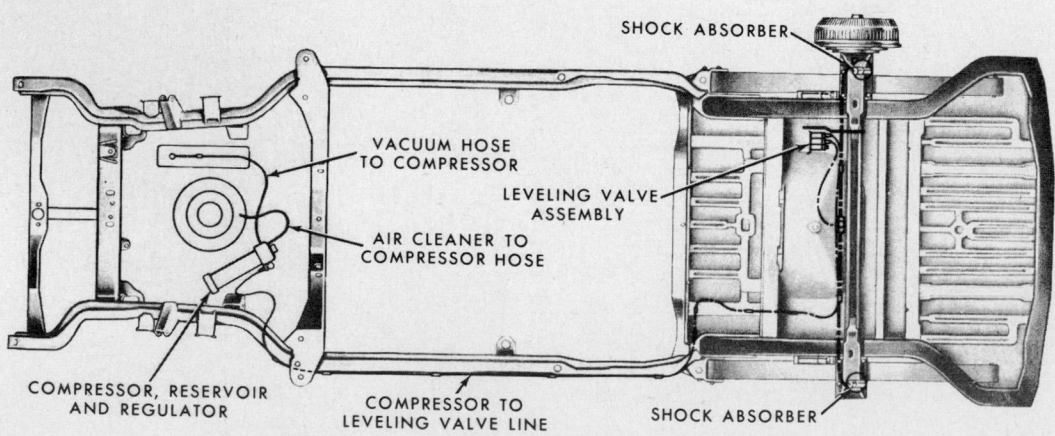

Automatic leveling system (© Cadillac Div. G.M. Corp.)

and install bolts and nuts. Do not tighten nuts at this time.

8. Install lower shock bolt and shock.
9. Jack up on rear axle and remove axle stands under frame side members.
10. With weight of car on axle only, tighten upper arm-to-crossmember nuts to 100 ft. lbs. and lower axle bracket nuts to 75 ft. lbs.
11. Install A.L.C. overtravel lever, lower car and inflate system to 140 psi.

NOTE: control arm pivot bolts must be tightened at standing height or ride rate will be affected.

12. Inspect brake lines for damage.

Lower Control Arm R & R— 1971-72

1. Jack up car.
2. Remove bolts and nuts that secure lower arm to axle and frame.
3. Remove lower control arm.
4. Install lower arm and tighten bolts to 100 ft. lbs.

Rear Coil Spring R & R— 1971-72

1. Remove both upper control arms from their axle mountings.
2. Disconnect both rear shocks at lower ends.
3. Disconnect brake hose and cap brake line.
4. Lower axle carefully, using a floor jack, until springs can be

removed.

Caution If axle is lowered beyond full rebound, springs can jump from their seats with considerable force. For this reason, lower axle only far enough to allow springs to be lightly compressed by hand and removed.

5. Inspect rubber insulators for damage.
6. Insert springs and jack up axle until springs are compressed.
7. Reconnect shocks and upper control arms.
8. Connect brake hose and bleed rear brake circuit.

Rear Axle Assembly

1967-70

The rear axle consists of a welded beam-type, drop center axle having spindles pressed into and bolted to the axle flanges. The rear wheels run on tapered roller bearings very similar to those used on the front wheels of Cadillac models other than the Eldorado.

1971-72

The rear axle was changed in 1971 to a straight, hollow tube design. The spindles still are pressed and bolted to the axle flanges and tapered roller bearings are used. The Track Master system, optional on 1971 and later Eldorado models, uses a hollow spindle through which the drive cables for the speed sensors run.

Removal—1967-70

1. Raise car, and remove rear wheels.
2. Remove rear brake drum, then hub assembly.
3. Disconnect brake lines and hose and parking brake cable.
4. Disconnect overtravel lever link from bracket on rear axle.
5. Remove spring guides that hold parking brake cable to center spring clamp.
6. Remove brake backing plates.
7. Supporting rear axle at center with hydraulic jack, remove four nuts on each side of spring clamp assemblies.
8. Lower jack and remove rear axle.

Removal—1971-72

1. Jack up rear of car and support on stands under frame rails.
2. Remove both tire and wheel assemblies.
3. Remove hubs as follows:
   a. Remove brake drums.
   b. If equipped with Track Master, remove three screws that secure drive cap, remove cap, retainer rings, spindle nut, washer and bearings.
   c. If equipped with standard axle, remove dust cap, cotter pin, spindle nut, washer and bearings.
   d. Pull hub off spindle.
4. Disconnect brake lines at wheel cylinders.
5. Disconnect rubber hose and cap

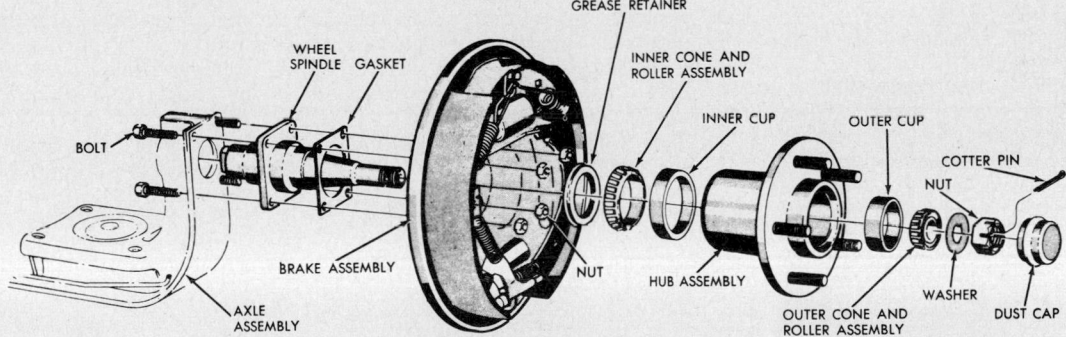

Rear axle disassembled—1967-70 (© Cad. Div. G.M. Corp.)

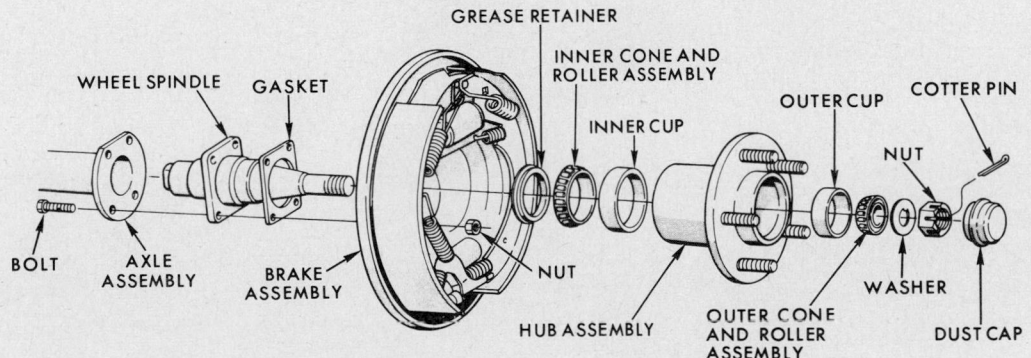

Rear axle disassembled—1971-72 (© Cad. Div. G.M. Corp.)

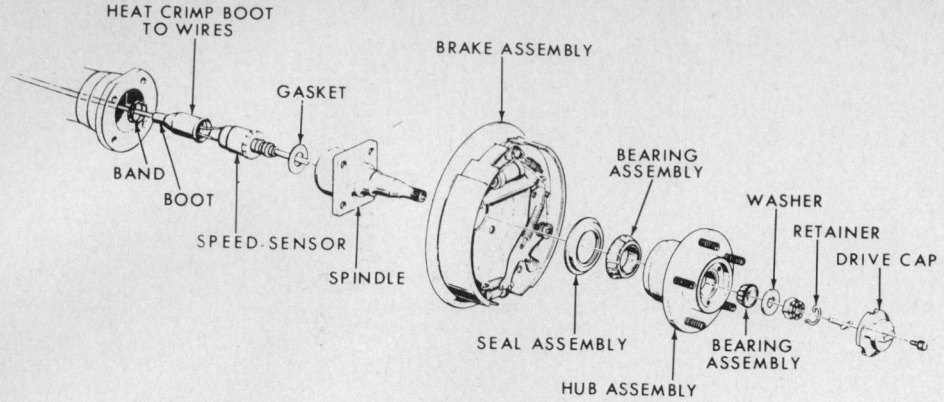

Rear axle disassembled—1971-72 with Track Master (© Cad. Div. G.M. Corp.)

to prevent brake fluid loss.

6. Disconnect overtravel link at axle bracket, then deflate shocks.
7. Remove brake backing plates and pull spindle using a slide hammer.

NOTE: make sure the sensor wiring is not damaged if equipped with T.M.

8. Disconnect brake lines from clips on axle.
9. If car is equipped with T.M., remove screw and clip that secures sensor cable to axle. Pull cable through ⅝ in. hole in axle and disconnect.
10. Disconnect lower shock bolts and position shocks out of the way.
11. Jack up on axle to relieve tension on upper control arm.
12. Remove bolts and nuts that secure upper control arms to axle.
13. Lower axle and remove coil springs. See Caution under *Rear Coil Spring R & R.*
14. Remove bolts and nuts that secure lower control arms to axle.
15. Remove brake junction from axle and rubber stop bumpers.
16. Remove axle from car.
17. To install, reverse removal procedure.

Drive Axles

Drive axles are a complete flexible assembly and consist of an axle shaft and an inner tri-pot joint and outer constant velocity joint. The inner tri-pot joint has complete flexibility, plus inward and outward movement. The outer constant velocity joint has complete flexibility only.

Drive Axle—Right Side

Removal—1967-68

1. Hoist car under lower control arms.

NOTE: battery should be disconnected.

2. Remove drive axle, cotter pin, nut and washer.
3. Using a wood-padded hammer,

tap on end of drive axle to unseat axle at hub asembly.

NOTE: install a piece of rubber hose over torsion bar connector at lower control arm to prevent tripot seal damage.

4. Remove inner constant velocity joint attaching bolts.

NOTE: on 1967-68 models, disconnect tie-rod end at steering knuckle and disconnect upper ball joint before proceeding to Step 5.

5. Slide drive axle inward and disengage outer joint from steering knuckle.
6. Rotate axle toward rear of car and guide it down and out.

Removal—1969-72

1. Follow Steps 1-4 of 1967-68 procedure.
2. Remove two output shaft support-to-engine bolts and one support-to-brace screw.
3. Rotate inboard end of axle rearward toward starter motor.
4. Slide output shaft straight out and remove.
5. Rotate drive axle inboard and toward front of car, guiding over front crossmember.

Caution Care must be exercised so that constant velocity joints do not turn to full extremes, and that seals are not damaged against shock absorber or stabilizer bar.

Installation—1967-68

1. Guide drive axle into position from underneath car. Lift it and slide it over lower control arm.
2. Insert splines into steering knuckle.
3. Reattach upper ball joint, not forgetting brake line clip. Tighten stud nut to 40 ft. lbs. and install cotter pin.
4. Attach brake line clip to frame.
5. Install six drive axle-to-output shaft screws and tighten to 65 ft. lbs.
6. Install washer and drive axle nut.
7. Remove protective piece of rubber hose from torsion bar connector.
8. Install wheel and tire.
9. Lower car to ground and tighten lug nuts to 105 ft. lbs. and drive axle nut to 105-110 ft. lbs.
10. Connect battery.

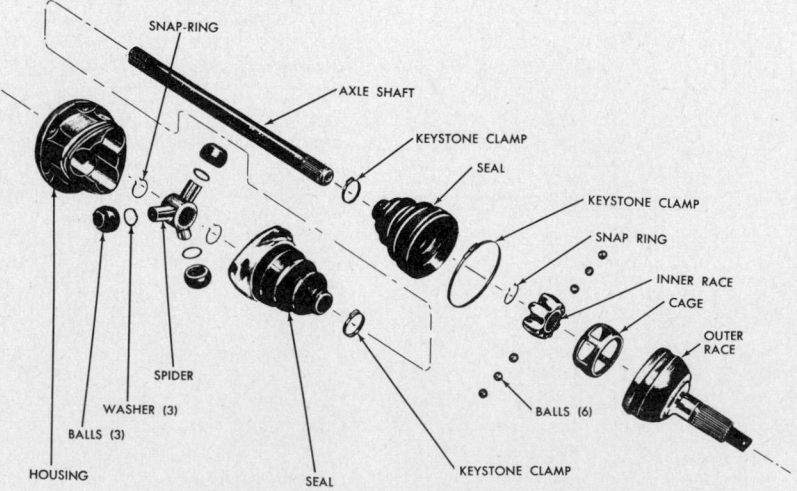

Drive axle exploded view (© Cadillac Div. G.M. Corp.)

Installation—1969-72

1. Carefully place right-hand drive axle assembly into lower control arm and enter outer race splines into knuckle.
2. Lubricate final drive output shaft seal, with wheel bearing grease.
3. Install right-hand output shaft into final drive and attach the support bolts to engine and brakes. Torque the bolts to 50 ft. lbs. (1969 and later).
4. Install brace.
5. Move right-hand drive axle assembly toward front of car and align with right-hand output shaft. Install attaching bolts and torque to 65 ft. lbs.
6. Install washer and nut on drive axle.
7. Remove floor stands and lower hoist.
8. Tighten wheel lugs to 105 ft. lbs. and drive axle nut to 105-110 ft. lbs. Install cotter pin.

Drive Axle—Left Side

Removal and Installation —1967-72

1. Hoist car under lower control arms.
2. Remove wheel and tire.
3. Remove drive axle cotter pin, nut and washer.
4. Install a piece of rubber hose over lower control arm torsion bar connector.
5. Remove six drive axle-to-output shaft screws and washers.
6. Loosen upper shock mounting bolt. Disconnect stabilizer bar link up to 1970.
7. Remove upper control arm ball joint cotter pin and nut.
8. Using hammer and brass drift, drive on knuckle until upper ball joint stud is free.
9. Remove brake hose bracket from frame.
10. Tip upper part of knuckle and support outward so that brake hose is not damaged.
11. Carefully guide drive axle assembly outboard.
   NOTE: care must be exercised so that constant velocity joints do not turn to full extremes and that seals are not damaged against shock absorber or stabilizer bar.
12. To install, reverse removal procedure. Tighten upper shock bolt to 75 ft. lbs., drive axle and wheel lug nuts to 105-110 ft. lbs., and output shaft-to-axle screws to 65 ft. lbs.

Constant Velocity Joint (Out of Car)

The constant velocity joints are to be replaced as a unit and are only disassembled for repacking and replacement of seals.

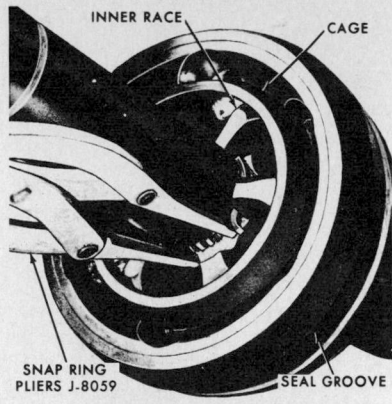

Removing outer axle joint
(© Cadillac Div. G.M. Corp.)

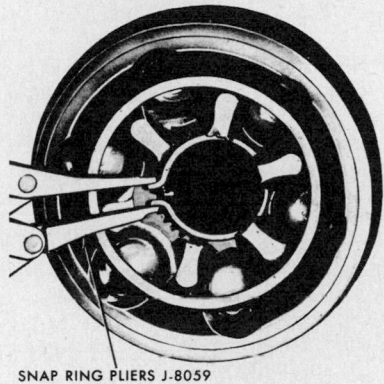

Removing inner race snap-ring
(© Cadillac Div. G.M. Corp.)

Outer C.V. Joint Disassembly

1. Insert axle assembly in vise. Hold by the mid-portion of the axle shaft.
2. Remove inner and outer seal clamps.
3. Slide seal down axle shaft to gain access to C. V. joint.
4. Using snap-ring pliers, spread retaining ring until C. V. joint can be removed from axle spline.
5. Remove retaining ring.
6. Slide seal from axle shaft.
7. Remove grease from constant velocity joint.
8. Holding constant velocity joint with one hand, tilt cage and inner race so that one ball can be removed. Continue until all six balls are removed.
9. Turn cage 90° and with large slot in cage aligned with land in outer race, lift out.
10. With cage and inner race assembly, turn inner race 90° to align with large hole in cage. Lift land on inner race up through large hole in cage and turn up and out to separate parts.

Assembly

1. Insert land of inner race into large hole in cage and pivot to install in cage.
2. Align inner race and pivot inner race 90° to align in outer race.

3. Insert balls into outer race one at a time until all six balls are installed. Inner race and cage will have to be tilted so that each ball can be inserted.
4. Pack constant velocity joint full of lubricant (Part No. 1050530).
5. Pack inside of seal with the same lubricant, until folds of seal are full.
6. Place small keystone clamp on axle shaft.
7. Install seal onto axle shaft.
8. Install retaining ring into inner race.
9. Insert axle shaft into splines of outer constant velocity joint until retaining ring secures shaft.
10. Position seal in slot of outer race.
11. Install large keystone clamp over seal and secure.
12. Install small keystone clamp over seal and secure.

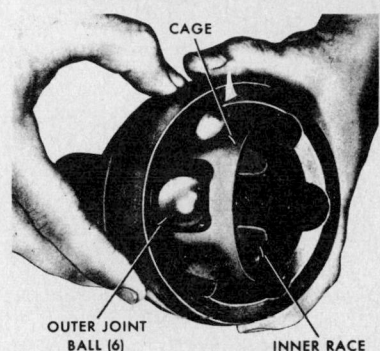

Removing balls from outer joint
(© Cadillac Div. G.M. Corp.)

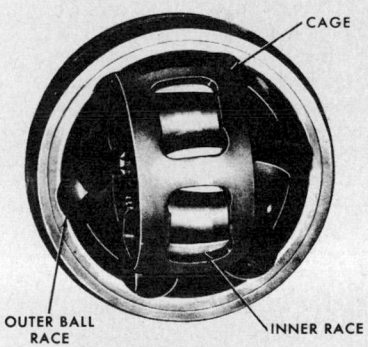

Removing cage and inner race
(© Cadillac Div. G.M. Corp.)

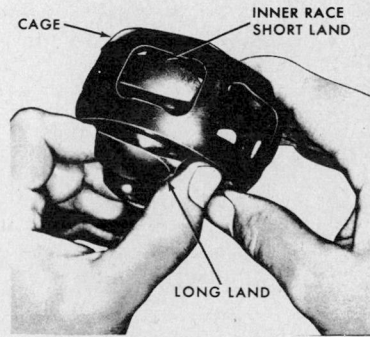

Removing inner race from cage
(© Cadillac Div. G.M. Corp.)

Inner Tri-pot Joint Disassembly

1. Insert axle assembly in vise. Clamp on mid-portion of axle shaft.
2. Remove small seal clamp.
3. Remove large end of seal from C. V. joint by prying out peened spots and driving off C. V. joint with hammer and chisel.
4. Slide the seal and adapter down the axle shaft until the tri-pot joint is exposed.

NOTE: the tri-pot housing is now free to slide off the joint. Use care to prevent the spider leg balls from sliding off the spider legs. Each leg ball contains multiple bearing rollers.

5. Cup one hand under the tri-pot joint to prevent dropping spider leg balls and rollers while sliding housing off of joint.
6. Remove spider leg ball.
7. Remove O-ring seal from outer housing.
8. Wipe excess grease from outer housing to gain access to snap ring and remove spider outer snap-ring.
9. With a plastic hammer, tap alternately on spider legs to drive spider off shaft.
10. Remove spider inner snap-ring.
11. Slide seal off axle shaft.
12. Remove rollers from spider leg balls.

Assembly

1. Insert axle assembly in a vise. Hold by mid-portion of axle shaft.
2. Place small keystone clamp on axle shaft.
3. Position seal on shaft.
4. Place spider inner snap-ring in position on shaft.
5. Apply lubricant to axle and the spider splines.
6. Align spider on axle shaft.
7. With a plastic hammer, tap alternately on spider legs to drive spider into position on axle shaft.
8. Install spider outer snap-ring on axle shaft.
9. Place O-ring on tri-pot joint housing.
10. Apply a thin coat of lubricant to inner race of leg balls, and install

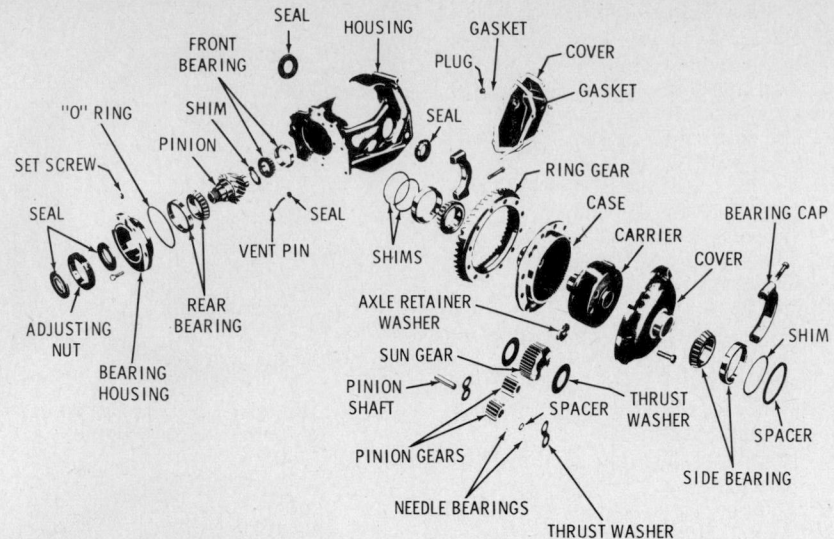

1967 final drive components (© Oldsmobile Div. G.M. Corp.)

leg ball rollers.
11. Apply lubricant to spider leg balls and legs.
12. Remove axle from vise then install washers and three spider leg balls, one at a time as a unit on the spider.

NOTE: when installing leg balls, use the leg ball washers as retainers for the spider rollers.

13. Pack inside of seal with special drive axle joint lubricant until the folds of the seal are full.
14. Pack housing with special drive axle joint lubricant and install by sliding housing over spider leg balls.
15. Position seal adapter over lip on joint housing and stake with blunt chisel.
16. Seat seal in groove on axle shaft, and secure keystone clamps.

Planetary-Type Differential

1967

This type differential replaces the conventional spider and beveled axle drive pinions with a planetary gear set to distribute torque to the respective drive axles.

Engine torque is transmitted from the power train, to the main drive pinion and ring gear, to the differential housing. Torque is then applied through the planetary and sun gear mechanism to both drive axles at variable speed requirements.

While the car is moving straight ahead, the planetary gears are fixed and rotate with the differential case and ring gear as a unit. However, when turning, the planetary gears revolve upon their individual axles with differential action, allowing the drive axles to rotate at different speeds.

This unit is not a controlled or lim-

ited slip differential. The unit normally is serviced as an assembly with the exception of the various seals.

Bevel Gear-Type Differential

Beginning 1968

Since 1968, a bevel gear-type differential is used on all front wheel drive models. This design supersedes the original planetary-type final drive. While unit removal and installation procedures are typical, the assembly, or its components are not interchangeable with the earlier design.

Overhauling the differential assembly is not encouraged. However, reconditioning procedures are found in later paragraphs of this final drive coverage. Differences in procedure are clearly indicated.

Output Shafts, Bearings and Seals

Right Side Removal

1. Disconnect battery.
2. Hoist car.
3. Place a short length of rubber

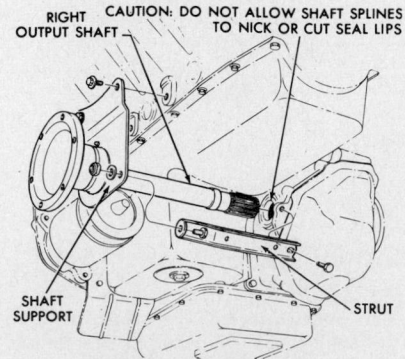

Output shaft, right side
(© Cadillac Div. G.M. Corp.)

Spider assembly (© Cadillac Div. G.M. Corp.)

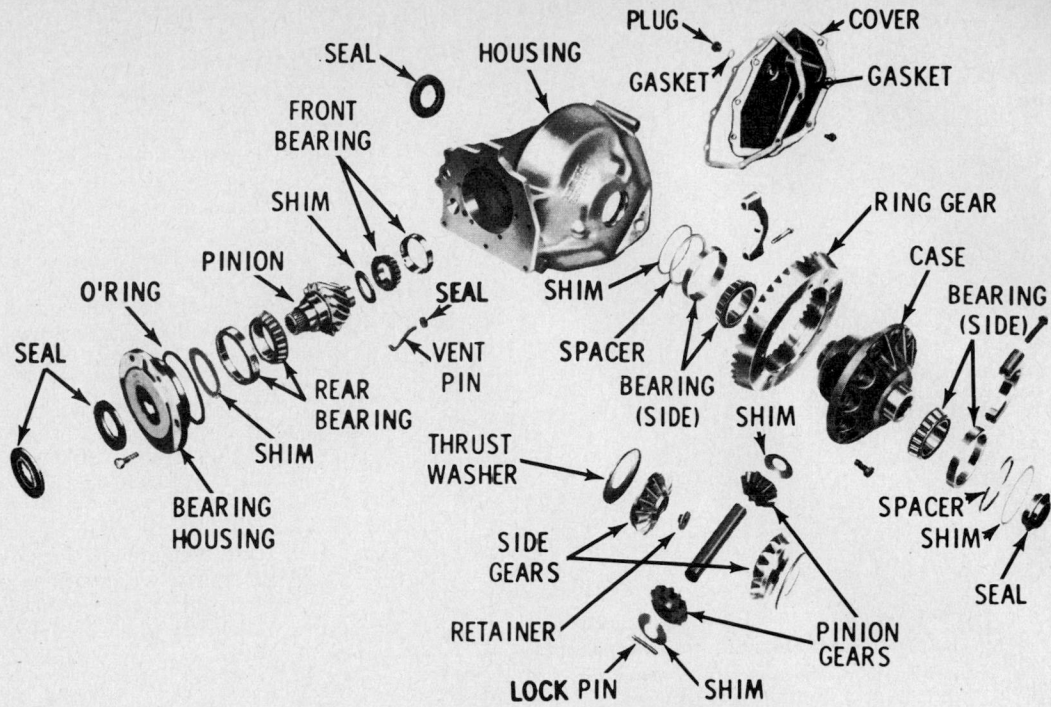

1968-72 final drive components (© Oldsmobile Div., G.M. Corp.)

hose over control arm torsion bar connector.

4. Disconnect right-hand drive axle.
5. Disconnect support from engine and brace. Loosen lower shock bolt.
6. Remove output shaft assembly.
7. If seal is to be removed, pry it out with a large screwdriver.
8. If output shaft bearing is to be removed, it can be removed as follows:
   a. Remove three self-tapping screws that secure bearing retainer.
   b. Clamp output shaft in a vise.
   c. Make two steel plates ¼x3x8 in. and install as illustrated.
   d. Install four ⅜—24 bolts about 5 in. long through output shaft flange.
   e. Tighten bolts alternately and bearing will be forced from its seat.

Installation

1. If output bearing was removed, assemble parts as illustrated.
2. Position assembly in a press and install bearing until seated.
3. Pack area between bearing and retainer with wheel bearing grease, then install slinger.
4. If seal was removed, it can now be installed.
5. Apply special seal lubricant to output shaft seal, then install output shaft into final drive, indexing the splines of both units.
6. Install support to engine and brace bolts.

NOTE: seat washers in old grooves in output shaft support to ensure output shaft alignment. If new support is installed, carefully center output shaft in support with bolts loosely installed, then tighten bolts to 50 ft. lbs. Do not allow shaft to hang unsupported in final drive.

7. Connect drive axle to output shaft. Tighten screws to 65 ft. lbs.
8. Remove protective rubber hose.
9. Connect battery, check engine oil level and check for oil leaks.

Left Side Removal

1. Remove right-hand output shaft assembly, as in previous paragraphs, on 1967 models.
2. Remove left drixe axle.
3. Using a 9/16 in. socket, remove left-hand output shaft retaining bolt and remove left-hand shaft.

4. If seal is to be removed, insert seal remover into seal and drive seal out with a hammer.

Installation

1. If seal was removed, install new seal.
2. Apply special seal lubricant to seal, then insert output shaft into final drive assembly, indexing splines of output shaft with splines of final drive.
3. Install left-hand output shaft retaining bolt and torque to 45 ft. lbs.
4. Install left drive axle.
5. Install right-hand output shaft, as described previously.

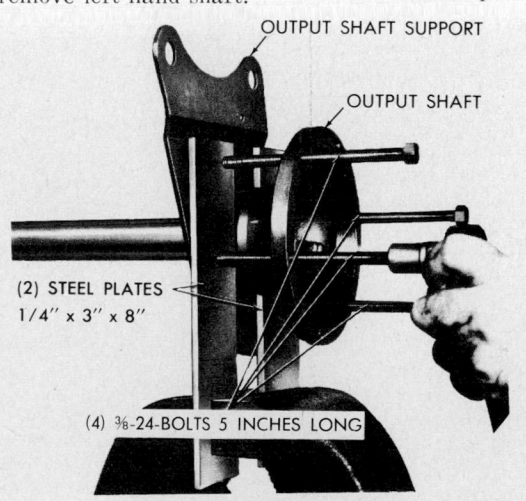

Removing output shaft bearing
(© Cad. Div. G.M. Corp.)

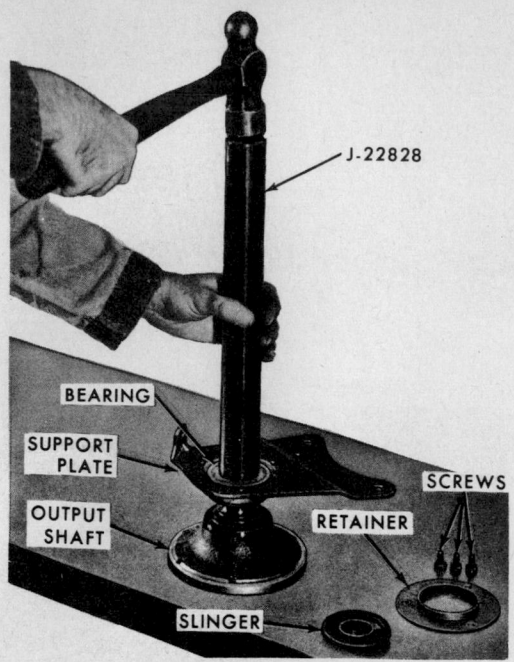

Installing output shaft support and bearing
(© Cad. Div. G.M. Corp.)

Final Drive

Removal

1. Disconnect battery.
2. Pump about one gallon of transmission fluid out of filler tube. Remove bolt on the bracket that secures filler tube and remove filler tube, plugging the filler tube hole.
3. Remove bolts A and B and nut H. (See illustration.)
4. Remove support bracket bolts.
5. Raise car and remove wheels and tires.
6. Install lengths of rubber hose on both lower torsion bar connectors.
7. Loosen twelve screws and washers that secure drive axles to output shafts.
8. Loosen, but do not remove, lower shock nut on right side.
9. Remove right drive axle and output shaft.
10. Remove six screws and lockwashers that secure left output shaft to axle.
11. Loosen screws that secure final drive cover to final drive. Allow lubricant to drain then remove screws and cover.
12. Compress left drive axle inner constant velocity joint and secure drive axle to frame.
13. Remove final drive support bracket.
14. Remove bolts C, D, E, and F and nut G.
15. Disengage final drive splines from transmission.
16. Remove final drive unit, permitting ring gear to rotate up over steering gear.
17. Remove transmission to final drive gasket and discard.

Installation

1. Positioning new gasket on transmission, install final drive unit, permitting ring gear to rotate up over steering linkage.
2. Align final drive splines with splines in transmission.
3. Align bolt studs G and H on transmission with holes in final drive.
4. Install bolts C, D, E and F and nut G finger tight.
5. Install support bracket on final drive unit.
6. Install other support brackets.
7. Install bolt in oil cooler lines clamp and tighten to 8 ft. lbs.
8. Tighten bolts C, D, E and F and nut G to 25 ft. lbs.
9. Reposition left drive axle and install screws to 65 ft. lbs.
10. Install right output shaft and axle.
11. Position final drive cover to final drive and install screws to 30 ft. lbs.
12. Fill final drive unit. Tighten lower shock nut to 75 lbs.
13. Install wheels and tires, tightening nuts finger tight.
14. Lower car and tighten wheel nuts to 105 ft. lbs.
15. Install bolts A and B and nut H, tightening to 25 ft. lbs.
16. Install new O-ring on transmission filler tube, remove plug in filler tube hole and install filler tube.
17. Connect battery.

Dismantling Drive Assembly

All Models

This is another area where adequate facilities are a must. Cadillac does not recommend disassembly of this unit unless proper special tools are available.

1. If available, install adapter J-22296-1 on differential holding fixture J-3289. Differential holding fixture must be modified to obtain clearance between fixture and final drive housing. Mount final drive in holding fixture.

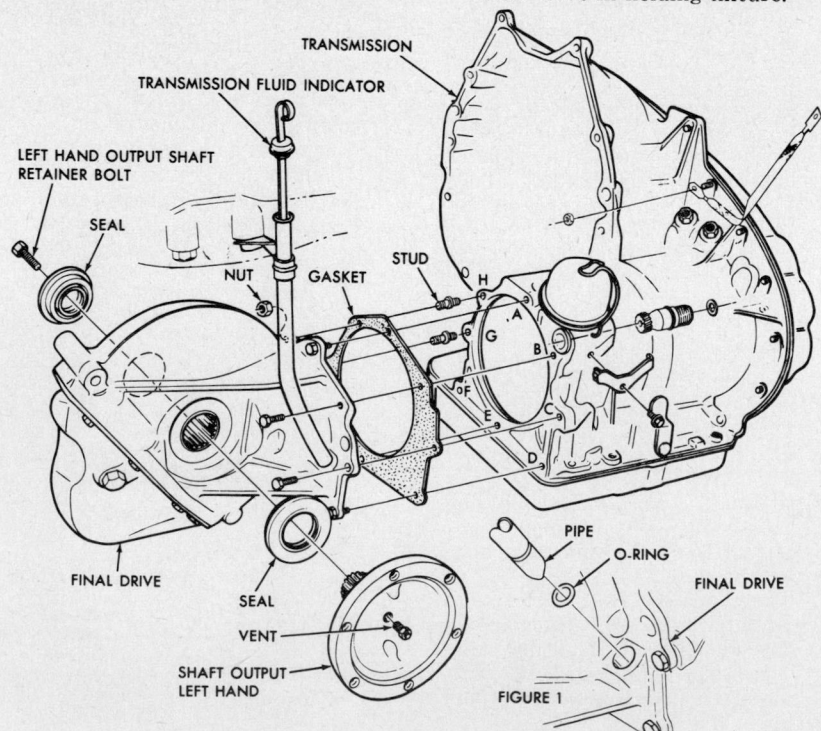

Final drive to transmission assembly (© Cadillac Div. G.M. Corp.)

2. Use a drain pan under the assembly. Remove the drain plug. Then, remove the cover attaching screws and remove the cover.
3. Rotate final drive until pinion points down, then check ring gear-to-pinion backlash with a dial indicator. Record backlash for reassembly. Check pinion and side bearing preload with tools, J-22208-1 and J-22208-2 with the help of a torque wrench. Record preload reading.
4. Remove side bearing caps.

NOTE: side bearing caps are of different size and can only be installed in one position.

5. Install spreader J-22196 on final drive, indexing the two guides on the spreader with the two holes on the carrier.
6. Turn the spreader screw to expand the spreader until the spacer and shims can be removed from between the small side of the bearing and the carrier.
7. Remove spreader from the carrier.
8. Remove the spacer and shims, then slide the case assembly to the left, away from the pinion gear. Remove case assembly from carrier. Check pinion bearing preload and record the reading.
9. Rotate carrier so the pinion is up.
10. Loosen set screw from adjusting nut.
11. Remove bearing housing bolts. Remove the drive pinion housing and remove the adjusting nut and housing from drive pinion. Remove rubber seal from bearing housing.
12. Remove rubber seal and vent wire from carrier.
13. With slide hammer J-2619 and tool J-22201, remove pinion front outer race.
14. Remove the output shaft oil seals.
15. Remove the two oil seals from the adjusting nut.
16. If necessary to remove pinion rear outer race, now is the time.

Pinion Bearings

All Models—Removal
1. Remove the pinion front bearing and selective shim. Bearing can be removed with a press.
2. Remove the pinion rear bearing.

Final Drive Case

All Models—Disassembly
1. If the side bearings are to be removed, it can best be done with tools J-22229-1, J-8433-1, and J-8416-1.
2. Mark ring gear, case and case cover, then remove all but two of the case cover to ring gear bolts. Leave two of the bolts 180° apart, loose.

3. Jar the assembly lightly on the bench to separate the halves of the case. Remove planet pinion carrier.
4. Clean all parts and examine all surfaces for wear or other damage.

Planetary-Type Pinion Gears

1967—Removal and Installation
1. Support the planetary pinion carrier assembly.
2. Press or drive the pinion pins out of the carrier.
3. Remove the pinion thrust washers, spacer, needle bearings, sun gear and thrust washers.

NOTE: the sun gear can be removed from only one opening of the carrier. This opening can be identified by the thinner wall at the carrier opening.

4. After removing the sun gear, the left axle retainer washer can be removed from the carrier.
5. Install by positioning loading tool J-22210 into planet pinion. Position a spacer washer over the loading tool, then install 24 needle bearings on each side of the spacer washer.
6. If the axle retainer washer was removed, install it at this time.
7. Position a thrust washer on each side of the sun gear, then insert the sun gear into carrier through large opening.
8. Position a thrust washer on each side of the planetary pinion, then insert planetary pinion into carrier.
9. Using a deep socket as a receiver, press pinion pin into carrier, until it bottoms.
10. Place a large punch in a vise, to be used as an anvil, and stake the opposite end of the pinion pin in three places.

Bevel-Type Pinion Gears

1968-72—Removal and Installation
1. After ring gear has been removed, drive lock pin from pinion shaft.
2. Push pinion shaft out of case.
3. Rotate one pinion gear and shim toward access hole in case, then remove.

NOTE: keep corresponding shims and pinion gear together for correct assembly.

4. Remove the other pinion and shim.
5. Remove side gears and thrust washers, keeping gears and washers in proper relationship for correct installation.

NOTE: the left-side gear has the threaded retainer which secures the (short) left output shaft. If threaded retainer is to be removed, use a brass drift to prevent trouble.

6. Upon assembling pinion and side

gears into the case, lubricate components with a quality E. P. lubricant.
7. Place side gear thrust washers over the side gear hubs and install side gears in case. Gear with threaded retainer belongs in left side of case.
8. Position one pinion (without shims) between side gears, then rotate gears until pinion is directly opposite from loading opening in case. Place other pinion between side gears so that the pinion shaft holes are in line; then rotate gears to make sure holes in pinions line up with holes in case.
9. If holes line up, rotate pinions back to loading opening to permit insertion of the pinion gear shims.
10. Install pinion shaft. Drive pinion shaft retaining lock pin into position.

Checking Pinion Depth

All Models
1. Install pinion front outer race. Drive race in until it bottoms.
2. Lubricate front bearing with final drive lubricant and install into front outer race.
3. Position tool J-21777-10 on the front bearing. Install tool J-21579 on final drive housing and retain with two bolts. Thread screw J-21777-13 into J-21579 until tip of screw engages tool J-21777-10. Torque tool J-21777-13 to 20 in. lbs. to preload the bearing.
4. Remove dial indicator post from tool J-21777-9 and install discs J-21777-11 and J-21777-12. Reinstall dial indicator post.
5. Place the gauging discs in the side bearing bores and install the side bearing caps.
6. Position the dial indicator on the mounting post of the gauge shaft with the contact button touching the indicator pad. Set dial indicator to zero, then depress the dial indicator until the needle rotates three-quarters of a turn clockwise. Tighten dial indicator.
7. Position the gauge shaft assembly in the carrier so that the dial indicator contact rod is directly over the gauging area of the gauge block, and the discs are seated fully in the side bearing bores.
8. Position gauge shaft so that the indicator rod contacts the gauging area. Rotate gauge rod back and forth until the indicator reads the greatest deflection. At the point of greatest deflection, set the indicator to zero. Repeat the rocking action to verify the zero setting.
9. After zero setting is obtained, rotate gauge shaft until the

indicator rod does not touch the gauging area. Read the pinion depth directly from the dial indicator.

10. Select the correct pinion shim to be used during assembly on the following basis:

    A. If a service pinion is being used, or a production pinion with no marking, the correct shim will have a thickness equal to the indicator gauge reading found in step 9.

    B. If a production pinion is used and marked +, the shim thickness indicated by the dial indicator on the pinion setting gauge must be increased by the amount etched on the pinion. If the pinion is marked —, the shim thickness indicated on the dial must be decreased by the amount etched on the pinion.

11. Remove pinion depth checking tools and front bearing from carrier.

Final Drive Case

All Models—Assembly

1. Install the planetary pinion carrier into the case.
2. With the case and cover alignment marks in index, insert four ring gear attaching bolts through case and cover. Align mark on ring gear with alignment marks on case and cover, then install ring and gear case. Alternately tighten the six attaching bolts to 85 ft. lbs.
3. If side bearings were removed, they can be installed now. Drive bearing on until it bottoms.
4. Install pinion rear bearing.
5. Position correct shim on drive pinion and install the drive pinion front bearing with tool J-21022 and a press.
6. Lubricate pinion bearings and install pinion into carrier.
7. Install seals into adjusting nut.
8. Install O-ring and vent pin on face of carrier. Torque attaching nuts to 35 ft. lbs.
9. Install seal protector J-22236 over drive pinion, then install the adjusting nut over the seal protector and thread into the housing.
0. Assemble tools as illustrated and adjust pinion bearing preload. The preload is 2 to 10 in. lbs. for new bearings, and 2 to 3 in. lbs. for used bearings. Adjust new bearing preload to 4 in. lbs. while rotating the pinion and checking preload until preload remains constant. When correct preload is obtained, tighten the set screw. Record preload reading because it will be used when making side bearing and preload adjustment. Leave the tools on pinion for side

bearing preload adjustment.

Side Bearing Preload Adjustment

All Models

Differential side bearing preload is adjusted by means of shims located between the side bearings and the carrier. One spacer is used on the right side only. Shims are used on both sides and come in thickness increments of .002 in. from .036 to .070 in. By changing the thickness of both side shims equally, ring gear and pinion backlash will not change.

1. Lubricate the side bearings with final drive lubricant.
2. Place differential in position in the carrier.
3. If the original ring gear and pinion are being used, subtract the reading obtained in Step 8 from the reading obtained in Step 3 of the Dismantling Drive Assembly procedure. This determines the original side bearing preload and will aid in determining whether thicker or thinner shims are needed to bring the side bearing preload to specifications.
4. Install original shim on left side and spacer on the right side.
5. Install the carrier spreader and apply just enough tension to allow the shim to be installed between the spacer and the carrier.
6. Release tension on the spreader, install side bearing caps, then check preload. Preload should be 15 to 20 in. lbs. for new bearings and 5 to 7 in. lbs. for old bearings over the pinion bearing preload obtained in Step 11, Final Drive Case Assembly.
7. If preload is not within specifications, select thicker or thinner shims to bring preload within limits.

Backlash Adjustment

All Models

1. Rotate differential case a few times to seat bearings, then mount dial indicator in order to read movement at the outer edge of one of the ring gear teeth.
2. Check backlash at three points around the ring gear. Backlash must not vary more than .002 in.
3. Backlash at the minimum point should be between .006 in. and .008 in. for all new gears. If original ring gear and pinion was installed, backlash should be set at the same reading obtained in Step 3 of Dismantling Drive Assembly procedure, if reading was within specifications.
4. If backlash was not within limits, correct by increasing thickness of one differential shim

and decreasing thickness of other side shim the same amount. This will not disturb differential side bearing preload. For each .001 in. change in backlash desired, transfer .002 in. shim thickness. To decrease backlash .001 in., decrease thickness of right shim .002 in. and increase thickness of left shim .002 in. To increase backlash .002 in. increase thickness of right shim .004 in. and decrease thickness of left shim .004 in.

5. When backlash is correct, remove spreader. Install bearing caps and bolts. Torque to 50 ft. lbs.
6. Install new output shaft seals.
7. Install new gasket on housing. Install cover, torque cover attaching bolts to 30 ft. lbs. Fill final drive to correct level with final drive lube.

Automatic Transmission

References

The Turbo Hydramatic transmission used on the Eldorado is a fully automatic transmission used for front wheel drive applications. It consists primarily of a three-element hydraulic torque converter, dual sprocket and link assembly, compound planetary gear set, three multiple-disc clutches, a sprag clutch, a roller clutch, two band assemblies, and an hydraulic control system. For major repair operations consult the Unit Repair Section.

Automatic Transmission R & R—1967-72

Removal

1. Disconnect the battery.
2. Remove the hood.
3. Remove the transmission dipstick, then remove the bolt holding the filler tube bracket to exhaust manifold and remove the filler tube. Discard the O-ring seal.
4. Remove bolts at locations A, B and C, holding the final drive case to the transmission. (See illustration).
5. Disconnect speedometer cable from the governor assembly, and unplug T.C.S. wiring if so equipped.
6. Disconnect oil cooler pipes at the transmission and at the radiator. Cap the pipes and plug connector holes in transmission and radiator.
7. Remove bolt holding the cooler pipe bracket to final drive bracket and position pipes outboard of governor assembly.

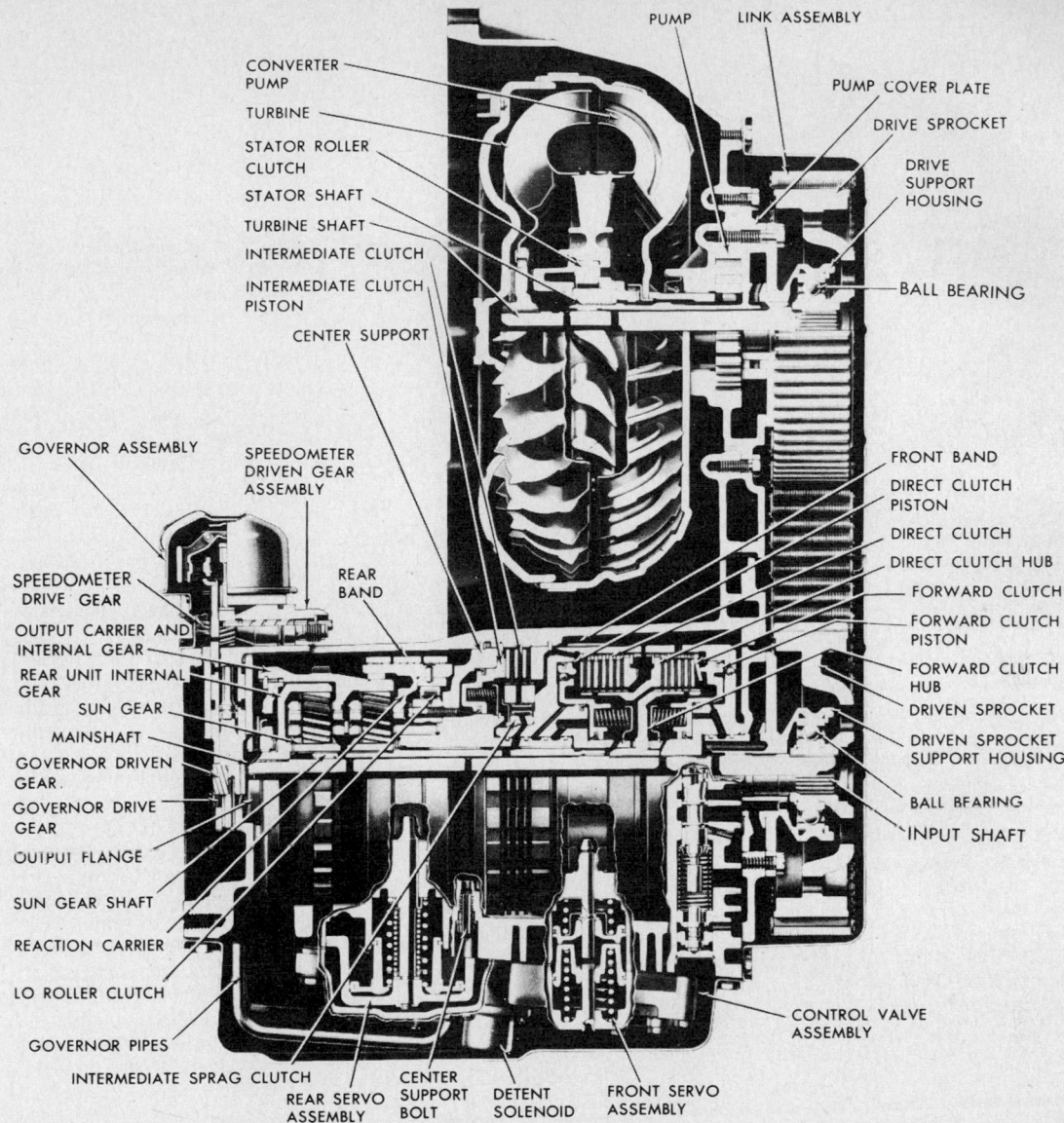

PUMP   LINK ASSEMBLY

CONVERTER PUMP

TURBINE

STATOR ROLLER CLUTCH

STATOR SHAFT

TURBINE SHAFT

INTERMEDIATE CLUTCH

INTERMEDIATE CLUTCH PISTON

CENTER SUPPORT

PUMP COVER PLATE

DRIVE SPROCKET

DRIVE SUPPORT HOUSING

BALL BEARING

GOVERNOR ASSEMBLY

SPEEDOMETER DRIVEN GEAR ASSEMBLY

SPEEDOMETER DRIVE GEAR

OUTPUT CARRIER AND INTERNAL GEAR

REAR UNIT INTERNAL GEAR

SUN GEAR

MAINSHAFT

GOVERNOR DRIVEN GEAR

GOVERNOR DRIVE GEAR

OUTPUT FLANGE

SUN GEAR SHAFT

REACTION CARRIER

LO ROLLER CLUTCH

GOVERNOR PIPES

INTERMEDIATE SPRAG CLUTCH

REAR BAND

REAR SERVO ASSEMBLY

CENTER SUPPORT BOLT

DETENT SOLENOID

FRONT SERVO ASSEMBLY

FRONT BAND

DIRECT CLUTCH PISTON

DIRECT CLUTCH

DIRECT CLUTCH HUB

FORWARD CLUTCH

FORWARD CLUTCH PISTON

FORWARD CLUTCH HUB

DRIVEN SPROCKET

DRIVEN SPROCKET SUPPORT HOUSING

BALL BEARING

INPUT SHAFT

CONTROL VALVE ASSEMBLY

Turbo-Hydramatic transmission components (© Cad. Div. G.M. Corp.)

8. Remove nut at location H, holding final drive to the transmission.
9. Remove bolts at locations I, J, K and L, holding transmission to engine and adapter plate.
10. Remove upper left bolt holding rear motor mount bracket to the transmission.
11. Remove bolt holding the ground strap to left side of cowl. Remove ground strap.
12. Remove upper left bolt holding converter cover plate to transmission, (use 7/16 in. socket with universal and extension to reach underneath the left exhaust manifold).

NOTE: loosen two screws holding A.L.C. compressor and position compressor out of the way.

13. Position cable with looped ends under engine intake manifold and hook looped ends to chain fall and cable, putting engine

mounts under tension.
14. Position safety chain over top of transmission.
15. Raise car and place on jack stands, adjusting chain fall as necessary.
16. Disconnect leads from starter.
17. Remove bolt at location O holding starter motor to transmission case and remove the ground strap.
18. While holding the starter, remove bolt at location P and remove starter.
19. Remove three remaining screws holding the converter cover plate to the transmission and remove the cover plate.
20. Position transmission jack, equipped with front end drive transmission adapter plate to transmission and install nut and bolt holding adapter brace to transmission at starter motor lower mounting bolt hole.

21. Disconnect electrical connector from transmission.
22. Remove vacuum line from vacuum modulator.
23. Secure transmission to transmission jack with safety chain.
24. Remove three flexplate-to-converter attaching bolts.
25. Remove bolts at locations M and N holding transmission to engine and adapter plate.
26. Remove cotter pin securing relay rod to manual yoke on left side of transmission and separate rod from yoke.
27. Remove bolts at locations D, E and F and nut at location G holding final drive to transmission.

NOTE: position a clean drain pan under a point where transmission and final drive meet to avoid leakage onto floor when the two units are separated.

28. Remove five bolts and washers holding the rear of acromat to

Transmission attaching bolt location—1967-72 (© Cadillac Div., G.M. Corp.)

front crossbar and frame horns and allow acromat to hang free.

29. Through access holes in bottom of front crossmember, remove two nuts and studs. Turn steering wheel to left lock.

30. Have a helper, using a large pry bar, shift engine forward, while mechanic uses small pry bar to help separate transmission from engine and final drive.

31. Following initial separation, allow transmission to drain at the separation.

32. Remove two bolts on right side, holding the rear motor mount to the transmission.

33. Through access holes in the bottom of transmission support bar, remove two bolts, one on each side, holding the rear motor mounts to transmission support bar, and position motor mounts and bracket rearward to underbody.

34. While helper pries and holds engine forward, move transmission rearward to disengage transmission case from dowels on engine adapter and to disengage final drive from studs on transmission case. Top of transmission should be tilted slightly rearward.

35. Slowly lower transmission, until converter is about half-way exposed from flexplate.

36. Install converter holding clamp, J-21366, using a 5/16 in.—18 nut to hold clamp screw to transmission case at location N.

Caution Converter holding clamp, J-21366, must be used to prevent the converter be-

coming disengaged when the transmission is removed.

37. Lower transmission from car.

Caution Rear motor mount bracket will follow transmission from car. To avoid damage or injury, remove bracket as soon as there is sufficient clearance.

38. Remove and discard final drive gasket and clean mounting surface of final drive.

Installation

1. Position transmission on jack, equipped with adapter plate, under the car.

2. Saturate new gasket with transmission fluid, then place gasket on final drive.

3. Position rear motor mount bracket on top of transmission support bar against underbody.

4. Raise transmission in place until converter is about half-way covered by flexplate, then remove converter holding clamp from transmission.

5. While helper pries engine forward with a pry bar, continue raising transmission, making sure the top of the transmission case clears splined input shaft of final drive, and position to engine.

6. Align the engine to the final drive, with the assistance of a helper by watching the following items:
   A. Studs on transmission case to mounting holes in final drive.
   B. Guide holes in transmission

case to dowels on adapter.
   C. Internal flange on final drive to transmission.

Caution Since engagement of splined final drive input shaft to transmission is hidden, care must be taken to avoid damaging transmission or final drive assembly.
   D. To help engagement of final drive splines, rotate one front wheel while helper holds the other.

NOTE: when alignment is complete and correct, the gap between the final drive and transmission should not exceed 1/4 in.

7. Loosely install bolts at locations D and F attaching transmission to final drive and bolt at location N attaching transmission to engine through adapter, alternately tightening bolts to avoid cocking the transmission. Do not torque bolts.

8. Working in the engine compartment, loosely install bolt at location J attaching transmission to adapter. Do not torque at this time.

9. Install bolt at location M holding transmission to adapter plate. Do not torque.

10. Position rear motor mount bracket to transmission and loosely install three bolts holding bracket to transmission.

NOTE: upper left bolt is installed from engine compartment.

11. Position rear engine mounts and bracket to transmission support bar, and loosely install bolts through access holes in bottom of bar, attaching mounts to bar.

12. Reposition engine assembly, as necessary, and install left bolt securing front motor mount to front cross bar. Torque front motor mount bolts to 30 ft. lbs.

13. Separate safety chain, remove nut and bolt securing jack adapter plate to transmission case and remove jack.

14. Torque the following bolts as specified:
   A. Rear engine mounts to transmission support bar, 55 ft. lbs.
   B. Rear engine mounts to transmission (two on right side), 55 ft. lbs.
   C. Transmission to adapter to engine, 30 ft. lbs.
   D. Transmission to adapter (location M), 30 ft. lbs.

Caution The following procedure for attaching the converter to the flexplate must be strictly followed to prevent improper installation and damage to flexplate and transmission.

15. Rotate converter until two of the three weld nuts on the converter line up with two of the three bolt holes in the flexplate. Position converter so that weld nuts are flush with flexplate. Be sure converter is not cocked and that pilot in center of converter is properly seated in crankshaft.

16. Install two flexplate to converter attaching bolts through access holes in flexplate and torque to 28 ft. lbs.

NOTE: bolts must be tightened at this time to assure proper alignment of converter.

17. Rotate flexplate and converter until third bolt hole is accessible. Install third bolt and torque to 28 ft. lbs.

18. Install vacuum hose on vacuum modulator assembly.

19. Install electrical connector to transmission connector.

20. Position converter cover plate to transmission case and install two lower and one upper right bolts holding the cover plate to the transmission. Torque to 5 ft. lbs.

21. Position the starter to the transmission case and install bolt at P position.

22. Position ground strap to transmission and install bolt holding the ground strap and starter to the transmission at location O. Torque bolts at locations O and P to 25 ft. lbs.

23. Install leads to starter motor.

24. Install bolts at locations C and E and a nut at G holding transmission to final drive.

25. Torque bolts at locations C through F to 25 ft. lbs.

26. Position acromat to front cross bar and frame horns and install five retaining bolts and washers.

27. Position relay rod to manual yoke and secure with a cotter pin.

28. Check operation of manual linkage and adjust, if necessary.

29. Disconnect chain fall and lower the car.

30. Remove cable from intake manifold and safety chain from transmission.

31. Install bolts at locations A and B and nut at location H holding transmission to final drive. Torque bolts to 25 ft. lbs.

32. Install upper left bolt holding converter cover plate to transmission in the manner described for removing it, the reversal of Step 12.

33. Install bolts at locations I, K and L, holding transmission to engine and adapter.

34. Torque bolts at locations I, J, K and L to 25 ft. lbs.

35. Tighten brass cooler pipe connectors at case to 28 ft. lbs. Clean connections and connect cooler pipes at transmission, us-

Removing sprocket snap-ring

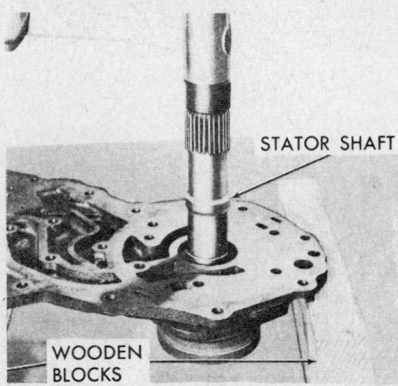

STATOR SHAFT

WOODEN BLOCKS

Removing drive sprocket support

⅛ INCH MASONITE

Removing tight sprockets

ing cooler pipe wrench J-21477. Torque to 28 ft. lbs.

36. Connect oil cooler pipes to radiator with the same wrench. Torque to 40 ft. lbs.

37. Install cooler pipe clamp.

38. Install speedometer cable to governor.

39. Install new O-ring on transmission filler tube and install filler tube through hole in final drive case.

40. Position transmission filler tube bracket to exhaust manifold and install retaining bolt.

41. Install body ground strap to firewall and secure it with a nut.

42. Connect battery.

43. Bring transmission to fluid level. Bring engine to operating temperature, then recheck fluid level.

44. Thoroughly check entire power train for oil and coolant leaks.

45. Install and align hood assembly.

Drive and Driven Sprockets for the Transmission Drive

References

If it should be necessary to replace either the drive sprocket, chain, or driven sprocket, the three unit combination must be replaced as a set. They are matched and are not to be serviced separately.

Removal

1. Remove 18 cover housing attaching bolts.

2. Remove cover housing and gasket. Discard the gasket.

3. Install J-4646 snap-ring pliers into sprocket bearing retaining snap-rings located under the drive and driven sprockets and remove snap-rings from retaining grooves in support housings.

NOTE: do not remove snap-rings from beneath the sprockets. Leave them in a loose position between the sprockets and the bearing assemblies.

4. Remove drive and driven sprockets, link assemblies, bearings and shaft simultaneously by alternately pulling upward on the drive and driven sprockets until the bearings are out of the drive and driven support housings.

NOTE: it may be necessary to pry up on the sprockets. Use care.

Caution Do not pry on the guide links or the aluminum case. Pry only on the sprockets.

5. Remove link assembly from drive and driven sprockets.

6. Remove two hook type oil seal rings from turbine shaft.

7. Inspect drive and driven sprocket bearing assemblies for rough or defective bearings.

NOTE: do not remove bearing assemblies from drive or driven sprockets unless they need replacement.

8. If removal of bearing assembly from drive and/or driven sprockets is necessary, proceed as follows:

   A. Remove sprocket to bearing assembly retaining snap-ring using tool J-5589, snap-ring pliers.

   B. Mount sprocket with turbine or input shaft placed in hole in work bench on two 2 x 4 x 10 in. pieces of wood.

   C. With a hammer and brass rod, drive the inner race al-

Removing sprockets and link assembly

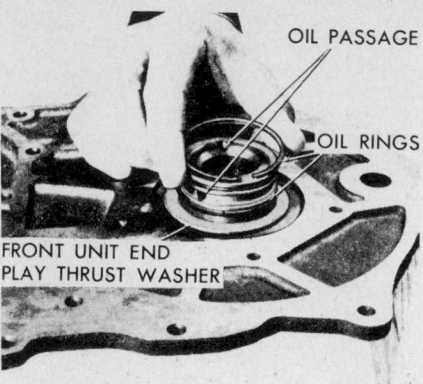

Installing oil rings on driven sprocket support

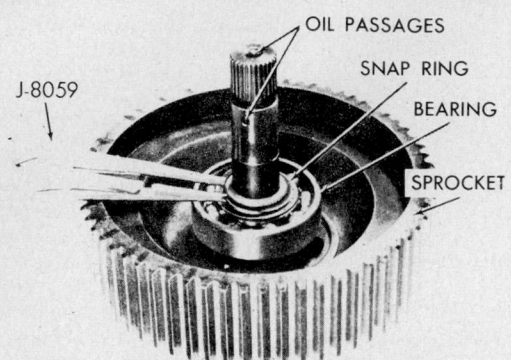

Removing sprocket bearing snap-ring

Installing driven sprocket support

ternately through each of the access openings until the bearing assembly is removed from the sprocket hub. Drive the sprocket, and turbine shaft and link assembly.

Inspection

1. Inspect drive sprocket teeth for nicks, burrs, scoring, gauling and excessive wear.
2. Inspect drive sprocket to ball bearing retaining snap-ring for damage.
3. Inspect drive sprocket ball bearing inner race mounting surface for damage.
4. Inspect turbine shaft for open lubrication passages. Run a tag wire through the passages to be sure they are open.
5. Inspect spline for damage.
6. Inspect the ground bushing journals for damage.
7. Inspect the two hook-type oil seal grooves for damage or excessive wear.
8. Inspect the turbine shaft for cracks or distortion.
9. Inspect the link assembly for damage or loose links.

NOTE: take particular notice of the guide links. They are the wide outside links on each side of the link assembly.

Driven Sprocket at Input Shaft

Inspection

1. Inspect driven sprocket teeth for nicks, burrs, scoring, gauling and excessive wear.
2. Inspect sprocket to ball bearing retaining snap-ring for damage.
3. Inspect ball bearing inner race mounting surface for damage.
4. Inspect input shaft for open lubrication holes. Run a tag wire through the holes to be sure they are open.
5. Inspect spline for damage.
6. Inspect ground bushing journals for damage.

Sprocket Bearings

Installation

1. Turn sprocket so that turbine or input shaft is pointing upward.
2. Install new sprocket bearing as follows:
   A. Install snap-ring, letter side down on shaft.
   B. Assemble bearing assembly on turbine or input shaft.
   C. Using tool, J-6133-A, drive the bearing assembly onto the hub of the sprocket until it is resting on the bearing seat of the sprocket.
   D. Install sprocket to bearing assembly retaining snap-ring into groove sprocket hub.
3. Install two hook-type oil seal rings on turbine shaft.

Front Unit End-Play Check

Make front unit end-play check as follows:

A. Install front unit end-play checking tool J-22241 into driven sprocket housing so that the urethane on the tool can engage the splines and the forward clutch housing. Let the tool bottom on the main shaft and then withdraw it approximately 1/16-1/8 in.
B. Remove two of the 5/16—18 bolts from the driven support housing.
C. Install 5/16—18 threaded hammer bolt with jam nut into one bolt hole in driven support housing.
NOTE: do not thread slide hammer bolt deep enough to interfere with forward clutch travel.
D. Mount dial indicator on rod and index indicator to register with the forward clutch drum that can be reached through second bolt removed from driven support housing.
E. Push end-play tool down to remove slack.
F. Push and hold output flange outward. Place a screwdriver in case opening at parking area and push upward on output carrier.
G. Place another screwdriver between the metal lip of the end-play tool and the drive sprocket housing. Now push upward on the metal lip of the end-play tool and read

THICKNESS	COLOR
.060-.064	Yellow
.071-.075	Blue
.082-.086	Red
.093-.097	Brown
.104-.108	Green
.115-.119	Black
.126-.130	Purple

NOTE: An oil soaked washer may tend to discolor so that it will be necessary to measure the washer with a set of one inch micrometers to determine its actual thickness.

Selective thrust washer chart—Eldorado
(© Cad. Div. G.M. Corp.)

the resulting end-play. This should be between .003-.024 in. The selective washer controlling this end play is the phenolic thrust washer located between the driven support housing and the forward clutch housing. If more or less washer thickness is required to bring the end-play within specifications, select the proper washer from the chart.

Radio

Procedures for removal and installation of radio may be found under instructions for same year model listed in the Cadillac section. On Eldorado models, it is not necessary to remove the defroster hose, otherwise the procedures for Cadillac apply.

Windshield Wipers

The windshield wiper system consists of the wiper motor and transmission assembly. It is similar to that used on other Cadillac models.

Transmission R & R

1967
1. Remove both wiper arm and blade assemblies.
2. Raise hood and remove nine screws that retain front and side edges of ventilator frame to cowl, noting locations of any shims.
   NOTE: to reach end screws, open doors and remove cover plates.
3. Carefully raise front edge of ventilator frame and disengage washer hoses.
4. Raise rear edge of frame and slide it forward. Remove vent frame and grill.
5. Remove two screws and cover plate on firewall.
6. Remove locknut that secures wiper crank to ball socket.
7. Remove three transmission mounting screws (each side) and both transmissions, after disengaging ball socket.
8. To install, reverse removal procedure, making sure ball socket is fully seated.

1968-70
1. Remove wiper arm and blade assemblies.
2. Remove screws that secure air inlet screen to cowl; remove screen.
3. Follow Steps 5-8 of 1967 procedure.
   NOTE: driver side transmission arm must point *down*, passenger side *up*.

1971-72
1. Raise hood and remove cowl vent screen.
2. Remove wiper arm and blade assembly from side being serviced.
3. Loosen, but do not remove, attaching nuts securing transmission drive linkage to motor crank arm. If only left transmission is being removed, it is not necessary to loosen right attaching nuts.
4. Disconnect transmission drive linkage from motor crank arm.
5. Remove the attaching screws of the transmission being serviced, then remove tranmission/s through plenum chamber opening.
6. To install, reverse removal procedure. Motor must be in "Park" position.

Motor R & R

See Cadillac section.

Heater System

Blower Assembly and Motor R & R

1967-70
1. Drain cooling system.
2. Remove rubber cooling hose from nipple and blower motor.
3. Disconnect blower motor electrical connector.
4. Remove five attaching screws and blower motor.
5. Remove left cowl-to-fender strut rod.
6. Remove heater hoses from blower case.
7. Disconnect Bowden cable from temperature door.
8. Disconnect connector from motor resistor.
9. Disconnect vacuum hoses, then remove twelve screws from blower case.
10. Pull blower assembly away from cowl and remove from car.
11. To install, reverse removal procedure, using a new gasket.

1971-72
See Cadillac section.

Heater Core R & R

1967-70
1. Remove heater blower motor and asembly.
2. Remove four screws, two on each side, that secure retaining clamps.
3. Remove retaining clamps and heater core.

1971-72
See Cadillac section.

Camaro, Chevelle, Chevy II, Monte Carlo

Index

YEAR IDENTIFICATION

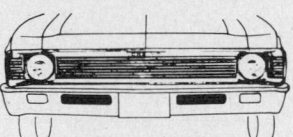

1965 Chevy II

1966 Chevy II

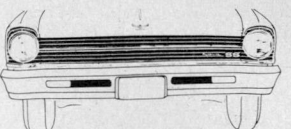

1967 Chevy II

1968-69 Chevy II

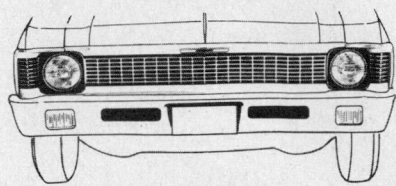

1970 Nova

1971 Nova

1965 Chevelle

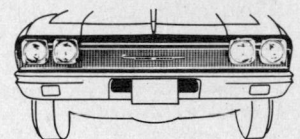

1966 Chevelle SS

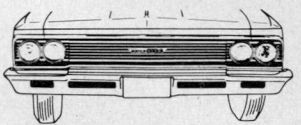

1966 Chevelle

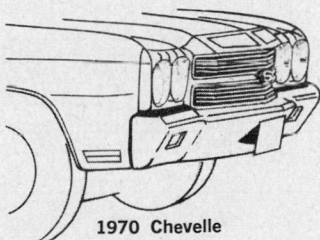

1967 Chevelle

1968 Chevelle

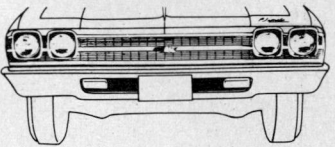

1969 Chevelle

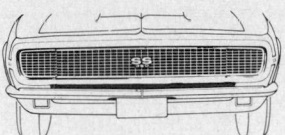

1970 Chevelle

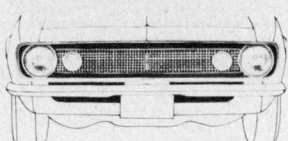

1971 Chevelle

1972 Chevelle

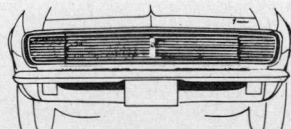

1967 Camaro SS

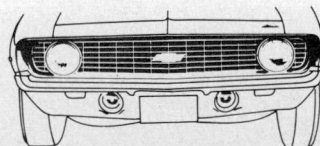

1967 Camaro

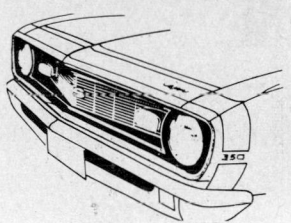

1968 Camaro SS

1968 Camaro

1969 Camaro

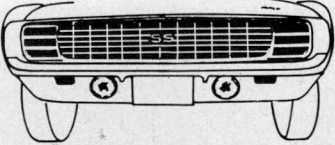

1969 Camaro SS

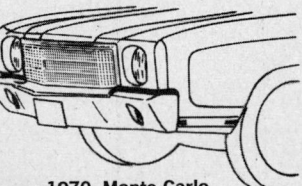

1970-71 Camaro

1972 Camaro

1970 Monte Carlo

1971 Monte Carlo

1972 Monte Carlo

FIRING ORDER

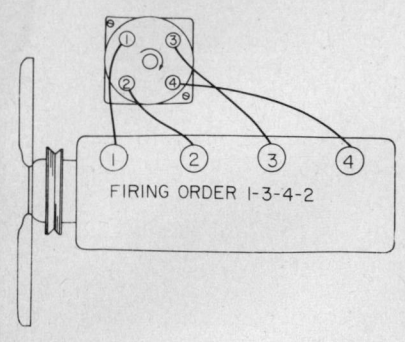

FIRING ORDER 1-3-4-2

153 4 cyl.

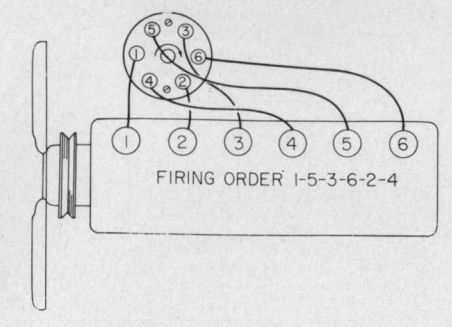

FIRING ORDER 1-5-3-6-2-4

194, 230, 250 6 cyl.

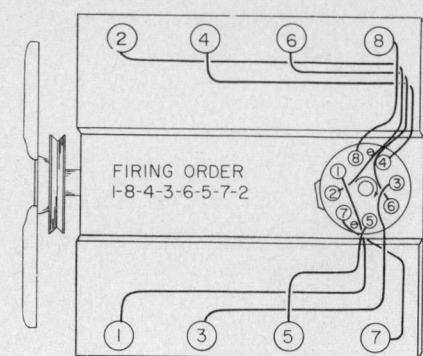

FIRING ORDER
1-8-4-3-6-5-7-2

283, 327, 350, 396, 400, 454 V8

CAR SERIAL NUMBER LOCATION

1965-67

Car serial number is found on a plate attached to the left front door hinge pillar.

1968-72

Car serial number is located on the top left-hand side of the instrument panel, visible through the windshield.

Car Serial Number Interpretation

A typical vehicle serial number tag yields manufacturer's identity, vehicle type, model year, assembly plant and production unit number when broken down as shown in the following chart.

Mfr. Identity[1]	Body Style[2]	Model Year[3]	Assy. Plant[4]	Unit No.[5]
1	5645	8	F	100025

1. Manufacturer's identity number assigned to all Chevrolet built vehicles.
2. Model Identification
3. Last number of model year (1968).
4. F-Flint
5. Unit numbering will start at 100,001 at all plants.

Engine Identification

Six Cylinder Engines

The production code letters immediately follow the engine serial number. The number is found on a pad at the front right-hand side of the cylinder block, just to the rear of the distributor.

V8 Engines

The production code letters immediately follow the engine serial number. The number is found on a pad at the front right-hand side of the cylinder block.

MODEL IDENTIFICATION

1965–67—Model Identification—Chevy II

Series	Model Number 4 Cyl.	Model Number 6 Cyl.	Model Number V8	Description
100	11111	11311	11411	2 dr. sedan, 6 passenger
	11169	11369	11469	4 dr. sedan, 6 passenger
		11335	11435	4 dr. station wagon, 2 seat
Nova		11569	11669	4 dr. sedan, 6 passenger
		11537	11637	2 dr. sport coupe, 5 passenger
		11535	11635	4 dr. station wagon, 2 seat
Nova SS		11737	11837	2 dr. sport coupe, 4 passenger

1968–72—Model Identification—Chevy Nova

Series	Model Number 4 Cyl.	Model Number 6 Cyl.	Model Number V8	Description
Nova	11127	11327	11427	2 dr. coupe, 5 passenger
	11169	11369	11469	4 dr. sedan, 6 passenger
Nova SS			11427	2 dr. coupe, 5 passenger

1965–67—Model Identification—Chevelle

Series	Model Number 6 Cyl.	Model Number V8	Description
Chevelle 300	13111	13211	2 dr. sedan, 6 passenger
	13169	13269	4 dr. sedan, 6 passenger
	13115	13215	2 dr. station wagon, 2 seat
Chevelle 300 Deluxe	13311	13411	2 dr. sedan, 6 passenger
	13369	13469	4 dr. sedan, 6 passenger
	13335	13435	4 dr. station wagon, 2 seat
Malibu	13569	13669	4 dr. sedan, 6 passenger
	13537	13637	2 dr. sport coupe, 5 passenger
	13567	13667	2 dr. convertible, 5 passenger
	13535	13635	4 dr. station wagon, 2 seat
Malibu SS	13737	13837	2 dr. sport coupe, 4 passenger
	13767	13867	2 dr. convertible, 4 passenger
El Camino	13380	13480	2 dr. sedan pickup, 3 passenger reg.
	13580	13680	2 dr. sedan pickup, 3 passenger deluxe

1968—Model Identification—Chevelle

Series	Model Number		Description
	6 Cyl.	V8	
Chevelle 300	13127	13227	2 dr. coupe, 5 passenger
Chevelle 300 Deluxe	13327	13427	2 dr. coupe, 5 passenger
	13337	13437	2 dr. sport coupe, 5 passenger
	13369	13469	4 dr. sedan, 6 passenger
Malibu	13535	13635	4 dr. station wagon, 2 seat
	13537	13637	2 dr. sport coupe, 5 passenger
	13539	13639	4 dr. sport sedan, 6 passenger
	13567	13667	2 dr. convertible, 5 passenger
	13569	13669	4 dr. sedan, 6 passenger
Nomad	13135	13235	4 dr. station wagon, 2 seat
Nomad Custom	13335	13435	4 dr. station wagon, 2 seat
Concours Estate Wagon	13735	13835	4 dr. station wagon, 2 seat
SS 396		13837	2 dr. sport coupe, 5 passenger
		13867	2 dr. convertible, 5 passenger
El Camino	13380	13480	2 dr. sedan pickup, 3 passenger
	13580	13680	2 dr. sedan pickup, 3 passenger
		13880	2 dr. sedan pickup, 3 passenger

1969–70—Model Identification—Chevelle

Series	Model Number		Description
	6 Cyl.	V8	
300 Deluxe	*13327	*13427	2 dr. coupe, 6 passenger
	*13337	*13437	2 dr. sport coupe, 5 passenger
	*13369	*13469	4 dr. sedan, 6 passenger
Malibu	*13537	*13637	2 dr. sport coupe, 5 passenger
	*13539	*13639	4 dr. sport sedan, 6 passenger
	*13567	*13667	2 dr. convertible, 5 passenger
	*13569	*13669	4 dr. sedan, 6 passenger
Station Wagons	13135①	13235②	Nomad, 4 dr. 2 seat
	13335③	13435④	Greenbrier, 4 dr. 2 seat
	13346	*13446	Greenbrier, 4 dr. 3 seat
	*13536	*13636	Concours, 4 dr. 2 seat
	13546	*13646	Concours, 4 dr. 3 seat
	—	*13836	Concours Estate, 4 dr. 2 seat
	—	*13846	Concours Estate, 4 dr. 2 seat
El Camino	*13380	*13480	2 dr. sedan pickup, 3 passenger
	*13580	*13680	2 dr. sedan pickup, 3 passenger
Monte Carlo*	—	13857	2 dr. sport coupe, 5 passenger
	—	13867	2 dr. convertible, 5 passenger

*—Applicable 1970 models.
① 13136—1970.
② 13236—1970.
③ 13336—1970.
④ 13436—1970.

1971–72—Model Identification—Chevelle

Series	Model Number		Description
	6 Cyl.	V8	
Chevelle	13337	13437	2 dr. sport coupe, 5 passenger
	13369	13469	4 dr. sedan, 6 passenger
Malibu	13537	13637	2 dr. sport coupe, 5 passenger
	13539	13639	4 dr. sport sedan, 6 passenger
	13567	13667	2 dr. convertible, 5 passenger
	13569	13669	4 dr. sedan, 6 passenger
Station Wagons	13136	13236	Nomad, 4 dr., 2 seat
	—	13436	Greenbrier, 4 dr., 2 seat
	—	13446	Greenbrier, 4 dr., 3 seat
	—	13636	Concours, 4 dr., 2 seat
	—	13646	Concours, 4 dr., 3 seat
	—	13836	Concours Estate, 4 dr., 2 seat
	—	13846	Concours Estate, 4 dr., 3 seat
El Camino	13380	13480	Standard 2 dr. sedan pick-up, 3 passenger
	—	13680	Custom 2 dr. sedan pick-up, 3 passenger
Monte Carlo	—	13857	2 dr. sport coupe, 5 passenger

1967–69—Model Identification—Camaro

Series	Model Number		Description
	6 Cyl.	V8	
Camaro	12337	12437	2 dr. sports coupe, 4 passenger
Camaro	12367	12467	2 dr. convertible, 4 passenger

1970–72—Model Identification—Camaro

Series	Model Number		Description
	6 Cyl.	V8	
Camaro	12387	12487	2 dr. sports coupe, 4 passenger

BATTERY AND STARTER SPECIFICATIONS

Year	Model	BATTERY			STARTERS						Brush Spring Tension (Oz.)
		Amp. Hours Capacity	Volts	Terminal Grounded	LOCK TEST			NO LOAD TEST			
					Amp.	Volts	Torque	Amps.	Volts	RPM	
1964	All Series	44	12	Neg.	Not Recommended			49–76	10.6	7,800	35
1965	All Series	44	12	Neg.	Not Recommended			49–76	10.6	7,800	35
1966–67	4 & 6 Cyl., V8—283	44	12	Neg.	Not Recommended			49–76	10.6	7,800	35
	V8—327, 396	61	12	Neg.	Not Recommended			65–100	10.6	4,200①	35
1968–69	4 Cyl., 6 Cyl., V8—307	45	12	Neg.	Not Recommended			—	10.6	—	35
	V8—302, 327, 350, 396	61	12	Neg.	Not Recommended			—	9	—	35
1970–72	4 Cyl., 6 Cyl., V8—307	45	12	Neg.	Not Recommended			50–80	9	5,500–10,500	35
	V8—350	61	12	Neg.	Not Recommended			55–80	9	3,500–6,000	35
	V8—402(396)	61	12	Neg.	Not Recommended			65–95	9	7,500–10,500	35
	V8—454	62	12	Neg.	Not Recommended			65–95	9	7,500–10,500	35

① —Camaro—230 & 327 cu. in. = 9,750

ENGINE IDENTIFICATION

Chevy II
Engine Identification Code, Location

4-6 Cyl.—Pad at front right-hand side of cylinder block at rear of distributor.
V8—pad at front right-hand side of cylinder block.

No. Cyls.	Cu. In. Displ.	Type	1965	1966	1967	1968	1969	1970	1971
4	153	M.T.	OA	OA		OA	AA		
4	153	M.T., HDC	OC	OC	OC	OC			
4	153	PG, Torque Dr.	OH	OH	OH	OH	AB		
4	153	M.T., Taxi	OG						
4	153	PG, Taxi	OG						
6	194	M.T.	OK	OK					
6	194	M.T., HDC	OM	OM	OM				
6	194	PG	OR	OR	OR				
6	194	M.T., Taxi	OQ						
6	194	PG, Taxi	OT						
6	194	M.T., PCV, Taxi							
6	194	PG, PCV, Taxi		OS					
6	194	PG, w/ex. EM		ZX	ZX				
6	194	w/ex. EM		ZY	ZY				
6	230	PG	PX	PX		BF			
6	230	PG, PCV							
6	230	w/ex. EM		PC					
6	230	PG, w/ex. EM		PG			AN		
6	230	HDC, AC				BB			
6	230	HDC				BC			
6	230	PG, AC				BH	AQ		
6	230	Hyd. 350					AO		
6	230	AC					AP		
6	230	Hyd. 350, AC					AR		
6	230	M.T.	LP	PV	PV		AM		
6	230	Torque Dr.					AN	CCD	
6	250	M.T., or OD			PC, PV	CB	BE	CCG, CRF	CCI, CCL
6	250	PG, w/ex. EM			PI, PX	CQ	BB	CCM	
6	250	PG, AC					BC		
6	250	Hyd. 350					BD	CCK	
6	250	AC					BF		
6	250	Hyd. 350, AC					BH		
6	250	Torque Dr.					BB, BC		
4	250	M.T.						CAA	
4	250	PG, TD						CAB	
8	283	M.T., 4-spd.	PL	PL	PL				
8	283	4-spd., AC	PM	PM	PM				
8	283	M.T., 3-spd.	PD	PD	PD				
8	283	3-spd., AC							
8	283	PG	PN	PN	PN				
8	283	PG, AC	PP	PP	PP				
8	283	PG, 4-BBL., AC	PB						
8	283	4-BBL.	PE	QA					
8	283	w/ex. EM		PE	PE				
8	283	AC		PF	PF				
8	283	4-BBL., AC	PG	QB					
8	283	w/ex. EM, AC		PG					
8	283	PG, 4-BBL.	PK	PK					
8	283	PG, AC, w/ex. EM		PO					
8	283	4-spd., w/ex. EM		PQ	PQ				
8	283	4-spd., AC, EM		PS					
8	283	PG, w/ex. EM		PU	PU				
8	283	4-BBL., EM		QC					
8	283	4-BBL., PG, EM		QD					
8	283	4-BBL., AC, EM		QE					
8	283	4-BBL., AC, PG, w/ex. EM		QF					

No. Cyls.	Cu. In. Displ.	Type	1965	1966	1967	1968	1969	1970	1971
8	307	M.T.				MB	DA	CNC	
8	307	SHP				ML			
8	307	PG				MM	DC	CNE	
8	307	Hyd. 350					DD	CNF	
8	307	4-spd.					DE	CND	
8	307	M.T.						CCA	CCA
8	307	PG						CCC	CCC
8	327	M.T.	ZA	ZA	ZA	MK			
8	327	M.T., HP	ZB						
8	327	w/ex. EM		ZB	ZB				
8	327	w/ex. EM, AC		ZC					
8	327	w/ex. EM, PG		ZD	ZD				
8	327	M.T., AC	ZE	ZE	ZE				
8	327	M.T., AC, HP	ZF						
8	327	PG, ex. EM, AC		ZF					
8	327	SHP, w/ex. EM		ZG					
8	327	SHP, w/ex. EM, AC		ZH					
8	327	SHP		ZI			ML		
8	327	SHP, AC		ZJ					
8	327	PG	ZK	ZK	ZK	MM			
8	327	PG, HP	ZL						
8	327	PG, AC	ZM	ZM	ZM				
8	327	PG, HP, AC	ZN						
8	350	M.T.					HA, HQ	CNI(250), CNJ(300)	
8	350	Hyd.					HB, HD	CNN(250), CRE(300)	
8	350	2-BBL.					HC		
8	350	PG					HE, HR	CNK, CNM	
8	350	PG, 2-BBL.					HF		
8	350	Hyd.					HS		
8	350	PG						CGB(250)	CGB
8	350	M.T.						CGK(300)	CGK
8	350	Hyd. 350						CGL(300)	CGL
8	350							CJD(300)	
8	350	M.T.						CJG(300)	
8	396	HP					JF		
8	396	SHP					JH, KA, KC		
8	396	HP, Hyd. 400					JI		
8	396	SHP. Hyd. 400					JL		
8	396	Hyd. 400					JM	CTW(350), CTY(375), CKN(325)	
8	396	PG					JU		
8	396	M.T.					KE	CTX(350), CKO(375)	
8	396	Hyd. 400#						CKP(375)	
8	396	M.T., HDC						CTZ(350), CKQ(375)	
8	396	M.T., HDC#						CKU(375)	
8	396	M.T.#						CKT(375)	
8	400	M.T.						CKR(330)	
8	400	M.T., HDC						CKS(300)	

AC—air conditioned.
HDC—heavy duty clutch.
HP—high performance engine.
SHP—special high performance engine.

PCV—positive crankcase ventilation.
OD—overdrive.
w/ex. EM, or EM—with exhaust emission.

M.T.—manual transmission.
PG—Powerglide transmission.
3 Spd.—three speed transmission.

4 Spd.—four speed transmission.
Hyd.—Hydramatic
#—Aluminum heads
TD—Torque Drive

Camaro
Engine Identification Code Location

Engine identification code letter follows immediately after engine seal number.
6 Cyl.—pad at front right-hand side of cylinder block at rear of distributor.
V8—pad at front right-hand side of cylinder block.

No. Cyls.	Cu. In. Displ.	Type	1967	1968	1969	1970	1971	No. Cyls.	Cu. Inc. Displ.	Type	1967	1968	1969	1970	1971
6	230	3 or 4 Spd.	LA	BA	AM	CCC		8	327	PG, w/ex. EM	MN				
6	230	3 or 4 Spd. AC	LB	BB				8	350	3 or 4 Spd.	MS	MS	HA,HQ	CNJ(300)	
6	230	3 or 4 Spd. w/ex. EM	LC					8	350	3 or 4 Spd. w/ex. EM	MT				
6	230	3 or 4 Spd. AC, w/ex. EM	LD					8	350	PG	MU	MU	HE,HR	CNK(300)	
6	230	PG, Torque Dr.	LE	BF	AN	CCD		8	350	PG, w/ex. EM	MV				
6	230	PG, AC	LH, LF	BH	AQ			8	350	Hyd.			HB,HS	CRE(300)	
6	230	Hyd. 350			AO			8	350	2-BBL.			HC	CNI(250)	
6	230	AC			AP			8	350	Hyd., 2-BBL.			HD	CNM(250)	
6	230	Hyd. 350, AC			AR			8	350	PG,2-BBL.			HF	CNN(250)	
6	230	PG, w/ex. EM	LG					8	350	370 H.P. (new Z28)			N.A.		
6	250	3 or 4 Spd.	LN	CM	BE			8	350	PG					CGB(245)
6	250	3 or 4 Spd. AC	LO	CN				8	350	Hyd. 400					CGR(330)
6	250	PG, w/ex. EM	LP					8	350	M.T.					CGK(270)
6	250	3 or 4 Spd. w/ex. EM	LQ												CJG(270)
6	250	AC		BF				8	350	Hyd. 350					CGL(270)
6	250	PG, Torque Dr.	FM	CQ	BB										CJD(270)
6	250	PG, AC	FR	CR	BC			8	350	M.T.					CJG(330)
6	250	PG, w/ex. EM	GP					8	396	M.T. & P.G.	MW	MW			
6	250	PG, AC, w/ex. EM	GQ		BC			8	396	Mt. & P.G. w/exh. EM.	MX				
6	250	Hyd. 350			BD			8	396	Hyd. 400	MY	MY	JG	CJI(350)	
6	250	Hyd. 350, AC			BH			8	396	Hyd. w/exh. EM.	MZ				
6	250	M.T.				CAA		8	396	SHP		MQ	JH		
6	250	PG				CCA		8	396	HP, Hyd.		MR	JI		
8	302	Z28		DZ	DZ*			8	396	SHP, ALUM. HEADS		MT			
8	307	M.T.			DA	CNC		8	396	HP		MX	JF		
8	307	P.G.			DC	CNE		8	396	PG			JB		
8	307	Hyd. 350			DD	CNF		8	396	M.T., ALUM. HEADS			JJ,KE		
8	307	4-spd.			DE	CND		8	396	SHP, Hyd. 400			JL	CJL(375)	
8	307	M.T.				CCA		8	396	Hyd. 400, ALUM. HEADS			JM		
8	307	PG				CCA		8	396	M.T.,			JU	CJF(350)	
8	327	3 or 4-spd (210)	MA	MA				8	396	M.T., SHP			KA,KC	CJH(375)	
8	327	3 or 4-spd. w/ex. EM	MB					8	400	Hyd. 400 (Mk. IV)				CTW(350),	
8	327	PG, (210 H.P.)	ME	ME										CKN(325),	
8	327	PG, w/ex. EM	MF											CTY(375)	
8	327	3 or 4 Spd. (275 H.P.)	MK					8	400	M.T. (MK. IV)				CTX(350),	
8	327	3 or 4 Spd. w/ex. EM	ML											CKO(375)	
8	327	PG (275 H.P.)	MM					8	400	Hyd. 400 (Mk. IV)					CLD(300)
								8	400	M.T. (MK. IV)					CLC(300)

AC—air conditioned.
HDC—heavy duty clutch.
HP—high performance.
SHP—special high performance.

M.T.—manual transmission.
PG—Powerglide transmission.
w/ex. EM—with exhaust emission.
4 BBL.—four barrel carburetor.

2 BBL.—two barrel carburetor.
Hyd.—Hydromatic transmission (350 or 400).
*—CNA = late production.

DELCOTRON AND AC REGULATOR SPECIFICATIONS

YEAR	MODEL	ALTERNATOR				REGULATOR					
		Field Current Draw @ 12V.	Output @ Generator RPM		Model	Field Relay			Regulator		
			2000	5000		Air Gap (In.)	Point Gap (In.)	Volts to Close	Air Gap (In.)	Point Gap (In.)	Volts at 125°
1965–67	1100693	2.2–2.6	27A	37A	1119515	.015	.030	2.3–3.7	.067	.014	13.5–14.4
	1100695	2.2–2.6	21A	32A	1119515	.015	.030	2.3–3.7	.067	.014	13.5–14.4
	1100794	2.2–2.6	27A	37A	1119515	.015	.030	2.3–3.7	.067	.014	13.5–14.4
1968	1100813	2.2–2.6	27A	37A	1119515	.015	.030	2.3–3.7	.067	.014	13.5–14.4
	1100693	2.2–2.6	27A	37A	1119515	.015	.030	2.3–3.7	.067	.014	13.5–14.4
1969	1100834	2.2–2.6	27A	37A	1119515	.015	.030	2.3–3.7	.067	.014	13.5–14.4
	1100836	2.2–2.6	27A	37A	1119515	.015	.030	2.3–3.7	.067	.014	13.5–14.4
1970	1100834	2.2–2.6	27A	37A	1119515	.015	.030	2.3–3.7	.067	.014	13.5–14.4
	1100837	2.2–2.6	27A	37A	1119515	.015	.030	2.3–3.7	.067	.014	13.5–14.4
1971	1100838	2.2–2.6	27A	37A	1119515	.015	.030	2.3–3.7	.067	.014	13.5–14.4
	1100839	2.2–2.6	27A	37A	1119515	.015	.050	2.3–3.7	.067	.014	13.5–14.4
1972											

① —13.0–13.6 @ 80°

Chevelle Engine Identification Code Location

Engine identification code letter follows immediately after engine serial number. 6 Cyl.—pad at front right-hand side of cylinder block at rear of distributor. V8—Pad at front right-hand side of cylinder block.

No. Cyls.	Cu. In. Displ.	Type	1965	1966	1967	1968	1969	1970	1971
6	194	M.T.	AA	AA					
6	194	HDC	AC	AC					
6	194	AC	AG	AG					
6	194	HDC, AC	AH	AH					
6	194	Taxi	AK						
6	194	PG	AL	AL					
6	194	PG, Taxi	AN						
6	194	PG, AC	AR	AR					
6	194	w/ex. EM		AS					
6	194	w/ex. EM, AC		AT					
6	194	PG, w/ex. EM		AX					
6	194	PG, w/ex. EM, AC		AY					
6	230	HDC			BC	BC	BC		
6	230	HDC, AC			BB	BB	BB		
6	230	PG				BF	BF		
6	230	PG, w/ex. EM		BL			AN		
6	230	Hyd., AC					AR		
6	230	PG, w/ex. EM, AC		BM					
6	230	Hyd.					AD		
6	230	w/ex. EM		BN					
6	230	w/ex. EM, AC		BO					
6	230	M.T.	CA	CA	CA	BA	AM		
6	230	M.T.	CB	CB					
6	230	3 Spd. AC			CB		AP		
6	230	PG	CC	CC	CC				
6	230	PG, AC	CD	CD	CD	BH	AQ		
6	250	3 Spd. or OD			CM	CM	BE	CCL	
6	250	3 Spd. AC			CN	CN	BF		
6	250	3 Spd. or OD w/ex. EM			CO				
6	250	3 Spd. AC w/ex. EM			CP				
6	250	PG			CQ	CQ	BB	CCM	
6	250	PG, AC			CR	CR	BC		
6	250	Hyd.					BD	CCK	
6	250	PG, w/ex. EM			CS				
6	250	Hyd., AC					BH		
6	250	PG, AC w/ex. EM			CT				
6	250	M.T.							CAA
8	283	3 Spd.	DA	DA	DA				
8	283	4 Spd.	DB	DB	DB				
8	283	PG	DE	DF	DE				
8	283	3 Spd., 4 Bbl.	DG	DG					
8	283	PG, 4 Bbl.	DH	DH					
8	283	w/ex. EM		DI	DI				
8	283	PG, w/ex. EM		DJ	DJ				
8	283	4 Spd., w/ex. EM		DK	DK				
8	283	4 Bbl., w/ex. EM		DL					
8	283	PG, 4 Bbl., w/ex. EM		DM					
8	283	HDC			DN				
8	307	Hyd.					DD	CNF	
8	307	M.T.				DA	DA	CNC	
8	307	4 Spd.				DE	DE	CND	
8	307	PG				DB	DC	CNE	
8	307	HDC					DN		
8	307	M.T.							CCA
8	327	M.T.	EA	EA	EA	EA			
8	327	HP	EB						
8	327	w/ex. EM		EB	EB				
8	327	SHP	EC			ES			
8	327	PG, w/ex. EM		EC	EC				
8	327	w/T. Ign.	ED						
8	327	3 or 4 Spd. (325 H.P.)			EP				
8	327	HDC, 3 or 4 Spd. w/ex. EM (325 H.P.)			ER				
8	327	HDC (325 H.P.)			ES	ES			
8	327	HDC (275 H.P.)			ED	ED			

No. Cyls.	Cu. In. Displ.	Type	1965	1966	1967	1968	1969	1970	1971
8	327	PG	EE	EE	EE	EE			
8	327	PG, HP	EF						
8	350	M.T.					HA		
8	350	Hyd.					HB		
8	350	2-BBL.					HC		
8	350	2-BBL., Hyd.					HD		
8	350	PG					HE	CNM(250)	
8	350	PG, 2-BBL.					HF		
8	350	M.T.					HP	CNI(250)	
8	350	M.T.					HR	CNJ(300)	
8	350	PG					HR	CNK(300)	
8	350	Hyd.					HS	CRE(300)	
8	350	M.T.							CGA(245)
8	350	PG							CGB(245)
8	350	M.T.							CGK(270)
8	350	Hyd. 350							CGL(270)
8	350	M.T.							CJD(270), CJJ(270)
8	396	HDC		ED	ED	ED	ED		
8	396	HP		EF	EF	EF	JC		
8	396	SHP				EG	JD		
8	396	w/ex. EM		EH	EH				
8	396	HP, w/ex. EM		EJ	EJ				
8	396	PG		EK	EK	EK	EK		
8	396	PG, HP		EL	EL	EL	EL		
8	396	PG, w/ex. EM		EM	EM				
8	396	PG, HP, w/ex. EM		EN	EN				
8	396	Hyd. (325 H.P.)			ET	ET	ET		
8	396	Hyd. (350 H.P.)			EU	EU	EU		
8	396	w/ex. EM (325 H.P.)					EV		
8	396	w/ex. EM (350 H.P.)					EW		
8	396	M.T.					JA	CTX(350), CKT(375), CKO(375)	
8	396	HP, 3-sp. Hyd. 400					JE		
8	396	Hyd. 400					JK	CTW(350)	
8	396	SHP, Hyd. 400 (#—CKP only)					KF	CTY(375), CKP(375), CKU(375)	
8	396	M.T.					KG		
8	396	Hyd. 400					KH	CKN(325)	
8	396	M.T., HP					KB		
8	396	M.T.					JV		
8	396	SHP, M.T.					KD		
8	396	M.T.					KI		
8	396	M.T., HDC						CTZ(350), CKQ(375)	
8	400	M.T. (330 H.P.)						CKR	
8	400	M.T., HDC (330 H.P.)						CKS	
8	400	Hyd. 350 (Mk. IV)							CLP(300)
8	400	Hyd. 400 (Mk. IV)							CLB(300)
8	400	M.T. (Mk. IV)							CLA(300)
8	400	4 Spd. (Mk. IV)							CLL(300)
8	400	M.T. Police (Mk. IV)							CLR(300)
8	400	M.T. (Mk. IV)							CLS(300)
8	454	M.T. (390 H.P.)						CRN, CRT	
8	454	Hyd. 400 (390 H.P.)						CRQ	
8	454	Hyd. 400 (450 H.P.)						CRR	
8	454	Hyd. 400 #(450 H.P.)						CRS	
8	454	M.T. (450 H.P.)						CRV	
8	400	M.T. (Mk. IV)							CPA(365), CPG(365), CPD(365), CPP(425)
8	400	M.T. (Mk. IV)							CPR(425)

AC—air conditioned.
HDC—heavy duty clutch.
HP—high performance.
SHP—special high performance.
M.T.—manual transmission.
OD—overdrive.
PG—powerglide transmission.
PCV—positive crankcase ventilation.
w/ex. EM—with exhaust emission.
w/T. Ign.—with transistor ignition.
4 Bbl.—four barrel carburetor.
Hyd.—Hydramatic.
#—Aluminum heads.

GENERAL CHASSIS AND BRAKE SPECIFICATIONS

YEAR	MODEL	CHASSIS		BRAKE CYLINDER SIZES				BRAKE DRUM Diameter (In.)	
		Overall Length (In.)	Tire Size	Master Cylinder (In.)		Wheel Cylinder—(In.)			
				Standard	Metallic	Front—	Rear	Front	Rear
1965	Chevy II, 4 Cyl.	182.9	6.00 x 13	1.0	.875	1.06	.875	9.5	9.5
	Chevy II, 6 Cyl.	182.9	6.50 x 13	1.0	.875	1.06	.875	9.5	9.5
	Chevy II, V8	182.9	6.95 x 14	1.0	.875	1.06	.875	9.5	9.5
	Chevy II, Sta. Wag.	182.9	7.00 x 13	1.0	.875	1.06	.875	9.5	9.5
	Chevelle, Exc. Wag.	196.6	6.95 x 14①	1.0	.875	1.06	.875	9.5	9.5
	Chevelle, Sta. Wag.	201.4	7.35 x 14①	1.0	.875	1.06	.875	9.5	9.5
1966	Chevy II, 4 Cyl.	183.0	6.50 x 13	1.0	.875	1.06	.875	9.5	9.5
	Chevy II, 6 Cyl.	183.0	6.50 x 13	1.0	.875	1.06	.875	9.5	9.5
	Chevy II, V8	183.0	6.95 x 14	1.0	.875	1.06	.875	9.5	9.5
	Chevy II, Wag.	187.4	6.95 x 14	1.0	.875	1.06	.875	9.5	9.5
	Chevelle, Exc. Wag.	197.0	6.95 x 14①	1.0	.875	1.06	.875	9.5	9.5
	Chevelle Wag.	197.6	7.75 x 14	1.0	.875	1.06	.875	9.5	9.5
1967	Chevy II, 4 Cyl. & 6 Cyl.	183.0	6.95 x 14	1.0	.875	1.06	.875	9.5	9.5
	Chevy II, V8	183.0	6.95 x 14	.875	.875	1.06	.875	9.5	9.5
	Chevy II, Wagon	187.4	6.95 x 14	1.0	.875	1.875	.875	9.5	9.5
	Chevelle, exc. Wag.	197.0	7.35 x 14②	1.0	.875	1.06	.938	9.5	9.5
	Chevelle, Wagon	199.9	7.75 x 14	1.125	.875	2.062	.938	9.5	9.5
	Camaro	184.6	7.35 x 14③	1.0	.875	1.125④	.875	9.5⑤	9.5
1968	Chevy II	187.7	7.35 x 14	1.00	.875	1.125	.875	9.5	9.5
	Chevy II w/Disc. Brakes	187.7	7.35 x 14	1.125	.875	2.062	.875	11 (Disc)	9.5
	Camaro	184.7	7.35 x 14	1.00	.875	1.125	.875	9.5	9.5
	Camaro w/Disc. Brakes	184.7	7.35 x 14	1.125	.875	2.062	.875	11 (Disc)	9.5
	Chevelle Coupes	196.8	7.35 x 14②	1.00	.875	1.125	.938	9.5	9.5
	Chevelle Sedans	200.8	7.35 x 14	1.00	.875	1.125	.938	9.5	9.5
	Chevelle Sta. Wag.	207.2	7.75 x 14	1.00	.875	1.125	.938	9.5	9.5
	Chevelle w/Disc. Brakes	—	—	1.125	—	2.062	.875	11 (Disc)	9.5
1969	Chevy II	189.4	7.35 x 14	1.0	—	1.125	.875	9.5	9.5
	Camaro	186.0	7.35 x 14	1.0	—	1.125	.875	9.5	9.5
	Chevelle Sedans	200.9	7.35 x 14	1.0	—	1.125	.875	9.5	9.5
	Chevelle, Coupe & Conv.	196.9	7.35 x 14	1.0	—	1.125	.875	9.5	9.5
	Chevelle Sta. Wag.	207.9	7.75 x 14	1.0	—	1.125	.875	9.5	9.5
	All w/Disc. Brakes	—	—	1.125	—	2.938	.875	11 (Disc)	9.5
1970–72	Chevy II	189.4	7.35 x 14	1.0	—	1.125	.875	9.5	9.5
	Camaro	188.0	7.35 x 14	1.125	—	2.938	.875	11 (Disc)	9.5
	Chevelle Sedans	201.2	7.35 x 14	1.0	—	1.125	.875	9.5	9.5
	Chevelle, Coupe & Conv.	197.2	7.35 x 14	1.0	—	1.125	.875	9.5	9.5
	Chevelle Sta. Wag.	206.5	7.75 x 14	1.0	—	1.125	.875	9.5	9.5
	All w/Disc. Brakes	—	—	1.125	—	2.938	.875	11 (Disc)	9.5
	Monte Carlo	205.8	G78 x 15⑥	1.125	—	2.938	.875	11 (Disc)	9.5

① —Models with 327 Engine—7.35 x 14.
With 396 Eng.—7.75 x 14.
② —396 cu. in. F70 x 14
③ —Camaro with 350 cu. in. option—D70 x 14

④ —Camaro with 350 cu. in. option 1⅛
⑤ —Camaro with front disc option = 11.0
⑥ —G70 x 15 base for 454 cu. in. engine.

GENERAL ENGINE SPECIFICATIONS

YEAR	CU. IN. DISPLACEMENT	CARBURETOR	ADVERTIZED HORSEPOWER @ RPM	ADVERTIZED TORQUE @ RPM (FT. LBS.)	A.M.A. HORSEPOWER	BORE & STROKE (IN.)	ADVERTIZED COMPRESSION RATIO	VALVE LIFTER TYPE	NORMAL OIL PRESSURE (PSI)
1965	4 Cyl.; 153	1-BBL.	90 @ 4000	152 @ 2400	24.0	3.875 x 3.25	8.5-1	Hyd.	35
	6 Cyl—194	1-BBL.	120 @ 4400	177 @ 2400	30.5	3.563 x 3.25	8.5-1	Hyd.	35
	6 Cyl—230	1-BBL.	140 @ 4400	215 @ 2000	36.0	3.875 x 3.25	8.5-1	Hyd.	35
	V8—283	2-BBL.	195 @ 4800	285 @ 2400	48.0	3.875 x 3.00	9.25-1	Hyd.	35
	V8—327	4-BBL.	250 @ 4400	350 @ 2800	51.2	4.000 x 3.25	10.5-1	Hyd.	35
	V8—327	4-BBL.	300 @ 5000	360 @ 3200	51.2	4.000 x 3.25	10.5-1	Hyd.	35
	V8—327	4-BBL.	350 @ 6000	360 @ 3200	51.2	4.000 x 3.25	11.0-1	Hyd.	35
1966	4 Cyl—153	1-BBL.	90 @ 4000	152 @ 2400	24.0	3.875 x 3.25	8.5-1	Hyd.	35
	6 Cyl—194	1-BBL.	120 @ 4400	177 @ 2400	30.5	3.563 x 3.25	8.5-1	Hyd.	35
	6 Cyl—230	1-BBL.	140 @ 4400	220 @ 1600	36.0	3.875 x 3.25	8.5-1	Hyd.	35
	V8—283	2-BBL.	195 @ 4800	285 @ 2400	48.0	3.875 x 3.00	9.25-1	Hyd.	45
	V8—283	4-BBL.	220 @ 4800	295 @ 3200	48.0	3.875 x 3.00	9.25-1	Hyd.	45
	V8—327	4-BBL.	275 @ 4800	355 @ 3200	51.2	4.000 x 3.25	10.5-1	Hyd.	45
	V8—327	4-BBL.	350 @ 5800	360 @ 3600	51.2	4.000 x 3.25	11.0-1	Hyd.	45
	V8—396	4-BBL.	325 @ 4800	410 @ 3200	53.6	4.094 x 3.76	10.25-1	Hyd.	60
	V8—396	4-BBL.	360 @ 5200	420 @ 3600	53.6	4.094 x 3.76	10.25-1	Hyd.	60
1967	4 Cyl—153	1-BBL.	90 @ 4000	152 @ 2400	24.0	3.875 x 3.25	8.5-1	Hyd.	35
	6 Cyl—194	1-BBL.	120 @ 4400	177 @ 2400	30.5	3.563 x 3.25	8.5-1	Hyd.	35
	6 Cyl—230	1-BBL.	140 @ 4400	220 @ 1600	36.0	3.875 x 3.25	8.5-1	Hyd.	35
	6 Cyl—250	1-BBL.	155 @ 4200	235 @ 1600	36.0	3.875 x 3.53	8.5-1	Hyd.	35
	V8—283	2-BBL.	195 @ 4800	285 @ 2800	48.0	3.875 x 3.00	9.25-1	Hyd.	45
	V8—327	4-BBL.	210 @ 4800	325 @ 3200	51.2	4.000 x 3.25	9.0-1	Hyd.	45
	V8—327	4-BBL.	275 @ 4800	355 @ 3200	51.2	4.000 x 3.25	10.25-1	Hyd.	45
	V8—327	4-BBL.	325 @ 4800	360 @ 3600	51.2	4.000 x 3.25	11.0-1	Hyd.	45
	V8—350	4-BBL.	295 @ 4800	380 @ 3200	51.2	4.000 x 3.48	10.25-1	Hyd.	45
	V8—396	4-BBL.	325 @ 4800	410 @ 3200	53.6	4.094 x 3.76	10.25-1	Hyd.	45
	V8—396	4-BBL.	350 @ 5200	420 @ 3600	53.6	4.094 x 3.76	10.25-1	Hyd.	45
1968	4 Cyl—153	1-BBL.	90 @ 4000	152 @ 2400	24.0	3.875 x 3.25	8.5-1	Hyd.	35
	6 Cyl—230	1-BBL.	140 @ 4400	220 @ 1600	36.0	3.875 x 3.25	8.5-1	Hyd.	35
	6 Cyl—250	1-BBL.	155 @ 4200	235 @ 1600	36.0	3.875 x 3.53	8.5-1	Hyd.	35
	V8—302	4-BBL.	290 @ 5800	290 @ 4200	51.2	4.000 x 3.00	11.0-1	Mech.	45
	V8—307	2-BBL.	200 @ 4600	300 @ 2400	48.0	3.875 x 3.25	9.0-1	Hyd.	45
	V8—327	2-BBL.	210 @ 4600	320 @ 2400	51.2	4.000 x 3.25	8.75-1	Hyd.	45
	V8—327	4-BBL.	275 @ 4800	355 @ 3200	51.2	4.000 x 3.25	10.0-1	Hyd.	45
	V8—327	4-BBL.	325 @ 5600	355 @ 3600	51.2	4.000 x 3.25	11.0-1	Hyd.	45
	V8—350	4-BBL.	295 @ 4800	380 @ 3200	51.2	4.000 x 3.48	10.25-1	Hyd.	45
	V8—396	4-BBL.	325 @ 4800	410 @ 3200	53.6	4.094 x 3.76	10.25-1	Hyd.	45
	V8—396	4-BBL.	350 @ 5200	415 @ 3400	53.6	4.094 x 3.76	10.25-1	Hyd.	45
	V8—396	4-BBL.	375 @ 5600	415 @ 3600	53.6	4.094 x 3.76	11.0-1	Mech.	45
1969	4 Cyl—153	1-BBL.	90 @ 4000	152 @ 2400	24.0	3.875 x 3.25	8.5-1	Hyd.	45
	6 Cyl—230	1-BBL.	140 @ 4400	220 @ 1600	36.0	3.875 x 3.25	8.5-1	Hyd.	45
	6 Cyl—250	1-BBL.	155 @ 4200	235 @ 1600	36.0	3.875 x 3.53	8.5-1	Hyd.	45
	V8—302	4-BBL.	290 @ 5800	290 @ 4200	51.2	4.000 x 3.00	11.0-1	Mech.	45
	V8—307	2-BBL.	200 @ 4600	300 @ 2400	48.0	3.875 x 3.25	9.0-1	Hyd.	45
	V8—350	4-BBL.	255 @ 4800	365 @ 3200	51.2	4.000 x 3.48	9.0-1	Hyd.	45
	V8—350	4-BBL.	300 @ 5000	380 @ 3200	51.2	4.000 x 3.48	10.25-1	Hyd.	45
	V8—396	4-BBL.	325 @ 4800	410 @ 3200	53.6	4.094 x 3.76	10.25-1	Hyd.	45

GENERAL ENGINE SPECIFICATIONS, continued

YEAR	CU. IN. DISPLACEMENT	CARBURETOR	ADVERTIZED HORSEPOWER @ RPM	ADVERTIZED TORQUE @ RPM (FT. LBS.)	A.M.A. HORSEPOWER	BORE & STROKE (IN.)	ADVERTIZED COMPRESSION RATIO	VALVE LIFTER TYPE	NORMAL OIL PRESSURE (PSI)
	V8—396	4-BBL.	350 @ 5200	415 @ 3400	53.6	4.094 x 3.76	10.25-1	Hyd.	45
	V8—396	4-BBL.	375 @ 5600	415 @ 3600	53.6	4.094 x 3.76	11.0-1	Mech.	45
1970	4 Cyl—153	1-BBL.	90 @ 4000	152 @ 2400	24.0	3.875 x 3.250	8.5-1	Hyd.	30–45
	6 Cyl—230	1-BBL.	140 @ 4400	220 @ 1600	36.0	3.875 x 3.250	8.5-1	Hyd.	30–45
	6 Cyl—250	1-BBL.	155 @ 4200	235 @ 1600	36.0	3.875 x 3.530	8.5-1	Hyd.	30–45
	V8—307	2-BBL.	200 @ 4600	300 @ 2400	48.0	3.875 x 3.250	9.0-1	Hyd.	30–45
	V8—350	2-BBL.	250 @ 4800	345 @ 2800	51.2	4.000 x 3.480	9.0-1	Hyd.	30–45
	V8—350	4-BBL.	300 @ 4800	380 @ 3200	51.2	4.000 x 3.480	10.25-1	Hyd.	30–45
	V8—350(Z28)	4-BBL.	360 @ 6000	380 @ 4000	51.2	4.000 x 3.480	11.0-1	Mech.	30–45
	V8—400	2-BBL.	265 @ 4400	390 @ 2400	54.5	4.125 x 3.750	8.5-1	Hyd.	30–45
	V8—396(402) (Mk. IV)	4-BBL.	350 @ 5200	415 @ 3400	54.5	4.125 x 3.760	10.25-1	Hyd.	30–45
	V8—400(402) (Mk. IV)	4-BBL.	330 @ 4800	410 @ 3200	54.5	4.125 x 3.760	10.25-1	Hyd.	30–45
	V8—454	4-BBL.	360 @ 4400	500 @ 3200	57.8	4.250 x 4.000	10.25-1	Hyd.	30–45
1971	6 Cyl—250	1-BBL.	145 @ 4200	230 @ 1600	36.0	3.875 x 3.530	8.5-1	Hyd.	30–45
	V8—307	2-BBL.	200 @ 4600	300 @ 2400	48.0	3.875 x 3.250	9.0-1	Hyd.	30–45
	V8—350	2-BBL.	245 @ 4800	350 @ 2800	51.2	4.000 x 3.480	8.5-1	Hyd.	30–45
	V8—350	4-BBL.	270 @ 4800	360 @ 3200	51.2	4.000 x 3.480	8.5-1	Hyd.	30–45
	V8—350 (Z28)	4-BBL.	330 @ 5600	360 @ 4000	51.2	4.000 x 3.480	8.5-1	Mech.	30–45
	V8—396(402) (Mk. IV)	4-BBL.	300 @ 4800	400 @ 3200	54.5	4.125 x 3.750	8.5-1	Hyd.	30–45
	V8—454	4-BBL.	425 @ 5600	475 @ 4000	57.8	4.250 x 4.000	9.0-1	Mech.	30–45
	V8—454	4-BBL.	365 @ 4800	465 @ 3200	57.8	4.250 x 4.000	8.5-1	Hyd.	30–45
1972	6 Cyl—250	1-BBL.	110 @ 4200①	②	36.0	3.875 x 3.53	8.5-1	Hyd.	30–45
	V8—307	2-BBL	140 @ 4600①	②	48.0	3.875 x 3.25	8.5-1	Hyd.	30–45
	V8—350	2-BBL.	165 @ 4800①	②	51.2	4.00 x 3.48	8.5-1	Hyd.	30–45
	V8—350	4-BBL.	210 @ 4800①	②	51.2	4.00 x 3.48	8.5-1	Hyd.	30–45
	V8—350 (Z28)	4-BBL.	275 @ 5600①	②	51.2	4.00 x 3.48	9.0-1	Mech.	30–45
	V8—402 (Mk. IV)	4-BBL.	208 @ 4800①	②	54.5	4.125 x 3.75	8.5-1	Hyd.	30–45
	V8—454	4-BBL.	285 @ 4800①	②	57.8	4.250 x 4.00	8.5-1	Hyd.	30–45

① —S.A.E. net H.P.
② —Torque information not available at press time.

TORQUE SPECIFICATIONS

YEAR	MODEL	CYLINDER HEAD BOLTS (FT. LBS.)	ROD BEARING BOLTS (FT. LBS.)	MAIN BEARING BOLTS (FT. LBS.)	CRANKSHAFT BALANCER BOLT (FT. LBS.)	FLYWHEEL TO CRANKSHAFT BOLTS (FT. LBS.)	MANIFOLD (FT. LBS.) Intake	MANIFOLD (FT. LBS.) Exhaust
1965–72	4 & 6-Cyl.	95	35	65	...	60	①	①
1965–67	V8—283-350	60-70	35	80	60②	60	30	①
1968–72	V8—302-400 (Small Block)	60-70	45	75②	60⑥	60	30	①
1965	V8—409	60-70	35-45	90-100	...	65	30	①
1965–72	V8—396-402 (Big Block)	80①	50	95③	85	65	30	①
1966–72	V8—427-454	80①	50④	100③	85	65	30	①

① —Aluminum Heads—Short bolts 65, Long bolts 75　　③ —Engines with 4-bolt mains—115　　⑤ —Center bolts—25-30, end bolts 15–20
② —Engines with 4-bolt mains—Outer bolts 65　　④ —7/16 bolts—70　　⑥ —Where applicable

CYLINDER HEAD BOLT TIGHTENING SEQUENCE

4 cylinder

6 cylinder

283, 302 (Z28), 307, 327, 350, 400 (small block) V8s

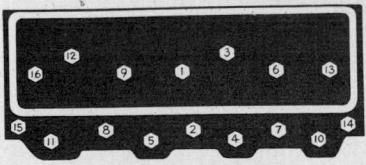

396, 400 (big block 402), 427, 454 V8s

TUNE-UP SPECIFICATIONS

YEAR	MODEL	SPARK PLUGS Type	Gap (In.)	DISTRIBUTOR Point Dwell (Deg.)	Point Gap (In.) Ⓐ	IGNITION TIMING (Deg.) ▲	CRANKING COMP. PRESSURE (Psi)	VALVES Tappet (Hot) Clearance (In.) Intake	Exhaust	Intake Opens (Deg.)	FUEL PUMP PRESSURE (Psi)	IDLE SPEED (Rpm) ★
1965	4—153 Cu. In.	46N	.035	31°–34°	.019	4B	130	■	■	34B	3–4½	500
	6—194 Cu. In.	46N	.035	31°–34°	.019	8B	130	■	■	34B	3–4½	500
	6—230 Cu. In.	46N	.035	31°–34°	.019	4B	130	■	■	49B	5–6½	500
	V8—283 Cu. In., 2-BBL.	45	.035	28°–32°	.019	4B	150	■	■	34B	5–6½	500
	V8—327 Cu. In. (250 H.P.)	44	.035	28°–32°	.019	4B	160	■	■	32B	5–6½	550
	V8—327 Cu. In. (300 H.P.)	44	.035	28°–32°	.019	8B	160	■	■	32B	5–6½	550
	V8—327 Cu. In. (350 H.P.)	44	.035	28°–32°	.019	8B	150	■	■	35B	5–6½	750
1966	4 Cyl.—153 Cu. In.	46N	.035	31°–34°	.019	4B	130	■	■	33½B	3–4½	575
	6 Cyl.—194 Cu. In.	46N	.035	31°–34°	.019	⊙**	130	■	■	62B	3–4½	500③
	6 Cyl.—230 Cu. In.	46N	.035	31°–34°	.019	4B	130	■	■	62B	3–4½	500
	V8—283 Cu. In.	45	.035	28°–32°	.019	4B	150	■	■	32½B	5–6½	500
	V8—327 Cu. In. (275 H.P.)	44	.035	28°–32°	.019	⊙	160	■	■	32½B	5–6½	500③
	V8—327 Cu. In. (350 H.P.)	44	.035	28°–32°	.019	10B	160	■	■	54B	5–6½	700
	V8—396 Cu. In.	43N	.035	28°–32°	.019	4B	160	■	■	40B	5–6½	550
	V8—396 Cu. In. (360 H.P.)	43N	.035	28°–32°	.019	4B	160	■	■	58B	5–6½	550
1967	4 Cyl.—153 Cu. In. (90 H.P.)	46N	.035	31°–34°	.019	4B	130	■	■	33½B	3–4½	500
	6 Cyl.—194 Cu. In. (120 H.P.)	46N	.035	31°–34°	.019	4B⊙	130	■	■	62B	3–4½	500⊙
	6 Cyl.—230 Cu. In. (140 H.P.)	46N	.035	31°–34°	.019	4B⊙	130	■	■	62B	3–4½	500⓪
	6 Cyl.—250 Cu. In. (155 H.P.)	46N	.035	31°–34°	.019	4B⊙	130	■	■	62B	3–4½	500⓪
	V8—283 Cu. In. (195 H.P.)	45	.035	28°–32°	.019	4B⊙	150	■	■	36B	5–6½	500⓪
	V8—327 Cu. In. (210 H.P.)	44	.035	28°–32°	.019	2B⓪	160	■	■	36B	5–6½	500⓪
	V8—327 Cu. In. (275 H.P.)	44	.035	28°–32°	.019	8B⊙	160	■	■	36B	5–6½	500⓪
	V8—327 Cu. In. (325 H.P.)	44	.035	28°–32°	.019	10B⊙	150	■	■	54B	5–6½	500⓪
	V8—350 Cu. In. (295 H.P.)	44	.035	28°–32°	.019	4B⊙	160	■	■	36B	5–6½	500⓪
	V8—396 Cu. In. (325 H.P.)	43N	.035	28°–32°	.019	4B⊙	160	■	■	40B	5–6½	500⓪
	V8—396 Cu. In. (350 H.P.)	43N	.035	28°–32°	.019	4B	160	■	■	56B	5–6½	500
	V8—396 Cu. In. (375 H.P.)	43N	.035	28°–32°	.019	4B	160	.024	.028	N.A.	5–8½	750●
1968	4 Cyl.—153 Cu. In. (90 H.P.)	46N	.035	31°–34°	.019	TDC①	130	■	■	17½B	3–4½	750●
	6 Cyl.—230 Cu. In. (140 H.P.)	46N	.035	31°–34°	.019	TDC①	130	■	■	16B	3–4½	700●
	6 Cyl.—250 Cu. In. (155 H.P.)	46N	.035	31°–34°	.019	TDC①	130	■	■	16B	3–4½	700●
	V8—302 Cu. In. (290 H.P.)	43	.035	28°–32°	.019	4B	190	.030	.030	N.A.	5–6½	900
	V8—307 Cu. In. (200 H.P.)	45S	.035	28°–32°	.019	2B	150	■	■	28B	5–6½	700●
	V8—327 Cu. In. (210 H.P.)	44	.035	28°–32°	.019	2A②	160	■	■	28B	5–6½	700●
	V8—327 Cu. In. (275 H.P.)	44	.035	28°–32°	.019	TDC①	160	■	■	28B	5–6½	700●
	V8—327 Cu. In. (325 H.P.)	44	.035	28°–32°	.019	4B	150	■	■	40B	5–6½	750
	V8—350 Cu. In. (295 H.P.)	44	.035	28°–32°	.019	TDC①	160	■	■	28B	5–8½	700●
	V8—396 Cu. In. (325 H.P.)	43N	.035	28°–32°	.019	4B	160	■	■	28B	5–8½	700●
	V8—396 Cu. In. (350 H.P.)	43N	.035	28°–32°	.019	TDC①	160	■	■	40B	7–8½	700●
	V8—396 Cu. In. (375 H.P.)	43N	.035	28°–32°	.019	4B	160	.024	.028	N.A.	5–8½	750
1969	4 Cyl. 153 Cu. In. (90 H.P.)	R46N	.035	31°–34°	.019	TDC④	130	■	■	17½B	3–4½	750⑦
	6 Cyl. 230 Cu. In. (140 H.P.)	R46N	.035	31°–34°	.019	TDC④	130	■	■	16B	3–4½	700⑤
	6 Cyl. 250 Cu. In. (155 H.P.)	R46N	.035	31°–34°	.019	TDC④	130	■	■	16B	3–4½	700⑥
	V8—302 Cu. In. (290 H.P.)	R43	.035	28°–32°	.019	4B	190	.030	.030	N.A.	5–6½	900
	V8—307 Cu. In. (200 H.P.)	R45S	.035	28°–32°	.019	2B	150	■	■	28B	5–6½	700⑦
	V8—350 Cu. In. (255 H.P.)	R44	.035	28°–32°	.019	TDC④	160	■	■	28B	5–6½	700⑦
	V8—350 Cu. In. (300 H.P.)	R44	.035	28°–32°	.019	TDC④	160	■	■	28B	5–6½	700⑦
	V8—396 Cu. In. (325 H.P.)	R44N	.035	28°–32°	.019	4B	160	■	■	28B	5–8½	800⑦

TUNE-UP SPECIFICATIONS, continued

YEAR	MODEL	SPARK PLUGS		DISTRIBUTOR		IGNITION TIMING (Deg.) ▲	CRANKING COMP. PRESSURE (Psi)	VALVES			FUEL PUMP PRESSURE (Psi)	IDLE SPEED (Rpm) ★
		Type	Gap (In.)	Point Dwell (Deg.)	Point Gap (In.) Ⓐ			Tappet (Hot) Clearance (In.) Intake	Exhaust	Intake Opens (Deg.)		
	V8—396 Cu. In. (350 H.P.)	R43N	.035	28°-32°	.019	TDC④	160	■	■	56B	5-8½	800⑦
	V8—396 Cu. In. (375 H.P.)	R43N	.035	28°-32°	.019	4B	160	.024	.028	N.A.	5-8½	750
1970	4 Cyl 153 Cu. In. (90 H.P.)	R46N	.035	31°-34°	.019	TDC④	130	■	■	17½B	3-4½	750⑦
	6 Cyl 230 Cu. In. (140 H.P.)	R46T	.035	31°-34°	.019	TDC④	130	■	■	16B	3-4½	750⑦
	6 Cyl 250 Cu. In. (155 H.P.)	R46T	.035	31°-34°	.019	TDC④	130	■	■	16B	3-4½	750⑦
	V8—307 Cu. In. (200 H.P.)	R43	.035	28°-32°	.019	2B⑧	150	■	■	28B	5-6½	700⑦
	V8—350 Cu. In. (250 H.P.)	R44	.035	28°-32°	.019	TDC④	160	■	■	28B	5-6½	750⑦
	V8—350 Cu. In. (300 H.P.)	R44	.035	28°-32°	.019	TDC④	160	■	■	28B	5-6½	700⑦
	V8—350 Cu. In. (370 H.P.)	R43	.035	28°-32°	.019	14B	190	.030	.030	43B	5-6½	750
	V8—396 Cu. In. (350 H.P.)	R44T	.035	28°-32°	.019	TDC④	160	■	■	56B	5-8½	700⑦
	V8—400 (265 H.P.)	R44	.035	28°-32°	.019	4B⑧	160	■	■	28B	5-8½	700⑦
	V8—400; 402 Cu. In. (330 H.P.) (Mk. IV)	R44T	.035	28°-32°	.019	4B⑧	160	■	■	28B	5-8½	700⑦
	V8—454 Cu. In. (360 H.P.)	R43T	.035	28°-32°	.019	6B	160	■	■	56B	5-8½	700⑦
1971-72	6 Cyl—250 Cu. In. (145 H.P.) ᶜ	R46TS	.035	31°-34°	.019	4B	130	■	■	16B	3-4½	550
	V8—307 Cu. In. (200 H.P.) ᶜ	R45TS	.035	29°-31°	.019	4B⑧	150	■	■	28B	5-6½	550-600
	V8—350 Cu. In. (245 H.P.) ᶜ	R45TS	.035	29°-31°	.019	2B⑨	160	■	■	28B	7-6½	550-600
	V8—350 Cu. In. (270 H.P.) ᶜ	R44TS	.035	29°-31°	.019	4B⑧	160	■	■	28B	7-8½	550-600
	V8—350 Cu. In. (330 H.P.) (Z-28) ᶜ	R44TS	.035	29°-31°	.019	8B⑩	150	.024	.030	42°40'B	7-8½	700
	V8—402 Cu. In. (Mk. IV) ᶜ	R44TS	.035	29°-31°	.019	8B	150	■	■	28B	7-8½	600
	V8—454 Cu. In. (365 H.P.) ᶜ	R42TS	.035	29°-31°	.019	8B	160	■	■	56B	7-8½	600
	V8—454 Cu. In. (425 H.P.) ᶜ	R42TS	.035	29°-31°	.019	8B⑩	150	.024	.028	44B	7-8½	700

★—with manual transmission in N and automatic in D.
▲—with vacuum advanced disconnected and plugged.
■—1 turn tighter than zero Lash.
Ⓐ—.016 in. (used)
**—8B std. engine; 3B man. trans; 8B Auto. trans.

⊚—1967—With California Air Injection:
  194 (120 H.P.)—2°B. @ 600-700 rpm.
  230 (140 H.P.)—4°B @ 700 rpm (500 w/Auto. trans.)
  250 (155 H.P.)—4°B @ 700 rpm (500 w/Auto. trans.)
  283 (195 H.P.)—TDC @ 700 rpm (600 w/Auto. trans.)
  327 (210 H.P.)—2°B @ 700 rpm (600 w/Auto. trans.)
  327 (275 H.P.)—6°B @ 700 rpm (600 w/Auto. trans.)
  327 (325 H.P.)—8°B @ 750 rpm
  327 (295 H.P.)—4°B @ 700 rpm (500 w/Auto. trans.)
  396 (325 H.P.)—4°B @ 700 rpm (500 w/Auto. trans.)

⊙—1966 With California Air Injection System:
  6 Cyl. 194, Dist. No. 1110360—8 B.
                1110373—3 B.
  V8—327 (275 H.P.) Dist. No. 1111152—8 B.
                  1111116—2 A.

①—w/A.T.—4B
②—w/A.T.—2B
③—With Calif. Air Injection—700 rpm.
●—4 Cyl. & V8 w/A.T., Idle 600 rpm.
  6 Cyl. w/A.T., Idle 500 rpm.
④—w/A.T.—4B
⑤—w/A.T.—2B
⑥—w/A.T.—500 rpm.
⑦—w/A.T.—600-650 rpm.
⑧—w/A.T.—8B
⑨—w/A.T.—6B
⑩—w/A.T.—12B
★—Not available in Cal.
A—After top dead center
B—Before top dead center
TDC—Top dead center
||—See engine decal for 1972.
ᶜ—1972 net H.P. 250 C.I.—110 H.P., 307 C.I.—140 H.P.* 350 C.I. 2-BBL.—165 H.P., 350 4-BBL.—210 H.P., 350 C.I.—228 275 H.P., 402 C.I.—260 H.P.*

CAUTION

General adoption of anti-pollution laws has changed the design of almost all car engine production to effectively reduce crankcase emission and terminal exhaust products. It has been necessary to adopt stricter tune-up rules, especially timing and idle speed procedures. Both of these values are peculiar to the engine and to its application, rather than to the engine alone. With this in mind, car manufacturers supply idle speed data for the engine and application involved. This information is clearly displayed in the engine compartment of each vehicle.

CRANKSHAFT BEARING JOURNAL SPECIFICATIONS

YEAR	MODEL	MAIN BEARING JOURNALS (IN.)				CONNECTING ROD BEARING JOURNALS (IN.)		
		Journal Diameter	Oil Clearance	Shaft End-Play	Thrust on No.	Journal Diameter	Oil Clearance	End-Play
1965	4 Cyl.—153	2.2983-2.2993	.0003-.0029	.002-.006	5	1.999-2.000	.0007-.0027	.009-.013
	6 Cyl.—194	2.2983-2.2993	.0003-.0029	.002-.006	7	1.999-2.000	.0007-.0027	.009-.013
	6 Cyl.—230	2.2983-2.2993	.0003-.0029	.002-.006	7	1.999-2.000	.0007-.0027	.009-.013
	V8—283	2.2978-2.2988	.0003-.0029 (1)	.002-.006	5	1.999-2.000	.0007-.0027	.009-.013
	V8—327	2.2978-2.2988	.0008-.0034 (1)	.002-.006	5	1.999-2.000	.0007-.0028	.009-.013
1966	4 Cyl.—153	2.2983-2.9993	.0003-.0029	.002-.006	5	1.999-2.000	.0007-.0027	.009-.013
	6 Cyl.—194	2.2983-2.2993	.0003-.0029	.002-.006	7	1.999-2.000	.0007-.0027	.009-.013
	6 Cyl.—230	2.2983-2.2993	.0003-.0029	.002-.006	7	1.999-2:000	.0007-.0027	.009-.013
	V8—283	(2)	.0003-.0029 (1)	.003-.011	5	1.999-2.000	.0007-.0027	.009-.013
	V8—327	(2)	.0003-.0034 (1)	.003-.011	5	1.999-2.000	.0007-.0028	.009-.013
	V8—396	(3)	(4)	.006-.010	5	2.199-2.200	.0007-.0028	.015-.021
1967	4 Cyl.—153	2.2983-2.2993	.0003-.0029	.002-.006	5	1.999-2.000	.0007-.0027	.009-.013
	6 Cyl.—194	2.2983-2.2993	.0003-.0029	.002-.006	7	1.999-2.000	.0007-.0027	.009-.013
	6 Cyl.—230	2.2983-2.2993	.0003-.0029	.002-.006	7	1.999-2.000	.0007-.0027	.009-.013
	6 Cyl.—250	2.2983-2.2993	.0003-.0029	.002-.006	7	1.999-2.000	.0007-.0027	.009-.013
	V8—283	(5)	(7)	.003-.011	5	1.999-2.000	.0007-.0027	.009-.013
	V8—327	(5)	(7)	.003-.011	5	1.999-2.000	.0007-.0028	.009-.013
	V8—350	2.24483-2.4493 (6)	.0008-.002 (8)	.003-.011	5	2.099-2.100	.0007-.0028	.009-.013
	V8—396	(3)	(4)	.006-.010	5	2.199-2.200	.0007-.0028	.015-.021
1968	4 Cyl.—153	2.2983-2.2993	.0003-.0029	.002-.006	5	1.999-2.000	.0007-.0027	.009-.013
	6 Cyl.—230	2.2983-2.2993	.0003-.0029	.002-.006	7	1.999-2.000	.0007-.0027	.009-.013
	6 Cyl.—250	2.2983-2.2993	.0003-.0029	.002-.006	7	1.999-2.000	.0007-.0027	.009-.013
	V8—302(Z28)	2.4479-2.4488	.0008-.003	.003-.011	5	2.099-2.100	.0007-.0028	.009-.013
	V8—307	2.4484-2.4493 (6)	.0008-.002 (8)	.003-.011	5	2.099-2.100	.0007-.0027	.009-.013
	V8—327	2.4484-2.4493 (6)	.0008-.002 (8)	.003-.011	5	2.099-2.100	.0007-.0028	.009-.013
	V8—350	2.4484-2.4493 (6)	.0008-.002 (8)	.003-.011	5	2.099-2.100	.0007-.0028	.009-.013
	V8—396	(9)	(11)	.006-.010	5	2.199-2.200	.0009-.0025	.015-.021
	V8—396(375 H.P.)	(10)	.0013-.0025 (12)	.006-.010	5	2.1985-2.1995	.0014-.003	.019-.025
1969	4 Cyl.—153	2.2983-2.2993	.0003-.0029	.002-.006	5	1.999-2.000	.0007-.0027	.009-.013
	6 Cyl.—230	2.2983-2.2993	.0003-.0029	.002-.006	7	1.999-2.000	.0007-.0027	.009-.013
	6 Cyl.—250	2.2983-2.2993	.0003-.0029	.002-.006	7	1.999-2.000	.0007-.0027	.009-.013
	V8—302(Z28)	2.4479-2.4488	.0008-.003	.003-.011	5	2.099-2.100	.0007-.0028	.009-.013
	V8—307	2.4479-2.4488	.0008-.002 (8)	.003-.011	5	2.099-2.100	.0007-.0027	.009-.013
	V8—327	2.4479-2.4488	.0008-.002 (8)	.003-.011	5	2.099-2.100	.0007-.0028	.009-.013
	V8—350	2.4479-2.4488	.0008-.002 (8)	.003-.011	5	2.099-2.100	.0007-.0028	.009-.013
	V8—396	(9)	(11)	.006-.010	5	2.199-2.200	.0009-.0025	.015-.021
	V8—396(375 H.P.)	(10)	.0013-.0025 (12)	.006-.010	5	2.1985-2.1995	.0014-.003	.019-.025
1970-72	6 Cyl.—250	2.2983-2.2993	.0003-.0029	.002-.006	7	1.999-2.000	.0007-.0027	.009-.014
	V8—307	2.4484-2.4493 (6)	(15)	.002-.006	5	2.099-2.100	.0007-.0028	.008-.014
	V8—350	2.4484-2.4493 (6)	(15)	.002-.006	5	2.099-2.100	.0007-.0028	.008-.014
	V8—396(402) (Mk. IV)	(13)	(16)	.006-.010	5	2.199-2.200	.0009-.0025	.015-.021
	V8—400 (19)	2.6584-2.6493 (18)	(16)	.006-.010	5	2.099-2.100	.0009-.0025	.015-.023
	V8—454	(14)	.0013-.0025 (17)	.006-.010	5	2.199-2.200	.0009-.0025	.015-.021

(1) No. 5—.0010-.0036

(2) No. 1—2.2987-2.2997
Nos. 2-4—2.2983-2.2993
No. 5—2.2978-2.2988

(3) Nos. 1-2—2.7487-2.7497
Nos. 3-4—2.7482-2.7492
No. 5—2.7478-2.7488

(4) Nos. 1-2—.0004-.002
Nos. 3-4—.0009-.0025
No. 5—.0013-.0029

(5) No. 1—2.2984-2.2993
Nos. 2-4—2.2983-2.2993
No. 5—2.2978-2.2988

(6) No. 5—2.4478-2.4488

(7) No. 1—.0008-.002
Nos. 2-4—.0018-.002
No. 5—.0010-.0036

(8) No. 5—.0018-.0034

(9) Nos. 1-2—2.7484-2.7493
Nos. 3-4—2.7481-2.7490
No. 5—2.7478-2.7488

(10) No. 1—2.7484-2.7493
Nos. 2-4—2.7481-2.7490
No. 5—2.7478-2.7488

(11) Nos. 1-2—.0010-.0022
Nos. 3-4—.0013-.0025
No. 5—.0015-.0031

(12) No. 5—.0015-.0031

(13) Nos. 1-2—2.7487-2.7496
Nos. 3-4—2.7481-2.7490
No. 5—2.7478-2.7488

(14) No. 1—2.7485-2.7494
Nos. 2-4—2.7481-2.7490
No. 5—2.7478-2.7488

(15) No. 1—.0003-.0015
Nos. 2-4—.0006-.0018
No. 5—.0008-.0023

(16) No. 1—.0007-.0019
Nos. 2-4—.0013-.0025
No. 5—.0024-.004

(17) No. 5—.0024-.004

(18) No. 5—2.6479-2.6488

(19) 1970 only (265 H.P.).

CAPACITIES

YEAR	MODEL	ENGINE CRANKCASE ADD 1 Qt. FOR NEW FILTER	TRANSMISSIONS Pts. TO REFILL AFTER DRAINING			DRIVE AXLE (Pts.)	GASOLINE TANK (Gals.)	COOLING SYSTEM (Qts.) WITH HEATER
			Manual		Automatic			
			3-Speed	4-Speed				
1965	4 Cyl.	3.5②	2	None	15.2	4	16	9
	6 Cyl.	4	2	None	15.2	4	16①	12
	V8—283	4	2	2.5	15.2	4	16①	17
	V8—327	4	2	2.5	15.2	4	16①	16③
1966	4 Cyl.	3.5②	2	None	15.2	3.5	16	9
	6 Cyl.	4	2	None	15.2	3.5	16①	12
	V8—283, 327	4	2	2.5	15.2	3.5	16①	17
	V8—396	4	2	2.5	15.2	3.5	20	22
1967	4 Cyl.	3.5②	3	None	17	3.5	16	9
	6 Cyl.	4	3	None	17	3.5	16①	11
	V8—283-327	4	3④	3	17	4	16①	16
	V8—350-396	4	3④	3	19	4	20①	23⑤
1968	4 Cyl.	3½②	3	None	17	3.5	18	9
	6 Cyl.	4	3	None	17	3.5	18⑥	12
	V8—302, 307, 327	4	3④	3	17	4	18⑥	16
	V8—350	4	3④	3	17	4	18	15
	V8—396	4	3④	3	19	4	18⑥	23
1969	4 Cyl.—153	3½②	3	None	17	⑧	18	9
	6 Cyl.—230, 250	4	3	None	17	⑧	18⑥	13
	V8—302, 307	4	3④	3	17⑦	⑧	18⑥	17
	V8—327	4	3④	3	19⑦	⑧	18⑥	17
	V8—350	4	3④	3	19	⑧	18⑥	16
	V8—396	4	3④	3	22	⑧	18⑥	23
1970	4 Cyl.—153	3½②	3	None	17	⑧	18	9
	6 Cyl.—230, 250	4	3	None	17⑦	⑧	18⑩	12
	V8—307	4	3	3	17⑦	⑧	18⑩	15
	V8—350	4	3	3	20⑨	⑧	18⑩	16
	V8—400(402)(Mk. IV)	4	None	3	22	⑧	⑩	23
	V8—400(402)	4	None	3	22	⑧	⑩	23
	V8—454	4	None	3	22	⑧	20	23
1971-72	6 Cyl.—250	4	3	—	17	⑧	⑪	12
	V8—307	4	3	—	17	⑧	⑪	15
	V8—350	4	3	3	17	⑧	⑪	16
	V8—402 (Mk. IV)	4	3	3	20.2	⑧	⑪	23
	V8—454	4	—	3	20.2	⑧	⑪	22

① —Chevy II—16 gal., Chevelle—20 gal., Camaro—18 gal.
② —Add 1 pint for new filter.
③ —300 H.P.—18 qts., 350 H.P.—19 qts.
④ —3 speed H.D. 3.5 pts.
⑤ —Camaro 15 qts.
⑥ —Chevelle 20 gals.
⑦ —3 Speed Auto. 20 pts.
⑧ 9.125 ring gear—3.5 pts
8.875 ring gear—4.0 pts.
⑨ —Turbohydramatic 400—22 pts.
⑩ —Camaro with 250 and larger eng.—19 gals.
Chevelle with 250 and larger eng.—20 gals.
⑪ —Chevelle, 19; Station wagon 18—Chevy II, 16— Camaro, 17; Monte Carlo, 18.

VALVE SPECIFICATIONS

YEAR AND MODEL	SEAT ANGLE (DEG.)	FACE ANGLE (DEG.)	VALVE LIFT INTAKE (IN.)	VALVE LIFT EXHAUST (IN.)	VALVE SPRING PRESSURE (VALVE OPEN) LBS. @ IN.	VALVE SPRING INSTALLED HEIGHT (IN.)	STEM TO GUIDE CLEARANCE (IN.)		STEM DIAMETER (IN.)	
							Intake	Exhaust	Intake	Exhaust
1965 4 Cyl.—153	46	45	.3350	.3350	175 @ 1.26	1.66	.0010-.0027	.0015-.0033	.3407-.3417	.3410-.3417
6 Cyl.-194	46	45	.3350	.3350	170 @ 1.33	1.66	.0010-.0027	.0015-.0033	.3407-.3417	.3410-.3417
6 Cyl.-230	46	45	.4070	.4070	175 @ 1.26	1.66	.0010-.0027	.0015-.0033	.3407-.3417	.3410-.3417
V8-283	46	45	.3987	.3987	175 @ 1.26	1.66	.0010-.0027	.0015-.0033	.3407-.3417	.3410-.3417
V8-327	46	45	.3987	.3987	175 @ 1.26	1.66	.0010-.0027	.0010-.0027	.3407-.3417	.3410-.3417
1966 4 Cyl.—153	46	45	.3973	.3973	175 @ 1.26	1.66	.0010-.0027	.0010-.0027	.3404-.3417	.3410-.3417
6 Cyl.—194	46	45	.3318	.3318	175 @ 1.33	1.66	.0010-.0027	.0010-.0027	.3410-.3417	.3410-.3417
6 Cyl.—230	46	45	.3318	.3318	175 @ 1.33	1.66	.0010-.0027	.0010-.0033	.3410-.3417	.3410-.3417
V8—283	46	45	.3987	.3987	175 @ 1.26	1.66	.0010-.0027	.0010-.0027	.3410-.3417	.3410-.3417
V8—327	46	45	.3987	.3987	175 @ 1.26	1.66	.0010-.0027	.0015-.0033	.3410-.3417	.3410-.3417
V8—327 (350 H.P.)	46	45	.4472	.4472	182 @ 1.21	1.66	.0010-.0027	.0015-.0033	.3410-.3417	.3410-.3417
V8—396	46	45	.3983	.3983	220 @ 1.46	1.88	.0010-.0027	.0010-.0027	.3715-.3722	.3713-.3720
V8—396 (360 H.P.)	46	45	.4614	.4800	315 @ 1.38	1.88	.0010-.0027	.0010-.0027	.3715-.3722	.3713-.3720
1967 4 Cyl.—153	46	45	.3973	.3973	175 @ 1.26	1.66	.0010-.0027	.0010-.0027	.3410-.3417	.3410-.3417
6 Cyl.—194	46	45	.3318	.3318	177 @ 1.33	1.66	.0010-.0027	.0010-.0027	.3410-.3417	.3410-.3417
6 Cyl.—230	46	45	.3880	.3880	177 @ 1.33	1.66	.0010-.0027	.0010-.0027	.3410-.3417	.3410-.3417
6 Cyl.—250	46	45	.3880	.3880	186 @ 1.27	1.66	.0010-.0027	.0010-.0027	.3410-.3417	.3410-.3417
V8—283	46	45	.3900	.4100	200 @ 1.25	1.66	.0010-.0027	.0010-.0027	.3410-.3417	.3410-.3417
V8—327 (210 & 275 H.P.)	46	45	.3900	.4100	200 @ 1.25	1.66	.0010-.0027	.0010-.0027	.3410-.3417	.3410-.3417
V8—327(325 H.P.)	46	45	.4472	.4472	200 @ 1.25	1.66	.0010-.0027	.0010-.0027	.3410-.3417	.3410-.3417
V8—350	46	45	.3900	.4100	200 @ 1.25	1.66	.0010-.0027	.0010-.0027	.3410-.3417	.3410-.3417
V8—396 (325 H.P.)	46	45	.3983	.3983	220 @ 1.46	1.88	.0010-.0027	.0010-.0027	.3715-.3722	.3713-.3720
V8—396 (350 H.P.)	46	45	.4614	.4800	315 @ 1.38	1.88	.0010-.0027	.0010-.0027	.3715-.3722	.3713-.3720
1968 4 Cyl.—153	46	45	.3973	.3973	175 @ 1.26	1.66	.0010-.0027	.0010-.0027	.3410-.3417	.3410-.3417
6 Cyl.—230	46	45	.3317	.3317	186 @ 1.27	1.66	.0010-.0027	.0017-.0027	.3410-.3417	.3410-.3417
6 Cyl.—250	46	45	.3880	.3880	186 @ 1.27	1.66	.0010-.0027	.0017-.0027	.3410-.3417	.3410-.3417
V8—307, 327 (210 & 275 H.P.)	46	45	.3900	.4100	198 @ 1.25	1.70	.0010-.0027	.0017-.0027	.3410-.3417	.3410-.3417
V8—302 (Z28)	46	45	.455	.455	200 @ 1.25	1.70	.0010-.0027	.0010-.0027	.3410-.3417	.3410-.3417
V8—327 (325 H.P.)	46	45	.4471	.4471	198 @ 1.25	1.70	.0010-.0027	.0017-.0027	.3410-.3417	.3410-.3417
V8—350	46	45	.3900	.4100	198 @ 1.25	1.70	.0010-.0027	.0017-.0027	.3410-.3417	.3410-.3417
V8—396 (325 H.P.)	46	45	.3983	.3983	215 @ 1.48	1.88	.0010-.0027	.0017-.0027	.3715-.3722	.3713-.3720
V8—396 (350 H.P.)	46	45	.4614	.4800	315 @ 1.38	1.88	.0010-.0027	.0017-.0027	.3715-.3722	.3713-.3720
1969 4 Cyl.—153	46	45	.3973	.3973	175 @ 1.26	1.66	.0010-.0027	.0010-.0027	.3410-.3417	.3410-.3417
6 Cyl.—230	46	45	.3317	.3317	175 @ 1.27	1.66	.0010-.0027	.0010-.0027	.3410-.3417	.3410-.3417
6 Cyl.—250	46	45	.3880	.3880	186 @ 1.27	1.66	.0010-.0027	.0010-.0027	.3410-.3417	.3410-.3417
V8—302 (Z28)	46	45	.455	.455	200 @ 1.25	1.70	.0010-.0027	.0010-.0027	.3410-.3417	.3410-.3417
V8—307, 350	46	45	.3900	.3900	200 @ 1.25	1.70	.0010-.0027	.0010-.0027	.3410-.3417	.3410-.3417
V8—396 (325 H.P.)	46	45	.3983	.3983	220 @ 1.46	1.88	.0010-.0027	.0010-.0027	.3715-.3722	.3715-.3722
V8—396 (350 H.P.)	46	45	.4614	.4800	235 @ 1.38	1.88	.0010-.0027	.0010-.0027	.3715-.3722	.3715-.3722
1970 4 Cyl.—153	46	45	.3973	.3973	175 @ 1.26	1.66	.0010-.0027	.0010-.0027	.3410-.3417	.3410-.3417
6 Cyl.—230	46	45	.3317	.3317	177 @ 1.33	1.66	.0010-.0027	.0010-.0027	.3410-.3417	.3410-.3417
6 Cyl.—250	46	45	.3880	.3880	186 @ 1.27	1.66	.0010-.0027	.0010-.0027	.3410-.3417	.3410-.3417
V8—307	46	45	.3900	.4100	200 @ 1.25	1.70	.0010-.0027	.0010-.0027	.3410-.3417	.3410-.3417
V8—350 (250, 300 H.P.) and 400, 402 (265 H.P.)	46	45	.3900	.4100	200 @ 1.25	1.70	.0010-.0027	.0010-.0027	.3410-.3417	.3410-.3417
V8—350 (370 H.P.)	46	45	.4586	.4850	200 @ 1.25	1.70	.0010-.0027	.0010-.0027	.3410-.3417	.3410-.3417
V8—396 (Mk. IV)	46	45	.4614	.4800	240 @ 1.38	1.88	.0010-.0027	.0010-.0027	.3715-.3722	.3715-.3722
V8—400 (402)	46	45	.3983	.3983	240 @ 1.38	1.88	.0010-.0027	.0010-.0027	.3715-.3722	.3715-.3722
V8—454 (360 H.P.)	46	45	.4614	.4800	240 @ 1.38	1.88	.0010-.0027	.0010-.0027	.3715-.3722	.3715-.3722

VALVE SPECIFICATIONS, continued

YEAR AND MODEL		SEAT ANGLE (DEG.)	FACE ANGLE (DEG.)	VALVE LIFT INTAKE (IN.)	VALVE LIFT EXHAUST (IN.)	VALVE SPRING PRESSURE (VALVE OPEN) LBS. @ IN.	VALVE SPRING INSTALLED HEIGHT (IN.)	STEM TO GUIDE CLEARANCE (IN.) Intake	STEM TO GUIDE CLEARANCE (IN.) Exhaust	STEM DIAMETER (IN.) Intake	STEM DIAMETER (IN.) Exhaust
1971–72	6 Cyl.—250	46	45	.3880	.3880	186 @ 1.27	1.66	.0010–.0027	.0010–.0027	.3410–.3417	.3410–.3417
	V8—307	46	45	.3900	.4100	200 @ 1.25	1.70	.0010–.0027	.0010–.0027	.3410–.3417	.3410–.3417
	V8—350 (245, 270 H.P.)	46	45	.3900	.4100	200 @ 1.25	1.70	.0010–.0027	.0010–.0027	.3410–.3417	.3410–.3417
	V8—350 (330 H.P.) (Z28)	46	45	.4586	.4850	200 @ 1.25	1.70	.0010–.0027	.0010–.0027	.3410–.3417	.3410–.3417
	V8—400 (402) (Mk. IV)	46	45	.3983	.4300	240 @ 1.38	1.88	.0010–.0027	.0010–.0027	.3713–.3720	.3713–.3720
	V8—454 (360 H.P.)	46	45	.4614	.4800	240 @ 1.38	1.88	.0010–.0027	.0010–.0027	.3713–.3720	.3713–.3720
	V8—454 (425 H.P.)	46	45	.5197	.5197	240 @ 1.38	1.88	.0010–.0027	.0010–.0027	.3715–.3722	.3713–.3720

*—Aluminum heads—45°.

WHEEL ALIGNMENT

YEAR	MODEL	CASTER Range (Deg.)	CASTER Pref. Setting (Deg.)	CAMBER Range (Deg.)	CAMBER Pref. Setting (Deg.)	TOE-IN (In.)	KING-PIN INCLINATION (Deg.)	WHEEL PIVOT RATIO Inner Wheel	WHEEL PIVOT RATIO Outer Wheel
1965	Chevy II	½P to 1½P	1P	0 to 1P	½P	¼ to ⅜	7	20	18¾
	Chevelle	1½N to ½N	1N	¼N to ¾P	¼P	1/16 to 3/16	8	20	18¾
1966	Chevy II	½P to 1½P	1P	0 to 1P	½P	¼ to ⅜	7	20	18¾
	Chevelle	1½N to ½N	1N	0 to 1P	½P	⅛ to ¼	8	20	18¾
1967	Chevy II	½P to 1½P	1P	0 to 1P	½P	⅛ to ¼	7	20	18¾
	Chevelle	1½N to ½N①	1N	0 to 1P	½P	⅛ to ¼	8¼	20	18¾
	Camaro	0 to 1P	½P	¼N to ¾P	¼P	⅛ to ¼	8¾	20	18¾
1968–69	Chevy II	0 to 1P	½P	¼N to ¾P	½P	⅛ to ¼	8¾	20	N.A.
	Chevelle	1½N to ½N①	1N	0 to 1P	½P	⅛ to ¼	8¼	20	18½
	Camaro	0 to 1P	½P	¼N to ¾P	½P	⅛ to ¼	8¾	20	N.A.
1970–71	Chevy II	0 to 1P	½P	¼N to ¾P	½P	⅛ to ¼	8¼–9¼	20	N.A.
	Chevelle, Monte Carlo	1½N to ½N①	1N	0 to 1P	½P	⅛ to ¼	7¾–8¾	20	N.A.
	Camaro	0 to 2P	1P	¼N to 1¾P	¾P	⅛ to ¼	10–11	20	N.A.
1972	Chevy II								
	Chevelle, Monte Carlo								
	Camaro								

①—SS 396 + El Camino—0 to 1P.
N—Negative.
P—Positive.

FUSES AND CIRCUIT BREAKERS

1963–60

Headlamps .... 15 AMP. CB
Instrument Lights .... 3 AMP. FUSE
Tail, stop, courtesy, glove box, license plate, dome light, clock .... 15 AMP. FUSE
Radio .... 2½ AMP. FUSE
Heater, back-up light, brake signal light .... 10 AMP. FUSE
Air conditioning—with heater .... 20 AMP. FUSE
Air conditioning blower .... 30 AMP. FUSE
Overdrive .... 15 AMP. FUSE

A circuit breaker in the light control switch protects the headlamp circuit, thus eliminating one fuse. A separate 30 amp. circuit breaker mounted on the firewall protects the power window, seat and top circuits. The under hood and spot lamp circuit is also protected by a separate 15 amp. inline fuse. Where current load is too heavy, the circuit breaker rapidly opens and closes, protecting the circuit until the cause is found and eliminated.

Fuses located in the fuse panel under the instrument panel are:

1969–70

Wiper/washer, 3-spd. A/T downshift ... SAE/SFE 25 AMP.
Back-up lamp, turn signal, cruise master, defogger, heater .... SAE/SFE 25 AMP.
Air conditioning—transmission control spark solenoid (1970) .... 3AG/AGC 25 AMP.
Radio, power window .... 3AG/AGC 10 AMP.
Tail, marker and fender lamps .... SAE/SFE 20 AMP.
Instrument lamps (Nova, Camaro and Chevelle) .... SAE/SFE 4 AMP.
Gauges and Tell-Tale Lamps .... 3AG/AGC 10 AMP.
Stop and Hazard .... SAE/SFE 20 AMP.
Clock, lighter, courtesy lamps, dome and luggage lamps .... SAE/SFE 20 AMP.

In-Line Fuses:
Air conditioning high blower speed fuse located in wire running from horn relay to A/C Relay
Comfortron and Four Season .... SAE 30 AMP.
Universal & All Weather (Nova) ..... SAE 20 AMP.

Fusible Links:
Pigtail lead at battery positive cable (except Corvette) ...... 14 gauge brown wire
Molded splice located at the horn relay .... 18 gauge black wire
Molded splice in voltage regulator #3 terminal wire .... 20 gauge orange wire
Molded splice in ammeter circuit (both sides of meter) .... 20 gauge orange wire

1971–72

Radio, TCS, Rear Defogger, Power window, 3-speed A/T downshift, Glove compartment light ...... 10 AMP.
Wiper/washer .... 25 AMP.
Stop lights, Warning flasher .... 20 AMP.
Heater, Air Conditioning .... 25 AMP.
Turn Signals, Back-Up lights, Cruise-master, Blocking relay .... 20 AMP.
Instrument, Dome lights, Anti-diesel, Blocking relays .... 2 AMP.
Instrument lamps (incl. A/T quadrant light) .... 3 AMP.
Gauges and Warning lights .... 10 AMP.
Clock, Cigarette lighter, Courtesy lights, Anti-diesel control, Deck lid, Lock, Anti-theft Alarm, Glove compartment, Dome lamps .... 25 AMP.
Tail, License, Marker, Luggage and Parking lights .... 20 AMP.

LIGHT BULBS

1965–68 Chevy II

Headlamp.............................. 6012; 40–50 W
Parking, tail, stop & turn signal .... 1157; 4–32 CP
Back-up lamps .... 1156; 32 CP
Gen., temp., oil, hi-beam indicator, clock ..... 1895; 2 CP
Dome lamp .... 211; 12 CP
License lamp............................. 67; 4 CP
Radio dial .... 1893; 3 CP
Instrument panel .... 1816; 3 CP
Traffic hazard .... 1445; 1 CP

1965–68 Chevelle

Headlamp (outer).................... 4002; 37½–55 W
Headlamp (inner).................... 4001; 37½ W
Instrument panel .... 1895; 2 CP
Other lamps same as Chevy II

1967–68 Camaro

Front parking & turn signals............. 1034; 4–32 CP
Instrument panel, temp., gen., oil, hi-beam
    indicator............................... 194; 2 CP

1969–72

LAMP USAGE	CANDLE POWER OR WATTAGE	BULB NUMBER
Headlamp unit		
Chevelle		
Outer—high beam	37½ Watts	4002
Outer—low beam	55 Watts	4002
Inner—high beam only	37½ Watts	4001
Nova & Camaro		
High beam	55 Watts	6012
Low beam	45 Watts	
Monte Carlo		
Parking lamp and directional signal		
Chevelle	3–32	1157
Camaro, Nova & Monte Carlo	3–32	1157NA
Tail, stop and directional signal	3–32	1157
Back-up lamp	32	1156
Instrument illumination lamps		
Chevelle (1970), Monte Carlo, Camaro	2	194
Chevelle (1969)	2	1895
Nova	3	168
Console instrument cluster (Nova)	2.5	1816
Temperature indicator (1969 Chevelle—2/1895)	2	194
Oil pressure indicator (1969 Chevelle—2/1895)	2	194
Generator indicator (1969 Chevelle—2/1895)	2	194
Hi-beam indicator		
Chevelle, Nova, Camaro	2	194
1969 Chevelle	2	1895
Directional indicator		
Chevelle, Nova, Camaro	2	194
1969 Chevelle	2	1895
Warning lamps		
1970 Nova—low fuel	2	194
Heater or A/C Control Panel		
Chevelle	1	1445
Nova, Camaro	2	1895
Glove compartment lamps		
Chevelle, Camaro, Nova		
Chevelle, Monte Carlo		
Dome and Courtesy Lamps		
Cartridge Type (All)	12	211
Bayonet Type	6	631
Seat Separator-Courtesy Lamp	6	212
1969 Compartment Lamp	1	1445
Side Marker-Front	2	194
Side Marker-Rear	2	194
License Plate Lamp	4	67
Radio Dial Lamp		
All AM Only Radios (all 1969 models use 2/1893)	2	293
All Tape Players and FM Radios	2	1893
Tape Player Lens Illumination Lamp (1970)	1	216
Stereo Indicator Lamp (1970)	.3	2182D
Automatic Transmission Control Indicator Lamp		
Chevelle (without seat separator) & Monte Carlo (w/o seat separator)		
Nova, Chevelle (with seat separator) & Monte Carlo (with seat separator)	2	194
Brake Alarm Lamp		
All except Corvette	2	194
1969 Chevelle	2	1895
Luggage Compartment Lamp	15	1003
Map Lamp (Mirror) (1969 models—6/562)	4	563
Underhood	15	93
Rear Window Defogger Lamp (1970)	2	194

Distributor

Caution When using an auxiliary starter switch for bumping the engine into position for timing or compression test, the primary distributor lead must be disconnected from the negative post of the ignition coil and the ignition switch must be on. Failure to do this may cause damage to the grounding circuit in the ignition switch.

4 and 6 Cylinder Models

Distributor design, (except for number of cam lobes and distributor cap) is similar for the unit(s) used on the OHV 4 and 6 engines. Mounting is on the forward right side of the engine. Both units use centrifugal and vacuum controlled advance mechanism. Direction of rotation (as viewed from the top) is clockwise for both models. Other pertinent distributor specifications can be found in the Tune-Up Specifications charts.

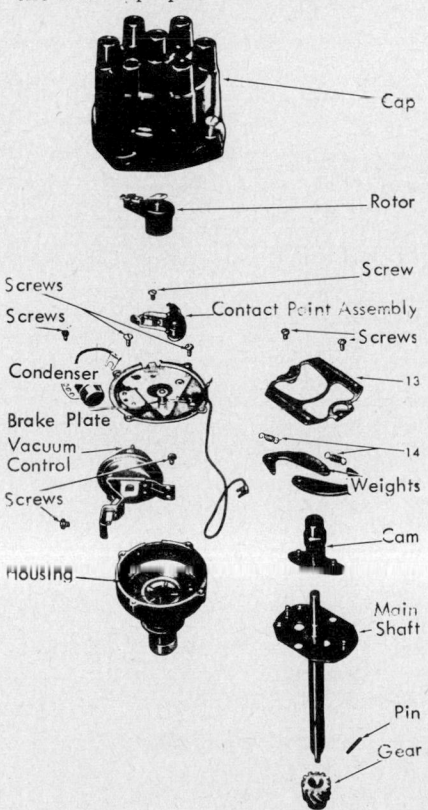

6 cylinder distributor exploded view—typical
(© Chevrolet Div. G.M. Corp.)

V8 Models

The distributor is located between the two banks of cylinders at the back of the block.

Distributor Removal

4 and 6 Cylinder Models

1. Remove distributor cap, primary wire and vacuum line at distributor.
2. Scribe a mark on the distributor body, locating the position of the rotor. Scribe another mark on the distributor body and engine block, showing the position of the body in the block.
3. Remove the distributor hold-down screw and lift the distributor up and out of the engine.

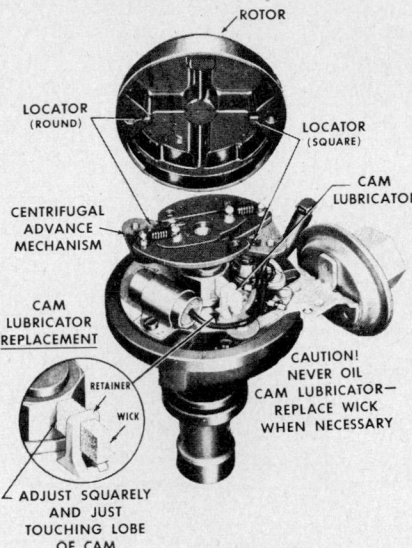

V8 distributor—typical (© G.M. Corp.)

V8 Models

The drive gear is attached to the distributor shaft. If it becomes necessary to remove the distributor, carefully mark the position of the rotor so that, if the engine is not turned after the distributor is taken out, the rotor can be returned to the position from which it was removed without difficulty.

To remove the distributor, take off the carburetor air cleaner, disconnect the coil primary wire and the vacuum line, remove the distributor cap, take out the single hold-down bolt located under the distributor body. With a pencil, mark the position of the body relative to the block, and then work the distributor up out of the block.

Distributor Installation

4 and 6 Cylinder Models

1. If the crankshaft was rotated, turn the engine until the piston of No. 1 cylinder is at the top of its compression stroke.
2. Position the distributor to the block so that the vacuum control unit is in its normal position.
3. Position the rotor to point toward the front of the engine (with distributor held out of the block, but in installed attitude). Turn rotor counterclockwise about one-eighth turn and push distributor down to engage camshaft drive. It may be necessary to move the rotor one way or the other to mesh the drive and driven gears properly.
4. While holding the distributor down in place, engage the starter a few times to make sure the oil pump shaft is engaged. Install hold-down clamp and bolt and snug up the bolt.
5. Once again, rotate the crankshaft until No. 1 cylinder is on the compression stroke and the harmonic balancer mark is on 0°.
6. Turn distributor body slightly until points open. Tighten distributor clamp bolt.
7. Place distributor cap in position and see that the rotor lines up with the terminal for the No. 1 spark plug.
8. Install cap, distributor primary wire, and double check plug wires in the cap towers.
9. Start engine and set timing according to the Tune-Up Specifications chart.
10. Reconnect vacuum hose to vacuum control assembly.

V8 Models

Remove No. 1 spark plug and, with finger on plug hole, crank the engine until compression is felt in No. 1 cylinder. Continue cranking until pointer lines up with the timing mark on the crankshaft pulley.

Position distributor in opening of the block in normal installed attitude; have rotor pointing to front of engine.

Turn the rotor counterclockwise about one-eighth of a turn (from straight front toward the left cylinder bank). Push the distributor down to engage the camshaft and while holding, turn the engine with the starter so that distributor shaft engages the oil pump shaft.

Return engine to compression stroke of No. 1 piston with timing mark on pulley aligned with the pointer. Adjust the distributor so that the points are opening. Install the cap being sure the rotor points to the contact for No. 1 spark plug. Connect the timing light and check that spark occurs as timing mark and pointer are aligned.

Generator, Regulator

AC generators and regulators are covered in the Unit Repair Section.

Delcotron Removal and Installation

1. Disconnect battery ground cable to prevent diode damage.
2. Disconnect Delcotron wiring.
3. Remove generator brace bolt. If power steering equipped, loosen pump brace and mount nuts. De-

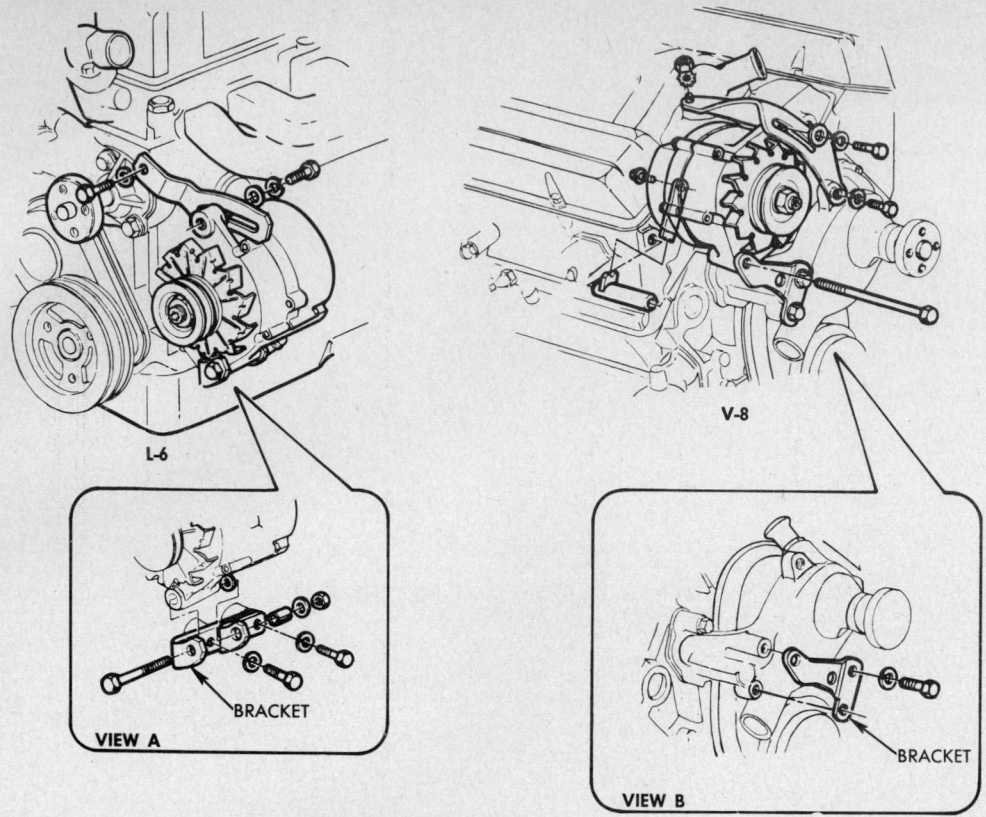

Delcotron installation (© Chev. Div. G.M. Corp.)

tach drive belt(s).
4. Support generator and **remove** mount bolt(s). Remove **unit** from vehicle.
5. Reverse procedure to install. Adjust drive belt to have ¼-½ in. play on longest run of belt.

AC Generator

The following are a few precautions to observe in servicing the Delcotron (AC) generator and the regulator.
1. When installing a battery, be **certain** that the ground polarity of the battery and the ground polarity of the generator and regulator are the same.
2. When connecting a booster battery, be sure to connect the **correct** battery terminals together.
3. When hooking up a charger, connect the correct charged leads to the battery terminals.
4. Never operate the generator on an open circuit. Be sure all connections in the charging circuit are tight.
5. Do not short across or ground any of the terminals on the generator or regulator.
6. Never polarize an AC system.

Battery, Starter

Information on the battery and starter will be found in the Battery

and Starter Specifications table.
A more general discussion of starters and their troubles can be found in the Unit Repair Section. The starter should require no lubrication or other maintenance between overhaul periods.

Starter Removal and Installation

1. Disconnect battery ground cable.
2. Raise and support vehicle.
3. Disconnect all wires at solenoid terminals. Note color coding of wires for reinstallation.
4. Remove starter front bracket and two mount bolts. On engines with solenoid heat shield, remove front bracket upper bolt and detach bracket from starter motor.
5. Remove front bracket bolt or nut. Rotate bracket clear. Lower starter front end first. Remove starter.
6. Reverse procedure to install. Torque mount bolts to 25-35 ft. lbs.

Instruments

Instrument Cluster Removal and Replacement

1965 Chevelle

1. Disconnect battery ground cable.
2. Remove upper mast jacket

clamp bolt and bend clamp away from steering column.
3. Disconnect speedometer cable. Disconnect oil pressure line at gauge on SS model.
4. Remove the screws that attach the console to the instrument panel and lean console forward onto the mast jacket. Remove radio knobs before removing console from panel.
5. Disconnect all cluster lamps, harness connectors, and two harness retaining clips from rear of cluster.
6. Lift console forward and upward to remove.
7. Unscrew and remove cluster from console.
8. Install by reversing removal procedure.

1966-67 Chevelle

1. Disconnect battery.
2. Remove steering coupling bolt and disconnect steering shaft from coupling.
3. Loosen mast jacket lower clamp.
4. On air-conditioned cars, remove air-conditioning center distribution duct.
5. Remove radio rear support bracket screw.
6. Remove mast jacket trim cover and support clamp.
7. Loosen set screw and remove transmission dial indicator (if so equipped).

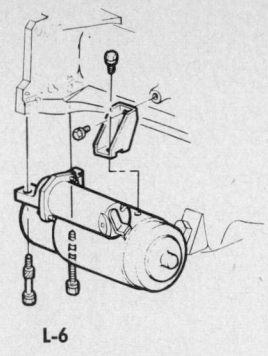

L-6

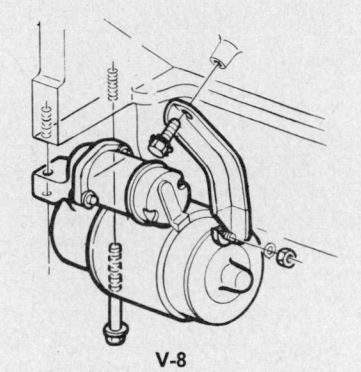

V-8

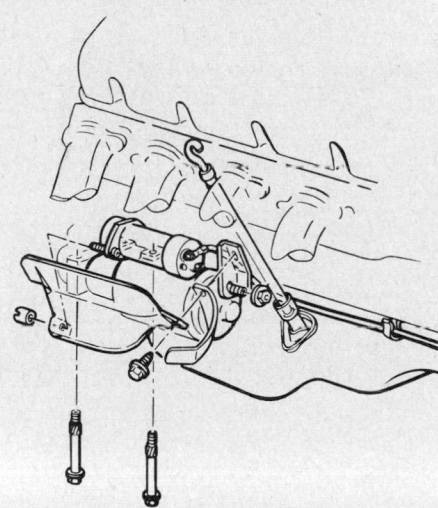

V-8 WITH SOLENOID HEAT SHIELD

Starter motor installation
(© Chev. Div. G.M. Corp.)

8. Disconnect speedometer shaft at speedometer head.
9. Remove the instrument panel attaching screws.
10. From under the console, remove the four lower retaining screws from the cluster housing.
11. With mast jacket padded, pull instrument panel from the console and lay forward on mast jacket.
12. Disconnect wiring harness, cluster lamps and wiring terminals from rear of cluster assembly.
13. Remove four screws holding the upper section of the cluster housing to panel and remove cluster from instrument panel.
14. Install by reversing removal procedure.

1968-69 Chevelle

1. Disconnect battery ground cable.
2. Remove ash tray and retainer.
3. Remove radio knobs, nuts, electrical connectors, and radio rear support. Remove radio.
4. Remove heater control screws, then push control head out of instrument panel.
5. Lower steering column. Remove automatic transmission indicator cable from steering column. Protect steering column with a cloth.
NOTE: see detailed procedure for column removal under *Steering*.
6. Remove instrument panel retaining screws at top, bottom, and sides of panel. Remove all attachments to the underside of the panel.
7. Lift panel up and back slightly, reach behind cluster to remove speedometer cable, support panel on protected steering column.
8. Remove clips at top of cluster rear cover and remove all connectors at rear of cluster. Remove oil pressure fitting from rear of oil pressure gauge, if so equipped.
9. Remove screws that secure twin window clusters to back of instrument panel and remove clusters.
10. Install by reversing procedure.
NOTE: see detailed procedure for column installation under *Steering*.

1970-72 Chevelle

1. Disconnect battery ground cable.
2. Lower steering column.
NOTE: see detailed procedure for column removal under *Steering*.
3. Disconnect parking brake hand release.
4. Disconnect speedometer cable.
5. Remove instrument panel pad.
6. Disconnect radio speaker bracket from instrument panel. Disconnect speaker wire from radio.
7. Disconnect air conditioning center outlet and control head.
8. Remove radio knobs, washers, bezels, and wiring.
9. Unbolt radio braces. Roll radio out from under instrument panel.
10. Remove six instrument panel bolts and roll out instrument panel with the help of an assistant.
11. Reverse procedure for installation.
NOTE: see detailed procedure for column installation under *Steering*.

1965 Chevy II

1. Disconnect battery ground cable.

2. Loosen and lower mast jacket from the dash panel.
3. Disconnect speedometer cable.
4. Remove the four screws that attach the cluster to the dash panel. Cluster may now be pulled clear of dash.
5. Remove the two harness retaining clips from rear of cluster.
6. Disconnect all indicator and illuminating bulb sockets. Remove cluster from vehicle.
7. Reverse procedure to install.

1966-67 Chevy II

1. Disconnect battery.
2. Remove transmission selector dial indicator assembly (if so equipped) and mast jacket upper support clamp.
3. Disconnect speedometer cable at speedometer head.
4. Remove screws holding the cluster to the console.
5. With the mast jacket well padded, pull cluster forward of console opening and disconnect all wires and lamp connections. Remove the cluster.
6. Install by reversing removal procedure.

1968 Chevy II, 1969-72 Nova

1. Disconnect battery ground cable.
2. Lower steering column.
NOTE: see detailed procedure for column removal under *Steering*.
3. Remove three screws above heater control securing it to instrument cluster.
4. Remove radio knobs, washers, bezel nuts, and front support.
5. Remove screws at top, bottom, and sides of cluster.
6. Tilt cluster forward. Reach behind to disconnect speedometer cable, speedminder, and electrical connectors. Remove screws and lift instrument assembly out of instrument carrier.
7. Reverse procedure to install.
NOTE: see detailed procedure for column installation under *Steering*.

1967-68 Camaro

1. Disconnect battery ground cable.
2. Remove mast jacket lower support screws at toe pan.
3. Remove mast jacket upper support bolts and allow steering column to rest on seat cushion.
4. Remove cluster attaching screws from face of panel and partially remove assembly from instrument panel.
5. Reaching behind cluster assembly, disconnect speedometer cable, speed warning device, and harness connector.
6. Remove assembly from instrument panel.
7. Install by reversing removal procedure.

1969 Camaro (Old Body Style)

1. Disconnect battery ground cable.
2. Remove:
   a. instrument panel pad
   b. air conditioning attachments
   c. radio brace attachments.
3. Lower steering column.
   NOTE: see detailed procedure for column removal under *Steering*.
4. Remove cluster attaching screws.
5. Disconnect:
   a. speedometer cable
   b. speed warning device
   c. wiring connectors.
6. Remove cluster assembly.
7. Reverse procedure to install.
   NOTE: see detailed procedure for column installation under *Steering*.

1970-72 Camaro (New Body Style)

1. Disconnect battery ground cable.
2. Remove six screws that secure trim cover beneath column. Two screws are above ash tray.
3. Reach up under the left side of the cluster and depress the headlight switch shaft retainer button, while gently pulling on knob.
4. Remove headlight switch retaining nut.
5. Remove cigarette lighter, then reach up behind right side of cluster and disconnect lighter wire and unscrew retainer from housing. Note the position of the grounding ring for proper installation.
6. Reach up under lower edge of cluster and remove one screw on each side of steering column.
7. Remove the four visible screws from the front of the cluster carrier.
8. Remove the screw that holds the wiper switch ground wire. The screw is fastened to the upper top left corner of the switch.
9. Carefully tilt carrier out, then reach behind and disconnect wiper and headlight switch wires.
10. Remove the eight screws that secure the lens assembly; remove lens.
11. Remove the four screws that secure the cluster.
12. Disconnect PRNDL indicator from column.
13. Reach behind cluster, depress speedo cable tang and tilt cluster forward.
14. Remove connectors from clock and printed circuit; free harness clips.
15. Lift out cluster and remove from car. The bulb holders, speedometer, clock, fuel gauge, and printed circuit are now accessible for service.
16. To install, reverse removal procedure.

1970-72 Chevelle SS, 1970-72 Monte Carlo

1. Disconnect battery ground cable.
2. Remove instrument panel pad.
3. Disconnect air conditioning center outlet and control head.
4. Disconnect radio speaker and brackets from cluster.
5. Disconnect speaker leads from radio.
6. Remove radio knobs, washers, bezels, and wiring.
7. Remove bolts from radio braces and roll radio out from under instrument panel.
8. Remove steering column cover.
9. Remove two steering column attaching bolts. Note the placement of shims.
10. Disconnect automatic transmission indicator cable from steering column housing and lower steering column.
11. Disconnect parking brake hand release rod attachment.
12. Remove six instrument panel attaching bolts and roll out panel assembly. An assistant is required for this operation.
13. Disconnect speedometer cable.
14. Remove instrument cluster lamp sockets.
15. Remove clock, fuel gauge, power top, and rear window defogger connectors from rear of instrument panel.
16. The printed circuit, speedometer, clock, fuel gauge, tachometer and bulbs are now accessible for service.
17. Reverse procedure to install.

Ignition Switch Replacement

1965-68 Chevy II, 1965 Chevelle

1. Disconnect battery.
2. Remove lock cylinder by placing in off position and inserting a wire in the small hole in cylinder face. While pushing on the wire, continue to turn cylinder counterclockwise. Pull cylinder from case.
3. Remove nut from passenger side of dash.
4. Pull switch from under dash and remove wiring connector.
5. To remove the theft resistant connector, the switch must be removed from under the dash. With screwdriver, depress tangs and separate the connector.
6. Install in reverse of above.

1966-68 Chevelle

1. Disconnect battery ground cable.
2. Remove:
   a. ash tray
   b. ash tray retainer
   c. Radio knobs, nuts, connectors, bracket, and radio.
3. Remove lock cylinder by positioning switch in Accessory position and inserting wire in hole in cylinder face. Push in wire and turn key counterclockwise to remove cylinder.
4. Remove bezel nut and pull out ignition switch.
5. Unsnap locking tangs on connector with a screwdriver. Unplug connector.
6. Reverse procedure to install.

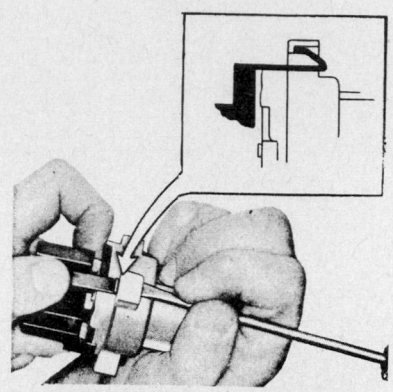

Unlocking ignition switch connector
(© G.M. Corp.)

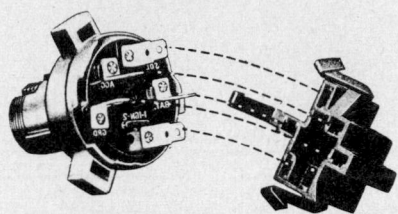

Separated ignition switch and connector—to 1968
(© G.M. Corp.)

1967-68 Camaro

This procedure is the same as that given above for the 1966-68 Chevelle, with the deletion of Step 2.

1969-72 All Models

All 1969-72 models have the ignition lock cylinder located in the upper right side of the steering column. The ignition switch is inside the channel section of the brake pedal support. The switch is inaccessible unless the steering column is lowered.

1969-72 ignition lock location

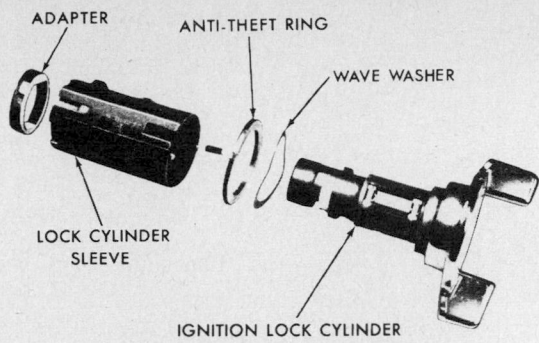

Ignition lock assembly—1969-72
(© Chev. Div. G.M. Corp.)

Lock Cylinder R & R—1969-72

1. Remove steering wheel and directional signal switch.
   NOTE: see *Steering*.
2. Place lock cylinder in Lock position up to 1970, Run position starting 1971.
3. Insert a small screwdriver into the turn signal housing slot. Keeping the screwdriver to the right side of the slot, break the housing flash loose and depress the spring latch at the lower end of the lock cylinder. Remove the lock cylinder.
4. To install, hold the lock cylinder sleeve and rotate the knob clockwise against the stop. Insert the cylinder into the housing, aligning the key and keyway. Hold a .070 in. drill between the lock bezel and housing. Rotate the cylinder counterclockwise, maintaining a light pressure until the drive section of the cylinder mates with the sector. Push in until the snap ring pops into the grooves. Remove drill. Check cylinder operation.

Ignition Switch R & R—1969-72

1. Lower steering column. The column must be carefully supported to prevent damage.
   NOTE: see *Steering*.
2. Remove lock cylinder as above.
   NOTE: pull actuating rod for switch up until a definite stop is felt, then push it down one detent to Lock position.

3. Remove two switch screws and switch assembly.
4. When replacing switch, make sure switch and lock are in Lock position. Do not use switch screws longer than the originals, or the compressibility feature of the column may be lost.

Lighting Switch Replacement
1965-68 Chevy II, 1967-72 Nova, 1967-69 Camaro and Chevelle

1. Disconnect battery.
2. Pull knob out to on position.
3. Reach under instrument panel and depress the switch shaft retainer, and remove knob and shaft assembly.
4. Remove the retaining ferrule nut.
5. Remove switch from instrument panel.
6. Disconnect the multi-plug connector from the switch.
7. Install in reverse of above.

1970-72 Chevelle, Monte Carlo

1. Disconnect battery ground cable.
2. Remove six screws and instrument panel pad.
3. Remove left radio speaker.
4. Pull knob to on position.
5. Reach behind instrument panel and depress switch shaft retainer. Remove knob and shaft assembly.
6. Remove ferrule nut and switch assembly from instrument panel.
7. Reverse procedure to install.

1970-72 Camaro

1. Disconnect battery negative cable.
2. Remove steering column lower cover (six screws).
3. Reach up under cluster on the left side and depress light switch shaft retainer, while pulling gently on shaft.
4. Remove nut that secures switch to cluster carrier.
5. Remove four cluster carrier screws in front and two from rear, then tilt right side of cluster out. Cigarette lighter grounding ring may have to be freed.
6. Unplug harness connector from switch.
7. Remove switch.
8. To install, reverse removal procedure. Make sure all ground connections are refastened.

Brakes

Description

General Motors cars have as standard equipment the duo-servo single anchor type service brake. Brake shoe linings are bonded and the shoes are self-adjusting. Segmented metallic brake linings are optional on some 1965 models. Drums are of cast iron.

Wheel cylinders are conventional double piston type.

Prior to 1967, the master cylinder consists of a single cylinder and reservoir mounted on the engine side of the firewall.

Since 1967, a dual type master cylinder is used. The front portion of the master cylinder supplies hydraulic pressure for the front wheels. Pressure for rear wheel brake application is supplied from the rear portion of the master cylinder.

More detailed information on this dual type of hydraulic brake system can be found in the Unit Repair Section.

As an option, both Bendix and Moraine power brakes are available. Data on these two power brakes can

Insert thin tool in this slot-Keep tool to right side of slot to break flash and depress lock cylinder retainer

Removing 1969-72 lock cylinder
(© Chevrolet Div., G.M. Corp.)

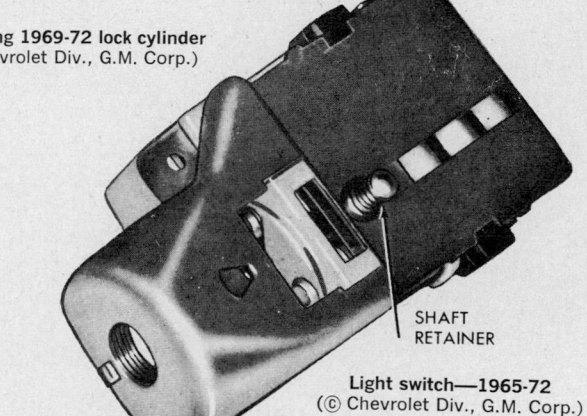

SHAFT RETAINER

Light switch—1965-72
(© Chevrolet Div., G.M. Corp.)

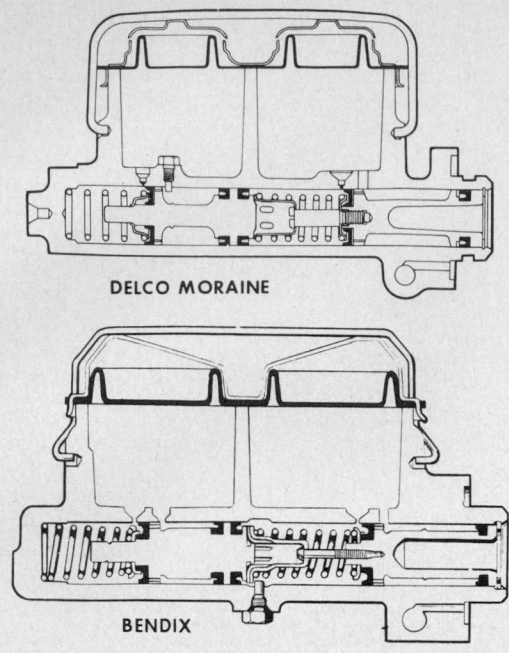

DELCO MORAINE

BENDIX

Dual type master cylinders, typical (© Chevrolet Div. G.M. Corp.)

be found in the Unit Repair Section.

Front wheel disc brakes are optional on some models starting 1966 and standard on the 1970-72 Camaro and SS454 Chevelle models. Repair procedures for disc brakes are given in the Unit Repair Section.

Parking Brake

The parking brake is hand operated by a lever attached to the dash panel, just to the right of the steering column on the 1965-67 Chevy II and pedal operated on all other models. It functions through an equalizer and cables to the rear brake shoes.

Parking Brake Adjustment

1965-72

1. Jack up rear of car and support with both rear wheels off floor.
2. Apply parking brake two

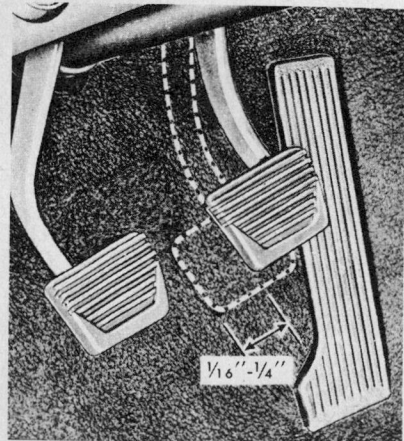

Brake pedal free play check
(© Chev. Div. G.M. Corp.)

notches from fully released position.
3. Loosen the equalizer front jam nut, then tighten rear nut until a light to moderate drag is felt when rear wheels are rotated.
4. Tighten jam nuts.
5. Fully release parking brake and rotate rear wheels—no drag should be felt.

Master Cylinder R & R

1965-72

1. Disconnect hydraulic line/s at master cylinder.
2. Remove the two retaining nuts and lockwashers that hold cylinder to firewall.
   NOTE: starting 1967, disconnect pushrod at brake pedal.
3. Remove the master cylinder, gasket and rubber boot.
4. Position master cylinder on firewall, making sure pushrod goes through the rubber boot into the piston.
   NOTE: starting 1967, reconnect pushrod clevis to brake pedal.
5. Install nuts and lockwashers.
6. Install hydraulic line/s, then check brake pedal free play.
7. Bleed brakes, as described in Unit Repair Section.
   NOTE: cars having disc brakes do not have a check valve in the front outlet port of the master cylinder. If one is installed, front discs will immediately wear out due to residual hydraulic pressure holding pads against rotor.

Brake Pedal Free Play Check

Caution Do not use this procedure for disc brakes.

The brake pedal has a definite stop, which is not adjustable. This stop consists of a rubber bumper at the release end of pedal travel. Before adjusting pushrod to master cylinder clearance, make sure the brake pedal returns freely to full release position and that spring has not lost tension.
1. Loosen jam nut on pushrod.
2. Turn pushrod as required to provide for a pedal movement of 1/16 to 1/4 in. before pushrod contacts master cylinder piston/s.
3. Tighten jam nut against clevis (14 ft. lbs.) and recheck movement.

Power Brake Booster R & R

1967-72 Except the Following Chevelle and Monte Carlo Models

1. Disconnect vacuum hose from vacuum check valve.
2. Disconnect hydraulic lines at master cylinder.
3. Disconnect pushrod at brake pedal assembly.
4. Remove nuts and lockwashers that secure booster to firewall and remove booster from engine compartment.
5. Install by reversing removal procedure. Make sure to check operation of stop lights and bleed brakes. Allow engine vacuum to build before applying brakes.

1969 Chevelle with Manual Transmission, 1970 Chevelle 116 in. Wheelbase Station Wagon, 1971-72 Chevelle and Monte Carlo—All

1. Remove master cylinder from vacuum booster.
2. Remove vacuum line from vacuum check valve.
3. On 1971-72 models, remove brake line clip from booster.
4. From inside vehicle, remove nuts and lockwashers that secure booster to firewall.
5. Push brake pedal to the floor. This will disengage booster from firewall and adequate clearance for removal of the pushrod pivot pin will be gained.
6. Remove clip from pivot pin, then remove power unit from car.
7. Install by reversing removal procedure. Make sure to check operation of stop lights and bleed brakes. Allow engine vacuum to build before applying brakes.

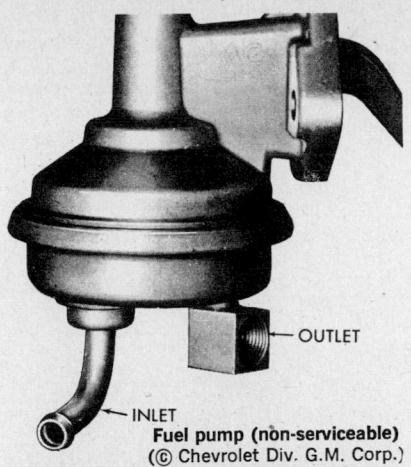

Fuel pump (non-serviceable)
(© Chevrolet Div. G.M. Corp.)

Fuel System

Fuel Pump

The fuel pump is the single action AC diaphragm type. Two types of fuel pumps are used; serviceable and non-serviceable. The serviceable type is used on all 1965 engines, 1966 inline engines without the A.I.R. emission control system, and 1966 283 and 327 V8's. The non-serviceable type is used on all other engines.

The pump is actuated by an eccentric located on the engine camshaft. On inline engines, the eccentric actuates the pump rocker arm. On V8 engines, a pushrod between the camshaft eccentric and the fuel pump actuates the pump rocker arm.

Fuel Pump R & R—1965-72

1. Disconnect fuel inlet and outlet lines at pump and plug pump inlet line.
2. Remove two pump mounting bolts and lockwashers; remove pump and gasket.
3. On all small-block engines, including Z28, if rocker arm pushrod is to be removed: take out the two adapter bolts and lockwashers and remove adapter and gasket.
4. On big-block V8 engines, 396, 402, 427, 454 cu. in., if rocker arm pushrod is to be removed:

take out pipe plug.
5. Install pump with new gasket coated with sealer. Coat mounting bolt threads with sealer and tighten bolts.

NOTE: on V8 engines, mechanical fingers or heavy grease can be used to hold pump pushrod in place during installation. Coat pipe plug threads or adapter gasket with sealer if pushrod was removed.

6. Connect inlet and outlet lines, start engine and check for leaks.

⏻ CHILTON TIME-SAVER

When replacing a fuel pump on a 283, 307, 327 or 350 cu. in. engine, considerable time can be saved as follows:

1. Before removing the old pump, remove the upper bolt from the engine's right front mounting boss. This bolt hole is in direct alignment with the fuel pump pushrod. The threaded bolt hole continues into the pump pushrod bore. The bolt acts as an oil plug.
2. Temporarily insert a longer bolt, (about $\frac{3}{8}$—16 x 2 in.) into the hole. Screw the bolt into the bore until it bottoms against the pump pushrod. (Don't tighten the bolt with a wrench or the rod can be damaged.)
3. The mechanic is now free to remove and install the fuel pump without worrying about fuel pump pushrod misalignment.

CAUTION: don't forget to reinstall original motor bolt.

Fuel Filter R & R

Glass Bowl Type—1965

1. Unscrew bail screw and remove bowl, gasket and paper element.
2. Discard element and clean bowl.
3. Install new element, using a new gasket. Do not overtighten bail

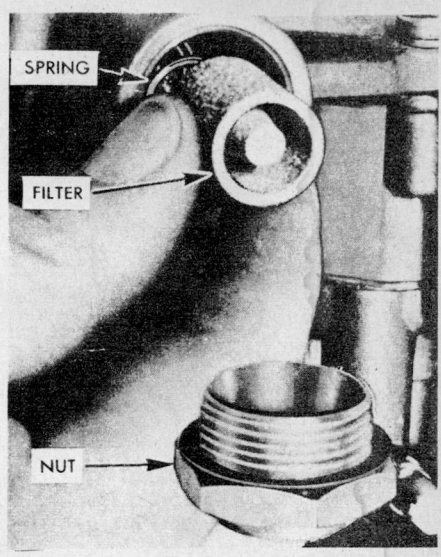

Bronze fuel filter (© Chev. Div. G.M. Corp.)

screw.

Paper and Bronze Types —1965-72

1. Disconnect fuel line connection at inlet of carburetor.
2. Remove inlet fuel filter nut from carburetor using a box wrench.
3. Remove filter element and spring.
4. If a bronze element, blow through cone end—element should allow air to pass freely.
5. Install element spring and new element into carburetor. Bronze elements are installed with small section of cone facing outward.
6. Install new gasket on fitting nut and install nut.
7. Install fuel line and tighten securely. Start engine and check for leaks.

Idle Speed and Mixture Adjustments

NOTE: the *Carburetor Usage Chart* will help in identifying the type of carburetor installed on a particular car. The carburetor illustrations show the locations of idle speed and mixture adjustment screws for each type carburetor.

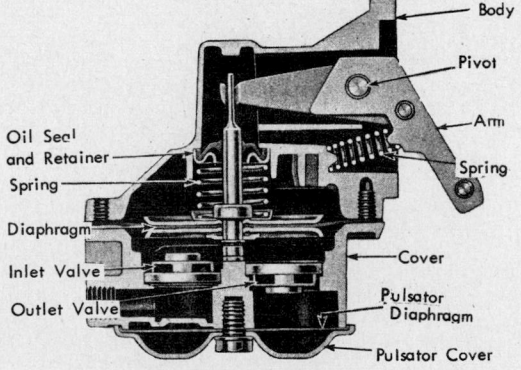

V8 fuel pump (serviceable) (© Chevrolet Div. G.M. Corp.)

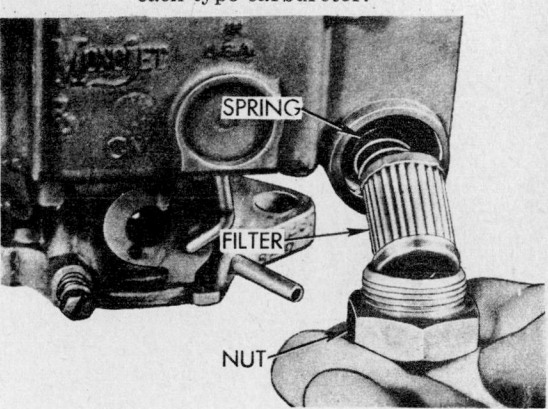

Paper guel filter (© Chev. Div. G.M. Corp.)

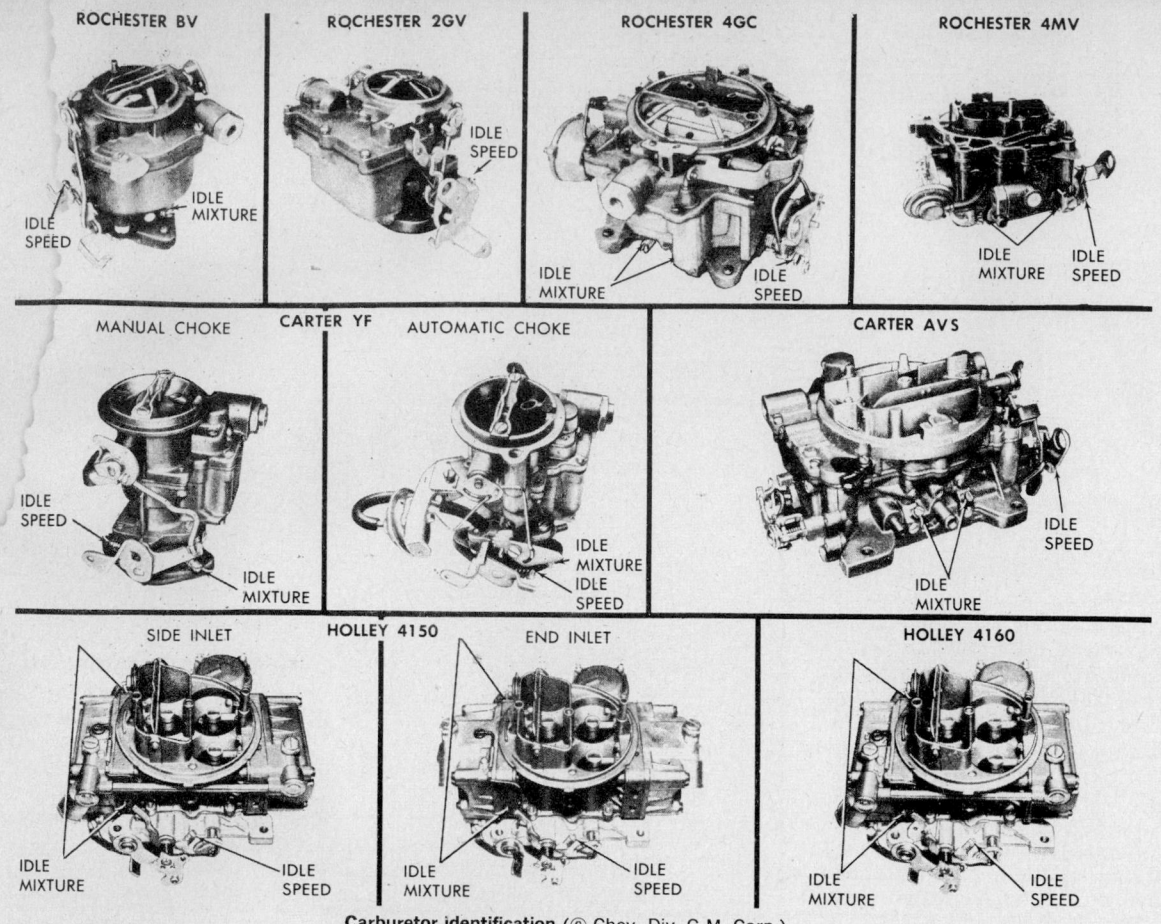

Carburetor identification (© Chev. Div. G.M. Corp.)

Carburetor Usage Chart

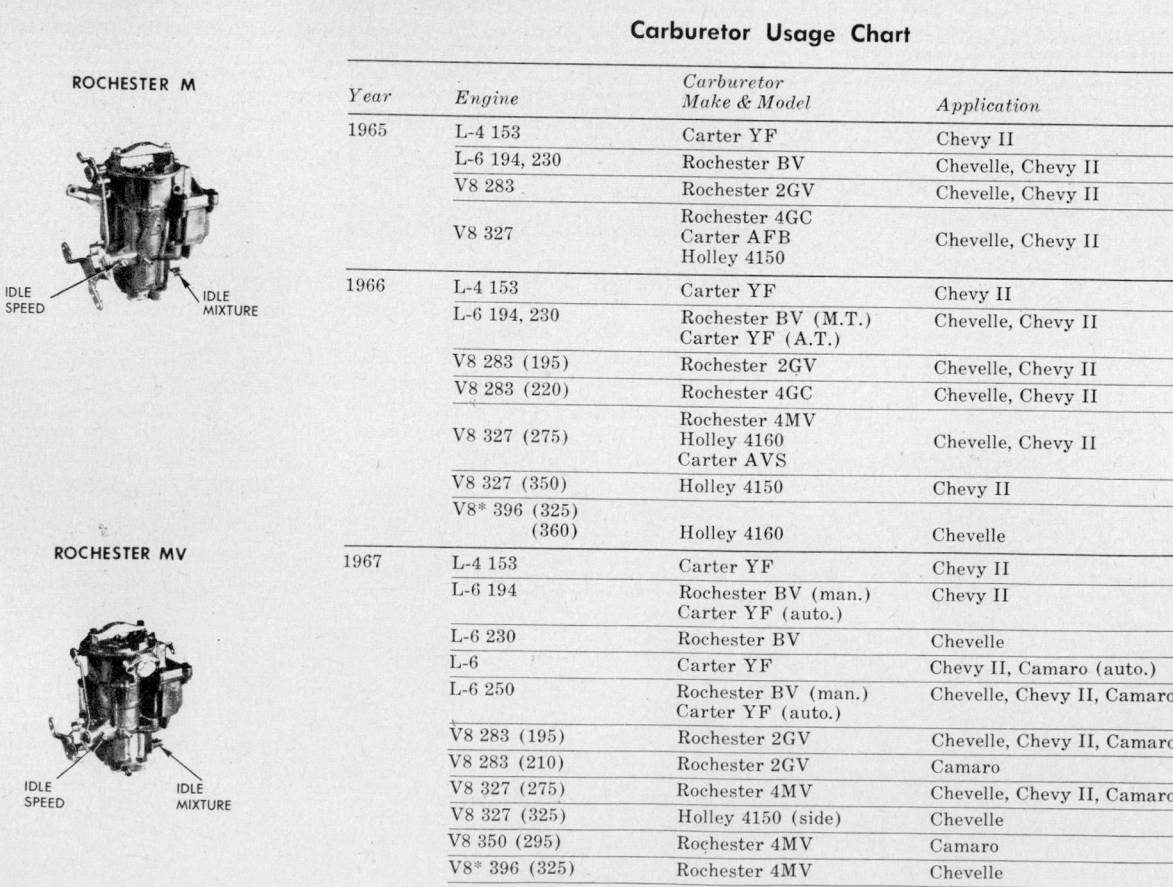

Year	Engine	Carburetor Make & Model	Application
1965	L-4 153	Carter YF	Chevy II
	L-6 194, 230	Rochester BV	Chevelle, Chevy II
	V8 283	Rochester 2GV	Chevelle, Chevy II
	V8 327	Rochester 4GC Carter AFB Holley 4150	Chevelle, Chevy II
1966	L-4 153	Carter YF	Chevy II
	L-6 194, 230	Rochester BV (M.T.) Carter YF (A.T.)	Chevelle, Chevy II
	V8 283 (195)	Rochester 2GV	Chevelle, Chevy II
	V8 283 (220)	Rochester 4GC	Chevelle, Chevy II
	V8 327 (275)	Rochester 4MV Holley 4160 Carter AVS	Chevelle, Chevy II
	V8 327 (350)	Holley 4150	Chevy II
	V8* 396 (325) (360)	Holley 4160	Chevelle
1967	L-4 153	Carter YF	Chevy II
	L-6 194	Rochester BV (man.) Carter YF (auto.)	Chevy II
	L-6 230	Rochester BV	Chevelle
	L-6	Carter YF	Chevy II, Camaro (auto.)
	L-6 250	Rochester BV (man.) Carter YF (auto.)	Chevelle, Chevy II, Camaro
	V8 283 (195)	Rochester 2GV	Chevelle, Chevy II, Camaro
	V8 283 (210)	Rochester 2GV	Camaro
	V8 327 (275)	Rochester 4MV	Chevelle, Chevy II, Camaro
	V8 327 (325)	Holley 4150 (side)	Chevelle
	V8 350 (295)	Rochester 4MV	Camaro
	V8* 396 (325)	Rochester 4MV	Chevelle
	V8* 396 (350)	Holley 4160	Chevelle

Carburetor Usage Chart

1968	L-4 153	Rochester M	Chevy II
	L-6 230, 250	Rochester MV	Chevelle, Chevy II, Camaro
	V8 302 (290 Z28)	Holley 4150	Camaro
	V8 307 (200)	Rochester 2GV	Chevelle, Chevy II
	V8 327 (210)	Rochester 2GV	Camaro
	V8 327 (250)	Rochester 4MV	Chevelle
	V8 327 (275)	Rochester 4MV	Chevelle, Chevy II, Camaro
	V8 327 (325)	Rochester 4MV	Chevelle, Chevy II
	V8 350 (295)	Rochester 4MV	Chevy II, Camaro
	V8* 396 (325)	Rochester 4MV	Chevelle, Chevy II
	V8* 396 (350)	Rochester 4MV	Chevelle, Chevy II
	V8* 396 (375)	Holley 4150	Chevelle, Chevy II
1969	L-4 153	Rochester M	Nova
	L-6 230, 250	Rochester MV	Chevelle, Nova, Camaro
	V8 302 (290 Z28)	Holley 4150	Camaro
	V8 307 (200)	Rochester 2GV (1¼")	Chevelle, Nova
	V8 327 (210)	Rochester 2GV (1¼")	Camaro
	V8 350 (300)	Rochester 4MV	Chevelle, Nova, Camaro
	V8* 396 (325)	Rochester 4MV	Chevelle, Camaro
	V8* 396 (350) (375)	Holley 4150	Chevelle, Nova, Camaro
1970 exc. below	L-4 153	Rochester M	Nova
	L-6 230	Rochester MV	Nova
	L-6 250	Rochester MV	Nova, Chevelle
	V8 307 (200)	Rochester 2GV (1¼")	Nova, Chevelle
	V8 350 (250)	Rochester 2GV (1½")	Chevelle, Monte Carlo, Chevelle
	V8 350 (300)	Rochester 4MV	Nova, Monte Carlo, Chevelle
	V8 400 (265)	Rochester 2GV (1½")	Monte Carlo
	V8* 400 (330)	Rochester 4MV	Monte Carlo, Chevelle (396)
	V8* 454 (360)	Rochester 4MV	Monte Carlo, Chevelle
	V8* 400 (350)	Rochester 4MV	Chevelle
1970½ and 1971	L-6 250	Rochester MV	Chevelle, Nova, Camaro
	V8 307 (200)	Rochester 2GV (1¼")	Chevelle, Nova, Camaro
	V8 350 (245)	Rochester 2GV	Nova, Monte Carlo, Chevelle, Camaro
	V8 350 (270)	Rochester 4MV	Nova, Monte Carlo, Chevelle, Camaro
	V8 350 (330 Z28)	Holley 4150	Camaro
	V8* 396/400 (300)	Rochester 4MV	Chevelle, Monte Carlo, Camaro
	V8* 454 (365)	Rochester 4MV	Monte Carlo, Chevelle
	V8* 454 (425)	Holley 4150	Monte Carlo, Chevelle

*—Mk. IV V8.

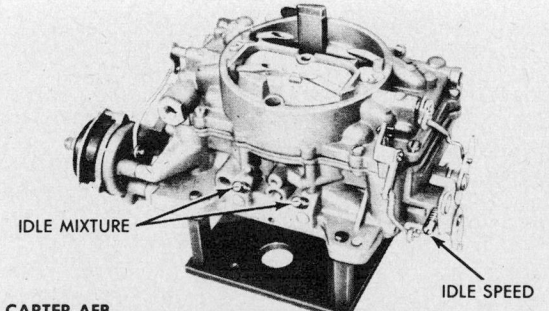

IDLE MIXTURE

IDLE SPEED

CARTER AFB

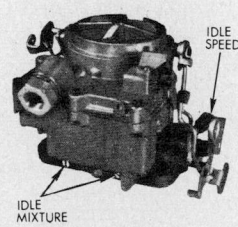

ROCHESTER 2GV (1-½)

IDLE SPEED

IDLE MIXTURE

1965-67 Without A.I.R.

Adjust with air cleaner removed.
1. Remove air cleaner.
2. Connect a tachometer and vacuum gauge to engine, set parking brake and place transmission in Neutral.
3. Turn in idle mixture screws until they gently seat, then back out 1½ turns.
4. Start engine and allow it to come to normal operating temperature. Make sure choke is fully open, then adjust idle speed screw to obtain specified idle speed (automatic in Drive, manual in Neutral).
5. Adjust idle mixture screw/s to obtain highest steady vacuum at specified idle speed, except for Rochester BV. For this carburetor, adjust idle mixture screw out ¼ turn from lean "drop off", the point where a 20-30 rpm drop is achieved by leaning the mixture.
NOTE: on carburetors having a hot idle compensator valve (A/C models), hold brass valve down with a pencil while making mixture adjustment.
6. Repeat Steps 4 and 5 if necessary.
7. Shut off engine, remove gauges and install air cleaner.

1967 With A.I.R.

Adjust with air cleaner removed.
1. Remove air cleaner.
2. Connect a tachometer and a vacuum gauge to engine, set parking brake and place transmission in Neutral.
3. Turn in idle mixture screw/s until they gently seat, then back out three turns.
4. Start engine and allow it to come up to normal operating temperature. Make sure choke is fully open, then adjust idle speed screw/s to obtain specified idle speed (automatic in Drive, manual in Neutral).
5. Turn the idle mixture screw/s clockwise (in) to the point where a 20-30 rpm drop in speed is achieved—this is the lean "drop off" point. Back out the screws ¼ turn from this point.
NOTE: during this adjustment, A/C should be off on L-4, L-6, 283, 327 and 350 engines. On 396 engines, A/C should be on and hot idle compensator pin depressed.
6. Repeat Steps 4 and 5 if necessary.
7. Shut off engine, remove gauges and install air cleaner.

1968-69

Adjust with air cleaner installed.
1. Turn in idle mixture screw/s until they seat gently, then back out three turns.
2. Start engine and allow it to come up to operating temperature. Make sure choke is fully open and preheater valve is open, then adjust idle speed screw to obtain specified idle speed (automatic in Drive, manual in Neutral).
NOTE: on A/C cars, turn off A/C *except* on L-4 and L-6 with auto transmission and 327 (325/350 H.P.) with manual transmission. On

these engines, idle is set with A/C on.

3. Adjust idle mixture screw/s to obtain highest steady idle speed, then readjust idle speed screw to obtain specified speed. On cars having idle stop solenoid, adjust as follows:

    a. Adjust idle speed to 500 rpm L-6 or 600 rpm V8 by turning hex on solenoid plunger.

    b. Disconnect wire at solenoid. This allows throttle lever to seat against idle screw.

    c. Adjust idle screw to obtain 400 rpm, then reconnect wire.

4. Adjust one mixture screw to obtain a 20 rpm drop in idle speed, then back out screw ¼ turn from this point.

5. Repeat Steps 3 and 4 for second mixture screw, if so equipped.

6. Readjust idle speed to obtain specified idle speed.

1970

Adjust with air cleaner installed.

1. Disconnect "FUEL TANK" line from vapor canister (E.E.C.).

2. Connect a tachometer to engine, start engine and allow it to come up to operating temperature. Make sure choke and preheater valves are fully open.

3. Turn off A/C and set parking brake. Disconnect and plug distributor vacuum line.

4. Make the following adjustments:

L-4 153

    a. Set mixture screw to obtain maximum idle rpm.

    b. Adjust idle speed screw to obtain 750 rpm for manual transmission (in Neutral), 650 rpm for automatic (in Drive).

    c. Adjust mixture screw to obtain a 20 rpm drop in idle speed, then back out ¼ turn from this point.

    d. Readjust idle speed to obtain specified rpm, then reconnect vacuum line.

L-6 230/250

    a. Turn in mixture screw until it gently seats, then back out screw four turns.

    b. Adjust solenoid screw to obtain 830 rpm for manual transmission (in Neutral) or 630 rpm for automatic (in Drive).

    c. Adjust mixture screw to obtain 750 rpm for manual transmission (in Neutral) or 600 rpm for automatic (in Drive).

    d. Disconnect solenoid wire and set idle speed to 400 rpm, then reconnect.

    e. Reconnect distributor vacuum line.

V8 307 and 400 (265 H.P.)

    a. Turn in mixture screws until they seat gently, then back out four turns.

    b. Adjust carburetor idle speed screw to obtain 800 rpm for manual transmission (in Neutral), or adjust solenoid screw to obtain 630 rpm for automatic transmission (in Drive).

    c. Adjust both mixture screws equally inward to obtain 700 rpm for manual transmission, 600 rpm for automatic (in Drive).

    d. On cars with automatic, disconnect solenoid wire, set carburetor idle screw to obtain 450 rpm and reconnect solenoid.

    e. Reconnect distributor vacuum line.

V8 350 (250 H.P.)

    a. Turn in mixture screws until they gently seat, then back out four turns.

    b. Adjust solenoid screw to obtain 830 rpm for manual transmission (in Neutral), 630 rpm for automatic (in Drive).

    c. Adjust both mixture screws equally inward to obtain 750 rpm for manual transmission or 600 rpm for automatic (in Drive).

    d. Disconnect solenoid wire, set carburetor idle screw to obtain 450 rpm and reconnect solenoid.

    e. Reconnect distributor vacuum line.

V8 350 (300 H.P.) and 400 (330 H.P.)

    a. Turn in both mixture screws until they gently seat, then back out four turns.

    b. Adjust carburetor idle screw to obtain 775 rpm for manual transmission, 630 rpm for automatic (in Drive).

    c. Adjust mixture screws equally to obtain 700 rpm for manual transmission, 600 rpm for automatic (in Drive).

    d. Reconnect distributor vacuum line.

V8 396 (350 H.P.) and 454 (360 H.P.)

    a. Turn in both mixture screws until they gently seat, then back out four turns.

    b. Adjust carburetor idle screw to obtain 700 rpm for manual transmission or 630 rpm for automatic (in

Drive).

    c. For cars with automatic transmission: adjust mixture screws equally to obtain 600 rpm with transmission in Drive.

    d. For cars with manual transmission: turn in *one* mixture screw until speed drops to 400 rpm, then adjust carburetor idle screw to obtain 700 rpm. Turn in the *other* mixture screw until speed drops 40 rpm, then regain 700 rpm by adjusting carburetor idle screw.

    e. Reconnect distributor vacuum line.

5. Disconnect tachometer and reconnect fuel vapor line.

1971-72

Adjust with air cleaner installed.

The idle stop solenoid is no longer used, having been replaced by the combination emission control valve. This valve is energized through the transmission to increase idle speed under conditions of high gear deceleration and to provide full vacuum spark advance during high gear operation. The valve is de-energized at curb idle and in the lower gears to provide a retarded spark under these conditions, the result of which is lower hydrocarbon emission. *The valve need not be adjusted unless the solenoid or throttle body is removed, or the carburetor overhauled.*

On all 1971 vehicles except those with solid lifter cams, i.e., 350/330 (LT-1 and Z28) and 454/425 (LS-6), idle limiter caps are installed on the mixture screws of the carburetors. Chevrolet does not recommend removing these caps, and does not recommend adjusting the mixture. Adjusting the mixture without the proper test gear will result in hydrocarbon emission levels in excess of the specified minimum

1. Follow Steps 1-3 of 1970 procedure.

2. Make the following adjustments:

L-6 250

    a. Adjust carburetor idle speed screw to obtain 550 rpm for manual transmission (in Neutral) or 500 rpm for automatic (in Drive). *Do not adjust solenoid screw.*

    b. Reconnect vapor line and distributor vacuum advance line.

V8 307 (200 H.P.) and 350 (245 H.P.)

    a. Adjust carburetor idle speed screw to obtain 600 rpm for manual transmission (in Neutral) with A/C off, or 550 rpm for automatic (in Drive) with A/C on. *Do not adjust solenoid screw.*

b. Reconnect vapor line and distributor vacuum advance line.

V8 350 (270 H.P.)

a. Adjust carburetor idle speed screw to obtain 600 rpm for manual transmission (in Neutral) with A/C off, or 550 rpm for automatic (in Drive) with A/C on. *Do not adjust solenoid screw.*

b. Place fast idle cam follower on second step of fast idle cam, turn A/C off and adjust fast idle to 1,350 rpm for manual transmission (in Neutral) or 1,500 rpm for automatic (in Park).

c. Reconnect vapor line and distributor vacuum advance line.

V8 350 (330 H.P. Z 28) and 454 (425 H.P.)

a. Adjust mixture screws to obtain maximum speed (rpm at idle), then adjust carburetor idle speed screw to obtain 700 rpm (manual in Neutral and automatic in Drive).

b. Turn in one mixture screw to obtain a 20 rpm drop in speed, then back out 1/4 turn.

c. Repeat Step "b" for other mixture screw, then reset idle to 700 rpm. *Do not adjust solenoid screw.*

d. Reconnect vapor line and distributor vacuum line.

V8 396 (300 H.P.) and 454 (365 H.P.)

a. Turn off A/C and adjust carburetor idle speed screw to obtain 600 rpm with manual transmission in Neutral and automatic in Drive. *Do not adjust solenoid screw.*

b. Place fast idle cam follower on second step of fast idle cam, turn off A/C and adjust fast idle to 1,350 rpm for manual transmission (in Neutral) or 1,500 rpm for automatic (in Park).

c. Reconnect vapor line and distributor vacuum line.

Combination Emission Control Valve Adjustment

1. Disconnect and plug distributor vacuum line.
2. Disconnect fuel tank line from vapor canister.
3. Extend the C.E.C. valve plunger to contact the throttle lever.
4. Adjust plunger length to obtain specified idle speed.
5. Reconnect fuel vapor line and distributor vacuum.

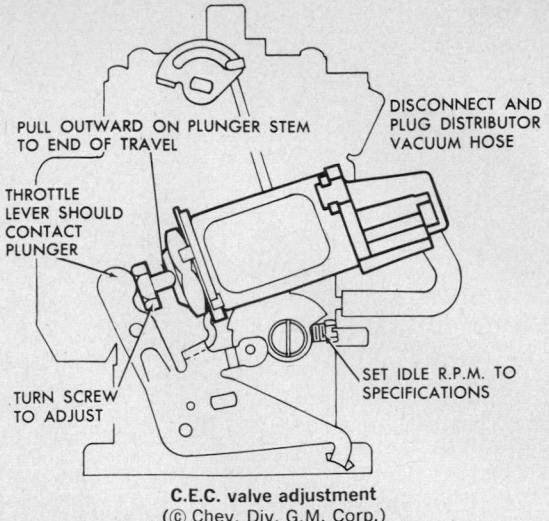

PULL OUTWARD ON PLUNGER STEM TO END OF TRAVEL

DISCONNECT AND PLUG DISTRIBUTOR VACUUM HOSE

THROTTLE LEVER SHOULD CONTACT PLUNGER

TURN SCREW TO ADJUST

SET IDLE R.P.M. TO SPECIFICATIONS

C.E.C. valve adjustment
(© Chev. Div. G.M. Corp.)

Exhaust System

Muffler Removal and Installation

1965-67

1. Remove U-clamp at center mounting.
2. Remove U-clamp at forward end of muffler pipe.
3. Disengage muffler at inlet and outlet ends.
4. To install, reverse removal procedure. Allow 3/4 in. clearance between muffler hanger and crossmember.

1968-72 Nova and Camaro

1. For single exhaust: remove U-clamp at muffler inlet.
2. For dual exhaust: remove U-clamps at muffler inlets and also at left-hand muffler outlet up to 1969.
3. Remove tailpipe hangers and disengage muffler/s from tailpipe/s and exhaust pipe/s.
4. Remove mufflers. It is recommended that tailpipe/s be replaced when replacing a muffler.
5. To install, reverse removal procedure. Do not tighten clamps and hangers until full clearance all around is obtained.

1968-72 Chevelle and Monte Carlo

1. Remove U-bolt clamp at muffler mounting.
2. Remove muffler from exhaust pipe by cutting the pipe with a torch or hacksaw. Cut cleanly and close to the muffler inlet for ample surface for muffler replacement.
3. Remove the muffler from the tail pipe with a hammer.
4. Replace with a new muffler and or tail pipe and exhaust pipe, as required.
5. Use existing hardware for replacement, plus a new U-bolt and two nuts to secure the muffler to the tail pipe.
6. Attach a new clamp assembly to the muffler and exhaust pipe.
7. Realign and check all clearances before tightening all fasteners.

Cooling System

A standard pressure cooling system is used on all models. The radiator cap is designed to maintain a cooling system pressure of about 13 or 15 psi above atmospheric. The water pump requires no attention except to make certain the air vent at the top of the hosing and the drain holes in the bottom do not become clogged.

Radiator Removal—1965-72

1. Drain radiator.
2. Disconnect hoses and oil cooler lines.
3. Remove radiator upper panel and shroud (if so equipped).
4. Remove radiator attaching bolts and lift radiator out of car.

Radiator Installation—1965-72

1. Slide radiator into position.
2. Install attaching bolts, shroud, and upper panel.
3. Install hoses and close drain.
4. Fill cooling system, run engine until operating temperature has been reached. Again fill cooling system and check for leaks.

Water Pump Removal and Installation—1965-72

1. Drain radiator. Loosen fan pulley bolts.
2. Disconnect heater hose, lower radiator hose, and bypass hose (as required) at water pump.
3. Remove Delcotron upper brace (V8 only), loosen swivel bolt, and remove fan belt.
NOTE: on Mark IV engines, disconnect power steering and A/C belts and pivot power steering pump to one side.
4. Remove fan blade assembly bolts, fan, and pulley. Thermostatic fan clutches must not be tilted on removal or the silicone fluid will leak out.
5. Remove pump bolts, pump, and gasket. On inline engines, pull the pump straight out to avoid impeller damage.
6. Reverse procedure to install.

Thermostat

When replacing thermostat, be sure to install unit with the spring and body toward the engine.

Engine

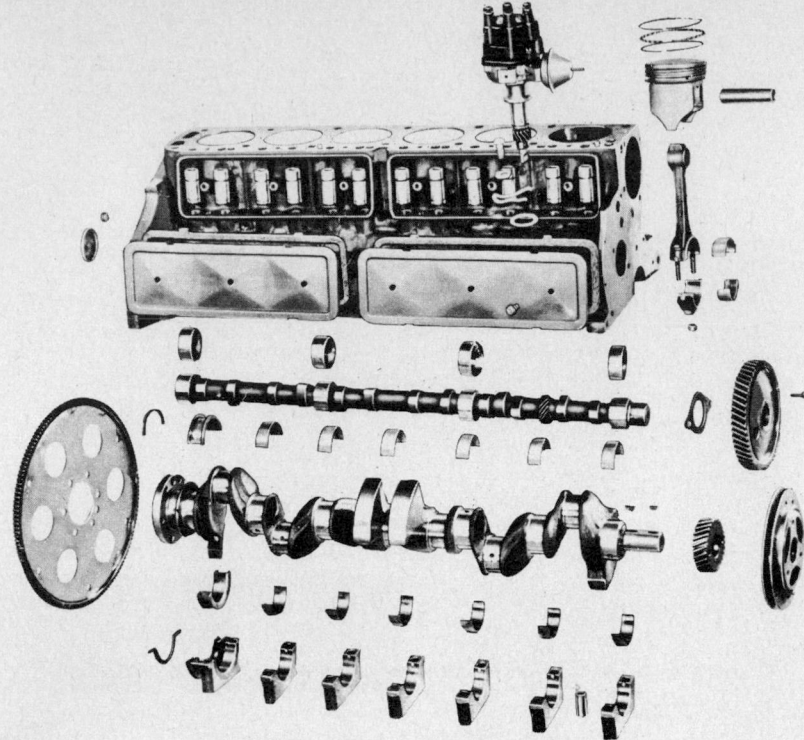

Exploded view, 6 cylinder engine, typical (© G.M. Corp.)

Four, six, and eight cylinder engines are used. The four cylinder engine is a 153 cu. in. inline design with five main bearings. The six cyclinder engines are also of the inline type, with seven main bearings. They are built in 230 and 250 cu. in. displacements. V8 engines are of two basic types. All engines of each type are generally similar in design and have some interchangeability of parts. The first type is the small V8 series. This includes the 283, 302, 307, 327, and 350 cu. in. engines. The second type is the large, or Mark IV, V8 series. This includes engines of 396, 400, and 454 cu. in. displacement. A small-block 400 cu. in. engine is also available in 2-BBL form. This engine must not be confused with the Mark IV 400, which is also called a "396" in some cars.

Pertinent engine data can be found in the General Engine Specifications chart.

Exhaust Emission Control

The air injector reactor (A.I.R.) system is used on all vehicles, with certain design exceptions, sold in California in 1966-67, and later on virtually all vehicles. This system uses a belt driven air pump to inject air into the exhaust ports. The effect of this is to drastically reduce the percentage of pollutants in the vehicle exhaust.

Beginning with the 1970 models, all General Motors cars use a complete system of emission controls. Some of the features of this system were introduced as in previous years, particularly on vehicles sold in California. In most cases, the features are introduced to comply with the strict California anti-air pollution standards, then later added to all vehicles. Features of the emission control systems are Positive Crankcase Ventilation (P.C.V.), Controlled Combustion System (C.C.S.), Evaporation Emission Control (E.E.C.), Transmission Controlled Spark (T.C.S.), and Combination Emission Control (C.E.C.).

P.C.V. uses intake manifold vacuum to draw crankcase vapors through a P.C.V. metering valve into the combustion chambers for burning.

C.C.S. increases combustion efficiency through leaner carburetor adjustments and revised distributor

Exploded view, typical V8 (© G.M. Corp.)

calibration. Thermostatically controlled air intakes are also used on most models.

E.E.C. reduces fuel vapor emission from the fuel tank and the carburetor float bowl by use of an air filter canister.

T.C.S. eliminates distributor vacuum advance in the low forward gears of both standard and automatic transmissions. This is done by means of solenoid operated vacuum valves.

The C.E.C. system, introduced in 1971, incorporates many features of the earlier T.C.S. system. The distributor vacuum advance feature is still eliminated in the low forward gears by use of the transmission and solenoid vacuum switches. Operation is slightly different, however, in that when the solenoid is in the non-energized position, rather than the energized position, the vacuum advance unit is shut off and the distributor is vented to the atmosphere. On C.E.C., venting is accomplished through a filter in the opposite end of the solenoid rather than through a direct hose connection to the carburetor air hose.

The T.C.S. system used a temperature override switch which allowed full vacuum advance in all gears until the engine was warm. This feature is incorporated into the C.E.C. system with an 82° F. temperature cut-off.

The C.E.C. solenoid is controlled by two switches and a time delay relay. The time delay relay energizes the solenoid for approximately 15 seconds after the ignition is turned on to allow full vacuum advance in all gears *independent* of temperature to eliminate stalling during "driveaway."

Engine dieseling is controlled by use of lower throttle blade openings (lower curb idle speeds). This has allowed the hot thermal override switch to be eliminated on all but the LS3 Camaro and two Corvette models (with automatic transmission and A/C). On these models, a solid-state time device engages the A/C compressor clutch for about 3 seconds after the ignition is shut off, the load from which effectively stalls the engine and prevents diesel overrun.

For diagnosis procedures, see the Unit Repair Section. Any of the methods of exhaust emission control requires close and frequent attention to tune-up factors of engine maintenance.

Since 1968, all car manufacturers post idle speeds and other pertinent data relative to the specific application in a conspicuous place in the engine compartment.

For details, consult the Unit Repair Section.

Engine R & R

NOTE: unless otherwise stated, the following operations cover the 4 cylinder, 6 cylinder and V8 engines.

Removal—1965-72

1. Raise car and place on jackstands.
2. Drain cooling system, transmission, and crankcase.
3. Scribe alignment marks on underside of hood and around hood hinges, and remove hood from hinges.
4. Disconnect coolant and heater hoses at engine attachment.
5. Disconnect battery cables at battery.
6. Remove radiator and shroud assembly. Remove fan and pulley.
7. Remove air cleaner.
8. Disconnect coil, starter and Delcotron wires, engine-to-body ground strap, oil pressure and engine temperature sender wires, and C.E.C. wire.
9. Disconnect gas tank line at fuel pump.
10. Disconnect accelerator control linkage at firewall.
11. Disconnect hand choke linkage (4 cylinder), and power brake vacuum line.
12. Disconnect exhaust pipe from manifold. On V8, disconnect crossover pipe.
13. Disconnect clutch shaft bracket at frame and disconnect clutch linkage. On automatic transmission models, remove transmission oil filler tube and plug the opening.
14. Attach engine lifting tool. Attach to hoist and secure the engine.
15. Remove driveshaft.
16. Remove and set aside power steering pump and air conditioning compressor. Do not disconnect hoses.
17. Remove engine rear mounting bolts.
18. Disconnect speedometer cable, transmission control rod linkage lower ends, T.C.S. switch, and transmission oil cooler lines.
19. Loosen front engine mounting bolts.
20. Raise engine slightly and remove bolts.
21. Remove transmission crossmember and free the transmission rear mounting.
22. Remove engine and transmission as a unit from the car.

Installation—1965-72

1. Bolt engine lifting tool to engine and lower engine and transmission into chassis as a unit. Guide engine to align front engine mounts with mounts on frame.
2. Install one rear transmission crossmember side bolt, swing crossmember up under transmission mount and install bolt in opposite side rail.
3. Align and install rear mount bolts.
4. Install engine front mount bolts and remove lifting tool from engine.
5. Install and connect all items in reverse order of engine removal procedure.

Separating Transmission and Clutch from Engine

Manual Transmission

1. Remove clutch housing cover plate screws.
2. Remove bolts holding clutch housing to engine block. Remove clutch housing and transmission assembly.
3. Remove starter and clutch housing cover plate.
4. Loosen clutch-to-flywheel bolts, alternately, until spring pressure is released. Remove all bolts, clutch disc and pressure plate assembly.
5. Re-attach transmission by reversing above process.

Automatic Transmission

1. Lower the engine and support it on suitable blocks.
2. Remove starter and converter housing underpan.
3. Remove flywheel-to-converter assembly attaching bolts.
4. Support transmission on blocks.
5. Remove transmission-to-engine mounting bolts.
6. With engine hoist attached, remove blocks from engine only and slowly guide the engine from the transmission.
7. Re-attach automatic transmission by reversing above process.

Cylinder Head

4 and 6 Cylinder Engines

Removal—1965-72

1. Drain cooling system and remove air cleaner. Disconnect P.C.V. hose.
2. Disconnect choke cable (4 cylinder), accelerator pedal rod at bell crank on manifold, and fuel and vacuum lines at carburetor.
3. Disconnect exhaust pipe at manifold flange, then remove manifold bolts and clamps and remove manifolds and carburetor as an assembly.
4. Remove fuel and vacuum line retaining clip from water outlet. Then disconnect wire harness from heat sending unit and coil, leaving harness clear of clips on rocker arm cover.
5. Disconnect radiator hose at water

outlet housing and battery ground strap at cylinder head.

6. Disconnect wires and remove spark plugs. On the 6 cylinder engine disconnect coil to distributor primary wire lead at coil and remove the coil.

7. Remove rocker arm cover. Back off rocker arm nuts, pivot rocker arms to clear push rods and remove push rods.

8. Remove cylinder-head bolts, cylinder head and gasket.

Installation—1965-72

1. Place a new cylinder-head gasket over dowel pins in cylinder block.

2. Guide and lower cylinder head into place over dowels and gasket.

3. Oil cylinder-head bolts, install and run them down snug.

4. Tighten the cylinder-head bolts a little at a time with a torque wrench in the correct sequence. Final torque should be 90 to 95 ft. lbs.

5. Install valve pushrods down through the cylinder-head openings and seat them in their lifter sockets.

6. Install rocker arms, balls and nuts and tighten rocker arm nuts until all pushrod play is taken up.

7. Install thermostat, thermostat housing and water outlet using new gaskets. Then connect radiator hose.

8. Install heat sending switch and torque to 15-20 ft. lbs.

9. Clean spark plugs or install new ones. Set gaps to .035 in.

10. Use new plug gaskets and torque to 20-25 ft. lbs.

11. Install coil (on six cylinder engine) then connect heat sending unit and coil primary wires, and connect battery ground cable at the cylinder head.

12. Clean surfaces and install new gasket over manifold studs. Install manifold. Install bolts and clamps and torque as specified.

13. Connect throttle linkage, and choke wire, (on four cylinder engine).

14. Connect P.C.V., fuel and vacuum lines and secure lines in clip at water outlet.

15. Fill cooling system and check for leaks.

16. Adjust valve lash.

17. Install rocker arm cover and position wiring harness in clips.

18. Clean and install air cleaner.

V8 Engines

Removal and Installation

1. Drain coolant. Remove air cleaner.

2. Disconnect:
   a. battery
   b. radiator and heater hose from manifold
   c. throttle linkage
   d. fuel line
   e. coil wires
   f. temperature sending unit
   g. power brake hose, distributor vacuum hose, and crankcase vent hoses.

3. Remove:
   a. distributor, marking position
   b. Delcotron upper bracket
   c. coil and bracket
   d. manifold attaching bolts
   e. intake manifold and carburetor.

4. Remove:
   a. rocker arm covers
   b. rocker arm nuts, balls, rocker arms, and push rods. These items must be replaced in their original locations.

5. Remove cylinder head bolts, cylinder head, and gasket.

6. Reverse procedure to install. Tighten head bolts evenly to the specified torque. On engines having steel gasket, use sealer on both sides. No sealer can be used on steel-asbestos gaskets.

Valve System

Chevrolet uses a hydraulically operated tappet system with adjustable rocker nuts to obtain zero lash.

Valve specifications may be obtained from the Valve Specifications chart and the Tune-up Specifications chart.

Hydraulic Valve Lifter Adjustment

In the case of disassembly, or any other cause for valve tappet adjustment, proceed as follows:

1. Adjust rocker arm nuts to eliminate lash. This must be done when lifter is on base of circle of cam.

2. Remove distributor cap and crank engine until distributor rotor points to No. 1 cylinder terminal, with points open.

The following valves can be adjusted with the engine in No. 1 firing position:

OHV 4—Intake No. 1, 2, Exhaust No. 1, 3

OHV 6—Intake No. 1, 2, 4, Exhaust No. 1, 3, 5

V8—Intake No. 1, 2, 5, 7, Exhaust No. 1, 3, 4, 8

3. Turn adjusting nut until all lash is removed from this particular valve train. This can be determined by checking pushrod side play while turning the adjustment. When all play has been removed, turn adjusting nut one more turn. This will place the lifter plunger in the center of its travel.

4. Follow steps 2 and 3 to adjust remaining valves.

The following valves can be adjusted with the engine in the No. 6 firing position (No. 4 on OHV 4):

OHV 4—Intake No. 3, 4, Exhaust No. 2, 4

OHV 6—Intake No. 3, 5, 6, Exhaust No. 2, 4, 6

V8—Intake No. 3, 4, 6, 8, Exhaust No. 2, 5, 6, 7

Readjust the lifters as follows with the engine hot and running.

1. Remove rocker arm covers and gaskets.

2. Place oil deflector clips on rocker arms.

3. With engine running at idle, back off rocker arm nut until it starts to clatter.

4. Turn nut down until clatter stops. This is the zero lash posi-

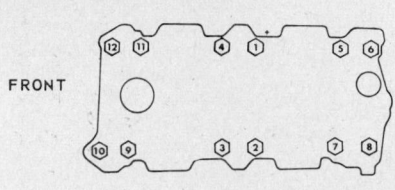

"SMALL V8"

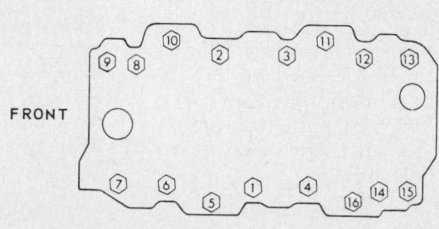

"MARK IV V8"

Intake manifold torque sequence—V8 engines (© Chev. Div. G.M. Corp.)

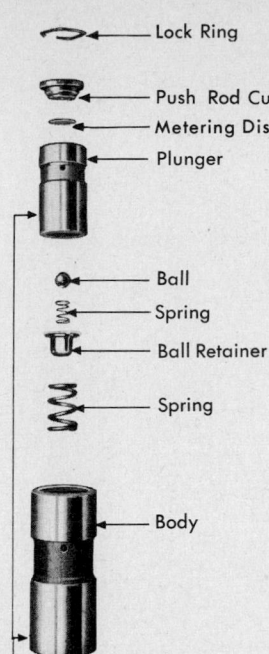

- Lock Ring
- Push Rod Cup
- Metering Disc
- Plunger
- Ball
- Spring
- Ball Retainer
- Spring
- Body

Plunger And Body Are Fitted Pairs And Must Not Be Mismated

tion.

5. Tighten nut down one-quarter turn. Pause ten seconds. Repeat additional quarter turns and ten second pauses until nut has been tightened down one full turn from the zero lash position.
6. Repeat steps 3, 4, and 5 for all rocker arms.
7. Remove oil deflector clips and replace rocker arm covers.

Mechanical Valve Lifter Adjustment

1. Set engine in No. 1 firing position.
2. Adjust the clearance between the valve stems and the rocker arms using a feeler gauge. Check the Tune-Up Specifications table for the proper clear-

ance. Adjust the following Valves in No. 1 firing position: Intake No. 2, 7, Exhaust No. 4, 8.
3. Turn crankshaft one-half revolution clockwise. Adjust the following valves: Intake No. 1, 8, Exhaust No. 3, 6.
4. Turn crankshaft one-half revo-

Adjusting valve clearance 6 cylinder
(© Chevrolet Div. G.M. Corp.)

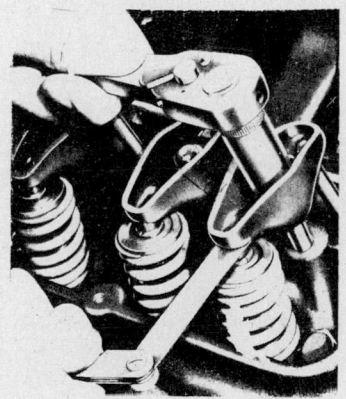

Adjusting valve clearance V8 with mechanical lifters
(© G.M. Corp.)

lution clockwise to No. 6 firing position. Adjust the following valves in No. 6 firing position: Intake No. 3, 4, Exhaust No. 5, 7.
5. Turn crankshaft one-half revolution clockwise. Adjust the following valves: Intake No. 5, 6, Exhaust No. 1, 2.
6. Run engine until normal operating temperature is reached. Reset all clearances, using deflectors.

Timing Cover

NOTE: the 6 cylinder engine uses a harmonic balancer that closely resembles the Chevrolet V8-type. The removal procedure for this dampener will be the same as that used for the Chevrolet V8. Driving the dampener back onto the crankshaft without supporting the pulley can cause damage. A replacing tool must be used during the reassembly operation.

Cover Removal and Installation

1. Drain and remove radiator.
2. Remove harmonic balancer, (6 and 8 cylinder) or a crankshaft pulley, (4 cylinder) using a puller.
3. Drain engine oil and remove oil pan. Remove V8 water pump.
4. Remove timing gear cover attaching screws, and cover and gasket.
5. Reverse procedure to install.

Caution The 6 and 8 cylinder engines use a harmonic balancer. Breakage may occur where the balancer has been hammered back onto the crankshaft. This balancer must be drawn back into place.

Oil Seal Replacement

1. After removing gear cover, pry oil seal out of front of cover with large screwdriver.

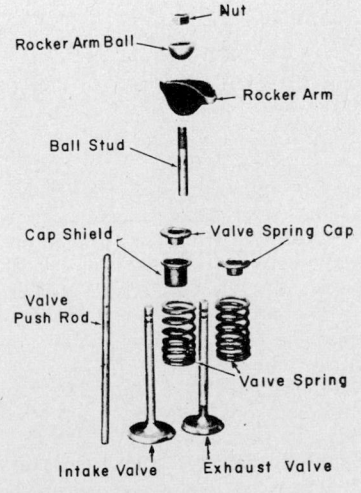

- Nut
- Rocker Arm Ball
- Rocker Arm
- Ball Stud
- Cap Shield
- Valve Spring Cap
- Valve Push Rod
- Valve Spring
- Intake Valve
- Exhaust Valve

V8 valve assembly (© G.M. Corp.)

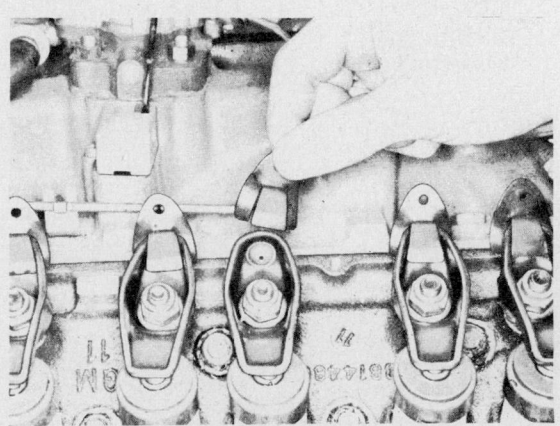

Oil deflector clips installed
(© Chevrolet Div. G.M. Corp.)

2. Install new lip seal with lip (open side of seal) inside and drive or press seal into place.

Inline Engine Camshaft Removal and Replacement

1965-69 Except Camaro

1. In addition to removing the timing gear cover, remove the grille assembly.
2. Remove valve cover and gasket, loosen all the valve rocker arm nuts and pivot the arms clear of the pushrods.
3. Remove distributor and fuel pump.
4. Remove coil, side cover and gasket. Remove pushrods and valve lifters.
5. Remove the two camshaft thrust plate retaining screws by working through holes in the camshaft gear.
6. Remove camshaft and gear assembly by pulling it out through the front of the block.

NOTE: if renewing either camshaft or camshaft gear, the gear must be pressed off the camshaft. The replacement parts must be assembled in the same manner (under pressure). In placing the gear on the camshaft, press the gear onto the shaft until it bottoms against the gear spacer ring. The end clearance of the thrust plate should be .001 to .005 in.

7. Install camshaft assembly in the engine.
8. Turn crankshaft and camshaft to align and bring the timing marks together. Push the camshaft into this aligned position. Install camshaft thrust plate-to-block screws and torque them to 6-7½ ft. lbs.
9. Runout on either crankshaft or camshaft gear should not exceed .003 in.
10. Backlash between the two gears should be between .004 and .006 in.
11. Install timing gear cover and gasket.
12. Install oil pan and gaskets.
13. Install harmonic balancer.

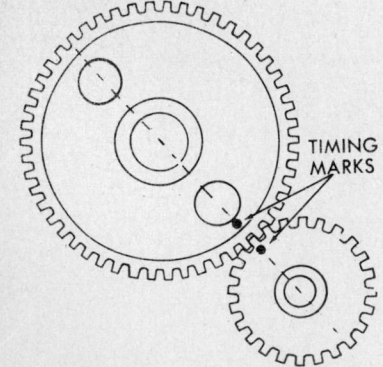

Timing mark, 4 and 6 cylinder

14. Line up keyway in balancer with key on crankshaft and drive balancer onto shaft until it bottoms against crankshaft gear.
15. Install valve lifters and pushrods. Install side cover with new gasket. Attach coil wires; install fuel pump.
16. Install distributor and set timing as described under distributor at the beginning of the section.
17. Pivot rocker arms over pushrods and lash the valves as described in a previous paragraph, Valve Tappets Adjustment.
18. Add oil to the engine. Install and adjust fan belt.
19. Install radiator or shroud.
20. Install grille assembly.
21. Fill cooling system, start engine and check for leaks.
22. Check and adjust timing.

1967-69 Camaro and All 1970-72 Models

Remove engine from car, then proceed as in *1965-69 Except Camaro*.

V8 Engine Camshaft Removal and Replacement

1. Remove intake manifold, valve lifters and timing chain cover (requires oil pan removal), as described in this section.
2. Remove grille, except on 1969-72 Nova and 1969 Camaro. On these models, remove both front motor mount bolts and right motor mount, then lower engine until it rests on frame.

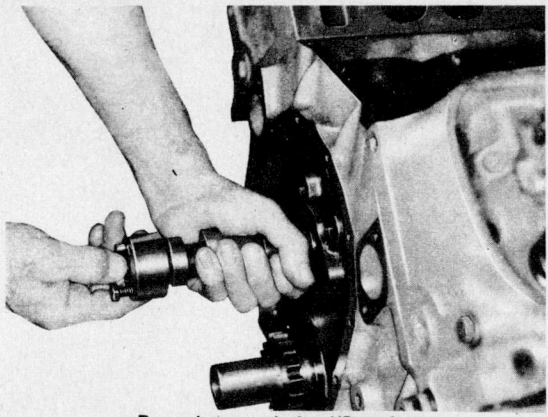

Removing camshaft—V8 engine
(© Chev. Div. G.M. Corp.)

3. On 1969-72 Nova and 1969 Camaro, remove the two center bolts and the one lower bolt that secure the hood latch support. This will give adequate clearance for the cam.
4. Remove fuel pump and pump pushrod.
5. Remove camshaft sprocket bolts, sprocket and timing chain. A light blow to the lower edge of a tight sprocket should free it (use a plastic mallet).
6. Install two 5/16—18 x 4 in. bolts

in cam bolt holes and pull cam from block.

7. To install, reverse removal procedure, aligning timing marks as illustrated.

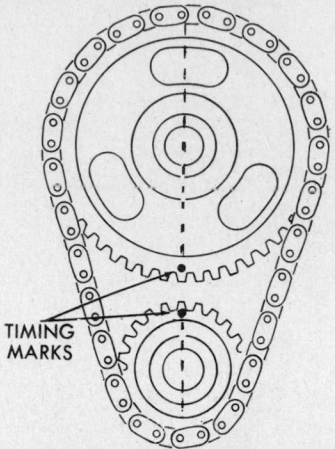

Timing mark, V8 engine

NOTE: cam lobes must be lubricated with Molykote or equivalent before installation. All cam journals are the same diameter, so make sure cam bearings are not dislodged during installation.

Timing Chain Replacement

V8 Models

V8 models are equipped with a timing chain. To replace the chain, remove the radiator core, water pump harmonic balancer, and the crankcase front cover. This will allow access to the timing chain. Crank the engine until the zero marks punched on both sprockets are closest to one another and in line between the shaft centers. Then, take out the three bolts that hold the camshaft gear to the camshaft. This gear is a light press fit on the camshaft and will come off readily. It is located by a dowel.

The chain comes off with the camshaft gear.

A gear puller will be required to

remove the crankshaft gear.

Without disturbing the position of the engine, mount the new crank gear on the shaft, then mount the chain over the camshaft gear. Arrange the camshaft gear in such a way that the timing marks will line up between the shaft centers and the camshaft locating dowel will enter the dowel hole in the cam sprocket.

Place the cam sprocket, with its chain mounted over it, in position on the front of the camshaft and pull up with the three bolts that hold it to the camshaft.

After the gears are in place, turn the engine two full revolutions to make certain that the timing marks are in correct alignment between the shaft centers.

Engine Lubrication

Oil Pan Removal—Inline Engines

1965-67 Chevy II

1. Disconnect battery ground strap at battery.
2. Drain oil from engine.
3. Disconnect all wires from starter. Remove starter.
4. Disconnect steering idler arm bracket at right hand frame rail. Swing linkage down for pan clearance.
5. On 6 cylinder only, remove front crossmember.
   NOTE: on station wagon, let stabilizer bar hang while removing crossmember.
6. Remove oil pan bolts, drop the pan and clean off gaskets and end seals.

1968-72 Nova, 1967-72 Camaro

1. Disconnect battery ground cable.
2. Remove front engine mount bolts.
   NOTE: 1970 up, remove upper radiator panel or side mount bolts.
3. Drain coolant. Remove radiator hoses.
4. Remove fan.
5. Drain engine oil.
6. Disconnect and remove starter.
7. Disconnect oil cooler lines and remove converter housing underpan.
8. Disconnect steering rod at idler lever. Swing linkage to one side for pan clearance.
9. Rotate crankshaft until timing mark on torsional damper is at 6:00 o'clock position.
10. Raise engine enough to insert 2 X 4 in. blocks under engine mounts.
11. Unbolt oil pan. On some models it may be necessary to remove the oil pump and intake pipe or

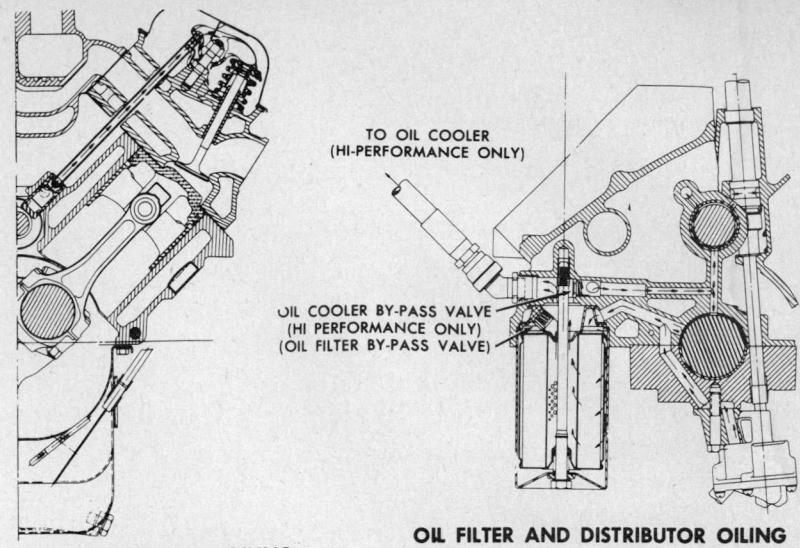

TO OIL COOLER
(HI-PERFORMANCE ONLY)

OIL COOLER BY-PASS VALVE
(HI PERFORMANCE ONLY)
(OIL FILTER BY-PASS VALVE)

VALVE MECHANISM OILING   **OIL FILTER AND DISTRIBUTOR OILING**

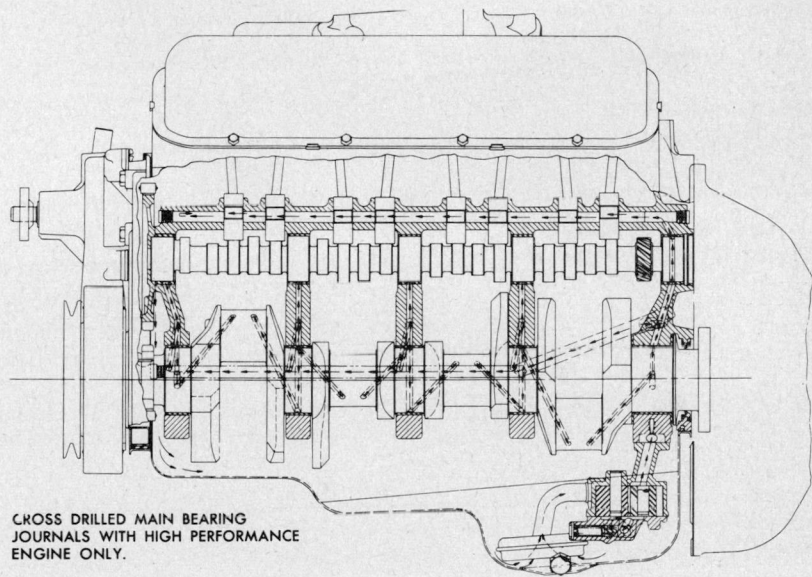

CROSS DRILLED MAIN BEARING
JOURNALS WITH HIGH PERFORMANCE
ENGINE ONLY.

CRANKCASE AND CRANKSHAFT OILING

Mark IV V8 lubrication (© G.M. Corp.)

remove the left engine mount for clearance. Lower pan.

1965-68 Chevelle, 1969 Chevelle with Standard Transmission

1. Remove engine from car.
2. Place engine on stands, supported at each front mount and at transmission extension.

Caution As a safety precaution, leave engine lift attached and most of the weight supported from above.

3. On cars equipped with automatic transmission, remove converter housing underpan.
4. Remove starter, then the oil pan.

1969 Chevelle with Automatic Transmission, 1970-72 Chevelle

1. Disconnect battery ground cable.
2. Remove radiator upper mounting panel. Place a piece of heavy cardboard between fan and radiator.
3. Remove starter. Disconnect fuel line.
4. Drain engine oil; disconnect brake line from front crossmember.
5. Remove converter housing underpan and splash shield.
6. Rotate crankshaft until timing mark on torsional damper is at 6:00 o'clock position.
7. Remove front engine mount through bolts.
8. Raise engine approximately

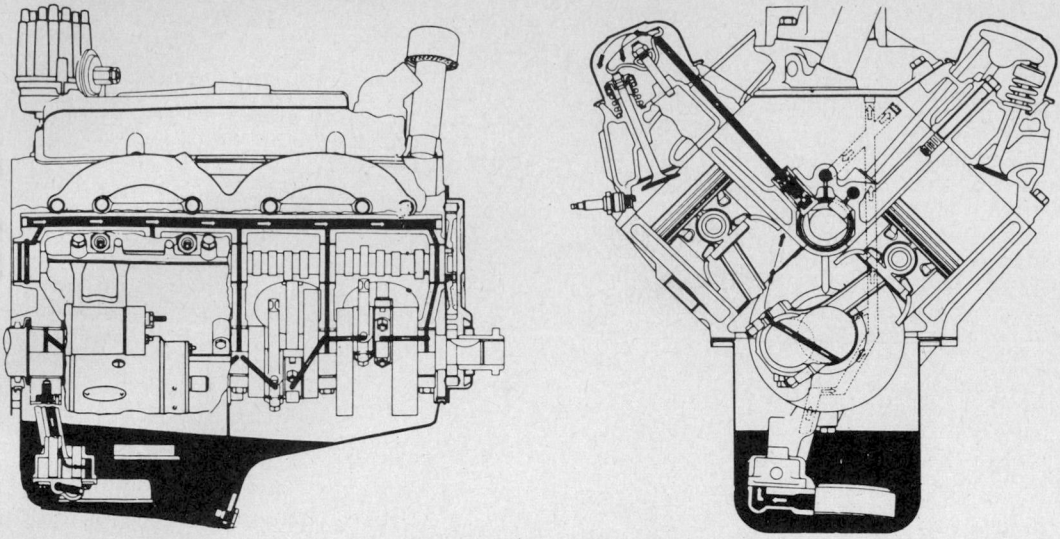

Oil passage diagram, small V8 engine (© G.M. Corp.)

three inches, remove engine mounts, and lower oil pan.

Oil Pan Removal—V8 Engines

1965-67 Chevy II

1. Disconnect battery ground cable.
2. Drain engine oil.
3. Disconnect and remove starter.
4. Disconnect steering idler arm bracket at right frame rail. Swing linkage down for clearance.
5. Disconnect exhaust pipes at manifolds.
6. Remove oil pan.

1965-68 Chevelle

This procedure is the same as that for 1965-68 Chevelle models with in-line engines.

1967-69 Camaro, 1968-72 Nova, 1969-72 Chevelle, 1970-72 Monte Carlo

1. Disconnect battery ground cable.
2. Remove distributor cap.
3. Remove radiator upper mounting panel.
4. Remove fan. On Mark IV engine models, place a piece of heavy cardboard between the radiator and fan.
5. Drain engine oil.
6. Disconnect exhaust or crossover pipes.
7. Remove converter housing underpan and splash shield.
8. On all except 1970-72 Chevelle, disconnect steering idler lever at the frame. Swing linkage down.
9. Rotate crankshaft until timing mark on torsional damper is at 6:00 o'clock position.
10. Remove starter.
11. On small V8, remove fuel pump.
12. Remove front engine mount through bolts.
13. Raise engine and insert blocks under engine mounts. Block thickness should be 2 in. for Nova and Camaro, and 3 in. for Chevelle.
14. Remove oil pan.

1969 Chevelle with 396 Engine or Manual Transmission, 1970-72 Chevelle 396, 454

1. Disconnect battery ground cable.
2. Remove:
   a. air cleaner
   b. dipstick
   c. distributor cap

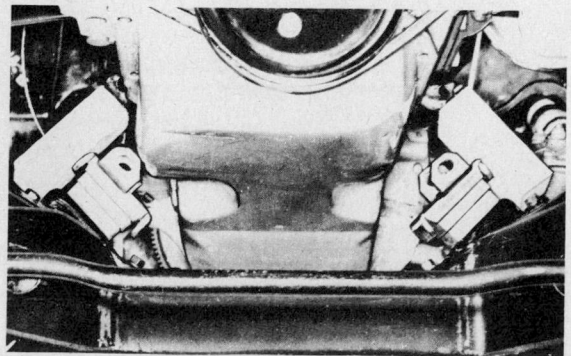

Installing blocks for oil pan removal—V8
(© Chev. Div. G.M. Corp.)

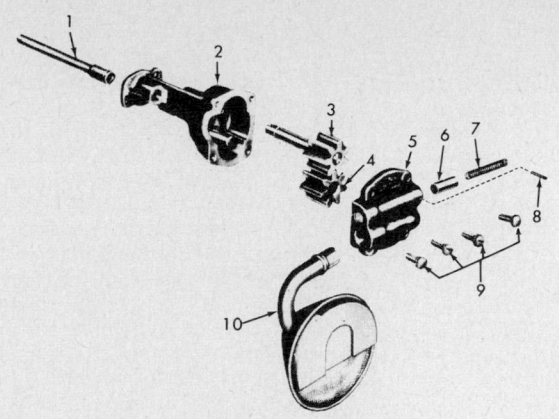

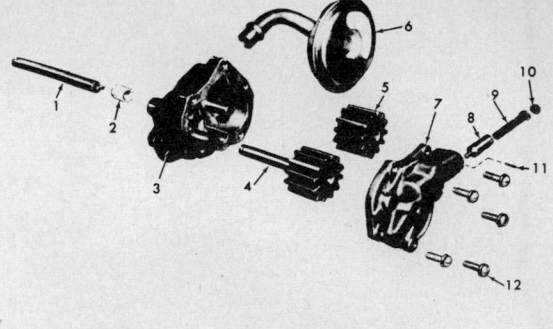

Oil pump—small block V8
(© Chev. Div. G.M. Corp.)

1 Shaft extension
2 Pump body
3 Drive gear and shaft
4 Idler gear
5 Pump cover
6 Pressure regulator valve
7 Pressure regulator spring
8 Retaining pin
9 Screws
10 Pickup screen and pipe

Oil pump—Mark IV V8
(© Chev. Div. G.M. Corp.)

1 Shaft extension
2 Shaft coupling
3 Pump body
4 Drive gear and shaft
5 Idler gear
6 Pickup screen and pipe
7 Pump cover
8 Pressure regulator valve
9 Pressure regulator spring
10 Washer
11 Retaining pin
12 Screws

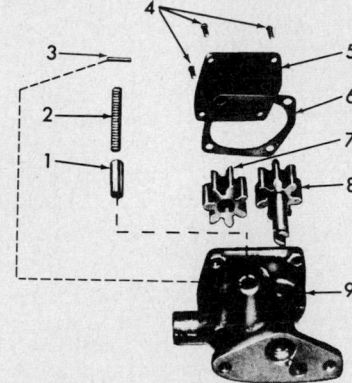

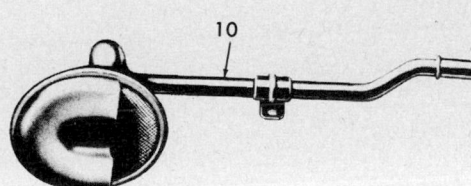

Oil pump—L6 engine (© Chev. Div. G.M. Corp.)

1 Pressure regulator valve
2 Pressure regulator spring
3 Retaining pin
4 Screws
5 Pump cover
6 Cover gasket
7 Idler gear
8 Drive gear and shaft
9 Pump body
10 Pickup screen and pipe

up engine. Move crossmember rearward.

13. Remove crossover or disconnect dual exhaust pipes.
14. Remove:
    a. flywheel housing cover
    b. transmission
    c. flywheel housing and throw-out bearing (manual transmission)
    d. front engine mount through bolts.
15. Raise rear of engine approximately 4 inches. Support engine by hoist.
16. Raise front of engine approximately 4 inches and insert 2 in. blocks under front engine mounts.
17. Rotate crankshaft until timing mark on torsional damper is at 6:00 o'clock position.
18. Unbolt and remove oil pan.

Oil Pump R & R

1. Remove oil pan.
2. Remove pump and pickup tube and screen assembly.
3. To install, reverse removal procedure.

Oil Pump Disassembly and Inspection

1. Remove pump cover screws, pump cover, and, on inline engines, gasket.
2. Remove idler and drive gears from pump body, after match-marking gears.
3. Remove pressure regulator valve retaining pin, pressure valve and related parts.
4. If pickup screen and tube needs to be replaced, mount pump in vise and extract old tube with pliers. This unit is serviced as an assembly.
5. Wash all parts in solvent and dry with compressed air.

d. radiator shroud and upper mounting panel.
3. On 396 models, place a piece of heavy cardboard between radiator and fan.
4. Disconnect engine ground straps. Remove fuel pump on 307 and 350 engines.
5. Disconnect accelerator control cable.
6. Drain oil. Remove filter on 307 and 350 engines.
7. Remove driveshaft and plug

rear of transmission.
8. Remove starter.
9. Disconnect transmission linkage at transmission or remove floor-shift lever.
10. Disconnect speedometer cable and back-up switch connector.
11. On manual transmission vehicles disconnect clutch cordon shaft at frame. On automatic transmission vehicles, disconnect cooler lines, detent cable, rod or switch wire, and modulator pipe.
12. Remove crossmember bolts. Jack

6. Inspect pump cover and housing for cracks or excessive wear.
7. Inspect gears for damage or excessive wear; check shaft for looseness in pump housing.
8. Check that pressure regulator valve fits properly without binding.
9. If any component parts are damaged, other than tube and screen, pump must be replaced as a unit.
10. To assemble, reverse disassembly procedure. Pack pump housing with petroleum jelly before installing cover.

Connecting Rods and Pistons

Removal

1. Drain crankcase and remove oil pan.
2. Drain cooling system and remove cylinder heads.
3. Remove any ridge or deposits from the upper end of cylinder bores with a ridge reamer.
4. Check rods and pistons for identification numbers and, if necessary, number them.
5. Remove connecting rod cap nuts and caps. Push the rods away from the crankshaft and install caps and nuts loosely to their respective rods.
6. Push piston and rod assemblies up and out of the cylinders.

Piston Ring Installation

1. Before replacing rings, inspect cylinder bores. If cylinder bore is in satisfactory condition, place each ring in its bore in turn and square it in bore with head of piston. Measure ring end gap. If gap is greater than limit, get new ring. If gap is less than limit, file end of ring to obtain correct gap.

Ring End Gap

	Compression Rings (in.)	Oil Rings (in.)
all inline engines, 283, 307, 350, 400, 454	.010-.020	.015-.055
302, 327	.013-.025	.015-.055
396, 427	.010-.030	.010-.030

2. Check ring side clearance by installing rings on piston, and inserting feeler gauge of correct dimension between ring and lower land. Gauge should slide freely around ring circumference without binding. Any wear will form a step on lower land.

Replace any pistons having high steps. Before checking ring side clearance be sure ring grooves are clean and free of carbon, sludge, or grit.

3. Space ring gaps at equal intervals around piston circumference. Be sure to install piston in its original bore. Install piston and rod assembly with connecting rod bearing tang slots on the side opposite the camshaft on V8 engines. Inline engine pistons must have the piston notch facing the front of the engine. Install short lengths of rubber tubing over connecting rod bolts to prevent damage to the rod journals. Install ring compressor over rings on piston. Lower piston and rod assembly into bore until ring compressor contacts block. Using wooden handle of hammer push piston into bore while guiding rod onto journal.

Ring Side Clearance

	Top Ring (in.)	Second Ring (in.)	Oil Ring (in.)
all inline engines, 283, 307, 400 (265 hp), 302, 327 (210, 250, 275 hp)	.0012-.0027	.0012-.0032	.000-.005
350 (215, 250 hp)	.0012-.0032	.0012-.0032	.002-.007
350 (300, 350, 370 hp), 327 (300, 325, 350 hp)	.0012-.0032	.0012-.0027	.000-.005
400 (330 hp), 454, 396, 427	.0017-.0032	.0017-.0032	.005-.0065

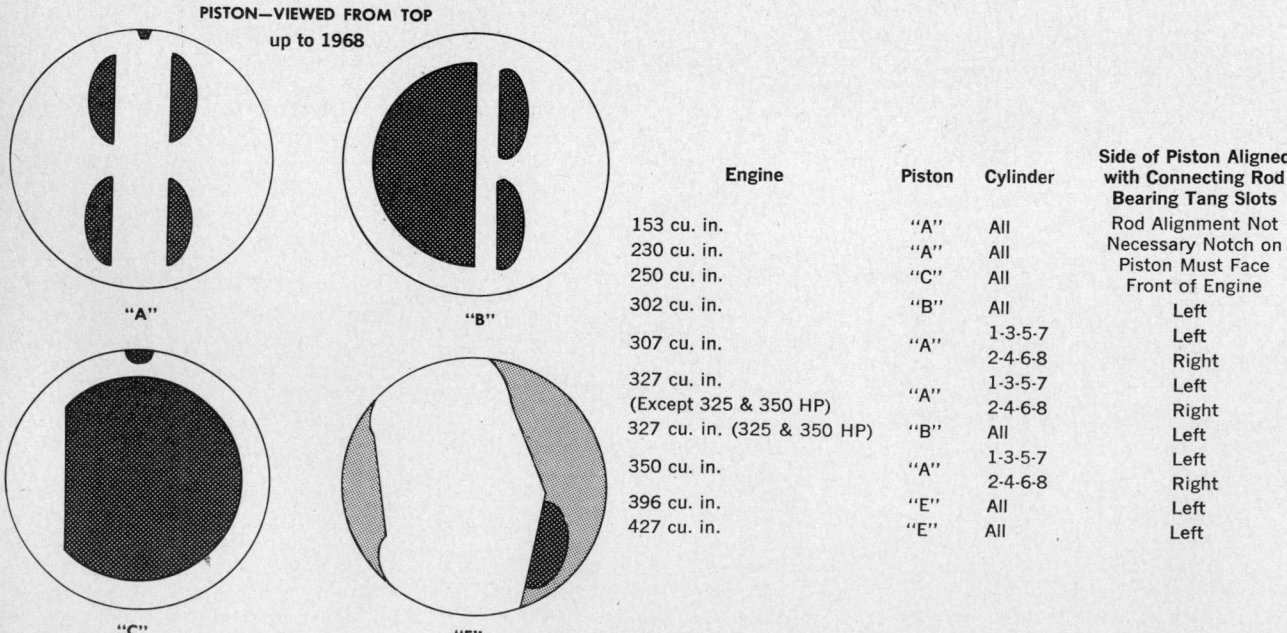

PISTON—VIEWED FROM TOP
up to 1968

Engine	Piston	Cylinder	Side of Piston Aligned with Connecting Rod Bearing Tang Slots
153 cu. in.	"A"	All	Rod Alignment Not Necessary Notch on Piston Must Face Front of Engine
230 cu. in.	"A"	All	
250 cu. in.	"C"	All	
302 cu. in.	"B"	All	Left
307 cu. in.	"A"	1-3-5-7	Left
		2-4-6-8	Right
327 cu. in. (Except 325 & 350 HP)	"A"	1-3-5-7	Left
		2-4-6-8	Right
327 cu. in. (325 & 350 HP)	"B"	All	Left
350 cu. in.	"A"	1-3-5-7	Left
		2-4-6-8	Right
396 cu. in.	"E"	All	Left
427 cu. in.	"E"	All	Left

Connecting rod—piston relationship
(© Chevrolet Div. G.M. Corp.)

PISTON—VIEWED FROM TOP
1969-70

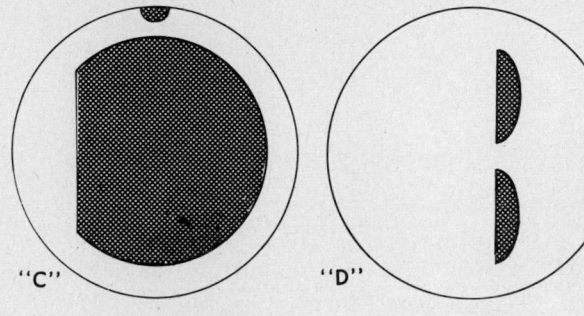

"A"   "B"

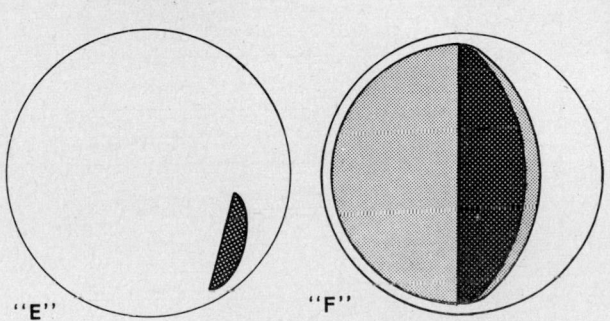

"C"   "D"

"E"   "F"

Engine	Piston	Cylinder	Side of Piston Aligned with Connecting Rod Bearing Tangs
153 cu. in.	"A"	All	Rod alignment not
230 cu. in.	"A"	All	necessary—notch on
250 cu. in.	"C"	All	piston must face
292 cu. in.	"C"	All	front of engine.
302 cu. in.	"F"	All	Left
307 cu. in.			
350 cu. in.		1-3-5-7	Left
(215 H.P. truck, 250 &	"A"	2-4-6-8	Right
300 HP. passenger)			
400 cu. in. (265 HP.)			
350 cu. in.			
(255 HP. truck)	"D"	All	Left
350 cu. in.			
(350 & 370 HP. passenger)	"F"	All	Left
366 cu. in.	"E"	All	Left
396 cu. in.	"B"	All	Left
400 cu. in.			
427 cu. in. (truck)	"E"	All	Left
427 cu. in. (passenger)	"B"	All	Left
454 cu. in.	"B"	All	Left

Connecting rod—piston relationship

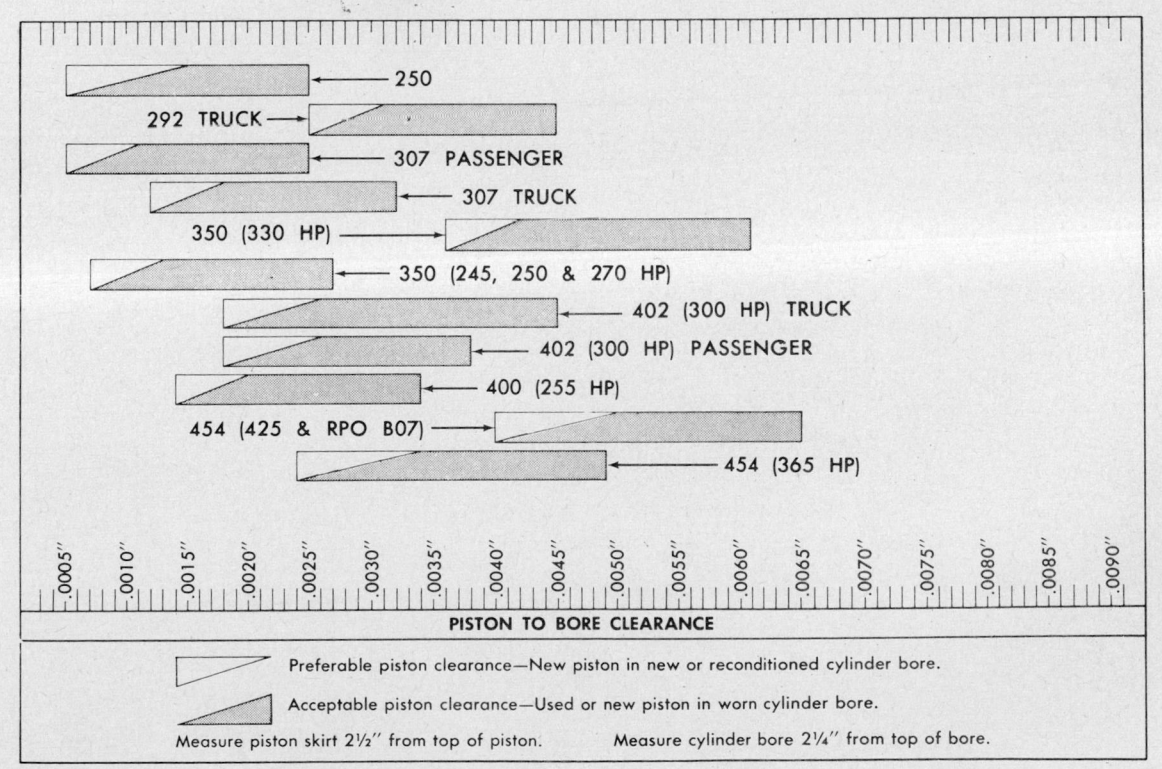

250
292 TRUCK →
307 PASSENGER
← 307 TRUCK
350 (330 HP) →
350 (245, 250 & 270 HP)
← 402 (300 HP) TRUCK
← 402 (300 HP) PASSENGER
← 400 (255 HP)
454 (425 & RPO B07) →
← 454 (365 HP)

.0005" .0010" .0015" .0020" .0025" .0030" .0035" .0040" .0045" .0050" .0055" .0060" .0065" .0070" .0075" .0080" .0085" .0090"

PISTON TO BORE CLEARANCE

Preferable piston clearance—New piston in new or reconditioned cylinder bore.

Acceptable piston clearance—Used or new piston in worn cylinder bore.

Measure piston skirt 2½" from top of piston.   Measure cylinder bore 2¼" from top of bore.

Piston-to-cylinder wall clearance—1971-72 (© Chev. Div. G.M. Corp.)

PISTON—VIEWED FROM TOP

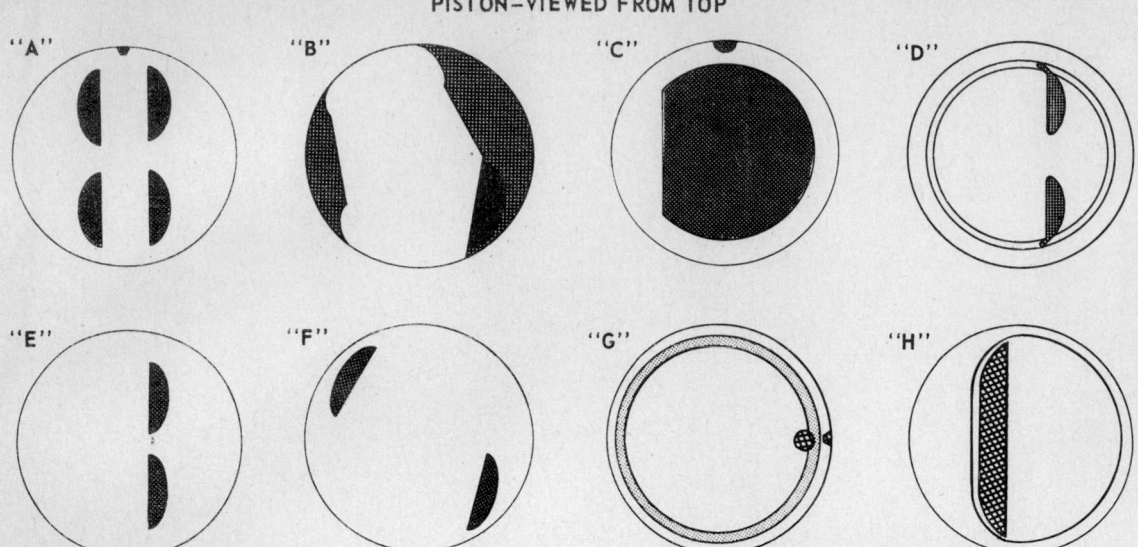

ENGINE	PISTON	CYLINDER	SIDE OF PISTON ALIGNED WITH CONNECTING ROD BEARING TANGS
250 CU. IN.	"C"	ALL	ALIGNMENT NOT NECESSARY NOTCH ON PISTON TOWARD FRONT OF ENGINE
292 CU. IN.			
307 CU. IN.	"A"	1-3-5-7	LEFT
		2-4-6-8	RIGHT
350 CU. IN. (215 HP.)	"D"	1-3-5-7	LEFT
		2-4-6-8	RIGHT
350 CU. IN. (245 HP.)			
350 CU. IN. (250 HP.)	"G"	1-3-5-7	LEFT
350 CU. IN. (270 HP.)		2-4 6-8	RIGHT
350 CU. IN. (330 HP.)	"H"	1-3-5-7	LEFT
		2-4-6-8	RIGHT
350 TRUCK (LPG)	"E"	1-3-5-7	LEFT
		2-4-6-8	RIGHT
400 CU. IN. (255 HP.)	"G"	1-3-5-7	LEFT
		2-4-6-8	RIGHT
402 CU. IN. (300 HP.)	"B"	1-3-5-7	LEFT
		2-4-6-8	RIGHT
454 CU. IN. (365 HP.)	"F"	1-3-5-7	LEFT
		2-4-6-8	RIGHT
454 CU. IN. (425 HP.)	"B"	1-3-5-7	LEFT
		2-4-6-8	RIGHT

Piston-to-connecting rod relationship—1971-72 (© Chev. Div. G.M. Corp.)

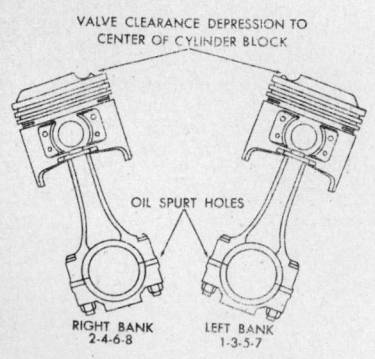

Piston and rod assembly—Mk. IV V8

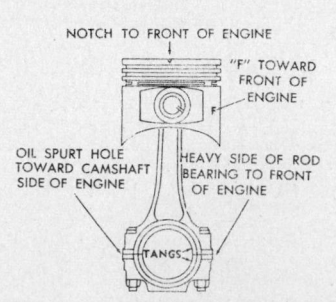

Piston and rod assembly, 4 and 6 cylinder

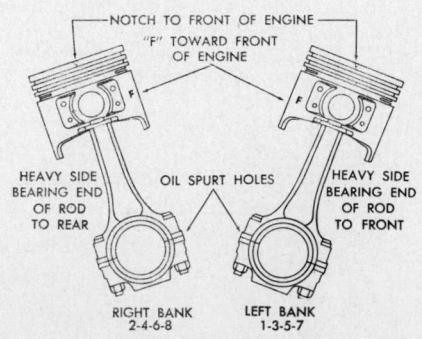

Piston and rod assembly—small block V8

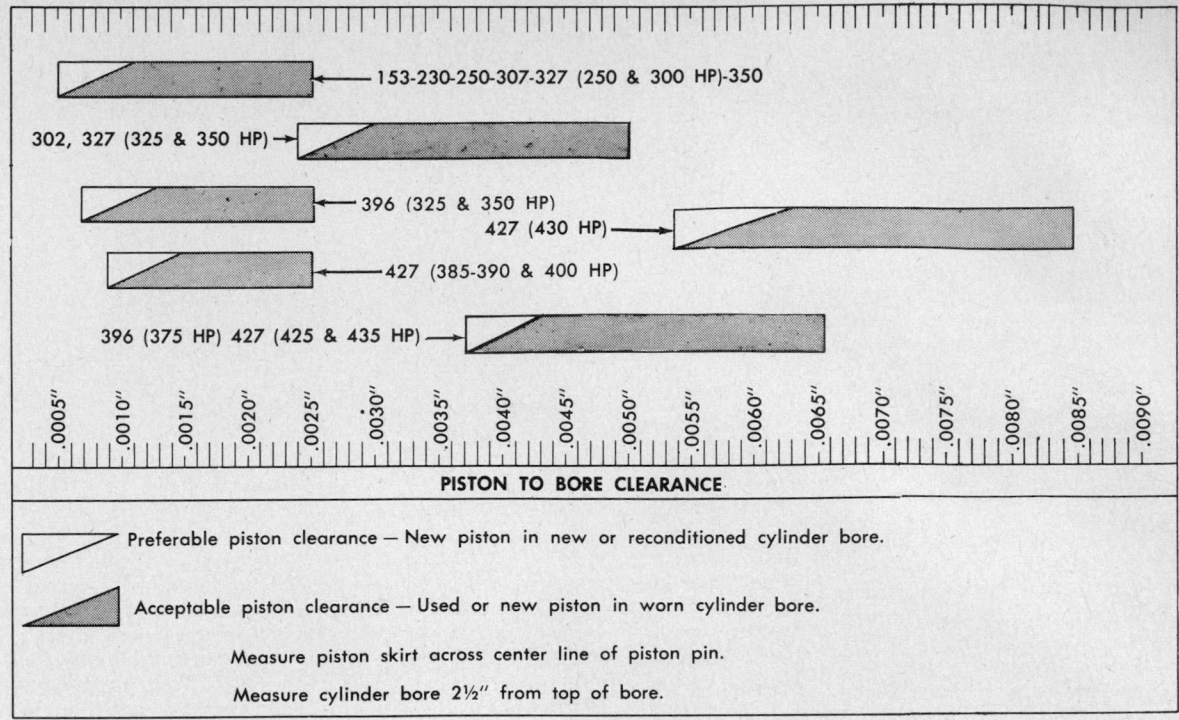

Piston—bore clearance, up to 1968 (© Chevrolet Div. G.M. Corp.)

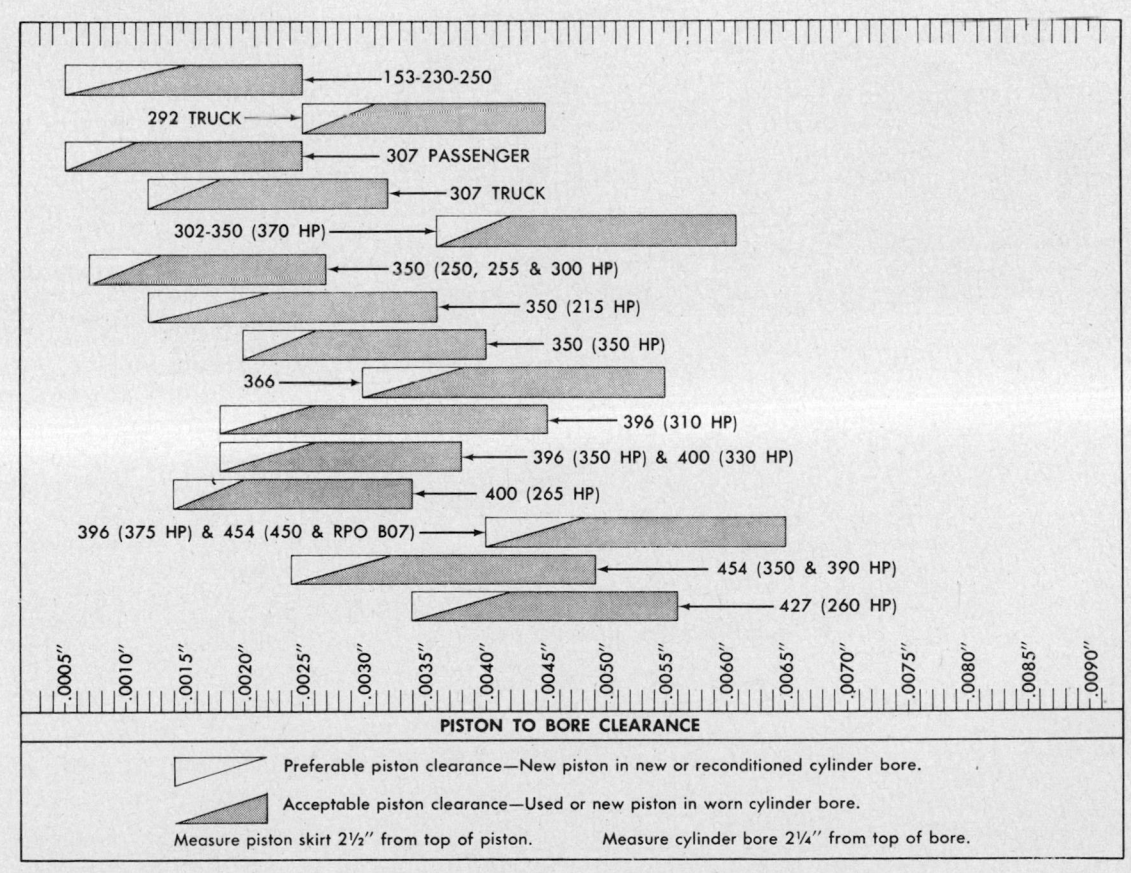

Piston—bore clearance, 1969-70 (© Chevrolet Div. G.M. Corp.)

Front Suspension

1965-67 Chevy II

Front suspension is an independent coil-spring, ball-joint-type with rubber bushed, pivoting upper and lower control arms. The coil springs are positioned at their lower ends on a pivoting spring seat bolted to the upper control arm. The upper end of the spring extends into spring towers formed in the front end sheet metal. Direct, double-acting shock absorbers are located inside the coil springs and are attached to the lower coil spring seat and to the upper bracket, accessible from the engine compartment.

Each lower control arm has a strut rod running diagonally forward to a brace attached between frame and radiator support. This strut rod provides for caster angle adjustment. Camber angle is adjusted by means of a cam-shaped lower control arm inner pivot bolt. A stabilizer rod, on station

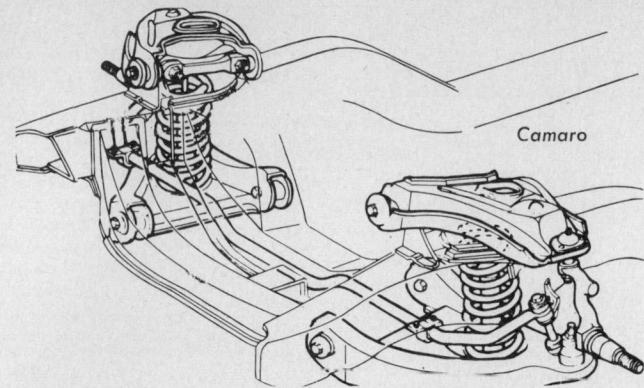

Front suspension—Nova 1968-70 Camaro to 1969
(© Chevrolet Div., G.M. Corp.)

of upper control arm inner support shaft shims.

Caster angle is adjusted by means of upper control arm inner support shaft shims.

Periodic maintenance of the front suspension includes lubrication of the four ball joints, spring seat lower pivot shafts and adjustment and lubrication of the front wheel bearings.

Further data on front end alignment can be obtained from the Front Wheel Alignment chart and from the Unit Repair Section.

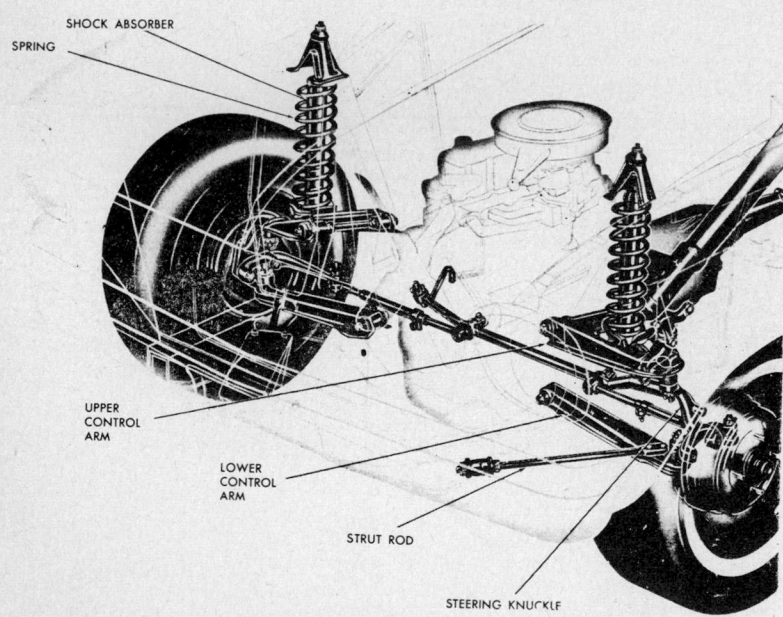

Front suspension, 1965-67 Chevy II (© G.M. Corp.)

wagons, connects the two lower control arms and is rubber mounted to the front crossmember. Front wheel bearings are tapered roller bearings.

Chevelle, Nova, Camaro and Monte Carlo

In these models, the springs ride on the lower control arms. Ball joints connect the upper and lower arms to the steering knuckle. Tapered roller wheel bearings are used.

Camber angle is adjusted by means

Coil Spring Replacement

1965-67 Chevy II—Coil Spring Removal

1. Raise car and remove wheel.
2. Support lower control arm with adjustable jackstand and raise slightly from full rebound position.
3. Remove shock absorber.
4. Insert spring compressor into upper spring tower so that lower U-bolt fits into shock absorber

mounting holes in spring seat. Secure the two lower studs to the spring seat with nuts.
5. Fit tool upper pilot to top of spring and compress the spring by tightening the upper nut. Compress spring until the screw is bottomed out.
6. Remove lower spring seat retaining nuts, lift spring and seat assembly from control arm and guide it down and out through fender skirt.

1965-67 Chevy II— Coil Spring Installation

1. Install new spring into tool and compress spring until screw is bottomed out.

NOTE: spring coil ends must be against spring stops in upper and lower seats.

2. Lift spring and tool assembly into place and position so that the upper spring stop is inboard.
3. Install lower spring seat to the control arm. Torque the nuts to 25-35 ft. lbs.
4. Loosen spring compressor until spring is properly seated in upper spring tower and remove the tool.
5. Install shock absorber.
6. Remove adjustable jackstand and install wheel and tire. Lower car to the floor.

Coil Spring R & R—1965-72 Chevelle, 1968-72 Nova, 1967-72 Camaro, 1970-72 Monte Carlo

1. Hold the shock absorber upper stem from turning, then disconnect the shock absorber at the top.
2. Support the car by the frame, so the control arms hang free, remove wheel assembly (replace one wheel nut to hold the brake drum) shock absorber, and stabilizer bar to lower control arm link.
3. Place a steel bar through the shock absorber mounting hole in the lower control arm so that the notch seats over the bottom spring coil and the bar extends

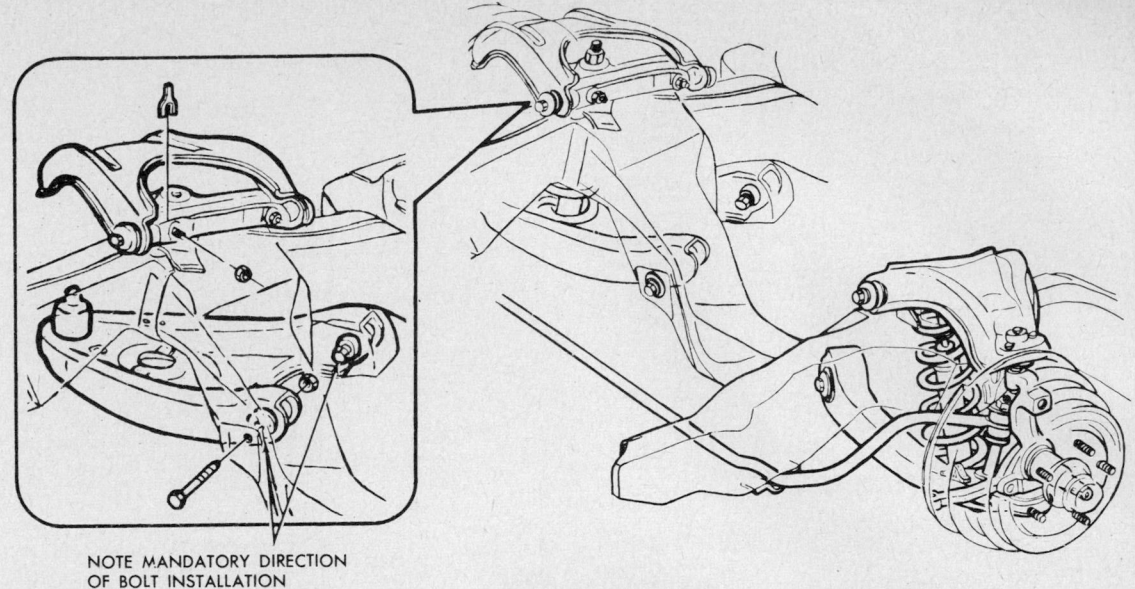

NOTE MANDATORY DIRECTION
OF BOLT INSTALLATION

Front suspension—Chevelle and Monte Carlo 1964-72 (ⓒ Chev. Div. G.M. Corp.

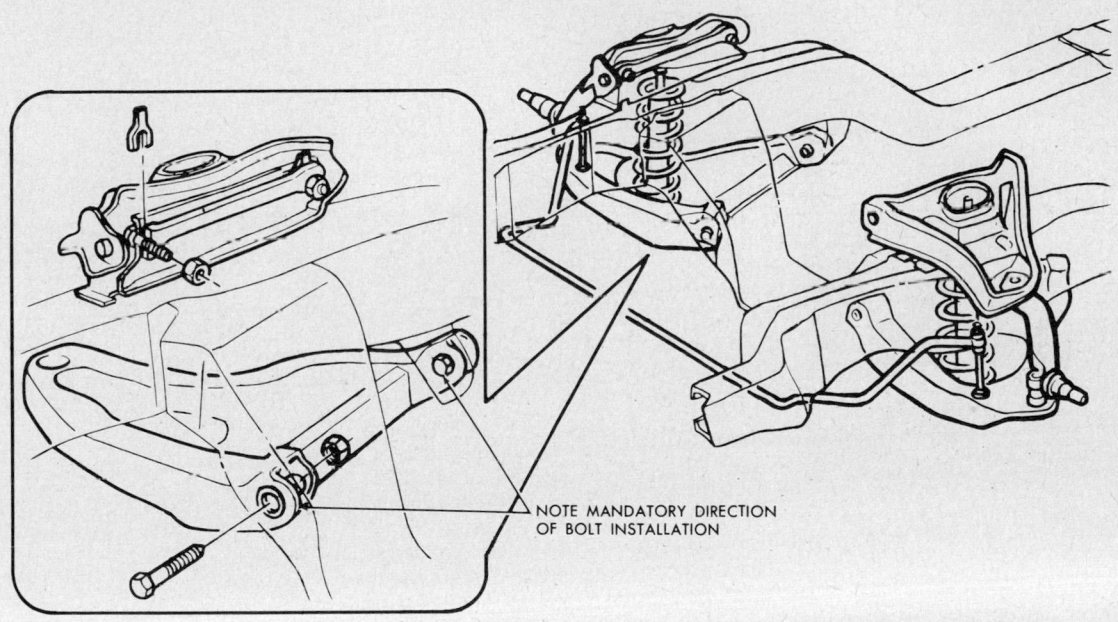

NOTE MANDATORY DIRECTION
OF BOLT INSTALLATION

Front suspension—Camaro 1970-72 (ⓒ Chev. Div. G.M. Corp.)

outboard beyond the end of the control arm and slightly toward the front of the car.

4. With a suitable jack, raise the end of the bar.

5. Remove lower ball stud cotter pin and nut, then remove the ball stud from the knuckle.

NOTE: place a chain around spring and through lower arm for safety.

6. Lower the jack supporting the steel bar and control arm until the spring can be removed.

7. Install by reversing removal procedure.

Jacking, Hoisting

1. Jack car at front spring seat of lower control arm. Jack car at rear axle housing except when equipped with rear stabilizer bar. On these models, jack at frame rails.

2. To lift at frame, use side rails in front of body floor pan and at rear corner at squared off corner of box ahead of rear wheel.

Steering Gear

Manual Steering Gear

Recirculating ball type gear is used on General Motors cars. Adjustment procedures are found in the Unit Repair Section.

Steering Gear R & R 1965-66 Chevy II

1. Remove pitman arm retaining nut. (Place an index mark on

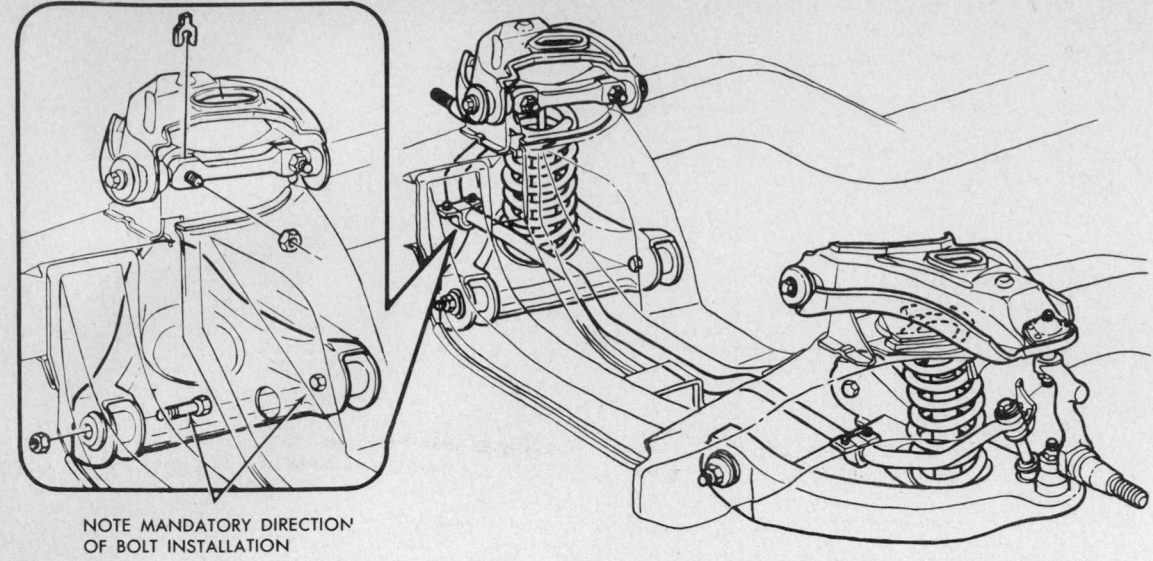

NOTE MANDATORY DIRECTION
OF BOLT INSTALLATION

Front suspension—Nova 1971-72 (© Chev. Div. G.M. Corp.)

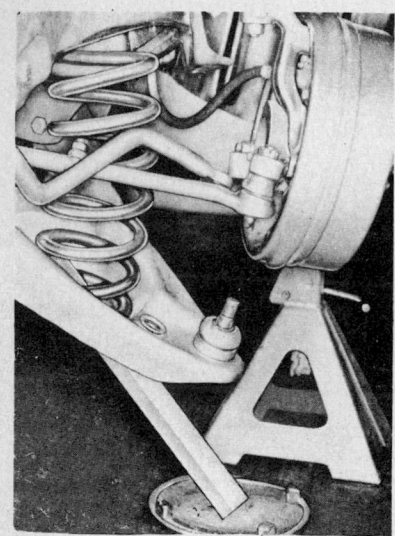

Front spring removal
(© Chevrolet Div. G.M. Corp.)

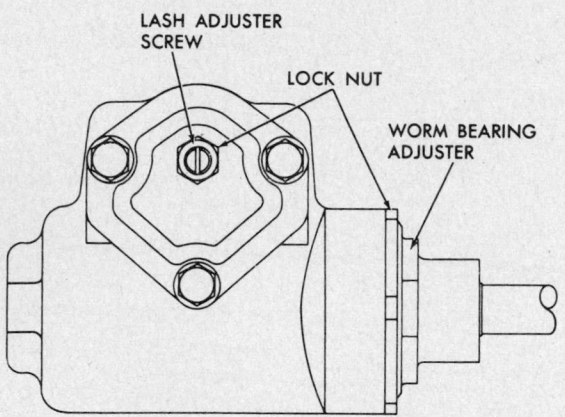

LASH ADJUSTER
SCREW

LOCK NUT

WORM BEARING
ADJUSTER

1967-70 Steering gear adjusting points
(© Chevrolet Div. G.M. Corp.)

pitman arm and sector shaft so that the two parts can be reassembled in the same register.)

2. Remove pitman arm from sector shaft.

3. Disconnect transmission linkage from shift lever (S).

4. Remove the two lower steering gear-to-frame mounting bolts.

5. Disconnect external electrical wires from horn junction, directional switch and back-up lamp switch (if so equipped).

6. Remove steering wheel.

7. Remove screws holding mast jacket hole seal to toe panel.

8. Remove mast jacket-to-steering gear clamp on cars equipped with automatic transmission.

9. Remove nuts from mast jacket-to-dash brace clamp.

10. Move mast jacket and steering gear assembly downward and away from dash, pivoting on remaining steering gear mounting bolt. Move front seat to the rear as far as possible. Pull steering and mast jacket toward you, rotating it so that shift levers will pass through the toe pan opening.

11. Reverse above procedure for installing.

All Models Except 1965-66 Chevy II

NOTE: on 1965-67 Chevelle, remove stabilizer to frame mounting brackets. Unbolt left front bumper bracket and brace from frame after marking location.

1. Disconnect steering shaft coupling.

2. Remove pitman arm with puller after marking relationship to shaft.

3. Remove bolts to frame. Remove steering gear.

4. Reverse procedure to install.

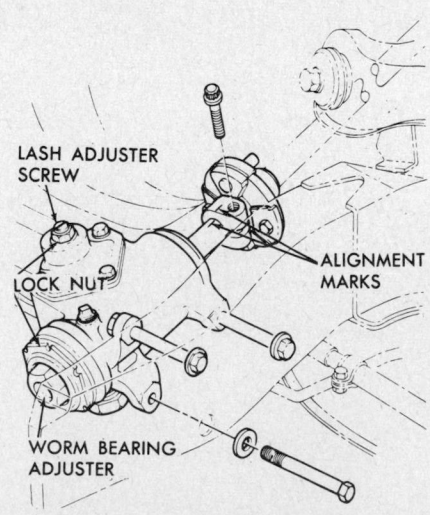

LASH ADJUSTER
SCREW

LOCK NUT

ALIGNMENT
MARKS

WORM BEARING
ADJUSTER

**Steering gear adjusting points,
1965-67 models**
(© Chevrolet Div., G.M. Corp.)

Power Steering Gear

Two types of power steering are used. The 1965-67 Chevy II uses the linkage assist type of gear with a pump delivering an assist to a power cylinder attached to the steering linkage.

All other models use an integral type of power steering gear. A pump delivers hydraulic pressure through two hoses to the steering gear itself.

Detailed service coverage is found in the Unit Repair Section.

Steering Column

Removal—1968

1. Disconnect wiring harness at column.
2. Disconnect neutral start and back-up light switch connections.
3. Remove steering wheel.
4. Remove nuts and washers that secure steering shaft to gear box.
5. Disconnect transmission linkage (column) at shift tube levers.
6. On Chevelle models: remove screws that secure mast jacket trim cover to instrument panel; remove trim cover.
7. Remove screws that hold upper and lower covers together; remove covers.
8. a. On Chevelle: remove screws that secure cover trim to dash panel, remove cover trim, then separate and remove inner and outer covers.
   b. On Camaro and Chevy II: fold grommet back on column, remove screws that hold upper and lower covers together, then remove covers from dash panel.
9. Support column and carefully remove screws, nuts and bolts that secure instrument panel mounting bracket to underside of panel. Remove wedge shims and save for installation.
10. Move back front seat as far as possible, then carefully lower steering column. Column cannot safely support its own weight without bending.

Installation—1968

1. Raise column into position and install wedge shims and bracket. Loosely install bracket bolts.
2. Secure flanged end of steering shaft to lower coupling.
3. Tighten instrument panel mounting bracket bolts and nuts to 30 ft. lbs.
4. On Chevelle: place mast jacket trim cover in position and secure.
5. Tighten shift indicator pointer setscrew.
6. a. On Chevelle: secure seal, inner and outer covers to

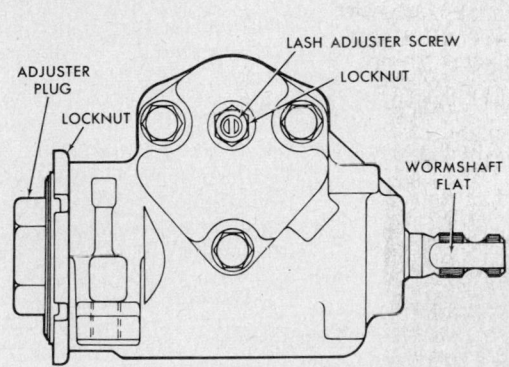

Steering gear adjustment points—1971-72
(© Chev. Div. G.M. Corp.)

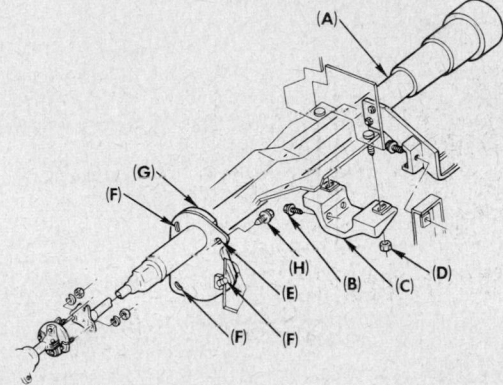

Steering column mounting—Camaro 1969-72
(© Chev. Div. G.M. Corp.)

D. 20 ft. lbs.
H. 35 in. lbs.

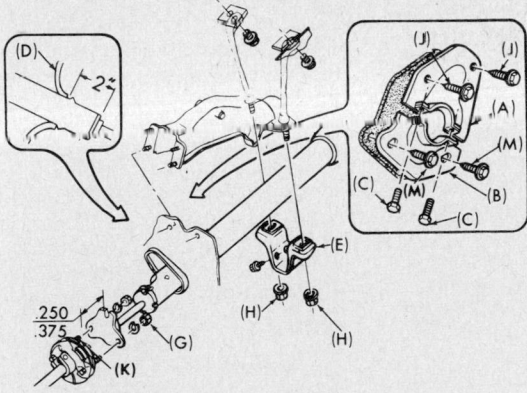

Steering column mounting—Nova 1969-72
(© Chev. Div. G.M. Corp.)

G. 20 ft. lbs.
H. 15 ft. lbs.
C. 35 in. lbs.
M. 35 in. lbs.
J. 35 in. lbs.

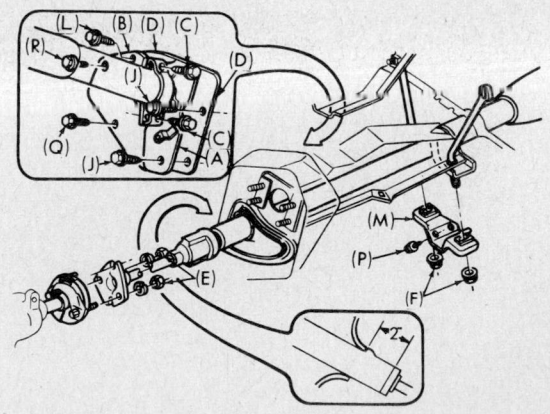

Steering column mounting—
Chevelle and Monte Carlo 1969-72
(© Chev. Div. G.M. Corp.)

E. 20 ft. lbs.
C. 35 in. lbs.
J,Q,R,L. 35 in. lbs.
F. 15 ft. lbs.

dash panel, fasten both covers together, and install trim cover.

b. On Camaro and Chevy II: secure seal, upper and lower covers to dash panel, fasten both covers together, and fold rubber boot against dash panel.

7. Connect transmission shift linkage, if removed.
8. Install steering wheel.
9. Connect column wiring harness plugs, then check back-up and neutral start switch adjustment.
10. Check that steering wheel is centered and that steering is properly adjusted.

Removal—1969-72

1. Disconnect battery ground cable.
2. Remove steering wheel.
3. Remove nuts and washers that secure flanged end of steering shaft to coupling.
4. Disconnect transmission shift linkage, or back drive linkage (floorshift), from shift tube levers.
5. Disconnect column wiring harness at connector. Disconnect neutral start switch and back-up light switch connectors.
6. Remove floor pan trim cover screws and cover.
7. a. On Chevelle, 1969 Camaro, Nova and Monte Carlo: remove the screws that secure the two halves of the floor pan cover; remove two halves and seal.
   b. On Camaro starting 1970: remove column plate to floor pan screws.
8. a. On Chevelle, 1969 Camaro, Nova and Monte Carlo: remove instrument panel trim cover screws and cover.
   b. On Camaro starting 1970: remove ash tray assembly and six steering column panel-to-instrument panel screws. Carefully lower panel and heater (or A/C) controls.
9. Remove automatic transmission shift indicator cable.
10. Move back front seat as far as possible.
11. Remove the two column bracket-to-instrument panel nuts and carefully lower the steering column.

Caution Any sharp blows to column will bend it. Column also cannot support its own weight.

Installation—1969-72

Chevelle, 116 in. Wheelbase Station Wagon, and Monte Carlo

1. Loosely assemble inner (A) and outer (B) dash covers to column

with two screws (C). Dash covers must be able to slide on column.
2. Glue cover seal (D) to outer cover (B).
3. Position rolled portion of dash seal (part of column assembly) at column lower reaction tab, 2 in. from bottom of jacket.
   NOTE: rolled portion of seal must be directed down column toward front of car and must remain in this position during and after column installation.
4. Position column in vehicle, install all electrical connections and position flange to joint and install lockwashers and nuts (E).
5. Loosely assemble nuts (F) to brace rods.
6. Position outer cover to dash and start screw (Q).
7. Install screw (L) and tighten to specified torque. Tighten screw (Q) to specified torque and install and tighten screw (R) to specified torque.
8. Tighten two clamp screws (C) to specified torque.
9. Install two inner cover screws (J) and tighten to specified torque.
10. Tighten two nuts (F) to specified torque.
11. Install the transmission indicator cable on column automatics.
12. Install the instrument panel trim cover.
13. Connect the transmission control linkage at the shift tube levers.
14. Install the steering wheel.
15. Connect the battery ground cable.
16. The following minimum clearances must be met:
    a. Upper control arm shaft to steering shaft—0.12 in.
    b. Engine to pot joint—0.37 in.
    c. Clutch linkage to pot joint—0.75 in.

Nova

1. Install upper (A) and lower (B) steering column to dash covers on column and tighten two screws (C) so that cover assembly is snug on column but still will move with respect to column.
2. Glue seal (D) (part of the column assembly) to upper (A) and lower cover (B).
3. Position rolled portion of dash panel seal (part of column assembly) at the column lower reaction tab 2 in. from bottom of jacket.
   NOTE: rolled portion of seal must be directed down column toward front of car and must remain in this position during and after column installation.

4. Position column in car, install all electrical connections and loosely install nuts (H).
5. Attach steering shaft flange to rag joint and tighten nuts (G) to specified torque.

Caution Do not tighten column to instrument panel unless vehicle is supported on its wheels or suspension.

6. Tighten two rearward mast jacket bracket nuts (H) to specified torque while holding joint to flange clearance dimension shown.
   NOTE: for remaining steps, upper cover (A) and lower cover (B) must move to established position of column which has been determined by joint and I.P. attachment.
7. Push upper (A) and lower (B) cover assembly to dash and line up all covers to dash attaching holes.
   NOTE: do not permit rolled section of seal (D) to reverse itself.
8. Holding both upper and lower cover assemblies against dash and column, install and tighten two screws (M) to the specified torque.
9. Tighten two screws (C) to specified torque.
10. Loosen two screws (M).
11. Tighten two screws (M) to specified torque.
12. Tighten two screws (J) to specified torque.
13. Remove plastic spacers (K) from flexible coupling pins.

Caution The alignment between the steering shaft and the steering gear must be such that a .04 in. gap (4-ply coupling) or a .07 in. gap (7-ply coupling) is maintained between the coupling rivets and the steering shaft flange with the steering shaft in straight ahead position and without torque on wheel. Less than .04 in. gap (4-ply) or .07 in. gap (7-ply) indicates that column must be realigned.

14. Install the transmission indicator cable on column automatics.
15. Install the instrument panel trim cover.
16. Connect the transmission control linkage.
17. Install the steering wheel.
18. Connect the battery ground cable.

Camaro

1. Position the column in the vehicle, install all electrical connections, position the shaft flange to flexible coupling and install the lockwashers and nuts (may be tightened to specified torque at any time).
2. Loosely assemble capsule nuts (D) to instrument panel studs.
3. Position plate (G) to floor pan and install screw (H) at (E)

net location and tighten to specified torque.

NOTE: align the column plate seal with the plate before tightening screw (H).

4. Tighten capsule nuts (D) to specified torque.
5. Install screws (H) at (F) slotted locations and tighten to specified torque.

NOTE: with the column installed, the following requirements must be met:

a. The flexible coupling must not be distorted due to the pot joint bottoming in either direction.
b. The steering wheel should be free to rotate from stop to stop (front wheels off the ground) with no lumpiness, stickiness or binding.
c. Steering column intermediate shaft to upper control arm forward bolt clearance must be .15 in. minimum.
d. If any of the above conditions exist, the column must be removed and checked for bent or damaged parts, incorrectly installed components or possible frame damage.
e. After correcting the complaint, repeat installation Steps 1-5.

6. Install the floor pan trim cover.
7. Install the steering column panel assembly to the instrument panel.
8. Install the ash tray.
9. Install the steering wheel.
10. Connect the transmission control linkage (back-drive linkage on floorshift models).
11. Connect the battery ground cable.

Clutch

A diaphragm type clutch assembly is used with all manual transmissions. A flat finger diaphragm clutch is used for normal service. V8 engines with four speed transmissions have a bent finger, centrifugal diaphragm clutch assembly. In this design the release fingers are bent back to gain a centrifugal boost and to insure quick re-engagement at high engine speeds. The centrifugal type clutch has the advantage of low pedal effort with high plate load. An optional heavy duty clutch assembly is used with some Mark IV engines. This unit is a dual plate bent finger diaphragm clutch.

The clutch release bearings used with the flat and bent finger diaphragms are not interchangeable. Using the flat finger release bearing with the bent finger clutch assembly

will result in slippage and rapid wear.

The only service adjustment necessary on the clutch is to maintain the correct pedal free play. Clutch pedal free play, or throwout bearing lash, decreases with driven disc wear.

Further information on clutches may be found in the Unit Repair Section.

Removal—1965-72

1. Support engine and remove transmission.
2. Disconnect clutch fork push rod and spring.
3. Remove flywheel housing.
4. Slide clutch fork from ball stud and remove fork from dust boot. Ball stud is threaded into clutch housing and may be replaced, if necessary.
5. Install an alignment tool to support the clutch assembly during removal. Mark flywheel and clutch cover for reinstallation, if they do not already have X marks.
6. Loosen clutch to flywheel attach-

ing bolts evenly, one turn at a time, until spring pressure is released. Remove bolts and clutch assembly.

Installation—1965-72

1. Clean pressure plate and flywheel face.
2. Support clutch disc and pressure plate with alignment tool. The driven disc is installed with the damper springs on the transmission side. The grease slinger is always on the transmission side.
3. Turn clutch assembly until mark on cover lines up with mark on flywheel, then install bolts. Tighten down evenly and gradually to avoid distortion.
4. Remove alignment tool.
5. Lubricate ball socket and fork fingers at release bearing end with high melting point grease. Lubricate recess on inside of throwout bearing and throwout fork groove with a light coat of graphite grease.
6. Install clutch fork and dust boot into housing. Install throwout

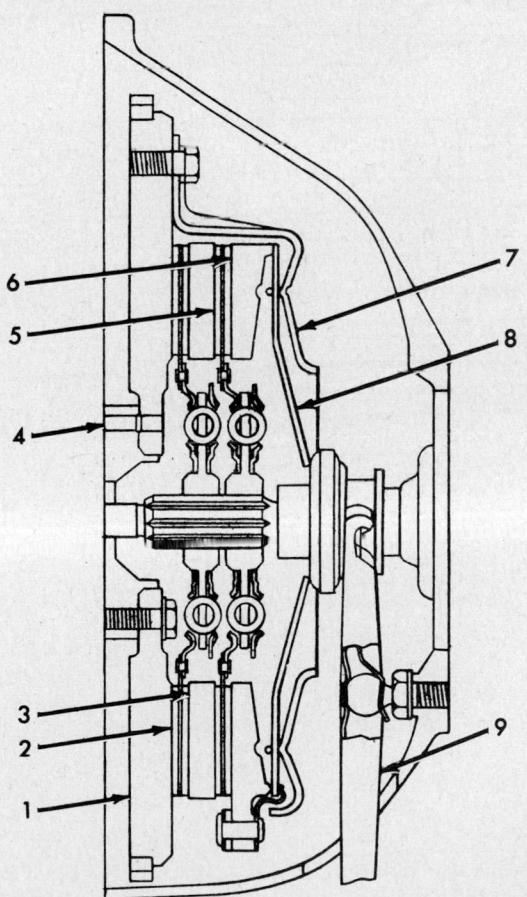

Dual disc clutch (© Chev. Div. G.M. Corp.)

1 Flywheel	4 Dowel hole	7 Cover
2 Front driven disc	5 Rear driven disc	8 Retracting spring
3 Front pressure plate	6 Rear pressure plate	9 Fork

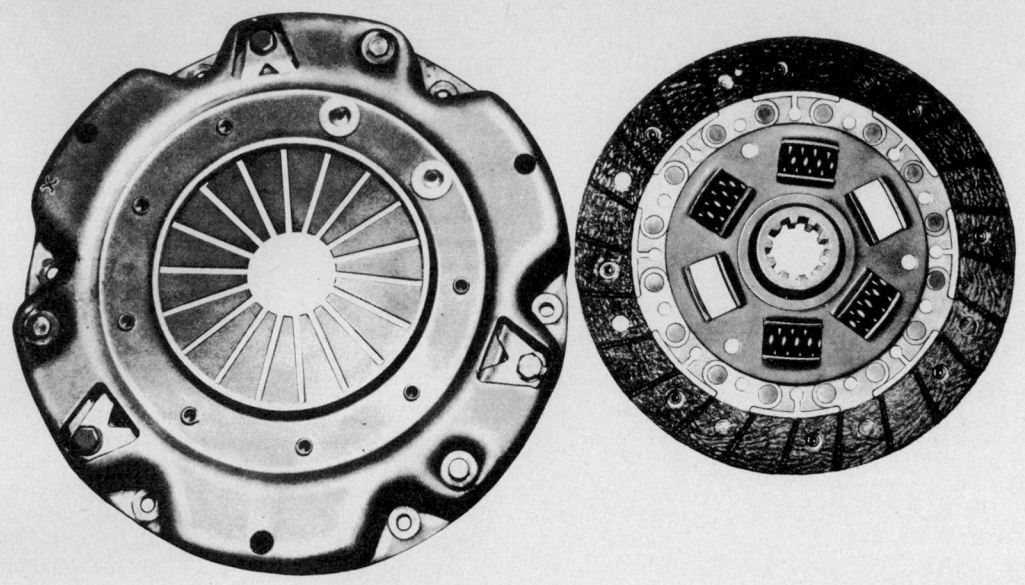

Single disc diaphragm clutch assembly (© Chevrolet Div., G.M. Corp.)

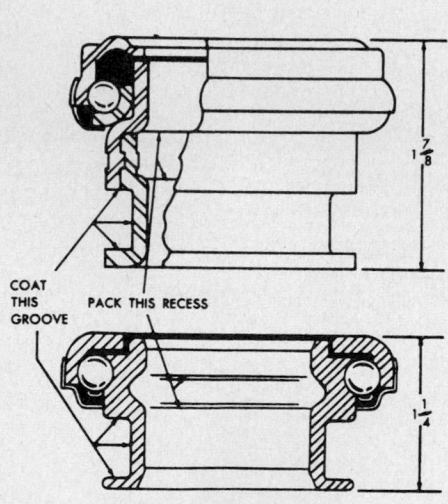

Clutch release bearing lubrication,
flat finger type at top,
bent finger type at bottom
(© Chevrolet Div. G.M. Corp.)

COAT THIS GROOVE

PACK THIS RECESS

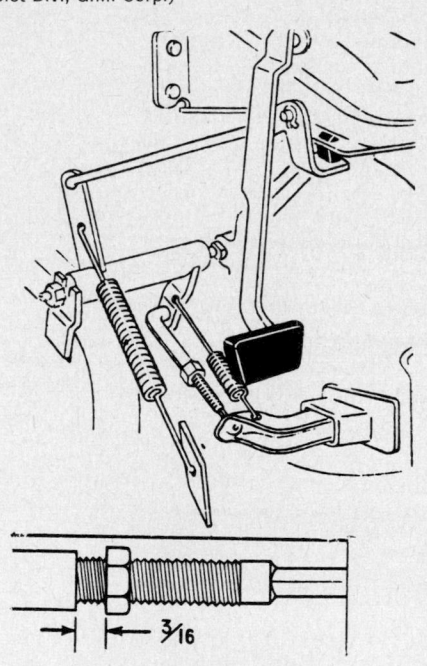

Clutch linkage, 1965-67 Chevelle
(© Chevrolet Div., G.M. Corp.)

bearing to throwout fork. Install flywheel housing. Install transmission.

7. Connect fork push rod and spring. Lubricate spring and pushrod ends.

8. Adjust shift linkage and clutch pedal free play.

Free Play Adjustment

This adjustment must be made under the vehicle on the clutch operating linkage. Free play is measured at the clutch pedal.

1. Disconnect return spring at clutch fork.

2. Hold clutch pedal up against stop. Loosen locknut.

3. Adjust pushrod to allow correct free play. Tighten locknut.

NOTE: see 1971-72 Camaro and Chevelle linkage illustration for alternate method.

4. Reinstall return spring and re-check free play.

Clutch Pedal Free Play

Vehicle	Free Play at Pedal Pad (in.)
1965 Chevelle, 1965 Chevy II	$\frac{3}{4}$-$1\frac{1}{8}$
1966 all models, 1967 Chevy II, 1971-72 Nova 1967 Chevelle	1-$1\frac{1}{2}$
1967-69 Camaro, 1968-70 Nova	1-$1\frac{1}{8}$
1968-72 Chevelle, 1970-72 Camaro	$1\frac{1}{8}$-$1\frac{3}{4}$

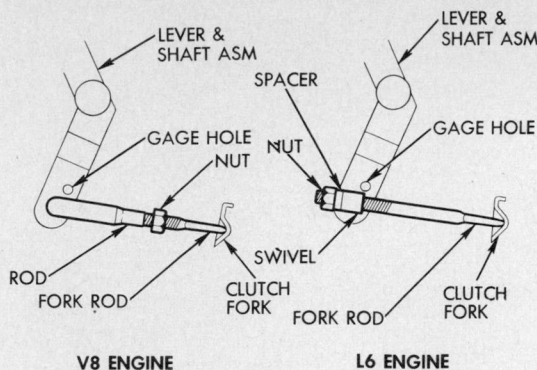

LEVER & SHAFT ASM
SPACER
GAGE HOLE
NUT NUT
ROD
FORK ROD
SWIVEL
CLUTCH FORK
FORK ROD

V8 ENGINE

LEVER & SHAFT ASM
GAGE HOLE
CLUTCH FORK

L6 ENGINE

Clutch pedal free play adjustment—typical 1968-72.
An alternate method of adjustment: remove return
spring, pull pedal back to rubber bumper and allow
throwout bearing to just contact fingers.
Adjust rod so that swivel fits into gauge hole and no
lash is in system, then install into lower hole.
(© Chev. Div. G.M. Corp.)

Clutch Start Switch

This switch, used on 1969-72 standard shift models, is operated by linkage from the clutch pedal arm, inside the vehicle. The function of the neutral start switch is to prevent the engine from being started unless the clutch pedal is fully depressed. There is no adjustment necessary for this switch.

Standard Transmission

Three and four speed transmissions are available on all models. Three speed transmissions from 1966 have all three forward gears synchronized; earlier models have only second and third gears synchronized. For 1966-72 models, a heavy duty three speed transmission is available.

All four speed transmissions have synchromesh in all forward gears. For 1966-72 models, a heavy duty four speed transmission is avilable.

A planetary overdrive, in combination with a three speed transmission, is available from 1966-69.

See the Unit Repair Section for transmission repairs, overdrive repairs, and Hurst shift linkage adjustments.

Transmission R & R Column Shift Models

1. Drain transmission.
2. Disconnect speedometer cable at transmission. Disconnect shift control rods from shift levers at the transmission.
3. Remove driveshaft.
4. Support rear of engine. Remove crossmember.
5. Remove two top transmission to clutch housing capscrews and install two long transmission guide pins in these holes.
6. Remove the two lower transmission mounting capscrews.
7. Slide the transmission straight back on the guide pins until the clutch gear is free of splines in the clutch disc.
8. Remove transmission from under car.
9. Install transmission in reverse order of removal.

Transmission R & R Floorshift Models

1. Remove shift lever trim plate and dust boot.
2. Remove shift lever assembly.
3. Raise car on a hoist, then disconnect speedometer cable at transmission.
4. Remove driveshaft, then support engine at the oil pan with a padded jack capable of supporting the engine weight when the transmission is removed.
5. Disconnect shift lever bracket. Remove all transmission shift levers and linkage.
6. Remove crossmember attaching bolts.
7. Loosen transmission crossmember and move rearward or remove.
8. Remove transmission-to-clutch housing retaining bolts and install two guide pins in top holes.
9. Slide transmission straight back to free the input shaft from the clutch hub.
10. When transmission has moved rearward enough, tilt front of transmission down and lower unit from car.
11. Install by reversing removal procedure.

Shift Linkage Adjustment

For adjustment on Hurst shift linkages, see the Unit Repair Section.

1965-68 Three Speed Column Shift

1. With transmission shifter rods disconnected at transmission levers, move both levers into neutral detents.
2. Move manual selector lever into neutral position.
3. Align first and reverse shifter tube lever with second and high shifter tube lever on the mast jacket. In some cases, a pin may be used to hold the levers in alignment.

NOTE: the key is engaged with the slot on the second and third shifter tube lever when selector lever is in the neutral position.

4. Loosen control rod clamp bolts. Install control rods on mast jacket shifter levers and secure with retaining clips.
5. Adjust length of first-reverse rod. Tighten clamp bolt.
6. Adjust length of second-third control rod. Tighten clamp bolt.
7. Shift through all positions to check adjustment, and to insure positive and full gear engagement.

1969-72 Three Speed Column Shift

1. With transmission in Reverse, place ignition switch in Off position up to 1970, Lock for 1971-72.
2. Loosen shift rod lock nuts.
3. Set transmission first-reverse lever in reverse position. Push up on first-reverse control rod to 1970, pull down for 1971-72 until column lever is in reverse detent position. Tighten first-reverse lock nut.
4. Shift column and transmission levers to neutral position. Insert a 3/16 in. dia rod into alignment holes in levers and alignment plate.
5. Tighten second-third locknut.
6. Remove alignment rod. Shift column lever to reverse. Turn key to Lock. Ignition switch must move freely to Lock position and it must not be possible to turn key to Lock when in any transmission position other than reverse. If this interlock binds, leave switch in Lock position and readjust first-reverse rod.
7. Check shifting.

1966-68 Three Speed Floorshift

1. Loosen shift rod locknuts.
2. Set shift lever in neutral and install locating pin into control lever bracket assembly. On some linkages, a flat locating gauge is used. This gauge is 1/8 thick X

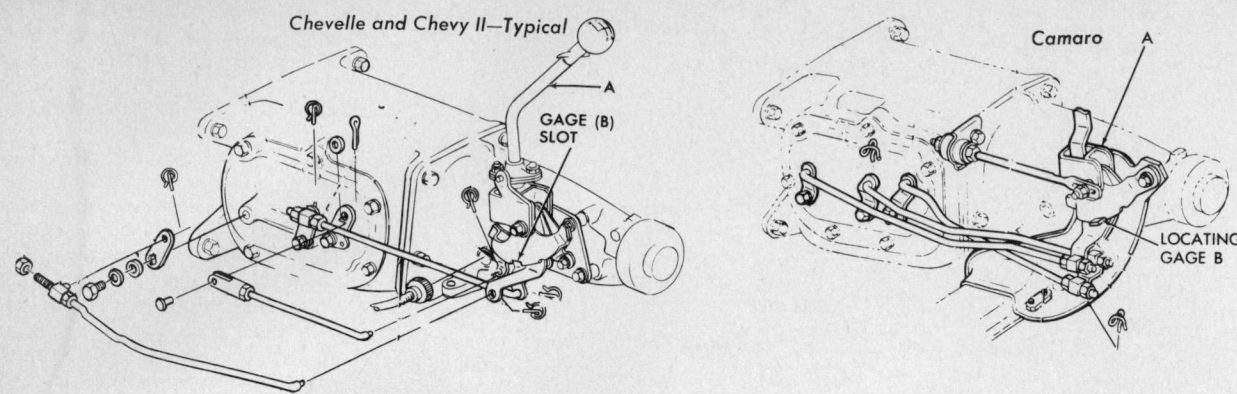

Chevelle and Chevy II—Typical

A

GAGE (B) SLOT

Camaro A

LOCATING GAGE B

Typical four speed floorshift linkage (© Chevrolet Div. G.M. Corp.)

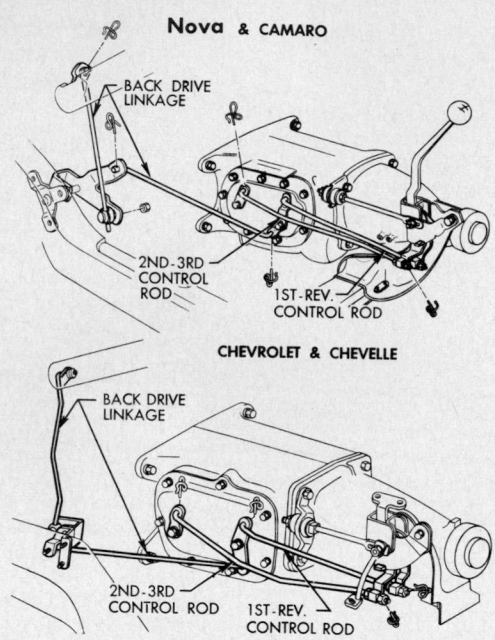

Nova & CAMARO

BACK DRIVE LINKAGE

2ND-3RD CONTROL ROD

1ST-REV. CONTROL ROD

CHEVROLET & CHEVELLE

BACK DRIVE LINKAGE

2ND-3RD CONTROL ROD

1ST-REV. CONTROL ROD

Typical three speed floorshift linkage, 1969-70
(© Chevrolet Div. G.M. Corp.)

41/64 wide X 3 in. long.

3. Place transmission shift levers in neutral positions.
4. Adjust length of control rods. Tighten locknuts.
5. Remove gauge or pin. Check shifting operation.

1969-72 Three Speed Floorshift

1. Turn ignition switch to Lock position up to 1970, Off starting 1971.
2. Loosen locknuts on shift rods and back drive rod.
3. Set transmission levers in neutral positions.
4. Set floorshift lever in neutral. Install locating gauge, $\frac{1}{8}$ thick X 41/64 wide X 3 in. long, into control lever bracket assembly.
5. Adjust length of shift rods. Tighten locknuts.
6. Remove locating gauge. Shift

into reverse.

7. Pull down slightly on back drive rod to remove any slack and tighten locknut. Ignition switch must move freely to Lock position and it must not be possible to turn key to Lock when in any transmission position other than reverse. If this interlock binds, leave the switch in Lock position and readjust back drive rod.
8. Check shifting operation.

1965-68 Four Speed Floorshift

1. Loosen shift rod clamp nuts or remove clevis pins.
2. Set transmission shift levers in neutral positions.
3. Insert locating gauge, $\frac{1}{8}$ thick X 41/64 wide X 3 in. long, into control lever bracket assembly.
4. Adjust length of shifting rods.

Tighten clamp nuts or replace clevis pins.

5. Remove gauge. Check shifting operation.

1969-72 Four Speed Floorshift

1. Place ignition switch in Lock position up to 1970, Off starting 1971.
2. Loosen locknuts at swivels on shift rods and back drive control rod.
3. Set transmission shift levers in neutral positions.
4. Shift lever into neutral. Insert locating gauge, $\frac{1}{8}$ thick X 41/64 wide X 3 in. long, into control lever bracket assembly.
5. Tighten shift rod locknuts and remove gauge.
6. Shift lever into reverse, then pull down slightly on back drive rod to remove slack. Tighten back drive rod locknut.
7. Ignition switch must move freely to Lock position and it must not be possible to turn key to Lock when in any transmission position other than reverse. Readjust back drive rod, if necessary.
8. Check for proper shifting operation.

Short Throw Shift Adjustment

Some four speed transmissions, primarily heavy duty units, have an adjustment for quicker shifting. The transmission levers have two control rod holes. Shift lever travel may be decreased by positioning the controls rods in the lower holes. This adjustment results in a tighter shift pattern and requires a slightly greater shifting effort.

Automatic Transmission

There are two basic automatic transmissions. The first is the two speed Powerglide, which is available up to 1972. A variation on the Powerglide, introduced in 1969, is

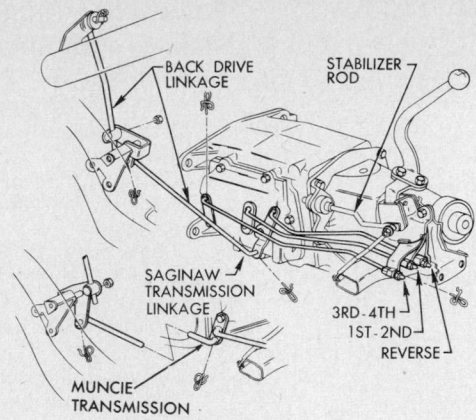

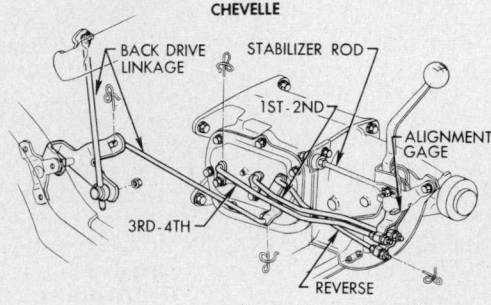

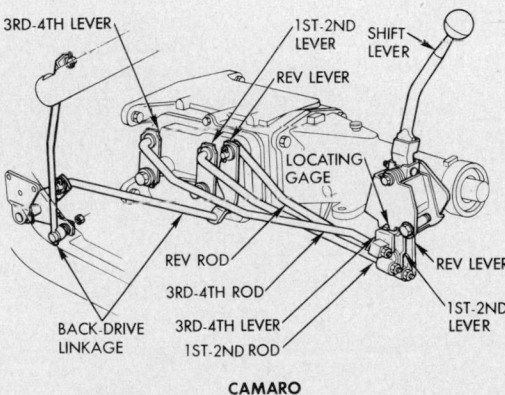

Transmission shift linkage—1971 illustrated
(© Chev. Div. G.M. Corp.)

the Torque Drive transmission. The Torque Drive unit is a Powerglide with the automatic shifting provisions removed. Torque Drive is shifted manually, but has no clutch. The second type is the three speed Turbo Hydra-Matic, used from 1966-72. This transmission is available in two load capacities, the Turbo Hydra-Matic 350 and the Turbo Hydra-Matic 400. This transmission is used in most General Motors vehicles.

Powerglide Shift Linkage Adjustment

1965-72 Column Shift

Check adjustment as follows:
1. The shift tube and lever assembly must be free in the mast jacket.
2. Lift the selector lever toward the steering wheel. Allow the selector lever to be positioned in Drive by the transmission detent.
3. Release selector lever. The selector lever should be prevented from engaging Low range unless the lever is lifted.
4. Lift the selector lever toward the steering wheel and allow the lever to be positioned in Neutral by the transmission detent.
5. Release the selector lever. The selector lever should now be prevented from engaging Reverse unless the lever is lifted. If the linkage is adjusted correctly, the selector lever should be prevented from moving beyond both the Neutral detent and the Drive detent unless the lever is lifted to pass over the mechanical stop

in the steering column.
Adjust as follows:
6. Loosen adjustment clamp at cross-shaft. Set transmission lever in drive by rotating lever counterclockwise to low detent, then clockwise one detent to drive.
7. Set selector lever in Drive. Remove any free play by holding cross-shaft upward and pulling shift rod downward.
8. Tighten clamp and recheck adjustment.
For 1969-72 models:
9. Place shift lever in Park and ignition switch in Lock. Loosen back drive rod clamp nut. Remove column lash and tighten clamp nut.
10. With selector lever in Park, the ignition key should move freely to Lock position. Lock position should be obtainable only when transmission is in Park.

1969-72 Torque Drive

1. Loosen swivel at idler lever.
2. Place transmission lever in Hi position.
3. Set shift lever at lower end of column up against first position stop.
4. Adjust rod in swivel and tighten retaining nut.
5. Place shift lever in Park and ignition switch in Lock. Loosen back drive rod clamp nut. Remove column lash and tighten clamp nut.
6. With selector lever in Park, the ignition key should move freely to Lock position. Lock position should be obtainable only when transmission is in Park.

1965-67 Chevelle Floorshift

1. Loosen adjustment nuts at swivel. Set transmission lever in drive position by moving counterclockwise to low detent, then clockwise one detent position to drive.
2. Set floorshift lever in Drive. Hold floorshift unit lower operating lever forward against shift lever detent.
3. Place a 7/64 (.11 in.) spacer between rear nut and swivel. Tighten rear nut against spacer.
4. Remove spacer and tighten front nut against swivel, locking swivel between nuts.

1965-68 Chevy II, 1969-72 Nova, 1967 Camaro Floorshift

This procedure is identical to that for 1965-67 Chevelle floorshift models, with the exception of the following steps:
3. Place a 3/32 (.09 in.) spacer between rear nut and swivel. Tighten rear nut against spacer.
5. Place shift lever in Park posi-

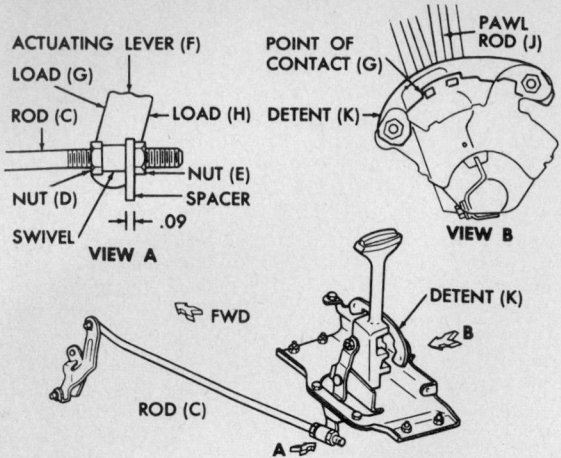

Automatic transmission rod operated floorshift linkage, Chevy II
(© Chevrolet Div., G.M. Corp.)

tion. Adjust column (back drive) rod. With shift lever in Park, the ignition key must move freely to Lock, and Lock position must not be obtainable in any transmission position other than Park.

1968-72 Chevelle, 1968-72 Camaro, 1970-72 Monte Carlo Floorshift

These models use a cable operated linkage.

1. Place shift lever in Drive position.
2. Disconnect cable from transmission lever. Place transmission lever in drive by rotating lever counterclockwise to low detent, then clockwise one detent to drive.
3. Measure distance from rearward face of attachment bracket to center of cable attachment pin. Adjust this dimension to 5.5 in. by loosening and moving cable end stud nut.

For 1969-72 models:

4. Place shift lever in Park and ignition switch in Lock position.
5. Loosen and adjust column (back drive) rod.

6. With selector lever in Park position, the ignition key should move freely to Lock position. Lock position should not be obtainable in any transmission position other than Park.

Turbo Hydra-Matic Shift Linkage Adjustment

The Turbo Hydra-Matic linkages are the same as those used on Powerglide models. Adjustments are the same, except that the transmission lever is adjusted to drive position by moving the lever clockwise to the low detent, then counterclockwise two detent positions to drive.

Powerglide Throttle Valve Linkage Adjustment
1965-66 V8, 1965-72 Inline Engines

1. Depress accelerator pedal.
2. Bellcrank on inline engines and carburetor lever on V8 engines must be at wide open throttle position.
3. Dash lever at firewall must be 1/64-1/16 in. off lever stop.
4. Transmission lever must be against transmission internal stop.
5. Adjust linkage to simultaneously obtain conditions in Steps 1-4, above.

1967-72 V8 Engines

1. Remove air cleaner.
2. Disconnect accelerator linkage at carburetor.
3. Disconnect both return springs.
4. Pull throttle valve upper rod forward until transmission is through detent.
5. Open carburetor to wide open throttle position. Adjust swivel on end of upper throttle valve rod so carburetor reaches wide open throttle position at the same time that the ball stud contacts the end of the slot in the upper throttle valve rod. A tolerance of 1/32 in. is allowable.

Turbo Hydra-Matic 350 Detent Cable Adjustment

The Turbo Hydra-Matic 350 has a detent, or downshift, cable between the carburetor linkage and the transmission.

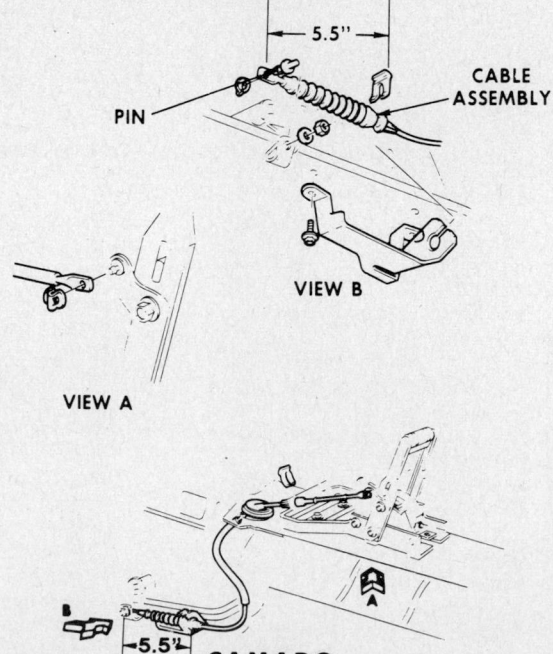

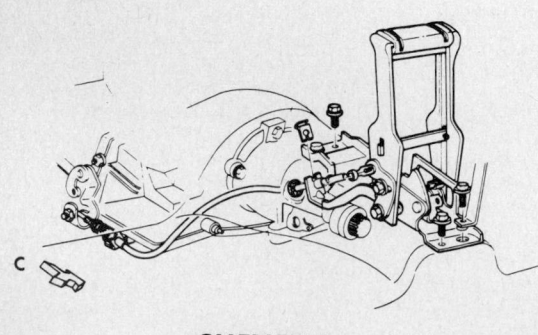

Automatic transmission cable operated floorshift linkage, Camaro and Chevelle
(© Chevrolet Div., G.M. Corp.)

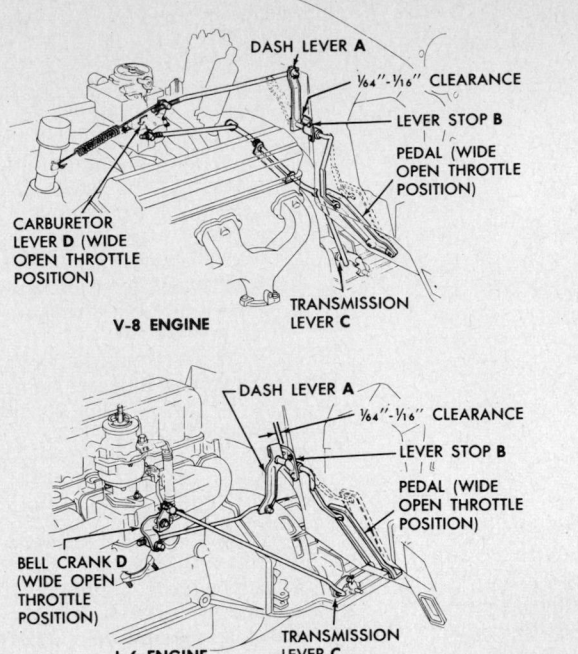

V-8 ENGINE

Powerglide throttle valve linkage adjustment, 1965-66 V8, 1965-72 inline engines
(© G.M. Corp.)

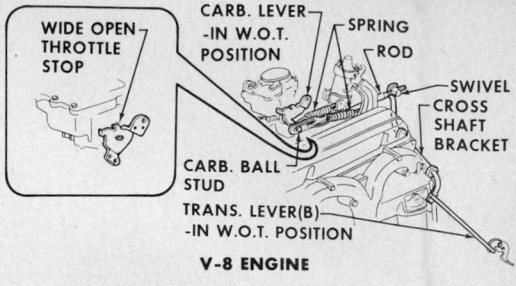

V-8 ENGINE

Powerglide throttle valve linkage, 1967-72 V8
(© Chevrolet Div., G.M. Corp.)

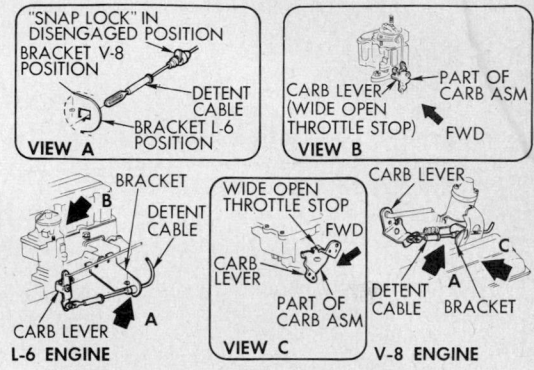

1969-72 Turbo Hydra-Matic 350 detent cable adjustment
(© Chevrolet Div., G.M. Corp.)

1969-72—All Models

1. Remove air cleaner.
2. Loosen detent cable screw or disengage snap lock.
3. Place carburetor lever in wide open throttle position. Make sure lever is against stop. On vehicles with Quadrajet carburetors, disengage the secondary lock out before placing lever in wide open throttle position.
   NOTE: detent cable must be pulled through detent position.
4. Engage snap lock or tighten detent screw.

Turbo Hydra-Matic 400 Detent Switch Adjustment

The Turbo Hydra-Matic 400 transmission has an electrical detent, or downshift, switch operated by the throttle linkage.

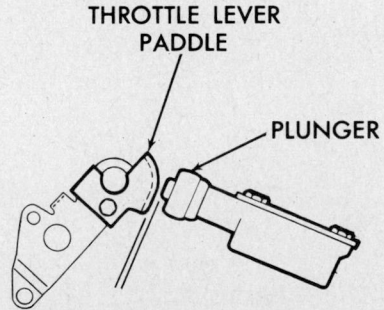

THROTTLE LEVER PADDLE

PLUNGER

Turbo Hydra-Matic 400 detent switch adjustment, 1968 Chevelle, 1969-72 Nova, 1968-72 Camaro
(© Chevrolet Div., G.M. Corp.)

1968 Chevelle and Camaro

1. Place carburetor lever in wide open position.
2. Place automatic choke in off position.
3. Fully depress switch plunger.
4. Adjust switch mounting to obtain distance between depressed switch plunger and throttle lever paddle of .05 in. for Chevelle and .20 in. for Camaro.

1969-72 Nova, 1969-72 Camaro

This procedure is the same as that for the 1968 Chevelle and Camaro, with the substitution of the following step:

4. Adjust switch mounting to obtain distance between depressed switch plunger and throttle lever paddle of .22-.24 in.

1969-72 Chevelle, 1970-72 Monte Carlo

1. Pull detent switch driver rearward until hole in switch body aligns with hold in driver. Insert a .092 in. dia. pin through the aligned holes to hold the driver in position.
2. Loosen mounting bolt.
3. Depress accelerator to wide open throttle position. Move switch forward until driver contacts accelerator lever.
4. Tighten mounting bolt. Remove pin.

Neutral Safety Switch

The neutral safety switch prevents the engine from being started in any transmission position except Neutral or Park. On column shift models, the switch is located on the upper side of the steering column under the instrument panel. On floorshift models, the switch is located inside the shift console.

Switch Replacement

1. Remove console for access on floorshift models.
2. Disconnect wiring connectors.
3. Remove switch.
4. Position shift lever in Drive. On column shift models, locate lever tang against transmission selector plate.
5. Align slot in contact support with hole in switch. Insert 3/32 in. dia. pin to hold support in place. Switch is now aligned in drive position.
6. Place contact support drive slot over drive tang. Install screws.
7. Remove pin. Connect wiring. Replace console.
8. Set parking brake and footbrake. Check to see that engine will start only in Drive or Neutral.

Turbo Hydra-Matic 350 R & R

1. Disconnect battery ground cable. Release parking brake.
2. Raise vehicle and drain oil.
3. On Camaro to 1969:
   a. disconnect parking brake ca-

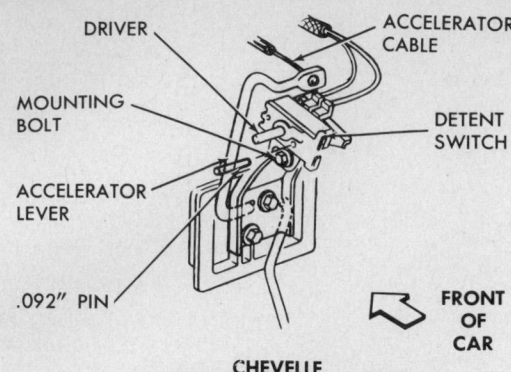

CHEVELLE
Turbo Hydra-Matic 400 detent switch adjustment,
1969-72 Chevelle and Monte Carlo
(© Chevrolet Div., G.M. Corp.)

bles
   b. remove convertible under-body reinforcement plate
   c. disconnect left exhaust pipe from manifold.
4. Remove driveshaft.
5. Disconnect:
   a. speedometer cable
   b. detent cable
   c. vacuum modulator line
   d. oil cooler lines
   e. shift linkage.
6. Support transmission.
7. Remove:
   a. crossmember
   b. converter underpan
   c. converter to flywheel bolts.
8. Loosen exhaust pipe to manifold bolts.
9. Lower transmission until jack is barely supporting it. Be careful that V8 distributor is not forced against firewall.
10. Remove:
    a. transmission to engine mounting bolts.
    b. oil filler tube.
11. Raise transmission to normal position. Support engine with a jack. Slide transmission to rear and then down. Use a strap to hold converter to transmission

or keep rear of transmission down to avoid losing converter.
12. Reverse procedure to install.

Turbo Hydra-Matic 400 R & R

This procedure is the same as that given above for the Turbo Hydra-Matic 350, with the substitution of the following step:
5. Disconnect:
   a. speedometer cable
   b. electrical lead to case connector
   c. vacuum line modulator
   d. oil cooler lines
   e. shift linkage.

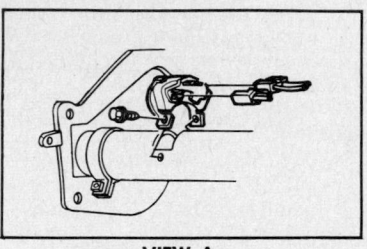

VIEW A

Powerglide R & R—1965-72

1. Raise car on hoist and drain oil.
2. Disconnect oil cooler and vacuum modulator lines and the speedometer drive cable at transmission. Fasten lines out of way.
3. Disconnect manual and throttle valve control lever rods from transmission.
4. Disconnect driveshaft.
5. Install suitable transmission lift equipment.
6. Disconnect engine rear mount on transmission extension, then remove transmission support crossmember.
7. Remove converter underpan, scribe flywheel-converter relationship for assembly. Remove converter-to-flywheel attaching bolts.
8. Support the engine at the oil pan rail with a jack or other suitable brace capable of supporting the engine weight when transmission is removed.
9. Lower rear of transmission slightly so that the upper transmission housing-to-engine attaching bolts can be reached by using a universal socket and a long extension. Remove upper bolts.
NOTE: make sure distributor does not hit firewall when lowering trans-

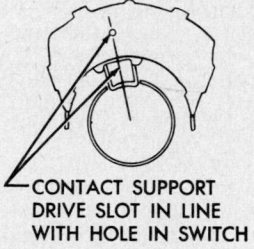

CONTACT SUPPORT
DRIVE SLOT IN LINE
WITH HOLE IN SWITCH

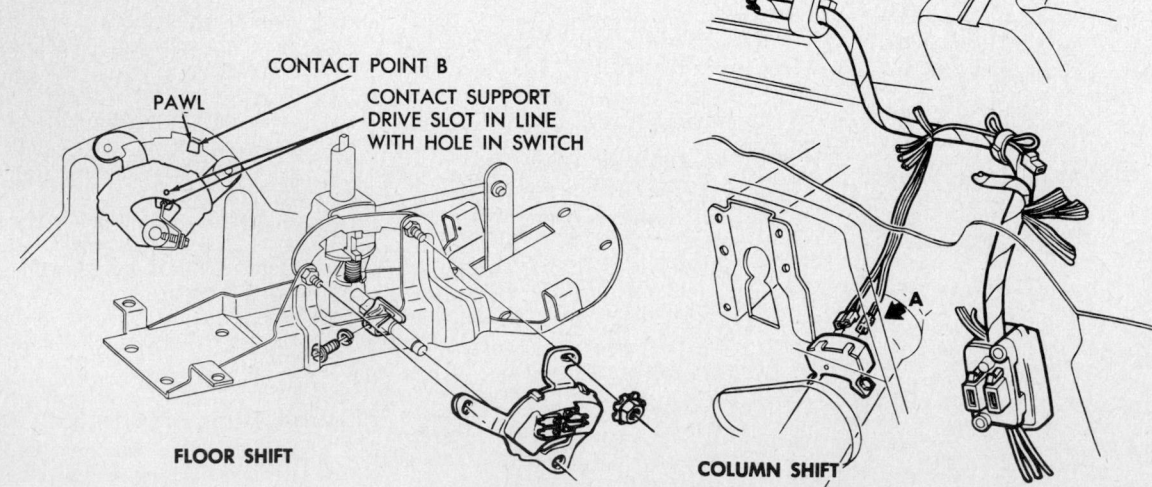

CONTACT POINT B
PAWL
CONTACT SUPPORT
DRIVE SLOT IN LINE
WITH HOLE IN SWITCH

FLOOR SHIFT

COLUMN SHIFT

Typical neutral safety switch installation (© Chevrolet Div. G.M. Corp.)

mission.

10. Remove remainder of transmission-to-housing bolts.
11. Remove transmission by moving it slightly to the rear and downward, then remove from beneath the car and transfer it to a work bench.

NOTE: watch the converter when moving the transmission rearward. If it does not follow the transmission, pry it free of the flywheel before proceeding.

Caution Use some sort of holding strap to keep the converter from falling out of the transmission during transmission removal and handling.

12. Install transmission in the reverse order of removal.

Drive Shaft, U Joints

A one piece, exposed type, tubular driveshaft is used on all models. The driveshaft has two cross and roller universal joints and a splined slip joint. The cross and roller universal joints may be of two types. The first is the Cleveland type which uses external snap rings for trunnion retention. The second is the Saginaw design in which the trunnions are retained by a nylon material which is injected into a groove in the yoke. A third type of driveshaft, introduced in 1971, employs a constant velocity joint at the axle end. It should be noted that this last type of joint is not serviceable.

See the Chevrolet Section for disassembly and repair of the universal joints.

Drive Axle, Suspension

The Chevelle and Monte Carlo have a coil spring rear suspension located by two lower control arms and two diagonally mounted upper control arms. Fore and aft axle movement is prevented by the lower control arms. Lateral movement is prevented by the upper control arms and the axle-to-frame tie-rod.

The Camaro, Chevy II, and Nova all have a leaf spring rear suspension. Some light duty models and all Chevy II models, up to 1967, have single leaf rear springs. Other models use the more conventional multiple leaf springs.

All models, starting 1968, use staggered shock absorbers to prevent axle hop on hard acceleration. The right shock absorber is mounted forward of the axle and the left shock absorber is mounted behind the axle.

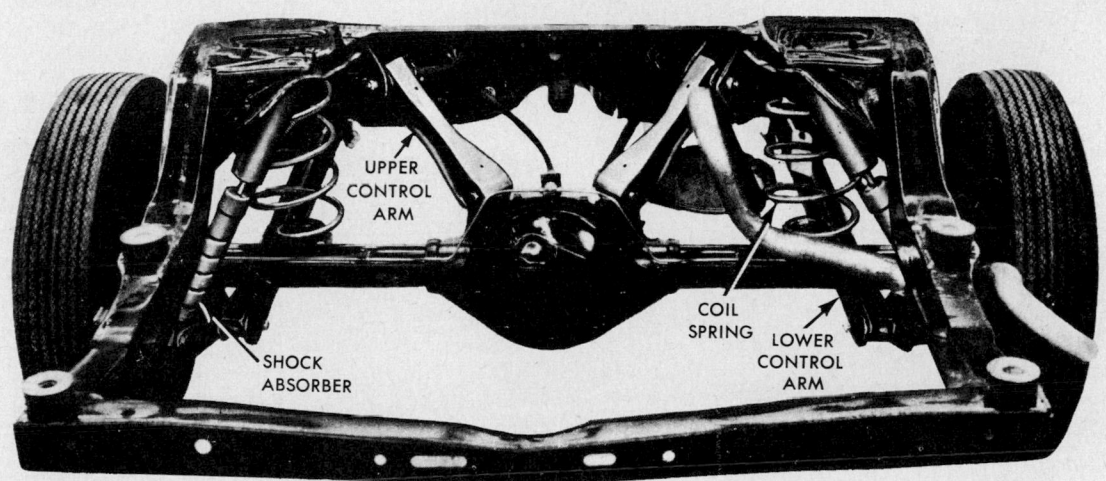

1968-72 Chevelle rear suspension (© Chevrolet Div., G.M. Corp.)

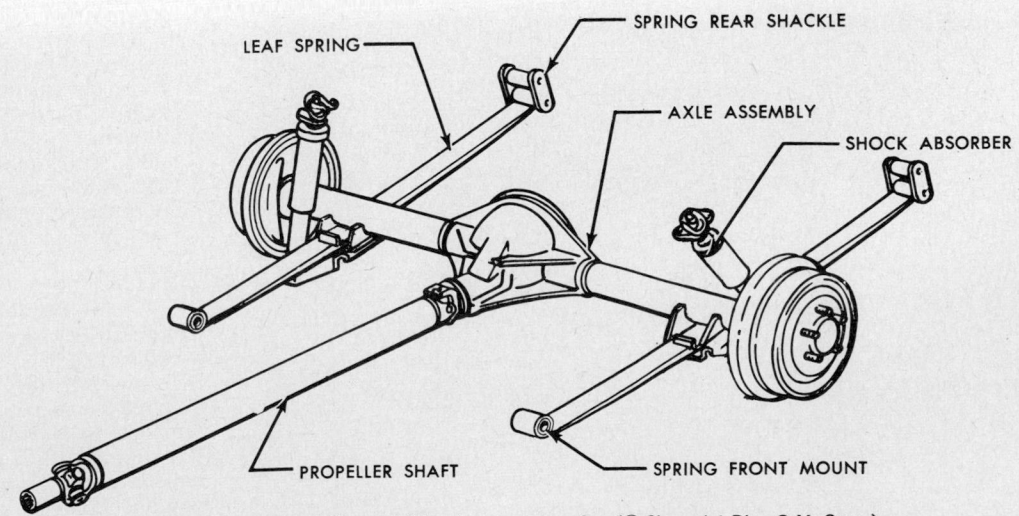

1968-72 Camaro and Chevy II (Nova) rear suspension (© Chevrolet Div., G.M. Corp.)

For repair details on rear axles, see the Unit Repair Section. For spring and shock absorber removal, see the Chevrolet Section.

Windshield Wipers

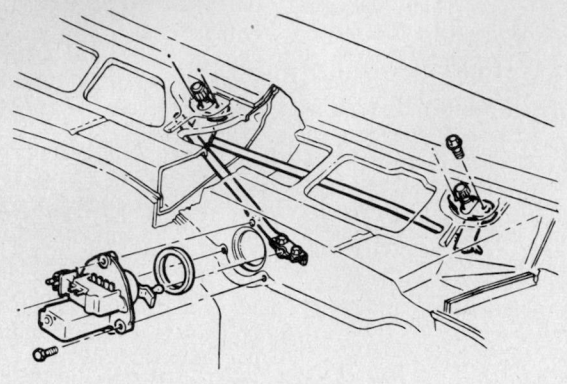

Wiper and motor linkage—Camaro (© Chevrolet Div., G.M. Corp.)

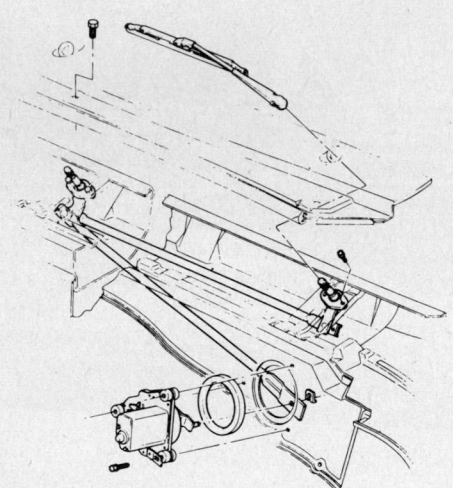

Wiper motor and linkage, 1965-67 Chevelle (© Chevrolet Div., G.M. Corp.)

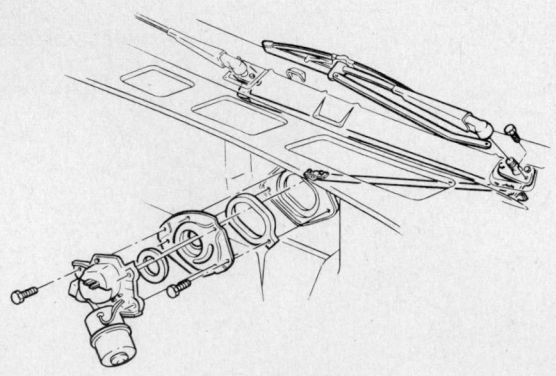

Chevelle recessed wipers
(© Chevrolet Div., G.M. Corp.)

Wiper Motor R & R

1965-67 Chevelle and Chevy II

1. Make certain wiper motor is in park position.
2. Working under instrument panel, remove transmission linkage from motor crank arm.
3. Disconnect electrical connectors and washer hoses.
4. Remove motor retaining bolts and remove motor.
5. Reverse procedure to install, checking sealing gaskets at motor.

1967 Camaro

1. Make certain wiper motor is in park position.
2. Disconnect washer hoses and electrical connectors.
3. Remove three motor bolts. Pull wiper motor assembly from cowl opening and loosen nuts retaining drive rod ball stud to crank arm.
4. Reverse procedure to install, checking sealing gaskets at motor.

1968-72 All Models

1. Make sure wiper motor is in park position.
2. Disconnect washer hoses and electrical connectors.
3. Remove the plenum chamber grille or access cover. Remove the nut retaining the crank arm to the motor assembly.
4. Remove the retaining screws or nuts and remove motor.
5. Reverse procedure to install, checking sealing gaskets at motor.

Wiper Transmission R & R

1965-67 Chevy II

1. Make certain wiper motor is in park position. Remove wiper arm and blade assemblies from transmission shaft.
2. Remove linkage from wiper crank arm. Remove left transmission link from right transmission.
3. Remove two screws securing transmission to cowl on one side. Remove transmission from under dash.
4. Reverse procedure to install, checking gasket.

1965-67 Chevelle

1. Make certain wiper motor is in park position. Remove wiper arm and blade assemblies from transmission shaft.
2. Remove plenum chamber grille.
3. Detach linkage from wiper crank arm.
4. Remove transmission retaining screws, lower assembly into plenum chamber, and remove unit.
5. Reverse procedure to install.

1967 Camaro, 1968-72 All Models

1. Make sure wiper motor is in park position.
2. Disconnect battery ground cable.
3. Remove wiper arm and blade assemblies from transmission. On articulated left arm assemblies, remove carburetor type clip retaining pinned arm to blade arm.

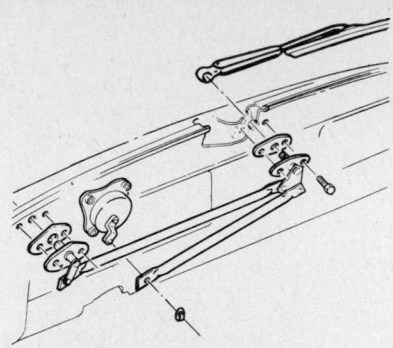

**Wiper transmission components
1965-67 Chevy II**
(© Chevrolet Div., G.M. Corp.)

4. Remove plenum chamber air intake grille or screen.
5. Loosen nuts retaining drive rod ball stud to crank arm and detach drive rod from crank arm.
6. Remove transmission retaining screws. Lower transmission and drive rod assemblies into plenum chamber.
7. Remove transmission and linkage from plenum chamber through cowl opening.
8. Reverse procedure to install, making sure wiper blade assemblies are installed in park position.

Radio

1965-72
1. Disconnect battery ground cable.
2. Remove ash tray and ash tray housing as necessary.
3. Remove knobs, controls, washers, trim plate, and nuts from radio.
4. Remove hoses from center air conditioning duct as necessary.
5. Disconnect all wiring leads.
6. Remove screw from radio rear mounting bracket and lower radio.
7. To install, reverse above procedure.

Heater System

Heater Core R & R

1965-67 Chevy II
1. Drain radiator.
2. From engine compartment, remove hoses from inlet and outlet connections.
3. Remove nuts around blower motor holding heater to dash panel.
4. From inside vehicle, remove glove compartment and glove compart-ment door.
5. Remove screws attaching heater distributor bracket to dash.
6. Remove screw holding case bracket to adaptor bracket.
7. Detach heater assembly from dash panel and adaptor assembly, then lower toward floor.
8. Disconnect all cable connections, wire connector and defroster hoses.
9. Remove assembly from vehicle.
10. Remove screws attaching core cover to heater.
11. Remove core mounting screws and remove core from heater.
12. Install in reverse of above.

1965-67 Chevelle
1. Drain radiator.
2. Remove heater hoses at connections beside air inlet assembly.
3. Remove cable and electrical connectors from heater and defroster assembly.
4. On engine side of dash, remove screws and nuts holding air inlet to dash panel.
5. Inside vehicle, pull entire assembly from the firewall and remove assembly from vehicle.
6. Remove core assembly retaining springs and remove core.
7. Install in reverse of above.

1968-72 All Models
1. Disconnect battery ground cable.
2. Drain radiator.
3. Disconnect heater hoses. Plug core inlet and outlet.
4. Remove nuts from air distributor duct studs on firewall.
5. On Chevy II, remove glove compartment and door assembly.
6. From under dash, drill out lower right hand distributor duct stud with a ¼ in. drill.
7. On 1970 and later Camaro: remove glove box and radio, then defroster duct to distributor duct screw.
8. Pull distributor duct from firewall mounting. Remove resistor wires. Lay duct on floor.
9. Remove core assembly from distributor duct.
10. Reverse procedure to install.

Heater Blower R & R

1965-67 Chevy II
1. Remove screws attaching the motor and blower to heater assembly.
2. Remove retainer attaching blower to motor shaft.
3. Install in reverse of above.

1965-67 Chevelle
1. Disconnect battery.
2. Unclip hoses from fender skirt.
3. Disconnect electrical feed from motor.
4. Turn vehicle front wheels to extreme right.
5. Remove right front fender skirt bolts and allow skirt to drop, resting it on top of tire. It may be wedged away from fender lower flange with block of wood to provide better access to bolts.
6. Remove screws attaching motor mounting plate to air inlet housing.
7. Remove screws attaching motor to mounting plate.
8. Remove clip attaching cage to shaft and remove blower motor.
9. Install in reverse of above.

1967-69 Camaro
1. Disconnect battery ground cable.
2. Disconnect hoses and wiring from fender skirt.
3. Remove wheel opening trim.
4. Remove rocker panel molding.
5. Loosen rear lower fender to body bolt.
6. Remove nine rearmost fender skirt attaching screws.
7. Pull lower rear edge of fender out. Pull skirt down. Place a block of wood between fender and skirt.
8. Remove blower to case attaching screws. Remove blower assembly.
9. Remove blower wheel retaining nut. Separate blower and motor.
10. Reverse procedure to install. Open end of blower should be away from motor.

1968 Chevy II, 1969 Nova, 1968-69 Chevelle, 1970-72 All Models
1. Disconnect battery ground cable.
2. Disconnect hoses and wiring from fender skirt.
3. Remove all fender skirt attaching bolts except those attaching skirt to radiator support.
4. Pull out, then down, on skirt. Place a block between skirt and fender.
5. Remove blower to case attaching screws. Remove blower assembly.
6. Remove blower wheel retaining nut and separate the motor and wheel.
7. Reverse procedure to install. Open end of blower should be away from motor.

Chevrolet and Corvette

Index

YEAR IDENTIFICATION

CHEVROLET

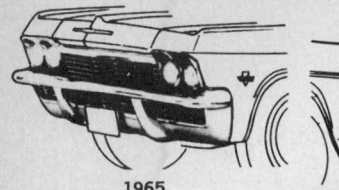
1965

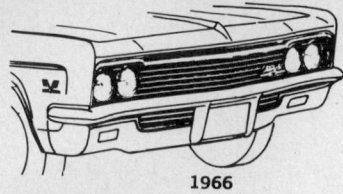
1966

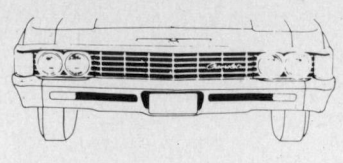
1967

1968

CHEVROLET

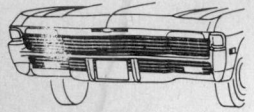
1968 Caprice

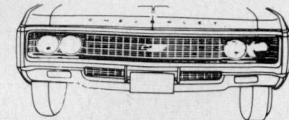
1969

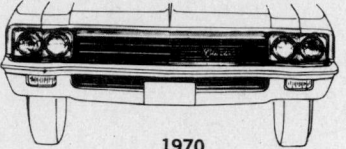
1970

1971

CHEVROLET   **CORVETTE**

1972 Caprice

1972 Impala

1965

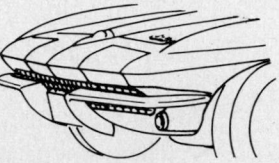
1966

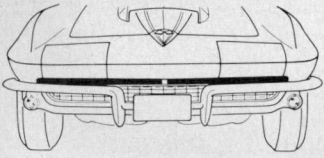
1967

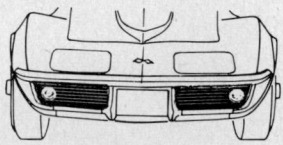
1968-69

1970-71

1972

FIRING ORDER

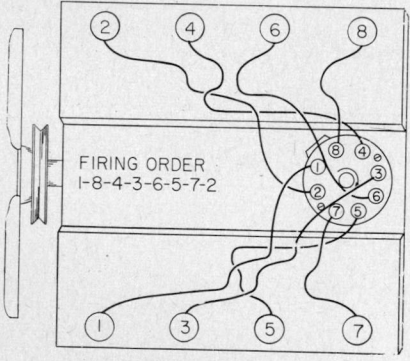
1965 409 cu. in.

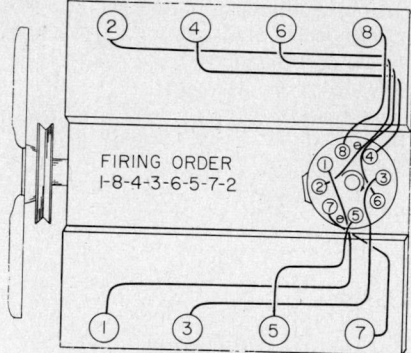
1965-72 283, 327, 350, 307, 396, 427, 400, 454 cu. in. V8

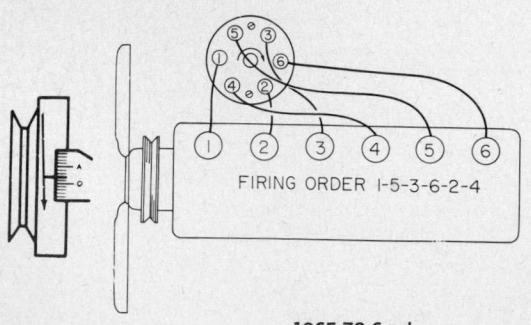
1965-72 6 cyl.

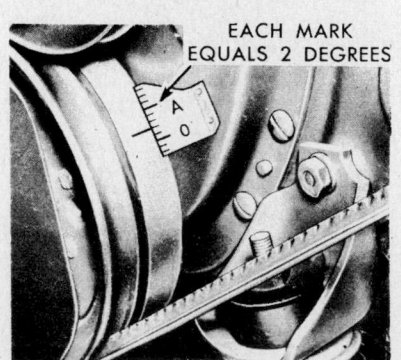
Ignition timing marks V8 engine
(© Chevrolet Div., G.M. Corp.)

CAR SERIAL NUMBER LOCATION

1965-67
Vehicle serial number is found on a plate attached to left front door hinge pillar.

1968-72
Vehicle serial number is found on a plate on the top left side of the instrument panel, visible through the windshield.

Car Serial Number Interpretation
A typical vehicle serial number tag yields manufacturer's identity, vehicle type, model year, assembly plant and production unit number when broken down as shown in the following chart.

Mfr. Identity[1]	Body Style[2]	Model Year[3]	Assy. Plant[4]	Unit No.[5]
1	5645	8	F	100025

1. Manufacturer's identity number assigned to all Chevrolet built vehicles.
2. Model Identification
3. Last number of model year (1968).
4. F-Flint
5. Unit numbering will start at 100,001 at all plants.

Engine Identification

Six Cylinder Engines
The production code letters immediately follow the engine serial number. The number is found on a pad at the front right-hand side of the cylinder block, just to the rear of the distributor.

V8 Engines
The production code letters immediately follow the engine serial number. The number is found on a pad at the front right-hand side of the cylinder block.

1965-68

Series	Model Number 6 Cyl.	Model Number V-8	Description
Biscayne	15311	15411	2 Dr. Sedan, 6 Passenger
	15369	15469	4 Dr. Sedan, 6 Passenger
	15335	15435	4 Dr. Station Wagon, 2 Seats
Bel Air	15511	15611	2 Dr. Sedan, 6 Passenger
	15569	15669	4 Dr. Sedan, 6 Passenger
	15535	15635	4 Dr. Station Wagon, 2 Seats
	15545	15645	4 Dr. Station Wagon, 3 Seats
Impala	16369	16469	4 Dr. Sedan, 6 Passenger
	16339	16439	4 Dr. Sports Sedan, 6 Passenger
	16337	16487	2 Dr. Sport Coupe, 5 Passenger
	16367	16467	2 Dr. Convertible, 5 Passenger
	16335	16435	4 Dr. Station Wagon, 2 Seats
	16345	16445	4 Dr. Station Wagon, 3 Seats
Impala SS	16537	16637	2 Dr. Sport Coupe, 4 Passenger
	16567	16667	2 Dr. Convertible, 4 Passenger

1965-68

Series	Model Number 6 Cyl.	Model Number V-8	Description
Caprice	—	16635	4 Dr. Custom Wagon—2-Seat
	—	16639	4 Dr. Custom Wagon, 6 Passenger
	—	16645	4 Dr. Custom Wagon, 3-Seat
	—	16647	2 Dr. Custom Coupe, 4 Passenger

1969-70

Series	Model Number 6 Cyl.	Model Number V-8	Description
Biscayne	*15311	*15411	2 Dr. Sedan
	15369	15469	4 Dr. Sedan
Bel Air	*15511	*15611	2 Dr. Sedan
	15569	15669	4 Dr. Sedan
Impala	16337	16437	2 Dr. Sport Coupe
	16339	16439	4 Dr. Sport Sedan
	—	16447	2 Dr. Custom Coupe
	—	16467	2 Dr. Convertible
	16369	16469	4 Dr. Sedan

1969-70

Series	Model Number 6 Cyl.	Model Number V-8	Description
Caprice	—	16639	4 Dr. Sport Sedan
	—	16647	2 Dr. Custom Coupe
Station Wagons	15336	15436	4 Dr. Brookwood 2-Seat
	15536	15636	4 Dr. Townsman 2-Seat
	15546	15646	4 Dr. Townsman 3-Seat
	—	16436	4 Dr. Kingswood 2-Seat
	—	16446	4 Dr. Kingswood 3-Seat
	—	16636	4 Dr. Kingswood Est. 2-Seat
	—	16646	4 Dr. Kingswood Est. 3-Seat

*Applicable to 1969 only.

1971-72

Series	Model Number 6 Cyl.	Model Number V8	Description
Biscayne	15369	15469	4 Dr. Sedan
Bel Air	15569	15669	4 Dr. Sedan
Impala	16357	16457	2 Dr. Sport Coupe
	—	16447	2 Dr. Custom Coupe
	—	16439	4 Dr. Sport Sedan
	—	16467	2 Dr. Convertible
	16369	16469	4 Dr. Sedan
Caprice	—	16639	4 Dr. Sedan
	—	16647	2 Dr. Coupe
Station Wagon	—	15435	Brookwood, 4 Dr., 2-seat
	—	15635	Townsman, 4 DR., 2-seat
	—	15645	Townsman, 4 Dr., 3-seat
	—	16435	Kingswood, 4 Dr., 2-seat
	—	16445	Kingswood, 4 Dr., 3-seat
	—	16635	Kingswood Estate, 4 Dr., 2-seat
	—	16645	Kingswood Estate, 4 Dr., 3-seat

Corvette
1965-72

Model No.	Description
19437	2 Dr. Sport Coupe, 2 Passenger
19467	2 Dr. Convertible, 2 Passenger

Chevrolet Engine Identification Code

No. Cyls.	Cu. In. Displ.	Type	1965	1966	1967	1968	1969	1970	1971
6	230	M.T.	FA						
6	230	M.T., HDC	FE						
6	230	M.T., AC	FL						
6	230	M.T., AC, HDC	FF						
6	230	PG	FM	FM					
6	230	PG, AC	FR						
6	230	Taxi, M.T.	FK						
6	230	Taxi, PG	FP						
6	250	PG, AC, w/ex. EM		GQ	GQ	CR	BO		
6	250	Taxi, PG, w/ex. EM		GR					
6	250	M.T.		FA	FA	CA	BA	CCG, CCH, CCZ, CRF, CRG	CAA
6	250	HDC, M.T.		FE	FE	CJ			
6	250	HDC, M.T., AC		FF	FF	CK			
6	250	M.T., AC		FL	FL	CN	BG		
6	250	Taxi, Police, M.T.			FK		BP	CCL	CAC
6	250	PG, TD			FM	CQ			CAB
6	250	PG, Taxi, Police			FP		BJ, BL	CCM	CAD
6	250	PG, AC		FR	FR	CR	BO		
6	250	AC		FV			BQ		
6	250	w/ex. EM		FY					
6	250	Taxi, w/ex. EM		FZ					
6	250	PG, w/ex. EM		GP	GP	CQ			
6	250	Hyd. 350, Police						CCK	
8	283	M.T.	GA	GA	GA				
8	283	PG	GF	GF	GF				
8	283	4 spd., w/ex. EM		GS	GS				
8	283	PG, w/ex. EM		GT	GT				
8	283	HDC				GU			
8	283	4-BBL.	GK	GW					
8	283	4-BBL., w/ex. EM		GX					
8	283	PG, 4-BBL., ex. EM		GZ					
8	283	4 spd.	GC	GC	GC				
8	283	w/ex. EM		GK	GK				
8	283	PG, 4-BBL.	GL	GL					
8	307	M.T.				DO			
8	307	4 spd. SS				DP			
8	307	HDC				DQ			
8	307	PG				DR			
8	327	M.T.	HA	HA	HA	HA	FA, FJ		
8	327	M.T., HP	HB						
8	327	w/ex. EM			HB	HB			
8	327	PG	HC	HC	HC	HC	FB, FK		
8	327	PG, HP	HD						
8	327	PG, w/ex. EM				HF	HF		
8	327	Hyd. 350				KL	FC, FL		
8	327	HDC				KE			
8	327	Hyd. 400					FH		
8	327	Police					FG		
8	327	M.T., Taxi					FY		
8	327	PG, Taxi					FZ		
8	327	Hyd. 350, Taxi					GA		
8	327	Hyd. 400, Taxi					GB		
8	350	PG					GE, HK		
8	350	Hyd. 350, 2-BBL.					HD, HM		
8	350	PG, 2-BBL.					HF, HL		
8	350	M.T.					HG, HD	CND (250), CNQ (300)	CGA (245)
8	350	Hyd. 400					HH, IA		
8	350	2-BBL.					HI		
8	350	Hyd. 400, 2-BBL.					HJ		
8	350	Hyd. 350					HN, HY	CNR (300), CNV (250)	
8	350	M.T.					HP, HT		
8	350	PG					HU	CNS (300), CNU (250)	CGB

No. Cyls.	Cu. In. Displ.	Type	1965	1966	1967	1968	1969	1970	1971
8	350	M.T., Taxi, 2-BBL.					IL		
8	350	PG, Taxi, 2-BBL.					IM		
8	350	Hyd. 350, Taxi, 2-BBL.					IN		CGJ
8	350	Hyd. 400, Taxi, 2-BBL.					IP		
8	350	M.T., Taxi, Police					IQ, IR	CNP (250)	CJB, CJH
8	350	PG, Taxi, Police					IS, IX	CNW (250)	
8	350	Hyd. 350, Taxi					IT, IY	CNT (300), CNX (250)	CGJ
8	350	Hyd. 400, Taxi					IV, IZ		
8	350	M.T., Taxi					IW		
8	396	M.T.	IA	IA	IA	IA	JT		
8	396	w/ex. EM		IB	IB				
8	396	M.T., w/ex. EM	IC						
8	396	PG, w/ex. EM		IC	IC				
8	396	M.T., SHP	IE						
8	396	PG	IG	IG	IG	IG			
8	396	PG, Trans. Ign.	II						
8	396	Hyd., w/ex. EM		IN	IN				
8	396	Hyd.		IV	IV	IV			
8	396	Hyd., Trans. Ign.	IW						
8	396	M.T., 2-BBL.					JN		
8	396	Hyd. 400, Police, 2-BBL.					JO		
8	396	2-BBL., Police					JP		
8	396	Hyd. 400, 2-BBL.					JQ		
8	396	M.T., Police					JR		
8	400	M.T. (265 H.P.)						CGR	
8	400	Hyd. 350						CLK (265)	
8	400	Hyd. 350 (Mk. IV)					CKR	CLP (300)	
8	400	M.T., Police (Mk. IV)					CKN	CLR (330)	
8	409	M.T., HP	JA						
8	409	M.T.	JB						
8	409	Trans. Ign.	JC						
8	409	Trans. Ign., HP	JD						
8	409	PG	JE						
8	409	PG, Trans. Ign.	JF						
8	427	M.T., HDC			IE, IX	IE			
8	427	SHP	ID			ID			
8	427	Hyd., w/ex. EM			IS	IS			
8	427	w/ex. EM	II	II					
8	427	M.T.	IH	IH	IH		MA		
8	427	Hyd.	IJ	IJ	IJ				
8	427	Hyd., HP, w/ex. EM	IO	IO					
8	427	SS Hyd.		IF					
8	427	HP					LA		
8	427	4-BBL.					LB		
8	427	Hyd. 400, HP					LC		
8	427	M.T., SHP					LD		
8	427	Hyd. 400, 4-BBL.					LE		
8	427	Hyd., Police, HP					LF		
8	427	M.T., Police, HP					LG, LZ, MB		
8	427	M.T., HP					LH, MC		
8	427	Hyd. 400					LI		
8	427	Hyd. 400, Police, 4-BBL.					LJ		
8	427	M.T., Police, 4-BBL.					LK		
8	427	Hyd. 400, SHP					LS		
8	427	M.T., Police					LY		
8	427	M.T., SHP					MD		
8	454	M.T.						CGV (345), CGU (390)	CPD (365)
8	454	M.T., Police						CGS (345), CGT (390)	CPG (365)

AC—Air conditioned.
HDC—Heavy duty clutch.
HP—High performance.
SHP—Special high performance.
M.T.—Manual transmission.
PG—Powerglide transmission.
Hyd.—Turbo-Hydramatic transmission.
w/ex. EM—With exhaust emission controls.
Trans. Ign.—Transistorized ignition.
TD—Torque Drive
M.T.—Manual Transmission

Corvette Engine Identification Code

No. Cyls.	Cu. In. Displ.	Type	1965	1966	1967	1968	1969	1970	1971
8	327	SHP, w/ex. EM		HD	HD				
8	327	HE	HE	HE	HE	HE			
8	327	HP	HF						
8	327	w/F.I.	HG						
8	327	SHP	HH						
8	327	w/ex. EM		HH	HH				
8	327	AC	HI						
8	327	HP, AC	HJ						
8	327	SHP, AC	HK						
8	327	T. Ign.	HL						
8	327	T. Ign., AC	HM						
8	327	w/F.I., T. Ign.	HN						
8	327	PG	HO	HO	HO				
8	327	T.H.				HO			
8	327	SHP, T.H.				HT			
8	327	PG, HP	HP						
8	327	PS, AC			HP				
8	327	4 Speed, AC, PS				HP			
8	327	PG, AC	HQ						
8	327	PG, HP, AC	HR						
8	327	PG, w/ex. EM		HR	HR				
8	327	SHP	HT	HT					
8	327	4 Speed			HT	HT			
8	327	SHP, AC	HU						
8	327	SHP, T. Ign.	HV						
8	327	SHP, T. Ign., AC	HW						
8	327	SHP, AC, W/ex. EM				KH			
8	350	HP					HW	CTN	
8	350	HP, AC					HX	CTO	
8	350	M.T.					HY	CTL	
8	350	T.H. 400					HZ	CTM	
8	350	HP, T. Ign.						CTP	
8	350	HP, T. Ign., AC						CTQ	
8	350	SHP						CTR	
8	350	SHP, T. Ign.						CTU	
8	350	SHP, T. Ign., M.T.						CTV	
8	350	M.T. (270 H.P.)							CGS
8	350	M.T. (330 H.P.)							CGZ

No. Cyls.	Cu. In. Displ.	Type	1965	1966	1967	1968	1969	1970	1971
8	350	Hyd. 400 (270 H.P.)							CGT
8	350	4-Spd. (330 H.P.)							CGY
8	396	SHP	IF						
8	427	SHP		IK					
8	427	HP (390 H.P.), T.H.		IL	IL	IL	LL, LM		
8	427	w/ex. EM (390 H.P.)		IM	IM				
8	427	SHP		IP		IT	LO		
8	427	(390 H.P.), T.H.		IQ	IQ	IQ			
8	427	PG, w/ex. EM (390 H.P.)		IR	IR				
8	427	SHP (435 H.P.)			IT	IR	LR		
8	427	Aluminum Heads (435 H.P.)			IU	IU	LP		
8	427	4 Speed w/ex. EM (435 H.P.)			JA				
8	427	4 Speed (400 H.P.)			JC				
8	427	PG or T.H. (400 H.P.)			JD	IO			
8	427	4 Speed (435 H.P.)			JE				
8	427	4 Speed, w/ex. EM (400 H.P.)			JF	IM			
8	427	PG w/ex. EM (400 H.P.)			JG				
8	427	Aluminum Heads w/ex. EM (435 H.P.)			JH				
8	427	HP, T.H. 400, 3-2-BBL.					LN		
8	427	HP, 3-2-BBL.					LQ		
8	427	SHP, HDC, 3-2-BBL.					LT		
8	427	Aluminum Heads, HDC					LU		
8	427	Aluminum Heads, T.H. 400					LW		
8	427	T.H. 400 (heavy duty)					LV		
8	427	SHP, T.H. 400					LX		
8	454	HP, 4-BBL., T.H. 400						CGW	
8	454	HP, 4-BBL.						CZU	
8	454	Heavy duty, 4-BBL.						CZL	
8	454	T.H. 400, 4-BBL.						CZN	
8	454	HP, 4-BBL., T. Ign.						CRI	
8	454	T.H. 400 (365 H.P.)							CPJ
8	454	M.T. (365 H.P.)							CPH
8	454	M.T. (425 H.P.)							CPW
8	454	T.H. 400 (425 H.P.)							CPX

AC—Air conditioned.
HP—High performance.
SHP—Special high performance.

M.T.—Manual transmission.
PG—Powerglide Transmission.
HDC—Heavy duty clutch.

PS—Power steering.
w/ex. EM—With exhaust emission.
w/F.I.—With fuel injection.

T. Ign.—With transistor ignition.
4 BBL.—Four barrel carburetor.
T.H.—With Turbo-Hydramatic.

WHEEL ALIGNMENT

YEAR	MODEL	CASTER Range (Deg.)	CASTER Pref. Setting (Deg.)	CAMBER Range (Deg.)	CAMBER Pref. Setting (Deg.)	TOE-IN (In.)	KING-PIN INCLINATION (Deg.)	WHEEL PIVOT RATIO Inner Wheel	Outer Wheel
1965-66	Chevrolet	1/4 N to 3/4 P	1/4 P	1/4 N to 3/4 P	1/4 P	1/8 to 1/4	7-8	20	20 1/4
	Corvette	1P to 2P ②	1 1/2 P	1/4 P to 1 1/4 P ③	3/4 P	7/32 to 11/32 ①	6 1/2 to 7 1/2	20	18 1/2
1967	Chevrolet	1/4 P to 1 1/4 P	1/4 P	1/4 P to 3/4 P	1/4 P	1/8 to 1/4	7-8	20	20 1/4
	Corvette	1/2 P to 1 1/2 P	1P	1/4 P to 1 1/4 P ③	3/4 P	3/16 to 5/16 ①	6 1/2 to 7 1/2	20	18 1/2
1968-69	Chevrolet	1/4 P to 1 1/4 P	1/4 P	1/4 N to 3/4 P	1/4 P	1/8 to 1/4	7-8	20	18
	Corvette	1/2 P to 1 1/2 P ④	1P	1/2 P to 1 1/4 P ⑤	3/4 P	3/16 to 5/16 ⑤	6 1/2 to 7 1/2	20	18 1/2
1970	Chevrolet	1/4 P to 1 1/4 P	1/4 P	1/4 N to 3/4 P	1/4 P	1/8 to 1/4	7-8	20	18
	Corvette	1/2 P to 1 1/2 P ④	1P	1/2 P to 1 1/4 P ⑤	3/4 P	3/16 to 5/16 ⑤	6 1/2 to 7 1/2	20	18 1/2
1971-72	Chevrolet	0 to 2N	1N	1/4 N to 1 1/4 P	1/2 P	1/16 to 5/16	9 1/2 to 10 1/2	N.A.	N.A.
	Corvette	0 to 2P ⑥	1P	0 to 1 1/2 P	3/4 P	3/16 to 5/16	6 1/2 to 7 1/2	N.A.	N.A.
	Station Wagons (116 in. WB)	1 1/2 N to 1/2 N	1N	1/4 P to 1 1/4 P	3/4 P	1/8 to 1/4	7 3/4 to 8 3/4	N.A.	N.A.

① —Rear wheels 1/16-3/16.
② —1966—1/2 P to 1 1/2 P.
③ —Rear wheels—1/2° ± 1/2°.
④ —W/pwr. steering: 1 3/4 P to 2 3/4 P.
⑤ —Rear wheel alignment: camber 1 3/8 N to 3/4 N toe-in 1/32-3/32.
⑥ —Power steering—1 1/4 P to 3 1/4 P.
N—Negative.
P—Positive.

GENERAL ENGINE SPECIFICATIONS

YEAR	CU. IN. DISPLACEMENT	CARBURETOR	ADVERTIZED HORSEPOWER @ RPM	ADVERTIZED TORQUE @ RPM (FT. LBS.)	A.M.A. HORSEPOWER	BORE AND STROKE (IN.)	ADVERTIZED COMPRESSION RATIO	VALVE LIFTER TYPE	NORMAL OIL PRESSURE (PSI)
1965	6 Cyl.—230	1-BBL.	140 @ 4400	220 @ 1600	36.0	3.875 x 3.250	8.50-1	Hyd.	45
	V8—283	2-BBL.	195 @ 4800	285 @ 2400	48.0	3.875 x 3.000	9.25-1	Hyd.	45
	V8—327	4-BBL.	250 @ 4400	350 @ 2800	51.2	4.000 x 3.250	10.5-1	Hyd.	45
	V8—327	4-BBL.	300 @ 5000	360 @ 3200	51.2	4.000 x 3.250	10.5-1	Hyd.	45
	V8—327	4-BBL.	350 @ 5300	360 @ 3600	51.2	4.000 x 3.250	11.0-1	Hyd.	45
	V8—327	4-BBL.	365 @ 6200	350 @ 4000	51.2	4.000 x 3.250	11.0-1	Mech.	45
	V8—327	Fuel Inj.	375 @ 6200	350 @ 4600	51.2	4.000 x 3.250	11.0-1	Mech.	45
	V8—396	4-BBL.	325 @ 4800	410 @ 3200	53.6	4.094 x 3.760	10.25-1	Hyd.	45
	V8—396	4-BBL.	425 @ 6400	415 @ 4000	53.6	4.094 x 3.760	11.00-1	Mech.	45
	V8—409	4-BBL.	340 @ 5000	420 @ 3200	59.5	4.313 x 3.500	10.0-1	Hyd.	45
	V8—409	4-BBL.	400 @ 5800	425 @ 3600	59.5	4.313 x 3.500	11.0-1	Mech.	45
1966	6 Cyl.—250	1-BBL.	150 @ 4200	235 @ 1600	36.0	3.875 x 3.530	8.5-1	Hyd.	45
	V8—283	2-BBL.	195 @ 4800	285 @ 2400	48.0	3.875 x 3.000	9.25-1	Hyd.	45
	V8—283	4-BBL.	220 @ 4800	295 @ 3200	48.0	3.875 x 3.000	9.25-1	Hyd.	45
	V8—327	4-BBL.	275 @ 4800	355 @ 3200	51.2	4.000 x 3.250	10.5-1	Hyd.	45
	V8—327	4-BBL.	300 @ 5000	360 @ 3200	51.2	4.000 x 3.250	10.5-1	Hyd.	45
	V8—327	4-BBL.	350 @ 5800	360 @ 3600	51.2	4.000 x 3.250	11.0-1	Hyd.	45
	V8—396	4-BBL.	325 @ 4800	410 @ 3200	53.6	4.094 x 3.760	10.25-1	Hyd.	60
	V8—427	4-BBL.	390 @ 5200	460 @ 3600	57.8	4.251 x 3.760	10.25-1	Hyd.	60
	V8—427	4-BBL.	425 @ 5600	460 @ 3600	57.8	4.251 x 3.760	11.00-1	Mech.	60
1967	6 Cyl.—250	1-BBL.	155 @ 4200	235 @ 1600	36.0	3.875 x 3.530	8.5-1	Hyd.	45
	V8—283	2-BBL.	195 @ 4800	285 @ 2400	48.0	3.875 x 3.000	9.25-1	Hyd.	45
	V8—327	4-BBL.	275 @ 4800	355 @ 3200	51.2	4.000 x 3.250	10.25-1	Hyd.	45
	V8—327	4-BBL.	300 @ 5000	360 @ 3400	51.2	4.000 x 3.250	10.25-1	Hyd.	45
	V8—327	4-BBL.	350 @ 5800	360 @ 3600	51.2	4.000 x 3.250	11.00-1	Hyd.	45
	V8—396	4-BBL.	325 @ 4800	410 @ 3200	53.6	4.094 x 3.760	10.25-1	Hyd.	65
	V8—427	4-BBL.	385 @ 5200	460 @ 3400	57.8	4.251 x 3.760	10.25-1	Hyd.	65
	V8—427	4-BBL.	390 @ 5400	460 @ 3600	57.8	4.251 x 3.760	10.25-1	Hyd.	65
	V8—427	3-2-BBL.	400 @ 5400	460 @ 3600	57.8	4.251 x 3.760	10.25-1	Hyd.	65
	V8—427	4-BBL.	425 @ 5600	460 @ 3800	57.8	4.251 x 3.760	11.0-1	Mech.	65
	V8—427	3-2-BBL.	435 @ 5800	460 @ 4000	57.8	4.251 x 3.760	11.00-1	Mech.	65
1968	6 Cyl.—250	1-BBL.	155 @ 4200	235 @ 1600	36.0	3.875 x 3.530	8.5-1	Hyd.	45
	V8—307	2-BBL.	200 @ 4600	300 @ 2400	48.0	3.875 x 3.250	9.0-1	Hyd.	45
	V8—327	4-BBL.	250 @ 4800	325 @ 3200	52.2	4.000 x 3.250	8.75-1	Hyd.	45
	V8—327	4-BBL.	275 @ 4800	355 @ 3200	51.2	4.000 x 3.250	10.0-1	Hyd.	45
	V8—327	4-BBL.	300 @ 5000	360 @ 3400	51.2	4.000 x 3.250	10.0-1	Hyd.	45
	V8—327	4-BBL.	350 @ 5800	360 @ 3600	51.2	4.000 x 3.250	11.0-1	Hyd.	45
	V8—396	4-BBL.	325 @ 4800	410 @ 3200	53.6	4.094 x 3.760	10.25-1	Hyd.	65
	V8—427	4-BBL.	385 @ 5200	460 @ 3400	57.8	4.251 x 3.760	10.25-1	Hyd.	65
	V8—427	4-BBL.	390 @ 5400	460 @ 3600	57.8	4.251 x 3.760	10.25-1	Hyd.	65
	V8—427	3-2-BBL.	400 @ 5400	460 @ 3600	57.8	4.251 x 3.760	10.25-1	Hyd.	65
	V8—427	3-2-BBL.	435 @ 5800	460 @ 4000	57.8	4.251 x 3.760	11.0-1	Mech.	65
1969	6 Cyl.—250	1-BBL.	155 @ 4200	235 @ 1600	36.0	3.875 x 3.530	8.5-1	Hyd.	35
	V8—327	2-BBL.	235 @ 4800	325 @ 2800	51.2	4.000 x 3.250	9.0-1	Hyd.	45
	V8—350	4-BBL.	255 @ 4800	365 @ 3200	51.2	4.000 x 3.480	9.0-1	Hyd.	45
	V8—350	4-BBL.	300 @ 4800	380 @ 3200	51.2	4.000 x 3.480	10.25-1	Hyd.	45
	V8—350	4-BBL.	350 @ 5600	380 @ 3600	51.2	4.000 x 3.480	11.0-1	Hyd.	45

GENERAL ENGINE SPECIFICATIONS, continued

YEAR	CU. IN. DISPLACEMENT	CARBURETOR	ADVERTIZED HORSEPOWER @ RPM	ADVERTIZED TORQUE @ RPM (FT. LBS.)	A.M.A. HORSEPOWER	BORE AND STROKE (IN.)	ADVERTIZED COMPRESSION RATIO	VALVE LIFTER TYPE	NORMAL OIL PRESSURE (PSI)
	V8—396	2-BBL.	265 @ 4800	400 @ 2800	53.6	4.094 x 3.760	9.0-1	Hyd.	45
	V8—396	4-BBL.	325 @ 4800	410 @ 3200	53.6	4.094 x 3.760	10.25-1	Hyd.	45
	V8—427	4-BBL.	335 @ 4800	470 @ 3200	57.8	4.251 x 3.760	10.25-1	Hyd.	45
	V8—427	4-BBL.	390 @ 5400	460 @ 3600	57.8	4.251 x 3.760	10.25-1	Hyd.	45
	V8—427	3-2-BBL.	400 @ 5400	460 @ 3600	57.8	4.251 x 3.760	10.25-1	Hyd.	45
	V8—427	3-2-BBL.	435 @ 5800	460 @ 4000	57.8	4.251 x 3.760	11.0-1	Mech.	45
1970	6 Cyl.—250	1-BBL.	155 @ 4200	235 @ 1600	36.0	3.875 x 3.530	8.5-1	Hyd.	30–45
	V8—350	2-BBL.	250 @ 4800	345 @ 2800	51.2	4.000 x 3.480	9.0-1	Hyd.	30–45
	V8—350	4-BBL.	300 @ 4800	380 @ 3200	51.2	4.000 x 3.480	10.25-1	Hyd.	30–45
	V8—350	4-BBL.	350 @ 5600	380 @ 3600	51.2	4.000 x 3.480	11.0-1	Hyd.	30–45
	V8—350	4-BBL.	370 @ 6000	380 @ 4000	51.2	4.000 x 3.480	11.0-1	Mech.	30–45
	V8—400	2-BBL.	265 @ 4400	400 @ 2400	54.4	4.125 x 3.750	9.0-1	Hyd.	30–45
	V8—454	4-BBL.	345 @ 4400	500 @ 3000	57.8	4.251 x 4.000	10.25-1	Hyd.	30–45
	V8—454	4-BBL.	390 @ 4800	500 @ 3400	57.8	4.251 x 4.000	10.25-1	Hyd.	30–45
	V8—454	4-BBL.	450 @ 5600	450 @ 5600	57.8	4.251 x 4.000	11.25-1	Mech.	30–45
1971-72②	6 Cyl.—250	1-BBL.	145 @ 4200	145 @ 4200②	36.0	3.875 x 3.53	8.5-1	Hyd.	40
	V8—350	2-BBL.	245 @ 4800	245 @ 4800②	51.2	4.00 x 3.48	8.5-1	Hyd.	40
	V8—350	4-BBL.	270 @ 4800	270 @ 4800②	51.2	4.00 x 3.48	8.5-1	Hyd.	40
	V8—350	4-BBL.	330 @ 5600	330 @ 5600②	51.2	4.00 x 3.48	9.0-1	Mech.	40
	V8—400	2-BBL.	255 @ 4800	255 @ 4800②	54.4	4.125 x 3.75	8.5-1	Hyd.	40
	V8—402 (Mk. IV)	4-BBL.	300 @ 4800	300 @ 4800②	54.4	4.125 x 3.76	8.5-1	Hyd.	40
	V8-454	4-BBL.	365 @ 4800	365 @ 4800②	57.8	4.251 x 4.00	8.5-1	Hyd.	40
	V8-454	4-BBL.	425 @ 5600	425 @ 5600②	57.8	4.251 x 4.00	9.0-1	Mech.	40

① —Special camshaft.
② —1972 S.A.E. Net H.P.: 250 C.I.—110 H.P., 350 C.I.—165 (2 Bbl.), 175 (4 Bbl.),
400 C.I.—170 H.P., 402 C.I.—208 H.P.*, 454 C.I.—285 H.P.*
* —Not available in California.

TORQUE SPECIFICATIONS

YEAR	MODEL	CYLINDER HEAD BOLTS (FT. LBS.)	ROD BEARING BOLTS (FT. LBS.)	MAIN BEARING BOLTS (FT. LBS.)	CRANKSHAFT BALANCER BOLT (FT. LBS.)	FLYWHEEL TO CRANKSHAFT BOLTS (FT. LBS.)	MANIFOLD (FT. LBS.) Intake	MANIFOLD (FT. LBS.) Exhaust
1965-72	4 & 6-Cyl.	95	35	65	...	60	①	①
1965-67	V8—283-350	60-70	35	80	60⑥	60	30	①
1968-72	V8—302-400 (Small Block)	60-70	45	75②	60⑥	60	30	①
1965	V8—409	60-70	35-45	90-100	...	65	30	①
1965-72	V8—396-402 (Big Block)	80①	50	95③	85	65	30	①
1966-72	V8—427-454	80①	50④	100③	85	65	30	①

① —Aluminum Heads—Short bolts 65, Long bolts 75
② —Engines with 4-bolt mains—Outer bolts 65
③ —Engines with 4-bolt mains—115
④ —⁷/₁₆ Rod bolts—70
⑤ —Center bolts—25-30, end bolts 15-20
⑥ —Where applicable

CYLINDER HEAD BOLT TIGHTENING SEQUENCE

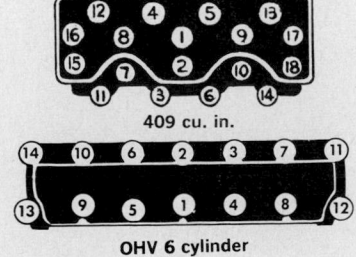

409 cu. in.

OHV 6 cylinder

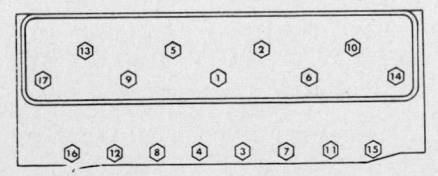

V8—283, 307, 327 and 350

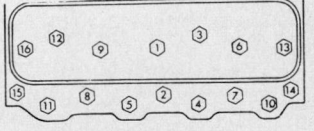

V8—396, 427, 454

TUNE-UP SPECIFICATIONS

YEAR	MODEL	SPARK PLUGS Type	Gap (In.)	DISTRIBUTOR Point Dwell (Deg.)	Point Gap (In.)	IGNITION TIMING (Deg.) ▲	CRANKING COMP. PRESSURE (Psi)	VALVES Tappet (Hot) Clearance (In.) Intake	Exhaust	Intake Opens (Deg.)	FUEL PUMP PRESSURE (Psi)	IDLE SPEED (Rpm) ★
1965	6 cyl.—230 Cu. In.	46N	.035	31°–34°	.019	4B	130	■	■	62B	3–4½	500
	V8—283 Cu. In.	45	.035	28°–32°	.019	4B	150	■	■	32½B	5–6½	500
	V8—327 Cu. In. Std.	44	.035	28°–32°	.019	4B	160	■	■	32½B	5–6½	500
	V8—327 Cu. In. (300 H.P.)	44	.035	28°–32°	.019	8B	160	■	■	32½B	5–6½	500
	V8—327 Cu. In. (350 H.P.)	44	.035	28°–32°	.019	8B	150	■	■	54B	5–6½	700
	V8—327 Cu. In. (365 H.P.)	44	.035	28°–32°	.019	10B	150	.030	.030	54B	5–6½	700
	V8—327 Cu. In. (Fuel Inj.)	44	.035	28°–32°	.019	12B	150	.030	.030	54B	5–6½	700
	V8—396 Cu. In. Std.	43N	.035	28°–32°	.019	4-6B	150	■	■	N.A.	5½	800
	V8—396 Cu. In. Hi. Perf.	43N	.035	28°–32°	.019	10B	150	.020	.024	N.A.	7½	800
	V8—409 Cu. In. Std.	43N	.035	28°–32°	.019	6B	150	■	■	38½B	7–8½	500
	V8—409 Cu. In. Opt.	43N	.035	28°–32°	.019	12B	150	.025 (10)	.025 (10)	50¾B	7–8½	700
1966	6 Cyl.—250 Cu. In.	46N	.035	31°–34°	.019	6B	130	■	■	62B	3–4½	500
	V8—283 Cu. In.	45	.035	28°–32°	.019	4B	150	■	■	32½B	5–6½	500
	V8—327 Cu. In. Std.	44	.035	28°–32°	.019	8B③	160	■	■	32½B	5–6½	500
	V8—327 Cu. In. (350 H.P.)	44	.035	28°–32°	.019	10B	150	■	■	54B	5–6½	700
	V8—396 Cu. In.	43N	.035	28°–32°	.019	4B	160	■	■	40B	5–6½	550
	V8—427 Cu. In. (390 H.P.)	43N	.035	28°–32°	.019	4B	160	■	■	58B	5–6½	550
	V8—427 Cu. In. (425 H.P.)	43N	.035	28°–32°	.019	8B	150	.020	.024	54B	5–6½	800
1967	6 cyl.—250 Cu. In.	46N	.035	31°–34°	.019	4B	130	■	■	62B	3–4½	500 ⑬
	V8—283 Cu. In. (195 H.P.)	45	.035	28°–32°	.019	4B⑩	150	■	■	36B	5–6½	500 ⑬
	V8—327 Cu. In. (275 H.P.)	44	.035	28°–32°	.019	8B⑪	160	■	■	38B	5–6½	500 ⑬
	V8—327 Cu. In. (300 H.P.)	44	.035	28°–32°	.019	6B⑩ ⑫	160	■	■	38B	5–6½	500 ⑬
	V8—327 Cu. In. (350 H.P.)	44	.035	28°–32°	.019	10B	150	■	■	54B	5–6½	700 ⑬
	V8—396 Cu. In. (325 H.P.)	43N	.035	28°–32°	.019	4B	160	■	■	40B	5–6½	500 ⑬
	V8—427 Cu. In. (385 H.P.)	43N	.035	28°–32°	.019	4B	160	■	■	56B	5–6½	550 ⑬
	V8—427 Cu. In. (390 H.P.)	43N	.035	28°–32°	.019	4B	160	■	■	56B	5–6½	550 ⑬
	V8—427 Cu. In. (400 H.P.)	43N	.035	28°–32°	.019	4B	160	■	■	56B	5–6½	550 ⑭
	V8—427 Cu. In. (425 H.P.)	43N	.035	28°–32°	.019	10B	150	.022	.024	44B	5–6½	1000
	V8—427 Cu. In. (435 H.P.)	43N	.035	28°–32°	.019	5B	150	.024	.028	44B	5–6½	750 ⑬
1968	6 Cyl.—250 Cu. In.	46N	.035	31°–34°	.019	TDC②	130	■	■	16B	3–4½	700④
	V8—307 Cu. In. (200 H.P.)	45S	.035	28°–32°	.019	2B	150	■	■	28B	5–6½	700⑧
	V8—327 Cu. In. (250 H.P.)	44S	.035	28°–32°	.019	4B	160	■	■	28B	5–6½	700⑧
	V8—327 Cu. In. (275 H.P.)	44	.035	28°–32°	.019	TDC②	160	■	■	28B	5–6½	700⑧
	V8—327 Cu. In. (300 H.P.)	44	.035	28°–32°	.019	4B	160	■	■	28B	5–6½	700⑧
	V8—327 Cu. In. (350 H.P.)	44	.035	28°–32°	.019	4B	150	■	■	40B	5–6½	750
	V8—396 Cu. In. (325 H.P.)	43N	.035	28°–32°	.019	4B	160	■	■	28B	5–6½	700⑧
	V8—427 Cu. In. (385 H.P.)	43N	.035	28°–32°	.019	4B	160	■	■	40B	5–8½	700⑧
	V8—427 Cu. In. (390 H.P.)	43N	.035	28°–32°	.019	4B	160	■	■	40B	5–8½	700⑧
	V8—427 Cu. In. (400 H.P.)	43N	.035	28°–32°	.019	4B	160	■	■	40B	5–8½	750⑧
	V8—427 Cu. In. (435 H.P.)	43N	.035	28°–32°	.019	4B	150	.024	.028	44B	5–8½	750
1969	6 cyl.—250 Cu. In.	R46N	.035	31°–34°	.019	TDC⑤	130	■	■	16B	3–4½	700⑦
	V8—327 Cu. In. (235 H.P.)	45S	.035	28°–32°	.019	2A⑥	160	■	■	28B	5–6½	700⑧

TUNE-UP SPECIFICATIONS, continued

YEAR	MODEL	SPARK PLUGS Type	Gap (In.)	DISTRIBUTOR Point Dwell (Deg.)	Point Gap (In.)	IGNITION TIMING (Deg.) ▲	CRANKING COMP. PRESSURE (Psi)	VALVES Tappet (Hot) Clearance (In.) Intake	Exhaust	Intake Opens (Deg.)	FUEL PUMP PRESSURE (Psi)	IDLE SPEED (Rpm) ★
	V8—350 Cu. In. (255 H.P.)	R44	.035	28°-32°	.019	TDC⑤	160	■	■	28B	5-6½	700⑧
	V8—350 Cu. In. (300 H.P.)	R44	.035	28°-32°	.019	TDC⑤	160	■	■	28B	5-6½	700⑧
	V8—350 Cu. In. (350 H.P.)	R44	.035	28°-32°	.019	4B	160	■	■	52B	5-6½	750
	V8—396 Cu. In. (265 H.P.)	R44N	.035	28°-32°	.019	TDC⑤	160	■	■	28B	5-6½	700⑧
	V8—427 Cu. In. (335 H.P.)	R44N	.035	28°-32°	.019	4B	160	■	■	28B	5-8½	800⑧
	V8—427 Cu. In. (390 H.P.)	R43N	.035	28°-32°	.019	4B	160	■	■	56B	5-8½	800⑤
	V8—427 Cu. In. (400 H.P.)	R43N	.035	28°-32°	.019	4B	160	■	■	56B	5-8½	800⑧
	V8—427 Cu. In. (435 H.P.)	R43N	.035	Transistor Ign.		4B	160	.024	.028	44B	5-8½	750
1970	6 Cyl.—250 Cu. In.	R46T	.035	31°-34°	.019	TDC⑤	130	■	■	16B	3-4½	750⑧
	V8—350 Cu. In. (250 H.P.)	R44	.035	28°-32°	.019	TDC⑤	160	■	■	28B	5-6½	750⑧
	V8—350 Cu. In. (300 H.P.)	R44	.035	28°-32°	.019	TDC⑤	160	■	■	28B	5-6½	700⑧
	V8—350 Cu. In. (350 H.P.)	R44	.035	28°-32°	.019	4B	160	■	■	52B	5-6½	750
	V8—350 Cu. In. (370 H.P.)	R43	.035	Transistor Ign.		14B	190	.030	.030	43B	5-6½	750
	V8—400 Cu. In. (265 H.P.)	R44	.035	28°-32°	.019	4B⑨	160	■	■	34B	5-8½	700⑧
	V8—454 Cu. In. (345 H.P.)	R44T	.035	28°-32°	.019	6B	160	■	■	30B	5-8½	600
	V8—454 Cu. In. (390 H.P.)	R43T	.035	28°-32°	.019	6B	160	■	■	56B	5-8½	700⑧
	V8—454 Cu. In. (450 H.P.)	R43T	.035	Transistor Ign.		4B	150	.024	.028	62B	5-8½	700
†1971-72	6 Cyl.—250 Cu. In.	R46T	.035	31°-34°	.019	4B	130	■	■	16B	3-4½	550
	V8—350 Cu. In. (245 H.P.)	R45TS	.035	28°-32°	.019	2B⑮	160	■	■	28B	7-8½	600⑦
	V8—350 Cu. In. (270 H.P.)	R44TS	.035	28°-32°	.019	4B⑨	160	■	■	28B	7-8½	600⑦
	V8—350 Cu. In. (330 H.P.)	R44TS	.035	28°-32°	.019	8B⑯	150	.024	.030	52B	7-8½	700
	V8—400 Cu. In. (255 H.P.)	R44TS	.035	28°-32°	.019	4B⑨	160	■	■	34B	7-8½	600⑦
	V8—402 Cu. In. (300 H.P.) (Mk. IV)	R44TS	.035	28°-32°	.019	8B	160	■	■	28B	7-8½	600
	V8—454 Cu. In. (365 H.P.)	R42TS	.035	28°-32°	.019	8B	160	■	■	30B	7-8½	600
	V8—454 Cu. In. (425 H.P.)	R42TS	.035	28°-32°	.019	8B⑥	160	.024	.028	56B	8	700⑧

★—with manual transmission in N and automatic in D. Add 50 rpm if equipped with air conditioning

▲—with vacuum advance disconnected. NOTE: These settings are only approximate. Engine design, altitude, temperature, fuel octane rating and the condition of the individual engine are all factors which can influence timing. The limiting advance factor must, therefore, be the "knock point" of the individual engine.

■—1 turn tighter than zero lash.

① —N.A. @ publication, see decal under hood for data.

⓪ —if exhaust emission equipped:
283 Cu. In., w/M.T. and A.I.R.—TDC.

② —w/A.T.—4B

③ —2A w/Auto. Trans.

④ —6 Cyl w/A.T.—Idle 600 rpm.

⑤ —w/Auto. Trans.—4°B.

⑥ —w/Auto. Trans.—2°B.

⑦ —w/Auto. Trans.—550 rpm.

⑧ —w/Auto. Trans.—600 rpm.

⑨ —w/Auto. Trans.—8°B.

A—After top dead center.

B—Before top dead center.

TDC—Top dead center.

⑩ —For sustained high speed driving—Intake .030 in., Exhaust .030 in.

⑪ —w/Auto. Trans. and A.I.R.—6B.

⑫ —w/Auto. Trans. and A.I.R.—4A.

⑬ —w/Auto. Trans. and A.I.R.—700 rpm.

⑭ —w/Auto. Trans. and A.I.R.—750 rpm.

⑮ —w/Auto. Trans.—6B.

⑯ —w/Auto. Trans.—12B.

† —On 1972 models consult the engine decal for timing and idle speed information.

CAUTION

General adoption of anti-pollution laws has changed the design of almost all car engine production to effectively reduce crankcase emission and terminal exhaust products. It has been necessary to adopt stricter tune-up rules, especially timing and idle speed procedures. Both of these values are peculiar to the engine and to its application, rather than to the engine alone. With this in mind, car manufacturers supply idle speed data for the engine and application involved. This information is clearly displayed in the engine compartment of each vehicle.

VALVE SPECIFICATIONS

YEAR AND MODEL	SEAT ANGLE (DEG.) ①	FACE ANGLE (DEG.)	VALVE LIFT INTAKE (IN.)	VALVE LIFT EXHAUST (IN.)	VALVE SPRING PRESSURE (VALVE OPEN) LBS. @ IN.	VALVE SPRING INSTALLED HEIGHT (IN.)	STEM TO GUIDE CLEARANCE (IN.)		STEM DIAMETER (IN.)	
							Intake	Exhaust	Intake	Exhaust
1965-66 6 Cyl.—230 Cu. In.*	46	45	.3318	.3318	175 @ 1.26	1.66	.0010-.0027	.0016-.0033	.3404-.3417	.3410-.3417
6 Cyl.—250 Cu. In.**	46	45	.3880	.3880	185 @ 1.27	1.66	.0010-.0027	.0010-.0027	.3410-.3417	.3410-.3417
V8—283 Cu. In.	46	45	.3987	.3987	175 @ 1.26	1.66	.0010-.0027	.0016-.0033	.3404-.3417	.3410-.3417
V8—327 Cu. In.	46	45	.3987	.3987	175 @ 1.26	1.66	.0010-.0027	.0016-.0033	.3404-.3417	.3410-.3417
V8—327 Cu. In. (350 H.P.)	46	45	.4472	.4472	175 @ 1.26	1.66	.0010-.0027	.0016-.0033	.3410-.3417	.3410-.3417
V8—327 Cu. In. (Fuel Inj.)	46	45	.4850	.4850	175 @ 1.26	1.66	.0010-.0027	.0016-.0033	.3410-.3417	.3410-.3417
V8—396 Cu. In. Std.	46	45	.3980	.3980	220 @ 1.46	1⁷⁄₈	.0005-.0024	.0012-.0029	.3715-.3722	.3713-.3720
V8—396 Cu. In. Hi. Perf.	46	45	.5000	.4960	315 @ 1.38	1⁷⁄₈	.0005-.0024	.0012-.0029	.3715-.3722	.3713-.3720
V8—409 Cu. In.	46	45	.4005	.4119	170 @ 1.33	1.66	.0010-.0027	.0015-.0032	.3715-.3722	.3710-.3717
V8—409 Cu. In. (400 H.P.)	46	45	.5567	.5567	330 @ 1.20	1.68	.0010-.0027	.0015-.0032	.3715-.3722	.3710-.3717
V8—427 Cu. In.	46	45	.4614	.4800	315 @ 1.38	1.88	.0010-.0027	.0015-.0032	.3715-.3722	.3713-.3720
V8—427 Cu. In. (425 H.P.)	46	45	.5197	.5197	315 @ 1.38	1.88	.0010-.0027	.0015-.0032	.3715-.3722	.3713-.3720
1967 6 Cyl.—250 Cu. In.	46	45	.3880	.3880	186 @ 1.27	1²¹⁄₃₂	.0010-.0027	.0010-.0027	.3410-.3417	.3410-.3417
V8—283 Cu. In.	46	45	.3900	.4100	200 @ 1.25	1⁵⁄₃₂	.0010-.0027	.0010-.0027	.3410-.3417	.3410-.3417
V8—327 Cu. In.	46	45	.3900	.4100	200 @ 1.25	1⁵⁄₃₂	.0010-.0027	.0010-.0027	.3410-.3417	.3410-.3417
V8—327 Cu. In. (300 H.P.)	46	45	.3900	.4100	200 @ 1.25	1⁵⁄₃₂	.0010-.0027	.0015-.0032	.3410-.3417	.3410-.3417
V8—327 Cu. In. (350 H.P.)	46	45	.4472	.4472	200 @ 1.25	1⁵⁄₃₂	.0010-.0027	.0015-.0032	.3410-.3417	.3410-.3417
V8—396 Cu. In.	46	45	.3983	.3983	220 @ 1.46	1⁷⁄₈	.0010-.0027	.0015-.0032	.3715-.3722	.3713-.3720
V8—427 Cu. In. (385, 390, 400 H.P.)	46	45	.4614	.4800			.0010-.0027	.0015-.0032	.3715-.3722	.3713-.3720
V8—427 Cu. In. (435 H.P.)	46	45	.5197	.5197	315 @ 1.38	1⁷⁄₈	.0010-.0027	.0015-.0032	.3715-.3722	.3713-.3720
1968 6 Cyl.—250 Cu. In.	46	45	.3880	.3880	186 @ 1.25	1.66	.0010-.0027	.0017-.0027	.3410-.3417	.3410-.3417
V8—307 Cu. In.	46	45	.3900	.4100	198 @ 1.25	1.70	.0010-.0027	.0017-.0027	.3410-.3417	.3410-.3417
V8—327 Cu. In. (Exc. 350 H.P.)	46	45	.3900	.4100	198 @ 1.25	1.70	.0010-.0027	.0017-.0027	.3410-.3417	.3410-.3417
V8—327 (350 H.P.)	46	45	.4472	.4472	198 @ 1.25	1.70	.0010-.0027	.0010-.0027	.3410-.3417	.3410-.3417
V8—396 Cu. In.	46	45	.3983	.3983	220 @ 1.46	1⁷⁄₈	.0010-.0027	.0015-.0032	.3715-.3722	.3713-.3720
V8—427 (Exc. 435 H.P.)	46	45	.4614	.4800	315 @ 1.38	1.88	.0010-.0027	.0015-.0032	.3715-.3722	.3713-.3722
V8—427 Cu. In. (435 H.P.)	46	45	.5197	.5197	315 @ 1.38	1.88	.0010-.0027	.0015-.0032	.3715-.3722	.3713-.3722
1969 6 Cyl. 250 Cu. In.	46	45	.3880	.3880	186 @ 1.27	1.66	.0010-.0027	.0015-.0032	.3410-.3417	.3410-.3417
V8—327, 350 Cu. In.	46	45	.3945	.3945	200 @ 1.25	1.70	.0010-.0027	.0010-.0027	.3410-.3417	.3410-.3417
V8—350 (350 H.P.)	46	45	.4500	.4600	200 @ 1.25	1.70	.0010-.0027	.0010-.0027	.3410-.3417	.3410-.3417
V8—396	46	45	.3983	.3983	220 @ 1.46	1⁷⁄₈	.0010-.0027	.0010-.0027	.3715-.3722	.3713-.3720
V8—427 (335 H.P.)	46	45	.3983	.3983	198 @ 1.32	1.88	.0010-.0027	.0010-.0027	.3715-.3722	.3713-.3720
V8—427 (390 & 400 H.P.)	46	45	.4614	.4800	312 @ 1.38	1.88	.0010-.0027	.0010-.0027	.3715-.3722	.3713-.3722
V8—427 (435 H.P.)	46	45	.5197	.5197	312 @ 1.38	1.88	.0010-.0027	.0010-.0027	.3715-.3722	.3713-.3722
1970 6 Cyl.—250 Cu. In.	46	45	.3880	.3880	186 @ 1.27	1.66	.0010-.0027	.0010-.0027	.3410-.3417	.3410-.3417
V8—350 Cu. In. (250, 300 H.P.)	46	45	.3900	.4100	200 @ 1.25	1.70	.0010-.0027	.0010-.0027	.3410-.3417	.3410-.3417
V8—350 Cu. In. (350 H.P.)	46	45	.4500	.4600	200 @ 1.25	1.70	.0010-.0027	.0010-.0027	.3410-.3417	.3410-.3417
V8—350 Cu. In. (370 H.P.)	46	45	.4586	.4850	200 @ 1.25	1.70	.0010-.0027	.0010-.0027	.3410-.3417	.3410-.3417
V8—400 Cu. In. (265 H.P.)	46	45	.3900	.4100	200 @ 1.25	1.70	.0010-.0027	.0010-.0027	.3410-.3417	.3410-.3417
V8—454 Cu. In. (345 H.P.)	46	45	.3983	.4300	240 @ 1.38	1.88	.0010-.0027	.0010-.0027	.3715-.3722	.3713-.3720
V8—454 Cu. In. (390 H.P.)	46	45	.4614	.4800	240 @ 1.38	1.88	.0010-.0027	.0010-.0027	.3715-.3722	.3713-.3720
V8—454 Cu. In. (450 H.P.)	46	45	.5197	.5197	315 @ 1.32	1.88	.0010-.0027	.0010-.0027	.3715-.3722	.3713-.3720
1971-72 6 Cyl.—250 Cu. In.	46	45	.3880	.3880	186 @ 1.27	1.66	.0010-.0027	.0010-.0027	.3410-.3417	.3410-.3417
V8—350 Cu.In. (245-270 H.P.)	46	45	.3900	.4100	200 @ 1.25	1.70	.0010-.0027	.0010-.0027	.3410-.3417	.3410-.3417
V8—350 Cu.In. (330 H.P.)	46	45	.4586	.4850	200 @ 1.25	1.70	.0010-.0027	.0010-.0027	.3410-.3417	.3410-.3417
V8—400 Cu. In. (255 H.P.)	46	45	.3983	.4300	240 @ 1.38	1.88	.0010-.0027	.0010-.0027	.3410-.3417	.3410-.3417
V8—402 Cu. In. (300 H.P.) (Mk. IV)	46	45	.3983	.4300	240 @ 1.38	1.88	.0010-.0027	.0010-.0027	.3715-.3722	.3713-.3720
V8—454 Cu. In. (365 H.P.)	46	45	.4614	.4800	240 @ 1.38	1.88	.0010-.0027	.0010-.0027	.3715-.3722	.3713-.3720
V8—454 Cu. In. (425 H.P.)	46	45	.5197	.5197	315 @ 1.38	1.88	.0010-.0027	.0010-.0027	.3715-.3722	.3713-.3720

*—1965 only.

**—1966 only.

① —45° w/Aluminum heads.

CRANKSHAFT BEARING JOURNAL SPECIFICATIONS

YEAR	MODEL	MAIN BEARING JOURNALS (IN.)				CONNECTING ROD BEARING JOURNALS (IN.)		
		Journal Diameter	Oil Clearance	Shaft End-Play	Thrust On No.	Journal Diameter	Oil Clearance	End-Play
1965	6 Cyl.—230 Cu. In.	2.2983–2.2993	.0003–.0029	.002–.006	7	1.9990–2.0000	.0007–.0027	.009–.013
	V8—283/327 Cu. In.	2.2978–2.2988	.0003–.0029	.002–.006	5	1.9990–2.0000	.0007–.0027	.009–.013
	V8—396 Cu. In. Std.	2.7487–2.7497 ①	.0004–.0020 ②	.006–.010	5	2.1990–2.2000	.0007–.0028	.015–.021
	V8—396 Cu. In. Hi. Perf.	2.7487–2.7497 ①	.0004–.0020 ②	.006–.010	5	2.1990–2.2000	.0007–.0028	.015–.021
	V8—409 Cu. In.	2.4980–2.4990 ③	.0006–.0032	.006–.010	5	2.1988–2.1998	.0009–.0030	.016–.020
1966–67	6 Cyl.—250 Cu. In.	2.2983–2.2993	.0003–.0029	.002–.006	7	1.9990–2.0000	.0007–.0027	.0085–.0135
	V8—283 Cu. In.	2.2987–2.2997 ④	.0003–.0029 ⑤	.003–.011	5	1.9990–2.0000	.0007–.0027	.009–.013
	V8—327 Cu. In.	2.2987–2.2997 ④	.0003–.0034 ⑤	.003–.011	5	1.9990–2.0000	.0007–.0028	.009–.013
	V8—396 Cu. In.	2.7487–2.7497 ①	.0004–.0020 ②	.006–.010	5	2.1990–2.2000	.0007–.0028	.015–.021
	V8—427 Cu. In.	2.7487–2.7497 ①	.0004–.0020 ②	.006–.010	5	2.1990–2.2000	.0007–.0028	.015–.021 ⑥
	V8—427 Cu. In. (435 H.P.)*	2.7487–2.7497 ①	.0004–.0020 ②	.006–.010	5	2.1990–2.2000	.0007–.0028	.019–.025
1968–1969	6 Cyl.—250 Cu. In.	2.2983–2.2993	.0003–.0029	.002–.006	7	1.9990–2.0000	.0007–.0027	.009–.013
	V8—307, 327 Cu. In.	2.4484–2.4493 ⑦	.0008–.0020 ⑧	.003–.011	5	2.0990–2.1000	.0007–.0028	.009–.013
	V8—350 Cu. In.**	2.4484–2.4493 ⑦	.0008–.0020 ⑧	.003–.011	5	2.0990–2.1000	.0007–.0028	.009–.013
	V8—396 Cu. In.	2.7484–2.7493 ⑨	.0010–.0022 ⑩	.006–.010	5	2.1990–2.2000	.0009–.0025	.015–.021
	V8—427 Cu. In.	2.7481–2.7490 ⑪	.0013–.0025 ⑫	.006–.010	5	2.1990–2.2000	.0009–.0025	.015–.021
	V8—427 Cu. In. (435 H.P.)	2.7481–2.7490 ⑪	.0013–.0025 ⑫	.006–.010	5	2.1985–2.1995	.0014–.0030	.019–.025
1970	6 Cyl.—250 Cu. In.	2.2983–2.2993	.0003–.0029	.002–.006	7	1.9990–2.0000	.0007–.0027	.009–.014
	V8—350 Cu. In.	2.4484–2.4493 ⑬	.0003–.0015 ⑭	.002–.006	5	2.0990–2.1000	.0007–.0028	.008–.014
	V8—400 Cu. In. (265 H.P.)	2.6509	.0008–.0020 ⑮	.002–.006	5	2.0990–2.1000	.0009–.0030	.008–.014
	V8—454 Cu. In.	2.7485–2.7494 ⑨	.0013–.0025 ⑯	.006–.010	5	2.1990–2.2000	.0009–.0025	.015–.021
	V8—454 Cu. In. (450 H.P.)	2.7481–2.7490 ⑪	.0013–.0025 ⑰	.006–.010	5	2.1985–2.1995	.0014–.0030	.019–.025
1971–1972	6 Cyl.—250 Cu. In.	2.2983–2.2993	.0003–.0029	.002–.006	7	1.9990–2.0000	.0007–.0027	.009–.014
	V8—350 Cu. In.	2.4484–2.4493 ⑬	.0008–.0020 ⑮	.002–.006	5	2.0990–2.1000	.0013–.0035	.008–.014
	V8—350 Cu. In. (330 H.P.)	2.7481–2.7490 ⑱	.0013–.0025 ⑲	.002–.006	5	2.0990–2.1000	.0013–.0035	.008–.014
	V8—400 Cu. In. (255 H.P.)	2.6484–2.6493 ⑳	.0008–.0020 ⑮	.002–.006	5	2.0990–2.1000	.0013–.0035	.008–.014
	V8—402 Cu. In. (300 H.P.) (Mk. IV)	2.7487–2.7496 ㉑	.0007–.0019 ㉒	.006–.010	5	2.1990–2.2000	.0009–.0025	.013–.023
	V8—454 Cu. In. (365 H.P.)	2.7485–2.7494 ㉓	.0013–.0025 ⑯	.006–.010	5	2.1990–2.2000	.0009–.0025	.015–.021
	V8—454 Cu. In. (425 H.P.)	2.7481–2.7490 ⑪	.0013–.0025 ⑰	.006–.010	5	2.1985–2.1995	.0009–.0025	.019–.025

① —No.'s 3, 4—2.7482–2.7492; No. 5—2.7478–2.7488.
② —No.'s 3, 4—.0009–.0025; No. 5—.0013–.0029.
③ —No. 5—2.4977–2.4987.
④ —No. 1 (1967)—2.2984–2.2993; No.'s 2, 3, 4—2.2983–2.2993; No. 5—2.2978–2.2988.
⑤ —No. 5—.0010–.0036.
⑥ —427 Cu. In. (425 H.P.)—.019–.025.
*—Not available in 1966.
⑦ —No. 5—2.4470–2.4488.
⑧ —No. 5—.0018–.0034.
⑨ —No.'s 3, 4—2.4781–2.7490; No. 5—2.7478–2.7488.
⑩ —No.'s 3, 4—.0013–.0025; No. 5—.0015–.0031.
⑪ —No. 5—2.7478–2.7488.
⑫ —No. 5—.0015–.0031.
**—Not available in 1968.

⑬ —No. 5—2.4479–2.4488.
⑭ —No.'s 2, 3, 4—.0006–.0018; No. 5—.0008–.0023.
⑮ —No.'s 2, 3, 4—.011–.0023; No. 5—.0017–.0033.
⑯ —No. 5—.0024–.0040.
⑰ —No. 5—.0029–.0045.
⑱ —w/Man. trans.—No. 5—2.7473–2.7483.
w/Auto. trans.—No. 1—2.7475–2.7484; No.'s 2, 3, 4—2.7481–2.740· No. 5—2.7473–2.7483.
⑲ —w/Man. trans.—No. 5—.0023–.0033.
w/Auto. trans.—No. 1—.0019–.0031; No.'s 2, 3, 4—.0013–.0025; No. 5—.0023–.0033.
⑳ —No. 5—2.6479–2.6488.
㉑ —No.'s 3, 4—2.7481–2.7490; No. 5—2.7473–2.7483.
㉒ —No.'s 2, 3, 4—.0013–.0025; No. 5—.0019–.0035.
㉓ —No.'s 2, 3, 4—2.7481–2.7490; No. 5—2.7478–2.7488.

BATTERY AND STARTER SPECIFICATIONS

| YEAR | MODEL | BATTERY | | | | STARTERS | | | | | | Brush Spring Tension (Oz.) |
| | | Ampere Hour Capacity | Volts | Group Number | Terminal Grounded | Lock Test | | | No-Load Test | | | |
						Amps.	Volts	Torque	Amps.	Volts	RPM	
1965-66	6 Cyl. & V8—283 Cu. In.	44	12	2SMR	Neg.	290	4.3	—	63	10.6	7,800	35
	V8—327 Cu. In.	61	12	2SMD	Neg.	330	3.5	—	83	10.6	4,350	35
	V8—396, 427 Cu. In.	61	12	2SMD	Neg.	Not Recommended			83	10.6	4,350	35
	V8—409 Cu. In.	70	12	2SMD	Neg.	330	2.0	—	83	10.6	4,350	35
1967	6 Cyl. & V8—283 Cu. In.	45	12	—	Neg.	Not Recommended			73	10.6	9,575	35
	V8—327 Cu. In.	61	12	—	Neg.	Not Recommended			83	10.6	4,250	35
	V8—396, 427 Cu. In.	61	12	—	Neg.	Not Recommended			85	10.6	9,900	35
1968	6 Cyl., V8—307, 327 (250 H.P.)	45	12	—	Neg.	Not Recommended			73	10.6	4,500	35
	V8, 327 (275 H.P.), 396, 427	61	12	—	Neg.	Not Recommended			85	10.6	10,000	35
	All Corvette Engs.	62	12	—	Neg.	Not Recommended			85	10.6	10,000	35
1969	6 Cyl., V8—327, 396	45	12	—	Neg.	Not Recommended			73	9	4,500	35
	V8—350, 427	61	12	—	Neg.	Not Recommended			85	9	10,000	35
	All Corvette Engs.	62	12	—	Neg.	Not Recommended			85	9	10,000	35
1970	6 Cyl.	45	12	—	Neg.	Not Recommended			50–80	9	5,500–10,500	35
	V8—350	51	12	—	Neg.	Not Recommended			55–80	9	3,500–6,000	35
	All Corvette Engs.	62	12	—	Neg.	Not Recommended			55–80	9	3,500–6,000	35
	V8—400	62	12	—	Neg.	Not Recommended			55–80	9	3,500–6,000	35
	V8—454	62	12	—	Neg.	Not Recommended			65–95	9	7,500–10,500	35
1971-72	6 Cyl.	45	12	—	Neg.	Not Recommended			50–80	9	5,500–10,500	35
	V8—350	61	12	—	Neg.	Not Recommended			65–95	9	7,500–10,500	35
	V8—400	61	12	—	Neg.	Not Recommended			65–95	9	7,500–10,500	35
	V8—402	61	12	—	Neg.	Not Recommended			65–95	9	7,500–10,500	35
	V8—454	76	12	—	Neg.	Not Recommended			65–95	9	7,500–10,500	35
	Corvette 350	62	12	—	Neg.	Not Recommended			65–95	9	7,500–10,500	35
	Corvette 454	76	12	—	Neg.	Not Recommended			65–95	9	7,500–10,500	35

DELCOTRON AND A.C. REGULATOR SPECIFICATIONS

| YEAR | MODEL | ALTERNATOR | | | REGULATOR | | | | | | |
| | | Field Current Draw @ 12V. | Output @ Generator RPM | | | Field Relay | | | Regulator | | |
			2000	5000	Model	Air Gap (In.)	Point Gap (In.)	Volts to Close	Air Gap (In.)	Point Gap (In.)	Volts at 125°
1965-67	1100693	2.2-2.6	27A	37A	1119515	.015	.030	2.3-3.7	.067	.014	13.5-14.4
	1100696	2.2-2.6	29A	42A	1119515	.015	.030	2.3-3.7	.067	.014	13.5-14.4
1968	1100693	2.2-2.6	27A	37A	1119515	.015	.030	2.3-3.7	.067	.014	13.5-14.4
	1100794	2.2-2.6	27A	37A	1119515	.015	.030	2.3-3.7	.067	.014	13.5-14.4
	1100696	2.2-2.6	29A	42A	1119515	.015	.030	2.3-3.7	.067	.014	13.5-14.4
1969	1100834	2.2-2.6	27A	37A	1119515	.015	.030	2.3-3.7	.067	.014	13.5-14.4
	1100836	2.2-2.6	27A	37A	1119515	.015	.030	2.3-3.7	.067	.014	13.5-14.4
	1100696	2.2-2.6	27A	37A	1119515	.015	.030	2.3-3.7	.067	.014	13.5-14.4
1970	1100834②	2.2-2.6	27A	37A	1119515	.015	.030	2.3-3.7	.067	.014	13.5-14.4
	1100900③	2.2-2.6	27A	37A	1119515	.015	.030	2.3-3.7	.067	.014	13.5-14.4
	1100901④	2.2-2.6	27A	37A	1119515	.015	.030	2.3-3.7	.067	.014	13.5-14.4
1971-72	1100544	4-4.5	②	②	1119515	.015	.030	1.5-3.2	.067	.014	13.8-14.8
	1100543 1100950	4-4.5	②	37A	1119515	.015	.030	1.5-3.2	.067	.014	13.8-14.8
	1100566 1100836 1100837	2.2-2.6	25A	35A	1119515	.015	.030	1.5-3.2	.067	.014	13.8-14.8
	1100843	2.2-2.6	33A	58A	1119515	.015	.030	1.5-3.2	.067	.014	13.8-14.8
	1100917	2.8-3.2	35A	59A	1119519	.030	.030	1.5-3.2	.067	.014	13.8-14.8
	1100567	2.2-2.6	28A	40A	1119515	.015	.030	1.5-3.2	.067	.014	13.8-14.8

① —At 1100 & 6500 rpm
② —Voltmeter not needed for cold output check. Load battery with carbon pile to obtain maximum output.

GENERAL CHASSIS AND BRAKE SPECIFICATIONS

| YEAR | MODEL | CHASSIS | | | BRAKE CYLINDER BORE | | BRAKE DRUM | |
| | | Overall Length (In.) | Tire Size | Master Cylinder (In.) | Wheel Cylinder Diameter (In.) | | Diameter (In.) | |
					Front	Rear	Front	Rear
CHEVROLET								
1965	Sedans	213.0	7.35 x 14② ③	1.0①	1³/₁₆	1.0	11	11
	Sta. Wag.	213.3	8.25 x 14	1.0①	1³/₁₆	1.0	11	11
	Conv.	213.0	7.75 x 14③	1.0①	1³/₁₆	1.0	11	11
1966	Sedans	213.2	7.35 x 14② ③	1.0①	1³/₁₆	1.0	11	11
	Conv.	213.2	7.75 x 14③	1.0①	1³/₁₆	1.0	11	11
	Sta. Wag.	212.4	8.55 x 14	1.0①	1³/₁₆	1.0	11	11
1967	Exc. Sta. Wag.	213.2	8.25 x 14	1.0①	1³/₁₆④	1.0	11⑤	11
	Sta. Wag.	212.4	8.85 x 14	1.0①	1³/₁₆④	1.0	11⑤	11
1968	Exc. Sta. Wag.	214.7	8.25 x 14	1.0①	1³/₁₆④	1.0	11⑤	11
	Sta. Wag.	213.9	8.55 x 14	1.0①	1³/₁₆④	1.0	11⑤	11
1969	Exc. Sta. Wag.	215.9	8.25 x 14	1.0⑥	1³/₁₆④	1.0	11⑤	11
	Sta. Wag.	216.7	8.85 x 14	1.0⑥	1³/₁₆④	1.0	11⑤	11
1970	Exc. Sta. Wag.	215.9	8.25 x 14	1.0⑥	1³/₁₆④	1.0	11⑤	11
	Sta. Wag.	216.7	8.85 x 14	1.0⑥	1³/₁₆④	1.0	11⑤	11
1971-72	Exc. Sta. Wag.	216.8	⑦	1.125	2.9375	.8125	11.86 (Disc)	11
	Sta. Wag.	223.2	L78 x 15	1.125	2.9375	1.0	11.86 (Disc)	12
CORVETTE								
1965-66	Conv.	175.1	7.75 x 15	1.0	1⁷/₈	1³/₈	11.75 (Disc)	11.75 (Disc)
	Coupe	175.1	7.75 x 15	⁷/₈	1⁷/₈	1.0	11.75	11.75
1967		175.1	7.75 x 15	1.0	1⁷/₈	1³/₈	11.75 (Disc)	11.75 (Disc)
1968-69		182.1	F70 x 15	1.0	1⁷/₈	1³/₈	11.75 (Disc)	11.75 (Disc)
1970		182.1	F70 x 15	1.0	1⁷/₈	1³/₈	11.75 (Disc)	11.75 (Disc)
1971-72		182.5	F70 x 15	1.0	1⁷/₈	1³/₈	11.75 (Disc)	11.75 (Disc)

① Metallic brakes — master cylinder bore — ⁷/₈.
② Models with 327 or 396 Eng. — 7.75 x 14.
③ Models with 409 or 427 Eng. — 8.25 x 14.
④ Disc 2¹⁵/₁₆.
⑤ Disc 11.75.

⑥ W/disc brakes — 1¹/₈.
⑦ All 6 Cyl. and Bel Air base V8 Models — F78 x 15
Impala and Caprice base V8 Models and all optional engines except
454 Cu. In. — G78 x 15.
454 Cu. In. engine Models — H78 x 15.

FUSES AND CIRCUIT BREAKERS

1965-68

Headlamps, parking lamps.................. 15 Amp. CB
Panel and accessory lamps................. 3 Amp. Fuse
Tail, dome, glove box, clock, stop, back-up,
   brake indicator, courtesy, stop lamps.... 10 Amp. Fuse
Heater (no air conditioning) .... 10 Amp. Fuse
Air conditioning (including heater)........ 20 Amp. Fuse
Radio.................................... 7½ Amp. Fuse

A circuit breaker in the light control switch protects the headlamp circuit, thus eliminating one fuse. A separate 30 Amp. circuit breaker mounted on the firewall protects the power window, seat and top circuits. The under hood and spot lamp circuit is also protected by a separate 15 Amp. inline fuse. Where current load is too heavy, the circuit breaker rapidly opens and closes, protecting the circuit until the cause is found and eliminated.

Fuses located in the fuse panel under the instrument panel are:

1969-70

Wiper/washer, 3-spd. A/T downshift... SAE/SFE 25 AMP.

Back-up lamp, turn signal, cruise
   master, defogger, heater .... SAE/SFE 25 AMP.
Air conditioning—transmission control
   spark solenoid .... 3AG/AGC 25 AMP.
Radio, power window .... 3AG/AGC 10 AMP.
Tail, marker and fender lamps........ SAE/SFE 20 AMP.
Instrument lamps..................... SAE/SFE 4 AMP.
Instrument lamps (Corvette) .... 1 AG/AGA 5 AMP.
Gauges and tell-tale lamps........... 3AG/AGC 10 AMP.
Stop and hazard..................... SAE/SFE 20 AMP.
Clock, lighter, courtesy lamps, dome
   and luggage lamps............... SAE/SFE 20 AMP.
In-Line Fuses
Air Conditioning Higher Blower Speed Fuse located in
   wire running from horn relay to A/C Relay
   Comfortron and Four Season ....SAE 30 AMP.
Fusible Links:
Pigtail lead at battery positive
   cable (except Corvette)...... 14 gauge brown wire
Molded splice at Solenoid "Bat"
   terminal (Corvette only) ..... 14 gauge brown wire
Molded splice located at the horn
   relay .... 16 gauge black wire

Molded splice in voltage regulator
   #3 terminal wire........... 20 gauge orange wire
Molded splice in ammeter circuit
   (both sides of meter)........ 20 gauge orange wire

1971-72

Radio, TCS, rear defogger, power window, 3-speed
   A.T. downshift, glove compartment light .. SAE 10 AMP.
Wiper/washer .... SAE 25 AMP.
Stop lights, warning flasher .... SAE 20 AMP.
Heater and air conditioning .... SAE 25 AMP.
Turn signals, back-up light, Cruise Master,
   blocking relay (A/C) .... SAE 20 AMP.
Instrument lights (Chevrolet) .... SAE 3 AMP.
Instrument lights (Corvette) .... SAE 5 AMP.
Gauges and warning lights .... SAE 10 AMP.
Clock, cigarette lighter, courtesy lights, anti-diesel
   control, deck lid, lock, anti-theft alarm, dome
   lamps .... SAE 25 AMP.
Tail lights, license plate light, side markers,
   luggage light, parking lights .... SAE 20 AMP.

CAPACITIES

YEAR	MODEL	ENGINE CRANKCASE ADD 1 Qt. FOR NEW FILTER	TRANSMISSIONS Pts. TO REFILL AFTER DRAINING			DRIVE AXLE (Pts.)	GASOLINE TANK (Gals.)	COOLING SYSTEM (Qts.) WITH HEATER
			Manual		Automatic			
			3-Speed ★	4-Speed				
CHEVROLET								
1965	6 Cyl.	4	2	None	18	4	20②	12
	V8—283 Cu. In.	4	2	2½	18	4	20②	17
	V8—327 Cu. In. (250 HP)	4	2	2½	18	4	20②	16
	V8—327 Cu. In. (300 HP)	4	2	2½	18	4	20②	18
	V8—396 Cu. In. Std.	4	2	2½	22	4	20	22
	V8—396 Hi. Perf.	5	2	2½	19	4	20	22
	V8—409 Cu. In.	4	2	2½	18	4	20②	22
1966	6 Cyl.—250 Cu. In.	4	2	None	18	4	20②	12
	V8—283 Cu. In.	4	2	2½	18	4	20②	17
	V8—327 Cu. In.	4	2	2½	18	4	20②	16
	V8—396 Cu. In.	4	2	2½	18③	4	20②	23
	V8—427 Cu. In.	4	2	2½	19	4	20②	24
1967	6 Cyl.—250 Cu. In.	4	3	None	17	3½	24	12
	V8—283 Cu. In.	4	3	3	17	3½	24	17
	V8—327 Cu. In.	4	3	3	19	4	24	15
	V8—396 Cu. In.	4	3½	3	19③	4	24	23
	V8—427 Cu. In.	4	3½	3	22	4	24	22
1968	6 Cyl.—250 Cu. In.	4	3	None	17	3½	24	11
	V8—307 Cu. In.	4	3	3	17	3½	24	16
	V8—327 Cu. In.	4	3	3	19	4	24	14
	V8—396 Cu. In.	4	3½	3	19③	4	24	21
	V8—427 Cu. In.	4	3½	3	22	4	24	21
1969	6 Cyl.—250 Cu. In.	4	3	None	17	⑤	24	12
	V8—327 Cu. In.	4	3	3	19③	⑤	24	17
	V8—350 Cu. In.	4	3½	3	19③	⑤	24	15
	V8—396 Cu. In.	4	3½	3	22	⑤	24	23
	V8—427 Cu. In.	4	3½	3	22	⑤	24	22
1970	6 Cyl.—250 Cu. In.	4	3	None	6⑦	⑤	25⑥	12
	V8—350 Cu. In. (250 H.P.)	4	3⑧	None	6½⑦	⑤	25⑥	16
	V8—400 Cu. In.	4	None	None	8⑦	⑤	25⑥	16
	V8—454 Cu. In.	4	None	None	8⑦	⑤	25⑥	22
1971-72	6 Cyl.—250 Cu. In.	4	3	None	6⑦	⑩	24⑪	12
	V8—350 Cu. In.	4	3	None	6.5⑨⑦	⑩	24⑪	16
	V8—400 Cu. In.	4	3	None	5⑦	⑩	24⑪	16
	V8—400 Cu. In. (Mk. IV)	4	None	None	8⑦	⑩	24⑪	23
	V8—454 Cu. In.	4	None	None	8⑦	⑩	24⑪	22

LIGHT BULBS

1965-68

Headlamp (outer)	4002; 37½-55 W
Headlamp (inner)	4001; 37½ W
Parking and front directional, tail and stop and rear directional	1157; 4-32 CP
Tail lamp (belair)	1155; 4 CP
Back-up lamp	1156; 32 CP
Instrument lamps, panel compartment, temperature, oil pressure, generator, hi-beam indicator, clock lamp	1895; 2 CP
A.T. quadrant, directional signal, ignition lock, heater control panel	1445; 1 CP
Dome lamp	1004; 15 CP
License plate lamp	1155; 4 CP
Radio dial lamp	1893; 2 CP
Brake alarm lamp	257; 2 CP

1969-72

LAMP USAGE	CANDLE POWER	BULB NUMBER
Headlamp unit		
Chevrolet & Corvette		
Outer—high beam	37½ Watts	4002
Outer—low beam	55 Watts	4002
Inner—high beam only	37½ Watts	4001
Parking lamp and directional signal		
Chevrolet	3-32	1157
Corvette	3-32	1157NA
Tail, stop and directional signal	3-32	1157
Backing lamp	32	1156
Instrument illumination lamps		
Chevrolet	2	194
Corvette	2	1895

CAPACITIES, continued

| YEAR | MODEL | ENGINE CRANKCASE ADD 1 Qt. FOR NEW FILTER | TRANSMISSIONS Pts. TO REFILL AFTER DRAINING | | | DRIVE AXLE (Pts.) | GASOLINE TANK (Gals.) | COOLING SYSTEM (Qts.) WITH HEATER |
| | | | Manual | | Automatic | | | |
			3-Speed★	4-Speed				
CORVETTE								
1965	V8—327 Cu. In. Std.	4	2	2½	18	4④	20	16½
	V8—327 Cu. In. Hi. Perf.	5	2	2½	18	4④	20	16½
	V8—396 Cu. In. Std.	4	2	2½	22	4④	20	22
	V8—396 Cu. In. Hi. Perf.	5	2	2½	19	4④	20	22
1966	V8—327 Cu. In.	5	2	2½	18	3½	20	19
	V8—427 Cu. In.	5	None	2½	None	3½	20	22
1967	V8—327 Cu. In.	5	3	3	19	3½	20	19
	V8—427 Cu. In.	5	None	3	19	3½	20	22
1968	V8—327 Cu. In.	4	3	4	22	4	20	14
	V8—427 Cu. In.	5	3	4	22	4	20	21
1969	V8—350 Cu. In.	4	3	3	22	4	20	15
	V8—427 Cu. In.	5	None	3	22	4	20	22
1970	V8—350 Cu. In.	4	None	3	22	4	20	15**
	V8—454 Cu. In.	5	None	3	22	4	20	22
1971-72	V8—350 Cu. In.	4	None	3	8⑦	4	18	⑫
	V8—454 Cu. In.	5	None	3	8⑦	4	18	⑫

★—Add 1 pt. for Overdrive.
① —Station Wagon—19.
② —Station Wagon—23½.
③ —With Turbo-Hydra-Matic—19 Pts. 1966, 22 Pts. 1967-70.
④ —1965—3½ Pts.
⑤ —8.125 ring gear 3.5 Pts.; 8.875 ring gear 4.0 Pts.
⑥ —Station Wagon—22.

⑦ —Case only—does not include converter.
⑧ —300 H.P.—None.
** —370 H.P.—18 Qts.
⑨ —350 Cu. In. (245 H.P.)—5 pts.
⑩ —850 ring gear 3.5 pts.; 8.875 ring gear 4.0 pts.
⑪ —Station wagons—23 (approx.)
⑫ —350 V8 (270 H.P.)—15 qts.; 350 V8 (330 H.P.)—18 qts.; 454 V8 (365 H.P.)—22 qts.; 454 V8 (425 H.P.)—20 qts.

LIGHT BULBS

1969-72 (continued)

LAMP USAGE	CANDLE POWER	BULB NUMBER
Temperature indicator	2	194
Oil pressure indicator	2	194
Generator indicator	2	194
Hi-beam indicator		
All except Corvette	2	194
Corvette	2	1895
Directional indicator		
All except Corvette	2	194
Corvette	2	1895
Cigarette lighter lamp		
Corvette	1	1445
Warning lamps		
Corvette—Door ajar	2	1895
Headlamps up	2	1895
Seat belts	2	1895
Chevrolet—low fuel	2	194
check doors	2	194
seat belt	2	194
Heater or A/C control panel		
Chevrolet	2	1895
Corvette	2.5	1816
Glove box lamps		
Chevrolet, without A/C & Corvette	2	1895
Chevrolet with A/C	2	1893

LAMP USAGE	CANDLE POWER	BULB NUMBER
Dome and courtesy lamps		
Cartridge type (all)	12	211
Bayonet type (exc. Corvette and station wagon third seat)	6	631
Corvette and station wagon third seat	6	90
Seat separator-courtesy lamp	6	212
Side marker-front	2	194
Side marker-rear	2	194
License plate lamp (exc. Corvette)	4	67
(Corvette)	4	97
Radio dial lamps		
All AM only radios	2	293
All tape players and FM radios	2	1893
Tape player lens illumination lamp	1	216
Stereo indicator lamp	.3	2182D
Automatic transmission control indicator lamp		
Chevrolet	2	194
Brake alarm lamp		
All except Corvette	2	194
Corvette	2	1895
Luggage compartment lamp	15	1003
Map lamp (mirror)	4	563
Underhood	15	93
Rear window defogger lamp	2	194

Distributor

Caution When using an auxiliary starter switch for bumping the engine into position for timing, the primary distributor lead must be disconnected from the negative post of the ignition coil and the switch must be in the On position. Failure to do this may cause damage to the grounding circuit in the ignition switch.

Distributor Removal

6 Cylinder Models

The distributor assembly is mounted on the right side of the block and is driven directly from the camshaft.

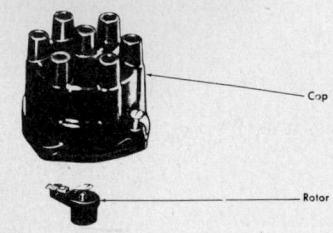

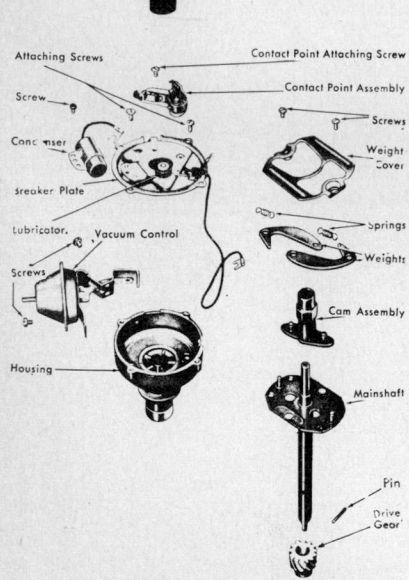

6-cylinder distributor, typical
(© Chevrolet Div. G.M. Corp.)

To remove the distributor, first detach the vacuum lines from the vacuum advance unit and lift off the distributor cap.

The distributor body is fastened to the block by a single cap screw which holds the octane selector plate down against the block. Scribe marks so that the distributor body and rotor can be installed in their original locations. Do not turn engine while the distributor is removed. Remove the retaining screw and lift the distributor out of the block.

V8 Models

The distributor is located between the two banks of cylinders at the back of the block.

The drive gear is attached to the

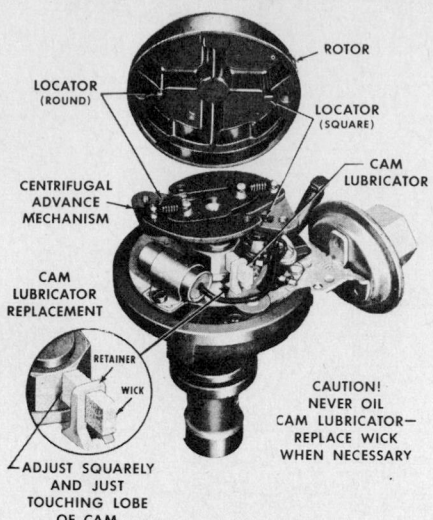

V8 distributor showing details of cam lubricator
(© Chevrolet Div. G.M. Corp.)

distributor shaft; therefore, if it becomes necessary to remove the distributor, carefully mark the position of the rotor. Then, if the engine is not turned after the distributor is taken out, it can be installed in the same position from which is was removed.

To remove the distributor, disconnect the carburetor air cleaner, disconnect the coil primary wire and the vacuum line, remove the distributor cap, take out the single hold-down bolt located under the distributor body, mark the position of the body relative to the block and then work the distributor up out of the block.

V8 Distributor Cam Lubricator Wick

If the car has gone 20,000 miles or more, the cam lubricator wick should be changed.

Take the distributor cap off. Using long-nose pliers, squeeze the wick assembly together at the base and lift it out. Wipe off the cam and install a new wick assembly so that the end of the wick touches the cam lobes. Overlubrication results when the wick presses too hard against the cam surface. Do not put oil on the wick. Install the distributor cap.

Distributor Installation (Engine Disturbed)

1. Turn crank until the No. 1 cylinder is at the top of its compression stroke. Remove the No. 1 spark plug to feel the compression.
2. Align the timing mark on the flywheel or vibration damper with the indicator.
3. With distributor body oriented in its normal position, hold the rotor pointing toward the front of the engine, then turn the rotor approximately ⅛ turn counterclockwise and push the distributor down until it engages the camshaft, rotating the shaft slightly if necessary.
   NOTE: on Mark IV engines there is a punch mark on the distributor drive gear which indicates the rotor position. Thus, the distributor may be installed with the cap in place. Align the punch mark 2° clockwise from the No. 1 cap terminal, then rotate the distributor body clockwise ⅛ turn counterclockwise and push the distributor down into the block.
4. Press down on the distributor and crank the engine to make sure the oil pump shaft is engaged.
5. Return the crankshaft to No. 1 cylinder compression stroke with the timing marks aligned.
6. Turn the distributor body counterclockwise until the points are just beginning to open, then

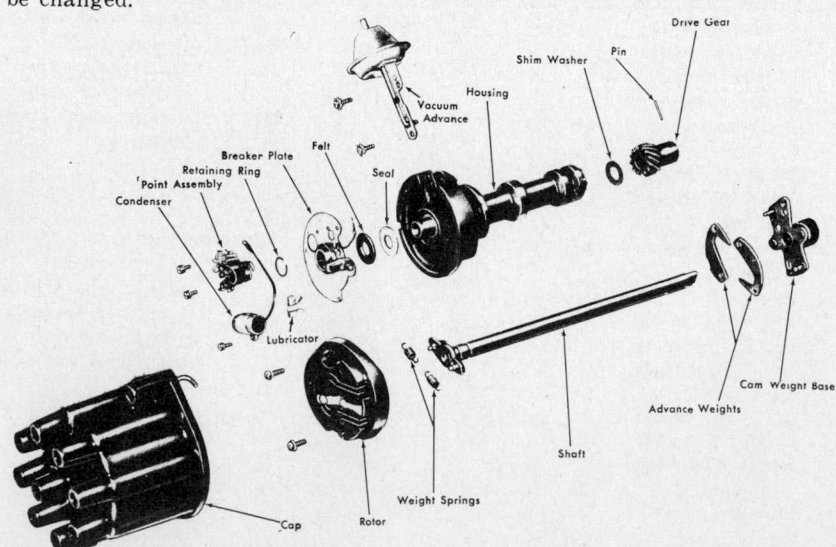

V8 distributor, typical (© Chevrolet Div. G.M. Corp.)

tighten the distributor clamp bolt.

7. Install the distributor cap, checking that the rotor points to the No. 1 terminal. Make sure that the spark plug wires are in their supports and are securely connected.

8. Connect distributor vacuum line and primary wire.

9. Start engine and set the timing.

Breaker Point Adjustment

Breaker point gap (dwell) adjustment is accomplished for 6-cylinder engines by loosening the point assembly attaching screw and turning the eccentric screw until correct gap clearance is obtained (use a feeler gauge). Tighten the point assembly attaching screws and install the distributor cap. Use a dwell meter, if available, to check the dwell angle, readjusting if necessary.

On V8 models there is a window in the distributor cap so that the dwell angle may be set while the engine is running. Use an Allen (hex) wrench to make the adjustment.

See Tune-Up Specifications at the beginning of this section for correct breaker point gap and dwell angle.

Caution On V8 models the distributor body is involved in the engine lubricating system. The lubricating circuit to the right bank valve train can be interrupted by mis-alignment of the distributor body. This can cause serious trouble and may be hard to diagnose. See Firing Order and Timing illustrations for correct distributor positioning.

Transistor Ignition

This system consists of a special distributor, an ignition pulse amplifier, and a special ignition coil. The distributor is similar in external appearance to the standard V8 distributor, but the internal construction bears little resemblance to the contact-point unit. An iron timer core replaces the breaker cam. This eight-lobed timer rotates inside a magnetic pick-up assembly, which replaces the contact points and condenser. The magnetic pick-up assembly consists of a ceramic permanent magnet, a steel pole piece, and a pick-up coil.

The magnetic pick-up assembly is mounted over the distributor shaft bearing, and is rotated by the vacuum advance unit to provide automatic spark advance. Centrifugal advance is provided by the rotating timer core, which is attached to normal advance weights. Troubleshooting is found in Unit Repair.

Removal

1. Disconnect pick-up coil connector.
2. Remove distributor cap.
3. Crank engine so that rotor points to No. 1 cylinder plug tower and timing mark on crankshaft pulley is indexed with pointer.
4. Remove distributor vacuum line.
5. Remove distributor hold-down bolt and clamp, then remove distributor.

Disassembly

1. Remove rotor.
2. Remove centrifugal weight springs.
3. Remove weights.
4. Remove roll pin, drive gear and washer.
5. Remove drive shaft.
6. Remove weight support and timer core from drive shaft.
7. Remove magnetic core assembly.

AC Generator (Delcotron)

The Delcotron, AC generator by Delco-Remy is used on Chevrolet vehicles.

Repair and test details on the Delcotron and its regulators can be found in the Unit Repair Section.

Caution Since the Delcotron and regulator are designed for use on a single polarity system, the following precautions must be observed:

1. The polarity of the battery, generator, and regulator must be matched and considered before making any electrical connections in the system.

2. When connecting a booster battery, be sure to connect the negative battery terminals with one another, and the positive battery terminals with one another.

3. When connecting a charger to the battery, connect the charger positive lead to the battery positive terminal. Connect the charger negative lead to the battery negative terminal.

4. Never operate the Delcotron on open circuit. Be sure that all connections in the circuit are clean and tight.

5. Do not short across or ground any of the terminals on the Delcotron regulator.

6. Do not attempt to polarize the Delcotron.

7. Do not use test lamps of more than 12 volts for checking diode continuity.

8. Avoid long soldering times when replacing diodes or transistors. Prolonged heat is damaging to these units.

9. Disconnect the battery ground terminal when servicing any AC system. This will prevent the possibility of accidentally reversing polarity.

Alternator R & R

1. Disconnect the battery cables from the battery terminals.
2. Disconnect and identify the wire leads from the alternator.
3. Remove the alternator brace bolt, then remove belt(s).
4. Remove the alternator pivot attaching bolt and remove alternator from vehicle.
5. To install, reverse the above procedure and adjust belt tension.

Battery, Starter

Detailed information on the battery and starter can be found in the Battery and Starter Specifications table of this section.

More information on batteries and starters can be found in the Unit Repair Section.

Starter R & R

1. Disconnect the battery and the wires from the solenoid.
2. Remove the starter mounting bolt and lock washers. On V8s, a stud nut and lock washer are at the front of the starter.
3. Pull starter forward and out of car.
4. To install, reverse the above procedure.

Instruments

Caution Disconnect battery while working on the speedometer or gauges.

Cluster R & R

All component parts of the dash instruments are contained within the instrument cluster. The cluster may be removed as a whole or the instruments can be removed separately, except the speedometer which requires removal of cluster. All the light bulb sockets are held by clips and can be easily snapped in or out of position. The fuel and temperature gauges and the speedometer are held in place by screws. See the Unit Repair Section for a discussion of gauges and instruments.

1965 Chevrolet

NOTE: on air conditioned models, the instrument panel console and cluster must be removed as an assembly.

1. Disconnect the battery ground cable.
2. Remove the steering wheel assembly: disconnect the turn signal switch harness, pull out the horn button or center ornament, remove the screws and receiving cup or horn ring, remove steering wheel nut and washer and remove the steering wheel with a puller.
3. Disconnect the speedometer cable at the speedometer.
4. Disconnect the cluster wiring multiple connector.
5. Remove left ash tray and retainer.
6. Remove the radio as described below in this section.
7. Remove the four upper attaching screws and the four lower attaching stud nuts. Note the position of the four lower stud mounting clips.
8. Carefully remove the instrument cluster.
9. Install in the reverse order of removal.

1966 Chevrolet

1. Disconnect battery.
2. Remove air-conditioning hose connecting left outlet to distributor duct.
3. Disconnect speedometer cable at the speedometer head.
4. Disconnect instrument panel wiring harness connector and clock or tachometer wiring lead connections at rear of cluster.
5. Remove radio control knobs, bezels and shaft retaining nuts. Push radio in to disengage shafts from panel openings.

NOTE: on rear-seat speaker models, disconnect fader control wiring from radio harness wiring.

6. Remove instrument panel compartment door and the compartment retaining screws.
7. Remove upper and lower instrument panel console retaining screws.
8. With adjacent painted surfaces protected, open right front door, roll console assembly forward and slide to the right to remove assembly from the car.

NOTE: at this point, all components (fuel gauge, speedometer, printed circuit, etc.) of the assembly may be serviced.

9. To separate instrument cluster assembly from the console, remove five screws in top of console

and four lower retaining nuts.
10. To install, reverse removal procedure.

1967 Chevrolet

1. Disconnect the battery ground cable.
2. Remove four screws and bezel from the top edge of the instrument console. Disengage tabs on the bezel from the clips on console.
3. Remove the eight cluster to console attaching screws and pull the cluster forward enough to disconnect the speedometer cable, wiring harness connector, clock and, if so equipped, speed warning device connectors and oil pressure line.
4. Remove the instrument cluster.
5. Install in the reverse order of removal.

1968 Chevrolet

1. Disconnect battery.
2. Unplug forward wiring harness from fuse panel and remove panel from firewall.
3. Remove screws retaining cluster to instrument panel.
4. From mast jacket, remove screws retaining column-mounted automatic transmission pointer cable.
5. From behind cluster, disconnect speedometer cable, harness connector, clock, speed warning device, defogger, convertible top or tail gate switches and vacuum hoses, if so equipped. If equipped with gauge pack, disconnect oil pressure line.
6. Using care to prevent scratching mast jacket, tip the top of cluster forward and remove from vehicle.
7. To install, reverse the removal procedure.

1969 Chevrolet

1. Disconnect the battery ground cable.
2. Remove the glove box and air conditioner center dash outlet.
3. Remove the four dash screws above the instruments and gently pull instrument panel pad loose from dash clips.
4. If so equipped, remove air conditioner lap cooler from under the steering column and stereo tape player.
5. Remove the three bolts from the underside of the dash.
6. Disconnect the shift indicator cable wire on the steering column.
7. Disconnect the radio wiring.
8. Lower the steering column.
9. Remove the instrument panel top attaching screws and gently lift and tilt the panel forward.
10. Disconnect speedometer cable (press snap retainer) and all

electrical connections.
11. Remove the six top illumination can attaching screws.
12. Remove the indicator bulb bezel: push in on the right side of each cover to expose the screws, then remove the bezel retaining screws (4).
13. Remove the rear cluster to carrier attaching screws and remove the cluster.
14. Install by reversing the removal procedure.

1970 Chevrolet

1. Disconnect the battery ground cable.
2. If applicable, remove the air conditioning lap cooler from under the steering column.
3. Lower the steering column, being sure to support it.
4. Remove the dash pad and, if applicable, disconnect the center air conditioning outlet hose.
5. Disconnect the shift indicator cable on the steering column and remove the indicator bulb bezel.
6. Remove shift indicator lamp housing.
7. Remove the radio.
8. Remove the instrument panel trim plate: the plate is held in place with snap-in studs on the left side, right side and to the right of the steering column. Use a hooked tool to pull the trim plate free.
9. Remove the air conditioner/ heater control assembly.
10. Remove the lower instrument cluster to bracket and parking brake pedal bracket screws.
11. Remove the ashtray and retaining bracket.
12. Remove the three screws at the top of the instrument cluster and tilt it forward.
13. Disconnect the speedometer cable and instrument wiring harness. The illumination cover must be removed to get at the wiring.
14. Remove the instrument cluster.
15. Installation is the reverse of the above procedure.

1971-72 Chevrolet

1. Disconnect the battery.
2. Remove the cigar lighter knob and the screw beneath it.
3. Pull out the headlight switch and remove screw in middle of shaft.
4. Remove the two screws in the lower corners and remove the shroud.
5. Remove the clock stem set knob.
6. Remove the lens and lens retaining strip. There are three screws holding the lens retaining strip.
7. Tilt the filter housing back and remove.

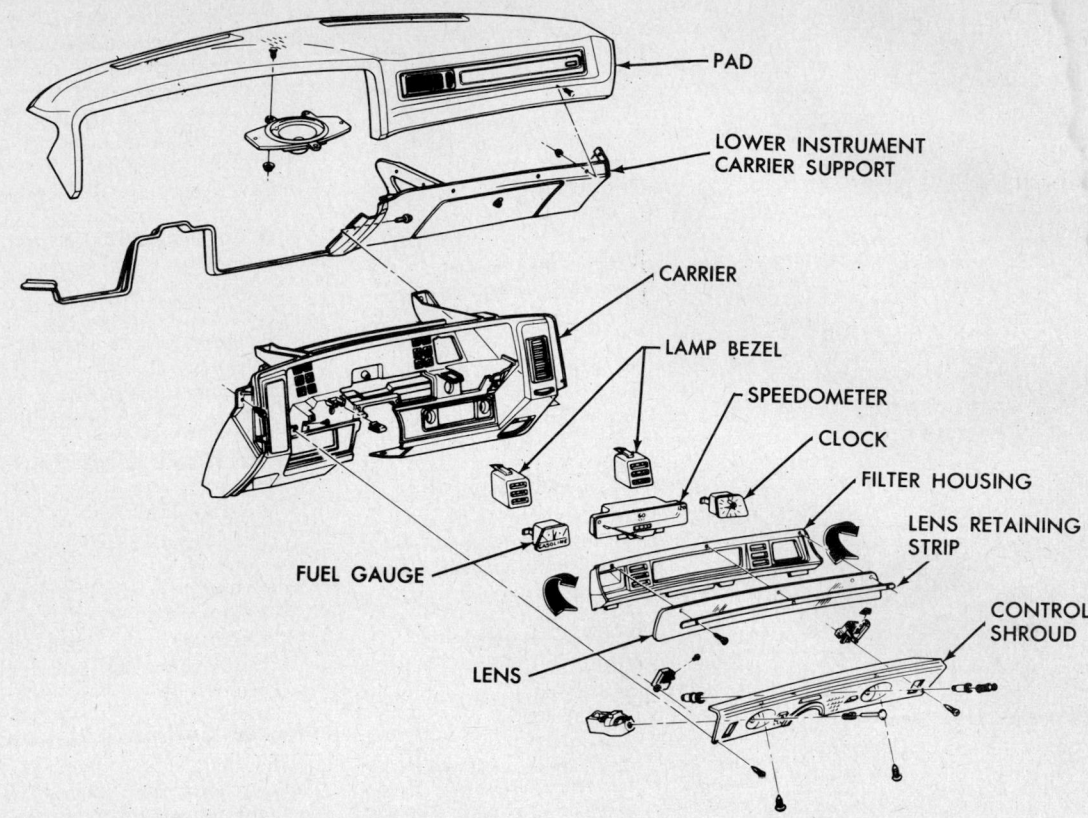

PAD

LOWER INSTRUMENT
CARRIER SUPPORT

CARRIER

LAMP BEZEL

SPEEDOMETER

CLOCK

FILTER HOUSING

LENS RETAINING
STRIP

CONTROL
SHROUD

FUEL GAUGE

LENS

8. The speedometer, fuel gauge and clock may be removed.
9. Install in the reverse of the above procedure.

1965-67 Corvette

1. Disconnect battery.
2. Remove mast jacket assembly.
3. Disconnect tachometer drive cable at distributor.
4. Disconnect cowl vent control cable brackets and the headlamp panel control switch from the instrument cluster.
5. Remove lighting switch and ignition switch, and disconnect ignition switch lamp support at instrument panel.
6. Disconnect parking brake lever support bracket at cowl cross-member.
7. Disconnect oil pressure line at oil pressure gauge, then remove the lead wires from ammeter, wiper switch and cigarette lighter. Disconnect trip odometer at mast jacket support.
8. Remove instrument cluster-to-dash retaining screws and pull cluster assembly slightly forward to make clearance for removal of speedometer cable, tachometer cable, cluster ground wire, fuse gauge lead wires and the remaining indicator and cluster illumi-

nating lamps.
9. Install by reversing the removal procedure.

1968-72 Corvette (Left-hand Section)

1. Disconnect battery.
2. Lower steering column.
3. Remove screws retaining left instrument panel to door opening, top of dash and left side of center instrument panel.
4. Unclip and remove floor console forward trim panel.
5. Pull cluster assembly forward to obtain clearance for removal of speedometer cable housing nut, tachometer cable housing nut, headlamp and ignition switch connectors and panel lamps.
6. To install, reverse removal procedure.

(Center Section)

1. Disconnect battery.
2. Remove screws from right side dash pad.
3. Remove clipped-in center floor console forward trim pads.
4. Remove radio knobs, bezel retaining nuts, aerial, speaker and electrical connections.
5. Remove radio, rear support bracket, and slide receiver out right side.

6. Remove upper center console trim plate screws, and tip trim plate forward for access to remove windshield wiper switch connector. Lift trim plate out.
7. Remove screws at left side of center console and nuts attached to underside of console studs.
8. Tilt console forward. Remove oil and electrical connections and lamps from rear of console.
9. Lift up and forward to remove console.
10. To install, reverse the removal procedure.

Ignition Switch Replacement

1965-68 All Models

1. Disconnect battery.
2. Remove cylinder by placing in lock position and insert stiff wire in small hole to depress plunger. Turn cylinder counterclockwise until cylinder can be removed.
3. Remove holding nut. (Tool J-7607 will assist.)
4. Pull switch from under dash and remove connectors.
5. Using a screwdriver, unsnap the locking tangs of the "theft resistant" connector.
6. Install in reverse of above.

1968 Corvette

The ignition switch replacement procedure is the same as that described above, except that the "CORVETTE" cover plate in the top center of the cluster assembly must be removed first.

1969-72 Chevrolet & Corvette

The switch is located inside the channel section of the brake pedal support and is completely inaccessible without first lowering the steer-

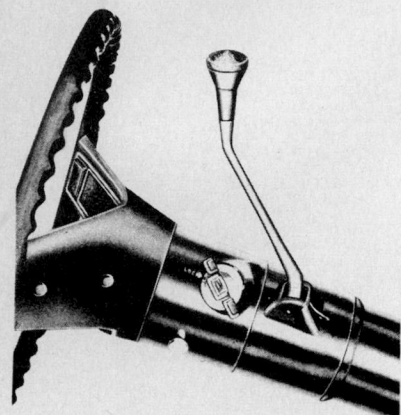

1969-70 ignition switch location

ing column. The switch is actuated by a rod and rack assembly. A gear on the end of the lock cylinder engages the toothed upper end of the rod.

1. Remove or lower the steering column as described under *Steering*. If steering column is lowered, be sure to properly support it.
2. Put the switch in "Lock" position. With the cylinder removed, the rod is in "Lock" position when it is in the next to the uppermost detent.
3. Remove the two switch screws and remove the switch assembly.
4. Before installing, place the new switch in "Lock" position and make sure the lock cylinder and actuating rod are in "Lock" position (second detent from the top).
5. Install the activating rod into the switch and assemble the switch on the column. Tighten the mounting screws. Use only the specified screws since overlength screws could impair the collapsibility of the column.
6. Reinstall the steering column.

Headlight Switch Replacement

1965-72 Except as Noted

1. Disconnect battery.
2. Pull knob out to on position.
3. Reach under instrument panel and depress the switch shaft retainer. Remove knob and shaft assembly.

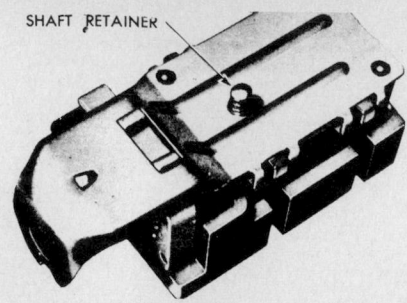

SHAFT RETAINER

Light switch shaft retainer
(© Chevrolet Div. G.M. Corp.)

4. Remove the retaining ferrule nut. (Tool J-4880 will assist.)
5. Remove switch from instrument panel.
6. Disconnect the multi-plug connector from the switch.
7. Replace in reverse of above. (In checking lights before installation, switch must be grounded to test dome light.)

1968 Corvette

The headlight switch replacement procedure is the same as that described immediately above, except that the instrument panel must be unscrewed and pulled forward to provide access to the switch. Also, when disconnecting the switch, identify the vacuum lines so that they can be correctly reconnected.

1969-72 Corvette

1. Disconnect the battery.
2. Remove mast jacket trim covers.
3. Unclip and remove the left forward console side trim panel.
4. Lower the steering column as described under *Steering*.
5. Remove the screws and washers which secure the left instrument panel to the door opening, the top of the dash and the left side of the center instrument cluster.
6. Pull the cluster assembly down and tilt it forward.
7. Depress the switch shaft retainer and remove the knob and shaft assembly.
8. Remove the switch retaining bezel.
9. Disconnect the vacuum lines, identifying them for correct reconnection.
10. Pry the connector from the switch.
11. Install in the reverse order of removal.

Brakes

Specific information on brake cylinder sizes can be found in the General Chassis and Brake Specifications table.

Brake adjustments, lining replacement, bleeding procedure, master and wheel cylinder overhaul can be found in the Unit Repair Section.

Information on troubleshooting and overhauling power brakes can be found in the Unit Repair Section.

Information on the grease seals which may need replacement can be found in the Unit Repair Section.

1967-72

Beginning with 1967 models, a dual hydraulic brake system is employed. The front and rear brakes are each separate systems with a common tandem master cylinder. In the event of a failure in either of the systems, the other will remain operable.

Power Brake Unit Removal

1. Remove vacuum hose from vacuum check valve.
2. Disconnect hydraulic lines at unit.
3. Disconnect push rod at brake pedal assembly.
4. Remove nuts and lockwashers that secure unit to firewall and remove unit.

Master Cylinder Removal

The pedals are pivoted from underneath the dash panel. The master cylinder is located on the engine side of the firewall.

1. To remove the master cylinder, disconnect the hydraulic lines, remove the clevis that connects the brake pushrod to the brake pedal from under the dash.
2. Remove the mounting bolts that hold the master cylinder to the firewall and lift off the master cylinder.
3. To install, reverse the above procedure.

Brake Pedal Free Travel Adjustment

The brake pedal stop is not adjustable, but brake pedal free travel is adjustable by setting the clearance between the pedal pushrod and the master cylinder.

1. Loosen the locknut on the pushrod.
2. Turn the pushrod until there is 1/16 to 1/4 in. pedal free travel (movement before the pushrod contacts the master cylinder pistons).
3. Tighten the locknut against the clevis and recheck the free travel.

Parking Brake Cable R & R

Before working under the dash to remove the front parking brake cable, disconnect the battery to avoid the possibility of shorting out any of the circuits.

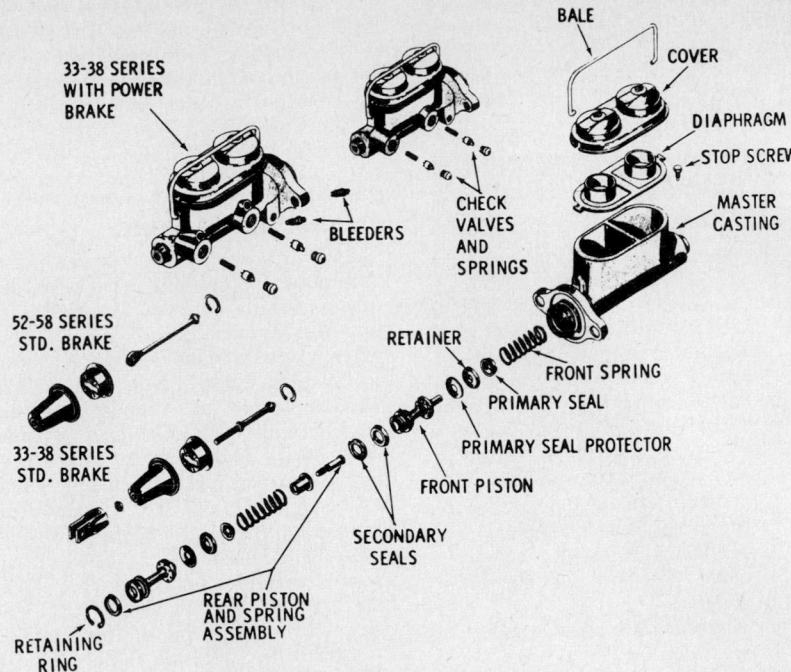

Master cylinder (Bendix). No front check valve with front disc brake.
(© Chevrolet Div., G.M. Corp.)

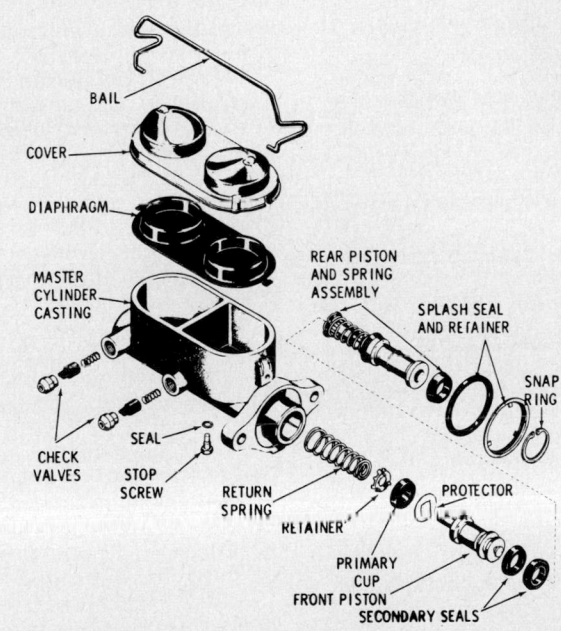

Master cylinder (Moraine). No front check valve with front disc brake.
(© Chevrolet Div., G.M. Corp.)

1965-70 Chevrolet

There are three parking brake cables: the front cable runs between the pedal assembly and the looped center cable; the center cable is a large loop, each end connected to the short rear cables and the center (forward) attached to the front cable with the equalizer; the rear cables are attached to brake shoe actuating levers.

To remove any of the cables, first release the brake pedal and loosen the equalizer adjusting nuts. The front cable slips into a clevis at the pedal lever and is connected to the equalizer by means of a threaded rod. The outer cable has locking fingers which secure it in a hole in the firewall.

The center cable is removed by disconnecting the equalizer, disconnecting each end from the rear cables and by removing it from the frame guides and hook. The rear cables are removed by disconnecting the forward end from the center cable, removing the retainers at the frame and by removing the rear end from the brake actuating levers. The brake drum and shoes must be removed to disconnect the rear cable from the actuating lever.

Adjust the parking brake after replacing any of the cables. Adjustment is made at the equalizer while the parking brake pedal is applied two notches from the full release position. Loosen the forward equalizer adjusting nut, tighten the rear nut until slight brake drag is obtained, then tighten the forward adjusting nut. Check operation after adjustment.

1971-72 Chevrolet

The parking brake cable design is essentially the same as that used in 1965-70 models with a forward, center and two rear cables. The front outer cable, however, is clipped to the pedal bracket. When replacing the front cable, tie a rope onto the top of the old cable and pull it through the cable route so that it may be used to pull the new cable into place. Remove the rear screws holding the inner fender panel to the fender to get at the cable grommet in the firewall. Adjustment is the same as that described for the 1965-70 models above.

1965 Corvette

To remove the front cable, release the parking brake and disconnect the cable ball end from the idler clevis at the equalizer. Remove the hand brake lever and the bracket clamps.

To remove the rear cable, disconnect the cable at the rear wheel flange plate and remove the cable ball out of the recess in the brake lever assembly clevis. Disconnect the clips and retainers along the frame and at the differential carrier support bracket. Disconnect the cable at the equalizer and remove the cable.

When assembling, lubricate the cables and all moving parts. To adjust the parking brake, first adjust the service brakes, then set the lever at four notches and adjust the equalizer nuts until drag is obtained at the rear brakes.

1966 Corvette

To remove the front cable, remove the three retainers. Disconnect the ball end from the idler lever at the equalizer. Remove the hand brake lever assembly and disconnect the ball end. Install in the reverse order of removal.

To remove the rear cable, remove the cable clip retainers at the frame rails. Disconnect the cable at the rear wheel flange plate and remove the ball end from the brake lever clevis. Disconnect the cables at the equalizer and remove.

Adjustment is made with the parking brake applied at two notches from the fully released position. Adjust the nuts at the equalizer until slight drag is felt at the rear wheels.

1967-72 Corvette

To remove the front cable, remove the parking brake lever and the pulley. Remove the cable ball end from the hand lever. Remove the seal grommet from the underbody cable hole and pull the cable out of the vehicle. Installation is the reverse of the removal procedure.

To remove the rear cables, remove the retainer clips at the frame and disconnect the cables at the rear flange plate. Remove the ball from the recess of the brake lever clevis and disconnect the cables from the equalizer. Install in the reverse order of removal.

Adjustment of the parking brake is made with the lever set at two notches from the fully released position. Tighten the equalizer adjusting nuts until slight drag is felt at the rear wheels.

Fuel System

Data on capacity of the gas tank can be found in the Capacities table. Data on correct engine idle speed and fuel pump pressure can be found in the Tune-up Specifications table.

Information covering operation and troubles of the fuel gauge is in the Unit Repair Section.

Fuel Pump

NOTE: two types of fuel pump are used; a serviceable type and a non-serviceable type.

To remove the fuel pump, disconnect the input flex line and the output line to the carburetor. The fuel pump then can be unbolted from the side of the block and lifted off. On V8 models, the pump is actuated by a pushrod in the block.

Beginning 1967

All Chevrolet engines are equipped with the non-serviceable type fuel pump. This pump is replaced as an assembly only.

Caution Fuel pump replacement V8. A fuel pump may fail to function at the time of replacement as a result of error in positioning or damage to the fuel pump pushrod of the V8 engine. This pushrod can slip out of place during the process of pump replacement and result in no pump action from the newly replaced unit. Before tightening the fuel pump to the engine, have someone spin the engine with the starter

while feeling the fuel pump body for movement. If the pump and pushrod are in correct position, movement will be felt in the pump as the pushrod pressure is applied and released from the pump arm.

⏻ CHILTON TIME-SAVER

283, 307, 327, and 350 cu. in.

When replacing a fuel pump on a 283, 307, 327 or 350 cu. in. engine, considerable time can be saved as follows:

1. Before removing the old pump, remove the upper bolt from the engine's right front mounting boss. This bolt hole is in direct alignment with the fuel pump pushrod. The threaded bolt hole continues into the pump pushrod bore. The bolt acts as an oil plug.
2. Temporarily insert a longer bolt, (about ⅜—16 x 2 in.) into the hole. Screw the bolt into the bore until it bottoms against the pump pushrod. (Don't tighten the bolt with a wrench or the rod can be damaged.)
3. The mechanic is now free to remove and install the fuel pump without worrying about fuel pump pushrod misalignment.

CAUTION: don't forget to reinstall original motor bolt.

396, 427 and 454 cu. in.

The design of these engines prevents the use of the method of simplifying fuel pump pushrod positioning while installing a fuel pump. However, to hold the pump pushrod in position while installing the fuel pump, the following works satisfactorily:

1. Clean oil from pushrod.
2. Pack a small quantity of non-fibrous grease in the area around the fuel pump pushrod to hold it in suspension long enough to position the fuel pump.
3. Install and check pump action, then torque attaching bolts.

Fuel Filters

Fuel filters are integral with the carburetor body. The filter element can be replaced as follows:

1. Disconnect the fuel line.
2. Remove the fuel filter nut from the carburetor.
3. Remove the filter element and spring. Blow through the filter end. If the air does not flow freely, replace the element. Do not attempt to clean the filter element.

4. Install the spring, then the element. Bronze filters in Holley carburetors must have the small section of the cone facing out.
5. Install the inlet fitting using a new gasket.
6. Install the fuel line.

Idle Speed and Mixture Adjustments

Idle mixture and speed adjustments are critical aspects of exhaust emission control. For a discussion of the various emission control systems see Exhaust Emission Control Systems later in this section. It is important that all tune-up instructions be carefully followed to ensure satisfactory engine performance and minimum exhaust pollution. The different combinations of emission systems application on the different engine models have resulted in a great variety of tune-up specifications. See the Tune-Up Specifications at the beginning of this section. Beginning in 1968, all models have a decal conspicuously placed somewhere in the engine compartment giving tune-up specifications.

When adjusting a carburetor with two idle mixture screws, adjust them alternately and evenly, unless otherwise stated.

See the Unit Repair Section for illustrations and adjustment specifications of Carter, Holley and Rochester carburetors. In the following adjustment procedures the term "lean roll" means turning the mixture adjusting screws in (clockwise) from optimum setting to obtain an obvious drop in engine speed (usually 20 rpm).

All 1965-66 and 1967 Without A.I.R.

Adjust with air cleaner removed.

1. Connect a tachometer and vacuum gauge to the engine, then set the parking brake and shift the manual transmission into Neutral, automatic into Drive.
2. Turn the idle mixture screw/s in until lightly seated, then back out 1½ turns.
3. With engine running, adjust the idle speed screw to obtain the specified rpm.
4. Adjust the idle mixture screw/s to obtain the highest steady manifold vacuum at the specified speed. If necessary, reset the idle speed screw while adjusting mixture.

NOTE: on air conditioned models, the air conditioner is turned on and the hot idle compensator valve is held closed while adjusting idle speed and mixture.

NOTE: on Rochester BV carburetors, turn the idle mixture screw to "lean roll" position, then back it out

¼ turn.

5. Final adjustment should be made with the air cleaner installed.
6. Remove tachometer and vacuum gauge.

1967 With A.I.R.

Adjust with air cleaner removed.

1. Connect a tachometer to the engine, place manual transmission in Neutral, automatic in Drive.
2. Turn idle mixture screw/s in until lightly seated, then back out 3 turns.
3. With engine running, adjust the idle speed screw to obtain the specified idle speed.
4. Adjust the idle mixture screw/s in to "lean roll" position, then back them out (rich) ¼ turn. Readjust the idle speed screw to keep the engine at the specified idle speed while adjusting the mixture.

NOTE: on air conditioned cars, turn the air conditioner off with L6, 283, 327 and 350 cu. in. engines. Air conditioner must be on and hot idle compensator held closed with 396 and 427 cu. in. engines.

5. Final adjustment should be made with the air cleaner installed.
6. Remove the tachometer.

All 1968-69

Adjust with air cleaner installed.

1. Turn the idle mixture screw/s in until lightly seated, then back out 3 turns.
2. With engine at operating temperature, adjust idle speed screw to obtain specified rpm, manual transmission in Neutral and automatic in Drive.

NOTE: on all 1968 models *except* L6 with automatic transmission and the 325 H.P. and 350 H.P. 327 cu. in. with manual transmission, the air conditioner is turned *off*. On the above-mentioned vehicles the air conditioner is left *on*. On 1969 models, turn the air conditioner either on or off according to the instructions on the tune-up decal.

3. Adjust one idle mixture screw to obtain the highest steady idle speed.
4. Adjust the idle speed screw to the speed specified on the tune-up decal.

NOTE: on models equipped with an idle solenoid, adjust the solenoid plunger hex to obtain 500 rpm on the L6 engine and 600 rpm on V8 engines. Disconnect the wire at the solenoid to de-energize it, allowing the throttle lever to contact the carburetor idle speed screw. Adjust the carburetor idle screw to obtain 400 rpm.

5. Adjust the mixture screw in to "lean roll" position, then back

out (rich) ¼ turn.

6. Repeat Steps 3, 4 and 5 for the other idle mixture screw for 2-BBL. and 4-BBL. engines.
7. Readjust the idle speed screw to obtain final specified rpm, if necessary.

1970 Chevrolet

Adjust with air cleaner installed.

If the vehicle is equipped with Evaporative Emission, disconnect the fuel tank line from the vapor canister while making the idle speed and mixture adjustments. Warm up the engine and leave it running with the choke and, if applicable, air cleaner damper door fully open and the air conditioning off.

250 Engine

1. Disconnect and plug the distributor vacuum hose at the distributor end.
2. Turn the idle mixture screw in until it lightly contacts the seat, back it out 4 turns.
3. Adjust the solenoid plunger to obtain 830 rpm (manual transmission in Neutral) or 630 rpm (automatic transmission in Drive).
4. Adjust mixture screw in to obtain 750 rpm (manual transmission in Neutral) or 600 rpm (automatic transmission in Drive).
5. Disconnect the solenoid wire and, with the solenoid plunger depressed, adjust the carburetor idle speed screw to obtain 400 rpm.
6. Reconnect the solenoid wire and distributor vacuum hose.

400 (265 H.P.) Engine

1. Disconnect and plug the distributor vacuum hose at the distributor end.
2. Turn the idle mixture screws in until they lightly contact the seats, then back them out 4 turns.
3. With manual transmission in Neutral, adjust the carburetor idle speed screw to obtain 800 rpm. With automatic transmission in Drive, adjust the solenoid plunger to obtain 630 rpm.
4. Adjust the idle mixture screws in equally to obtain 700 rpm (manual transmission in Neutral) or 600 rpm (automatic transmission in Drive).
5. If equipped with automatic transmission, disconnect the solenoid wire and, with solenoid plunger depressed, set the carburetor idle speed screw to obtain 450 rpm.
6. Reconnect the solenoid wire and the distributor vacuum hose.

350 (250 H.P.) Engine

1. Disconnect and plug the distributor vacuum hose at the distributor end.
2. Turn the idle mixture screws in until they lightly contact the seats, then back them out 4 turns.
3. With manual transmission in Neutral, adjust the solenoid plunger to obtain 830 rpm. With automatic transmission in Drive, adjust the solenoid plunger to obtain 630 rpm.
4. Adjust the idle mixture screws in equally to obtain 750 rpm (manual transmission in Neutral) or 600 rpm (automatic transmission in Drive).
5. Disconnect the solenoid wire and, with the solenoid plunger fully depressed, set the carburetor idle speed screw to obtain 450 rpm.
6. Reconnect the solenoid wire and distributor vacuum hose.

350 (300 H.P.) Engine

1. Disconnect the vacuum hose at the distributor and plug the hose.
2. Turn the idle mixture screws in until they lightly contact the seats, then back them out 4 turns.
3. With manual transmission in Neutral, adjust the carburetor idle speed screw to obtain 775 rpm. With automatic transmission in Drive, adjust the carburetor idle speed screw to obtain 630 rpm.
4. Adjust the mixture screws in equally to obtain 700 rpm (manual transmission in Neutral) or 600 rpm (automatic transmission in Drive).
5. Reconnect the distributor vacuum hose.

454 (450 H.P.) Engine

1. *Remove the air cleaner.*
2. Disconnect the distributor vacuum hose at the distributor and plug the hose.
3. Adjust the mixture screws for maximum idle speed.
4. With manual transmission in Neutral, adjust the carburetor idle speed screw to obtain 750 rpm. With automatic transmission in Drive, adjust the carburetor idle speed screw to obtain 700 rpm.
5. Turn one idle mixture screw to obtain a 20 rpm drop in idle speed, then back the screw out ¼ turn. Repeat for the second idle mixture screw.
6. Repeat Step 4 above.
7. Reconnect the distributor vacuum hose and install the air cleaner.

*454 (345 H.P.) and
454 (390 H.P.) Engines*

1. Disconnect the distributor vacuum hose at the distributor and plug the hose.
2. Turn the idle mixture screws in until they are lightly seated, then back them out 4 turns.
3. With automatic transmission in Drive, adjust the carburetor idle speed screw to obtain 630 rpm. Adjust the idle mixture screws in equally to obtain 600 rpm.
4. With manual transmission in Neutral, adjust the carburetor idle speed screw to obtain 700 rpm. Turn one of the mixture screws in until the engine speed drops to 400 rpm. Readjust the idle speed screw to obtain 700 rpm. Turn in the other mixture screw until the engine speed drops 40 rpm. Readjust the idle speed screw to obtain 700 rpm.
5. Reconnect the distributor vacuum hose.

1970 Corvette

Adjust with air cleaner installed.
If the vehicle is equipped with Evaporative Emission, disconnect the fuel tank line from the vapor canister while making the idle speed and mixture adjustments. Warm up the engine and leave it running while adjusting. The choke valve and, if applicable, air cleaner damper door should remain open. Leave the air conditioning off.

350 (300, 350 and 370 H.P.) Engines

1. Adjust the idle mixture screws equally to obtain maximum idle speed.
2. On the 300 H.P. engine with manual transmission in Neutral adjust the idle speed screw to obtain 700 rpm. On the 300 H.P. engine with automatic transmission in Drive, adjust the idle speed screw to obtain 600 rpm.
3. On the 350 and 370 H.P. engines, adjust the idle speed screw to obtain 750 rpm with the manual transmission in Neutral.

*427 (390 H.P. and 400 H.P.)
Without Air Conditioning*

1. Adjust the idle mixture screws to obtain the maximum idle rpm.
2. On the 390 H.P. engine with manual transmission in Neutral, adjust the idle speed screw to obtain 800 rpm. On the 390 engine with automatic transmission in Drive, adjust the idle speed screw to obtain 600 rpm.
3. On the 400 H.P. engine with manual transmission in Neutral, adjust the idle speed screw to obtain 750 rpm. On the 400 H.P. engine with automatic transmission in Drive, adjust the idle

speed screw to obtain 600 rpm.

*427 (390 and 400 H.P.)
With Manual Transmission
and Air Conditioning*

1. Turn the air conditioning off and disconnect the wire from the idle-stop solenoid.
2. Adjust the idle mixture screws to obtain the maximum idle speed.
3. With transmission in Neutral, adjust the idle speed screw to obtain 550 rpm.
4. Turn each idle mixture screw in to obtain a 20 rpm drop, then back out each screw ¼ turn.
5. Turn on the air conditioning and reconnect the wire to the idle-stop solenoid.
6. Adjust the solenoid plunger to obtain 1,000 rpm.

*427 (390 and 400 H.P.)
with Automatic Transmission
and Air Conditioning*

1. Turn the air conditioning on.
2. Adjust the mixture screws to obtain the maximum idle speed.
3. Adjust the solenoid plunger to obtain 650 rpm with the transmission in Drive.
4. Adjust each mixture screw to obtain a 20 rpm drop in engine speed, then back out each screw ¼ turn.
5. Readjust the solenoid plunger to obtain 650 rpm.
6. Disconnect the solenoid wire and, with the plunger depressed, adjust the carburetor idle speed screw to obtain 500 rpm.
7. Reconnect the solenoid wire.

427 (430 and 435 H.P.) Engines

1. Adjust the idle mixture screws alternately and evenly to obtain the maximum smooth idle speed.
2. With the automatic transmission in Drive, adjust the solenoid plunger to obtain 750 rpm.
3. With the manual transmission in Neutral, adjust the carburetor idle speed screw to obtain 750 rpm (435 H.P.) or 1,000 rpm (430 H.P.).
4. Disconnect the solenoid wire (automatic transmission models only) and, with the solenoid plunger fully depressed, adjust the carburetor idle speed screw to obtain 500 rpm.
5. If necessary, readjust the carburetor idle screw (manual transmission) or the solenoid plunger (automatic transmission) to obtain the speeds specified in Steps 2 and 3.

All 1971—Initial Adjustments

Adjust with air cleaner installed.
The following initial idle adjustments are part of the normal engine tune-up. There is a tune-up

decal placed conspicuously in the engine compartment outlining the specific procedure and settings for each engine application. Follow all of the instructions when adjusting the idle. These tuning procedures are necessary to obtain the delicate balance of variables for the maintenance of both reliable engine performance and efficient exhaust emission control.

NOTE: all engines except the 350 (330 H.P.) and 454 (425 H.P.) have limiter caps on the mixture adjusting screws. The idle mixture is preset and the limiter caps installed at the factory in order to meet emission control standards. Do not remove these limiter caps unless all other possible causes of poor idle condition have been thoroughly checked out. Procedures for setting the idle mixture with the limiter caps removed are described under the heading "Complete Adjustment" later on.

The solenoid used on 1971 carburetors is different from the one used on earlier models. Combination Emission Control System (C.E.C. solenoid) valve regulates distributor vacuum as a function of transmission gear position.

Caution The C.E.C. solenoid is adjusted only after: 1) replacement of the solenoid, 2) major carburetor overhaul, or 3) after the throttle body is removed or replaced.

Instructions for C.E.C. solenoid plunger adjustment follow the "Complete Adjustment".

All initial adjustments described below are made:

1. With the engine warmed up and running.
2. With the choke fully open.
3. With the fuel tank line disconnected from the Evaporative Emission canister on all models except the Corvette.
4. With the fuel tank gas cap removed on the Corvette.
5. With the vacuum hose disconnected at the distributor and plugged.

Be sure to reconnect the distributor vacuum hose and to connect the fuel tank to evaporative emission canister line or install the gas cap when idle adjustments are complete.

250 6-Cylinder Engine

Adjust the carburetor idle speed screw (NOT the solenoid plunger) to obtain 550 rpm (manual transmission in Neutral) or 500 rpm (automatic transmission in Drive).

*350 and 400 (2-BBL) and
350 (4-BBL Quadrajet) Engines*

Adjust the carburetor idle speed screw (NOT the solenoid plunger) to obtain 600 rpm (manual transmission in Neutral with the air conditioner off) or 550 rpm (automatic transmission in Drive with the air conditioner on).

350 and 454 (4-BBL Holley) Engines —Corvette

1. Adjust the carburetor idle speed screw (NOT the solenoid plunger) to obtain 700 rpm (manual transmission in Neutral or automatic transmission in Drive).
2. Adjust the idle mixture screws alternately to obtain the maximum smooth idle speed.
3. Adjust one of the idle mixture screws to obtain a 20 rpm drop ("lean roll"), then back it out ¼ turn.
4. Repeat Step 4 above for the other idle mixture screw.
5. Readjust the carburetor idle speed screw to obtain 700 rpm if necessary.

402 and 454 (4-BBL Quadrajet) Engines

Turn the air conditioner off. Adjust the carburetor idle speed screw (NOT the solenoid plunger) to obtain 600 rpm (manual transmission in Neutral or automatic transmission in Drive).

All 1971—Complete Adjustment

The adjustment of the idle mixture requiring the removal of the limiter caps is only made after carburetor overhaul, throttle body part replacement, mixture needle part replacement or limiter cap and needle removal. Before proceeding, follow the tuning instructions on the tune-up decal (refer to "All 1971—Initial Adjustment").

1. Turn the idle mixture screw/s in until lightly contact the seat, then back out 4 turns.
2. Referring to the chart ("Idle Mixture Adjustment"), adjust the idle speed screw (NOT the solenoid plunger) to obtain the "initial idle speed" listed in Column #1.
3. Hook-up a CO (carbon monoxide) gas analyzer to the vehicle.
4. Adjust the idle mixture screw (both screws equally on 2- and 4-BBL carburetors) to obtain the specified %CO reading (Column #3).
5. Readjust the idle speed screw (NOT the solenoid plunger) to obtain the specified "final idle speed" (Column #2).
6. Install service idle mixture screw limiter cap/s on the idle mixture screws (except on Holley carburetors).
7. Reconnect the distributor vacuum hose.
8. Reconnect the fuel tank vapor hose or, on Corvettes, install the fuel tank cap.

NOTE: if a CO analyzer is unavailable, the following alternate procedure may be used to adjust the idle mixture.

1. Turn the idle mixture screw/s in until lightly seated, then back out 4 full turns.
2. Adjust the carburetor idle speed screw (NOT the solenoid plunger) to obtain the "initial idle speed" (see Column #1 of "Idle Mixture Adjustment" chart).
3. Adjust the idle mixture screw/s to obtain the "final idle speed" (see Column #2 in the "Idle Mixture Adjustment" chart).
4. Install service idle limiter cap/s on mixture screws.
5. Reconnect the distributor vacuum hose and fuel vapor line.

1971 C.E.C. Valve Adjustment

This adjustment is made only after: 1) replacement of the solenoid; 2) major overhaul of the carburetor; or 3) after the throttle body is removed and replaced.

Perform the "Initial Adjustments" described above and the tune-up as described on the tune-up decal before preceding with the C.E.C. valve adjustment. Warm up the engine and leave it running while making the adjustment, leaving manual transmission in Neutral or automatic transmission in Drive. Turn the air conditioner off, remove the fuel tank cap (Corvette only), disconnect the fuel tank vapor line from the canister (all but Corvette) and disconnect the distributor vacuum hose from the distributor and plug the hose.

1. Manually extend the C.E.C. valve plunger to contact the throttle lever.
2. Adjust the plunger length to obtain the idle speed specified in Column #4 of the "Idle Mixture Adjustment" table.
3. Reconnect the fuel tank vapor hose and the distributor vacuum hose.

Exhaust System

Muffler, Exhaust Pipe and Tail Pipe

On Chevrolet models, the exhaust pipe (manifold to muffler) is welded to the muffler and all other connections are clamped with U-bolts. All exhaust systems are hung with rubber brackets.

Components should be replaced whenever there is evidence of broken or damaged parts, deterioration, broken seams or loose connections which may cause leaks. Exhaust system pipes and resonators rearward of the muffler should be replaced whenever a new muffler is installed. When replacing the muffler, cut the exhaust pipe as close to the muffler inlet as possible to provide enough pipe for attaching the replacement muffler.

Make sure that the exhaust system components have at least ¾ in. clearance from the floor pan to avoid possible overheating. Install U-bolt clamps at a 90° angle to the slots in the muffler or resonator inlets and outlets.

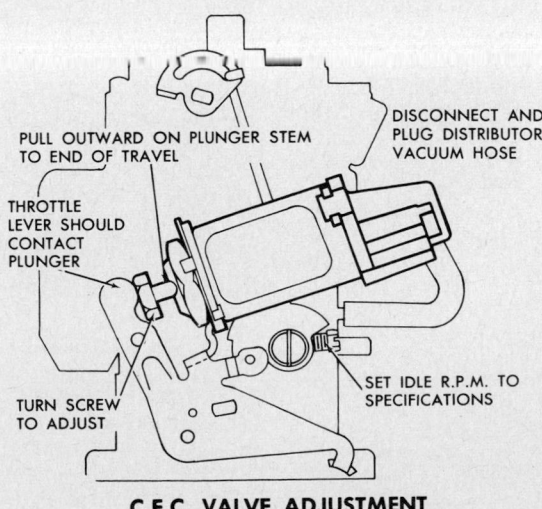

C.E.C. VALVE ADJUSTMENT

1971 C.E.C. valve adjustment (© Chev. Div., G.M. Corp.)

1971 Idle Mixture Adjustment

Transmission	Engine	#1 Initial Idle Speed (rpm)	#2 Final Idle Speed (rpm)	#3 % CO @ Idle	#4 CEC Valve Engine Speed (rpm)
Manual	250 6-Cyl.	625	550	1.0	850
	400 (255 H.P.)	700	600	0.5	900
	350 (270 H.P.)	675	600	1.0	900
	402 (300 H.P.)	675	600	1.0	850
	454 (365 H.P.)	675	600	1.0	850
Automatic	250 6-Cyl.	530	500	1.0	650
	400 (255 H.P.)	580	550	0.5	650
	350 (270 H.P.)	580	550	0.5	650
	402 (300 H.P.)	630	600	1.0	650
	454 (365 H.P.)	630	600	1.0	650
Manual	350 (330 H.P.)	*	700	*	900
	454 (425 H.P.)	*	700	*	900
Automatic	350 (330 H.P.)	*	700	*	750
	454 (425 H.P.)	*	700	*	750

*These engines are equipped with A.I.R. and do not have idle limiter caps.

Cooling System

Chevrolet engine cooling systems function at high pressure for increased cooling efficiency. The radiator cap has both pressure and vacuum relief valves.

Cooling system capacities for the various models can be found in the Capacities table at the beginning of this section. Information on the water temperature gauge can be found in the Unit Repair Section.

The thermostat is located inside a housing on the front of the cylinder head on six-cylinder engines and between the intake manifold and the cylinder head (forward) on V8 engines.

Caution When replacing a thermostat, it is sometimes possible to install it in the reverse position. The spring-loaded end of the unit must be installed toward the engine.

Water Pump R & R

1. Drain the radiator and loosen the fan pulley bolts.
2. Disconnect the heater hose, lower radiator hose and, if applicable, the bypass hose at the water pump.
3. On V8 engines, remove the Delcotron upper brace. Loosen the swivel bolt and remove the fan belt.
4. On Mark IV engines, disconnect the power steering and air conditioning belts and swivel the power steering pump to one side.
5. Remove the fan blade and pulley. Replace a bent or damaged fan.

NOTE: thermostatic fan clutches must be kept in an "in-car" position. When removed from the car the assembly should be supported so that the clutch disc remains in a vertical plane to prevent silicone fluid leakage.

6. Remove the water pump attaching bolts and, if applicable, the power steering-to-pump bolts and remove the pump and gasket.

NOTE: on six-cylinder engines, pull the pump straight out of the block first to avoid damage to the impeller.

7. Install the pump assembly using a new gasket. Coat the gasket on both sides with sealer. Tighten the 5/16 in. bolts to 15 ft. lbs. (six-cylinder) and the 3/8 in. bolts (V8) to 30 ft. lbs.
8. Install the pulley and fan.
9. On Mark IV engines, install the power steering and air conditioning bolts.
10. Connect the hoses and fill the cooling system.
11. On V8 engines, install the Delcotron upper brace and fan belt. Install the power steering pump bolt.
12. Adjust the belts, then start the engine and check for leaks.

Radiator Core Removal

Chevrolet

1. Drain the cooling system.
2. Disconnect the radiator upper and lower hoses and, if applicable, transmission coolant lines.
3. Remove the radiator upper panel if so equipped.
4. If there is a radiator shroud in front of the radiator, the radiator and shroud are removed as an assembly.

5. If there is a fan shroud, remove the shroud attaching screws let the shroud hang on the fan.
6. Remove the radiator attaching bolts and remove the radiator.
7. Installation is the reverse of the removal procedure.

Fan Shroud—1965-67 Corvette

1. Drain the radiator.
2. Raise the hood and install a bolt in the hole of the hood support bracket.
3. Disconnect the upper radiator hose and the supply tank hose at the radiator connection.
4. Remove the six shroud bolts.
5. Carefully remove the shroud.
6. Install in reverse order of removal.

Aluminum Radiator—1965-67 Corvette

1. Remove the fan shroud as described above.
2. Disconnect the lower radiator hose.
3. Remove the radiator upper mount bracket, then lift out radiator.
4. To install, reverse the removal procedure.

Copper Radiator—1966-67 Corvette

1. Scribe the location of the hood panel bracket, then remove the hood panel assembly.
2. Drain the radiator and disconnect the hoses.
3. Remove the fan.
4. Remove the four bolts along the top of the radiator support, the right and left radiator holddown clamps and the shroud center bracket.
5. Remove the horns and bolts retaining the fan shroud to the radiator support.
6. Remove the radiator and fan shroud from the vehicle.
7. Installation is the reverse of the removal procedure.

Radiator—1968-72 Corvette

1. Drain the radiator.
2. Raise the hood and insert a bolt in the hole of the hood support.
3. Remove the radiator inlet and outlet hoses and, if applicable, the transmission coolant hoses.
4. If applicable, remove the supply tank hose at the radiator connection.
5. Remove the shroud to radiator support bracket screws (the L88 engine does not have a fan shroud).
6. Remove the shroud to radiator baffle bracket screws and let the shroud rest on the fan.
7. Remove the radiator upper support bracket screws and carefully lift the radiator from the

car.

8. Install in the reverse order of removal.

Engine

Engine application and specification tables may be found at the beginning of this section.

The following service procedures apply to all engines, except where differences are specified. The 396, 400, 427 and 454 V8 (Mark IV series) are essentially the same engine. Similarly, the 283, 302, 307, 327 and 350 series engines all utilize the same block design.

Exhaust Emission Control

Positive Crankcase Ventilation

In this system, crankcase vapors are drawn into the intake manifold and burned as part of the engine combustion. The "positive" ventilation uses a vented-mesh oil filler cap for clean air intake to the crankcase and the "close positive" system draws clean air from the carburetor air cleaner.

The ventilation flow is regulated by the PCV valve. To check the operation of the valve:

1. Connect a tachometer and vacuum gauge to the engine.
2. Start the engine and adjust the idle speed and mixture.
3. Disconnect the ventilation hose at the valve, block the opening of the valve and note the engine rpm change.
4. A change of less than 50 rpm indicates that the PCV valve is plugged and must be replaced.

For a more complete discussion of crankcase ventilation systems, see Sections 3 and 4 under Exhaust Emission Controls in the Unit Repair Section.

Air Injection Reactor

The A.I.R. (K-19) system is employed on various 1966-72 models. Carburetors and distributors used on A.I.R.-equipped engines are designed particularly for these engines and are not interchangeable with those used on engines without A.I.R.

The system functions by injecting air into the exhaust ports, thus facilitating the spontaneous combustion of carbon monoxide and unburnt hydrocarbons in the exhaust gases.

For a complete description of the A.I.R. system, see Exhaust Emission Systems in the Unit Repair Section.

Controlled Combustion System

This system increases combustion efficiency by means of leaner carburetor mixtures and revised distributor calibration. On most installations, thermostatically controlled air cleaner intakes draw warm air from an exhaust manifold shroud.

Particular attention must be paid to the tuning of C.C.S. equipped engines to maintain performance and efficient exhaust emission control. The Controlled Combustion System is more thoroughly discussed under Exhaust Emission Systems in the Unit Repair Section.

Evaporative Emission Control

Beginning in 1970, a fuel vapor control system was installed on many vehicles. This system is designed to reduce fuel vapor emission. The canister filter should be replaced every 12 months or 12,000 miles. To remove the canister and replace the filter, proceed as follows:

1. Note the positions of the hoses, then disconnect them from the canister.
2. Loosen the clamps and remove the canister.
3. Remove the bottom of the canister and pull out the filter.
4. Install a new filter and assemble the bottom to the canister.
5. Install the canister and tighten the clamp bolts.
6. Install the hoses in their original positions.

Idle Speed Solenoid

1968-69 models may have an idle speed solenoid on the carburetor. Due to the leaner carburetor settings required for emission control, the engine may have a tendency to "diesel" or "run-on" after the ignition is turned off. The carburetor solenoid, energized when the ignition is on, maintains the normal idle speed. When the ignition is turned off, the solenoid is de-energized and permits the throttle valves to fully close, thus preventing run-on. For adjustment of carburetors with idle solenoids, see "Idle Speed and Mixture Adjustments."

Transmission Controlled Spark

See the Unit Repair Section, Exhaust Emission Systems, for a description of the TCS solenoid used on most 1970 models.

Combustion Emission Control System

All 1971 models are equipped with a C.E.C. solenoid which controls distributor vacuum as a function of transmission gear engagement and

Exploded view, V8 engine external parts, typical (© Chevrolet Div. G.M. Corp.)

which provides a higher idle speed when energized. See "Idle Speed and Mixture Adjustments" for solenoid plunger adjustment procedure.

Engine R & R

1. Remove the hood. Scribe lines around the hinges so that the hood can be installed in its original location.
2. Remove the air cleaner.
3. Disconnect the battery cables at the battery.
4. Remove the radiator and shroud.
5. Remove the fan blade and pulley.
6. Disconnect wires at:
   a. C.E.C. solenoid.
   b. Coil.
   c. Temperature switch.
   d. Delcotron.
   e. Starter solenoid.
   f. Oil pressure sending unit.
7. Disconnect:
   a. Accelerator linkage at the pedal.
   b. Oil pressure gauge line, if so equipped.
   c. Exhaust pipes at the manifold flanges.
   d. Engine cooler lines, if so equipped.
   e. Vacuum line to the power brake unit, if so equipped.
   f. Fuel line (front tank) at the fuel pump.
8. Remove the power steering pump, leaving the hoses attached to the pump.
9. Raise the car on a hoist.
10. Drain the cooling system and the crankcase.
11. Remove the driveshaft.
    NOTE: if a plug for the driveshaft opening in the transmission is not available, drain the transmission.
12. Disconnect:
    a. Shift linkage at the transmission.
    b. Speedometer cable at the transmission.
    c. Transmission cooler lines, if so equipped.
    d. TCS switch at the transmission.
13. On vehicles with synchromesh transmissions, disconnect the clutch linkage at the cross-shaft then remove the cross-shaft at the frame bracket.
14. Lower the vehicle and remove the rocker arm covers and install engine lifting adapter on the cylinder heads.
15. Raise the engine enough to take the weight off the front mounts, then remove the front mount through bolts.
16. Remove the rear mount to crossmember bolts.
17. Raise the engine enough to take the weight off the rear mount, then remove the crossmember.
    NOTE: on Chevrolets it is neces-

sary to remove the mount from the transmission before the crossmember can be removed.
18. Remove the engine/transmission assembly as a unit.
19. To remove the clutch and transmission from the engine:
    a. Remove the clutch housing cover plate screws.
    b. Remove the clutch housing to engine attaching bolts, then, remove the transmission and clutch housing as a unit.

Caution Do not let the weight of the transmission hang on the spline because the clutch disc may be easily damaged.

    c. Remove the starter and clutch housing rear cover plate.
    d. Loosen the clutch mounting bolts one turn at a time (to prevent distortion of the clutch cover) until the spring pressure is released. Remove all the bolts, clutch disc and pressure plate assembly.
20. To remove the automatic transmission:
    a. Remove the starter and the converter housing underpan.
    b. Remove the flywheel to converter attaching bolts.
    c. Supporting both the engine and transmission, remove the transmission to engine mounting bolts.
    d. Slowly guide the engine from the transmission.

Manifolds

Combination Manifold Used on 6 Cylinder Engines

All Chevrolet six cylinder engines are equipped with a combination intake and exhaust manifold. The exhaust manifold is equipped with a heat riser valve which, when the engine is cold, deflects the hot exhaust gases against the intake manifold to assist in rapid warm up.

If the engine doesn't seem to warm up properly or, when operated at a high speed, acts lean, it is a good idea to check this heat riser valve to be certain that it is functioning freely. Failure of the heat riser valve to open will increase the time required to warm the engine. Failure of the heat riser valve to close after the manifold is hot will cause the engine to run lean.

To remove the manifold assembly, disconnect the exhaust pipe flange and remove all connections to the carburetor. Take off the vacuum lines at the manifold and at the carburetor.

Remove the carburetor, and the manifold may be unbolted from the side of the cylinder head using socket wrenches and box wrenches. If neces-

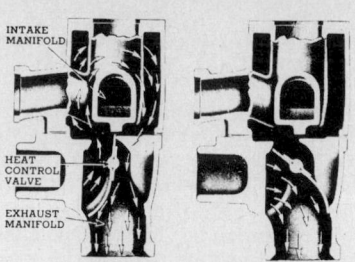

Manifold heat valve used on 6 cylinder engines
(© Chevrolet Div. G.M. Corp.)

sary to remove either exhaust or intake manifolds they may be separated by removing one bolt and two nuts at center of assembly.

Before reinstalling the manifold, thoroughly clean out the ports to avoid turbulence, particularly on the intake manifold.

Intake Manifold R & R—V8

1. Remove the air cleaner.
2. Drain the radiator.
3. Disconnect:
   a. Battery cables at the battery.
   b. Upper radiator and heater hoses at the manifold.
   c. Crankcase ventilation hoses as required.
   d. Fuel line at the carburetor.
   e. Accelerator linkage at the pedal lever.
   f. Vacuum hose at the distributor.
   g. Power brake hose at the carburetor base or manifold, if applicable.
   h. Ignition coil and temperature sending switch wires.
4. Remove the distributor cap and scribe the rotor position relative to distributor body.
5. Remove the distributor.
6. If applicable, remove the Delcotron upper bracket.
7. Remove the manifold to head attaching bolts, then remove the manifold and carburetor as an assembly.
8. If the manifold is to be replaced, transfer the carburetor (and mounting studs), water outlet and thermostat (use a new gasket), heater hose adapter and, if applicable, the choke coil.
9. Before installing the manifold, thoroughly clean the gasket and seal surfaces of the cylinder heads and manifold.
10. Install the manifold end seals, folding the tabs if applicable, and the manifold/head gaskets, using a sealing compound around the water passages.
11. When installing the manifold, care should be taken not to dislocate the end seals. It is helpful to use a pilot in the distributor opening. Tighten the manifold bolts to 30 ft. lbs. in the se-

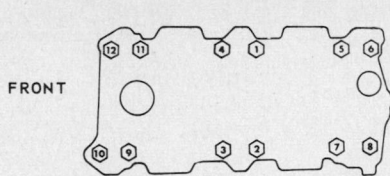 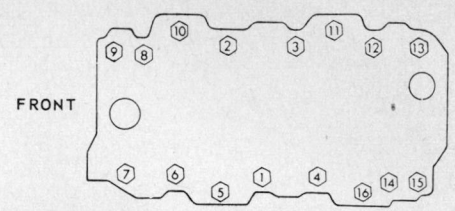

Intake manifold tightening sequence (left—small block V8; right—Mk. IV V8)
(© Chev. Div., G.M. Corp.)

quence illustrated.

12. Install the ignition coil.

13. Install the distributor with the rotor in its original location as indicated by the scribe line. If the engine has been disturbed, refer to "Distributor R&R" above.

14. If applicable, install the Delcotron upper bracket and adjust the belt tension.

15. Connect all components disconnected in Step 3 above.

16. Fill the cooling system, start the engine, check for leaks and adjust the ignition timing and carburetor idle speed and mixture.

Exhaust Manifold R & R—V8

1. If equipped with A.I.R., remove the air injector manifold assembly. The ¼ in. pipe threads in the manifold are straight threads. Do not use a ¼ in. tapered pipe tap.

2. Disconnect the battery.

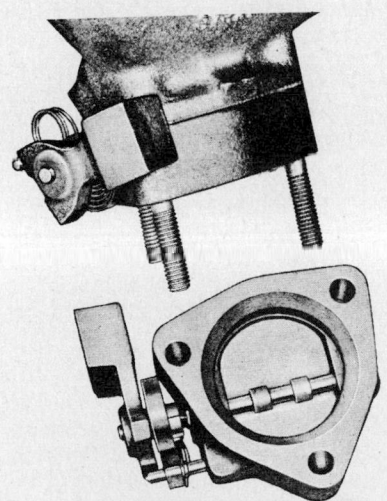

Manifold heat valve used on V8 engines
(© Chevrolet Div. G.M. Corp.)

3. If applicable, remove the air cleaner pre-heater shroud.

4. Remove the exhaust pipe flange nuts, then hang the pipe with wire.

5. Remove the manifold mounting bolts (end bolts first), then remove the manifold.

6. To install, clean the mating surfaces, then install the manifold with the center bolts first. Install the end bolts, then tighten all bolts to 20 ft. lbs.

7. To complete installation, reverse Steps 1 through 3.

Cylinder Head

R & R

6 Cylinder Models

To remove the cylinder head, detach the air cleaner and all rods, lines and vacuum tubes at the carburetor and manifold.

NOTE: if the engine is equipped with an exhaust emission control system, the injector connections must be disconnected at the cylinder head. Disconnect any interfering components and tie back out of the way.

When installing, do not use sealer on the composition steel asbestos gasket. Coat the threads of the head bolts with sealing compound before installation. Tighten the head bolts in sequence (see the illustration at the beginning of this section) a little at a time until each is torqued to 95 ft. lbs. Install all components which were removed. Adjust the valve mechanism as described later.

Caution The ¼ in. pipe threads at the cylinder head air injection nozzles are a straight pipe thread. Do not use a ¼ in. tapered pipe tap. Hoses used in this air injection system are of special material. Do not substitute.

1. Unbolt the manifold from the cylinder head, but not from the exhaust pipe flange. The manifold is simply pulled away from the head.

2. Remove the engine side plate covers and the gas lines at the fuel pump. Unbolt and lift off the rocker cover, disconnect the oil line leads to the rockers.

3. The rocker levers are supported separately and may be left intact until the head is removed.

4. Unbolt and lift off the cylinder head.

V8 Models

1. Remove the intake manifold as described above.

2. Remove the exhaust manifolds as described above.

3. Back off the rocker arm nuts and pivot the rocker arms out of the way so that the pushrods can be removed. Identify the

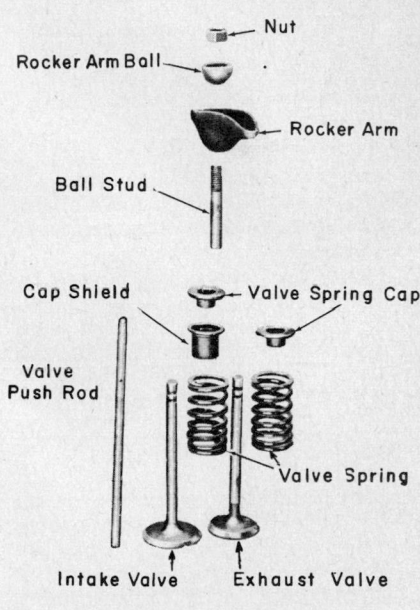

V8 engine valve system
(© Chevrolet Div. G.M. Corp.)

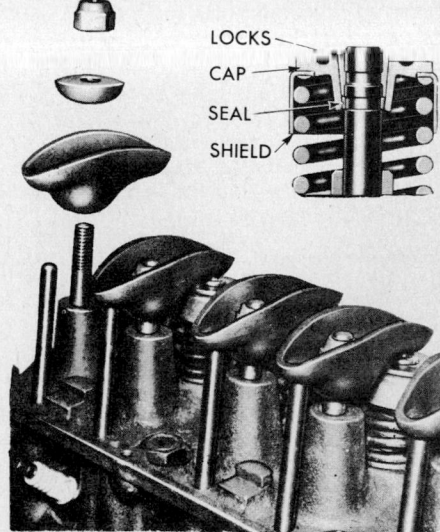

6-cylinder head and rocker arm assembly, 230 cu. in. engine
(© Chevrolet Div. G.M. Corp.)

pushrods so that they can be reinstalled in their original locations.

4. Remove the cylinder head bolts and cylinder heads.

5. Install using new gaskets. The head gasket is installed with the bead up.

NOTE: coat a STEEL gasket on both sides with sealer. If a STEEL ASBESTOS gasket is used, do not apply sealer. Clean the bolt threads, apply sealing compound and install the bolts finger tight.

6. Tighten the head bolts a little at a time in the sequence illustrated in the Specifications at the beginning of this section. Tighten to a final torque of 65 ft. lbs. (small V8) or 85 ft. lbs. (Mark IV).

7. Install the exhaust and intake manifolds as described previously.

8. Adjust the valves as described later.

Rocker Arm R & R

Rocker arms are removed by removing the adjusting nut. Be sure to adjust valve lash after replacing rocker arms.

Rocker arm studs that have damaged threads or are loose in the cylinder heads may be replaced with new studs available in 0.003 in. and 0.013 in. oversize. Do not attempt to install an oversize stud without reaming the stud bore. Studs are press-fit.

NOTE: if engine is equipped with the A.I.R. exhaust emission control system, the interfering components of the system must be removed. Disconnect the lines at the air injection nozzles in the exhaust manifolds.

Valve System

Hydraulic and mechanical valve lifter applications for the various engines are listed in the General Engine Specifications table at the beginning of this section. Valve tappet clearances are listed in the Tune-Up Specifications table. Complete valve specifications are found in the Valve Specifications table.

Valve Tappet Adjustment

Hydraulic Lifters

On six-cylinder engines, crank the engine until the distributor rotor

points to the No. 1 firing position and the breaker points are just opening. The following valves may be adjusted:

No. 1	exhaust	intake
No. 2		intake
No. 3	exhaust	
No. 4		intake
No. 5	exhaust	

To adjust the rest of the valves, crank the engine until the distributor rotor points to the No. 6 firing position and the breaker points are just opening. The following valves may be adjusted:

No. 2	exhaust
No. 3	intake
No. 4	exhaust
No. 5	intake
No. 6	exhaust intake

On V8 engines, crank the engine until the No. 1 piston is at TDC of its compression stroke (the compression can be felt by placing a finger over the spark plug hole or by feeling the valves as the timing mark passes "0"—if the valves don't move, the No. 1 piston is at the top of its compression stroke). With the crankshaft in this position the following valves may be adjusted:

Exhaust—1, 3, 4, 8
Intake—1, 2, 5, 7

Rotate the crankshaft one full revolution until the timing pointer is again aligned with the "0". With the crankshaft thus in No. 6 cylinder firing position, the following valves may be adjusted:

Exhaust—2, 5, 6, 7
Intake—3, 4, 6, 8

Adjustment is made by backing off the rocker arm adjusting nut until there is play in the pushrod. Tighten the nut to remove the pushrod clearance (this can be felt by rotating the pushrod with the fingers while tightening the adjusting nut). When the pushrod cannot be freely turned, tighten the nut one additional turn to place the hydraulic lifter in the center of its travel. No further adjustment is required.

Mechanical Lifters

Position the crankshaft for No. 1, then No. 6 cylinder firing positions as described for adjusting hydraulic lifters above. In the case of mechanical lifters, however, use a feeler gauge between the rocker arm and the valve stem to obtain the correct clearance. The final valve lash setting is made with the engine running at normal

operating temperature. Specified valve lash (hot) can be found in the Tune-Up Specifications at the beginning of this section.

Valve Guides

Valve guides are integral with the cylinder head. Valve guide bores may be reamed to accommodate the standard oversize valve stems. Maximum allowable valve stem to guide bore clearance is .0027 in.

Valve Replacement

With cylinder head on bench and the rockers removed, compress the valve spring and remove the valve lock, seal, spring cap and spring.

Line the valve springs up on a flat surface. All should be the same height. Replace those that do not match with new.

When reinstalling the valves in the head, some asbestos washers with loading springs are available. These washers are placed over the intake valve stems onto the top of the valve guide before installation of the regular valve spring. These washers effect a good seal when the guides are not badly worn.

Check that the contact between the seal at the end of the valve stem and the spring cap is air tight. The closed coil portion of the valve spring contacts the cylinder head.

Timing Case

Crankshaft Pulley Replacement

NOTE: to prevent vibration damper damage, it is important that a tool similar to factory tool J-22197 be used on engines, except the 396 cu. in. engine, to install the damper. When installing the damper on the 396 engine, tool J-21058, or equivalent, should be used.

6 Cylinder Models

1. Remove the radiator core and the fan belt. Remove accessory drive pulley and belt, if so equipped.

2. Use a screw-type puller to remove the balancer-pulley assembly.

V8 Models

1. Drain radiator and disconnect the hoses. Take off the fan belt, and the fan pulley assembly. Remove the battery.

2. Remove the fan shroud. Remove the radiator core. Unbolt the pulley portion of the balancer-pulley assembly.

3. Install screw-type puller and remove the balancer portion from the crankshaft.

Timing Case Cover and Front Oil Seal Replacement

NOTE: the timing case cover oil

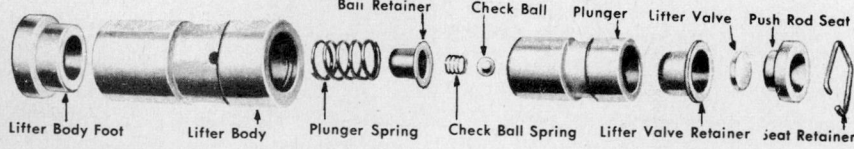

Lifter Body Foot   Lifter Body   Plunger Spring   Check Ball Spring   Lifter Valve Retainer   Seat Retainer

Ball Retainer   Check Ball   Plunger   Lifter Valve   Push Rod Seat

Typical hydraulic lifter exploded (© Chevrolet Div. G.M. Corp.)

seal may be replaced without removing the case cover on all Corvettes and Chevrolets.

After gaining access to the oil seal, pry the old seal out of the cover with a screwdriver. Then, lubricate the new seal and drive it into place with tool J-8340, or equivalent.

6 Cylinder Models

1. Remove the crankshaft pulley. Remove the oil pan.
2. Remove the timing case cover attaching screws and the two bolts that are installed from inside the engine through the front main bearing cap to hold the cover at the bottom.
3. Remove the cover and gasket. Pry the old seal out of the front side of the cover with a large screwdriver.
4. Install the new seal so that the open end of the seal is toward the inside of the cover. When reinstalling, be careful that cover is positioned to hold seal concentric to the shaft.
5. Tighten the screws and the two bolts inside the engine to 6-7½ ft. lbs.

V8 Models

1. Remove the crankshaft pulley. Remove the oil pan. Remove the water pump. Remove the screws holding the timing case cover to the block and remove the cover and gaskets.
2. Use a large screwdriver to pry the old seal out of the front face of the cover.
3. Install the new seal so that open end is toward the inside of the cover.
4. Check that the timing chain oil slinger is in place against the crankshaft sprocket.
5. Install the cover carefully onto the locating dowels.
6. Tighten the attaching screws to 6-8 ft. lbs.

Timing Gear Replacement

6 Cylinder Engines

Chevrolet timing gears are arranged so that (unless deliberately disturbed) the valve timing will remain as set at the factory. Unless the gears are badly worn or seriously damaged, the valve timing will remain constant within reasonable limits.

If it becomes necessary to replace the timing gears due to wear or damage, remove the radiator core, disconnect the front motor mounts and jack up the front of the engine. Remove the fan belt, fan pulley, oil pan and timing case cover.

NOTE: the manufacturer recommends that the camshaft be removed from the car in order to remove and replace the gear in an arbor press.

Sometimes when the gear is being pressed on in place on the car, damage results to the thrust washer in back of the cam gear. Unfortunately, this damage is not noticed until the engine is started.

To replace the gear by removing the camshaft, remove the rocker arm assemblies and the distributor, take out all of the pushrods and all of the lifters. The camshaft may then be pulled out toward the front of the engine. It will be necessary to retime the ignition.

Runout of the timing gear should not exceed .004 in. Backlash between the two gears should not be less than .004 in. nor more than .006 in. End clearance of the thrust plate should be .001 to .005 in.

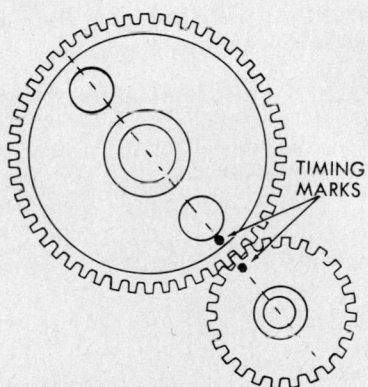

Timing mark alignment, 6 cylinder

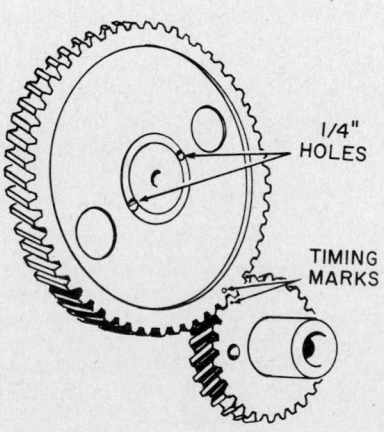

Time-saver for fast removal

A different approach to this situation, and certainly a quicker one, is as follows:

1. Very carefully center punch and drill two ¼ in. holes in opposite sides of the camshaft gear hub, as illustrated.
2. Break the fiber part of the camshaft gear away from the steel hub.
3. Split the steel hub with a cold chisel at the drilled holes.
4. Remove broken camshaft gear and clean entire timing case area.
5. Place the new gear on the camshaft to line up with the keyway and the gear timing marks.
   NOTE: be sure to allow for the helical cut on the gear when aligning the marks for timing.
6. Have a reliable helper, with the aid of a pinch bar, buck up against one of the camshaft lobes from underneath. (The success of the job depends upon this man's care in holding forward thrust on the camshaft. Failure on his part will allow the camshaft to be forced back and dislodge the oil sealing expansion plug in the back at the rear of the camshaft.)
7. With the aid of a 1¼ in. socket and a lead hammer, tap the new gear into place on the camshaft.

CAUTION: the use of a dial indicator will reduce the possibility of driving the gear too far onto the camshaft. This would alter the desired camshaft thrust clearance of .001 to .005 in. Use care when approaching the final position of the gear on the shaft, because it is impossible to increase the thrust clearance without pulling the new gear. In the absence of a dial indicator, this end thrust can be measured with a feeler gauge. In this case, the thrust clearance is to be measured between the camshaft gear hub and the thrust plate. A feeler gauge strip, inserted in either of the two large gear holes, will reach this point.

Timing Chain Replacement

V8 Models

To replace the chain, remove the radiator core, water pump, the harmonic balancer and the crankcase front cover. This will allow access to the timing chain. Crank the engine until the timing marks on both sprockets are nearest each other and in line between the shaft centers. Then take out the three bolts that hold the camshaft gear to the camshaft. This gear is a light press fit on the camshaft and will come off easily. It is located by a dowel.

The chain comes off with the camshaft gear.

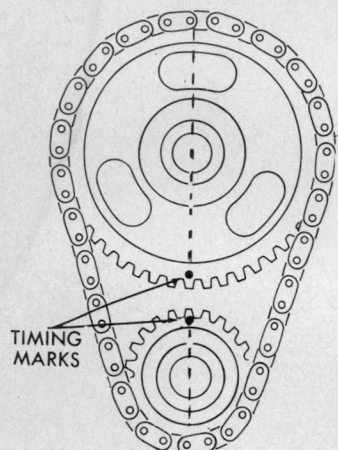

TIMING MARKS

Timing mark alignment, V8

A gear puller will be required to remove the crankshaft gear.

Without disturbing the position of the engine, mount the new crankshaft gear on the shaft, and mount the chain over the camshaft gear. Arrange the camshaft gear in such a way that the timing marks will line up between the shaft centers and the camshaft locating dowel will enter the dowel hole in the cam sprocket.

Place the cam sprocket, with its chain mounted over it, in position on the front of the car and pull up with the three bolts that hold it to the camshaft.

After the gears are in place, turn the engine two full revolutions to make certain that the timing marks are in correct alignment between the shaft centers.

End-play of the V8 camshaft is zero.

Pistons and Connecting Rods

Connecting Rod Bearings

Chevrolet *does not recommend* adjusting the slip-in type rod bearing. However, this bearing may be adjusted for normal wear by installing a taper or feather type shim between the lower bearing shell and the bearing cap.

Assembling Piston to Connecting Rod

6 Cylinder Engines

Where split skirt-type pistons are being installed, the split in the skirt of the piston should be placed opposite the clamp screw of the wristpin. This is also opposite the number on the bottom of the connecting rod.

Where solid skirt slipper-type pistons are being replaced, it is unimportant which way the piston is mounted onto the connecting rod. However, if the old pistons are being reinstalled, the piston should be carefully marked before it is detached from the connecting rod in order that it may be replaced on the same side from which it was removed.

V8 Engines

Pistons are marked with a cast depression at the top of the piston and also the letter F on the piston strut. This depression and F always go toward the front.

For the left bank, pistons Nos. 1, 3, 5, and 7, the heavy flange at the bottom of the connecting rod goes on the side of the piston having the depression and F mark. For the right bank, cylinders Nos. 2, 4, 6, and 8, the heavy flange on the connecting rod goes to the side opposite the stamped letter F and the cast depression in the top of the piston.

Assembling Piston and Rod Assembly to the Engine

6 Cylinder Models

When assembling the rods to the pistons and installing the pistons in their respective bores, be sure that the flange, or heavy side of the rod at

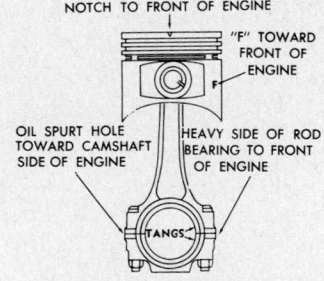

NOTCH TO FRONT OF ENGINE

"F" TOWARD FRONT OF ENGINE

OIL SPURT HOLE TOWARD CAMSHAFT SIDE OF ENGINE

HEAVY SIDE OF ROD BEARING TO FRONT OF ENGINE

TANGS

Correct relation of piston to rod, 6-cylinder 230 and 250 cu. in. engines

the bearing end, is toward the front of the piston (cast depression in top of piston head). The oil hole in the connecting rod goes toward the camshaft side of the engine.

V8 Models

Place the piston and rod assemblies into the cylinder so that the depression cast into the top of the piston (and the letter F stamped on the boss of the piston) face front. Double check that the pistons are in the correct bank by noting that on the left bank, pistons Nos. 1, 3, 5 and 7, the heavy flange on the connecting rod

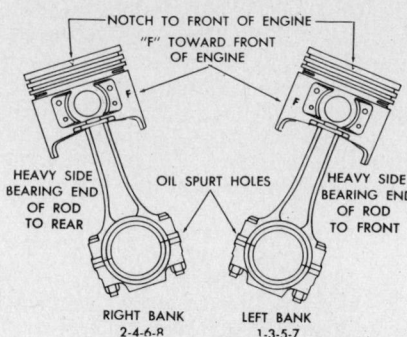

NOTCH TO FRONT OF ENGINE

"F" TOWARD FRONT OF ENGINE

HEAVY SIDE BEARING END OF ROD TO REAR

OIL SPURT HOLES

HEAVY SIDE BEARING END OF ROD TO FRONT

RIGHT BANK 2-4-6-8

LEFT BANK 1-3-5-7

Correct relation of piston to rod (283, 307, 327 and 350 cu. in. engines)

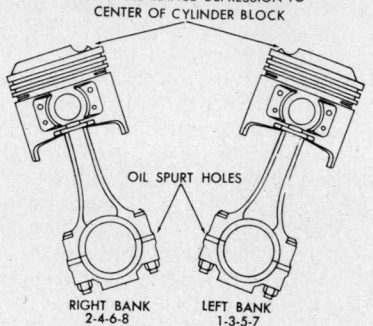

VALVE CLEARANCE DEPRESSION TO CENTER OF CYLINDER BLOCK

OIL SPURT HOLES

RIGHT BANK 2-4-6-8

LEFT BANK 1-3-5-7

Correct relation of piston to rod (396, 427, and 454 cu. in. engines)

will also face forward, but on the right bank, cylinders Nos. 2, 4, 6 and 8, the heavy flange on the connecting rod will face toward the rear.

Piston Rings

Replacement

Before replacing rings, inspect cylinder bores.

1. Using internal micrometer measure bores both across thrust faces of cylinder and parallel to axis of crankshaft at minimum of four locations equally spaced. The bore must not be out of round by more than 0.005 in. and it must not "taper" more than 0.010 in. "Taper" is the difference in wear between two bore measurements in any cylinder. Bore any cylinder beyond limits of out of roundness or taper to diameter of next available oversize piston that will clean up wear. The recommended clearances are given in the chart.

2. If bore is within limits dimensionally, examine bore visually. It should be dull silver in color and exhibit pattern of machining cross hatching intersecting at about 45 degrees. There should be no scratches, tool marks, nicks, or other damage. If any such damage exists, bore cylinder to clean up damage and

then to next oversize piston diameter. Polished or shiny places in the bore are known as glazing. Glazing causes poor lubrication, high oil consumption and ring damage. Remove glazing by honing cylinders with clean, sharp stones of No. 180-220 grit to obtain surface finish of 15-35 RMS. Use a hone also to obtain correct piston clearance and surface finish in any cylinder that has been bored.

3. If cylinder bore is in satisfactory condition, place each ring in bore in turn and square it in bore with head of piston. Measure ring gap. If ring gap is greater than limit, get new ring. If ring gap is less than limit, file end of ring to obtain correct gap.

4. Check ring side clearance by in-

⏻ CHILTON TIME-SAVER

This or any other machining operation should be done with the cylinder block completely disassembled. Hot tank cylinder block after honing or boring. To remove minor glazing when honing equipment is not available, run emery cloth back and forth across glazed area perpendicular to axis of bore. Scrub block and bores thoroughly with soap and water to remove all grit after using emery cloth.

NOTE: the emery cloth method should be used only as a last resort as it is a method much inferior to honing.

---

stalling rings on piston, and inserting feeler gauge of correct dimension between ring and lower land. Gauge should slide freely around ring circumference without binding. Any wear will form a step on lower land. Replace any pistons having high steps. Before checking ring side clearance be sure ring grooves are clean and free of carbon, sludge, or grit.

5. Space ring gaps at equidistant intervals around piston circumference. Be sure to install piston in its original bore. Install short lengths of rubber tubing over connecting rod bolts to prevent damage to rod journal. Install ring compressor over rings on piston. Lower piston rod assembly into bore until ring compressor contacts block. Using wooden handle of hammer push piston into bore while guiding rod onto journal.

Piston and Ring Specifications

Displacement (cu. in.)	Advertised Brake H.P.	Piston clearance (Prod.) (in.)	Piston clearance (Service Max.) (in.)	Compression Ring Groove clearance (in.) Top (Prod.)	Second (Prod.)	Service (high prod. limit)	Compression Ring Gap (in.) Top (Prod.)	Second (Prod.)	Service (high prod. limit)	Oil Ring Groove clearance (in.) Prod.	Service	Oil Ring Gap (in.) Prod.	Service (high prod. limit)
153	90	.0005-.0015	.0025	.0012-.0027	.0012-.0032	+.001	.010-.020	.010-.020	+.01	.000-.005	+.001	.015-.055	+.01
230	140	.0005-.0015	.0025	.0012-.0027	.0012-.0032	+.001	.010-.020	.010-.020	+.01	.000-.005	+.001	.015-.055	+.01
250	155	.0005-.0015	.0025	.0012-.0027	.0012-.0032	+.001	.010-.020	.010-.020	+.01	.000-.005	+.001	.015-.055	+.01
283, 307, 327	All	.0005-.0011	.0025	.0012-.0027	.0012-.0032	+.001	.010	.020	+.01	.000-.005	+.001	.015-.055	+.01
350	250	.0007-.0013	.0027	.0012	.0032	+.001	.010-.020	.013-.025	+.01	.002-.007	+.001	.015-.055	+.01
350	300	.0007-.0013	.0027	.0012-.0032	.0012-.0027	+.001	.010-.020	.013-.025	+.01	.000-.005	+.001	.015-.055	+.01
350	350	.0020-.0026	.0036	.0012-.0032	.0012-.0027	+.001	.010-.020	.013-.023	+.01	.000-.005	+.001	.015-.055	+.01
350	370	.0036-.0042	.0061	.0012-.0032	.0012-.0027	+.001	.010-.020	.013-.023	+.01	.000-.005	+.001	.015-.055	+.01
396	350	.0018-.0026	.0038	.0017-.0032	.0017-.0032	+.001	.010-.020	.010-.020	+.01	.0005-.0065	+.001	.010-.030	+.01
396	375	.0036-.0046	.0065	.0017-.0032	.0017-.0032	+.001	.010-.020	.010-.020	+.01	.0005-.0065	+.001	.010-.030	+.01
400	265	.0014-.0020	.0034	.0012-.0027	.0012-.0032	+.001	.010-.020	.010-.020	+.01	.000-.005	+.001	.015-.055	+.01
400	330	.0018-.0026	.0038	.0017	.0032	+.001	.010-.020	.010-.020	+.01	.0005-.0065	+.001	.015-.055	+.01
409	340	.0009-.0015	.0045	.0017-.0032	.0017-.0032	+.001	.010-.020	.010-.020	+.01	.0012-.0050	+.001	.015-.055	+.01
409	400	.0035-.0042	.0045	.0017-.0032	.0017-.0032	+.001	.010-.020	.010-.020	+.01	.0012-.0050	+.001	.015-.055	+.01
409	425	.0035-.0042	.0045	.0017-.0032	.0017-.0032	+.001	.010-.020	.010-.020	+.01	.0012-.0050	+.001	.015-.055	+.01
427	390	.0024-.0034	.0045	.0017-.0032	.0017-.0032	+.001	.010-.020	.010-.020	+.01	.0005-.0065	+.001	.010-.030	+.01
427	400	.0024-.0034	.0045	.0017-.0032	.0017-.0032	+.001	.010-.020	.010-.020	+.01	.0005-.0065	+.001	.010-.030	+.01
427	430	.0058-.0068	.0080	.0017-.0032	.0017-.0032	+.001	.010-.020	.010-.020	+.01	.0005-.0065	+.001	.010-.030	+.01
427	435	.0040-.0050	.0065	.0017-.0032	.0017-.0032	+.001	.010-.020	.010-.020	+.01	.0005-.0065	+.001	.010-.030	+.01
454	345	.0024-.0034	.0049	.0017-.0032	.0017-.0032	+.001	.010-.020	.010-.020	+.01	.0005-.0065	+.001	.015-.055	+.01
454	360	.0024-.0034	.0049	.0017-.0032	.0017-.0032	+.001	.010-.020	.010-.020	+.01	.0005-.0065	+.001	.015-.055	+.01
454	390	.0024-.0034	.0049	.0017-.0032	.0017-.0032	+.001	.010-.020	.010-.020	+.01	.0005-.0065	+.001	.015-.055	+.01
454	450	.0040-.0050	.0065	.0017-.0032	.0017-.0032	+.001	.010-.020	.010-.020	+.01	.0005-.0065	+.001	.015-.055	+.01

Caution Some pistons, such as those used in the 454, 396 or 427 engines with high lift camshafts, have a peculiar head shape. Where the standard piston is equipped with a gabled, or double slanted top, the high torque piston top has only one slanted side. This is a means of raising compression ratio.

Use care in assembly because the piston head is clearance-bored to allow for the valve head.

Engine Lubrication

Oil Pan Removal

Chevrolet 6 Cylinder Manual Transmission

The oil pan can be removed, either after removing engine, or as follows:
1. Drain radiator and oil pan.
2. Disconnect gas tank line at fuel pump and upper and lower radiator hoses.
3. Remove clutch housing-to-engine block bolt above dowel on right side.
4. Raise vehicle on hoist or place on jack stands.
5. Rotate engine to align distributor rotor No. 3 and No. 5 plug wires. (This locates No. 6 crank throw part way up.)
6. Remove starter and flywheel front cover plate.
7. Remove front mount through bolts.
8. Jack front of engine. (Tool J-6987 on balancer will aid.) Raise as far as possible always using care by checking various dash and body tunnel clearances.
9. Remove front engine mount frame bracket on right side and remove oil filter where necessary.
10. Remove oil pan screws and lower pan to frame.
11. Remove oil pump to gain clearance, then remove oil pan by sliding and rotating front to right and then to rear, and down at an angle. (On certain earlier models, these procedures may be varied in some self-evident areas.)
12. Install in reverse of above.
NOTE: gasket can be replaced by completely removing pan from vehicle.

Chevrolet 6 Cylinder Automatic Transmission

1. Drain radiator and crankcase.
2. Disconnect gas tank line at fuel pump, and radiator hoses at radiator.
3. Remove clutch housing-to-engine block bolt above dowel pin on each side.
4. Rotate engine to align distributor between No. 3 and No. 5 plug

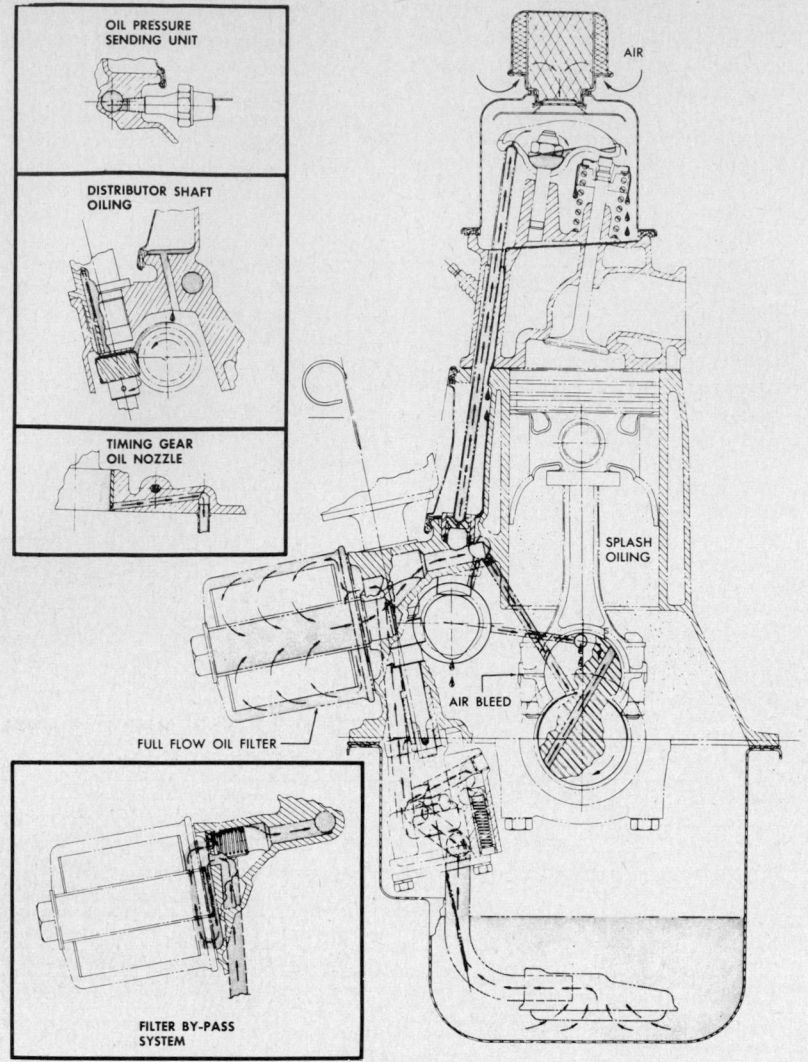

230 cu. in. 6-cylinder engine lubrication (© Chevrolet Div. G.M. Corp.)

wires. (This locates No. 6 crank throw part way up.)
5. Raise vehicle on hoist or on jack stands.
6. Remove converter cover pan, and starter assembly.
7. Follow Steps 7 through 12, listed above.

Chevrolet—V8 (Except. 409 Cu. In. 1965)

1. Disconnect battery positive cable.
2. Remove distributor cap from distributor to prevent breakage against firewall.
3. Drain cooling system. Remove radiator hoses, and remove oil dipstick and tube, where necessary.
4. Remove fan blade assembly.
5. Raise car, and drain engine oil.
6. Remove bolts from engine front mounts. Disconnect and remove starter.
7. On cars with automatic transmissions, remove converter housing underpan.
8. Disconnect steering rod at idler lever and swing linkage down for

pan clearance.
9. Rotate crankshaft until timing mark on the damper is at six o'clock position.
10. Using a block of wood and a suitable jack, raise engine enough to insert 2 x 4 in. wood blocks under engine mounts then lower engine onto blocks.
11. Remove engine oil pan.
12. Install by reversing removal procedures.
NOTE: the 396, 427 and 454 cu. in. engines use three ¼ in. attaching bolts at crankcase front cover; one at each corner, and one at the lower center.

Corvette

1. Disconnect battery, and remove dipstick and tube.
2. Raise car and support on stands. Drain engine oil.
3. Remove starter and flywheel underpan.
4. Disconnect steering idler arm and lower steering linkage.
5. Remove oil pan and discard gas-

kets and seals.

6. On high performance engines, the oil baffle must be removed before additional operations can be performed.

NOTE: on the 427 and 454 cu. in. engine, the oil pan has three ¼ in. attaching bolts at crankcase front cover; one at each front corner, and one at lower center.

7. Install by reversing removal procedure.

1965 409 Cu. In. V8

It is necessary to remove engine to remove oil pan.

Oil Filter

The oil filter is located under the engine at the left side just forward of the flywheel housing and is accessible from underneath the car.

Torque on the filter should be 25 ft. lbs. This is equivalent to one and one-third turns after the filter has been brought up snug to the case.

Oil Pump Replacement

On all Chevrolet engines, the oil pump is located in the oil pan, and it is driven by a tang from the distributor shaft.

On six-cylinder engines, the pump is flange-mounted to the under side of the crankcase with two cap screws.

On V8 models, the oil pump is bolted to the rear, main bearing cap. Oil is fed from the pump up through the rear, main bearing cap.

Oil Pump Disassembly

1. Remove the oil pump from the engine to the bench.
2. Detach the oil pickup screen and clean it up thoroughly with a reliable solvent. Remove the cover from the oil pump and slide off the idler gear.

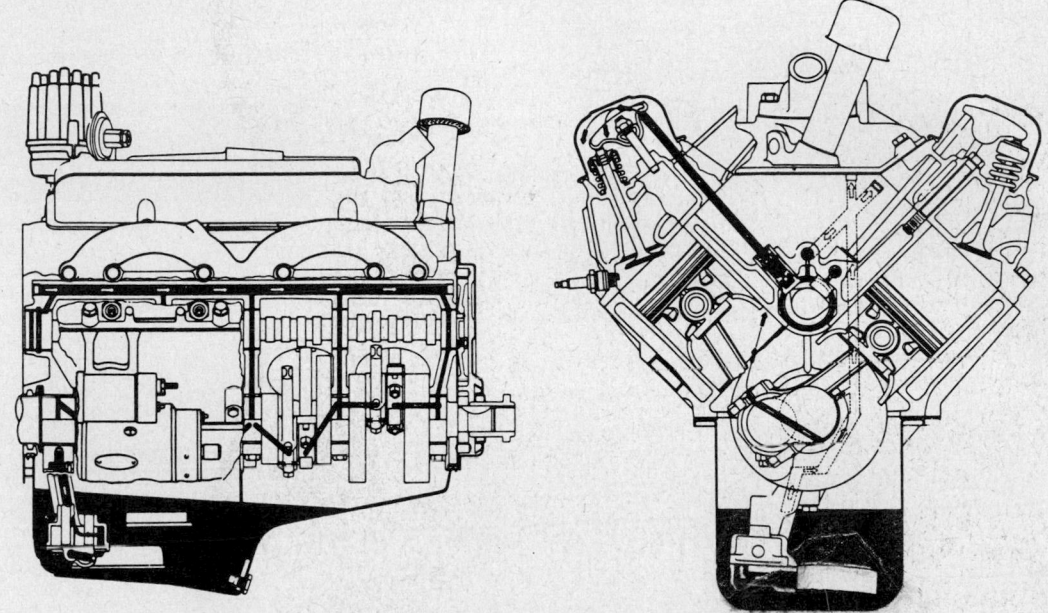

283, 307, 327 and 350 cu. in. V8 engine lubrication (© Chevrolet Div. G.M. Corp.)

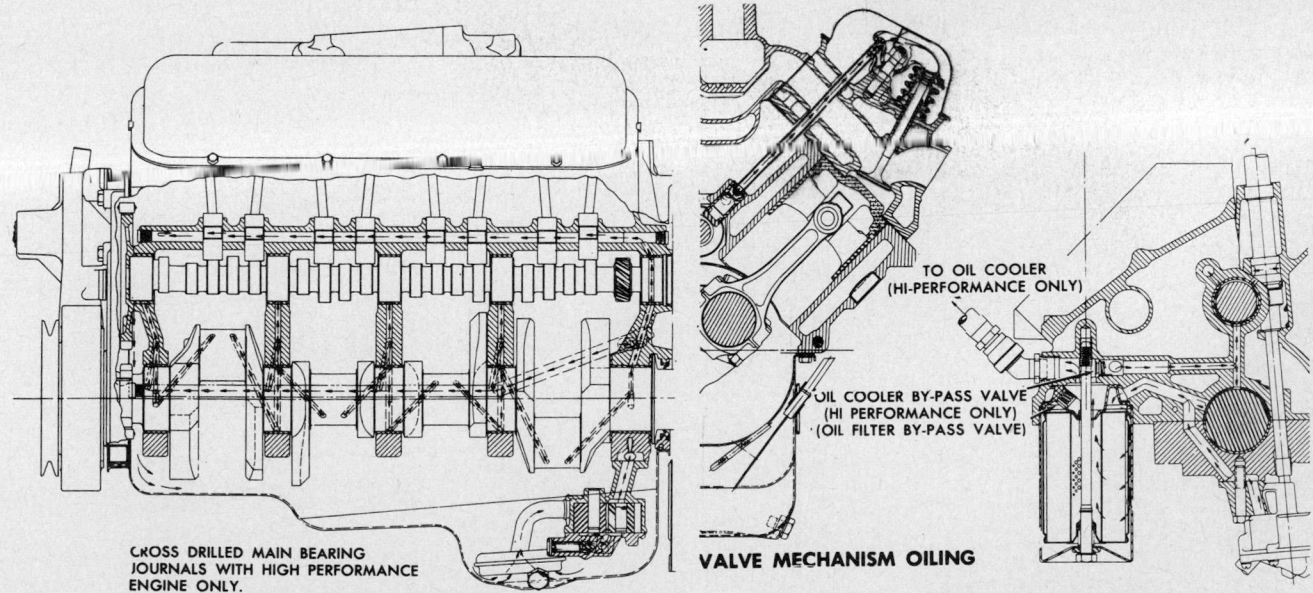

CROSS DRILLED MAIN BEARING JOURNALS WITH HIGH PERFORMANCE ENGINE ONLY.

CRANKCASE AND CRANKSHAFT OILING

TO OIL COOLER (HI-PERFORMANCE ONLY)

OIL COOLER BY-PASS VALVE (HI PERFORMANCE ONLY) (OIL FILTER BY-PASS VALVE)

VALVE MECHANISM OILING

OIL FILTER AND DISTRIBUTOR OILING

396 and 427 cu. in. V8 lubrication (© Chevrolet Div., G.M. Corp.)

3. With the main drive gear still left keyed to the shaft, thoroughly clean the inside of the oil pump. Examine the inside of the pump body for deep scores or scratches, and the cover plate for scores or scratches. Replace the idler gear and check the clearance between the idler gear and the drive gear teeth at the point where they mesh. This clearance should not exceed .002-.003 in. The clearance around the outer rim of either of the gears should not exceed .002-.003 in.

4. If any of the parts are scored or badly worn and the engine develops low oil pressure, replace the gears and/or the housing, whichever shows wear.

Rear Main Bearing Oil Seal Replacement

Wick Type Seal

1. Remove oil pan and oil pump. Remove rear main bearing cap, discarding lower seal.

2. Loosen the remaining bearing caps to allow the crankshaft to drop a slight amount. If the shaft does not drop, place a lever between the shaft and block and force the crankshaft down into the space provided.

3. Using a screwdriver, push the seal out of upper bearing so end can be grabbed with pliers and pulled out. Wiggle the crankshaft slightly to aid this operation.

4. Use the lower bearing cap to form the new upper seal into a semi-circle. Insert a wire (soft tag-type) through the seal about ¼ in. from the end. Wrap the wire around the end of the seal so it has a good grip.

5. Use a light coat of vaseline to lubricate the seal and insert the

wire into the seal groove and up and over the crankshaft. Pull the seal gently into position. It may be necessary to rotate the crankshaft to aid in getting the seal placed. With seal centered in the opening, cut off the ends so that they stick out 1/64 in. beyond the parting surface.

6. Install the lower seal in the groove and roll into place. Cut the small portions of the ends that protrude from the groove flush with the surface of the bearing cap. Install bearing cap over the crankshaft onto the block.

Neoprene Seal

1. Remove rear main bearing cap and pry old seal from groove. Insert new seal with lubricant only on the lip. Do not get oil on the glue-treated parting line surfaces. Lip faces front of engine.

2. Using a hammer and small punch, revolve the upper half of the seal until it protrudes far

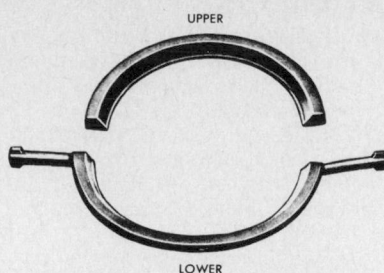

Rear main bearing oil seal, 6 cylinder (© Chevrolet Div. G.M. Corp.)

enough to remove with pliers.

3. Oil the seal except at the glue-treated ends and, using a hammer handle, roll the seal into place in the block.

4. These seals are made to size and require no trimming. Install the lower half over the crankshaft and in place onto the block.

Front Suspension

Figures covering the caster, cam-

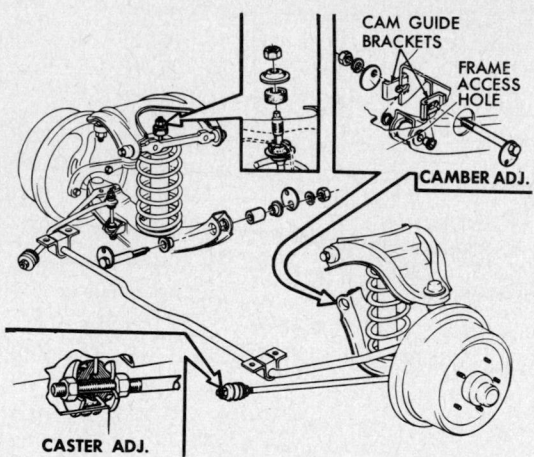

Front suspension, 1965-67 (© Chevrolet Div. G.M. Corp.)

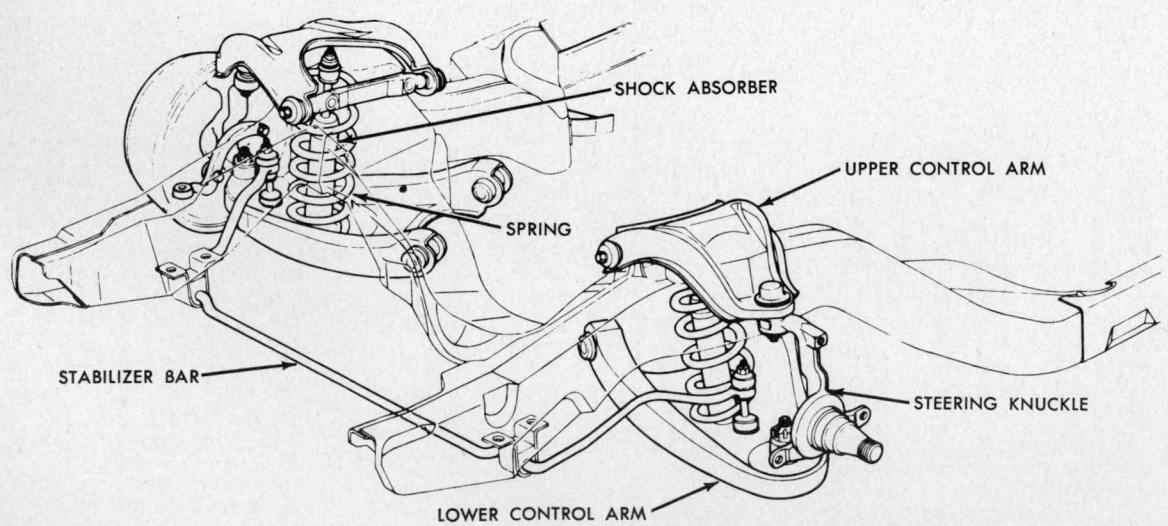

Front suspension, Chevrolet 1968-72

ber, toe-in, kingpin inclination, and turning radius can be found in the Wheel Alignment table of this section.

Tire sizes can be found in the General Chassis and Brake Specifications Table of this section.

Front Springs R & R

Chevrolet

1. Remove shock absorber upper stem retaining nut and grommet.
2. Support the car by the frame so that the control arms hang free. Remove the wheel assembly, shock absorber, stabilizer to lower control arm link, strut rod to lower control arm attaching nuts, bolts and lockwashers, and the tie-rod end.
3. Scribe the position of the inner pivot camber adjusting cam bolt and then remove the nut, lock washer and outer cam.
4. Install a steel bar through the shock absorber mounting hole in the lower control arm so that the notch in the bar seats over the bottom spring coil and the bar extends inboard and under the inner bushing. Fit a 5 in. wood block between the bar and the lower arm inner support bushing.
5. With a floor jack, raise the end of the steel bar enough to remove tension from the inner pivot cam bolt. The bolt can then be removed.
6. Carefully lower the inner end of the control arm. Tension on the spring must be removed before the spring can be taken out of the car.
7. Remove the spring.
8. Install by reversing removal procedure.

Corvette—1965-67

1. Support car by the frame to allow control arms to swing free. Remove wheel assembly, stabilizer bar and shock absorber.
   Loosen lower ball joint to steering knuckle nut, and the two lower control arm cross-shaft bushing bolts.
2. Place tool J-6874-1 across top of sixth coil of the spring. Then, loosely secure tool J-6874-2 to the upper shoe, with attaching capscrews and lockwashers. The upper shoe V notch and lower shoe raised land should contact the spring.
3. Insert tool J-6874 up through center of spring and attach to upper and lower shoe assembly.
4. Position spacers under shock absorber mounting hole and against bottom of lower control arm. Install special bearing washer and tool J-6874-5. Locate bearing against spacer and large

washer against bearing. Feed screw up through large washer bearing and spacer and thread into tool J-6874 and tighten.
5. Center shoe assembly on spring and tighten screw until a very slight compression is exerted on the spring. Then, firmly tighten the two capscrews holding the upper and lower shoes to lock these shoes to the spring.
6. Tighten the spring compressor enough to permit the spring to clear the spring tower, then remove the lower ball joint to steering knuckle nut.
7. Disconnect lower ball joint from the steering knuckle and lower control arm while the spring is compressed. Immediately release compression on spring by backing off the tool screw. Release spring and tool and remove the spring.
8. Install by reversing the removal procedure.

Corvette—1968-72

1. Raise car on hoist and remove nut, retainer and grommet from top of shock absorber. Support car so that control arms swing free.
2. Disconnect stabilizer bar from lower control arm and remove shock absorber.
3. Bolt spring remover tool (J-22944) to a suitable jack and place it under the lower control arm bushings so that the bushings seat in the grooves of the tool.
4. Remove cross shaft rear retaining nut and the two front retaining bolts.
5. Slowly release jack, swing control arm forward, then remove spring.
6. Install by reversing procedure above.

Upper Ball Joint R & R

1. Raise the car on a hoist.
2. Remove the tire and wheel assembly.
3. Support the lower control arm with a jack.
4. Remove the upper ball stud nut.
5. Remove the ball stud from the knuckle.
6. Chisel or grind off the ball joint mounting rivets.
7. Drill out the ball stud attaching holes to accept the service ball joint attaching bolts.
8. Install the ball joint with the nuts and bolts supplied with the new joint.
9. Install the lube fitting in the new joint.
10. Mate the upper control arm to the steering knuckle and install the ball stud through the knuckle boss.
11. Tighten the ball stud nut to 50

ft. lbs. plus whatever is necessary to align the cotter pin holes. Install the cotter pin.
12. Install the wheel and lower the vehicle.

Lower Ball Joint R & R

NOTE: on the 1971-72 Corvette, the lower ball joint removal and installation is the same as that described for the upper ball joint above. For all others:

1. Raise the vehicle on a hoist and remove the wheel. On vehicles equipped with disc brakes, remove the caliper assembly.
2. Support the lower control arm with a jack.
3. Loosen the lower ball stud nut. Break the ball stud loose. Remove the ball stud nut.
4. Remove the ball stud from the steering knuckle.
5. The ball joint in 1965-70 models is attached with rivets which must be chiseled or ground off. Beginning with 1971 models, the ball joint is pressed in and must be pressed out.
6. Install the new ball joint, using the bolts supplied with the service ball joint (drill out the rivet hoses to accommodate the mounting bolts) on 1965-70 models. The thick-headed bolt is installed on the forward side of the control arm. Press in the ball joint on 1971 and later models.
7. Install the ball stud in the steering knuckle boss. This may be done by raising the lower control arm with the jack.
8. Install the nut on the ball stud, tightening to 80-90 ft. lbs.
9. Install the lube fitting.

Lower Control Arm R & R

1. Remove the spring as described above.
2. Remove the ball stud from the steering knuckle as described above.
3. Remove the control arm pivot bolts and remove the control arm. On some Corvettes, the pivot bolt is secured to the frame with two bolts.
4. To install, reverse the above procedure.

Upper Control Arm R & R

1. Raise the vehicle on a hoist.
2. Support the outer end of the lower control arm, with a jack.
3. Remove the wheel.
4. Separate the upper ball joint from the steering knuckle as described above under "Upper Ball Joint R&R"
5. Remove the control arm shaft to frame nuts.

NOTE: tape the shims together and identify them so that they can be installed in the positions from which they were removed.

6. Remove the bolts which attach the control arm shaft to the frame and remove the control arm. Note the positions of the bolts.
7. Install in the reverse order of removal. Make sure the shaft to frame bolts are installed in the same position they were in before removal and that the shims are in their original positions. Tighten the shaft to frame bolts to 85 ft. lbs. on the Chevrolet and to 55 ft. lbs. on the Corvette. The control arm shaft nuts are torqued to 60 ft. lbs.

Steering Knuckle R & R

1. Raise the vehicle on a hoist.
2. Support the lower control arm with a jack.
3. Remove the wheel.
4. Remove the brake drum and backing plate or the caliper, disc and splash shield. Do not disconnect the brake hydraulic line and do not let the backing plate or caliper hang by the hydraulic line.
5. Remove the upper and lower ball studs from the steering knuckle as described above.
6. Install in the reverse order of removal, referring to "Ball Joint R&R" above if necessary.

Jacking, Hoisting

When jacking the car, place the jack at the spring seat of the lower control arm in the front and at the axle housing in the rear. A bumper jack may also be used.

To hoist the car, position the hoist arms at the frame side rails immediately in front of the rear wheels and immediately behind the front wheels.

Steering Gear

Steering Gear R & R

1. On 1965-66 models, remove the steering coupling lower clamp bolt and spread the clamp slightly. On 1967 Corvettes, loosen the clamp bolt and slide the coupling upper flange upward on the steering shaft. On 1967-72 Chevrolets and 1968-72 Corvettes, remove the retaining nuts, lockwashers, and bolts at the steering coupling to steering shaft flange.
2. Remove the pitman arm nut and washer from the pitman shaft and mark the relation of the arm to the shaft.
3. Using a puller, remove the pitman arm.

4. Remove the steering gear mounting bolts and remove the gear.
5. To install, reverse the above procedure. Be sure to install the pitman arm in its original position. Be sure that the coupling flange is properly aligned before installing the bolts. Tighten the pitman shaft nut to 180 ft. lbs. on the Chevrolet and to 140 ft. lbs. on the Corvette. Tighten the steering coupling bolts to 20 ft. lbs.

Power Steering Gear R & R

Installation and removal of power steering gears is the same as that described for manual steering gears above, with the addition of disconnecting and reconnecting the hydraulic lines. Cap both hoses and steering gear outlets to prevent foreign material from entering the system.

Power Steering—Corvette

The steering power assist system on all Corvettes incorporates a control valve between the pitman arm and the relay rod and a power cylinder attached to the relay rod.

Control Valve R & R

The rubber seal for the control valve ball stud (to which the pitman arm connects) may be replaced without removing the control valve. Remove the pitman arm, then remove the bolt and clamp which retain the ball stud. When installing the new seal, make sure the lips of the seal mate with the clamp.

To remove the control valve:

1. Raise the front of the car and place it on stands.
2. Remove the relay rod to control valve clamp bolt.
3. Disconnect and drain the hydraulic hoses.
4. Remove the ball stud nut and disconnect the control valve from the pitman arm.
5. Unscrew the control valve from the relay rod.

6. To install, reverse the above procedure. Bleed the hydraulic system as described below. Grease the ball joint.

Power Cylinder R & R

1. Place the car on a hoist.
2. Disconnect the two hydraulic lines, letting them drain.
3. Remove the cotter pin, nut, retainer and grommet from the power cylinder rod end. Inspect the grommet in the bracket, replacing if necessary.
4. Remove the cotter pin, nut and ball stud at the relay rod and remove the power cylinder.
5. To install, reverse the removal procedure. Bleed the hydraulic system as described below. Grease the ball joint.

Bleeding Power Steering System

1. Fill the fluid reservoir.
2. Let the fluid stand undisturbed for two minutes, then crank the engine for about two seconds. Refill reservoir if necessary.
3. Repeat Steps 1 and 2 above until the fluid level remains constant after cranking the engine.
4. Raise the front of the car until the wheels are off the ground, then start the engine. Increase the engine speed to about 1,500 rpm.
5. Turn the wheels to the left and right, checking the fluid level and refilling if necessary.

Steering Linkage R & R

There are two tie-rods on all models, activated by the relay rod. Tie-rod ends are threaded and clamped in order that the steering can be adjusted. Ball studs are used to connect linkages. When disconnecting ball stud connections, loosen the nut, then strike the female linkage as illustrated. When assembling or adjusting the tie-rods, make sure that the tie-rod ends are in alignment in their ball studs before tightening the clamp.

Control valve ball stud seal—Corvette
(© Chev. Div., G.M. Corp.)

Pitman Shaft Seal R & R

The pitman shaft seal can be replaced without removing the steering gear from the vehicle as follows:

1. Place the steering wheel in center position.
2. Remove the bolts which secure the gear side housing, then remove the pitman shaft and side cover as a unit.
3. Remove the pitman shaft seal from the steering gear body.
4. Grease the new seal and drive it into place with a suitable socket.
5. Install the side cover and pitman shaft assembly, being careful not to damage the new seal and

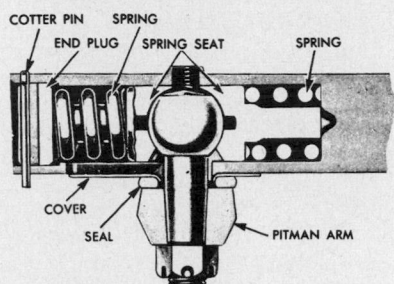

Pitman arm attachment to relay rod
(© Chevrolet Div. G.M. Corp.)

using a new cover gasket.
6. Install the side cover retaining bolts.

Steering Column Removal

1969-72 All Models

1. Disconnect the battery ground cable.
2. Remove the steering wheel.
3. Disconnect the steering shaft flange from the flexible coupling.
4. Disconnect the shift linkage (backdrive linkage on floor shift models) from the column shift tube levers.
5. Disconnect all wiring.
6. Remove the floor pan trim cover.
7. On Chevrolet models, remove the two halves of the floor pan cover. On Corvettes, remove the two nuts which secure the floor pan bracket to the mounting studs.
8. Remove the instrument trim panel cover.

9. If so equipped, remove the transmission indicator cable.
10. Move the front seat back as far as possible to give maximum working room.
11. Remove the two column bracket-to-instrument panel nuts. Carefully remove the column. Have a helper guide the lower shift levers through the firewall opening.

Steering Column Installation

1969-70 Chevrolet

1. Loosely assemble the inner (A) and outer (B) dash covers on the column with screws (C and D).
2. Glue the cover seal (E) to the bottom of the outer cover (B).
3. Position the lower center portion of the cover seal (E) onto the column as illustrated.

NOTE: the rolled portion of the seal must be downward and remain in that position all through installation.

4. Position the column in the car and loosely install mast jacket bracket retaining nuts (H).
5. Connect all wiring.
6. Install flexible coupling bolts, tightening to 20 ft. lbs.
7. While holding the column to maintain a flex joint to flange clearance of 0.250-0.375 in., tighten the two mast jacket bracket retaining nuts to 20 ft. lbs. on Chevrolet models and to 15 ft. lbs. on Corvettes.
8. Position inner (A) and outer (B) cover on the dash and line up all the screwholes.
9. Holding both covers against the column, tighten the inner cover screws (K).
10. Tighten screw (C) to 35 in. lbs., then screw (D) to 35 in. lbs.
11. Loosen the two screws (K), then tighten screws (L) to 35 in. lbs.
12. Tighten screws (K) to 35 in. lbs.

Caution Check the alignment of the steering column by making sure that there is a 0.040 in. gap maintained between the coupling

rivets and the steering shaft flange while the steering is in the straight-ahead position and there is no torque on the steering wheel. If the gap is less than 0.040 in., the steering column must be realigned.

13. If applicable, install the transmission indicator cable.
14. Install the instrument panel trim cover.
15. Connect the transmission control linkage at the shift tube levers.
16. Install the steering wheel.
17. Connect the battery ground cable.

1971-72 Chevrolet

1. Assemble the lower dash cover (A) to seal (B) with the three carrots (parts of the seal).
2. Loosely assemble the upper (C) and lower (B) dash cover with the two screws (D) so that cover is loose enough to slide up and down the column.
3. Install instrument panel bracket (M) to the steering column, tightening the four bolts (P) to 15 ft. lbs.
4. Position the column in the car and install the flex coupling flange lockwashers and nuts (E), tightening to 20 ft. lbs.
5. Loosely install the two nuts (F) at the instrument panel bracket (M).
6. Position the lower cover to the dash and loosely install screw (J) in the lower left hand hole.
7. Install screw (L) in the lower right hand elongated hole, tightening to 35 in. lbs.
8. Tighten screw (J) in lower left hand hole to 35 in. lbs.
9. Tighten the left hand upper to lower cover screw (D) to 35 in. lbs.
10. Install screw (Q) in the left hand outer cover, tightening to 35 in. lbs.
11. Tighten the clamp screw (D) to 35 in. lbs.
12. Install the three remaining upper cover screws (R), tightening to 35 in. lbs.

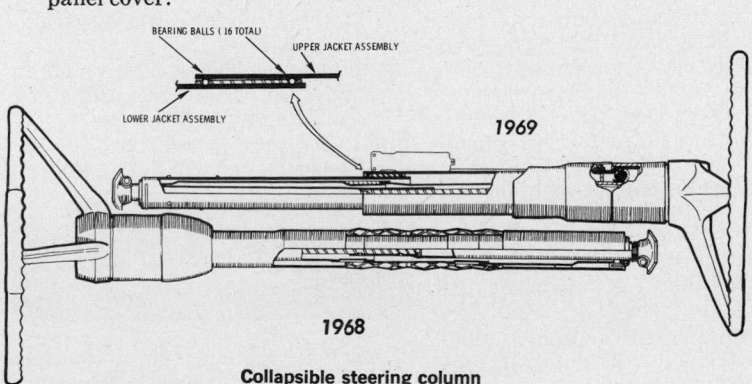

Collapsible steering column

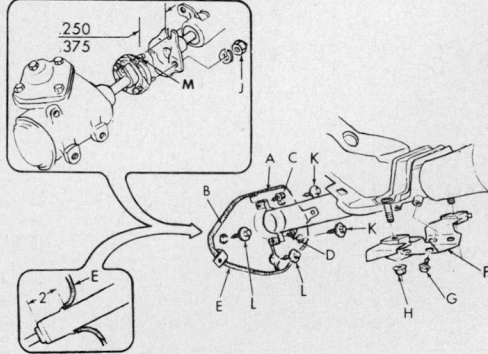

1969-70 Chevrolet steering column mounting
(© Chev. Div., G.M. Corp.)

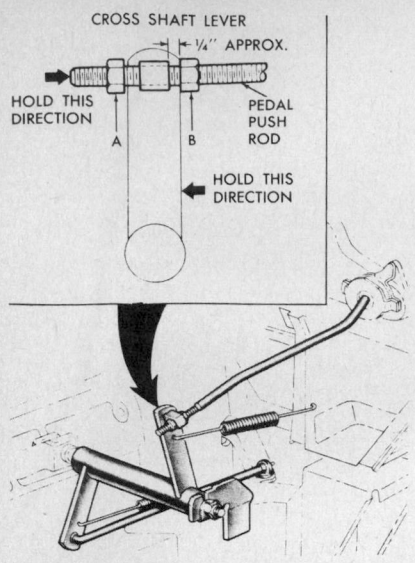

CROSS SHAFT LEVER

¼" APPROX.

HOLD THIS DIRECTION

A   B

PEDAL PUSH ROD

HOLD THIS DIRECTION

Typical clutch linkage
(© Chevrolet Div. G.M. Corp.)

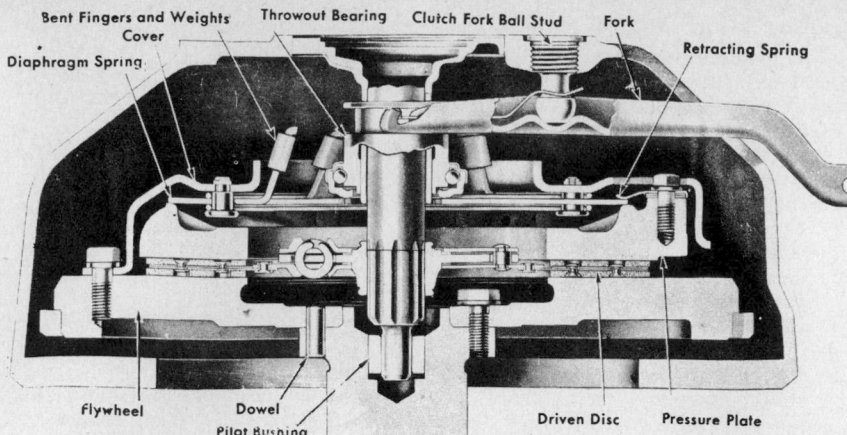

Bent Fingers and Weights Cover — Throwout Bearing — Clutch Fork Ball Stud — Fork

Diaphragm Spring — Retracting Spring

Flywheel — Dowel — Pilot Bushing — Driven Disc — Pressure Plate

Typical V8 clutch cross-section (© Chevrolet Div. G.M. Corp.)

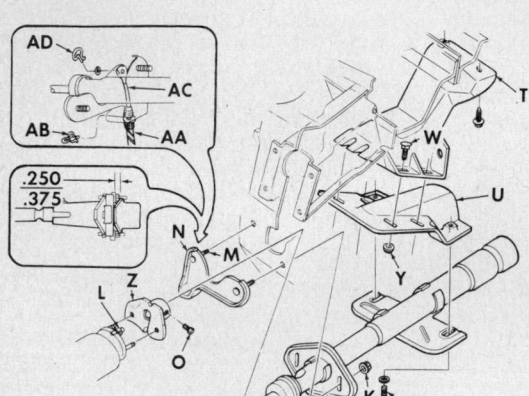

AD
AC
AB   AA

.250
.375

N
M
Z
L
O
K   H

1969-72 Corvette steering column mounting
(Chev. Div., G.M. Corp.)

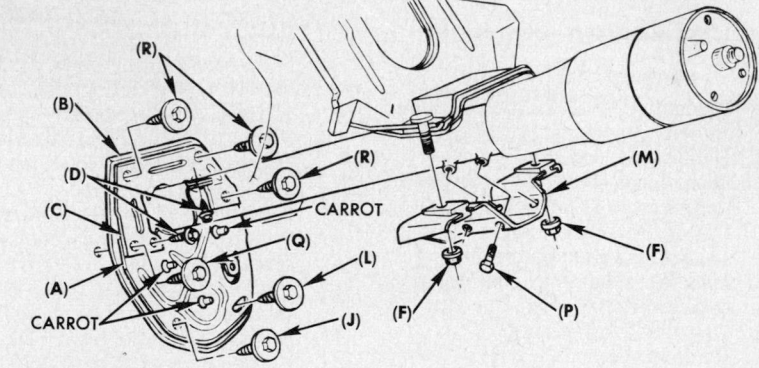

T
W
U
Y

1971-72 Chevrolet steering column mounting (© Chev. Div., G.M. Corp.)

13. Tighten the two instrument panel bracket nuts (F) to 20 ft. lbs.
14. If applicable, install the transmission indicator cable.
15. Install the instrument panel trim cover.
16. Connect the transmission control linkage at the shift tube levers.
17. Install the steering wheel.
18. Connect the battery ground cable.

1969-72 Corvette

1. Assemble the support (U) to the bracket (T) with the bolts (W) and nuts (Y), leaving the bolts loose.
2. Install the upper end of the rag joint (Z) to the steering gear, tightening the screws to 20 ft. lbs.
3. Position the column assembly in the car, sliding the splined end into the upper end of the rag joint (Z).
4. Connect all wiring.
5. Start the two steering column bracket screws (H).
6. If applicable, install the transmission control cable bracket (N) with bolt (M) and hold it in place.
7. Install the nuts (K) while holding the steering column so that there is a 0.300 ± 0.050 in. clearance between the mast jacket and the inside of the hollow of the instrument panel. Tighten nuts (K) to 15 ft. lbs., then pull back the support (U) to fit the column in its present position.

Caution Do not tighten the column to the instrument panel until the weight of the car is on the wheels or suspension.

8. Maintaining the rag joint dimension illustrated, tighten the upper rag joint flange pinch bolt (O) to 20 ft. lbs.

9. If applicable, attach the backdrive cable sheath (AA) to the transmission control cable bracket (N) with the spring clip (AB), then attach the inner cable (AC) to the lever on the steering column with the retainer (AD).
10. Secure the column lower plate to the front of the dash, tightening the nuts (K) to 35 in. lbs.
11. Install the steering wheel.
12. Connect the battery ground cable.

Clutch

Clutches are of the diaphragm spring type. The throwout bearing is a ball bearing with no provision for lubrication. The throwout fork pivots on a ball stud which is mounted in the rear face of the bellhousing.

Clutch Pedal Free-Travel

The pedal should travel 1 in. to 1½ in. for Chevrolet, 1¼ in. to 2 in. for standard Corvette and 2 in. to 2½ in. for heavy duty Corvette before the throw-out bearing engages the diaphragm spring.

This should be checked at the pedal by hand; ¾ in. true free-travel of the bearing will approximate 1 in. feel at the pedal.

The adjustment is made on the fork pushrod running from the lever and shaft assembly to the clutch fork. On some models, the adjustment is made at the fork end by changing the position of two jam nuts. On other models, the adjustment is made at the front end of the rod by turning an adjustable swivel. On this type, one turn of the swivel equals approximately 3/16 in. at the pedal. The adjustment can be made by holding the fork pushrod rearward to remove all lash, then adjusting the swivel to line up a conical point stamped on the swivel with a dimple stamped on the lever to which it attaches.

Clutch Pedal Height

The top of the clutch pedal pad should be at least 7 in. above the deadener felt glued to the metal floor pan. Do not measure to the floor mat.

If less than 7 in., cut off the rubber pedal stop to obtain proper pedal height. On some models, the rubber pedal stop is fastened to a metal piece held to the instrument panel brace by a bolt and nut. A slotted hole in the brace allows for adjustment of the bumper holding piece.

If more than 7 in. of pedal travel occurs, it may be that the diaphragm spring is being overstressed.

Clutch R & R

All Models

1. Support the engine and remove the transmission as described in "Manual Transmission R&R."
2. Disconnect the clutch fork pushrod and spring.
3. Remove the flywheel housing.
4. Slide the clutch fork from the ball stud and remove the fork from the dust boot. The ball stud is threaded into the clutch housing and is easily replaced, if necessary.
5. Install a clutch pilot tool.
NOTE: look for the assembly markings "X" on the flywheel and the clutch cover (pressure plate assembly). If there are none, scribe marks to identify the position of the clutch cover relative to the flywheel.
6. Loosen the clutch cover bolts

evenly until the spring pressure is relieved, then remove the bolts and clutch assembly.
7. Before installing, clean the pressure plate and the flywheel face.
8. Position the disc and pressure plate assembly on the flywheel and install a pilot tool.
NOTE: the disc on six-cylinder engines is installed with the springs

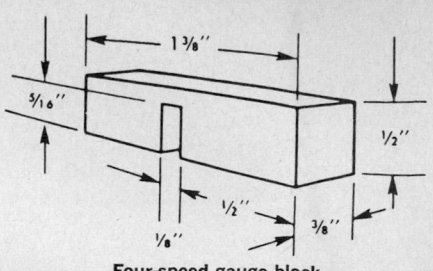

Four-speed gauge block
(© Chevrolet Div. G.M. Corp.)

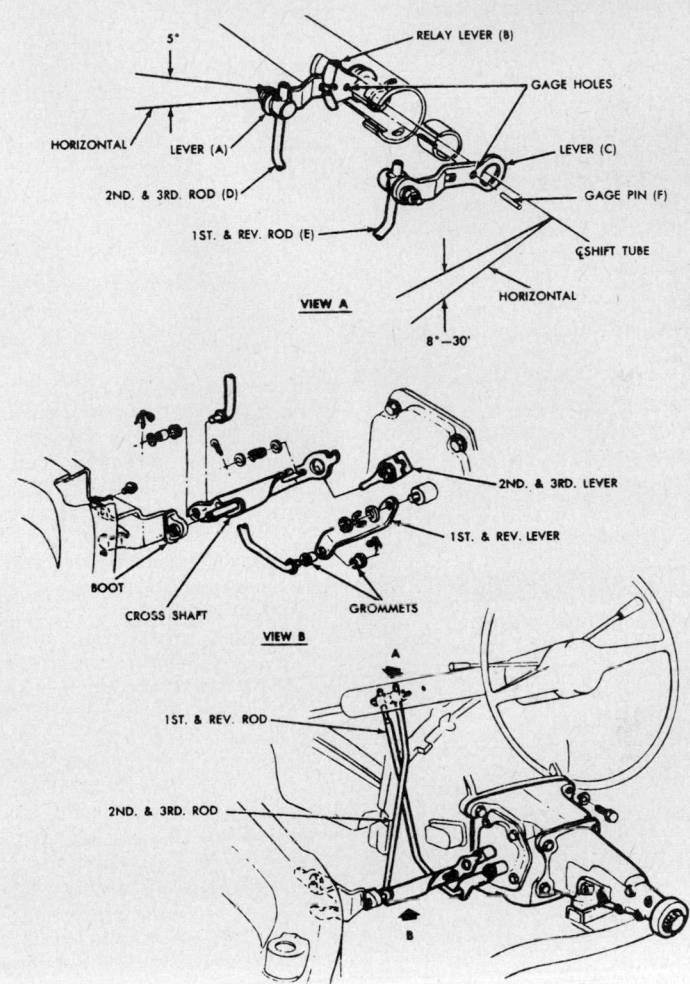

Heavy duty 3-speed linkage adjustment (© Chevrolet Div. G.M. Corp.)

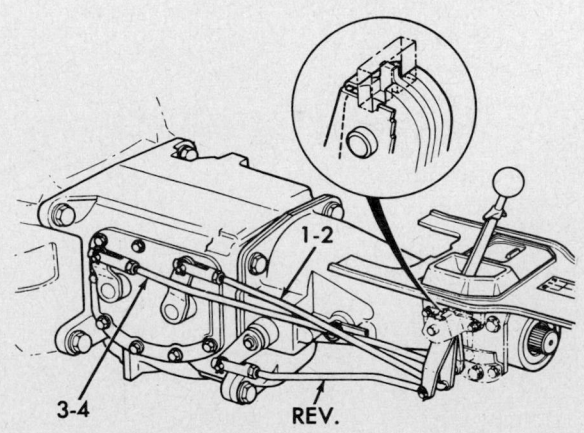

Four-speed transmission gearshift linkage (© Chevrolet Div. G.M. Corp.)

facing the flywheel. On V8 engines, the grease slinger must face the transmission.

9. Install the pressure plate assembly bolts. Make sure the mark on the cover is aligned with the mark on the flywheel. Tighten the bolts alternately and evenly to 35 ft. lbs.
10. Remove the pilot tool.
11. Remove the release fork and lubricate the ball socket and the fork fingers at the throwout bearing with graphite or Moly Grease. Reinstall the release fork.
12. Lubricate the inside recess and the fork groove of the throwout bearing with a light coat of graphite or Moly Grease.
13. Install the clutch release fork and dust boot in the clutch housing and the throwout bearing on the fork, then install the flywheel housing. Tighten flywheel housing bolts to 30 ft. lbs.
14. Connect the fork pushrod and spring.
15. Adjust the shift linkage as described later.
16. Adjust the clutch pedal free play as described previously.

Standard Transmission

Transmission refill capacities are in the Capacities table of this section.

Troubleshooting and repair of manual transmissions is covered in the Unit Repair Section.

Shift Linkage Adjustment

Three-Speed

1. Loosen swivel attaching nuts on shifter rod-to-lever attachments at bottom of steering column.
2. Move both control rods until transmission levers are in neutral detents.
3. Move manual selector lever to neutral position.
4. Engage second and third shifter lever at bottom of steering column with relay lever.
5. Center the levers in the mast jacket by measuring from edge of slot in jacket to edge of slot in spacer at each side of lever.
6. Adjust swivel on end of second and third shifter control rod until swivel enters hole in lever. Install swivel and insert retaining clip.
7. Move first and reverse lever on tube until lug on lever lines up with slot in relay lever.
8. Adjust swivel on end of first and reverse control rod until swivel enters hole in lever. Install swivel and insert retaining clip.
9. Move selector lever through all

positions of shift to check adjustment and smoothness of operation.

Four-Speed—1965

The four-speed transmission gearshift linkage uses three shift rods and levers. Adjustment can be made with the aid of a simple gauge block J-9574. An alternative method is to have an assistant hold the manual shifter lever firmly in the neutral position.

Four-Speed—1966-72

Since 1966, two makes of four-speed transmission are used, Muncie and Saginaw. Linkage adjustments, however, are typical. A gauge block 1/8 in. thick by 41/64 in. wide and 3 in. long should be used to locate and maintain neutral detent position of the shift lever while making linkage adjustments.

Adjustment Procedure

1. Remove three screws holding the chrome ring to the floor pan and remove.
2. Remove three screws holding the boot and retainer to the floor pan, then slide boot up the shift rod.
3. Place transmission in neutral and install gauge block (or have assistant hold the manual shift lever in neutral).
4. Remove the cotter pin, anti-rattle washer, and clevis pin at each of the three shift levers.
5. On each shift rod, adjust the threaded clevis to permit free entry of the clevis pin into the hole in the transmission lever. This adjustment is critical.
6. Lubricate shift rod clevis pin and connect clevises to shift levers.
7. Remove gauge block (if used) and check for freedom and ease of shifting. If any one of the shifts is not smooth, one of the clevises may require one-half turn.
8. Reinstall gearshift manual lever boot and chrome ring to floor pan.

Transmission Removal (Except Corvette)

1. Raise the car on a hoist and drain the transmission. Disconnect the speedometer cable and the control levers. Disconnect the propeller shaft. Remove two bolts attaching the center bearing to the frame. Remove nuts and U-bolts retaining the rear universal joint bearing to the differential pinion drive flange. Move the propeller shaft rearward to the left and under the rear axle housing to withdraw the front universal joint from the transmission output shaft. Remove the transmission rear mounting pad bolts and unbolt the support member from the frame.

2. On all models, remove the two top transmission-to-clutch housing cap screws, and insert guide pins to keep the weight of the transmission from falling on the clutch assembly.
3. Remove the lower transmission-to-clutch housing cap screws. Slide the transmission straight back on the guide pins until the input shaft of the transmission is free of the clutch.
4. Remove the transmission from under the car.
5. Install in reverse order of removal.

Transmission Removal (Corvette)

1965-67

1. Disconnect battery.
2. Disassemble shift control lever assembly.
3. Raise car on a hoist.
4. Place a block of wood between the top of the differential housing and the underbody.
5. Disconnect differential carrier front support from the frame bracket at the biscuit mount.
6. Pry the carrier down, while removing the two center mounting bolts from the carrier front support.
7. Pivot carrier support downward for access to propeller shaft U-joint.
8. Disconnect propeller shaft U-joints, front and rear.
9. Disconnect parking brake cable from ball socket at idler lever near center of underbody.
10. Remove propeller shaft.
11. Remove heat deflectors from right and left exhaust pipes.
12. Remove left bank exhaust pipe. Remove right bank exhaust pipe and heat riser.
13. Disassemble transmission mount as follows:
    A. Remove two bolts that hold rear mount cushion to rear mount bracket.
    B. Support engine under the oil pan (with a well padded jack) and raise engine to take weight off rear mount cushion.
    C. Remove the three transmission mount bracket-to-crossmember bolts, and remove mount bracket.
    D. Remove the two bolts from mount pad to transmission case, and remove rubber mount cushion and exhaust pipe yoke.
14. Disconnect transmission linkage by removing shift levers at transmission.
15. Disconnect speedometer cable at transmission.
16. Remove two bolts to disconnect

the transmission gearshift control lever and bracket assembly from its adapter plate on side of transmission.

17. Lower transmission assembly from the car, letting the gearshift lever slide down through the dust boot in the console.
18. Remove transmission - to - clutch housing attaching bolts.
19. Remove transmission rearward from the clutch and rotate the assembly to gain access to the three flathead machine screws in the control lever bracket adapter plate. Rotate transmission back to upright position.
20. Slowly lower rear of engine until tachometer drive cable at distributor clears the ledge across front of dash.
21. Slide transmission rearward out of clutch, then tip front of transmission down and lower the assembly out of the car.
22. Install by reversing removal procedure.

1968-72

1. Disconnect the battery ground cable.
2. Remove the shifter ball and "T" handle.
3. Remove the console trim plate.
4. Raise the vehicle on a hoist.
5. Remove the right and left exhaust pipes.
6. Disconnect the driveshaft at the transmission, lower the driveshaft and remove the slip yoke from the transmission.
7. Remove the rear mount to bracket bolts, then jack the engine enough to raise the transmission from the mount.
8. Remove the transmission linkage mounting bracket to frame bolts.
9. Remove the bolts attaching gearshift assembly to mounting bracket and remove the mounting bracket. Remove the shifter mechanism with the rods attached.
10. Disconnect the shift levers at the transmission.
11. Disconnect the speedometer cable and the TCS switch wiring.
12. Remove the transmission mount bracket.
13. Remove the transmission to clutch housing retaining bolts and the lower left extension bolt.
14. Pull the transmission rearward until it is clear of the clutch housing, then rotate it clockwise while pulling to the rear. Carefully lower the rear of the engine until the tachometer drive cable at the distributor just clears the firewall.

Caution The tachometer cable is easily damaged if it hits the firewall. Slide the transmission rearward until it clears the clutch, then tilt the front of it down and lower it from the car.

15. Installation is the reverse of removal. Adjust the shift linkage.

Automatic Transmission

Transmission removal and replacement and linkage adjustments are covered in the following paragraphs. For test procedures, transmission overhaul and other detailed information see Unit Repair Section.

Neutral Safety Switch Adjustment

In all models the adjustment is made with the shift lever in Drive position. Loosen the switch mounting screws. Align the slot in the contact support with the hole in the switch and insert a 3/32 in. pin to hold the support in place.

On column shift models, place the contact support drive slot over the shifter tube drive tang and tighten the screws.

On Corvettes, the shift control lever must be disconnected from the control rod and the shift control knob removed. Then remove the trim plate to get at the switch. Proceed as described in the first paragraph above, then place the contact support drive slot over the drive tang. Tighten the switch mounting screws, then remove the pin. Reinstall the shift control lever and trim plate.

On Chevrolet models with floor shift, the ash tray, trim plate assembly and indicator lens and housing must be removed from the console before proceding as described in the first paragraph above. Clamp the control lever pawl against the contact point of the detent. Tighten the switch mounting screws, then remove the pin and reinstall all the console components which were removed.

Linkage Adjustments

Column Shift—All Models

1. Make sure that the shift lever works freely in the mast jacket.
2. Check for proper linkage adjustment:
   a. Pull the selector lever back and allow the lever to be positioned in Drive by the transmission detent.
   NOTE: do not use the indicator pointer as a reference. The indicator pointer will be adjusted after the linkage.
   b. Release the lever. The lever should not go into Low range unless it is lifted.
   c. Lift the shift lever and allow the lever to be positioned in Neutral by the transmission detent.
   d. Release the lever. The lever should not go into Reverse unless it is lifted.
   e. If the selector lever can move beyond the Neutral and Drive detents without being lifted, then the mechanical stops in the steering column are not coordinated with the transmission detents and adjustment is required.

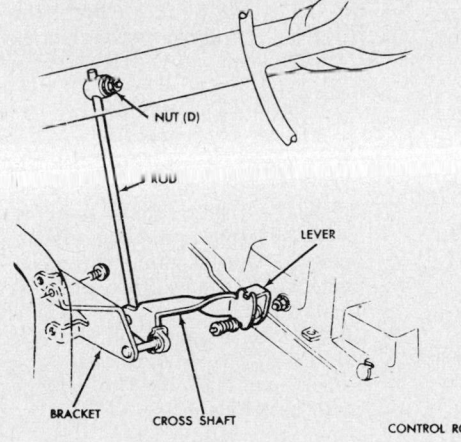

CONTROL ADJUSTMENT

1. Set transmission lever in "Drive" position.
2. Set shift tube & lever assby. in "Drive" position.
3. Tighten nut (D) to 10 ft. lbs.
4. Check shift pattern in all ranges. Readjust if necessary.

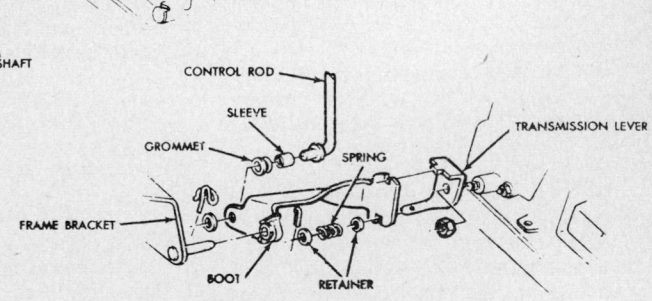

Turbo-hydramatic, column linkage adjustment ⓒ Chevrolet Div. G.M. Corp.)

3. To adjust, place the selector lever in Drive as determined by the transmission detent.
4. Loosen the adjustment clamp or swivel at the cross-shaft and po-

LINKAGE ADJUSTMENT

1. Set lever (D) & control lever (E) in "Drive" detent.

2. Apply Forward load (Y) on lever (G) to Fully seat lever (E) in "Drive".

3. Place a 7/64" spacer (H) between nut (A) & Swivel (J), run nut (A) to spacer. Remove spacer & apply rearward load (X) until lever (G) touches nut (A). Tighten nut B.

4. Check shift pattern in all ranges, readjust if required.

Turbo-hydramatic, console linkage adjustment (© Chevrolet Div. G.M. Corp.)

sition the selector lever in Drive.
5. With the selector lever in Drive and the transmission lever in Drive detent position, tighten the clamp or swivel bolt.
6. Repeat Step 2 above to check for proper adjustment.
7. If necessary, readjust the selector pointer to agree with the transmission detents.
8. Readjust the neutral safety switch if necessary.
9. When properly adjusted:
   a. From Reverse to Drive position travel, the transmission detent must be noted and related to the indicated position on the dial.
   b. In Drive and Reverse positions, the selector lever must drop back into position freely when lifted.

1965-67 Corvette (Powerglide)

Disconnect the clevis at the bottom of the selector lever. Put the transmission in Park detent and the selector lever in Park. Adjust the clevis until the clevis pin will fit eas-

ily in the holes, then secure it with washer and cotter pin. Check the operation of the shift mechanism in all positions.

1968-72 Corvette (Turbo-Hydramatic)

1. Disconnect the pushrod at the transmission lever.
2. With the transmission lever in Drive detent and the selector lever in Drive, rotate the pushrod until the hole lines up with the lever pin.
3. Install the pushrod on the pin and install the retainer clip.
4. Check operation of the linkage in all positions.

Powerglide

Transmission R & R

All Models

1. Raise the car on a hoist and drain the transmission.
2. Disconnect at the transmission:
   a. Vacuum modulator line.

   b. Oil cooler lines, if so equipped. Tie the lines out of the way.
   c. Speedometer cable.
   d. Shift linkage.
   e. Throttle valve linkage.
   f. Driveshaft.
3. Install a transmission jack under the transmission.
4. Disconnect the rear mount on the transmission extension.
5. Disconnect the transmission support crossmember and slide it rearward.
6. Remove the converter underpan. The flywheel and converter are assembled to balance, so scribe marks to indicate their relative positions for reassembly.
7. Remove the converter to flywheel attaching bolts.
8. Support the engine at the oil pan rail with a jack or brace.
9. Lower the rear of the transmission slightly to gain access to the upper transmission housing to engine attaching bolts. Remove the bolts.

Caution Do not lower the transmission too far on models with V8 engines. The distributor may hit the firewall.

10. Remove the rest of the transmission housing to engine bolts.
11. Move the transmission slightly to the rear and downward, then remove it from under the car.

NOTE: make sure that the converter is coming off with the transmission. If it gets stuck, pry it free from the flywheel before removing the transmission.

Caution Do not let the converter fall off the transmission. Keep the transmission tilted forward end up until a holding strap or strong wire can be installed to hold the converter on.

12. To install, raise the transmission into place with a transmission jack.
13. Remove the converter holding strap or wire and install the upper transmission housing to engine bolts. Install the rest of the bolts, tightening to 35 ft. lbs.
14. Remove the support from the engine, then raise the transmission to final position.

NOTE: the light side of the converter and the heavy side of the flywheel must be aligned for balance. Align the white flywheel balance mark with the blue converter mark. The marks scribed during removal should align the converter and the flywheel in the same way.

15. After aligning the flywheel and converter, install the bolts, tightening to 15-20 ft. lbs. on 1965-67 models and to 30-35 ft. lbs. on 1968-72 models.
16. Install the converter underpan.
17. Install the transmission support crossmember to the frame and the transmission.
18. Remove the transmission jack and install the driveshaft.
19. Connect:
    a. Shift linkage.
    b. Throttle valve linkage.
    c. Oil cooler lines, if so equipped.
    d. Vacuum modulator line.
    e. Speedometer cable.
20. Fill the transmission with fluid.
21. Check the transmission for proper operation and leakage.
22. Check the shift linkage, adjusting if necessary.

Throttle Valve Adjustment

1965-66 All Models
1967-72 6-Cylinder

Adjustment is made with the throttle pedal completely depressed and the bellcrank (six-cylinder) or carburetor lever (V8) in wide open position.

Adjust the length of the linkage to obtain a 1/64 in. to 1/16 in. clearance between the lever on the firewall and its stop when the transmission lever is against its stop.

1967-72 V8

1. Remove the air cleaner and disconnect:
   a. Accelerator linkage at the carburetor.
   b. Accelerator return spring.
   c. Throttle valve rod return spring.
2. Pull the throttle valve upper rod forward until the transmission is through detent and place the carburetor in wide open position. The carburetor must reach wide open position at the same time that the ball stud contacts the end of the slot in the upper throttle valve rod.
3. Adjust the swivel on the end of the upper throttle valve rod to obtain the setting described in Step 2 above. Allowable tolerance is approximately 1/32 in.
4. Connect and adjust the carburetor linkage.

Turbo-Hydramatic

Detent Switch Adjustment

1969-72 350 (Chevrolet)

1. Disengage the snap lock on the detent cable.
2. Place the carburetor in wide open position (lever against the stop). On Quadrajet carburetors, disengage the secondary locknut before placing the lever in wide open position.

NOTE: detent cable must be through detent.

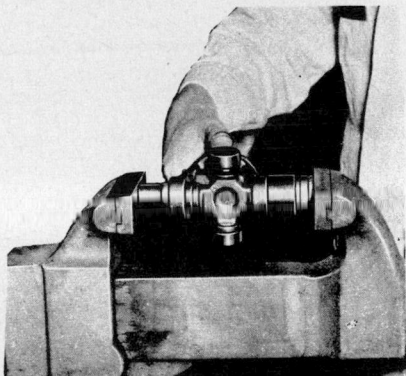

Assembling universal joint
(© Chev. Div., G.M. Corp.)

3. Holding the carburetor in wide open position, push the snap lock on the detent cable downward until the top is flush with the cable.

1968-72 400 (Corvette)

The detent switch is located on the carburetor.

1. Pull the detent switch driver rearward until the hole in the switch body aligns with the hole in the driver.
2. Insert a 0.092 in. pin through the aligned holes to a depth of 0.10 in. to hold the driver in position.
3. Loosen the switch mounting bolt.
4. With the throttle held in wide open position, move the switch forward until the driver contacts the accelerator lever.
5. Tighten the mounting bolt and remove the pin.

1968-72 400 (Chevrolet)

The detent switch is located on the carburetor.

1. Loosen the switch mounting bolt.
2. Holding the throttle in wide open position (choke fully open), depress the detent switch plunger until it bottoms in the switch. Move the switch toward the throttle lever paddle until there is a clearance of 0.23 ± 0.01 in. (1969-72 models), 0.20 in. (1968 models with 396 or 427 engine) or 0.05 in. (1968 models with 307 or 327 engine) between the face of the lever paddle and the depressed detent switch plunger.
3. Tighten the switch mounting bolts.

Transmission R & R

1. Disconnect battery, then raise the car.
2. Remove drive shaft.
3. Disconnect speedometer cable at transmission, electrical lead at transmission connector, vacuum line at modulator, and oil cooler pipes.
4. Disconnect shift control linkage.
5. Support transmission with suitable transmission jack.
6. Disconnect rear mount from frame crossmember.
7. Remove two bolts at each end of frame crossmember and remove crossmember.
8. Remove oil cooler lines, vacuum modulator line and detent solenoid connector wire at transmission.
9. Remove converter underpan.
10. Remove converter to flywheel bolts.
11. Loosen exhaust pipe to manifold bolts about 1/4 in., then lower transmission until jack is just supporting it.
12. Remove transmission to engine mounting bolts and remove oil filler tube at transmission.
13. Raise transmission to its normal position, support engine with a jack and slide transmission rearward, then lower it away from the car.

NOTE: use converter holding tool J-5384, or suitable substitute, to keep from losing converter from transmission while handling the assembly.

14. Install by reversing the removal procedure.

Drive Shaft, U Joints

Driveshafts are of a one-piece design, using Carden type universal joints. The universal joints are lubsealed at the factory and require no periodic maintenance. The front yoke is splined, providing a slip joint for slight length variations in the drive line. There is a damper on some models: this damper is not serviced separately.

Two basic universal joints are used. The Dana or Cleveland type uses snap-ring bearing cap retainers. The Saginaw uses injection molded plastic to retain the bearing caps. On the Saginaw type there is a snap-ring groove in the bearing housing inboard of the yoke to hold the bearings in place.

Driveshaft R & R

Disconnect the rear universal joint flange. On some models, the bearing caps are bolted directly to the differential flange with clamps or U-bolts. Pull the front yoke from the transmission. Watch for oil leaks from the transmission output housing. Install in the reverse order of removal.

Universal Joint R & R

Dana and Cleveland Type

1. Remove the driveshaft.
2. Remove the snap-rings from the trunnion yoke.
3. Using a vise and suitably sized sockets, press on the trunnion until the bearing cap is almost out. Grasp the cap in the vise and work it out of the yoke. Repeat the above procedure for the rest of the bearing caps.
4. Pack the rollers in grease and fill the grease reservoir.
5. To install, position the trunnion in the yoke and partially install one bearing cap. Start the trunnion in the bearing cap and partially install the other cap. Align the trunnion with the caps and press into place.
6. If necessary, repeat Step 5 above for the other yoke.
7. Install the snap-rings.
8. Install the driveshaft in the vehicle.

Saginaw Type

Remove and install the bearing caps and trunnion as described for the Dana and Cleveland type universal joints. On an original universal joint, however, the bearing

caps will be secured in the yokes with injected plastic. The plastic will shear when the bearing caps are pressed. Service snap-rings are installed in the groove on the inside (of yoke) of the installed caps.

Drive Axle, Suspension

Coil Type Rear Springs (Chevrolet)

1965-72 R & R

1. Raise rear of vehicle and place jack stands under frame. Support weight of vehicle at rear axle housing separately from above frame position.
2. Remove both rear wheels.
3. With car supported as in Step 1, and springs compressed by weight of vehicle:
   a. Disconnect both rear shocks from anchor pin lower connection.
   b. Loosen the upper control arm(s) rear pivot bolt (do not remove the nut).
   c. Loosen both left and right lower control arm rear attachment (do not disconnect from axle brackets).

d. Remove rear suspension tie rod from stud on axle tube.

4. Slightly loosen the nut on the bolt that retains the spring and seat to control arm at lower seat of both rear springs. When bolt has been backed off the maximum distance, all threads of the nut should still be engaged on the bolt.

Caution Under no condition should the nut, at this time, be removed from the bolt in the seat of either spring.

5. Slowly lower the rear axle assembly, allowing the axle to swing down, carrying the springs out of the upper seat. This provides access for spring removal.
6. Remove the lower seat attaching parts from each spring, then remove springs from vehicle.
7. Position springs in upper seat and install lower seat parts on control arm. Install nut of spring retaining bolt finger-tight.

NOTE: Omit lockwasher under the special high carbon bolt, so that sufficient threads will be available to start the nut. Lockwashers will be installed later.

8. Alternately raise the axle slightly and retighten the nut on each spring lower seat bolt. Continue

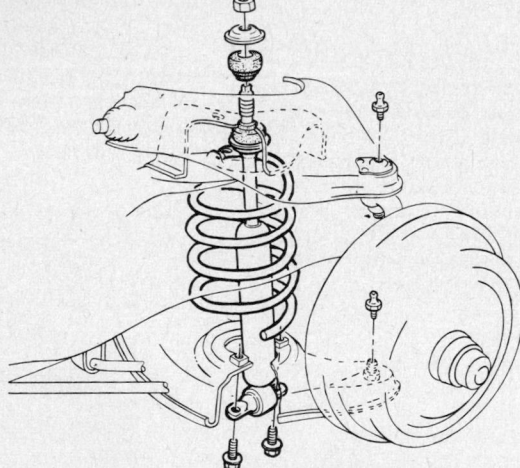

Installing shock absorber—typical
(© Chevrolet Div. G.M. Corp.)

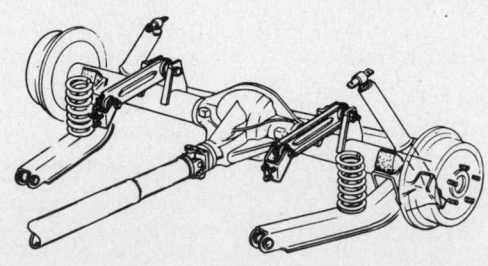

Chevrolet rear suspension (© Chevrolet Div. G.M. Corp.)

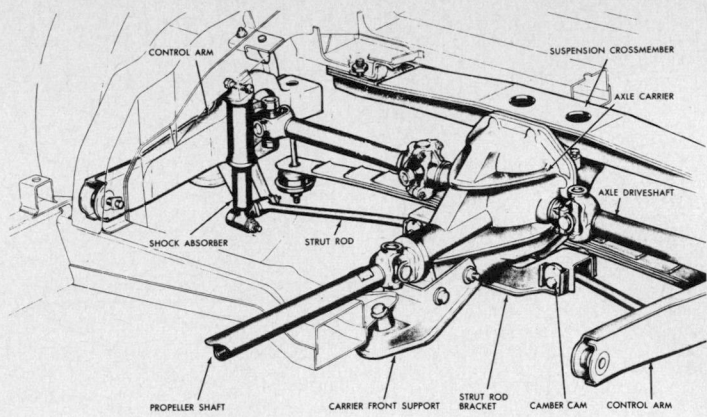

Corvette rear suspension (© Chevrolet Div. G.M. Corp.)

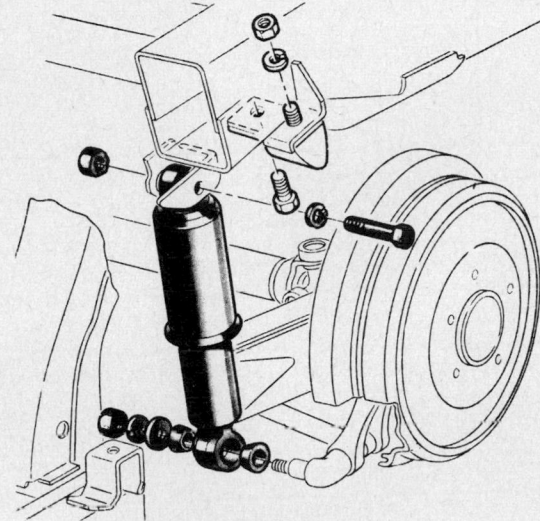

Shock absorber installation, Corvette
(© Chevrolet Div. G.M. Corp.)

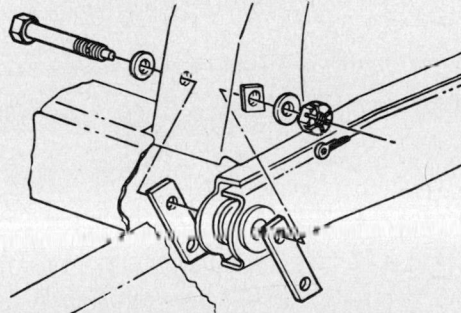

Toe-in adjustment shim location, Corvette
(© Chevrolet Div., G.M. Corp.)

in until the weight is fully supported on the jack or lift. With spring now completely compressed to approximate curb position, completely position the springs in the lower seats by torquing the nut on the lower seat bolt.

9. Reconnect shock absorbers, torque rear attachment of upper and lower control arms, and reconnect the axle tie-rod.

10. While still jacked under axle, remove the nut from the lower seat bolt of one rear spring and install lockwasher and replace nut and tighten. Similarly in-stall lockwasher at other spring.

11. Install rear wheels and lower car to floor.

Transverse Leaf Rear Spring (Corvette)

1965-72 R & R

1. Raise car and support it by the frame, slightly forward of torque control pivot points. Remove wheel assemblies.

2. Place floor jack under spring near link bolt, and raise spring until nearly flat.

3. Tie the end of the spring to the suspension crossmember to hold

this flat attitude, with a 1/4 in. or 5/16 in. chain and grab hook wrapped around the spring and crossmember. To prevent chain slipping, use a C-clamp on the spring adjacent to the chain.

4. Remove link bolt and rubber bushings.

5. Support and raise spring end, as before, and remove chain.

6. Carefully lower jack to completely relax spring.

7. Repeat foregoing procedure on the other side of car.

8. Remove four bolts and washers attaching the spring at the center.

9. Remove spring from car.

10. Install by reversing removal procedure.

Leaf Spring R & R Chevrolet 126 In. W.B. Station Wagon
1971-72

1. Raise the vehicle on a hoist and place an adjustable jack under the axle.

2. Raise the axle until all tension is relieved from the spring.

3. Disconnect the shock absorber from the spring retainer plate.

4. Remove the upper shackle retaining bolt, then the front spring eye bolt.

5. Remove the spring/axle U-bolts, lower plate, spring pads, and spring.

6. Remove the shackle from the spring.

7. Before installing the spring, install the shackle on the rearward end.

8. Place the upper cushion on the spring, then insert the front of the spring into the frame and attach the rear shackle, leaving the bolt loose.

9. Install the lower spring pad and retainer plate, tightening the U-bolt nuts to 40 ft. lbs.

10. Tighten the rear shackle bolts to 80 ft. lbs.

11. Tighten the front eye bolt to 115 ft. lbs.

12. Attach the shock absorber to spring retainer plate, tightening to 65 ft. lbs.

13. Remove the jack and lower the vehicle.

Strut Rod and Bracket (Corvette)

Rear Wheel Camber Adjustment

Due to the design of this rear suspension, it is important that the strut rod and rear wheel camber adjusting specifications and procedures be included.

Rod and Bracket—Removal

1. Raise car on a hoist.

2. Disconnect shock absorber lower

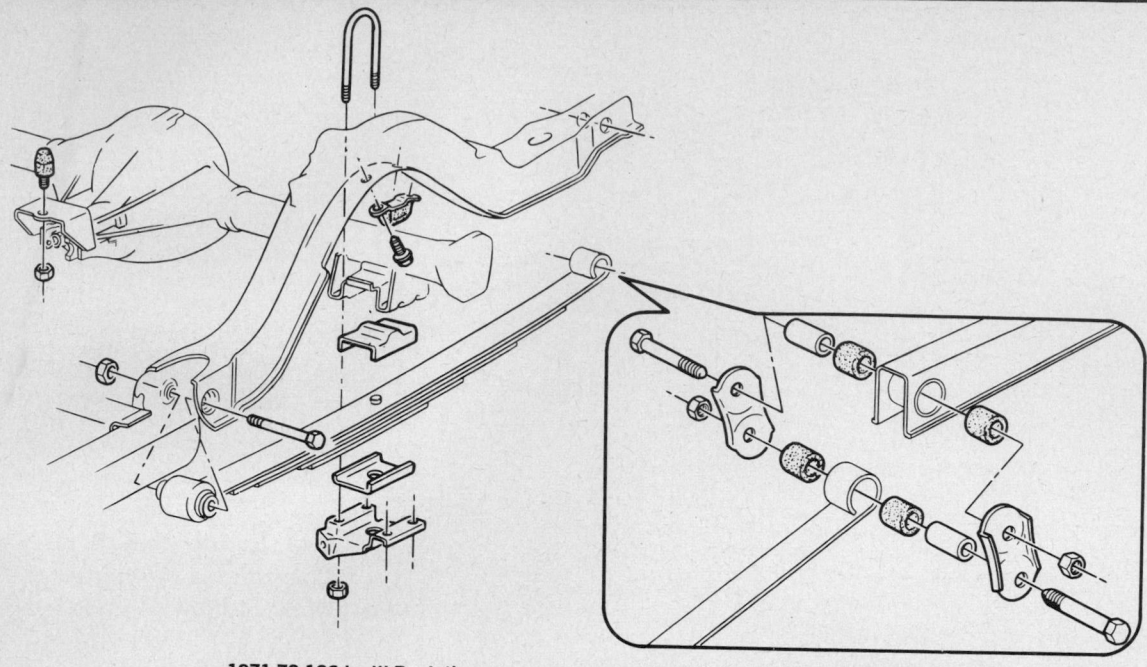

1971-72 126 in. W.B. station wagon rear suspension (© Chev. Div., G.M. Corp.)

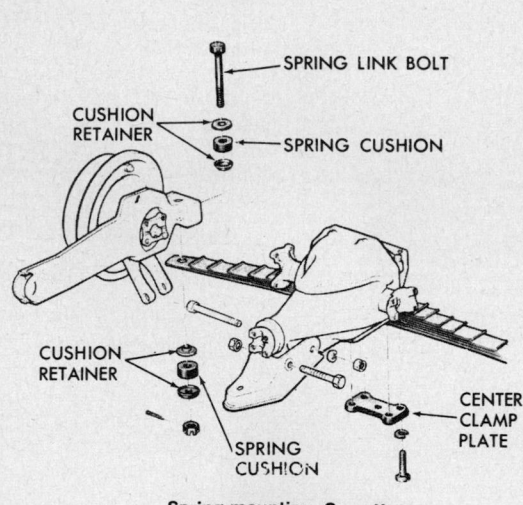

SPRING LINK BOLT

CUSHION RETAINER

SPRING CUSHION

CUSHION RETAINER

SPRING CUSHION

CENTER CLAMP PLATE

Spring mounting, Corvette
(© Chevrolet Div. G.M. Corp.)

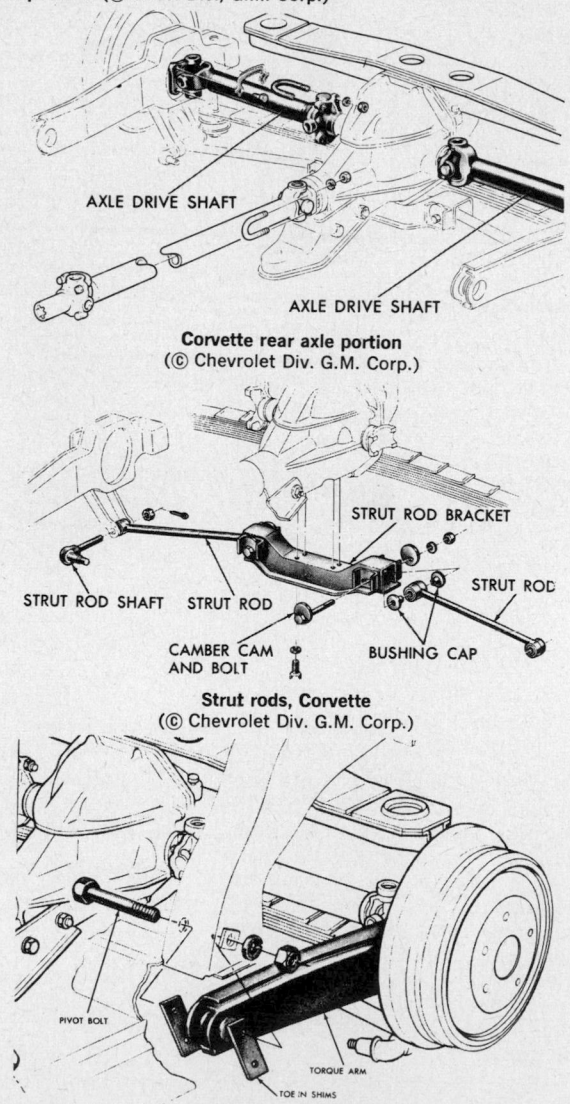

AXLE DRIVE SHAFT

AXLE DRIVE SHAFT

Corvette rear axle portion
(© Chevrolet Div. G.M. Corp.)

STRUT ROD BRACKET

STRUT ROD

STRUT ROD SHAFT   STRUT ROD

CAMBER CAM AND BOLT

BUSHING CAP

Strut rods, Corvette
(© Chevrolet Div. G.M. Corp.)

PIVOT BOLT

TORQUE ARM

TOE IN SHIMS

Torque control arm, Corvette
(© Chevrolet Div. G.M. Corp.)

eye from strut rod shaft.

3. Remove strut rod shaft cotter pin and nut. Withdraw shaft by pulling toward the front of the car.

4. Mark related position of camber adjustment, so that adjustment is maintained upon reassembly.

5. Loosen camber bolt and nut. Remove four bolts holding strut rod bracket to carrier and lower the bracket.

6. Remove cam bolt and cam bolt assembly. Pull strut down out of bracket and remove bushing caps.

7. Inspect strut rod bushings for wear and replace where necessary. Replace strut rod if it is bent or damaged in any way.

8. Install by reversing removal procedure.

9. Check rear wheel camber and adjust to specifications.

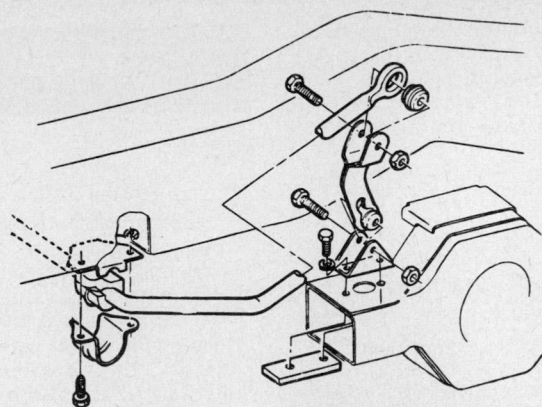

Stabilizer shaft installation, Corvette
(© Chevrolet Div. G.M. Corp.)

Torque Control Arm R & R (Corvette)

1. Disconnect spring on the side from which the torque arm is to be removed. Follow procedure for Springs R & R 1964-69, Corvette.
   NOTE: if so equipped, disconnect stabilizer rod from torque arm.
2. Remove shock absorber lower eye from strut rod shaft.
3. Disconnect and remove strut rod shaft and swing strut rod down.
4. Remove four bolts holding the axle driveshaft to spindle flange and disconnect drive shaft.
5. Disconnect brake line at wheel cylinder inlet or caliper and from torque arm. Disconnect parking brake cable.
6. Remove torque arm pivot bolt and toe-in shims, then pull torque arm out of frame. Tape shims together to assure relationship for reassembly.
7. To install, place torque arm in frame opening.
8. Position toe-in shims in original location on both sides of torque arm. Install pivot bolt and lightly tighten at this time.
9. Raise axle driveshaft into position and install to drive flange. Torque bolts to 75 ft. lbs.
10. Raise strut into position and insert strut rod shaft so that flat lines up with flat in spindle support fork. Install nut and torque to 80 ft. lbs.
11. Install shock absorber lower eye and tighten nut to 35 ft. lbs.
12. Connect spring end as outlined under Leaf Type Rear Springs—Corvette, 1964-69 R & R.
    NOTE: if car is so equipped, connect stabilizer shaft.
13. Install brake drum or disc and caliper, and wheel. Then lower the car. Tighten torque pivot bolt to 50 ft. lbs.
14. Bleed brakes and check camber and toe-in.

Drive Axle, Suspension

Rear drive axle overhaul procedures can be found in the Unit Repair Section. Rear axle lubricant capacities are listed in the Capacities table at the beginning of this section.

Rear Axle Assembly Removal

Chevrolet

1. Jack up the back of the car to allow sufficient room to work, then place another jack under the rear axle housing. Disconnect the driveshaft.
2. Remove the single bolt which holds the center support arm to the rear of the axle banjo housing.
3. Remove the wheel assemblies, disconnect the shocks at the lower end, and then slowly lower the rear axle housing.
4. Remove the bolt on each side which holds the torque arm to the rear axle housing, disconnect the hand brake cable and the hydraulic line and the T fitting over the rear axle housing. Then, slide the housing assembly out from underneath the vehicle.
5. Install in the reverse order of removal.

Corvette, 1965-72

Corvette is equipped with an independent rear suspension. The differential is solidly attached to the car frame, the rear wheels being driven through tubular rear axles, each fitted with two universal joints. A transverse, multiple leaf rear spring provides rear suspension. Brake torque and driving forces are transmitted through radius arms to the frame. The spring supports vertical loads, while lateral forces, on turns etc., are taken by the axles and control rods to the fixed differential and to the frame.

1. Raise the vehicle on a hoist.
2. Disconnect the spring and link bolts.

3. Disconnect the axle shafts at the carrier by removing the U-bolts on the universal joint trunnions.
4. Disconnect the carrier front support bracket at the frame crossmember.
5. Disconnect the driveshaft at the companion flange.
6. Scribe marks indicating the cam and bolt relative location on the strut rod bracket and loosen the cam bolts.
7. Remove the four bolts which secure the bracket to the carrier lower surface and drop the bracket. Remove the camber cam bolts and swing the strut rods up and out of the way.

8. Remove the eight carrier to cover bolts, loosening the bolts gradually to permit the lubricant to drain out.
9. Pull the carrier partially out of the cover, drop the nose to clear the crossmember, then gradually work the carrier down and out.
10. To install, clean the carrier cover and grease the gasket surface.
11. Using a new gasket and two ½-13 x 1-¼ in. studs as aligning studs, raise the carrier into position.
12. Install the carrier to cover bolts, tightening securely.
13. Install the driveshaft to the companion flange, tightening the clamp bolts securely.
14. Install the rubber cushion on the bracket and position to the frame crossmember. Install the nut, tightening to 50 ft. lbs.
15. Install the axle trunnions to the yokes with the U-bolts.
16. Assemble the strut rods to the bracket and raise the bracket into position under the carrier. Install the four bolts, tightening to 35 ft. lbs.
17. Move the camber cams to the marked locations and tighten the cam nuts.
18. Connect the spring end link bolts.
19. Fill the housing with lubricant to the level of the filler hole.

Positraction Differential

No special attention is required in this area, except with the lubricant used.

Under no circumstances use anything but special G.M. Positraction lubricant.

Failure to follow these instructions may result in permanent damage to the unit.

Windshield Wipers

Motor R & R

These models may be equipped with vacuum or electric motors. Power transmission may be through cable, or through levers and links.

1965-67 Chevrolet

1. Make sure the battery is disconnected and the wiper motor is in parked position.
2. Remove washer hoses, if present, and all electrical connectors.
3. Remove plenum chamber ventilator grille.
4. Disconnect transmission drive linkage from wiper motor crank arm.
5. Remove motor retaining bolts, then remove the motor.
6. Install motor by reversing the removal procedure.

NOTE: make sure the wiper motor is properly grounded.

1965-67 Corvette

1. Disconnect battery.
2. Remove ignition distributor shielding and left bank plug wire vertical shield.
3. Disconnect left bank plug wire bracket-to-manifold, position assembly to one side.
4. Disconnect ignition resistor at firewall, then remove washer pump inlet and outlet hose at pump valve assembly.
5. Remove ignition distributor cap and position to one side, then disconnect washer pump and motor assembly wires.
6. Remove glove compartment door and compartment.
7. Make sure wiper arms and motor are both in parked position. Remove transmission retaining clip and disconnect both transmission and spacer from crank arm.
8. Remove four wiper motor-to-dash wall mounting bolts and remove wiper motor from the car.
9. Install motor by reversing removal procedure.

1968-72 Corvette and Chevrolet

1. With wiper motor in park position and hood open, disconnect the washer hoses and all wiring from the motor assembly.
2. Remove the plenum chamber grill on Corvettes or the access cover on Chevrolet models.
3. Loosen the nuts which retain the drive link to the crank arm ball stud on Chevrolet models. Remove the nut which retains the crank arm to the motor assembly on Corvette models.
4. On Corvettes, remove the ignition shield and distributor cap. Remove and identify the left bank spark plug leads.
5. Remove the motor mounting screws or nuts and remove the motor.
6. To install, reverse the above procedure.

Transmission R & R

1965-67 Chevrolet

1. With the wiper motor in parked position, remove shroud top ventilator grille.
2. Detach transmission drive linkage from wiper motor assembly.
3. Remove screws holding transmission to body, then lower transmission into plenum chamber.
4. Remove the assembly from the plenum chamber.
5. To install, reverse the removal procedure.

1965-67 Corvette

1. Remove wiper block and arm assembly from transmission.
2. Remove glove compartment door and compartment.
3. Remove three transmission-to-cowl retaining screws.
4. Remove wiper transmission retaining clip and remove transmission from crank arm. Then, remove transmission through the glove compartment opening.
5. To install, reverse removal procedure.

1968-72 Chevrolet and Corvette

1. Open the hood and disconnect the battery.
2. Make sure that the wiper motor is in park position.
3. On Corvette models, remove the rubber plug from the front of the wiper door actuator, then insert a screwdriver, pushing the internal piston rearward to open the door.
4. Remove the wiper arm and blade. On the articulated left hand arm assembly, remove the retaining clip from the pin on the drive arm.
5. Remove the plenum chamber air intake grill or screen.
6. Loosen the nuts which retain the drive rod ball stud to the crank arm and detach the drive rod from the crank arm.
7. Remove the transmission retaining screws or nuts, then lower the drive rod assemblies into the plenum chamber.
8. Remove the transmission and linkage from the plenum chamber through the cowl opening.
9. To install, reverse the above procedure.

Radio

R & R

1966-72 Chevrolet

1. Disconnect battery.
2. Remove ash tray, retainer attaching screws and retainer.
3. Remove heater control panel retaining screws and push panel assembly from console.

NOTE: if interference between control panel and radio is met, loosen radio retaining nuts.

4. Remove radio control knobs, bezels and retaining nuts.
5. Disconnect radio wiring harness, and antenna lead-in.
6. Remove radio rear brace attaching screw, and remove radio from the car.
7. Remove speaker retaining bolt and remove speaker.
8. To install, reverse removal procedure.

1966-72 Corvette Coupe

1. Disconnect battery.
2. Remove right and left door sill plates and kick pads.
3. Disconnect right and left side radio-to-speaker connectors.
4. Remove right side dash pad.
5. Remove right and left console forward trim pads.
6. Remove bolt and remove the heater floor outlet duct by pulling it through left hand opening.
7. From front of console, tape radio push buttons in depressed position. From rear of console, disconnect electrical connector, brace and antenna lead-in.
8. Remove radio knobs and bezel retaining nuts. Push radio assembly forward and remove from rear through right side opening.
9. Install by reversing procedure above.

1966-72 Corvette Convertible

1. Disconnect batery.
2. Remove right instrument panel pad.
3. Disconnect speaker connectors.
4. Remove wiper switch trim plate screws to gain access to switch connector and remove connector and trim plate from cluster assembly.
5. Unclip and remove right and left console forward trim pads and remove forwardmost screw on right and left side of console.
6. Inserting a flexible drive socket between the console and metal horseshoe brace, remove the nuts from the two studs on the lower

edge of the console cluster. Remove the remaining screws that retain the cluster assembly to the instrument panel.

7. From rear of console, disconnect electric connector, brace and antenna lead-in.
8. Remove radio knobs and bezel retaining nuts.
9. Pull radio assembly forward and remove through right side opening.
10. Install by reversing procedure above.

Heater System

Heater Blower R & R

1965-72 Chevrolet

1. Disconnect battery.
2. Unclip hoses from fender skirt.
3. Disconnect electrical feed from motor.

4. Turn vehicle front wheels to extreme right.
5. Remove right front fender skirt bolts and allow skirt to drop, resting it on top of tire. It may be wedged away from fender lower flange with block of wood to provide better access to bolts.
6. Remove screws attaching motor mounting plate to air inlet housing.
7. Remove screws attaching motor to mounting plate.
8. Remove clip attaching cage to shaft and remove blower motor.
9. Install in reverse of above.

1965-72 Corvette

1. Remove the radiator supply tank from its retaining straps. Move it out of the way. Disconnect the battery.
2. Remove blower motor electrical connectors.
3. Scribe a reference mark on the blower motor mounting plate and

the blower motor.

4. Remove the five screws that mount the blower mounting plate to the blower inlet assembly.
5. Withdraw the blower assembly from the inlet assembly.
6. Install in reverse of removal procedure.

Heater Core R & R

1. Drain radiator.
2. Remove heater hoses at connections beside air inlet assembly.
3. Remove cable and electrical connectors from heater and defroster assembly.
4. On engine side of dash, remove screws and nuts holding air inlet to dash panel.
5. Inside vehicle, pull entire assembly from firewall and remove assembly from vehicle.
6. Remove core assembly retaining springs and remove core.
7. Install in reverse of above.

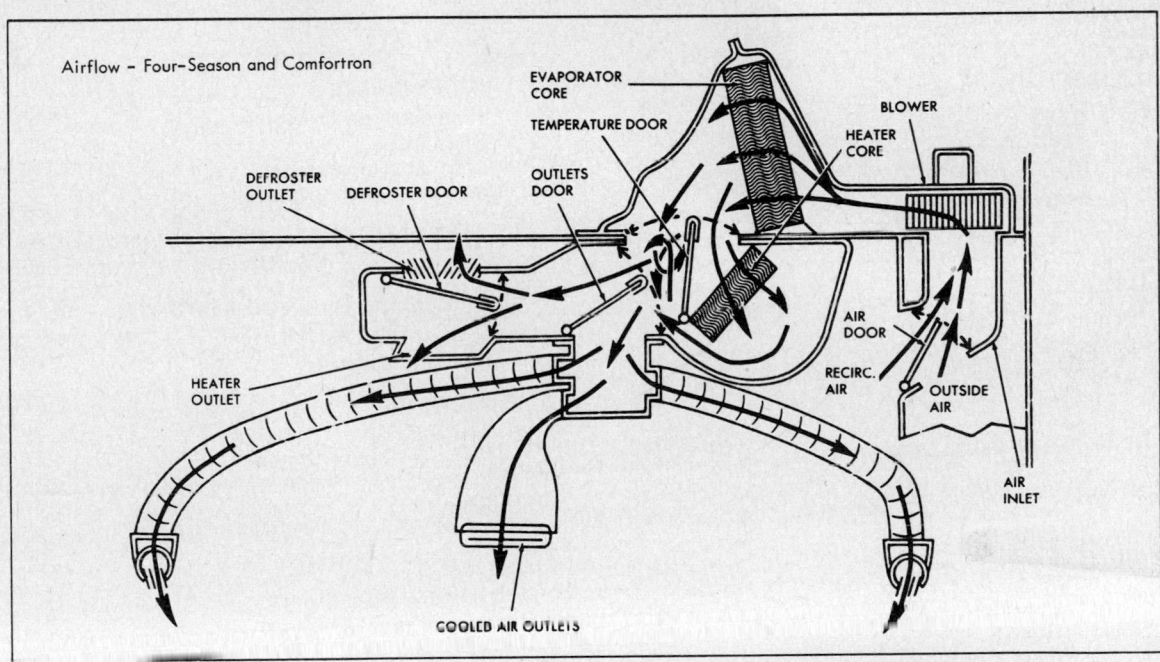

Airflow - Four-Season and Comfortron

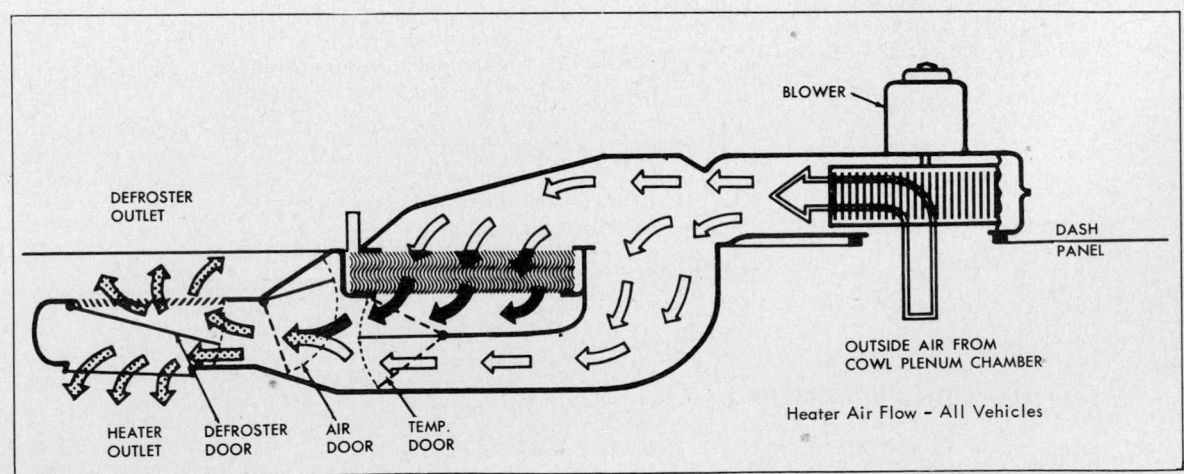

Heater Air Flow - All Vehicles

Chrysler and Chrysler Imperial

Index

YEAR IDENTIFICATION

CHRYSLER

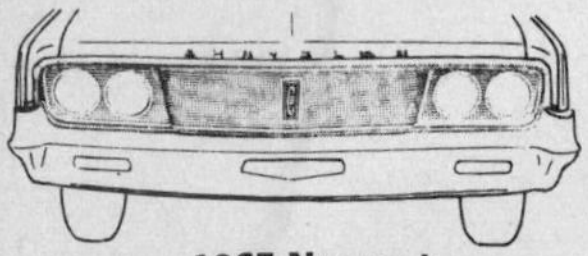

1965 Newport

1965 "300"

1965 New Yorker

1966 Newport

1966 "300"

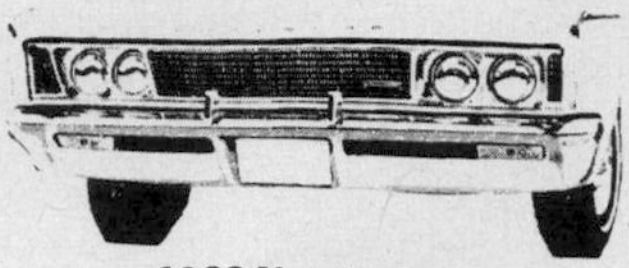

1966 New Yorker

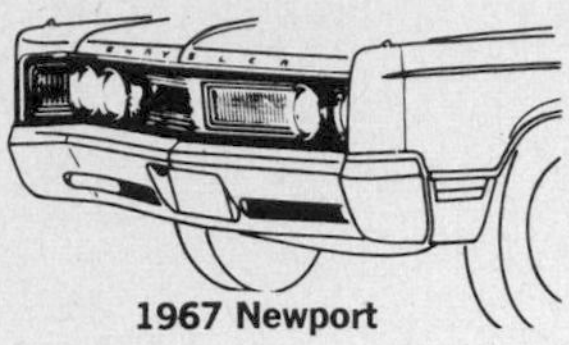

1967 Newport

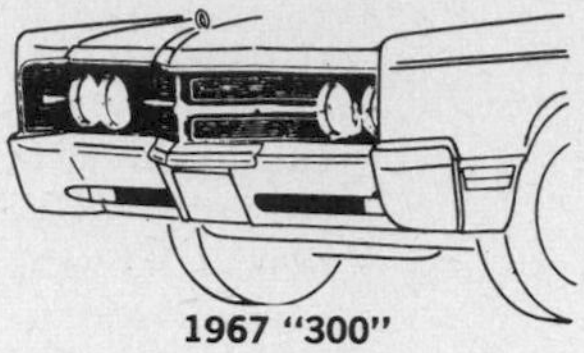

1967 "300"

1967 New Yorker

1968 Newport

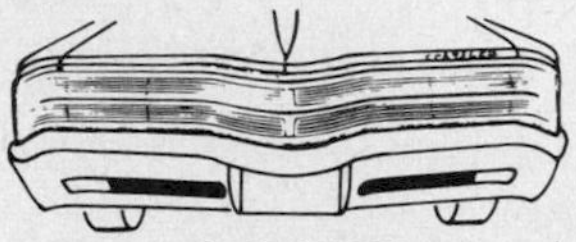

1968 "300"

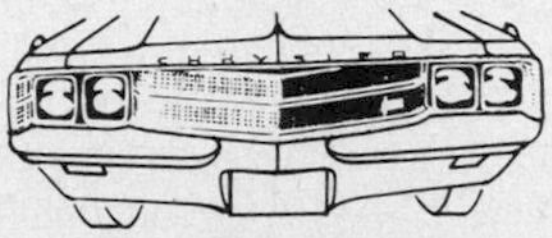

1968 New Yorker

1969 Newport

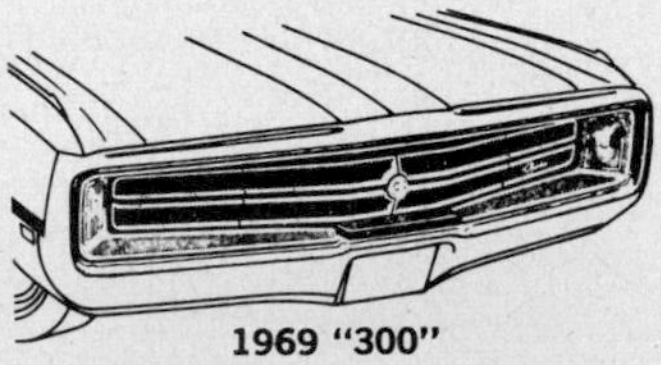

1969 "300"

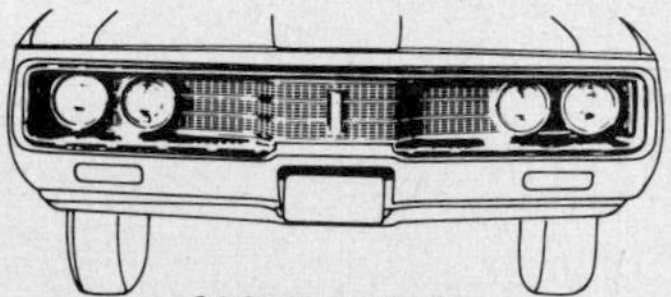

1969 New Yorker

1970 Newport Custom

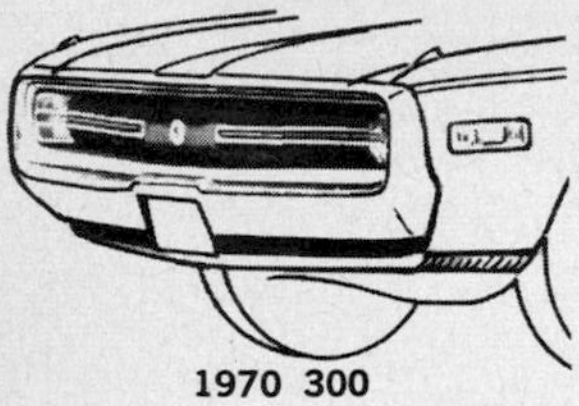

1970 300

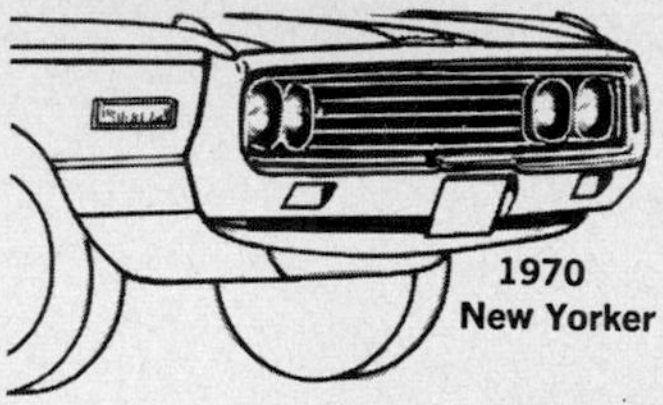

1970 New Yorker

1971 Newport

1972 Newport

1972 New Yorker

IMPERIAL

1965

1966

1967

1968

1969

1970 Imperial LeBaron

1971 Le Baron

1972 Le Baron

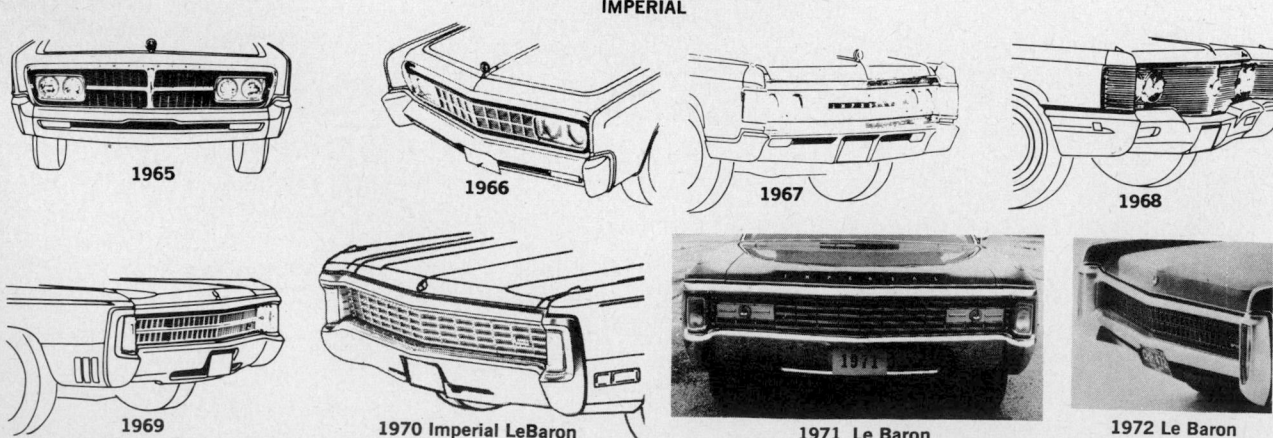

CAR SERIAL NUMBER LOCATION

1965

The vehicle number is located on a metal plate attached to the left front door hinge pillar.

All vehicle numbers contain ten digits. They are interpreted as follows:

First: Make of vehicle.
Second: Model of vehicle.
Third: Year built.
Fourth: Assembly plant. (3 = Detroit; 6 = Delaware)
Last six: Sequence production number.

The starting serial numbers are as follows:

Chrysler Models
AC-1 Newport
.........C1-5 (3 or 6) 100001
AC-2 300 ..C2-5 (3 or 6) 100001
AC-3 New Yorker
.........C3-5 (3 or 6) 100001
AC-2 300L C4-5 (3 or 6) 100001
AC-3 New Yorker (sta. wgn.)
.........C7-5 (3 or 6) 100001
AC-1 Newport (sta. wgn.)
.........C5-5 (3 or 6) 100001
Police
.........C9-5 (3 or 6) 100001

Imperial Models
AY-2 Crown Y2-53100001
AY-3 LeBaron Y3-53100001

1966

Vehicle number location same as 1965. All vehicle numbers now contain thirteen digits. They are interpreted as follows:

First: Car line (make). (C = Chrysler; Y = Imperial)
Second: Price class. (see note 1)
Third: Body type. (see note 2)
Fourth: Body type. (see note 2)
Fifth: Engine displacement. (see note 3)
Sixth: Model year.
Seventh: Assembly plant. (3 = Jefferson, 6 = Newark, 8 = Export)
Last six: Production sequence number.
Note 1: E = economy; L = low; M = medium; H = high; P = premium.
Note 2: 23 = 2-dr. hardtop; 27 = convt.; 41 = 4-dr. sdn.; 42 = 4-dr. town sdn.; 43 = 4-dr. hardtop; 45 = 2-seat sta. wgn.; 46 = 3-seat sta. wgn.
Note 3: F = 383 cu. in.; G = 413 cu. in.; J = 440 cu. in.

Chrysler Models
Newport BC-1
300 ....BC-2
New Yorker BC-3

Imperial Models
Crown BY-3
LeBaron BY-3

1967

Vehicle number location same as 1965. Vehicle number interpretation code same as 1966, with the following exceptions:
(1) Body type 42 is deleted.
(2) G = 383 cu. in.; J = 440 cu. in.; K = Spec. Ord. 8.

1968

Vehicle number is located on a plate on the left side of the instrument panel, visible through the windshield. Vehicle number interpretation code same as 1966, with the following exceptions:
(1) Body type 42 is deleted.
(2) Premium price class is deleted.
(3) G = 383 cu. in.; H = 383 High perf.; K = 440 cu. in.; L = 440 cu. in. high perf.; M = Spec. Ord. 8.
(4) C = Jefferson assembly plant; F = Newark assembly plant.

Chrysler Models
Newport DC-1
Newport Custom DC-1
300 ....DC-2
New Yorker DC-3

Imperial Models
Crown DY-1
LeBaron DY-1

1969-70

Vehicle number location same as 1968. Vehicle number interpretation code same as 1968.

Chrysler Models
Newport
Newport Custom
300
New Yorker
Town and Country

Imperial Models
Imperial

1970

Vehicle number location same as 1968. Vehicle number interpretation code same as 1968.

Chrysler Models
Newport
Newport Custom
300
New Yorker
Town and Country

Imperial
Crown
Le Baron

1971

Vehicle number location same as 1968. Vehicle number interpretation code same as 1968.

Chrysler Models
Newport
Newport Custom
300
New Yorker
Town and Country

Imperial
Le Baron

FIRING ORDER

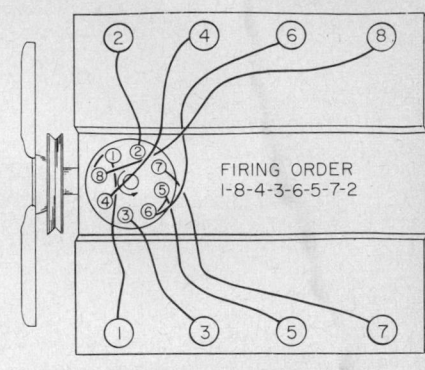

FIRING ORDER
1-8-4-3-6-5-7-2

1965-72—all V8

Engine Identification

On 1965-67 engines, the engine number is stamped on a boss on the top of the engine block, in back of the water pump. On 1968 and later engines, the engine number is stamped on the engine block oil pan rail at the left rear corner below the starter opening. Engines are as follows:

1965
Newport, AC-1 383
Chrysler 300, AC-2 383
Chrysler 300L, AC-2 413
New Yorker, AC-3 413
Imperial, AY-1 413

1966
Newport, BC-1 383
Chrysler 300, BC-2 383
New Yorker, BC-3 440
Imperial, BY-1 440

1967
Newport, CC-1 383
Newport Custom, CC-1 383
300, CC-2 440
New Yorker, CC-3 440
Imperial Crown, CY-1 440
Imperial LeBaron, CY-1 440

1968
Newport, DC-1 ....383, 440
Newport Custom, DC-1 .383, 440
300, DC-2 440
New Yorker, DC-3 440
Imperial Crown, DY-1 440
Imperial LeBaron, DY-1 ...440

1969
Newport, LB
  383 cu. in. (2-BBL., std. cam)
Newport, LB
  383 cu. in. (4-BBL., std. cam)
Newport, RB
  440 cu. in. (4-BBL., spl. cam)
300, LB
  440 cu. in. (4-BBL., std. cam)
300, RB
  440 cu. in. (4-BBL., spl. cam)
New Yorker, RB
  440 cu. in. (4-BBL., std. cam)

New Yorker, RB
  440 cu. in. (4-BBL., spl. cam)
Imperial, RB
  440 cu. in. (4-BBL., std. cam)

1970

Newport, Town & Country
  Std. LB, 383, 2-BBL., std. cam,
  single exhaust
  Opt. LB, 383, 4-BBL., std.
  cam, dual exhaust
  Opt. RB, 440, 4-BBL., spec.
  cam, dual exhaust

300
  Std. LB, 440, 4-BBL., std.
  cam, single exhaust
  Opt. RB, 440, 4-BBL., spec.
  cam, dual exhaust
New Yorker
  Std. RB, 440, 4-BBL., std.
  cam, single exhaust
  Opt. RB, 440, 4-BBL., spec.
  cam, dual exhaust
Imperial
  RB, 440, 4-BBL., std. cam,
  single exhaust

1971

Newport, Newport Custom
  Std. LB, 383, 2 BBL., std. cam
  Opt. LB, 383, 4 BBL., spec. cam
  Opt. RB, 440, 4 BBL., spec. cam
300, New Yorker
  Std. RB, 440, 4 BBL., Std. cam
  Opt. RB, 440, 4 BBL., spec. cam
Town and Country
  Std. LB, 383, 2 BBL., std. cam
  Opt. LB, 383, 4 BBL., spec. cam
  Opt. RB, 440, 4 BL., Std. cam
Imperial
  Std. RB, 440, 4 BBL., std. cam

GENERAL ENGINE SPECIFICATIONS

YEAR	CU. IN. DISPLACEMENT	CARBURETOR	ADVERTIZED HORSEPOWER @ RPM	ADVERTIZED TORQUE @ RPM (FT. LBS.)	A.M.A. HORSEPOWER	BORE AND STROKE (IN.)	ADVERTIZED COMPRESSION RATIO	VALVE LIFTER TYPE	NORMAL OIL PRESSURE (PSI)
1965	V8—383	2-BBL.	270 @ 4400	390 @ 2800	57.8	4.250 x 3.375	9.2-1	Hyd.	60
	V8—383	4-BBL.	330 @ 4600	425 @ 2800	57.8	4.250 x 3.375	10.0-1	Hyd.	60
	V8—413	4-BBL.	340 @ 4600	470 @ 2800	56.1	4.188 x 3.750	10.1-1	Hyd.	60
	V8—413	2-4-BBL.	360 @ 4800	470 @ 3200	56.1	4.188 x 3.750	10.1-1	Mech.	60
1966	V8—383	2-BBL.	270 @ 4400	390 @ 2800	57.8	4.250 x 3.375	9.2-1	Hyd.	55
	V8—383	4-BBL.	325 @ 4800	425 @ 2800	57.8	4.250 x 3.375	10.0-1	Hyd.	55
	V8—440	4-BBL.	350 @ 4400	480 @ 2800	59.7	4.320 x 3.750	10.0-1	Hyd.	55
1967	V8—383	2-BBL.	270 @ 4400	390 @ 2800	57.8	4.250 x 3.375	9.2-1	Hyd.	55
	V8—383	4-BBL.	325 @ 4800	425 @ 2800	57.8	4.250 x 3.375	10.0-1	Hyd.	55
	V8—440	4-BBL.	350 @ 4400	480 @ 2800	59.7	4.320 x 3.750	10.0-1	Hyd.	55
	V8—440	4-BBL.	375 @ 4600	480 @ 3200	59.7	4.320 x 3.750	10.0-1	Hyd.	55
1968	V8—383	2-BBL.	290 @ 4400	380 @ 2400	57.8	4.250 x 3.375	9.2-1	Hyd.	55
	V8—383	4-BBL.	330 @ 5000	425 @ 3200	57.8	4.250 x 3.375	10.0-1	Hyd.	55
	V8—440	4-BBL.	350 @ 4400	480 @ 2800	59.7	4.320 x 3.750	10.1-1	Hyd.	55
	V8—440	4-BBL.	375 @ 4600	480 @ 3200	59.7	4.320 x 3.750	10.1-1	Hyd.	55
1969	V8—383	2-BBL.	290 @ 4400	380 @ 2400	57.8	4.250 x 3.375	9.2-1	Hyd.	55
	V8—383	4-BBL.	330 @ 5000	425 @ 3200	57.8	4.250 x 3.375	10.0-1	Hyd.	55
	V8—440	4-BBL.	350 @ 4400	480 @ 2800	59.7	4.320 x 3.375	10.1-1	Hyd.	55
	V8—440	4-BBL.	375 @ 4600	480 @ 3200	59.7	4.320 x 3.375	10.1-1	Hyd.	55
1970	V8—383	2-BBL.	290 @ 4400	390 @ 2800	57.8	4.250 x 3.375	8.7	Hyd.	45-65①
	V8—383	4-BBL.	330 @ 5000	425 @ 3200	57.8	4.250 x 3.375	9.5	Hyd.	45-65①
	V8—440	4-BBL.	350 @ 4400	480 @ 2800	59.7	4.320 x 3.375	9.7	Hyd.	45-65①
	V8—440	4-BBL.	375 @ 4600	480 @ 3200	59.7	4.320 x 3.375	9.7	Hyd.	45-65①
1971	V8—360	2-BBL.	255 @ 4000	360 @ 2400	51.2	4.000 x 3.580	8.7-1	Hyd.	45-65①
	V8—383	2-BBL.	290 @ 4400	390 @ 2800	57.8	4.250 x 3.375	8.7-1	Hyd.	45-65①
	V8—383	4-BBL.	330 @ 5000	425 @ 3200	57.8	4.250 x 3.375	9.5-1	Hyd.	45-65①
	V8—440	4-BBL.	350 @ 4400	480 @ 2800	59.7	4.320 x 3.750	9.7-1	Hyd.	45-65①
	V8—440	4-BBL.	375 @ 4600	480 @ 3200	59.7	4.320 x 3.750	9.5-1	Hyd.	45-65①
1972	V8—360	2-BBL.	175@4000	285@2400	51.2	4.000 x 3.580	8.8-1	Hyd.	45-65①
	V8—400	2-BBL.	190@4400	310@2400	60.3	4.342 x 3.375	8.2-1	Hyd.	45-65①
	V8—440	4-BBL.	225@4400 ②③	345@3200 ②③	59.7	4.320 x 3.750	8.2-1	Hyd.	45-65①

① — @ 2,000 rpm.
② — Calif. emission package: 216 H.P. @ 4400 RPM, 340 ft. lbs. @ 3200 RPM.
③ — Dual snorkel air cleaner: 230 H.P. @ 4400 RPM, 355 ft. lbs. @ 2800 RPM.
   Dual exhaust: 245 H.P. @ 4400 RPM, 360 ft. lbs. @ 3200 RPM.

CRANKSHAFT BEARING JOURNAL SPECIFICATIONS

YEAR	MODEL	MAIN BEARING JOURNALS (IN.)				CONNECTING ROD BEARING JOURNALS (IN.)		
		Journal Diameter	Oil Clearance	Shaft End-Play	Thrust On No.	Journal Diameter	Oil Clearance	End-Play
1965	V8—383 Cu. In.	2.625	.0010	.0045	3	2.375	.0010	.013
	V8—413 Cu. In.	2.750	.0010	.0045	3	2.375	.0010	.013
1966-72	V8—360 Cu. In.	2.810	.0005-.0025	.002-.007	3	2.125	.0005-.0020	.010-.018
	V8—383 Cu. In.	2.625	.0005-.0020	.002-.007	3	2.38	.0005-.0020	.009-.017
	V8—400 Cu. In.	2.625	.0005-.0020	.002-.007	3	2.375	.0005-.0025	.009-.017
	V8—440 Cu. In.	2.750	.0005-.0020	.002-.010	3	2.38	.0007-.0032	.009-.017

TUNE-UP SPECIFICATIONS

YEAR	MODEL	SPARK PLUGS		DISTRIBUTOR		IGNITION TIMING (Deg.) ▲	CRANKING COMP. PRESSURE (Psi)	VALVES		Intake Opens (Deg.)	FUEL PUMP PRESSURE (Psi)	IDLE SPEED (Rpm) ★
		Type	Gap (In.)	Point Dwell (Deg.)	Point Gap (In.)			Tappet (Hot) Clearance (In.) Intake	Exhaust			
1965	V8—383 Cu. In.; Std.	J14Y	.035	30°	.017	10B	140	Zero	Zero	13B	4½	500
	V8—383 Cu. In.; Hi. Perf.	J10Y	.035	30°	.017	10B	150	Zero	Zero	24B	4½	500
	V8—413 Cu. In.	J12Y	.035	30°	.017	10B	150	Zero	Zero	24B	4½	500
	V8—413 Cu. In.; Hi. Perf.	J10Y	.035	①	.017	10B	150	.015	.024	25B	4½	500
1966	V8—383 Cu. In.; Std., 2-BBL.	J14Y	.035	30°	.017	12½B⊚	140	Zero	Zero	13B	4½	500②
	V8—383 Cu. In.; 4-BBL.	J13Y	.035	30°	.017	12½B⊚	150	Zero	Zero	18B	4½	500②
	V8—440 Cu. In.; 4-BBL.	J13Y	.035	30°	.017	12½B⊚	150	Zero	Zero	18B	4½	500②
1967	V8—383 Cu. In.; Std. 2-BBL.	J14Y	.035	30°	.017	12½B⊚	145	Zero	Zero	16B	4½	500②
	V8—383 Cu. In.; 4-BBL.	J13Y	.035	30°	.017	12½B⊚	145	Zero	Zero	16B	4½	500②
	V8—440 Cu. In.; 4-BBL.	J13Y	.035	30°	.017	12½B⊚	145	Zero	Zero	18B	4½	500②
	V8—440 Cu. In.; Hi. Perf.	J11Y	.035	30°	.017	12½B⊚	145	Zero	Zero	19B	4½	500②
1958	V8—383 Cu. In.; 2-BBL., M.T.	J14Y	.035	30°	.017	TDC	145	Zero	Zero	18B	4½	650
	V8—383 Cu. In.; 2-BBL., A.T.	J14Y	.035	30°	.017	7½B	145	Zero	Zero	18B	4½	650
	V8—383 Cu. In.; 4-BBL. M.T.	J11Y	.035	30°	.017	5B	145	Zero	Zero	18B	4½	650
	V8—383 Cu. In.; 4-BBL., A.T.	J11Y	.035	30°	.017	TDC	145	Zero	Zero	18B	4½	650
	V8—440 Cu. In., M.T.	J13Y	.035	30°	.017	TDC	145	Zero	Zero	18B	4½	650
	V8—440 Cu. In., A.T.	J13Y	.035	30°	.017	7½B	145	Zero	Zero	18B	4½	600
	V8—440 Cu. In.; Hi. Perf.	J11Y	.035	30°	.017	5B	145	Zero	Zero	21B	4½	650
1969	V8—383 Cu. In.; 2-BBL., M.T.	J14Y	.035	32°	.017	TDC	145	Zero	Zero	18B	4½	650
	V8—383 Cu. In.; 2-BBL., A.T.	J14Y	.035	32°	.017	7½B	145	Zero	Zero	18B	4½	650
	V8—383 Cu. In.; 4-BBL., A.T.	J11Y	.035	32°	.017	5B	145	Zero	Zero	18B	4½	650
	V8—440 Cu. In.	J13Y	.035	32°	.017	7½B	145	Zero	Zero	18B	4½	650
	V8—440 Cu. In.; Hi. Perf.	J11Y	.035	32°	.017	5B	145	Zero	Zero	21B	4½	650
1970	V8—383 Cu. In.; 2-BBL., M.T.	J14Y	.035	28.5-32.5⑤	.016-.021	10B⑦	100③	Zero	Zero	18B	3½-5	750
	V8—383 Cu. In.; 2-BBL., A.T.	J14Y	.035	28.5-32.5⑤	.016-.021	12½B⑦	100③	Zero	Zero	18B	3½-5	650
	V8—383 Cu. In.; 4-BBL., A.T.	J11Y	.035	28.5-32.5⑤	.016-.021	12½B④⑦	110③	Zero	Zero	18B	3½-5	700
	V8—440 Cu. In.	J13Y	.035	28.5-32.5⑤	.016-.021	12½B④⑦	110③	Zero	Zero	18B	3½-5	650
	V8—440 Cu. In.; Hi. Perf.	J11Y	.035	28.5-32.5⑤	.016-.021	12½B④⑦	110③	Zero	Zero	21B	3½-5	800
1971	V8—360 Cu. In.; M.T.	N10Y	.035	28.5-32.5⑤	.016-.021	2.5B⑥	100③	Zero	Zero	16B	3½-5	750
	V8—360 Cu. In.; A.T.	N10Y	.035	28.5-32.5⑤	.016-.021	2.5B⑥	100③	Zero	Zero	16B	3½-5	700
	V8—383 Cu. In.; 2-BBL., M.T.	J14Y	.035	28.5-32.5⑤	.016-.021	2.5B⑥	100③	Zero	Zero	18B	3½-5	750
	V8—383 Cu. In.; 2-BBL., A.T.	J14Y	.035	28.5-32.5⑤	.016-.021	2.5B⑥	100③	Zero	Zero	18B	3½-5	700
	V8—383 Cu. In.; 4-BBL., A.T.	J11Y	.035	28.5-32.5⑤	.016-.021	2.5B⑥	110③	Zero	Zero	18B	3½-5	700
	V8—440 Cu. In. Std.	J13Y	.035	28.5-32.5⑤	.016-.021	2.5B⑥	110③	Zero	Zero	18B	3½-5	750
	V8—440 Cu. In.; Hi. Perf.	J11Y	.035	28.5-32.5⑤	.016-.021	5B⑥	110③	Zero	Zero	21B	3½-5	800
1972	V8—360 Cu. In.	N13Y	.035	28.5-32.5①⑨	.014-.019⑦	TDC⑦	100⑦	Zero	Zero	16B	5-7	750⑩
	V8—400 Cu. In.; 2-BBL.	J11Y	.035	28.5-32.5⑨	.016-.021⑨	5B⑥	100③	Zero	Zero	18B	3½-5	700⑩
	V8—440 Cu. In.; 4-BBL. (Calif.)	J11Y	.035	⑨	⑨	⑧⑥	100③	Zero	Zero	18B	3½-5	700⑩
	V8—440 Cu. In.; 4-BBL.	J11Y	.035	28.8-32.5⑤⑨	.016-.021⑨	⑧⑥	110③	Zero	Zero	18B	3½-5	750⑩

▲ With vacuum advance disconnected and plugged. Ignition timing values may vary from state to state due to state and federal exhaust emission standards. See engine decal for confirmation of timing data.

⊚—1966 with Cleaner Air Package (California). Set at 5°A. 1967, manual transmission TDC; automatic transmission 5°B.

①—With double point set, total cam angle = 34°.

②—With Cleaner Air Package, 625 rpm.

③—Minimum.

④—10B for M.T.

⑤—When setting dwell, disconnect vacuum advance line and distributor solenoid.

⑥—When timing engine, disconnect vacuum advance line only

⑦—When timing engine, disconnect vacuum advance line and distributor solenoid wire.

⑧—With dist. 3656341: 10°B; With dist. 3656347: 5°B.

⑨—Electronic ignition std. in Calif. and on Imperial, optional rest of U.S.A.

⑩—See decal for idle speed adjusting procedure.

A—After top dead center.
B—Before top dead center.
TDC—Top dead center.
A.T.—Automatic transmission.
M.T.—Manual transmission.
★—See text for procedure.

CAUTION

General adoption of anti-pollution laws has changed the design of almost all car engine production to effectively reduce crankcase emission and terminal exhaust products. It has been necessary to adopt stricter tune-up rules, especially timing and idle speed procedures. Both of these values are peculiar to the engine and to its application, rather than to the engine alone. With this in mind, car manufacturers supply idle speed data for the engine and application involved. This information is clearly displayed in the engine compartment of each vehicle.

GENERAL CHASSIS AND BRAKE SPECIFICATIONS

| YEAR | MODEL | CHASSIS | | BRAKE CYLINDER BORE | | | BRAKE DRUM | |
| | | Overall Length (In.) | Tire Size | Master Cylinder (In.) | Wheel Cylinder Diameter (In.) | | Diameter (In.) | |
					Front	Rear	Front	Rear
1965	Newport sed.	218.2	8.25 x 14	1.0	1.125	.9375	11	11
	Npt. St. W., 300 & N.Y. sdn.	218.2⑤	8.55 x 14	1.0	1.125	.9375	11	11
	New Yorker, sta. wag.	219.0	8.85 x 14	1.0	1.125	.9375	11	11
	Imperial	227.8	9.15 x 15	1.0	1.125	.9375	11	11
1966	Newport	218.2	8.25 x 14①	1.0	1.125	.9375	11	11
	"300"	218.2	8.55 x 14	1.0	1.125	.9375	11	11
	New Yorker	218.2	8.55 x 14	1.0	1.125	.9375	11	11
	Newport & N.Y. sta. wag.	219.0	9.00 x 14	1.0	1.125	.9375	11	11
	Imperial	227.0	9.15 x 15	1.0	1.125	.9375	11	11
	All with Disc. Brake	—	8.45 x 15①	1.125	2.375	.8750	11.87	11
1967	Newport	219.3	8.25 x 14	1.0	1.125④	.9375	11②	11
	New Yorker	219.3	8.55 x 14	1.0	1.125④	.9375	11②	11
	"300"	223.4	8.55 x 14	1.0	1.125④	.9375	11②	11
	Imperial	224.7	9.15 x 15	1.0③	1.125④	.9375	11②	11
	Sta. Wag., 2 Seat	219.5	8.85 x 15	1.0③	1.125④	.9375	11②	11
	Sta. Wag., 3 Seat	220.3	8.85 x 15	1.0③	1.125④	.9375	11②	11
1968	Newport	219.2	8.55 x 14	1.0	1.125	.9375	11	11
	New Yorker	219.2	8.55 x 14	1.0	1.125	.9375	11	11
	"300"	221.7	8.55 x 14	1.0	1.125	.9375	11	11
	Imperial (Disc.)	224.5	9.15 x 15	1.125	2.375	.9375	11.76	11
	Sta. Wag., 2 Seat	219.5	8.85 x 14	1.0	1.125	.9375	11	11
	Sta. Wag., 3 seat	220.3	8.85 x 14	1.0	1.125	.9375	11	11
	Disc. Brakes (exc. wag.)	—	8.45 x 15	1.125	2.375	.9375	11.76	11
	Disc. Brakes (sta. wag.)	—	8.85 x 15	1.125	2.375	.9375	11.76	11
1969	Newport	224.7	8.55 x 15	1.0	1.125	.9375	11	11
	New Yorker	224.7	8.55 x 15	1.0	1.125	.9375	11	11
	"300"	224.7	8.55 x 15	1.0	1.125	.9375	11	11
	Imperial (Disc.)	229.7	9.15 x 15	1.125	2.375	.9375	11.76	11
	Disc. Brakes exc. wag.	—	8.45 x 15	1.0	2.375	.9375	11.76	11
	Disc. Brakes sta. wag.	—	8.85 x 15	1.125	2.375	.9375	11.76	11
1970	Newport	224.7	H78 x 15	1.0	1.187	.9375	11	11
	New Yorker	224.7	J78 x 15	1.0	1.187	.9375	11	11
	"300"	224.7	H78 x 15	1.0	1.187	.9375	11	11
	Imperial (Disc.)	229.7	L84 x 15	1.125	2.75	.9375	11.75	11
	Disc. Brakes	—	—	1.125	2.75	.9375	11.75	11
	Sta. wagon	224.8	L84 x 15	1.0	1.125	.9375	11	11
1971	Newport, 300	224.6	H78 x 15	1.03	1.187⑥	.9375	11⑦	11
	New Yorker (Disc.)	224.6	J78 x 15	1.03	2.75	.9375	11.75	11
	Sta. Wag. (Disc.)	224.8	L84 x 15	1.03	2.75	.9375	11.75	11
	Imperial (Disc.)	229.7	L84 x 15	1.125	2.75	.9375	11.75	11
1972	Newport Royal	224.1	⑧	1.03	2.75	.9375	11.6⑨	11
	Newport Custom	224.1	⑧	1.03	2.75	.9375	11.6⑨	11
	New Yorker	224.9	⑧	1.03	2.75	.9375	11.6⑨	11
	Town & Country	224.8	L84 x 15	1.03	2.75	.9375	11.6⑨	11
	New Yorker Brougham	224.9	⑧	1.03	2.75	.9375	11.6⑨	11
	Imperial LeBaron	229.5	L84 x 15	1.03	2.75	.9375	11.6⑨	11

① —Disc. Brakes—Sedans & Conv. 8.15 x 15, w/AC 8.45 x 15.
② —Disc. Brakes—11.87
③ —Disc. Brakes—1⅛
④ —Disc. Brakes—2.375
⑤ —Newport Sta. Wag.—219.0

⑥ —Disc. Brakes—2.75
⑦ —Disc. Brakes—11.75
⑧ —With 360 V8: G78 x 15 std.; with 400 V8: H78 x 15 std.; with 440 V8: J78 x 15 std.
⑨ —Disc brakes std. starting 1972.

WHEEL ALIGNMENT

YEAR	MODEL	CASTER Range (Deg.)	CASTER Pref. Setting (Deg.)	CAMBER Range (Deg.)	CAMBER Pref. Setting (Deg.)	TOE-IN (In.)	KING-PIN INCLINATION (Deg.)	WHEEL PIVOT RATIO Inner Wheel	WHEEL PIVOT RATIO Outer Wheel
1965	Manual Steering	1N-0	½N	①	①	3/32-5/32	5-7	21½	20
	Power Steering	¼P-1¼P	¾P	①	①	3/32-5/32	5-7	21½	20
1966	Manual Steering	1N-0	½N	②	②	3/32-5/32	7½③	20	18.8④
	Power Steering	¼P-1¼P	¾P	②	②	3/32-5/32	7½③	20	18.8④
1967	Chrysler, Manual	1N-0	½N	②	②	3/32-5/32	7½	20	18.8
	Chrysler, Power	¼P-1¼P	¾P	②	②	3/32-5/32	7½	20	18.8
	Imperial, Power	¼P-1¼P	¾P	②	②	3/32-5/32	9	20	17.9
1968	Manual Steering	1N-0	½N	②	②	3/32-5/32	7½③	20	18.8
	Power Steering	¼P-1¼P	¾P	②	②	3/32-5/32	7½⑤	20	18.8⑥
1969	Man, Pow. exc. Imperial	1N-0	½N	②	②	3/32-5/32	7½⑤	20	18.8
	Power Steering Imperial	¼P-1¼P	¾P	②	②	3/32-5/32	9	20	17.9
1970-72	Manual Steering	½N ± 9/16	½N	⑦	⑧	⅛ ± 1/16	9	20	18.8
	Power Steering—Chrysler	½N ± 9/16 ⑨	½N	⑦	⑧	⅛ ± 1/16	9	20	18.8
	Power Steering—Imperial	¾P ± 9/16	¾P	⑦	⑧	⅛ ± 1/16	9	20	17.9

①—Camber range and preferred setting: Set right side at ⅛N-⅛P with 0 preferred. Set left side at ⅛P to ⅜P with ¼ preferred.
②—Left side—P¼ to P¾. Preferred P½. Right side—0 to P½. Preferred P¼.
③—Imperial 6½ degrees.
④—Imperial 18.5 degrees.
⑤—Imperial 9 degrees.
⑥—Imperial 17.9.
⑦—Left side—½P ± ¼; Right side—¼P ± ¼.
⑧—Left side—½P; Right side—¼P.
⑨—1971-72—¾P + ½
N—Negative.
P—Positive.

VALVE SPECIFICATIONS

YEAR AND MODEL		SEAT ANGLE (DEG.)	FACE ANGLE (DEG.)	VALVE LIFT INTAKE (IN.)	VALVE LIFT EXHAUST (IN.)	VALVE SPRING PRESSURE (VALVE OPEN) LBS. @ IN.	VALVE SPRING INSTALLED HEIGHT (IN.)	STEM TO GUIDE CLEARANCE INTAKE	STEM TO GUIDE CLEARANCE EXHAUST	STEM DIAMETER INTAKE	STEM DIAMETER EXHAUST
1965	V8-383	45	45	.392	.390	195 @ 1 15/32	1⅞	.001-.003	.002-.004	.372-.373	.371-.372
	V8-413 Std.	45	45	.430	.430	195 @ 1 15/32	1⅞	.001-.003	.002-.004	.372-.373	.371-.372
	V8-413 Hi. Perf.	45	45	.444	.450	225 @ 1 7/16	1⅞	.001-.003	.002-.004	.372-.373	.371-.372
1966	V8-383, 2-BBL.	45	45	.392	.390	195 @ 1 15/32	1 55/64	.001-.003	.002-.004	.372-.373	.371-.372
	V8-383, 440, 4-BBL.	45	45	.425	.435	200 @ 1 7/16	1 55/64	.001-.003	.002-.004	.372-.373	.371-.372
1967	V8-383, 2-BBL.	45	45	.425	.435	200 @ 1 7/16	1 55/64	.001-.003	.002-.004	.372-.373	.371-.372
	V8-383, 440, 4-BBL.	45	45	.425	.435	200 @ 1 7/16	1 55/64	.001-.003	.002-.004	.372-.373	.371-.372
	V8-440, 4-BBL. Hi. Perf.	45	45	.450	.458	246 @ 1 23/64	1 55/64	.001-.003	.002-.004	.372-.373	.371-.372
1968-69	V8-383, 2-BBL.	45	45	.425	.435	200 @ 1 7/16	1 55/64	.001-.003	.002-.004	.372-.373	.371-.372
	V8-383, 4-BBL.	45	45	.425	.435	200 @ 1 7/16	1 55/64	.001-.003	.002-.004	.372-.373	.371-.372
	V8-440	45	43	.425	.435	200 @ 1 7/16	1 55/64	.001-.003	.002-.004	.372-.373	.371-.372
	V8-440 Hi. Perf.	45	45	.450	.458	230 @ 1 13/32	1 55/64	.001-.003	.002-.004	.372-.373	.371-.372
1970	V8-383, 2-BBL.	45	45	.425	.437	200 @ 1 7/16	1 55/64	.001-.003	.002-.004	.372-.373	.371-.372
	V8-383, 4-BBL.	45	45	.425	.437	234 @ 1 7/16	1 55/64	.001-.003	.002-.004	.372-.373	.371-.372
	V8-440	45	45	.425	.437	234 @ 1 7/16	1 55/64	.001-.003	.002-.004	.372-.373	.371-.372
	V8-440 Hi. Perf.	45	45	.450	.458	234 @ 1 7/16	1 55/64	.001-.003	.002-.004	.372-.373	.371-.372
1971	V8-360, 2-BBL.	①	①	.410	.412	189 @ 1 9/32	1 41/64	.001-.003	.002-.004	.372-.373	.371-.372
	V8-383, 2-BBL.	44½-45	45-45½	.425	.437	200 @ 1 27/64	1 55/64	.001-.003	.002-.004	.372-.373	.371-.372
	V8-383, 4-BBL.	44½-45	45-45½	.450	.437	234 @ 1 25/64	1 55/64	.001-.003	.002-.004	.372-.373	.371-.372
	V8-400	44½-45	45-45½	.434	.434	200 @ 1 7/16	1 55/64	.001-.003	.002-.004	.372-.373	.371-.372
	V8-440	44½-45	45-45½	.425	.437	234 @ 1 25/64	1 55/64	.001-.003	.002-.004	.372-.373	.371-.372
	V8-440, Hi. Perf.	44½-45	45-45½	.450	.465	234 @ 1 25/64	1 55/64	.001-.003	.002-.004	.372-.373	.371-.372
1972	V8-360	①	①	.410	.412	195 @ 1 15/64	1 21/32	.001-.003	.002-.004	.372-.373	.371-.372
	V8-400	44½-45	45-45½	.434	.430	200 @ 1 27/64	1 55/64	.001-.003	②	.372-.373	③
	V8-440	44½-45	45-45½	.434	.430	200 @ 1 27/64	1 55/64	.001-.003	②	.372-.373	③

①—Intake: seat 44½-45, face 45-45½. Exhaust: seat 44½-45, face 47-47½.
②—Hot end: .002-.0037. Cold end: .001-.0027.
③—Hot end: .3713-.3720. Cold end: .3723-.3730.

AC GENERATOR AND REGULATOR SPECIFICATIONS

YEAR	MODEL	ALTERNATOR			REGULATOR			
		Field Current Draw @ 12 V.	Current Output	Model	Point Gap (in.)	Air Gap (In.)	Voltage at 140°F.
1965-67	Standard	2.3-2.7	35 Amp.	2098300	.015	.050	13.4-14.0
	Heavy Duty	2.3-2.7	40 Amp.	2098300	.015	.050	13.4-14.0
1968-69	Standard	2.3-2.7	37 Amp.	2098300	.015	.050	13.4-14.0
	W/Air Cond.	2.3-2.7	46 Amp.	2098300	.015	.050	13.4-14.0
1970-71	Standard	2.38-2.75	34.5 ± 3 Amp.	3438150	-----Not Adjustable-----		13.3-14.0
	Heavy Duty and/or Air. Cond.	2.38-2.75	44.5 ± 3 Amp.	3438150	-----Not Adjustable-----		13.3-14.0
1972	3438804 (Chrysler)	2.4-2.7	41 Amp.	3438150	-----Not Adjustable-----		13.8-14.4①
	3438811 (Imperial)	2.4-2.7	50 Amp.	3438150	-----Not Adjustable-----		13.8-14.4①

① — @ 80°F.

BATTERY AND STARTER SPECIFICATIONS

YEAR	MODEL	BATTERY			STARTERS						Brush Spring Tension (Oz.)
					Lock Test		No-Load Test				
		Ampere Hour Capacity	Volts	Terminal Grounded	Amps.	Volts	Torque	Amps.	Volts	RPM	
1965-66	①	59	12	Neg.	400	4.0	8.5	78	11.0	3,800	34
	②	70	12	Neg.	450	4.0	24.0	90	11.0	2,175	34
1967-69	383, 440—W.O./Air Cond.	59	12	Neg.	425	4.0	24.0	90	11.0	2,300	40
	All others	70	12	Neg.	425	4.0	24.0	90	11.0	2,300	40
1970-72	360, 383, 400 V8	59	12	Neg.	400-450	4.0	—	90	11.0	1,925-2,600	32-36
	440 V8	70	12	Neg.	400-450	4.0	—	90	11.0	1,925-2,600	32-36

① — Except New Yorker, Imperial and 300 hi. perf.
② — New Yorker, Imperial and 300 hi. perf.

CAPACITIES

YEAR	MODEL	ENGINE CRANKCASE ADD 1 Qt. FOR NEW FILTER	TRANSMISSIONS Pts. TO REFILL AFTER DRAINING			DRIVE AXLE (Pts.)	GASOLINE TANK (Gals.)	COOLING SYSTEM (Qts.) WITH HEATER
			Manual ③		Automatic			
			3-Speed	4-Speed				
1965	Town & Country	4	5	7½	19½	4	22	17
	Imperial	5	None	None	19½	4	23	17
	Others	4	5	7½	19½	4	25	17
1966	Imperial	5	None	None	18½	4	23	18
	Town & Country	4	6	None	18½	4	22	17
	Others	4	6	None	18½	4	25	17
1967	Imperial	5	None	None	18½	4	25	18
	Town & Country	4	None	None	18½	4	22	17
	Others	4	6½	None	18½	4	25	17
1968	Imperial	4	None	None	18½	4	24	18②
	Town & Country	4	None	None	18½	4	22	17②
	Others	4	6	None	18½	4	24	17②
1969	Imperial	4	None	None	18½	4	24	19②
	Town & Country	4	None	None	18½	4	23	17③
	Others	4	6	None	18½	4	24	17②
1970	Imperial	4	None	None	19	4.4	24	⑥
	440 Hi. Perf.	6	None	None	19	4.4	⑤	⑥
	Others	4	4¾	None	④	4.4	⑤	⑥
1971	Imperial	4	None	None	19	4.5	23	17.5
	Chrysler	4	4¾	None	④	4.5	23	⑦
1972	Imperial	4	None	None	19	4.5	23	16
	Chrysler	4	None	None	⑧	4.5	23	16

② — Add 1½ qts. for rear seat heater.
③ — Use SAE 80 or 90 gear oil in warm weather. For year-round use, it is permissible to use automatic transmission fluid, type A, suffix A.
④ — 383 2-BBL.—19; 383 4-BBL;—16; 440—19, 360—16.
⑤ — Exc. sta. wag.—24; sta. wag.—23.

⑥ — 383 2-BBL.—14.5; w/AC—16; Chrysler 383 4-BBL. and all 440—15.5; w/AC—17; Imperial—16.5.
⑦ — 360—15.5, w/AC—16; 383 and 400—14.5, w/AC 15; 440—15.5, w/AC 17.
⑧ — 360—16.3; 400—19.0.

TORQUE SPECIFICATIONS

YEAR	MODEL	CYLINDER HEAD BOLTS (FT. LBS.)	ROD BEARING BOLTS (FT. LBS.)	MAIN BEARING BOLTS (FT. LBS.)	CRANKSHAFT BALANCER BOLT (FT. LBS.)	FLYWHEEL TO CRANKSHAFT BOLTS (FT. LBS.)	MANIFOLD (FT. LBS.)	
							Intake	Exhaust
1965–72	V8—All except 360 Cu. In.	65–75	40–45	80–85	▲	55–65	40	30
1971–72	V8—360 Cu. In.	95	45	85	*	55	35	30

▲—Crankshaft Pulley Bolt:
Vibration damper bolts—15 ft. lbs. for 1965-69; 9 ft. lbs. for 1970-72.
Bolt in end of crankshaft—135 ft. lbs.

*—Crankshaft pulley bolt:
Vibration damper bolts—200 in. lbs.
Bolt in end of crankshaft—135 ft. lbs.

CYLINDER HEAD BOLT TIGHTENING SEQUENCE

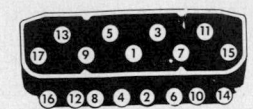

1965-72—all V8 except 360

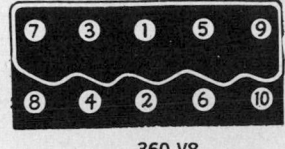

360 V8

FUSES AND CIRCUIT BREAKERS

1965–69

Lighting system . . . . 15 Amp. CB
Top, power windows, power seats . . . . 30 Amp. CB
Dome, stop, trunk, park, tail lamps . . . . 20 Amp. Fuse
Cigarette lighter, glove compartment . . . . . . 20 Amp. Fuse
Instrument panel lamps . . . . 2 Amp. Fuse
Air conditioner or heater . . . . 20 Amp. Fuse
Air conditioner, rear . . . . 20 Amp. CB
Windshield wiper (1-speed) Chrys. . . . . 5 Amp. CB
Windshield wiper (2-speed) Chrys. . . . . 7 Amp. CB
Windshield wiper (2-speed) Imp. . . . . 6 Amp. CB
Radio . . . . 7½ Amp. Fuse

1970–72

Accessory and turn signal . . . . 20 Amp. (Imperial)
Accessories . . . . 20 Amp. (Chrysler)
Headlight sentinel . . . . 20 Amp.
Cigarette lighter . . . . 20 Amp.

Console . . . . 20 Amp. (Chrysler)
Emergency flasher . . . . 20 Amp. (Chrysler)
Emergency flasher and stop lights . . . . 20 Amp. (Imperial)
Headlight dimmer . . . . 4 Amp.
Heater or A/C blower motor . . . . 20 Amp.
Instrument lights . . . . 5 Amp. (Chrysler)
Instrument lights . . . . 5 Amp. (Imperial)
Low fuel warning relay . . . . 5 Amp. (Imperial)
Radio and back-up lights . . . . 20 Amp.

LIGHT BULBS

1965–69

Electroluminescent lighting used on some of the instruments.

Headlamp (dual type) (inner) . . . . 4001; 37½ W
Headlamp (dual type) (outer) . . . . 4002; 37½–50 W
Beam indicator, glove box, map lamp . . . . 57; 1 CP
Hand brake, warning lamp . . . . 90; 1 CP
Front and rear parking, stop, front and rear
  turn signal lamps . . . . 1034; 32–4 CP
License plate lamp . . . . 67; 3 CP
Map and dome lamps . . . . 1004; 15 CP
Back-up lamps . . . . 1073; 32 CP
Transmission push-button, clock light . . . . 57; 2 CP
Transmission selector, auto-pilot lamps . . . . 1816; 2.85 CP
Radio dial . . . . 1893; 2 CP
Trunk lamp . . . . 1003; 15 CP
Tachometer w/console . . . . 1893; 2 CP

1970

	CHRYSLER	IMPERIAL
Arm rest lamp		1445
Ash Tray	1445(2)	*1445(2)
Auto-temp	*(168)	*(704)
Back-up lights	1156(2)	1156(2)
Brake system warning light . . .	57	57
Clock	*(168)	*(704)
Cornering light	1293	1293

Dome and/or "C" pillar
  light 550
Door and pocket panel
  and/or reading light 90 90
Fasten belts indicator 57 57
Fender mounted turn signal
  indicator . . . . 330(2) . . . 1813(2)
Gear selector indicator
  (column) . . . . *(168) . . . *(704)
Gear selector with console . . . . 57 . . . . —
Glove compartment . . . . 1891 . . . 1891
Heater and/or A/C Control . . . *168 . . . *(704)
High beam indicator 57 57
Instrument cluster and
  speedometer illumination . . *(168) . . . *(704)(4)
Ignition lamp . . . . 1445 . . . 1445
License light . . . . 67(1)-67(2) . 67

	Station Wagon	
Lock doors indicator	158	
Map lamp	90	90
Oil pressure indicator	57	Gauge
Open door indicator		57
Panel rheostat valve	24 Ohms	12 Ohms
Park and turn signal (front) . . .	1157(2)	1157NA
Portable reading light		89
Radio	*(168)	*(704)
Sealed beam—Hi-beam (No. 1) . . .	4001	4001

Sealed beam—Hi-low beam
  (No. 2) . . . . 4002 . . . 4002
Sentry signal 57 57
Side marker . . . . 1895(4) . . 1895(4)
Stereo indicator . . . . 1445 . . . 1445
Switch lighting . . . . *(168) . . *(704)
Tail light (only) . . . . 1095(2) . . 1095
Tail, stop and turn signal . . . . 1157(2) . . 1157(6)
Temperature indicator . . . . 57(2) . . . —
Trunk and/or under hood
  light . . . . 1004 . . . 1004
Turn signal indicator (panel) . . *57-168 . . —

*Included in instrument cluster lighting.

NOTE: All of the above bulbs are brass base. Aluminum base bulbs are not approved and not to be used.

1971–72

Same as 1970 except the following:

Ash Tray	1892(2)	1892(2)
Fasten belt indicator	—	158
High beam indicator	—	158
Lock doors indicator	57	158
Map lamp	57	158
Panel rheostat valve	15.5 Ohms	15.5 Ohms
Trunk and/or under hood light . . .	1003	1003

Distributor

Detailed information, direction of rotation, cylinder numbering, firing order, point gap, point dwell, timing mark location, spark plugs, spark advance and idle speed will be found in the Specifications tables.

Distributor Removal and Installation

Removal Procedure

Disconnect vacuum advance hose and primary wire. Lift off distributor cap. Mark edge of housing to aid in locating position of rotor for reinstalling. Remove the hold-down bolt, lock plate and distributor.

Installation Procedure

If engine has been turned after removal, make sure No. 1 piston is at top dead center and install the distributor so that the rotor is pointing to No. 1 firing position. Install the lock plate and screw, but not tightly. Rotate the crankshaft to align the specified degree mark on the crankshaft pulley with the pointer. Rotate distributor until contacts are opening. Tighten the hold-down bolt and reconnect the primary lead and the vacuum pipe. Check that timing is correct, using a timing light.

Generator, Regulator

Detailed facts on the alternator are in the Alternator and Regulator Specifications table.

General information on generator and regulator repair and troubleshooting is in the Unit Repair Section.

Alternator R&R

1. Disconnect battery ground cable.
2. Disconnect alternator output "BATT" and field "FLD" leads. Disconnect ground wire.
3. Remove mounting bolts. Remove alternator.
4. Reverse procedure for installation. Adjust drive belt to have ¼ in. deflection at the center of the longest run between pulleys.

Caution   Under no circumstances should the alternator circuit be polarized.

Battery, Starter

Detailed information on the battery and starter is found in the Battery and Starter Specifications table.

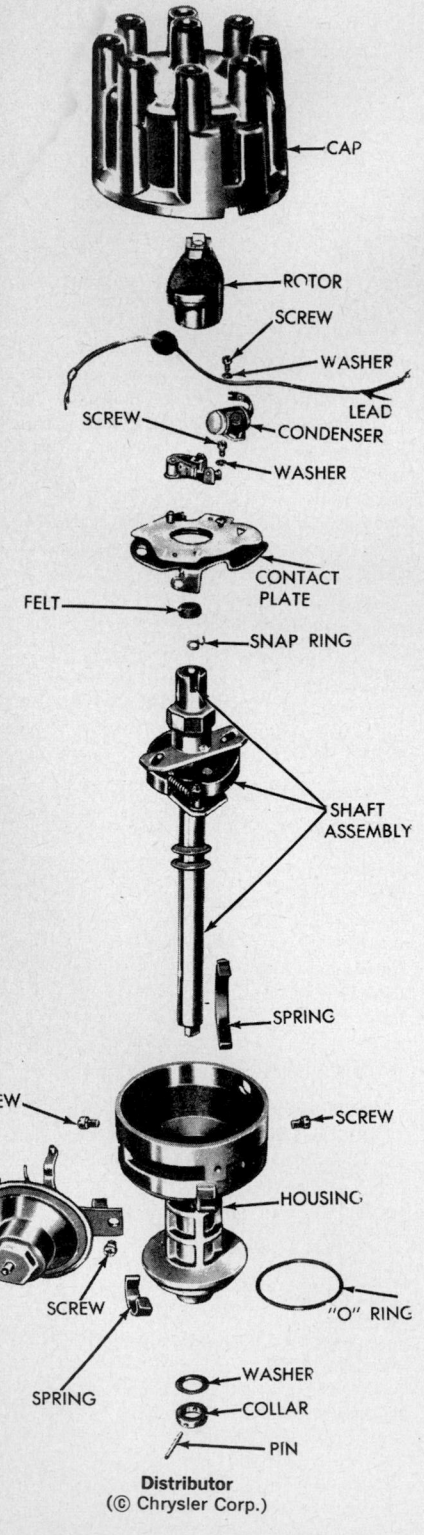

Distributor
(© Chrysler Corp.)

CAP
ROTOR
SCREW
WASHER
LEAD
SCREW
CONDENSER
WASHER
FELT
CONTACT PLATE
SNAP RING
SHAFT ASSEMBLY
SPRING
SCREW
SCREW
HOUSING
SCREW
"O" RING
SPRING
WASHER
COLLAR
PIN

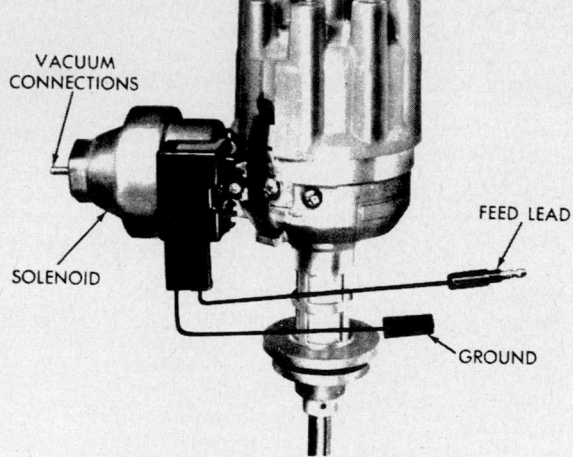

Distributor with solenoid retard mechanism
(© Chrysler Corporation)

VACUUM CONNECTIONS
SOLENOID
FEED LEAD
GROUND

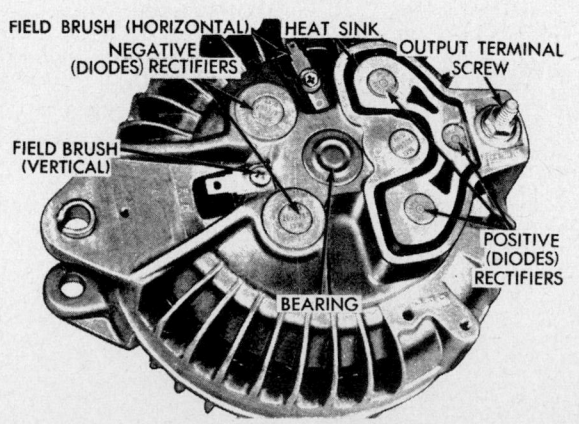

Alternator assembly
(© Chrysler Corporation)

FIELD BRUSH (HORIZONTAL)
HEAT SINK
NEGATIVE (DIODES) RECTIFIERS
OUTPUT TERMINAL SCREW
FIELD BRUSH (VERTICAL)
POSITIVE (DIODES) RECTIFIERS
BEARING

More information can be found in the Unit Repair Section.

Starter R & R

Disconnect battery and starter wires. If equipped with automatic transmission, slide cooler tube bracket off stud. Remove attaching bolts and lift out starter.

Instruments

Instrument Cluster Removal

1965-66 Imperial

The instrument cluster is serviced in three separate sections. When servicing the cluster, it is necessary to remove only the section containing the desired unit.

1. Disconnect the battery ground cable.
2. Remove screws attaching instrument cluster chrome bezel to instrument cluster. Remove bezel.
3. Remove trip odometer knob, clock reset knob, and temperature control level knob.
4. Remove lens from cluster.
5. Remove screws attaching cluster face plate to cluster. Remove face plate.
6. To remove speedometer: Disconnect speedometer and odometer reset cables from under instrument panel. Remove four speedometer to cluster screws. Remove speedometer.
7. To remove printed circuit assembly: Remove assembly to cluster screws. Pull assembly forward. Disconnect printed circuit connector. Remove assembly to service fuel, oil, temperature, and ammeter gauges.
8. To remove clock: Remove screws. Pull clock forward and disconnect wire. Remove clock.
9. To install reverse above procedure.

1967-68 Imperial

1. Disconnect battery ground cable.
2. Tape top of steering column to prevent scratching.
3. Remove four steering column trim plate screws. Remove cover.
4. Loosen allen screw on right underside of steering column. Push gear selector forward and rotate clockwise to remove.
5. Remove steering column upper clamp.
6. Remove air conditioning left spot cooler hose by releasing. alligator clamp at the connection.
7. Remove four upper bezel screws. Remove four lower bezel screws from lower left corner of bezel, each side of steering column, and inside the ash tray.
8. Raise lower edge of bezel. Disconnect electrical connectors. Remove vacuum hose from rear air switch.
9. Remove bezel with spot cooler hose attached.
10. Remove odometer reset cable bezel nut. Push cable up into panel.
11. Remove eight cluster mounting screws. Pull cluster out, bottom edge first. Disconnect printed circuit connector, speedometer cable, and ammeter wires. Remove cluster.
12. Reverse procedure for installation.

1969-70 Imperial

1. Disconnect battery ground cable.
2. Remove left ash tray and radio.
3. Remove heater controls.
4. Disconnect vent control cables at fresh air doors.
5. Remove:

a. vent control.
b. map lamp.
c. lamp panel assembly.
d. cluster accessory bezel.
e. steering column cover.
f. gear shift indicator.
g. steering column clamp.
h. cover screws at floor panel.
6. Lower steering column.
7. Disconnect speedometer cable.
8. Remove five upper cluster mounting screws. Remove five lower cluster mounting screws through access holes in lower instrument panel.
9. Move cluster to the right. Push right end toward front and turn top down. Pull left end of cluster out of panel.
10. Disconnect all wiring and connectors. Remove cluster.
11. Reverse procedure to install.

1971-72 Imperial and Chrysler

1. Remove map lamp panel and map lamp.
2. Remove headlight switch.
3. Remove radio and ATC control.
4. Remove the four screws that attach the steering column cover to the steering column and remove the cover.
5. Remove the gear shift indicator pointer.
6. Remove the three duffy plate mounting screws, the steering column ground wire and attaching nut and the three upper steering column attaching nuts, then, lower the steering column.
7. Disconnect the speedometer cable from the speedometer head.
8. Remove the screw that attaches the ATC in-car sensor to the instrument cluster bezel and remove the sensor housing from the bezel.
9. Remove the clock assembly

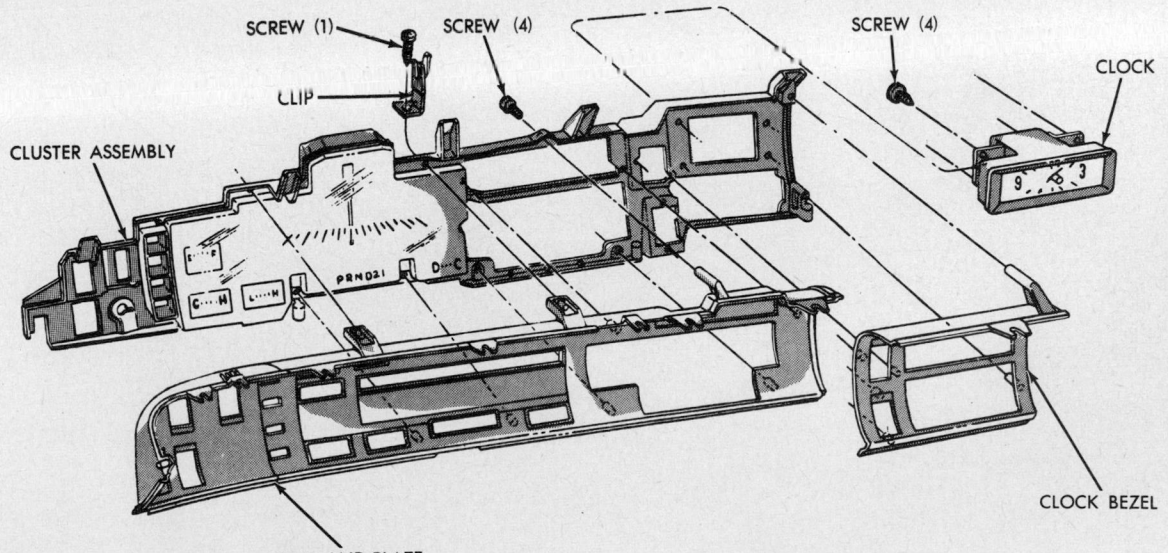

1970 Imperial instrument cluster and bezel (© Chrysler Corporation)

(Imperial only).

10. Working through the access hole in the lower panel, remove the six lower cluster attaching screws.
11. Working over the cluster, remove the five upper cluster attaching screws.
12. Disconnect all accessible electrical connectors from the cluster.
13. To remove the cluster, move it rearward, then, position the cluster so the bottom of the cluster can be removed from the dash in a horizontal position. Disconnect any electrical connectors that are still attached to the cluster as the cluster is removed from the dash.
14. Reverse above procedure to install.

1965-66 Chrysler

1. Disconnect battery ground cable
2. Remove steering column cover.
3. Disconnect gear shift indicator link.
4. Remove column clamp. Loosen column lower support plate. Lower steering column.
5. Remove steering column upper filler.
6. Disconnect speedometer, odometer, and circuit board connector.
7. Remove ignition switch and accessory switch.
8. Remove lower and upper cluster trim bezels.
9. Remove cluster retaining screws. Lower cluster and disconnect ammeter wires. Remove cluster.
10. To install, reverse above procedure.

1967-68 Chrysler

1. Disconnect battery ground cable.
2. Remove steering column cover.
3. Protect steering column.
4. Disconnect gear shift indicator link.
5. Remove column lower support plate bolts. Remove column upper clamp. Lower steering column.
6. Remove warning light bezel mounting screws. Pull bezel out slightly. Disconnect wiring. Remove bezel.
7. Remove four upper and four lower screws from instrument cluster bezel. Pull bezel out slightly. Disconnect electrical connectors. Remove bezel.
8. Disconnect odometer reset cable and speedometer cable.
9. Remove eight cluster mounting screws.
10. Pull cluster out to disconnect ammeter, gas gauge, clock, and cluster lighting lamps. Remove cluster.
11. Reverse procedure to install.

1969-70 Chrysler

1. Disconnect battery ground cable.
2. Remove lower steering column cover.
3. Remove gear shift indicator pointer.
4. Disconnect turn signal wiring connector.
5. Remove three outside floor plate mounting bolts, ground strap from steering column support, and three steering column clamp support nuts. Lower steering column.
6. Remove left ash tray and radio.
7. Remove heater controls and vent controls.
8. Remove map lamp and lamp panel.
9. From under instrument panel, remove four mounting screws from right end accessory switch cover.
10. Disconnect speedometer cable.
11. Remove wiring harness from clip on left of column support.
12. Remove four upper cluster mounting screws. Remove four lower cluster mounting screws through access holes in the lower panel.
13. Move cluster right, rotating the right end of cluster toward front and down. Roll top of cluster down and rock slightly to the left. Disconnect wiring. Roll cluster out from instrument panel.
14. Reverse procedure for installation.

Ignition Switch Replacement

1965-66 Imperial

1. Remove lower steering column cover plate.
2. Remove accessory switch knobs.
3. Remove screw attaching left end of bezel to instrument panel. This screw may be reached from inside steering column opening.
4. Remove screw in switch well.
5. Lift off bezel.
6. Remove mounting nut from ignition switch.
7. From under panel, pull switch down, disconnect wiring and remove switch from under panel.
8. Install in reverse of above.

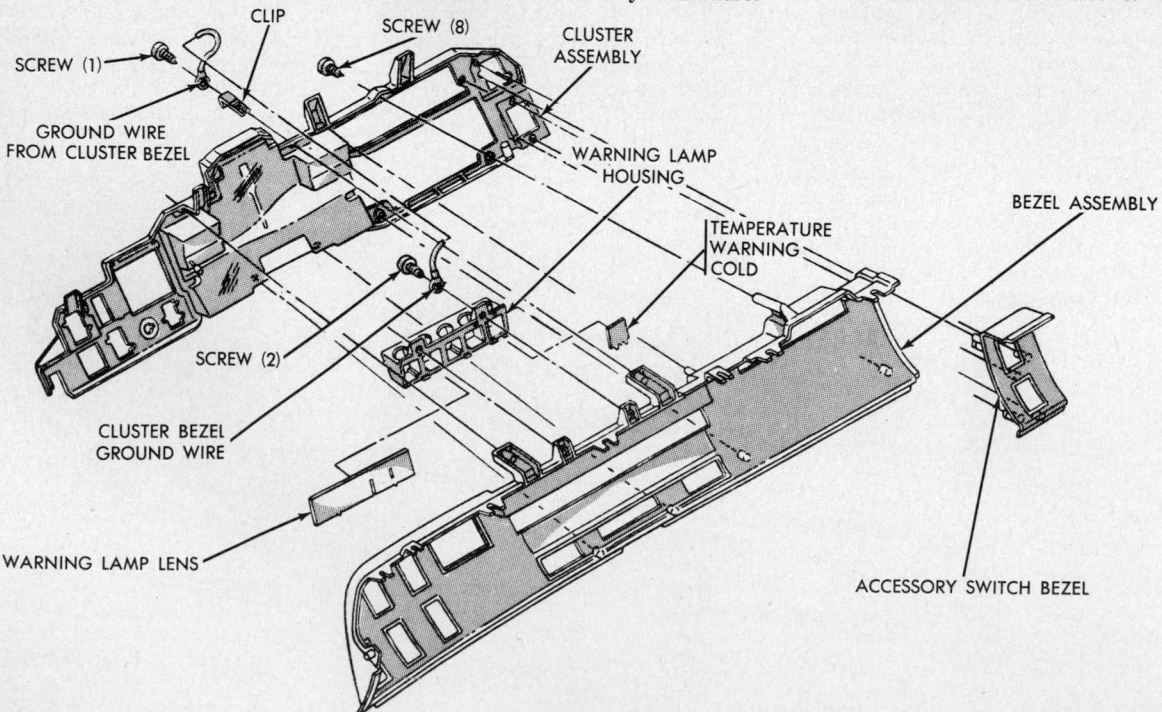

SCREW (1)

CLIP

SCREW (8)

CLUSTER ASSEMBLY

GROUND WIRE FROM CLUSTER BEZEL

WARNING LAMP HOUSING

TEMPERATURE WARNING COLD

BEZEL ASSEMBLY

SCREW (2)

CLUSTER BEZEL GROUND WIRE

WARNING LAMP LENS

ACCESSORY SWITCH BEZEL

1969 Chrysler instrument cluster and bezel (© Chrysler Corporation)

1965-66 Chrysler
1967-69 All Models
1. Remove switch bezel nut.
2. Push switch through panel.
3. Disconnect wiring connector.
4. Remove switch.
5. To install, reverse procedure. Align key on switch with slot in panel.

1970-72 Standard Steering Column
1. Disconnect ground cable from battery.
2. Remove steering wheel.
3. Remove turn signal lever.
4. Remove turn signal switch and upper bearing retainer.
5. Remove ignition key lamp assembly.
6. Remove snap ring. Remove three bearing housing to lock housing screws.
7. Pull bearing housing from shaft. Remove bearing lower snap-ring.
8. Pry sleeve off steering shaft lock plate hub to expose pin.
9. Press, do not hammer, pin from shaft.
10. Remove lock plate from shaft.
11. Remove buzzer switch and lock lever guide plate.
12. Lock switch and remove key. Insert a stiff wire into lock cylinder release hole, push in to release lock retainer, and pull lock cylinder out.
13. Remove three retaining screws and ignition switch assembly.
14. Reverse procedure for installation.

1970-72 Tilt Steering Column
1. Disconnect ground cable from battery.
2. Remove steering wheel.
3. Remove turn signal lever.
4. Remove gearshift lever pivot pin and tilt release lever, and turn signal switch lever.
5. Press down lock plate and carrier and remove C-ring. Remove lock plate, carrier and spring.
6. Remove three turn signal switch attaching screws, place shift bowl in low position, and remove switch and wiring. (The shift bowl is the section to which the shift lever is attached.)
7. Remove buzzer switch.
8. Lock switch and remove key.
9. Insert a small screwdriver into the slot next to the switch mounting screw boss (right-hand slot) and depress spring latch at bottom of slot. Remove lock.
10. Remove housing cover.
11. Install tilt release lever and place column in full up position.
12. Insert screwdriver into tilt spring retainer slot, press in approximately 3/16 in., turn approximately 1/8 turn counter-

clockwise until ears align with housing grooves, and remove spring and guide.
13. Remove seat and upper bearing race.
14. Remove ignition switch mounting screws and switch.
15. Reverse procedure for installation. For further information on the tilting steering column, refer to the Unit Repair Section.

Headlight Switch Replacement
1965-66 Imperial
1. Remove lower steering column cover plate.
2. Remove headlight switch knob, stem assembly and windshield-wiper switch knob.
3. Remove screw that attaches right end of switch bezel. This screw can be reached from inside the steering column opening.
4. Remove headlight switch retaining nut, using a spanner wrench.
5. Lift off switch bezel.
6. Remove light switch and wiper switch stem light seals.
7. Remove switch mounting nut.
8. Pull switch down from under panel and disconnect wiring.
9. Install in reverse of above.

1965-66 Chrysler
All switches on the instrument panel or in the clusters can be serviced from under the panel by removing the knob, mounting nut and bezel, and disconnecting the wires.

1967-68 All Models
1. Remove the instrument cluster bezel as outlined above under instrument Cluster Removal.
2. Remove headlamp switch from rear of bezel.
3. Install in reverse of above.

1969-70 All Models
1. Remove instrument cluster as outlined above under Instrument Cluster Removal.
2. Remove headlamp switch from rear of cluster.
3. Install in reverse of above.

1971-72 All Models
1. If equipped with air conditioning, remove the left air conditioning duct.
2. Remove the headlight switch shaft and knob by pulling the switch to the On position, reaching under the dash, and depressing the button on the bottom of the headlight switch case. Pull the knob and shaft from the switch.
3. Remove the sentinel and automatic dimmer control knobs if equipped with automatic headlight dimmer.
4. Remove the headlight switch attaching nut.

5. Remove the headlight switch from under the dash and disconnect the wires.
6. Reverse above procedure to install.

Brakes

Beginning 1966
Front wheel disc brakes are used on front wheels of some models. Information on this type of brake is in the Unit Repair Section.

Beginning 1967
A compound brake system is used on all models. This system is, in effect, two independent hydraulic systems, one for the front brakes and another for the rear brakes. The master cylinder has two pistons in tandem and two fluid outlets. The front outlet tube is connected to the hydraulic system safety switch and to the rear brakes. The rear outlet tube is also connected to the safety switch and the front brakes. In the event of a pressure loss in either branch of the system, the safety switch causes a warning light to be illuminated on the instrument panel.

Power Brakes
The power brake unit features a direct pedal connection to a vacuum unit mounted on the firewall with a master cylinder directly mounted to a vacuum booster.

This vacuum-suspended system

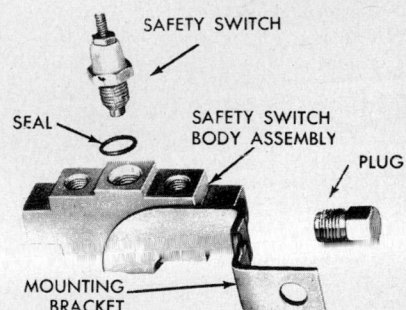

Hydraulic system safety switch
(© Chrysler Corp.)

utilizes engine intake manifold vacuum and atmospheric pressure for its power boost to the master cylinder.

Master Cylinder Removal
1. Disconnect fluid lines. On disc brake cylinders, plug brake outlets to prevent leakage.
2. Remove nuts attaching master cylinder to cowl panel or to power brake unit.
3. Disconnect pedal push rod (non-power brakes) from brake pedal.
4. Remove master cylinder from vehicle.
5. Reverse procedure to install.

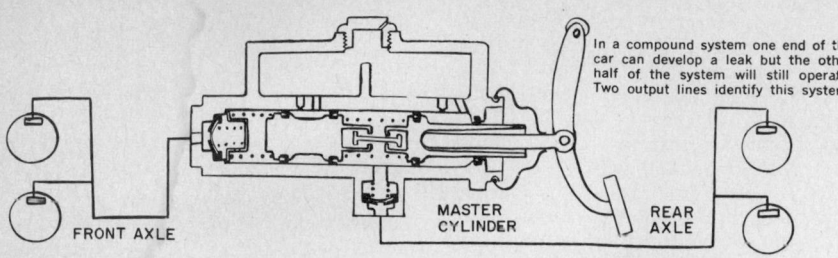

In a compound system one end of the car can develop a leak but the other half of the system will still operate. Two output lines identify this system.

FRONT AXLE

MASTER CYLINDER

REAR AXLE

Dual master cylinder, typical—1967-70

6. Bleed brake system.

Power Brake Booster R & R

1. Remove the nuts attaching the master cylinder to the brake booster and position the master cylinder out of the way. If the brake lines do not have enough slack to allow the master cylinder to be moved without kinking the brake lines, it will be necessary to disconnect the brake lines.
2. Disconnect the vacuum hose from the brake booster.
3. Working under the dash, remove the attaching nut and bolt from the brake booster pushrod and disconnect the pushrod from the brake pedal. On linkage type power brake boosters, remove the lower pivot mounting bolt.
4. Remove the four nuts and washers that attach the brake booster to the interior side of the firewall.
5. Remove the booster from under the hood.
6. Reverse above procedure to install.
7. If the brake lines were disconnected, bleed the brake system.

Parking Brake Adjustment

1. Raise and support vehicle. Release parking brake lever. Loosen cable adjusting nut.
2. Tighten cable adjusting nut until a slight drag is felt while rotating wheel.
3. Loosen cable adjusting nut until both rear wheels can be rotated freely. Back off cable adjusting

nut two full turns.
4. Apply parking brake several times. Check to see that rear wheels rotate freely without dragging.

Fuel System

Carburetors

Since 1965, Chrysler and Imperial models have used four types of carburetors: Stromberg, Ball and Ball, Carter and Holley. Stromberg WWC3 carburetors were used from 1965-67 on 383 V8s without Chrysler's Clean Air Package. Two-venturi models of the Ball and Ball BBD carburetor still are in production for 383 V8 engines. Two similar models of the Carter four-venturi carburetor have been used: 1965-67 vehicles used an AFB model, and 1968 and later vehicles have been equipped with an AVS model. Since 1968, some 440 V8s have been equipped with Holley 4150 model four-venturi carburetors, and the 1971 360 V8 is equipped with a Holley 2200 two-venturi carburetor.

Some 1966-67 and all 1968 and later carburetors incorporate modifications to reduce engine exhaust emissions. Carburetor modifications for 1966-69 are part of Chrysler's Cleaner Air Package, and 1970 and

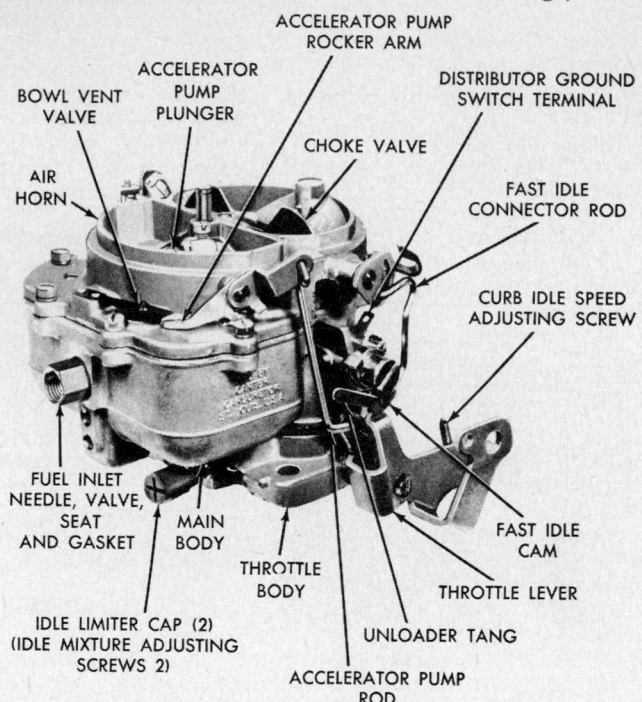

ACCELERATOR PUMP ROCKER ARM

BOWL VENT VALVE

ACCELERATOR PUMP PLUNGER

DISTRIBUTOR GROUND SWITCH TERMINAL

CHOKE VALVE

AIR HORN

FAST IDLE CONNECTOR ROD

CURB IDLE SPEED ADJUSTING SCREW

FUEL INLET NEEDLE, VALVE, SEAT AND GASKET

MAIN BODY

THROTTLE BODY

FAST IDLE CAM

THROTTLE LEVER

IDLE LIMITER CAP (2) (IDLE MIXTURE ADJUSTING SCREWS 2)

UNLOADER TANG

ACCELERATOR PUMP ROD

Ball and Ball carburetor (© Chrysler Corporation)

later models are part of the Cleaner Air System. The only carburetor changes used with the Cleaner Air Package are the installation of carburetor idle mixture limiter stops on the idle mixture adjustment screws, and leaner carburetor mixtures. With the Cleaner Air System, in addition to the above mentioned changes, faster acting chokes were added and, on some models, solenoid operated throttle stops and distributor retard mechanisms. The throttle stop raises the engine idle speed to reduce exhaust emissions, but de-energizes when the ignition is shut off to prevent the engine from dieseling. The distributor retard solenoid is acti-

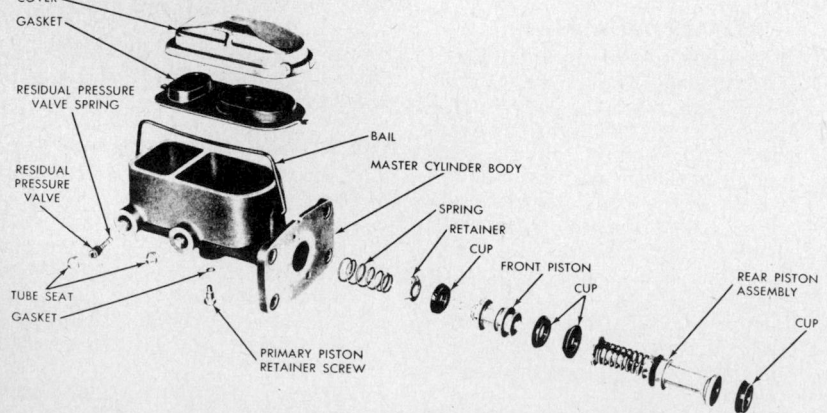

COVER

GASKET

RESIDUAL PRESSURE VALVE SPRING

RESIDUAL PRESSURE VALVE

BAIL

MASTER CYLINDER BODY

SPRING

RETAINER

CUP

FRONT PISTON

CUP

REAR PISTON ASSEMBLY

CUP

TUBE SEAT

GASKET

PRIMARY PISTON RETAINER SCREW

Dual type master cylinder (exploded view) with disc brakes

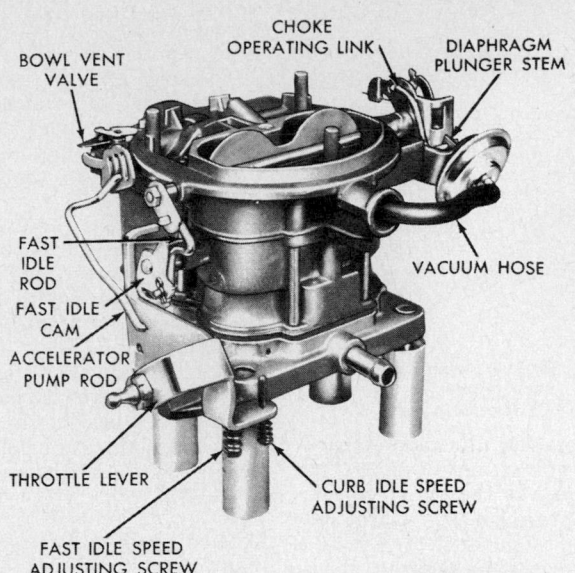

BOWL VENT VALVE

CHOKE OPERATING LINK

DIAPHRAGM PLUNGER STEM

FAST IDLE ROD

FAST IDLE CAM

ACCELERATOR PUMP ROD

VACUUM HOSE

THROTTLE LEVER

CURB IDLE SPEED ADJUSTING SCREW

FAST IDLE SPEED ADJUSTING SCREW

Stromberg carburetor (© Chrysler Corporation)

vated when the idle speed adjustment screw returns to the curb idle position and contacts a sensor mounted on the carburetor. These carburetors also incorporate an internally mounted hot idle compensator which opens to induct additional air into the carburetor during low speed-high temperature operation.

Idle Speed and Mixture Adjustments

NOTE: 1966-67 CAP carburetors are identified by a green tag, mounted on air horn.

1965-67 Without CAP

Adjust with air cleaner removed.
1. Run the engine at fast idle to stabilize engine temperature.

2. Make sure the choke plate is fully released.
3. Attach a tachometer of known accuracy to the engine.
4. If equipped with air conditioning, turn the air conditioner ON.
5. Adjust the carburetor idle speed screw to obtain a curb idle speed of 500 rpm (550 rpm if equipped with air conditioner).
6. Turn the two idle mixture screws in or out to obtain the highest rpm possible. After obtaining the highest rpm, turn each mixture screw clockwise until the engine speed starts to drop, then, turn each screw in a counterclockwise direction just enough to regain the lost rpm.
7. If the mixture adjustment proce-

dure has changed the curb idle speed, readjust the idle speed.

1966-72 with CAP or CAS

Adjust with air cleaner installed.
1. Run engine at fast idle to stabilize engine temperature.
2. Make sure the choke plate is fully released.
3. Attach a tachometer of known accuracy to the engine.
4. Connect an exhaust gas analyzer to the engine and insert the probe as far into the tailpipe as possible. On vehicles with dual exhaust, insert the probe into the left tailpipe as this is the side without a heat riser valve.
5. Check ignition timing and adjust it as required to conform to specifications.
6. If equipped with air conditioning, turn the air conditioner OFF.
7. Place the transmission in the Neutral position.
8. Turn the idle speed screw or electric solenoid plunger to adjust engine idle speed to specifications.
9. Turn each idle mixture adjustment screw 1/16 turn richer (counterclockwise). Wait 10 seconds and observe the reading on the exhaust gas analyzer. Continue this procedure until the meter indicates a definite increase in the richness of the mixture.

NOTE: this step is very important. A carburetor that is set too lean will cause the exhaust gas analyzer to give a false reading indicating a rich mixture. Because of this, the carburetor must first be known to have a rich mixture to verify the reading on

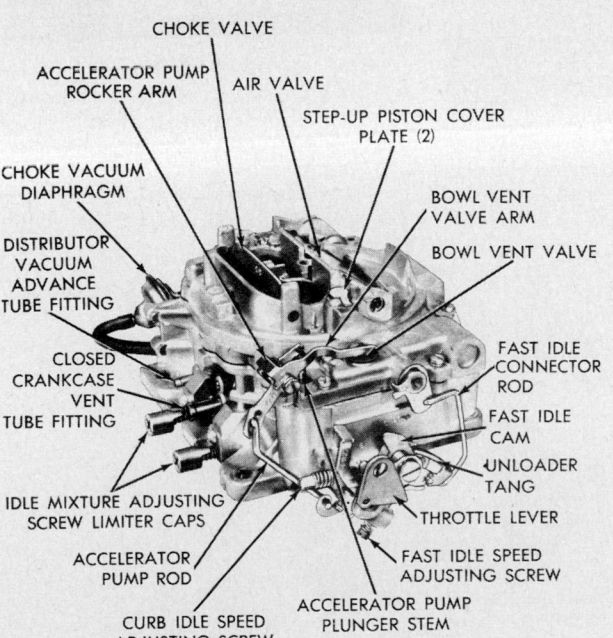

CHOKE VALVE

ACCELERATOR PUMP ROCKER ARM

AIR VALVE

STEP-UP PISTON COVER PLATE (2)

CHOKE VACUUM DIAPHRAGM

DISTRIBUTOR VACUUM ADVANCE TUBE FITTING

CLOSED CRANKCASE VENT TUBE FITTING

BOWL VENT VALVE ARM

BOWL VENT VALVE

FAST IDLE CONNECTOR ROD

FAST IDLE CAM

UNLOADER TANG

IDLE MIXTURE ADJUSTING SCREW LIMITER CAPS

ACCELERATOR PUMP ROD

CURB IDLE SPEED ADJUSTING SCREW

ACCELERATOR PUMP PLUNGER STEM

THROTTLE LEVER

FAST IDLE SPEED ADJUSTING SCREW

Carter AVS carburetor (© Chrysler Corporation)

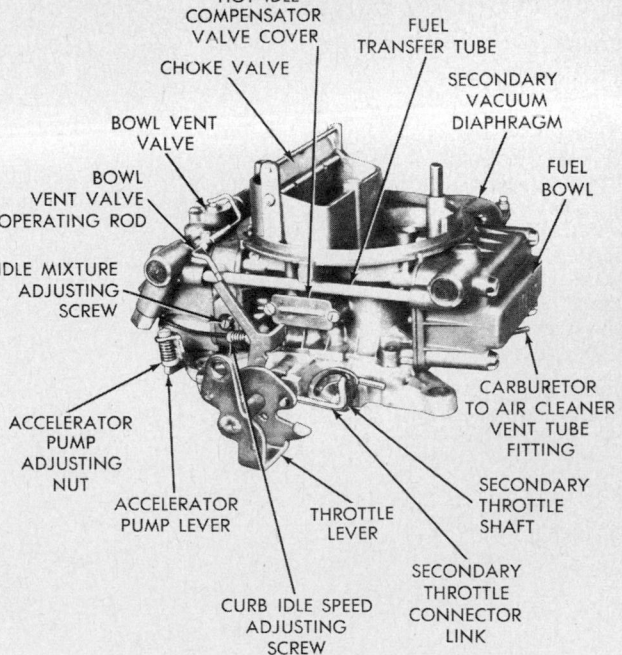

HOT IDLE COMPENSATOR VALVE COVER

FUEL TRANSFER TUBE

CHOKE VALVE

SECONDARY VACUUM DIAPHRAGM

BOWL VENT VALVE

FUEL BOWL

BOWL VENT VALVE OPERATING ROD

IDLE MIXTURE ADJUSTING SCREW

ACCELERATOR PUMP ADJUSTING NUT

CARBURETOR TO AIR CLEANER VENT TUBE FITTING

ACCELERATOR PUMP LEVER

THROTTLE LEVER

SECONDARY THROTTLE SHAFT

CURB IDLE SPEED ADJUSTING SCREW

SECONDARY THROTTLE CONNECTOR LINK

Holley carburetor (© Chrysler Corporation)

the exhaust gas analyzer.

10. After verifying the reading obtained on the meter, adjust the mixture screws to get an air-/fuel ratio of 14.2. Turn the mixture screws counterclockwise (richer) to lower the meter reading and clockwise (leaner) to raise the meter reading.

11. If the mixture adjustment procedure has changed the curb idle speed, readjust the idle speed.

Rough Idle and Low Speed Surge

Rough idle and low speed surge can be the result of improper balance of the idle mixture adjustment in the right and left carburetor bores. To correct this condition, perform the following operation.

1. Remove the plastic caps from the idle mixture screws in the base of the carburetor (Ball and Ball or Carter) or from the sides of the primary metering block (Holley).

2. Perform Steps 1-8 of the idle speed and mixture adjustment procedure.

3. Turn both mixture screws clockwise until they are lightly seated.

4. On Ball and Ball carburetors, turn both mixture screws 1½ turns counterclockwise. On Carter and Holley carburetors, turn both mixture screws 2-3 turns counterclockwise.

5. Start the engine and perform Steps 9-11 of the idle speed and mixture adjustment procedure.

6. Install the plastic limiter caps on the mixture screws.

NOTE: in order to obtain a smooth idle, it is important that both mixture adjustment screws are adjusted an equal number of turns from the fully seated position.

Vapor Separator

The 440 high performance engine is equipped with a vapor separator mounted between the carburetor and the fuel pump.

Serviced only as a unit, the vapor separator consists of a steel can containing a filter screen. It has an inlet from the fuel pump and an outlet to the carburetor. It also has a metered vapor bleed hole which is piped back to the fuel tank.

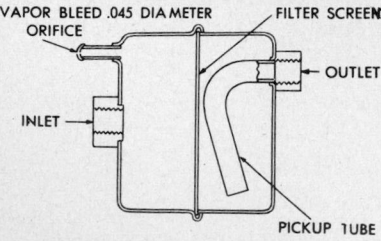

Sectional view of vapor separator
(© Chrysler Corp.)

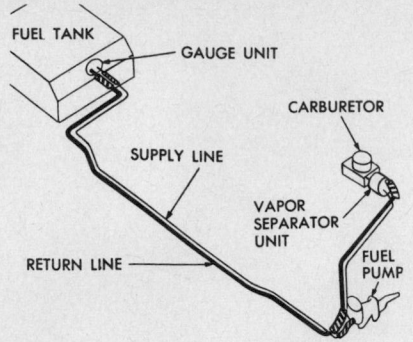

Schematic showing piping to vapor separator
(© Chrysler Corp.)

When operating, the vapor separator is full of fuel. Any vapor that may form goes to the top of the can and, passing through the metered orifice, returns to the fuel tank.

The unit cannot be serviced. If vaporlock is evident, remove the return line at the top of the unit and pass a thin wire through the orifice to clear it.

Fuel Pump

The standard fuel pump on Chrysler and Imperial models is of pressed steel construction and cannot be disassembled for service. A repairable fuel pump is optional for some 1968 to present models. This type is easily recognized by the assembling screws. The fuel pump is driven by an eccentric on the camshaft and a short pushrod.

Fuel Filter

An inline fuel filter is used near the carburetor. This filter is the throwaway type and cannot be cleaned. To assure an unrestricted fuel supply, the filter should be replaced at least every 24,000 miles, and more frequently if fuel contamination is suspected.

Exhaust System

The single exhaust system used on Chrysler and Imperial models consists of three parts: an exhaust pipe, a muffler and a tailpipe. A straight-

through type resonator if fitted integrally in the tailpipe.

The dual exhaust system used on Chrysler and Imperial models consists of six parts: an exhaust pipe, a muffler and integral inlet pipe, and a tailpipe; mounted on each side of the chassis.

On all models, the exhaust pipe is mounted to the muffler by means of a flange-type connection. A heat riser valve is incorporated in the right-side exhaust manifold. A thermostatic spring closes a plate in the exhaust manifold during cold engine operation to direct exhaust gases to a heat chamber beneath the carburetor mounting flange to help vaporize the fuel mixture. As the engine reaches operating temperature, the thermostatic spring retracts and allows the exhaust gases to flow freely from the manifold.

Replacement

To replace any component of the exhaust system, remove the clamp/s or flange/s that attach it to the pipe/s or manifold/s it mounts to. Remove the attaching parts from the exhaust system hanger that mounts the part to be replaced to the underbody. Using a torch or air chisel, separate the part to be replaced from the rest of the exhaust system.

NOTE: many muffler-tailpipe assemblies are welded together; before removing any parts, determine if the replacement parts are serviced separately or as an assembly. If the service parts are sold separately, it will be necessary to cut the weld on the original parts and separate them.

Cooling System

Water Pump R & R

1. Drain cooling system. Remove fan shroud, if so equipped.

2. Loosen the power steering pump, idler pulley, and alternator. Remove all belts.

3. Remove fan, spacer or fluid

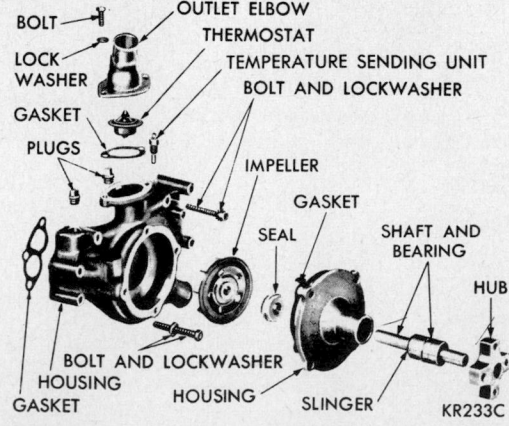

Water pump—383, 413 and 440 cu. in. (© Chrysler Corp.)

drive, and pulley.

4. Remove pump attaching bolts.
5. Reverse procedure to install. Torque pump attaching bolts to 30 ft. lbs. and fan nuts to 15 ft. lbs. Adjust power steering belt, fan belt, and alternator belt.

Thermostat R & R

1. Drain cooling system down to thermostat level or below.
2. Remove upper radiator hose from thermostat housing at top of water pump housing.
3. Remove thermostat housing and thermostat. Discard gasket.
4. Using a new gasket, install thermostat so pellet end is toward engine.
5. Replace upper hose and fill radiator with coolant to 1¼ in. below filler neck.

Radiator Core R & R

1. Drain coolant.
2. On automatic transmission vehicles, disconnect oil cooler lines at radiator bottom tank.
3. Remove upper and lower hoses.
4. Remove shroud from radiator.
5. Remove radiator attaching screws and lift out radiator.
6. Reverse procedure to install.

Engine

Positive Crankcase Ventilation

All models are equipped with a

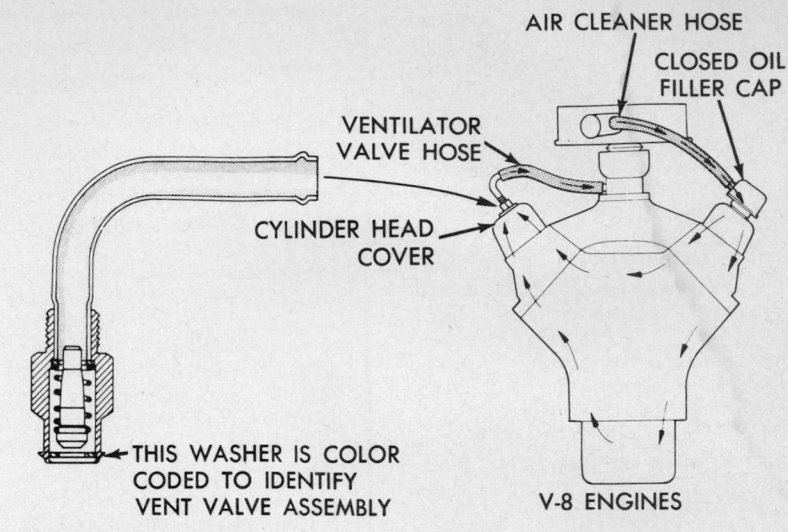

THIS WASHER IS COLOR CODED TO IDENTIFY VENT VALVE ASSEMBLY

FLOW CONTROL VALVE

Fully closed ventilation system (© Chrysler Corp.)

positive crankcase ventilation system. Air is drawn into the engine through the oil filler cap and circulated through the engine. The air and vapors are drawn out of the engine through the rocker arm cover, a flow control valve, and the intake manifold, into the combustion chambers where they are consumed.

Vehicles sold in California from 1965 to 1967, and all vehicles from 1968 on, have a fully closed crankcase ventilation system. This

fully closed system is the same as that described above, except that intake air is drawn from the carburetor air cleaner into a closed oil filler cap.

Exhaust Emission Control

From 1966 to 1969, Chrysler Corporation uses the C.A.P. system of exhaust emission control. The C.A.P. system utilizes carburetor modifications and a second vacuum-operated distributor timing regulation mechanism.

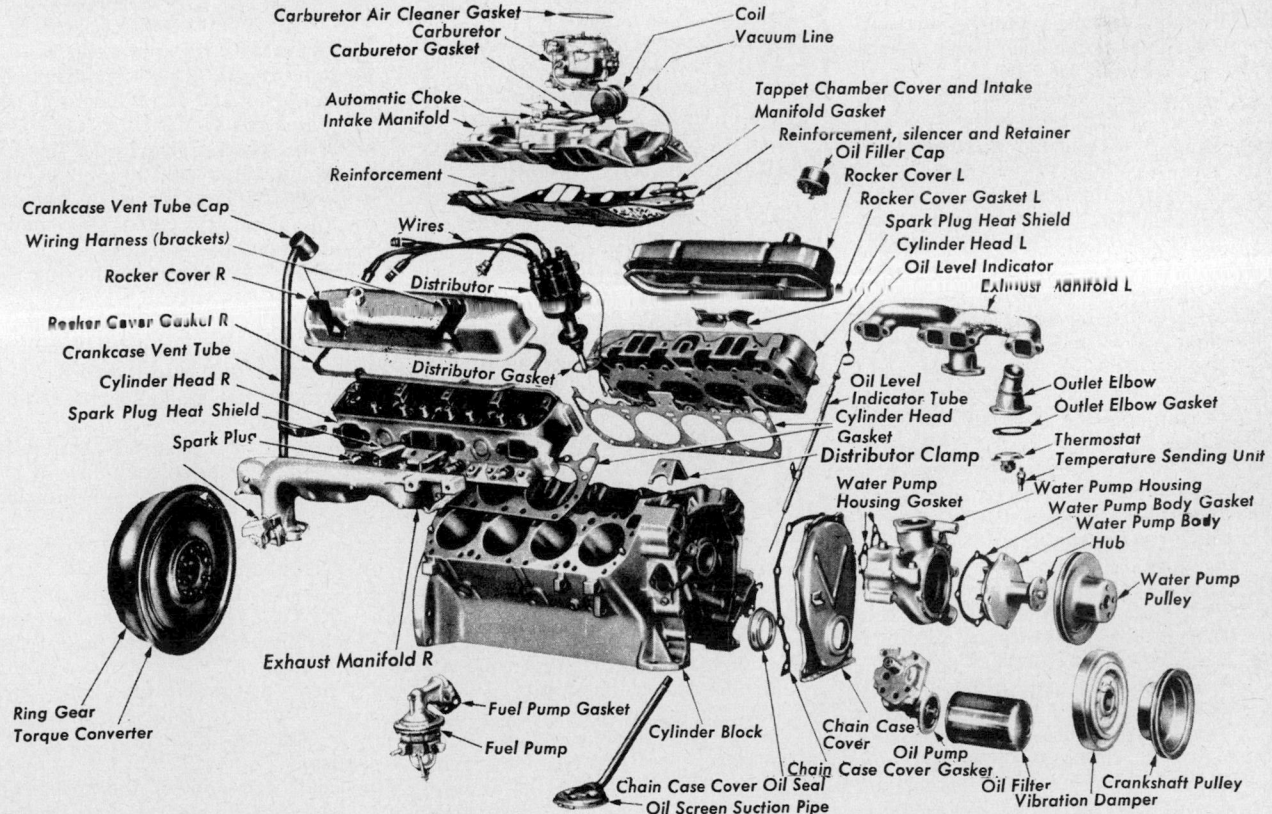

1965-70 engine external parts (© Chrysler Corp.)

Since 1970, a cleaner air system, C.A.S., is used. This system uses heated intake air; various carburetor modifications including leaner mixtures, a fast acting choke, an external idle mixture limiter, and a solenoid throttle stop; solenoid operated distributor retard; and reduced compression ratios.

Engine Description

The Chrysler and Imperial use Chrysler Corporation's "B" block type engines. The "B" block type engines are divided into two series, the low block series and the high block series. These series differ in block deck height, main bearing journal size, connecting rod length, and pushrod length. In other respects, these engines are similar and have a number of interchangeable parts. The 383 cu. in. engine is a low block engine. The 413 and 440 cu. in. engines are high block engines. These engines are all conventional overhead valve V8's with wedge shaped combustion chambers and deep blocks extending well below the crankshaft centerline. In 1971, a 400 cu. in., low compression engine was introduced as an option for some Chrysler models.

Engine Removal

1965-72

1. Scribe outline of hood hinge brackets and remove hood.
2. Drain cooling system. Remove battery.
3. Remove all hoses, fan shroud, and disconnect oil cooler lines, then remove radiator.
4. Disconnect fuel lines and wires attached to engine units.
5. Remove air cleaner and carburetor.
6. If equipped with air conditioning and/or power steering, remove the unit from the engine and position it out of the way *without disconnecting the lines.*
7. Attach lifting sling to the engine.
8. Raise the vehicle on a hoist and install an engine support fixture to support the rear of the engine.
9. Drain the transmission and torque converter.
10. Disconnect the exhaust pipes from the exhaust manifolds.
11. Remove the driveshaft.
12. Disconnect the transmission linkage and any wiring or cables that attach to the transmission.
13. Remove the engine rear support crossmember and remove the transmission from the vehicle.
14. Remove the bolts that attach the motor mounts to the chassis.
15. Lower the vehicle and attach a chain hoist or other lifting device to the engine.

⏱ CHILTON TIME-SAVER

This is the manufacturer's recommended procedure for engine assembly removal. It is possible to remove the engine without removing the transmission. If the engine is removed without removing the transmission, care must be exercised not to allow the weight of the engine to rest on torque converter hub. To remove the engine, follow this procedure: perform Steps 1-7, connect a remote control starter switch to the engine, raise the vehicle on a hoist, remove the inspection plate from the bellhousing, crank the engine to gain access to the four torque converter-to-driveplate attaching nuts and remove the nuts. Remove the bolt that mounts the transmission filler tube bracket to the engine. Remove the bolts that attach the transmission to the engine. When removing the engine, place a block of wood on the lifting point of a floor jack and position the jack under the transmission. As the engine is removed from the engine compartment, raise and lower the jack so the angle of the transmission will duplicate as nearly as possible the angle of the engine. When the engine is reinstalled in the vehicle, keep in mind that the crankshaft bolt circle, the inner and outer circle of holes in the drive plate, and the four tapped holes in the front face of the converter all have one hole offset. To insure proper engine-torque converter balance, the torque converter must be mounted to the drive plate at the same point it was originally installed.

16. Raise the engine and carefully remove it from the vehicle.
17. Reverse above procedure to install.

Manifolds

Intake Manifold R & R —All Models

1. Drain cooling system.
2. Remove carburetor air cleaner, and fuel line.
3. Disconnect accelerator linkage.
4. Remove vacuum control tube at carburetor and distributor.
5. Disconnect the spark plug wires from the spark plugs and remove the distributor cap and wires from the engine as an assembly. Disconnect the coil primary wires. Remove the heater

hose from the intake manifold. Disconnect the crankcase vent hose from the carburetor.
6. Disconnect heat indicator sending unit wire.
7. Remove intake manifold. Reverse procedure to install. Torque manifold bolts to correct figure from Torque Specifications Table.

Exhaust Manifold R & R— All Models

1. Remove spark plugs.
2. Remove alternator from right cylinder head.
3. Disconnect exhaust pipe from exhaust manifold.
4. Unbolt manifold from cylinder head. Slide manifold off studs and away from cylinder head.

Caution If an exhaust manifold mounting stud comes out of the cylinder head with the nut, install a new stud in the head, applying sealer to the coarse thread end. If this procedure is not followed, water leaks may develop around the stud.

5. Reverse procedure to install. Torque manifold bolts to correct figure from Torque Specifications Table. Tighten exhaust pipe bolts to 40 ft. lbs.

Cylinder Head

Removal and Installation

All Engines

1. Drain the cooling system.
2. Remove the intake manifold by following the procedure outlined under Intake Manifold R&R.
3. If the right-side cylinder head is to be removed, disconnect the negative battery cable, remove the alternator mounting bolts, and position the alternator out of the way without removing the wires.
4. Remove the spark plugs to avoid breaking them during removal.
5. Remove the valve covers, then remove the rocker arm assemblies.
6. Remove the pushrods and keep them in order so they may be returned to their original location in the engine.
7. Remove the exhaust manifolds from the heads.
8. Remove the 17 bolts that attach the cylinder head to the engine block, and remove the head from the engine.
9. Clean all gasket mounting surfaces and check all surfaces with a straight edge to verify flatness.
10. Coat both sides of the new head gasket with sealer and install the cylinder head and gasket on

the engine. Tighten all cylinder head bolts in sequence to 40 ft. lbs., then to 70 ft. lbs.

11. Reverse Steps 1-7 to complete installation. When installing the rocker arm assemblies, tighten each bolt several turns at a time so the hydraulic lifters will gradually be compressed. Tighten the rocker shaft bolts to 25 ft. lbs.

Rocker Arm Installation

1. Install pushrods, small end first.
2. Install rocker shaft assembly, being sure to install the long stamped steel retainers in the number two and four positions. Install rocker shafts so that the 3/16 in. dia. rocker arm lubrication holes point downward into the rocker arm, toward the valve end of the rocker arms. This is

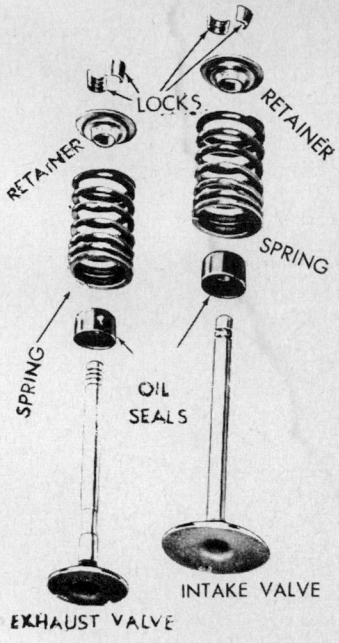

Valve assembly
(© Chrysler Corp.)

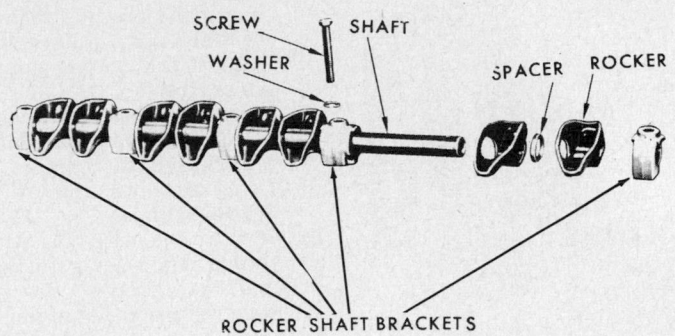

Rocker shaft assembly (© Chrysler Corp.)

Rocker Shaft Removal

1. Remove the carburetor air cleaner and pull the wires off the spark plugs. Remove the rocker covers.

NOTE: on 1965-66 Imperial models equipped with air conditioning, the crankshaft must be rotated until the No. 8 exhaust valve is open to provide adequate clearance to remove the right-side rocker arm cover.

2. Loosen the rocker shaft retaining bolts, gradually and alternately, until all valve spring tension has been relieved. Remove rocker shaft bolts and retainers. Then, lift off rockers and shaft as an assembly.

necessary to provide proper lubrication.

3. Gradually tighten rocker shaft bolts to 25 ft. lbs., allowing time for tappets to bleed down to their operating length.
4. Install rocker covers with new gaskets. Torque to approximately 40 in. lbs.

Valve System

Valves

Detailed information on the valves and valve guides is in the Valve Specifications table.

Valve Guides

Separate valve guides are not used.

The guide is cast, integrally, with the cylinder head.

In cases of excessive stem-to-guide clearance, valves with oversize stems are available in the following increments: .005 in., .015 in. and .030 in. When installing valves with oversize stems, the guides must be reamed. Reamers to accommodate the oversize stems are available.

Caution Do not attempt to ream the valve guides in their present worn state to .030 in., or even .015 in., in one step. To maintain original bore angle, it is important to use step reaming procedures of .005 in., .015 in., then, if necessary, .030 in.

Hydraulic Tappet Removal

The tappet can be removed without removing the intake manifold or cylinder heads by following this procedure:

1. Remove rocker arm covers.
2. Remove rocker arms and shaft assembly.
3. Remove pushrods and place them in their respective places, on the bench, to retain their identity.
4. Slide tappet puller through pushrod opening in the cylinder head, and seat the tool firmly in the head of the tappet.
5. Pull tappet out of bore with a twisting motion.
   If all tappets are to be removed, store them in their respective holes in a holder to ensure proper location at the time of assembly.

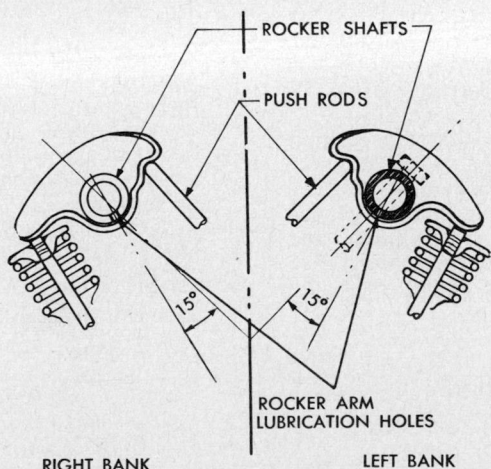

Rocker arm positioning (© Chrysler Corp.)

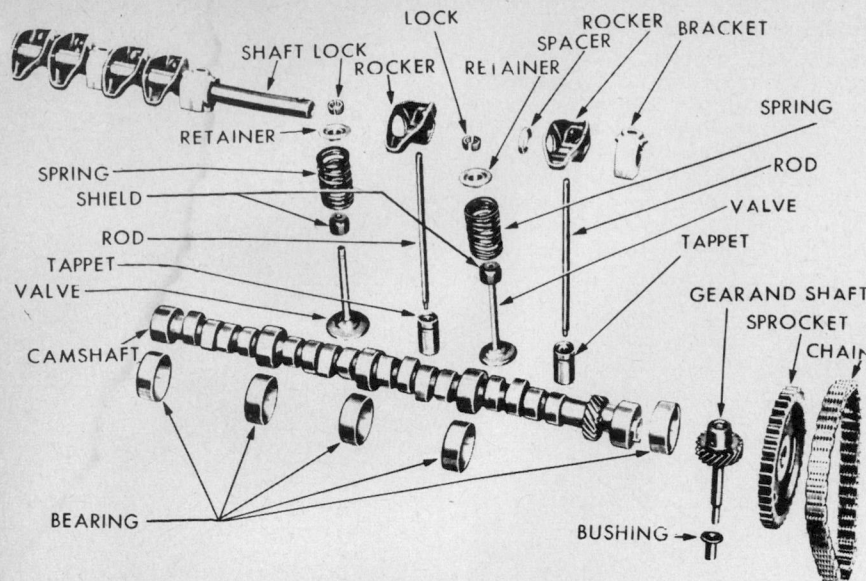

Valve train (© Chrysler Corp.)

NOTE: a diamond-shaped symbol on the engine numbering pad indicates that some tappet bodies are .008 in. oversize.

Checking Valve Timing

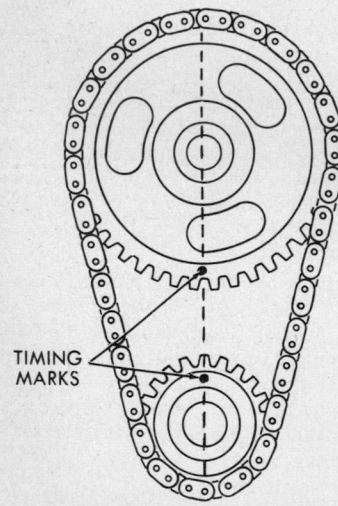

TIMING MARKS

Timing mark alignment

1. Turn crankshaft until No. 6 exhaust valve is closing and No. 6 intake valve is opening.
2. Insert a ¼ in. spacer between rocker arm pad and stem tip of No. 1 intake valve.
3. Install a dial indicator so plunger contacts valve spring retainer as nearly perpendicular as possible.
4. Allow spring load to bleed tappet down. Zero the indicator.
5. Turn the crankshaft clockwise until the intake valve has lifted the amount specified in the accompanying chart. The timing, read at the timing indicator on the chain case cover, should read from 10 degrees BTDC to 2 de-

grees ATDC.
6. If the reading is not within the specified limits: Inspect timing sprocket index marks, inspect timing chain for wear, and check accuracy of timing indicator marks.
7. Turn crankshaft counterclockwise until valve is closed. Do not turn crankshaft any further clockwise, as the valve spring might bottom, causing serious damage. Remove indicator and spacer.

Timing Chain, Cover and Camshaft

Timing Chain and Cover R & R

1. Drain the cooling system.
2. Disconnect the upper and lower radiator hoses from the engine. Disconnect the transmission cooler lines from the radiator.
3. If equipped with a fan shroud, remove it from the radiator and position it rearward over the fan.
4. Remove the radiator attaching screws and remove the radiator from the vehicle.
5. Remove the bolts that attach the fan to the water pump and remove the fan, fan spacer (if so equipped) and pulley from the engine.

6. Disconnect the negative battery cable. Remove the bolts that attach the alternator mounting bracket to the engine and remove the alternator and bracket from the engine and position them out of the way with the wires attached.
7. If equipped with power steering, remove the bolts that attach the power steering pump mounting bracket to the engine. Remove the pump and bracket from the engine and position them out of the way with the lines attached.
8. Remove the water pump from the engine.
9. Remove the bolt and washer that attaches the vibration damper to the crankshaft.
10. Using a puller, remove the vibration damper.
11. Remove the bolts that attach the timing chain cover to the block and the front of the oil pan. Remove the cover from the engine.
12. To check timing chain slack, place a scale next to the timing chain to detect any movement of the chain. Place a torque wrench and socket on the camshaft sprocket attaching bolt. Apply either 30 ft. lbs. (if cylinder heads are installed on the engine) or 15 ft. lbs. (cylinder heads removed) of force to the bolt and rotate the bolt in the direction of crankshaft rotation to remove all slack from the chain. While applying torque to the camshaft sprocket bolt, the crankshaft should not be allowed to rotate. It may be necessary to block the crankshaft to prevent rotation. Position the scale over the edge of a timing chain link and apply an equal amount of torque in the opposite direction. If the movement of the chain exceeds 3/16 in., replace the chain.
13. To remove the timing chain, crank the engine until the timing marks on the sprockets are aligned, remove the bolt that attaches the cam sprocket to the camshaft, and slide the chain and both sprockets forward and remove them from the engine as an assembly.
14. Reverse above procedure to install.

Camshaft R & R

1. Remove the timing chain and

Valve Timing

	Measurement for Standard Engines (in.)		Measurement for High Performance Engines (in.)
1965	.013		.034 (413)
1966	.013	(383-2 bbl.)	.034 (383, 440-4 bbl.)
1967-72	.025		.033 (440)

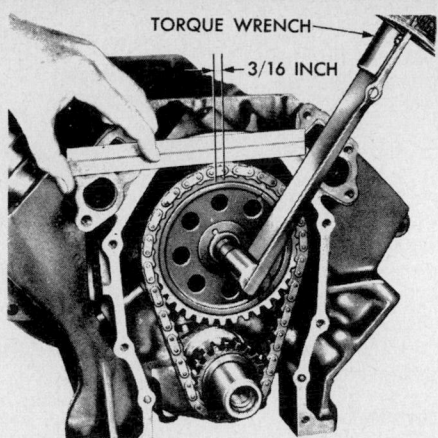

Checking timing chain slack
(© Chrysler Corporation)

cover.
2. Remove the intake manifold.
3. Remove the rocker arm covers and rocker arm assemblies.
4. Remove the pushrods and valve lifters and keep them in order so they may be returned to their original location in the engine.
5. Remove the distributor and distributor pump driveshaft.
6. Remove the fuel pump from the engine and position it out of the way without disconnecting the fuel lines.
7. Remove the camshaft from the engine. Use care not to damage the lobes during removal.
8. Reverse above procedure to install, lubricating the cam before installation.

NOTE: when installing the camshaft and timing chain, do not allow the camshaft to contact the welch plug in the rear of the engine block as this could loosen the plug in the engine.

Engine Lubrication

Oil Pump

Removal
1. Remove oil pan and filter assembly.
2. Remove oil pump from bottom side of engine.

Disassembly
1. Remove filter base and oil seal ring.
2. Remove pump rotor and shaft. Lift out outer pump rotor.
3. Remove oil pressure relief valve plug. Lift out spring and relief valve plunger.

Inspection
1. Clean all parts thoroughly in solvent.
2. Inspect mating face of oil pump cover. Replace cover if face is scratched or grooved.
3. Lay straight edge across oil pump cover face. If .0015 feeler gauge can be inserted between cover and straight edge, replace cover.
4. Measure outer rotor. If rotor length is less than 0.943 in., replace rotor. If rotor diameter is less than 2.469 in., replace rotor.
5. Measure inner rotor. If rotor length is less than 0.942 in., replace rotor.
6. Install outer rotor in pump body. Holding rotor to one side, measure clearance between rotor and body. If clearance is greater than 0.014 in., replace pump body.
7. Install inner rotor into pump body. Place straight edge across body between bolt holes. If feeler gauge thicker than .004 in. can be inserted between rotors and body, replace body.
8. Measure clearance between tips

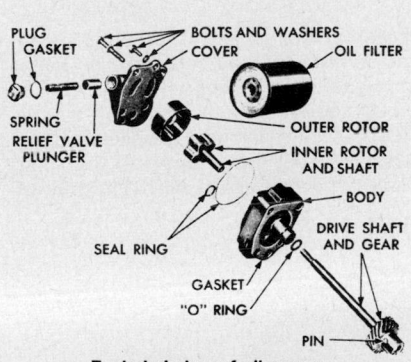

Exploded view of oil pump
(© Chrysler Corp.)

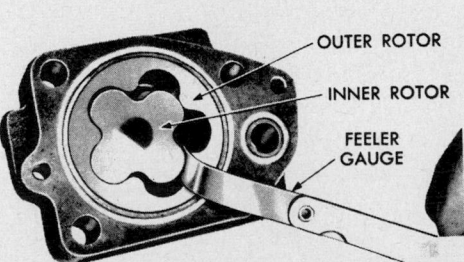

Measuring clearance between oil pump rotors
(© Chrysler Corp.)

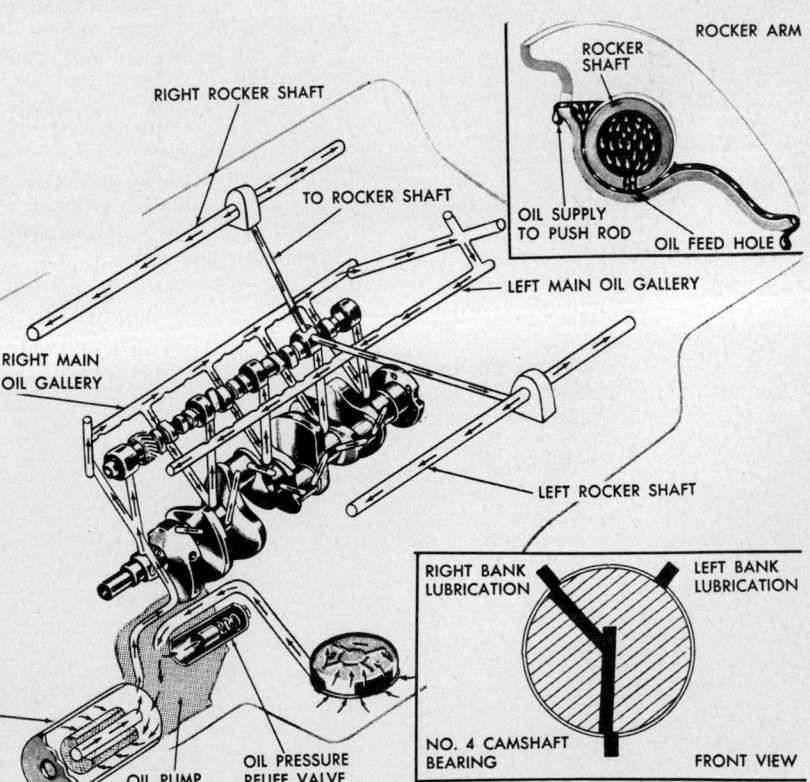

Engine lubrication (© Chrysler Corp.)

of inner and outer rotors where they are opposed. If clearance exceeds .010 in., replace inner and outer rotors.

Assembly and Installation

1. Assemble pump using new parts as required.
2. Install new seal rings between filter base and body. Torque bolts to 10 ft. lbs.
3. Install new O-ring seal on pilot of oil pump before attaching oil pump to cylinder block.
4. Install oil pump on engine using a new gasket. Tighten attaching bolts to 30 ft. lbs. Install oil filter assembly and oil pan.

Oil Pan Removal and Installation

From under the car, disconnect the exhaust pipes at the exhaust manifolds. Loosen the clamp at the Y connection where the two exhaust pipes come together, and remove the Y exhaust pipes. With dual exhaust, disconnect both pipes at manifolds. Disconnect the steering idler arm and let the steering linkage drop down out of the way. Remove the transmission (or converter) dust shield at the front of the flywheel housing.

Remove the bolts that hold the oil pan to the block. Turn the crankshaft in order to get the front counterweight out of the way and turn the pan counterclockwise to clear the oil pump screen. Then, slide the oil pan backward and down. Reverse procedure to install pan.

Pistons, Connecting Rods and Main Bearings

Rod and Piston Assembly Removal

1. Remove the cylinder head and oil pan. Select two pistons in the down position, insert a good cylinder ridge reamer into those two cylinders and remove the ring ridge.
2. Turn the crankshaft until two other pistons are in the same down position and repeat the ridge-removing operation.
3. From underneath the car, select two connecting rods in the down position, take off the locking device (cotter pin or pal nut) and remove the two lower connecting rod nuts. Tap the cap of the connecting rod gently, and slide it off the two bolts. Push that rod and piston assembly up toward the top of its bore, and immediately replace the cap on the bottom of the rod running

the two nuts up finger tight. This is a precaution to prevent mixing the caps up or getting them on the bottom of the connecting rod the wrong way.
4. Before pushing the rod and piston assembly up out of the bore, or immediately after, check to ascertain if the number of the connecting rod is stamped on the bottom of the rod. If it is not, either file or mark the rod with the cylinder number so that it can be replaced in the cylinder from which it was removed.

Piston Ring Replacement

Before replacing rings, inspect cylinder bores.

1. If cylinder bore is in satisfactory condition, place each ring in its bore in turn and square it in the bore with the head of a piston. Measure ring end gap. If ring gap exceeds limits, try another ring. If ring gap is too small, file end of ring to obtain correct gap.
2. Check ring side clearance by installing rings on piston, and inserting feeler gauge between ring and lower land. Gauge should slide freely around ring circumference without binding. Any wear will show as a step on the lower land. Replace any pistons having high steps.
3. Space ring gaps at equidistant intervals around piston circumference. Be sure to install piston in its original bore. Install short lengths of rubber tubing over connecting rod bolts to prevent damage to rod journal. Install ring compressor over rings on piston. Lower piston and rod assembly into bore until ring compressor contacts block. Using wooden handle of hammer push piston into bore while guiding rod onto journal.

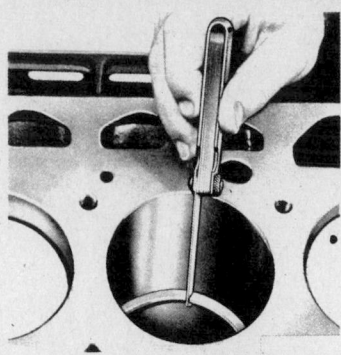

Measuring piston ring end gap

Measuring piston ring side clearance

Rod and Piston Assembly Installation

The pistons are assembled to the engine with the V notch in the head of the piston toward the front.

Rear Main Bearing Oil Seal

Service replacement seals are of split rubber type composition. This type of seal makes it possible to replace the upper half of the rear main oil seal without removing the engine from the car. When installing rubber seals, they must be replaced as a set and can not be combined with the rope type rear main seal. The follow-

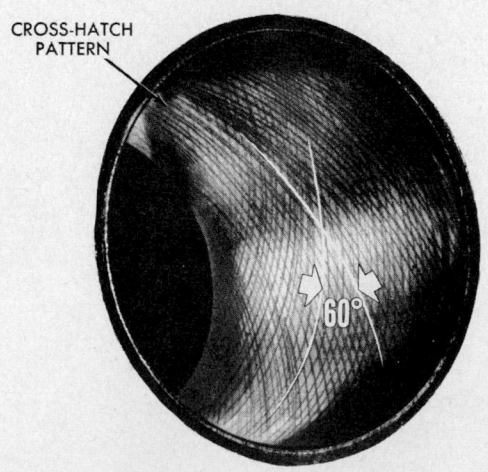

CROSS-HATCH PATTERN

60°

Cylinder wall cross-hatching pattern
(© Chrysler Corp.)

Piston Ring End Gap

	Top Compression Ring Gap (in.)	Bottom Compression Ring Gap (in.)	Oil Control Ring Gap (in.)
1965	.013-.025	.013-.025	.013-.055
1966-67	.013-.025	.013-.025	.015-.055
1968-72	.013-.023	.013-.023	.015-.055

Piston Ring Side Clearance

	Top Compression Ring Side Clearance (in.)	Bottom Compression Ring Side Clearance (in.)	Oil Control Ring Side Clearance (in.)
1965	.0015-.0030	.0015-.0040	.009
1966	.0015-.0040	.0015-.0040	.0002-.0050
1967-72	.0015-.0040	.0015-.0040	.0000-.0050

ing procedure is for removing the rope type seal and replacing it with the rubber type seal.

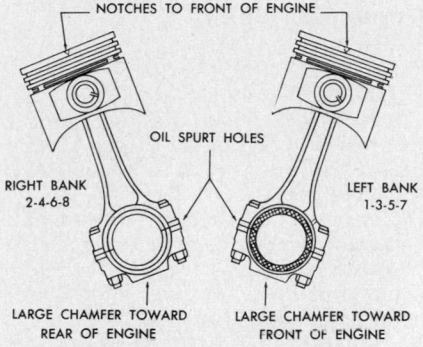

Piston and connecting rod assembly

Replacement

1. Remove the oil pan.
2. Remove the rear seal retainer and the rear main bearing cap.
3. Remove the lower rope seal by prying from the side with a small screwdriver.
4. To remove the upper rope seal, drive up on either exposed end of the seal with a 6 in. piece of 3/16 in. brazing rod. When the opposite end of the seal starts to protrude from the block, have an assistant grasp it with pliers and gently pull it from the block while the opposite end is being driven.
5. Wipe crankshaft clean and lightly oil crankshaft and new seal before installing seal.
6. Loosen all main bearing caps slightly to lower the crankshaft which will ease installation.

Caution Do not allow the crankshaft to drop enough to permit the main bearings to become displaced on the crankshaft.

7. Hold the seal tightly against the crankshaft with the thumb (with paint stripe to the rear) and install the seal in the block groove. Rotate the crankshaft if necessary while installing the seal in the groove. *Make sure the sharp edges on the block groove*

do not cut or nick the rear of the seal.

8. Install lower half of seal (with paint stripe to the rear) into the lower seal retainer.
9. Install rear main bearing cap.
10. Tighten all main bearing caps to specification.

NOTE: make sure all main bearings are located in their proper position before tightening the main bearing caps.

Side Seal Installation

Perform the following operations as rapidly as possible. The side seals are made from a material that expands quickly when oiled.

1. Apply mineral spirits or diesel fuel to the side seals. Failure to pre-oil the seals will result in an oil leak.
2. Install seals in the seal retainer grooves immediately.
3. Install seal retainer and tighten screws to 30 ft. lbs.

Front Suspension

Torsion Bar Springs

Contrary to appearance, the torsion bars are not interchangeable from right to left. They are marked with an R or an L, according to their location.

Torsion Bar Removal and Replacement

Removal

1. Raise the vehicle so the front suspension drops to the limit of its downward travel.
2. Remove the upper control arm rebound bumper if so equipped.
3. On all models except 1967-72

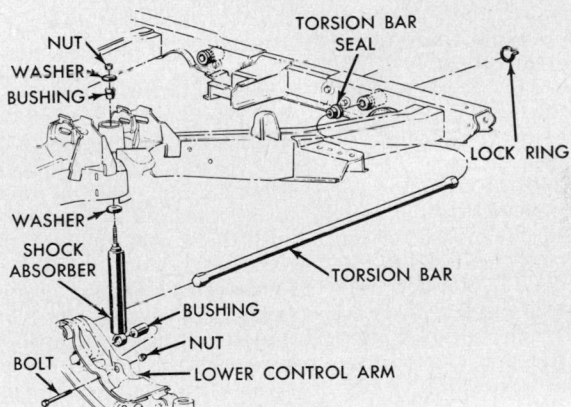

1965-70 Chrysler torsion bar
(© Chrysler Corp.)

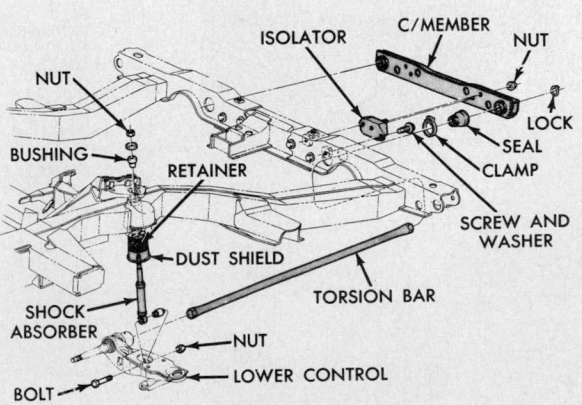

1967-70 Imperial torsion bar
(© Chrysler Corp.)

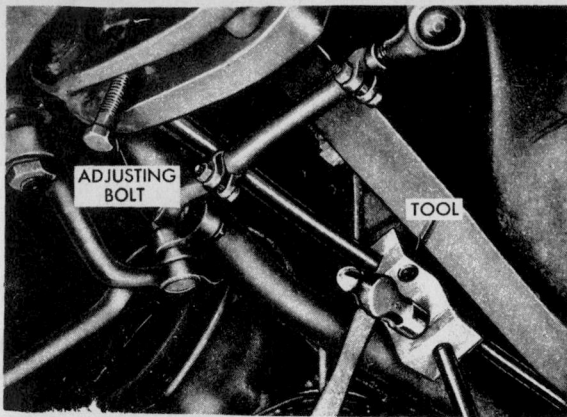

Removing the torsion bar
(© Chrysler Corporation)

Imperials, remove the tension from the torsion bar to be replaced by turning the anchor adjusting bolt in a counterclockwise direction and removing the adjusting bolt and swivel. On 1967-72 Imperials, release the load on both torsion bars by turning each anchor adjusting bolt in a counterclockwise direction. This is necessary because the rubber insulator rear crossmember would be under load and could possibly cause severe damage or personal injury.

4. Slide rear anchor balloon seal off of the rear anchor and remove the lockring from the anchor.
5. On all models except 1965-66 Imperials, remove the torsion bar from the vehicle by sliding it rearward and out of the torsion bar rear anchor. On 1965-66 Imperials, slide the torsion bar rearward until the forward end disengages from the lower control arm. Remove the torsion from the vehicle by sliding it for-

ward and downward until it disengages from the rear anchor. It may be necessary to attach a tool to the torsion bar and drive it rearward to disengage it from the lower control arm.

If it is necessary to attach a tool to the torsion bar to remove it and the same torsion bar is to be installed in the car again, care must be exercised not to crack or badly mar the surface of the torsion bar as this could lead to premature torsion bar failure.

Caution Installation

1. Position the torsion bar in the chassis and apply a coating of chassis lubricant to both ends.
NOTE: on 1965-66 Imperials, to install the torsion bar, turn the bar until the anchor end is positioned approximately 120° (eight o'clock or four o'clock position) down from the frame and engage the front end of the bar in the hex opening in the lower control arm. If the anchor end is not installed in this position, it

will be impossible to adjust the front suspension to the correct height after the torsion bar is installed.
2. Install the lockring in the anchor, making sure it is seated in the groove.
3. Pack the annular opening in the rear anchor completely full of chassis lubricant and position the lip of the balloon seal in the groove of the anchor.
4. On all models except 1965-66 Imperials, turn the adjusting bolt in a clockwise direction to place a load on the torsion bar. On 1965-66 Imperials, turn the adjusting bolt until approximately 1 in. of threads are showing above the swivel.
5. Lower the vehicle to the floor and adjust front end height as required.

Upper Ball Joint

Replacement

1. Raise the vehicle by placing a floor jack under the lower control arm. Place the lifting point of the jack as close as possible to the wheel.
2. Remove the wheel, tire and drum as an assembly. On models with disc brakes, remove the tire and wheel, remove the disc brake pads, remove the disc brake caliper from the steering knuckle and position the caliper out of the way with the brake line attached. Remove the brake rotor from the steering knuckle.
3. Remove the nut that attaches the upper ball joint to the steering knuckle and, using a suitable tool, loosen the ball joint stud from the steering knuckle.
4. Unscrew the upper ball joint from the upper control arm and remove it from the vehicle.
5. Position new ball joint on the upper control arm, screw the ball joint into the control arm

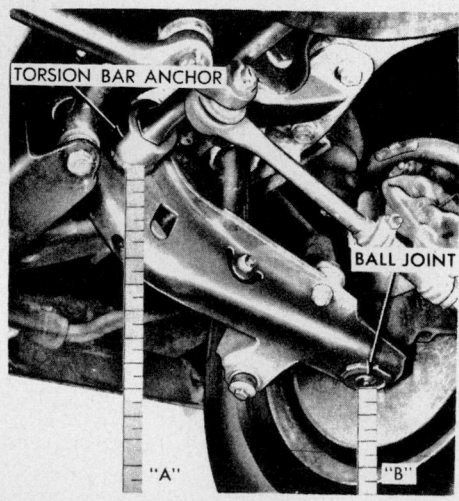

Measuring front suspension height, 1967-70 Imperial
(© Chrysler Corp.)

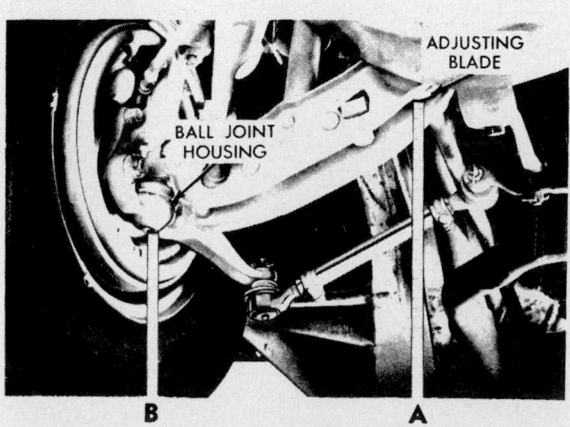

Measuring front suspension height, 1965-70 Chrysler
(© Chrysler Corp.)

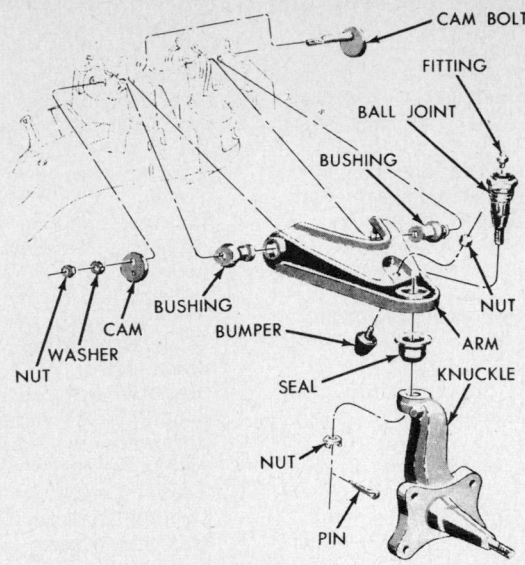

Chrysler upper control arm (© Chrysler Corporation)

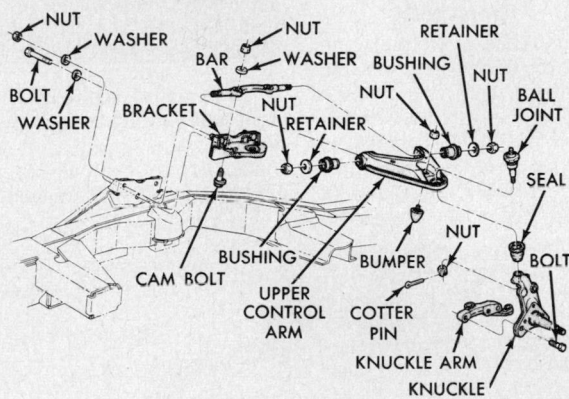

Imperial upper control arm 1967-71
(© Chrysler Corporation)

until it bottoms on the control arm and tighten the ball joint to a minimum of 125 ft. lbs.

NOTE: when installing a ball joint, make certain the ball joint threads engage those of the upper control arm squarely if the original control arm is being used.

6. Position a new seal on the ball joint stud and install the seal in the ball joint making sure the seal is fully seated on the ball joint housing.

7. Position ball joint stud in the steering knuckle and install the retaining nut.

8. Lubricate ball joint and, if replacement ball joint is equipped with knock-off type grease fitting, break off that portion of the fitting over which the lubrication gun was installed.

9. If equipped with disc brakes, install the rotor, caliper and brake pads. Install the tire and wheel.

10. Lower the vehicle and adjust

front suspension height as required.

Lower Ball Joint

Inspection

1. Raise the front of the vehicle by placing a floor jack under the lower control arm. Position the lifting point of the jack as close to the wheel as possible.

2. Have an assistant raise and lower the tire and wheel assembly and observe any movement at the lower ball joint.

3. On 1965-66 Imperials and 1965-67 Chryslers, replace the ball joint if the axial (up and down) play of the ball joint housing arm in relation to the ball joint stud exceeds 0.050 in. On 1968-72 Chryslers, replace the ball joint if the axial play exceeds 0.070 in. On 1967-72 Imperials, the lower ball joints are pre-loaded and, if any free

play exists, the lower ball joint-control arm assembly must be replaced.

Removal— 1965-72 Chrysler and 1965-66 Imperial

The lower ball joint is integral with the steering arm and is not serviced separately.

1. Raise the vehicle on a hoist so the front suspension will drop to the downward limit of its travel.

2. Remove the upper control arm rebound bumper if so equipped.

3. Remove all load from the torsion bar that is attached to the same side of the vehicle as the ball joint to be replaced by turning the torsion bar adjusting bolt in a counterclockwise direction.

4. Remove the tire, wheel, and brake drum from the vehicle as an assembly. If equipped with disc brakes, remove the tire and wheel. Remove the brake pads, and remove the caliper from the steering knuckle and position it out of the way with the brake line attached. Remove the rotor from the spindle.

5. Remove the two lower bolts that attach the steering arm-ball joint assembly to the brake assembly mounting plate.

6. Using a suitable tool, disconnect the tie rod end from the steering arm.

7. Remove the ball joint stud retaining nut and cotter pin.

8. Using a suitable tool, separate and remove the ball joint from the lower contol arm.

Installation

1. Position ball joint-steering arm assembly on the steering knuckle and install the two retaining bolts.

2. Insert the ball joint stud in the lower control arm and install the retaining nut and cotter pin.

3. Position the tie rod end in the steering knuckle and install the retaining nut and cotter pin.

4. Place a load on the torsion bar by turning the adjusting bolt in a clockwise direction.

5. Install the tire, wheel and brake drum assembly. If equipped with disc brakes, install the rotor, caliper, brake pads and tire and wheel assembly.

6. Lower vehicle and install upper control arm rebound bumper if so equipped.

7. Check and adjust front suspension height as required.

Removal—1967-72 Imperial

Lower ball joints on these Imperial models are serviced only as ball joint-control arm assemblies.

1. Raise the vehicle on a hoist so

the front suspension drops to the downward limit of its travel.

2. Remove the wheel and tire as an assembly.

3. Remove the load from *both* torsion bars by turning the adjusting bolts in a counterclockwise direction.

4. Disconnect the shock absorber from the lower control arm and position the shock out of the way. Disconnect the strut bar from the lower control arm.

5. Disconnect the brake hose from the caliper.

6. Remove the lower ball joint retaining nut and cotter pin.

7. Using a suitable tool, separate the ball joint stud from the steering knuckle.

8. Remove the nut and washer that attaches the lower control arm pivot shaft to the frame.

9. Using a brass drift and hammer, tap the end of the pivot shaft to loosen it (the shaft is a tapered fit in the front crossmember).

10. Remove the lower control arm and shaft from the vehicle as an assembly.

11. Position the control arm assembly in a press with the hex opening for the torsion bar in the up position and place a support under the outer edge of the control arm.

12. Insert a brass drift in the hex opening and press the shaft out of the control arm. The bushing inner arm will remain on the shaft.

13. Remove the torsion bar adjusting bolt and swivel from the control arm.

Installation

1. Position a new bushing on the pivot shaft (flange end of the bushing first) and seat the bushing on the shoulder of the pivot shaft.

2. Press the shaft and bushing assembly into the new control arm.

3. Install the torsion bar adjusting bolt and swivel on the new control arm.

4. Position a new seal on the ball joint and install the seal. To ease installation of the seal, the ball joint stud should be perpendicular to the body of the ball joint.

5. Position the control arm assembly on the crossmember in approximate operating position and install the nut and washer. *Do not tighten the nut until the full weight of the vehicle is on the wheels.*

6. Insert the lower ball joint stud in the steering knuckle and install the retaining nut and cotter pin.

7. Install the strut bar rear bushing and retainer on the strut bar

and insert the strut bar through the crossmember.

8. Install the front strut bar bushing and retainer on the strut bar and install the retaining nut finger tight only.

9. Position the rear of the strut bar over the lower control arm and install the bumper and plate.

10. Connect the shock absorber to the lower control arm and install the retaining nut finger tight. Place a load on each torsion bar by turning the adjusting bolt clockwise.

11. Connect the brake line to the disc brake caliper and bleed the brakes.

12. Install the tire and wheel assembly.

13. Lower the vehicle to the floor. Tighten the strut bar, shock absorber and lower control arm attaching nuts.

14. Check and adjust front end height as required.

Front Height Adjustment

1. Jounce vehicle several times, releasing it on downward motion.

2. Measure distance A. For 1965-66 Imperial models, this is measured from the lowest point of the lower control arm bushing housing to the floor. For 1965-72

Chrysler models, the measurement is taken from the lowest point of the adjusting blade. For 1967-72 Imperial models, measure from the lowest point of the front torsion bar anchor at the rear of the lower control arm flange.

3. Measure distance B. This is the distance between the lowest point of the lower ball joint housing and the floor.

4. Subtract distance A from distance B to obtain front suspension height.

5. Measure the other side. There should be no more than $\frac{1}{8}$ in. difference in height from one side to the other.

6. Adjust height, as necessary, by turning torsion bar adjusting bolt clockwise to increase height and counterclockwise to decrease height.

Jacking, Hoisting

Jack car at front under lower control arm and at rear under axle housing.

To lift at frame, use adapters so that contact will be made at points

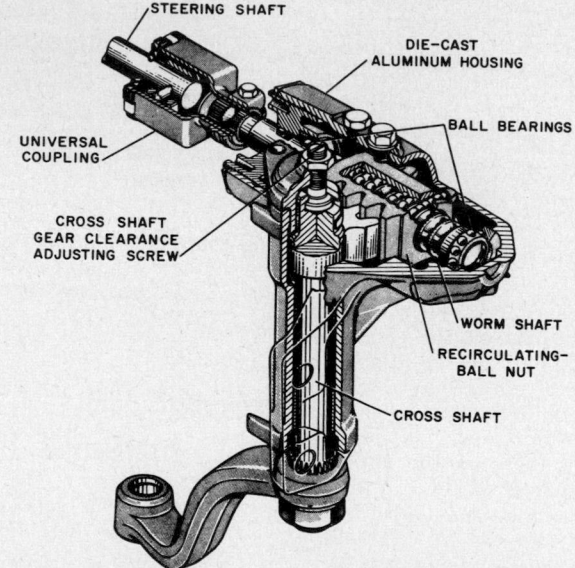

1965-70 manual steering gear (© Chrysler Corp.)

Front Suspension Height

	Suspension Type	Chrysler (in.)	Imperial (in.)
1965-66	Standard	$1\frac{1}{8} \pm \frac{1}{8}$	$2 \pm \frac{1}{8}$
	Heavy Duty	$1\frac{1}{8} \pm \frac{1}{8}$	$2\frac{3}{8} \pm \frac{1}{8}$
	Limousine		$2\frac{3}{8} \pm \frac{1}{8}$
1967-72	Standard	$1\frac{1}{8} \pm \frac{1}{8}$	$1\frac{3}{4} \pm \frac{1}{8}$
	Heavy Duty	$1\frac{1}{8} \pm \frac{1}{8}$	

shown. Lifting pad must extend beyond sides of supporting structure.

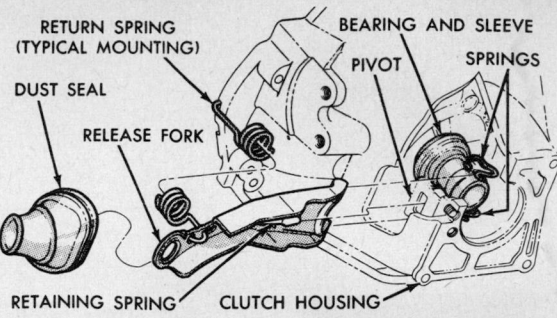

Clutch release fork, bearing and sleeve (© Chrysler Corp.)

Steering Gear

Manual Steering Gear
Instructions covering the adjustment of the steering gear are in the Unit Repair Section.

Power Steering Gear
Troubleshooting and repair instructions covering power steering gear is given in the Unit Repair Section.

Manual Steering Gear Removal and Installation

1965
1. Remove steering arm retaining nut. Pull off steering arm.
2. Remove bolt from coupling clamp at upper end of steering gear wormshaft.
3. Loosen steering column jacket to instrument panel clamp. Slide the column assembly up far enough to disengage the coupling from the wormshaft.
4. Remove three steering gear housing bolts and remove steering gear from under vehicle.
5. Reverse procedure to install.
6. Tighten mounting bolts to 80 ft. lbs. and coupling bolt to 33 ft. lbs. Tighten steering arm nut to 120 ft. lbs.

1966
This procedure differs from that for 1965 models only in the substitution of the following steps:
2. Remove pin from coupling clamp at upper end of steering gear wormshaft.
6. Tighten mounting bolts to 80 ft. lbs. and steering arm nut to 120 ft. lbs.

1967
1. Remove steering gear arm retaining nut and lockwasher. Remove arm with puller.
2. Disconnect column shift gear selector linkage.
3. Remove pin from coupling clamp at upper end of steering gear wormshaft.

4. Loosen steering column jacket to instrument panel clamp. Slide the column assembly up far enough to disengage the coupling from the wormshaft.
5. Remove column lower support plate to floor pan bolts.
6. Remove housing bolts. Remove steering gear.
7. Reverse procedure to install.
8. Torque mounting bolts to 80 ft. lbs. and steering arm nut to 120 ft. lbs.

1968
Modify the procedure for 1967 models by the substitution of the following step:
8. Torque mounting bolts to 80 ft. lbs. and steering arm nut to 175 ft. lbs.

1969
Modify the procedure for 1967 models by substitution of the following step:
8. Torque mounting bolts to 100 ft. lbs. and steering arm nut to 175 ft. lbs.

1970-72
1. Remove energy absorbing steering column. See Unit Repair Section for this procedure.
2. Remove steering arm nut and lockwasher. Pull off steering arm.
3. Remove frame mounting bolts. Remove steering gear.
4. Reverse procedure to install. Torque mounting bolts to 100 ft. lbs. and steering arm nut to 180 ft. lbs. When installing steering gear in vehicle, be sure that vehicle wheels are straight ahead and that steering gear is centered.

Clutch

The only practical service possible on the clutch assembly is adjusting the pedal free play. All other service requires the removal of the clutch assembly

If the clutch assembly is being removed because of chatter or malfunction, it is advisable to check to see if there is any oil leaking from the rear main bearing or from the transmission. Oil on the clutch facings will produce a noticeable chatter, or slipping.

Clutch Pedal Free Play (Throw-out Bearing Clearance)
This adjustment is done at the adjusting nut on the clutch release rod. There should be 1 in. free-travel of the pedal before the throw-out bearing strikes the fingers of the clutch.

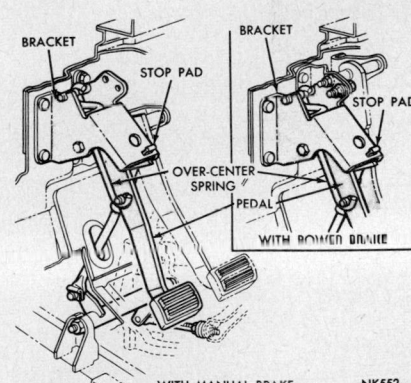

Clutch pedal and linkage—1965-70

Clutch Assembly Removal
Remove the driveshaft. Disconnect the gear shift control rods and the speedometer cable. Support the back of the transmission and remove the bolts that hold the transmission to the bell housing.

Some shops prefer to replace the two upper bolts with two long pilots so the transmission can be slid straight back on the pilots. This eliminates the risk of bending the clutch disc.

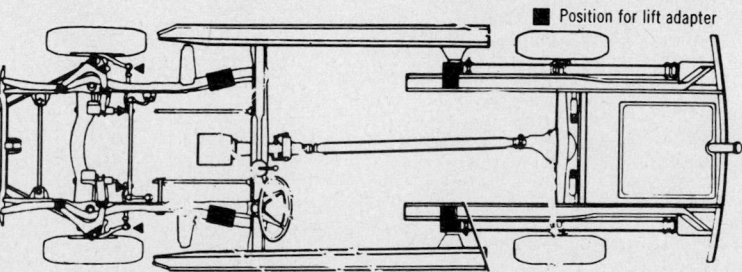

■ Position for lift adapter

Positioning lift adapter (© Chrysler Corp.)

On all models, remove the transmission assembly, the clutch housing lower pan and the clutch throw-out fork. The clutch cover assembly should be stamped, showing its relation to the flywheel so that it can be reassembled in the same position from which it was removed. The cover bolts should be removed, a few turns at a time, in order to avoid springing the clutch cover.

Standard Transmission

Transmission refill capacities are in the Capacities table.

See Unit Repair Section for overhaul procedures.

Transmission Removal and Installation

1. Disconnect all attaching parts at the transmission.
2. Remove driveshaft.
3. Support the rear of the engine on a padded jack and take off the transmission crossmember.
4. Detach the transmission from the clutch housing and move down and out of the car.
5. Reverse procedure for installation.

Shift Linkage Adjustment
1965 Four Speed Floorshift

1. Remove the shift boot attaching screws, and slide the boot up on the shift lever.
2. Disconnect all the shift rods at the adjusting swivels.

3. Bend a ¼ in. diameter rod to a right angle. Insert through the aligning holes in the control rod levers. This locks all three levers in neutral positions.
4. Adjust the length of the three shift rods until the swivel stub shafts match the control rod lever holes. Install the stub shafts and secure with clips.
5. Remove the ¼ in. diameter aligning rod.
6. With transmission hand shift lever in third or fourth speed detent position, adjust the lever stop screws (front and rear) to provide from .020-.040 in. clearance between the lever and the stops. Tighten adjusting screw locknuts.

7. Test linkage adjustment for ease of shifting and crossover operation.

Caution Accuracy of adjustment is very important because there is no reverse gear interlock to prevent engaging two gears at the same time.

8. Slide the boot down the shift lever shaft to the floor and tighten with attaching screws.

1965 Column Shift

1. Disconnect second-third rod from column lever and first-reverse rod from transmission lever. Position both transmission levers in neutral positions.

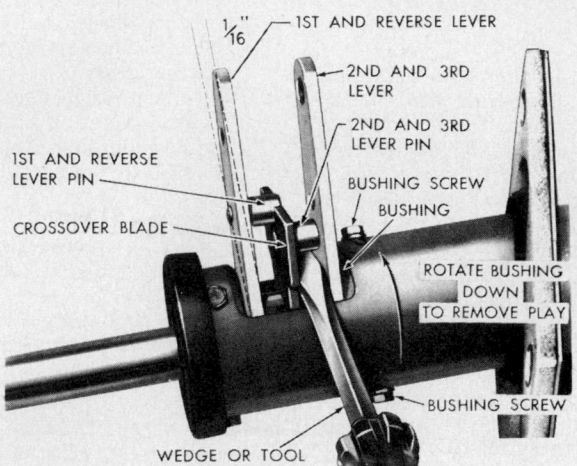

Holding crossover blade in neutral position, 1964-70 column shift
(© Chrysler Corp.)

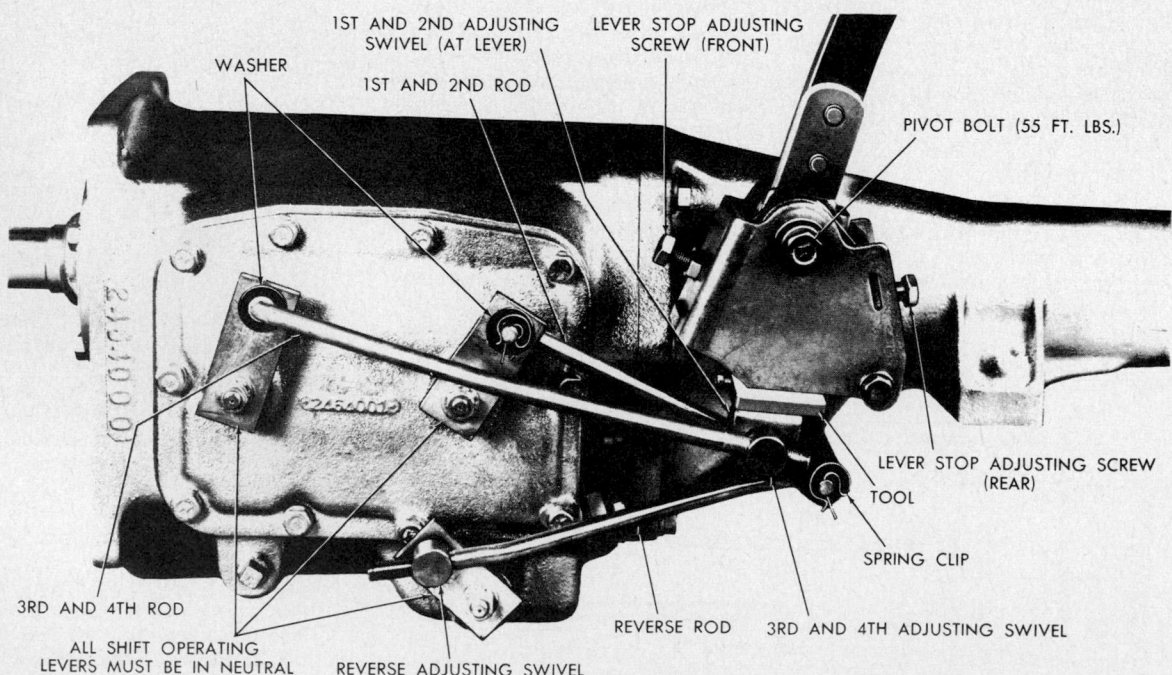

Four speed linkage, 1964-65 (© Chrysler Corp.)

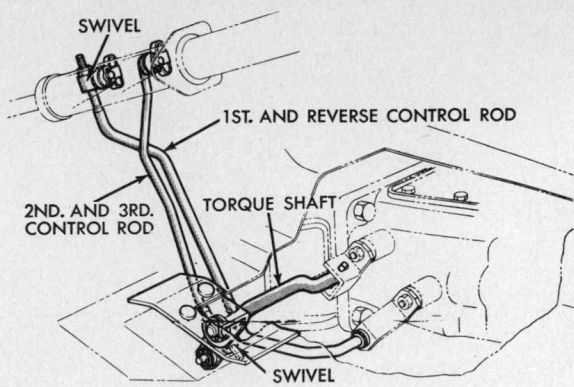

Column shift linkage, 1965-69
(© Chrysler Corp.)

2. If ends of lower column levers can be moved more than 1/16 in. up and down, loosen the two upper bushing screws (just above the lever slot) and rotate the bushing downward to remove play. Tighten screws.
3. Use a screwdriver between the crossover blade and second-third lever, to engage the crossover blade with both lever pins.
4. Adjust the length of each control rod and connect the rods.
5. Remove screwdriver and check shifting.

1966-69 Column Shift

These models have an interlock to prevent engaging two gears at once. Add the following steps to the 1965 Column Shift adjustment procedure:

6. Shift transmission into neutral. Make sure clutch free play is correct.
7. Loosen clutch interlock rod swivel clamp bolt. Hold clutch pedal to fully returned position. Slide swivel along interlock rod to engage pawl with lever. Tighten clamp bolt.
8. Disengage clutch. Shift transmission halfway between neutral and first. Let out clutch pedal. The interlock should only allow the pedal to return to one or two inches from the floor.

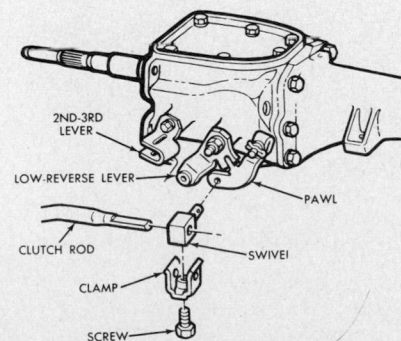

Three-speed interlock—1966-69
(© Chrysler Corp.)

1970-71 Column Shift

1. Disconnect both shift rods from transmission levers. Check that transmission levers are in neutral positions.
2. Move shift lever to line up locating slots in bottom of steering column shift housing and bearing housing. Install suitable tool in slot and lock ignition switch.
3. Place screwdriver between crossover blade and second-third lever so that both pins are engaged by crossover blade.
4. Set first-reverse transmission lever in reverse position. Adjust rod length and connect the rod.
5. Remove gearshift housing locating tool. Unlock ignition switch. Shift column lever to neutral position.
6. Install and adjust length of second-third rod.
7. Remove screwdriver. Steering column should lock in reverse but not in second position.

Automatic Transmission

Anti-Stall Adjustment

The anti-stall consists of a diaphragm and a plunger with a small orifice. The air trapped behind the diaphragm is bled out at a specific rate by the orifice. The device acts to keep the throttle from snapping shut during the last 1/4 in. of travel.

To check, open the throttle by hand and release. The closing of the throttle should be visibly slowed by the action of the anti-stall.

To adjust, have the engine at operating temperature and set adjusting screw so that the plunger has 1/16 in. travel after the throttle is fully closed.

Neutral Start Switch

The neutral switch is mounted in the transmission case on all models.

When the transmission manual lever is placed in either the Park or Neutral position, a cam, which is attached to the transmission throttle lever inside the transmission, contacts the neutral start switch and provides a ground to complete the starter solenoid circuit. On late model Chryslers and Imperials, the back-up light switch has been incorporated into the neutral switch. The combination neutral and back-up light switch can be identified by the three electrical terminals on the rear of the switch. On this type of switch, the center terminal is for the neutral switch and the two outer terminals are for the back-up lights.

NOTE: in order for the neutral start switch to function properly, the transmission manual linkage must be properly adjusted and the actuater cam in the transmission must be centered in the neutral switch mounting hole in the transmission.

Shift Linkage Adjustment

There are two basic types of Torqueflite linkages used in Chrysler and Imperial vehicles. A cable linkage is used on 1965 models, and a rod linkage is used on 1966-70 models. Adjustment procedures for both types are given below.

1965 Column Selector

1. Have an assistant hold the selector lever firmly in the 1 (Low) position.
2. Hold the gearshift control cable guide centered in the hole of the transmission case and apply light pressure to bottom the assembly in the low detent. Rotate the adjustment wheel clockwise until it contacts the case squarely. Turn the wheel counter-clockwise to line up an adjustment hole with the screw hole in the case. Counting this hole as number one, turn the wheel counter-clockwise until the fifth hole lines up with the screw hole.

1965 Console Selector

1. With the selector lever in Reverse, look through the console clearance hole to see if scribe mark on control lever lines up with center of sprag lever guide pin. To adjust, loosen locknut and rotate cam to align scribe mark with center of guide pin. Hold in position and torque cam locknut to 95 in. lbs.

1966-69 Console Selector, 1966-69 Column Selector

1. Place selector lever in Park. Loosen control rod swivel clamp.
2. Move selector to rear of Park detent.
3. Check that transmission lever is in park position. Tighten swivel clamp screw to 100 in. lbs.

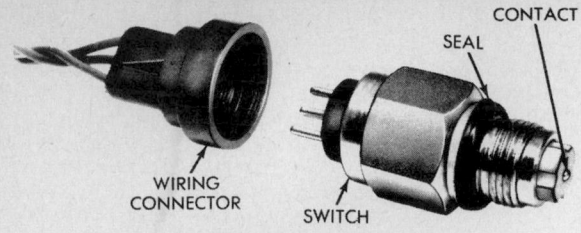

Combination neutral start and back-up light switch
(© Chrysler Corporation)

WIRING CONNECTOR
SWITCH
SEAL
CONTACT

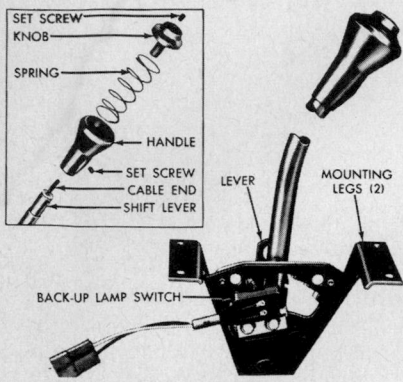

Automatic transmission console shifter—
1965-70
(© Chrysler Corp.)

SET SCREW
KNOB
SPRING
HANDLE
SET SCREW
CABLE END
SHIFT LEVER
LEVER
MOUNTING LEGS (2)
BACK-UP LAMP SWITCH

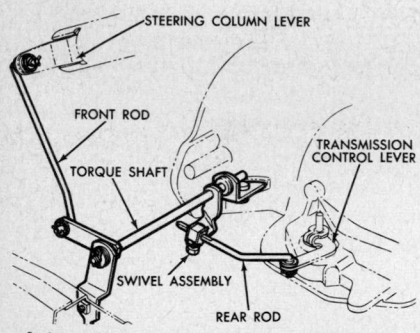

Automatic transmission columnshift linkage
—1966 Chrysler and 1967-69 All
(© Chrysler Corp.)

STEERING COLUMN LEVER
FRONT ROD
TORQUE SHAFT
TRANSMISSION CONTROL LEVER
SWIVEL ASSEMBLY
REAR ROD

1965 Console selector adjustment
(© Chrysler Corp.)

SELECTOR LEVER IN REVERSE
SCRIBE MARK
GUIDE PIN
CAM
LOCK NUT
PARKING LOCK CABLE

1970-72 Console Selector, 1970-72 Column Selector

1. Free adjustable rod ends.
2. Place selector lever in Park. Lock steering column. On console selector, line up locating slots in bottom of shift housing and bearing housing. Hold in place with a suitable tool.
3. Move selector to rear of Park detent.
4. Set adjustable rods to proper length.
5. Check adjustment:
   a. Detents and gate stops should be positive.
   b. Selector lever must not remain out of detent position when placed against gate and then released.
   c. Key start must occur with selector lever held against Park gate.

Throttle Linkage Adjustment

1965-70 Manual Transmission Models

1. Apply multi-purpose grease lightly to all linkage friction points.

2. Disconnect choke at carburetor. Set carburetor on slow idle position.
3. Adjust position of cable housing ferrule in clamp to remove slack from cable. Back off ferrule ¼ in. to provide ¼ in. cable slack at idle.
4. Connect choke rod.

1965-66 Chrysler with Automatic Transmission
1967-68 All Automatic Transmission Models

1. Apply multi-purpose grease lightly to all linkage friction points.
2. Disconnect return spring and slotted transmission rod from carburetor lever pin. Disconnect transmission intermediate rod ball socket from upper bellcrank ball end.
3. Disconnect choke. Set carburetor on slow idle position.
4. Place a 3/16 in. dia. rod in holes in the engine mounted bellcrank and lever. Adjust intermediate transmission rod at upper end. The ball socket must line up with the ball end with rod held up-

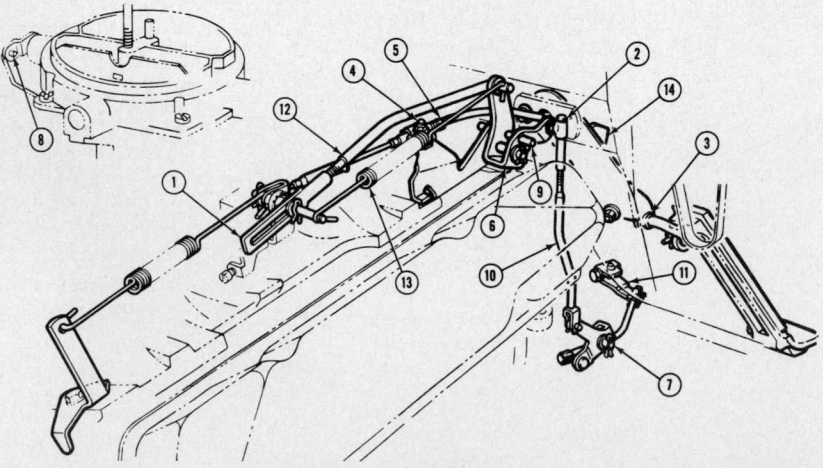

1967 throttle linkage—all automatic transmission (© Chrysler Corp.)

ward against the transmission stop. Assemble ball socket to ball end.

5. Remove 3/16 in. rod from upper bellcrank and lever.

6. Hold carburetor rod forward against transmission stop and adjust so that rear end of adjusting link slot just contacts the carburetor lever pin. Lengthen

carburetor rod two full turns.

7. Assemble slotted link to carburetor.

8. Adjust cable housing ferrule in clamp to remove all cable slack. Back off ferrule 1/4 in.

9. Connect choke rod.

1965-66 Imperial Automatic Transmission Models

1. Apply multi-purpose grease lightly to linkage friction points.

2. Disconnect return spring and slotted transmission rod from carburetor lever pin.

3. Disconnect choke. Set carburetor on slow idle position.

4. Hold transmission lever forward

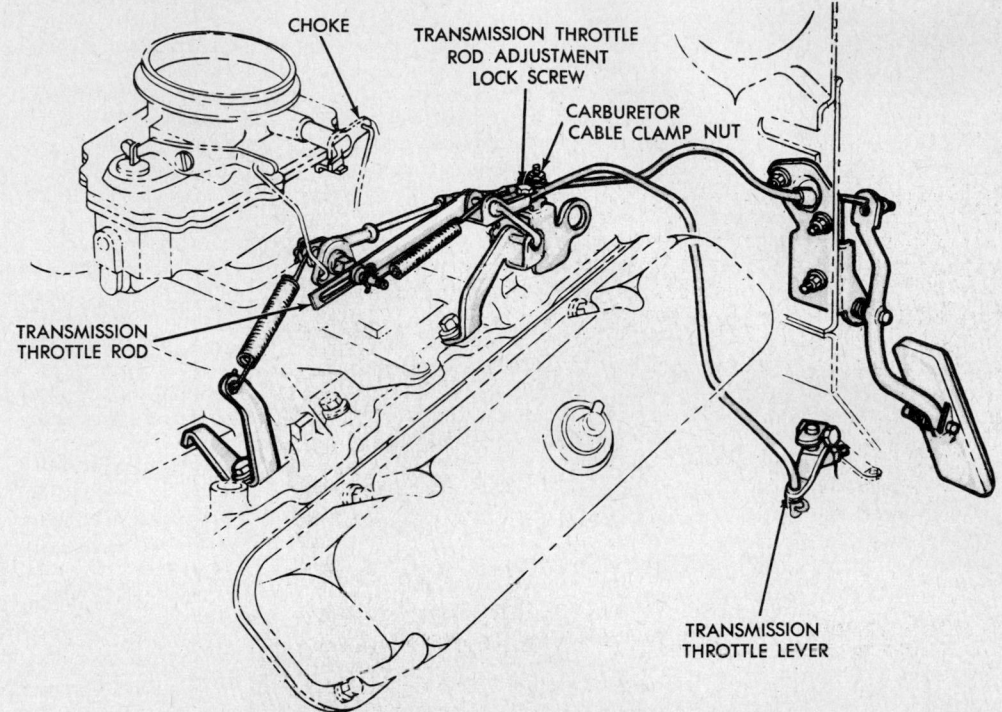

Throttle linkage, all 1970 automatic transmission models (© Chrysler Corp.)

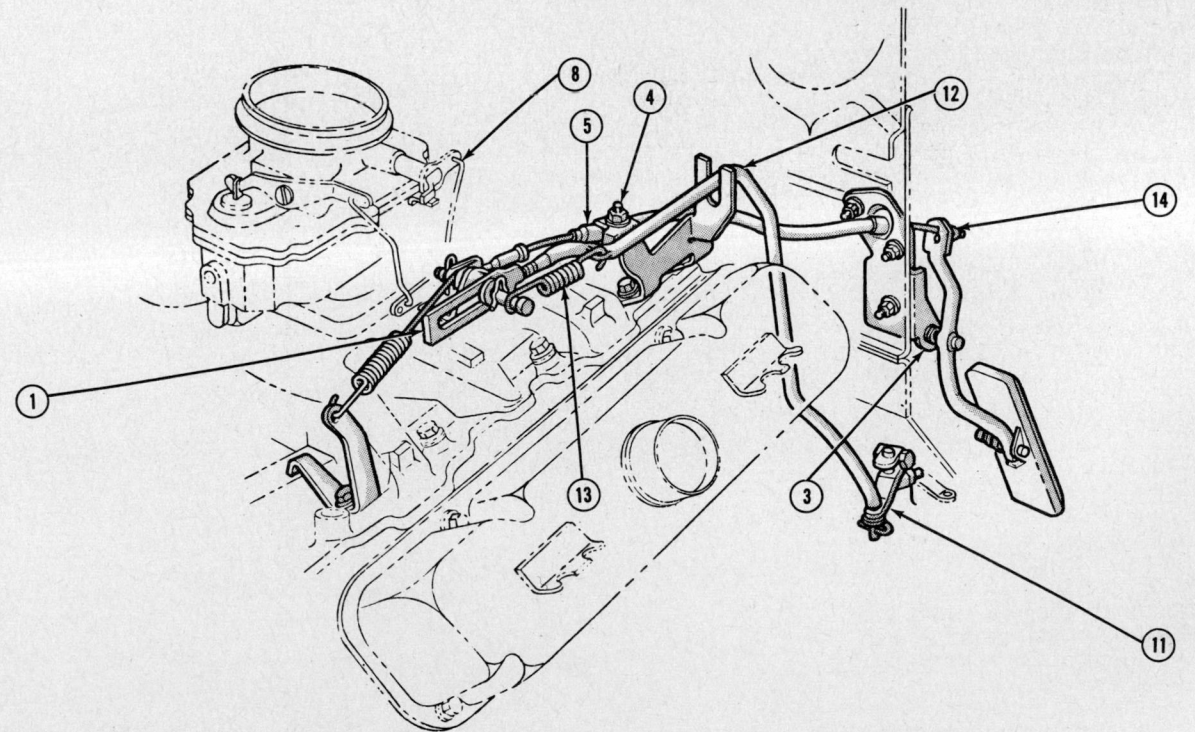

Throttle linkage, all 1969 automatic transmission models (© Chrysler Corp.)

against stop. Adjust length of transmission rod so that rear end of adjusting link slot just contacts the carburetor lever pin. Lengthen the rod one full turn.

5. Replace slotted adjustment rod on carburetor lever pin. Replace transmission linkage return spring.

6. Adjust position of cable housing ferrule in clamp to remove all cable slack. Back off ferrule ¼ in.

7. Connect choke rod.

1969-71 Automatic Transmission Models

This procedure is the same as that outlined above for the 1965-66 Imperial Automatic Transmission Models with the substitution of the following steps:

2. Disconnect return spring.

4. Loosen transmission throttle rod adjustment lock screw. Hold transmission lever firmly forward against stop. On engines with solenoid idle stops, the solenoid plunger must also be in its fully extended position. Adjust transmission rod length by pulling forward on the slotted link so that rear edge of slot is against carburetor lever pin. Tighten locking screw.

5. Replace transmission linkage return spring.

Transmission Removal and Installation

1965 All Models

The transmission and converter must be removed as an assembly or the converter drive plate, front pump bushing, and oil seal will be damaged. The drive plate will not support a load; therefore, none of the weight of the transmission should be allowed to rest on the plate during removal.

1. Raise and support vehicle.
2. Connect a remote control starter switch to solenoid so that engine may be rotated from under vehicle.
3. Disconnect high tension cable from coil.
4. Place selector lever in park position.
5. Remove converter front cover plate for access to drain plug and mounting bolts.
6. Rotate engine to bring drain plug to six o'clock position.
7. Drain converter and transmission.
8. Mark converter and drive plate to locate position in reassembly. Matching is made positive by offsetting one of the holes in plate and in converter.
9. Rotate engine to five and seven o'clock positions and remove two drive plate bolts. Then rotate en-

gine and remove remaining bolts. Do not rotate converter or drive plate by prying because this can distort the drive plate. Also, the starter should never be engaged if the drive plate is not attached to the converter with at least one bolt, or if the transmission case to engine block bolts have been loosened.

10. Disconnect battery ground cable.
11. Remove starting motor assembly.
12. Disconnect neutral starting switch wire.
13. Remove gearshift control cable to transmission adjusting wheel lock screw. Pull cable out of transmission case as far as possible. It may be necessary to back off on the adjusting wheel a few turns.
14. Insert small screwdriver above and slightly to right of gearshift cable. Disengage cable adapter lock spring by pushing screwdriver to right while pulling outward on cable.
15. Disconnect throttle rod from relay lever at left side of the transmission.
16. Disconnect oil cooler lines at transmission and remove oil filler tube.
17. Remove speedometer pinion and sleeve.
18. Loosen parking lock cable clamp bolt where cable enters the cover. Tap end of bolt lightly to release hold on cable. Remove housing cover lower plug. Insert screwdriver through hole and gently exert pressure against projecting portion of cable lock spring and withdraw lock cable.
19. Disconnect driveshaft at the rear universal joint and pull shaft assembly out of extension housing. (Except Imperial models.) Remove driveshaft center bearing housing bolts and slide shaft rearward to disengage front joint from front yoke. (Imperial models)
20. Remove rear engine mount insulator-to-extension housing bolts.
21. Install rear support fixture at

engine and raise engine slightly.

22. Remove attaching bolts and the crossmember.
23. Place proper jack under transmission to support assembly.
24. Attach small C-clamp to edge of converter to hold converter in place as transmission is removed.
25. Remove converter housing retaining bolts and carefully work the transmission rearward off engine block dowels. Disengage converter hub from end of crankshaft.
26. Lower transmission jack, remove transmission and converter as an assembly.
27. Remove C-clamp and carefully slide converter out of transmission.
28. Install in reverse of above. It is important that front pump rotors properly align to engage the front pump inner lugs. An aligning tool is necessary. The converter hub hole in crankshaft should be coated with wheel bearing lubricant.

1966 All Models, 1967-72 Chrysler

This procedure is the same as that for 1965 All Models outlined above, with the substitution of the following steps:

13. Disconnect gear selector rods from transmission.
14. Delete Step 14.
18. Delete Step 18.

1967-72 Imperial

This procedure is the same as that for 1965 All Models, with the substitution of the following steps:

13. Disconnect gear selector rods from transmission.
14. Delete Step 14.
18. Delete Step 18.
23. Place jack under transmission to support assembly. Through openings on rear side of torsion bar rear anchor crossmember, remove four large bolts securing rubber isolators to center crossmember. Remove six additional bolts securing center crossmember, then remove crossmember from stub frame. Do not remove

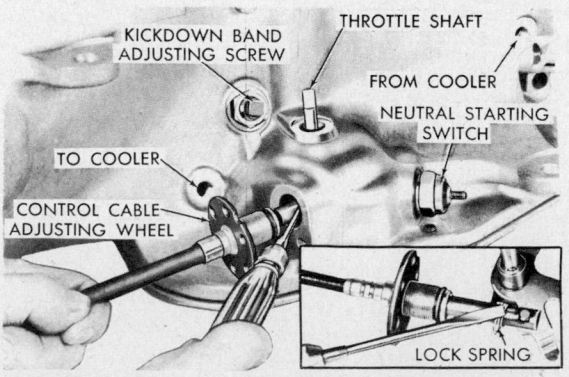

Removing gearshift control cable (© Chrysler Corp.)

rear anchor crossmember from the torsion bars.

U Joints, Drive Lines

All Chrysler from 1965 and Imperial from 1967 models use one piece driveshafts with two universal joints. All 1965 Chrysler manual transmission models have a ball and trunnion joint at the front and a cross and roller joint at the rear. 1965 Chrysler automatic transmission models and all 1966-72 Chrysler models have two cross and roller joints, with a slip spline at the front universal joint. 1967-70 Imperials have two constant velocity universal joints with a sliding yoke at the front.

All 1965-66 Imperials have two piece driveshafts with three universal joints, a support bearing forward of the center joint, and a sliding spline. 1965-66 models have two constant velocity joints and a cross and roller joint at the front.

Refer to the Dodge-Plymouth Section for disassembly and repair details on ball and trunnion and cross and roller universal joints.

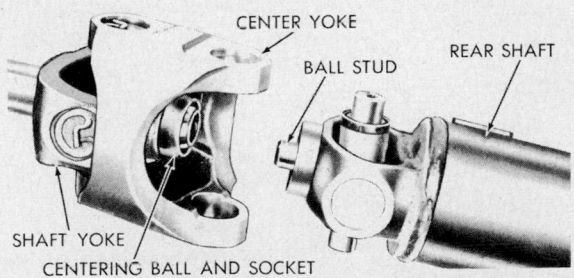

Center constant velocity universal joint, 1965-66 Imperial
(© Chrysler Corp.)

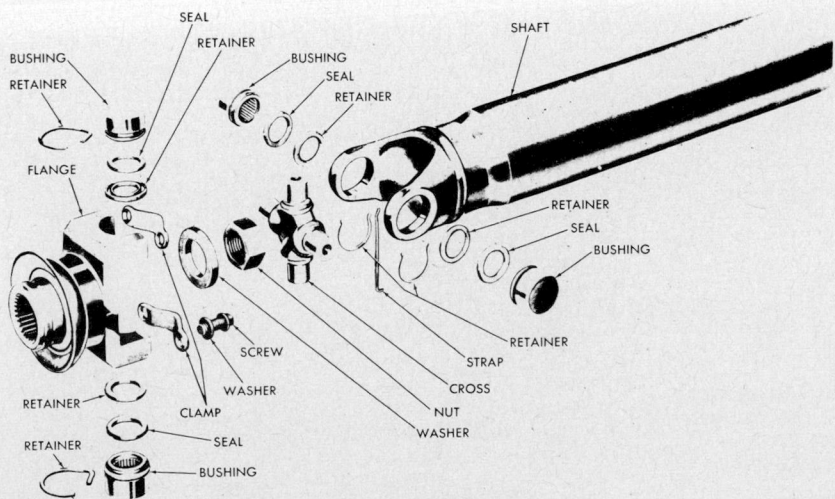

Rear cross and roller U-joint (© Chrysler Corp.)

Constant Velocity Universal Joint

Disassembly

Remove the driveshaft and, before disassembling any parts, mark the joints for proper indexing at the time of assembly.

1. Remove four screws and lockwashers. Remove spline yoke.
2. Remove two loose bearings from centering socket yoke.
3. Remove snap-rings holding the bearing assemblies in the center socket yoke shaft, and center yoke bores.
4. Press bearing assemblies from the yokes by using a 3/4 in. socket as a remover and a pipe or socket with an inside diameter of not less than 1 1/16 in. as a receiver on the opposite bearing. With the aid of a press or vise, press one of the rear yoke bearings about 3/8 in. out of the yoke.
5. Clamp the exposed bearing in the vise and drive the yoke from the bearing with a brass drift.
6. Using the same procedure, press the exposed end of the cross to force the bearing on the opposite end about 3/8 in. out of the yoke. Remove the bearing from the yoke as previously described in Step 5.
7. Remove the remaining set of bearings from the propeller shaft yoke in the same way.
8. With the shaft held in the vise, press in on the yoke shaft and work the center joint off the cross.
9. Remove the cross from the propeller shaft yoke. Remove centering stud spring from the propeller shaft.
10. Remove the four roller bearing assemblies to separate the yoke shaft from the center yoke, as previously described.

If it is necessary to remove the centering ball and socket assembly, proceed as follows:

11. Carefully pry the centering ball seal assembly from the yoke shaft.
12. Remove seal from the centering stud seal retainer and the bearing rollers from the centering ball.
13. Fill the cavity behind the centering ball and inside the ball with lithium base grease.
14. Insert a rod, slightly smaller than the inside diameter of the centering ball, into the ball, then strike it sharply with a hammer. The force applied should force the ball and retainer from the yoke.

Assembly

1. Position the centering assembly in the yoke with the large diameter hole up, and press it firmly into its seat.
2. Apply grease on the inside surface of the centering ball. Install the 34 rollers. Install the centering stud seal in the ball.
3. Install centering ball seal assembly on the yoke and press firmly into place.
4. Coat the inside surfaces of the bearing races with the same grease, and install the 32 rollers. Also, pack the reservoirs in the ends of the cross with the same grease.
5. Place the cross in the shaft yoke. Insert one bearing assembly in the bearing bore of the shaft yoke. With the bar stock or socket used as a remover when disassembling, press the bearing into the bore. At the same time, guide the cross into the bearing. Press the bearing into the yoke far enough to install the snap-ring. Install the snap-ring. Reverse the position of the yoke and install the opposite bearing and snap-ring in the same manner.
6. Place the center yoke on the cross installed in the shaft yoke. Install the two bearings and snap-rings in the yoke, as previously described.
7. Install the cross and two bearings

in the shaft yoke, in the same manner as previously described. Install snap-rings.

8. Install centering stud spring on the centering stud, (large end first). Apply grease to the stud.
9. Position the cross in the center universal joint of the propeller shaft while guiding the centering ball on the centering stud, applying pressure at the same time. Work the center yoke over the cross. Don't damage the cross seals.
10. Install the two bearing assemblies in the rear bores of the center yoke, as previously described. Install snap-rings.
11. Coat the splines of the center socket yoke with grease.
12. Install slip spline yoke on the constant velocity joints with screws and lockwashers. Tighten to 300 in. lbs.

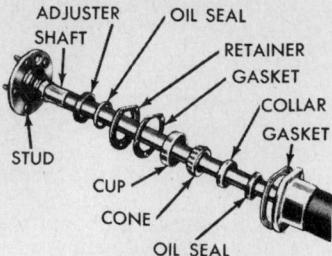

Rear axle (disassembled)
(© Chrysler Corp.)

nuts and U-bolts. Remove the spring plate.
5. Loosen and remove the nuts holding the front spring hanger to the front body mounting bracket.
6. Remove the rear spring hanger bolts and let the spring drop far enough to pull the front spring hanger bolts out of the body mounting bracket.

7. Remove the front pivot bolt from the front spring hanger.
8. Loosen and remove rear shackle nuts and remove the rear shackle from the spring.
9. Remove rear spring from the vehicle.
10. Reverse above procedure to install. When installing the front and rear pivot nuts and bolts, do not tighten the bolts until the vehicle has been lowered to the floor and weight is on the wheels.

Radio

Removal and Installation

1965-66 Imperial

1. Disconnect battery ground cable.
2. Remove ash tray screws. Lower ash tray assembly and disconnect turn signal flasher and ash tray light. Remove ash tray.

Drive Axle, Suspension

Troubleshooting and Adjustment

General instructions covering the troubles of the drive axle and how to repair and adjust it, together with information on installation of rear axle bearings and grease seals, are given in the Unit Repair Section.

Capacities of the drive axle are given in the Capacities table.

Rear Spring R & R

1. Raise the vehicle on a hoist.
2. Place jack stands under the differential and lower the vehicle until the weight is removed from the rear springs.
3. Disconnect the rear shock absorber.
4. Loosen and remove the U-bolt

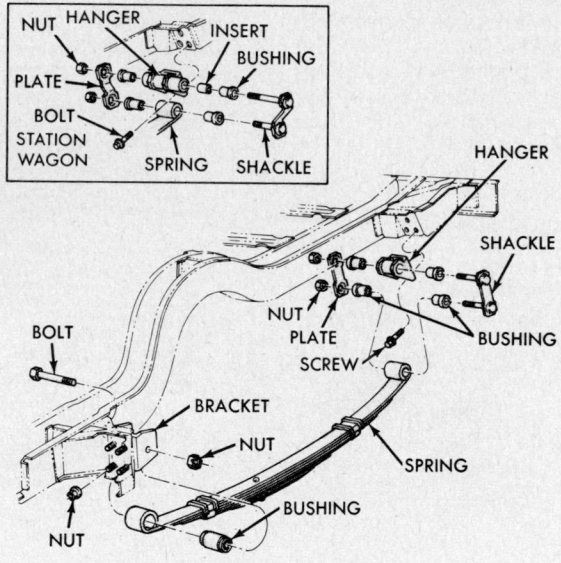

Chrysler rear spring (© Chrysler Corporation)

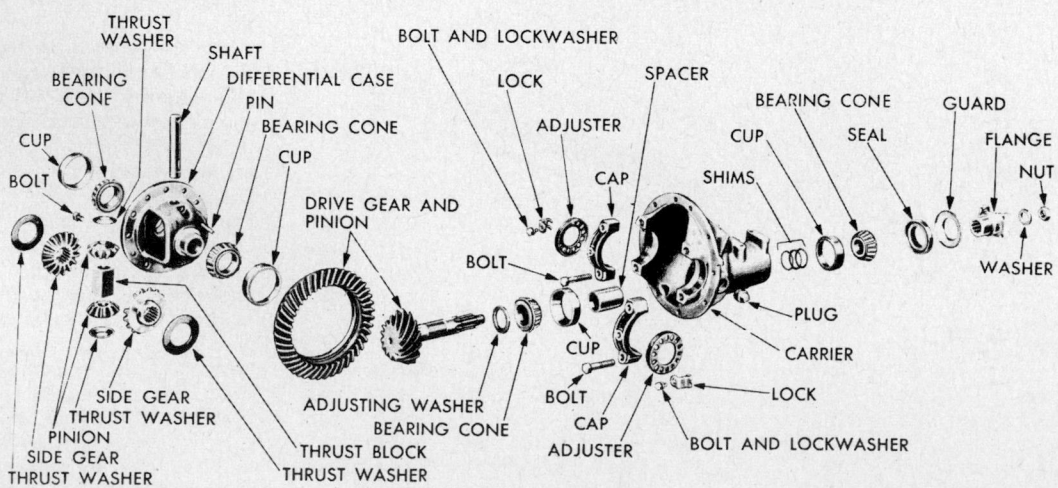

Differential (disassembled) (© Chrysler Corp.)

3. Remove lower radio bracket.
4. Disconnect radio wiring.
5. Remove instrument panel pencil brace, just left of radio.
6. Remove radio knobs and mounting nuts.
7. Pull radio out of panel and rotate so radio face is to right of vehicle. Remove radio from under instrument panel.
8. Reverse procedure to install.

1965-66 Chrysler

1. Disconnect battery ground cable.
2. On air conditioned models, remove center outlet hose.
3. Remove ash tray and housing assembly.
4. Remove radio knobs and mounting nuts.
5. Disconnect radio wiring.
6. Remove mounting bracket.
7. Remove radio through ash tray assembly opening.
8. Reverse procedure to install.

1967-68 Imperial

1. Disconnect battery ground cable.
2. Remove air conditioning duct and hoses.
3. Disconnect heater blower motor wire connectors from resistor.
4. Disconnect radio wiring.
5. Remove radio support bracket.
6. Remove radio knobs and mounting nuts. Slide radio down and to the right. Rotate front of radio up and remove.
7. Reverse procedure to install.

1967 Chrysler

1. Disconnect battery ground cable.
2. Remove ash tray and housing.
3. Remove air conditioning ducts and hoses.
4. Remove bezels next to map light.
5. Remove two upper radio bezel screws now exposed and remove screw in lower center edge of bezel.
6. Disconnect antenna cable. Remove radio mounting screws from instrument panel.
7. Remove support bracket screw at lower lip of instrument panel and loosen nut on mounting stud at back of radio.
8. Rotate rear edge of radio out and down enough to disconnect speaker and feed wires. Remove radio.
9. Reverse procedure to install.

1968 Chrysler

1. Disconnect battery ground cable.
2. Remove ash tray. Lower ash tray housing. Disconnect two ash tray lights and remove housing.
3. Remove heater temperature control knob.
4. Remove blower switch connector.
5. Remove heater control plate attaching nuts and drop controls down to ash tray opening.
6. Disconnect electrical connections, vacuum switch connector, and bowden cable.
7. Remove heater controls through ash tray opening.
8. Remove fader cover plate and reverberator cover plate.
9. Open glove compartment and remove center bezel (three screws).
10. Remove radio mounting nuts.
11. Remove radio mounting bracket.
12. Disconnect radio wiring.
13. Tilt radio toward instrument panel and slightly toward right to disconnect stereo plug, if so equipped. Remove radio through ash tray opening.
14. Reverse procedure to install.

1969-72 All Models

1. Disconnect battery ground cable.
2. Remove left ash tray.
3. Remove steering column cover.
4. Unscrew stereo tape reset knob, if so equipped.
5. Disconnect radio wiring.
6. Move defroster vacuum actuator to facilitate radio removal.
7. Remove two radio mounting screws through access openings in lower instrument panel. On search-tune and AM radios, remove knobs, bezels, and nuts.
8. Remove radio support bracket mounting screw from lower reinforcement. Support radio.
9. Remove radio support bracket. Remove radio from under instrument panel.
10. Reverse procedure to install.

Windshield Wipers

Wiper Motor Removal and Installation

1965 Imperial

1. Disconnect battery ground cable.
2. Remove left air conditioning spot cooler hose.
3. Remove right defroster hose.
4. Remove right instrument panel lower reinforcement to windshield wiper motor mounting bracket pencil brace.
5. Remove glove compartment on air conditioned models.
6. Pivot defroster control vacuum actuator down out of the way.
7. Disconnect motor wiring.
8. Disconnect right and left wiper links at the wiper pivots.
9. Remove nuts attaching wiper motor mounting bracket to cowl panel.
10. Remove wiper motor, motor mounting bracket, and wiper links as an assembly from under the instrument panel.

11. Reverse procedure to install.

1965-66 Chrysler, 1967-68 All Models

1. Disconnect battery ground cable.
2. Remove wiper arm and blade assemblies.
3. Remove windshield lower moulding.
4. Remove cowl grille panel.
5. Remove drive crank arm retaining nut and drive crank. Disconnect motor wiring.
6. Remove three nuts mounting motor to bulkhead and remove motor.
7. Reverse procedure to install.

1966 Imperial

1. Disconnect battery ground cable.
2. Remove air conditioning right spot cooler hose and distribution duct.
3. Remove instrument panel lower reinforcement to windshield wiper motor mounting bracket pencil brace.
4. Disconnect motor wiring.
5. Remove both left and right link to pivot retainers.
6. Remove three motor bracket mounting nuts.
7. Work motor and link assembly out from under panel toward right side of vehicle.
8. Remove links and motor mounting bracket.
9. Reverse procedure to install.

1969-70 All Models

1. Disconnect battery ground cable.
2. Lift the wiper arm and insert a .090 pin or drill. Pull wiper arm from shaft with a rocking motion.
3. Remove windshield lower moulding.
4. Remove cowl screen.
5. Remove drive crank arm retaining nut and drive crank. Disconnect motor wiring.
6. Remove three mounting nuts. Remove motor.
7. Reverse procedure to install.

1971-72 All Models with Concealed Wipers

1. Disconnect the negative battery cable.
2. Lift the latch on each wiper arm and remove the arms and blades as an assembly.
3. Remove the cowl screen.
4. Remove the drive crank retaining nut and drive crank.
5. Disconnect the lead wires from the wiper motor.
6. Remove the three wiper motor mounting bolts and remove the motor from the vehicle.
7. Reverse above procedure to install. When installing the wiper arms and blades, make sure the wiper motor is in the Park position.

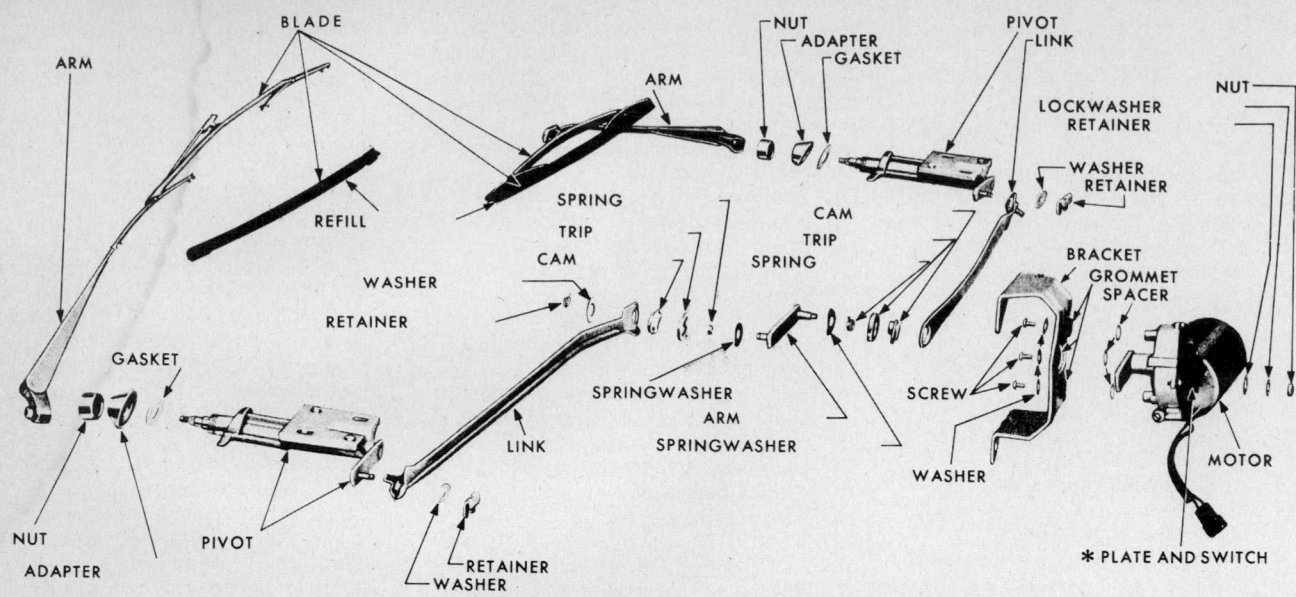

1965-66 Imperial windshield wiper linkage (© Chrysler Corporation)

Wiper Transmission

1965-66 Imperial

The best way to service the windshield wiper linkage on these models is to remove the wiper motor and linkage from under the dash as an assembly and perform any required service with the assembly on the bench. To disassemble and reassemble the linkage follow the illustration.

1965-66 Chrysler

Removal

1. Remove the wiper arm and blade assemblies.
2. Remove the lower windshield moulding.
3. Remove the cowl screen.
4. With the wiper system in the Park position, remove the retainer clip from the end of the wiper motor drive crank and pin. On models with variable speed wipers, remove the cover from the mechanism to gain access to the clip.
5. Remove the spring washer and drive link from the drive crank pin.
6. Remove the retaining clip from the connecting link pin on the right pivot.
7. Remove the nuts that attach the left pivot to the body of the vehicle.
8. Remove the links and left pivot through the cowl panel opening.

Installation

1. Position the links and left pivot on the cowl.
2. Install the bushing and connecting link on the right pivot and install the retaining clip. Make sure the clip is fully seated on the pivot pin.

3. Install the left pivot in the body of the vehicle.
4. Position the motor end of the drive link on the motor drive crank pin and install the spring washer and retaining clip. On models with variable speed wipers, make certain the boot retainer, parking spring, spring release and cam (O ring, release spring, retainer and cam on 1965 models) are in the proper position.
5. On vehicles with variable speed wipers, install the cover mechanism.
6. Install the cowl grille, the lower windshield moulding and the wiper arm and blade assemblies.

1967-68 All Models

1. Remove the wiper arm and blade assemblies.
2. Remove the lower windshield moulding.
3. Remove the cowl grille.
4. Remove the nut or clip that at-

taches the crank arm to the wiper motor output pin.
5. Remove the clip, felt and brass washer from the right pivot and remove the connecting link from the right pivot.
6. Remove the bolts that attach the left pivot to the body of the vehicle.
7. Remove the links and left pivot from the vehicle through the cowl opening.
8. Reverse above procedure to install.

1969-70 All Models and 1971-72 with Concealed Wipers

1. Insert a 0.090 in. pin in the base of each wiper arm and remove the arm and blade assemblies from the wiper pivots.
2. On 1969 models, remove the windshield lower moulding.
3. Remove the cowl screen.
4. Remove the crank arm retaining nut and crank arm from the wiper motor.

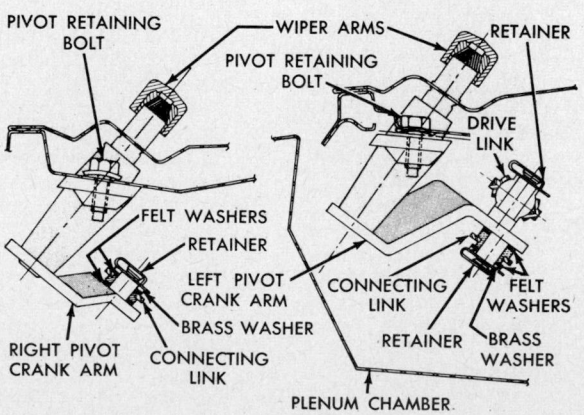

1968 Chrysler windshield wiper pivots
(© Chrysler Corporation)

5. Remove the bolts that attach the right and left pivots to the body of the vehicle.
6. Remove the links and pivots as an assembly through the cowl opening.
7. Reverse above procedure to install.

Heater System

Heater Blower R & R

1965-66 Imperial
1. Disconnect battery ground cable.
2. Disconnect heater ground wire at wiper motor mounting bracket.
3. Disconnect heater wires from harness connector.
4. Disconnect vacuum hoses from units (where used).
5. Remove hoses from attaching clips.
6. Remove valve capillary coil from opening in housing (driver's compartment).
7. Remove clips from housing.
8. Remove screws attaching heater duct to dash panel (left of vent door, below heater on passenger side, and wiper motor right link pivot).
NOTE: disconnect wiper right link at pivot to expose housing screws.
9. Remove housing and blower by pulling down and out.
10. Remove blower, mounting plate, and motor.
11. Install in reverse of above.

1965-66 Chrysler, 1967-68 All Models
1. Disconnect battery ground cable.
2. Disconnect water hoses at dash panel (engine side). Plug heater hose fittings to prevent spilling water in passenger area.
3. Under instrument panel, remove

bracket from top of heater to dash.
4. Remove defroster hoses at heater, and disconnect vacuum lines at heater.
5. Disconnect wiring at heater blower motor resistor.
6. Remove glove compartment.
7. Disconnect control cable at heater end.
8. Unclamp flexible connector at right end of heater. Do not remove connector from cowl side.
9. Pull carpet or mat from under instrument panel.
10. From engine compartment, remove nuts mounting the assembly to the instrument panel.
11. Pull heater toward rear to clear mounting studs from dash. Rotate heater assembly until studs are down, then remove heater.
12. Disconnect wiring from heater assembly to blower motor.
13. Remove motor cooler tube.
14. Remove heater back plate.
15. Remove fan from motor shaft.
16. Remove blower motor from back plate.
17. Install in reverse of above.

1969-72 All Models
The blower motor is mounted to the engine side housing under the right front fender between the inner fender shield and the fender. The inner fender shield must be removed to service the blower motor.

Heater Core R & R

1965-66 Imperial
1. Disconnect battery ground cable.
2. Drain cooling system.
3. Disconnect heater hoses at heater.
4. Remove screws attaching heater housing to instrument panel.
5. **Remove housing and core as an assembly.**
6. Remove mastic to expose housing.

7. Remove core from outer housing.
8. Install in reverse of above.

1965-66 Chrysler, 1967-68 All Models
1. Follow Steps 1 through 11 under Heater Blower R&R, 1965-66 Chrysler, 1967-68 All Models.
2. Remove heater cover plate.
3. Remove screws attaching heater core to heater, and remove core.
4. Install in reverse of above.

1969-72 All Models
1. Disconnect battery ground cable. Drain coolant.
2. Disconnect heater hoses and plug fittings.
3. Slide front seat back. Unplug antenna from radio.
4. Remove vacuum hoses from trunk lock, if so equipped.
5. Disconnect blower motor resistor block.
6. Remove vacuum hoses from defroster actuator and heater shut off door actuator.
7. Swing support bracket up out of the way.
8. Remove four retaining nuts from studs on engine side housing.
9. Remove locating bolt from bottom center of passenger side housing.
10. Roll or tip housing out from under instrument panel.
11. Remove temperature control cable retaining clip and cable from heat shut off door crank.
12. From inside housing, remove two retaining nuts from right side of heater core and four screws from outside of housing.
13. Remove core tube locating metal screw from top of housing.
14. Carefully pull heater core out of housing.
15. Reverse procedure to install.

Dodge and Plymouth

Index

YEAR IDENTIFICATION
DODGE

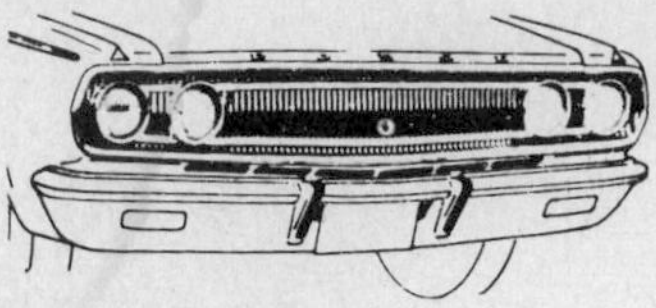

1965 550

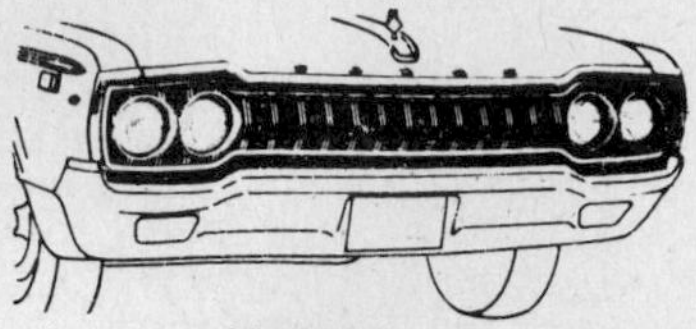

1965 880

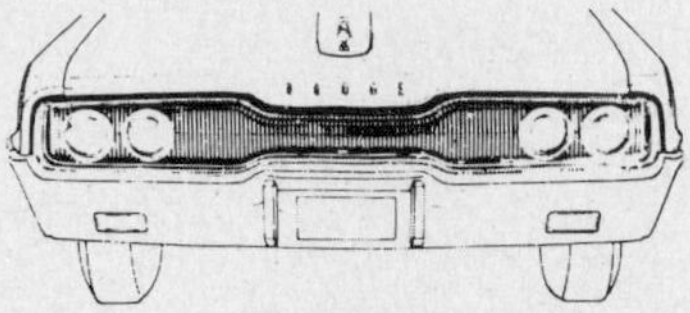

1966 Polara

1966 Coronet

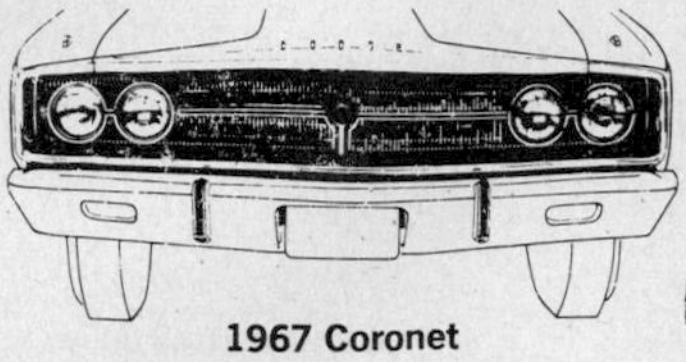

1967 Coronet

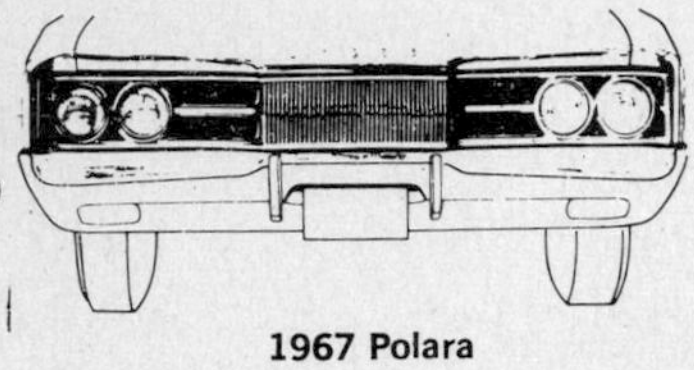

1967 Polara

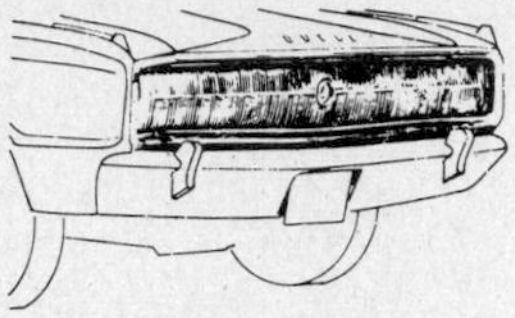

1967 Charger

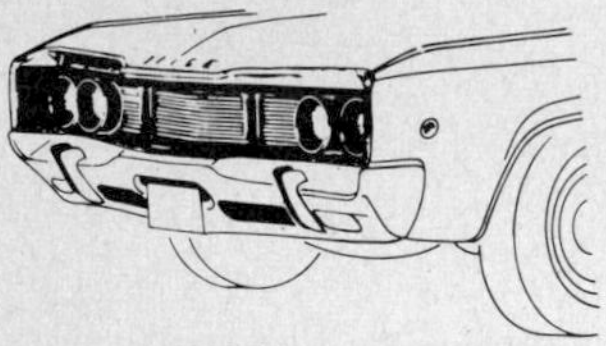

1968 Polara

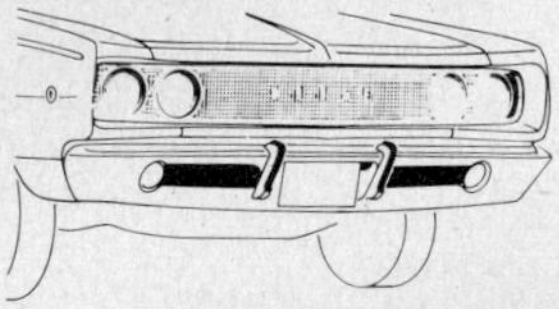

1968 Coronet

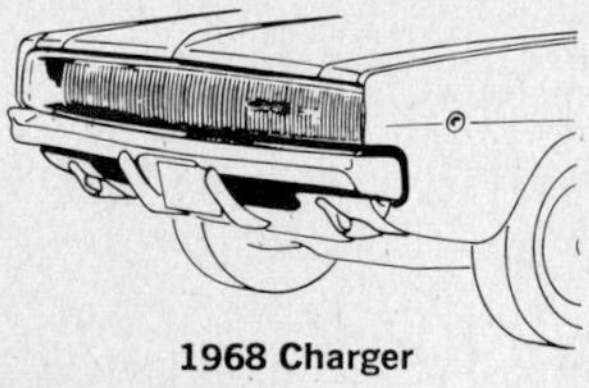

1968 Charger

1969 Polara

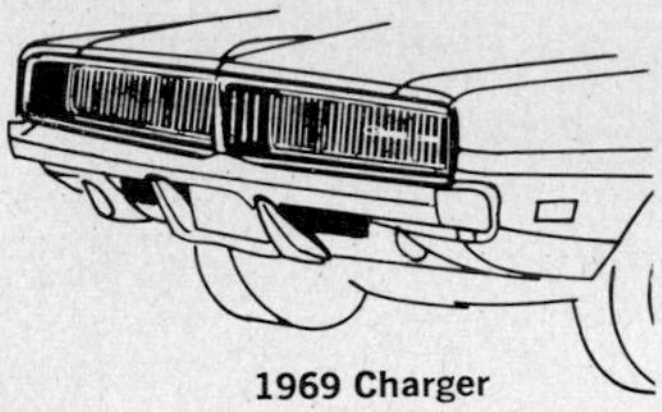

1969 Charger

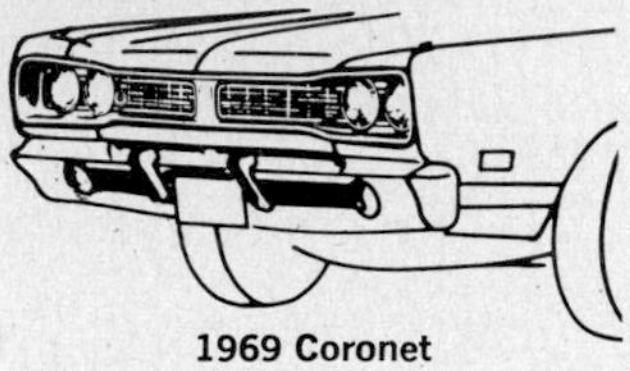

1969 Coronet

1970 Coronet 500

1970 Polara

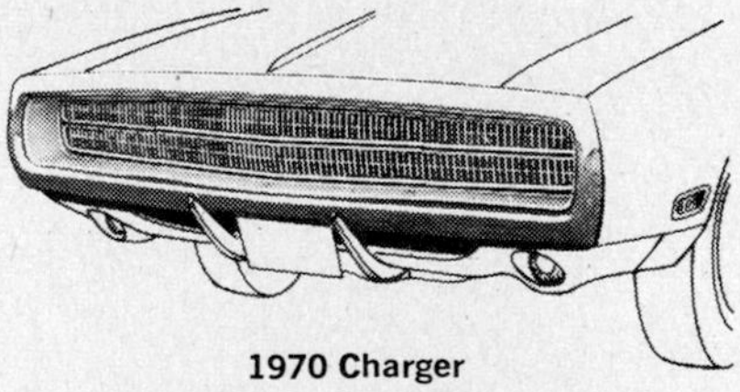

1970 Charger

1970 Coronet 440

1971 Coronet

1971 Charger

1971 Polara

1972 Coronet

1972 Monaco

1972 Charger

1972 Polara

YEAR IDENTIFICATION

PLYMOUTH

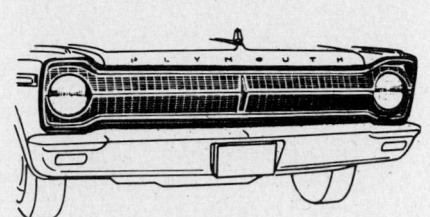
1965

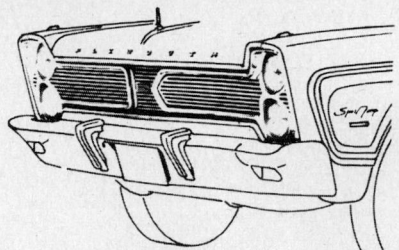
1966 Fury

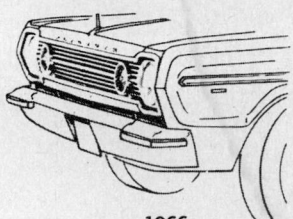
1966

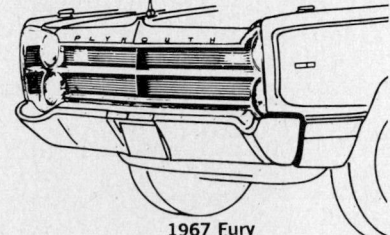
1967 Fury

1967

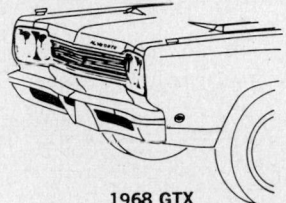
1968 Fury

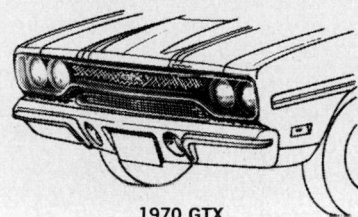
1968 GTX

1968 Road Runner

1969

1969

1970 GTX

1970 Plymouth Fury

1971 Satellite

1971 Roadrunner

1971 Fury

1972 Satellite

1972 Sebring

1972 Road Runner

1972 Fury

FIRING ORDER

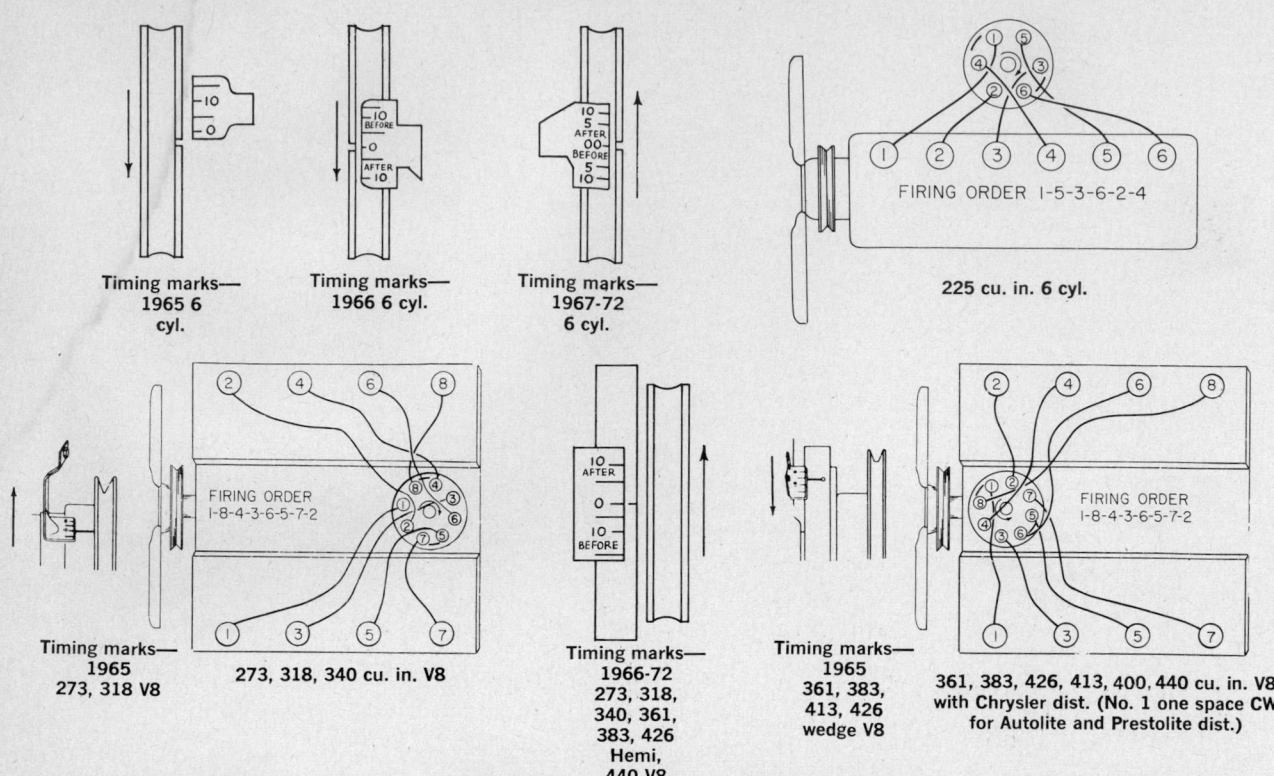

Timing marks—1965 6 cyl.

Timing marks—1966 6 cyl.

Timing marks—1967-72 6 cyl.

FIRING ORDER 1-5-3-6-2-4

225 cu. in. 6 cyl.

Timing marks—1965 273, 318 V8

FIRING ORDER 1-8-4-3-6-5-7-2

273, 318, 340 cu. in. V8

Timing marks—1966-72 273, 318, 340, 361, 383, 426 Hemi, 440 V8

Timing marks—1965 361, 383, 413, 426 wedge V8

FIRING ORDER 1-8-4-3-6-5-7-2

361, 383, 426, 413, 400, 440 cu. in. V8 with Chrysler dist. (No. 1 one space CW for Autolite and Prestolite dist.)

CAR SERIAL NUMBER LOCATION AND ENGINE IDENTIFICATION

Car Serial Number Location

1965-67

Plate on left front door hinge post.

1968-71

Top of instrument panel, visible through windshield.

Model Identification

1965

The ten digit vehicle identification number is interpreted as follows:
First digit—car line
D—Polara, 880, and Monaco
P—Fury
R—Belvedere
W—Coronet eight cyl.
4—Coronet six cyl.
Second digit—price class
1—Polara, Belvedere I, Fury I, and low priced Coronet
2—Fury II
3—880, Belvedere II, Fury III, and high priced Coronet
4—Monaco, Satellite, Sport Fury, and premium Coronet
5—Polara station wagon, Belvedere I station wagon, Fury I station wagon, and low priced Coronet station wagon

6—Fury II station wagon
7—880 station wagon, Belvedere II station wagon, Fury III station wagon and high priced Coronet station wagon.
8—taxi
9—police
Third digit—model year
Fourth digit—assembly plant
Sixth to tenth digits—sequential serial number

1966

The thirteen digit vehicle identification number is interpreted as follows:
First digit—car line
D—Polara and Monaco
P—Fury
R—Belvedere
W—Coronet
Second digit—price class
E—economy
L—low
H—high
P—premium
K—police
T—taxi
S—VIP
M—medium
Third and fourth digits—body type
21—two door sedan
23—two door hardtop
27—convertible
29—two door sports hardtop
41—four door sedan
42—four door hardtop
43—four door hardtop
45—station wagon
46—station wagon

Fifth digit—engine
B—225 six
C—273
D—318
E—361
F—383
H—426
Sixth digit—model year
Seventh digit—assembly plant
Eighth to tenth digits—sequential serial number

1967

First digit—car line
D—Polara and Monaco
P—119 in. wheelbase Plymouth
R—116 in. wheelbase Plymouth
W—Coronet
X—Charger
Second digit
E—economy
L—low
M—medium
H—high
P—premium
K—police
T—taxi
S—VIP
Third and fourth digits—body type
21—two door sedan
23—two door hardtop
27—convertible
29—two door sports hardtop
41—four door sedan
43—four door hardtop
45—two seat station wagon
46—three seat station wagon
Fifth digit—engine
B—225 six
C—special six

D—273
E—318
F—383
G—383 high performance
H—426 Hemi
J—440
K—440 special order
L—440 high performance
Sixth digit—model year
Seventh digit—assembly plant
Eighth to tenth digits—sequential
  serial number

1968

The thirteen digit vehicle identifi-
cation number is interpreted as fol-
lows:
First digit—car line
  D—Polara and Monaco
  P—119 in. wheelbase Plymouth
  R—116 in. Plymouth
  W—Coronet
  X—Charger
Second digit—price class
  E—economy   K—police
  L—low   T—taxi
  H—high   S—special
  M—medium   O—super stock
  P—premium
Third and fourth digits—body type
  21—two door sedan
  23—two door hardtop
  27—convertible
  29—two door sports hardtop
  41—four door sedan
  43—four door hardtop
  45—two seat station wagon
  46—three seat station wagon
Fifth digit—engine
  B—225 six
  C—special six
  D—273
  F—318
  G—383
  H—383 high performance
  J—426 Hemi
  K—440
  L—440 high performance
  M—special V8
Sixth digit—model year
Seventh digit—assembly plant
Eighth to tenth digits—sequential
  serial number

1969

The thirteen digit vehicle identifi-
cation number is interpreted as fol-
lows:
First digit—car line
  D—Polara and Monaco
  P—Fury 119 in. wheelbase
  R—Satellite 116 in. wheelbase
  W—Coronet
  X—Charger
Second digit—price class
  E—economy   K—police
  L—low   T—taxi
  M—medium   S—special
  H—high   O—super stock
  P—premium   X—fast top
Third and fourth digits—body style
  21—two door sedan
  23—two door hardtop
  27—convertible
  29—two door sport hardtop

41—four door sedan
43—four door hardtop
45—two seat station wagon
46—three seat station wagon
Fifth digit—engine
  B—225 six
  C—special six
  D—273
  F—318
  G—383
  H—383 high performance
  J—426 Hemi
  K—440
  L—440 high performance
  M—special V8
Sixth digit—model year
Seventh digit—assembly plant
Eighth to tenth digits—sequential
  serial number

1970-72

The thirteen digit vehicle identifica-
tion number is interpreted as fol-
lows:
First digit—car line
  D—Polara and Monaco
  P—Fury
  R—Satellite

SERIAL NUMBER LOCATION

1965-67
Plate on left front hinge pillar.

1968-72
Plate on left top side of dash seen through windshield.

W—Coronet
X—Charger
Second digit—price class
  L—low   N—N.Y. taxi
  M—medium   T—taxi
  H—high   S—special
  P—premium   O—super stock
  K—police
Third and fourth digits—body style
  21—two door sedan
  23—two door hardtop
  27—convertible
  29—Charger
  41—four door sedan
  43—four door hardtop
  45—six passenger station wagon
  46—nine passenger station wagon
Fifth digit—engine
  C—225 six   R—426 Hemi
  E—special six T—440
  G—318   U—440 high per
  L—383   V—440 six pack
  N—383 high perf Z—special order V8
Sixth digit—model year
Seventh digit—assembly plant
Eighth to tenth digits—sequential
  serial number

ENGINE IDENTIFICATION CODE

A—Stamped on right front of block below cylinder head at coil.
B—Left side front of block below head.
C—Right side top front of block at distributor.
D—Top front of block left of water pump.
E—Left side top front of block behind thermostat housing.
F—Stamped on block pan rail left rear at starter.

YEAR	ENGINE	CODE	LOCATION
1965	6 Cyl.—225	A225	A
	8 Cyl.—273	A273	B
	8 Cyl.—318	A318	B
	8 Cyl.—361	A361	C
	8 Cyl.—383	A383	C
	8 Cyl.—426 Wedge	A426	E
1966	6 Cyl.—225	B225	A
	8 Cyl.—273	B273	B
	8 Cyl.—318	B318	B
	8 Cyl.—383	B383	C
	8 Cyl.—426 Hemi	BH426	D
	8 Cyl.—440	B440	E
1967	6 Cyl.—225	C225	A
	8 Cyl.—273	C273	B
	8 Cyl.—318	C318	B
	8 Cyl.—383	C383	C
	8 Cyl.—426 Hemi	CH426	D
	8 Cyl.—440	C440	E
1968-70	6 Cyl.—225	225	A
	8 Cyl.—273 (68-69)	273	B
	8 Cyl.—318	318	B
	8 Cyl.—383	383	F
	8 Cyl.—383 Hi. Perf.	383	F
	8 Cyl.—426 Hemi	426	F
	8 Cyl.—440	440	F
	8 Cyl.—440 Hi. Perf.	440	F
1971-72	6 Cyl.—225	225	A
	8 Cyl.—318	318	B
	8 Cyl.—340	340	B
	8 Cyl.—360	360	B
	8 Cyl.—383	383	F
	8 Cyl.—383 Hi. Perf.	383	F
	8 Cyl.—400	400	F
	8 Cyl.—426 Hemi	426	F
	8 Cyl.—440	440	F
	8 Cyl.—440 Hi. Perf.	440	F

CRANKSHAFT BEARING JOURNAL SPECIFICATIONS

YEAR	MODEL	MAIN BEARING JOURNALS (IN.)				CONNECTING ROD BEARING JOURNALS (IN.)		
		Journal Diameter	Oil Clearance	Shaft End-Play	Thrust On No.	Journal Diameter	Oil Clearance	End-Play
1965-72	L6—225	2.7495-2.7505	.0005-.0015	.002-.007	3	2.1865-2.1875	.0005-.0015	.006-.012
	V8—273	2.4495-2.5005	.0005-.0015	.002-.007	3	2.1240-2.1250	.0005-.0015	.006-.014
	V8—318	2.4495-2.5005	.0005-.0015	.002-.007	3	2.1240-2.1250	.0005-.0015	.006-.014
	V8—340	2.4495-2.5005	.0005-.0015	.002-.007	3	2.1240-2.1250	.0005-.0025	.006-.014
	V8—360	2.8095-2.8105	.0005-.0015	.002-.007	3	2.1240-2.1250	.0005-.0015	.006-.014
	V8—361	2.6245-2.6255	.0005-.0015	.002-.007	3	2.3740-2.3750	.0005-.0015	.009-.017
	V8—383	2.6245-2.6255	.0005-.0015	.002-.007	3	2.3740-2.3750	.0005-.0015	.009-.017
	V8—400	2.6245-2.6255	.0005-.0015	.002-.007	3	2.3740-2.3750	.0005-.0020	.006-.014
	V8—413, 426	2.7495-2.7505	.0005-.0015	.002-.007	3	2.3740-2.3750	.001-.002	.006-.012
	V8—426 Hemi	2.7495-2.7505	.0015-.0030	.002-.007	3	2.3740-2.3750	.0007-.0025	.009-.017
	V8—440	2.7495-2.7505	.0005-.0015	.002-.007	3	2.3740-2.3750	.0007-.0020	.009-.017

TUNE-UP SPECIFICATIONS

YEAR	MODEL AND CU. IN. DISPLACEMENT	SPARK PLUGS		DISTRIBUTOR		IGNITION TIMING (Deg.) ▲	CRANKING COMP. PRESSURE (Psi)	VALVES		Intake Opens (Deg.)	FUEL PUMP PRESSURE (Psi)	IDLE SPEED (Rpm) ★
		Type	Gap (In.)	Point Dwell (Deg.)	Point Gap (In.)			Tappet Clearance (In.)				
								Intake	Exhaust			
1965	6 Cyl.—225	N14Y	.035	42	.020	2½B	125	.010H	.020H	10B	4½	550
	V8—273 M.T.	N14Y	.035	30	.017	5B	135	.013H	.021H	14B	6½	500
	V8—273 A.T.	N14Y	.035	30	.017	10B	135	.013H	.021H	14B	6½	500
	V8—273 4-BBL.	J10Y	.035	30③	.017	10B	135	.013H	.021H	14B	6½	600
	V8—318 M.T.	J14Y	.035	30	.017	5B	140	.013H	.021H	19B	6	550
	V8—318 A.T.	J14Y	.035	30	.017	10B	140	.013H	.021H	19B	6	475
	V8—361	J14Y	.035	30	.017	10B	140	Zero	Zero	13B	4½	500
	V8—383 2-BBL.	J14Y	.035	30	.017	10B	140	Zero	Zero	13B	4½	500
	V8—383 4-BBL.	J10Y	.035	30③	.017	10B	145	Zero	Zero	24B	4½	550
	V8—413 Std.	J14Y	.035	30	.017	12½B	145	Zero	Zero	14B	4½	500
	V8—413 Spec. Cam	J10Y	.035	30③	.017	10B	155	Zero	Zero	14B	4½	500
	V8—426	J10Y	.035	30③	.017	10B	145	.028C	.032C	24B	4½	500
1966	6 Cyl.—225	N14Y	.035	42½	.020	2½B ⊙	125	.010H	.020H	10B	4½	550②
	V8—273 M.T. 2-BBL.	N14Y	.035	30	.017	5B ⊙	135	.013H	.021H	14B	6	500①
	V8—273 A.T. 2-BBL.	N14Y	.035	30	.017	10B ⊙	135	.013H	.021H	14B	6	500①
	V8—273 4-BBL.	N10Y	.035	29③	.017	10B ⊙	150	.013H	.021H	14B	6	500①
	V8—318 M.T.	J14Y	.035	30	.017	5B ⊙	140	.013H	.021H	19B	6	500②
	V8—318 A.T.	J14Y	.035	30	.017	10B ⊙	140	.013H	.021H	19B	6	500②
	V8—361, 383 2-BBL.	J14Y	.035	30	.017	12½B ⊙	140	Zero	Zero	13B	4½	500②
	V8—383 4-BBL.	J13Y	.035	30	.017	12½B ⊙	150	Zero	Zero	18B	4½	500②
	V8—426 Hemi	J13Y	.035	30	.017	12½B ⊙	150	.028C	.032C	30B	4½	500②
	V8—440 4-BBL.	J13Y	.035	30	.017	12½B ⊙	150	Zero	Zero	18B	4½	500②
1967	6 Cyl.—225	N14Y	.035	42½	.020	5B	125	.010H	.020H	10B	4½	550
	6 Cyl.—225 Exh. Em.	N14Y	.035	42½	.020	TDC	135	.013H	.021H	14B	6	650
	V8—273 M.T. 2-BBL.	N14Y	.035	30	.017	5B ⊙	135	.013H	.021H	14B	6	500①
	V8—273 A.T. 2-BBL.	N14Y	.035	30	.017	10B ⊙	135	.013H	.021H	14B	6	650
	V8—318 M.T. 2-BBL.	N14Y	.035	30	.017	5B ⊙	140	Zero	Zero	14B	6	500①
	V8—318 A.T. 2-BBL.	N14Y	.035	30	.017	10B ⊙	140	Zero	Zero	14B	6	500①
	V8—383 M.T. 2-BBL.	J14Y	.035	30	.017	12½B	140	Zero	Zero	16B	4½	550
	V8—383 M.T. Exh. Em. 2-BBL.	J14Y	.035	30	.017	TDC	140	Zero	Zero	16B	4½	650
	V8—383 A.T. 4-BBL.	J13Y	.035	30	.017	12½B	150	Zero	Zero	16B	4½	550
	V8—383 A.T. Exh. Em. 4-BBL.	J13Y	.035	30	.017	5B	150	Zero	Zero	16B	4½	650
	V8—426 Hemi	N10Y	.035	30	.017	12½B	150	.028C	.032C	30B	7¼	750
	V8—426 Hemi Exh. Em.	N10Y	.035	30	.017	TDC	150	.028C	.032C	30B	7¼	750
	V8—440	J11Y	.035	30	.017	12½B	150	Zero	Zero	19B	4½	650
	V8—440 M.T. Exh. Em.	J11Y	.035	30	.017	TDC	150	Zero	Zero	16B	4½	650
	V8—440 A.T. Exh. Em.	J11Y	.035	30	.017	5B	150	Zero	Zero	16B	4½	650

TUNE-UP SPECIFICATIONS, continued

YEAR	MODEL AND CU. IN. DISPLACEMENT	SPARK PLUGS Type	Gap (In.)	DISTRIBUTOR Point Dwell (Deg.)	Point Gap (In.)	IGNITION TIMING (Deg.) ▲	CRANKING COMP. PRESSURE (Psi)	VALVES Tappet Clearance (In.) Intake	Exhaust	Intake Opens (Deg.)	FUEL PUMP PRESSURE (Psi)	IDLE SPEED (Rpm) ★
1968	6 Cyl.—225	N14Y	.035	42	.020	TDC	135	.010H	.020H	10B	4½	650
	V8—273 M.T.	N14Y	.035	30	.017	5A	135	Zero	Zero	10B	6	700
	V8—273 A.T.	N14Y	.035	30	.017	2½A	135	Zero	Zero	10B	6	650
	V8—318 M.T.	N14Y	.035	30	.017	5A	140	Zero	Zero	10B	6	650
	V8—318 A.T.	N14Y	.035	30	.017	2½A	140	Zero	Zero	10B	6	600
	V8—383 2-BBL. M.T.	J14Y	.035	30	.017	TDC	150	Zero	Zero	18B	4½	650
	V8—383 2-BBL. A.T.	J14Y	.035	30	.017	7½B	150	Zero	Zero	18B	4½	600
	V8—383 4-BBL. M.T.	J11Y	.035	30	.017	TDC ④	150	Zero	Zero	18B	4½	650
	V8—383 4-BBL. A.T.	J11Y	.035	30	.017	5B	150	Zero	Zero	18B	4½	650
	V8—426	N10Y	.035	⑥	.017	TDC	175	.028C	.032C	36B	7½	750
	V8—440 (HP) M.T.	J11Y	.035	⑥	.017	TDC	150	Zero	Zero	21B	6¾	650
	V8—440 A.T.	J13Y	.035	30	.017	7½	150	Zero	Zero	18B	4½	600
	V8—440 (HP) A.T.	J11Y	.035	⑥	.017	5B	150	Zero	Zero	21B	6¾	650
1969	6 Cyl. 225	N14Y	.035	44	.020	TDC	135	.010H	.020H	10B	4½	650
	V8—318	N14Y	.035	32	.017	TDC	140	Zero	Zero	10B	6	650
	V8—383, 2-BBL. M.T.	J14Y	.035	32	.017	TDC	150	Zero	Zero	18B	4½	650
	V8—383, 2-BBL. A.T.	J11Y	.035	32	.017	7½B	150	Zero	Zero	18B	4½	600
	V8—383, 4-BBL. M.T.	J11Y	.035	32	.017	TDC	150	Zero	Zero	18B	4½	650
	V8—383, 4-BBL. A.T.	J11Y	.035	32	.017	5B	150	Zero	Zero	18B	4½	600
	V8—383, Hi. Perf. M.T.	J11Y	.035	⑥	.017	TDC	150	Zero	Zero	21B	4½	650
	V8—383, Hi. Perf. A.T.	J11Y	.035	⑥	.017	5B	150	Zero	Zero	21B	4½	600
	V8—426	N10Y	.035	⑥	.017	TDC	175	.028C	.028C	36B	7½	750
	V8—440 Std. Eng.	J13Y	.035	32	.017	7½B	150	Zero	Zero	18B	4½	650
	V8—440 Hi. Perf. M.T.	J11Y	.035	⑥	.017	TDC	150	Zero	Zero	21B	4½	650
	V8—440 Hi. Perf. A.T.	J11Y	.035	32	.017	5B	150	Zero	Zero	21B	4½	650
1970	6 Cyl.—225	N14Y	.035	41–46	.017–.023	TDC ± 2½	100⑨	.010	.020	10B	3½–5	⑦
	V8—318	N14Y	.035	30–34	.014–.019	TDC ± 2½	100⑨	Zero	Zero	10B	5–7	⑧
	V8—383, 2-BBL., M.T.	J14Y	.035	28½–32½	.016–.021	TDC ± 2½	100⑨	Zero	Zero	18B	3½–5	650
	V8—383, 4-BBL., A.T.	J11Y	.035	28½–32½	.016–.021	2½B	110⑨	Zero	Zero	18B ⑩	3½–5	750
	V8—383, 2-BBL., A.T.	J14Y	.035	28½–32½	.016–.021	2½B ± 2½	100⑨	Zero	Zero	18B	3½–5	750
	V8—383, 4-BBL., M.T.	J11Y	.035	28½–32½	.016–.021	TDC ± 2½	110⑨	Zero	Zero	18B ⑩	3½–5	750
	V8—426 Hemi, M.T.	N10Y	.035	27–32	.014–.019	TDC ± 2½	110⑨	⑪	⑪	36B	7–8½	900
	V8—426 Hemi, A.T.	N10Y	.035	27–32	.014–.019	5B ± 2½	110⑨	⑪	⑪	36B	7–8½	900
	V8—440 Std. Eng., M.T.	J13Y	.035	27–32	.014–.019	5B	110⑨	Zero	Zero	18B	3½–5	900
	V8—440 Std. Eng., A.T.	J13Y	.035	27–32	.014–.019	5B	110⑨	Zero	Zero	18B	3½–5	650
	V8—440, Hi. Perf., M.T.	J11Y	.035	28½–32½	.016–.021	TDC ± 2½	110⑨	Zero	Zero	21B	7–8½	900
	V8—440, Hi. Perf., A.T.	J11Y	.035	28½–32½	.016–.021	2½B ± 2½	110⑨	Zero	Zero	21B	7–8½	800
	V8—440 Six Pack	J11Y	.035	③	.014–.019	5B ± 2½	110⑨	Zero	Zero	21B	7–8½	900 ⑫
1971	6 Cyl.—225	N14Y	.035	41–46	.017–.023	2½B	100⑨	.010	.020	10B	3½–5	700 ⑦
	V8—318	N13Y	.035	30–34	.014–.019	TDC	100⑨	Zero	Zero	10B	5–7	750 ⑧
	V8—340, M.T.	N9Y	.035	27–32③	.014–.019	5B	110⑨	Zero	Zero	22B	5–7	900
	V8—340, A.T.	N9Y	.035	30–34	.014–.019	5B	110⑨	Zero	Zero	22B	5–7	900
	V8—360, 2-BBL., M.T.	N13Y	.035	30–34	.014–.019	2½B	100⑨	Zero	Zero	16B	5–7	750
	V8—360,2-BBL., A.T.	N13Y	.035	30–34	.014–.019	2½B	100⑨	Zero	Zero	16B	5–7	700
	V8—383, 2-BBL., M.T.	J14Y	.035	28½–32½	.014–.019	TDC	100⑨	Zero	Zero	18B ⑩	3½–5	650
	V8—383, 2-BBL., A.T.	J14Y	.035	28½–32½	.014–.019	2½B	100⑨	Zero	Zero	18B ⑩	3½–5	750
	V8—383, 4-BBL., M.T.	J11Y	.035	28½–32½	.014–.019	TDC	110⑨	Zero	Zero	18B ⑩	3½–5	700

TUNE-UP SPECIFICATIONS, continued

| YEAR | MODEL | SPARK PLUGS | | DISTRIBUTOR | | IGNITION TIMING (Deg.) ▲ | CRANKING COMP. PRESSURE (Psi) | VALVES | | Intake Opens (Deg.) | FUEL PUMP PRESSURE (Psi) | IDLE SPEED (Rpm) ★ |
| | | Type | Gap (In.) | Point Dwell (Deg.) | Point Gap (In.) | | | Tappet (Hot) Clearance (In.) | | | | |
								Intake	Exhaust			
	V8—383, 4-BBL., A.T.	J11Y	.035	28½–32½	.014–.019	2½B	110⑨	Zero	Zero	18B ⑩	3½–5	650
	V8—426 Hemi, M.T.	N10Y	.035	28–32	.014–.019	TDC	110⑨	⑪	⑪	36B	7–8½	900
	V8—426 Hemi, A.T.	N10Y	.035	28–32	.014–.019	2½B	110⑨	⑪	⑪	36B	7–8½	900
	V8—440, Regular Fuel	J11Y	.035	28½–32½	.016–.021	5B	110⑨	Zero	Zero	18B	3½–5	900⑦
	V8—440, Hi. Perf., M.T.	J11Y	.035	28½–32½	.016–.021	TDC	110⑨	Zero	Zero	21B	6–7⅓	900
	V8—440, Hi. Perf., A.T.	J11Y	.035	28½–32½	.016–.021	2½B	110⑨	Zero	Zero	21B	6–7½	800
	V8—440 3 x 2-BBL.	J11Y	.035	27–32③	.014–.019	5B	110⑨	Zero	Zero	21B	6–7½	900
1972	6 Cyl.—225	N14Y	.035	41–46	.017–.023	2½B	100⑨	.010	.020	10B	3½–5	700⑦
	V8—318	N13Y	.035	30–34	.014–.019	TDC	100⑨	Zero	Zero	10B	5–7	750⑧
	V8—340	N9Y	.035	⑤	⑤	⑤	110⑨	Zero	Zero	22B	5–7	⑤
	V8—360	N13Y	.035	30–34	.014–.019	2½B	100⑨	Zero	Zero	16B	5–7	750⑧
	V8—400, M.T.	J11Y	.035	28–32	.014–.019	⑤	100⑨	Zero	Zero	18B ⑩	3½–5	⑤
	V8—400, A.T.	J11Y	.035	28–32	.014–.019	2½B	100⑨	Zero	Zero	18B ⑩	3½–5	⑤
	V8—440, Regular Fuel	J11Y	.035	28–32	.016–.021	5B	100⑨	Zero	Zero	18B	3½–5	⑤

★—With manual transmission in N and automatic in D. Add 50 rpm if equipped with air conditioning.

▲—With vacuum advance disconnected. NOTE: These settings are only approximate. Engine design, altitude, temperature, fuel octane rating and the condition of the individual engine are all factors which can influence timing. The limiting advance factor must, therefore, be the "knock point" of the individual engine.

⓪—With Cleaner Air Package (California) 5° ATDC.

①—With Cleaner Air Package manual trans. 700, auto. 650.

②—With Cleaner Air Package manual trans. 650, auto. 650.

③—Both sets—37–42.

④—383 Cu. In. high performance—Ign. 7½°, and mechanical lifters at .016 and .028 in. cold.

⑤—See engine decal.

⑥—Dual points, 27°–31°—both sets, 36°–40°.

⑦—A.T.—650.

⑧—A.T.—700.

⑨—Minimum.

⑩—Super Bee and Road Runner—21B.

⑪—See text.

⑫—With solenoid throttle stop connected.

B—Before top dead center.

A—After top dead center.

A.T.—Automatic transmission.

M.T.—Manual transmission.

CAUTION

General adoption of anti-pollution laws has changed the design of almost all car engine production to effectively reduce crankcase emission and terminal exhaust products. It has been necessary to adopt stricter tune-up rules, especially timing and idle speed procedures. Both of these values are peculiar to the engine and to its application, rather than to the engine alone. With this in mind, car manufacturers supply idle speed data for the engine and application involved. This information is clearly displayed in the engine compartment of each vehicle.

ALTERNATOR AND AC REGULATOR SPECIFICATIONS

| YEAR | | ALTERNATOR | | | REGULATOR | | | |
	Model	Field Current Draw @ 12 V.	Current Output @ 1250 Engine RPM	Model	Point Gap (In.)	Air Gap (In.)	Voltage at 140°F.
1965–69	6 Cyl.—225	2.38–2.75	26 ± 3 Amps.	2098300①	.015	.050	13.4–14.0
	V8 Std.—All	2.38–2.75	34.5 ± 3 Amps.				
	Heavy Duty, A/C	2.38–2.75	44 ± 3 Amps.④	2444980②	.015	.032–.042	13.2–14.2
1970–72	6 Cyl.—225	2.38–2.75	26 ± 3 Amps.	3438150③	③	③	13.3–14.0
	V8 Std.—All	2.38–2.75	34.5 ± 3 Amps.				
	Heavy Duty, A/C	2.38–2.75	44.5 ± 3 Amps.④				

① Chrysler built—used interchangeably with 2444980.

② Essex wire built—used interchaneibly with 2098300.

③ Electronic type.

④ 51 ± 3 Amps.—Special equipment.

TORQUE SPECIFICATIONS

YEAR	MODEL	CYLINDER HEAD BOLTS (FT. LBS.)	ROD BEARING BOLTS (FT. LBS.)	MAIN BEARING BOLTS (FT. LBS.)	CRANKSHAFT BALANCER BOLT (FT. LBS.)	FLYWHEEL TO CRANKSHAFT BOLTS (FT. LBS.)	MANIFOLD (FT. LBS.) Intake	MANIFOLD (FT. LBS.) Exhaust
1965–72	Slant 6	65	45	85	Press	55	10●	10
	273, 318, 340, 360 V8	95	45	85	▲	55–65	40	25
	361, 383, 400, 413, 426 Wedge, 440 V8	70	45	85	▲	55	40–50	30
	426 Hemi	70–75	75	100●●	135	70	See Text	35

●—Intake to exhaust—17–20 ft. lbs. ▲—Balancer bolts—15 ft. lbs.
●●—Crossbolts—45 ft. lbs. End of crankshaft bolt—135 ft. lbs.

GENERAL ENGINE SPECIFICATIONS

YEAR	CU. IN. DISPLACEMENT	CARBURETOR	ADVERTISED HORSEPOWER @ RPM	ADVERTISED TORQUE @ RPM (FT. LBS.)	A.M.A. HORSEPOWER	BORE & STROKE (IN.)	ADVERTISED COMPRESSION RATIO	VALVE LIFTER TYPE	NORMAL OIL PRESSURE (PSI)
1965	6 Cyl.—225	1-BBL.	145 @ 4000	215 @ 2400	27.7	3.400 x 4.125	8.40:1	Mech.	55
	V8—273	2-BBL.	180 @ 4200	260 @ 1600	42.0	3.625 x 3.310	8.80:1	Mech.	55
	V8—273	4-BBL.	235 @ 5200	280 @ 4000	42.0	3.625 x 3.310	10.50:1	Mech.	55
	V8—318	2-BBL.	230 @ 4400	340 @ 2400	48.9	3.910 x 3.310	9.00:1	Mech.	55
	V8—361	2-BBL.	265 @ 4400	380 @ 2400	54.0	4.125 x 3.375	9.00:1	Hyd.	55
	V8—383	2-BBL.	270 @ 4400	390 @ 2800	57.8	4.250 x 3.375	9.20:1	Hyd.	55
	V8—383	4-BBL.	330 @ 4600	425 @ 2800	57.8	4.250 x 3.375	10.00:1	Hyd.	55
	V8—413	4-BBL.	340 @ 4600	470 @ 2800	57.1	4.188 x 3.750	10.10:1	Hyd.	55
	V8—413	4-BBL.	360 @ 4800	470 @ 3200	57.1	4.188 x 3.750	10.30:1	Mech.	55
	V8—426 Wedge	2 x 4-BBL.	365 @ 4800	470 @ 3200	57.8	4.250 x 3.750	10.30:1	Hyd.	55
	V8—426 Wedge	2 x 4-BBL.	425 @ 6000	480 @ 4600	57.8	4.250 x 3.750	12.50:1	Mech.	55
1966	6 Cyl.—225	1-BBL.	145 @ 4000	215 @ 2400	27.7	3.400 x 4.125	8.40:1	Mech.	55
	V8—273	2-BBL.	180 @ 4200	260 @ 1600	42.0	3.625 x 3.310	9.00:1	Mech.	55
	V8—273	4-BBL.	235 @ 5200	280 @ 4000	42.0	3.625 x 3.310	10.50:1	Mech.	55
	V8—318	2-BBL.	230 @ 4400	340 @ 2400	48.9	3.910 x 3.310	9.00:1	Mech.	55
	V8—361	2-BBL.	265 @ 4400	380 @ 2400	54.0	4.125 x 3.375	9.00:1	Hyd.	55
	V8—383	2-BBL.	270 @ 4400	390 @ 2800	57.8	4.250 x 3.375	9.20:1	Hyd.	55
	V8—383	4-BBL.	325 @ 4800	425 @ 2800	57.8	4.250 x 3.375	10.0:1	Hyd.	55
	V8—426 Hemi	4-BBL.	425 @ 5000	490 @ 4000	57.8	4.250 x 3.750	10.25:1	Hyd.	55
	V8—440	4-BBL.	350 @ 4400	480 @ 2800	59.7	4.320 x 3.750	10.0:1	Hyd.	55
1967	6 Cyl.—225	1-BBL.	145 @ 4000	215 @ 2400	27.7	3.400 x 4.125	8.40:1	Mech.	55
	V8—273	2-BBL.	180 @ 4200	260 @ 1600	42.0	3.625 x 3.310	9.20:1	Mech.	55
	V8—318	2-BBL.	230 @ 4400	340 @ 2400	48.9	3.910 x 3.310	9.20:1	Hyd.	55
	V8—383	2-BBL.	270 @ 4400	390 @ 2800	57.8	4.250 x 3.375	9.20:1	Hyd.	55
	V8—383	4-BBL.	325 @ 4000	425 @ 2800	57.8	4.250 x 3.375	10.00:1	Hyd.	55
	V8—426 Hemi	2 x 4-BBL.	425 @ 5000	490 @ 4000	57.8	4.250 x 3.750	10.25:1	Mech.	55
	V8—440	4-BBL.	350 @ 4400	480 @ 2800	59.7	4.320 x 3.750	10.00:1	Hyd.	55
	V8—440	4-BBL.	375 @ 4600	480 @ 3200	59.7	4.320 x 3.750	10.00:1	Hyd.	55
1968	6 Cyl.—225	1-BBL.	145 @ 4000	215 @ 2400	27.7	3.400 x 4.125	8.40:1	Mech.	55
	V8—273	2-BBL.	190 @ 4400	260 @ 2000	42.0	3.625 x 3.310	9.00:1	Hyd.	55
	V8—318	2-BBL.	230 @ 4400	340 @ 2400	48.9	3.910 x 3.310	9.20:1	Hyd.	55
	V8—383	2-BBL.	290 @ 4400	390 @ 2800	57.8	4.250 x 3.375	9.20:1	Hyd.	55
	V8—383	4-BBL.	330 @ 5000	425 @ 3200	57.8	4.250 x 3.375	10.00:1	Hyd.	55
	V8—426 Hemi	2 x 4-BBL.	425 @ 5000	490 @ 5000	57.8	4.250 x 3.750	10.25:1	Mech.	55
	V8—440	4-BBL.	350 @ 4400	480 @ 2800	59.7	4.320 x 3.750	10.10:1	Hyd.	55
	V8—440	4-BBL.	375 @ 4600	480 @ 3200	59.7	4.320 x 3.750	10.10:1	Hyd.	55
1969	6 Cyl.—225	1-BBL.	145 @ 4000	215 @ 2400	27.7	3.400 x 4.125	8.40:1	Mech.	55
	V8—318	2-BBL.	230 @ 4400	340 @ 2400	48.9	3.910 x 3.310	9.20:1	Hyd.	55
	V8—383	2-BBL.	290 @ 4400	390 @ 2800	57.8	4.250 x 3.375	9.20:1	Hyd.	55
	V8—383	4-BBL.	330 @ 5000	425 @ 3200	57.8	4.250 x 3.375	10.00:1	Hyd.	55
	V8—383	4-BBL.	335 @ 5200	425 @ 3400	57.8	4.250 x 3.375	10.00:1	Hyd.	55

GENERAL ENGINE SPECIFICATIONS, continued

YEAR	CU. IN. DISPLACEMENT	CARBURETOR	ADVERTIZED HORSEPOWER @ RPM	ADVERTIZED TORQUE @ RPM (FT. LBS.)	A.M.A. HORSEPOWER	BORE & STROKE (IN.)	ADVERTIZED COMPRESSION RATIO	VALVE LIFTER TYPE	NORMAL OIL PRESSURE (PSI)
	V8—426 Hemi	2-4-BBL.	425 @ 5000	490 @ 4000	57.8	4.250 x 3.750	10.25:1	Mech.	55
	V8—440	4-BBL.	350 @ 4400	480 @ 2800	59.7	4.320 x 3.750	10.10:1	Hyd.	55
	V8—440	4-BBL.	375 @ 4600	480 @ 3200	59.7	4.320 x 3.750	10.10:1	Hyd.	55
1970	6 Cyl.—225	1-BBL.	145 @ 4000	215 @ 2400	27.7	3.400 x 4.125	8.40:1	Mech.	45–60
	V8—318	2-BBL.	230 @ 4400	320 @ 2000	48.9	3.910 x 3.310	8.8:1	Hyd.	45–65
	V8—383	2-BBL.	290 @ 4400	390 @ 2800	57.8	4.250 x 3.375	8.7:1	Hyd.	45–65
	V8—383	4-BBL.	330 @ 5000	425 @ 3200	57.8	4.250 x 3.375	9.5:1	Hyd.	45–65
	V8—383 Hi Perf.	4-BBL.	335 @ 5200	425 @ 3400	57.8	4.250 x 3.375	9.5:1	Hyd.	45–65
	V8—426 Hemi	2 x 4-BBL.	425 @ 5000	490 @ 4000	57.8	4.250 x 3.750	10.25:1	Hyd.	45–65
	V8—440	4-BBL.	350 @ 4400	480 @ 2800	59.7	4.320 x 3.750	9.7:1	Hyd.	45–65
	V8—440	3 x 2-BBL.	390 @ 4700	490 @ 3200	59.7	4.320 x 3.750	10.5:1	Hyd.	45–65
1971	6 Cyl.—225	1-BBL.	145 @ 4000	215 @ 2400	27.7	3.400 x 4.125	8.4:1	Mech.	45–60
	V8—318	2-BBL.	230 @ 4400	320 @ 2000	48.9	3.910 x 3.310	8.6:1	Hyd.	45–65
	V8—340	4-BBL.	275 @ 5000	340 @ 3200	52.2	4.040 x 3.310	10.2:1	Hyd.	45–65
	V8—360	2-BBL.	255 @ 4400	360 @ 2400	51.2	4.000 x 3.580	8.7:1	Hyd.	45–65
	V8—383	2-BBL.	275 @ 4400	375 @ 2800	57.8	4.250 x 3.375	8.5:1	Hyd.	45–65
	V8—383 Hi. Perf.	4-BBL.	300 @ 4800	410 @ 3400	57.8	4.250 x 3.375	8.5:1	Hyd.	45–65
	V8—426 Hemi	2 x 4-BBL.	425 @ 5000	490 @ 4000	57.8	4.250 x 3.750	10.2:1	Hyd.	45–65
	V8—440	4-BBL.	335 @ 4400	460 @ 3200	59.7	4.320 x 3.750	8.5:1	Hyd.	45–65
	V8—440 Hi. Perf.	4-BBL.	370 @ 4600	480 @ 3200	59.7	4.320 x 3.750	9.5:1	Hyd.	45–65
	V8—440	3 x 2-BBL.	385 @ 4700	490 @ 3200	59.7	4.320 x 3.750	10.3:1	Hyd.	45–65
1972	6 Cyl.—225	1-BBL.	110 @ 4000 ①	185 @ 2000 ①	27.7	3.400 x 4.125	8.4:1	Hyd.	45–60
	V8—318	2-BBL.	150 @ 4000	260 @ 1600	48.9	3.910 x 3.310	8.6:1	Hyd.	45–65
	V8—340	4-BBL.	240 @ 4800	290 @ 3600	52.2	4.040 x 3.310	8.5:1	Hyd.	45–65
	V8—360	2-BBL.	175 @ 4000	285 @ 2400	51.2	4.000 x 3.580	8.8:1	Hyd.	45–65
	V8—400	2-BBL.	190 @ 4400	310 @ 2400	60.3	4.342 x 3.375	8.2:1	Hyd.	45–65
	V8—400	4-BBL.	255 @ 4800 ② ③	340 @ 3200 ② ③	60.3	4.342 x 3.375	8.2:1	Hyd.	45–65
	V8—440	4-BBL.	225 @ 4400 ④ ⑤	345 @ 3200 ④ ⑤	59.7	4.320 x 3.750	8.2:1	Hyd.	45–65
	V8—440	4-BBL.	280 @ 4800 ⑥ ⑦	375 @ 3200 ⑥ ⑦	59.7	4.320 x 3.750	8.2:1	Hyd.	45–65
	V8—440	3 x 2-BBL.	330 @ 4800	410 @ 3600	59.7	4.320 x 3.750	10.3:1	Hyd.	45–65

① —Calif. emission package: 97 H.P. @ 4000 RPM, 180 ft. lbs. @ 2000 RPM.
② —Calif. emission package: 246 H.P. @ 4800 RPM, 335 ft. lbs. @ 3200 RPM.
③ —Fresh air package: 265 H.P. @ 4800 RPM, 345 ft. lbs. @ 3200 RPM
   (N.A. in Calif.).
④ —Calif. emission package: 216 H.P. @ 4400 RPM, 340 ft. lbs. @ 3200 RPM.
⑤ —Dual snorkel air cleaner: 230 H.P. @ 4400 RPM, 355 ft. lbs. @ 2800 RPM.
   Dual exhaust: 245 H.P. @ 4400 RPM, 360 ft. lbs. @ 3200 RPM.
⑥ —Calif. emission package: 271 H.P. @ 4800 RPM, 370 ft. lbs. @ 3200 RPM.
⑦ —Fresh air package: 290 H.P. @ 4800 RPM, 380 ft. lbs. @ 3200 RPM
   (N.A. in Calif.).

CYLINDER HEAD BOLT TIGHTENING SEQUENCE

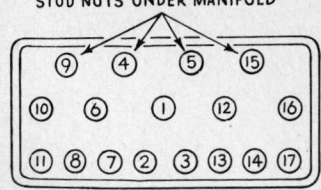

426 Hemi V8

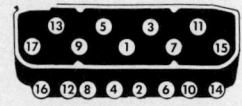

361, 383, 400 ,413,
426 wedge, 440 V8

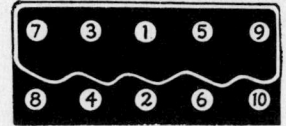

360 V8

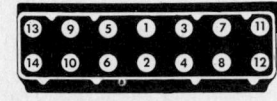

225 6 cyl.

VALVE SPECIFICATIONS

YEAR AND MODEL	SEAT ANGLE (DEG.)	FACE ANGLE (DEG.)	VALVE LIFT INTAKE (IN.)	VALVE LIFT EXHAUST (IN.)	VALVE SPRING PRESSURE (VALVE OPEN) LBS. @ IN.	VALVE SPRING INSTALLED HEIGHT (IN.)	STEM TO GUIDE CLEARANCE (IN.) Intake	Exhaust	STEM DIAMETER (IN.) Intake	Exhaust
1965 6 Cyl.—225 Cu. In.	45	①	.375	.360	145 @ $1\frac{15}{16}$	$1\frac{11}{16}$	.001–.003	.002–.004	.372–.373	.371–.372
V8—273 2-BBL.	45	45	.395	.405	145 @ $1\frac{5}{16}$	$1\frac{11}{16}$	.001–.003	.002–.004	.372–.373	.371–.372
V8—273 4-BBL.	45	45	.415	.425	177 @ $1\frac{5}{16}$	$1\frac{11}{16}$	.001–.003	.002–.004	.372–.373	.371–.372
V8—318 Cu. In.	45	45	.397	.403	145 @ $1\frac{5}{16}$	$1\frac{11}{16}$	.001–.003	.002–.004	.372–.373	.371–.372
V8—361 Cu. In.	45	45	.392	.390	195 @ $1\frac{15}{32}$	$1\frac{55}{64}$	.001–.003	.002–.004	.372–.373	.371–.372
V8—383 Cu. In.	45	45	.430	.430	195 @ $1\frac{15}{32}$	$1\frac{55}{64}$	.001–.003	.002–.004	.372–.373	.371–.372
V8—426 Cu. In.	45	45	.430	.430	195 @ $1\frac{15}{32}$	$1\frac{55}{64}$	.001–.003	.002–.004	.372–.373	.371–.372
1966 6 Cyl.—225 Cu. In.	45	②	.395	.395	145 @ $1\frac{15}{16}$	$1\frac{11}{16}$	.001–.003	.002–.004	.372–.373	.371–.372
V8—273 2-BBL.	45	45	.395	.405	145 @ $1\frac{5}{16}$	$1\frac{11}{16}$	.001–.003	.002–.004	.372–.373	.371–.372
V8—273 4-BBL.	45	45	.415	.425	177 @ $1\frac{5}{16}$	$1\frac{11}{16}$	.001–.003	.002–.004	.372–.373	.371–.372
V8—318 Cu. In.	45	45	.397	.403	145 @ $1\frac{5}{16}$	$1\frac{11}{16}$	.001–.003	.002–.004	.372–.373	.371–.372
V8—361 Cu. In.	45	45	.392	.390	195 @ $1\frac{15}{32}$	$1\frac{55}{64}$	.001–.003	.002–.004	.372–.373	.371–.372
V8—383 2-BBL.	45	45	.392	.390	195 @ $1\frac{15}{32}$	$1\frac{55}{64}$	.001–.003	.002–.004	.372–.373	.371–.372
V8—383 4-BBL.	45	45	.425	.435	195 @ $1\frac{15}{32}$	$1\frac{55}{64}$	.001–.003	.002–.004	.372–.373	.371–.372
V8—426 Hemi	45	45	.480	.460	184 @ $1\frac{13}{32}$	$1\frac{55}{64}$	.002–.004	.003–.005	.309	.308
V8—440 Cu. In.	45	45	.425	.437	200 @ $1\frac{7}{16}$	$1\frac{55}{64}$	.001–.003	.002–.004	.372–.373	.371–.372
1967 6 Cyl.—225 Cu. In.	45	②	.395	.395	145 @ $1\frac{7}{16}$	$1\frac{11}{16}$	.001–.003	.002–.004	.372–.373	.371–.372
V8—273 2-BBL.	45	45	.395	.405	145 @ $1\frac{5}{16}$	$1\frac{11}{16}$	.001–.003	.002–.004	.372–.373	.371–.372
V8—273 4-BBL.	45	45	.415	.425	177 @ $1\frac{5}{16}$	$1\frac{11}{16}$	.001–.003	.002–.004	.372–.373	.371–.372
V8—318 Cu. In.	45	45	.390	.390	177 @ $1\frac{5}{16}$	$1\frac{11}{16}$	.001–.003	.002–.004	.372–.373	.371–.372
V8—383 2-BBL.	45	45	.425	.437	195 @ $1\frac{15}{32}$	$1\frac{55}{64}$	.001–.003	.002–.004	.372–.373	.371–.372
V8—383 4-BBL.	45	45	.425	.437	200 @ $1\frac{7}{16}$	$1\frac{55}{64}$	.001–.003	.002–.004	.372–.373	.371–.372
V8—426 Hemi	45	45	.480	.460	184 @ $1\frac{13}{32}$	$1\frac{55}{64}$	.002–.004	.003–.005	.309	.308
V8—440 4-BBL.	45	45	.425	.437	200 @ $1\frac{7}{16}$	$1\frac{55}{64}$	.001–.003	.002–.004	.372–.373	.371–.372
V8—440 Hi. Perf.	45	45	.450	.465	246 @ $1\frac{23}{64}$	$1\frac{55}{64}$	.001–.003	.002–.004	.372–.373	.371–.372
1968 6 Cyl.—225 Cu. In.	45	①	.395	.395	145 @ $1\frac{5}{16}$	$1\frac{11}{16}$	.001–.003	.002–.004	.372–.373	.371–.372
V8—273 Cu. In.	45	45	.372	.400	177 @ $1\frac{5}{16}$	$1\frac{11}{16}$	.001–.003	.002–.004	.372–.373	.371–.372
V8—318 Cu. In.	45	45	.372	.400	177 @ $1\frac{5}{16}$	$1\frac{11}{16}$	.001–.003	.002–.004	.372–.373	.371–.372
V8—383 2-BBL.	45	45	.425	.437	200 @ $1\frac{7}{16}$	$1\frac{55}{64}$	.001–.003	.002–.004	.372–.373	.371–.372
V8—383 4-BBL.	45	45	.450	.465	225 @ $1\frac{7}{16}$	$1\frac{55}{64}$	.001–.003	.002–.004	.372–.373	.371–.372
V8—383 Hi. Perf.	45	45	.450	.465	230 @ $1\frac{13}{32}$	$1\frac{55}{64}$	.002–.004	.003–.005	.309	.308
V8—426 Hemi	45	45	.490	.480	280 @ $1\frac{3}{8}$	$1\frac{55}{64}$	.002–.004	.003–.005	.372–.373	.371–.372
V8—440 4-BBL.	45	45	.425	.435	200 @ $1\frac{7}{16}$	$1\frac{55}{64}$	.001–.003	.002–.004	.372–.373	.371–.372
V8—440 Hi. Perf.	45	45	.450	.458	230 @ $1\frac{13}{32}$	$1\frac{55}{64}$	.001–.003	.002–.004	.372–.373	.371–.372
1969 6 Cyl.—225 Cu. In.	45	①	.395	.395	145 @ $1\frac{5}{16}$	$1\frac{11}{16}$	.001–.003	.002–.004	.372–.373	.371–.372
V8—318 Cu. In.	45	①	.372	.400	177 @ $1\frac{5}{16}$	$1\frac{11}{16}$	.001–.003	.002–.004	.372–.373	.371–.372
V8—383 2-BBL.	45	45	.425	.437	200 @ $1\frac{7}{16}$	$1\frac{55}{64}$	.001–.003	.002–.004	.372–.373	.371–.372
V8—383 4-BBL.	45	45	.425	.437	246 @ $1\frac{23}{64}$	$1\frac{55}{64}$	.001–.003	.002–.004	.372–.373	.371–.372
V8—383 Hi. Perf.	45	45	.450	.465	246 @ $1\frac{23}{64}$	$1\frac{55}{64}$	.002–.004	.003–.005	.309	.308
V8—426 Hemi	45	45	.490	.480	280 @ $1\frac{3}{8}$	$1\frac{55}{64}$	.002–.004	.003–.005	.372–.373	.371–.372
V8—440 4-BBL.	45	45	.425	.435	200 @ $1\frac{7}{16}$	$1\frac{55}{64}$	.001–.003	.002–.004	.372–.373	.371–.372
V8—440 Hi. Perf.	45	45	.450	.458	246 @ $1\frac{23}{64}$	$1\frac{55}{64}$	.001–.003	.002–.004	.372–.373	.371–.372

VALVE SPECIFICATIONS, continued

YEAR AND MODEL		SEAT ANGLE (DEG.)	FACE ANGLE (DEG.)	VALVE LIFT INTAKE (IN.)	VALVE LIFT EXHAUST (IN.)	VALVE SPRING PRESSURE (VALVE OPEN) LBS. @ IN.	VALVE SPRING INSTALLED HEIGHT (IN.)	STEM TO GUIDE CLEARANCE (IN.)		STEM DIAMETER (IN.)	
								Intake	Exhaust	Intake	Exhaust
1970	6 Cyl.—225 Cu. In.	45	①	.395	.395	156 @ 1¼	1¹¹⁄₁₆	.001–.003	.002–.004	.372–.373	.371–.372
	V8—318 Cu. In.	45	①	.372	.400	177 @ 1⁵⁄₁₆	1¹¹⁄₁₆	.001–.003	.002–.004	.372–.373	.371–.372
	V8—383 2-BBL.	45	45	.425	.437	200 @ 1⁷⁄₁₆	1⁵⁵⁄₆₄	.001–.003	.002–.004	.372–.373	.371–.372
	V8—383 4-BBL.	45	45	.425	.437	234 @ 1²³⁄₆₄	1⁵⁵⁄₆₄	.001–.003	.002–.004	.372–.373	.371–.372
	V8—383 Hi Perf.	45	45	.450	.465	234 @ 1²³⁄₆₄	1⁵⁷⁄₆₄	.001–.003	.002–.004	.372–.373	.371–.372
	V8—426 Hemi	45	45	.490	.480	310 @ 1³⁄₈	1⁵⁵⁄₆₄	.002–.004	.003–.005	.309	.308
	V8—440 4-BBL.	45	45	.425	.437	200 @ 1⁷⁄₁₆	1⁵⁵⁄₆₄	.001–.003	.002–.004	.372–.373	.371–.372
	V8—440 Hi Perf.	45	45	.450	.465	234 @ 1²³⁄₆₄	1⁵⁵⁄₆₄	.001–.003	.002–.004	.372–.373	.371–.372
	V8—440 3 x 2-BBL.	45	45	.450	.465	310 @ 1³⁄₈	1⁵⁵⁄₆₄	.001–.003	.002–.004	.372–.373	.371–.372
1971	6 Cyl.—225 Cu. In.	45	①	.406	.414	156 @ 1¼	1¹¹⁄₁₆	.001–.003	.002–.004	.372–.373	.371–.372
	V8—318 Cu. In.	45	①	.373	.400	③	1¹¹⁄₁₆	.001–.003	.002–.004	.372–.373	.371–.372
	V8—340 Cu. In.	45	①	.430	.445	244 @ 1¹⁄₁₅	1¹¹⁄₁₆	.001–.003	.002–.004	.372–.373	.371–.372
	V8—360 Cu. In.	45	①	.410	.412	③	1¹¹⁄₁₆	.001–.003	.002–.004	.372–.373	.371–.372
	V8—383 2-BBL.	45	45	.425	.435	200 @ 1⁷⁄₁₆	1⁵⁵⁄₆₄	.001–.003	.002–.004	.372–.373	.371–.372
	V8—383 Hi Perf.	45	45	.450	.465	234 @ 1²³⁄₆₄	1⁵⁷⁄₆₄	.001–.003	.002–.004	.372–.373	.371–.372
	V8—426 Hemi	45	45	.490	.481	310 @ 1³⁄₈	1⁵⁵⁄₆₄	.002–.004	.003–.005	.309	.308
	V8—440 Regular Fuel	45	45	.425	.437	200 @ 1⁷⁄₁₆	1⁵⁵⁄₆₄	.001–.003	.002–.004	.372–.373	.371–.372
	V8—440 Hi Perf.	45	45	.450	.465	234 @ 1²³⁄₆₄	1⁵⁵⁄₆₄	.001–.003	.002–.004	.372–.373	.371–.372
	V8—440 3 x 2-BBL.	45	45	.450	.465	310 @ 1²³⁄₆₄	1⁵⁵⁄₆₄	.001–.003	.002–.004	.372–.373	.371–.372
1972	6 Cyl.—225 Cu. In.	45	①	.406	.414	156 @ 1¼	1¹¹⁄₁₆	.001–.003	.002–.004	.372–.373	.371–.372
	V8—318 Cu. In.	45	①	.373	.400	③	1¹¹⁄₁₆	.001–.003	.002–.004	.372–.373	.371–.372
	V8—340 Cu. In.	45	①	.430	.445	244 @ 1¹⁄₅	1¹¹⁄₁₆	.001–.003	.002–.004	.372–.373	.371–.372
	V8—360 Cu. In.	45	①	.410	.412	③	1¹¹⁄₁₆	.001–.003	.002–.004	.372–.373	.371–.372
	V8—400 2-BBL.	45	45	.434	.434	200 @ 1⁷⁄₁₆	1⁵⁵⁄₆₄	.001–.003	.002–.004	.372–.373	.371–.372
	V8—400 Hi Perf.	45	45	.450	.465	234 @ 1²³⁄₆₄	1⁵⁷⁄₆₄	.001–.003	.002–.004	.372–.373	.371–.372
	V8—440 Regular Fuel	45	45	.425	.437	200 @ 1⁷⁄₁₆	1⁵⁵⁄₆₄	.001–.003	.002–.004	.372–.373	.371–.372

① —Intake 45; Exhaust 43.
② —Intake 45; Exhaust 47.
③ —Intake—189 @ 1⁵⁄₁₆, Exhaust—200 @ 1⁷⁄₁₆.

BATTERY AND STARTER SPECIFICATIONS

YEAR	MODEL	BATTERY Ampere Hour Capacity	Volts	Terminal Grounded	Model Number	STARTERS Lock Test Amps.	Volts	Torque	No-Load Test Amps.	Volts	RPM	Brush Spring Tension (oz.)
1965–69	225, 318 std., 273 std.,	48	12	Neg.	2095753	350	4.0	—	78	11.0	3,800	32–48
	361, 383 std.,	59	12	Neg.	2095150	400–450	4.0	—	90	11.0	1,925–2,400	32–48
	426, 440 std., opt. all others	70	12	Neg.	1889100①	350	4.0	8.5	78	11.0	3,800	32–36
	426 Hemi	70	12	Neg.	2642930②	310–445	4.0	—	78	11.0	3,800	32–36
1970–72	225, 318, 340, 360 std.	46	12	Neg.	2875560③	400–450	4.0	—	90	11.0	1,925–2,600	32–36
	360, 383, 400 std.	59	12	Neg.								
	426, 440 std., opt. all others	70	12	Neg.								

① Taxi 225 cu. in. with 11 in. clutch—1965–72.
② 426 Hemi.
③ All engines—1970–72.

WHEEL ALIGNMENT

YEAR	MODEL		FRONT END HEIGHT ▲ (In.)	CASTER		CAMBER		TOE-IN (In.)	KING PIN INCLINATION (Deg.)	WHEEL PIVOT RATIO	
				Range (Deg.)	Pref. Setting (Deg.)	Range (Deg.)	Pref. Setting (Deg.)			Inner Wheel	Outer Wheel
1965	Belvedere Satellite	M.S.	$1\frac{3}{4} \pm \frac{1}{8}$ ②	0–1N	$\frac{1}{2}$N	①	①	$\frac{3}{32} - \frac{5}{32}$	$6\frac{1}{2}$	20	17.8
	Belvedere Satellite	P.S.	$1\frac{3}{4} \pm \frac{1}{8}$ ②	$\frac{1}{4}$P–$1\frac{1}{4}$P	$\frac{3}{4}$P	①	①	$\frac{3}{32} - \frac{5}{32}$	$6\frac{1}{2}$	20	17.8
	Fury, 880 Monaco	M.S.	$1\frac{3}{8} \pm \frac{1}{8}$ ③	0–1N	$\frac{1}{2}$N	①	①	$\frac{3}{32} - \frac{5}{32}$	9	20	18.8
	Fury, 880 Monaco	P.S.	$1\frac{3}{8} \pm \frac{1}{8}$ ③	$\frac{1}{4}$P–$1\frac{1}{4}$P	$\frac{3}{4}$P	①	①	$\frac{3}{32} - \frac{5}{32}$	9	20	18.8
	Coronet	M.S.	$1\frac{3}{4} \pm \frac{1}{8}$ ② ④	0–1N	$\frac{1}{2}$N	①	①	$\frac{3}{32} - \frac{5}{32}$	$7\frac{1}{2}$	20	17.8
	Coronet	P.S.	$1\frac{3}{4} \pm \frac{1}{8}$ ② ④	$\frac{1}{4}$P–$1\frac{1}{4}$P	$\frac{3}{4}$P	①	①	$\frac{3}{32} - \frac{5}{32}$	$7\frac{1}{2}$	20	17.8
1966	Coronet, Belvedere, Satellite	M.S.	$1\frac{7}{8} \pm \frac{1}{8}$	0–1N	$\frac{1}{2}$N	①	①	$\frac{3}{32} - \frac{5}{32}$	$7\frac{1}{2}$	20	17.8
	Coronet, Belvedere, Satellite	P.S.	$1\frac{7}{8} \pm \frac{1}{8}$	$\frac{1}{4}$P–$1\frac{1}{4}$P	$\frac{3}{4}$P	①	①	$\frac{3}{32} - \frac{5}{32}$	$7\frac{1}{2}$	20	17.8
	Fury, 880, Monaco	M.S.	$1\frac{1}{8} \pm \frac{1}{8}$	0–1N	$\frac{1}{2}$N	①	①	$\frac{3}{32} - \frac{5}{32}$	$7\frac{1}{2}$	20	18.8
	Fury, 880, Monaco	P.S.	$1\frac{1}{8} \pm \frac{1}{8}$	$\frac{1}{4}$P–$1\frac{1}{4}$P	$\frac{3}{4}$P	①	①	$\frac{3}{32} - \frac{5}{32}$	$7\frac{1}{2}$	20	18.8
1967–69	Coronet, Charger, Belvedere, Satellite	M.S.	$1\frac{7}{8} \pm \frac{1}{8}$	0–1N	$\frac{1}{2}$N	①	①	$\frac{3}{32} - \frac{5}{32}$	$7\frac{1}{2}$	20	17.8
	Coronet, Charger, Belvedere, Satellite	P.S.	$1\frac{7}{8} \pm \frac{1}{8}$	$\frac{1}{4}$P–$1\frac{1}{4}$P	$\frac{3}{4}$P	①	①	$\frac{3}{32} - \frac{5}{32}$	$7\frac{1}{2}$	20	17.8
	Fury, Monaco, Polara	M.S.	$1\frac{3}{8} \pm \frac{1}{8}$ ⑤	0–1N	$\frac{1}{2}$N	①	①	$\frac{3}{32} - \frac{5}{32}$	$7\frac{1}{2}$	20	18.8
	Fury, Monaco, Polara	P.S.	$1\frac{3}{8} \pm \frac{1}{8}$ ⑤	$\frac{1}{4}$P–$1\frac{1}{4}$P	$\frac{3}{4}$P	①	①	$\frac{3}{32} - \frac{5}{32}$	$7\frac{1}{2}$	20	18.8
1971–72	Coronet, Charger, Satellite, Belvedere	M.S.	$1\frac{7}{8} \pm \frac{1}{8}$	$\frac{1}{2}$N ± $\frac{1}{2}$	$\frac{1}{2}$N	①	①	$\frac{3}{32} - \frac{5}{32}$	$7\frac{1}{2}$	20	17.8
	Coronet, Charger, Satellite, Belvedere	P.S.	$1\frac{7}{8} \pm \frac{1}{8}$	$\frac{3}{4}$P ± $\frac{1}{2}$	$\frac{3}{4}$P	①	①	$\frac{3}{32} - \frac{5}{32}$	$7\frac{1}{2}$	20	17.8
	Polara, Monaco, Fury	M.S.	$1\frac{3}{8} \pm \frac{1}{8}$ ⑤	$\frac{1}{2}$N ± $\frac{1}{2}$	$\frac{1}{2}$N	①	①	$\frac{3}{32} - \frac{5}{32}$	$7\frac{1}{2}$	20	18.8
	Polara, Monaco, Fury	P.S.	$1\frac{3}{8} \pm \frac{1}{8}$ ⑤	$\frac{1}{2}$N ± $\frac{1}{2}$	$\frac{3}{4}$P	①	①	$\frac{3}{32} - \frac{5}{32}$	$7\frac{1}{2}$	20	18.8

▲—Fr procedure, see text.
M.S.—Manual steering.
P.S.—Power steering.

N—Negative.
P—Positive.
①—Left—$\frac{1}{4}$P–$\frac{3}{4}$P; $\frac{1}{2}$P preferred. Right—0–$\frac{1}{2}$P; $\frac{1}{4}$P preferred.

②—Heavy duty—$2\frac{1}{8} \pm \frac{1}{8}$.
③—Fury sta. wag., Monaco, Polara, Custom 880—$1\frac{1}{8} \pm \frac{1}{8}$.
④—Sta. wag.—$1\frac{3}{4} \pm \frac{1}{8}$.
⑤—Monaco, Polara—$1\frac{1}{8} \pm \frac{1}{8}$.

GENERAL CHASSIS AND BRAKE SPECIFICATIONS, DODGE

YEAR	MODEL	CHASSIS		BRAKE CYLINDER BORE			BRAKE DRUM	
		Overall Length (In.)	Tire Size	Master Cylinder (In.)	Wheel Cylinder Diameter (In.)		Diameter (In.)	
					Front	Rear	Front	Rear
1965	Coronet Pass.	204.3	7.35 x 14	1.000	1.125	.9375	10.00	10.00
	Coronet Sta. Wag.	209.3	7.75 x 14	1.000	1.125	.9375	10.00	10.00
	Polara Exc. Sta. Wag.	212.3	8.25 x 14	1.000	1.125	.9375	11.00	11.00
	Polara Sta. Wag.	217.1	8.55 x 14	1.000	1.125	.9375	11.00	11.00
	Custom 880 and Monaco	212.3	8.25 x 14	1.000	1.125	.9375	11.00	11.00
	Custom 880 Sta. Wag.	217.1	8.55 x 14	1.000	1.125	.9375	11.00	11.00
1966	Coronet, 6 Cyl. Sed.	203.2	6.95 x 14	1.000	1.125	.9375	10.00	10.00
	Coronet, 6 Cyl. Conv.	203.2	7.35 x 14	1.000	1.125	.9375	10.00	10.00
	Coronet, V8 Sed. and Conv.	203.2	7.35 x 14	1.000	1.125	.9375	10.00	10.00
	Coronet, Sta. Wag., 2 Seat	207.9	7.75 x 14	1.000	1.125	.9375	10.00	10.00
	Coronet, Sta. Wag., 3 Seat	209.0	8.25 x 14	1.000	1.125	.9375	10.00	10.00
	Polara and Monaco, Exc. Sta. Wag.	213.3	8.25 x 14	1.000①	1.125⑦	.9375③	11.00	11.00
	Station Wagon	217.1	8.55 x 14	1.000①	1.125⑦	.9375③	11.00	11.00
1967	Coronet, Exc. Sta. Wag.	219.6	7.35 x 14	1.000①	1.125⑦	.9375	10.00	10.00
	Coronet, Sta. Wag., 2 Seat	207.9	8.25 x 14	1.000①	1.125⑦	.9375	10.00	10.00
	Coronet, Sta. Wag., 3 Seat	210.4	8.25 x 14	1.000①	1.125⑦	.9375	10.00	10.00
	Charger	203.6	7.35 x 14	1.000①	1.125⑦	.9375	10.00	10.00
	Polara and Monaco, Exc. Sta. Wag.	219.6	8.25 x 14	1.000①	1.125⑦	.9375③	11.00	11.00
	Polara and Monaco, Sta. Wag.	221.3	8.45 x 15	1.000①	1.125⑦	.9375③	11.00	11.00
1968–69	Coronet, Exc. Sta. Wag.	206.6	7.35 x 14	1.000	1.125	.9375	10.00⑤	10.00⑤
	Coronet, Sta. Wag.	210.0	8.25 x 14	1.000	1.125	.9375	10.00⑤	10.00⑤
	Charger	208.0	F70 x 14	1.000	1.125	.9375	10.00⑤	10.00⑤
	Polara and Monaco, Exc. Sta. Wag.	219.0	8.25 x 14	1.000	1.125	.9375	11.00	11.00
	Polara and Monaco, Sta. Wag., 2 Seat	219.6	8.55 x 14	1.000	1.125	.9375	11.00	11.00
	Polara and Monaco, Sta. Wag., 3 Seat	220.0	8.55 x 14	1.000	1.125	.9375	11.00	11.00
	Coronet and Charger (Disc Brakes)	—	—	1.125	2.000	.9375	11.04	10.00
	Polara and Monaco (Disc Brakes)	—	8.15 x 15④	1.125	⑥	.9375	11.76	11.00
1970	Coronet, 6 Cyl., Exc. Sta. Wag.	209.2	F78 x 14	1.000	1.125	.9375	10.00	10.00
	Coronet, V8 318 & 383, Exc. Sta. Wag.	209.2	G78 x 14	1.000	1.125	.9375	10.00⑦	10.00⑦
	Coronet, V8 426 & 440, Exc. Sta. Wag.	209.2	F70 x 14	1.000	1.125	.9375	11.00	11.00
	Coronet, Sta. Wag.	211.7	G78 x 14	1.000	1.125	.9375	11.00	11.00
	Charger, 6 Cyl.	208.0	F78 x 14	1.000	1.125	.9375	10.00	10.00
	Charger, V8 318	208.0	G78 x 14	1.000	1.125	.9375	10.00	10.00
	Charger, V8 426 & 440	208.0	F70 x 14	1.000	1.125	.9375	11.00	11.00
	Polara & Monaco, Exc. Sta. Wag.	219.9	H78 x 15	1.000	1.125	.9375	11.00	11.00
	Polara & Monaco, Sta. Wag., 2-seat	223.9	J78 x 15	1.000	1.125	.9375	11.00	11.00
	Polara & Monaco, Sta. Wag., 3-seat Exc. 318	223.9	L78 x 15	1.000	1.125	.9375	11.00	11.00
	Polara & Monaco, Sta. Wag., 3-seat 318	223.9	J78 x 15	1.000	1.125	.9375	11.00	11.00
	Coronet & Charger (Disc Brakes)	—	—	1.125	2.750	.9375	10.72	11.00
	Polara & Monaco (Disc Brakes)	—	—	1.125	2.750	.9375	11.75	11.00

GENERAL CHASSIS AND BRAKE SPECIFICATIONS, DODGE

YEAR	MODEL	CHASSIS			BRAKE CYLINDER BORE			BRAKE DRUM	
		Overall Length (In.)	Tire Size	Master Cylinder (In.)	Wheel Cylinder Diameter (In.)			Diameter (In.)	
					Front	Rear		Front	Rear
1971–72	Coronet/Charger, 2 Door 225 & 318 Cu. In.	205.4	E78 x 14	1.000	1.187	.9375		10.00 ⑧	10.00 ⑧
	Coronet/Charger, 2 Door 340, 383, & 400 Cu. In.	205.4	F70 x 14	1.000	1.187	.9375		10.00 ⑧	10.00 ⑧
	Coronet/Charger, 2 Door 440 Cu. In.	205.4	G60 x 15	1.000	1.187	.9375		11.00	11.00
	Coronet, 4 Door	207.0	F78 x 14	1.000	1.187	.9375		10.00 ⑧	10.00 ⑧
	Coronet, Sta. Wag.	213.4	H78 x 14	1.000	1.187	.9375		11.00	11.00
	Polara and Monaco, exc. Sta. Wag.	220.2	H78 x 15 ⑨	1.000	1.187	.9375		11.00	11.00
	Polara and Monaco Sta. Wag.	223.5	J78 x 15 ⑩	1.000	1.187	.9375		11.00 ⑪	11.00 ⑪
	Coronet/Charger, Polara, Monaco (Disc Brakes)	—	—	1.000	2.750	.9375		11.75 ⑫	11.00

① —Disc brakes—Budd type—1.125 in.
② —Disc brakes—Budd type—2.375 in., Kelsey-Hayes 1.638 in, Bendix 2.000.
③ —When car is equipped with front discs—.875 in.
④ —Station Wagons—8.45 x 15 in.
⑤ —11 in. std. on Coronet R/T; opt. w/V8—426 and 440.
⑥ —1969—2.750 in.
⑦ —V8 383 high perf.—11 in.
⑧ —11.00 in. optional.
⑨ —G78 x 15 w/6 Cyl. & V8-2BBL.
⑩ —L84 x 15 w/engines larger than 318 cu. in. on Monaco.
⑪ —Disc brakes std. w/engines larger than 360 cu. in.
⑫ —Coronet/Charger—10.72.

GENERAL CHASSIS AND BRAKE SPECIFICATIONS PLYMOUTH

YEAR	MODEL	CHASSIS			BRAKE CYLINDER BORE			BRAKE DRUM	
		Overall Length (In.)	Tire Size	Master Cylinder (In.)	Wheel Cylinder Diameter (In.)			Diameter (In.)	
					Front	Rear		Front	Rear
1965	Belvedere, Satellite	203.4	7.35 x 14 ▲	1.000	1.125	.9375		10.00	10.00
	Fury	209.4	7.35 x 14 ●	1.000	1.125	.9375		10.00	10.00
	Sports Fury	209.4	7.75 x 14 ●	1.000	1.125	.9375		10.00	10.00
1966	6 Cyl. Belvedere, Satellite	200.5	6.95 x 14 †	1.000	1.125	.9375		10.00	10.00
	V8	200.5	7.35 x 14 †	1.000	1.125	.9375		10.00	10.00
	6 Cyl. Fury	209.8	7.35 x 14 ‡	1.000	1.125	.9375		11.00	11.00
	V8	209.8	7.75 x 14 ‡	1.000	1.125	.9375		11.00	11.00
	Disc Brakes, Kelsey-Hayes	—	—	1.000	1.625	.9375		11.00	11.00
	Disc. Brakes, Budd	—	—	1.125	2.375	.9375		11.00	11.00
1967	6 Cyl. Belvedere, Satellite	200.5 †	7.35 x 14 †	1.000 ②	1.125 ③	.9375		10.00 ⑤	10.00
	V8	200.5 ①	7.35 x 14 ①	1.000 ②	1.125 ③	.9375		10.00 ⑤	10.00
	Fury	213.1 ‡	7.75 x 14 ‡	1.000 ②	1.125 ④	.9375		11.00 ⑥	11.00
	V8 Belvedere—GTX	200.5	7.75 x 14	1.000 ②	1.125 ③	.9375		11.00 ⑥	11.00
1968	Belvedere, Satellite (STD.)	202.7	8.25 x 14	1.000	1.125	.9375		10.00	10.00
	GTX, Opt. 426 & 440	202.7	8.55 x 14	1.000	1.125	.9375		11.00	11.00
	Belvedere & Satellite sta. wag.	208.0	8.15 x 14	1.000	1.125	.9375		10.00	10.00
	Belvedere & Satellite (disc brakes)	202.7	—	1.125	2.00	.9375		11.04 (Disc)	10.00
	Fury & V.I.P.	213.0	8.25 x 14	1.000	1.125	.9375		11.00	11.00
	Suburban (two-seat)	216.0	8.55 x 14	1.000	1.125	.9375		11.00	11.00
	Suburban (three-seat)	217.0	8.55 x 14	1.000	1.125	.9375		11.00	11.00
	Suburban (disc brakes)	—	8.45 x 15	1.125	2.375	.9375		11.76 (Disc)	11.00
	Fury models (disc brakes)	213.0	8.15 x 15	1.125	2.375	.9375		11.76 (Disc)	11.00

GENERAL CHASSIS AND BRAKE SPECIFICATIONS
PLYMOUTH

YEAR	MODEL	CHASSIS Overall Length (In.)	CHASSIS Tire Size	BRAKE CYLINDER BORE Master Cylinder (In.)	Wheel Cylinder Diameter (In.) Front	Wheel Cylinder Diameter (In.) Rear	BRAKE DRUM Diameter (In.) Front	BRAKE DRUM Diameter (In.) Rear
1969	Satellite							
	6 Cyl. exc. sta. wag.	202.7	7.35 x 14	1.000	1.125	.9375	10.00	10.00
	Sta. wag.	208.0	8.25 x 14	1.000	1.125	.9375	10.00	10.00
	V8, exc. below	202.7	7.35 x 14	1.000	1.125	.9375	10.00 (7)	10.00 (7)
	V8, sta. wag.	208.0	8.25 x 14	1.000	1.125	.9375	10.00	10.00
	V8, Road Runner	202.7	F70 x 14	1.000	1.125	.9375	11.00	11.00
	V8, GTX	202.7	F70 x 14	1.000	1.125	.9375	11.00	11.00
	Disc Brakes	—	—	1.125	2.000	.9375	(Disc)	10.00
	Fury							
	6 Cyl. exc. sta. wag.	214.5	7.75 x 15	1.000	1.125	.9375	11.00	11.00
	Sta. wag.	219.1	8.85 x 15	1.000	1.125	.9375	11.00	11.00
	V8, exc. below	214.5	7.75 x 15	1.000	1.125	.9375	11.00	11.00
	V8, sta. wag.	219.1	8.85 x 15	1.000	1.125	.9375	11.00	11.00
	Disc Brakes	—	—	1.125	2.750	.9375	(Disc)	11.00
1970	Satellite & Belvedere, exc. Sta. Wag.	204.0	(8)	1.000 (15)	1.187	.9375	10.00 (14)	10.00 (14)
	Satellite & Belvedere, Sta. Wag.	209.1	G78 x 14	1.000	1.187	.9375	11.00	11.00
	Fury, exc. Sta. Wag.	214.9	F78 x 15 (12)	1.000	1.187	.9375	11.00	11.00
	Fury Sta. Wag.	220.6	J78 x 15	1.000	1.187	.9375	11.00	11.00
	Disc Brakes	—	—	1.125	2.750	.9375	11.75 (11)	11.00
1971–72	Satellite, 2 Door 225 & 318 Cu. In.	203.2	E78 X 14	1.000	1.187	.9375	10.00 (14)	10.00 (14)
	Satellite, 2 Door 340, 383, & 400 Cu. In.	203.2	F70 x 14	1.000	1.187	.9375	10.00 (14)	10.00 (14)
	Satellite, 2 Door 440 Cu. In.	203.2	G60 x 15	1.000	1.187	.9375	11.00	11.00
	Satellite, 4 Door	204.6	F78 x 14	1.000	1.187	.9375	10.00 (14)	10.00 (14)
	Satellite, Sta. Wag.	210.9	H78 x 14	1.000	1.187	.9375	11.00	11.00
	Fury, all Exc. Sta. Wag.	215.1	F78 x 15 (12)	1.000	1.187	.9375	11.00	11.00
	Fury, Sta. Wag.	220.2	J78 x 15 (13)	1.000	1.187	.9375	11.00	11.00
	Satellite & Fury, Disc Brakes	—	—	1.000	2.750	.9375	11.75 (11)	11.00

▲—Option & station wagon—7.75 x 14.
●—Optional—8.25 x 14.
  Station wagon—8.55 x 14.
†—Sta. Wag. two-seat 7.75 x 14, three-seat 8.25 x 14, Overall Length 207.
‡—St. Wag. 8.55 x 14, overall length—two-seat 216.1—three-seat 217.4.
①—Sta. wag. 8.25 x 14, overall length—two-seat 207.1—three-seat 208.8.
②—Disc brakes—1.125 in.
③—Disc brakes—2 in.
④—Disc brakes 2.375 in.
⑤—Disc brakes 11.188 in.

⑥—Disc brakes 11.875 in.
⑦—383 hi. perf., 426, 440—11 inches.
⑧—225 and 318—F78 x 14; 426 and 440—F70 x 14.
⑩—225, 318 and 383 except high perf.—10 in.; 383 high perf. 426 and 440—11 in.
⑪—Satellite and Belvedere—10.72.
⑫—G78 x 15 and H70 x 15 optional.
⑬—L84 x 15 optional.
⑭—11.00 in. optional.
⑮—426 Hemi—1.125 in.

CAPACITIES

YEAR	MODEL	ENGINE CRANKCASE ADD 1 Qt. FOR NEW FILTER	TRANSMISSIONS Pts. TO REFILL AFTER DRAINING			DRIVE AXLE (Pts.)	GASOLINE TANK (Gals.)	COOLING SYSTEM (Qts.) WITH HEATER
			Manual 3-Speed	Manual 4-Speed	Automatic			
1965	6 Cyl.—225	4	6.00	None	17.00	4.00	19.00[1]	13.00
	V8—273	4	4.50	7.50	19.50	4.00	19.00[1]	18.00
	V8—318	4	4.50	7.50	19.50	4.00	19.00[1]	21.00
	V8—361	4	4.50	7.50	19.50	4.00	19.00[1]	17.00
	V8—383	4	4.50	7.50	19.50	4.00	19.00[1]	17.00
	V8—413, 426	4	4.50	7.50	19.50	4.00	19.00[1]	17.00
1966	6 Cyl.—225	4	6.50	None	16.00	2.00[5]	19.00[1]	13.00[4]
	V8—318	4	6.00	9.00	18.50	4.00	25.00[6]	22.00[7]
	V8—383	4	6.00	9.00	18.50	4.00	25.00[6]	18.00[8]
	V8—426 Hemi	6	None	9.00	18.50	4.00	25.00[6]	18.00[8]
1967	6 Cyl.—225	4	6.50	None	16.00	2.00[5]	19.00	13.00[4]
	V8—273	4	6.50	8.00	16.00	[9]	19.00	19.00[10]
	V8—318	4	6.50	8.50	18.50	[9]	19.00	18.00[11]
	V8—318 Police	4	6.50	8.50	18.50	[9]	19.00	19.00[10]
	V8—383	4	6.50	8.50[12]	18.50	[9]	19.00, 25.00[6]	17.00[11]
	V8—440	4	6.50	8.50[12]	18.50	[9]	19.00, 25.00[6]	17.00[11]
	V8—426 Hemi	6	None	8.50[12]	18.50	[9]	19.00, 25.00[6]	18.00
1968	6 Cyl.—225	4	6.5	None	15.50	[9]	19.00	13.00[4]
	V8—273	4	5.75	8.00	15.50	[9]	19.00	18.00[11]
	V8—318	4	5.75	8.00	15.50	[9]	19.00[15]	18.00[11]
	V8—318 Police	4	5.75	8.00	18.50	[9]	19.00	19.00[11]
	V8—383	4	5.75	9.00	18.50[13]	[9]	19.00[15]	17.00[11]
	V8—426 Hemi	6	None	9.00	16.00	[9]	19.00	18.00
	V8—440	4	5.75	9.00	18.50[13]	[9]	19.00[15]	17.00[14] [11]
1969	6 Cyl.—225	4	6.50	None	15.50	[9]	19.00	13.00[16]
	V8—318	4	6.00	None	15.50[19]	[9]	19.00[15]	16.00[17]
	V8—318 Police	4	6.00	7.50	18.50	[9]	19.00	19.00
	V8—383	4	6.00	7.50[8]	18.50[13]	[9]	19.00[15]	16.00[11]
	V8—383 Police	4	6.00	7.50	18.50	[9]	19.00	17.00
	T8—426 Hemi	6	None	7.50[18]	16.00	[9]	19.00	18.00
	V8—440	4	6.00	7.50[18]	18.50[13]	[9]	19.00[15]	17.00[14] [11]
1970	6 Cyl.—225	4	4.75[21]	None	17.00	[9]	[2]	13.00[16]
	V8—318	4	4.75[21]	None	17.00	[9]	[2]	16.00[17]
	V8—383	4	4.75[21]	7.50	19.00[20]	[9]	[2]	14.50[16]
	V8—426 Hemi	6	None	7.50	16.80	[9]	[2]	17.00
	V8—440	4	4.75[21]	7.50	19.00	[9]	[2]	17.00[22]
	V8—440 3 x 2 BBL.	6	None	7.50	19.00	[9]	[2]	17.00
1971	6 Cyl.—225	4	4.75	None	17.00	[9]	[3]	13.00[16]
	V8—318	4	4.75	None	17.00	[9]	[3]	16.00[17]
	V8—340	4	4.75	7.50	16.30	4.50	21.00	14.50
	V8—360	4	4.75	None	16.30	4.50	23.00	15.50
	V8—383	4	4.75	7.50	19.00[20]	[9]	[3]	14.50[16]
	V8—426 Hemi	6	None	7.50	16.80	[9]	19.00	17.00
	V8—440	4[23]	4.75[21]	7.50	19.00	[9]	[3]	17.00[22]

CAPACITIES

YEAR	MODEL	ENGINE CRANKCASE ADD 1 Qt. FOR NEW FILTER	TRANSMISSIONS Pts. TO REFILL AFTER DRAINING			DRIVE AXLE (Pts.)	GASOLINE TANK (Gals.)	COOLING SYSTEM (Qts.) WITH HEATER
			Manual		Automatic			
			3-Speed	4-Speed				
1972	6 Cyl.—225	4	4.75	None	17.00	⑨	③	13.00 ⑬
	V8—318	4	4.75	None	17.00	⑨	③	16.00 ⑰
	V8—340	4	4.75	7.50	16.30	4.50	21.00	14.50
	V8—360	4	4.75	None	16.30	4.50	23.00	15.50
	V8—400	4	4.75	7.50	19.00 ⑳	⑨	③	14.50 ⑯
	V8—440	4 ㉓	4.75	7.50	19.00	⑨	③	17.00

① Station wagon—21.
② Intermediate—19.00, Full size—23.00.
③ Intermediate—21.00, Full size—23.00.
④ With air cond. or heavy duty rad.—14.00
⑤ Station wagon and 1967 Sure-Grip—4.00.
⑥ Station wagon—22.00.
⑦ With air cond., trailer pack, or heavy duty rad. —23.00
⑧ With air cond., trailer pack, or heavy duty rad. —19.00.
⑨ 7¼ in. axle, 2.00; 8¼ in. axle, 4.40; 8¾ in axle, 4.4. 9¾ in. axle, 5.50.

Axle	Fillter Location	Cover fastening
7¼ in.	Cover	9 bolts
8¼ in.	Carrier, right side	10 bolts
8¾ in.	Carrier, right side	Welded
9¾ in.	Cover	10 bolts

⑩ With air cond., trailer pack, or heavy duty rad. —20.00.
⑪ With air cond., trailer pack, or heavy duty rad. —add 1 Qt.
⑫ All Plymouth Fury—9.00.
⑬ High performance—15.50.

⑭ —With manual transmission—18.00.
⑮ Polara, Monaco, Fury—23.00 except station wagon. Station wagon—22.00.
⑯ Add 2 Qts. for air cond. or heavy duty rad.
⑰ Add 3 Qts. for air cond. or heavy duty rad.
⑱ All Plymouth Fury—7.75.
⑲ A904 transmission—17.00.
⑳ High performance—16.30.
㉑ All synchro 3-sp.—use Dexron A.T. Fluid.
㉒ Fury—15.50.
㉓ 440 w/3 x 2 BBL.—6.

LIGHT BULBS

DODGE

1965

	Coronet	Polara, Monaco, Custom 880
Sealed beam—low beam	4002	4002
Sealed beam—high beam	4001	4001
Tail, stop & turn signal	1034	1034
Tail light	—	—
Park & turn signal	1034	1034
Back up lights	1073	1073
License light	67	67
Trunk and/or under hood	1004	1004
Glove compartment	1891	1891
Radio	1893	1893
Gear shift indicator	1445	53X
Handbrake indicator	57	257
Dome lamp	1004	1004
Map lamp	90	1004
Heater and/or AC cont. P/B	1892	53X
Turn signal indicator	158	158
High beam indicator	158	57
Oil pressure warning light	158	158
Instrument cluster illumination	158	158
Ignition switch	—	1445
Ash tray	—	53X
Auto pilot	—	57
Door and/or pocket panel	—	90

1966

	Polara, Monaco	Coronet
Ash tray	53X	—
Auto pilot	57	—
Back-up lights	1073	1073
Clock	158	(a)
Dome lights	1004	1004
Door and/or pocket	90	90
Emergency flasher	57	57
Fender mounted turn signals	1893	—
Gear selector indicator	53X	1445
Gear selector with console	57	57
Glove compartment	1891	1891

Handbrake indicator	257	57	
Heater and/or A. C. control	53X	—	
High beam indicator	57	158	
Instrument cluster illumination	158	158-57	
Ignition switch	1445	—	
License light	67	67	
Map light	1004	90	
Oil pressure indicator	158	158	
Panel and/or ridge light	90	90	
Park and turn signal	1034A	—	
Radio	1893	1893	
Sealed beam—hi-beam (No. 1)	4001	4001	
Sealed beam—lo-beam sealed beam —hi-lo beam (No. 2)	4002	4002	
Tachometer with console	57	57	
Tail lights	67	—	
Tail stop and turn signal	1034	1034	
Trunk and/or under hood light	1004	1004	
Turn signal indicator	158	158	

(a) In instrument cluster lighting.

1967

	Polara, Monaco	Coronet	Charger
Air conditioning control	*	1445	EL
Back-up lights	1073	1141	1141
Brake system warning light	158	257	257
Clock	*	*	57
Dome and/or "C" pillar light	1004	1004	1004
Door, pocket panel and/or reading light	90	90	90
Fender mounted turn signal indicator	1893	1893	330
Gear selector indicator	*	1445	1445
Gear selector with console	57	57	53X
Glove compartment	1891	1891	1891
Handbrake indicator	158	257	257
High beam indicator	150	158	57

Instrument cluster			
illumination	158	158	EL
License light	67	67	67
Map light	90	90	90
Oil pressure indicator	158	158	Gauge
Park and turn signal	1034	1034	1034
Portable reading light	90	—	—
Radio	1893	1893	EL
Sealed beam—hi-beam (No. 1)	4001	4001	4001
Sealed beam—hi-lo beam (No. 2)	4002	4002	4002
Tachometer	1816	1816	EL
Tail light	67	67	—*
Tail, stop and turn signal	1034	1034	1034
Trunk and/or under hood light	1004	1004	1004
Turn signal indicator (panel)	158	158	57
Ash tray	53X	—	—
Auto pilot	1445, 1892		
Ignition switch	53X	—	

*Included in instrument cluster lighting.
EL—Electroluminescent lighting.

1968

	Polara, Monaco	Coronet	Charger
Air conditioning indicator	1445	1892	1892
Ash tray	1445	1445	1445
Back-up lights	1073 (Sta. Wagon— 1141)	1073 (1141— Sta. Wagon)	1073
Brake system warning light	158	158	57
Clock	*	57	***
Courtesy lamp	—	89	89
Dome and/or "C" pillar light	1004	1004	1004

LIGHT BULBS DODGE

Door, pocket panel and/or reading light ..	90	90	90
Fender mounted turn signal indicator......	330, 1893	330	**
Gear selector indicator......	*	1445	—
Gear selector with console.......	57	57	57
Glove compartment........	1891	1891	1891
High beam indicator......	158	158	57
Ignition lamp	53X	1445	1445
Instrument cluster illumination ...	57	158	57-158
License light.....	67	67	67
Map light........	90	90	90
Oil pressure indicator.....	158	158	Gauge
Park and turn signal	1034	1034	1034
Radio..........	1816	1816	1816
Sealed beam—hi-beam (No. 1)..	4001	4001	4001
Sealed beam—hi-lo beam (No. 2)........	4002	4002	4002
Side marker......	1895	1895	1895
Tachometer......	1816	57	*
Tail, stop and turn signal	1034	1034	1034
Trunk and/or under hood light	1004	1004	1004
Turn signal Indicator (panel)	158	158	57
Auto. temp	53X	—	—
Cornering lights ..	1195P	—	—
Tail light	1095	—	—

*Included in instrument cluster lighting.
***Hood mounted.
***Not lighted.

High beam indicator	158	158	57
Ignition lamp	1445	1445	1445
Instrument cluster illumination ...	**158(4)	**158(4)	**57(3) 158(3)
License light.....	67	67	67
Map light	90	90	90
Oil pressure indicator	158	158	Gauge
Park and turn signal	1157(2)	1157(2)	1157A(2)
Radio	**1816	**1816	**1816
Radio with tape ..	—	**1815	—
Reverse 4-speed transmission indicator	—	53	53
Sealed beam—hi-beam (No. 1)	4001	4001	4001
Sealed beam—hi-lo beam (No. 2)	4002	4002	4002
Tachometer	—	**57	*
Tail, stop and turn signal	1157(2)	1157(2)	1157(4)
Trunk and/or under hood light	1004	1004	1004
Turn signal indicator (panel) ..	158(2)	158(2)	57(2)
Air cond. controls	**1892(2)	—	—
Auto. temp. buttons.......	**1893(2)	—	—
Auto. temp. thumbwheel ..	**53	—	—
Cornering lights..	1195(2)	—	—
Heater controls ..	**1892(2)	—	—
Side marker.....	67(2)	—	—
Stereo indicator..	1445	—	—
Super lite indicator	1445	—	—
Tail light	1095(2)	—	—
Switch lighting...	1892	—	—

*Included in instrument cluster lighting.
**Headlamp rheostat dimming.
***Hood mounted.

Oil pressure indicator.....	158	158	158
Park and turn signal......	1157(2)	1157(2)	1157(2)
Radio	**1816	1816	1816
Radio with tape.........	—	1815	—
Reverse 4-speed transmission indicator	—	53	53
Sealed beam—hi-beam (No. 1)	4001	4001	4001
Sealed beam—hi-lo beam (No. 2).........	4002	4002	4002
Seat belt indicator	—	53	53
Tachometer.............	—	57	—
Tail, stop and turn signal ..	1157(2)	1157(2)	1157(2)
Trunk and/or under hood light..........	1004	1004	1004
Turn signal indicator (panel)................	158(2)	158	158
Air cond. controls	**1892(2)	—	—
Auto. temp. buttons	**1893(2)	—	—
Auto. temp. thumbwheel ..	**53	—	—
Cornering lights	1195(2)	—	—
Heater controls...........	**1892(2)	—	—
Side marker	67(2)	—	—
Stereo indicator	1445	—	—
Super lite indicator.......	1445	—	—
Tail light	1095(2)	—	—
Switch lighting	1892	—	—

*Included in instrument cluster lighting.
**Headlamp rheostat dimming.
***Hood mounted.

1969

	Polara, Monaco	Coronet	Charger
Air conditioning indicator	—	**1892(2)	**1892(2)
Ash tray	**1445	**1892	**53
Back-up lights ...	1156(2)	1156(2)	1156(2)
Brake system warning light..	158	158	57
Clock..........	*	**57	*
Courtesy lamp ...	90	89	89
Dome and/or "C" pillar light	551	1004	1004
Door, pocket panel and/or reading light ..	90	90	90
Fender mounted turn signal indicator	330(2)	330(2)	1816(2)***
(Tail lamp only) ..	—	—	1095(2)
Gear selector indicator	**57	**1445	**1445
Gear selector with console ..	**57	**57	**57
Glove compartment........	1891	1891	1891

1970

	Polara, Monaco	Coronet	Charger
Air conditioning indicator .	—	1892	1892
Ash tray.............	**1445	1445	1445
Back-up lights..........	1156(2)	1156(2)	1156(2)
Brake system warning light.................	158	158	57
Clock	*	57	57
Courtesy lamp..........	90	89	89
Dome and/or "C" pillar light...........	551	1004	1004
Door, pocket panel and/or reading light.........	90	90	90
Fender mounted turn signal indicator........	330(2)	330(2)	330(2)
(Tail lamp only)..........	—	—	1095
Gear selector indicator....	**57	161	161
Gear selector with console	**57	57	57
Glove compartment	1891	1891	1891
High beam indicator	158	158	57
Ignition lamp	1445	1445	1445
Instrument cluster illumination	**158(4)	158	57,158
License light	67	67	67
Map light	90	90	90

1971–72

	Coronet/ Charger	Polara/ Monaco
Air conditioner and auto-temp.............	53	*
Ash tray	1445	1445
Auxilliary switch............	—	1445
Back-up.................	1156	1156
Brake system warning.......	158	57
Clock.....................	*	*
Cornering	—	1293
Courtesy	—	90
Dome	1004	211-2
Door ajar.................	1892	57
Fender turn-signal	330	220
Front park and turn-signal	1157	1157
Gear selector (column).......	161	*
Gear selector (console)	57	57
Glove compartment	57	57
Instrument cluster	158**	1893
Ignition	1445	1445
License	67	67
Low fuel	1892	57
Map and courtesy	562	—
Oil pressure	158	57
Pocket panel..............	90	90
Radio	1815	*
Reverse 4-speed transmission indicator.....	53	53
Sealed beam (No. 1).........	4001	4001
Sealed beam (No. 2).........	4002	4002
Side maker, front...........	195	1895
Side marker, rear (Sta. Wag.)	1893	1893
Stero indicator	—	1445
Switches	1892	1892
Stop, tail, and turn-signal	1157	1157
Trunk and underhood	1003	1003
Tarn-signal indicator	158	57

*—Included in instrument cluster lighting.
**—57 with Rallye instrument cluster.

LIGHT BULBS Plymouth

1965-66

	Belvedere, Satellite	Fury I, II, III
Sealed beam—lo-beam	—	4002
Sealed beam—hi-beam	—	4001
Single beam 2 filament	6012	—
Tail, stop & turn signal	1034	1034
Park & turn signal	1034A	1034A
Back-up lamps	1073	1073
License lamp	67	67
Trunk and/or under hood lamp	1004	1004
Glove compartment	1891	1891
Radio	1893	1893
Transmission gear shift control	1445	—
Handbrake indicator	57	256
Dome lamp	1004	1004
Map lamp	90	90
Clock	—	57
Heater and/or A.C. control	—	57
Turn signal indicator	158	57
High beam indicator	158	158
Oil pressure indicator	158	158
Instrument and speedometer cluster illumination	57, 158	158
Emergency flasher	57	57
Auto pilot	—	1816
Gear selector with console	57	57

1967

	Belvedere, Satellite	Fury I, II, III
Air conditioning indicator	1893	FL
Auto pilot	—	1445 & 1892
Brake system warning light	257	57
Clock	57	—
Dome and/or "C" pillar light	1004	1004
Door, pocket panel and/or reading light	90	90
Fender mounted turn signal indicator	330	330
Gear selector indicator	1445	FL
Gear selector with console	57	57
Glove compartment	1891	1891
Handbrake indicator	57	57
High beam indicator	158	57
Instrument cluster illumination	158	1893
Ignition switch	—	1445
License light	67	67
Map light	90	90
Oil pressure indicator	158	57
Park and turn signal	1034A	1034
Portable reading light	—	90
Radio	1893	FL
Sealed beam—hi-beam (No. 1)	4001	4001
Sealed beam—hi-lo beam (No. 2)	4002	4002
Tail, stop and turn signal	1034	1034
Trunk and/or under hood light	1004	1004
Turn signal indicator (panel)	158	57

FL—Floodlighted

1968

	Belvedere, Satellite	Fury I, II, III
Air conditioning indicator	1892*	FL
Ash receiver	1445*	FL
Back-up lights	1073	1073
Brake system warning light	158	57
Clock	57	—
Courtesy lamp	89	—
Dome and/or "C" pillar light	1004	1004
Door, pocket panel and/or reading light	90	90
Fender mounted turn signal indicator	330	330M
Gear selector indicator	1445	FL
Gear selector with console	57	57

	Belvedere, Satellite	Fury, V.I.P.
Glove compartment	1891	1891
High beam indicator	158	57
Instrument cluster illumination	158	1893
Ignition switch	1445	1445
License light	67	67
Map light	90	1445
Oil pressure indicator	158	57
Park and turn signal	1034	1034NA
Radio	1816	FL
Sealed beam—hi-beam (No. 1)	4001	4001
Sealed beam—hi-lo beam (No. 2)	4002	4002
Side Marker	1895	1895
Tachometer	57	FL
Tachometer with console	—	1816
Tail, stop and turn signal	1034	1034
Trunk and/or under hood light	1004	1004
Turn signal indicator (panel)	158	57

FL—Floodlighted

*Included in instrument cluster.

1969

	Belvedere, Satellite	Fury, V.I.P.
Air conditioner control and auto-temp	**1892 (2)	**1893 (FL)
Ash receiver	**1892	**1445
Back-up lights	1156 (2)	1156 (2)
Brake system warning indicator	158	57
Clock	** 57	**1893 (FL)
Cornering lights	—	1293 (2)
Courtesy lamp	89	—
Dome lamp	1004	551
Pocket panel lamp	90	90
Fender mounted turn signal indicator	330 (2)	330 (2)
Gear selector indicator	**1445	**1893 (FL)
Gear selector with console	** 57	** 57
Glove compartment	1891	1891
High beam indicator	158	1892
Instrument cluster and speedometer illumination	** 158 (4)	**1893 (FL)
Ignition lamp	1445	1445
License light	67	704
Map and courtesy lamp	90	90
Oil pressure indicator	158	57
Park and turn signal	1157 (2)	1157 (2)
Radio	**1816	**1893 (FL)
Radio with tape	**1815	—
Sealed beam—hi-beam (No. 1)	4001	4001
Sealed beam—hi-lo beam (No. 2)	4002	4002
Stereo indicator	—	1445
Switch lighting	—	**1893 (FL)
Tachometer	** 57	**1893 (FL)
Tail, stop and turn signal	1157 (2)	1157 (2)
Trunk and/or under hood lamp	1004	1004
Turn signal indicator (panel)	158 (2)	57 (2)
Reverse 4-speed transmission indicator	53	53
Heat control	—	1893

FL—Floodlighted
NA—Not Available
*—Included in instrument cluster lighting
**—Headlamp rheostat dimming

1970

	Belvedere, Satellite	Fury, V.I.P.
Air conditioner control and auto-temp	1892	1893
Ash receiver	1445	1445
Back-up lights	1156	1156
Brake system warning indicator	158	57
Clock	57	1893

	Belvedere, Satellite	Fury
Cornering lights	—	1293
Courtesy lamp	89	—
Dome lamp	1004	550
Pocket panel lamp	90	90
Fender mounted turn signal indicator	330	330
Gear selector indicator	161	1893
Gear selector with console	57	57
Glove compartment	1891	1891
High beam indicator	158	1892
Instrument cluster and speedometer illumination	158	1893
Ignition lamp	1445	1445
License light	67	67
Map and courtesy lamp	90	90
Oil pressure indicator	158	57
Park and turn signal	1157	1157
Radio	1816	1893
Radio with tape	1815	—
Sealed beam—hi-beam (No. 1)	4001	4001
Sealed beam—hi-lo beam (No. 2)	4002	4002
Switch lighting	—	1893
Tachometer	57	1893
Tail, stop and turn signal	1157	1157
Trunk and/or under hood lamp	1004	1004
Turn signal indicator (panel)	158	57
Reverse 4-speed transmission indicator	53	53
Heat control	—	1893

1971-72

	Belvedere, Satellite	Fury
Air conditioner control and auto-temp	53	*
Ash tray	1445	1445
Back-up	1156	1156
Brake system warning	158	57
Clock	*	*
Cornering	—	1293
Courtesy	—	90
Dome	1004	211-2
Door	—	90
Door ajar	1892	1892
Fender turn-signal	330-2	330-2
Front park and turn-signal	1157	1157
Gear selector (column)	161	*
Gear selector (console)	57	*
Glove compartment	1891	1891
High beam	158	1891
Instrument cluster	158**	1893
Ignition	1445	1445
License	67	1445
Low fuel	1892	—
Map	562	—
Oil pressure	158	57
Pocket panel	90	90
Radio	1816	*
Reverse 4-speed transmission indicator	53	53
Sealed beam (No. 1)	4001	4001
Sealed beam (No. 2)	4002	4002
Side marker	194	1895
Stereo indicator	1445	1445
Switches	1892	1892
Tail, stop, and turn-signal	1157	1157
Turn-signal indicator	158	57

*—Included in instrument cluster lighting.
**—57 with Rallye instrument cluster.

FUSES AND CIRCUIT BREAKERS
DODGE

1965

FUSES

Radio	3 AG/AGC; 5 AMP
Heater or air cond.	3 AG/AGC; 20 AMP
Accessories	3 AG/AGC; 20 AMP
Cigar lighter	3 AG/AGC; 20 AMP
Tail, stop, dome	3 AG/AGC; 20 AMP
Instrument lights	3 AG/AGC; 2 AMP—Dart
	3 AMP—Coronet
	4 AMP—Polara, Monaco, 880
Rear Air conditioning (Polara, Monaco, 880 only)	3 AG/AGC; 20 AMP

CIRCUIT BREAKERS

Winshield wiper—variable speed (integral with wiper switch)	7½ AMP
	(6—Coronet)
Windshield wiper—single speed (integral with wiper switch)	5 AMP
Lighting system (integral with headlight)	15 AMP
	(20—Coronet)
Power windows, power seats, top lift (behind left front kick panel)	30 AMP
Door locks (Polara, Monaco, 880 only) (behind left front kick panel)	15 AMP

1966

FUSES

Accessories	3 AG/AGC; 20 AMP
Cigar lighter	3 AG/AGC; 20 AMP
Heater or air cond.	3 AG/AGC; 20 AMP
Instrument lights	3 AG/AGC; 4 AMP—Polara, Monaco
	3 AMP—Coronet
Radio	3 AG/AGC; 5 AMP
Tail, stop, dome	3 AG/AGC; 20 AMP
Rear air cond. (Monaco, Polara only)	3 AG/AGC; 20 AMP

CIRCUIT BREAKERS

Door locks (behind left front kick panel)	15 AMP
Lighting system (integral with headlight)	20 AMP
Power windows, power seats, top lift and tail gate (behind left front kick panel)	30 AMP
Windshield wiper—single speed (integral with wiper switch)	5 AMP
Variable speed (integral with wiper switch)	7½ AMP
	(6 Coronet)

1967

FUSES

Accessories	20 AMP
Cigar lighter (front)	20 AMP
Console*	20 AMP
Emergency flasher**	20 AMP
Heater or air conditioning	20 AMP
Instruments	4 AMP
Radio	5 AMP
Tail, stop, dome**	20 AMP

*Inline fuse.

**Emergency flasher and stoplight use same inline fuse.

***Dome light and front cigar lighther on same fuse.

CIRCUIT BREAKERS

Cigar lighter—rear (behind left front cowl trim panel)	15 AMP
Convertible top (behind left front cowl trim panel)	30 AMP
Door locks (behind left front cowl trim panel)	15 AMP
Headlights (integral with headlight swtich)	20 AMP
Power seats (behind left front cowl trim panel)	30 AMP
Power tailgate (behind left front cowl trim panel)	30 AMP
Power windows (behind left front cowl trim panel)	30 AMP
Windshield wiper (integral with wiper switch)	7.5 AMP

1968
FUSES

	Monaco, Polara	Coronet, Charger
Accessories	20 AMP	20 AMP
Cigar lighter (front) and dome lamp	20 AMP	20 AMP
Console (inline fuse; Monaco, Polara)	20 AMP	20 AMP
Emergency flasher	20 AMP	20 AMP
Heater or air conditioning	20 AMP	20 AMP
Instruments	4 AMP	3 AMP
Radio and back-up lamps	5 AMP	5 AMP
Tail and stop lamps	20 AMP	20 AMP

CIRCUIT BREAKERS

	Monaco	Polara
Cigar lighter—rear (behind left front cowl trim panel)	15 AMP	15 AMP
Convertible top (behind left front cowl trim panel)	30 AMP	30 AMP
Door locks (behind left front cowl trim panel)	15 AMP	15 AMP
Headlights (integral with headlight switch)	20 AMP	20 AMP
Power seats (behind left front cowl trim panel)	30 AMP	30 AMP
Power tailgate (behind left front cowl trim panel)	30 AMP	30 AMP
Power windows (behind left front cowl trim panel)	30 AMP	30 AMP
Windshield wiper (integral with wiper switch)	7.5 AMP	7.5 AMP

	Coronet	Charger
Convertible top (instrument panel cluster behind ammeter)	30 AMP	30 AMP
Headlights (integral with headlight switch)	20 AMP	15 AMP
Power tailgate (instrument panel cluster behind ammeter)	30 AMP	—
Power windows (instrument panel cluster behind ammeter)	30 AMP	30 AMP
Windshield wipers (integral with wiper switch)	6 AMP	6 AMP

1969–70
FUSES

Accessories	20 AMP
Console	20 AMP
Emergency flasher	20 AMP
Heater or air conditioning	20 AMP
Instrument lamps	3 AMP
Radio and back-up lamps	7.5 AMP
Stop and dome	20 AMP
Tail and cigar lighter	20 AMP

CIRCUIT BREAKERS

	Monaco	Polara
Cigar lighter—rear (on fuse block)	30 AMP	30 AMP
Convertible top (on fuse block)	30 AMP	30 AMP
Door locks (behind right front cowl trim panel)	15 AMP	15 AMP
Headlights (integral with headlight switch)	20 AMP	20 AMP
Power seats (on fuse block)	30 AMP	30 AMP
Power tailgate (on fuse block)	30 AMP	30 AMP
Power windows (on fuse block)	30 AMP	30 AMP
Windshield wiper (integral with wiper switch)	7.5 AMP	7.5 AMP

	Coronet	Charger
Convertible top (instrument panel cluster behind ammeter)	30 AMP	30 AMP
Headlights (integral with headlight switch)	20 AMP	20 AMP
Power tail gate (instrument panel cluster behind ammeter)	30 AMP	—
Power windows (instrument panel cluster behind ammeter)	30 AMP	30 AMP
Windshield wipers (integral with wiper switch (3-speed)	7.5 AMP	7.5 AMP
(2-speed)	6.0 AMP	6.0 AMP

1971–72
FUSES

Accessories	20 AMP
Console	20 AMP
Stop lights/dome lights	20 AMP
Emergency flasher	20 AMP
Heater/air conditioner	20 AMP
Instrument lights	5 AMP
Miscellaneous	20 AMP
Radio/back-up lights	20 AMP

CIRCUIT BREAKERS

	Coronet/ Charger	Polara/ Monaco
Concealed headlamps (integral with relay, left end of instrument panel)	5 AMP	—
Door locks (on fuse block)	—	15 AMP
Front seat back latch (on fuse block)	—	15 AMP
Headlights (integral with h/l switch)	20 AMP	20 AMP
Power seats (on fuse block)	—	30 AMP
Power tailgate (on fuse block)	30 AMP	30 AMP
Power windows (on fuse block)	30 AMP	30 AMP
Tailgate lock (on fuse block)	15 AMP	—
Windshield wiper (integral w/wiper switch) 2-speed	6 AMP	6 AMP
3-speed	7½ AMp	7½ AMP

FUSES AND CIRCUIT BREAKERS
PLYMOUTH

1965–66
FUSES

Radio	5 AMP
Heater or air conditioning	20 AMP
Accessories	20 AMP
Cigar lighter	20 AMP
Tail, stop, dome	20 AMP
Instrument lamps	*

*AV-1 and AV-2—2 ampere; AR-1 and AR-2—3 ampere; AP-1 and AP-2—4 ampere.

CIRCUIT BREAKERS

Winshield wiper—variable speed (integral with wiper switch)	*
Windshield wiper—single speed (integral with wiper switch)	5 AMP
Lighting system (integral with headlamp switch)	15 AMP
Power windows, power seats, top lift (behind left front kick panel)	30 AMP
Electric door locks (behind left front kick panel)	15 AMP

*AR-1 and AR-2—6 ampere; AP-1 and AP-2—7½ ampere.

1967
FUSES

Accessories	20 AMP
Cigar lighter (front)	20 AMP
Console*	20—All
Emergency flasher**	20 AMP
Heater or air conditioner	20 AMP
Instrument lights	3—Belvedere and Satellite
	4—Fury and V.I.P.
Radio	5 AMP
Tail, stop, dome	20 AMP

*Inline fuse.

**Stop light and emergency flasher use same inline fuse on Fury and V.I.P. models only.

CIRCUIT BREAKERS

	Belvedere Satellite	Fury V.I.P.
Cigar lighter—rear (behind left front cowl trim panel)	—	15 AMP
Convertible top (*integral with top lift switch)	30 AMP	30 AMP
Door locks (behind left front cowl trim panel)	—	15 AMP
Headlights (integral with headlight switch)	20 AMP	20 AMP
Power seats (behind left front cowl trim panel)	—	30 AMP
Power tailgate (*integral with tailgate switch)	30 AMP	30 AMP

Power windows (**behind left front cowl trim panel)	30 AMP	30 AMP
Windshield wipers (integral with wiper switch)	6 AMP	7.5 AMP

*Behind left front cowl trim panel in Fury and V.I.P. models.

**Integral with top lift switch on Belvedere or Satellite convertible models.

1968
FUSES

	Belvedere Satellite	Fury V.I.P.
Accessories	20 AMP	20 AMP
Cigar lighter (front) and dome light	20 AMP	20 AMP
Console (inline fuse)	—	20 AMP
Emergency flasher	—	20 AMP
Heater or air conditioner	20 AMP	20 AMP
Instrument lights	3 AMP	4 AMP
Radio and back-up lamps	5 AMP	5 AMP
Tail stop (and emergency flasher—except Fury and VIP)	20 AMP	20 AMP

CIRCUIT BREAKERS

	Belvedere Satellite	Fury V.I.P.
Cigar lighter—rear (behind left front cowl trim panel)	—	15 AMP
Convertible top (integral with top lift switch, behind left front cowl trim panel in Fury and V.I.P. models.)	—	30 AMP
Convertible top (instrument panel cluster behind ammeter)	30 AMP	—
Door locks (behind left front cowl trim panel)	—	15 AMP
Headlights (integral with headlight switch)	20 AMP	20 AMP
Power seats (behind left front cowl trim panel)	—	30 AMP
Power tailgate (instrument panel cluster behind ammeter)	30 AMP	30 AMP
Power windows (instrument panel cluster behind ammeter)	30 AMP	30 AMP
Windshield wipers (integral with wiper switch)	6 AMP	7.5 AMP

1969–70
FUSES

	Belvedere Satellite	Fury VIP
Accessory	20 AMP	20 AMP
Console	—	20 AMP
Emergency flasher	20 AMP	20 AMP

	Belvedere Satellite	Fury VIP
Heater and air conditioner	20 AMP	20 AMP
Instrument lamps	3 AMP	3 AMP
Radio and back-up lamps	7.5 AMP*	7.5 AMP*
Stop and dome lamps	20 AMP	20 AMP
Tail lamps and cigar lighter	20 AMP	20 AMP

*—1970—20

CIRCUIT BREAKERS

	Belvedere Satellite	Fury VIP
Convertible (on fuse block integral with switch)	30 AMP	30 AMP
Door locks (behind right front cowl trim panel)	15 AMP	15 AMP
Headlights (integral with headlamp switch)	20 AMP	20 AMP
Power seats (on fuse block)	—	30 AMP
Power tail gate (on fuse block)	30 AMP	30 AMP
Power windows (on fuse block)	30 AMP	30 AMP
Windshield wipers (integral with wiper switch)	7.5 AMP	7.5 AMP

1971–72
FUSES

Accessories	20 AMP
Console	20 AMP
Stop lights/dome light	20 AMP
Emergency flasher	20 AMP
Heater/air conditioner	20 AMP
Instrument lights	5 AMP
Miscellaneous	20 AMP
Radio/back-up lights	20 AMP
Tail lamps	20 AMP

CIRCUIT BREAKERS

	Belvedere/ Satellite	Fury
Concealed headlamps (integral with relay, left end of instrument panel)	—	5 AMP
Door locks (on fuse block)	—	15 AMP
Front seat back latch (on fuse block)	—	15 AMP
Headlights (integral with h/l switch)	20 AMP	20 AMP
Power seats (on fuse block)	—	30 AMP
Power tailgate (on fuse block)	30 AMP	30 AMP
Tailgate lock (on fuse block)	15 AMP	—
Windshield wiper (integral w/wiper switch)		
2-speed	6 AMP	6 AMP
3-speed	7½ AMP	7½ AMP

Distributor

Detailed information on distributor drive, direction of distributor rotation, cylinder numbering, firing order, point gap, point dwell, timing mark location, spark plugs, and spark advance will be found in the Specification Tables.

Distributor Assembly Removal

1. Take off the cap and wire assembly.
2. Disconnect the primary coil wire and vacuum control tube.
3. Mark the distributor and rotor relative positions.
4. Loosen the distributor mounting and lift out the distributor.

NOTE: to simplify reinstallation, do not disturb the engine while the distributor is out.

5. Reinstall by reversing the above procedure.

Distributor Replacement (When Engine has been Disturbed)

Slant 6 Engine

1. Remove No. 1 spark plug and, with the thumb closing the hole, rotate the engine until No. 1 piston is up on compression at top dead center. This is determined by the pressure on the thumb and the DC mark on the crankshaft pulley hub.
2. Rotate the rotor to a position just ahead of the No. 1 distributor cap terminal.

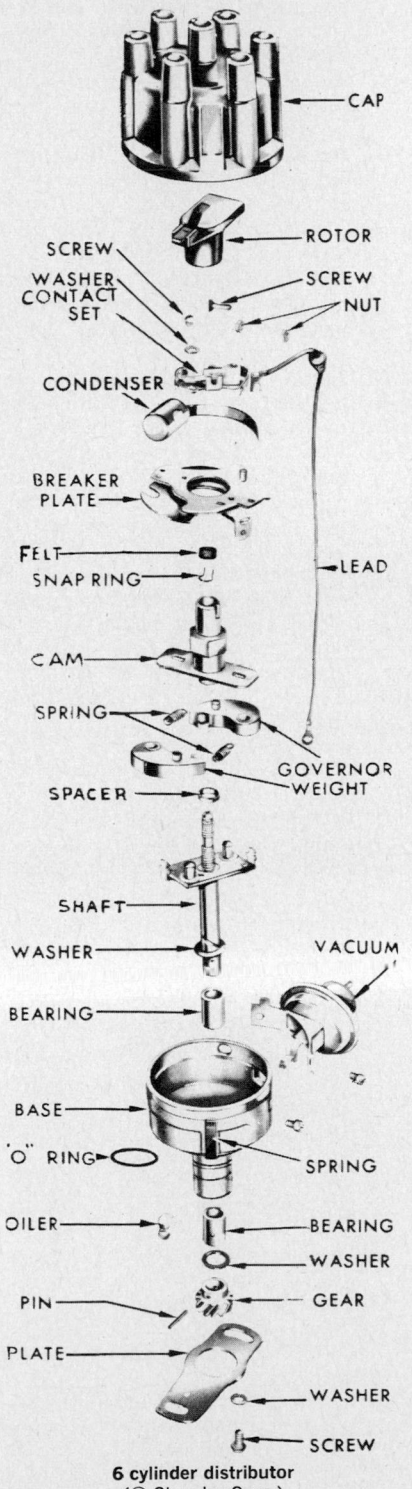

6 cylinder distributor
(© Chrysler Corp.)

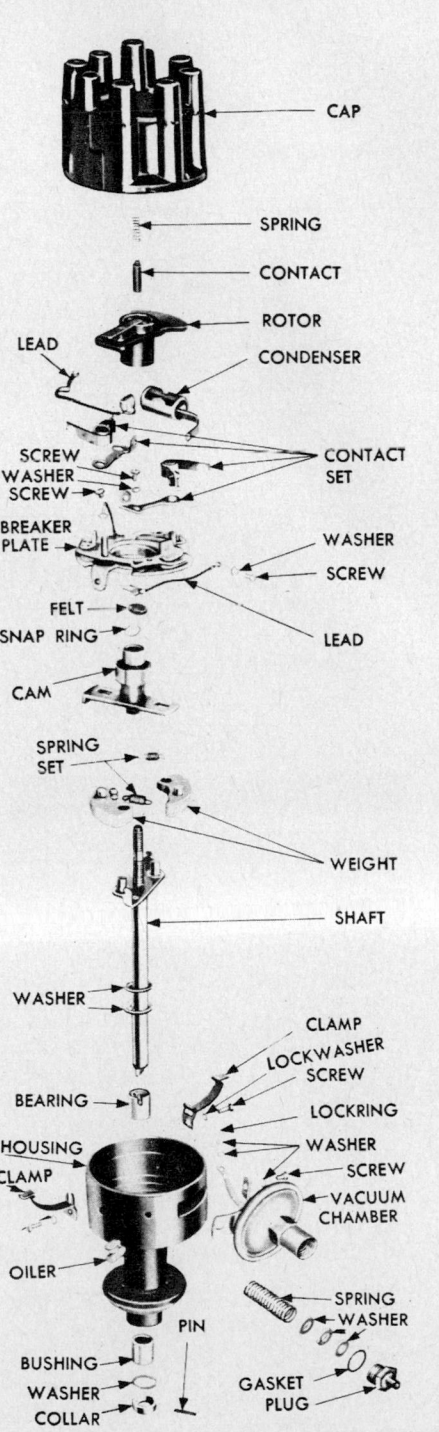

V8 distributor (Autolite-Prestolite)

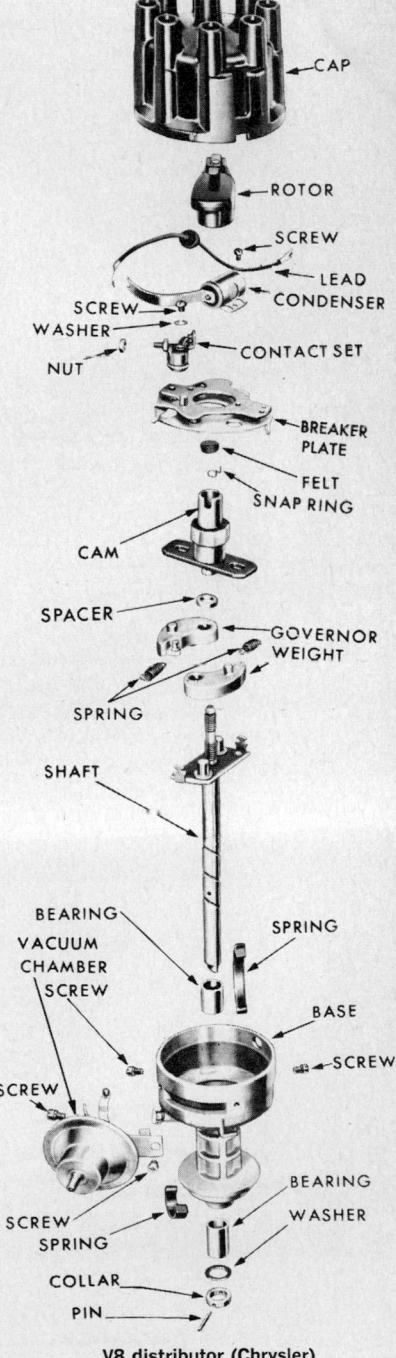

V8 distributor (Chrysler)

3. Lower the distributor into the opening, engaging distributor gear with drive gear on camshaft. With distributor fully seated on engine, rotor should be under the cap No. 1 tower with distributor contacts just opening.

4. Install cap, tighten hold-down arm screw and check timing with a timing light.

V8 Engine

Rotate the crankshaft until No. 1 cylinder is at top dead center. The pointer on the chain case cover should be over the DC mark on the crankshaft pulley. The slot in the intermediate shaft which carries the gear that drives the oil pump and the distributor, should be parallel with the crankshaft.

Hold the distributor over the mounting pad on the cylinder block so that the distributor body flange coincides with the mounting pad and the rotor points to the No. 1 cylinder firing position.

Install the distributor while holding the rotor in position, allowing it to move only enough to engage the slot in the drive gear.

Spark Plug Wires

The spark plug wires have a non-metallic, spring-type conductor for improved radio noise suppression. Care should be taken not to jerk the cables off the spark plugs or out of the distributor cap towers (especially if the engine is hot) for the cable may pull out of its terminal.

Check cables for excessive resistance or open circuit. Replace if over 30,000 ohm resistance.

Resistor-type spark plugs are not to be used with resistor-type cables—poor engine performance will result.

If radio develops excessive noise or if there is a pronounced engine miss, check for defective (broken) cables.

Alternator

Removal

To remove alternator:
1. Disconnect battery.
2. Disconnect Bat. and Fld. leads from alternator.
3. Remove alternator by removing two mounting bolts and belt tensioner bracket bolt.
4. To reinstall: reverse the above.
Never attempt to polarize an alternator, and never short the regulator.

Starter

Starter R & R

Disconnect battery and starter wires. Remove attaching bolts and lift out starter.

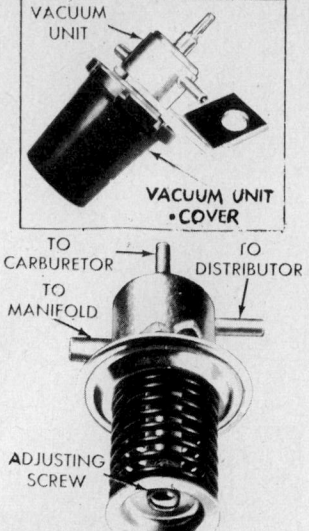

Distributor vacuum unit
(© Chrysler Corp.)

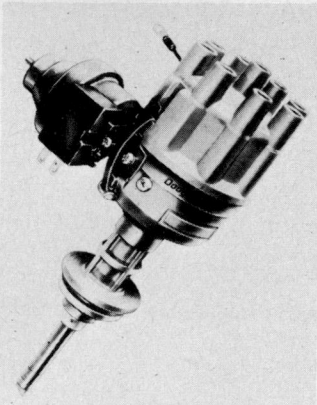

High performance distributor with solenoid retard
(© Chrysler Corp.)

Instruments

Removal

1965 Models Except Dodge 880
1. Disconnect battery.
2. From below dash remove retaining nuts and washers holding cluster to panel.
3. Disconnect wires and connectors.
4. Protect steering column with cloth to prevent scratching.
5. Carefully pull cluster from front of panel.
NOTE: an ammeter is used in connection with models using alternators.
6. Reinstall: Reverse the above.

1966-67 Belvedere and Satellite
1. Disconnect battery.
2. Disconnect speedometer cable, remove steering column cover and steering column clamp.
3. Remove six screws in upper and lower face of cluster bezel. Pull cluster out far enough to remove multiple connectors from headlamp and wiper switches and printed circuit board. Remove ammeter gauge wires, heater switch wires and control cables.
4. Remove cluster. Reverse procedure to install.

1966-68 Fury and VIP
1. Disconnect battery.
2. Remove eight instrument cluster light panel retaining screws, remove panel and rest panel on top of trim pad. It is not necessary to disconnect wire.
3. Remove heater or air conditioning control knobs, and check reset knob.
4. Remove six bezel retaining screws and remove bezel.
5. Remove four screws from steering column cover and drop cover with vent controls attached.
6. In vehicles with automatic transmission and column shift, remove gear selector link nut, spring washer and bolt.
7. Remove four stereo speaker grille screws and place speaker on top of instrument panel.
8. Disconnect speedometer cable, and remove five cluster mounting screws. Raise cluster slightly, roll upper edge out and disconnect ammeter leads.
9. With cluster face down disconnect fuel and temperature gauge wires and high beam, oil pressure, and turn signal light sockets.
10. Remove cluster. Reverse procedure to install.

Polara, Custom 880, Monaco—1965-66
1. Disconnect battery.
2. Disconnect speedometer cable.
3. Remove cluster mounting screws and roll cluster out.
4. Disconnect printed circuit plug and remove cluster.
5. Reinstall in reverse of above.

1966 Coronet
1. Disconnect battery, and tape top of steering column for scratch protection.
2. If air-conditioned, remove left spot cooler, duct and hose, and the fuse block.
3. Disconnect speedometer cable at head.
4. Remove steering column support bracket, then lower column support plate at firewall.
5. Remove radio knobs, mounting nuts, ash tray housing and the lighter.
6. From under the dash, remove mounting nut next to the heater blower switch.
7. Remove headlight switch knob and bezel by depressing release

button on headlight switch and pulling out on headlight switch knob. Do not remove switch from the panel.

8. Loosen set screw in wiper switch knob and remove the switch bezel. Do not remove switch from panel.

9. Remove four instrument cluster retaining screws and pull cluster out far enough to disconnect printed circuit board and ignition switch multiple connectors. Disconnect the two ammeter wires and remove from car.

10. Install by reversing removal procedure.

NOTE: all instruments may be serviced after removing the four screws holding the cluster bezel to the cluster housing and the ignition switch. Remove the temperature or fuel gauge terminal nuts from the printed circuit board. The alternator gauge is serviced in the same way from the cluster housing. The printed circuit board is serviced after the instruments, voltage limiter, light bulbs and four retaining screws are removed.

1966-67 Charger and 1967 Coronet

1. Disconnect battery.
2. Tape steering column to protect paint.
3. Remove heater control knobs and radio knobs and mounting nuts.
4. Open glove box door.
5. Disconnect speedometer cable.
6. Remove wiring harness from clips at steering column bracket.
7. Remove eight Phillips head screws from upper and lower lips of cluster bezel on Coronets or seven Phillips head screws on Chargers.
8. Carefully pull cluster out and to the right far enough to reach around left end of cluster and disconnect printed circuit multiple connector.
9. Remove ammeter wires and clock light on Coronets. On Chargers, remove wires from each gauge including tachometer. Disconnect panel lighting (white wire).
10. Roll top of cluster down while working to right over open glove box door. Remove Cluster. Reverse procedure to install.

1967-68 Polara and Monaco, 1968-70 Coronet, Belvedere, and Satellite

1. Disconnect battery.
2. Remove steering column trim cover by removing four screws.
3. Roll carpet back and remove lower mounting plate.
4. Remove steering column clamp.
5. Remove upper trim moulding, if so equipped, and left side trim moulding and left side trim plate, if so equipped.

6. Remove radio trim plate, and four switch bezel mounting screws, and switch bezel.
7. Remove ignition switch.
8. Remove center air conditioning register cover, if so equipped.
9. Remove lower trim pad by removing six screws from under panel and four screws from front panel.
10. Disconnect speedometer cable.
11. Remove six cluster mounting screws, and rock cluster out.
12. Disconnect wiring and remove cluster. Reverse procedure to install.

1968-70 Charger

1. Disconnect battery.
2. Remove steering column opening cover, steering column lower support plate, and steering column upper clamp.
3. Disconnect speedometer cable.
4. Remove five screws mounting cluster to panel.
5. Release wire harness from three retaining clips, and rock cluster out of panel far enough to disconnect wiring at ammeter, switches, tachometer or clock, light bulbs, and printed circuit. Roll out instrument panel. Reverse procedure to install.

1969-70 Polara and Monaco

1. Disconnect battery.
2. Remove steering column cover.
3. Remove gear shift indicator from column.
4. Remove lower column floor plate by removing three bolts.
5. Remove three upper column mounting nuts.
6. Lower steering and let wheel rest on seat.
7. Remove switch bezel, radio bezel.
8. Remove cluster trim pad and trim pad.
9. Disconnect clock reset cable at instrument panel lower reinforcement.
10. Disconnect clock electrical lead.
11. Remove five cluster assembly mounting screws.
12. Roll cluster out slightly and disconnect speedometer cable.
13. Disconnect gear shift indicator lamp.
14. Disconnect main harness from cluster.
15. Disconnect alternator gauge electrical leads and remove cluster. Reverse procedure to install.

1969-70 Fury and VIP

1. Disconnect battery.
2. Remove nine panel screws, and disconnect and remove light panel.
3. Remove steering column cover.
4. Remove radio trim bezel.
5. Remove left trim bezel and/or spot cooler.

6. Remove left and center air conditioner ducts, if so equipped.
7. From under panel disconnect leads to switches and clock, lamp assemblies, and speedometer cable.
8. Remove gear shift indicator pointer from column.
9. Tape column to protect paint.
10. Remove column upper clamp and lower support.
11. Lower column and rest on seat cushion.
12. Remove eight screws mounting cluster to instrument panel. Roll cluster out. Disconnect electrical connections to high beam indicator, fuel gauge, ammeter, and temperature gauge. Remove cluster. Reverse procedure to install.

1971-72 Coronet, Charger and Satellite

1. Disconnect the negative battery cable.
2. Remove the ash tray.
3. Remove the radio control knobs and mounting nuts.
4. Remove the radio.
5. Remove the heater control panel.
6. Remove the upper steering column mounting clamp and lower the steering column.
7. Remove the instrument cluster attaching screws.
8. Disconnect the speedometer cable from the speedometer head.
9. Pull the instrument cluster forward and disconnect the wiring as the connections become accessible.
10. Reverse above procedure to install.

1971-72 Polara, Monaco and Fury

1. Disconnect the negative battery cable.
2. Remove the lamp panel.
3. Remove the steering column cover.
4. Remove the radio cover bezel.
5. Remove the instrument panel left trim bezel and spot cooler (if so equipped).
6. If equipped with air conditioning, remove the left-side duct and center air conditioning connector.
7. Working under the dash, disconnect all electrical leads from the cluster and disconnect the speedometer cable from the speedometer head.
8. Remove the gear shift indicator pointer from the steering column.
9. Tape steering column to protect the paint finish.
10. Remove the three steering column upper clamp nuts and the three bolts from the steering column lower support at the floor.

11. Lower the steering column and allow it to rest on the front seat cushion.
12. Remove the eight screws that attach the instrument cluster to the instrument panel. Roll the cluster forward and disconnect any electrical connections still attached to the cluster as they become accessible.
13. Remove the cluster from the vehicle.
14. Reverse above procedure to install.

Speedometer Removal

1965 Plymouth, 1965-66 Coronet, and 1969-70 Belvedere and Satellite

After removing instrument cluster, remove speedometer by taking out two mounting screws.

1966-68 Plymouth, 1966-72 Charger, 1967-72 Coronet, and 1967-68 Monaco and Polara

1. Remove instrument cluster.
2. With cluster face down remove cluster bezel to cluster housing screws and separate the two.
3. On some models remove temperature, fuel and ammeter gauges to gain clearance.
4. Remove two screws and rubber washers, and withdraw speedometer. Reverse procedure to install.

1969-70 Fury and VIP

1. Remove instrument cluster.
2. Remove gearshift indicator housing from cluster by removing two screws.
3. Remove cluster assembly from bezel assembly by removing four screws.
4. Remove cluster lens from cluster housing by turning up two upper cluster mounting pads.
5. Remove two mounting screws and remove speedometer. Reverse procedure to install.

1965-66 Dodge 880, Monaco, and Polara

1. Disconnect battery.
2. Disconnect speedometer cable.
3. Remove three screws that attach speedometer cluster to housing.
4. Roll cluster out and disconnect printed circuit plug.
5. Remove cluster.

1969-70 Monaco and Polara

1. Remove the instrument cluster.
2. Remove the gear selector indicator housing from the instrument cluster.
3. Remove the instrument cluster bezel from the cluster.

4. Remove the lens from the cluster housing.
5. Remove the screws that attach the speedometer head to the instrument cluster and remove the speedometer from the cluster.
6. Reverse above procedure to install.

Tachometer—Charger

The tachometer is removed from the instrument cluster housing after bezel and housing are separated. The electroluminescent light wire is disconnected from the tachometer dial and the four mounting screws are removed from the back of the housing.

Headlight Switch R & R

1965-66 Belvedere, Satellite and Coronet

1. Working under the dash, disconnect the multiple connector from the rear of the headlight switch.
2. Press the release button on the body of the headlight switch and pull the control knob and shaft from the switch.
3. Remove the bezel nut that attaches the headlight switch to the dash and remove the switch.
4. Reverse above procedure to install.

1965-66 Fury, Polara and Monaco

1. Remove the instrument cluster.
2. Disconnect the multiple connector from the rear of the headlight switch.
3. Press the release knob on the body of the headlight switch and pull the control knob and shaft from the switch.
4. Remove the bezel nut that attaches the headlight switch to the dash and remove the switch.
5. Reverse above procedure to install.

1967-68 Belvedere, Satellite, Coronet and 1967 Charger

1. Remove the screw that attaches the fuse box to the dash and position the fuse box out of the way.
2. Disconnect the multiple connector from the rear of the headlight switch.
3. Press the release button on the body of the headlight switch and pull the control knob and shaft from the switch.
4. Remove the bezel nut that attaches the headlight switch to the dash and remove the switch.

1968 Charger

1. Remove the instrument cluster.
2. Disconnect the multiple connector from the rear of the switch.
3. Disconnect the vacuum hose from the heater.

4. Remove the two screws that attach the headlight switch to the dash and remove the switch.
5. Reverse above procedure to install.

1967-68 Fury, VIP, Polara and Monaco

1. Remove the screw that attaches the fuse box to the dash and position the fuse box out of the way.
2. Remove the two screws that attach the headlight switch to the rear of the dash.
3. Disconnect the multiple connector from the rear of the headlight switch and remove the switch.

1969-72 All Models

1. Disconnect the multiple connector from the rear of the headlight switch. On models with air conditioning, it may be necessary to disconnect the ducts to gain access to the wiring.
2. Remove the two screws that attach the headlight switch to the dash and remove the headlight switch from the vehicle.
3. Reverse above procedure to install.

Ignition Switch R & R

1965-69 All Models

1. Disconnect the multiple connector from the rear of the switch.
2. Remove the bezel nut that attaches the ignition switch to the dash and remove the switch.

1970-72 All Models
See Chrysler section.

Brakes

Brake Information

Specific information on brake cylinder sizes can be found in the General Chassis and Brake Specifications table.

Information on brake adjustments, lining replacement, disc brakes, bleeding procedure, master and wheel cylinder overhaul can be found in the Unit Repair Section.

Information on troubleshooting and overhauling power brakes can be found in the Unit Repair Section.

Information on the grease seals which may need replacement can be found in the Unit Repair Section.

Beginning 1967

Since 1967, a tandem-type master cylinder has been used on all models. This design divides the brake hydraulic system into two independent and hydraulically separated halves.

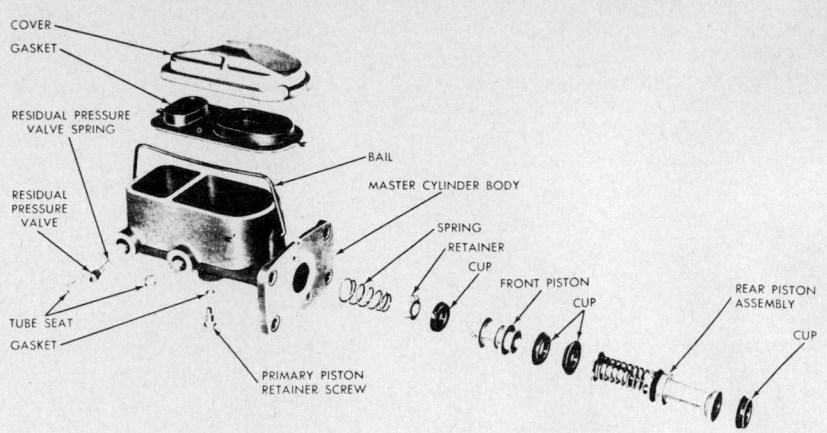

Dual type master cylinder used with disc brakes (© Chrysler Corp.)

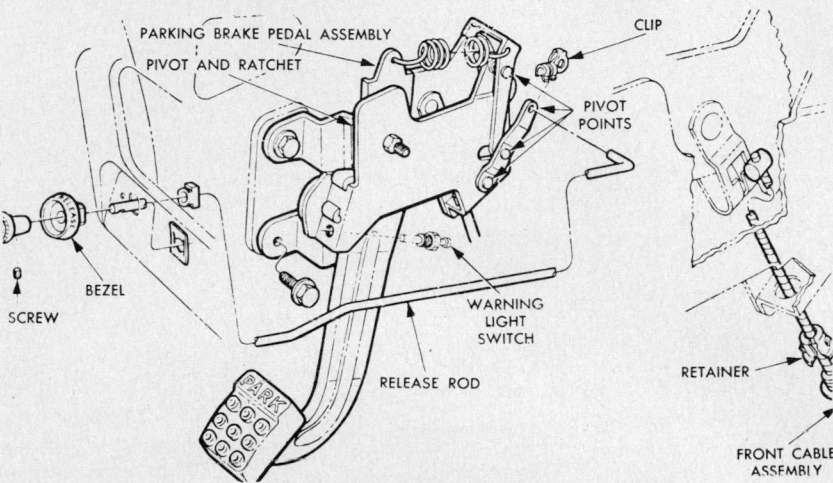

Parking brake control (© Chrysler Corp.)

Details and repair procedures on this tandem system may be found in the Unit Repair Section.

Master Cylinder Removal

1965-66

The master cylinder is mounted on the front side of the firewall under the hood.

1. Disconnect the brake pushrod and stop light wires from under the dash, remove the brake line, unbolt the master cylinder from the dash panel.

1967-72

1. Disconnect front and rear brake tubes from master cylinder.

NOTE: on drum brake master cylinders, residual pressure valves will keep cylinder from draining, but front brake outlet (rearmost) must be plugged on disc brake master cylinders.

2. Remove nuts that attach master cylinder to cowl panel or power brake unit.
3. On manual drum brakes, disconnect pedal pushrod from brake pedal.
4. Slide master cylinder straight out from cowl or power brake unit.

Disc Brakes

Since 1965, disc brakes have been available on front wheels of some models. Complete service procedures are covered in the Unit Repair Section.

Parking Brake Adjustment

1. Release parking brake lever and loosen cable adjusting nut to ensure cable is slack. Before loosening cable adjusting nut, clean threads with wire brush and lubricate.
2. Tighten cable adjusting nut until a slight drag is felt while rotating wheel. Loosen cable enough to allow both wheels to rotate freely. Back off cable adjusting nut two full turns.
3. Apply and release parking brake several times. Test to see that rear wheels rotate freely without grabbing.

Power Brake

1965-72

Various types of power brakes are used. One is the vacuum-type, using a master cylinder and pedal linkage of the reaction type. A vacuum cylinder is combined with a conventional master cylinder.

Another is a tandem-diaphragm-type, consisting of a self-contained vacuum hydraulic power unit.

The basic elements are vacuum power chamber with a front and rear shell, a center plate, front and rear diaphragm, pushrod and diaphragm return spring.

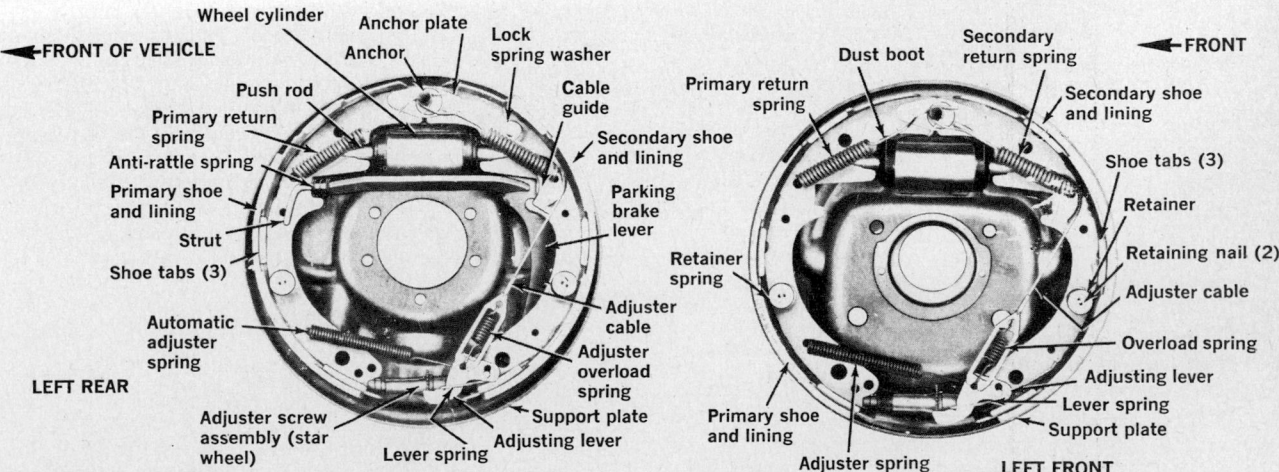

Drum brakes, showing major components (© Chrysler Corp.)

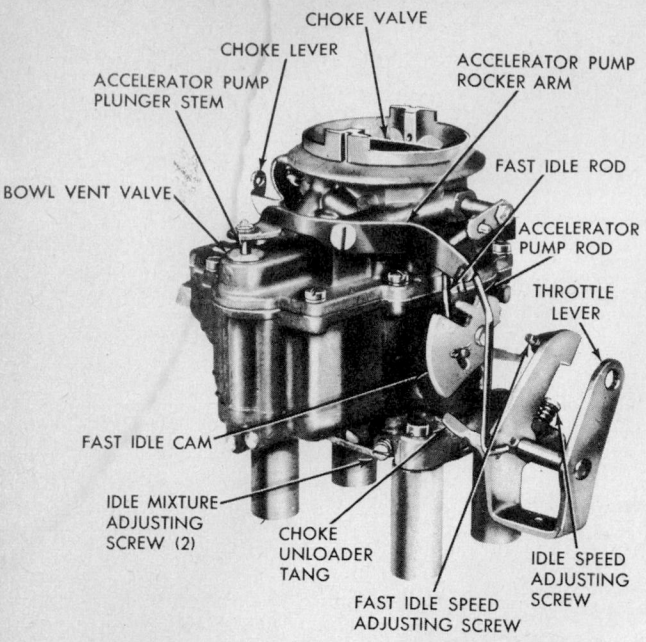

CHOKE VALVE
CHOKE LEVER
ACCELERATOR PUMP PLUNGER STEM
ACCELERATOR PUMP ROCKER ARM
FAST IDLE ROD
BOWL VENT VALVE
ACCELERATOR PUMP ROD
THROTTLE LEVER
FAST IDLE CAM
IDLE MIXTURE ADJUSTING SCREW (2)
CHOKE UNLOADER TANG
FAST IDLE SPEED ADJUSTING SCREW
IDLE SPEED ADJUSTING SCREW

Stromberg carburetor adjustments (© Chrysler Corporation)

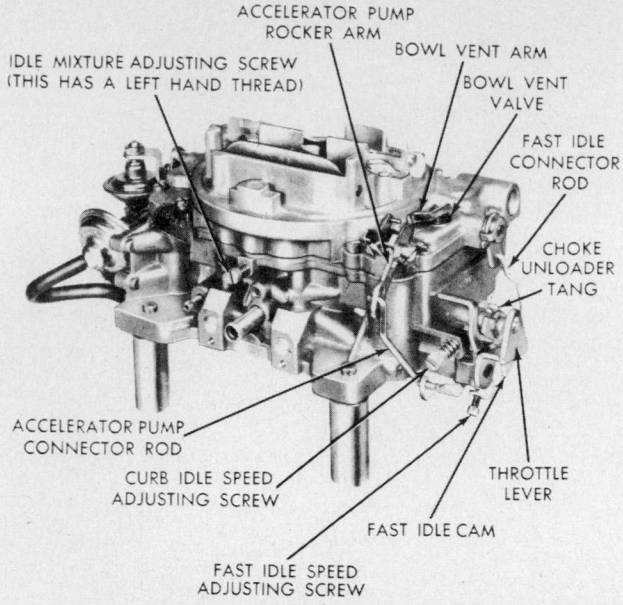

ACCELERATOR PUMP ROCKER ARM
BOWL VENT ARM
BOWL VENT VALVE
IDLE MIXTURE ADJUSTING SCREW (THIS HAS A LEFT HAND THREAD)
FAST IDLE CONNECTOR ROD
CHOKE UNLOADER TANG
ACCELERATOR PUMP CONNECTOR ROD
CURB IDLE SPEED ADJUSTING SCREW
THROTTLE LEVER
FAST IDLE CAM
FAST IDLE SPEED ADJUSTING SCREW

1968-69 Carter AVS carburetor adjustments (© Chrysler Corporation)

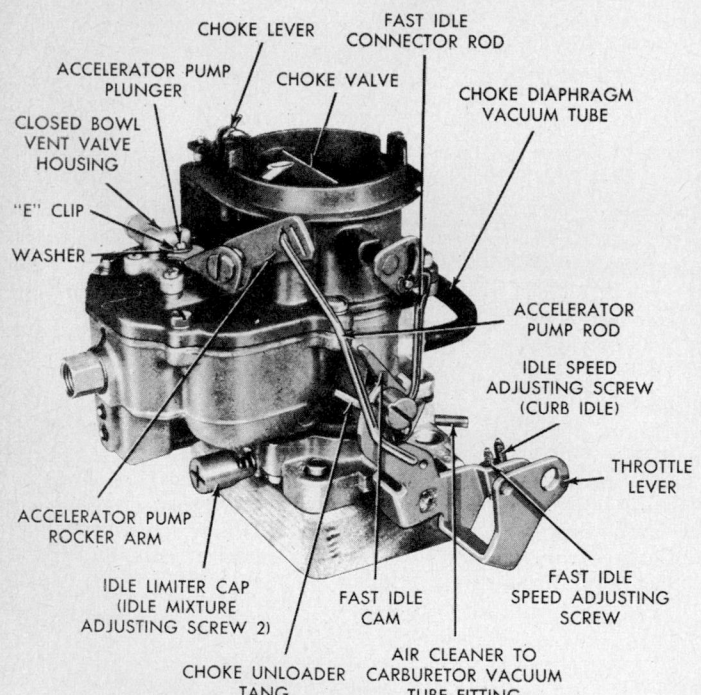

CHOKE LEVER
FAST IDLE CONNECTOR ROD
ACCELERATOR PUMP PLUNGER
CHOKE VALVE
CLOSED BOWL VENT VALVE HOUSING
CHOKE DIAPHRAGM VACUUM TUBE
"E" CLIP
WASHER
ACCELERATOR PUMP ROD
IDLE SPEED ADJUSTING SCREW (CURB IDLE)
THROTTLE LEVER
ACCELERATOR PUMP ROCKER ARM
IDLE LIMITER CAP (IDLE MIXTURE ADJUSTING SCREW 2)
FAST IDLE CAM
FAST IDLE SPEED ADJUSTING SCREW
CHOKE UNLOADER TANG
AIR CLEANER TO CARBURETOR VACUUM TUBE FITTING

Ball & Ball carburetor adjustments (© Chrysler Corporation)

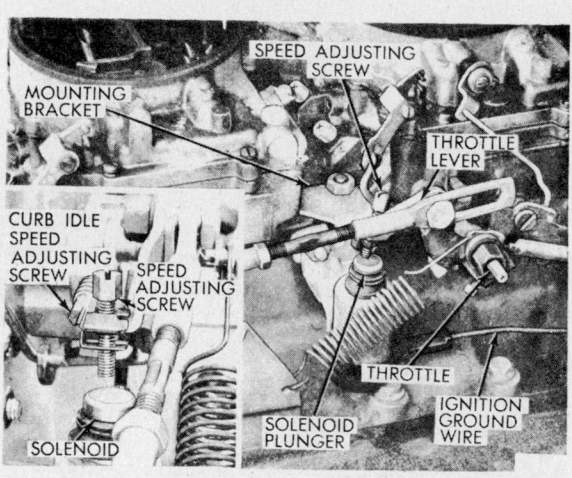

MOUNTING BRACKET
SPEED ADJUSTING SCREW
THROTTLE LEVER
CURB IDLE SPEED ADJUSTING SCREW
SPEED ADJUSTING SCREW
THROTTLE
SOLENOID
SOLENOID PLUNGER
IGNITION GROUND WIRE

Solenoid throttle positioner adjustment (© Chrysler Corporation)

A control valve integral with the diaphragms regulates the amount of application.

For information on reconditioning see Unit Repair Section.

Fuel System

Carburetors

Since 1965, Dodge and Plymouth models have used many different types of carburetors. However, the adjustment procedure for all these carburetors, with a few exceptions, is the same. Some 1966-67 and all 1968 and later carburetors incorporate modifications to reduce engine exhaust emissions. Carburetor modifications for 1966-69 are part of Chrysler's Cleaner Air Package, and 1970 and later models are part of the Cleaner Air System. The only carburetor changes used with the Cleaner Air Package are the installation of carburetor mixture limiter stops on the carburetor idle mixture adjustment screws, and leaner carburetor mixtures. With the Cleaner Air System, in addition to the above mentioned changes, faster acting chokes were added and, on some models, solenoid operated throttle stops and distributor retard mechanisms. The throttle stop raises the engine idle speed to reduce engine emissions, but de-energizes when the ignition is shut off to prevent the engine from dieseling. The distributor retard solenoid is activated when the idle speed adjustment screw returns to the curb idle position and contacts a sensor, mounted on the carburetor, which retards ignition timing while the engine is at idle. These carburetors also incorporate an internally mounted hot idle compensator which opens to induct additional air into the carburetor during low speed, high temperature operation.

Both the 426 Hemi and the 440 engines are available with multiple carburetor options. The 426 Hemi is

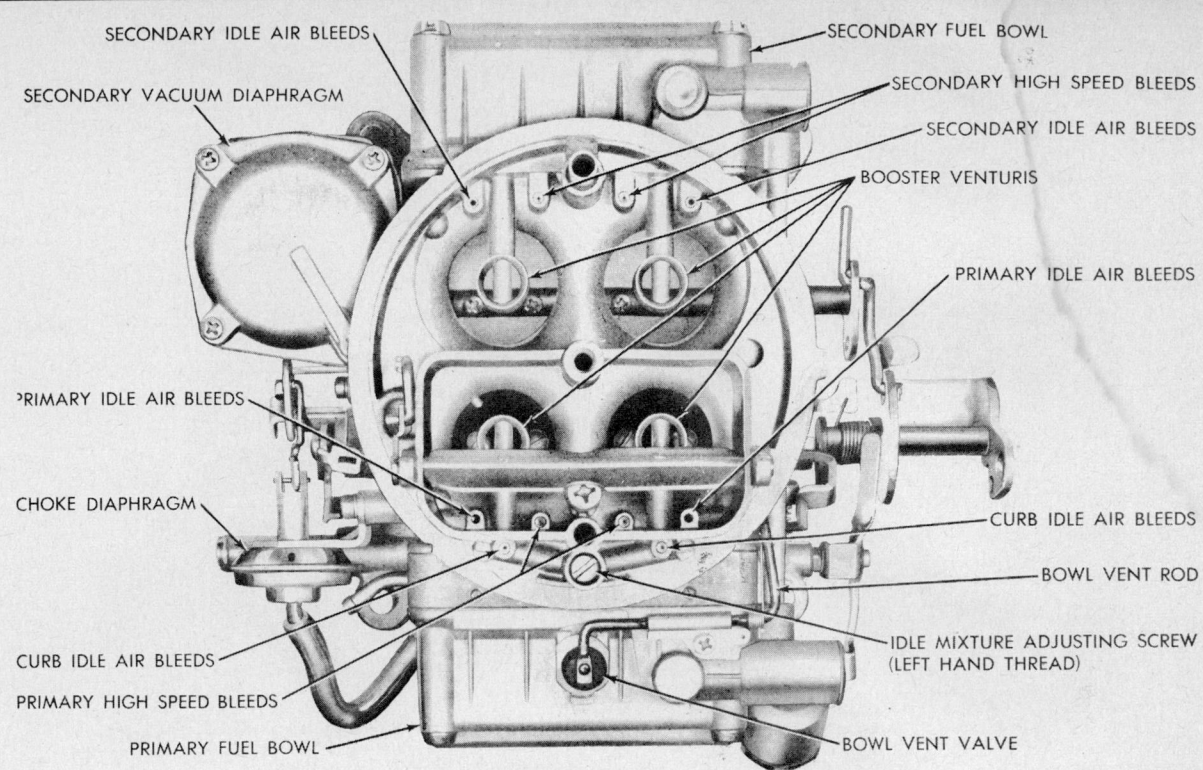

SECONDARY IDLE AIR BLEEDS

SECONDARY VACUUM DIAPHRAGM

SECONDARY FUEL BOWL

SECONDARY HIGH SPEED BLEEDS

SECONDARY IDLE AIR BLEEDS

BOOSTER VENTURIS

PRIMARY IDLE AIR BLEEDS

PRIMARY IDLE AIR BLEEDS

CHOKE DIAPHRAGM

CURB IDLE AIR BLEEDS

BOWL VENT ROD

IDLE MIXTURE ADJUSTING SCREW
(LEFT HAND THREAD)

CURB IDLE AIR BLEEDS

PRIMARY HIGH SPEED BLEEDS

PRIMARY FUEL BOWL

BOWL VENT VALVE

1968-69 Holley carburetor adjustments (© Chrysler Corporation)

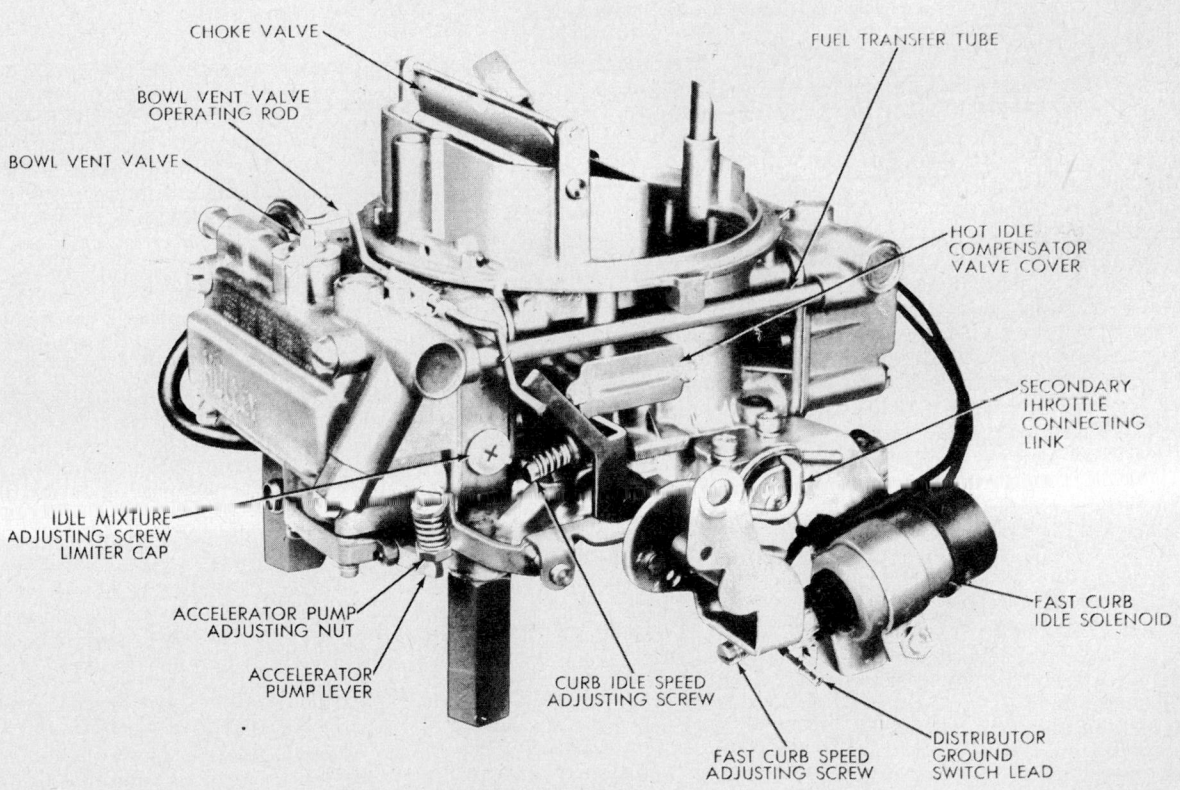

CHOKE VALVE

FUEL TRANSFER TUBE

BOWL VENT VALVE
OPERATING ROD

BOWL VENT VALVE

HOT IDLE
COMPENSATOR
VALVE COVER

SECONDARY
THROTTLE
CONNECTING
LINK

IDLE MIXTURE
ADJUSTING SCREW
LIMITER CAP

ACCELERATOR PUMP
ADJUSTING NUT

ACCELERATOR
PUMP LEVER

CURB IDLE SPEED
ADJUSTING SCREW

FAST CURB
IDLE SOLENOID

FAST CURB SPEED
ADJUSTING SCREW

DISTRIBUTOR
GROUND
SWITCH LEAD

1970-71 Holley carburetor adjustments (© Chrysler Corporation)

equipped with two Carter AFB carburetors. Both of these carburetors have complete idle systems which must be adjusted and synchronized to obtain a satisfactory engine idle. The 440 Six Pack engine is equipped with three Holley 2300 two-venturi carburetors. Only the center carburetor on this engine is equipped with an idle system and the inboard and outboard carburetors contain no idle adjustments.

Idle Speed and Mixture Adjustments

NOTE: 1966-67 CAP carburetors can be identified by a green tag attached to the air horn.

1965-67 Without CAP

Adjust with air cleaner removed.

1. Run engine at fast idle to stabilize engine temperature.
2. Make sure the choke plate is fully released.
3. Attach a tachometer of known accuracy to the engine.
4. If equipped with air condition-

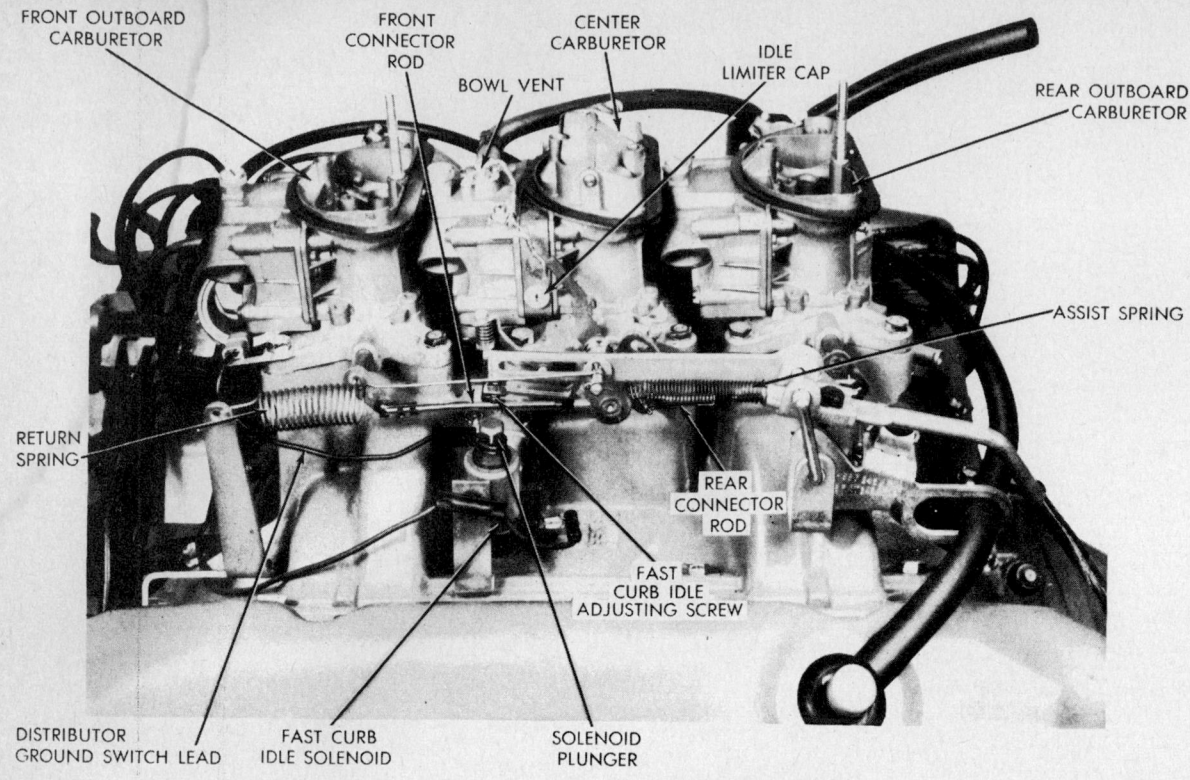

Holley Six Pack carburetor adjustments (© Chrysler Corporation)

ing, turn the air conditioner ON.
5. On models with six cylinder engine, turn the headlights on high beam.
6. Adjust the carburetor idle speed screw to obtain a curb idle speed of 500 rpm (550 if equipped with air conditioner).
7. Turn the idle mixture screws in or out to obtain the highest rpm possible. After obtaining the highest rpm, turn each idle mixture screw clockwise until the engine speed starts to drop, then turn the mixture screw counterclockwise just enough to regain the lost rpm.
8. If the mixture adjustment procedure has changed the curb idle speed, adjust the idle speed.

1966-72 with CAP or CAS Except 426 Hemi

Adjust with air cleaner installed.
NOTE: this is the basic carburetor adjustment procedure, any specific exceptions are listed below.
1. Run engine at fast idle to stabilize engine temperature.
2. Make sure choke plate is fully released.
3. Attach a tachometer of known accuracy to the engine.
4. Connect an exhaust analyzer to the engine and insert the probe as far into the tailpipe as possible. On vehicles with dual exhaust, insert the probe into the left tailpipe as this is the side without the heat riser valve.
5. Check ignition timing and ad-

just it as required to conform to specification.
6. If equipped with air conditioning, turn the air conditioner OFF.
7. Place the transmission in the Neutral position. Make sure the hot idle compensator valve is fully seated in the closed position.
8. Turn the engine idle speed adjustment screw in or out to adjust idle speed to specification. If equipped with an electric solenoid throttle positioner, turn the solenoid adjusting screw in or out to obtain specified rpm. Then, adjust the curb idle speed screw until it just touches the stop on the carburetor body. Now, back the curb idle speed adjusting screw out one full turn.
9. Turn each idle mixture adjustment screw 1/16 turn richer (counterclockwise). Wait 10 seconds and observe the reading on the exhaust gas analyzer. Continue this procedure until the meter indicates a definite increase in the richness of the mixture.

NOTE: this step is very important. A carburetor that is set too lean will cause the exhaust gas analyzer to give a false reading indicating a rich mixture. Because of this, the carburetor must first be known to have a rich mixture to verify the reading on the exhaust gas analyzer.

10. After verifying the reading obtained on the meter, adjust the mixture screws to get an air/fuel ratio of 14.2:1. Turn the mixture screws clockwise (leaner) to raise the meter reading or counterclockwise (richer) to lower the meter reading.

1968-69 383 and 440 V8

The carburetors used on these engines (Ball & Ball 2V, Carter 4V or Holley 4V) have lead or cup plugs installed over the idle mixture screws and an additional off idle mixture control screw added to the body of the carburetor. When adjusting the carburetor idle speed and mixture, use the off idle adjustment screw to alter the idle speed air/fuel mixture so it conforms to the 14.2:1 ratio specified. If unable to obtain an acceptable engine idle by adjusting this screw, refer to the procedure to correct rough idle and low speed surge.

Rough Idle and Low Speed Surge— All 1966-72 Except Hemi
Rough idle and low speed surge can be the result of improper balance of the idle mixture adjustment in the right and left carburetor bores. To correct this condition, perform the following operation.
1. On 1968-69 383 or 440 V8, remove the lead plugs from the two limiter screws in the base of the carburetor (Ball & Ball or Carter) or the cup plugs from the sides of the primary metering body (Holley). The best way

to remove the lead plugs is with a small drill and easy-out. Use a sharp punch to remove cup plugs from a Holley carburetor.

2. On all other models, remove the plastic limiter caps from the idle mixture adjustment screws.

3. Perform Steps 1-8 of the idle speed and mixture adjustment procedure.

4. On 1968-69 383 or 440 V8, turn the single off idle mixture adjustment screw counterclockwise (richer) until it is seated, then turn it clockwise (lean) ¾ turn. Do not disturb this adjustment during the remaner of this procedure.

5. Turn both idle mixture adjustment screws clockwise until they are lightly seated. On some models, the idle mixture screws have a prevailing torque feature which causes the screws to become more difficult to turn as they approach the seated position.

6. On Ball & Ball carburetors, turn both idle mixture screws 1½ turns counterclockwise. On Carter and Holley carburetors, turn both idle mixture screws 2-3 turns counterclockwise.

7. Start the engine and perform Steps 9-11 of the idle speed and mixture adjustment procedure.

NOTE: in order to obtain a smooth idle, it is important that both mixture adjustment screws are adjusted an equal number of turns from the fully seated position.

8. Install lead plugs, cup plugs, or plastic caps on the idle mixture screws.

426 Hemi

Because each carburetor is equipped with a complete idle system, accurate carburetor synchronization is very important. After adjusting the idle speed and mixture, it should be rechecked and rebalanced as required in the outside ambient temperature after a road test.

Adjust with air cleaner removed.

1. Run engine at fast idle to stabilize engine temperature.
2. Make sure the choke plate is fully released.
3. Attach a tachometer of known accuracy to the engine.
4. If equipped with a hot idle compensator valve, make sure it is fully seated in the closed position.
5. Place the transmission in the Neutral position.
6. Turn the idle speed adjustment screws in or out to adjust the engine idle speed to specification. If equipped with an electric solenoid throttle positioner, turn the solenoid adjusting screw in or out to obtain specified engine idle speed. Then, turn the curb

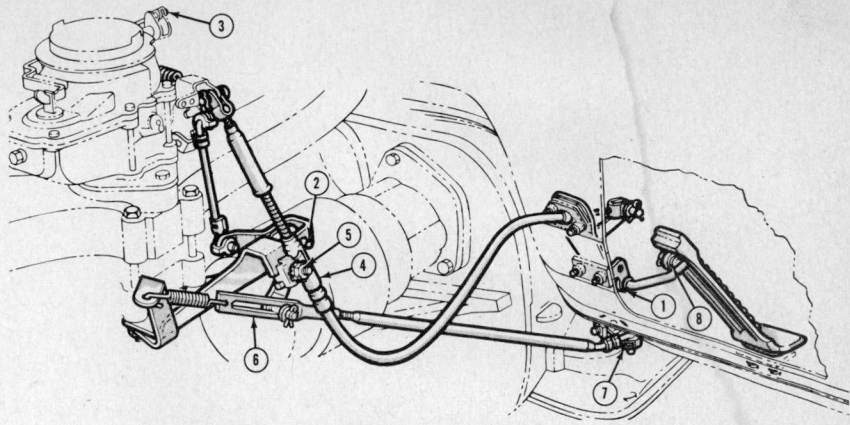

Linkage—1965-68 Coronet and Plymouth six cylinder (© Chrysler Corp.)

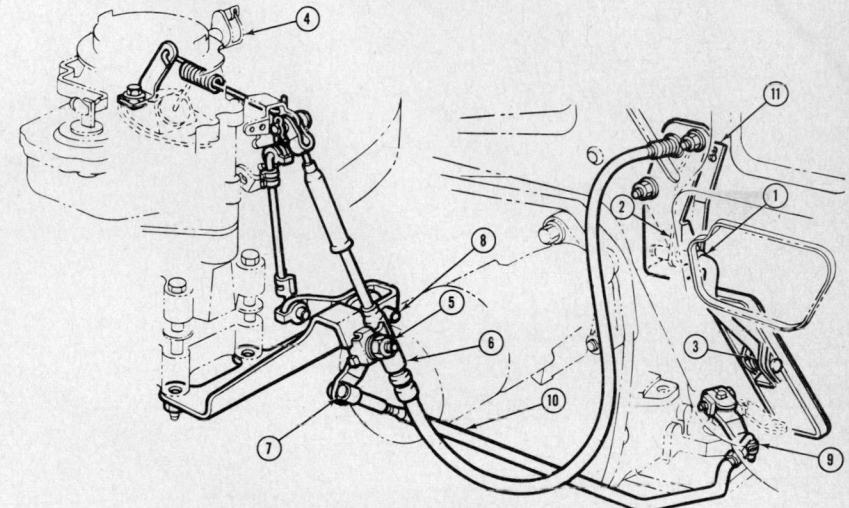

Linkage—1967 six cylinder (© Chrysler Corp.)

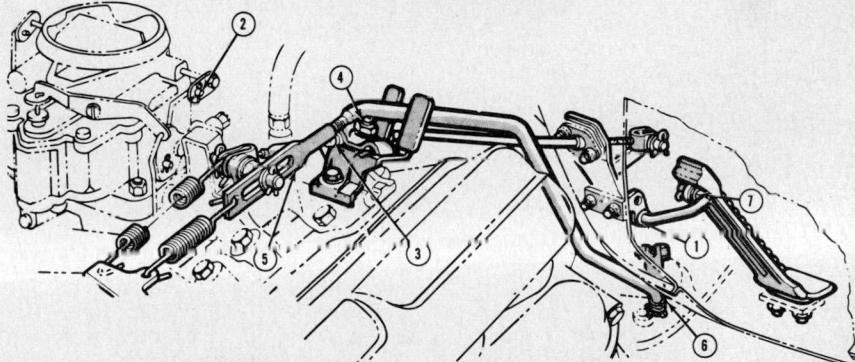

Linkage—1965 Coronet and Plymouth 273-318 (© Chrysler Corp.)

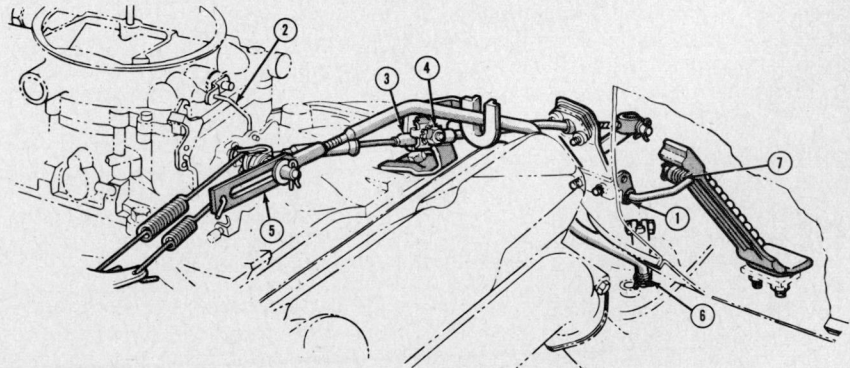

Linkage—1965 Plymouth (© Chrysler Corp.)

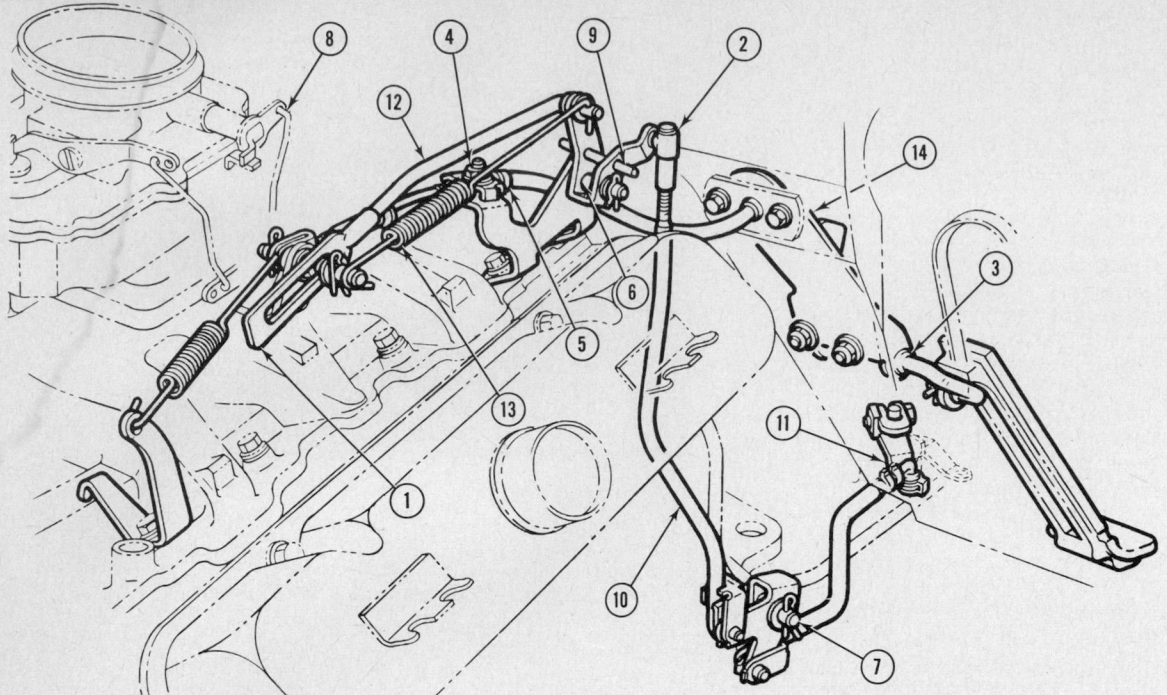

1965 273 engines with automatic and 1964 and some 1965 318 engines with automatic
(© Chrysler Corp.)

idle speed adjusting screw clockwise until it just touches the stop on the carburetor throttle body. Next, back the curb idle speed adjusting screw out one full turn.

7. Adjust each idle mixture screw to obtain the highest rpm possible. Repeat this operation until all four mixture adjustment screws have been properly adjusted and balanced.

8. If the idle mixture adjustment procedure has changed the engine idle speed, adjust the idle speed.

Fuel Pump Removal

All Models

Remove all lines at the fuel pump, and the pump-to-block mounting screws. Remove the pump.

Throttle Linkage Adjustment

1965-70 Dodge and Plymouth Six with Automatic Transmission

1. Apply thin film of multi-purpose grease on the ends of the accelerator shaft (1) where it turns in the bracket, nylon roller (8) at pedal and bellcrank pin (2).
2. Disconnect return spring and slotted transmission rod (6) from the bellcrank lever pin.
3. Block choke in open position. Open throttle to fast idle cam and then return to curb idle position.
4. Hold transmission lever forward (7) against its stop (rod or lever must not be moved vertically) and adjust transmission rod at

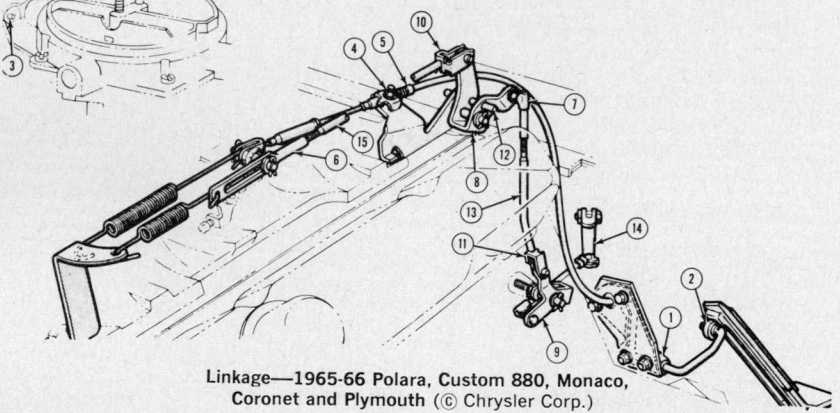

Linkage—1965-66 Polara, Custom 880, Monaco, Coronet and Plymouth (© Chrysler Corp.)

threaded adjustment (6) at upper end. Rear of slot should contact bellcrank lever pin without exerting any force.
5. Lengthen rod by two full turns.
6. Assemble slotted adjustment (6) to bellcrank pin with washer and retainer pin and reconnect return spring. Check to be sure slotted adjuster link (6) returns to the full forward position.
7. Loosen cable clamp nut (5) and adjust position of cable housing ferrule (4) in clamp so that all slack is removed from the cable with the carburetor at curb idle. To remove slack, move ferrule (4) away from carburetor lever.
8. Back off ferrule (4) ¼ in. to provide ¼ in. cable slack at idle. Tighten clamp nut (5).
9. Remove choke blocking.

1965-68 Dodge and Plymouth Six with Manual Transmission

1. Apply thin film of multi-purpose grease on the ends of the acceler-

ator shaft (1) where it turns in the bracket and nylon roller at pedal (8).
2. Block choke in open position and operate throttle to be sure throttle returns to curb idle.
3. Follow steps 7, 8, and 9 above, under Automatic Transmission. (See illustration.)

1965 Dodge and Plymouth 273 Engine with Automatic Transmission and some 1965 Dodge and Plymouth 318 Engines with Automatic Transmission

1. Apply thin film of multi-purpose grease on both ends of accelerator shaft (1) where it turns in the bracket and the nylon roller (7) at pedal.
2. Disconnect return spring and slotted transmission rod (5) from carburetor lever pin.
3. Block choke in open position and operate throttle to be sure throttle returns to curb idle.

4. Hold transmission lever (6) forward against its stop (rod or lever must not be moved vertically) and adjust length of transmission rod at threaded adjustment (5). Rear of slot should contact Carburetor lever pin without exerting any force.

5. Lengthen rod by two full turns.

6. Assemble slotted adjustment (5) to carburetor lever pin and install washer and retainer pin. Connect linkage return spring. Check to be sure slotted adjuster link (5) returns to full forward position.

7. Loosen cable clamp nut (4) and adjust ferrule in clamp to remove all slack with the carburetor at curb idle.

8. Back off ferrule (3) ¼ in. This provides ¼ in. cable slack at idle. Tighten cable clamp nut (4).

9. Remove choke blocking.

1965 Dodge and Plymouth 273 Engines with Automatic, and 1964 and some 1965 318 Engines with Automatic

1. Apply thin film of multi-purpose grease on both ends of accelerator shaft (1) where it turns in the bracket; and the nylon roller (7) at pedal.

2. Block choke open and operate throttle to be sure throttle returns to curb idle.

3. Follow steps 7, 8 and 9 under Automatic Transmission. (See illustration.)

1965 Coronet and Plymouth with 361, 383 or 426 cu. in. Engine and Automatic Transmission

Follow procedure listed for 273 and 318 cu. in. Engines and Automatic Transmissions.

1965 Coronet and Plymouth with 361, 383 or 426 cu. in. Engine and Manual Transmission

Follow procedure listed for 273 and 318 cu. in. Engines and Manual Transmissions.

1965-66 Polara, Custom 880, Monaco with all Engines and Automatic Transmission and 1966 Coronet and Plymouth 318, 361, 383 Engines with Automatic, and some 1965 Coronet and Plymouth 318, 361, 383 and 426 Engines with Automatic

1. Apply thin film of multi-purpose grease on both ends of accelerator shaft (1), nylon roller (2), upper and lower pivot points (8) and (9) at bellcranks, and clipped ends of transmission linkage (10-11).

2. Disconnect return spring, slotted transmission rod (6) from lever pin. Disconnect intermediate rod ball socket (7) from upper bell-crank ball end.

3. Block choke open and operate throttle returns to full curb idle.

4. With a 3/16 in. x 4 in. rod (12) placed in the upper engine mounted bellcrank and lever (8) adjust the length of the intermediate rod (13) by threaded upper end adjustment. The socket (7) must line up with the ball, with the rod held against the transmission stop (14).

5. Assemble ball socket (7) to ball end and remove gauge rod (12).

6. Hold carburetor rod (15) forward against transmission stop (14) and adjust its length at the slotted link (6) so that rear of slot (6) just contacts the carburetor lever pin.

7. Lengthen carburetor rod (15) two full turns at link (6).

8. Assemble link (6) to carburetor.

9. Loosen cable clamp nut (4) and adjust cable position in clamp so that all slack is removed from cable at curb idle.

10. Back off ferrule (5) ¼ in. This provides ¼ in. cable slack at idle and retighten cable clamp nut (4).

11. Remove choke block.

1965-66 Polara, 880, and Monaco with all Engines and Manual Transmissions, and 1966 Coronet and Plymouth 318, 361, and 383 Engines with Manual Transmissions, and some 1965 Coronet and Plymouth 318, 361, and 383 Engines with Manual Transmission

1. Follow steps 1, 3, 9, 10 and 11 listed under Automatic Transmission.

1967-72 Dodge and Plymouth 318, 383, 400 and 440 Engines with Automatic Transmission

1. Apply a thin film of multi-purpose grease at all points of bell crank, throttle cable and linkage movement.

2. Disconnect choke at the carburetor, or block the choke valve in fully open position. Open throttle slightly to release fast idle cam, then return carburetor to curb idle.

3. Hold, or wire, the transmission lever (11) firmly forward against its stop, while performing the next four steps of adjustment.

4. With a 3/16 in. diameter rod (9) placed in the holes provided in upper bell crank (6) and lever, adjust transmission rod (10) by means of adjustment (2) at upper end. The ball socket (2) must line up with the ball end with a

slight downward effort on the rod.

5. Assemble ball socket (2) to ball end and remove the 3/16 in. locating rod from upper bell crank lever (6).

6. Disconnect return spring (13), then adjust length of carburetor rod (12) by pushing rearward on the rod lightly and turning the threaded adjustment (1). The rear end of slot should contact carburetor pin without exerting forward force on pin when slotted adjuster link (1) is in its normal operating position against lever pin nut.

7. Assemble slotted adjustment (1) to carburetor lever pin and install washer and retainer pin. Assemble transmission linkage return spring (13) in place.

8. Remove wire holding the transmission lever, then check transmission linkage for freedom of operation. Move slotted adjuster link (1) to full rearward position, then be sure it returns to its full forward position.

9. Loosen cable clamp nut (4), adjust position of cable housing ferrule (5) in the clamp so that all slack is removed from the cable at curb idle. To remove slack from cable, move cable (5) in the clamp in a direction away from the carburetor lever.

10. Back off ferrule (5) ¼ in. This provides free play between front edge of accelerator shaft lever and the dash bracket. Tighten cable clamp nut (4) to 45 in. lb.

11. Connect choke (8) rod or remove blocking fixture.

1967-72 Coronet and Belvedere 273 and 318 Engines with Automatic Transmission

1. Apply thin film of multi purpose grease on accelerator shaft (3) where it turns in bracket, ball-end, and support (14) at rear end of throttle cable.

2. Disconnect choke (8) at carburetor or block choke valve in full open position. Open throttle slightly to release fast idle cam, then return carburetor to idle.

3. Hold or wire transmission lever (11) firmly forward against stop while performing next four steps.

4. With 3/16 in. rod (9) placed in holes provided in upper bellcrank and lever, adjust length of intermediate transmission rod (10) by means of threaded adjustment at upper end. The ball socket (2) must line up with ball end with a downward effort on rod.

5. Assemble ball socket (2) to ball end and remove 3/16 in. rod from upper bell crank and lever.

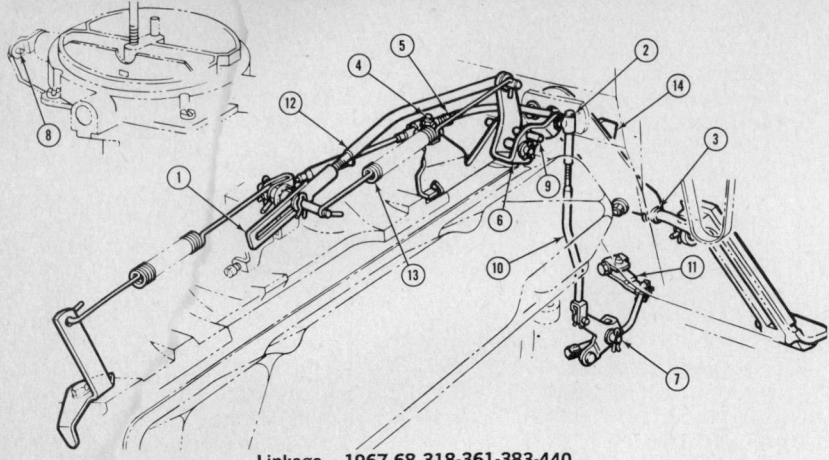

Linkage—1967-68 318-361-383-440
(© Chrysler Corp.)

6. Disconnect return spring (13), then adjust length of carburetor rod (12) by pushing rearward on rod with slight effort and turning threaded adjustment (1). The rear end of the slot should contact carburetor lever pin without exerting any forward force on pin when slotted adjuster link (1) is in its normal operating position against lever pin nut.

7. Assemble slotted adjustment (1) to carburetor lever pin and install washer and retainer pin. Assemble transmission linkage return spring (13) in place.

8. Remove wire securing transmission lever, then check transmission linkage freedom of operation and move slotted adjuster link (1) to full rearward position.

9. Loosen cable clamp nut (4). Adjust position of cable housing ferrule (5) in clamp so that all slack is removed from cable with carburetor at an idle. To remove slack from cable, move ferrule (5) in the clamp away from carburetor levers.

10. Back off ferrule (5) ¼ in. This provides ¼ in. free play between front edge of accelerator shaft lever and dash bracket. Tighten cable clamp nut (4) to 45 in. lbs.

11. Connect choke (8) or remove blocking fixture.

1967-68 Coronet and Belvedere 273 and 318 Engines with Manual Transmission

1. Apply light film of multi-purpose grease on accelerator shaft (3) where it turns in bracket, ball-end, and support (14) at rear end of throttle.

2. Disconnect choke (8) at carburetor or block choke valve in full open position. Open throttle slightly to release fast idle cam, then return carburetor to curb idle.

3. Loosen cable clamp nut (4). Adjust position of cable housing ferrule (5) in the clamp so that all slack is removed from cable with carburetor at an idle. To remove slack from cable, move

ferrule (5) in the clamp away from carburetor lever.

4. Back off ferrule (5) ¼ in. This provides ¼ in. cable slack at idle. Tighten cable clamp nut (4) to 45 in. lbs.

5. Connect choke (8) rod or remove blocking fixture.

1967-68—All Models, 318, 383, 440—Manual Transmission

1. Apply a thin film of multi-purpose grease to all points of bell crank, throttle cable and linkage movement.

2. Disconnect choke at carburetor, or block the choke valve in fully open position. Open throttle slightly to release fast idle cam, then return carburetor to curb idle.

3. Loosen cable clamp (4), adjust position of cable housing ferrule (5) in the clamp so that all slack is removed from cable with carburetor at curb idle. To remove slack from cable, move ferrule (5) in the clamp in the direction away from the carburetor lever.

4. Back off ferrule (5) ¼ in. This provides cable slack at idle. Tighten cable clamp nut (4) to 45 in. lb.

5. Connect choke rod at carburetor, or remove locking fixture.

1967-71—All Models, 426 (Hemi.) Engine—Automatic Transmission

1. Apply a thin film of multi-purpose grease to all points of bell crank and throttle linkage.

2. Block choke valve in open position. Open throttle to release fast idle cam, then return carburetor to curb idle.

3. Hold or wire transmission lever (10) forward against its stop, while performing the next four steps of adjustment.

4. With a 3/16 in. diameter rod (8) placed in holes provided in bell crank and lever (15), adjust length of transmission rod (9) by means of threaded upper end. The ball socket must line up with the ball end while the rod is held upward against the transmission stop (10).

5. Assemble ball socket to ball end and remove the 3/16 in. positioning rod (8) from upper bell crank and lever (15).

6. Disconnect return spring (11), adjust length of rod (20) by pushing rearward on rod and turning threaded adjuster link (2). The rear end of the slot should contact carburetor lever stud without exerting any forward force on the stud when slotted adjuster link is in its normal operating position.

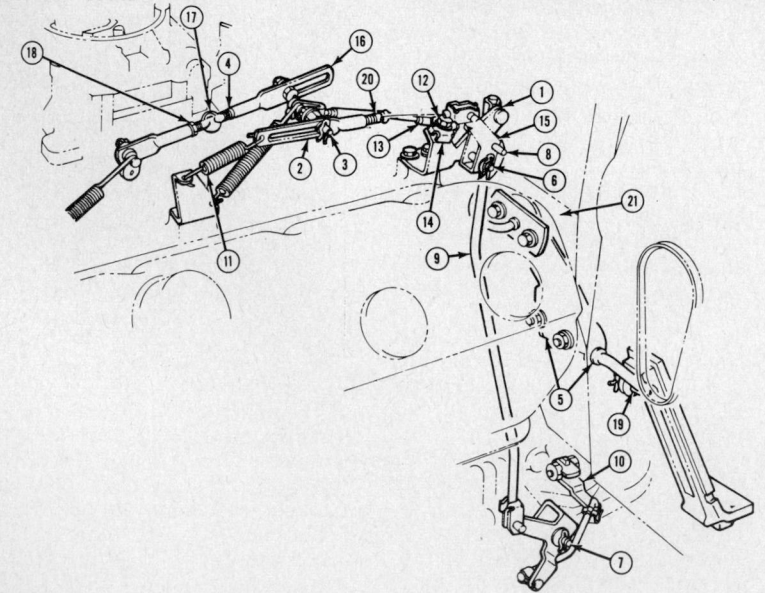

Linkage—426 Hemi (© Chrysler Corp.)

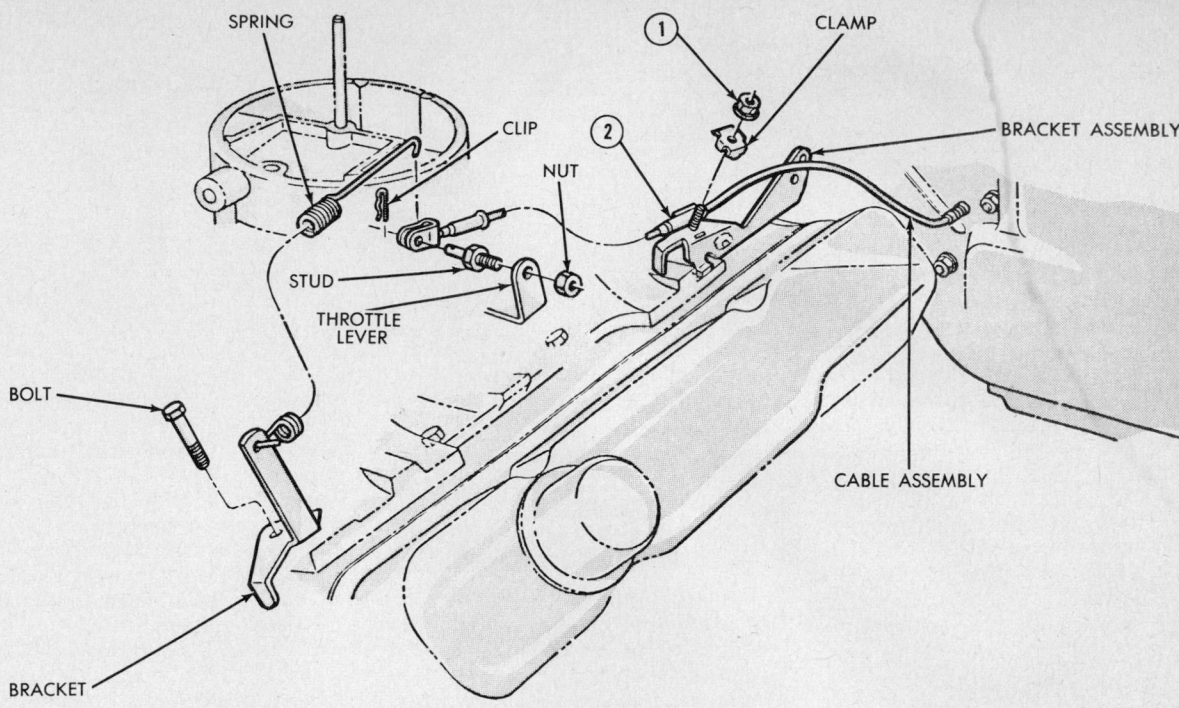

Linkage adjustment 1969-72—all engines with manual transmission except 426 Hemi
(© Chrysler Corp.)

7. Assemble slotted adjuster link (2) to carburetor lever stud and install washer and retainer pin. Assemble transmission linkage return spring (11) in place.

8. Remove wire holding transmission lever, then check transmission linkage for freedom of operation. Move slotted adjuster link (2) to full rearward position, then allow it to return slowly. Be sure it returns to full forward position against the stud.

9. Loosen cable clamp nut (12), adjust position of cable housing ferrule (13) in the clamp (14) so that all slack is removed from the cable with rear carburetor at curb idle. To remove slack from cable, move ferrule (13) in clamp (14) in direction away from carburetor lever.

10. Back off ferrule (13) ¼ in. This will provide free play between front edge of accelerator shaft lever and dash bracket. Tighten clamp (14) to 45 in. lbs.

11. Route cable so it does not interfere with carburetor rod (20) or upper bell crank (15) through full throttle travel.

12. Attach carburetor rod assembly (4) between the carburetors with slotted rod end (16) attached to outboard side of inboard lever on rear carburetor. With rear carburetor at wide-open throttle, adjust length of connector rod (4) so that front carburetor is also at wide open throttle. To lengthen rod (4), turn adjusting stud (17) clockwise as viewed from front of engine. Tighten

lock nut (18).

13. Remove choke valve blocking fixture.

1969-72 Dodge and Plymouth —All Engines with Manual Transmission, Except 426 Hemi

1. Apply thin film of multi-purpose grease on accelerator shaft where it turns in the bracket, ball end, and socket at rear end of throttle cable.

2. Disconnect choke at carburetor or block choke valve in full open position. Open throttle slightly to release fast idle cam, then return carburetor to idle.

3. Loosen cable clamp nut (1). Adjust position of cable housing ferrule (2) in clamp so that all slack is removed from cable with carburetor at idle. To remove slack from cable, move ferrule (2) in clamp away from carburetor lever.

4. Back off ferrule (2) ¼ in. to provide ¼ in. cable slack at idle. Tighten cable clamp nut to 45 in. lbs.

5. Connect choke rod or remove blocking fixture.

1971-72 —All Models, 426 (Hemi) Engine—Manual Transmission

1. Apply a thin film of multi-purpose grease to all points of bell crank and throttle linkage.

2. Block choke valve open, then open throttle slightly to release fast idle cam. Return carburetor to curb idle.

3. Loosen cable clamp nut (12), adjust position of cable housing ferrule (13) in clamp (14) so that all slack is removed from cable with rear carburetor at curb idle. To remove slack, move ferrule (13) in clamp (14) in the direction away from the carburetor lever.

4. Back off ferrule (13) ¼ in. This provides free play between front edge of accelerator shaft lever and the dash bracket. Tighten clamp (14) to 45 in. lbs.

5. Attach carburetor rod (4) assembly between the carburetors with slotted rod end (16) attached to outboard side of inboard lever on rear carburetor. With rear carburetor at wide-open throttle, adjust length of connector rod (4) so that front carburetor is also at wide-open throttle. To lengthen rod (4), turn adjusting stud (17) clockwise as viewed from front of engine. Tighten lock nut (18).

6. Remove choke valve blocking fixture.

Exhaust System

Manifold Heat Valve

A heat riser control is incorporated in the exhaust manifold to regulate the amount of heat bypassing the intake manifold heat chamber.

The most common service required by the heat riser control is to keep it free to turn against its thermostat spring.

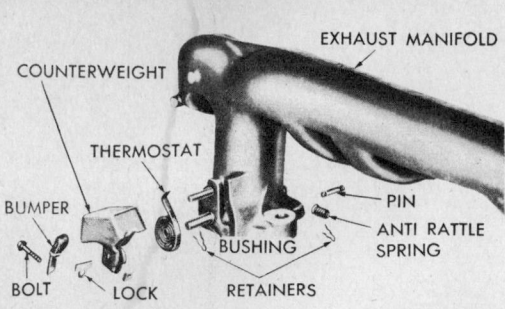

V8 manifold heat valve (© Chrysler Corp.)

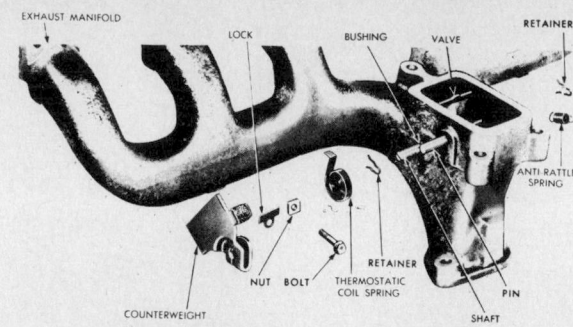

Slant 6 manifold heat valve (© Chrysler Corp.)

If difficulty is noticed in the warm-up period, or if after the car has become warm it seems to run lean, check the heat riser valve to make certain that it is turning freely on its shaft. If it is not, before removing the manifold, try to loosen it up with the use of a good penetrating oil. If this fails to loosen it, it may be necessary to remove the manifold in order to free the heat riser valve.

Exhaust Pipe, Muffler and Tail Pipe

6 Cylinder Models

The oval muffler used on all models is of the straight-through type. When installing a new muffler, the word, front, stamped at one end is installed toward the front of the car.

If difficulty is experienced in separating the muffler from the exhaust and/or tail pipe, soak the joint for a few minutes with a good penetrating oil or a rust dissolving fluid.

The exhaust pipe can be removed by detaching it at the manifold and at the exhaust pipe flange, and it can be threaded out through the back.

Sometimes this is a little difficult since it requires careful threading to get it through.

The tail pipe can be removed by detaching it from its hangers and removing the rear muffler clamp.

Access to the exhaust flange bolt is either from under the hood or under the car, using a long extension on a socket wrench.

V8 Models With Single Exhaust

A Y-type exhaust pipe is used to connect the two manifolds to a single exhaust line.

The Y connection can be taken down by removing the bolts that hold its flanges to the two exhaust flanges. A U-type clamp is used to hold the Y connection to the exhaust pipe.

Dual Exhaust System

The dual exhaust system is available on all V8 models. The dual system is two separate systems, each going to its separate manifold, and there is no crossover pipe. Otherwise, the service on the exhaust system is exactly the same as

it is for the single muffler standard production car.

Cooling System

Cooling System Information

Detailed information on cooling system capacity can be found in the Capacities table.

Information on the water temperature gauge can be found in the Unit Repair section.

Water Pump Removal

1. Drain cooling system. Remove upper half of fan shroud if so equipped or set one piece shroud back on engine.
2. Loosen power steering pump, idler pulley and alternator. Remove all belts.
3. Remove fan, spacer or fluid drive, and pulley.

Caution Do not place a fluid drive unit with the shaft pointing downwards. Silicone fluid will drain into fan drive bearing and ruin grease.

4. Remove bolts attaching water pump to housing. Remove water pump and discard gasket.

Thermostat

On all models, the thermostat is located in the water outlet elbow just under the upper radiator hose connection.

Caution Be sure to install thermostat with the bellows or spring toward the engine.

Engine

Dodge and Plymouth Engines 1965-72

The standard equipment engine in most Dodge and Plymouth car models is the 225 cu. in. slant six. Although this engine has a very long stroke by modern standards, it presents a low profile because the entire block is canted 30 degrees on the right.

The 273 cu. in. and 318 cu. in. engines are Chrysler Corporation's "A"

block series of V8s. The oldest of the current "A" blocks, the 318, originally used polyspherical combustion chambers. When the 273 was introduced in 1964, it had the simpler wedged shaped combustion chambers, and in 1967 the 318 adopted them also. In 1971, a low compression 360 cu. in. V8 was added to the list of "A" block engines available.

Chrysler Corporation's "B" block series is really two series of engines, the low-block series and the raised-block series. These series differ in block deck height, main journal diameter, connecting rod length, and pushrod length. Otherwise these engines are similar and many parts interchange. The 361 and 383 cu. in. engines are low-block engines, and the 413, 426 wedge head, and the 440 cu. in. V8s are raised-block engines. All these engines are conventional V8s with wedge shaped combustion chambers and deep blocks that extend well below crankshaft centerline.

The 426 Hemi is Dodge and Plymouth's largest, heaviest, most complicated, and most powerful engine. It is basically a "B" series, raised-block engine, but with so many differences that it must be treated as a completely seperate engine. It has hemispherical combustion chambers with 2.25 in. intake and 1.95 in. exhaust valves actuated by rocker arms mounted on separate intake and exhaust rocker shafts. The spark plugs are centrally located in the combustion chambers, and aluminum tubes protect the plugs and wires from oil where they pass through the rocker covers. Because of the huge intake ports, there is no room for head bolts on the intake side. Instead studs are mounted in the head which extend down into the valley between the cylinder heads. To reduce piston side thrust, Hemis use longer connecting rods than other raised-block "B" engines, and to strengthen the lower end, the main caps are crossbolted. The Hemi engine was discontinued in 1971 and is no longer available.

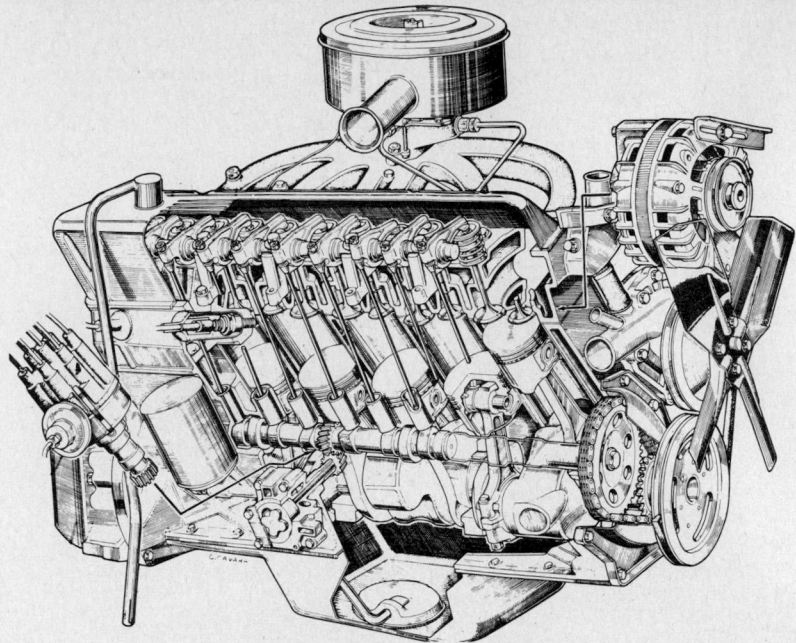

225 cu. in. engine (© Chrysler Corp.)

426 Hemi V8 engine (© Chrysler Corp.)

ifications, ignition timing controls, and reduced engine compression ratios.

Engine R & R

1. Scribe the outline of the hood hinge brackets on the bottom of the hood and remove the hood.
2. Drain the cooling system and remove the radiator.
3. Remove the battery.
4. Remove the fuel line from the fuel pump and plug the line.
5. Remove all wires and hoses that attach to the engine.
6. If equipped with air conditioning and/or power steering, remove the unit from the engine and position it out of the way *without disconnecting the lines*.
7. Attach lifting sling to the engine. On models equipped with a 426 Hemi engine, never attempt to remove the engine with the lifting sling attached to the intake manifold.
8. Raise the vehicle on a hoist and install an engine support fixture to support the rear · of the engine.
9. On automatic transmission models, drain the transmission and torque converter. On standard transmission models, disconnect the clutch torque shaft from the engine.
10. Disconnect the exhaust pipe/s from the exhaust manifold/s.
11. Remove the driveshaft.
12. Disconnect the transmission linkage and any wiring or cables that attach to the transmission.
13. Remove the engine rear support crossmember and remove the transmission.
14. Remove the bolts that attach the motor mounts to the chassis.
15. Lower the vehicle and attach a chain hoist or other lifting device to the engine.
16. Raise the engine and carefully remove it from the vehicle.
17. Reverse above procedure to install.

Manifolds

Combination Manifold Removal

6 Cylinder Models

Remove all leads to the carburetor —vacuum, gasoline and throttle. Detach the exhaust manifold at the flange and, using socket and box wrenches, unbolt the manifold from the side of the block.

Exhaust Emission Control

Positive Crankcase Ventilation

All models are equipped with a positive crankcase ventilation system which draws air into the engine through the oil filler cap and circulates it through the engine. The air combines with vapors in the crankcase and exits the engine through a metering valve mounted in the rocker arm cover. The air-vapor mixture then re-enters the engine through the carburetor or intake manifold and passes into the combustion chamber where it is burned.

Cleaner Air Package (CAP)

Some 1966-67 and all 1968-69 models use this package to reduce engine exhaust emissions. Changes include the addition of limiters to the carburetor idle mixture screws, leaner carburetor mixtures and vacuum controlled ignition timing retard mechanisms.

Cleaner Air System (CAS)

All 1970 and later models are equipped with this type of exhaust emission control. This system consists of: heated carburetor air cleaner intake ducts, carburetor mod-

⏻ CHILTON TIME-SAVER

This is the manufacturer's recommended procedure for engine assembly removal. It is possible to remove the engine without removing the transmission. If the engine is to be removed from the vehicle without removing the transmission, care must be exercised not to allow the weight of the engine to rest on the torque converter hub (automatic transmission) or transmission input shaft (standard transmission).

To remove the engine without removing the transmission, use the following operation. Peform Steps 1-7 and 10 of the above operation. If the vehicle is equipped with an automatic transmission, attach a remote starter switch to the engine, remove the inspection plate from the bellhousing, crank the engine to gain access to the torque converter-to-driveplate attaching nuts and remove the nuts. If the vehicle is equipped with a manual transmission, disconnect the clutch torque shaft from the engine block and the clutch linkage from the adjustment rod. Remove the bolt that attaches the transmission filler tube to the engine (automatic transmission). Support the transmission and re-move the bolts that attach the transmission to the engine or clutch bellhousing. When removing the engine, place a block of wood on the lifting point of a floor jack and position the jack under the transmission. As the engine is removed from the vehicle, raise and lower the jack as required so the angle of the transmission duplicates as nearly as possible the angle of the engine.

When installing the engine into a vehicle with an automatic transmission, keep in mind that the crankshaft flange bolt circle, the inner and outer circle of holes in the driveplate, and the four tapped holes in the front face of the converter all have one hole offset. To ensure proper engine-torque converter balance, the torque converter must be mounted to the driveplate in the same location in was originally installed.

When installing the engine into a vehicle with a manual transmission, it may be necessary to disconnect the driveshaft and turn the transmission output shaft, with the transmission in gear, to get the transmission input shaft splines to mesh with the inner hub on the clutch disc.

Typical water pump—B block engines
(© Chrysler Corp.)

10. Remove screws attaching heat shield and outlet tube to rear face of intake manifold and remove tube and shield.
11. Remove intake manifold, coil and carubretors as an assembly.

Rocker Shaft Removal

Six Cylinder
1. Remove closed ventilation system (PCV).
2. Remove rocker arm cover and gasket.
3. Remove rocker shaft bolts and retainers.
4. Remove rocker shaft assembly.

273 and 318 Engines
1. Disconnect spark plug wires.
2. Disconnect closed ventilation system (PCV).
3. Remove rocker cover and gasket.
4. Remove five rocker shaft bolts and retainers.
5. Remove rocker shaft assembly.

361, 383, 413, and 440 Engines
1. Remove rocker arm cover and gasket.
2. Remove rocker shaft bolts and retainers and remove rocker shaft assembly.

426 Hemi
1. Remove air cleaner, and distributor cap with spark plug cables and secondry coil cable as an assembly.
2. Grasp secondary cables at plastic spark covers and pull covers straight out.
3. Remove spark plugs.
4. On left bank, disconnect brake lines at master cylinder, and remove cotter pin and clevis pin from linkage in back of power brake.
5. Remove four nuts attaching booster to mounting bracket and remove power brake and master cylinder assembly.
6. Remove rocker covers and gaskets.
7. Remove five bolts that attach rocker shafts assembly on each head.

Exhaust Manifolds

V8 Models
Disconnect the exhaust manifold at the pipe flange. Access to these bolts is underneath the car.

The exhaust manifold mounting bolts are very difficult to reach. Unless the operator is particularly adept at working in close spaces, it might be an excellent idea to loosen the front engine mounting bolts and jack the engine up a little to gain some clearance so that the manifold can be taken off more readily.

It is generally considered quicker to jack up the engine about an in. than it is to attempt to take the exhaust manifold off with the engine in place on the car.

Intake Manifold Removal

All Engines Except 426 Hemi
1. Drain cooling system and disconnect battery.
2. Remove the air cleaner and fuel line from the carburetor.
3. Disconnect accelerator linkage.
4. Remove vacuum control between carburetor and distributor.
5. Remove distributor cap and wires.
6. Disconnect coil wires, temperature sending unit wire, heater hoses, and bypass hose.
7. Remove intake manifold, ignition coil, and carburetor as an assembly.

426 Hemi
1. Drain cooling system and disconnect battery.
2. Remove the air cleaner and fuel lines from the carburetors.
3. Disconnect accelerator linkage.
4. Remove vacuum control between carburetor and distributor. Remove distributor cap and wires.
5. Disconnect coil wires, heater hoses and bypass hose.
6. Remove two stud nuts and washers which retain intake manifold inlet heat tube to right hand exhaust header.
7. Remove screws attaching upper end of inlet tube to rear face of intake manifold.
8. Remove inlet tube and discard gaskets. Install new gaskets at assembly.
9. Remove nut, washer, and bolt from tube clamp at exhaust pipe. Remove clamp from outlet tube.

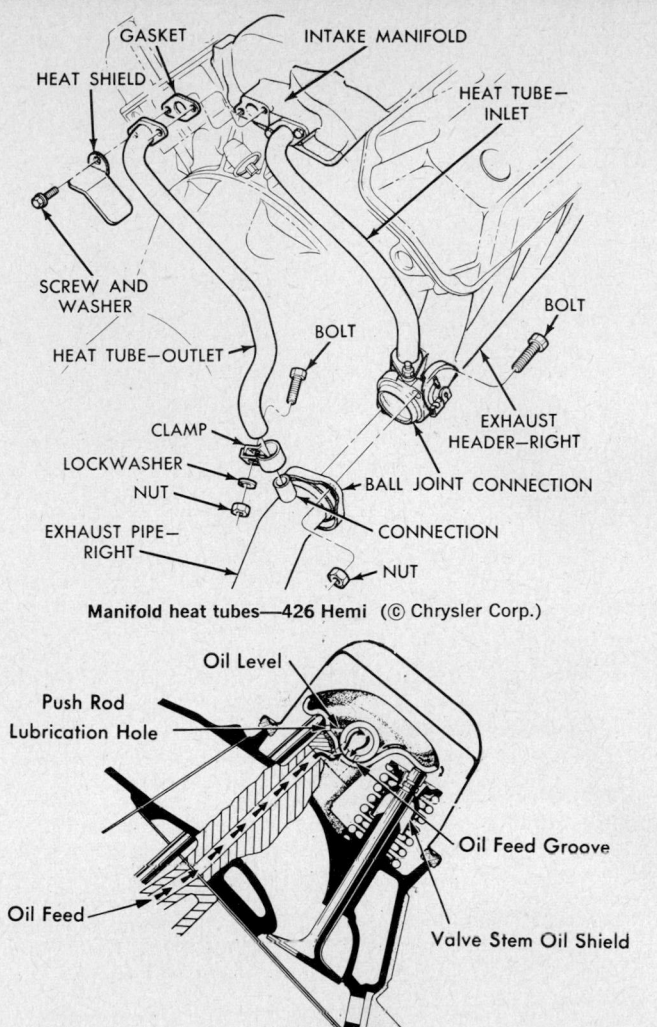

Manifold heat tubes—426 Hemi (ⓒ Chrysler Corp.)

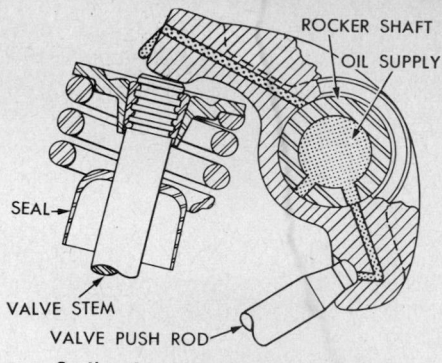

Section through rocker shaft showing
oil supply bores—1965-66 318 V8
(ⓒ Chrysler Corp.)

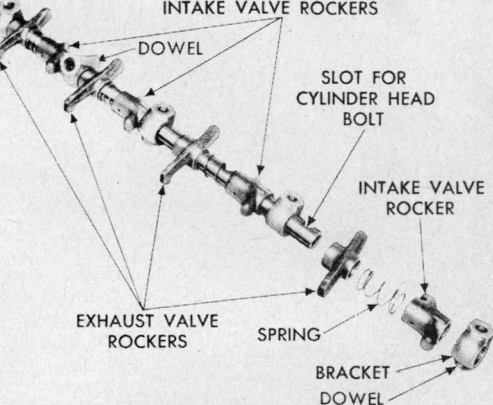

1965-66 318 V8 rocker shaft
(ⓒ Chrysler Corp.)

Rocker and shaft oil supply—B block engines (ⓒ Chrysler Corp.)

NOTE: these rocker shaft assembly bolts pass through the head and into the block. Anytime rocker shaft assembly is removed, remove that head, fit a new gasket, reassemble and torque.

8. Lift off rocker shafts assembly.

Cylinder Head

Removal

Six Cylinder

1. Drain cooling system.
2. Remove air cleaner and fuel line.
3. Remove vacuum line at carburetor and distributor.
4. Disconnect accelerator linkage.
5. Disconnect spark plug wires by pulling straight out in line with plugs.
6. Disconnect heater hose and by-pass hose clamp.
7. Disconnect temperature sending wire.
8. Disconnect exhaust pipe at exhaust manifold flange.
9. Remove intake and exhaust manifold as an assembly.

10. Remove closed vent system (PCV) and rocker cover.
11. Remove rocker shaft assembly.
12. Remove pushrods in sequence and save them to re-install in original bores.
13. Remove 14 head bolts.
14. Remove head.
15. Remove spark plugs and tubes.

273 and 318 Engines

1. Drain cooling system and disconnect battery.
2. Remove intake manifold.
3. Remove exhaust manifolds.
4. Remove rocker shaft assemblies.
5. Remove pushrods in sequence and save them to install in their original bores.
6. Remove ten head bolts from each cylinder head.

361, 383, 413, and 440 Engines

1. Drain cooling system and disconnect battery.
2. Remove alternator, air cleaner, and fuel line.
3. Remove intake manifold.
4. Remove tappet chamber cover.

5. Remove rocker covers and gaskets.
6. Remove exhaust manifolds.
7. Remove rocker shaft assemblies.
8. Remove pushrods in sequence and save them to install in their original bore.
9. Remove 17 head bolts from each cylinder head and remove heads.

426 Hemi—Removal and Installation

1. Remove rocker covers.
2. Remove rocker shaft assemblies.
3. Remove intake manifold.
4. Disconnect exhaust headers, and tie out of way.
5. Remove eight lower head bolts. Remove the nuts from the four cylinder studs inside of the tappet chamber.
6. Remove heads. Do not set heads on studs at any time. Because of the unusual use of rocker shaft bolts as head bolts follow installation procedure carefully.
7. Coat new head gasket with sealer and install with raised bead towards block.
8. Install cylinder heads taking care not to damage studs.
9. Install nuts on cylinder head studs and short cylinder head bolts in outer bolt holes, but do not tighten either.
10. Install pushrods in their original bores. The short rods go in the

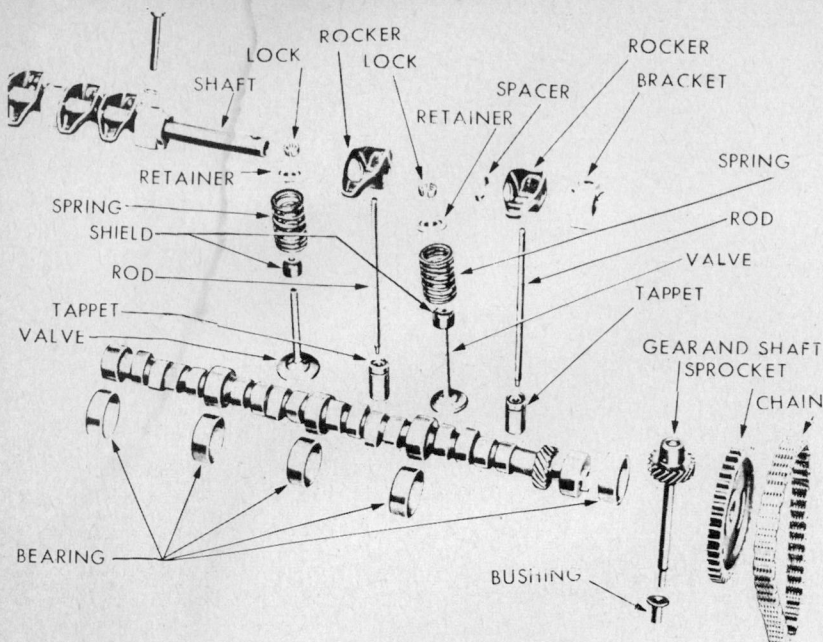

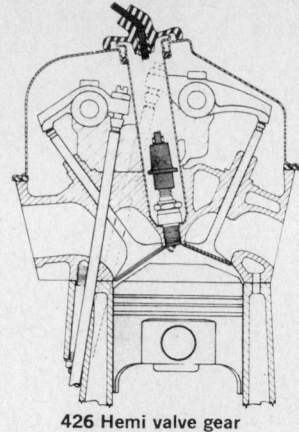

426 Hemi valve gear
(© Chrysler Corp.)

Valve train components—B block engines (© Chrysler Corp.)

upper holes and the long rods go in the lower holes.

11. Position rocker shafts assemblies on heads and install five long head bolts in each after lining up pushrods with rockers.
12. Torque bolts and stud nuts in sequence given at front of section.
13. Adjust valve lash on 1965-69 Hemis.
14. Install headers with new gaskets and torque to 35 ft. lbs.
15. Install new rocker cover gaskets and install rocker covers. Tighten nuts to 10 ft. lbs.
16. Gap plugs to 0.035 in. Slide spark plug tube shields over tubes. With six in. extension install spark plugs and tubes. Torque to 30 ft. lbs. Do not drop or bang spark plugs for this may change gap.
17. Install manifold.

Valve System

Hydraulic Lifter Adjustment Except 426 Hemi

To be certain the hydraulic lifter is operating some place near the middle of its stroke, the Chrysler Corporation recommends that the length of the valve stem protruding from the cylinder head be checked with gauge C-3061 (engines with two rocker shafts) or C-3684 (engines with one rocker shaft.) However, if this gauge is not available an emergency check can be made by turning the engine until the valve being checked is in the fully closed position and the lifter is on the bottom of the cam. Depress the pushrod to force the lifter to leak down. While held in this position, there should be from .060 in. to .210 in. between the

rocker arm pad and the end of the valve stem.

Tappet Adjustment—426 Hemi

1. Adjust ignition timing to TDC.
2. Mark crankshaft damper with chalk at TDC and 180° opposite TDC.
3. Rotate crankshaft until No. 1 cylinder is at TDC and points are just opening.

4. Adjust intake tappets on No. 2 and No. 7 cylinders and exhaust tappets on No. 4 and No. 8 cylinders. On 1965-69 engines, adjust the intake valves to have a clearance of .028 in. and the exhaust valves .032 in. with the engine COLD. On 1970-71 engines, adjust the valves to have zero lash, then tighten the adjustment screw an additional 1½ turns. Tighten the locknuts to 25 ft. lbs.
5. Rotate crankshaft 180° in normal direction of rotation until points open to fire No. 4 cylinder.
6. Adjust intake tappets on No. 1 and No. 8 cylinders and exhaust tappets on No. 3 and No. 6 cylinders as in Step 4.

Torquing Hemi head stud nuts
(© Chrysler Corp.)

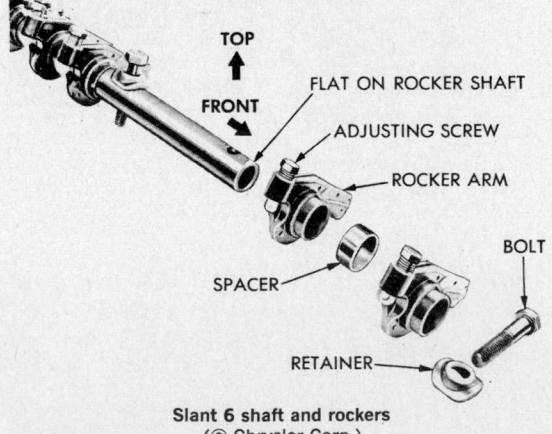

Slant 6 shaft and rockers
(© Chrysler Corp.)

7. Rotate crankshaft 180° in normal direction of rotation until points open to fire No. 6 cylinder.
8. Adjust intake tappets on No. 3 and No. 4 cylinders and exhaust tappets on No. 5 and No. 7 cylinders as in Step 4.
9. Rotate crankshaft 180° in normal direction of rotation until points open to fire No. 7 cylinder.
10. Adjust intake tappets on No. 5 and No. 6 cylinders and exhaust tappets on No. 1 and No. 2 cylinders as in Step 4.
11. Set ignition timing to operating specifications and install rocker covers.

Tappet Adjustment— 6 Cylinder Engine

1. Start the engine and allow it to idle for 5 minutes.
2. Remove the rocker arm cover.
3. Start the engine and adjust the intake valves to have a clearance of 0.010 in. and the exhaust 0.020 in. with the engine HOT.

Valve Guides

Dodge and Plymouth engines do not have separate valve guides. They do have, however, 0.005, 0.015, and 0.030 in. oversize valves (stem diameter). To use these, ream the worn guides to the smallest oversize that will clean up wear. Always start with the smallest reamer and proceed in steps to the largest, as this maintains the concentricity of the guide with the valve seat.

As an alternate procedure, some local automotive machine shops bore out the stock guides and replace them with bronze or cast iron guides which are of stock internal dimensions.

Hydraulic Tappets

Removal—All Except 426 Hemi

Tappets may be removed without removing manifold or cylinder heads, as follows:

1. Remove rocker covers and rocker shaft assembly.
2. Remove pushrods and identify to insure correct installation into original bore.
3. Slide magnetic or claw tool through opening in cylinder head and seat tool firmly in head of tappet.
4. Pull tappet out of bore with a twisting motion.

NOTE: all tappets must be installed in their original bores.

Timing Cover, Chain and Camshaft

Timing Chain and Cover R&R

1. Drain the cooling system.
2. Disconnect the upper and lower

⏱ CHILTON TIME-SAVER

The following is a method for replacing valve springs, oil seals or spring retainers without removing the cylinder head.

1. Entirely dismantle a spark plug and save the threaded shell.
2. To this shell, braze or weld an air chuck.
3. Remove the valve rocker cover. Remove the rocker arm from the affected valve.
4. Remove the spark plug from the affected cylinder.
5. Turn the crankshaft to bring the piston of this cylinder down, away from possible contact with the valve head. Sharply tap the valve retainer to loosen the valve lock.
6. Turn the crankshaft to bring the piston in this cylinder to the exact top of its compression stroke.
7. Screw in the chuck-equipped spark plug shell.
8. Hook up an air hose to the chuck and turn on the pressure (about 200 lbs.).
9. With a strong and constant supply of air holding the valve closed, compress the valve spring and remove the lock and retainer.
10. Make the necessary replacements and reassemble.

NOTE: it is important that the operation be performed exactly as stated, in this order. The piston in the affected cylinder must be on exact top center to prevent air pressure from turning the crankshaft.

---

radiator hoses from the engine. Disconnect the transmission cooler lines from the radiator.
3. If equipped with a fan shroud, remove it from the radiator and position it rearward over the fan.
4. Remove the radiator attaching screws and remove the radiator from the vehicle.
5. Remove the bolts that attach the fan to the water pump and remove the fan, fan spacer (if so equipped) and pulley from the engine.
6. Disconnect the negative battery cable. Remove the bolts that attach the alternator mounting bracket to the engine and remove the alternator and bracket from the engine and position them out of the way with the wires attached.
7. If equipped with power steering, remove the bolts that attach the power steering pump mounting bracket to the engine. Remove the pump and bracket from the engine and position them out of the way with the lines attached.
8. Remove the water pump from the engine.
9. Remove the bolt and washer that attaches the vibration damper to the crankshaft.
10. Using a puller, remove the vibration damper.
11. Remove the bolts that attach the timing chain cover to the block and the front of the oil pan. Remove the cover from the engine.
12. To check timing chain slack, place a scale next to the timing chain to detect any movement in the chain. Place a torque wrench and socket on the camshaft sprocket attaching bolt. Apply either 30 ft. lbs. (if cylinder heads are installed on the engine) or 15 ft. lbs. (cylinder heads removed) of force to the

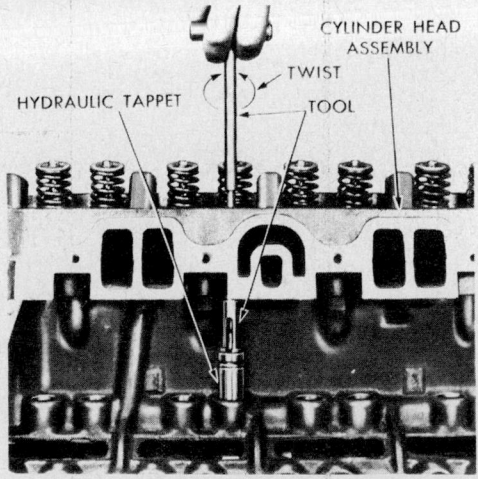

Removal of hydraulic tappets
(© Chrysler Corp.)

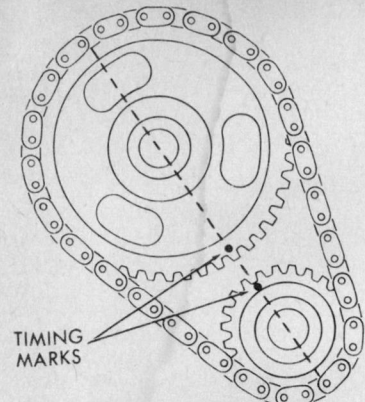

6 cyl. timing mark alignment

TIMING MARKS

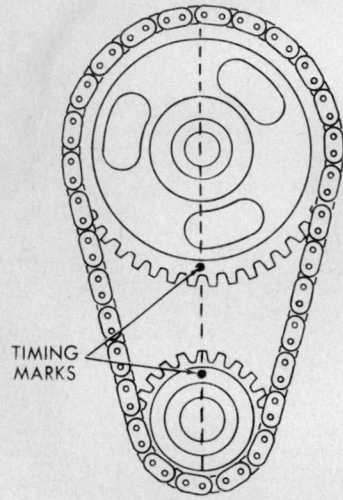

V8 timing mark alignment

TIMING MARKS

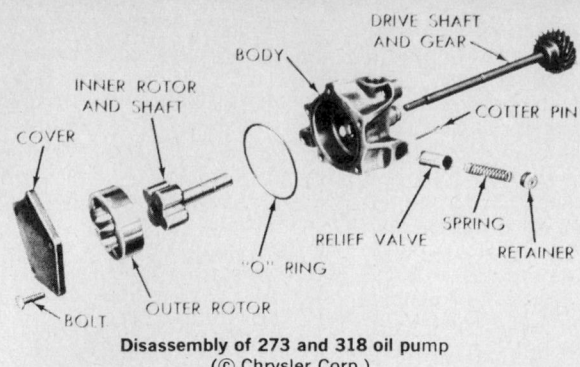

Disassembly of 273 and 318 oil pump
(© Chrysler Corp.)

INNER ROTOR AND SHAFT · BODY · DRIVE SHAFT AND GEAR · COVER · COTTER PIN · RELIEF VALVE · SPRING · RETAINER · "O" RING · OUTER ROTOR · BOLT

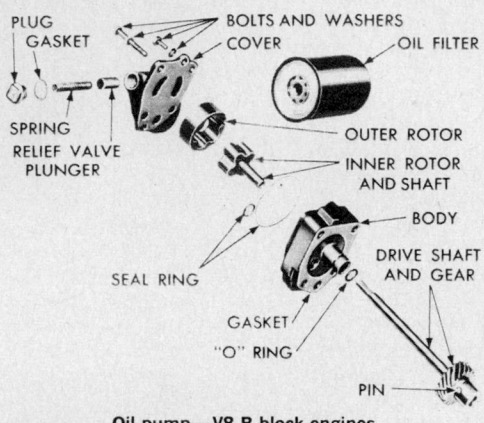

Oil pump—V8 B block engines
(© Chrysler Corp.)

PLUG · GASKET · BOLTS AND WASHERS · COVER · OIL FILTER · SPRING · RELIEF VALVE PLUNGER · OUTER ROTOR · INNER ROTOR AND SHAFT · BODY · DRIVE SHAFT AND GEAR · SEAL RING · GASKET · "O" RING · PIN

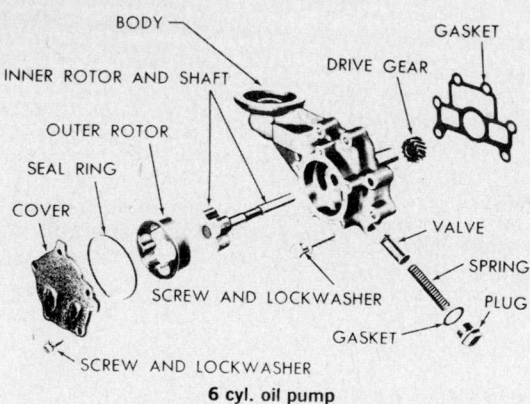

6 cyl. oil pump
(© Chrysler Corp.)

BODY · INNER ROTOR AND SHAFT · DRIVE GEAR · GASKET · OUTER ROTOR · SEAL RING · COVER · VALVE · SPRING · PLUG · SCREW AND LOCKWASHER · GASKET · SCREW AND LOCKWASHER

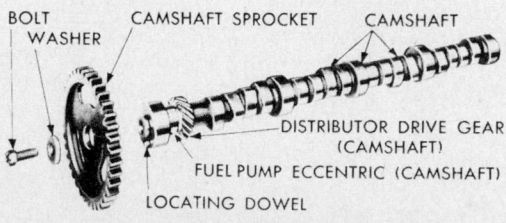

Camshaft and sprocket—273-318 V8
(© Chrysler Corp.)

BOLT · WASHER · CAMSHAFT SPROCKET · CAMSHAFT · DISTRIBUTOR DRIVE GEAR (CAMSHAFT) · FUEL PUMP ECCENTRIC (CAMSHAFT) · LOCATING DOWEL

bolt and rotate the bolt in the direction of crankshaft rotation to remove all slack from the chain. While applying torque to the camshaft sprocket bolt, the crankshaft should not be allowed to rotate. It may be necessary to block the crankshaft to prevent rotation. Position the scale over the edge of a timing chain link and apply an equal amount of torque in the opposite direction. If the movement of the chain exceeds 3/16 in., replace the chain.

13. To remove the timing chain, crank the engine until the timing marks on the sprockets are aligned, remove the bolt that attaches the cam sprocket to the camshaft, and slide the chain and both sprockets forward and remove them from the engine as an assembly.

14. Reverse above procedure to install.

Camshaft R&R

1. Remove the timing chain and cover.
2. Remove the intake manifold.
3. Remove the rocker arm covers and rocker arm assemblies.

4. Remove the pushrods and valve lifters and keep them in order so they can be returned to their original location in the engine.
5. Remove the distributor and distributor-oil pump driveshaft.
6. Remove the fuel pump from the engine and position it out of the way without disconnecting the fuel lines.
7. Remove the camshaft from the engine. Use care not to damage the lobes during removal.
8. Reverse above procedure to install, lubricating the cam before installation.

NOTE: when installing the camshaft and timing chain, do not allow the camshaft to contact the welch plug in the rear of the engine block as this could loosen the plug.

Engine Lubrication

Oil Pan Removal

Slant 6

1. Remove the tie-rod at the steering and idler arms.
2. Remove the two front engine mounting bolts.
3. Remove left side support, connecting converter housing and cylinder block.
4. Raise the engine about two inches.
5. Drain engine oil.
6. Remove oil pan bolts, lower the pan to the rear.

NOTE: do not turn the oil pick-up out of position.

V8 Engines

1. Disconnect the negative battery cable. Remove the oil dipstick.
2. Raise the vehicle on a hoist and drain the crankcase.
3. Disconnect the steering center link from the idler arm and the Pitman arm.
4. Disconnect the exhaust pipes from the exhaust manifolds. On models equipped with a 361, 383, 400, 413, 426, or 440 V8, disconnect the exhaust pipe/s from the muffler inlet pipe/s and remove.
5. Remove the engine to torque converter left housing strut.
6. On models equipped with a 361, 383, 400, 413, 426, or 440 V8, remove the torque converter dust shield.
7. Remove the oil pan bolts and the oil pan. Turn the crankshaft as required to get the oil pan to clear the crankshaft counterweights during removal.

Oil Pump Removal

Six Cylinder

1. Drain radiator, disconnect upper and lower hoses, and remove fan shroud.

2. Raise vehicle on hoist, support front of engine with jackstand placed under right front corner of oil pan, and remove engine mount bolts. Do not support engine at crankshaft pulley or vibration damper.
3. Raise engine approximately 1½ to 2 in.
4. Remove oil filter, oil pump attaching bolts, and pump assembly.

273, 318, 340 and 360 Engines

1. Remove oil pan.
2. Remove oil pump from rear main bearing cap.

361, 383, 400, 413, 440, and 426 Hemi Engines

1. Remove oil pan and filter assembly.
2. Remove oil pump from bottom side of engine.

Oil Pump Disassembly

Six Cylinder

1. Remove pump cover and seal ring.
2. Press off drive gear. Support gear to keep load off aluminum body.
3. Remove pump rotor and shaft and lift out outer pump rotor.
4. Remove oil pressure relief valve plug and lift out spring and retainer.

273, 318, 340 and 360 Engines

1. Remove cotter pin from relief valve, drill ⅛ in. hole into relief valve cap, and insert self threading sheet metal screw into cap.
2. Clamp sheet metal screw in vise, and, supporting oil pump body, tap body with soft-headed hammer until cap comes out. Discard cap and remove spring and relief valve.
3. Remove oil pump cover bolts and lock washers and lift off cover.
4. Discard oil seal ring.
5. Remove pump motor and shaft and remove outer rotor.

361, 383, 400, 413, 440, and 426 Hemi

1. Remove filter base and oil seal ring.
2. Remove pump rotor and shaft and lift out outer pump rotor.
3. Remove oil pressure relief valve plug and lift out spring and relief valve plunger.

Oil Pump Inspection— All Engines

1. Clean all parts thoroughly in solvent.
2. Inspect mating surface of oil pump cover. Mating face should be smooth with no scratches or grooving. Replace if scratched or

grooved.
3. Lay straight edge across oil pump cover face. If 0.0015 in. feeler gauge can be inserted between cover and straight edge, replace cover.
4. Measure outer rotor. If rotor length is less than 0.649 in. for six cylinder, 0.825 in. for 273, 318, 340 and 360 V8s, or 0.943 in. for larger V8s, replace rotor. If rotor diameter is less than 2.469 in. for either sixes or eights replace rotor.
5. Measure inner rotor. If rotor length is less than 0.649 in. for six cylinder, 0.825 in. for 273, 318, 340 and 360 V8s, or 0.942 in. for larger V8s, replace rotor.
6. Install outer rotor in pump body and holding against one side of body measure clearance between rotor and body. If clearance is greater than 0.014 in., replace oil pump body.
7. Install inner rotor into pump body and place straight edge across pump body between bolt holes. If feeler gauge greater than 0.004 in. can be inserted between rotors and body, replace oil pump body.
8. Measure clearance between tips of inner and outer rotor where they are opposed. If clearance exceeds 0.010 in., replace inner and outer rotors.

Oil Pump Assembly and Installation

Six Cylinder

1. Assemble pump using new parts as required.
2. Install new seal rings between cover and body. Tighten cover bolts to 95 in. lbs.
3. Install pump on engine. Tighten attaching bolts to 200 in. lbs.
4. Lower engine and install engine mount bolts.
5. Replace fan shroud, connect upper and lower hoses, and fill radiator.

273, 318, 340 and 360 V8s

1. Assemble pump using new parts as required.
2. Install new seal rings between cover and body. Tighten cover bolts to 95 in. lbs.
3. Fill pump with oil to prime it and install pump and strainer on rear main bearing cap. Tighten bolts to 35 ft. lbs.
4. Replace oil pan.

361, 383, 400, 413, 440, and 426 Hemi V8s

1. Assemble pump using new parts as required.
2. Install new seal rings between filter base and body. Torque bolts to 10 ft. lbs.

3. Install new O-ring seal on pilot of oil pump before attaching oil pump to cylinder block.

4. Install oil pump on engine using new gasket and tightening bolts to 30 ft. lbs. Install oil filter assembly and oil pan.

Pistons, Connecting Rods and Main Bearings

Rod and Piston Assembly Removal

All Models

1. Remove the cylinder head and oil pan.

2. Insert a good cylinder ridge reamer into the top of the bores accessible without turning the crankshaft, and remove the ridge. Detach the tool, turn the crankshaft, reattach the tool and remove the ridge on the next cylinder. Continue this process until all cylinder ridges have been removed.

Caution This is not a boring bar, so merely remove the ridge.

3. From underneath the car, select the connecting rods in the down position, and remove the locking device (pawl nut or cotter pin). Take off the two nuts that hold the cap to the lower end of the connecting rod. Tap the cap gently and slide it off the end of the bolts. Be careful not to lose the lower half of the rod bearing.

4. Start the connecting rod and piston assembly up toward the top of the bore, but, before pushing it out, replace the cap so that there isn't the slightest chance of it getting mixed up or put on in the wrong way.

5. At this point, note whether the number of the cylinder is stamped on the connecting rod, and, if it is not, some provision will have to be made to mark the rod, such as a file mark or a punch mark. Push the rod and piston assembly up until the rings snap out of the cylinder.

6. When assembling pistons to connecting rods, and the assemblies to the engine, on the slant 6, be sure to locate the squirt hole to the proper side. The 1965-66 engine using cast iron block has the piston head notch at the front, with the oil squirt hole to the right side of the engine. Where aluminum blocks are used, the piston head notch is front with the oil squirt hole to the left side of the engine.

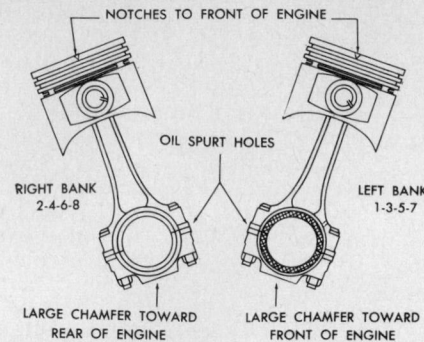

NOTCHES TO FRONT OF ENGINE

OIL SPURT HOLES

RIGHT BANK 2-4-6-8

LEFT BANK 1-3-5-7

LARGE CHAMFER TOWARD REAR OF ENGINE

LARGE CHAMFER TOWARD FRONT OF ENGINE

Relation of piston and rod—all V8s

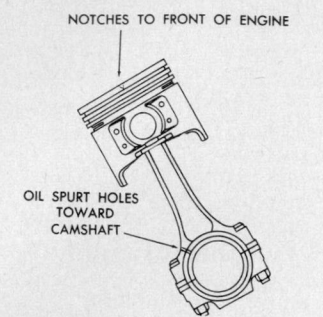

NOTCHES TO FRONT OF ENGINE

OIL SPURT HOLES TOWARD CAMSHAFT

Relation of piston and rod—slant 6

Piston Rings

Replacement

1. If cylinder bore is in satisfactory condition, place each ring in bore (in turn) and align using the head of a piston. Measure the ring end gap with feeler gauges; if gap is greater than limit, use new ring; if gap is less than limit, file end of ring to obtain correct gap. The correct ring gaps are found in the chart.

2. Check ring side clearance by installing rings onto piston and inserting feeler gauge of correct thickness between ring and lower land. Gauge should slide freely around ring circumference without binding. Any wear will usually show up as a step on the lower land; replace any pistons having high steps. Ring side clearance is found in the chart.

3. Space ring gaps at equidistant intervals around piston circumference. Be sure to install piston into its original bore. Install short lengths of rubber tubing over connecting rod bolts to prevent rod journal damage, then install ring compressor over rings on piston and lower piston-rod assembly into bore until ring compressor contacts block. Using a woden hammer handle, push piston into bore while guiding rod onto journal.

Rear Main Bearing Oil Seal

Service replacement seals are of split rubber type composition. This type of seal makes it possible to replace the upper half of the rear main

oil seal without removing the engine from the car. When installing rubber seals, they must be replaced as a set and cannot be combined with the rope type rear main seal. The following procedure is for removing the rope type seal and replacing it with the rubber type seal.

Replacement

NOTE: on vehicles with a 426 Hemi engine, remove the transmission and vibration damper in addition to the procedure listed below.

1. Remove the oil pan.

2. Remove the rear seal retainer and the rear main bearing cap.

3. Remove the lower rope seal by prying from the side with a small screwdriver.

4. To remove the upper rope seal, drive up on either exposed end of the seal with a 6 in. piece of 3/16 in. brazing rod. When the opposite end of the seal starts to protrude from the block, have an assistant grasp it with pliers and gently pull it from the block while the opposite end is being driven.

5. Wipe crankshaft clean and lightly oil crankshaft and new seal before installing seal.

6. Loosen all main bearing caps slightly to lower the crankshaft which will ease installation.

Caution Do not allow the crankshaft to drop enough to permit the main bearings to become displaced on the crankshaft.

7. Hold the seal tightly against the crankshaft with the thumb (with paint stripe to the rear) and install the seal in the block groove. Rotate the crankshaft if necessary while installing the seal in the groove. *Make sure the sharp edges on the block groove do not cut or nick the rear of the seal.*

8. Install lower half of seal (with paint stripe to the rear) into the lower seal retainer.

9. Install rear main bearing cap.

10. Tighten all main bearing caps to specification.

NOTE: make sure all main bearings are located in their proper position before tightening the main bearing caps.

Front Suspension

Upper Ball Joint

Replacement

1. Raise the vehicle by placing a floor jack under the lower control arm. Place the lifting point of the jack as close as possible to the wheel.

2. Remove the wheel, tire and

Ring end gap (in.)

Year and Engine	Top compression	Bottom compression	Oil control
1965 six	0.010-0.020	0.010-0.020	0.015-0.062
1966-70 six	0.010-0.020	0.010-0.020	0.015-0.055
1965-70 273, 318	0.010-0.020	0.010-0.020	0.015-0.055
1965 big V8s	0.013-0.025	0.013-0.025	0.013-0.025
1966-67 big V8s	0.013-0.025	0.013-0.025	0.015-0.055
1968-72 big V8s	0.013-0.023	0.013-0.023	0.015-0.055

Ring side clearance (in.)

Year and Engine	Top compression	Bottom compression	Oil control
1965 six	0.0015-0.0040	0.0015-0.0040	0.009 max.
1965 all V8	0.0015-0.0030	0.0015-0.0040	0.009 max.
1966-72 six and 273, 318, 340 and 360 V8s	0.0015-0.0040	0.0015-0.0040	0.0002-0.0050
1966 361, 383, 413	0.0015-0.0040	0.0015-0.0040	0.0002-0.0050
1967-72 383, 440, 400 V8s	0.0015-0.0040	0.0015-0.0040	0.0000-0.0050
1966-71 Hemi	0.0010-0.0030	0.0010-0.0030	0.0002-0.0050

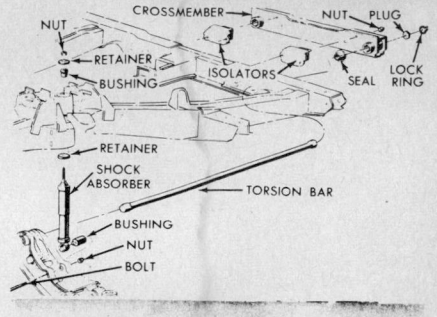

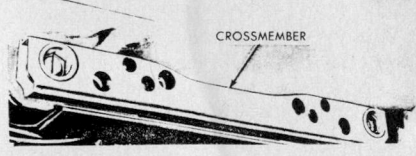

Torsion bar suspension—1965-72
(© Chrysler Corp.)

drum as an assembly. On models with disc brakes, remove the tire and wheel, remove the disc brake pads, remove the disc brake caliper from the steering knuckle and position the caliper out of the way with the brake line attached. Remove the brake rotor from the steering knuckle.

3. Remove the nut that attaches the upper ball joint to the steering knuckle and, using a suitable tool, loosen the ball joint stud from the steering knuckle.

4. Unscrew the upper ball joint from the upper control arm and remove it from the vehicle.

5. Position new ball joint on the upper control arm, screw the ball joint into the control arm until it bottoms on the control arm and tighten the ball joint to a minimum of 125 ft. lbs.

NOTE: when installing a ball joint, make certain the ball joint threads engage those of the upper control arm squarely if the original control arm is being used.

6. Position a new seal on the ball joint stud and install the seal in the ball joint making sure the seal is fully seated on the ball joint housing.

7. Position ball joint stud in the steering knuckle and install the retaining nut.

8. Lubricate ball joint and, if replacement ball joint is equipped with knock-off type grease fitting, break off that portion of the fitting over which the lubrication gun was installed.

9. If equipped with disc brakes, install the rotor, caliper and brake pads. Install the tire and wheel.

10. Lower the vehicle and adjust front suspension height as required.

Lower Ball Joint

Inspection

1. Raise the front of the vehicle by placing a floor jack under the lower control arm. Position the lifting point of the jack as close to the wheel as possible.

2. Have an assistant raise and lower the tire and wheel assembly and observe any movement at the lower ball joint.

3. On 1965-67 models, replace the ball joint if the axial (up and down) play of the ball joint housing arm in relation to the ball joint stud exceeds 0.050 in. On 1968-72 models, replace the ball joint if the axial play exceeds 0.070 in.

Removal

The lower ball joint is integral with the steering arm and is not serviced separately.

1. Raise the vehicle on a hoist so the front suspension will drop to the downward limit of its travel.

2. Remove the upper control arm rebound bumper if so equipped.

3. Remove all load from the torsion bar that is attached to the same

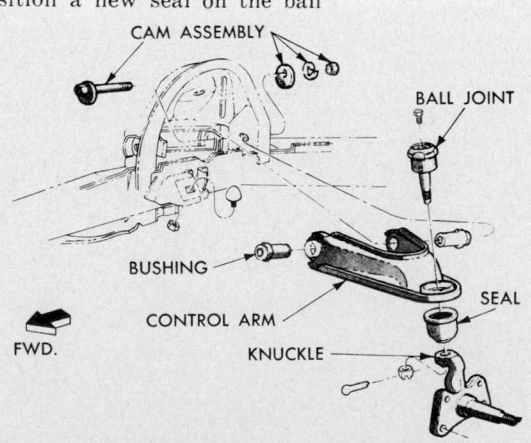

Upper control arm—Belvedere, Satellite, Coronet and Charger
(© Chrysler Corporation)

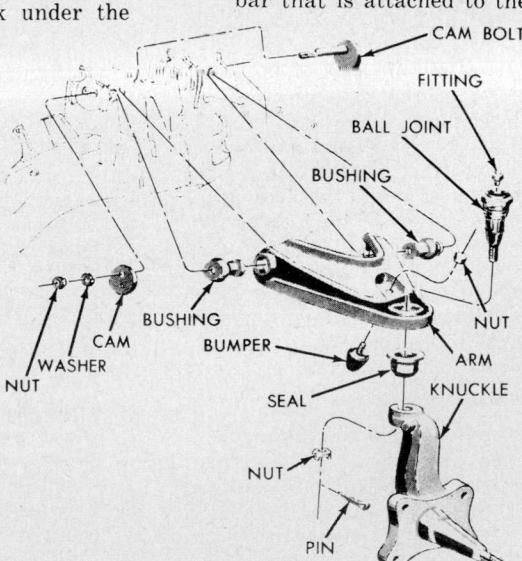

Upper control arm—Fury, Polara and Monaco
(© Chrysler Corporation)

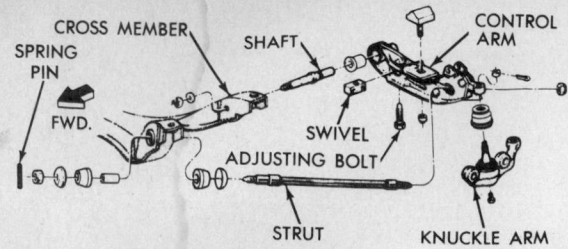

Lower control arm—Belvedere, Satellite, Coronet and Charger
(© Chrysler Corporation)

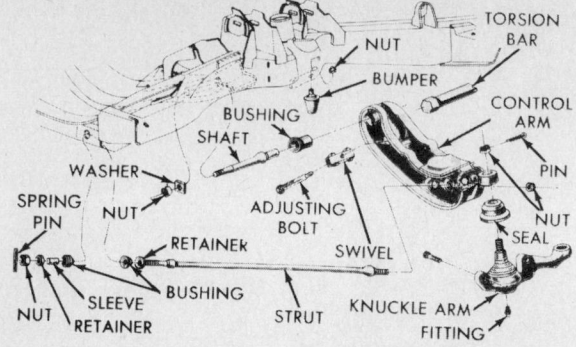

Lower control arm—Fury, Polara and Monaco
(© Chrysler Corporation)

side of the vehicle as the ball joint to be replaced by turning the torsion bar adjusting bolt in a counterclockwise direction.

4. Remove the tire, wheel, and brake drum from the vehicle as an assembly. If equipped with disc brakes, remove the tire and wheel, remove the brake pads, and remove the caliper from the steering knuckle and position it out of the way with the brake line attached. Remove the rotor from the spindle.

5. Remove the two lower bolts that attach the steering arm-ball joint assembly to the brake assembly mounting plate.

6. Using a suitable tool, disconnect the tie-rod end from the steering arm.

7. Remove the ball joint stud retaining nut and cotter pin.

8. Using a suitable tool, separate and remove the ball joint from the lower control arm.

Installation

1. Position ball joint-steering arm assembly on the steering knuckle and install the two retaining bolts.

2. Insert the ball joint stud in the lower control arm and install the retaining nut and cotter pin.

3. Position the tie-rod end in the steering knuckle and install the retaining nut and cotter pin.

4. Place a load on the torsion bar by turning the adjusting bolt in a clockwise direction.

5. Install the tire, wheel and brake drum assembly. If equipped with disc brakes, install the rotor, caliper, brake pads and tire and wheel assembly.

6. Lower vehicle and install upper control arm rebound bumper if so equipped.

7. Check and adjust front suspension height as required.

Front Height

Adjustment. (Without Gauge)

1. Jounce the car and measure from the lower ball joint to the floor (measurement A).

2. Measure from the control arm torsion bar spring anchor housing to the floor, (measurement B).

3. Subtract A from B. The difference should be as shown in specification table.

4. Measure the other side in the same way.

5. Adjust by turning the torsion bar anchor adjusting nut, clockwise to raise, and counterclockwise to lower.

Torsion Bar Springs

Contrary to appearance, the torsion bars are not interchangeable from right to left. They are marked with an R or an L, according to their location.

Removal

1. Lift the car by the body only so that the front suspension is free of all load. If the car is to be raised with jacks, place jack under center of frame crossmember and raise until suspension is free of all load.

2. Release load from torsion bar by backing off anchor adjusting nuts. Remove the adjusting nut and swivel bolt.

3. Remove the lower control arm strut.

4. Remove the lock spring from the rear of torsion bar rear anchor.

5. Install the front of the torsion suitable clamp, and remove torsion bar rearward by striking the clamping tool with a hammer.

Caution Do not apply heat to the front or rear anchors. Do not scratch or otherwise mar the skin of the torsion bar during removal or installation.

6. Remove the clamping tool and slide the rear anchor balloon seal off the front end of the bar.

7. Remove torsion bar by sliding the bar rearward and out through the rear anchor.

Installation

1. Clean the hex openings of both front and rear anchors, also clean the male ends of the torsion bar.

2. Feed the torsion bar through the rear anchor.

3. Slide the balloon-type seal over the torsion bar, with the large cupped side of the seal facing the rear.

4. Coat both ends of the torsion bar with multi-purpose grease.

5. Install the front of the torsion bar in the lower control arm.

6. Install the lock ring in the rear anchor, then move torsion bar rearward until the bar contacts the lock ring.

7. Position swivel bolt on the control arm and hold in place while installing the adjusting nut and seat. Tighten the adjustment about 10 turns before lowering car to the floor.

8. Pack the annular opening in the rear anchor with multi-purpose grease. Slide the rear anchor balloon-type seal into position over the rear anchor until the lip of the seal fits in the groove.

9. Install lower control arm strut.

10. Lower car to the floor and adjust front suspension height.

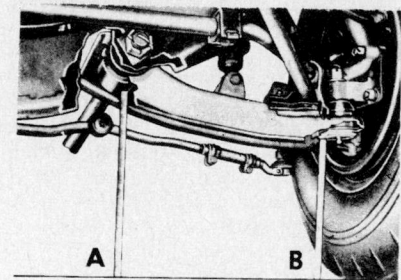

Checking front suspension height at ball joint and lower control arm
(© Chrysler Corp.)

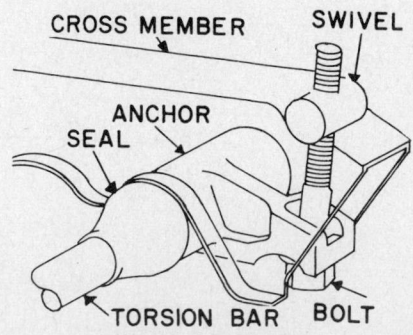

Torsion bar adjustment bolt
(© Chrysler Corp.)

Jacking, Hoisting

Jack car at front lower control arm and at rear under axle housing.

To lift at frame, use adapters so that contact will be made at points shown. Lifting pads must extend beyond sides of supporting structure.

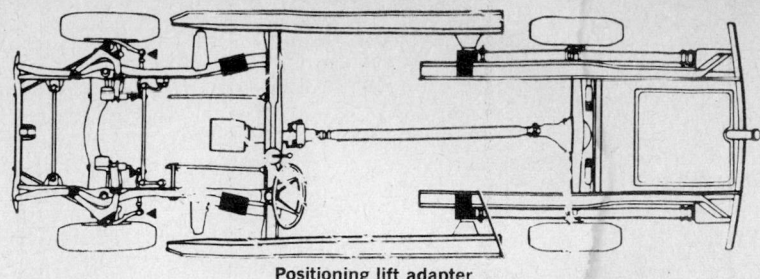

Positioning lift adapter

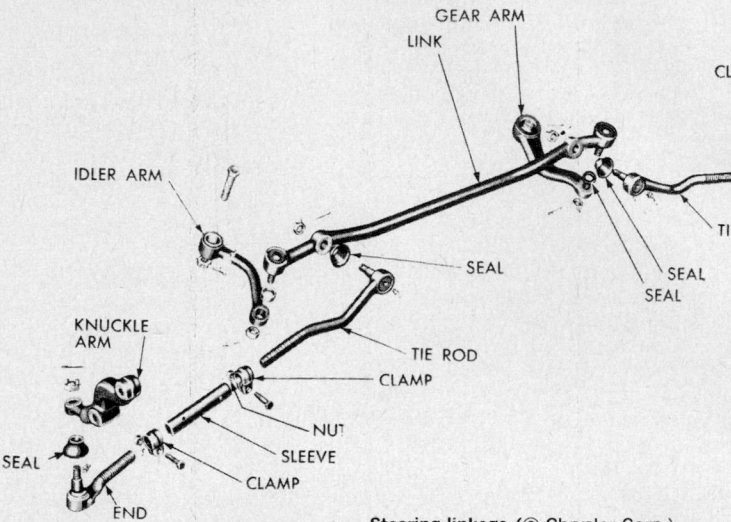

Steering linkage (© Chrysler Corp.)

Steering Gear

Gear Assembly Removal

The steering gear assembly can be removed without removing the column.

1965-69

1. Remove the pin or bolt that attaches the coupling on the steering shaft to the steering gear worm gear.
2. Pull back the carpet and remove the screws that attach the steering column mounting plate to the floor pan.
3. Loosen the steering column-to-instrument panel attaching clamp bolts enough to disengage the tab on the clamp from the slot in the steering column jacket.
4. On 1965-66 models equipped with standard transmission, and on all 1967-69 models, disconnect the shift linkage from the shift tube.
5. Slide the steering column upward to disengage the steering shaft coupling from the steering gear worm gear.
6. Remove the nut that attaches the Pitman arm to the steering gear and, using a puller, remove the steering arm from the steering gear.
7. On models equipped with a 426 Hemi engine, remove the battery, the battery tray and the left motor mount attaching stud nut and washer.
8. If equipped with power steering, disconnect the lines from the steering gear and plug them to prevent fluid spillage.
9. Remove the bolts that attach the steering gear to the chassis and remove the steering gear. On models with a six cylinder engine, remove the steering gear from the engine compartment. On all V8 models except the 426 Hemi, remove the steering gear from under the vehicle. On models with a 426 Hemi, jack the engine up 1½ in. and rotate the steering gear forward and remove it from under the hood through the battery tray opening.
10. To install steering gear, position it on the chassis and install the attaching bolts. Align the master spline on the steering gear worm gear (12 o'clock position) with the master spline on the steering shaft coupling, making sure the front wheels and the steering wheel are in the straight ahead position.

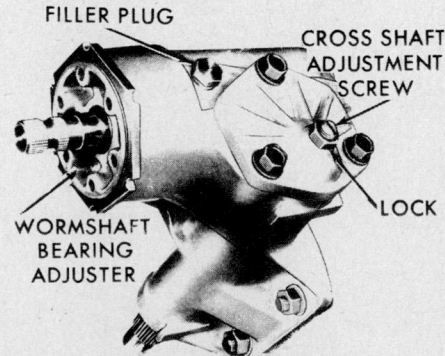

Steering gearbox adjustment
(© Chrysler Corp.)

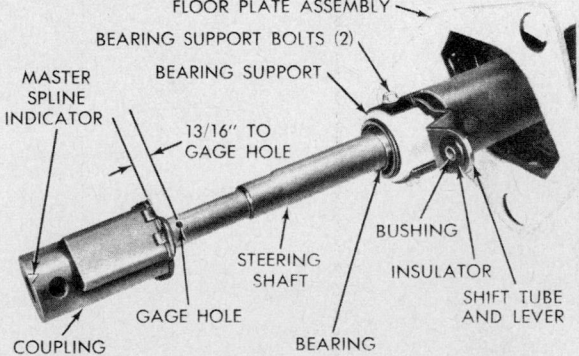

Steering column lower end (© Chrysler Corporation)

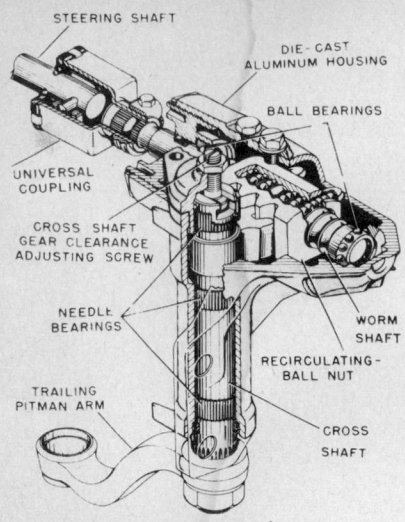

1965-70 manual steering gear
(© Chrysler Corp.)

11. Install the pin or bolt that attaches the coupling to the worm gear.

12. Position the steering column on the instrument panel and loosely install the nuts or bolts that attach the steering column bracket to the dash. Move the column up or down in the instrument panel support until the dimension between the steering shaft coupling and the gauge hole in the steering shaft is 13/16 in.

1970-72

To prevent damage to the energy absorbing steering column, it is necessary to completely detach the column from the floor and the instrument panel before the steering gear

is removed.

1. Disconnect the negative battery cable.
2. Disconnect the linkage from the bottom of the steering column.
3. Remove the steering shaft lower coupling-to-worm gear roll pin.
4. Disconnect the wiring connectors at the steering column.
5. Remove the horn ring ornament assembly.
6. Disconnect the wire from the horn switch. Remove the screws that attach the horn ring and switch to the steering wheel and remove the ring and switch.
7. Remove the steering wheel attaching nut and washer and, using a puller, remove the steering wheel from the steering shaft.
8. Remove the turn signal lever.
9. Remove the screws that attach the steering column base plate to the floor pan. Remove the finish plate from under the instrument panel to expose the steering column mounting bracket.
10. On Fury, Polara and Monaco models, remove the automatic transmission shift indicator pointer from the shift tube bracket.
11. Remove the nuts or bolts that attach the steering column bracket to the instrument panel support. If shims are used between the bracket forward leg and the panel support, they must be installed in the same location when the column is installed.
12. Carefully pry steering shaft lower coupling from the steering

gear worm shaft and remove the steering column assembly from the vehicle. Use care not to scratch or damage the column during removal.

13. Remove the nut and washer that attaches the Pitman arm to the steering gear.
14. Using a puller, remove the steering arm from the gear.
15. Remove the bolts that attach the steering gear to the chassis and remove the gear from the vehicle.
16. To install the steering gear, position it on the chassis and install the retaining bolts. Align the master spline on the worm gear (12 o'clock position) with the master spline on the steering shaft coupling, making sure the front wheels and the steering wheel are in the straight ahead position.
17. Install the pin that attaches the coupling to the worm gear.
18. Position the steering column on the instrument panel and loosely install the nuts or bolts that attach the steering column bracket to the dash. Move the steering column and bracket up or down in the instrument panel support until the dimension between the steering shaft coupling and the gauge hole in the steering shaft is 13/16 in.

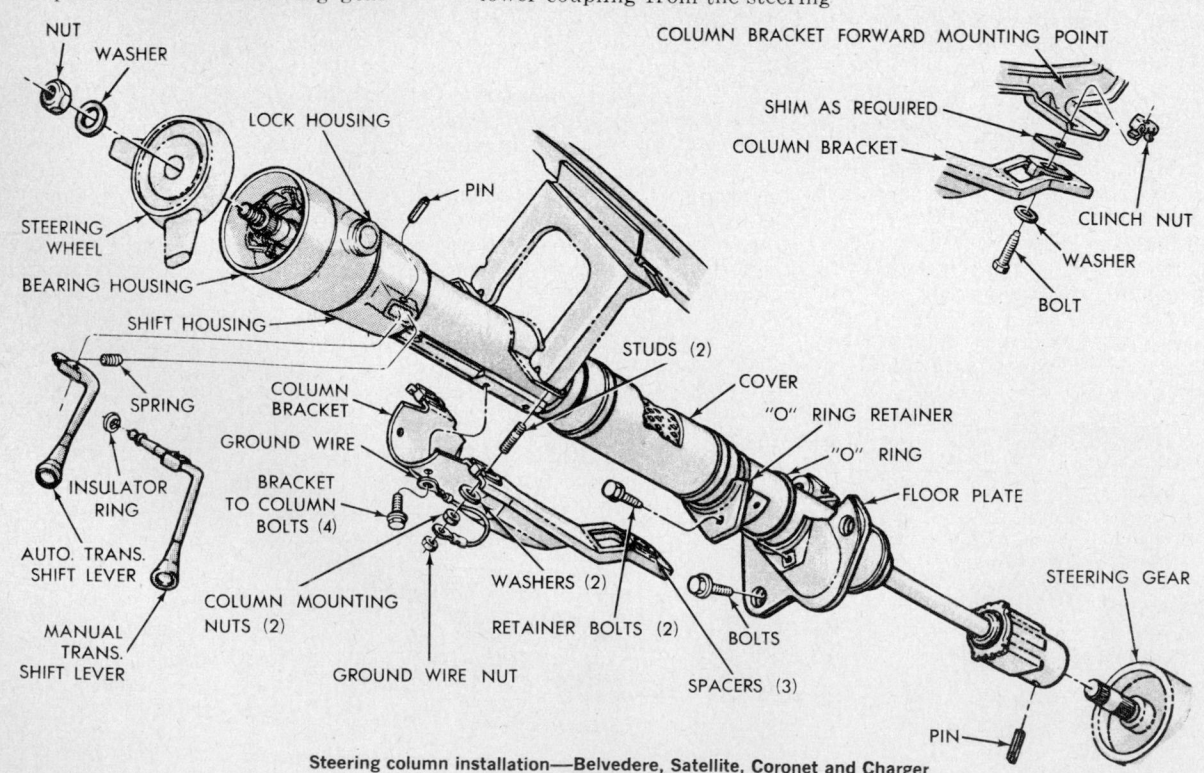

Steering column installation—Belvedere, Satellite, Coronet and Charger
(© Chrysler Corporation)

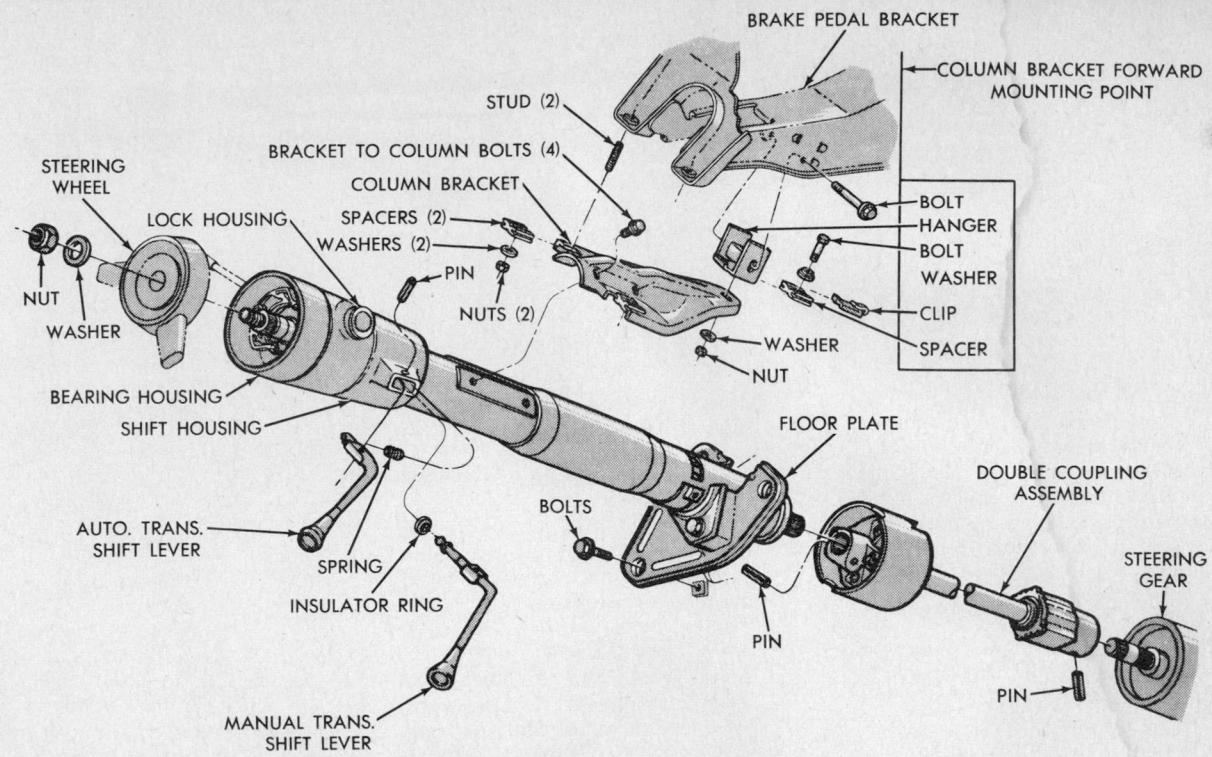

STEERING WHEEL

LOCK HOUSING

NUT

WASHER

BEARING HOUSING

SHIFT HOUSING

AUTO. TRANS. SHIFT LEVER

SPRING

INSULATOR RING

MANUAL TRANS. SHIFT LEVER

STUD (2)

BRACKET TO COLUMN BOLTS (4)

COLUMN BRACKET

SPACERS (2)

WASHERS (2)

PIN

NUTS (2)

BOLTS

PIN

BRAKE PEDAL BRACKET

COLUMN BRACKET FORWARD MOUNTING POINT

BOLT
HANGER
BOLT
WASHER
CLIP
SPACER

WASHER

NUT

FLOOR PLATE

DOUBLE COUPLING ASSEMBLY

STEERING GEAR

PIN

Steering column installation—Fury, Polara and Monaco (© Chrysler Corporation)

Clutch

Pedal Clearance Adjustment

All Models

1. Inspect condition of clutch pedal rubber stop. If stop is damaged, install new stop.
2. On six cylinder models disconnect the interlock rod by loosening rod swivel screw.
3. Adjust fork rod by turning self-locking self-adjusting nut to provide 5/32 in. free movement at end of fork. This movement will provide prescribed one inch play at pedal.

6 Cylinder

1. On six cylinder models. place transmission in neutral. The interlock pawl will enter slot in first-reverse lever.
2. Loosen swivel clamp bolt and slide swivel on rod to enter pawl. Install washers and clip. Hold interlock pawl forward and tighten swivel clamp bolt to 100 in. lbs. Clutch pedal must be in full return position during the adjustment.
3. Disengage clutch and shift half way to first or reverse. Clutch should now be held down by interlock to within one or two in. of floor.

Clutch Assembly Removal

The clutch assembly comes out

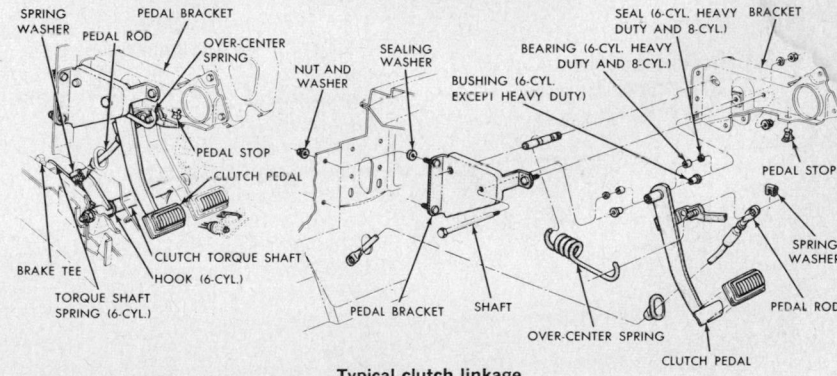

SPRING WASHER
PEDAL ROD
PEDAL BRACKET
OVER-CENTER SPRING
NUT AND WASHER
SEALING WASHER
BUSHING (6-CYL. EXCEPT HEAVY DUTY)
BEARING (6-CYL. HEAVY DUTY AND 8-CYL.)
SEAL (6-CYL. HEAVY DUTY AND 8-CYL.) BRACKET
PEDAL STOP
CLUTCH PEDAL
PEDAL STOP
CLUTCH PEDAL
CLUTCH TORQUE SHAFT HOOK (6-CYL.)
BRAKE TEE
TORQUE SHAFT SPRING (6-CYL.)
PEDAL BRACKET
SHAFT
OVER-CENTER SPRING
SPRING WASHER
PEDAL ROD

Typical clutch linkage

through the bottom of the flywheel housing.

1. Remove the transmission as described in the following transmission sections.
2. Remove the clutch underpan and the clutch throwout bearing and sleeve. Matchmark the clutch cover to flywheel. Reaching up from the bottom, remove the bolts that hold the clutch cover to the flywheel, a little at a time so as not to spring the cover. When all pressure is removed, remove the bolts and take the clutch out through the bottom of the flywheel housing.

Transmissions

Synchromesh Transmission Removal

Dodge and Plymouth have used

four synchromesh manual transmissions in recent years. Six cylinders use a three speed, top cover transmission with synchromesh on second and third. V8s up to 1970 use a similar three speed, top cover transmission with synchromesh on second and third. 1970-72 V8s use a new fully synchromesh, side cover three speed. All Dodge and Plymouth four speed cars use a fully synchromesh, side cover four speed.

Top Cover Three Speeds

1. Split the front universal joint and remove all attaching parts from the transmission, such as speedometer cable, ground cables, shift levers and rods, hand brake cables, etc.
2. Place a jack under the back of the engine and take a slight load on the jack. Remove the bolts that hold the transmission to the frame crossmember, then

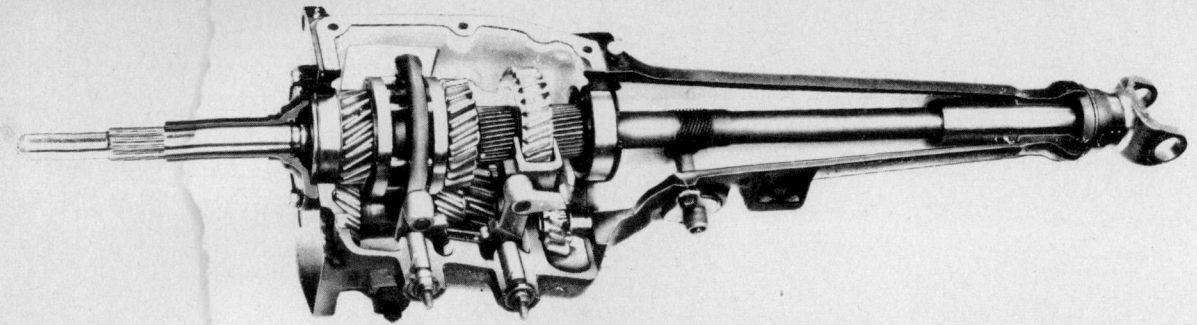

3-speed top cover manual transmission (© Chrysler Corp.)

take out the bolts that hold the crossmember to the frame. Let the crossmember come down.

3. Remove the two upper bolts that hold the transmission to the bell housing and replace them with two long pilot studs. Remove the two bottom bolts and slide the transmission assembly back along the two upper pilot studs until the clutch shaft clears the clutch hub. Slide off the end of the pilot shafts and lower to the floor.

4. Reverse the above for installation. Be sure not to allow the transmission to hang after the pinion has entered the clutch disc.

Fully Synchromesh, Side Cover Three Speed

1. Remove shift rods from transmission levers.
2. Drain transmission fluid.
3. Disconnect drive shaft at rear universal joint. Mark both parts for reassembly.
4. Carefully pull yoke out of transmission extension.
5. Disconnect speedometer and backup lights.
6. Remove part of exhaust if it blocks transmission.
7. Raise engine slightly and block in

place.
8. Support transmission with jack, and remove crossmember.
9. Remove transmission to clutch housing bolts.
10. Slide transmission to rear until drive pinion shaft clears. Clear clutch disc, lower transmission, and remove from vehicle.

Four Speed

1. Raise vehicle on a hoist and drain transmission.
2. Disconnect all shift controls from transmission levers. Remove three bolts securing shift unit to extension housing.
3. Disconnect propeller shaft at rear universal joint. Carefully pull yoke out of transmission extension.
4. Disconnect speedometer cable and backup light switch leads.
5. Disconnect left exhaust pipe or dual exhausts. Disconnect parking brake cable.
6. Raise engine slightly and block in place.
7. Disconnect transmission extension from crossmember.
8. Remove crossmember.
9. Support transmission with jack. Remove clutch housing to transmission bolts.
10. Slide transmission to rear until

drive pinion shaft clears clutch disc.
11. Lower transmission and remove from vehicle.

Manual Shift Adjustments
Column Mounted Shifter

Three Speed 1965-67 Dodge and Plymouth

1. With the second and third con-

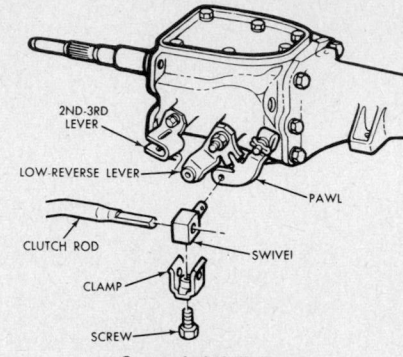

3-speed shift linkage
(© Chrysler Corp.)

trol rod disconnected from the lever on the column, and first and reverse control rod disconnected at the transmission lever, position both transmission levers in neutral.

2. Check for axial freedom of the shift levers in the column. If the outer ends of the levers move up or down along the column axis over 1/16 in., loosen the two upper bushing screws and rotate the plastic bushing, downward, until all of the axial play is eliminated. Retighten bushing screws.

3. Wedge a screwdriver between the crossover blade and the second and third lever, so that the crossover blade is engaged with both lever crossover pins.

4. Adjust the swivel on the end of second and third rod until the stub shaft of the swivel enters the hole in the column lever. Install washers and clip. Tighten swivel lock nut to 70 in. lbs.

5. Slide the clamp and swivel on the end of the first and reverse control rod until the swivel stub shaft enters the hole in the transmission lever. Install washers and clip. Tighten the swivel clamp bolt to 100 in. lbs.

Three Speed 1968-69 Coronet, Charger and Belvedere

1. Remove second-third swivel from steering column lever and first-reverse swivel from transmission lever.

4-speed transmission
(© Chrysler Corp.)

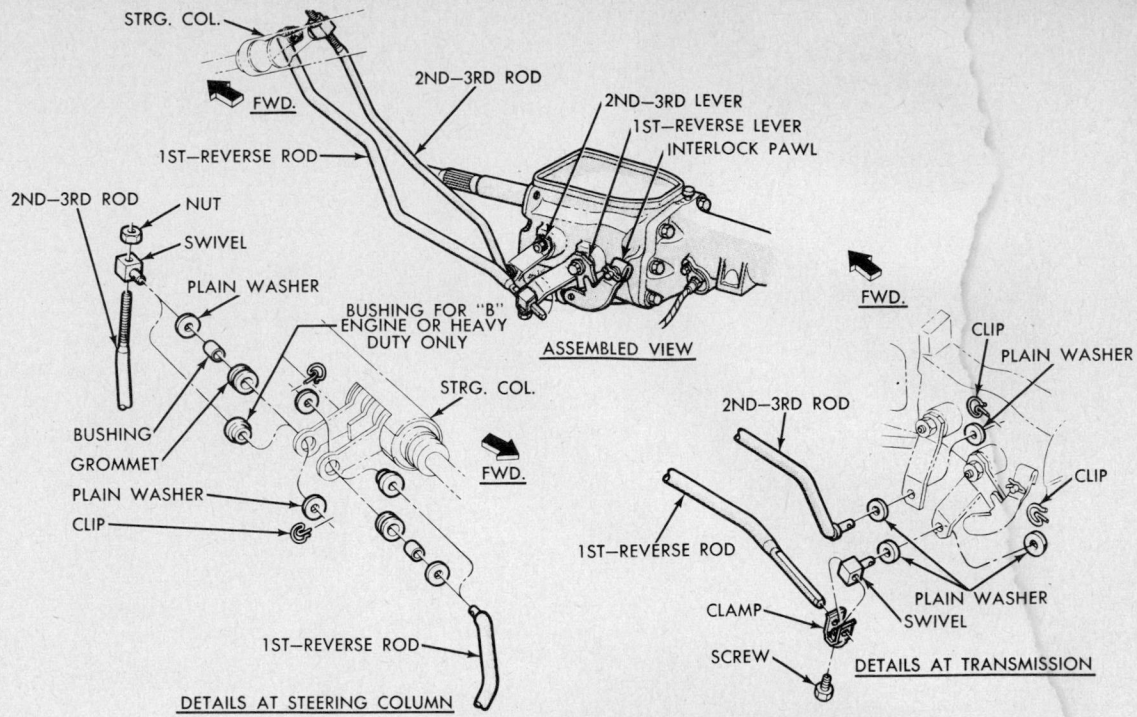

1968-69 Coronet, Charger, and Belvedere gearshift linkage (© Chrysler Corp.)

2. Make sure transmission shift levers are in neutral (middle detent) position.

3. Loosen lock nut and adjust second-third swivel so it will enter second-third lever at steering column while hand lever on steering column is held 12 degrees above horizontal position. Install washers and clip. Tighten swivel nut to 70 in. lbs.

4. Place screwdriver or suitable tool between cross-over blade and second-third lever at steering column so that both lever pins are engaged by cross-over blade.

5. Adjust first reverse rod swivel by loosening clamp bolt and sliding swivel along rod so it will enter first-reverse lever at transmission. Install washers and slip. Tighten swivel bolt to 100 in. lbs.

6. Remove tool from cross-over blade at steering column and shift through all gears to check adjustment and cross over smoothness.

Three Speed 1968-69 Polara, Monaco, and Fury

1. Remove first-reverse rod swivel from steering column and second-third rod swivel from torque shaft lever.

2. Make sure transmission shift levers are in neutral (middle de-

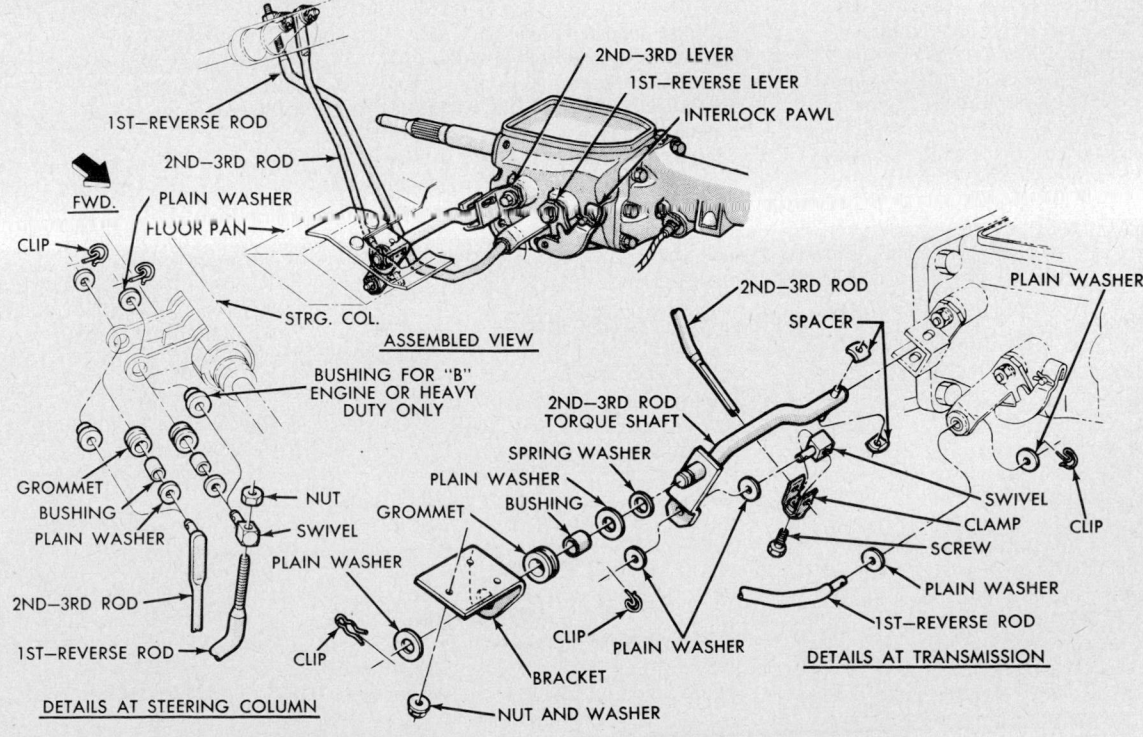

1968-69 Polara, Monaco, Fury and VIP gearshift linkage (© Chrysler Corp.)

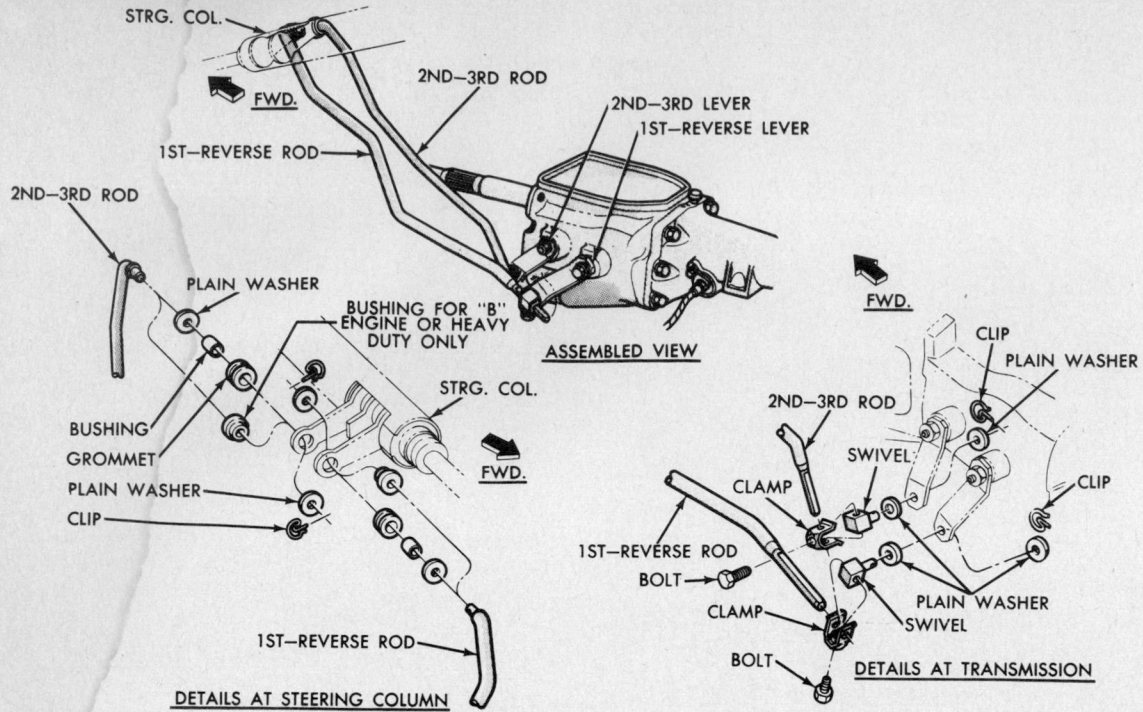

1970-72 three speed gearshift linkage (© Chrysler Corp.)

tent) position.

3. Adjust second-third rod swivel by loosening clamp bolt and sliding swivel along rod so it will enter torque shaft lever while hand lever on steering column is held 12 degrees above horizontal position. Install washers and clip. Tighten swivel clamp bolt to 100 in. lbs.

4. Place screwdriver or suitable tool between cross-over blade and second-third lever at steering column so that both lever pins are engaged by cross-over blade.

5. Adjust first-reverse rod swivel by loosening lock nut and turning swivel so it will enter first-reverse lever at steering column. Install washers and clip. Tighten swivel lock nut to 70 in. lbs.

6. Remove tool from cross-over blade at steering column and shift through all gears to check adjustment and cross-over smoothness.

Three Speed 1970-72

1. Remove both shift rod swivels from transmission shift levers. Make sure transmission shift levers are in neutral (middle detent) position.

2. Move shift lever to line up locating slots in bottom of steering column shift housing and bearing housing. Install suitable tool in slot and lock ignition switch.

3. Place screwdriver or suitable tool between crossover blade and second-third lever at steering column so that both lever pins are engaged by cross-over blade.

4. Set first-reverse lever on transmission to reverse position (rotate clockwise).

5. Adjust first-reverse rod swivel by loosening clamp bolt and sliding swivel along rod so it will enter first-reverse lever at transmission. Install washers and clip. Tighten swivel bolt to 100 in. lbs.

6. Remove gearshift housing locating tool, unlock ignition switch, and shift column lever into neutral position.

7. Adjust second-third rod swivel by loosening clamp bolt and sliding swivel along rod so it will enter second-third lever at transmission. Install washers and clip. Tighten swivel bolt to 100 in. lbs.

8. Remove tool from crossover blade at steering column, and shift through all gears to check adjustment and cross-over smoothness.

Floor Mounted Shifter

1965 Four Speed

1. Remove the shift boot attaching screws, and slide the boot up on the shift lever. If the shifter is not equipped with alignment holes, have an assistant hold the shifter in the true Neutral position.

2. Disconnect all the shift rods at the adjusting swivels.

3. Bend a ¼ in. diameter rod to a right angle, and insert through the aligning holes in the control rod levers and the slots provided in the gear shift support.

4. Adjust the length of the shift

rods until the swivel stub shafts match the control rod lever holes. Install the stub shafts and secure with clips.

5. Remove the ¼ in. diameter aligning rod.

6. With transmission hand shift lever in third or fourth speed detent position, adjust the lever stop screws (front and rear) to provide from .020 to .040 in. clearance between the lever and the stops. Tighten adjusting screw locknuts.

7. Test linkage adjustment for ease of shifting and crossover operation.

Caution   Accuracy of adjustment is very important because there is no reverse gear interlock to prevent engaging two gears at the same time.

8. Slide the boot down the shift lever shaft to the floor and secure with attaching screws.

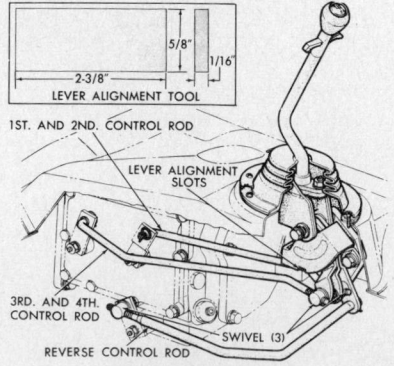

4-speed shift linkage
(© Chrysler Corp.)

1966-72 Three and Four Speed

Many Dodge and Plymouth four speed transmissions use Hurst shift linkages. To adjust these linkages, see Hurst Shift Linkage section. Adjust Chrysler Corporation linkages as follows.

1. Make up a lever aligning tool from 1/16 in. thick metal as in illustration.
2. With transmission in neutral, disconnect all control rods from the transmission levers.
3. Insert lever aligning tool through the slots in the levers and against the back plate. This locks the levers in neutral.
4. With all transmission levers in neutral, adjust the length of the control rods so they enter the transmission levers freely without rearward or forward movement.
5. Install control rod flat washers and retainers. Remove the aligning tool.
6. Check linkage for ease of shifting into all gears and for ease of crossover.

Automatic Transmission

TORQUEFLITE B (aluminum case) transmissions are used with the Slant 6 and V8 models up to 1965.

TORQUEFLITE (A-727-A and B) is a version of the Torqueflite B, but with no rear pump, and is used in all models beginning 1966.

Gearshift Linkage Adjustment Column Shift 1965-72

1. Place gearshift selector lever in PARK position and loosen control rod swivel clamp screw a few turns.

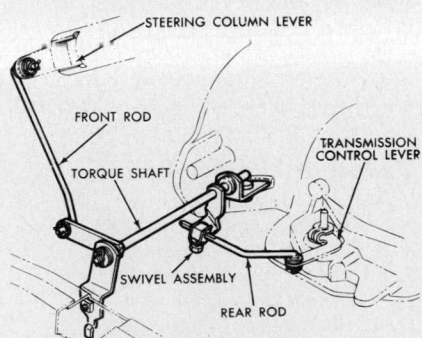

Automatic transmission column shift linkage
(© Chrysler Corp.)

2. Move transmission lever all the way to rear (in PARK detent).
3. With control lever on transmission in PARK position detent and selector lever in PARK position, tighten swivel clamp screw.

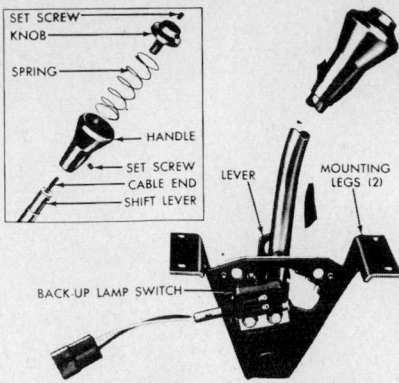

Automatic transmission console shifter
(© Chrysler Corp.)

Gearshift Linkage Adjustment Console Shift 1965-72

1. Place gearshift selector lever in PARK position and loosen lower rod swivel clamp screw a few turns.
2. Move transmission lever all the way to rear (in PARK detent).
3. With control lever on transmission in PARK position detent, and selector lever in PARK position, tighten swivel clamp screw or adjusting lever bolt securely.

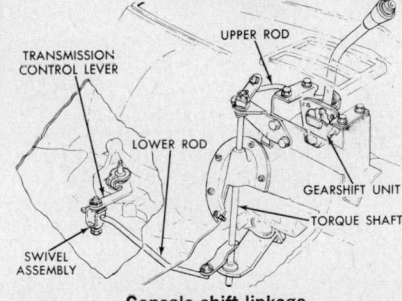

Console shift linkage
(© Chrysler Corp.)

Neutral Start Switch

The neutral switch is mounted in the transmission case on all models. When the transmission manual lever is placed in either the Park or Neutral position, a cam, which is attached to the transmission throttle lever inside the transmission, contacts the neutral start switch and provides a ground to complete the starter solenoid circuit. On late model Dodges and Plymouths, the back-up light switch has been incorporated into the neutral switch. The combination neutral and back-up light switch can be identified by the three electrical terminals on the rear of the switch. On this type of switch, the center terminal is for the neutral switch and the two outer terminals are for the back-up lights.

NOTE: in order for the neutral start switch to function properly, the transmission manual linkage must be properly adjusted and the actuator cam in the transmission must be centered in the neutral switch mounting hole in the transmission.

Removal and Installation

Remove transmission and torque converter as an assembly or the converter drive plate, pump bushing, and oil seal will be damaged. The drive plate will not support a load, therefore, do not allow weight of transmission to rest on drive plate.

1. Connect remote control starter switch to starter solenoid and position switch so engine can be rotated from under vehicle.
2. Disconnect secondary (High Tension) cable from ignition coil.
3. Remove cover plate from in front of converter to provide access to converter drain plug and mounting bolts.
4. Rotate engine with remote control starter switch to bring drain plug to six o'clock position. Drain torque converter and transmission.
5. Mark converter and drive plate to aid in reassembly. There is an offset hole in crankshaft flange bolt circle, inner and outer circle of holes in drive plate, and four tapped holes in front face of converter so their parts will be installed in original position.
6. Rotate engine with remote control switch to locate two converter to drive plate bolts at five and seven o'clock positions. Remove bolts, rotate engine and remove two more bolts. Do not

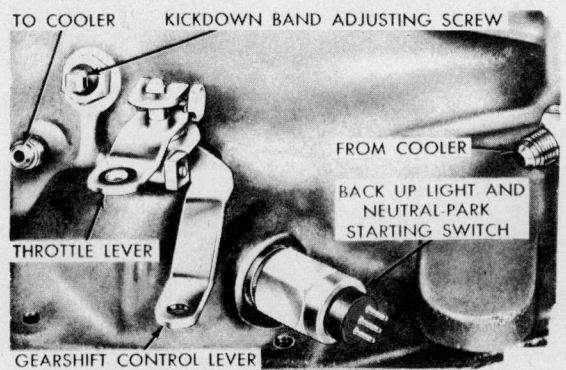

Combination neutral start and back up light switch
(© Chrysler Corporation)

rotate converter by prying as this will distort drive plate. Do not engage starter if drive plate is not attached to converter with at least one bolt or if transmission to block bolts have been loosened.

7. Disconnect battery.
8. Remove starter.
9. Disconnect wire from neutral start switch.
10. Disconnect gearshift rod from transmission lever. Remove gearshift torque shaft from transmission housing and left side rail. On console shifts, remove two bolts securing gearshift torque shaft lower bracket to extension housing. Swing bracket out of way for transmission removal. Disconnect gearshift rod from transmission lever.
11. Disconnect throttle rod from bellcrank at left side of transmission bell housing.
12. Disconnect oil cooler lines at transmission and remove oil filler tube. Disconnect speedometer cable.
13. Disconnect drive shaft at rear universal joint. Carefully pull shaft assembly out of extension housing.
14. Remove transmission mount to extension housing bolts.
15. Raise engine slightly and block in place.
16. Remove crossmember attaching bolts and remove crossmember.
17. Support transmission with jack.
18. Attach a small C-clamp to edge of converter housing to hold converter in place during removal of transmission.
19. Remove converter housing retaining bolts. Carefully work transmission to rear off engine dowels and disengage converter hub from end of crankshaft.
20. Lower and remove transmission. Remove C-clamp and remove converter. Reverse procedure to install.

U Joints, Drive Lines

Cross- and Bearing-Type Joint Disassembly

The cross- and bearing-type joint can be identified easily since the joint is not covered.

1. To disassemble the joint, remove the four bolts that hold the two bearing assemblies to the companion flange and knock the bearings off the flange.
2. To remove the bearings from the yoke, first remove the bearing retainer lock washers or C-washers, then pressing on one of the bearings, drive the bearing in

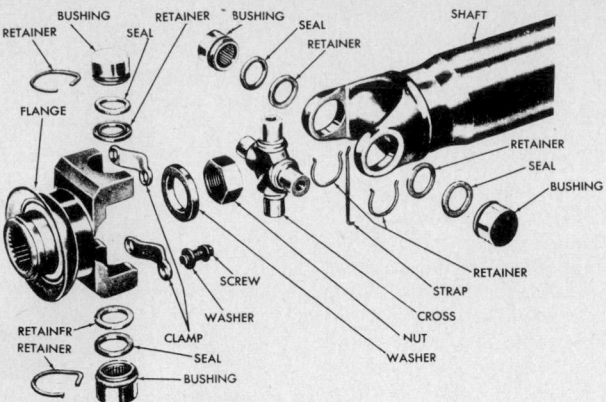

Exploded view—cross and bearing type universal joint
(© Chrysler Corp.)

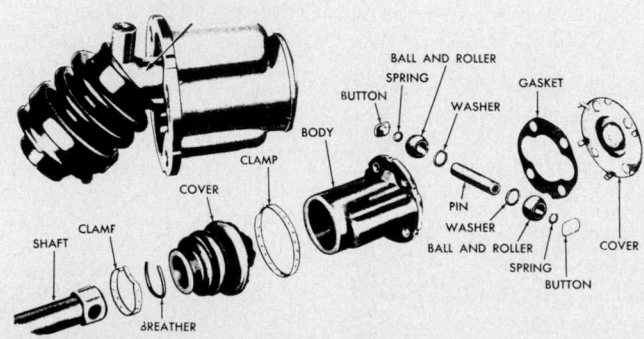

Exploded view—ball and trunnion type universal joint
(© Chrysler Corp.)

toward the center of the joint. This will force the cross to push the opposite bearing out of the universal joint yoke. After it has been pushed all the way out of the yoke, pull up the cross slightly and pack some washers under it. Then press on the end of the cross from which the bearing was just removed to force the first bearing out of the yoke.
3. Perhaps the easiest way to reassemble is to start both bearing retainers into the yoke at the same time, hold the cross carefully in the fingers and squeeze both bearings in a vise or heavy C-clamp. Driving the bearings into place usually cocks the little rollers, greatly reducing the life of the bearings.
4. Reinstall the locking devices.

Ball- and Trunnion-Type Joint Disassembly

The housing of the ball- and trunnion-type joint is held to its companion flange by four bolts. Remove the four bolts and pry the cover assembly backward away from the companion flange so that the shaft can be lowered. If two ball and trunnion type joints are used, both must be disconnected from their companion flanges in order to get the driveshaft over to the bench.

Remove the grease cover which will release the centering spring.

Remove the centering button spring and the ball and roller assemblies from the cross pin. Supporting the propeller shaft ball, press out the cross pin.

The cover and boot assembly can then be slid off the end of the propeller shaft.

Some models use a cross- and bearing-type joint at the rear joint, and a ball- and trunnion-type at the front.

Ball- and trunnion-type universal joints do not require a slip yoke since the driveshaft can work back and forth in the universal joint housing.

Driveshaft Center Bearing

Some models use a three universal joint drive line having two driveshafts and a center support bearing. The center support bearing and housing assembly are removed with the front driveshaft.

Split the rear universal joint and remove the rear driveshaft.

Disconnect the front driveshaft at the transmission flange and remove the bolts that hold the center bearing housing to the frame. Take off the center bearing housing, together with the front shaft.

On the bench, remove the nut that holds the center universal joint flange to the driveshaft and, with a puller,

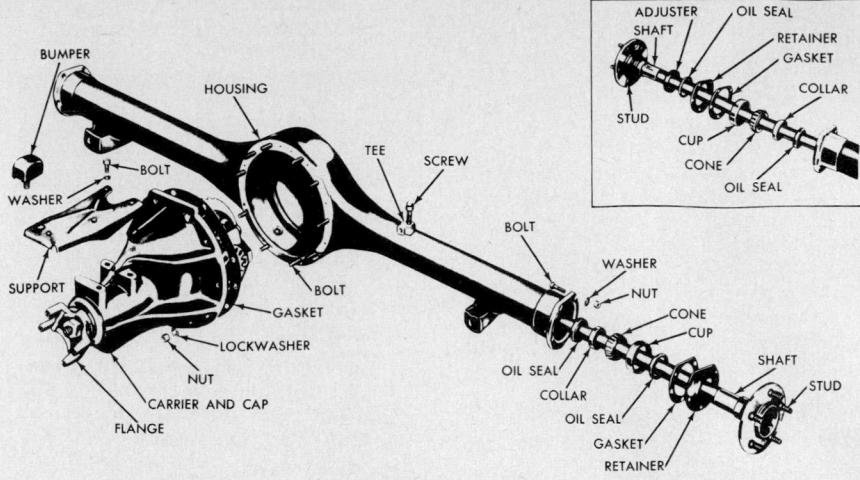

8¾ in. rear axle—1965-72 (© Chrysler Corp.)

draw off the flange. The bearing and housing assembly can then be pulled off the front of the shaft.

Rear Axles, Suspension

Troubleshooting and Adjustment

General instructions covering the troubles of the drive axle and how to repair and adjust it, together with information on installation of rear axle bearings and grease seals, are given in the Unit Repair Section.

Capacities of the drive axle are given in the Capacities tables.

Rear Shock Absorber Replacement

On all models, a direct acting shock absorber is used. To remove it, simply detach at the top and bottom and lift off the car.

Rear Spring Replacement

On all models, the rear spring is hung on the frame at the front and through a shackle at the rear end.

To remove the spring, first remove the shock absorber and take the weight off the car on a jack stand in front of the rear spring, high enough so that the rear axle will hang from its springs. Then, place a jack under the axle and take some of the download off the spring.

Remove the four nuts that hold the U-bolt to the axle housing, and let the lockplate fall down.

Take out the two nuts that hold the rear shackle, the top one to the frame, the bottom one to the spring, and drive off the rear shackle.

Remove the single bolt that holds the spring at the front, and lower the spring to the floor.

Rear Axle Assembly Removal

To remove the rear axle assembly on all models, detach the brake line at the T-fitting, detach the rear univer-sal joint, remove the rear shock absorbers, remove the nuts that hold the U-bolts to the rear springs and rear axle housing and disconnect the spring at the back link. Let the spring drop to the floor.

Jack stand should be placed on the frame in front of the front spring, or the body should be raised with a chain block attached to the back bumper.

If it is difficult or impossible to raise the car sufficiently high to let the rear wheels pass under the fenders, the rear wheels can be removed. Roll the rear axle assembly out from underneath the car.

On models that use a rear torsion bar, it will be necessary to detach the torsion bar before removing the axle.

Replace the rear axle assembly by reversing the removal procedure.

Radio

Radio Removal

1965 Coronet and Belvedere

On vehicles equipped with air conditioning, service radio through glove box opening in instrument panel.
1. Disconnect battery.
2. Remove radio control knobs.
3. From under instrument panel disconnect radio feed wire at fuse block.
4. Disconnect antenna and radio speaker leads.
5. Remove screw attaching radio mounting bracket to instrument panel lower reinforcement.
6. Loosen top screw on radio mounting bracket and remove mounting bracket.
7. From front of radio remove two nuts attaching radio to the instrument panel and remove radio. Reverse procedure to install.

1965 Dodge 880, Polara, Monaco, and Plymouth Fury
1. Disconnect battery.
2. Remove radio knobs.
3. Remove radio mounting nuts.
4. From under instrument panel disconnect speaker leads, radio feed wire, and antenna lead cable at radio.
5. Remove radio to instrument panel bracket and remove radio. Reverse procedure to install.

1966 Dodge Polara, Monaco and Plymouth Fury 1967 Belvedere and Satellite
1. Disconnect battery.
2. Remove control knobs and two mounting nuts.
3. On air-conditioned cars, remove spot cooler hoses and distribution duct, then disconnect speaker, power supply and antenna leads.
4. Remove radio support bracket.
5. Rotate front end of radio down and remove radio from under the dash panel.

1966-67 Coronet and Charger and 1966 Belvedere
1. Disconnect battery.
2. Remove upper half of glove compartment and disconnect wires from speaker.
3. Remove radio knobs and two mounting nuts.
4. Disconnect both defroster hoses at the heater.
5. Disconnect antenna cable and radio feed wires at connector.
6. Loosen radio support bracket retaining nut at radio and remove support bracket mounting screw from lower edge of instrument panel.
7. Remove radio from under instrument panel.
8. To install, reverse removal procedure.

1967 Polara and Monaco
1. Disconnect battery.
2. Remove heater or air-conditioner knobs.
3. Remove five center bezel retaining screws (3 in underside of lip and 2 in face of bezel.) Remove the bezel.
4. Remove ash tray and housing.
5. Disconnect right defroster hose at heater outlet. Tie hose out of way.
6. From ash tray opening, remove two heater or air-conditioner control mounting nuts and move the control assembly out of the way. It is not necessary to disconnect control cables.
7. Disconnect radio feed wires and antenna cable from the radio.
8. Remove two radio mounting screws from front of panel. Remove radio.

NOTE: on air-conditioned cars, the distribution duct must be removed.
9. To install, reverse removal procedure.

1967-68 Fury and VIP

1. Remove instrument cluster bezel. See Instrument Cluster Removal in this section.
2. From under panel, loosen radio support bracket nut at upper end.
3. Disconnect feed wires, speaker wires, and antenna cable at radio.
4. From front of instrument panel, remove three radio mounting screws and lift radio out of panel.
5. With radio on bench, remove knobs and four lens retaining screws. Remove lens. Reverse procedure to install.

1968 Polara and Monaco

1. Disconnect battery.
2. Disconnect cigar lighter lead and remove ash tray and housing.
3. Remove automatic temperature control, if so equipped.
4. Remove center air outlets, if so equipped.
5. Remove radio mounting bracket. (Loosen one nut at radio, remove one screw in lower reinforcement, and swing bracket toward glove box to clear area for radio removal.)
6. Remove eight bezel mounting screws (three in upper center trim bezel, three in upper right trim bezel, and two in lower center trim bezel).
7. Pull bezel out slightly and disconnect fader control harness and remove two fader control mounting screws from rear of fader and reverberator, if so equipped.
8. Remove reverberator knob, if so equipped.
9. Slide center trim bezel out of upper moulding toward cluster.
10. Remove two radio mounting screws.
11. Reach through ash tray opening and disconnect antenna leads and electrical leads.
12. Remove radio from panel by tipping radio down and lowering through ash tray opening. Reverse procedure to install.

1968-70 Charger

1. Disconnect battery.
2. Remove radio finish plate.
3. On air conditioned vehicles, remove lower center air duct, left air duct, and upper center duct
4. Remove radio mounting bracket.
5. Remove two screws mounting radio to front of instrument panel.
6. Disconnect antenna and speaker leads.

7. Remove radio from under panel. Reverse procedure to install.

1968-70 Coronet and 1969-70 Belvedere and Satellite

1. Disconnect battery.
2. Remove radio upper trim panel.
3. Remove radio finish plate.
4. Remove radio rear mounting nut from mounting bracket.
5. Disconnect electrical wiring and antenna lead.
6. Remove two mounting screws from front of instrument panel.
7. Remove radio from instrument panel.

1968 Belvedere and Satellite and 1969-70 Polara and Monaco

1. Disconnect battery.
2. Remove automatic temperature control, if so equipped.
3. Remove radio bezel.
4. Remove two radio mounting bolts at front of instrument panel.
5. Remove air conditioner duct, if so equipped.
6. Disconnect electrical leads and antenna lead.
7. Loosen radio mounting bracket stud nut and slide radio and stud towards front of car from mounting bracket.
8. Carefully remove radio from under panel to avoid damaging electrical leads from main harness or automatic temperature control asperator tube. Reverse procedure to install.

1969-72 Fury, VIP, and 1971-72 Polara and Monaco

1. Disconnect battery.
2. Remove nine lamp panel mounting screws, lower lamp panel assembly slightly, disconnect lamp harness from main harness, and remove lamp panel from instrument panel.
3. Remove steering column cover.
4. Remove radio trim bezel mounting screws and bezel.
5. Remove center lower air conditioner duct, if so equipped.
6. Disconnect electrical leads and antenna lead at radio.
7. Remove radio support mounting bracket.
8. Remove two radio mounting bolts.
9. Move radio down through bottom of instrument panel carefully to avoid damage to vacuum hoses and electrical leads. Reverse procedure to install.

1971-72 Satellite, Coronet and Charger

1. Disconnect the negative battery cable.
2. Remove the ash tray.
3. Remove the radio control knobs and retaining nuts.

4. Disconnect the lead wires from the radio and remove the radio from the vehicle.

Windshield Wipers

Motor R & R

1965-70 Fury, Polara and Monaco

1. Remove the windshield wiper arm and blade assemblies. On 1969-70 models insert a 0.090 in. pin in the hole in the base of the wiper arm to release the assemblies from the pivots.
2. Remove the windshield lower moulding.
3. Remove the cowl grille.
4. Remove the nut that attaches the wiper link to the wiper motor drive pin or crank and disconnect the link from the motor.
5. Disconnect the wiper motor wiring at the multiple connector.
6. Remove the nuts that attach the wiper motor to the cowl panel and remove the motor through the cowl grille opening.

1965 Belvedere, Satellite and Coronet

NOTE: on models equipped with air conditioning, the wiper motor must be serviced through the glove box opening in the instrument panel.
1. Working under the dash, remove the clips that attach the wiper drive links to the wiper pivots. Lift the wiper links off the pivot pins.
2. Disconnect the wiper motor wiring at the multiple connector.
3. Remove the support brace that connects the wiper motor mounting bracket to the instrument panel.
4. Remove the four nuts that attach the wiper motor mounting bracket to the studs on the cowl panel.
5. Remove the wiper motor, mounting bracket and linkage from under the dash by pulling the assembly down and to the right. Remove the assembly from the vehicle through the right door opening.

1966 Belvedere, Satellite and Coronet

1. Disconnect the negative battery cable.
2. Disconnect the wiper motor wiring at the multiple connector (engine side of the firewall).
3. Remove the three wiper motor mounting nuts and pull the motor out far enough to gain access to the drive crank.

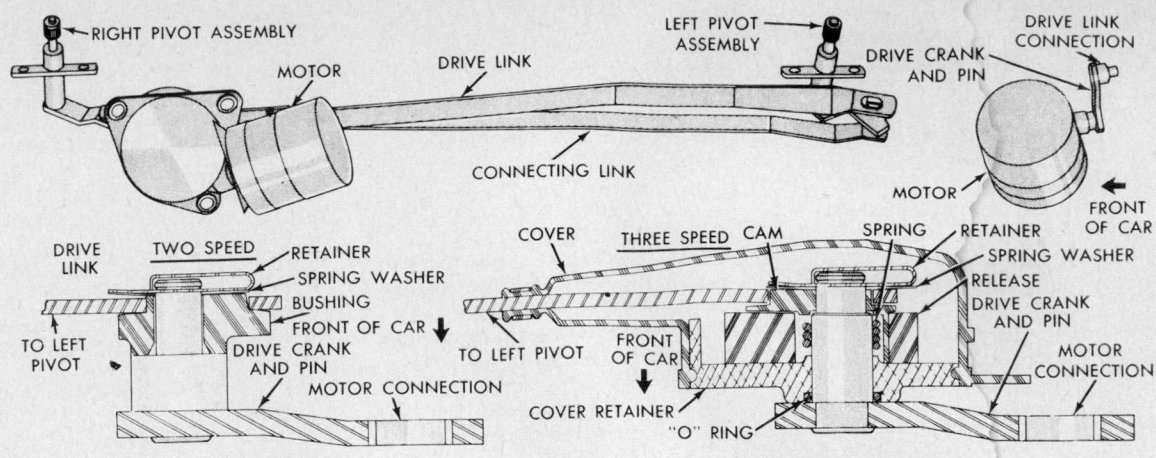

Windshield wiper system—Fury, Polara and Monaco (© Chrysler Corporation)

4. Rotate the crank until the drive link retainer is accessible.
5. Using a short screwdriver, carefully pry the lip of the retainer over the drive link pivot pin and remove the retainer and spring washer.
6. Remove the motor from the vehicle.

1967-70 Belvedere, Satellite, Coronet and Charger and All 1971-72 with Non-Concealed Wipers

1. Disconnect the negative battery cable.
2. Disconnect the wiper motor wiring at the multiple connector.
3. On models without air conditioning, working under the dash, remove the nut that attaches the drive link to the wiper motor and disconnect the drive link from the motor. Remove the nuts that attach the wiper motor to the studs in the cowl panel and remove the motor from the vehicle.
4. On models equipped with air conditioning, remove the instrument cluster to gain access to the left wiper pivot. Remove the drive link retaining clip from the left pivot. Remove the drive link and felt washer from the left pivot. Remove the wiper motor mounting nuts. Work the motor off the mounting studs far enough to gain access to the nut that attaches the drive link to the wiper motor. *Do not force or pry the wiper motor off the mounting studs as this could damage the wiper drive link.* Using a 1/2 in. open end wrench, remove the motor crank arm nut. Remove the arm from the wiper motor and remove the motor from the vehicle.

All 1971-72 with Concealed Wipers

See Chrysler section.

Linkage

1965-70 Belvedere, Satellite, Coronet and Charger

If car is air-conditioned, remove glove compartment to gain access to right pivot retainer.

1. Disconnect the negative battery cable. Remove the wiper arm and blade assemblies.
2. Remove the link retaining clip from the right pivot. On 1966-67 models, remove the fuse box and position it out of the way.
3. Remove wiper motor mounting nuts and pull motor out far enough to remove drive link from drive crank arm.
4. From under the panel, remove left pivot mounting nuts and right pivot retainer.
5. Remove the two links and left pivot as an assembly from under the panel or through the glove compartment.

1965-69 Fury, Polara and Monaco

1. Remove the wiper arm and blade assemblies.
2. Remove the windshield lower moulding.
3. Remove the cowl grille.
4. To remove the right pivot, disconnect the connecting link from the pivot, remove the bolts that attach the pivot to the cowl and remove the pivot.
5. To remove the left pivot, disconnect the connecting link from

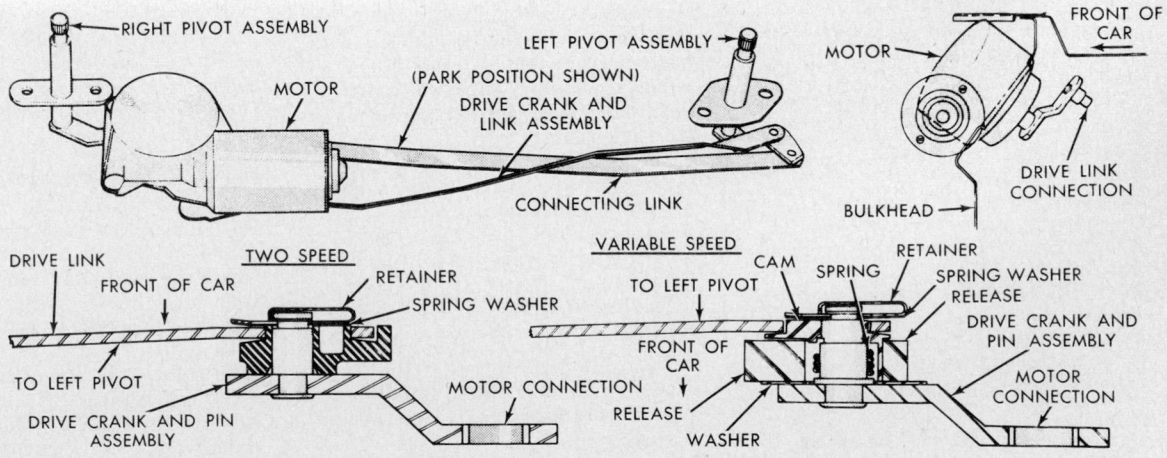

Windshield wiper system—Satellite, Belvedere, Coronet and Charger
(© Chrysler Corporation)

the right pivot. Disconnect the drive crank from the wiper motor. Remove the bolts that attach the left pivot to the cowl and remove the pivot and links through the cowl opening.

1970 Fury, Polara and Monaco

1. Remove the wiper arm and blade assemblies.
2. Remove the cowl screen.
3. Remove the crank arm nut and crank arm from the wiper motor.
4. Remove the bolts that attach the right and left pivots to the body.
5. Remove the pivots and linkage from the vehicle as an assembly through the cowl opening.

1971-72 All Models with Non-Concealed Wipers

1. Remove the wiper arm and blade assemblies.
2. If equipped with air conditioning, remove the left spot cooler duct to gain access to the left wiper pivot. Remove the glove box to gain access to the right wiper pivot.
3. Insert a wide blade screwdriver between the wiper link and the pivot crank arm and gently pry the link and plastic bushing from the pivot.
4. Remove the nut that attaches the pivot to the body of the vehicle and remove the pivot.

1971-72 All Models with Concealed Wipers

See Chrysler section.

Heater System

Heater Assembly R & R

1965 Belvedere, Satellite and Coronet

1. Disconnect battery.
2. Drain cooling system below heater hose level and disconnect heater hoses.
3. Remove air intake duct from blower.
4. Remove screw holding blower to plenum bracket.
5. Disconnect actuator lines.
6. Disconnect heater wires from left side of heater.
7. Disconnect heater ground wire.
8. Remove control lever cable from control valve.
9. Remove defroster tubes from heater housing.
10. From engine compartment, remove nuts and washers attaching heater assembly to dash panel.
11. Remove heater to dash panel attaching screws.
12. Remove assembly from car.
13. Remove control valve screws and

remove valve by pulling it straight out from housing. The valve is held to core by use of an O-ring.
14. Remove heater to core screws and remove core assembly.
15. Install in reverse of above.

1965 Fury

1. Disconnect battery.
2. Disconnect heater hoses at dash panel. Plug heater hose fittings to prevent coolant spillage.
3. Under instrument panel, remove bracket, top of heater to dash.
4. Remove defroster hoses at heater.
5. Disconnect wires at blower motor resistor.
6. Remove glove compartment.
7. Disconnect cables at heater end.
8. Unclamp flexible connector at right end of heater. Do not remove connector.
9. Pull carpet or mat from under instrument panel.
10. From engine compartment, remove nuts attaching heater assembly to dash panel.
11. Pull assembly toward rear of vehicle until studs are clear of panel. Rotate heater assembly until studs are down and remove heater from under instrument panel.
12. Install in reverse of above.

1965 Dodge Except Coronet; 1966-70 Belvedere, Satellite, Coronet and Charger

1. Drain radiator and disconnect battery.
2. Remove the glove box.
3. Disconnect heater hoses at bulkhead. Plug hose fittings on heater to prevent spilling coolant on trim when removing heater.
4. From under instrument panel remove heater to cowl support bracket.
5. Remove defroster hoses and disconnect wiring from heater motor resistor.
6. Disconnect fresh air vent control and shut off door cables at heater from under instrument panel. Reaching through glove box, disconnect temperature control door cable.
7. From inside engine compartment, remove three nuts that mount heater to bulkhead.
8. Rotate heater assembly until mounting studs are up and carefully remove heater from under instrument panel.
9. Reverse procedure to install.

1966-68 Fury, Polara and Monaco

1. Disconnect battery.
2. Disconnect hoses from heater and plug fittings to prevent coolant from leaking and spilling on

inside of body when removed.
3. Remove bracket from top of heater to dash panel.
4. Remove defroster hoses at heater and vacuum actuator hose.
5. Disconnect wire at blower motor resistor.
6. Remove glove compartment.
7. Disconnect control cable at heater end.
8. Unclamp connector at right end of heater. Do not remove connector.
9. Pull carpet or mat from under instrument panel.
10. From inside engine compartment, remove nuts that attach heater assembly to dash panel.
11. Pull heater toward rear to clear mounting studs from dash panel and rotate heater until studs are down, then remove heater from panel.

1969-72 Fury, Polara and Monaco

1. Disconnect battery and drain radiator.
2. Disconnect heater hoses at dash panel. Plug hose fittings on heater to prevent spilling coolant on trim.
3. Slide front seat back to allow room.
4. Disconnect radio antenna.
5. Disconnect electrical conductors from blower motor resistor block on face of housing.
6. Remove vacuum hoses from trunk lock if so equipped.
7. Remove control cables from defroster door crank and heat shut off door crank.
8. Remove bottom retaining nut from support bracket and swing bracket up and out of way.
9. In engine compartment remove four retaining nuts from studs on engine side housing.
10. Remove locating bolt from bottom center of passenger side housing.
11. Roll or tip housing out from under instrument panel.
12. Remove temperature control cable retaining clip and cable from heat shut off door crank.

1971-72 Satellite, Coronet and Charger

1. Disconnect the negative battery cable.
2. Drain the cooling system.
3. Disconnect the heater hoses from the heater core tubes at the dash panel. Plug the core tubes to prevent spilling coolant on the interior of the car.
4. Remove the three mounting nuts from the studs around the blower motor and remove the flange and air seal.
5. Disconnect the antenna lead

wire from the radio and position it out of the way.

6. Remove the screw that attaches the housing to the support rod for the plenum. It is located on the right-side of the housing above the outside air opening.
7. Disconnect the three air door cables.
8. Disconnect the wires from the blower motor resistor.
9. Tip the heater assembly down and out from under the dash.

Blower Motor

1965 Belvedere, Satellite and Coronet

1. Disconnect battery.
2. Disconnect heater ground wire.
3. Loosen air intake duct clamp at blower end and remove duct from blower assembly.
4. Remove screw which holds blower to plenum.
5. Remove blower assembly from housing.
6. From inside housing, disconnect blower assembly wires.
7. Install in reverse of above.

1965 Fury, Polara and Monaco 1966-68 All Models 1969-72 Belvedere, Satellite, Coronet and Charger

1. Remove heater as outlined in Heater Removal.
2. Disconnect wiring from blower motor to heater assembly.
3. Remove motor cooler tube.
4. Remove heater back plate assembly from heater.
5. Remove fan from motor shaft.
6. Remove blower motor from back plate.

1969-72 Fury, Polara and Monaco

The blower motor is mounted to the engine side housing under the right front fender, between the inner fender shield and the fender. The inner fender shield must be removed to service the blower motor.

1. Raise the hood and remove all brackets and clips that attach to the inner fender shield under the hood.
2. Raise the car on a hoist and remove the right front tire and wheel assembly.
3. From under the fender, remove the bolts that attach the inner fender shield to the fender.
4. Remove the fender shield from the vehicle.
5. Disconnect the blower motor wiring at the multiple connector.
6. Remove the nuts that attach the blower motor to the heater housing and remove the blower motor.

Heater Core

1965 Belvedere, Satellite and Coronet

1. Remove the heater assembly.
2. Remove the heater hot water control valve attaching screw. Pull the valve straight up and remove it from the heater housing. The valve is held into the heater core by an O-ring.
3. Remove the heater core attaching screws and remove the core.

1965 Fury, Polara and Monaco 1966-68 All Models 1969-70 Belvedere, Satellite, Coronet and Charger

1. Remove the heater assembly.
2. Remove the heater cover plate.
3. Remove the screws that attach the heater core to the heater assembly and remove the core.

1969-72 Fury, Polara and Monaco

1. Remove the heater assembly.
2. From inside the heater assembly, remove the two retaining nuts from the right-side of the heater core.
3. Remove the four heater core attaching screws from the outside of the heater housing.
4. Remove the heater core locating metal screw from the top of the heater housing.
5. Carefully pull the heater core from the heater housing.

1971-72 Belvedere, Satellite, Coronet and Charger

1. Remove the heater assembly.
2. Remove the screws that attach the front cover to the heater housing.
3. Cut sponge rubber plenum-to-housing air seal in two places, where the front cover separates the cover from the housing.
4. Remove the one core tube retaining screw from behind the heater housing, between the heater core tubes.
5. Remove the sponge rubber gaskets from the heater core tubes. Remove the heater core from the heater housing.

Fairlane, Falcon, Mustang, Comet, Cougar, Montego, Maverick, Torino

Index

YEAR IDENTIFICATION

FAIRLANE AND TORINO

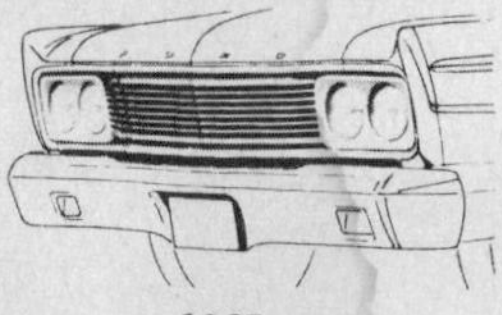

1965    1966 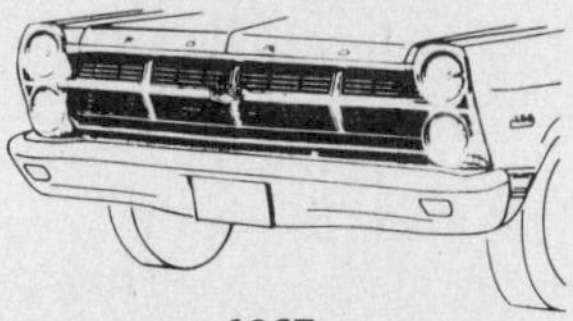   1967

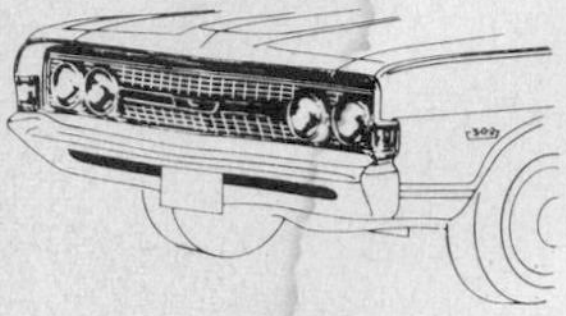

1968 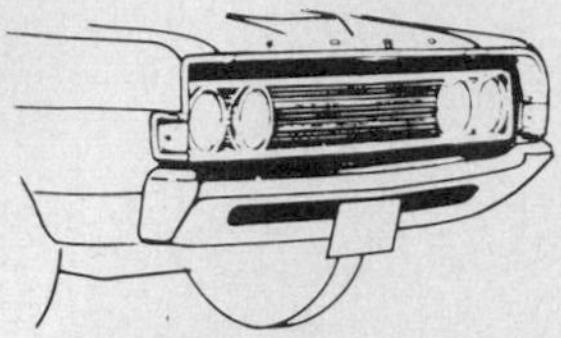   1969 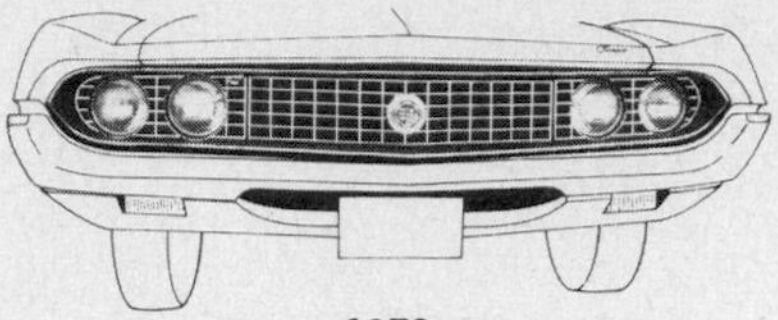   1970

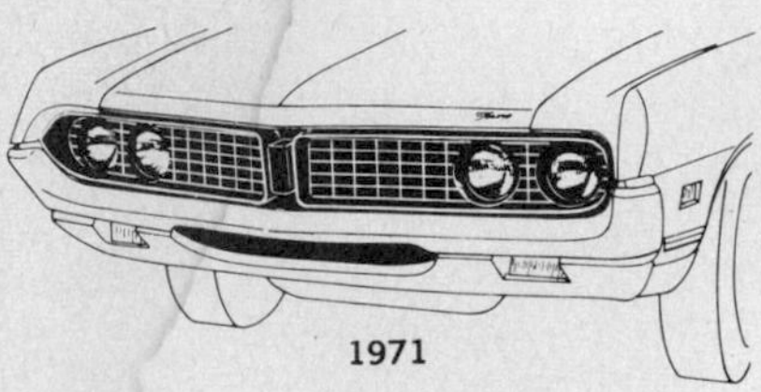

1971

1972 Torino    1972 Gran Torino

FALCON

1965    1966

1967 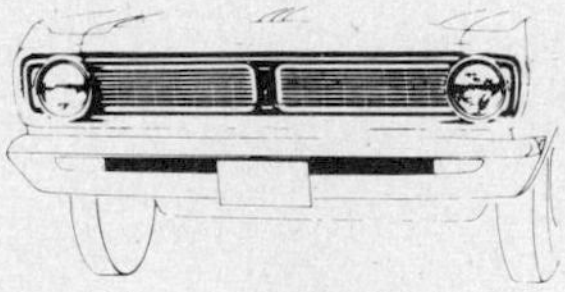   1968 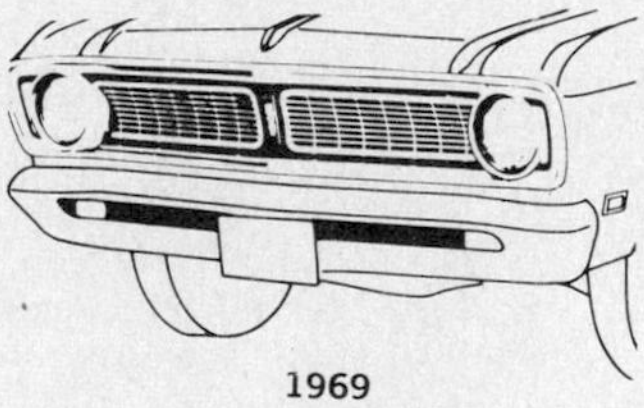   1969

COUGAR

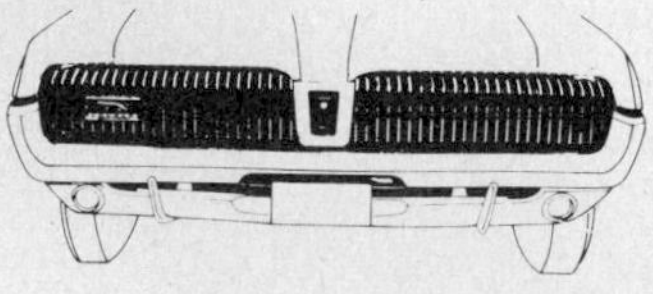

1967 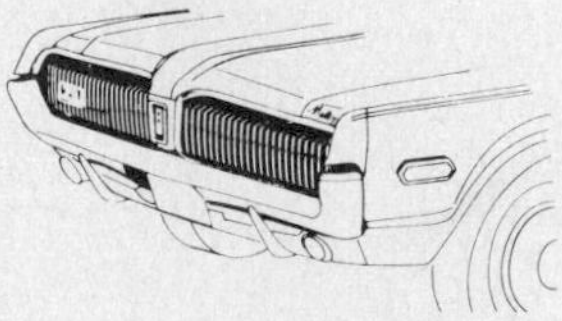   1968 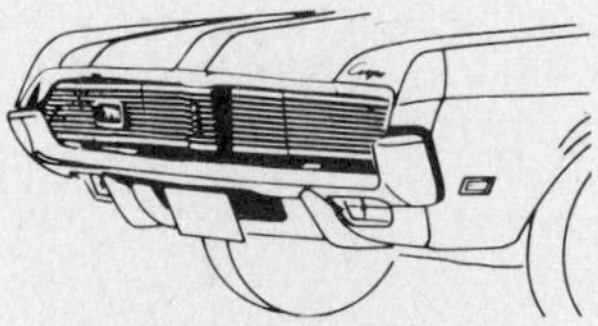   1969

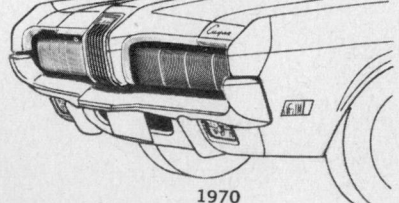
1970

1971

1972 XR-7

YEAR IDENTIFICATION

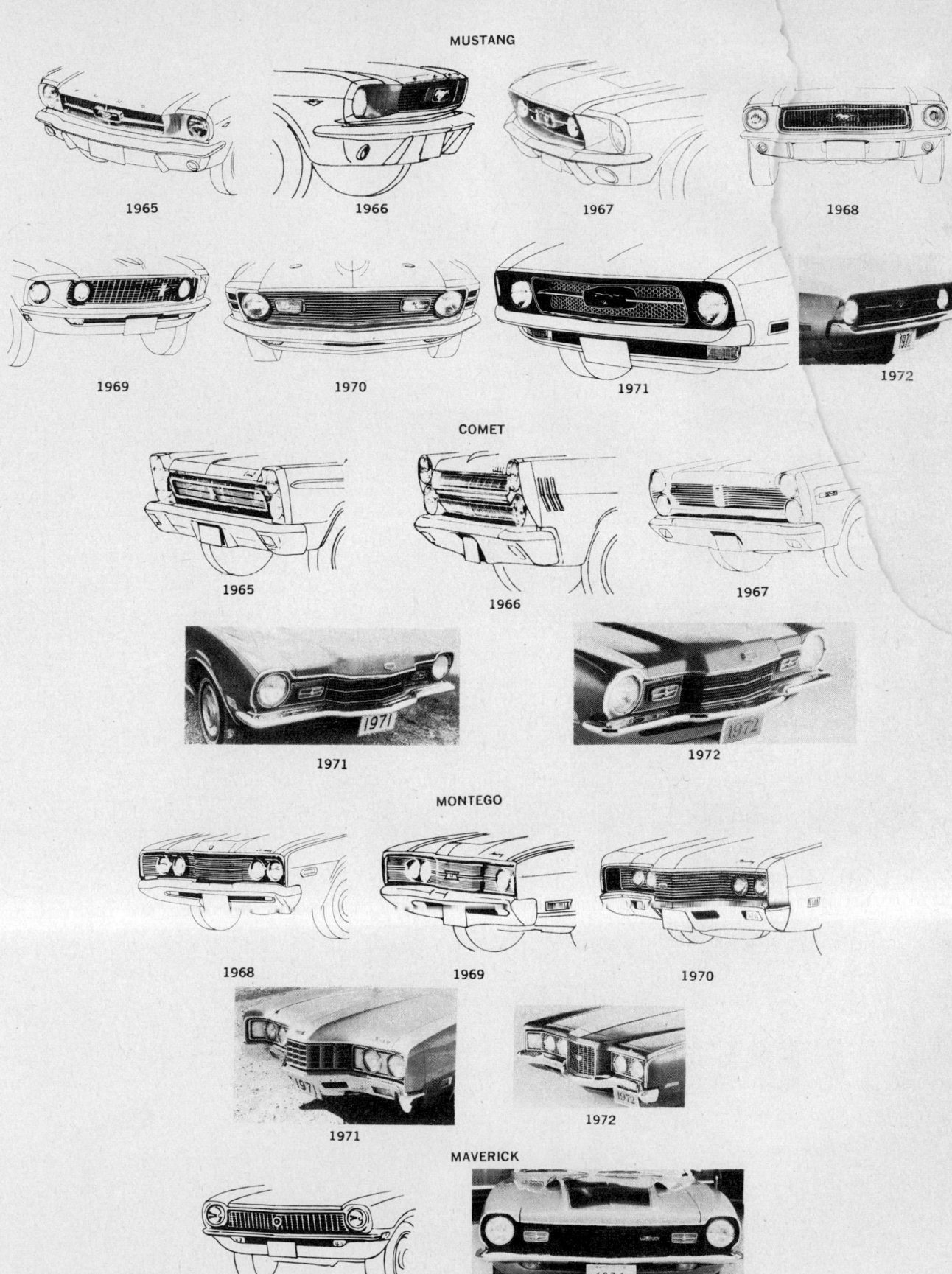

MUSTANG

1965   1966   1967   1968

1969   1970   1971   1972

COMET

1965   1966   1967

1971   1972

MONTEGO

1968   1969   1970

1971   1972

MAVERICK

1970-72   1971-72 Grabber

FIRING ORDER

1968-72
289, 302 V8
timing marks

1968-72
390, 427,
428, 429 V8
timing marks

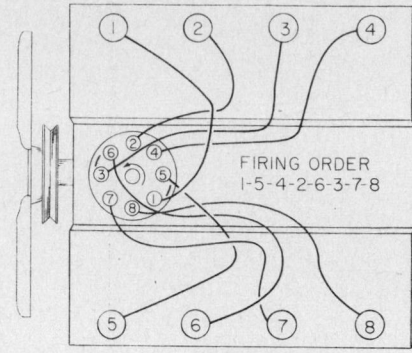

FIRING ORDER
1-5-4-2-6-3-7-8

All V8 except 351

1965-67
390, 427 V8
timing marks

1965-67
260, 289 V8
timing marks

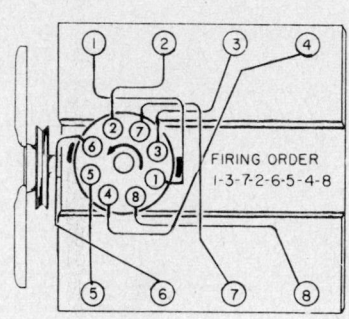

FIRING ORDER
1-3-7-2-6-5-4-8

351 V8

1968-72
6 cyl.
timing marks

BTC   TC   ATC

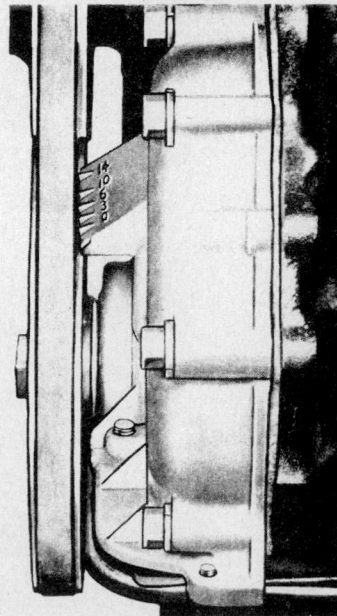

1965-67
6 cyl.
timing marks

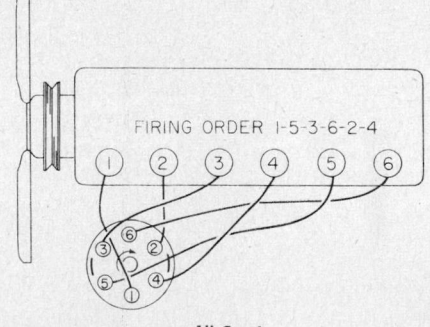

FIRING ORDER 1-5-3-6-2-4

All 6 cyl.

YEAR IDENTIFICATION
FIRING ORDER
CAR SERIAL NUMBER
LOCATION AND
ENGINE
IDENTIFICATION

1965-67

Engine is identified through car serial number. Serial numbers, and other pertinent information, are to be found on a plate riveted to the rear edge of the left front door.

The engine number is stamped on the top surface of the engine block near the crankcase breather pipe, front left side.

The car serial number is composed of eleven digits, the first five giving the year, assembly plant, body serial code (2 digits), model and engine type. The second six digits are a sequential serial number.

1968-72

The serial number is on a plate attached to the top of the instrument panel, visible through the windshield. The plate is interpreted as per the illustrations.

Vehicle Certification Label 1970-72

The vehicle certification label is located on the rear of the driver's door. The upper half of the label contains the name of the manufacturer, the month and year of manufacture, and the certification statement. For interpretation of the lower half of the label, see the illustration.

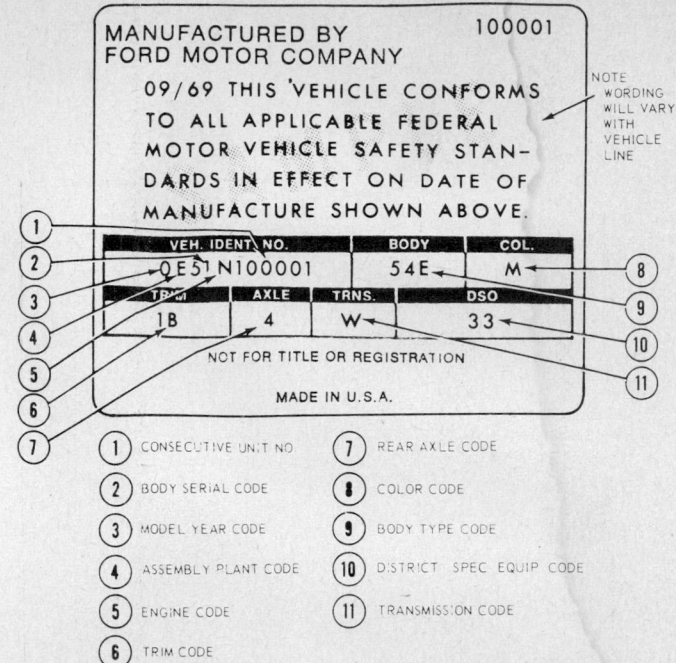

1. CONSECUTIVE UNIT NO.
2. BODY SERIAL CODE
3. MODEL YEAR CODE
4. ASSEMBLY PLANT CODE
5. ENGINE CODE
6. TRIM CODE
7. REAR AXLE CODE
8. COLOR CODE
9. BODY TYPE CODE
10. DISTRICT SPEC EQUIP CODE
11. TRANSMISSION CODE

Vehicle certification label—1970-72

Typical vehicle identification number (VIN) tab

1 Model year code
2 Assembly plant code
3 Body serial code
4 Engine code
5 Consecutive unit number
6 Body type code
7 Color code
8 Trim code
9 Date code
10 District—special equipment code
11 Rear axle code
12 Transmission code

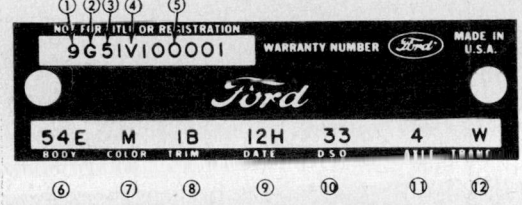

Engine number and code location, V8 engines

CRANKSHAFT BEARING JOURNAL SPECIFICATIONS

YEAR	MODEL	MAIN BEARING JOURNALS (IN.)				CONNECTING ROD BEARING JOURNALS (IN.)		
		Journal Diameter	Oil Clearance	Shaft End-Play	Thrust On No.	Journal Diameter	Oil Clearance	Side Clearance
1965-72	6 Cyl.—170	2.2482-2.2490	.0005-.0022	.004-.008	3	2.1232-2.1240	.0008-.0024	.003-.010
	6 Cyl.—200	2.2482-2.2490	.0005-.0022	.004-.008	5	2.1232-2.1240	.0008-.0024	.003-.010
	6 Cyl.—250	2.3982-2.3990	.0005-.0022	.004-.008	5	2.1232-2.1240	.0008-.0024	.003-.010
	V8—302, 289	2.2482-2.2490	.0005-.0024⑤	.004-.008	3	2.1228-2.1236①	.0008-.0026②	.010-.020
	V8—351W	2.2994-3.0002	.0013-.0030	.004-.008	3	2.3103-2.3111	.0008-.0026	.010-.020
	V8—351C	2.7484-2.7492	.0009-.0026	.004-.010	3	2.3103-2.3111	.0008-.0026	.010-.020
	V8—390	2.7484-2.7492	.0008-.0020	.004-.010	3	2.4380-2.4388	.0008-.0030	.010-.020
	V8—427	2.7484-2.7492	.0010-.0031	.004-.010	3	2.4380-2.4388	.0013-.0032	.010-.020
	V8—428	2.7484-2.7492	.0010-.0020	.004-.010	3	2.4380-2.4388	.0010-.0030	.010-.020
	V8—429	2.9994-3.0002	.0005-.0025③	.004-.008	3	2.4992-2.5000	.0008-.0028④	.010-.020

① —Boss 302—2.1222-2.1230.
② —Boss 302—.0015-.0025.
③ —Boss 429—.0010-.0025.
④ —Boss 429—.0015-.0025.
⑤ —302—.001-.0018 No. 1 bearing only.

Engine Codes

1965

U	6 cyl. 170 cu. in.	K	8 cyl. 289 cu. in.
T	6 cyl. 200 cu. in.	*4	6 cyl. 170 cu. in.
F	8 cyl. 260 cu. in.	*6	8 cyl. 260 cu. in.

*Low Compression

1966

A	8 cyl. 289 cu. in. 4V Prem.	Y	8 cyl. 390 cu. in. 2V
C	8 cyl. 289 cu. in. 2V Reg.	Z	8 cyl. 390 cu. in. 4V
K	8 cyl. 289 cu. in. Hi-Perf.	*2	6 cyl. 200 cu. in. 1V
T	6 cyl. 200 cu. in. 1V	*3	8 cyl. 289 cu. in. 2V

*Low Compression

1967

U	6 cyl. 170 cu. in. 1V	K	8 cyl. 289 cu. in. Hi-Perf.
T	6 cyl. 200 cu. in. 1V	Y	8 cyl. 390 cu. in. 2V
*2	6 cyl. 200 cu. in. 1V	H	8 cyl. 390 cu. in. 2V
*3	8 cyl. 289 cu. in. 2V	S	8 cyl. 390 cu. in. 4V
C	8 cyl. 289 cu. in. 2V	W	8 cyl. 427 cu. in. 4V Hi-Perf.
A	8 cyl. 289 cu. in. 4V Prem.	R	8 cyl. 427 cu. in. 8V Hi-Perf.

*Low Compression

1968

U	6 cyl. 170 cu. in. 1V	*6	8 cyl. 302 cu. in. 2V
T	6 cyl. 200 cu. in. 1V	J	8 cyl. 302 cu. in. 4V
*2	6 cyl. 200 cu. in. 1V	Y	8 cyl. 390 cu. in. 2V
C	8 cyl. 289 cu. in. 2V	X	8 cyl. 390 cu. in. 2V Prem.
F	8 cyl. 302 cu. in. 2V	S	8 cyl. 390 cu. in. 4V GT
		W	8 cyl. 427 cu. in. 4V Hi-Perf.

*Low Compression

1969

U	6 cyl. 170 cu. in. 1V	F	8 cyl. 302 cu. in. 2V
T	6 cyl. 200 cu. in. 1V	*6	8 cyl. 302 cu. in. 2V
*2	6 cyl. 200 cu. in. 1V	D	8 cyl. 302 cu. in. 2V Police
L	6 cyl. 250 cu. in. 1V	H	8 cyl. 351 cu. in. 2V ①
*3	6 cyl. 250 cu. in. 1V	M	8 cyl. 351 cu. in. 4V ①
		#S	8 cyl. 390 cu. in. 4V
		Q	8 cyl. 428 cu. in. 4V CJ
		SR	8 cyl. 428 cu. in. 4V CJ

*Low Compression
#Improved Performance
S Ram Air Induction

1970

U	6 cyl. 170 cu. in. 1V	G	8 cyl. 302 cu. in. 4V Boss
T	6 cyl. 200 cu. in. 1V	H	8 cyl. 351 cu. in. 2V ①
*2	6 cyl. 200 cu. in. 1V	M	8 cyl. 351 cu. in. 4V ①
L	6 cyl. 250 cu. in. 1V	Q	8 cyl. 428 cu. in. 4V CJ
*3	6 cyl. 250 cu. in. 1V	#R	8 cyl. 428 cu. in. 4V CJ
F	8 cyl. 302 cu. in. 2V	N	8 cyl. 429 cu. in. 4V
*6	8 cyl. 302 cu. in. 2V	C	8 cyl. 429 cu. in. 4V CJ

D	8 cyl. 302 cu. in. 2V Taxi	#J	8 cyl. 429 cu. in. 4V CJ
		Z	8 cyl. 429 cu. in. 4V Boss

*Low Compression
#Ram Air Induction

1971

U	6 cyl. 170 cu. in. 1V	M	8 cyl. 351 cu. in. 4V
T	6 cyl. 200 cu. in. 1V	Q	8 cyl. 351 cu. in. 4V CJ*
L	6 cyl. 250 cu. in. 1V	N	8 cyl. 429 cu. in. 4V
F	8 cyl. 302 cu. in. 2V	C	8 cyl. 429 cu. in. 4V CJ
H	8 cyl. 351 cu. in. 2V	J	8 cyl. 429 cu. in. 4V CJ●

*Also known as 351 GT
●Ram Air Induction

Transmission Codes

1964-65

1	Three speed manual	4	Three speed automatic
3	Two speed automatic	5	Four speed manual

1966

1	Three speed manual	5	Four speed manual
4	Three speed automatic type C6	6	Three speed automatic type C4

1967

1	Three speed manual	5	Four speed manual
2	Overdrive	W	Automatic C4
3	Three speed manual	U	Automatic C6

1968

1	Three speed manual	W	Automatic C4
5	Four speed manual	U	Automatic C6

1969

1	Three speed manual	Y	Automatic MX
5	Four speed manual-wide ratio	X	Automatic FMX
6	Four speed manual-close ratio	Z	Automatic C6 Special for Police
W	Automatic C4		and trailer towing
U	Automatic C6		

1970-71

1	Three speed manual	W	Automatic C4
5	Four speed manual-wide ratio	U	Automatic C6
6	Four speed manual-close ratio	X	Automatic FMX
V	Semi-Automatic stick shift	Z	Automatic C6 Special for Police
			and trailer towing

① —All 351 4V engines are Cleveland engines. Both Windsor and Cleveland versions of the 351 2V engine are available. The quickest method of engine identification is to disconnect a spark plug wire at the spark plug and examine the size of the spark plug. Windsor engines are equipped with standard 18mm spark plugs. Cleveland engines are equipped with smaller 14mm spark plugs.

CYLINDER HEAT BOLT TIGHTENING SEQUENCE

289, 302, 302 Boss, 351W,
351C (similar bolt pattern),
390, 427, 428, 429, 429 Boss
(similar bolt pattern) cu. in. V8

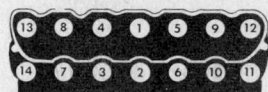

170, 200, 250 cu. in. 6 cyl.

TORQUE SPECIFICATIONS

YEAR	MODEL	CYLINDER HEAD BOLTS (FT. LBS.)*	ROD BEARING BOLTS (FT. LBS.)	MAIN BEARING BOLTS (FT. LBS.)	CRANKSHAFT BALANCER BOLT (FT. LBS.)	FLYWHEEL TO CRANKSHAFT BOLTS (FT. LBS.)	MANIFOLD (FT. LBS.) Intake	MANIFOLD (FT. LBS.) Exhaust
1965-68	6 Cyl.	70-75	19-24	60-70	85-100	75-85	None	13-18
	V8—260, 289, 302	65-70	19-24①	60-70	70-90	75-85	12-15②	15-20
	V8—390, 428	80-90	40-45	95-105	70-90	75-85	32-35	18-24
	V8—427	100-110	53-58	95-105	70-90	75-85	32-35	18-24
1969	6 Cyl.	70-75	19-24	60-70	85-100	75-85	—	13-18
	V8—302	65-72	19-24	60-70	70-90	75-85	23-25	12-16
	V8—351W	95-100	40-45	95-105	70-90	75-85	23-25	18-24
	V8—390	80-90	40-45	95-105	70-90	75-85	32-35	18-24
	V8—428	80-90	53-58	95-105	70-90	75-85	32-35	18-24
1970-72	6 Cyl.	70-75	19-24③	60-70	85-100	75-85	—	13-18
	V8—302	65-72	19-24④	60-70⑤	70-90	75-85	23-25	12-16
	V8—351	95-100	40-45	95-105	70-90	75-85	23-25 (⁵⁄₁₆) 28-32 (³⁄₈)	18-24
	V8—428	80-90	53-58	95-105	70-90	75-85	32-35	18-24
	V8—429	130-140	40-45	95-105⑥	70-90	75-85	25-30	28-33
	V8—429 Boss	90-95	85-90	70-80	70-90	75-85	25-30	28-33

① —289 High perf. 40-45.
② —1966-68, 20-22 FT. LBS.
③ —250—21-26.
④ —302 Boss—40-45.
⑤ —302 Boss—outer bolts 35-40.
⑥ —⁷⁄₁₆ in. bolts—70-80.
* —Tighten cylinder head bolts in three steps.

BATTERY AND STARTER SPECIFICATIONS

YEAR	MODEL	BATTERY Ampere Hour Capacity	BATTERY Volts	BATTERY Terminal Grounded	STARTERS Lock Test Amps.	STARTERS Lock Test Volts	STARTERS Lock Test Torque	STARTERS No-Load Test Amps.	STARTERS No-Load Test Volts	STARTERS No-Load Test RPM	Brush Spring Tension (Oz.)
1965	6 Cyl.—All	40	12	Neg.	540	4.2	14.0	50	12	9,500	45
	V8—All	55	12	Neg.	670	6.0	15.5	70	12	9,500	45
1966	6 Cyl.	45	12	Neg.	460	5	9.0	70	12	9,500	40
	V8	55	12	Neg.	670	5	15.5	70	12	9,500	40
	Option	70	12	Neg.	670	5	15.5	70	12	9,500	40
	Option	80	12	Neg.	670	5	N.A.	70	12	9,500	40
1967-72	6 Cyl.—170 Cu. In.	45	12	Neg.	460	5	9.0	50	12	9,500	40
	6 Cyl.—200 Cu. In.	45	12	Neg.	670	5	15.5	70	12	9,500	40
	V8—exc. below	55	12	Neg.	460①	5	9.0②	70	12	9,500	40
	V8—351 4-BBl	70	12	Neg.	460①	5	9.0②	70	12	9,500	40
	V8—428, 429	80	12	Neg.	460①	5	9.0②	70	12	9,500	40

① —4½ in. diameter starter—670.
② —4½ in. diameter starter—15.5.

AC GENERATOR AND REGULATOR SPECIFICATIONS

YEAR	MODEL	ALTERNATOR Field Current Draw @ 12V.	ALTERNATOR Output @ 6500 Generator RPM	REGULATOR Field Relay Air Gap (In.)	REGULATOR Field Relay Point Gap (In.)	REGULATOR Volts to Close	REGULATOR Air Gap (In.)	REGULATOR Point Gap (In.)	REGULATOR Volts at 125°
1965-69	Autolite	2.8-3.3	38A	—	—	2.5	.049-.056	.017-.022	13.8-14.4
	Autolite	2.9-3.1	42A	.012-.022	.015-.022	2.5	.049-.056	.017-.022	13.8-14.4
	Autolite	2.9	45A	.015	—	2.5-4	.052	.019	13.8-14.6
	Autolite	2.9	55A	.015	—	2.5-4	.052	.019	13.8-14.6
	Leece-Neville	2.9	53A	.012	.025	7.0	.047	.019	14.1-14.9
1970-72	Autolite Purple	2.4	38A			2.0-4.2			13.5-15.3
	Autolite Orange	2.9	42A			2.0-4.2			13.5-15.3
	Autolite Red	2.9	55A			2.0-4.2			13.5-15.3
	Autolite Green	2.9	61A			2.0-4.2			13.5-15.3
	Autolite Black	2.9	65A			2.0-4.2			13.5-15.3

TUNE-UP SPECIFICATIONS

YEAR	MODEL	SPARK PLUGS		DISTRIBUTOR		IGNITION TIMING (Deg.) ▲	CRANKING COMP. PRESSURE (Psi)	VALVES Tappet (Hot) Clearance (In.)		Intake Opens (Deg.)	FUEL PUMP PRESSURE (Psi)	IDLE SPEED (Rpm) ★
		Type	Gap (In.)	Point Dwell (Deg.)	Point Gap (In.)			Intake	Exhaust			
1965	6 Cyl.—Exc. 200	BF82	.034	37.5°	.025	8B	170	Hyd.	Hyd.	13B	4½	500
	6 Cyl.—Exc. 200 Auto.	BF82	.034	37.5°	.025	12B	170	Hyd.	Hyd.	13B	4½	485
	6 Cyl.—200 Auto. Trans.	BF82	.034	37.5°	.025	12B	150	Hyd.	Hyd.	6B	4½	485
	V8—260 Std. Trans.	BF42	.034	27.0°	.015	6B①	150	Hyd.	Hyd.	21B	5	575
	V8—260 Auto. Trans.	BF42	.034	27.0°	.015	10B①	150	Hyd.	Hyd.	21B	5	500
	V8—289 Std. Trans.	BF42	.034	27.0°	.015	6B②	150	Hyd.	Hyd.	20B	5	575
	V8—289 Auto. Trans.	BF42	.034	27.0°	.015	8B	150	Hyd.	Hyd.	20B	5	500
	V8—289 Hi Perf.	BF32	.034	27.0°	.020	10B	200	.018	.018	46B	5	750
1966	6 Cyl. 170, 200 M.T.	BF82	.034	39.0°	.025	6B⊙	170	Hyd.	Hyd.	13B	4½	500
	6 Cyl. 170, 200 A.T.	BF82	.034	39.0°	.025	12B⊙	170	Hyd.	Hyd.	13B	4½	500
	V8—289 M.T.	BF42	.034	27.0°	.017	6B⊙	150	Hyd.	Hyd.	20B	5	600
	V-8, 289 A.T.	BF42	.034	27.0°	.017	6B⊙	150	Hyd.	Hyd.	20B	5	500
	V-8, 289 Hi Perf.	BF32	.030	31.0°	.020	12B	200	.018	.018	46B	5	750
	V-8, 390 M.T.	BF42	.034	27.0°	.017	10B⊙	180	Hyd.	Hyd.	26B	5	600
	V-8, 390 A.T.	BF42	.034	28.0°	.017	10B⊙	180	Hyd.	Hyd.	26B	5	500
1967	6 Cyl.—170, 200 M.T.	BF82	.034	37.0°	.025	6B⊙	170	Hyd.	Hyd.	9B	4½	600
	6 Cyl.—170, 200 A.T.	BF82	.034	37.0°	.025	12B⊙	170	Hyd.	Hyd.	9B	4½	525
	V8—289, 2-BBL.	BF42	.034	27.0°	.017	6B⊙	150	Hyd.	Hyd.	16B	5	600
	V8—289, 4-BBL.	BF42	.034	27.0°	.017	6B⊙	150	Hyd.	Hyd.	16B	5	600
	V8—289 Hi-Perf.	BF32	.034	31.0°	.020	12B⊙	200	.019	.021	46B	5	750
	V8—390, 2-BBL. M.T.	BF42	.034	26.0°	.017	10B⊙	180	Hyd.	Hyd.	16B	5	600
	V8—390, 2-BBL. A.T.	BF42	.034	26.0°	.017	10B⊙	180	Hyd.	Hyd.	16B	5	500
	V8—390, 4-BBL. M.T.	BF32	.034	26.0°	.017	12B⊙	180	Hyd.	Hyd.	20B	5	575
	V8—390, 4-BBL. A.T.	BF32	.034	26.0°	.017	12B⊙	180	Hyd.	Hyd.	20B	5	500
	V8—427, Transistor—All	BF32	.030	23.0°	.020	8B	180	.025	.025	48B	5	800
1968	6 Cyl. 170, 200	BF82	.034	37.0°	.027	6B	170	Hyd.	Hyd.	9B	4½	600
	V8—289 M.T.	BF42	.034	27.0°	.017	6B	150	Hyd.④	Hyd.④	9B	5	625
	V8—289 A.T.	BF42	.034	27.0°	.017	6B	150	Hyd.	Hyd.	9B	5	525
	V8—302	BF42	.034	27.0°	.017	6B	150	Hyd.	Hyd.	15B	5	650③
	V8—390 2-BBL.	BF32	.034	27.0°	.020	6B	180	Hyd.	Hyd.	13B	5	650
	V8—390 4-BBL.	BF32	.034	27.0°	.020	6B	180	Hyd.	Hyd.	18B	5	650
	V8—427	BF32	.034	27.0°	.020	6B	180	Hyd.	Hyd.	18B	5	650
1969	6 Cyl. 170, 200	BF82	.034	37.0°	.027	6B	170	Hyd.	Hyd.	9B	4½	①
	6 Cyl. 250	BF82	.034	40.0°	.025	6B	⑲	Hyd.	Hyd.	10B	5	⑤ ⑯
	V8—302, 2-BBL. A.T.	BF42	.034	29.0°	.017	6B	⑲	Hyd.	Hyd.	16B	5	550
	V8—302, 2-BBL. M.T.	BF42	.034	27.0°	.021	6B	⑲	Hyd.	Hyd.	16B	5	650
	V8—351, 2-BBL.	BF42	.034	29.0°	.017	6B	⑲	Hyd.	Hyd.	11B	5	⑰
	V8—351, 4-BBL.	BF32	.034	29.0°	.017	6B	⑲	Hyd.	Hyd.	11B	5	⑱
	V8—390, 4-BBL. A.T.	BF32	.034	29.0°	.017	6B	⑲	Hyd.	Hyd.	16B	5	550
	V8—390, 4-BBL. M.T.	BF42	.034	29.0°	.017	6B	⑲	Hyd.	Hyd.	16B	5	650-700
	V8—428, 4-BBL. A.T. CJ	BF32	.034	29.0°	.017	6B	⑲	Hyd.	Hyd.	18B	5	650
	V8—428, 4-BBL. M.T. CJ	BF32	.034	29.0°	.017	6B	⑲	Hyd.	Hyd.	18B	5	700

CAUTION

General adoption of anti-pollution laws has changed the design of almost all car engine production to effectively reduce crankcase emission and terminal exhaust products. It has been necessary to adopt stricter tune-up rules, especially timing and idle speed procedures. Both of these values are peculiar to the engine and to its application, rather than to the engine alone. With this in mind, car manufacturers supply idle speed data for the engine and application involved. This information is clearly displayed in the engine compartment of each vehicle.

TUNE-UP SPECIFICATIONS, continued

YEAR	MODEL	SPARK PLUGS Type	Gap (In.)	DISTRIBUTOR Point Dwell (Deg.)	Point Gap (In.)	IGNITION TIMING (Deg.) ▲	CRANKING COMP. PRESSURE (Psi)	VALVES Tappet (Hot) Clearance (In.) Intake	Exhaust	Intake Opens (Deg.)	FUEL PUMP PRESSURE (Psi)	IDLE SPEED (Rpm) *
1970	6 Cyl. 170, 200	BF82	.035	37.0°	.027	6B	(19)	Hyd.	Hyd.	9B	4½	(11)
	6 Cyl. 250	BF82	.035	40.0°	.025	6B	(19)	Hyd.	Hyd.	10B	5	(12)
	V8—302, 2-BBL. A.T.	BF42	.035	(9)	(9)	6B	(19)	Hyd.	Hyd.	16B	5	600/500 (5)
	V8—302, 2-BBL. M.T.	BF42	.035	(9)	(9)	6B	(19)	Hyd.	Hyd.	16B	5	800/500 (5)
	V8—302 Boss	AF32	.035	30-33°	.020 (10)	16B	(19)	.025	.025	40B	5-6	800/500 (5)
	V8—351, 2-BBL. A.T.	BF42 (6)	.035	(9)	(9)	10B	(19)	Hyd.	Hyd.	11B	5	600/500 (5) (8)
	V8—351, 2-BBL. M.T.	BF42 (6)	.034	(9)	(9)	10B	(19)	Hyd.	Hyd.	11B	5	700/500 (5)
	V8—351, 4-BBL. A.T. (7)	AF32	.035	(9)	(9)	6B	(19)	Hyd.	Hyd.	14B	5	600/500 (5) (8)
	V8—351, 4-BBL. M.T. (7)	AF32	.035	(9)	(9)	6B	(19)	Hyd.	Hyd.	14B	5	700/500 (5)
	V8—428, 4-BBL. A.T. CJ	BF32	.035	(9)	(9)	6B	(19)	Hyd.	Hyd.	18B	5	(14) (5)
	V8—428, 4-BBL. M.T. CJ	BF32	.035	(9)	(9)	6B	(19)	Hyd.	Hyd.	18B	5	(14) (5)
	V8—429 Boss	AF32	.035	30-33°	.020 (10)	10B	(19)	.013C	.013C	40B	6-8	700/500 (5)
	V8—429, 4-BBL. CJ	AF32	.035	(9)	(9)	10B	(19)	Hyd.	Hyd.	32B	6-8	850/500 (5) (13)
	V8—429, 4-BBL. SCJ	AF32	.035	(9)	(9)	10B	(19)	.019	.019	40½B	6-8	(13) (5)
1971-72	6 Cyl. 170, 200	BRF42	.035	37°	.027	6B	(19)	Hyd.	Hyd.	9B	4½	11
	6 Cyl. 250	BRF42	.035	37°	.026	6B	(19)	Hyd.	Hyd.	10B	5	12
	V8—302, 2-BBL. A.T.	BRF42	.035	(9)	(9)	16B	(19)	Hyd.	Hyd.	16B	5 (8)	600/500
	V8—302, 2-BBL. M.T.	BRF42	.035	(9)	(9)	6B	(19)	Hyd.	Hyd.	16B	5	800/500
	V8—351, 2 BBL. A.T.	BRF42 (6)	.035	(9)	(9)	6B	(19)	Hyd.	Hyd.	12B	5 (8)	600/500
	V8—351, 2-BBL. M.T.	BRF42 (6)	.035	(9)	(9)	6B	(19)	Hyd.	Hyd.	12B	5	800/500
	V8—351, 4-BBL. A.T.	ARF42	.035	(9)	(9)	6B	(19)	Hyd.	Hyd.	18B	5	600/500
	V8—351, 4-BBL. M.T.	ARF42	.035	(9)	(9)	6B	(19)	Hyd.	Hyd.	18B	5	800/500
	V8—429, 4-BBL.	BRF42	.035	(9)	(9)	4B	(19)	Hyd.	Hyd.	16B	5 (8)	600/500
	V8—429, 4-BBL. CJ	ARF 32	.035	(9)	(9)	10B	(19)	Hyd.	Hyd.	32B	6-8	850/500
	V8—429, 4-BBL. SCJ	ARF 32	.035	(9)	(9)	10B	(19)	.019	.019	40B	6-8	850/500

*—See text for procedure.

▲—With vacuum advance disconnected and plugged. NOTE: These settings are only approximate. Engine design, altitude, temperature, fuel octane rating and the condition of the individual engine are all factors which can influence timing. The limiting advance factor must, therefore, be the "knock point" of the individual engine.

B—Before top dead center.

CJ—Cobra Jet.

A.T.—Automatic transmission.

M.T.—Manual transmission.

(1)—Mustang—4B.

(2)—Mustang—8B.

(3)—550 rpm with automatic.

(4)—High perf. engine—Intake = .019 in.; Exhaust = .021 in.

(5)—Higher idle speed with solenoid throttle positioner energized, lower with it disconnected.

(6)—ARF42 on Cleveland engine.

(7)—Cleveland built engine.

(8)—600 rpm on models not equipped with a solenoid throttle positioner.

(9)—Dual diaphragm unit—one set of points = 24-29° dwell, .021 point gap. Single diaphragm unit—one set of points = 26-31° dwell, .017 point gap.

(10)—Dual points.

(11)—M.T.—750
A.T.—550

(12)—M.T.—750/500
A.T.—600/500

(13)—A.T.—600

(14)—M.T.—725/500 } 725 w/o A/C
A.T.—675/500 } 675 w/o A/C.

(15)—M.T.—650/500
A.T.—700/500

(16)—M.T.—700 w/o A/C
700/500 with A/C
A.T.—550 w/o A/C
550/430 with A/C

(17)—M.T.—650
A.T.—550

(18)—M.T.—675
A.T.—575

(19)—When checking compression, take the highest reading and compare it to the lowest. The lowest reading must be within 75% of the highest.

(ᵒ)—1966 with Thermactor system:
Timing—170, 200, 289 = TDC
390 = 6B
Idle speed—M.T. = 625 rpm
A.T. = 550-575 for 170 & 200
475-500 for 289 & 390

(ᵒ)—1967 with Thermactor system:
Timing—170 = TDC
200 = 5B
289 = TDC
289 High perf. & 390 = 6B

VALVE SPECIFICATIONS

YEAR AND MODEL	SEAT ANGLE (DEG.)	FACE ANGLE (DEG.)	VALVE LIFT INTAKE (IN.)	VALVE LIFT EXHAUST (IN.)	VALVE SPRING PRESSURE (VALVE OPEN) LBS. @ IN.	VALVE SPRING INSTALLED HEIGHT (IN.)	STEM TO GUIDE CLEARANCE (IN.) Intake	Exhaust	STEM DIAMETER (IN.) Intake	Exhaust
1965										
6 Cyl.—200	45	44	.348	.348	142-158 @ 1.222	$1\frac{9}{16}$-$1\frac{39}{64}$	.0008-.0025	.0018-.0035	.3100-.3107	.3090-.3097
6 Cyl.—170	45	44	.348	.348	112-122 @ 1.222	$1\frac{9}{16}$-$1\frac{39}{64}$	.0008-.0025	.0018-.0035	.3100-.3107	.3090-.3097
V8—289	45	44	.380	.380	161-178 @ 1.380	$1\frac{3}{4}$-$1\frac{25}{32}$	.0010-.0027	.0020-.0037	.3416-.3423	.3406-.3413
V8—260	45	44	.368	.380	161-177 @ 1.390	$1\frac{3}{4}$-$1\frac{25}{32}$	.0008-.0025	.0018-.0035	.3100-.3107	.3090-.3097
1966										
6 Cyl.—170, 200	45	44	.348	.348	142-158 @ 1.222	$1\frac{9}{16}$-$1\frac{39}{64}$	.0008-.0025	.0010-.0027	.3100-.3107	.3098-.3105
V8—289	45	44	.368	.380	161-177 @ 1.390	$1\frac{3}{4}$-$1\frac{25}{32}$	.0010-.0027	.0020-.0037	.3416-.3423	.3406-.3413
V8—289 H.P.	45	44	.471	.457	235-260 @ 1.320	$1\frac{3}{4}$-$1\frac{25}{32}$	.0010-.0027	.0020-.0037	.3416-.3423	.3406-.3413
V8—390	45	44	.408	.408	233-257 @ 1.380	$1\frac{13}{16}$-$1\frac{27}{32}$	.0010-.0024	.0010-.0024	.3711-.3718	.3711-.3718
1967										
6 Cyl.—170	45	44	.348	.348	142-158 @ 1.222	$1\frac{9}{16}$-$1\frac{39}{64}$	.0008-.0025	.0010-.0027	.3100-.3107	.3098-.3105
6 Cyl.—200	45	44	.367	.367	142-158 @ 1.222	$1\frac{9}{16}$-$1\frac{39}{64}$	.0008-.0025	.0010-.0027	.3100-.3107	.3098-.3105
V8—289①	45	44	.368	.381	174-192 @ 1.270	$1\frac{5}{8}$-$1\frac{11}{16}$	.0010-.0027	.0010-.0027	.3416-.3423	.3416-.3423
V8—289②	45	44	.426	.425	171-189 @ 1.230	$1\frac{5}{8}$-$1\frac{11}{16}$	.0010-.0027	.0010-.0027	.3416-.3423	.3416-.3423
V8—289 H.P.	45	44	.477	.477	235-260 @ 1.320	$1\frac{3}{4}$-$1\frac{25}{32}$	.0010-.0027	.0010-.0027	.3416-.3423	.3416-.3423
V8—390	45	44	.440	.440	209-231 @ 1.380	$1\frac{13}{16}$-$1\frac{27}{32}$	.0010-.0024	.0010-.0024	.3711-.3718	.3711-.3718
V8—390GT	45	44	.481	.490	255-280 @ 1.320	$1\frac{51}{64}$-$1\frac{53}{64}$	.0010-.0024	.0010-.0024	.3711-.3718	.3711-.3718
V8—427	30 int. 45 exh.	29 int. 44 exh.	.500	.500	255-280 @ 1.320	$1\frac{51}{64}$-$1\frac{53}{64}$	.0010-.0024	.0020-.0034	.3711-.3718	.3701-.3708
1968										
6 Cyl.—170, 200	45	44	.348	.348	142-158 @ 1.222	$1\frac{9}{16}$-$1\frac{39}{64}$	.0008-.0025	.0010-.0027	.3100-.3107	.3098-.3105
V8—289, 302	45	44	.368	.381	171-189 @ 1.230	$1\frac{5}{8}$-$1\frac{11}{16}$	.0010-.0027	.0015-.0032	.3416-.3423	.3411-.3418
V8—390 2-V	45	44	.427	.430	209-231 @ 1.380	$1\frac{13}{16}$-$1\frac{27}{32}$	.0010-.0024	.0015-.0032	.3711-.3718	.3706-.3713
V8—390GT	45	44	.481	.490	255-280 @ 1.320	$1\frac{51}{64}$-$1\frac{53}{64}$	.0010-.0024	.0015-.0032	.3711-.3718	.3706-.3713
V8—427	30 int. 45 exh.	29 int. 44 exh.	.481	.490	255-280 @ 1.320	$1\frac{51}{64}$-$1\frac{53}{64}$	.0010-.0024	.0020-.0034	.3711-.3718	.3701-.3708
1969										
6 Cyl.—170, 200	45	44	.348	.348	142-158 @ 1.222	$1\frac{9}{16}$-$1\frac{39}{64}$	.0008-.0025	.0010-.0027	.3100-.3107	.3098-.3105
6 Cyl.—250	45	44	.368	.368	142-158 @ 1.222	$1\frac{9}{16}$-$1\frac{39}{64}$	.0008-.0025	.0010-.0027	.3100-.3107	.3098-.3105
V8—302	45	44	.368	.381	171-189 @ 1.230	$1\frac{5}{8}$-$1\frac{11}{16}$	.0010-.0027	.0010-.0027	.3416-.3423	.3411-.3418
V8—351W	45	44	.418	.448	204-226 @ 1.340	$1\frac{25}{32}$-$1\frac{13}{16}$	.0010-.0027	.0010-.0027	.3416-.3423	.3706-.3713
V8—390 H.P.	45	44	.481	.490	209-231 @ 1.380	$1\frac{13}{16}$-$1\frac{27}{32}$	.0010-.0027	.0015-.0032	.3711-.3718	.3706-.3713
V8—428CJ	30 int. 45 exh.	29 int. 44 exh.	.481	.490	255-280 @ 1.320	$1\frac{51}{64}$-$1\frac{53}{64}$	.0010-.0027	.0015-.0032	.3711-.3718	.3706-.3713
V8—428CJ③	30 int. 45 exh.	29 int. 44 exh.	.481	.490	255-280 @ 1.320	$1\frac{51}{64}$-$1\frac{53}{64}$	.0010-.0027	.0015-.0032	.3711-.3718	.3706-.3713
1970-72										
6 Cyl.—170, 200	45	44	.348	.348	142-158 @ 1.222	$1\frac{9}{16}$-$1\frac{5}{8}$	.0008-.0025	.0010-.0027	.3100-.3107	.3098-.3105
6 Cyl.—250	45	44	.368	.368	142-158 @ 1.222	$1\frac{9}{16}$-$1\frac{5}{8}$	.0008-.0025	.0010-.0027	.3100-.3107	.3098-.3105
V8—302	45	44	.368	.381	171-189 @ 1.230	$1\frac{5}{8}$-$1\frac{21}{32}$	.0010-.0027	.0010-.0027	.3416-.3423	.3411-.3418
V8—302 Boss	45	44	.477	.477	299-331 @ 1.320	$1\frac{13}{16}$-$1\frac{27}{32}$	.0010-.0027	.0015-.0032	.3416-.3423	.3411-.3418
V8—351W	45	44	.418	.448	204-226 @ 1.340	$1\frac{3}{4}$-$1\frac{13}{16}$	.0010-.0027	.0010-.0027	.3416-.3423	.3411-.3418
V8—351C 2-V	45	44	.407	.407	199-221 @ 1.420	$1\frac{13}{16}$-$1\frac{27}{32}$	.0010-.0027	.0015-.0032	.3416-.3423	.3411-.3418
V8—351C 4-V	45	44	.427	.427	271-299 @ 1.320	$1\frac{13}{16}$-$1\frac{27}{32}$	.0010-.0027	.0015-.0032	.3416-.3423	.3411-.3418
V8—351 CJ	45	44	.480	.488	275-285 @ 1.370	$1\frac{13}{16}$-$1\frac{27}{32}$	.0010-.0027	.0015-.0032	.3416-.3423	.3411-.3418
V8—428CJ	30 int. 45 exh.	29 int. 44 exh.	.481	.490	255-280 @ 1.320	$1\frac{13}{16}$-$1\frac{27}{32}$	.0015-.0032	.0015-.0032	.3711-.3718	.3706-.3713
V8—428CJ③	30 int. 45 exh.	29 int. 44 exh.	.481	.490	255-280 @ 1.320	$1\frac{13}{16}$-$1\frac{27}{32}$	.0015-.0032	.0015-.0032	.3711-.3718	.3706-.3713
V8—429CJ	30 int. 45 exh.	29 int. 44 exh.	.500	.500	294-330 @ 1.320	$1\frac{13}{16}$-$1\frac{27}{32}$	.0010-.0027	.0020-.0034	.3416-.3423	.3411-.3418
V8—429SCJ	30 int. 45 exh.	29 int. 44 exh.	.515	.515	294-330 @ 1.320	$1\frac{13}{16}$-$1\frac{27}{32}$	.0010-.0027	.0020-.0034	.3416-.3423	.3411-.3418
V8—429 Boss	30 int. 45 exh.	29 int. 44 exh.	.478	.505	300-330 @ 1.320	$1\frac{13}{32}$-$1\frac{27}{32}$	.0010-.0024	.0020-.0034	.3711-.3718	.3701-.3708

① —Some engines with early Thermactor exhaust emission and all engines not having Thermactor.

② —Late production with Thermactor.

③ —Ram Air.

CAPACITIES

YEAR	MODEL	ENGINE CRANKCASE ADD 1 Qt. FOR NEW FILTER	TRANSMISSIONS Pts. TO REFILL AFTER DRAINING Manual 3-Speed	4-Speed	Automatic	DRIVE AXLE (Pts.)	GASOLINE TANK (Gals.)	COOLING SYSTEM (Qts.) WITH HEATER
1965	6 Cyl.—170 Cu. In.	3½	2½	4½	15	2½	③	10½
	6 Cyl.—200 Cu. In.	3½	2½	4½	15	2½	③	17
	V8—289 Cu. In.	4	3½	3½	17	4½	③	16
	Fairlane 6 Cyl.	3½	2½	4½	17	4½	16	9½
	Fairlane V8—289	4	3½	3½	17	4½	16	15
	Fairlane V8—289 Hi Perf.	4	None	3½	17	5	16	15
	Mustang, 6 Cyl.	3½	2½	4½	15	2½	16	9½
	Mustang, V8	4	3½	4	17	4½	16	15
1966	Falcon 6 Cyl.	3½	2	None	15	2½	16①	9½
	Falcon V8—289	4	3½	4	17¾	4½	16①	15
	Comet & Fairlane 6 Cyl.	3½	2	None	15	4½	20	9½
	Comet & Fairlane V8—289	4	3½	4	17¾	4½	20	15
	Comet & Fairlane V8—390	4	3½	4	26	4½	20	20½
	Mustang 6 Cyl.—200	3½	2	4	15	2½	16	9½
	Mustang V8—289	4	3½	4	17¾	4½	16	15
1967	Falcon 6 Cyl.	3½	2	None	15¾	2½	16①	9½
	Falcon V8—289	4	3½	4	17¾	4½	16①	15
	Comet & Fairlane 6 Cyl.	3½	2	None	15¾	4½	20	9½
	Comet & Fairlane V8—289	4	3½	4	17¾	4½	20	15
	Comet & Fairlane V8—390	4	3½	4	26	4½	20	20½
	Mustang V8—289	4	None	4	17¾	5	17	15
	Cougar V8—289	4	3½	4	17¾	4	17	15
	Cougar V8—390	4	3½	4	26	5	17	20½
	All V8—427	5	None	4	None	5	20	19½
1968	Comet & Fairlane 6 Cyl.	3½	3½	None	16	4	20	9½
	Comet & Fairlane—289, 302	4	3½	4	18	4	20	15
	Comet & Fairlane—390, 427	4	3½	4	26	5	20	20½
	Falcon 6 Cyl.	3½	3½	None	16	2	16	9½
	Falcon V8	4	3½	4	26	4	16①	15
	Mustang 6 Cyl.	3½	3½	None	16	2½	16	9½
	Mustang V8	4	3½	4	26④	5⑤	16	20½⑥
	Cougar V8—302	4	3½	4	18	4	17	15
	Cougar V8—390, 427	4	3½	4	26	5	17	20½
	Montego 6 Cyl.	3½	3½	None	16	2½	20	9½
	Montego V8	4	3½	4	26④	5⑤	20	20½⑥
1969	6 Cyl. 170	3½	3½	None	16	2½	16	9¼
	6 Cyl. 200	3½	3½	None	16	2½	⑦	9½
	6 Cyl. 250	3½	3½	None	18	4	⑦	10
	V8—302	4	3½	4	18	4	⑦	15
	V8—351W	4	3½	4	22	5	⑦	15
	V8—390	4	3½	4	25½	5	⑦	20½
	V8—428	4	3½	4	25½	5	⑦	20½
1970-72	6 Cyl. 170	3½	3½	None	16	2½	16	9½
	6 Cyl. 200	3½	3½	None	16	2½	⑦	9½
	6 Cyl. 250	3½	3½	None	18	4	⑦	11.3⑪
	V8—302⑬	4	3½	4	18	4	⑦	15⑭
	V8—351W and 351C	4	3½	4	22	5	⑦	15.5⑧
	V8—428	4	3½	4	25½	5	⑦	19.3
	V8—429	4⑩ ⑫	None	4	25½	5	⑦	19⑨

① Ranchero and wagon—20 gal.
② Fairlane—16 gal.
③ 1965 Falcon—16 gal.; 1965 Comet—20 gal.
④ V8 289 and 302—18 pts.
⑤ V8 289 and 302—4 pts.
⑥ V8 289 and 302—15 qts.
⑦ Falcon and Maverick—16 gal. Mustang and Falcon wagon—20 gal. Fairlane, Montego and Cougar—20 gal. Torino and Montego wagon and Ranchero—18 gal.
⑧ —1970 Mustang and Cougar—14.6
⑨ —CJ and SCJ—19.6.
⑩ —SCJ—6 (includes 1 qt. for filter and 1 qt. for oil cooler).
⑪ —1970 Mustang 9.8
⑫ —Boss 429—8 (incl. 2 qts. for filter and cooler.)
⑬ —Add an additional qt. for Boss 302 oil cooler.
⑭ —1970 Mustang—13.5 gal.

GENERAL CHASSIS AND BRAKE SPECIFICATIONS

YEAR	MODEL	CHASSIS		Master Cylinder (In.)	BRAKE CYLINDER BORE Wheel Cylinder Diameter (In.)		BRAKE DRUM Diameter (In.)	
		Overall Length (In.)	Tire Size		Front	Rear	Front	Rear
1965	6 Cyl.—Falcon Sedan	181.6	6.00 x 13	1.0	1 1/16	13/16	9	9
	Falcon Sta. Wag.	190.0	6.45 x 14	1.0	1 1/8	7/8	9	9
	Comet Sedan	195.3	6.95 x 14	1.0	1 1/16	13/16	9	9
	Comet Sta. Wag.	195.3	6.95 x 14	1.0	1 1/8	7/8	9	9
	V8—Falcon Sedan	181.6	6.45 x 14	1.0	1 1/8	29/32	10	10
	Falcon Sta. Wag.	190.0	6.95 x 14	1.0	1 1/8	15/16	10	10
	Comet Sd., Ex. Cali.	195.3	6.95 x 14	1.0	1 1/8	29/32	10	10
	Comet Caliente	195.3	6.95 x 14	1.0	1 1/8	29/32	10	10
	Comet Sta. Wag.	195.3	6.95 x 14	1.0	1 1/8	15/16	10	10
	Mustang, All	181.6	6.50 x 13†	1.0	1 1/8 ■	29/32	10■	10
	Fairlane, Exc. Sta. Wag.	198.4	6.95 x 14☆	1.0	1 1/8	29/32	10	10
	Fairlane, Sta. Wag.	203.2	7.35 x 14	1.0	1 3/32	15/16	10	10
1966	6 Cyl.—Falcon; Sedan	184.3	6.50 x 13	1.0	1 1/16	27/32	9	9
	Falcon; Sta. Wag.	198.7	7.35 x 14	1.0	1 1/16	27/32	9	9
	Comet; Sedan	203 *	6.95 x 14	1.0	1 1/16	27/32	9	9
	Comet; Sta. Wag.	199.9	7.75 x 14	1.0	1 1/16	27/32	9	9
	V8—Falcon; Sedan	184.3	6.95 x 14	1.0	1 1/8	29/32	10	10
	Falcon; Sta. Wag.	198.7	7.35 x 14	1.0	1 1/8	29/32	10	10
	Comet; Sedan	203 *	6.95 x 14●	1.0	1 1/8	29/32	10	10
	Comet; Sta. Wag.	199.9	7.75 x 14	1.0	1 1/8	29/32	10	10
	Mustang; All	181.6	6.95 x 14	1.0▲	1 1/8 ■	29/32	10■●●	10●●
	Fairlane 6 & 8; Exc. Wag.	197.0	6.95 x 14	1.0	1 1/8	29/32	10	10
	Fairlane, Sta. Wag.	199.8	6.95 x 14	1.0	1 1/8	29/32	10	10
	Fairlane V8—390	197.0	7.35 x 14	1.0	1 1/8	29/32	10	10
1967-68	6 Cyl.—Falcon (Sedan)	184.3	6.50 x 13	1.0②	1 1/16	27/32	9	9
	6 Cyl.—Falcon (Sta. Wag.)	198.7	7.75 x 14	1.0②	1 3/32 ⑫	15/16	10■	10
	V8—Falcon (Sedan)	184.3	6.95 x 14	1.0②	1 1/8 ⑫	29/32	10■	10
	V8—Falcon (Sta. Wag.)	198.7	7.75 x 14	1.0②	1 3/32 ⑫	15/16	10■	10
	6 Cyl.—Fairlane (Sedan)	197.0	7.35 x 14	1.0⑦	1 1/8 ⑫	29/32	10■	10

WHEEL ALIGNMENT

YEAR	MODEL	CASTER Range (Deg.)	CASTER Pref. Setting (Deg.)	CAMBER Range (Deg.)	CAMBER Pref. Setting (Deg.)	TOE-IN (In.)	KING-PIN INCLINATION (Deg.)	WHEEL PIVOT RATIO Inner Wheel	Outer Wheel
1965	Falcon & Comet	0 to 1P	1/2 P	1/4 N to 1 1/4 P	1/2 P	1/4 to 5/16	7	20 3/4	20
	Fairlane (1965)	1N to 1P	0	1/2 N to 1P	1/4 P	3/32 to 11/32	7 3/4	20	17 1/2
	6 Cyl.—Mustang	3/4 P to 1 3/4 P	1 1/4 P	0 to 1P	1/2 P	1/4 to 5/16	7	20	19
	V8—Mustang	1/4 N to 3/4 P	1/4 P	0 to 1P	1/2 P	1/4 to 5/16	7	20	18 3/4
1966	Falcon	1N to 1P	0	1/2 N to 1P	1/4 P	1/8 to 3/8	7 3/4	20	17 3/4
	Fairlane & Comet	1N to 1P	0	1/2 N to 1P	1/4 P	3/32 to 11/32	7 1/2	20	17 1/2
	6 Cyl. Mustang	0 to 2P	1P	1/4 N to 1 1/4 P	1/2 P	1/8 to 3/8	7	20	18 7/8 ①
	V8 Mustang	1N to 1P	0	1/4 N to 1 1/4 P	1/2 P	1/8 to 3/8	6 7/8	20	19 1/4 ①
1967	Comet, Falcon, Fairlane	1N to 0	1/2 N	1/4 N to 3/4 P	1/4 P	1/4 ± 1/16	7 1/2	20	17 3/4
	Cougar, Mustang	1/4 N to 3/4 P	1/4 P	1/2 P to 1 1/2 P	1P	3/16 ± 1/16	6 3/4	20	18 3/4
1968	Comet, Falcon, Fairlane, ② Montego	1 1/2 N to 1/2 P	1/2 N	1/2 N to 1P	1/4 P	1/4 ± 1/16	7	20	18 1/4
	Cougar & Mustang	3/4 N to 1 1/4 P	1/4 P	1/4 P to 1 3/4 P	1P	1/4 ± 1/16	6 3/4	20	18 3/4
1969	Falcon, Torino, Montego	1 3/4 N to 1/4 P	3/4 N	1/2 N to 1P	1/4 P	3/16 ± 1/16	7	20	18 1/8
	Cougar & Mustang	3/4 N to 1 1/4 P	1/4 P	1/4 P to 1 3/4 P	3/4 P	3/16 ± 1/16	6 3/4	20	18 3/4
1970-72	Montego, Falcon, Torino	1 1/4 N to 1/4 N	3/4 N	1/2 N to 1P	1/4 P	1/4 ± 1/16	7 2/3 ②	20	③
	Cougar & Mustang	1N to 1P	0	0 to 1 1/2 P⑤	1P	3/16 ± 1/16	6 3/4	20	18°40'
	Maverick, Comet	1 1/2 N to 1/2 P	1/2 N	1/2 N to 1/4 P	1/4 P	3/16 ± 1/16	6 3/4	20	18 3/4 ④

① —V8 power steering—18 3/4°; 6 cyl. power steering—20 1/4°. ③ —Falcon—18°6'; others with manual steering—17°19'; power steering—17°49'. ⑤ —1970 models—1/4 P to 1 3/4 P

② —Falcon—6 2/3.

④ —18.2° for power steering.

N—Negative.
P—Positive.

GENERAL CHASSIS AND BRAKE SPECIFICATIONS, continued

YEAR	MODEL	CHASSIS		BRAKE CYLINDER BORE			BRAKE DRUM	
		Overall Length (In.)	Tire Size	Master Cylinder (In.)	Wheel Cylinder Diameter (In.) Front	Rear	Diameter (In.) Front	Rear
	6 Cyl.—Fairlane (Sta. Wag.)	199.9	7.75 x 14	1.0[2]	$1\frac{3}{32}$	$\frac{15}{16}$	10■	10
	V8—Fairlane (Sedan)	197.0	7.35 x 14	1.0[2]	$1\frac{1}{8}$	$\frac{29}{32}$	10■	10
	V8—Fairlane (Sta. Wag.)	199.9	7.75 x 14	1.0[2]	$1\frac{3}{32}$	$\frac{15}{16}$	10■	10
	6 Cyl.—Mustang	183.6	7.35 x 14	1.0	$1\frac{1}{16}$[9]	$\frac{27}{32}$	10	10
	V8—Mustang	183.6	7.35 x 14	1.0	$1\frac{1}{8}$[9]	$\frac{7}{8}$	10■	10
	6 Cyl.—Comet (Exc. 2 Door Sedan)	203.5	7.35 x 14	1.0[2]	$1\frac{1}{8}$[9]	$\frac{29}{32}$	10■	10
	6 Cyl.—Comet (2 Door Sedan)	196.4	7.35 x 14	1.0[2]	$1\frac{1}{8}$[9]	$\frac{29}{32}$	10■	10
	6 Cyl.—Comet (Sta. Wag.)	199.9	7.75 x 14	1.0[2]	$1\frac{3}{32}$[9]	$\frac{15}{16}$	10■	10
	V8—Comet (Exc. 2 Door Sedan)	203.5	7.35 x 14	1.0[2]	$1\frac{1}{8}$[9]	$\frac{29}{32}$	10■	10
	V8—Comet (2 Door Sedan)	196.4	7.35 x 14	1.0[2]	$1\frac{1}{8}$[9]	$\frac{29}{32}$	10■	10
	V8—Comet (Sta. Wag.)	199.9	7.75 x 14	1.0[2]	$1\frac{3}{32}$[9]	$\frac{15}{16}$	10■	10
	V8—Cougar (289, 302 Engine)	190.3	7.35 x 14[3]	1.0	$1\frac{1}{8}$[9]	$\frac{7}{8}$	11.4[1]	10
	V8—Cougar (390, 427 Engine)	190.3	7.35 x 14[3]	1.0	$1\frac{3}{32}$[9]	$\frac{13}{16}$	11.4[1]	10
	6 Cyl. Montego	206.1	7.35 x 14	1.0[2]	$1\frac{1}{8}$[9]	$\frac{29}{32}$	10	10
	V8—Montego	206.1	7.35 x 14[3]	1.0[2]	$1\frac{3}{32}$[9]	$\frac{7}{8}$	10	10
1969	Cougar	193.8	[4]	1.0[2]	$1\frac{3}{32}$[9]	$\frac{7}{8}$	10■	10
	Falcon 6 Cyl.—200	184.3	[4]	1.0[2]	$1\frac{1}{16}$[9]	$\frac{27}{32}$	9■	9
	Falcon Sta. Wag.	198.7	[4]	1.0[2]	$1\frac{3}{32}$[9]	$\frac{15}{16}$	10■	10
	Falcon Pass. Car, Exc. 6 Cyl.—200	184.3	[4]	1.0[2]	$1\frac{1}{8}$[9]	$\frac{7}{8}$	10■	10
	Fairlane & Montego, Pass. 250, 302	201.1[5]	[4]	1.0[2]	$1\frac{1}{8}$[9]	$\frac{7}{8}$	10■	10
	Fairlane & Montego, P & C, 351, 390	201.1[5]	[4]	1.0[2]	$1\frac{3}{32}$[9]	$\frac{7}{8}$	10■	10
	Fairlane & Montego, Conv. exc. above	201.1[5]	[4]	1.0[2]	$1\frac{3}{32}$[9]	$\frac{7}{8}$	10■	10
	Fairlane Sta. Wagons	203.9	[4]	1.0[2]	$1\frac{3}{32}$[9]	$\frac{15}{16}$	10■	10
	Mustang 6 Cyl.	187.4	[4]	1.0	$1\frac{1}{16}$[9]	$\frac{27}{32}$	9	9
	Mustang V8—302	187.4	[4]	1.0	$1\frac{1}{8}$[9]	$\frac{7}{8}$	10■	10
	Mustang V8 exc. 302	187.4	[4]	1.0	$1\frac{3}{32}$[9]	$\frac{7}{8}$	10■	10
1970	Cougar	196.1	[4]	1.0	$1\frac{1}{8}$[9]	$\frac{29}{32}$	10■	10
	Falcon 6 Cyl. Sedan	206.2	[4]	1.0	$1\frac{1}{16}$	$\frac{27}{32}$	9	9
	Falcon Sta. Wag.	209.0	[4]	1.0	$1\frac{1}{8}$[9]	$\frac{31}{32}$	10■	10
	Falcon V8 Sedan	206.2	[4]	1.0	$1\frac{1}{8}$[9]	$\frac{29}{32}$	10■	10
	Torino & Montego Sedan	206.2[6]	[4]	1.0[2]	$1\frac{1}{8}$[9]	$\frac{29}{32}$	10■	10
	Torino & Montego Sta. Wagon	209.0[7]	[4]	1.0[2]	$1\frac{1}{8}$[9]	$\frac{31}{32}$	10■	10
	Maverick 6 Cyl.	179.4	[4]	1.0	$1\frac{1}{16}$	$\frac{27}{32}$	9	9
	Mustang 6 Cyl.	187.4	[4]	1.0	$1\frac{1}{16}$	$\frac{27}{32}$	9	9
	Mustang V8	187.4	[4]	1.0	$1\frac{1}{8}$[9]	$\frac{7}{8}$[10]	10■	10
1971-72	Cougar	196.7	[4]	1.0	$1\frac{1}{8}$[10]	$\frac{29}{32}$	10■	10
	Mustang 6 Cyl.	189.5	[4]	1.0	$1\frac{1}{8}$[9]	$\frac{7}{8}$	10■	10
	Mustang V8	189.5	[4]	1.0	$1\frac{1}{8}$	$\frac{29}{32}$	9	10
	Maverick 6 Cyl.	179.4[8]	[4]	1.0	$1\frac{1}{16}$	$\frac{27}{32}$	9	9
	Maverick V8	179.4[8]	[4]	1.0	$1\frac{1}{8}$	$\frac{7}{8}$	10	10
	Comet—6 Cyl.	181.8[8]	[4]	1.0	$1\frac{1}{16}$	$\frac{27}{32}$	10■	9
	Comet—302 V8	181.8[8]	[4]	1.0	$1\frac{1}{8}$	$\frac{7}{8}$	10■	10
	Montego, Torino, Falcon Sedans	206.2[6]	[4]	1.0[2]	$1\frac{1}{8}$[9]	$\frac{29}{32}$	10■	10
	Montego, Torino, Falcon Sta. Wagons	209.0[7]	[4]	1.0[2]	$1\frac{1}{8}$[9]	$\frac{31}{32}$	10■	10

†—Optional—6.95 x 14
■—Disc brakes 11.3 in.
*—202 Series—195.9
●—With V8—390, 7.35 x 14 & 7.75 x 14
▲--With Pwr. Brakes—.875
● ●—6 Cyl. 9 in. Drums
☆—V8 Models—7.35 x 14
[1]—Disc front.
[2]—0.9375 in. when equipped with power brakes or disc brakes.
[3]—GT Models F70 x 14
[4]—All tire information posted in each individual car.
[5]—Montego—206.2
[6]—Montego—209.9
[7]—Montego—211.8
[8]—4-dr. sedan—188.7
[9]—Disc Brakes—2.38
[10]—351, 390, 428 V8—$\frac{27}{32}$ in.

GENERAL ENGINE SPECIFICATIONS

YEAR	CU. IN. DISPLACEMENT	CARBURETOR	ADVERTIZED HORSEPOWER @ RPM	ADVERTIZED TORQUE @ RPM (FT. LBS.)	A.M.A. HORSEPOWER	BORE AND STROKE (IN.)	ADVERTIZED COMPRESSION RATIO	VALVE LIFTER TYPE	NORMAL OIL PRESSURE @ 2000 RPM (PSI)
1965-66	6 Cyl.—170	1-BBL.	105 @ 4400	158 @ 2400	29.4	3.500 x 2.940	9.1-1	Hyd.	35-60
	6 Cyl.—200	1-BBL.	120 @ 4400	185 @ 2400	32.5	3.680 x 3.126	9.2-1	Hyd.	35-60
	V8—289	2-BBL.	200 @ 4400	282 @ 2400	51.2	4.000 x 2.870	9.3-1	Hyd.	35-60
	V8—289	4-BBL.	225 @ 4800	305 @ 3200	51.2	4.000 x 2.870	10.0-1	Hyd.	35-60
	V8—289	4-BBL.	271 @ 6000	312 @ 3400	51.2	4.000 x 2.870	10.5-1	Mech.	35-55
	V8—390	2-BBL.	265 @ 4400	401 @ 2600	52.49	4.050 x 3.780	9.5-1	Hyd.	35-55
	V8—390	4-BBL.	315 @ 4600	427 @ 2800	52.49	4.050 x 3.780	10.5-1	Hyd.	35-55
	V8—390	4-BBL.	335 @ 4800	427 @ 3200	52.49	4.050 x 3.780	10.5-1	Hyd.	35-55
1967	6 Cyl.—170	1-BBL.	105 @ 4400	158 @ 2400	29.4	3.500 x 2.940	9.1-1	Hyd.	35-55
	6 Cyl.—200	1-BBL.	120 @ 4400	190 @ 2400	32.5	3.680 x 3.130	9.2-1	Hyd.	35-55
	V8—289	2-BBL.	200 @ 4400	282 @ 2400	51.2	4.000 x 2.870	9.3-1	Hyd.	35-55
	V8—289	4-BBL.	225 @ 4800	305 @ 3200	51.2	4.000 x 2.870	9.8-1	Hyd.	35-55
	V8—289	4-BBL.	271 @ 6000	312 @ 3400	51.2	4.000 x 2.870	10.0-1	Mech.	35-55
	V8—390	2-BBL.	265 @ 4400	401 @ 2600	52.49	4.050 x 3.780	9.5-1	Hyd.	35-55
	V8—390	4-BBL.	315 @ 4600	427 @ 2800	52.49	4.050 x 3.780	10.5-1	Hyd.	35-55
	V8—390	4-BBL.	335 @ 4800	427 @ 3200	52.49	4.050 x 3.780	10.5-1	Hyd.	35-55
	V8—427	4-BBL.	410 @ 5600	476 @ 3400	57.33	4.233 x 3.781	11.1-1	Mech.	35-65
	V8—427	2-4-BBL.	425 @ 6000	480 @ 3700	57.33	4.233 x 3.781	11.1-1	Mech.	35-65
1968	6 Cyl.—170	1-BBL.	100 @ 4400	156 @ 2400	29.40	3.500 x 2.940	8.7-1	Hyd.	35-60
	6 Cyl.—200	1-BBL.	115 @ 3800	190 @ 2200	32.50	3.680 x 3.130	8.8-1	Hyd.	35-60
	V8—289	2-BBL.	195 @ 4400	280 @ 2400	51.20	4.000 x 2.870	8.7-1	Hyd.	35-60
	V8—302	2-BBL.	210 @ 4600	295 @ 2600	51.20	4.000 x 3.000	9.0-1	Hyd.	35-60
	V8—302	4-BBL.	230 @ 4800	310 @ 2800	51.20	4.000 x 3.000	10.0-1	Hyd.	35-60
	V8—390	2-BBL.	265 @ 4400	390 @ 2600	52.49	4.050 x 3.780	9.5-1	Hyd.	35-60
	V8—390	4-BBL.	325 @ 4800	427 @ 3200	52.49	4.050 x 3.780	10.5-1	Hyd.	35-60
	V8—427	4-BBL.	390 @ 5600	460 @ 3200	57.30	4.236 x 3.780	10.9-1	Hyd.	35-60
1969	6 Cyl.—170	1-BBL.	105 @ 4400	158 @ 2400	29.40	3.500 x 2.940	9.1-1	Hyd.	35-60
	6 Cyl.—200	1-BBL.	120 @ 4400	190 @ 2400	32.50	3.680 x 3.130	8.8-1	Hyd.	35-60
	6 Cyl.—250	1-BBL.	155 @ 4000	240 @ 1600	32.50	3.680 x 3.910	9.0-1	Hyd.	35-60
	V8—302	2-BBL.	210 @ 4400	275 @ 2400	51.20	4.000 x 3.000	9.5-1	Hyd.	35-60
	V8—351	2-BBL.	250 @ 4600	355 @ 2600	51.20	4.000 x 3.500	9.5-1	Hyd.	35-60
	V8—351	4-BBL.	290 @ 4800	385 @ 3200	51.20	4.000 x 3.500	10.7-1	Hyd.	35-60
	V8—390	4-BBL.	320 @ 4800	427 @ 3200	52.49	4.050 x 3.780	10.5-1	Hyd.	35-60
	V8—428 CJ	4-BBL.	335 @ 5200	440 @ 3400	54.59	4.130 x 3.980	10.6-1	Hyd.	35-60
1970	6 Cyl.—170	1-BBL.	105 @ 4400	156 @ 2200	29.40	3.502 x 2.940	8.7-1	Hyd.	35-60
	6 Cyl.—200	1-BBL.	120 @ 4000	190 @ 2000	32.50	3.682 x 3.126	8.7-1	Hyd.	35-60
	6 Cyl.—250	1-BBL.	155 @ 4400	240 @ 1600	32.50	3.682 x 3.190	9.0-1	Hyd.	35-60
	V8—302	2-BBL.	210 @ 4400	295 @ 2400	51.2	4.000 x 3.000	9.5-1	Hyd.	35-60
	V8—302 Boss	4-BBL.	290 @ 5800	290 @ 4300	51.2	4.000 x 3.000	10.5-1	Mech.	35-60
	V8—351W or C	2-BBL.	250 @ 4600	355 @ 2600	51.2	4.000 x 3.500	9.5-1	Hyd.	35-60
	V8—351C	4-BBL.	300 @ 5400	380 @ 3400	51.2	4.000 x 3.500	11.0-1	Hyd.	35-60
	V8—428 CJ	4-BBL.	335 @ 5200	440 @ 3400	54.58	4.130 x 3.984	10.6-1	Hyd.	35-60
	V8—429	4-BBL.	360 @ 4600	476 @ 2800	60.80	4.360 x 3.590	10.5-1	Hyd.	35-60
	V8—429 CJ	4-BBL.	370 @ 5400	450 @ 3400	60.83	4.360 x 3.590	11.3-1	Hyd.	35-60
	V8—429 SCJ	4-BBL.	375 @ 5400	450 @ 3400	60.83	4.360 x 3.590	11.3-1	Mech.	35-60
	V8—429 Boss	4-BBL.	375 @ 5200	450 @ 3400	60.83	4.360 x 3.590	10.5-1	Mech.	45-60

GENERAL ENGINE SPECIFICATIONS, continued

YEAR	CU. IN. DISPLACEMENT	CARBURETOR	ADVERTIZED HORSEPOWER @ RPM	ADVERTIZED TORQUE @ RPM (FT. LBS.)	A.M.A. HORSEPOWER	BORE AND STROKE (IN.)	ADVERTIZED COMPRESSION RATIO	VALVE LIFTER TYPE	NORMAL OIL PRESSURE @ 200 RPM (PSI)
1971	6 Cyl.—170	1-BBL.	100 @ 4200	148 @ 2200	29.40	3.502 x 2.940	8.7-1	Hyd.	35–60
	6 Cyl.—200	1-BBL.	115 @ 4000	180 @ 2200	32.5	3.682 x 3.126	8.7-1	Hyd.	35–60
	6 Cyl.—250	1-BBL.	145 @ 4000	232 @ 1600	32.5	3.682 x 3.190	9.0-1	Hyd.	35–60
	V8—302	2-BBL.	210 @ 4600	296 @ 2600	51.2	4.000 x 3.000	9.0-1	Hyd.	35–60
	V8—351	2-BBL.	240 @ 4600	350 @ 2600	51.2	4.000 x 3.500	9.0-1	Hyd.	35–60
	V8—351	4-BBL.	285 @ 5400	370 @ 3400	51.2	4.000 x 3.500	9.7-1	Hyd.	35–60
	V8—351 CJ*	4-BBL.	280 @ 5800	345 @ 3400	51.2	4.000 x 3.500	9.0-1	Hyd.	35–60
	V8—351 HO	4-BBL.	330 @ 5800	380 @ 4300	51.2	4.000 x 3.500	11.5-1	Mech.	35–60
	V8—429	4-BBL.	360 @ 4600	476 @ 3000	60.80	4.360 x 3.590	10.5-1	Hyd.	35–60
	V8—429 CJ	4-BBL.	370 @ 5400	450 @ 3400	60.83	4.360 x 3.590	11.3-1	Hyd.	35–60
	V8—429 SCJ	4-BBL.	375 @ 5400	450 @ 3400	60.83	4.360 x 3.590	11.3-1	Mech.	35–60
1971½-72	6 Cyl.—170	1-BBL.	100 @ 4200 ①	148 @ 2200 ①	29.40	3.502 x 2.940	8.7-1 ①	Hyd.	35–60
	6 Cyl.—200	1-BBL.	115 @ 4000 ①	180 @ 2200 ①	32.5	3.682 x 3.126	8.7-1 ①	Hyd.	35–60
	6 Cyl.—240	1-BBL.	145 @ 4000 ①	232 @ 1600 ①	32.5	3.682 x 3.190	9.0-1 ①	Hyd.	35–60
	V8—302	2-BBL.	210 @ 4600 ①	296 @ 2600 ①	51.2	4.000 x 3.000	9.0-1 ①	Hyd.	35–60
	V8—351	2-BBL.	240 @ 4600 ①	350 @ 2600 ①	51.2	4.000 x 3.500	9.0-1 ①	Hyd.	35–60
	V8—351	4-BBL.	255 @ 4800 ①	360 @ 3000 ①	51.2	4.000 x 3.500	9.0-1 ①	Hyd.	35–60
	V8—351 CJ*	4-BBL.	280 @ 5800 ①	345 @ 3400 ①	51.2	4.000 x 3.500	9.0-1 ①	Hyd.	35–60

*Also known as 351 GT.

①—1971½ advertized horsepower and torque ratings are shown in tables. 1972 S.A.E. net horsepower, compression ratios or net torque ratings were not available at press time, however, they will be substantially lower than 1971½ figures, since they are based on S.A.E. J245 standards, representing actual output of the engine installed in any particular vehicle.

LIGHT BULBS
1965–66

Unit	Candela ① or Wattage	Trade Number	Unit	Candela ① or Wattage	Trade Number
Headlight no. 1 (inner or lower)	37.5 W.	4001	Turn signal (inst. panel)	2 C.	1895
Headlight no. 2 (outer or upper)	37.5/50 W.	4002	Illumination		
Headlight (Falcon-Mustang)	40/50 W.	6012	Instruments	2 C.	1895
Fog light (Mustang)	35 W.	4415	Clock	2 C.	1895
Front turn signal/parking	32 C.	1157	Heater control	2 C.	1895
Rear turn signal and stop/tail	32 C.	1157	Hi-beam indicator	2 C.	1895
License plate	4 C.	1155	Speedometer	2 C.	1895
Back-up lights (Falcon sdn)	32 C.	1156	Glove compartment	2 C.	1895
Back-up lights (Falcon sta. wag.)	32 C.	1076	Glove compartment (Mustang console)	1.5 C.	1445
Back-up lights (Mustang)	21 C.	1142	Courtesy light (ins. panel)	6 C.	631
Spot light	30 W.	4405	Radio pilot light (Fairlane)	2 C.	1892
Luggage compartment	6 C.	631	Radio pilot light (Mustang)	1.9 C.	1891
Luggage compartment (Fairlane)	15 C.	93	Radio pilot light (Falcon)	2 C.	1891
Cargo light (wagon—Comet)	15 C.	1003	Radio dial (Comet)	2 C.	1895
Engine compartment (Comet)	15 C.	93	Arm rest courtesy (Fairlane)	6 C.	631
Dome light	15 C.	1003	Courtesy light (front door—Comet)	4 C.	1155
Warning lights			Courtesy light (fast back—Mustang)	15 C.	1003
Oil and generator	2 C.	1895	Courtesy light (Falcon conv.)	6 C.	631
Park brake (Comet—Mustang)	1 C.	257	Ash receptacle (Fairlane)	1.5 C.	1445
Park brake	2 C.	1895	Courtesy light (Mustang console)	3 C.	1816
Seat belt (Fairlane)	1.6 C.	257	Clock (Mustang rally pac)	3 C.	1816
Seat belt (Comet—Falcon)	2 C.	1895	Tachometer (Mustang—rally pac)	2 C.	1895
Emergency flasher	2 C.	1895	Automatic transmission control	2 C.	1895
Alternator	2 C.	1895	Map light	6 C.	631

①—Candela is the new international term for candlepower

MERCURY INTERMEDIATE, FALCON, FAIRLANE, AND MUSTANG
1967

Light Description	Mercury Intermediate		Falcon		Fairlane		Mustang	
	Bulb No.	Candela or Wattage	Bulb No.	Candela or Wattage	Bulb No.	Candela or Wattage	Bulb No.	Candela or Wattage
Ash receptacle or cigar lighter					1445	1.5 C.	1895	2 C.
Backup lights—sedan	1156	32 C.	1156	32 C.	1156	32 C.	1142	21 C.
station wagon	1156	32 C.	1076	32 C.	1156	32 C.		
Courtesy lamp (console)							1895	2 C.
(convertible and inst. panel)	631	6 C.	631	6 C.	631	6 C.	631	6 C.
(door mounting or armrest)	631	6 C.			631	6 C.	1004 ⑤	15 C.
Cargo lamp (station wagon)	1003	15 C.	1003	15 C.	1003	15 C.		
Dome lamp	1003	15 C.	1003	15 C.	1003	15 C.	1003	15 C.
Engine compartment	631	6 C.	631	6 C.	631	6 C.	631	6 C.
Glove compartment or console	1895	2 C.	1895	2 C.	1895	2 C.	1445	1.5 C.
Headlamps hi-lo beam (outer or upper)	4002	37.5–50 W	6012	40–50 W	4002	37.5–50 W	6012 ④	40–50 W
hi beam (inner or lower)	4001	37.5 W			4001	37.5 W		
License lamp	97	4 C.	97	4 C.	97	4 C.	97	4 C.
Luggage compartment	631	6 C.	631	6 C.	631	6 C.	631	6 C.
Map light	631	6 C.	631	6 C.	631	6 C.	631	6 C.
Park and turn signal lamp	1157-A	4-32 C.	1157	4-32 C.	1157	4-32 C.	1157-A	4-32 C.
Spotlight (4.4 in. dia.)	4405	30 W	4405	30 W	4405	30 W	4405	30 W
Taillight, stop and turn signal lamp	1157	4-32 C.	1157	4-32 C.	1157	4-32 C.	1157	4-32 C.
Instrument panel illumination								
Clock & ignition key	1895	2 C.	1816	3 C.	1895	2 C.	1895 ①	2 C.
Control nomenclature	1895	2 C.	1895	2 C.	1895	2 C.	1895	2 C.
Gages and speedometer	1895	2 C.	1895	2 C.	1895	2 C.	1895	2 C.
Radio dial light	1893	1.9 C.	1445	1.5 C.	1895	2 C.	1893	1.9 C.
Tachometer	1895	2 C.	1895	2 C.	1895	2 C.	1895	2 C.
Trans control selector indicator	1445	1.5 C.	1445	1.5 C.	1445	1.5 C.	1445	1.5 C.
Turn signal indicators (L and R) ③	1895	2 C.	1895	2 C.	1895	2 C.	1895	2 C.
Warning lights, panel or lamp kits								
Emergency flasher	1895	2 C.	1895	2 C.	1895	2 C.	1895	2 C.
Hi-beam indicator	1895	2 C.	1895	2 C.	1895	2 C.	1895	2 C.
Oil press., alt., and temp warning	1895	2 C.	1895	2 C.	1895	2 C.	1895	2 C.
Parking brake warning	1895	2 C.	1895	2 C.	1895	2 C.	257	1.6 C.
Seat belt warning	1895	2 C.	1895	2C ②	257	1.6 C.	1891	2 C.

① —1816 (3C.) for Rally PAC ② —1895G bulb for States of Minnesota and Wisconsin ⑤ —Fastback 1004 15C. for door mounted light
② —R.P.O. ④ —Fog light 4415 (35W)

COUGAR
1967

Light Description	Bulb No.	Candela or Wattage	Light Description	Bulb No.	Candela or Wattage
Headlight-hi-lo beam (outer)	4002	37.5 & 50 Watts	Gages	1895	2 C.
Headlight-hi beam (inner)	4001	37.5 Watts	Hi-beam	1895	2 C.
Front parking and turn signal	1157A	4-32C.	Turn signal	1895	2 C.
Rear and stop and turn signal	1157	4-32C.	Clock	1895	2 C.
License plate	97	4 C.	Turn signal indicator ①	1895-G	2 C.
Map light	631	6 C.	Courtesy light	631	6 C.
"C" pillar light	1003	15 C.	Hand brake signal	1895	2 C.
Auto-trans. quadrant	158	2 C.	Radio AM	1893	1.9 C.
Turn signal indicator	53X	1 C.	Spotlight	4405	30 Watts
Door courtesy	1816	3 C.	Console light	1816	3 C.
Luggage compartment	631	6 C.	Low fuel warning	1445	1.5 C.
Glove compartment	631	6 C.	Emergency flasher warning	1445	1.5 C.
Back-up light	1156	32 C.	Door lock warning	256	1.6 C.
Dome	1816	3 C.	Seat belt warning	1445	1.5 C.
Speedometer	1445	1.5 C.			

① —For States of Minnesota and Wisconsin

FALCON, FAIRLANE, MONTEGO, AND MUSTANG
1968

Light Description	Montego		Falcon		Fairlane		Mustang	
	Bulb No.	Candela or Wattage	Bulb No.	Candela or Wattage	Bulb No.	Candela or Wattage	Bulb No.	Candela or Wattage
Ash receptacle or cigar lighter					1445	1.5C.	1895	2C.
Backup lights—sedan	1156	32C.	1156	32C.	1156	32C.	1142	21C.
station wagon	1156	32C.	1076	32C.	1156	32C.	—	—
Courtesy lamp (console)							1816	3C.
(convertible and inst. panel)	631	6C.	631	6C.	631	6C.	631	6C.
(door mounting or armrest)	631	6C.	—	—	631	6C.	631	6C.
Cargo lamp (station wagon)	1003	15C.	1003	15C.	1003	15C.	—	—
Dome lamp	1003	15C.	1003	15C.	1003	15C.	1003	15C.
Engine compartment	631	6C.	631	6C.	631	6C.	631	6C.
Glove compartment or console	1895	2C.	1895	2C.	1895	2C.	1895	2C.
Headlamps—hi-lo beam (outer)	4002	37.5-50W	6012	40-50W	4002	37.5-50W	6012 ◯	40-50W
hi beam (inner)	4001	37.5W	—	—	4001	37.5W	—	—
License lamp	97	4C.	97	4C.	97	4C.	97	4C.
Luggage compartment	631	6C.	631	6C.	631	6C.	631	6C
Map light	631	6C.	631	6C.	631	6C.	631	6C.
Park and turn signal lamp	1157-A	4-32C.	1157-NA	4-32C.	1157-NA	4-32C.	1157-A	4-32C.
Spotlight (4.4 in. dia.)	4405	30W	4405	30W	4405	30W	4405	30W
Taillight, stop and turn signal lamp	1157	4-32C.	1157	4-32C.	1157	4-32C.	1157	4-32C.
Instrument panel illumination								
Clock & ignition key	1895	2C.	1816	3C.	1895	2C.	1895②	2C.
Control nomenclature	1895	2C.	1895	2C.	1895	2C.	1895	2C.
Gages and speedometer	194	2C.	194	2C.	194	2C.	1895	2C.
Radio dial light	1893	1.9C.	1893	1.9C.	1893	1.9C.	1893	1.9C.
Tachometer	1895	2C.	1895	2C.	1895	2C.	1895	2C.
Trans. control selector indicator	161	1C.	161	1C.	161	1C.	1893	1.9C.
Turn signal indicators (L and R)	194	2C.	194	2C.	194	2C.	1895	2C.
Warning lights, panel or lamp kits								
Emergency flasher	194	2C.	194	2C.	194	2C.	1895	2C.
Hi-beam indicator	194	2C.	194	2C.	194	2C.	1895	2C.
Oil press., alt., and temp warning	194	2C.	194	2C.	194	2C.	1895	2C.
Parking brake warning ③	194	2C.	1895	2C.	1895	2C.	256	1.6C.
Seat belt warning	1895	2C.	1895	2C.	1895	2C.	—	—
Ignition key	—	—	1895	2C.	—	—	—	—
Front side marker	1178-A	4C.	1178-A	4C.	—	—	1178-A	4C.
Turn signal indicator (mounted on hood) ③	—	—	—	—	—	—	53X	1C.

① — Fog light 4415 (35W)   ② —1816 (3C.) for rally pac   ③ —R.P.O.

COUGAR
1968

Light Description	Bulb No.	Candela or Wattage	Light Description	Bulb No.	Candela or Wattage
Headlight—hi-lo beam (outer)	4002	37.5 & 50 Watts	Gages	1895	2C.
Headlight—hi beam (inner)	4001	37.5 Watts	Hi-beam	1895	2C.
Front parking and turn signal	1157A	4-32C.	Turn signal	1895	2C.
Rear and stop and turn signal	1157	4-32C.	Clock	1895	2C.
License plate	97	4C.	Turn signal indicator	1895	2C.
Map light	631	6C.	Courtesy light	631	6C.
"C" pillar light	1003	15C.	Hand brake signal	1895	2C.
Auto-trans. quadrant	1445	1.5C.	Radio AM	1893	1.9C.
Door courtesy	1816	3C.	Spotlight	4405	30 Watts
Luggage compartment	631	6C.	Console light	1816	3C.
Glove compartment	631	6C.	Low fuel warning	1895	2C.
Back-up light	1156	32C.	Door lock warning	257	1.6C.
Front side marker	97N.A.	4C.	Seat belt warning	1895	2C.
Speedometer	1895	2C.			

1969

Light Description	Montego		Falcon		Fairlane		Mustang		Cougar	
	Bulb No.	Candela or Wattage	Bulb No.	Candela or Wattage	Bulb No.	Candela or Wattage	Bulb No.	Candela or Wattage	Bulb No.	Candela or Wattage
Ash receptacle or cigar lighter			1445	1.5C.	1445	1.5C.			1445	1.5C.
Auxiliary instrument cluster					1895	2C.				
Back-up lights										
sedan	1156	32C.	1156	32C.	1156	32C.	1142	21C.	1156	32C.
station wagon	1157	32C. 4C.	1076	32C.	1156	32C.				
Cargo light (station wagon)	1003	15C.	1003	15C.	1003	15C.				
Courtesy light										
C-pillar							1003	15C.	1003	15C.
floor console							1445	1.5C.	1816	3C.
convertible or inst. panel	631	6C.	631	6C.	631	6C.	631	6C.	631	6C.
door mounted							212	6C.	212	6C.
Cruise light (speed control)									1895	2C.
Dome light	1003	15C.	1003	15C.	1003	15C.	1003	15C.		
Door ajar indicator	1895	2C.	1895	2C.	1895	2C.			194	2C.
Door ajar indicator (convenience pkg.)									257	1.6C.
Engine compartment	631	6C.	631	6C.	631	6C.	631	6C.	631	6C.
Fog light					4415	35W	4415	35W		
Fog light switch					53X	1C.	53X	1C.		
Front park and turn signal light	1157A	3-32C.	1157	3-32C.	1157NA②	3-32C.	1157A	3-32C.	1157A	3-32C.
Front side marker	1178A	4C.	1178A	4C.			1178A	4C.	194A	2C.
Glove compartment	1891	2C.	1891	2C.	1891	2C.	1891	2C.	1891	2C.
Headlights										
hi-lo beam	4002	37.5-50W	6012	40-50W	4002	37.5-50W	4002	37.5-50W	4002	37.5-50W
hi-beam	4001	37.5W			4001	37.5-5W			4001	37.5W
Hi-beam indicator	194	2C.	194	2C.	194	2C.	194	2C.	194	2C.
Ignition key			1895	2C.	1895	2C.			1895	2C.
Instrument panel illumination										
clock	1895	2C.			1895	2C.	1895	2C.	1895	2C.
control nomenclature heater and A/C			1895	2C.	1895	2C.	1895	2C.	1895	2C.
gauges and speedometer	194	2C.	194	2C.	194	2C.	194	2C.	194	2C.
tachometer							1895	2C.		
License light	97	4C.	97	4C.	97	4C.	97	4C.	97	4C.
Low fuel indicator	1895	2C.	1895	2C.	1895	2C.			194	2C.
Low fuel indicator (convenience pkg.)									1895	2C.
Luggage compartment	631	6C.	631	6C.	631	6C.	631	6C.	631	6C.
Map light	631	6C.	631	6C.	631	6C.			1816	3C.
Oil press., service brakes, alternator and temp. indicator	194	2C.	194	2C.	194	2C.	194	2C.	194②	2C.
Parking brake indicator					257	1.6C.	256	1.6C.	194④	2C.
Parking brake indicator (convenience pkg.)	1895	2C.	257	1.6C.	1895	2C.			256③	1.6C.
Radio dial light	1893	1.9C.	1893	1.9C.	1893	1.9C.	1893	1.9C.	1893	1.9C.
AM/FM stereo dial light	1892	1.3C.			1892	1.3C.	1892	1.3C.	1892	1.3C.
Rear side marker	194	2C.	194	2C.	194	2C.	194	2C.	194	2C.
Roof console							631	6C.		
Seat belt indicator	1895	2C.	1895	2C.	1895	2C.	1895	2C.	194	2C.
Seat belt indicator (convenience pkg.)							1891	2C.	1891	2C.
Spotlight (4.4 inch diameter)	4405	30W	4405	30W	4405	30W	4405	30W	4405	30W
Taillight, stop and turn signal light	1157	3-32C.	1157	3-32C.	1157	3-32C.	1157A	3-32C.	1157	3-32C.
Trans. control selector indicator (column mounted)	161	1C.	161	1C.	161	1C.	1893	1.9C.	1445	1.5C.
Trunk light (portable)	1003	15C.	1003	15C.	1003	15C.	1003	15C.	1003	15C.
Turn signal indicators (L and R)	194	2C.	194	2C.	194	2C.	194	2C.	194	2C.
Turn signal indicator (mounted on hood)					1895	2C.	1895	2C.		

① — Candela is the international term for candle power.　　③ — Except XR7.
② — Service brake indicator light only.　　④ — XR7.

FAIRLANE
1970

Light Description	Candle Power or Wattage	Trade No.
Standard Equipment		
Headlamps—hi & lo	37.5 & 50 Watts	4002
Headlamps—hi-beams	37.5 Watts	4001
Front park/turn/side marker	3-32 c.p.	1157A①
Rear tail/stop/turn sedan	3-32 c.p.	1157
sta. wagon	3-32 c.p.	1157
Back-up lamps	32 c.p.	1156
License plate lamp	4 c.p.	97
sta. wagon	4 c.p.	97
Dome lamp	12 c.p.	105
Hoot mtd. turn signals (GT)	2 c.p.	1895
Emergency flashers—included in front & rear turn signals		
Front side marker	2 c.p.	194
Rear side marker	2 c.p.	194
Instrument Panel Cluster	2 c.p.	194
Courtesy lamp (conv. only)	Fuse type	562
Hi-beam indicator	2 c.p.	194
Turn signal indicators	2 c.p.	194
Warning lights (oil, alt., brake system)	2 c.p.	194
Fuel gauge—speedometer	2 c.p.	194
Heater (or A/C opt.) bar.	2 c.p.	1895
Clock (optional)	2 c.p.	1895
Deluxe seat belt (option)	2 c.p.	1895

Light Description	Candle Power or Wattage	Trade No.
Emergency flasher indicators— included in turn signal indicators		
Optional Equipment		
Courtesy lamp	6 c.p.	631
Fog lamps—clear	35 Watts	4415
Fog lamp switch	1 c.p.	53X
Glove compartment	2 c.p.	1891
Spotlight—4.4″ dia.	30 Watts	4405
Radio pilot light (AM radio)	1.9 c.p.	1893
Tachometer	2 c.p.	1895
Auto. trans. quadrant	1.5 c.p.	1445
Console lamp	3 c.p.	1816
Luggage comp. light	12 c.p.	105
Floor shift quadrant	1.5 c.p.	1445
Parking brake—warning	2 c.p.	1895
Engine compartment	6 c.p.	631
Portable trunk lamp	15 c.p.	1003
Aux. inst. cluster	2 c.p.	1895
Map lamp	6 c.p.	631
Cargo lamp—sta. wag.	12 c.p.	105
AM/FM (MPX) radio	1.9 c.p.	1893
Hood mtd. turn signals (optional with hi perf. eng.)	2 c.p.	1895
Ash tray	1.5 c.p.	1445
Headlights—on	2 c.p.	1859

① —Amber.

MONTEGO
1970

Lamp Description	Candle Power or Wattage	Trade No.
Standard Equipment		
Headlamps		
hi-lo beam	37.5 & 50 Watts	4002
hi-beam	37.5 Watts	4001
Front park and turn	3-32 c.p.	1157A
Rear, stop and turn (passenger)	3-32 c.p.	1157
Rear, stop and turn (station wagon)	3-32 c.p.	1157
License plate lamp	4 c.p.	97
Dome lamp	12 c.p.	105
Back-up lamp	32 c.p.	1156
Front side marker	2 c.p.	194
Rear side marker	2 c.p.	194
Instrument Panel		
Warning lights	2 c.p.	194
Instrument (speed-o & gauges)	2 c.p.	194
Hi-beam	2 c.p.	194

Lamp Description	Candle Power or Wattage	Trade No.
Radio dial	2 c.p.	1893
Turn signal	2 c.p.	194
Clock	2 c.p.	1895
Instrumentation package	2 c.p.	194
Ashtray	1.5 c.p.	1445
PRND21 (column)	1.5 c.p.	1445
Accessory Equipment		
Glove compartment	2 c.p.	1891
Luggage compartment	12 c.p.	105
Engine compartment	6 c.p.	631
Spot lamp	30 Watt	4405
Courtesy lamp (in instr. panel)	6 c.p.	562
Cargo lamp (wagon)	12 c.p.	105
Tachometer	2 c.p.	1895
Cluster	2 c.p.	1895

COUGAR
1970

Lamp Description	Candle Power or Wattage	Trade No.	Lamp Description	Candle Power or Wattage	Trade No.
Headlamps—hi & lo	37.5 & 50 Watts	4002	Glove compartment	3 c.p.	1816
Headlamps—highbeam	37.5 Watts	4001	**Warning Lamps**		
Front park and turn signal	3-32 c.p.	1157A	**All Except XR-7 Models**		
Rear tail, stop and turn signal	3-32 c.p.	1157	Low "Fuel"	2 c.p.	1895
Front side markers	4 c.p.	97NA	"Door" ajar	1.6 c.p.	257
Rear side markers	2 c.p.	194	Seat belts	2 c.p.	1895
License plate lamp	4 c.p.	97	"Park" brake	2 c.p.	194
Auto. trans. quadrant	1.5 c.p.	1445	"Brakes"	2 c.p.	194
Luggage compartment	6 c.p.	631	"Lights"	2 c.p.	194
Back-up lamp	32 c.p.	1156	"Alternator"	2 c.p.	194
Courtesy lamps—under panel	6 c.p.	562	"Oil"	2 c.p.	194
Courtesy lamps—pillar	12 c.p.	105	**XR-7 Models**		
Courtesy lamps—door	6 c.p.	212	Low "Fuel"	2 c.p.	194
Console lamp	3 c.p.	1816	"Door" ajar	2 c.p.	194
Instrument Panel			Seat "belts"	2 c.p.	194
Speedometer	2 c.p.	194	"Park" brake	2 c.p.	194
Gauges	2 c.p.	194	"Brakes"	2 c.p.	194
Hi-beam	2 c.p.	194	"Lights"	2 c.p.	194
Turn signal indicators	2 c.p.	194	**Optional Equipment**		
Clock	2 c.p.	1895	Heater—air conditioner control	1.5 c.p.	1445
Cluster illumination	2 c.p.	194	Radio AM	1.9 c.p.	1893
Ash tray	1.5 c.p.	1445	Radio AM-FM	1.9 c.p.	1893
Ash tray—console	1.3 c.p.	1892	Radio AM-tape player	1.9 c.p.	1893
Map lamp	3 c.p.	1816	Engine compartment	6 c.p.	631
			Spotlight	30 Watt	4405

FALCON AND MAVERICK
1970

Lamp Description	Candle Power or Wattage	Trade No.	Lamp Description	Candle Power or Wattage	Trade No.
Standard Equipment			**Optional Equipment**		
Headlamps	40-50 Watts	6012	Spotlight—4.4" dia.	30 Watts	4405
Front part/turn signal (Maverick)	3-32 c.p.	1157A	Air cond. controls	2 c.p.	1895
Front park/turn signal (Falcon)	3-32 c.p.	1157	Radio pilot light	1.9 c.p.	1893
Rear tail/stop/turn	3-32 c.p.	1157	Auto. trans. quadrant	1.5 c.p.	1445
Back-up light	32 c.p.	1156	Tachometer light (round)	2 c.p.	1895
Back-up light (Falcon station wagon)	32 c.p.	1076	Hood mounted (Maverick)	2 c.p.	57
License plate lamp	4 c.p.	97	Luggage comp. light (Maverick)	6 c.p.	631
Dome lamp	12 c.p.	105	Seat belt warning (Maverick)	2 c.p.	1895
Front & rear side marker lamp	2 c.p.	194	Falcon only courtesy light (inst. panel)	6 c.p.	562
Instrument Panel			Clock light	3 c.p.	1816
Hi-beam indicator	2 c.p.	194	Luggage comp. light	12 c.p.	105
Turn signal indicators	2 c.p.	194	Portable trunk light	15 c.p.	1003
Warning lights (oil, alt., hot, brakes)	2 c.p.	194	Parking brake warning	16 c.p.	257
Speedometer & fuel gauge	2 c.p.	194	Engine compt.	6 c.p.	631
Heater controls	2 c.p.	1895	Map light	6 c.p.	631
Ash tray light (Maverick)	1.5 c.p.	1445	Cargo light	12 c.p.	105

MUSTANG
1970

Light Description	Candle Power or Wattage	Trade No.	Light Description	Candle Power or Wattage	Trade No.
Standard Equipment			**Optional Equipment**		
Headlamps—hi & lo	40-50 Watts	6012	Ash tray (console)	1.3 c.p.	1892
Front park & turn signal	3-32 c.p.	1157②	Ash tray (instrument panel)	1.5 c.p.	1445
Front side marker	4 c.p.	97②	Courtesy lamp	6 c.p.	631
Rear tail stop/turn signal	3-32 c.p.	1157	Fog lamps	35 Watts	4415
Four way emergency flashers— included in front & rear turn signals			Fog lamp—switch	1 c.p.	53X
			Map lamp	15 c.p.	1004
Back-up lamp	32 c.p.	1156	Spotlight 4.4" dia.	30 Watts	4405
License plate lamp	4 c.p.	97	R & L turn signal indicators (outside— in hood scoop) all except Grande hardtop	1 c.p.	53X
Courtesy lamp—Fastback 64 "C" pillar	12 c.p.	105			
Courtesy lamp—under inst. pnl. (63 & 76)	Fuse type	562	Radio pilot light (AM radio)	1.9 c.p.	1893
Dome courtesy (65 only)	12 c.p.	105	Warning light—brake	1.6 c.p.	256
Hood mtd. turn signals (Mach I)	1 c.p.	53X	Conv. pkg. seat belt	2 c.p.	1891
Rear side marker lamp	2 c.p.	194	Trans. control selector indicator	1.5 c.p.	1445
Instrument Panel			Headlights on	1.6 c.p.	0000
Hi-beam indicator	2 c.p.	194	Luggage compt. lamp	6 c.p.	631
Turn signal indicators	2 c.p.	194	Engine compt. lamp	6 c.p.	631
Turn signal indicators are also emergency flasher indicators			Portable trunk lamp	15 c.p.	1003
			Clock	2 c.p.	1895
*Warning lights—oil, alt. & Brakes①	2 c.p.	194	AM/FM (MPX) radio	1.9 c.p.	1893
Glove compt./light	2 c.p.	1891	Warning light belts	2 c.p.	1891
Instruments	2 c p	194	Door courtesy r.p.o.	6 c.p.	212
Seat belt warning light r.p.o.	1.5 c.p.	1445	Radio AM-stereo type	9 c.p.	1893
Heater control	2 c.p.	1895			

① — Oil and alternator warning lights used with tachometer installation only.

② — Natural amber.

1971–72

EXTERIOR LIGHTS

LAMP DESCRIPTION	COUGAR	TORINO	RANCHERO	COMET	MAVERICK	MONTEGO	MUSTANG	CANDLE POWER OR WATTAGE	TRADE NO.
Back-up Lamps		2	2		2		2	32 CP	1156
	2			2		2		32 CP	1076
Headlamps Hi Beam	2	2	2				2	37.5 Watts	4001
Headlamps Hi & Lo				2	2		2	40 & 50 Watts	4012
	2	2	2				2	37.5 & 50 Watts	4002
License Plate Light (Car)	1	1	1	1	1	1	1	4 CP	97
License Plate Light (Wagon)		2					1	4 CP	97
Luggage Compartment	1	1		1	1	1	1	6 CP	631
Parking & Turn Signal-Front	2	2	2	2	2	2	2	3-32 CP	1157
Rear-Stop & Turn Signal	6	2	2	2	2		4	3-32 CP	1157
Rear-Stop & Turn (Hi-Series)					4			3-32 CP	1157
Rear-Stop & Turn (Lo-Series)							2	3-32 CP	1157
Rear-Stop & Turn (Wagon)		2					2	3-32 CP	1157
Side Marker Lamp—(Front)	2	2	2	2	2	2		1 CP	161
Side Marker Lamp—(Front)							2	2 CP	194
Side Marker Lamp—(Rear)		2	2	2	2	2		1 CP	161
Side Marker Lamp—(Rear)	2						2	2 CP	194
Sport Lamps					2	2		3-32 CP	1157-A
Sport Lamps							2	15 CP	96

INTERIOR LIGHTS

LAMP DESCRIPTION	COUGAR	TORINO	RANCHERO	COMET	MAVERICK	MONTEGO	MUSTANG	CANDLE POWER OR WATTAGE	TRADE NO.
Cargo Lamp (S/W)		1					1	12 CP	105
Clock		2				2		2 CP	1895
Clock (Console)	2				2		2	2 CP	194
Console Lamp	1						1	.75 CP	1892
Courtesy Lamp (I/P)	2						2	6 CP	631
		2	2		2			6 CP	562
Courtesy Lamp (C Pillar)	2							12 CP	105
Dome Light	1	1	1	1	1	1	2	12 CP	105
Glove Compartment		1				1		2 CP	1893
		1					1	2 CP	1895
Map Light		1						6 CP	631
	1						1	6 CP	212

FUSES AND CIRCUIT BREAKERS
1965–66

Function	Location	Falcon Comet	Fairlane	Mustang
		Rating Type	Rating Type	Rating Type
Dome courtesy-map cargo	Fuse panel	7½ SFE	7½ SFE	7½ SFE
Tail-park license	Light switch	15 C.B.	15 C.B.	15 C.B.
Stop light	Light switch	15 C.B.	15 C.B.	15 C.B.
Clock	Fuse panel	7½ SFE	7½ SFE	7½ SFE
Back-up	Fuse panel	14 SFE	14 SFE	14 SFE
Turn signals (act as a circuit breaker)				
Radio	Fuse panel (acc. socket)	14 SFE	14 SFE	14 SFE
Heater	Fuse panel	14 SFE	14 SFE	14 SFE
Heater and PRNDL dial	Fuse panel heater socket			14 SFE
Cigar lighter	Fuse panel	14 SFE	14 SFE	14 SFE
Cigar lighter and emergency warning flasher	Fuse panel cigar lighter socket	20 SFE	20 SFE	20 SFE
Tachometer	Fuse panel (dome socket)	7½ SFE	7½ SFE	7½ SFE
Convertible top	Between starter relay & junction block	Safety link	Safety link	Safety link
Power window—power seat	On starter relay	20 C.B.	20 C.B.	20 C.B.
Overdrive	Clips to overdrive relay	20 SFE	20 SFE	20 SFE
Seat belt warning	Fuse panel acc. socket	14 SFE	14 SFE	14 SFE
Windshield washer (two speed wiper)		14 SFE	14 SFE	
Windwhield washer (single speed wiper)		14 SFE	14 SFE	14 SFE
Windshield washer (two speed wiper)	Wiper switch			12 C.B.
Windshield wiper	Wiper switch	6 (S. Sp.) C.B. 7 (2 Sp.) C.B. (Falcon) 7 Intermittent	6 (S. Sp.) C.B. 7 (2 Sp.) C.B.	5 (S. Sp.) C.B. 12 (2 Sp.) C.B.
Light-instrument panel	Fuse panel instrument LP socket	2½ AGA	2½ AGA	2½ AGA
Light-instrument cluster	connected into 15 C.B. light switch	2½ AGA	2½ AGA	2½ AGA
Light-clock		2½ AGA	2½ AGA	2½ AGA
Light-tachometer		2½ AGA	2½ AGA	2½ AGA
Light-ash receptacle		2½ AGA	2½ AGA	2½ AGA
Light-PRNDL dial		2½ AGA	2½ AGA	
Light-PRNDL dial (console only)	Fuse panel acc. socket	14 SFE	14 SFE	
Light-luggage compartment	Fuse panel	7½ SFE	7½ SFE	7½ SFE
Light-door open warning	Fuse panel		7½ SFE	
Light-glove box	Fuse panel	7½ SFE	7½ SFE	7½ SFE
Light-spotlight	In line	7½ SFE	7½ SFE	7½ SFE
Light-headlights	Light switch	18 Comet C.B. 12 Falcon C.B.		
Emergency warning flasher	Fuse panel	14 SFE	14 SFE	14 SFE
Horns	Light switch	15 C.B.	15 C.B.	15 C.B.
Air conditioner (integrated)	On ign. switch	25 C.B.	25 C.B.	25 C.B.
Back light control	At starter relay	20 C.B.	20 C.B.	
Economy air conditioner	In line	15 AGC	15 AGC	15 AGC
Motor windshield wiper	Circuit breaker integral with motor	C.B.	C.B.	C.B.
Motor convertible top		C.B.	C.B.	C.B.
Motor power window		C.B.	C.B.	C.B.
Motor power seat		C.B.	C.B.	C.B.

MERCURY INTERMEDIATE, FALCON, FAIRLANE, COUGAR AND MUSTANG
1967

Fuse Panel Circuits	Protective Device—Fuses in Amperes				
	Mercury Intermediate	Falcon	Fairlane	Cougar	Mustang
Ash tray light	AGA-2.5	AGA-2.5	AGA-2.5	AGA-2.5	AGA-2.5
Back up light	SFE-14	SFE-14	SFE-14	SFE-14	SFE-14
Cargo light	SFE-7.5	SFE-7.5	SFE-7.5	SFE-7.5	SFE-7.5
Cigar lighter	SFE-20	SFE-20	SFE-20	SFE-20	SFE-20
Clock	SFE-20	—	SFE-20	SFE-7.5	SFE-7.5
Clock light	AGA-2.5	—	AGA-2.5	AGA-2.5	AGA-2.5
Courtesy lights	SFE-7.5	SFE-7.5	SFE-7.5	SFE-7.5	SFE-7.5
Dome lights	SFE-7.5	SFE-7.5	SFE-7.5	SFE-7.5	SFE-7.5
Door ajar warning (door open warning, Fairlane taxi)	—	—	SFE-7.5	SFE-14	SFE-7.5
Emergency warning flasher	SFE-20	SFE-20	SFE-20	SFE-14	SFE-20
Glove box light	SFE-7.5	SFE-7.5	SFE-7.5	SFE-7.5	SFE-7.5
Heater and defroster	SFE-14	SFE-14	SFE-14	SFE-14	SFE-14
Instrument panel and cluster lights	AGA-2.5	AGA-2.5	AGA-2.5	AGA-2.5	AGA-2.5
Luggage compartment light	SFE-7.5	SFE-7.5	SFE-7.5	SFE-7.5	SFE-7.5
Map light	SFE-7.5	SFE-7.5	SFE-7.5	SFE-7.5	SFE-7.5
Radio	SFE-14	SFE-14	SFE-14	SFE-14	SFE-14
Radio light	AGA-2.5	AGA-2.5	AGA-2.5	AGA-2.5	AGA-2.5
Seat belt warning light (inst. or safety conv. panel)	SFE-14	SFE-14	SFE-14	SFE-7.5	SFE-7.5
Seat belt warning—Cougar model 65B only	—	—	—	SFE-14	—
Tachometer light	AGA-2.5	—	AGA-2.5	AGA-2.5	AGA-2.5
Transmission selector light	AGA-2.5	AGA-2.5	AGA-2.5	SFE-14	SFE-14
Turn signals	SFE-14	SFE-14	SFE-14	SFE-14	SFE-14
Windshield washers	SFE-14	SFE-14	SFE-14	—	—

Miscellaneous Circuits	Location	Protective Device—Fuse or Circuit Breaker (C.B.) in Amperes				
		Mercury Intermediate	Falcon	Fairlane	Cougar	Mustang
Headlights	In headlight switch	18 C.B.	12 C.B.	18 C.B.	18 C.B.	12 C.B.
Tail lights, stop lights, license lights, parking lights and horns	In headlight switch	15 C.B.	15 C.B.	15 C.B.	15 C.B.	15 C.B.
Tail lights (Cougar)	Near left rear light assy.	—	—	—	5 C.B.	—
Emergency warning flasher	Windshield wiper bracket	—	—	—	15 C.B.	—
Windshield wipers	Windshield wiper switch	6 C.B.	6 C.B.	6 C.B.	6 C.B.	6 C.B.
Intermittent windshield wipers	Windshield wiper switch	7 C.B.	—	—	—	—
Convertible top	Between starter relay and junction block	Safety link	—	Safety link		Safety link
Power windows, power seats and back window control	On starter relay	20 C.B.	20 C.B.	20 C.B.	—	—
Overdrive	Clip to overdrive relay	—	—	SFE-20	—	—
Air conditioner (integrated)	Acc. terminal ignition switch	25 C.B.	25 C.B.	25 C.B.	25 C.B.	25 C.B.
Air conditioner (economy)	In-line from acc. terminal of ignition switch	AGC-15	AGC-15	AGC-15	AGC-15	AGC-15
Speed control	In-line from acc. terminal of ignition switch	—	—	—	SFE-7.5	SFE-7.5
Motors: windshield wiper, convertible top, power windows and power seats	Integral part of motor	C.B.	C.B.	C.B.	C.B.	C.B.
Transmission selector light (console)	In-line	AGW-4	AWG-4	AGW-4	—	—
Parking brake warning	In-line	AGW-4	AGW-4	AGW-4	SFE-7.5	SFE-7.5

COUGAR, FAIRLANE, FALCON, MONTEGO AND MUSTANG

1968

Fuse Panel Circuits	Protective Device—Fuses in Amperes				
	Cougar	Fairlane	Falcon	Montego	Mustang
Ash tray light	AGA-2.5	SFE-4	SFE-4	SFE-4	AGA-2.5
Back up light	SFE-14	SFE-20	SFE-20	SFE-20	SFE-14
Cargo light	SFE-7.5	SFE-14	SFE-14	SFE-14	SFE-7.5
Cigar lighter	SFE-14	SFE-20	SFE-20	SFE-20	SFE-14
Clock	SFE-7.5	SFE-20	—	SFE-20	SFE-7.5
Clock light	AGA-2.5	SFE-4	—	SFE-4	AGA-2.5
Courtesy light	SFE-7.5	SFE-14	SFE-14	SFE-14	SFE-7.5
Defogger (cartridge in feed line for Cougar & Mustang)	SFE-7.5	SFE-20	SFE-20	SFE-20	SFE-7.5
Door ajar warning (door open warning, Fairlane taxi)	SFE-14	SFE-14	SFE-14	SFE-14	SFE-7.5
Dome light	SFE-7.5	SFE-14	SFE-14	SFE-14	SFE-7.5
Emergency warning flasher	—	SFE-20	SFE-20	SFE-20	SFE-20
Engine compartment light	—	—	—	—	SFE-7.5
Fog lights (bracket at fuse panel)	—	—	—	—	10 Amp. C.B.
Glove compartment light	SFE-7.5	SFE-14	SFE-14	SFE-14	SFE-7.5
Heater and defroster (30 AMP. req'd for A/C) ①	SFE-14	SFE-14	SFE-14	SFE-14	SFE-14
Instrument panel and cluster lights	AGA-2.5	SFE-4	SFE-4	SFE-4	AGA-2.5
Luggage compartment light	SFE-7.5	SFE-14	SFE-14	SFE-14	SFE-7.5
Map light	SFE-7.5	SFE-14	SFE-14	SFE-14	SFE-7.5
Radio and stereo tape	SFE-14	SFE-20	SFE-20	SFE-20	SFE-14
Radio light	AGA-2.5	SFE-4	SFE-4	SFE-4	AGA-2.5
Seat belt warning light (inst. or conv. control panel)	SFE-7.5	SFE-14	SFE-14	SFE-14	SFE-7.5
Seat belt warning light (inst. or conv. control panel)	SFE-14	—	—	—	—
Swing-tilt steering wheel (cartridge in feed line)	SFE-7.5	—	—	—	SFE-7.5
Tachometer light	AGA-2.5	SFE-4	—	SFE-4	AGA-2.5
Tilt steering wheel (cartridge in feed line)	SFE-7.5	—	—	—	SFE-7.5
Transmission selector light	SFE-14	SFE-4	SFE-4	SFE-4	SFE-14
Turn signals (cartridge in feed line)	SFE-15	SFE-20	SFE-20	SFE-20	SFE-14
Windshield washers	—	SFE-20	SFE-20	SFE-20	—

① —Located in fuse panel.

Miscellaneous Circuits	Location	Protective Device—Fuse or Circuit Breaker (C.B.) in Amperes				
		Montego	Falcon	Fairlane	Cougar	Mustang
Headlights	In headlight switch	18 C.B.	12 C.B.	18 C.B.	18 C.B.	12 C.B.
Tail lights, stop lights, license lights, parking lights, horns & marker lights	In headlight switch	15 C.B.	15 C.B.	15 C.B.	15 C.B.	15 C.B.
Tail lights (Cougar)	Near left rear light assy.	—	—	—	5 C.B.	—
Emergency warning flasher	Bracket at fuse panel	—	—	—	15 C.B.	—
Windshield wipers	Windshield wiper switch	6 C.B.	6 C.B.	6 C.B.	6 C.B.	6 C.B.
Intermittent windshield wipers	Windshield wiper switch	7 C.B.	—	—	—	—
Convertible top	Between starter relay and junction block	Safety Link	—	Safety Link	—	Safety Link
Power windows, power seats and back window control	On starter relay	20 C.B.	20 C.B.	20 C.B.	—	—
Air conditioner (integrated)	① ◐	①	①	①	②	②
Speed control	In-line from acc. terminal of ignition switch	—	—	—	SFE-7.5	SFE-7.5
Motors: windshield wiper, convertible top, power windows and power seats	Integral part of motor	C.B.	C.B.	C.B.	C.B.	C.B.
Transmission selector light (console)	In-line	AGW-4	AGW-4	AGW-4	—	—
Parking brake warning	In-line	AGW-4	AGW-4	AGW-4	SFE-7.5	SFE-7.5

① ◐—30 amp. fuse in fuse panel.   ◐—30 amp. fuse in bracket attached to fuse panel.

COUGAR, FALCON, FAIRLANE, MONTEGO AND MUSTANG   **1969**

Circuits	Location	Protective Device Fuse or Circuit Breaker (C.B.) in Amperes				
		Cougar	Fairlane	Falcon	Montego	Mustang
Ash tray light		SFE 4	SFE 14	SFE 14	SFE 14	SFE 4
Back-up light		AGC or SFE 20	AGC or SFE 20	AGC or SFE 20	AGC or SFE 20	AGC or SFE 20
Cigar lighter	Fuse panel	SFE 14	AGC or SFE 20	AGC or SFE 20	AGC or SFE 20	AGC or SFE 20
Clock feed		SFE 14	AGC or SFE 20	AGC or SFE 20	AGC or SFE 20	SFE 14
Convertible top feed	Between starter relay and junction block	Fuse Link ○	20 C.B.	—	20 C.B. ○	Fuse Link
Convertible top motor	Integral part of motor	C.B.	C.B.	C.B.	C.B.	C.B.

Courtesy lights
  C pillar
  Cargo
  Console (Fairlane and Montego only) door
  Dome
  Glove compartment
  Luggage compartment
  Map light
	Fuse panel	SFE 14	SFE 14	SFE 14	SFE 14	SFE 14

Emergency flashers		15 C.B. ②	AGC or SFE 20	AGC or SFE 20	AGC or SFE 20	AGC or SFE 20
Engine compartment light	Cartridge in feed line	SFE 7.5	SFE 7.5	SFE 7.5	SFE 7.5	SFE 7.5
Fog lights	Bracket at fuse panel	—	10 C.B.	—	—	10 C.B.
Headlights	In headlight switch	18 C.B.	18 C.B.	18 C.B.	18 C.B.	18 C.B.
Heater and defroster	Fuse panel	SFE 14	SFE 14	SFE 14	SFE 14	SFE 14
Heater and defroster with air conditioner	Fuse panel	8 AG or AGX 30	8 AG or AGX 30	8 AG or AGX 30	8 AG or AGX 30	8 AG or AGX 30
Horns	In headlight switch	15 C.B.	15 C.B.	15 C.B.	15 C.B.	15 C.B.
Indicator lights (convenience control panel) Door ajar		AGC or SFE 20	—	—	—	AGC or SFE 20
Dual brake		—	SFE 14 ①	SFE 14 ①	SFE 14 ①	—
Engine temperature		—	SFE 14 ①	SFE 14 ①	SFE 14 ①	—
Low fuel	Fuse panel	AGC or SFE 20	—	—	—	AGC or SFE 20
Oil		—	SFE 14 ①	SFE 14 ①	SFE 14 ①	—
Seat belt (instrument or convenience control panel)		AGC or SFE 20	SFE 14 ①	SFE 14 ③	SFE 14 ③	AGC or SFE 20

Instrumental panel lights
  Clock light
  Heater controls
  Radio
	Fuse panel	SFE 4	SFE 14	SFE 14	SFE 4	SFE 4

License lights
  Marker lights
  Parking lights
	In headlight switch	15 C.B. ②	15 C.B.	15 C.B.	15 C.B.	15 C.B.

Power backlight	Attached to starting motor relay	—	20 C.B.	20 C.B.	20 C.B.	—
Power backlight motor	Integral with motor	—	C.B.	C.B.	C.B.	—
Power backlight relay feed	Fuse panel	—	AGC or SFE 20	AGC or SFE 20	—	—
Power seats	On starter relay	20 C.B.	AGC or SFE 20 in Fuse panel	20 C.B.	20 C.B.	20 C.B.
Power seats motors	Integral part of motor	C.B.	C.B.	C.B.	C.B.	C.B.
Power window	Attached to starting motor relay	20 C.B.	20 C.B.	—	20 C.B.	20 C.B.
Power window motor	Integral with motor	C.B.	C.B.	—	C.B.	C.B.
Power window relay feed	Fuse panel	AGC or SFE 20	AGC or SFE 20	—	AGC or SFE 20	AGC or SFE 20
PRNDL (auto. trans.)	Fuse panel	—	SFE 14	SFE 14	SFE 14	—
Radio and/or stereo tape feed	Fuse panel	—	AGC or SFE 20	—	AGC or SFE 20	—
Speed control		AGC or SFE 20	—	—	—	AGC or SFE 20
Stop lights	In headlight switch	15 C.B. ②	15 C.B.	15 C.B.	15 C.B.	15 C.B.
Swing-tilt steering wheel	Fuse panel	AGC or SFE 20	—	—	—	AGC or SFE 20
Taillights	In headlight switch	15 C.B.	15 C.B.	15 C.B.	15 C.B.	15 C.B.
Transmission selector light	Fuse panel	AGC or SFE 20	SFE 4	SFE 4	SFE 4	AGC or SFE 20

① —Attached to starting motor relay   ② —Bracket attached to L.H. lower instrument panel   ③ —Instrument panel mounted light uses AGC or SFE 20

COUGAR, FALCON, FAIRLANE, MONTEGO AND MUSTANG   **1969**

Circuits	Location	Protective Device Fuse or Circuit Breaker (C.B.) in Amperes				
		Cougar	Fairlane	Falcon	Montego	Mustang
Turn signals	Fuse panel	AGC or SFE 20	AGC or SFE 20	AGC or SFE 20	AGC or SFE 20	AGC or SFE 20
Windshield washers	Fuse panel					
Windshield wipers	Windshield wiper switch	6 C.B.	8 C.B.	8 C.B.	8 C.B.	6 C.B.
Windshield wiper motor	Integral part of motor	C.B.	C.B.	C.B.	C.B.	C.B.

MUSTANG, COUGAR, FALCON, MAVERICK, FAIRLANE and MONTEGO **1970**

Circuits	Location	Protective Device Fuse or Circuit Breaker (C.B.) in Amperes				
		Cougar	Fairlane	Falcon/Maverick	Montego	Mustang
Ash tray light	Fuse panel	SFE 4	SFE 4	SFE 4	SFE 4	SFE 4
Automatic seat back latch release			AGC or SFE 20			
Back-up light		AGC or SFE 15	AGC or SFE 15	AGC or SFE 15	AGC or SFE 20	AGC or SFE 15
Cigar lighter		SFE 14	AGC or SFE 20	AGC or SFE 20	AGC or SFE 20	SFE 14
Clock feed		SFE 14	AGC or SFE 20	AGC or SFE 20	AGC or SFE 20	SFE 14
Convertible top feed	Attached to starting motor relay	20 C.B.	20 C.B.		20 C.B.	20 C.B.
Convertible top motor	Integral part of motor	C.B.	C.B.	C.B.	C.B.	C.B.
Courtesy lights C pillar / Cargo / Console (Fairlane and Montego only) door / Dome / Glove compartment / Luggage compartment / Map light	Fuse panel	SFE 14	SFE 14	SFE 14	SFE 14	SFE 14
Emergency flashers	Fuse panel	15 C.B. ⑦	AGC or SFE 20	AGC or SFE 20	AGC or SFE 20	AGC or SFE 20
Emission control and/or throttle solenoid		SFE 14	SFE 14		SFE 14	SFE 14
Engine compartment light	Cartridge in feed line	SFE 7.5			SFE 7.5	SFE 7.5
Headlights	In headlight switch	18 C.B.	18 C.B.	12 C.B.	18 C.B.	12 C.B.
Heater and defroster	Fuse panel	SFE 14	SFE 14	SFE 14	SFE 14	SFE 14
Heater and defroster with air conditioner	Fuse panel	8 AG or AGX 30	8 AG or AGX 30 ④	8 AG or AGX 30	8 AG or AGX 30	8 AG or AGX 30
Horns	In headlight switch	15 C.B.	15 C.B.	15 C.B.	15 C.B.	15 C.B.
Indicator lights (convenience control panel) door ajar	Fuse panel	AGC or SFE 15				
Dual brake	Fuse panel		SFE 14	SFE 14⑤	SFE 14	
Engine temperature	Fuse panel		SFE 14	SFE 14⑤	SFE 14	
Low fuel	Fuse panel	AGC or SFE 15				
Oil	Fuse panel		SFE 14	SFE 14⑤	SFE 14	
Seat belt (instrument or convenience control panel)	Fuse panel	AGC or SFE 15	SFE 14①	SFE 14①	AGC or SFE 20	AGC or SFE 15
Instrument panel lights	Fuse panel	SFE 4	SFE 4	SFE 4	SFE 4	SFE 4
Clock light	Fuse panel					
Heater and A/C controls	Fuse panel					
Radio	Fuse panel					
Windshield wiper/washer controls	Fuse panel		SFE 4		SFE 4	
License lights	In headlight switch	15 C.B.	15 C.B.	15 C.B.	15 C.B.	15 C.B.
Marker lights						
Parking lights						
Parking brake indicator light	Fuse panel					AGC or SFE 15
Power backlight	Attached to starting motor relay		20 C.B.	20 C.B.⑤	20 C.B.	
Power backlight motor	Integral with motor		C.B.	C.B. ⑤	C.B.	
Power backlight relay feed	Fuse panel		AGC or SFE 20	AGC or SFE 20⑤		
Power seats	On starter relay				20 C.B.	
Power seats motors	Integral part of motor				C.B.	
Power tailgate	Attached to starting motor relay		20 C.B.			
Power tailgate motor	Integral part of motor		C.B.			
Power window	Attached to starting motor relay	20 C.B.	20 C.B.		20 C.B.	

MUSTANG, COUGAR, FALCON, MAVERICK, FAIRLANE and MONTEGO
1970

Circuits	Location	Protective Device Fuse or Circuit Breaker (C.B.) in Amperes				
		Cougar	Fairlane	Falcon/Maverick	Montego	Mustang
Power window motor	Integral with motor	C.B.	C.B.		C.B.	
Power window relay feed	Fuse panel	AGC or SFE 15	AGC or SFE 20	AGC or ⑤ SFE 20	AGC or SFE 20	
PRNDL (auto. trans.)	Fuse panel	15 C.B. ①	SFE 4	SFE 4	SFE 4	15 C.B. ①
Radio and/or stereo tape feed	Fuse panel	AGC or SFE 15	AGC or SFE 15	AGC or SFE 15	AGC or SFE 20	AGC or SFE 15
Rear window defogger	Fuse panel	AGC or SFE 15	AGC or SFE 20	AGC or SFE 20	AGC or SFE 20	
Spotlight	Cartridge in feed wire	SFE 7.5	SFE 7.5			
Stop lights	In headlight switch	15 C.B. ②	15 C.B.	15 C.B.	15 C.B.	15 C.B.
Taillights	In headlight switch	15 C.B.	15 C.B.	15 C.B.	15 C.B.	15 C.B.
Transmission selector light	Fuse panel	15 C.B. ①	SFE 4	SFE 4	SFE 4	15 C.B. ①
Turn signals Windshield washers	Fuse panel	AGC or SFE 20	AGC or SFE 20	AGC or SFE 20	AGC or SFE 20	AGC or SFE 15
Windshield wipers	Windshield wiper switch	6 C.B.	8 C.B.	8 C.B.	8 C.B.	6 C.B.
Windshield wiper motor	Integral part of motor	C.B.	C.B.	C.B.	C.B.	C.B.

① —Integral with headlight switch   ③ —Instrument panel mounted light used AGC or SFE 20   ⑤ —Falcon only
② —Bracket attached to L.H. lower instrument panel   ④ —Economy dealer-installed A/C used AGC or SFE 20

1971-72
MUSTANG AND COUGAR

CIRCUIT	CIRCUIT PROTECTION AND RATING	LOCATION	CIRCUIT	CIRCUIT PROTECTION AND RATING	LOCATION
Headlamps Mustang Cougar	12 AMP C.B. 18 AMP C.B.	Integral with lighting switch	Power windows Power seat Power top & Heated back-lite	20 AMP C.B.	On starter relay
Parking lamps Marker lamps License lamps Tail lamps (R.P.O. PRNDL Lamp)	15 AMP C.B.	Integral with lighting switch	W/S wiper (2 spd.)	7 AMP C.B.	In W/S wiper switch
			Intermittent W/S wiper (RPO)	7 AMP C.B.	
			Front seat back latch solenoid	C.B.	Integral with solenoid
Engine compt. lamp	7.5 AMP Fuse (SFE 7.5)	Cartridge in feed line	Window motor Seat motor Top motor	C.B.	In motor
Stop lamps	15 AMP C.B.	On relay panel above glove box			

MONTEGO, TORINO AND RANCHERO

CIRCUIT	CIRCUIT PROTECTION AND RATING	LOCATION	CIRCUIT	CIRCUIT PROTECTION AND RATING	LOCATION
Headlamps	18 AMP C.B.	Integral with lighting switch	Engine compt. lamp	7.5 AMP Fuse (SFE - 7.5)	Cartridge in feed line
Parking lamps Marker lamps License lamps Tail lamps Horns & Stop lamps	15 AMP C.B.		Power windows Back-lite Power seat (Mont.) Power top (Torino)	20 AMP C.B.	On starter relay
W/S wiper (2 Spd.)	7 AMP C.B.	In W/S wiper switch	Window motor Seat motor Top motor	C.B.	In motor
Intermittent W/S wiper	7 AMP C.B.				

MAVERICK AND SMALL COMET

CIRCUIT	CIRCUIT PROTECTION AND RATING	LOCATION
Headlights	12 AMP C.B.	
Horn, stop, front & rear marker, front parking, rear and license lights	15 AMP C.B.	Integral with lighting switch
Windshield wiper circuit	6 AMP C.B.	Integral with W/S wiper switch

Distributor

Description

There are three different types of distributor used, the vacuum advance, as used with 6-cylinder engines, the dual advance distributor, as used with the V8 standard production engines and the centrifugal advance distributor, used on some of the high performance engines.

In 1968 all models adopted the dual advance distributor to provide more accurately timed ignition and cleaner, smog-free exhaust. Some of these distributors have dual diaphragm vacuum advance mechanisms. These have two vacuum lines to the distributor bellows, one to advance the timing during high speed road use, and one to retard the timing at idle. On engines using dual advance distributors before 1967, it was customary to check initial advance with a timing light and with the vacuum line connected. Since 1967 any attempt to check the timing without disconnecting and plugging the vacuum lines will give inaccurate readings.

6-Cylinder Vacuum Advance

Ignition timing changes are entirely satisfied by the action of the breaker plate. The position of the plate is controlled by a vacuum-actuated diaphragm working against the tension of two accurately calibrated breaker plate springs. The diaphragm moves the breaker plate counterclockwise to advance the spark. The springs tend to counteract this movement to return timing to a retarded position. Cam and rotor rotation are clockwise as viewed from the top.

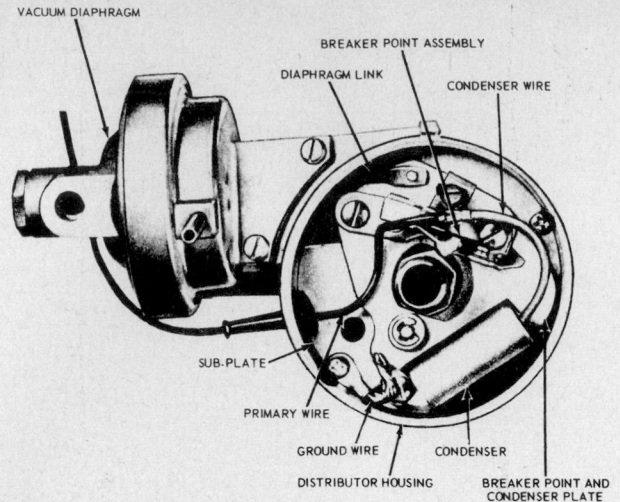

Breaker plate installed—6 cylinder engine, dual diaphragm distributor (© Ford Motor Co.)

Dual Advance

The dual advance distributor has two independently operated spark-timing control systems. A governor-type and a vacuum-type control are used on each distributor of standard production engines. Centrifugal weights cause the cam to advance or rotate ahead, relative to the distributor shaft.

The vacuum control mechanism operates through a spring loaded diaphragm and movable breaker plate, about the same as the vacuum advance distributor.

The 289, high performance (4-bbl. carb.) engine is equipped with centrifugal advance only.

Distributor Removal

1. Remove distributor cap. Disconnect the primary wire at the coil and the vacuum control line at the distributor.
2. Scribe a mark on the distributor body, showing position of the rotor. Then, scribe another mark on the distributor body and engine block, showing the position of the body in the block. These marks can be used to advantage when reassembling the distributor in an undisturbed engine.
3. Remove the screw, lockwasher and hold-down clamp. Pull the distributor out of the block. Do not rotate crankshaft while distributor is out of block because it will then be necessary to re-time ignition.

Distributor Installation

1. If ignition timing is required, rotate the crankshaft to bring No. 1 piston to T.D.C. of its compression stroke.
2. Position distributor in the block with the rotor at No. 1 firing position. Be sure that the oil pump intermediate driveshaft is prop-

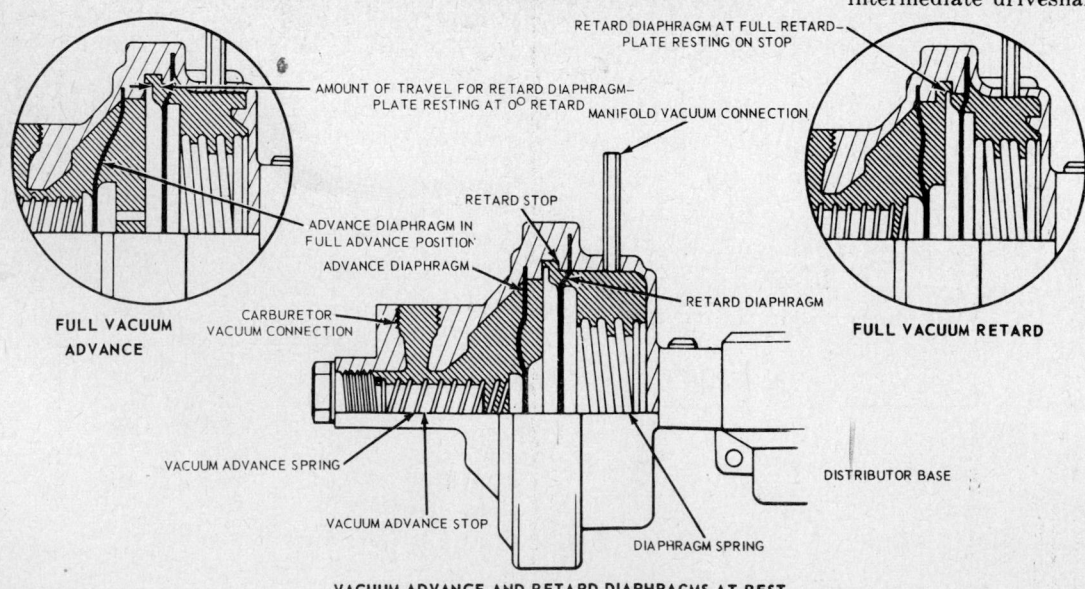

Dual diaphragm vacuum advance mechanism (© Ford Motor Co.)

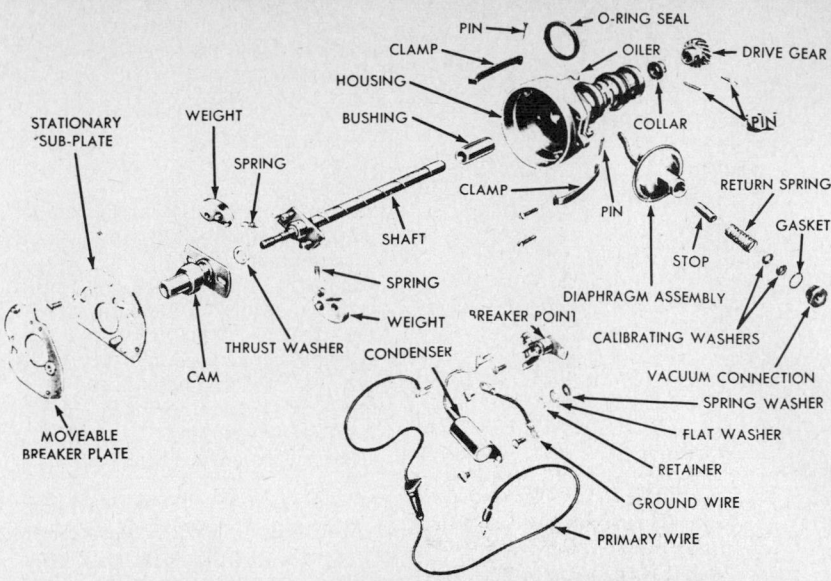

Typical dual advance distributor (© Ford Motor Co.)

erly seated in the oil pump.

3. Install, but do not tighten, the distributor retaining clamp and screw.
4. Rotate the distributor body clockwise until the breaker points start to open.
5. Tighten the retaining clamp screw.
6. Install distributor cap.
7. Connect distributor primary wire.
8. Start engine and run long enough to obtain engine operating temperature.
9. Idle engine to 500 rpm. Then, with a timing light, check the timing marks at the front pulley and make necessary corrections.
10. Connect the vacuum control line to the distributor and check advance characteristics with the timing light when the engine is accelerated.

V8 Centrifugal Advance

Follow procedure as in the Dual Advance type, eliminating the vacuum control items.

Distributor Modulator

Many post-1970 Ford engines are equipped with a distributor modulator system to reduce engine emis-

Distributor installation—6 cyl.
(© Ford Motor Co.)

sions. It consists of four major components: a speed sensor, a thermal switch, an electronic control amplifier and a three way solenoid valve. The operation of this system is explained in the Exhaust Emission Control Section in the rear of this manual.

Alternator, Regulator

The AC generator is covered in the Unit Repair Section.

Caution Since the AC generator and regulator are designed for use on only one polarity system, the following precautions must be observed:

1. The polarity of the battery, generator and regulator must be matched and considered before making any electrical connections in the system.
2. When connecting a booster battery, be sure to join the negative battery terminals together and the positive battery terminals together.
3. When connecting a charger to the battery, connect the charger positive lead to the battery positive terminal. Connect the charger negative lead to the battery negative terminal.
4. Never operate the AC generator on open circuit. Be sure that all connections in the circuit are clean and tight.
5. Do not short across or ground any of the terminals on the AC generator.
6. Do not attempt to polarize the AC generator.
7. Do not use test lamps of more than 12 volts for checking diode continuity.
8. Avoid long soldering times when replacing diodes or transistors. Prolonged heat is damaging to these units.
9. Disconnect the battery ground terminal when servicing any AC system. This will prevent the possibility of accidental reversing of polarity.

Alternator R & R

1. Disconnect the battery ground cable.
2. Loosen the alternator mounting bolts and remove the adjustment arm to alternator attaching bolt. Disengage the alternator belt.
3. Remove the electrical connectors from the alternator and remove the alternator. On 1967 model Cougars, it is necessary to remove the alternator mounting

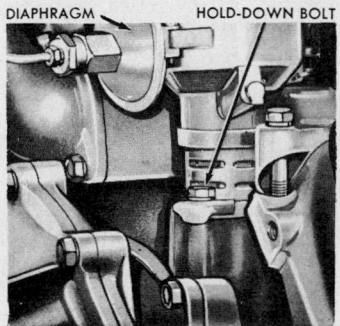

Distributor installation—V8
(© Ford Motor Co.)

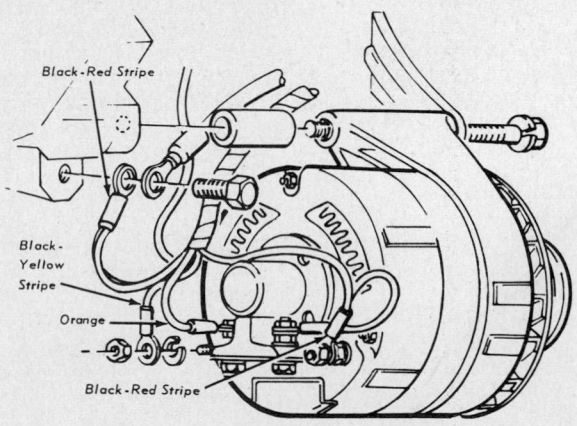

Typical alternator mounting
(© Ford Motor Co.)

bolts and the alternator wiring ground bolt from engine to gain access to the electrical connectors.

4. Reverse above procedure to reinstall.

Starter

The starter is a four-brush, series-parallel wound unit. The circuit is completed by means of a relay controlled switch which is part of the ignition switch.

Removal and Installation

Due to interference of the exhaust inlet pipe on some models, the steering idler arm must be lowered to provide clearance for starter removal.

1. Disconnect the starter cable at the starter terminal, remove the flywheel housing to starter retaining screws. Remove the starter assembly and the rubber dust ring.
2. Position the rubber dust ring on the flywheel housing.
3. Position the starter assembly to the flywheel housing, and begin on the starter retaining screws. On a car with an automatic transmission, the transmission dipstick tube bracket is mounted under the starter side mounting bolt. Snug all bolts, then tighten to 15 ft. lbs. tightening the middle bolt first.

Instruments

Cluster R & R

1965-67 Falcon and Comet and 1966 Mustang

1. Disconnect the battery cable.
2. Disconnect speedometer cable.
3. Remove the screws retaining the instrument cluster assembly to the instrument panel and tilt the cluster forward.
4. Disconnect the wiring and the bulb sockets. Remove the cluster assembly.

NOTE: all individual instruments may be removed and serviced at this time.

5. To reinstall, reverse the removal procedure.

1966-67 Fairlane

1. Disconnect the battery ground cable.
2. Remove the radio, knobs and nuts.
3. Disconnect the speedometer cable.
4. Remove the screws from the cluster assembly and position it outward.
5. Disconnect the bulbs, constant voltage regulator and ground

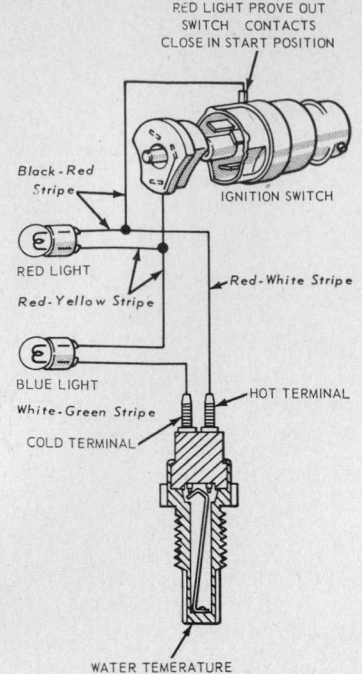

RED LIGHT PROVE OUT SWITCH CONTACTS CLOSE IN START POSITION

Black-Red Stripe

IGNITION SWITCH

RED LIGHT

Red-Yellow Stripe

Red-White Stripe

BLUE LIGHT

White-Green Stripe

HOT TERMINAL

COLD TERMINAL

WATER TEMERATURE SENDING UNIT

Temperature gauge circuit
(© Ford Motor Co.)

wire, clock, and fuel gauge. Move the cluster assembly to a bench.

6. Remove the clock knob and the screws holding the rear cluster cover which retains the speedometer, clock, fuel gauge, and bulbs for the alternator, oil pressure, and hot and cold water temperature.

NOTE: at this point, the individual instruments may be removed for servicing.

7. To reinstall, reverse the removal procedure.

1967-68 Cougar and Mustang

1. Disconnect battery.
2. Cover steering column.
3. Remove instrument panel front pad assembly retaining screws and remove pad assembly.
4. Remove four screws retaining heater control assembly to instrument panel and position control assembly outward.
5. Reaching through heater control opening, disconnect speedometer cable from speedometer.
6. Remove three ash tray receptacle retaining screws.
7. Disconnect cigar lighter element wiring connector and remove ash tray receptacle.
8. Reaching through ash tray opening, remove nut and washer which retain inboard end of instrument cluster to instrument panel.
9. Remove seven external screws retaining instrument cluster to instrument panel.
10. Position cluster assembly to outward, disconnect two multiple

connectors and remove instrument cluster. Reverse procedure to install.

1968 Fairlane

1. Disconnect battery.
2. Remove instrument panel cover assembly.
3. Remove right instrument panel shield assembly retaining screws and remove shield.
4. Remove five screws retaining cluster assembly and move cluster out.
5. Disconnect speedometer, tachometer, if so equipped, and multiple plug from printed circuit and remove cluster.
6. Reverse procedure to install.

1968 Falcon and 1969 Fairlane and Montego—1970 Falcons with 184 In. Overall Length Use This Procedure, 1970-71 Falcons with 203 In. Overall Length Use 1970 Fairlane Procedure

1. Disconnect battery.
2. Open glove compartment and remove glove compartment retaining screws. Remove glove box.
3. Reaching through glove compartment opening, remove nut that retains pad to instrument panel.
4. Remove retaining screws along lower right of pad and retaining screws above instrument cluster.
5. Raise pad assembly, disconnect speaker wires and remove pad assembly.
6. Remove five screws retaining instrument cluster to instrument panel and move cluster out.
7. Disconnect speedometer cable, heater control cables, and heater illumination bulb. Disconnect switch plug and multiple plug to printed circuit. Remove clamp retaining heater cables to control and remove cluster.
8. Reverse procedure to install.

1968 Montego and Comet

1. Disconnect battery.
2. Remove glove box liner retaining screws and remove glove box.
3. Reaching through glove box opening, remove two nuts retaining pad to panel.
4. Remove two pad retaining screws from top of instrument cluster.
5. Remove seven pad retaining screws from along bottom of pad.
6. Lift up pad and disconnect radio speaker wires and clock wires. Remove pad.
7. Remove eight screws retaining cluster to instrument panel.
8. Move cluster out and disconnect speedometer cable, multiple plug to cluster, multiple plug to con-

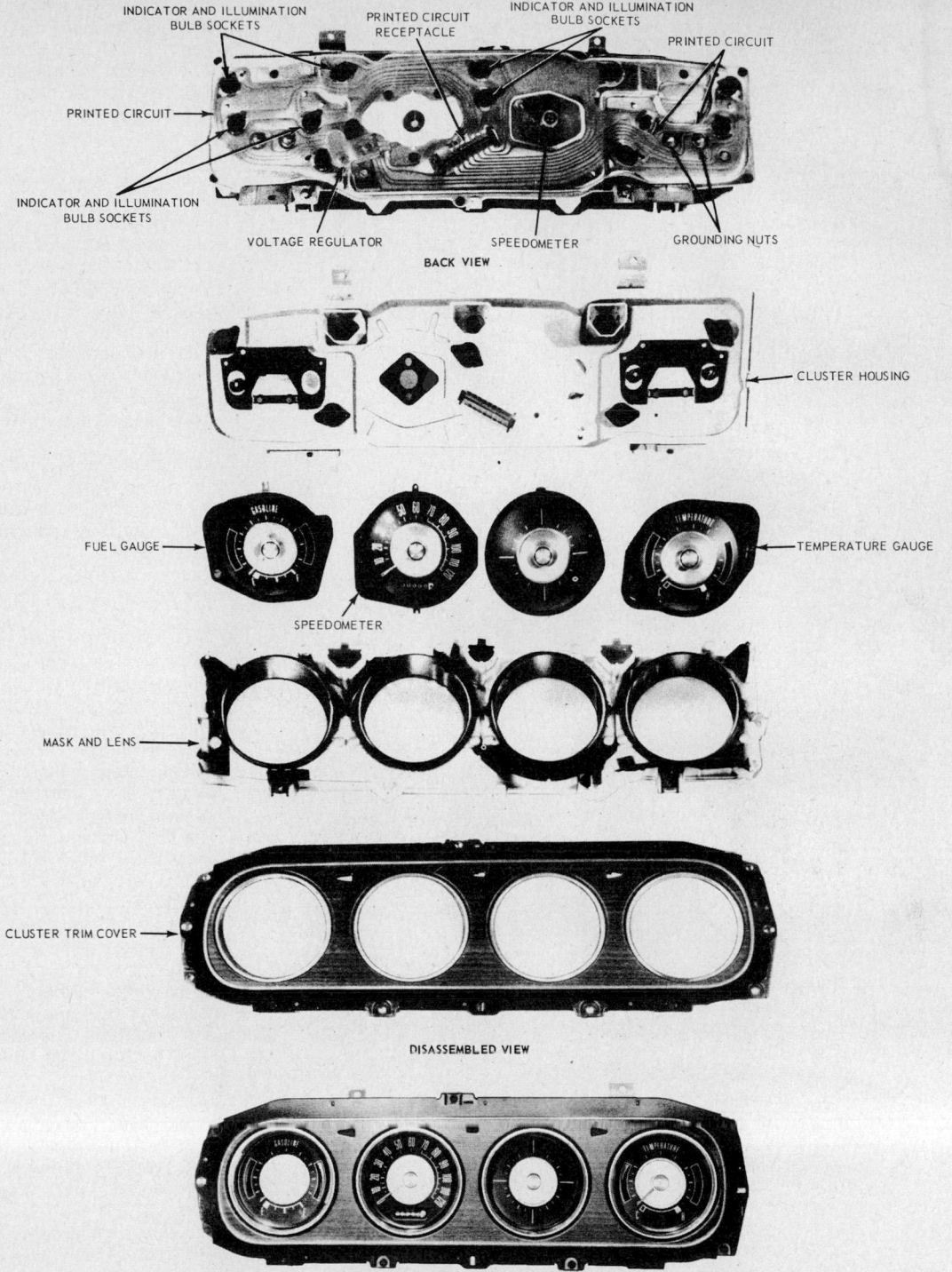

INDICATOR AND ILLUMINATION BULB SOCKETS

PRINTED CIRCUIT RECEPTACLE

INDICATOR AND ILLUMINATION BULB SOCKETS

PRINTED CIRCUIT

PRINTED CIRCUIT

INDICATOR AND ILLUMINATION BULB SOCKETS

VOLTAGE REGULATOR

SPEEDOMETER

GROUNDING NUTS

BACK VIEW

CLUSTER HOUSING

FUEL GAUGE

TEMPERATURE GAUGE

SPEEDOMETER

MASK AND LENS

CLUSTER TRIM COVER

DISASSEMBLED VIEW

ASSEMBLED VIEW

1969-70 Cougar instrument cluster—typical (© Ford Motor Co.)

venience lights, if so equipped and heater control cables and switch.

9. Disconnect clock, if so equipped, and remove cluster. Reverse procedure to install.

1969-72 Cougar and Mustang

1. Disconnect battery.
2. Remove cluster opening finish panel from pad assembly below instrument cluster (two screws).
3. Remove right and left lower end mouldings for access to pad retaining screws at lower ends of instrument panel.
4. Remove three pad retaining screws from top inner edge of pad to pad support.
5. Remove two retaining screws from right and left lower pad end.
6. Remove three retaining screws from lower right pad to instrument panel.
7. Pull pad assembly back, disconnect clock and courtesy light wires behind right side of pad and remove pad assembly. On XR7 models, disconnect multiple connector behind center of pad before removing pad.
8. Remove six screws retaining cluster to instrument panel and withdraw cluster slightly.

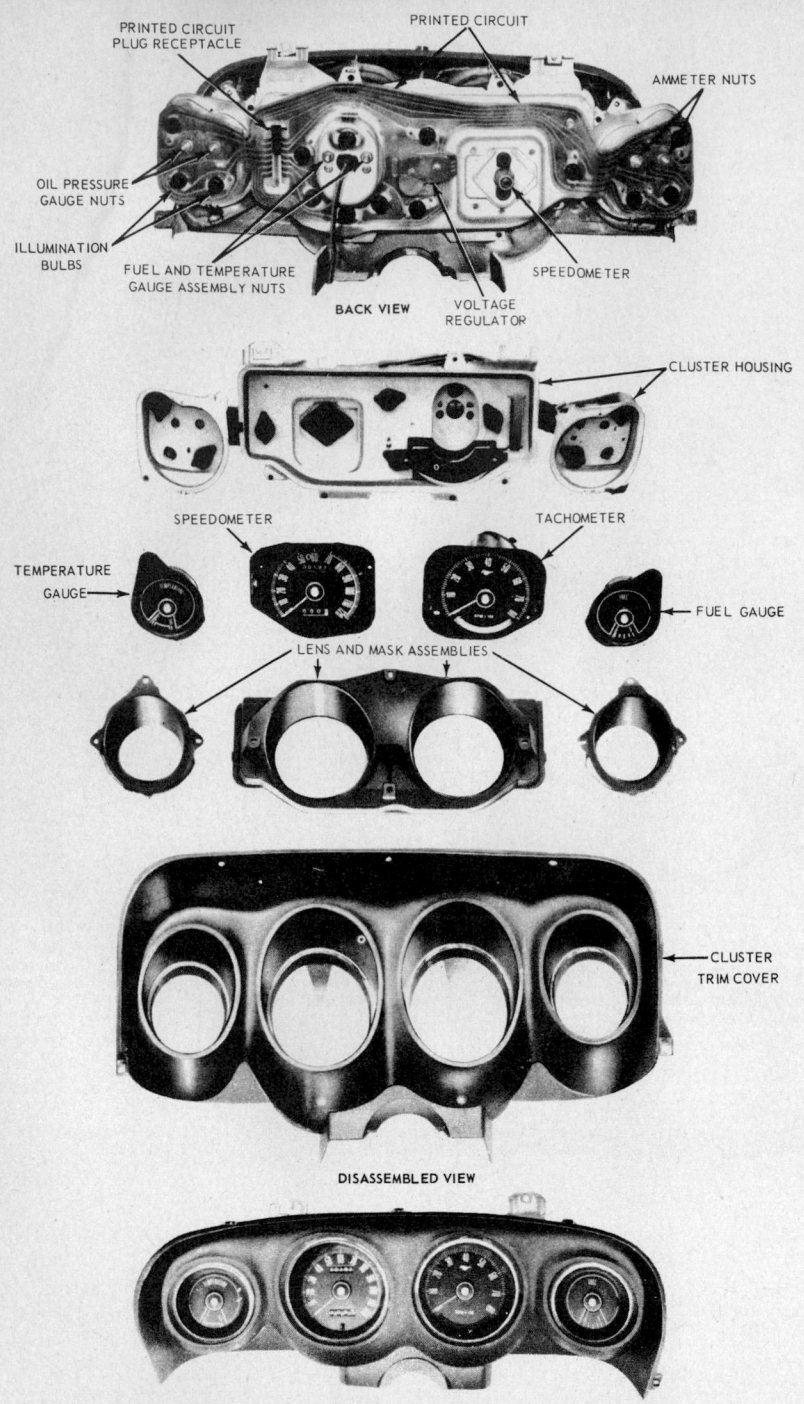

BACK VIEW

PRINTED CIRCUIT PLUG RECEPTACLE

PRINTED CIRCUIT

AMMETER NUTS

OIL PRESSURE GAUGE NUTS

ILLUMINATION BULBS

FUEL AND TEMPERATURE GAUGE ASSEMBLY NUTS

VOLTAGE REGULATOR

SPEEDOMETER

CLUSTER HOUSING

SPEEDOMETER

TACHOMETER

TEMPERATURE GAUGE

FUEL GAUGE

LENS AND MASK ASSEMBLIES

CLUSTER TRIM COVER

DISASSEMBLED VIEW

ASSEMBLED VIEW

1969-70 Mustang instrument cluster—typical (© Ford Motor Co.)

9. Disconnect multiple plug to printed circuit, and tachometer plug if so equipped.
10. Disconnect speedometer cable by pressing on flat surface of plastic connector and pulling cable away from speedometer.
11. Remove cluster. Reverse procedure to install.

1969-72 Maverick

1. Disconnect battery.
2. From under instrument panel disconnect speedometer cable by pressing flat surface of plastic connector and pulling cable away from head.
3. Remove two retaining screws at top of cluster and swing cluster down from panel.
4. Disconnect multiple connector plug from printed circuit at back of cluster.
5. Remove cluster by disengaging brackets on cluster lower edge from slots in panel.

1970-72 Fairlane

1. Disconnect battery.
2. Remove one retaining screw

from lower edge of dash pad at left of instrument cluster.
3. Remove five pad to instrument panel screws across bottom edge of pad to right of cluster.
4. Pull pad and retainer assembly free from clips on instrument panel.
5. Disconnect speaker and remove pad.
6. Remove four screws that retain cluster to panel and move cluster part way out of panel.
7. Disconnect speedometer cable, multiple plug to printed circuit and feed plug to tachometer or clock, if so equipped.
8. Disengage three wiring harness connected light bulb and socket assemblies from their receptacles.
9. Disconnect cable and five vacuum hoses from heater control, and feed plug to heater control switch and connector to heater control light.
10. Remove cluster. Reverse procedure to install.

1970-72 Montego and Cyclone

1. Disconnect battery.
2. Remove glove box for access and remove heater control panel by removing two retaining screws.
3. Disconnect two wires to light bulbs in heater control.
4. Remove two screws and left finish panel from pad.
5. Remove four retaining screws at lower right side and one screw at far left side of instrument panel pad.
6. Pull pad and retainer assembly free from clips on instrument panel.
7. On Cyclone Spoilers and other models with auxiliary instrument clusters, disconnect feed plugs to auxiliary cluster and tachometer.
8. Disconnect radio speaker and remove pad.
9. Remove four cluster to instrument panel retaining screws and move cluster part way out of panel.
10. Disconnect speedometer cable and cluster feed plug from its receptacle in printed circuit.
11. Disconnect electrical plug to clock and remove cluster. Reverse procedure to install.

1970-71 Cyclone Spoiler Auxiliary Instrument Cluster

This item is also optional in other models.
1. Perform steps 1-9 in Instrument Cluster removal.
2. Remove four cluster to pad retaining nuts from mounting studs.
3. Remove auxiliary cluster. Reverse procedure to install.

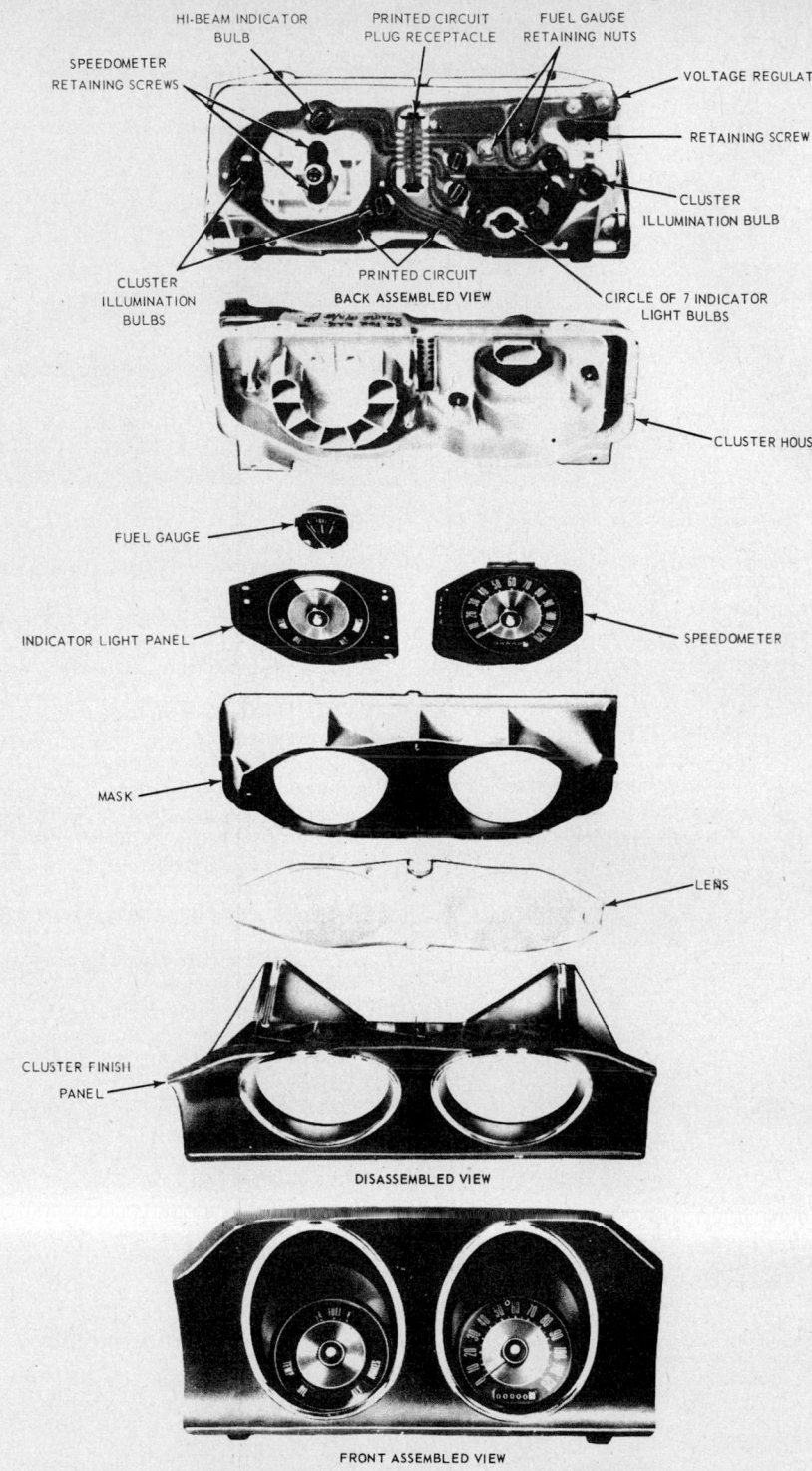

HI-BEAM INDICATOR BULB

PRINTED CIRCUIT PLUG RECEPTACLE

FUEL GAUGE RETAINING NUTS

SPEEDOMETER RETAINING SCREWS

VOLTAGE REGULATOR

RETAINING SCREW

CLUSTER ILLUMINATION BULB

CLUSTER ILLUMINATION BULBS

PRINTED CIRCUIT

BACK ASSEMBLED VIEW

CIRCLE OF 7 INDICATOR LIGHT BULBS

CLUSTER HOUSING

FUEL GAUGE

INDICATOR LIGHT PANEL

SPEEDOMETER

MASK

LENS

CLUSTER FINISH PANEL

DISASSEMBLED VIEW

FRONT ASSEMBLED VIEW

Maverick instrument cluster (© Ford Motor Co.)

Speedometer Head R & R

1965-67 Falcon and Comet and 1966 Mustang

1. Disconnect battery.
2. Disconnect speedometer cable at the head.
3. Remove instrument cluster assembly.
4. Remove six screws holding the instrument cluster back plate as-sembly and remove the back plate.
5. Remove the speedometer head attaching screws and remove head.
6. Install in reverse of removal pro-cedure.

1966-67 Fairlane

1. Disconnect battery.
2. Remove radio knobs, mounting nuts and radio.
3. Disconnect speedometer cable.
4. Remove the screws holding the cluster assembly to the instru-ment panel. Position the cluster assembly outward.
5. Disconnect bulbs, constant vol-tage regulator and its ground wire, the clock and fuel gauge.
6. Remove the cluster assembly.
7. Remove the clock knob and the screws holding the rear cluster cover.
8. Remove the screws holding the speedometer head to the cover and the four rubber insulators. Remove the speedometer head.
9. Install by reversing above pro-cedure.

1967-68 Cougar and Mustang

1. Disconnect battery.
2. Remove instrument cluster.
3. Remove nine rear cluster hous-ing retaining screws and remove rear cluster housing and gauges.
4. Remove two speedometer retain-ing nuts and remove speedome-ter. Reverse procedure to install.

1968-69 Fairlane

1. Disconnect battery.
2. Remove instrument cluster.
3. Remove eight button clips re-taining lens and mask to cluster. Oil and alternator finish covers and four rubber spacers will come off with mask and lens.
4. Remove two screws retaining speedometer and remove speed-ometer. Reverse procedure to install.

1968-69 Falcon

1. Disconnect battery.
2. Remove instrument cluster.
3. Remove heater control knobs and remove eight screws retain-ing instrument cluster rear housing and remove rear hous-ing.
4. Remove three screws retaining speedometer and remove speed-ometer. Reverse procedure to install.

1968-69 Montego and Comet

1. Disconnect battery.
2. Remove instrument cluster.
3. Remove heater control and switch knobs.
4. Remove seven screws retaining back of cluster and remove clus-ter back.
5. Remove two screws and remove speedometer. Reverse procedure to install.

1969-72 Mustang

1. Disconnect battery.
2. Remove instrument cluster.
3. Separate left and right instru-ment rear housings from printed circuit by removing three bulbs and two retaining nuts in each

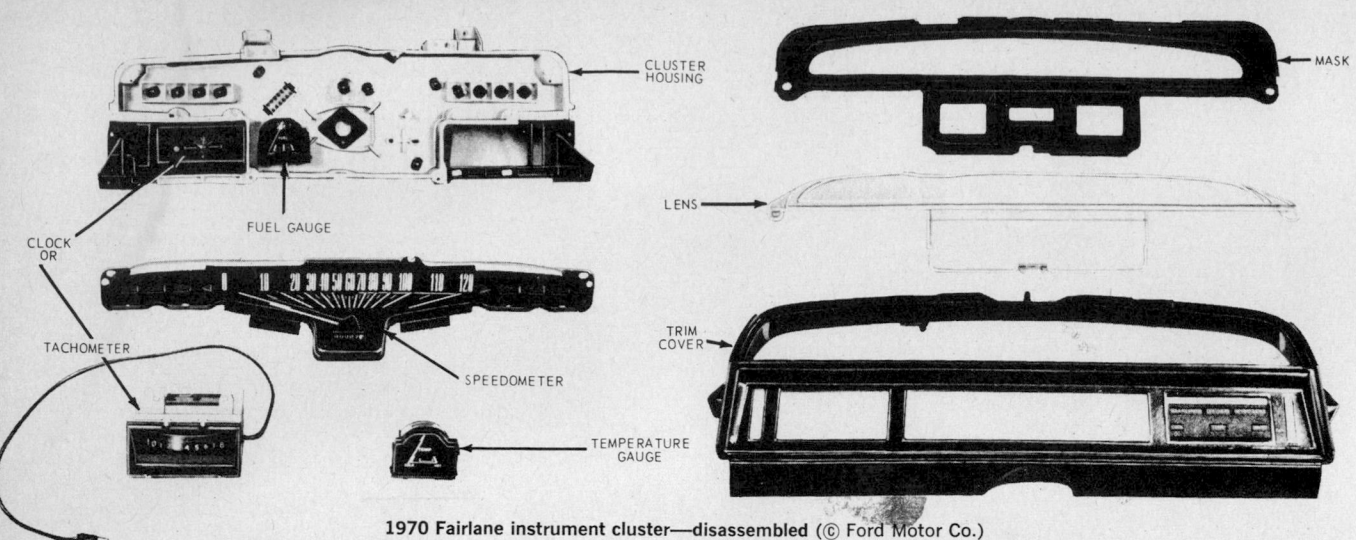

1970 Fairlane instrument cluster—disassembled (© Ford Motor Co.)

housing.

4. Remove center instrument rear housing from cluster by removing four screws. Printed circuit remains attached to housing.
5. Remove two retaining screws and remove speedometer. Reverse procedure to install.

1969-72 Cougar

1. Disconnect battery and remove

instrument cluster.
2. Remove mask and lens from cluster.
3. Separate front and rear cluster housing assemblies. Reverse procedure to install.

1969-72 Maverick

1. Disconnect battery.
2. Remove instrument cluster.
3. Remove four retaining screws

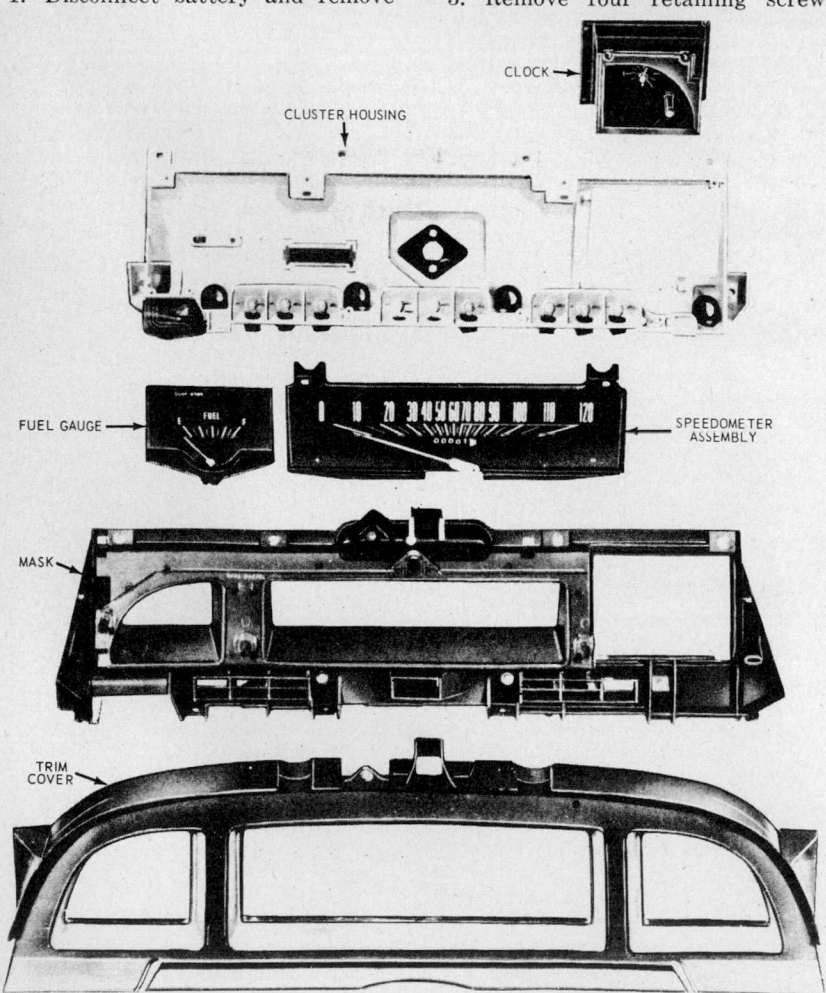

1970 Montego and Cyclone instrument cluster—disassembled (© Ford Motor Co.)

and separate cluster housing from finish panel.
4. Remove two retaining screws and remove speedometer.
5. Reverse procedure to install.

1970-72 Fairlane

1. Disconnect battery.
2. Remove instrument cluster.
3. Remove retaining screws at back of cluster.
4. Remove three retaining screws at front of cluster.
5. Pull speedometer out from front. Reverse procedure to install.

1970-72 Montego

1. Disconnect battery.
2. Remove instrument cluster.
3. Remove seven retaining screws and remove cover from front of cluster.
4. Remove mask and lens assembly from instrument cluster by removing eight screws.
5. Remove retaining screws at back of cluster and pull speedometer from front of cluster. Reverse procedure to install.

Lock Cylinder Replacement

1965-69

1. Insert key and turn to Acc. position.
2. With stiff wire in hole, depress lock pin and rotate cylinder counterclockwise, then pull out cylinder.

1970-72

1. Disconnect the negative battery cable.
2. On cars with a fixed steering column, remove the steering wheel trim pad and the steering wheel. Insert a stiff wire into the hole located in the lock cylinder housing. On cars with a tilt steering wheel, this hole is located on the outside of the steering column

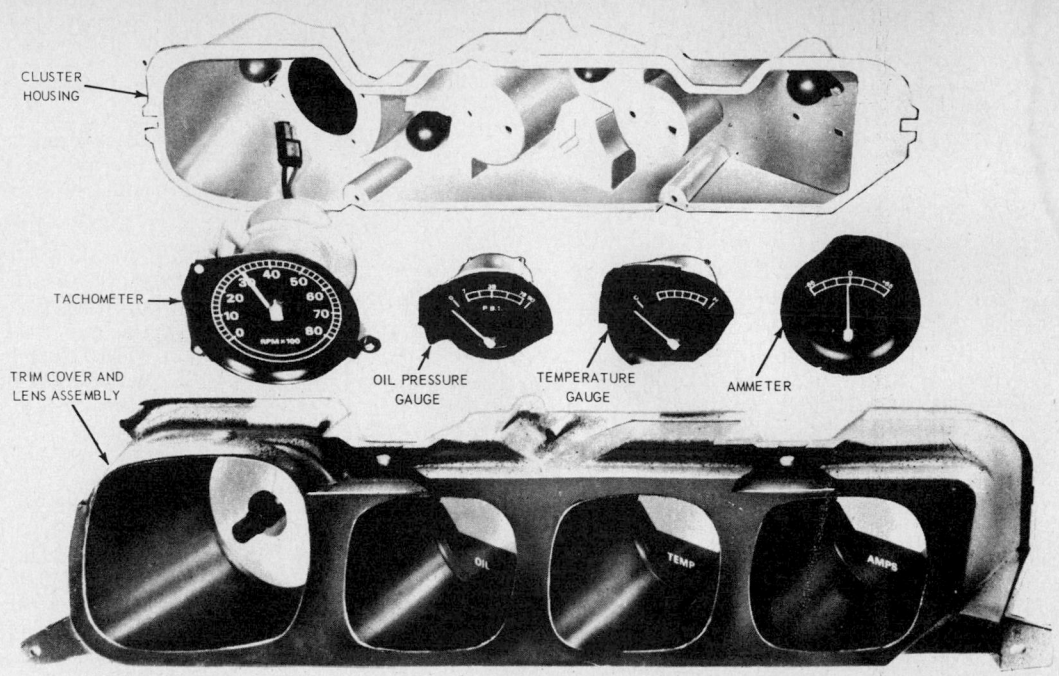

CLUSTER HOUSING

TACHOMETER

TRIM COVER AND LENS ASSEMBLY

OIL PRESSURE GAUGE

TEMPERATURE GAUGE

AMMETER

1970 Cyclone spoiler instrument cluster—disassembled (© Ford Motor Co.)

near the emergency flasher button and it is not necessary to remove the steering wheel.

3. Place the gear shift lever in Reverse on standard shift cars and in Park on cars with automatic transmission, and turn the ignition key to the ON position.

4. Depress wire and remove lock cylinder and wire.

5. Insert new cylinder into housing and turn to the OFF position. This will lock the cylinder into position.

6. Reinstall steering wheel and pad.

7. Connect negative battery cable.

Ignition Switch Replacement

1965-69

1. Remove cylinder as above.

2. Press in on rear of switch and rotate the switch one-eighth turn counterclockwise. Remove the bezel, switch and spacer.

3. Remove nut from back of switch. Remove the accessory and gauge feed wires from accessory terminal. Pull insulated plug from rear of switch.

4. Install in reverse of above.

1970-72

See Lincoln Continental section.

Lighting Switch Replacement

1965-72

1. Disconnect battery.

2. Remove knob and shaft by pressing release knob button on switch housing and with knob in full on position.

3. Remove mounting nut, then switch.

4. Remove junction box from switch.

5. Install in reverse of above.

KNOB RELEASE BUTTON

Headlight switch
(© Ford Motor Co.)

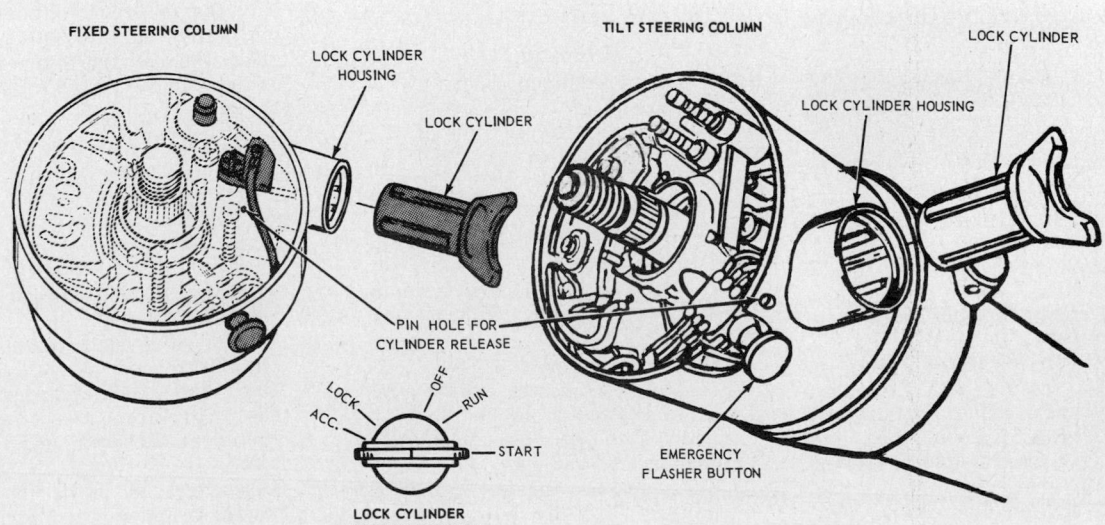

FIXED STEERING COLUMN

TILT STEERING COLUMN

LOCK CYLINDER HOUSING

LOCK CYLINDER

LOCK CYLINDER HOUSING

LOCK CYLINDER

PIN HOLE FOR CYLINDER RELEASE

LOCK
ACC.
OFF
RUN
START

LOCK CYLINDER OPERATING PATTERN

EMERGENCY FLASHER BUTTON

Lock cylinder replacement with locking column (© Ford Motor Co.)

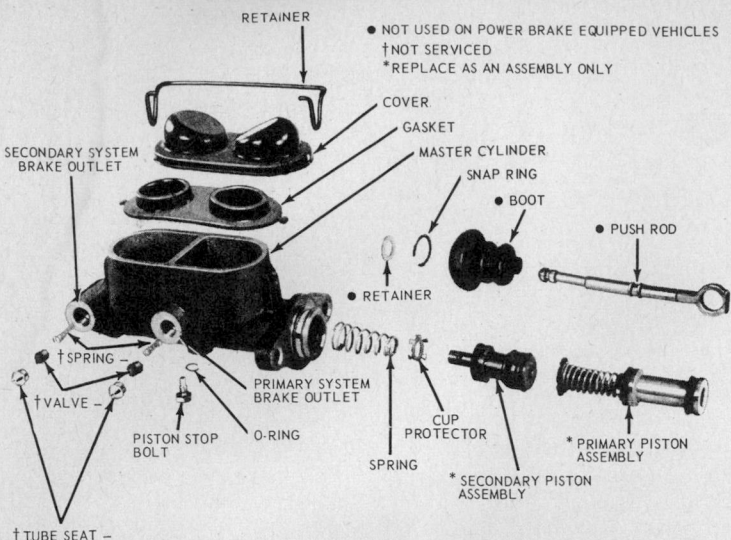

RETAINER
- NOT USED ON POWER BRAKE EQUIPPED VEHICLES
† NOT SERVICED
* REPLACE AS AN ASSEMBLY ONLY

COVER
GASKET
MASTER CYLINDER
SNAP RING
• BOOT
• PUSH ROD

SECONDARY SYSTEM
BRAKE OUTLET

• RETAINER

† SPRING

† VALVE

PISTON STOP
BOLT   O-RING

PRIMARY SYSTEM
BRAKE OUTLET

CUP
PROTECTOR

SPRING

* PRIMARY PISTON
ASSEMBLY

* SECONDARY PISTON
ASSEMBLY

† TUBE SEAT

Dual master cylinder—drum brakes (© Ford Motor Co.)

Neutral Safety and Back-Up Light Switch Assembly—Automatic Transmission

1965-72

Ford small cars throughout this period have used the same neutral switches and back up switches as full sized Fords.

See Ford section for a complete breakdown of years, transmissions, and adjustments.

Back-Up Light Switch—Manual Transmission

1965-72

The back-up light switch may be located in either one of two places. The back-up light switch location, on cars with column shift selector and linkage controls, is at the bottom of the column.

The back-up light switch location, on cars with consoles and floor shift selector, is on the left side of the transmission back at the shift control bracket.

Brakes

Single-anchor, internal-expanding hydraulic brakes are standard on all models.

An independent parking brake operates the rear wheel brake shoes through a mechanical cable linkage.

Self-Adjusting Brakes

The self-adjusting brake mechanism consists of a cable, cable guide, adjuster lever, and adjuster spring. The cable is hooked over the anchor pin at the top and is connected to the lever at the bottom. The cable is connected to the secondary brake shoe by means of the cable guide. The ad-

juster spring is hooked to the primary brake shoe and to the lever.

The automatic adjuster operates only when the brakes are applied while the car is moving rearward.

With the car moving rearward and the brakes applied, the wrapping action of the shoes following the drum forces the upper end of the primary shoe against the anchor pin. Action of the wheel cylinder moves the upper end of the secondary shoe away from the anchor pin. Movement of the secondary shoe causes the cable to pull the adjusting lever upward and against the end of a tooth on the adjusting screw star wheel. Upward travel of the lever increases as lining wear increases. When the lever can move far enough upward to pass over the end of the tooth, the adjuster spring pulls the lever downward causing the star wheel to turn and expand the shoes. The star wheel is turned one tooth at a time as the linings progressively wear.

Master Cylinder

1965-66

The master cylinder consists of a single cylinder and reservoir, mounted on the engine side of the firewall.

Master Cylinder R & R
Standard Brakes

1. Disconnect the rubber boot from the rear of the master cylinder in the passenger compartment.
2. Disconnect the brake line from the master cylinder.
3. Remove the master cylinder retaining bolts from the firewall and lift the cylinder away from the pushrod and boot.
4. To reinstall master cylinder, guide it carefully onto the pushrod and replace mounting bolts.
5. Connect the brake line to the

master cylinder, but leave the brake line fitting loose.
6. Fill the master cylinder, and with the brake line loose, slowly bleed the air from the cylinder using the foot pedal.
7. Tighten the line at the master cylinder and refill to within ¼ in. of the top.

Power Brakes

1. Disconnect the brake line from the master cylinder.
2. Remove the two nuts and lock-washers that attach the master cylinder to the brake booster.
3. Remove the master cylinder from the booster.
4. Reverse above procedure to reinstall.
5. Fill master cylinder and bleed entire brake system.
6. Refill master cylinder.

Beginning 1967

Since 1967, a tandem-type master cylinder has been used on all models. This design divides the brake hydraulic system into two independent and hydraulically separated halves.

Dual Master Cylinder R & R

Standard Brakes

1. Working under the dash, disconnect the master cylinder pushrod from the brake pedal. The pushrod cannot be removed from the master cylinder.
2. Disconnect the stoplight switch wires and remove the switch from the brake pedal, using care not to damage the switch.
3. Disconnect the brake lines from the master cylinder.
4. Remove the attaching screws from the firewall and remove the master cylinder from the car.
5. Reinstall in reverse of above order, leaving the brake line fittings loose at the master cylinder.
6. Fill the master cylinder, and with the brake lines loose, slowly bleed the air from the master cylinder using the foot pedal.

Power Brakes

Use same procedure as 1965-66.

Power Brakes

Power Unit Removal

1. Working inside the car below the instrument panel, disconnect booster valve operating rod from the brake pedal assembly.
2. Open the hood, and disconnect the wires from the stop light switch at the brake master cylinder.
3. Disconnect the brake line at the master cylinder outlet fitting.
4. Disconnect manifold vacuum hose from the booster unit.

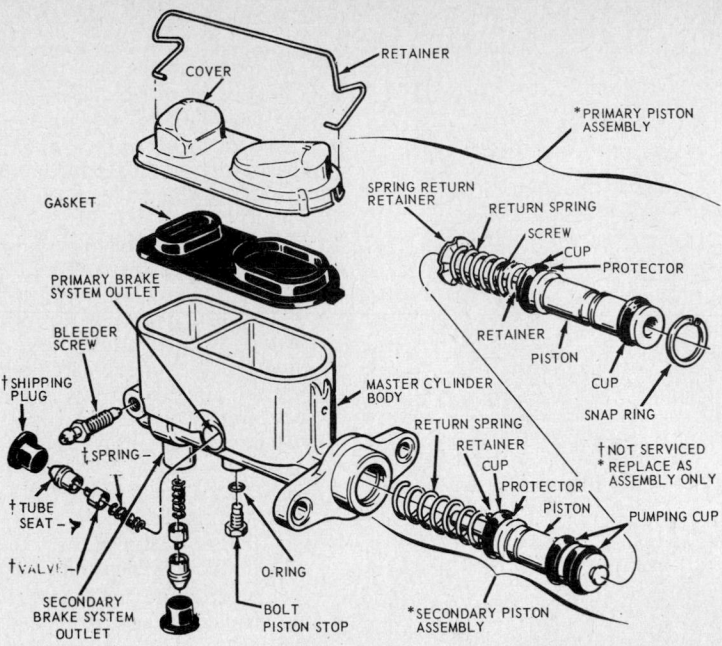

Dual master cylinder—disc brakes (© Ford Motor Co.)

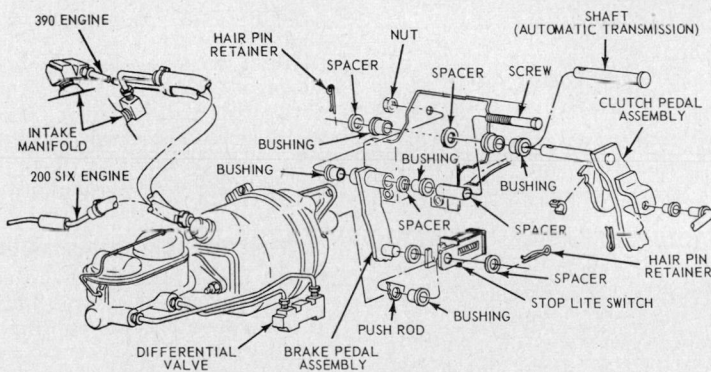

Vacuum brake booster installation (© Ford Motor Co.)

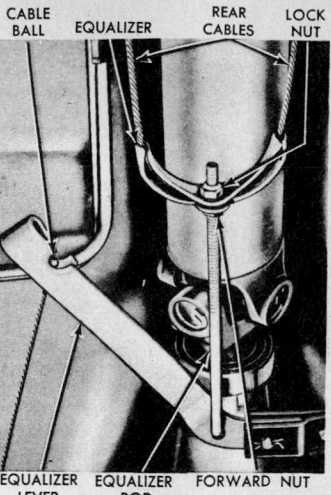

Parking brake linkage
(© Ford Motor Co.)

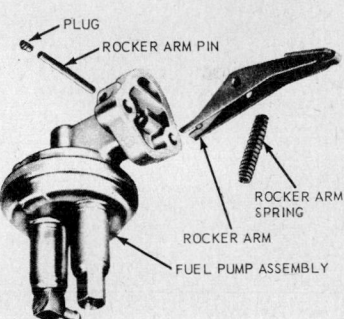

6 cylinder fuel pump
(© Ford Motor Co.)

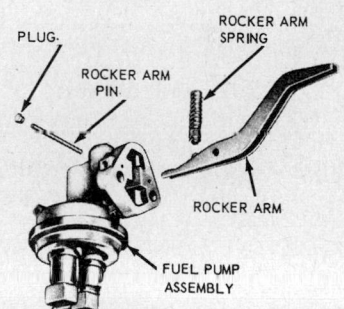

V8 fuel pump
(© Ford Motor Co.)

5. Remove the four bracket-to-dash panel attaching bolts.
6. Remove the booster and bracket assembly from the dash panel, sliding the valve operating rod out from the engine side of the dash panel.

Power Unit Installation

1. Mount the booster and bracket assembly to the dash panel by sliding the valve operating rod in through the hole in the dash panel, and installing the attaching bolts.
2. Connect manifold vacuum hose to the booster.
3. Connect the brake line to the master cylinder outlet fitting.
4. Connect stop light switch wires.
5. Working inside the car below the instrument panel, install the rubber boot on the valve operating rod at the passenger side of the dash panel.
6. Connect the valve operating rod to the brake pedal with the bushings, eccentric shoulder bolt, and nut.

Disc Brakes

Since 1965, disc brakes have been available on front wheels of some models. Complete Service Procedures are covered in the Unit Repair Section.

Parking Brake Adjustment

In most cases, a rear brake shoe adjustment will provide satisfactory parking brake action. However, if parking brake cables are excessively loose after releasing the handbrake, proceed as follows:

1. Pull up the handle to the third notch.
2. Loosen locknut on equalizer rod under the car. Then loosen the nut in front of the equalizer, several turns.
3. Turn the locknut forward against the equalizer until the cables are just tight enough to stop forward rotation of the wheels.
4. When cables are properly adjusted, tighten both nuts against the equalizer.
5. Release the handle and feel for freeness of rear wheels.

Fuel System

Data on capacity of the gas tank is in the Capacities table.

Data on fuel pump pressure will be found in the Tune-up Specifications table. Both the above tables can be found in this car section.

Information covering operation and diagnosis of the fuel gauge will be found in the Unit Repair Section.

Fuel Pump

Description

A single-action, permanently sealed Carter fuel pump is used on all models. On 6-cylinder engines the

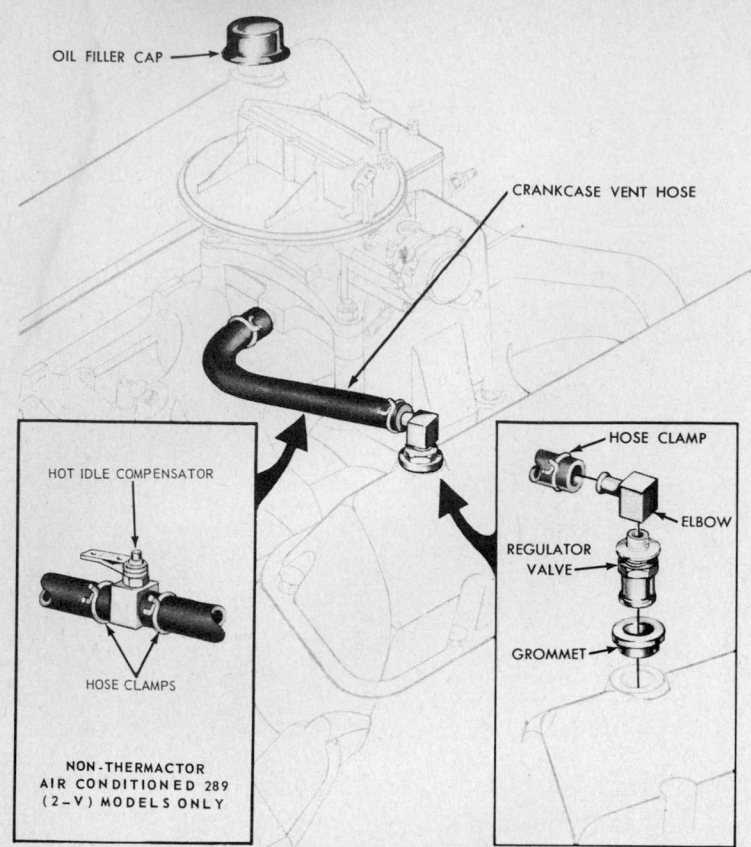

OIL FILLER CAP

CRANKCASE VENT HOSE

HOT IDLE COMPENSATOR

HOSE CLAMPS

NON-THERMACTOR
AIR CONDITIONED 289
(2-V) MODELS ONLY

HOSE CLAMP

ELBOW

REGULATOR
VALVE

GROMMET

Typical hot idle compensator installation (© Ford Motor Co.)

fuel pump is located on the lower, left center of the engine block. The V8 fuel pump is mounted on the left side of the cylinder front cover.

R & R—All Models

1. Remove the inlet and outlet lines from the pump.
2. Remove the fuel pump retaining screws and remove the pump and gasket.
3. Clean all gasket material from the pump mounting surface on the engine, and apply a coat of oil-resistant sealer to the new gasket.
4. Position pump on engine and install retaining screws.
5. Reinstall lines, start engine and check for leaks.

NOTE: if resistance is felt while positioning the fuel pump on the block, the camshaft eccentric is in the high position. To ease installation, connect a remote engine starter switch to the engine and "tap" remote switch until resistance fades.

Fuel Filter

All 1965 models have a replaceable fuel filter cartridge located in a container mounted on the bottom of the fuel pump. All models since 1966 have used a non-serviceable inline fuel filter which is located at the carburetor fuel inlet.

Carburetor

Ford uses eight types of carburetors: Autolite 1100, Carter YF and RBS (1-barrel), Autolite 2100 (2-barrel), Autolite 4100, Autolite 4300, and Holley 4150 and 4150C (4-barrel).

Idle Speed and Mixture Adjustments

1965-67: Adjust with air cleaner removed.

1967-72: Adjust with air cleaner installed.

This is the procedure for adjusting all carburetors, any exceptions are listed below.

1. Run engine at fast idle to equalize operating temperature.
2. Make sure the choke plate is fully released.
3. Turn headlights on high beam.
4. If engine is equipped with hot idle compensator valve, make sure it is fully seated in the closed position.
5. Attach tachometer of known accuracy to the engine.
6. On cars equipped with air conditioning, 1965-69 models (except 200 CI 6-cylinder and 302 V8 engines with automatic transmission) set idle speed with air conditioner turned ON. On all 1970 and later models the idle speed is set with the air conditioner turned OFF.

7. On 1967 and later models equipped with a temperature sensing valve in the distributor vacuum line, remove and plug the vacuum hoses from the distributor to the valve and from the intake manifold to the valve, at the valve located in the intake manifold.
8. Make sure the dashpot is working freely and not binding.
9. If it is not possible to adjust the idle speed with the air cleaner installed, the engine idle speed must be rechecked after installing the air cleaner. On cars with vacuum controlled heat ducts in the air cleaner, the vacuum line must be plugged if the carburetor is to be adjusted with the air cleaner removed.
10. On 1969 and later model cars for which the specifications list two idle speeds, the first speed listed is obtained by adjusting the electric solenoid on the carburetor, and the second by disconnecting the solenoid and adjusting the carburetor idle screw in the normal manner.

NOTE: with the electric solenoid disengaged, the carburetor adjusting screw must make contact with the throttle shaft to prevent the throttle plates from jamming in the throttle bore when the engine is shut off.

Fuel Mixture Adjustment

1. On 1965-67 models turn the mixture screws clockwise until engine speed begins to drop, then back out until engine reaches highest rpm.
2. On 1968 and later models with idle mixture limiters, adjust to obtain the highest rpm possible. Limiter caps should not be removed.
3. If satisfactory idle is not obtained following this procedure, refer to additional carburetor adjustments listed in the Exhaust Emission Controls Section in the Unit Repair Section of this book.

Dashpot Adjustment

Type A Dashpots

1. Adjust throttle to fast idle position and turn dashpot adjusting screw out until it is clear of dashpot plunger assembly.
2. Turn screw in until it contacts plunger. Then turn dashpot adjusting screw in specified number of turns against plunger.

NOTE: Not all engines are equipped with dashpots, and not all are adjusted in this manner. This chart applies only to models mentioned.

Year, Engines and Models	No. of Turns
1965-66 six cylinder automatic vehicles	3½
1967 Falcon with 170 six cylinder, automatic and without emission control	3½
1967 Comet, Fairlane, Falcon, and Mustang with 200 six cylinder and automatic and without emission control	3½
1967 Comet, Fairlane, Falcon and Mustang with six cylinder, auto transmission, and emission control	2
1969 Falcon and Mustang 200 six cylinder with automatic	2¼
1969 Falcon and Mustang 200 six cylinder with manual transmission	3¼

Type B Dashpots

1. With engine idle speed and mixture properly adjusted and with engine at operating temperature, loosen dashpot lock nut.
2. Hold throttle in closed position and depress dashpot plunger. Measure clearance between plunger and cam. Adjust dashpot nut to give proper clearance.

NOTE: Not all engines have dashpots and not all are adjusted in this manner. This chart applies only to models mentioned.

Type C Dashpots

Some models are equipped with solenoid operated dashpots. These are not adjusted.

Exhaust System

Description

The exhaust system consists of a muffler inlet pipe, an inlet extension pipe, and a muffler (with integral outlet pipe). The muffler inlet pipe used with V8 engines is the Y-type, in which the inlet pipe from the left exhaust manifold crosses over beneath the transmission. It is welded to the inlet pipe from the right exhaust manifold.

Muffler and Outlet Pipe

Removal

1. Remove inlet extension pipe clamp at muffler.
2. Remove bolts that attach the rear end of the muffler to the frame-mounted bracket.
3. Separate the muffler from the inlet extension pipe and remove the muffler and outlet pipe assembly.

Installation

1. Slide the new muffler and outlet pipe assembly on the inlet extension pipe. Position the inlet extension pipe clamp.
2. Position the muffler and outlet

pipe assembly to the frame-mounted bracket and install the retaining bolts. Tighten inlet extension pipe clamp.
3. Start engine and check exhaust system for leaks.

Inlet Pipe

Removal

1. Remove inlet pipe clamp at inlet extension pipe.
2. Remove two nuts and lock washers holding the inlet pipe to the exhaust manifold (both exhaust manifolds on the V8 engines).
3. Pull the inlet pipe/s down and remove the inlet pipe from the inlet extension pipe.

Installation

1. Clean the gasket surfaces of the exhaust manifold/s.
2. Install a new gasket over the studs of the exhaust manifold/s.
3. Slide the new inlet pipe into the inlet extension pipe. Then posi-

Year, Model and Engine	Clearance Manual (in.)	Automatic (in.)
1965 Two barrel carb.		5/64
1965 Four barrel carb.		5/16
1966 Two barrel carb.		0.060-0.090
1966 Four barrel carb.		0.060-0.090
1967 Falcon with 170 six and emission control		⅛
1967 289 2 V without emission control		0.060-0.090
1967 289 2 V with emission control	0.110-0.140	0.110-0.140
1967 390 2V with emission control when equipped with dashpot	0.080-0.110	0.110-0.140
1967 390 2V without emission control	⅛	⅛
1967 289 4V with emission control	⅛	⅛
1967 390 4V when equipped with dashpot		⅛
1969 Montego, Fairlane and Mustang 250 six except when solenoid equipped	0.080	
1969 302 2V	⅛	⅛
1969 351 Windsor 2V	7/64	
1969 351 Windsor 4V	3/32	
1969 390 4V	⅛	
1969 428 CJ	0.100	0.100
1969 Falcon 170 six	0.100	0.100
1970-71 170 and 200 six cylinder if so equipped	7/64	7/64
1970-71 Montego, Fairlane, and Mustang 250 six		7/32
1970 302 2V without air conditioning		⅛
1970-71 351 Windsor 2V without air conditioning		⅛
1970-71 351 Cleveland 2V without air conditioning		⅛
1970-71 351 Cleveland 4V without air conditioning		0.080
1970 429 4V Montego and Fairlane	0.070	0.070
1970 428 CJ without air conditioning	0.140	0.200

tion the inlet pipe clamp.
4. Position the inlet pipe on the studs of the exhaust manifold/s. Then, install the lock washers and nuts. Tighten the nuts.
5. Tighten inlet pipe clamp.
6. Start engine and check exhaust system for leaks.

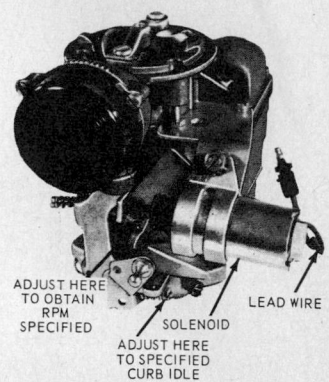

ADJUST HERE TO OBTAIN RPM SPECIFIED · LEAD WIRE · SOLENOID · ADJUST HERE TO SPECIFIED CURB IDLE

Solenoid equipped Carter YF carburetor adjustments
(© Ford Motor Co.)

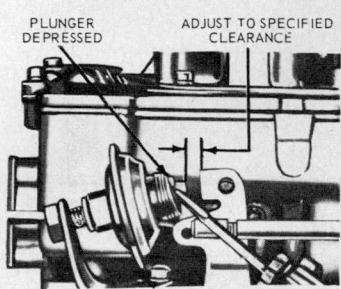

PLUNGER DEPRESSED · ADJUST TO SPECIFIED CLEARANCE

Anti-stall dashpot adjustment
(© Ford Motor Co.)

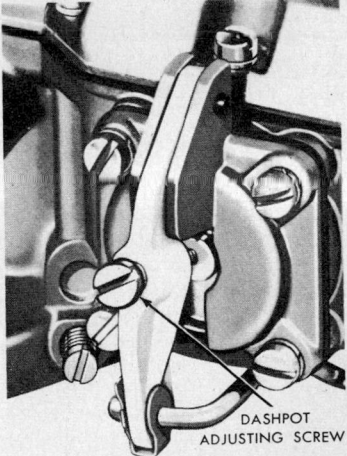

DASHPOT ADJUSTING SCREW

ADJUST THROTTLE TO HOT IDLE POSITION PRIOR TO ADJUSTING DASHPOT

Type A dashpot adjustment
(© Ford Motor Co.)

Inlet Extension Pipe

Removal

1. Remove muffler and outlet pipe assembly by following directions given in Muffler and Outlet Pipe, Removal.

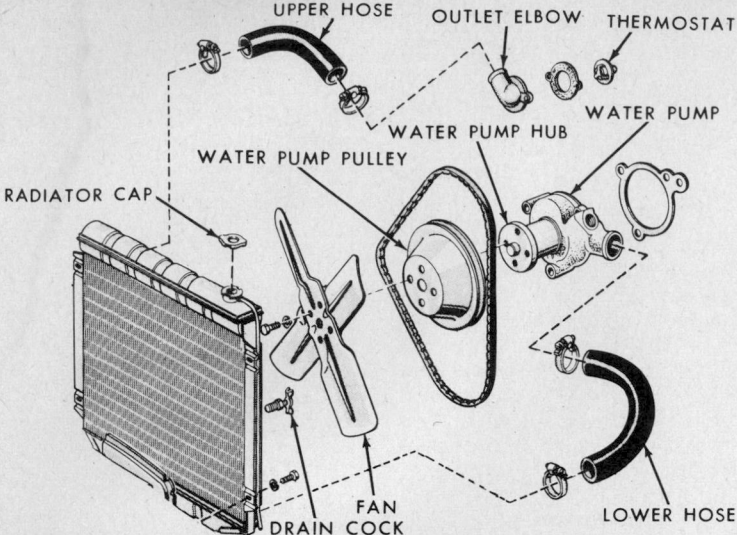

UPPER HOSE   OUTLET ELBOW   THERMOSTAT

WATER PUMP HUB   WATER PUMP

WATER PUMP PULLEY

RADIATOR CAP

FAN

DRAIN COCK   LOWER HOSE

Radiator and related parts (© Ford Motor Co.)

2. Remove the clamps at the inlet pipe and at the frame-mounted bracket. Remove the inlet extension pipe.

Installation

1. Slide the new inlet extension pipe on the inlet pipe.
2. Position the clamps at the inlet pipe and at the frame mounted bracket. Tighten the clamps.
3. Install the muffler and outlet pipe assembly by following Steps 1 through 3 of Muffler and Outlet Pipe, Installation.

Cooling System

Both the 6-cylinder and V8 engines employ cooling systems that are basically similar.

In the 6-cylinder engine, coolant flows from the cylinder head, past the thermostat (if it is open) and into the radiator upper tank. In the V8 engine, coolant from each cylinder head flows through water passages in the intake manifold, then past the thermostat (if it is open) and into the radiator upper tank.

The standard thermostat operating temperature is 185°-192°F. However, a low reading thermostat of 157°-162°F is available for use with non-permanent-type anti freeze solutions.

A single water pump assembly is used. The pump has a sealed bearing integral with the water pump shaft. The bearing requires no lubrication. There is a bleed hole in the water pump housing. This is not a lubrication hole.

Radiator

Removal
1. Drain cooling system.
2. Disconnect upper and lower hoses

at the radiator.
3. On automatic transmission-equipped cars, disconnect oil cooler lines at radiator.
4. On vehicles equipped with a fan shroud, remove the shroud retaining screws and position the shroud out of the way.
5. Remove radiator attaching bolts and lift out the radiator.

Installation

1. If a new radiator is to be installed, transfer the petcock from the old radiator to the new one. On cars equipped with automatic transmissions, transfer the oil cooler line fittings from the old radiator to the new one.
2. Position the radiator and install, but do not tighten, the radiator support bolts. On cars equipped with automatic transmissions, connect the oil cooler lines. Then tighten the radiator support bolts.
3. On vehicles equipped with a fan shroud, reinstall the shroud.
4. Connect the radiator hoses. Close the radiator petcock. Then fill and bleed the cooling system.
5. Start the engine and bring to operating temperature. Check for leaks.
6. On cars equipped with automatic transmissions, check the cooler lines for leaks and interference. Check transmission fluid level.

Water Pump R & R
1. Drain cooling system.
2. On 351C and 400 V8, disconnect the negative battery cable.
3. On cars with power steering, remove the drive belt, models with 352, 390, 427, or 428 engines, remove the power steering mounting retaining screws and remove the pump and bracket as an assembly and position it out of the way.

4. If the vehicle is equipped with air conditioning, remove the idler pulley bracket and air conditioner drive belt.
5. On engines with Thermactor, remove the belt; on 1968 models, remove the pump.
6. Disconnect the lower radiator hose and heater hose from the water pump.
7. On cars equipped with a fan shroud, remove the retaining screws and position the shroud rearward.
8. Remove the fan and spacer from the engine, and if the car is equipped with a fan shroud, remove the fan and shroud from the engine as an assembly.
9. Loosen alternator mounting bolts, remove the alternator belt and remove the alternator adjusting arm bracket from the water pump.
10. Loosen bypass hose at water pump.
11. Remove water pump retaining screws and remove pump from engine.
12. Clean any gasket material from the pump mounting surface, and on 429 V8 remove the water pump backing plate and replace the gasket.
NOTE: the 240 and 250 CI 6-cylinder engines originally use a one-piece gasket for the cylinder front cover and water pump. Trim away the old gasket at the edge of the cylinder cover and replace with service gasket.
13. Remove the heater hose fitting from the old pump and install it on the new pump.
14. Coat both sides of the new gasket with a water-resistant sealer, then re-install pump reversing the above procedure.

Engine

1965-72
There are three different six-cylinder engines available in intermediate size Ford products: the 170, the 200 and the 250 cu. in. engines. These engines are all of the same family, and the only great difference among them is their bore and stroke. One distinguishing characteristic that makes these engines easily identifiable is the fact that the intake manifold is cast as an integral part of the cylinder head.

Optional V8 engines for these models are very numerous, and like the family of six-cylinder engines, there is a great amount of similarity among them.

The most widely used are the 260, 289, and 302 V8s. These are remarkably compact engines with stud-mounted rockers and wedge-shaped

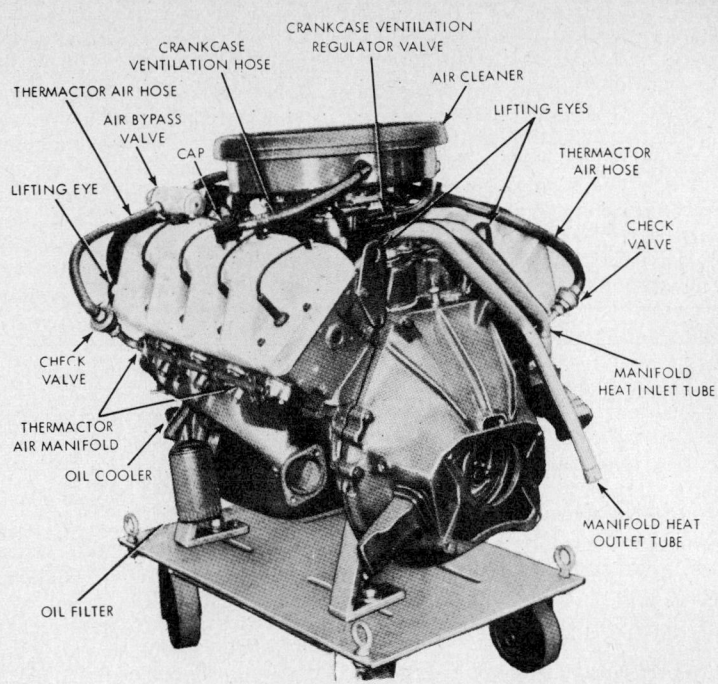

Boss 429 V8 (© Ford Motor Co.)

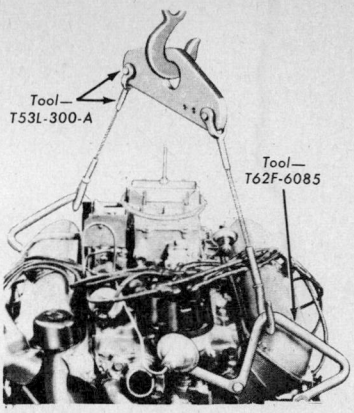

V8 engine lifting brackets and sling
(© Ford Motor Co.)

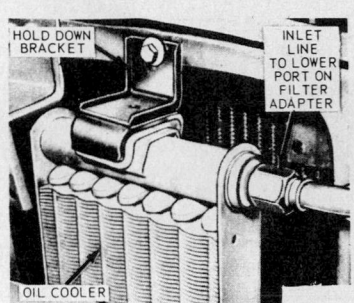

Engine oil cooler
(© Ford Motor Co.)

6 cyl. engine lifting hook
(© Ford Motor Co.)

combustion chambers. Complete information on repairing these engines is in the Ford-Thunderbird section. The 260 V8 was dropped from production in 1965, while the 289 V8 was discontinued in 1969.

In 1969, Ford Motor Company introduced a longer stroke, higher block version of the 302 engine. This engine is the 351 Windsor engine and features the wedge-shaped combustion chambers and stud-mounted rockers of the small block engine in a new intermediate sized block. See the Ford-Thunderbird section for information on this engine.

In 1970, Ford Motor Company added the 351 Cleveland engine. The 351 Cleveland engine has the same bore and stroke as the Windsor engine, and there most of the resemblance ends. It has different main bearing size, larger valves, smaller plugs, semi-hemispherical combustion chambers and more power. It is used concurrently with the Windsor engine and is found in many of the same models. The Cleveland engine is treated in this section.

The Boss 302 V8 was eliminated from production in 1971, and it was replaced by a high-performance version of the 351 Cleveland engine. It is designated as the 351 HO (High Output) engine.

In late 1966, Ford installed the 390 cu. in. V8 in The Cyclone GT and Fairlane GT. This V8 was soon joined by other large Y block V8s, the 427 and the 428 Cobra Jet. These big V8s were installed in small numbers in every intermediate and compact Ford Motor Company product, with

the exception of the Maverick and the Falcon. See the Mercury section for information on these engines.

To qualify for Trans-American sedan racing, Ford built a small number of Mustangs and Cougars in 1969-70 equipped with a special Boss 302 V8. This is essentially a 302 cu. in. engine of the 260-289 family, topped by cylinder heads from the 351 Cleveland engine. This engine is also treated in this section.

In 1970 some Mercury Montegos and Cyclones and Fairlanes use the 429 V8. This V8 comes in three forms. The first is the 429 4V engine, which is the same as is used in full sized Mercury and Ford cars. The second is the 429 CJ engine which uses stronger rods, big valve heads, smaller 14 mm. plugs, and an ignition governor set at 5,800 rpm. The third is the 429 Super CJ, which is similar to the 429 CJ except for forged pistons, four bolt main caps, solid lifters, and a 6,000 rpm governor. Despite the substantial differences between these engines, they are serviced in the same manner—see the Mercury section.

In 1969 and 1970 Ford released about one thousand Mustangs and Cougars powered by the Boss 429 engine. This engine is based loosely on the 429 engines discussed above, but its features are so individual it must be covered separately. It has modified hemispherical combustion chambers, very large valves and ports, valve seats canted in two planes, rockers with individual rocker shafts, and O-rings and chevron seals in lieu of head gaskets. The heads are of aluminum, the valves take special valve

seals, the main bearings have four bolt main caps, and the spark plugs pass through the rocker covers. In short, this is a very special engine that demands special procedures found in this section.

Exhaust Emission Control

In compliance with anti-pollution laws, the Ford Motor Company has adopted a distributor and a modified carburetor with some engine changes, to reduce terminal exhaust fumes to an acceptable level. This method is known as Ford's Improved Combustion (IMCO) System.

The plan supersedes (in most cases) the previous method used to conform to 1966-67 California laws. The new system phases out (except with stick shift and special purpose engine applications) the thermactor, or afterburner type of exhaust treatment.

The IMCO concept utilizes broader, yet more critical, distributor control and carburetor modification.

Since 1968, all car makers have posted idle speeds and other pertinent data, relative to the specific engine car application in a conspicuous place in the engine compartment.

For details on the IMCO system, consult the Unit Repair Section.

Engine Removal

1. Scribe the hood hinge outline on the under-hood, disconnect the hood and remove.
2. Drain the entire cooling system and crankcase.
3. Remove the air cleaner, disconnect the battery at the cylinder head. On automatic transmission equipped cars, disconnect oil cooler lines at the radiator.
4. Remove upper and lower radiator hoses and remove radiator. If equipped with air conditioning, unbolt compressor and position compressor out of way with refrigerant lines intact. Unbolt and lay refrigerant radiator forward without disconnecting refrigerant lines. On some 428 CJ engines and all 429 Super CJ, Boss 302, and Boss 429 engines disconnect inlet and outlet lines from engine oil cooler, remove hold-down bracket and remove cooler.
5. Remove fan, fan belt and upper pulley.
6. Disconnect the heater hoses at the water pump and the carburetor spacer.
7. Disconnect the generator wires at the generator, the starter cable at the starter, the accelerator rod at the carburetor and, on the 6-cylinder engine, the choke control cable at the carburetor.
8. Disconnect fuel tank line at the fuel pump and plug the line.
9. Disconnect the coil primary wire at the coil. Disconnect wires at the oil pressure and water temperature sending units.
10. Remove the starter and dust seal.
11. On a car equipped with a manual-shift transmission, remove the clutch retracting spring. Disconnect the clutch equalizer shaft and arm bracket at the underbody rail and remove the arm bracket and equalizer shaft.
12. Raise the car. Remove the flywheel or converter housing upper retaining bolts through the access holes in the floor pan.
13. Disconnect the exhaust pipe or pipes at the exhaust manifold. Disconnect the right and left motor mount at the underbody bracket. Remove the flywheel or converter housing cover.
14. On a car with manual shift, remove the flywheel housing lower retaining bolts.
15. On a car equipped with automatic transmission, disconnect throttle valve vacuum line at the intake manifold, disconnect the converter from the flywheel. Remove the converter housing lower retaining bolts. On a car with power steering, disconnect power steering pump from cylinder head. Put drive belt and wire steering pump out of the way.
16. Lower the car. Support the transmission and flywheel or converter housing with a jack.
17. Attach an engine lifting hook. Lift the engine up and out of the compartment and onto an adequate workstand.

Engine Installation

1. Place a new gasket over the studs of the exhaust manifold/s.
2. Attach engine sling and lifting device. Lift engine from workstand.
3. Lower the engine into the engine compartment. Be sure the exhaust manifold/s is in proper alignment with the muffler inlet pipe/s, and the dowels in the block engage the holes in the flywheel housing.
   On a car with automatic transmission, start the converter pilot into the crankshaft.
   On a car with manual-shift transmission, start the transmission main drive gear into the clutch disc. If the engine hangs up after the shaft enters, rotate the crankshaft slowly (with transmission in gear) until the shaft and clutch disc splines mesh.
4. Install the flywheel or converter housing upper bolts.
5. Install engine support insulator to bracket retaining nuts. Disconnect engine lifting sling and remove lifting brackets.
6. Raise front of car. Connect exhaust line/s and tighten attachments.
7. Position dust seal and install starter.
8. On cars with manual-shift transmissions, install remaining flywheel housing-to-engine bolts. Connect clutch release rod. Position the clutch equalizer bar and bracket, and install retaining bolts. Install clutch pedal retracting spring.
9. On cars with automatic transmissions, remove the retainer holding the converter in the housing. Attach the converter to the flywheel. Install the converter housing inspection cover and the remaining converter housing retaining bolts.
10. Remove the support from the transmission and lower the car.
11. Connect engine ground strap and coil primary wire.
12. Connect water temperature gauge wire and the heater hose at coolant outlet housing. Connect ac-

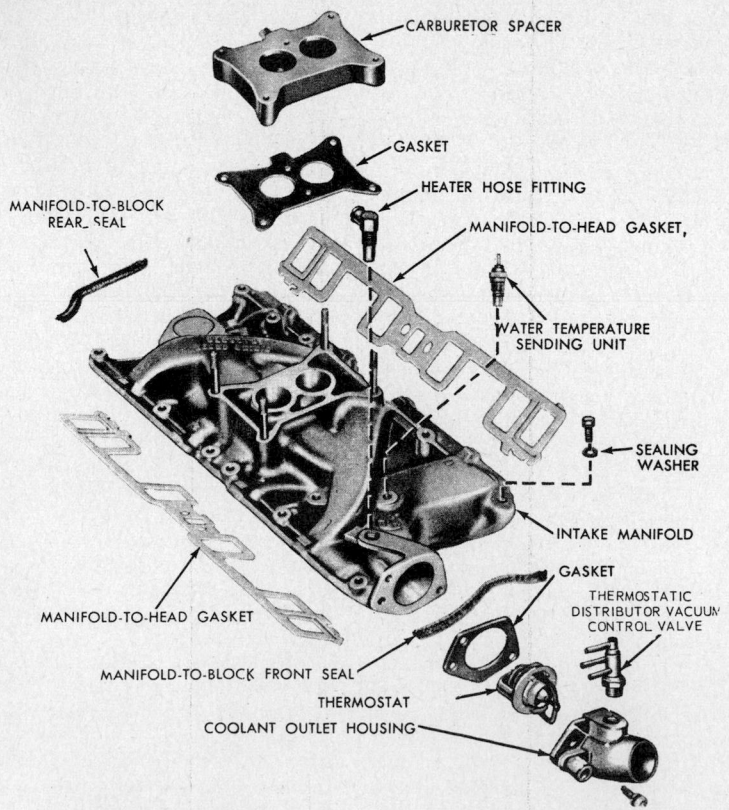

Intake manifold assembly—289, 302, 351 Windsor V8s (© Ford Motor Co.)

celerator rod at the bellcrank.

13. On cars with automatic transmission, connect the transmission filler tube bracket. Connect the throttle valve vacuum line.

14. On cars with power steering, install the drive belt and power steering pump bracket. Install the bracket retaining bolts. Adjust drive belt to proper tension.

15. Remove plug from the fuel tank line. Connect the flexible fuel line and the oil pressure sending unit wire.

16. Install the pulley, belt, spacer, and fan. Adjust belt tension.

17. Tighten generator adjusting bolts. Connect generator wires and the battery ground cable.

18. Install radiator. Connect radiator hoses. On air conditioned cars, install compressor and refrigerant radiator. On some 428 CJ engines, and all 429 Super CJ, Boss 302, and Boss 429 engines, install engine oil cooler and hold-down bracket and connect inlet and outlet lines.

19. On cars with automatic transmission, connect oil cooler lines.

20. Install oil filter. Connect heater hose at water pump, after bleeding the system.

21. Bring crankcase to level with correct grade of oil. Run engine at fast idle and check for leaks. Install air cleaner and make final engine adjustments.

22. Install and adjust hood.

23. Road-test car.

Intake Manifold Removal

6 Cylinder

170, 200 and 250 cu. in. sixes have intake manifolds that are integral with the cylinder head and cannot be removed.

260, 289 and 302 V8

See Ford–Thunderbird Section.

390, 427, and 428 V8

See Mercury Section.

429, 429 CJ, and 429 Super CJ V8s

See Mercury Section.

351 Windsor V8

See Ford–Thunderbird Section.

302 Boss, 351 Cleveland and 351 HO V8s

1. Drain cooling system and remove air cleaner. On Boss 302 engine, disconnect Thermactor air hose from check valve at rear of intake manifold and loosen hose clamp at hose bracket. Remove air hose and Thermactor air by-pass valve from bracket and position out of way.

2. Disconnect accelerator linkage and accelerator downshift linkage, if so equipped, and position out of way. On Boss 302, disconnect choke cable from carburetor.

3. Disconnect high tension lead and wires from coil. Disconnect engine wire loom and position out of way.

4. Disconnect spark plug wires from spark plugs by grasping, twisting, and pulling molded cap only. Remove distributor cap and wire assembly.

5. Remove carburetor fuel inlet line.

6. Disconnect distributor vacuum hoses from distributor. Remove hold-down bolt and remove distributor.

7. Disconnect radiator upper hose from coolant outlet housing and disconnect temperature sender wire.

8. Loosen clamp on water pump by-pass hose at coolant outlet housing and slide hose off outlet housing.

9. Disconnect crankcase vent hose (PCV) at rocker cover.

10. If vehicle is air conditioned, remove compressor to intake manifold brackets.

11. Remove intake manifold and carburetor as an assembly. Discard all used gaskets and clean all mating surfaces.

12. Reverse procedure to install.

Boss 429 V8

1. Disconnect battery.

2. Drain cooling system.

3. Disconnect heater hose from manifold.

4. Disconnect positive crank case ventilation (PCV) hose from right-hand rocker cover. Disconnect and tag all vacuum lines from rear of intake manifold.

5. Twist and pull the molded spark plug wire cap from each plug. Remove plug wires from brackets on rocker covers.

6. Disconnect high tension lead from coil and remove distributor cap and wires from distributor as an assembly.

7. Disconnect accelerator linkage from carburetor. Remove bolts that attach accelerator linkage bellcrank. Disconnect linkage spring and position linkage to one side.

8. Disconnect all distributor vacuum lines from carburetor and vacuum control valves and tag them.

9. Disconnect carburetor fuel line.

10. Disconnect wiring harness from coil battery terminal, temperature sender unit, oil pressure sending unit, and other connections as necessary. Disengage

wiring harness from retaining clips at left rocker cover bolts. Move harness out of way.

11. Disconnect Thermactor air by-pass valve from mounting bracket and place it to one side.

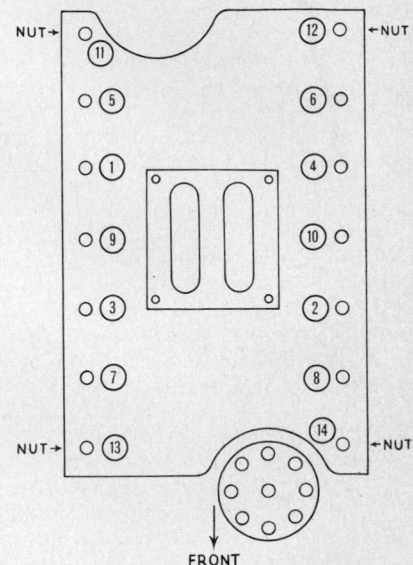

Tightening procedure

12. Remove coil and bracket assembly.

13. Disconnect manifold heat inlet and outlet tubes from rear of manifold and from exhaust pipe.

14. Remove distributor from engine.

15. Remove intake manifold attaching bolts.

16. Remove manifold and carburetor as an assembly. Discard used gaskets.

17. To install intake manifold, reverse above procedure—the manifold should be torqued in place as shown in the illustration.

Exhaust Manifold Removal R & R

6 Cylinder Engines

1. Remove the air cleaner and heat duct body.

2. Disconnect the muffler inlet pipe and remove the choke hot air tube from the manifold.

3. Bend the exhaust manifold attaching bolt lock tabs back, remove the bolts and the manifold.

4. Clean all manifold mating surfaces and place a new gasket on the muffler inlet pipe.

5. Reinstall manifold by reversing above procedure, torque attaching bolts in sequence from the centermost bolt outward.

V8 Engines—Except 428 CJ and 429 Boss

1. On right exhaust manifold, remove the air cleaner, automatic choke heat tube and air cleaner heat ducts.

2. Disconnect the exhaust manifold(s) from the muffler inlet pipe(s).
3. Remove the manifold attaching bolts and remove the manifold(s).
4. Reverse above procedure to reinstall, using new inlet pipe gaskets.

NOTE: to remove the left side exhaust manifold from a car equipped with a 351 C engine, it is necessary to remove the oil filter and the transmission selector cross-shaft or clutch linkage and equalizer shaft bracket, depending on transmission type.

428 CJ Engine

This procedure is for removing both manifolds. If only one manifold is to be removed, do not remove any equipment located on or near the opposite side of the engine.

1. Remove the air cleaner, heat tubes, choke and vacuum lines from the manifold.
2. Remove the air cleaner heat tube mounting studs and the three forward attaching bolts from the right-side manifold.
3. Raise the car on a hoist, and remove the idler arm bracket from the frame.
4. Disconnect the starter cable and remove the starter motor.
5. Remove the remaining right-side manifold attaching bolts.
6. Disconnect all exhaust system hangers and lower the exhaust system.
7. Remove the inlet pipes from the manifolds.
8. On vehicles with manual transmission, remove the clutch linkage and equalizer bracket from the engine.
9. Disconnect the Pitman arm from the steering sector shaft and, on vehicles with power steering, remove the steering control valve bracket from the frame.
10. Lower the car, disconnect the steering shaft flex joint, unbolt and remove the steering gear box assembly from the frame.
11. Raise the car again and disconnect and remove both motor mounts and the rear crossmember support attaching bolts.
12. Position a jack under the engine and, using a piece of wood under the oil pan, raise the engine slightly.
13. Remove remaining manifold attaching bolts and remove the manifolds.
14. Clean all gasket surfaces and, using new inlet pipe gaskets, reverse above procedure to reinstall manifolds.

429 Boss Engine

1. Remove the battery ground cable.

2. Remove the valve covers.
3. Disconnect the Thermactor air manifolds from the check valves.
4. Remove the air manifolds from the exhaust manifolds.
5. With the car on a hoist, remove the 8 exhaust manifold attaching bolts and disconnect the muffler inlet pipes.
6. Disconnect the clutch linkage and equalizer bracket from the engine.
7. Work the manifolds rearward and remove them through the engine compartment.
8. Clean all gasket surfaces and install new gaskets on the muffler inlet pipes.
9. Reinstall the manifold, working them into position from under the vehicle.

Cylinder Head

6 Cylinder Removal

1. Drain cooling system, remove the air cleaner and disconnect the battery cable at the cylinder head.
2. Disconnect exhaust pipe at the manifold end, spring the exhaust pipe down and remove the flange gasket.
3. Disconnect the fuel and vacuum lines from the carburetor. Disconnect the intake manifold line at the intake manifold.
4. Disconnect the accelerator and retracting spring at the carburetor. Disconnect the manually operated choke cable (if so equipped).
5. Disconnect the carburetor spacer outlet line at the spacer. Disconnect the radiator upper hose and the heater hose at the water outlet elbow. Disconnect the radiator lower hose and the heater hose at the water pump.
6. Disconnect the distributor vacuum control line at the distributor. Disconnect the gas filter line on the inlet side of the filter and the vacuum line at the fuel pump. Remove these three lines as an assembly, then remove the windshield wiper line at the vacuum pump, (if so equipped).

7. Disconnect the spark plug wires and remove the plugs.
8. Remove the rocker arm cover.
9. Back off all of the tappet adjusting screws to relieve tension on the rocker shaft. Loosen the rocker arm shaft attaching bolts and remove the rocker arm and shaft assembly. Remove the valve pushrods, in order, and keep them that way.
10. Remove one cylinder-head bolt from each end of the head (at opposite corners) and install cylinder head guide studs. Remove the remaining cylinder head bolts and lift off the cylinder head.

To help in removal and installation of cylinder head, two 6 in. x 7/16—14 bolts with heads cut off and the head end slightly tapered and slotted for installation and removal, with a screwdriver, will reduce the possibility of damage during head replacement. These guide studs make a handy tool during head removal and gasket and head replacement.

6-Cylinder Installation

1. Clean the cylinder head and block surfaces. Be sure of flatness and no surface damage.
2. Apply cylinder head gasket sealer to both sides of the new gasket and slide the gasket down over the two guide studs in the cylinder block.

NOTE: apply gasket sealer only to steel shim head gaskets. Steel-asbestos composite head gaskets are to be installed without any sealer.

3. Carefully lower the cylinder head over the guide studs. Place the exhaust pipe flange on the manifold studs (new gasket).
4. Coat the threads of the end bolts for the right side of the cylinder head with a small amount of water-resistant sealer. Install, but do not tighten, two head bolts at opposite ends to hold the head gasket in place. Remove the guide studs and install the remaining bolts.
5. Cylinder head torquing should proceed in three steps and in prescribed order. Tighten to 55 ft.

Removing rocker arm assembly—6 cyl. (© Ford Motor Co.)

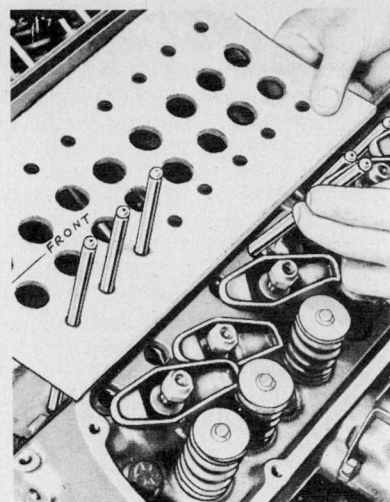

Pushrod removal—289, 302, and 351 Windsor V8s
(© Ford Motor Co.)

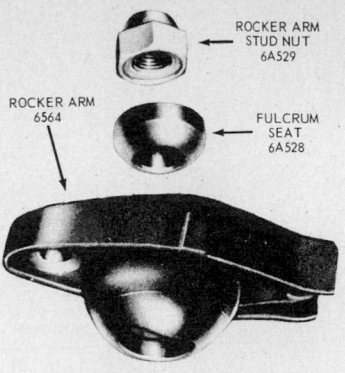

289, 302, and 351 Windsor rocker arm assembly
(© Ford Motor Co.)

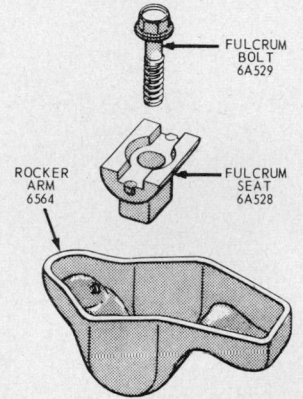

351 Cleveland V8 rocker arm assembly
(© Ford Motor Co.)

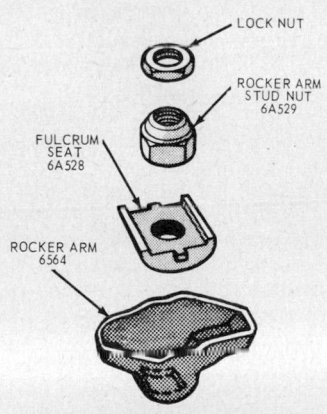

Boss 302 rocker arm assembly
(© Ford Motor Co.)

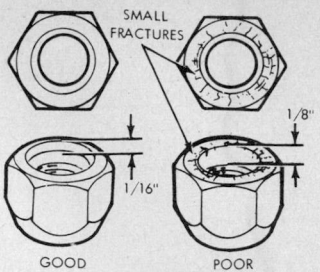

Rocker arm stud nut inspection
(© Ford Motor Co.)

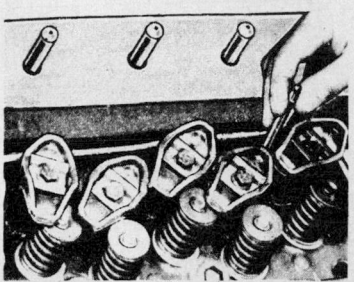

Removing push rods—351 Cleveland V8
(© Ford Motor Co.)

lbs., then give them a second tightening to 65 ft. lbs. The final step is to 75 ft. lbs., at which they should remain undisturbed.

6. Lubricate both ends of the pushrods and install them in their original locations.
7. Apply a petroleum jelly-type lubricant to the rocker arm pads and the valve stem tips and position the rocker arm shaft assembly on the head. Be sure the oil holes in the shaft are in a down position.
8. Tighten all the rocker shaft retaining bolts to 30-35 ft. lbs. and do a preliminary valve adjustment (make sure there are no tight valve adjustments).
9. Hook up the exhaust pipe.
10. Reconnect the heater and radiator hoses.
11. Reposition the distributor vacuum line, the carburetor gas line and the intake manifold vacuum line on the engine. Hook them up to their respective connections and reconnect the battery cable to the cylinder head.

12. Connect the accelerator rod and retracting spring. Connect the choke control cable and adjust the choke.
13. Reconnect the vacuum line at the distributor. Connect the fuel inlet line at the fuel filter and the intake manifold vacuum line at the vacuum pump. Connect the windshield wiper vacuum line to the other side of the vacuum pump.
14. Lightly lubricate the spark plug threads, install them and torque to 25 ft. lbs. Connect spark plug wires and be sure the wires are all the way down in their sockets.
15. Fill the cooling system and bleed. Run the engine for about ½ hour at a good fast idle to stabilize all engine parts temperatures.

16. Adjust engine idle speed and idle fuel-air adjustment.
17. Reset valve tappet adjustment to .016 in. for a hot adjustment of both intake and exhaust valves on those engines not using hydraulic lifters.
18. Coat one side of a new rocker cover gasket with oil-resistant sealer. Lay the treated side of the gasket on the cover and install the cover. Be sure the gasket seals evenly all around the cylinder head.

260, 289, 302 and 351 Windsor V8

See Ford–Thunderbird Section.

390, 427, 428, 429, 429CJ, and 429 Super CJ V8s

See Mercury Section.

302 Boss, 351 HO and 351 Cleveland V8s

1. Remove intake manifold.
2. Remove attaching bolts and remove rocker covers.
3. Remove rocker arm lock nuts, stud nuts, fulcrum seats and rockers from Boss 302. Remove rocker arm fulcrum bolts, fulcrum seats and rockers from 351 Cleveland engines.

NOTE: if cylinder head is not to be disassembled, loosen rocker arms and pivot them sideways to clear pushrods.

4. Remove pushrods in sequence and save to replace in original bores.
5. If left cylinder head is to be removed, unbolt power steering pump, if any, from cylinder head. On Boss 302, remove ignition coil.
6. If right cylinder head is to be removed, remove alternator mounting bolt bracket and spacer. On 351 Cleveland, remove ground wire at back of cylinder head.
7. Disconnect exhaust manifolds from head pipes.
8. Remove cylinder head attaching bolts and lift cylinder heads from block. Remove and discard head gasket.
9. On Boss 302 engine, reverse procedure to install heads—adjust valve clearances.
10. On 351 Cleveland engines, position head gasket over cylinder dowels on block. Position cylin-

Removing spark plug wires on Boss 429 (© Ford Motor Co.)

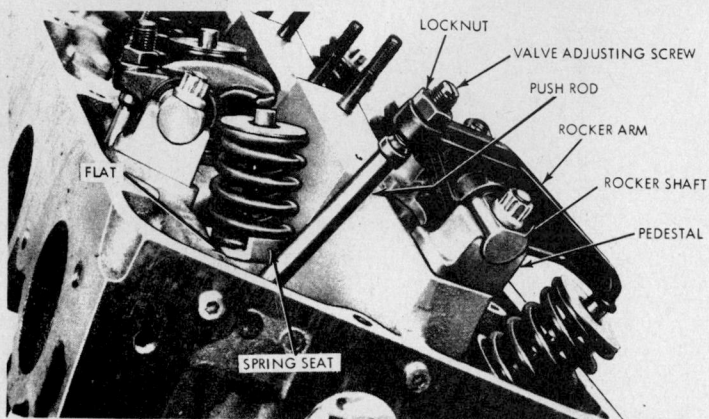

Boss 429 valve gear (© Ford Motor Co.)

der head on block and install attaching bolts.

11. Tighten all bolts in sequence at front of section to 50 ft. lbs., then tighten bolts in sequence to 60 ft. lbs. Finally torque to specification.
12. Clean pushrods in solvent and blow out oil passage in pushrod with compressed air if available. Roll pushrods across flat surface to check for straightness. Discard bent pushrods, do not attempt to straighten them.
13. Lubricate and install pushrods into their original bores.
14. Lubricate top of valve stem, rocker arm, and fulcrum seat.
15. Position No. 1 piston on TDC at end of compression stroke. Install rocker arms, fulcrum seats, and fulcrum bolts on following valves: No. 1 intake, No. 1 exhaust, No. 4 intake, No. 3 exhaust, No. 8 intake, and No. 7 exhaust. Torque fulcrum bolts to 17-23 ft. lbs.
16. Rotate engine 180° clockwise and install rocker arms, fulcrum seats, and fulcrum bolts on No. 3 intake, No. 2 exhaust, No. 7 intake, and No. 6 exhaust.
17. Rotate crankshaft 270° clockwise and install rocker arms, fulcrum seats and fulcrum bolts on No. 2 intake, No. 4 exhaust, No. 5 intake, No. 5 exhaust, No.

6 intake, and No. 8 exhaust.
NOTE: be sure fulcrum seat base is inserted in its slot on cylinder head before torquing fulcrum bolt.
18. Connect exhaust manifolds at muffler inlet pipes. Torque nuts to 18-24 ft. lbs.
19. If right cylinder head was removed, install alternator mounting bracket through bolt and air cleaner inlet duct on right head assembly. Connect ground wire at rear of head. Adjust belt tension.
20. Apply oil resistant sealer to one side of new rocker cover gasket. Lay cemented side of gaskets in place in covers. Install rocker covers.
21. If left cylinder head was removed on power steering equipped vehicle, install drive belt and power steering pump bracket. Install bracket attaching bolts. Adjust drive belts.
22. Install intake manifold.

Boss 429 Removal

1. Disconnect battery.
2. Remove cap that connects crankcase ventilation hose (PCV) to left rocker cover.
3. Remove air cleaner.
4. If removing right head, remove crankcase ventilation hose.
5. Lift each plug wire from bracket.

6. Disconnect wires from spark plugs by twisting and pulling on molded duct caps.
7. If removing left head, disconnect brake master cylinder from booster and move it to one side to provide clearance.
8. Remove rocker cover attaching nuts and bolts.
9. Lift rocker covers from heads.
10. Clean gasket material from covers and heads.
11. Remove intake manifold.
12. Back off all rocker arm adjusting screws.
13. Remove all rocker shaft attaching nuts from rocker shafts.

NOTE: each rocker on a Boss 429 engine has its own individual rocker shaft.

14. Remove rocker arms, shafts and pedestals. Keep them in sequence so that they can be installed in their original position.
15. Lift pushrods from cylinder head. Keep them in sequence to install into their original bores.
16. Disconnect exhaust head pipe from exhaust manifold.
17. Disconnect air hose from thermactor check valve on head being removed.
18. Remove ten cylinder head bolts. Connect lifting sling to lifting eye at each end of cylinder head, and lift cylinder head from block with hoist.
19. Remove all rubber and steel gaskets from head and block.
20. Clean cylinder block and head mating surfaces.

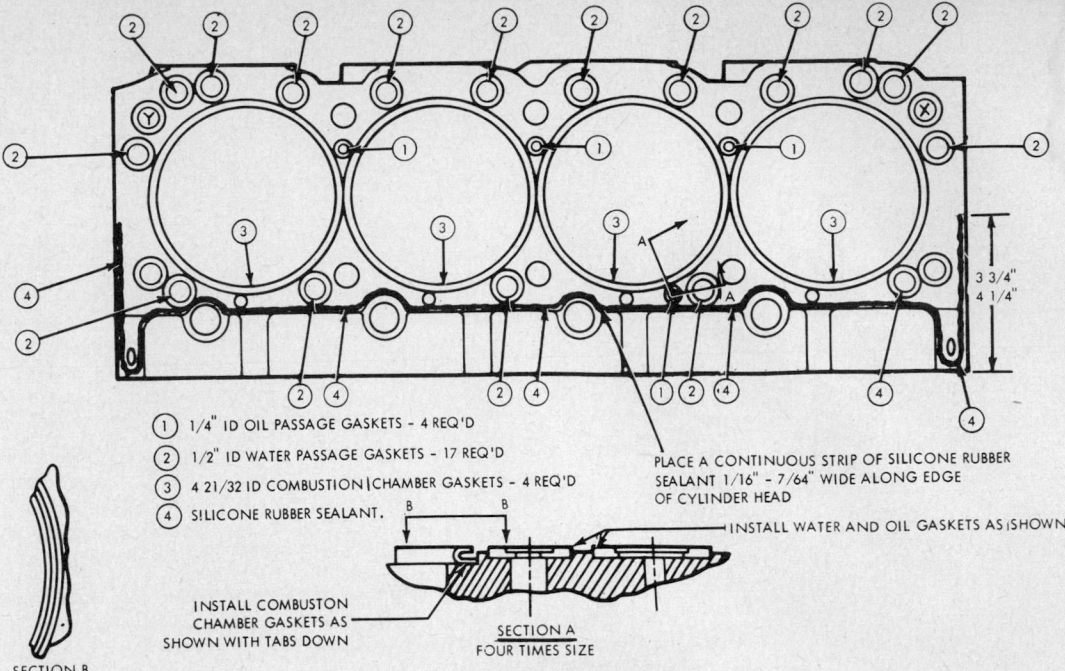

① 1/4" ID OIL PASSAGE GASKETS - 4 REQ'D
② 1/2" ID WATER PASSAGE GASKETS - 17 REQ'D
③ 4 21/32 ID COMBUSTION CHAMBER GASKETS - 4 REQ'D
④ SILICONE RUBBER SEALANT.

PLACE A CONTINUOUS STRIP OF SILICONE RUBBER SEALANT 1/16" - 7/64" WIDE ALONG EDGE OF CYLINDER HEAD

INSTALL WATER AND OIL GASKETS AS SHOWN

INSTALL COMBUSTION CHAMBER GASKETS AS SHOWN WITH TABS DOWN

SECTION A
FOUR TIMES SIZE

SECTION B

Boss 429 cylinder head gasket location (© Ford Motor Co.)

Boss 429 Installation

1. Wipe head and block surfaces with chlorathane.
2. Coat upper end of cylinder head and block with silicone rubber primer (Dow Corning A-4094 or equivalent). Coat gasket counter bores with quick drying adhesive sealer to prevent dropping gaskets while installing head.
3. Position four combustion chamber gaskets in counterbores with tabs seated down. Locate tabs by rotating gasket between finger and thumb to feel tabs.
4. Press four 1/4 in. ID gaskets into cylinder head counter bores with stepped side facing up.
5. Press seventeen 1/2 in. ID gaskets into cylinder head counter bores with stepped side facing up.
6. Apply a continuous strip of sealant along top edge of cylinder head.
7. Install guide pin at each end of cylinder block.
8. Lower cylinder head into place over guide pins. Take care not to drop any gaskets.
9. Install but do not tighten eight attaching bolts and flat washers.
10. Remove two guide pins and install two remaining bolts and washers.
11. Torque attaching bolts in sequence shown at front of section to 55-60 ft. lbs. Then torque to 75-80 ft. lbs. Finally torque to 90-95 ft. lbs.
12. Connect Thermactor air to check valve.
13. Connect lead pipe to exhaust manifold.
14. Lubricate both ends of pushrods and install.
15. Lubricate rocker arms and shafts with engine oil and install with loosened adjusting screws. Do not torque shafts down at this time.
16. Rotate crank shaft damper until No. 1 piston is at TDC at end of compression stroke.
17. Install distributor in cylinder block with rotor at No. 1 firing position and points just beginning to open. Install hold-down clamp and bolt.
18. Torque rocker shaft nuts on No. 1 cylinder intake and exhaust to 12-15 ft. lbs. If engine is equipped with a solid lifter camshaft, adjust valve clearance to specification (cold) using feeler gauge or valve gapper between rocker arm and valve stem tip. Torque adjusting screws in place. If engine is equipped with an hydraulic lifter camshaft, loosen locknut and turn in adjusting screw on No. 1 cylinder intake and exhaust rocker until all clearance is removed. Rotate pushrod with fingers while tightening adjusting screw to determine point when clearance is removed. Tighten adjusting screws 1/16 turn further. Hold adjusting screws in place and torque locknuts to 20-30 ft. lbs.
19. Rotate crankshaft 90° to position No. 5 piston at TDC and repeat step 18 for No. 5 intake and exhaust rockers.
20. Rotate crank shaft 90° and repeat procedure in Step 18 for each cylinder in firing order (1-5-4-2-6-3-7-8).
21. Remove distributor.
22. Coat one side of new rocker cover gasket with oil resistant sealer and lay cemented side in place on cover.
23. Install cover. Make sure gasket seats evenly all around cover.
24. Tighten cover attaching bolts evenly and alternately in two steps. Then torque cover bolts to 12-15 ft. lbs. Wait two minutes and retorque to 12-15 ft. lbs.
25. Install intake manifold.
26. Connect each spark plug wire to its respective plug. Insert plug wires into brackets on valve cover.
27. Install cap and crank case ventilation hose (PCV) on valve cover.
28. If installing left head, install master cylinder on booster.
29. Install air cleaner and connect battery.

Valve System

The 6-cylinder engines are equipped with tubular pushrods and barrel type tappets. Valve lash is controlled by self locking adjusting screws.

V8 engines, except the 289 and 427 high performance, use hydraulic tappets. The pushrods in the V8s also transfer oil under pressure to the friction areas of the rocker arms.

6-Cylinder Hydraulic Valve Adjustment

The following procedure is performed with the engine running.

1. After the engine has been brought to operating temperature, remove the valve cover.
2. With engine at normal idle speed, back off the valve rocker arm adjusters, one at a time, until the rocker arm starts to clatter.
3. Turn the arm adjuster down until the clatter stops.

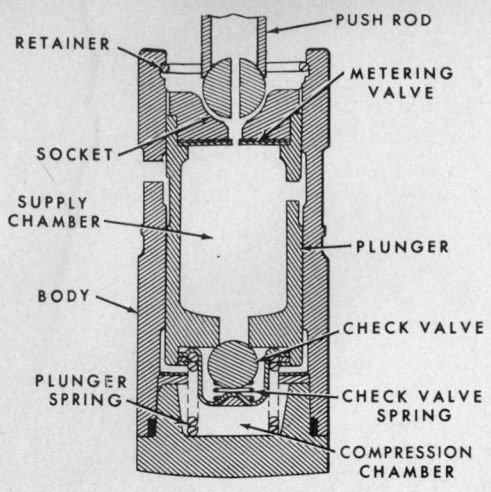

RETAINER — PUSH ROD — METERING VALVE

SOCKET

SUPPLY CHAMBER — PLUNGER

BODY — CHECK VALVE

PLUNGER SPRING — CHECK VALVE SPRING — COMPRESSION CHAMBER

Hydraulic tappet
(© Ford Motor Co.)

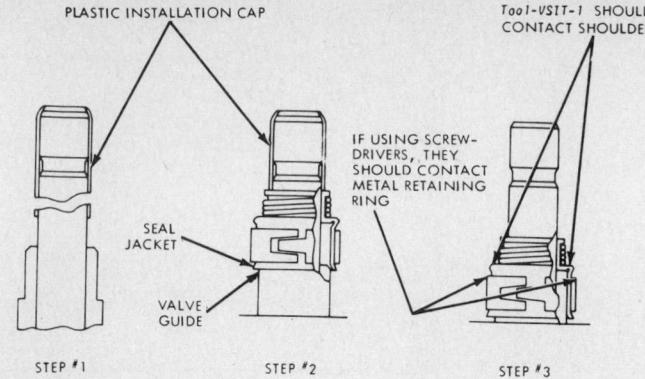

PLASTIC INSTALLATION CAP

Tool-VSIT-1 SHOULD CONTACT SHOULDER

IF USING SCREW-DRIVERS, THEY SHOULD CONTACT METAL RETAINING RING

SEAL JACKET

VALVE GUIDE

STEP #1   STEP #2   STEP #3

STEP #1 WITH VALVES IN HEAD. PLACE PLASTIC INSTALLATION CAP OVER END OF VALVE STEM.

STEP #2 START VALVE STEM SEAL CAREFULLY OVER CAP. PUSH SEAL DOWN UNTIL JACKET TOUCHES TOP OF GUIDE.

STEP #3 REMOVE PLASTIC INSTALLATION CAP. USE INSTALLATION TOOL-VSIT-1 OR SCREWDRIVERS TO BOTTOM SEAL ON VALVE GUIDE.

Installing valve stem seals—Boss 429 (© Ford Motor Co.)

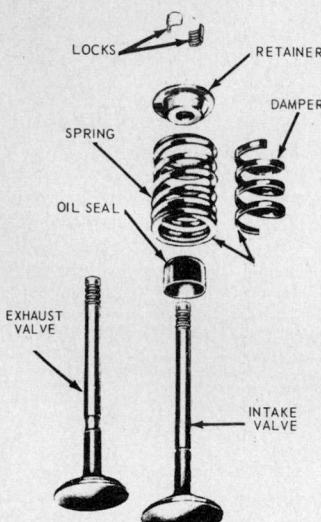

LOCKS — RETAINER

DAMPER

SPRING

OIL SEAL

EXHAUST VALVE

INTAKE VALVE

Valve assembly—351 Cleveland V8
(© Ford Motor Co.)

LOCKS

RETAINER

DAMPER SPRING

VALVE SPRING

OIL SEAL

EXHAUST VALVE

SPRING SEAT

INTAKE VALVE

Valve assembly—Boss 302 V8
(© Ford Motor Co.)

4. Continue to turn down the adjuster exactly one turn. This will force the hydraulic lifter piston into the approximate center of its travel.

5. Install valve rocker cover.

On models with non-adjustable rockers, the pushrods must be changed to secure proper lifter position.

V8 Hydraulic Valve Adjustment

All V8 engines with hydraulic valve lifters have non-adjustable valves. 352, 390, 427, and 428 engines use rocker arm shaft assemblies, while all other V8's have individually mounted rocker arms. The only way the valves on these engines can be adjusted is by installing .060 over or undersize pushrods.

NOTE: on all engines with individually mounted rocker arms, if the original factory valve setting has been disturbed by removal of any valve system component it is necessary to retorque the rocker arms using the procedure outlined in the Ford section under Preliminary Valve Adjustment.

V8 Mechanical Valve Lifter Adjustment

1. Run engine to bring to operating temperature.
2. Remove rocker covers.
3. Insert a feeler guage of specified thickness between the rocker arm and valve, and with engine running, adjust rocker arm to obtain desired clearance.
4. Reinstall rocker cover.

Disassembly of Cylinder Heads

1. Remove cylinder heads.
2. Compress valve springs using valve spring compressor.
3. Remove valve locks or keys.

4. Release valve springs.
5. Remove valve springs, retainers, oil seals, and valves. On Boss 302 and Boss 429 engines, remove valve spring seals also.

NOTE: if a valve does not slide out of the guide easily check end of stem for mushrooming or heading over. If head is mushroomed, file off excess, remove and discard valve. If valve is not mushroomed, lubricate stem of valve, remove, and check for stem wear or damage.

Valve Seals—Boss 429

The Boss 429 uses special valve seals which require special handling. To remove, grasp bottom edge of valve seal with Perfect Circle tool No. VSIT-1 or equivalent and pull seal from valve. To install, place plastic installation cap that comes with seal kit over valve stem. Start seal carefully over cap. Push seal down until jacket touches top of guide. Remove plastic installation cap. Grasp valve seal with Perfect Circle tool and push seal on to valve guide until it bottoms. If tool is not available, place two small screwdrivers about 90° from gap in metal retaining ring and push seal downward until it bottoms.

Valve Guides

Ford Motor Company engines use integral valve guides. Mercury and Ford dealers offer valves with oversize stems for worn guides. To fit these, enlarge valve guide bores with valve guide reamers to an oversize that cleans up wear. If a large oversize is required it is best to approach that size in stages by using a series of reamers of increasing diameter. This helps to maintain the concentricity of the guide bore with the valve seat. The correct valve guide to stem clearance is at front of this section.

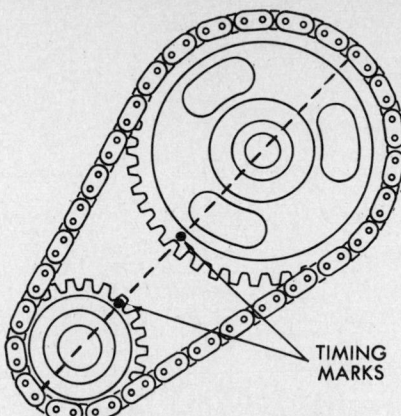

Timing mark alignment—6 cyl.

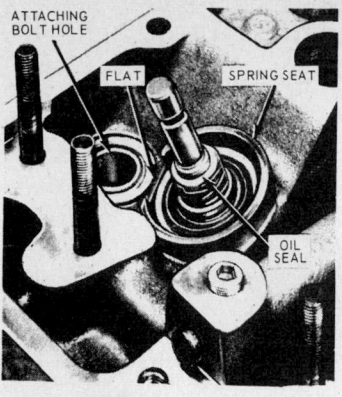

Valve spring seal and oil seal location—
Boss 429
(© Ford Motor Co.)

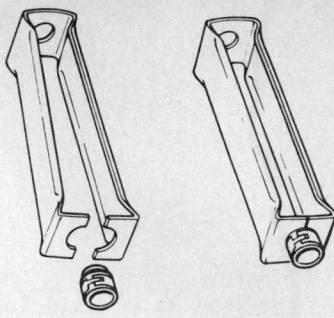

Boss 429 valve stem seal tool
(© Ford Motor Co.)

Checking timing chain deflection
(© Ford Motor Co.)

As an alternative, some local automotive machine shops will fit replacement guides that use standard stem valves.

Timing Cover and Chain

6-Cylinder Cover and Chain

Removal

1. Drain the cooling system and crankcase.
2. Disconnect the upper radiator hose from the intake manifold and the lower hose from the water pump. On cars with automatic transmission, disconnect the cooler lines from the radiator.
3. Remove the radiator, fan and pulley, and engine drive belts. On models with air conditioning, remove the condenser retaining bolts and position the condenser forward. *Do not disconnect the refrigerant lines.*
4. On 170 and 200 cu. in. engines remove the cylinder front cover retaining bolts and front oil pan bolts and gently pry the cover away from the block. On 250 engines, it is necessary to remove the oil pan before removing the front cover.
5. Remove the crankshaft pulley bolt and use a puller to remove the vibration damper.
6. With a socket wrench of the proper size on the crankshaft

pulley bolt, gently rotate the crankshaft in a clockwise direction until all slack is removed from the left side of the timing chain. Scribe a mark on the engine block parallel to the present position of the left side of the chain. Next, turn the crankshaft in a counterclockwise direction to remove all the slack from the right side of the chain. Force the left side of the chain outward with the fingers and measure the distance between the reference point and the present position of the chain. If the distance exceeds 1/2 inch, replace the chain and sprockets.

7. Crank the engine until the timing marks are aligned as shown in the illustration. Remove the bolt, slide sprocket and chain forward and remove as an assembly.

Installation

1. Position the sprockets and chain on the engine, making sure that the timing marks are aligned.
2. Reinstall the front cover, applying oil resistant sealer to the new gasket.
NOTE: on 170 and 200 engines, trim away the exposed portion of the old oil pan gasket flush with front of the engine block. Cut and position the required portion of a new gasket to the oil pan, applying sealer to both sides of it.
3. On 250 engines, reinstall the oil pan.
4. Install the fan, pulley and belts. Adjust belt tension.
5. Install the radiator, connect the radiator hoses and transmission cooling lines. If equipped with air conditioning, install the condenser.
6. Fill the crankcase and cooling system. Start the engine and check for leaks.

V8 crankshaft damper removal
(© Ford Motor Co.)

V8 Cover and Chain

Removal

1. Drain cooling system, remove air cleaner and disconnect the battery.
2. Disconnect radiator hoses and remove the radiator.
3. Disconnect heater hose at water pump. Slide water pump by-pass hose clamp toward the pump.
4. Loosen generator mounting bolts at the generator. Remove the generator support bolt at the water pump. Remove Thermactor pump on 428 CJ, 429 Super CJ, Boss 302, and Boss 429 engines.
5. Remove the fan, spacer, pulley, and drive belt.
6. Remove pulley from crankshaft pulley adapter. Remove cap screw and washer from front end of crankshaft. Remove crankshaft pulley adapter with a puller.

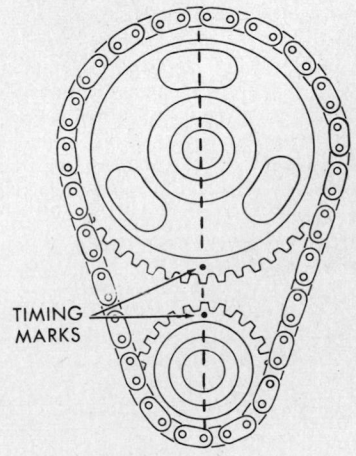

TIMING MARKS

Timing mark alignment—V8

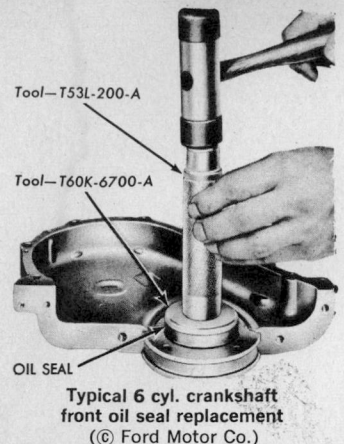

Tool—T53L-200-A

Tool—T60K-6700-A

OIL SEAL

**Typical 6 cyl. crankshaft
front oil seal replacement**
(© Ford Motor Co.)

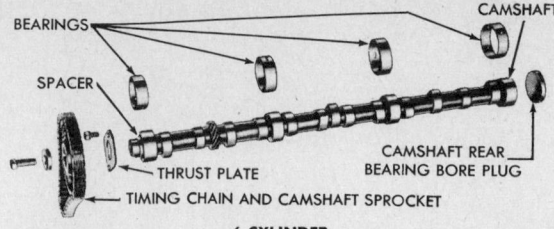

BEARINGS

CAMSHAFT

SPACER

THRUST PLATE

CAMSHAFT REAR
BEARING BORE PLUG

TIMING CHAIN AND CAMSHAFT SPROCKET

6 CYLINDER

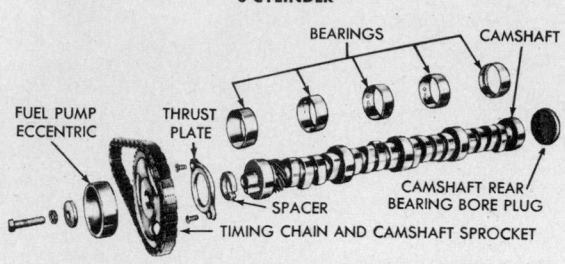

BEARINGS

CAMSHAFT

FUEL PUMP
ECCENTRIC

THRUST
PLATE

SPACER

CAMSHAFT REAR
BEARING BORE PLUG

TIMING CHAIN AND CAMSHAFT SPROCKET

8 CYLINDER
Camshaft and related parts (© Ford Motor Co.)

7. Disconnect fuel pump outlet line at the pump. Remove fuel pump retaining bolts and lay the pump to the side.

8. Remove the front cover attachbolts. On the 351C engine, it is necessary to remove the oil pan before the front cover can be removed.

9. Remove the crankshaft oil slinger if so equipped.

10. Check timing chain deflection, using the procedure outlined in Step 6 of the six cylinder cover and chain removal.

11. Crank engine until sprocket timing marks are aligned as shown in valve timing illustration.

12. Remove crankshaft sprocket cap screw, washers, and fuel pump eccentric. Slide both sprockets and chain forward and off as an assembly.

V8 Cover and Chain

Installation

1. Position sprockets and chain on the camshaft and crankshaft with both timing marks on a centerline. Install fuel pump eccentric, washers and sprocket attaching bolt. Torque the sprocket attaching bolt to 30-35 ft. lbs.

2. Install crankshaft front oil slinger.

3. Clean front cover and mating surfaces of old gasket material.

4. Coat a new cover gasket with sealer and position it on the block.
NOTE: on all except 351C engines, trim away the exposed portion of the oil pan gasket flush with the cylinder block. Cut and position the required portion of a new gasket to the oil pan, applying sealer to both sides of it. On 351C engines, after installing the cylinder front cover, install the oil pan using a new gasket.

5. Install front cover, using a crankshaft-to-cover alignment tool. Torque attaching bolts to 12-15 ft. lbs.

6. Install fuel pump, torque attaching bolts to 23-28 ft. lbs., connect fuel pump outlet tube.

7. Install crankshaft pulley adapter and torque attaching bolt to 70-90 ft. lbs. Install crankshaft pulley.

8. Install water pump pulley, drive belt, spacer and fan.

9. Install generator support bolt at the water pump. Tighten generator mounting bolts. Adjust drive belt tension. Install Thermactor pump if so equipped.

10. Install radiator and connect all coolant and heater hoses. Connect battery cables.

11. Refill and bleed cooling system.

12. Start engine and operate at fast idle to operating temperature.

13. Check for leaks, install air cleaner. Adjust ignition timing and make all final adjustments.

6 & 8 Cylinder Cover Seal R & R

It is a recommended practice to replace the cover seal any time the front cover is removed.

1. With the cover removed from the car, drive the old seal from the rear of cover with a pin-punch. Clean out the recess in the cover.

2. Coat the new seal with grease and drive it into the cover until it is fully seated. Check the seal after installation to be sure the spring is properly positioned in the seal.

Camshaft R & R

6 Cylinder Engines

1. Remove the cylinder head as directed in that section.

2. Remove the cylinder front cover, timing chain and sprockets as outlined in the preceding section.

3. Disconnect and remove the grille. On Mustang models, remove the gravel deflector.

4. Using a magnet, remove the valve lifters and keep them in order so that they can be installed in their original positions.

5. Remove the camshaft thrust plate and remove the camshaft by pulling it from the front of the engine. Use care not to damage the camshaft lobes or journals while removing the cam from the engine.

6. Before installing the camshaft, coat the lobes with Lubriplate and the journals and all valve parts with heavy oil.

7. Reverse above procedure to install, following recommended torque settings and tightening sequences.

V8 Engines

1. Remove the intake manifold as outlined previously.

2. Remove the cylinder front cover, timing chain and sprockets as directed previously.

3. Remove the grille, and, on models with air conditioning, remove the condenser retaining bolts and position it out of the way. *Do not disconnect refrigerant lines.*

4. Remove the rocker arm covers.

5. On 352, 390, 427 and 428 engines it is necessary to remove the rocker arm shafts to remove the intake manifold. On all other engines with individually mounted rocker arms, loosen the rocker arm fulcrum bolts and rotate the rocker arms to the side.

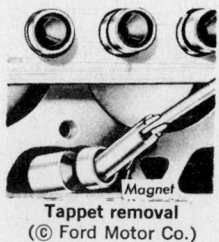

Magnet

Tappet removal
(© Ford Motor Co.)

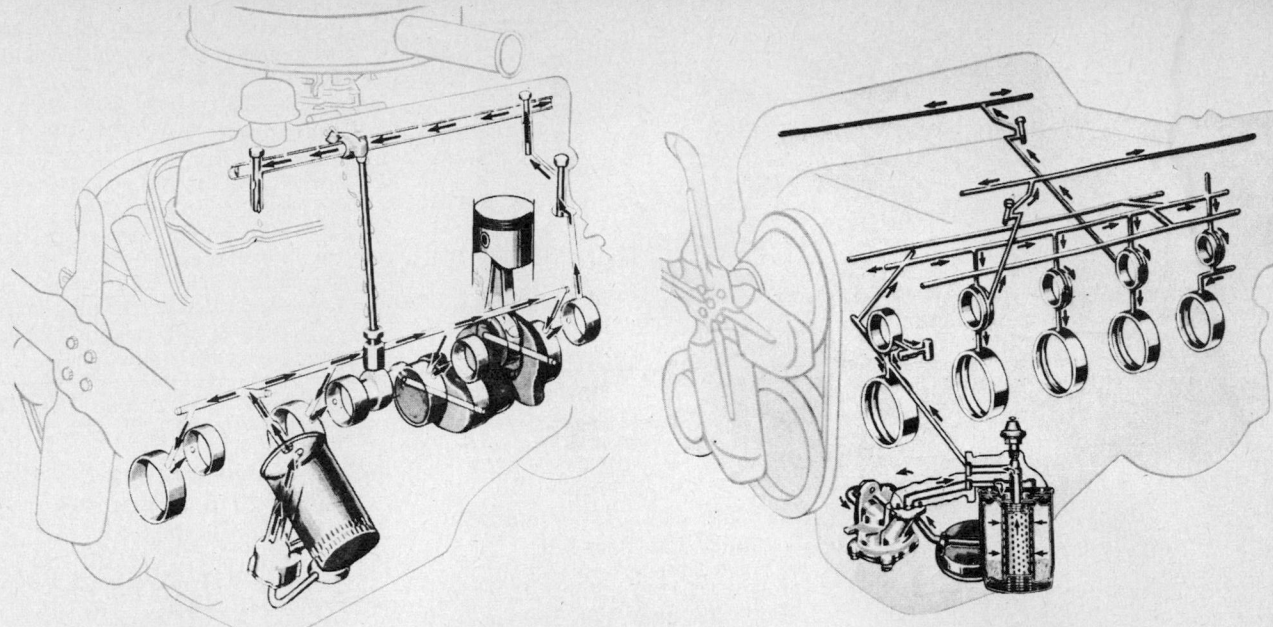

6 cyl. engine lubrication (© Ford Motor Co.)

390, 427 and 428CJ V8s engine lubrication (© Ford Motor Co.)

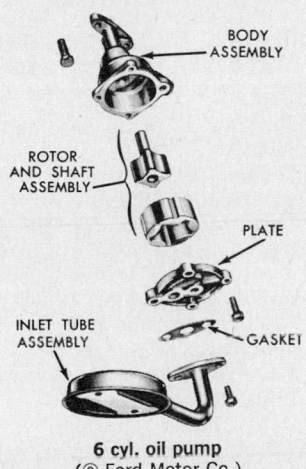

6 cyl. oil pump
(© Ford Motor Co.)

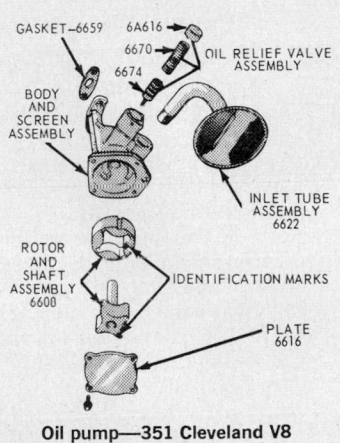

Oil pump—351 Cleveland V8
(© Ford Motor Co.)

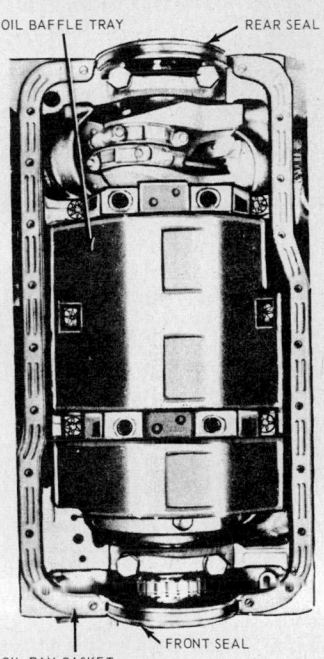

Oil baffle tray—Boss 302
(© Ford Motor Co.)

6. Remove the pushrods and lifters and keep them in order so that they can be installed in their original positions.
7. Remove the camshaft thrust plate and washer if so equipped. Remove the camshaft from the front of the engine. Use care not to damage camshaft lobes or journals while removing the cam from the engine.
8. Before installing the camshaft, coat the lobes with Lubriplate and the journals and valve parts with heavy oil.
9. Reverse above procedure to install.

NOTE: on engines with individually mounted rocker arms, it is necessary to perform a preliminary valve adjustment before starting the engine.

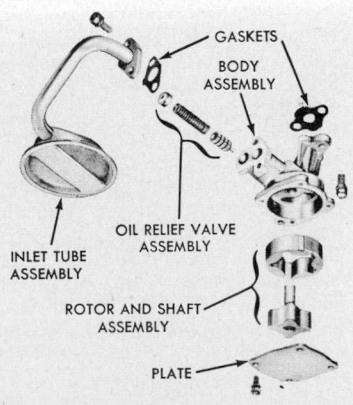

289, 302, Boss 302, and
351 Windsor V8s oil pump
(© Ford Motor Co.)

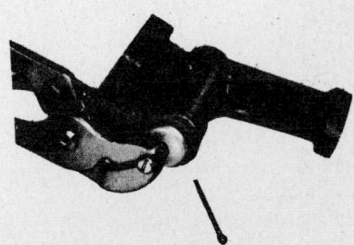

Removing oil pump relief valve—429 V8s
(© Ford Motor Co.)

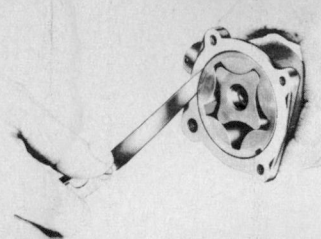

Measuring clearance between outer rotor and housing
(© Ford Motor Co.)

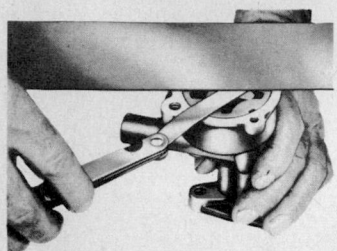

Measuring rotor end play
(© Ford Motor Co.)

Engine Lubrication

All engines are equipped with full-flow-type oil filters to condition the oil before it reaches the main bearings. The filter is equipped with an internal, relief, by-pass valve as a safety precaution. The system of lubrication is best shown in the illustrations.

Under normal driving conditions, engine oil and oil filter should be changed at 6,000 mile intervals. However, adverse driving conditions, dusty operation, short trips, winter driving, etc., may justify the change at much shorter intervals.

Oil Pan R & R

NOTE: on certain engine-chassis combinations, interference will be encountered between the oil pan and oil pump while attempting to remove the oil pan. If this occurs, lower the oil pan and reach inside it and remove the two bolts retaining the oil pump and pickup tube to the engine block. Lower the pump and pickup tube assembly into the pan and remove it with the pan.

6 Cylinder

1. Drain crank case, and remove dipstick and flywheel inspection plate.
2. In Mustangs, disconnect stabilizer bar and pull downwards out of way.
3. Remove one bolt, loosen other and swing No. 2 crossmember out of way.
4. Remove oil pan. Reverse procedure to install.

Oil pump and inlet tube installed— 351 Cleveland V8
(© Ford Motor Co.)

260, 289, 302, 351 Windsor, and 302 Boss V8s

See Ford–Thunderbird Section.

390, 427 and 428 Engines

See Ford–Thunderbird Section.

429 4V, 429 CJ, 429 Super CJ, and Boss 429

See Mercury Section.

351 Cleveland V8 in Cougar and Mustang

1. Remove dip stick, raise vehicle, and drain crank case.
2. Disconnect starter cable, remove starter.
3. Remove stabilizer bar.
4. Remove two bolts retaining No. 2 crossmember and remove crossmember.
5. Remove pan bolts, turn crank shaft for maximum clearance, and remove pan. Reverse procedure to install.

351 Cleveland V8 in Fairlane and Montego

1. Remove dipstick.
2. Remove fan shroud bolts and position fan shroud over pan.
3. Raise vehicle, drain crank case, disconnect starter cable, and remove starter.
4. Remove stabilizer bar attaching bolts, and lower sway bar for clearance.
5. Remove engine front support bolts.
6. Raise engine and place wood block between engine supports and chassis brackets.
7. Remove oil pan attaching bolts.
8. Move automatic transmission oil cooler lines, if any, out of way and remove pan. Reverse procedure to install.

Oil Pump

Removal—6 Cylinder

1. Remove oil pan.
2. Remove oil pump inlet tube and screen assembly.

3. Remove oil pump attaching bolts and remove oil pump gasket and intermediate shaft.

Removal—260, 289, 302, 351 Windsor and Boss 302 V8s

1. Remove oil pan.
2. Remove oil pump pickup tube and screen from oil pump.
NOTE: it is not necessary to remove oil baffle tray on Boss 302 engines to do this job.
3. Remove oil pump attaching bolts and remove oil pump, gasket, and intermediate drive shaft.

Removal—390, 427, and 428 V8

See Mercury Section.

Removal—429 4V, 429 CJ, 429 Super CJ and Boss 429

See Mercury Section.

Removal—351 Cleveland V8

1. Remove oil pan.
2. Remove oil pump attaching bolts and remove oil pump with pickup tube and screen, gasket, and intermediate shaft.

Oil Pump Disassembly Except 429 4V, 429 CJ, 429 Super CJ, and Boss 429 V8s

1. Remove oil pump inlet tube and gasket.
2. Remove cover attaching screws and remove cover.
3. Remove inner rotor and shaft assembly and remove outer rotor.
4. Insert a self threading sheet metal screw into relief valve chamber cap and pull cap out of chamber.
5. Remove relief valve spring and plunger.

Oil Pump Disassembly 429 4V, 429 CJ, 429 Super CJ, and Boss 429 V8s

1. Remove four screws and washer securing pump cover and remove cover.
2. Remove inner rotor and shaft assembly and outer rotor.
3. Remove stake marks which secure relief valve plug.
4. Insert self tapping metal screw in relief valve plug.
5. Use pliers to remove plug and remove spring and relief valve.

Inspection—All Engines

1. Examine inner rotor, outer rotor, and pump body for wear or damage.
2. Examine mating surface of cover for wear, scoring, grooving, or warping. Replace damaged cover.
3. Install outer rotor in pump body, and holding rotor against one side, measure clearance between rotor and body. Clearance should be 0.006-0.013 in. If clearance is

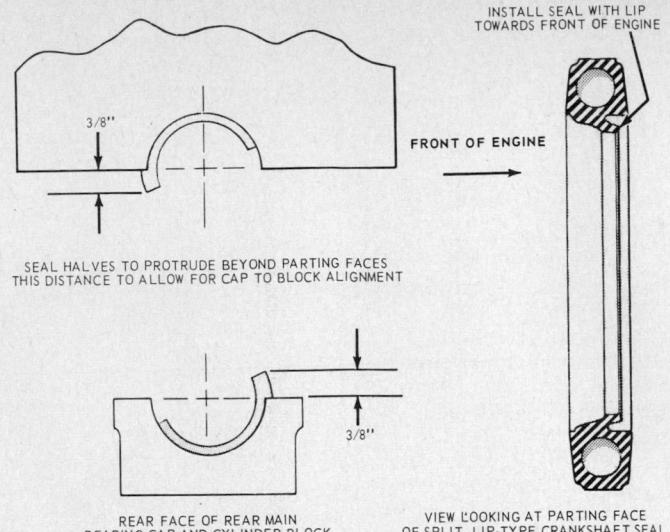

SEAL HALVES TO PROTRUDE BEYOND PARTING FACES
THIS DISTANCE TO ALLOW FOR CAP TO BLOCK ALIGNMENT

REAR FACE OF REAR MAIN
BEARING CAP AND CYLINDER BLOCK

VIEW LOOKING AT PARTING FACE
OF SPLIT, LIP-TYPE CRANKSHAFT SEAL

Installing split lip type rear oil seal (© Ford Motor Co.)

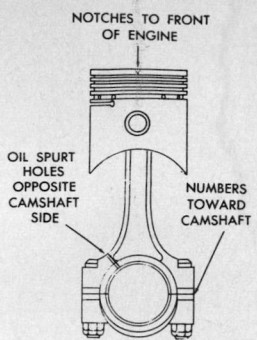

Piston and rod assembly—6 cyl.

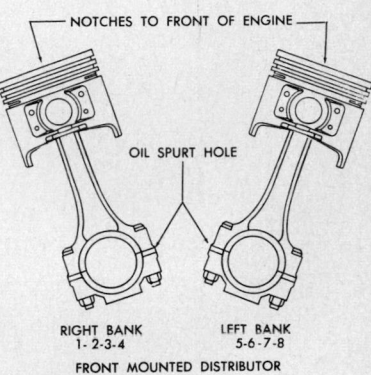

Piston and rod assembly—V8 289 cu. in.

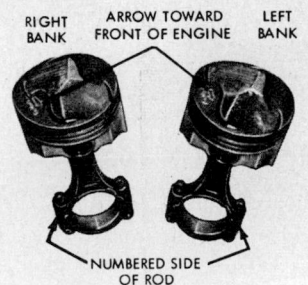

Piston and rod assembly—351 Cleveland and Boss 302 V8s (© Ford Motor Co.)

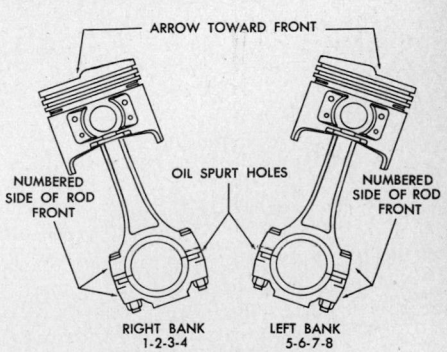

Piston and rod assembly—390, 427, and 428CJ V8s

excessive, replace worn or damaged part or parts.

4. Install inner rotor and shaft in pump body. Place straight edge over pump body and rotors, and measure clearance between straight edge and rotors. Clearance should be 0.0011-0.0041 in. If clearance is excessive, replace rotors.

NOTE: the inner rotor and shaft, and the outer rotor, are replaceable only as an assembly.

5. Check drive shaft to housing bearing clearance by measuring OD of drive shaft journal area and ID of bearing. Clearance should be 0.0015-0.0029 in.
6. Inspect relief valve for collapsed or worn condition. Check relief valve for scoring and for free operation in bore.

Oil Pump Assembly Except 429 4V, 429 CJ, 429 Super CJ, Boss 429 V8s

1. Clean and oil all parts.
2. Install oil pressure relief valve plunger, spring, and new cap.
3. Install outer rotor and inner rotor and shaft assembly. Be sure identification marks on inner and outer rotors are aligned.
4. Install cover and torque cover attaching screws to 6-9 ft. lbs. on six cylinders, and 9-12 ft. lbs. on V8s.
5. Position new gasket and oil inlet tube on oil pump and install attaching bolts.

Oil Pump Assembly — 429 4V, 429 CJ, 429 Super CJ, and Boss 429

1. Install relief valve, spring, and plug in pump body. Press plug inward until it seats, then stake in place.

NOTE: the relief hole in plug must not be covered or obstructed.

2. Install outer rotor and inner rotor and shaft in body.
3. Install cover and four screws and washers.
4. Torque cover screws to 6-9 ft. lbs.

Installation—All Engines

1. Prime oil pump by filling inlet on outlet port with engine oil and rotating shaft of pump to distribute it.
2. Position intermediate drive shaft into distributor socket.
3. Position new gasket on pump body and insert intermediate drive shaft into pump body.
4. Install pump and intermediate shaft as an assembly.

NOTE: do not force pump if it does not seat readily. The drive shaft may be misaligned with the distributor shaft. To align rotate intermediate drive shaft into a new position.

5. Install and torque oil pump attaching screws to 12-15 ft. lbs. on six cylinder, 20-25 ft. lbs. on V8s.
6. Install oil pan.

Rear Crankshaft Oil Seal R & R

1967-69 390, 427, and 428 and all 1970 and Later Engines

1. Remove the oil pan, and, if required, the oil pump.
2. Loosen all main bearing caps allowing the crankshaft to lower slightly.

NOTE: the crankshaft should not be allowed to drop more than 1/32 in.

3. Remove the rear main bearing cap and remove the seal from the cap and block.
4. Carefully clean the seal grooves

in the cap and block with solvent.

5. Soak the new seal halves in clean engine oil.

6. Install the upper half of the seal in the block with the undercut side of the seal toward the front of the engine. Slide the seal around the crankshaft journal until 3/8 in. protrudes beyond the base of the block.

7. Repeat above procedure on lower seal, allowing an equal length of the seal to protrude beyond the opposite end of the bearing cap.

8. Install rear bearing cap and torque all main bearings to specifications. Apply sealer only to the rear of the seals.

9. Dip the bearing cap side seals in oil, then immediately install them. Do not use any sealer on the side seals. Tap the seals into place and do not clip the protruding ends.

10. Install the oil pump and pan. Fill the crankcase with oil, start engine check for leaks.

All Other Engines

The manufacturer recommends the engine be removed from the car and the crankshaft pulled to replace the seals. An aftermarket tool is available to replace some of these seals with the engine in the car.

Connecting Rods and Pistons

Removal

1. Drain crankcase and remove oil pan. Remove oil baffle tray if so equipped.

2. Drain cooling system and remove cylinder head or heads.

3. Remove any ridge and/or deposits from the upper end of cylinder bores with a ridge reamer.

4. Check rods and pistons for identification numbers and, if necessary, number them.

5. Remove connecting rod cap nuts and caps. Push the rods away from the crankshaft and install caps and nuts loosely to their respective rods.

6. Push piston and rod assemblies up and out of the cylinders.

Installation

1. Lightly coat pistons, rings and cylinder walls with light engine oil.

2. With bearing caps removed, install pieces of protective rubber hose on bearing cap bolts.

3. Install each piston in its respective bore, using thread guards on each assembly. Guide the rod bearing into place on the crankcase journal.

4. Remove thread guards from con-

necting rods and install lower half of bearing and cap. Check clearances.

5. Install oil pan.

6. Install cylinder head.

7. Refill crankcase and cooling system.

8. Start engine, bring to operating temperature and check for leaks.

Piston Rings

Replacement

Before replacing rings, inspect cylinder bores.

1. If cylinder bore is in satisfactory condition, place each ring in bore in turn and square it in bore with head of piston. Measure ring gap. If ring gap is greater than limit, get new ring. If ring gap is less than limit, file end of ring to obtain correct gap.

2. Check ring side clearance by installing rings on piston, and inserting feeler gauge of correct dimension between ring and lower land. Gauge should slide freely around ring circumference without binding. Any wear will form a step on lower land. Replace any pistons having high steps. Before checking ring side clearance be sure ring grooves are clean and free of carbon, sludge, or grit.

3. Space ring gaps at equidistant intervals around piston circumference. Be sure to install piston in its original bore. Install short lengths of rubber tubing over connecting rod bolts to prevent

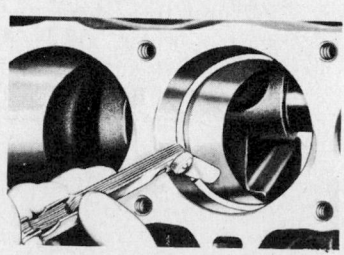

1. OUT-OF-ROUND = DIFFERENCE BETWEEN **A** AND **B**
2. TAPER = DIFFERENCE BETWEEN THE **A** MEASUREMENT AT TOP OF CYLINDER BORE AND THE **A** MEASUREMENT AT BOTTOM OF CYLINDER BORE

Taper and out of roundness
(© Ford Motor Co.)

damage to rod journal. Install ring compressor over rings on piston. Lower piston rod assembly into bore until ring compressor contacts block. Using wooden handle of hammer, push piston into bore while guilding rod onto journal.

Measuring ring side clearance
(© Ford Motor Co.)

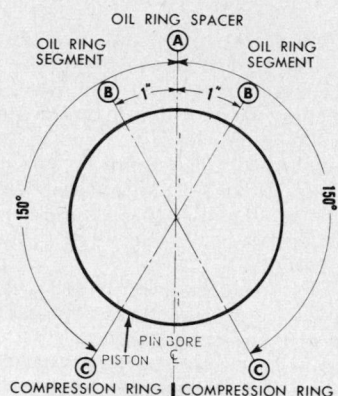

Ring gap spacing
(© Ford Motor Co.)

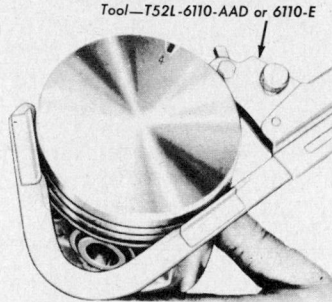

Cleaning ring grooves
(© Ford Motor Co.)

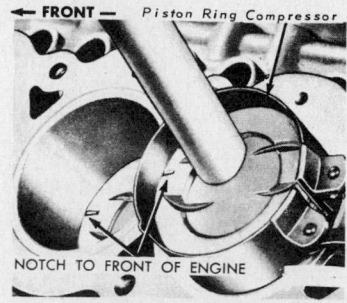

Installing piston
(© Ford Motor Co.)

Measuring piston ring gap
(© Ford Motor Co.)

Piston Clearance

Year and Engine	Minimum (in.)	Maximum (in.)
1965-71 Sixes	0.0014	0.0021
1965-66 260 and 289 V8s	0.0014	0.0022
1965-67 289 High Performance	0.0030	0.0038
1967-71 289, 302 and 351 Windsor V8s	0.0018	0.0026
1966-71 390 and 428 CJ V8s	0.0015	0.0023
1967 427 V8①	0.0042	0.0066
1968 427 V8②	0.0030	0.0038
1969-70 Boss 302	0.0034	0.0042
1970-71 351 Cleveland	0.0014	0.0022
1970-71 429 4V V8	0.0014	0.0022
1970 429 CJ, 429 Super CJ, and Boss 429 V8s	0.0030	0.0038

① Solid lifter high performance version.
② Hydraulic lifter street version

Ring Gaps

Year and Engine	Top Compression (in.)		Bottom Compression (in.)		Oil Control (in.)	
	Min.	Max.	Min.	Max.	Min.	Max.
1965-71 289, 302, Boss 302, 351 Windsor, and 351 Cleveland V8s	0.010	0.020	0.010	0.020	0.015	0.069
1966-71 Six	0.010	0.020	0.010	0.020	0.015	0.055
1966-68 390 V8	0.010	0.031	0.010	0.020	0.015	0.066
1967 427 V8	0.010	0.031	0.010	0.020	0.015	0.066
1968 427 V8	0.018	0.028	0.010	0.025	0.015	0.055
1968-70 428 CJ, 429 4 V, 429 CJ, 429 Super CJ, and Boss 429 V8s	0.010	0.020	0.010	0.020	0.010	0.035
1969-71 390	0.010	0.020	0.010	0.020	0.015	0.055

Ring, Side Clearance

Year and Engine	Top Compression (in.)			Bottom Compression (in.)			Oil Control
	Min.	Max.	Replace	Min.	Max.	Replace	
1965 Sixes	0.0019	0.0036	0.006	0.0020	0.0040	0.006	Snug
1965 260 and 289 V8s	0.0019	0.0036	0.006	0.0010	0.0040	0.006	Snug
1966 170 Six	0.0009	0.0026	0.006	0.0020	0.0040	0.006	Snug
1966 200 Six	0.0019	0.0036	0.006	0.0020	0.0040	0.006	Snug
1966-67 289 V8	0.0019	0.0036	0.006	0.0020	0.0040	0.006	Snug
1966-67 390 V8	0.0020	0.0040	0.006	0.0020	0.0040	0.006	Snug
1967 427 V8	0.0024	0.0041	0.006	0.0020	0.0040	0.006	Snug
1968-71 All	0.0020	0.0040	0.006	0.0020	0.0040	0.006	Snug

Front Suspension

The front coil springs are mounted on top of the upper control arm to a tower in the sheet metal of the body. This type of mounting provides good stability. The lower arm and stabilizing strut substitute for the conventional A frame and serve to guide the lower part of the spindle through its cycle of up-and-down movement. The rod-type stabilizing strut is mounted between two rubber buffer pads at the front end to cushion fore and aft thrust of suspension. The effective length of this rod is variable and must be considered in maintenance. Ball joints are of the usual steel construction.

General information covering the front suspension, and how to adjust it, together with information on installation of front wheel bearings and grease seals, are given in the Unit Repair Section.

Definitions of the points of steering geometry are covered in the Unit Repair Section. This article also covers troubleshooting front end geometry and irregular tire wear.

Figures covering the caster, camber, toe-in, kingpin inclination, and turning radius can be found in the Front Wheel Alignment table of this section.

Tire size figures can be found in the General Chassis and Brake Specifications table of this section.

Front Spring

Removal

1. Raise hood and remove shock absorber upper mounting bracket bolts.
2. Raise front of vehicle, and place safety stands under inboard ends of lower control arms.
3. Remove shock absorber lower attaching nuts, washers and insulators.
4. Lift shock absorber and upper bracket from spring tower.
5. Remove wheel cover on hub cap.
6. Remove grease cap, cotter pin, nut lock, adjusting nut, and outer bearing.
7. Pull wheel, tire and hub and drum off spindle as an assembly.
8. Install spring compressor as

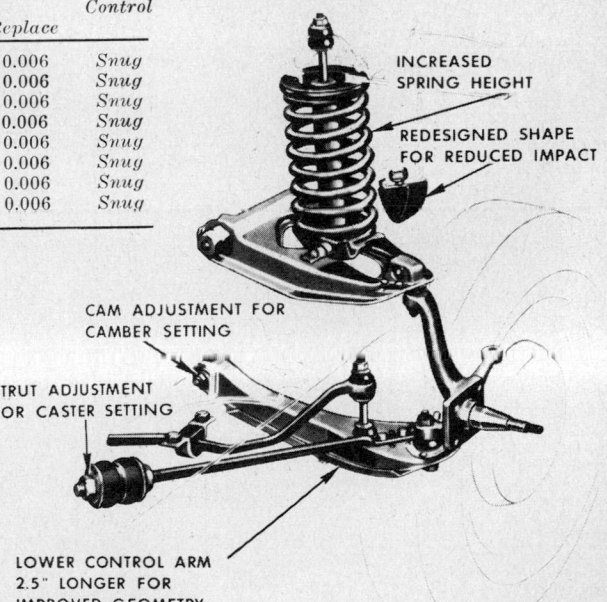

INCREASED SPRING HEIGHT

REDESIGNED SHAPE FOR REDUCED IMPACT

CAM ADJUSTMENT FOR CAMBER SETTING

STRUT ADJUSTMENT FOR CASTER SETTING

LOWER CONTROL ARM 2.5" LONGER FOR IMPROVED GEOMETRY

Caster and camber adjustment points (© Ford Motor Co.)

shown in figures.
9. Compress spring until all tension is removed from control arms.
10. Remove two upper control arm attaching nuts and swing control arm out board.
11. Release spring compressor and remove.
12. Remove spring.

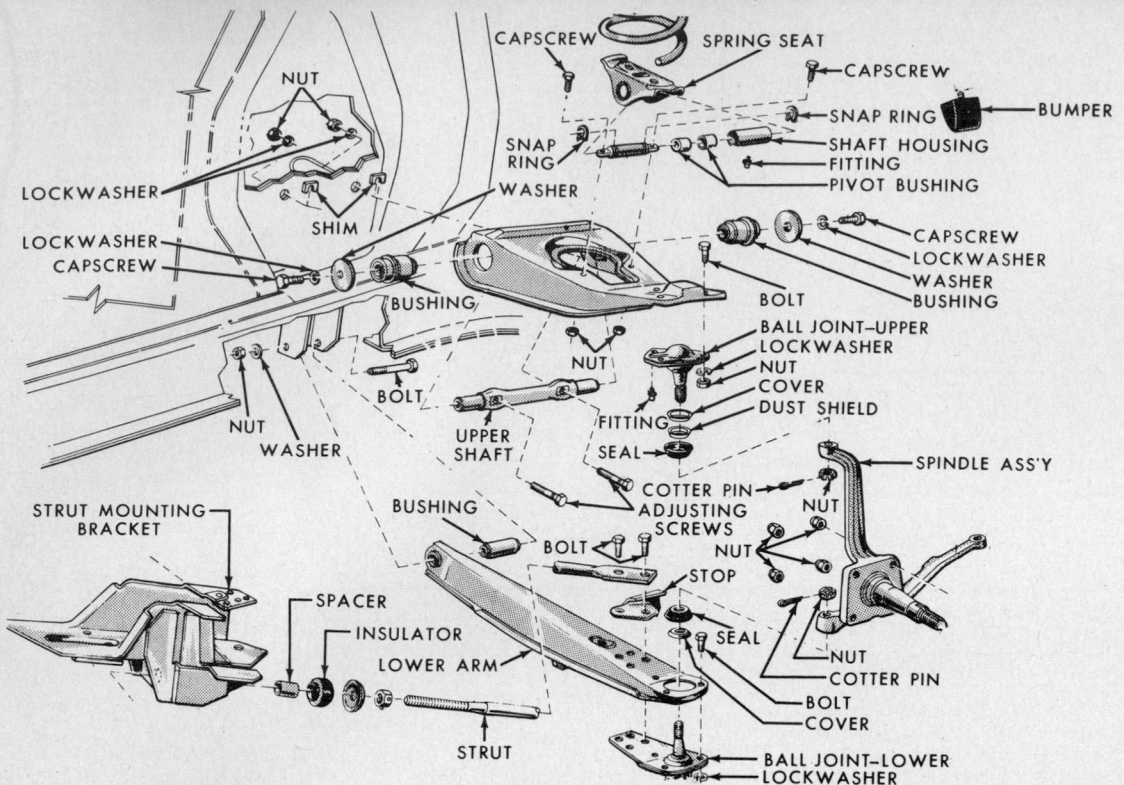

Typical front suspension (© Ford Motor Co.)

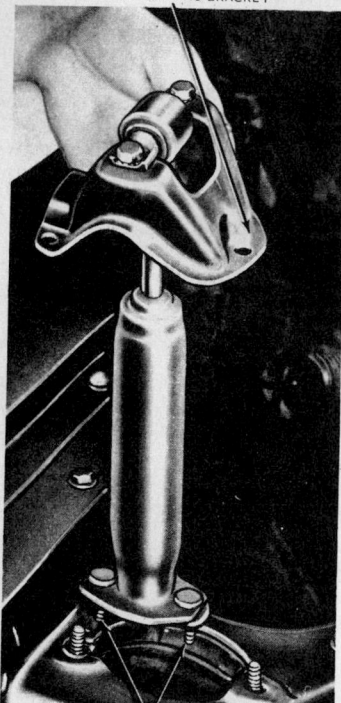

Removing shock absorber and
bracket assembly
(© Ford Motor Co.)

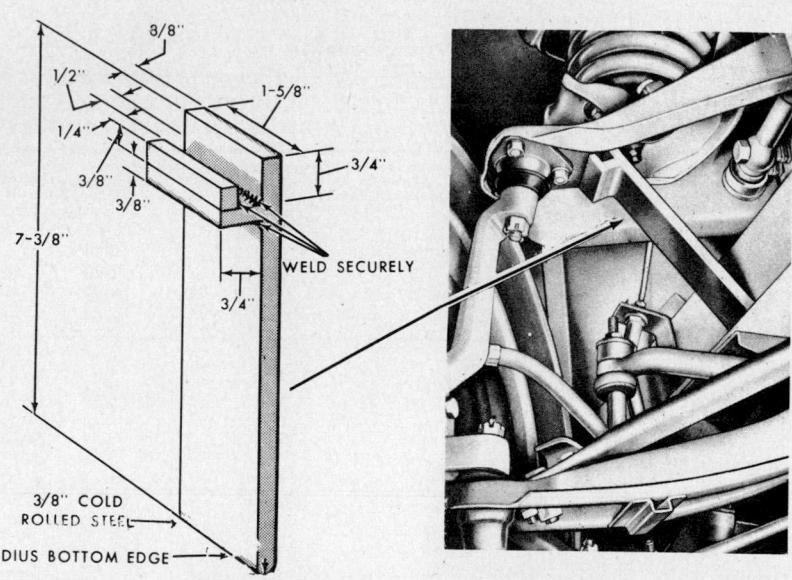

Upper control arm support (© Ford Motor Co.)

Installation

1. Place upper spring insulator on spring and secure in place with tape.
2. Position spring in spring tower and compress with spring compressor.
3. Swing upper control arm in board and install attaching nuts.

Torque nuts to 75-100 ft. lbs. on 1966-70 Montego, Fairlane, Comet, Falcon, and Maverick and 1967-70 Cougar and Mustang, 55-75 ft. lbs. on 1964-66 Mustangs, and 65-90 ft. lbs. on 1964-65 Comets and Falcons.
4. Release spring pressure and guide spring into upper arm spring seat. The end of the spring must be not more than ½ in. from tab on spring seat.
5. Remove spring compressor and position wheel, tire, and hub and drum on spindle.
6. Install bearing, washer and adjusting nut.

7. On disc brake cars, loosen adjusting nut three turns, and rock wheel hub and rotor assembly in and out to push disc brake pads away from rotor.
8. While rotating wheel, hub and drum assembly, torque adjusting nut to 17-25 ft. lbs. to seat bearing.
9. With 1⅛ in. box wrench back off adjusting nut ½ turn, and tighten nut to 10-15 in. lbs. or finger tight.
10. Position lock on adjusting nut and install new cotter pin. Bend ends of pin around castellated

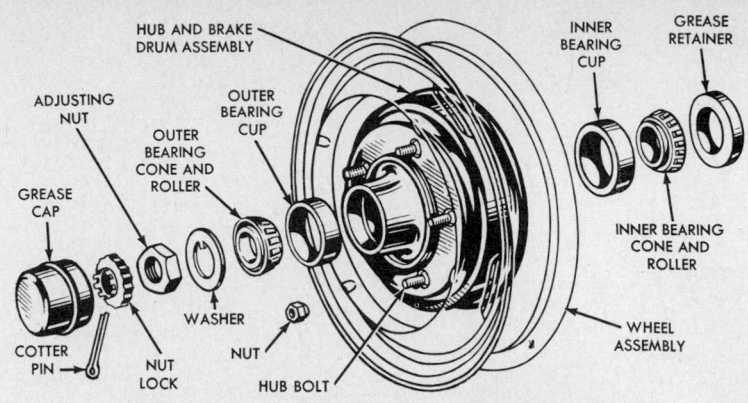

Front hub, bearings, and grease retainers (© Ford Motor Co.)

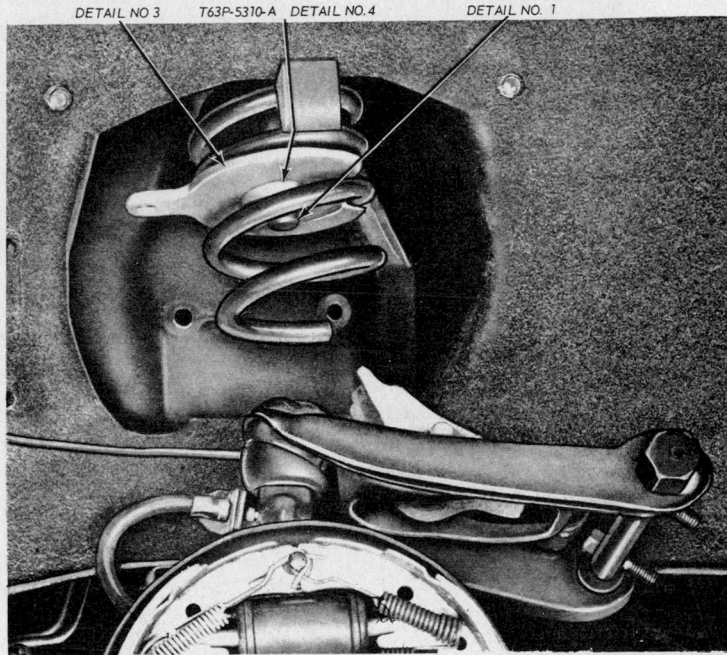

Compressing spring (© Ford Motor Co.)

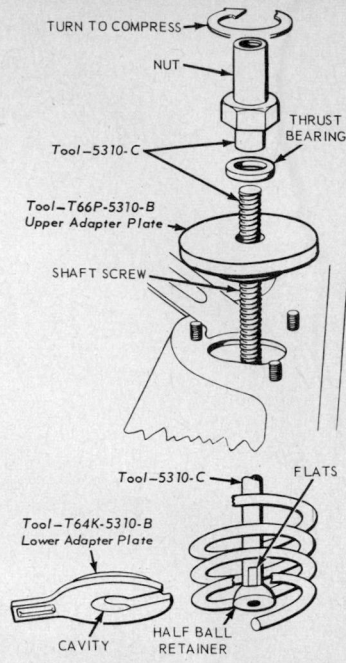

Spring compressor
(© Ford Motor Co.)

Replacement

1. Position an upper control arm support between the upper arm and side rail as shown in the illustration.
2. Raise the vehicle, position jack stands and remove the wheel and tire.
3. Remove the stabilizer bar to link attaching nut and disconnect the bar from the link.
4. Remove the link bolt from the lower arm.
5. Remove the strut bar to lower attaching nuts and bolts.
6. Remove the lower ball joint cotter pin and back off the nut. Using a suitable tool, loosen the ball joint stud in the spindle.
7. Remove the nut from the arm and lower the arm.
8. Remove the lower arm to underbody cam attaching parts and remove the arm.
9. To install, position the lower arm in the underbody and install the ball joint and cam attaching parts loosely.
10. Install the stabilizer and strut and torque the attaching parts to specifications.
11. Torque the lower arm pivot and ball joint stud to specifications.
12. Lower the car and remove the upper arm support.
13. Front end alignment must be rechecked.

Upper Ball Joint

Inspection

1. Raise the vehicle on a hoist or floor jack so that the front wheels hang in full down position.

---

flange of nut lock.

11. Check front wheel rotation and install grease cap and hub cap.
12. Install shock absorber and upper bracket assembly, making sure shock absorber lower studs have insulators and are in pivot plate holes.
13. Install nuts and washers on lower studs and torque to 8-12 ft. lbs. on 1970 and later models and 12-17 ft. lbs. on 1965-69 models.
14. Install nuts on shock absorber upper bracket and torque to 10-15 ft. lbs. on Cougars, Mustangs, and Mavericks, 20-28 ft. lbs. on 1966-1970 Montegos, Fairlanes, Comets, and Falcons, and 15-25 ft. lbs. on 1965 Comets and Falcons.
15. Lower car.

Lower Ball Joint

On all intermediate size Ford cars, the lower ball joint is an integral part of the lower control arm. If the lower ball joint is defective the entire lower control arm must be replaced.

Inspection

1. Raise the vehicle on a hoist or floor jack so that the front wheel falls to the full down position.
2. Have an assistant grasp the bottom of the tire and move the wheel in and out.
3. As the wheel is being moved, observe the lower control arm where the spindle attaches to it.
4. Any movement between the lower part of the spindle and the lower control arm indicates a bad control arm which must be replaced.

NOTE: during this check, the upper ball joint will be unloaded and may move; this is normal and not an indication of a bad ball joint. Also, do not mistake a loose wheel bearing for a worn ball joint.

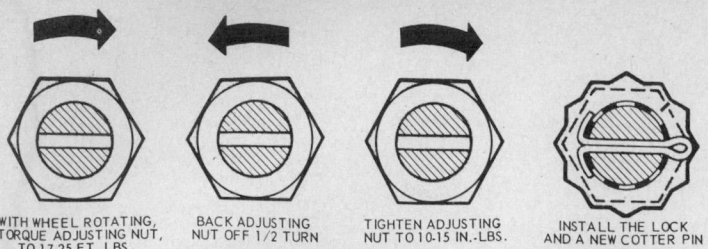

WITH WHEEL ROTATING, TORQUE ADJUSTING NUT, TO 17-25 FT. LBS.   BACK ADJUSTING NUT OFF 1/2 TURN   TIGHTEN ADJUSTING NUT TO 10-15 IN.-LBS.   INSTALL THE LOCK AND A NEW COTTER PIN

Adjusting wheel bearings (© Ford Motor Co.)

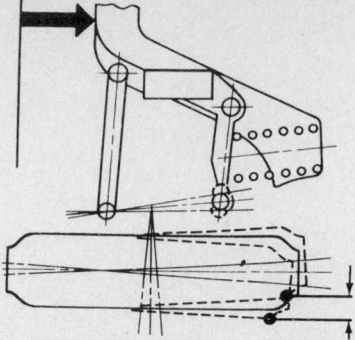

Measuring upper ball joint radial play
(© Ford Motor Co.)

2. Have an assistant grasp the wheel top and bottom and apply alternate in and out pressure to the top and bottom of the wheel.
3. Radial play of 1/4 in. is acceptable measured at the inside of the wheel adjacent to the upper arm.

NOTE: this radial play measurement is multiplied at the outer circumference of the tire and should not be measured here. Measure only at the inside of the wheel.

Replacement

1. Position support between the upper arm and frame rail as shown in illustration.
2. Raise the vehicle and remove the tire and wheel.
3. Remove the upper ball joint cotter pin and loosen the nut.
4. Using a suitable tool, loosen the ball joint in the spindle.
5. Remove the three ball joint retaining rivets using a large chisel.
6. Remove the nut from the ball joint stud and remove the ball joint.
7. Clean and remove all burrs from the ball joint mounting area of the control arm before installing

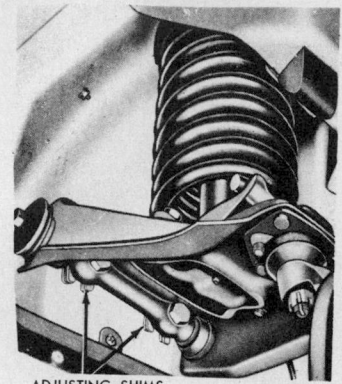

ADJUSTING SHIMS
Upper control arm assembly
(© Ford Motor Co.)

new ball joint.
8. Install the ball joint in the upper arm using the service part nuts and bolts. Do not attempt to rivet a new ball joint to the arm.
9. Install and torque the ball joint stud nut and install the cotter pin.
10. Lubricate the new joint with a hand type grease gun only, using an air pressure gun may loosen the ball joint seal.
11. Install wheel, lower vehicle and

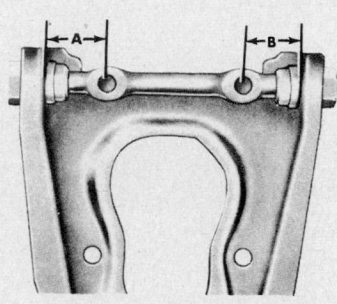

Centering upper A-arm inner shaft
(© Ford Motor Co.)

remove upper arm support.
12. Check front end alignment.

Upper Control Arm

Replacement

1. Remove the shock absorber and upper mounting bracket from the car as an assembly.
2. Raise the vehicle and remove the

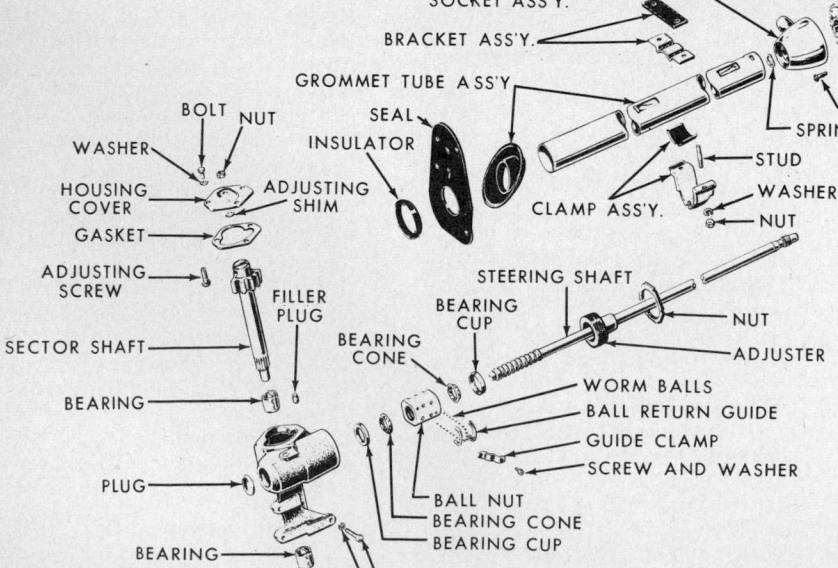

SHIFT LEVER SOCKET ASS'Y.
BRACKET ASS'Y.
GROMMET TUBE ASS'Y
BOLT   NUT
WASHER
HOUSING COVER
GASKET
ADJUSTING SCREW
SECTOR SHAFT
BEARING
PLUG
BEARING
OIL SEAL
SECTOR SHAFT ARM
SEAL
INSULATOR
ADJUSTING SHIM
FILLER PLUG
BEARING CONE
CLAMP ASS'Y.
STUD
WASHER
NUT
STEERING SHAFT
BEARING CUP
NUT
ADJUSTER
WORM BALLS
BALL RETURN GUIDE
GUIDE CLAMP
SCREW AND WASHER
BALL NUT
BEARING CONE
BEARING CUP
BOLT
LOCKWASHER
LOCKWASHER
NUT
NUT
SPRING
SLEEVE
BUSHING
NUT
FLANGE ASS'Y.
FLANGE BOLT
SPRING WASHER

Typical steering gear and related parts (© Ford Motor Co.)

wheel and tire as an assembly.
3. Install spring compressor tool.
4. Place a safety stand under the lower arm.
5. Remove the cotter pin from the upper ball joint stud and loosen the nut.
6. Using a suitable tool, loosen the ball joint in the spindle, then, remove the nut and lift the stud from the spindle.
7. Remove the upper arm attaching nuts from the engine compartment, and remove the upper arm.
8. To install the arm, position it on the mounting bracket and install the attaching nuts on the inner shaft attaching bolts.

NOTE: the original equipment keystone-type lockwashers must be used with the inner shaft attaching nuts and bolts.

9. Install the upper ball joint stud in the spindle and tighten the nut to specifications. Install a new cotter pin.
10. Remove spring compressor and position spring on upper arm. Install wheel and check front end alignment.

⏱ CHILTON TIME-SAVER

When upper control arm bushings become low on lubrication, they become very noisy. This can often be corrected by lubrication and it is not necessary to replace the bushings. On early models that do not contain grease plugs it is necessary to drill and tap the bushing to accept a grease fitting. On later models with grease plugs it is difficult to remove the plug and grease the bushing with conventional tools. Ford Motor Co. has available through its dealers an upper A-arm lubrication kit which greatly eases the performance of this operation.

Steering Gear

The steering gear is of the worm and recirculating ball type. The sector shaft is straddle-mounted in the cover above the gear and a housing-mounted roller bearing below the gear. The steering linkage consists of a Pitman arm, a steering (Pitman) arm to idler arm rod, an idler arm and tie-rods. Power steering is available as an option and it is the non-internal type, meaning that the pump provides assist to the steering linkage and hydraulically assisted steering gear.

Adjustment and R & R

See Unit Repair Section under Manual Steering.

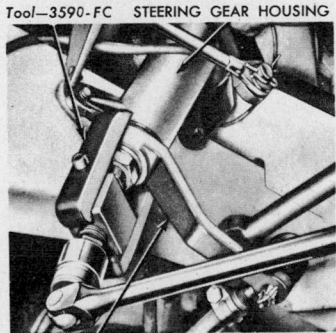

Tool-3590-FC STEERING GEAR HOUSING

SECTOR SHAFT ARM (PITMAN ARM)
Sector shaft arm removal
(© Ford Motor Co.)

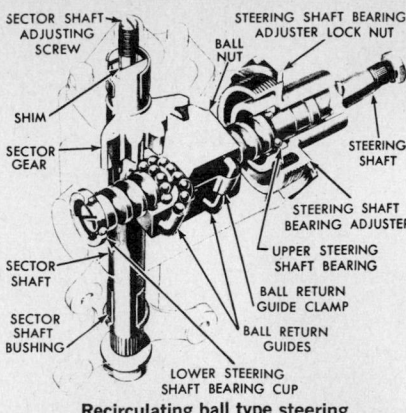

SECTOR SHAFT ADJUSTING SCREW

SHIM

SECTOR GEAR

SECTOR SHAFT

SECTOR SHAFT BUSHING

STEERING SHAFT BEARING ADJUSTER LOCK NUT

BALL NUT

STEERING SHAFT BEARING ADJUSTER

STEERING SHAFT

STEERING SHAFT BEARING ADJUSTER

UPPER STEERING SHAFT BEARING

BALL RETURN GUIDE CLAMP

BALL RETURN GUIDES

LOWER STEERING SHAFT BEARING CUP

Recirculating ball type steering
(© Ford Motor Co.)

Jacking, Hoisting

Jack car at front under spring seat of lower control arm. Jack car at rear axle housing close to differential case.

Twin post lifts—front adapters must be carefully placed, large enough to cover entire spring seat area. Rear adapters or forks must be placed under axle not more than one in. outboard from welds near differential housing.

Frame contact lifts—place adapters as shown in diagram. Be sure that pads cover at least 12 sq. in. in area.

Hoist contact area—front
(© Ford Motor Co.)

Hoist contact area—rear
(© Ford Motor Co.)

Clutch

Pedal Adjustment—1965

1. To check pedal assist spring tension, measure the distance between the inside radius of the spring hook and the front face of the link. This distance should be 1 3/16 in. Turn the nut on the retainer to get proper pedal assist.
2. Measure the total pedal travel. If the total travel is not within 6-6½ in., move the pedal bumper and bracket up or down, as necessary.
NOTE: Always check and adjust total travel before checking free travel.
3. To check pedal free travel, start to depress the pedal slowly until the release fingers contact the release bearing. Measure this distance with a rule. The difference between this reading and the reading when the pedal is released is free travel. To obtain the required ⅞-1⅛ in. free travel, loosen the pedal-to-equalizer-rod nuts and rotate the equalizer bar, as needed. Then secure both equalizer bar nuts.

Pedal Adjustment—1966-72

1. Disconnect clutch return spring from release lever.
2. Loosen release lever rod locknut and adjusting nut.
3. Move clutch release lever rearward until release bearing lightly contacts clutch pressure plate release fingers.
4. Adjust rod length until rod seats in release lever pocket.
5. Insert specified feeler gauge between adjusting nut and swivel sleeve. Tighten adjusting nut against gauge.
6. Tighten lock nut against adjusting nut, taking care not to disturb adjustment. Torque locknut to 15-20 ft. lbs. and remove feeler gauge.
7. Install clutch return spring.
8. Check free travel at pedal. Readjust if necessary to obtain specified travel. Moving adjusting nut away from swivel sleeve increases travel. Moving adjusting nut toward swivel sleeve decreases travel.
9. As final check, measure pedal free travel with transmission in neutral and engine running at 3,000 rpm. If pedal travel is not minimum of ½ in., readjust free travel.

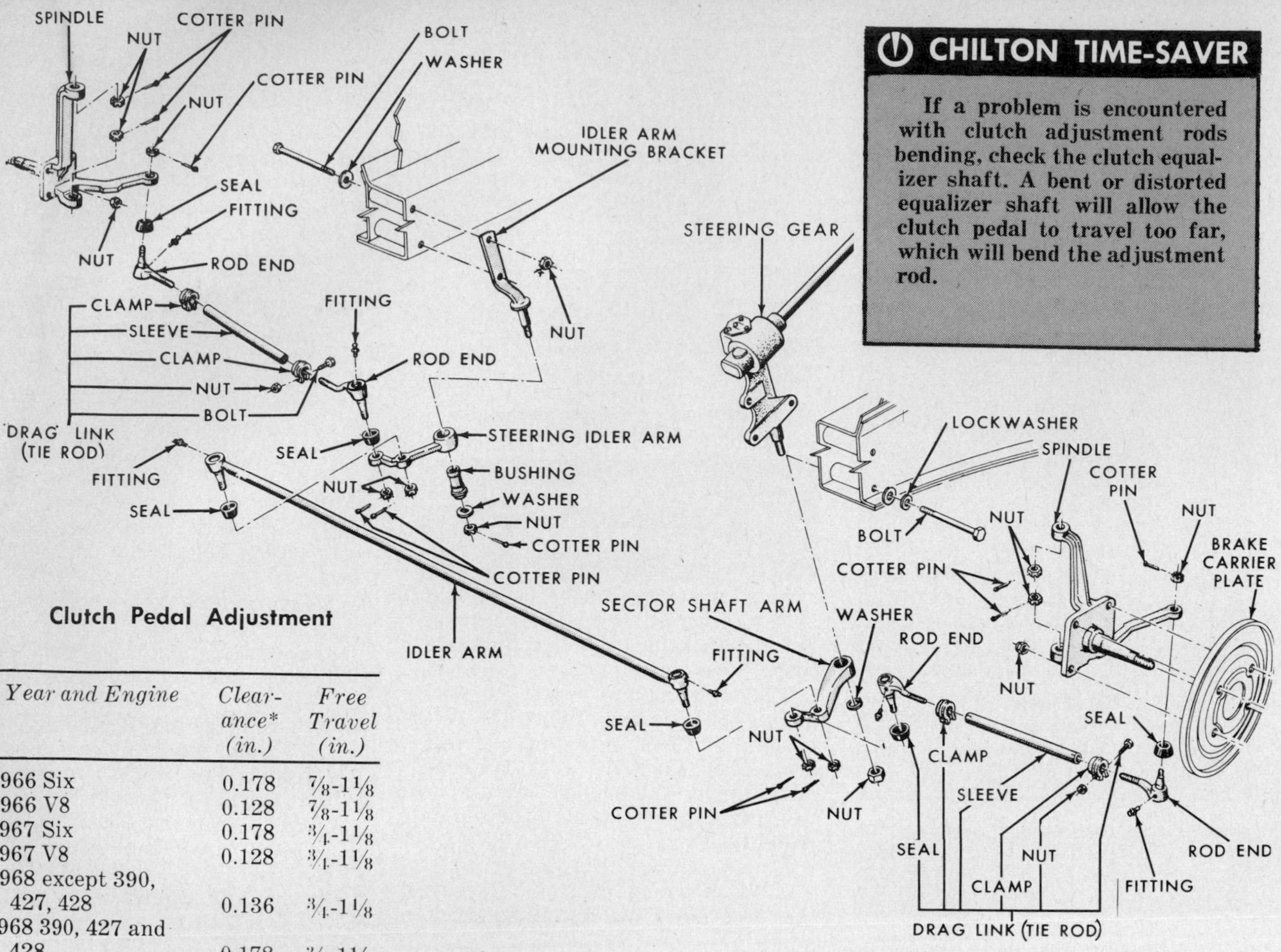

SPINDLE
COTTER PIN
NUT
COTTER PIN
NUT
BOLT
WASHER
IDLER ARM MOUNTING BRACKET
SEAL
FITTING
NUT
ROD END
CLAMP
SLEEVE
CLAMP
NUT
BOLT
DRAG LINK (TIE ROD)
FITTING
ROD END
NUT
STEERING GEAR
SEAL
STEERING IDLER ARM
BUSHING
WASHER
NUT
COTTER PIN
COTTER PIN
FITTING
SEAL
NUT
IDLER ARM
LOCKWASHER
SPINDLE
COTTER PIN
NUT
NUT
BOLT
BRAKE CARRIER PLATE
COTTER PIN
SECTOR SHAFT ARM
WASHER
ROD END
FITTING
NUT
SEAL
SEAL
NUT
CLAMP
SLEEVE
COTTER PIN
NUT
SEAL
NUT
ROD END
CLAMP
FITTING
DRAG LINK (TIE ROD)

Typical steering linkage (© Ford Motor Co.)

CHILTON TIME-SAVER

If a problem is encountered with clutch adjustment rods bending, check the clutch equalizer shaft. A bent or distorted equalizer shaft will allow the clutch pedal to travel too far, which will bend the adjustment rod.

Clutch Pedal Adjustment

Year and Engine	*Clearance* (in.)*	*Free Travel (in.)*
1966 Six	0.178	7/8-1 1/8
1966 V8	0.128	7/8-1 1/8
1967 Six	0.178	3/4-1 1/8
1967 V8	0.128	3/4-1 1/8
1968 except 390, 427, 428	0.136	3/4-1 1/8
1968 390, 427 and 428	0.178	3/4-1 1/8
1969-72 except 390, 428 and 429	0.136	7/8-1 1/8
1969-72 390, 428 and 429	0.178	7/8-1 1/8

* Between adjusting nut and swivel sleeve

Clutch and/or Transmission Removal

1. Disconnect and remove starter and dust ring, if the clutch is to be removed.
2. Raise the car.
3. Disconnect the driveshaft at the rear universal joint and remove the driveshaft.

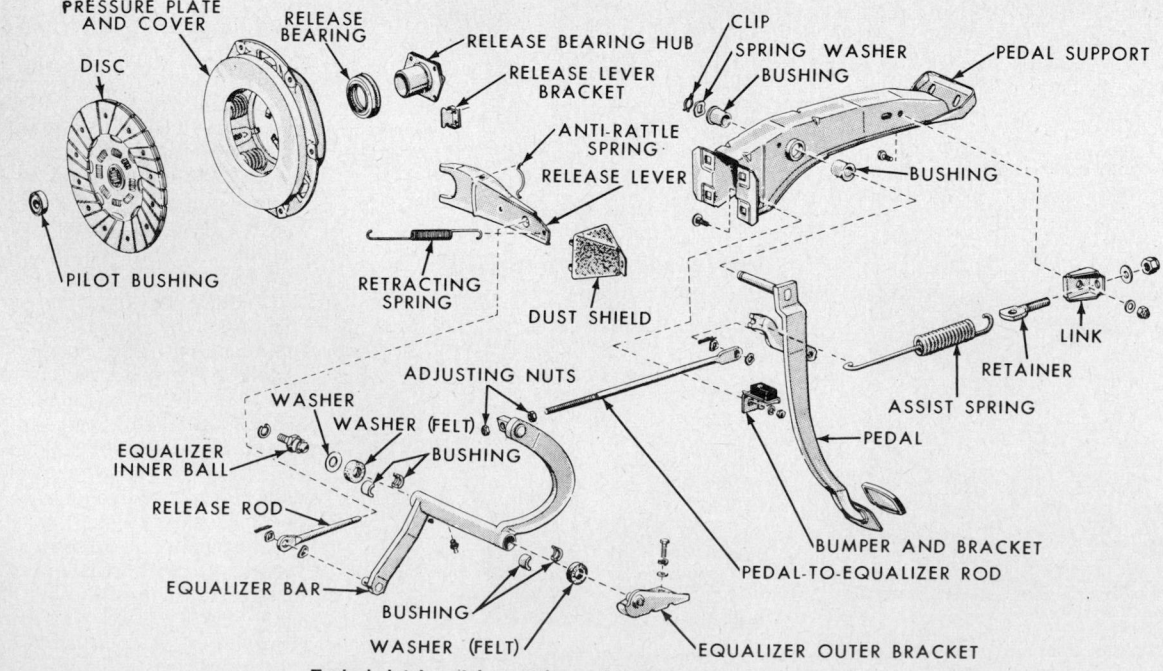

PRESSURE PLATE AND COVER
RELEASE BEARING
RELEASE BEARING HUB
DISC
RELEASE LEVER BRACKET
CLIP
SPRING WASHER
BUSHING
PEDAL SUPPORT
ANTI-RATTLE SPRING
RELEASE LEVER
BUSHING
PILOT BUSHING
RETRACTING SPRING
DUST SHIELD
LINK
RETAINER
ADJUSTING NUTS
WASHER
WASHER (FELT)
ASSIST SPRING
EQUALIZER INNER BALL
BUSHING
PEDAL
RELEASE ROD
BUMPER AND BRACKET
EQUALIZER BAR
PEDAL-TO-EQUALIZER ROD
BUSHING
WASHER (FELT)
EQUALIZER OUTER BRACKET

Typical clutch pedal mounting and linkage (© Ford Motor Co.)

4. Disconnect the speedometer cable at the transmission extension.
5. Disconnect the gear shift rods from the transmission shift levers. If car is equipped with four speed, remove bolts that secure shift control bracket to extension housing.
6. Remove the bolt holding the extension housing to the rear support, and remove the muffler inlet pipe bracket to housing bolt.
7. Remove the two rear support bracket insulator nuts from the underside of the crossmember. Remove crossmember.
8. Place a jack (equipped with a protective piece of wood) under the rear of the engine oil pan. Raise the engine, slightly.
9. Remove transmission - to - fly-wheel-housing bolts. Thread two guide studs into the bottom attaching bolt holes.
NOTE: on 429 cu. in. engines the upper left-hand transmission attaching bolt is a seal bolt. Carefully note its position so that it may be reinstalled in its original position.
10. Slide the transmission back and out of the car.
11. Remove release lever retracting spring and disconnect pedal at the equalizer bar.
12. Remove bolts that secure engine rear plate to front lower part of bellhousing.
13. Remove bolts that attach bell housing to cylinder block and remove housing and release lever as a unit.
14. Loosen six pressure plate cover attaching bolts evenly to release spring pressure. Mark cover and flywheel to facilitate reassembly in same position.
15. Remove six attaching bolts while holding pressure plate cover. Remove pressure plate and clutch disc.

Clutch and/or Transmission Installation

1. Wash flywheel surface with alcohol.

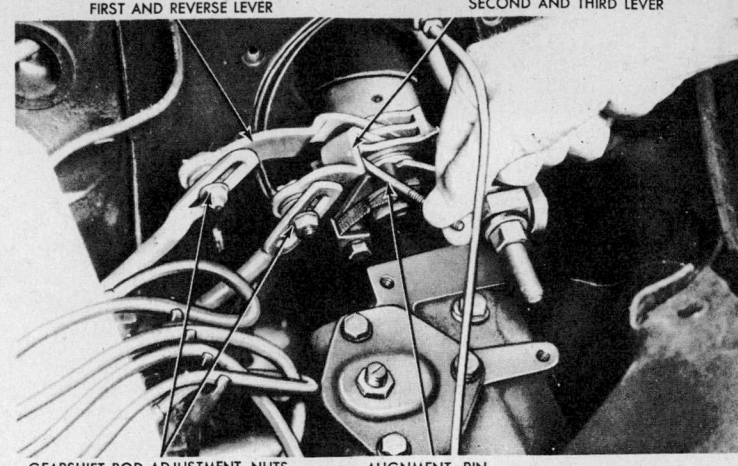

FIRST AND REVERSE LEVER   SECOND AND THIRD LEVER

GEARSHIFT ROD ADJUSTMENT NUTS   ALIGNMENT PIN

Manual transmission column shift adjustment 1965 and 1968-70 (© Ford Motor Co.)

2. Attach the clutch disc and pressure plate assembly to the fly-wheel with the bolts finger tight.
3. Align the clutch disc with the pilot bushing. Torque cover bolts to 23-28 ft. lbs. on 1965-66 vehicles and to 12-20 ft. lbs. on 1967-72 vehicles.
4. Lightly lubricate the release lever fulcrum ends. Install the release lever in the flywheel housing and install the dust shield.
5. Apply very little lubricant on the release bearing retainer journal. Attach the release bearing and hub on the release lever.
6. Install the flywheel housing and torque the attaching bolts to 40-50 ft. lbs. on all 1965 vehicles and on the 1966-72 V8s. Torque 1966-72 sixes to 23-33 ft. lbs. Install the dust cover and torque the bolts to 17-20 ft. lbs.
7. Connect the release rod and the retracting spring. Connect the pedal - to - equalizer - rod at the equalizer bar.
8. Install starter and dust ring.
9. Start the transmission extension housing up and over the rear support. After moving the trans-

mission back just far enough for the pilot shaft to clear the clutch housing, move it upward and into position on the transmission guide studs.
10. Move the transmission forward and into place against the fly-wheel housing.
11. Remove guide studs and attach the transmission with a torque of 37-42 ft. lbs. on all cars except 1965-66 six cylinder four speed. Torque 1965-66 six cylinder four speed to 40-45 ft. lbs.
12. Slowly lower the engine onto the crossmember.
13. Install and torque the insulator-to-crossmember nuts to 25-35 ft. lbs. on all 1965-69 vehicles except 1968-69 390, 427 and 428 CJ Cougars and Mustangs. Torque 1968-69 390, 427 and 428 CJ Cougars and Mustangs to 30-42 ft. lbs. Torque 1972 Montegos, 1970-72 Fairlanes and Mavericks to 30-50 ft. lbs. and 1970-72 Cougars and Mustangs to 25-35 ft. lbs.
14. Connect gear shift rods and the speedometer cable.
15. Hook up the drive shaft.
16. Refill transmission to proper level.

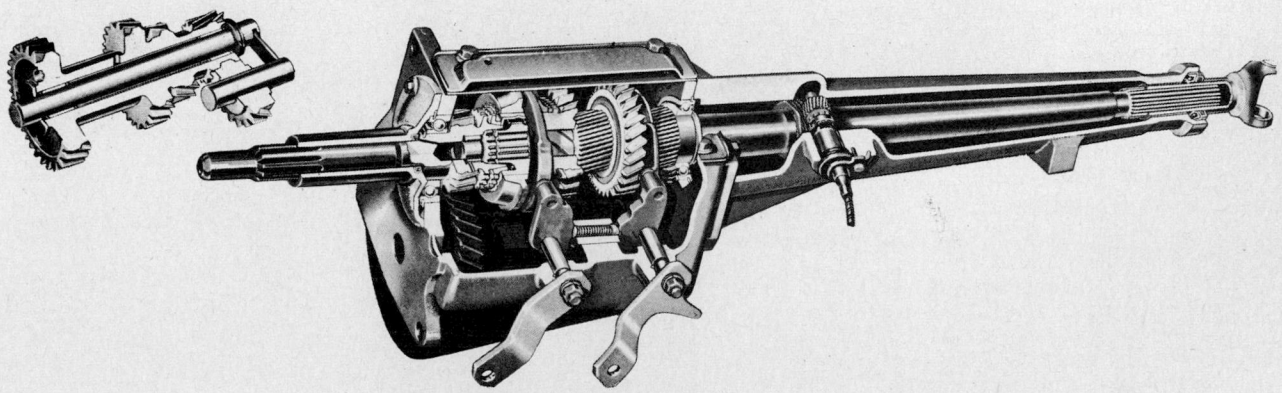

3-speed synchromesh transmission (© Ford Motor Co.)

Standard Transmission

There are five manual transmission used during the 1965-72 period: (1) a light duty, top cover, three speed with a non-synchromesh low gear used on 1965-67 six cylinders, (2) a heavy duty, top cover, fully synchromesh three speed used on 1965-67 V8s and on all 1968-72 three speed applications, (3) a medium duty, top cover, overdrive transmission with non-synchromesh low gear used on some 1965-67 Fairlane 289 2V V8s, (4) a light duty, side cover fully synchromesh, Dagenham-built four speed used on 1965-66 six cylinders, (5) a heavy duty, top cover, fully synchromesh, Ford-built four speed used on 1965-72 V8s.

Three-Speed Column Shift Linkage Adjustment

With the transmission in neutral, the shift lever should be in a horizontal plane and parallel to the instrument panel line. Corrective adjustments should be made at the gear shift rods.

1965 and 1968-72

1. Place lever in neutral.
2. Loosen two gear shift rod adjustment nuts.
3. Insert 3/16 in. diameter alignment pin through first and reverse gear shift lever and second and third gear shift lever. Align levers to insert pin.
4. Tighten gear shift rod adjustment nuts, and remove pin.
5. Check gear lever for smooth crossover.

1966-67

1. Place lever in neutral.
2. Loosen two gear shift rod adjustment nuts.
3. Insert locally fabricated tool in slot provided in lower steering column. See figure for manufacturing dimensions of tool. Align levers to insert tool.
4. Tighten gear shift rod adjustment nuts, and remove tool.
5. Check gear lever for smooth crossover.

Three Speed Floor and Console Shift Linkage

1. Loosen three shift linkage adjustment nuts.
2. Install a ¼ in. diameter alignment pin through control bracket and levers.
3. Tighten three shift linkage adjustment nuts and remove alignment pin.
4. Check gear lever for smooth crossover.

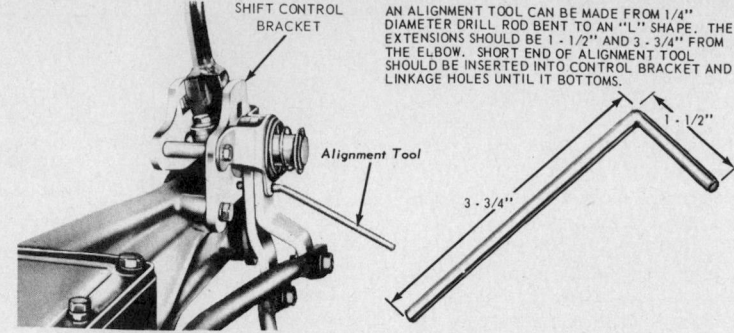

Manual transmission floor or console shift adjustment (© Ford Motor Co.)

Four-Speed Linkage— Dagenham Four Speed

1. Place shifter lever in neutral position, then raise car on a hoist.
2. Insert a ¼ in. rod into the alignment holes of the shift levers.
3. If the holes are not in exact alignment, check for bent connecting rods or loose lever lock nuts at the rod ends. Make replacements or repairs, then adjust as follows.
4. Loosen the three rod-to-lever retaining lock nuts and move the levers until the ¼ in. gauge rod will enter the alignment holes. Be sure that the transmission shift levers are in neutral and the reverse shifter lever is in the neutral detent.
5. Install the shift rods and torque the lock nuts to 15 to 20 ft. lbs.
6. Remove the ¼ in. gauge rod.
7. Operate the shift levers to assure correct shifting.
8. Lower the car and road test.

Four Speed Linkage

See Ford–Thunderbird Section.

Transmission Lock Rod Adjustment

1970 and later models with floor or console mounted shifters and manual transmissions incorporate a transmission lock rod which prevents the shifter from being moved from the reverse position when the ignition lock is in the OFF position. The lock rod connects the shift tube in the steering column to the transmission

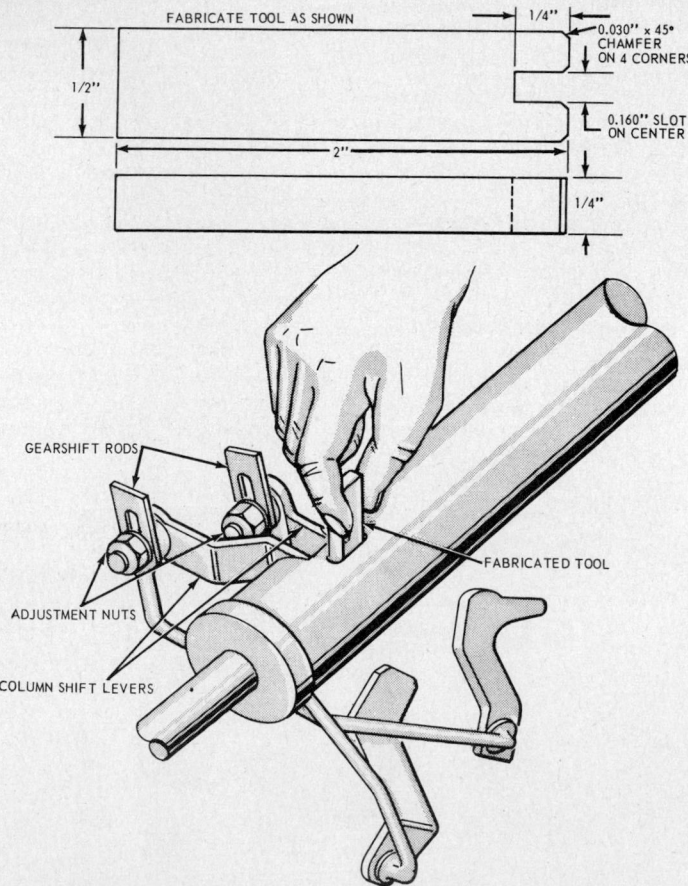

Manual transmission column shift adjustment 1966-67 (© Ford Motor Co.)

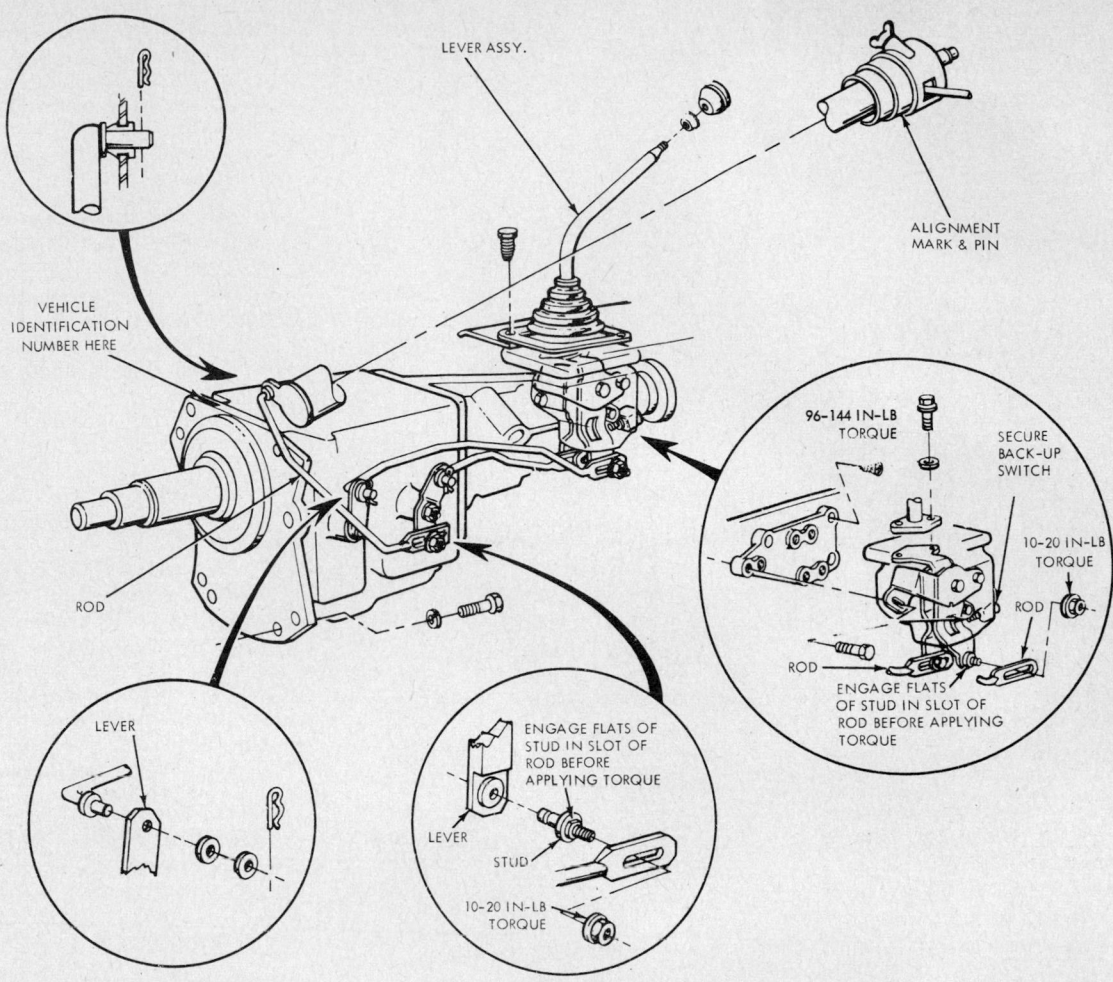

VEHICLE IDENTIFICATION NUMBER HERE

LEVER ASSY.

ALIGNMENT MARK & PIN

96-144 IN-LB TORQUE

SECURE BACK-UP SWITCH

10-20 IN-LB TORQUE

ROD

ROD

ENGAGE FLATS OF STUD IN SLOT OF ROD BEFORE APPLYING TORQUE

ROD

LEVER

ENGAGE FLATS OF STUD IN SLOT OF ROD BEFORE APPLYING TORQUE

LEVER

STUD

10-20 IN-LB TORQUE

Three-speed floor mounted shift linkage and lock rod (© Ford Motor Co.)

reverse lever. The lock rod cannot be properly adjusted until the manual linkage adjustment is correct.

1. With the transmission selector lever in the neutral position, loosen the lock rod adjustment nut on the transmission reverse lever.
2. Insert a .180 in. diameter rod (No. 15 drill bit) in the gauge pin hole located at the 6 o'clock position on the steering column socket casting, directly below the ignition lock.
3. Manipulate the pin until the casting will not move with the pin inserted.
4. Torque the lock rod adjustment rod to 10-20 ft. lbs.
5. Remove the pin and check the linkage operation.

Automatic Transmission

Three different automatic transmissions are used in Ford compact and intermediate cars: a C4, a C6, and a FMX. The C4 is a light duty transmission used on six cylinder and small block V8 engines. The FMX is an intermediate duty transmission used on medium duty V8s. The C6 is a heavy duty transmission used on high-performance and large displacement V8 engines. A semi-automatic version of the C4, the C4S, is available on the Maverick.

C4 Three-Speed Automatic

Throttle Linkage Adjustment

Initial Adjustments

1. Apply parking brake and place selector lever at N.
2. Run engine at normal idle speed. If engine is cold, run engine at fast idle speed (about 1200 rpm) until it reaches normal operating temperature. When engine is warm, slow it down to normal idle speed.
3. Connect tachometer to engine.
4. Adjust engine idle speed to specified rpm with transmission selector lever at D or D_1 or D_2.
5. The carburetor throttle lever must be against hot idle speed adjusting screw at specified idle speed in D or D_1 or D_2.

1965 Comet and Falcon— Final Adjustments

1. With engine off, check accelerator pedal for height of 4¼ in. measured from top of pedal to floor pan. To obtain correct height, adjust accelerator connecting link.
2. With engine off, loosen lock nut at adjustable upper end of downshift rod.
3. With carburetor choke in off position, depress accelerator pedal to the floor. Block pedal to hold it in wide open position.
4. Adjust downshift rod to place rod in kickdown detent position.
5. Back off adjustment to allow about 1/16 in. of free travel in bell crank assembly. Tighten

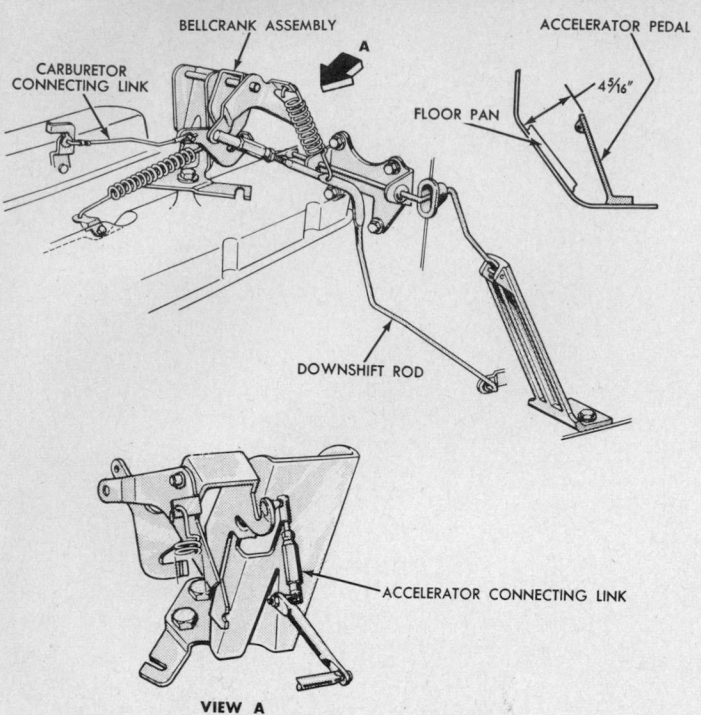

Throttle linkage adjustment C4 transmission 1965 Comet and Falcon (© Ford Motor Co.)

lock nut and release accelerator pedal.

1967-69 Mustang and Cougar Sixes and V8s, 1966-68 Comet, Montego, and Fairlane Sixes and 1966-69 Falcon Sixes and V8s—Final Adjustments

1. With engine off, check accelerator pedal for height of 4½ in. measured from top of pedal at pivot point to floor pan. To obtain correct pedal height, adjust accelerator connecting link at point A in figure.
2. With engine off disconnect downshift control cable at point B from accelerator shaft lever.
3. With carburetor choke in off position, depress accelerator to floor. Block pedal to hold it in wide open position.
4. Rotate downshift lever C counterclockwise to place it against internal stop.
5. With lever held in this position, and all slack removed from cable, adjusting trunnion so that it wil lslide into accelerator shaft lever. Turn one additional turn clockwise, then secure it to lever with retaining clip.
6. Remove block to release carburetor linkage.

1965-66 Mustange Sixes and V8s—Final Adjustments

1. With engine stopped and accelerator pedal in normal idle position, check pedal for height of $3\frac{7}{8}$ in. Be sure fast idle cam is not contacting fast idle screw of carburetor.
2. To check for free pedal travel, depress accelerator pedal to full throttle position (carburetor throttle lever against full throttle stop). Release pedal and recheck pedal height.
3. If necessary, adjust pedal height. On six cylinder engines, disconnect carburetor return spring and carburetor rod. Adjust length of rod to bring pedal height within specifications. Connect carburetor rod, tighten jam nut and install return spring. On V8 engines, disconnect carburetor return springs and carburetor rod where it connects to the accelerator shaft. Adjust length of rod to bring pedal height within specifications. Connect carburetor rod and return spring.
4. On six cylinder engines, disconnect downshift cable return spring at transmission, carburetor return spring at manifold

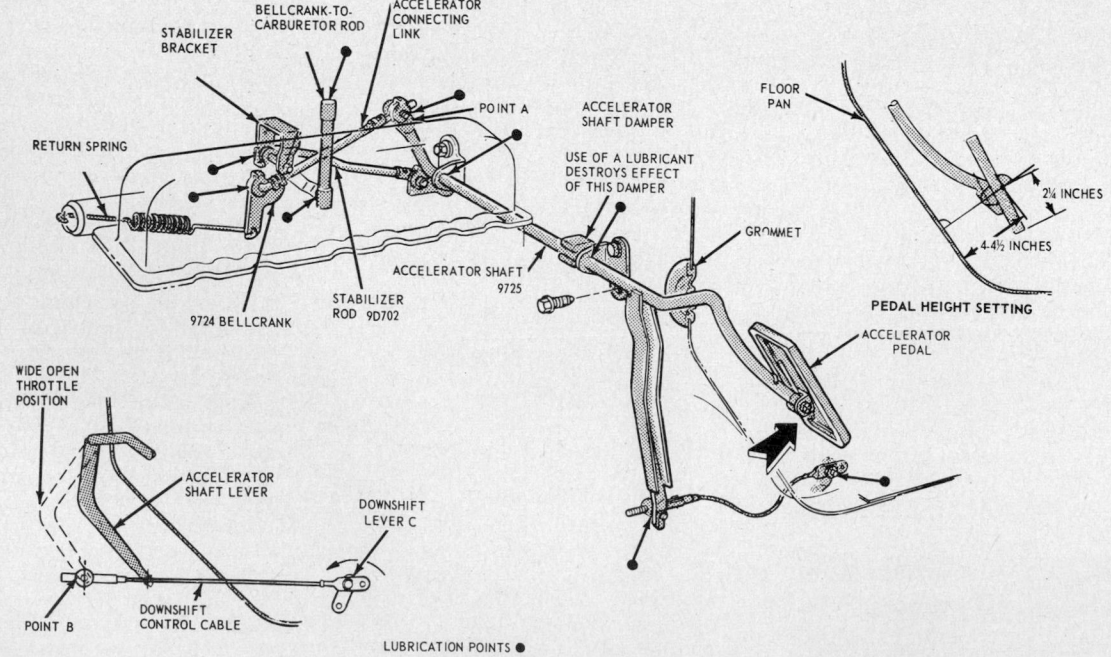

Throttle linkage adjustment C4 transmission 1966-68 Montego, Comet, and Fairlane, and 1966-69 Falcon with six cylinder
(© Ford Motor Co.)

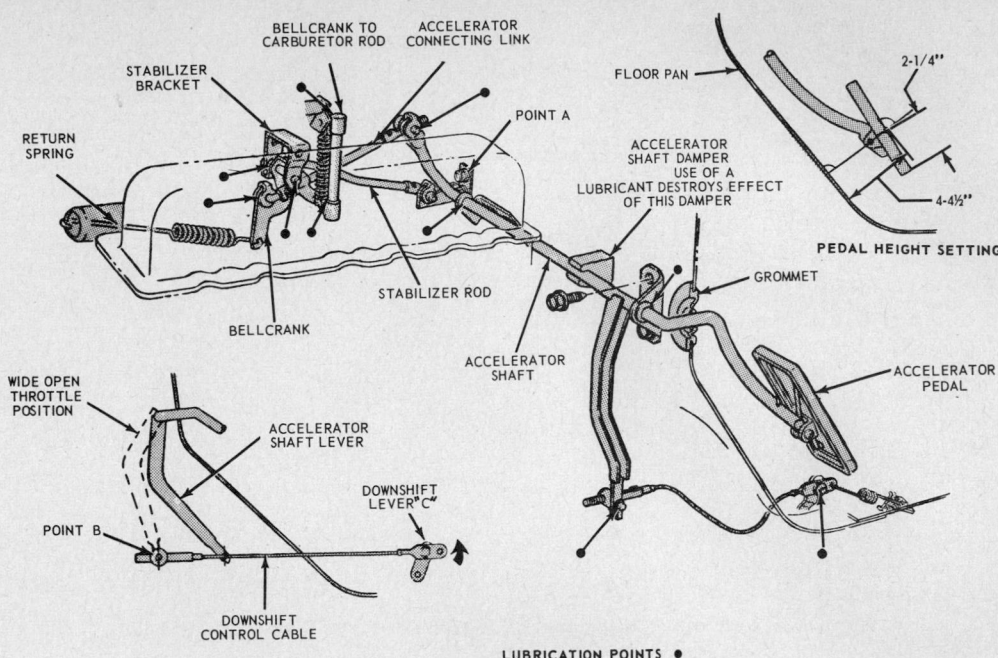

Throttle linkage adjustment C4 transmission 1967-68 Mustang six (© Ford Motor Co.)

and downshift cable where it connects to the accelerator shaft.

5. Position downshift lever in downshift position (carburetor wide open).

6. Hold downshift lever on transmission against stop in counter clockwise direction (downshift position).

7. Adjust trunnion on downshift cable where it connects to the accelerator shaft so that it aligns with hole in downshift lever, then install attaching clip.

8. Install return springs.

9. On V8 engines, disconnect downshift return spring at bellcrank, carburetor return spring, and downshift lever at the bellcrank.

10. Hold carburetor rod in wide open position. The step in rod should place bellcrank in downshift position.

11. Hold downshift lever rod in downward position. This places transmission lever in downshift position.

12. Adjust downshift lever trunnion at the bellcrank so that it aligns with hole in bellcrank. Install trunnion and retaining clip.

13. Release levers and install carburetor rod and bellcrank.

1966-69 Comet, Montego, and Fairlane with V8 Engine, 1969 Montego and Fairlane with Six Cylinder Engine—Final Adjustment

1. Disconnect bellcrank to carburetor rod at point C and accelerator connecting link from throttle shaft at point B.

2. Disconnect stabilizer rod from stabilizer at point B.

3. Insert 1/4 inch diameter pin through stabilizer and bracket.

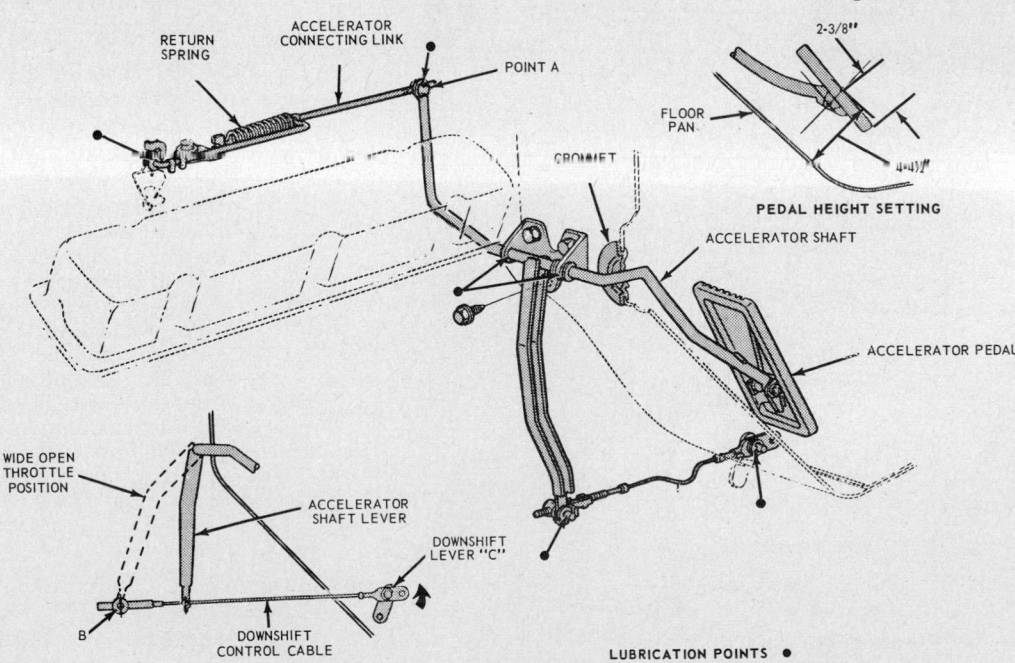

Throttle linkage adjustment C4 transmission 1967-68 Cougar and Mustang V8
(© Ford Motor Co.)

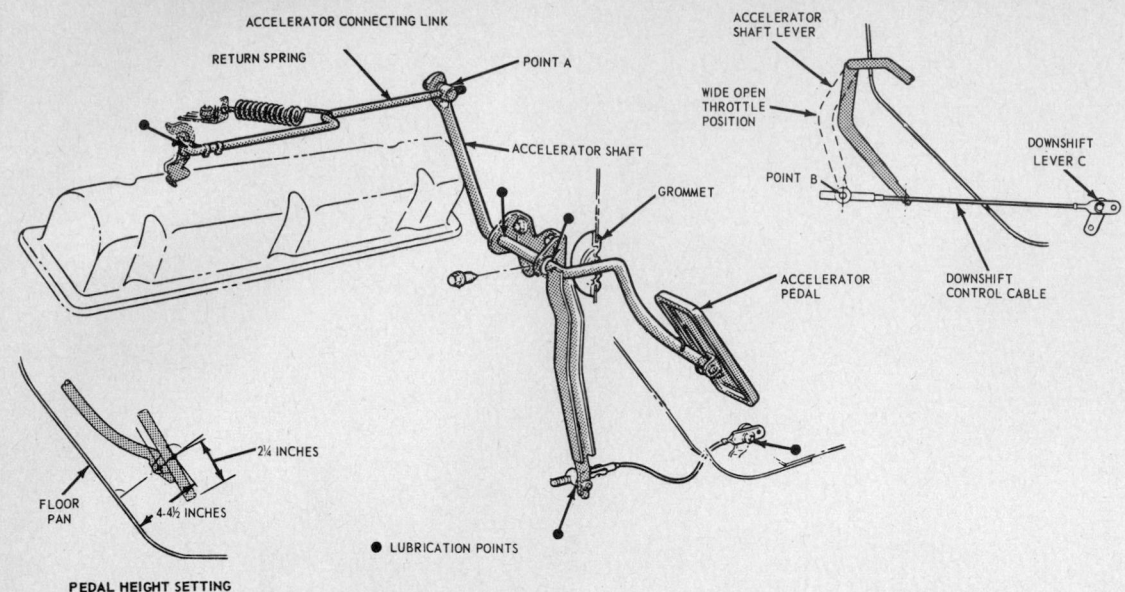

Throttle linkage adjustment C4 transmission 1966-69 Falcon V8 (© Ford Motor Co.)

4. Adjust length of stabilizer rod so that trunnion enters stabilizer freely. Secure stabilizer rod with retaining clip.

5. Secure carburetor to bellcrank rod to bell crank with attaching clip at point C.

6. Adjust length of accelerator rod connecting link to obtain accelerator pedal height of 4-4½ in. measured from top of pedal at pivot point. Connect accelerator connecting link to accelerator shaft with retaining clip after proper accelerator pedal height is obtained.

7. With engine off, disconnect downshift control cable at point D from accelerator shaft lever.

8. Rotate downshift lever E counter clockwise to place it against internal stop.

9. With lever held in this position, and all slack removed from cable, adjust trunnion so that it will slide into downshift lever. Turn it one additional turn clockwise, then secure it to accelerator shaft lever with retaining clip..

10. Remove block to release accelerator linkage.

1969-70 Mustang Six Cylinder, and 1970 Montego, Fairlane, and Maverick Six Cylinder— Final adjustments

1. Disconnect throttle return spring and remove trunnion and cable at bellcrank.

2. Hold transmission in full downshift against stop.

3. Hold carburetor throttle lever wide open against stop.

4. Adjust trunnion at bellcrank until ball stud on shaft and ball stud receiver on cable align. Then turn trunnion one full additional turn to increase length.

5. Release transmission and carburetor to normal free position.

6. Install throttle return spring.

1969-72 Cougar and Mustang V8s, and 1970-72 Montego and Fairlane V8s—Final Adjustments

1. Disconnect throttle and downshift return springs.

2. Hold carburetor throttle lever in

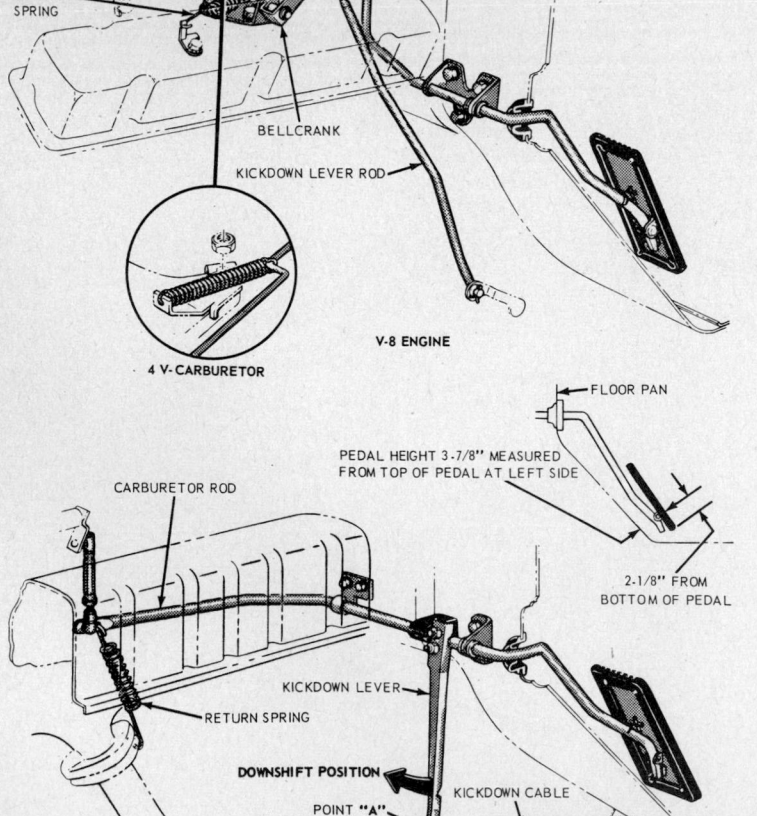

Throttle linkage adjustment C4 transmission 1965-66 Mustang (© Ford Motor Co.)

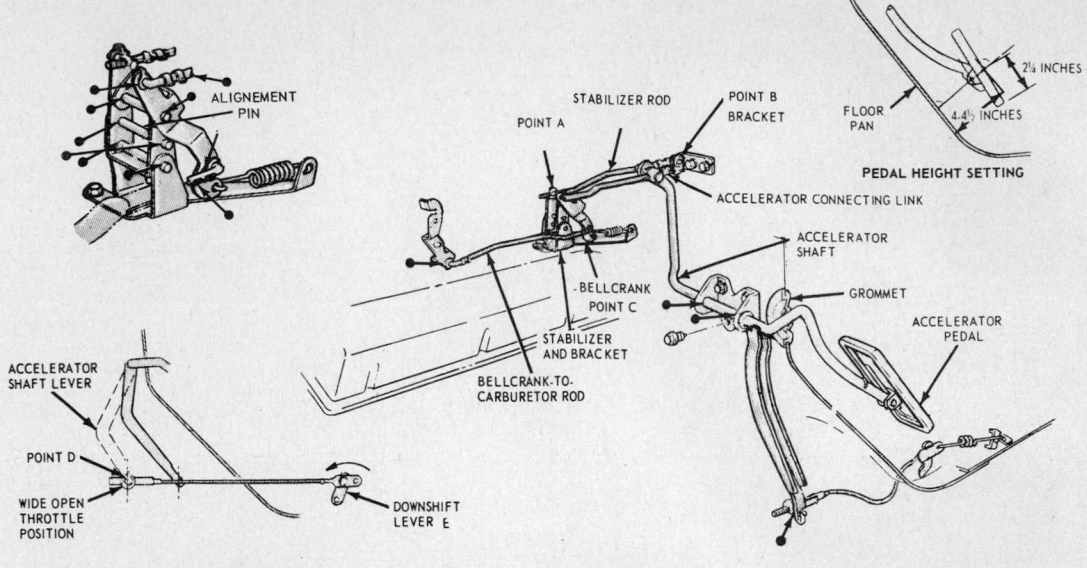

Throttle linkage adjustment C4 transmission 1966-69 Montego, Comet, Falcon, and Fairlane
(© Ford Motor Co.)

wide open position against stop.

3. Hold transmission in full down-shift position against internal stop.

4. Turn adjustment screw on carburetor downshift lever to within 0.040-0.080 in. of contacting pickup surface of carburetor throttle lever.

5. Release transmission and carburetor to normal free positions.

6. Install throttle and downshift return springs.

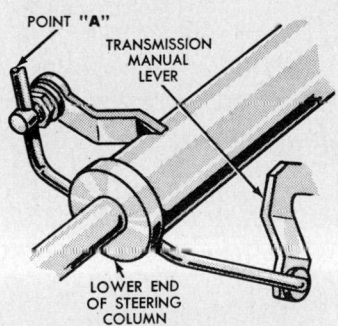

Typical column shift 1964-68
(© Ford Motor Co.)

Manual Linkage Adjustment

1965-72 Column Shift

1. With engine stopped, loosen clamp at shift lever at point A so that shift rod is free to slide in clamp.

2. Place transmission shift lever into D or D₁ (large dot) position. On Maverick with semi-automatic transmission, place lever in Hi.

3. Shift manual lever at transmission into D, D₁, or Hi. Detent

position. D on two speed transmission and D_1 on 1965-66 three speed transmission is second from rear. On 1967 and later transmissions, D or Hi is third detent from rear.

4. Tighten clamp on shift rod at point A to 10-20 ft. lbs.

5. Check pointer alignment and transmission operation for all selector lever positions.

Floor or Console Shift

1. Place transmission shift lever in D, (large dot) on most 1966 cars and D on some 1966 and all 1967 and later cars.

2. Raise vehicle and loosen manual lever shift rod retaining nut. Move transmission lever to D_1 or D position. On most 1966 transmissions, D_1 is fifth detent from rear. On 1966 Cyclone and Fairlane GT's with select shift and on all 1967 and later cars, D is fourth detent from rear.

3. With transmission shift lever

and transmission manual lever in position, tighten nut at point A to 10-20 ft. lbs.

4. Check transmission operation for all selector lever detent positions.

NOTE: since 1970, all models with a floor or console mounted selector lever have incorporated a transmission lock out rod to prevent the transmission selector from being moved out of the PARK position when the ignition lock is in the OFF position. The lock rod connects the shift tube in the steering column to the transmission manual lever. The lock rod cannot be properly adjusted until the manual linkage adjustment is correct.

Lock Rod Adjustment

1. With the transmission selector lever in the DRIVE position, loosen the lock rod adjustment nut on the transmission manual lever.

2. Insert a .180 in. diameter rod

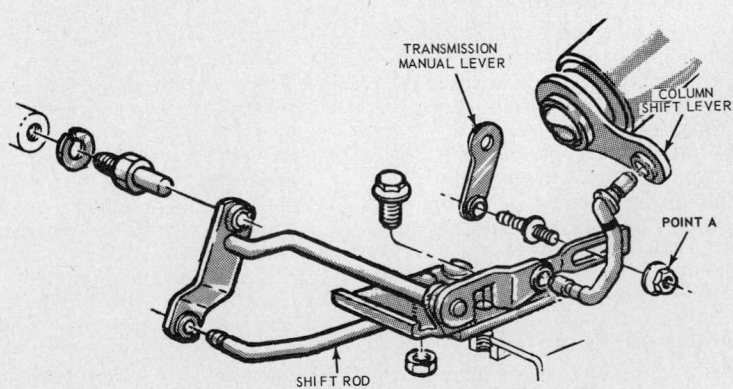

Typical column shift 1969-70 (© Ford Motor Co.)

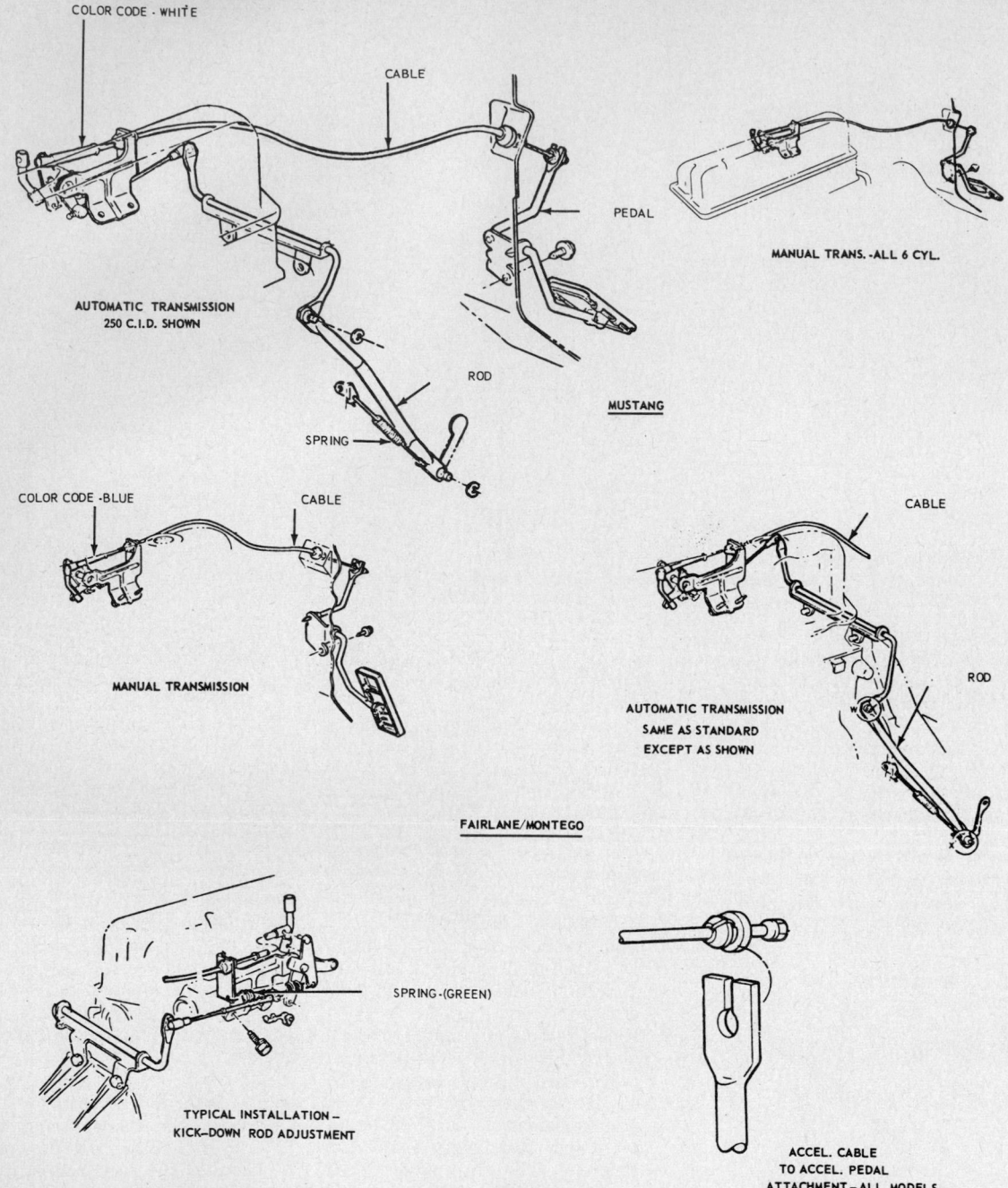

COLOR CODE - WHITE

CABLE

PEDAL

MANUAL TRANS.-ALL 6 CYL.

AUTOMATIC TRANSMISSION
250 C.I.D. SHOWN

ROD

MUSTANG

SPRING

COLOR CODE -BLUE

CABLE

CABLE

MANUAL TRANSMISSION

AUTOMATIC TRANSMISSION
SAME AS STANDARD
EXCEPT AS SHOWN

ROD

FAIRLANE/MONTEGO

SPRING-(GREEN)

TYPICAL INSTALLATION –
KICK–DOWN ROD ADJUSTMENT

ACCEL. CABLE
TO ACCEL. PEDAL
ATTACHMENT – ALL MODELS

Throttle linkage adjustment 1969-70 Mustang six and 1970 Montego and Fairlane six
(© Ford Motor Co.)

(No. 15 drill bit) in the gauge pin hole in the steering column socket casting, it is located at the 6 o'clock position directly below the ignition lock.
3. Manipulate the pin so that the casting will not move when the pin is fully inserted.
4. Torque the lock rod adjustment nut to 10-20 ft. lbs.
5. Remove the pin and check the linkage operation.

Transmission Removal

1. Raise vehicle and remove converter cover attaching bolts, at lower side of converter housing.

Remove cover.
2. Remove two converter drain plugs. Drain fluid from converter. Install converter drain plugs.
3. Remove drive shaft and install extension housing seal replacement tool or plug extension housing to prevent loss of transmission fluid.
4. Remove vacuum line hose from transmission vacuum unit. Disconnect vacuum line from retaining clip.
5. Remove two extension housing to crossmember attaching bolts.
6. Remove speedometer cable from

extension housing.
7. Disconnect exhaust pipe flange from manifolds.
8. Remove parking brake cable from equalizer lever.
9. Loosen transmission pan bolts and drain fluid at one corner of pan. Tighten attaching bolts after fluid has drained.
10. Disconnect fluid cooler lines from transmission case.
11. Remove manual and downshift rods from transmission control levers.
12. On 1969-70 Mustangs, disconnect neutral start switch wires from retaining clamps and con-

STANDARD TRANSMISSION

CABLE

SNAP IN FITTING

MAVERICK CABLE INSTALLATION

C4 Transmission Installation Torques

	Ft. Lbs.
Converter housing	
engine six cylinder	23-33
engine V8	40-50
Crossmember attaching bolts, 170 six	14-24
Extension housing	
Crossmember bolts, 170 six	30-35
Crossmember attaching bolts, 200 and 250 sixes	10-20
Crossmember bolts, 200 and 250 sixes	30-35
Crossmember attaching bolts, 260, 289, 302, Boss 302, 351 Windsor, and 351 Cleveland V8s in Montego, Comet, Fairlane and Falcons	50-70
Crossmember bolts, 260, 289, 302, Boss 302, 351 Windsor, and 351 Cleveland V8s	30-45
Flywheel—Converter bolts	23-33
Transmission filler tube	
Transmission case	32-42

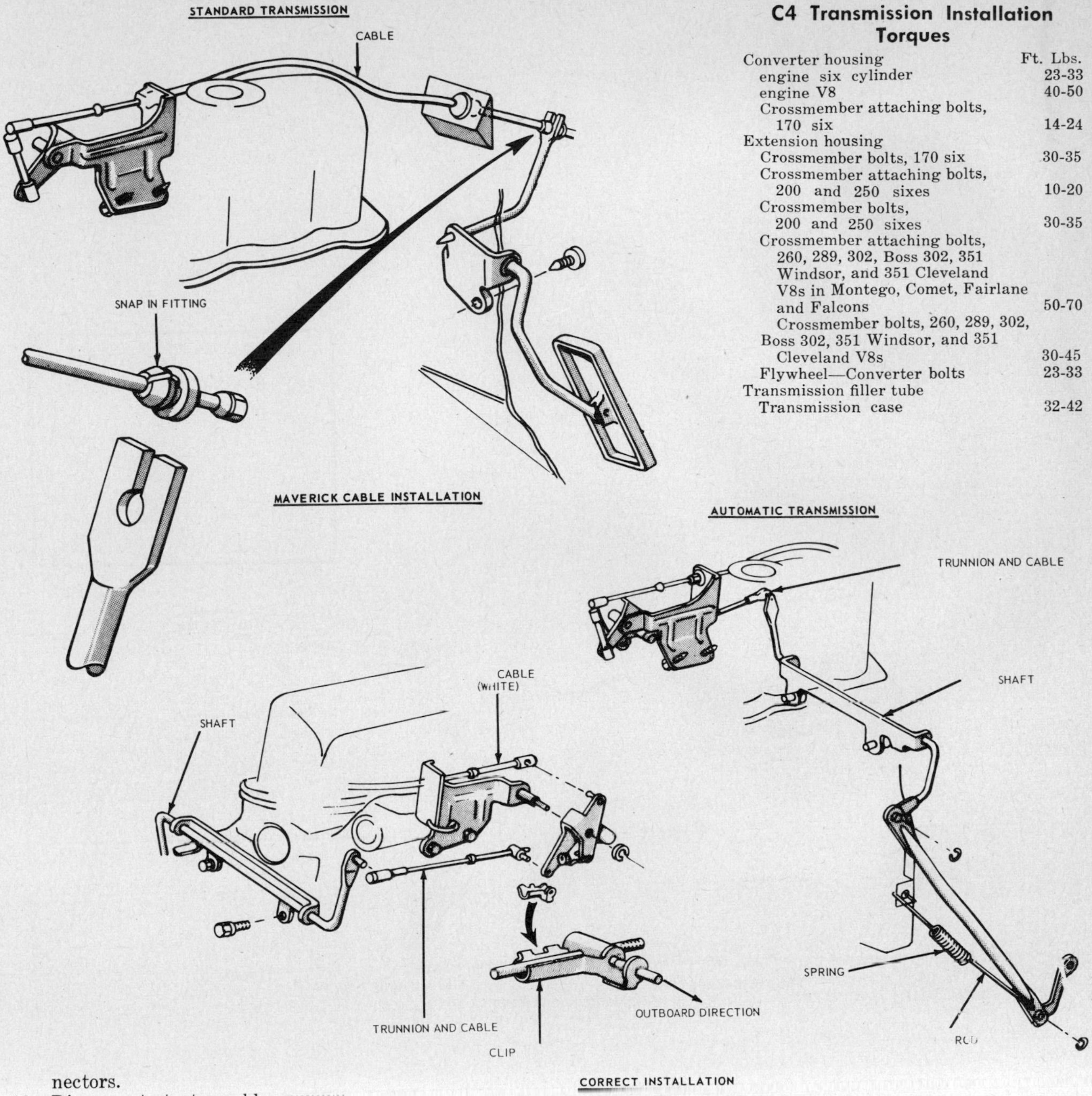

AUTOMATIC TRANSMISSION

TRUNNION AND CABLE

SHAFT

CABLE (WHITE)

SHAFT

SPRING

ROD

TRUNNION AND CABLE

CLIP

OUTBOARD DIRECTION

CORRECT INSTALLATION

Throttle linkage adjustment—1969-70 Maverick (© Ford Motor Co.)

nectors.

13. Disconnect starter cable, remove starter attaching bolts, and remove starter from converter housing.

14. Lift fluid filler tube from case.

15. Remove four converter to flywheel attaching nuts.

16. Place transmission jack to support transmission and secure transmission to jack with safety chain.

17. Remove four crossmember attaching bolts and lower crossmember.

18. Remove five converter housing attaching bolts and lower transmission from car.

Transmission Replacement

Reverse removal procedure to install transmission and use torque values given in chart.

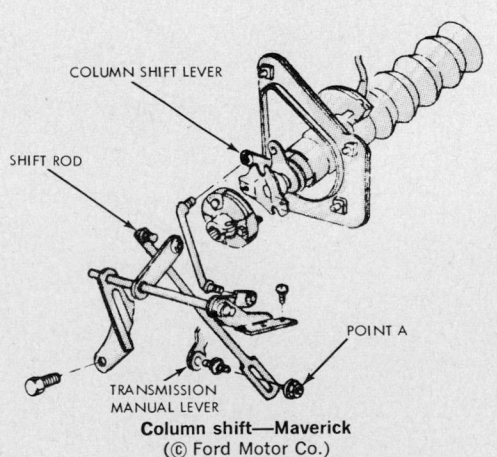

COLUMN SHIFT LEVER

SHIFT ROD

POINT A

TRANSMISSION MANUAL LEVER

Column shift—Maverick
(© Ford Motor Co.)

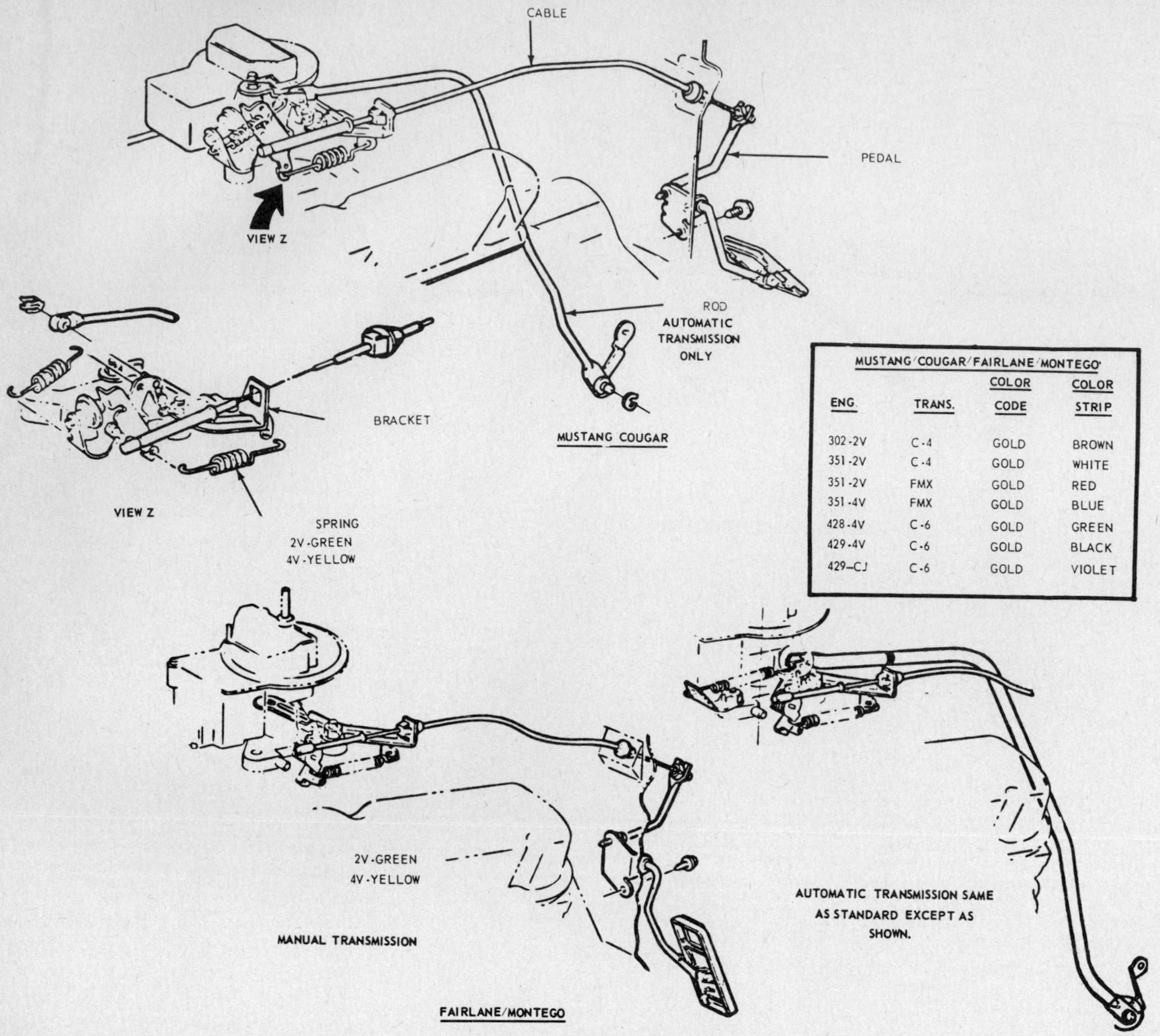

CABLE

PEDAL

VIEW Z

ROD
AUTOMATIC
TRANSMISSION
ONLY

MUSTANG COUGAR

BRACKET

VIEW Z

SPRING
2V-GREEN
4V-YELLOW

MUSTANG/COUGAR/FAIRLANE/MONTEGO			
ENG.	TRANS.	COLOR CODE	COLOR STRIP
302-2V	C-4	GOLD	BROWN
351-2V	C-4	GOLD	WHITE
351-2V	FMX	GOLD	RED
351-4V	FMX	GOLD	BLUE
428-4V	C-6	GOLD	GREEN
429-4V	C-6	GOLD	BLACK
429-CJ	C-6	GOLD	VIOLET

2V-GREEN
4V-YELLOW

MANUAL TRANSMISSION

AUTOMATIC TRANSMISSION SAME
AS STANDARD EXCEPT AS
SHOWN.

FAIRLANE/MONTEGO

**Throttle linkage adjustment—1969-72 Cougar and Mustang V8s, and
1972 Montego and Fairlane V8s**
(© Ford Motor Co.)

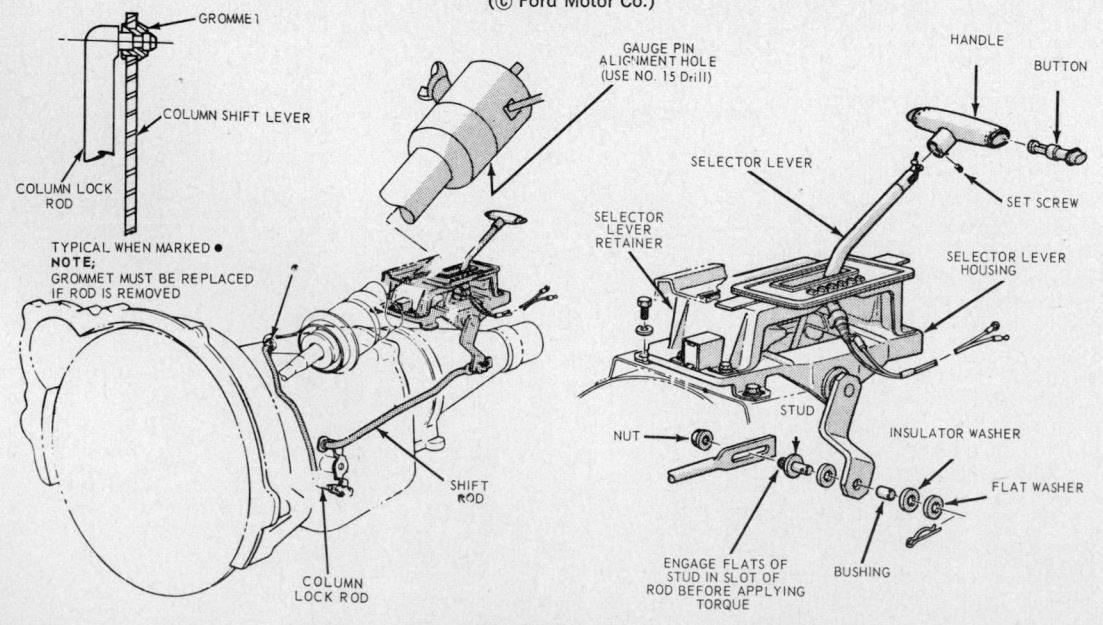

GROMMET

COLUMN SHIFT LEVER

COLUMN LOCK
ROD

TYPICAL WHEN MARKED ●
NOTE:
GROMMET MUST BE REPLACED
IF ROD IS REMOVED

GAUGE PIN
ALIGNMENT HOLE
(USE NO. 15 Drill)

HANDLE

BUTTON

SELECTOR LEVER

SET SCREW

SELECTOR
LEVER
RETAINER

SELECTOR LEVER
HOUSING

STUD

NUT

INSULATOR WASHER

FLAT WASHER

SHIFT
ROD

BUSHING

COLUMN
LOCK ROD

ENGAGE FLATS OF
STUD IN SLOT OF
ROD BEFORE APPLYING
TORQUE

**Automatic transmission floor mounted shift linkage and lock rod—
Mustang and Cougar** (© Ford Motor Co.)

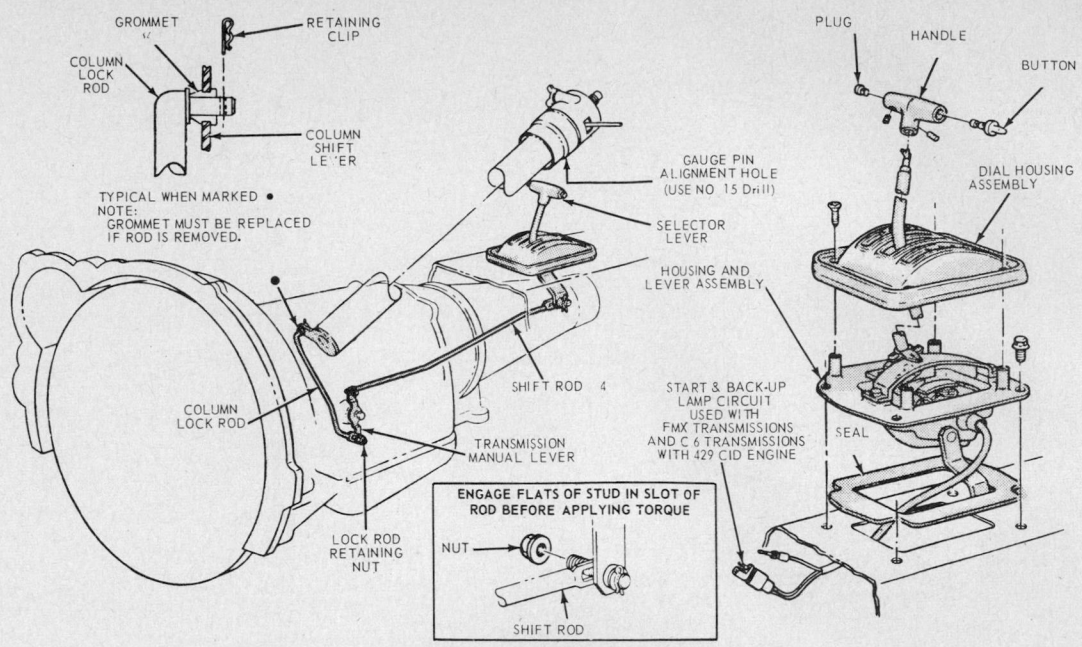

Automatic transmission floor mounted shift linkage and lock rod—
Fairlane and Montego (© Ford Motor Co.)

C6 Three-Speed Automatic

Throttle and Downshift Linkage

Initial Adjustments

See C4 three speed automatic.

1966-68 Montego, Comet, and Fairlane with 390, 427 Engines —Final Adjustments

1. Disconnect bellcrank to carburetor rod at point C and accelerator rod from throttle shaft at point B.
2. Disconnect stabilizer rod from stabilizer at point A.
3. Insert ¼ in. diameter pin through stabilizer and bracket.
4. Adjust length of stabilizer rod so that trunnion enters stabilizer freely. Secure stabilizer rod with retaining clip.
5. Secure carburetor to bellcrank rod to bellcrank with attaching clip at point C.
6. Adjust length of accelerator rod to obtain accelerator pedal height of 4-4½ in. measured at pedal.
7. Connect accelerator rod to accelerator shaft with retaining clip after proper accelerator pedal height has been established.
8. With engine off, disconnect downshift rod from lever at point D.
9. With carburetor choke in off position, depress accelerator pedal to floor; block pedal to hold it in

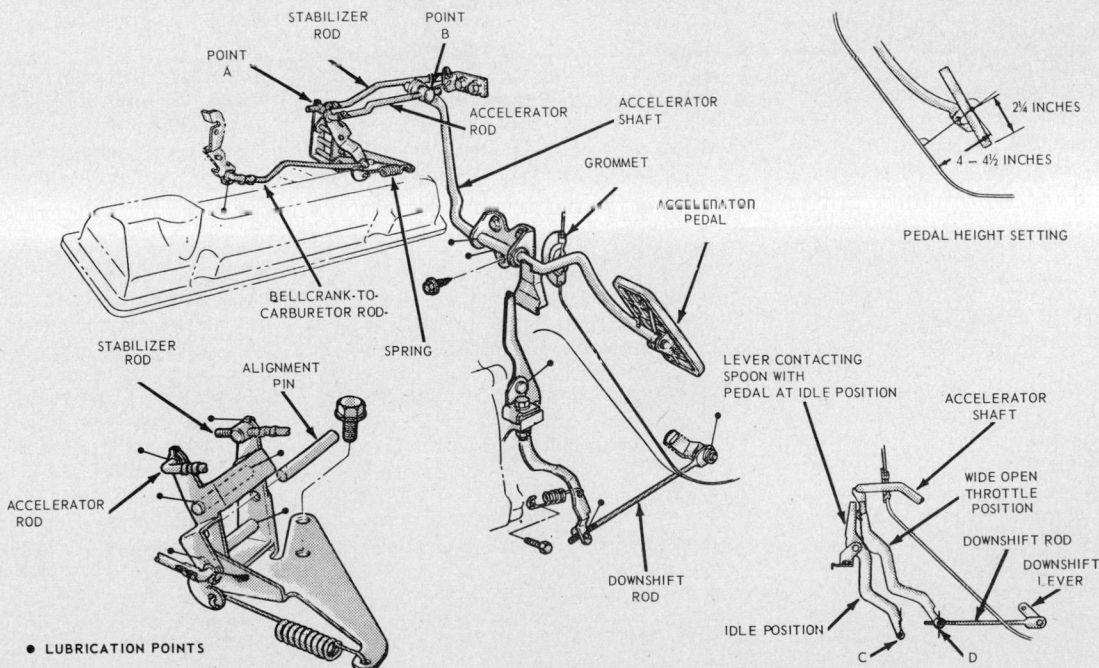

Throttle linkage adjustment—C6 transmission 1966-68 Montego, Comet and
Fairlane with 390, 427
(© Ford Motor Co.)

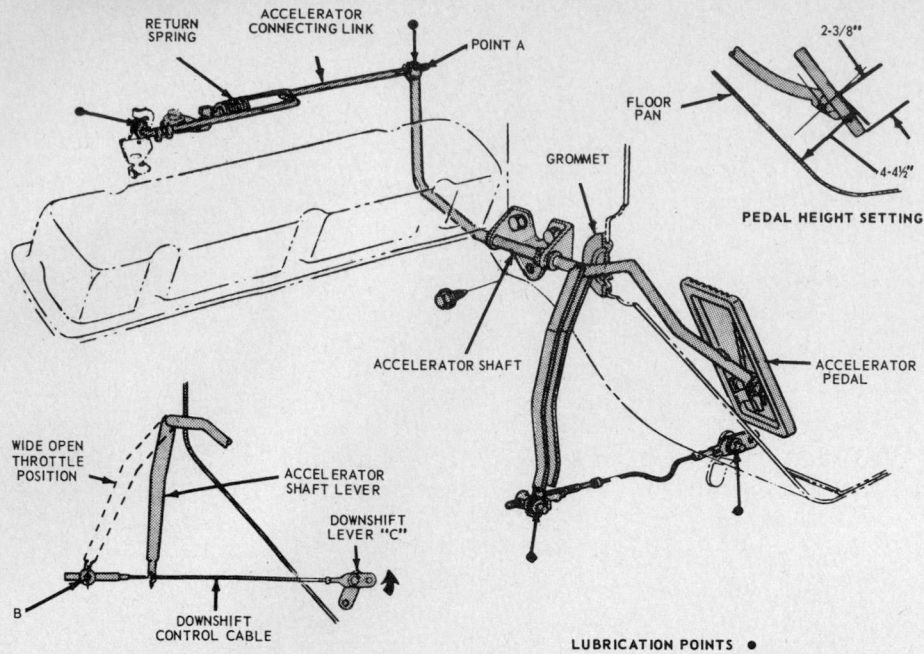

Throttle linkage adjustment—C6 transmission 1967-68 Cougar and Mustang with 390, 427
(© Ford Motor Co.)

open position.

10. Rotate downshift lever on transmission in counter clockwise direction to place it against internal stop.

11. Adjust trunnion at point D so that it enters downshift lever freely.

12. Turn it one additional turn counter clockwise to lengthen rod. Secure it to lever with retaining clip.

13. Remove block from accelerator pedal.

1967-68 Cougar and Mustang with 390, 427 Engines— Final Adjustments

1. With engine off, check accelerator pedal for height of 4½ in. measured from top of pedal at pivot point to floor pan. To obtain correct pedal height, adjust accelerator connecting link at point A.

2. With engine off, disconnect downshift control cable at point B and from accelerator shaft lever.

3. With carburetor choke in off position, depress accelerator pedal to floor. Block pedal to hold it in wide open position.

4. Rotate downshift lever C counter clockwise to place it against internal stop.

5. With lever held in this position, and with all slack removed from cable, adjust trunnion so that it will slide into accelerator shaft lever. Turn it one turn clockwise, then secure it to lever with retaining clip.

6. Remove block to release accelerator linkage.

1969-72 All Models—Final Adjustments

See C4 Three Speed Automatic under 1969-72 Cougar V8.

Manual Linkage Adjustment, Transmission Lock Rod Adjustment

See C4 Three Speed Automatic.

Transmission Removal and Replacement—Beginning 1966

1. Raise hood and disconnect starter neutral switch wires.

2. Disconnect the transmission oil filler tube from the manifold.

3. Raise the car and remove the bolts that attach the reinforcement plate at the rear of the transmission oil pan. Remove the plate.

4. With a drain pan under the transmission, loosen the transmission oil pan bolts and slowly drain and remove the pan. After all of the oil is out of the transmission, reinstall the pan, using about four bolts.

5. Remove two bolts that attach the cover to the lower end of the converter housing.

6. Remove two drain plugs from the converter housing and allow it to drain.

7. Remove four nuts that attach the converter to the drive plate.

8. Lift the filler tube from the transmission case.

9. Disconnect starter cable, then remove the starter.

10. Disconnect fluid cooler lines from transmission.

11. Disconnect vacuum hose from the diaphragm.

12. Disconnect manual and downshift rods from the transmission.

13. Disconnect speedometer cable from extension housing.

14. Remove the three bolts that hold the manual and downshift control rod splash shield to the side rail and remove the shield.

15. Remove lower bellcrank bracket lower attaching bolt. Pivot the bracket to allow the bellcrank to hang free.

16. Pry upper bellcrank out of converter housing and allow it to hang free.

17. Disconnect the driveshaft from the rear axle and remove it from the transmission.

18. Remove converter housing-to-cylinder block lower attaching bolts.

19. Loosen parking brake adjusting nut at the equalizer and remove the retracting spring. Disconnect rear brake cables and remove the equalizer.

20. Remove the two nuts that attach the engine rear mounts to the crossmember.

21. Place a transmission jack under the transmission and raise it just high enough to remove the weight from the crossmember.

22. Remove crossmember-to-frame attaching nuts and remove the crossmember.

23. Remove engine rear support-to-extension housing attaching bolts and remove support.

24. Secure the transmission to the

jack with a safety chain. Lower the transmission and remove the upper converter housing-to-cylinder block attaching bolts.

25. Move the transmission away from the cylinder block. Lower it and remove it from under the car.

26. Remove the converter and mount the transmission in a holding fixture.

27. Replace the transmission by reversing removal procedure.

NOTE: transmission and servicing procedures are in the Unit Repair Section.

FMX Automatic Transmission

Since 1969, the FMX transmission has been used in some intermediate size Fords. It is usually used in conjunction with the 351 V8 engine. The adjustments are the same as used with the C4 transmission. The removal and replacement procedure is also the same as the C4, with the exception that the transmission can be removed without removing the torque converter and housing from the engine. To accomplish this, simply remove the transmission-to-housing bolts instead of removing the transmission-to-engine attaching bolts.

U Joints, Drive Lines

Rear Universal Joint Removal

The rear universal joint has two pillow blocks which are bolted to the pinion shaft flange.

Take out the four bolts that hold the bearing blocks to the pinion shaft and gently tap off the bearing blocks.

Lower the back end of the drive shaft and the front end can be slid out of the back of the transmission together with the transmission yoke portion of the front universal joint.

Carry the assembly—the front universal joint complete, the driveshaft

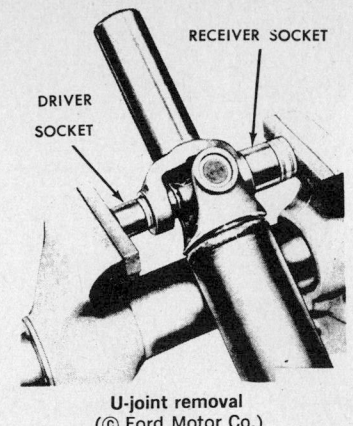

U-joint removal
(© Ford Motor Co.)

and the rear universal joint—to the bench and remove the cross from the rear universal joint by taking out the lock rings from the inner side of the bearings. Using a large punch or an arbor press, drive one of the bearings in toward the center, which will force out the opposite bearing.

When it is pressed out far enough to grip it with a pair of pliers, grip it and pull it out of the driveshaft yoke.

Now drive the cross in the opposite direction until the opposite bearing has been driven far enough out for gripping with a pair of pliers.

When both bearings have been taken out, the cross can be lifted from between the two yokes.

Front Universal Joint Removal

Follow the procedure given above for the rear universal joint but leave the rear universal joint cross in place on the driveshaft if it is not to be removed.

Remove the lock rings from the inner side of two opposite bearings and press on the outer side of one of the bearings, forcing the cross over, which will force the bearing on the opposite side out of its yoke.

Remove the bearing which was forced out of the yoke and then press the cross in the opposite direction to press the other bearing out.

Repeat this procedure on the third and fourth bearings.

When installing the new bearings in the universal joint yoke, it is possible to put them in with a driver of some type, but it is recommended that this work be done in an arbor press since a heavy jolt on the needle bearings can very easily misalign them, which will greatly shorten their life.

Drive Axle, Suspension

Types

There are three types of Ford axles used in compact and intermediate cars. The most prevalent is the integral carrier axle which uses a 7¼ in. ring and pinion gear. This is found on six cylinder models exclusively. All work on the differential or ring gear is done through an inspection plate on the back of the housing. The easiest way to work on this type is to remove the entire housing.

Most V8 models use a medium duty axle with an 8 in. ring gear. Large V8s use a heavy duty axle with 8¾ and 9 in. ring gears. These two axles have removable carrier assemblies which contain the ring gear and pinion and differential. Therefore most repairs can be done without removing the axle housings from the car. One unique Ford Motor Company feature of these two larger axles is the straddle mounted pinion in which the pinion gear is supported on both sides by a bearing. This has been a Ford feature since Model T days.

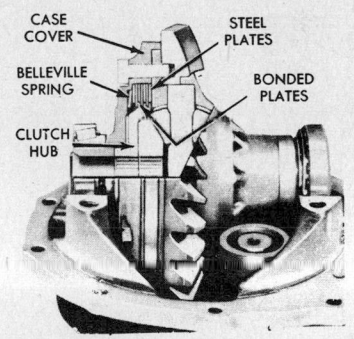

Locking type differential
(© Ford Motor Co.)

Troubleshooting and Adjustments

General instructions covering troubles of the drive axle with repair methods and adjustments are in the Unit Repair Section.

Integral Carrier Rear Axle
Removal

1. Raise the car and support it under the rear frame member.
2. Drain lubricant from the axle.
3. Disconnect driveshaft at pinion flange.
4. Disconnect lower end of shock

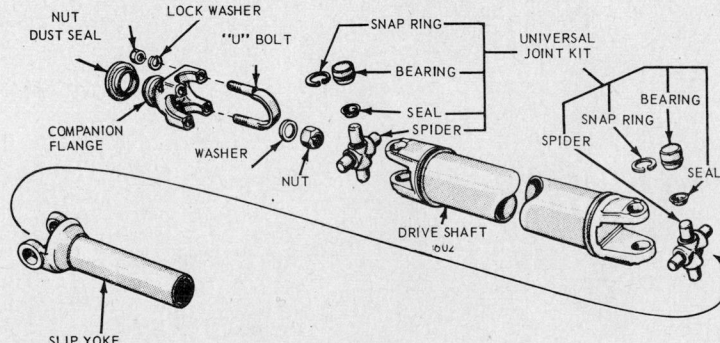

Driveshaft and universal joint assembly (© Ford Motor Co.)

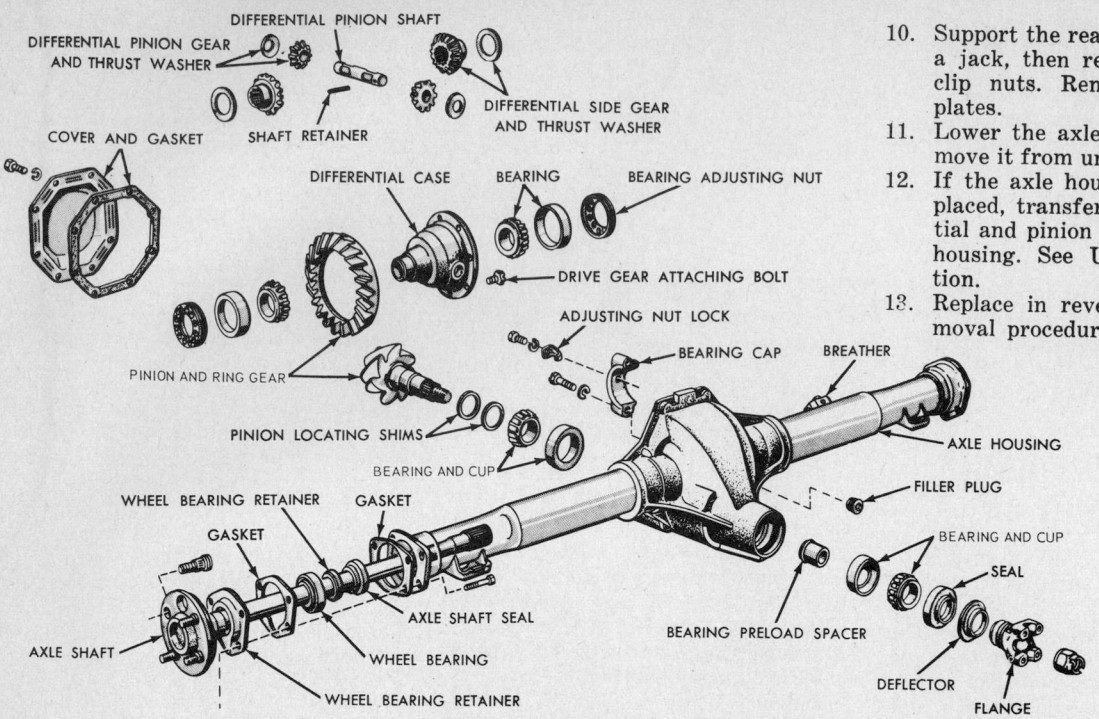

DIFFERENTIAL PINION SHAFT

DIFFERENTIAL PINION GEAR AND THRUST WASHER

COVER AND GASKET

SHAFT RETAINER

DIFFERENTIAL SIDE GEAR AND THRUST WASHER

DIFFERENTIAL CASE

BEARING

BEARING ADJUSTING NUT

DRIVE GEAR ATTACHING BOLT

ADJUSTING NUT LOCK

BEARING CAP

BREATHER

PINION AND RING GEAR

PINION LOCATING SHIMS

BEARING AND CUP

AXLE HOUSING

FILLER PLUG

WHEEL BEARING RETAINER

GASKET

GASKET

BEARING AND CUP

SEAL

AXLE SHAFT SEAL

AXLE SHAFT

WHEEL BEARING

WHEEL BEARING RETAINER

BEARING PRELOAD SPACER

DEFLECTOR

FLANGE

Rear axle assembly—6 cyl. (© Ford Motor Co.)

10. Support the rear axle housing on a jack, then remove the spring clip nuts. Remove spring clip plates.

11. Lower the axle housing and remove it from under the car.

12. If the axle housing is being replaced, transfer all the differential and pinion parts to the new housing. See Unit Repair Section.

13. Replace in reverse order of removal procedure.

absorbers.

5. Remove wheels, brake drums and both axle shafts.

6. Remove vent hose from rear axle vent tube and remove the tube from brake tube connection and axle housing.

7. Without opening the brake hydraulic system, remove the T-fitting from the axle housing. Remove the brake line clip from the axle housing.

8. Remove axle shaft oil seals.

9. Remove both brake backing plates and tie them back and out of the way. The brake lines and parking brake cables are still attached to the backing plates.

Removable Carrier Rear Axle

Removal

1. Remove the carrier assembly from the axle housing as outlined in following paragraph.

2. With safety stands under the rear frame members, disengage brake line from the axle housing

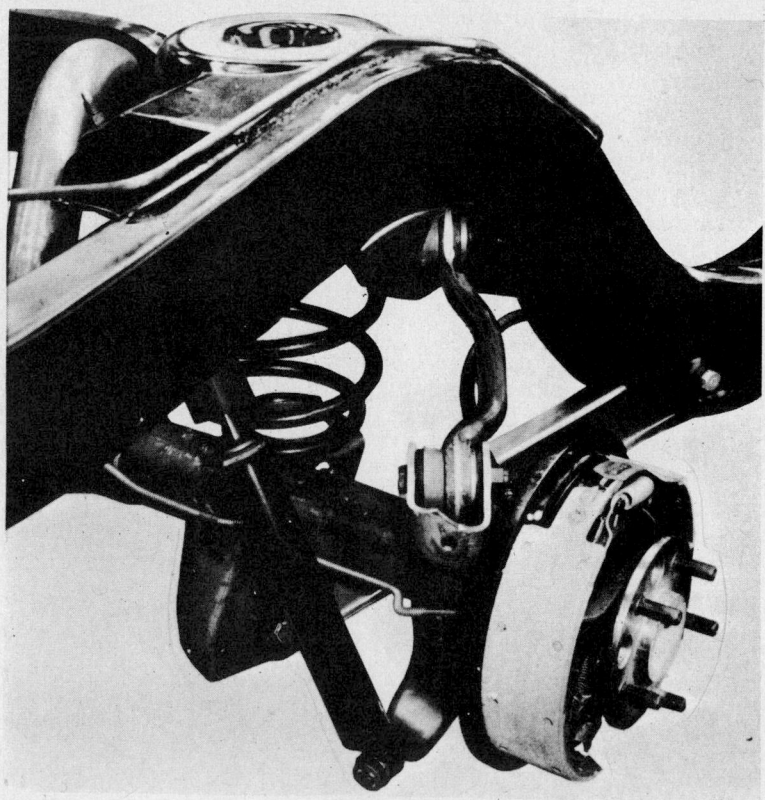

1972 rear suspension (© Ford Motor Co.)

and keep clear.

3. Disconnect vent tube from axle housing.
4. Remove the brake carrier plate assemblies from the axle housing and support them out of the way. Do not open the line.
5. Disconnect each rear shock absorber from spring clip plate and position out of the way.
6. Lower rear axle slightly to reduce some tension. Disconnect the axle from the springs.
7. Remove rear axle from under the car.
8. Replace in reverse order of removal.

Differential Carrier R & R

1. Raise the car and support on stands. Remove rear wheel and tire assemblies.
2. Remove the two rear brake drums from the axle shaft flange studs.
3. Working through the hole provided in each axle flange, remove the rear wheel bearing retaining plate attaching nuts. Pull both axle shafts out of the axle housing. Install a nut on one of the brake carrier plate retaining bolts to hold the plate to the axle housing after the shaft has been removed. Whenever an axle shaft has been removed, the wheel bearing oil seal must be replaced.
4. Scribe the driveshaft end yoke and the U-joint flange to insure proper position at assembly. Disconnect driveshaft at the rear U-joint, and remove the driveshaft from the transmission.
5. With a drain pan under the carrier, remove the carrier retaining nuts and the carrier.
6. Replace carrier by reversing removal procedure.

NOTE: for differential carrier service procedures, see Unit Repair Section.

Radio

1965-66 All Models

1. Pull the radio and control knobs off. Remove the nuts and washers retaining the radio to the instrument panel.
2. Disconnect the antenna lead at the right side of the radio.
3. Disconnect the speaker lead.
4. Disconnect the radio lead wire at the fuse panel, and disconnect the pilot light wire. Remove the lead wire from the retaining clips.
5. Remove the radio right support bracket to radio retaining bolt. Remove the radio left support bracket to radio retaining nut (one bracket only on the Bendix radio).
6. Remove the radio assembly from the instrument panel.

7. Position the radio to the instrument panel, and install the washers and retaining nuts at the knob shafts. Be sure the radio mounting stud enters the support bracket.
8. Install the radio support bracket retaining nut and bolt. Tighten all mounting nuts to 25 in. lbs. torque.
9. Connect the antenna lead to the radio.
10. Connect the radio speaker lead and the pilot light lead.
11. Connect the radio power lead and the pilot light lead.
12. Install the radio control knobs.
13. Check the radio operation and adjust the antenna trimmer.

1967 Comet, Falcon and Fairlane

1. Disconnect negative cable from battery.
2. Pull radio control knobs off and remove nuts and washers that attach radio to instrument panel.
3. Disconnect antenna lead at right side of radio (at back of AM-FM radio).
4. Disconnect speaker lead.
5. Disconnect radio lead wire and dial light wire from quick disconnects.
6. Remove radio support bracket.
7. Remove radio from instrument panel.
8. To install, position radio in instrument panel and install washers and attaching nuts at knob shafts. Be sure radio mounting stud enters support bracket.
9. Install radio support bracket.
10. Connect antenna lead to radio.
11. Connect radio speaker lead.
12. Connect radio power lead and dial light lead.
13. Install radio control knobs.
14. Connect battery.
15. Check radio operation.

1967-68 Cougar and Mustang without Console

1. Disconnect battery.
2. Remove rear support bracket attaching nut.
3. Remove four screws that attach bezel and receiver to instrument panel.
4. Move receiver rearward away from instrument panel.
5. Disconnect antenna, speaker, and power leads and remove receiver from instrument panel.
6. To install, position radio under instrument panel and connect speaker, antenna, and power leads.
7. Secure receiver to instrument panel with attaching screws.
8. Secure rear support bracket to receiver with attaching nut.
9. Connect battery.
10. Check operation of radio.

1967-68 Cougar and Mustang with Console

1. Disconnect battery.
2. Remove two screws attaching right and left supports to support bracket.
3. Remove console assembly.
4. Disconnect radio wiring and antenna lead.
5. Remove control knobs from radio.
6. Remove two nuts and washers from radio shafts and remove radio.
7. To install, position radio in opening and install nuts and washers on control shafts.
8. Install control knobs.
9. Connect radio wires and antenna lead cable.
10. Install console assembly.
11. Install two screws attaching right and left support to support bracket.
12. Connect battery.

1968-72 Montego, Fairlane, and Falcon

1. Disconnect battery.
2. Pull radio control knobs off shafts.
3. Remove radio support to instrument panel attaching screw.
4. Remove two bezel nuts from radio control shafts.
5. Lower radio and disconnect antenna, speaker, and power leads. Remove radio.
6. To install, connect antenna, speaker and power leads to radio.
7. Position radio in instrument panel and install two bezel nuts. Torque bezel nuts to 30-35 in. lbs.
8. Install radio support bracket to instrument panel attaching screw and torque to 30-35 in. lbs.
9. Connect battery.
10. Adjust antenna trimmer, if necessary.
11. Install radio control knobs and set push buttons for desired stations.

1969-72 Cougar and Mustang

1. Disconnect battery.
2. Pull control knobs, discs, and sleeve from radio control shafts.
3. Remove radio applique from instrument panel.
4. Remove right and left finish panels.
5. Remove two mounting plate attaching screws.
6. Pull radio out of instrument panel and disconnect wires from radio.
7. Remove mounting plate and rear support from radio.
8. Remove radio.
9. To replace, install mounting plate and rear support on radio.

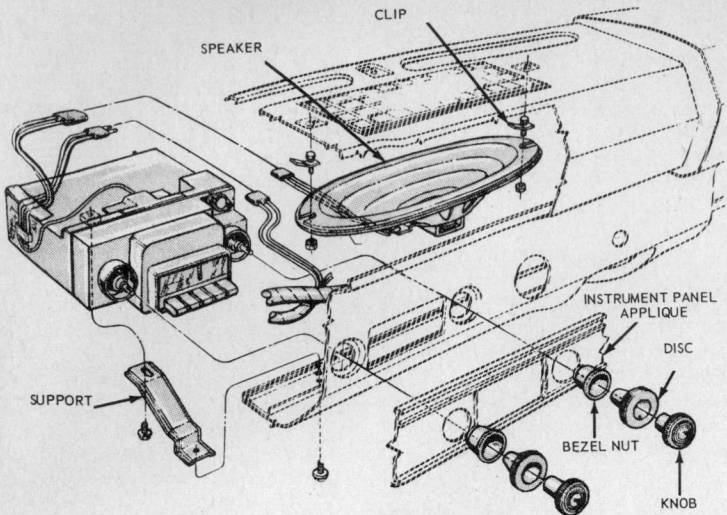

Radio removal—1968-70 Montego, Comet, Fairlane, and Falcon (© Ford Motor Co.)

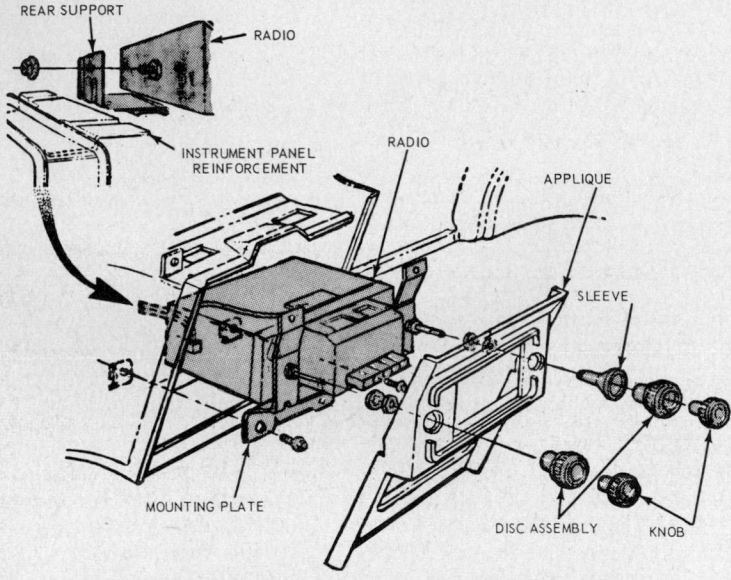

Radio removal—1969-70 Cougar and Mustang (© Ford Motor Co.)

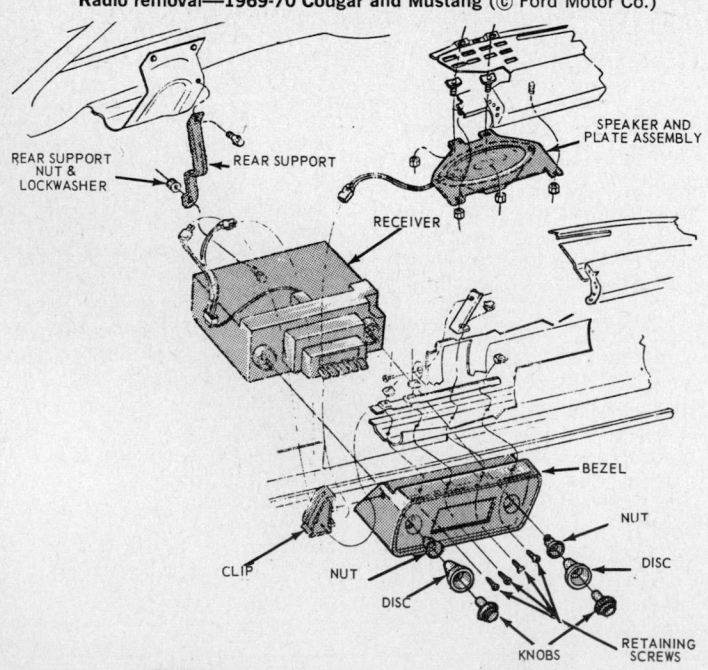

Radio removal—Maverick (© Ford Motor Co.)

10. Position radio near opening and connect wires to radio.
11. Install jumper wire to ground radio to instrument panel.
12. Connect battery and check operation of radio.
13. Adjust antenna trimmer.
14. Disconnect battery and remove jumper cable.
15. Insert radio and wires into panel opening. Be sure radio rear support slips over instrument panel reinforcement.
16. Install mounting plate attaching screws.
17. Install left and right finish panels.
18. Install radio applique, sleeve, discs, and control knobs.
19. Connect radio ground cable and set push buttons.

1970-72 Maverick and Comet

1. Disconnect battery.
2. Remove radio rear support nut and lock washer.
3. Remove four radio to instrument panel retaining screws.
4. Pull radio from instrument panel and disconnect antenna, speaker, and power leads.
5. Remove radio.
6. Remove knob and disc assemblies from radio shafts.
7. Remove two bezel retaining nuts and remove bezel.
8. To install radio, position bezel on radio and install two bezel retaining nuts.
9. Install disc and knob assemblies on radio shafts.
10. Connect antenna, speaker. and power connectors.
11. Position radio so that rear support mounting bolt enters hole in rear support mounting bracket.
12. Install four radio to instrument panel retaining screws.
13. Install radio rear support nut and lock washer.
14. Place speaker and power wire harnesses in clip on bezel.
15. Connect battery and check operation of radio.
16. Adjust selector buttons for desired stations.

Windshield Wipers

Motor R & R

1965-66 Comet, Falcon, and Mustang

1. Disconnect harness from wiper motor.
2. Remove three bolts retaining wiper motor and mounting bracket assembly to dash panel.
3. Lower assembly and disconnect wiper links at motor.
4. Remove motor and bracket as-

sembly.

5. To install, assemble motor and bracket assembly and connect wiper links to motor.
6. Install motor and bracket assembly on dash by installing three retaining bolts.
7. Connect harness connector to wiper motor.
8. Connect battery and check operation of wiper motor.

1966 Fairlane

1. Disconnect wiper links drive arm from wiper motor drive shaft under instrument panel.
2. Disconnect wiring leads from motor.
3. Remove wiper motor mounting bolts and remove motor.
4. To install, apply sealer around edge of motor mounting bracket and around each bracket bolt hole. Place motor against dash and install mounting bolts.
5. Attach wiring leads.
6. Place wiper link drive arm on motor drive shaft and install nut.

1967-69 Montego, Comet, Falcon, and Fairlane

1. Disconnect wiper motor wire connector.
2. Remove wiper arm and blade assemblies.
3. Remove cowl top grille panel retaining screws and remove cowl top grille.
4. Remove wiper link retaining clip from wiper motor arm.
5. Remove four wiper motor retaining bolts and remove wiper motor and mounting bracket.
6. To install position wiper motor

and mounting bracket against dash panel and install four retaining bolts.
7. Place wiper link on motor drive arm and install retaining clip.
8. Install cowl top grille panel.
9. Connect wiper motor wiring connectors.
10. Check motor operation.

1967-68 Cougar and Mustang

1. Disconnect battery.
2. Remove courtesy light. If car is air conditioned, lower air conditioner to floor.
3. Disconnect wiper motor plug connector.
4. Remove nut retaining pivot arm and wiper arms to motor.
5. Remove bolts and star washers retaining motor to mounting bracket, and remove motor.
6. To install motor, attach motor to mounting bracket with bolts and star washers.
7. Position pivot arm and wiper arms on motor and install retaining nut.
8. Connect motor wire plug and battery.
9. Check motor operation and install courtesy light and air conditioner.

1969-70 Cougar and Mustang

1. Remove wiper arm and blade assemblies from pivot shafts and disconnect left side washer hose at T fitting on cowl grille.
2. Remove eight screws and remove cowl top grille.
3. Motor is located inside left fresh air plenum chamber. Disconnect motor ground wire by removing one screw at forward edge of

plenum chamber.
4. Disconnect motor wire at plug and push it back into plenum chamber.
5. Disconnect linkage drive arm from motor output arm crank pin by removing retaining clip.
6. Remove three bolts that retain motor to mounting bracket, rotate motor output arm 180 degrees, and remove motor.
7. Before installing motor, rotate output arm 180 degrees. Before connecting linkage drive arm to motor, turn ignition to ACC position to allow motor to go to park position.

1970-72 Montego, Falcon, and Fairlane, 1971-72 Mustang and Cougar

1. Disconnect battery and wiper motor connector.
2. Remove cowl top left vent screen by removing four retaining drive pins.
3. Remove wiper link retaining clip from wiper motor arm.
4. Remove three wiper motor retaining bolts, and remove wiper motor and mounting bracket.
5. To install motor, place wiper motor and mounting bracket against dash panel and install three retaining bolts.
6. Position wiper link on motor drive arm, and install connecting clip. Be sure to force clip locking flange into locked position as shown in figure.
7. Install cowl top vent screen and secure with four drive pins.
8. Check motor operation and connect wiring plugs.

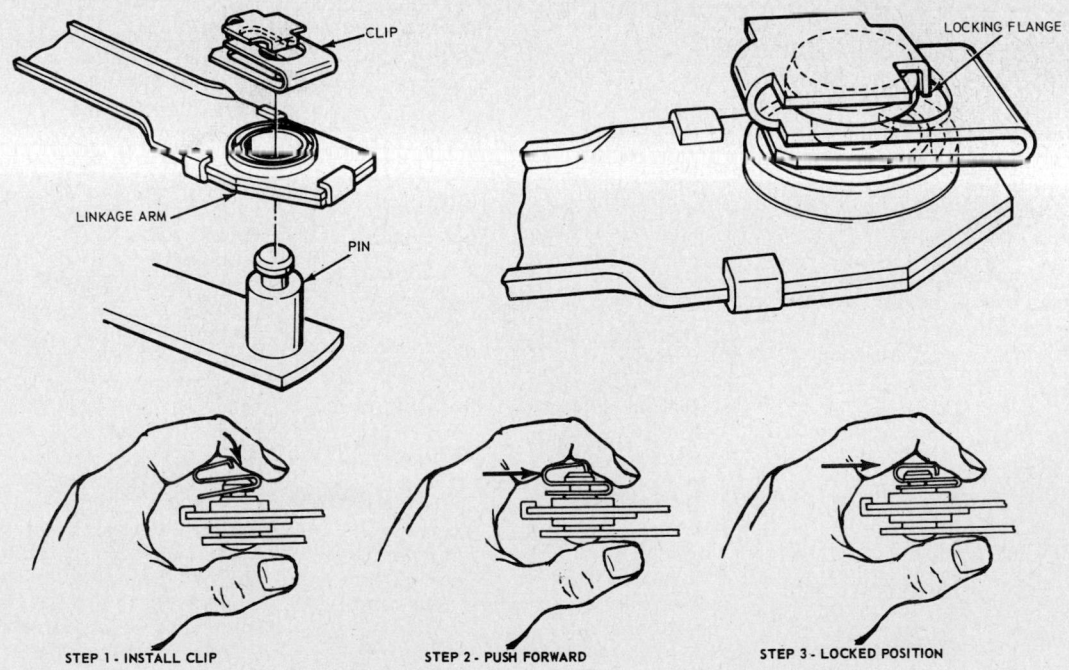

STEP 1 - INSTALL CLIP   STEP 2 - PUSH FORWARD   STEP 3 - LOCKED POSITION

Installation of windshield wiper connecting clips (© Ford Motor Co.)

1970-72 Maverick and Comet

1. Remove instrument cluster.
2. If air conditioned, remove center connector and duct assembly. Remove mounting bracket screw behind center duct, disconnect assembly from plenum chamber and left duct, and pull center connector and duct assembly out through cluster opening.
3. Working through cluster opening, disconnect two pivot shaft links from motor drive arm by removing retaining clip.
4. Disconnect wiring plug at motor, remove three retaining bolts, and remove motor through cluster opening.
5. To install motor, bolt motor to mounting plate with three retaining bolts.
6. Connect right pivot shaft link to motor and then connect left pivot shaft link. Lock clip as shown.
7. On air conditioned vehicles, insert end of center connector and duct assembly near mounting bracket into left duct and opposite end into plenum chamber.
8. Secure assembly with mounting bracket screw.
9. Install instrument cluster, and check operation of wiper motor.

Pivot Shaft and Linkage R & R

1965-66 Comet, Falcon, Fairlane, and Mustang

1. Remove windshield wiper blade and arm assembly.
2. Remove pivot shaft retaining nut, bezel, and gasket.
3. Disconnect wiper link from motor, and remove link and pivot shaft assembly.
4. To install, place pivot shaft and link assembly on cowl and wiper motor. Connect link to motor.
5. Install pivot shaft through cowl and install gasket, bezel, and retaining nut.
6. Install wiper arm and blade assembly.

1967-69 Montego, Comet, Falcon, and Fairlane

1. Remove wiper arms and blades.
2. Remove cowl top grille retaining screws and remove cowl top grille.
3. Remove clip retaining drive arm to pivot.
4. Remove three retaining screws from each pivot and remove pivot shaft and link assembly.
5. To install, position pivot shaft and link assembly in the cowl and install pivot shaft retaining screws.
6. Place left link on motor drive arm and install retaining clip.
7. Install wiper arms and blades,

and check wiper operation.
8. Install cowl top grille panel.

1967-68 Cougar and Mustang— Left Side

1. Disconnect battery.
2. Remove wiper arm and blade assembly.
3. Remove four screws that retain heater control to instrument panel and move heater control outward.
4. Remove clip that retains link to motor drive.
5. Working through heater control opening, remove three pivot shaft retaining bolts.
6. Remove pivot and link out through heater control opening.
7. To install, put a new gasket on pivot.
8. Install pivot through heater control opening, and install three retaining bolts.
9. Install clip that retains link to motor drive.
10. Install heater control assembly.
11. Install arm and blade assembly.

1967-68 Cougar and Mustang— Right Side

1. Disconnect battery.
2. Remove wiper arm and blade assembly.
3. Remove glove box liner retaining screws and remove glove box liner.
4. Working through glove box opening, remove three bolts which retain pivot assembly to cowl panel.
5. Remove clip which retains link to wiper motor drive and remove pivot and link assembly out through glove box opening.
6. To install, put new gasket on pivot.
7. Install pivot and link assembly through glove box opening and install three pivot retaining bolts.
8. Install link retaining clip on wiper motor drive.
9. Install glove box liner.
10. Connect battery and install wiper arm and blade.

1969-70 Cougar and Mustang

1. Disconnect battery.
2. Remove wiper arm and blade assemblies from pivot shafts.
3. Disconnect washer hose at T fitting on cowl grille.
4. Remove eight screws and remove cowl top grille.
5. Disconnect linkage drive arm from motor output arm crank pin by removing retaining clip.
6. Remove clip and disconnect right link from right arm and pivot shaft assembly.
7. Remove three retaining screws and remove right arm and pivot shaft assembly.

8. Remove three screws retaining left arm and pivot shaft.
9. Lift out pivot shaft and arm, left link, and linkage drive arm as one assembly. Assembly comes out to right.
10. When installing pivot shaft assemblies, tighten retaining bolts to 3-7 ft. lbs. Install left pivot shaft and linkage first. Be sure linkage connecting clips are forced into locked position as shown in figure.

1970-72 Maverick and 1971-72 Comet—Left Side

1. Remove instrument cluster.
2. Remove wiper arm and blade assembly from pivot shaft.
3. Working through cluster opening, disconnect both pivot shaft links from motor drive arm by removing retaining clip.
4. Remove three bolts that retain left pivot shaft assembly to cowl and take left pivot shaft assembly out through cluster opening.
5. Before installing, cement new gasket on pivot shaft mounting flange. Tighten retaining bolts to 3-7 ft. lbs. After installing pivot shaft and link assembly to cowl connect right pivot shaft link to motor drive arm first, and then connect left link. Be sure connecting clip is locked as shown in figure.

1970-72 Maverick and 1971-72 Comet—Right Side

1. Disconnect battery.
2. Remove wiper arm and blade assembly from pivot shaft.
3. If car is air conditioned, remove right duct assembly. Unclip duct from right connector, slide left end out of plenum chamber, and lower duct assembly out from under instrument panel.
4. From under instrument panel, disconnect first left and then right pivot shaft link from motor drive arm by removing remaining clip.
5. Reaching between utility shelf and instrument panel, remove three bolts that retain right pivot shaft and link assembly to cowl. Lower assembly out from under instrument panel.
6. Before installing, cement new gasket to pivot shaft mounting flange. After installing pivot shaft and link assembly to cowl, be sure right pivot shaft link is connected to motor drive arm before left pivot shaft link. Be sure connecting clip is in locked position as shown in figure.

Heater System

Heater R & R

1965 Fairlane

1. Partially drain cooling system.
2. Disconnect the fresh-air inlet cable at instrument panel.
3. Disconnect right-air inlet boot at blower housing.
4. Disconnect defroster valve control cable at plenum chamber.
5. Disconnect defroster hoses at the outlets.
6. Disconnect heater wires from resistor and disconnect the motor wire.
7. Disconnect heater hoses at the firewall.
8. Remove plenum chamber retaining nuts at firewall and lay assembly on floor.
9. Disconnect heat control valve cable at the valve and remove assembly from car.
10. Install in reverse of above.

1965 Comet and Falcon and 1965-66 Mustang

1. Partially drain cooling system.
2. Remove glove compartment.
3. Disconnect three control cables.
4. Disconnect defroster hoses at plenum.
5. Disconnect heater hoses at water pump and carburetor heater and remove hoses from retaining clips. On 8-cylinder models remove hoses from choke clip.
6. Disconnect motor wire and ground wire-to-dash panel retaining screw.
7. Remove heater and motor assembly retaining nuts from dash panel.
8. Disconnect fresh-air inlet boot and pull heater assembly from panel.
9. Install in reverse of above.

1969-70 Cougar and Mustang

1. Disconnect battery and drain coolant.
2. Remove instrument panel pad.
3. Remove glove compartment liner and door.
4. Remove air distribution duct from heater.
5. Disconnect control cables from heater assembly.
6. Disconnect wires from blower motor resistor.
7. Remove right courtesy light located on underside of instrument panel, if so equipped.
8. Remove heater support to dash panel retaining screw.
9. Disconnect vacuum hoses and remove power air vent duct, if so equipped.
10. Remove blower motor ground wire grounding screw.

11. Disconnect heater hoses from heater at dash panel.
12. Working in engine compartment, remove five heater assembly retaining nuts.
13. Remove instrument panel to cowl attaching screws.
14. Remove instrument panel right side brace.
15. Pull heater assembly and right side of instrument panel rearward, and remove heater assembly. Reverse procedure to install.

1966-72 Montego, Comet, Fairlane, Falcon and All Intermediate 1971-72

1. Drain coolant.
2. Disconnect both heater hoses at dash.
3. Remove nuts retaining heater assembly to dash.
4. Disconnect temperature and defroster cables at heater.
5. Disconnect wires from resistor, and disconnect blower motor wires and clip retaining heater assembly to defroster nozzle.
6. Remove glove box.
7. Remove bolt and nut right air duct control to instrument panel. Remove nuts retaining right air duct and remove duct assembly.
8. Remove heater assembly to bench.

1967-68 Cougar and Mustang

1. Disconnect battery and drain coolant.
2. Disconnect heater hoses at engine.
3. Loosen screws at choke housing and position hose out.
4. Remove nuts retaining heater to dash.

5. Remove screw retaining ground wire at dash and disconnect two wires. Remove glove box liner.
6. Disconnect defroster hoses, temperature control cable, defroster control cable, and heat control cable.
7. Remove screw retaining heater to air intake.
8. Remove heater assembly from vehicle pulling hose through dash.

1970-72 Maverick and 1971-72 Comet

1. Drain the cooling system and disconnect the negative battery cable.
2. Disconnect the blower ground wire (black) from the fender apron.
3. Disconnect the heater hoses from the engine block.
4. Remove the five heater assembly to firewall attaching bolts from the firewall.
5. Working inside the car, remove the ignition switch and plate from the package tray and remove the tray from the dash.
6. Remove the right kick panel and remove the package tray bracket.
7. Disconnect the heater control cables from the heater.
8. Disconnect the defroster air duct from the top of the heater.
9. Disconnect the heater blower motor lead wires from the resistor at the bottom of the heater.
10. Remove the one screw from the bracket that mounts the heater to the dash.
11. Remove the heater from the car by pulling the heater hoses

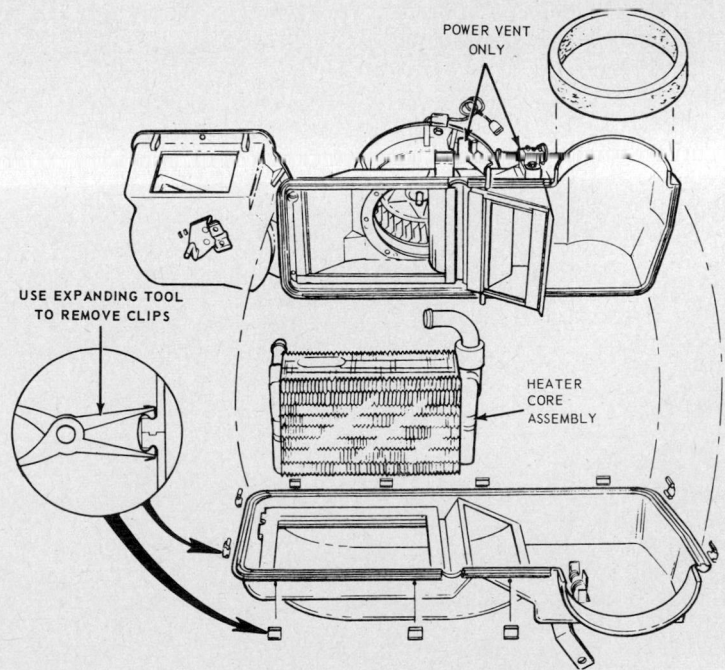

POWER VENT ONLY

USE EXPANDING TOOL TO REMOVE CLIPS

HEATER CORE ASSEMBLY

Heater core removal—1969-72 Cougar and Mustang (© Ford Motor Co.)

through the firewall, then disconnecting them from the heater.

Heater Core R & R

1965 Comet, Fairlane and Falcon and 1965-66 Mustang

1. Remove heater as above.
2. Remove clips retaining housing halves and separate the halves.
3. Lift core from housing chamber.
4. Install in reverse of above.

1969-70 Cougar and Mustang 1970-72 Maverick and Comet

1. Remove heater assembly.
2. Remove air inlet seal from heater assembly.
3. Remove eleven clips from heater assembly flange and separate heater assembly housing.
4. Remove heater core from heater assembly housing. Reverse procedure to install.

1966-72 Montego, Fairlane, Falcon, 1966-67 Comet, and 1971-72 Mustang and Cougar

The heater core is located in the heater case in a diagonal position. It is serviced through an opening in the back plate. Remove heater core cover and pad and remove core. Reverse procedure to install.

Blower Motor R & R

The blower motor on all models is located inside the heater assembly. To replace the blower motor, remove the heater assembly from the car following the steps in the above procedures. Once the heater assembly is removed, it is a simple operation to remove the motor attaching bolts and remove the motor. On all pre-1966 cars, the blower cage must be removed from the motor before the motor can be removed. On all post-1966 models, the motor and cage are removed as an assembly.

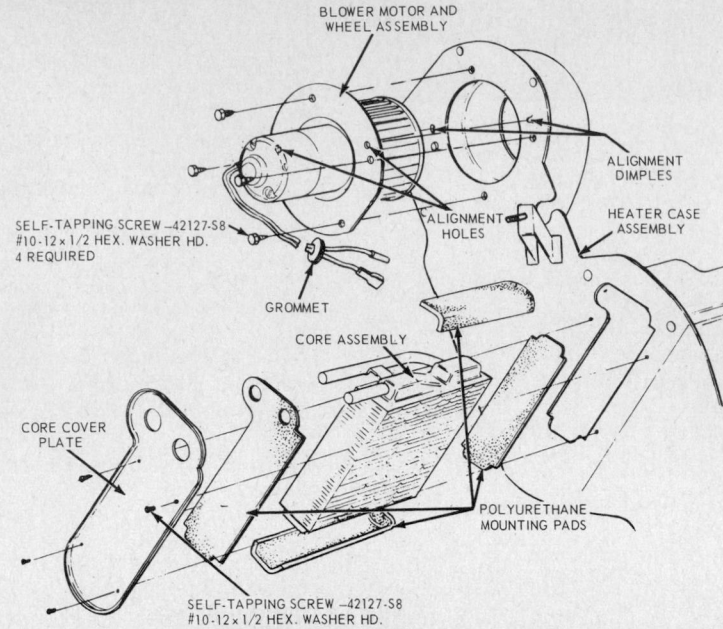

Heater, blower motor and core assemblies—
1966-72 Montego, Comet, Fairlane, Falcon, and Maverick
(© Ford Motor Co.)

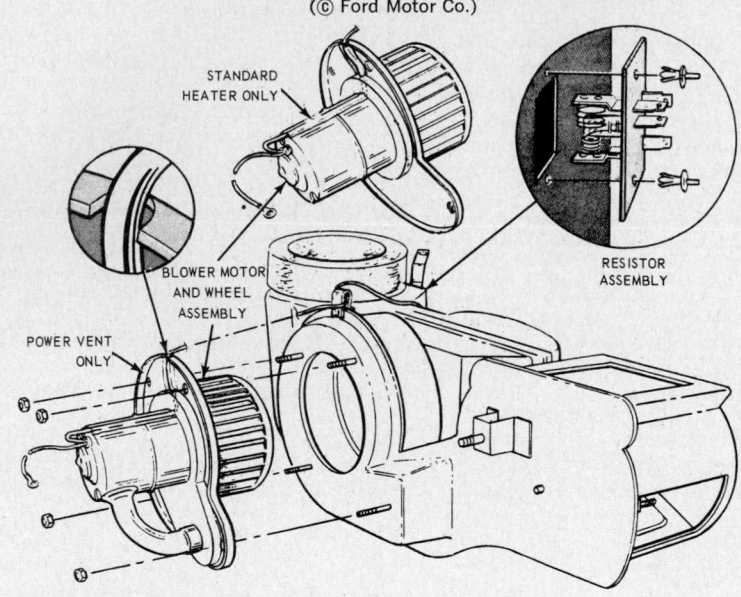

Heater blower and motor installation—1969-72 Cougar and Mustang (© Ford Motor Co.)

YEAR IDENTIFICATION

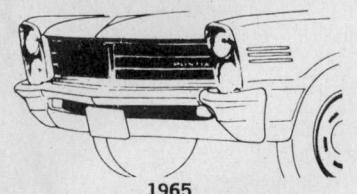
1965

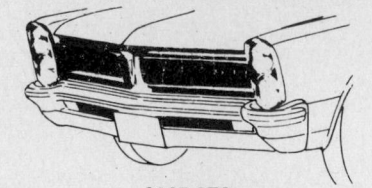
1965 GTO

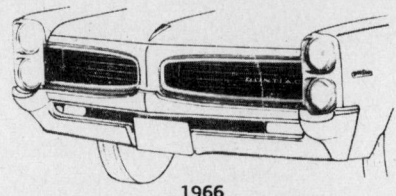
1966

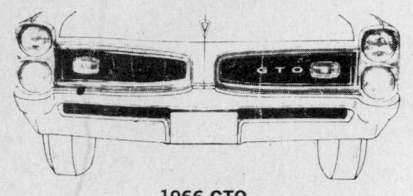
1966 GTO

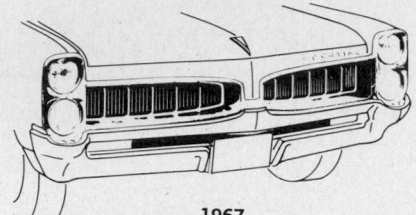
1967

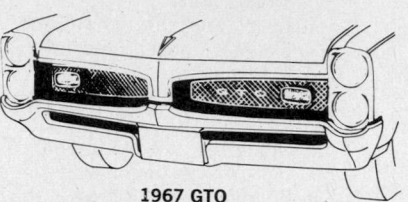
1967 GTO

1967 Firebird

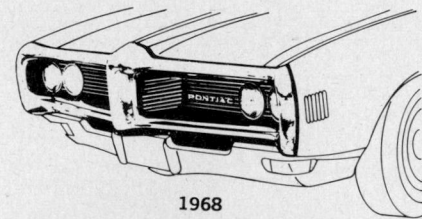
1968

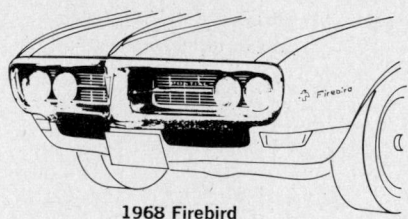
1968 Firebird

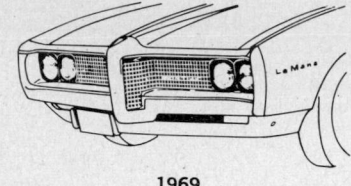
1969

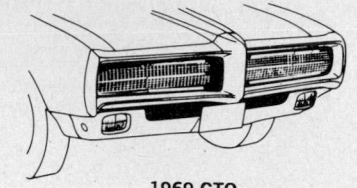
1969 GTO

1969 Firebird

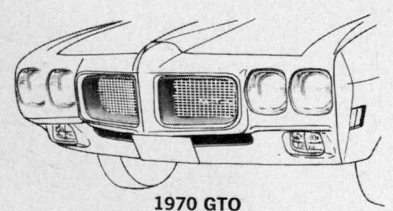
1970 GTO

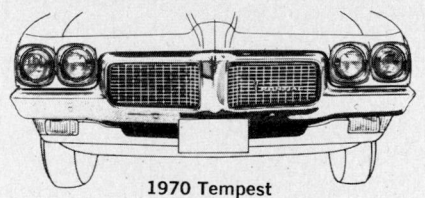
1970 Tempest

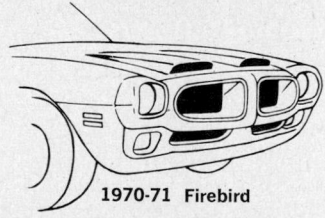
1970-71 Firebird

1971 Tempest

1971 GTO

1972 Tempest

1972 GTO

1971-72 Ventura II

FIRING ORDER

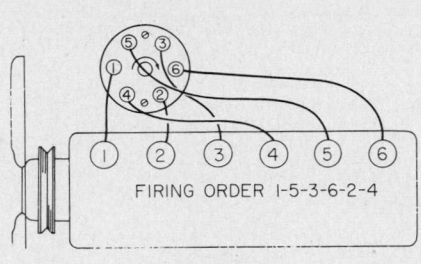

FIRING ORDER 1-5-3-6-2-4

1965-72 6 cyl.

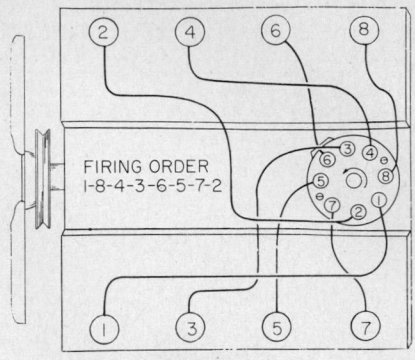

FIRING ORDER
1-8-4-3-6-5-7-2

1965-72 V8

CAR SERIAL NUMBER LOCATION

1965-67

The car serial number is on a plate attached to the left front door hinge pillar. The number is interpreted below:

1968-72

The car serial number is located on a plate attached to the top of the instrument panel, left-hand side, visible through the windshield. The number is interpreted as follows:

1965-72

First digit: Car division
Second and third digits: Series number
Fourth and fifth digits: Body style code
Sixth digit: Year manufactured
Seventh digit: Plant
Eighth digit: Engine used (1 = V8; 6 = 6 cyl.)
Ninth to thirteenth digits—sequential serial number

Engine Identification

The engine number, on V8 engines, is located on a machined pad on the right-hand bank of the engine block.

The engine production code is stamped immediately below this number.

On six cylinder engines, the engine code is stamped on the cylinder head-to-block contact surface behind the oil filler pipe.

Use the following charts to find your engine and its special equipment.

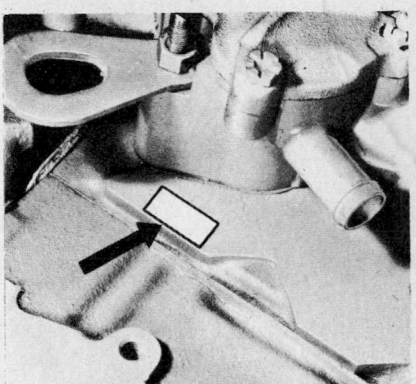

Engine number and code location— 1965-69 V8 engines

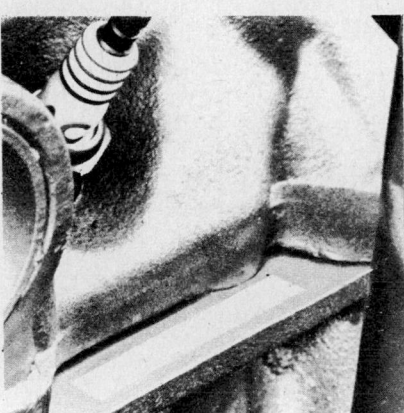

6-cyl. engine serial number location

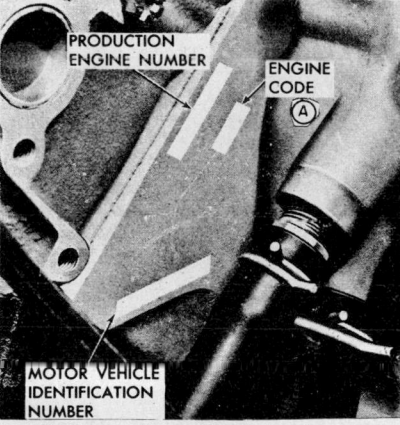

PRODUCTION ENGINE NUMBER

ENGINE CODE Ⓐ

MOTOR VEHICLE IDENTIFICATION NUMBER

Engine number and code location— 1970-72 V8 engines

WHEEL ALIGNMENT

YEAR	MODEL	CASTER		CAMBER		TOE-IN (In.)	KING-PIN INCLINATION (Deg.)	WHEEL PIVOT RATIO	
		Range (Deg.)	Pref. Setting (Deg.)	Range (Deg.)	Pref. Setting (Deg.)			Inner Wheel	Outer Wheel
1965-69	Exc. Firebird	2N to 1N	1½N	¼N to ¾P	¼P	0 to ⅛	9.0	20	18.25
1967-69	Firebird	0 to 1P	½P	¼N to ¾P	¼P	⅛ to ¼	8.25-9.25	20	—
1970-71	Tempest, LeMans	1N to 2N	1½N	¼N to ¾P	¼P	0 to ⅛	9	20	22
	Station Wagon	1½N to 2½N	2N	¼N to ¾P	¼P	0 to ⅛	9	20	22
	Firebird	½N to 1½N	1N	¼P to 1¼P	¾P	⅛ to ¼	8.25-9.25	20	22
1971-72	Tempest, Le Mans	1N to 2N	1½N	½N to ½P	0	¹⁄₁₆ to ³⁄₁₆	9	20	22
	Firebird	½N to ½P	0	½N to 1½P	1P	⅛ to ¼	8.25-9.25	20	22
	Ventura II	0 to 1P	½P	¼ to ¾P	¼P	⅛ to ¼	...	20	22

N—Negative.
P—Positive.

1965–67 ENGINE IDENTIFICATION CODES

No. Cyls.	Cu. In. Displ.	Type	1965	1966	1967
6	230	A.T., 1 BBL.		ZG	ZG
6	215	3 Spd., M.T., 1 BBL.	ZK		
6	230	3 Spd., M.T., 1 BBL.		ZK	ZK
6	215	A.T., 1 BBL.	ZL		
6	230	A.T., 4 BBL. w/Ex. Em.			ZL
6	215	A.T., 1 BBL.	ZM		
6	230	A.T., 1 BBL.		ZM	ZM
6	215	3 Spd., M.T., 1 BBL.	ZN		
6	250	A.T., 1 BBL.		ZN	ZN
6	215	3 Spd., M.T., 1 BBL.	ZR		
6	230	M.T., 4 BBL. w/Ex. Em.			ZR
6	215	3 Spd., M.T., 1 BBL.	ZS		
6	230	3 Spd., M.T., 1 BBL.		ZS	ZS
8	400	3 Spd., M.T., 4 BBL.			WT
8	389	3 Spd., M.T., 3–2 BBL.		WV	
8	400	4 BBL. w/Ex. Em.			WV
8	389	3 Spd., M.T., 4 BBL.		WW	
8	400	M.T., 4 BBL. w/Ex. Em.			WW
8	326	3 Spd., M.T., 2 BBL.		WX	
8	326	3 Spd., M.T., 2 BBL. w/Ex. Em.			WX
8	326	3 Spd., M.T., 2 BBL.	WP	WP	WP
8	326	3 Spd., M.T., 4 BBL.	WR	WR	WR
8	389	3 Spd., M.T., 3–2 BBL.	WS	WS	
8	400	3 Spd., M.T., 4 BBL.			WS
8	389	3 Spd., M.T., 4 BBL.	WT	WT	
8	389	A.T., 4 BBL.		XE	
8	400	A.T., 4 BBL. w/Ex. Em.			XE
8	326	A.T., 2 BBL. w/Ex. Em.			XF
8	326	A.T., 4 BBL. w/Ex. Em.			XG
8	400	A.T., 2 BBL. w/Ex. Em.			XL
8	400	A.T., 2 BBL.			XM
8	400	A.T., 4 BBL.			XP
8	326	M.T., 4 BBL. w/Ex. Em.			XR
8	400	M.T., 4 BBL.			XS
8	400	A.T., 4 BBL. w/Ex. Em.			YI
8	326	A.T., 2 BBL.	YN	YN	
8	326	A.T., 4 BBL.	YP	YP	
8	400	A.T., 4 BBL. w/Ex. Em.			YQ
8	389	A.T., 3–2 BBL.	YR	YR	
8	400	M.T., 4 BBL. w/Ex. Em.			YR
8	389	A.T., 4 BBL.	YS	YS	
8	400	A.T., 4 BBL. (335 HP)			YS
8	400	A.T., 4 BBL. (360 HP)			YZ
6	215	3 Spd., M.T., 1 BBL.	ZD		
6	230	3 Spd., M.T., 4 BBL.		ZD	ZD
6	215	A.T., 1 BBL.	ZE		
6	230	A.T., 4 BBL.		ZE	ZE
6	230	3 Spd., M.T., 1 BBL.		ZF	ZF

1968 FIREBIRD ENGINE IDENTIFICATION

DISPLACEMENT	HORSEPOWER	ENGINE CODE	MANUAL	AUTOMATIC	1-BBL	2-BBL	QUADRAJET	9.0	9.2	10.5	10.75	9777254	9779066	9779067	9779068	9785744	9790826	9792539	1110430	1110431	1111281	1111282	1111447	1111270	1111449	SINGLE	STD. TWO	H.D. TWO (SPEC.)	RAM AIR
250 Cu. In. (six)	175	ZK	X		X			X										X	X							X			
	175	ZN		X	X			X										X	X							X			
	215	ZD	X				X	X									X			X							X		
	215	ZE		X			X	X									X		X								X		
350 Cu. In. (V8)	265	WC	X			X			X			X										X				X			
	265	YJ		X		X			X			X										X					X		
	320	WK	X				X		X						X								X				X		
	320	YM		X			X		X						X							X					X		
400 Cu. In. (V8)	335	XN		X			X			X					X		X											•	X
	335	WQ	X				X			X					X		X											•	X
	335	WI	X				X			X					X	X												•	X
	335	WZ	X				X			X				X	X													•	X
	330	YW		X			X			X					X		X										X	•	
	330	YT		X			X			X					X		X										X	•	

• With 60 PSI Oil Pump Spring
All Cars Use CCS

1968 TEMPEST ENGINE IDENTIFICATION

DISPLACEMENT	HORSEPOWER	ENGINE CODE	TRANS. MANUAL	AUTOMATIC	CARB. 1-BBL	2-BBL	QUADRAJET	COMP. 8.6	9.0	9.2	10.5	10.75	CAM 9777254	9779067	9779068	9785744	9790826	9792539	DIST 1110430	1110431	1111281	1111282	1111447	1111272	1111270	1111449	VS SINGLE	STD. TWO	H.D. TWO (SPEC.)	RAM AIR
250 Cu. In. (six)	175	ZK	X		X				X								X		X								X			
	175	ZN		X	X				X								X		X								X			
	215	ZO	X				X			X								X		X								X		
	215	ZE		X			X			X								X		X								X		
350 Cu. In. (8A)	265	WD	X			X			X				X								X							X		
	265	YN		X		X			X				X								X							X		
	320	WR	X				X				X		X										X					X		
	320	YP		X			X				X		X									X						X		
400 Cu. In. (8A)	265	XM		X		X	X						X												X			X		
	360	WT	X				X					X				X	X												•	X
	350	YS		X			X					X				X	X										•	X		
	360	WS	X				X					X					X	X									•	X		
	350	YZ		X			X					X				X	X										•	X		
	360	XS	X				X					X					X	X									•			X
	360	XP		X			X					X			X		X										•			X

• With 60 PSI Oil Pump Spring
All Cars Use CCS

1969 TEMPEST ENGINE IDENTIFICATION

HP	ENGINE CODE	DISP 250	350	400	TRANS MANUAL	AUTOMATIC	CARB 1 BBL (MV)	2 BBL (2GV)	4 BBL (4MV)	COMP 8.6:1	9.0:1	9.2:1	10.5:1	10.75:1	CAM 9790826	9792539	9796327	9777254	9785744	9779067	9779068	9794041	DIST 1110474	1110475	1111940	1111946 (b)	1111942	1111952 (b)	1111941 (b)	1111960	VS SINGLE	STD.-DUAL	H.D.-DUAL	H.D. SPEC.-DUAL	RAM AIR IV-DUAL	SMALL VALVE	LARGE VALVE
175	(a)ZK ZC	X			X		X				X				X									X							X					X	
175	(a)ZN ZF	X				X	X	X			X				X									X							X					X	
230	(a)ZD ZH	X			X			X				X					X						X									X				X	
215	(a)ZE ZL	X				X		X				X					X						X									X				X	
265	(a)XR XS		X		X			X				X						X							X							X				X	
(c) 265	(a)YN YU		X			X		X				X						X							X							X				X	
265	(a)WP WU		X		X			X				X						X												X			X				X
330	XU		X		X			X			X							X			(d)								X	X				X	X
330	WV		X		X			X			X						X			(e)								X	X				X	X
350	YS			X	X			X				X				X					X								X						X	X
350	WT			X	X	X		X				X				X					X								X						X	X
366	YZ			X	X	X		X				X				X					X								X						X	X
366	WS			X	X	X		X				X	X								X								X						X	X
265	(a)XM XX		X		X		X				X					X								X								X				X	
370	XP			X		X		X				X						X			X								X					X	X
370	WW			X	X	X		X				X						X			X								X					X	X

(a) Early production (small valve) engines with 30° intake valve seat angle. Later production (small valve) engines use 45° intake valve seat. NOTE: all large valve engines use 30° intake valve seat.

(b) Uses hardened drive gear for use with 60 psi oil pump and high tension distributor points.

(c) Two speed (M31) if equipped with A/C; Turbo-Hydramatic (M38) optional without A/C.

(d) Uses distributor 1111965

(e) Uses distributor 1111966

1969 FIREBIRD ENGINE IDENTIFICATION

HORSEPOWER	ENGINE CODE	DISPLACEMENT 250	350	400	TRANS. MANUAL	AUTOMATIC	CARB. 1 BBL (MV)	2 BBL (2GV)	4 BBL (4MV)	COMP. RATIO 9.0:1	9.2:1	10.5:1	10.75:1	CAMSHAFT 9790826	9792539	9796327	9777254	9779067	9779068	9794041	DISTRIBUTOR 1110474	1110475	1111941 (b)	1111942	1111945	1111946 (b)	1111952 (b)	1111960	VALVE SPRINGS SINGLE	STD.-DUAL	H.D.-DUAL	H.D. SPEC.-DUAL	RAM AIR IV-DUAL	CYL. HEAD SMALL VALVE	LARGE VALVE
175	ZC (a) ZK	X			X		X			X				X									X							X					X	
175	ZF (a) ZN	X				X	X			X				X									X							X					X	
230	ZH (a) ZD	X			X			X			X					X					X										X				X	
215	ZL (a) ZE	X				X		X			X						X				X										X				X	
265	WM (a) WC		X		X			X			X						X													X				X	
265	XB (a) XL		X		X			X			X						X						X							X				X	
(c) 265	YE (a) YJ		X		X			X			X						X						X							X				X	
325	WN			X		X			X			X				X												X					X	
325	XC			X	X				X			X					X						X					X					X	
330	WZ			X	X	X			X				X				X											X					X	
330	YT			X	X				X				X				X					X							X				X	
335	WQ			X	X				X				X			X											X					X	
335	YW			X	X				X				X		X							X					X					X	
345	WH			X	X				X				X					X		X									X	X	X	
345	XN			X	X				X				X					X		X									X	X	X	

(a) Early production (small valve) engines with 30° intake valve seat angle. Later production (small valve) engines use 45° intake valve seat. NOTE: all large valve engines use 30° intake valve seat.

(b) Uses hardened drive gear for use with 60 psi oil pump and high tension distributor points.

(c) Two speed (M31) if equipped with A/C; Turbo-Hydramatic (M38) optional without A/C.

(d) Uses distributor 1111965

(e) Uses distributor 1111966

1970 TEMPEST ENGINE IDENTIFICATION

HORSEPOWER	ENGINE CODE	DISPLACEMENT 250	350	400	455	TRANS. MANUAL	AUTOMATIC	CARB. 1 BBL (MV)	2 BBL (GV)	4 BBL (4MV)	COMP. RATIO 8.5:1	8.8:1	10.0:1	10.25:1	10.5:1	CAMSHAFT 9777254 (U)	9779066 (N)	9779067 (P)	9779068 (S)	9794041 (T)	DISTRIBUTOR 1110463	1110464	1112008	1112007	1111148 (4)	1111176 (4)	1112009 (4)	1112012 (4)	1112011 *	VALVE SPRINGS SINGLE	STD.-DUAL	H.D. SPEC.-DUAL	RAM-AIR IV-DUAL	CYL. HEAD SMALL VALVE	LARGE VALVE
155	ZB ①	X				X		X			X					X					X									X				X	
155	ZG ①	X					X	X			X					X					X									X				X	
255	WU		X			X			X			X				X							X								X			X	
255	YU		X				X		X			X				X							X								X			X	
366	WS ②			X		X				X			X				X												†			X			X
350	WT			X		X				X				X			X							X							X			X
370	WW ③			X		X				X				X				X						X						X				X
370	XP ③			X			X			X				X				X						X						X				X
265	XX			X			X		X						X							X								X			X	
330	XV			X			X			X			X		X							X								X			X	
350	YS			X			X			X			X			X							X								X			X
366	YZ ②			X			X			X				X			X							X				X				X
370	WA			X	X	X	X			X			X				X						X						X				X
370	YC			X	X	X	X			X			X			X							X						X				X

① L-6 camshaft usage is 3864897 for both manual and automatic transmissions.

† WS Engine uses 1112024 Distributor.

② Ram Air III

③ Ram Air IV

④ Uses hardened drive gear for use with 60 psi oil pump and high tension distributor points.

* Uses cadmium gear for use with R.A. IV only.

1970 FIREBIRD ENGINE IDENTIFICATION

HORSEPOWER	ENGINE CODE	250	350	400	MANUAL	AUTOMATIC	1 BBL (MV)	2 BBL (2GV)	4 BBL (4MV)	8.5:1	8.8:1	10.0:1	10.25:1	10.5:1	3864897	9777254 (U)	9779067 (P)	9779068 (S)	9794041 (T)	1110463	1110464	1111148$	1111176$	1112007	1112008	1112009$	1112013*	1112024$	SINGLE	STD.-DUAL	H.D.-DUAL	H.D. SPEC.-DUAL	SUPER DUTY-DUAL	SMALL VALVE	LARGE VALVE
155	ZB	X			X		X			X					X					X										X					X	
155	ZG	X				X	X			X					X						X										X				X	
255	WU		X		X			X			X					X								X						X					X	
255	YU		X			X		X			X					X									X						X				X	
265	XX			X		X		X			X					X										X					X				X	
330	WT			X	X	X			X			X					X								X					X					X
330	YS			X		X			X		X						X					X									X					X
345	WS¶			X	X	X			X				X					X										X					X			X
345	YZ¶			X		X			X				X					X									X						X			X
370	WH§			X	X	X			X					X					X										X					X		X
370	XN§			X		X			X					X					X										X					X		X

¶ RAM AIR III
§ RAM AIR SUPER DUTY
* Uses cadmium gear for use with R.A. Super Duty only.
$ Uses hardened drive gear.

1971 TEMPEST ENGINE IDENTIFICATION

ENGINE CODE	Engine No. (Last Two Digits)	HORSEPOWER	"A" SERIES	250 L-6	350 V-8	400 V-8	455 V-8	MANUAL (3-Speed)	MANUAL (4-speed)	AUTOMATIC	MV (1Bbl.)	2GV (2 Bbl.)	4MV (4 Bbl.)	8.5:1	8.0:1	8.2:1	8.4:1	PRESSED-IN	THREADED	SINGLE	DUAL (STD.)	DUAL (H.D.)	SMALL	LARGE	3864897	483555 (W)	9779066 (N)	9779067 (P)	9779068 (S)	HIGH-BALL (STD.)	HIGH-BALL*	LOW-BALL	1110489	1112069	1112068	1112070	1112072	1112073	1112083	1112089	1112090
ZB	63	145	X	X				X			X			X				X		X			X		X	X				X			X								
ZG	64	145	X	X						X	X			X				X		X			X		X	X				X			X								
WR	94	250	X		X			X				X			X			X			X		X		X	X				X							X				
WN	90	250	X		X			X				X			X			X			X		X		X	X				X											X
WU	92	250	X		X					X		X			X			X			X		X		X	X				X							X				
YP	98	250	X		X					X		X			X			X			X		X		X	X				X											X
YU	96	250	X		X					X		X			X			X			X		X		X	X					X							X			
WP	97	250	X		X					X		X			X			X			X		X		X	X					X							X			
XR	95	250	X		X					X		X			X			X			X		X		X	X				X											X
YN	99	250	X		X					X		X			X			X			X		X		X	X				X											X
WT	78	300	X			X		X				X				X		X			X			X	X		X			X					X						
WK	74	300	X			X			X			X				X		X			X			X	X		X			X					X						
XX%	73	265	X		X					X			X	X			X			X		X		X	X	X				X								X			
YX	71	265	X		X					X			X	X			X			X		X		X	X	X				X									X		
YS	79	300	X		X					X		X			X		X			X		X		X	X		X			X						X					
WL†	18	335	X				X	X	X			X				X			X			X		X	X				X		X									X	
WC†	15	335	X				X		X	X		X				X			X			X		X	X				X		X								X		
YC+	19	325	X				X			X		X				X	X				X		X	X			X				X							X			
YE†	16	335	X				X			X		X				X		X			X		X	X				X		X							X			

*Lifter Body with Cast-Iron Foot
**"YU" is used with M35 transmission; "XR" is used with M38 transmission.
†455 H.O. Engine
%Man. Trans. Models use WS engine code
+ Man. Trans. Models use WJ engine code
& Man. Trans. Models use WG engine code

1971 FIREBIRD ENGINE IDENTIFICATION

			Model Usage	Displacement				Transmission			Carburetor			Compression Ratio				Rocker Arm Stud		Valve Spring			Valve Size		Camshaft					Valve Lifter			Distributor								
Engine Code	Engine No. (Last Two Digits)	Horsepower	"F" Series	250 L-6	350 V-8	400 V-8	455 V-8	MANUAL (3-Speed)	MANUAL (4-Speed)	AUTOMATIC	MV (1 Bbl.)	2GV (2 Bbl.)	4MV (4 Bbl.)	8.5:1	8.0:1	8.2:1	8.4:1	PRESSED-IN	THREADED	SINGLE	DUAL (STD.)	DUAL (H.D.)	SMALL	LARGE	3864897	483555 (W)	9779066 (N)	9779067 (P)	9779068 (S)	HIGH-BALL (STD.)	HIGH-BALL*	LOW-BALL	1110489	1112069	1112068	1112070	1112072	1112073	1112083	1112089	1112090
CAA	51	145	X	X				X			X			X				X		X			X		X					X			X								
CAB	52	145	X	X						X	X			X				X		X			X		X					X			X								
WR	94	250	X		X			X				X			X			X			X		X			X				X									X		
WN	90	250	X		X			X				X			X			X			X		X			X				X											X
WU	92	250	X		X				X			X			X			X			X		X			X				X									X		
YP	98	250	X		X				X			X			X			X			X		X			X				X											X
YU	96	250	X		X					X		X			X			X			X		X			X				X								X			
WP	97	250	X		X					X		X			X			X			X		X			X				X											X
XR	95	250	X		X					X		X			X			X			X		X				X			X							X				
YN	99	250	X		X					X		X			X			X			X		X				X			X											X
WT	78	300	X			X		X					X			X			X		X			X				X			X					X				
WK	74	300	X			X			X				X			X			X			X		X				X			X				X	X				
XX%	73	265	X			X			X				X			X			X			X		X					X		X					X				
YX	71	265	X			X				X			X			X		X		X			X			X				X									X		
YS	79	300	X			X				X			X			X			X		X			X					X		X					X				
WL†	18	335	X				X	X					X				X	X		X			X					X		X							X	X	
WC†	15	335	X				X		X				X				X		X			X		X					X		X							X	X	
YC+	19	325	X				X			X			X				X	X			X		X				X			X							X			
YE†	16	335	X				X			X			X				X	X			X		X					X		X							X			

* Lifter Body with Cast-Iron Foot
** "YU" is used with M35 transmission; "XR" is used with M38 transmission.
† 455 H.O. Engine

% Man. Trans. Models use WS engine code
+ Man. Trans. Models use WJ engine code
& Man. Trans. Models use WG engine code

1971 VENTURA ENGINE IDENTIFICATION

Cylinder Heads group comprises COMP. RATIO, ROCKER ARM STUD and VALVE SPRING.

		DISPLACEMENT		TRANSMISSION		CARBURETOR		COMP. RATIO	ROCKER ARM STUD	VALVE SPRING		CAMSHAFT		VALVE LIFTER	DISTRIBUTOR		
ENGINE CODE	HORSEPOWER	250 L-6	307 V-8	MANUAL	AUTOMATIC	MV	2GV	8.5:1	PRESSED-IN	SINGLE	DUAL	3864897	3896929	HIGH BALL	1110489	1112005	1112039
CAA	145	X		X		X		X	X	X		X		X	X		
CAB	145	X			X	X		X	X	X		X		X	X		
CCA	200		X	X			X	X	X		X		X	X		X	
CCC	200		X		X		X	X	X		X		X	X			X

CRANKSHAFT BEARING JOURNAL SPECIFICATIONS

YEAR	MODEL	MAIN BEARING JOURNALS (IN.)				CONNECTING ROD BEARING JOURNALS (IN.)		
		Journal Diameter	Oil Clearance	Shaft End-Play	Thrust On No.	Journal Diameter	Oil Clearance	End-Play
1965-66	6 Cyl.	2.30	.0003–.0029	.002–.006	7	2.000	.0007–.0027	.008–.014
	V8—326	3.00	.0005–.0020	.0035–.0085	4	2.250	.0005–.0025	.006–.011 ①
	V8—389	3.00	.0005–.0020	.0035–.0085	4	2.250	.0005–.0025 ②	.006–.011 ①
1967	6 Cyl.	2.30	.0003–.0019	.002–.006	7	2.000	.0007–.0027 ③	.0085–.0135
	V8—326	3.00	.0002–.0017	.0035–.0085	4	2.250	.0005–.0025	.006–.011 ①
	V8—400	3.00	.0002–.0017	.0035–.0085	4	2.250	.0005–.0026	.006–.011 ①
1968	6 Cyl.	2.30	.0003–.0019	.002–.006	7	2.000	.0007–.0027 ③	.0085–.0135
	V8—350	3.00	.0002–.0017	.0035–.0085	4	2.250	.0005–.0025	.006–.011 ①
1969	V8—400	3.00	.0002–.0017	.0035–.0085	4	2.250	.0005–.0026	.006–.011 ①
	6 Cyl.	2.30	.0003–.0019	.002–.006	7	2.000	.0007–.0027 ③	.0085–.0135
	V8—350	3.00	.0002–.0017 ④	.0035–.0085	4	2.250	.0005–.0025	.006–.011 ①
	V8—400	3.00	.0002–.0017 ④	.0035–.0085	4	2.250	.0005–.0026 ⑤	.006–.011 ①
1970	6 Cyl.	2.30	.0003–.0029	.002–.006	7	2.000	.0007–.0027	.009–.013
	V8—350	3.00	.0002–.0017	.0035–.0085	4	2.250	.005–.0025	.012–.017 ①
	V8—400	3.00	.0002–.0017 ⑥	.0035–.0085	4	2.250	.0005–.0026 ⑤	.012–.017 ①
	V8—455	3.25	.0005–.0021	.0035–.0085	4	2.250	.0010–.0031	.012–.017 ①
1971-72	6 Cyl.	2.2983-2.2993	.0003–.0029	.002–.006	7	2.000	.0007–.0027	.009–.014
	V8—307 C	⑦	⑧	.002–.006	5	2.099-2.100	.0013–.0035	.002–.006 ①
	V8—350 P	3.00	.0002–.0017	.003–.009	4	2.250	.0005–.0025	.012–.017 ①
	V8—350 C	⑦	⑧	.002–.006	5	2.099-2.100	.0013–.0035	.002–.006 ①
	V8—400	3.00	.0002–.0017	.003–.009	4	2.250	.0005–.0025	.012–.017 ①
	V8—455	3.25	⑨	.003–.009	4	2.250	.0025–.0025	.012–.017 ①

① —Total for 2 connecting rods.
② —.0005–.0026 in 1966.
③ —.0007–.0028 on 6 Cyl. 4-BBL. engine option.
④ —.0012–.0028 on Ram Air IV engine option.
⑤ —.0015–.0031 on Ram Air IV engine option.

⑥ —No.'s 1, 2, 3, 4 on Ram Air IV option—.0007–.0023.
No.'s 1, 2, 3, 4 on Ram Air IV option—.0012–.0028.
No. 5 on Ram Air IV option—.0007–.0022.
⑦ —No.'s 1, 2, 3, 4—2.4484-2.4493.
No. 5—2.4479-2.4488.

⑧ —No. 1—.0008–.0020
No.'s 2, 3, 4—.0011–.0023
⑨ —w/small valve—.0003–.0019
w/large valve—.0005–.0021
P —Pontiac engine.
C —Chevrolet engine.

BATTERY AND STARTER SPECIFICATIONS

YEAR	MODEL	BATTERY				STARTERS			
							No-Load Test		Brush Spring Tension (Oz.)
		Ampere Hour Capacity	Volts	Group Number	Terminal Grounded	Amps.	Volts	RPM	
1965	6 Cyl.	44	12	17MI	Neg.	49–76	10.6	6,200-9,400	35
	V8—Std.	53	12	2SMB	Neg.	65–120	10.6	3,600-5,400	35
	V8—w/AC	61	12	2SMB	Neg.				35
1966	6 Cyl.	44	12	17MI	Neg.	49–76	10.6	6,200-9,600	35
	326—V8	53	12	2SMB	Neg.	65–100	10.6	3,600-5,100	35
	389—V8	61	12	2SBM	Neg.	Not Recommended			35
1967-69	6 Cyl.	44*	12	17MI	Neg.	49–76	10.6	6,200-9,600	35
	326, 350—V8	53*	12	2SM	Neg.	65–100	10.6	3,600-5,100	35
	400—V8	61	12	2SM	Neg.	Not Recommended			35
1970-71	6 Cyl.	45*	12	17MI	Neg.	Not Recommended			35
	6 Cyl.—								
	Ventura II	45	12	17MI	Neg.	50–80	9.0	5,500-10,500	35
	V8—								
	Ventura II	61	12	2SM	Neg.	50–80 ①	9.0 ①	5,500-10,500 ①	35
	V8—350 P	53*	12	25M	Neg.	Not Recommended			35
	V8—400, 455	61	12	2SM	Neg.	Not Recommended			35

*—61 amp. battery used w/AC or H.D. battery option.
① —350 V8—65-95 amps., 9.0 volts, 7,500-10,500 rpm.
P—Pontiac engine.

GENERAL ENGINE SPECIFICATIONS

YEAR	CU. IN. DISPLACEMENT	CARBURETOR	ADVERTIZED HORSEPOWER @ RPM	ADVERTIZED TORQUE @ RPM (FT. LBS.)	A.M.A. HORSEPOWER	BORE AND STROKE (IN.)	ADVERTIZED COMPRESSION RATIO	VALVE LIFTER TYPE	NORMAL OIL PRESSURE (PSI)
1965	215(OHV)6	1-BBL.	140 @ 4200	206 @ 2000	33.7	3.75 x 3.25	8.6:1	Hyd.	35
	326 V8	2-BBL.	250 @ 4600	333 @ 2800	44.3	3.72 x 3.75	9.2:1	Hyd.	35
	326 V8	4-BBL.	285 @ 5000	359 @ 3200	44.3	3.72 x 3.75	10.5:1	Hyd.	35
	389 V8	4-BBL.	335 @ 5000	431 @ 3200	52.8	4.06 x 3.75	10.75:1	Hyd.	35
	389 V8	3-2-BBL.	360 @ 5200	424 @ 3600	52.8	4.06 x 3.75	10.75:1	Hyd.	35
1966	230 (OHC)6	1-BBL.	165 @ 4700	216 @ 2600	36.0	3.88 x 3.25	9.0:1	Hyd.	35
	230 (OHC)6	4-BBL.	207 @ 5200	228 @ 3800	36.0	3.88 x 3.25	10.5:1	Hyd.	35
	326 V8	2-BBL.	250 @ 4600	333 @ 2800	44.3	3.72 x 3.75	9.2:1	Hyd.	35
	326 V8	4-BBL.	285 @ 5000	359 @ 3200	44.3	3.72 x 3.75	10.5:1	Hyd.	35
	389 V8	4-BBL.	335 @ 5000	431 @ 3200	52.8	4.06 x 3.75	10.75:1	Hyd.	35
	389 V8	3-2-BBL.	360 @ 5200	424 @ 3600	52.8	4.06 x 3.75	10.75:1	Hyd.	35
1967	230 (OHC)6	1-BBL.	165 @ 4700	216 @ 2600	36.0	3.88 x 3.25	9.0:1	Hyd.	35
	230 (OHC)6	4-BBL.	215 @ 5200	240 @ 3800	36.0	3.88 x 3.25	10.5:1	Hyd.	35
	326 V8	2-BBL.	250 @ 4600	333 @ 2800	44.3	3.72 x 3.75	9.2:1	Hyd.	35
	326 V8	4-BBL.	285 @ 5000	359 @ 3200	44.3	3.72 x 3.75	10.5:1	Hyd.	35
	400 V8	2-BBL.	255 @ 4400	397 @ 2400	54.3	4.12 x 3.75	8.6:1	Hyd.	35
	400 V8	4-BBL.	325 @ 4800	410 @ 3400	54.3	4.12 x 3.75	10.75:1	Hyd.	35
	400 V8	4-BBL.	325 @ 5200	410 @ 3600	54.3	4.12 x 3.75	10.75:1	Hyd.	35
	400 V8	4-BBL.	335 @ 5000	441 @ 3400	54.3	4.12 x 3.75	10.75:1	Hyd.	35
	400 V8	4-BBL.	360 @ 5400	438 @ 3600	54.3	4.12 x 3.75	10.75:1	Hyd.	35
	400 V8	4-BBL.	360 @ 5100	438 @ 3600	54.3	4.12 x 3.75	10.75:1	Hyd.	35
1968	250 (OHC)6	1-BBL.	175 @ 4800	240 @ 2600	36.0	3.88 x 3.53	9.0:1	Hyd.	31
	250 (OHC)6	4-BBL.	215 @ 5200	255 @ 3800	36.0	3.88 x 3.53	10.5:1	Hyd.	31
	350 V8	2-BBL.	265 @ 4600	355 @ 2800	48.0	3.88 x 3.75	9.2:1	Hyd.	35
	350 H.O. V8	4-BBL.	320 @ 5100	380 @ 3200	48.0	3.88 x 3.75	10.5:1	Hyd.	35
	400 V8	2-BBL.	265 @ 4600	335 @ 2800	54.3	4.12 x 3.75	9.2:1	Hyd.	35
	400 V8	4-BBL.	330 @ 4800	430 @ 3300	54.3	4.12 x 3.75	10.75:1	Hyd.	35
	400 H. O. V8	4-BBL.	335 @ 5000	430 @ 3400	54.3	4.12 x 3.75	10.75:1	Hyd.	35
	400 (Ram Air)V8	4-BBL.	335 @ 5300	430 @ 3600	54.3	4.12 x 3.75	10.75:1	Hyd.	35
	400 H. O. V8	4-BBL.	360 @ 5100	445 @ 3600	54.3	4.12 x 3.75	10.75:1	Hyd.	35
	400 (Ram Air)V8	4-BBL.	360 @ 5400	445 @ 3800	54.3	4.12 x 3.75	10.75:1	Hyd.	35
1969	250 (OHC)6	1-BBL.	175 @ 4800	240 @ 2600	36.0	3.88 x 3.53	9.0:1	Hyd.	35
	250 (OHC)6	4-BBL.	215 @ 5200	255 @ 3800	36.0	3.88 x 3.53	10.5:1	Hyd.	35
	250 (OHC)6	4-BBL.	230 @ 5400	260 @ 3600	36.0	3.83 x 3.53	10.75:1	Hyd.	35
	350 V8	2-BBL.	265 @ 4600	355 @ 2800	48.0	3.88 x 3.75	9.2:1	Hyd.	35
	350 V8	4-BBL.	325 @ 5100	380 @ 3200	48.0	3.88 x 3.75	10.5:1	Hyd.	35
	350 V8	4-BBL.	330 @ 4800	380 @ 3200	48.0	3.88 x 3.75	10.5:1	Hyd.	35
	400 V8	2-BBL.	265 @ 4600	397 @ 2400	54.3	4.12 x 3.75	8.6:1	Hyd.	35
	400 V8	4-BBL.	330 @ 4800	430 @ 3300	54.3	4.12 x 3.75	10.75:1	Hyd.	35
	400 V8	4-BBL.	335 @ 5000	430 @ 3400	54.3	4.12 x 3.75	10.75:1	Hyd.	35
	400 V8	4-BBL.	345 @ 5400	430 @ 3700	54.3	4.12 x 3.75	10.75:1	Hyd.	35
	400 V8	4-BBL.	350 @ 5000	445 @ 3000	54.3	4.12 x 3.75	10.75:1	Hyd.	35
	400 V8	4-BBL.	366 @ 5100	445 @ 3600	54.3	4.12 x 3.75	10.75:1	Hyd.	35
	400 V8	4-BBL.	370 @ 5500	445 @ 3900	54.3	4.12 x 3.75	10.75:1	Hyd.	35
1970	250(OHV)6	1-BBL.	155 @ 4200	235 @ 1600	36.0	3.87 x 3.53	8.5:1	Hyd.	35
	350 V8	2-BBL.	255 @ 4600	355 @ 2800	48.0	3.88 x 3.75	8.8:1	Hyd.	35
	400 V8	2-BBL.	265 @ 4600	397 @ 2400	54.3	4.12 x 3.75	8.8:1	Hyd.	35
	400 V8	4-BBL.	330 @ 4800	445 @ 2900	54.3	4.12 x 3.75	10.00:1	Hyd.	35
	400 Ram Air	4-BBL.	345 @ 5400	430 @ 3700	54.3	4.12 x 3.75	10.75:1	Hyd.	35
	400 V8	4-BBL.	350 @ 5000	445 @ 3000	54.3	4.12 x 3.75	10.25:1	Hyd.	35
	400 Judge	4-BBL.	366 @ 5100	445 @ 3600	54.3	4.12 x 3.75	10.50:1	Hyd.	35
	400 Ram Air IV	4-BBL.	370 @ 5500	445 @ 3900	54.3	4.12 x 3.75	10.50:1	Hyd.	35
	455 V8	4-BBL.	360 @ 4300	500 @ 2700	55.2	4.15 x 4.21	10.25:1	Hyd.	35

GENERAL ENGINE SPECIFICATIONS

YEAR	CU. IN. DISPLACEMENT	CARBURETOR	ADVERTIZED HORSEPOWER @ RPM	ADVERTIZED TORQUE @ RPM (FT. LBS.)	A.M.A. HORSEPOWER	BORE AND STROKE (IN.)	ADVERTIZED COMPRESSION RATIO	VALVE LIFTER TYPE	NORMAL OIL PRESSURE (PSI)
1971	250 (OHV)6	1-BBL.	145 @ 4200	230 @ 1600	36.0	3.87 x 3.53	8.5:1	Hyd.	30-45
	307 V8	2-BBL.	200 @ 4600	300 @ 2400	48.0	3.87 x 3.25	8.5:1	Hyd.	40-45
	350 V8	2-BBL.	250 @ 4400	350 @ 2400	48.0	3.88 x 3.75	8.0:1	Hyd.	30-40
	400 V8	2-BBL.	265 @ 4400	400 @ 2400	54.3	4.12 x 3.75	8.2:1	Hyd.	55-60
	400 V8	4-BBL.	300 @ 5000	430 @ 3400	54.3	4.12 x 3.75	8.2:1	Hyd.	55-60
	455 V8	4-BBL.	325 @ 4400	455 @ 3200	55.2	4.15 x 4.21	8.2:1	Hyd.	55-60
	455 V8HO	4-BBL.	335 @ 4800	480 @ 3600	55.2	4.15 x 4.21	8.4:1	Hyd.	55-60
1972	250(OHV)6	1-BBL.	110 @ 3800★	185 @ 1600★	36.0	3.87 x 3.53	8.5:1	Hyd.	30-45
	307 V8	2-BBL.	140 @ 4400★	235 @ 2400★	48.0	3.87 x 3.25	8.5:1	Hyd.	40-45
	350 V8①	2-BBL.	160 @ 4400★	270 @ 2000★	48.0	3.87 x 3.75	8.0:1	Hyd.	30-40
	350 V8②	2-BBL.	175 @ 4400★	275 @ 2000★	48.0	3.87 x 3.75	8.0:1	Hyd.	30-40
	400 V8①	2-BBL.	175 @ 4000★	310 @ 2400★	54.3	4.12 x 3.75	8.2:1	Hyd.	30-40
	400 V8②	2-BBL.	200 @ 4000★	325 @ 2400★	54.3	4.12 x 3.75	8.2:1	Hyd.	30-40
	400 V8①	4-BBL.	200 @ 4000★	295 @ 2800★	54.3	4.12 x 3.75	8.2:1	Hyd.	55-60
	400 V8②	4-BBL.	250 @ 4400★	325 @ 3200★	54.3	4.12 x 3.75	8.2:1	Hyd.	55-60
	455 V8①	4-BBL.	220 @ 3600★	350 @ 2400★	55.2	4.15 x 4.21	8.2:1	Hyd.	55-60
	455 V8②	4-BBL.	250 @ 3600★	375 @ 2400★	55.2	4.15 x 4.21	8.2:1	Hyd.	55-60
	455 V8 HO	4-BBL.	300 @ 4000★	415 @ 3200★	55.2	4.15 x 4.21	8.4:1	Hyd.	55-60

★—SAE net rating.   ①—Single exhaust.   ②—Dual exhaust.

TORQUE SPECIFICATIONS

YEAR	MODEL	SPARK PLUGS (FT. LBS.)	CYLINDER HEAD BOLTS (FT. LBS.)	ROD BEARING BOLTS (FT. LBS.)	MAIN BEARING BOLTS (FT. LBS.)	CRANKSHAFT BALANCER BOLT (FT. LBS.)	FLYWHEEL TO CRANKSHAFT BOLTS (FT. LBS.)	MANIFOLD (FT. LBS.) Intake	MANIFOLD (FT. LBS.) Exhaust
1965-69	6 Cyl.	15-25	85-100	30-35	60-70	PRESSED ON	60-70	25-40	15-25
	V8	15-25	85-100	40-46	90-110▲	130-190	85-100	20-35	30-45
1970-72	6 Cyl.	15	95	35	65	PRESSED ON	60	25-30③	25
	V8 P	25	95	43	90-110	160	95	40	30
	V8—307 C	15	65	45	75	60	60	30	20
	V8—350 C①	15	65	45	75	60	60	30	20②

▲—Rear main—120 ft. lbs.   P—Pontiac engine.   ②—Inside bolts—30 ft. lbs.
C—Chevrolet engine used in Ventura II.   ①—Not available until 1972.   ③—End-bolts—15-20 ft. lbs.

CYLINDER HEAD BOLT TIGHTENING SEQUENCE

V8

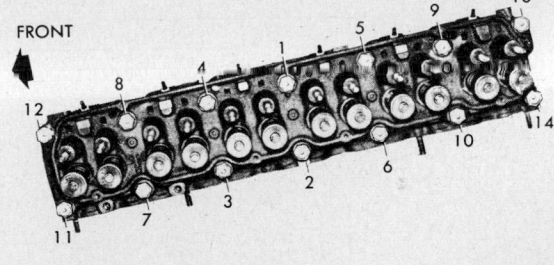

1970 OHV 6 cyl.

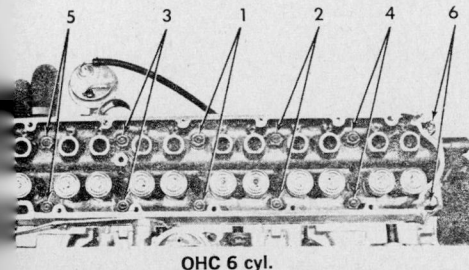

OHC 6 cyl.

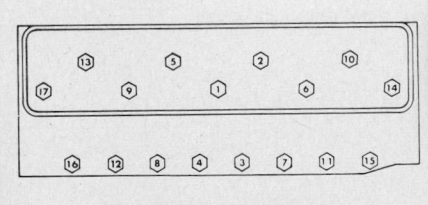

1971-72 Chevrolet 307 and 350 Cu. In. engines

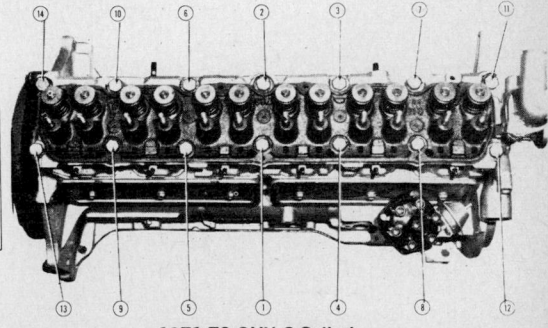

1971-72 OHV 6 Cylinder

TUNE-UP SPECIFICATIONS

YEAR	MODEL	SPARK PLUGS		DISTRIBUTOR		IGNITION TIMING (Deg.) ▲	CRANKING COMP. PRESSURE (Psi) ★	VALVES		Intake Opens (Deg.)	FUEL PUMP PRESSURE (Psi)	IDLE SPEED (Rpm) ★
		Type	Gap (In.)	Point Dwell (Deg.)	Point Gap (In.)			Tappet (Hot) Clearance (In.)				
								Intake	Exhaust			
1965	6 Cyl	46N	.035	31–34	.016	4B	*	Zero	Zero	18B	5–6.5	500
	V8—326 Cu.In.	45S	.035	28–32	.016	6B	*	Zero	Zero	22B	5–6.5	500
	V8—389 Cu.In.	45S	.035	28–32	.016	6B	*	Zero	Zero	23B	5–6.5	500
1966	6 Cyl., 1-BBL., OHC	44S	.035	31–34	.016	5B	*	Zero	Zero	12B	4–5.5	500 ①
	6 Cyl., 4-BBL., OHC	45S	.035	31–34	.016	5B	*	Zero	Zero	20B	4–5.5	500 ①
	V8—326 Cu. In.	45S	.035	28–32	.016	6B	*	Zero	Zero	22B	5–6.5	500 ①
	V8—389 Cu. In., 4-BBL.	45S	.035	28–32	.016	6B	*	Zero	Zero	23B	5–6.5	500 ①
	V8—389 Cu. In., 3 2-BBL.	45S	.035	28–32	.016	6B	*	Zero	Zero	31B	5–6.5	500 ①
1967	6 Cyl., 1-BBL., OHC	44N	.035	31–34	.016	5B	*	Zero	Zero	7B	4–5.5	500 ②⑤
	6 Cyl., 4-BBL., OHC	44N	.035	31–34	.016	5B⑥	*	Zero	Zero	14B	4–5.5	500 ②⑤
	V8—326 Cu. In.	45S	.035	28–32	.016	6B	*	Zero	Zero	22B	5–6.5	500 ②⑤
	V8—400 Cu. In., 255 H.P.	44S	.035	28–32	.016	6B	*	Zero	Zero	22B	5–6.5	500 ⑤
	V8—400 Cu. In., 335 H.P.	44S	.035	28–32	.016	6B	*	Zero	Zero	④	5–6.5	600 ③⑤
	V8—400 Cu. In., 360 H.P.	44S	.035	28–32	.016	6B	*	Zero	Zero	31B	5–6.5	600 ③⑤
	V8—400 Cu. In., 360 H.P., Ram Air	44S	.035	28–32	.016	6B	*	Zero	Zero	38B	5–6.5	600 ③⑤
1968	6 Cyl., 1 and 4-BBL., OHC	44N	.035	31–34	.016	TDC⑦	*	Zero	Zero	14B	4–5.5	700 ⑪
	V8—350 Cu. In., 265 H.P.	45S	.035	28–32	.016	9B	*	Zero	Zero	22B	5–6.5	700 ⑫
	V8—350 Cu. In., 320 H.P., Firebird, Tempest H.O.	45S	.035	28–32	.016	9B	*	Zero	Zero	⑧	5–6.5	850 ⑬
	V8—400 Cu. In., 265 H.P.	44S	0.35	28–32	.016	9B	*	Zero	Zero	22B	5–6.5	700 ⑫
	V8—400 Cu. In., 330 H.P.	44S	.035	28–32	.016	9B	*	Zero	Zero	23B	5–6.5	850 ⑬
	V8—400 Cu. In., 335 H.P., Firebird H.O.	44S	.035	28–32	.016	9B	*	Zero	Zero	⑨	5–6.5	850 ⑬
	V8—400 Cu. In., 335 H.P., Firebird Ram Air	44S	.035	28–32	.016	9B	*	Zero	Zero	⑩	5–6.5	1000 ⑬
	V8—400 Cu. In., 360 H.P., GTO H.O.	44S	.035	28–32	.016	9B	*	Zero	Zero	⑨	5–6.5	850 ⑬
	V8—400 Cu. In., 360 H.P., GTO Ram Air	44S	.035	28–32	.016	9B	*	Zero	Zero	⑩	5–6.5	1000 ⑬
1969	6 Cyl., 1 and 4-BBL., OHC	R44S	.035	31–34	.016	TDC⑦	*	Zero	Zero	14B ⑭	4–5.5	500 ⑯
	V8—350 Cu. In., 265 H.P.	R46S	.035	28–32	.016	9B	*	Zero	Zero	22B	5–6.5	850 ⑬
	V8—350 Cu. In., 325 H.P., Firebird, Tempest H.O.	R45S	.035	28–32	.016	9B	*	Zero	Zero	⑮	5–6.5	1000 ⑬
	V8—350 Cu. In., 330 H.P.	R45S	.035	28–32	.016	9B	*	Zero	Zero	22B	5–6.5	1000 ⑬
	V8—400 Cu. In., 265 H.P.	R45S	.035	28–32	.016	9B	*	Zero	Zero	22B	5–6.5	850 ⑬
	V8—400 Cu. In., 330 H.P.	R44S	.035	28–32	.016	9B	*	Zero	Zero	23B	5–6.5	1000 ⑬
	V8—400 Cu. In., 335 H.P., Firebird H.O.	R44S	.035	28–32	.016	9B	*	Zero	Zero	⑨	5–6.5	1000 ⑬
	V8—400 Cu. In., 345 H.P., Firebird Ram Air IV	R44S	.035	28–32	.016	15B	*	Zero	Zero	42B	5–6.5	1000 ⑰
	V8—400 Cu. In., 350 H.P.	R45S	.035	28–32	.016	9B	*	Zero	Zero	23B	5–6.5	1000 ⑬
	V8—400 Cu. In., 366 H.P., GTO Ram Air	R44S	.035	28–32	.016	9B	*	Zero	Zero	⑩	5–6.5	1000 ⑰
	V8—400 Cu. In., 370 H.P., GTO Ram Air IV	R44S	.035	28–32	.016	15B	*	Zero ㉖	Zero ㉖	42B	5–6.5	1000 ⑰

TUNE-UP SPECIFICATIONS

YEAR	MODEL	SPARK PLUGS		DISTRIBUTOR		IGNITION TIMING (Deg.) ▲	CRANKING COMP. PRESSURE (Psi)	VALVES		Intake Opens (Deg.)	FUEL PUMP PRESSURE (Psi)	IDLE SPEED (Rpm) ★
		Type	Gap (In.)	Point Dwell (Deg.)	Point Gap (In.)			Tappet (Hot) Clearance (In.)				
								Intake	Exhaust			
1970	6 Cyl., 1, OHV	R46T	.035	31–34	.019	18 ⑱	*	Zero	Zero	16B	4–5	750 ⑫
	V8–350 Cu. In., 255 H.P.	R46S	.035	28–32	.016	9B	*	Zero	Zero	22B	5–6.5	800 ⑬
	V8–400 Cu. In., 265 H.P.	R46S	.035	28–32	.016	9B	*	Zero	Zero	22B	5–6.5	850 ⑬
	V8–400 Cu. In., 330 H.P.	R45S	.035	28–32	.016	9B	*	Zero	Zero	30B	5–6.5	1050 ⑲
	V8–400 Cu. In., 345 H.P., Firebird Ram Air	R44S	.035	28–32	.016	9B	*	Zero	Zero	31B	5–6.5	1050 ⑲
	V8–400 Cu. In., 350 H.P.	R45S	.035	28–32	.016	9B	*	Zero	Zero	23B	5–6.5	1050 ⑲
	V8–400 Cu. In., 366 H.P., GTO Ram Air	R44S	.035	28–32	.016	9B	*	Zero	Zero	31B	5–6.5	1050 ⑲
	V8–400 Cu. In., 370 H.P., GTO Ram Air IV	R44S	.035	28–32	.016	15B	*	Zero ㉖	Zero ㉖	42B	5–6.5	1000 ⑰
	V8–455 Cu. In., 360 H.P.	R44S	.035	28–32	.016	9B	*	Zero	Zero	⑨	5–6.5	1050 ⑲
1971–1972	6 Cyl., OHV	R46TS††	.035	31–34	.016 ⑳	4B	130–140	Zero	Zero	16B	4–5	550 ㉓
	V8–307 Cu. In., 200 H.P.	R45TS††	.035	28–32	.016 ⑳	4B	150	Zero	Zero	28B	5–6.5	600 ㉔
	V8–350 Cu. In., 250 H.P.†	R47S††	.035	28–32	.016 ⑳	8B	120–160	Zero	Zero	㉑	5–6.5	800 ⑫
	V8–400 Cu. In., 265 H.P.	R47S††	.035	28–32	.016 ⑳	12B	120–160	Zero	Zero	26B	5–6.5	600 ㉕
	V8–400 Cu. In., 300 H.P.	R46S††	.035	28–32	.016 ⑳	12B	120–160	Zero	Zero	23B	5–6.5	650
	V8–455 Cu. In., 325 H.P.	R46S††	.035	28–32	.016 ⑳	12B	120–160	Zero	Zero	23B	5–6.5	600 ㉓
	V8–455 Cu. In., 335 H.P.	R46S††	.035	28–32	.016 ⑳	12B	120–160	Zero	Zero	31B	5–6.5	600 ㉕

▲—With vacuum advance disconnected. NOTE: these settings are only approximate. Engine design, altitude, temperature, fuel octane rating and the condition of the individual engine are all factors which can influence timing.

★—With manual transmission in N and automatic transmission in D. Add 50 rpm for air conditioning.

① —California A.I.R. system—600 rpm.

B—Before Top Dead Center.

TDC—Top Dead Center.

② —w/M.T.—600 rpm.

*—Lowest cylinder reading with 80% of highest.

③ —w/M.T.—700 rpm.

④ —w/M.T.—23B; w/A.T.—30B.

⑤ —6 Cyl. w/A.I.R. and A.T.—600 rpm; w/A.I.R. and M.T.—700 rpm. V8 w/A.I.R. and M.T.—700 rpm; w/A.I.R. and A.T.—600 rpm.

⑥ —6 Cyl. w/A.I.R., 1-BBL. only—TDC.

⑦ —6 Cyl., 4-BBL.—5B.

⑧ —w/M.T.—30B; w/A.T.—23B.

⑨ —w/M.T.—31B; w/A.T.—23B.

⑩ —w/M.T.—38B; w/A.T.—31B.

⑪ —6 Cyl., 4-BBL.—800 rpm; all 6 Cyl. w/A.T.—600 5 pm.

⑫ —w/A.T.—600 rpm.

⑬ —w/A.T.—650 rpm.

⑭ —6 Cyl., 4-BBL. w/A.T.—22B.

⑮ —w/M.T.—38B; w/A.T.—23B.

⑯ —6 Cyl. w/M.T. and 4-BBL.—500 rpm. All 6 Cyl. w/A.I.—500 rpm.

⑰ —w/A.T.—750 rpm.

⑱ —6 Cyl. w/M.T.—TDC @ 700 rpm. 6 Cyl. w/A.T. 4B @ 550 rpm.

⑲ —w/A.T.—675 rpm.

⑳ —.019 in. (new).

㉑ —26B w/camshaft no. 483555; 30B w/camshaft no. 9779066.

㉒ —w/A.T.—8B.

㉓ —w/A.T.—500 rpm.

㉔ —w/A.T.—550 rpm.

㉕ —w/A.T.—700 rpm.

†—Two 350 Cu. In. (250 H.P.) engines will be used in 1972. The Ventura II will use a Chevrolet 350 Cu. In. version, while Tempest, LeMans, and Firebird will use a Pontiac version.

††—1972 engines use smaller diameter spark plugs with tapered seats.

㉖ —Ram Air IV engines use limited travel hydraulic lifters. See Car Section for details.

CAUTION

General adoption of anti-pollution laws has changed the design of almost all car engine production to effectively reduce crankcase emission and terminal exhaust products. It has been necessary to adopt stricter tune-up rules, especially timing and idle speed procedures. Both of these values are peculiar to the engine and to its application, rather than to the engine alone. With this in mind, car manufacturers supply idle speed data for the engine and application involved. This information is clearly displayed in the engine compartment of each vehicle.

VALVE SPECIFICATIONS

YEAR AND MODEL	SEAT ANGLE (DEG.)	FACE ANGLE (DEG.)	VALVE LIFT INTAKE (IN.)	VALVE LIFT EXHAUST (IN.)	VALVE SPRING PRESSURE (VALVE OPEN) LBS. @ IN.	VALVE SPRING INSTALLED HEIGHT (IN.)	STEM TO GUIDE CLEARANCE (IN.) Intake	STEM TO GUIDE CLEARANCE (IN.) Exhaust	STEM DIAMETER (IN.) Intake	STEM DIAMETER (IN.) Exhaust
1965 6 Cyl.—215	46	45	.334	.334	171 @ 1.326	1 21/32	.0010–.0027	.0020–.0037	.340	.340
V8—326	①	②	.370	.406	③	1 19/32	.0021–.0038	.0026–.0043	.340	.340
V8—326 H.O.	①	②	.370	.406	④	1 19/32	.0021–.0038	.0026–.0043	.340	.340
V8—389	①	②	.406	.408	⑤	1 19/32	.0021–.0038	.0026–.0043	.340	.340
1966 6 Cyl.—230, OHC, 1-BBL.	①	②	.400	.400	192 @ 1.183	1 37/64	.0021–.0038	.0026–.0043	.340	.340
6 Cyl.—230, OHC, 4-BBL.	①	②	.438	.438	⑥	1 37/64	.0021–.0038	.0026–.0043	.340	.340
V8—326, 2-BBL.	①	②	.370	.406	③	1 19/32	.0021–.0038	.0026–.0043	.340	.340
V8—326, 4-BBL.	①	②	.370	.406	④	1 19/32	.0021–.0038	.0026–.0043	.340	.340
V8—389, 4-BBL.	①	②	.406	.408	⑤	1 19/32	.0021–.0038	.0026–.0043	.340	.340
V8—389, 3-2-BBL.	①	②	.409	.409	⑦	1 19/32	.0021–.0038	.0026–.0043	.340	.340
1967 6 Cyl.—230, OHC, 1-BBL.	①	②	.400	.400	⑨	1 37/64	.0016–.0033	.0021–.0038	.340	.340
6 Cyl.—230, OHC, 4-BBL.	①	②	.438	.438	⑩	1 37/64	.0016–.0033	.0021–.0038	.340	.340
6 Cyl.—230 (Firebird) 1-BBL.	①	②	.440	.400	⑨	1 37/64	.0016–.0033	.0021–.0038	.340	.340
6 Cyl.—230 (Firebird) 4-BBL.	①	②	.428	.438	⑩	1 37/64	.0016–.0033	.0021–.0038	.340	.340
V8—326, 2 and 4-BBL.	①	②	.375	.410	⑪	1 19/32	.0016–.0033	.0021–.0038	.340	.340
V8—400, 2-BBL., 255 H.P.	①	②	.375	.410	⑪	1 19/32	.0016–.0033	.0021–.0038	.340	.340
V8—400, 325 H.P.	①	②	.410	.413⑧	⑫	1 19/32	.0016–.0033	.0021–.0038	.340	.340
V8—400, 325 H.P. Ram Air	①	②	.413	.413	⑬	1 19/32	.0016–.0033	.0021–.0038	.340	.340
V8—400, 335 H.P.	①	②	.410	.413⑧	⑫	1 19/32	.0016–.0033	.0021–.0038	.340	.340
V8—400, 360 H.P. Ram Air	①	②	.413	.413	⑬	1 19/32	.0016–.0033	.0021–.0038	.340	.340
V8—400, 360 H.P., GTO H.O.	①	②	.414	.413	⑭	1 19/32	.0016–.0033	.0021–.0038	.340	.340
1968 6 Cyl.—250, 1-BBL., OHC	①	②	.400	.400	⑯	1.63	.0016–.0033	.0021–.0038	.3412–.3419	.3407–.3414
6 Cyl.—250, 4-BBL., OHC	①	②	.438	.438	⑰	1.63	.0016–.0033	.0021–.0038	.3412–.3419	.3407–.3414
V8—350 (265 H.P.) and V8—400 (265 H.P.)	①	②	.376	.412	⑱	1 37/64	.0016–.0033	.0021–.0038	.3412–.3419	.3407–.3414
V8—350 H.O. (320 H.P)	①	②	.410	.413⑧	⑲	1 37/64	.0016–.0033	.0021–.0038	.3412–.3419	.3407–.3414
V8—400 (330 H.P.)	①	②	.410	.413	⑳	1 9/16	.0016–.0033	.0021–.0038	.3412–.3419	.3407–.3414
V8—400 H.O. (330 and 360 H.P.)	①	②	.414⑮	.413	㉑	1 9/16	.0016–.0033	.0021–.0038	.3412–.3419	.3407–.3414
V8—400 Ram Air (335 and 360 H.P.)	①	②	.413⑧	.413	㉒	1.71	.0016–.0033	.0021–.0038	.3412–.3419	.3407–.3414
1969 6 Cyl.—250, 1-BBL., OHC	45	44	.400	.400	⑯	1.63	.0016–.0033	.0021–.0038	.3412–.3419	.3407–.3414
6 Cyl.—250, 4-BBL., OHC	45	44	.438	.438	⑰	1.63	.0016–.0033	.0021–.0038	.3412–.3419	.3407–.3414
V8—350 (265 H.P.) and V8—400 (265 H.P.)	45	44	.376	.412	⑱	1 37/64	.0016–.0033	.0021–.0038	.3412–.3419	.3407–.3414
V8—350 H.O. (335, 330 H.P.)	㉓	㉓	.414⑮	.413	㉔	1 19/32	.0016–.0033	.0021–.0038	.3412–.3419	.3407–.3414
V8—400 (330, 350 H.P.)	㉓	㉓	.410	.413	㉕	1 9/16	.0016–.0033	.0021–.0038	.3412–.3419	.3407–.3413
V8—400 (335 H.P.)	㉓	㉓	.414⑮	.413	㉖	1 19/32	.0016–.0033	.0021–.0038	.3412–.3419	.3407–.3413
V8—400 Ram Air (366 H.P.)	㉓	㉓	.414⑮	.413	㉔	1 19/32	.0016–.0033	.0021–.0038	.3412–.3419	.3407–.3414
V8—400 Ram Air IV (345, 370 H.P.)	㉓	㉓	.520	.520	㉗	1.82	.0016–.0033	.0021–.0038	.3412–.3419	.3407–.3414
1970 6 Cyl.—250, 1-BBL., OHV	46	45	.388	.388	180-192 @ 1.27	1 21/32	.0010–.0027	.0010–.0027	.3410–.3417	.3410–.3417
V8—350 (255 H.P.) and V8—400 (265 H.P.)	45	44	.376	.412	⑱	1 37/64	.0010–.0027	.0010–.0027	.3410–.3417	.3410–.3417
V8—400 (330 H.P.)	45	44	.410	.414	⑲ *	1 37/64	.0016–.0033	.0021–.0038	.3412–.3417	.3407–.3414
V8—400 Ram Air (345 H.P.)	㉓	㉓	.520	.520	㉗	1.82	.0016–.0033	.0021–.0038	.3412–.3417	.3407–.3414
V8—400 (350 H.P.)	①	②	.410	.413	㉘	1 19/32	.0016–.0033	.0021–.0038	.3412–.3417	.3407–.3414
V8—400 Ram Air (366 H.P.)	①	②	.414	.413	㉙	1 19/32	.0016–.0033	.0021–.0038	.3412–.3417	.3407–.3414
V8—400 Ram Air IV (370 H.P.)	①	②	.527	.527	㉚	1 13/16	.0016–.0033	.0021–.0038	.3412–.3417	.3407–.3414
V8—455 (360 H.P.)	①	②	.414⑮	.413	㉛	1 9/16	.0016–.0033	.0021–.0038	.3412–.3417	.3407–.3414
1971-72 6 Cyl.—250, 1-BBL., OHV	46	45	.388	.388	180-192 @ 1.27	1 21/32	.0010–.0027	.0015–.0032	.3410–.3417	.3410–.3417
V8—307 (200 H.P.)c	46	45	.260	.273	194-206 @ 1.25	1 23/32	.0010–.0027	.0012–.0029	.3410–.3417	.3410–.3417
V8—350 (250 H.P.) p	45	44	.376	.412	⑱	1 37/64	.0016–.0033	.0021–.0038	.340	.340
V8—350 (245 H.P.) c	46	45	.260	.273	194-206 @ 1.25	1 23/64	.0010–.0027	.0012–.0029	.3410–.3417	.3410–.3417
V8—400 (265 H.P.)	45	44	.376	.412	⑱	1 37/64	.0016–.0033	.0021–.0038	.340	.340
V8—400 (300 H.P.)	①	②	.410	.413	⑲ *	1 37/64	.0016–.0033	.0021–.0038	.340	.340
V8—455 (325 H.P.)	①	②	.410	.413	⑲	1 37/64	.0016–.0033	.0021–.0038	.340	.340
V8—455 (335 H.P.)	①	②	.414	.413	㉕	1 19/32	.0016–.0033	.0021–.0038	.340	.340

(See footnotes on next page)

CAPACITIES

YEAR	MODEL	ENGINE CRANKCASE ADD 1 Qt. FOR NEW FILTER	TRANSMISSIONS Pts. TO REFILL AFTER DRAINING			DRIVE AXLE (Pts.)	GASOLINE TANK (Gals.)	COOLING SYSTEM (Qts.) WITH HEATER
			Manual		Automatic			
			3-Speed	4-Speed				
1965	6 Cyl.—215 Cu. In.	4.0	3.0	3.75	15.0	3.0	21.5	13.5
	V8—326 Cu. In.	5.0	3.0	3.75	15.0	3.0	21.5	20.5
	V8—389 Cu. In.	5.0	3.0	3.75	15.0	3.0	21.5	20.5
1966	6 Cyl.—230 Cu. In.	5.0	2.8	2.5	15.0	3.0	21.5	13.5
	V8—326 Cu. In.	5.0	2.8	2.5	15.0	3.0	21.5	20.5
	V8—389 Cu. In.	5.0	2.8	2.5	15.0	3.0	21.5	20.0
1967	6 Cyl.—230 Cu. In.	5.0	2.8	2.5	15.0	3.0	21.5●	12.7
	V8—326 Cu. In.	5.0	2.8	2.5	15.0	3.0	21.5●	18.6
	V8—400 Cu. In.	6.0	2.8	2.5	19.0	3.0	21.5●	17.8
1968	6 Cyl.—250 Cu. In.	5.0	3.5	3.5	15.0	3.0	21.5●	12.1
	V8—350 Cu. In.	5.0	3.5■	2.5	15.0	3.0	21.5●	18.6
	V8—400 Cu. In.	5.0	2.8	2.5	19.0①	3.0	21.5●	17.8
1969	6 Cyl.—250 Cu. In.	4.5	3.5	3.5	15.0	3.0	21.5●	12.0
	V8—350 Cu. In.	5.0	3.5■	2.5	15.0	3.0	21.5●	19.5
	V8—400 Cu. In.	5.0	2.8	2.5	19.0①	3.0	21.5●	18.5
1970-72	6 Cyl.—250 Cu. In.	4.0	3.5③	...	20.0	3.0②	21.5●●	12.4
	V8—307 Cu. In.	4.0	3.5	—	20.0	3.5	18.0	15.5
	V8—350 Cu. In.	5.0	3.5	2.5	19.25④	3.0②	21.5●●	19.5
	V8—400 Cu. In.	5.0	2.8	2.5	19.0	3.0②	21.5●●	18.6
	V8—455 Cu. In.	5.0	2.8	2.5	19.0	3.0②	21.5	18.0

■—Lemans, 2¾ Pts.
●—Firebird, Gasoline Tank—18.5 Gal.
①—"350" Trans.-20
②—5 Pts. w/8.875 in ring gear; 4.25 on Firebird
●●—Firebird, Gasoline Tank—17.0 gal.
③—Saginaw 3-spd; 3-spd. Muncie-2.8.
④—6 Cyl.—21.0.

(Footnotes for Valve Specifications Chart on previous page)

① —Intake—30°; Exhaust—45°.
② —Intake—29°; Exhaust—44°.
③ —Intake: Inner—57-64 @ 1.196; Outer—106-114 @ 1.216.
　 Exhaust: Inner—60-67 @ 1.160; Outer—111-119 @ 1.180.
④ —Intake: Inner—86-93 @ 1.196; Outer—121-131 @ 1.216.
　 Exhaust: Inner—92-98 @ 1.160; Outer—127-137 @ 1.180.
⑤ —Intake: Inner—92-98 @ 1.160; Outer—127-137 @ 1.180.
　 Exhaust: Inner—92-98 @ 1.158; Outer—127-138 @ 1.178.
⑥ —Intake and Exhaust: Inner—101-108 @ 1.123; Outer—132-142 @ 1.143.
⑦ —w/M.T.—Intake: Inner—110-120 @ 1.16; Outer—128-138 @ 1.177.
　　　Exhaust: Inner—110-120 @ 1.157; Outer—128-138 @ 1.177.
　 w/A.T.—Intake: Inner—92-99 @ 1.157; Outer—128-138 @ 1.177.
　　　Exhaust: Inner—92-99 @ 1.157; Outer—128-138 @ 1.177.
⑧ —.414 in. w/A.T.
⑨ —Intake and Exhaust: Outer—184-200 @ 1.183.
⑩ —Intake and Exhaust: Inner—87-93 @ 1.191; Outer—122-132 @ 1.211.
⑪ —Intake: Inner—87-93 @ 1.191; Outer—122-132 @ 1.211.
　 Exhaust: Inner—93-99 @ 1.156; Outer—128-138 @ 1.176.
⑫ —w/M.T.—Intake and Exhaust: Inner—93-99 @ 1.156; Outer—128-138 @ 1.176.
　 w/A.T.—Intake and Exhaust: Inner—93-99 @ 1.152; Outer—128-138 @ 1.176.
⑬ —Intake and Exhaust: Outer—231-247 @ 1.173.
⑭ —w/M.T.—Intake: Inner—111-121 @ 128-138 @ 1.172.
　　　Exhaust: Inner—111-121 @ 1.153; Outer—128-138 @ 1.173.
　 w/A.T.—Intake: Inner—93-99 @ 1.152; Outer—128-138 @ 1.172.
　　　Exhaust: Inner—93-99 @ 1.153; Outer—128-138 @ 1.173.
⑮ —.410 in. w/A.T.
⑯ —Intake and Exhaust: Outer—166-176 @ 1.23.
⑰ —Intake: Inner—59-65 @ 1.152; Outer—116-128 @ 1.20.
　 Exhaust: Inner—59-65 @ 1.16; Outer—116-128 @ 1.20.
⑱ —Intake: Inner—89-99 @ 1.17; Outer—123-133 @ 1.21.
　 Exhaust: Inner—94-104 @ 1/13; Outer—129-139 @ 1.17.
⑲ —w/M.T.—Intake: Inner—94-104 @ 1.132; Outer—128-138 @ 1.17.
　　　Exhaust: Inner—95-105 @ 1.129; Outer—129-139 @ 1.17.

　 w/A.T.—Intake: Inner—94-104 @ 1.13; Outer—128-138 @ 1.17.
　　　Exhaust: Inner—95-105 @ 1.13; Outer—129-139 @ 1.17.
⑳ —w/M.T.—Intake: Inner—118-128 @ 1.112; Outer—132-142 @ 1.151.
　　　Exhaust: Inner—118-128 @ 1.108; Outer—132-142 @ 1.148.
　 w/A.T.—Intake: Inner—97-107 @ 1.112; Outer—132-142 @ 1.151.
　　　Exhaust: Inner—98-108 @ 1.108; Outer—132-142 @ 1.148.
㉑ —w/M.T.—Intake: Inner—119-129 @ 1.107; Outer—133-143 @ 1.147.
　　　Exhaust: Inner—118-128 @ 1.108; Outer—132-142 @ 1.148.
　 w/A.T.—Intake: Inner—97-107 @ 1.112; Outer—132-142 @ 1.151.
　　　Exhaust: Inner—98-108 @ 1.108; Outer—133-143 @ 1.148.
㉒ —w/M.T.—Intake and Exhaust: Inner—88-98 @ 1.23; Outer—182-198 @ 1.30.
　 w/A.T.—Intake: Inner—88-98 @ 1.228; Outer—183-199 @ 1.298.
　　　Exhaust: Inner—88-98 @ 1.229; Outer—182-198 @ 1.229.
㉓ —Intake—29° Seat, 30° Face; Exhaust—45° Seat, 44° Face.
㉔ —w/M.T.—Intake: Inner—96-106 @ 1.107; Outer—193-207 @ 1.177.
　 w/A.T.—Intake: Inner—96-106 @ 1.11; Outer—192-206 @ 1.178.
　 w/A.T., M.T.—Exhaust: Inner—96-106 @ 1.108; Outer—192-206 @ 1.178.
㉕ —Intake: Inner—98-108 @ 1.111; Outer—132-142 @ 1.151.
　 Exhaust: Inner—98-108 @ 1.108; Outer—133-143 @ 1.148.
㉖ —w/M.T.—Intake and Exhaust: Inner—96-106 @ 1.10; Outer—193-207 @ 1.177.
　 w/A.T.—Intake: Inner 97-107 @ 1.111; Outer—132-143 @ 1.151.
　　　Exhaust: Inner—98-108 @ 1.108; Outer—133-143 @ 1.148.
㉗ —Intake and Exhaust: Inner—105-115 @ 1.23; Outer—214-228 @ 1.30.
㉘ —Intake: Inner—118-128 @ 1.11; Outer—125-139 @ 1.18.
　 Exhaust: Inner—118-128 @ 1.108; Outer—125-139 @ 1.18.
* —w/A.T. only.
㉙ —Intake and Exhaust: Inner—119-129 @ 1.107; Outer—126-140 @ 1.177.
㉚ —Intake and Exhaust: Inner—106-116 @ 1.22; Outer—216-230 @ 1.29.
㉛ —w/M.T.—Intake: Inner—98-108 @ 1.107; Outer—133-143 @ 1.147.
　 w/A.T.—Intake: Inner—97-107 @ 1.111; Outer—132-142 @ 1.151.
　 w/M.T., A.T.—Exhaust: Inner—98-108 @ 1.108; Outer—133-143 @ 1.148.
p—Pontiac Engine
c—Chevrolet engine in 1972 Ventura II

AC GENERATOR AND REGULATOR SPECIFICATIONS

| YEAR | ALTERNATOR | | | REGULATOR | | | | | | |
| | Part Number | Field Current Draw @ 12 V. | Output at Generator RPM 5000 | Field Relay | | | | Regulator | | |
				Part Number	Air Gap (In.)	Point Gap (In.)	Volts to Close	Air Gap (In.)	Point Gap (In.)	Volts at 125°
1965	1100714	2.2–2.6	37	1119515	.015	.030	1.5–3.2	.067	.014	13.5–14.4
	1100716									
	1100729									
	1100701		55							
	1100707									
	1100728									
	1100726									
	1100727		42							
	1100702①	4.0–4.5	60	1116366	. . .	. . .	. . .	. . .	. . .	13.4–14.1
	1100703①									
1966	1100761	2.2–2.6	37	1119515	.015	.030	1.5–3.2	.067	.014	13.5–14.4
	1100704									
	1100760		55							
	1100700									
	1100741①	4.0–4.5	60	1116368	. . .	. . .	. . .	. . .	. . .	13.4–14.1
	1100702①									
1967–69	1100761	2.2–2.6*	37	1119515②	. . .	. . .	. . .	. . .	. . .	13.5–16.0
	1100704									
	1100832③									
	1100830③		55							
	1100700									
	1100760									
1970	1100704	2.2–2.6	37	1119515	. . .	. . .	. . .	. . .	. . .	13.5–16.0
	1100888									
	1100905									
	1100700		55							
	1100891									
	1100892									
	1100906									
	1100895		61							
1971–72	1100550	4.0–4.5	37	1119515	. . .	. . .	. . .	. . .	. . .	13.8–14.8
	1100920									
	1100927									
	1100566④									
	1100836④									
	1100920		55							
	1100928									
	1100843④		61							
	11001015		80							

① —w/Transistor ignition.

② —Transistor regulator 1116368 optional equipment until 1968.

③ —Integrated Circuit Generator (C.S.I.—no external regulator) optional on 1969 Firebird.

*—4.0–4.5 on alternator no.'s 1100832 and 1100830.

④ —Used only on Ventura II.

GENERAL CHASSIS AND BRAKE SPECIFICATIONS

YEAR	MODEL	CHASSIS			BRAKE CYLINDER BORE			BRAKE DRUM	
		Overall Length (In.)	Tire Size	Master Cylinder Bore (In.)	Wheel Cylinder Diameter (In.)			Diameter (In.)	
					Front	Rear		Front	Rear
1965	All Exc. Safari & GTO	206.1	6.95 x 14 ▲	1.0	1.125	.9375		9.5	9.5
	Safari	204.4	7.35 x 14 ■	1.0	1.125	.9375		9.5	9.5
	GTO	206.1	7.75 x 14	1.0	1.125	.9375		9.5	9.5
1966	All Exc. Sta. Wag. & G.T.O.	206.4	6.95 x 14	.875	1.125	.9375		9.5	9.5
	Station Wagon	203.6	7.75 x 14	.875	1.125	.9375		9.5	9.5
	G.T.O.	206.4	7.75 x 14	.875	1.125	.9375		9.5	9.5
1967	All Exc. Sta. Wag. & G.T.O.	206.6	7.75 x 14	1.0	1.125	.875		9.5	9.5
	Station Wagon	203.4	7.75 x 14	1.0	1.125	.875		9.5	9.5
	G.T.O.	206.6	F-70 x 14	1.125 ●	2.6875 ●	.875		11.0 ●	9.5
	Firebird	188.8	E-70 x 14	1.0	1.125	.875		9.5	9.5
1968	Tempest, Custom, LeMans	204.7	8.25 x 14*	1.0	1.125	.875		9.5	9.5
	Safari Wagon	211.0	8.25 x 14*	1.0	1.125	.875		9.5	9.5
	GTO	200.7	G-70 x 14	1.0	1.125	.875		9.5	9.5
	Firebird	188.8	F-70 x 14*	1.0	1.125	.875		9.5	9.5
	All w/Disc Brakes	—	—	1.125	2.0625	.875		11.12	9.5
1969	Tempest, Custom, LeMans	205.5	8.25 x 14*	1.0	1.125	.875		9.5	9.5
	Safari Wagon	211.0	8.25 x 14*	1.0	1.125	.875		9.5	9.5
	GTO	201.2	G-70 x 14	1.0	1.125	.875		9.5	9.5
	Firebird	191.1	F-70 x 14*	1.0	1.125	.875		9.5	9.5
	All w/Disc Brakes	—	—	1.125	2.9375	.875		10.94	9.5
1970	Tempest, Custom, LeMans	205.5	8.25 x 14*	1.0	1.125	.875		9.5	9.5
	Safari Wagon	210.6	8.25 x 14*	1.0	1.125	.875		9.5	9.5
	GTO, Judge	201.2	G-70 x 14	1.0	1.125	.875		9.5	9.5
	Firebird, Trans Am	192.6	E-70 x 14*	1.125 ●	2.0625 ●	.875		11.0 ●	9.5
	All w/Disc Brakes	—	—	1.125	2.9375	.875		11.0	9.5
1971–72	Tempest, Custom, LeMans	206.8 ■	E78 x 14 ▲	1.0	1.125	.875		9.5	9.5
	Safari Wagon	210.9	H78 x 14	1.0	1.125	.875		9.5	9.5
	GTO, Judge	203.3	G70 x 14	1.0	1.125	.875		9.5	9.5
	Firebird, Trans Am	191.6	E78 x 14†	1.0	1.125	.875		9.5	9.5
	Ventura II	194.5	E78 x 14	1.0	1.125	.875		9.5	9.5
	All w/Disc Brakes	—	—	1.125	2.9375	.875		10.94	9.5

■ —202.8 on 2-dr models.
▲ —Le Mans, Lemans Sport—F78 x 14; G78 x 14 std. on V8 models w/AC.
† —F60 x 15 bias belted std. on Trans Am

● —Disc Brakes.
* —Tempest 6 Cyl.—7.75 x 14.
Firebird 6 Cyl. 1-BBL. E-70 x 14.

LIGHT BULBS

1965	1966	1967	1968	1969	1970	1971-72	
			Bulb Number (Quantity)				
1445(1)	1445(1)	1445(1)	1445(1)	1445	—	—	Ash tray
1156(2)	1156(2)	1156(2)	1156	1156	1156▲	1156■■	Back-up
1895(2)	1895(2)	1895(2)	1895	1895	1895	1895	Clock
—	—	1895(1)	1895	1895	—	—	Console compartment
—	—	—	—	—	—	—	Cornering
1899(1)	1899(1)	89(1)	89	89	89	89★	Courtesy
68(2)	68(2)	89(1)	89(1)	89(1)	89	89	Courtesy (console)
211(1)	211(1)	211(1)	211(1)	211(1)	211-1	211-1	Dome
1891(1)	1891(1)		—	—	—	—	Glove compartment
4001(2)	4001(2)	Type 2(2)	Type 2(2)	Type 2(2)	Type 2(2)	Type 2▲▲	Headlamp (high beam)
4002(2)	4002(2)	Type 1(2)	Type 1(2)	Type 1(2)	Type 1(2)	Type 1▲▲	Headlamp (low beam)
1895(1)	1895(1)	1445(2)	1445	1445	1895	1895	Heater/air conditioner
1895	1895	1891	1891	1891	1895	1895†	Instrument cluster
1895	1895	—	—	—	—	—	Instrument floodlight
67(1)	67(1)	67(1)	67(1)	67(1)	67	67	License
—	—	—	—	—	1004	—	Map
1157A(2)	1157A(2)	1157A(2)	1157A	1157A	1157	1157	Parking
1895(1)	1895(1)	1895	1895	1895	1895	1895■	Radio
—	—	—	—	—	—	—	Rear quarter
—	—	—	—	—	—	—	Rear window defogger
1445(1)	1445(1)	1445	1445	1893	1893	1893	Shift quadrant (column)
—	—	1445	1445	1445	1445	1445	Shift quadrant (console)
—	—	—	1895	194A	194A	194A	Side marker (front)
—	—	—	1893●	194A	194	194	Side marker (rear)
1157	1157	1157	1157	1157	1157	1157	Stop
1157(2)	1157(2)	1157	1157	1157	1157	1157	Tail
1003(1)	1003(1)	89	89	89	1003●●	1003●●	Trunk
1157A(2)	1157A(2)	1157A(2)	1157	1157	1157	1157	Turn signal
93(1)	93(1)	93	1003	1003	1003	1003	Underhood
1895	1895	1895	194	194	194	194	Warning (dash lights)
4404(1)	4404(1)	4404(1)	—	—	—	—	Spot light
1445(1)	1445(1)	1445(1)	—	—	1445	1445	Cigarette lighter light
1895	1895	194(2)	194	194	194	194	Turn signal indicator
—	—	1895	194	194	194	194	Ignition lock
194	194	194	194	194	194	194	Tachometer

●—Firebird—1895
●●—Tempest—89
▲—Firebird—1157
▲▲—Ventura II—6014

■—Ventura II—293
■■—Ventura II—1157
★—Ventura II—211
†—Ventura II, console cluster—1816.

FUSES AND CIRCUIT BREAKERS

	1965	1966	1967	1968	1969	1970	1971-72
			Fuse Type — Amperage				
A/C controls lamp	AGC-4	AGC-4	AGC-4	AGC-4	AGC-4	SFE-4	SFE-4
A/C power, blower motor	AGA-20	AGA-20	AGC-30	AGC-30	AGC-30	AGC-30	AGC-30
Ash tray lamps	AGC-4	AGC-4	AGC-4	AGC-4	AGC-4	SFE-4	SFE-4
Back-up lamps	AGC-20	AGC-20	SFE-20	SFE-20	SFE-20	SFE-20	SFE-20
Cigarette lighter	AGC-20	AGC-20	SFE-20	SFE-20	SFE-20	SFE-20	SFE-20
Cigarette lighter lamp	...	...	AGC-4	AGC-4	AGC-4	SFE-4	SFE-4
Clock lamp	AGC-4	AGC-4	AGC-4	AGC-4	AGC-4	SFE-4	SFE-4
Clock power	AGC-20	AGC-20	SFE-20	SFE-20	SFE-20	SFE-20	SFE-20
Console comp. lamp	AGC-20	AGC-20	SFE-20	SFE-20	SFE-20	...	...
Console courtesy lamp	AGC-20	AGC-20	SFE-20	SFE-20	SFE-20	...	...
Cruise control	AGC-20	AGC-20	SFE-20	SFE-20	SFE-20	AGC-10	AGC-10
Turn signals	AGC-15	AGC-20	AGC-10	SFE-20	SFE-20	SFE-20	SFE-20
Dome light	AGC-10	AGC-20	SFE-20	SFE-20	SFE-20	SFE-20	SFE-20
Downshift switch	...	...	SFE-20	AGC-10	AGC-10	...	...
Heater controls lamp	AGC-4	AGC-4	AGC-4	AGC-4	AGC-4	SFE-4	SFE-4
Heater blower motor	AGA-20	AGC-20	SFE-20	AGC-25	AGC-25	AGC-25	AGC-25
Instrument lamps	AGC-4	AGC-4	AGC-4	AGC-4	AGC-4	SFE-4	SFE-4
Instrument panel lamp	AGC-20	AGC-20	SFE-20	SFE-20	SFE-20	SFE-20	SFE-20
Instrument panel courtesy lamp	AGC-20	AGC-20	SFE-20	SFE-20	SFE-20	SFE-20	SFE-20
License lamp	AGC-10	AGC-20	SFE-20	SFE-20	SFE-20	SFE-20	SFE-20
Trunk lamp	AGC-10	AGC-10	SFE-20	SFE-20	SFE-20	SFE-20	SFE-20
Brake warning lamp	AGA-20	AGC-20	SFE-20	SFE-20	SFE-20	AGC-10	AGC-10
Power antenna	AGA-20	AGC-20	SFE-20	SFE-20	SFE-20	...	...
Power seat C.B.	40	40	40	40	40	40	40
Power tail gate window C.B.	40	40	40	40	40	40	40
Power windows C.B.	40	40	40	40	40	40	40
Radio lamp	AGC-4	AGC-4	AGC-4	AGC-4	AGC-4	SFE-4	SFE-4
Radio power	AGW-2.5	AGW-2.5	AGC-10	AGC-10	AGC-10	AGC-10	AGC-10
Rear window defogger	AGA-20	AGA-20	SFE-20	SFE-20	SFE-20	AGC-25	AGC-25
Speedometer safeguard	...	...	SFE-20	SFE-20	SFE-20	AGC-25	AGC-25
Shift quadrant lamp	AGC-4	AGC-4	AGC-4	AGC-4	AGC-4	SFE-4	SFE-4
Spot lamp	AGC-20	AGC-20	SFE-20	...	...	...	...
Stop lamp	AGC-15	AGC-15	SFE-20	SFE-20	SFE-20	SFE-20	SFE-20
Tachometer	IAG-1	IAG-1	AGC-4	AGC-4	AGC-4	SFE-4	SFE-4
Tail lamps	AGC-10	AGC-10	SFE-20	SFE-20	SFE-20	SFE-20	SFE-20
Underhood lamp	AGC-20	AGC-20	SFE-20	SFE-20	SFE-20	SFE-20	SFE-20
Windshield washer pump, motor	AGC-20	AGC-20	SFE-20	AGC-25	AGC-25	AGC-25	AGC-25

C.B. — Circuit breaker.

Distributor

Removal

1. Disconnect distributor primary the distributor is removed from wire.
2. Remove distributor cap. (Unlatch the cap by using a screwdriver to disengage the latches.)
3. Crank engine so the rotor is in No. 1 position and the crankshaft pulley timing mark in line with the pointer.
4. Disconect vacuum line at distributor.
5. Remove distributor clamp screw and hold-down clamp.
6. Lift out distributor and distributor-to-block gasket. Notice the slight rotation of the rotor as the block.

Installation—If Engine Has Been Disturbed

1. With No. 1 piston coming up on compression stroke, continue cranking the engine until the pulley timing mark indexes with the stationary mark.
2. Position the distributor to the opening in the block with reference to the firing order sequence shown in the firing order illustrations of this section.
3. Point the rotor toward distributor cap No. 1 tower location. Then, slightly retard the distributor rotor position.
4. Press down on distributor housing until seated, clamp unit in place.
5. Check initial timing centrifugal and vacuum advance characteristics and engine vacuum.

Transistor Ignition

This system consists of a special distributor, an ignition pulse amplifier, and a special ignition coil. The distributor is similar in external appearance to the standard V8 distributor, but the internal construction bears little resemblance to the contact-point unit. An iron timer core replaces the breaker cam. This eight-lobed timer rotates inside a magnetic pick-up assembly, which replaces the contact points and condenser. The magnetic pick-up assembly consists of a ceramic permanent magnet, a steel pole piece, and a pick-up coil.

The magnetic pick-up assembly is mounted over the distributor shaft bearing, and is rotated by the vacuum advance unit to provide automatic spark advance. Centrifugal advance is provided by the rotating timer core, which is attached to normal advance weights. Troubleshooting is found in the Unit Repair Section.

Removal

1. Disconnect pick-up coil connector.
2. Remove distributor cap.
3. Crank engine so that rotor points to No. 1 cylinder plug tower and timing mark on crankshaft pulley is indexed with pointer.
4. Remove distributor vacuum line.
5. Remove distributor hold-down bolt and clamp, then remove dis-

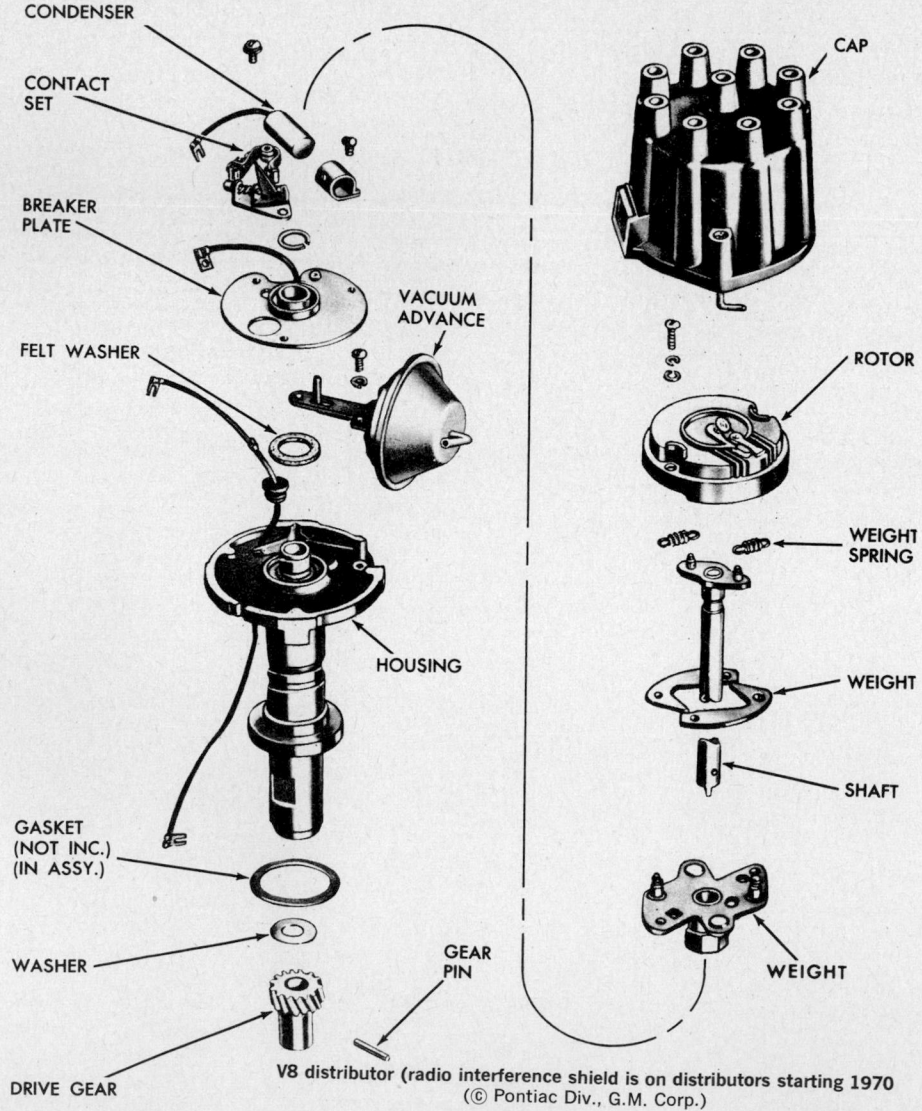

CONDENSER

CONTACT SET

BREAKER PLATE

FELT WASHER

VACUUM ADVANCE

HOUSING

GASKET (NOT INC.) (IN ASSY.)

WASHER

DRIVE GEAR

GEAR PIN

CAP

ROTOR

WEIGHT SPRING

WEIGHT

SHAFT

WEIGHT

V8 distributor (radio interference shield is on distributors starting 1970
(© Pontiac Div., G.M. Corp.)

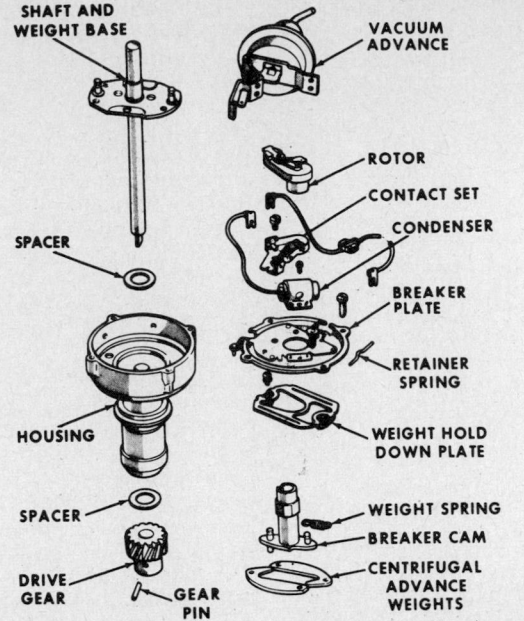

Six-cylinder distributor
(© Pontiac Div. G.M. Corp.)

Labels: SHAFT AND WEIGHT BASE, VACUUM ADVANCE, ROTOR, CONTACT SET, CONDENSER, BREAKER PLATE, RETAINER SPRING, WEIGHT HOLD DOWN PLATE, WEIGHT SPRING, BREAKER CAM, CENTRIFUGAL ADVANCE WEIGHTS, SPACER, HOUSING, SPACER, DRIVE GEAR, GEAR PIN

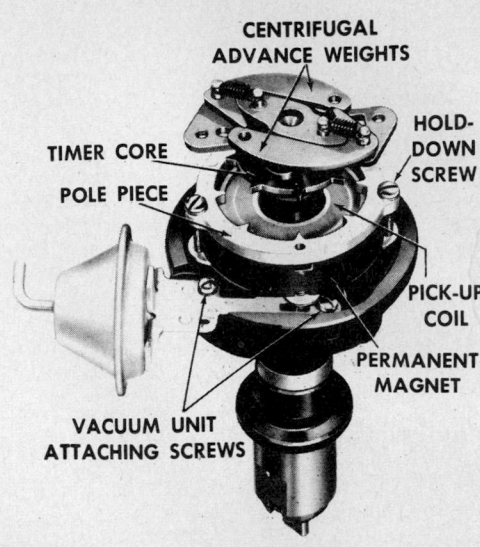

Transistor ignition distributor
(© Pontiac Div. G.M. Corp.)

Labels: CENTRIFUGAL ADVANCE WEIGHTS, HOLD-DOWN SCREW, TIMER CORE, POLE PIECE, PICK-UP COIL, PERMANENT MAGNET, VACUUM UNIT ATTACHING SCREWS

tributor.

Disassembly

1. Remove rotor.
2. Remove centrifugal weight springs.
3. Remove weights.
4. Remove roll pin, drive gear and washer.
5. Remove drive shaft.
6. Remove weight support and timer core from drive shaft.
7. Remove magnetic core assembly.
8. Disengage leads from primary connector.
9. Remove coil assembly.
10. Remove magnetic core support plate retaining ring; remove plate.
11. Remove felt and brass washer, then remove vacuum advance unit.

AC Generator (Delcotron)

An alternating current generator is used. This unit is the Delco-Remy, Delcotron or Transistor C.S.I. unit. The purpose of this unit is to satisfy the increase in electrical loads that have been imposed upon the car battery by modern conditions of traffic and driving patterns.

These charging systems are covered in the Unit Repair Section of this manual.

Caution Since the Delcotron and regulator are designed for use on only one polarity system, the following precautions must be observed:

1. The polarity of the battery, generator and regulator must be considered before making any electrical connections with the system.
2. When connecting a booster battery, be sure to connect the negative battery terminals respectively, and the positive battery terminals respectively.
3. When connecting a charger to the battery, connect the charger positive lead to the battery positive terminal. Connect the charger negative lead to the battery negative terminal.
4. Never operate the Delcotron on open circuit. Be sure that all connections in the circuit are clean and tight.
5. Do not short across or ground any of the terminals on the Delcotron regulator.
6. Do not attempt to polarize the Delcotron.
7. Do not use test lamps of more than 12 volts for checking diode continuity.
8. Avoid long soldering times when replacing diodes or transistors. Prolonged heat is damaging to these units.
9. Disconnect the battery ground terminal when servicing any AC system. This will prevent the possibility of accidental reversal of polarity.

Alternator R & R—1965-72

1. Disconnect positive battery cable.
2. Remove alternator wires or connector.
3. Loosen adjusting bolt.
4. Remove V-belt. On power steering six, loosen A. I. R. pump.
5. Remove alternator retaining bolts or thru bolt.
6. Remove alternator.
7. To install, reverse removal procedure. Tighten bracket bolt on non-A/C cars to 10-25 ft. lbs., all other bolts to 25-35 ft. lbs.

Battery, Starter

Battery

A Delco 12 volt battery is used in all models.

Starter

The starter circuit consists of the battery, battery cables, starting motor, starter motor solenoid switch, ignition-starter switch and the neutral safety switch, (used on cars with automatic transmission).

The starting motor and solenoid assembly is mounted on the flywheel housing.

The solenoid switch closes the circuit between the battery and the starting motor. It also operates the shift lever that moves the drive pinion into mesh with the flywheel ring gear.

Starter Removal—Six

1. Disconnect positive battery cable.
2. Disconnect solenoid wires.
3. Disconnect starter brace, if so equipped.
4. Remove starter-to-engine bolts and starter.

Starter Removal—V8

1. Jack up car and support on axle stands.
2. Follow Steps 1-4 of six-cylinder procedure, working from underneath car.

Instruments

The instrument cluster includes the speedometer head, the generator charge indicator, the oil pressure indicator and the temperature indicator. Also, the fuel gauge, light switch, wiper and washer switch, starter and ignition switch and the cigarette lighter.

Cluster Removal and Installation

1965 Tempest

1. Disconnect battery.
2. Remove upper retaining nuts.
3. Remove screws at lower edge of cluster.
4. Remove screws from lower steering column bezel.
5. Disconnect speedometer cable.
6. Pull cluster and housing out from instrument panel to gain access to wiring.
7. Starting at the top, remove bulbs and wiring.
8. Remove screws holding cluster to housing and remove the cluster.
9. To install, reverse above procedure.

1966-68 Tempest

1. Disconnect battery.
2. Remove screws holding bezel and cluster assembly to instrument panel.
3. Remove speedometer cable.
4. Disconnect heater control cables.
5. Lower steering column by removing trim plate and loosening nuts on column bracket.
6. Pull cluster and bezel away from instrument panel to gain access to wiring and other connections.
7. Remove bulbs, wiring and other connections, as necessary.
8. Remove screws holding the cluster to the bezel. Remove cluster.
9. Install by reversing removal procedure.

1969-70 Tempest

1. Disconnect battery.
2. Remove glove compartment and, on 1970 models, lower panel trim.
3. Disconnect speedometer cable, wire connectors at headlight switch, wipers, turn signals, ignition switch, heater, air conditioner, and printed circuit board.

4. Remove lower column trim and disconnect heater cable; remove lower air conditioner duct, if necessary.
5. Lower steering column.
6. Remove three instrument panel screws at gauge clusters.
7. Remove three upper right instrument panel nuts.
8. Remove ground strap retaining screws, if present, then disconnect harness conduit.
9. Remove cluster retaining screws, then cluster.
10. To install, reverse removal procedure.
NOTE: it may be necessary to shift the instrument panel around to gain access to some wiring.

1971-72 Tempest and GTO

1. Disconnect battery cable and remove lower A/C duct, if so equipped.
2. Remove lower instrument panel trim and glove box.
3. Lower steering column.
4. Disconnect speedometer cable and heater cable (at case).
5. Remove three instrument panel screws at gauges and three nuts at upper right.
6. Remove lower instrument panel bolts at right and left of column.
7. Pull crash pad away from column, then disconnect printed circuit.
8. Remove harness retaining screws, cluster screws and cluster.
9. To install, reverse removal procedure.

1967-69 Firebird

1. Disconnect battery.
2. Remove lower instrument panel cover.
3. Remove ashtray bracket screws, radio retaining nuts, and glove compartment.
4. Disconnect heater control cables and wires.
5. Disconnect speedometer cable, then remove upper left-hand vent duct connector.
6. Disconnect headlight switch shaft.
7. Remove screws across top and bottom of instrument panel and the nut on the right-hand side (stud through dash).
8. Loosen toe plate screws, remove lower column support nuts, and drop steering column.
9. Pull panel out far enough to reach behind it, then disconnect printed circuit board, windshield wipers, and cigarette lighter.
10. Remove ground straps and cluster retaining screws.
11. Carefully remove cluster.
12. To install, reverse removal procedure, making sure steering column is properly aligned.

1970-72 Firebird

1. Disconnect battery and remove upper instrument panel trim plate.
2. Remove lower instrument panel trim and bracket at column.
3. Loosen two steering column nuts and lower column.
4. Remove cluster screws, pull out cluster, and disconnect speedometer cable and wiring for printed circuit.
5. To install, reverse removal procedure.

1971-72 Ventura II

1. Disconnect battery cable and remove steering column cover trim.
2. Remove three screws that retain heater or A/C control to panel.
3. Remove radio control knobs, bezels and nuts.
4. Remove screws at top, bottom and side of carrier (where it is secured to instrument panel pad).
5. Disconnect shift indicator cable at shift bowl, then remove two steering column to instrument panel nuts.
6. Remove toe plate cover and five toe plate-to-cowl screws, lower steering column from panel and protect it with a towel.
7. Remove ground wire screw under left side of pad, above kickpad, then disconnect speedometer cable.
8. Tilt cluster and carrier to the rear, disconnect printed circuit and ground connections and allow assembly to rest on column.
9. Remove cluster screws and cluster from carrier.
10. To install, reverse removal procedure.
NOTE: a mandatory column alignment procedure must be followed to ensure integrity of collapsible column. See the procedure for the 1971 Nova in this manual; columns are similar.

Ignition Switch R & R—1965-68

1. Remove switch from the dash by unscrewing the switch ferrule with a special spanner wrench, tool J-5893-A.
2. Remove switch from back of instrument panel and disconnect wires.
3. Replace switch by reversing above method.

Ignition Switch R & R—1969-72

The ignition and steering wheel locking switch is located just below the gear selector lever on the steering column.

1. Disconnect battery.

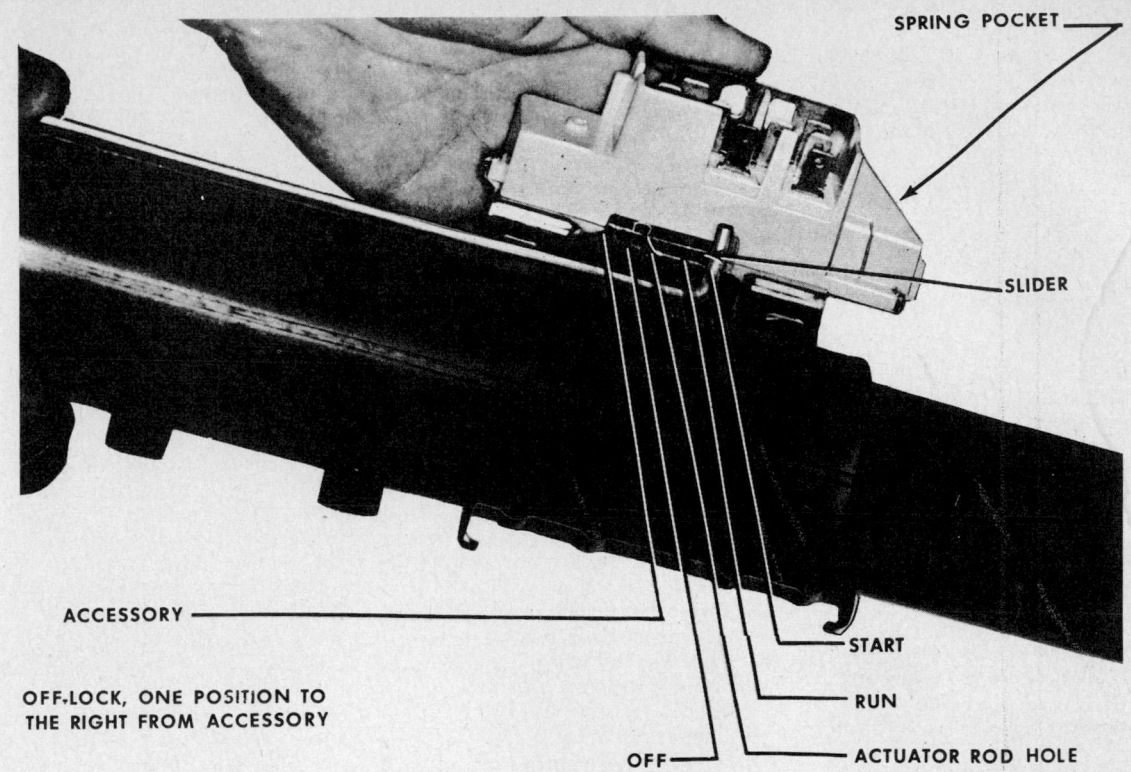

SPRING POCKET

SLIDER

ACCESSORY

OFF-LOCK, ONE POSITION TO
THE RIGHT FROM ACCESSORY

START

RUN

OFF

ACTUATOR ROD HOLE

1969-72 ignition lock switch (© Pontiac Div. G.M. Corp.)

2. Loosen toe pan screws.
3. Remove column to panel nuts, lower steering column, and disconnect switch wire connectors.
4. Remove switch attaching screws and switch.
5. To install, move key lock to OFF-LOCK position.

6. Move actuator rod hole in switch to OFF-LOCK position.
7. Install switch, with rod in hole, then reverse removal procedure.

Switch Adjustment—Standard Column

1. Place switch in OFF position.

2. Position switch on column, then move slider to extreme left (toward wheel).
3. Move slider back two positions to the right of ACCESSORY position.
4. Place key in any run position and shift transmission into any position but Park for automatics or Reverse for manual.
5. Position lock toward ACCESSORY with a light finger pressure and secure switch.

Switch Adjustment—Tilt Column

1. Place key in ACCESSORY position; leave key in lock.
2. Loosen switch mounting screws.
3. Push switch upward toward wheel to make certain it is in ACCESSORY detent.
4. Hold key in full counter clockwise ACCESSORY position and tighten switch mounting screws.
5. Switch is properly adjusted if: it will go into ACCESSORY position, the key can be removed when in lock, and switch will go into START position.

Lock Cylinder Replacement —1965-68

1. Disconnect battery, then insert key.
2. Remove lock cylinder by placing in off position and inserting wire into small hole in cylinder face. While pushing in on wire, continue to turn cylinder counterclockwise, then pull cylinder from case.

Spring Pocket

Actuator Rod Hole

Slider

Accessory
**Off-Lock, One position to the
left from accessory**

Off
Run
Start

Adjusting ignition switch—1969-72 tilt column (© Pontiac Div. G.M. Corp.)

Lock Cylinder Replacement
—1969-72
1. Remove steering wheel.
2. Pull turn signal switch up far enough to allow access to spring latch slot.
3. Place key in RUN position, insert a thin screwdriver into the slot next to the switch mounting screw boss and depress spring latch.
4. Remove lock from housing. Thin flash of metal over slot is easily broken.
5. To install, first hold lock cylinder sleeve and rotate knob clockwise against stop.
6. Lay a 1/16 in. drill on housing surface next to housing bore.
7. Insert cylinder into housing bore, aligning keyway, and push in to abutment.
8. Rotate knob counterclockwise, pushing in slightly, until cylinder mates with sector.
9. Push in until spring latch pops into groove, then remove drill.

Caution If lock cylinder is forced beyond its normal latched position, complete disassembly of upper bearing assembly will be necessary to free it.

Lighting Switch Replacement
—1965-72
1. Disconnect battery.
2. Pull knob to on position.
3. Reach under instrument panel and depress the switch shaft retainer (see illustration), then remove knob and shaft assembly.
   NOTE: disconnect vacuum hose on vacuum-operated headlamp models.
4. Remove retaining ferrule nut.
5. Remove switch from instrument panel.
6. Disconnect multi-plug connector from switch.
7. Install in reverse of above. (In checking lights before installation, switch must be grounded to test dome lights on some models).

Brakes

Standard brakes are of the duo-servo, self-adjusting type. The self-adjusting feature operates only when the brakes are applied with car moving in reverse. When the brakes are applied, friction between the primary shoe and the drum causes the primary shoe to bear against the anchor pin. Hydraulic pressure in the wheel cylinder forces the upper end of the secondary shoe away from the anchor pin. As this moves, the upper end of the adjuster lever is prevented from moving by the actuating link attached to the anchor pin, thus forcing the lower end of the lever against the star wheel. If the linings are worn, the adjuster lever moves the star wheel a predetermined distance to maintain the proper shoe-to-drum clearance.

Metallic brake linings, used on some early high-performance models, never should be installed on cars equipped with standard brake drums unless the drums are radius ground and honed to a special finish. See the Unit Repair Section of this manual for more information on metallic brake linings.

Since 1967, a dual-type master cylinder has been used. For detailed information on this type cylinder, see Unit Repair Section.

The parking brake uses a foot-operated control lever, enclosed cables, rear wheel brake shoe levers and struts to the rear wheel shoes. The parking brake is released by pulling the release lever.

Information on brake adjustments, lining replacement, bleeding procedure, master and wheel cylinder overhaul can be found in the Unit Repair Section.

Information on the grease seals which may need replacement can be found in the Unit Repair Section.

Disc Brakes

From 1967, single-piston, sliding-caliper disc brakes have been available as optional equipment on most models (standard with high performance packages and Firebird starting 1970). These brakes have a vented, cast-iron rotor with two braking surfaces.

Disc brakes need no adjustment because, during operation, the application and release of hydraulic pressure causes the piston and caliper to move only slightly. In the released position, the pads do not move very far from the rotor thus, as pads wear down, the piston simply moves farther out of the caliper bore and the caliper repositions itself on its mounting bolts to maintain proper pad-to-rotor clearance.

A metering valve in the front brake circuit prevents the discs from operating until about 75 psi exists in the system. This enables the rear drum brakes to operate in synchronization with the front discs and reduces the possibility of unequal brake application and premature lock-up. A proportioning valve in the rear brake circuit of some models accomplishes the same purpose. Starting 1971, a two- or three-function combination valve replaces the separate units used previously. The pressure required to operate front brakes is now 110-150 psi. Disc brake pads should be examined for wear every 12,000 miles. See the Unit Repair Section of this manual for service procedures.

Parking Brake Adjustment
—1965-72

The automatic self-adjusting feature incorporated in the rear brake mechanism normally maintains

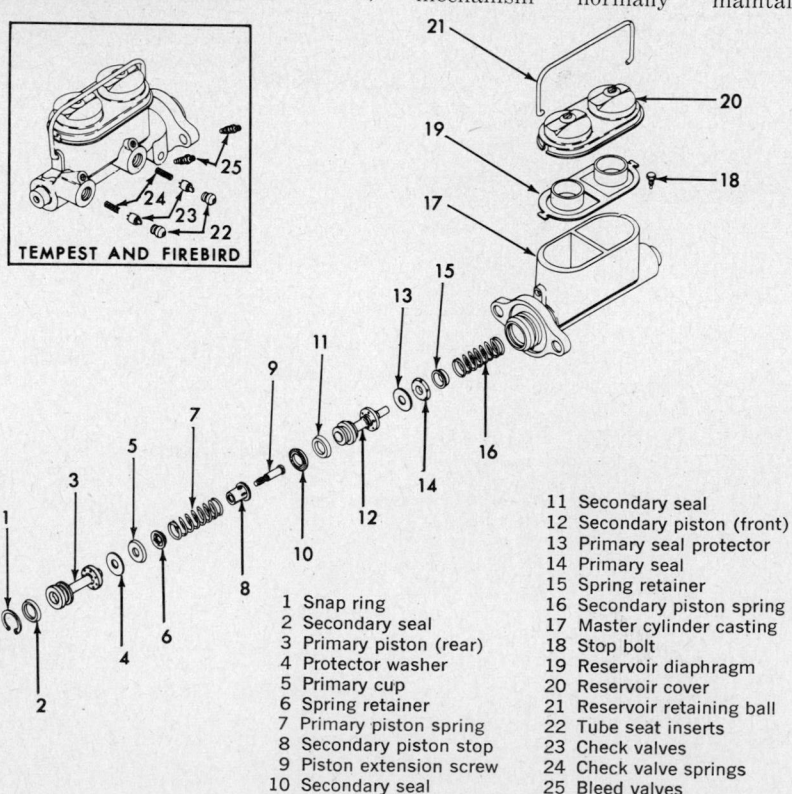

TEMPEST AND FIREBIRD

1 Snap ring
2 Secondary seal
3 Primary piston (rear)
4 Protector washer
5 Primary cup
6 Spring retainer
7 Primary piston spring
8 Secondary piston stop
9 Piston extension screw
10 Secondary seal
11 Secondary seal
12 Secondary piston (front)
13 Primary seal protector
14 Primary seal
15 Spring retainer
16 Secondary piston spring
17 Master cylinder casting
18 Stop bolt
19 Reservoir diaphragm
20 Reservoir cover
21 Reservoir retaining ball
22 Tube seat inserts
23 Check valves
24 Check valve springs
25 Bleed valves

Dual master cylinder (© Pontiac Div. G.M. Corp.)

proper parking brake adjustment. For this reason, the rear brake adjustment must be checked before any adjustment of the parking brake cables is done. Check the parking brake mechanism and cables for free movement and lubricate all working surfaces before proceeding.

Caution It is very important that the parking brake cables are not too tight. If the cables are too tight, they create a drag and position the secondary shoes so that the self-adjusters continue to operate in compensation for drag wear. The result is rapidly worn rear brake linings.

1. Jack up both rear wheels.
2. Push parking brake pedal 5-7 notches from full release position (for Tempest and GTO up to 1970), 2 notches (Firebird up to 1970), or 4-8 notches for all series starting 1971.
3. Loosen rear equalizer locknut and adjust forward nut until light rear brake drag is felt as wheels are rotated by hand.
4. Tighten locknut and release parking brake pedal; no drag should be felt.

Master Cylinder R & R

1965-72

1. Disconnect hydraulic line/s at master cylinder; disconnect clevis at pedal.
2. Remove the two retaining nuts and lockwashers that hold cylinder to firewall.
3. Remove the master cylinder, gasket and rubber boot.
4. Position master cylinder on firewall; reconnect pushrod clevis to brake pedal.
5. Install nuts and lockwashers.
6. Install hydraulic line/s, then check brake pedal free play.
7. Bleed brakes, as described in Unit Repair Section.

NOTE: cars having disc brakes do not have a check valve in the front outlet port of the master cylinder. If one is installed, front discs will

immediately wear out due to residual hydraulic pressure holding pads against rotor.

Fuel System

Fuel System Information

Data on capacity of the gas tank will be found in the Capacities table. Data on correct engine idle speed and fuel pump pressure will be found in the Tune-Up Specifications table. Both tables can be found in this section.

Information covering operation and troubles of the fuel gauge will be found in the Unit Repair Section.

The carburetor is Rochester or Carter, but varies with the application. See Unit Repair Section.

Idle Stop Adjustment

Adjust plunger to obtain specified idle speed. Disconnect wires and observe operation of solenoid. The plunger should drop back to allow the carburetor idle screw to contact the idle cam; engine speed should drop to lower, "solenoid inactive" idle speed. NOTE: idle stop unit must be disconnected when setting ignition timing on six-cylinder and Ram Air engines.

Fuel Pump

The fuel pump is of the single action diaphragm-type and is equipped with a pulsation dampening chamber for stabilizing fuel flow.

A vapor diverter is incorporated into the fuel pumps used on air conditioned V8 and 4-BBL. models. The fuel pump is not repairable and must be replaced as a unit if defective.

Fuel Pump R & R—1965-72

1. Disconnect fuel inlet, outlet and vapor return lines at pump and plug pump inlet line.
2. Remove two pump mounting bolts and lockwashers; remove pump and gasket.

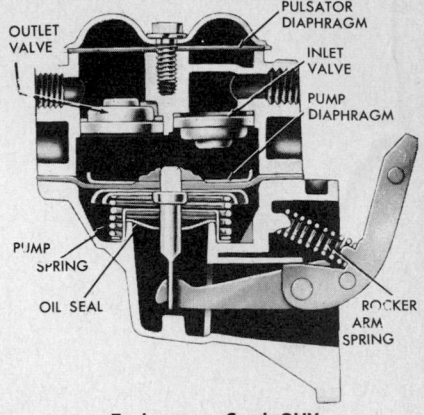

Fuel pump—6 cyl. OHV
(© Pontiac Div. G.M. Corp.)

3. On Ventura II V8 engines, if rocker arm pushrod is to be removed: take out the two adapter bolts and lockwashers and remove adapter and gasket.
4. Install pump with new gasket coated with sealer. Coat mounting bolt threads with sealer and tighten bolts.

NOTE: on Ventura II V8 engines, mechanical fingers or heavy grease can be used to hold pump pushrod in place during installation. Coat pipe plug threads or adapter gasket with sealer if pushrod was removed.

5. Connect inlet and outlet lines, start engine and check for leaks.

Fuel Filter

Paper and Bronze Types— 1965-72

1. Disconnect fuel line connection at inlet of carburetor.
2. Remove inlet fuel filter nut from carburetor using a box wrench.
3. Remove filter element and spring.
4. If a bronze element, blow through cone end—element should allow air to pass freely.
5. Install element spring and new element into carburetor. Bronze elements are installed with small section of cone facing outward.
6. Install new gasket on fitting nut and install nut.

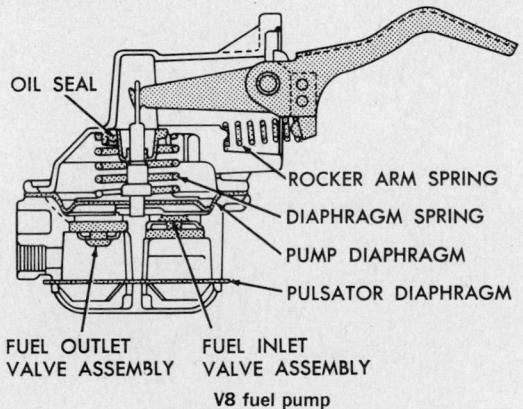

V8 fuel pump
(© Pontiac Div., G.M. Corp.)

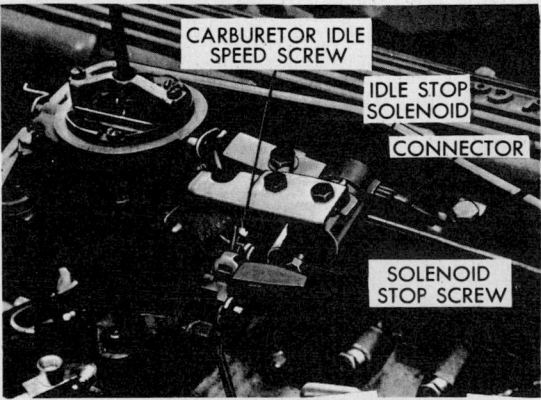

Idle stop solenoid—six-cylinder type shown
(© Pontiac Div. G.M. Corp.)

7. Install fuel line and tighten securely. Start engine and check for leaks.

⏻ CHILTON TIME-SAVER

Ventura II
307 and 350 cu. in.

When replacing a fuel pump on a 307 or 350 cu. in. engine, considerable time can be saved as follows:

1. Before removing the old pump, remove the upper bolt from the engine's right front mounting boss. This bolt hole is in direct alignment with the fuel pump pushrod. The threaded bolt hole continues into the pump pushrod bore. The bolt acts as an oil plug.
2. Temporarily insert a longer bolt, (about ⅜—16 x 2 in.) into the hole. Screw the bolt into the bore until it bottoms against the pump pushrod. (Don't tighten the bolt with a wrench or the rod can be damaged.)
3. The mechanic is now free to remove and install the fuel pump without worrying about fuel pump pushrod misalignment.

CAUTION: don't forget to reinstall original motor bolt.

Idle Speed and Mixture Adjustments

1965-67 (BV, 2GC, AFB, 4MV, Tri-Power)

Adjust with air cleaner installed.

1. Turn in idle mixture screw/s until lightly seated, then back out 1 turn for 1966 AFB, 2 turns for 1967 4MV, 1½ turns for others.
2. Set parking brake, place transmission in Neutral, connect a tachometer.
3. Start engine and allow it to warm up to normal operating temperature. Choke must be open and engine off fast idle.
4. Depress hot idle compensator pin on six-cylinder models with A/C and all V8 with automatic transmission. Place transmission in Neutral for manual, Drive for automatic.
5. Adjust idle speed screw to obtain specified idle speed, making sure hot idle compensator is still depressed.
   NOTE: only center carb needs adjustment on GTO Tri-Power 389.
6. Adjust mixture screw/s to obtain highest idle speed with best quality idle. "Missing" usually

means mixture is too lean; "loping," too rich.

7. Reset idle speed screw to obtain specified idle speed.
8. Adjust idle speed-up device on six-cylinder A/C models as follows:
   a. Turn on A/C.
   b. Adjust diaphragm plunger screw to obtain 540-560 rpm (1965 auto.), 580-600 rpm (1965 manual), 500 rpm (1966-67 auto. without A.I.R.), 600 rpm (1966-67 auto. with A.I.R. and manual without A.I.R.), or 700 rpm (1966-67 manual with A.I.R.).

1968-69

Adjust with air cleaner installed.

V8 Engines

1. Turn in idle mixture screws until lightly seated, then back out 4 turns (2-BBL.) or 6 turns (4-BBL.).
2. Connect a tachometer, start engine and allow it to warm up to normal operating temperature. On automatic transmision, A/C cars, turn off A/C.
3. Place automatic in Drive, manual in Neutral. With idle stop solenoid energized, adjust mixture screws for best lean idle speed.
4. Adjust idle stop solenoid screw to obtain specified idle speed for all 1968 and only 1969 Ram Air; use idle screw for all other 1969 cars.
5. Disconnect idle stop solenoid, then adjust idle speed screw on carburetor to obtain 650 rpm idle for manual transmission 4-BBL., 500 rpm for all others.
   NOTE: do not re-adjust mixture screws.
6. Place fast idle lever on top step of cam and adjust fast idle speed.

L-6 Engines

1. Turn in mixture screws until they lightly seat, then back out 5 turns.
2. Start engine, connect tachometer, and allow engine to warm up to normal operating temperature. On automatic transmission cars, place selector in Drive and turn off A/C, if so equipped.
3. Adjust idle stop solenoid screw to obtain 610 rpm for auto. transmission (1-BBL. and 4-BBL.), 730 rpm for manual transmission 1-BBL., 830 rpm for 1968 manual transmission 4-BBL., or 880 rpm for 1969 manual transmission 4-BBL.
4. Turn mixture screws clockwise to obtain 600 rpm for auto. transmission (1-BBL. and 4-BBL.), 700 rpm for manual

transmission 1-BBL., 800 rpm for 1968 manual transmission 4-BBL., or 850 rpm for 1969 manual transmission 4-BBL.

5. Disconnect idle stop solenoid and adjust idle speed screw on carburetor to obtain 600 rpm for manual transmission 4-BBL., 500 rpm for all others.
   NOTE: don't disturb idle mixture screws or stop solenoid after this point.
6. Reconnect solenoid and adjust fast idle speed.

1970

Adjust with air cleaner installed.

1. On California cars, remove fuel filler cap.
2. Disconnect and plug distributor vacuum advance hose.
3. Plug hot idle compensator on all automatic transmission V8's with Quadrajet (4 MV) carburetor *except* Ram Air III and IV. Also plug compensator on all L-6 and V8 2-BBL. with automatic and A/C.
4. With automatic in Drive, manual in Neutral, adjust curb idle speed as follows:

L-6 and Ram Air IV

a. With idle stop solenoid energized, adjust solenoid screw to obtain 830 rpm for L-6, 1,000 rpm for R.A. IV, 630 rpm for automatic L-6, and 750 rpm for automatic R.A. IV.
b. Adjust mixture screws equally to obtain lean best idle at 1,000 rpm for manual R.A. IV, 750 rpm for automatic R.A. IV, 750 rpm for manual L-6, and 600 rpm for automatic L-6.
c. Disconnect solenoid wire and adjust carburetor idle speed screw to obtain 400 rpm for L-6, 500 rpm for R.A. IV automatic, and 650 rpm for R.A. IV manual.

350, 400, 455 Engines

a. Back out mixture screws 3-5 turns from lightly seated positions.

b. Adjust carburetor idle speed screw to obtain 850 rpm for manual 350 and 400 2-BBL., 1,050 rpm for manual 400 and 455 4-BBL., or 675 rpm for all automatic 350, 400, 455 engines.

c. Lean mixture screws equally (turn in) to obtain 800 rpm for manual 350 and 400 2-BBL., 950 rpm for manual 400 and 455 4-BBL., or 650 rpm for all automatic 350, 400, 455 engines.

1971

Adjust with air cleaner installed. The idle stop solenoid is no longer used, having been replaced by the combination emission control vavle. This valve is energized through the transmission to increase idle speed under conditions of high gear deceleration and to provide full vacuum spark advance during high gear operation. The valve is de-energized at curb idle and in the lower gears to provide a retarded spark under these conditions, the result of which is lower hydrocarbon emission. *The valve need not be adjusted unless the solenoid or throttle body is removed, or the carburetor overhauled.*

307, 350, 400, 455 V8 Engines

1. Disconnect carburetor "EVAP" hose from vapor storage canister.
2. Disconnect and plug carburetor-to-vacuum (distributor vacuum) solenoid hose at solenoid. Disconnect throttle solenoid wire on 4-BBL. manual transmission engines.
3. Set dwell and timing (in that order) at specified idle speed.
4. Adjust carburetor speed screw to obtain specified idle speed, automatic in Drive, manual in Neutral.
5. On 4-BBL. manual transmission models, reconnect throttle solenoid wire, manually extend solenoid screw and adjust to specified idle rpm.
6. Place automatic in Park, manual in Neutral and check fast idle speed with screw on top step of cam. Adjust fast idle screw to obtain 1,700 rpm. NOTE: 2-BBL. carburetors are not adjustable for fast idle.
7. Reconnect distributor vacuum and vapor storage hoses.

L-6 Engine

1. Disconnect fuel tank "EVAP" hose from vapor storage canister.
2. Disconnect and plug distributor vacuum advance hose.
3. Set dwell and timing (in that order) at specified idle speed.
4. Adjust carburetor idle speed screw to obtain 550 rpm for manual, 500 rpm for automatic (in Drive). Do not adjust solenoid screw.
5. Place automatic in Park and manual in Neutral, then place fast idle cam tang on top step of fast idle cam and check fast idle speed. Adjust to obtain 2,400 rpm.

Alternate Procedure—L-6 and V8

If the carburetor has been overhauled, or the plastic locks removed from the mixture screws, the following procedure must be used to adjust idle speed and mixture. It must be emphasized that the manufacturer does not recommend this procedure as a substitute for the preceding methods, in that exhaust emission quality can be adversely affected unless the proper test equipment is available.

1. Turn in mixture screw/s until lightly seated, then back out 3½ turns.
2. Start engine and adjust carburetor idle speed screw to obtain a speed 25 rpm above specified idle (automatic), 75 rpm higher for L-6 and 2-BBL. V8 (manual), or 100 rpm higher for 4-BBL. V8 (manual).
3. Turn mixture screw/s in equally until specified idle speed is obtained. At this point, a CO meter should be employed to adjust mixture. A reading of 1.0% or less must be maintained.
4. Shut off engine and install new limiter caps
5. Adjust fast idle speed, as described previously.

C.E.C. Valve Adjustment

1. With engine runing at specified slow idle, manually extend C.E.C. plunger to contact throttle lever.
2. Adjust plunger length to obtain 850 rpm for L-6 manual, 650 rpm for L-6 and 307 automatic, 900 rpm for 307 manual, or 1,000 rpm for 400 4-BBL. and 455 H.O. 4-BBL. with manual transmission.

Exhaust System

Crossover Pipe R & R —V8 Engine

1. Remove four bolts holding exhaust crossover pipe to exhaust manifold.
2. Remove clamp connecting exhaust crossover pipe to exhaust pipe.
3. Remove exhaust crossover pipe from car.
4. Replace exhaust crossover pipe by reversing the above steps. Torque bolts connecting the crossover pipe to the manifold to 15-25 ft. lbs. Torque nuts on clamp to 33 ft. lbs.

Exhaust Pipe R & R
OHV Six—1965, 1970-72

1. Remove two bolts from exhaust manifold flange.
2. Cut pipe in front of muffler, or remove clamp.
3. Remove exhaust pipe.
4. Replace pipe by reversing the above steps. Clamp new pipe in front of muffler; tighten flange bolts to 22-30 ft. lbs., 15 ft. lbs. for 1971-72.

Standard OHC Six—1966-69

1. Remove two bolts from manifold flange.
2. Loosen exhaust pipe to muffler U-clamp on Tempest, intermediate pipe on Firebird.
3. Remove exhaust pipe from car.
4. To install, reverse removal procedure, tightening flange bolts to 35 ft. lbs., exhaust pipe U-clamp nuts to 18 ft. lbs.

NOTE: coat all slip joints with sealer before installation.

High Performance OHC Six —1966-69

1. Loosen front (behind muffler) and rear tailpipe supports.
2. Loosen exhaust pipe to muffler U-clamp.
3. Disconnect muffler from exhaust

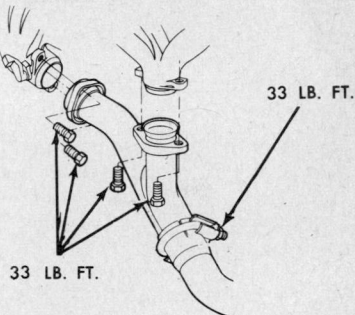

High performance OHC 6 exhaust manifold bolts. Bolts should be tightened to 25 ft. lbs. for 1969 engines.
(© Pontiac Div. G.M. Corp.)

pipe by pulling muffler and tailpipe to the rear.
4. Loosen U-clamp that secures exhaust pipe to manifold Y-pipe.
5. Remove exhaust pipe.
6. Remove four bolts that hold Y-pipe to exhaust manifold; remove Y-pipe.
7. To install, reverse removal procedure, tightening Y-pipe to manifold bolts to 33 ft. lbs. (25 ft. lbs.—1969), Y-pipe to exhaust pipe U-clamp bolts to 33 ft. lbs., front muffler U-clamp and tailpipe U-clamp to 18 ft. lbs., and resonator U-clamp to 33 ft. lbs.

NOTE: coat all slip joints with sealer before installation.

All V8 Single Exhaust—1965-72

1. Loosen crossover to exhaust pipe U-clamp.
2. Disconnect crossover pipe from exhaust pipe by pulling exhaust or intermediate pipe to the rear.
3. Loosen front U-clamp on muffler and remove exhaust pipe.
4. To install, reverse removal procedure, tightening muffler U-clamp to 18 ft. lbs., crossover to exhaust pipe U-clamp to 33 ft. lbs., manifold flange bolts to 25 ft. lbs. (15 ft. lbs. for 307 V8).

NOTE: coat all slip joints with sealer before installation. Tighten one manifold flange bolt finger-tight

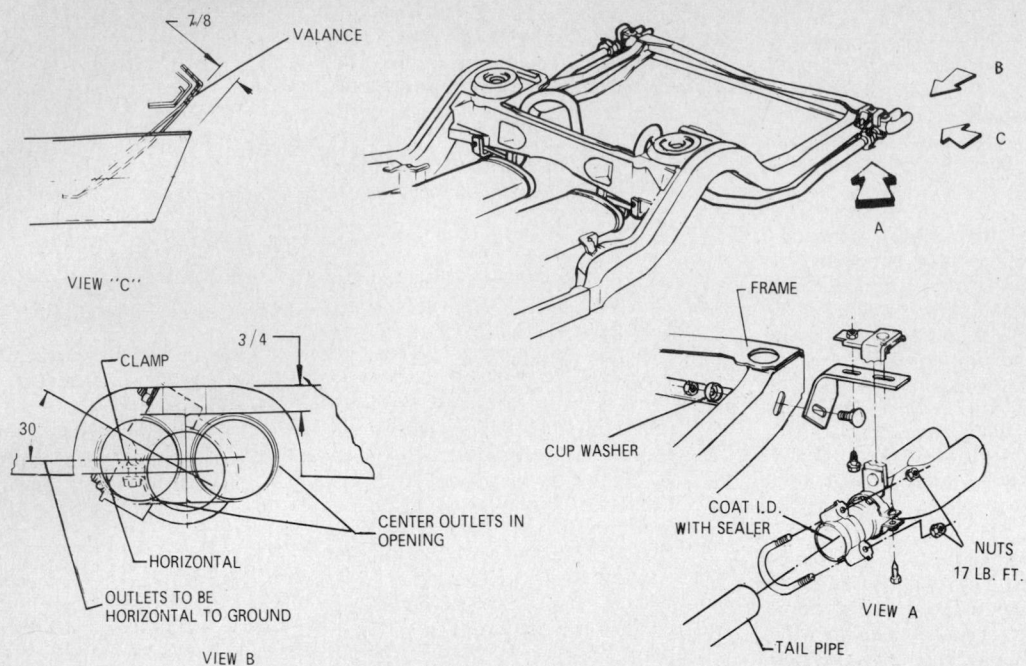

1970-71 GTO exhaust extension alignment (© Pontiac Div., G.M. Corp.)

before tightening the other bolt with a wrench (each side).

All V8 Dual Exhaust—1965-72

1. Remove two or three nuts or bolts (depending on engine) from manifold flange.
2. Remove U-clamp at front of muffler.
3. Remove exhaust pipe/s.
4. To install, reverse removal procedure, tightening manifold flange bolts to 25-35 ft. lbs. and muffler front U-clamp nuts to 15-20 ft. lbs.

NOTE: it may be necessary to loosen resonator (if so equipped), remove tailpipe, and remove front muffler on some models.

Vacuum-Operated Exhaust —1970 GTO 400

A vacuum-operated exhaust system is available on 1970 GTO 400 models, unless equipped with California evaporative control system or Ram Air.

The dual mufflers are equipped with vacuum-operated servos attached to the front of each muffler. An actuator rod is connected to the diaphragm of each servo and passes through each muffler to operate spring-loaded valves. When the switch under the steering column is actuated (pulled out), vacuum on the servo diaphragms pulls the spring-loaded valves away from the muffler end baffle pipes, thus allowing exhaust to pass directly into the rear muffler chambers.

A vacuum reservoir tank, located on the left front inner fender panel, supplies vacuum to the system when engine vacuum is not available and during acceleration.

GTO Exhaust Extensions —1970-71

The dual-outlet exhaust extensions used on this model must be properly aligned to prevent rattling. (See illustrations.)

Cooling System

Radiator—1965-66 Tempest and GTO

A top-tank, down-flow unit is used. A drain cock is located at the inside lower left-hand corner of the radiator. The core is of the down-flow-tube and center-type, and is constructed of copper.

Radiator R & R—1965-66 Tempest and GTO

1. Drain cooling system.
2. Disconnect overflow, upper and lower radiator hoses.
3. Remove radiator fan shield.
4. Remove radiator.
5. To replace, reverse removal steps.

Radiator—1967-72 Tempest, GTO and Ventura II

A cross-flow radiator is used instead of a conventional down-flow and center type. With the cross-flow design, coolant flows horizontally through the core and the tanks are located on each side.

Advantages of the cross-flow radiator are improved cooling capability, more effective cooling surface area, and a low silhouette.

Automatic transmission radiators have oil coolers built into the right-hand tank, air-conditioned and high-performance models have greater cooling capacity than standard. The drain cock is located at the inside, lower left-hand corner of the radiator.

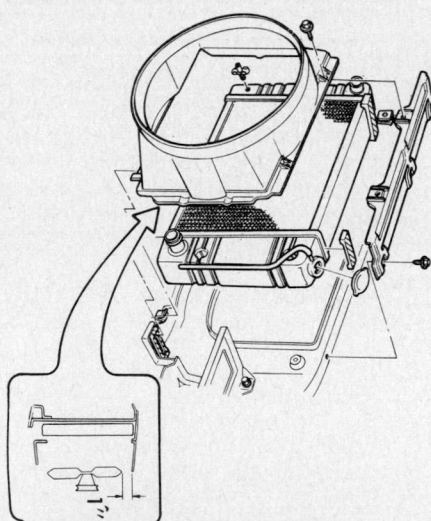

Radiator installation—1971-72 Ventura II (© Pontiac Div. G.M. Corp.)

Radiator R & R—1967-72 Tempest, GTO and Ventura II

1. Drain coolant.
2. Remove fan shield assembly.
3. Disconnect upper and lower hoses.
4. Disconnect and plug oil cooler lines, if equipped with automatic transmission.

NOTE: on 1969 Tempest models remove fan blade, then remove entire radiator and shroud as an assembly.

5. Remove fan shroud, if installed.
6. Lift radiator straight up and out of car.
7. To install, reverse removal procedure, making sure lower cradles are properly located and automatic transmission is full.

Radiator R & R—1967-72
Firebird

1. Disconnect battery.
2. Drain coolant, then disconnect upper and lower hoses.
3. Disconnect and plug oil cooler lines, if equipped with automatic transmission.
4. Remove upper fan shield (six cylinder) or upper shroud bracket (V8).
5. Remove radiator hold-down bolts and lift radiator and shroud assembly from car.
6. To install, reverse removal procedure, making sure automatic transmission fluid level is correct. Tighten hold-down bolts to 12 ft. lbs.

Water Pump R & R

All Engines

The pump cover is die-cast, and into it the water pump bearing outer race is fitted. Therefore, the cover, shaft bearing and hub are not replaceable. The shaft seal and impeller are the only replaceable parts of the water pump. V8 water pumps are serviced as an assembly only.

1. Drain cooling system.
2. Remove fan belt and pulley or pulleys from the pump hub.
3. Disconnect hose from the pump inlet and heater hose from nipple. Remove pump assembly and gasket from timing chain cover.
   NOTE: remove upper front timing cover and two accessory drive housing bolts on OHC six engine. Tighten water pump hold down bolts to 20 ft. lbs. for six-cylinder, 15 ft. lbs. for V8, engine. OHC six accessory drive housing and upper timing cover bolts must be tightened to 15 ft. lbs. only.
4. Check pump shaft bearings for end-play or roughness of operation. If bearings are not in serviceable condition, the assembly must be replaced.

Thermostat R & R

1. Drain coolant to below thermostat level.
2. Disconnect upper hose and remove water outlet assembly.
3. Replace by reversing the above steps. Torque attaching bolts to 20-30 ft. lbs.
4. Refill to 3 in. below filler neck and bleed cooling system.

Engine

Six-Cylinder Engine

1965

A 215 cu. in. OHV six, similar to Chevrolet, is used.

1966-69

A 230 and 250 cu. in. overhead camshaft (OHC) engine is used. While most of the service procedures are the same as for the previous six cylinder engine, there are, however, some areas that are different. These areas will be covered in their regular departments.

1970-72

A 250 cu. in. OHV six, similar to Chevrolet, replaces the OHC six cylinder engine. This engine is used in the Ventura II as a base engine.

V8 Engine

In 1965-66, four engines were offered. Two were 326 cu. in. displacement, and the other two, used exclusively in the GTO, were 389 cu. in. engines having either a single four-barrel carburetor or a triple-two-barrel set-up.

In 1967, the two 326 cu. in. V8's were kept in the engine lineup, but the old 389 was replaced by three versions of the new 400 cu. in. V8. In 1968 and 1969, the 400 engine was retained, although the Ram Air version of this engine was given four-bolt main caps due to the increased performance. In 1968, an all-new 350 cu. in. engine of Pontiac design was introduced. This engine is used as the standard base engine up to the present.

In 1970, the 400 cu. in. engine was available in two Ram Air versions for use in the GTO—the Ram Air III and IV. For the first time, a high output version of the 455 cu. in. engine, also with four-bolt main caps, was made available in the GTO. This engine was used in the Trans Am Firebird and GTO Judge in 1971.

The 1971 Ventura II has, as an option, a 307 cu. in. V8 of Chevrolet design. This engine was supplemented in 1972 by a two-barrel version of the Chevrolet 350 cu. in. V8, which must not be confused with the Pontiac-designed engine of the same displacement that is used concurrently throughout the line.

Exhaust Emission Control

Beginning 1968

In compliance with anti-pollution laws involving all of the continental United States, the General Motors Corporation has elected to adopt a special system of terminal exhaust treatment. This plan supersedes (in most cases) the method used to conform to 1966-67 California laws. The new system cancels out (except with stick shift and special purpose engine applications) the use of the A.I.R. method previously used.

The new concept, Combustion Control System (C.C.S.) utilizes engine modification, with emphasis on carburetor and distributor changes. Any of the methods of terminal exhaust treatment require close and frequent attention to tune-up factors of engine maintenance.

Since 1968, all car manufacturers have posted idle speeds and other pertinent data relative to the specific engine-car application in a conspicuous place in the engine compartment.

Beginning 1970

The more stringent 1970 laws require tighter control of emissions. Crankcase emissions are controlled by the Closed Positive Crankcase Ventilation System, and exhaust emissions by the engine Controlled Combustion System (C.C.S.), in conjunction with the new Transmission Controlled Spark System (T.C.S.).

In addition, cars sold in California are equipped with an Evaporation Control System that limits the amount of gasoline vapor discharged into the atmosphere (usually from the carburetor and fuel tank).

The T.C.S. system consists of a transmission switch, a solenoid valve, and a temperature switch. Under normal conditions, the system permits the vacuum distributor (spark) advance to operate only in high gear (both manual and automatic transmissions). When the engine temperature is below 85°F., or above 220°F., however, the system allows the vacuum advance to operate normally.

The C.E.C. system, introduced in 1971 on the Ventura II, incorporates many features of the earlier T.C.S. system. The distributor vacuum advance feature is still eliminated in the low forward gears by use of the transmission and solenoid vacuum switches. Operation is slightly different, however, in that when the solenoid is in the non-energized position, rather than the energized position, the vacuum advance unit is shut off and the distributor is vented to the atmosphere. On C.E.C., venting is accomplished through a filter in the opposite end of the solenoid rather than through a direct hose connection to the carburetor air hose.

The T.C.S. system used a temperature override switch which allowed full vacuum advance in all gears until the engine was warm. This feature is incorporated into the C.E.C. system with an 82° F. temperature cut-off.

The C.E.C. solenoid is controlled by two switches and a time delay relay. The time delay relay energizes the solenoid for approximately 15 seconds after the ignition is turned on to allow full vacuum advance in all gears *independent* of temperature to eliminate stalling during "driveaway.'"

Engine dieseling is controlled by use of lower throttle blade openings (lower curb idle speeds).

On A/C, automatic transmission models, a solid-state time device engages the A/C compressor clutch for about 3 seconds after the ignition is shut off, the load from which effectively stalls the engine and prevents diesel overrun.

For diagnosis procedures, see the Unit Repair Section.

Engine R & R

1965 6 Cylinder and 1965-66 V8

1. Remove hood.
2. Drain cooling system and remove radiator.
3. Disconnect heater hoses at the engine.
4. Disconnect wiring harness at generator, ignition coil, starter solenoid, heater blower, thermogauge and oil pressure switch.
5. Disconnect ground strap at both sides of the engine.
6. Disconnect fuel line at fuel pump.
7. Disconnect vacuum modulator line at automatic transmission and power brake vacuum line.
8. Remove front fender cross brace.
9. Remove fan and fan pulley.
10. Disconnect accelerator rod at firewall.
11. Raise front of car.
12. Disconnect exhaust pipe at manifold.
13. Disconnect clutch and shift linkage on synchromesh, oil filler tube on automatic.
14. Disconnect rear U-joint bolts and remove driveshaft. Plug the end of the extension housing with rags to prevent oil loss. Disconnect speedometer cable at transmission then remove starter on 1965 models.
15. Disconnect engine support at crossmember, then lower car.
16. Raise engine with chain hoist, then remove transmission rear mount from crossmember. Move forward to clear the firewall and heater.
17. Lift and remove engine and transmission.
18. Replace by reversing the removal procedure.

1966-72 6 Cylinder and 1967-72 V8

1. Disconnect battery.
2. Drain cooling system.
3. Scribe alignment marks on hood and remove hood from hinges.
4. Disconnect engine wiring har-

ness and ground straps.
5. Remove air cleaner and fan shield or shroud.
6. Disconnect radiator and heater hoses.
7. If equipped with manual transmission, remove radiator.
8. Remove fan and fan pulley.

NOTE: if equipped with power steering and/or air conditioning, disconnect and swing aside pump/compressor *without* disconnecting hoses.

9. Disconnect accelerator linkage and support bracket.
10. Disconnect automatic transmission vacuum modulator line and power brake vacuum line at carburetor.

NOTE: on Firebird models up to 1969 with air conditioning, remove wiper motor.

11. Jack up front of car and drain engine oil.
12. Disconnect fuel lines at pump.
13. Disconnect exhaust pipes.
14. Disconnect starter wires.
15. If equipped with automatic transmission, remove converter cover and three converter retaining bolts, then slide converter to the rear.
16. If equipped with manual transmission, disconnect clutch linkage and remove clutch cross-shaft.

NOTE: remove starter and lower flywheel cover on 1970-72 V8s and L-6 from 1971.

17. Remove four lower bellhousing bolts (two per side).
18. Disconnect transmission filler tube support (automatic) and starter wire shield from cylinder heads.
19. Remove two front motor mount-to-frame bolts.
20. Lower car to floor then, using a jack and a wood block, support the transmission.
21. Remove two remaining bellhousing bolts.
22. Raise transmission slightly, using the jack and wood block, then, using a chain hoist, remove the engine.
23. To install, reverse removal procedure. Install the two upper bellhousing bolts first (with jack still under transmission).

NOTE: do not lower engine completely until jack and wood block are removed.

Cylinder Head

1965 and 1970-72 6 Cylinder

Removal

1. Drain cooling system, remove air cleaner. Disconnect radiator hoses.
2. Disconnect accelerator pedal rod at bellcrank, fuel and vacuum lines at carburetor. Disconnect exhaust pipe at manifold flange.
3. Remove manifold-to-cylinder

head attaching bolts and manifolds.
4. Remove rocker arm cover assembly, temperature sender and coil wires.
5. Loosen rocker arm nuts and rotate rocker arms so the pushrods can be removed.
6. Remove pushrods and store them so they can be installed in their original locations.
7. Disconnect spark plug wires.
8. Remove cylinder head bolts.
9. Lift off the head.
10. Remove cylinder head gasket.

Installation

1. Position new cylinder head gasket on block, on locating dowels.
2. Place cylinder head in position.
3. Install cylinder head attaching bolts. Torque to 95 ft. lbs.
4. Install pushrods in original location and position.
5. Position rocker arms and torque rocker arm nuts to 15-25 ft. lbs., further tighten until valve train play is removed, with lifter on base circle of cam, then tighten one more turn.
6. Install rocker arm cover.
7. Install manifold-to-cylinder head bolts and torque to 30 ft. lbs. (center) and 15-20 ft. lbs. (end).
8. Install pushrod cover and crankcase breather outlet pipe.
9. Connect all wires, hoses and linkage; fill cooling system and check for leaks.
10. Connect spark plug wires.

1966-69 6 Cylinder OHC

Removal

1. Drain cooling system and remove air cleaner.
2. Disconnect accelerator pedal cable at bellcrank on manifold, and fuel and vacuum lines at carburetor.
3. Disconnect exhaust pipe at manifold flange, then remove manifold bolts and clamps and remove manifolds and carburetor as an assembly.
4. Remove timing belt top front cover.
5. Align timing marks, remove belt tension then remove belt from camshaft sprocket.
6. Remove rocker arm cover assembly.
7. Remove timing belt upper front cover mounting support bracket and rear lower cover.
8. Disconnect spark plug wires.
9. Remove rocker arms and hydraulic valve lash adjusters. Keep rocker arms and hydraulic lash adjusters in proper sequence for exact location for installation.
10. Remove cylinder head bolts and gasket.
11. Clean gasket surfaces and carbon from cylinder head and block.

Installation

When installing new head, transfer all serviceable parts to new head using new seals on intake and exhaust manifold gaskets.

1. Place new cylinder head gasket in position over dowels in cylinder block.
2. Guide cylinder head into place over dowels and gasket.
3. Start all cylinder head bolts in threads.

NOTE: bolts are of two different lengths. When inserted into proper holes, all bolts will project an equal distance from the head. Do not use sealer of any kind on threads.

4. Tighten cylinder head a little at a time with a torque wrench. Tighten center bolts and then the end bolts. Final torque should be 90-100 ft. lbs.
5. Reverse Steps 1-9 of removal to complete installation procedure.

1965-72 V8

Removal

1. Remove intake manifold, valley cover, and rocker arm cover.
2. Loosen all rocker arm retaining nuts and pivot rockers off pushrods.
3. Remove pushrods and place in order.
4. Remove exhaust pipe flange bolts.

NOTE: on 1968-70 air-conditioned Firebird models, remove compressor hold-down bolts and move compressor aside *without* disconnecting hoses.

5. Remove battery ground strap and engine ground strap on left head; engine ground strap and automatic transmission oil filler tube bracket on right head.
6. Remove cylinder head bolts and head, with exhaust manifold attached.

NOTE: left head must be maneuvered to clear power steering and power brake units except on Ventura II.

NOTE: on 1968-70 air-conditioned Firebird models, the right motor mount-to-frame bolt must be removed and the engine jacked up about 2 in. to gain access to the right rear rocker arm cover bolt and cylinder head bolt.

Installation

1. Check head surface for straightness, then place a new head gasket on block.

CAUTION: on 1968-70 air-conditioned Firebird models, install right rear head bolt into head *before* placing head on block.

NOTE: bolts are of three different lengths on all V8s. When bolts are properly installed, they will project an equal distance from head.

2. Install all bolts and tighten evenly to specified torque.
3. Install pushrods in original posi-

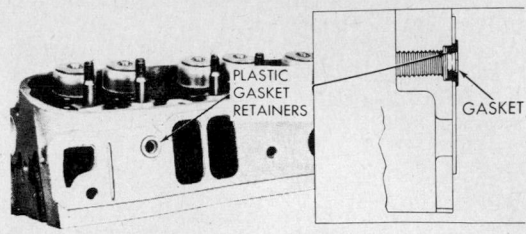

Intake manifold gaskets can be held in place using plastic retainers, available at Pontiac dealers
(© Pontiac Div. G.M. Corp.)

tions.

4. Position rocker arms over pushrods and tighten ball retaining nuts to 20 ft. lbs. (except Ram Air IV and 1970 Ram Air Super Duty engines; see special procedure).
5. Replace rocker arm cover.
6. Replace valley cover.
7. Replace ground straps, oil filler tube bracket, intake manifold, and right motor mount bolt (on A/C Firebird models).
8. Install exhaust pipe flange nuts.

NOTE: most left and right cylinder heads are interchangeable within a single year, large-and small-valve heads should not be used on the same engine.

Intake Manifold R & R —1965-72 V8 Except Ventura II 307, 350

1. Drain radiator and block.

NOTE: there are petcocks on each side of block; jack up rear of car 15-18 in. to drain completely.

2. Remove air cleaner and upper radiator hose.
3. Disconnect heater hose.
4. Disconnect temperature gauge wire, then remove two spark plug wire brackets from manifold.
5. Disconnect power brake vacuum and distributor vacuum lines.

NOTE: vacuum retard line is located at lower rear of vacuum unit on some exhaust emission distributors.

6. Disconnect fuel line at carburetor.
7. Disconnect crankcase vent hose and accelerator linkage.
8. Remove bolts that secure accelerator linkage bracket, then remove intake manifold bolts and nuts.
9. Remove manifold and gasket.

CAUTION: make sure O-ring between intake manifold and timing chain cover is in place.

10. To install, reverse removal procedure, tightening timing chain cover to manifold bolts to 10-20 ft. lbs., manifold hold-down bolts and nuts evenly to 40-45 ft. lbs.

Intake Manifold R & R— 1971-72 Ventura II 307, 350 V8

1. Drain water from radiator and both sides of block.

2. Disconnect battery cables, upper radiator hose, accelerator linkage, carburetor fuel line, coil and temperature sender wires.
3. Disconnect power brake hose at carburetor base and spark advance hose at distributor.
4. Disconnect PCV hoses, then remove distributor cap and matchmark rotor and housing.
5. Remove distributor hold-down clamp and pull out distributor.
6. Remove upper alternator bracket and coil.
7. Remove manifold-to-head bolts, then remove manifold from engine.
8. To install, reverse removal procedure. Stick manifold end seals in position with sealer and tighten manifold bolts to 30 ft. lbs.

Intake and Exhaust Manifold R & R—1965 and 1970-72 OHV 6 Cylinder, 1966-69 OHC 6 Cylinder

1. Remove air cleaner.
2. Disconnect accelerator linkage and return spring.
3. Disconnect fuel and vacuum lines at carburetor; disconnect choke rod.
4. Disconnect exhaust pipe at manifold flange.
5. Remove manifold bolts and clamps, then remove manifolds.

NOTE: intake manifold can be separated from exhaust manifold by removing one bolt and two nuts. These fasteners should be tightened to 15-30 ft. lbs. after the manifolds are bolted to the engine.

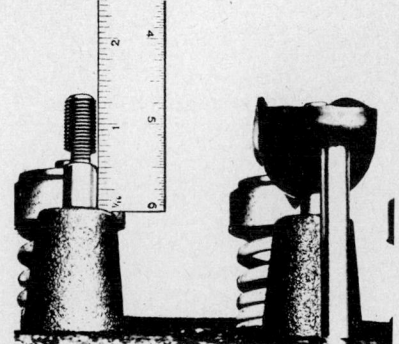

Rocker stud height—OHV 6 cyl.
(© Pontiac Div. G.M. Corp.)

6. To install, reverse removal procedure, tightening center clamp bolts to 25-30 ft. lbs., end bolts to 15-20 ft. lbs. (for OHV engines), or all bolts to 30 ft. lbs. (for OHC engines).

Rocker Arm Stud R & R

1965 and 1970-72 OHV 6 Cylinder

1. Remove rocker cover and rocker arm.
2. File two slots 3/32-1/8 in. deep on opposite sides of stud. Bottom of slots should be ½ in. from top of stud hole.
3. Place spacer washer (or tool J-6392-3) over stud, then position a stud remover (or tool J-6392-1) on stud and tighten securely.
4. Place a spacer (socket or J-6392-2) over the stud remover, then thread a 7/8 in. nut on stud remover and turn in until stud pulls from head.
5. If an oversize stud is to be used (0.003 and 0.013 in. oversize

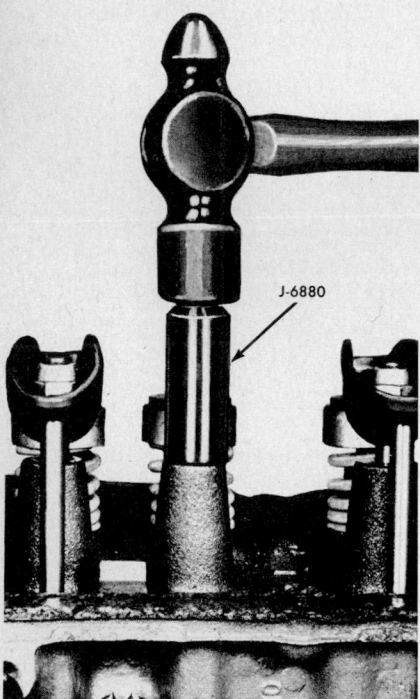

Installing rocker arm stud—OHV 6 cyl.
(© Chevrolet Div. G.M. Corp.)

studs are available), ream stud hole to proper size.
6. To install, coat press-fit area of stud with axle lube, then press or hammer into place.
NOTE: the factory recommends that tool J-6880 be used for this job. This tool is simply a sleeve that is held in place with an Allen screw—it protects the threads from damage. Any homemade tool similar to the one illustrated will work if care is exercised. Do not hammer directly on the stud, because it is hardened to the point where it will fracture if sub-

Removing rocker arm stud—V8
(© Pontiac Div. G.M. Corp.)

jected to shock.

1965-72 V8 Except GTO and Ventura II

Caution This procedure can be used **only** on engines with pressed-in rocker studs. GTO and some special high performance engines have screwed-in rocker studs which are easily identified by their hex head lower portion. Another common stud-securing procedure on standard engines is "pinning" pressed-in studs by drilling through the stud boss and stud and inserting an interference-fit roll pin. Make sure any such pins are removed before attempting the following procedure.

1. Disconnect battery and drain cooling system.
2. Remove rocker cover.
3. Pack oily rags around stud holes and engine openings.
4. Remove rocker arm and pushrod, then file two slots 3/32-1/8 in. deep on opposite sides of the stud. The top of the slots should be ¼-3/8 in. below thread travel.
5. Place a spacer washer (or tool J-8934-3) over the stud, then position stud remover (or tool J-8934-1) on stud and tighten Allen screws.
6. Place a spacer (socket or J-8934-2) over the remover, then thread a 7/8 in. nut on stud remover and turn in until stud pulls from head.
7. If an oversize stud is to be used (0.003 in. oversize studs are available), ream stud hole to the proper size, then clean chips from area.
8. To install, refer to Step 6 of OHV 6 cylinder stud replacement procedure, substituting factory tool number J-23342 for J-6880.
NOTE: valve adjustment for Ram Air IV engines is covered later in this section.

GTO Screwed-In Rocker Studs

1. Remove rocker cover.
2. Remove rocker arm and nut.
3. Remove stud, using a deep socket.
4. Install new stud, tightening to 50 ft. lbs.

1971-72 Ventura II V8

1. Remove rocker cover.
2. Place a stack of 3/8 in. washers over stud so that about 8-10 threads show.
3. Thread a 3/8—24 nut onto stud and turn it down with a wrench until stud begins to move. It will be necessary to remove nut and add more washers as the stud comes out.
NOTE: Stud can be rethreaded to 3/8—16 if it's stripped.
4. To install, coat the stud with hypoid lube, then press in using tool J-6880, as for OHV six.

Cylinder Head Disassembly

1. Remove cylinder heads, as previously described.
2. Compress valve springs, using valve spring compressor.
3. Remove valve locks or keys.
4. Release valve springs.
5. Remove valve springs, retainers, oil seals, and valves.
NOTE: if a valve does not slide out of the guide easily, check end of stem for mushrooming or heading over. If head is mushroomed, file off excess material, remove and discard valve. If valve is not mushroomed, lubricate stem, remove valve and check guide for galling.

Valves

Valve Guides

Pontiac engines have integral valve guides. Pontiac offers valves with oversize stems for worn guides (0.001, 0.003 and 0.005 in. being available for most engines). To fit these, enlarge valve guide bores with valve guide reamers to an oversize that cleans up wear. If a large oversize is required, it is best to approach that size in stages by using a series of reamers of increasing diameter. This helps to maintain the concentricity of the guide bores with the valve seats. The correct valve stem to guide clearance is given in the Valve Specifications table at the beginning of this section.

Compressing valve spring with tool J22263.1—OHC 6 cyl.
(© Pontiac Div. G.M. Corp.)

As an alternate procedure, some local automotive machine shops fit replacement guides that use standard stem valves.

The following is a method for replacing valve springs, oil seals or spring retainers without removing the cylinder head.

1. **Entirely dismantle a spark plug and save the threaded shell.**
2. **To this shell, braze or weld an air chuck.**
3. **Remove the valve rocker cover. Remove the rocker arm from the valve to be worked on.**
4. **Remove the spark plug from the cylinder to be worked on.**
5. **Turn the crankshaft to bring the piston of this cylinder down, away from possible contact with the valve head. Sharply tap the valve retainer to loosen the valve lock.**
6. **Then turn the crankshaft to bring the piston in this cylinder to the Exact Top of its Compression Stroke.**
7. **Screw in the chuck-equipped spark plug shell.**
8. **Hook up an air hose to the chuck and turn on the pressure (about 200 lbs.).**
9. **With a strong and constant supply of air holding the valve closed, compress the valve spring and remove the lock and retainer.**
10. **Make the necessary replacements and reassemble.**

NOTE: it is important that the operation be performed exactly as stated, in this order. The piston in the cylinder must be on exact top-center to prevent air pressure from turning the crankshaft.

Checking valve spring installed height—6 cyl.
(© Pontiac Div. G.M. Corp.)

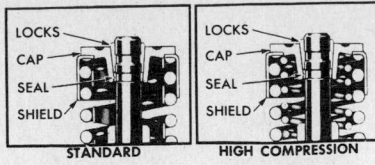

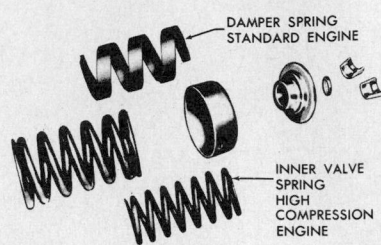

Typical valve spring assemblies
(© Pontiac Div. G.M. Corp.)

Hydraulic Valve Lifter Disassembly

Disassemble lifters for cleaning only; no repairs are permitted.

1. Grasp lock ring with needle nose pliers and remove. (Depress plunger to gain clearance.)
2. Remove pushrod cup, metering valve disc, and upper metering disc (if any). Do not bend metering disc.
3. Remove plunger assembly and plunger spring.
4. Remove spring, check valve retainer and check valve from plunger.
5. Clean all parts in solvent (lacquer thinner) and reassemble.

NOTE: internal parts are **not** interchangeable between lifters.

1966-69 6 Cylinder OHC Lash Adjuster (Valve Tappet)

This engine is equipped with hydraulic valve lash adjusters. These adjusters are located in the cylinder head and serve as a fulcrum of the rocker arms, and locate the rocker arms accurately with the camshaft lobes. This lash adjuster is identical to that of a lifter used in a conventional pushrod engine. However, the lash adjuster remains stationary to maintain adjustment at all times.

These adjusters are to be serviced in the same manner as conventional hydraulic tappets.

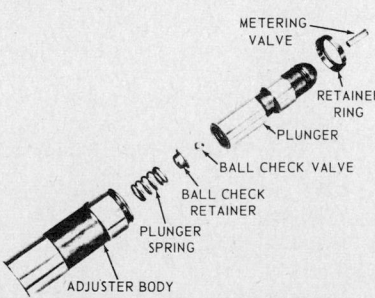

6 cyl. OHC valve lash adjuster
(© Pontiac Div. G.M. Corp.)

R & R

1. Remove rocker cover assembly.
2. Remove rocker arm and hydraulic lash adjuster assemblies, keeping them in proper order for correct installation in original positions.

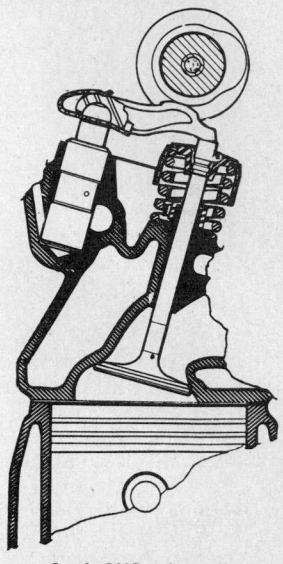

6 cyl. OHC valve train
(© Pontiac Div. G.M. Corp.)

3. If lash adjuster sticks in its bore, proceed as follows:
   a. Remove rocker arm.
   b. Fill vent hole adjacent to lifter with SAE 30 oil.
   c. Insert a 4 in. length of 3/16 in. diameter rod into the vent hole and strike the end of the rod sharply with a hammer.

NOTE: the hydraulic pressure generated in this operation should be sufficient to dislodge even the most stubborn adjuster.

4. To install, reverse removal procedure, with the exception of Step 3.

Valve Adjustment—Ram Air IV and Super Duty Engine

With this engine, it is not possible to adjust valves by tightening the rocker arm adjusting nut until it seats on the shoulder of the rocker arm. To adjust these limited travel lifters with the engine installed in the car, proceed as follows: (If engine has been removed, use other procedure.)

Engine In Car

1. Tighten rocker arm adjusting nuts so that pushrods will not jump out of place when engine is started.
2. Start engine and retighten rocker arm on any valve that is clattering. Tighten just until noise disappears.

NOTE: oil deflector clips are a help in this operation; they are available through automotive parts jobbers.

3. Allow engine to run until nor-

mal operating temperature is achieved, then loosen each rocker arm adjusting nut until clattering begins. Retighten nut until noise disappears (this brings pushrod slightly into top of lifter travel) and, with adjusting nut in this position, tighten locknut to 30-40 ft. lbs.

Engine Out of Car

1. Rotate crankshaft until No. 1 piston is at TDC on compression stroke and distributor rotor points to No. 1 spark plug wire cap tower. Timing mark should be aligned with "O" on timing cover.
2. Tighten rocker arm adjusting nuts on No. 1 cylinder rockers to obtain 0.008 in. clearance between rocker arms and valve stems.
3. Tighten adjusting nuts an additional 1/8 turn ±5°, then tighten locknuts to 30-40 ft. lbs.
4. Rotate crankshaft 90°, in normal direction of rotation, to bring next piston in firing order (No. 8) to TDC on compression stroke, then complete Steps 2 and 3.
5. Continue as in Step 4 for the rest of the cylinders; firing order is 1-8-4-3-6-5-7-2.

Timing Case

Timing Gear Cover and Oil Seal R & R

1965 and 1970-72 OHV 6 Cylinder

1. Drain cooling system and disconnect radiator hoses at radiator.
2. Remove fan and water pump pulley.
3. Remove radiator and fan belt.
4. Remove harmonic balancer, using a puller.
5. Loosen oil pan bolts and allow pan to rest against front crossmember.
6. Remove timing gear cover bolts, then remove cover and gasket.
7. Pry out oil seal using a screwdriver.
   NOTE: seal can be replaced with cover installed.
8. Install new seal, with lip toward inside of cover. Drive it into place, using proper seal installer or an old wheel bearing outer race.
9. Inspect oil nozzle for damage and replace if necessary, then clean all gasket surfaces.
10. Install cover and gasket (stick gasket to block with Vaseline or wheel bearing grease), making sure cover is centered properly on crankshaft end.
    NOTE: the factory uses a centering tool (J-21742) for this job.
11. Tighten cover bolts to 7 ft. lbs.,

then install oil pan and harmonic balancer.

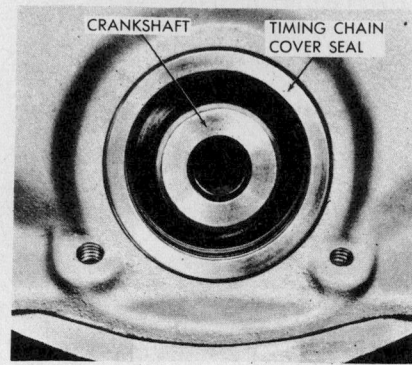

Timing chain cover oil seal
(© Pontiac Div. G.M. Corp.)

1965-72 V8 Except Ventura II

1. Drain radiator and cylinder block.
2. Loosen alternator adjusting bolts.
3. Remove fan, fan pulley, and accessory drive belts.
4. Disconnect radiator hoses.
5. Remove fuel pump.
   NOTE: not necessary if only seal is being replaced.
6. Remove harmonic balancer bolt and washer.
7. Remove harmonic balancer.
   NOTE: do not pry on rubber-mounted balancers. Seal can be removed, using a screwdriver, at this point. Install new seal with lip inward.
8. Remove front four oil pan to timing cover bolts.
9. Remove timing cover bolts and nuts and cover to intake manifold bolt.
10. Pull cover forward and remove.
11. Remove O-ring from recess in intake manifold, then clean all gasket surfaces.
12. To replace seal, pry it out of the cover using a screwdriver. Install the new seal with lip inwards.
    NOTE: seal can be replaced with cover installed.
13. To install, reverse removal procedure, making sure all gaskets are replaced. Tighten four oil pan bolts to 12 ft. lbs., harmonic balancer bolt to 160 ft. lbs., and fan pulley bolts to 20 ft. lbs.

1971-72 Ventura II V8

1. Remove oil pan, as outlined later in this section.
2. Lower engine back onto motor mounts.
3. Remove harmonic balancer, using a puller.
4. Remove water pump, as outlined previously.
5. Remove timing cover bolts and cover.
6. Install by reversing removal procedure. Tighten cover bolts to 80 in. lbs.

Timing Belt, Crankshaft Sprocket, or Lower Crankcase Cover Seal R & R—1966-69 OHC 6 Cylinder

Radiator removal, at this point, is a distinct advantage for this operation.

1. Remove upper front timing cover.
2. Align timing marks.
3. Remove fan and water pump pulley.
4. Remove harmonic balancer.
5. Remove timing belt lower front cover.
6. Loosen accessory drive mounting bolts to provide slack in timing belt.
7. Remove timing belt.
8. Remove crankshaft timing belt flange and sprocket.
9. Carefully remove seal from crankcase cover.
10. Install new seal, with lip of seal inward, using seal installer J-22260.
11. Replace crankshaft timing belt sprocket and flange.
12. Align timing marks and replace timing belt.
13. Replace timing belt lower cover and harmonic balancer.
14. Adjust timing belt tension.
15. Replace water pump pulley and fan.
16. Replace timing belt upper front cover.

Front Crankcase Cover and Gasket R & R—1966-69 OHC 6 Cylinder

1. Remove timing belt sprocket, as described above.
2. Remove four front oil pan-to-crankcase cover retaining bolts.
3. Loosen remaining oil pan bolts, as necessary, to provide clearance between crankcase cover and oil pan.
4. Remove five front crankcase cover attaching bolts.
5. Remove front crankcase cover and gasket, clean off the old gasket.
6. Inspect cover seal for wear or distortion.
7. Using new gasket installed over dowels and, if necessary, new seal, reverse removal procedures, torque oil pan and crankcase cover bolts to 10-15 ft. lbs.

Housing Assembly, Oil Pump, Distributor and Fuel Pump— 1966-69 OHC 6 Cylinder

The housing is unique, and consists of the oil pump, distributor and the fuel pump. The oil filter is also attached to this housing. The housing carries the drive sprocket for the above units and is used as a tensioner for the timing belt.

Oil Pressure Regulator R & R

1. Remove cap washer and spring from housing assembly.
2. Using magnet, remove valve from housing assembly.
3. Install valve on spring and install as an assembly.
4. Install cap washer.

Oil Pump R & R

1. Remove oil pump cover and gasket.
2. Remove drive gear and driven gear.
3. Install gears.
4. Replace cover using new gasket. Torque attaching bolts to 15-25 ft. lbs.

9. Align timing marks and install timing belt.
10. Connect fuel lines to fuel pump.
11. Replace distributor cap, vacuum lines and wires.
12. Adjust timing belt tension, see timing belt adjustment.
13. Replace timing belt top front cover.

Distributor and Oil Pump Drive Housing (Except Oil Pump) Disassembly and Assembly

1. Remove housing assembly.
2. Observe and record location of sprocket timing mark and position of distributor rotor. Remove distributor.

5. Inspect shaft assembly, seal and bearing.
6. If necessary to replace bearing or seal, use tool J-22264 and slide hammer to remove seal, or bearing and seal together.
7. Use tools J-22267-1 and J-22267-2 to install seal.
8. Reassemble by reversing Steps 1 through 4.

NOTE: substitute tools can be made by duplicating tools in illustrations.

1966-69 OHC Timing Belt Adjustment

1. Remove timing belt top front cover.
2. Using J-22232-2 calibration bar, set the pointer of timing belt tension fixture J-22232-1 to zero.

NOTE: this calibration must be performed before each use of J-22232 fixture to insure an accurate timing belt adjustment.

3. Remove camshaft sprocket to camshaft bolt and install J-22232-1 (tension fixture) on the belt with the rollers on the outside (smooth) surface of belt. Thread the fixture mounting bolt into camshaft sprocket bolt location, finger-tight.
4. Squeeze indicator end (upper) of fixture and quickly release so the fixture assumes released or relaxed position.
5. With J-22232-1 installed, as above, adjust accessory drive housing up or down, as required, to obtain a tension adjustment indicator reading centered in the green range, with drive housing mounting bolts torqued to 15 ± 3 ft. lbs.
6. Remove tension fixture and install sprocket retaining bolt, making sure bolt threads and washers are free of dirt.
7. Install upper front timing belt cover.

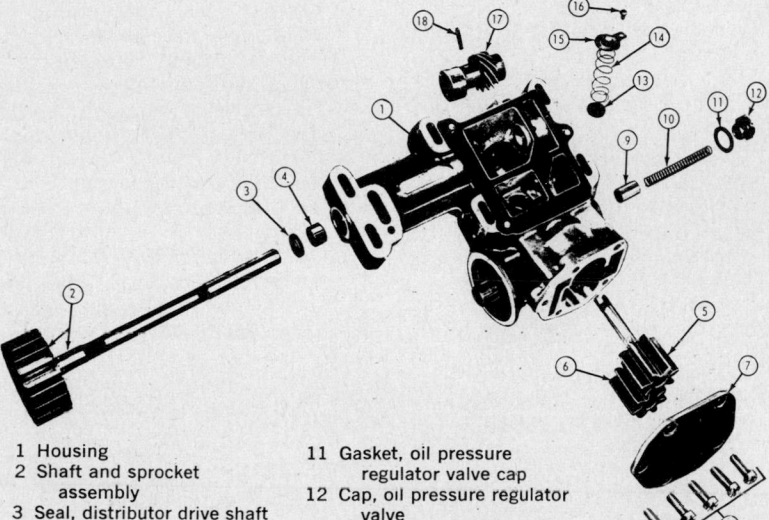

1 Housing
2 Shaft and sprocket assembly
3 Seal, distributor drive shaft
4 Bearing, distributor drive
5 Gear and shaft assembly oil pump drive
6 Gear, oil pump driven cover, oil pump
7 Cover, oil pump
8 Bolt, oil pump cover to housing
9 Valve, oil pressure regulator
10 Spring, oil pressure regulator

11 Gasket, oil pressure regulator valve cap
12 Cap, oil pressure regulator valve
13 Seat, oil filter by-pass valve
14 Spring, oil filter by-pass valve
15 Retainer, oil filter by-pass valve
16 Screw, oil filter by-pass valve retainer
17 Gear and eccentric
18 Pin, distributor oil and fuel pump gear and eccentric

OHC 6 cyl. oil pump housing and distributor drive assembly
(© Pontiac Div. G.M. Corp.)

Housing Assembly R & R

1. Remove timing belt top front cover.
2. Align timing marks.
3. Loosen six housing assembly from cylinder block retaining bolts.
4. Remove timing belt from camshaft sprocket and distributor drive.
5. Disconnect fuel lines from fuel pump.
6. Remove distributor cap, vacuum lines and wires from distributor.
7. Remove housing by removing six retaining bolts.
8. Install, using a new gasket, and loosely install housing assembly to cylinder block with six retaining bolts.

3. Remove fuel pump eccentric and distributor drive gear retaining pin.
4. Remove shaft and sprocket assembly from housing.

J 22264

Removing seal from OHC 6 distributor and oil pump drive housing
(© Pontiac Div. G.M. Corp.)

Camshaft R & R

1965 and 1970-72 OHV 6 Cylinder

1. Drain cooling system.

2. Remove radiator, fan, and water pump pulley.
3. Remove grill.
4. Remove valve cover and gasket, then loosen rocker arm nuts and pivot rockers out of the way.
5. Remove pushrods.
6. Remove distributor, fuel pump, and spark plugs.
7. Remove coil, pushrod (tappet gallery) covers and gasket; reach in and remove tappets, keeping them in order.
8. Remove harmonic balancer, then loosen oil pan bolts and allow pan to drop.
9. Remove timing gear cover.
10. Remove two camshaft thrust plate bolts by rotating cam gear

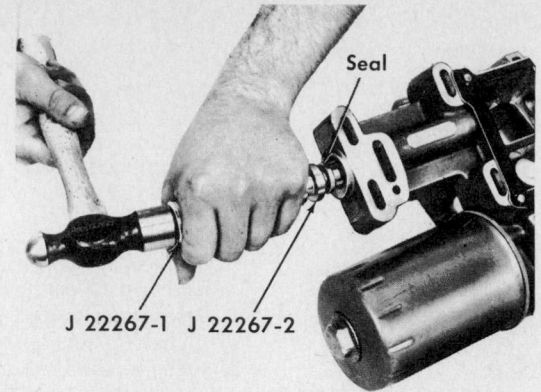

J 22267-1   J 22267-2

Installing seal into OHC 6 distributor and oil pump drive housing
(© Pontiac Div. G.M. Corp.)

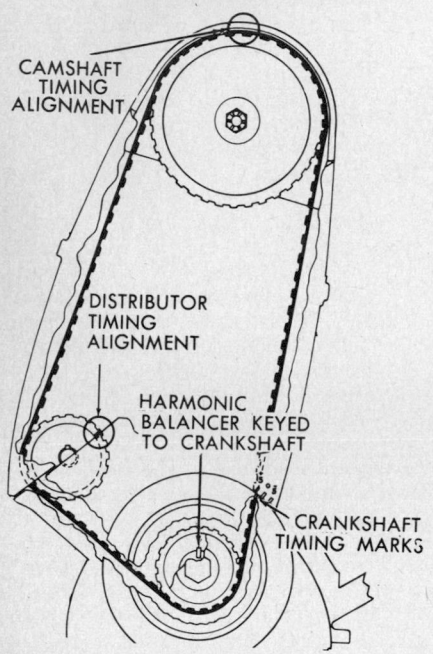

CAMSHAFT TIMING ALIGNMENT

DISTRIBUTOR TIMING ALIGNMENT

HARMONIC BALANCER KEYED TO CRANKSHAFT

CRANKSHAFT TIMING MARKS

OHC 6 cyl. timing mark alignment

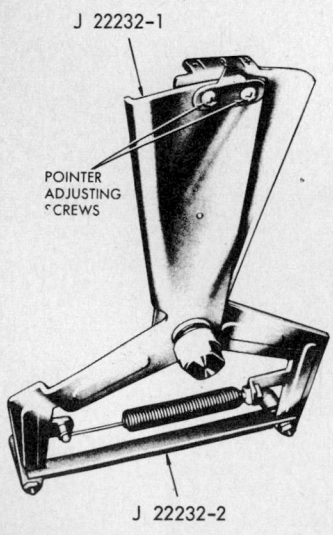

J 22232-1

POINTER ADJUSTING SCREWS

J 22232-2

OHC 6 cyl. timing belt adjustment with tool J-22232
(© Pontiac Div. G.M. Corp.)

holes to gain clearance.
11. Remove the camshaft by pulling it straight forward.
NOTE: do not wiggle the camshaft; cam bearings could be dislodged.
12. If cam gear is to be replaced, press it from the shaft using an arbor press.
CAUTION: thrust plate must be positioned so that Woodruff key does not damage it during removal.
13. New cam gear must be pressed onto the shaft, with the shaft supported in back of the front bearing journal.
NOTE: the thrust plate end-play should be 0.001-0.005 in. If less than 0.001 in., replace spacer ring; if greater than 0.005 in., replace thrust plate.
14. Carefully install the camshaft into the engine, then turn crankshaft and camshaft so that timing marks coincide; tighten thrust plate bolts to 5-8 ft. lbs.
15. Check camshaft and crankshaft gear runout using a dial indicator. Cam gear runout should not

exceed 0.004 in., crank gear should not exceed 0.003 in.
NOTE: if runout is excessive, remove gear and clean burrs from shaft.
16. Check gear backlash using a dial indicator; it should not exceed 0.006 in. and should not be less than 0.004 in.
17. To complete installation, reverse Steps 1-9.
NOTE: install distributor with No. 1 piston at TDC on compression stroke so that vacuum diaphragm faces forward and rotor points to No. 1 spark plug wire cap tower. Make sure oil pump drive shaft is properly indexed with distributor drive shaft.

1965-72 V8 Except Ventura II

1. Drain cooling system and remove air cleaner.
2. Disconnect all water hoses, vacuum lines and spark plug wires.
3. Disconnect accelerator linkage, temperature gauge wire, and fuel lines.
4. Remove hood latch brace.
5. Remove PCV hose, then remove rocker covers.
NOTE: on air-conditioned models, remove alternator and bracket.
6. Remove distributor, then remove intake manifold.
7. Remove valley cover.
8. Loosen rocker arm nuts and pivot rockers out of the way.
9. Remove pushrods and lifters (keep them in proper order).
10. Remove harmonic balancer, fuel pump, and four oil pan to timing cover bolts.
11. Remove timing cover and gasket, then remove fuel pump eccentric and bushing.
12. Align timing marks, then remove timing chain and sprockets.
13. Remove camshaft thrust plate.
14. Remove camshaft by pulling straight forward, being careful not to damage cam bearings in the process.
NOTE: it may be necessary to jack up the engine slightly to gain clearance, especially if motor mounts are worn.

Checking OHV 6 camshaft gear backlash
(© Chevrolet Div. G.M. Corp.)

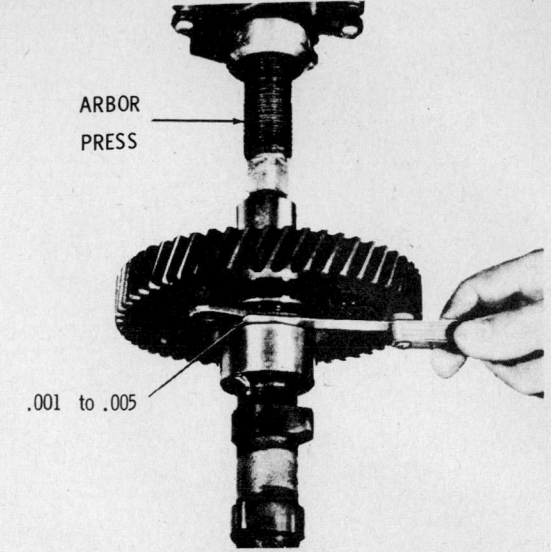

ARBOR PRESS

.001 to .005

Installing OHV 6 camshaft gear and checking thrust plate end-play
(© Chevrolet Div. G.M. Corp.)

Checking OHV 6 camshaft gear runout
(© Chevrolet Div. G.M. Corp.)

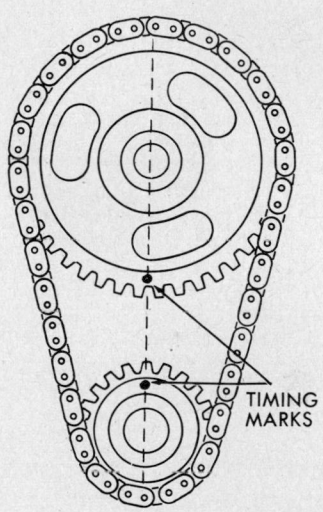

TIMING MARKS

V8 timing mark alignment

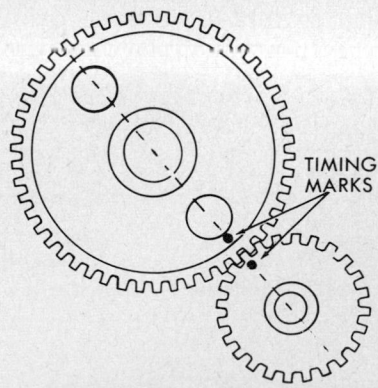

TIMING MARKS

OHV 6 cyl. timing mark alignment

15. Install new camshaft, with lobes and journals coated with heavy (SAE 50-60) oil, into the engine, being careful not to damage cam bearings.
NOTE: most specialty cams come with a special "break-in" lubricant for the lobes and journals; if such lubricant is available, use it instead of heavy oil.
16. Install camshaft thrust plate and tighten bolts to 20 ft. lbs.
17. To install, reverse Steps 1-12, tightening sprocket bolts to 40 ft. lbs., timing cover bolts and nuts to 30 ft. lbs., oil pan bolts to 12 ft. lbs., and harmonic balancer bolt to 160 ft. lbs.

1971-72 Ventura II V8

1. Remove intake manifold, valve lifters and timing chain cover (requires oil pan removal), as described in this section.

2. Remove the two center bolts and the one lower bolt that secure the hood latch support. This will give adequate clearance for the cam. Remove radiator.
3. Remove fuel pump and pump pushrod.
4. Remove camshaft sprocket bolts, sprocket and timing chain. A light blow to the lower edge of a tight sprocket should free it (use a plastic mallet).
5. Install two 5/16—18 x 4 in. bolts in cam bolt holes and pull cam from block.
6. To install, reverse removal procedure, aligning timing marks as illustrated.
NOTE: cam lobes must be lubricated with Molykote or equivalent before installation. All cam journals are the same diameter, so make sure cam bearings are not dislodged during installation.

1966-69 OHC 6 Cylinder

1. Remove camshaft sprocket and seal.
2. Remove rocker cover assembly.
3. Using an adapter and a slide hammer, drive camshaft to the

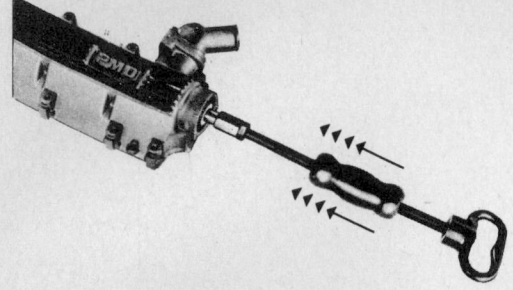

Removing camshaft with slidehammer—OHC 6
(© Pontiac Div. G.M. Corp.)

INDEX THRUST WASHER
TANG IN HOLE IN ROCKER
ARM COVER

Camshaft thrust washer position—OHC 6
(© Pontiac Div. G.M. Corp.)

rear. Make sure bearing surfaces are not damaged during this operation.

4. Disconnect slide hammer and remove camshaft from rear of rocker cover.
5. Remove thrust washer, retaining washer, and bolt from rear of camshaft.
6. Clean and inspect all parts for wear or damage, then inspect bearing surfaces for wear or scoring.
7. Clean camshaft oil passages.
8. To install, reverse removal procedure making sure thrust washer is installed as illustrated. Tighten retaining bolt to 40 ft. lbs.
9. Check camshaft end-play, using a dial indicator on the front sprocket; end-play should be 0.003-0.009 in. and is controlled by the camshaft bore plug.

NOTE: lubricate camshaft lobes and rockers with special lubricant, available at Pontiac dealers. Tighten rocker cover bolts and nuts to 15 ft. lbs. from center outward.

Engine Lubrication

Oil Pan R & R

1965 OHV 6 Cylinder and 1965-66 V8

1. Drain crankcase and cooling system, then remove engine and transmission from vehicle as a complete assembly.
2. Remove the oil pan bolts, then the pan.
3. To install, reverse removal procedure.

1967-70 V8 and 1971 Tempest with Manual Transmission

1. Remove engine from car, as previously described.
2. Remove oil pan bolts.
3. Remove oil pan.

NOTE: 1970 Tempest V8 oil pan can be removed, in some cases, in a manner similar to 1968-69 Firebird V8.

1968-69 Firebird V8

1. Disconnect battery cable at battery.
2. Remove distributor cap and fan shield.
3. Remove fan and fan pulley on air-conditioned models.
4. Disconnect engine ground straps.
5. On air-conditioned models, remove compressor and swing it out of the way without disconnecting hoses.
6. Jack up front of car and drain engine oil.
7. Disconnect steering idler arm from frame.
8. Remove exhaust crossover pipe on single exhaust cars; disconnect exhaust pipes at manifold flanges on dual exhaust cars.
9. Remove starter motor, starter motor bracket, and flywheel cover.
10. Support engine with a chain hoist, then remove motor mounts and loosen rear transmission mount.

NOTE: it may be necessary, in individual cases, to remove the rear transmission mount.

11. Remove oil pan bolts, raise engine about 4½ in., and move engine forward about 1½ in.
12. Remove oil pan by rotating clockwise (to clear oil pump) and pulling down.
13. To install, reverse removal procedure.

1970½ Firebird and All 1971-72 V8 Models

1. Rotate engine until timing mark is at 2:00 o'clock position.
2. Disconnect battery cables.
3. Remove fan. On Ventura II V8, remove only the fan shroud and tilt power steering pump out of the way.
4. Move all water hoses and wiring out of the way.
5. Raise car and drain engine oil. Disconnect idler arm from frame and pitman arm from shaft on Firebird starting 1970½.
6. Disconnect exhaust pipe/s at manifold.
7. Remove starter and bracket, then remove flywheel inspection cover.
8. Support engine with a wood-padded jack.
9. Remove both frame-to-motor mount bolts.
10. Jack up engine for clearance, then remove oil pan bolts and pan.
11. To install, reverse removal procedure. Tighten pan bolts to 12 ft. lbs.

1970-72 OHV 6 Cylinder

1. Remove upper radiator shield assembly.
2. Disconnect negative battery cable.
3. Jack up front of car and drain engine oil.
4. Disconnect exhaust pipe at manifold flange.
5. Remove starter motor and flywheel cover.
6. Raise engine slightly, using a chain hoist, then remove both front motor mount to frame bolts and right motor mount.
7. Remove oil pan bolts, then raise engine and remove oil pan.
8. To install, reverse removal procedure.

NOTE: bolts into timing gear cover should be installed last. They are installed at an angle and holes line up after rest of oil pan bolts are tightened finger-tight.

1966-69 6 Cylinder OHC Removal

1. Disconnect battery.
2. Remove air cleaner assembly.
3. On air conditioned cars, remove compressor from mounting brackets and position to one side.
4. Inspect all water hoses and wiring harness for routing and possible interference. (Engine is

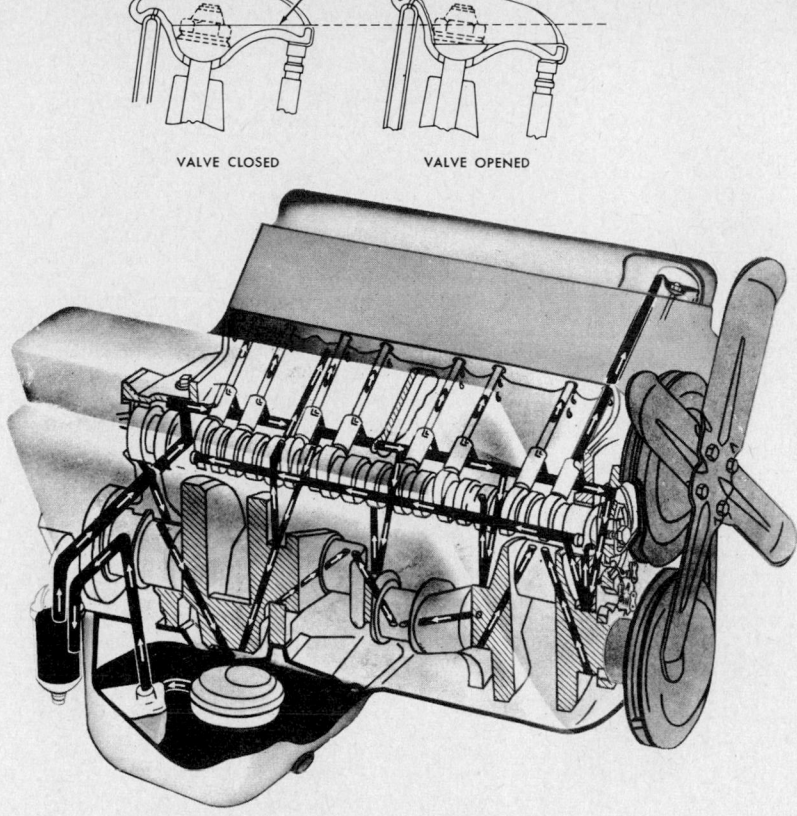

STATIC OIL LEVEL

VALVE CLOSED   VALVE OPENED

V8 oil flow (© Pontiac Div. G.M. Corp.)

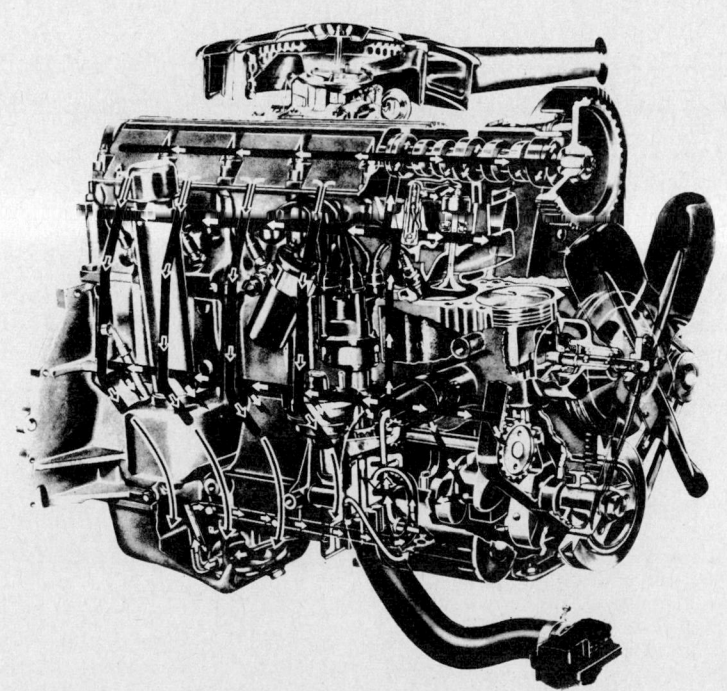

OHC 6 cyl. oil flow
(© Pontiac Div. G.M. Corp.)

raised at least 4½ in. on Tempest, 2 in. on Firebird.)

NOTE: before raising the car, prop the hood open at least 6 in. to ensure enough clearance between timing belt cover and inner hood panel.

5. Raise car and drain crankcase.
6. Remove starter assembly and flywheel cover.
7. Reroute or disconnect any wiring between bellhousing and floor pan to insure against damage when bellhousing contacts pan.
8. Loosen transmission insulator to crossmember retaining bolts.
9. Remove right and left engine insulator to frame bracket through-bolts.
10. Rotate harmonic balancer until timing mark is at bottom. (This properly positions crankshaft counterweights.)
11. Bolt engine support bracket, tool J-22345 to front of harmonic balancer.
12. With suitable equipment, raise engine at J-22345 until insulators clear frame brackets.
13. Remove oil pan bolts.
14. Raise engine. Apply a rearward force on the engine-transmission assembly until oil pan clears the flywheel housing. Then, remove the oil pan.

1966-69 6 Cylinder OHC Installation

1. Install new gasket on oil pan.
2. Apply enough rearward force on engine-transmission assembly to allow oil pan to clear flywheel housing.
3. Install oil pan and torque retaining bolts to 10-15 ft. lbs.
4. Lower engine, remove engine support bracket and install engine insulator bracket to frame through-bolts.
5. Tighten transmission insulator to crossmember bolts to 25-35 ft. lbs.
6. Replace flywheel cover and starter assembly.
7. Lower the car.
8. On air-conditioned cars, install compressor and adjust belt tension.
9. Replace air cleaner assembly.
10. Refill crankcase.
11. Connect battery.

Oil Pump R & R
V8 and 6 Cylinder Engines Except 6 Cylinder OHC

1. Remove engine oil pan. (See previous procedure.)
2. Remove pump attaching screws and carefully lower the pump, while removing the pump drive shaft.
3. Reinstall in reverse order.

NOTE: OHC 6 cylinder oil pump R & R is covered earlier in this section.

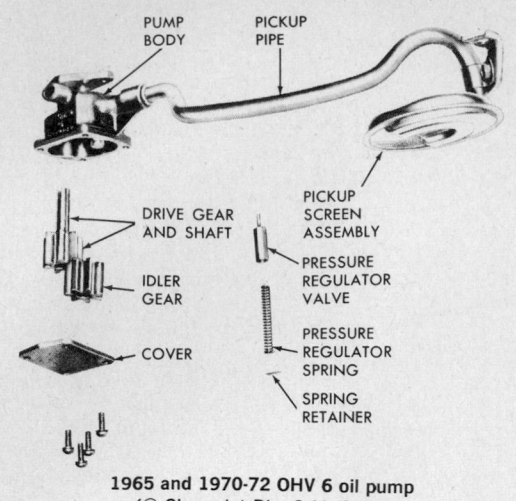

1965 and 1970-72 OHV 6 oil pump
(© Chevrolet Div. G.M. Corp.)

1965-72 6 cylinder engines,
including OHC   0.015 in. compression
              0.035 in. oil
1965-67 326 V8 and 1965-66 389

V8 engines	No. 1	0.021 in.
	No. 2	0.019 in.
	oil	0.035 in.

1967 326 V8, 1967-69 400 V8 and
   1968-72 350 V8 engines
         0.019 in. compression
         0.035 in. oil

1970-72 400 V8 engine	No. 1	0.019 in.
	No. 2	0.015 in.
	oil	0.035 in.
1970-72 455 V8 engine	No. 1	0.021 in.
	No. 2	0.015 in.
	oil	0.035 in.

Clean ring grooves, using a commercial groove cleaner or a broken ring, then install rings. Space ring gaps equally around piston circumference and check ring to groove clearance. The following figures apply to all V8 and six-cylinder engines:

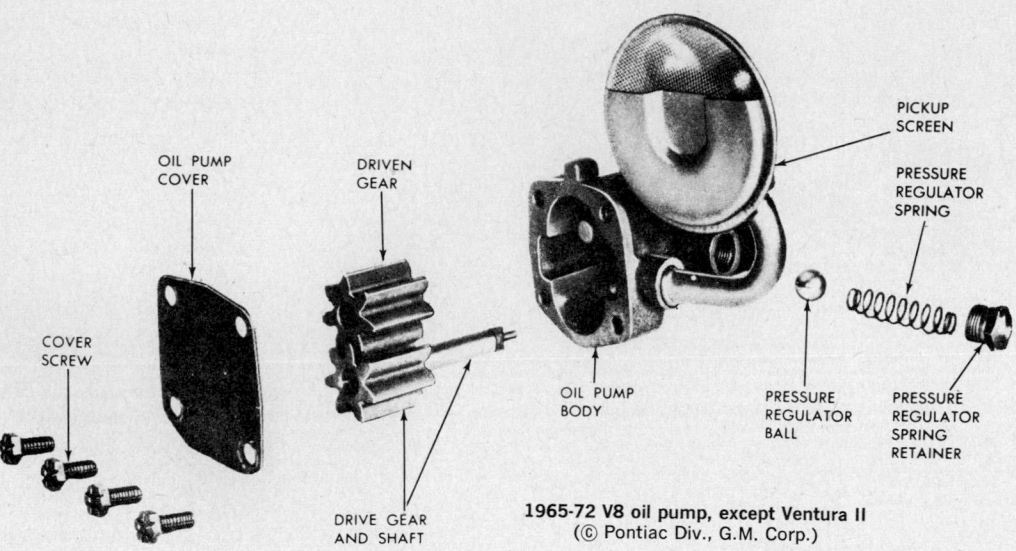

1965-72 V8 oil pump, except Ventura II
(© Pontiac Div., G.M. Corp.)

Oil Pump Disassembly, Inspection and Assembly

1. Remove pressure regulator spring.
2. Remove cover hold-down bolts and cover.
3. Remove driven gear and drive gear, then remove drive shaft.
4. Clean all parts in solvent, especially pump pickup screen.
   NOTE: do not remove or loosen oil pickup tube or screen.
5. Inspect regulator spring for distortion, wear, or cracks.
6. Inspect regulator ball for damage.
7. Inspect pump components for wear.
8. To assemble, first install drive and driven gears, then install cover.
   NOTE: it is a good idea to pack pump with Vaseline for proper priming.
9. Turn drive shaft by hand to make sure it turns freely.
10. Install regulator ball, spring, and retainer.

NOTE: pressure regulator springs are normally 50 psi and are used with unplated gears. GTO oil pumps up to and including 1969, and all Ram Air IV oil pumps to 1970, use 60 psi springs in conjunction with cadmium plated gears. In 1970-72, some 4-BBL. engines use a 60 psi spring and phosphate coated iron gears. Never use higher pressure springs with unplated gears, and never try to increase oil pressure by changing spring length.

Piston Rings

If cylinder bore is in satisfactory condition, place each ring in bore, in turn, and square it in bore using a piston top. Measure the ring end gap with feeler gauges. If gap is greater than that specified, get new ring; if gap is less than that specified, file end of ring to bring within tolerance. Clearances are as follows:

No. 1	0.0015-0.0030 in.
No. 2	0.0015-0.0035 in.
oil	0.0005-0.0055 in.

Ventura II V8 307/350

No. 1	0.0012-0.0027 in.
No. 2	0.0012-0.0032 in.
oil	0.002 - 0.007 in.

Lower rod and piston asemblies, one at a time, into bore until ring compressor contacts block. Using wooden hammer handle, push piston into bore while guiding rod onto journal.

Front Suspension

Description

Ball joints, located at the outer ends of the upper and lower control arms, act as pivot points for both the vertical movement of the wheel and rotation of the steering knuckle. The spherical joints have a fixed boot grease seal to protect against dirt and water. Steering knuckles and spindles are one-piece forgings.

Rubber bushings at the upper inner control arm ends pivot on shafts attached to the frame. By varying shim thickness at this point, caster and camber adjustments are accomplished. The inner ends of the lower control arms are also rubber mounted, and are attached to the front crossmember through brackets.

The upper ends of the coil springs are seated in the frame, while the lower ends rest on the lower control arms. Double-action shock absorbers are located inside the coil springs, the rubber insulated upper end of each unit being fastened to the frame, the similarly insulated lower end to the lower control arm.

For increased roll stability, a stab-

PISTON TO CYLINDER WALL CLEARANCE (IN.)

Engine	At Top Land	At Skirt Top	At Skirt Bottom
1965-215 OHV	.0320-.0420	.0005-.0011*	.0004-.0017
1970-72 250 OHV 6	.0345-.0435	.0005-.0011†	—
1966-69 230/250 OHC 6	.0250-.0303	.0022-.0028△	.0017-.0033
1965-66 326 V8	.0310-.0410	.0005-.0021‡	.0006-.0018
1967-68 326 V8	.0248-.0301	.0022-0028△	.0017-.0033
1965-66 389 V8	.0177-.0230	.0005-0021‡	.0017-.0033
1967-68 400 V8	.0177-.0230	⌠.0025-0031△ (67) / ⌡.0022-0028△ (68)	.0017-.0033
1969 400 V8	.0170-.0210	.0025-.0031△	.0020-.0036
All Ram Air IV V8	.0330-.0420	.0055-.0061△	.0040-.0057
1970-72 400 V8	.0170-.0210	.0025-.0033△	.0020-.0038
1968-69 350 V8	.0240-.0290	.0022-.0028△	.0017-.0033
1970-72 350 V8	.0240-.0290	.0025-.0033△	.0020-.0038
1970-72 455 V8	.0240-.0290	.0025-.0033◎	.0020-.0038
1971-72 307 Ventura II	.0235-.0325	.0005-.0015**	—
1972 350 Ventura II	.0235-.0325	.0007-.0017††	—

* 2.16 in. below piston top.
† 2.44 in. below piston top.
△ 1.11 in. below piston top.
◎ 1.08 in. below piston top

‡ 1.18 in. below piston top (.0007-.0013 in. preferred).
** 1.675 in. below piston top.
†† 1.560 in. below piston top.

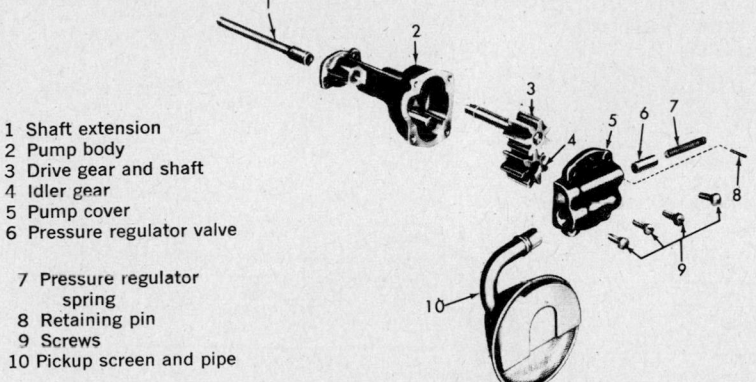

1 Shaft extension
2 Pump body
3 Drive gear and shaft
4 Idler gear
5 Pump cover
6 Pressure regulator valve

7 Pressure regulator spring
8 Retaining pin
9 Screws
10 Pickup screen and pipe

Oil pump components—1971-72 Ventura II V8
(© Pontiac Div. G.M. Corp.)

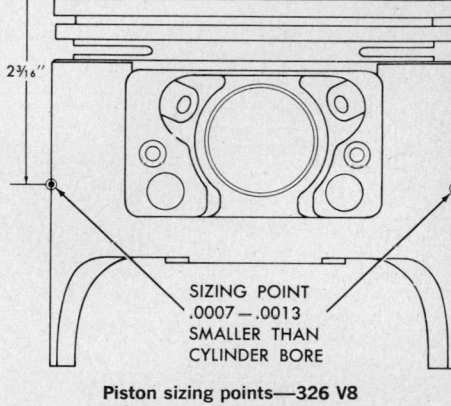

SIZING POINT
.0007—.0013
SMALLER THAN
CYLINDER BORE

Piston sizing points—326 V8
(© Pontiac Div. G.M. Corp.)

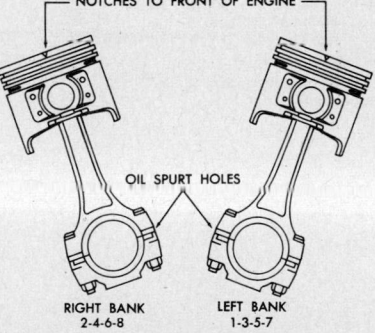

NOTCHES TO FRONT OF ENGINE

OIL SPURT HOLES

RIGHT BANK 2-4-6-8   LEFT BANK 1-3-5-7

**V8 piston and rod assembly, except Ventura II.
See Camaro section for small-block V8
piston and rod assembly.**

NOTCH & "F" TOWARD FRONT OF ENGINE

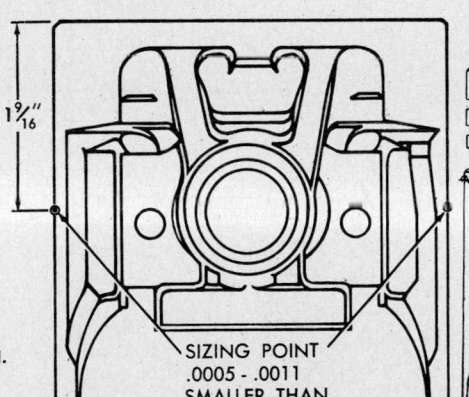

SIZING POINT
.0005 - .0011
SMALLER THAN
CYLINDER BORE

Piston sizing points—OHV 6

SIZING POINT

**Piston sizing points—OHC 6 and all V8 except 326
and Ventura II** (© Pontiac Div., G.M. Corp.)

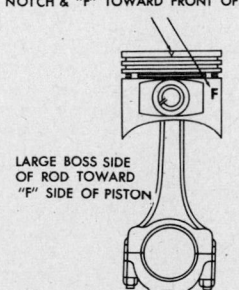

LARGE BOSS SIDE
OF ROD TOWARD
"F" SIDE OF PISTON

Piston and rod assembly—6 cyl.

ilizer bar is rubber mounted to the frame and is connected to the lower control arms via links at each end.

The Ventura II front suspension is similar to the Tempest, the main difference being that the stabilizer bar mounting brackets are located by two clamps and sleeves mounted to the inboard ends. The gap between the sleeve and bracket never should exceed 1/8 in. See the Unit Repair

Section for wheel alignment procedures.

Coil Spring R & R—1965 Tempest and GTO

1. Place car on a hoist which supports car at side rails. The front control arms must be allowed to swing free, and must be positioned so that the control arms may be raised or lowered with

the hoist.

2. Remove shock absorber and wheel.
3. Disconnect stabilizer bar from control arm, then disconnect tie-rod.
4. Place stand under control arm and take up slightly on spring compression.
5. Remove lower ball stud from steering knuckle.
6. Carefully raise hoist until spring is free. Remove the spring.
7. To install, reverse removal procedure, tightening tie-rod to 30-45 ft. lbs., lower ball joint to 85-100 ft. lbs, and upper ball joint (if removed) to 55-70 ft. lbs.

Coil Spring R & R—1966-68 Tempest and GTO

1. Jack up car to allow lower control arm to hang free. Support car on jack stands under the frame side rails.
2. Remove wheel and brake drum.
3. Remove shock absorber.

4. Disconnect stabilizer bar from lower control arm.
5. Insert a spring compressing tool through the shock absorber mounting holes and compress the coil spring until it lifts from its seat.
   NOTE: a spring compressor can be fabricated using a length of threaded rod, a support plate and a support hook.
6. Remove backing plate and swing it out of the way.
7. Disconnect lower ball joint stud and swing steering knuckle out of the way.
8. Pull lower control arm down far enough to remove spring.
9. To install, reverse removal procedure.
   NOTE: spring must be compressed before installation.

Coil Spring R & R—1967-72 Firebird, 1969-72 Tempest, GTO, and Ventura II

1. Jack up car and support on jack stands at frame side rails.
2. Remove shock absorber.
3. Disconnect stabilizer bar at lower control arm.
4. Support lower control arm with a hydraulic floor jack, then remove the two inner control arm to front crossmember bolts.
5. Carefully lower the control arm, allowing the spring to relax.
6. Reach in and remove spring.
   NOTE: this is probably the best all-around procedure and it can be used, with some slight modification, for all models from 1965.

Upper Control Arm Removal

1. Support car weight at outer end of lower control arm.
2. Remove wheel and tire.
3. Remove cotter pin and nut from upper control arm ball stud.
4. Remove the stud from the knuckle with a pry bar, while tapping with a hammer.
5. Remove two nuts that hold the

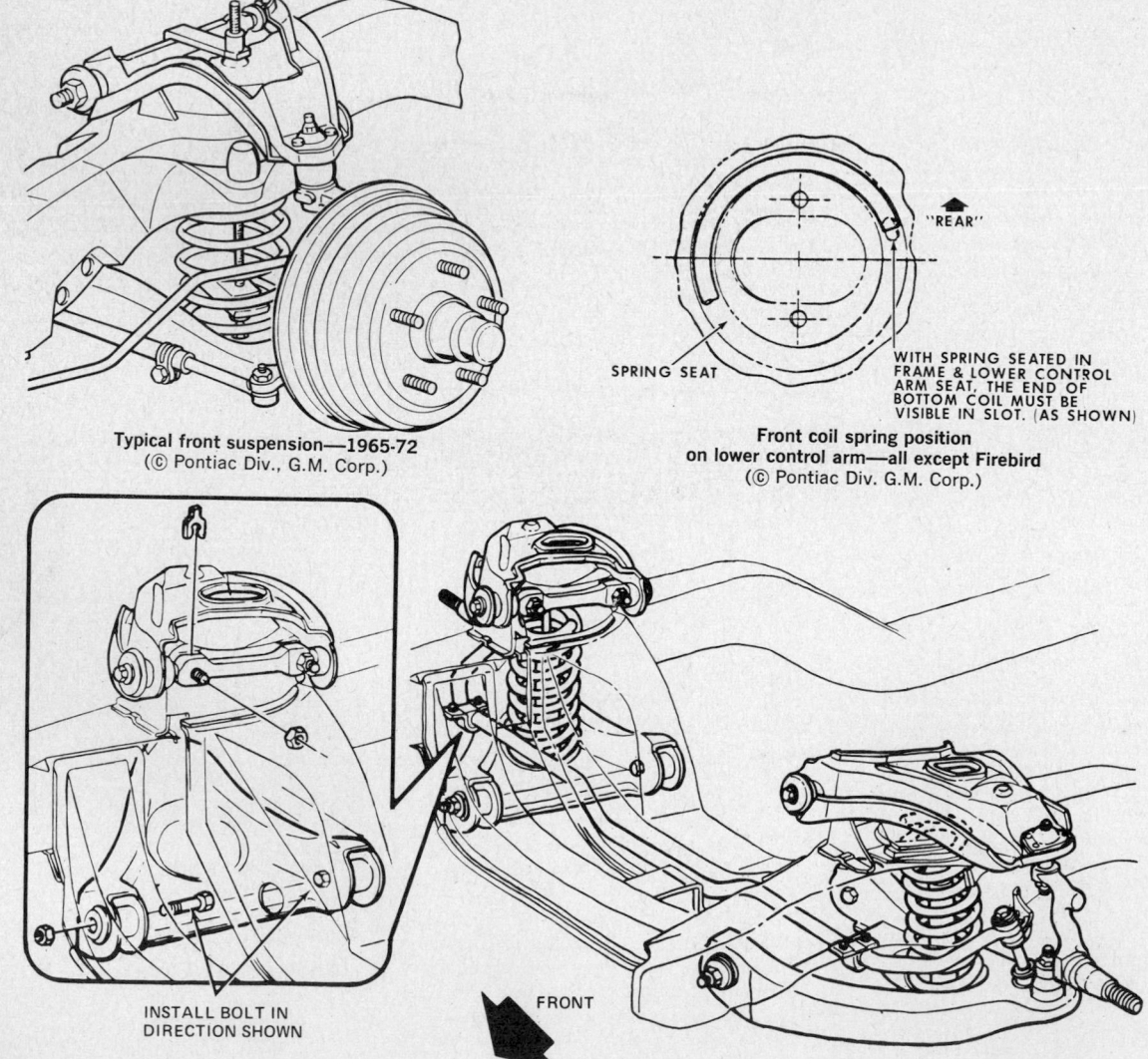

Typical front suspension—1965-72
(© Pontiac Div., G.M. Corp.)

"REAR"

SPRING SEAT

WITH SPRING SEATED IN
FRAME & LOWER CONTROL
ARM SEAT, THE END OF
BOTTOM COIL MUST BE
VISIBLE IN SLOT. (AS SHOWN)

Front coil spring position
on lower control arm—all except Firebird
(© Pontiac Div. G.M. Corp.)

INSTALL BOLT IN
DIRECTION SHOWN

FRONT

Front suspension—1971-72 Ventura II (© Pontiac Div. G.M. Corp.)

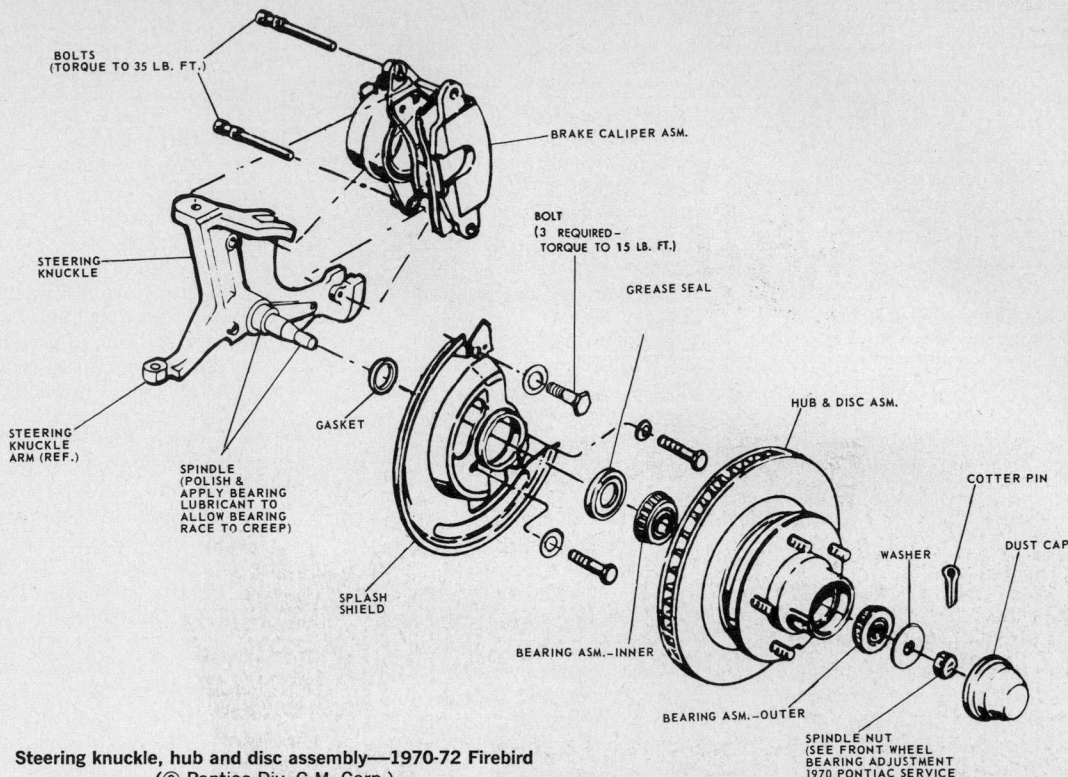

BOLTS
(TORQUE TO 35 LB. FT.)

BRAKE CALIPER ASM.

STEERING
KNUCKLE

BOLT
(3 REQUIRED -
TORQUE TO 15 LB. FT.)

GREASE SEAL

STEERING
KNUCKLE
ARM (REF.)

HUB & DISC ASM.

COTTER PIN

SPINDLE
(POLISH &
APPLY BEARING
LUBRICANT TO
ALLOW BEARING
RACE TO CREEP)

GASKET

WASHER

DUST CAP

SPLASH
SHIELD

BEARING ASM.-INNER

BEARING ASM.-OUTER

SPINDLE NUT
(SEE FRONT WHEEL
BEARING ADJUSTMENT
1970 PONTIAC SERVICE
MANUAL)

Steering knuckle, hub and disc assembly—1970-72 Firebird
(© Pontiac Div. G.M. Corp.)

upper control arm cross-shaft to front crossmember. Count number of shims at each bolt.

NOTE: on V8 Firebird models up to 1969 with air conditioning, swing compressor out of the way.

Upper Ball Joint Removal

1. Prickpunch the center of the four rivets.
2. Drill through the heads of these rivets.
3. Chisel off rivet heads and tap out rivets with a punch.

Upper Ball Joint Installation

1. Install new ball joint against top side of upper control arm. Secure joint to control arm with the four special alloy bolts and nuts furnished with the replacement part.
2. Torque these bolts and nuts to 10-12 ft. lbs.

NOTE: use special bolts only.

Upper Control Arm Installation

1. Install bolts through holes and install upper control arm to crossmember.
2. Secure two nuts and washers to the bolts holding the upper control arm shaft to front crossmember. Install same number of shims as removed at each bolt. Torque bolts to 50 ft. lbs.
3. Lubricate ball joint with chassis lube.
4. Install ball joint stud through knuckle. Install nut, and torque to 50 ft. lbs.
5. Install wheel and tire assembly.

6. Lower car to floor.
7. Bounce car to neutralize front end suspension and torque pivot shaft nuts to 50 ft. lbs. on Tempest, 35 ft. lbs. on Firebird.
8. Be sure to recheck caster and camber.

Lower Control Arm and Ball Joint R & R

1. Remove coil spring and lower control arm inner bolts.
2. Separate lower ball joint from steering knuckle by prying, while hammering sharply on steering knuckle.
3. Press lower ball joint from lower control arm using suitable arbors and a large bench vise.
4. To install, reverse removal procedure, tightening lower ball joint stud nut to 85-90 ft. lbs.

NOTE: if only ball joint is to be removed, remove brake caliper or hub and backing plate, with jack under lower arm. Begin with Step 2.

Jacking, Hoisting

Jack car at front spring seats of lower control arms. Jack car at rear under axle housing.

Manual Steering Gear

NOTE: see Unit Repair Section.

Steering Gear Box R & R

1. Disconnect pitman arm from pit-

man shaft.

NOTE: the factory recommends a special puller be used, although the arm can be removed, in some cases, by using a pry bar and a hammer.

2. Matchmark the worm shaft flange and steering shaft, then disconnect lower flange.
3. Remove the three steering gear box to frame bolts, then the gear box.
4. To install, reverse removal procedure, tightening frame bolts to 70-90 ft. lbs.

In-Car Adjustment

There are two adjustments on the steering gear, worm bearing preload and pitman shaft overcenter adjustment.

The wheel should turn smoothly through its entire range. Roughness indicates internal trouble requiring disassembly. Binding (especially in straight ahead position) indicates too tight an adjustment. See the Unit Repair Section.

Power Steering Gear

For detailed information on the power steering and pump, see Unit Repair Section.

Clutch

A single-plate, dry-disc, diaphragm-spring clutch is used on all Tempest, Firebird, GTO and Ventura II models. The clutch assembly consists of the driven plate, the pressure plate,

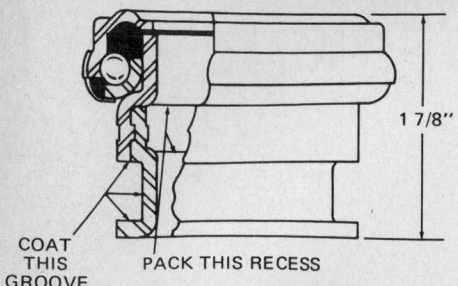

COAT
THIS
GROOVE   PACK THIS RECESS

1 7/8"

**Clutch throwout bearing used on
1971-72 Ventura II. This bearing is
different from the one used on
400 and 455 cu. in. engines**
(© Pontiac Div. G.M. Corp.)

and the release mechanism. Grooves on both sides of the driven plate prevent the plate's sticking to the flywheel and pressure plate due to vacuum.

Two types of diaphragm type pressure plates are used—a bent finger type, for the high performance OHC six-cylinder and V8s of more than 350 cu. in. displacement, and a flat finger type, for low performance V8s and six-cylinder standard engines. The diaphragm spring design is such that no overcenter spring is required.

The clutch release mechanism consists of a ball thrust (throwout) bearing and various linkage configurations (for the various models) to control this bearing. The throwout bearing slides on the front transmission extension housing (nose piece), which is concentric with and encloses the transmission main drive gear. When pedal pressure is applied, the clutch fork pivots on its ball socket, through linkage action, and the inner

end of the fork forces the throwout bearing against the release levers.

A clutch safety switch prevents engine cranking unless the clutch is disengaged (on 1969-72 models). The only periodic clutch service required, other than adjustment for normal wear, is the lubrication of all linkage pivot points every 6,000 miles.

Removal—1965-72

1. Raise car and support on jackstands.
2. Support rear of engine with jackstand.
3. Remove driveshaft.
4. Remove rear crossmember bolts from frame and transmission mounts, and remove crossmember.

NOTE: see transmission removal procedure for procedure variations.

5. Disconnect transmission shift linkage, speedometer cable and clutch return spring. Clutch fork pushrod will now hang free.
6. Remove clutch housing cover plate screws and let plate hang from starter gear housing.
7. Lower engine enough to gain access to clutch housing bolts at engine block, then remove all but uppermost bolt.
8. Hold transmission and clutch housing assembly against block over dowel pins while removing last bolt. Remove transmission and clutch housing as an assembly.
9. Matchmark pressure plate and flywheel with paint to make sure correct balance is maintained.
10. Loosen the six cover plate at-

taching screws, a little at a time, until clutch diaphragm spring tension is released. Remove bolts, clutch assembly and pilot tool.

Installation—1965-72

1. The clutch bearing is an oil-impregnated type bearing pressed into the crankshaft. Inspect and renew, if necessary.
2. Install clutch disc with long hub forward (toward flywheel).
3. Install pressure plate and cover assembly, then align clutch disc by inserting pilot tool, or old transmission mainshaft, into splines. Align mark on clutch cover with mark on flywheel, then align nearest bolt holes.
4. Install bolts in every other hole in cover and tighten alternately. Then, install remaining three bolts, tighten all six to 25 ft. lb. (35 for Ventura II).
5. Remove clutch pilot tool and check to see that it can be reinserted and moved freely.
6. Install clutch fork and dust boot into clutch housing. Lubricate throwout bearing with graphite grease.
7. Complete the reassembly of clutch housing and transmission by reversing removal method. Tighten housing bolts to 40 ft. lbs. (30 for Ventura II).
8. Adjust shifter and clutch release linkage.

Clutch Pedal Adjustment —1965-72

1. Disconnect return spring.
2. With pedal against stop, loosen

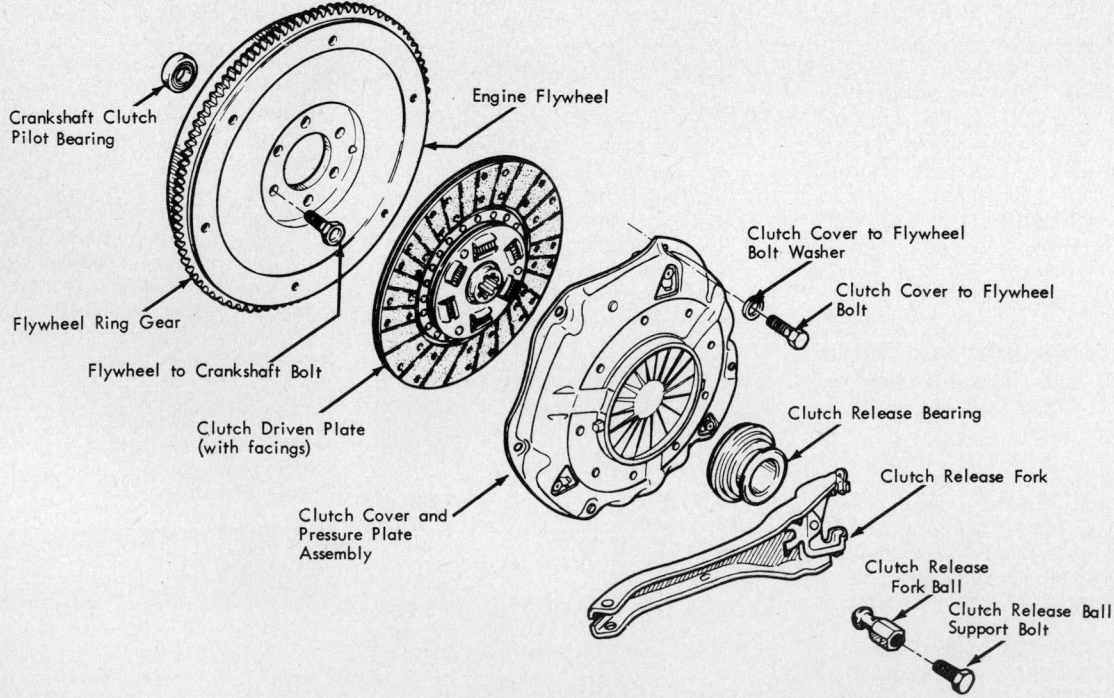

Crankshaft Clutch
Pilot Bearing

Engine Flywheel

Flywheel Ring Gear

Flywheel to Crankshaft Bolt

Clutch Driven Plate
(with facings)

Clutch Cover and
Pressure Plate
Assembly

Clutch Cover to Flywheel
Bolt Washer

Clutch Cover to Flywheel
Bolt

Clutch Release Bearing

Clutch Release Fork

Clutch Release
Fork Ball

Clutch Release Ball
Support Bolt

Typical diaphragm spring clutch assembly (© Pontiac Div., G.M. Corp.)

locknut to allow adjusting rod to be turned out of swivel (V8), or pushrod (6 cyl.), until the throwout bearing contacts the release fingers in the pressure plate.

3. Turn adjusting rod into swivel or pushrod 3½ turns (3 turns for Ventura II) ; tighten locknut to 8-12 ft. lbs. for 1965-68, 30 ft. lbs. for 1969-72.

4. Install return spring and check pedal lash; it should be approximately 1 in.

Pilot Bearing and Flywheel Replacement—1965-72

1. Remove transmission and clutch.
2. Using a small cold chisel, remove stake marks which hold pilot bearing in the flywheel.
3. Pull the old bearing out of the flywheel, using a slide hammer if necessary.
4. With new bearing held in place, shielded side toward transmission, gently tap on bearing until it enters the flywheel until flush. Stake in at least two places, using a prick punch.
5. If flywheel is removed, make sure to matchmark the flywheel and crankshaft flange.
6. To install, reverse removal procedure, tightening flywheel bolts to 95 ft. lbs.

NOTE: flywheel bolts do not need lockwashers.

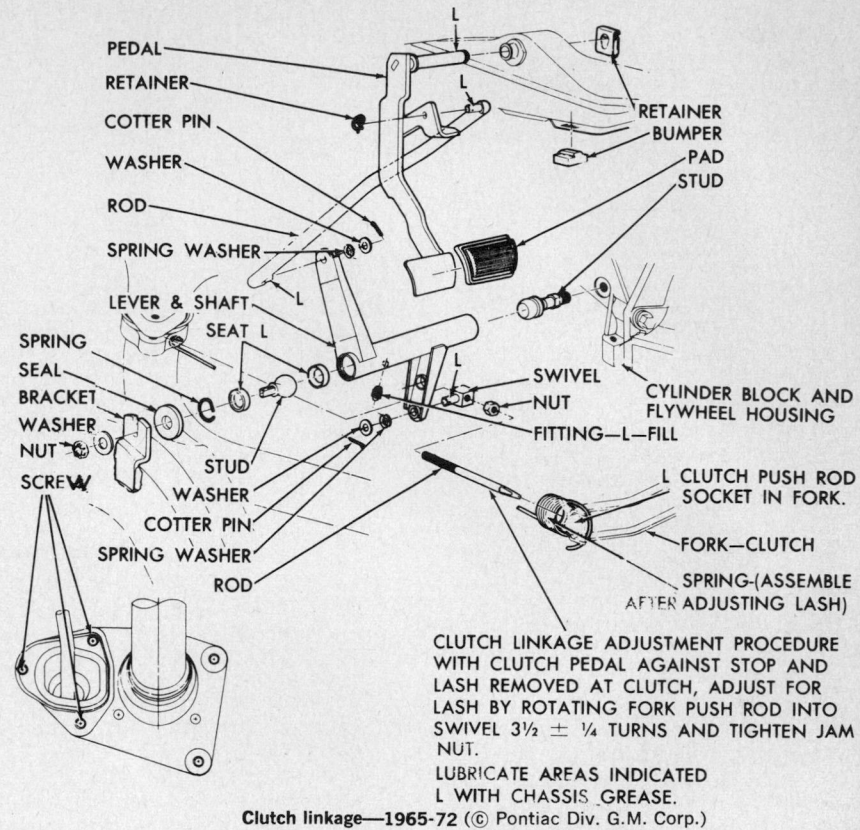

Clutch linkage—1965-72 (© Pontiac Div. G.M. Corp.)

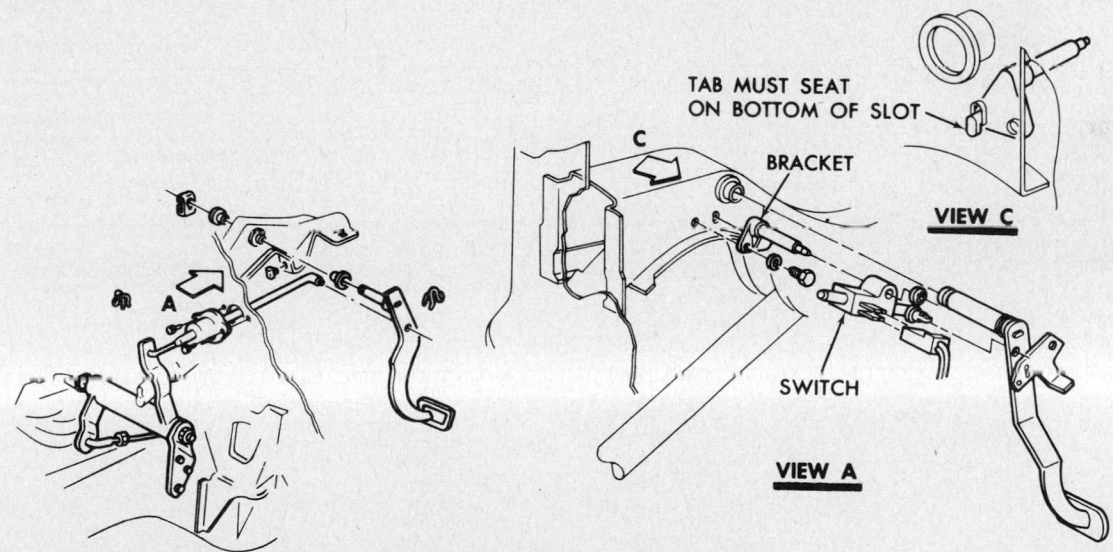

Upper clutch linkage—1971-72 Ventura II (© Pontiac Div. G.M. Corp.)

Three-Speed Manual Transmission

Linkage Adjustment—Column

1965-66
See illustrations.

1967-68 Saginaw Transmission
See illustrations.

1969-72 Saginaw Transmission, Except Firebird from 1970

1. Place gearshift lever in Reverse and lock ignition.
2. On Tempest, loosen swivel clamp bolt (C) at rear transmission shift lever (1st and Reverse) and bolt (D) at equalizer shaft and lever assembly. (See view B in illustration)
3. On Firebird, loosen swivel clamp nut (C) at rear transmission shift lever (1st and Reverse) as illustrated in view C in illustration, then loosen nut (D) at idler lever.
4. Position front transmission shift lever (2nd and 3rd) in Neutral and rear transmission shift lever (1st and Reverse) in Reverse.
5. Tighten swivel clamp bolt (C) or nut (C) to 20 ft. lbs., then unlock

steering column and shift into Neutral.

6. Align lower gearshift levers (on column) (E and F) in Neutral position, then insert a 0.185 in. diameter gauge pin through hole in lower control levers.

7. Tighten swivel clamp bolt (D) or nut (D) to 20 ft. lbs., then remove gauge pin and check shift pattern.

1970-72 Firebird with Saginaw Transmission

1. Place lever in Reverse and lock ignition.
2. Loosen both swivel clamp nuts.
3. Place front transmission shift lever in Neutral.
4. Place rear transmission lever in Reverse.
5. Tighten both swivel clamp nuts to 20 ft. lbs., unlock column and check shift pattern.

1971-72 Ventura II

1. Follow Steps 1-3 of Firebird procedure.
2. Pull down slightly on 1st-Rev rod to remove slack, then tighten swivel clamp nut at 1st-Rev lever to 20 ft. lbs.
3. Unlock steering column and shift into Neutral. Align column levers and insert a .185-.186 in. gauge pin through alignment holes.

4. Position 2nd-3rd transmission lever in Neutral, then tighten swivel clamp nut to 20 ft. lbs.
5. Remove gauge pin and check shift pattern and ignition lock. With lever in Reverse, key must move to LOCK freely. This should not be possible in any other gear.

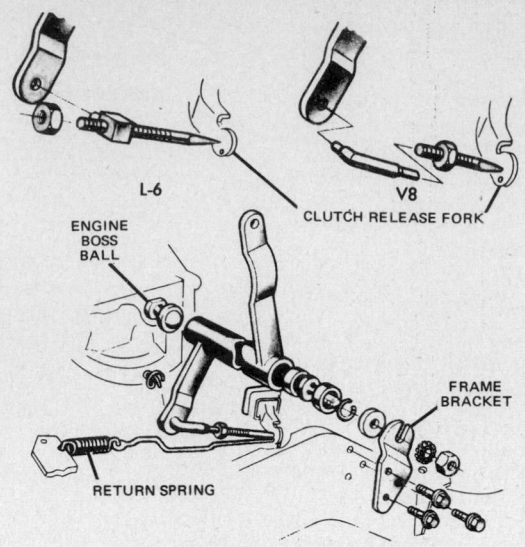

Lower clutch linkage—1971-72 Ventura II
(© Pontiac Div. G.M. Corp.)

Linkage Adjustment—Floor
1965-66

1. Place gearshift lever in Neutral.
2. Loosen two swivel nut assemblies.
3. Insert a 1/4 in. drill rod into bracket and lever assembly and align shift levers in Neutral position.

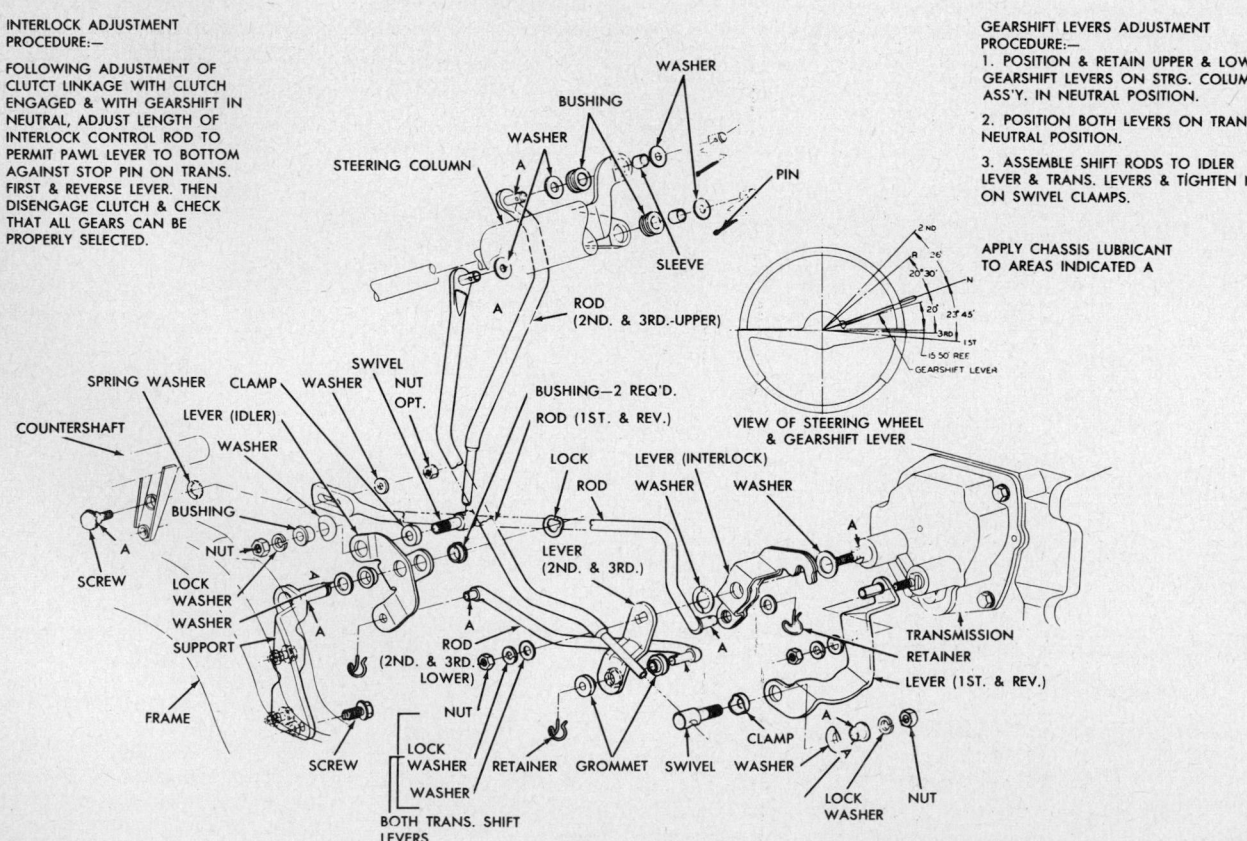

Gearshift column linkage—1967-70 Tempest with Saginaw transmission
(© Pontiac Div., G.M. Corp.)

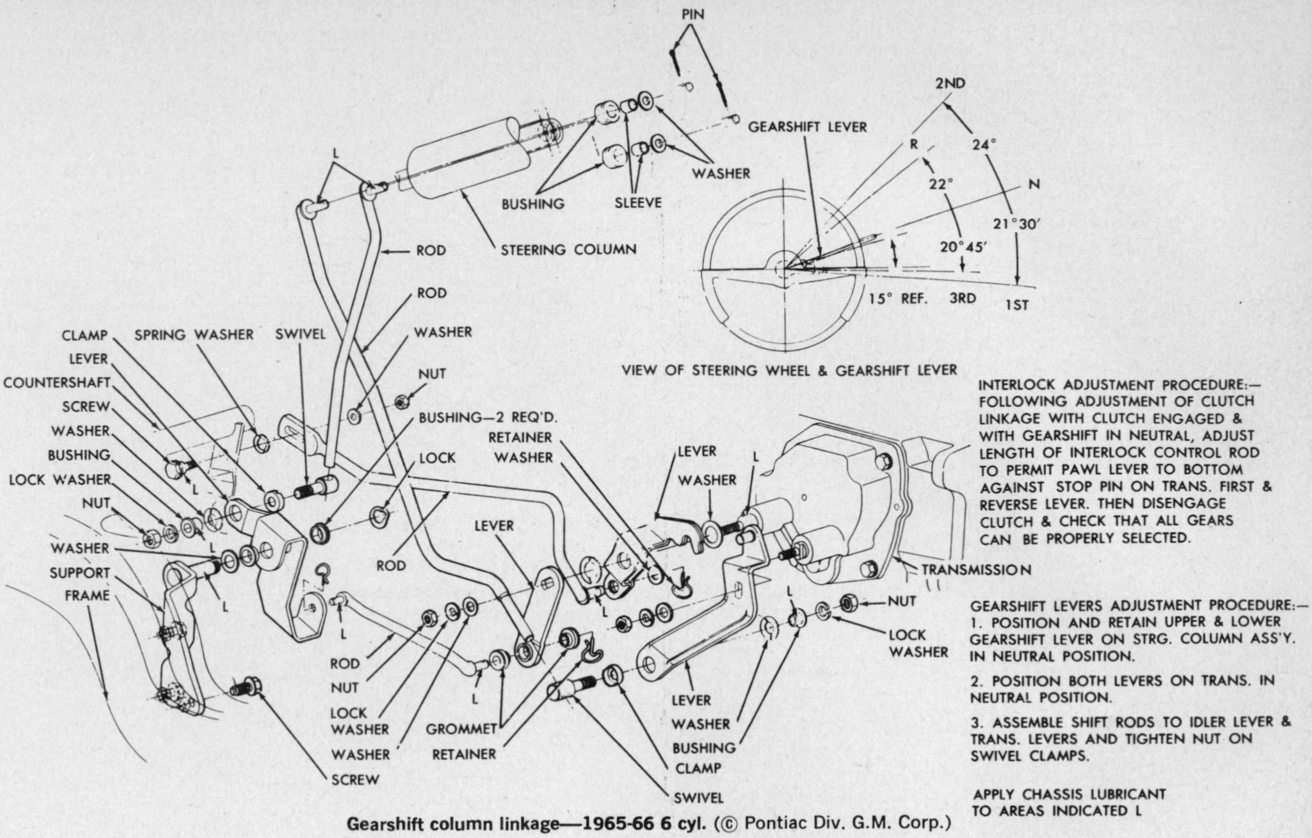

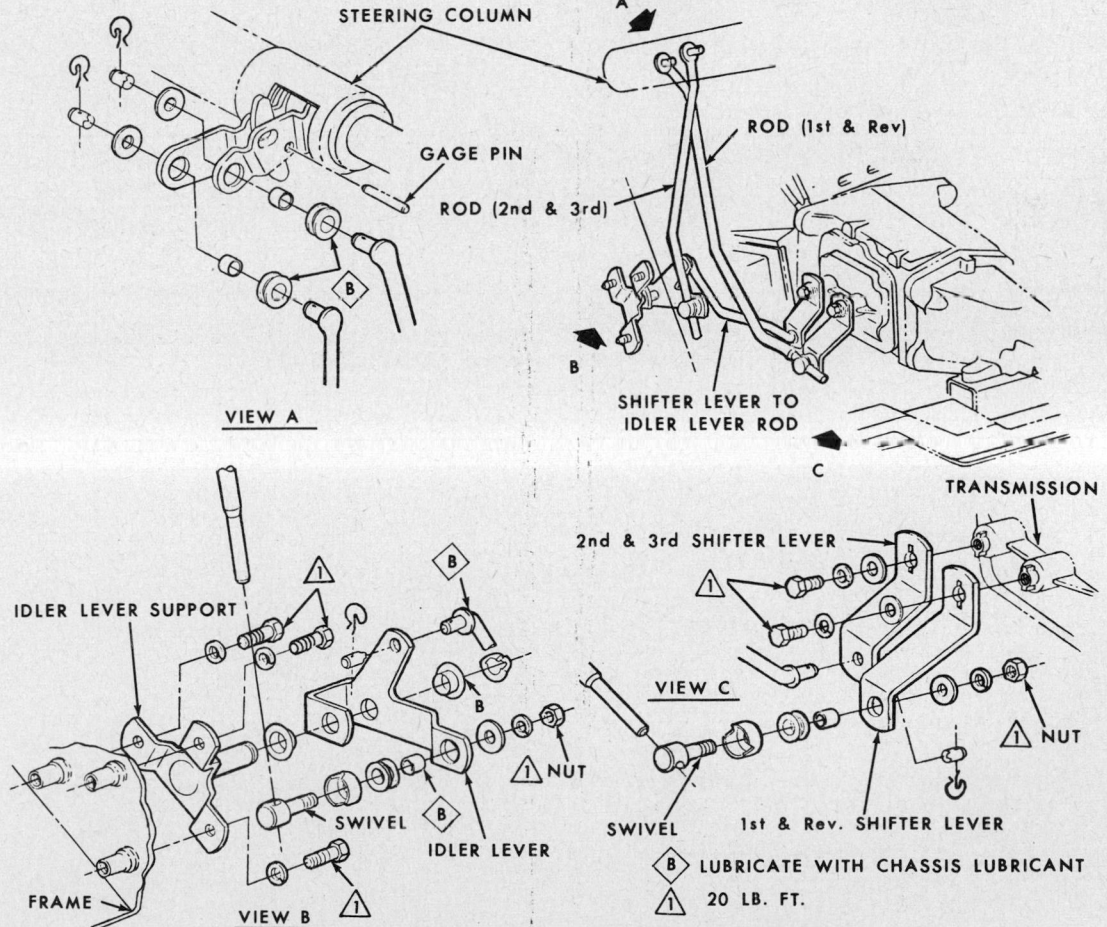

PIN

GEARSHIFT LEVER

WASHER

BUSHING **SLEEVE**

ROD

STEERING COLUMN

ROD

2ND

R 24°

22° N

21°30'

20°45'

15° REF. 3RD 1ST

VIEW OF STEERING WHEEL & GEARSHIFT LEVER

CLAMP **SPRING WASHER** **SWIVEL**

LEVER **WASHER**

COUNTERSHAFT **NUT**

SCREW **BUSHING—2 REQ'D.**

WASHER **RETAINER**

BUSHING **LOCK** **WASHER**

LOCK WASHER **LEVER**

NUT **LEVER** **WASHER**

WASHER **ROD**

SUPPORT **NUT**

FRAME **LOCK WASHER**

ROD

NUT

LOCK WASHER

WASHER

SCREW

GROMMET

RETAINER

LEVER

WASHER

BUSHING

CLAMP

SWIVEL

TRANSMISSION

NUT

LOCK WASHER

INTERLOCK ADJUSTMENT PROCEDURE:—
FOLLOWING ADJUSTMENT OF CLUTCH
LINKAGE WITH CLUTCH ENGAGED &
WITH GEARSHIFT IN NEUTRAL, ADJUST
LENGTH OF INTERLOCK CONTROL ROD
TO PERMIT PAWL LEVER TO BOTTOM
AGAINST STOP PIN ON TRANS. FIRST &
REVERSE LEVER. THEN DISENGAGE
CLUTCH & CHECK THAT ALL GEARS
CAN BE PROPERLY SELECTED.

GEARSHIFT LEVERS ADJUSTMENT PROCEDURE:—
1. POSITION AND RETAIN UPPER & LOWER
GEARSHIFT LEVER ON STRG. COLUMN ASS'Y.
IN NEUTRAL POSITION.

2. POSITION BOTH LEVERS ON TRANS. IN
NEUTRAL POSITION.

3. ASSEMBLE SHIFT RODS TO IDLER LEVER &
TRANS. LEVERS AND TIGHTEN NUT ON
SWIVEL CLAMPS.

APPLY CHASSIS LUBRICANT
TO AREAS INDICATED L

Gearshift column linkage—1965-66 6 cyl. (© Pontiac Div. G.M. Corp.)

STEERING COLUMN A

GAGE PIN

ROD (2nd & 3rd)

ROD (1st & Rev)

B

**SHIFTER LEVER TO
IDLER LEVER ROD**

VIEW A B

C

TRANSMISSION

2nd & 3rd SHIFTER LEVER

IDLER LEVER SUPPORT

VIEW C

NUT

NUT

SWIVEL

SWIVEL

1st & Rev. SHIFTER LEVER

IDLER LEVER

FRAME

VIEW B

B **LUBRICATE WITH CHASSIS LUBRICANT**

20 LB. FT.

Gearshift column linkage—1967-68 Firebird with Saginaw transmission
(© Pontiac Div. G.M. Corp.)

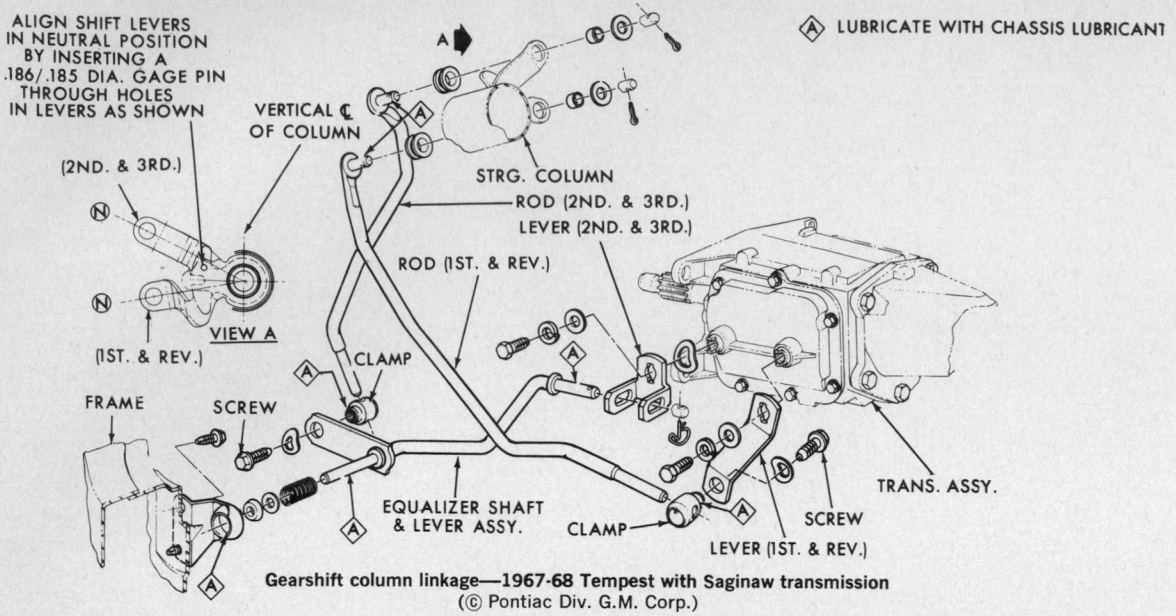

ALIGN SHIFT LEVERS IN NEUTRAL POSITION BY INSERTING A .186/.185 DIA. GAGE PIN THROUGH HOLES IN LEVERS AS SHOWN

LUBRICATE WITH CHASSIS LUBRICANT

VERTICAL ℄ OF COLUMN

A

STRG. COLUMN
ROD (2ND. & 3RD.)
LEVER (2ND. & 3RD.)
ROD (1ST. & REV.)

(2ND. & 3RD.)

(1ST. & REV.)

VIEW A

CLAMP

FRAME

SCREW

TRANS. ASSY.

EQUALIZER SHAFT & LEVER ASSY.

CLAMP

SCREW

LEVER (1ST. & REV.)

Gearshift column linkage—1967-68 Tempest with Saginaw transmission
(© Pontiac Div. G.M. Corp.)

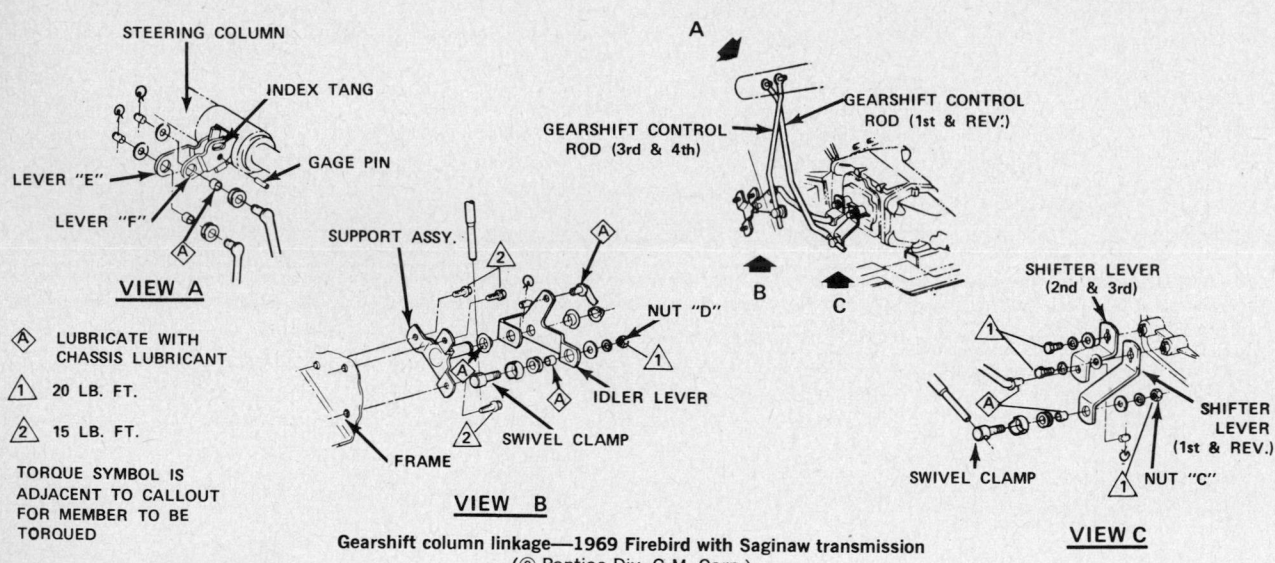

STEERING COLUMN

INDEX TANG

GAGE PIN

LEVER "E"

LEVER "F"

VIEW A

LUBRICATE WITH CHASSIS LUBRICANT

20 LB. FT.

15 LB. FT.

TORQUE SYMBOL IS ADJACENT TO CALLOUT FOR MEMBER TO BE TORQUED

SUPPORT ASSY.

NUT "D"

IDLER LEVER

FRAME

SWIVEL CLAMP

VIEW B

A

GEARSHIFT CONTROL ROD (3rd & 4th)

GEARSHIFT CONTROL ROD (1st & REV.)

B

C

SHIFTER LEVER (2nd & 3rd)

SWIVEL CLAMP

SHIFTER LEVER (1st & REV.)

NUT "C"

VIEW C

Gearshift column linkage—1969 Firebird with Saginaw transmission
(© Pontiac Div. G.M. Corp.)

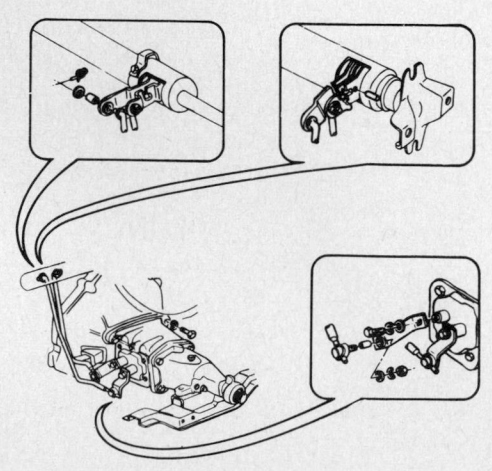

Column shift linkage adjustment—Ventura II
(© Pontiac Div. G.M. Corp.)

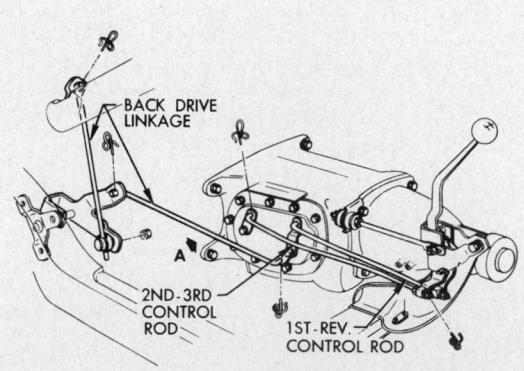

BACK DRIVE LINKAGE

A

2ND-3RD CONTROL ROD

1ST-REV. CONTROL ROD

Floorshift adjustment—Ventura II
(© Pontiac Div. G.M. Corp.)

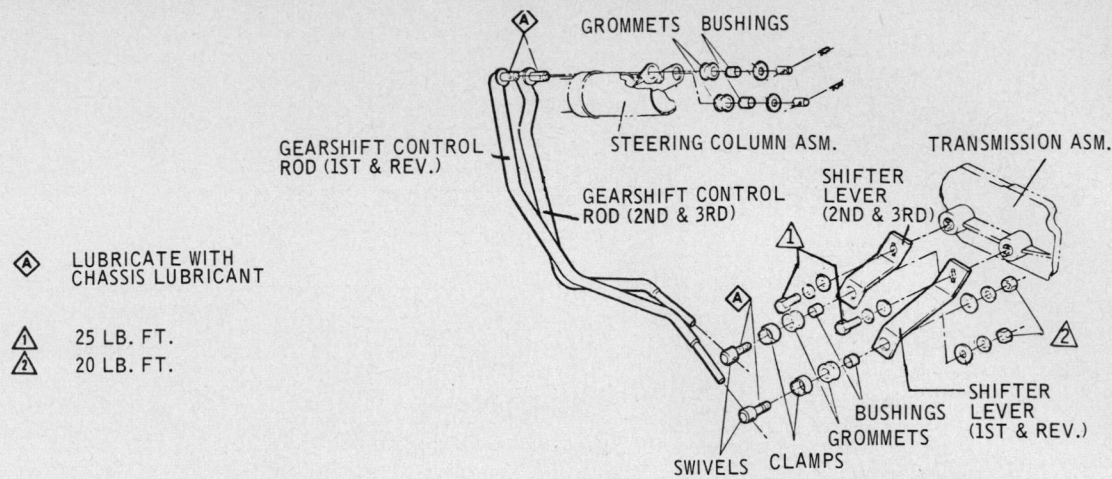

Column shift linkage—1970-71 Firebird with Saginaw transmission
(© Pontiac Div. G.M. Corp.)

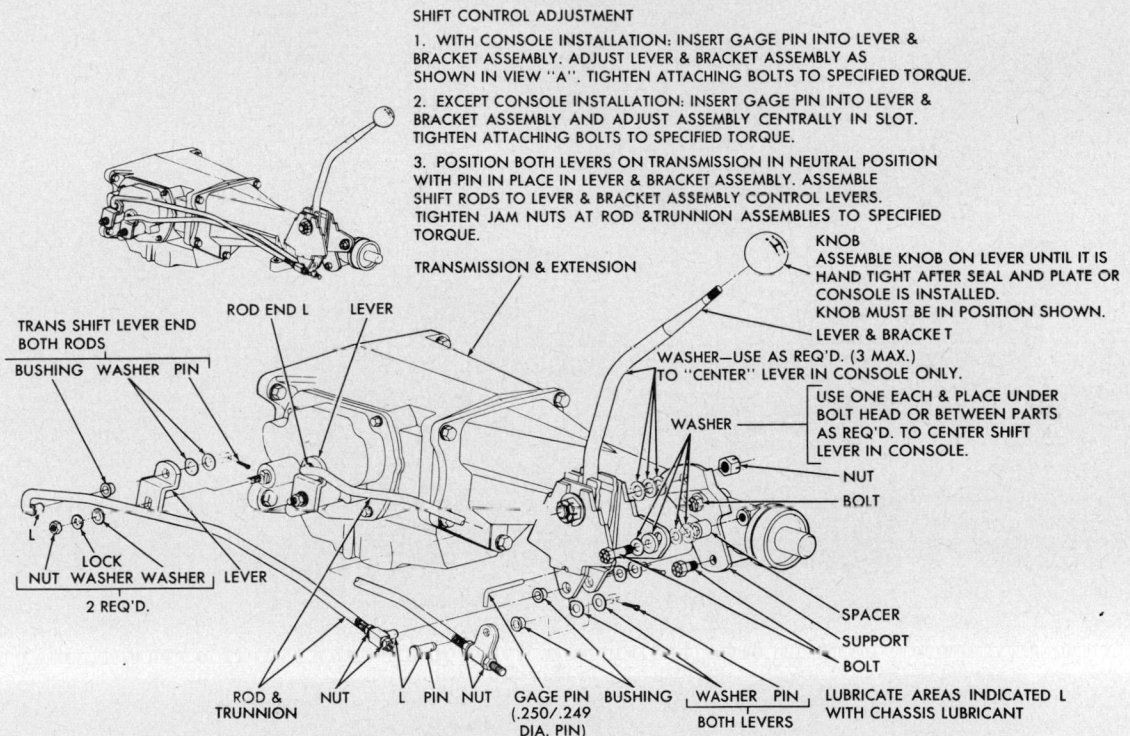

SHIFT CONTROL ADJUSTMENT

1. WITH CONSOLE INSTALLATION: INSERT GAGE PIN INTO LEVER & BRACKET ASSEMBLY. ADJUST LEVER & BRACKET ASSEMBLY AS SHOWN IN VIEW "A". TIGHTEN ATTACHING BOLTS TO SPECIFIED TORQUE.

2. EXCEPT CONSOLE INSTALLATION: INSERT GAGE PIN INTO LEVER & BRACKET ASSEMBLY AND ADJUST ASSEMBLY CENTRALLY IN SLOT. TIGHTEN ATTACHING BOLTS TO SPECIFIED TORQUE.

3. POSITION BOTH LEVERS ON TRANSMISSION IN NEUTRAL POSITION WITH PIN IN PLACE IN LEVER & BRACKET ASSEMBLY. ASSEMBLE SHIFT RODS TO LEVER & BRACKET ASSEMBLY CONTROL LEVERS. TIGHTEN JAM NUTS AT ROD &TRUNNION ASSEMBLIES TO SPECIFIED TORQUE.

Gearshift floor linkage—1965-66 Tempest 3-speed transmission (© Pontiac Div. G.M. Corp.)

4. Position transmission shift levers in Neutral position.
5. Tighten swivel nut assemblies to 8-12 ft. lbs.
6. Remove gauge pin and check shift pattern.

1967-68 Saginaw Transmission

See illustrations. Procedure same as 1965-66 except that locknuts must be tightened to 30 ft. lbs.

1967-68 H.D. Dearborn Transmission

See illustrations.

1969 and 1970-72 Saginaw and H.D. Dearborn Transmission

1. Place gearshift lever in Neutral.
2. Loosen swivel clamp on gearshift control rod (see Back Drive Linkage illustrations).
3. Loosen trunnion locknuts on 1st-Reverse and 2nd-3rd transmission control rods.
4. Insert a 1/4 in. drill rod into shifter assembly.
5. If gearshift lever is not properly aligned with floor opening (view C):
   a. *Console*—loosen two shifter to support bolts and align shifter as in view C in illustration; tighten bolts.
   b. *Without console*—loosen two

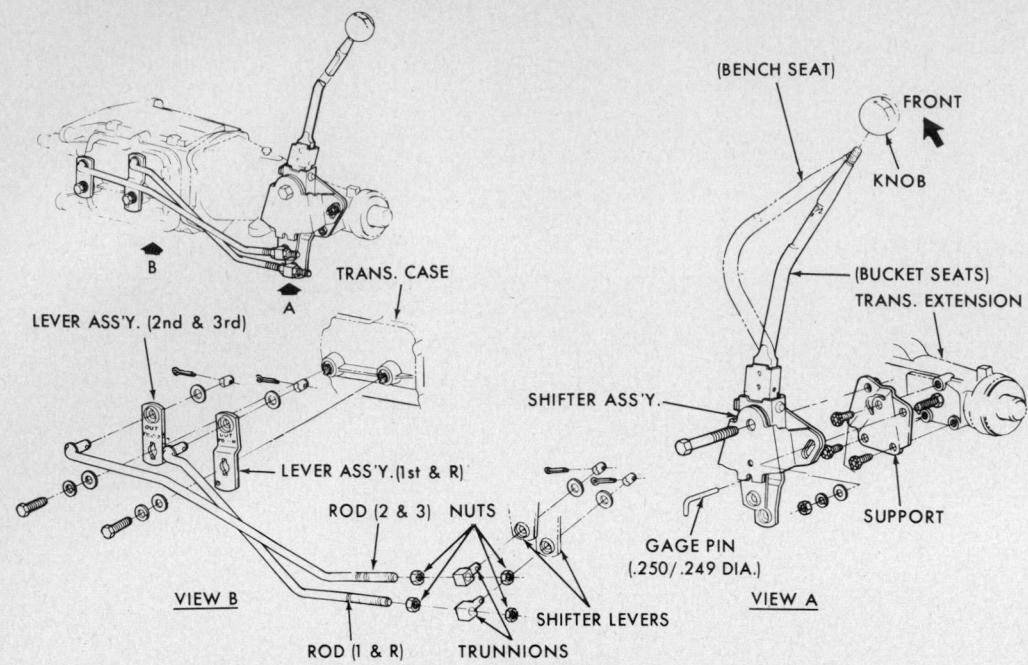

Gearshift floor linkage—1967-72 Tempest and Firebird with Saginaw 3-speed transmission
(© Pontiac Div., G.M. Corp.)

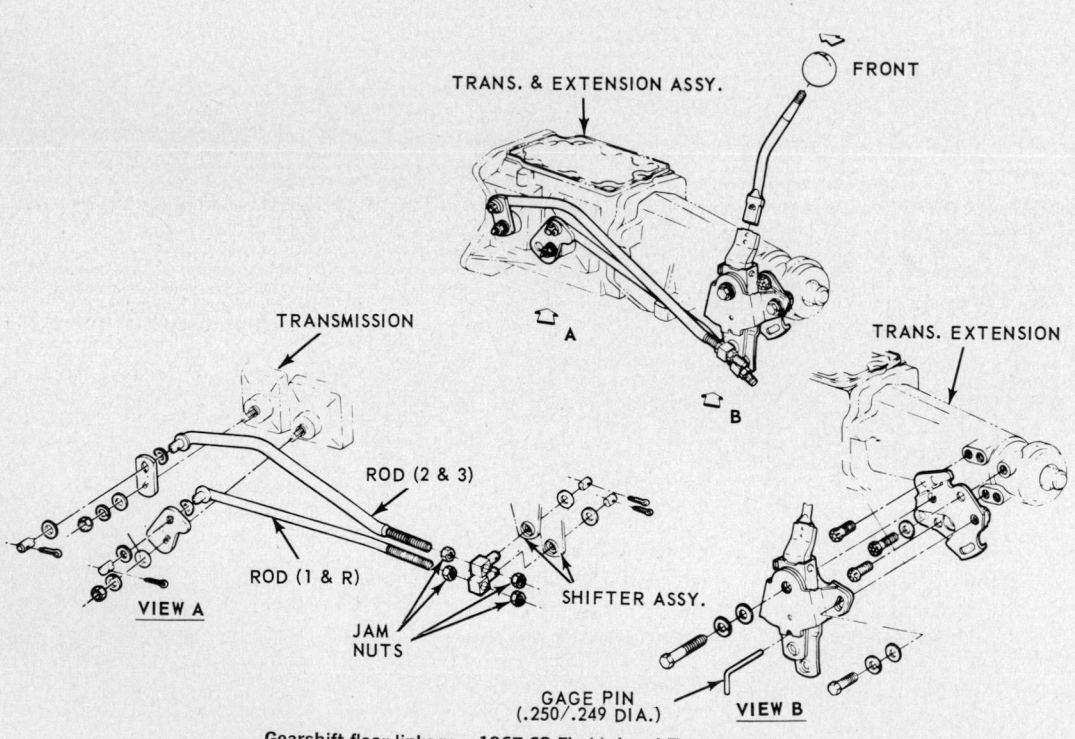

Gearshift floor linkage—1967-68 Firebird and Tempest with
H.D. Dearborn 3-speed transmission
(© Pontiac Div., G.M. Corp.)

shifter to support bolts and center shifter in boot; tighten bolts.

6. Position both transmission shift levers in Neutral and tighten locknuts to 30 ft. lbs. (25 ft. lbs. 1971).

7. Remove gauge pin and check shift pattern.

8. Place gearshift lever in Reverse, then place steering column lower lever in Lock position and lock ignition.

9. Push up (pull down—Ventura II) on gearshift control rod to take up lash in column lock mechanism, then tighten adjusting swivel clamp to 20 ft. lbs.

1970-72 H.D. Muncie Transmission

See illustrations. Procedure is the same as Saginaw and H.D. Dearborn transmission linkage adjustment. Tighten swivel clamp nuts to 20 ft. lbs. (Tempest) and 25 ft. lbs. (Firebird).

NOTE: the 1970 Saginaw transmis-

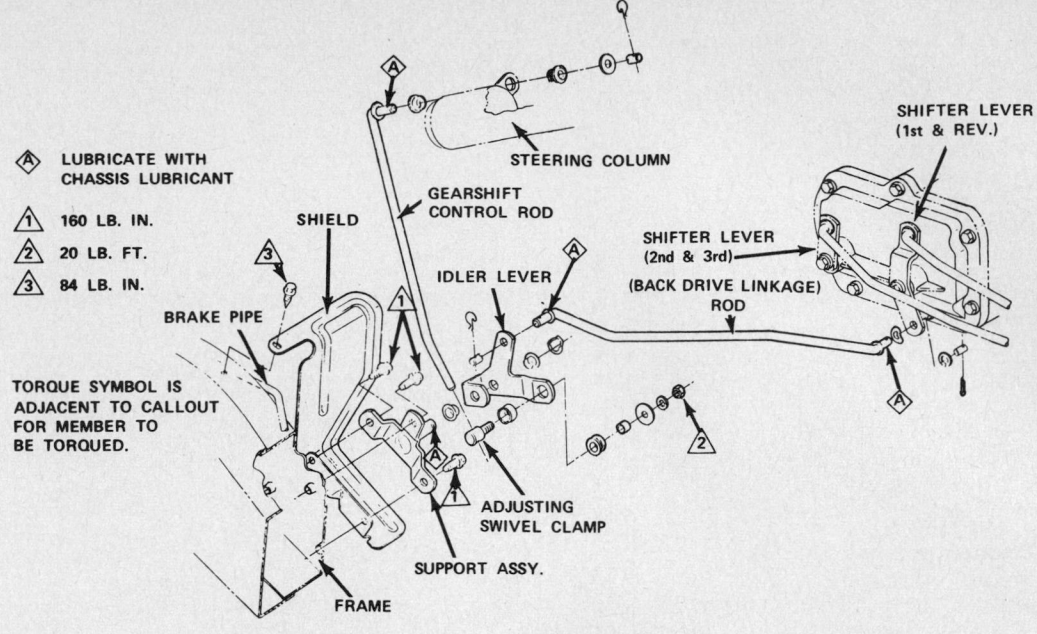

LUBRICATE WITH
CHASSIS LUBRICANT

160 LB. IN.

20 LB. FT.

84 LB. IN.

TORQUE SYMBOL IS
ADJACENT TO CALLOUT
FOR MEMBER TO
BE TORQUED.

SHIELD

BRAKE PIPE

STEERING COLUMN

GEARSHIFT
CONTROL ROD

IDLER LEVER

SHIFTER LEVER
(1st & REV.)

SHIFTER LEVER
(2nd & 3rd)

(BACK DRIVE LINKAGE)
ROD

ADJUSTING
SWIVEL CLAMP

SUPPORT ASSY.

FRAME

Back drive floor linkage—1969 Firebird with 3-speed transmission
(© Pontiac Div., G.M. Corp.)

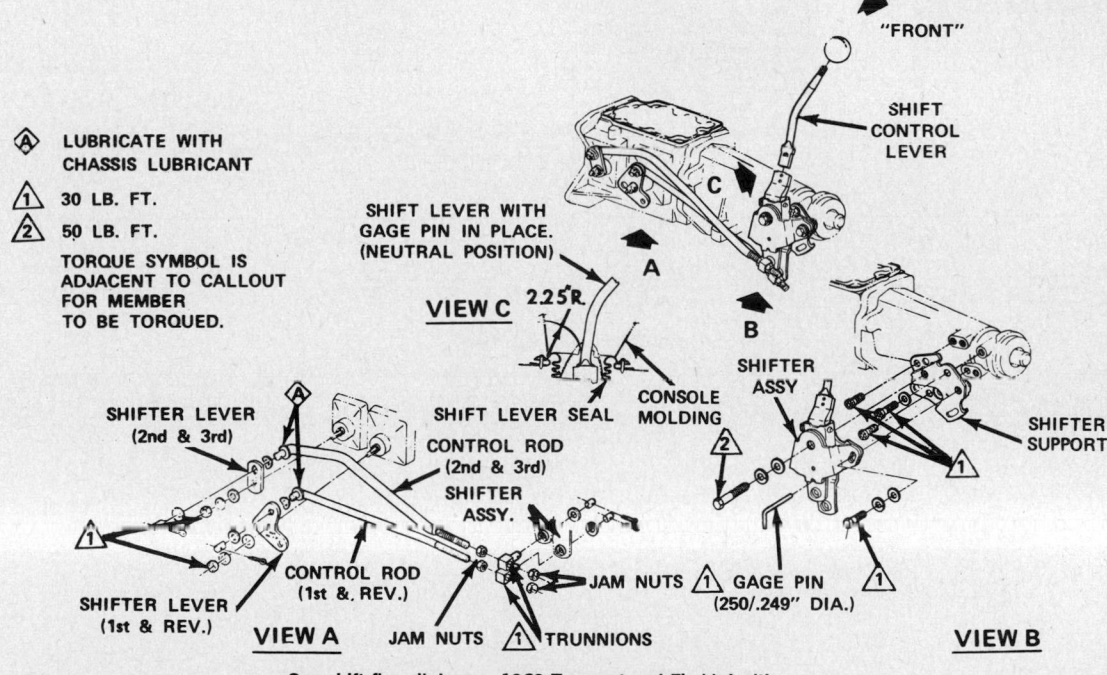

LUBRICATE WITH
CHASSIS LUBRICANT

30 LB. FT.

50 LB. FT.

TORQUE SYMBOL IS
ADJACENT TO CALLOUT
FOR MEMBER
TO BE TORQUED.

"FRONT"

SHIFT
CONTROL
LEVER

SHIFT LEVER WITH
GAGE PIN IN PLACE.
(NEUTRAL POSITION)

VIEW C   2.25 R

CONSOLE
MOLDING

C

A

B

SHIFTER
ASSY.

SHIFTER
SUPPORT

SHIFTER LEVER
(2nd & 3rd)

CONTROL ROD
(2nd & 3rd)

SHIFTER
ASSY.

CONTROL ROD
(1st & REV.)

JAM NUTS

GAGE PIN
(250/.249" DIA.)

SHIFTER LEVER
(1st & REV.)

VIEW A   JAM NUTS   TRUNNIONS

VIEW B

Gearshift floor linkage—1969 Tempest and Firebird with
H.D. Dearborn 3-speed transmission
(© Pontiac Div., G.M. Corp.)

sion is not available with floorshift, except on Firebird models.

Four-Speed Manual Transmission

Linkage Adjustment—Floor

1965-68 All

1. Place gearshift lever in Neutral.
2. Loosen three swivel nut assemblies.

3. Insert a 1/4 in. drill rod into gauge pin hole in shifter.
4. Position transmission shift levers in Neutral.
5. Install swivel assemblies, adjusting length so that they fit into transmission shift levers without binding; tighten swivel nuts to 8-12 ft. lbs. up to 1966, 30 ft. lbs. for 1967-68.
6. Remove gauge pin and check shift pattern.

1969-72 Muncie and 1969 Saginaw Transmission

1. Place gearshift lever in Neutral.
2. Loosen adjusting swivel clamp on gearshift control rod.
3. For 1969 Saginaw, loosen trunnion locknuts on 1st-2nd and Reverse shift rods, then disconnect trunnion from lever (view A), Loosen locknuts for Muncie-equipped 1969 up Tempest, GTO, Firebird.

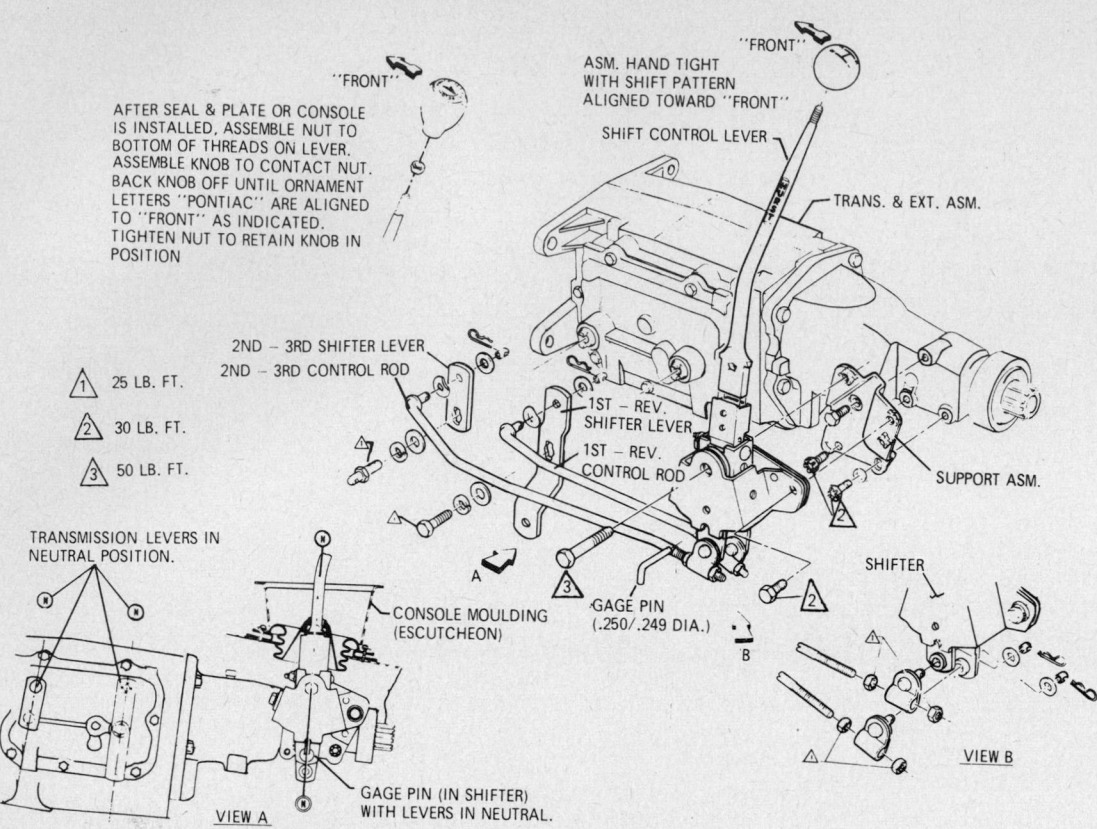

AFTER SEAL & PLATE OR CONSOLE IS INSTALLED, ASSEMBLE NUT TO BOTTOM OF THREADS ON LEVER. ASSEMBLE KNOB TO CONTACT NUT. BACK KNOB OFF UNTIL ORNAMENT LETTERS "PONTIAC" ARE ALIGNED TO "FRONT" AS INDICATED. TIGHTEN NUT TO RETAIN KNOB IN POSITION

"FRONT"

ASM. HAND TIGHT WITH SHIFT PATTERN ALIGNED TOWARD "FRONT"

"FRONT"

SHIFT CONTROL LEVER

TRANS. & EXT. ASM.

2ND – 3RD SHIFTER LEVER
2ND – 3RD CONTROL ROD

1ST – REV. SHIFTER LEVER
1ST – REV. CONTROL ROD

SUPPORT ASM.

△1 25 LB. FT.
△2 30 LB. FT.
△3 50 LB. FT.

TRANSMISSION LEVERS IN NEUTRAL POSITION.

CONSOLE MOULDING (ESCUTCHEON)

GAGE PIN (.250/.249 DIA.)

SHIFTER

GAGE PIN (IN SHIFTER) WITH LEVERS IN NEUTRAL.

VIEW A

VIEW B

Gearshift floor linkage—1970-71 with H.D. Muncie 3-speed transmission
(© Pontiac Div., G.M. Corp.)

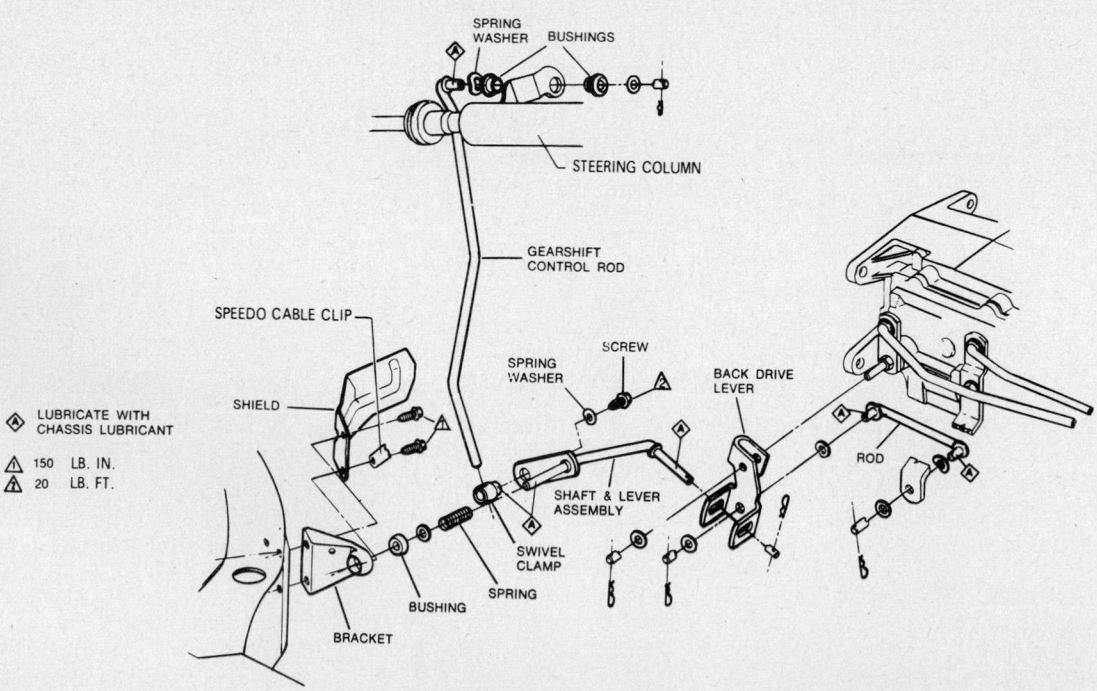

SPRING WASHER

BUSHINGS

STEERING COLUMN

GEARSHIFT CONTROL ROD

SPEEDO CABLE CLIP

SPRING WASHER

SCREW

BACK DRIVE LEVER

SHIELD

ROD

◇ LUBRICATE WITH CHASSIS LUBRICANT
△ 150 LB. IN.
△ 20 LB. FT.

SHAFT & LEVER ASSEMBLY

SWIVEL CLAMP

BUSHING

SPRING

BRACKET

Back drive floor linkage—1970-71 with H.D. Muncie 3-speed transmission
(© Pontiac Div., G.M. Corp.)

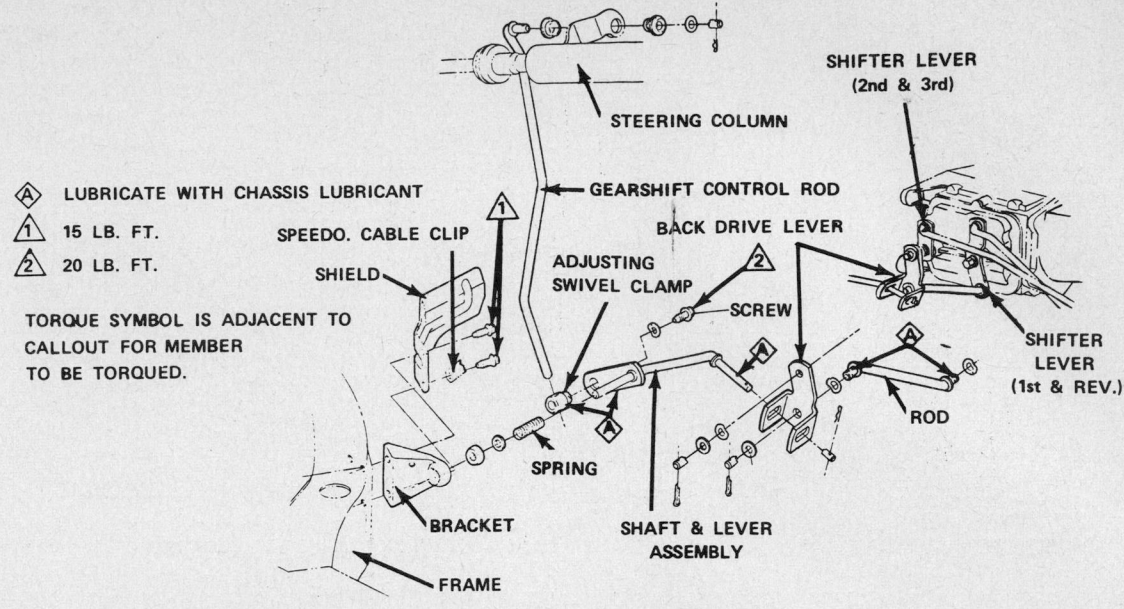

LUBRICATE WITH CHASSIS LUBRICANT

15 LB. FT.

20 LB. FT.

TORQUE SYMBOL IS ADJACENT TO CALLOUT FOR MEMBER TO BE TORQUED.

SPEEDO. CABLE CLIP

SHIELD

STEERING COLUMN

GEARSHIFT CONTROL ROD

BACK DRIVE LEVER

ADJUSTING SWIVEL CLAMP

SCREW

SHIFTER LEVER (2nd & 3rd)

SHIFTER LEVER (1st & REV.)

ROD

SPRING

BRACKET

SHAFT & LEVER ASSEMBLY

FRAME

Back drive floor linkage—1969 Tempest with 3-speed transmission
(© Pontiac Div. G.M. Corp.)

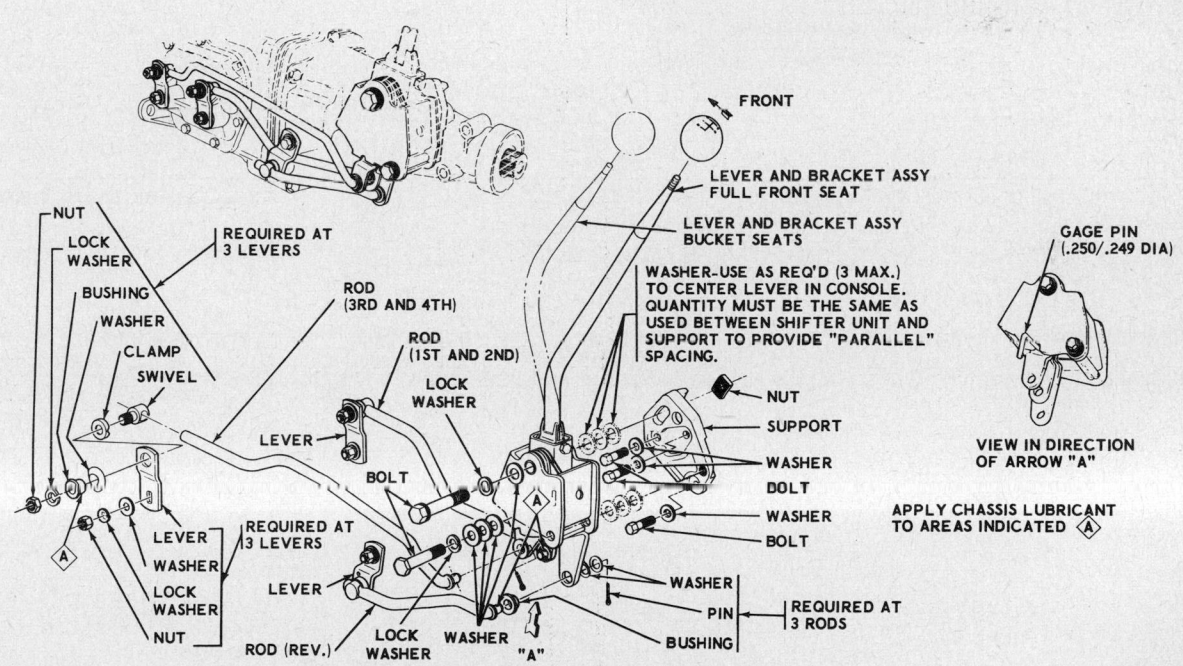

NUT
LOCK WASHER
BUSHING
WASHER
CLAMP
SWIVEL

REQUIRED AT 3 LEVERS

ROD (3RD AND 4TH)

ROD (1ST AND 2ND)

LOCK WASHER

LEVER

BOLT

FRONT

LEVER AND BRACKET ASSY FULL FRONT SEAT

LEVER AND BRACKET ASSY BUCKET SEATS

WASHER-USE AS REQ'D (3 MAX.) TO CENTER LEVER IN CONSOLE. QUANTITY MUST BE THE SAME AS USED BETWEEN SHIFTER UNIT AND SUPPORT TO PROVIDE "PARALLEL" SPACING.

NUT
SUPPORT
WASHER
BOLT
WASHER
BOLT

GAGE PIN (.250/.249 DIA)

VIEW IN DIRECTION OF ARROW "A"

APPLY CHASSIS LUBRICANT TO AREAS INDICATED

LEVER
WASHER
LOCK WASHER
NUT

REQUIRED AT 3 LEVERS

LEVER

ROD (REV.)

LOCK WASHER

WASHER

"A"

WASHER
PIN
BUSHING

REQUIRED AT 3 RODS

Gearshift floor linkage—typical 1965-66 4-speed transmission (© Pontiac Div. G.M. Corp.)

4. Insert a 1/4 in. drill rod into gauge pin hole in shifter.
5. If gearshift lever is not properly aligned with floor opening (view C-1969, view A-1970 up):
   a. *Console*—loosen two shifter to support bolts and align shifter as per illustration; tighten

   bolts.
   b. *Without console*—loosen two shifter to support bolts and center shifter in boot; tighten bolts.
6. Place transmission shift levers in Neutral and tighten locknuts to 30 ft. lbs. for 1969 Saginaw.

7. Align trunnion with hole in 3rd-4th shifter lever, insert trunnion and secure with washer and cotter pin for 1969 Saginaw. Tighten locknuts to 30 ft. lbs. for 1969 up Muncie.

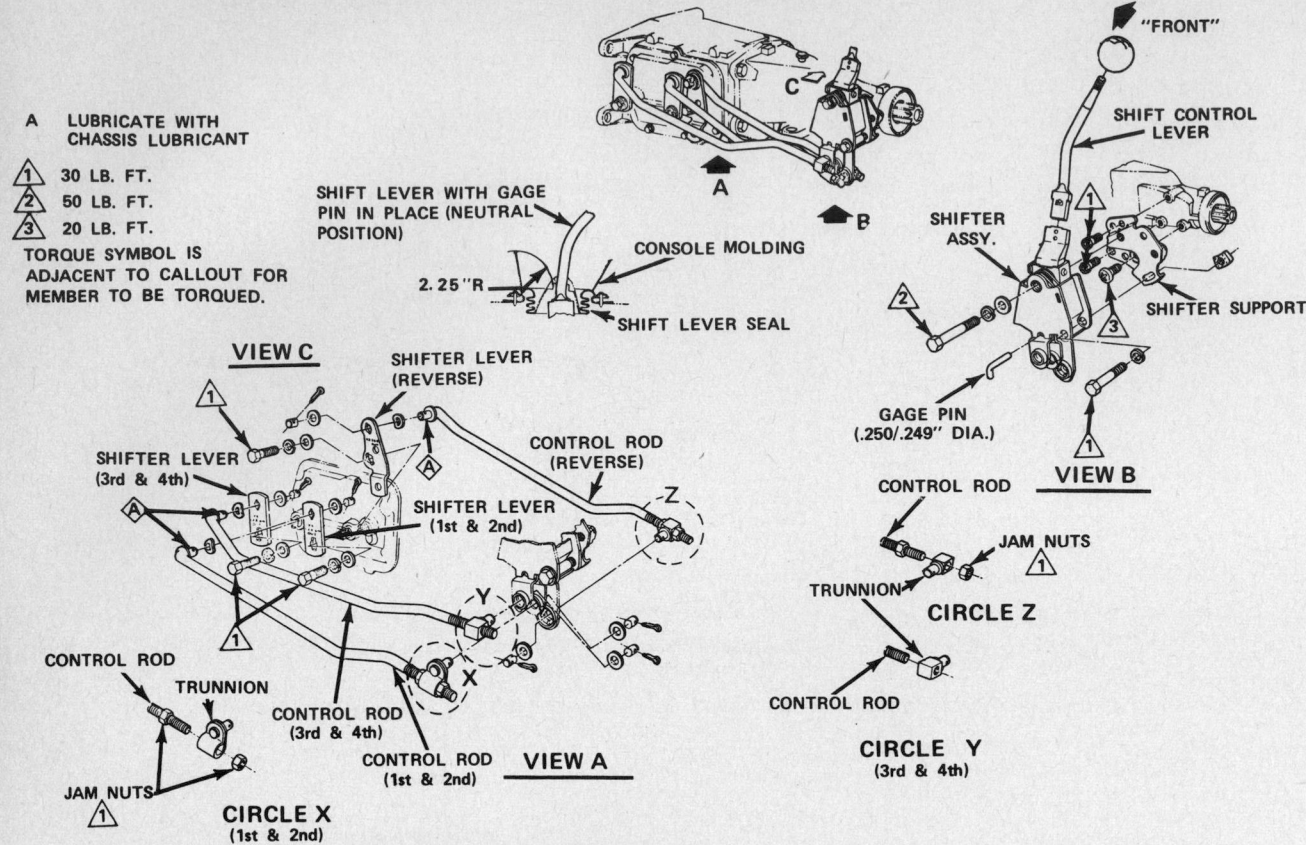

A   LUBRICATE WITH
CHASSIS LUBRICANT

△1   30 LB. FT.
△2   50 LB. FT.
△3   20 LB. FT.

TORQUE SYMBOL IS
ADJACENT TO CALLOUT FOR
MEMBER TO BE TORQUED.

SHIFT LEVER WITH GAGE
PIN IN PLACE (NEUTRAL
POSITION)

2.25"R

CONSOLE MOLDING

SHIFT LEVER SEAL

"FRONT"

SHIFT CONTROL
LEVER

SHIFTER
ASSY.

SHIFTER SUPPORT

GAGE PIN
(.250/.249" DIA.)

VIEW B

VIEW C

SHIFTER LEVER
(REVERSE)

SHIFTER LEVER
(3rd & 4th)

SHIFTER LEVER
(1st & 2nd)

CONTROL ROD
(REVERSE)

CONTROL ROD
(3rd & 4th)

CONTROL ROD
(1st & 2nd)

VIEW A

CONTROL ROD

TRUNNION

JAM NUTS

CIRCLE X
(1st & 2nd)

CONTROL ROD

TRUNNION

JAM NUTS

CIRCLE Z

CONTROL ROD

CIRCLE Y
(3rd & 4th)

Gearshift floor linkage—typical Saginaw 4-speed transmission (© Pontiac Div., G.M. Corp.)

A   LUBRICATE WITH
CHASSIS LUBRICANT

△1   30 LB. FT.
△2   50 LB. FT.
△3   20 LB. FT.
△4   25 LB. FT.

CALLOUT FOR MEMBER TO BE TORQUED.
TORQUE SYMBOL IS ADJACENT TO

2.25"R

SHIFT LEVER WITH
GAGE PIN IN PLACE
(NEUTRAL POSITION)

CONSOLE MOLDING

VIEW C   SHIFT LEVER SEAL

"FRONT"

SHIFT CONTROL LEVER

SHIFTER
ASSY.

SHIFTER
SUPPORT

GAGE PIN
(250/.249 DIA.)

VIEW B

CONTROL ROD

TRUNNION

JAM NUTS △1

CIRCLE Z
REVERSE

SHIFTER LEVER
(1st & 2nd)

SHIFTER LEVER
(3rd & 4th)

SHIFTER LEVER
(REVERSE)

CONTROL ROD

TRUNNION

CONTROL ROD
(REVERSE)

CIRCLE Y
(3RD-4TH)

CONTROL ROD

JAM NUTS △1

TRUNNION

CIRCLE X
(1ST-2ND)

CONTROL ROD
(1st & 2nd)

CONTROL ROD
(3rd & 4th)

VIEW A

Gearshift floor linkage—Muncie 4-speed transmission (© Pontiac Div., G.M. Corp.)

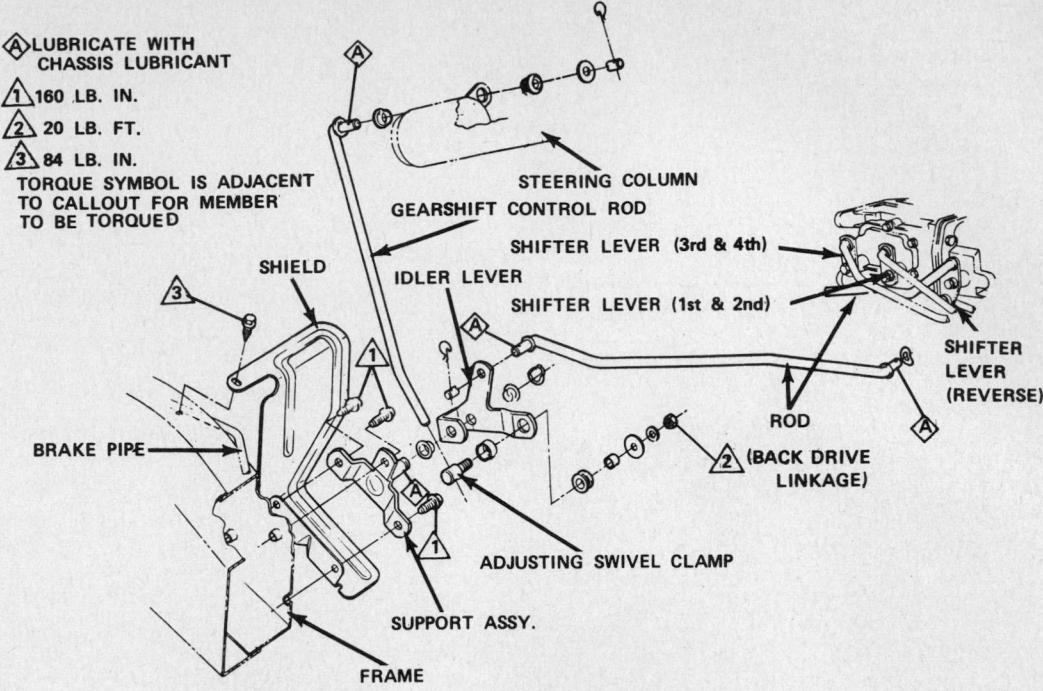

△A LUBRICATE WITH CHASSIS LUBRICANT
△1 160 LB. IN.
△2 20 LB. FT.
△3 84 LB. IN.
TORQUE SYMBOL IS ADJACENT TO CALLOUT FOR MEMBER TO BE TORQUED

SHIELD

BRAKE PIPE

STEERING COLUMN
GEARSHIFT CONTROL ROD
IDLER LEVER
SHIFTER LEVER (3rd & 4th)
SHIFTER LEVER (1st & 2nd)
SHIFTER LEVER (REVERSE)
ROD
(BACK DRIVE LINKAGE)
ADJUSTING SWIVEL CLAMP
SUPPORT ASSY.
FRAME

Typical back drive floor linkage—Muncie 4-speed transmission illustrated
(© Pontiac Div., G.M. Corp.)

8. Remove gauge pin and check shift pattern.
9. Place gearshift lever in Reverse, set steering column lower lever in Lock position and lock ignition.
10. Push up on gearshift control rod to take up lash in steering column lock mechanism, then tighten adjusting swivel clamp nut to 20 ft. lbs.

Automatic Transmission

Transmission R & R—1965-72

1. Raise car and provide support for front and rear of car.
2. Disconnect front exhaust pipe bolts at the exhaust manifold and at the connection of the intermediate exhaust pipe location (single exhaust only.) On dual exhaust, the exhaust pipes need not be removed, just loosened.
3. Remove driveshaft.
4. Place suitable jack under transmission and fasten transmission securely to jack.
5. Remove vacuum modulator hose from vacuum modulator, then remove T.C.S. wire.
6. Loosen cooler line bolts and separate cooler lines from transmission.
7. Remove transmission mounting pad to crossmember bolts.
8. Remove transmission crossmember support to frame rail bolts. Remove crossmember.
9. Disconnect speedometer cable.
10. Loosen shift linkage and downshift cable.

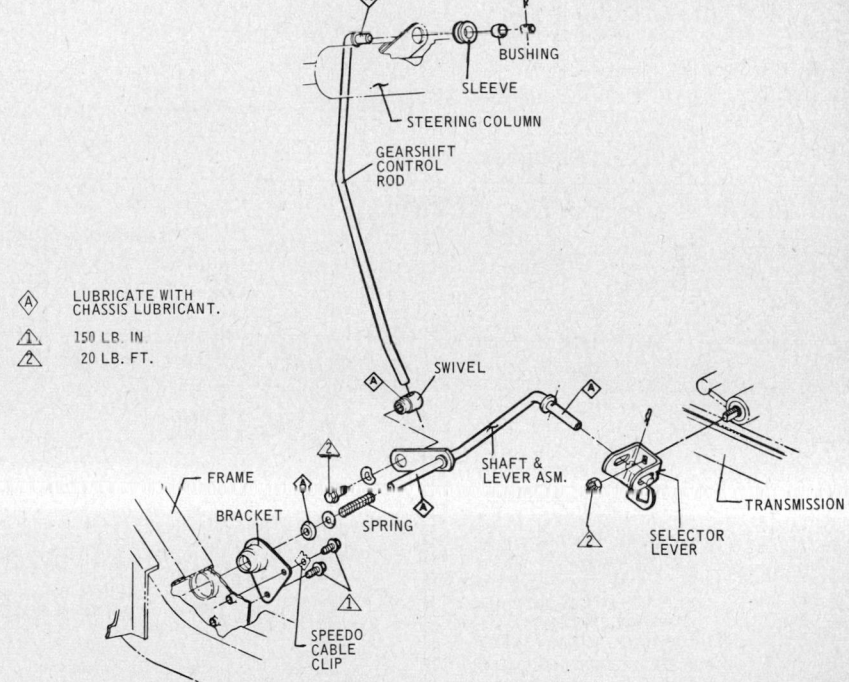

◇A LUBRICATE WITH CHASSIS LUBRICANT.
△1 150 LB. IN.
△2 20 LB. FT.

BUSHING
SLEEVE
STEERING COLUMN
GEARSHIFT CONTROL ROD
SWIVEL
FRAME
BRACKET
SPRING
SHAFT & LEVER ASM.
TRANSMISSION
SELECTOR LEVER
SPEEDO CABLE CLIP

Turbo-Hydramatic column linkage—1970-72 Firebird. M-35 linkage is similar.
(© Pontiac Div. G.M. Corp.)

11. Disconnect and remove transmission filler pipe.
12. Support engine at oil pan.
13. Remove transmission flywheel cover pan.
14. Mark flywheel and converter pump for reassembly in same positions, and remove converter pump to flywheel bolts.
15. Remove transmission case to engine block bolts.
16. Move transmission rearward to provide clearance between converter pump and crankshaft.
17. Lower transmission and move to bench.
18. To install, reverse removal procedure.

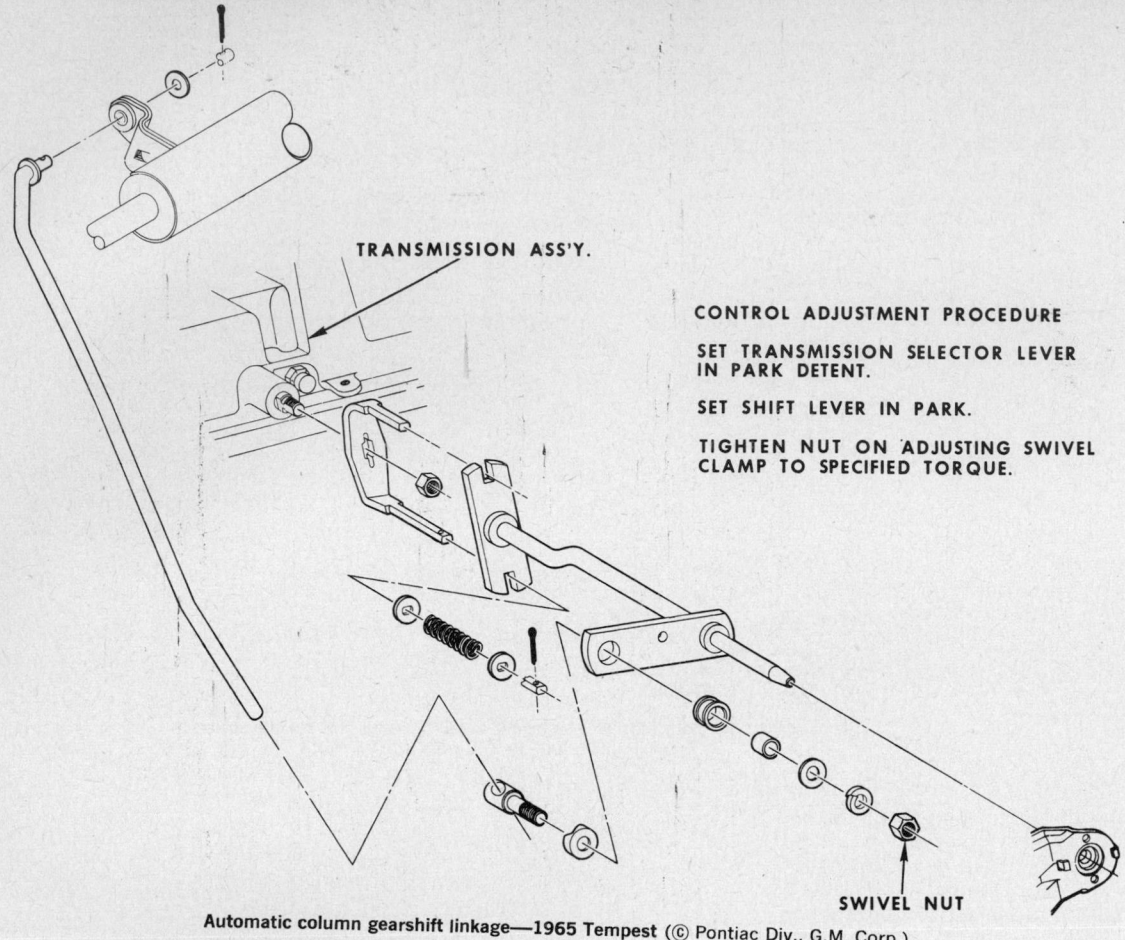

TRANSMISSION ASS'Y.

CONTROL ADJUSTMENT PROCEDURE

SET TRANSMISSION SELECTOR LEVER IN PARK DETENT.

SET SHIFT LEVER IN PARK.

TIGHTEN NUT ON ADJUSTING SWIVEL CLAMP TO SPECIFIED TORQUE.

SWIVEL NUT

Automatic column gearshift linkage—1965 Tempest (© Pontiac Div., G.M. Corp.)

TRANSMISSION

TRANSMISSION SELECTOR LEVER

DR

VIEW B

ADJUSTING GAGE NEUTRALIZER SWITCH

STEERING COLUMN

STEERING COLUMN

VIEW SHOWING SWITCH INSTALLATION

STARTER NEUTRALIZER SWITCH INSTALLATION

1. POSITION GEARSHIFT LEVER IN "DRIVE" POSITION. (SEE VIEW A)

2. INSERT SWITCH "DRIVE TANG" IN SHIFTER TUBE SLOT AND ASSEMBLY SWITCH TO STEERING COLUMN JACKET.

3. INSERT ADJUSTING GAGE IN SWITCH. MOVE GEAR SELECTOR TO "PARK" POSITION & REMOVE ADJUSTING GAGE.

ROD

VERTICAL ₵ OF STEERING COLUMN

ADJUST SLOT

₵ OF HOLE IN SWITCH ASSEMBLY

SWITCH "DRIVE TANG" IN DRIVE POSITION

PK

RESET SLOT

DR

J-22701 NEUTRALIZER SWITCH GAUGE SET (5)

VIEW A

SUPPORT

LEVER

A

NUT

TRANSMISSION

B

ROD

SELECTOR LEVER

SWIVEL CLAMP

BRACKET

FRAME

△ LUBRICATE AREAS INDICATED WITH CHASSIS LUBRICANT

Turbo-Hydramatic column gearshift linkage—1967-68 Firebird (© Pontiac Div. G.M. Corp.)

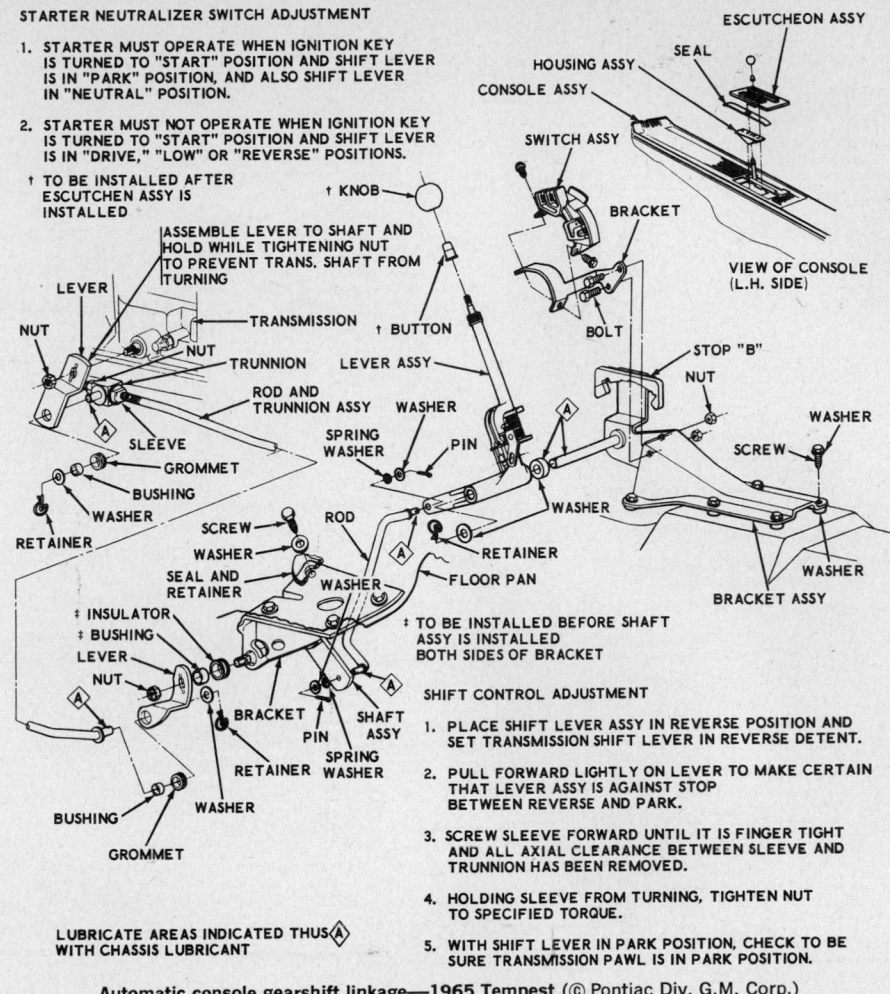

STARTER NEUTRALIZER SWITCH ADJUSTMENT

STARTER NEUTRALIZER SWITCH ADJUSTMENT

1. STARTER MUST OPERATE WHEN IGNITION KEY IS TURNED TO "START" POSITION AND SHIFT LEVER IS IN "PARK" POSITION, AND ALSO SHIFT LEVER IN "NEUTRAL" POSITION.

2. STARTER MUST NOT OPERATE WHEN IGNITION KEY IS TURNED TO "START" POSITION AND SHIFT LEVER IS IN "DRIVE," "LOW" OR "REVERSE" POSITIONS.

† TO BE INSTALLED AFTER ESCUTCHEN ASSY IS INSTALLED

ESCUTCHEON ASSY

HOUSING ASSY SEAL

CONSOLE ASSY

SWITCH ASSY

† KNOB

ASSEMBLE LEVER TO SHAFT AND HOLD WHILE TIGHTENING NUT TO PREVENT TRANS. SHAFT FROM TURNING

BRACKET

VIEW OF CONSOLE (L.H. SIDE)

LEVER

NUT

TRANSMISSION

NUT

TRUNNION

ROD AND TRUNNION ASSY

BOLT

† BUTTON

LEVER ASSY

WASHER

STOP "B"

NUT

WASHER

SLEEVE

GROMMET

BUSHING

WASHER

RETAINER

SPRING WASHER

PIN

SCREW

WASHER

SCREW

ROD

RETAINER

WASHER

WASHER

BRACKET ASSY

SEAL AND RETAINER

WASHER

FLOOR PAN

‡ TO BE INSTALLED BEFORE SHAFT ASSY IS INSTALLED BOTH SIDES OF BRACKET

‡ INSULATOR

‡ BUSHING

LEVER

NUT

BRACKET

PIN

SHAFT ASSY

SPRING WASHER

RETAINER

BUSHING

WASHER

GROMMET

SHIFT CONTROL ADJUSTMENT

1. PLACE SHIFT LEVER ASSY IN REVERSE POSITION AND SET TRANSMISSION SHIFT LEVER IN REVERSE DETENT.

2. PULL FORWARD LIGHTLY ON LEVER TO MAKE CERTAIN THAT LEVER ASSY IS AGAINST STOP BETWEEN REVERSE AND PARK.

3. SCREW SLEEVE FORWARD UNTIL IT IS FINGER TIGHT AND ALL AXIAL CLEARANCE BETWEEN SLEEVE AND TRUNNION HAS BEEN REMOVED.

4. HOLDING SLEEVE FROM TURNING, TIGHTEN NUT TO SPECIFIED TORQUE.

5. WITH SHIFT LEVER IN PARK POSITION, CHECK TO BE SURE TRANSMISSION PAWL IS IN PARK POSITION.

LUBRICATE AREAS INDICATED THUS △A WITH CHASSIS LUBRICANT

Automatic console gearshift linkage—1965 Tempest (© Pontiac Div. G.M. Corp.)

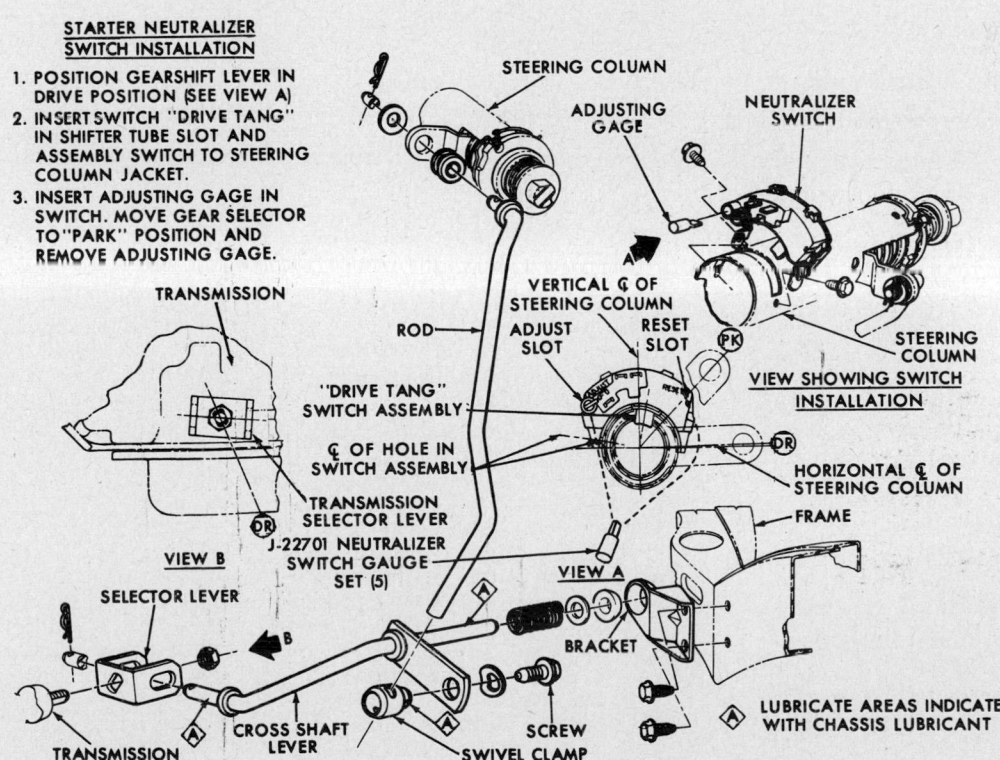

STARTER NEUTRALIZER SWITCH INSTALLATION

1. POSITION GEARSHIFT LEVER IN DRIVE POSITION (SEE VIEW A)

2. INSERT SWITCH "DRIVE TANG" IN SHIFTER TUBE SLOT AND ASSEMBLY SWITCH TO STEERING COLUMN JACKET.

3. INSERT ADJUSTING GAGE IN SWITCH. MOVE GEAR SELECTOR TO "PARK" POSITION AND REMOVE ADJUSTING GAGE.

STEERING COLUMN

ADJUSTING GAGE

NEUTRALIZER SWITCH

TRANSMISSION

ROD

VERTICAL ₵ OF STEERING COLUMN

ADJUST SLOT

RESET SLOT

STEERING COLUMN

VIEW SHOWING SWITCH INSTALLATION

"DRIVE TANG" SWITCH ASSEMBLY

₵ OF HOLE IN SWITCH ASSEMBLY

TRANSMISSION SELECTOR LEVER

J-22701 NEUTRALIZER SWITCH GAUGE SET (5)

HORIZONTAL ₵ OF STEERING COLUMN

FRAME

VIEW B

SELECTOR LEVER

VIEW A

BRACKET

TRANSMISSION CASE BOSS

CROSS SHAFT LEVER

SCREW

SWIVEL CLAMP

LUBRICATE AREAS INDICATED WITH CHASSIS LUBRICANT

Turbo-Hydramatic column gearshift linkage—1967-68 GTO (© Pontiac Div. G.M. Corp.)

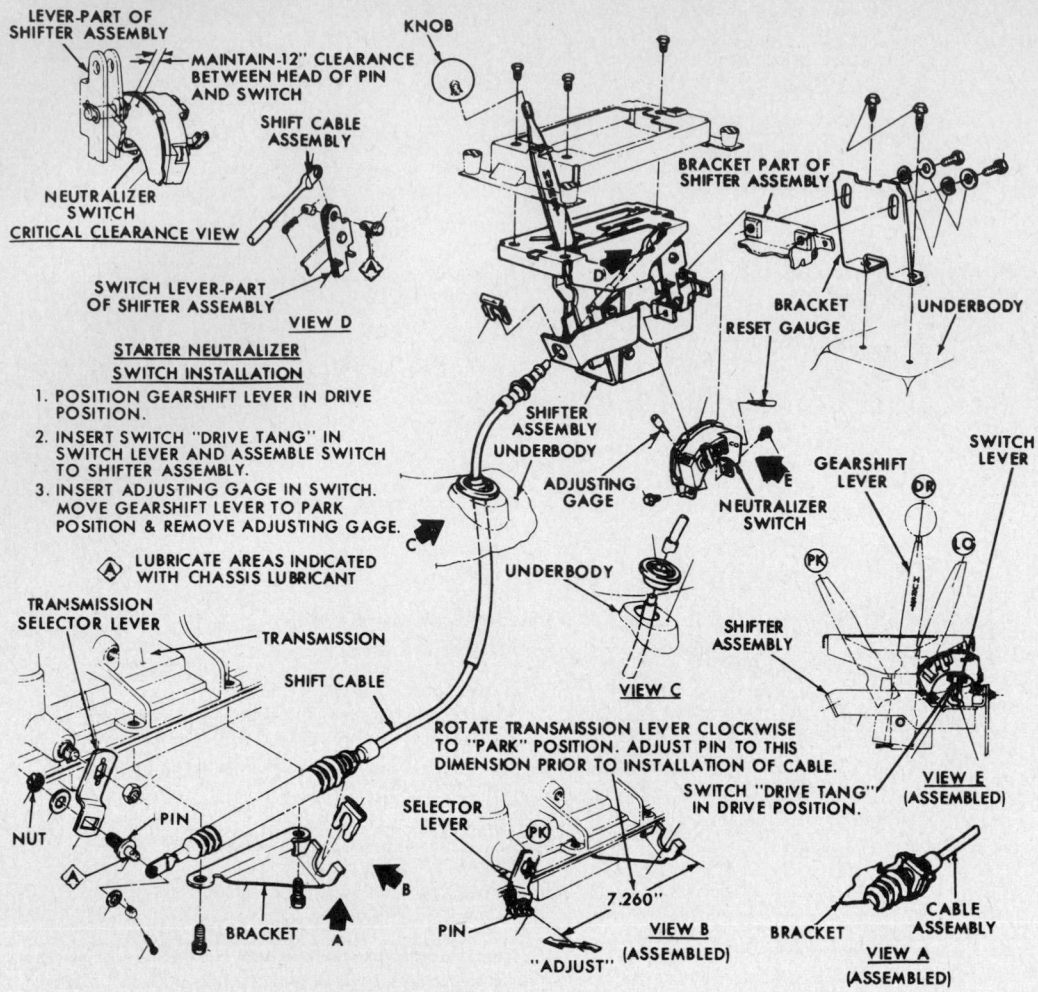

Turbo-Hydramatic console gearshift linkage—1967-68 GTO (© Pontiac Div. G.M. Corp.)

Shift Linkage Adjustment
1965-68

See illustrations.

All Turbo-Hydramatic Column —1969-72
Two-Speed (M-35) Column —1969-72

1. Loosen screw (nut on Firebird) on adjusting swivel clamp.
2. Place gearshift lever in Park and lock ignition.
3. Place transmission shift lever in Park detent (rotate clockwise, see illustrations).
4. Push up on gearshift control rod until lash is taken up in steering column lock mechanism, then tighten screw or nut on swivel clamp to 20 ft. lbs. (30 ft. lbs. on 1969 Firebird).

Turbo-Hydramatic Console —1969-72

1. Disconnect shift cable from transmission shift lever by removing nut from pin.
2. Adjust back drive linkage (as in Step 4, above).

3. Unlock ignition and rotate transmission shift lever counter-clockwise two detents.
4. Place console lever in Neutral and move against forward Neutral stop.
5. Assemble shift cable and pin to transmission shift lever so that no binding exists, then tighten nut to 30 ft. lbs. (20 ft. lbs.—1970-72).

Two-Speed (M-35) Console —1969-72

1. Disconnect shift cable from transmission shift lever pin.
2. Place console lever in Park and lock ignition.
3. Rotate transmission shift lever clockwise to Park position and push up on control rod to take up slack.
4. Tighten swivel to 30 ft. lbs. (20—1970 up).
5. Unlock ignition and rotate range lever on transmission counter-clockwise two positions.
6. Place shift lever in Neutral and move forward against Neutral stop.

7. Assemble shift cable and pin to transmission lever (free fit) and tighten pin nut to 30 ft. lbs. up to 1969, 20 ft. lbs. thereafter.

Turbo-Hydramatic (M-38) Console —1971-72 Ventura II

1. Loosen both swivel nuts (B and C) on control rod (E).
2. Place transmission lever (F) in Drive. (Full CCW to Low, then CW two positions).
3. Set pawl rod (K) into Drive notch.
4. Apply load (Y) on actuating lever (D) until pawl rod (K) contacts detent at (Z).
5. Place a 0.094 in. spacer between nut (B) and swivel. Run in nut (B) until it hits spacer, then release load Y and tighten nut (C) to 40 in. lbs.
6. Place transmission shift lever (F) in Park and lock ignition.
7. Losen nut (H) at idler lever (J), then remove play by rotating shift lever downward. Tighten nut (H) to 20 ft. lbs.

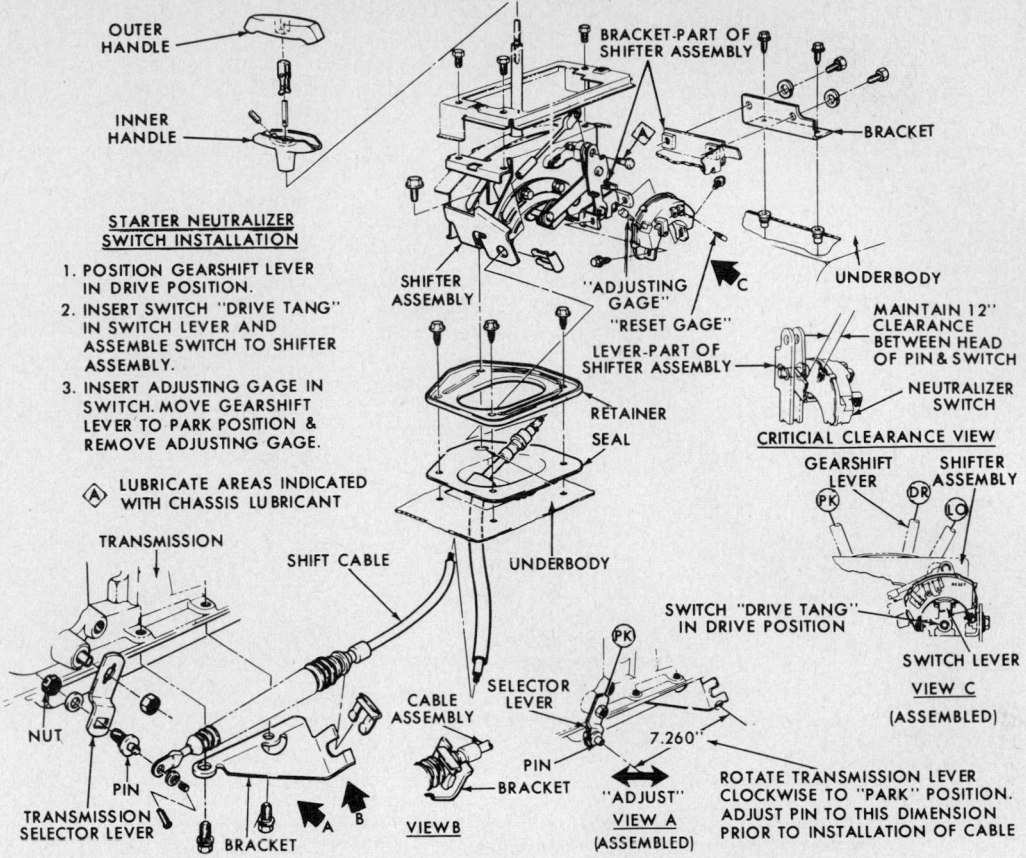

1. POSITION GEARSHIFT LEVER IN DRIVE POSITION.
2. INSERT SWITCH "DRIVE TANG" IN SWITCH LEVER AND ASSEMBLE SWITCH TO SHIFTER ASSEMBLY.
3. INSERT ADJUSTING GAGE IN SWITCH. MOVE GEARSHIFT LEVER TO PARK POSITION & REMOVE ADJUSTING GAGE.

Ⓐ LUBRICATE AREAS INDICATED WITH CHASSIS LUBRICANT

MAINTAIN 12" CLEARANCE BETWEEN HEAD OF PIN & SWITCH

CRITICIAL CLEARANCE VIEW

SWITCH "DRIVE TANG" IN DRIVE POSITION

VIEW C (ASSEMBLED)

7.260"

ROTATE TRANSMISSION LEVER CLOCKWISE TO "PARK" POSITION. ADJUST PIN TO THIS DIMENSION PRIOR TO INSTALLATION OF CABLE

Turbo-Hydramatic console gearshift linkage—1967-68 Firebird (© Pontiac Div. G.M. Corp.)

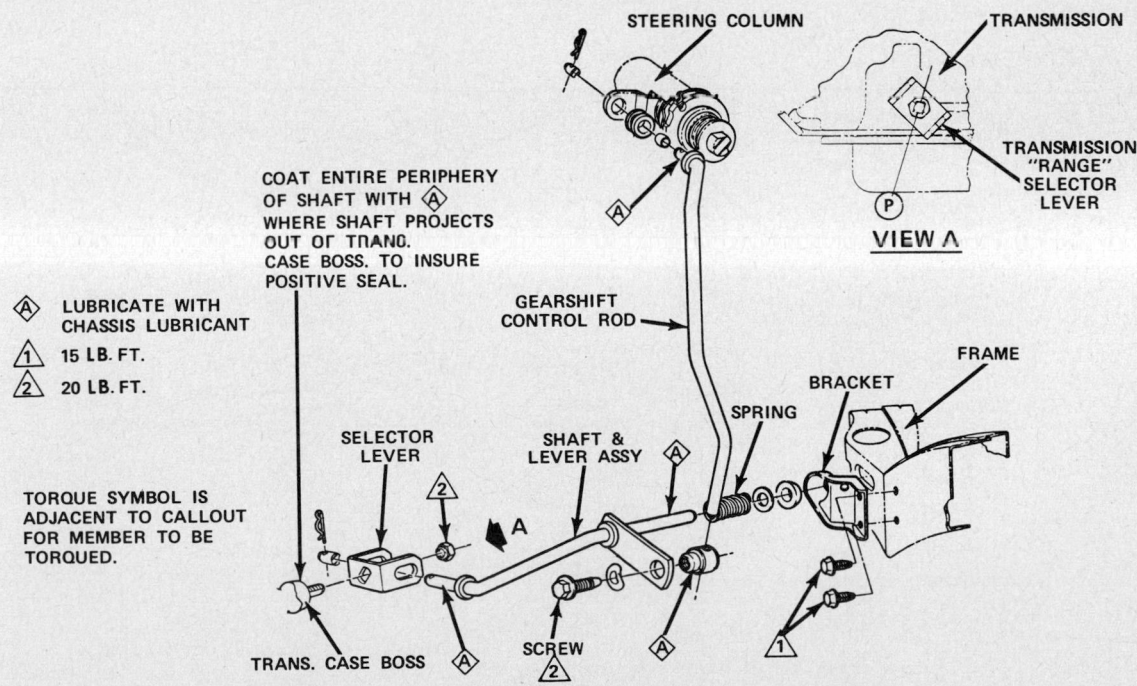

COAT ENTIRE PERIPHERY OF SHAFT WITH Ⓐ WHERE SHAFT PROJECTS OUT OF TRANS. CASE BOSS. TO INSURE POSITIVE SEAL.

Ⓐ LUBRICATE WITH CHASSIS LUBRICANT
△1 15 LB. FT.
△2 20 LB. FT.

TORQUE SYMBOL IS ADJACENT TO CALLOUT FOR MEMBER TO BE TORQUED.

VIEW A

Turbo-Hydramatic column gearshift linkage—1969-70 Tempest and GTO
Two-speed automatic column gearshift linkage—1969-70 Tempest
(© Pontiac Div. G.M. Corp.)

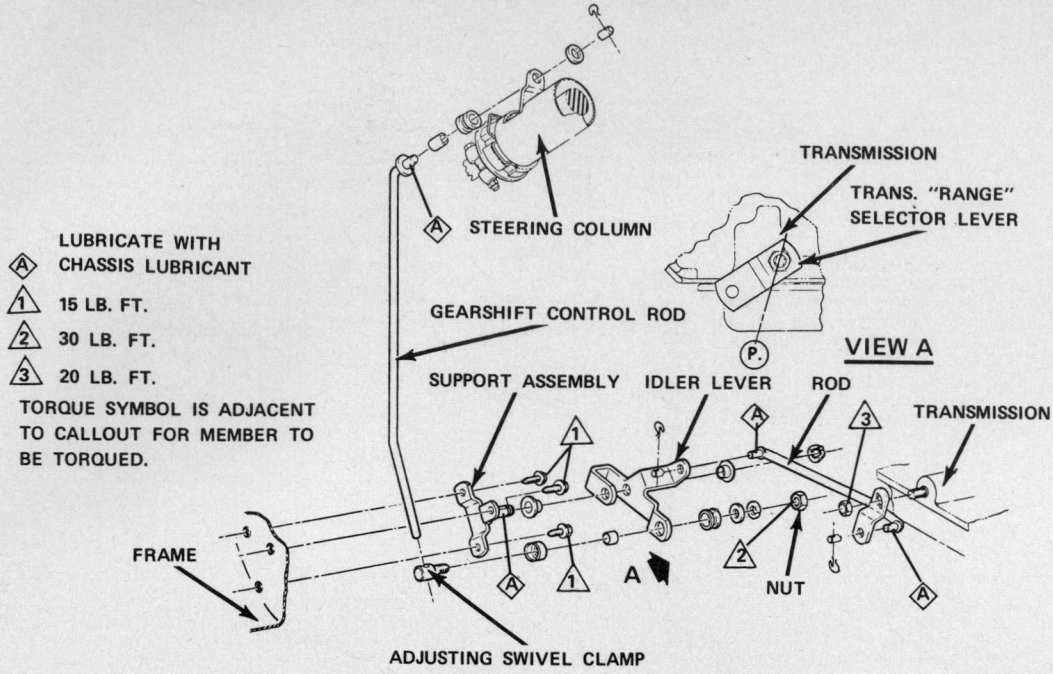

LUBRICATE WITH CHASSIS LUBRICANT

△A LUBRICATE WITH CHASSIS LUBRICANT

△1 15 LB. FT.

△2 30 LB. FT.

△3 20 LB. FT.

TORQUE SYMBOL IS ADJACENT TO CALLOUT FOR MEMBER TO BE TORQUED.

Turbo-Hydramatic column gearshift linkage—1969 Firebird
Two-speed automatic column gearshift linkage—1969 Firebird
(© Pontiac Div. G.M. Corp.)

Downshift Cable Adjustment —1969-72

Tempest

1. With engine off and throttle butterflies closed (off fast idle), position retainer against insert on cable (from inside car).
2. To adjust, grasp accelerator pedal lever adjacent to downshift cable and pull carburetor cable to wide open throttle position. Check for full cable travel.

Firebird

1. With engine off and throttle butterflies closed (off fast idle), position the retainer (under the hood) rearward against washer and insert (or Snap Lock up).

2. To adjust, push carburetor extension lever to wide open throttle position and check for full cable travel.

Ventura II

1. Disengage the Snap Lock on the detent cable.
2. Place carburetor lever at wide open position, against stop.

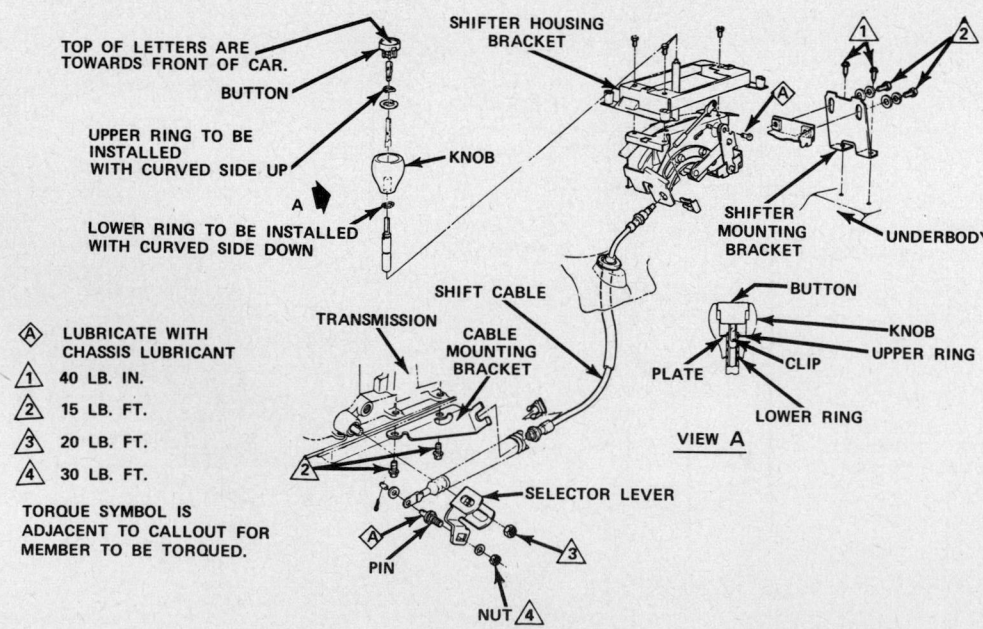

△A LUBRICATE WITH CHASSIS LUBRICANT

△1 40 LB. IN.

△2 15 LB. FT.

△3 20 LB. FT.

△4 30 LB. FT.

TORQUE SYMBOL IS ADJACENT TO CALLOUT FOR MEMBER TO BE TORQUED.

Typical Turbo-Hydramatic console gearshift and two-speed automatic console gearshift linkage—1969-72
(© Pontiac Div., G.M. Corp.)

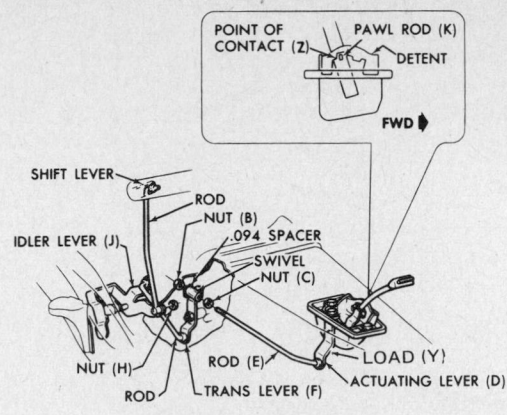

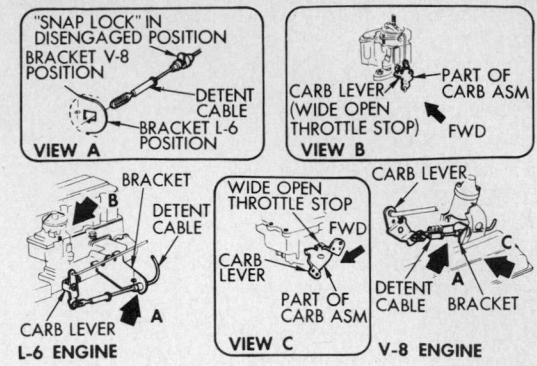

Console shift linkage—Ventura II
with Turbo-Hydramatic
(© Pontiac Div. G.M. Corp.)

Detent cable adjustment—Ventura II
(© Pontiac Div. G.M. Corp.)

3. With detent cable through detent, push Snap Lock downward until its top is flush with the cable.

Throttle Valve (TV) Linkage Adjustment—Two-Speed (M-35) 1970-72

6 Cylinder Models

1. Remove air cleaner.
2. Disconnect TV control rod swivel and clip from carburetor lever, then disconnect TV return spring from bellhousing.
3. Push TV control rod rearward until transmission TV lever is against internal transmission stop.
4. Holding TV control rod in this position, hold carburetor lever in wide open throttle position and adjust TV control rod swivel so that pin freely enters hole in carburetor lever without binding.
5. Secure swivel, connect return spring and check linkage action for binding.
6. Install air cleaner.

V8 Models

1. Remove air cleaner.
2. Disconnect accelerator linkage at carburetor.
3. Disconnect throttle and TV rod return springs.
4. Pull TV rod forward until transmission is through detent, hold in this position and open carburetor butterflies to wide open position.
5. The butterflies must reach wide open position at the same time that the ball stud contacts end of slot in upper TV rod (± 1/32 in.).
6. If necessary, adjust swivel end of upper TV rod.
7. Connect linkage and springs, then check linkage for binding.
8. Install air cleaner.

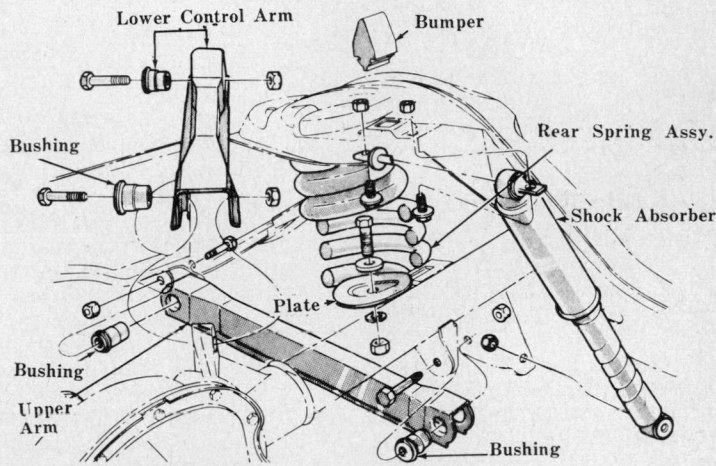

Coil spring rear suspension—1965-72 (© Pontiac Div., G.M. Corp.)

Rear Axles, Suspension

1965-72 Tempest and GTO

The rear wheels are fastened to axle shafts within a Salisbury-type, solid axle housing. The axle housing is connected to the frame by a four-link suspension system, consisting of two upper and two lower control arms pivoted in rubber at each end. These control arms locate the axle laterally and axially with relation to the frame, and oppose torque reaction under acceleration and braking.

Two coil springs are mounted between seats in the frame and axle housing to carry the load of the vehicle. A steel stabilizer bar is mounted on some GTO models to improve side roll stability. This bar attaches to the lower control arms and is positioned under the axle housing.

Shock absorbers are direct double-action hydraulic units and are mounted between the lower control arms and the frame.

1968-72 Firebird and 1971-72 Ventura II

Firebird models use dual multiple-leaf springs and two hydraulic shock absorbers mounted between the lower spring seats and the floor pan. The shocks are staggered, the right shock in front of, and the left shock behind, the axle tubes to reduce spring wind-up under acceleration and braking.

A steel stabilizer bar is used on Formula and Trans Am models to improve side roll stability. This bar is mounted in rubber and is supported by brackets under each shock and spring anchor plate. Two strut supports connect the bar to the frame side rails.

The Ventura II suspension is similar to that used on the Firebird, except that single leaf rear springs are utilized. These springs have a dampener strapped ten inches behind the front spring eye to lessen oscillations under loading.

Rear Axle Housing R & R —Coil Springs

1. Jack up the back of the car to allow sufficient room to work, then place another jack under the rear axle housing.
2. Disconnect the driveshaft.

3. Remove both axle shafts, wire backing plates out of the way, and remove brake hose bracket and brake line.

NOTE: it may be necessary to remove the axle cover and remove the "C" lock retaining the axle shaft. (See Drive Axles, Unit Repair Section.)

4. Disconnect the shocks at the lower end, then slowly lower the rear axle housing until springs can be removed.
5. Remove the bolt on each side which holds the torque arm to the rear axle housing, disconnect lower control arms.
6. Slide the housing assembly out.
7. To install, reverse removal procedure, tightening shock nuts to 55-75 ft. lbs., upper and lower control arm bolts to 75-100 ft. lbs. (nuts to 60-85 ft. lbs.), U-joint bolts to 14-20 ft. lbs.

NOTE: tighten nuts and bolts to specification with car on ground and suspension fully loaded. Do not exceed 20 ft. lbs. on U-joint bolts, or bearings can be distorted.

Rear Axle Housing R & R —Leaf Springs

1. Follow Steps 1-3 in *Rear Axle Housing R&R—Coil Springs.*
2. Disconnect shock absorbers.
3. Disconnect rear spring from its shackles and brackets and lower rear axle housing.
4. Remove axle housing from beneath vehicle.
5. To install, reverse removal procedure, connecting front spring eyes first. Tighten bracket nuts to 100 ft. lbs. and shackle pin nuts to 50 ft. lbs.

NOTE: tighten nuts and bolts to specification with car on ground and suspension fully loaded. Do not exceed 20 ft. lbs. on U-joint bolts, or bearings can be distorted.

Spring Dampener R & R— Ventura II

1. Jack up rear of car.
2. Install C-clamp over damper.

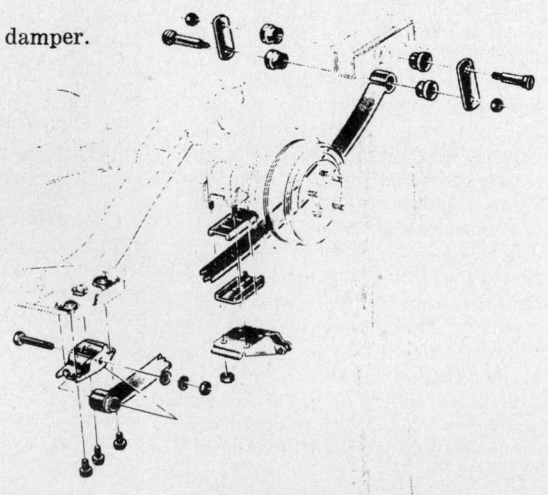

Rear spring installation—Ventura II
(© Pontiac Div. G.M. Corp.)

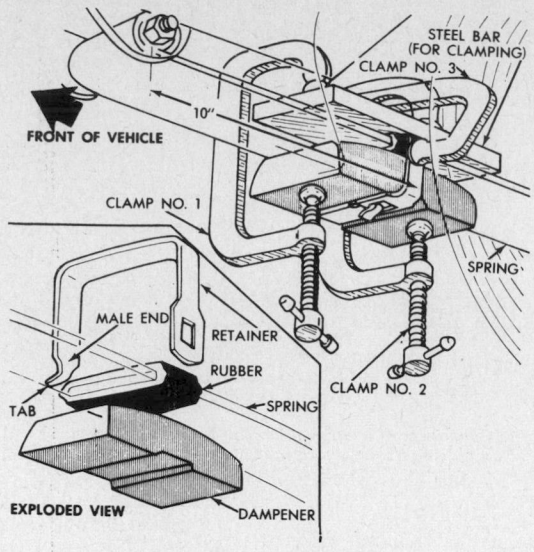

Spring dampener installation—Ventura II
(© Pontiac Div. G.M. Corp.)

3. Straighten retainer tab.
4. Remove C-clamp, retainer, damper and rubber cushion.
5. Install rubber cushion 10 in. behind centerline of front eye.
6. Install damper, then place a steel bar (1 x 2 x 6 in.) on top of cushion and retainer.
7. Install two C-clamps as illustrated, then tighten clamps No. 1 and No. 2 equally until equal rubber deflection is noted. Install clamp No. 3 and tighten to obtain additional compression.
8. Bend male end of retainer toward spring until flush. Repeat Step 7 to press female end of retainer into position, then lock tab.
9. Remove clamps and steel bar, test dampener retention and lower car.

Windshield Wipers

Motor R & R

1965-72

1. Remove hoses and wire terminals that are connected to wiper unit.
2. Remove clip that secures wiper crank to wiper transmission arm.

NOTE: this clip is under instrument panel on 1965-66 models, under leaf screen on depressed-park motors, and accessible only after firewall bolts are removed on some standard motors. On some models, the wiper arm must be removed to facilitate motor removal.

3. Remove screws that secure wiper assembly to firewall.
4. Install a gasket on the motor.
5. Position wiper assembly on firewall and secure.
6. Connect wire terminals and hoses.
7. Connect wiper crank with wiper transmission arm.

Wiper Transmission R & R

1965-72

1. Remove arm and blade assemblies.
2. Remove fresh air intake grille.
3. Remove wiper transmission retaining screws.
4. Loosen, but do not remove, wiper transmission crank to linkage nuts.
5. Remove wiper transmissions and linkage, through cowl opening.
6. To install, reverse above procedure. Make sure wiper blades are in park position after they are installed.

Radio

Radio R & R

1965-70

1. Disconnect antenna and power leads, remove tape deck and multiplex.
2. Loosen hex screws and remove knobs.
3. Remove escutcheon retaining nuts.
4. Remove screw that holds receiver to panel bracket, then remove ash tray.
   NOTE: with air conditioner, outlet duct and bezel must be removed.
5. Remove speaker by disconnecting output connector and mounting bracket screws.
6. Reverse above procedure to reinstall.
   NOTE: this procedure is very general, and some combinations of accessories may require slight modifications.

1970½-72 Firebird

1. Disconnect battery.
2. Remove glove box, glove box door and lower right A/C duct.
3. Remove radio knobs, nuts and trim plate.
4. Disconnect antenna and power lines.
5. Disconnect speaker leads, then remove radio bracket and radio from passenger side of dashboard.
6. To install, reverse removal procedure.

1971-72 Tempest and Ventura II

1. Disconnect battery. Remove lower A/C duct on Tempest.
2. Remove radio knobs, bezels and hex nuts.
3. Remove support bracket bolt.
4. Disconnect electrical and antenna leads; remove radio from under dash.
5. To install, reverse removal procedure.

Heater System

Heater Blower R & R

1965 Tempest & GTO

1. Hoist front of car.
2. Remove right front wheel.
3. Remove right front headlamp.
4. Remove right front fender.
5. Disconnect wire at blower.
6. Remove blower motor attaching screws and assembly.
7. Install in reverse of above.

1966-67 Tempest & GTO

1. Disconnect battery. On six cylinder models, loosen and reposition battery to provide clearance between front fender and fender inner panel.
2. Disconnect heater blower wire at blower.
3. Remove blower motor to blower housing bolts.
4. Remove motor and impeller assembly from the blower housing and position with impeller facing toward engine below right hood hinge.
5. Remove blower to impeller retaining nut and washer, then separate.
6. Move motor, then impeller, separately along top of fender panel to front opening, then remove.
7. Install by reversing removal procedure.

1968-69 Tempest & GTO, 1969 Firebird, 1971-72 Ventura II

1. Remove battery and battery tray.
2. Remove inner fender skirt.
   NOTE: on 1971-72 Ventura II, remove fender skirt attaching bolts and pry skirt away far enough to insert a wooden block. This should give sufficient clearance.
3. Remove blower power wire.
4. Remove blower retaining screws and blower.
5. To install, reverse removal procedure.
   NOTE: if duct was removed, make sure it is properly sealed during installation.

1967-68 Firebird

1. Disconnect battery cables, then remove battery and battery tray.
2. Unclip heater hoses from fender skirt.
3. Scribe alignment marks at hood hinges, then remove hood.
4. Remove right front fender and skirt as an assembly.
5. Disconnect blower power wire.
6. Remove blower screws and blower.
7. To install, reverse removal procedure.
   NOTE: if duct was removed, make sure it is properly sealed during installation.

1970-72 Tempest, Firebird, & GTO

1. Jack up front of car and remove right front wheel.
2. Cut access hole along stamped outline on right fender skirt, using an air chisel.
3. Disconnect blower power wire.
4. Remove blower.
5. To install, reverse removal procedure, covering access hole with a metal plate secured with sealer and sheet metal screws.

Heater Core R & R

1965 Tempest & GTO

1. Drain radiator.
2. Remove glove compartment.
3. Disconnect hoses at heater.
4. Disconnect control cables at core and case assembly.
5. Remove wire connector from resistor assembly at top left side of heater outlet duct by prying connector up with flat screwdriver.
6. Remove nuts that hold heater to air inlet duct, and remove heater assembly.
7. Remove core and case assembly.
8. Install in reverse of above.

1966-67 Tempest & GTO

1. Drain radiator and remove glove compartment.
2. Disconnect heater hoses at the heater.
3. Disconnect heater control cables at heater.
4. Remove front wheel.
5. Remove wire connector from resistor at top left side of heater air outlet by prying connector up with a screwdriver.
6. Cut a one inch hole in the skirt.
7. Remove six nuts from the heater to air inlet duct and remove heater.
8. Install by reversing removal procedure.
9. Patch the skirt hole.

1968 Tempest and GTO

1. Disconnect heater hoses at heater.
2. Remove glove compartment.
3. Remove five nuts which secure heater to firewall.
4. Pull case from firewall, then disconnect cables and wire connector from resistor.

1967-1972 Firebird, 1969-72 Tempest & GTO

1. Drain radiator.
2. Disconnect heater hoses at air inlet assembly.

NOTE: the water pump hose goes to top heater core pipe, the other hose (from rear of right cylinder head on V8, center of block on 6) goes to the lower heater core pipe.

3. Remove nuts from core studs on firewall (under hood).

NOTE: on 1970-72 Firebird, remove glove box and door, then remove heater outlet from case. Remove defroster duct screw on all 1971-72 models.

4. From inside the car, pull the heater assembly from the firewall.
5. Disconnect control cables and wires, then remove heater assembly.
6. To remove core, unhook retaining springs.
7. To install, reverse removal procedure, making sure core is properly sealed during installation.

1971-72 Ventura II

1. Disconect battery.
2. Drain radiator, disconnect heater hoses at core and plug core tubes.
3. Remove nuts from core case studs on firewall.
4. Remove glove box and glove box door.
5. From inside car, drill out lower right hand heater case stud with ¼ in. drill.
6. Pull entire heater case, with core, from firewall.
7. Disconnect Bowdin cables and blower resistor connector, then remove case from car.
8. Remove core from case.
9. To install, reverse removal procedure. Use sealer around core and replace drilled stud with new screw and Pal nut.

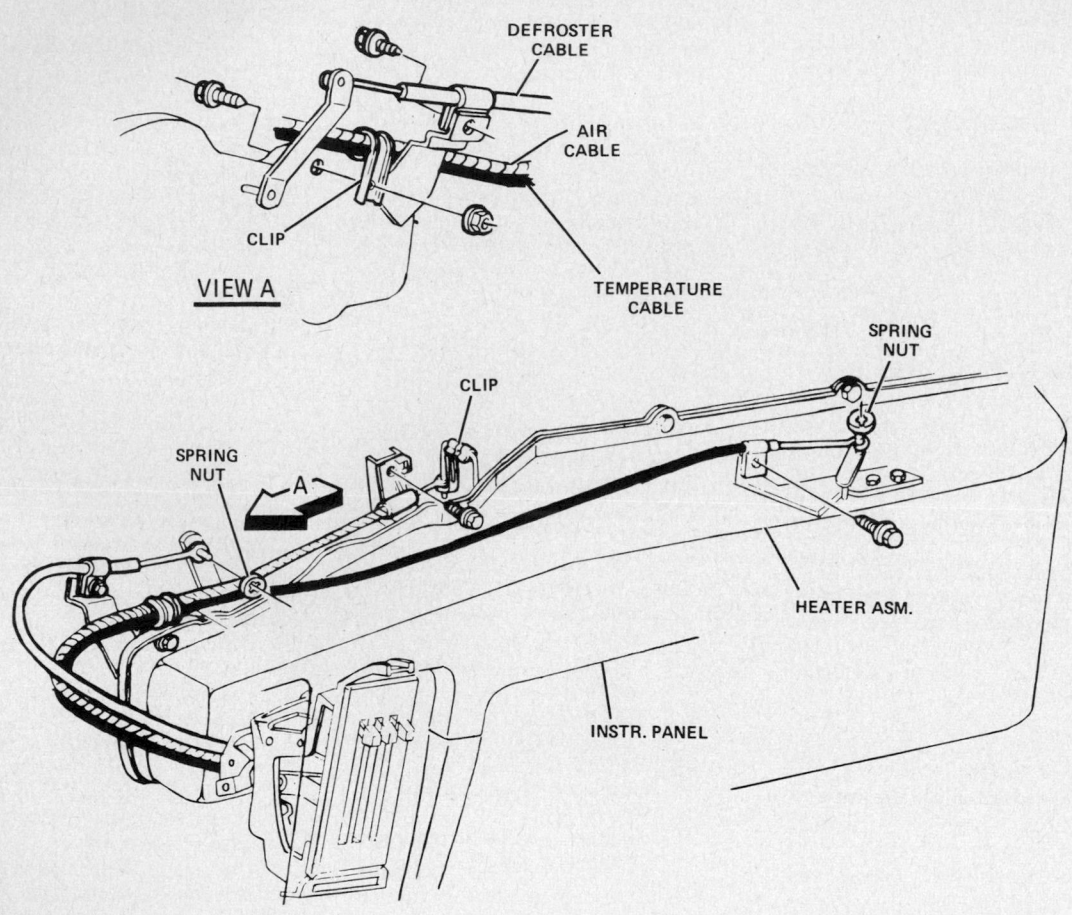

Heater Cable Routing

Index

YEAR IDENTIFICATION

FORD

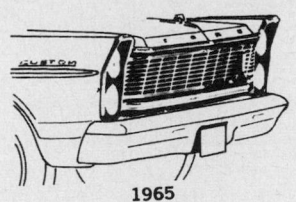
1965

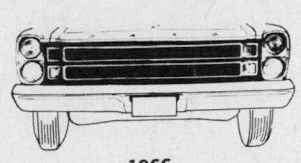
1966

1967

1968

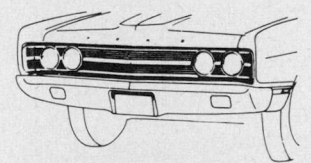
1969

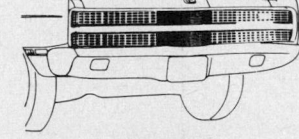
1969 LTD

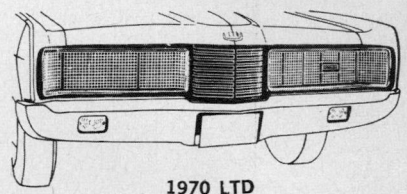
1970 LTD

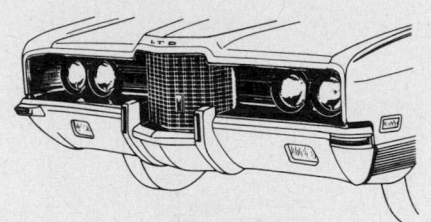
1971 LTD

1972 Galaxie

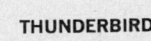
1972 LTD

THUNDERBIRD

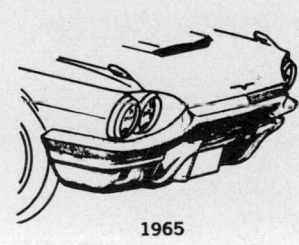
1965

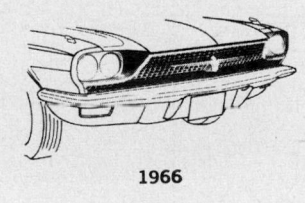
1966

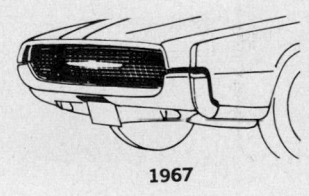
1967

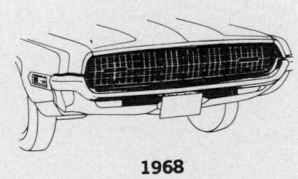
1968

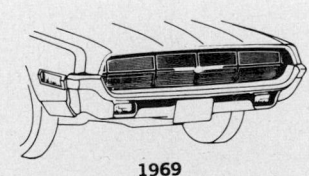
1969

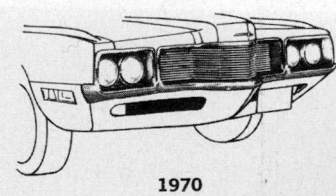
1970

1972

YEAR IDENTIFICATION

MERCURY

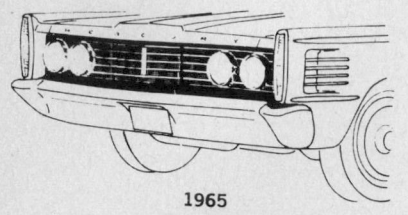

1965

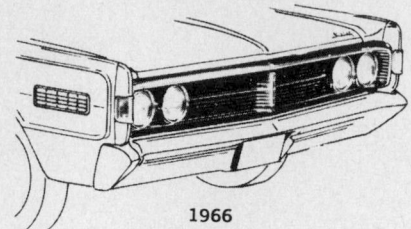

1966

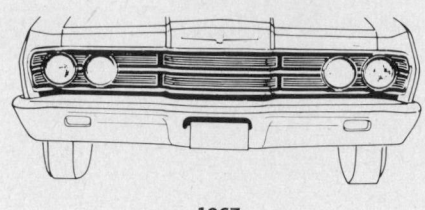

1967

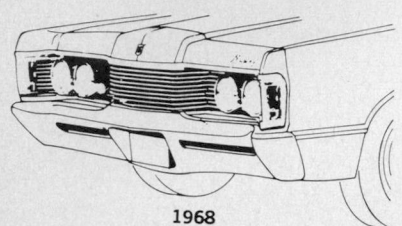

1968

1969

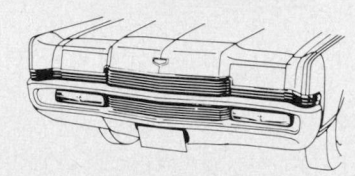

1969 (Marquis)

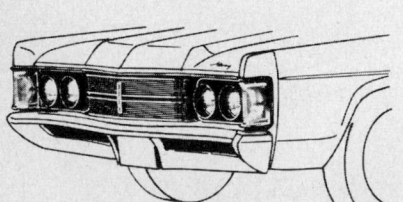

1970 Monterey

1970 Marquis Brougham

1971

1972 Monterey

1972 Marquis

FIRING ORDER

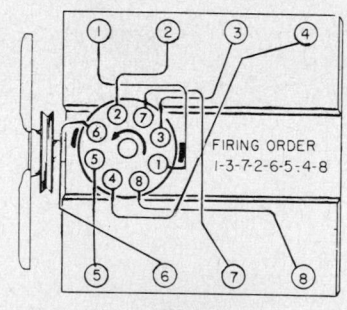

FIRING ORDER
1-3-7-2-6-5-4-8

V8 351 cu. in.

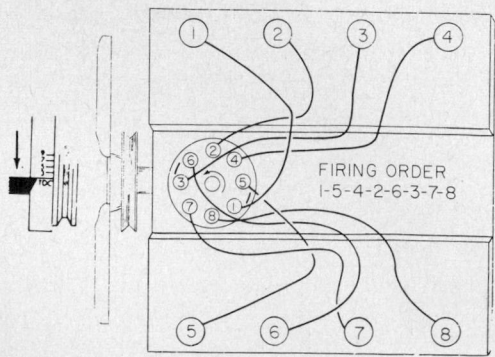

FIRING ORDER 1-5-4-2-6-3-7-8

V8 except 351 cu. in.

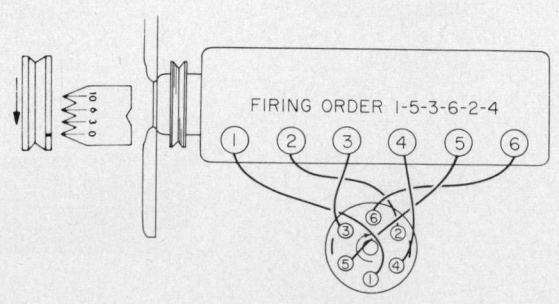

FIRING ORDER 1-5-3-6-2-4

240 cu. in. 6 cyl.

CAR SERIAL NUMBER LOCATION AND ENGINE IDENTIFICATION

1965-67

Engine is identified through car serial number. Serial numbers, and other pertinent information, are on a plate riveted to the rear edge of the left front door pillar.

The engine number is stamped on the top surface of the engine block near the crankcase breather pipe, front left side.

The car serial number is composed of eleven digits, interpreted as illustrated. The production year code is the last digit of the model year in which the vehicle was produced. (For example, "6" = 1966, "9" = 1969). The fifth digit, a letter, represents the engine identification code. (See table.)

1968-72

The serial number can be found on a plate attached to the top of the instrument panel, visible through the windshield. Information for identification remains essentially the same as for 1965-67 models.

Vehicle Certification Label —1970-72

The label is located on the rear of the driver's door. The upper portion contains the name of the manufacturer, the month and year of manufacture, and the certification statement. The lower portion of the label is interpreted in the illustration.

Engine Identification Code

CU. IN. DISPL.	TYPE	YEAR AND CODE						
		1965	1966	1967	1968	1969	1970	1971
240-6	1-BBL.	V	V	V	V	V	V	V
240-6	Police	B	B	B	B	B	B	B
240-6	Taxi	E	E	E	E	E	E	E
289-V8	2-BBL.	C	C	C				
302-V8	2-BBL.				F	F	F	F
302-V8	Taxi				D	D	D	D
351-V8	2-BBL.①						H	H
352-V8	4-BBL.	X	X					
390-V8	2-BBL.	Y	Y	Y	Y	Y	Y	Y
390-V8	2-BBL.②	H	H	H	X	X		
390-V8	4-BBL.	Z	Z	Z	Z			
400-V8	2-BBL.							S
410-V8	4-BBL.		M	M				
427-V8	4-BBL.	W	W	W				
427-V8	8-BBL.	R	R	R				
428-V8	4-BBL.		Q	Q	Q			
428-V8	Police		P	P	P	P	P	
429-V8	2-BBL.					K	K	K
429-V8	4-BBL.				N	N	N	N
429-V8	Police							P

① —All 1970 351 2-BBL. engines have Windsor heads. 1971 351 2-BBL. engines are a mixture of Cleveland and Windsor designs. The quickest method of engine identification is to disconnect a spark plug wire at the spark plug and examine the size of the plug. Windsor engines are equipped with standard 18mm spark plugs. Cleveland engines are equipped with smaller 14mm spark plugs.

② —Premium fuel engine used in Mercurys equipped with automatic transmission.

Typical vehicle identification number (VIN) tab

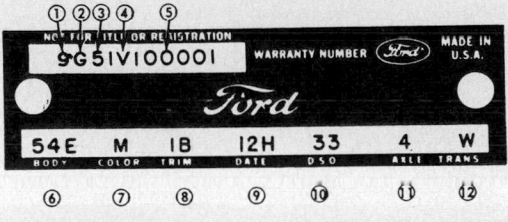

1 Model year code
2 Assembly plant code
3 Body serial code
4 Engine code
5 Consecutive unit number
6 Body type code
7 Color code
8 Trim code
9 Date code
10 District—special equipment code
11 Rear axle code
12 Transmission code

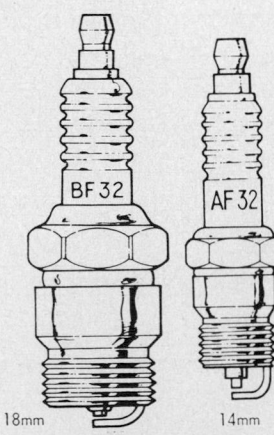

18mm   14mm
Left—Windsor spark plug
Right—Cleveland spark plug

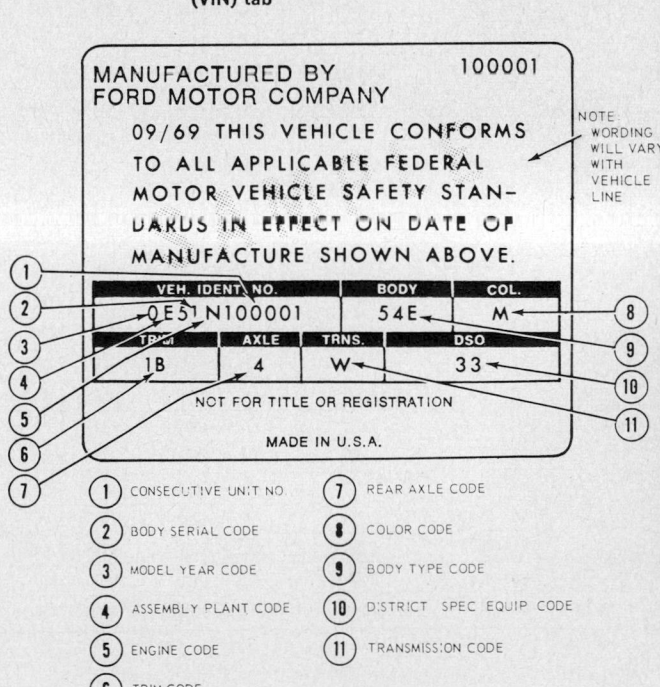

1970-72 Vehicle Certification Label

GENERAL ENGINE SPECIFICATIONS

YEAR	CU. IN. DISPLACEMENT	CARBURETOR	ADVERTIZED HORSEPOWER @ RPM	ADVERTIZED TORQUE @ RPM (FT. LBS.)	A.M.A. HORSEPOWER	BORE AND STROKE (IN.)	ADVERTIZED COMPRESSION RATIO	VALVE LIFTER TYPE	OIL PRESSURE @ 2000 RPM (PSI)
1965	6 Cyl.—240	1-BBL.	155 @ 4200	239 @ 2200	38.40	4.000 x 3.180	8.75-1	Hyd.	35-60
	V8—289	2-BBL.	200 @ 4400	282 @ 2400	51.20	4.000 x 2.870	9.3-1	Hyd.	35-55
	V8—352	4-BBL.	250 @ 4400	352 @ 2800	51.20	4.000 x 3.500	9.3-1	Hyd.	35-55
	V8—390▲	2-BBL.	250 @ 4400	378 @ 2400	52.5	4.050 x 3.781	9.4-1	Hyd.	35-55
	V8—390	4-BBL.	300 @ 4600	427 @ 2800	52.49	4.050 x 3.781	10.1-1	Hyd.	35-55
	V8—390	4-BBL.	330 @ 5000	427 @ 3200	52.49	4.050 x 3.781	10.1-1	Mech.	35-55
	V8—427	2-4-BBL.	425 @ 6000	480 @ 3700	57.33	4.233 x 3.781	11.1-1	Mech.	40-55
1966	6 Cyl.—240	1-BBL.	150 @ 4000	234 @ 2200	38.40	4.000 x 3.180	9.2-1	Hyd.	35-60
	V8—289	2-BBL.	206 @ 4400	282 @ 2400	51.20	4.000 x 2.870	9.3-1	Hyd.	35-55
	V8—352	4-BBL.	250 @ 4400	352 @ 2800	51.20	4.000 x 3.500	9.3-1	Hyd.	35-55
	V8—390	2-BBL.	265 @ 4400	401 @ 2600	52.49	4.050 x 3.781	9.5-1	Hyd.	35-55
	V8—390▲	2-BBL.	275 @ 4400	405 @ 2600	52.49	4.050 x 3.781	9.5-1	Hyd.	35-55
	V8—390	4-BBL.	315 @ 4600	427 @ 2800	52.49	4.050 x 3.781	10.5-1	Hyd.	35-55
	V8—410	4-BBL.	330 @ 4600	444 @ 2800	52.5	4.050 x 3.980	10.5-1	Hyd.	35-55
	V8—427	4-BBL.	410 @ 5600	476 @ 3400	57.33	4.233 x 3.781	11.1-1	Mech.	40-55
	V8—427	2-4-BBL.	425 @ 6000	480 @ 3700	57.33	4.233 x 3.781	11.1-1	Mech.	40-55
	V8—428	4-BBL.	345 @ 4600	462 @ 2800	54.48	4.130 x 3.980	10.5-1	Hyd.	35-55
	V8—428 ★	4-BBL.	360 @ 5400	459 @ 3200	54.48	4.130 x 3.980	10.5-1	Hyd.	35-70
1967	6 Cyl.—240	1-BBL.	155 @ 4200	239 @ 2200	38.40	4.000 x 3.180	9.2-1	Hyd.	35-60
	V8—289	2-BBL.	200 @ 4400	282 @ 2400	51.20	4.000 x 2.870	9.3-1	Hyd.	35-55
	V8—390	2-BBL.	265 @ 4400	401 @ 2600	52.5	4.050 x 3.784	9.5-1	Hyd.	35-65
	V8—390 ▲	2-BBL.	275 @ 4400	405 @ 2600	52.49	4.050 x 3.781	9.5-1	Hyd.	35-65
	V8—390	4-BBL.	315 @ 4600	427 @ 2800	52.49	4.050 x 3.781	10.5-1	Hyd.	35-65
	V8—410	4-BBL.	330 @ 4600	444 @ 2800	52.5	4.050 x 3.980	10.5-1	Hyd.	35-65
	V8—427	4-BBL.	410 @ 5600	476 @ 3400	57.33	4.233 x 3.781	11.1-1	Mech.	40-55
	V8—427	2-4-BBL.	425 @ 6000	480 @ 3700	57.33	4.233 x 3.781	11.1-1	Mech.	40-55
	V8—428	4-BBL.	345 @ 4600	462 @ 2800	54.58	4.130 x 3.980	10.5-1	Hyd.	35-65
	V8—428★	4-BBL.	360 @ 5400	459 @ 3200	54.48	4.130 x 3.980	10.5-1	Hyd.	45-70
1968	6 Cyl.—240	1-BBL.	150 @ 4000	234 @ 2200	38.40	4.000 x 3.180	9.2-1	Hyd.	35-60
	V8—302	2-BBL.	210 @ 4600	300 @ 2600	51.20	4.000 x 3.000	9.0-1	Hyd.	35-60
	V8—390	2-BBL.	270 @ 4400	390 @ 2600	52.49	4.050 x 3.781	9.5-1	Hyd.	35-60
	V8—390▲	2-BBL.	280 @ 4400	403 @ 2600	52.49	4.050 x 3.781	10.5-1	Hyd.	35-60
	V8—390	4-BBL.	315 @ 4600	427 @ 2800	52.49	4.050 x 3.781	10.5-1	Hyd.	35-60
	V8—428	4-BBL.	340 @ 5400	462 @ 2800	54.58	4.130 x 3.980	10.5-1	Hyd.	35-60
	V8—428★	4-BBL.	360 @ 5400	459 @ 3200	54.58	4.130 x 3.980	10.5-1	Hyd.	35-60
	V8—429	4-BBL.	360 @ 4600	480 @ 2800	60.80	4.360 x 3.590	10.5-1	Hyd.	45
1969	6 Cyl.—240	1-BBL.	150 @ 4000	234 @ 2200	38.40	4.000 x 3.180	9.2-1	Hyd.	35-60
	V8—302	2-BBL.	210 @ 4400	295 @ 2400	51.20	4.000 x 3.000	9.5-1	Hyd.	35-60
	V8—390	2-BBL.	270 @ 4400	390 @ 2600	52.49	4.050 x 3.781	9.5-1	Hyd.	35-60
	V8—390▲	2-BBL.	280 @ 4400	430 @ 2600	52.49	4.050 x 3.781	10.5-1	Hyd.	35-60
	V8—428★	4-BBL.	360 @ 5400	459 @ 3200	54.58	4.130 x 3.980	10.5-1	Hyd.	35-60
	V8—429	2-BBL.	320 @ 4400	460 @ 2200	60.80	4.360 x 3.590	10.5-1	Hyd.	35-60
	V8—429	4-BBL.	360 @ 4600	476 @ 2800	60.80	4.360 x 3.590	11.0-1	Hyd.	35-60
1970	6 Cyl.—240	1-BBL.	150 @ 4000	234 @ 2200	38.40	4.000 x 3.180	9.2-1	Hyd.	35-60
	V8—302	2-BBL.	210 @ 4400	295 @ 2400	51.20	4.000 x 3.000	9.5-1	Hyd.	35-60
	V8—351	2-BBL.	250 @ 4600	355 @ 2600	51.20	4.000 x 3.500	9.5-1	Hyd.	35-60
	V8—390	2-BBL.	270 @ 4400	390 @ 2600	52.54	4.050 x 3.781	9.5-1	Hyd.	35-60
	V8—428★	4-BBL.	360 @ 5400	459 @ 3200	54.58	4.130 x 3.980	10.5-1	Hyd.	35-60
	V8—429	2-BBL.	320 @ 4400	460 @ 2200	60.80	4.360 x 3.590	10.5-1	Hyd.	35-60
	V8—429	4-BBL.	360 @ 4600	480 @ 2800	60.80	4.360 x 3.590	10.5-1	Hyd.	35-60

GENERAL ENGINE SPECIFICATIONS

YEAR	CU. IN. DISPLACEMENT	CARBURETOR	ADVERTIZED HORSEPOWER @ RPM	ADVERTIZED TORQUE @ RPM (FT. LBS.)	A.M.A. HORSEPOWER	BORE AND STROKE (IN.)	ADVERTIZED COMPRESSION RATIO	VALVE LIFTER TYPE	OIL PRESSURE @ 2,000 RPM (PSI)
1971	6 Cyl.—240	1-BBL.	140 @ 4000	230 @ 2200	38.40	4.000 x 3.180	8.9-1	Hyd.	35-60
	V8—302	2-BBL.	210 @ 4600	296 @ 2600	51.20	4.000 x 3.000	9.0-1	Hyd.	35-60
	V8—351	2-BBL.	240 @ 4600	350 @ 2600	51.20	4.000 x 3.500	9.0-1	Hyd.	35-60
	V8—390	2-BBL.	255 @ 4400	376 @ 2600	52.54	4.052 x 3.784	8.6-1	Hyd.	35-65
	V8—400	2-BBL.	260 @ 4400	400 @ 2200	51.20	4.000 x 4.000	9.0-1	Hyd.	50-70
	V8—429	2-BBL.	320 @ 4400	460 @ 2200	60.83	4.360 x 3.590	10.5-1	Hyd.	35-75
	V8—429	4-BBL.	360 @ 4600	480 @ 2800	60.83	4.360 x 3.590	10.5-1	Hyd.	35-75
	V8—429★	4-BBL.	370 @ 5400	450 @ 3400	60.83	4.360 x 3.590	11.3-1	Hyd.	35-70
1971½–72	6 Cyl.—240	1-BBL.	① 140 @ 4400	① 230 @ 2200	38.40	4.000 x 3.180	—	Hyd.	35-60
	V8—302	2-BBL.	① 210 @ 4600	① 296 @ 2600	51.20	4.000 x 3.000	—	Hyd.	35-60
	V8—351	2-BBL.	① 240 @ 4600	① 350 @ 2600	51.20	4.000 x 3.500	—	Hyd.	35-60
	V8—400	2-BBL.	① 260 @ 4400	① 400 @ 2200	51.20	4.000 x 4.000	—	Hyd.	50-70
	V8—429	2-BBL.	① 320 @ 4400	① 460 @ 2200	60.83	4.362 x 3.590	—	Hyd.	35-70
	V8—429	4-BBL.	① 360 @ 4600	① 480 @ 2800	60.83	4.362 x 3.590	—	Hyd.	35-70

▲—Premium fuel engine used in Mercurys equipped with automatic transmission.

★—Police Intercepter engine.

①—1971½ advertized horsepower and torque ratings are shown in tables. 1972 S.A.E. net horsepower, compression ratios or net torque ratings were not available at press time, however, they will be substantially lower than 1971½ figures, since they are based on S.A.E. J245 standards, representing actual output of the engine installed in any particular vehicle.

BATTERY AND STARTER SPECIFICATIONS

YEAR	MODEL	BATTERY				STARTERS ⓐ						Brush Spring Tension (Oz.)
						Lock Test			No Load Test			
		Ampere Hour Capacity	Volts	Group Number	Terminal Grounded	Amps.	Volts	Torque	Amps.	Volts	RPM	
1965	6 Cyl.	45	12	22HF	Neg.	670	5	15.5	70	12	9,500	40
	V8—289, 352	45	12	22HF	Neg.	670	5	15.5	70	12	9,500	40
	V8—390	55	12	24F	Neg.	670	5	15.5	70	12	9,500	40
	V8—427	70	12	27F	Neg.	580	5	14.8	110	12	5,200	48
1966	6 Cyl.	45	12	22HF	Neg.	670	5	15.5	70	12	9,500	40
	V8—289, 352, 390	45*	12	22HF	Neg.	670	5	15.5	70	12	9,500	40
	V8—428	80	12	27HF	Neg.	670	5	15.5	70	12	9,500	40
1967	6 Cyl.	45	12·	22HF	Neg.	670	5	15.5	70	12	9,500	40
	V8—289, 390	45*	12	22HF	Neg.	670	5	15.5	70	12	9,500	40
	V8—428	80	12	27HF	Neg.	670	5	15.5	70	12	9,500	40
1968–69	6 Cyl.	45	12	22HF	Neg.	670	5	15.5	70	12	9,500	40
	V8—302	55‡	12	24F	Neg.	670	5	15.5	70	12	9,500	10
	V8—390	45●	12	22HF	Neg.	670	5	15.5	70	12	9,500	40
	V8—428	80	12	27HF	Neg.	670	5	15.5	70	12	9,500	40
	V8—429	80	12	27HF	Neg.	700	5	15.5	70	12	9,500	40
1970	6 Cyl.	45	12	21R	Neg.	670	5	15.5	70	12	9,500	40
	V8—302, 351	55‡	12	24F	Neg.	670	5	15.5	70	12	9,500	40
	V8—390	45●	12	21R	Neg.	670	5	15.5	70	12	9,500	40
	V8—428, 429	80	12	27HF	Neg.	700	5	15.5	70	12	11,000	40
1971–72	6 Cyl.	45▲	12	21R	Neg.	670	5	15.5	70	12	9,500	40
	V8—302	45▲	12	21R	Neg.	670	5	15.5	70	12	9,500	40
	V8 351	45●	12	21R	Neg.	670	5	15.5	70	12	9,500	40
	V8 400	70	12	27F	Neg.	700	5	15.5	70	12	11,000	40
	V8 429	80	12	27HF	Neg.	700	5	15.5	70	12	11,000	40

ⓐ—Starter specifications in table are for 4½ in. starter. Starter specifications for all models with a 4 in. diameter starter are:

					460	5	9.0	70	12	40

★—55 Amp. with automatic transmission or air conditioning.

‡—70 Amp. with air conditioning.

●—55 Amp. with automatic transmission, 70 Amp. with air conditioning.

▲—55 Amp. with air conditioning.

TUNE-UP SPECIFICATIONS

YEAR	MODEL	SPARK PLUGS		DISTRIBUTOR		IGNITION TIMING (Deg.) ▲	CRANKING COMP. PRESSURE (Psi)	VALVES		Intake Opens (Deg.)	FUEL PUMP PRESSURE (Psi)	IDLE SPEED (Rpm)
		Type	Gap (In.)	Point Dwell (Deg.)	Point Gap (In.)			Tappet (Hot) Clearance (In.) Intake	Exhaust			
1965	6 Cyl.—240 Cu. In.; M.T.	BF42	.034	37	.025	6B	150–200	Zero	Zero	23B	4.5	475
	6 Cyl.—240 Cu. In.; A.T.	BF42	.034	37	.025	8B	150–200	Zero	Zero	23B	4.5	475
	V8—289 Cu. In.; M.T.	BF42	.034	27	.015	6B	130–170	Zero	Zero	20B	5.0	575
	V8—289 Cu. In.; A.T.	BF42	.034	27	.015	10B	130–170	Zero	Zero	20B	5.0	500
	V8—352 Cu. In.; M.T.	BF42	.034	27	.015	6B	160–200	Zero	Zero	22B	5.0	500
	V8—352 Cu. In.; A.T.	BF42	.034	27	.015	10B	160–200	Zero	Zero	22B	5.0	475
	V8—390 Cu. In.; M.T.	BF42	.034	27	.015	4B	170–210	Zero	Zero	26B	5.0	500
	V8—390 Cu. In.; A.T.	BF42	.034	27	.015	6B	170–210	Zero	Zero	26B	5.0	500
	V8—427 Cu. In.; M.T.	BF32	.030	35	.020	8B	160–200	.025H	.025H	5A	6.0	700
1966	6 Cyl.—240 Cu. In.; M.T.	BTF42	.034	39	.025	6B ①	150–200	Zero	Zero	23B	5.0	525 ①
	6 Cyl.—240 Cu. In.; A.T.	BTF42	.034	39	.025	12B ①	150–200	Zero	Zero	23B	5.0	525
	V8—289 Cu. In.	BF42	.034	28	.017	6B ①	130–170	Zero	Zero	20B	5.0	Ⓐ
	V8—352 Cu. In.	BF42	.034	28	.017	10B	160–200	Zero	Zero	22B	6.0	Ⓐ
	V8—390 and 410 Cu. In.	BF42	.034	28	.017	10B ①	170–210	Zero	Zero	26B	6.0	Ⓐ
	V8—427 Cu. In.	BF32	.034	23	.020	8B	160–200	.025H	.025H	5A	6.0	800
	V8—428 Cu. In.	BF42	.030	28	.017	10B ①	170–210	Zero	Zero	16B	6.0	Ⓐ
1967	6 Cyl.—240, M.T.	BF42	.034	39	.025	6B ①	150–200	Zero	Zero	12B	5.0	525 ①
	6 Cyl.—240, A.T.	BF42	.034	39	.025	10B ①	150–200	Zero	Zero	12B	5.0	500
	V8—289, All	BF42	.034	28	.015	6B ①	130–170	Zero	Zero	15B	5.0	525
	V8—390, 2-BBL., A.T.	BF42	.034	28	.017	10B ①	160–200	Zero	Zero	16B	5.0	500
	V8—390 and 410, 4-BBL., M.T.	BF42	.034	28	.017	10B ①	170–210	Zero	Zero	16B	5.0	575
	V8—390 and 410, 4-BBL., A.T.	BF42	.034	28	.017	10B ①	170–210	Zero	Zero	16B	5.0	500
	V8—427 All	BF32	.030	23	.020	8B	160–200	.025H	.025H	48B	6.0	800
	V8—428 All	BF42	.034	28	.017	10B ①	170–210	Zero	Zero	16B	6.0	600
1968	6 Cyl.—240	BF42	.034	39	.025	6B	150–200	Zero	Zero	12B	5.0	Ⓐ
	V8—302	BF32	.034	27	.021	6B	130–170	Zero	Zero	16B	5.0	625 ●●
	V8—390, 2-BBL.	BF32	.034	27	.021	6B	160–200	Zero	Zero	13B	6.0	625 ●●
	V8—390, 4-BBL.	BF32	.034	27	.021	6B	170–210	Zero	Zero	16B	6.0	625 ●●
	V8—428	BF32	.034	27	.021	6B	170–210	Zero	Zero	16B	6.0	625 ●●
	V8—428, P.I.	BF32	.034	27	.021	6B	170–210	Zero	Zero	18B	6.0	600
	V8—429	BF42	.034	27	.021	6B	180–200	Zero	Zero	16B	6.0	550
1969	6 Cyl.—240	BF42	.034	39	.027	6B	‡	Zero	Zero	12B	5.0	775/550 ●●
	V8—302, 2-BBL.	BF42	.034	27	.021	6B	‡	Zero	Zero	16B	5.0	625 ●●
	V8—390, 2-BBL.	BF42	.034	27	.021	6B	‡	Zero	Zero	13B	5.0	625 ●●
	V8—428, 4-BBL., P.I.	BF32	.034	29	.021	6B	‡	Zero	Zero	18B	6.0	550
	V8—429, 2-BBL.	BF42	.034	29	.021	6B	‡	Zero	Zero	16B	6.0	550
	V8—429, 4-BBL.	BF42	.034	29	.021	6B	‡	Zero	Zero	16B	6.0	550
1970	6 Cyl.—240	BF42	.034	39	.027	6B	‡	Zero	Zero	10B	4–6	800/500 ●●
	V8—302, 2-BBL.	BF42	.034	27	.021	6B	‡	Zero	Zero	16B	4–6	①
	V8—351, 2-BBL.	BF42	.034	27	.021	6B	‡	Zero	Zero	11B	4–6	②
	V8—390, 2-BBL.	BF42	.034	27	.021	6B	‡	Zero	Zero	13B	5–6	③
	V8—428, 4-BBL., P.I.	BF32	.035	24–29	.021	6B	‡	Zero	Zero	18B	5–6	600 ④
	V8—429, 2-BBL.	BF42	.034	27	.021	6B	‡	Zero	Zero	6B	5.5–6.5	⑤
	V8—429, 4-BBL.	BF42 ⑥	.034	27	.021	6B	‡	Zero	Zero	6B	5.5–6.5	⑤

TUNE-UP SPECIFICATIONS

YEAR	MODEL	SPARK PLUGS		DISTRIBUTOR		IGNITION TIMING (Deg.) ▲	CRANKING COMP. PRESSURE (Psi)	VALVES		Intake Opens (Deg.)	FUEL PUMP PRESSURE (Psi)	IDLE SPEED (Rpm)
		Type	Gap (In.)	Point Dwell (Deg.)	Point Gap (In.)			Tappet (Hot) Clearance (In.)				
								Intake	Exhaust			
1971–72	6 Cyl.—240	BRF42	.034	38	.027	6B	‡	Zero	Zero	18B	4–6	①
	V8—302, 2-BBL.	BRF42	.034	27	.021	6B	‡	Zero	Zero	16B	4–6	②
	V8—351, 2-BBL.	BRF42⑧	.034	27	.021	6B	‡	Zero	Zero	11B	4–6	⑦
	V8—390, 2-BBL.	BRF42	.034	27	.021	6B	‡	Zero	Zero	13B	5.5–6.5	③
	V8—400, 2-BBL.	ARF42	.034	27	.021	6B	‡	Zero	Zero	17B	5.5–6.5	④
	V8—429, 2-BBL.	BRF42	.034	27	.021	4B	‡	Zero	Zero	16B	5.5–6.5	600④
	V8—429, 4-BBL.	BRF42	.034	27	.021	4B	‡	Zero	Zero	16B	5.5–6.5	600④
	V8—429, 4-BBL., P.I.	ARF32	.034	30	.017	10B	‡	Zero	Zero	32B	5.5–6.5	600④

B—Before top dead center.
TDC—Top dead center.
A.T.—Automatic Transmission.
M.T.—Manual Transmission.
★—See text for procedure.
P.I.—Police Interceptor.
▲—With vacuum advance disconnected and plugged. NOTE: These settings are only approximate. Engine design, altitude, temperature, fuel octane rating and the condition of the individual engine are all factors which can influence timing.
‡—When checking compression, take the highest compression reading and compare it to the lowest reading. The lowest reading must be within 75% of the highest.
Ⓐ—M.T.—600
  A.T.—500
●●—A.T. 550 RPM

⑥—1966 with thermactor system:
  timing: 6 Cyl. & V8 289—TDC
  idle speed: 6 Cyl. M.T.—650 rpm
  V8 352—635, 289—600
  V8 390 A.T.—500
⑨—1967 with thermactor system:
  6 Cyl. M.T.—TDC A.T.—4B
  V8—289 exc. Hi Per.—TDC
  V8—289—Hi Per.—12B
  V8—390, 410, 428—6B
①—500—A.T. With solenoid throttle positioner, 800/500—M.T., 600/500—A.T.
②—575—A.T. With solenoid throttle positioner, 700/500—M.T., 600/500—A.T.
③—575—A.T. With solenoid throttle positioner, 750/500—M.T., 600/500—A.T.
④—With solenoid throttle positioner, 600/500.
⑤—600—A.T. With solenoid throttle positioner, 850/500—M.T.
⑥—Thunderbird use BRF42.
⑦—351W: 575—A.T. With solenoid throttle positioner, 775/500—M.T., 600/500—A.T. 351C: 600—A.T. With solenoid throttle positioner, 700/500—M.T., 600/500—A.T.
⑧—351C use ARF42.

CAUTION

General adoption of anti-pollution laws has changed the design of almost all car engine production to effectively reduce crankcase emission and terminal exhaust products. It has been necessary to adopt stricter tune-up rules, especially timing and idle speed procedures. Both of these values are peculiar to the engine and to its application, rather than to the engine alone. With this in mind, car manufacturers supply idle speed data for the engine and application involved. This information is clearly displayed in the engine compartment of each vehicle.

WHEEL ALIGNMENT

YEAR	MODEL	CASTER		CAMBER		TOE-IN (In.)	KING-PIN INCLINATION (Deg.)	WHEEL PIVOT RATIO	
		Range (Deg.)	Pref. Setting (Deg.)	Range (Deg.)	Pref. Setting (Deg.)			Inner Wheel	Outer Wheel
1964	Ford	1N to 1P	0	0 to 1¼P	⅝P	⅛ to ¼	7⅛	20	17½
	T-Bird	¾N to 2¼N	1½N	0 to ¾P	⅜P	⅛ to ¼	7⅜	20	18¾
1965	Ford, Mercury	0 to 2P	1P	¼N to 1P	½P	1/32 to 7/32	7	20	17½
	T-Bird	3¼N to 1¼N	1½N	¾N to 1P	½P	1/32 to 9/32	7	20	19½
1966	Ford, Mercury	½N to ½P	1P	¼N to ¾P	¼P	⅛ to ¼	7	20	17½
	T-Bird	2½N to ½P	1½N	¼N to 1¼P	½P	⅛ to ¼	7	20	19½
1967	Ford, Mercury	½P to 1½P	1P	¼N to 1¼P	¾P	1/16 to 3/16	7¾	20	18⅛
	T-Bird	½N to 1½P	½P	½P to 1½P	1P	⅛ to ¼	7¾	20	18⅛
1968–69	Ford, Mercury	0 to 2P	1P	¼N to 1¼P	¾P	⅛ to ¼	7¾	20	18⅛
	T-Bird	0 to 2P	1P	¼N to 1¼P	½P	1/16 to 5/16	7¾	20	18¼
1970–72	All Models	0 to 2P	1P	¼N to 1¼P	½P	1/16 to 5/16	7¾	20	19 5/32

N—Negative.
P—Positive.

VALVE SPECIFICATIONS

YEAR AND MODEL	SEAT ANGLE (DEG.) In.	SEAT ANGLE (DEG.) Ex.	FACE ANGLE (DEG.)	VALVE LIFT INTAKE (IN.)	VALVE LIFT EXHAUST (IN.)	VALVE SPRING PRESSURE (VALVE OPEN) LBS. @ IN.	VALVE SPRING INSTALLED HEIGHT (IN.)	STEM TO GUIDE CLEARANCE (IN.) Intake	STEM TO GUIDE CLEARANCE (IN.) Exhaust	STEM DIAMETER (IN.) Intake	STEM DIAMETER (IN.) Exhaust
1965 6 Cyl.—240 Cu. In.	45	45	45	.376	.400	190 @ 1.33	1.700	.001–.0027	.001–.0027	.3416–.3423	.3416–.3423
V8—289 Cu. In.; All	45	45	45	.368	.380	170 @ 1.39	1.780	.001–.0027	.002–.0037	.3416–.3423	.3406–.3413
V8—352 Cu. In.; All	45	45	45	.408	.408	190 @ 1.42	1.820	.001–.0024	.001–.0024	.3711–.3718	.3711–.3718
V8—390 Cu. In.; All	45	45	45	.408	.408	200 @ 1.42	1.820	.001–.0024	.001–.0024	.3711–.3718	.3721–.3728
V8—427 Cu. In.; All	30	45	②	.500	.500	200 @ 1.42	1.820	.001–.0024	.002–.0034	.3711–.3718	.3701–.3708
1966 6 Cyl.—240 Cu. In.	45	45	45	.376	.400	190 @ 1.33	1.700	.001–.0027	.001–.0027	.3416–.3423	.3416–.3423
V8—289 Cu. In.	45	45	45	.368	.380	170 @ 1.39	1.780	.001–.0027	.002–.0037	.3406–.3423	.3416–.3413
V8—352 Cu. In.	45	45	45	.381	.381	190 @ 1.42	1.820	.001–.0024	.001–.0024	.3711–.3718	.3711–.3718
V8—390, 410, 428 Cu. In.	45	45	45	.438	.438	240 @ 1.38	1.820	.001–.0024	.001–.0024	.3711–.3718	.3711–.3718
V8—427 Cu. In.	30	45	②	.514	.514	270 @ 1.32	1.820	.001–.0024	.002–.0034	.3711–.3718	.3701–.3708
V8—428 Cu. In., P.I.	45	45	45	.514	.514	270 @ 1.32	1.820	.001–.0024	.001–.0024	.3711–.3718	.3711–.3718
1967 6 Cyl.—240 Cu. In.	45	45	45	.376	.400	190 @ 1.33	1.700	.001–.0027	.001–.0027	.3416–.3423	.3416–.3423
V8—289 Cu. In.	45	45	45	.368	.380	180 @ 1.29	1.660	.001–.0027	.001–.0027	.3416–.3423	.3416–.3423
V8—390, 410 Cu. In.	45	45	45	.437	.437	220 @ 1.38	1.820	.001–.0024	.001–.0024	.3711–.3718	.3711–.3718
V8—427 Cu. In.	30	45	②	.500	.500	240 @ 1.32	1.820	.001–.0024	.002–.0034	.3711–.3718	.3701–.3708
V8—428 Cu. In.	45	45	45	.437	.437	220 @ 1.38	1.820	.001–.0024	.001–.0024	.3711–.3718	.3711–.3718
V8—428 Cu. In., P.I.	45	45	45	.481	.490	240 @ 1.32	1.820	.001–.0024	.001–.0024	.3711–.3718	.3711–.3718
1968–69 6 Cyl.—240 Cu. In.	45	45	45	.376	.400	190 @ 1.33	1.580	.001–.0027	.001–.0027	.3416–.3423	.3411–.3418
V8—302 Cu. In.	45	45	45	.368	.381	180 @ 1.23	1.660	.001–.0027	.0015–.0032	.3416–.3423	.3411–.3418
V8—390 Cu. In. 2-BBL.	45	45	45	.427	.430	220 @ 1.38	1.820	.001–.0024	.001–.0032	.3711–.3718	.3706–.3713
V8—390 Cu. In. 4-BBL.	45	45	45	.437	.437	220 @ 1.38	1.820	.001–.0024	.001–.0032	.3711–.3718	.3706–.3713
V8—428 Cu. In.	45	45①	①	.437	.437	220 @ 1.38	1.820	.001–.0024	.001–.0032	.3711–.3718	.3706–.3713
V8—428 Cu. In. Interceptor	45	45①	①	.481	.490	270 @ 1.32	1.820	.001–.0024	.001–.0032	.3711–.3718	.3706–.3713
V8—429 Cu. In.	45	45	45	.443	.486	250 @ 1.36	1.820	.001–.0027	.001–.0027	.3416–.3423	.3416–.3423
1970 6 Cyl.—240 Cu. In.	45	45	45	.376	.400	190 @ 1.33	1.700	.001–.0027	.001–.0027	.3416–.3423	.3416–.3423
V8—302 Cu. In.	45	45	45	.368	.381	180 @ 1.23	1.660	.001–.0027	.001–.0027	.3416–.3423	.3411–.3418
V8—351 Cu. In.	45	45	45	.418	.448	215 @ 1.34	1.790	.001–.0027	.001–.0027	.3416–.3423	.3411–.3418
V8—390 Cu. In.	45	45	45	.427	.430	220 @ 1.38	1.820	.001–.0027	.001–.0032	.3711–.3718	.3706–.3713
V8—428 Cu. In., P.I.	45	45	45	.481	.490	240 @ 1.32	1.820	.001–.0024	.001–.0024	.3711–.3718	.3711–.3718
V8—429 Cu. In.	45	45	45	.443	.486	250 @ 1.36	1.820	.001–.0027	.001–.0027	.3416–.3423	.3716–.3723
1971–72 6 Cyl.—240 Cu. In.	45	45	45	.376	.400	197 @ 1.30	1.700	.0010–.0027	.0010–.0027	.3416–.3423	.3416–.3423
V8—302 Cu. In.	45	45	45	.368	.380	180 @ 1.23	1.640	.0010–.0027	.0015–.0032	.3416–.3423	.3411–.3418
V8—351W Cu. In.	45	45	45	.418	.448	215 @ 1.34	1.790	.0010–.0027	.0015–.0032	.3416–.3423	.3411–.3418
V8—351C Cu. In.	45	45	45	.407	.407	210 @ 1.42	1.820	.001–.0027	.001–.0032	.3416–.3423	.3411–.3418
V8—390 Cu. In.	45	45	45	.427	.430	220 @ 1.38	1.820	.0010–.0027	.0015–.0032	.3711–.3718	.3706–.3713
V8—400 Cu. In.	45	45	45	.427	.433	220 @ 1.38	1.820	.0010–.0027	.0015–.0032	.3416–.3423	.3411–.3418
V8—429, Cu. In. 2-4-BBL.	45	45	45	.442	.486	229 @ 1.33	1.810	.0010–.0027	.0010–.0027	.3416–.3423	.3416–.3423
V8—429 Cu. In., P.I.	30	45	②	.500	.500	315 @ 1.32	1.820	.001–.0027	.001–.0027	.3416–.3423	.3416–.3423

① —Beginning mid-year 1968, the 428 Cu. In. engine, except Police, used 30° intake valve seat angle and 29° intake face angle.

② —Intake 29°, exhaust 44°
P.I.—Police Interceptor.

GENERAL CHASSIS AND BRAKE SPECIFICATIONS

YEAR	MODEL	CHASSIS		BRAKE CYLINDER BORE			BRAKE DRUM	
		OVERALL LENGTH (In.)	TIRE SIZE	MASTER CYL. (In.)	WHEEL CYL. (In.) Front	Rear	DIAMETER (In.) Front	Rear
1965	Ford Sedan	210.0	7.35 x 15	1.0①	$1^3/_{32}$	$^{15}/_{16}$	11.03	11.03
	Ford Wagon	210.0▲	8.15 x 15	1.0①	$1^3/_{32}$	$^{15}/_{16}$	11.03	11.03
	Mercury Sedan	218.4	8.15 x 15	1.0①	$1^3/_{32}$	$^{31}/_{32}$	11.03	11.03
	Mercury Wagon	214.5	8.15 x 15	1.0①	$1^1/_{16}$	$^{31}/_{32}$	11.03	11.03
	Thunderbird	205.4	8.15 x 15	$^{15}/_{16}$	$1^3/_{32}$	$^{15}/_{16}$	11.03	11.03
1966	Ford Sedan	210.0	7.35 x 15	1.0①	$1^3/_{32}$●	$^{31}/_{32}$	11.03★	11.03
	Ford Wagon	210.9	8.15 x 15	1.0①	$1^1/_{16}$●	$^7/_8$	11.03★	11.03
	Mercury Sedan	220.4	8.15 x 15	1.0①	$1^3/_{32}$●	$^{31}/_{32}$	11.03★	11.03
	Mercury Wagon	216.5	8.15 x 15	1.0①	$1^1/_{16}$●	$^{31}/_{32}$	11.03★	11.03
	Thunderbird	205.4	8.15 x 15	$^{15}/_{16}$	$1^{15}/_{16}$	$^{15}/_{16}$	11.78D	11.03
1967	Ford Sedan	213.0	7.75 x 15⑥	1.0②	$1^3/_{32}$●	$^{31}/_{32}$	11.03★	11.03
	Ford Wagon	213.9	8.45 x 15	1.0②	$1^3/_{32}$●	$^{15}/_{16}$	11.03★	11.03
	Mercury Sedan	218.5	8.15 x 15	1.0②	$1^3/_{32}$●	$^{15}/_{16}$	11.03★	11.03
	Mercury Wagon	213.8	8.15 x 15	1.0②	$1^3/_{32}$●	$^{15}/_{16}$	11.03★	11.03
	Thunderbird	206.9③	8.15 x 15	1.0	$1^{15}/_{16}$	$^{15}/_{16}$	11.87D	11.03
1968	Ford Sedan	213.9	7.75 x 15④	1.0	$1^3/_{32}$§	$^{31}/_{32}$	11.03 ·	11.03
	Ford Wagon	216.5	8.45 x 15	1.0	$1^3/_{32}$§	$^{15}/_{16}$	11.03 ·	11.03
	Mercury Sedan	220.1	8.15 x 15	1.0	$1^3/_{32}$§	$^{15}/_{16}$	11.03 ·	11.03
	Mercury Wagon	215.4	8.45 x 15	1.0	$1^3/_{32}$§	$^{15}/_{16}$	11.03 ·	11.03
	Thunderbird	212.5	8.15 x 15	1.0	$2^3/_4$	$^{15}/_{16}$	11.72D	11.03
1969	Ford Sedan	213.9	7.75 x 15④	1.0	$1^3/_{32}$§	$^{15}/_{16}$	11.03 ·	11.03
	Ford Wagon	216.5	8.45 x 15	1.0	$1^3/_{32}$§	$^{15}/_{16}$	11.03 ·	11.03
	Mercury Sedan	221.8	H78 x 15	1.0	$1^1/_4$§	$^{15}/_{16}$	11.03 ·	11.03
	Mercury Wagon	221.8	H70 x 15	1.0	$1^1/_4$§	$^{15}/_{16}$	11.03 ·	11.03
	Thunderbird	212.5	8.15 x 15	1.0	$2^3/_4$	$^{15}/_{16}$	11.72D	11.03
1970	Ford Sedan	214.0	F78 x 15⑧	1.0	$1^1/_8$§	$^{15}/_{16}$	11.03 ·	11.03
	Ford Wagon	216.9	H78 x 15	1.0	$1^1/_8$§	$^{15}/_{16}$	11.03 ·	11.03
	Mercury Sedan	221.8	G78 x 15	1.0	$1^1/_8$§	$^{15}/_{16}$	11.03 ·	11.03
	Mercury Wagon	218.0	H78 x 15	1.0	$1^1/_8$§	$^{15}/_{16}$	11.03 ·	11.03
	Thunderbird	212.5	215 x 15	1.0	$2^3/_4$	$^{15}/_{16}$	11.72D	11.03
1971-72	Ford Sedan	216.2	F78 x 15⑤	1.0	$1^1/_8$§	$^{15}/_{16}$	11.03 ·	11.03
	Ford Wagon	219.2	H78 x 15	1.0	$1^1/_8$§	$^{15}/_{16}$	11.03 ·	11.03
	Mercury Sedan	224.7	G78 x 15	1.0	$1^1/_8$§	$^{15}/_{16}$	11.03 ·	11.03
	Mercury Wagon	220.4	H78 x 15	1.0	$1^1/_8$§	$^{15}/_{16}$	11.03 ·	11.03
	Thunderbird	212.5	215 x 15	1.0	$2^3/_4$	$^{15}/_{16}$	11.72D	11.03

▲—10 passenger wagon—210.9.
●—With disc brakes—1.938.
★—With disc brakes—11.87.
§—With disc brakes—$2^3/_4$.
·—With disc brakes—11.72.

①—With power brakes—.875.
②—With power brakes—.937.
③—4 Door Landau—209.4.
④—With 302 engine—8.25-15.
with 390 engine—8.55-15.
with 429 engine—H70-15.

⑤—With 302, 351, or 390 engine—H78 x 15.
with 429 engine—H70 x 15.
⑥—With 289 engine—8.15 x 15.
with 390 or 428 engine—8.45 x 15.
D—Disc Brakes

AC GENERATOR AND REGULATOR SPECIFICATIONS

YEAR	ALTERNATOR			REGULATOR	Field Relay			Regulator		
	Part No. or Manufacturer	Field Current @ 12 V.	Output @ Generator RPM	Part No. or Manufacturer	Air Gap (in.)	Point Gap (in.)	Volts to Close	Air Gap (in.)	Point Gap (in.)	Volts @ 75°
1965	Autolite	2.8–3.3	42	Autolite	.018	N.A.	2.5–4	.052	.020	14.1–14.9
	Autolite	2.8–3.3	45							
	Autolite	2.8–3.3	55							
	Leece-Nevelle	2.8–3.3	53	Leece-Nevelle	.010	.019	1.6–2.6	.050	.019	14.1–14.9
				Leece-Nevelle	.012	.025	6.2–7.2	.050	.019	14.1–14.9
	Leece-Nevelle	2.8–3.3	60							
1966	Autolite	2.9	42	Autolite	0.014	N.A.	2.5–4	.053	.020	14.1–14.9
	Autolite	2.9	45	Autolite transistor	①	①	2.5–4	①	①	14.1–14.9
	Autolite	2.9	55							
	Leece-Nevelle	2.9	53	Leece-Nevelle 53 Amp only	.010	.019	1.6–2.6	.050	.019	14.1–14.9
	Leece-Nevelle	4.6	60	Leece-Nevelle 53 and 60 Amp	.012	.025	6.2–7.2	.050	.019	14.1–14.9
	Leece-Nevelle	2.9	60							
1967	Autolite	2.5	38	Autolite	.014	N.A.	2.5–4	N.A.	N.A.	13.9–14.9
	Autolite	2.9	42							
	Autolite	2.9	45							
	Autolite	2.9	55							
	Autolite	4.6	60	Autolite Transistor	①	①	2.5–4	①	①	13.9–14.9
	Leece-Nevelle	2.9	53	Leece-Nevelle 53 Amp only	.010	.019	1.6–2.6	.050	.019	13.9–14.9
	Leece-Nevelle	2.9	65	Leece-Nevelle 53 and 60 Amp	.012	.025	6.2–7.2	.050	.019	13.9–14.9
1968	Autolite C6AF10300C	2.9	42	Autolite	①	①	4.2–9.0	①	①	13.5–15.3
	Autolite C6AF10300G	2.9	55							
	Autolite C6TF10300F	2.9	65							
	Leece-Nevelle	2.9	65	Leece-Nevelle	0.012	0.025	6.2–7.2	0.047	0.019	13.9–14.9
1969	Autolite	2.9	42	Autolite	①	①	4.2–9.0	①	①	13.5–15.3
	Autolite	2.9	55							
	Autolite	2.9	65							
	Leece-Nevelle	2.9	65	Leece-Nevelle	0.012	0.025	6.2–7.2	0.047	0.019	13.9–14.9
1970–72	Autolite	2.9	42	Autolite	①	①	2.0–4.2	①	①	13.5–15.3
	Autolite	2.9	55							
	Autolite	2.9	61							
	Autolite	2.9	65							
	Leece-Nevelle	2.9	65	Leece-Nevelle	.012	.025	6.2–7.2	.047	.019	13.9–14.9

① —Transistorized regulator—not adjustable.

CAPACITIES

YEAR	MODEL	ENGINE CRANKCASE ADD 1 Qt. FOR NEW FILTER	TRANSMISSIONS Pts. TO REFILL AFTER DRAINING			DRIVE AXLE (Pts.)	GASOLINE TANK (Gals.) ▲	COOLING SYSTEM (Qts.) WITH HEATER
			Manual		Automatic (Pts.)			
			3-Speed	4-Speed				
1965	6 Cyl.	4	3	None	17	5	20	16
	V8, 289	4	3	4	17	5	20	16
	V8, 352	5	3	4	20	5	20	20½
	V8, 390, 427	5	3	4	20	5	20	20½
	T-Bird	5	None	None	20	5	20	20½
1966	6 Cyl.	4	3½	None	20	5	25	13
	V8—289	4	3½	None	20	5	25	15
	V8—352	5	3½·	None	20	5	25	20½
	V8—390	4	3½	4	20	5	25	20½
	V8—427	5	None	4	None	5	25	20½
	V8—410, 428	4	None	4	26	5	25	20½
	T-Bird	4	None	None	26*	5	22	20½
1967	6 Cyl.	4	3½	None	20	5	25	13
	V8—289	4	3½	None	20	5	25	15
	V8—390, 410	4	3½	4	26	5	25	20½
	V8—427	5	None	4	None	5	25	20½
	V8—428	4	None	4	26	5	25	20½
	T-Bird	4	None	None	26*	5	22	20½
1968-69	6 Cyl.	4	3½	None	20½	5	25	14
	V8—302	4	3½	None	22	5	25	15
	V8—390	4	3½	4	22①	5	25	20½
	V8—428	4	None	4	26	5	25	20
	V8—429	4	None	None	26	5	25②	20½
1970	6 Cyl.—240	4½	3½	None	22	5	24½	14.4
	V8—302	4	3½	None	22	5	24½	15.4
	V8—351	4	3½	None	22	5	24½	16.5
	V8—390	4	3½	None	26	5	24½	20.1
	V8—428	4	None	4	26	5	24½	20.1
	V8—429	4	None	None	26	5	24½	18.6
	V8—429 T-Bird	4	None	None	26	5	24	19.4
1971-72	6 Cyl.—240	4	3.5	None	20.5	5	22½	14.1
	V8—302	4	3.5	None	20.5	5	22½	15.4③
	V8—351	4	3.5	None	22	5	22½	16.5④
	V8—390	4	None	None	26	5	22½	20.1⑤
	V8—400	4	None	None	26	5	22½	17.6⑥
	V8—429	4	None	None	26	5	22½	18.6
	V8—429 T-Bird	4	None	None	26	5	22½	19.4

① —C6-26 pts.
② —Thunderbird—24 gals.
③ —With A/C—15.6.
④ —With A/C—16.8
⑤ —With A/C—20.5.
⑥ —With A/C—18.2.
▲—1965 sta. wgn.—20 gals.
1966-69 sta. wgn.—20 gals.
1970-72 sta. wgn.—22 gals.
*—Cruise-o-matic—20 pts.

CRANKSHAFT BEARING JOURNAL SPECIFICATIONS

YEAR	MODEL	MAIN BEARING JOURNALS (IN.)				CONNECTING ROD BEARING JOURNALS (IN.)		
		Journal Diameter	Oil Clearance	Shaft End-Play	Thrust On No.	Journal Diameter	Oil Clearance	SIDE CLEARANCE
1965	6 Cyl.—240 Cu. In.	2.3982-2.3990	.0008-.0024	.004-.008	5	2.1232-2.1236	.0009-.0029	.006-.013
	V8—289 Cu. In.	2.2486-2.2490	.0007-.0030	.004-.008	3	2.1232-2.1236	.0009-.0029	.006-.016
	V8—427 Cu. In.	2.7488-2.7492	.0010-.0031	.004-.010	3	2.4384-2.4388	.0013-.0032	.014-.024
	V8—Exc. Above	2.7488-2.7492	.0006-.0027	.004-.010	3	2.4384-2.4388	.0007-.0028	.006-.024
1966	6 Cyl.—240 Cu. In.	2.3982-2.3990	.0005-.0024	.004-.008	5	2.1228-2.1236	.0006-.0022	.006-.013
	V8—289 Cu. In.	2.2482-2.2490	.0005-.0024	.004-.008	3	2.1228-2.1236	.0008-.0026	.010-.020
	V8—352 Cu. In.	2.7484-2.7492	.0005-.0025	.004-.010	3	2.4380-2.4388	.0008-.0026	.010-.020
	V8—390, 410 Cu. In.	2.7484-2.7492	.0005-.0025	.004-.010	3	2.4380-2.4388	.0008-.0026	.010-.020
	V8—427 Cu. In.	2.7484-2.7492	.0007-.0031	.004-.010	3	2.4380-2.4388	.0013-.0032	.014-.024
	V8—428 Cu. In.	2.7484-2.7492	.0005-.0025	.004-.010	3	2.4380-2.4388	.0008-.0026	.010-.020
1967	6 Cyl.—240 Cu. In.	2.3986-2.3990	.0008-.0024	.004-.008	5	2.1228-2.1236	.0006-.0026	.006-.013
	V8—289 Cu. In.	2.2482-2.2490	.0005-.0022	.004-.008	3	2.1228-2.1236	.0007-.0028	.010-.020
	V8—390, 410 Cu. In.	2.7484-2.7492	.0005-.0025	.004-.010	3	2.4380-2.4388	.0007-.0028	.014-.020
	V8—427 Cu. In.	2.7484-2.7492	.0007-.0031	.004-.010	3	2.4380-2.4388	.0013-.0032	.014-.024
	V8—428 Cu. In.	2.7484-2.7492	.0008-.0012	.004-.010	3	2.4380-2.4388	.0008-.0022	.014-.020
1968	6 Cyl.—240 Cu. In.	2.3986-2.3990	.0008-.0024	.004-.008	5	2.1232-2.1246	.0007-.0028	.014-.020
	V8—302 Cu. In.	2.2486-2.2490	.0005-.0024	.004-.008	3	2.1232-2.1246	.0007-.0028	.014-.020
	V8—390, 427, 428, 429 Cu. In.	2.7488-2.7492	.0008-.0012	.004-.008	3	2.4384-2.4388	.0007-.0028	.014-.020
1969	6 Cyl.—240 Cu. In.	2.3982-2.3990	.0005-.0015	.004-.008	5	2.1228-2.1236	.0008-.0015	.006-.013
	V8—302 Cu. In.	2.2482-2.2490	.0005-.0015	.004-.008	3	2.1228-2.1236	.0008-.0015	.010-.020
	V8—390 Cu. In.	2.7484-2.7492	.0013-.0025	.004-.010	3	2.4380-2.4388	.0008-.0015	.010-.020
	V8—428 Cu. In.	2.7484-2.7492	.0010-.0020	.004-.010	3	2.4380-2.4388	.0020-.0030	.010-.020
	V8—429 Cu. In.	2.9994-3.0002	.0005-.0015	.004-.008	3	2.4992-2.5000	.0008-.0015	.010-.020
1970	6 Cyl.—240 Cu. In.	2.3982-2.3990	.0005-.0015	.004-.008	5	2.1228-2.1236	.0008-.0026	.006-.013
	V8—302 Cu. In.	2.2482-2.2490	.0005-.0015	.004-.008	3	2.1228-2.1236	.0008-.0026	.010-.020
	V8—351 Cu. In.	2.994-2.3002	.0013-.0025	.004-.008	3	2.3103-2.3111	.0008-.0026	.010-.020
	V8—390 Cu. In.	2.7484-2.7492	.0005-.0025	.004-.008	3	2.4380-2.4388	.0008-.0026	.010-.020
	V8—428 Cu. In.	2.7484-2.7492	.0008-.0020	.004-.008	3	2.4380-2.4388	.0008-.0026	.010-.020
	V8—429 Cu. In.	2.9994-3.0002	.0005-.0025	.004-.008	3	2.4992-2.5000	.0008-.0026	.010-.020
1971-72	6 Cyl.—240 Cu. In.	2.3982-2.3990	.0005-.0022	.004-.008	5	2.1228-2.1236	.0008-.0024	.006-.013
	V8—302 Cu. In.	2.2482-2.2490	.0005-.0024①	.004-.008	3	2.1228-2.1236	.0008-.0026	.010-.020
	V8—351 Cu. In.	2.9998②	.0012-.0029③	.004-.008	3	2.3103-2.3111	.0007-.0025	.010-.020
	V8—390 Cu. In.	2.7484-2.7492	.0008-.0020	.004-.008	3	2.4380-2.4388	.0010-.0030	.010-.020
	V8—400 Cu. In.	2.9994-3.0002	.0009-.0026	.004-.008	3	2.3103-2.3111	.0008-.0026	.010-.020
	V8—429 Cu. In.	2.9994-3.0002	.0005-.0025	.004-.008	3	2.4992-2.500	.0008-.0028	.010-.020

① —.0001-.0020 No. 1 bearing only.
② —351 C engine—2.7484-2.7492.
③ —351 C engine—.0009-.0026.

TORQUE SPECIFICATIONS

YEAR	MODEL	CYLINDER HEAD BOLTS (FT. LBS.)	ROD BEARING BOLTS (FT. LBS.)	MAIN BEARING BOLTS (FT. LBS.)	CRANKSHAFT BALANCER BOLT (FT. LBS.)	FLYWHEEL TO CRANKSHAFT BOLTS (FT. LBS.)	MANIFOLD (FT. LBS.) Intake	MANIFOLD (FT. LBS.) Exhaust
1965-66	6 Cyl.—240 Cu. In.	70-75	40-45	60-70	135-145	75-85	25	25
	V8—289; 6 Cyl. 240 Cu. In.	65-70	19-24■	60-70	70-90▲	75-85	13$\frac{1}{2}$	15$\frac{1}{2}$
	V8—352, 390, 410, 428 Cu. In.	80-90	40-45	95-105	70-90	75-85	33$\frac{1}{2}$	15
	V8—427 Cu. In.	100-110	53-58	95-105	70-90	75-85	33$\frac{1}{2}$	15
1967-68	6 Cyl.—240 Cu. In.	70-75	40-45	60-70	130-145	75-85	25	25
	V8—289, 302 Cu. In.	65-70	19-24	60-70	70-90	75-85	21	15$\frac{1}{2}$
	V8—390 410, 428, 429 Cu. In.	80-90	40-45	95-105	70-90	75-85	33$\frac{1}{2}$	15$\frac{1}{2}$
	V8—427 Cu. In.	100-110	53-58	95-105	70-90	75-85	33$\frac{1}{2}$	15$\frac{1}{2}$
1969	6 Cyl.—240 Cu. In.	70-75	40-45	60-70	130-150	75-85	25	25
	V8—302 Cu. In.	65-72	19-24	60-70	70-90	75-85	24	14
	V8—390, 428 Cu. In.	80-90	40-45	95-105	70-90	75-85	33$\frac{1}{2}$	21
	V8—429 Cu. In.	130-140	40-45	95-105	70-90	75-85	27$\frac{1}{2}$	30$\frac{1}{2}$
1970	6 Cyl.—240 Cu. In.	70-75	40-45	60-70	130-150	75-85	25	25
	V8—302 Cu. In.	65-72	19-24	60-70	70-90	75-85	24	14
	V8—351 Cu. In.	95-100	40-45	95-105	70-90	75-85	23-25	18-24
	V8—390, 428 Cu. In.	80-90	**	95-105	70-90	75-85	32-35	18-24
	V8—429 Cu. In.	130-140	40-45	95-105	70-90	75-85	27$\frac{1}{2}$	30$\frac{1}{2}$
1971-72	6 Cyl.—240 Cu. In.	70-75	40-45	60-70	130-150	75-85	25	25
	V8—302 Cu. In.	65-72	19-24	60-70	70-90	75-85	24	14
	V8—351 Cu. In.	95-100	40-45	95-105	70-90	75-85	23-25	18-24①
	V8—390 Cu. In.	80-90	40-45	95-105	70-90	75-85	32-35	18-24
	V8—400 Cu. In.	95-105	40-45	95-105	70-90	75-85	27-33	12-16
	V8—429 Cu. In.	130-140	40-45	95-105	70-90	75-85	27$\frac{1}{2}$	30$\frac{1}{2}$

▲—6 Cyl. 240 Cu. In. = 135-145.
■—6 Cyl. 240 Cu. In. = 40-45.
**—390—40-45; 428—53-58.
①—351C engine—12-16.
●—Tighten cylinder head bolts in 3 steps: the first 20 ft. lbs. less than maximum torque, the second 10 ft. lbs. less than maximum torque, and the third maximum torque.

CYLINDER HEAD BOLT TIGHTENING SEQUENCE

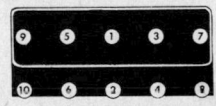

V8 (big block)

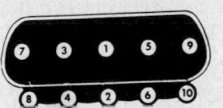

V8 289, 302 and 351

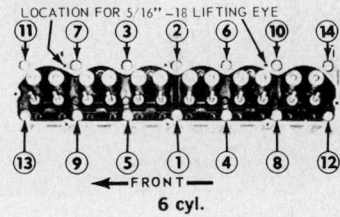

LOCATION FOR 5/16"—18 LIFTING EYE

6 cyl.

LIGHT BULBS

1965, MERCURY

Unit	Candela* or Wattage	Trade Number
Headlight no. 1 (inner)	37.5W	4001
Headlight no. 2 (outer)	37.5/50W	4002
Front turn signal/parking	4/32C.	1157-A
Rear turn signal & stop/tail	4/32C.	1157
License plate	4C.	1155
Back-up lights	21C.	1156
Spot light	30W	4405
Dome light	15C.	1003
Instrument panel indicators		
Hi beam	2C.	158
Oil pressure gauge	2C.	158
Ammeter	2C.	158

Unit	Candela* or Wattage	Trade Number
Turn signal	2C.	1895
Parking brake warning	2C.	257
Illumination		
Speedometer	2C.	158
Cluster	2C.	158
Heater control	2C.	158
Clock	2C.	1895
Radio dial	2C.	1891
Courtesy and/or Map (door mounted)	15C.	1003
Automatic transmission control	1C.	161

*Candela is the new international term for candlepower.

1965, FORD and THUNDERBIRD

Unit	Candela* or Wattage	Trade Number
Headlight no. 1 (lower)	37.5 W.	4001
Headlight no. 2 (upper)	37.5/50 W.	4002
Front turn signal/parking	4/32 C.	1157-A
Rear turn signal & stop/tail	4/32 C.	1157
License plate	4 C.	1155
Back-up lights	32 C.	1156
Spot light	30 W.	4405
Dome light	15 C.	1003
Instrument panel indicators		
Hi beam	2 C.	1895
Oil pressure, coolant temp. hot/cold	2 C.	1895
Alternator	2 C.	1895

Unit	Candela* or Wattage	Trade Number
Turn signal	2 C.	1895
Parking brake warning	2 C.	257
Illumination		
Speedometer	1.5 C.	1895
Cluster	2 C.	1895
Heater control panel	2 C.	1895
Clock	2 C.	1895
Radio dial	3 C.	1816
Courtesy and/or Map (door mounted)	15 C.	1003
Automatic transmission control	1 C.	161

*Candela is the new international term for candlepower.

1966, FORD and THUNDERBIRD

Standard equipment		
Hi-lo beam	37.5 & 50 Watts	4002
Hi beam	37.5 Watts	4001
Front parking and turn indicator	4–32 C.	1157
Rear lamp, stop and turn indicator (sedan)	4–32 C.	1157
(sta. wag.)	4–32 C.	1157
License plate lamp	4 C.	1155
Courtesy lamp (convertible)	6 C.	631
Dome lamp	15 C.	1003
Courtesy lamp (door mountings)	15 C.	1003
Courtesy lamp ("C" pillar)	15 C.	1003
Console lamp	6 C.	631
Courtesy lamp	12 C.	211
Instrument panel		
Instruments	2 C.	1895
Indicator hi beam	2 C.	1895
Warning lights (oil & generator temperature hot/cold)	2 C.	1895
Park brake rel. warning light	2 C.	1895
Heater control panel (fresh air)	3 C.	1895
L & R turn indicator	2 C.	1895
Accessory equipment		
Back-up lamps	32 C.	1156
Radio pilot light	2 C.	1891
Spotlight 4.4" diameter	30 Watts	4405
Clock	3 C.	1816
Automatic transmission	1 C.	161
Luggage compartment	15 C.	93
Cigar lighter	2 C.	1895
Engine compartment	6 C.	631
Tachometer	2 C.	1895
Trans. control selector indicator	1.5 C.	1445
Safety package		
Door lock	2 C.	1895
Low fuel	2 C.	1895
Door-warning open	2 C.	1895
Emergency flasher	2 C.	1895
Seat belt	2 C.	1895

①—Candela is the new International term for candlepower.

1966, MERCURY

Unit	Candela ① or Wattage	Trade Number
Standard equipment		
Hi-lo beam	37.5 & 50 Watts	4002
Hi-beam	37.5 Watts	4001
Front park and turn signal lamp	4–32C.	1157
Rear lamp and stop and turn signal (pass. car)	4–32C.	1157
Dome lamp	15C.	1003
License lamp	4C.	1155
Courtesy lamp (convertible)	6C.	631
Cargo lamp (sta. wag. 77B)	15C.	1003
Back-up lamp (sta. wag. & pass. car)	21C.	1141
Rear, stop and turn (station wagon)	4–32C.	1157
Courtesy lamp (door mounting)	15C.	1003
Auto. trans. selector	2C.	1895
Instrument panel		
Medallion light	1.5C.	1445
Gages, speedometer	2C.	158
Hi-beam indicator	2C.	158
L & R signal indicator	2C.	158
Glove compartment	2C.	1895
Automatic transmission	1C.	161
Control nomenclature	2C.	1895
Speedometer pointer	1.5C.	1445
Rear window/top nomenclature	2C.	1895
W/S wiper nomenclature	2C.	1895
Lights nomenclature	2C.	1895
Dome lamp—swivel	15C.	1003
Dome lamp—swivel	6C.	631
Courtesy lamp ("C" pillar reverse back)	15C.	1003
Courtesy lamp ("C" pillar, fastback)	6C.	631
Cornering lamp	50C.	1195
Heater control	2C.	1895
Accessory equipment		
Warning indicator panel	2C.	1895
Warning indicator panel	1.6C.	257
Clock	3C.	1816
Engine compartment lamp	15C.	93
Radio pilot light	1.9C.	1893
Radio on-off light (AM-FM only)	1.3C.	1892
Instrument warning lamp kit	2C.	1895
Luggage compartment lamp	6C.	631
Spotlamp (4.40 diameter)	30 Watts	4405
Air conditioner	2C.	1895
Cargo lamp (station wagon)	15C.	1003
Parking brake warning	1.6C.	257
Back-up lamp	21C.	1141
Courtesy lamp (instrument panel)	6C.	631
Oil temp. warning	1.6C.	257
Cigar lighter	2C.	1895
Tachometer	2C.	1895
Trans. control selector indicator	1.5C.	1445

①—Candela is the new international term for candlepower

1967, MERCURY

Light Description	Bulb No.	Candela or Wattage
Cargo lamp (station wagon)	1003	15C.
Cornering lamp (Mercury)	1195	50C.
Dome lamp	1003①	15C.
Engine compartment	93	15C.
Glove compartment	1816	3C.
Headlamps		
Hi-lo beam (outer or upper)	4002	37.5-50W
Hi beam (inner or lower)	4001	37.5W
License lamp	97	4C.
Luggage compartment	631	6C.
Map light	631	6C.
Park and turn signal lamp	1157-A	4-32C.
Spotlight (4.4 inch dia.)	4405	30W
Taillight, stop and turn signal	1157	4-32C.
Door lock warning	1895	2C.
Emergency flasher	1895	2C.
Hi-beam indicator	158	2C.
Low fuel warning	158	2C.
Oil press., alt and temp warning	158	2C.
Parking brake warning	257	1.6C.
Seat belt warning	158	2C.
Ash receptacle or cigar lighter	1445	1.5C.
Back-up lamps	1156	32C.
Courtesy lamp	631	6C.
("C" pillar)	①	
(Console)	1816	3C.
(Convertible and inst. panel)	631	6C.
(Door mounting or armrest)	631	6C.
Clock and ignition key	1816	3C.
Control nomenclature (ex heater)	1895②	2C.
Control, right and left	158②	2C.
Gauges and speedometer	158	2C.
Heater control	1895	2C.
Radio dial light		
AM	1893	1.9C.
AM-FM	1893	1.9C.
Tachometer	1895	2C.
Trans. control selector indicator (console)	1445③	1.5C.
Turn signal indicators (L and R)	158	2C.

①—631 (6C.) for dual swivel dome lights, 1003 (15C.) for swivel dome lights.

②—1445 (1.5C.) for speedometer pointer and medallion.

③—161 (1C.) for automatic transmission.

1967, FORD and THUNDERBIRD

Light Description	Ford Bulb No.	Ford Candela or Wattage	Thunderbird Bulb No.	Thunderbird Candela or Wattage	Light Description	Ford Bulb No.	Ford Candela or Wattage	Thunderbird Bulb No.	Thunderbird Candela or Wattage
Cargo lamp (station wagon)	1003	15C.	...	...	Seat belt warning	158	2C.	1891	2C.
Dome lamp	1003	15C.	...	...	Ash receptacle or cigar lighter	1895	2C.	1895	2C.
Engine compartment	631	6C.	...	...	Back-up lamps	1156	32C.	1076	32C.
Glove compartment	1895	2C.	631	6C.	Courtesy lamp	211	12C.	...	...
Headlamps hi-lo beam (outer or upper)	4002	37.5–50W	4002	37.5–50W	"C" pillar	1003	15C.	1003	15C.
hi beam (inner or lower)	4001	37.5W	4001	37.5W	Console	1816	3C.	...	...
License lamp	97	4C.	97	4C.	Convertible and inst. panel	631	6C.	...	...
Luggage compartment	93	15C.	631	6C.	Door mounting or armrest	1004	15C.	211	12C.
Map light	...	...	211	12C.	Clock and ignition key	1816	3C.	158	2C.
Park and turn signal lamp	1157-A	4–32C.	1157-A	32C.	Control nomenclature (ex heater)	1895	2C.	1891②	2C.
Spotlight (4.4 inch dia.)	4405	30W	4405	30W	Control, right and left	1895	2C.	①	
Taillight, stop and turn signal	1157	4–32C.	1157	32C.	Gauges and speedometer	1816	3C.	1445	1.5C.
Door lock warning	1895	2C.	256	1.6C.	Heater control	158	2C.	...	...
Emergency flasher	1895	2C.	1891	2C.	Radio dial light AM	1893	1.9C.	1891	2C.
Hi-beam indicator	158	2C.	158	2C.	AM-FM	1893	1.9C.	1892	1.3C.
Low fuel warning	158	2C.	1891	2C.	Tachometer	1895	2C.	1895	2C.
Oil press., alt and temp warning	158	2C.	158	2C.	Trans. control selector indicator (console)	1445③	1.5C.	158	2C.
Parking brake warning	257	1.6C.	1895	2C.	Turn signal indicators (L and R)	158	2C.	53 X ④	1C.

①—1445 (1.5C.) for speedometer, 1895 (2C.) for gauges.
②—1816 (3C.) for identification light.
③—161 (1C.) for automatic transmission.
④—1895 (2C.) for turn signal, 1895G (2C.) for Minnesota and Wisconsin.

1968, MERCURY

Unit	Candela① or Wattage	Trade Number	Unit	Candela① or Wattage	Trade Number	Unit	Candela① or Wattage	Trade Number
Standard equipment			Instrument panel			Engine compartment lamp	6C.	631
Headlamps			Gauges, speedometer	2C.	194	Radio pilot light	1.9C.	1893
Hi-lo beam	37.5 & 50 Watts	4002	Hi-beam indicator	2C.	194	Instrument warning lamp kit	2C.	1895
			L & R signal indicator	2C.	194	Luggage compartment lamp	6C.	631
Hi-beam	37.5 Watts	4001	Glove compartment	3C.	1816	Spotlamp (440 diameter)	30 Watts	4405
Front park and turn signal lamp	4-32C.	1157NA	Automatic transmission	2C.	158	Air conditioner	2C.	1895
Rear lamp and stop and turn signal (pass. car)	4-32C.	1157	Control nomenclature	2C.	1895	Cargo lamp (station wagon)	15C.	1003
Dome lamp	15C.	1003	Speedometer pointer	2C.	194	Parking brake warning	2C.	194
License lamp	4C.	97	Rear window/top nomenclature	2C.	1895	Back-up lamp	32C.	1156
Courtesy lamp (convertible)	6C.	631	W/S wiper nomenclature	2C.	1895	Courtesy lamp (instrument panel)	6C.	631
Cargo lamp (sta. wag. 77B)	15C.	1003	Lights nomenclature	2C.	1895	Tachometer	2C.	1895
Back-up lamp (sta. wag. & pass. car)	32C.	1156	Front side marker	4C.	97NA	Trans. control selector indicator	2C.	158
Rear, stop and turn (sta. wag.)	4 & 32C.	1157	Courtesy lamp ("C" pillar)	15C.	1003	Speed control indicator	2C.	194
Courtesy lamp (door mounting)	6C.	631	Heater control	2C.	1891	Map light	3C.	1816
Auto. trans. selector	2C.	158	Accessory equipment			Ash tray light	2C.	194
			Warning indicator panel	2C.	1891	Fog lights (amber)	35 Watts	4415A
			Warning indicator panel	1.6C.	256	Fog light switch	1C.	161
			Clock	2C.	194			

①—Candela is the new international term for candlepower.

1968, FORD

Unit	(1) Candela Or Wattage	Trade Number
Standard equipment		
Headlamp		
Hi-lo beam	37.5 & 50 Watts	4002
Hi-beam	37.5 Watts	4001
Front parking, side marker and turn indicator	4-32 C.	1157
Rear lamp and stop and turn indicator		
sedan	4-32 C.	1157
sta. wag.	4-32 C.	1157
License plate lamp	4 C.	97
Courtesy lamp (convertible)	6 C.	631
Dome lamp	15 C.	1003
Courtesy lamp (door mounting)	6 C.	631
Courtesy lamp ("C" pillar)	15 C.	1003
Console lamp	3 C.	1816
Cargo lamp (sta. wag.)	15 C.	1003
Instrument panel		
Instruments	2 C.	1895
Indicator hi beam	2 C.	1895
Warning lights (oil & generator temperature hot/cold)	2 C.	1895
Park brake rel. warning light	2 C.	257
Heater control panel (fresh air)	2 C.	1895
L & R turn indicator	2 C.	1895
Accessory equipment		
Back-up lamps	32 C.	1156
Radio pilot light	1.9 C.	1893
Spotlight 4.4" diameter	30 Watts	4405
Clock	3 C.	1816
Automatic transmission	2 C.	158
Luggage compartment	6 C.	631
Engine compartment	6 C.	631
Tachometer	2 C.	1895
Trans. control selector indicator	1.5 C.	1445
Safety package		
Low fuel	2 C.	1895
Door-warning open	2 C.	1895
Emergency flasher	2 C.	1895
Seat belt	2 C.	1895

(1) Candela is the new international term for candlepower.

1968, THUNDERBIRD

Light Description	Bulb No.	Candela or Wattage (1)
Headlights—hi & lo	4002	37.5 & 50 W
Headlights—hi beams	4001	37.5 W
Front park & turn signal	1157A	4-32 C.
Rear tail/stop/turn signal	1157	4-32 C.
Back-up light	1156	32 C.
License plate light	97	4 C.
Roof quarter light	1003	15 C.
Glove compartment	1895	2 C.
Auto. trans. select. ind. fixed & tilt column	1445	1.5 C.
Door courtesy light	212 or 212-1	6 C.
Map light	212 or 212-1	6 C.
Luggage compartment	631	6 C.
Front side marker	97NA ②	4 C.
Instrument panel courtesy light	631	6 C.
Hi-beam indicators	194	2 C.
Turn signal indicators	194	2 C.
Warning—brakes & belts	194	2 C.
Ignition switch	194	2 C.
Instruments	194	2 C.
Heater controls	1895	2 C.
Control nomenclature rear vent & wipers	194	2 C.
Fog lights—clear	4415	35 W
Fog light switch	53X	1 C.
Spotlight—4.4 inch diameter	4405	30 W
Manual A/C control	1895	2 C.
ATC control	1895	2 C.
Radio pilot light	1893	1.9 C.
Park brake signal	1895	2 C.
Safety convenience package		
Low fuel warning	1891	2 C.
Door ajar warning	256	1.6 C.
Seat belt warning	1891	2 C.
Emergency flasher warning	1891	2 C.
Cigar lighter	1895	2 C.
Engine compartment	631	6 C.
Portable trunk light	1003	15 C.
Auxiliary instrument center	1895	2 C.
Tachometer	1895	2 C.
Supplemental stop light	1156	32 C.

① —Candela is the international term for candlepower.

② —Natural amber color.

1969, MERCURY

Light Description	Bulb No.	Candela ① or Wattage
Air conditioner control	1895	2C.
Ash tray light	1445	1.5C.
Auto. trans. selector (column mounted)	1445	1.5C.
Auxiliary instrument cluster	1895	2C.
Back-up light	1156	32C.
Cargo light (station wagon)	1003	15C.
Convenience indicator panel	1891	2C.
Convenience indicator panel	256	1.6C.
Courtesy light (C pillar)	1003	15C.
Courtesy light (door mounting)	212	6C.
Dome light	1003	15C.
Engine compartment light	631	6C.
Fog lights (amber)	4415A	35W
Fog light switch	161	1C.
Front park and turn signal light (high series) ②	1157A	3-32C.
Front park, side marker and turn signal light (lo series) ②	1157NA	3-32C.
Front side marker (high series) ②	1178A	4C.
Luggage compartment light	631	6C.
Map light	1816	3C.
Parking brake indicator	194	2C.
Radio		
AM/FM/MPX dial light	1891	2C.
Pilot light	1893	1.9C.
Stereo jewel light	1892	1.3C.
Rear side marker	194	2C.
Gauges, speedometer	194	2C.
Glove compartment	1816	3C.
Headlights—hi beam	4001	37.5W
Headlights—hi-lo beam	4002	37.5 & 50W
Heater control	1895	2C.
Indicator lights		
Alternator	194	2C.
Brakes	194	2C.
Cold	194	2C.
Door ajar	256	1.6C.
High beam	194	2C.
Hot	194	2C.
Lights on	256	1.6C.
Low fuel	1891	2C.
Oil	194	2C.
Instrument indicator light kit	1895	2C.
L & R signal indicator	194	2C.
License light	97	4C.
Rear stop light (high series) ②	1156	32C.
Rear tail, stop, and turn signal	1157	3-32C.
Rear tail light (high series) ②	1095	4C.
Rear window/top nomenclature	1895	2C.
Speed control indicator	161	1C.
Spot light (4.40 diameter)	4405	30W
Trunk light (portable)	1003	15C.

① —Candela is the international term for candle power.

② —High series Mercury models are: Marquis, Brougham Marauder and Marquis Colony Park. All other Mercury models are low series.

1969, FORD

Light Description	Bulb No.	Candela or Wattage①
AM/FM radio	1891	2 C.
AM/FM/stereo radio	1892	1.3C.
Air conditioner control	1895	2C.
Ash tray receptacle	1445	1.5C.
Automatic transmission selector (column mtd)	194	2C.
Auxiliary instrument cluster charge indicator	1895	2C.
Back-up lights	1156	32C.
Cargo light (station wagon)	1003	15C.
Clock	1895	2C.
Courtesy light (54C, 57F)	631	6C.
Courtesy light (65A)	212	6C.
Courtesy light (C pillar)	1003	15C.
Courtesy light (convertible)	631	6C.
Dome light	1003	15C.
Door ajar (convenience group)	1895	2C.
Emergency flasher	1156	32C.
Engine compartment	631	6C.
Seat belt (convenience group or instrument panel)	1895	2C.
Speed control actuator indicator	161	1C.
Spotlight 4.4 inch diameter	4405	30 W
Trans. control selector indicator (floor shift)	1445	1.5C.
Trunk light (portable)	1003	15C.
Fog lights (clear)	4415	35W
Fog light switch	53X	1C.
Front parking and turn indicator	1157	3-32C.
Front-side marker	1178-A	4C.
Glove compartment	1816	3C.
Headlight hi-beam	4001	37.5W
Headlight—hi-lo beam	4002	37.5 & 50W
Heater control panel (fresh air)	1895	2C.
Ignition switch	1895	2C.
Indicator hi-beam	194	2C.
Indicator lights (oil & alternator temperature hot/cold brakes)	194	2C.
Instruments	194	2C.
L & R turn indicator	194	2C.
License plate light	97	4C.
Low fuel (convenience group)	1895	2C.
Luggage compartment	631	6C.
Park brake release indicator light	257	1.6C.
Park brake release indicator light (convenience group)	1895	2C.
Radio pilot light	1895	2C.
Rear light and stop and turn indicator	1157	3-32C.
Rear-side marker	194	2C.

①—Candela is the international term for candlepower.

1969, THUNDERBIRD

Light Description	Bulb No.	Candela or Wattage①
ATC control	1895	2C.
Auto. trans. select. ind. fixed & tilt column	1445	1.5C.
Back-up light	1156	32C.
Brakes & belts indicator	194	2C.
Cigar lighter	1895	2C.
Control nomenclature: rear vent & wipers	194	2C.
Cornering light	97A or 1195	4C. 50C.
Door ajar indicator	256	1.6C.
Door courtesy light	211 or 211-1	12C.
Emergency flasher	1891	2C.
Engine compartment	631	6C.
Fog lights—clear	4415	35 W
Fog light switch	53X	1C.
Front park & turn signal	1157A	3-32C.
Front side marker	1178A	4C.
Glove compartment	1895	2C.
Headlights—hi & lo	4002	37.5 & 50 W
Headlights—hi-beams	4001	37.5 W
Heater controls	1895	2C.
Hi-beam indicators	194	2C.
Ignition switch	161	1C.
Instrument panel courtesy light	631	6C.
Instruments	194	2C.
License plate light	97	4C.
Low fuel indicator	1891	2C.
Luggage compartment	631	6C.
Manual A/C control	1895	2C.
Map light	212	6C.
Parking brake signal	1895	2C.
Radio pilot light	1893	1.9C.
AM/FM stereo pilot light	1892	1.3C.
Rear-side marker	194	2C.
Rear tail/stop/turn signal	1157	3-32C.
Roof quarter light	1003	15C.
Seat belt indicator	1891	2C.
Spotlight—4.4 inch diameter	4405	30W
Supplemental stop light	1156	32C.
Trunk light (portable)	1003	15C.
Turn signal indicators	168A	3C.

①—Candela is the international term for candlepower.

1970, FORD

Light Description	Candle Power or Wattage	Trade No.
Standard equipment		
Headlamps—hi and lo	37.5-50 w	4002
Headlamps—hi beam	37.5 w	4001
Front park & turn signal & emergency flasher	3-32 C.	1157A
Front side marker lamp	2C.	194
Rear tail/stop/turn signal sedan	3-32C.	1157
Rear tail/stop/turn signal sta. wgn.	3-32C.	1157
Rear side marker/lower bulb	12C.	105
Back-up lamps sedans	32C.	1156
sta. wgn.	32C.	1076
License plate lamp	4C.	97
Dome lamp 62, 71, 54A, B & E, 57B	12C.	105
Courtesy lamp "C" pillars 68, 65, 57, 54C	12C.	105
Instrument courtesy lamp convertible	6C.	631
Cargo lamps sta. wgn. models 71A/B/C, 71E; optional, 71D/H/J	12C.	105
Door courtesy 65A	6C.	212
Door courtesy 54C, 57F	6C.	631
Rear side marker lamp	2C.	194
Instrument panel		
Cluster	2C.	1895
Cluster lights	2C.	194
Glove box lamp	3C.	1816
Hi-beam indicators	2C.	194
Turn signal indicators	2C.	194
Warning lights, (oil, alt., temp., brakes)	2C.	194
Seat belt warning (R.P.O.)	2C.	1891
Open door warning (taxis)	2C.	1895
Parking brake release warning (optional)	1.6C.	257
Instruments	2C.	194
Clock or block cover	2C.	1895
Heater control panel	2C.	1895
Optional equipment		
Spotlight	30 w	4405
Fog lamps, clear	35 w	4415
Fog lamp switch	1C.	53X
Air conditioner control	2C.	1895
AM-dual channel	1.9C.	1893
AM-radio	1.9C.	1893
Defogger, rear window	2C.	1895
Electric defroster, rear window	2C.	1895
Headlights on	1.6C.	256
Ash tray lamp (std. on some models)	2 C.	1891
AM/FM radio dial light (MPX)	2C.	1891
AM/FM/MPX stereo jewel	1.3C.	1892
AM stereo tape	1.9C.	1893
Convenience package		
Low fuel	2C.	1895
Door ajar	2C.	1895
Seat belt	2C.	1895
Parking brake	2C.	1891
Glove compartment	3C.	1816
Speed control actuator indicator	1C.	161
Luggage compartment	6C.	631
Portable trunk lamp	15C.	1003
Engine compartment	6C.	631
Floor shift-PRND21	1.5C.	1895
Auxiliary inst. cluster (charge indicator)	2C.	1895

1970, MERCURY

Light Description	Candle Power or Wattage	Trade No.
Standard equipment headlamps		
Hi-lo beam	37.5 & 50W	4002
Hi-beam	37.5W	4001
Front park and turn signal lamp	3-32 c.p.	1157
Rear lamp and stop and turn signal (pass. car)	3-32 c.p.	1157
Dome lamp	12 c.p.	105
License lamp	4 c.p.	97
Courtesy lamp (conv.)	6 c.p.	631
Cargo lamp (sta. wag.)	12 c.p.	105
Back-up lamp (sta. wag. & pass. car)	32 c.p.	1156
Rear stop and turn (sta. wag.)	3-32 c.p.	1157
Rear running lamp (sta. wag.)	4 c.p.	1095
Courtesy lamp (door mtd.)	6 c.p.	212
Courtesy lamp ("C" pillar)	12 c.p.	105
Courtesy lamp—inst. panel	6 c.p.	631
Front & rear side marker	2 c.p.	194
Instrument panel		
Gauges, speedometer	2 c.p.	194
Hi-beam indicator	2 c.p.	194
Warning lights		
Oil	2 c.p.	194
Alternator	2 c.p.	194
Hot	2 c.p.	194
Brakes	2 c.p.	194
Seat belt	2 c.p.	194
Parking brake	2 c.p.	194
Defog	2 c.p.	194
L & R signal indicator	2 c.p.	194
Glove compartment	3 c.p.	1816
Select-shift transmission selector—column & console	2.5 c.p.	1445
Courtesy lamp (inst. panel)	6 c.p.	631
Ash tray—inst. panel	1.5 c.p.	1445
Heater control	1.5 c.p.	1445
Accessory equipment		
Clock	2 c.p.	194
Engine compartment lamp	6 c.p.	631
Radio and stereo tape pilot light	2 c.p.	1893
AM/FM Multiplex and AM Pilot	2 c.p.	1893
Luggage compartment lamp	6 c.p.	631
Spotlamp (4.40 dia.)	30W	4405
Air conditioner	2 c.p.	1895
Fog lamps (amber)	35W	4415A
Fog lamp switch (illum.)	1 c.p.	161
Map lamp	3 c.p.	1816
Tachometer	2 c.p.	1895

1970, THUNDERBIRD

Light Description	Candle Power or Wattage	Trade No.
Standard equipment		
Headlamps—hi & lo	37.5 & 50 w.	4002
Headlamps—hi beams	37.5 w.	4001N
Front park and turn signal	3-32C.	1157A
Rear tail/stop/turn signal	3-32C.	1157
License plate	4C.	97
Floor console ash tray	1.5C.	1445
"C" pillar	12C.	105
Auto. trans. quadrant	1.5C.	1445
Door courtesy	6C.	212
Luggage compartment	6C.	631
Glove compartment	2C.	1895
Back-up lamps	32C.	1156
Front side marker	2C.	194A
Front cornering lamp	50C.	1196
Front side marker lamp	2C.	194
Cigar lighter	1.5C.	1445
Rear side marker lamp	2C.	194
Instrument panel		
Map	6C.	212
Brake and belt warnings	2C.	194
Glove compartment	2C.	1895
Instrument panel courtesy	6C.	631
Ash tray	1.5C.	1445
Hi-beam indicator	2C.	194
Turn signal indicators	2C.	168A
Instruments	2C.	194
Control nomenclature—		
Wiper/Washer	2C.	194
Heater-A/C Controls	2C.	1895
Optional equipment		
Supplemental parking lamps	6C.	90
Fog lights	35 w.	4415
Fog lights switch	1C.	53X
Radio pilot light (All)	1.9C.	1893
Spotlight	30 W.	4405
Parking brake signal	2C.	1895
Engine compartment	6C.	631
Portable trunk lamp	15C.	1003
High level taillamps	32C.	1156
Convenience check group		
Low fuel	2C.	1891
Lights on	2C.	1891
Door ajar	2C.	1891
Seat belt	2C.	1891
Rear window electric Defrost warning	1.3C.	1892

1971–72, FORD and MERCURY

Light Description	Candle Power or Wattage	Trade No.
Back-up lamps	32 CP	1156
Cargo lamp (Wagon)	12 CP	105
Clock	2 CP	1895
Cornering lamp	50 CP	1196
Courtesy lamp (Door)	6 CP	212
Courtesy lamp (Dash)	6 CP	631
Courtesy lamp (C pillar)	12 CP	105
Dome lamp	6 CP	90
Glove compartment	.7 CP	1445
Headlamps—High beam	37.5 W	4001
Headlamps—Low beam	37.5 & 50 W	4002
License plate lamp	4 CP	97
Luggage compartment	6 CP	631
Map lamp	6 CP	212
Parking & turn signal—front	3-32 CP	1157 NA
Turn signal & stop lamp—rear	3-32 CP	1157
Rear running lamp (Wagon)	12 CP	105
Side marker lamps—front	2 CP	194
Side marker lamps—rear		
Ford	2 CP	194
Mercury	4 CP	97
Wagon	12 CP	105

1971–72, THUNDERBIRD

Light Description	Candle Power or Wattage	Trade No.
Back-up lamps	32 CP	1156
Console lamp	.75 CP	1892
Cornering lamps	50 CP	1196
Courtesy lamp (Door)	6 CP	212
Courtesy lamp (Dash)	6 CP	90
Courtesy lamp (C pillar)	12 CP	105
Glove compartment	2 CP	1895
Headlamp—High beam	37.5 W	4001
Headlamp—Low beam	37.5 & 50 W	4002
License plate lamp	4 CP	97
Luggage compartment	6 CP	631
Map lamp	6 CP	212
Overhead console	2 CP	1891
Parking & turn signal—front	3-32 CP	1157 NA
Turn signal & stop lamp—rear	3-32 CP	1157
Side marker lamps—front	1 CP	161
Side marker lamps—rear	1 CP	161
Supplemental park lamps	15 CP	94

FUSES AND CIRCUIT BREAKERS

1965, All Models

Circuit	Protective Device	Location
Headlights	18 Amp. circuit breaker	Incorporated in lighting switch
Instrument panel, transmission indicator and ash receptacle lights	AGA-5 Fuse	Fuse panel
Turn signals and back-up lights, radio, single-speed washer motor	SFE-14 Fuse	Fuse panel
dual-speed washer motor	12 Amp. circuit breaker	Incorporated in washer switch
Seat belt warning, emergency warning	SFE-20 Fuse	Fuse panel
Heater blower, power antenna, door open warning	SFE-20	Fuse panel
Electric windshield wiper (single-speed) (dual-speed) (intermittent—Mercury)	6 Amp. circuit breaker 12 Amp. circuit breaker 7 Amp. circuit breaker	Incorporated in wiper switch
Cigar lighter	SFG-14 Fuse	Fuse panel
Air conditioner (integrated system)	25 Amp. circuit breaker	On ignition switch
Spot light	SFE-7.5 Fuse	Cartridge in feed wire
Overdrive	AGC-15 Fuse	On overdrive relay
Clock, dome, courtesy, map, cargo, trunk, glove box	SFE-9 Fuse	Fuse panel
Tail, park, license plate, and horns	15 Amp. circuit breaker	Incorporated in lighting switch
Speed control	SFE 14 Amp. fuse	Cartridge in feed wire
Transistorized ignition	AGA-2 fuse	Cartridge in feed wire
Top control motor feed, power windows and seat, back lite	20 Amp. circuit breaker	At starter relay
Air conditioner economy		Cartridge in feed wire

1966, All Models

Circuit	Circuit Protection		Location
	Rating	Trade No.	
Power assists			
Convertible top circuit	14 gage wire Fuse link	(C6AB-14A094-A)	In wiring near starter relay
Convertible top with power option(s)	20 Amp. C.B. replaces fuse link		On starter relay
Power windows including backlite & tailgate	20 Amp. C.B.		
Power seats (four- and six-way)	20 Amp. C.B.		
Air conditioning circuit			
Air conditioner (economy)	15 Amp.	AGC 15	Fuse cartridge in feed wire
Air conditioner (selectair)	25 Amp. C.B.		On back of ignition switch at accessory terminal
Miscellaneous circuits			
Overdrive	20 Amp. fuse	AGC 15	On overdrive relay
Transistorized ignition	2 Amp. fuse	AGA 2	Fuse cartridge in feed wire
Speed control	14 Amp. fuse	SFE 14	
Spotlight	7.5 Amp. fuse	SFE 7.5	
Automatic headlamp dimmer	4 Amp. fuse	AGA 4	
Seat belt warning and parking brake warning	No protection		
Gauge circuits			
Charge indicator	No protection		
Oil pressure indicator			
Engine water—cold			
Engine water—hot			
Motors			
Windshield wiper motor	Circuit		Integral with motor
Convertible top motor	breaker		
Power window motor			
Power seat motor			

1966, All Models

Circuit	Circuit Protection		Location
	Rating	Trade No.	
Headlamp circuit			
Headlamps	18 Amp. C.B.		Integral with lighting switch.
High beam indicator lamp			
Rear lamps (tail lights & stop lights)	15 Amp. C.B.		
Front parking lamps			
Ignition switch lamp			
License lamp			
Horns			
Dome lamp circuit			
Dome lamp	9 Amp. fuse	SFE 9	On fuse panel (dome socket).
Courtesy lamps			
Cargo lamp			
Glove compartment lamp			
Luggage compartment lamp			
Clock			
Instrument panel illumination	4 Amp. fuse①	AGA 4①	Fuse panel (instrument panel socket) This circuit is connected into the light switch rheostat.
Clock light			
Instrument cluster lights			
Ash tray light			
PRNDL—Console or column light			
Radio light			
Heater control lights			
Heater circuit			
Heater and defroster motor	20 Amp. fuse	SFE 20 or AGC 20	Fuse panel (heater socket).
Safety convenience panel lamps			
Low fuel warning			
Seat belt warning			
Door ajar warning			
Door unlock warning			
Power antenna			
Station wagon under seat heater			
Open door warning			
Cigar Lighter Circuit			
Cigar lighter	14 Amp. fuse	SFG 14	Fuse panel (cigar lighter socket).
Cigar lighter plus Emergency warning option (hang-on or convenience panel)	20 Amp. fuse (replaces 14 Amp. cigar fuse)	SFE 20	
Radio Circuit			
Radio	14 Amp. fuse	SFE 14	Fuse panel (radio socket).
Back-up lamps			
Single speed washers			
Turn signal circuit			(After fuse flasher protects circuit for turn signal).
Windshield Wipers			
Single speed wipers	6 Amp. C.B.		Integral with windshield wiper switch.
Dual speed wipers and washers	12 Amp. C.B.		
Intermittent wipers	7 Amp. C.B.		

① —Mercury—5 Amp. fuse, AGA 5

1967, FORD and MERCURY

Circuit	Protective Device-Fuse or Circuit Breaker (C.B.) in Amperes	Location
Headlights	18 C.B.	Integral with light switch
High beam indicator	18 C.B.	Integral with light switch
Horns, tail- and stoplights, parking lights	15 C.B.	
Ignition switch light and license light	15 C.B.	Integral with light switch
Clock, and lamps for dome, cargo	SFE 9	Fuse panel
Courtesy, glove and luggage compartments		
Lights for clock, radio, heater control, ash tray	AGA 4	
Instrument cluster, transmission selector (console or column)		Fuse panel
Heater and defroster motor, power antenna, stationwagon underseat heater, and warning lamps for low fuel, seat belt, door ajar, door lock, and cornering lamp	SFE 20 or AGC 20	Fuse panel
Cigar lighter	SFE 14	Fuse panel
Cigar lighter and emergency warning (hang-on or conv. panel)	SFE 20	Fuse panel
Radio, back-up lights, single speed washers, turn signals	SFE 14	Fuse panel (after fuse, flasher protects circuit for turn signal)
Dual speed wipers and washers (Ford)	12 C.B.③	Integral with windshield wiper switch
Convertible top circuit	Fuse link ①	In wiring near starter relay
Convertible top with power option(s)	20 C.B. replaces link	On starter relay
Power windows (including backlite and tailgate)	20 C.B.	
Power seats (four- and six-way)	20 C.B.	
Air conditioner (economy)	AGC 15	Fuse cartridge in feed wire
Air conditioner (selectair)	25 C.B.	②
Overdrive	AGC 15	On overdrive relay
Speed control	AGA 5	Fuse cartridge in feed wire
Spotlight	SFE 7.5	Fuse cartridge in feed wire
Automatic headlight dimmer	AGW 4	Fuse cartridge in feed wire
Seat belt warning and parking brake warning	SFE 7.5	Fuse cartridge in feed wire
Indicators for charge, oil press., engine coolant hot and cold	No protection	
Windshield wiper motor, convertible top motor, power window motor and power seat motor	Circuit breaker	Integral with motor

① —14 gage wire (C6AB-14A094-A) ③ —Mercury intermittent wipers 6 C.B.
② —On back of ignition switch at accessory terminal

1967, THUNDERBIRD

Circuit	Protective Device-Fuse or Circuit Breaker (C.B.) in Amperes	Location
Electric antenna	SFE 14	Fuse panel
Low fuel level warning	7.5 SFE, AGW	Fuse panel
Speed control, seat belt warning	AGW 4	Fuse panel
Radio	SFE, AGW 7.5	Fuse panel
Windshield washer, backup lights, door open warning	SFE, AGW, 4AG 7.5	Fuse panel
Turn signal	AGC, 3AG 15	Fuse panel
Instrument panel lights, ash receptacle light	SFE 6	Fuse panel
Trans. indicator light (PRNDL), glove box light	SFE 6	Fuse panel
Interior lights, dome, courtesy, map, luggage comp, clock	SFE 14	Fuse panel
Cigar lighter	SFE 15	Fuse panel
Emergency warning indicator	SFE 20	Fuse panel
Rear light wire	5-C.B.	Rear panel-LH rear of quarter panel
Tail lights, parking lights, license light	15-C.B.	In headlight switch
Headlights	18-C.B.	In headlight switch
Stoplights	15-C.B.	Fuse panel
Heater, air conditioner	30-C.B.	Fuse panel
Electric windows, electric seats, horns	20-C.B.	Fuse panel
Windshield wiper	Hydraulically operated	No. fuse or circuit breaker

1968, FORD and MERCURY

Circuit	Circuit Protection		Location
	Rating	Trade No.	
Headlamp circuit			
Headlight	18 Amp. C.B.		Integral with lighting switch
High beam indicator light			
Rear lamps (tail lights & stop lights)	15 Amp. C.B.		
Front parking and side marker light			
Ignition switch light			
License light			
Horns			
Dome lamp circuit			
Dome lamp	9 Amp. fuse	SFE 9	On fuse panel (dome socket)
Courtesy light			
Cargo light			
Map light			
Glove compartment light			
Luggage compartment light			
Clock			
Tachometer			
Instrument panel illumination			
Mercury	5 Amp. fuse①	AGA 5 ①	Fuse panel (instrument panel socket). This circuit is connected into the light switch rheostat
Clock light			
Instrument cluster lights			
Ash tray light			
PRNDL—console or column light			
Radio light			
Heater control lights			
Heater circuit			
Heater and defroster motor	20 Amp. fuse	SFE 20 or AGC 20	Fuse panel (heater socket)
Safety convenience panel lamps:			
Low fuel warning			
Seat belt warning			
Door ajar warning			
Door unlock warning			
Power antenna			
Station wagon under seat heater			
Defogger and spot light			
Cigar lighter plus emergency warning	20 Amp. fuse	SFE 20	Fuse panel
Radio circuit			
Radio	14 Amp. fuse	SFE-14	Fuse panel (radio socket)
Back-up lamps			
Single speed washers			
Intermittent speed washers			
Turn signal circuit			(After fuse flasher protects circuit for turn signal)
Seat belt warning, parking brake, door ajar			
Windshield wipers			Integral with windshield wiper switch
Intermittent wipers (Mercury) Dual speed wipers (Ford)	7.5 Amp. C.B. (two-speed)		
Power assists Convertible top circuit	14 gage wire fuse link	(C6AB-14A094-A)	In wiring near starter relay
Convertible top with power option(s)	20 Amp. C.B. replaces fuse link		On starter relay
Power windows including backlite & tailgate	20 Amp. C.B.		
Power seats (four- and six-way)	20 Amp. C.B.		

1968, FORD and MERCURY

Circuit	Circuit Protection		Location
	Rating	Trade No.	
Air conditioning circuit			
Air conditioner (Economy)	15 Amp.	AGC 15	Fuse cartridge in feed wire
Air conditioner (Selectair)	25 Amp. C.B.		Center flange of instrument panel
Miscellaneous circuits:			
Speed control	5 Amp. fuse	AGA 5	Fuse cartridge in feed wire
Spotlight	20 Amp. fuse	SFE 20	Fuse panel (heater socket)
Automatic headlamp dimmer	4 Amp. fuse	SFE 4 7.5	Fuse cartridge in feed wire
Parking brake warning	14 Amp. fuse	SFE 24	Fuse panel (accessory socket)
Motors:			
Windshield wiper motor	Circuit breaker		In switch
Convertible top motor			
Power window and backlite motor			
Power seat motor			

① —Ford—4 Amp. fuse—AGA 4

1968, THUNDERBIRD

Circuit	Location	Protective Device
Dome, courtesy, map, glove compt., luggage compt. and movable steering column	Fuse panel	SFE 14①
Tail, park, license, marker, and supplemental taillights	In headlight switch	15 C.B.
Stop light and emergency flashers	Right side of dash panel	20 C.B.
Clock and stereo tape player	Fuse panel	SFE 15
Back-up lights and W/S washer	Fuse panel	SFE 7.5
Turn signal	Fuse panel	SFE 15
Radio and rear window defogger	Fuse panel	SFE 7.5
Heater—air conditioner	Right side of dash panel	30 C.B.
Instrument panel and PRNDL lights, ash tray lights	Fuse panel	SFE 6
Cigar lighter	Fuse panel	SFE 20
Power radio antenna	Fuse panel	3AG 10
Speed control, seat belt and door opening warning	Fuse panel	SFE 4
Low fuel warning	Fuse panel	SFE 7.5
Headlights	In headlight switch	18 C.B.
Horns, power windows, power seats and power reclining seat	Fuse panel	20 C.B.
Ammeter light	Fuse panel	SFE 14
Dual brake warning system	Fuse panel	SFE 6
Load circuit	Terminal junction block and starter motor relay	Fuse link

① —With movable steering column use SFE-20

1969, THUNDERBIRD

Circuit	Location	Protective Device①
Ammeter circuit		SFE 14
Ash tray lights		SFE 6
Back-up lights		SFE 7.5
Cigar lighter (front and rear)	Fuse panel	AGC or SFE 20
Clock feed		3AG or AGC 15
Cornering lights		7AG or AGW 15
Courtesy lights		8AG or AGX 20
Footwell		
Glove compartment		
Luggage compartment		
Map		
Dual brake warning system		SFE 6
Electric seat motors	Integral part of motor	CB.
Electric window motors		
Emergency flashers	Right side of dash panel	20 CB.
Four-horn circuit	Cartridge in feed line	AGC or SFE 20
Headlights	In headlight switch	18 CB.
Headlights on buzzer circuit	Integral with lighting switch	15 CB.
Heated back window	Attached to brake pedal support	20 CB.
Heater—air conditioner	Right side of dash panel	30 CB.
Horns	Circuit breaker panel RH. dash panel	20 CB.
Indicator lights		
Door ajar	Fuse panel	SFE 7.5
Low fuel		
Seat belt (console)		

Circuit	Location	Protective Device 1
Instrument panel lights	Fuse panel	SFE 6
Dual brakes indicator		
Heater control		
Ignition switch PRND21		
Radio dial		
Seat belt (instrument panel)		
Stereo tape player		
License	In headlight switch	15 C.B.
Marker		
Movable steering column	Fuse panel	8AG or AGX 20
Park	In headlight switch	15 C.B.
Power antenna	Fuse panel	3AG or AGC 10
Power seats	Circuit breaker Panel R.H. dash panel	20 C.B.
Power windows		
Power window relay feed		30 C.B.
Radio	Fuse panel	SFE 7.5
Rear window defogger		
Speed control, seat belt		7AG or AGW 15
Stereo tape player feed		3AG or AGC 15
Stoplight	Right side of dash panel	20 C.B.
Supplemental stop light circuit	Fuse panel	8 AG or AGX 20
Taillights	In headlight switch	15 C.B.
Turn signals	Fuse panel	7AG or AGW 15
Windshield washer	Fuse panel	SFE 7.5

① —Fuse or circuit breaker (C.B.) in amperes.

1969, FORD and MERCURY

Circuit	Location	Protective Device [1]	Circuit	Location	Protective Device [1]	Circuit	Location	Protective Device [1]
Air conditioner feed	Center of instrument panel flange	25 C.B.	Power seat feed	On starter relay	20 C.B.	License lights Lights on buzzer	Integral with lighting switch	15 C.B.
Air conditioner feed (dealer installed)	Cartridge in feed line at accy. terminal of fuse panel	AGC or SFE 20	Power seat motors	In motor	C.B.	Low fuel indicator	Fuse panel—left side of dash	AGC or SFE 20
			Power top feed	On starter relay	20 C.B.	Luggage compartment		SFE 14
Ammeter Fuse panel		SFE 4	Power top motor Power window motors	In motor	C.B.	Marker lights	Integral with lighting switch	15 C.B.
Antenna—electric Back-up lights Cigar lighter		AGC or SFE 20	Power window relay feed	Fuse panel—left side of dash	AGC or SFE 20	Power window supply	On starter relay	20 C.B.
Clock feed		SFE 14	Headlights and high beam indicator	Integral with lighting switch	18 C.B.	Radio feed Rear window defogger Seat belt indicator	Fuse panel—left side of dash	AGC or SFE 20
Courtesy lights C pillar Cargo Dome Door Glove compartment Instrument panel Map	Fuse panel left side of dash	SFE 14	Heated back window	On starter relay	20 C.B.	Speed control	Cartridge in feed line at accy. terminal of fuse panel	AGA 5
			Heater—defroster motor	Fuse panel—left side of dash	SFE 14			
Door ajar indicator Emergency flasher		AGC or SFE 20	Horns Ignition switch light	Integral with lighting switch	15 C.B.	Stop lights Taillights	Integral with lighting switch	15 C.B.
Open door indicator	Fuse panel—left side of dash	SFE 14 AGC or	Instrument panel lights Clock Gauges Heater control PRNDL Radio	Fuse panel—left side of dash	SFE 4	Windshield washer	Fuse panel—left side of dash	AGC or SFE 20
Parking brake indicator		SFE 20				Windshield wiper-washer	In wiper switch	10 C.B.
Parking lights	Integral with lighting switch	15 C.B.						

[1] —Fuse or circuit breaker (C.B.) in Amperes.

1970, MERCURY

Circuit	Location	Circuit Breaker (C.B.) or Fuse in Amperes	Circuit	Location	Circuit Breaker (C.B.) or Fuse in Amperes	Circuit	Location	Circuit Breaker (C.B.) or Fuse in Amperes
Headlights	Integral with light switch	18 C.B.	Inteval windshield wipers	Mounted to lower center flange of instrument panel	8.25 C.B.		center flange of instrument panel	
Rear tail lights Front parking lights License light Side marker Horns Headlight buzzer Stop lights	Integral with light switch	15 C.B.	Convertible top Power windows	On starter relay	20 C.B.	Stop lights	Mounted to lower R.H. flange of instrument panel	20 C.B.
			Rear window defroster & seat back latch Power seats	On starter relay	20 C.B.	Motors—protected by integral circuit breakers Power seat Power window Convertible top	In motor	C.B.
Windshield wipers	Integral with wiper switch	7 C.B.	Air conditioner	Mounted to lower	25 C.B.			

1970, FORD

Circuit	Location	Circuit Breaker (C.B.) or Fuse in Amperes
Headlights	Integral with light switch	18 C.B.
Rear tail lights Front parking lights License light Side marker Horns Headlight buzzer Stop lights	Integral with light switch	15 C.B.
Windshield wipers	In windshield wiper switch	10 C.B.
Interval windshield wipers	Upper center of instr. panel near blower switch	8.25 C.B.
Convertible top Power Windows	On starter relay	20 C.B.
Rear window defroster & seat back latch Power seats	On starter relay	20 C.B.
Air conditioner	Upper center instrument panel near blower switch	30 C.B.
Air conditioner dealer installed	Cartridge in feed line attached to accy. terminal fuse panel	20 fuse
Motors—protected by integral circuit breakers Power seat Power window Convertible top	In motor	C.B.

1970-72, THUNDERBIRD

Circuit	Rate	Location	Circuit	Rate	Location
Parking lights License light Tail lights Marker lights Headlight buzzer Motors	15 AMP	In headlight switch	Power seat Power windows	Integral	In motor assembly
			Headlight circuit	18 AMP	In headlight switch
			Windshield wiper	Integral	In wiper switch
			Rear window defroster	20 AMP	On brake pedal support

1971-72, FORD and MERCURY

Circuit	Circuit Protection and Rating	Location
Headlamps	18 Amp. C.B.	Integral with lighting switch
Parking lamps Marker lamps License lamps Tail lamps Horns	15 Amp. C.B.	
Windshield wipers	8.25 Amp. C.B.	In headlight switch
Stop lamps	15 Amp. C.B.	Mounted on lower center of instrument panel flange
Air conditioner	30 Amp. C.B.	
Air conditioner—dealer installed	20 Amp. Fuse	Feed line to fuse panel
Power windows Backlite Power seat Power top	20 Amp. C.B.	On starter relay
Deck lid release (Mercury)	6 Amp. C.B.	Instrument panel between glove box and ash tray
Window motor Seat motor Top motor	C.B.	In motor

Distributor

R & R

All 6 Cylinder

First, mark the position of the rotor and body and, to remove it, lift off the cap and wire assembly, disconnect the ignition primary wire, disconnect the vacuum line to the carburetor, remove the distributor hold-down bolt and pull the distributor out of the side of the block.

All V8s

On these models, the distributor is located in the front of the engine and is easily accessible.

First, mark the position of the rotor, also the position of the body with relation to the block. Disconnect the ignition primary wire, the vacuum lead, the distributor cap, then take out the hold-down bolt that holds the distributor down in the block and lift it up out of the block.

Do not disturb the engine after the distributor has been removed in case it should disturb the ignition timing.

Ignition Timing

If the timing relationship has been disturbed, proceed to retime the ignition as follows: bring No. 1 cylinder up into the firing position. This can be checked by removing the spark plug, placing your thumb in the spark plug hole, then cranking the engine until the compression attempts to blow by your thumb. Now, slowly bring the crankshaft around until the T.D.C. mark on the crankshaft pulley lines up with the pointer. This is the approximate firing position for No. 1 cylinder.

Remove the distributor cap and mark on the outside of the distributor the position of the rotor. The wire from No. 1 spark plug should be placed in the socket just above the rotor. Now, working in the direction of the distributor rotation, place the spark plug wires into the cap according to the firing order of the engine.

Viewed from above, rotation of distributor for six cylinder engine is clockwise; for eight cylinder, counterclockwise.

Ignition Primary Resistor

A resistance wire is used between the ignition switch and the coil. Any time difficulty is experienced with the ignition system, it is a good idea to check the resistor.

Generator, Regulator

Most cars are equipped with alternating current generators. This charging system is different from the

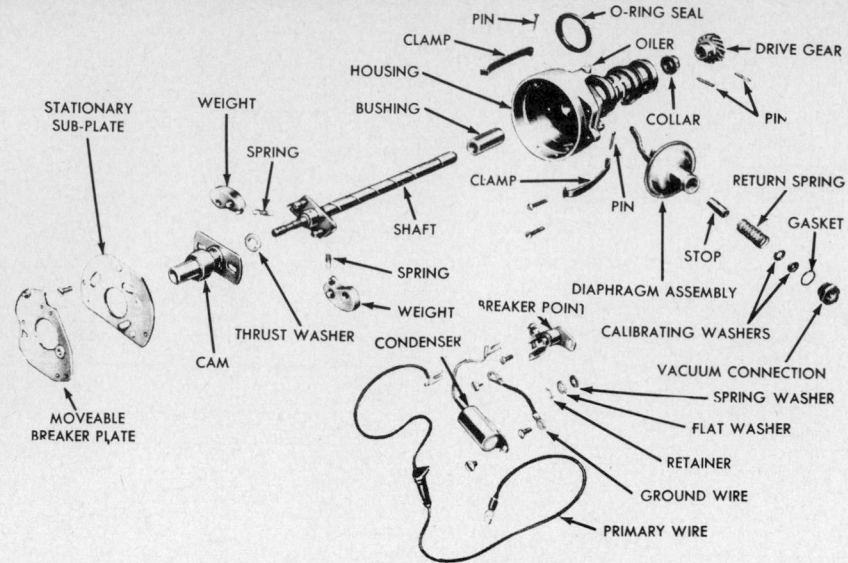

Dual advance distributor (© Ford Motor Co.)

DC circuit and requires certain precautions.

1. Reversing battery connections will cause damage to the one-way electrical valves, the rectifiers.
2. Booster battery connections must be made as follows: the negative terminal of the booster battery must be connected to the negative terminal of the car battery. The positive terminal of the booster battery must be connected to the positive terminal of the car battery.
3. Fast chargers should never be used as boosters to start AC circuit-equipped cars.
4. When servicing the battery with a fast charger, always disconnect car battery cables.
5. Never attempt to polarize an AC generator.

Complete alternator servicing data is in the Unit Repair Section.

Alternator R & R

1. Disconnect the negative battery cable.
2. Loosen the alternator mounting bolts, remove the alternator to adjusting arm bolt and remove the belt.
3. Remove the alternator mounting bolt and spacer, position the alternator so that the wire connectors can be disconnected and remove the alternator.

NOTE: on alternators with integral regulators mounted on the back of the alternator housing, press the sides of the retainer clip and remove the wire from the regulator.

4. Reverse above procedure to reinstall, applying pressure only to the front of the alternator housing when tightening the drive belt.

Regulator R & R

1. Disconnect the negative battery

cable. On 1969 and later Fords the regulator is located behind the battery and it is necessary to remove the battery to remove the regulator.

2. Remove the regulator mounting screws and wires, then remove the regulator.
3. On vehicles with integral regulator, remove the alternator to adjusting arm bolt and the drive belt.
4. Swing the alternator down, remove the terminal covers from the regulator and remove the regulator attaching nuts.
5. Press the sides of the retainer clip and remove the retaining clip and supply wire. Remove the regulator.
6. Reverse above procedure to reinstall.

Fuse Link

Since 1970, all Ford products have incorporated a fuse link in the charging system. The fuse link is a short length of insulated wire, several gauge sizes smaller than the system it protects. The fuse link blows out if a booster battery is hooked into the system incorrectly, or if a component of the electrical system is shorted to ground. When the fuse link blows, it leaves an open circuit in the charging system and the alternator will not charge the battery. A blown fuse link can be indentified by bare wire ends or bubbled insulation. It is located in the engine wire harness on or near the starter solenoid and is marked FUSE LINK.

Battery, Starter

Starter R & R

1. Disconnect the negative battery cable.

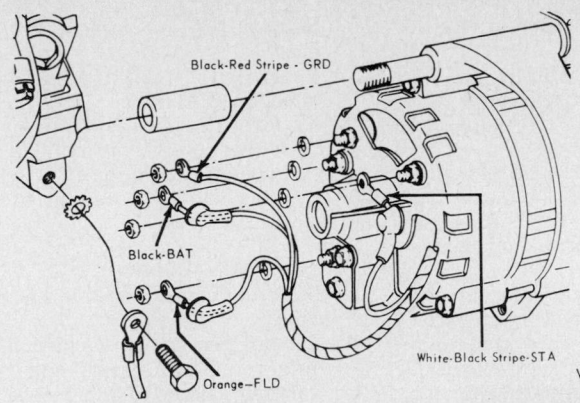

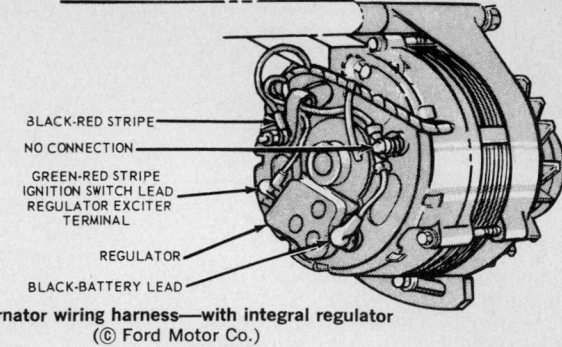

Typical alternator installation (© Ford Motor Co.)

Alternator wiring harness—with integral regulator
(© Ford Motor Co.)

2. Disconnect the starter cable from the starter.
3. Remove the starter mounting bolts.
4. Manipulate the starter so that it can be lowered through the steering linkage. On some engine/chassis combinations this can be done by turning the steering wheel all the way to the right; on others it will be necessary to remove the idler arm bracket attaching bolts and lower the assembly away from the engine.
5. Reverse above procedure to reinstall.

Speedometer Head Removal

1965-66 Ford

1. Disconnect battery, and cover steering column.
2. Remove retaining screws from instrument panel cluster pad and retainer.
3. Remove screws from upper and lower instrument panel cluster cover. Remove cover.
4. Remove radio knobs.
5. Remove friction pins retaining the instrument cluster lens and mask.
6. Disconnect the speedometer cable.
7. On 1966 models, remove the clock.
8. Remove retaining screws from the speedometer retaining bracket, and remove the bracket.
9. Remove screws retaining speedometer head, remove the standoffs from the locating posts and the speedometer head.
10. To reinstall, reverse the removal procedure.

1967 Ford

1. Disconnect battery.
2. Remove instrument panel pad.
3. Remove clock reset knob.
4. Remove four screws retaining warning light housing, disconnect fuel gauge, and remove warning light housing.

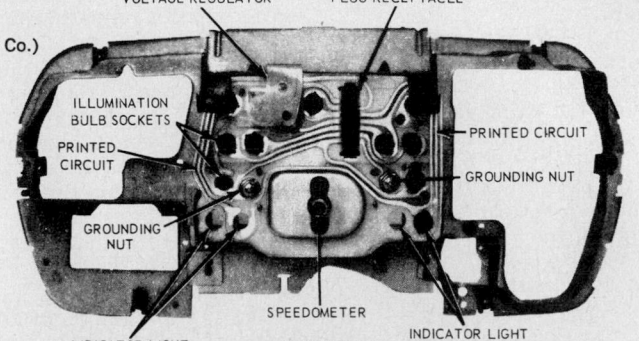

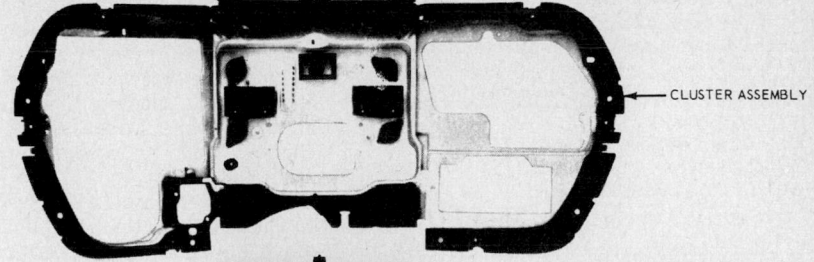

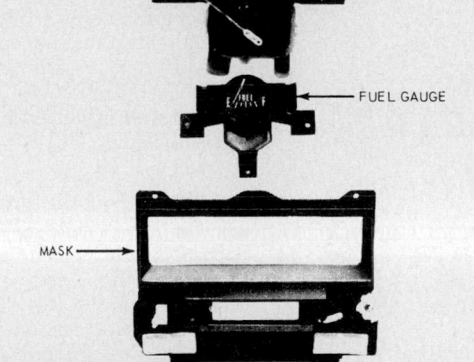

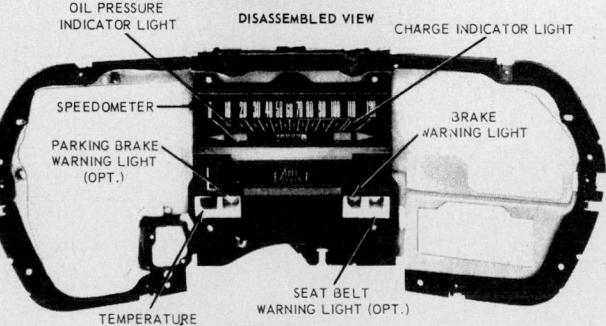

1970 Ford instrument cluster (© Ford Motor Co.)

5. Remove eight friction pins retaining instrument cluster and mask. Remove lens.
6. Remove rubber spacers.
7. Remove three screws retaining speedometer assembly. Disconnect speedometer cable and remove speedometer.

1968 Ford

1. Disconnect battery.
2. Remove right and left windshield mouldings.
3. Pry moulding from right side of instrument panel pad covering the pad retaining screws.
4. Pry off two access covers located above the speedometer lens and on underside of pad.
5. Remove screws retaining instrument panel pad, and remove pad.
6. Remove radio knobs.
7. Remove button clips retaining instrument cluster mask and lens, and remove mask and lens.
8. Disconnect speedometer cable.
9. Remove screws retaining instrument panel lower pad and remove pad.
10. Remove screws from clock retainer and clock and position clock forward.
11. Remove plate under speedometer and two rubber spacers and screws retaining speedometer assembly.
12. Remove speedometer.

1969-72 Ford

1. Remove upper part of instrument panel by removing screws along lower edge, two screws in each of the defroster registers, and disconnecting the radio speaker.
2. Remove cluster opening finish panels from each side of instrument cluster.
3. Disconnect plugs to printed circuit, radio, heater and A/C fan, windshield wipers and washers, and any other electrical connection to cluster.
4. Disconnect heater and A/C control cables and speedometer cable.
5. Remove all knobs from instrument panel if required.
6. Remove instrument cluster trim cover.
7. Remove mounting screws and remove cluster.
8. Remove speedometer from cluster.

1965-66 Thunderbird

1. Disconnect the battery ground cable. Then, cover the steering column and panel where necessary to prevent paint damage.
2. Remove the radio knobs and bezel.
3. Remove headlight switch control knob and bezel nut.

4. Remove the instrument finish panel.
5. Remove the headlight switch mounting screws and push the switch toward the front of the car.
6. Remove the console panel finish moulding cap, and remove the screws retaining the left lower half of the instrument cluster housing assembly.
7. Remove the clock housing retaining screws and rotate the clock housing upward and rearward to expose the two tab screws retaining the instrument panel upper moulding.
8. Remove screws from the instrument panel upper moulding and the screws under the cluster. Pull the moulding away from the instrument panel for access to the cluster screws. Tape the tabs to prevent scratches.
9. Remove the instrument indicator cover retaining screws and remove the covers.
10. Through the indicator openings, remove the screws retaining the lower cluster to the upper cluster. Position the instrument indicator covers on the instruments to prevent damage.
11. Remove the screws retaining the speedometer cluster to the instrument panel at the top of the cluster, and pull speedometer from cluster.
12. Disconnect the cable and all wires to the speedometer head and remove the speedometer cluster.
13. Remove the speedometer housing-to-cluster mounting screws and remove housing assembly.
14. Remove the screws retaining the speedometer housing cover to the speedometer assembly and remove the speedometer.
15. To reinstall, reverse the removal procedure.

1967 Thunderbird

1. Loosen the Allen screw at the bottom of the speedometer pod.
2. Remove the pod retaining screws from the top of the pod.
3. Carefully pull the speedometer and pod straight out and away from the dash.
4. Remove the three retaining screws and remove the speedometer from the front housing.
5. Remove the two screws and remove the speedometer from the rear housing.
6. Remove the speedometer cable and remove the speedometer from the car.
7. Reverse above procedure to install.

1968 Thunderbird

1. Disconnect the negative battery cable.

2. Remove the instrument cluster bezel.
3. Remove the clock adjustment knob, mask and lens.
4. Remove the three speedometer attaching screws and remove the speedometer from the car.
5. Reverse above procedure to install.

1969 Thunderbird

1. Disconnect the negative battery cable.
2. Remove the six air conditioning duct retaining screws and pull the duct rearward.
3. Remove the two screws from the applique on the left side of the cluster.
4. Remove the three screws between the cluster hood and crash pad.
5. Remove the four screws from the lower windshield moulding and remove the moulding.
6. Remove the two screws and nuts from the forward edge of the crash pad.
7. Disconnect the radio speaker lead and remove the crash pad.
8. Remove the radio knob and bezel.
9. Remove the heater controls and windshield wiper control knobs.
10. Remove the four nuts and retainers on the shafts of the radio, heater, and wiper controls.
11. Remove the eight screws from the lower control housing and lower the housing.
12. Remove the screws from the instrument panel finish cover and remove the cover.
13. Remove the odometer reset knob.
14. Remove the screws retaining the lower edge of the upper cluster finish panel.
15. Remove the four screws retaining the upper edge of the upper cluster finish cover and remove the cover.
16. Remove the right-hand air conditioning register.
17. Disconnect the speedometer cable through the register opening.
18. Remove the three screws retaining the speedometer head to the cluster and remove the speedometer head.

1970-72 Thunderbird

1. Disconnect the negative battery cable.
2. Remove the screws retaining the instrument cluster cover bezel to the instrument panel.
3. Remove the bezel and the clock knob.
4. Remove the speedometer lens retainers and remove the lens.
5. Remove the speedometer attaching screws and pull the speedometer head forward.

6. Remove the screws attaching the speedometer cable retainer to the cluster and disengage the speedometer cable by pressing on the flat part of the plastic collar.
7. Reverse above procedure to reinstall.

1965-66 Mercury

On 1965-66 Mercurys, once finish panel is removed, all instruments are readily accessible and removable.
1. Disconnect battery.
2. Remove headlight knob and bezel nut, wiper knob and bezel nut, air conditioner and heater knobs and radio knobs.
3. Remove retaining screws from finish panel and slightly move panel out from instrument cluster.
4. Disconnect wires from air conditioner and heater, and remove finish panel.
5. Disconnect and remove speedometer.

1967-68 Mercury

1. Disconnect battery.
2. Remove control knobs from heater, radio, clock, wipers, and headlights.
3. Remove four retaining screws around speedometer bezel and remove bezel.
4. Remove screws retaining right and left finish panels and remove panels.
5. Remove four button retainers from speedometer dial cover and remove speedometer dial.
6. Remove four screws retaining speedometer, and move speedometer out a little.
7. Disconnect speedometer cable and instrument voltage regulator. Remove speedometer and housing.
8. Remove two nuts retaining speedometer to housing and remove speedometer. Reverse procedure to install speedometer.

1969-70 Mercury

1. Disconnect battery.
2. Remove wiper knob and bezel, cigarette lighter element and finish panel.
3. Remove retaining screws and remove left and right end finish panels.
4. Remove screw that attaches lower pad to upper pad at each end.
5. Remove screws that retain upper finish panel to its support at each defroster opening. Remove six upper finish panel to pad screws, and lift off upper finish panel.
6. Remove four screws that attach upper pad and retainer assembly to pad supports and remove upper pad assembly.

7. Remove two screws that attach right half of lower pad and retainer assembly to pad supports, remove screws that attach left half of lower pad to lower left instrument panel, and remove lower pad and retainer assembly.
8. Remove windshield wiper nut.
9. Remove bracket from left end of pad support.
10. Remove cigarette lighter and bracket assembly.
11. Remove five pad support to instrument panel screws and three lower left-hand panel to instrument panel screws, and remove pad support and lower panel as an assembly.
12. From behind instrument panel, disconnect plug to printed circuit, clock, and any other electrical connection.
13. Disconnect speedometer cable and remove instrument cluster from instrument panel. Reverse procedure to install cluster.

1971-72 Mercury

1. Disconnect the negative battery cable.
2. Remove the eight screws retaining the dash pad and map light.
3. Disconnect the radio speaker and map light.
4. Remove the instrument panel pad and upper finish panel.
5. Disconnect the speedometer cable and all electrical connections from the rear of the instrument cluster.
6. Remove the four cluster attaching screws and remove the cluster from the dash.
7. Remove the clock reset knob.
8. Remove the eight screws from the rear of the cluster which attach the mask and housing to the back plate.
9. Remove the housing and remove the mask by pressing down on the retaining tab on the lower right corner of the back plate.
10. Remove the two screws attaching the speedometer and remove the speedometer.
11. Reverse above procedure to install.

Ford, Mercury and T-Bird Ignition Lock Cylinder Replacement

1965-69

1. Insert key and turn to Acc. position.
2. With stiff wire in hole, depress lock pin and rotate cylinder counterclockwise, then pull out cylinder.

1970-72

1. Disconnect the negative battery cable.

2. On cars with a fixed steering column, remove the steering wheel trim pad and the steering wheel. Insert a stiff wire into the hole located in the lock cylinder housing. On cars with a tilt steering wheel, this hole is located on the outside of the steering column near the emergency flasher button and it is not necessary to remove the steering wheel.
3. Place the gear shift lever in Reverse on standard shift cars and in Park on cars with automatic transmission, and turn the ignition key to the ON position.
4. Depress wire and remove lock cylinder and wire.
5. Insert new cylinder into housing and turn to the OFF position. This will lock the cylinder into position.
6. Reinstall steering wheel and pad if removed.
7. Connect negative battery cable.

Ignition Switch Replacement

1965-69

1. Remove cylinder as above.
2. Unscrew the bezel from the ignition switch and remove switch from panel.
3. Remove insulated plug from rear of switch.
4. Install in reverse of above.

1970-72

See Lincoln Section.

Headlight Switch R & R

All Except 1970 Mercury

1. Disconnect the negative battery cable.
2. On 1971-72 Ford and Mercury, remove the instrument panel pad, speedometer head, and instrument cluster. (See Speedometer Head R&R).
3. Pull the headlight switch control knob to the full ON position and press the release knob on the switch. With the knob depressed, pull the knob and shaft from the switch.
4. Remove the wire connector from the back of the switch and, if equipped with headlight doors, remove the vacuum hoses. On 1967-69 Mercury, remove the wire harness bracket.
5. Remove the bezel retaining nut and remove the switch from the dash. On 1971-72 Fords the switch is attached to the dash with three screws instead of a bezel nut.
6. Reverse above procedure to reinstall. When installing the headlight switch control knob and shaft, turn the shaft in the switch until a distinct click is heard, locking the shaft in place.

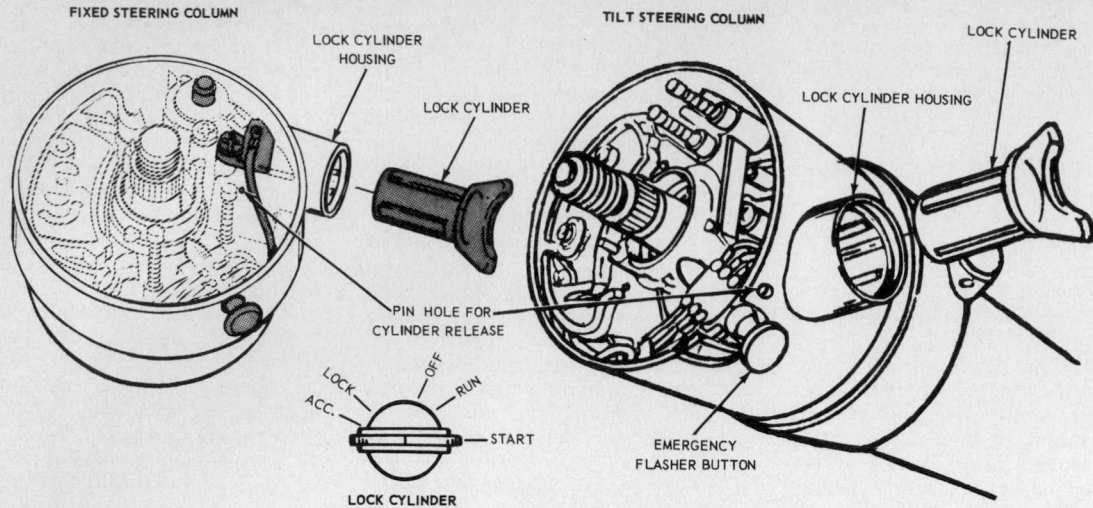

FIXED STEERING COLUMN

TILT STEERING COLUMN

LOCK CYLINDER HOUSING

LOCK CYLINDER

LOCK CYLINDER

LOCK CYLINDER HOUSING

LOCK CYLINDER

PIN HOLE FOR CYLINDER RELEASE

EMERGENCY FLASHER BUTTON

LOCK CYLINDER OPERATING PATTERN

LOCK ACC. OFF RUN START

Post-1970 lock cylinder replacement (© Ford Motor Co.)

KNOB RELEASE BUTTON

Typical headlight switch
(© Ford Motor Co.)

1970 Mercury

1. Remove the battery ground cable.
2. Working under the dash, remove the wire connector from the back of the headlight switch. If equipped with headlight doors, remove the vacuum hoses from the switch.
3. Remove the four switch retaining screws and remove the switch from the dash.
4. Reverse above procedure to install.

Brakes

All models have single anchor, internal expanding, self adjusting shoe brakes on the rear wheels. On models without disc brakes, the front brakes are identical to the rear brakes with the exception of parking brake hardware. Front disc brakes have been available as an option since 1965. 1965-67 disc brakes have dual piston, anchored calipers. 1968 and later vehicles have single piston, floating calipers. 1965-66 cars with standard brakes have a single cylinder and reservoir, mounted on the firewall. All 1965-66 vehicles with disc brakes and all 1967 and later cars have dual reservoir master cylinders and brake systems in which the front and rear brake hydraulic systems are separate and independent of each other.

Master Cylinder

1965-66

The master cylinder consists of a single cylinder and reservoir, mounted on the engine side of the firewall.

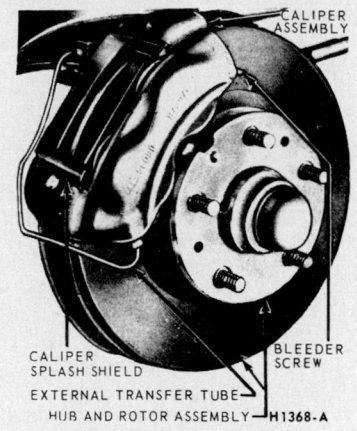

CALIPER ASSEMBLY

CALIPER SPLASH SHIELD

BLEEDER SCREW

EXTERNAL TRANSFER TUBE

HUB AND ROTOR ASSEMBLY — H1368-A

Disc brake caliper assembly
(© Ford Motor Co.)

Master Cylinder R & R

Standard Brakes

1. Disconnect the rubber boot from the rear of the master cylinder in the passenger compartment.
2. Disconnect the brake line from the master cylinder.
3. Remove the master cylinder retaining bolts from the firewall and lift the cylinder away from the pushrod and boot.
4. To reinstall master cylinder, guide it carefully onto the pushrod and replace mounting bolts.
5. Connect the brake line to the master cylinder, but leave the brake line fitting loose.
6. Fill the master cylinder, and with the brake line loose, slowly bleed the air from the cylinder using the foot pedal.
7. Tighten the line at the master cylinder and refill to within ¼ in. of the top.

Power Brakes

1. Disconnect the brake line from the master cylinder.
2. Remove the two nuts and lockwashers that attach the master cylinder to the brake booster.
3. Remove the master cylinder from the booster.
4. Reverse above procedure to reinstall.
5. Fill master cylinder and bleed entire brake system.
6. Refill master cylinder.

Dual Master Cylinder R&R

Standard Brakes

1. Working under the dash, disconnect the master cylinder pushrod from the brake pedal. The pushrod cannot be removed from the master cylinder.
2. Disconnect the stoplight switch wires and remove the switch from the brake pedal, using care not to damage the switch.
3. Disconnect the brake lines from the master cylinder.
4. Remove the attaching screws from the firewall and remove the master cylinder from the car.
5. Reinstall in reverse of above order, leaving the brake line fittings loose at the master cylinder.
6. Fill the master cylinder, and with the brake lines loose, slowly bleed the air from the master cylinder using the foot pedal.

Power Brakes

Use same procedure as 1965-66.

Brake Booster R & R

1. Working from inside the car, beneath the instrument panel, remove the booster pushrod from the brake pedal.
2. Disconnect the stop light switch wires and remove the switch from the brake pedal. Use care not to damage the switch during removal.

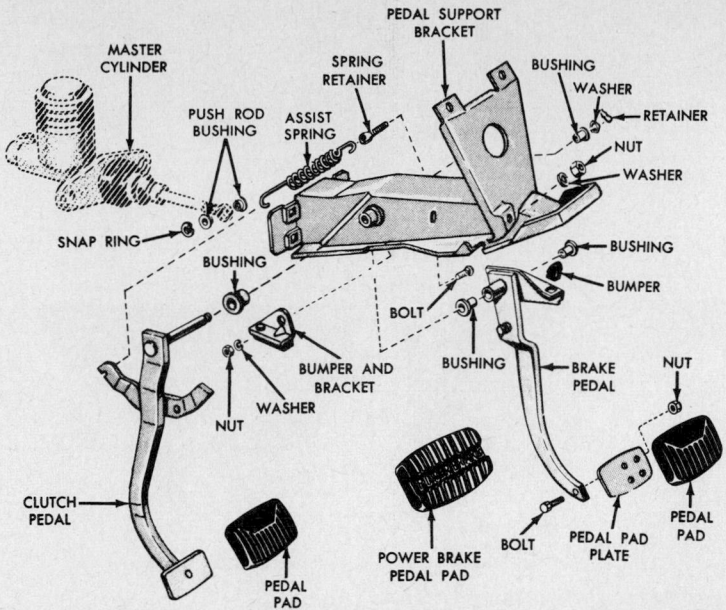

Pedal assembly and related parts (© Ford Motor Co.)

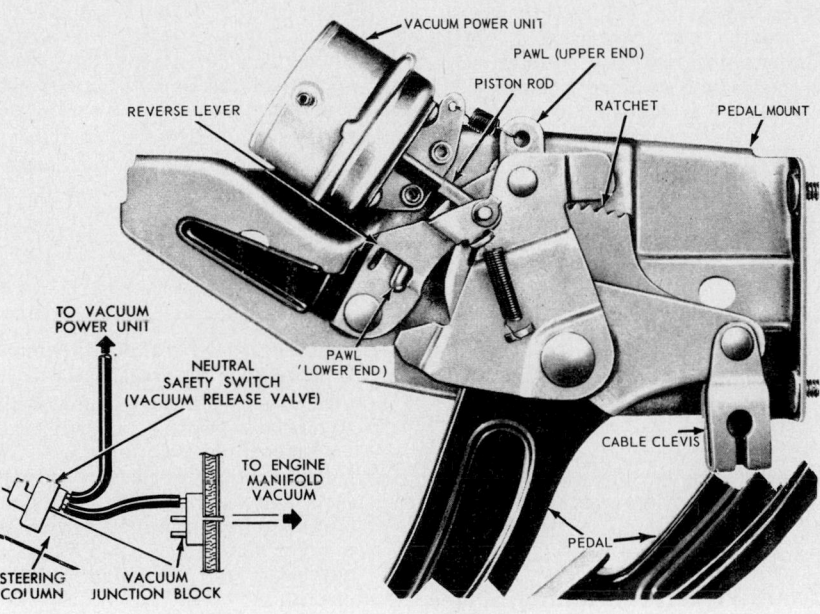

Vacuum release parking brake (© Ford Motor Co.)

3. Raise the hood and remove the master cylinder from the booster without disconnecting the brake lines. Carefully position the master cylinder out of the way, being careful not to kink the brake lines.
4. Remove the manifold vacuum hose from the booster.
5. Remove the booster to firewall attaching bolts and remove the booster from the car.
6. Reverse above procedure to reinstall.

Parking Brake Adjustment

1. Raise the vehicle on a hoist with the transmission in Neutral and the parking brake fully released.
2. Tighten the adjusting nut against the cable equilizer until the rear brakes drag when the wheels are turned.
3. Loosen up on the adjustment nut until the brakes are fully released.

Fuel System

Fuel Pump

Description

A single-action, permanently sealed Carter fuel pump is used on all models. On 6-cylinder engines, the fuel pump is located on the lower left center of the engine block. The V8 fuel pump is mounted on the left side of the cylinder front cover.

R&R—All Models

1. Remove the inlet and outlet lines from the pump.
2. Remove the fuel pump retaining screws and remove the pump and gasket.
3. Clean all gasket material from the pump mounting surface on the engine, and apply a coat of oil-resistant sealer to the new gasket.
4. Position pump on engine and install retaining screws.
5. Reinstall lines, start engine and check for leaks.

NOTE: if resistance is felt while positioning the fuel pump on the block, the camshaft eccentric is in the high position. To ease installation, connect a remote engine starter switch to the engine and "tap" remote switch until resistance fades.

Fuel Filter

All 1965 models have a replaceable fuel filter cartridge located in a container mounted on the bottom of the fuel pump. All models since 1966 have used a non-serviceable inline fuel filter which is located at the carburetor fuel inlet.

⏻ CHILTON TIME-SAVER

Rear Brake Drum Removal

Occasional cases of rear wheel drums, frozen to the rear axle flange, require much time and effort to remove without damage.

If a rear drum resists normal efforts to remove by tapping, try the following method:

1. Drive two or three of the serrated hub bolts out of the drum and into the brake shoe area.

2. With an old screwdriver or other suitable wedge forced between the drum and axle flange through these bolt holes, tap and wedge the drum from the axle flange.

3. After the drum is removed, the bolts can be recovered and returned to their respective places in the axle flange.

Any damage to the drum can usually be corrected by a few taps with a hammer.

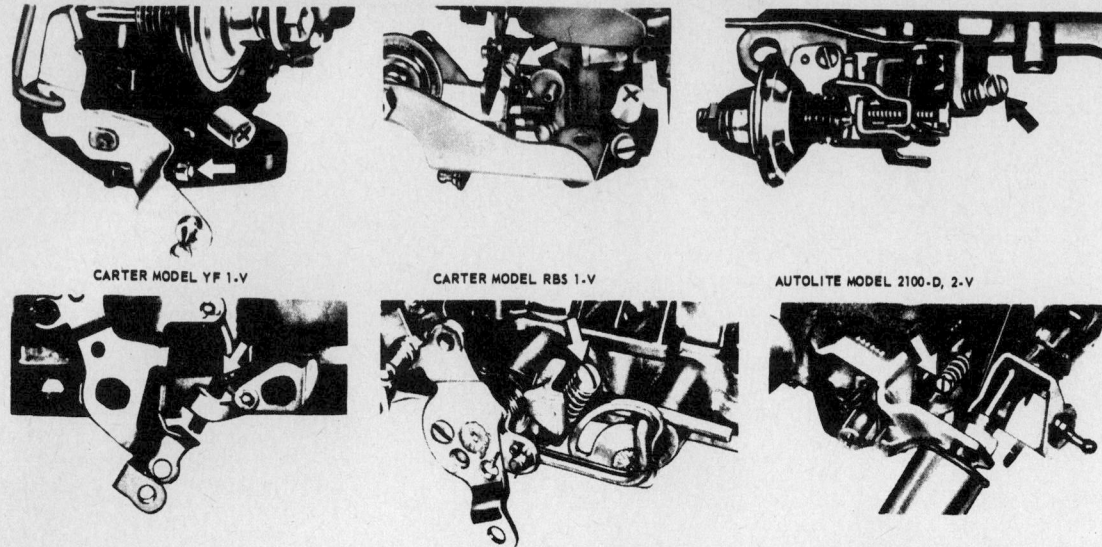

CARTER MODEL YF 1-V   CARTER MODEL RBS 1-V   AUTOLITE MODEL 2100-D, 2-V

AUTOLITE MODEL 4300 4-V   HOLLEY MODEL 4150C 4-V   ROCHESTER MODEL 4 MV

Idle speed adjusting screws (© Ford Motor Co.)

Carburetor

Ford uses eight types of carburetors: Autolite 1100, Carter YF and RBS (1-barrel), Autolite 2100 (2-barrel), Autolite 4100, Autolite 4300, and Holley 4150 and 4150C (4-barrel).

Idle Speed Adjustment

1965-67: Adjust with air cleaner removed.

1968-71: Adjust with air cleaner installed.

This is the procedure for adjusting all carburetors, any exceptions are listed below.

1. Run engine at fast idle to equalize operating temperature.
2. Make sure the choke plate is fully released.
3. Turn headlights on high beam.
4. If engine is equipped with hot idle compensator valve, make sure it is fully seated in the closed position.
5. Attach tachometer of known accuracy to the engine.
6. On cars equipped with air conditioning, 1965-69 models (except 200 CI 6-cylinder and 302 V8 engines with automatic transmission) set idle speed with air conditioner turned ON. On all 1970 and later models the idle speed is set with the air conditioner turned OFF.
7. On 1967 and later models equipped with a temperature sensing valve in the distributor vacuum line, remove and plug the vacuum hoses from the distributor to the valve and from the intake manifold to the valve, at the valve located in the intake manifold.
8. Make sure the dashpot is working freely and not binding.

9. If it is not possible to adjust the idle speed with the air cleaner installed, the engine idle speed must be rechecked after installing the air cleaner. On cars with vacuum controlled heat ducts in the air cleaner, the vacuum line must be plugged if the carburetor is to be adjusted with the air cleaner removed.
10. On 1969 and later model cars for which the specifications list two idle speeds, the first speed listed is obtained by adjusting the electric solenoid on the carburetor, and the second by disconnecting the solenoid and adjusting the carburetor idle screw in the normal manner.

NOTE: with the electric solenoid disengaged, the carburetor adjusting screw must make contact with the throttle shaft to prevent the throttle plates from jamming in the throttle bore when the engine is shut off.

Fuel Mixture Adjustment

1. On 1965-67 models, turn the mixture screws clockwise until engine speed begins to drop, then back out until engine reaches highest rpm.
2. On 1968 and later models with idle mixture limiters, adjust to obtain the highest rpm possible. Limiter caps should not be removed.
3. If satisfactory idle is not obtained following this procedure, refer to additional carburetor adjustments listed in the Exhaust Emission Systems Section in the Unit Repair Section of this book.

Dashpot Adjustment 1965-67 Six Cylinder

1. Adjust throttle position to fast idle position and turn dashpot

adjusting screw out until it is clear of dashpot plunger assembly.
2. Turn in screw until it contacts plunger. Then turn in screw specified number of turns against plunger.

Models	Number of Turns
1965 240 six	3¼—3 3/4
1966 240 six	3½
1967 240 six	
without emission control	6
with emission control	2

3. Check accelerator pump setting.

Dashpot Adjustment All Others

1. With engine idle speed and mixture properly adjusted and with engine at operating temperature, loosen dashpot locknut.
2. Hold throttle in closed position and depress dashpot plunger. Measure clearance between plunger and cam. Adjust dashpot adjusting nut to give proper clearance.
3. Tighten locknut and check setting of accelerator pump.

Cooling System

Radiator R & R

1. Drain the cooling system.
2. Remove the upper and lower radiator hoses from the radiator.
3. On models with a fan shroud, remove the shroud attaching screws and move the shroud rearward to gain clearance.
4. If equipped with automatic transmission, remove the cooler lines from the radiator.
5. Remove radiator attaching screws and remove radiator from the car.
6. Reverse above procedure to in-

stall.

7. Fill cooling system, run engine at fast idle and check for leaks.

Water Pump R & R

1. Drain the cooling system.
2. On 351C and 400 V8, disconnect the negative battery cable.
3. On cars with power steering, remove the drive belt; models with 352, 390, 427 and 428 engine, remove the power steering mounting retaining screws and remove the pump and bracket as an assembly and position it out of the way.
4. If vehicle is equipped with air conditioning, remove the idler pulley and drive belt from the engine.
5. Disconnect the lower radiator hose, heater hose and bypass hose from the water pump.
6. On cars with a fan shroud, remove the shroud retaining screws and position the shroud rearward over the fan.
7. Remove the fan attaching screws and remove the fan, fan spacer and shroud from the engine compartment.
8. Loosen the alternator mounting bolts and remove the belt.
9. Remove any accessory mounting brackets from the water pump.
10. Remove the water pump mounting bolts and remove the pump from the engine.
11. Clean all gasket surfaces, and on 429 V8 remove the water pump backing plate and replace the gasket.
    NOTE: the 240 6-cylinder engine originally had a one-piece gasket for the cylinder front cover and the water pump. Trim away the old gasket at the edge of the cylinder cover and replace with service gasket.
12. Remove the water pump fitting from the old pump and install it in the new pump.
13. Coat both sides of the new gasket with water resistant sealer, then install pump by reversing above procedure.

Exhaust System

All exhaust systems consist of three basic components: a pipe (called a muffler inlet pipe) that carries exhaust gases from the exhaust manifold(s) to the midpoint of the chassis, a pipe (called an inlet pipe extension) that carries the gases from the inlet pipe to the muffler which is mounted behind the rear axle, and a muffler and self-contained outlet pipe. On some models with dual exhaust, a resonator is pieced into the inlet pipe extension. On 6-cylinder models the inlet pipe is a

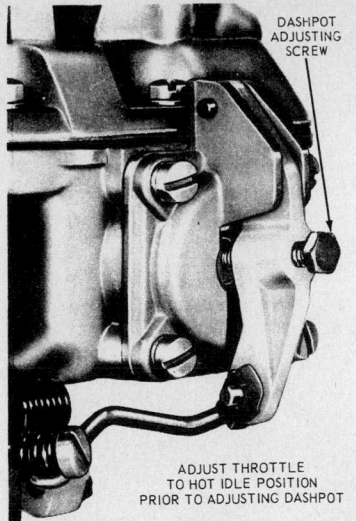

DASHPOT ADJUSTING SCREW

ADJUST THROTTLE TO HOT IDLE POSITION PRIOR TO ADJUSTING DASHPOT

Dashpot— 1965-67 6 cylinder
(© Ford Motor Co.)

straight pipe that runs directly rearward from the exhaust manifold; on V8s with single exhaust, the inlet pipe is a Y-shaped pipe that joins the pipes coming from each manifold into a common pipe, on V8s with dual exhaust, the inlet pipe is an H-shaped pipe in which each exhaust manifold has its own complete exhaust system, but is joined together with a balance tube at the inlet pipe to equalize pressure.

To replace any component of the exhaust system, simply remove the clamp(s) or flange(s) that attach it to the pipe(s) or manifold(s) it mounts to. Remove the attaching parts from the exhaust system hangers and lower the exhaust system. Using a torch or air chisel, separate the part to be replaced from the rest of the exhaust system.

NOTE: many inlet pipe extension-muffler assemblies are welded together; before removing any parts, determine if the replacement parts are serviced as an assembly or separately. If the service parts are sold separately, it will be necessary to cut the weld on the original parts and separate them.

Engine

The only 6-cylinder engine available on full size Ford products is the 240 cu. in. version. The intake manifolding on this six is mounted conventionally on the right-hand side and is detachable, unlike the intake manifolding on Ford sixes in smaller cars. The 289, 302, 351W V8 engines are the most popular engines in full sized Fords. The 289 and 302 are identical in exterior appearance and are notably compact, about 20 in. across. The larger displacement

Dashpot Adjustment

Model	Manual	Clearance (in.) Automatic
1965 two barrel carburetors		5/64
1965 four barrel carburetors		5/16
1966 two barrel carburetors		0.060 - 0.090
1966 four barrel carburetors		0.060 - 0.090
1967 289 2V with emission control		0.110 - 0.140
1967 390 2V with emission control		0.080 - 0.110
1967 390 4V with emission control		1/8
1967 428 4V with emission control		1/8
1967 428 Police with emission control		1/8
1968 240 Six without thermactor pump		0.080
1968 240 Six with thermactor pump		0.100
1968 302 2V		0.125
1968 390 2V		0.125
1968 390 4V		0.093
1968 428 4V		0.093
1968 428 Police with thermactor pump		0.109
1969 240 six	0.080	0.080
1969 302 2V	1/8	1/8
1969 351 2V	7/64	—
1969 351 4V	3/32	—
1969 390 2V	1/8	1/8
1969 390 4V	1/8	—
1969 428 Police	—	7/64
1969 429 2V	—	1/8
1969 429 4V	3/32	—
1970 240 1V		7/64
1971-72 240 1V		0.100
1970-72 302, 351, 429 2V		1/8
1970-72 429 4V		0.100

NOTE: many models are equipped with a solenoid instead of a dashpot.

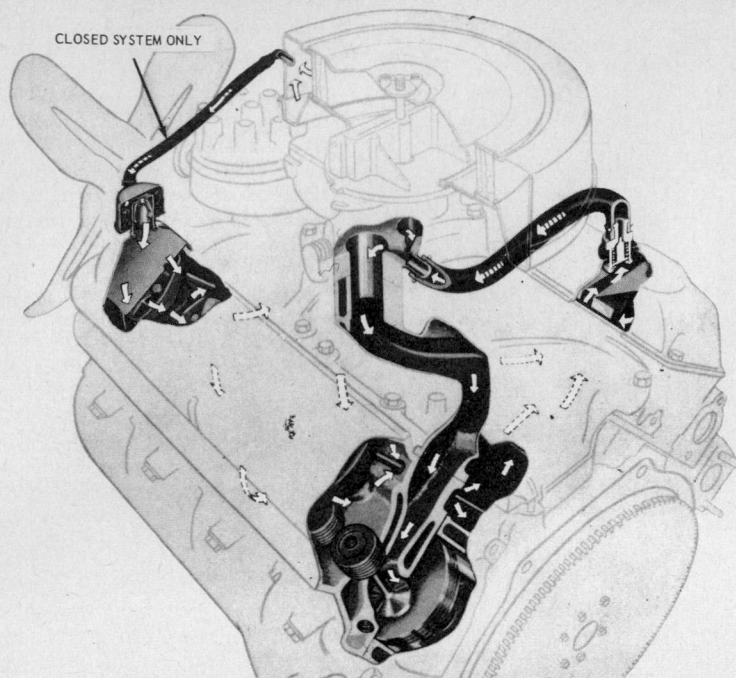

CLOSED SYSTEM ONLY

289 V8 positive crankcase ventilation system (© Ford Motor Co.)

351W is wider and bulkier although nearly identical in layout and conformation. All three have trapezoidal shaped valve covers. The 352, 390, 427 and 428 family of engines is recognizable by its unusual intake manifold that extends under valve covers. The engines of this family are identical in exterior appearance. These engines are used widely in full size Fords and the 390 engine was standard equipment in Thunderbirds from 1961 to 1968, with the 428 as an option in 1966 and 1967.

The 429 engine is the first of a new series of big block Ford engines. At present, it is available in two-barrel and four-barrel versions. The engine is identifiable by its great bulk, and by the tunnel port configuration noticeable in the shape of its intake manifold.

Exhaust Emission Control

In compliance with anti-pollution laws, the Ford Motor Company has adopted a distributor and a modified carburetor with some engine changes to reduce terminal exhaust fumes to an acceptable level. This method is known as Ford's Improved Combustion System (IMCO).

The plan supersedes (in most cases) the previous method used to conform to 1966-67 California laws. The new system phases out (except with stick shift and special purpose engine applications) the thermactor, or afterburner type of exhaust treatment.

The IMCO concept utilizes broader, yet more critical, distributor control and carburetor modification.

Since 1968, all car makers have posted idle speeds and other pertinent data relative to the specific engine application in a conspicuous place in the engine compartment.

Many post-1970 Ford engines are equipped with a distributor modulator system to reduce engine emissions. It consists of four major components: a speed sensor, a thermal switch, an electronic control amplifier and a three way solenoid valve. This is called the DISTOVAC system.

Detailed information on all emission control systems can be found in the Unit Repair Section in the rear of this book.

Engine Removal

1. Scribe the hood hinge outline on the underside of the hood, disconnect the hood and remove.
2. Drain the entire cooling system and oil from engine oil pan.
3. Remove the air cleaner, disconnect the battery at the cylinder head. On automatic transmission-equipped cars, disconnect oil cooler lines at the radiator.
4. Remove the upper and lower radiator hoses from the engine and, if the engine is equipped with a fan shroud, disconnect the shroud from the radiator and position it rearward. Remove the radiator from the car.
5. Remove the fan attaching screws and remove the fan, fan spacer and shroud from the engine as an assembly. Loosen and remove all drive belts.
6. Disconnect the heater hoses from the engine. If the vehicle is equipped with power steering, remove the pump from the engine and position it out of the way.

7. Remove the alternator mounting bolts and ground wire from the block and remove the alternator. Disconnect the carburetor and kickdown linkage from the engine.
8. On models with power brakes, remove the vacuum line from the engine. On cars with air conditioning, remove the compressor mounting bracket from the engine and position the compressor out of the way without disconnecting the refrigerant lines.
  NOTE: if the compressor lines do not have enough slack to move the compressor out of the way without disconnecting the refrigerant lines, the air conditioning system must be evacuated, using the required tools, before the refrigerant lines can be disconnected.
9. Disconnect fuel tank line at the fuel pump and plug the line.
10. Disconnect the coil primary wire at the coil. Disconnect wires at the oil pressure and water temperature-sending units.
11. Remove the starter and dust seal.
12. On a car equipped with a manual-shift transmission, remove the clutch retracting spring. Disconnect the clutch equalizer shaft and arm bracket at the underbody rail and remove the arm bracket and equalizer.
13. Raise the car. Remove the flywheel or converter housing upper retaining bolts through the access holes in the floor pan.
14. Disconnect the exhaust pipe or pipes at the exhaust manifold. Disconnect the right and left motor mount at the underbody bracket. Remove the flywheel or converter housing cover.
15. On a car with manual shift, remove the flywheel housing lower retaining bolts.
16. On a car with automatic transmission, disconnect throttle valve vacuum line at the intake manifold, disconnect the converter from the flywheel. Remove the converter housing lower retaining bolts. On a car with power steering, disconnect power steering pump from cylinder head. Remove drive belt and wire steering pump out of the way.
17. Lower the car. Support the transmission and flywheel or converter housing with a jack.
18. Attach an engine lifting hook. Lift the engine up and out of the compartment and onto an adequate work stand.

Engine Installation

1. Place a new gasket over the studs of the exhaust manifold/s except on 352, 390, 427 and 428 engines.
2. Attach engine sling and lifting device. Then lift engine from work stand.

3. Lower the engine into the engine compartment. Be sure the exhaust manifold/s properly line up with the muffler inlet pipe/s and the dowels in the block engage the holes in the flywheel housing.

On a car with automatic transmission, start the converter pilot into the crankshaft.

On a car with manual-shift transmission, start the transmission main drive gear into the clutch disc. If the engine hangs up after the shaft enters, rotate the crankshaft slowly (with transmission in gear) until the shaft and clutch disc splines mesh.

4. Install the flywheel or converter housing upper bolts.

5. Install engine support insulator to bracket retaining nuts. Disconnect engine lifting sling and remove lifting brackets.

6. Raise front of car. Connect exhaust line/s and tighten attachments.

7. Position dust seal and install starter.

8. On cars with manual-shift transmissions, install remaining flywheel housing-to-engine bolts. Connect clutch release rod. Position the clutch equalizer bar and bracket and install retaining bolts. Install clutch pedal retracting spring.

9. On cars with automatic transmissions, remove the retainer holding the converter in the housing. Attach the converter to the flywheel. Install the converter housing inspection cover. Install the remaining converter housing retaining bolts.

10. Remove the support from the transmission and lower the car.

11. Connect engine ground strap and coil primary wire.

12. Connect water temperature gauge wire and the heater hose at coolant outlet housing. Connect accelerator rod at the bellcrank.

13. On cars with automatic transmission, connect the transmission filler tube bracket. Connect the throttle valve vacuum line.

14. On cars with power steering, install the drive belt and power steering pump bracket. Install the bracket retaining bolts. Adjust drive belt to proper tension.

15. Remove plug from the fuel tank line. Connect the flexible fuel line and the oil pressure sending unit wire.

16. Install the pulley, belt spacer, and fan. Adjust belt tension.

17. Install the alternator and the negative battery cable.

18. In vehicles with power brakes, connect vacuum line at intake manifold. On cars with air conditioning, install compressor on mounting bracket.

19. Install radiator. Connect radiator hoses.

20. On cars with automatic transmissions, connect oil cooler lines.

21. Install oil filter. Connect heater hose at water pump, after bleeding the system.

22. Bring crankcase to level with correct grade of oil. Run engine at fast idle and check for leaks. Install air cleaner and make final engine adjustments.

23. Install and adjust hood.

24. Road test car.

Engine Manifolds

Intake and Exhaust Manifold Removal—All 6-Cylinder

1. Remove the air cleaner. Remove the carburetor linkage and kick down linkage from the engine.

2. Disconnect the fuel line from the carburetor and all vacuum lines from the manifolds.

3. Remove the negative battery cable, then remove the alternator mounting bolts and remove the alternator from the engine with the wires attached.

4. Disconnect the muffler inlet pipe from the engine.

5. Remove the manifold attaching parts from the engine, and remove the two manifolds as an assembly.

6. To separate the manifolds, remove the carburetor and then remove the nuts that secure the manifolds together.

7. Clean all gasket areas and reverse above procedure to install; using all new gaskets.

Intake Manifold Removal—All V8

1. Drain the cooling system.

2. Disconnect the upper radiator hose from the thermostat housing and the bypass hose from the manifold.

3. Remove the air cleaner and ducts.

4. Remove the distributor cap and wires from the engine. Mark the position of the distributor rotor in relationship to the intake manifold, remove the primary wire from the coil, then remove the distributor hold-down bolt and the distributor.

5. Remove all vacuum lines from the intake manifold and remove the temperature sending unit wire.

6. Disconnect the fuel line and any vacuum lines from the carburetor.

7. Remove all carburetor linkage and kickdown linkage that attaches to the intake manifold.

8. On 352, 390, 427 and 428 engines, remove the valve covers, the rocker arm assemblies and the pushrods. The rocker arms should be removed by backing off each of the four bolts two turns in sequence from front to back. Keep pushrods in order so that they can be installed in their original position.

9. Remove the manifold attaching bolts and remove the manifold. If it is necessary to pry the manifold to loosen it from the engine, use care not to damage any gasket sealing surfaces.

10. Clean all gasket surfaces and firmly cement new gaskets in place. The gaskets should be securely locked in place before attempting to install the manifold.

11. Reverse above procedure to reinstall.

Exhaust Manifold Removal—All V8

1. If the right-side manifold is to be removed, disconnect the choke heat tube, remove the air cleaner and ducts.

2. On models with 427 V8, to remove the left manifold, remove the clutch linkage and brackets from the engine block. If the right side is to be removed, disconnect and lower the idler arm, and remove the motor support attaching nuts and raise the engine several inches.

3. On 1965 Thunderbirds, to remove the left manifold, remove the power steering pump and dipstick tube.

4. On 1966 Thunderbirds, to remove the right manifold, disconnect and remove the starter and disconnect the engine supports so the engine can be raised several inches to gain clearance.

5. On vehicles with 351C and 400 V8s, to remove the left manifold, remove the oil filter. If equipped with an automatic transmission remove the transmission selector lever cross-shaft from the engine block. If equipped with a manual transmission, disconnect the

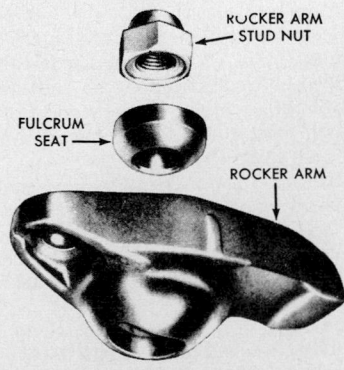

Rocker arm—1965-69 6 cyl. and 289 cu. in. V8

(© Ford Motor Co.)

equalizer shaft bracket and clutch linkage from the engine.

6. Disconnect the manifolds from the muffler inlet pipes.

7. If the manifold attaching bolts are installed with locking washers, bend back the tabs on the washers.

8. Remove the manifold to cylinder head attaching bolts, and remove the manifolds from the car.

9. Clean all gasket surfaces, and reverse above procedure to install; using all new gaskets.

Cylinder Head

6-Cylinder Head Removal

1. Drain coolant and remove air cleaner. Disconnect battery cable at cylinder head.

2. Disconnect exhaust pipe at manifold.

3. Disconnect accelerator retracting spring, choke control cable and accelerator rod at carburetor.

4. Disconnect fuel line and distributor control vacuum line at the carburetor.

5. Disconnect coolant tubes from carburetor spacer. Disconnect coolant and heater hoses.

6. Disconnect distributor control vacuum line at distributor and fuel inlet line at the filter. Remove lines as an assembly.

7. On an engine equipped with positive crankcase ventilation, disconnect the emission exhaust tube.

8. Disconnect spark plug wires at the plugs and the small wire from the temperature-sending unit. On an engine equipped with an exhaust emission control system, disconnect the air pump hose at the air manifold assembly. Unscrew the tube nuts and remove the air manifold. Disconnect the anti-backfire valve air and vacuum lines at the intake manifold. On a car equipped with power brakes, disconnect the brake vacuum line at the intake manifold.

9. Remove rocker arm cover.

10. On 240 cu. in. engines, loosen the rocker arm stud nut so that the rocker arm can be rotated to one side. Remove valve pushrods and keep them in sequence.

11. Remove one cylinder-head bolt from each end and install two 7/16 in. x 14 guide studs.

12. Remove remaining cylinder head bolts, then remove cylinder head.

6-Cylinder Head Installation

1. Clean head and block surfaces.

2. Apply sealer to both sides of head gasket. Position gasket over guide studs or dowel pins.

NOTE: apply gasket sealer only to steel shim head gaskets. Steel-asbestos composite head gaskets are to be installed without any sealer.

3. Install new gasket on the exhaust pipe flange.

4. Lift the cylinder head over the guide studs and slide it carefully into place while guiding the exhaust manifold studs into the exhaust pipe flange.

5. Coat cylinder-head attaching bolts with water-resistant sealer and install (but do not tighten) the head bolts.

6. Torque the head, in proper sequence, and in three progressive steps to 75 ft. lbs.

7. Lubricate both ends of the pushrods and insert them in their original bores and sockets.

8. Lubricate valve stem tips and rocker arm pads.

9. On engines beginning 1965, position the rocker arms and tighten the stud nuts enough to hold the pushrods in position. Adjust valve lash, as outlined later.

10. Do a preliminary, cold, valve lash adjustment.

11. Install exhaust pipe-to-manifold nuts and lockwashers. Torque to 17-22 ft. lbs.

12. Connect radiator and heater hoses. Connect coolant tubes at the carburetor spacer.

13. Connect distributor vacuum line and the carburetor fuel line. Connect battery cable to cylinder head.

14. On engines equipped with positive crankcase ventilation, clean components thoroughly and install.

NOTE: on engines equipped with an exhaust emission control system, install the air manifold assembly on the cylinder head. Connect the air pump outlet hose to the air manifold. Connect the anti-backfire valve, air and vacuum lines to the intake manifold.

15. Connect accelerator rod pull-back spring. Connect choke control cable and the accelerator rod at the carburetor.

16. Connect distributor control vacuum line at distributor. Connect carburetor fuel line at fuel filter.

17. Connect temperature - sending unit wire at sending unit. Connect spark plug wires.

18. Completely fill and bleed the cooling system.

19. Run engine for a minimum of 30 minutes at 1200 rpm to stabilize engine temperature. Then, check for coolant and oil leaks.

20. Adjust engine idle mixture and speed. Check valve lash and adjust, if necessary.

21. Install valve rocker arm cover, then the air cleaner.

V8 Heads, 352, 390, 427, 428, Removal

1. Remove intake manifold as previously described.

2. Remove any remaining accessories.

3. Disconnect the muffler inlet pipes from the manifolds.

4. Unbolt and remove heads.

V8 Heads, 289, 302, 351 and 429 cu. in., Removal

1. Remove the intake manifold and carburetor as an assembly.

2. Remove rocker arm covers.

3. On cars equipped with air conditioning, isolate and remove the compressor.

4. If the left cylinder head is involved on a car with power steering, remove the steering pump and bracket and remove the drive belt: Tie assembly out of the way.

5. If the left cylinder head is involved on a car equipped with exhaust emission control system, disconnect the hose from the air manifold on the left cylinder head.

6. If the right head is involved, remove the alternator mounting bracket bolt and spacer, ignition coil and air cleaner inlet duct from the right cylinder head.

7. If the right cylinder head is to be removed on an engine equipped with an exhaust emission control system, remove the air pump and bracket. Disconnect the hose from the right cylinder head.

8. Disconnect the exhaust manifold/s at the exhaust pipe/s.

9. Loosen rocker arm stud nuts so that the arms can rotate to the side to clear the pushrods. Remove the pushrods. On 351 engines, remove exhaust manifold to get access to lower cylinder head bolts.

10. Remove cylinder-head bolts and lift off cylinder head.

V8 Heads Installation

Reverse above procedure, (see valve lash adjustment under Valve System, in the following paragraphs).

Valve System

All engines used in full-size Ford products, with the exception of the 1965-66 427 V8, are equipped with hydraulic valve lifters. Valve systems with hydraulic valve lifters operate with zero clearance in the valve train, and because of this the rocker arms are nonadjustable. The only means by which valve system clearances can be altered is by installing

.060 in. over- or undersize pushrods; but, because of the hydraulic lifter's natural ability to compensate for slack in the valve train, all components of the valve system should be checked for wear if there is excessive play in the system.

When a valve in the engine is in the closed position, the valve lifter is resting on the base circle of the camshaft lobe and the pushrod is in its lowest position. To remove this additional clearance from the valve train, the valve lifter expands to maintain zero clearance in the valve system. When a rocker arm is loosened or removed from the engine, the lifter expands to its fullest travel. When the rocker arm is reinstalled on the engine, the proper valve setting is obtained by tightening the rocker arm to a specified limit. But with the lifter fully expanded, if the camshaft lobe is on a high point it will require excessive torque to compress the lifter and obtain the proper setting. Because of this, when any component of the valve system has been removed, a preliminary valve adjustment procedure must be followed to ensure that when the rocker arm is reinstalled on the engine and tightened, the camshaft lobe for that cylinder is in the low position.

Preliminary Valve Adjustment

6-Cylinder

1. Crank the engine until the TDC mark on the crankshaft damper is aligned with timing pointer on the cylinder front cover.
2. Scribe a mark on the damper at this point.
3. Scribe two more marks on the damper, each equally spaced from the first mark (see illustration).
4. With the engine on TDC of the compression stroke, (mark A aligned with the pointer) back off the rocker arm adjusting nut until there is end-play in the pushrod. Tighten the adjusting nut until all clearance is removed, then tighten the adjust-

ing nut one additional turn on 1969 and later models and ¾ of a turn on all 1965-68. To determine when all clearance is removed from the rocker arm, turn the pushrod with the fingers. When the pushrod can no longer be turned, all clearance has been removed.

5. Repeat this procedure for each valve, turning the crankshaft 1/3 turn to the next mark each time and following the engine firing order of 1-5-3-6-2-4.

289 and 1968-69 302 V8

NOTE: this procedure for the 289 and early 302 V8 engines is designed for engines in which the rocker arm mounting studs do *not* incorporate a positive stop shoulder on the mounting stud. These engines were originally equipped with this kind of stud. However, due to production differences, it is possible some 289 or early 302 engines may be encountered that *are* equipped with positive stop rocker arm mounting studs. Before following this procedure, verify that the rocker arm mounting studs do not incorporate a positive stop shoulder. On studs without a positive stop, the shank portion of the stud that is exposed just above the cylinder head is the same diameter as the threaded portion, at the top of the stud, to which the rocker arm retaining nut attaches. If the shank portion of the stud is of greater diameter than the threaded portion, this identifies it as a positive stop rocker arm stud and the procedure for the 351 engine should be followed.

1. Crank the engine until #1 cylinder is at TDC of the compression stroke and the timing pointer is aligned with the mark on the crankshaft damper.
2. Scribe a mark on the damper at this point.
3. Scribe three more marks on the damper, dividing the damper into quarters (see illustration).
4. With mark A aligned with the timing pointer, adjust the valves on #1 cylinder by backing off

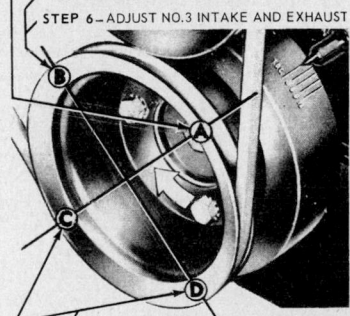

STEP 1—SET NO. 1 PISTON ON T.D.C. AT END OF COMPRESSION STROKE ADJUST NO. 1 INTAKE AND EXHAUST

STEP 4— ADJUST NO. 6 INTAKE AND EXHAUST

STEP 2— ADJUST NO. 5 INTAKE AND EXHAUST

STEP 3— ADJUST NO. 3 INTAKE AND EXHAUST

STEP 5— ADJUST NO. 2 INTAKE AND EXHAUST

STEP 6— ADJUST NO. 4 INTAKE AND EXHAUST

Position of crankshaft for valve adjustment —6 cylinder
(© Ford Motor Co.)

STEP 1—SET NO.1 PISTON ON T.D.C. AT END OF COMPRESSION STROKE —ADJUST NO.1 INTAKE AND EXHAUST

STEP 5— ADJUST NO.6 INTAKE AND EXHAUST

STEP 2— ADJUST NO.5 INTAKE AND EXHAUST

STEP 6— ADJUST NO.3 INTAKE AND EXHAUST

STEP 4— ADJUST NO.2 INTAKE AND EXHAUST

STEP 8— ADJUST NO.8 INTAKE AND EXHAUST

STEP 3— ADJUST NO.4 INTAKE AND EXHAUST

STEP 7— ADJUST NO.7 INTAKE AND EXHAUST

Position of crankshaft for valve adjustment —289 V8
(© Ford Motor Co.)

With No. 1 at TDC at end of compression stroke make a chalk mark at points B and C approximately 90 degrees apart.

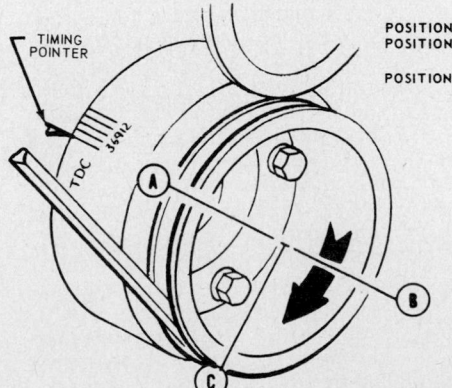

TIMING POINTER

POSITION A — No. 1 at TDC at end of compression stroke.
POSITION B — Rotate the crankshaft 180 degrees (one half revolution) clockwise from POSITION A.
POSITION C — Rotate the crankshaft 270 degrees (three quarter revolution) clockwise from POSITION B.

Position of crankshaft for valve adjustment—302, 351, 400 and 429 V8
(© Ford Motor Co.)

the adjusting nut until the push-rod has free play in it. Then, tighten the nut until there is no free play in the rocker arm. This can be determined by turning the pushrod while tightening the nut; when the pushrod can no longer be turned, all clearance has been removed. After the clearance has been removed, tighten the nut an additional ¾ of a turn.

5. Repeat this procedure for each valve, turning the crankshaft ¼ turn to the next mark each time and following the engine firing order of 1-5-4-2-6-3-7-8.

351, 400, 429 and 1970-72 302 V8

1. Crank the engine until #1 cylinder is at TDC of the compression stroke and the timing pointer is aligned with the mark on the crankshaft damper.
2. Scribe a mark on the damper at this point.
3. Scribe two additional marks on the damper (see illustration).
4. With the timing pointer aligned with mark A on the damper, tighten the following valves to the specified torque:
   302 and 429- No. 1, 7 and 8 Intake; No. 1, 5 and 4 Exhaust
   351 and 400- No. 1, 4 and 8 Intake; No. 1, 3 and 7 Exhaust
5. Rotate the crankshaft 180° to point B and tighten the following valves:
   302 and 429- No. 5 and 4 Intake; No. 2 and 6 Exhaust
   351 and 400- No. 3 and 7 Intake; No. 2 and 6 Exhaust
6. Rotate the crankshaft 270° to point C and tighten the following valves:
   302 and 429- No. 2, 3 and 6 Intake; No. 7, 3 and 8 Exhaust
   351 and 400- No. 2, 5 and 6 Intake; No. 4, 5 and 8 Exhaust
7. Rocker arm tighten specifications are: 302 and 351W—tight-

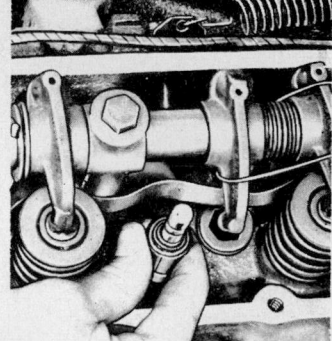

Valve stem seal removal
(© Ford Motor Co.)

en nut until it contacts the rocker shoulder, then torque to 18-20 ft. lbs.; 351C and 400—tighten bolt to 18-25 ft. lbs.; 429—tighten nut until it contacts rocker shoulder, then torque to 18-22 ft. lbs.

352, 390, 428 and 1967 427

1. Position the left rocker arm and oil deflector assembly on the head, making sure the oversize bolt is installed in the second rocker arm stand from the front of the engine.
2. Install each rocker arm stand attaching bolt finger tight, then, working from the front of the engine back, tighten each bolt two turns at a time until the rocker arm is mounted on the head.
3. Torque the bolts to 40-45 ft. lbs.
4. Position the right rocker arm and oil deflector assembly on the head, making sure the oversize bolt is installed in the third rocker arm stand from the front of the engine.
5. Repeat Steps 2 and 3 on the right side, this time working from the rear of the engine forward.

Mechanical Adjustable Valve Adjustment—Primary Step

1. Make primary valve adjustment in the following manner, and continue to install rocker covers and fill cooling system.
   NOTE: tappets must be adjusted while on the low radius of the cam.
2. If the distributor has not been disturbed and ignition timing is reasonably correct, proceed as follows: rotate crankshaft until the distributor rotor points to No. 1 plug wire tower of the distributor cap. Adjust valves in cylinder firing order according to rotor position.
3. If the distributor is out of time or has been removed from the engine: turn the crankshaft until No. 1 piston is at the top of its compression stroke, (intake valve of No. 6 cylinder just beginning to open), and the crankshaft damper is on T.D.C. Make three chalk marks on the crankshaft damper, 120° apart, starting with T.D.C. These marks will divide crankshaft travel into three parts, or six segments, of each engine cycle. Valve adjustment can then be made in firing sequence, beginning with No. 1 on T.D.C. and progressing through the regular order of firing by advancing one chalk mark, (120 crankshaft degrees) at a time.

Mechanical Adjustable Valves Adjustment—Final Step

NOTE: be sure engine is at regular operating temperature by running at least thirty minutes.

1. With engine idling, check valve clearance with a feeler gauge. Adjust clearance, if necessary, to .016 in. (hot) for both intake and exhaust.

⏻ CHILTON TIME-SAVER

Tappet Removal

To remove and replace tappets from 352, 390, 427, and 428 engines without removing the intake manifold, first remove rocker covers and rocker assembly. Then remove pushrods from their bores. Locate tappet or tappets to be moved by shining a light through pushrod bores. Use a magnet or claw tool to seize tappet and withdraw it through pushrod bore. It may be necessary on some tappets to move them over and draw them through a larger adjoining pushrod bore, but tappets should always be replaced in their original holes.

Valve Guides

Valve guides on all engines are an integral part of the cylinder head casting. If valve guides become worn, they can be reamed oversize or bronze replacement bushings can be installed. Oversize valves are available with stem diameters .003, .015, and .030 in. larger than standard. If the guides are to be reamed more than .003 in. oversize, they must be reamed in steps starting with .003 in. and progressing until the desired diameter is achieved.

NOTE: when valve guides become worn, the excessive clearance between the valve and the head can allow the valve to tap on the cylinder head and emit a noise very similar to the noise a defective valve lifter emits. When checking the valve system to locate a noise, and the lifters are not defective and no excessive clearances exist in the valve train, the valve guides should be checked for wear.

Timing Case

Timing Gear Cover Removal

6-Cylinder Engines

1. Drain the cooling system and the crankcase.
2. Remove the radiator from the car.
3. Loosen and remove all engine drive belts.

4. On vehicles with power steering, disconnect the pump mounting bracket from the cylinder front cover and position the pump and bracket out of the way.

5. On models with air conditioning, remove the condenser mounting bolts and position the condenser out of the way. *Do not disconnect the refrigerant lines.*

6. Disconnect and remove the fan and fan spacer.

7. Remove any accessory drive pulleys from the crankshaft damper. Remove the capscrew and washer from the crankshaft end; then, using a puller, remove the crankshaft damper.

8. Remove the alternator adjusting arm bolt and position the arm out of the way.

9. Remove the starter cable and attaching bolts, and remove the starter.

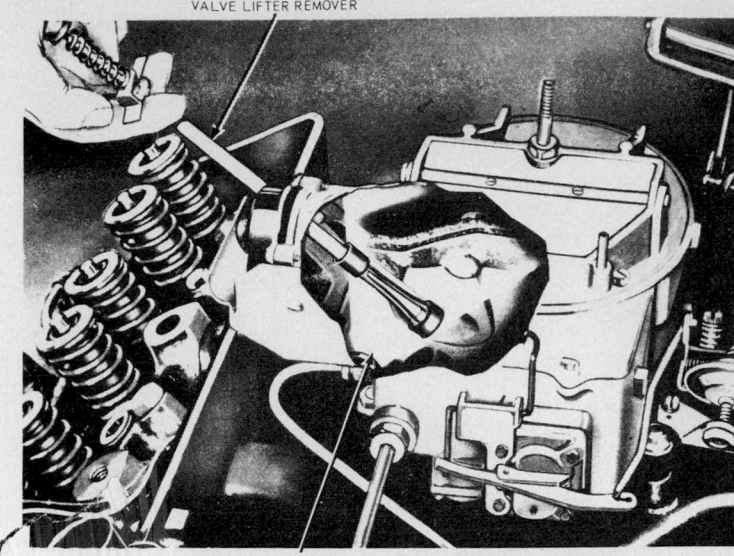

Removing valve lifter—intake manifold installed (© Ford Motor Co.)

⏱ CHILTON TIME-SAVER

Frequently valves become bent or warped, or their seats become blocked with carbon or other material. Left unattended, these situations can cause burnt valves, damaged cylinder heads and other expensive trouble. To detect leaking valves early, perform this test whenever the cylinder head is removed.

1. **After removing head, replace spark plugs. Removing spark plugs before removing heads eliminates breakage.**

2. **Place head on bench with valves, springs, retainers, and keys installed—combustion chambers up.**

3. **Pour enough gasoline into each combustion chamber to completely cover both valves. Watch combustion chambers for two minutes for any air bubbles that indicate leakage.**

10. Remove the engine front support insulator to intermediate support bracket nuts on both supports. Remove the engine rear support insulator to crossmember bolt and insulator to transmission extension housing bolts. Raise the transmission and remove the support insulator. Lower the transmission to the crossmember.

11. Raise the engine and place 2 in. thick blocks of wood between both supports and brackets.

12. Remove the oil pan bolts, and lower the oil pan. Reach inside the oil pan and remove the two oil pump to block bolts, and lower the pump and screen into

the pan. Turn the crankshaft as required to gain clearance and remove the oil pan.

13. Remove the front cover attaching bolts and remove the cover from the engine.

14. Reverse above procedure to install.

Timing Gear and/or Camshaft Replacement

6-Cylinder

1. Remove the timing case cover.

2. Mark the location of the grille center support and hood lock assembly in relation to the radiator support. Remove the grille, center support, and hood lock as an assembly.

3. Remove the air cleaner and valve cover.

4. Disconnect the fuel pump outlet line and remove the fuel pump from the engine.

5. Loosen the rocker arm nuts and position the rocker arms to the side so the pushrods can be removed. Keep the pushrods in order so that they can be returned to their original location in the engine.

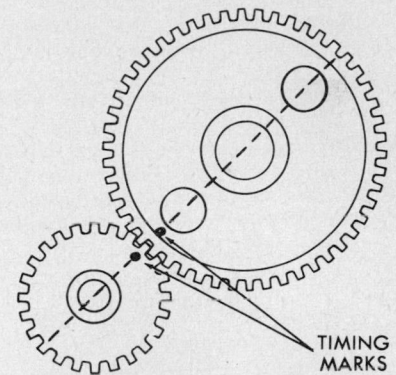

Timing mark alignment—240 6 cyl.

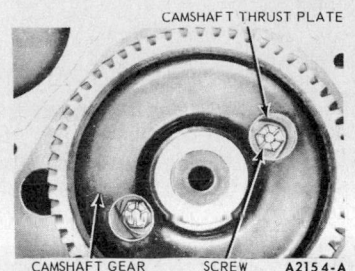

Camshaft gear removal—240 cu. in. 6 cyl. (© Ford Motor Co.)

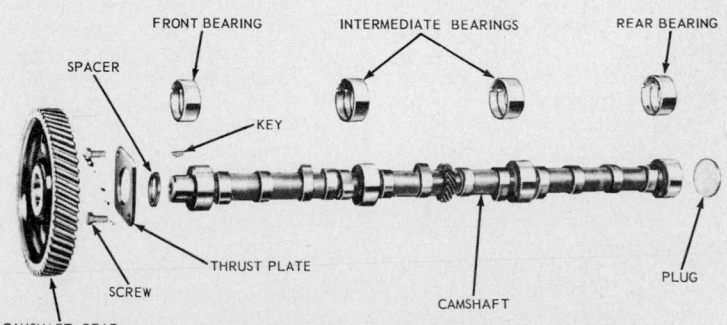

Camshaft and related parts—240 cu. in. 6 cyl. (© Ford Motor Co.)

6. Remove the pushrod cover from the side of the engine, and, using a magnet, remove the lifters from their bores. Keep the lifters in order so they can be returned to their original location in the engine.

7. Rotate the engine until the timing marks are aligned on the timing gears.

8. Remove the camshaft thrust plate screws.

9. Remove the camshaft by pulling it out the front of the engine. Use care not to damage the camshaft lobes or journals while removing the cam from the engine.

10. Place the camshaft/gear assembly in a press and press the cam from the gear.

11. Position new gear on camshaft and press into position.

12. Using a puller, remove the crankshaft timing gear.

13. Using a suitable tool, press the new gear onto the crankshaft.

14. Before installing the camshaft in the engine, coat the lobes with Lubriplate and the journals and all valve train components with heavy oil.

15. Reverse above procedure to install, following recommended torque settings and performing preliminary valve adjustment before starting engine.

Tool—T64T-6306-A
Tool—T65L-6306-A   A2152-A

Camshaft gear installation—240 cu. in. 6 cyl.
(© Ford Motor Co.)

V8 Cover and Chain

Removal

1. Drain the cooling system and crankcase.

2. Disconnect the negative battery cable.

3. If equipped with a fan shroud, disconnect it from the radiator and position it rearward.

4. Remove the radiator. Remove the fuel pump.

5. Remove the fan attaching bolts, remove the fan, fan spacer and shroud from the engine.

6. Loosen and remove all engine drive belts.

7. Remove the power steering pump mounting bracket and position the pump and bracket out of the way.

8. If equipped with air conditioning, remove the compressor and condenser and position them out of the way. *Do not disconnect the refrigerant lines.*

9. Disconnect the alternator adjusting arm from the engine and position it out of the way.

10. If equipped with Thermactor, remove the pump from the engine.

11. Disconnect the heater hose and bypass hose from the water pump.

12. Remove any accessory drive pulleys from the crankshaft damper and remove the crankshaft front

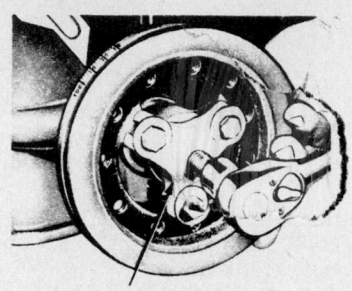

Removing crankshaft damper
(© Ford Motor Co.)

bolt and washer.

13. Using a puller, remove the crankshaft damper from the engine.

14. On 352, 390, 427 and 428 V8, use a suitable tool to pull the crankshaft sleeve away from the cylinder front cover. Remove the sleeve from the engine.

15. Remove the front cover attaching bolts and the front oil pan bolts.

16. Remove the cover from the engine.

17. Remove the crankshaft front oil slinger.

18. To check timing chain free play, rotate the crankshaft in a clockwise direction until all slack is removed from the left side of the chain. Scribe a mark on the engine parallel to the present position of the chain. Next, rotate the crankshaft in a counterclockwise direction to remove all the slack from the right side of the chain. Force the left side of the chain outward with the fingers and measure the distance between the present position of the chain and the reference mark on the engine. If the distance exceeds ½ in., replace the chain and sprockets.

19. To replace the chain and sprockets, crank the engine until the timing marks are aligned as shown in the illustration.

20. Remove the camshaft sprocket attaching bolt and remove the chain and sprockets from the engine by sliding them forward as an assembly.

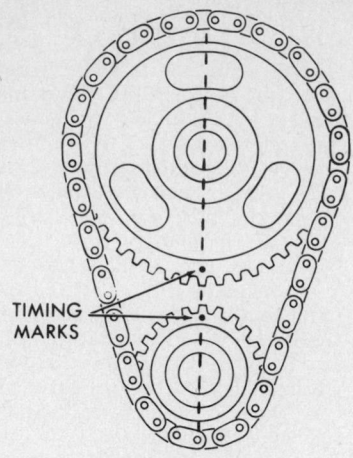

TIMING MARKS

Timing mark alignment— V8 front mounted distributor

Installation

1. Position the chain and sprockets on the engine, making sure that the timing marks on the sprockets are aligned.

2. Clean all gasket surfaces. Trim away the exposed portion of the oil pan gasket flush with the front of the block.

3. Cut and position the required portion of a new gasket to the oil pan, applying sealer to both sides of it.

4. Reinstall the front cover, applying oil resistant sealer to the new gasket.

5. Install the components that were removed from the engine by reversing the removal procedure.

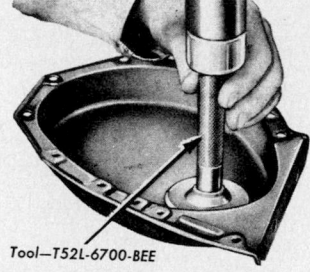

Tool—T52L-6700-BEE

Timing case oil seal installation—6 cyl.
(© Ford Motor Co.)

Timing Case Oil Seal Replacement

All Models

To replace the oil seal, it is necessary to take off the timing case cover and drive the seal out with a pin punch. Clean out the recess in the cover and install a new seal using a special driving tool.

Coat the new seal with grease to reduce friction when installing and starting the car.

V8 Camshaft Replacement

1. Remove the intake manifold.

2. Remove the cylinder front cover, timing chain and sprockets as outlined previously.

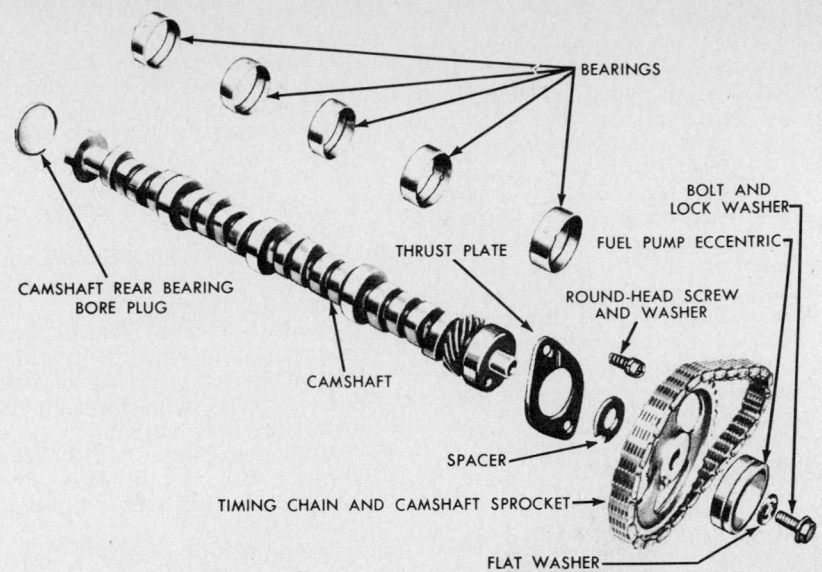

V8 camshaft and related parts (© Ford Motor Co.)

3. Remove the rocker arm covers.
4. On 352, 390, 427 and 428 engines it is necessary to remove the rocker arm shafts to remove the intake manifold. On all other engines with individual rocker arms, loosen the rocker arm fulcrum bolts and rotate the rocker arms to the side.
5. Remove the pushrods and lifters and keep them in order so that they can be installed in their original location.
6. Remove the camshaft thrust plate and washer if so equipped. Remove the camshaft from the front of the engine. On certain engine/chassis combinations it may be necessary to remove the grille to gain adequate clearance to remove the camshaft. Use care not to damage the camshaft lobes or journals while removing the cam from the engine.
7. Before installing the camshaft in the engine, coat the lobes with Lubriplate and the journals and all valve train components with heavy oil.
8. Reverse above procedure to install.
9. On all engines with individually mounted rocker arms, a preliminary valve adjustment must be performed before starting the engine.

Engine Lubrication

6 Cylinder—No Oil Pressure

Some instances of no oil pressure have occurred on the 6-cylinder engine.

Design characteristics and wear bring about the failure responsible for this condition.

The gear-type oil pump is entirely within the crankcase, in line with,

and driven by, the distributor gear through a hex shaft.

This shaft is pinned in the lower end of the distributor driveshaft by a roll pin. The bottom end of the hex shaft seats in the female end of the oil pump drive. It is possible for the roll pin to shear or work out of place. This will allow the hex driveshaft to slip down and out of the distributor drive and cause oil pump failure.

Oil Pan Removal

1965-72—6 Cylinder

1. Drain crankcase and cooling system.
2. Disconnect upper hose at outlet elbow and lower hose at radiator. Remove radiator.
3. Disconnect flexible fuel line at fuel pump.
4. With automatic transmission, disconnect kickdown rod at bell-crank assembly. On car with standard transmission, disconnect clutch linkage.
5. Raise car on hoist.
6. Disconnect starter cable at starter. Remove retaining bolts and remove starter.
7. Remove nuts on both engine front support insulator-to-support bracket.
8. Remove bolt and insulator, rear support insulator-to-crossmember and insulator-to-transmission extension housing.
9. Raise transmission, remove support insulator, lower transmission to crossmember.
10. Raise engine with transmission jack and place 3-in. thick wood blocks between both front support insulators and intermediate support brackets.
11. Remove oil pan retaining bolts and oil pump mounting bolts. With oil pump in pan, rotate

crankshaft as needed to remove pan.
12. Install in reverse of above.

CHILTON TIME-SAVER

In the event of no-oil-pressure, remove the distributor and check the condition of this hex drive. If the above situation exists, it may be possible to recover the hex shaft with the aid of a magnet or a mechanical finger tool. If recovery is possible, the shaft can be reattached to the distributor with a new roll pin. The alternative is to drop the oil pan and remove the oil pump to retrieve the hex.

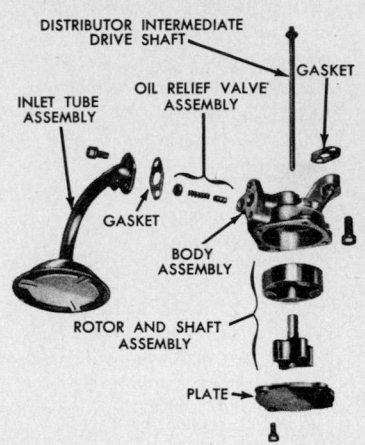

Oil pump for V8 with distributor at the front (© Ford Motor Co.)

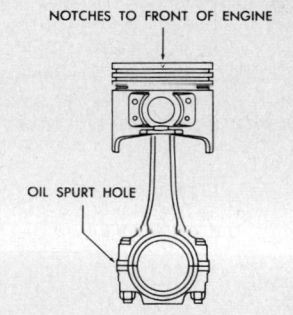

Piston and rod assembly—6 cyl.

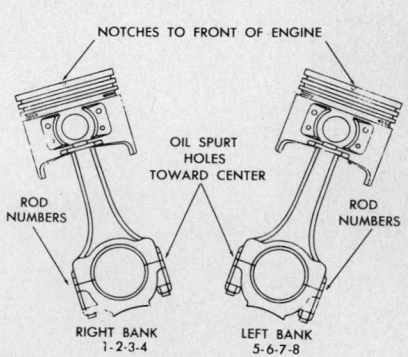

Piston and rod assembly—V8

1965-72—289, 302, 351 Cu. In. V8

1. Remove oil level dipstick. Drain oil pan.
2. Disconnect stabilizer bar from lower control arms, and pull ends down.
3. Remove oil pan attaching bolts and position pan on front cross-member.
4. Remove one oil inlet tube bolt and loosen the other to position tube out of way to remove pan.
5. Turn crankshaft as required for clearance to remove pan.
6. Install in reverse of above.

1965-72—V8s Except 289, 302, 351 Cu. In.

1. Raise car and place safety stands in position. Drain oil from crankcase.
2. Disconnect stabilizer bar links and pull ends down. On models equipped with a fan shroud, remove the shroud from the radiator and position it rearward over the fan.
3. Remove nuts and lockwashers from engine front support insulator-to-intermediate support bracket.
4. Install block of wood on jack and position jack under leading edge of pan.
5. Raise engine approximately 1¼ in. and insert a 1-in. block between insulators and crossmember. Remove floor jack.
6. Remove oil pan attaching screws and lower pan to frame cross-member.
7. Turn crankshaft to obtain clearance between crankshaft counterweight and rear of pan.
8. Remove oil pump attaching bolts.
9. Position tube and screen out of the way and remove the pan.
10. Install in reverse of above.

Connecting Rods and Pistons

Removal

All Models

Take off the cylinder heads and oil

pan. Select the pistons in the down position and, using a good cylinder ridge reamer, remove the ridge from the top of these cylinders. Turn the crankshaft and repeat this reaming operation until all of the cylinders have been ridge-reamed.

From underneath the car, remove the two bolts from the connecting rod cap on the rods that are in the down position. Push the connecting rod and piston assembly part way up the bore and immediately replace the cap on the bottom of the connecting rod. This is to eliminate the possibility of losing the bearing or getting the caps mixed up.

Inspection of Pistons

All Models

Carefully inspect the pistons, particularly the thrust face, for scratches or scores. Do not confuse an ordinary wear pattern with scoring. Scoring on the piston is generally accompanied by a comparable scoring on the cylinder walls, whereas the wear pattern usually leaves a perfectly smooth and, in fact, somewhat glassy cylinder wall.

Cylinders showing the slightest scoring will have to be rebored and pistons with scores will have to be resized or replaced.

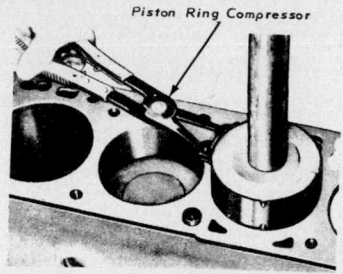

Piston Ring Compressor

Installing piston (© Ford Motor Co.)

Installation of Pistons

1. Coat the piston, rings, and cylinder wall with light engine oil.
2. With bearing caps removed, install pieces of protective rubber hose on each bearing cap bolt to prevent them from scoring any internal engine parts during installation.
3. Using a piston ring compressor tool, install each piston in the bore it was removed from.
4. Remove the thread guards from the connecting rods, position the upper bearing insert on the rod, and carefully guide the rod onto the crankshaft journal.
5. Install the lower half of the bearing cap and insert on the crankshaft and tighten to specification.
6. Check connecting rod side clearance.

Piston Rings

Replacement

Each piston is fitted with 3 piston rings: an upper and lower compres-

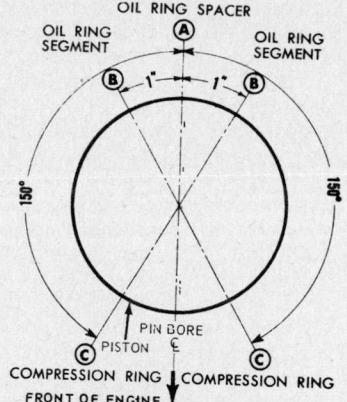

Piston ring spacing (© Ford Motor Co.)

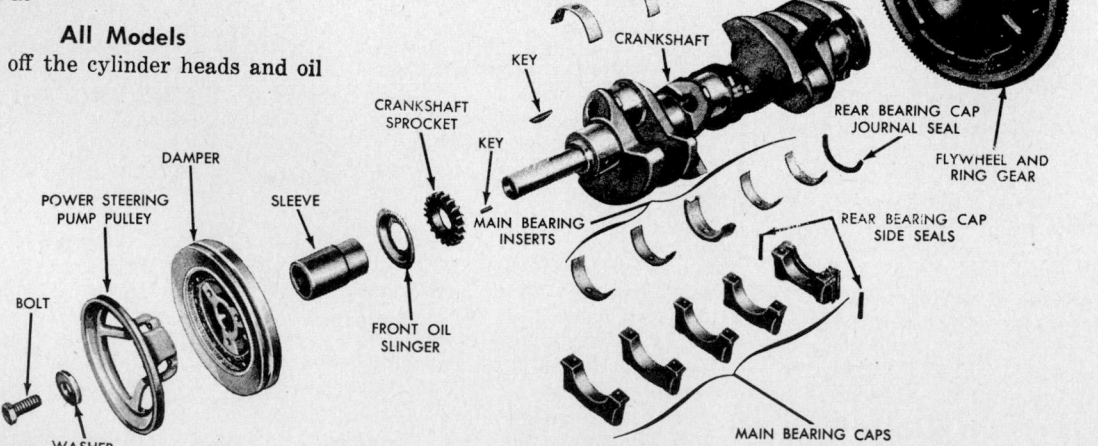

V8 crankshaft and related parts (© Ford Motor Co.)

sion ring which seals the combustion chamber of the engine so that the expanding gases of the power stroke do not escape, and an oil control ring which prevents cylinder wall lubricating oil from entering the combustion chamber. Due to the great amount of pressure and high temperature present in the piston area during combustion, piston ring clearances are very critical. Before replacing piston rings, piston and cylinder wall dimensions must first be checked; for even new piston rings cannot seal a piston or cylinder wall that is worn beyond specifications.

1. Using an internal micrometer, measure cylinder wall taper and out-of-roundness.
2. Measure piston outside diameter and subtract this measurement from the cylinder bore diameter obtained in above step. The result of this subtraction will give piston to wall clearance which also must be within specification.
3. If the cylinder wall and piston measurements are within specifications, and new rings are to be installed, hone the cylinder to the proper finish.
4. Position each ring in the cylinder bore it is to be used in and square it with the cylinder wall by gently pushing it downward with an inverted piston.
5. Using a feeler gauge of correct thickness, measure the ring end gap. If it exceeds specifications, try another ring, if it is less than specifications file the end of the ring to correct.
6. Install the rings on the pistons and measure piston ring-to-piston side clearance.

NOTE: before installing piston rings, the ring grooves on the piston should be thoroughly cleaned of all foreign material.

7. Space ring gaps on piston as shown in illustration.

Piston to Cylinder Wall Clearance

Year and Engine	Min. (in.)	Max. (in.)
1965-72 240 Six	0.0014	0.0022
1965-66 289 V8	0.0014	0.0022
1967-72 289, 302, and 351W	0.0018	0.0026
1965-72 352, 390, and 428	0.0015	0.0023
1969-72 351C, 400, and 429	0.0014	0.0022
1965-67 427	0.0042	0.0066

Rear Main Bearing Oil Seal

1965-69 Except 390, 427, and 428 V8 and 240 6-Cylinder

On both 6 and 8 cylinder models, a packing-type seal is used in back of the rear main bearing. To replace the upper half of the seal, it is necessary to remove the crankshaft. The lower half of the seal may be replaced by

Piston Ring End Gap

Year and Engine	Top Compression Min. Max. (in.)		Oil Ring Min. Max. (in.)	
1965-72 240 Six	0.010	0.020	0.015	0.055
1965-72 289, 302, 351, and 400	0.010	0.020	0.015	0.069
1965 352, 390 and 427	0.010	0.020	0.015	0.066
1966-68 390 and 427	0.010	0.031	0.015	0.066
1969-72 390	0.010	0.020	0.015	0.055
1966 428	0.010	0.033	0.015	0.066
1967-68 428	0.010	0.020	0.015	0.066
1969-70 429	0.010	0.020	0.010	0.035
1971-72 429	0.010	0.020	0.015	0.055

End Gap for all Bottom Compression Rings is: 0.010 to 0.020

Piston Ring Side Clearance

Year and Engine	Top Compression Min. Max. (in.)		Lower Compression Min. Max. (in.)	
1965-67 240 Six and 289	0.0019	0.0036	0.002	0.004
1968-72 240 Six and 302	0.002	0.004	0.002	0.004
1965 352, 390 and 427	0.0024	0.0041	0.002	0.004
1966-72 352, 390 and 428	0.002	0.004	0.002	0.004
1966-67 427	0.0024	0.0041	0.002	0.004
1969-72 351, 400 and 429	0.002	0.004	0.002	0.004

Oil Ring Side Clearance for all Engines is "snug".
If Piston Ring Side Clearance exceeds 0.006 in. the piston must be replaced.

taking down the rear main bearing cap and inserting new packing, letting the packing protrude approximately 1/16 in. above the cap at either side. Bolt the cap into place and immediately take it down to determine if the seal has riveted over. If it has riveted over, trim just the riveted portion with a razor blade, and bolt the cap back up again. Remove the cap again to determine if the main bearing cap is seating properly in the block. The reason for permitting the oil seal packing to protrude is so that it will tend to compress the upper half of the packing more tightly into the retainer in the cylinder block. In this way it is sometimes possible to prevent leaks at the rear main bearing without replacing the upper half of the oil seal.

1967-69 390, 427, 428 and All 1970-72

1. Loosen all main bearing cap bolts, lowering crankshaft slightly but not more than 1/32 in.
2. Remove rear main cap, and remove upper and lower halves of seal. On block half of seal, use seal removing tool or insert a small metal screw into end of seal with which to draw it out.
3. Clean seal grooves with solvent and dip replacement seal in clean engine oil.
4. Install upper seal half in its groove in block with lip toward front of engine by rotating it on seal journal of crankshaft until approximately 3/8 in. protrudes below parting surface.
5. Tighten other main caps and torque to specification.

6. Install lower seal half in rear main cap with lip to front and approximately 3/8 in. of seal protrudes to mate with upper seal.
7. Install rear main cap and torque.
8. Dip side seals in engine oil and install them. Tap seals in last half inch if necessary. Do not cut protruding ends of seals.

1965-69 6-Cylinder

If the rear main bearing oil seal is the only operation involved, it can be replaced in the car according to the following procedure.

NOTE: if the oil seal is being replaced in conjunction with a rear main bearing replacement, the engine must be removed from the car.

1. Remove the starter.
2. On cars equipped with automatic transmissions, remove the transmission. On cars equipped with manual shift transmissions, remove the transmission, clutch, flywheel and engine rear cover plate.
3. With an awl, punch holes in the main bearing oil seal, on opposite sides of the crankshaft and just above the bearing cap to cylinder block split line. Insert a sheet metal screw in each hole. With two large screwdrivers, pry the oil seal out.
4. Clean the oil recess in the cylinder block, main bearing cap and the crankshaft sealing surface.
5. Lubricate the entire oil seal. Then, install and drive the seal into its seat .005 in. below the face of the cylinder block with tool T-65L-6701-A.
6. The remaining procedure is the reverse of removal.

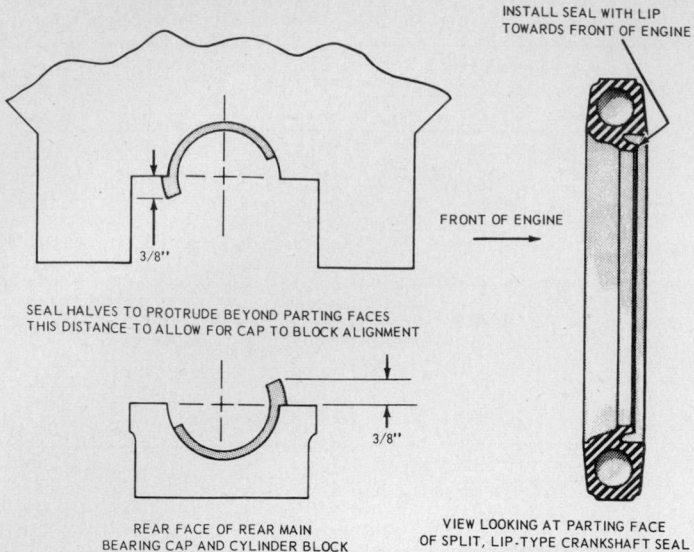

INSTALL SEAL WITH LIP
TOWARDS FRONT OF ENGINE

FRONT OF ENGINE

3/8"

SEAL HALVES TO PROTRUDE BEYOND PARTING FACES
THIS DISTANCE TO ALLOW FOR CAP TO BLOCK ALIGNMENT

3/8"

REAR FACE OF REAR MAIN
BEARING CAP AND CYLINDER BLOCK

VIEW LOOKING AT PARTING FACE
OF SPLIT, LIP-TYPE CRANKSHAFT SEAL

Installing split-lip type rear main oil seal (© Ford Motor Co.)

Front Suspension

Coil Spring and Lower Control Arm R & R

Except 1965-66 T-Bird

1. Raise car and support with stands placed back of lower arms.
2. If equipped with drum type brakes, remove the wheel and brake drum as an assembly. Remove the brake backing plate attaching bolts and remove the backing plate from the spindle. Wire the assembly back out of the way.
3. If equipped with disc brakes, remove the wheel from the hub. Remove two bolts and washers that hold the caliper and brake hose bracket to the spindle. Remove the caliper from the rotor and wire it back out of the way. Then, remove the hub and rotor from the spindle.
4. Disconnect lower end of the shock absorber and push it up to the retracted position.
5. Disconnect stabilizer bar link from the lower arm.
6. Remove cotter pins from the upper and lower ball joint stud nuts.
7. Remove two bolts and nuts holding the strut to the lower arm.
8. Loosen the lower ball joint stud nut two turns. Do not remove this nut.
9. Install spreader tool T57P-3006-A between the upper and lower ball joint studs.
10. Expand the tool until the tool exerts considerable pressure on the studs. Tap the spindle near the lower stud with a hammer

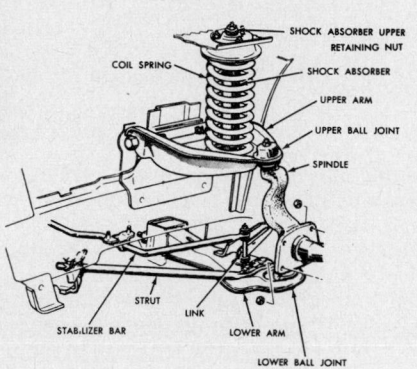

SHOCK ABSORBER UPPER
RETAINING NUT

COIL SPRING

SHOCK ABSORBER

UPPER ARM

UPPER BALL JOINT

SPINDLE

STRUT

LINK

STABILIZER BAR

LOWER ARM

LOWER BALL JOINT

T-Bird front suspension—1965-66
(© Ford Motor Co.)

to loosen the stud in the spindle. Do not loosen the stud with tool pressure only.

11. Position floor jack under the lower arm and remove the lower ball joint stud nut.
12. Lower floor jack and remove the spring and insulator.
13. Remove the A-arm to crossmember attaching parts, and remove the arm from the car.
14. Reverse above procedure to install. If lower control arm was replaced because of damage, check front end alignment.

T-Bird—1965-66

1. Raise the car and position stands under the suspension lower arms.
2. Remove wheel and brake assembly as described in Steps 2 and 3 of the previous procedure.
3. Raise the car slightly in order to lower the suspension upper arm. Install spring tool T63P-5310-A. Slide the tool bearing and upper plate over the shaft screw against the shaft nut. Insert the tool assembly through the upper opening in the spring housing so that the shaft screw goes through the top of the coil spring. The tool upper plate holes must accommodate the studs in the frame spring tower.
4. From under the car, place the tool lower plate under the fourth

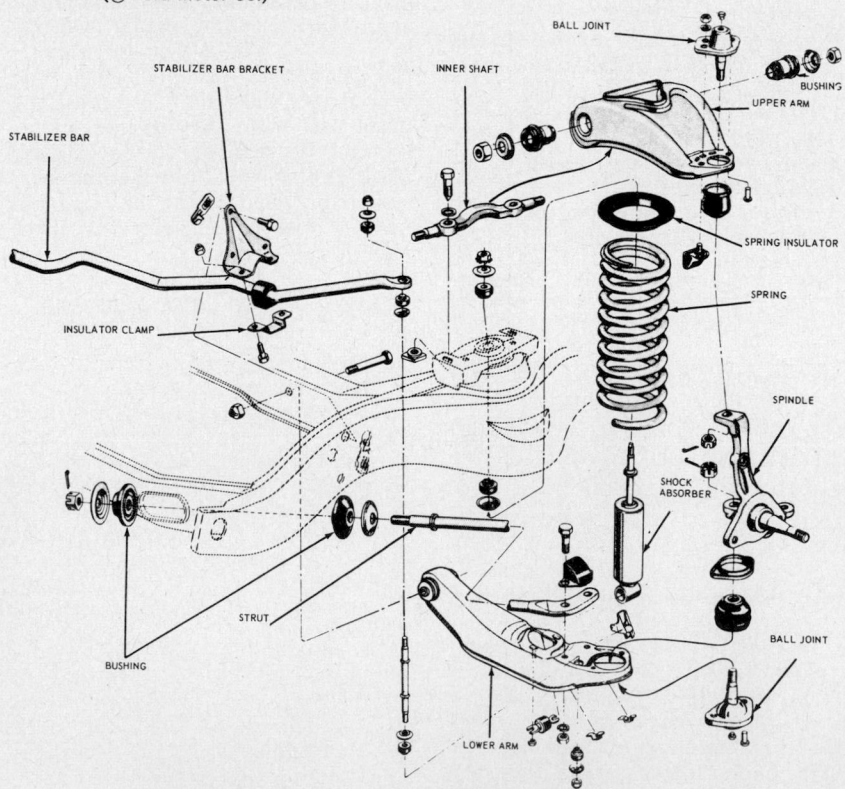

BALL JOINT

BUSHING

UPPER ARM

STABILIZER BAR BRACKET

INNER SHAFT

SPRING INSULATOR

STABILIZER BAR

SPRING

INSULATOR CLAMP

SPINDLE

SHOCK ABSORBER

STRUT

BUSHING

BALL JOINT

LOWER ARM

Typical front suspension—1965-70 (© Ford Motor Co.)

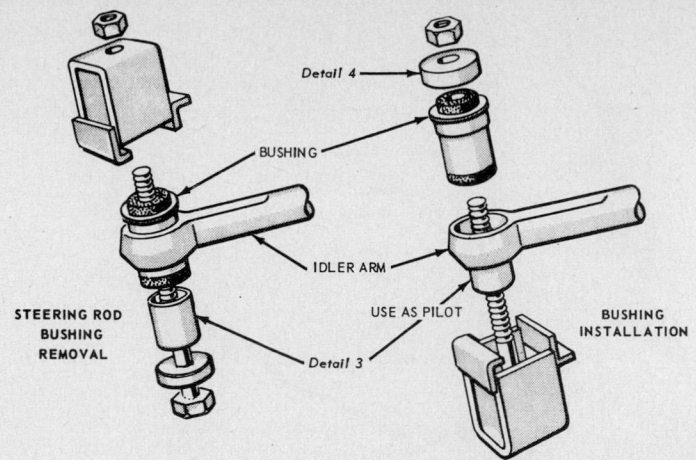

STEERING ROD BUSHING REMOVAL

Detail 4

BUSHING

IDLER ARM

USE AS PILOT

Detail 3

BUSHING INSTALLATION

Installing idler arm bushing (© Ford Motor Co.)

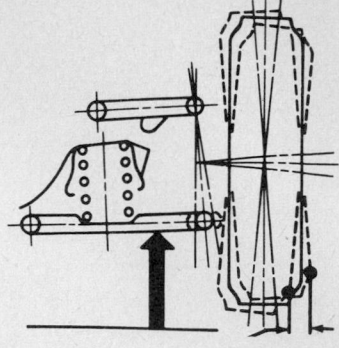

Measuring lower ball joint radial play
(© Ford Motor Co.)

spring coil from the bottom. Secure the plate to the coil by installing the tool retainer in the groove in the shaft screw.

5. Insert a ½ in. square flex-handle wrench in the drive hole in the lower plate to prevent the tool with spring from turning. While holding the tool, compress the spring by turning the tool shaft nut clockwise.

6. Remove the two nuts and lock washers that attach the upper arm inner shaft to the chassis, and swing the arm out of the way. The arm pivots on the ball joint.

7. Remove the bolt that holds the clip and brake line to the chassis, then move the brake line out of the way.

8. Disconnect the stabilizer bar from the link at both left- and right-hand suspension lower arms by removing the bar-to-link attaching nuts and upper bushings. Position the bar out of the way.

9. Fully release the spring tension by turning the tool shaft nut counterclockwise. Hold the lower plate of the tool with the ½ in. square drive wrench so that the tool will not turn or snap loose during spring release.

10. Remove the spring tool, then remove the spring from the car.

11. Install by reversing above procedure.

Lower Ball Joint

Inspection

1. Raise the vehicle by placing a floor jack under the lower arm; or, raise the vehicle on a hoist and place a jack stand under the lower arm and lower the vehicle onto it to remove the preload from the lower ball joint.

2. Have an assistant grasp the wheel top and bottom and apply alternate in and out pressure to the top and bottom of the wheel.

3. Radial play of ¼ in. is acceptable measured at the inside of the wheel adjacent to the lower arm.
NOTE: this radial play is multiplied at the outer circumference of the tire and should be measured only at the inside of the wheel.

Replacement

1. Raise the vehicle on a hoist and allow the front wheels to fall to their full down position.

2. Drill a ⅛ in. hole completely through each ball joint attaching rivet.

3. Use a ⅜ in. drill in the pilot hole to drill off the head of the rivet.

4. Drive the rivets from the lower arm.

5. Place a jack under the lower arm and lower the vehicle about 6 in.

6. Remove the lower ball joint stud cotter pin and attaching nut.

7. Using a suitable tool, loosen the ball joint from the spindle and remove the ball joint from the lower arm.

8. Clean all metal burrs from the lower arm and install the new ball joint, using the service part nuts and bolts to attach the ball joint to the lower arm. Do not attempt to rerivet the ball joint once it has been removed.

9. Check front end alignment.

Upper Ball Joint

Inspection

1. Raise the vehicle by placing a floor jack under the lower arm. Do not allow the lower arm to hang freely with the vehicle on a hoist or bumper jack.

2. Have an assistant grasp the bottom of the tire and move the wheel in and out.

3. As the wheel is being moved, observe the upper control arm where the spindle attaches to it. Any movement between the upper part of the spindle and the upper ball joint indicates a bad

ball joint which must be replaced.
NOTE: during this check the lower ball joint will be unloaded and may move; this is normal and not an indication of a bad ball joint. Also, do not mistake a loose wheel bearing for a defective ball joint.

Replacement

1. Raise the vehicle on a hoist and allow the front wheels to fall to their full down position.

2. Drill a ⅛ in. hole completely through each ball joint attaching rivet.

3. Using a large chisel, cut off the head of each rivet and drive them from the upper arm.

4. Place a jack under the lower arm and lower the vehicle about 6 in.

5. Remove the cotter pin and attaching nut from the ball joint stud.

6. Using a suitable tool, loosen the ball joint stud from the spindle and remove the ball joint from the upper arm.

7. Clean all metal burrs from the upper arm and install the new ball joint, using the service part nuts and bolts to attach the ball joint to the upper arm. Do not attempt to rerivet the ball joint once it has been removed.

8. Check front end alignment.

Upper Control Arm

Replacement

1. Raise the vehicle on a hoist.

2. If equipped with drum brakes remove the tire, wheel and brake drum as an assembly. If equipped with disc brakes, remove the tire and wheel.

3. Remove the cotter pin and attaching nut from the ball joint stud.

4. Using a suitable tool, loosen the upper ball joint from the spindle.

5. Place a jack under the lower arm and lower the vehicle about 6 in.

6. Remove the upper arm inner shaft attaching bolts and remove

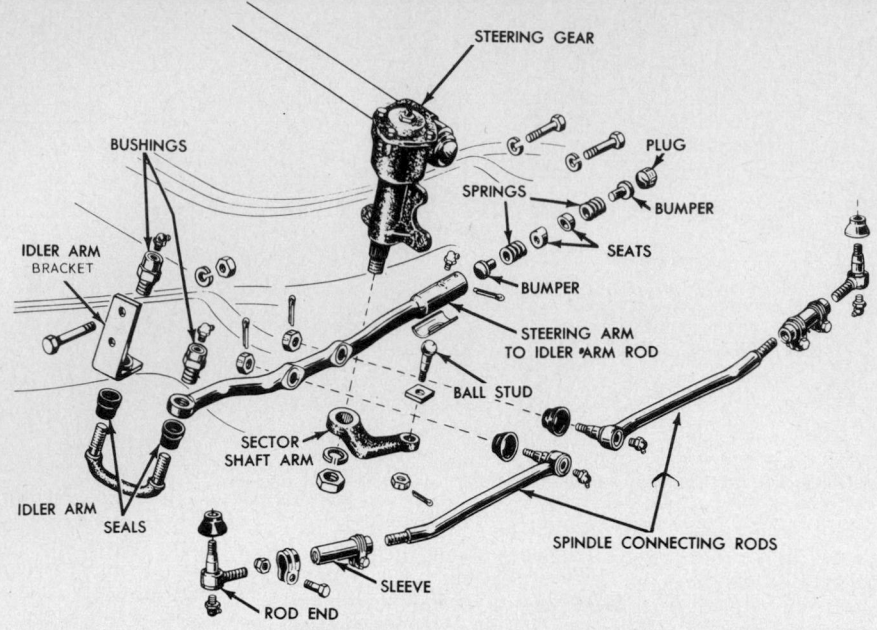

Typical steering linkage (© Ford Motor Co.)

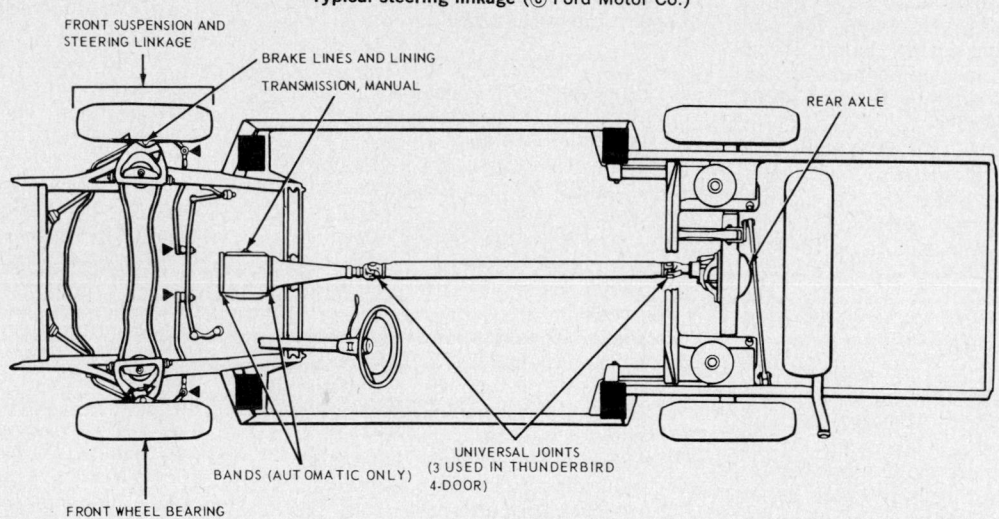

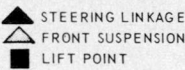

▲ STEERING LINKAGE
△ FRONT SUSPENSION
■ LIFT POINT

Ford hoist lifting positions (© Ford Motor Co.)

the arm and shaft from the chassis as an assembly.
7. Reverse above procedure to install.
8. Adjust front end alignment.

Steering Gear

The steering gear on all models with manual steering is the worm and recirculating ball type. The sector shaft is straddle mounted in the cover above the gear and a housing mounted roller bearing below the gear.

Since 1965, all full-size Fords, Mercurys and Thunderbirds with power steering have used integral type power steering. On this type of steer-

ing, hydraulic assist is provided directly to the steering gear, eliminating all hoses and hardware which was previously mounted under the chassis. The most common type of steering gear used with integral power steering is the Ford torsion bar model. The torsion bar type power steering unit includes a worm and one-piece rack piston, which is meshed with the gear teeth on the steering sector shaft. In certain limited applications a Saginaw Rotary Valve type power steering unit is used. In this unit, the rack-piston nut is of one piece design and is geared to the steering sector shaft.

All removal, adjustment and overhaul operations are contained in the Unit Repair Section of this book;

listed under manual steering and power steering respectively.

Jacking, Hoisting

Ford and Mercury (Except 1965-66 T-Bird)

1. Jack car at front spring seats of lower control arms, and at rear axle housing close to differential case.
2. To lift at frame, use adapters so that contact will be made at points shown. Adapters should support at least 12 sq. in.

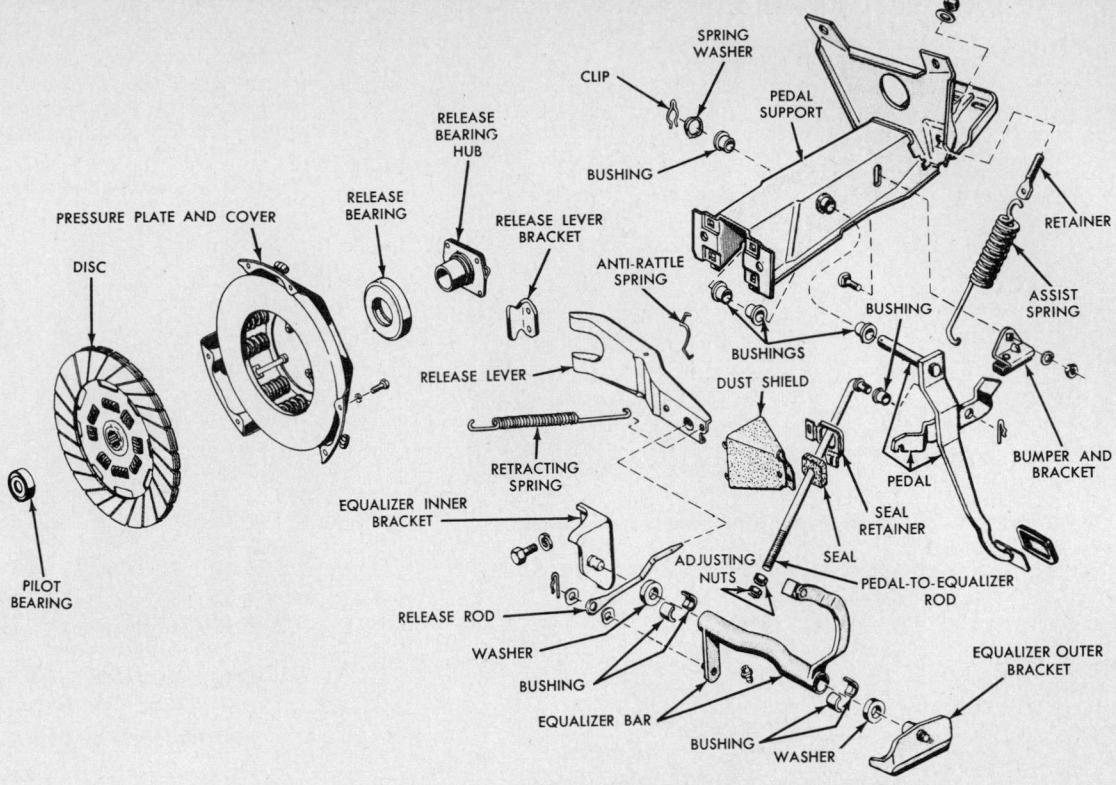

Exploded view of the complete clutch and pedal assembly (© Ford Motor Co.)

T-Bird—1965-66

1. (With twin post lift) Front: place adapters to contact lower suspension arms. Rear: place forks not more than one in. from the circular welds near the differential housing.
2. (With frame contact lift) Place adapters at points shown on diagram and covering an area not less than 24 sq. in.

Clutch

Clutch Pedal Adjustment

1. Disconnect the clutch return spring from the release lever.
2. Loosen the release lever adjusting nut and locknut.
3. Move the clutch release lever rearward until the throwout bearing can be felt to lightly contact the pressure plate fingers.
4. Adjust the rod length until the rod seats in the pocket in the release lever.
5. Insert a feeler gauge of specified thickness between the adjusting nut and swivel sleeve. Tighten the nut against the feeler gauge. Correct feeler gauge thicknesses are: 1965—0.375 in., 1966-67— 0.206 in., 1968—0.120 in., 1969-72—0.194 in.
6. Tighten the locknut against the adjusting nut, being careful not to disturb the adjustment.

7. Connect the clutch return spring.
8. Make a final check with the engine running at 3000 rpm, and transmission in neutral. Under this condition, centrifugal weights on release fingers may reduce the clearance. Readjust, if necessary, to obtain at least ½ in. free-play while maintaining the 3000 rpm to prevent fingers contacting release bearing. This is important.

Clutch and/or Transmission R & R

1. Raise the vehicle on a hoist.
2. Disconnect the driveshaft from the rear U-joint flange and slide the front yoke from the transmission.
3. Insert a cap or rag in the transmission extension housing to prevent fluid leakage.
4. Disconnect the speedometer cable and shifter linkage from the transmission. On models with a four-speed transmission, remove the shifter mounting bracket from the extension housing.
5. On models with a three-speed transmission, disconnect the transmission mount from the crossmember. If equipped with a four-speed transmission, remove the front parking brake cable from the crossmember and remove the crossmember from the car.

6. Remove the bolts that mount the transmission to the bellhousing. On 429 V8s, the upper left-hand transmission attaching bolt is a seal bolt. Carefully note its location so that it may be returned to its original position.
7. Move the transmission rearward until the input shaft clears the bellhousing and lower it from the car.
8. Disconnect the clutch release lever return spring.
9. If equipped with a one-piece aluminum bellhousing, remove the starter and remove the bellhousing from the engine. If equipped with a cast iron bellhousing, remove only the inspection cover from the bottom of the bellhousing.
10. Loosen the 6 pressure plate attaching bolts evenly to release spring pressure, and remove the clutch assembly from the car.
11. To install, position clutch assembly on flywheel and install each pressure plate attaching bolt finger tight.
12. Insert a transmission pilot shaft or other suitable tool to align the clutch disc with the flywheel and alternately tighten the pressure plate attaching bolts until the plate is secured to the flywheel.
13. Reverse above procedure to install transmission and driveshaft.

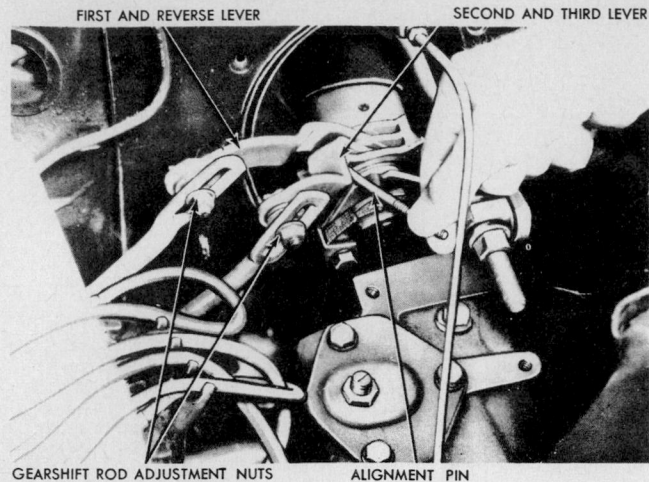

Gearshift linkage adjustment 3-speed transmission (© Ford Motor Co.)

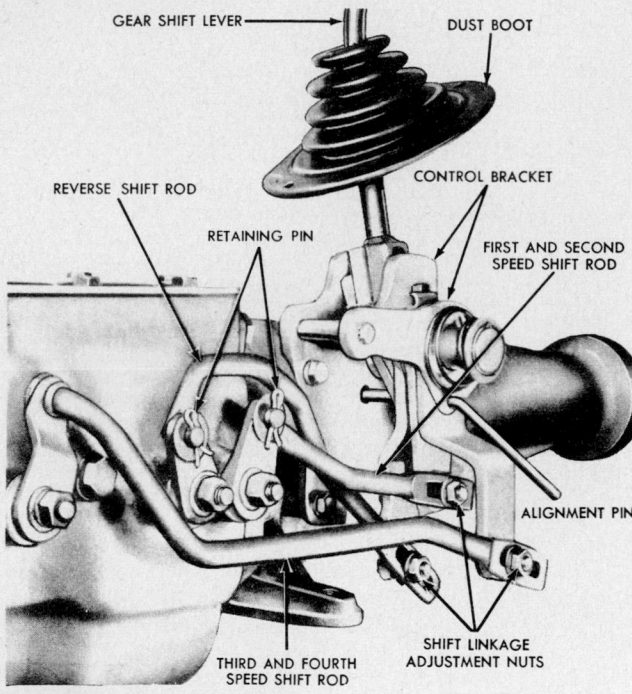

Adjusting shift linkage, 4-speed transmission (© Ford Motor Co.)

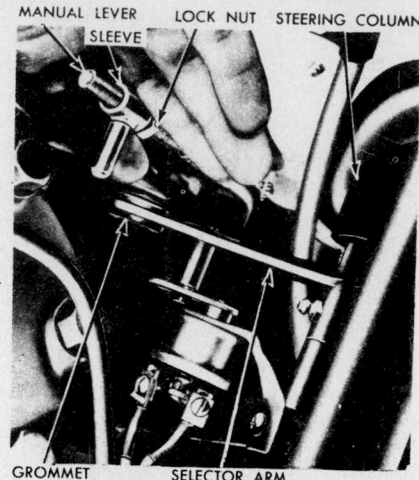

Adjusting manual control valve linkage
(© Ford Motor Co.)

BOTTOM VIEW OF SWITCH

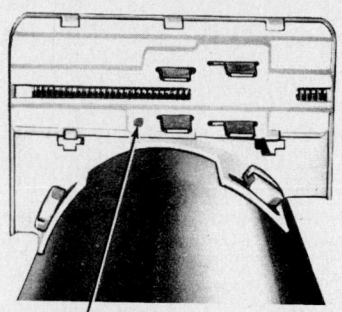

Neutral start switch—1964-67 Cruise-o-matic
(© Ford Motor Co.)

Transmissions

Manual Transmission Linkage Adjustment

Column Mounted

1. Place the gear shift lever in the Neutral position.
2. Loosen the two gear shift adjustment nuts on the shift linkage.
3. Insert a 3/16 in. alignment tool through the first and reverse lever, the second and third gear shift lever, and the two holes in the lower casing. An alignment tool can be fabricated from 3/16 in. rod bent to an L shape. The extension that is to be inserted into the levers should be 1 in. in length from the elbow.
4. Manipulate the levers so the alignment tool will move freely through the alignment holes.
5. Tighten the two gear shift rod adjustment nuts.
6. Remove the tool and check linkage operation.

Floor Mounted

1. Place hand shifter lever in neutral position, then raise car on a hoist.
2. Insert a 1/4 in. rod into the alignment holes of the shift levers.
3. If the holes are not in exact alignment, check for bent connecting rods or loose lever locknuts at the rod ends. Make replacements or repairs, then adjust as follows.
4. Loosen the three rod-to-lever retaining locknuts and move the levers until the 1/4 in. gauge rod will enter the alignment holes. Be sure that the transmission shift levers are in neutral, and the reverse shifter lever is in the neutral detent.
5. Install shift rods and torque locknuts to 12-15 ft. lbs. on 1965 transmissions and 18-23 ft. lbs. on 1966-72 transmissions.
6. Remove the 1/4 in. gauge rod.
7. Operate the shift levers to assure correct shifting.
8. Lower the car and road-test.

Transmission Lock Rod Adjustment

1970 and later models with floor or console mounted shifters and manual transmissions incorporate a transmission lock rod which prevents the shifter from being moved from the reverse position when the ignition lock is in the OFF position. The lock rod connects the shift tube in the steering column to the transmission reverse lever. The lock rod cannot be properly adjusted until the manual linkage adjustment is correct.

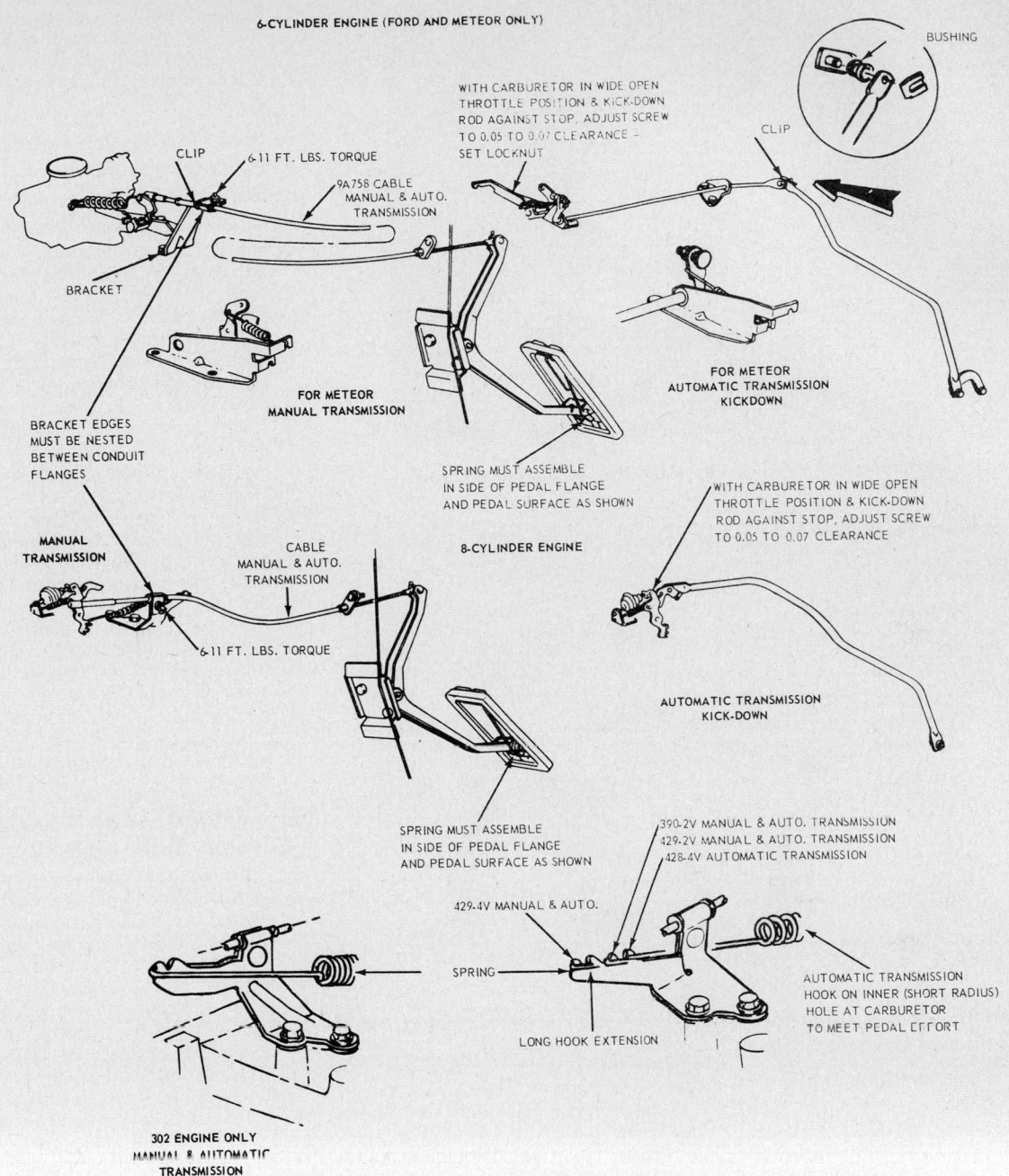

6-CYLINDER ENGINE (FORD AND METEOR ONLY)

BUSHING

CLIP

CLIP

6-11 FT. LBS. TORQUE

WITH CARBURETOR IN WIDE OPEN THROTTLE POSITION & KICK-DOWN ROD AGAINST STOP, ADJUST SCREW TO 0.05 TO 0.07 CLEARANCE – SET LOCKNUT

9A758 CABLE MANUAL & AUTO. TRANSMISSION

BRACKET

FOR METEOR MANUAL TRANSMISSION

FOR METEOR AUTOMATIC TRANSMISSION KICKDOWN

BRACKET EDGES MUST BE NESTED BETWEEN CONDUIT FLANGES

MANUAL TRANSMISSION

CABLE MANUAL & AUTO. TRANSMISSION

8-CYLINDER ENGINE

SPRING MUST ASSEMBLE IN SIDE OF PEDAL FLANGE AND PEDAL SURFACE AS SHOWN

WITH CARBURETOR IN WIDE OPEN THROTTLE POSITION & KICK-DOWN ROD AGAINST STOP, ADJUST SCREW TO 0.05 TO 0.07 CLEARANCE

6-11 FT. LBS. TORQUE

AUTOMATIC TRANSMISSION KICK-DOWN

SPRING MUST ASSEMBLE IN SIDE OF PEDAL FLANGE AND PEDAL SURFACE AS SHOWN

390-2V MANUAL & AUTO. TRANSMISSION
429-2V MANUAL & AUTO. TRANSMISSION
428-4V AUTOMATIC TRANSMISSION

429-4V MANUAL & AUTO.

SPRING

AUTOMATIC TRANSMISSION HOOK ON INNER (SHORT RADIUS) HOLE AT CARBURETOR TO MEET PEDAL EFFORT

LONG HOOK EXTENSION

302 ENGINE ONLY MANUAL & AUTOMATIC TRANSMISSION

Manual linkage adjustment—1969-70 (© Ford Motor Co.)

1. With the transmission selector lever in the neutral position, loosen the lock rod adjustment nut on the transmission reverse lever.
2. Insert a .180 in. diameter rod (No. 15 drill bit) in the gauge pin hole located at the 6 o'clock position on the steering column socket casting, directly below the ignition lock.
3. Manipulate the pin until the casting will not move with the pin inserted.
4. Torque the lock rod adjustment nut to 10-20 ft. lbs.
5. Remove the pin and check the linkage operation.

Automatic Transmission

Manual Linkage Adjustment

1. With engine off, loosen clamp at shift lever so shift rod is free to slide.
2. Position selector lever in D1 position (large green dot) on dual range transmissions. On select shift transmission (P R N D 2 1) position lever in D position.
3. Shift lever at transmission into D1 detent position on dual range transmissions or into D position on select shift transmissions.

NOTE: D1 position is second from rear on all dual range transmissions. D position is third from rear on all column shift select shift transmissions and 1966-68 console shift select shift transmissions. D position is fourth from rear on 1969-72 console shift select shift transmissions.

4. Tighten clamp and torque nut to 8-13 ft. lbs. on 1965-68 column shifts and 10-20 ft. lbs. on 1969-72 column shifts. Torque 1965-68 console shift nuts to 20-25 ft. lbs. and 1969-72 console shift nuts to 10-20 ft. lbs.

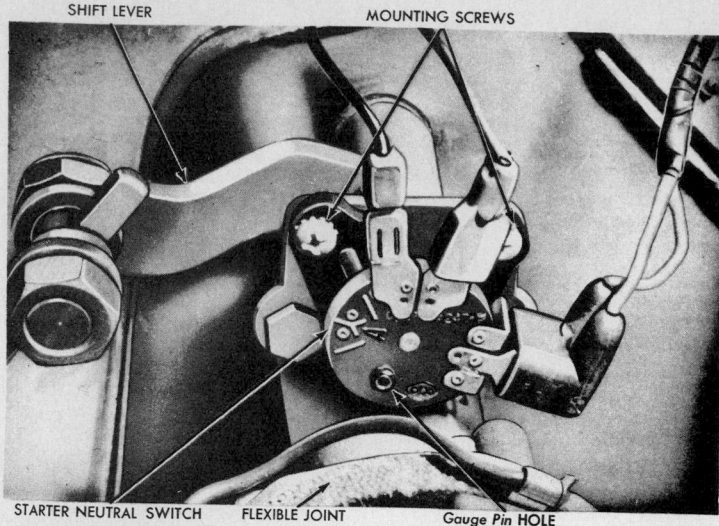

Neutral start switch—column mounted C4 and C6 1965-67 (© Ford Motor Co.)

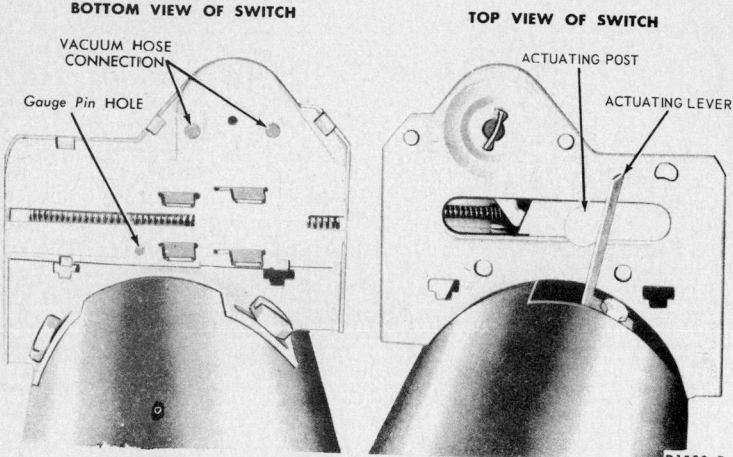

Neutral start switch—T-Bird (© Ford Motor Co.)   D1502-B

Neutral Start Switch Adjustment —1965-67 Except Console Shift Cruise-O-Matics and All 1967 Console Shifts

1. With manual linkage properly adjusted, try to engage starter in each position on quadrant. Starter should engage only in Park and Neutral positions.
2. To adjust, loosen screws that locate switch on steering column.
3. Place shift lever in neutral detent.
4. Rotate switch until gauge pin (No. 43 drill) can be inserted in gauge pin hole 31/64 in.
5. Tighten down locating screws and check starter engagement in each position as in Step 1.

Neutral Start Switch Adjustment —Column Shift 1968-72

1. With manual linkage properly adjusted, try to engage starter in each position on quadrant. Starter should engage only in neutral or park position.

2. Place shift lever in neutral detent.
3. Disconnect start switch wires at plug connector. Disconnect vacuum hoses, if any. Remove screws securing neutral start switch to steering column and remove switch. Remove actuator lever along with Type III switches.
4. With switch wires facing up, move actuator lever fully to the left and insert gauge pin (No. 43 drill) into gauge pin hole at point A. See accompanying figure. On Type III switch, be sure gauge pin is inserted a full 1/2 in.
5. With pin in place, move actuator lever to right until positive stop is engaged.
6. On Type I and Type II switches, remove gauge pin and insert it at point B. On Type III switches, remove gauge pin, align two holes in switch at point A and reinstall gauge pin.
7. Reinstall switch on steering col-

umn. Be sure shift lever is engaged in neutral detent.
8. Connect switch wires and vacuum hoses and remove gauge pin.
9. Check starter engagement as in Step 1.

Neutral Start Switch Adjustment —1965-66 Console Shift Cruiso-matics and 1967 Console Shift C4 and C6 Transmissions

1. With manual linkage properly adjusted, try to engage starter in each position on quadrant. Starter should engage only in Neutral or Park position.
2. Remove handle from shift lever and chrome trim panel from top of console.
3. Place lever in Neutral, remove quadrant retaining screws and indicator light, and lift quadrant from console.
4. Loosen switch attaching screws, and move shift lever back and forth until gauge pin (No. 43 drill) can be inserted into gauge pin holes.
5. Place shift lever in neutral position, and slide switch back and forward until switch actuating lever contacts shift lever.
6. Reassemble shift quadrant in console.
7. Check starter engagement as in Step 1.

Neutral Start Switch Adjustment —Console Shift 1968-72

1. With manual linkage properly adjusted, try to engage starter at each position on quadrant. Starter should engage only in Neutral and Park positions.
2. Remove shift handle from shift lever, and console from vehicle.
3. Loosen switch attaching screws, and move shift lever back and forward until gauge pin (No. 43 drill) can be inserted fully.
4. Place shift lever firmly against neutral detent stop and slide switch back and forward until switch lever contacts shift lever.
5. Tighten switch attaching screws, and check starter engagement as in Step 1.
6. Reinstall console and shift linkage.

Lock Rod Adjustment

Since 1970, all models with a floor or console mounted selector lever have incorporated a transmission lock out rod to prevent the transmission selector from being moved out of the Park position when the ignition lock is in the Off position. The lock rod connects the shift tube in the steering column to the transmission manual lever. The lock rod cannot be properly adjusted until the manual linkage adjustment is correct.

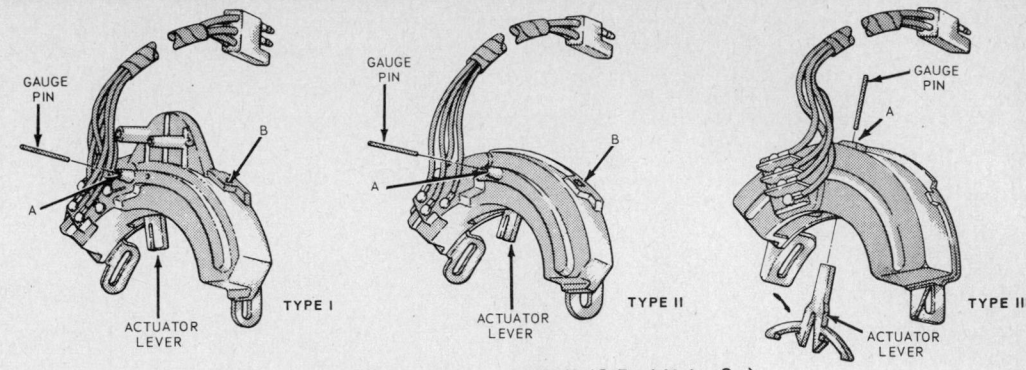

Neutral start switches—1968-70 (© Ford Motor Co.)

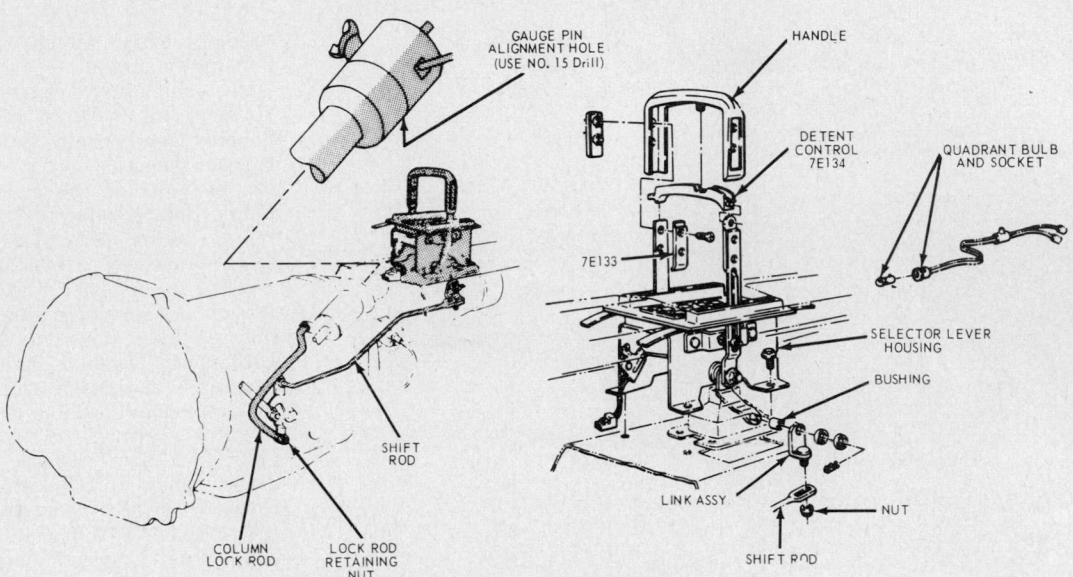

Floor mounted automatic transmission linkage (© Ford Motor Co.)

1. With the transmission selector lever in the Drive position, loosen the lock rod adjustment nut on the transmission manual lever.
2. Insert a .180 in. diameter rod (No. 15 drill bit) in the gauge pin hole in the steering column socket casting, it is located at the 6 o'clock position directly below the ignition lock.
3. Manipulate the pin so that the casting will not move when the pin is fully inserted.
4. Torque the lock rod adjustment nut to 10-20 ft. lbs.
5. Remove the pin and check the linkage operation.

Throttle Linkage Adjustments

All 1965-68 Throttle and Downshift Linkage

1. Apply the parking brake and place selector lever in N.
2. Run engine at fast idle until it reaches normal operating temperature. Then, slow it down to normal idle.
3. Connect a tachometer to the engine.
4. Adjust engine to specified idle speed with selector in D1 or D2. Due to the vacuum parking brake release (if so equipped), the parking brake will not hold while selector is in D1 or D2. Keep service brake applied.
5. When satisfied that idle speed is correct, stop engine and adjust dashpot clearance. Check clearance between dashpot plunger and throttle lever.
6. With engine stopped, disconnect carburetor return spring from throttle lever and loosen accelerator cable conduit attaching clamp.
7. With accelerator pedal to floor and throttle lever wide open, slide cable conduit to rear (to left on six cylinder engine) to remove slack from cable. Tighten clamp.
8. Disconnect downshift lever return spring and hold throttle lever wide open. Depress downshift rod to "through detent stop". Set downshift lever adjusting screw against throttle lever.
9. Connect carburetor return spring and downshift lever return spring.

All Beginning 1969

1. Disconnect downshift lever return spring.
2. Hold throttle shaft lever wide open, and hold downshift rod against "through detent stop".
3. Adjust downshift screw to provide 0.050-0.070 in. clearance between screw and throttle shaft lever. On 240 cu. in. engine, tighten locknut.
4. Connect downshaft lever return spring.

C4 Automatic Transmission R&R

1. Raise vehicle and remove three converter cover attaching bolts and remove cover.
2. Remove two converter drain plugs, drain converter and reinstall plugs.
3. Remove drive shaft and plug of extension housing.
4. Remove vacuum line hose from vacuum unit and from attaching clip.
5. Remove extension housing to crossmember attaching bolts.
6. Remove speedometer cable.
7. Disconnect exhaust pipes from manifolds.
8. Remove parking brake cable from equalizer lever.

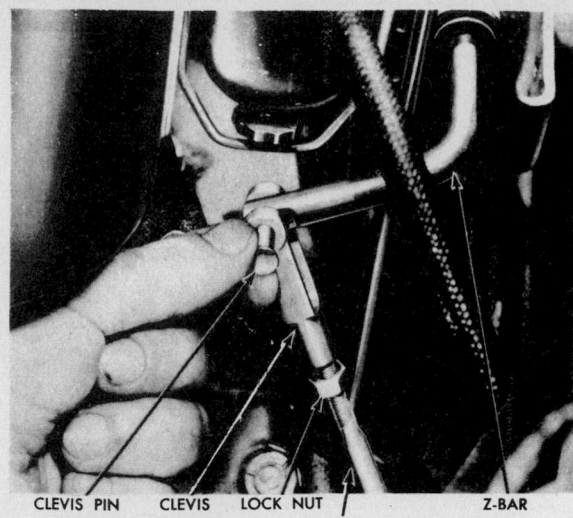

CLEVIS PIN   CLEVIS   LOCK NUT   Z-BAR
THROTTLE CONTROL ROD

Adjusting throttle valve control rod (© Ford Motor Co.)

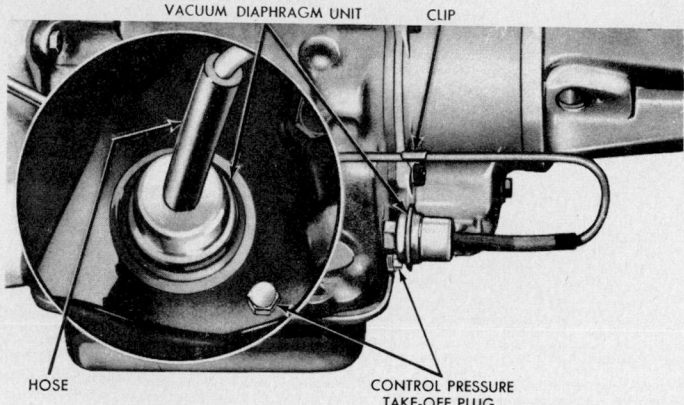

VACUUM DIAPHRAGM UNIT   CLIP

HOSE   CONTROL PRESSURE TAKE-OFF PLUG

Vacuum diaphragm and control pressure connecting point (© Ford Motor Co.)

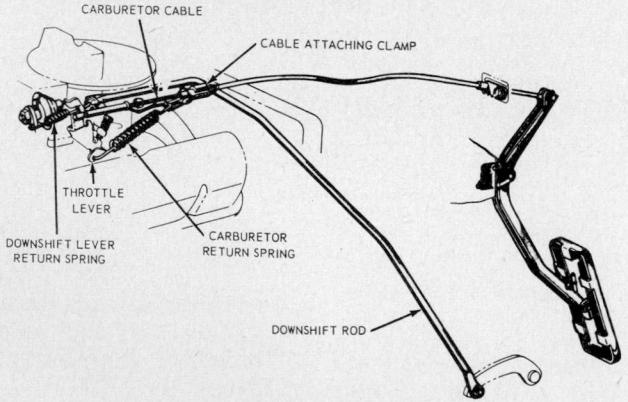

CARBURETOR CABLE
CABLE ATTACHING CLAMP
THROTTLE LEVER
DOWNSHIFT LEVER RETURN SPRING
CARBURETOR RETURN SPRING
DOWNSHIFT ROD

Throttle linkage—V8 1965-69 (© Ford Motor Co.)

CLAMP   CARBURETOR CABLE AND CABLE CONDUIT
CARBURETOR RETURN SPRING
DOWNSHIFT LEVER RETURN SPRING
DOWNSHIFT ROD
ACCELERATOR PEDAL

Throttle linkage—6 cyl. 1965-69 (© Ford Motor Co.)

9. Remove fluid filler tube and drain transmission fluid.
10. Disconnect oil cooler lines.
11. Remove all linkages from transmission.
12. Disconnect starter cable and remove starter.
13. Remove four torque converter to flywheel attaching nuts.
14. Position jack to support transmission and secure with safety chain. Remove four crossmember bolts and lower crossmember.

15. Remove converter to engine bolts. Lower transmission and remove from car.
16. Reverse above procedure to install transmission.

Cruise-o-matic Automatic Transmission R&R

After 1967, Cruise-o-matics are designated as FMX or MX transmissions, depending on application.
1. Remove two upper bolts and lock

washers which attach converter housing to engine.
2. Raise vehicle, remove cover from lower front side of converter housing, and drain fluid from transmission.
3. Remove one of converter drain plugs. Rotate converter 180° and remove other plug. Do not attempt to turn converter with wrench on converter stud nuts.
4. Disconnect filler tube from transmission case.
5. Disconnect vacuum hose from vacuum diaphragm unit and from extension housing clip.
6. Remove flywheel to converter nuts and flat washers. Install drain plugs in converter and torque to 15-28 ft. lbs. Install converter housing front plate to hold converter when removing transmission.
7. Disconnect and remove starter.
8. Disconnect oil cooler lines and remove vent tube.
9. Disconnect all linkages.
10. Disconnect speedometer and remove drive shaft.
11. Support transmission on stand, remove transmission mount bolts, and remove crossmember.
12. Support rear of engine, remove remaining engine attaching bolts, and lower transmission.
13. Reverse above procedure to install transmission.

C6 Automatic Transmission R&R

1. Raise vehicle and drain transmission and converter.
2. Remove driveshaft and plug extension housing.
3. Disconnect and remove starter.
4. Remove four converter to flywheel attaching nuts.
5. Disconnect parking brake front cable from equalizer.
6. Remove two crossmember to frame attaching bolts.
7. Remove two transmission mount bolts.
8. Disconnect all linkages.
9. Disconnect exhaust pipes from manifolds.

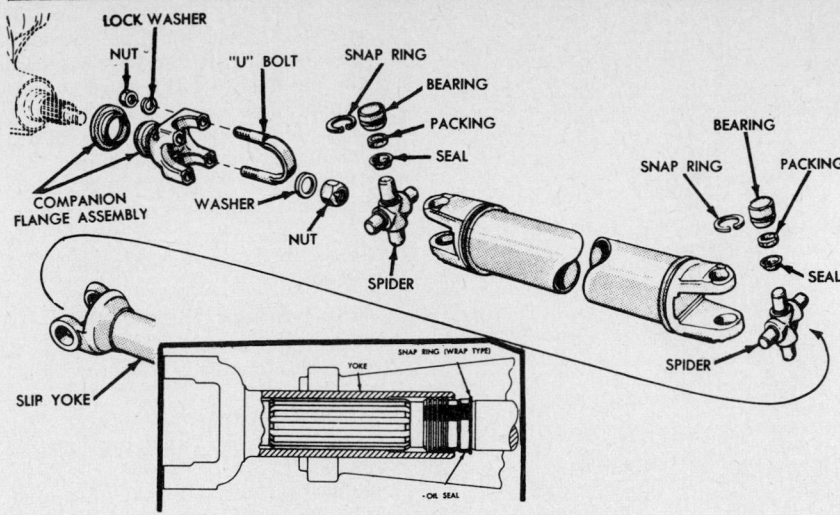

LOCK WASHER
NUT
"U" BOLT
SNAP RING
BEARING
PACKING
SEAL
BEARING
SNAP RING
PACKING
SEAL
COMPANION FLANGE ASSEMBLY
WASHER
NUT
SPIDER
SPIDER
SLIP YOKE
YOKE
SNAP RING (WRAP TYPE)
OIL SEAL

Driveshaft and universal joint (© Ford Motor Co.)

10. Raise transmission on transmission jack.
11. Disconnect parking brake cables from equalizer.
12. Remove crossmember and lower transmission to gain access to oil cooler lines.
13. Disconnect oil cooler lines from transmission and disconnect vacuum line from vacuum diaphragm and retaining clip.
14. Disconnect speedometer at transmission.
15. Remove bolt that secures transmission filler tube to engine block and remove tube.
16. Secure transmission to jack with chain.
17. Remove converter housing to engine bolts.
18. Move transmission back and down to clear vehicle.
19. Reverse procedure to install transmission.

Drive Shaft, U Joints

Rear Joint Removal Ford, Mercury and 1965-67 T-Bird

The universal joints on all Fords in this section are of the cross- and needle-bearing-type.

The rear universal joint has two pillow blocks which are bolted to the pinion shaft flange.

Take out the four bolts that hold the bearing blocks to the pinion shaft and gently tap off the bearing blocks.

Lower the back end of the driveshaft and the front end can be slid out of the back of the transmission together with the transmission yoke portion of the front universal joint.

Carry the assembly—the front universal joint complete, the driveshaft and the rear universal joint crossover—to the bench and remove the cross from the rear universal joint by

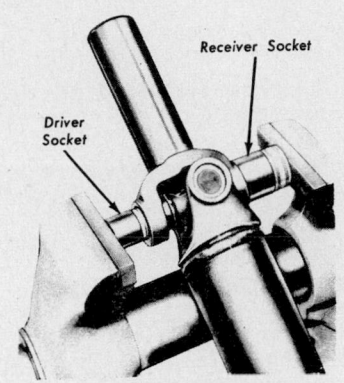

Receiver Socket
Driver Socket

U-joint removal
(© Ford Motor Co.)

taking out the lock rings from the inner side of the bearings. Using a large punch or an arbor press, drive one of the bearings in toward the center forcing out the opposite bearing.

When the bearing is pressed out far enough, grip it with a pair of pliers and pull it out of the driveshaft yoke.

Now, drive the cross in the opposite direction until the remaining bearing has been driven out far enough for a purchase with a pair of pliers.

When both bearings have been taken out, the cross can be lifted from between the two yokes.

Front Universal Joint Removal —Ford, Mercury and 1965-67 T-Bird

Follow the procedure given above for the rear universal joint, but leave the rear universal joint cross in place on the driveshaft if it is not to be removed.

Remove the lock rings from the inner side of two opposite bearings and press on the outer side of one of the bearings, forcing the crossover. This will force the bearing on the opposite side out of its yoke.

Remove the forced-out bearing and press the cross in the opposite direc-

tion to force the other bearing out.

Repeat this procedure on the third and fourth bearings.

When installing the new bearings in the universal joint yoke, it is possible to put them in with a driver of some type, but it is recommended that this work be done in an arbor press since a heavy jolt on the needle bearings can very easily misalign them.

Double Cardan Universal Joints

Since 1968, all Thunderbirds have used a driveshaft with a double Cardan U-Joint. Each of the two Cardan joints consist of two universal joints, a centering socket yoke and a center yoke. Bearing cups are retained by injected plastic; but, repair kits contain replacement snap-rings. This driveshaft mounts to the differential pinion flange by means of a circular companion flange.

Replacement

1. Mark the position of the companion flange in relation to the pinion flange so the driveshaft may be returned to its original location.
2. Disconnect the companion flange from the pinion flange.
3. Pull the driveshaft rearward until the front yoke clears the transmission extension housing and remove the driveshaft from the car.
4. Mark the position of the spiders, the center yoke and the centering socket yoke in relation to the companion flange. *The spiders must be assembled with the bosses in their original position to provide proper clearance.*
5. If the universal joints have been previously replaced and are retained with snap-rings, remove the snap-rings.
6. Using a press or large punch, drive one of the bearing caps on the U-Joint to be replaced toward the center of the driveshaft. Remove the bearing cap opposite the cap being driven as it emerges from the driveshaft. Repeat this procedure until all the bearing caps have been removed, then, remove the spider.
7. To disassemble the ball socket from the yoke, insert a screwdriver into the centering ball socket and pry out the rubber seal. Remove the retainer, three piece ball seat, washer and spring from the ball socket.
8. Reverse above procedure to install, making sure all parts are mounted in their original location.

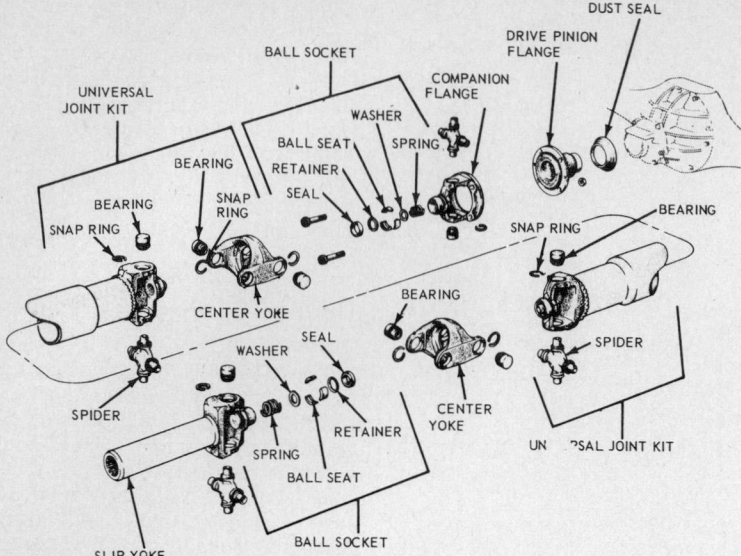

UNIVERSAL JOINT KIT
BALL SOCKET
BALL SEAT
BEARING
RETAINER
SNAP RING
SEAL
BEARING
SPRING
SNAP RING
BEARING
CENTER YOKE
SEAL
WASHER
SPIDER
RETAINER
SPRING
BALL SEAT
BALL SOCKET
SLIP YOKE
DUST SEAL
DRIVE PINION FLANGE
COMPANION FLANGE
WASHER
SPRING
BEARING
SNAP RING
BEARING
SPIDER
CENTER YOKE
UN___SAL JOINT KIT

Driveshaft with double Cardan universal joints (© Ford Motor Co.)

Rear Suspension

1965-72

The rear suspension is a coil-link design. Large, low-rate coil springs are mounted between rear axle pads and frame supports. Parallel lower arms extend forward of the spring seats to rubber frame anchor to accommodate driving and breaking forces. A third link is mounted between the axle and the frame to control torque reaction forces from the rear wheels.

Lateral (side sway) motion of the rear axle is controlled by a rubber bushed rear track bar, linked laterally between the axle and frame.

Rear Springs R & R

1. Place car on hoist and lift under rear axle housing. Place jack stands under frame side rails.
2. Disconnect track bar at the rear axle housing bracket.
3. Disconnect rear shock absorbers from the rear axle housing brackets.
4. Disconnect hose from axle housing vent.
5. Lower hoist with axle housing until coil springs are released.
6. Remove spring lower retainer with bolt, nut, washer and insulator.
7. Remove spring with large rubber insulator pads from car.
8. Install in reverse of above.

Rear Shock Absorber Replacement

Rear shock absorbers on all Fords are straddle-mounted and are held to rubber bushings at both the top and bottom connections. Simply remove the nuts from the top and bottom of the shock absorber and lift the shock absorber off the car.

Radio

Removal and Installation

1965-66 Except Thunderbird

1. Disconnect battery ground at the battery.
2. On cars with air-conditioning, disconnect air-conditioning ducts from the plenum and remove the nozzle adapter plate.
3. Remove radio knobs.
4. Remove the nut holding the bracket to the radio and position the bracket away from the radio. On cars with air-conditioning, remove the bracket.
5. Disconnect the antenna, speaker, power and pilot light leads from the radio.
6. Remove the two radio to mounting plate mounting bolts from under the instrument panel.
7. Remove the radio from under the instrument panel. Be careful not to damage the radio pointer on the sub dial.
8. Install by reversing removal procedure.

1965-66 Thunderbird

1. Pry off the right and left side console mouldings. Remove both console moulding retainers.
2. Pry off the right and left instrument panel chrome mouldings.
3. Remove the six screws and two bolts retaining the right and left side finish panels to the instrument panel. Pull the finish panels away from the Thrument panel.
4. Remove the screws holding the right and left side console finish panels. Remove the finish panels.
5. Remove the two screws holding the lower end of the radio to the support brackets.
6. Remove radio knobs and the bezel mounting nuts and washers.
7. Disconnect the antenna and speaker connectors and remove the radio.
8. Install by reversing removal procedure.

1967 Except Thunderbird

1. Disconnect battery.
2. Remove cigarette lighter and radio knobs.
3. Remove instrument cluster retaining screws and instrument cluster.
4. Remove radio support nut and two bolts which retain radio in cluster.
5. Move radio out of cluster and disconnect antenna, speaker and power leads.
6. Reverse procedure to install radio.

1967-69 Thunderbird

1. Disconnect battery.
2. Remove inspection cover plate beneath steering wheel.
3. If necessary remove vacuum motor on inboard tilt swing column to provide clearance. Place shift lever in any position but Park before removing motor.
4. Remove two knobs and discs from radio.
5. Rpmove sleeve or fader control and two hex mounting nuts from radio shafts.
6. Remove radio rear support bracket.
7. Slide radio forward and down toward inspection hole.
8. Disconnect all leads and remove radio.
9. Reverse procedure to install radio.

1968 Ford

1. Disconnect battery.
2. Remove mouldings from windshield pillars.
3. Unsnap mouldings from right side of instrument panel pad.
4. Remove two pop off access covers from cluster area.
5. Remove four screws attaching right half of pad to instrument panel.
6. Remove two screws attaching left side of pad to instrument panel above cluster.
7. Remove one screw attaching each end of instrument panel lower pad to upper pad and remove upper pad from vehicle.
8. Pull all knobs from radio control shafts.
9. Remove ten retaining buttons and remove lens and mask from instrument cluster.

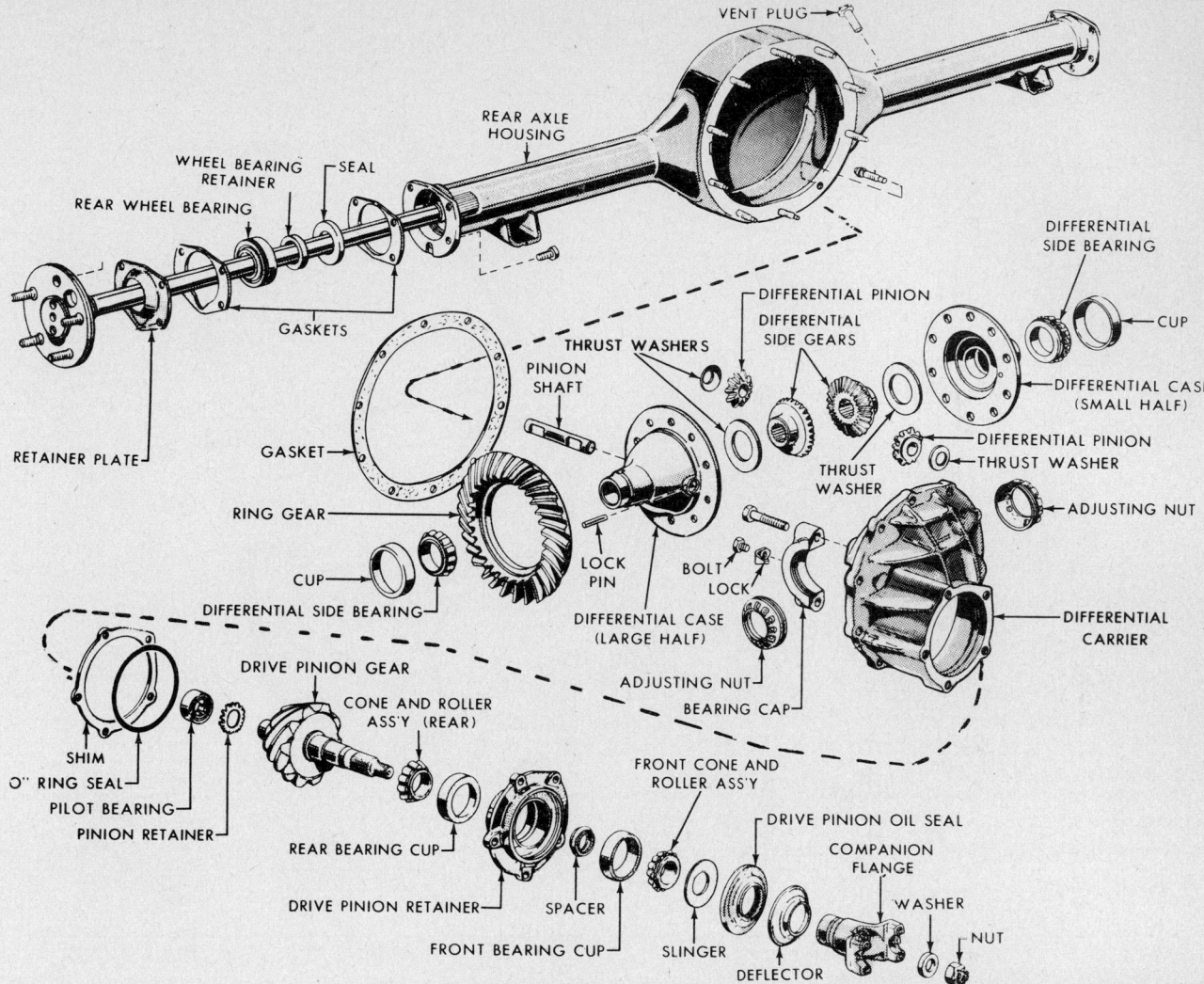

Rear axle components (© Ford Motor Co.)

10. Remove two screws from black-out **cover** at right of speedometer and **remove cover.**
11. Remove four screws attaching radio front plate to instrument cluster.
12. Pull radio out and disconnect leads.
13. Reverse procedure to install radio.

1968 Mercury

1. Disconnect the negative battery cable.
2. Pull the radio control knobs from the radio.
3. Remove the four screws attaching the bezel around the speedometer and remove the bezel.
4. Pull the windshield wiper control knob off the shaft.
5. Remove the clock and heater knobs.
6. Remove the nut attaching the radio to the rear support.
7. Remove the four screws attaching the cluster right finish cover and remove the cover.
8. Remove the four screws attaching the radio and mounting plate

to the instrument panel. Pull the radio out from the instrument panel and disconnect the radio leads from the radio.
9. Remove the mounting plate from the radio. Reverse above procedure to install.

1969-70 Mercury

1. Disconnect battery.
2. Remove radio knobs and remove nut from radio shaft.
3. Remove radio rear support nut and nut retaining radio to instrument panel.
4. Lower radio and disconnect antenna, radio, power, and speaker lead wires.
5. Remove radio. Reverse procedure to install radio.

1969-70 Ford

1. Remove radio knobs and wiper and washer knobs.
2. Remove lighter and pull off heater switch knobs.
3. Remove ten screws retaining instrument panel trim cover assembly and remove.
4. Remove lower rear radio support bolt.

5. Remove three nuts retaining radio in instrument panel and pull radio halfway out.
6. Disconnect all leads and remove radio.
7. Reverse procedure to install radio.

1970-72 Thunderbird

Use procedure under 1970-71 Mark III.

1971-72 Ford and Mercury

1. Disconnect the negative battery cable.
2. Remove the radio knobs and the nuts retaining the radio cover bezel.
3. Remove the bezel and the nut retaining the fader control to the bezel.
4. Remove the upper and lower radio support brackets and bolts.
5. Disconnect all leads from the radio.
6. Remove the two nuts retaining the radio to the instrument panel and remove the radio.
7. Reverse above procedure to install.

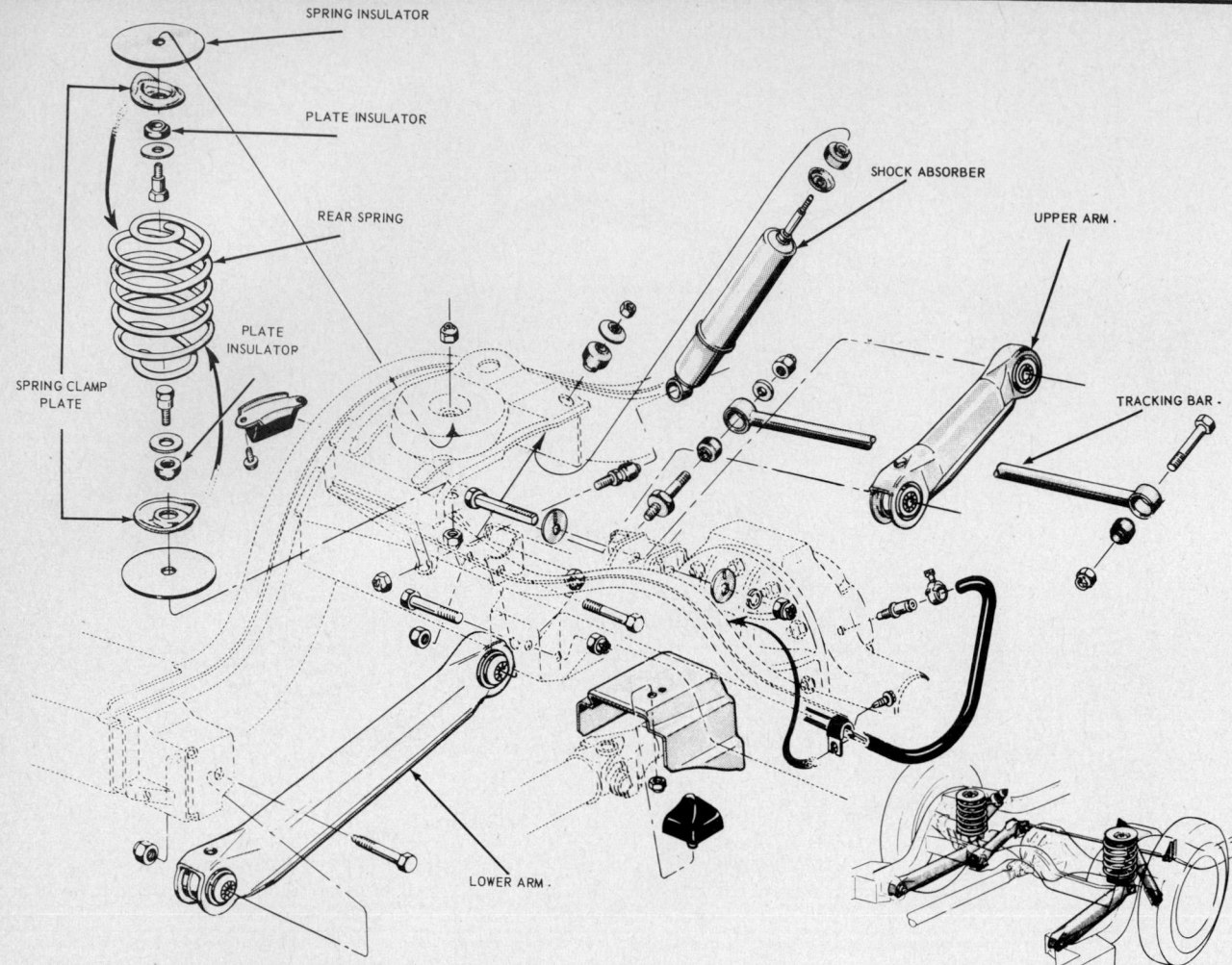

SPRING INSULATOR

PLATE INSULATOR

REAR SPRING

SHOCK ABSORBER

UPPER ARM .

PLATE INSULATOR

TRACKING BAR .

SPRING CLAMP PLATE

LOWER ARM .

Rear suspension—beginning 1965 (© Ford Motor Co.)

Windshield Wipers

Motor R & R

Ford, 1965-72

1. Disconnect the negative battery cable.
2. Remove the wiper arm and blade assemblies from the pivot shafts.
3. On 1966-70 models, remove the cowl grille. On 1971-72 vehicles, remove the left side cowl grille.
4. Disconnect the wiper links at the wiper output pin by removing the retaining clip.
5. Disconnect the wire leads from the motor. On 1965-68 models the leads are located under the hood; and, on 1969-72 cars they are located under the dash.
6. On 1965-68 models, remove the motor and bracket attaching bolts from the engine side of the firewall and remove the motor from the car. On 1969-72 models, remove the motor attaching bolts from under the dash and remove the motor.
7. Reverse above procedure to install.

NOTE: before installing the wiper arms and blades, operate the wiper motor to ensure the pivot shafts are in the park position when the arms and blades are installed.

T-Bird, 1965-72 Except 1970

This motor works by hydraulic pressure taken from the power steering system. During wiper operation, a part of the fluid supply is bypassed through the wiper motor by a valve on the motor.

1. Remove wiper arm and blade assemblies, pivot shaft nuts and bezels.
2. Remove the cowl top panel.
3. Disconnect both pivot shaft links at the wiper motor.
4. Remove carburetor air cleaner.

Caution If the engine has been running recently, watch out for hot fluid in the wiper system.

5. Disconnect the lines at the wiper motor.
6. Remove wiper motor mounting screws.
7. Disconnect the Tcontrol cable from the motor, then remove the motor.

8. If replacing the wiper motor, transfer all fittings.
9. Position motor to the bracket area, connect and adjust the control cable.
10. Start the lines in the fittings, position the motor on its mount and install attaching screws. Tighten fittings.
11. Connect the links to the wiper motor arm.
12. Start engine and check operation of wiper motor. Stop engine and bring power steering reservoir to level.
13. Reinstall cowl top panel.
14. Install bezels, nuts and wiper arm assemblies. Install the air cleaner.

T-Bird, 1970

1970 Thunderbirds used electric, two-speed wipers instead of the usual hydraulic type.

1. Disconnect the negative battery cable.
2. Disconnect the windshield washer hose. Remove the three retaining bolts and pull the cowl grille from under the two clips.
3. Disconnect the wiper motor leads from the engine side of the

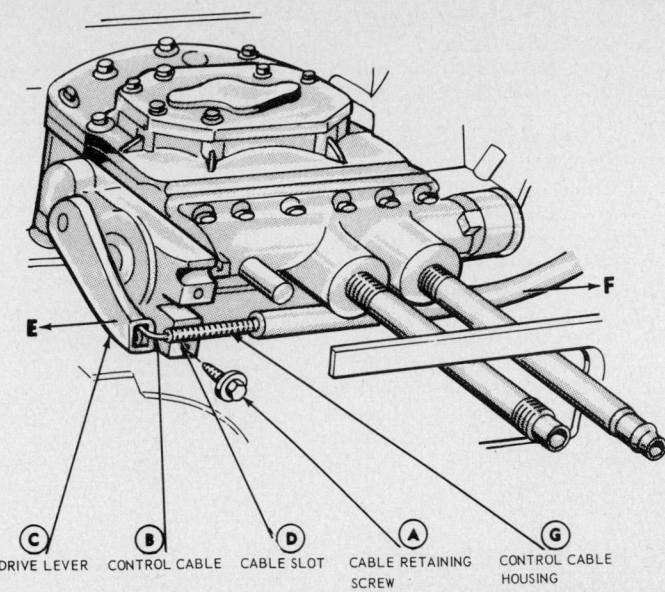

Hydraulic windshield wiper motor (© Ford Motor Co.)

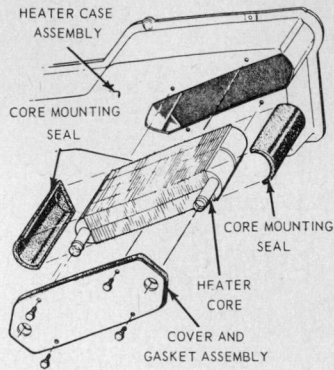

Ford heater core installation
(© Ford Motor Co.)

firewall and push the wiring and insulating grommet through the hole in the firewall.

4. Remove the four motor to dash retaining bolts.

5. Lift the wiper motor out and, at the same time, pull the wiper arm and blade assembly to the left to gain access to the wiper output pin.

6. Remove the clip and disconnect the wiper links from the motor.

7. Remove the three motor-to-mounting plate bolts and remove the motor.

8. To reinstall, first position the wire harness and grommet in the hole in the firewall, then reverse above procedure.

Transmission or Linkage R & R

1965-72 All Models

1. Disconnect the battery ground cable.

2. Remove the wiper arms and blades from the pivots as an assembly. On Thunderbird be sure to remove the tension arm retaining clip from the stud on the left pivot.

3. Remove the cowl grille from the car.

4. Disconnect the linkage arm from the drive arm by removing the clip.

5. Remove the pivot attaching screws from the cowl and remove the pivot from the cowl.
NOTE: on 1969-72 Fords and Mercurys, to remove the left wiper transmission, it is first necessary to loosen the attaching screws on the right wiper arm pivot.

Heater System

Heater Core R & R

1965-72 Ford and Mercury

1. Partially drain cooling system.
2. Remove heater hoses at core.
3. Remove retaining screws, core cover and seal from plenum.
4. Remove core from plenum.
5. Install in reverse of above, applying a thin coat of silicone to the pads.

T-Bird 1965-66

1. Partially drain cooling system.
2. Disconnect hoses from heater core.
3. Remove lower instrument panel.
4. Remove right-hand trim panel from console.
5. Disconnect defroster hoses at heater.
6. Disconnect Bowden control cables from heater control head and from fresh-air door on heater.
7. Disconnect wiring.
8. Under hood, remove nuts holding heater to dash.
9. Remove rear support screw near the fresh air intake.
10. Ease heater to floor of car. Use care not to spill coolant on carpets.
11. Install in reverse of above.

T-Bird 1967-72

1. Remove the hood and air cleaner.
2. Drain the cooling system.
3. Remove the heater hoses and po-

sition the hoses and hot water valve out of the way.
4. Disconnect the vacuum hose from the top of the heater case and position it out of the way.
5. Remove the transmission dip stick and tube assembly from the transmission.
6. Disconnect the blower motor lead wires.
7. Remove the heater core case cover and remove the core from the case.
8. Reverse above procedure to install.

Heater Blower Motor R & R

1965-66 Thunderbird

1. Working under the hood, remove the wiring leads from the motor.
2. Remove the blower motor mounting screws and remove the motor from the cowl.

1967-72 Thunderbird

1. Working inside the car, remove the right kick panel cover.
2. Remove the screws attaching the fresh air duct and remove the duct from the car.
3. Reach inside the cowl panel and disconnect the blower motor wire leads.
4. Still working inside the cowl panel, remove the one screw attaching the blower motor to the mounting plate. Rotate the motor mounting plate clockwise to disengage it from the heater case.
5. Remove the blower motor and wheel assembly from the car by guiding it out of the opening in the cowl panel.

1965-67 Ford and Mercury

1. Open the hood and mark the location of the hood hinges on the hood. Remove the hood attaching bolts and remove the hood.

2. Remove the retaining nut and bolt and remove the right hood hinge support.

3. Remove the retaining bolts and remove the right hood hinge and support as an assembly.

4. Disconnect the heater motor wires.

5. Remove the heater motor mounting screws and on 1967 models remove the motor from the car. On 1965-66 models, remove the rear upper fender and hood bumper bolt; then, lift the rear of the fender ¼ in. and remove the motor from the car.

6. Reverse above procedure to install.

1968, '69 and '71-72 Ford and Mercury

1. Disconnect the negative battery cable.

2. Disconnect the blower motor wire leads under the hood.

3. Remove any parts mounted on the inside of the right fender apron.

4. Raise the vehicle on a hoist and remove the right front wheel.

5. Remove the fender apron-to fender attaching bolts and lower the fender apron.

6. Insert a block of wood between the apron and the fender to gain working space.

7. Reach inside the fender apron and remove the blower motor mounting plate attaching screws.

8. Remove the blower motor, wheel and mounting plate from inside the fender as an assembly.

9. Reverse above procedure to install.

1970 Ford and Mercury

1. Open the hood and mark the location of the hood hinges on the hood. Remove the hood from the car.

2. Remove the right hood hinge assembly from the car.

3. Disconnect the right fender attaching bolts and remove the fender from the car.

4. Disconnect the blower motor wire leads.

5. Remove the blower motor mounting plate attaching screws and remove the blower motor, wheel and mounting plate from the car as an assembly.

6. Reverse above procedure to install.

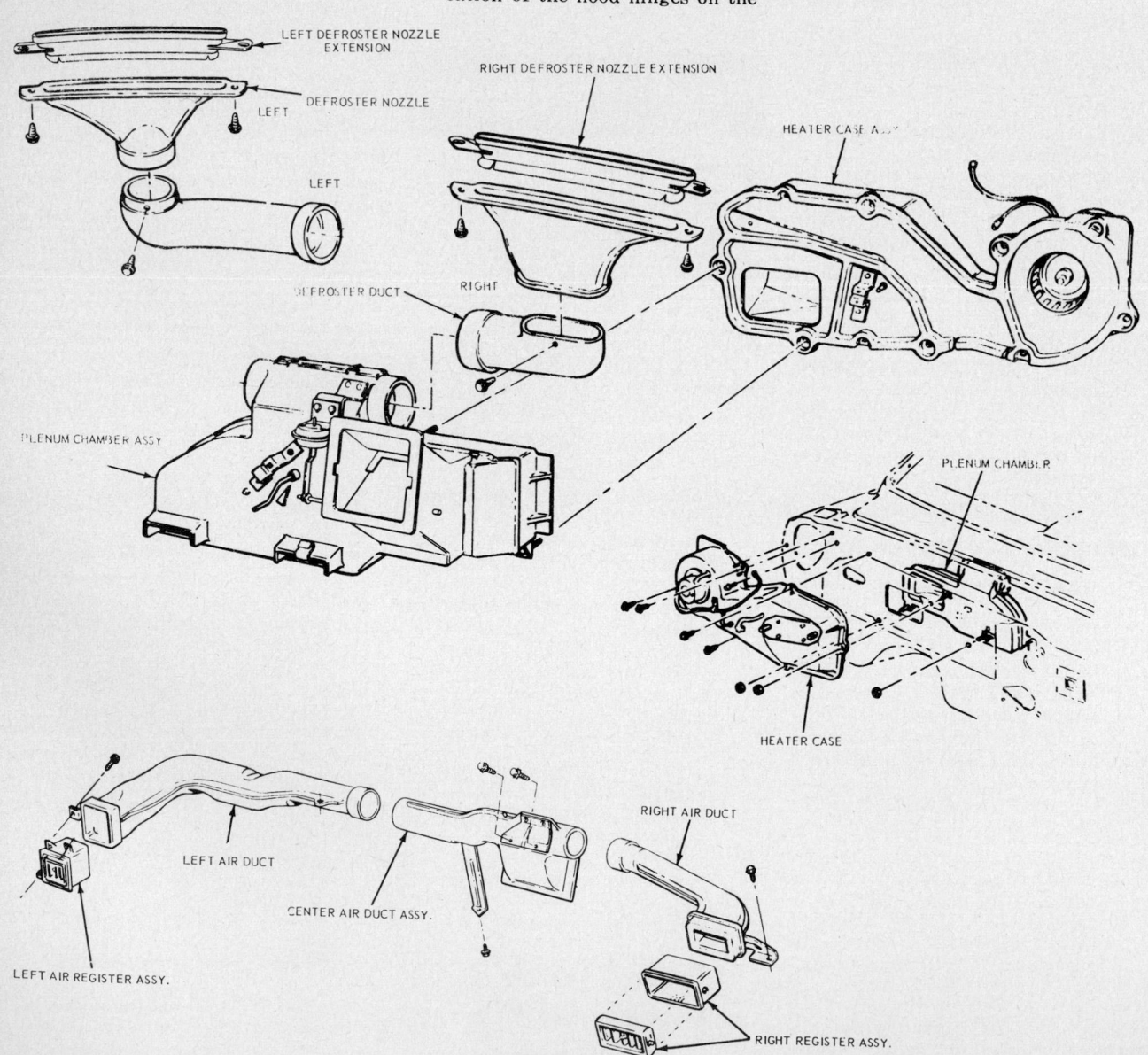

Index

YEAR IDENTIFICATION

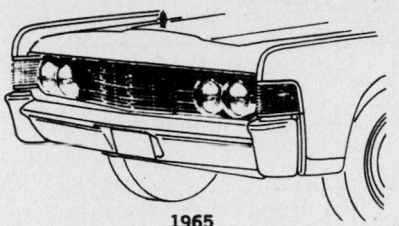

1965

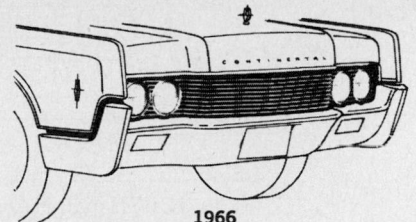

1966

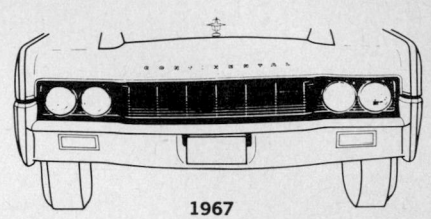

1967

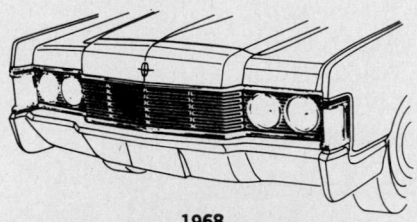

1968

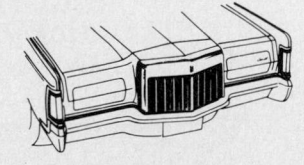

1969 Mark III

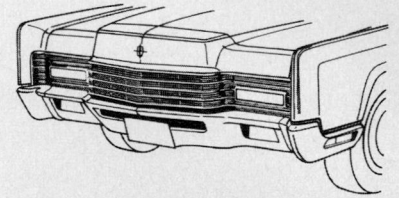

1970 Continental

1970 Mark III

1971 Lincoln Continental

1971 Continental Mark III

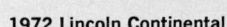

1972 Lincoln Continental

1972 Continental Mark IV

FIRING ORDER

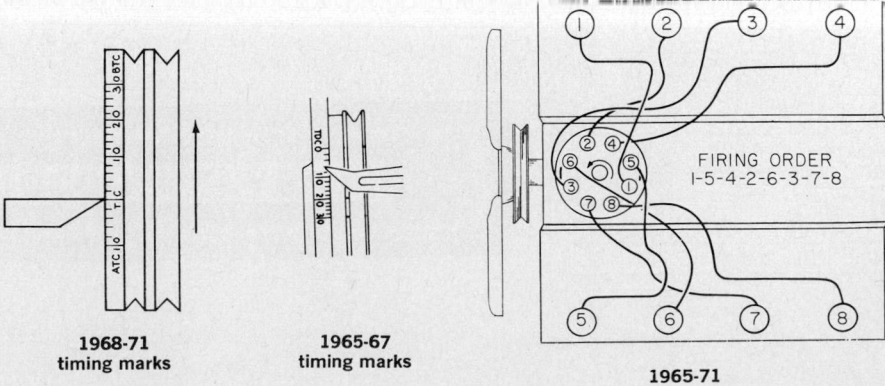

1968-71 timing marks

1965-67 timing marks

FIRING ORDER 1-5-4-2-6-3-7-8

1965-71

CAR SERIAL NUMBER LOCATION

1965-68

The vehicle number is stamped on a plate attached to the left front door hinge post. The engine number and vehicle number are identical.

1969-72

The vehicle number is stamped on an aluminum tab riveted to the top of the instrument panel, visible through the driver's side windshield. The serial number contains eleven digits. They are interpreted as follows:

First: Model year code. (9 = 1969, 0 = 1970, 1 = 1971, 2 = 1972)
Second: Assembly plant code.
Third and fourth: Body serial code.
Fifth: Engine code. (A = 460 cu. in.)
Last six: Consecutive unit number.

Vehicle Certification Label

1970-72

The vehicle certification label is attached to the left-hand door jamb. This label has, on its upper portion, the name of the manufacturer, the month and year of manufacture, and the certification statement. The label also shows the vehicle identification number, which must match that on the dashboard. See the illustration for interpretation of the label.

Engine Identification

No. Cyls.	Cu. In. Displ.	Type	YEAR AND CODE						
			1965	1966	1967	1968	1969	1970	1971
8	460	4-BBL.					A	A	A
8	462	4-BBL.		G	G	G			
8	430	4-BBL.	N						

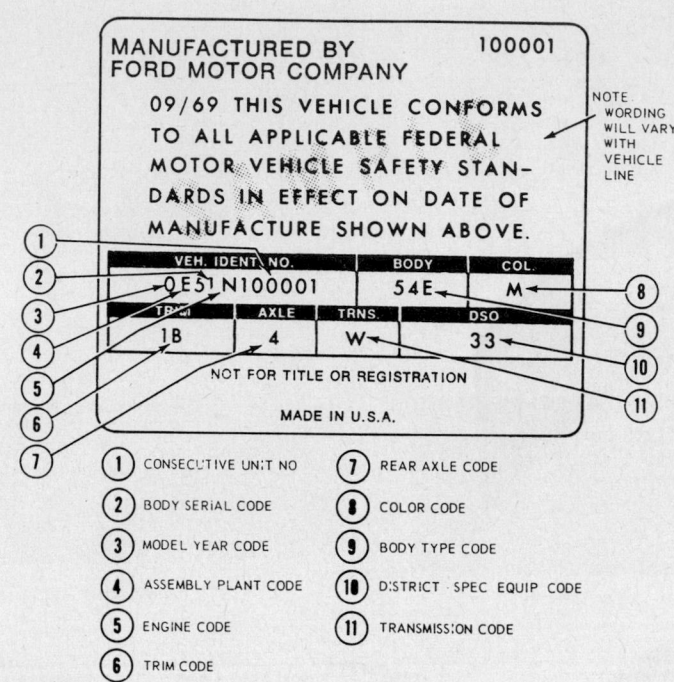

Vehicle certification label—1970-72

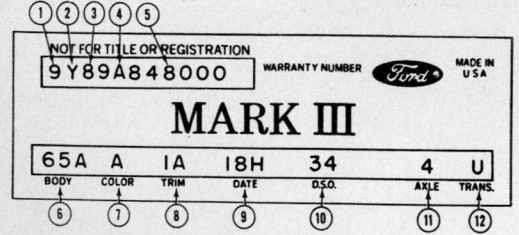

1 Model year code
2 Assembly plant code
3 Body serial code
4 Engine code
5 Consecutive unit number
6 Body type code
7 Color code
8 Trim code
9 Date code
10 District—special equipment code
11 Rear axle code
12 Transmission code

TUNE-UP SPECIFICATIONS

YEAR	MODEL	SPARK PLUGS Type	Gap (In.)	DISTRIBUTOR Point Dwell (Deg.)	Point Gap (In.)	IGNITION TIMING (Deg.) ▲	CRANKING COMP. PRESSURE (Psi)	VALVES Tappet (Hot) Clearance (In.) Intake	Exhaust	Intake Opens (Deg.)	FUEL PUMP PRESSURE (Psi)	IDLE SPEED (Rpm) ★
1965	All	BF42	.035	26–28	.015	6B	180	Zero	Zero	22B	5–6	465
1966–67	Std. Ign.	BTF42	.034	26–31	.017	10B	180	Zero	Zero	20B	5–6	500 ⊙
	Transistor Ign.	BTF42	.034	22–24	.020	10B	180	Zero	Zero	20B	5–6	500 ⊙
1968	All	BTF42	.034	24–29	.021	6B	180	Zero	Zero	20B	5–6	550
1968–69	460 Cu. In.	BF42	.034	26–31	.017	10B	190	Zero	Zero	16B	4–5	600 ③
1970–72	460 Cu. In.	BF42	.032–.036	27–31.5	.017–.021	10B	190 ①	Zero	Zero	16B	5.5–6.5	590 ②

★—With manual transmission in N and automatic in D.
▲—With vacuum advance disconnected. NOTE: These settings are only approximate. Engine design, altitude, temperature, fuel octane rating and the condition of the individual engine are all factors which can influence timing. The limiting advance factor must, therefore, be the "knock point" of the individual engine.

⊙—500–525 with Thermactor system.
B—Before top dead center.
①—Lowest reading must be at least 75% of the highest.
②—With lights on and A/C off.
③—1969—550, in Drive w/A.C. and lights on.

Caution

General adoption of anti-pollution laws has changed the design of almost all car engine production to effectively reduce crankcase emission and terminal exhaust products. It has been necessary to adopt stricter tune-up rules, especially timing and idle speed procedures. Both of these values are peculiar to the engine and to its application, rather than to the engine alone. With this in mind, car manufacturers supply idle speed data for the engine and application involved. This information is clearly displayed in the engine compartment of each vehicle.

GENERAL ENGINE SPECIFICATIONS

YEAR	CU. IN. DISPLACEMENT	CARBURETOR	ADVERTIZED HORSEPOWER @ RPM	ADVERTIZED TORQUE @ RPM (FT. LBS.)	A.M.A. HORSEPOWER	BORE & STROKE (IN.)	ADVERTIZED COMPRESSION RATIO	VALVE LIFTER TYPE	NORMAL OIL PRESSURE (PSI)
1965	430	4-BBL.	320 @ 4600	465 @ 2600	59.7	4.300 x 3.700	10.1:1	Hyd.	50
1966–68	462	4-BBL.	340 @ 4600	485 @ 2800	61.4	4.380 x 3.830	10.25:1	Hyd.	45
1968–69	460	4-BBL.	365 @ 4600	500 @ 2800	60.8	4.360 x 3.850	10.5:1	Hyd.	35–60 ①
1970–71	460	4-BBL.	365 @ 4600 ②	500 @ 2800 ②	60.8	4.362 x 3.850	10.5:1	Hyd.	35–75 ①
1972	460	4-BBL.	②	②	60.8	4.362 x 3.850	②	Hyd.	35–75 ①

①—At 2,000 rpm.
②—Not available at press time

VALVE SPECIFICATIONS

YEAR AND MODEL		SEAT ANGLE (DEG.) IN.	FACE ANGLE (DEG.) EX.	VALVE LIFT INTAKE (IN.)	VALVE LIFT EXHAUST (IN.)	VALVE SPRING PRESSURE (VALVE OPEN) LBS. @ IN.	VALVE SPRING INSTALLED HEIGHT (IN.)	STEM TO GUIDE CLEARANCE (IN.) Intake	Exhaust	STEM DIAMETER (IN.) Intake	Exhaust
1965	430 Cu. In.	45 45	44	.408	.408	220–240 @ 1.39	1.64	.0008–.0018	.0020–.0030	.3711–.3722	.3701–.3709
1966–68	462 Cu. In.	45 45	44	.442	.442	220–240 @ 1.39	1.65	.0008–.0025	.0010–.0027	.3710–.3717	.3708–.3715
1968–69	460 Cu. In.	45 45	44	.442	.486	240–266 @ 1.33	1.81	.0010–.0027	.0010–.0027	.3416–.3423	.3416–.3423
1970	460 Cu. In.	44½–45	45½–45¾	.442	.486	240–266 @ 1.33	1.81	.0010–.0027	.0010–.0027	.3416–.3423	.3416–.3423
1971–72	460 Cu. In.	44½–45	45½–45¾	.442	.486	240–266 @ 1.33	1.81	.0010–.0027	.0010–.0027	.3416–.3423	.3416–.3423

CRANKSHAFT BEARING JOURNAL SPECIFICATIONS

YEAR	MODEL	MAIN BEARING JOURNALS (IN.) Journal Diameter	Oil Clearance	Shaft End-Play	Thrust On No.	CONNECTING ROD BEARING JOURNALS (IN.) Journal Diameter	Oil Clearance	End-Play
1965–68	430, 462 Cu. In.	2.8994–2.9002	.0016	.006	3	2.5992–2.6001	.0016	.006
1968–72	460 Cu. In.	2.9994–3.0002	.0005–.0025	.004–.008	3	2.4992–2.5000	.0008–.0026	.010–.020 ①

①—Both rods.

GENERAL CHASSIS AND BRAKE SPECIFICATIONS

YEAR	MODEL	CHASSIS			BRAKE CYLINDER BORE			BRAKE DRUM	
		Overall Length (In.)	Tire Size	Master Cylinder (In.)	Wheel Cylinder Diameter (In.)			Diameter (In.)	
					Front	Rear		Front	Rear
1965	All	216¹/₃	9.15 x 15	1.0	1¹⁵/₁₆	¹⁵/₁₆		11.87 Disc	11.03■
1966	All	220.9	9.15 x 15	1.0	1¹⁵/₁₆	¹⁵/₁₆		11.87 Disc	11.03■
1967–69	All Exc. Mark III	220.9①	9.15 x 15	1.0	1¹⁵/₁₆	¹⁵/₁₆		11.96 Disc	11.09②
1968–69	Mark III	216.1	8.55 x 15	1.0	2³/₄	¹⁵/₁₆		11.72 Disc	11.03■
1970–72	All Exc. Mark III, IV	225.0	9.15 x 15	1.0	1¹⁵/₁₆	¹⁵/₁₆		11.72 Disc	11.03
1970–72	Mark III, IV	216.1	225R15	1.0	2.755	¹⁵/₁₆		11.72 Disc	11.03■

■—Refinishing Limit—11.090.
①—1969, 224.2.
②—Refinishing Limit—11.150.

AC GENERATOR AND REGULATOR SPECIFICATIONS

YEAR	MODEL	ALTERNATOR				REGULATOR						
		Field Current Draw @ 12V.	Output @ Alternator RPM		Model	Field Relay			Regulator		
			900	6500		Air Gap (In.)	Point Gap (In.)	Volts to Close	Air Gap (In.)	Point Gap (In.)	Volts at 125°
1965	Ford Std.	2.9–3.1	10	40	Ford	.020	.019	2½–4	.052	.020	13.8–14.6
	Ford Opt.	2.9–3.1	10	42	Ford	.020	.019	2½–4	.052	.020	13.8–14.6
	Ford Opt.	2.8–3.3	10	55	Ford	.018	.019	2–3	.052	.020	13.8–14.6
1966–67	Autolite	4.4–4.8	10	60	Autolite	.014	—	2½–4	.052	.020	13.8–14.6
1968–69	Autolite	2.9–3.1	22	55	Autolite	.018	.019	2½–4	.052	.020	13.3–15.3
1970–72	Autolite① DOLF—10300	2.9–3.1	22	55	Autolite	Transistor Type				N.A.	13.3–14.6
	Autolite② DOAF—10300	2.8–3.3	28	65	Autolite	Transistor Type				N.A.	13.8–15.3

①—Integral regulator.
②—Opt.; required with heated back window.

BATTERY AND STARTER SPECIFICATIONS

YEAR	MODEL	BATTERY			STARTERS						
		Ampere Hour Capacity	Volts	Terminal Grounded	Lock Test			No-Load Test			Brush Spring Tension (Oz.)
					Amps.	Volts	Torque	Amps.	Volts	RPM	
1965	All	80	12	Neg.	670	4.0	15.5	70	12.0	9,500	40
1966–69	All	85	12	Neg.	670	5.0	15.5	70	12.0	9,500	40
1970–72	All	85	12	Neg.	Not Recommended			70	12.0	—	40

WHEEL ALIGNMENT

YEAR	MODEL	CASTER		CAMBER		TOE-IN (In.)	KING-PIN INCLINATION (Deg.)	WHEEL PIVOT RATIO	
		Range (Deg.)	Pref. Setting (Deg.)▲	Range (Deg.)	Pref. Setting (Deg.)■			Inner Wheel	Outer Wheel
1965–69	Continental	2¼ N–¾ N	1½ N	0–¾ P	½ P	¹/₁₆–³/₁₆	7³/₄	20	17³/₄
1968–70	Mark III	½ P–1½ P	1	0–1 P	½ P	¹/₈–¼	7³/₄	20	19.3
1970	Continental	2¼ N–¾ N	1½ N	¹/₈ P–⁵/₈ P	½ P	0–¹/₁₆	7³/₄	20	18½
1971–72	Continental	2½ N to ½ N	1½ N	¼ N–1¼ N	½ P	0–¼	7⁷/₈	20	18¹/₁₂
	Mark III, IV	0–2 P	1	¼ N–1¼ P	½ P	¹/₁₆–⁵/₁₆	7³/₄	20	19¼

■—Not to vary more than ½ degree from one side to the other.
▲—Not to vary more than ¼ degree from one side to the other.
N—Negative.
P—Positive.

CAPACITIES

YEAR	MODEL	ENGINE CRANKCASE ADD 1 Qt. FOR NEW FILTER	TRANSMISSIONS Pts. TO REFILL AFTER DRAINING			DRIVE AXLE (Pts.)	GASOLINE TANK (Gals.)	COOLING SYSTEM (Qts.) WITH HEATER
			Manual		Automatic			
			3-Speed	4-Speed				
1965	All Models	5	None	None	23	4.8	24	25
1966-67	All Models	5	None	None	26	5.5	25.5	23
1968-69	462 Cu. In.	5	None	None	27	5.0	25.5	23.5
1968-69	Mark III	4	None	None	26.5	5.0	25.5	19.3
1970-72	Mark III, IV	4	None	None	26	5.0	24②	19.4
1970-72	460 Cu. In.	4	None	None	26	5.0	24.5①	19.6③

①—1970 w/Evap. Emission—23.5; 1971-72—22.5.
②—1970 w/Evap. Emission—22.5; 1971-72—22.5.
③—1971-72—19.4.

TORQUE SPECIFICATIONS

YEAR	MODEL	CYLINDER HEAD BOLTS (FT. LBS.)	ROD BEARING BOLTS (FT. LBS.)	MAIN BEARING BOLTS (FT. LBS.)	CRANKSHAFT BALANCER BOLT (FT. LBS.)	FLYWHEEL TO CRANKSHAFT BOLTS (FT. LBS.)	MANIFOLD (FT. LBS.)	
							Intake	Exhaust
1965-68	430, 462 Cu. In.	125-135①	40-45	95-105	75-90	75-85	23-28	15-21
1968-72	460 Cu. In.	130-140②	40-45	95-105	70-90	75-85	25-30	28-33

①—1966-68 462 Cu. In. 135-145.
②—In three steps: Step 1—70-80
Step 2—100-110
Step 3—130-140

CYLINDER HEAD BOLT TIGHTENING SEQUENCE

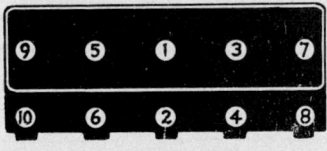

1965-72

CIRCUIT PROTECTION—1968 LINCOLN

Circuit	Location	Protective Device	Circuit	Location	Protective Device
Cigar lighter (front)	Fuse panel	AGC 15	Warning lights: open door, deck lid open, seat belt	Fuse panel	SFE 7.5
Cigar lighter (rear)	Fuse panel	AGC 15			
Interior lights: dome, courtesy, map, glove box and luggage compartment and clock feed	Fuse panel	SFE 14	Heater and air-conditioner	R.H. cowl side panel	30 C.B.
			Electric seats and horns	R.H. cowl side panel	30 C.B.
			Electric windows	R.H. cowl side panel	20 C.B.
Electric antenna	Fuse panel	AGC 10	Stoplights and emergency warning	R.H. cowl side panel	10 C.B.
Instrument panel lights, trans. indicator light (PRNDL)	Fuse panel	SFE 6	Taillights, license light, parking lights, ash tray light	In headlight switch	15 C.B.
Speed control, pwr. window by-pass switch, A/C and heater relay, defogger blower	Fuse panel	SFE 14	Headlights	In headlight switch	18 C.B.
			Power circuit	Terminal junction block and starter motor relay	Fuse assy. (fuse link wire) (6-in. long no. 14 gauge wire)
Radio	Fuse panel	SFE 7.5			
Back-up lights, windshield washer, turn signals	Fuse panel	SFE 15	Windshield wiper	Hydraulically operated	(No fuse or circuit breaker)

CIRCUIT PROTECTION 1968–69 MARK III

Circuit	Circuit Protection—Fuse or Circuit Breaker (C.B.)		Location
	Rating	Trade No.	
Headlight Circuit	18 Amp. C.B.		Integral with Lighting Switch
Tail Lights, Running Lights, License Plate Light, Parking Lights, Marker Lights	15 Amp. C.B.		Integral with Lighting Switch
Instrument Panel and Instrument Cluster Illumination	6 Amp.	SFE 6	Fuse Panel
Clock Feed, Courtesy Lights, Luggage Compartment Light, Glove Compartment Light, Map Light and Reading Lights	14 Amp. ①	SFE 14 ①	Fuse Panel
Warning Lights (except Low Fuel Warning)	7.5 Amp.	SFE 7.5	Fuse Panel
Low Fuel Warning	7.5 Amp.	SFE 7.5	Fuse Panel
Windshield Washer and Back-Up Lights	7.5 Amp.	SFE 7.5	Fuse Panel
Turn Signal	7.5 Amp.	SFE 7.5	Fuse Panel
Ammeter	14 Amp.	SFE 14	Fuse Panel
Speed Control	7.5 Amp.	SFE 7.5	Fuse Panel
Radio	7.5 Amp.	SFE 7.5	Fuse Panel
Power Antenna	10 Amp.	3AG 10	Fuse Panel
Front Cigar Lighter and Stereo	15 Amp.	SFE 15	Fuse Panel
Rear Cigar Lighter	15 Amp.	SFE 15	Fuse Panel
Power Seats, Windows and Horns	30 Amp. C.B.		Circuit Breaker Panel (Seat and window motors also protected by integral circuit breakers)
Stop Lights and Emergency Warning	10 Amp. C.B.		Circuit Breaker Panel
Heater and Air Conditioner	30 Amp. C.B.		Circuit Breaker Panel
Charging Circuit	Fusible Link		NFusible Link Block (below starter relay in engine compartment)
Headlight Dimmer	4 Amp.		Fuse Cartridge in Feed Wire
Anti-Skid Brake Control	3 Amp.	SFE3	Fuse Panel

① —Use 20 Ampere SFE 20 fuse if equipped with moveable steering column.

CIRCUIT PROTECTION—1965–67 LINCOLN

Circuit	Location	Protective Device-Fuse Or Circuit Breaker (C.B.) In Amperes	Circuit	Location	Protective Device-Fuse Or Circuit Breaker (C.B.) In Amperes
Cigar lighter (front)	Fuse panel	AGC 15	Top control neutral relay	R.H. cowl side panel	10 C.B.
Cigar lighter (rear)	Fuse panel	AGC 15	Stoplights and emergency warning	R.H. cowl side panel	15 C.B.
Interior lights: dome, courtesy, map, glove box and luggage compartment	Fuse panel	SFE 14	Taillights, license light, parking lights, ash tray light	In headlight switch	15 C.B.
Electric antenna	Fuse panel	AGC 10	Headlights	In headlight switch	18 C.B.
Instrument panel lights, trans. indicator light (PRNDL)	Fuse panel	SFE 6	Upper back panel motor control	In luggage comp't.	30 C.B.
Speed control	Fuse panel	SFE 14	Deck lock control and top lock motor control	In luggage comp't.	30 C.B.
Radio	Fuse panel	SFE 7.5	Top control motor feed	Terminal junction block and starter motor relay	Fuse assy (fuse link wire) (6-in. long no. 12 gauge wire)
Back-up lights and windshield washer	Fuse panel	SFE 15			
Turn signals	Fuse panel	SFE 15			
Warning lights: open door, deck lid open, seat belt	Fuse panel	SFE 5	Power circuit	Terminal junction block and starter motor relay	Fuse assy (fuse link wire) (6-in. long no. 14 gauge wire)
Heater and air-conditioner	R.H. cowl side panel	30 C.B.			
Electric seats and horns	R.H. cowl side panel	30 C.B.	Windshield wiper	Hydraulically operated (no fuse or circuit breaker)	
Electric windows	R.H. cowl side panel	20 C.B.			

CIRCUIT PROTECTION—1969 LINCOLN CONTINENTAL

Circuit	Location	Protective Device	Circuit	Location	Protective Device
Ash receptacle light (front)	Fuse panel	SFE 14	Instrument panel lights: clock, defogger indicator, fuel gauge, heater/defroster and A/C control lights, radio dial light, speed control indicator	Fuse panel	SFE 6
Ash receptacle light (rear)	In headlight switch	15 C.B.			
Back-up lights	Fuse panel	7AG or AGW 15			
Cigar lighter (front)	Fuse panel	3AG or AGC 15			
Cigar lighter (rear)	Fuse panel	3AG or AGC 15	License light	In headlight switch	15 C.B.
Clock feed	Fuse panel	SFE 14	Marker lights	In headlight switch	15 C.B.
Courtesy lights: dome, map, glove box, luggage compartment, reading lights, C pillar lights	Fuse panel	SFE 14	Power window motors	Integral part of motor	C.B.
			Radio	Fuse panel	SFE 7.5
Defogger motor	Fuse panel	SFE 14	Speed control circuit	Fuse panel	SFE 14
Electric antenna	Fuse panel	3AG or AGC 10	Stereo tape player	Fuse panel	SFE 7.5
Emergency flasher	R.H. cowl side panel	15 C.B.	Stop lights	R.H. cowl side panel	15 C.B.
Headlights	In headlight switch	18 C.B.	Taillights	In headlight switch	15 C.B.
Heater and air-conditioner	R.H. cowl side panel	30 C.B.	Transmission indicator light (PRNDL)	Fuse panel	SFE 6
Horns	R.H. cowl side panel	30 C.B.	Turn signals	Fuse panel	7 AG or AGW 15
Ignition switch light	Integral with lighting switch	15 C.B.	Windshield washer	Fuse panel	7 AG or AGW 15
			Optional equipment power circuit	Terminal junction block and starter motor relay	Fuse assembly (fuse link wire) (7 inch long no. 14 gauge wire)
Indicator lights: brake, deck lid open, engine temperature, low fuel, oil pressure, open door, seat belt	Fuse panel	SFE 7.5			
			Parking lights	In headlight switch	15 C.B.
			Power seats	R.H. cowl side panel	30 C.B.
			Power seats motors	Integral part of motor	C.B.
			Power windows	R.H. cowl side panel	20 C.B.
			Power window by-pass switch	Fuse panel	SFE 14

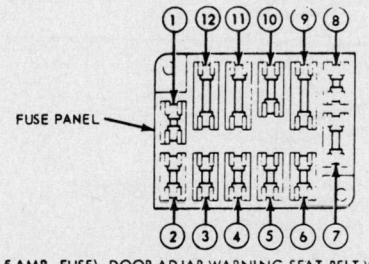

FUSE PANEL →

LOCATED IN RIGHT SIDE
OF GLOVE BOX
IN BACK OF
REMOVABLE COVER

① (7.5 AMP. FUSE) DOOR ADJAR WARNING SEAT BELT WARNING BRAKE SYS. WARNING
ENGINE TEMP FUEL GAUGE

② (7.5 AMP. FUSE) LOW FUEL WARNING

③ (7.5 AMP. FUSE) POWER WINDOW SAFETY RELAY COIL FEED,

④ (7.5 AMP. FUSE) BACK-UP LAMPS SPEED CONTROL

⑤ (7.5 AMP. FUSE) TURN SIGNALS

⑥ (7.5 AMP. FUSE) WINDSHIELD WASHER REAR WINDOW DEFOGGER

⑦ (SPARE OR 3 AMP. FUSE) SURE-TRACK BRAKE SYS.

⑧ (6 AMP. FUSE) ILLUMINATION LAMPS INSTRUMENT PANEL CLUSTER RADIO PRND 21
HEATER/A.C. CONTROLS ASH TRAY

⑨ (15 AMP. FUSE) POWER ANTENNA

⑩ (14 AMP. FUSE) COURTESY LAMPS, CLOCK FEED, LUGGAGE COMPT. LAMP,
GLOVE COMPT. LAMP, ENGINE COMPT. LAMP,
MAP LAMP AND REAR READING LAMPS

⑪ (15 AMP. FUSE) FRONT LIGHTERS, RADIO AND STEREO TAPE

⑫ (15 AMP. FUSE) REAR LIGHTERS

Fuse panel—1970-71 Mark III

① BLANK OR 20 AMP. FOR HEATED BACKLITE

② (20 AMP.) POWER WINDOWS

③ (30 AMP.) HEATER, A/C

④ (10 AMP.) STOP LIGHTS, EMERGENCY FLASHER

⑤ (30 AMP.) HORNS POWER SEATS AND A/C
HIGH SPEED BLOWER

Circuit breaker panel—1970-71 Mark III
(in 1971 No. 2 is 1, 3 is 2 and 3 is spare)

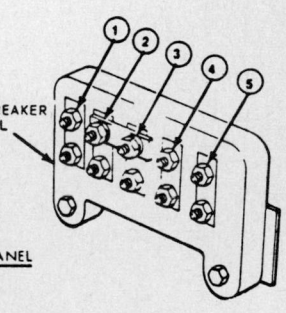

CIRCUIT BREAKER
PANEL

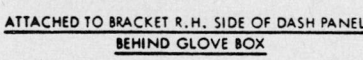

ATTACHED TO BRACKET R.H. SIDE OF DASH PANEL
BEHIND GLOVE BOX

FUSES AND CIRCUIT BREAKERS NOT IN PANEL— 1970–72 LINCOLN CONTINENTAL

Circuit	Rate	Location	Circuit	Rate	Location
Automatic headlamp dimmer	4 AMP SFE-4	In-line fuse	Headlights, headlight door open warning light	18 AMP C.B.	In headlight switch
Parking lights, license light, tail lights, ash receptacle light, marker lights	15 AMP C.B.	In headlight switch	Motors, power seat, power windows	C.B.	In motor assembly
			Windshield wiper	7.5 AMP Fuse ①	In wiper switch
			Seat Back latch solenoid	C.B.	In solenoid

① 1971-72—8.25

FUSES AND CIRCUIT BREAKERS NOT IN PANEL— 1970–72 MARK III, IV

Circuit	Rate	Location	Circuit	Rate	Location
Parking lights, license light, tail lights, marker lights, headlight buzzer, motors	15 AMP	In headlight switch	Headlight circuit	18 AMP	In headlight switch
			Windshield wiper	Integral	In wiper switch
			Rear window defroster	20 AMP	On brake pedal support
Power seat, power windows	Integral	In motor assembly			

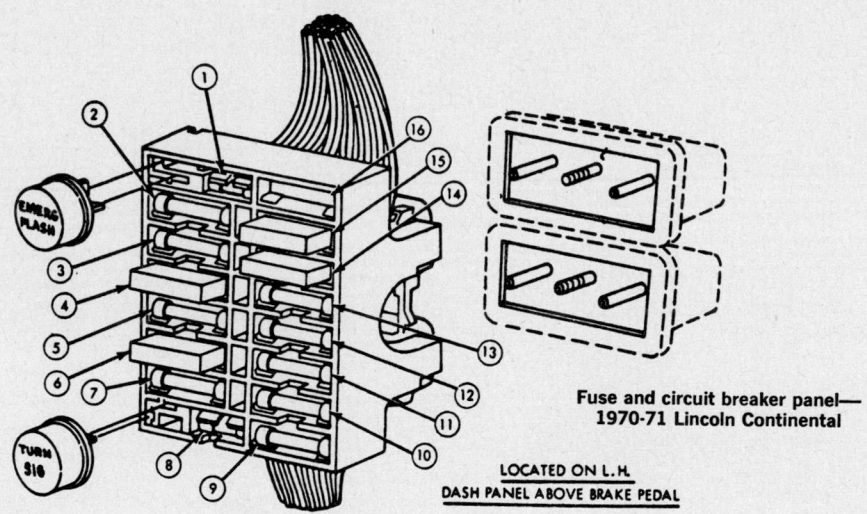

Fuse and circuit breaker panel— 1970-71 Lincoln Continental

LOCATED ON L. H.
DASH PANEL ABOVE BRAKE PEDAL

① (SPARE) OR (3 AMP. FUSE) SURE TRACK (BRAKE SKID CONTROL)
② (7.5 AMP. FUSE) WARNING LAMPS, DOOR AJAR, DECK LID OPEN, LOW FUEL, SEAT BELT, DUAL BRAKE
③ (20 AMP. FUSE) CIGAR LIGHTER (FRONT), DOOR LOCK SOLENOID
④ (20 AMP. C.B.) STOPLAMPS & EMERGENCY WARNING SYSTEM
⑤ (20 AMP. FUSE) CIGAR LIGHTER (REAR)
⑥ (30 AMP. C.B.) POWER SEAT, HORNS
⑦ (15 AMP. FUSE) COURTESY LAMPS, DOORS, "C" PILLAR READING, LUGGAGE COMPT., MAP, GLOVE BOX, & CLOCK FEED, SEAT BACK LATCH CONTROL, DOME LAMP

⑧ (6 AMP. FUSE) (INSTR. PANEL LAMPS) UPPER & LOWER CLUSTER ILLUM. CLOCK, HTR. & A/C, W/S WIPER, MAP LAMP SWITCH ILLUM., RADIO LAMP & PRNDL LAMP
⑨ (7.5 AMP. FUSE) SPEED CONTROL, DEFOGGER, W/S WASHER & SEAT BELT WARNING (STD.)
⑩ (15 AMP. FUSE) TURN SIGNAL & CORNERING LAMPS & BACK-UP LAMPS
⑪ (25 AMP. FUSE) HEATED BACK WINDOW
⑫ (7.5 AMP. FUSE) POWER WINDOW SAFETY RELAY COIL FEED
⑬ (7.5 AMP. FUSE) RADIO, POWER ANTENNA & STEREO TAPE PLAYER
⑭ (20 AMP. C.B.) POWER WINDOWS
⑮ (30 AMP. C.B.) AIR CONDITIONER, HEATER & DEFROSTER
⑯ (SPARE)

1965–67 LINCOLN CONTINENTAL

Light Description	Bulb No.	Candlepower or Wattage	Light Description	Bulb No.	Candlepower or Wattage
Engine compartment	93	15 C.P.	Ash receptacle or cigar lighter	1445	1.5 C.P.
Glove compartment	1895	2 C.P.	Back-up lamps	1156	32 C.P.
Headlamps hi-lo beam (outer or upper)	4002	37.5-50W	Courtesy lamp	631	6 C.P.
hi beam (inner or lower)	4001	37.5W	("C" pillar)	1003	15 C.P.
License lamp	97	4 C.P.	(console)	1895	2 C.P.
Luggage compartment	631	6 C.P.	(door mounting or armrest)	212	6 C.P. (fuse type)
Map light	631	6 C.P.	Clock and ignition key	158	2 C.P.
Park and turn signal lamp	1157-A	4-32 C.P.	Control nomenclature (ex. c. heater)	158	2 C.P.
Taillight, stop and turn signal	1157	32 C.P.	Control, right and left	1895	2 C.P.
Door lock warning	158	2 C.P.	Gages and speedometer	158	2 C.P.
Emergency flasher	158	2 C.P.	Heater control	158	2 C.P.
Hi-beam indicator	158	2 C.P.	Radio dial light AM	1893	1.9 C.P.
Low fuel warning	1895	2 C.P.	AM-FM	1893	1.9 C.P.
Oil press., alt and temp warning	158	2 C.P.	Trans. control selector indicator	1445	1.5 C.P.
Parking brake warning	158	2 C.P.	Turn signal indicators (L and R)	158	2 C.P.
Seat belt warning	158	2 C.P.	Trunk warning	158	2 C.P.
Utility lamp (double end) dealer	1155	4 C.P.	Cruise control indicator	158	2 C.P.
accessory	1143	32 C.P.			

1968 LINCOLN CONTINENTAL

Light Description	Bulb No.	Candela or Wattage ①	Light Description	Bulb No.	Candela or Wattage ①
Engine compartment	631	6C.	Courtesy light (roof)	631	6C.
Glove compartment	1895	2C.	(quarter)	1003	15C.
Headlights hi-lo beam	4002	37.5-50W	(console)	1895	2C.
hi beam	4001	37.5W	(door mounting or armrest)	212	6C. (fuse type)
License light	97	4C.	Clock and ignition key	1895	2C.
Luggage compartment	631	6C.	Control nomenclature (ex. C. heater)	1895	2C.
Map light	212	6C.	Control, right and left	1895	2C.
Park and turn signal light	1157NA②	4—32C.	Gauges and speedometer	194	2C.
Taillight, stop and turn signal	1157	4—32C.	Heater control	1895	2C.
Door lock warning	1895	2C.	Radio dial light AM	1893	1.9C.
Emergency flasher	1895	2C.	AM-FM	1893	1.9C.
Hi-beam indicator	1895	2C.	Trans. control selector indicator (tilt)	1445	1.5C.
Low fuel warning	1895	2C.	Turn signal indicators (L and R)	1895	2C.
Oil press., alt. and temp. warning	1895	2C.	Trunk warning	1895	2C.
Seat belt warning	1895	2C.	Cruise control indicator	1445	1.5C.
Utility light (double end) dealer	1155	4C.	Trans. control selector indicator (fixed)	194	2C.
accessory	1143	32C.	Spotlight	4405	30 W
Ash receptacle or cigar lighter	1445	1.5C.	Manual A/C control	1895	2C.
Back-up lights	1156	32C.	ATC control	1895	2C.

① — Candela is the international term for candlepower.
② — Natural amber color.

1969 MARK III

Light Description	Bulb No.	Candela or Wattage	Light Description	Bulb No.	Candela or Wattage
ATC control	1895	2C.	Hi-beam indicators	194	2C.
Auto. trans. select. ind.—fixed & tilt column	1445	1.5C.	Ignition switch	161	1C.
			Instrument panel courtesy light	631	6C.
Back-up light	1156	32C.	Instruments	194	2C.
Brakes & belts indicator	194	2C.	License plate light	97	4C.
Cigar lighter	1895	2C.	Low fuel indicator	194	2C.
Control nomenclature: rear vent & wipers	194	2C.	Luggage compartment	90	6C.
			Manual A/C control	1895	2C.
Door ajar indicator	1891	2C.	Map light	212	6C.
Door courtesy light	211 or 211-1	12C.	Parking brake signal	1895	2C.
Emergency flasher	1891	2C.	Radio pilot light	1893	1.9C.
Engine compartment	631	6C.	AM/FM stereo pilot light	1892	1.3C.
Fog lights—clear	4415	35 W	Rear-side marker	97	4C.
Fog light switch	53X	1C.	Rear tail/stop/turn signal	1157	3–32C.
Front park & turn signal	1157NA	3–32C.	Roof quarter light	1003	15C.
Front side marker	1178A	4C.	Seat belt indicator	1891	2C.
Glove compartment	1895	2C.	Trunk light (portable)	1003	15C.
Headlights—hi & lo	4002	37.5 & 50 W	Trunk open indicator	1891	2C.
Headlights—hi-beams	4001	37.5 W	Turn signal indicators	168A	3C.
Heater controls	1895	2C.			

1969 LINCOLN CONTINENTAL

Light Description	Bulb No.	Candela or Wattage	Light Description	Bulb No.	Candela or Wattage
Ash receptacle or cigar lighter	1445	1.5C.	Luggage compartment	631	6C.
ATC control	1895	2C.	Manual A/C control	1895	2C.
Back-up lights	1156	32C.	Map light	212	6C.
Clock and ignition key	1895	2C.	Oil press., alt. and temp indicator	1895	2C.
Courtesy light			Park and turn signal light	1157NA ①	3–32C.
C pillar	1003	15C.	Radio dial light		
glove compartment	1895	2C.	AM	1893	1.9C.
door	212	6C.	AM/FM	1891	2C.
Cruise control indicator	1445	1.5C.	AM/FM stereo	1892	1.3C.
Door lock warning	1895	2C.	Seat belt indicator	1895	2C.
Engine compartment	631	6C.	Side marker lights (front)	1178A	4C.
Glove compartment	1895	2C.	Side marker lights (rear)	194	2C.
Headlights			Speed control actuator indicator	1445	1.5C.
hi-lo beam	4002	37.5–50W	Spotlight	4405	30W
hi beam	4001	37.5W	Taillight, stop and turn signal	1157	3–32C.
Heater control	1895	2C.	Trans. control selector indicator (fixed)	158	2C.
Hi-beam indicator	1895	2C.	Trans. control selector indicator (tilt)	1445	1.5C.
Instrument cluster illumination	1895	2C.	Trunk light (portable)	1003	15C.
License light	97	4C.	Trunk open indicator	1895	2C.
Low fuel indicator	1895	2C.	Turn signal indicators (L and R)	1895	2C.

① —Natural amber color.

1970–72 LINCOLN CONTINENTAL

Light Description	Trade No.	Candle Power or Wattage	Light Description	Trade No.	Candle Power or Wattage
Headlamps			L & R turn signal indicator	1895	2 c.p.
hi-lo beam	4002	37.5 & 50 watts	Hi beam indicator	1895	2 c.p.
hi-beam	4001	37.5	Heater control	1895	2 c.p.
Front parking lamps and turn signal	1157A	3–32 c.p.	Courtesy lamp	631	6 c.p.
Front side marker	194-A ①	2 c.p. ①	Illumination	1895	2 c.p.
Rear side marker	1895 ①	2 c.p. ①	Speedometer	1895	2 c.p.
Rear lamp, stop and turn signal	1157	3–32 c.p.	Clock	1895	2 c.p.
Rear seat reading	105	12 c.p.	Ash tray (instr. panel and rear)	1445	1.5 c.p.
Luggage compartment	631	6 c.p.	Door lock nomenclature	1895	2 c.p.
License plate	97	4 c.p.	Low fuel warning	1895	2 c.p.
Back-up lamp	1156	32 c.p.	Auto. trans. ind. lamp	1445	1.5 c.p.
Courtesy lamp (door) 4-door	212	6 c.p. fuse type	Radio AM signal seeking	1893	1.9 c.p.
Courtesy lamp (C pillar)	105	12 c.p.	Radio AM-FM Stereo	1891	2.0 c.p.
Map	212	6 c.p.	Radio AM-stereo tape	1893	1.9 c.p.
*212-1 used in 2-door models			Engine compartment	631	6 c.p.
Instrument panel			Speed control illumination	1445	1.5 c.p.
Warning lights	1891	2 c.p.	Headlamp door open	194	2 c.p.
Glove compartment	1895	2 c.p.			

① — 1971-72—161, 1 c.p.

1970–72 MARK III, IV

Light Description	Trade No.	Candle Power or Wattage	Light Description	Trade No.	Candle Power or Wattage
Headlight—hi-lo beam	4002	37.5 & 50 W	Overhead console warning lights	1891	2 c.p.
hi beam	4001	37.5 W	Courtesy lights	631	6 c.p.
Front park & turn signal	1157NA	3–32 c.p.	Hi-beam indicator	194	2 c.p.
Rear tail/stop/turn signal	1157	3–32 c.p.	Turn signal indicators	168-A	3 c.p.
Back up light	1156	32 c.p.	Warning lights, brake & low fuel	194	2 c.p.
License plate light	97	4 c.p.	Warning light, rear window defroster	1892	1.3 c.p.
Rear seat reading light	105	12 c.p.	Instrument illumination light	194	2 c.p.
Glove compartment light	1895	2 c.p.	Radio dial light	1893	1.9 c.p.
Transmission control selector			Heater/air cond./auto. temp.		
indicator light	1445	1.5 c.p.	control light	1895	2 c.p.
Door courtesy lights	212	6 c.p.	Wiper control lights	194	2 c.p.
Map light	212	6 c.p.	Cigar lighter light	1895	2 c.p.
Front side marker light	97NA	4 c.p.	Speed control light	53X	1 c.p.
Rear side marker light	97	4 c.p.	Ash tray light	1445	1.5 c.p.
Luggage compartment light	90	6 c.p. ①	Courtesy lamp (I/p)	90	6 c.p.
			Courtesy lamp (C pillar)	105	12 c.p.

① — 1971-72—631, 6 c.p.

Distributor

Distributor Removal

The distributor is located at the front of the engine between the cylinder banks.

Remove the carburetor air cleaner, take off the ignition primary lead and the vacuum advance lead. Carefully mark the position of the rotor in relation to the body of the distributor, and mark the position of the body of the distributor relative to the chamber cover. Remove the hold-down bolt and lift out distributor. The marks are made so that the distributor can be reinstalled without having to retime the ignition.

Ignition Timing

The ignition timing is marked on the vibration damper and it is recommended that a stroboscopic-type timing light be used to determine the exact point of ignition.

Ignition Retiming

If the timing relationship has been disturbed, retime the ignition as follows: bring No. 1 cylinder up to the firing position. This can be checked by removing the spark plug, placing your thumb in the spark plug hole and then cranking the engine until the compression attempts to blow by your thumb. Now, slowly bring the crankshaft around until the T.D.C. mark on the crankshaft pulley lines up with the pointer. This is the approximate firing position for No. 1 cylinder.

Remove the distributor cap and mark the position of the rotor on the outside of the distributor. The wire from No. 1 spark plug should be placed in the socket just above the rotor. Now, working in the direction of distributor rotation, place the spark plug wires into the cap according to the firing order of the engine.

Alternator, Regulator

Facts on the alternator and the regulator are in the Alternator and Regulator Specifications table.

General information on alternator and regulator repair and troubleshooting is in the Unit Repair Section under the heading Basic Electrical Diagnosis.

Alternator

Cars are equipped with alternating current generators. This charging system is different from the DC circuit, and requires certain precautions.

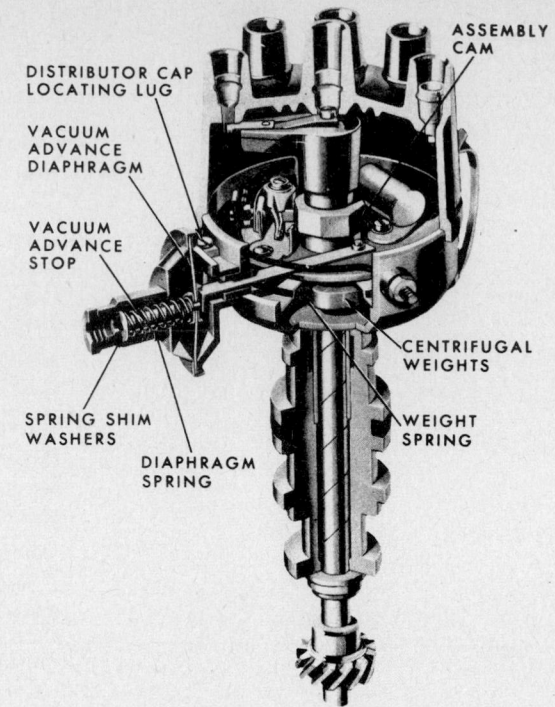

Distributor (© Ford Motor Co.)

1. Reversing battery connections will cause damage to the one-way electrical valves, the rectifiers.
2. Booster battery connections must be made as follows: the negative terminal of the booster battery must be connected to the negative terminal of the car battery. The positive terminal of the booster battery must be connected to the positive terminal of the car battery.
3. Fast charges should never be used as boosters to start AC circuit equipped cars.
4. When servicing the battery with a fast charger, always disconnect car battery cables.
5. Never attempt to polarize an AC generator.

Complete alternator servicing data is in the Unit Repair Section.

Alternator R & R

1. Disconnect the negative battery cable.
2. Loosen the alternator mounting bolts, remove the alternator to adjusting arm bolt and remove the belt.
3. Remove the alternator mounting bolt and spacer, position the alternator so that the wire connectors can be disconnected and remove the alternator.

NOTE: on alternators with integral regulators mounted on the back of the alternator housing, press the sides of the retainer clip and remove the wire from the regulator.

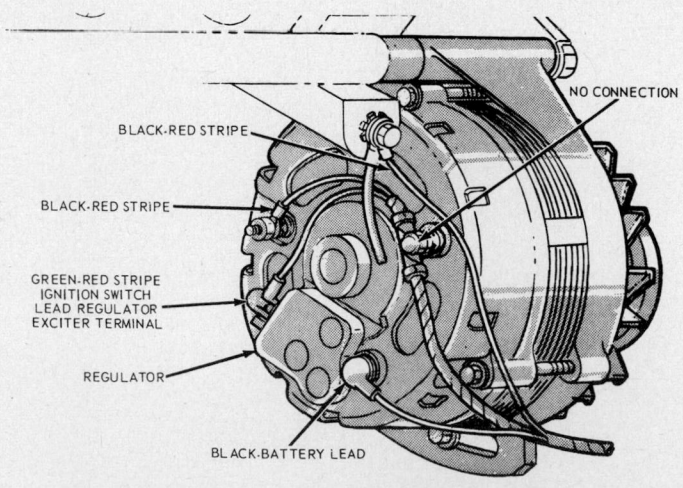

Alternator installation with integral regulator (© Ford Motor Co.)

4. Reverse above procedure to reinstall, applying pressure only to the front of the alternator housing when tightening the drive belt.

Regulator R & R

1. Disconnect the negative battery cable.
2. Remove the regulator mounting screws and wires, then remove the regulator.
3. On vehicles with integral regulator, remove the alternator to adjusting arm bolt and the drive belt.
4. Swing the alternator down, remove the terminal covers from the regulator and remove the regulator attaching nuts.
5. Press the sides of the retainer clip and remove the retaining clip and supply wire. Remove the regulator.
6. Reverse above procedure to reinstall.

Fuse Link

Since 1970, all Ford products have incorporated a fuse link in the charging system. The fuse link is a short length of insulated wire, several gauge sizes smaller than the system it protects. The fuse link blows out if a booster battery is hooked into the system incorrectly, or if a component of the electrical system is shorted to ground. When the fuse link blows, it leaves an open circuit in the charging system and the alternator will not charge the battery. A blown fuse link can be identified by bare wire ends or bubbled insulation. It is located in the engine wire harness on or near the starter relay and is marked FUSE LINK.

Starter

Starter R & R

Disconnect starter cable, raise car, turn front wheels fully to the right. Remove the two bolts attaching the steering idler arm, remove starter mounting bolts. Remove starter.

Instruments

1965 Cluster Removal

1. Disconnect battery.
2. Remove heater, air conditioner, blower and radio control knobs.
3. Remove the screws holding instrument bezel to panel and remove bezel.
4. Remove the finish molding from upper edge of instrument panel.
5. Remove screws from trim collar at steering column and remove collar.

6. Remove screws from right and left lower panel end plates.
7. Remove screws from plate over steering column and remove plate.
8. Remove lock cylinder from ignition switch.
9. Remove screws from upper edge of lower instrument panel.
10. Remove jam nuts and disconnect speedometer trip reset and clock reset from lower edge of lower panel.
11. Remove hood lock release control handle and bracket from lower panel.
12. Remove speed control head and mounting bracket from lower panel.
13. Remove fuse block cover plate in glove compartment, and remove screws holding fuse block to lower panel.
14. Disconnect compartment courtesy light.
15. Disconnect rear deck lid lock release control handle.
16. Remove instrument switch from lower panel. Do not disconnect wires.
17. Remove headlight switch. Do not disconnect wires.
18. Remove knob from wiper control lever.
19. Remove wiper control bezel, wiper and washer control from panel.
20. Remove bolts at right and left sides of lower panel to inner cowl panel.
21. Remove ash tray and disconnect tray light and lighter leads.
22. Remove lower panel from car.
23. Reinstall by reversing the above procedure.

1966-69 Cluster Removal Except Mark III

1. Disconnect battery.
2. Remove six screws in air conditioning register casting assembly and pull register rearward until it hangs on ducts.
3. Remove three screws between cluster hood and crash pad.
4. Remove four screws in lower windshield moulding and remove moulding.
5. Remove two screws and two nuts in forward edge of crash pad.
6. Disconnect radio speaker lead and remove crash pad.
7. Remove radio knobs and bezels.
8. Remove heater, air conditioning control, and windshield wiper control knobs.
9. Remove four nuts and four retainers on shafts of radio, heater, air conditioning, and windshield wiper control.
10. Remove eight screws in lower control housing and drop housing.
11. Remove four screws from under-

side of instrument panel attaching finish cover and remove cover.
12. Remove odometer reset knob.
13. Remove three screws retaining lower edge of upper cluster finish panel.
14. Remove four screws retaining upper edge of upper cluster finish panel.
15. Remove nine screws retaining mask and lens to cover and remove mask and two piece lens.
16. Remove eight screws retaining speedometer dial plate to cover and remove dial. Reverse procedure to install.

1970-72 Cluster Removal Except Mark III

1. Remove instrument panel pad. Do not remove cluster trim cover, if only instrument cluster is to be removed.
2. Reach under instrument panel and disconnect instrument cluster printed circuit plug from receptacle.
3. From passenger side of instrument panel, remove cluster to cluster housing retaining screws and swing cluster away from housing.
4. From underside of housing unhook pointer control cable from PRNDL pointer lever.
5. Remove cable retaining clip (one nut) from cluster and remove cluster from vehicle.

1968-71 Mark III Instrument Cluster R&R

Removal

1. Disconnect battery ground cable.
2. Remove five attaching screws from upper edge of instrument cluster pad and retainer assembly. Remove the pad and retainer from face of instrument cluster.
3. Remove clock knob. Remove eight push-type retainer buttons from the instrument cluster mask and remove the mask.
4. Remove three screws holding the speedometer to the cluster and pull the speedometer from the cluster. Disconnect the two speedometer cable-to-cluster retaining screws and clamps, release the tab of the plastic retainer and remove it from the cable. If equipped with speed control, disconnect speedometer cable at speed-control-unit instead.
5. Remove eight screws holding the instrument cluster to the instrument panel. Remove the three screws holding the rear vent and wiper control pod. Pull the cluster and pod out of the panel.
6. Disconnect the multiple connector and the low fuel warning

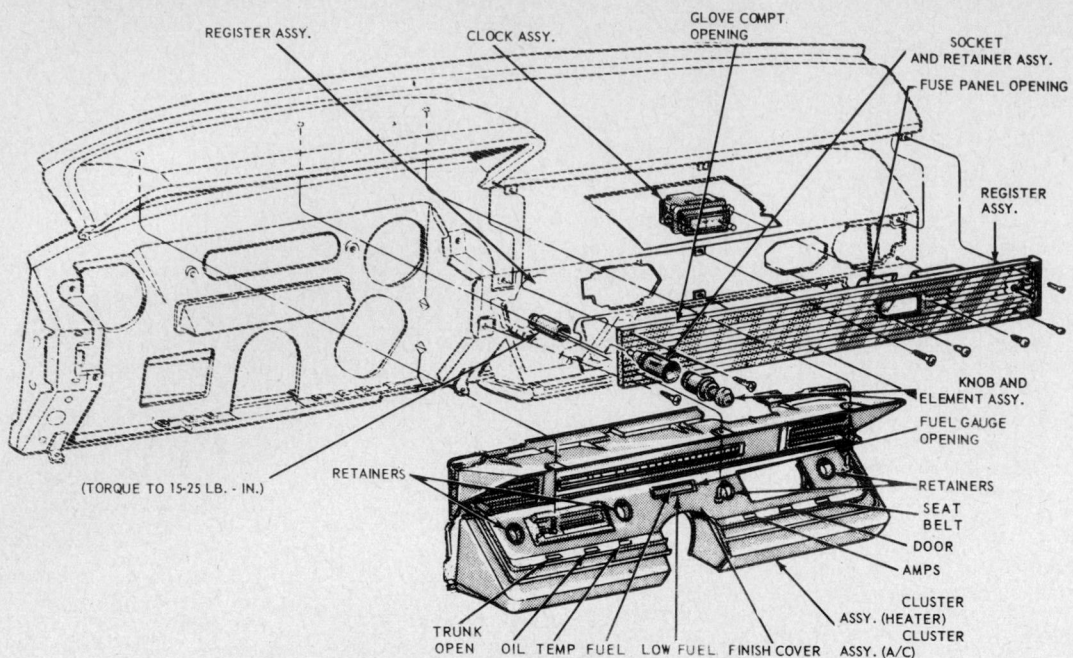

REGISTER ASSY.

CLOCK ASSY.

GLOVE COMPT.
OPENING

SOCKET
AND RETAINER ASSY.

FUSE PANEL OPENING

REGISTER
ASSY.

KNOB AND
ELEMENT ASSY.

FUEL GAUGE
OPENING

RETAINERS

RETAINERS
SEAT
BELT
DOOR
AMPS

CLUSTER
ASSY. (HEATER)
CLUSTER
ASSY. (A/C)

(TORQUE TO 15-25 LB. - IN.)

TRUNK
OPEN   OIL TEMP FUEL LOW FUEL FINISH COVER

Lower control housing—1966-69 (© Ford Motor Company)

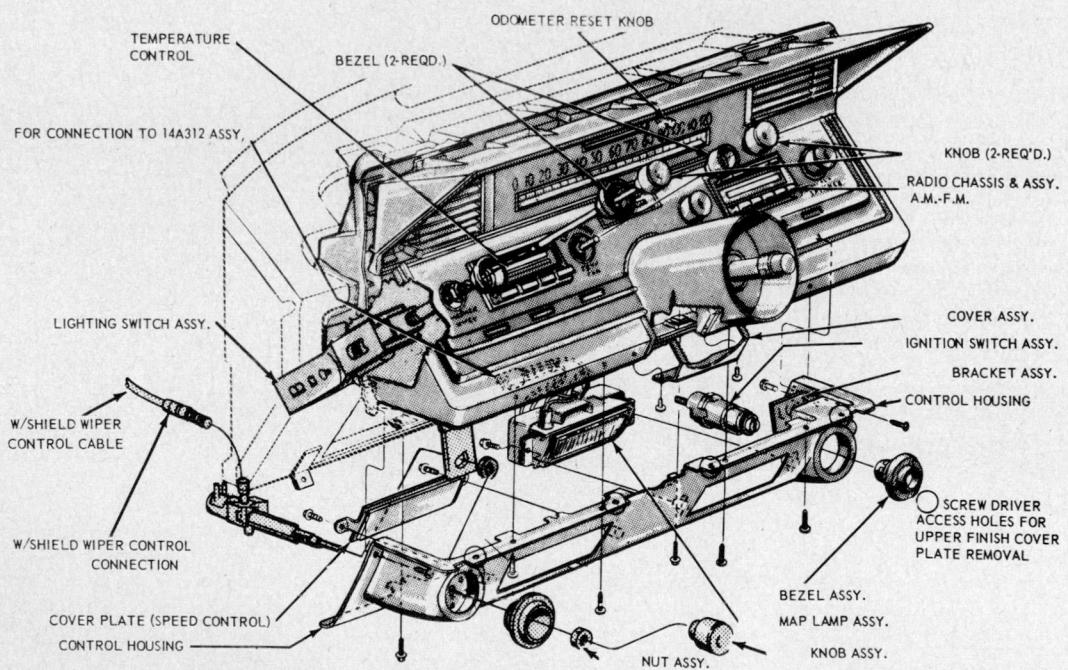

TEMPERATURE
CONTROL

BEZEL (2-REQD.)

ODOMETER RESET KNOB

FOR CONNECTION TO 14A312 ASSY.

KNOB (2-REQ'D.)

RADIO CHASSIS & ASSY.
A.M.-F.M.

LIGHTING SWITCH ASSY.

COVER ASSY.
IGNITION SWITCH ASSY.
BRACKET ASSY.
CONTROL HOUSING

W/SHIELD WIPER
CONTROL CABLE

SCREW DRIVER
ACCESS HOLES FOR
UPPER FINISH COVER
PLATE REMOVAL

W/SHIELD WIPER CONTROL
CONNECTION

BEZEL ASSY.
MAP LAMP ASSY.

COVER PLATE (SPEED CONTROL)

CONTROL HOUSING

NUT ASSY.

KNOB ASSY.

Typical instrument panel cluster—1966-69 (© Ford Motor Company)

lights at the printed circuit. Then, remove the instrument cluster.

Installation

1. Connect instrument cluster multiple connector to the printed circuit. Install the low fuel warning and dual brake warning lights to the cluster.
2. Guide the speedometer cable through the cluster housing and install the plastic retainer to the cable.

3. Position the instrument cluster to the panel and insert the eight retainer screws. Insert the two speedometer cable retaining screws and clamps.
4. Position the speedometer to the cluster and insert the three retaining screws. Connect the speedometer cable to the speed-control-unit, if so equipped.
5. Position the rear vent and wiper control pod to the panel and insert the three retaining screws.
6. Position the instrument cluster

mask and install the eight push-type retainer buttons. Install the clock knob.
7. Position instrument cluster pad and retainer assembly to the face of the cluster and insert the five screws holding the upper edge of the pad to the instrument panel pad.
8. Connect battery ground cable.

Speedometer R & R
1965

1. Disconnect battery.

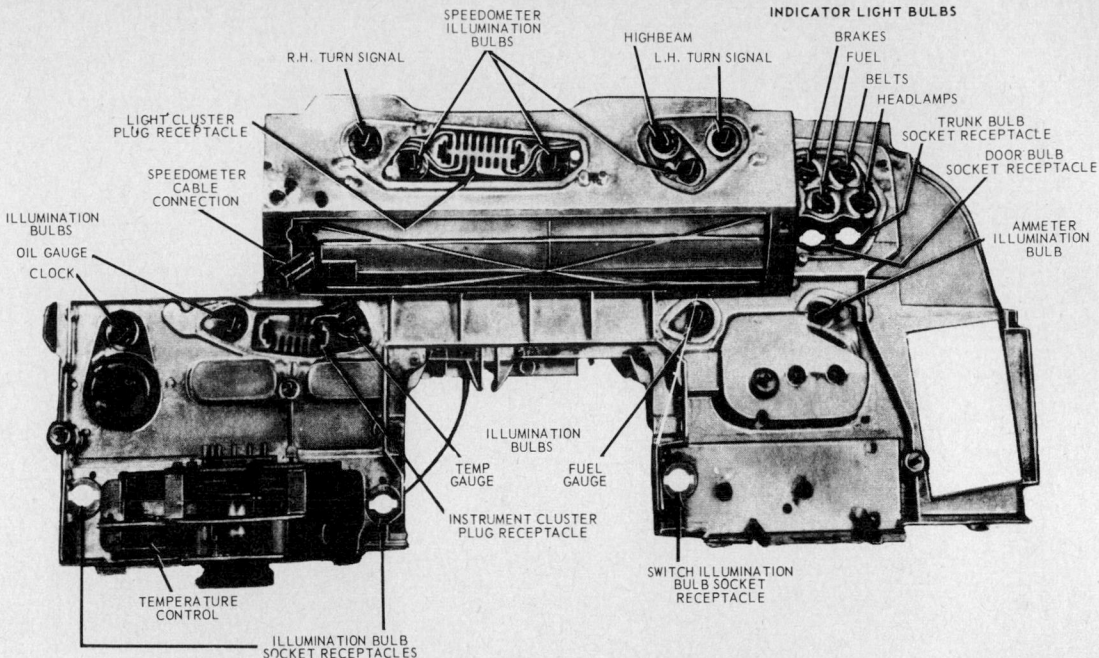

SPEEDOMETER
ILLUMINATION
BULBS

INDICATOR LIGHT BULBS

R.H. TURN SIGNAL

HIGHBEAM

L.H. TURN SIGNAL

BRAKES
FUEL
BELTS
HEADLAMPS

LIGHT CLUSTER
PLUG RECEPTACLE

TRUNK BULB
SOCKET RECEPTACLE

DOOR BULB
SOCKET RECEPTACLE

SPEEDOMETER
CABLE
CONNECTION

AMMETER
ILLUMINATION
BULB

ILLUMINATION
BULBS

OIL GAUGE

CLOCK

ILLUMINATION
BULBS

TEMP
GAUGE

FUEL
GAUGE

INSTRUMENT CLUSTER
PLUG RECEPTACLE

SWITCH ILLUMINATION
BULB SOCKET
RECEPTACLE

TEMPERATURE
CONTROL

ILLUMINATION BULB
SOCKET RECEPTACLES

1970 Lincoln Continental instrument cluster—rear view (© Ford Motor Company)

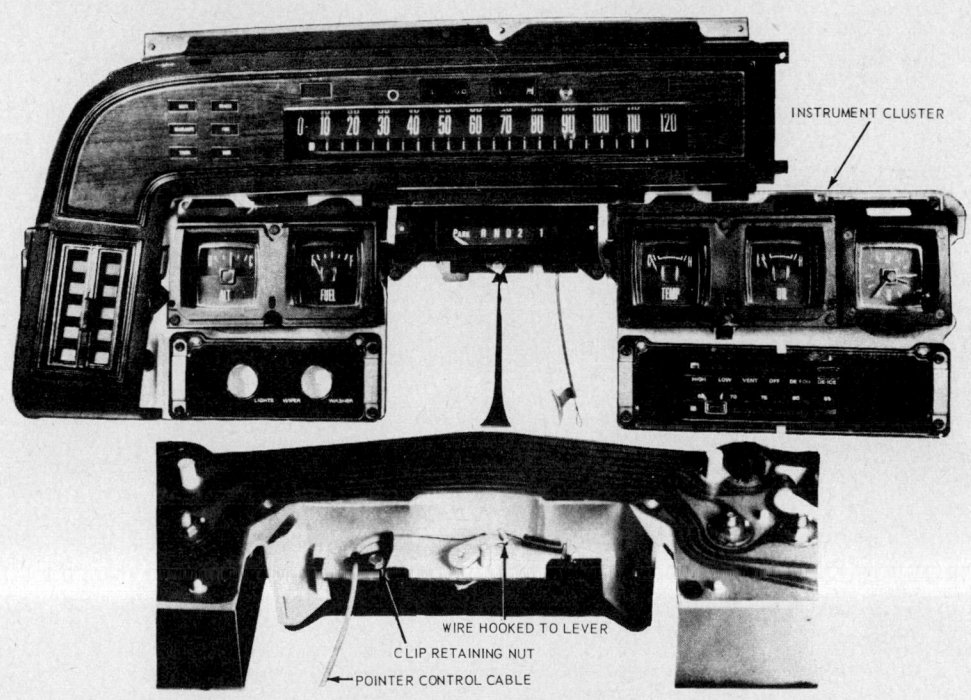

INSTRUMENT CLUSTER

WIRE HOOKED TO LEVER

CLIP RETAINING NUT

POINTER CONTROL CABLE

1970 Lincoln Continental instrument cluster—front view (© Ford Motor Company)

2. Remove heater, air conditioner, blower and radio control knobs.
3. Remove screws holding plate over steering column. Remove plate.
4. Remove screws holding instrument panel bezel to panel and remove the bezel.
5. Disconnect speedometer reset control cable from instrument panel.
6. Remove speedometer to panel retaining screws, position speedometer out of panel and dis-

nect cable. Remove speedometer and reset cable as a unit.
7. Reinstall by reversing the above.

1966-69 Except Mark III
1. Disconnect battery.
2. Remove six screws from the air-conditioner register casting. Pull register rearward until it is free.
3. Remove two screws in the applique on the left side of cluster.
4. Remove two screws between cluster hood and crash pad.
5. Remove four screws in the lower

windshield moulding, and the moulding.
6. Remove two screws and two nuts from the forward edge of the crash pad.
7. Disconnect radio speaker lead and remove crash pad.
8. Remove radio knobs and bezels.
9. Remove heater and air conditioner control knobs.
10. Remove four nuts and retainers on shafts of the radio, heater, air-conditioner and wiper controls.

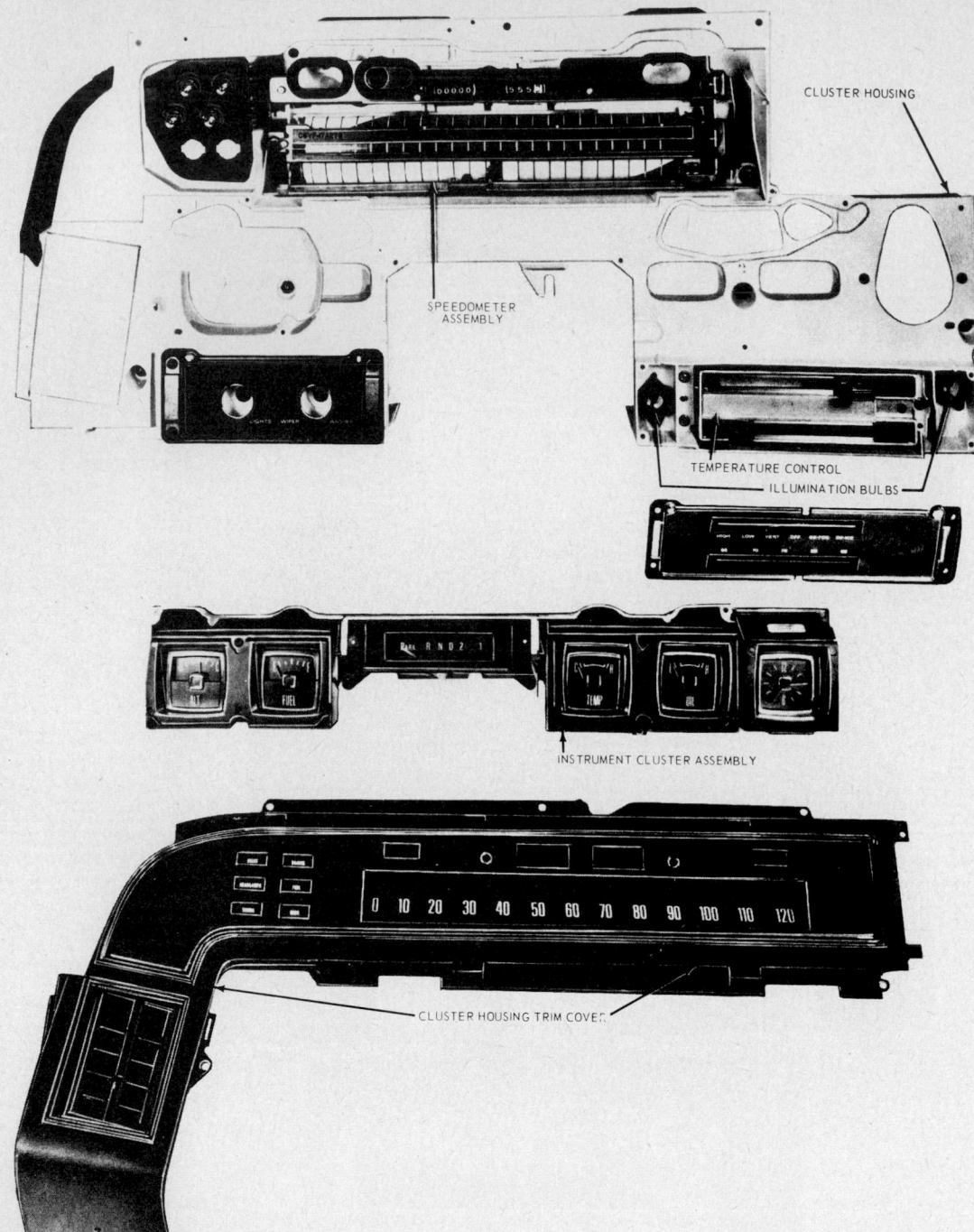

Disassembly of 1970 Lincoln Continental instrument cluster (© Ford Motor Company)

11. Remove eight screws from the lower control housing and lower the housing.
12. Remove four screws from the underside of the instrument panel attaching the finish cover, and remove cover.
13. Remove odometer reset knob.
14. Remove three screws holding the lower edge of the upper cluster finish panel.
15. Remove four screws holding the upper edge of the upper cluster finish cover and remove cover.
16. Remove four screws holding the right-hand cluster air-condition-

ing register. Disconnect hose and remove it.
17. Disconnect speedometer cable at the head.
18. Remove three screws that hold the head to the cluster housing, and remove the speedometer head.

1970-72 Except Mark III

1. Remove retaining screws and remove cluster housing trim panel from cluster housing.
2. Reach up behind instrument panel and disconnect speedometer cable.

3. Remove speedometer to cluster housing retaining screws.
4. Lift speedometer from cluster housing.

1968-71 Mark III

To remove speedometer, follow Steps 1 through 3 under Instrument Cluster R & R.

4. Remove the three screws holding the speedometer to the cluster and pull the speedometer head from the cluster. Transfer the speedometer mounting plate to the replacement speedometer (assuming that a new unit is to

be installed). Install the speed-ometer with the three retaining screws. Complete the installation by following Steps 6 through 8 under Instrument Cluster Instal-lation.

Ignition Lock R & R

See Ford section

Ignition Switch R & R

1966-69 Except Mark III

1. Disconnect battery.
2. Remove eight screws from lower control housing, drop the hous-ing.
3. Remove nut holding the wiring connector at the ignition switch and remove connector.
4. Unscrew the bezel and remove the switch.

1968-69 Mark III

1. Disconnect battery.
2. Insert ignition key in switch. Turn key to accessories position. Insert a paper clip end in the hole at the edge of the lock tumbler cylinder. Lightly depress the clip end while turning the key counterclockwise past the accessory position. This will release the lock cylinder from the switch assembly. Pull out the lock cylinder with the key. If only the lock cylinder is to be replaced, proceed to Step 8.
3. Remove bezel nut with special tool T65L-700-A.
4. Lower switch assembly, and re-move accessory wire retaining nut. Depress the tabs securing the multiple connector to the rear of the switch with a modified tool 18918-A. Modification of the tool consists of grinding the inside of the tool jaws to produce more clearance around the rear of the switch. Pull multiple connector from switch and remove the switch.
5. To install the switch, depress tabs on multiple connector and plug connector into the switch assem-bly. Be sure tabs lock into place.
6. Position switch in its retainer and install bezel nut.
7. Insert key in the switch assembly and turn the key to accessory po-sition. Place cylinder and key in switch. Push cylinder into the switch until it is fully seated, then turn key to lock position. Check by turning key to verify lock cyl-inder operation.
8. Reconnect battery.

1970-72 All

1. Disconnect battery.
2. Remove shrouding from steering column, and detach and lower steering column from brake sup-port bracket.
3. Disconnect switch wiring at mul-tiple plug.
4. Remove two nuts that retain switch to steering column.
5. Detach switch plunger from switch actuator rod and remove switch.
6. To re-install switch, place both locking mechanism at top of col-umn and switch itself in lock po-sition for correct adjustment. To hold column in lock position, place automatic shift lever in PARK or manual shift lever in reverse, and turn to LOCK and remove key. New switches are held in lock by plastic shipping pins. To pin existing switches, pull switch plunger out as far as it will go and push back in to first detent. Insert $3/32$ in. diam-eter wire in locking hole in top of switch.
7. Connect switch plunger to switch actuator rod.

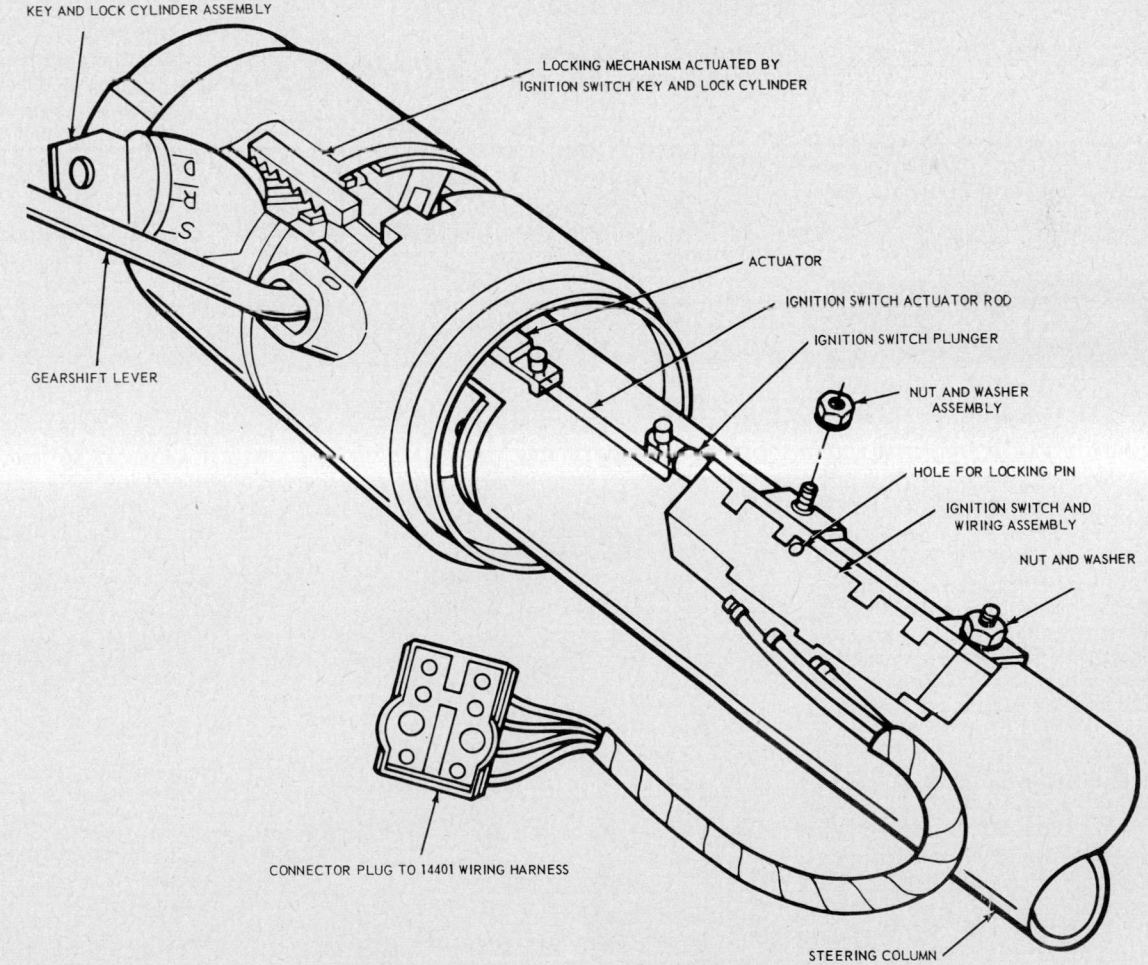

KEY AND LOCK CYLINDER ASSEMBLY

LOCKING MECHANISM ACTUATED BY IGNITION SWITCH KEY AND LOCK CYLINDER

ACTUATOR

IGNITION SWITCH ACTUATOR ROD

IGNITION SWITCH PLUNGER

NUT AND WASHER ASSEMBLY

HOLE FOR LOCKING PIN

IGNITION SWITCH AND WIRING ASSEMBLY

NUT AND WASHER

GEARSHIFT LEVER

CONNECTOR PLUG TO 14401 WIRING HARNESS

STEERING COLUMN

Ignition switch—1970 Lincoln (© Ford Motor Company)

8. Position switch on column and install attaching nuts. Do not tighten them.
9. Move switch up and down to locate mid position of rod lash, and then tighten nuts.
10. Remove locking pin or wire.
11. Attach steering column to brake support bracket and install shrouding.

Lighting Switch Replacement

Except Mark III
1. Disconnect battery.
2. Remove knob and shaft by pressing release knob button on switch housing and with knob in full on position.
3. Remove moulding nut from switch.
4. Remove junction block from switch.
5. Install in reverse of above.

Mark III
1. Disconnect battery ground cable.
2. Remove seven screws holding lower finish panel to lower side of instrument panel.
3. Remove control knob and shaft from headlight switch. This is done by pressing the release button on the underside of the switch (with shaft pulled all the way out).
4. Remove bezel and nut from headlight switch.
5. Remove two screws from switch-to-instrument panel.
6. Remove switch from panel. Disconnect wire multiple connector and vacuum hoses from the switch.
7. Install by reversing removal procedure.

Brakes

Since 1965, all Lincoln models have been equipped with front power disc brakes. All rear brakes are of the conventional shoe design. All 1965-66 models use a single reservoir master cylinder. All 1967 and later vehicles are equipped with dual reservoir master cylinders. The front and rear brake hydraulic systems are independent of each other on vehicles with dual master cylinders. The disc brake calipers on 1965-69 Lincoln cars utilize dual pistons, while 1970 and later models incorporate single piston calipers.

Master Cylinder R & R

1965-66
1. Disconnect the brake lines from the master cylinder.
2. Remove the two nuts and lockwashers that attach the master cylinder to the brake booster.
3. Pull the master cylinder forward

until it clears the booster pushrod, then remove it from the car.
4. Reverse above procedure to install, making sure the pushrod is firmly seated in the booster before installing the master cylinder.
5. Fill the master cylinder with extra-heavy duty fluid and bleed the brake system.

1967-72
1. Disconnect the brake lines from the master cylinder.
2. Remove the two nuts and lockwashers that attach the master cylinder to the brake booster.
3. Slide the master cylinder forward until it clears the booster pushrod, then remove the master cylinder from the car.
4. Reverse above procedure to install; but, leave the brake lines loose on the master cylinder.
5. Fill the master cylinder with extra-heavy duty fluid and, using the foot pedal, slowly bleed the air from the master cylinder.
6. Tighten the brake lines, fill the master cylinder, then, bleed the brake system at the front and then the rear wheels.
7. Refill master cylinder.

Power Brake Booster R & R

1965-66
1. Disconnect the negative battery cable.
2. Disconnect the brake lines from the master cylinder.
3. Remove the two retaining nuts and lockwashers and remove the master cylinder from the brake booster.

4. Disconnect the vacuum hose from the booster.
5. To increase working room, remove the power steering return line from the steering gear and plug the line.
6. Remove the two nuts and bolts that mount the fender apron brace to the cowl, and remove the brace and the belt that attaches the power steering and air conditioning hoses to the brace.
7. Working under the dash, disconnect and remove the stop light switch and pushrod from the brake pedal. Use care not to damage the stop light switch during removal.
8. Remove the nuts that retain the booster to the firewall from the interior side of the firewall.
9. Remove the booster from under the hood.
10. Reverse above procedure to install.

1967-68
1. Disconnect the negative battery cable.
2. Remove the two bolts that attach the brake pressure differential valve to the fender apron.
3. Remove the two nuts that attach the master cylinder to the booster and position the master cylinder out of the way with the brake lines attached. Use care when moving the master cylinder so that the brake lines do not become kinked.
4. Disconnect the vacuum hose at the booster.
5. Remove the two nuts and bolts that attach the fender apron

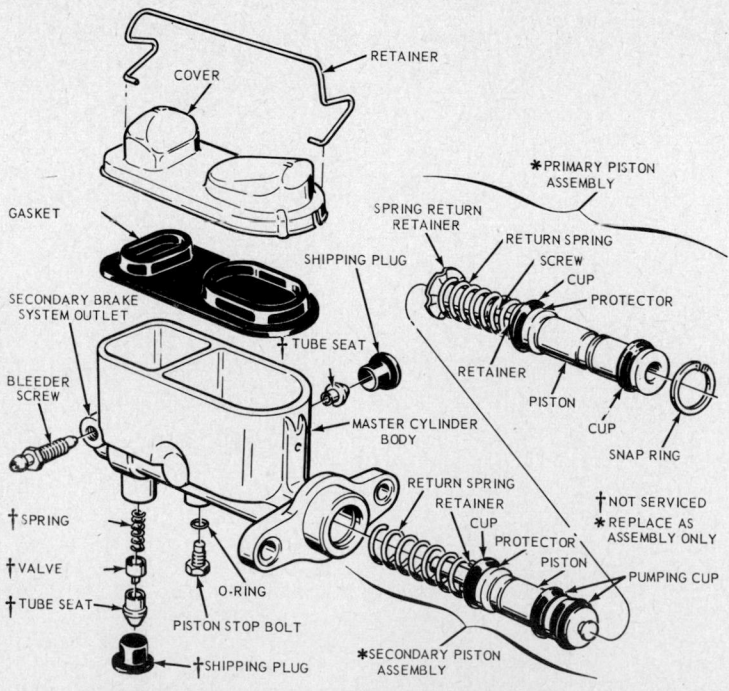

Dual type master cylinder (© Ford Motor Co.)

brace to the cowl and remove the brace.

6. Remove the clip and attaching bolt that secures the air conditioning hose to the hood latch and position the air conditioning hose out of the way.
7. Working under the dash, disconnect and remove the stop light switch and pushrod from the brake pedal. Use care not to damage the stop light switch during removal.
8. Remove the nuts that retain the booster to the firewall from the interior side of the firewall.
9. Remove the booster from under the hood.
10. Reverse above procedure to install.

1969-72

1. Disconnect the vacuum hose from the booster.
2. Remove the two nuts and lockwashers that mount the master

Parking Brake Cable Adjustment

1. Fully release the parking brake pedal.
2. Raise the car on a hoist.
3. Adjust the pedal cable to about 10 in., measured from the cable attachment at the crossmember to the cable adjusting nut.
4. Depress the parking brake pedal one notch from normal, released position.
5. Loosen locknut on equalizer rod and turn the forward nut inward toward the front of the car until a moderate drag is felt when turning the rear wheels.
6. Holding forward nut in position, tighten locknut. Lock the adjustment at the equalizer.
7. Release parking brake, and make sure that the brake shoes return to the fully released position.

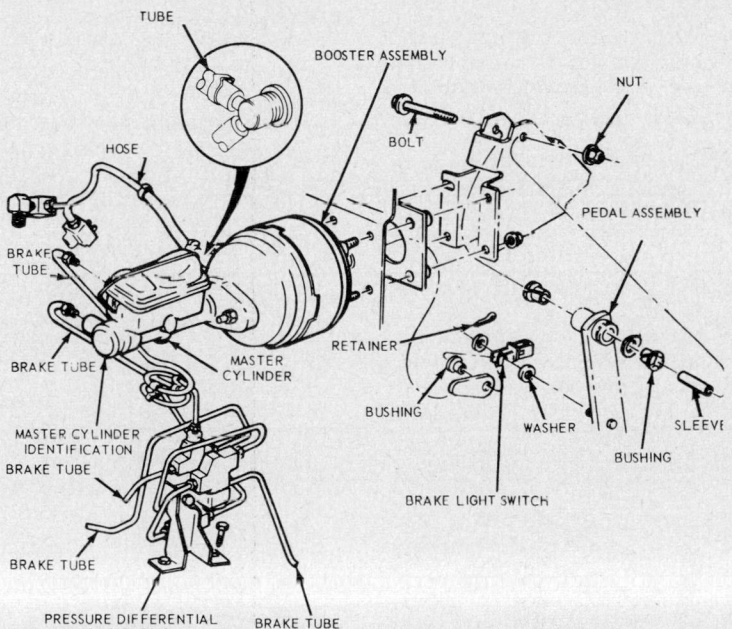

Brake pedal and booster installation (© Ford Motor Co.)

cylinder to the booster and move the master cylinder out of the way with the lines attached. Use care not to kink the brake lines.

3. Working under the dash, disconnect and remove the stop light switch and pushrod from the brake pedal. Use care not to damage the switch during removal.
4. Remove the four booster to firewall attaching nuts from the interior side of the firewall.
5. Remove the booster from under the hood.
6. Reverse above procedure to install.

Brake Adjustment—Rear Brakes Only

The automatic adjusters operate only when the brakes are applied as the car is moving rearward. The wraparound action of the shoes following the drum while moving rearward forces the upper end of the primary shoe against the anchor pin and the secondary shoe away from the anchor pin.

The link holds the top of the actuator stationary, forcing the actuator to pivot on the secondary shoe. The pivoting action forces the pawl downward against the end of a tooth on the star wheel adjusting screw which

turns the star wheel and expands the shoes.

The greater the clearance between the brake drum and the lining, the greater the travel of the secondary shoe away from the anchor. The more the secondary shoe moves, the greater the adjustment. When the brakes are adjusted correctly, there will not be sufficient travel of the secondary shoe to permit the actuator to pivot and force the pawl to engage against the end of a tooth of the star wheel adjusting screw, and turn the wheel to expand the shoe.

When the brakes are applied as the car is moving forward, the self-adjuster does not operate because the wraparound action of the shoes forces the secondary shoe against the anchor pin.

Whenever removing or replacing a star wheel assembly, special care must be exercised to be certain that the correct star wheel assembly is installed on the right brake drum to enable the self-adjuster to function properly.

Fuel System

Carburetor

Two different carburetors have been used on Lincoln engines since 1965: the 430 and 462 V8s are equipped with a Carter carburetor, while the 460 V8 uses a model 4300 Autolite carburetor.

Idle Speed Adjustment

1. 1965-68 Carter Carburetor: *Adjust with air cleaner removed.* 1968-71 4300 Carburetor: *Adjust with air cleaner installed.* If it is not possible to adjust carburetor idle speed with the air cleaner installed, the engine idle speed must be rechecked after installing the air cleaner. On models with vacuum controlled heat ducts in the air cleaner, the vacuum line must be plugged if the carburetor is to be adjusted with the air cleaner removed.
2. Run engine at fast idle to equalize operating temperature.
3. Make sure the choke plate is fully released.
4. Turn headlights on high beam.
5. Tape hot idle compensator so that it is fully seated in the closed position.
6. On vehicles equipped with air conditioning, all models EXCEPT 1969, set the idle speed with the air conditioner turned OFF. 1969 models, set the idle speed with the air conditioner turned ON.
7. Remove and plug the vacuum line to the parking brake release, then, set the parking brake and

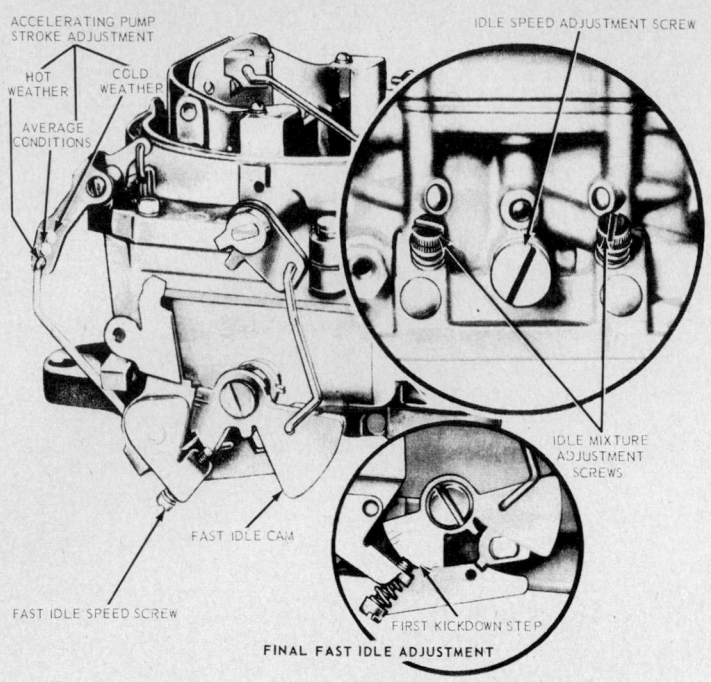

Carter carburetor adjustments (© Ford Motor Co.)

put the transmission in the Drive position.

8. Attach a tachometer of known accuracy to the engine.

9. Adjust the idle speed screw or solenoid to obtain specified rpm. On Carter carburetors, turn the idle speed adjusting screw in to decrease speed and out to increase engine speed. On Autolite

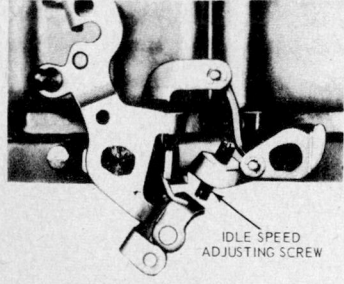

Autolite carburetor idle speed adjustment
(© Ford Motor Co.)

carburetors, turn the idle adjusting screw in to increase speed and out to decrease speed. On carburetors with an electric solenoid, turn the solenoid plunger to the right to increase idle speed and to the left to decrease it.

NOTE: There are two engine idle speeds listed for cars with solenoid equipped carburetors. The first or higher speed is adjusted as explained above, the second is adjusted with the solenoid electrical lead disconnected, by turning the adjustment screw on the side of the carburetor. With the solenoid disconnected, the idle adjusting screw must contact the

throttle shaft or the throttle plates may become jammed in the throttle bores of the carburetor when the engine is shut off.

Fuel Mixture Adjustment

1. On engines with Carter carburetors, turn the mixture screws clockwise until engine idle becomes rough, then, back out adjustment screws until engine reaches highest rpm.

2. On Autolite carburetors with idle mixture limiter caps, follow the same procedure, but, final adjustment must be made with the caps installed.

3. If adjusting the idle mixture has altered engine idle speed, reset idle speed to specification.

NOTE: if a smooth idle cannot be obtained following this procedure, refer to additional carburetor adjustments listed in the exhaust emission systems section in the Unit Repair Section of this book.

Dashpot Adjustment

Carter Carburetor

1. With the carburetor idle speed adjusted to specification, measure the distance between the dashpot lever and the top surface of the carburetor. If the distance is not within specs bend the dashpot lever to correct.

2. With the carburetor in the full open position, measure the distance between the dashpot lever and the top surface of the carburetor. If the distance is not within specs, bend the rear end of the dashpot lever to correct.

Autolite Carburetor

1. With the carburetor idle speed adjusted to specification, depress the plunger of the dashpot with a screwdriver. Measure the distance between the tip of the plunger and the carburetor throttle lever. If the distance is not within specs, loosen the dashpot locknut and turn the dashpot to adjust.

Dashpot Adjustments

Carter Carburetor	#1 setting	#2 setting
All except 1966	1/8 in.	7/16 in.
1966	1/8 in.	5/16 in.

Autolite Carburetor		
1968-69	3/32 in.	
1970-71	1/10 in.	

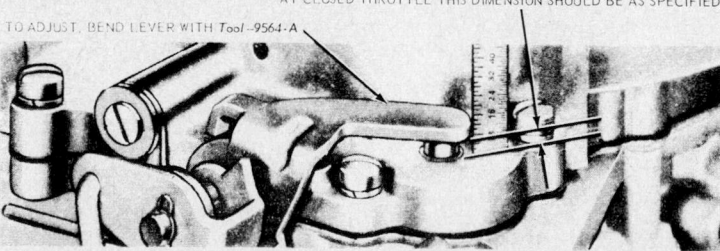

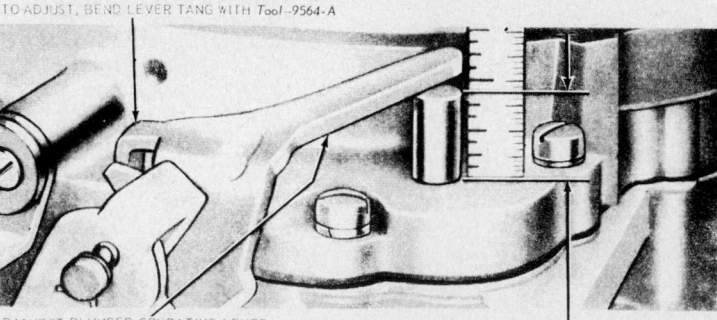

Carter carburetor anti-stall dashpot adjustments (© Ford Motor Co.)

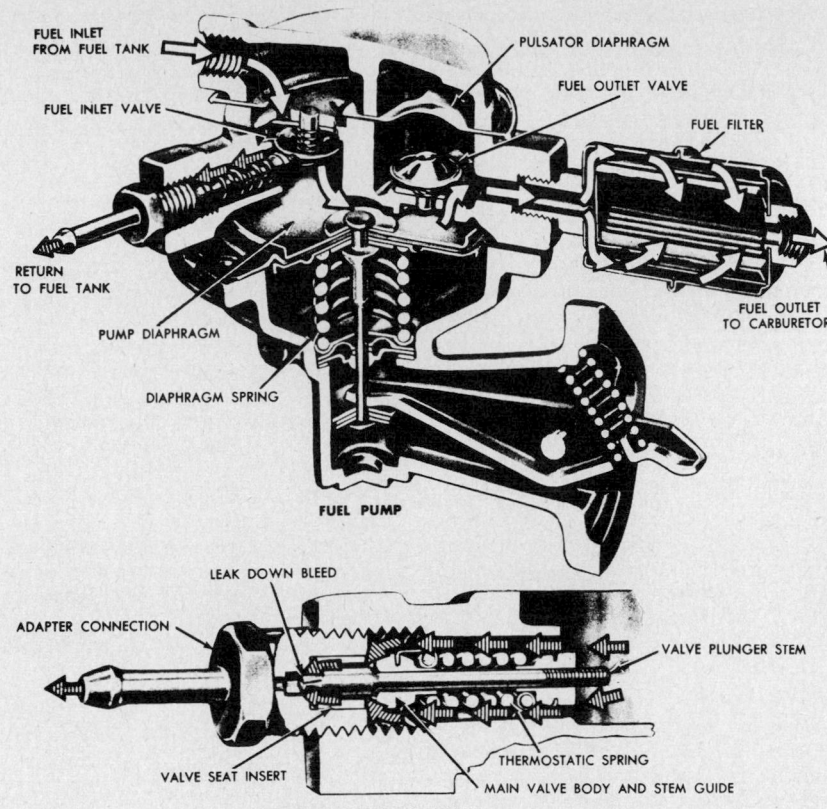

Fuel pump and thermostatic valve (© Ford Motor Co.)

Fuel Pump Removal

1965-68

The fuel pump is mounted on the top portion of the engine front cover.

To remove the pump, disconnect the fuel and vapor discharge connections. The pump can then be unbolted and lifted off.

On power-steering models, the bolts are accessible from under the car.

1968-72 460 Engine

The fuel pump is mounted on the left side of the cylinder front cover.

A separate in-line fuel filter is used. The filter cannot be serviced. Renew it in case of obstruction. This pump is spring loaded in opposition to camshaft eccentric lobe action, and is conventional.

The pump is Carter-built and cannot be serviced.

Exhaust System

Description

1965-69 Lincoln Continental

All models are equipped with a three-piece, dual exhaust system. It consists of a resonator inlet pipe, a resonator and integral crossover pipe assembly and a muffler on each side of the chassis.

1969-72 Lincoln Continental

All models are equipped with a three-piece, single exhaust system. It consists of a Y shaped muffler inlet pipe, a muffler and self-contained outlet pipe and a resonator and tailpipe assembly.

1969-71 Mark III

All models are equipped with a two-piece, dual exhaust system. It consists of an H shaped resonator inlet pipe, and a one piece resonator, resonator outlet pipe, muffler and tailpipe assembly for each side of the chassis.

Replacement

To replace any component of the exhaust system, simply remove the clamp (s) or flange (s) that attach it to the pipe (s) or manifold (s) it mounts to. Remove the attaching parts from the exhaust system hangers and lower the exhaust system. Using a torch or air chisel, separate the part to be replaced from the rest of the exhaust system.

NOTE: many inlet pipe-resonator-muffler assemblies are welded together; before removing any parts, determine if the replacement parts are serviced separately or as an assembly. If the service parts are sold separately, it will be necessary to cut the weld on the original parts and separate them.

Cooling System

Radiator Removal

1. Drain the cooling system.
2. Disconnect the upper and lower radiator hoses from the radiator.
3. Disconnect the transmission cooler lines from the radiator.
4. If the air conditioner condenser attaches to the radiator, remove the retaining bolts and position the condenser out of the way. *Do not disconnect the refrigerant lines.*
5. If equipped with a fan shroud, disconnect it from the radiator and position it rearward over the fan.
6. Remove the radiator mounting bolts, and remove the radiator from the car.
7. Reverse above procedure to install.

Water Pump Removal

430 and 462 Engines

1. Drain cooling system and disconnect battery.
2. On air conditioned cars, remove fan drive clutch, fan, and compressor drive pulley as an assembly.
3. Remove radiator supply tank.
4. If not air conditioned, remove fan and spacer.
5. Loosen clamp securing bypass hose.
6. Remove alternator splash shield.
7. Loosen alternator adjusting bracket and mounting bracket bolts. Push alternator inward and remove bolts.
8. Disconnect radiator outlet and heater hose at water pump.
9. Remove water pump retaining bolts. Position dip stick tube bracket and power steering pump bracket to allow clearance.
10. Remove water pump.

460 Engine

1. Drain cooling system.
2. Remove bolts retaining fan assembly to water pump.
3. Remove radiator shroud and fan.
4. On air conditioned cars, loosen compressor drive belt.
5. Loosen alternator mounting bolts and remove alternator drive belt.
6. Remove water pump pulley.
7. Disconnect radiator lower hose, heater hose, and bypass hose at water pump.
8. Remove water pump bolts and remove water pump.

Engine

Lincoln Engines—1965-1972

The 1965 Lincoln used a bulky, heavy

430 cu. in. V8. Big though it was, this engine was admirably suited for use in a luxury car. The engine was characterized by a relatively short stroke, a deep Y-block construction, and most unusual cylinder heads. The head mating surface was flat with no indentation for a combustion chamber, and was mounted on the block at approximately 60° to the axis of the bore. The angle between the cylinder head and the piston formed the combustion chamber.

In 1966 Lincoln increased the bore to 4.380 in. and the stroke to 3.830 in. for 462 cu. in. This engine continued in use through 1968.

During 1968 the 460 cu. in. engine was introduced. Throughout that year it was mixed indiscriminately with the 462 engine in Lincoln production, only the new Mark III used the 460 exclusively. Because of this mixing and because the bore, 4.36 in., and stroke, 3.85 in., and displacement are close to those of the older engine, many people confuse the two. The new engine differs substantially. It has canted valves, stud mounted rocker arms, semi-hemispherical combustion chambers, tunnel ports, a block split at crankshaft centerline, an intake manifold that replaces the valley cover, and a much lighter weight. Since 1969 this engine has been used exclusively.

Valve System

Description
See Ford section.

Preliminary Valve Adjustment

430 and 462 V8s
See Ford section, under 352 V8.

1968 460 V8
See Ford section, under 289 V8.

1969-72 460 V8
See Ford section, under 429 V8.

CHILTON TIME-SAVER

The following is a method for replacing valve springs, oil seals or spring retainers without removing the cylinder head.
1. Entirely dismantle a spark plug and save the threaded shell.
2. To this shell, braze or weld an air chuck.
3. Remove the valve rocker cover. Remove the rocker arm from the valve to be worked on.
4. Remove the spark plug from the cylinder to be worked on.
5. Turn the crankshaft to bring the piston of this cylinder down, away from possible contact with the valve head. Sharply tap the valve retainer to loosen the valve lock.
6. Then turn the crankshaft to bring the piston in this cylinder to the Exact Top of its Compression Stroke.
7. Screw in the chuck-equipped spark plug shell.
8. Hook up an air hose to the chuck and turn on the pressure (about 200 lbs.).
9. With a strong and constant supply of air holding the valve closed, compress the valve spring and remove the lock and retainer.
10. Make the necessary replacements and reassemble.

NOTE: it is important that the operation be performed exactly as stated, in this order. The piston in the cylinder must be on exact top-center to prevent air pressure from turning the crankshaft.

Valve Guides

Lincolns use integral valve guides. Lincoln dealers offer valves with oversize stems for worn guides. To fit these, enlarge valve guide bores with valve guide reamers to an oversize that cleans up wear. If a large oversize is required, it is best to approach that size through stages by using a series of reamers of increasing diameters. This helps to maintain the concentricity of the guide bore with the valve seat. The correct valve guide to stem clearance is in front of this section. As an alternative, some local automotive machine shops will fit replacement guides that use standard stem valves.

Exhaust Emission Control

In compliance with anti-pollution laws, the Ford Motor Company has adopted a distributor and a modified carburetor with some engine changes, to reduce terminal exhaust fumes to an acceptable level. This method is known as Ford's Improved Combustion System (IMCO).

The plan supersedes (in most cases) the previous method used to conform to 1966-67 California laws. The new system phases out (except

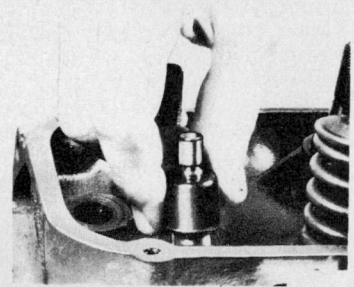

Replacing valve stem seal
(© Ford Motor Co.)

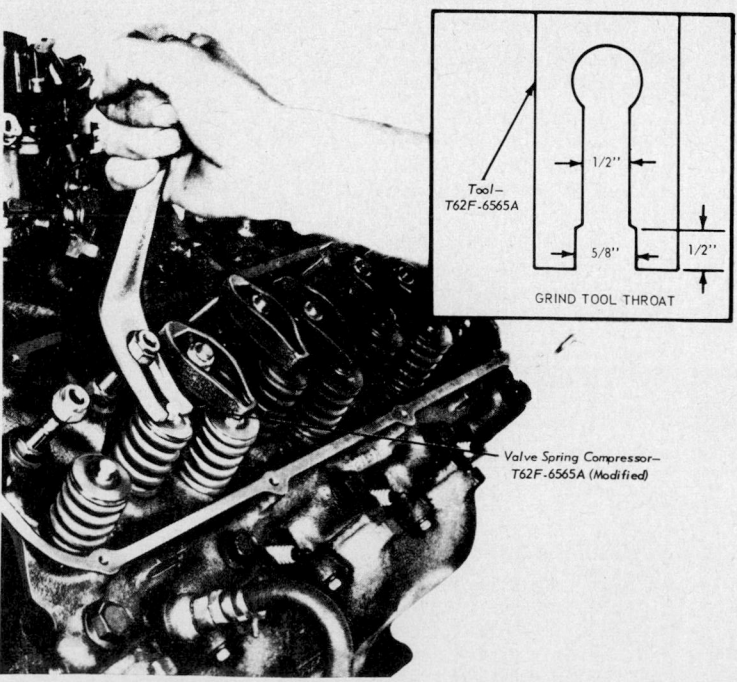

GRIND TOOL THROAT

Valve Spring Compressor—
T62F-6565A (Modified)

Compression valve spring in chassis (© Ford Motor Co.)

with stick shift and special purpose engine applications) the thermactor, or afterburner type of exhaust treatment.

The IMCO concept utilizes broader, yet more critical, distributor control through carburetor modification.

Since 1968, all car makers have posted idle speeds and other pertinent data, relative to the specific engine application in a conspicuous place in the engine compartment.

For details on the IMCO system, consult the Unit Repair Section.

Engine Removal

1965-72

Engine R & R is for the engine only, without the transmission attached.

1. Raise the hood, and cover or mask all parts of the car that could be scratched during R & R procedures.
2. Set the parking brake and raise the car. Put stands beneath the underbody front crossmember.
3. Drain the engine cooling system and the engine oil pan.
4. Scribe the hinge outline on the underside of the hood. Remove hood.
5. If the engine is equipped with an exhaust emission control system, remove the crankcase vent filter from the air cleaner. Remove carburetor air cleaner and air inlet duct assembly. Disconnect the battery ground.
6. Remove both engine radiator hoses.
7. Disconnect heater hoses at intake manifold and water pump. Disconnect power brake and power booster line from the intake manifold connection and position it to one side.
8. Disconnect heater vacuum hose from the intake manifold.
9. Disconnect automatic transmission vacuum line at the intake manifold.
10. Remove transmission tube slotted bracket from the right rear exhaust manifold mounting stud.
11. Disconnect battery ground strap at cylinder block.
12. Disconnect primary wires at the coil. Disconnect wires from temperature-sending unit and the fast idle solenoid (air-conditioned cars).
13. Disconnect wire from oil pressure-sending unit. Detach wiring loom from valve rocker arm cover and position it out of the way.
14. Disconnect transmission fluid lines at the radiator. Remove transmission fluid filter from underbody side member (if car is so equipped).
15. Remove fuel hose mounting

bracket from radiator. Remove heat shield from fuel pump. Disconnect hoses from fuel pump.
16. On air-conditioned cars, remove fan drive clutch to water pump pulley retaining bolts. Remove fan drive clutch, fan and compressor pulley from the car as a unit.
17. Remove fan blade and spacer assembly from water pump pulley.
18. On vehicles equipped with air conditioning, disconnect the compressor electrical lead and remove the compressor mounting bracket attaching bolts. Remove the compressor from the engine and position it out of the way without disconnecting the refrigerant lines.

Caution If the compressor refrigerant lines do not have enough slack to position the compressor out of the way without disconnecting the refrigerant lines, the air conditioning system will have to be evacuated by a trained air conditioning serviceman. Under no circumstances should an untrained person attempt to disconnect the air conditioning refrigerant lines.

19. Remove the alternator mounting bolts and position the alternator out of the way without disconnecting the wires.
20. Disconnect the transmission and accelerator linkage at the bellcrank. Secure the linkage to the dash panel for engine clearance purposes.
21. Remove access cover from the converter housing. Remove underbody splash shield at lower front of transmission.
22. Remove resonator inlet pipes from the exhaust manifolds.
23. Remove the power steering pump mounting bracket from the engine and position the pump and bracket out of the way.
24. Remove the nuts and washers that hold the engine front support insulators to the underbody side members.
25. Remove the starter attaching bolts. Remove the starter.
26. Detach the oil cooler inlet and outlet transfer line retaining clip from the cylinder block.
27. Remove the flywheel to converter retaining nuts.
28. Remove lower converter housing to cylinder block retaining bolts.
29. Install a transmission support under the transmission.
30. Remove the upper converter housing to cylinder block retaining bolts.
31. Attach engine lifting eyes to the exhaust manifolds.
32. Install lifting sling and attach to chain hoist. With plenty of help,

carefully raise and remove engine from car.
33. Install by reversing removal procedure.

Intake and Exhaust Manifold(s)

Intake Manifold R & R

1. Drain the cooling system.
2. Disconnect the upper radiator hose from the thermostat housing and the bypass hose from the intake manifold. On 430 and 462 V8, disconnect and remove the radiator surge tank from the intake manifold.
3. Remove the air cleaner and ducts from the engine.
4. Disconnect the spark plug wires from the spark plugs and remove the distributor cap and wires from the engine as an assembly. On models equipped with a 460 V8, mark the position of the distributor rotor in relation to the intake manifold, remove the primary wire from the coil and the distributor hold-down bolt, then, remove the distributor from the engine.
5. Remove all vacuum lines from the intake manifold and the wire from the temperature sending unit.
6. Disconnect all fuel and vacuum lines from the carburetor.
7. Remove all carburetor and kickdown linkage that attaches to the intake manifold.
8. Remove the manifold attaching bolts and remove the manifold. If it is necessary to pry the manifold to loosen it from the engine, use care not to damage any gasket sealing surfaces.
9. Clean all gasket surfaces and cement new gaskets firmly in place. The gaskets should be firmly locked in place before attempting to install the manifold.
10. Reverse above procedure to install.

Exhaust Manifold Removal— 430 and 462 Engines

1. Remove air cleaner and air inlet duct assembly. Block rear wheels and set parking brake. Raise front of car and install safety stands.
2. Disconnect the exhaust manifold/s at the resonator inlet pipe/s.
3. Detach the engine front support insulators from the underbody side members.
4. Place a jack under the front edge of the oil pan. Raise the front of the engine about 2 in. to make clearance for removal of the exhaust manifold/s.

Caution, When raising the engine, use care to prevent forcing the engine against the automatic temperature control case (if so equipped) in the engine compartment. Position 2 in. wood blocks between the front support insulators and underbody side members. Remove the jack and let the engine rest on the wood blocks.

5. Unlock and remove the manifold lower retaining bolts. Remove safety stands and lower the car.
6. Remove the two automatic choke tubes from the right exhaust manifold.
7. If the engine is equipped with an exhaust emission control system, remove the air hose/s from the air manifold/s.
8. Unlock and remove the exhaust manifold retaining nuts, manifold/s and gasket/s.
9. Install by reversing the above procedure.

Exhaust Manifold Removal— 460 Engine

1. Remove air cleaner and warm air duct assembly to remove right exhaust manifold.
2. Disconnect manifolds at exhaust pipe.
3. Remove retaining bolts and washers, and remove manifolds and lifting brackets.

Cylinder Head

Rocker Assembly Removal— 430 and 462 Engines

1. Raise the hood and remove the carburetor air cleaner. Disconnect the ignition wires where they cross over the rocker cover. Remove the rocker cover and carefully scrape off its gasket.
2. Now, working a little at a time, loosen the bolts that hold the rocker brackets to the cylinder head so that the tension of the valve springs will be left off, a little at a time. Once the tension is released, remove the screws and lift the rocker assemblies up off the cylinder head.
3. If the rockers are to be disassembled, they should be laid out carefully on a bench, disassembled and marked so that they can be reassembled in the same position as before. Rocker assemblies are installed in reverse order of removal, following procedure under Preliminary Valve Adjustment.

1968-72—460 Engine Rocker Assemblies

These rocker arms are of the pedestal-mounted-type and are removable, one at a time.

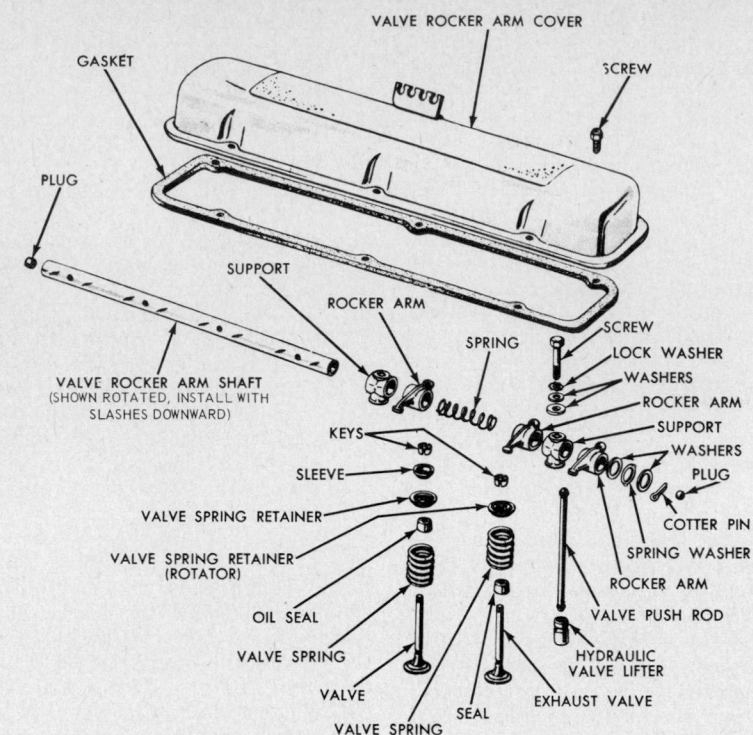

Rocker shaft and valve components—430 and 462 V8 (© Ford Motor Co.)

Removal

1. If removing a rocker arm assembly from the right cylinder head, partially drain the cooling system and disconnect heater water tubes at the water pump and intake manifold. Remove tube assembly retaining bolts and move tube assembly out of the way. Remove crankcase ventilation regulator valve and hose from valve rocker arm cover. Remove air cleaner and duct assembly.
   If removing an arm assembly from the left side, take off oil filler cap and air supply hose from valve rocker cover.
2. Disconnect plug wires at spark plugs. Twist, then pull, on molded cap of wire only. Do not pull the wire. Remove wires from bracket on the valve rocker arm covers and pull wires out of the way.
3. Remove rocker arm covers.
4. Remove rocker arm stud nut, fulcrum seat, and rocker arm.
   NOTE: rocker arm studs that are broken, or have bad threads, should be replaced.
   If the stud is broken, flush with the head, drill and use an easy-out.
   When installing the new stud, lubricate the threads, then torque to 65-75 ft. lbs.

Installation

1. Apply lubriplate to top of valve stem.
2. Lubriplate fulcrum seat and socket. Install rocker arm, fulcrum seat and stud nut. Perform

preliminary valve adjustment.
3. Adjust valve clearance according to recommendations.
4. Clean rocker arm covers and cylinder head gasket surfaces.
5. Apply oil-resistant sealer to one side of new cover gaskets. Apply cemented side of gaskets in rim of covers.
6. Position covers on cylinder heads. Install and torque cover bolts to 2½-4 ft. lbs. Two minutes later, retorque attaching bolts to same specifications.
7. Route spark plug wires in brackets on valve rocker covers. Reconnect plug wires.
8. Install heater tube assembly, if disconnected, and fill cooling system.
9. On the right valve rocker arm cover, install crankcase ventilation regulator valve and hose.
10. Install air cleaner and duct, and adjust assembly, if removed. On the left rocker arm cover, install oil filler cap and air supply hose.

Cylinder Head Removal

1. Drain the cooling system.
2. On 1966-67 Lincolns, remove the battery.
3. If the right side cylinder head is to be removed from a 430 or 462 engine, remove the horns and mounting brackets and the transmission filler tube support brace.
4. On vehicles equipped with a 430 or 462 V8, disconnect the spark plug wires from the spark plugs,

and remove distributor cap and wires from the engine as an assembly. Mark the position of the distributor rotor in relation to the intake manifold, disconnect the distributor primary wire from the coil, remove the distributor hold-down bolt and remove the distributor from the engine.

5. Remove the intake manifold from the engine, following the procedure outlined under Intake Manifold R&R.

6. On 430 and 462 engines, remove the pushrod chamber cover from the engine.

7. If the right cylinder head is to be removed, disconnect the negative battery cable, loosen the alternator mounting bolts, remove the bolt attaching the alternator to the cylinder head and swing the alternator downward with the wires attached.

8. If the left cylinder head is to be removed, remove the air conditioning compressor and mounting bracket from the head and position them out of the way without disconnecting the refrigerant lines. Remove the power steering pump and mounting bracket from the head and position them out of the way without disconnecting the lines.

9. Remove the valve covers. On 430 and 460 engines remove the rocker arm assemblies from the engine. On 460 engines, loosen each rocker arm and turn them to the side.

10. Remove the pushrods from the engine and keep them in order so they can be returned to their original location's in the engine.

11. Remove the exhaust manifold to resonator inlet pipe attaching bolts.

12. Remove the cylinder head attaching bolts and remove the head(s) from the engine.

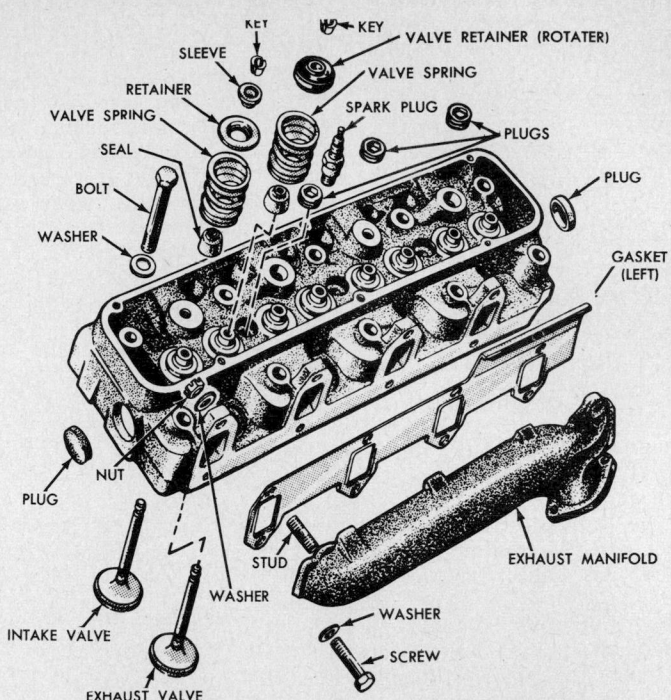

Cylinder head and parts layout—430 and 462 V8 (© Ford Motor Co.)

Cylinder head removal 460 V8 (© Ford Motor Company)

Disassembly of cylinder head
(© Ford Motor Company)

13. Reverse above procedure to install, tightening the head bolts to specification in three steps and performing a preliminary valve adjustment before starting engine.

Timing Case Cover, Chain and Sprockets

Timing Case Cover Removal
430 and 462 Engines

1. Drain entire engine cooling system. Remove the hood.

2. Disconnect all radiator hoses and the overflow pipe from the coolant supply tank.

3. Remove the bolt securing the supply tank brace, engine ground strap and battery ground cable to the water pump. Remove supply tank thermostat and gasket. Loosen coolant by-pass hose at water pump.

4. On a car equipped with air-conditioning, loosen the compressor support bracket bolts. Remove the drive belt, then, remove the fan drive clutch and fan assembly and the compressor drive pulley as a unit.

5. Loosen the alternator, remove the fan and alternator drive belts. Remove the fan blade assembly, spacer and mounting bolts from the water pump pulley as a unit.

6. Disconnect the dipstick tube bracket at the water pump. Remove the steering pump reservoir bracket from the water pump and loosen the remaining bracket mounting bolts to allow clearance for removal of the water pump.

7. Remove the water pump. Remove the crankshaft damper attaching bolt. Remove the damper.

8. Disconnect power steering lines at the pump and plug the lines. Remove bolts holding the power steering reservoir to the front cover.

9. Remove the crankshaft damper key and remove the power steering pump.
10. Remove the shield from the fuel pump, fuel lines from the pump; remove the pump. Remove the cup-type plug from the top of the cylinder front cover by using a long punch. Remove the fuel pump pushrod.
11. Remove the oil pan.
12. If timing chain is to be replaced, perform Steps 16-18 under 460.

460 Engine Removal

1. Drain cooling system and crankcase.
2. Remove oil pan and oil pump.
3. Remove fan blades from water pump shaft.
4. Remove radiator (fan) shroud.
5. Disconnect all radiator hoses at engine. Disconnect oil cooler lines.
6. Remove radiator.
7. Loosen alternator. Loosen air conditioner idler pulley. Remove drive belts with water pump pulley.
8. Remove air conditioner compressor (do not open compressor lines to expose the sealed air-conditioner system to atmosphere).
9. Remove crankshaft pulley attaching bolt and washer. Remove damper and remove Woodruff key from crankshaft.
10. Disconnect power steering pressure line at pump. Drain fluid.

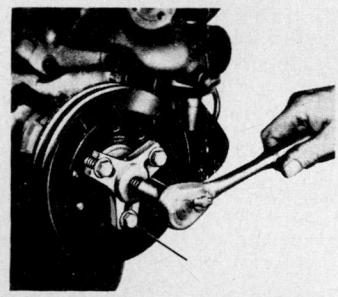

Removing crankshaft vibration damper
(© Ford Motor Co.)

11. Remove steering pump.
12. Loosen by-pass hose at water pump. Disconnect heater hose at pump.
13. Disconnect and plug fuel inlet line at fuel pump. Disconnect fuel line at carburetor fuel pump. Remove fuel pump.
14. Remove front cover-to-block attaching bolts. Remove front cover and water pump as an assembly. Discard gasket.
15. If a new front cover is to be installed, change the water pump at this time.
16. Check timing chain deflection, at this time, by rotating crankshaft

in a clockwise direction enough to take up the slack on the right hand side of the chain (as facing the open chain). Establish a reference mark on the block and measure from this point to the left side of the chain. This measurement when deflected should not exceed ½ in. If deflection is more than ½ in., replace chain and both sprockets.
17. If chain and sprockets are being removed, crank the engine until timing marks on the sprockets

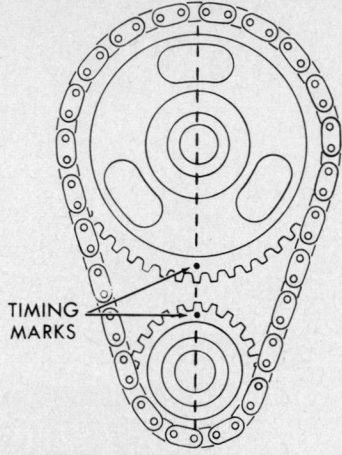

Valve timing alignment marks

are at their closest related points and on a center line with both crankshaft and camshaft centers.
18. Remove camshaft sprocket capscrew, washer, and fuel pump eccentric. Slide off timing chain, sprockets and chain as an assembly.

460 Engine Installation

1. Install chain and sprockets as an assembly with sprocket timing marks directly toward each other and on a centerline with the crankshaft and camshaft.
2. Install fuel pump eccentric, washer, and attaching cap screw. Torque camshaft sprocket attaching screw to 40-45 ft. lbs. Lubricate chain and sprockets with engine oil.
3. After cleaning mating surfaces, coat the areas with oil-resistant sealer and position gasket on cylinder block.
4. Position cover over crankshaft and slide cover on against cylinder block. Coat cover retaining screws with oil-resistant sealer and install screws. Torque attaching screws to 10-13 ft. lbs.
5. Apply lubriplate to oil seal rubbing surface of steering pump inner hub. Apply mixture of white lead and oil to crankshaft stub in preparing damper installation. Install power steering pump.

6. Install crankshaft damper Woodruff key and press on crankshaft damper. Do not hammer damper into place. Install damper retainer screw and washer. Torque to 75-90 ft. lbs.
7. Coat new fuel pump gasket with oil-resistant sealer and place on fuel pump. Install fuel pump. Connect fuel lines to fuel pump.
8. Install oil pump and oil pan.
9. Install air-conditioner compressor and water pump.
10. Install water pump pulley and all drive belts.
11. Position radiator to lower support, position upper support to radiator retaining bolts. Connect air coolant hoses. Connect oil cooler lines.
12. Place fan assembly inside radiator shroud and set in position on water pump hub. Install shroud to radiator screws and tighten. Insert and tighten fan attaching screws.
13. Adjust belt tension. Tighten alternator retaining bolts and compressor idler pulley.
14. Fill and bleed cooling system. Fill crankcase.
15. Run engine at fast idle and check for coolant and oil leaks. Set ignition timing.

Engine Lubrication

Oil Pan Removal

430 and 462 Engines

1. Position No. 1 piston to 15° B.T.D.C. Remove the oil dipstick.
2. Disconnect the fan shroud and place it over the fan.
3. Set the parking brake, then raise the car. The car must be supported in a manner that will not interfere with the lowering of the pan.
4. Drain crankcase.
5. Remove generator splash shield. Disconnect engine lateral restrictor.
6. To provide clearance, remove engine front support insulator to underbody side member retaining nuts. With a block of wood on a floor jack under the front edge of the oil pan, raise the engine about an inch. Insert a ½ in. block of wood between the insulators and the underbody side members. Remove the floor jack.
7. Remove the end attachments of the front stabilizer bar and rotate the ends of the bar downward to position the center of the bar up away from the oil pan.
8. Remove oil pan attaching bolts. Free the oil pan from the cylinder block. Remove the two bolts that hold the oil pump pick-up tube and screen assembly to the

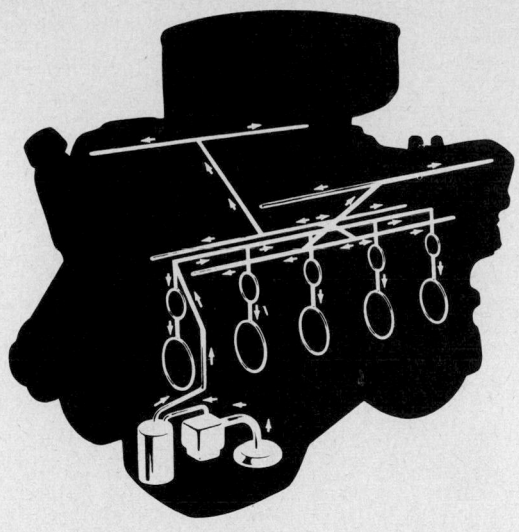

Lubrication system—430 and 462 V8 (© Ford Motor Co.)

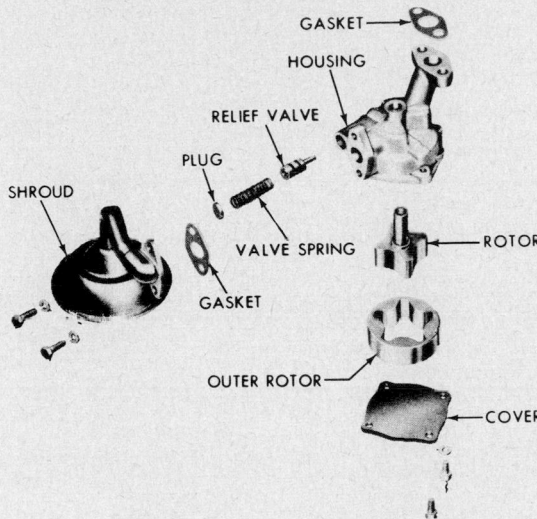

GASKET
HOUSING
RELIEF VALVE
PLUG
SHROUD
VALVE SPRING
ROTOR
GASKET
OUTER ROTOR
COVER

Disassembled oil pump (© Ford Motor Co.)

oil pump, and allow the tube and screen to drop into the oil pan. Remove the oil pan.

9. Install the oil pan by reversing the removal procedure.

1968-69 460 Engine

1. Disconnect radiator shroud.
2. Raise car on a hoist and drain crankcase.
3. Disconnect idler arm from underbody.
4. Loosen starter mounting bolts.
5. Remove cylinder block to converter housing bolts.
6. Disconnect engine front support insulators from underbody crossmember. Place floor jack under front of oil pan (block of wood between jack and oil pan). Raise engine just enough to insert 1 in. wood blocks between insulators and underbody side members. Remove floor jack.
7. Remove end attachments of front stabilizer bar and rotate ends of

bar down to raise center of bar. Remove oil filter.
8. Remove oil pan mounting bolts and lower oil pan to underbody crossmember. Remove splash shield from right side of oil pan.
9. Disconnect pressure line at power steering pump. Remove bolts holding the pump to cylinder front cover and rotate pump to clear the oil pan. Remove the oil pan.
10. Install oil pan in reverse order of removal and torque attaching bolts to 6-9 ft. lbs. Torque oil pump-to-cylinder block bolts to 20-25 ft. lbs.

1970-72 460 Engine

1. Disconnect the negative battery cable.
2. Disconnect the fan shroud from the radiator and position it rearward over the fan.
3. Drain the crankcase and remove the oil filter.
4. On Mark III models, disconnect

the oil cooler lines from the radiator. Remove the bolt that attaches the oil cooler line bracket to the cylinder block.
5. Remove the end attachments of the front stabilizer bar and rotate the ends downward.
6. Remove the starter attaching bolts.
7. Remove the motor mount to chassis attaching bolts and raise the engine several inches.
8. Place blocks of wood between the motor mounts and the chassis.
9. Remove the converter housing to engine block support bracket bolts and remove the brackets.
10. Remove the oil pan attaching bolts and remove the pan from the engine. On Mark III models, it will be necessary to move the oil cooler lines out of position to remove the pan.
11. Clean all gasket mounting surfaces and reverse above procedure to install.

Connecting Rods and Pistons

Rod and Piston Assembly

Removal

On all Lincoln Continental and Mark II models, the rod and piston assemblies are removed through the top of the block.

Remove the oil pan and cylinder heads.

Start with any pistons that are down and remove the ring ridge from the top of the cylinder wall with a ring ridge reamer or a bearing scraper.

From underneath the car, take off the lower half of the connecting rod on those rods from which the cylinder ridge has been removed. Carefully mark the cap so that it can be replaced in the same position on the same rod, or install the cap on the rod immediately.

Push the upper half of the rod and piston assembly up out of the top of the block.

Repeat on the rest of the cylinders and piston assemblies.

Installation

1. Coat the piston, rings, and cylinder wall with light engine oil.
2. With bearing caps removed, install pieces of protective rubber hose on each bearing cap bolt to prevent them from scoring any internal engine parts during installation.
3. Using a piston ring compressor tool, install each piston in the bore it was removed from.

Piston Ring Compressor

ARROW TOWARD FRONT OF ENGINE

Piston installation
(© Ford Motor Company)

4. Remove the thread guards from the connecting rods, position the upper bearing insert on the rod, and carefully guide the rod onto the crankshaft journal.
5. Install the lower half of the bearing cap and tighten to specifications.
6. Check connecting rod side clearance.

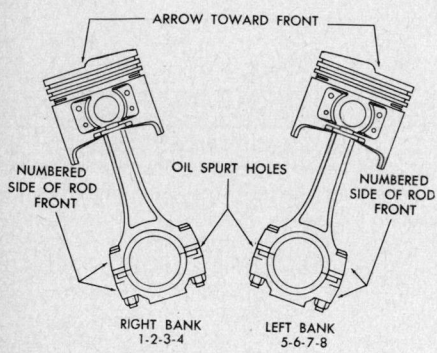

ARROW TOWARD FRONT

NUMBERED SIDE OF ROD FRONT — OIL SPURT HOLES — NUMBERED SIDE OF ROD FRONT

RIGHT BANK 1-2-3-4   LEFT BANK 5-6-7-8

**Correct relation of piston to rod—
430 and 462 V8**

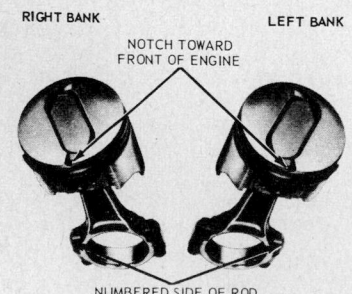

RIGHT BANK   LEFT BANK

NOTCH TOWARD FRONT OF ENGINE

NUMBERED SIDE OF ROD

Correct piston and rod positions 460 engines
(© Ford Motor Company)

Piston Rings

Replacement

Each piston is fitted with 3 piston rings: an upper and lower compression ring which seals the combustion chamber of the engine so that the expanding gases of the power stroke do not escape, and an oil control ring

which prevents cylinder wall lubricating oil from entering the combustion chamber. Due to the great amount of pressure and high temperature present in the piston area during combustion, piston ring clearances are very critical. Before replacing piston rings, piston and cylinder wall dimensions must first be checked; for even new piston rings cannot seal a piston or cylinder wall that is worn beyond specifications.

1. Using an internal micrometer, measure cylinder wall taper and out-of-roundness.

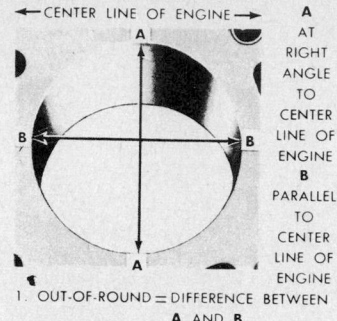

← CENTER LINE OF ENGINE →

A AT RIGHT ANGLE TO CENTER LINE OF ENGINE
B PARALLEL TO CENTER LINE OF ENGINE

1. OUT-OF-ROUND = DIFFERENCE BETWEEN **A** AND **B**
2. TAPER = DIFFERENCE BETWEEN THE **A** MEASUREMENT AT TOP OF CYLINDER BORE AND THE **A** MEASUREMENT AT BOTTOM OF CYLINDER BORE

Cylinder bore out of roundness and taper
(© Ford Motor Company)

2. Measure piston outside diameter and subtract this measurement from the cylinder bore diameter obtained in above step. The result of this subtraction will give piston to wall clearance which also must be within specification.
3. If the cylinder wall and piston measurements are within specifications, and new rings are to be installed, hone the cylinder to the proper finish.
4. Position each ring in the cylinder bore it is to be used in and square it with the cylinder wall by gently pushing it downward with an inverted piston.
5. Using a feeler gauge of correct thickness, measure the ring end

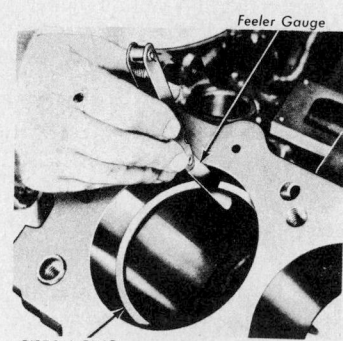

Feeler Gauge

PISTON RING

Checking ring gap
(© Ford Motor Company)

gap. If it exceeds specifications, try another ring, if it is less than specifications file the end of the ring to correct.
6. Install the rings on the pistons and measure piston ring to piston side clearance.

NOTE: before installing piston rings, the ring grooves on the piston

Checking ring side clearance
(© Ford Motor Company)

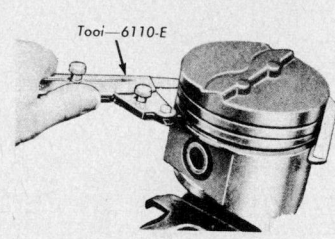

Tooi—6110-E

Cleaning ring grooves
(© Ford Motor Company)

should be thoroughly cleaned of all foreign material.
7. Space ring gaps on piston as shown in illustration.

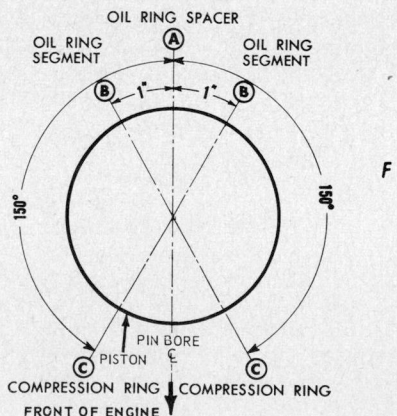

OIL RING SPACER

OIL RING SEGMENT (A) OIL RING SEGMENT

(B) (B)

150° 150°

F

PIN BORE

PISTON (C) (C)

COMPRESSION RING   COMPRESSION RING

FRONT OF ENGINE

Spacing piston rings (© Ford Motor Co.)

Rear Main Bearing Oil Seal

1965-69

The rear main bearing oil seal on 1965-69 models is a packing-type seal which requires the removal of the crankshaft to replace the upper half.

The lower half may be replaced, however, by removing the crankshaft rear main bearing cap and inserting a new packing into the packing retainer. It is sometimes possible to correct an oil leak at the rear main bearing by installing new packing in the lower half of the main bearing cap and letting it protrude approximately 1/16 in. above the cap surface. The cap is then bolted up to the cylinder block and is immediately taken down. If the packing has riveted over, the riveted portion is cut off.

Again, bolt the cap into place and keep repeating this cycle until it is either necessary to cut off the packing or the bearing cap finally seats.

The object of letting the seal protrude is to compress the upper portion of the rear main bearing seal to prevent a leak at that point.

Rear Crankshaft Oil Seal R & R

1970-72

1. Remove the oil pan, and, if required, the oil pump.

2. Loosen all main bearing caps allowing the crankshaft to lower slightly.

   NOTE: the crankshaft should not be allowed to drop more than 1/32 in.

3. Remove the rear main bearing cap and remove the seal from the cap and block.

4. Carefully clean the seal grooves in the cap and block with solvent.

5. Soak the new seal halves in clean engine oil.

6. Install the upper half of the seal in the block with the undercut side of the seal toward the front of the engine. Slide the seal around the crankshaft journal until 3/8 in. protrudes beyond the base of the block.

7. Repeat above procedure on lower seal, allowing an equal length of the seal to protrude beyond the opposite end of the bearing cap.

8. Install rear bearing cap and torque all main bearings to specifications. Apply sealer only to the rear of the seals.

9. Dip the bearing cap side seals in oil, then immediately install them. Do not use any sealer on the side seals. Tap the seals into place and do not clip the protruding ends.

10. Install the oil pump and pan. Fill

Ring Gaps (in.)			
Year and Engine	Top Compression	Bottom Compression	Oil Control
1965-66 430 and 462	0.010-0.020	0.010-0.020	0.015-0.066
1967-68 462	0.010-0.035	0.010-0.020	0.015-0.066
1968 460	0.010-0.031	0.010-0.031	0.015-0.066
1969-72 460	0.010-0.020	0.010-0.020	0.010-0.035

Side Clearance (in.)			
Year and Engine	Top Compression	Bottom Compression	Oil Control
1965-68 430 and 462	0.0020-0.0035	0.0020-0.0035	Snug
1968-72 460	0.0020-0.0040	0.0020-0.0040	Snug

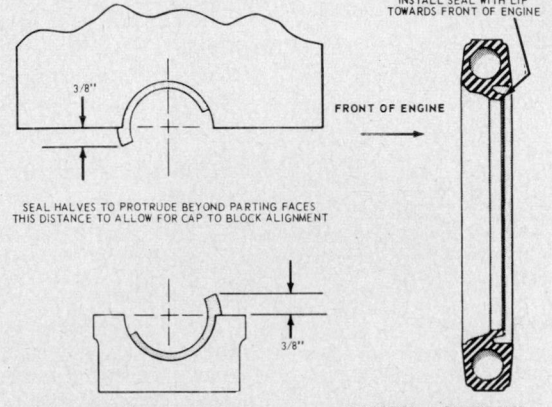

INSTALL SEAL WITH LIP TOWARDS FRONT OF ENGINE

FRONT OF ENGINE

SEAL HALVES TO PROTRUDE BEYOND PARTING FACES THIS DISTANCE TO ALLOW FOR CAP TO BLOCK ALIGNMENT

REAR FACE OF REAR MAIN BEARING CAP AND CYLINDER BLOCK

VIEW LOOKING AT PARTING FACE OF SPLIT, LIP-TYPE CRANKSHAFT SEAL

1970-71 rear main seal installation (© Ford Motor Co.)

⏻ CHILTON TIME-SAVER

Top Half, Rear Main Bearing Oil Seal Replacement

All Models

The following method has proven a distinct advantage in most cases.

1. Drain engine oil and remove oil pan.

2. Remove rear main bearing cap.

3. With a 6 in. length of 3/16 in. brazing rod, drive up on either exposed end of the top half of oil seal. When the opposite end of the seal starts to protrude, have a helper grasp it with pliers and pull, gently, while the driven end is being tapped. It is surprising how easily most of these seals can be removed by this method.

Fabric-Type Seal Installation

1. Obtain a 12 in. piece of copper wire (about the same gauge as that used in the strands of an insulated battery cable).

2. Thread one strand of this wire through the new seal, about ½ in. from the end, bend back and make secure.

3. Thoroughly saturate the new seal with engine oil.

4. Push the copper wire up through the oil seal groove until it comes down on the opposite side of the bearing.

5. Pull (with pliers) on the protruding copper wire while the crankshaft is being turned and the new seal is slowly fed into place.

   CAUTION: this snaking operation slightly reduces the diameter of the new seal and care will have to be used to keep the seal from slipping too far through the top half of the bearing.

6. When an equal amount of seal is extending from each side, cut off the copper wire close to the seal and tamp both ends of the seal up into the groove (this will tend to expand the seal again).

   NOTE: don't worry about the copper wire left in the groove. It is too soft to cause damage.

7. Replace the seal in the cap in the usual way, and replace the oil pan.

the crankcase with oil, start engine check for leaks.

Jacking, Hoisting

Drive-On Hoist

Care should be exercised when driving the car on to a hoist because the body may contact the upright flanges on the hoist with subsequent damage. The approach ramp should be built up slightly if the angle of approach is too steep.

Rail-Type Hoist

The forks which contact the rear axle must be carefully positioned to avoid damage to the shock absorbers.

Forklift Hoist

The rear post fork, if not adjustable to width, may require special adapters to avoid damaging the rear shock absorbers.

Frame Contact Hoist

Particular care must be exercised when using a frame contact hoist. Specific areas marked on the underbody are designated as hoisting areas.

The lifting areas at the front of the vehicle are clearly designated by corrugated metal plates. These plates are bolted to the underbody midway between the front edge of the door and the rear edge of the front fender wheel opening. The front hoist pads or adapter arms, must be positioned on these corrugated plates.

The lifting areas at the rear of the vehicle are located at the edge of the underbody approximately 15 in. forward of the front edge of the rear wheel opening cover panel. The rear hoist pads, or adapter arms, must not be positioned forward of this point.

Floor Jack (Support)

Various acceptable jacking locations are available when it is necessary to raise any one portion of the vehicle. However, when jacking against sheet metal, a wood block 2 x 4 of suitable length should be placed between the jack and the sheet metal to prevent damaging or deforming the metal. Do not attempt to raise one entire side of the body by placing a jack midway between the front and rear wheels. This procedure will probably result in permanent damage.

Jacking at the Front

Each wheel can be raised independently by placing a floor jack under the spring seat pocket in the lower suspension arm.

Jacking at the Rear

Each wheel can be raised independently by placing a floor jack under the rear axle housing.

Bumper Jack

The bumper jack lifting points are similar to those specified in previous models. There is a mounting bracket at the underside edge at the front and rear bumpers for a bumper jack.

Front Suspension

Front Spring and Lower Arm

Removal and Replacement
1965-69 Except Mark III

1. Raise the car. Place a support under each underbody side rail to the rear of the lower arm, in the lifting pad area.
2. Remove wheel and tire assembly, then, remove the hub and drum. On disc brake-equipped cars: remove two bolts and washers that attach the caliper to the spindle.

Remove the caliper from the rotor and wire it to the underbody. Remove the hub and rotor from the spindle.

3. Loosen splash shield to provide clearance at the end of the arm when it is lowered.
4. Remove the shock absorber, and disconnect the stabilizing strut from the lower arm. Disconnect the stabilizer bar from the suspension bar.
5. Remove the cotter pin and loosen the castellated nut attaching the lower ball joint to the spindle.
6. Place a box wrench over the lower end of the ball joint remover tool between the two spindle pivot points. (The tool should seat firmly against the ends of both studs, and not against the lower stud nut.)
7. Turn the wrench until both studs are under tension, then, rap the spindle near the lower stud to loosen the stud from the spindle. Do not loosen the stud with tool pressure alone.
8. Place a jack under the outer end of the lower arm and raise the arm several inches.
9. Install spring compressor tool inside the spring with the jaws of the tool toward the center of the car.
10. Remove the nut from the ball

MEASURE FROM UNDERSIDE OF
CROSS MEMBER POCKET, ADJACENT TO
FRONT SIDE OF JOUNCE BUMPER
BRACKET, TO TOP OF DRAG STRUT FLAT

FRONT RIDE HEIGHT (INCHES)	
NORMAL	5¾
MAXIMUM	6⅛
MINIMUM	5⁵⁄₁₆

POINT A

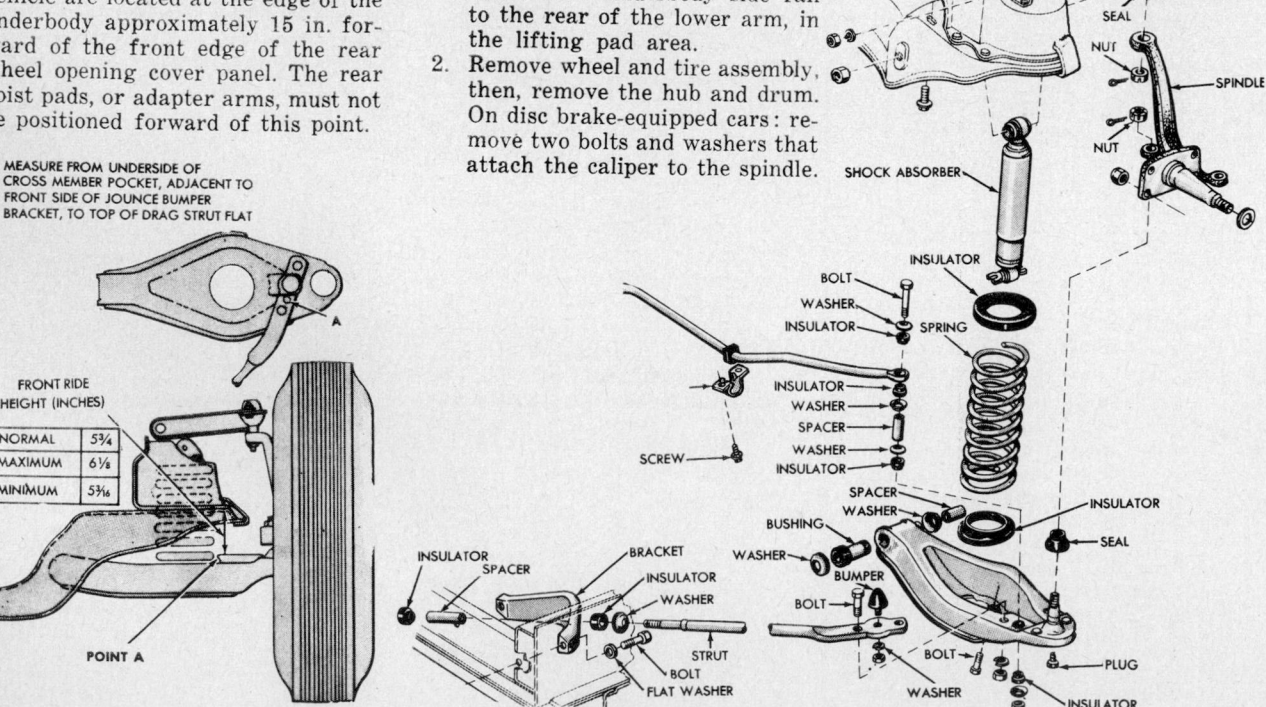

Front suspension—1965-69 except Mark III Ⓒ Ford Motor Co.

joint stud. Lower the jack until the spindle and spring are free, and remove the spring and insulators.

11. Remove the lower arm to crossmember nut, bolt, washers, and spacer, then remove arm.

12. Install by reversing the removal procedure.

Front Spring Removal—1968-71 Mark III and 1970-72 Continental

1. Raise vehicle and support front end of frame with jack stands.
2. Place jack under lower arm to support it.
3. Disconnect lower end of shock absorber from lower arm.
4. Remove bolts that attach strut and rebound bumper to lower arm.
5. Disconnect lower end of sway bar stud from lower arm
6. Remove nut and bolt that secures inner end of lower arm to crossmember.
7. Lower jack slowly to relieve spring pressure on lower arm then remove spring.

Ball Joints

See Ford section.

Steering Gear

Steering Gear Assembly Removal (From Car)

1965

1. Disconnect the power gear hoses. Remove the bolts that hold the flexible coupling to the steering gear flange, raise the car and remove the pitman arm.
2. Disconnect the exhaust pipe at the flange.
3. Clamp the front wheels to the extreme right position and take out the cap screws that secure the gear assembly to the under body front side member. Remove the gear.
4. The gear is reinstalled in the reverse of the procedure which removed it.

1966-67

1. Disconnect pressure and return line from steering gear. Cap each line and plug inlets in steering gear.
2. Remove ground strap from steering gear housing.
3. Remove bolt that attaches flex coupling to steering gear.
4. Remove bolt that attaches left brace to torque box. Loosen bolt that secures brace to side rail and swing brace to one side.
5. Remove pitman arm from sector shaft.
6. Remove pipe between manifold and resonator.
7. Disconnect linkage rod from equalizer shaft. Remove equalizer stud from side rail. Move equalizer shaft up and out of way. Do not lose stud or bushings.
8. Remove bolt from lower end of fender splash shield. Move splash shield to one side to gain access to steering gear.
9. Remove three steering gear attaching bolts. Support gear be-

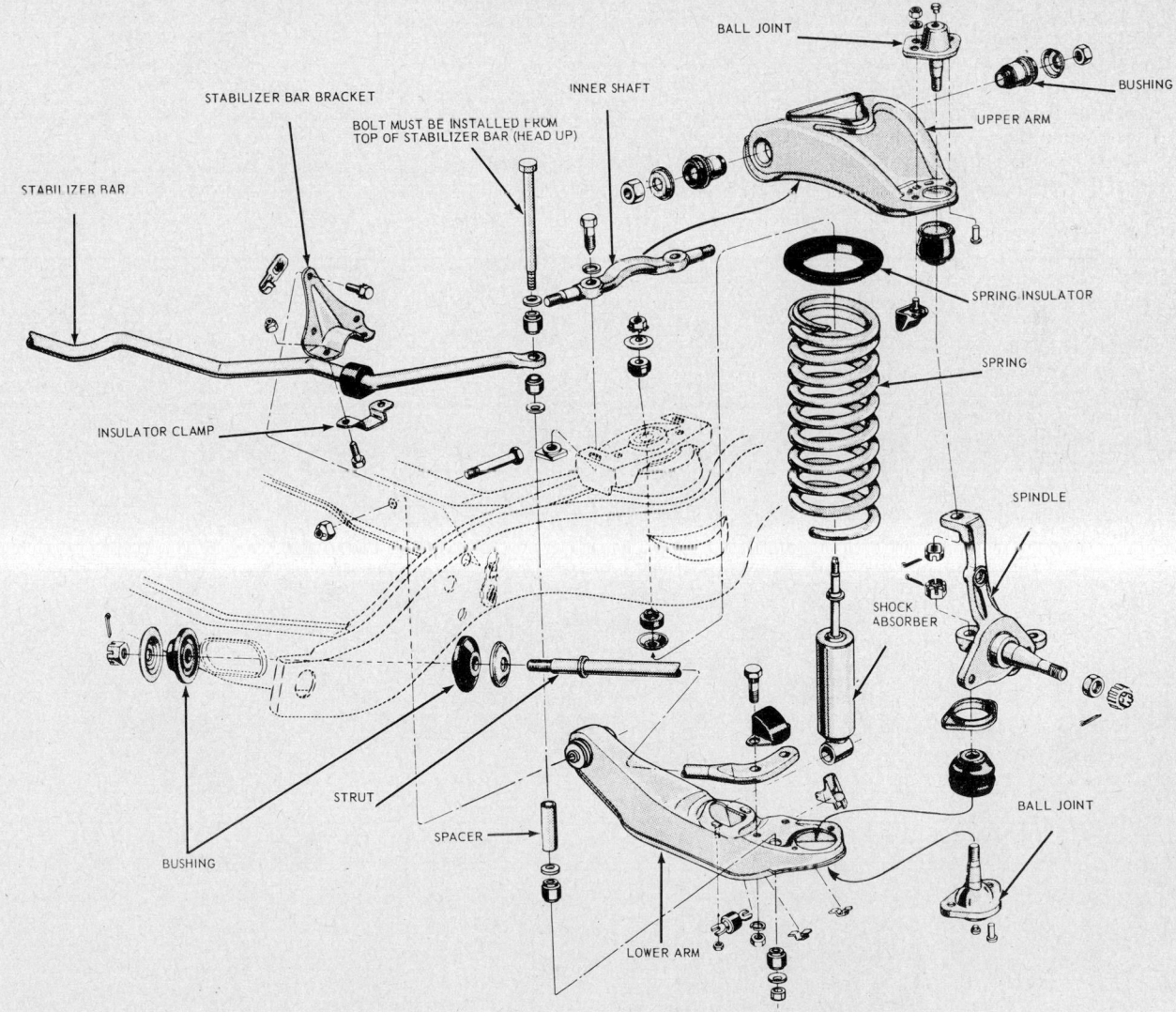

1970-72 Lincoln Continental and 1968-71 Mark III (© Ford Motor Co.)

fore completely removing last bolt.

10. Move steering gear down to free it from flex joint. Rotate it counterclockwise to provide clearance between side rail and engine.

11. Remove steering gear and remove three pads from gear. Reverse procedure to install.

1968-72

1. Disconnect hydraulic lines from the steering gear. Plug lines and ports to protect from leaking and the entry of dirt.

2. Remove the two bolts that hold the flex coupling to the steering gear and to the column.

3. Raise the car and remove the sector shaft attaching nut.

4. Remove pitman arm from the sector shaft.

5. Support steering gear, then remove the three steering gear attaching bolts.

6. Work the steering gear free of the flex coupling and remove it from the car.

7. If the flex coupling stayed on the input shaft, lift it off the shaft at this time.

8. Install by sliding the flex coupling into place on the steering shaft. Turn steering wheel so that the spokes are in the horizontal position.

9. Center the steering gear input shaft.

10. Slide the steering gear input shaft into the flex coupling and into place on the frame side rail. Install the three attaching bolts and torque them to specifications.

11. Be sure that the front wheels are in a straight ahead position, then install the pitman arm on the sector shaft. Install and tighten the sector shaft to pitman arm attaching nut to 150-225 ft. lbs.

12. Move the flex coupling into place on the input shaft and steering column shaft, install and tighten attaching bolts.

13. Connect and tighten the fluid pressure and the return lines to the steering gear.

14. Fill the power steering pump and cycle the steering gear by turning the steering wheel through both extremes of its travel.

15. Check for leaks and again check fluid level. Be sure required level is maintained.

Automatic Transmission

Twin-Range Turbo-Drive

Downshift Rod Adjustment —1965

1. With ignition key off, push ac-

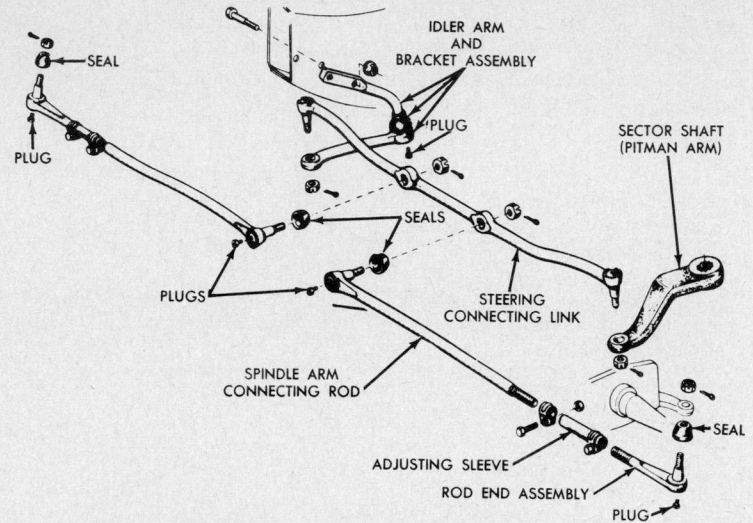

Disassembled view of typical steering linkage (© Ford Motor Co.)

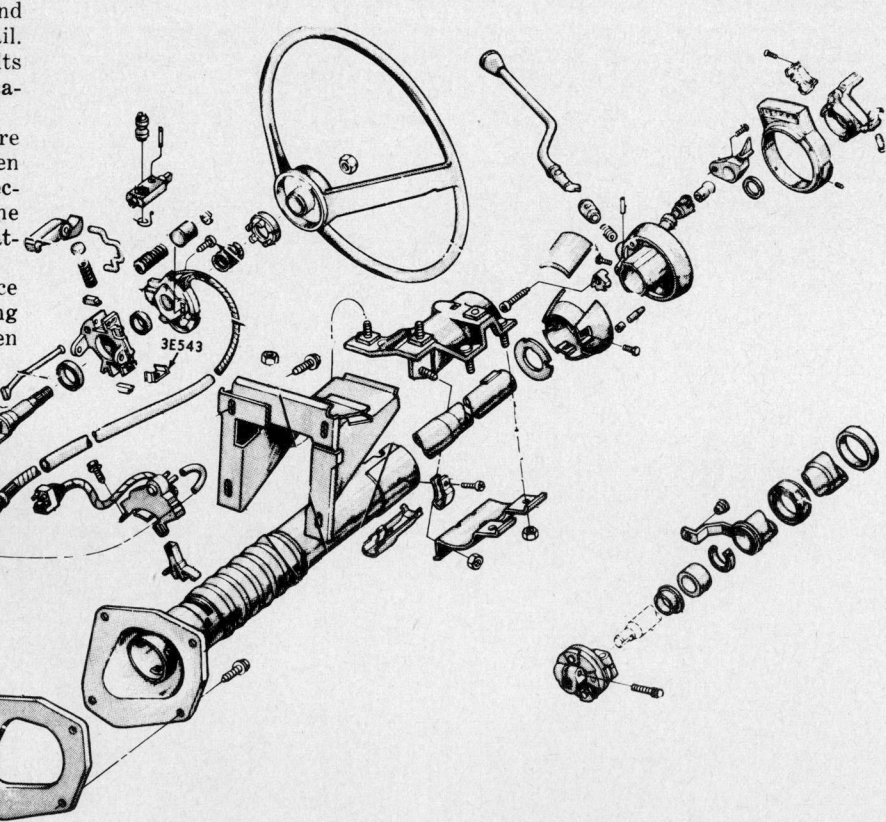

Steering column, automatic transmission and shift mechanism tilt wheel

celerator to full kickdown position. Check position of bellcrank slot and pin. The pin must be within 3/32 in. from the top of the bellcrank slot. (Release accelerator pedal when making adjustment.)

2. It is important that no binding exists at either end of downshift rod. If downshift rod is not vertical and free, binding will result and travel will be restricted. After adjustment, tighten jam nuts.

3. With the accelerator again depressed, the top of the bellcrank pin must be within 3/32 in. from the top of the bellcrank slot. To adjust, disconnect the downshift rod at F. Lengthen or shorten the rod, as needed, to obtain correct linkage travel.

Manual Linkage Adjustment —1965

1. Raise the car. Disconnect the manual shift rod from the clevis at the clevis pin.

2. Lower the car and position the selector lever so the pointer is against the stop in D2 range. (This position must be maintained throughout the manual adjustment.)

3. Position the detent lever in the third position (D2 detent) from the bottom. (The second detent is D1 and the bottom detent is low.)

4. Adjust the manual shift rod clevis so the clevis pin enters the clevis detent and lever freely. Lengthen the clevis one full turn and reassemble.

5. Check the position of the pointer

in each range. If the pointer does not line up with the letters in each range, adjust the letters. Do not adjust the linkage to correct pointer register with letters.

C-6 Dual Range

Beginning 1966

Downshift Rod

1. Loosen the locknut on the downshift rod. Disconnect rod from the ballstud on the bellcrank assembly by sliding the spring clip off the end of the rod.

2. Pull upward and hold the downshift rod against the transmission internal stop. Adjust length of rod until the hole in the rod is aligned with the ballstud on the bellcrank assembly.

3. Lengthen the downshift rod one turn and position it on the ballstud. Slide the spring clip over the end of the rod to lock the rod to the ballstud. Tighten locknut securely.

4. Be sure the bellcrank outer bracket is against the stop pin. If it is not, lengthen the downshift rod one turn. If the rod is too long, there will be no upshift.

Manual Linkage Adjustment

1. If the car is equipped with a tilt wheel steering, position the column up as far as possible. With the engine off, place the selector lever against the stop in the D1 (large dot) position.

Raise the car, and remove linkage splash shield.

2. Disconnect the adjustable link from the transmission manual shift lever on the transmission.

3. Be sure the transmission shift is fully engaged in D1, the second detent from the bottom. The bottom detent is L (low).

4. Loosen locknut on adjustable link, then pull down on the link to hold the selector lever against the D1 stop. Adjust the link by turning the lower end until the hole in the link aligns with the stud on the transmission manual lever. Connect it to the transmission shift lever.

5. Check selector lever through all positions to secure correct adjustment.

Neutral Safety and Back-Up Light Switch Adjustment

1965

1. With manual lever properly adjusted, loosen the two switch attaching bolts.

2. With the transmission lever in neutral, rotate the switch and insert the gauge pin A (No. 43 drill shank end) into the gauge pin holes of the switch. The gauge pin must be inserted to a full 13/64 in. into all three gauge holes of the switch.

3. Torque the switch attaching bolts to 55-75 ft. lbs. Then, remove gauge pin from the switch.

4. Check operation of the switch. The engine should start only with the selector lever in neutral and park. The back-up light should burn only with the selector in reverse.

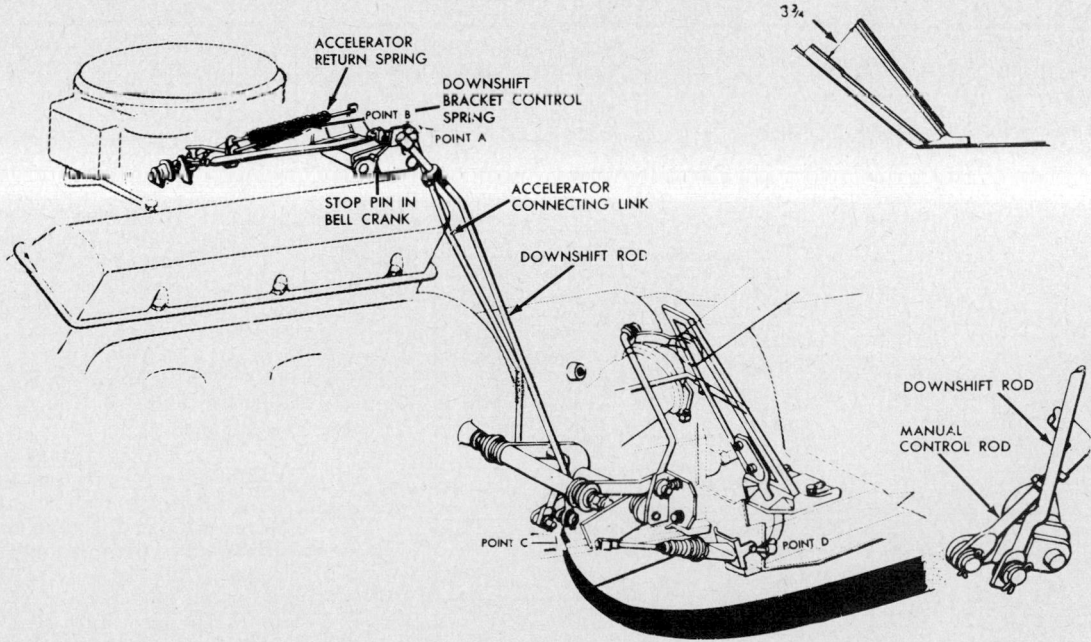

Typical linkage adjustments (© Ford Motor Co.)

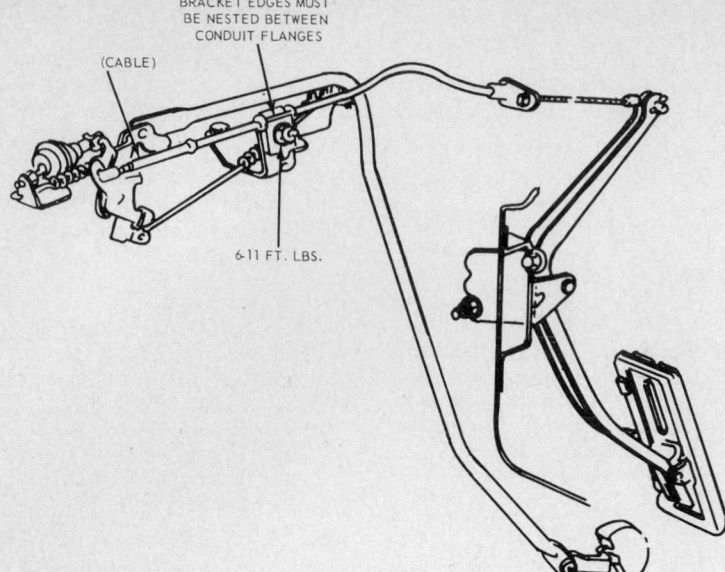

Throttle and downshift linkage—Mark III (© Ford Motor Company)

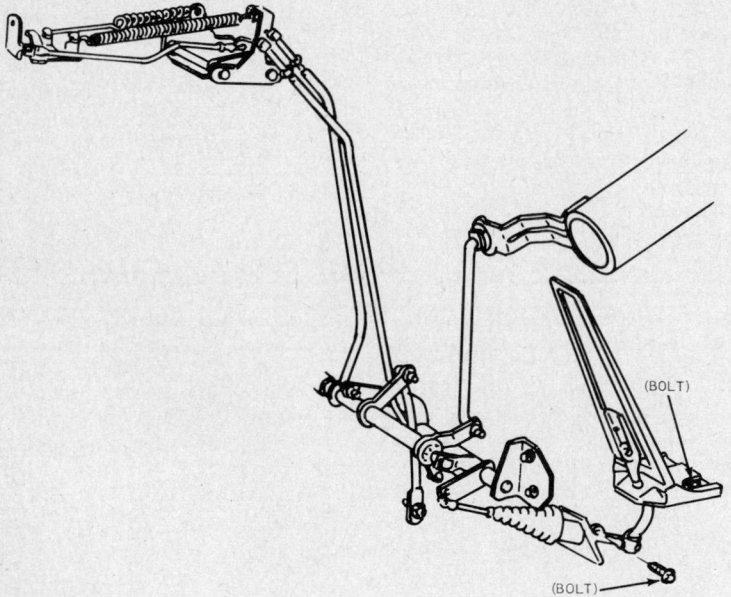

Throttle and downshift linkage—1966-70 Continental (© Ford Motor Company)

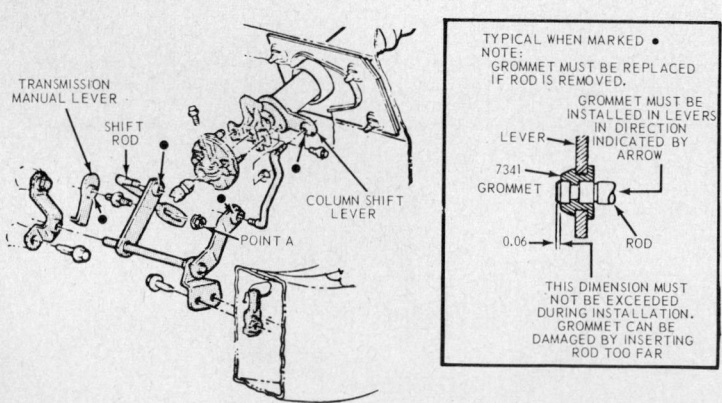

Transmission manual linkage, Lincoln Continental (© Ford Motor Co.)

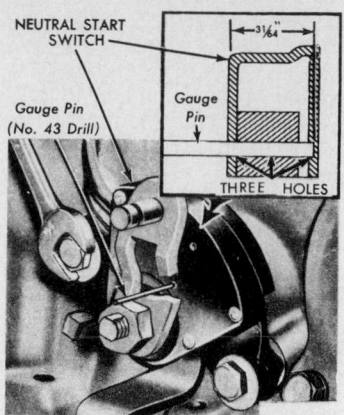

Neutral start switch—1966-67
(© Ford Motor Company)

1966-67

1. With manual linkage properly adjusted, try to engage starter in each position on quadrant. Starter should engage only in park and neutral positions.
2. To adjust loosen screws that locate switch on steering column.
3. Place shift lever in neutral detent.
4. Rotate switch until gauge pin (No. 43 drill) can be inserted into gauge pin hole $31/64$ in.
5. Tighten down locating screws and check starter engagement in each position as in step one.

1968-72

1. With manual linkage properly adjusted, try to engage starter in each position on quadrant. Starter should engage only in park or neutral positions.
2. Place shift lever in neutral detent.
3. Disconnect start switch wires at plug connector. Disconnect vacuum hoses if any. Remove screws securing neutral start switch to steering column and remove switch. Remove actuator lever along with Type III switches.
4. With switch wires facing up move actuator lever fully to the left and insert gauge pin (No. 43 drill) into gauge pin hole at point A. See accompanying figure. On Type III switch, be sure gauge pin is inserted a full $1/2$ in.
5. With pin in place, move actuator lever to right until positive stop is engaged.
6. On Type I and Type II switches remove gauge pin and insert it at point B. On Type III switches remove gauge pin, align two holes in switch at point A and reinstall gauge pin.
7. Reinstall switch on steering column. Be sure shift lever is engaged in neutral detent.
8. Connect switch wires and vacuum hoses and remove gauge pin.

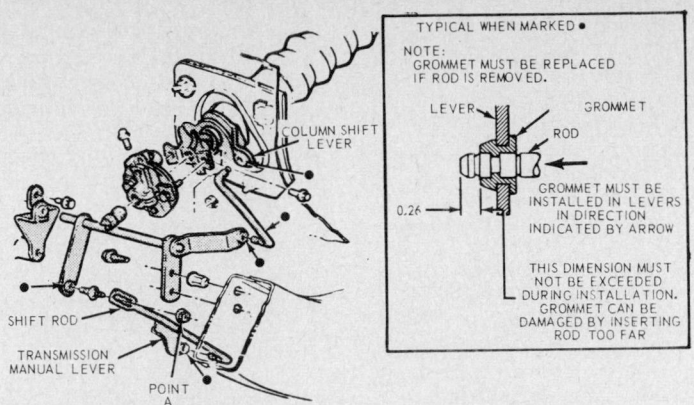

Transmission manual linkage, Mark III (© Ford Motor Co.)

9. Check starter engagement as in Step 1.

Transmission Removal & Replacement

1965 Turbo-Drive

To remove the transmission from any Lincoln or Lincoln Continental, it is necessary to remove the gear box and converter housing assembly as a unit. Two additional converter housing-to-transmission case bolts are located behind the converter assembly, and are not accessible until after the converter has been removed.

Refer to illustration for identity of underbody components.

1. Raise the hood and disconnect accelerator linkage (downshift rod) from bellcrank.
2. Remove two upper bolts and one bolt from right side of converter housing to engine block.

3. Remove one inner upper bolt attaching the starter motor to the converter housing.
4. Install remote control starter switch to the starter solenoid and put the transmission in neutral. Raise the car.
5. Disconnect the engine stabilizer bar bracket from the converter housing. (See illustration.) Remove converter housing lower plate.
6. Drain the converter.
7. Disconnect the fluid filler tube at the transmission and drain transmission.
8. Remove exhaust crossover pipe.
9. Disconnect oil cooler lines at transmission.
10. Index the rear universal joint and pinion flange to help upon reassembly. Disconnect propeller shaft at rear universal joint and remove the shaft.
11. Disconnect parking brake cables and the spring from equalizer bar. Remove the bar.
12. Remove two remaining bolts from starter motor to converter housing. Disconnect starter cable from electrical power box. Slide starter motor forward over the crossmember and secure out of

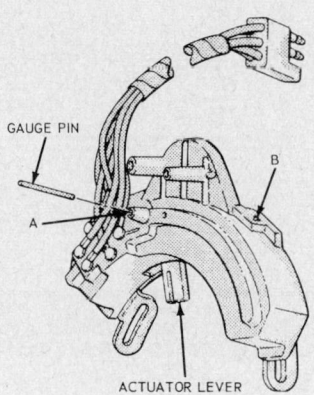

Neutral start switch—1968-72 (© Ford Motor Co.)

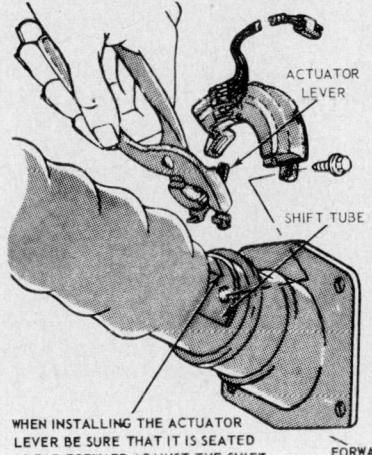

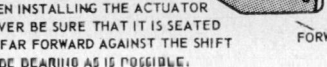

WHEN INSTALLING THE ACTUATOR LEVER BE SURE THAT IT IS SEATED AS FAR FORWARD AGAINST THE SHIFT TUBE BEARING AS IS POSSIBLE.

FORWARD

Removing or installing switch actuator—1968-70 (© Ford Motor Company)

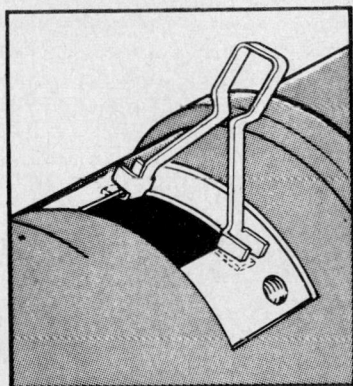

ACTUATOR LEVER INSTALLED

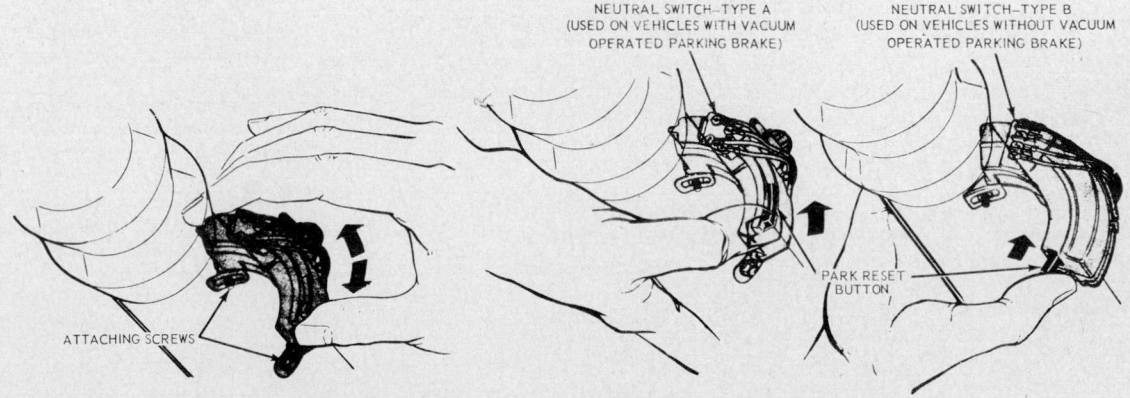

Adjusting neutral start switch—1968-72 (© Ford Motor Co.)

the way.

13. Remove control linkage splash shield. Disconnect manual and throttle control linkage from the transmission.
14. Disconnect speedometer at transmission.
15. Remove nut and washer from engine rear mount lower stud.
16. Secure transmission jack under, and raise the transmission off the rear mount crossmember. (See illustration.)
17. Remove two attaching bolts from the rear mount to the transmission extension housing.
18. Remove four attaching bolts and nuts from the crossmember to underbody brackets. (See illustration.)
19. Remove the rear mount from the crossmember. Then, remove the crossmember by sliding it over the left exhaust pipe to the rear of the left mounting bracket.
20. Lower the transmission jack slightly, and remove the remaining three converter housing to engine block bolts.
21. Move transmission toward the rear, lower, and remove from under the car.
22. Remove converter from converter housing.
23. Remove six bolts holding the converter housing to transmission case. Remove converter housing.

NOTE: replace transmission by reversing the above procedure.

For further detail and overhaul data on transmissions, see Unit Repair Section.

1966-69 C-6

The R & R procedure is essentially the same as for the earlier Turbodrive transmissions. However, factory recommendations are as follows:

1. Raise hood and disconnect starter neutral switch wires.
2. Disconnect the transmission oil filler tube from the manifold.
3. Raise the car and remove the bolts that attach the reinforcement plate at the rear of the transmission oil pan. Remove the plate.
4. With a drain pan under the transmission, loosen the transmission oil pan bolts and slowly drain and remove the pan. After all of the oil is out of the transmission, reinstall the pan, using about four bolts.
5. Remove two bolts that attach the cover to the lower end of the converter housing.
6. Remove two drain plugs from the converter housing and allow it to drain.
7. Remove four nuts that attach the converter to the drive plate.
8. Lift the filler tube from the transmission case.

9. Disconnect starter cable, then, remove the starter.
10. Disconnect fluid cooler lines from transmission.
11. Disconnect vacuum hose from the diaphragm.
12. Disconnect manual and downshift rods from the transmission.
13. Disconnect speedometer cable from extension housing.
14. Remove the three bolts that hold the manual and downshift control rod splash shield to the side rail and remove the shield.
15. Remove lower bellcrank bracket lower attaching bolt. Pivot the bracket to allow the bellcrank to hang free.
16. Pry upper bellcrank out of converter housing and allow it to hang free.
17. Disconnect the driveshaft from the real axle and remove it from the transmission.
18. Remove converter housing-to-cylinder block lower attaching bolts.
19. Loosen parking brake adjusting nut at the equalizer and remove the retracting spring. Disconnect rear brake cables and remove the equalizer.
20. Remove the two nuts that attach the engine rear mounts to the crossmember.
21. Place a transmission jack under the transmission and raise it just high enough to remove the weight from the crossmember.
22. Remove crossmember-to-frame attaching nuts and remove the crossmember.
23. Remove engine rear support-to-extension housing attaching bolts and remove support.
24. Secure the transmission to the jack with a safety chain. Lower the transmission and remove the upper converter housing-to-cylinder block attaching bolts.
25. Move the transmission away from the cylinder block. Lower it and remove it from under the car.
26. Remove the converter and mount the transmission in a holding fixture.
27. Replace the transmission by reversing removal procedure.

NOTE: transmission and servicing procedures can be found in the Unit Repair Section.

1968-71, Mark III
Transmission R&R

The C-6 transmission is used, as in previous models, however some modifications warrant some R & R procedure changes.

Removal

1. From the engine compartment,

remove the fluid filler tube bracket attaching screw that secures it to the rear of the right cylinder head. Lift tube and dipstick from the transmission.
2. Remove the starting motor upper attaching bolt using a long extension.
3. Remove the two converter housing upper attaching bolts.
4. Raise the car on a hoist.
5. Remove dust shield from the front end of the converter housing.
6. Crank engine until one of the converter drain plugs is accessible. Remove the plug.
7. Crank engine until the other plug is at the bottom. Place a drain pan to catch the fluid.
8. Remove the driveshaft.
9. Remove the side rail support brace attaching bolts and remove the brace.
10. After the fluid has drained from the converter, replace the plug.
11. Place drain pan under the transmission pan and loosen the pan attaching bolts. Allow the fluid to drain. Finally, remove all of the pan bolts except two on the same side. After the fluid has drained, install the bolts on the opposite side of the pan to hold it in place.
12. Remove converter-to-flywheel attaching nuts.
13. Disconnect downshift linkage from the transmission downshift lever.
14. Remove the selector rod from the manual shift lever.
15. Remove the two screws that attach the shift rod bellcrank bracket to the converter housing and remove the bracket.
16. Disconnect the vacuum diaphragm hose from the upper end of the vacuum tube.
17. Disconnect the speedometer cable from the extension housing and place it out of the way.
18. Remove the starting motor-to-lower attaching bolts and place the motor to one side.
19. Disconnect the two oil cooler lines from the right side of the transmission. Remove the idler arm attaching bolts and lower the arm.
20. Disconnect the muffler inlet pipes at the exhaust manifold and allow the pipes to hang.
21. Remove the vibration absorber from the extension housing.
22. Remove the two engine rear support-to-extension housing attaching bolts.
23. Place transmission jack under the transmission and raise it just enough to remove the weight from the support.
24. Remove two support attaching bolts and remove the support.

25. Lower the jack just enough to remove the weight.
26. Remove the four remaining converter housing-to-cylinder block attaching bolts and the accelerator linkage stop from the left side of the housing.
27. Carefully lower the transmission and remove it from under the car.
28. Remove the converter, then mount the transmission in a holding fixture.

Installation

1. Install in reverse of removal procedure. Torque converter drain plugs to 14-28 ft. lbs.
2. Install converter on stator support.
3. Secure transmission on a transmission jack.
4. Rotate converter so that the studs and drain plugs are aligned with their holes in the flywheel.
5. Move transmission toward the cylinder block until they contact each other. Install and torque the attaching bolts to 40-50 ft. lbs. Before tightening the center bolt on the left side, make sure that the accelerator linkage stop bracket is properly positioned so that the left upper bolt may be installed later.
6. Connect the fluid cooler lines to their fittings on the right side of the transmission.
7. Raise the transmission and install the engine rear support and tighten the bolts. Be sure that the handbrake equalizer is in position.
8. Lower transmission and remove the jack.
9. Install engine rear support-to-extension housing attaching bolts.
10. Install driveshaft.
11. Connect speedometer cable to extension housing.
12. Position starting motor on the converter housing and secure it with the two lower bolts.
13. Install the torque converter-to-flywheel attaching nuts and torque to 20-30 ft. lbs.
14. Install converter housing dust shield.
15. Secure the frame side rail support brace with the attaching bolts and lock washers.
16. Connect the downshift rod to the transmission downshift lever.
17. Connect the vacuum diaphragm hose to the upper end of the vacuum tube.
18. Install a new grommet in the manual lever. Then, secure the manual selector rod to the lever.
19. Position the vibration absorber to the transmission extension housing and secure it with the three attaching bolts.
20. Connect the muffler inlet pipes to the exhaust manifolds.
21. Lower the car and install the two converter housing upper bolts. Torque them to specifications.
22. Install starter motor upper bolt.
23. Place a new O-ring on the end of the fluid filler tube and insert it in the transmission case. Secure the tube to the right cylinder head wih the attaching screw and lock washer.
24. Fill the transmission to the proper level with the specified amount of fluid.
25. Adjust manual and throttle linkage as required.

1970-72 Lincoln Continental Transmission R & R

1. Raise hood and remove transmission dipstick.
2. Raise vehicle on hoist and remove bolt that secures transmission filler tube to cylinder head.
3. Remove bolts that attach reinforcement plate at rear of transmission oil pan, and remove plate.
4. Remove three bolts that attach manual and downshift control rod splash shield to side rail and remove shield.
5. Place drain pan under transmission. Loosen all transmission pan attaching bolts and allow fluid to drain. Remove pan. After fluid is drained, replace pan.
6. Remove two bolts that attach cover to lower end of converter housing.
7. Remove two front support bracket bolts at converter housing.
8. Remove drain plug from converter and allow to drain.
9. Remove four nuts that attach converter to flywheel.
10. Lift fluid filler tube from transmission case.
11. Remove two idler arm bracket bolts from frame side rail and allow idler arm to hang free.
12. Disconnect starter cable, and remove starter.
13. Disconnect oil cooler lines from transmission.
14. Disconnect vacuum hose from diaphragm.
15. Loosen parking brake adjuster nut at equalizer and remove retracting spring. Disconnect rear brake cables and remove equalizer from bracket.
16. Disconnect speedometer cable from extension housing.
17. Disconnect driveshaft from transmission flange and position out of way.
18. Disconnect downshift rod from downshift lever.
19. Remove manual selector rod from selector lever.
20. Remove lower bell crank.
21. Pry upper bell crank out of converter housing.
22. Remove cooler lines from clip on cylinder head.
23. Remove converter housing to cylinder block lower attaching bolts.
24. Remove two nuts that attach engine rear mounts to crossmember.
25. Place transmission jack under transmission and raise it enough to remove weight from crossmember.
26. Remove engine rear support to extension housing attaching bolts and remove supports.
27. Remove crossmember.
28. Secure transmission to jack with safety chain.
29. Lower transmission and remove upper converter housing to cylinder block attaching bolts.
30. Move transmission away from cylinder block.
31. Lower transmission and remove from vehicle.
32. Remove converter. Reverse procedure to install.

U Joints, Drive Lines

Since 1965, all Lincoln models have been equipped with Carden universal joints at the front end of the driveshaft. 1965 models had a conventional universal joint at the rear of the driveshaft. 1966-69 models had Carden universal joints at the rear of driveshaft which attached to the the differential by means of a conventional pinion flange. In 1970 a companion flange was added to the rear of the driveshaft.

Each Carden universal joint consists of two universal joints, a centering socket yoke or companion flange, and a center yoke.

Driveshaft and Universal Joint R & R

1. Mark the position of the centering socket yoke or companion flange in relation to the pinion flange so the driveshaft can be returned to its original location.
2. Disconnect the centering socket yoke or companion flange from the pinion flange.
3. Pull the driveshaft rearward until it clears the transmission extension housing and remove the driveshaft from the car.
4. Mark the position of the spiders, the center yoke, and the centering socket or companion flange. *The spiders must be assembled with the bosses in their original location to provide proper clearance.*
5. Remove the snap-rings that re-

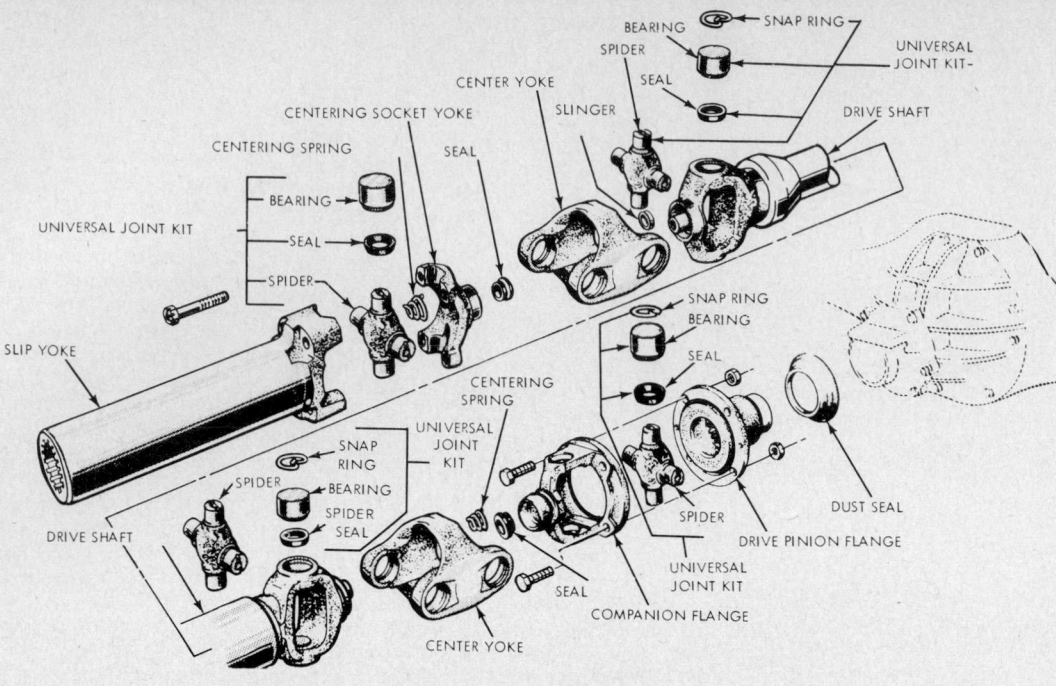

Driveshaft with Dana double Carden universal joints (© Ford Motor Co.)

tain the spider bearing caps.

6. Using a suitable tool, drive one of the bearing caps on the U-joint to be replaced toward the center of the driveshaft. If the bearing cannot be driven all the way out of the yoke, pull it from the driveshaft using lock-pliers; or, position the protruding bearing cap in the jaws of a vise and, using a soft hammer, drive the center yoke away from the bearing cap.

7. Repeat Step 6 until all bearing caps have been removed, then, remove the spiders.

8. To remove the centering socket or companion flange, pull it from its mounting stud and remove the rubber seal.

Caution When removing a universal joint that mounts to the driveshaft proper, use care when driving the universal joint out of the center yoke. If the universal joint is driven too far, the oil slinger on the front of the driveshaft yoke will be driven against the inside of the center yoke, damaging the oil slinger.

Rear Axles, Suspension

Rear Spring Replacement

1965-69 Except Mark III

Longitudinal leaf springs are used on these models.

They are held with a single bolt at

the front, and with a shackle at the back.

Take the weight of the car on a frame in front of the rear spring. Unbolt and remove the rear shackle. Disconnect the rear shock absorber and remove the four U-bolts from each side of the spring saddle where the spring is held to the rear axle housing. Lower the spring to the ground, remove the nut that holds the front pin in the frame bracket and drive the front spring pin out.

The spring can then be slid from under the car.

Replace in reverse of the procedure which removed it.

1968-71 Mark III and 1970-72 Continental

Coil springs are used at rear suspension.

The rear suspension is a coil-link design. Large, low-rate coil springs are mounted between rear axle pads

and frame supports. Parallel lower arms extend forward of the spring seats to rubber frame anchor to accommodate driving and braking forces. A third link is mounted between the axle and the frame to control torque reaction forces from the rear wheels.

Lateral (side sway) motion of the rear axle is controlled by a rubber bushed rear track bar, linked laterally between the axle and frame.

1. Place car on hoist and lift under rear axle housing. Place jack stands under frame side rails.
2. Disconnect track bar at the rear axle housing bracket.
3. Disconnect rear shock absorbers from the rear axle housing brackets.
4. Disconnect hose from axle housing vent.
5. Lower hoist with axle housing until coil springs are released.
6. Remove spring lower retainer with

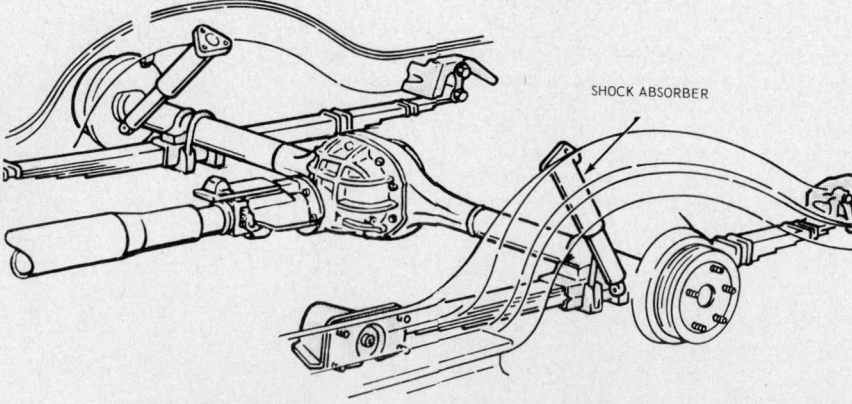

Rear suspension—1965-69 except Mark III

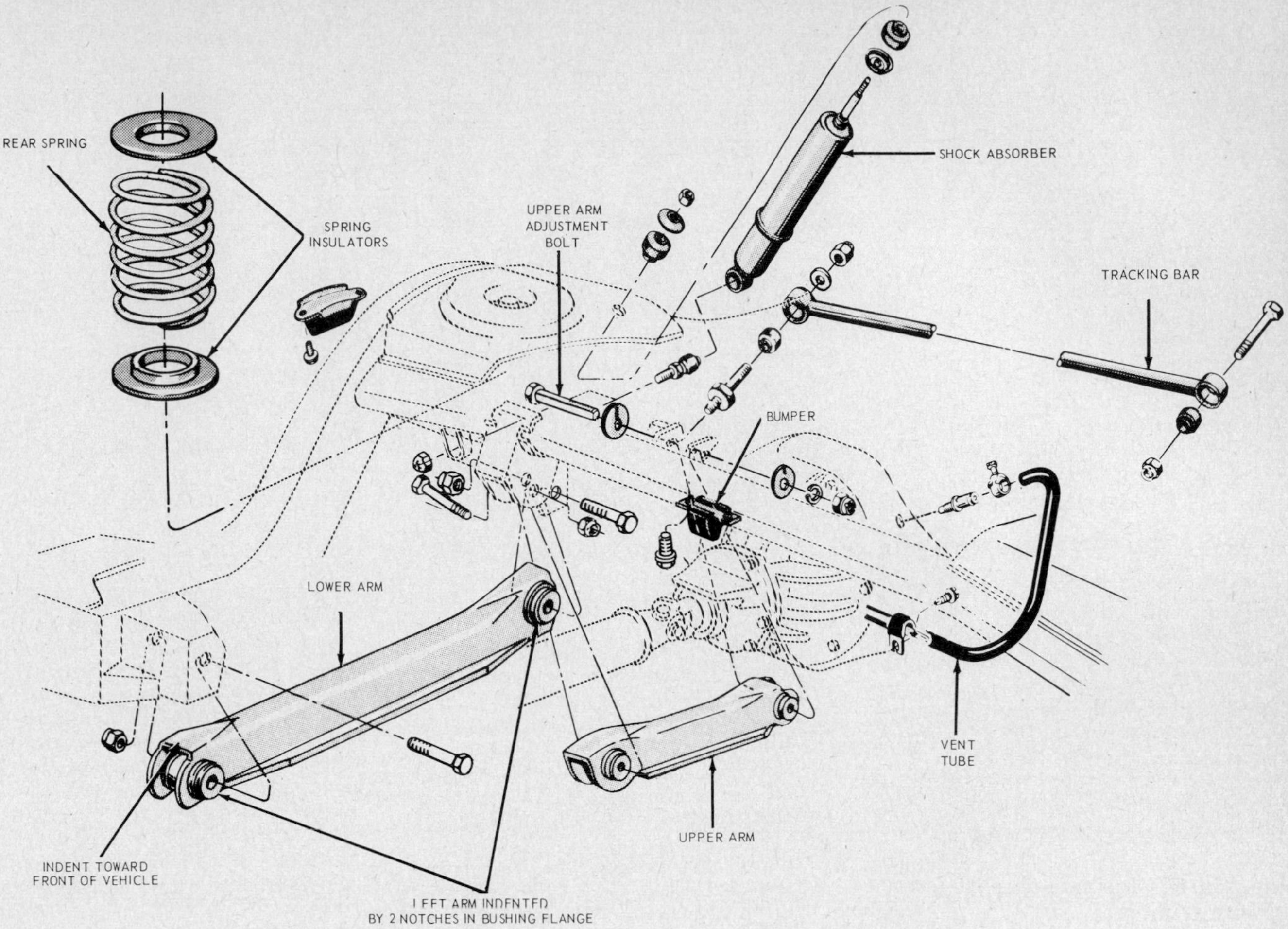

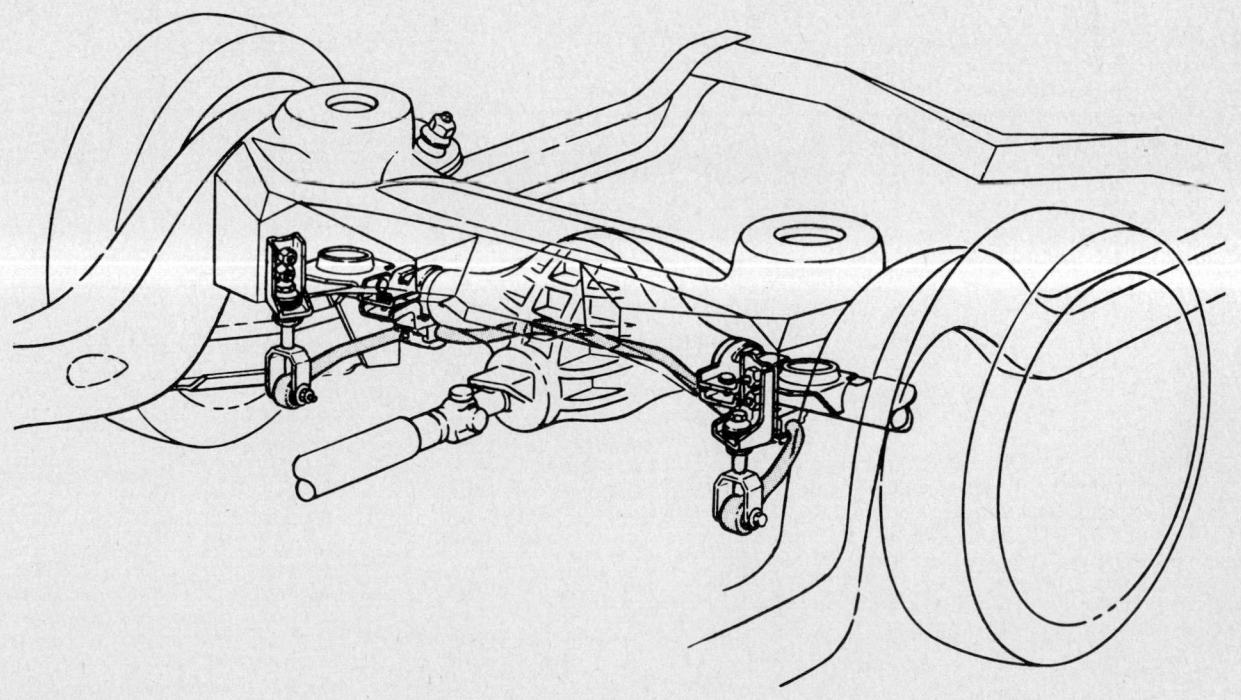

REAR SPRING

SPRING INSULATORS

UPPER ARM ADJUSTMENT BOLT

SHOCK ABSORBER

TRACKING BAR

BUMPER

LOWER ARM

UPPER ARM

VENT TUBE

INDENT TOWARD FRONT OF VEHICLE

LEFT ARM INDENTED BY 2 NOTCHES IN BUSHING FLANGE

1970-72 Lincoln Continental and 1968-71 Mark III (© Ford Motor Co.)

1972 Continental Mark IV rear suspension (© Ford Motor Company)

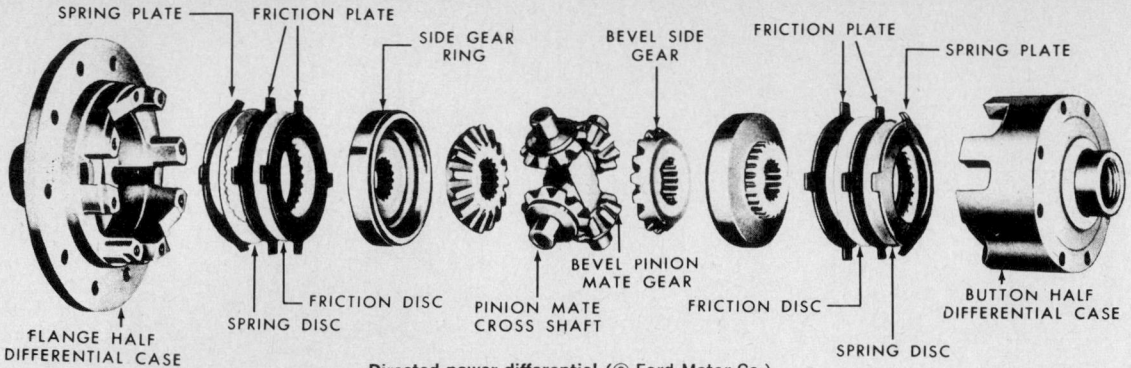

Directed power differential (© Ford Motor Co.)

bolt, nut, washer and insulator.
7. Remove spring with large rubber insulator pads from car.
8. Install in reverse of above.

Shock Absorber Replacement

Mark III and 1970 Continental

Rear shock absorbers on all cars are straddle mounted and are held to rubber bushings at both the top and bottom connections. Simply remove the nuts from the top and bottom of the shock absorber and lift the shock absorber off the car.

Axle Assembly Removal

1965-69 Except Mark III

To remove the rear axle on these models, take the weight of the car on the frame in front of the rear spring and split the rear universal joint. Disconnect the brake hoses and brake lines, and the shock absorbers, unbolt and remove the rear spring back shackles.

Remove the four U-bolts that hold the spring to the axle housing and disconnect the shock absorber.

Lower both springs to the floor, and the rear axle assembly can be slid out from under the car.

Mark III and 1970-72 Continental

The Mark III and 1970-72 Continental axle is not removed as an assembly.

1. Raise vehicle on hoist and remove wheels.
2. Remove rear hubs and drums. Back off brake shoes if drums do not come easily.
3. Remove nuts that secure rear wheel bearing retainer through hole in axle housing flange.
4. Pull each axle out of housing using properly designed puller. Do not damage oil seals.
5. Secure brake carrier plate to axle housing with one attaching nut.
6. Remove drive shaft.
7. Clean housing around carrier to prevent ingress of dirt.
8. Remove carrier nuts and drain housing.

9. Remove carrier.
10. Position safety stands under frame rear members, and support axle housing with floor jack or hoist.
11. Disengage brake line from clips that hold it on axle.
12. Disconnect vent tube from rear axle housing.
13. Remove brake backing plates and secure them with wire. Do not disconnect brake line.
14. Disconnect lower studs of shocks from axle.
15. Remove retaining nut and washer and disconnect track bar from mounting stud on axle housing.
16. Lower axle housing until springs are released.
17. Lift out springs.
18. Remove nuts, washers, and pivot bolts that connect lower arms to axle. Disconnect arms from axle.
19. Remove pivot bolt, nut, lock washer, and two eccentric washers.
20. Lower axle housing and remove from vehicle. Reverse procedure to install.

Radio

Radio R & R

1965

1. Disconnect battery.
2. Remove control knobs and two jam nuts and lock washers retaining outer bezel.
3. Remove outer bezel and four screws and large bezel.
4. Remove two screws attaching center trim panel to support and slide panel away from windshield.
5. Disconnect feed and lamp connectors, and antennae lead in.
6. Remove three attaching screws and pull radio and support out of instrument panel.
7. Discover speaker leads.
8. Remove two jam nuts and washers and remove support.
To reinstall: reverse the above.

1966-69 Except Mark III

1. Disconnect battery.
2. Remove eight screws in the lower control housing.
3. Disconnect lead from the speaker/s.
4. Disconnect power antenna lead.
5. Disconnect lead to the foot operated switch for AM-FM radios on cars so equipped.
6. Disconnect one two-way disconnect for power and pilot light.
7. Remove the two knobs and two bezels on the selector shafts. Remove the two nuts and two retainers on the selector shafts.
8. Remove the two screws holding the radio bracket to the lower reinforcement on the instrument panel.
9. Remove the two nuts and washers from the selector shafts. Disconnect the antenna lead and remove the radio.
10. To install, reverse the above.

1968-71—Mark III

Removal

1. Disconnect ground from battery.
2. Pull knobs off the control shafts.
3. Remove the cover plate located below the steering column.
4. Remove nut from the right radio control shaft.
5. Remove six screws and the trim applique from in front of the radio.
6. Remove the nut and washer from the right radio control shaft.
7. Remove screw attaching the front left side of the radio to the instrument panel.
8. Remove the radio support attaching screw.
9. Disconnect the radio power wires and speaker wires at the connectors.
10. Disconnect the antenna lead-in cable and remove the radio.

Installation

1. Connect the power, speaker, and antenna leads to the radio.
2. Position radio to instrument panel and install the attaching screw at the left front side of the

radio.

3. Install the washer and nut on the radio right control shaft.
4. Install radio rear support attaching screw.
5. Position the trim applique to the instrument panel and install the six attaching screws.
6. Install the nut on the radio right control shaft.
7. Install the discs, felt washer and knobs on the radio control shafts.
8. Install cover plate below the steering column.
9. Connect the ground cable to the battery.
10. Check operation of radio and set the push buttons.

1970-72 Continental

1. Disconnect battery.
2. Remove map light assembly.
3. Remove right and left inspection covers.
4. Remove lower instrument panel pad.
5. Remove glove box, open ashtray, and leave it open.
6. Remove glove box switch.
7. Through glove box opening remove two nuts retaining radio finish panel to instrument panel.
8. Remove radio knobs.
9. Remove two screws at top of finish panel. Position panel out and disconnect cigar lighter and light from right panel.
10. Through glove box opening remove nut from lower right corner of center finish panel.
11. Remove radio top support nut and three mounting screws. Pull radio out. Disconnect power leads and antenna cable. Remove radio. Reverse procedure to install.

Windshield Wipers

Motor R & R

1965-69

The wiper motor is hydraulically operated by oil pressure from the power steering pump via the steering gear.

1. Remove washer coordinator hose from bottom of wiper motor.
2. Remove oil return, feed and control lines from wiper motor.
3. Disconnect wiper control cable at the wiper motor.
4. Remove two screws holding the wiper motor to the auxiliary drive mounting plate. Remove wiper motor.
5. Install motor by reversing the removal procedure.
6. Refill the power steering system and bleed the lines.

1970-72 Continental

1. Disconnect battery.

2. Remove wiper arm and blade assemblies from pivot shafts.
3. Remove left cowl screen for access.
4. Disconnect linkage drive arm from motor output arm crank pin by removing retaining clip.
5. Disconnect two push on wire connectors from the motor.
6. From engine side of dash, remove three bolts that retain motor and remove motor. Reverse procedure to install.

1970 Mark III

1. Disconnect battery.
2. Disconnect washer hose, remove three retaining bolts, and pull cowl top grille out from under two clips.
3. Disconnect connector plugs from wiring harness at engine side of dash panel. Push wiring and plugs along with grommet through hole in dash.
4. Remove four motor to cowl retaining bolts. Lift motor out, and at the same time pull wiper arm and blade assembly to left for access to motor crank pin clip. Remove clip and disconnect drive link from motor crank pin. Remove three retaining bolts and separate motor from mounting plate and cover and wiring harness assembly. Reverse procedure to install.

1971 Mark III

See 1971-72 Thunderbird.

Transmission R & R

1965-69

Auxiliary Drive

1. Remove both wiper arms and blades from the pivot assemblies.
2. Remove the ventilation grille and screen.
3. Remove both washer nozzles.
4. Disconnect the pivot shaft drive arm from the auxiliary drive.
5. Remove the four screws and the auxiliary drive assembly.
6. To install, reverse the removal procedure.

Wiper Pivot

1. Remove the windshield wiper arms and blades.
2. Remove the cowl top ventilation grille and screen.
3. Right hand: disconnect the drive arm from the pivot shaft assembly.
4. Left hand: disconnect the drive arm from the right hand pivot assembly and the drive arm from the auxiliary drive assembly.
5. Remove the pivot shaft retaining capscrews and nuts.
6. Remove the pivot shaft and housing from the car.
7. To install, reverse the removal procedure.

1970-72 Continental

1. Disconnect battery.
2. Remove wiper arm and blade assemblies from pivot shafts.
3. Remove cowl screens for access.
4. Disconnect left linkage arm from drive arm by removing clip.
5. Remove three bolts retaining left pivot shaft assembly through cowl opening.
6. Disconnect linkage drive arm from motor crank pin by removing clip.
7. Remove three bolts that connect drive arm pivot shaft assembly to cowl. Remove pivot shaft drivearm and rightarm as an assembly. Reverse procedure to install.

1970 Mark III

1. Disconnect battery.
2. Disconnect washer hose, remove three retaining bolts, and pull cowl top grille out from under two clips.
3. Remove wiper arm and blade assemblies.
4. To remove left pivot shaft, loosen right pivot shaft retaining bolts, and remove left pivot shaft retaining bolts. Remove connecting clip, and disconnect left pivot shaft link from right pivot shaft crank pin. Work left pivot shaft and link assembly toward right and out through cowl opening.
5. To remove right pivot shaft, remove three retaining bolts and disconnect linkage from crank pin by removing clip. Lift pivot shaft assembly from cowl. Reverse procedure to install.

1971 Mark III

1. Remove the wiper arm and blade assemblies. Be sure to remove the tension arm retaining clip from the tension arm retaining stud on the left pivot assembly.
2. Remove the retaining screws and remove the cowl grille. Disconnect the washer hoses.
3. Remove the clip retaining the link assembly to the motor.
4. Remove the screws that attach the pivot shaft and link assembly to the cowl and remove the pivot shaft and link assembly.
5. Reverse above procedure to install.

Heater System

Heater Core Removal

1966-69 Continental

1. Disconnect battery, remove air cleaner, and drain coolant from system.
2. Disconnect hoses at heater core.

3. Remove harness clamp on top of evaporator-heater case.
4. Remove temperature blender door variable actuator.
5. Remove heater core cover plate retaining screws and cover plate.
6. Lift out heater core. Reverse procedure to install.

1968-71 Mark III

1. Remove hood and air cleaner and drain engine coolant.
2. Disconnect both hydraulic lines at wiper motor and position them to one side on 1968-69 Mark III.
3. Disconnect heater hoses at heater core and position hoses and water valve away from housing.
4. Disconnect vacuum supply hose on top of housing and remove oil pressure sending unit from back of engine.
5. Remove transmission dip stick and tube assembly.
6. Disconnect multiple connector leading to icing switch.
7. Remove evaporator housing front cover.
8. Remove heater core housing cover.
9. Remove heater core retaining bracket and remove heater core.

1970-72 Continental

1. Drain engine coolant.
2. Disconnect vacuum junction valve from dash panel and move valve and vacuum hoses away from case.
3. Disconnect speed control servo and bracket assembly if so equipped from dash panel and move it away from case.
4. Disconnect multiple connector from blower resistor and remove harness from clip on case.
5. Disconnect heater hoses from heater case and remove hose support clamp from case. Move hoses and water valve away from case.
6. Remove seven case cover to case flange attaching screws and wire harness clip.
7. Remove six cover to back plate stud nuts.
8. Remove one upper case to dash panel mounting screw.
9. Remove two case to dash panel mounting stud nuts, one on inboard mounting flange and one below case on lower flange.
10. Carefully move heater core assembly forward to clear mounting studs and lift it up and out of vehicle.
11. Remove two spring clips from core tubes on front of core cover.
12. Remove three screws from core end plate and remove plate.
13. Remove heater core and mounting gasket assembly from core cover and remove gasket from core. Reverse procedure to install.

Heater Blower Removal

1966-69 Continental

The blower motor is mounted in the right fender well.

1. Remove right fender splash shield secured with six bolts.
2. Remove four screws retaining

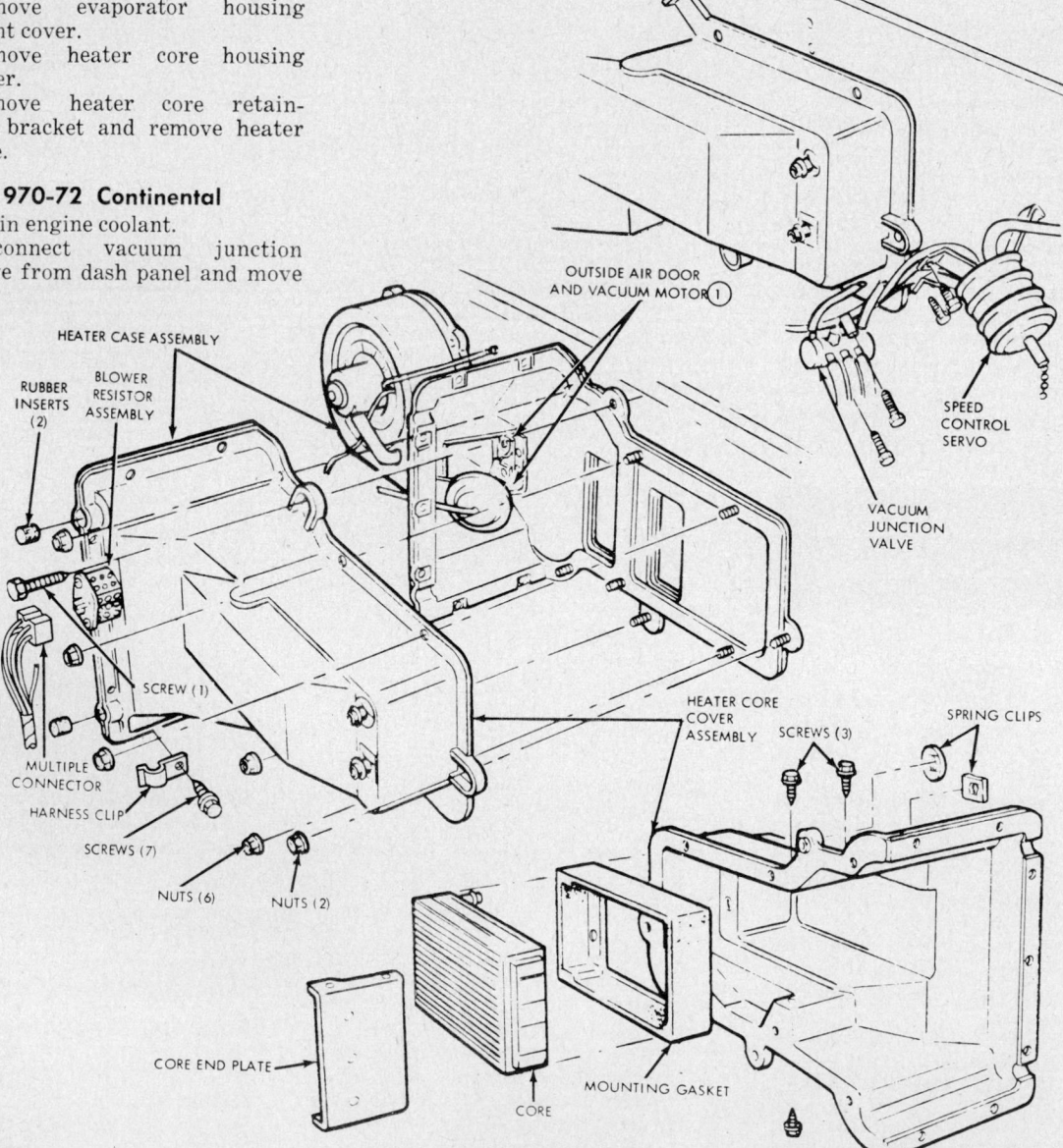

Heater core removal—1970-72 Lincoln Continental (© Ford Motor Co.)

blower motor to housing.
3. Disconnect electrical leads and remove motor.
4. Remove four nuts retaining motor housing to air door assembly and remove one nut through motor opening.
5. Remove housing and disassemble boot.
6. From inside car, remove right cowl trim panel and remove three screws retaining air door assembly to cowl.
7. From under fender remove screw at top.
8. Disconnect vacuum hose and remove air door assembly. Reverse procedure to install.

1968-71 Mark III
1. Remove right cowl side trim panel.
2. Remove screws retaining duct to cowl side panel and sound baffle and remove duct.
3. Disconnect lead wire to blower motor.
4. Remove one screw from motor mounting plate, rotate motor mounting plate clockwise to unlock plate from case and remove motor and wheel assembly through opening in cowl side of panel. Reverse procedure to install.

1970-72 Continental
1. Remove hood.
2. Remove right hood hinge and right fender inner support brace as an assembly.
3. Disconnect blower motor air cooling tube from motor.
4. Disconnect motor lead wire from harness and ground wire from dash panel.
5. Disconnect rear section of right front fender panel apron from fender around wheel opening and remove two lower fender to cowl mounting screws.
6. Separate fender apron from fender wheel opening so that apron can be pushed downward away from blower motor.
7. Remove four blower motor plate screws. Move motor and wheel forward out of blower scroll and remove assembly through opening while applying pressure to fender apron to enlarge opening at hinge area. Reverse procedure to install.

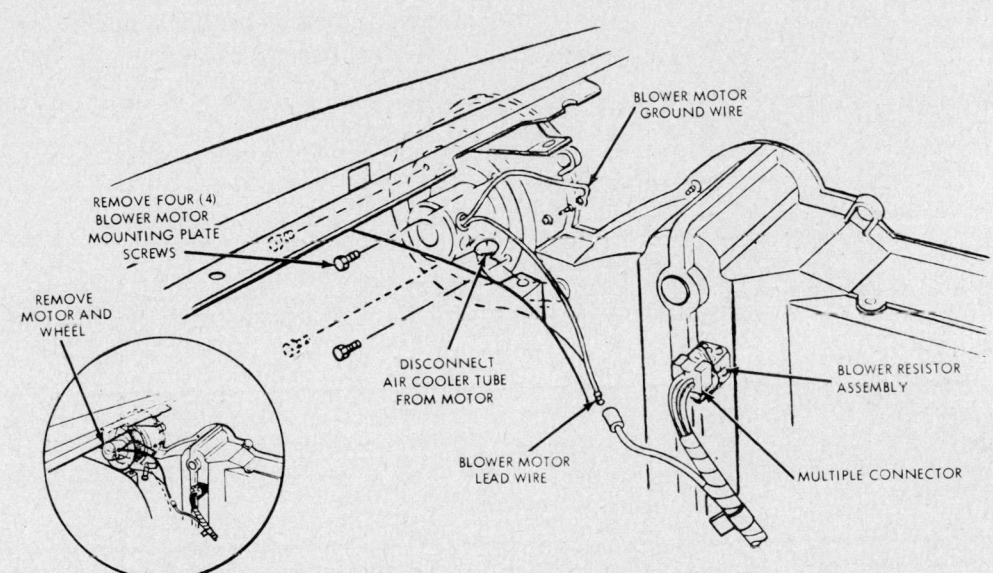

Heater blower removal—1970-72 Lincoln Continental (© Ford Motor Co.)

Oldsmobile and F-85

Index

608

YEAR IDENTIFICATION

OLDS

1965 Starfire 88

1965 98

1965 Jetstar

1966 Dynamic 88

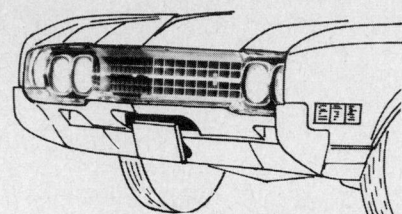

1966 98

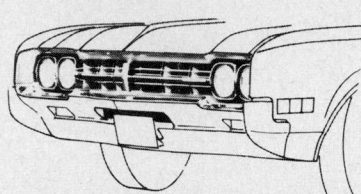

1966 Starfire 88

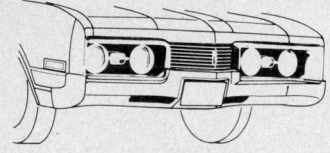

1967 Delta 88

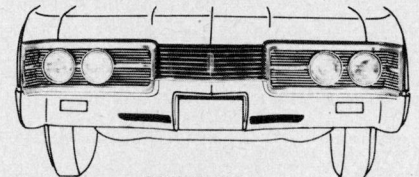

1967 Delmont

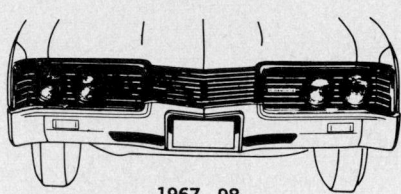

1967 98

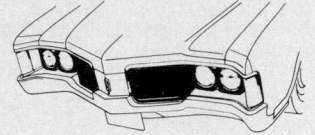

1968 88 - 98

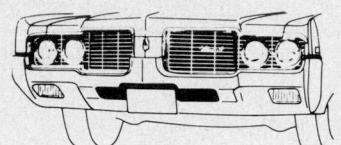

1969 88

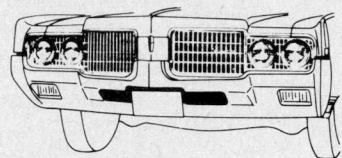

1969 98

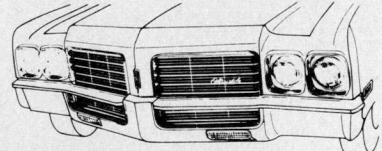

1970 98 Series

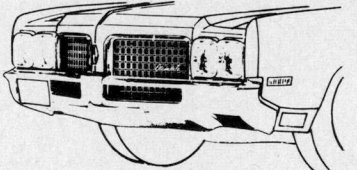

1970 Delta 88

1971 Delta 88

1971 98

1972 Delta 88

1972 98

YEAR IDENTIFICATION

F-85

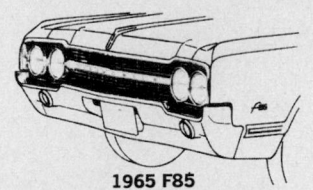
1965 F85

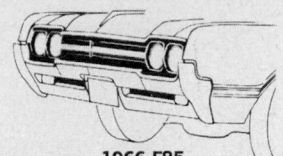
1966 F85

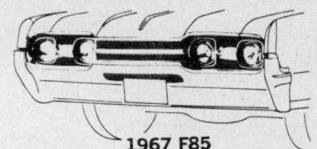
1967 F85

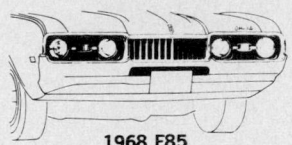
1968 F85

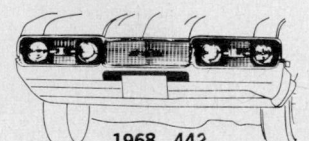
1968 442

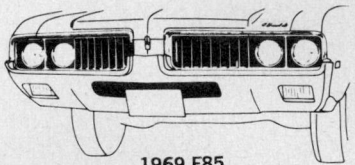
1969 F85

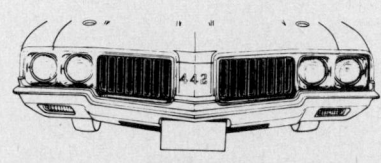
1970 4-4-2

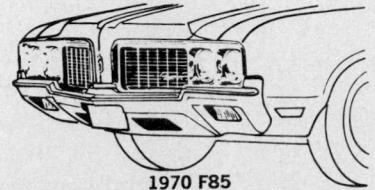
1970 F85

1971 Cutlass S

1971 Cutlass Supreme

1972 Cutlass S

1972 Cutlass Supreme

FIRING ORDER

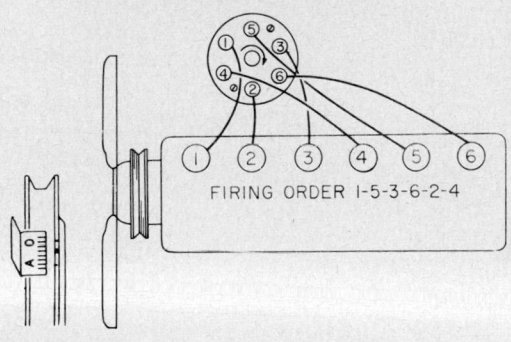

FIRING ORDER 1-5-3-6-2-4

1966-71 OHV 6 cyl.

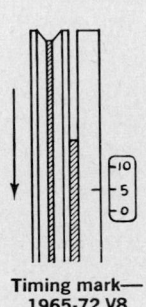
Timing mark—
1965-72 V8

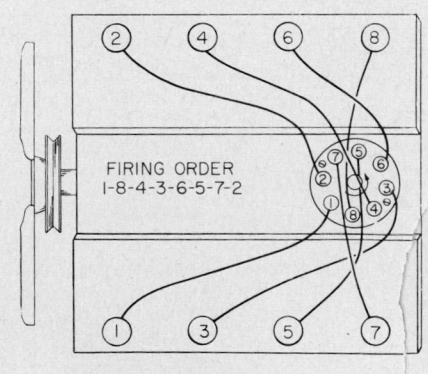
FIRING ORDER
1-8-4-3-6-5-7-2

1965-72 330, 350, 400, 425, 455 V8

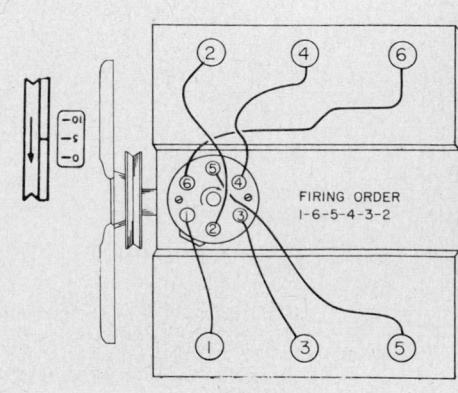
FIRING ORDER
1-6-5-4-3-2

1965 V6

CAR SERIAL NUMBER LOCATION

1965-67
Located on left front door hinge pillar.

1968-72
Left side of instrument panel, visible through windshield.

1965-72
First digit—Oldsmobile Division
Second digit indicates series
Third digit indicates engine
   Odd no. = 1965—V6,
   1966-71—L6
   Even no. = V8

Fourth and fifth digits indicate body type
Sixth digit indicates year

Seventh digit (letter) indicates plant
Eighth to tenth digits—sequential serial number

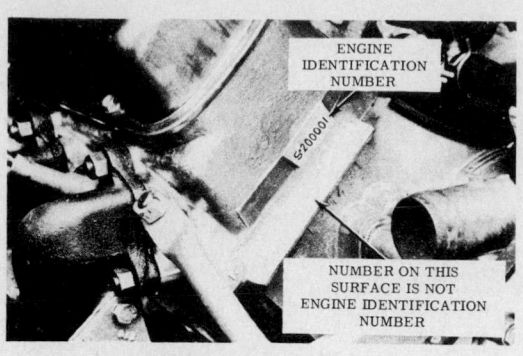

V8 engine identification code location— 1965-67

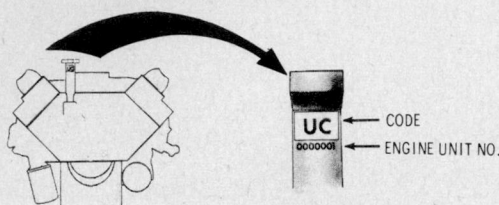

V8 engine identification code location— 1968-72

OLDS ENGINE IDENTIFICATION

YEAR	ENGINE	PRODUCTION CODE	CODE LOCATION
1965	425 V8 2-BBL.	M	B
	425 V8 4-BBL.	N	B
	330 V8	U	B
1966	425 V8 2-BBL.	M	B
	425 V8 4-BBL.	N	B
	330 V8	V, X	B
1967	425 V8 2-BBL.	P	B
	425 V8 4-BBL.	R	B
	330 V8	V, X	B
1968-69	350 V8 2-BBL.	TB, TD, TL	C
	350 V8 4-BBL.	TN	C
	455 V8 2-BBL.	UA, UB	C
	455 V8 4-BBL.	UN, UO	C
	455 V8 2-BBL. (low comp.)	UC, UD, UJ	C
1970	350 V8 2-BBL.	QA, QI, QJ, TC, TD, TL	C
	350 V8 4-BBL. 10.25 CR	QN, QP, QV	C
	350 V8 4-BBL. 10.5 CR	QD, QX	C
	455 V8 2-BBL. 9.0 CR	UC, UD, UJ	C
	455 V8 2-BBL. 10.25 CR	TX, TY	C
	455 V8 4-BBL., 10.25 CR	TP, TQ, TU, TV, TW, UN, UO	C
	455 V8 4-BBL. 10.5 CR	TS, TT	C
	455 V8 4-BBL. 10.25 CR W 33	UL	C
1971	350 V8 2-BBL.	TE, TD, TC	C
	455 V8 2-BBL.	UC, UD, UE	C
	455 V8 4-BBL.	UN, UO, US, UT	C
1972	350 V8 2-BBL.	H	C
	350 V8 BBL.	K	C
	455 V8 4-BBL.	T	C
	455 V8 4-BBL.	U ①	C
	455 V8 4-BBL.	W	C

Code location: B—Stamped on machined pad at front of right cylinder head.
   C—Tape attached directly to front of oil fill tube.
   ①—With Dual Exhaust

F-85 AND CUTLASS ENGINE IDENTIFICATION

YEAR	ENGINE	PRODUCTION CODE	CODE LOCATION
1965	225 V6	LH	C
	330 V8	U	D
	440 V8	W	D
1966	250 L6 1-BBL.	F	B
	250 L6	T	B
	330 V8	V, X	D
	400 V8	V	D
1967	250 L6 1-BBL.	F	B
	330 V8	V, X	D
	400 V8	V	D
1968-69	250 L6 1-BBL.	VA, VB, VE, VF	B
	350 V8 2-BBL.	QA, QB, QI, QJ	E
	350 V8 4-BBL. ①	QN, QP, QV, QX	E
	400 V8 2-BBL.	QL	E
	400 V8 4-BBL.	QR, QS, QW	E
	400 V8 4-BBL. (W30)	QT, QU	E
1970	250 L6 1-BBL.	VB, VF	B
	350 V8 2-BBL.	QA, QI, OJ TC, TD, TL	E
	350 V8 4-BBL.	QN, QP, QU	E
	350 V8 4-BBL. (W31)	QD, QX	E
	455 V8 2-BBL.	TY, TX	E
	455 V8 4-BBL.	TW, TV, TU, TQ, TP	E
	455 V8 4-BBL. (W30)	TS, TT	E
1971	250 L6 1-BBL.	ZB, ZG	B
	350 V8 2-BBL.	QI, QA, QJ	E
	350 V8 4-BBL.	QB, QO, QN, QP	E
	455 V8 2-BBL.	UC, UD	E
	455 V8 4-BBL.	TQ, TP, TU, TN, TW, TV, TA	E
	455 V8 4-BBL. (W30)	TS, TB, TT, TL	E
1972	350 V8 2-BBL.	H	E
	350 V8 2-BBL.	J ②	E
	350 V8 4-BBL.	K	E
	350 V8 4-BBL.	M ②	E
	455 V8 4-BBL.	U	E
	455 V8 4-BBL.	V	E
	455 V8-W30	X	E

Code location: B—Right side of engine block, directly behind distributor.
   C—Right cylinder head-to-block deck face.
   D—Stamped on machined pad at front of right cylinder head.
   E—Tape attached directly to front of oil fill tube.
   ①—QX = W31 engine.
   ②—With dual exhaust.

VALVE SPECIFICATIONS

YEAR AND MODEL		SEAT ANGLE (DEG.)	FACE ANGLE (DEG.)	VALVE LIFT INTAKE (IN.)	VALVE LIFT EXHAUST (IN.)	VALVE SPRING PRESSURE (VALVE OPEN) LBS. @ IN.	VALVE SPRING INSTALLED HEIGHT (IN.)	STEM TO GUIDE CLEARANCE (IN.) INTAKE	STEM TO GUIDE CLEARANCE (IN.) EXHAUST	STEM DIAMETER (IN.) INTAKE	STEM DIAMETER (IN.) EXHAUST
1965	V6—225	45	45	.391	.401	168 @ 1.26	1.64	⑦	⑦	.3407–.3412	.3402–.3407③
	V8—330	45	45	.401	.401	180–194 @ 1.27	1.67	.0010–.0027	.0015–.0032	.3425–.3432	.3420–.3427
	V8—425, 400	45	45	.429	.429	180–194 @ 1.27	1.67	.0010–.0027	.0015–.0032	.3425–.3432	.3420–.3427
1966–67	L6—250	45	45	.388	.388	180–192 @ 1.27	1.66	.0010–.0027	.0010–.0027	.3410–.3417	.3410–.3417
	V8—330	45	46	.401	.401	180–194 @ 1.27	1.67	.0010–.0027	.0015–.0032	.3425–.3432	.3420–.3427
	V8—400	①	①	.431④	.433④	180–194 @ 1.27	1.67	.0010–.0027	.0015–.0032	.3425–.3432	.3420–.3427
	V8—425	45⑤	45⑤	.429	.429	180–194 @ 1.27	1.67	.0010–.0027	.0015–.0032	.3425–.3432	.3420–.3427
1968–69	L6—250	45	45	.388	.388	180–192 @ 1.27	1.66	.0010–.0027	.0010–.0027	.3410–.3417	.3410–.3417
	V8—350	45	46	.400	.400	180–194 @ 1.27	1.67	.0010–.0027	.0015–.0032	.3425–.3432	.3420–.3427
	V8—350 (W31)	45	46	.475	.475	180–194 @ 1.27	1.67	.0010–.0027	.0015–.0032	.3425–.3432	.3420–.3427
	V8—400, 2-BBL.	①	①	.430	.432	180–194 @ 1.27	1.67	.0010–.0027	.0015–.0032	.3425–.3432	.3420–.3427
	V8—400, 4-BBL.	①	①	.472	.472	180–194 @ 1.27	1.67	.0010–.0027	.0015–.0032	.3425–.3432	.3420–.3427
	V8—455	45	46	.435	.435	180–194 @ 1.27	1.67	.0010–.0027	.0015–.0032	.3425–.3432	.3420–.3427
1970	L6—250	45	45	.388	.388	180–192 @ 1.27	1.66	.0010–.0027	.0010–.0027	.3410–.3417	.3410–.3417
	V8—350	45	46	.400	.400	180–194 @ 1.27	1.67	.0010–.0027	.0015–.0032	.3425–.3432	.3420–.3427
	V8—350(W31)	45	46	.475	.475	180–194 @ 1.27	1.67	.0010–.0027	.0015–.0032	.3425–.3432	.3420–.3427
	V8—455	45	46	.435	.435	180–194 @ 1.27	1.67	.0010–.0027	.0015–.0032	.3425–.3432	.3420–.3427
	V8—455 (W33, W30)	①	①	.472	.472	180–194 @ 1.27	1.67	.0010–.0027	.0015–.0032	.3425–.3432	.3420–.3427
1971–72	L6—250	46	45	.388	.388	180–192 @ 1.27	1.66	.0010–.0027	.0010–.0027	.3410–.3417	.3410–.3417
	V8—350	45⑥	46	.400	.400	180–194 @ 1.27	1.67	.0010–.0027	.0015–.0032	.3425–.3432	.3420–.3427
	V8—455	45⑥	46	.435	.435	180–194 @ 1.27	1.67	.0010–.0027	.0015–.0032	.3425–.3432	.3420–.3427
	V8—455 (W33, W30)	45⑥	46	.472	.472	180–194 @ 1.27	1.67	.0010–.0027	.0015–.0032	.3425–.3432	.3420–.3427

① —Intake—30° seat, 30° face.
  Exhaust—45° seat, 46° face.
② —Guide tapers from top to bottom with bigger dimension at top.
  Intake .001–.003
  Exhaust .0015–.0035
③ —Guide tapers from top to bottom with bigger dimension at top.
④ —.472 on cars with manual transmissions.
⑤ —30° on 1966 425 V8.
⑥ —30° Exhaust seats, all 1972 except California.

AC GENERATOR AND REGULATOR SPECIFICATIONS

YEAR	Part No.	ALTERNATOR Field Current Draw @ 12V.	ALTERNATOR Amp Output @ Engine RPM 750 RPM	ALTERNATOR Amp Output @ Engine RPM 3000 RPM	Part No.	REGULATOR Field Relay Air Gap (In.)	Field Relay Point Gap (In.)	Field Relay Volts to Close	Regulator Air Gap (In.)	Regulator Point Gap (In.)	Regulator Volts at 125°
1965–66	1100705	2.2–2.6	12	37	1119515	.015	.030	6.3–8.3	.060	.014	13.5–14.4
	1100696	2.2–2.6	15	42	1119515	.015	.030	6.3–8.3	.060	.014	13.5–14.4
	1100704	2.2–2.6	12	37	1119515	.015	.030	6.3–8.3	.060	.014	13.5–14.4
	1100699	2.2–2.6	15	42	1119515	.015	.030	6.3–8.3	.060	.014	13.5–14.4
	1100686	2.2–2.6	20	55	1119515	.015	.030	6.3–8.3	.060	.014	13.5–14.4
1967–70	1100767	2.2–2.6	12	37	1119515	.015	.030	6.3–8.3	.060	.014	13.5–14.4
	1100880	2.2–2.6	12	37	Transistor type, integral with alternator, no adjustment.						
	1100734	2.2–2.6	12	42	1119515	.015	.030	6.3–8.3	.060	.014	13.5–14.4
	1100878	2.2–2.6	12	42	1119515	.015	.030	6.3–8.3	.060	.014	13.5–14.4
	1100907	2.2–2.6	12	55	1119515	.015	.030	6.3–8.3	.060	.014	13.5–14.4
1971–72	1100566	2.2–2.6	11	37	1119515	.015	.030	6.3–8.3	.060	.014	13.5–14.4
	1100767	2.2–2.6	12	37	1119515	.015	.030	6.3–8.3	.060	.014	13.5–14.4
	1100888	2.2–2.6	11	37	1119515	.015	.030	6.3–8.3	.060	.014	13.5–14.4
	1100934	2.2–2.6	11	37	Transistor type, integral with alternator, no adjustment.						
	1100567	2.2–2.6	11	42	1119515	.015	.030	6.3–8.3	.060	.014	13.5–14.4
	1100734	2.2–2.6	12	42	1119515	.015	.030	6.3–8.3	.060	.014	13.5–14.4
	1100568	2.2–2.6	11	55	1119515	.015	.030	6.3–8.3	.060	.014	13.5–14.4
	1100569	2.2–2.6	11	55	1119515	.015	.030	6.3–8.3	.060	.014	13.5–14.4
	1100935	2.2–2.6	11	55	Transistor type, integral with alternator, no adjustment.						
	1100570	2.2–2.6	11	61	1119515		.030	6.3–8.3	.060	.014	13.5–14.4
	1100553	2.2–2.6	11	63	1119515	.015	.030	6.3–8.3	.060	.014	13.5–14.4

GENERAL ENGINE SPECIFICATIONS

YEAR	CU. IN. DISPLACEMENT	CARBURETOR	ADVERTIZED HORSEPOWER @ RPM	ADVERTIZED TORQUE @ RPM (FT. LBS.)	A.M.A. HORSEPOWER	BORE AND STROKE (IN.)	ADVERTIZED COMPRESSION RATIO	VALVE LIFTER TYPE	NORMAL OIL PRESSURE (PSI)
1965	V6—225	1-BBL.	155 @ 4400	225 @ 2400	33.8	3.750 x 3.400	9.00:1	Hyd.	35
	V8—330	2-BBL.	250 @ 4800	335 @ 2800	49.6	3.938 x 3.385	9.00:1	Hyd.	35
	V8—330	4-BBL	315 @ 5200	360 @ 3600	49.6	3.938 x 3.385	10.25:1	Hyd.	35
	V8—425	2-BBL.	280 @ 4400	425 @ 2400	54.0	4.125 x 3.975	9.00:1	Hyd.	35
	V8—425	2-BBL.	310 @ 4400	450 @ 2400	54.0	4.125 x 3.975	10.25:1	Hyd.	35
	V8—425	4-BBL.	360 @ 4800	470 @ 2800	54.0	4.125 x 3.975	10.25:1	Hyd.	35
	V8—425	4-BBL.	370 @ 4800	470 @ 3200	54.0	4.125 x 3.975	10.50:1	Hyd.	35
1966	L6—250	1-BBL.	155 @ 4200	240 @ 2000	36.0	3.875 x 3.530	8.50:1	Hyd.	35
	V8—330	2-BBL.	250 @ 4800	335 @ 2800	49.6	3.938 x 3.385	9.00:1	Hyd.	35
	V8—330	4-BBL.	320 @ 5200	360 @ 3600	49.6	3.938 x 3.385	10.25:1	Hyd.	35
	V8—400	4-BBL.	350 @ 5000	440 @ 3600	51.2	4.000 x 3.975	10.50:1	Hyd.	35
	V8—425	2-BBL.	310 @ 4400	450 @ 2400	54.0	4.125 x 3.975	10.25:1	Hyd.	35
	V8—425	4-BBL.	365 @ 4800	470 @ 3200	54.0	4.125 x 3.975	10.25:1	Hyd.	35
	V8—425	4-BBL.	375 @ 4800	470 @ 3200	54.0	4.125 x 3.975	10.50:1	Hyd.	35
1967	L6—250	1-BBL.	155 @ 4200	240 @ 2000	36.0	3.875 x 3.530	8.50:1	Hyd.	35
	V8—330	2-BBL.	250 @ 4800	335 @ 2800	49.6	3.938 x 3.385	9.00:1	Hyd.	35
	V8—330	2-BBL.	260 @ 4800	355 @ 2800	49.6	3.938 x 3.385	10.25:1	Hyd.	35
	V8—330	4-BBL.	310 @ 5200	340 @ 3600	49.6	3.938 x 3.385	9.00:1	Hyd.	35
	V8—330	4-BBL.	320 @ 5200	360 @ 3600	49.6	3.938 x 3.385	10.25:1	Hyd.	35
	V8—400	4-BBL.	350 @ 5000	440 @ 3600	51.2	4.000 x 3.975	10.50:1	Hyd.	35
	V8—425	2-BBL.	300 @ 4400	430 @ 2400	54.0	4.125 x 3.975	9.00:1	Hyd.	35
	V8—425	2-BBL.	310 @ 4400	450 @ 2400	54.0	4.125 x 3.975	10.25:1	Hyd.	35
	V8—425	4-BBL.	365 @ 4800	470 @ 3200	54.0	4.125 x 3.975	10.25:1	Hyd.	35
	V8—425	4-BBL.	375 @ 4800	470 @ 3200	54.0	4.125 x 3.975	10.50:1	Hyd.	35
1968	L6—250	1-BBL.	155 @ 4200	240 @ 2000	36.0	3.875 x 3.530	8.50:1	Hyd.	35
	V8—350	2-BBL.	250 @ 4400	355 @ 2600	52.7	4.057 x 3.385	9.00:1	Hyd.	35
	V8—350	4-BBL.	300 @ 4800	390 @ 3600	52.7	4.057 x 3.385	10.25:1	Hyd.	35
	V8—350	4-BBL.	310 @ 4800	390 @ 3200	52.7	4.057 x 3.385	10.25:1	Hyd.	35
	V8—400	2-BBL.	290 @ 4600	425 @ 2400	47.9	3.870 x 4.250	9.00:1	Hyd.	45
	V8—400	4-BBL.	350 @ 4800	440 @ 3200	47.9	3.870 x 4.250	10.50:1	Hyd.	45
	V8—400	4-BBL.	360 @ 5400	440 @ 3600	47.9	3.870 x 4.250	10.50:1	Hyd.	45
	V8—455	2-BBL.	310 @ 4200	490 @ 2400	54.5	4.125 x 4.250	9.00:1	Hyd.	35
	V8—455	4-BBL.	320 @ 4200	500 @ 2400	54.5	4.125 x 4.250	10.25:1	Hyd.	35
	V8—455	4-BBL.	365 @ 4600	510 @ 3000	54.5	4.125 x 4.250	10.25:1	Hyd.	35
1969	L6—250	1-BBL.	155 @ 4200	240 @ 2000	36.04	3.875 x 3.530	8.50:1	Hyd.	35
	V8—350	2-BBL.	250 @ 4400	355 @ 2600	52.7	4.057 x 3.385	9.00:1	Hyd.	35
	V8—350	4-BBL.	310 @ 4800	390 @ 3200	52.7	4.057 x 3.385	10.25:1	Hyd.	35
	V8—350 (W31)	4-BBL.	325 @ 5400	360 @ 3600	52.7	4.057 x 3.385	10.50:1	Hyd.	35
	V8—400	4-BBL.	325 @ 4600	440 @ 3000	47.9	3.870 x 4.250	10.50:1	Hyd.	45
	V8—400	4-BBL.	350 @ 4800	440 @ 3200	47.9	3.870 x 4.250	10.50:1	Hyd.	45
	V8—400	4-BBL.	360 @ 5400	440 @ 3600	47.9	3.870 x 4.250	10.50:1	Hyd.	45
	V8—455	2-BBL.	310 @ 4200	490 @ 2400	54.5	4.125 x 4.250	9.00:1	Hyd.	35
	V8—455	4-BBL.	365 @ 4600	510 @ 3000	54.5	4.125 x 4.250	10.25:1	Hyd.	35
	V8—455	4-BBL.	390 @ 5000	500 @ 3200	54.5	4.125 x 4.250	10.25:1	Hyd.	35
1970	L6—250	1-BBL.	155 @ 4200	240 @ 2000	36.04	3.875 x 3.530	8.50:1	Hyd.	35
	V8—350 (L65)	2-BBL.	250 @ 4400	355 @ 2600	52.7	4.057 x 3.385	9.00:1	Hyd.	35
	V8—350 (L74)	4-BBL.	310 @ 4800	390 @ 3200	52.7	4.057 x 3.385	10.25:1	Hyd.	35
	V8—350 (W31)	4-BBL.	325 @ 5400	360 @ 3600	52.7	4.057 x 3.385	10.50:1	Hyd.	35
	V8—455 (L33)	2-BBL.	320 @ 4200	500 @ 2400	54.5	4.125 x 4.250	10.25:1	Hyd.	35
	V8—455 (L31)	4-BBL.	365 @ 4600	510 @ 3000	54.5	4.125 x 4.250	10.25:1	Hyd.	35
	V8—455 (W33)	4-BBL.	390 @ 5000	500 @ 3200	54.5	4.125 x 4.250	10.25:1	Hyd.	35
	V8—455 (W30)	4-BBL.	370 @ 5400	500 @ 3600	54.5	4.125 x 4.250	10.50:1	Hyd.	35
	V8—455 (L30)	2-BBL.	310 @ 4200	490 @ 2400	54.5	4.125 x 4.250	9.00:1	Hyd.	35

GENERAL ENGINE SPECIFICATIONS, continued

YEAR	CU. IN. DISPLACEMENT	CARBURETOR	ADVERTIZED HORSEPOWER @ RPM	ADVERTIZED TORQUE @ RPM (FT. LBS.)	A.M.A. HORSEPOWER	BORE AND STROKE (IN.)	ADVERTIZED COMPRESSION RATIO	VALVE LIFTER TYPE	NORMAL OIL PRESSURE (PSI)
1971	L6—250	1-BBL.	145 @ 4200	230 @ 2000	36.4	3.875 x 3.530	8.0:1	Hyd.	30–50
	V8—350	2-BBL.	240 @ 4200	350 @ 2400	52.7	4.057 x 3.385	8.5:1	Hyd.	30–50
	V8—350	4-BBL.	260 @ 4600	360 @ 3200	52.7	4.057 x 3.385	8.5:1	Hyd.	30–50
	V8—455	2-BBL.	280 @ 4000	445 @ 2000	54.5	4.125 x 4.250	8.5:1	Hyd.	30–50
	V8—455	4-BBL.	320 @ 4400	460 @ 2800	54.5	4.125 x 4.250	8.5:1	Hyd.	30–50
	V8—455	4-BBL.	340 @ 4600	460 @ 3200	54.5	4.125 x 4.250	8.5:1	Hyd.	30–50
	V8—455 (W30)	4-BBL.	350 @ 4700	460 @ 3200	54.5	4.125 x 4.250	8.5:1	Hyd.	30–50
1972	V8—350	2-BBL.	160(175)*	275(295)*	52.7	4.057 x 3.385	8.5:1	Hyd.	30–50
	V8—350	4-BBL.	180(220)*	275(300)*	52.7	4.057 x 3.385	8.5:1	Hyd.	30–50
	V8—455 A.T.	4-BBL.	250*	370*	54.5	4.125 x 4.250	8.5:1	Hyd.	30–50
	V8—455 S.T.	4-BBL.	270*	370*	54.5	4.125 x 4.250	8.5:1	Hyd.	30–50
	V8—455 (W30)	4-BBL.	300*	410*	54.5	4.125 x 4.250	8.5:1	Hyd.	30–50
	V8—455	4-BBL.	225(250)*	360(370)*	54.5	4.125 x 4.250	8.5:1	Hyd.	30–50
	V8—455 Toro.	4-BBL.	250*	375*	54.5	4.125 x 4.250	8.5:1	Hyd.	30–50

*With dual exhaust.

TORQUE SPECIFICATIONS

YEAR	MODEL	CYLINDER HEAD BOLTS (FT. LBS.)	ROD BEARING BOLTS (FT. LBS.)	MAIN BEARING BOLTS (FT. LBS.)	CRANKSHAFT BALANCER BOLT (FT. LBS.)	FLYWHEEL TO CRANKSHAFT BOLTS (FT. LBS.)	MANIFOLD (FT. LBS.) Intake	MANIFOLD (FT. LBS.) Exhaust
1965-72	6—Cyl., all	95	35	65	Press fit	60	20–30	20–30
	V8, all	80	42	120②	160 min	①	23–35	20–25

① —A.T. 60 ft. lbs.; M.T. 90 ft. lbs.
② —V8-330, 350—80 on No. 1-4, 120 on No. 5.

CYLINDER HEAD BOLT TIGHTENING SEQUENCE

1965 V6

1966-71 OHV 6 cyl.

1965-72 330, 350, 400, 425, 455 V8

CRANKSHAFT BEARING JOURNAL SPECIFICATIONS

YEAR	MODEL	MAIN BEARING JOURNALS (IN.) Journal Diameter	Oil Clearance	Shaft End-Play	Thrust On No.	CONNECTING ROD BEARING JOURNALS (IN.) Journal Diameter	Oil Clearance	End-Play
1965-66	V6—225	2.4995	.0012	.006	2	2.000	.0013	.010
	V8—330	2.4995	.0012	.006	3	2.1238-2.1248	.0013	.007
	V8—400, 425	3.0000	.0020	.006	3	2.500	.0015	.007
1967-70	L6—250	2.2988	.0003–.0029	.002–.006	7	1.999-2.000	.0007–.0027	.0085–.0135
	V8—330	2.4995	.0015–.0031	.004–.006	3	2.1238-2.1248	.0015–.0030	.002–.013
	V8—350	2.4995	.0005–.0021①	.004–.008	3	2.1238-2.1248	.0004–.0033	.002–.013
	V8—455	3.0000	.0005–.0021②	.004–.008	3	2.4988-2.4998	.0004–.0033	.002–.013
1971-72	L6—250	2.2988	.0003–.0029	.002–.006	7	1.999-2.000	.0007–.0027	.0085–.0135
	V8—350	2.4995	.0005–.0021①	.004–.008	3	2.1238-2.1248	.0004–.0033	.002–.013
	V8—455	3.0000	.0005–.0021②	.004–.008	3	2.4988-2.4998	.0004–.0033	.002–.013

★—No. 5, .0027.
① —No. 5, .0015–.0031
② —No. 5, .0020–.0034

TUNE-UP SPECIFICATIONS

YEAR	MODEL	SPARK PLUGS		DISTRIBUTOR		IGNITION TIMING (Deg.) ▲	CRANKING COMP. PRESSURE (Psi)	VALVES Tappet (Hot) Clearance (In.)		Intake Opens (Deg.)	FUEL PUMP PRESSURE (Psi) ●	IDLE SPEED (Rpm) ★
		Type	Gap (In.)	Point Dwell (Deg.)	Point Gap (In.)			Intake	Exhaust			
1965	F-85, V6—All	44S	.035	30	.016	5B	160	Zero	Zero	24B	$4\frac{1}{2}$-$5\frac{3}{4}$	550
	F-85, V8—2-BBL.	45S	.035	30	.016	$7\frac{1}{2}$B	180	Zero	Zero	22B	$7\frac{1}{2}$-$8\frac{1}{2}$	550
	F-85, V8—4-BBL.	44S	.035	30	.016	$7\frac{1}{2}$B	180	Zero	Zero	22B	$7\frac{1}{2}$-$8\frac{1}{2}$	550
	Jetstar 88, 2-BBL.	45S	.030	30	.016	$7\frac{1}{2}$B	180	Zero	Zero	24B	$5\frac{1}{2}$	550
	Jetstar 88, 4-BBL.	44S	.030	30	.016	$7\frac{1}{2}$B	180	Zero	Zero	24B	$5\frac{1}{2}$	550
	Dynamic 88, 2-BBL.	45S	.030	30	.016	$7\frac{1}{2}$B	170	Zero	Zero	21B	$5\frac{1}{2}$	850
	Series 98	44S	.030	30	.016	5B	180	Zero	Zero	21B	$5\frac{1}{2}$	850
	Jetstar-1, Starfire	44S	.030	30	.016	5B	180	Zero	Zero	21B	$5\frac{1}{2}$	850
1966	F-85, OHV 6, 1-BBL.	46N	.035	32	.019	5B	130	Zero	Zero	62B	$4\frac{1}{2}$●	500
	F-85, V8, 2-BBL.	45S	.030	30	.016	$7\frac{1}{2}$B	180	Zero	Zero	22B	$7\frac{1}{2}$-$8\frac{1}{2}$	550
	F-85, V8, 4-BBL.	44S	.030	30	.016	$7\frac{1}{2}$B	180	Zero	Zero	22B	$7\frac{1}{2}$-$8\frac{1}{2}$	550
	F-85, V8, 4-4-2, 4-BBL.	44S	.030	30	.016	$7\frac{1}{2}$B	190	Zero	Zero	21B	6	600
	Jetstar 88, 2-BBL.	44S	.030	30	.016	$7\frac{1}{2}$B	180	Zero	Zero	24B	$7\frac{3}{4}$-9	550
	Jetstar 88, 4-BBL.	44S	.030	30	.016	$7\frac{1}{2}$B	180	Zero	Zero	24B	$7\frac{3}{4}$-9	550
	Dynamic 88, 2-BBL.	44S	.030	30	.016	$7\frac{1}{2}$B	170	Zero	Zero	21B	$7\frac{3}{4}$-9	500
	Dynamic 88, 4-BBL.	44S	.030	30	.016	$7\frac{1}{2}$B	180	Zero	Zero	21B	$7\frac{3}{4}$-9	550
	Delta 88, 2-BBL.	44S	.030	30	.016	$7\frac{1}{2}$B	170	Zero	Zero	21B	$7\frac{3}{4}$-9	600
	Delta 88, 4-BBL.	44S	.030	30	.016	$7\frac{1}{2}$B	180	Zero	Zero	21B	$7\frac{3}{4}$-9	600
	Starfire, 4-BBL.	44S	.030	30	.016	$7\frac{1}{2}$B	180	Zero	Zero	21B	$7\frac{3}{4}$-9	600
1967	L6—250, 1-BBL. (155 HP)	46N	.035	32	.016	5B	130	Zero	Zero	62B	$4\frac{1}{2}$●	500
	V8—330, 2-BBL. (250 HP)	45S	.030	30	.016	$7\frac{1}{2}$B	180	Zero	Zero	12B ①	8	550
	V8—330, 2-BBL. (260 HP)	44S	.030	30	.016	$7\frac{1}{2}$B	180	Zero	Zero	21B	8	550
	V8—330, 4-BBL. (310 HP)	44S	.030	30	.016	$7\frac{1}{2}$B	180	Zero	Zero	21B	8	550
	V8—330, 4-BBL. (320 HP)	44S	.030	30	.016	$7\frac{1}{2}$B	180	Zero	Zero	21B	8	550
	V8—400, 4-4-2 (350 HP)	44S	.030	30	.016	$7\frac{1}{2}$B	180	Zero	Zero	30B ②	7	600
	V8—425, 2-BBL. (300 HP)	44S	.030	30	.016	5B	160	Zero	Zero	21B	8	550
	V8—425, 2-BBL. (310 HP)	44S	.030	30	.016	$7\frac{1}{2}$B	180	Zero	Zero	21B	8	550
	V8—425, 4-BBL. (365 HP)	44S	.030	30	.016	$7\frac{1}{2}$B	180	Zero	Zero	21B	8	550
	V8—425, 4-BBL. (375 HP)	44S	.030	30	.016	$7\frac{1}{2}$B	190	Zero	Zero	21B	8	550
1968	L6—250, M.T. (155 HP)	46N	.035	32	.016	4B	130	Zero	Zero	16B	$3\frac{1}{2}$-$4\frac{1}{2}$	650
	L6—250, A.T. (155 HP)	46N	.035	32	.016	6B	130	Zero	Zero	16B	$3\frac{1}{2}$-$4\frac{1}{2}$	550
	V8—350, 2-BBL. (250 HP)	45S	.030	30	.016	5B	160	Zero	Zero	16B	$5\frac{1}{2}$-7	650■
	V8—350, 4-BBL. (300 HP)	44S	.030	30	.016	$7\frac{1}{2}$B	180	Zero	Zero	16B	$5\frac{1}{2}$-7	650■
	V8—350, 4-BBL. (310 HP)	44S	.030	30	.016	$7\frac{1}{2}$B	180	Zero	Zero	16B	$5\frac{1}{2}$-7	650■
	V8—400, 2-BBL. (290 HP)	44S	.030	30	.016	TDC	180	Zero	Zero	21B	$5\frac{1}{2}$-7	725
	V8—400, 4-BBL. (350 HP)	44S	.030	30	.016	TDC	180	Zero	Zero	30B	$5\frac{1}{2}$-7	725
	V8—400, 4-BBL. (360 HP)	44S	.030	30	.016	TDC	180	Zero	Zero	30B	$5\frac{1}{2}$-7	725
	V8—455, 2-BBL. (310 HP)	45S	.030	30	.016	10B	180	Zero	Zero	20B	$5\frac{1}{2}$-7	550
	V8—455, 2-BBL. (320 HP)	45S	.030	30	.016	10B	180	Zero	Zero	20B	$5\frac{1}{2}$-7	550
	V8—455, 4-BBL. (365 HP)	45S	.030	30	.016	10B	190	Zero	Zero	20B	$5\frac{1}{2}$-7	550
1969	L6—250, M.T. (155 HP)	46N	.030	35	.016	TDC	130	Zero	Zero	16B	$3\frac{1}{2}$-4	700
	L6—250, A.T. (155 HP)	46N	.030	35	.016	4B	130	Zero	Zero	16B	$3\frac{1}{2}$-4	500
	V8—350, 2-BBL. (250 HP)	45S	.030	30	.016	6B	180	Zero	Zero	16B	$5\frac{1}{2}$-7	850
	V8—350, 4-BBL. (310 HP)	44S	.030	30	.016	8B	180	Zero	Zero	16B	$5\frac{1}{2}$-7	850
	V8—350, 4-BBL. (325 HP)	44S	.030	30	.016	12B	180	Zero	Zero	16B	$5\frac{1}{2}$-7	850
	V8—400, 4-BBL. (325 HP)	44S	.030	30	.016	8B ③	180	Zero	Zero	56B	5-8	850
	V8—400, 4-BBL. (350 HP)	44S	.030	30	.016	8B ③	180	Zero	Zero	56B	5-8	850
	V8—400, 4-BBL. (360 HP)	44S	.030	30	.016	8B ③	180	Zero	Zero	56B	5-8	850
	V8—455, 2-BBL. (310 HP)	45S	.030	30	.016	6B	180	Zero	Zero	20B	5-8	850
	V8—455, 4-BBL. (365 HP)	44S	.030	30	.016	8B	180	Zero	Zero	20B	5-8	850
	V8—455, 4-BBL. (390 HP)	44S	.030	30	.016	10B	190	Zero	Zero	20B	5-8	850

TUNE-UP SPECIFICATIONS, continued

YEAR	MODEL	SPARK PLUGS		DISTRIBUTOR		IGNITION TIMING (Deg.) ▲	CRANKING COMP. PRESSURE (Psi)	VALVES			FUEL PUMP PRESSURE (Psi)	IDLE SPEED (Rpm) ★
		Type	Gap (In.)	Point Dwell (Deg.)	Point Gap (In.)			Tappet (Hot) Clearance (In.)		Intake Opens (Deg.)		
								Intake	Exhaust			
1970	L6—250, M.T. (155 HP)	R46T	.035	31–34	.019	TDC	130	Zero	Zero	16B	4–5	750
	L6—250, A.T. (155 HP)	R46T	.035	31–34	.019	4B	130	Zero	Zero	16B	4–5	600
	V8-350, 2-BBL. (250 HP)	R46S	.030	30	.016	10B④	180	Zero	Zero	16B	5½-6½	750⑤
	V8-350, 4-BBL. (310 HP)	R45S	.030	30	.016	10B	180	Zero	Zero	16B	5½-6½	650⑤
	V8-350, 4-BBL. (325 HP)	R45S	.030	30	.016	14B	180	Zero	Zero	40B	5½-6½	750⑥
	V8—455, 2-BBL. (310 HP)	R46S	.030	30	.016	8B	180	Zero	Zero	20B	5-6½	675⑤
	V8—455, 4-BBL. (365 HP)	R45S	.030	30	.016	8B	180	Zero	Zero	20B	5-6½	575
	V8—455, 4-BBL. (390 HP)	R44S	.030	30	.016	12B	190	Zero	Zero	24B	5-6½	600
1971	L6—250	R46TS	.035	31–34	.019	4B	100①	Zero	Zero	16B	4–5	550
	V8—350 2-BBL.	R46S	.035	30	.016	10B	100①	Zero	Zero	14B	5½-6½	750⑥
	V8—350 4-BBL., A.T.	R46S	.035	30	.016	12B	100①	Zero	Zero	14B	5½-6½	600
	V8—350 4-BBL., M.T.	R45S	.035	30	.016	10B	100①	Zero	Zero	30B	5½-6½	750
	V8—455 2-BBL.	R46S	.035	30	.016	8B	100①	Zero	Zero	20B	5½-6½	750⑥
	V8—455 4-BBL.	R46S	.035	30	.016	8B	100①	Zero	Zero	20B	5½-6½	750⑥
	V8—455 (340 HP)	R46S	.035	30	.016	10B	100①	Zero	Zero	22B	6	600
	V8—455 (W30)	R45S	.035	30	.016	12B⑦	100①	Zero	Zero	30B	6	750⑥
1972	V8—350 2-BBL.	R46S	.035	30	.019	8° @ 1100 RPM.	100①	Zero	Zero	14B	5½-6½	**
	V8—350 4-BBL., A.T.	R46S	.035	30	.019	12° @ 1100 RPM.	100①	Zero	Zero	14B	5½-6½	**
	V8—350 4-BBL., M.T.	R45S	.035	30	.019	8° @ 1100 RPM.	100①	Zero	Zero	30B	5½-6½	
	V8—455 4-BBL. A.T.	R46S	.035	30	.019	8° @ 1100 RPM	100①	Zero	Zero	20B	5½-6½	**
	V8—455 Std. W30	R455	.035	30	.019	10° @ 1100 RPM	100①	Zero	Zero	22B	6	**
	V8—455 (W30) A.T.	R45S	.035	30	.019	10° @ 850 RPM.	100①	Zero	Zero	30B	6	**

★ With manual transmission in N and automatic in D. If equipped with air conditioning add 50 rpm.

▲—With vacuum advance disconnected. NOTE: These settings are only approximate. Engine design, altitude, temperature, fuel octane rating and the condition of the individual engine are all factors which can influence timing.

●—If equipped with exhaust emission control—5½-7.

■—550 rpm with automatic transmission.

①—Vista Cruiser = 21B.

②—Auto. transmission = 21B.

③—Std. transmission = 2B.

B—Before top dead center.

TDC—Top dead center.

A.T.—Automatic transmission.

M.T.—Manual transmission.

④—10B for intermediate cars with 350 2-BBL. (250 HP). 8B for full size cars with 350 2-BBL. (250 HP).

⑤—575 rpm for A.T.

⑥—600 rpm for A.T.

⑦—10B automatic transmission.

⑧—Minimum.

**—See engine decal.

Caution

General adoption of anti-pollution laws has changed the design of almost all car engine production to effectively reduce crankcase emission and terminal exhaust products. It has been necessary to adopt stricter tune-up rules, especially timing and idle speed procedures. Both of these values are peculiar to the engine and to its application, rather than to the engine alone. With this in mind, car manufacturers supply idle speed data for the engine and application involved. This information is clearly displayed in the engine compartment of each vehicle.

GENERAL CHASSIS AND BRAKE SPECIFICATIONS

YEAR	MODEL	CHASSIS		BRAKE CYLINDER BORE			BRAKE DRUM	
		Overall Length (In.)	Tire Size	Master Cylinder (In.)	Wheel Cylinder Diameter (In.)		Diameter (In.)	
					Front	Rear	Front	Rear
1965	F-85/Cutlass	204.4	6.95 x 14 ①	1.00	1.00	⁷/₈	9.5	9.5
	Std. Sta. Wag.	202.7	7.35 x 14 ①	1.00	1.00	⁷/₈	9.5	9.5
	Vista Cruiser	207.7	7.75 x 14	1.00	1.00	⁷/₈	9.5	9.5
	88 Series	216.9	7.74 x 14 ②	1.00	1¹/₈	1.00	9.5	9.5
	98 Series	222.9	8.55 x 14	1.00	1¹/₈	1.00	11.0	11.0
1966	F-85/Cutlass/442	204.0	6.95 x 14 ①	1.00	1¹/₈	⁷/₈	9.5	9.5
	Std. Sta. Wag.	204.3	7.75 x 14	1.00	1¹/₈	⁷/₈	9.5	9.5
	Vista Cruiser	209.5	8.25 x 14	1.00	1¹/₈	⁷/₈	9.5	9.5
	88 Series	217.0	8.25 x 14 ②	1.00	1¹/₈	1.00	11.0	11.0
	98 Series	222.9	8.55 x 14 ③	1.00	1¹/₈	1.00	11.0	11.0
1967	F-85/Cutlass/442	204.0	7.75 x 14	1.00	1¹/₁₆	⁷/₈ ④	9.5	9.5
	Std. Sta. Wag.	204.3	7.75 x 14	1.00	1¹/₁₆	⁷/₈	9.5	9.5
	Vista Cruiser	209.5	8.25 x 14	1.00	1¹/₁₆	¹⁵/₁₆	9.5	9.5
	88 Series	217.8	8.25 x 14	1.00	1¹/₈	1.00	11.0	11.0
	98 Series	223.0	8.85 x 14	1.00 ⑤	1¹/₈ ⑥	1.00	11.0	11.0
	Disc Brakes, F-85 & 442	—	—	1¹/₈	2¹/₁₆	¹³/₁₆	11.0	9.5
	Disc Brakes, 88 & 98	—	—	1¹/₈	1¹⁵/₁₆	1.00	11⁷/₈	11.0
1968	F-85/Cutlass, 2-Door	201.6	7.75 x 14 ⑦	1.00	1¹/₈	¹⁵/₁₆	9.5	9.5
	442	201.6	F70 x 14 ⑦	1.00	1¹/₈	¹⁵/₁₆	9.5	9.5
	F-85/Cutlass, 4-Door	205.6	7.75 x 14 ⑦	1.00	1¹/₈	¹⁵/₁₆	9.5	9.5
	Std. Sta. Wag.	212.5	7.75 x 14 ⑦	1.00	1¹/₈	¹⁵/₁₆	9.5	9.5
	Vista Cruiser	217.5	8.25 x 14 ⑦	1.00	1¹/₈	¹⁵/₁₆	9.5	9.5
	88 Series	217.8	8.55 x 14 ⑧	1.00	1³/₁₆	1.00	11.0	11.0
	98 Series	223.7	8.85 x 14 ⑨	1.00	1³/₁₆	1.00	11.0	11.0
	Disc Brakes, F85 & 442	—	—	1¹/₈	2¹/₁₆	¹³/₁₆	11.0	9.5
	Disc Brakes, 88 & 98	—	—	1¹/₈	1¹⁵/₁₆	1.00	11⁷/₈	11.0
1969	F-85/Cutlass, 2-Door	201.9	7.75 x 14 ⑩	1.00	1¹/₈	¹⁵/₁₆	9.5	9.5
	442	201.9	F70 x 14	1.00	1¹/₈	¹⁵/₁₆	9.5	9.5
	F-85/Cutlass, 4-Door	205.9	7.75 x 14 ⑩	1.00	1¹/₈	¹⁵/₁₆	9.5	9.5
	Std. Sta. Wag.	212.6	8.25 x 14 ⑪	1.00	1¹/₈	¹⁵/₁₆	9.5	9.5
	Vista Cruiser	217.6	8.55 x 14 ⑪	1.00	1¹/₈	1.00	9.5	9.5
	88 Series	218.6	8.55 x 15 ⑫	1.00	1³/₁₆	1.00	9.5	9.5
	98 Series	224.4	8.85 x 15 ⑫	1.00	1³/₁₆	1.00	9.5	9.5
	Disc Brakes, all exc. 88 & 98	—	—	1¹/₈	2¹⁵/₁₆	¹⁵/₁₆ ⑬	10.9	9.5
	Disc Brakes, 88 & 98	—	—	1¹/₈	2¹⁵/₁₆	1.00	11.8	11.0
1970	F-85/Cutlass, 2-Door	203.4	G78 x 14 ⑭	1.00	1¹/₈	⁷/₈	9.5	9.5
	442	203.2	G70 x 14 ⑮	1.00	1¹/₈	⁷/₈	9.5	9.5
	F-85/Cutlass, 4-Door	207.4	G78 x 14 ⑭	1.00	1¹/₈	⁷/₈	9.5	9.5
	Std. Sta. Wag.	213.2	H78 x 14	1.00	1¹/₈	¹⁵/₁₆	9.5	9.5
	Vista Cruiser	218.2	H78 x 14	1.00	1¹/₈	1.00	9.5	9.5
	88 Series	218.5	H78 x 14	1.00	1³/₁₆	¹⁵/₁₆	11.0	11.0
	98 Series	224.4	J78 x 14	1.00	1³/₁₆	¹³/₁₆	11.0	11.0
	Disc Brakes, all exc. 88 & 98	—	—	1¹/₈	2¹⁵/₁₆	⁷/₈ ⑬	11.0	9.5
	Disc Brakes, 88 & 98	—	—	1¹/₈	2¹⁵/₁₆	¹⁵/₁₆	11.9	11.0
1971-72	F-85/Cutlass, 2-Door	203.6	G78 x 14 ⑭	1.00	1¹/₈	⁷/₈	9.5	9.5
	442	203.6	G70 x 14 ⑮	1.00	1¹/₈	⁷/₈	9.5	9.5
	F-85/Cutlass, 4-Door	207.6	G78 x 14 ⑭	1.00	1¹/₈	⁷/₈	9.5	9.5
	Std. Sta. Wag.	213.3	H78 x 14	1.00	1¹/₈	⁷/₈	9.5	9.5
	Vista Cruiser**	218.3	H78 x 14	1¹/₈	2¹⁵/₁₆	1.00	11.0	9.5
	88 Series**	220.2	H78 x 15	1¹/₈	2¹⁵/₁₆	¹⁵/₁₆	11.9	11.0
	Custom Cruiser**	225.3	L78 x 15	1¹/₈	2¹⁵/₁₆	1.00	11.9	11.0
	98 Series**	226.1	J78 x 15	1¹/₈	2⁵/₁₆	¹⁵/₁₆	11.9	11.0
	Disc Brakes, all F-85 series	—	—	1¹/₈	2¹⁵/₁₆	⁷/₈	11.0	9.5

CAPACITIES

YEAR	MODEL	ENGINE CRANKCASE ADD 1 Qt. FOR NEW FILTER	TRANSMISSIONS Pts. TO REFILL AFTER DRAINING			DRIVE AXLE (Pts.)	GASOLINE TANK (Gals.)	COOLING SYSTEM (Qts.) WITH HEATER
			Manual		Automatic			
			3-Speed	4-Speed				
1965	F-85, V6	4	2	$2\frac{1}{2}$	18	$2\frac{1}{2}$	20	11
	F-85, V8	4	2	$2\frac{1}{2}$	18	$2\frac{1}{2}$	20	17
	Jetstar 88	4	2	$2\frac{1}{4}$	18	3	25	17
	All others	4	3	$2\frac{1}{4}$	18	$4\frac{3}{4}$	25	18
1966	F-85, L6	4	$3\frac{1}{2}$	None	18	$3\frac{3}{4}$	20	$11\frac{3}{4}$
	F-85, V8	4	$3\frac{1}{2}$	$2\frac{1}{4}$	18	$3\frac{3}{4}$	20●	$15\frac{1}{4}$
	442, V8	4	5	$2\frac{1}{4}$	18	$3\frac{3}{4}$	20	$16\frac{1}{4}$
	Jetstar 88	4	5	$2\frac{1}{4}$	18	$3\frac{3}{4}$	25	17
	All others	4	5	$2\frac{1}{4}$	18	$5\frac{1}{2}$	25	$17\frac{1}{2}$
1967	F-85, L6	4	$3\frac{1}{2}$	None	19	$3\frac{1}{2}$	20	$11\frac{3}{4}$.
	F-85, V8	4	$3\frac{1}{2}$	$2\frac{1}{4}$	19	$3\frac{1}{2}$	20	$15\frac{1}{4}$
	442 (400 Eng.)	4	5	$2\frac{1}{4}$	23	3	20	$16\frac{1}{4}$
	Series with 425 Eng.	4	5	$2\frac{1}{4}$	23	$5\frac{1}{4}$	25	$17\frac{1}{2}$
	Vista Cruiser (330 Eng.)	4	$3\frac{1}{2}$	$2\frac{1}{4}$	19	$3\frac{1}{2}$	24	$15\frac{1}{4}$
	Delmont, All	4	5	$2\frac{1}{4}$	19■	3	25	$16\frac{1}{2}$
1968-69	L6	4	$3\frac{1}{2}$	None	19	$3\frac{3}{4}$	20	$12\frac{1}{2}$
	V8—350	4	$3\frac{1}{2}$	$2\frac{1}{4}$	19	$3\frac{3}{4}$	20	$15\frac{1}{4}$
	V8—400 (442)	4	5	$2\frac{1}{4}$	23	$3\frac{3}{4}$	20	$16\frac{1}{4}$
	V8—455	4	$3\frac{1}{2}$	None	23	$5\frac{1}{4}$	25	$17\frac{1}{2}$
1970-72	L6	4	$3\frac{1}{2}$	None	20	$4\frac{1}{4}$	20	$12\frac{1}{2}$
	V8—350	4	$3\frac{1}{2}$	$3\frac{1}{2}$	20	$4\frac{1}{4}$	20① ③	$15\frac{1}{4}$
	V8—455	4	$4\frac{1}{2}$	$3\frac{1}{2}$	23	$5\frac{1}{4}$	25② ③	17

●—1967 Vista Cruiser—24.
■—When Equipped with 425 Engine—23.

①—88 Series with 350 V8—25.
②—Cutlass and 442 with 455 V8—20.
③—Station Wagons—23.

WHEEL ALIGNMENT

YEAR	MODEL	CASTER		CAMBER		TOE-IN (In.)	KING-PIN INCLINATION (Deg.)	WHEEL PIVOT RATIO	
		Range (Deg.)	Pref. Setting (Deg.)	Range (Deg.)	Pref. Setting (Deg.)			Inner Wheel	Outer Wheel
1965-67	F-85 Series	$\frac{1}{2}$N to 2N	$1\frac{1}{2}$N	$\frac{1}{4}$N to $\frac{1}{2}$P	$\frac{1}{4}$P	$\frac{1}{8}$ to $\frac{3}{16}$	$7\frac{1}{2}$–8	23	20
	88 & 98 Series	$\frac{1}{2}$N to $1\frac{1}{2}$N	$\frac{1}{2}$N	$\frac{1}{4}$N to $\frac{1}{2}$P	$\frac{1}{4}$P	$\frac{1}{8}$ to $\frac{3}{16}$	10	23	20
1968-69	F-85 Series	$\frac{1}{2}$N to 2N	$1\frac{1}{4}$N①	$\frac{1}{4}$N to $\frac{1}{2}$P	$\frac{1}{8}$P	$\frac{1}{8}$ to $\frac{1}{4}$	9	20	$18\frac{3}{4}$
	88 & 98 Series	$\frac{1}{2}$N to $1\frac{1}{2}$N	$1\frac{1}{4}$N①	$\frac{1}{4}$N to $\frac{1}{2}$P	$\frac{1}{8}$P	$\frac{1}{8}$ to $\frac{3}{16}$	11	20	$18\frac{1}{2}$
1970	F-85 Series	$\frac{1}{2}$N to 2N	$1\frac{1}{4}$N①	$\frac{1}{4}$N to $\frac{1}{2}$P	$\frac{1}{8}$P	$\frac{1}{8}$ to $\frac{1}{4}$	9	20	$18\frac{3}{4}$
	88 & 98 Series	$\frac{1}{2}$N to $1\frac{1}{2}$N	$1\frac{1}{4}$N①	$\frac{1}{4}$N to $\frac{1}{2}$P	$\frac{1}{8}$P	$\frac{1}{8}$ to $\frac{3}{16}$	11	20	$18\frac{1}{2}$
1971-72	F-85 Series	$\frac{3}{4}$N to $1\frac{3}{4}$N	$1\frac{1}{4}$N	$\frac{3}{4}$N to $\frac{3}{4}$P*	$\frac{1}{4}$P*	0 to $\frac{1}{16}$	9	20	19②
	88 & 98 Series	$\frac{1}{2}$P to $1\frac{1}{2}$P	1P	$\frac{3}{4}$N to $\frac{3}{4}$P*	$\frac{1}{4}$P*	0 to $\frac{1}{16}$	$10\frac{1}{2}$	20	$18\frac{1}{2}$

*—Right side to be $\frac{1}{2}$° more neg. than left side. Range—$\frac{3}{4}$ N to $\frac{1}{4}$ P. Pref.
setting—$\frac{1}{4}$ N.
①—Power Steering—$\frac{3}{4}$ N.

②—Power steering—18.
N—Negative.
P—Positive.

*—Larger drum brakes optional on most models.
**—Disc brakes standard.
①—7.75 x 14 standard 442, optional F-85/Cutlass.
②—8.55 x 14 optional.
③—8.85 x 14 optional.
④—1.00 in. on 442.

⑤—$\frac{7}{8}$ in. with metallic lining.
⑥—$1\frac{3}{16}$ in. with metallic lining.
⑦—205R14 radial optional.
⑧—8.45 x 15 or 225R15 radial with disc brakes.
⑨—8.85 x 15 or 225R15 radial with disc brakes.
⑩—F78 x 14 & F70 x 14 optional.

⑪—H78 x 14 optional.
⑫—J78 x 15 optional.
⑬—1.00 in. on Vista Cruiser.
⑭—G70 x 14 optional.
⑮—G60 x 15 optional.

BATTERY AND STARTER SPECIFICATIONS

YEAR	MODEL	BATTERY						STARTERS				
		Ampere Hour Capacity	Volts	Terminal Grounded	Lock Test			No-Load Test			Brush Spring Tension (Oz.)
					Amps.	Volts	Torque	Amps.	Volts	RPM	
1965-66	6—Cyl.	44	12	Neg.	Not Recommended			85	10.6	4,500-6,000	35
	V8—330	61	12	Neg.	Not Recommended			80	10.6	5,000	35
	V8—400, 425	70	12	Neg.	Not Recommended			62	10.6	6,000-8,000	35
1967-72	6—Cyl.	44	12	Neg.	Not Recommended			50-80	9-10.5	6,000-10,000	35
	V8—350	62	12	Neg.	Not Recommended			50-80	9-10.5	5,000-6,000	35
	V8—400, 425, 455	72, 73, 75	12	Neg.	Not Recommended			50-80	9-10.5	5,000-6,000	35

FUSES AND CIRCUIT BREAKERS— OLDSMOBILE

1965	1966	1967	1968	1969	1970	1971-72	
SFE-20/25	SFE-20/30	SFE-20/30	SFE-20	SFE-20	SFE-20	C-B	Accessory relay
AGC-25	AGC-30	AGC-30	AGC-25	AGC-25	AGC-25	AGC-25	Air conditioner
SFE-9	SFE-9	SFE-9	SFE-20	SFE-20	SFE-20	SFE-20	Back-up lights
SFE-20	SFE-20	SFE-20	AGC-25	AGC-25	AGC-25	AGC-25	Courtesy lights
—	AGA-3	AGA-3	SFE-20	5A, I-L	5A, I-L	58, I-L	Cruise control
SFE-20	SFE-20	SFE-20	AGC-25	AGC-25	AGC-25	AGC-25	Dome lights
—	—	—	SFE-20	SFE-20	SFE-20	SFE-20	Emergency flashers
C-B	C-B	C-B	C-B	C-B	C-B	C-B	Headlights
SFE-20	SFE-20	SFE-29	AGC-25	AGC-25	AGC-25	AGC-25	Heater
SFE-9	SFE-9	SFE-9	AGC-10	AGC-10	AGC-10	AGC-10	Instruments
AGA-3	AGA-3	AGA-3	SFE-4	SFE-4	SFE-4	SFE-4	Instrument panel lights
SFE-9	SFE-9	SFE-9	AGC-10	AGC-10	AGC-10	AGC-10	Radio
SFE-20	SFE-20	SFE-20	SFE-20	SFE-20	SFE-20	SFE-20	Stop lights
—	—	SFE-20	AGC-25	AGC-25	AGC-25	AGC-25	Rear window defogger
SFE-2	—	—	—	2A, I-L	2A, I-L	2A, I-L	Tachometer
SFE-9	AGW-15	AGW-15	SFE-20	SFE-20	SFE-20	SFE-20	Tail lights
SFE-9	SFE-9	SFE-9	AGC-10	AGC-10	AGC-10	AGC-10	Transmission control
—	—	—	SFE-20	SFE-20	SFE-20	SFE-20	Turn signals
SFE-9	SFE-9	SFE-9	AGC-25	AGC-25	AGC-25	AGC-25	Trunk/underhood lights
SFE-20	SFE-20	SFE-20	SFE-20	AGC-25	AGC-25	AGC-25	Wipers

C-B—Circuit breaker.
I-L—In-line.

FUSES AND CIRCUIT BREAKERS F-85

1965	1966	1967	1968	1969	1970	1971-72	
SFE-20	SFE-20	SFE-20	SFE-20	SFE-20	SFE-20	SFE-20	Accessory relay
AGC-25	AGC-25	AGC-25	AGC-25	AGC-25	AGC-25	AGC-25	Air conditioner
SFE-9	SFE-9	SFE-9	SFE-20	SFE-20	SFE-20	SFE-20	Back-up lights
SFE-20	SFE-20	SFE-20	AGC-25	AGC-25	AGC-25	AGC-25	Courtesy lights
—	—	—	SFE-20	5A, I-L	5A, I-L	5A, I-L	Cruise control
SFE-20	SFE-20	SFE-20	AGC-25	AGC-25	AGC-25	AGC-25	Dome lights
—	—	—	SFE-20	SFE-20	SFE-20	SFE-20	Emergency flashers
C-B	C-B	C-B	C-B	C-B	C-B	C-B	Headlights
SFE-20	SFE-20	SFE-20	AGC-25	AGC-25	AGC-25	AGC-25	Heater
SFE-9	SFE-9	SFE-9	AGC-10	AGC-10	AGC-10	AGC-10	Instruments
AGA-3	AGA-3	AGA-3	SFE-4	SFE-4	SFE-4	SFE-4	Instrument panel lights
SFE-9	SFE-9	SFE-9	AGC-10	AGC-10	AGC-10	AGC-10	Radio
SFE-20	SFE-20	SFE-20	SFE-20	SFE-20	SFE-20	SFE-20	Stop lights
—	—	—	AGC-25	AGC-25	AGC-25	AGC-25	Rear window defogger
AGA-2	AGA-2	AGA-2	—	2A, IL	2A, I-L	2A, I-L	Tachometer
SFE-9	SFE-9	SFE-9	SFE-20	SFE-20	SFE-20	SFE-20	Tail lights
SFE-9	SFE-9	SFE-9	AGC-10	AGC-10	AGC-10	AGC-10	Transmission control
—	—	—	SFE-20	SFE-20	SFE-20	SFE-20	Turn signals
—	SFE-9	SFE-20	AGC-25	AGC-25	AGC-25	AGC-25	Trunk/underhood lights
SFE-20	SFE-20	SFE-20	SFE-20	AGC-25	AGC-25	AGC-25	Wipers

C-B—Circuit breaker.   I-L—In-line.

LIGHT BULBS—Oldsmobile

1965	1966	1967	1968	1969	1970	1971-72	
1445	1445	1445	1445	1445	1445	1445	Ash tray
1156	1156	1156	1156	1156	1156①	1156①	Back-up
1893	1893	1893	1893	1816	1816	1893	Clock
1895	1895	1895	1895	1895	1895	—	Console compartment
—	1195	1195	1293	1293	1293	1293	Cornering
90	90	90	90	90	90	97	Courtesy
90	90	90	97	97	97	—	Courtesy (console)
1004	1004	1004	211	211	211	211	Dome
1895	1895	212	212	212	212	563	Glove compartment
4001	4001	4001	4001	4001	4001	4001	Headlamp (high beam)
4002	4002	4002	4002	4002	4002	4002	Headlamp (low beam)
1895	1895	1895	1445	1895	1895	1895	Heater/air conditioner
194	194	194	194	194	194	168	Instrument cluster
—	—	—	—	—	—	1893	Instrument floodlight
97	97	97	97	97	97	97	License
90	90	—	562	563	563	563	Map
1157	1157	1157 NA	1157 NA	1157 NA	1157 NA	1157 NA	Parking
1893	1893	1893	1893	1893	1893	1893	Radio
90	90	90	90	90	90	212	Rear quarter
—	—	—	—	—	1445	1445	Rear window defogger
1893	1893	1816	1816	1445	1816	1816	Shift quadrant (column)
1445	1445	1895	1895	1895	1445	—	Shift quadrant (console)
—	—	—	97A	194A	194	194	Side marker (front)
—	—	—	194	194	194	194	Side marker (rear)
1157 A	1157 A	1157	1157	1157	1157	1157	Stop
1157 A	1157 A	1157	1157	1157	1157	1157	Tail
—	631	631	631	631	631	631	Trunk
1157	1157	1157 NA	1157 NA	1157 NA	1157 NA	1157 NA	Turn signal
—	631	631	631	631	631	631	Underhood
158	158	158	161/168	168	161/168	161②	Warning (dash lights)

①—1157 used in 88 series.   ②—194 for low fuel warning.

LIGHT BULBS—F-85

1965	1966	1967	1968	1969	1970	1971–72	
1445	1445	1445	1445	1445	1445	1445	Ash tray
1156	1156	1156	1156	1156	1156	—	Back-up
1893	1816	1816	1893	1893	1893	1893	Clock
1895	1895	1895	1895	1895	1895	1895	Console compartment
—	—	—	—	—	—	—	Cornering
90	90	90	90	90	90	90	Courtesy
90	90	90	97	97	97	97	Courtesy (console)
211	211	211	211	211	211	211	Dome
1893	1895	1895	1893	1893	212	563	Glove compartment
4001	4001	4001	4001	4001	4001	4001	Headlamp (high beam)
4002	4002	4002	4002	4002	4002	4002	Headlamp (low beam)
1895	1445	1445	1445	1445	161	161	Heater/air conditioner
194	194	194	194	194	194	194	Instrument cluster
—	—	—	—	—	—	161	Instrument floodlight
97	97	97	97	97	97	97	License
—	—	—	562	563	563	563	Map
1157	1157	1157	1157 NA	1157 NA	1157 NA	1157 NA	Parking
1893	1893	1893	1893	1893	1445	1445	Radio
—	—	—	212	212	212	212	Rear quarter
—	—	—	—	—	—	1445	Rear window defogger
1445	1445	1816	1816	1445	1816	1816	Shift quadrant (column)
—	—	1445	1895	1895	1445	1445	Shift quadrant (console)
—	—	—	194A	194A	194	194	Side marker (front)
—	—	—	194	194	194	194	Side marker (rear)
1157	1157	1157	1157	1157	1157	1157	Stop
1157	1157	1157	1157	1157	1157	1157	Tail
—	—	—	631	631	631	631	Trunk
1157	1157	1157	1157 NA	1157 NA	1157 NA	1157 NA	Turn signal
—	—	—	—	631	631	631	Underhood
158	158	158	161/168	161/168	161/168	161/168	Warning (dash lights)

Distributor

Distributors on V8 engines have a window in the cap so that the point gap (dwell angle) may be adjusted with an Allen wrench while the engine is running. When installing a new contact point set, only the gap is adjusted; the spring tension and point alignment are pre-adjusted.

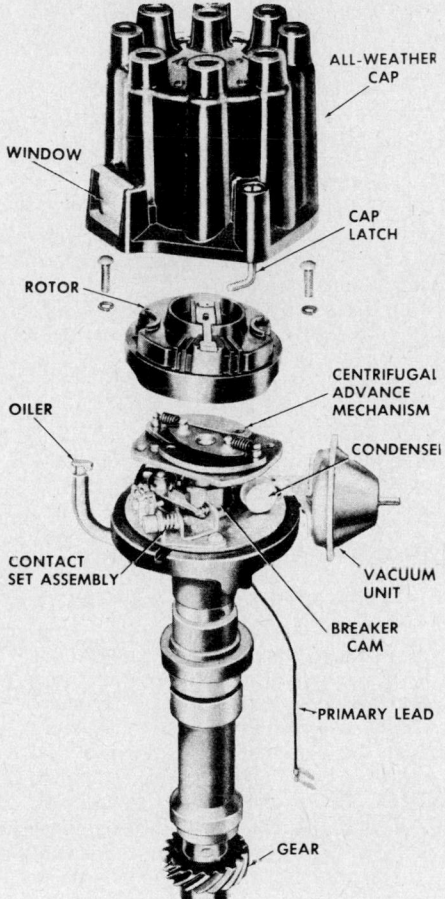

Distributor details, externally adjusted type
(© Oldsmobile Div. G.M. Corp.)

Distributor Removal

V6 and V8

1. Remove distributor cap, primary wire and vacuum line at the distributor.
2. Scribe a mark on the distributor body, locating the position of the rotor, and scribe another mark on the distributor body and engine block, showing the position of the body in the block.
3. Remove the hold-down screw and lift the distributor out of the block.
   NOTE: the distributor cam on the V6 engine has different sized lobes for some cylinders. Each spark plug wire must always remain in its original distributor cap terminal.

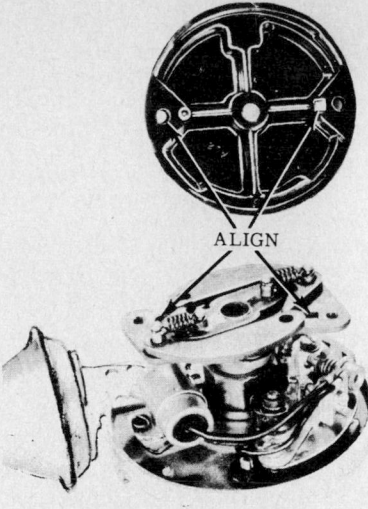

ALIGN

Rotor installation
(© Oldsmobile Div. G.M. Corp.)

Distributor Installation

1. If engine has been disturbed, rotate the crankshaft to bring the piston of No. 1 cylinder to the top of its compression stroke.
2. Position the distributor in the block with the rotor at No. 1 firing position. Make sure the oil pump intermediate driveshaft is properly seated in the oil pump.
3. Install the distributor lock but do not tighten.
4. Rotate the distributor body clockwise until the breaker points are starting to open. Tighten the retaining screw.
5. Connect the primary wire and the vacuum line to the distributor, then install distributor cap.
6. Start the engine and check the timing and dwell angle.

OHV 6

The distributor assembly is mounted on the right side of the block and is driven directly from the camshaft.

To remove the distributor, first detach the vacuum lines to the vacuum advance unit and lift off the distributor cap. Scribe a mark on the distributor indicating rotor position and a mark on the block indicating distributor position.

The distributor body is held to the block by a single cap screw that holds the octane selector plate down against the block. Remove the retaining screw and lift the distributor out of the block.

Alternator

1965-72

The charging system consists of the Delco-Remy Delcotron AC generator and a conventional relay-type regulator. Starting in 1969, the Del-

cotron in the 442 model is equipped with a built-in transistorized regulator unit. This regulator is a completely electronic sealed unit and cannot be adjusted.

See "Basic Electrical Diagnosis" in the Unit Repair Section for charging system test and component overhaul procedures.

Caution Since the Delcotron and regulator are designed for use on only one polarity system, the following precautions must be observed:

1. The polarity of the battery, generator, and regulator must be matched and considered before making any electrical connections in the system.
2. When connecting a booster battery, be sure to connect the negative battery terminals together and the positive battery terminals together.
3. When connecting a charger to the battery, connect the charger positive lead to the battery positive terminal. Connect the charger negative lead to the battery negative terminal.
4. Never operate the Delcotron on open circuit. Be sure that all connections in the circuit are clean and tight.
5. Do not short across or ground any of the terminals on the Delcotron regulator.
6. Do not attempt to polarize the Delcotron.
7. Do not use test lamps of more than 12 volts for checking diode continuity.
8. Avoid long soldering times when replacing diodes or transistors. Prolonged heat is damaging to these units.
9. Disconnect the battery ground terminal when servicing any A.C. system. This will prevent the possibility of accidental reversing of polarity.

Battery, Starter

Specifications on the battery and starter are in the Battery and Starter Specifications table.

See "Basic Electrical Diagnosis" in the Unit Repair Section for starter motor service procedures.

Starter R & R

1965-69 Except 400 Cu.In. Engine

1. Disconnect battery.
2. Noting positions of wires, disconnect starter wiring.

3. If equipped with manual transmission, remove flywheel cover.
4. Remove upper support attaching bolt.
5. Remove two mounting bolts and remove starter.
6. Install by reversing the above procedure.

1967-69 400 Cu. In. Engine

1. Disconnect battery.
2. Disconnect clutch return spring at clutch release yoke.
3. Disconnect exhaust pipe from left manifold.
4. Loosen upper and remove lower starter to block brace bolts.
5. Remove two starter to brace block bolts.
6. Move starter forward and downward, then disconnect wires from three starter terminals.
7. Remove starter.
8. Install by reversing the above procedure.

1970-72

1. Disconnect battery and hoist car.
2. Remove upper support attaching bolt.
3. Remove flywheel housing cover.
4. Remove two starter mounting bolts.
5. Lower starter, disconnect wiring, and remove starter.
6. Install by reversing the above procedure.

Instruments

Removal and Installation— Except F-85

1965-67

1. Disconnect battery.
2. Remove windshield side garnish moldings on 1965-66 models.
3. Remove steering column clamp.
4. If equipped with air conditioning, remove manifold and hoses.
5. Remove shift indicator needle.
6. Disconnect electrical leads.
7. Remove following from panel without disconnecting.
   a. Cruise control head.
   b. Ignition switch.
   c. Temperature control assembly.
8. Remove attaching screws and remove panel.
9. Install by reversing procedure above.

1968-69

1. Disconnect battery.
2. If equipped with air conditioning, remove manifold.
3. Remove trim pad below steering column and remove shift indicator needle.
4. Remove fuel gauge, speedometer and clock clusters. Remove

radio.
5. Remove screws from heater or air conditioning control, positioning control behind panel.
6. If equipped with cruise control, disconnect wiring, remove cable, and remove assembly from panel.
7. Remove ignition switch cylinder, then escutcheon, leaving switch connected to wiring.
8. Remove headlight switch control and wiper knobs with escutcheons leaving switches connected to wiring.
9. Disconnect wire connectors from accessory switches, lighter and map lamp.
10. Remove ash tray.
11. If equipped with air conditioning, remove left outlet housing by removing the knob and screw.
12. Remove panel attaching screws.
13. Install by reversing procedure above.

1970

1. Disconnect battery.
2. Remove headlight switch knob and escutcheon, leaving switch behind panel with wiring attached.
3. Remove heater or air conditioning control, positioning behind panel. Do not disconnect wiring, hoses or cables.
4. Remove glove compartment and remove trim cap.
5. Remove shift indicator needle, if so equipped.
6. Remove attaching screw and bolts.
7. Disconnect wire connectors.
8. Remove screws attaching main wiring harness.
9. Disconnect speedometer cable.
10. Remove nuts from steering column bracket and lower column until wheel rests on seat.
11. Remove screws from panel to column support.
12. Remove attaching screws above cluster.
13. Remove panel assembly by moving toward right side of car.
14. Install by reversing procedure above.

Instrument Panel Removal— F-85

1965-67

1. Disconnect battery.
2. Disconnect speedometer cable, wiring connectors and clip.
3. If equipped with air conditioning, disconnect cables, vacuum hoses, duct and manifold.
4. Remove screws that secure steering column and nuts that secure column clamp and lower column.
5. Remove attaching nuts and remove panel with controls attached.
6. Install by reversing procedure above.

1968-69

1. Disconnect battery.
2. Remove glove compartment as illustrated.
3. If equipped with air conditioning, remove right and left ducts and manifold.
4. Remove screws from heater or air conditioning control. Do not disconnect hoses or cables.
5. Disconnect antenna lead-in and speaker connector at radio.
6. Disconnect wiring connectors.
7. Remove escutcheon from ignition switch, positioning switch behind dash.
8. Disconnect speedometer cable.
9. Remove bolt attaching wiring harness clamp.
10. Remove trim cap below steering column.
11. Remove bolts and nuts attaching steering column, lowering column until wheel rests on seat.
12. Remove panel.
13. Install by reversing procedure above.

1970

Instruments can be removed after instrument trim panel is removed. Trim panel is removed by removing attaching screws and pulling top of panel rearward, then up.

Instrument Cluster Removal

1971-72 F-85, Cutlass, 442

Each of the three instrument clusters (speedometer, fuel gauge or clock/tachometer) is removed separately. The instrument trim panel which surrounds all three clusters must be removed first. Always disconnect the battery cable. Remove three cluster attaching screws then pull out the cluster and disconnect the wiring. When removing the speedometer cluster from a vehicle with an automatic transmission column shift, remove the panel below the steering column and disconnect the shift indicator clip. The speedometer cable must also be disconnected.

When installing the cluster, be sure that two of the attaching screws go through the holes in the ground straps.

1971-72 88, 98

1. Disconnect the battery and remove the panels directly under the steering column and to the lower left.
2. Remove the shift indicator needle.
3. Disconnect the speedometer cable, then turn ignition switch to "RUN" and shift lever in "Drive".
4. Remove the four cluster attaching screws.
5. Pull out the cluster far enough so that the multiple wiring con-

nector (printed circuit) can be disconnected, then remove the cluster.

Printed Circuit Removal

1. Remove all cluster lamp sockets, and circuit attaching screws.
2. Remove hex nuts from fuel gauge mounting studs.
3. Lift printed circuit from cluster.

Printed Circuit Installation

When installing, reverse removal procedure. Do not overtighten attaching screws or nuts. This could cause cracking and opening the circuit.

Ignition Switch Replacement

1965-68

1. Disconnect battery.
2. Place switch in off position and insert wire in small hole in cylinder face. While pushing in on wire turn cylinder counterclockwise and pull cylinder from case.
3. Remove nut from passenger side of dash.
4. Pull switch from under dash and remove wiring connector.

5. To remove theft resistant connector, where used, switch must be out from under dash. With screwdriver, depress tangs and separate the connector.
6. Install in reverse order of above.

1969-72

1. Disconnect negative battery cable.
2. Place ignition switch in "ACC" position (1969), "RUN" position (1970) or 'OFF-UNLOCKED' (1971-72).
3. Remove toe pan cover (if applicable) and loosen toe clamp bolts.
4. Remove lower instrument panel trim and toe pan trim panel.
5. Remove automatic transmission shift indicator needle.
6. Remove steering column dash bracket and let steering wheel rest on the driver's seat.
7. Remove two switch attaching screws and lift switch off actuator rod.
8. Disconnect wiring.
9. To install, check that lock

cylinder is still in "ACC" (1969), "RUN" (1970) or "OFF-UNLOCKED" (1971-72) position and move sliding portion of switch until switch hole is positioned as illustrated. Hold the switch in this position with a 0.090 in. pin as illustrated.
10. Connect the wiring to the switch.
11. Position switch over actuator rod, install attaching screws (tighten to 3 ft. lbs.) and remove the 0.090 in. pin.
12. Reverse Steps 1 through 6 to complete installation.

Headlight Switch Replacement

1965-68

1. Disconnect battery.
2. Pull knob out to on position.
3. Reach under instrument panel, depress the switch shaft retainer, and remove knob and shaft assembly.
4. Remove retaining ferrule nut.
5. Remove switch from instrument panel.
6. Disconnect the multi-plug connector from the switch.

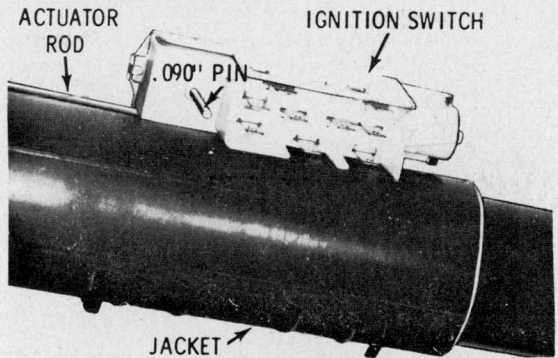

Holding ignition switch in position—1969-71
(© Olds. Div. G.M. Corp.)

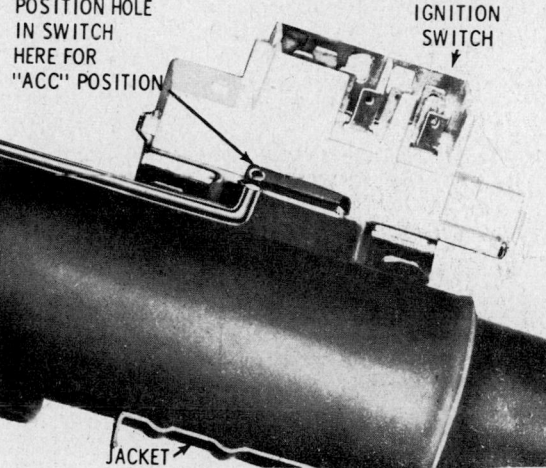

Ignition switch in "ACC" position—1969
(© Olds. Div. G.M. Corp.)

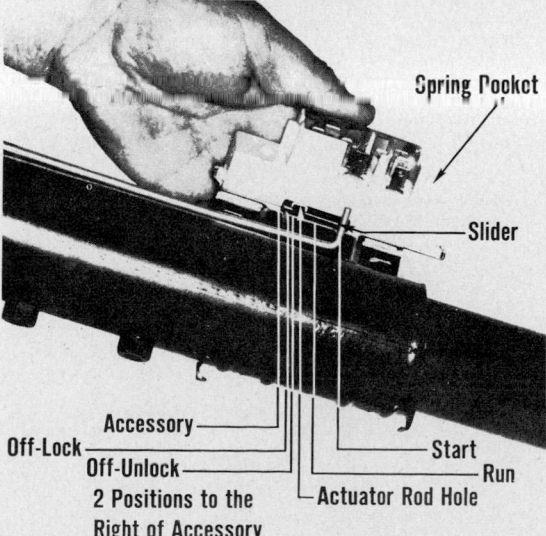

Ignition switch in "Off-Unlocked" position—1971
(© Olds. Div. G.M. Corp.)

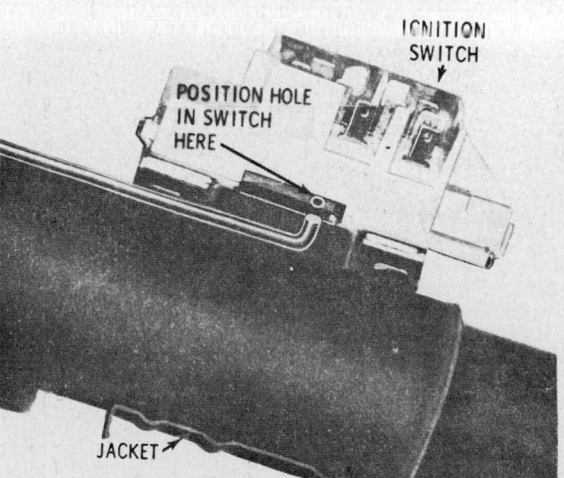

Ignition switch in "RUN" position—1970
(© Olds. Div. G.M. Corp.)

7. Install in reverse of above. (In checking lights before installation, switch must be grounded to test dome lights).

1969-72

1. Disconnect the battery.
2. On 1971-72 88 and 98 models, remove the left-hand control panel from the dash.
3. Pull the switch to "ON" position, then depress the spring-loaded button on the switch body and pull knob out of the switch.
4. Remove the escutcheon.
5. Remove the switch from behind the panel and disconnect the multiple connector.
6. Install in the reverse order of the above procedure.

Brakes

Specific information on brake lining sizes is in the General Chassis and Brake Specifications table.

Information on brake adjustments, lining replacement, bleeding procedure, master and wheel cylinder overhaul is in the Unit Repair Section.

Information on overhauling power brakes is in the Unit Repair Section.

Information on the grease seal replacement is in the Unit Repair Section.

Beginning 1967, a dual-type master cylinder is used. For detailed information on this type cylinder, see Unit Repair Section.

1969-72

A single-cylinder disc brake is used on the front wheels of some models. Information on this brake is in the Unit Repair Section.

Brake Pedal Travel

1965-66

Before adjusting the brakes, make certain there is ½ in.—¾ in. free pedal travel (measured at the toeboard). This adjustment is made at the master-cylinder pushrod.

1967-72

There are no brake pedal adjustments on these models.

Parking Brake Cable Adjustment

1. Release parking brake. Check for proper pedal clearance.
2. Adjust rear cables by tightening equalizer adjusting nut to obtain heavy drag at rear brakes.
3. Loosen equalizer adjusting nut seven full turns. Tighten locknut.

Master Cylinder R & R

1. Disconnect and cap or plug hydraulic lines.

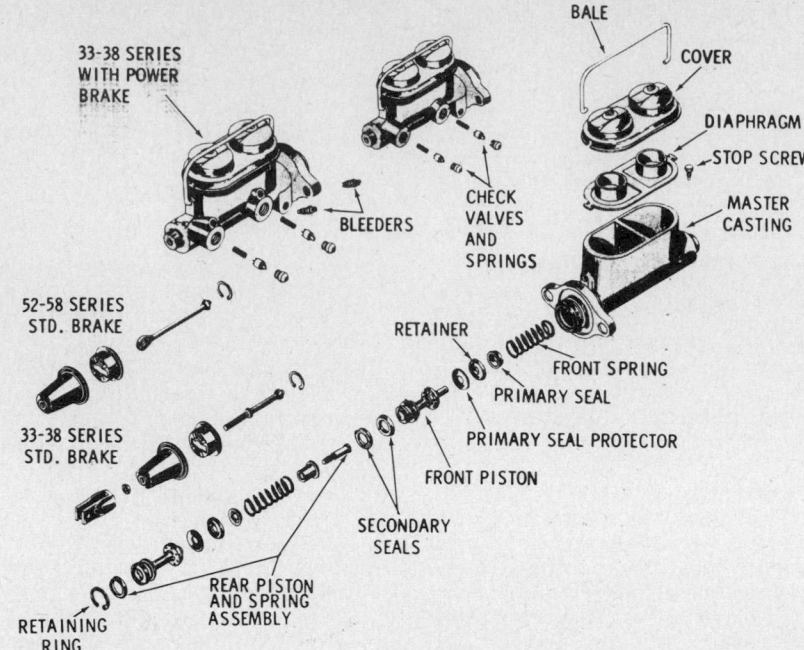

Master cylinder (Moraine)
(© Oldsmobile Div. G.M. Corp.)

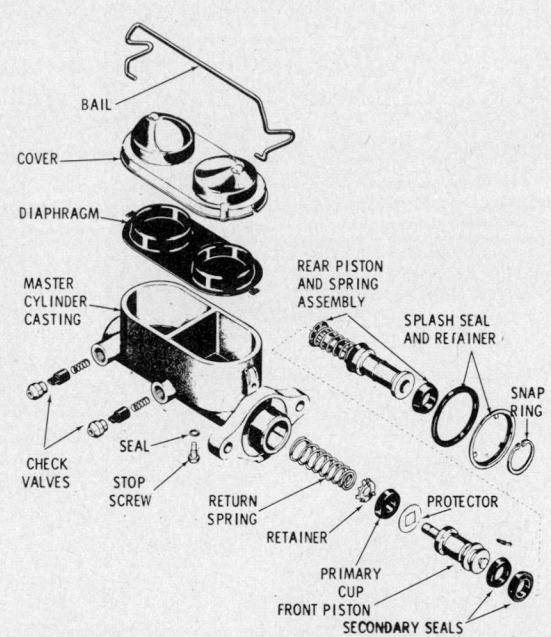

Master cylinder (Bendix)—no check valve with front disc brakes
(© Oldsmobile Div., G.M. Corp.)

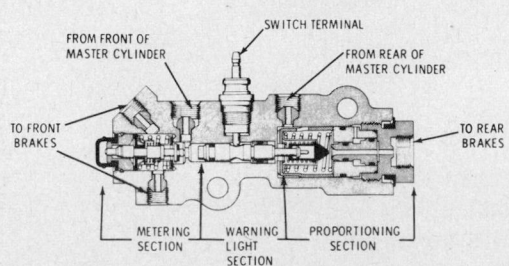

Combination valve with warning light switch
(© Olds. Div. G.M. Corp.)

2. If there is no power booster unit, remove the pushrod - to - pedal clevis pin.

3. Remove the attaching bolts and master cylinder.

4. Install in the reverse order of removal. Fill with fluid and bleed.

Power Brake Unit

The master cylinder and power booster are removed as a unit. Disconnect vacuum and hydraulic lines. Disconnect the pushrod from the brake pedal. Remove the vacuum unit mounting stud nuts and remove the assembly. Install in the reverse order of removal, tightening the mounting nuts to 28 ft. lbs. Fill the master cylinder reservoir with fluid.

Warning Switch

Whenever there is a significant difference in pressure between the front disc or drum and rear drum systems, a piston in the combination valve activates the warning light switch, thus indicating a failure in one of the hydraulic systems. In the event of combination valve malfunction, no attempt should be made to repair the valve. The complete valve assembly must be replaced.

Fuel System

Gas tank capacities may be found in the Capacities table at the beginning of this section. See "Dash Gauges and Indicators" in the Unit Repair Section for a discussion of fuel gauge operation.

Idle Speed and Mixture Adjustments

1965-69 All Models

Adjust with air cleaner removed.

Warm up the engine, remove the air cleaner, disconnect the air cleaner vacuum hose at the intake manifold, plug manifold fitting, disconnect the vacuum distributor hose and plug the hose. With automatic transmission in Drive and manual transmission in neutral, adjust the throttle stop screw and idle mixture screws alternately to obtain the best idle at the specified rpm. See Rochester Carburetor Adjustment table in the Unit Repair Section for the correct idle speed.

Adjust the throttle closing solenoid, if so equipped, as described in Step 5 of the 1970 1-BBL adjustment below.

Install and reconnect all components and recheck the idle speed.

1968-69 1-BBL (250 Cu. In.)

Adjust with air cleaner removed.

Idle adjustments on these models are the same as those described for the 1970 model with the excep-

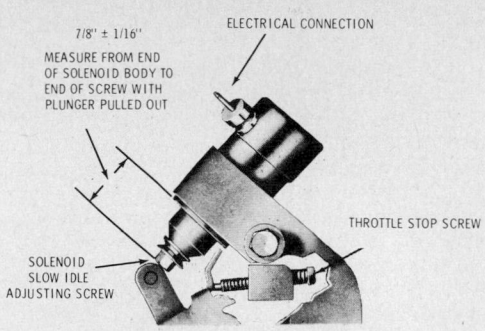

Adjusting throttle closing solenoid—1970 1-BBL
(© Olds. Div. G.M. Corp.)

tion of the mixture adjustment. Follow the 1970 procedure but, instead of Steps 6 through 8, adjust the mixture as follows:

1. Adjust slow idle screw and mixture screw alternately to obtain the best idle at:

   575 rpm: 1968 with auto trans in Drive

   725 rpm: 1968 with manual trans in neutral

   625 rpm: 1969 with auto trans in Drive

   775 rpm: 1969 with manual trans in neutral

   NOTE: plug hot idle compensator hole with a pencil eraser.

2. Turn idle mixture screw in to obtain a 20-25 rpm reduction for final idle speed.

1970 1-BBL (250 Cu. In.)

Adjust with air cleaner removed.

The throttle closing solenoid on this model carburetor is wired to the ignition switch. When the ignition is turned off, the solenoid de-energizes, allowing the throttle plates to close completely and thus preventing running-on after the ignition switch is turned off. To adjust the carburetor idle, proceed as follows:

1. Remove the air cleaner and disconnect the air cleaner vacuum hose at the base of the carburetor. Plug the hose fitting.

2. Disconnect the vacuum hose at the distributor and plug the hose.

3. Start the engine and let it warm up. Place the transmission in Drive or neutral. The choke should be fully open, the fast idle follower off the cam and the throttle stop screw should be off the cam. Make sure the solenoid wire is connected.

4. If the engine stalls or idles roughly, check for possible vacuum leaks. The idle mixture screws are preset at the factory and should not be adjusted unless absolutely necessary. If poor idle condition persists, proceed with Steps 6 through 8 below.

5. The distance between the end of the solenoid plunger screw and the solenoid body must be 13/16 to 15/16 in. when the solenoid is energized (plunger fully ex-

tended). If adjustment is required, set the idle at 575 rpm with the throttle stop screw. Loosen the solenoid bracket clamp and adjust by turning the screw in the plunger. Locate the solenoid in the bracket clamp so that the plunger is lightly against the carburetor lever when the solenoid is energized and so that the solenoid terminal is 30° toward the rear. Tighten the clamp. Back off the throttle stop screw until it no longer contacts the stop.

6. Turn the engine off. Turn the idle mixture adjusting screw in until it is lightly seated, then back it out four turns. Start the engine.

7. Adjust the solenoid slow idle adjusting screw to obtain 830 rpm (manual transmission in neutral) or 630 rpm (automatic transmission in Drive).

8. Plug the hot idle compensator hole located inside the air horn with a pencil eraser and turn the idle mixture screw in to obtain 750 rpm (manual transmission in neutral) or 600 rpm (automatic transmission in Drive). Remove the pencil eraser.

9. Turn the throttle stop screw until it just contacts the throttle lever.

10. Disconnect the solenoid wire and adjust the throttle stop screw to obtain 400 rpm with manual transmission in neutral or automatic transmission in Drive. Do not readjust the idle mixture.

11. Reconnect the solenoid wire, unplug and reconnect the distributor vacuum hose, unplug and reconnect the vacuum hose at the base of the carburetor, install the air cleaner and connect the air cleaner hose.

12. Make sure the hot air adapter and the ventilation tube are connected and properly seated.

1970 2-BBL and 4-BBL

Adjust with air cleaner removed.

1. Warm up engine and leave it running.

2. Remove air cleaner, disconnect the air cleaner vacuum hose at

the intake manifold and plug the fitting on the manifold.

3. Disconnect the vacuum hose at the distributor and plug the hose.
4. Stop engine, turn off the air conditioner and restart the engine.
5. Make sure choke is fully open.
6. With automatic transmission in Drive or manual transmission in neutral, adjust idle speed as specified in the first column of the table.

NOTE: idle mixture screws have been preset at the factory and should not be adjusted unless absolutely necessary. Check all other possible causes of poor idle before adjusting mixture screws.

7. Turn idle mixture screws all the way in until lightly bottomed, then turn back out 6 full turns, except on 350 cu. in. engine (not W-31) with the 4-barrel, which are backed out 4 turns.
8. Set the throttle screw until the specified rpm is obtained (left-hand column of table below). Automatic transmission in Drive and manual transmission in neutral.
9. Turn each mixture screw in (clockwise) equally in 1/4 turn increments until proper slow (final) idle is obtained (right-hand column of table below).
10. Unplug and connect distributor vacuum hose and install air cleaner and air cleaner hose.
11. Be sure hot air adapter and ventilation tube are connected and seated properly.

Slow Idle Adjustment

Trans/Engine	Initial RPM	Final Slow Idle
2-BBL.		
Automatic—		
350, 455	620	575
Manual—350	800	750
Manual—455	720	675
4-BBL.		
Automatic—350	625	575
Manual—350	725	650
Automatic—W-31	*	750
Manual—W-31	*	625
Automatic—455	700	600
Manual—455	*	750
Automatic—W-30	675	650
Manual—W-30	*	750
Automatic—455 (88, 98 only)	650	575
Automatic, Manual— W-33	625	600

* Adjust only to final slow idle speed.

1971 1-BBL (250 Cu. In.)

Adjust with air cleaner installed.
The following adjustments must be made in the order presented below. First set idle as follows:
1. Warm up the engine and make sure the choke is full open.
2. Disconnect the fuel tank hose

from the vapor canister.

3. Disconnect the distributor vacuum hose and plug the hose leading to the carburetor.
4. Set the dwell and timing at the specified rpm.
5. Adjust the carburetor idle speed screw to obtain :

500 rpm : auto trans (in Drive), without air conditioner.

550 rpm : manual trans (in neutral), without air conditioner

575 rpm : auto trans (in Drive), with air conditioner (off)

600 rpm : manual trans (in neutral), with air conditioner (off)

NOTE: do not adjust solenoid screw.
6. Reconnect distributor vacuum hose and fuel tank hose.

The idle mixture is set at the factory and the adjusting screw capped in order that the fuel-air mixture remains adjusted to meet government emission standards. The mixture should only be adjusted in the case of major carburetor overhaul or, after an exhaustive check of other likely causes of poor engine performance, it is apparent the idle mixture is not correct. To adjust idle mixture :
1. Connect a CO (carbon monoxide) meter to the exhaust system.
2. Disconnect fuel hose at the canister and plug hose.
3. Remove idle limiter cap from the idle mixture adjusting screw.
4. Adjust idle mixture screw to obtain a "CO" reading of 1% with the engine idling at specified idle speed.
5. Install a new limiter cap on the idle mixture adjusting screw.
6. Connect the fuel hose to the canister.

If a CO meter is unavailable, the following alternate method may be followed to adjust the idle mixture :
1. Follow the instructions on the vehicle tune-up sticker before proceeding. (Distributor vacuum hose disconnected and fuel tank vent hose disconnected.)
2. Remove mixture limiter cap and turn screw until it is lightly bottomed in its seat, then back out 4 full turns.
3. Adjust idle speed adjusting screw to obtain an idle speed of 530 rpm (automatic transmission) or 630 rpm (manual transmission).
4. Adjust mixture screw in (leaner) until the engine speed drops 20-30 rpm.
5. Install limiter cap on the idle mixture screw.
6. Reconnect distributor vacuum hose and fuel tank vapor hose.

The idle stop solenoid has been replaced by a combination emission

control (C.E.C.) valve which, when energized by the transmission, acts as a throttle stop by increasing the idle speed during high gear operation. The C.E.C. valve also provides for spark advance during high gear operation and retarded spark for lower gears and at idle. Adjustment is made only after the solenoid has been replaced, the carburetor has been overhauled or the throttle body has been removed. Adjust C.E.C. valve as follows :
1. Follow instructions on tune-up sticker.
2. Start engine, turn air conditioner off and put transmission in "Drive" or neutral.
3. Disconnect vacuum hose to distributor and plug hose.
4. Disconnect the fuel tank hose from canister.
5. Pull out solenoid plunger until it contacts the throttle lever, then adjust plunger length to obtain 650 rpm (automatic transmission) or 850 rpm (manual transmission) with plunger extended.
6. Remove plug from the distributor hose and reconnect distributor hose and fuel tank canister hose.
7. Check slow idle speed.

1971 2-BBL and 4-BBL

Adjust with air cleaner removed.
1. Warm up engine and leave it running.
2. Remove air cleaner, disconnect air cleaner hose at the isntake manifold and plug the fitting.
3. Make sure the choke is open and the air conditioner if off.
4. Disconnect the carburetor hose from the vapor canister and on the 2-barrel plug the hose. Do not plug the hose on the 4-barrel.
5. Disconnect the distributor vacuum hose at the distributor and plug the hose.
6. Set the dwell and timing.
7. Adjust the carburetor idle screw to obtain 750 rpm (manual transmission in neutral) or 600 rpm (automatic transmission in Drive).

NOTE: idle mixture screws have been preset at the factory and capped. Remove the caps only in the case of major overhaul, throttle body removal or when all other possible causes of poor idle condition have been thoroughly checked.

8. To adjust the idle mixture, stop the engine, connect a CO (carbon monoxide) meter to the exhaust system and turn the idle mixture screws until they are lightly seated. Back out the idle mixture screws 6 full turns, then start engine and adjust the screws equally to obtain a good idle at the specified rpm with a maximum CO reading of 0.6% on the 2-barrel and 0.3% on the

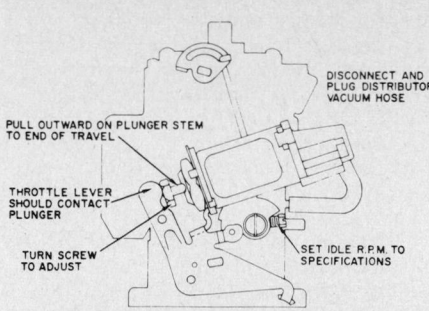

Adjusting C.E.C. valve—1971 1-BBL
(© Olds. Div. G.M. Corp.)

4-barrel. Temporarily install the air cleaner and check that the CO concentration does not exceed the specified level, readjusting idle mixture screws if necessary.

9. Install new idle limiter caps.
10. Reinstall and reconnect everything which was removed or disconnected in Steps 1 through 5.

Fuel Filter

All carburetors have a fuel filter which is integral with the carburetor body. To replace the filter element, remove the fuel inlet line, then remove the inlet fitting and pull out the filter element. Be careful when tightening the brass fitting because the threads are easily stripped.

Fuel Pump Removal

Disconnect the fuel and vacuum lines, remove the two mounting bolts and remove the pump and gasket.

Exhaust System

All exhaust pipes are retained to the manifold with a flange and two bolts or studs. The rest of the pipes, mufflers and resonators are held to-gether with U-bolt clamps. When inspecting the exhaust system, check for holes in the mufflers and resonators and check that the drain holes are facing down and are not clogged.

The exhaust system is suspended from the frame with rubber dampened hangers. Exhaust system components should have at least ¾ in. clearance from the floor pan to avoid possible overheating.

Tighten exhaust pipe to manifold flange bolts or stud nuts to 18 ft. lbs., U-bolts clamp nuts to 15 ft. lbs. and pipe hangers to 10 ft. lbs.

Cooling System

Detailed information on cooling system capacity is in the Capacities table.

Information on the water temperature gauge is in the Unit Repair Section.

Thermostatic Vacuum Switch

If equipped with exhaust emission control and air-conditioning, a thermostatic vacuum switch is used to increase ignition timing advance at idle when higher coolant temperatures are encountered. This change from part to full vacuum advance at engine idle, tends to improve cooling at idle.

If a heating condition exists at idle speeds only, disconnect the distributor vacuum hose at the thermostatic switch. When engine temperature is above 230° F., there should be no vacuum at this port at idle. If engine temperature is above 230° F. and vacuum is present at port D, check distributor advance.

Radiator Core Removal

NOTE: on models with an oil cooler, the oil cooler lines will have to be disconnected and capped.

On models with the horns attached to the core brackets, remove the horns.

The radiator core can be removed from all Oldsmobile models without taking off the water pump. Remove the radiator upper baffle plate, shroud, radiator hoses, headlight wires, hood cables, and unbolt the core assembly from its support. Slide shroud over the fan. Lift out the raciator core. It may be necessary to rotate the fan blades in order to keep them out of the way.

Water Pump Removal

Drain the cooling system and loosen the generator and power steering belts, remove the fan and fan pulley, disconnect hoses, remove bolts

TIP FUEL PUMP AND POSITION ARM UNDER FUEL PUMP ECCENTRIC

Installing fuel pump
(© Oldsmobile Div. G.M. Corp.)

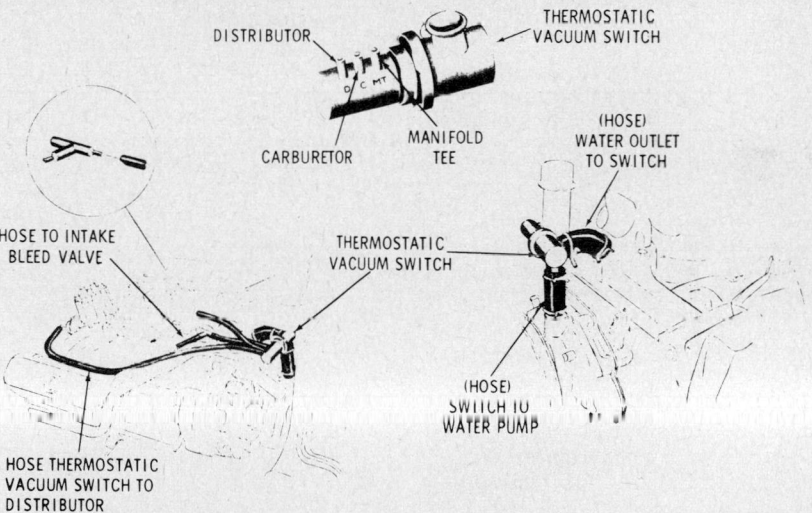

Thermostatic vacuum switch K-19 (© Oldsmobile Div. G.M. Corp.)

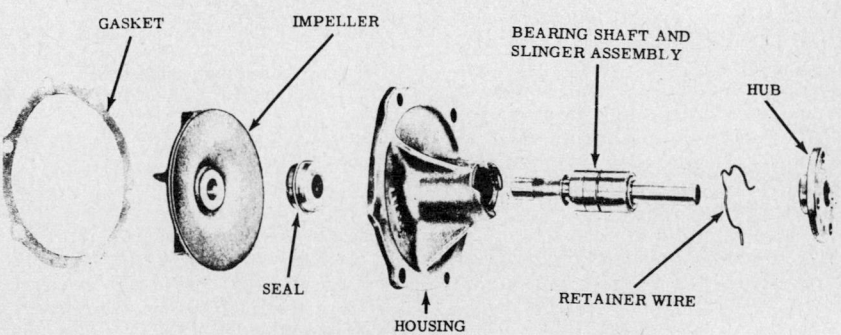

Water pump (© Oldsmobile Div. G.M. Corp.)

that hold the water pump to front of engine and lift off pump.

Only one side of the gasket should be coated with gasket compound when reinstalling.

Dip the bolts in sealer before inserting them in the pump.

Engine

Engine Removal

1965-72 V6 and V8

1. Drain cooling system, remove hood, and disconnect battery.
2. Disconnect radiator hoses, heater hoses, vacuum and power steering hoses, starter cable at junction block, engine to ground strap, fuel hose from fuel line, wiring and accelerator linkage.
3. Remove fan and fan pulley, coils and upper radiator support.
4. Raise car on hoist.
5. Disconnect exhaust pipes at manifold.
6. Remove torque converter cover and install a converter holding tool.
7. Remove engine mount thru bolts and support the engine. On F-85 models, install engine support bar (BT-6424). On older models, install engine support bar (BT-3016). Use adapters (BT-6424-2).
8. Lift engine and secure transmission chain support to frame.
9. Remove three converter to flywheel attaching bolts.
10. Remove six transmission to engine bolts.
11. Lower the car.
12. Secure chain lift (BT-6606) to engine, disconnect engine support bar and remove engine.

1965-72 OHV 6 Engine

1. Drain cooling system and the engine oil.
2. Remove carburetor air cleaner, disconnect battery, remove hood.
3. Remove radiator shroud, fan blade and pulley.
4. Disconnect wires at starter solenoid, generator, temperature switch, oil pressure switch and at the coil.
5. Disconnect accelerator linkage at the manifold, exhaust pipe at manifold, fuel pump (from tank) at fuel pump, vacuum line to power brake unit at manifold and power steering pump lines at the pump.
6. Raise car on a hoist.
7. Remove propeller shaft. (Either drain or plug the rear end of the transmission to prevent oil leakage.)
8. Disconnect shift linkage and the

speedometer cable at the transmission.
9. On manual shift transmission equipped cars, disconnect clutch linkage at cross shaft, then remove cross shaft engine bracket.
10. Remove transmission assembly.
11. Remove front mount thru bolts.
12. Attach chain lift (BT-6606) and raise engine to take weight off front mounts, then remove rear mount bolts.
13. Remove engine assembly from car.
14. Install by reversing removal procedure.

Engine Manifolds

Intake Manifold Removal

All V8 Models

Remove the carburetor air cleaner, drain the radiator and disconnect the upper radiator hose. Remove the spark plugs and disconnect the spark plug wire supports. Remove distributor cap and high tension wires. Disconnect the throttle, vacuum and gas lines from the carburetor and take off the carburetor. If equipped with power steering, remove pump and bracket. Remove the bolts that hold the intake manifold to the two cylinder heads. The coil can be left on the intake manifold.

On the 400 and 425 cu. in. engines it may be necessary to remove the distributor to provide clearance for manifold removal. On the 455 cu. in. engine it will be necessary to remove the oil filler tube.

Install in the reverse order of removal, tightening all bolts first to 15 ft. lbs., then to 35 ft. lbs. in the se-

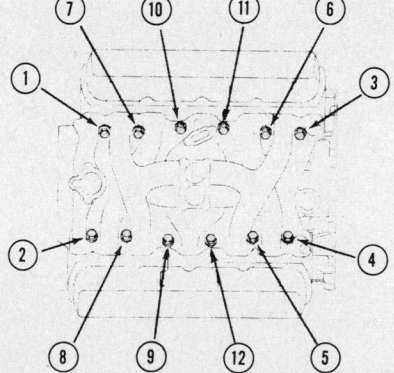

Intake manifold bolt tightening sequence—V8
(© Olds. Div. G.M. Corp.)

quence illustrated. Coat all gasket surfaces with sealer.

F-85 V6

1. Drain cooling system.
2. Remove carburetor air cleaner. Disconnect throttle return from the carburetor. Disconnect and remove the coil.
3. Disconnect temperature indica-

tor wire from sending unit.
4. Disconnect accelerator and transmission linkage at carburetor. Disconnect throttle return spring.
5. Slide front thermostat by-pass hose clamp back on the hose. Disconnect upper radiator hose at outlet.
6. Disconnect heater hose at the temperature control valve inlet. Force the end of the hose down to permit coolant to drain from intake manifold.
7. Remove 12 manifold-to-head attaching bolts.
8. Remove intake manifold and carburetor as an assembly by sliding rearward to disengage the thermostat by-pass hose from the water pump. Remove intake manifold gasket sound absorber.
9. Be sure there is no coolant present. Then remove intake manifold gasket clamps and remove the gasket. Remove rubber gasket seal.
10. Install by reversing above procedure. Torque to 25-30 ft. lbs.

Exhaust Manifold Removal

F-85 V6

(Cylinder heads off)
1. Remove exhaust manifold-to-exhaust pipe attaching bolts.
2. On the right side, remove generator rear attaching bolt.
3. Unlock and remove exhaust manifold-to-cylinder-head bolts. Remove the manifold.
4. Install by reversing above. Torque to 18-24 ft. lbs.

All V8 Models

Remove the bolts from the exhaust manifold flanges on both sides and take off the crossover pipe. On the right side, remove generator and bracket. Remove shroud if so equipped. Remove the bolts that hold the exhaust manifold to the cylinder head and lift off the exhaust manifolds.

On some models with the 455 cu. in. engine, the starter will have to be removed to work on the left-hand exhaust manifold. On other models with the 455 cu. in. engine, the front wheel will have to be removed in order to gain access to the right-hand manifold through the opening in the fender inner panel. When installing, tighten the manifold-to-head attaching bolts to 25 ft. lbs. torque, tightening those in the center first.

OHV 6 Models

This engine uses a combined intake and exhaust manifold, equipped with thermostatic heat-riser valve.

To remove the manifold assembly disconnect the exhaust pipe flange and remove all connections to the carburetor. Take off the vacuum lines on the manifold and also at the carburetor.

Remove the carburetor and unbolt the manifold.

Before reinstalling the manifold, thoroughly clean out the ports to prevent turbulence, particularly in the intake manifold.

Exhaust Emission Control

The A.I.R. (Air Injection Reactor "K-19") emission control system is designed to reduce unburnt hydrocarbons in the engine exhaust. An air pump forces filtered air into the exhaust port of each cylinder, thereby spontaneously oxidizing the carbon monoxide and unburnt hydrocarbons.

The General Motors Corporation has adopted a special system of terminal exhaust treatment. This plan supersedes (in most cases) the method used to conform to 1966-67 California laws. The new system cancels out (except with stick shift and special purpose engine applications) the use of the A.I.R. method previously used.

The new concept, combustion control system (C.C.S.) utilizes engine modification, with emphasis on carburetor and distributor changes. Any of the methods of terminal exhaust treatment requires close and frequent attention to tune-up factors of engine maintenance.

All car manufacturers post idle speeds and other pertinent data relative to the specific engine-car application in a conspicuous place in the engine compartment.

For details, consult the Unit Repair Section.

Evaporative Emission Canister

1970-72 models are equipped with Evaporative Emission System which prevents fuel vapor loss to the atmosphere. The carbon canister stores vapors from the fuel tank vent system and is inside the right front fender on V8 equipped cars and inside the left front fender on 6-cylinder models. The fiber filter located in the bottom of the canister should be replaced every 12,000 miles. To remove the canister, remove the hoses and loosen the bracket clamp screw.

Cylinder Head

Rocker Shaft Removal

V6

1. Remove the bolts that hold the rocker cover assembly to the cylinder head and lift off the rocker cover.
2. A little at a time, loosen the bolts that hold the rocker brackets to the cylinder head, and lift off the rocker assemblies.
3. If the pushrods are to be pulled

up through the cylinder head, be careful to break the seal created by the oil at the lifter plunger in order to prevent pulling the lifter plunger up with the push rod.

4. On some models it may be necessary to loosen the heater motor and core assembly in order to pull out the pushrods in No. 8 cylinder. Do not bend the pushrod in any way in order to force it past the heater motor.

This condition varies with body styles. When installing, tighten rocker arm shaft bracket bolts to 35 ft. lbs.

V8

Install the pairs of rocker arms for each cylinder only when the lifters are off the cam lobe and the valves are closed. Lubricate all pivot and rocker arm wear points with Lubriplate. Torque the hardened flanged retaining bolts to 25 ft. lbs. (20 ft. lbs. on the 1965-66 engines).

OHV 6

Rocker arms are mounted individually on studs and retained by rounded nuts. With the lifters off the cam lobes, tighten the retaining nut until zero lash is obtained (this can be felt by turning the pushrod by hand until it cannot be rotated). Tighten the nut one more turn.

Cylinder Head Removal

V8 and V6

1. Drain the radiator. It is possible to drain enough of the coolant from the block to remove the heads by raising the rear wheels at least 24 in.

2. Remove the intake manifold and carburetor as an assembly.
3. Remove exhaust manifold(s).
4. Loosen or remove any accessory brackets which interfere.
5. Remove the valve cover.
6. On the V6 remove the rocker arm shaft. On V8 engines, remove rocker arm bolts, pivots, rocker arms and pushrods. Scribe the pivots and identify the rocker arms and pushrods so that they may be installed in their original locations.
7. Remove cylinder head bolts and cylinder head(s).
8. Install in the reverse order of removal. It is recommended that the head gasket be coated on both sides with sealer. Dip head bolts in oil before installing. Tighten all head bolts in the correct sequence to 60-70 ft. lbs., then again in sequence to the specified torque. See Specifications at the beginning of this section for correct head bolt torque and tightening sequence.

OHV 6 Engine

1. Drain cooling system and remove manifold assembly and valve mechanism.
2. Remove fuel and vacuum line from retaining clip and disconnect wires from temperature sending units.
3. Disconnect upper radiator hose and battery ground strap.
4. Remove coil.
5. Remove cylinder head bolts, then head and gasket.

Install in the reverse order of removal. See Specifications at the beginning of this section for correct head bolt torque and tightening sequence.

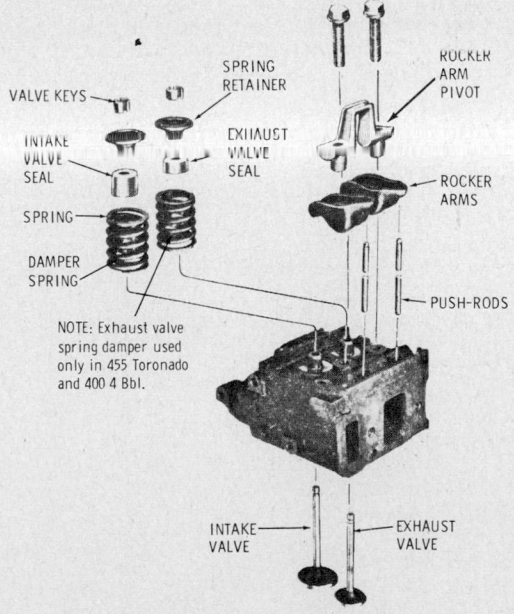

Valve and cylinder head assembly—V8
(© Olds. Div. G.M. Corp.)

Valve System

Hydraulic lifters are used on all engines. These lifters are not interchangeable. To remove hydraulic lifters, first remove intake manifold and rocker assemblies, then pull out lifters.

Hydraulic lifters operate normally under conditions of zero valve lash. See "Rocker Shaft Removal" above for valve lash adjustment.

Rocker arm lubrication is provided by means of oil feed through the pushrods on V8 engines and through the rocker arm shaft on the V6.

Valve guides are not replaceable, but may be reamed to 0.003 in., 0.005 and 0.013 in. oversize. Occassionally a valve guide bore will be oversize as manufactured. These are marked on the inboard side of the cylinder heads on the machined surface just above the intake manifold. To ream a 0.010 in. oversize valve guide bore, use the 0.013 in. oversize reamer. Service valves are available in five different stem diameters: Standard, 0.003 oversize, 0.005 oversize, 0.010 oversize and 0.013 oversize.

Valve Springs

All Models

The easiest and quickest way to check a valve spring is to lay the spring on a flat, level surface and compare its free length with that of a new valve spring. If a new valve spring is not available, lay all the springs alongside each other to see if they are all the same length.

If they vary in length, they must be checked either on a spring compression type checker or tested for free length against a new valve spring.

Timing Case

Valve Timing Procedure

V8 and V6

On all Oldsmobile models except the L6, a chain is used to drive the camshaft. The construction is such that the chain can be worn even badly without seriously affecting the valve timing. If the chain is worn badly enough to cause the timing to jump or it becomes necessary to replace either the chain or the sprockets or both, proceed as follows:

1. Remove the timing case cover and take off the camshaft gear.

NOTE: the fuel pump operating cam is bolted to the front of the camshaft sprocket and the sprocket is located on the camshaft by means of a dowel.

2. Remove the timing chain and the camshaft sprocket and, if the crankshaft sprocket is to be replaced, remove it also at this time.
3. Reinstall the crankshaft sprocket

being careful to start it with the keyway in perfect alignment since it is rather difficult to correct for misalignment after the gear has been started on the shaft. Turn the timing mark on the crankshaft gear until it points directly toward the center of the camshaft. Mount the timing chain over the camshaft gear and start the camshaft gear up on to its shaft with the timing marks as close as possible to each other and in line between the shaft centers. Rotate the cam-

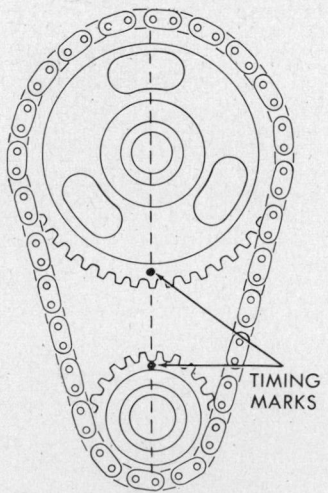

Timing marks—except inline 6

shaft to align the shaft with the new gear.

A dowel pin is used for alignment. Secure the camshaft gear and check to see that the mark on the crankshaft sprocket and the mark on the camshaft sprocket are as described above. Valves timed in this manner are correct regardless of which piston is at top center. It may be necessary, however, to retime the ignition since there is a possibility it will be 180° out of position.

Front Cover R & R

V8 Engines

The timing case cover and the water pump housing are a one-piece casting.
1. Drain the cooling system and disconnect the radiator and heater hoses, remove the radiator core, the fan blades and the pulley.
2. Remove the vibration damper.
3. Place a jack under the engine, take a light load on the jack and remove the two bolts that attach the front of the engine to the frame.
4. Remove the oil pan (see Engine Lubrication section). Crank the engine until No. 3 or No. 7 cylinder is in the firing position. This will be when the distributor rotor points to the wire leading to No. 3 or No. 7 spark plug.
5. Take off the fuel pump. Remove the front cover attaching bolts and lift the cover assembly off the front of the engine.
6. Install in the reverse order of removal. Tighten self-tapping water pump attaching screws to 13 ft. lbs., 5/16 in. front cover attaching bolts to 25 ft. lbs. and the four bottom bolts (cover plate) to 35 ft. lbs.

V6 Engines

The cover includes part of the water pump, oil pump and filter mounting and mounting for fuel pump.

1. Drain cooling system.
2. Disconnect heater hose, by-pass hose and both radiator hoses. Disconnect oil pressure switch wire.
3. Remove crankshaft pulley, fan and fan pulley, and all belts.
4. Remove distributor cap, vacuum hose, generator and mounting bracket.
5. Remove fuel pump hoses, fuel pump and two front oil pan bolts.
6. Remove nine cover-to-block attaching bolts and remove cover.

NOTE: whenever the front cover is removed, it is necessary to remove the oil pump cover and to completely pack the pump gear housing with petrolatum. This is to prime the oil pump and ensure immediate oil pressure to engine parts.

7. Install new cover gasket with a good sealing compound.
8. Install the cover.
9. Oil attaching bolts and install. Torque evenly to 30-35 ft. lbs.
10. Apply special seal lubricant on pulley seal surface.
11. Install pulley, pulley bolt and pull the pulley into place. Torque to 140-160 ft. lbs.
12. Connect oil pressure switch.
13. Install generator mounting bracket and adjust the link.
14. Install fuel pump, using a new gasket and sealer.
15. Oil fuel pump bolts and torque to 20-25 ft. lbs.
16. Connect fuel lines.
17. Install distributor (see distributor paragraph in this section.)
18. Connect vacuum advance hose and primary wire.
19. Install distributor cap and wires.
20. Connect all of the hoses.
21. Install fan pulley, fan and four bolts, torquing to 20 ft. lbs.
22. Install and adjust belts.
23. Refill and bleed cooling system.

1966-72, OHV 6 Models

1. Remove the crankshaft pulley. Remove the oil pan.
2. Remove the timing case cover attaching screws and the two bolts that are installed from inside the engine through the front main bearing cap to hold the cover at the bottom.
3. Remove the cover and gasket. Pry the old seal out of the front side of the cover with a large screwdriver.
4. Install the new seal so that the open end of the seal is toward the inside of the cover. When reinstalling, be careful that cover is positioned to hold seal concentric to the shaft.
5. Tighten the screws and the two bolts inside the engine to 6-7½ ft. lbs.

Front Cover Oil Seal

Removal and Installation (Cover not removed)

1. Remove belts.
2. Remove pulley and hubs.
3. Carefully pry out old seal with screwdriver or thin punch, using care not to damage shaft surface.
4. Coat outside diameter of new seal with proper sealer.
5. Drive in seal with proper tool, using care not to distort it nor damage mating surfaces or shaft.
6. Reinstall removed parts and adjust belts.

⏻ CHILTON TIME-SAVER

A different approach to this situation, and certainly a quicker one, is as follows:

1. **Very carefully center punch and drill two ¼ in. holes in opposite sides of the camshaft gear hub.**
2. **Break the fiber part of the camshaft gear away from the steel hub.**
3. **Split the steel hub with a cold chisel at the two newly drilled holes.**
4. **Remove broken camshaft gear and clean entire timing case area.**
5. **Place the new gear on the camshaft to line up with the keyway and the gear timing marks.**

NOTE: be sure to allow for the helical cut on the gear when aligning the marks for timing.

6. **Have a reliable helper, with the aid of a pinch bar, buck up against one of the camshaft lobes from underneath. (The success of the job depends upon this man's care in holding forward thrust on the camshaft. Failure on his part will allow the camshaft to be forced back and dislodge the oil sealing expansion plug in the back at the rear of the camshaft.)**
7. **With the aid of a 1¼ in. socket and a lead hammer, tap the new gear into place on the camshaft.**

CAUTION: The use of a dial indicator will reduce the possibility of driving the gear too far onto the camshaft. This would alter the desired camshaft thrust clearance of .001 in. to .005 in. Use care when approaching the final position of the gear on the shaft because It Is Impossible to increase the thrust clearance without pulling the new gear. In the absence of a dial indicator, this end thrust can be measured with a feeler gauge. In this case the thrust clearance is to be measured between the camshaft gear hub and the thrust plate. A feeler gauge strip, inserted in either of the two large gear holes, will reach this point.

Timing Gear Replacement

1966-72, OHV 6 Engines—F-85

Timing gears are arranged so that (unless deliberately disturbed) the valve timing will remain as set at the factory. Unless the gears are badly worn or seriously damaged, the valve timing will remain constant within reasonable limits.

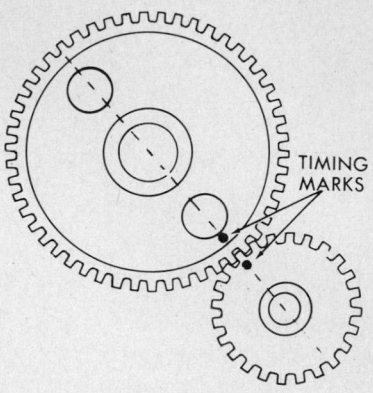

Timing marks—inline 6

If it becomes necessary to replace the timing gears due to wear or damage, remove the radiator core, disconnect the front motor mounts and jack up the front of the engine. Remove the fan belt, fan pulley, oil pan and timing case cover.

NOTE: it is recommended that the camshaft be removed from the car in order to remove and replace the gear in an arbor press.

To replace the gear by removing the camshaft, remove the rocker arm assemblies and the distributor, take out all of the pushrods and take out all of the lifters. The camshaft may then be pulled out toward the front of the engine. It will be necessary to retime the ignition.

Runout of the timing gear should not exceed .004 in. Backlash between the two gears should not be less than .004 in. nor more than .006 in. Endplay of the thrust plate should be .001-.005 in.

Engine Lubrication

Oil Pan R & R

All 1965-71 Olds and F-85 350, 425 and 455 Cu. In. Engines All 1970-72 F-85 Except 455 Cu. In.

1. Disconnect the negative battery cable and remove the dipstick.
2. On 1968-72 models, remove the upper radiator support and fan shroud attaching screws.
3. Raise the car on a hoist and drain the crankcase.
4. On F-85, Cutlass, 442 and Vista Cruiser models, disconnect the exhaust pipe from the right exhaust manifold. On 88 and 98 models lower the relay rod by disconnecting the idler arm or pitman arm.
5. Disconnect the engine mounts and carefully jack the front of the engine up as far as possible using a suitable tool. The special

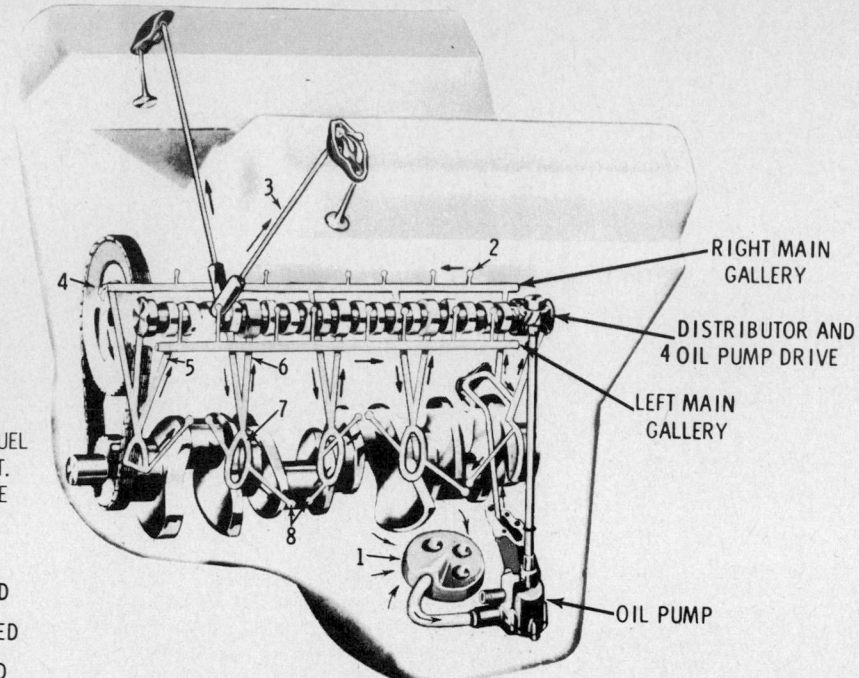

1. OIL PICK-UP
2. LIFTER FEED
3. ROCKER ARM VALVE TIP FEED
4. SPLASH LUBE TO TIMING CHAIN, FUEL PUMP CAM & DIST. & OIL PUMP DRIVE
5. LEFT MAIN GALLERY FEED
6. CAM BEARING FEED
7. MAIN BEARING FEED
8. ROD BEARING FEED

RIGHT MAIN GALLERY

DISTRIBUTOR AND OIL PUMP DRIVE

LEFT MAIN GALLERY

OIL PUMP

Engine lubrication —V8 (© Olds Div. G.M. Corp.)

lifting tool bolts to the front of the block.

6. Remove crossover pipe and starter.
7. Remove oil pan attaching bolts, rotate the crankshaft until the No. 1 crankshaft throw is up, then remove the oil pan.
8. When installing, apply sealer to both sides of pan gasket and install on block. Install the front and rear (rubber) seals. Install the pan, tightening 5/16 in. bolts to 15 ft. lbs. and 1/4 in. bolts to 10 ft. lbs.
9. Reverse Steps 1 through 6 to complete installation.

1969 400 Cu. In.
1970-72 F-85 455 Cu. In.

1. Disconnect the negative battery cable and disconnect the fan shroud.
2. Raise the car on a hoist and drain the crankcase.
3. Remove the driveshaft.
4. Disconnect the exhaust pipe and starter.
5. Install a rear engine support bar and remove the flywheel housing inspection cover.
6. Disconnect modulator line, speedometer cable, oil cooler lines, solenoid wire and linkage.
7. Remove transmission crossmember, transmission and flywheel.
8. Raise the front of the engine.
9. Remove the right engine mount and raise the engine 2 in. Install a wedge block.
10. Loosen the left engine mount-to-block bolts enough to allow

for the removal of the oil pan bolts.

11. Remove the oil pan bolts, free the pan from the block and disconnect the oil pump.
12. Remove the oil pan and pump.
13. To install, clean all gasket surfaces and apply sealer to both sides of the pan gaskets. Install the gaskets on the block.
14. Install front and rear (rubber) seals.
15. Hold the oil pan in approximate position and install the oil pump, tightening bolts to 35 ft. lbs.
16. Install the oil pan, tightening 5/16 in. bolts to 15 ft. lbs. and 1/4 in. bolts to 10 ft. lbs.
17. Install the flywheel.
18. Remove the wedge block and tighten engine mount to engine block bolts to 50 ft. lbs.
19. Remove front engine support tool and install the transmission.
20. Install transmission crossmember and remove the rear engine support tool.
21. Connect modulator lines, speedometer cable, oil cooler lines, solenoid wire and linkage.
22. Connect the starter and exhaust pipe.
23. Install the driveshaft.
24. Lower car and fill the crankcase.
25. Connect the fan shroud and connect the battery negative cable.

1966-68 400 Cu. In.

1. Disconnect the battery negative cable and remove the upper radiator baffle.
2. Remove driveshaft, transmission

crossmember, transmission and flywheel.

3. Disconnect the left exhaust pipe and the starter.
4. Disconnect the right engine mount. Raise both the front and rear of the engine, tilting it to the left and using the left engine mount as a pivot.
5. Install a rear engine support bar, inserting a 1 in. block between the bar and the right rear corner on the oil pan to obtain additional lift on the right side.
6. Raise the front of the engine. The engine must rock when raised.
7. Raise the right side of the engine approximately 2½ in. and insert a block between the upper and lower right engine mounts.
8. Remove the support bar from the rear of the engine.
9. Remove oil pan attaching bolts and remove oil pan toward the rear of the engine. No. 1 and No. 2 connecting rod journals should be at 4 or 7 o'clock position as viewed from the front of the engine.
10. To install, follow Step 8 of the 350, 425, and 455 cu. in. engine procedure and reverse Steps 1 through 8 above.

1966-72 OHV 6

1. Disconnect battery positive cable, fuel flex line at the fuel pump and starter leads at the starter.
2. Remove upper radiator support and bracket to upper hose. On cars with air conditioning,

remove the fan and clutch assembly.

3. Remove front motor mount bracket to motor mount bolts.

4. Raise the car on a hoist and drain crankcase.

5. Disconnect automatic transmission linkage and remove flywheel cover and starter.

6. Disconnect exhaust pipe at the manifold.

7. Position timing mark notch at the 6 o'clock position.

8. Raise the engine with a jack at the crankshaft damper and remove the right engine mount with bracket.

9. Remove the oil pan attaching bolts and the oil pan. It may be necessary to raise the engine further to get the pan out. Be careful not to damage cowl mounted parts.

10. To install, reverse the above procedure. Use new gaskets.

Oil Pump

On all engines except the V6, the oil pump is mounted to the bottom of the block and is accessible only by removing the oil pan. On the V6 however, the oil pump is attached to the timing (front) cover and may be removed easily after removing the oil filter.

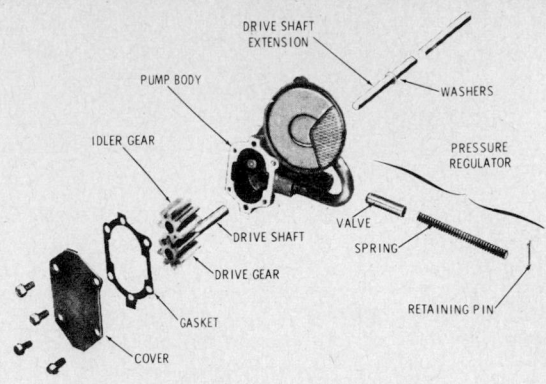

Oil pump—V8 (© Olds. Div. G.M. Corp.)

On OHV 6 and V8 engines, remove the oil pan as described in the previous paragraph, then unbolt and remove the oil pump and screen as an assembly. On the OHV 6 the pickup tube has a bolt-attached bracket.

To disassemble the oil pump, remove the cover attaching screws, cover and pump gears. On V8 engines the driveshaft extension has a rubber washer which cannot be removed. If the washer is damaged or not positioned 1-11/32 in. from the end of the shaft, replace the shaft and washer as an assembly. Remove the pressure regulating valve retaining pin, spring and related parts. Clean all components thoroughly in solvent. Replace scored or damaged gears.

If the end clearance between the gears and the cover is excessive (over 0.006″), the gears and cover must be replaced. Replace drive gear and shaft if the shaft is loose in its bore. Check that the pressure regulator valve operates freely in its bore. The pickup tube and screen are serviced as an assembly.

Rear Main Bearing Oil Seal

V8 Engine

The crankshaft need not be removed to replace the rear main bearing upper oil seal. Drain the crankcase and remove the oil pan and rear main bearing cap. Using a blunt-ended tool, drive the upper seal into its groove on each side until it is tightly packed. This is usually 1/4-3/4 in. Cut pieces of new seal 1/16 in. longer than required to fill the grooves and install, packing into place. Carefully trim any protruding seal, being sure not to scratch or damage the bearing surface. Install a new seal in the bearing cap and install cap, tightening bolts to 120 ft. lbs. Install the oil pan.

Top Half, Rear Main Bearing Oil Seal Replacement

The following method has proven a distinct advantage in most cases.

1. Drain engine oil and remove oil pan.

2. Remove rear main bearing cap.

3. With a 6 in. length of 3/16 in. brazing rod, drive up on either exposed end of the top half oil seal. When the opposite end of the seal starts to protrude, have a helper grasp it with pliers and pull gently while the driven end is being tapped. It is surprising how easily most of these seals can be removed by this method.

New Woven Fabric-Type Seal Installation

1. Obtain a 12 in. piece of copper wire (about the same gauge as that used in the strands of an insulated battery cable).

2. Thread one strand of this wire through the new seal, about 1/2 in. from the end, bend back and make secure.

3. Thoroughly saturate the new seal with engine oil.

4. Push the copper wire up through the oil seal groove until it comes down on the opposite side of the bearing.

5. Pull (with pliers) on the protruding copper wire while the crankshaft is being turned and the new seal is slowly fed into place.

CAUTION: this snaking operation slightly reduces the diameter of the new seal and care will be used to keep the seal from slipping too far through the top half of the bearing.

6. When an equal amount of seal is extending from each side, cut off the copper wire close to the seal and tamp both ends of the seal up into the groove. This will tend to expand the seal again.

NOTE: don't worry about the copper wire left in the groove, it is too soft to cause damage.

7. Replace the seal in the cap in the usual way and replace the oil pan.

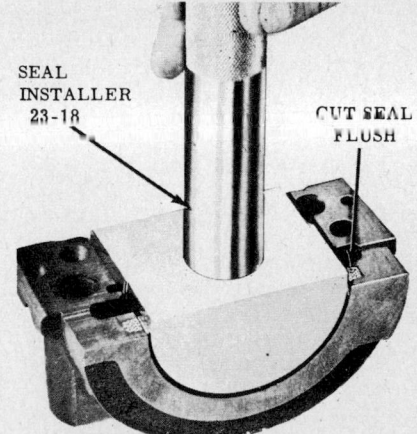

SEAL INSTALLER 23-18

CUT SEAL FLUSH

Installing oil seal
(© Oldsmobile Div. G.M. Corp.)

OHV 6 Engine—1966-72

The rear main bearing oil seal is of moulded design and can be replaced (both halves) without removal of the crankshaft.

NOTE: always replace both halves as a unit. Install with the lip facing toward front of the engine.

1. With oil pan removed, remove the rear main bearing cap.
2. Remove oil seal from the groove by lifting the end tab, then clean seal groove.
3. Lubricate the lip and O.D. of a new seal with engine oil. Keep oil off the parting line surface.
4. Insert seal into cap and roll into place with fingers. Use light pressure on the seal to prevent cutting the O.D. of the seal with the sharp edges of the groove. Be sure the tabs of the seal are properly located in the cross grooves.
5. To remove upper half of seal, use a small hammer to tap a brass pin punch on one end of seal until it protrudes far enough to be removed with pliers.
6. Lubricate the lip and O.D. of a new seal with engine oil. Keep oil off parting line surface. Gradually push with a hammer handle, while turning crankshaft, until seal is rolled into place. Be careful that seal bead on O.D. of seal is not cut.
7. Install rear main bearing cap (with new seal) and torque to specifications. Be sure cross seal tabs are in place and properly seated.

Connecting Rods And Pistons

Piston Assembly Removal

1. Remove cylinder head.
2. Remove oil pan.
3. Examine cylinder bores for top ridge. If ridge exists, remove it before taking pistons out.
4. Number all the pistons, connecting rods and caps. Starting at the front, the right bank is numbered 2-4-6-8. The left bank is numbered, 1-3-5-7.
With the V6 engine, the right bank is numbered 2-4-6; the left bank, 1-3-5, from the front. The OHV inline 6 engine has an order of 1-2-3-4-5-6.
5. With No. 4 crankpin straight down, remove cap and bearing shell from No. 1 connecting rod. Install connecting rod bolt guides to hold upper half of the bearing shell in place.
6. Push piston and rod assembly up out of the cylinder. Then remove bolt guides and reinstall cap and bearing shell on the rod.
7. Remove the remaining rod and piston assemblies in the same manner.
8. Carefully remove oil rings with piston ring expander.
9. Carefully press out the old pin.

NOTE: check the cylinder bores for out-of-round, taper or other damage. Any cylinders requiring attention may be bored or honed the same as any conventional cast iron cylinder block. Maximum allowable taper is .010 in.

Fitting Rings and Pins

1. When new rings are installed without reboring the cylinders, cylinder wall glaze should be broken. This can be done by using the finest grade stones in a cylinder hone.
2. New piston rings must be checked for clearance in piston grooves and for cap in cylinder bores.
3. When fitting new rings to new pistons the side clearance for compression rings should be .002 to .004 in. for V8 and .003 to .005 in. for 6 cylinder engines. Side clearance of the oil ring should be .0001 to .0051 for V8 engines through 1967, .0035 to .0095 for 6 cylinder engines through 1967, .001 to .005 for later 6 cylinder and 350 cu. in. V8, .001 to .010 for 400 cu. in. V8 and .002 to .008 for 455 cu. in. V8.
4. Check end gap of compression rings by placing them in the bore in which they will operate. Then push them to the bottom of the bore with a piston. Now measure the end gap in each ring. The end gap should be no less than .015 in.
5. If piston pin bosses are worn out of round or oversize, the piston and pin should be replaced. Oversize pins are not practical because the pin is a press fit in the connecting rod. Piston pins must fit the piston with an easy finger push at 70°F.
6. In assembling the piston to the connecting rod, a press is ideal. However, substitutes are available that will serve the purpose.
7. If the rod assembly is to go into the left bank, the boss on the rod and cap go toward the rear of the engine. If the rod assembly is to go into the right bank, the boss on the rod and cap go toward the front of the engine. In both cases, the connecting rod bearing oil spurt holes point up.

Connecting Rod Bearings

1. Remove connecting rod cap with bearing shell. Wipe all oil from the bearing area.
2. Place a piece of plastigage lengthwise along the bottom center of the lower bearing shell. Then install cap with bearing shell and torque the bolt nuts to specifications.

NOTE: do not turn crankshaft.

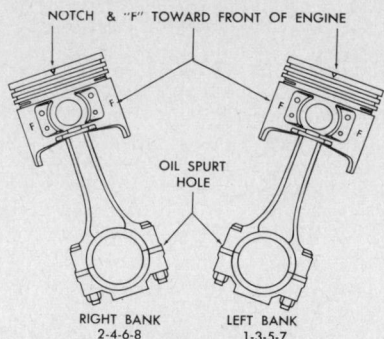

Piston and rod assembly—V8 except 215

3. Remove the cap and shell. The gauge material will be found flattened and adhering to either the bearing shell or the crankpin. Do not remove it.
4. Using the scale that comes with the gauge, measure the flattened gauge material at its widest point. The number within the graduation which comes closest to the width of the gauging material indicates the bearing to crankpin clearance in thousandths of an inch.
5. Desired clearance for a new bearing is given in the specifications. If the bearing has been in service, it is wise to install a new bearing if clearance exceeds .0035 in.
6. If a new bearing is required, try a standard, then each undersize bearing in turn until one is found that is within specifications.
7. With the proper bearing selected,

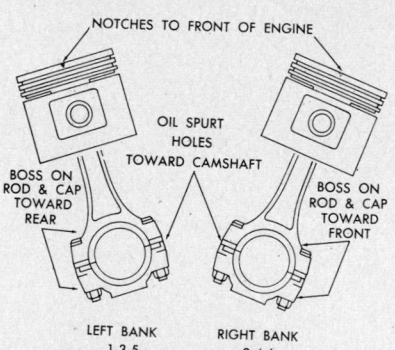

Piston and rod assembly—V6 225

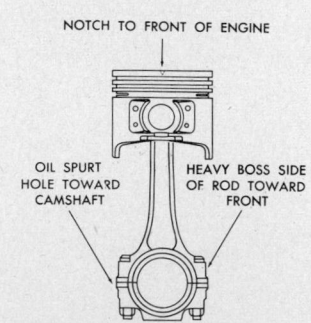

Piston and rod assembly—inline 6

clean off the gauging material, reinstall the bearing cap and torque.

8. After the bearing cap has been torqued, it should be possible to move the connecting rod back and forth on the crankpin, the extent of end clearance.

Piston Assembly Installation

1. Carefully assemble the piston to the connecting rod (press in the pin).
2. Remove piston and rod from the press. Rock the piston on the pin to be sure pin or piston boss was not damaged during the pressing operation.
3. Install ring expander in lower ring groove. Position the ends of the expander above the piston pin where groove is not slotted. The ends of the expander must butt together.
4. Install oil ring rails over expander with gaps up on same side of piston as oil spurt hole in connecting rod.
5. Install compression rings, (with a ring expander) in top and center groove.
6. Coat all bearing surfaces, rings and piston skirt with engine oil.
7. Position the crankpin of the cylinder being worked on, down.
8. Remove connecting rod bearing cap and with upper bearing shell correctly seated in the rod, install connecting rod bolt guides.
9. Make sure the gaps in the two oil ring rails are up toward the center of the engine. Make sure the gaps of the compression rings are not in line with each other or the oil ring rails. Be sure the ends of the oil ring spacer-expander are butted and not overlapped.
10. With a good ring compressor, install the piston and rod assembly into the cylinder bore and carefully tap down until the rod bearing is solidly seated on the crankpin.
11. Remove the connecting rod bolt guides and install cap and lower bearing shell. Torque to 30-35 ft. lbs.
12. Install other piston and rod assemblies in the same manner. When the assemblies are all installed, the oil spurt holes will be up. The rib on the edge of the rod cap will be on the same side as the conical boss on the connecting rod web. These marks will be toward the other connecting rod on the same crankpin.
13. Accumulated end clearance between rod bearings on any crankpin should be .006 in.—.014 in.
14. Install oil screen and oil pan.
15. Install cylinder heads.

NOTE: before starting a new or reconditioned engine, it is advisable to pack the oil pump with petroleum jelly to insure pump priming for immediate lubrication. See Engine Front Cover Installation in this section.

Front Suspension

Front wheel alignment procedures, ball joint checks, wheel bearing and seal replacement procedures can be found in the Unit Repair Section.

Overall length, brake cylinder and tire size figures are in the General Chassis and Brake Specifications table.

Upper Control Arm R & R

1965-68 F-85

1. Raise car and place stands under frame.
2. Remove tire and wheel.
3. Place floor jack under lower control arm spring seat.
4. Remove ball joint stud from steering knuckle, by removing cotter pin and nut and with tool J-8806 or equivalent, press joint loose from knuckle.

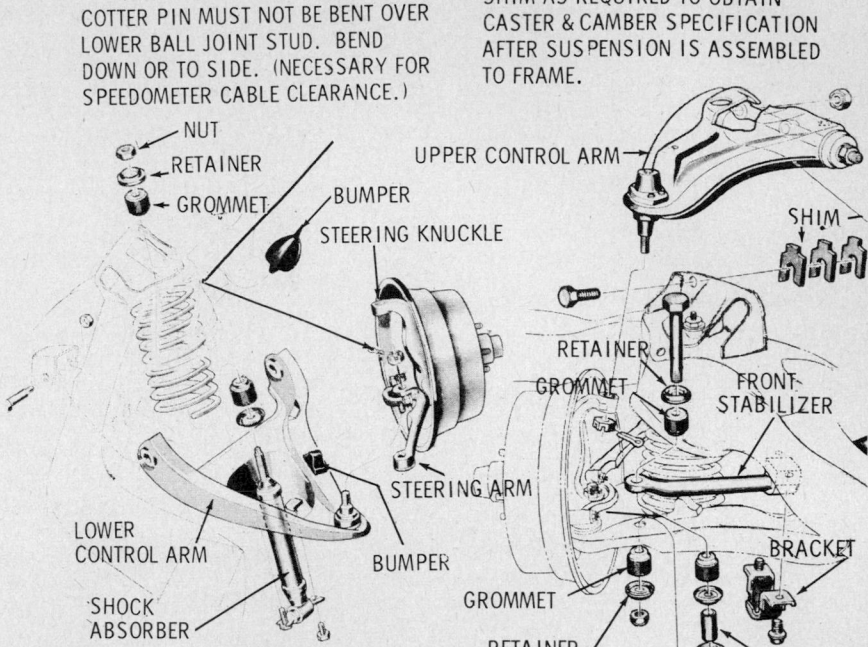

COTTER PIN MUST NOT BE BENT OVER LOWER BALL JOINT STUD. BEND DOWN OR TO SIDE. (NECESSARY FOR SPEEDOMETER CABLE CLEARANCE.)

SHIM AS REQUIRED TO OBTAIN CASTER & CAMBER SPECIFICATION AFTER SUSPENSION IS ASSEMBLED TO FRAME.

1965-72 front suspension—except F-85 (© Oldsmobile Div., G.M. Corp.)

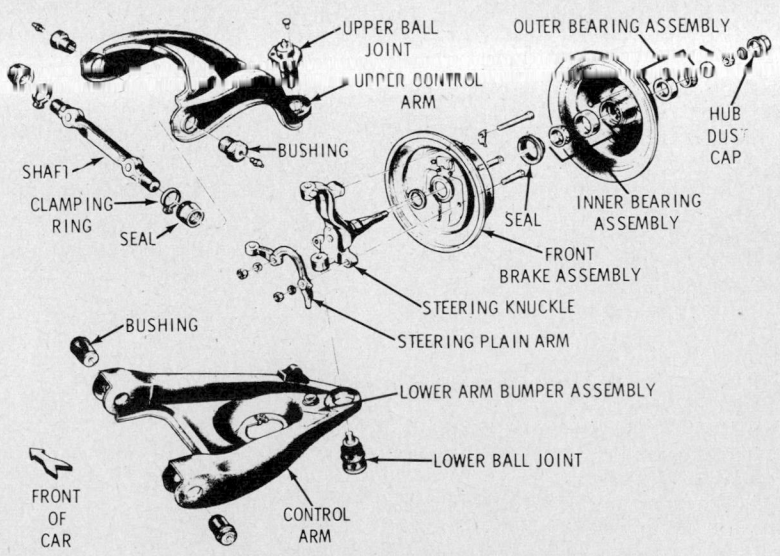

1965-72 front suspension—F-85 (© Oldsmobile Div., G.M. Corp.)

5. Support hub assembly and remove upper arm by sliding shaft
off end of bolts.

NOTE: mark or locate alignment
shims for easier reassembly.

6. Attach arm assembly to frame
using original shims. Torque to
65 ft. lbs.

7. Install ball joint. Torque nut to
40 ft. lbs. (minimum).

8. Install hub, drum and wheel
assembly and lower car to floor.

Lower Control Arm and/or Front Spring R & R

All Models

1. Raise front of car and support by
stands under frame.
2. Remove tire and wheel.
3. Disconnect stabilizer link from
lower arm.
4. Remove shock absorber.
5. Place floor jack under lower arm,
between spring seat and ball
joint. Tool BT-6505 may be
used to compress spring.
6. Disconnect lower control arm ball
joint from knuckle.
7. Slowly lower floor jack until
spring is fully extended and remove spring.
8. To reinstall, tape insulator to top
of spring.
9. While holding spring and insulator against pilot in front cross
bar, tilt spring so it will pivot in
lower arm. Rotate spring so
bottom coil will index with edge
of hole in arm spring seat. Spring
should not cover any portion of
hole.
10. With floor jack positioned between seat and ball joint, raise
arm until ball joint is tight in
knuckle. Install ball joint nut and
tighten to 35-60 ft. lbs.
11. Install shock absorber.
12. Connect stabilizer link.
13. Install wheel and lower car.

Upper Control Arm R & R

Except 1965-68 F-85

1. Raise car and place stands under
frame.
2. Remove tire and wheel.
3. Remove speedometer cable from
knuckle where so equipped.
4. Place floor jack under lower control arm spring seat.
5. Remove ball joint stud from
steering knuckle, by removing
cotter pin and nut and with tool
J-8806 or equivalent, press joint
loose from knuckle.
6. Disconnect ground strap from
control arm.
7. Support hub assembly and remove upper arm by sliding shaft
off end of bolts.

NOTE: mark or locate alignment
shims for easier reassembly.

8. It is necessary to remove upper
control arm attaching bolts to
gain clearance to remove arm assembly. Tap bolt down with
brass drift. Pry bolt up with box
wrench. Using a suitable pry
bar and block of wood, pry bolts
from frame.

9. Remove control arm from car.
10. To reinstall, position bolts loosely
in frame and install pivot shaft
on bolts.
11. Install lock washers and nuts and
with brass drift, drive attaching
bolts into frame.
12. Install alignment shims, placing
them in position from which they
were removed. Torque nuts to 70
ft. lbs.
13. Connect ball joint and torque to
40 ft. lbs.
14. Attach ground strap.
15. Install speedometer cable and
wheel and tire and lower car to
floor.

Jacking, Hoisting

When supporting car on floor jack
or floor stand, the car should be supported at the suspension points only.
Under no condition should the car be
supported at extreme ends of frame
or side rail.

When using frame contact lift,
position contact pads to lift the side
rails at points shown on diagram.

Never use bumper jack other than
that provided with car.

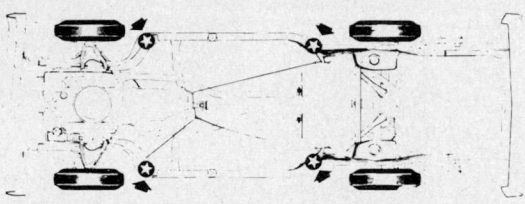

LIFT POINTS

Hoist contact points (© Oldsmobile Div. G.M. Corp.)

Steering Gear

Horn and Steering Wheel

Round center horn caps are removed by prying out. The horn pan
on deluxe steering wheels is removed
by either pulling down and out or by
removing screws from underneath.
Disconnect the battery when working
on the horn.

Extreme caution must be exercised
when removing the steering wheel:
the energy absorbing column is held
rigid by plastic fasteners which easily shear or loosen when abnormal
pressure is applied. Use a steering
wheel pulling tool. Carefully torque
steering wheel retaining nut to 35 ft.
lbs. when installing.

Steering Linkage

On all models two short tie-rods
are attached to either end of a cen-
tral relay rod. The pitman shaft has
a vertical axis and the pitman arm
rotates through a horizontal plane.
The tie-rods have ball studs at each
end and have an adjustable middle
section which is secured with clamps.

Use a suitable puller to remove the
pitman arm from the pitman shaft.
When assembling, install the pitman

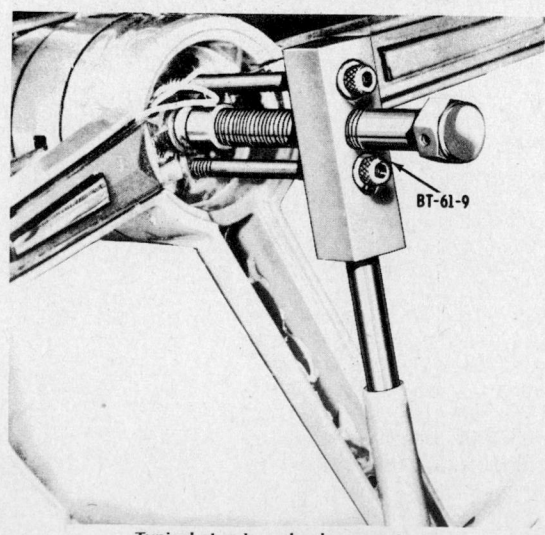

BT-61-9

Typical steering wheel removal
(© Oldsmobile Div. G.M. Corp.)

arm with the front wheels in the straight-ahead position and the steering wheel centered. Tighten the pitman arm retaining nut to 150 ft. lbs.

Whenever the tie-rod end is assembled to the tie-rod, make sure that an equal number of threads are exposed at each end of the tie rod sleeve. Tighten tie-rod clamp bolts to 15-20 ft. lbs. When disconnecting a linkage joint, never pry a wedge between the joint and the attached part. Always use a puller. When removing a tie-rod from a steering arm, loosen the ball stud nut, then tap the end of the steering arm with a hammer to free the tie-rod. Always use new seals when reassembling. Tighten tie-rod joint nuts to 45 ft. lbs.

Toe-in and steering wheel spoke alignment is obtained by turning the adjusting sleeves on the tie-rods which in turn lengthen or shorten the tie-rod assemblies.

Manual Steering

Instructions for the overhaul of the steering gear can be found in the Unit Repair Section.

Removal

1. Remove flex coupling flange attaching nuts and lockwashers.
2. Raise front of car and support under outer ends of lower control arms.
3. Remove pitman shaft nut and pull pitman arm from shaft with suitable puller.
4. Remove gear to frame mounting bolts. Clear speedometer cable and any linkage parts from interference and remove gear assembly from car.
5. Reinstall in reverse of the above. Torque gear to frame nuts to 60-80 ft. lbs. Torque pitman arm nut to 100-120 ft. lbs.

Power Steering

Troubleshooting and repair instructions for power steering gears are in the Unit Repair Section.

Power Steering Gear Removal

Disconnect the power steering hoses and remove the four bolts that hold the coupling to the power gear. Remove the nut from the cross-shaft and pull off the pitman arm.

From underneath the vehicle, remove the bolts that attach the power gear assembly to the frame and let the power gear come down through the bottom.

Power Steering Pump Removal

Remove and cap the two hoses that run through the pump, loosen the clamp bolts so that the pump can be slid along its adjusting slot and take the belt off. Remove the three

bolts that hold the pump bracket to the cylinder heads and lift off the pump.

Pitman Shaft Seal Replacement (with power steering gear in place in car)

1. Disconnect pitman arm from pitman shaft. Clean end of pitman shaft and housing. Tape the splines of the pitman shaft to keep them from cutting the seal. Use only one layer of tape. Too much tape will prevent passage of the seal. Using lock ring pliers, remove the seal retaining ring.
2. Start the engine and turn the steering wheel to the right so that the oil pressure in the housing will force the seals out. Catch the seal and the oil in a container. Turn off the engine when the two seals are out.
3. Inspect the two old seals for damage to the rubber covering on the outside diameter. If it seems scored or scratched, inspect the housing for burrs, etc. and remove them before installing the new seals.
4. Lubricate the two new seals with petroleum jelly. Put the one with a single lip in first, then put in a washer, drive seal in far enough to permit installation of double lip seal, washer and the seal retaining ring. The first seal is not supposed to bottom in its counterbore.
5. Fill reservoir to proper level, start engine, turn wheel to right, and check for leaks.
6. Remove the tape and reinstall the pitman arm. Tighten nut to 90-110 ft. lbs.

When installing a new belt, the tension should be set so that the pulley will slip in the belt when 40-45 ft. lbs. torque is applied to pulley nut. With a used belt the torque should be 30-35 ft. lbs.

Clutch

Clutch Pedal Adjustment

The clutch pedal should be adjusted so that there is 3/4 to 1 in. freeplay at the clutch pedal before the throwout bearing engages the clutch fingers. This adjustment is made under the car at the adjustable clutch rod just in front of the throwout fork. Loosen the jam nut and turn the adjusting screw until the desired clearance is obtained, then tighten the jam nut.

Clutch Removal

1. Remove transmission as described under Standard Transmission.

2. Remove clutch throwout bearing.
3. Disconnect release rod from fork. Disconnect boot from opening.
4. Release fork from ball stud and remove fork.
5. Mark clutch cover and flywheel for reassembly indexing.
6. Remove clutch cover attaching bolts. Be sure to loosen equally and gradually around cover to relieve unequal pressure on cover.
7. Lift out clutch assembly.
8. Assemble in reverse of above.

Standard Transmission

See the Capacities Table at the beginning of this section for manual transmission refill capacities. For manual transmission overhaul procedures, see the Unit Repair Section.

Transmission Removal

1. Disconnect throttle linkage and raise car. If applicable, disconnect T.C.S. switch.
2. Remove driveshaft.
3. Install engine support bar with appropriate adapter.
4. On console equipped floorshifts, disconnect shifter assembly at transmission, allowing this unit to remain in car. On regular floorshifts, remove floor pan seal. Insert a feeler gauge, remove shift lever and remove shifter with transmission.
   NOTE: this information does not pertain to column shifts.
5. Disconnect parking brake cables and remove cross support bar.
6. Disconnect speedometer cable.
7. Remove transmission upper and lower bolts.
8. Slide transmission rearward and remove. On models equipped with dual exhaust, it may be necessary to disconnect left exhaust pipe at the manifold.
9. Install by reversing procedure above.

Shift Linkage Adjustment

1965-68 3-Speed Column Shift

1. With transmission in neutral, loosen the swivel nuts on the shift rods at the transmission. Make sure that the shift rods are free to move in the swivels.
2. Insert a 3/16 in. rod through the shift levers and into the upper hole of the column bracket.
3. With transmission levers in neutral, tighten the swivel nuts to 23 ft. lbs.
4. Remove the 3/16 in. rod and check that the column shift levers are exactly in line, adjusting one of them if necessary.

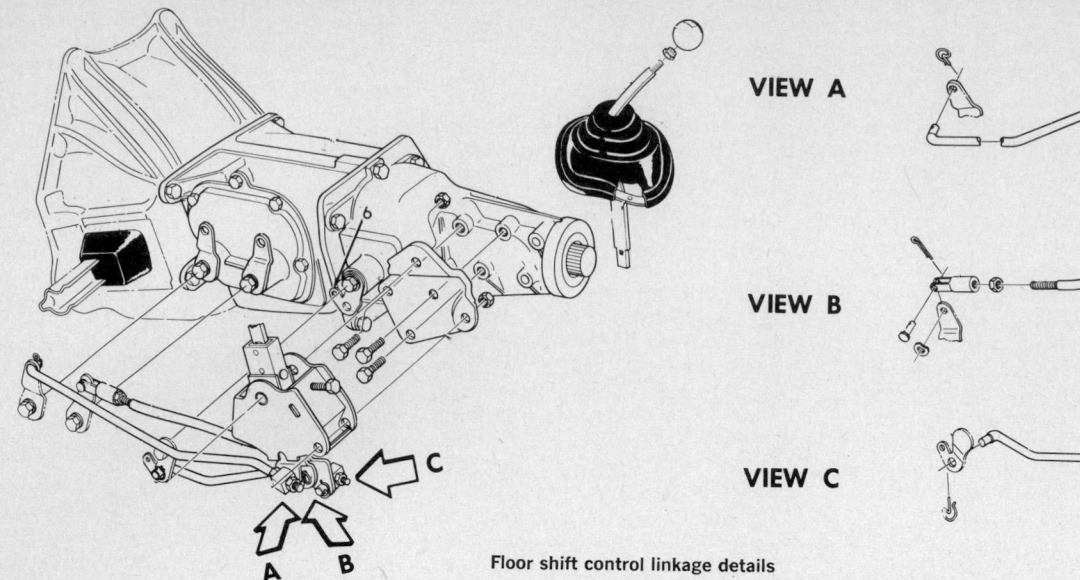

VIEW A

VIEW B

VIEW C

Floor shift control linkage details

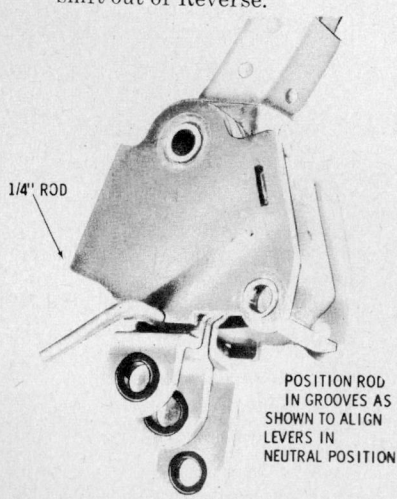

1/4" ROD

POSITION ROD
IN GROOVES AS
SHOWN TO ALIGN
LEVERS IN
NEUTRAL POSITION

Adjusting shift linkage—4-Speed
(© Olds. Div. G.M. Corp.)

5. Check the operation of the shift linkage.

1969-72 3-Speed Column Shift

1. With the transmission in reverse and the car raised on a hoist, loosen the swivel bolts on the shift rods at the transmission.
2. Check that the shift rods move freely in the swivels, then push up on the reverse shift rod until the detent in the column is felt and tighten the swivel bolt for the first-reverse rod to 20 ft. lbs.
3. With transmission in neutral, insert a 3/16 in. rod through the second-third shift lever and into the alignment hole. Tighten the swivel bolt for the second-third shift lever to 20 ft. lbs.
4. Lower the car and check the shift operation.
5. Place transmission in Reverse and the ignition in LOCK position. Check that the key can be removed, the wheel not turned and the transmission will not shift out of Reverse.

6. Turn the ignition to RUN position and place the transmission in second gear. Check that the ignition key cannot be removed and that the steering wheel will turn.

3- and 4-Speed Floor Shift

The linkage adjustment procedure is the same as that described above for the column shift type, with the exception that the shift levers are aligned with a 1/4 in. rod.

Automatic Transmission

Complete overhaul procedures for the Turbo-Hydramatic 350 and 400 automatic transmission can be found in the Unit Repair Section.

Transmission Removal
Turbo Hydra-Matic 400

1. Remove flywheel cover.
2. Remove torque converter attaching bolts.
   NOTE: mark flywheel and converter so they can be installed in same position.
3. Install engine support bar.
4. Disconnect solenoid wires and manual shift linkage at side of transmission.
5. Disconnect oil cooler lines, vacuum modulator line and filler pipe.
6. Disconnect parking brake cable.
7. Remove driveshaft assembly.
8. Disconnect exhaust pipe bracket at rear of crossmember.
9. Position jack under transmission.
10. Remove crossmember.
11. Remove transmission to block attaching bolts.
12. Move transmission away from engine, using tool (J-21364) to hold converter in place.

13. Lower transmission and remove from car.
14. Install by reversing procedure above.

Turbo Hydra-Matic 350

1. Inside the car, slide the clip on the downshift cable to the end of the cable.
2. Remove transmission oil level dipstick.
3. Hoist car.
4. Remove bolt and remove downshift cable from link, plugging hole.
5. Remove transmission cooler lines.
6. Remove flywheel cover pan and three bolts holding the converter to the flywheel.
7. Disconnect modulator line and the transmission controlled spark switch, if so equipped.
8. Remove speedometer clip and driven gear, plugging hole.
9. Remove cotter pin and manual shift linkage.
10. Remove driveshaft.
11. Remove transmission mount support bolts at transmission mount and frame.
12. Raise transmission with a jack and remove support.
13. Lower transmission slightly and remove transmission to engine bolts.
14. Remove transmission by lowering and moving rearward, using a special tool to hold converter.
15. Install by reversing procedure above.

Jetaway

1. Remove transmission filler pipe.
2. Raise car on hoist.
3. Disconnect transmission control.
4. Disconnect manual rod from transmission lever.
5. Remove propeller shaft assembly.
6. Remove flywheel dust cover.

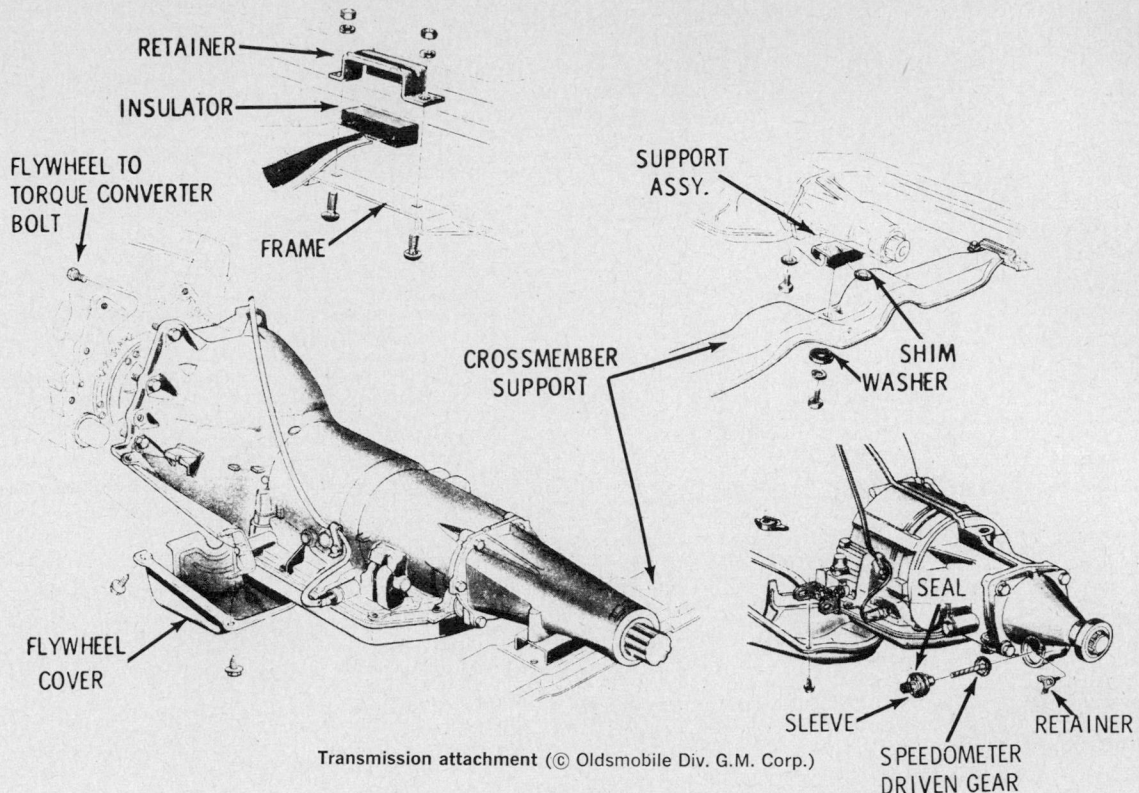

Transmission attachment (© Oldsmobile Div. G.M. Corp.)

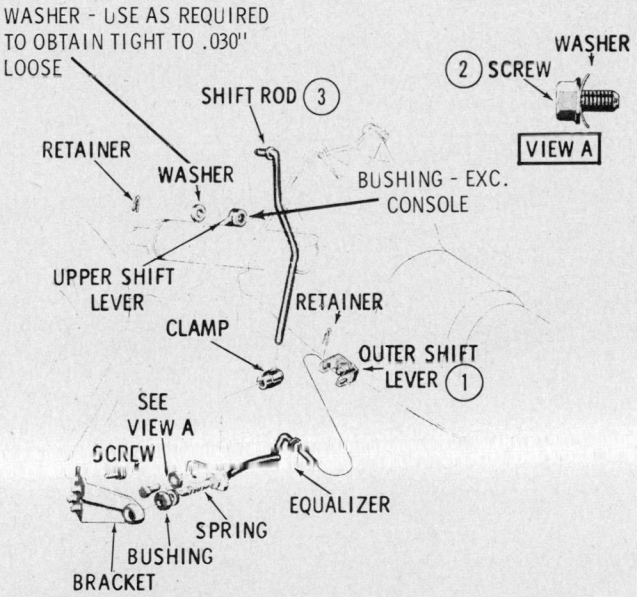

Column shift linkage adjustment for Turbo Hydra-matic transmission
(© Oldsmobile Div. G.M. Corp.)

SHIFT ROD ADJUSTMENT

1. Set transmission outer lever in drive position.
2. Hold upper shift lever against drive position stop in upper steering column (do not raise lever).
3. Tighten screw in clamp on lower end of shift rod to specified torque.
4. Check Operation:
   A. With key in "run" position and transmission in "reverse" be sure that key cannot be removed and that steering wheel is not locked.
   B. With key in "lock" position and shift lever in "park," be sure that key can be removed, that steering wheel is locked, and that the transmission remains in park when the steering column is locked.

7. Install engine support bar.
8. Remove bolts at rear transmission mount.
9. Remove attaching brackets and remove cross support bar.
10. Disconnect oil cooler lines and cap immediately.
11. Disconnect modulator line.
12. Disconnect speedometer cable.
13. Remove three flywheel to converter attaching bolts.
14. Support transmission with unit lift and remove transmission to flywheel housing bolts.
15. Remove transmission by moving rearward and lowering from car, using a special tool to hold converter in place.
16. Install by reversing procedure above.

Shift Linkage Adjustment

Turbo Hydra-Matic and Jetaway

The proper linkage adjustment is obtained by positioning the shift lever in the D or Drive position at the column or console, whichever the case, and positioning the manual lever in the D detent at the transmission. See the illustrations for procedure.

U Joints, Drive Lines

Cross and bearing-type universals

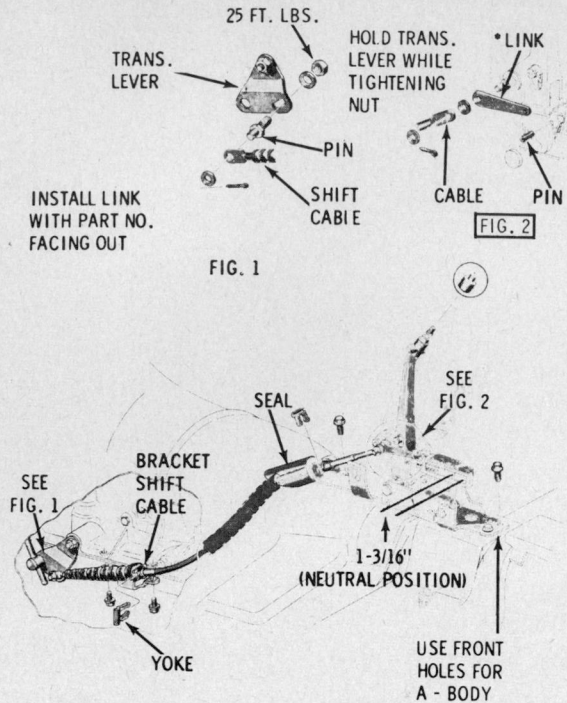

TRANS. LEVER

25 FT. LBS.

HOLD TRANS. LEVER WHILE TIGHTENING NUT

*LINK

PIN

SHIFT CABLE

CABLE   PIN

FIG. 2

INSTALL LINK WITH PART NO. FACING OUT

FIG. 1

SEE FIG. 2

SEAL

BRACKET SHIFT CABLE

SEE FIG. 1

1-3/16" (NEUTRAL POSITION)

YOKE

USE FRONT HOLES FOR A - BODY

Console shift linkage adjustment for Turbo Hydra-Matic transmission
(© Oldsmobile Div. G.M. Corp.)

SHIFT CABLE ADJUSTMENT

1. Loosen shift rod clamp screw, loosen pin in transmission manual lever.
2. Place shift lever in "P" position, place transmission manual lever in "P" position and ignition key in lock position.
3. Pull shift rod lightly against lock stop and tighten clamp screw.
4. Move pin in manual transmission lever to give "free pin" fit and tighten attaching nut.
5. Check Operation:
   A. Move shift handle into each gear position and see that transmission manual lever is also in detent position.
   B. With key in "run" position and transmission in "reverse," be sure that key cannot be removed and that steering wheel is not locked.
   C. With key in "lock" position and transmission in "park," be sure that key can be removed and that steering wheel is locked.

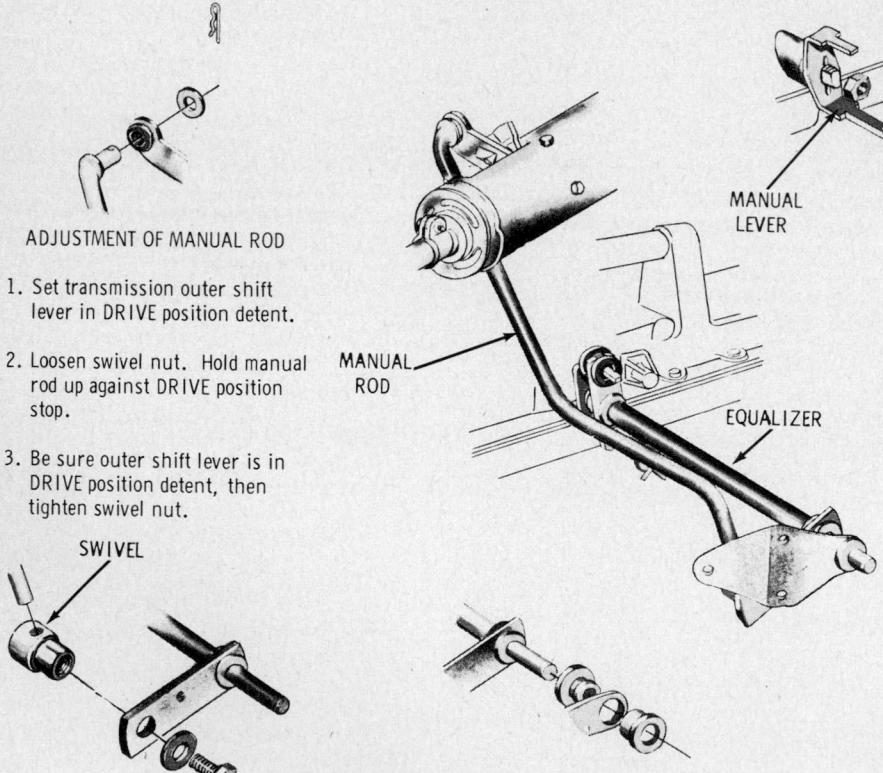

ADJUSTMENT OF MANUAL ROD

1. Set transmission outer shift lever in DRIVE position detent.

2. Loosen swivel nut. Hold manual rod up against DRIVE position stop.

3. Be sure outer shift lever is in DRIVE position detent, then tighten swivel nut.

SWIVEL

MANUAL LEVER

MANUAL ROD

EQUALIZER

Column shift linkage adjustment for Jetaway transmission (© Oldsmobile Div. G.M. Corp.)

yokes by two lock plates, one on each side.

5. Take out the nut that holds the lock plate in position and lift off the lock plate. The bearing can then be driven from one side across to the other which will drive the opposite side bearing out. Once the opposite side bearing has been removed, drive on the cross, itself, to drive out the first bearing.

6. It is recommended, when reinstalling bearings, that an arbor press or a very heavy C-clamp be used, because driving on them distorts the outer race of the needle bearings.

Drive Shaft Torque

U-bolts 16 ft. lbs. Center bearing to body 14 ft. lbs. Slip yoke nut 50-75 ft. lbs.

Constant Velocity Joint

This joint consists of two universal joints closely coupled with a coupling yoke. There is a centering ball socket between the two joints which maintains their relative position. The ball is integral with the shaft and, if

are used on all Oldsmobile models.

Driveshaft and Universal Joint Removal

1. Remove the four bolts that hold the rear universal filler blocks to the pinion shaft flange and pry the universal joint off the pinion flange, lowering the back end of

the shaft to the floor.

2. Tape the bearing blocks to the universal joints so that they don't get lost or dirty.

3. The front end of the shaft can then be slid off the back of the transmission shaft and carried to the bench.

4. The bearings are held into the

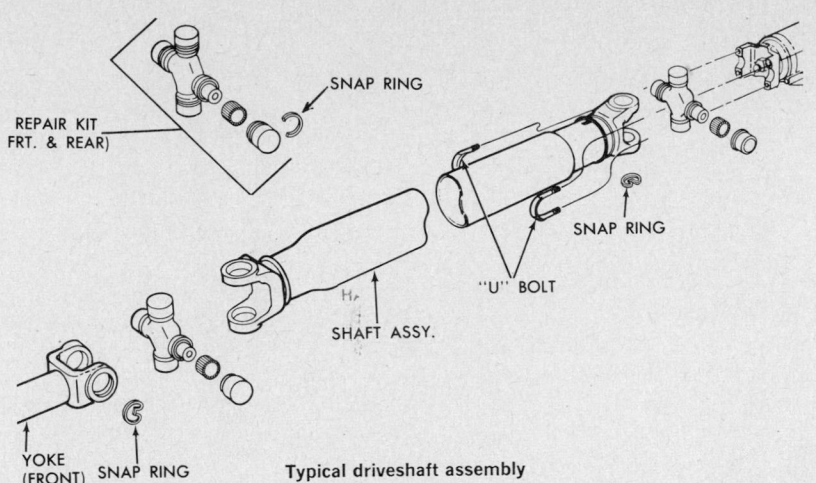

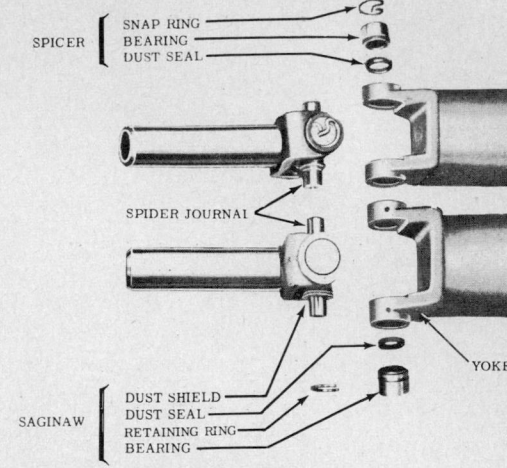

Typical driveshaft assembly

NOTE: RETAINING RINGS ARE USED ON SAGINAW WITH
SERVICE REPLACEMENT BEARINGS ONLY.

Driveshaft identification

damaged, the entire driveshaft must be replaced. The ball socket is integral with the flange yoke. The spring loaded ball seats are replaceable.

To disassemble the C.V. joint, first mark the relation of the flange yoke and driveshaft yoke, coupling ball support tube yoke. The cross bearing cups are pressed out in the usual manner, but they must be disassembled in the following sequence: rear of coupling yoke (2), differential flange yoke (2), front end of the coupling yoke (2) and driveshaft (2). Reassemble in the reverse of the order.

Drive Axle, Suspension

Differential overhaul procedures may be found in the Unit Repair Section.

Rear Shock Absorber Replacement

To replace the rear shock absorber, first raise the car and support the rear axle to prevent stretching of the brake hose. Then remove the nut from the lower end of the shock and tap the shock free from the bracket. To disconnect the shock at the top, remove the bolt or bolts and remove the shock.

NOTE: on extended station wagons, a retainer and grommet will be removed with the nut at the top.

Rear Coil Spring Replacement

1. Disconnect the shock absorber link and raise the car enough to take the pressure off the

coil spring and, reaching down through the coil spring, remove the bolt that holds the bottom of the spring to the insulating pad on the rear axle.
2. Working through the coil spring upward, take out the upper bolt that holds the spring to the frame at the top.
3. If the car has been raised sufficiently, the spring can be lifted out.

Improved Traction Axle Identification

The following is a simple way to distinguish between the standard and the improved type units.
1. Raise both rear wheels off the ground.
2. With the parking brake off, turn one wheel forward (by hand) and note the direction of rotation

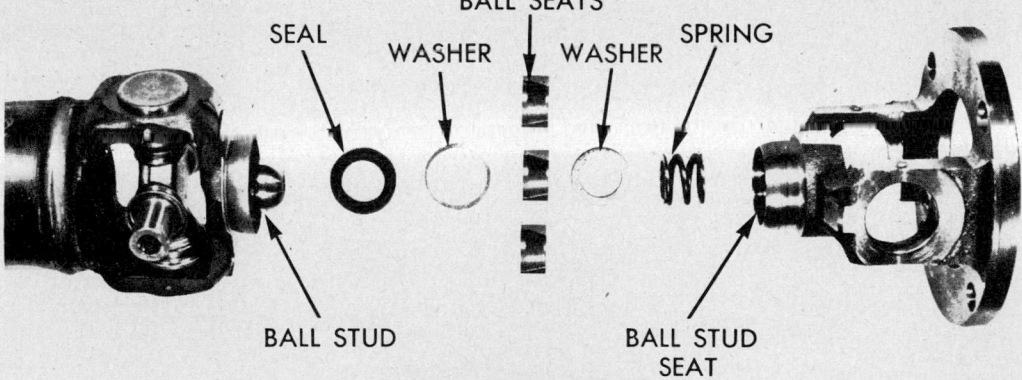

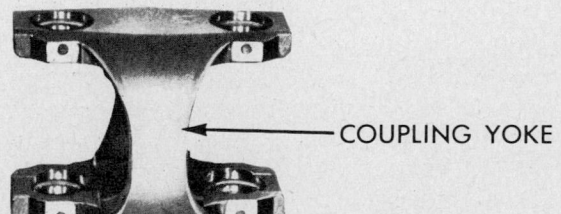

Constant velocity joint (©Olds. Div. G.M. Corp.)

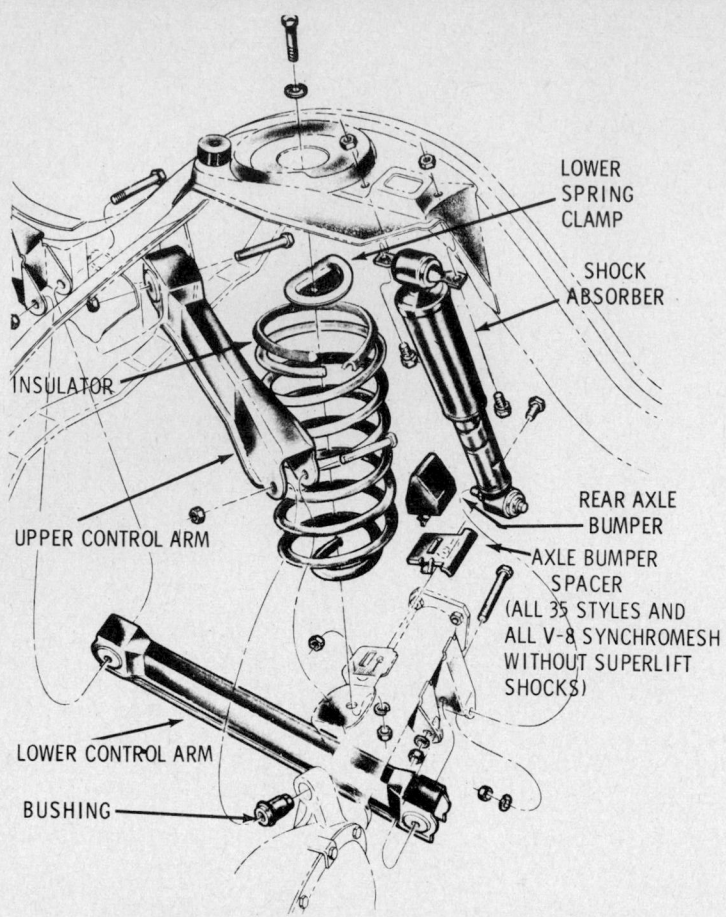

LOWER SPRING CLAMP

SHOCK ABSORBER

INSULATOR

UPPER CONTROL ARM

REAR AXLE BUMPER

AXLE BUMPER SPACER (ALL 35 STYLES AND ALL V-8 SYNCHROMESH WITHOUT SUPERLIFT SHOCKS)

LOWER CONTROL ARM

BUSHING

1965-71 rear suspension (© Oldsmobile Div., G.M. Corp.)

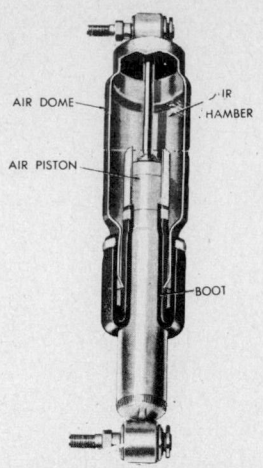

AIR DOME

IR HAMBER

AIR PISTON

BOOT

Superlift shock absorber
(© Oldsmobile Div. G.M. Corp.)

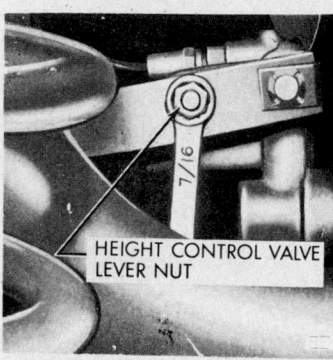

7/16

HEIGHT CONTROL VALVE LEVER NUT

Height control valve lever nut
(© Oldsmobile Div. G.M. Corp.)

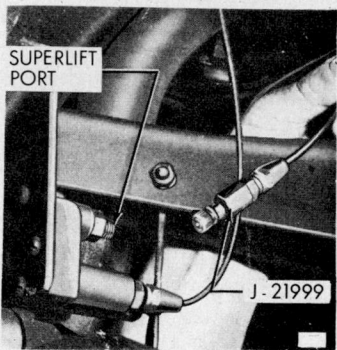

SUPERLIFT PORT

J - 21999

Superlift air supply line removal
(© Oldsmobile Div. G.M. Corp.)

of the other wheel.

3. If the other wheel turns in the same direction as the one being turned, the rear axle is of the improved type.

4. If the other wheel turns in the opposite direction, the axle is of standard design.

Rear Axle R & R

1. Depending on the model, remove fender panels, rear wheels, drums, axle shafts, resonator assembly and tail pipe, anything which is in the way. Raise the car on a hoist.

2. Unclip the brake hydraulic lines from the axle housing and remove the junction block from the housing.

3. Wire the brake backing plates to the frame.

4. Support the frame with stands and lower the axle housing assembly.

5. Remove the stabilizer bar, if so equipped.

6. Remove coil springs or remove the U-bolts from leaf spring.

7. Disconnect driveshaft.

8. Disconnect the control arm attaching bolts at the differential

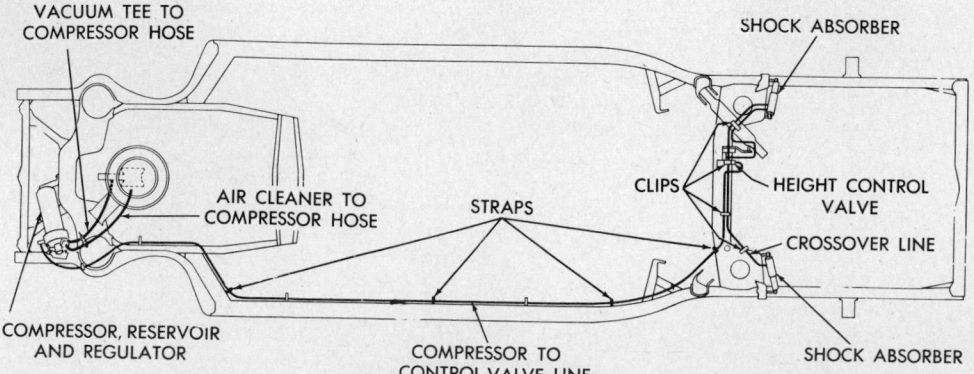

VACUUM TEE TO COMPRESSOR HOSE

SHOCK ABSORBER

AIR CLEANER TO COMPRESSOR HOSE

STRAPS

CLIPS

HEIGHT CONTROL VALVE

CROSSOVER LINE

COMPRESSOR, RESERVOIR AND REGULATOR

COMPRESSOR TO CONTROL VALVE LINE

SHOCK ABSORBER

Automatic Level Control (© Oldsmobile Div. G.M. Corp.)

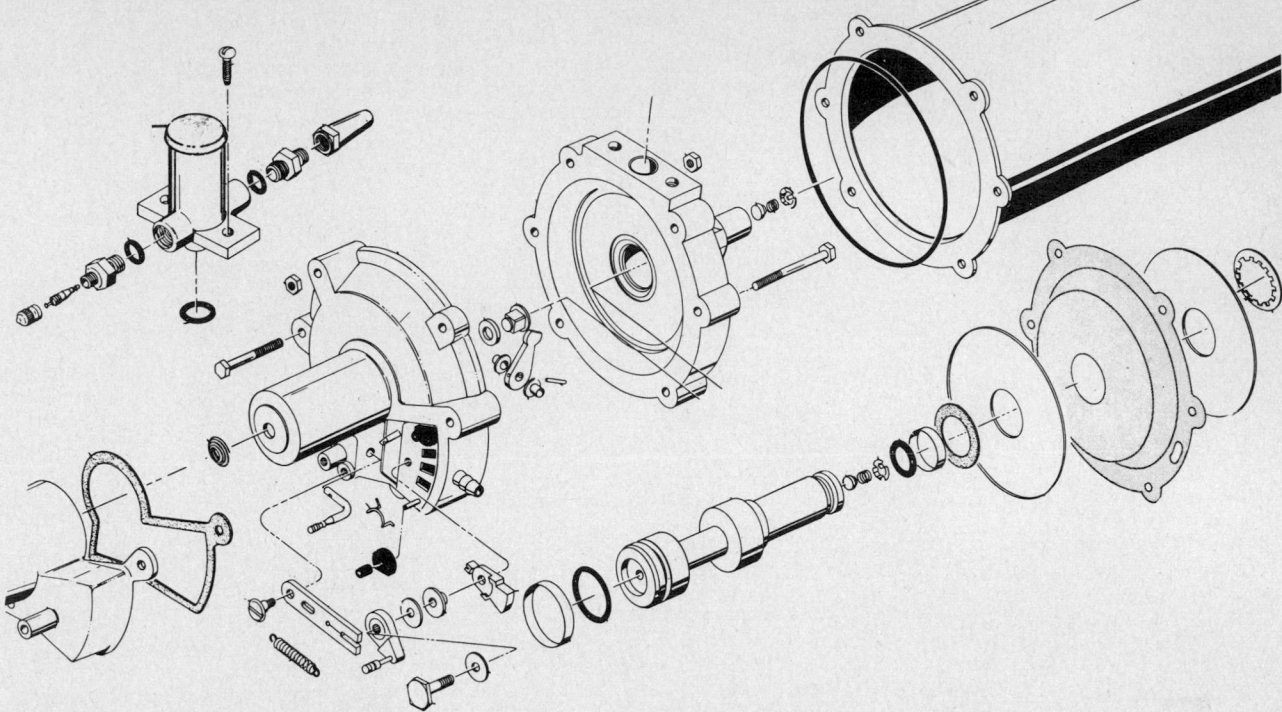

Superlift shock absorber, air compressor, regulator and reservoir details

housing.

9. On cars with leaf springs, remove the rear shackle and lower the spring. Remove bolt from spring front bushing and remove each spring.
10. Remove axle assembly.
11. To install, reverse the above procedure.

Automatic Level Control

The system consists of a vacuum-operated air compressor, connected to a control valve mounted at rear suspension crossmember. The valve is then connected to Superlift rear shock absorbers.

The Superlift shock absorber is essentially a conventional shock absorber enclosed in an air chamber. A pliable nylon-reinforced neoprene boot seals the air dome to air piston. It will extend or retract under the pressure controlled by the valve.

As load is added to the vehicle, the control valve admits air under pressure to these shock absorbers, lifting vehicle to normal position. As load is reduced the valve releases air and lowers vehicle to the previous normal level.

The valve is connected by a link to the right rear upper control link. A deflection of at least 1/2 in. is required to make it operative.

A delay mechanism is built into the valve housing. This requires 4 to 15 seconds to cause valve to operate. It prevents operation during normal road motion.

Pressure at the shock absorber units is kept equal by means of the line connecting the two units, with only one unit connected directly to the control valve. This keeps approximately 8 to 15 psi on shock absorber units at all times. The pressure is released at the control valve and the equalizing pressure is maintained through a check valve at the release fitting.

The compressor is located at the engine compartment. It is operated by vacuum surge through a line connected just forward of the carburetor insulator connection. Air at atmospheric pressure is taken into the compressor through a line connected to the air cleaner. The compressed air from the compressor is supplied to a reservoir and then to the control valve.

Any service work on this system or other parts of the vehicle that may deflate the system will require reinflation to approximately 140 psi.

All lines are 1/8 in. diameter flexible black tubing. In working on this system, use care not to kink this tubing. Keep tubing away from the exhaust system.

Radio

Removal and Installation

1. Disconnect battery.
2. If equipped with air conditioning, remove cool air manifold.
3. Remove defroster manifold.
4. Remove radio knobs, washers or rear speaker control.
5. Remove radio attaching nuts and escutcheons.
6. Disconnect all wiring and antenna lead-in.
7. Remove radio support bracket attaching screw(s), if applicable.
8. Remove radio from rear of instrument panel.
9. Install by reversing removal procedure.

Windshield Wipers

Motor R & R

1. Disconnect drive link from crank arm under the instrument panel by removing the retaining clip.
2. Disconnect harness connector from motor terminals and disconnect washer hoses, if so equipped.
3. Remove three attaching screws, then lift motor assembly from cowl, guiding the crank arm out of the hole in the cowl panel.
4. Install by reversing removal procedure.

Wiper Transmission R & R

1. Remove wiper arms and blades.
2. Raise the hood and remove cowl vent screen or grill.
3. On some models it may be necessary to remove the glove box.
4. Loosen, but do not remove, the transmission drive link to motor crankarm attaching nuts and disconnect drive link from the crankarm.

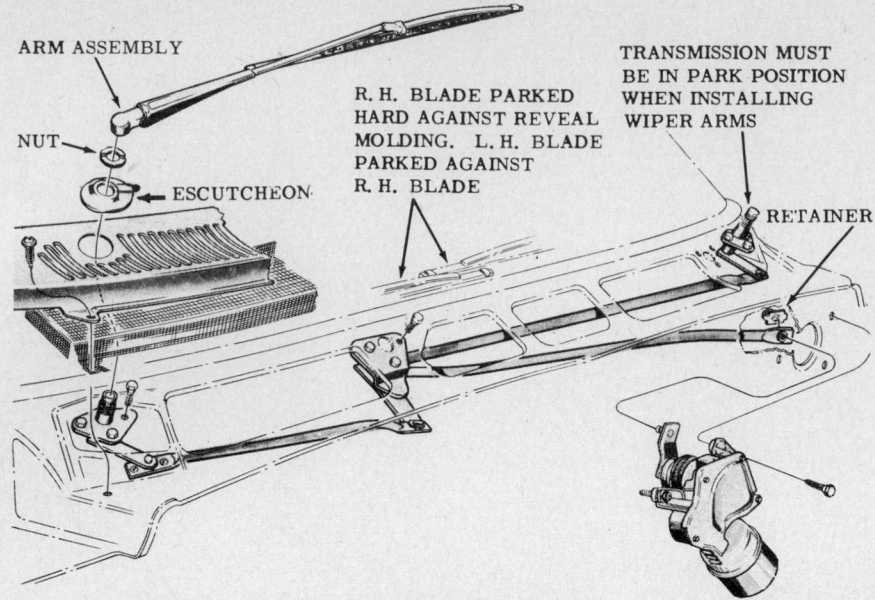

ARM ASSEMBLY

NUT

ESCUTCHEON

R. H. BLADE PARKED
HARD AGAINST REVEAL
MOLDING. L. H. BLADE
PARKED AGAINST
R. H. BLADE

TRANSMISSION MUST
BE IN PARK POSITION
WHEN INSTALLING
WIPER ARMS

RETAINER

2-speed overlap wiper—except F-85 (© Oldsmobile Div. G.M. Corp.)

5. Remove right and left transmission to body attaching screws and guide the transmission and linkage assembly out through cowl plenum chamber opening.
6. To install, reverse the above procedure.

HeaterSystem

1971-72 88 and 98

To remove the heater case and core, disconnect the battery and remove the four heater case to dash panel attaching nuts. Drain the radiator enough so that the heater hoses may be disconnected. Disconnect the control cables and vacuum hose. Remove the defroster duct to case attaching screw and the right half of the right hand dash trim panel. Remove the heater case from

the car. The heater core may now be removed from the case. Install in reverse order of removal.

To remove the blower motor, disconnect the battery and remove the right front wheel. Remove the canister or battery. Remove the three filler plate to radiator support screws, the filler plate to wheelhouse attaching screws and the filler plate. Remove the blower attaching screws and the connector. Remove the blower. Installation is the reverse of the removal procedure.

1969-72 F-85, Cutlass, 442, Vista-Cruiser

To remove the heater blower and inlet assembly, remove the right front fender filler panel. Disconnect the blower motor wiring. Remove the attaching nuts and screws and remove the heater assembly. The blower motor may be removed from the inlet assembly by removing the

ATTACHING NUTS

Blower and air inlet attachment
(© Oldsmobile Div. G.M. Corp.)

attaching screws. Installation is the reverse of the removal procedure.

To remove the core from the heater case, drain the radiator, disconnect the heater hoses and remove the five attaching nuts. To gain access to the lower nut it will be necessary to disconnect the right fender at the bottom and wedge it away from the body. Disconnect the wiring and the three control cables and remove the case assembly from the dash. Remove the core retainer and core. Install in reverse of the above procedure.

1970 88 and 98

To remove the heater case and core, remove the glove box. Disconnect the wiring, vacuum lines and defroster hoses from the heater case. Drain the radiator enough so that the heater hoses can be disconnected. Remove the blower assembly attaching screws and remove the heater case from inside the car. Remove the heater core from the case. Install in the reverse of the above procedure.

To remove the blower motor, dis-

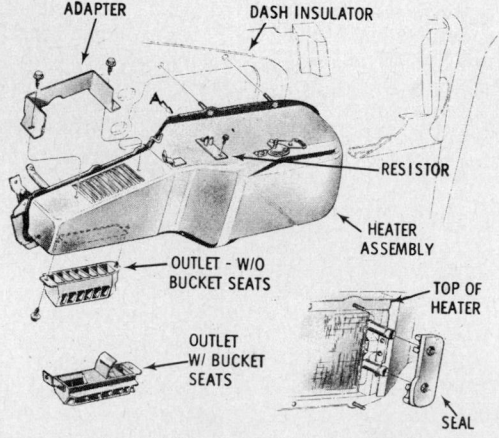

ADAPTER

DASH INSULATOR

RESISTOR

HEATER ASSEMBLY

OUTLET - W/O BUCKET SEATS

OUTLET W/ BUCKET SEATS

TOP OF HEATER

SEAL

Heater assembly
(© Oldsmobile Div., G.M. Corp.)

connect the blower feed wire. Remove the fender filler panel bolts and move the filler panel forward and inward. Remove the blower assembly attaching nuts and screws. Push the heater case studs back so that they do not protrude through the dash. Push down on the inner fender panel and remove the blower assembly. Remove the blower motor attaching screws and remove the blower. When installing, use a bead of sealer around the heater inlet.

1969 88 and 98,
1968 All Models,
1965-67 88 and 98

To remove the heater case and core, remove the glove box. Disconnect the wiring, vacuum lines and defroster hoses from the heater case. Drain the radiator enough so that the heater hoses and gasket may be removed. Remove the blower assembly attaching screws and nuts and, from inside the car, remove the heater case. Remove the heater core from the case. Install in the reverse order of the above procedure.

To remove the blower assembly, disconnect the blower feed wire. To reach the upper sheet metal screw, construct a 3 foot length of $\frac{3}{8}$ drive extensions and a 7/16 socket, then feed the tool through the opening between the fender filler and the fender forward of the right front wheel. Use sealing compound to hold the screw when removing or installing. Remove the remaining attaching nuts and screws. Push the heater case studs back until the studs do not protrude through the dash. Remove the fender to dash panel attaching screw just over the blower assembly case and remove the two bolts from the bottom rear of the fender. Keep track of the shims. Push down on the inner fender panel and remove the blower assembly. The blower motor may be removed from the blower assembly at this point. Install in reverse order of the removal procedure.

1965-67 F-85, Cutlass, Jetstar 88

To remove the blower and inlet assembly, remove the right front wheel and disconnect the motor wiring. Remove the attaching nuts and screws. The lower outboard nut can be removed by drilling a $\frac{3}{4}$ in. hole through the fender panel at the dimple provided in the fender filler panel. When finished with the job, plug the hole with a rubber grommet. Remove the assembly and remove the blower motor from the assembly.

To remove the heater core and case, disconnect the heater hoses and remove the five attaching nuts. Remove the lower outboard nut as described in the preceding paragraph. Disconnect the wiring, control cables and remove the case. To remove the core, remove the retainer and pry the clip on the other side. Installation is the reverse of the removal procedure.

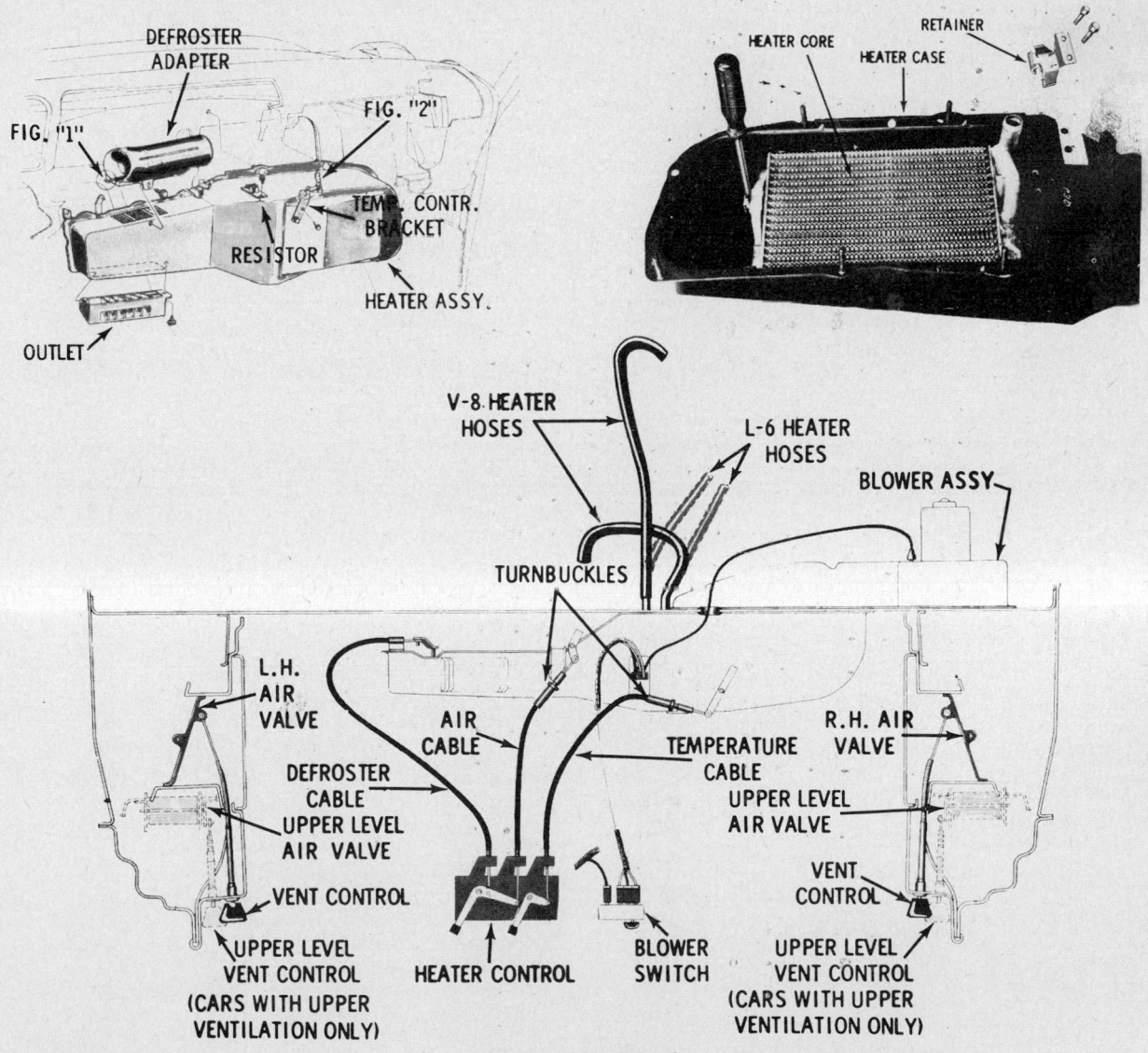

Heater Control Cables

Oldsmobile Toronado

Index

NOTE: Information not given in this section will be found under that given for the same year models and same year and displacement engines in the Oldsmobile section.

YEAR IDENTIFICATION

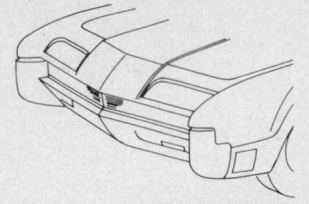

1966

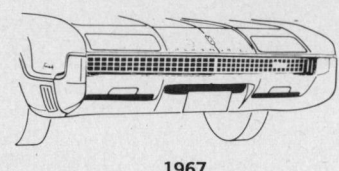

1967

1968

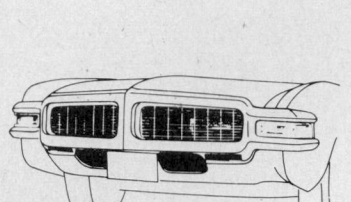

1969

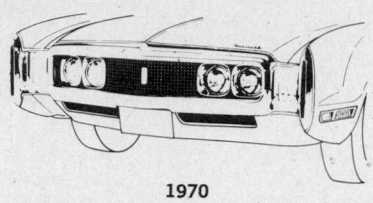

1970

1971

1972

FIRING ORDER

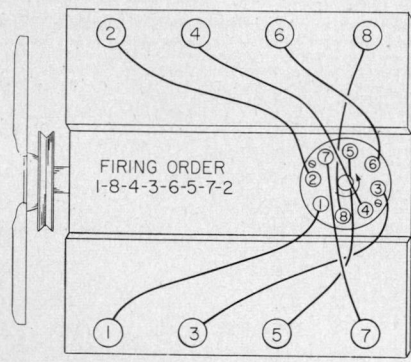

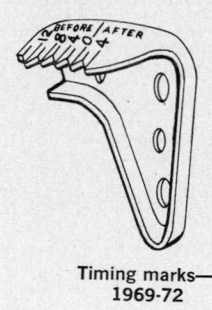

Timing marks—
1969-72

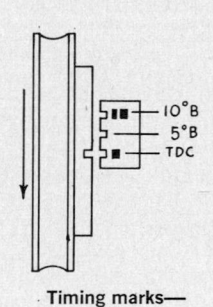

Timing marks—
1966-67

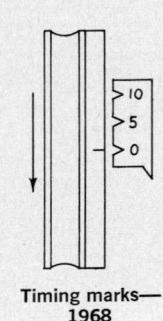

Timing marks—
1968

CAR SERIAL NUMBER LOCATION AND ENGINE IDENTIFICATION

Vehicle Identification Number

1966-67

The plate is located on the left front door pillar. Interpretation of the serial number is seen in the illustration. All Toronado models, Series 39687, are built in the Lansing plant in these years. Starting serial numbers for the standard Toronado and Deluxe Toronado are 394877M600001 and 396877M600002 respectively (for 1967 models).

1968-71

The identification plate is located on the dashboard, and can be seen through the left-hand side of the windshield. Interpretation of the number is the same as for 1966-67 models.

1972

The vehicle identification plate is located on the left side of the dashboard, visible through the windshield. Serial number interpretation is illustrated.

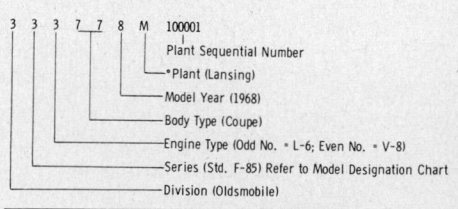

*Series	Letter	Plant
3100 through 4800	M	Lansing, Michigan
	Z	Fremont, California
	G	Framingham, Mass. (Early Production)
	E	Linden, New Jersey
5400 through 6600	M	Lansing, Michigan
	X	Kansas City, Kansas
	E	Linden, New Jersey
	C	Southgate, California
	D	Atlanta, Georgia
8400 through 9400	M	Lansing, Michigan
3100 through 4400	(Number) 1	Oshawa, Canada

Vehicle identification number interpretation—
1966-71

Engine Identification

1966-67

The engine identification number is stamped on a pad on the front of the right cylinder head. The code suffix letter is found in the chart. All engines are 425 cu. in. displacement.

1968-72

The engine identification number is found on a tape attached to the oil breather tube. The code letters are found in the chart. All engines are 455 cu. in. displacement.

Toronado Engine Identification Code

No. Cyls.	Cu. In. Displ.	YEAR AND CODE						
		1966	1967	1968	1969	1970	1971	1972
8	425	T	T					
8	455			US, UV, UT, UW	US, UW, UT, UV	(S, US, UT-Std.) (O, UW, UV—W34)	(S—Std.) (US, UT—Opt.)	W

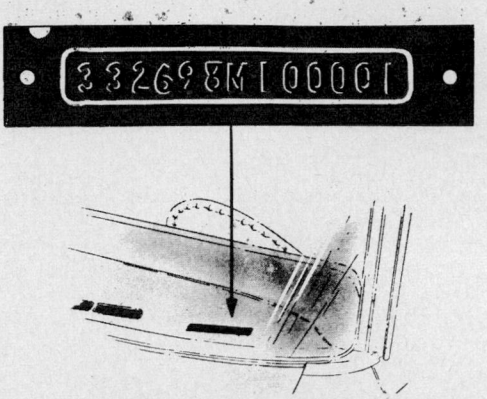

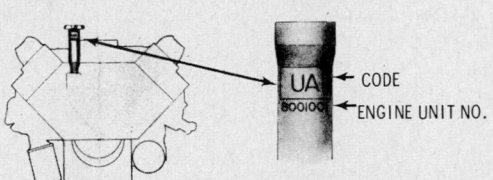

Engine code and unit number tag—1968-72

Vehicle identification number plate—1968-72

1972 OLDSMOBILE
VEHICLE IDENTIFICATION NUMBERS

3 J 67 X 2 M 100001

DIVISIONAL CODE — SERIES — BODY TYPE — ENGINE USAGE — MODEL YEAR — PLANT CODE — PLANT SEQUENTIAL NUMBER

Vehicle identification number interpretation—1972

GENERAL ENGINE SPECIFICATIONS

YEAR	CU. IN. DISPLACEMENT	CARBURETOR	ADVERTIZED HORSEPOWER @ RPM	ADVERTIZED TORQUE @ RPM (FT. LBS.)	A.M.A. HORSEPOWER	BORE & STROKE (IN.)	ADVERTIZED COMPRESSION RATIO	VALVE LIFTER TYPE	NORMAL OIL PRESSURE (PSI)
1966-67	V8—425 Cu. In.	4-BBL.	385 @ 4800	475 @ 3200	54.0	4.125 x 3.975	10.50:1	Hyd.	30-45①
1968	V8—455 Cu. In.	4-BBL.	375 @ 4600	510 @ 3000	54.5	4.126 x 4.250	10.25:1	Hyd.	30-45①
	V8—455 Cu. In.	4-BBL.	400 @ 4800	500 @ 3200	54.5	4.126 x 4.250	10.25:1	Hyd.	30-45①
1969	V8—455 Cu. In.	4-BBL.	365 @ 4600	510 @ 3000	54.5	4.126 x 4.250	10.25:1	Hyd.	30-45①
	V8—455 Cu. In.	4-BBL.	390 @ 5000	500 @ 3200	54.5	4.126 x 4.250	10.25:1	Hyd.	30-45①
1970	V8—455 Cu. In.	4-BBL.	375 @ 4600	510 @ 3000	54.5	4.126 x 4.250	10.25:1	Hyd.	30-45①
	V8—455 Cu. In. (W34)	4-BBL.	400 @ 5000	500 @ 3200	54.5	4.126 x 4.250	10.25:1	Hyd.	30-45①
1971	V8—455 Cu. In.	4-BBL.	350 @ 4400	465 @ 2800	54.5	4.126 x 4.250	8.5:1	Hyd.	30-45①
1972	V8—455 Cu. In.	4-BBL.	250②	375②	54.5	4.126 x 4.250	8.5:1	Hyd.	30-45①

①—At 1500 rpm.
②—Horsepower and torque ratings are SAE net ratings.

VALVE SPECIFICATIONS

YEAR AND MODEL	SEAT ANGLE (DEG.)	FACE ANGLE (DEG.)	VALVE LIFT INTAKE (IN.)	VALVE LIFT EXHAUST (IN.)	VALVE SPRING PRESSURE (VALVE OPEN) LBS. @ IN.	VALVE SPRING INSTALLED HEIGHT (IN.)	STEM TO GUIDE CLEARANCE (IN.)		STEM DIAMETER (IN.)	
							Intake	Exhaust	Intake	Exhaust
1966-67 V8—425 Cu. In.	①	②	.431	.433	180-194 @ 1.27	1.670	.0010-.0027	.0015-.0032	.3432-.3425	.3427-.3420
1968-69 V8—455 Cu. In.	①	②	.435	.435	180-194 @ 1.27	1.670	.0010-.0027	.0015-.0032	.3432-.3425	.3427-.3420
1970 V8—455 Cu. In.	③	③	.435	.435	180-194 @ 1.27	1.670	.0010-.0027	.0015-.0032	.3432-.3425	.3427-.3420
V8—455 Cu. In. (W34)	④	④	.472	.472	180-194 @ 1.27	1.670	.0010-.0027	.0015-.0032	.3432-.3425	.3427-.3420
1971-72 V8—455 Cu. In.	③	③	.440	.440	180-194 @ 1.27	1.670	.0010-.0027	.0015-.0032	.3432-.3425	.3427-.3420

①—Intake 30°, Exh. 45°.
②—Intake 30°, Exh. 45°.
③—Intake & Exh. Seat 45°, Intake & Exh. Face 46°.
④—Intake 30°, Exh. 45°.
⑤—Intake 30°, Exh. 46°.

TUNE-UP SPECIFICATIONS

YEAR	MODEL AND CU. IN. DISPLACEMENT	SPARK PLUGS		DISTRIBUTOR		IGNITION TIMING (Deg.) ▲	CRANKING COMP. PRESSURE (Psi)	VALVES			Intake Opens (Deg.)	FUEL PUMP PRESSURE (Psi) ★	IDLE SPEED (Rpm) ★
		Type	Gap (In.)	Point Dwell (Deg.)	Point Gap (In.)			Tappet (Hot) Clearance (In.)					
								Intake	Exhaust				
1966	425 Cu. In.	44S	.030	30°	.016	7½B	180	Zero	Zero	21B	7½	850
1967	425 Cu. In.	44S	.030	30°	.016	7½B	180	Zero	Zero	21B	7½	850
1968	455 Cu. In.	44S	.030	30°	.016●	7½B	180	Zero	Zero	20B	7	850
1969	455—4-BBL. (365 HP)	44S	.030	30°	.016	8B	180	Zero	Zero	20B	7	850
	455—4-BBL. (390 HP)	44S	.030	30°	.016	10B	190	Zero	Zero	20B	7	850
1970	455—4-BBL. (375 HP)	R44S	.030	30°	.016	8B	180	Zero	Zero	22B	5½-7	600
	455—4-BBL. (400 HP)	R44S	.030	30°	.016	12B	190	Zero	Zero	24B	5½-7	600
1971-72	455—4-BBL. (350 HP)	R46S	.040	29-31	.016	10B	100①	Zero	Zero	22B	6	600

★—With automatic in D.

▲—With vacuum advance disconnected. NOTE: These settings are only approximate. Engine design, altitude, temperature, fuel octane rating and the condition of the individual engine are all factors which can influence timing. The limiting advance factor must, therefore, be the "knock point" of the individual engine.

●—W/transistor ign.—.045 in.

B—Before top dead center.

①—Minimum—Lowest must be within 80% of highest.

Caution

General adoption of anti-pollution laws has changed the design of almost all car engine production to effectively reduce crankcase emission and terminal exhaust products. It has been necessary to adopt stricter tune-up rules, especially timing and idle speed procedures. Both of these values are peculiar to the engine and to its application, rather than to the engine alone. With this in mind, car manufacturers supply idle speed data for the engine and application involved. This information is clearly displayed in the engine compartment of each vehicle.

GENERAL CHASSIS AND BRAKE SPECIFICATIONS

YEAR	MODEL	CHASSIS		BRAKE CYLINDER BORE			BRAKE DRUM	
		Overall Length (In.)	Tire Size	Master Cylinder (In.)	Wheel Cylinder Diameter (In.)		Diameter (In.)	
					Front	Rear	Front	Rear
1966	Toronado Cpe.	211.0	8.85 x 15▲	⅞	1⅛	⅞	11.00	11.00
1967	Toronado Cpe.	211.0	8.85 x 15▲	1.0	1⅛■	⅞	11.00①	11.00
1968	Toronado Cpe.	211.4	8.85 x 15	1.0	1⅛■	⅞	11.00①	11.00
1969	Toronado Cpe.	214.8	8.85 x 15④	1.0②	1⅛③	⅞	11.00①	11.00
1970	Toronado Cpe.	214.3	J78 x 15	1⅛	2¹⁵⁄₁₆	¹⁵⁄₁₆	10.88 disc	11.00
1971-72	Toronado Cpe.	219.9	J78 x 15	1⅛	2¹⁵⁄₁₆	¹⁵⁄₁₆	10.88 disc	11.00

▲—Opt.—9.15 x 15

■—Disc = 2.06 in.

①—Disc = 11¹⁹⁄₆₄ in.

②—Disc = 1¹⁄₁₆ in.

③—Disc = 2¹⁵⁄₁₆ in.

④—J78 x 15 Optional.

CRANKSHAFT BEARING JOURNAL SPECIFICATIONS

YEAR	MODEL	MAIN BEARING JOURNALS (IN.)				CONNECTING ROD BEARING JOURNALS (IN.)		
		Journal Diameter	Oil Clearance	Shaft End-Play	Thrust On No.	Journal Diameter	Oil Clearance	End-Play
1966-67	V8—425 Cu. In.	3.0000	②	.004–.008	3	2.4988-2.5003	.0004-.0033	.002–.013①
1968-72	V8—455 Cu. In.	3.0000	②	.004–.008	3	2.4988-2.4998	.0004-.0033	.002–.013①

①—Both rods.

②—Nos. 1-4—.0021-.005.
　No. 5—.002-.0034.

CAPACITIES

YEAR	MODEL	ENGINE CRANKCASE ADD 1 Qt. FOR NEW FILTER	TRANSMISSIONS Pts. TO REFILL AFTER DRAINING			DRIVE AXLE (Pts.)	GASOLINE TANK (Gals.)	COOLING SYSTEM (Qts.) WITH HEATER
			Manual 3-Speed	4-Speed	Automatic			
1966-69	Toronado Cpe.	5	None	None	④	②	24	17.5②
1970-72	Toronado Cpe.	5	None	None	④	③	24	18①

① —18.5 with A/C.
② —16.5 without heater; 18.0 with A/C.
③ —1966-68—4.5; 1969-72—4.0.
④ —1966—24; 1967—24 dry, 5½ refill; 1968—24 dry, 8 refill; 1969—24 dry,
　　8 refill; 1970-72—24 dry, 8 refill.

TORQUE SPECIFICATIONS

YEAR	MODEL	CYLINDER HEAD BOLTS (FT. LBS.)	ROD BEARING BOLTS (FT. LBS.)	MAIN BEARING BOLTS (FT. LBS.)	CRANKSHAFT BALANCER BOLT (FT. LBS.)	DRIVEPLATE TO CRANKSHAFT BOLTS (FT. LBS.)	MANIFOLD (FT. LBS.) Intake	Exhaust
1966-67	V8—425 Cu. In.	80	42	80-120▲	50	60	35	25
1968-72	V8—455 Cu. In.	80	42	120	160	60	35	25

▲—Nos. 1 thru 4—80. No. 5—120.

CYLINDER HEAD BOLT TIGHTENING SEQUENCE

1966-72

BATTERY AND STARTER SPECIFICATIONS

YEAR	MODEL	BATTERY Ampere Hour Capacity	Volts	Terminal Grounded	STARTER No-Load Test Amps.	Volts	RPM	Brush Spring Tension (Oz)
1966	425 cu. in.	73	12	Neg.	70-105	10.6	3,800	35
1967	425 cu. in.	73	12	Neg.	70-105	10.6	3,800	35
1968-71	455 cu. in.	75	12	Neg.	70-105	10.6	3,800	35

AC GENERATOR AND REGULATOR SPECIFICATIONS

YEAR	PART NO.	ALTERNATOR Field Current Draw @ 12V.	Output	Part No.	REGULATOR Field Relay Air Gap (In.)	Point Gap (In.)	Volts to Close	Regulator Air Gap (In.)	Point Gap (In.)	Volts at 125°
1966	1100842	2.2-2.6	42	1119515	.015	.030	6.3-8.3	.060	.014	13.5-14.4
	1100694	2.2-2.6	55	1119515	.015	.030	6.3-8.3	.060	.014	13.5-14.4
1967	1100842	2.2-2.6	42	1119515	.015	.030	6.3-8.3	.060	.014	13.5-14.4
1968-69	1100734	2.2-2.6	42	1119515	.015	.030	6.3-8.3	.060	.014	13.5-14.4
	1100777	2.2-2.6	55	1119515	.015	.030	6.3-8.3	.060	.014	13.5-14.4
1970	1100878	2.2-2.6	42	1119515	.015	.030	6.3-8.3	.060	.014	13.5-14.4
	1100907	2.2-2.6	55	1119515	.015	.030	6.3-8.3	.060	.014	13.5-14.4
1971-72	1100567	2.2-2.6	42	1119515	.015	.030	6.3-8.3	.060	.014	13.5-14.4
	1100570	2.2-2.6	61	1119515	.015	.030	6.3-8.3	.060	.014	13.5-14.4

LIGHT BULBS

1966–69

Speedometer indicator, high beam indicator
fuel, temperature, ammeter, turn signal
oil pressure warning, parking brake
warning.. 194; 2 CP
Heater, air conditioning...................... 1895; 2 CP
Radio dial... 1893; 2 CP
Ignition switch, ash tray, cruise control...... 1445; 1 CP
Electric clock.................................... 1816; 2.5 CP
FM-AM Indicator.............................. 2182D; .3 CP
Underhood, trunk............................... 631; 6 CP
Courtesy.. 90; 6 CP
Rear quarter lamps, door lights, glove
compartment..................................... 212; 6 CP
Headlamp—upper beam................. L-4001; 37½ W
Headlamp—upper & lower beam ... L-4002; 37½ & 55 W
License... 97; 4 CP
Parking & turn signal................... 1157A; 4 & 32 CP
Tail & stop................................... 1157; 4 & 32 CP
Back-up.. 1156; 32 CP
Cornering lamp.............................. 1195; 50 CP

1970

Ident. No.	Quan.	C.P.	Usage
194	3	2	Speedometer, odometer and shift indicator
194	1	2	High beam indicator
194	2	2	Fuel, temperature, ammeter and oil gauge
194	2	2	Turn signal indicator
194	1	2	Brake warning light
194	1	2	Generator warning
194	1	2	Eng. temp.—stop engine warning
168	1	2.5	Oil pressure warning
1895	1	2	Heater, ventilation & air cond. control
1895	1	2	Console compartment
1445	1	1	HMT shift indicator—console only

257	1	2	Engine temperature indicator —hot
1445	1	1	Ash tray light
1445	1	1	Cruise control "on" light
1445	1	1	Rear window defogger "on" light
1445	4	1	Nameplate lights
1445	1	1	Auxiliary high beam indicator
1445	2	1	Electric clock
1893	1	2	Radio dial
563	1	4	Mirror map lamp
631	1	6	Underhood
631	1	6	Trunk
90	2	6	Courtesy
68	2	3	Front seat back
97	1	4	Courtesy light—console
212	4	6	Rear quarter lamps
212	4	6	Door lights
212	1	6	Glove box

1970 EXTERNAL LAMPS

97	1	4	License
1157NA	2	3 & 32	Parking & turn signal
1157	4	3 & 32	Tail and stop
194	2	2	Side marker—front
194	2	2	Side marker—rear
1157	2	32	Back up
1195	2	50	Cornering lamp
L-4001	2	37½ Watt	Headlamp—upper beam
L-4002	2	37½ & 55 Watt	Headlamp—upper & lower beam

1971–72

Ident. No.	Quant.	C.P.	Usage
168	3	3	Instrument Cluster Lighting
161	2	2	Turn Signal Indicator
194	1	2	Low Fuel Indicator

161	1	1	Generator Warning
161	1	1	Brake Warning Light
161	1	1	High Beam Indicator
161	1	1	Eng. Temp. Indicator (Hot)
161	1	1	Oil Pressure Warning
1816	2	2.5	Inst. Panel Floodlights (Toronado Right Side)
1893	4	2	Inst. Panel Floodlights (Toronado Left Side)
1445	1	1	Ash Tray
1893	1	2	Radio Dial (Except AM/FM/Stereo/Tape)
564	1	2	Radio Dial (AM/FM/Stereo/Tape)
1816	1	2.5	Electric Clock
631	1	6	Underhood
631	1	6	Trunk
212	1	6	Rear Load Area
563	1	4	Map Lamp—Panel
97	2	4	Courtesy
212	2	6	Side Roof or Rear Quarter
212	4	6	Courtesy/Warning Lamps
211	1	12	Dome
563	1	4	Glove Box

1971–72 EXTERNAL LAMPS

97	1	4	License
1157NA	2	3 & 32	Parking & Turn Signal
1157	4	3 & 32	Tail and Stop
142456	4	21	Upper Level Stop and Tail
194	2	2	Side Marker—Front
194	2	2	Side Marker—Rear
1157	2	32	Back Up
1195	2	50	Cornering Lamp
L-4001	2	37½ Watt	Headlamp—Upper Beam
L-4002	2	37½ Watt & 55 Watt	Headlamp—Upper & Lower Beam

WHEEL ALIGNMENT

YEAR	MODEL	CASTER		CAMBER		TOE-IN (In.)	KING-PIN INCLINATION (Deg.)	WHEEL PIVOT RATIO	
		Range (Deg.)	Pref. Setting (Deg.)	Range (Deg.)	Pref. Setting (Deg.)			Inner Wheel	Outer Wheel
1966–67	All	1½N to 2½N	2N	¼N to ½P	⅛P	0 to ¹⁄₁₆	11	20	18¼
1968–69	All	1½N to 2½N	2N	¼N to ½P	⅛P	0 to ¹⁄₁₆	11	20	18¼
1970	All	1¾N to 2¾N	2¼N	¼N to ½P	⅛P	0 to ¹⁄₁₆	11	20	18¼
1971–72	All	1½N to 2½N	2N	¼N to ¾P ① ¾N to ¼P ②	¼P ① ¼N ②	0 ± ¹⁄₁₆	11	—	—

N—Negative.
P—Positive.

① —Left side (to be ½ P more than right side).
② --Right side.

FUSES AND CIRCUIT BREAKERS

1966–69

Radio, back-up lamps, fuel gauge, oil pressure indicator lamp, parking brake lamp, transmission control, temperature gauge lamp, cornering lamp, glove compartment lamp, underhood lamp . . . . SFE-9 Amp. Fuse

License lamp, tail lamps, trunk lamp . . . AGW-15 Amp Fuse

Ash tray lamp, clock lamp, cruise control lamp heater, ventilator and comfortron lights . . . . AGA-3A Amp. Fuse

Heater . . . . SFE-20 Amp. Fuse

Heater w/A.C. ACE-30 Amp. Fuse

Heater w/rear window defroster . . . . . . ACE-30 Amp. Fuse

Cruise control relay, power antenna, power windows . . . . SFE-20 Amp. Fuse

Power seat relay . . . . AGC-30 Amp. Fuse

Windshield wiper, stop lamps . . . . SFE-20 Amp. Fuse

Cigar lighter, clock, courtesy lamps rear quarter lamps, rear seat lamps. AGC-30 Amp. Fuse

Headlamps . . . . CB

Air conditioner . . . . CB

Electric seat and/or window motors . . . . CB

1970

Application	Name of Fuse Circuit on Fuse Block	Fuse Type and Amps
Heater, air conditioning	Htr.-A/C	AGC-25
Stop lamps, hazard warning lamps	Stop-Haz.	SFE-20
Trunk lamp, trunk release		
Lighter		
Clock		
Courtesy lamps		
Rear quarter lamps	Clk. Ltr.-Ctsy.	AGC-25
Rear seat lighter		
Glove box lamp		
Headlamp "off" delay (night watch)		
Rear lamp		
Underhood lamp		
Cornering lamp	Tail	AGW-15
License lamp		
Side marker lamps		
Radio	Radio	SAE-9
Power windows		
Cruise control	Pwr.-Relay	SFE-20
Mirror map lamp		
Windshield wiper	Wiper	AGC-25
Instrument panel lamp	Inst. Lps.	SAE-4
Transmission control	Gauges-Trans.	SAE-9
Back-up lamp		
Park brake lamp	Back-Up	SAE-9
Turn signal flasher		

1971–72

Application	Name of Fuse Circuit on Fuse Block	Fuse Type and Amps.
Heater, A/C defogger	Htr.-A/C	AGC-25
Dome, cigarette lighter, clock, courtesy, trunk, glove box, Trunk release, headlight "off" delay, mirror map light	Clk. Ltr.-Ctsy.	AGC-25
Cornering, tail, side marker, license, underhood lights	Tail	SFE-20
Stop, hazard warning lights	Stop-Haz.	SFE-20
Instrument panel lights	Inst. Lps.	SFE-4
Elec. windows, seats	Accsy-Pwr. Rly.	40 AMP. C.B.
Radio, Tape player	Radio	AGC-10
Windshield wipers	Wiper	AGC-25
Turn sigs., back-up, Cruise controls	Dir. Sig.-Back-up	SFE-20
Transmission control, park brake	Gauges-Trans.	AGC-10

Distributor

Detailed information on distributor drive, direction of distributor rotation, cylinder numbering, firing order, point gap, point dwell, timing mark location, spark plugs, spark advance, and idle speed are in the specifications tables of this section.

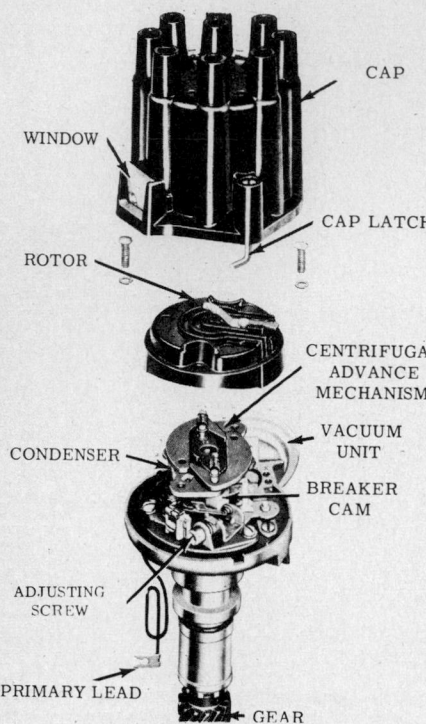

Distributor details
(© Oldsmobile Div. G.M. Corp.)

Distributor Removal

1966-72

Remove the air cleaner, distributor cap and wire assembly. Mark the position of the rotor in relation to the body and the body in relation to the block. Do not move the engine after the distributor is removed. Disconnect the vacuum line at the distributor and remove the primary wire. Take out the bolt that holds the distributor to the block and lift off the distributor.

These models are fitted with an externally adjusted distributor having a window in the distributor cap. Final adjustment of the breaker points is done with the engine running.

The breaker points are set roughly to the correct gap, the distributor installed on the vehicle and the engine started and run at fast idle.

Attach a dwell meter to the distributor.

Raise the window in the cap and, with the engine running, turn the adjusting screw with an Allen wrench until a point dwell of 30° is obtained. If a dwell meter is not available, turn the screw inward until the en-

gine slows down, then outward until the engine slows down, counting the number of turns between the two positions. Set the points midway between these two positions.

AC Generator (Delcotron)

The Delco-Remy Delcotron is used on all models. For testing and service procedures for this charging system, see Basic Electrical Diagnosis in the Unit Repair Section.

Removal and Installation

Disconnect the battery negative cable. The alternator is mounted in the front of the engine above the right bank of cylinders. Disconnect and identify the wires from the alternator. Loosen the top adjusting bracket bolt, let the alternator swing down, then remove the bottom swivel bolt. When installing, be sure to tighten the belt tension.

Caution Since the Delcotron and regulator are designed for use on a one polarity system, the following precautions must be observed:

1. The polarity of the battery, generator and regulator must be considered and matched before making any electrical connections to the system.

2. When connecting a booster battery, be sure to connect the negative battery terminals together and the positive battery terminals together.

3. When connecting a charger to the battery, connect the charger positive lead to the battery positive terminal. Connect the charger negative lead to the battery negative terminal.

4. Never operate the Delcotron on open circuit. Be sure that all connections in the circuit are clean and tight.

5. Do not short across or ground any of the terminals on the Delcotron regulator.

6. Do not attempt to polarize the Delcotron.

7. Do not use test lamps of more than 12 volts for checking diode continuity.

8. Avoid long soldering times when replacing diodes or transistors. Prolonged heat is damaging to these units.

9. Disconnect the battery ground terminal when servicing any AC system. This will prevent the possibility of accidental reversal of polarity.

Battery, Starter

See the Specifications at the beginning of this section for battery and starter specifications. Starter overhaul procedures can be found in the Unit Repair Section, Basic Electrical Diagnosis.

Starter Removal and Installation

1. Disconnect the battery and raise the car.
2. Remove the two attaching bolts and move the starter for easier access to the wires.
3. Identify the positions of the wires and disconnect the wires from the starter.
4. Remove starter.
5. Installation is the reverse of the above procedure

Instruments

Dash Instrument Panel Removal

1966-68

1. Disconnect battery.
2. If equipped with Cruise Control, disconnect cable at the regulator.
3. Remove screws from right-hand and left-hand lower trim panels.
4. Remove transmission indicator needle.
5. Remove nuts and clamps from column to upper reinforcement. Column may rest on front seat cushion.
6. Loosen bolts at the side, approximately ¼ in.
7. Speedometer cable and radio lead-in should be disconnected from behind control panel.
8. Remove screws at the top of the control panel.
9. If equipped with air-conditioner, disconnect outlet hose.

NOTE: all components of the control panel can be removed at this time for any service required.

10. Disconnect main wiring harness from components.
11. Remove bolts that were originally loosened ¼ in. in Step 6.
12. Remove control panel.
13. Install by reversing the removal procedure.

1969-70

The instrument panel on these models is basically the same as the one used previously. To remove and install the panel, follow the above procedure and include the following steps:

1. If equipped with the tilt and travel steering wheel, the steer-

attach the speedometer to the cluster base and remove the speedometer.

4. Install in reverse order of removal.

Ignition Switch R & R

1966-68

1. Remove control panel.
2. Turn switch to Acc. position.
3. Insert a paper clip into the small hole in the front side of the switch and depress, while turn-

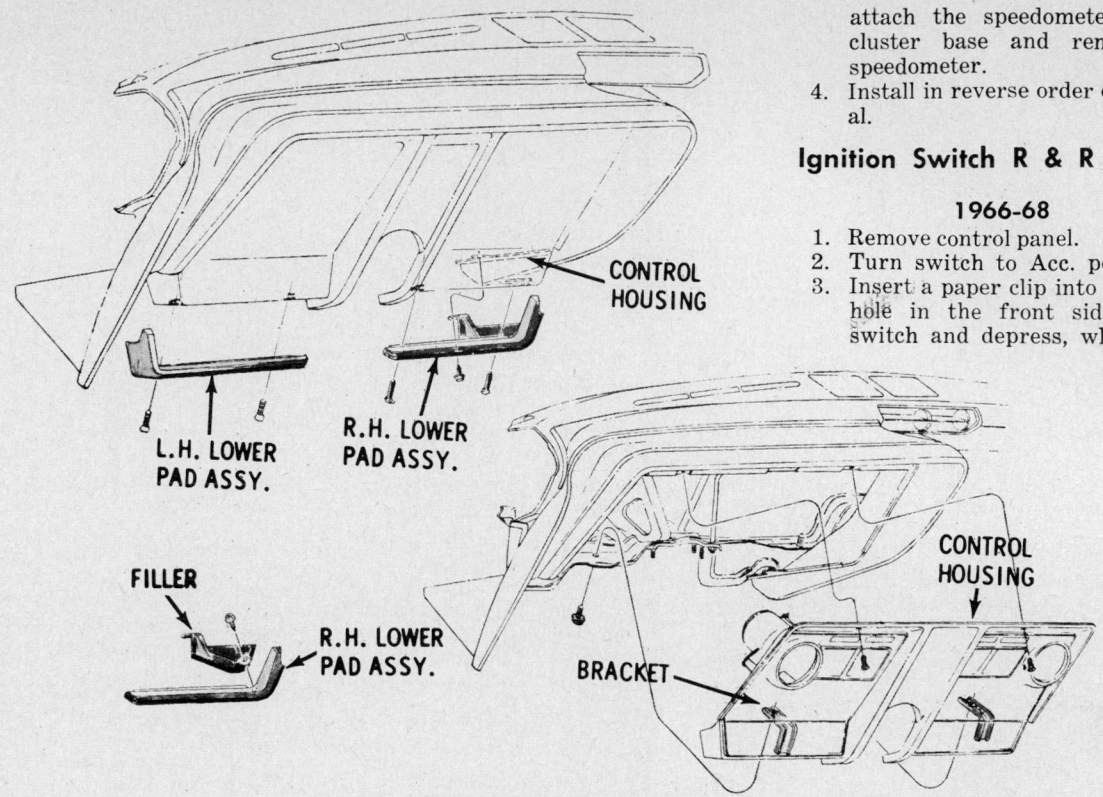

Control panel attachment (© Oldsmobile Div. G.M. Corp.)

ing column need not be disconnected but merely tilted down to its lowest position.

2. While holding the panel tilted outward, disconnect all electrical connectors: all printed circuit multiple connectors, radio, clock, lighter, headlight switch, wiper and washer switch and accessory switches.
3. Remove the heater or air conditioner control panel and remove the panel without disconnecting the wiring.

1971-72

1. Disconnect the battery.
2. Remove the steering column bottom trim cover.
3. Remove the left lower trim panel.
4. Remove the shift indicator needle and disconnect the speedometer cable.
5. If equipped with cruise control, disconnect at the cruise control regulator and push about 6 in. of cluster face housing.
6. Put ignition switch to "RUN" position and shift lever in "Drive."
7. Remove the panel side and top (outboard) attaching screws.
8. Pull the panel out and disconnect the multiple connector. If equipped with cruise control, disconnect the speedometer cable.
9. Installation is the reverse of removal.

Speedometer Cable

Removal—1966-67

1. Remove right-hand lower trim panel.
2. Disconnect cable at speedometer.
3. Disconnect cable at transmission.
4. Remove cable.
5. Reinstall by reversing the above procedure.

1968-72

1. Remove instrument panel.
2. Disconnect cable at speedometer.
3. Remove cable.
4. Install by reversing removal procedure.

Speedometer Head R & R

1966-70

1. Remove control panel, refer to Dash Instrument Panel Removal.
2. Disconnect printed circuits. (There are three connectors).
3. Remove radio.
4. Remove eight cover-to-cluster attaching screws.
5. Remove four attaching bolts, cover to speedometer head.
6. Install by reversing the above procedure.

1971-72

1. Remove the instrument panel as described above.
2. Remove the four screws which attach the cluster base to the cluters face housing.
3. Remove the two screws which

ing the key counterclockwise. The lock should pop out.

4. Remove escutcheon.
5. Remove switch from backside of instrument panel and remove wiring connector.
6. Install by reversing above procedure.

1969-72

1. Disconnect the negative battery cable.
2. Place the ignition switch in "ACC" position (1969), "RUN" position (1970) or "OFF-UNLOCKED" (1971-72).
3. Remove the toe pan cover (if applicable) and loosen the toe clamp bolts. Ilustrations may be found in the Oldsmobile, F-85 Section.
4. Remove the lower instrument panel trim and toe pan trim panel.
5. Remove the automatic transmission shift indicator needle.
6. Remove the steering column dash bracket and let the steering wheel rest on the driver's seat.
7. Remove the two switch attaching screws and lift the switch off the actuator rod.
8. Disconnect the wiring.
9. To install, check that the lock cylinder is still in "ACC" (1969), "RUN" (1970) or "OFF-UNLOCKED" (1971-72) position and move the sliding portion of the switch until the switch hole is positioned as illus-

trated. Hold the switch in this position with a 0.090 in. pin as illustrated.

10. Connect the wiring to the switch.

11. Position the switch over the actuator rod, install the attaching screws (tighten to 3 ft. lbs.) and remove the 0.090 in. pin.

12. Reverse Steps 1 through 6 to complete installation.

Headlight Switch R & R

1966-70

1. Remove lower left-hand trim panel.
2. Remove knob by first pulling the knob out to the headlight position, then depressing the spring-loaded button on switch body. Then, pull knob out of switch assembly.
3. Remove escutcheon nut.
4. Remove headlamp switch from rear of control panel.
5. Disconnect wiring and vacuum hoses.
6. Installation is the reverse of removal.

1971-72

The left hand control panel must be removed in order to remove the headlight switch.

1. Disconnect the battery.
2. Pry the floor lamp lens and lamp assembly out with a thin screwdriver.
3. Remove the screws from the left side of the lower steering trim and from the left hand trim panel.
4. Remove the nut and screw from the temperature cable on the bottom of the air conditioner or heater control.
5. Remove the ground wire attaching screw from the left hand panel lower brace.
6. Remove the four control panel attaching screws and remove the panel.
7. Remove the multiple connector from the headlight switch.
8. Pull the switch to "ON" position and push in on the small button on the switch, then pull the switch knob and shaft from the switch.
9. Remove the escutcheon from the switch and remove switch.
10. Install in reverse order of removal.

Brakes

Detailed information on brakes can be found in the General Chassis and Brake Specifications table at the beginning of this section. Brake adjustment, brake lining replacement, hydraulic cylinder overhaul

and bleeding procedures can be found in the Unit Repair Section. Power brake overhaul procedures can be found in the Unit Repair Section.

On 1967 and 1968 models, the 4-piston Delco Moraine power front disc brake became available as an option. In 1969 it was replaced by the single piston disc brake. On 1970-72 models, the single piston Delco Moraine power front disc brakes are standard equipment. Beginning in 1967, a dual hydraulic system is used. A distributor assembly actuates a warning light switch whenever there is a failure in one of the hydraulic systems. Up to 1970, a balance valve in the rear system is used to proportion the hydraulic pressure to the rear wheels when more than 310 psi is required at the front (disc brake) wheels. On 1971-72 models, the distributor and balance functions are integrated in the combination valve assembly. Service procedures for the Delco Moraine single cylinder disc brake are found in the Unit Repair Section.

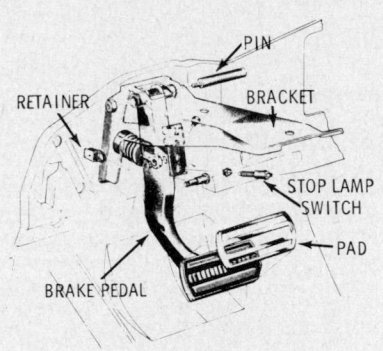

Brake pedal assembly
(© Oldsmobile Div. G.M. Corp.)

Brake Pedal Clearance

1966 Only

Before adjusting the brakes, make certain there is ½ in.—¾ in. free pedal travel (measured at the toeboard). This adjustment is made at the master cylinder pushrod.

Brake Pedal Travel

Maximum allowable brake pedal travel on 1966-70 models is 1-⅞ in. On 1971-72 models maximum allowable travel is 2½ in. To bring pedal travel within specifications, adjust self-adjusting brakes by driving the car back backward and forward alternately and applying the brakes. If pedal travel does not decrease, either the linings are excessively worn or the self-adjusting mechanism is frozen.

Parking Brake Adjustment

1. Release the parking brake.
2. Check hydraulic brake pedal travel, adjusting if necessary.

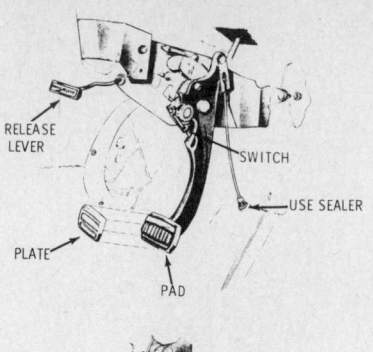

Parking brake assembly
(© Oldsmobile Div. G.M. Corp.)

3. Tighten the equalizer adjusting nut until heavy resistance is felt when rotating the rear wheels forward, then back off the adjusting nut seven full turns.

Parking Brake Outer Cable R & R

1. Disconnect the cable at the connector.
2. Remove the conduit bracket retainer.
3. Remove the rear wheel and brake drum.
4. Disconnect the cable from the actuating lever and install a corbin type hose clamp over the conduit retainer fingers.
5. Tap on the conduit lightly to remove it from the backing plate.
6. Install in the reverse order of removal.

Master Cylinder R & R

1. Disconnect and plug hydraulic lines.
2. Remove the attaching nuts and remove the master cylinder from the power unit.

Power Cylinder Removal

1. From inside the car, detach the brake pushrod from the brake pedal.
2. Detach the vacuum hose at the vacuum cylinder and disconnect the hydraulic line from the front of the slave cylinder.
3. Remove the four nuts that hold the vacuum unit up to the toeboard and remove the unit.
4. Install in reverse order of removal. Bleed system.

Fuel System

Gas tank capacities can be found in the Capacities table at the beginning of this section. See Dash Gauges and Indicators in the Unit Repair Section for fuel gauge troubleshooting. See Tune-Up Specifications at the beginning of this section for correct idle speed and fuel pump operating pressure.

Carburetor

Idle Speed and Mixture Adjustments

1966-69
Adjust with air cleaner removed.
1. Warm up the engine and remove the air cleaner.
2. Disconnect the air cleaner vacuum hose at the intake manifold, plug the manifold fitting, disconnect the vacuum distributor hose and plug the hose.
3. With the transmission in Drive, adjust the throttle stop screw and idle mixture screws alternately to obtain the best idle at the specified rpm. Hold the hot idle compensator closed while making the adjustment.
4. On 1969 models, turn each mixture screw in to obtain a 10-15 rpm drop (20-30 rpm drop for both screws), then back each screw out 1/4 turn.
5. Do not idle more than 5 minutes while adjusting rpm. Install the air cleaner and recheck the idle. Install and connect all the rest of the components.

1970
Adjust with air cleaner removed.
1. Warm up the engine and leave it running.
2. Remove the air cleaner, disconnect the air cleaner vacuum hose at the intake manifold and plug the fitting on the manifold.
3. Disconnect the vacuum hose at the distributor and plug the hose.
4. Stop the engine, turn off the air conditioner and restart the engine.
5. Make sure the choke is fully open.
6. With the transmission in Drive, hold the hot idle compensator closed and adjust the throttle stop screw to obtain 600 rpm.
NOTE: the idle mixture screws have been preset at the factory and should not be adjusted unless absolutely necessary. Check all other possible causes of poor idle condition before adjusting the mixture screws.
7. To adjust the idle mixture, turn the mixture adjusting screws all the way in until lightly bottomed, then turn back out 6 full turns.
8. Set the throttle screw until 675 rpm is obtained. Transmission should be in Drive.

9. Turn each mixture screw in (clockwise) equally in 1/4 turn increments until 600 rpm is obtained.
10. Unplug and connect the distributor vacuum hose and install the air cleaner and air cleaner hose.
11. Be sure that the hot air adapter and ventilation tube are connected and seated properly.

1971
Adjust with air cleaner removed.
1. Warm up the engine and leave it running.
2. Remove the air cleaner, disconnect the air cleaner hose at the intake manifold and plug the fitting.
3. Make sure the choke is open and the air conditioner is off.
4. Disconnect the carburetor hose from the vapor canister. Do not plug the hose.
5. Disconnect the distributor vacuum hose at the distributor and plug the hose.
6. Set the dwell and timing.
7. Adjust the carburetor idle screw to obtain 600 rpm with the transmission in Drive.
NOTE: idle mixture screws have been preset at the factory and capped. Remove the caps only in the case of major overhaul, throttle body removal or when all other possible causes of poor idle condition have been thoroughly checked.
8. To adjust the idle mixture, stop the engine, connect a CO (carbon monoxide) meter to the exhaust system and turn the idle mixture screws in until they are lightly seated. Then back out the mixture screws 6 full turns. Start the engine and adjust the screws equally to obtain a good idle at the specified rpm with a maximum CO reading of 0.3%. Temporarily install the air cleaner and check the CO reading: if it exceeds 0.3%, readjust it.
9. Install new idle limiter caps.
10. Reinstall and reconnect everything that was removed or disconnected in Steps 1 through 5.

Fuel Pump Removal

1966-68
The fuel pump is located in front of the right bank of cylinders.
Disconnect the fuel and vacuum lines, take out the two mounting bolts that hold it to the timing case cover and lift off the pump.

1969-72
A new fuel pump features a large fuel reservoir, with a filter element within the pump housing.

Evaporative Emission Canister
1970-72 models are equipped with

an Evaporative Emission System that prevents fuel vapor loss to the atmosphere. The carbon canister stores vapors from the fuel tank vent system. The canister is located inside the left front fender filler panel. The fiber filter located in the bottom of the canister should be replaced every 12,000 miles.
To remove the canister:
1. Remove the air induction hose from the air cleaner and inlet duct.
2. Remove the two hoses on the top of the carbon canister.
3. Loosen the canister bracket clamp screw.
4. Remove the carbon canister.
5. Installation is the reverse of the above procedure.

Fuel Filter
All carburetors have a fuel filter that is integral with the carburetor body. To replace the filter element, remove the fuel inlet line, then remove the inlet fitting and pull out the filter element. When installing new filter element, tighten the inlet fitting gently.

Exhaust System

Exhaust pipes are retained to the manifold with a flange and two bolts or studs. The rest of the exhaust system components are held together with U-bolt clamps. When inspecting the exhaust system, check for rust holes in the mufflers and resonators and check that the drain holes are facing down and are not clogged.

The exhaust system is suspended from the frame with rubber damp-ened hangers. All of the pipes, mufflers or resonators should have at least 3/4 in. clearance from the floor pan to prevent the possibility of over-heating.

Tighten exhaust pipe to manifold flange bolts or stud nuts to 18 ft. lbs., U-bolt clamp nuts to 15 ft. lbs. and pipe hanger bolts to 10 ft. lbs.

Cooling System

Cooling System Information
Detailed information on cooling system capacity is in the Capacities table of this section.

Information on the water temperature gauge is in the Unit Repair Section.

Thermostatic Vacuum Switch
If equipped with exhaust emission control and air-conditioning, a thermostatic vacuum switch is used to

increase ignition timing advance at idle when higher coolant temperatures are encountered. This change, from part to full vacuum advance at engine idle, tends to improve cooling at idle.

If a heating condition exists at idle speeds only, disconnect the distributor vacuum hose at the thermostatic switch. When engine temperature is above 230° F., there should be no vacuum at this port at idle. If engine temperature is above 230° F., and vacuum is present at port D, check distributor advance.

Radiator R & R

1. Drain the cooling system.
2. Remove the upper radiator baffle.
3. Detach the fan shroud and set it on the fan.
4. Remove the upper, lower and overflow hoses.
5. Disconnect and cap the automatic transmission oil cooler lines.
6. Lift the radiator core out of the car.
7. To install, reverse the above procedure. Be sure that the lower support seals are correctly positioned. Fill the cooling system.

Water Pump Removal

Drain the cooling system and loosen the generator and power steering belts. Remove the fan and fan pulley, then remove bolts that hold the water pump to front of engine. Lift off the pump.

Only one side of the gasket should be coated with gasket compound when reinstalling.

Dip the bolts in sealer before inserting them into the pump.

Thermostat

On all engines, the thermostat is located under the water outlet elbow in the water manifold at the front of the block.

Engine

General engine specifications, crankcase capacities, torque specifications and valve specifications may be found at the beginning of this section.

Exhaust Emission Control

1966-67 models are equipped with the A.I.R. (Air Injection Reactor) emission control system. This system is designed to reduce unburnt hydrocarbons in the engine exhaust. An air pump forces filtered air into the exhaust port of each cylinder, thereby spontaneously oxidizing the carbon monoxide and unburnt hydrocarbons.

1968-72 models are equipped with the C.C.S. (Controlled Combustion System) emission control system. In conjunction with more refined ignition advance and retard mechanisms and carburetor tuning, the C.C.S. air intake system reduces pollutants in the exhaust. Whenever the engine compartment temperature is below 85°F., a vacuum diaphragm closes the external air cleaner intake. Air intake is then restricted to the hot air ducts which envelop the exhaust manifolds. See the Unit Repair Section for details.

Intake and Exhaust Manifolds

See the Oldsmobile-F-85 section for intake and exhaust manifold removal and installation procedures.

Cylinder Head

Cylinder head removal and installation, rocker arm and valve mechanism service procedures may be found in the Oldsmobile-F-85 section.

Hydraulic Lifters

Hydraulic lifters are used on all engines. These lifters are not interchangeable. To remove hydraulic lifters, first remove the intake manifold and rocker assemblies and pushrods (keep them in order), then pull out the lifters (keep them in sequence so that they may be reinstalled in their original locations).

Hydraulic lifters operate normally under conditions of zero valve lash.

Rocker arm lubrication is provided by means of oil feed through the pushrods.

Valve guides are not replaceable, but may be reamed to 0.003 in., 0.005 in. and 0.013 in. oversize. Occassionally a valve guide bore will be oversize as manufactured. These are marked on the inboard side of the cylinder head on the machined surface just above the intake manifold. To ream a 0.010 in. oversize valve guide bore, use the 0.013 in. reamer. Service valves are available in five different stem diameters: Standard, 0.003 in. oversize, 0.005 in. oversize, 0.010 in. oversize and 0.013 in. oversize.

Engine R & R

Removal

1. Drain radiator.
2. Remove hood, marking hinge for reassembly.
3. Disconnect battery.
4. Disconnect radiator hoses and cooler lines, heater hoses, vacuum hoses, engine to body ground strap, fuel hose from fuel line, wiring and accelerator cable. Remove air conditioner compressor and power steering pump without disconnecting lines and set them aside.
5. Remove coil, throttle control switch bracket, radiator support and radiator. Remove air cleaner.
6. Raise the car.
7. Disconnect exhaust pipes at manifold. Loosen, but do not remove, upper left flywheel cover attaching bolt (this will require 30 in. of wrench extension).
8. Disconnect wires and remove starter.
9. Remove torque converter cover and remove three bolts securing the converter to flywheel. Scribe marks on converter and flywheel for reassembly.

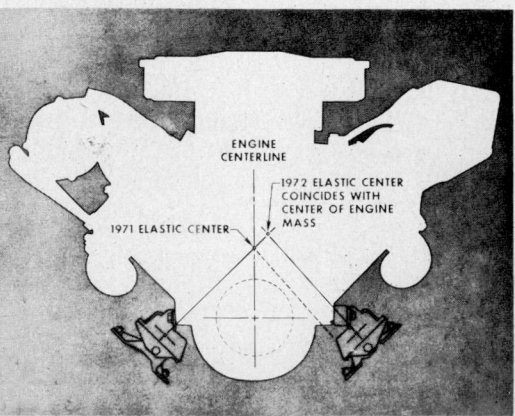

New mounts on 1972 Oldsmobile engines cause elastic center to coincide with center of engine mass.

(© Olds. Div., G.M. Corp.)

10. Attach a final drive supporting tool (BT-6322) to support final drive assembly.
11. Remove two attaching bolts from right output shaft support bracket and one through bolt attaching final drive to engine block on the left side. Scribe around the washers for correct reassembly.
12. Remove engine mount to crossmember nuts and front engine mount nuts.
13. Lower the car.
14. Support engine by using a lifting fixture (BT-6606).
15. Remove six bolts, transmission to engine.
16. Using suitable lifting device, lift engine from car.

Caution If car is to be moved, install converter holding tool (J-21654).

17. To install, reverse removal procedure.

Engine Lubrication

Oil Pan R & R

1966-67

1. Remove engine assembly.
2. Remove dipstick.
3. Drain oil and remove filter assembly.
4. Remove mount from front cover.
5. Remove oil pan attaching bolts and remove oil pan.
6. Apply a good sealer to both sides of pan gaskets and install on block.
7. Install front and rear seal.
8. Wipe lubricant on seal area and install pan. Torque 5/16 in. bolts to 15 ft. lbs. and 1/4 in. bolts to 10 ft. lbs.
9. Reinstall mount to front cover and oil filter assembly.
10. Reinstall engine and fill crankcase as explained in charts.

1968-70

1. Disconnect battery and remove dipstick.
2. Remove upper radiator support screws and fan shroud screws.
3. Hoist car and drain oil.
4. Disconnect engine mounts and jack front of engine up as far as possible.
5. Remove crossover pipe and starter.
6. Remove oil pan attaching bolts and remove oil pan.
7. Install in reverse order of removal, using new gaskets with sealer on both sides.

1971-72

The engine must be removed from the vehicle in order to remove the oil pan. Follow the procedure described for 1966-67 models above.

Oil Pump R & R

Remove the oil pan as described above. Remove the oil baffle. Remove the oil pump to rear main bearing cap attaching bolts, then remove the pump and drive shaft extension. See "Oil Pump" in the Oldsmobile-F-85 section for service procedures.

Rear Main Oil Seal Replacement

Whether or not the engine must be removed from the vehicle in order to replace the rear main bearing oil seal depends upon the removal of the oil pan. See "Oil Pan R & R" above. Remove the oil pan and rear main bearing cap. Using a blunt-ended tool, drive the upper seal into its groove on each side until it is tightly packed. This is usually 1/4—3/4 in. Cut pieces of the old lower bearing cap seal 1/16 in. longer than the distance each side of the upper seal was compressed. Install these pieces into each side of the upper seal seat, packing them into place. Carefully trim any protruding seal, being sure not to scratch or damage the bearing surface. Install a new seal in the bearing cap and install the cap, tightening bolts to 120 ft. lbs. Install the oil pan.

Timing Case

Timing case and front cover services require the removal of the engine.

Front Cover R & R

1. Remove the engine from the car.
2. Remove all belts, fan, fan pulley, crankshaft pulley and harmonic balancer.
3. Drain the crankcase and remove the oil pan.
4. Remove front cover attaching bolts and remove front cover, timing indicator and water pump assembly.
5. When installing, use a new gasket, applying sealer around the water holes.
6. Apply oil to bolt and thread holes, then tighten self-tapping water pump attaching bolts to 13 ft. lbs., 5/16 in. bolts to 25 ft. lbs. and the bottom three bolts and one stud to 50 ft. lbs.
7. Complete installation by following Steps 1 through 3 above in reverse order. Tighten crankshaft pulley bolt to 160 ft. lbs.

Front Cover Oil Seal R & R

The front cover oil seal may be replaced without removing the front cover from the engine and without removing the engine.
1. Remove the belts.
2. Remove the crankshaft pulley and harmonic balancer.

3. Using a seal puller (tool BT-6406), remove the oil seal.
4. Apply sealer to the outside diameter of the seal, then install the seal with tool BT-6405. Tighten the installing tool until there is a 0.005 in. clearance between the tool and the front cover.
5. Install the crankshaft harmonic balancer and pulley, tightening the pulley attaching bolt to 160 ft. lbs. and the pulley bolts to 20 ft. lbs.
6. Install and adjust the belts.

Timing Gear R & R

1. Remove the front cover as described above (the engine must be removed from the car).
2. Remove the fuel pump.
3. Remove the fuel pump eccentric.

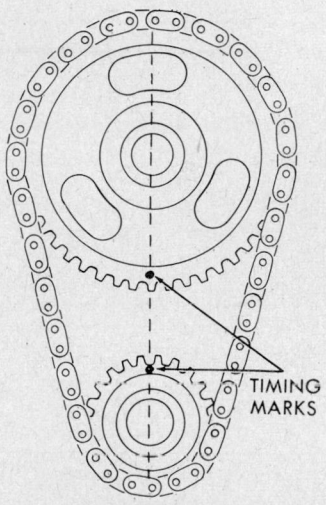

Valve timing alignment marks

4. Remove the oil slinger, cam gear and timing chain.
5. Remove the crankshaft gear and key.
6. Install the camshaft gear, crankshaft gear and timing chain as an assembly, with the timing marks aligned as illustrated.
7. Install the fuel pump eccentric with the cupped side out, tightening the attaching bolt to 160 ft. lbs.
8. Drive in the crankshaft key with a brass hammer until it bottoms.
9. Install the oil slinger.
10. Install the fuel pump and front cover, then install the engine.

Camshaft R & R

1. Remove the engine from the car, then remove the oil pan and front cover.
2. Remove valve covers, rocker arms, pushrods and hydraulic lifters, keeping the pushrods and lifters in order so that they can be installed in their original positions.
3. Remove the intake manifold.
4. Remove the oil filler pipe and

water temperature switch.

5. Remove the fuel pump, fuel pump eccentric, camshaft gear, oil slinger and timing chain.

6. Carefully remove camshaft by sliding it out the front of the engine.

7. To install the camshaft, coat the bearings with Concentrate No. 582099 or 1050800 or equivalent, then, with camshaft and crankshaft gears properly aligned, install the camshaft in the engine.

8. Complete installation by reversing Steps 1 through 5, referring to front cover and timing gear procedures above.

Rod and Main Bearings

NOTE: it is necessary to remove the engine in order to service the bearing area.

Main Bearing Replacement

1. Remove the oil pan and oil pump.

2. Use Plastigauge to measure individual bearing clearances. If clearance is in excess of 0.0035 in. on any journal, both shells must be replaced. It is possible to have more than one bearing size in the same engine. Tighten bearing cap bolts to 120 ft. lbs. when using the Plastigauge.

3. To replace the bearing, remove the bearing cap and lower shell.

4. Insert a flattened cotter pin or roll out pin in the oil passage hole in the crankshaft, then rotate the crankshaft in the direction opposite to cranking rotation. The upper shell should roll out.

5. Check the journals for scoring and out-of-round. Maximum out-of-round is 0.0015 in.

6. Clean journal and bearing cap thoroughly, then place new upper shell (with tang in proper position) on the journal and turn it into place with a flattened cotter pin or roll out pin. Install lower shell in the bearing cap and install cap, tightening cap bolts to 120 ft. lbs. Apply Special Lubricant No. 1050169 or equivalent to the thrust flanges of No. 3 bearing shells before installation. Install a new upper and lower rear oil seal when replacing No. 5 bearing.

7. Install oil pump and oil pan, then install the engine.

Connecting Rods and Pistons

To service the pistons and rod bearings, remove the engine from the car and remove the oil pan, oil pump and cylinder heads. When replacing pistons and rod bearings, complete one cylinder at a time to insure that all parts are reinstalled in their original positions.

Use a ridge reamer to remove the ridge from the cylinder bore above the ring travel before removing the piston and rod assembly.

When replacing rod bearings, first clean and check the journal for scoring and out-of-round. Maximum allowable out-of-round is 0.0015 in. If measuring clearance with Plastigage, place the piece of Plastigage in the center of the lower-bearing shell and tighten the bearing cap bolts to 42 ft. lbs. Maximum allowable bearing clearance is 0.0035 in. Measure the rod side clearance by spreading the rods apart with a screwdriver and inserting a feeler gauge. Side clearance should be 0.002 to 0.011 in. Assemble the rod such that the bearing shell tangs, rod oil spit hole and bearing cap tang notch are all in the center of the engine V. Lubricate the bearing shells with engine oil before installation.

Maximum allowable cylinder bore taper is 0.001 in. Piston to cylinder bore clearance should be 0.001 to 0.002 in. If new rings are to be installed in the old pistons, thoroughly clean out the ring grooves. Ring gap should be 0.013 to 0.023 in. for the compression rings and 0.015 to 0.055 in. for the oil rings. Measure the gap with the ring positioned at the bottom of the ring travel in the cylinder bore.

All cylinder rod nuts are tightened to 42 ft. lbs.

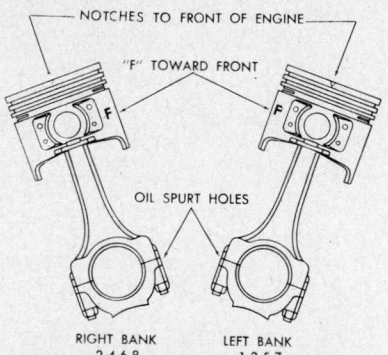

Piston and rod assembly—425 cu. in. (letter "F" is on skirt cutaway on 455 cu. in.)

Correct piston and rod assembly position on the 425 cu. in. engine is with the letter "F" on the side of the piston facing toward the front of the engine; and on the 455 cu. in. engine with the letter "F" on the bottom of the inside skirt facing the front of the engine.

Front Suspension

Description

The front suspension consists of control arms, stabilizer bar, shock absorbers and a right and left torsion bar. Torsion bars are used in place of conventional coil springs. The front end of the torsion bar is attached to the lower control arm. The rear of torsion bar is mounted into an adjustable arm at the torsion bar crossmember. The carrying height of the car is controlled by this adjustment.

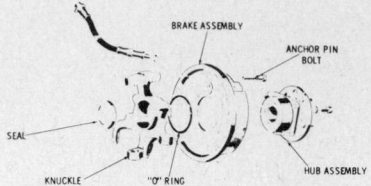

Front hub assembly—1966-69
(© G.M. Corp.)

Wheel Hub (Front) Removal and Installation

1. Carefully pull drum from hub assembly.

2. Remove drive axle cotter pin, nut and washer. Remove disc, if so equipped.

3. Position access slot in hub assembly so each of the attaching bolts can be removed.

4. Position spacer tool (J-22237) and install front hub puller (J-21579) and slide hammer (J-2619).

5. Remove hub assembly.

6. To install, reverse removal procedure.

NOTE: O.D. of bearing must be lubricated with E.P. chassis lubricant. Use care when installing hub assembly over drive axle splines.

Disc R & R

1970-72

1. Siphon off about two-thirds of the fluid in the front reservoir of the master cylinder. Do not empty the reservoir or it will be necessary to bleed the system.

2. Hoist the car and remove the wheel.

3. Position piston compressor tool on the caliper and tighten the screw until the piston bottoms and the shoes are backed off the disc.

4. Remove the two caliper to knuckle attaching bolts and carefully lift the caliper from the disc. Support it so that the hose is not kinked or stretched.

5. Mark the hub and disc so that they will be correctly positioned when installed, then pull evenly on the disc to remove.

6. To install, reverse the above procedure. Make sure that the disc is positioned according to the marks made during removal. Tighten the caliper attaching bolts to 35 ft. lbs. and the wheel

nuts to 115 ft. lbs. Fill the front reservoir of the master cylinder and check the action of the brakes.

Steering Knuckle O-Ring Seal

1966-68

Replacement of seal with wheel removed.
1. Remove hub and drum.
2. Remove upper ball joint cotter pin and nut.
3. Remove brake line hose clip from ball joint stud.
NOTE: do not loosen ball joint stud.
4. Bend lock plate on anchor bolt up and remove anchor bolt.
5. Carefully lift brake backing plate outboard over end of axle shaft and support brake hose so that it is not damaged.
6. Remove O-ring seal.
7. To install, reverse removal procedure.

Knuckle Seals—1969-72

Right-Hand Seal Removal
1. Hoist car under lower control arms.
2. Remove drive axle cotter pin, nut and washer.
3. Remove oil filter element.
4. Remove inner C. V. joint attaching bolts and push joint outward and rearward to disengage from output shaft.
5. Remove output shaft.
6. Remove drive axle assembly.
7. Pry seal from knuckle.

Left-Hand Seal Removal
1. Hoist car under lower control arms.
2. Remove wheel and drum.
3. Remove drive axle cotter pin, nut and washer.
4. Remove tie-rod end cotter pin and nut.
5. Split tie-rod.
6. Place support block between drive axle and lower control arm.
7. Remove upper control arm ball joint cotter pin and nut. Remove brake hose clip from ball joint stud.
8. Using hammer and brass drift, drive on knuckle until ball joint stud is free.
9. Install spacer between lower ball joint seal and knuckle.
10. Remove lower ball joint from knuckle, using a puller.
11. Remove knuckle.
12. Pry seal from knuckle.

Steering Knuckle Removal
1. Remove hub and drum or disc.
2. Remove upper ball joint cotter pin and nut. Remove caliper starting 1969.
3. Remove brake line hose clip

from ball joint stud.
NOTE: do not loosen ball joint stud.
4. Bend lock plate on anchor bolt up and remove anchor bolt of cars with drum brakes.
5. Carefully lift brake backing plate outboard over end of axle shaft and support brake hose so that it is not damaged.
NOTE: it is not necessary to remove dust shield on cars with disc brakes.
6. Place rubber pad over lower control arm torsion bar connector to protect C.V. joint seal.
7. Using a brass drift and hammer loosen upper ball joint stud.
8. Remove cotter pin and nut from tie-rod end.
9. Using brass drift and hammer, remove tie-rod end from knuckle.
10. Remove cotter pin and nut from lower ball joint.
11. Carefully place ball joint puller adapter between ball joint seal and knuckle.
12. Remove lower ball joint from knuckle.
13. Remove knuckle.
14. Knuckle seal can be pried from the knuckle at this time.

Steering Knuckle Installation
1. Using seal installer, install seal into knuckle. Seal should be packed with chassis grease.
2. Install lower ball joint stud into knuckle and attach nut. Do not tighten nut at this time.
3. Install tie-rod and stud into knuckle and attach nut. Do not tighten nut at this time.
4. Install upper ball joint stud into knuckle and attach nut. Do not tighten nut at this time.
5. Install backing plate onto knuckle with anchor bolt and lock plate. Do not tighten nut at this time.
6. Remove upper ball joint attaching nut and install brake line hose clip.
7. Torque ball joint nuts to a minimum of 40 ft. lbs. up to 1969, 85 ft. lbs. starting 1970. Never back off to install cotter pins.
NOTE: cotter pin on upper ball joint must be bent up, only, to prevent interference with C. V. joint seal.
8. Torque tie-rod end to 30 ft. lbs. and install cotter pin.
9. Torque anchor bolt to 135 ft. lbs. on drum brake models, and bend lock plate onto flat of bolt head.
10. Install drum or disc and wheel; install drive axle nut.
12. Remove floor stand and lower car.
13. Be sure to check camber, caster and toe-in, and adjust if necessary. Tighten drive axle and lug nuts to 105-110 ft. lbs.

Torsion Bar Removal

1966
1. Hoist car and place floor stands under front frame horns. Lower front hoist.
2. Slide seal at rear of torsion bar forward.
3. Install torsion bar remover and installer on the crossmember support. Align pin of tool in hole in crossmember. Turn center screw until seated in dimple of torsion adjusting arm.
4. Using a socket on the torsion bar adjusting bolt, turn counter-clockwise; counting the number of turns necessary to remove.
NOTE: number of turns to remove the adjusting bolt will be used when installing.
5. Remove adjusting bolt and nut.
6. Turn center screw of tool until torsion bar is completely relaxed.
7. Place a block of wood 6 x 6 x 8 in. on hoist and raise under lower control arm until drive axle is horizontal.
8. Remove stabilizer bolt, nut, grommets, retainers and spacer. Discard the bolt.
9. Place a daub of paint on the bottom side of the torsion bar.
10. Slide torsion bar forward until it bottoms in lower control arm. Adjusting arm will drop out.
NOTE: do not mark, scratch, or in any way damage the surface of the torsion bar. Replacement will be necessary if such conditions exist.
11. Remove bolt from crossmember on the side you are removing torsion bar.
12. Remove center bolt assembly from tool BT-6601.
13. Raise crossmember and twist rearward until torsion bar clears member.
14. Slowly raise lower control arm until maximum height is obtained. Care must be exercised so the floor stands are not dislodged.
15. Raise center crossmember until contact is made with floor pan.
16. Pull rearward on torsion bar with hands only, until torsion bar is out of lower control arm. It may be necessary to use air, blowing into nut of lower control arm, to relieve the vacuum caused by grease.

1967-68
1. Hoist car under the lower control arms.
2. Slide seal at rear of torsion bar forward.
3. Install torsion bar remover and installer on the torsion bar crossmember. Position the tool center bolt in the dimple on the torsion adjusting arm.
4. Turn the torsion adjusting bolt counter-clockwise, counting the

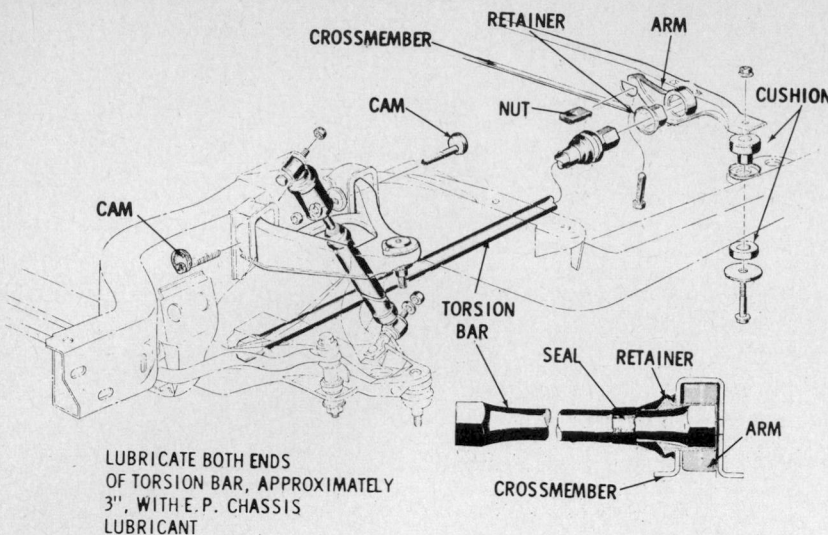

LUBRICATE BOTH ENDS
OF TORSION BAR, APPROXIMATELY
3", WITH E.P. CHASSIS
LUBRICANT

Front suspension torsion bar   (© Olds. Div., G.M. Corp.)

number of turns necessary to remove it.

5. Remove the torsion adjusting
nut, and turn the center bolt of
the removal and installation tool
until the torsion bar is completely relaxed.

6. Slide the torsion bar forward
until it bottoms in the control
arm. The adjusting arm will drop
out.

7. Remove the bolt from the crossmember on the side from which
you are removing the torsion
bar.

8. Raise the crossmember and twist
it rearward until the torsion bar
is free.

9. Support the frame horns with
stands, and lower the hoist until
the control arms are hanging
freely.

10. Remove the lower control arm
rear bushing bolt.

11. Pry the lower control arm downward until the torsion bar can be
pulled out.

Removing torsion bar
(© Oldsmobile Div. G.M. Corp.)

1969-72

1. Hoist car and support at lift
points.
2. Place torsion bar remover and installer so that center screw is
seated in dimple of torsion adjusting arm.
3. Remove torsion bar adjusting bolt, counting number of
turns necessary.
4. Turn center screw of tool until
torsion bar is completely relaxed.
5. Disconnect stabilizer link.
6. Disconnect shock absorber from
lower control arm.
7. Remove bolts from lower control
arm to frame.
8. Pry lower control arm from
frame and move forward until
torsion bar and adjusting arm
can be removed.

Torsion Bar Installation

1966

1. Lubricate both ends of torsion
bar for approximately 3 in. with

extreme pressure chassis lubricant.
2. With daub of paint, in the same
location as when removed, insert torsion bar into lower control bar nut and push forward
until bar bottoms.
3. Pry crossmember back, then
align torsion bar with hole in
crossmember.
4. Lower crossmember and install
torsion bar removal and installation tool.
5. Lower front lower control arm
until drive axle is horizontal.
6. Install torsion bar arm and pull
torsion bar rearward until fully
seated in arm.
7. Install crossmember bolt through
rubber mounting and torque to
40 ft. lbs.
8. Lower front lower control arm
and remove 6 x 6 x 8 in. block.
9. Install new bolt into stabilizer
bar to lower control arm. Torque
to 14 ft. lbs., cut off bottom of
bolt so that ¼ in. is remaining
below nut.
10. Using removal and installation
tool, tighten up torsion bar arm
to install lock plate under arm
and through crossmember.
11. Lubricate threads of torsion bar
adjuster bolt with extreme pressure chassis lubricant and turn
nut the same number of turns
used to remove.
12. Remove installation tool.
13. Raise front hoist and remove
floor stands from front frame
horns. Lower car to floor.
14. Check ride height. Correct by
turning torsion bar adjusting
bolt.

1967-68

1. Lubricate both ends of the torsion bar (approximately 3 in.)
with extreme pressure chassis
lubricant.
2. Install the torsion bar in the
lower control arm, pushing it
forward until it bottoms.
3. Pry the crossmember back, and
align the torsion bar with the
hole in the crossmember.
4. Position the lower control arm,
and install the bolt and nut. Do
not torque.
5. Raise the hoist, and remove the
frame stands.
6. Install the torsion bar adjusting
arm in the crossmember, and
pull the torsion bar rearward
until fully seated in the arm.
7. Install the crossmember bolt and
torque to 40 ft. lbs.
8. Install the torsion bar removal
and installation tool on the crossmember, with the center bolt
seated in the dimple on the adjusting arm.
9. Tighten the tool center bolt, and
install the adjusting nut under
the arm in the crossmember.

10. Lubricate the adjusting bolt threads with extreme pressure chassis lubricant, and install the same number of turns that it was backed out.
11. Lower the car to the ground, and torque the control arm bolt to 80 ft. lbs.

1969-72

1. Lubricate both ends of torsion bar for approximately 3 in. with extreme pressure chassis lubricant.
2. Position adjusting arm into crossmember, insert torson bar into adjusting arm and lower control arm, then position lower control arm into frame brackets and install nuts and bolts loosely.
3. Connect shock to lower control arm, tightening nut to 80 ft. lbs.
4. Connect stabilizer bar to lower control arm. Torque nut to 15 ft. lbs. and cut off bolt ¼ in. below nut.
5. Place torsion bar remover and installer over crossmember and tighten center screw.
6. Raise hoist under lower control arms.
7. Torque lower control arm bushing nuts to 90 ft. lbs.
8. Check ride height and adjust if necessary.

Upper Control Arm Removal

NOTE: the upper control arm is serviced as an assembly, less bushings.
1. Hoist car and remove wheel.
2. Remove upper shock attaching bolt.
3. Remove cotter pin and nut on upper ball joint.
4. Disconnect brake hose clamp from ball joint stud.
5. Separate upper ball joint stud from steering knuckle.
6. Remove upper control arm cam assemblies and remove control arm from car by guiding shock absorber through access hole in arm.

Upper Control Arm Installation

1. Guide upper control arm over shock absorber and install bushing ends into frame horns.
2. Install cam assemblies.
NOTE: front cam is mounted up, rear cam is mounted down.
3. Install ball joint stud into knuckle.
4. Install brake hose clip onto ball joint stud.
5. Install ball joint nut. Torque to 40 ft. lbs. and insert cotter pin, crimp.
NOTE: cotter pin must be crimped toward upper control arm to prevent interference with outer C. V. joint seal.
6. Install upper shock, attaching bolt and nut. Torque to 75 ft. lbs.

7. Install wheel.
8. Lower hoist.
9. Check camber, caster and toe-in, and adjust if necessary.

Upper Control Arm Bushing Removal (On the Car)

NOTE: the upper control arm bushings can be removed and installed on or off the car.
1. Hoist car under lower control arms and remove wheel.
2. Disconnect upper shock absorber attaching bolt.
3. Remove cam assemblies from control arms.
4. Move control arms out of frame horns and attach bushing removal tools.

Upper Control Arm Bushing Installation (On the Car)

1. Install tools and press bushings into control arm.
2. Move control arm into frame horns and install cam assemblies. Front cam is installed with the bolt in the lower position. Rear cam is installed with the bolt in the upper position.
3. Connect upper shock attaching bolt. Torque to 75 ft. lbs.
4. Replace wheel and lower car.
5. Align front wheels.

Lower Control Arm Removal —Right Side 1966-68

1. Remove drive axle assembly.
2. Hoist car and place floor stands under frame horns.
3. Relax the torsion bar. Refer to Torsion Bar Removal.
4. Remove wheel.
5. Remove shock absorber.
6. Disconnect stabilizer bar from lower control arm. Discard the bolt.
7. Place a spacer between stabilizer bar and tie rod.
8. Remove cotter pin and nut from lower ball joint stud.
9. Remove the ball joint stud from spindle.
10. Remove lower control arm bushing bolts and, with the aid of a helper, remove lower control arm and torsion bar, as an assembly. Torsion bar arm will drop out at this time.
11. Carefully slide torsion bar from lower control arm and store in a safe clean place.

Lower Control Arm Installation —Right Side 1966-68

1. Lubricate both ends of torsion bar for approximately 3 in., with extreme pressure chassis lubricant.
2. Install torsion bar into nut of lower control arm.

3. With the aid of a helper, lift torsion bar and lower control arm assembly up until torsion bar will engage arm in crossmember and bushing ends of lower control arm engage frame horn.
NOTE: make sure daub of paint on torsion bar is in the same position as when removed.
4. Install lower control arm bushing bolts and nuts. Do not torque.
5. Install lower control arm ball joint stud into knuckle. Install and torque to 40 ft. lbs.
6. Remove spacer from between stabilizer bar and tie rod.
7. Using a new bolt, connect stabilizer bar to lower control arm. Refer to illustration for correct sequence of grommets, retainers and spacer. Torque to 14 ft. lbs. Cut bolt off ¼ in. below nut.
8. Install shock absorber. Torque upper bolts to 75 ft. lbs., lower nut to 75 ft. lbs.
9. Install wheel.
10. Position torsion bar removal and installation tool over torsion bar crossmember and tighten center bolt until adjustment nut can be positioned through crossmember. Lubricate adjuster bolt with E. P. chassis lubricant and turn in the same number of turns noted during removal.
11. Raise hoist under lower control arms and remove floor stands.
12. Install right-hand drive axle assembly.
13. Torque lower control arm bushing bolts to 75 ft. lbs.
14. Check caster, camber and toe-in.

Lower Control Arm Removal —Left Side 1966-68

1. Remove drive axle assembly. Refer to Drive Axle Assembly Removal—Left Hand.
2. Place floor stands under frame horns.
3. Lower hoist slowly until floor stands are seated and hoist is still under lower control arm.
4. Remove shock absorber and bolt from stabilizer bar to lower control arm. Discard the bolt.
5. Completely relax the torsion bar. Refer to Torsion Bar Removal.
6. Lower front hoist to floor.
7. With the aid of a helper, remove lower control arm attaching bolts and carefully lower control arm and torsion bar as an assembly. Torsion bar arm will drop out at this time.
8. Carefully slide torsion bar from lower control arm and store in a safe clean place.

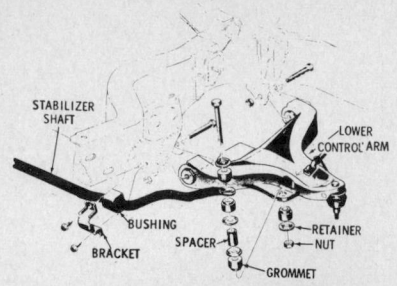

Lower control arm and related components
(© Oldsmobile Div. G.M. Corp.)

Lower Control Arm Installation —Left Side 1966-68

1. Lubricate both ends of torsion bar with extreme pressure chassis lubricant for approximately 3 in.
2. Install torsion bar into nut of lower control arm.
3. With the aid of a helper, lift torsion bar and lower control arm assembly up until torsion bar will engage arm in crossmember and bushing ends of lower control arm engage frame horn.

   NOTE: make sure daub of paint on torsion bar is in the same position as when removed.
4. Install lower control arm bushing bolts and nuts. Do not torque.
5. Position torsion bar removal and installation tool over torsion bar crossmember and tighten center bolt until lower control arm is in a horizontal plane.
6. Install drive axle. Refer to Drive Axle Installation—Left Side.
7. Install shock absorber. Torque upper bolt to 75 ft. lbs., lower nut to 75 ft. lbs.
8. Using a new bolt, connect stabilizer bar to lower control arm. Refer to illustration for correct sequence of grommets, retainers and spacer. Torque to 14 ft. lbs. Cut bolt off 1/4 in. below nut.
9. Continue to tighten center bolt of tool until adjustment nut can be positioned through crossmember. Lubricate adjuster bolt with E. P. chassis lubricant and turn in the same amount of turns noted during removal.
10. Install drum and wheel.
11. Remove floor stands and lower hoist.
12. Torque lower control arm bushing bolt to 75 ft. lbs.
13. Check caster, camber and toe-in.

Lower Control Arm R & R —1969-72

1. Hoist car and support at lift points. Remove wheel assembly.
2. Place torsion bar remover and installer over crossmember so that center screw is seated in dimple of torsion adjusting arm.
3. Remove torsion bar adjusting

bolt and nut, counting the number of turns necessary.

NOTE: this number of turns will be used when installing, to obtain initial carrying height.
4. Turn center screw of tool until torsion bar is completely relaxed.
5. Disconnect shock absorber and stabilizer link from lower control arm.
6. Remove drive axle nut.
7. Remove cotter pin and nut from lower ball joint stud.
8. Remove ball joint stud from knuckle, using puller.
9. Push drive axle in and pull knuckle outward to gain clearance, then remove lower control arm from knuckle and torsion bar.
10. Install by reversing removal procedure. Check and adjust ride height if necessary.

Lower Control Arm Bushing Removal

1. Hoist car on a two post lift.
2. Disconnect upper shock attaching bolt.
3. Remove stabilizer link bolt and discard the bolt.
4. Place floor stands under frame horns. Lower front lift to floor.

   NOTE: on 1971-72 models, the frame brace must be unbolted and moved away from the lower control arm mounts.
5. Install torsion bar removal and installation tool.
6. Remove lower control arm bushing bolts and lower control arm until free of frame horns.
7. Install bolts through rear bushing and press out bushing.

   NOTE: Because of the torsion bar nut attachment to the lower control arm, it will be necessary to use a hardened 1/2—20 nut, to remove the front bushing.

Lower Control Arm Bushing Installation

1. Install tools and press rear bushing into lower control arm.

   NOTE: Because of the torsion bar nut attachment to the lower control arm, it will be necessary to use a hardened 1/2-20 nut, to install the front bushing.
2. Raise lower control arm into frame horns and install bushing bolts and nuts. Do not torque.
3. Turn center bolt of tool into dimple of torsion bar arm until adjusting nut can be inserted through center frame support. Turn adjusting bolt clockwise the same number of turns needed to remove. Remove tool.
4. Raise front lift under lower control arms, and remove floor stands.

5. Connect upper shock attaching bolt and nut. Torque to 75 ft. lbs.
6. Using a new bolt, attach stabilizer link bolt to lower control arm. Torque to 14 ft. lbs.
7. Lower car and torque lower control arm bushing bolts to 75 ft. lbs.

Ball Joint Vertical Check

1. Raise the car and position floor stands under the left and right lower control arm, as near as possible to each lower ball joint. Car must be stable and should not rock on floor stands.
2. Position dial indicator to register vertical movement at wheel hub.
3. Place a pry bar between the lower control arm and the outer race of the C.V. joint and pry down on the bar. Care must be used so that the drive axle seal is not damaged. The vertical reading must not exceed .125 in.

Ball Joint Horizontal Check

1. Place car on floor stands, as outlined in Step 1 in the Vertical Check.
2. Position dial indicator at the rim of the wheel, to indicate side play.
3. Grasp wheel with the hands, top and bottom, and push in on the bottom of the tire while pulling out at the top. Read gauge, then reverse the push-pull procedure. Horizontal deflection on the gauge should not exceed .125 in. at the wheel rim. This procedure checks both the upper and lower ball joints.

Lower Control Arm Ball Joint Removal

1. Remove knuckle.
2. Using hack saw, saw the three rivet heads off.
3. Using a 7/32 in. bit, drill side rivets 3/16 in. deep.
4. Using hammer and punch, drive center rivet out of the control arm.

Lower Control Arm Ball Joint Installation

1. Install service ball joint into control arm and torque bolts and nut.
2. Install knuckle.

Lower Control Arm Ball Joint Seal Removal

The lower ball joint seal can be installed with lower control arm either in or out of the car.
1. Remove steering knuckle. Refer to Knuckle Removal.
2. Using hammer and chisel, drive seal from ball joint.
3. Wipe grease from ball joint and stud.

Lower Control Arm
Ball Joint Seal Installation

1. Position new seal over ball joint stud.
2. Lubricate jaws of seal installer and carefully slide jaw between seal and retainer.
3. Tap lightly with hammer on center bolt of tool until retainer is fully seated.
4. Install knuckle.
5. Lubricate the ball joint fitting until grease appears from seal.

Stabilizer Bar Removal

1. Remove link bolts, nuts, grommets, spacers and retainers from lower control arm. Discard bolts.
2. Remove two bolts which attach dust shield to frame, both sides.
3. Remove bracket to frame attaching bolts and remove stabilizer bar from front of car.

Stabilizer Bar Installation

Reverse removal procedure.
NOTE: new link bolts are torqued to 14 ft. lbs., then cut off ¼ in. from nut.

Torsion Bar Crossmember Removal

1. Raise car on a two post hoist and place floor stand under front torque boxes. Lower front hoist.
2. Disconnect parking brake cable and equalizer, and clip at torsion bar crossmember. Pull cable through the crossmember.
3. Relax torsion bars. Refer to Torsion Bar Removal.
4. Remove torsion bar removal and installation tool.
5. Slide both torsion bars forward until they bottom in lower control arm nut.

6. Remove bolts from torsion bar crossmember to frame.
7. Raise torsion bar crossmember, remove rubber cushions from frame horns.
8. Disconnect hangers at muffler and tail pipes.
9. Move torsion bar crossmember to the right or left side until member clears frame, then remove.

Torsion Bar Crossmember Installation

1. Insert torsion bar crossmember above frame on right side of car and position left side over frame horn.
2. Raise crossmember so that rubber cushions can be installed.
3. Lubricate ends of torsion bars with extreme pressure chassis lubricant for about 3 in.
4. Raise crossmember up and toward rear of car. Raise torsion bars until they enter hole provided for them in crossmember.
5. Install adjuster arms into crossmember and slide torsion bars toward the rear of car until fully seated against rear edge of crossmember.
6. Install rebound cushions, bolts, washers and nuts through frame and crossmember. Torque to 40 ft. lbs.
7. Position torsion bar installation and removal tool over crossmember and tighten center bolt until nut can be inserted through crossmember.
8. Lubricate adjuster bolt with extreme pressure chassis lubricant and turn the same number of turns required to remove it.
9. Remove tool.
10. Install seals over retainers at

rear of torsion bars.
11. Insert parking brake cable through crossmember. Install clip at crossmember.
12. Connect parking brake cable to equalizer.
13. Connect and tighten muffler and tail pipe hangers.
14. Hoist car and remove floor stands.
15. Lower car.
16. Check parking brake cable adjustment. Adjust as necessary.

Front End Alignment

Carrying height is controlled by the adjustment setting of the torsion bar adjusting bolt. Clockwise rotation of the bolt increases the front height. It is very important that this height be considered and made correct before further steering geometry is established. Car must be on a level surface, gas tank full or a compensating weight added. Front seat must be all the way to the rear and tires inflated properly. All doors must be closed and no passengers or additional weight should be in the car or trunk.

1. Check rocker panel to ground dimension, as illustrated. Front and rear reading to ground should be as follows. Front to rear and side to side should be within ¾ in.

	Front	Rear
1966	8 in.	8⅛ in.
1967-68	8 in.	8¼ in.
1969-70	8 in.	8 in.
1971-72	8¾ in.	9 in.

2. Align car on wheel alignment equipment as follows:
3. Raise front end and check wheel runout. Set and center the run-

CAR ON LEVEL SURFACE
FUEL TANK FULL
TRUNK EMPTY
FRONT SEAT REARWARD
DOORS CLOSED
TIRES AT CORRECT PRESSURE

TO ADJUST FRONT CARRYING HEIGHT
RAISE CAR AT FRONT CROSSMEMBER
TO RELIEVE STRAIN ON ADJUSTING
BOLT. LUBRICATE ADJUSTING BOLT
BEFORE ATTEMPTING TO CHANGE
CARRYING HEIGHT.

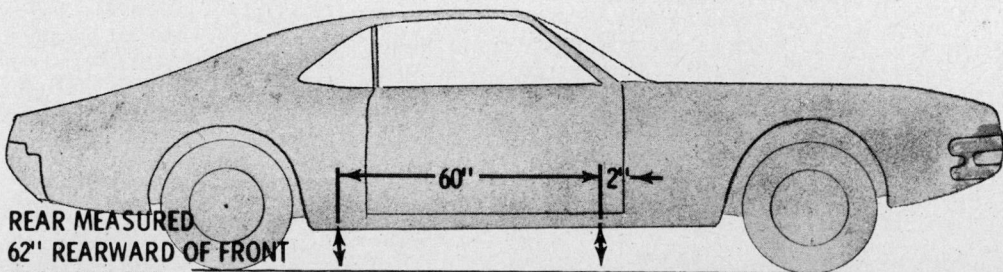

REAR MEASURED
62" REARWARD OF FRONT
EDGE OF DOOR
SPEC. 8' + 1/2" OR -1" ROCKER PANEL TO FLOOR

FRONT TO REAR - WITHIN 3/4"
SIDE TO SIDE - WITHIN 3/4"

FRONT MEASURED 2" REARWARD OF
FRONT EDGE OF DOOR
SPEC. 8" + 1/2" OR - 1" MEASURED FROM
ROCKER PANEL TO FLOOR.

Adjusting carrying height (© Oldsmobile Div. G.M. Corp.)

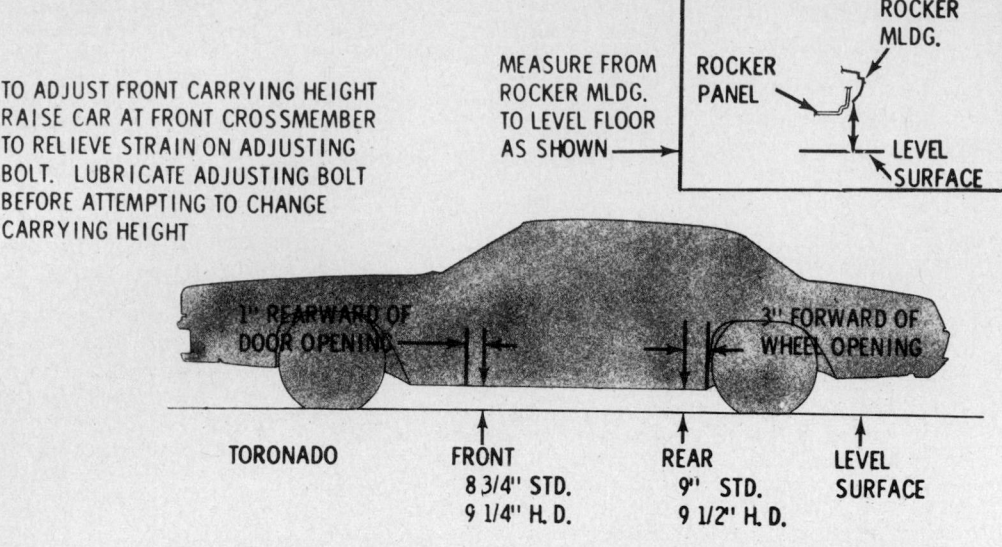

TO ADJUST FRONT CARRYING HEIGHT
RAISE CAR AT FRONT CROSSMEMBER
TO RELIEVE STRAIN ON ADJUSTING
BOLT. LUBRICATE ADJUSTING BOLT
BEFORE ATTEMPTING TO CHANGE
CARRYING HEIGHT

MEASURE FROM
ROCKER MLDG.
TO LEVEL FLOOR
AS SHOWN

ROCKER
MLDG.

ROCKER
PANEL

LEVEL
SURFACE

1" REARWARD OF
DOOR OPENING

3" FORWARD OF
WHEEL OPENING

TORONADO   FRONT   REAR   LEVEL
            8 3/4" STD.   9" STD.   SURFACE
            9 1/4" H.D.   9 1/2" H.D.

FRONT TO REAR +1/2" TO -3/4"
SIDE TO SIDE 3/4" MAX.
FRONT TO REAR SLOPE +3/4"

MEASURE WITH FULL GAS TANK SEAT
REARWARD, TIRE PRESSURE CORRECT,
DOOR CLOSED AND TRUNK EMPTY

Adjusting carrying height—1971-72 (© Oldsmobile Div., G.M. Corp.)

out, then lower the car.

4. Loosen nuts on inboard side of upper control arm cam bolts.
5. Check camber and adjust if necessary with rear cam bolt.
6. Take the caster reading. Use camber reading scale for making this adjustment.
   A. Turn rear bolt so camber reading is 1/4° more than original setting, for every 1° of caster change needed for correct reading. Turn to plus side of camber if caster is negative and to negative camber if caster is positive.
   B. Turn the front cam bolts so camber will return to the original proper setting.
   C. Recheck caster reading.
   NOTE: if a problem exists, and you should run out of cam in the attempt to gain correct reading:
   A. Turn front cam bolt so high part of cam is pointing up.
   B. Turn rear cam bolt so high part of cam is pointing down.
   This is a location to start from and a correct setting should be obtainable with the above procedure.
   NOTE: torque upper control arm cam nuts to 95 ft. lbs.; hold head of bolt securely. Any movement of the cam will affect final setting and you will have to recheck caster and camber adjustment.
7. Toe-in adjustment is as follows.
   A. Center steering wheel, raise car and check wheel runout.
   B. Loosen tie rod end nuts, and adjust to proper setting.
   C. Tighten tie rod end nuts. Torque nuts 20 ft. lbs. Position tie rod clamps so open-

ings of clamps are facing up. This is a very necessary setting. Interference and possible trouble with front end linkage could occur if clamps snag anything while turning.

Drive Axles

Drive axles are a complete flexible assembly and consist of an axle shaft with an inner and outer constant velocity joints. Right axle shaft has a torsional damper mounted in the center. The inner constant velocity joint has complete flexibility, plus inward and outward movement. The outer constant velocity joint has complete flexibility only.

Beginning 1967

Beginning 1967, Tri-pot inboard drive joints replace the ball spline Rzeppa joints of 1966 production. These joints consist of a three-pronged trunnion spider, needle bearing mounted balls, a universal housing, axle shaft, and rubber boot. This joint combines constant velocity universal action with axial slip motion.

Drive Axle Removal
—Right Side

1. Hoist car under lower control arms.
2. Remove drive axle cotter pin, nut and washer.
3. Remove oil filter.
4. Remove inner constant velocity joint attaching bolts.
5. Push inner constant velocity joint outward enough to disengage the right-hand final drive output shaft, then move rearward.
6. Remove right-hand output shaft bracket bolts to engine and final drive.
7. Remove right-hand output shaft and drive axle assembly.

Caution Care must be exercised so that constant velocity joints do not turn to full extremes, and that seals are not damaged against shock absorber or stabilizer bar.

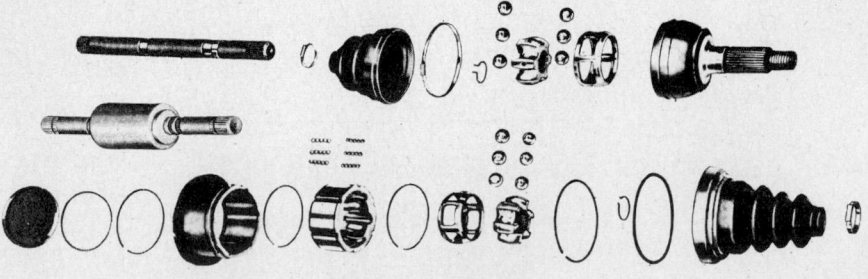

Drive axle assembly

Drive Axle Installation —Right Side

1. Carefully place righthand drive axle assembly into lower control arm and enter outer race splines into knuckle.
2. Lubricate final drive output shaft seal, with special seal lubricant part No. 1050169.
3. Install right-hand output shaft into final drive and attach the support bolts to engine and brakes. Torque the bolts to 50 ft. lbs.
4. Move right-hand drive axle assembly toward front of car and align with right-hand output shaft. Install attaching bolts and torque to 65 ft. lbs.
5. Install oil filter.
6. Install washer and nut on drive axle. Torque to 60 ft. lbs. on 1966 models and to 150 ft. lbs. on 1967-72 models, then insert cotter pin.
7. Remove floor stands and lower hoist.
8. Check engine oil. Add if necessary.

Drive Axle Removal —Left Side

1. Hoist car under lower control arms.
2. Remove wheel and, if equipped with drum brakes, remove drum. If equipped with disc brakes, remove disc.
3. Remove drive axle cotter pin, nut and washer.
4. On 1966-69 models only, position access slot in hub assembly so that each of the attaching bolts can be removed. It will be necessary to push aside adjuster lever to remove one of the bolts.
5. On 1966-69 models only, install a slide hammer with adapter on the hub.
6. On 1966-69 models only, remove hub assembly. It will again be necessary to push aside adjuster lever for clearance for hub assembly.
7. Remove tie-rod end cotter pin and nut.
8. Remove the tie-rod end from the knuckle with a puller.
9. Remove bolts from drive axle assembly and left output shaft. Insert a spacer between the axle shaft and lower control arm.
10. Remove upper control arm ball joint cotter pin and nut.
11. Using hammer and brass drift, drive on knuckle until upper ball joint stud is free.
12. Using puller, remove lower ball joint from knuckle. Care must be exercised so that ball joint does not damage drive axle seal.
14. Remove knuckle and support, so that brake hose is not damaged.
15. Carefully guide drive axle assembly outboard.

NOTE: care must be exercised so that constant velocity joints do not turn to full extremes and that seals are not damaged against shock absorber or stabilizer bar.

Drive Axle Installation —Left Side

1. Carefully guide left-hand drive axle assembly onto lower control arm and into position on spacer.
2. Insert lower control ball joint stud into knuckle and attach nut. Do not torque.
3. Center left-hand drive axle assembly in opening of knuckle and insert upper ball joint stud.
4. Place brake hose clip over upper ball joint stud and install nut. Do not torque.
5. Insert tie-rod end stud into knuckle and attach nut. Torque to 45 ft. lbs. on 1966-69 models and 35 ft. lbs. on 1970-72 models. Install cotter pin and crimp.
6. On 1966-69 models, lubricate hub assembly bearing O.D. with E.P. grease and install. Torque to 65 ft. lbs.
7. Align inner constant velocity joint with output shaft and install attaching bolts. Torque to 65 ft. lbs.
8. Torque upper and lower ball joint stud nuts to 40 ft. lbs. Install cotter pins and crimp.

NOTE: upper ball joint cotter pin must be crimped toward upper control arm to prevent interference with outer constant velocity joint seal.

9. Install drive axle washer and nut. Torque to 60 ft. lbs. on 1966-69 models and 150 ft. lbs. on 1970-72 models. Install cotter pin and crimp.
10. Install drum, if applicable, and wheel.
11. Remove floor stands and lower hoist.
12. Check camber, caster and toe-in and adjust if necessary. Refer to Front End Alignment.

Constant Velocity Joint (Out of Car)

The constant velocity joints are to be replaced as a unit and are only disassembled for repacking and re-

RETAINING CUP
"O" RING SEAL
RETAINING RING
OUTER HOUSING
RETAINING RING
INNER HOUSING
BALLS (30)
RETAINING RING
CAGE
INNER RACE
BALLS (6)
RETAINING RING
"O" RING SEAL
SEAL
CLAMP

AXLE SHAFT
CLAMP
SEAL
CLAMP
RETAINING RING
INNER RACE
BALLS (6)
CAGE
OUTER RACE

Left-hand drive axle assembly (© Oldsmobile Div. G.M. Corp.)

placement of seals.

Outer C. V. Joint Disassembly

1. Insert axle assembly into vise. Hold by the mid-portion of the axle shaft.
2. Remove inner and outer seal clamps.
3. Slide seal down axle shaft to gain access to C. V. joint.
4. Using snap-ring pliers, spread retaining ring until C. V. joint can be removed from axle spline.
5. Remove retaining ring.
6. Slide seal from axle shaft.
7. Remove grease from constant velocity joint.
8. Holding constant velocity joint with one hand, tilt cage and inner race so that one ball can be removed. Continue until all six balls are removed.
9. Turn cage 90° and, with large slot in cage aligned with land in inner race, lift out.
10. With cage and inner race assembly, turn inner race 90° in line with large hole in cage. Lift land on inner race up through large hole in cage and turn up and out to separate parts.

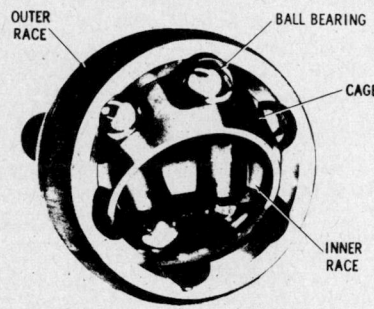

Removing balls from outer race
(© Oldsmobile Div. G.M. Corp.)

Outer C. V. Joint Assembly

1. Insert land of inner race into large hole in cage and pivot to install into cage.
2. Align inner race and pivot inner race 90° to align in outer race.
3. Insert balls into outer race one at a time until all six balls are installed. Inner race and cage will have to be tilted so that each ball can be inserted.
4. Pack constant velocity joint full of lubricant, part No. 1050530.
5. Pack inside of seal with the same lubricant, until folds of seal are full.
6. Place small keystone clamp on axle shaft.
7. Install seal onto axle shaft.
8. Install retaining ring into inner race.
9. Insert axle shaft into splines of outer constant velocity joint until retaining ring secures shaft.
10. Position seal in slot of outer race.

Installing balls into outer race
(© Oldsmobile Div. G.M. Corp.)

11. Install large keystone clamp over seal and secure.

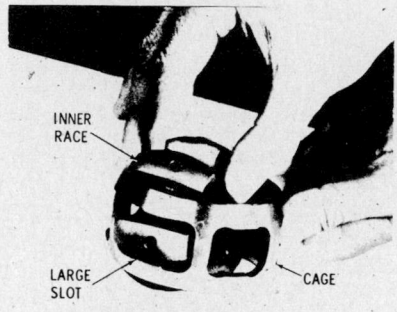

Removing inner race
(© Oldsmobile Div. G.M. Corp.)

1966 Inner C. V. Joint Disassembly

1. Insert axle assembly into vise. Clamp on mid-portion of axle shaft.
2. Remove small seal clamp.
3. Remove large end of seal from C. V. joint by prying out peened spots and driving off C. V. joint with hammer and chisel.
4. Slide seal down shaft until C. V. joint is disassembled. Remove O-ring from outer housing.
5. Wipe all grease from C. V. joint.
6. Remove axle shaft retaining ring.
7. Remove retaining ring from interior of ball spline outer housing.
8. Remove ball spline outer housing from ball spline inner housing being careful not to drop or lose balls, five in a line with six rows, total 30.
9. Follow disassembly of outer C. V. joint from Steps 4 through 9 for inner C. V. joint.
10. Remove grease from inside of ball spline outer housing.
11. Using wood block, carefully drive along outer edges from inside of ball spline outer housing and remove retaining cup.
12. Remove O-ring from interior of ball spline outer housing.

13. Remove retaining ring from interior of ball spline outer housing.
14. Remove O-ring from exterior of ball spline outer housing.
15. Remove two retaining rings from ball spline inner housing.

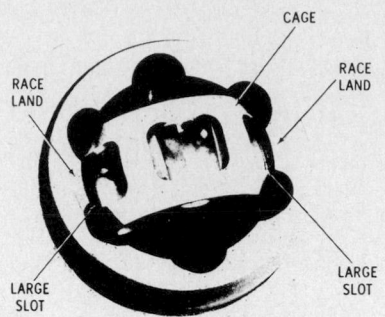

Positioning cage
(© Oldsmobile Div. G.M. Corp.)

1966 Inner C. V. Joint Assembly

1. Install two retaining rings onto inner spline housing.
2. Install retaining ring into groove of outer spline housing.
3. Install O-ring into inner groove of outer spline housing. Lubricate O-ring with special seal lubricant, part No. 1050169.
4. Install cover into outer spline housing using a press.
5. Insert land of inner race into large hole in case and pivot to install in cage.
6. Align inner race and cage and install into inner spline housing.
7. Insert balls into inner spline housing, one at a time, until all six balls are in. Inner race and cage will have to be tilted so that each ball can be inserted.
8. Install inner spline housing into outer spline housing. Raise inner spline housing and install five balls into each spline. (Six splines.)
9. Lower inner spline housing into outer spline housing and install retaining ring into groove at top of outer spline housing.
10. Install retaining ring into inner race.
11. Pack C. V. joint full of lubricant, part No. 1050530.
12. Place small keystone clamp on axle shaft.
13. Pack inside of seal with lubricant, part No. 1050530, until folds of seal are full.
14. Install seal onto axle shaft.
15. Install O-ring onto outer spline housing.
16. Insert axle shaft into splines of inner race until retaining ring secures shaft.
17. Insert drive axle assembly into a press and peen seal in six places, equally spaced.

18. Remove drive axle from press.
19. Position seal in groove of axle shaft until inner constant velocity joint is fully extended.
20. Install keystone clamp and secure.

1967-72 Inner C. V. Joint Disassembly

1. Place axle in a vise, clamping on the mid-portion of the axle shaft.
2. Remove the small seal clamp.
3. Remove the large end of the seal from C. V. joint with a hammer and chisel.
4. Carefully slide the seal down the axle shaft.
5. Carefully lift the housing assembly from the spider assembly and remove the O-ring from the housing outer surface. Use a rubber band to hold the three balls on the spider.
6. Remove the retaining ring from the end of the axle shaft.
7. Slide the spider assembly from the shaft.
8. Remove the inner retaining ring from the axle shaft.
9. Slide the seal off the axle shaft.
10. Remove the cover from the housing, prying with a screwdriver.
11. Remove the O-ring from the housing.
12. Remove the three balls from the spider, being careful not to lose the needle bearings. There are 53 needles per ball.

1967-72 Inner C. V. Joint Assembly

1. Slide a new seal clamp onto the axle shaft, to be installed after the seal is positioned.
2. Pack the new seal full with lubricant No. 1050802 or equivalent.
3. Position the retaining ring on the axle shaft inner slot.
4. Install the needle bearings (53) in the balls, packing with grease.
5. Install the three balls on the spider. Use a rubber band to hold them in place on the spider.
6. Position the spider assembly on the axle shaft and install the retaining ring.
7. Install a new O-ring in the outer groove in the housing.
8. Remove the rubber band from the spider assembly and push the spider assembly into the housing.
9. Lubricate the housing outer groove O-ring with seal lubricant No. 1050169 or equivalent and slide the seal into position, lightly tapping it into place with a soft hammer and staking in six evenly spaced places. Be careful not to cut the O-ring with the metal portion of the seal.

10. Position seal into groove on the axle shaft and install the clamp.
11. Extend the axle shaft until the seal is at maximum length.
12. Fill the housing with lubricant No. 1050802 or equivalent.
13. Install a new O-ring in the housing and lubricate the O-ring with seal lubricant No. 1050169 or equivalent.
14. Install the cover into the housing.

Drixe Axle Disassembly

1. Remove drive axle assembly.
2. Remove outer C. V. joint seal clamps.
3. Remove inner C. V. joint seal by prying out peened spots and driving off seal.
4. Slide seals inboard on shaft.
5. Using snap-ring pliers, spread retaining rings until both C. V. joints can be removed from axle shaft.
6. Remove seals from axle.

Drive Axle Assembly

1. Pack seals with lubricant, part No. 1050530.
2. Place outer C. V. joint seal on axle, with keystone clamps in position on seal.
3. Insert axle into outer C. V. joint until retaining ring locks axle into position.
4. Position seal and clamps and secure keystone clamps.
5. Place inner C. V. joint seal on axle with keystone clamp in position on seal.
6. Insert axle into inner C. V. joint until retaining ring locks axle into position.
7. Place axle assembly into press. Press seal into position and peen to secure.
8. Secure small keystone clamp with seal in position.
9. Install drive axle assembly.

Differential

Planetary-Type

1966-67

This type differential replaces the conventional spider and beveled axle drive pinions with a planetary gear set to distribute torque to the respective drive axles.

Engine torque is transmitted from the power train, to the main drive pinion and ring gear, to the differential housing. Torque is then applied through the planetary and sun gear mechanism to both drive axles at variable speed requirements.

While the car is moving straight ahead, the planetary gears are fixed and rotate with the differential case and ring gear, as a unit. However, when turning, the planetary gears revolve upon their individual axes with differential action, allowing the drive axles to rotate at different speeds.

This unit is not a controlled or limited slip differential.

Bevel Gear-Type

1968-72

Since 1968, a bevel gear-type differential is used on all front-wheel drive models. This design supersedes the original planetary gear-type final drive. While unit removal and installation procedures are typical, the assembly is not interchangeable with the 1966-67 design.

Overhauling the differential assembly is not encouraged. However, reconditioning procedures are given in later paragraphs of this final drive coverage. Differences in procedure will be clearly indicated.

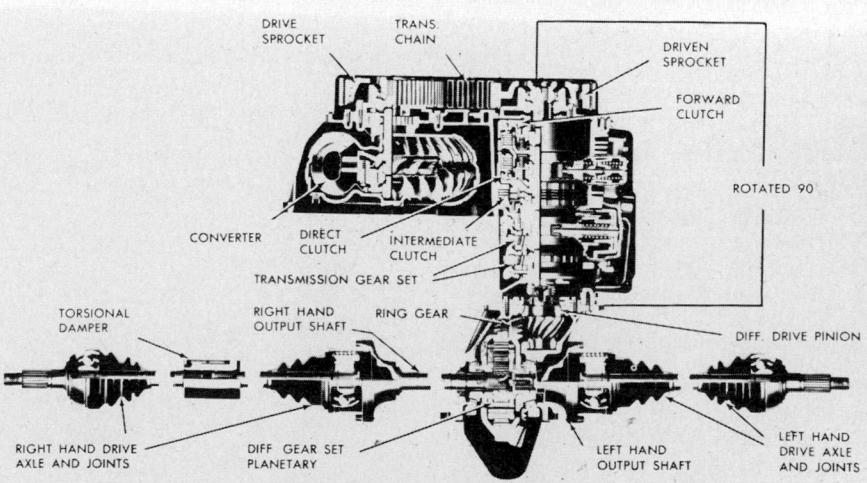

Power train cross-section—1966-67 (© Oldsmobile Div. G.M. Corp.)

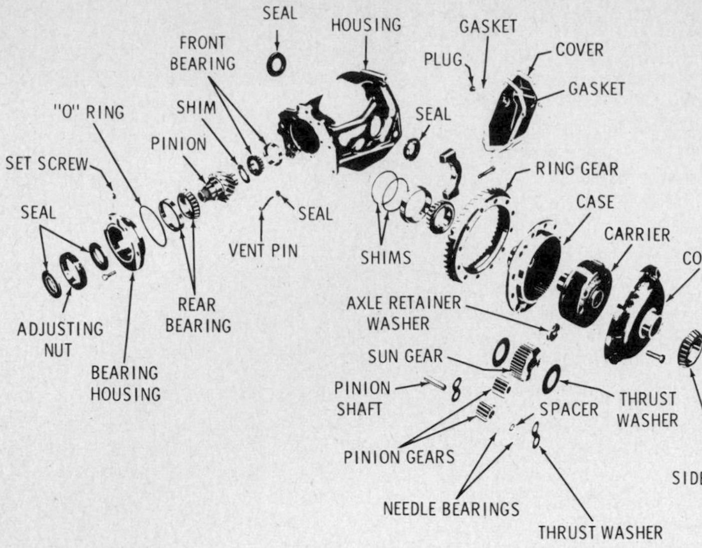

SEAL
FRONT
BEARING
HOUSING
SEAL
GASKET
PLUG
COVER
GASKET
"O" RING
SHIM
SEAL
SET SCREW
PINION
SEAL
RING GEAR
SEAL
VENT PIN
CASE
BEARING CAP
ADJUSTING
NUT
REAR
BEARING
SHIMS
CARRIER
COVER
BEARING
HOUSING
AXLE RETAINER
WASHER
SHIM
SUN GEAR
SPACER
PINION
SHAFT
THRUST
WASHER
PINION GEARS
SPACER
NEEDLE BEARINGS
SIDE BEARING
THRUST WASHER

Final drive component—1966-67 (© Oldsmobile Div. G.M. Corp.)

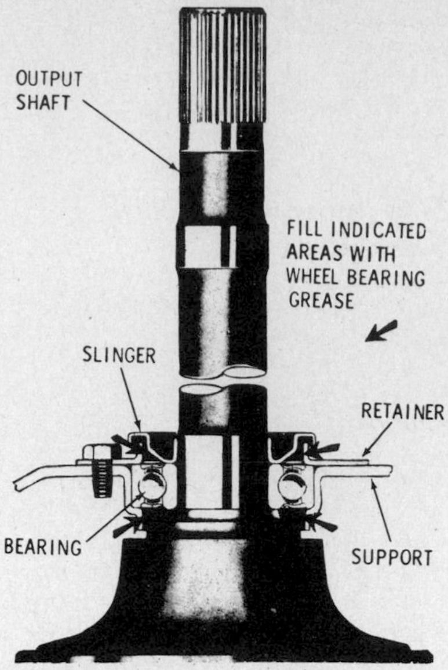

OUTPUT
SHAFT
FILL INDICATED
AREAS WITH
WHEEL BEARING
GREASE
SLINGER
RETAINER
BEARING
SUPPORT

Assembly of right-hand output shaft
(© Oldsmobile Div. G.M. Corp.)

SEAL
HOUSING
PLUG
COVER
FRONT
BEARING
GASKET
GASKET
SHIM
O'RING
PINION
SEAL
RING GEAR
SEAL
SHIM
CASE
BEARING
(SIDE)
SEAL
VENT
PIN
SPACER
REAR
BEARING
BEARING
(SIDE)
SHIM
SHIM
THRUST
WASHER
SPACER
SHIM
SIDE
GEARS
SEAL
BEARING
HOUSING
RETAINER
PINION
GEARS
LOCK PIN
SHIM

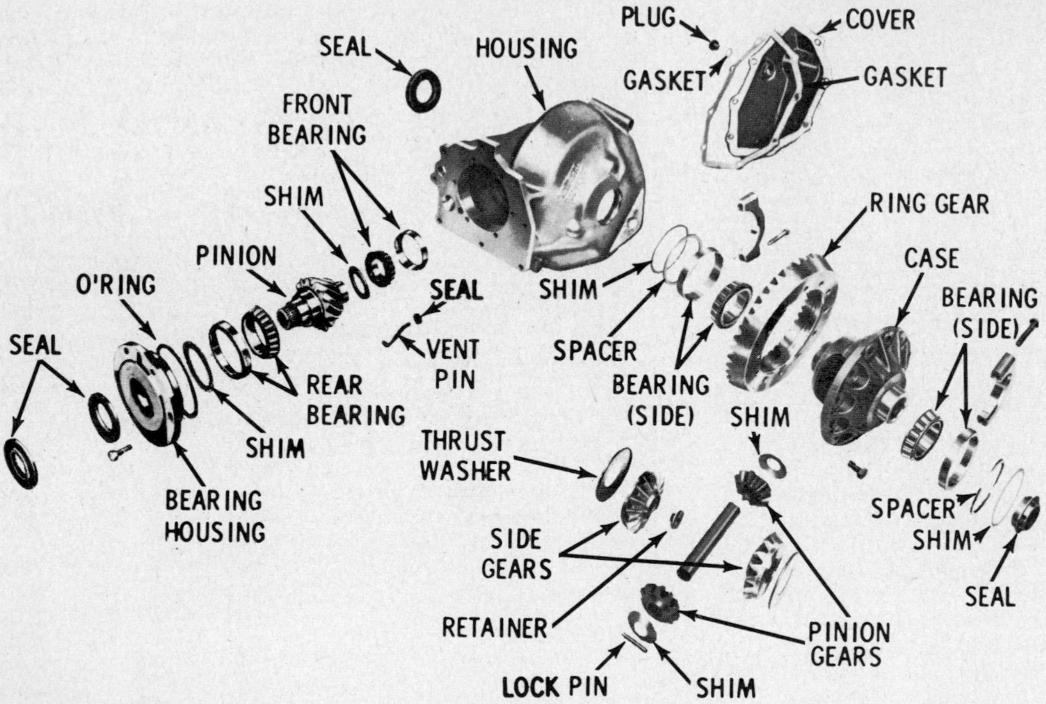

Final drive components—1968-72 (© Oldsmobile Div., G.M. Corp.)

Output Shafts, Bearings and Seals

Right Side Removal

1. Disconnect battery.
2. Hoist car.
3. Remove engine oil filter.
4. Disconnect right-hand drive axle.
5. Disconnect support from engine and brace.
6. Remove output shaft assembly.
7. If seal is to be removed, install seal remover J-943 into seal and drive seal out with a hammer.
8. If output shaft bearing is to be removed, use a press.

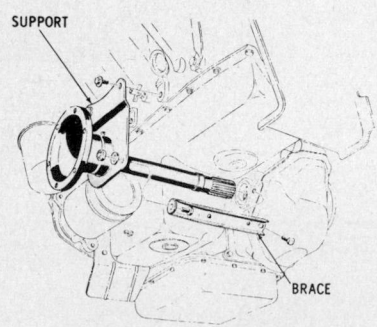

SUPPORT

BRACE

Right-hand output shaft
(© Oldsmobile Div. G.M. Corp.)

Right Side Installation

1. If output bearing was removed, assemble parts as illustrated.
2. Position assembly in a press and install bearing until seated.
3. Pack area between bearing and retainer with wheel bearing grease, then install slinger.
4. If seal was removed, it can now be installed.
5. Apply special seal lubricant to output shaft seal, then install output shaft into final drive, indexing the splines of both units.
6. Install support to engine and brace bolts.

7. Connect drive axle to output shaft.
8. Install engine oil filter.
9. Connect battery, check engine oil level and check for oil leaks.

Left Side Removal

The left-hand output shaft can normally be removed only after removing the final drive assembly from the car. However, if the left-hand axle assembly has been removed for any reason, the output shaft and seal can be removed as follows:

1. Remove left hand drive axle assembly, as described above.
2. Using a 9/16 in. socket, remove left-hand output shaft retaining bolt and left-hand shaft.
3. Install left-hand output shaft tool J-943 into seal and drive out with a hammer.

Left Side Installation

1. If seal was removed, install new seal.
2. Apply special seal lubricant to seal, then insert output shaft into final drive assembly, indexing splines of output shaft with splines of final drive.
3. Install left-hand output shaft retaining bolt and torque to 45 ft. lbs.
4. Install left-hand axle as described above.

Final Drive

Removal

1. Disconnect battery.
2. See illustration. Remove bolts A, B, and C. Nut D must be removed with a special wrench, such as MAC S-147.
   NOTE: it may be necessary to remove the transmission filler tube to gain clearance.

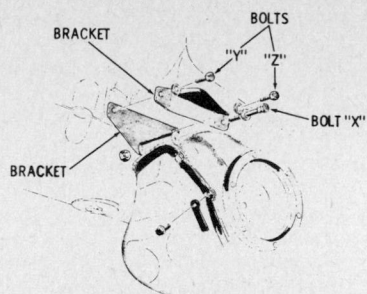

Disconnecting final drive from engine
(© Oldsmobile Div. G.M. Corp.)

3. Hoist the car. If a two post hoist is used, the car must be supported with floor stands at the front frame rails and the front post lowered.
4. Disconnect right and left drive axles from the output shafts.
5. Remove engine oil filter.
6. Disconnect brace from final drive, then disconnect right-hand output shaft assembly from engine.
7. Remove output shaft assembly from final drive.
8. See illustration. Remove bolt X and loosen bolts Y and Z.
9. Remove final drive cover and allow lubricant to drain.
10. Position transmission lift with adapter for final drive. Install an anchor bolt through final drive housing and lift pad.
11. See illustration. Remove bolts E, F, and G, and nut from H.
12. Move transmission lift toward front of car to disengage final drive splines from transmission.
13. Lower transmission lift and remove final drive from lift.
14. Using a 9/16 in. socket, remove the left output shaft retainer bolt, then pull output shaft from final drive.
15. Remove transmission to final drive gasket.

Installation

1. Apply special seal lubricant to both output shaft seals.
2. Install the left output shaft into the final drive. Retain with bolt and torque to 45 ft. lbs.
3. Position final drive on transmission lift and install an anchor bolt through the housing and lift pad.
4. Apply a thin film of special seal lubricant on the transmission side of the new final drive to transmission gasket. Then position gasket on the transmission.
5. Raise the transmission lift. Align the two bolt studs D and H on the transmission with their mating holes in the final drive. Move final drive until it mates with the transmission.

Caution It may be necessary to rotate the left output shaft to align the splines on the final drive with the splines of the transmission output shaft.

6. Install bolts E, F, and G and nut H finger tight.
7. Install bolt X and torque to 75 ft. lbs. Tighten and torque bolts Y and Z to 50 ft. lbs.
8. Loosen and remove lift from final drive.
9. Position a new cover gasket on the final drive, then install cover. Torque cover bolts to 30 ft. lbs.
10. Install right output shaft into final drive, indexing splines of output shaft with splines of final drive. Install mounting bracket and brace bolts and tighten.
11. Connect drive axles to output shafts.
12. Install oil filter.
13. Raise hoist, remove stands and lower car.
14. If filler tube was removed, attach a new O-ring and install filler tube.
15. Install bolts A, B, and C and nut D. Torque all final drive to transmission bolts to 25 ft. lbs. Torque nuts to about 25 ft. lbs.
16. Connect battery.
17. Fill final drive with four and one-half pints of lubricant, part No. 1050015.
18. Check engine oil level. Start engine and check transmission fluid level.
19. Check for any oil leaks.

Drive Unit Disassembly

Adequate facilities are a must for this service.

1. If available, install adapter J-22296-1 onto differential holding fixture J-3289. Differential holding fixture must be modified to obtain clearance between fixture and final drive housing. Mount final drive in holding fixture.

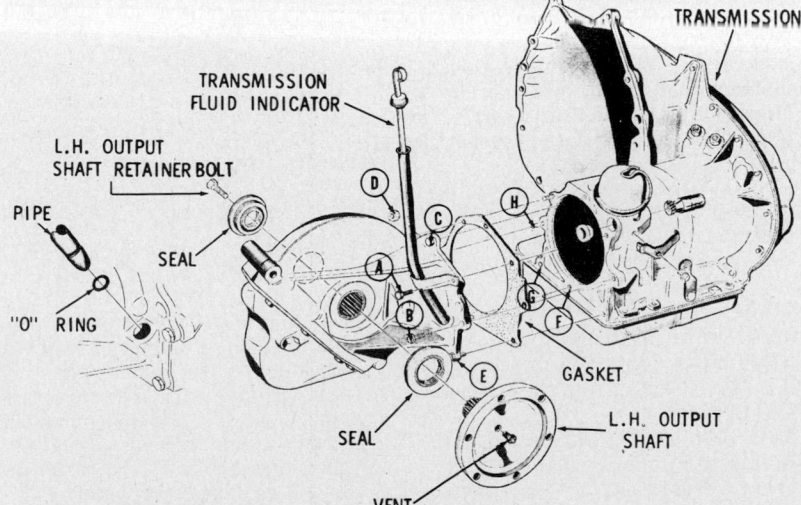

Transmission attachment bolts (© Oldsmobile Div. G.M. Corp.)

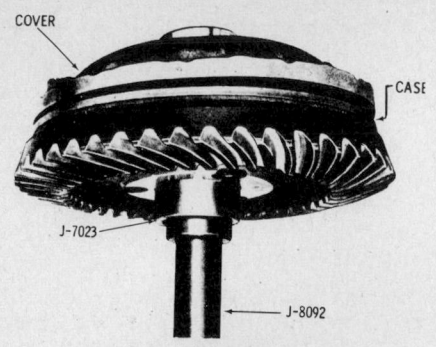

Separating case halves
(© Oldsmobile Div. G.M. Corp.)

2. Use a drain pan under the assembly. Remove the drain plug. Then, remove the cover attaching screws and cover.
3. Rotate final drive until pinion points down, then check ring gear to pinion backlash with a dial indicator. Record backlash for reassembly. Check pinion and side bearing pre-load with tools, J-22208-1 and J-22208-2, with the help of a torque wrench. Record pre-load reading.
4. Remove side bearing caps.
NOTE: side bearing caps are of different size and can only be installed in one position.
5. Install spreader J-22196 onto final drive, indexing the two guides on the spreader with the two holes on the carrier.
6. Turn the spreader screw to expand the spreader until the spacer and shims can be removed from between the small side of the bearing and the carrier.
7. Remove spreader from the carrier.
8. Remove the spacer and shims, then slide the case assembly to the left, away from the pinion gear. Remove case assembly from carrier. Check pinion bearing preload and record the reading.
9. Rotate carrier so the pinion is up.
10. Loosen set screw from adjusting nut.
11. Remove bearing housing bolts. Remove the drive pinion housing and remove the adjusting nut and housing from drive pinion. Remove rubber seal from bearing housing.
12. Remove rubber seal and vent wire from carrier.
13. With slide hammer J-2619 and tool J-22201, remove pinion front outer race.
14. Remove the output shaft oil seals.
15. Remove the two oil seals from the adjustment nut.
16. If necessary, remove pinion rear outer race.

Pinion Bearing Removal

1. Remove the pinion front bearing

and selective shim. Bearing can be removed with a press.
2. Remove the pinion rear bearing.

Final Drive Case Disassembly

1. If the side bearings are to be removed, use tools J-22229-1, J-8433-1, and J-8416-1.
2. Mark ring gear, case and case cover, then remove all but two of the case cover to ring gear bolts. Loosen, but do not remove, two of the bolts 180° apart.
3. Jar the assembly lightly on the bench to separate the two halves of the case. Remove pinion carrier.
4. Clean all parts and examine all surfaces for wear or other damage.

Pinion Gears, Planetary-Type Removal and Installation

1966-67

(See Final Drive Components)
1. Support the planetary pinion carrier assembly.
2. Press or drive the pinion pins out of the carrier.
3. Remove the pinion thrust washers, spacer, needle bearings, sun gear and thrust washers.
NOTE: the sun gear can be removed from only one opening of the carrier. This opening can be identified by the thinner wall at the carrier opening.
4. After removing the sun gear, the left axle retainer washer can be removed from the carrier.
5. Install by installing loading tool J-22210 into planet pinion. Position a spacer washer over the loading tool, then install 24 needle bearings on each side of the spacer washer.
6. If the axle retainer washer was removed, install it at this time.
7. Position a thrust washer on each side of the sun gear, then insert the sun gear into carrier through large opening.
8. Position a thrust washer on each side of the planet pinion, then insert planet pinion into carrier.
9. Using a deep socket as a receiver, press pinion pin into carrier, until it bottoms.
10. Place a large punch in a vise, to be used as an anvil, and stake the opposite end of the pinion pin in three places.

Pinion Gears, Bevel-Type Removal and Installation

1. After ring gear has been removed, drive lock pin from pinion shaft.
2. Push pinion shaft out of case.
3. Rotate one pinion gear and shim toward access hole in case, then remove.
NOTE: keep corresponding shims

and pinion gear together for correct assembly.
4. Remove the other pinion and shim.
5. Remove side gears and thrust washers, keeping gears and washers in proper relationship for correct installation.
NOTE: the left-side gear has the threaded retainer that secures the (short) left output shaft. If threaded retainer is to be removed, use a brass drift to prevent trouble.
6. Upon assembling pinion and side gears into the case, lubricate components with a quality extreme pressure lubricant.
7. Place side gear thrust washers over the side gear hubs and install side gears into case. Gear with threaded retainer belongs in left side of case.
8. Position one pinion (without shims) between side gears, then rotate gears until pinion is directly opposite from loading opening in case. Place other pinion between side gears so that the pinion shaft holes are in line; then rotate gears to make sure holes in pinions line up with holes in case.
9. If holes line up, rotate pinions back to loading opening just enough to permit insertion of the pinion gear shims.
10. Install pinion shaft. Drive pinion shaft retaining lock pin into position.

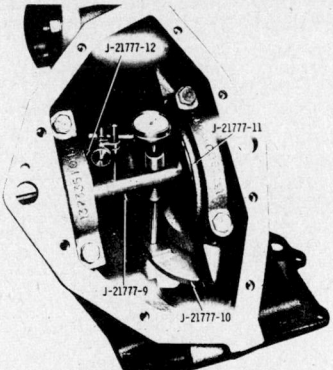

Checking pinion depth
(© Oldsmobile Div. G.M. Corp.)

Checking Pinion Depth

1. Install pinion front outer race. Drive race in until it bottoms.
2. Lubricate front bearing with final drive lubricant and install into front outer race.
3. Position tool J-21777-10 on the front bearing. Install tool J-21579 onto final drive housing and retain with two bolts. Thread screw J-21777-13 into J-21579 until tip of screw engages tool J-21777-10. Torque tool J-21777-13 to 20 in. lbs. to pre-load the bearing.
4. Remove dial indicator post from tool J-21777-9 and install discs

J-21777-11 and J-21777-12. Reinstall dial indicator post.

5. Place the gauging discs in the side bearing bores and install the side bearing caps.

6. Position the dial indicator on the mounting post of the gauge shaft with the contact button touching the indicator pad. Set dial indicator to zero, then depress the dial indicator until the needle rotates three-quarters of a turn clockwise. Tighten dial indicator.

7. Position the gauge shaft assembly in the carrier so that the dial indicator contact rod is directly over the gauging area of the gauge block, and the discs are seated fully in the side bearing bores.

8. Position gauge shaft so that the indicator rod contacts the gauging area. Rotate gauge rod back and forth until the indicator reads the greatest deflection. At the point of greatest deflection, set the indicator to zero. Repeat the rocking action to verify the zero setting.

9. After zero setting is obtained, rotate gauge shaft until the indicator rod does not touch the gauging area. Read the pinion depth directly from the dial indicator.

10. Select the correct pinion shim to be used during assembly on the following basis:
    A. If a service pinion is being used, or a production pinion with no marking, the correct shim will have a thickness equal to the indicator gauge reading found in Step 9.
    B. If a production pinion is being used and it is marked + or −, the correct shim will be determined as follows:
    If the pinion is marked +, the shim thickness indicated by the dial indicator on the pinion setting gauge must be increased by the amount etched on the pinion. If the pinion is marked −, the shim thickness indicated on the dial must be decreased by the amount etched on the pinion.

11. Remove pinion depth checking tools and front bearing from carrier.

Final Drive Case Assembly

1. Install the pinion carrier into the case.

2. With the case and cover alignment marks indexed, insert four ring gear attaching bolts through case and cover. Align mark on ring gear with alignment marks on case and cover, then install ring gear onto case. Tighten the six attaching bolts alternately. Torque bolts to 85 ft. lbs.

3. If side bearings were removed, they can be installed now. Drive bearing on until it bottoms.

4. Install pinion rear bearing.

5. Position correct shim on drive pinion and install the drive pinion front bearing with tool J-21022 and a press.

6. Lubricate pinion bearings and install pinion into carrier.

7. Install seals into adjusting nut.

8. Install O-ring and vent pin onto face of carrier. Torque attaching nuts to 35 ft. lbs.

9. Install seal protector J-22236 over drive pinion, then install the adjusting nut over the seal protector and thread into the housing.

10. Assemble tools, as illustrated, and adjust pinion bearing preload. The preload is 2-10 in. lbs. for new bearings, and 2-3 in. lbs. for used bearings. Adjust new bearing preload to 4 in. lbs. while rotating the pinion and checking preload. Adjust until preload remains constant. When correct preload is obtained, tighten the set screw. Record preload reading as it will be used when making side bearing preload adjustment. Leave the tools on pinion for side bearing preload adjustment.

Side Bearing Preload Adjustment

Differential side bearing preload is adjusted by means of shims located between the side bearings and the carrier. One spacer is used on the right side only. Shims are used on both sides and come in thickness increments of .002 in. from .036 to .070 in. By changing the thickness of both side shims equally, ring gear and pinion backlash will not change.

1. Lubricate the side bearings with final drive lubricant.

2. Place differential in position in the carrier.

3. If the original ring gear and pinion are being used, subtract the reading obtained in Step 8 from the reading obtained in Step 3 of the Final Drive Disassembly procedure. This determines the original side bearing preload and will aid in determining whether thicker or thinner shims are needed to bring the side bearing preload to specifications.

4. Install original shim onto left side and spacer onto the right side.

5. Install the carrier spreader and apply just enough tension to allow the shim to be installed between the spacer and the carrier.

6. Release tension on the spreader, install side bearing caps, then check preload. Preload should be

15-20 in. lbs. for new bearings and 5-7 in. lbs. for old bearings over the pinion bearing preload obtained in Step 11, Final Drive Case Assembly.

7. If pre-load is not within specifications, select thicker or thinner shims to bring preload within limits.

Checking backlash
(© Oldsmobile Div. G.M. Corp.)

Backlash Adjustment

1. Rotate differential case a few times to seat bearings, then mount dial indicator in order to read movement at the outer edge of one of the ring gear teeth.

2. Check backlash at three points around the ring gear. Lash must not vary more than .002 in.

3. Backlash at the minimum point should be .006-.008 in. for all new gears. If original ring gear and pinion were installed, backlash should be set at the same reading obtained in Step 3 of Final Drive Disassembly procedure, if reading was within specifications.

4. If backlash was not within limits, correct by increasing thickness of one differential shim and decreasing thickness of other side shim the same amount. This will not disturb differential side bearing preload. For each .001 in. change in backlash desired, transfer .002 in. shim thickness. To decrease backlash .001 in., decrease thickness of right shim .002 in. and increase thickness of left shim .002 in. To increase backlash .002 in. increase thickness of right shim .004 in. and decrease thickness of left shim .004 in.

5. When backlash is correct, remove spreader. Install bearing caps and bolts. Torque to 65 ft. lbs.

6. Install new output shaft seals.

7. Install new gasket onto housing. Install cover, torque cover attaching bolts to 30 ft. lbs. Fill final drive to correct level.

Automatic Transmission

The Turbo-Hydramatic transmission used on the Toronado is a fully automatic transmission used for front-wheel drive applications. It consists primarily of a three element hydraulic torque converter, dual sprocket and link assembly, compound planetary gear set, three multiple disc clutches, a sprag clutch, a roller clutch, two band assemblies and hydraulic control system. For major repair operations on this transmission, consult the Unit Repair Section of this manual.

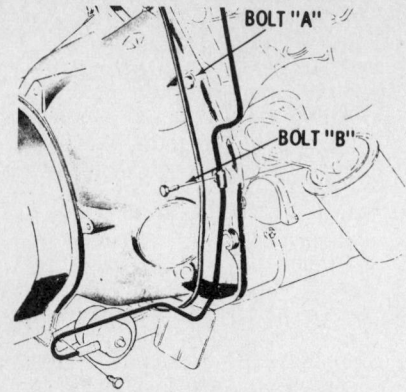

Transmission to engine attachment
(© Oldsmobile Div. G.M. Corp.)

SHIFT LINKAGE ADJUSTMENT

1. POSITION SELECTOR LEVER IN "D"
2. OBTAIN ZERO CLEARANCE AT COLUMN SHIFT LEVER.
3. LOOSEN BOLT "A".
4. WITH SELECTOR LEVER AND TRANSMISSION LEVER IN "D", TORQUE BOLT "A" TO 20 FT. LBS.
5. CHECK NEUTRAL SAFETY SWITCH ADJUSTMENT.

Shift linkage adjustments (© Oldsmobile Div. G.M. Corp.)

Linkage Adjustments

See illustration for manual linkage adjustment.

Automatic Transmission Removal

1. Disconnect battery.
2. Disconnect oil cooler lines at transmission and speedometer

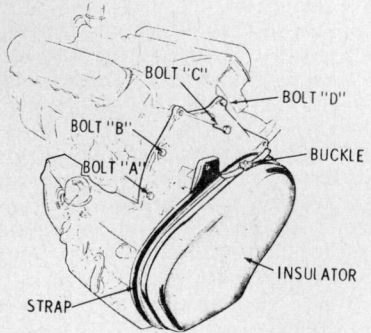

Transmission to engine attachment
(© Oldsmobile Div. G.M. Corp.)

cable at governor.
3. Install engine support bar.
4. Remove nut D and bolts A, B and C as in illustration. A special wrench, such as MAC S-147, must be used to remove nut D on 1966-67 models.

5. Remove bolts A, B, C and D as in illustrations.
6. Loosen flywheel cover plate bolt A. (See illustration.)
7. Raise the car on a hoist.
8. Disconnect starter wiring, then remove starter.
9. Remove bolts B, C and D from flywheel cover plate.
10. Remove flywheel to converter bolt E. Rotate flywheel until all bolts are removed.
11. Disconnect vacuum modulator line and stator wiring.
12. Install transmission lift.

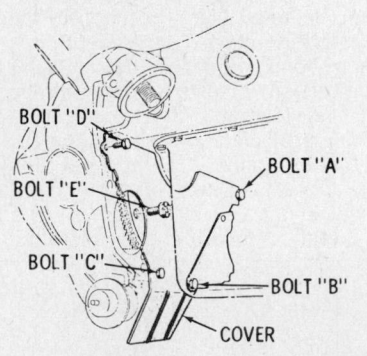

Transmission to converter attachment (© Oldsmobile Div. G.M. Corp.)

13. Remove shift linkage.
14. Remove bolts E, F, G and nut from H. (See illustration.)
NOTE: when the last three transmission to final drive bolts are removed, a quantity of oil will be lost.
15. Remove bolts A and B. (See illustration.)
16. Remove the two upper engine mount brackets to transmission bolts A and B. (See illustration.)
17. Remove the four brackets to engine mount bolts.
18. Slide transmission rearward and down. Engine mount bracket will follow transmission down. Install converter holding tool J-21654.
19. After transmission is removed from car, the link assembly cover insulator can be removed or installed.

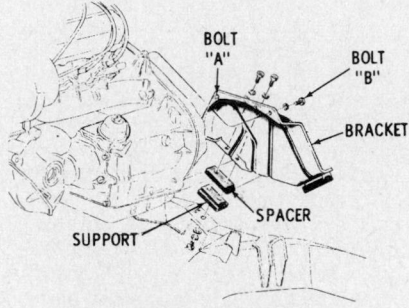

Engine mount attachment
(© Oldsmobile Div. G.M. Corp.)

Automatic Transmission Installation

When installing the transmission, the motor mount bracket must be positioned loosely on the link assembly cover until the transmission is in place. Then reverse removal procedure. Torque the bolts as follows:
Engine to torque converter housing —30 ft. lbs.
Engine bracket to transmission—55 ft. lbs.
Engine bracket to rubber mount—55 ft. lbs.
Oil cooler lines to transmission—30 ft. lbs.
Final drive to transmission nuts and bolts—25 ft. lbs.
Torque converter to flywheel bolts— 30 ft. lbs.

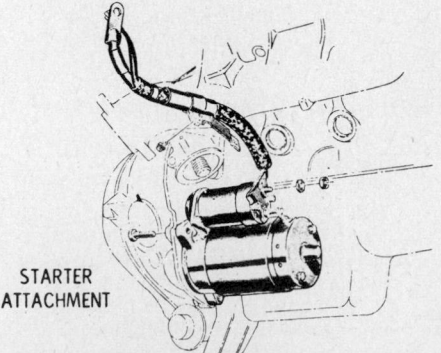

STARTER ATTACHMENT

Flywheel housing cover—5 ft. lbs.
Starter to transmission—30 ft. lbs.

After the transmission is installed, check transmission oil level. Refer to capacity chart at the beginning of this car section.

Drive and Driven Sprockets for the Transmission Drive

If it should be necessary to replace either the drive sprocket, chain, or driven sprocket, the three unit combination must be replaced as a set. They are matched and are not to be serviced separately.

Removal

1. Remove cover housing attaching bolts.
2. Remove cover housing and gasket. Discard the gasket.
3. Install J-4646 snap-ring pliers into sprocket bearing retaining snap-rings located under the drive and driven sprockets, then remove snap-rings from retaining grooves in support housings.
   NOTE: do not remove snap-rings from beneath the sprockets. Leave them in a loose position between the sprockets and the bearing assemblies.
4. Remove drive and driven sprockets, link assemblies, bearings and shaft simultaneously by alternately pulling upward on the drive and driven sprockets until the bearings are out of the drive and driven support housings.
   NOTE: it may be necessary to pry up on the sprockets. Use care.

Caution Do not pry on the guide links or the aluminum case. Pry only on the sprockets.

5. Remove link assembly from drive and driven sprockets.
6. Remove two hook-type oil seal rings from turbine shaft.
7. Inspect drive and driven sprocket bearing assemblies for rough or defective bearings.
   NOTE: do not remove bearing assemblies from drive or driven sprockets unless they need replacement.
8. If removal of bearing assembly from drive and/or driven sprockets is necessary, proceed as follows:
   A. Remove sprocket to bearing assembly retaining snap-ring using tool J-5589, (snap-ring pliers).
   B. Mount sprocket with turbine or input shaft placed in hole in work bench on two 2 x 4 x 10 in. pieces of wood.
   C. With a hammer and brass rod, drive the inner race alternately through each of the access openings until the bearing assembly is removed

from the sprocket hub. Drive the sprocket, then turbine shaft and link assembly.

Inspection

1. Inspect drive sprocket teeth for nicks, burrs, scoring, galling and excessive wear.
2. Inspect drive sprocket to ball bearing retaining snap-ring for damage.
3. Inspect drive sprocket ball bearing inner race mounting surface for damage.
4. Inspect turbine shaft for open lubrication passages. Run a tag wire through the passages to make sure they are open.
5. Inspect spline for damage.
6. Inspect the ground bushing journals for damage.
7. Inspect the two hook-type oil seal grooves for damage or excessive wear.
8. Inspect the turbine shaft for cracks or distortion.
9. Inspect the link assembly for damage or loose links.
   NOTE: take particular notice of the guide links. They are the wide outside links on each side of the link assembly.

Installation

Install by reversing removal procedures.

Driven Sprocket at Input Shaft Inspection

1. Inspect driven sprocket teeth for nicks, burrs, scoring, galling and excessive wear.
2. Inspect sprocket to ball bearing retaining snap-ring for damage.
3. Inspect ball bearing inner race mounting surface for damage.
4. Inspect input shaft for open lubrication holes. Run a tag wire through the holes to make sure they are open.
5. Inspect spline for damage.
6. Inspect ground bushing journals for damage.

Sprocket Bearing Installation

1. Turn sprocket so that turbine or input shaft is pointing upward.
2. Install new sprocket bearing as follows:
   A. Install snap-ring, letter side down to shaft.
   B. Assemble bearing assembly on turbine or input shaft.
   C. Using drift (J-6133-A), drive the bearing assembly onto the hub of the sprocket until it is resting on the bearing seat of the sprocket.
   D. Install sprocket to bearing assembly retaining snap-ring into groove sprocket hub.
3. Install two hook-type oil seal rings onto turbine shaft.

Checking front unit end-play
(© Oldsmobile Div. G.M. Corp.)

THICKNESS	COLOR
.060 - .064	Yellow
.071 - .075	Blue
.082 - .086	Red
.093 - .097	Brown
.104 - .108	Green
.115 - .119	Black
.126 - .130	Purple

Front unit end-play selective washer thickness

Front Unit End-Play Check

1. Install front unit end-play checking tool, (J-22241), into driven sprocket housing so that the urethane on the tool can engage the splines and the forward clutch housing. Let the tool bottom on the main-shaft, then withdraw it approximately $1/16$-$1/8$ in.
2. Remove two of the 5/16—18 bolts from the driven support housing.
3. Install 5/16—18 threaded slide hammer bolt with jam nut into one bolt hole in driven support housing.
   NOTE: do not thread slide hammer bolt deep enough to interfere with forward clutch travel.
4. Mount dial indicator on rod and index indicator to register with the forward clutch drum which can be reached through second bolt removed from driven support housing.
5. Push end-play tool down to remove slack.
6. Push and hold output flange outward. Place a screwdriver in case opening at parking pawl area and push upward on output carrier.
7. Place another screwdriver between the metal lip of the end-play tool and the drive sprocket housing. Now, push upward on the metal lip of the end-play tool and read the resulting end-play. This should be .003-.024 in. The selective washer controlling this end-play is the phenolic thrust washer located between the driven support housing and the forward clutch housing. If more or less washer thickness is required to bring the end-play within specifications, select the proper washer from the the chart.

Rear Suspension

Some 1971-72 models are equipped with True-Track Braking (JL9 option). This is an electrically controlled rear brake equalizing system. The wheel speed sensors are mounted under the spindles, each with a driveshaft which runs through the spindle to attach to the grease cap.

Care must be taken when removing the rear spindle or the rear assembly not to break the sensor wiring or damage the sensor unit.

An illustration of the axle and sensor may be found in the Cadillac Eldorado Section.

All 1971-72 models have a straight tubular axle housing instead of the I-beam drop axle used on 1966-70 models.

following precautions should be taken:

1. The cones must be a slip fit on the spindle.
2. Inside of cones should be lubricated to make sure the cone creeps on the spindle.
3. Spindle nut must be a free-running fit on the threads.
4. Adjustment of rear wheel bearings should be made by continuously revolving the wheel while torquing the nut as follows:

A. Torque adjusting nut to 25-30 ft. lbs. to seat all components thoroughly.

B. Back off nut one-half turn, then retighten finger tight.

C. If unable to insert cotter pin at this position, back off to nearest castellation.

4. Remove four attaching bolts on center clamp assembly.
5. Lift center clamp up, shock will hold it in position.
6. On 1966-67 models, remove resonator bracket attaching bolts to frame and allow resonator to hang loose.
7. Lower jack until axle is free from spring.
8. Remove shackle assembly from spring and body.
9. Remove bolt from front of rear spring and remove spring.
10. If spring bushing is worn, remove and replace it.

Rear Leaf Spring Installation

1966-70

To install, reverse removal procedure.

A. Front bushing is a press fit. Replacement will require an arbor press.

B. Torque resonator bracket attaching bolts to 14 ft. lbs.

C. Torque four spring center clamp assembly bolts to 30 ft. lbs.

D. Install wheel, torque to 115 ft. lbs.

E. Remove all supports and, with car on the ground, torque rear shackle bolts to 40 ft. lbs. and front spring bolt to 75-80 ft. lbs.

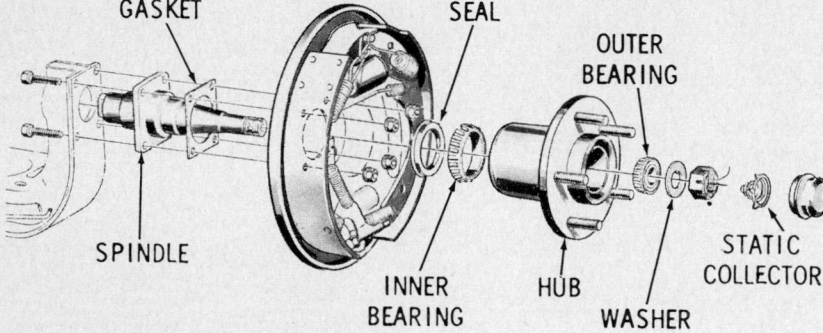

Rear hub assembly 1966-70 (© Oldsmobile Div., G.M. Corp.)

Rear Wheel Spindle R & R

1. Support the rear of the car with stands.
2. Remove the wheel, drum and hub assembly.
3. Disconnect the brake line fitting at the wheel cylinder.
4. Remove the four spindle attaching bolts and tie the backing plate out of the way.
5. On 1971-72 models, pull the spindle with a slide hammer.
6. On 1966-70 models, place a jack under the axle and remove the four bolts from the center spring clamp assembly. Remove the rubber insulator and lower the axle enough with the jack to provide working room for the spindle removal. Either drive the spindle out from behind or use a pulling tool.
7. To install, reverse the removal procedure. Install spindle with the keyway up, tightening the four bolts progressively one turn at a time. Adjust the rear wheel bearing.

Wheel Bearing Adjustment

For the rear wheel tapered roller bearings to be correctly adjusted, the

Rear Leaf Spring Removal

1966-70

1. Raise car and support on frame pad. With jack under axle, remove wheel.
2. Remove nut only from front of rear spring.
3. Remove two attaching nuts on rear shackle (outer). Remove rear shackle (outer).

Rear Coil Spring R & R

1971-72

1. With the car supported with floor stands, position a hoist under the tube assembly and raise it enough to relieve the tension on the shock absorber.
2. Disconnect the shock absorbers at the tube assembly.
3. Carefully lower the tube assembly until the springs are fully extended.

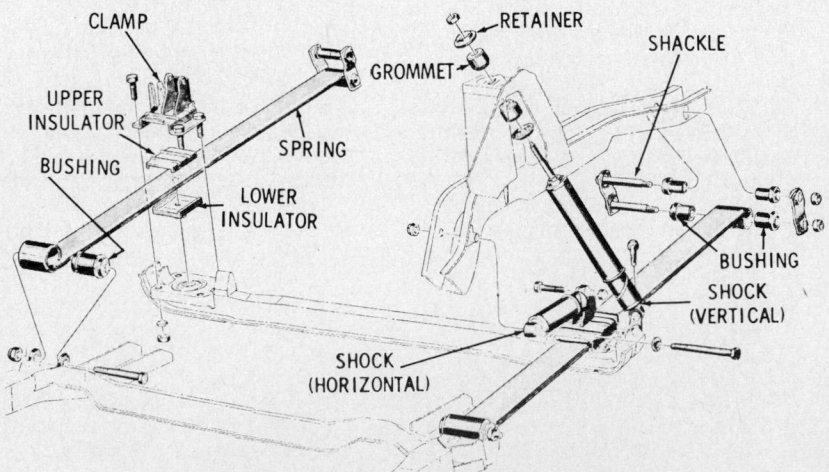

Rear suspension 1966-70 (© Oldsmobile Div., G.M. Corp.)

Caution Do not stretch the brake hydraulic hose.

4. Remove the springs and insulators.

5. When installing, place the insulator on top of the spring and install the spring with the identification tag next to the tube assembly.

6. Hoist the tube assembly and connect the shock absorber, tightening the lower nut to 65 ft. lbs.

Rear Axle R & R

1966-70

1. Lift car and support at both rear frame pads.
2. Remove wheels, drum and hub assemblies.
3. Disconnect brake lines and parking brake cable.
4. Remove backing plate attaching bolts and let backing plates rest on floor.
5. With jack under center of axle, remove eight attaching bolts from center spring clamp assemblies.
6. Disconnect brake hose.
7. Lower jack and remove axle.
8. Install in the reverse order of removal.

1971-72

1. With the car supported at the frame with stands and a hoist under the tube axle assembly, remove the wheels.
2. Disconnect:
   a. Brake lines at the wheel cylinders.
   b. Parking brake cable at the equalizer.
   c. Rubber brake hose from underbody bracket.
   d. Shock absorbers at the tube assembly.
3. Carefully lower the hoist under the tube assembly and remove the springs.
4. Remove the backing plate and tie out of the way.
5. Remove the four bolts which at-

tach the suspension arms to the tube assembly.

6. If installing a new tube, transfer the spindles, brake tubing, rubber bumpers, bushings and, if so equipped, the True-Track units and wiring to the new tube. Install in the reverse order of removal.

Radio

R & R

1966-70

1. Disconnect battery.
2. Remove both lower cluster panels.
3. Remove steering column attaching nuts and lower bracket.
4. Remove shift indicator needle.
5. Disconnect speedometer cable.
6. Remove attaching nuts from cluster lower brackets, leaving brackets attached to the instrument panel.
7. Remove two upper instrument panel screws and lay cluster assembly on steering column.
8. Remove radio knobs, washers or rear seat speaker control.
9. Remove radio attaching nuts and escutcheons.
10. Disconnect all wiring and antenna lead-in.
11. Remove lower radio support bracket attaching nut.
12. Remove radio from instrument panel.
13. Install by reversing the removal procedure.

1971-72

1. Loosen the ground strap at the lower tie bar.
2. Remove the radio support bracket nut at the rear of the radio.
3. Disconnect the three lights from the bezel.
4. Remove the four bezel attaching

screws and pull the bezel forward as far as possible.

5. Disconnect all wiring from the radio.
6. Remove the radio knobs, attaching nuts and escutcheons, then remove the radio.
7. Installation is the reverse of the removal procedure. The antenna trimmer must be adjusted when the radio is installed.

Windshield Wipers

The windshield wiper system consists of the wiper motor and transmission assembly. It is very similar to that used on other Oldsmobile models. See the Oldsmobile, F-85 Section.

Heater System

R & R

1. Disconnect blower feed and resistor wiring.
2. Disconnect vacuum hoses from the air inlet and forced vent diaphragms.
3. Disconnect temperature cable from temperature door lever.
4. Disconnect heater hoses. Keep open ends of hoses above engine coolant level to prevent loss of coolant.
5. Remove heater assembly attaching screws.
6. Remove heater assembly from the cowl.
7. If heater core is to be removed, it can be removed at this time.
8. To install, reverse the removal procedure. Be sure to apply sealer to the mounting face of the heater assembly.

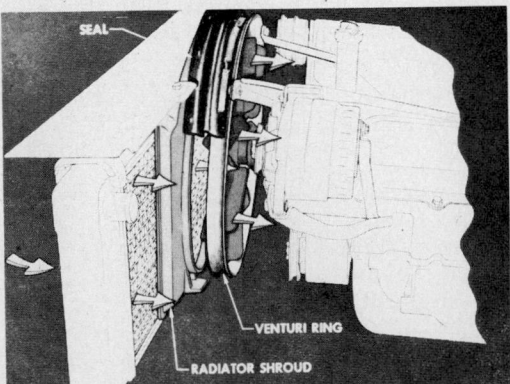

1972 Oldsmobile Toronado venturi fan shroud.
(© Olds. Div., G.M. Corp.)

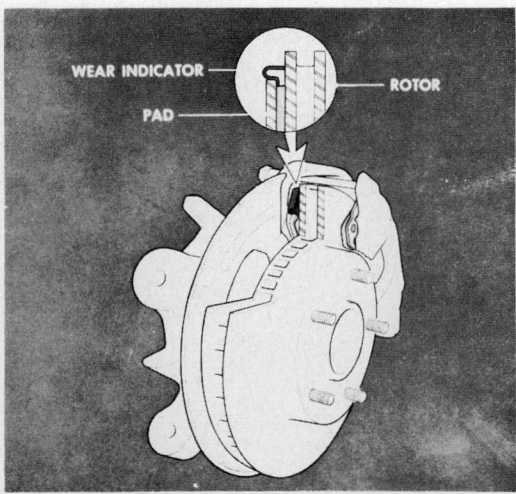

1972 Oldsmobile disc brake wear indicator.
(© Olds. Div., G.M. Corp.)

Pinto

Index

FIRING ORDER

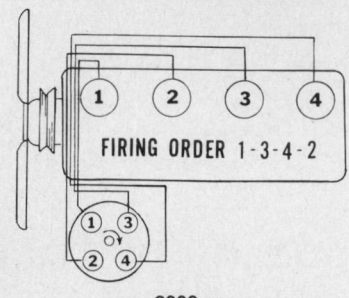

1600 cc.

FIRING ORDER 1-2-4-3

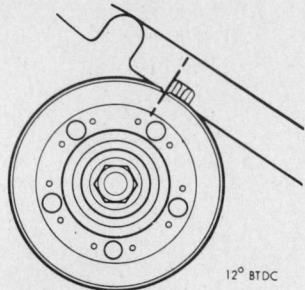

2000 cc.

FIRING ORDER 1-3-4-2

Timing Marks—1600 cc. engine

12° BTDC

YEAR IDENTIFICATION

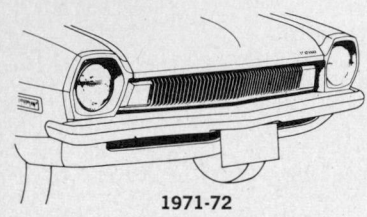

1971-72

CAR SERIAL NUMBER LOCATION AND ENGINE IDENTIFICATION

Vehicle Identification Number

The Vehicle Identification Number is located on a tab mounted on the upper left-hand corner of the dashboard, visible through the windshield. The VIN also appears on the Vehicle Certification Label, and is interpreted according to the illustration of this label.

Vehicle Certification Label

The Vehicle Certification Label is located on the rear edge of the drivers door. Alteration or removal of this label will result in its destruction, or the appearance of the word VOID.

Engine Identification

Engine code W indicates a 1600 cc. engine, X indicates a 2000 cc. engine. The engine code is the fifth digit of the Vehicle Identification number.

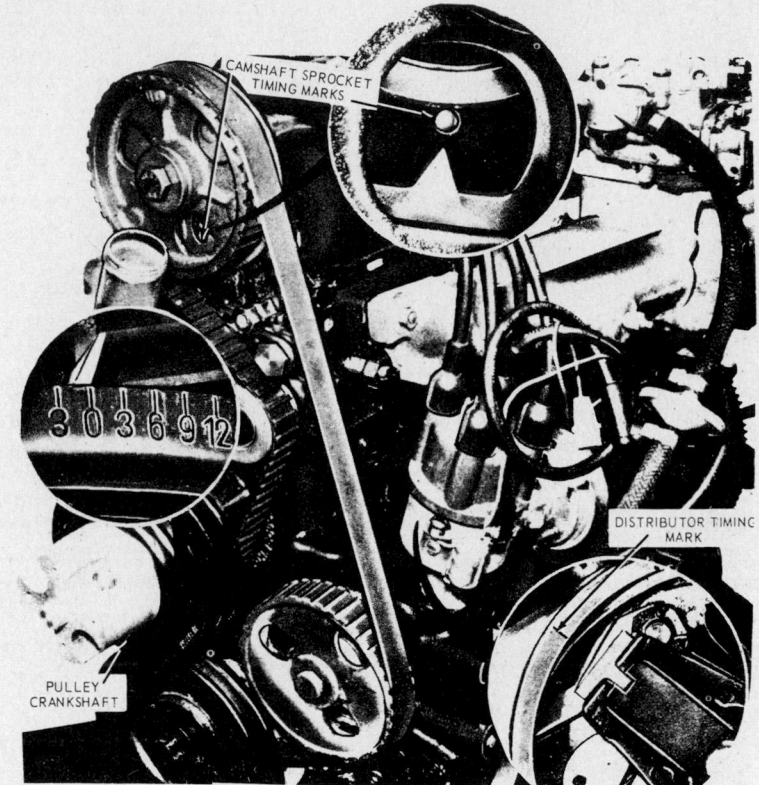

Timing Marks—2000 cc. engine

Vehicle Identification Number Plate

1. CONSECUTIVE UNIT NO.
2. BODY SERIAL CODE
3. MODEL YEAR CODE
4. ASSEMBLY PLANT CODE
5. ENGINE CODE
6. TRIM CODE
7. REAR AXLE CODE
8. COLOR CODE
9. BODY TYPE CODE
10. DISTRICT - SPECIAL EQUIPMENT CODE
11. TRANSMISSION CODE

Vehicle Certification Label

GENERAL ENGINE SPECIFICATIONS

YEAR	CU. IN. DISPLACEMENT	CARBURETOR	ADVERTIZED HORSEPOWER @ RPM	ADVERTIZED TORQUE @ RPM (FT. LBS.)	A.M.A. HORSEPOWER	BORE & STROKE (IN.)	ADVERTIZED COMPRESSION RATIO	VALVE LIFTER TYPE	NORMAL OIL PRESSURE (PSI)
1971-72	97.6	Autolite, 1-BBL.	75 @ 5000	96 @ 3000	16.3	3.188 x 3.056	8.0:1	Mech.	35 ②
	122.0	Weber 32/36DFAV	100 @ 5600	120 @ 3600	20.4	3.575 x 3.029	9.0:1	OHC ①	50 ③

① Cam follower.   ② At 1,000 rpm.   ③ At 1,500 rpm.

TUNE-UP SPECIFICATIONS

YEAR	MODEL	SPARK PLUGS		DISTRIBUTOR		IGNITION TIMING (Deg.) ▲	CRANKING COMP. PRESSURE (Psi)	VALVES		Intake Opens (Deg.)	FUEL PUMP PRESSURE (Psi)	IDLE SPEED (Rpm)
		Type (Auto Lite)	Gap (In.)	Point Dwell (Deg.)	Point Gap (In.)			Tappet (Cold) Clearance (In.) Intake	Exhaust			
1971-72	1600 cc	AGS-22	.023-.027	38-42	.024-.026	12B ②	④	.010	.017	17B	3½-4½	800/500 ⑤
	2000 cc	BRF-32	.032-.036	38-42	.024-.026	6B ①	④	.008 ③	.010 ③	18B	3½-4½	750 M.T. 650 A.T.

▲—With vacuum advance disconnected.
B—Before top dead center.
①—At 650 rpm in Drive (A.T.); 750 rpm in Neutral (M.T.).

②—At 900 rpm.
③—Between cam and follower.
A.T.—Automatic Transmission.

M.T.—Manual Transmission.
④—Lowest within 75% of highest.
⑤—Higher Speed with solenoid energized.

CAUTION

General adoption of anti-pollution laws has changed the design of almost all car engine production to effectively reduce crankcase emission and terminal exhaust products. It has been necessary to adopt stricter tune-up rules, especially timing and idle speed procedures. Both of these values are peculiar to the engine and to its application, rather than to the engine alone. With this in mind, car manufacturers supply idle speed data for the engine and application involved. This information is clearly displayed in the engine compartment of each vehicle.

GENERAL CHASSIS AND BRAKE SPECIFICATIONS

YEAR AND MODEL		CHASSIS		BRAKE CYLINDER BORE				BRAKE DRUM	
		Overall Length (In.)	Tire Size	Master Cylinder (In.)		Wheel Cylinder Diameter (In.)		Diameter (In.)	
				Std.	Power	Front	Rear	Front	Rear
1971-72	Two-door sedan	163.0	6.00 x 13 ①	.9375	N.A.	1.000 ②	.7187	9.00 ③	9.00
	Three-door sedan	163.0	6.00 x 13 ①	.9375	N.A.	1.000 ②	.7187	9.00 ③	9.00

①—Optional sizes: A78 x 13; A70 x 13.   ③—Disc rotor diameter—9.30.
②—2.125 for disc brakes.   N.A.—Not available.

AC GENERATOR AND REGULATOR SPECIFICATIONS

YEAR	MODEL	ALTERNATOR				REGULATOR						
		Brush Spring Pressure (Oz.)	Output		Model	Field Relay			Regulator			
			Volts	Amps.		Air Gap (In.)	Point Gap (In.)	Volts to Close	Air Gap (In.)	Point Gap (In.)	Volts @ 50-125°F
1971-72	DOZF-B	—	13.5-15.3	38	DOAF-A	Not Adjustable		2.5-4.0	Not Adjustable		13.5-15.3
	DOAF-G	—	13.5-15.3	42	DOAF-A	Not Adjustable		2.5-4.0	Not Adjustable		13.5-15.3

CRANKSHAFT BEARING JOURNAL SPECIFICATIONS

YEAR AND MODEL		MAIN BEARING JOURNALS (IN.)				CONNECTING ROD BEARING JOURNALS (IN.)		
		Journal Diameter	Oil Clearance	Shaft End-Play	Thrust On No.	Journal Diameter	Oil Clearance	End-Play
1971-72	1600 cc	2.1253-2.1261	.0005-.0015	.003-.011	3	1.9368-1.9376	.001-.0015	.004-.010
	2000 cc	2.2432-2.2440	.0005-.0015	.004-.008	—	2.0464-2.0772	.001-.0015	.010-.024

Ignition System

Distributor

1600 cc

The Autolite distributor is mounted on the right-hand side of the engine and is gear-driven by the camshaft. It incorporates both centrifugal and vacuum advance mechanisms. The vacuum *advance* action is controlled by carburetor vacuum, while the vacuum *retard* action is controlled by intake manifold vacuum. The **IMCO** system, described in more detail in the Unit Repair Section, is used to control exhaust emissions.

2000 cc

The 2000 cc engine is equipped with a Bosch dual diaphragm, dual-advance distributor. It is located on the left side of the engine and rotates in a clockwise direction. The ignition condenser is mounted externally on the body of the distributor.

Removal

1. Unsnap the two clips and remove the distributor cap.
2. Disconnect the vacuum lines from the distributor.
3. Matchmark the distributor housing and the engine block, then scribe another mark on the housing to indicate the rotor position.

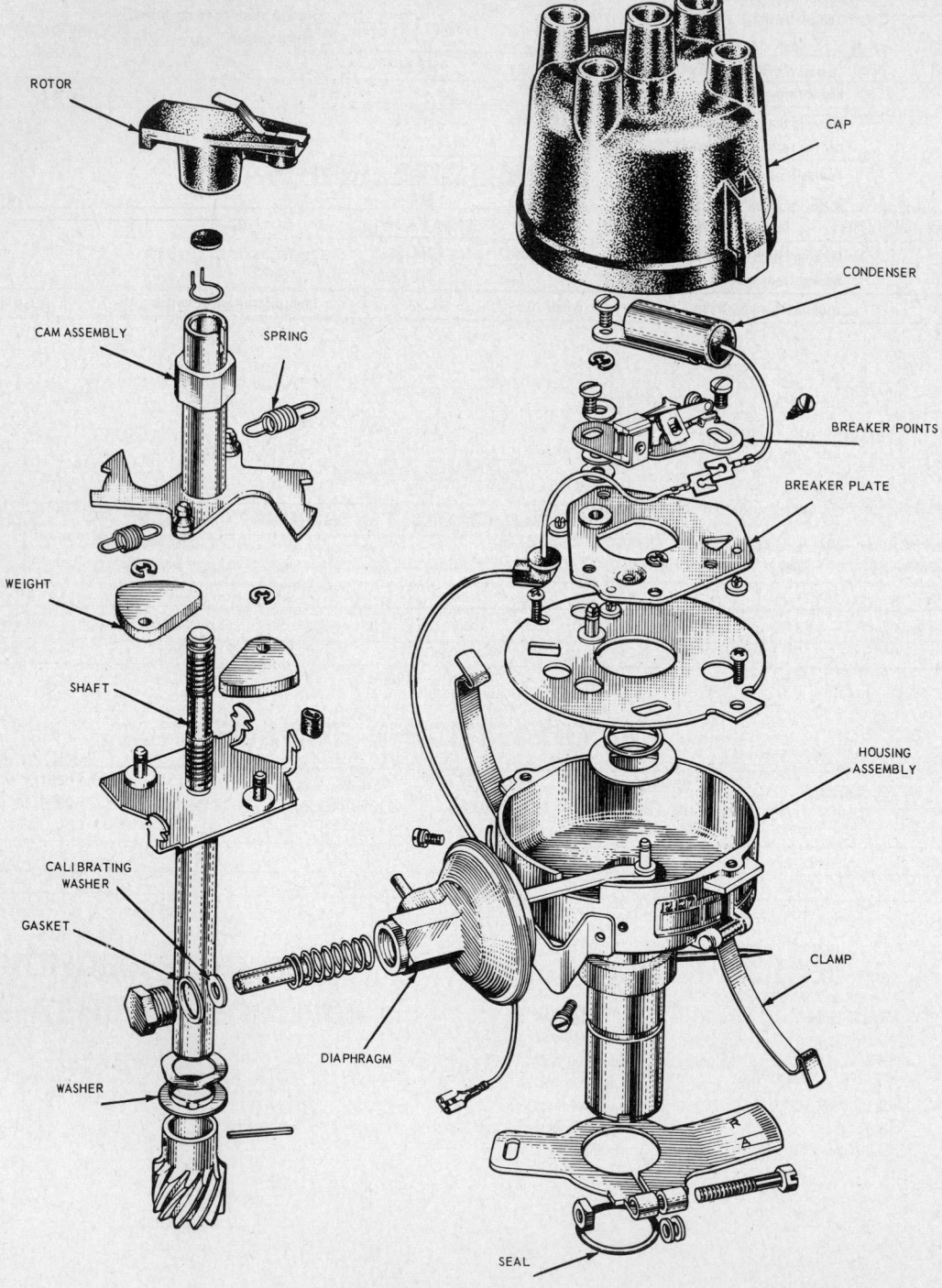

ROTOR

CAM ASSEMBLY   SPRING

WEIGHT

SHAFT

CALIBRATING WASHER

GASKET

DIAPHRAGM

WASHER

CAP

CONDENSER

BREAKER POINTS

BREAKER PLATE

HOUSING ASSEMBLY

CLAMP

SEAL

Distributor (© Ford Motor Co.)

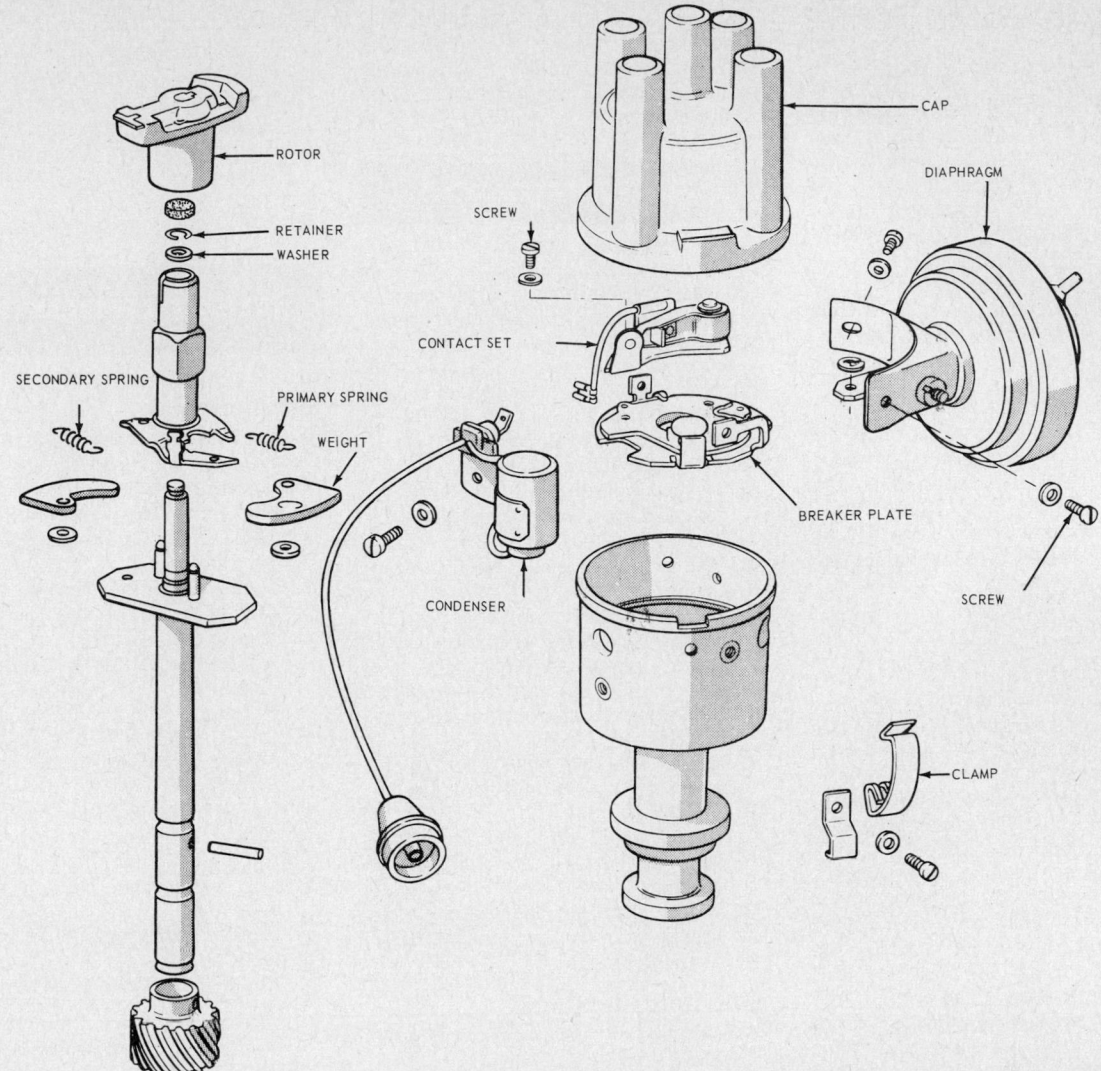

ROTOR

RETAINER

WASHER

SECONDARY SPRING

PRIMARY SPRING

WEIGHT

CONDENSER

SCREW

CAP

DIAPHRAGM

CONTACT SET

BREAKER PLATE

SCREW

CLAMP

Bosch distributor (© Ford Motor Co.)

4. Remove the bolt that holds the distributor, then carefully pull out the unit.

Disassembly—1600

1. Remove the condenser lead and condenser, then remove wires from points.
2. Remove breaker point assembly.
3. Remove the snap-ring on the vacuum unit pivot post, then remove the two breaker plate hold-down screws and the breaker plate.
4. Remove the large snap-ring on the pivot post.
5. Remove the flat washer, the two wave washers, and the upper contact breaker plate.
NOTE: it may be necessary to move the breaker plate to disengage the hold-down pin from the slot in the lower plate. There is a grounding spring between the two breaker plates which must be reinstalled for proper distributor operation.
6. Remove the primary wire rub-

ber grommet, then remove the governor weights.
7. Unclip the advance springs, first noting which spring goes to each post.
8. Remove the vacuum unit, then remove the felt cam spindle pad.
9. Remove the snap-ring and the cam spindle, making sure to mark the slot where the advance stop is located.
10. Remove the drive gear retaining pin, using a pin punch, then remove the drive gear and the two washers located above it.
11. Remove shaft, plate, and thrust washers from the distributor housing.
12. Remove the vacuum unit end bolt and pull out the vacuum spring, stop, and shims.

Assembly—1600

1. Assemble the vacuum spring, stop, and shims; install bolt and seal ring.

2. Slide thrust washers onto the distributor shaft below the plate, then fit the shaft and plate to the distributor housing and slide on the thrust washer, wave washer, and gear. Install retaining pin.
NOTE: if a new gear or shaft is installed, a new retaining pin hole must be drilled. The new gear has a pilot hole as supplied.
3. Install the distributor cam spindle, making sure the advance stop is in the correct slot, and secure with snap-ring. Place a new felt wick, moistened with oil, in the cam spindle top.
4. Install vacuum unit, then reconnect the springs to their original posts.
5. Lightly lubricate the governor weight pivots with grease, then install them with the flat sides toward cam spindle; secure them with spring clips.
6. Install the primary wire rubber grommet, connect the grounding spring to the pivot post, then in-

stall upper breaker plate. The hold-down spindle must enter the "keyhole" slot.

7. Hold this assembly in place using the two spring washers, flat washer, and large snap-ring.

8. Check the clearance between the two breaker plates, using a feeler gauge, at the point underneath the nylon bearing nearest the hold-down pin; clearance should not exceed 0.010 in.

NOTE: to reduce clearance, thread the nut further onto the hold-down screw.

9. Position and secure the breaker plate assembly in the housing.

10. Install the snap-ring onto the end of the vacuum unit pivot post, then lubricate the cam spindle with a tiny amount of Lubriplate or equivalent.

11. Install points and condenser and adjust point gap.

Installation

1. Align matchmarks, if engine has not been disturbed, and install distributor.

NOTE: keep in mind that the helical gear will tend to rotate the distributor as it is pushed down.

2. If engine has been disturbed, turn crankshaft until No. 1 piston is at TDC on compression stroke and timing marks are aligned. With the vacuum unit pointing towards the back of the engine approximately 45° from crankshaft centerline, and rotor pointing to No. 2 spark plug wire tower, insert the distributor into the engine.

3. Adjust contact breaker points and ignition timing.

Ignition Timing Adjustment

1. Adjust contact breaker points to specification, with the rubbing block on the highest part of the cam spindle lobe.

2. Connect the leads of a strobe-type timing light to the battery and to No. 1 spark plug wire.

NOTE: a small nail, inserted into the distributor cap tower, makes a good hook-up terminal.

3. Clean the timing marks on the front cover and on the crankshaft pulley.

4. Start the engine and allow it to idle at 600 rpm, distributor vacuum lines disconnected and plugged.

5. Shine the timing light on the index area—timing should be set at 12° BTDC for IMCO-equipped 1600 models and 6° on 2000.

NOTE: to advance timing, loosen

distributor clamp and rotate distributor opposite normal distributor rotation; to retard timing, rotate in the same direction as distributor normally rotates.

Alternator

The charging system consists of the battery, which will be covered separately, the alternator, the regulator and the wires and cables required to connect these units.

Some precautions that should be taken into consideration when working on this, or any other, AC charging system are as follows:

1. Never switch battery polarity.

2. When installing a battery, always connect the grounded terminal first.

3. Never disconnect the battery while the engine is running.

4. If the molded connector is disconnected from the alternator, do not ground the hot wire.

5. Never run the alternator with the main output cable disconnected.

6. Never electric weld around the car without disconnecting the alternator.

7. Never apply any voltage in excess of battery voltage during testing.

8. Never "jump" a battery for starting purposes with more than 12 volts.

Alternator Removal

1. Disconnect the battery negative cable.

2. Disconnect the alternator connectors.

3. Loosen the three mounting bolts and tilt the alternator in towards the engine.

4. Remove the fanbelt, then remove the mounting bolts and the alternator.

Alternator Installation

1. Position the alternator and loosely install the mounting bolts.

2. Install fanbelt, hold alternator so as to place tension on the belt (½ in. deflection at belt midpoint), then tighten mounting bolts.

3. Connect alternator wires and the battery cable.

Battery, Starter

The Pinto is equipped with an Autolite positive engagement starter. Internal starter repair procedures can be found in the Unit Repair Section.

R&R

1. Raise the vehicle on a hoist.

2. Disconnect the starter cable from the starter motor.

3. Remove the starter attaching bolts and move the starter forward and remove it from the car.

4. Reverse above procedure to install.

Instruments

Cluster Removal and Installation

1. Reach under the dash and disconnect the speedometer cable by pressing on the flat surface of the connector while pulling the cable away from the speedometer head.

2. Remove the two screws that attach the top of the instrument cluster to the dash.

3. Slide the top of the instrument cluster forward and lift it up to disengage the mounting pins in the bottom of the instrument cluster from the brackets in the dash.

4. Reach inside the instrument cluster opening and disengage the multiple connector plug from the instrument cluster printed circuit.

5. Remove the cluster from the dash.

6. Reverse above procedure to install.

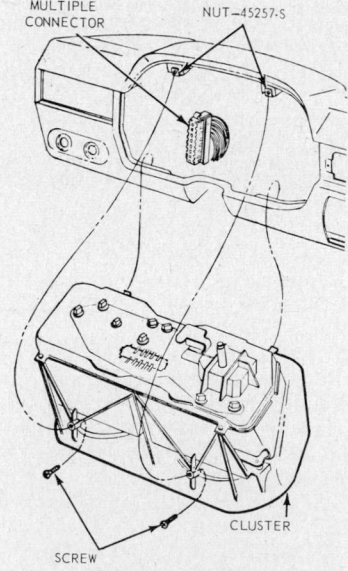

Instrument cluster removal
(© Ford Motor Co.)

Headlight Switch R&R

1. Remove the instrument cluster.

2. Disconnect the battery ground cable.

3. Remove the headlight switch control knob, shaft and retaining nut.

4. Disconnect the multiple connector from the switch and remove the switch from instrument cluster opening.
5. Reverse above procedure to install.

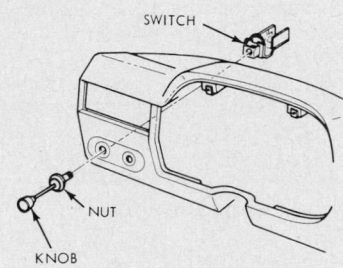

Headlight switch removal
(© Ford Motor Co.)

Ignition Switch

Removal

1. To gain access to the switch, remove the steering column shroud and disconnect and lower the steering column from the brake support bracket.
2. Disconnect the negative battery cable.
3. Disconnect the switch wiring at the multiple connector.
4. Remove the two nuts that retain the ignition switch to the steering column.
5. Remove the pin that connects the switch plunger to the actuating rod and remove the switch.

Installation

1. When installing the ignition switch, both the switch and the ignition lock must be in the LOCK position. The manual parts can be held in place by turning the ignition lock cylinder to the LOCK position with the transmission in PARK (automatic transmission) or REVERSE (standard transmission). To hold the switch in the LOCK position, insert a pin in the hole on the top of the switch, after manually moving the switch to the lock position.
2. Position the hole in the end of the switch plunger to the hole in the actuator and install the connecting pin.
3. Position the ignition switch on the steering column, and install, but do not tighten the retaining nuts.
4. Move the switch up and down on the steering column to find the mid-point of the actuating rod lash, then tighten the switch retaining nuts.
5. Remove the locking pin from the switch and install the steering column and shroud.

Ignition Lock Cylinder R&R

See Fairlane section.

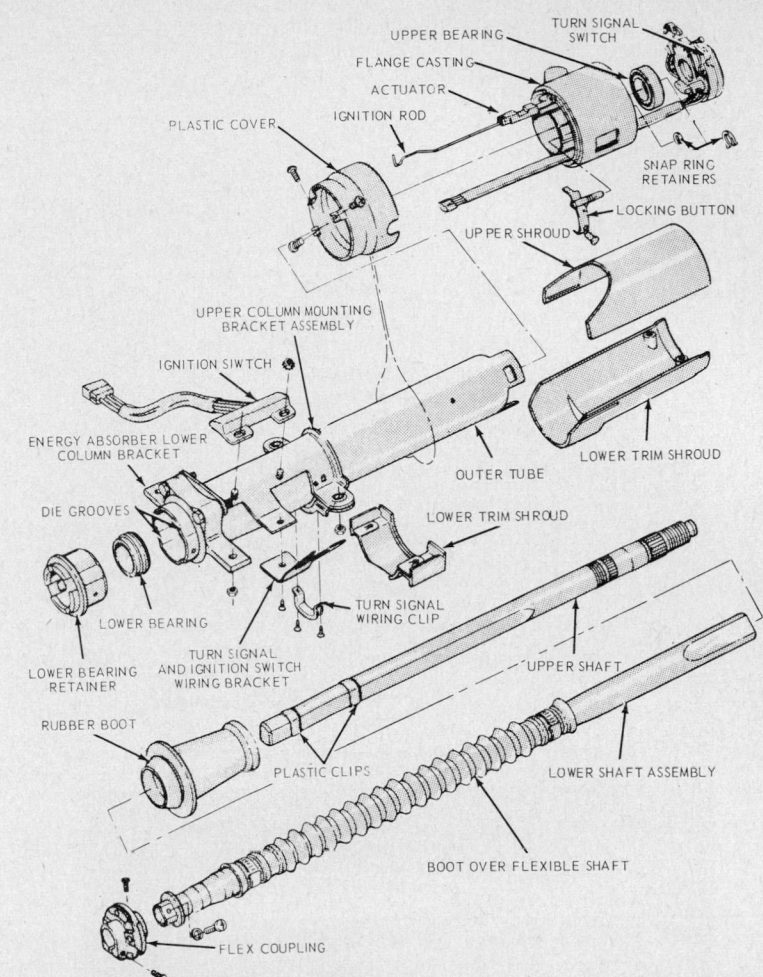

Steering column disassembled (© Ford Motor Co.)

Brakes

The drum brake system incorporates single anchor, internal expanding and self adjusting brake assemblies. The brake hydraulic system employs a dual reservoir master cylinder, a pressure differential valve and a single cylinder, dual piston wheel cylinder mounted on each backing plate. Front disc brakes are available as an option.

The parking brake is operated through a floor-mounted lever located between the front seats. Pulling the lever transmits force through a two cable linkage to operate the rear drum brakes. A self-adjusting feature operates when there is excessive clearance between the brake shoes and drums.

Master Cylinder Removal

1. Working under the dash, disconnect the stop light switch wires from the stop light switch and remove the switch and master cylinder pushrod from the brake pedal. Use care not to damage the stop light switch during removal.
2. Raise the hood and remove the brake lines from the master cylinder.
3. Remove the capscrews and lockwashers that attach the master cylinder to the firewall and remove the master cylinder.
4. Reverse above procedure to install, but, leave the brake lines loose on the master cylinder.
5. Fill the master cylinder with Extra Heavy Duty Brake Fluid.
6. Bleed the master cylinder by slowly depressing the foot pedal.
7. Refill master cylinder and bleed the front, then the rear, brakes.

Parking Brake Adjustment

1. Fully release the parking brake.
2. Place the transmission in Neutral and raise the rear of the vehicle until the rear wheels clear the floor.
3. Tighten the adjusting nut on the equalizer rod until the rear brakes drag when the rear wheels are turned.
4. Loosen the adjusting nut until

the rear wheels can be turned without the rear brakes dragging.

5. Lower the rear of the vehicle and check the operation of the parking brake.

stage is actuated by mechanical linkage when the primary throttle plates reach an opening of approximately 45°. The primary stage includes a curb idle system, accelerator pump system, idle transfer system, main

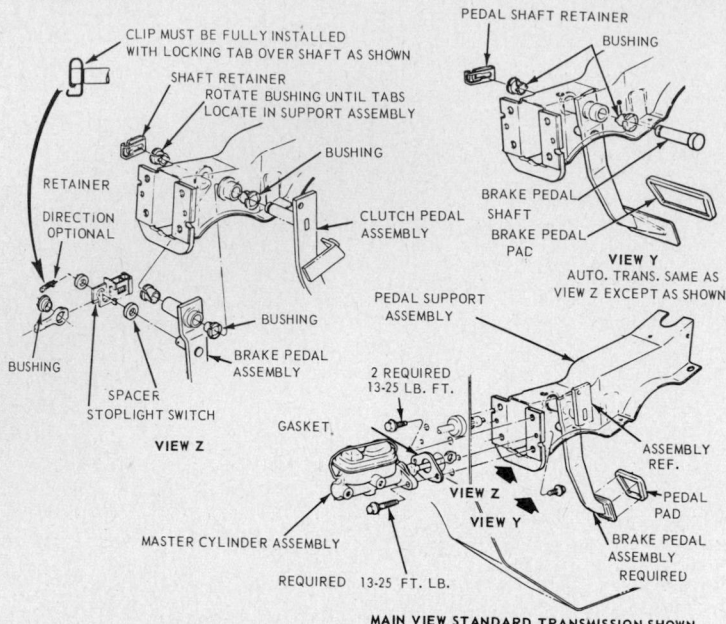

Master cylinder and brake pedal installation (© Ford Motor Co.)

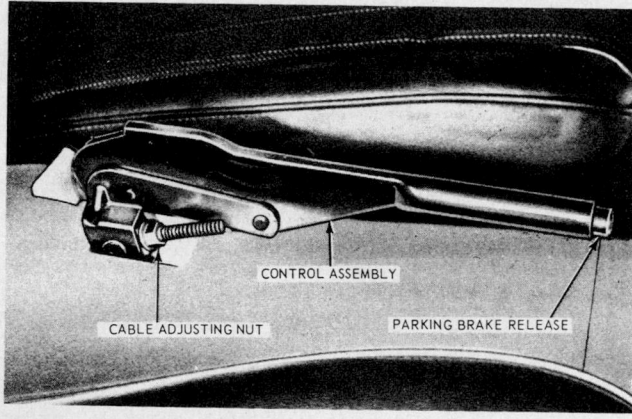

Parking brake adjustment (© Ford Motor Co.)

Fuel System

Carburetor

The carburetor used on the 1600 cc engine is an Autolite single-barrel downdraft unit having idle, main, power valve, and accelerator pump systems. Cars equipped with exhaust emission controls have a tamper-proof slow-running volume screw that limits the rich mixture setting.

The 2000 cc Pinto engine is equipped with an Autolite model 5200 carburetor. The 5200 model is a two stage, two venturi carburetor. The primary stage venturi bore is of smaller diameter than the secondary stage venturi bore. The secondary

metering system and power enrichment system.

The secondary stage includes a transfer system, main metering system and power system. Both stages share a common fuel bowl.

On both carburetors, the automatic choke is mounted on the carburetor housing. It has a bimetallic thermostatic coil which winds up when cold and unwinds when hot. A vacuum diaphragm and spring controls the initial operation of the choke. Engine coolant flowing through a choke water cover heats the bimetal coil and controls the final choke opening.

Carburetor R&R

1. Lift the hood and remove the air cleaner.

2. Disconnect fuel and vacuum lines at the carburetor.

3. Disconnect decel valve line at carburetor.

4. Disconnect accelerator linkage, drain cooling system, and disconnect automatic choke.

5. Remove carburetor hold-down nuts and washers and the carburetor.

6. To install, reverse removal procedure, using a new gasket.

Idle Speed and Mixture Adjustments

Adjust with air cleaner installed, high beams on, A/C off.

1600 cc

Accurate adjustment of the carburetor requires the use of an exhaust gas analyzer. Using the analyzer, adjust for a 13.4-13.9 air/fuel ratio at specified rpm.

If an analyzer is not available, the carburetor can be roughly adjusted in the following manner:

1. Connect a tachometer between coil-to-distributor primary wire and ground. Adjust idle to specified rpm, turning the curb idle screw.

2. Adjust the lower idle screw to obtain maximum rpm—do not break the limit stop.

3. Screw in the lower idle screw to obtain a 20-40 rpm drop from the maximum idle speed.

4. Reset the idle speed, if necessary, using the curb idle screw to obtain specified rpm.

2000 cc

1. Run the engine at fast idle to stabilize engine temperature.

2. Connect a tachometer of known accuracy to the engine.

3. On vehicles with a manual transmission, place the transmission selector in the Neutral position. On vehicles with an automatic transmission, set the parking brake and place the transmission selector in the Drive position.

4. Adjust the curb idle screw to obtain a curb idle speed of 750 rpm on a vehicle with a manual transmission, or 650 rpm on a vehicle with an automatic transmission.

5. Turn the idle mixture adjusting screw inward to obtain the smoothest idle possible within the range of the idle limiter.

In some cases, rough idle coupled with erratic shift pattern can be caused by improper attachment of the battery ground cable to the engine bellhousing. The cable, when improperly routed, can cause the transmission vacuum line to become disconnected at the transmission. To

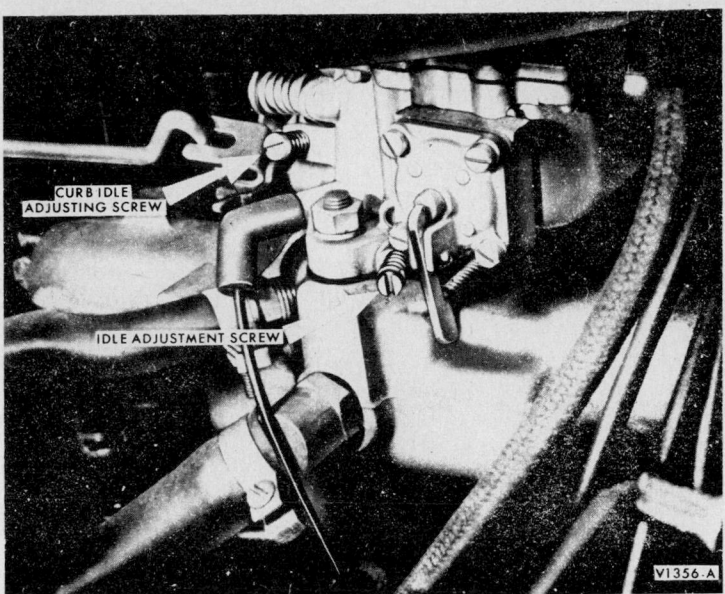

Carburetor adjustment—1600 (© Ford Motor Co.)

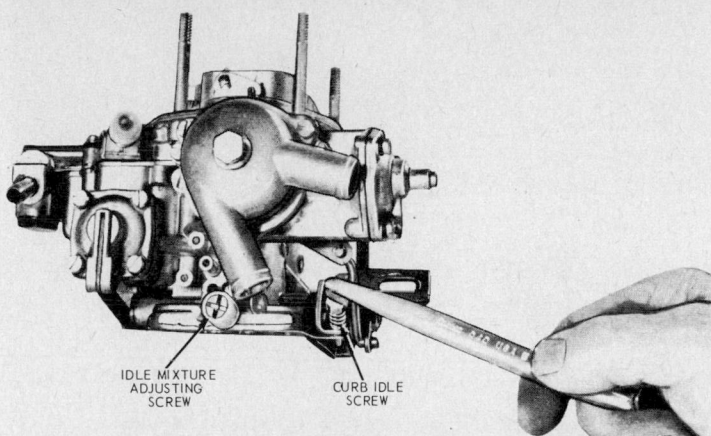

Autolite 5200 carburetor idle adjustments (© Ford Motor Co.)

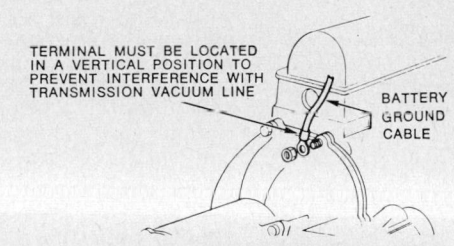

Battery ground cable location
(© Ford Motor Co.)

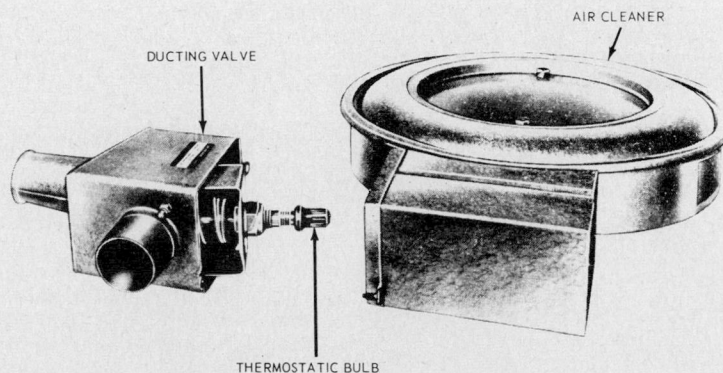

Air cleaner and duct assembly (© Ford Motor Co.)

provide proper clearance, rotate the cable so that it is in a vertical position where it attaches to the engine block.

Air Cleaner Assembly

The air cleaner used on the Pinto has a temperature-operated valve and duct assembly built-in, the failure of which will reduce the effectiveness of the emission control system.

The system is designed to provide heated air (+90° F.) to the carburetor during normal operation. A thermostatic bulb is connected through a spring-loaded linkage to a flap valve. This valve is designed to shut off the flow of hot air when underhood temperatures approach 110° F.

Testing

With the duct and valve assembly installed, the flap valve should be in the **up** position, shutting off the cold air intake, so long as ambient air temperature is below 85°F. If the valve is not in the **up** position, check for valve wear or breakage in the duct. The entire duct and valve assembly must be replaced as a unit if wear is in evidence.

To further test the unit, remove it from the car and immerse the thermostatic bulb in water. Heat the water to 85°F., allow the temperature to stabilize for about five minutes, then observe valve—it should be in the **up** position. Increase water temperature to 110°F. and again wait five minutes. The flap valve should be in the **down** position to shut off the hot air. If the flap does not work as indicated, the thermostatic bulb must be replaced as a unit.

Fuel Pump

1600 cc

A diaphragm-type mechanical fuel pump, mounted on the right-hand side of the engine, supplies fuel to the carburetor under pressure. The pump is driven by the camshaft and is permanently sealed.

2000 cc

A diaphragm-type mechanical fuel pump, mounted on the left-front of the cylinder block, supplies fuel to the carburetor under pressure. The pump is actuated by a rod which is driven by an eccentric on the auxiliary shaft and is permanently sealed.

Removal and Installation

1. Disconnect the fuel lines from the fuel pump and plug the inlet line from the gas tank to prevent gas leakage.
2. Remove the fuel pump retaining screws and remove the pump.
3. On 2000 cc engines, remove the fuel pump actuating rod.

4. Clean all gasket mounting surfaces.

5. On 2000 cc engines, install the fuel pump actuating rod.

6. Apply oil-resistant sealer to the fuel pump, position the pump on the engine and install the retaining screws.

NOTE: on 1600 cc engines, make sure the fuel pump rocker arm is riding on the camshaft eccentric.

7. Connect the fuel lines to the fuel pump, start the engine and check for leaks.

Evaporative Emission Control System

All Pintos are equipped with a fuel vapor control system. The system has four major components—the fuel tank, the vapor separator, the three-way control valve, and the vapor absorbing charcoal canister. The fuel tank is equipped with a non-vented filler cap and has the vapor separator welded to its top side. The vapor separator cannot be serviced separately if defective—the entire fuel tank must be replaced.

The tank fuel filler neck is double-sealed and, in addition to fulfilling its primary function of receiving fuel, vents air through a secondary chamber and indicates fuel level.

tank as fuel is consumed (to prevent tank collapse).

The primary function of the three-way control valve is the control of fuel fill level. As fuel level rises, vapor is discharged into the atmosphere through the fill control tube and the space between the inner filler tube and the outer neck. When the

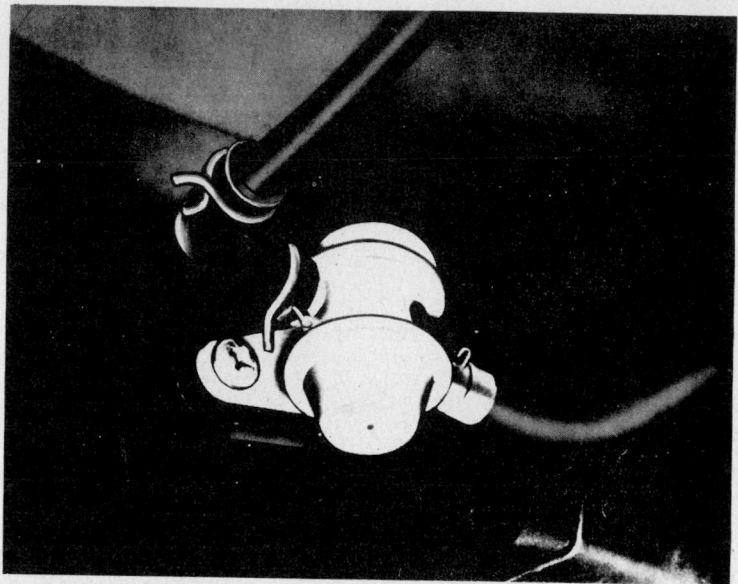

Three-way control valve (©️ Ford Motor Co.)

maintained, when full, at approximately 90% of full tank volume to allow for thermal expansion.

When thermal expansion takes place, vapor flows when a vapor pressure of 0.3 to 0.65 psi is developed in the line from the separator unit. The vapor passes through the now open three-way control valve, through the

Charcoal canister—tighten center bolt to 15-18 ft. lbs. (©️ Ford Motor Co.)

The vapor separator (see illustration) serves to prevent the entry of liquid fuel into the three-way control valve supply line.

The three-way control valve has three internal valves—a check valve to regulate fuel control (0.3-0.65 psi), a safety pressure relief valve to permit vapor blow-off in case of a plugged vapor line, and a vacuum relief air valve to replace air in the

fuel level is high enough to cover the fill control tube orifice, vapor can no longer escape and the filler tube begins to fill up. At this point, neither vapor nor fuel can flow through the system to the check valve, since at least 0.3 psi is required to open the valve and the pressure head in the filler is still insufficient. The tank level is therefore controlled by the level in the fill control tube and is

system, to the charcoal canister in the engine compartment. Vapor is there absorbed by the activated charcoal until the car is started, whereupon the "stored" vapor is sucked through a connecting hose into the air cleaner and burned.

If the line should become restricted (between charcoal canister and check valve), the vapor pressure is permitted to rise to 0.7 to 1.5 psi, at which point the pressure relief valve portion of the three-way control valve opens to allow the vapor to pass into the atmosphere.

The vacuum relief valve portion of the three-way control valve always remains closed until a pressure differential of 0.25 psi is reached (between atmospheric pressure and vacuum in tank). When this point is reached, the valve opens to the atmosphere and air is allowed to pass into the tank, through a filter, until pressure balance is achieved.

Exhaust System

The Pinto uses a single exhaust system. It consists of an exhaust manifold outlet pipe, and muffler and inlet pipe assembly. The 1600 cc engine exhaust manifold mounts on the left side of the engine, while the 2000 cc engine exhaust manifold mounts to the right side of the engine.

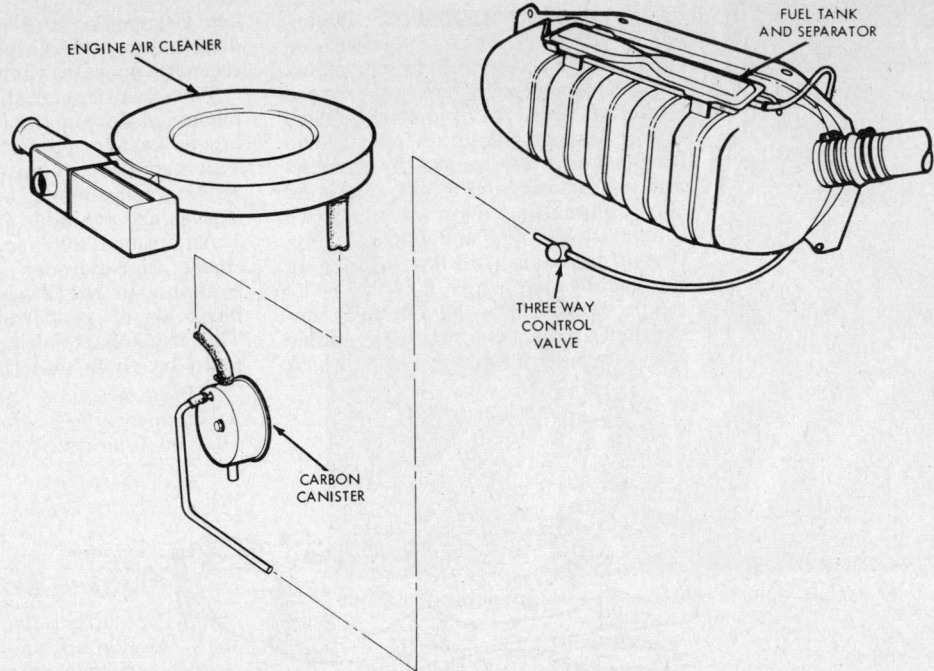

ENGINE AIR CLEANER

FUEL TANK AND SEPARATOR

THREE WAY CONTROL VALVE

CARBON CANISTER

Evaporative emission control system schematic (© Ford Motor Co.)

Exhaust Manifold Outlet Pipe R&R

1. Raise the vehicle on a hoist.
2. Remove the clamp that attaches the manifold outlet pipe to the engine bellhousing bracket.
3. Support the rear of the exhaust system and remove the clamp that attaches the exhaust manifold outlet pipe to the muffler inlet pipe.
4. Remove the nuts that attach the manifold outlet pipe to the manifold.
5. Remove the outlet pipe from the car.
6. Reverse above procedure to install, using a new exhaust manifold flange gasket.

Muffler and Inlet Pipe Assembly R&R

1. Raise the vehicle on a hoist so that the rear axle housing will drop to the limit of its travel.
2. Remove the clamp that attaches the manifold outlet pipe to the muffler inlet pipe.
3. Remove the standard attaching parts from the exhaust system hangers, lower the exhaust system and pull the muffler and inlet pipe assembly rearward and remove it from the car.
4. Reverse above procedure to install.

Cooling System

The cooling system consists of the water pump, fan, thermostat, radia-

tor, and connecting lines. Coolant is circulated from the bottom of the radiator up through the water pump and into the cylinder block and cylinder head to the thermostat. If the engine is at operating temperature (or hotter), the coolant is returned to the radiator top tank, from where it flows down through the radiator tubes to be cooled by air. If the engine is cold, the coolant flows through a bypass hose to allow the coolant in the block and head to warm up quickly.

Water Pump R&R

1600 cc

1. Lift the hood, then drain the cooling system.
2. Remove lower radiator hose and heater hose from water pump.
3. Loosen alternator adjusting and mounting bolts, pivot alternator toward engine, and remove V-belt.
4. Remove fan and pulley, then remove pump bolts and pump.
5. To install, reverse removal procedure, tightening alternator bolt to 15-18 ft. lbs.
   NOTE: use a new gasket, with Permatex.

2000 cc

1. Drain the cooling system.
2. Disconnect the heater hose and the lower radiator hose from the water pump.
3. Loosen the alternator attaching bolts and remove the alternator drive belt.
4. If engine is equipped with a fan

shroud, remove the bolts that attach it to the radiator and position it rearward over the fan.
5. Remove the fan attaching bolts, then, remove the fan, fan spacer, pulley and fan shroud (if so equipped) from the engine as an assembly.
6. Remove the camshaft drive belt cover.
7. Remove the water pump attaching bolts, then, remove the water pump from the engine.
8. Clean all gasket material from the cylinder block.
9. Coat new gasket with water-resistant sealer and reverse above procedure to install.

Radiator R&R

1. Lift the hood and drain the cooling system.
2. If equipped with an automatic transmission, disconnect the transmission cooler lines from the bottom of the radiator. If equipped with a fan shroud, remove the bolts that attach it to the radiator and position it rearward over the fan.

   NOTE: radiator cap should be opened to allow pressure release.
3. Disconnect radiator top and bottom hoses, remove hold-down bolts, and lift out radiator.
4. Remove the overflow hose from the filler neck.
5. To install, reverse removal procedure.

   NOTE: cap should be left off with engine running to allow air to bleed out of system.

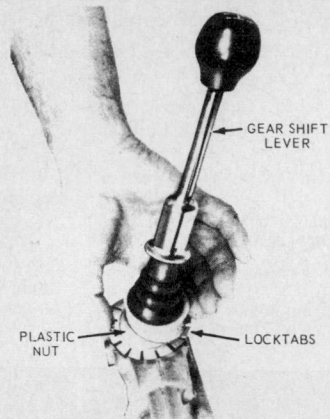

Removing plastic dome nut from shift linkage
(© Ford Motor Co.)

8. Disconnect and remove the driveshaft. Place rags in the extension housing to prevent loss of lubricant.
9. Disconnect the back up light switch wires and remove the switch.
10. Remove the clutch release lever dust cover.
11. Disconnect the clutch cable from the clutch release lever.
12. Remove the starter motor attaching bolts and position the motor out of the way.
13. Remove the speedometer cable-to-transmission attaching screw and remove the cable and gear from the transmission. Plug the opening in the transmission to prevent lubricant spillage.
14. Support the rear of the engine with a jack and remove the crossmember-to-body attaching bolts.
15. Remove the bolts that attach the crossmember to the transmission extension housing and remove the crossmember from the car.
16. Lower the engine to gain working room, and remove the remaining flywheel housing-to-engine attaching bolts.
17. Slide the transmission rearward and remove it from the car.
18. If the clutch is to be removed, loosen the six pressure plate attaching bolts evenly to release spring pressure gradually. If the same pressure plate and cover are to be reused, mark the position of the pressure plate and flywheel so they can be returned to their original location.
19. Remove the pressure plate attaching bolts and remove the pressure plate and clutch from the car.

Installation

1. Position the clutch and pressure plate on the flywheel and install the attaching bolts loosely.
NOTE: the three dowel pins on the flywheel must be aligned with the

pressure plate.
2. Align the clutch assembly, using a pilot shaft or other suitable tool, and alternately tighten the bolts.
3. Position the transmission and flywheel assembly on the studs on the cylinder block and install the retaining bolts.
4. Reverse removal procedure to install remaining equipment.

Standard Transmission

Transmission R&R

See *Clutch, Clutch Housing, and Transmission R&R* in this car section.

Automatic Transmission

Downshift Linkage Adjustment

1. Disconnect the downshift lever return spring.
2. Hold the throttle shaft lever in the wide open position. Hold the downshift rod against the through detent stop. Adjust the downshift screw to obtain 0.050-0.070 in. clearance between the screw tip and the throttle shaft lever tab.
3. Connect the downshift lever return spring.

Manual Linkage Adjustment

1. Place the transmission selector lever in the Drive position.
2. Raise the vehicle on a hoist and loosen the manual linkage shift rod at the selector lever.
3. Move the transmission manual lever to the Drive position (fourth detent position from the rear of the transmission).
4. Tighten the nut on the manual linkage shift rod to 10-20 ft. lbs.
5. Lower the car and check transmission operation.

Neutral Start Switch Adjustment

1. Place the transmission selector

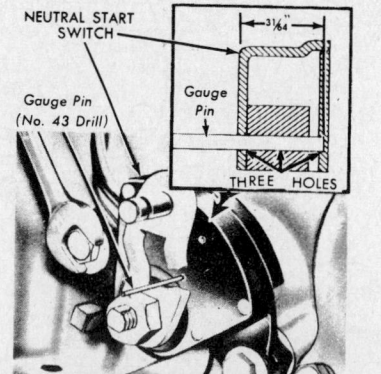

Neutral start switch adjustment
(© Ford Motor Co.)

lever in the Neutral position.
2. Raise the vehicle on a hoist and loosen the two bolts that attach the neutral switch to the transmission.
3. Rotate the switch until a gauge pin (shank end of a #43 drill bit) can be inserted through the gauge pin holes in the switch. The gauge pin must be inserted a full 31/64 in. into the switch, through all three holes in the switch.
4. Tighten the switch retaining bolts to 50-75 in. lbs. and remove the pin.

Transmission R&R

1. Remove the two upper converter housing-to-engine attaching nuts.
NOTE: two 10mm x 3/8 in. studs are used to attach the upper part of the converter housing to the engine block. If the studs are removed, make sure they are reinstalled with the metric threads in the engine block.
2. Remove the bolt that attaches the transmission filler tube support bracket to the engine block. Remove the filler tube from the transmission, then remove it from the car.
3. Raise the vehicle on a hoist and remove the converter housing inspection cover.
4. Place a drain pan under the converter housing and remove the converter drain plug. Reinstall plug in converter after all the fluid has drained out.
5. Place a drain pan under the transmission oil pan and loosen the pan attaching bolts. Drain the fluid from one corner of the pan. After the fluid has drained, tighten the pan bolts.
6. Disconnect the driveshaft from the pinion flange and slide the yoke from the transmission extension housing. Remove the driveshaft from the car.
7. Remove the vacuum hose from the transmission modulator valve and disengage the hose from the positioning clip on the transmission.
8. Remove the engine support-to-crossmember nut.
9. Remove the speedometer cable from the extension housing.
10. Disconnect the oil cooler lines from the transmission case.
11. Disconnect the transmission rod at the manual lever. Disconnect the downshift rod and spring at the downshift lever.
12. Disconnect the neutral start switch connectors and retaining clamps.
13. Turn the crankshaft as required, and remove the four converter-to-flywheel attaching nuts.
14. Position a transmission jack under the transmission and se-

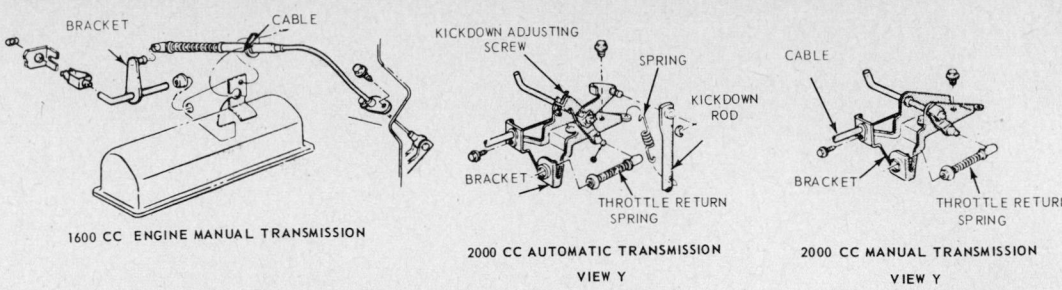

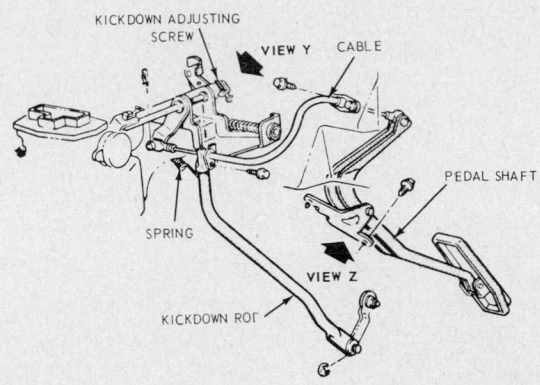

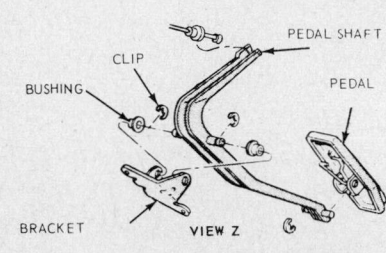

1600 CC ENGINE MANUAL TRANSMISSION

2000 CC AUTOMATIC TRANSMISSION
VIEW Y

2000 CC MANUAL TRANSMISSION
VIEW Y

Throttle linkage (© Ford Motor Co.)

cure the transmission to the jack with a chain.

15. Remove the bolts that attach the crossmember to the frame and remove the crossmember.

16. Remove the bolts that attach the starter motor to the converter housing and position the starter out of the way.

17. Remove the remaining converter housing-to-engine attaching bolts.

18. Move the transmission rearward to disengage the converter from the flywheel and remove the transmission from the car.

Installation

1. Install the two studs that attach the upper part of the converter housing to the engine block if they were removed.

NOTE: be sure to install the studs with the metric threads in the engine block.

2. Raise the transmission into position and install the converter housing-to-engine attaching bolts. Be sure the downshift spring bracket is installed on the upper left side of the converter housing-to-engine bolt.

3. Tighten the converter housing-to-engine attaching bolts to 23-33 ft. lbs.

4. Reverse Steps 1-16 of the removal procedure to complete installation.

Drive Shaft, U Joints

U-Joint R&R

1. Raise the vehicle on a hoist.

2. Mark the position of the rear driveshaft yoke in relation to the pinion flange so the driveshaft can be returned to its original location.

3. Disconnect the rear U-Joint from the pinion flange and remove the loose bearing caps. Pull the driveshaft rearward until it clears the transmission extension housing. Remove the driveshaft from the car.

4. Place the driveshaft in a vise and remove the snap-rings from the U-Joint to be removed.

5. Using a suitable tool, drive one of the bearing caps on the U-Joint to be removed toward the center of the driveshaft.

6. Remove the opposite bearing cap from the one being driven as it emerges from the driveshaft.

7. Repeat Step 6 until all bearing caps have been removed.

8. Remove the U-Joint spider from the driveshaft.

9. To install, position the spider in the driveshaft and drive the bearing caps onto the spider.

10. Install the snap-rings in the driveshaft.

11. Reinstall the driveshaft in its original location in the car.

Rear Suspension

The rear suspension consists of conventional three-leaf, longitudinal, semi-elliptic springs, located asymmetrically to the rear axle carrier and fastened by U-bolt clamps. Standard telescopic shock absorbers control vertical rebound.

Rear Shock Absorber R&R

1. Disconnect the lower end of the shock absorber from the spring plate.

2. Remove the three bolts retaining the shock absorber mounting bracket at the upper end of the shock.

3. Compress and remove shock from car.

4. Transfer mounting bracket to new shock.

5. Position shock absorber on car and install attaching parts.

Rear Spring R&R

1. Disconnect the lower end of the shock absorber from the spring plate and position the shock out of the way.

2. Raise the vehicle on a hoist and place supports under the axle and the underbody.

3. Remove the spring plate attaching nuts from the U bolts. Remove the spring plate.

4. Disconnect and remove the rear shackle from the spring.

5. Remove the front hanger bolt and nut from the eye of the spring. Remove the spring from the car.

6. Reverse above procedure to install.

NOTE: all used attaching parts must be discarded and replaced with new parts.

Drive Axles

The rear axle assembly is an integral-type housing, hypoid design, with the centerline of the pinion set below the centerline of the ring gear.

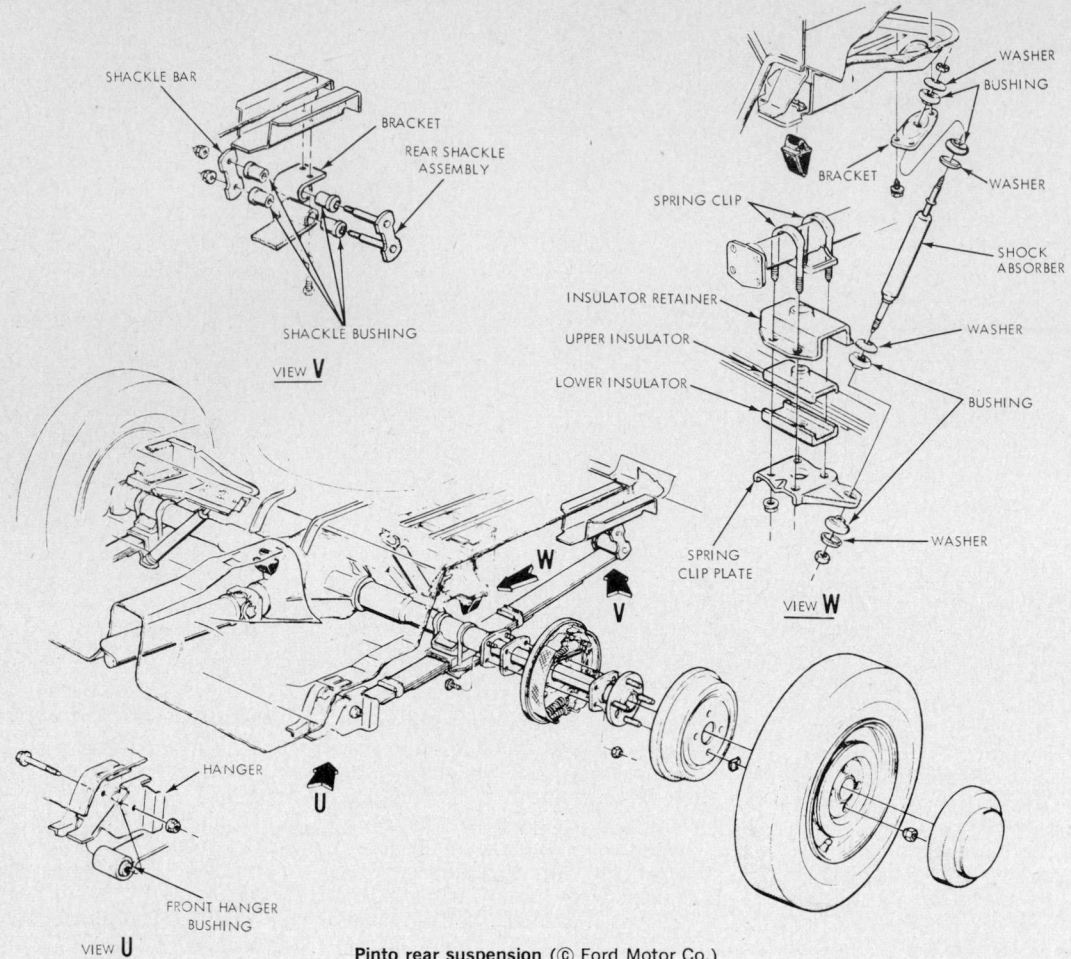

SHACKLE BAR

BRACKET

REAR SHACKLE
ASSEMBLY

SHACKLE BUSHING

VIEW **V**

WASHER

BUSHING

BRACKET

WASHER

SPRING CLIP

SHOCK
ABSORBER

INSULATOR RETAINER

UPPER INSULATOR

LOWER INSULATOR

WASHER

BUSHING

WASHER

SPRING
CLIP PLATE

VIEW **W**

HANGER

FRONT HANGER
BUSHING

VIEW **U**

Pinto rear suspension (© Ford Motor Co.)

The semi-floating axle shafts are positioned in the housing by ball bearings and a bearing retainer at the outer ends of the axle housing.

A cover on the rear of the differential housing provides access for inspection and repairs.

Rear Axle Bearing R&R

1. Remove the rear wheel and brake drum.
2. Working through the hole in the axle shaft flange, remove the four nuts that secure the axle bearing retainer.
3. Remove the axle shaft, using care not to damage the oil seal.
4. Using a large chisel, slot the axle bearing retaining ring and remove the bearing from the axle.
5. Press a new bearing into place on the axle shaft.
6. Install axle in housing and install the bearing retainer and attaching nuts.
7. Install the brake drum and wheel.

Axle Housing R&R

1. Raise the vehicle on a hoist and remove the driveshaft.
2. Disconnect the lower ends of the shock absorbers.

3. Remove the rear wheels and brake drums.
4. Disconnect and remove the vent hose from the housing and the brake junction.
5. Remove the brake line T-fitting

from the housing.
6. Support the axle housing and remove the rear springs.
7. Lower the axle housing and remove it from the car.
8. If the axle housing is being re-

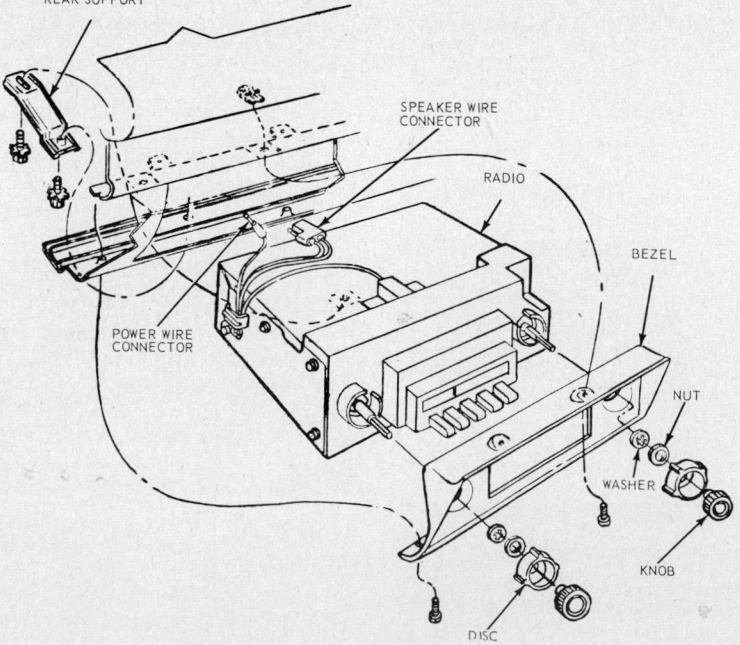

REAR SUPPORT

SPEAKER WIRE
CONNECTOR

RADIO

BEZEL

POWER WIRE
CONNECTOR

NUT

WASHER

KNOB

DISC

Radio installation (© Ford Motor Co.)

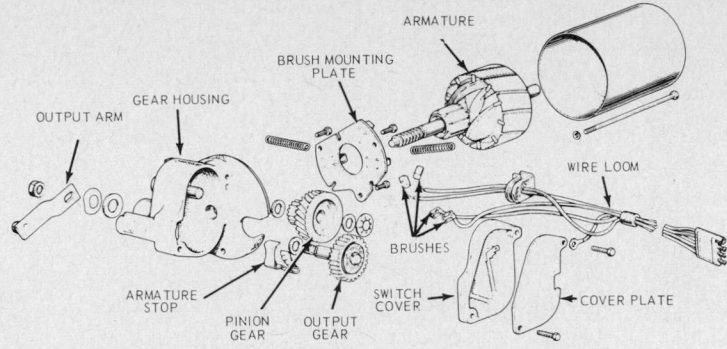

ARMATURE

BRUSH MOUNTING
PLATE

GEAR HOUSING

OUTPUT ARM

WIRE LOOM

BRUSHES

ARMATURE
STOP

PINION
GEAR

OUTPUT
GEAR

SWITCH
COVER

COVER PLATE

Wiper motor disassembled (© Ford Motor Co.)

placed, transfer all component parts.

9. Reverse above procedure to install.

Radio

R&R

1. Disconnect the negative battery cable.
2. Remove the bolt that mounts the radio to the radio support.
3. Remove the four screws attaching the radio cover bezel to the instrument panel.
4. Pull the radio from the instrument panel and disconnect the radio lead wires.
5. Remove the radio from the car.
6. Reverse above procedure to install.

Windshield Wipers

Motor R&R

1. Loosen the two nuts and disconnect the wiper pivot shaft and link assembly from the motor drive arm ball.
2. Remove the three motor attaching screws and lower the motor away from the left side of the dash.
3. Disconnect the wiper motor wires and remove the wires.
4. To install, position the motor under the dash and install the wires.
5. Position the motor to the dash and install the retaining screws.
6. Position the wiper pivot shaft and link assembly to the motor drive arm ball and tighten the two nuts.

Linkage R&R

1. Remove the windshield wiper arms and blades from the pivot shafts.
2. Loosen the two nuts retaining the wiper pivot shaft and link assembly to the motor drive arm ball.
3. Remove the three screws attach-

ing each pivot shaft.

4. Remove the pivot shaft and link assembly from under the left side of the dash.
5. Reverse above procedure to install.

Heater System

Heater Assembly R&R

1. Drain the cooling system and disconnect the negative battery cable.
2. Disconnect the blower motor ground wire (black) at the engine side of the dash panel.
3. Disconnect the heater hoses at the engine block.
4. Remove the four nuts that attach the heater assembly to the dash, from the engine side of the dash.
5. Working inside the car, remove

the glove box.

6. Disconnect the control cables from the heater.
7. Remove the snap-rivet that attaches the forward side of the defroster air duct to the heater assembly. Move the air duct back into the defroster nozzle and disengage it from the tabs on the heater box. Tilt the forward edge of the duct up and forward to disengage it from the nozzle, and remove it from the left side of the heater assembly.
8. Remove the heater assembly to dash panel support bracket mounting screw and remove the heater assembly. At the same time, pull the heater hoses through the dash panel. Then, disconnect the hoses from the heater core in the case.

Blower Motor

1. Remove the heater assembly.
2. Disconnect the blower motor lead wire from the resistor. Remove the four blower motor mounting plate attaching nuts and remove the motor and wheel.

Heater Core

1. Remove the heater assembly.
2. Remove the compression gasket from the cowl air inlet and remove the eleven clips from the case. Separate the case and remove the heater core.

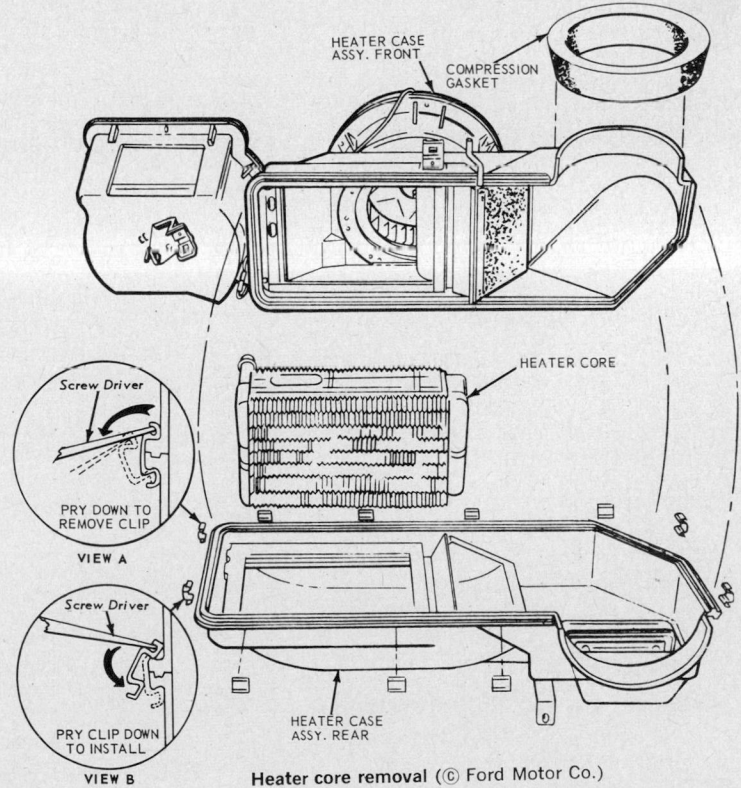

HEATER CASE
ASSY. FRONT

COMPRESSION
GASKET

HEATER CORE

Screw Driver

PRY DOWN TO
REMOVE CLIP

VIEW A

Screw Driver

PRY CLIP DOWN
TO INSTALL

VIEW B

HEATER CASE
ASSY. REAR

Heater core removal (© Ford Motor Co.)

Pontiac, Grand Prix

Index

YEAR IDENTIFICATION

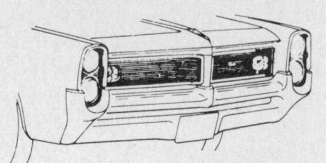

1965 Grand Prix

1965

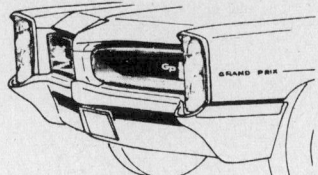

1966 Grand Prix

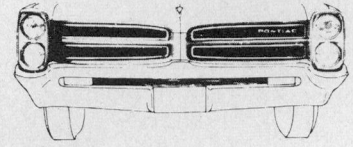

1966

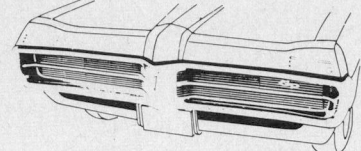

1967 Grand Prix

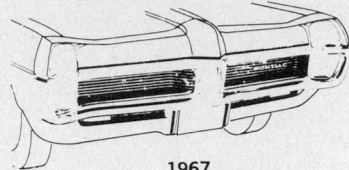

1967

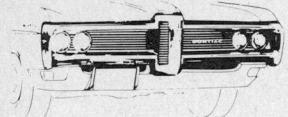

1968

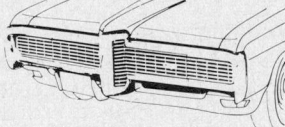

1968 Grand Prix

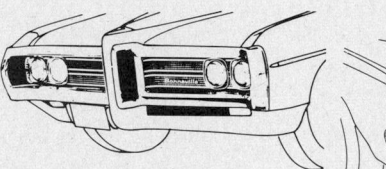

1969

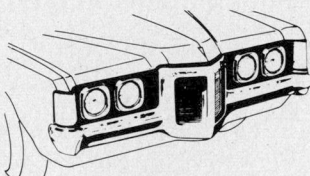

1969 Grand Prix

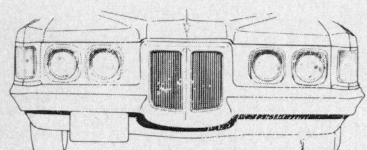

1970 Grand Prix

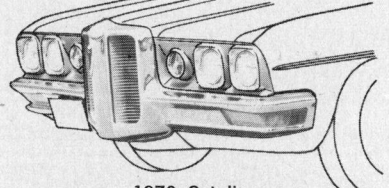

1970 Catalina

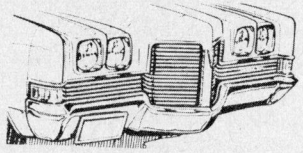

1971 Pontiac

1971 Grand Prix

1972 Pontiac

1972 Grand Prix

FIRING ORDER

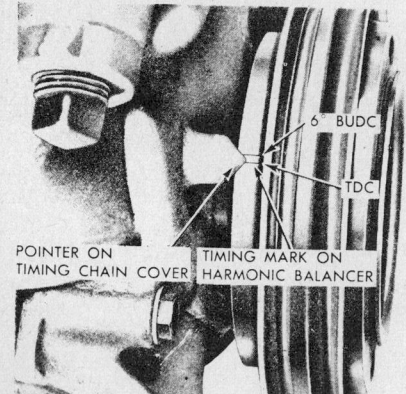

Ignition timing marks—1965
(© Pontiac Div., G.M. Corp.)

Ignition timing marks—1966-72
(© Pontiac Div., G.M. Corp.)

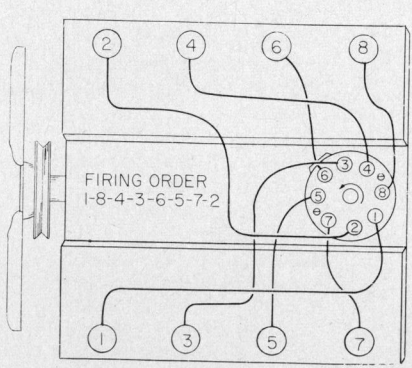

FIRING ORDER
1-8-4-3-6-5-7-2

1965-72 V8

CAR SERIAL NUMBER LOCATION

1965-67

Car serial number is on the left front door pillar. This number is interpreted below.

1968-72

Car serial number is located on the upper left-hand side of the instrument panel, visible through the windshield. The number is interpreted as follows:

1965-72

First digit: Car division
Second and third digits: Series number
Fourth and fifth digits: Body style code
Sixth digit: Year manufactured
Seventh digit: Plant
Eighth digit: Engine used (1 = V8; 6 = 6 cyl.)
Ninth to thirteenth digits—sequential serial number

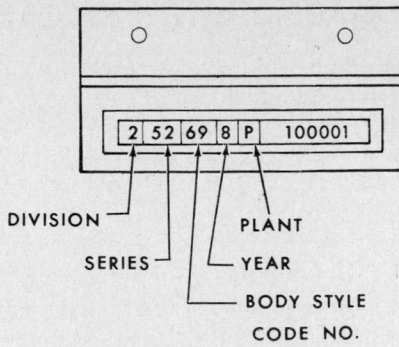

Typical vehicle serial number

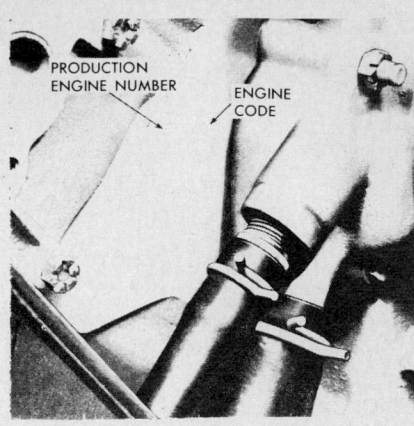

Engine serial number location

Engine Identification

1965-72

The engine production number is found on the front of the right bank of cylinders, stamped into the block.

The engine production code is stamped on a machined pad just beneath this number. Refer to the charts for engine code interpretation.
First digit: Pontiac Division.
Second and third digit: Model series.
Fourth and fifth digit: Body style.
Sixth digit: Year manufactured.
Seventh digit: Plant.

Engine Production Codes 1965–66

No. Cyls.	Cu. In. Displ.	Type	1965	1966	1967	No. Cyls.	Cu. In. Displ.	Type	1965	1966	1967
8	389	3 Spd., M.T., 2 Bbl.	WA	WA		8	428	M.T., 4 Bbl., 2 + 2, Exh. Em.			XK
8	400	M.T., 2 Bbl.			WA	8	400	M.T., 4 Bbl., Exh. Em.			XY
8	400	M.T., 2 Bbl. H.D.C.			WB	8	400	M.T., 4 Bbl.			XZ
8	389	3 Spd., M.T., 4 Bbl.	WD			8	400	A.T., 2 Bbl.			YA
8	400	M.T., 4 Bbl., Exh. Em.			WD	8	400	A.T., 2 Bbl., Exh. Em.			YB
8	389	3 Spd., M.T., 4 Bbl.		WE		8	400	A.T., 2 Bbl.			YC
8	400	M.T., 4 Bbl.			WE	8	400	A.T., 2 Bbl., AC			YD
8	389	3 Spd., M.T., 3-2 Bbl.	WF			8	400	A.T., 4 Bbl., H.D.C.			YE
8	400	A.T., 2 Bbl., AC			WF	8	400	A.T., 4 Bbl., AC, H.D.C.			YF
8	421	3 Spd., M.T., 4 Bbl.	WG	WG		8	389	A.T., 4 Bbl., AC	YF	YF	
8	428	M.T., 4 Bbl., 2 + 2			WG	8	421	A.T., 4 Bbl.	YH	YH	
8	421	3 Spd., M.T., 3-2 Bbl.	WH	WH		8	400	A.T., 4 Bbl.			YH
8	421	3 Spd., M.T., 3-2 Bbl.	WJ	WJ		8	421	A.T., 3-2 Bbl.	YI	YI	
8	420	M.T., 4 Bbl.			WS	8	421	3 Spd., M.T., 3-2 Bbl.	YK		
8	421	3 Spd., M.T., 4 Bbl.		WK		8	421	A.T., 3-2 Bbl.		YK	
8	428	A.T., 4 Bbl., Exh. Em.			WL	8	428	A.T., 4-Bbl. 2 + 2			YK
8	400	M.T., 2 Bbl., Exh. Em.			WM	8	400	A.T., 4 Bbl., Exh. Em.			YL
8	400	M.T., 2 Bbl., Exh. Em.			WN	8	421	A.T., 4 Bbl.	YT		
8	389	3 Spd., M.T., 2 Bbl.	XA			8	389	A.T., 2 Bbl.	YU		
8	400	M.T., 2 Bbl.			XA	8	400	A.T., 2 Bbl., Exh. Em.			YU
8	389	A.T., 2 Bbl.	XB			8	389	A.T., 2 Bbl., AC	YV		
8	400	A.T., 2 Bbl.			XB	8	400	A.T., 2 Bbl., AC			YV
8	389	A.T., 4 Bbl.	XC			8	389	A.T., 4 Bbl.	YW		
8	400	A.T., 4 Bbl.			XC	8	400	A.T., 4 Bbl., Exh. Em., H.D.C.			YW
8	428	A.T., 4 Bbl., Exh. Em., 2 + 2			XD	8	389	A.T., 4 Bbl., AC	YX		
8	400	A.T., 4 Bbl.			XH	8	400	A.T., 4 Bbl., Exh. Em., AC, H.D.C.			YX
8	400	A.T., 4 Bbl., AC			XJ	8	428	M.T., 4 Bbl., Exh. Em., 2 + 2			YV

AC—Air conditioned.
A.T.—Automatic transmission.

M.T.—Manual transmission.
2 Bbl.—Two barrel carburetor.

4 Bbl.—Four barrel carburetor.
H.D.C.—Heavy duty clutch.

1968 ENGINE CODES AND SPECIAL EQUIPMENT

Column groups: TRANS-MISSION (MANUAL, AUTOMATIC) · CARBURETOR (2-BBL, QUADRAJET) · COMPRESSION RATIO (8.6, 10.5, 10.75) · CAMSHAFT (9777254, 9779066, 9779067, 9779068) · STANDARD DISTRIBUTOR (1111272, 1111270, 1111449, 1111300, 1111448, 1111435, 1111450) · VALVE SPRINGS (STD.-TWO, H.D. TWO (SPEC.)) · SPECIAL EXHAUST MANIFOLDS

DISPLACEMENT	HP	ENGINE CODE	MANUAL	AUTOMATIC	2-BBL	QUADRAJET	8.6	10.5	10.75	9777254	9779066	9779067	9779068	1111272	1111270	1111449	1111300	1111448	1111435	1111450	STD.-TWO	H.D. TWO (SPEC.)	SPECIAL EXHAUST MANIFOLDS
400 Cu. In. Engine	290	WA	X		X			X			X							X			X		
	290	WB	X		X			X			X							X			X		
	265	YA		X	X		X			X				X							X		
	290	YC		X	X			X				X		X							X		
	340	YE		X		X		X		X							X				X		
	350	XZ	X			X		X				X					X				X		
	350	XH		X		X		X		X							X				X		
428 Cu. In. Engine	375	WG	X			X		X					X						X		X	X	
	390	WJ	X			X			X			X			●							X	X
	375	YH		X		X		X				X								X	X		
	390	YK		X		X			X			X			●						X		X

●—With 60 psi oil pump spring. All cars use CCS.

1969 ENGINE CODES AND SPECIAL EQUIPMENT

Column groups: DISPLACEMENT (400, 428) · TRANS-MISSION (MANUAL, AUTOMATIC) · CARBURETOR (2-BBL (2GV), 4-BBL (4MV)) · COMPRESSION RATIO (8.6:1, 10.5:1, 10.75:1) · CAMSHAFT (9777254, 9779066, 9779067, 9779068) · DISTRIBUTOR (1111253, 1111940, 1111946 (e), 1111952 (e), 1111960, 1111959) · VALVE SPRINGS (H.D.-DUAL, H.D. SPEC.-DUAL) · CYLINDER HEAD (SMALL VALVE, LARGE VALVE)

400	428	HP	ENGINE CODE	MANUAL	AUTOMATIC	2-BBL (2GV)	4-BBL (4MV)	8.6:1	10.5:1	10.75:1	9777254	9779066	9779067	9779068	1111253	1111940	1111946 (e)	1111952 (e)	1111960	1111959	H.D.-DUAL	H.D. SPEC.-DUAL	SMALL VALVE	LARGE VALVE
X		290	(a) WA / WD	X		X			X		X						X				X		X	
X		265	(a) YA / YB		X	X		X			X					X					X		X	
X		290	(a) WB / WE	X		X			X		X						X				X		X	
X		290	(a) YC / YD		X		X		X		X				X						X		X	
	X	360	WG		X		X		X				X						X		X			X
	X	360	(a) YL / YH		X		X		X			X							X			X		X
	X	390	WJ	X			X			X				X				X				X			X
	X	360	(b) XK		X		X		X				X						X			X		X
	X	360	(e) XE / (c) XJ		X		X		X				X						X			X	X	
	X	390	YK		X		X			X			X				X				X			X
X		350	(d) WX	X			X		X				X				X				X			X
X		350	(d) XH		X		X		X			X		X						X			X
	X	370	(d) WF		X		X		X				X					X			X	X		X
	X	370	(d) XF		X		X		X			X				X				X	X		X
	X	390	(d) WL	X			X			X				X			X				X			X
	X	390	(d) XG		X		X			X			X					X		X			X
X		265	(d) YF		X	X		X			X				X					X		X	
X		340	(d) XZ		X		X		X		X				X					X		X	

(a) Early production (small valve) engines with 30° intake valve seat angle. Later production (small valve) engines use 45° intake valve seat. NOTE: All large valve engines use 30° intake valve seat.

(b) Police Freeway Enforcer.

(c) Police Highway Patrol.

(d) Gran Prix.

(e) Uses special hardened drive gear. (With 60 psi oil pump.)

1967 ENGINE CODES AND SPECIAL EQUIPMENT

HORSEPOWER	ENGINE CODE	DISP. TRANS 400	428	MANUAL	AUTOMATIC	CARB. 2-BBL	4-BBL	QUADRAJET	COMP. RATIO 7.9	8.6	10.5	10.75	CAMSHAFT 9779254(U)	9779066(N)	9779067(P)	9779068(S)	STD. DIST. 1111250	1111254	1111237	1111253	1111242	1111183	1111252	1111261	1111243	1111244	BKR LESS 1111245	1111251	1111180	1111255	VALVE STD. TWO	H.D. TWO	H.D. SPECIAL	AIR COND.	A.I.R. SYSTEM	C.C.S.	SPECIAL EXHAUST MANIFOLDS
265	WA	X		X		X				X			X							X											X						
265	WB	X		X		X				X			X							X											X						
333	WD	X		X			X				X				X		X														X				X		
333	WE	X		X			X				X				X				X												X			0			
260	XB	X			X	X			X				X							X											X						
293	XC	X		X		X			X					X						X											X						
350	XH	X		X		X				X				X									X								X			0			
350	XJ	X		X		X				X				X									X								X			0	X		
350	XY	X		X		X				X					X										X						X					X	
350	XZ	X		X		X				X					X								X						X		X			0			
265	YA	X			X	X			X				X							X											X						
265	YB	X			X	X			X				X											X							X					X	
290	YC	X			X					X			X								X										X			0			
290	YD	X			X					X			X							X											X			0	X		
325	YE	X			X		X			X				X						X											X			0			
325	YF	X			X		X			X			X							X											X			0			
360	WG		X	X	X		X			X			X							X														0	X		
376	WJ		X	X			X					X	X●							X							●			0	X				X		X
376	Y3		X	X	X		X					X	X●							X							●			0	X					X	X
360	Y2		X	X	X		X			X				X						X											X			0		X	
376	XK		X	X	X		X					X			X				●											X	X	X				
360	YH		X	X	X		X			X				X						X											X			0			
376	YK		X	X	X		X					X	X●							X							●			0	X						X
360	YY		X	X	X		X			X				X			X														X					X	

●—With 60 PSI oil pump spring
0—Optional

1970 ENGINE CODES AND SPECIAL EQUIPMENT

HORSEPOWER	ENGINE CODE	USAGE PONTIAC	GRAND PRIX	DISPLACEMENT 350	400	455	TRANS MANUAL	AUTOMATIC	CARB 2 BBL (2GV)	4 BBL (4MV)	COMP. RATIO 8.8:1	10.0:1	10.25:1	CAMSHAFT 9777254(U)	9779066(N)	9779067(P)	9779068(S)	DISTRIBUTOR 1112008	1112007	1111148★	1111176★	1111105	1112012★	VALVE SPRINGS STD. DUAL	CYL. HEAD SMALL VALVE	LARGE VALVE
225	W7	X		X					X		X			X				X						X	X	
255	X7	X		X				X	X		X			X				X						X	X	
290	WE	X			X		X		X			X				X		X						X	X	
350	WX		X		X		X			X		X				X				X				X		X
350	XH		X		X			X		X		X				X					X			X		X
330	XZ	X			X			X		X	X					X						X		X	X	
265	YB	X	X	X				X	X		X				X			X						X	X	
290	YD	X		X				X	X			X			X			X						X	X	
370	WG	X	X			X	X			X			X			X							X	X	X	X
370	XF	X	X			X				X			X				X						X	X	X	X
360	YH	X				X				X	X						X					X			X	X

★—Uses hardened drive gear for use with 60 psi oil pump and high tension distributor points.

1971 Engine Codes and Special Equipment

ENGINE CODE	HORSEPOWER	"B" SERIES	"G" SERIES	250 L-6	350 V-8	400 V-8	455 V-8	MANUAL (3 Speed)	MANUAL (4 Speed)	AUTOMATIC	MV (1 Bbl.)	2GV (2 Bbl.)	4MV (4 Bbl.)	8.5:1	8.0:1	8.2:1	8.4:1	PRESSED-IN	THREADED	SINGLE	DUAL (STD.)	DUAL (H.D.)	SMALL	LARGE	3864897	483555 (W)	9779066 (N)	9779067 (P)	9779068 (S)	HIGH-BALL (STD.)	HIGH-BALL*	LOW-BALL	1110489	1112069	1112068	1112070	1112071	1112072	1112073	1112083
WR	250	X			X			X				X			X			X			X		X		X					X										X
YU	250	X			X					**		X			X			X			X		X		X					X				X						
XR	250	X			X					**		X			X			X			X		X			X				X				X						
WT	300		X			X		X					X		X				X		X			X		X						X					X				
WK	300		X			X			X				X		X				X		X			X		X						X					X				
XX%	265	X			X					X			X		X			X			X		X		X					X							X			
YS	300	X	X			X				X			X		X				X		X			X			X				X							X		
YC+	325	X	X				X			X			X		X				X		X			X				X			X								X	
YG &	280	X				X				X		X			X				X		X			X					X		X							X		

*—Lifter Body with Cast-Iron Foot
**—"YU" is used with M35 transmission; "XR" is used with M38 transmission.
%—Man. Trans. Models use WS engine code
+—Man. Trans. Models use WJ engine code
&—Man. Trans. Models use WG engine code

BATTERY AND STARTER SPECIFICATIONS

YEAR	MODEL	BATTERY Ampere Hour Capacity	Volts	Group Number	Terminal Grounded	Lock Test Amps.	Lock Test Volts	Lock Test Torque	No-Load Test Amps.	No-Load Test Volts	No-Load Test RPM	Brush Spring Tension (Oz.)
1965–66	with Synchromesh	53	12	2SM	Neg.	Not Recommended			100	10.6	3,600	35
	with Hydramatic	61	12	2SM	Neg.	Not Recommended			120	10.6	4,700	35
	Hvy. Duty Opt. ▲	70	12	25M	Neg.	Not Recommended			Not Recommended			35
1967–68	with Synchromesh	53	12	2SM	Neg.	Not Recommended			100	10.6	4,350	35
	with Hydramatic	61	12	2SM	Neg.	Not Recommended			120	10.6	4,350	35
	Hvy. Duty Opt.	70	12	25T	Neg.	Not Recommended			Not Recommended			35
1969	Std.	61	12	R59	Neg.	Not Recommended			Not Recommended			35
	H.D.†	70	12	R69	Neg.	Not Recommended			Not Recommended			35
	Grand Prix	61	12	R59	Neg.	Not Recommended			Not Recommended			35
1970	350 Cu. In. Std.	53	12	Y59	Neg.	Not Recommended			Not Recommended			35
	400 Cu. In. Std.; 350, 400 Cu. In.*	61	12	R59	Neg.	Not Recommended			Not Recommended			35
	455 Cu. In. Std.; 350, 400 Cu. In. H.D.†	62	12	R59S	Neg.	Not Recommended			Not Recommended			35
	455 Cu. In. H.D.†	76	12	R79W	Neg.	Not Recommended			Not Recommended			35
1971–72	350 Cu. In. Std.	53	12	Y59	Neg.	Not Recommended			Not Recommended			35
	400 Cu. In. Std.; 350, 400 Cu. In.*	61	12	R59	Neg.	Not Recommended			Not Recommended			35
	455 Std.; 350, 400 Cu. In. H.D.; 455 Cu. In.*	62	12	R89S	Neg.	Not Recommended			Not Recommended			35
	455 Cu. In. H.D.†	76	12	R89W	Neg.	Not Recommended			Not Recommended			35

▲—1966
*—With A/C and/or Rear Window Defroster
†—Heavy Duty Option

TUNE-UP SPECIFICATIONS

YEAR	MODEL	SPARK PLUGS		DISTRIBUTOR		IGNITION TIMING (Deg.) ▲	CRANKING COMP. PRESSURE (Psi)	VALVES		Intake Opens (Deg.)	FUEL PUMP PRESSURE (Psi)	IDLE SPEED (Rpm) ★
		Type	Gap (In.)	Point Dwell (Deg.)	Point Gap (In.)			Tappet (Hot) Clearance (In.) Intake	Exhaust			
1965-66	V8—Std. Eng., M.T.	45S	.035	30	.016	6B	145	Zero	Zero	22B	5-6½	500
	V8—Std. Eng., A.T.	45S	.035	30	.016	6B	160	Zero	Zero	30B	5-6½	500
	V8—389 (425E)	45S	.035	30	.016	6B	160	Zero	Zero	14B	5-6½	500
	V8—389 (425A)	45S	.035	30	.016	6B	160	Zero	Zero	29B	5-6½	500
	V8—421 Cu. In., Std.	45S●	.035	30	.016	6B	160	Zero	Zero	23B	5-6½	500
	V8—421 Cu. In., Opt.	45S●	.035	30	.016	6B	160	Zero	Zero	31B	5-6½	600
1967	V8—400, 2-BBL.	45S	.035	30	.016	6B ⊙	160	Zero	Zero	22B	5-6½	600■
	V8—400, 4-BBL., M.T.	45S	.035	30	.016	6B ⊙	160	Zero	Zero	23B	5-6½	600■
	V8—400, 4-BBL., A.T.	45S	.035	30	.016	6B ⊙	160	Zero	Zero	30B	5-6½	500■
	V8—428, 4-BBL.	44S	.035	30	.016	6B ⊙	160	Zero	Zero	23B	5-6½	700
	V8—428, H.O.	44S	.035	30	.016	6B ⊙	160	Zero	Zero	31B	5-6½	700
1968	V8—400, 2-BBL. (L. Comp.)	45S	.035	30	.016	9B	150-170	Zero	Zero	22B	5-6½	800☆ ⑩
	V8—400, 2-BBL., M.T.	45S	.035	30	.016	9B	185-210	Zero	Zero	30B	5-6½	800 ⑩
	V8—400, 2-BBL., A.T.	45S	.035	30	.016	9B	185-210	Zero	Zero	23B	5-6½	600 ⑩
	V8—400, 4-BBL., M.T.	45S	.035	30	.016	9B	185-210	Zero	Zero	23B	5-6½	850 ⑩
	V8—400, 4-BBL., A.T.	45S	.035	30	.016	9B	185-210	Zero	Zero	30B	5-6½	600 ⑩
	V8—428, 4-BBL.	44S	.035	30	.016	9B	185-210	Zero	Zero	23B⑤	5-6½	850☆ ⑩
	V8—428, H.O., M.T.	44S	.035	30	.016	9B	185-210	Zero	Zero	23B	5-6½	850 ⑩
	V8—428, H.O., A.T.	44S	.035	30	.016	9B	185-210	Zero	Zero	23B	5-6½	650 ⑩
1969	V8—400, 2-BBL. (Low C.)	R45S	.035	30	.019	9B	150-170	Zero	Zero	22B	5-6½	850⑨
	V8—400, 2-BBL., M.T.	R45S	.035	30	.019	9B	185-210	Zero	Zero	30B	5-6½	850
	V8—400, 2-BBL., A.T.	R45S	.035	30	.019	9B	185-210	Zero	Zero	22B	5-6½	650
	V8—400, 4-BBL., M.T.	R45S	.035	30	.019	9B	185-210	Zero	Zero	23B	5-6½	1000 ⑩
	V8—400, 4-BBL., A.T.	R45S	.035	30	.019	9B	185-210	Zero	Zero	30B⑥	5-6½	650 ⑩
	V8—428, M.T.	R44S	.035	30	.019	9B	185-210	Zero	Zero	23B	5-6½	1000
	V8—428, A.T.	R44S	.035	30	.019	9B	185-210	Zero	Zero	30B⑦	5-6½	650
	V8—428, H.O., M.T.	R44S	.035	30	.019	9B	185-210	Zero	Zero	31B	5-6½	1000
	V8—428, H.O., A.T.	R44S	.035	30	.019	9B	185-210	Zero	Zero	23B	5-6½	650

▲—With vacuum advance disconnected and plugged. NOTE: These settings are only approximate. Engine design, altitude, temperature, fuel octane rating and the condition of the individual engine are all factors which can influence timing. The limiting advance factor must, therefore, be the "knock point" of the individual engine.

★—With manual transmission in N and automatic in D.

●—1966, V8—421; 44S.

■—100 rpm higher on exhaust emission cars.

⊙—Engines equipped with emission control systems—initial timing the same as standard.

☆—V8—400, 2-BBL. (Low Comp.)—M.T.—800 rpm; A.T.—600 rpm. V8—428, 4-BBL., M.T.—850 rpm, A.T.—650 rpm.

B—Before top dead center.

†—1972 engines use smaller diameter spark plugs with tapered seats.

① —800—M.T. 650—A.T.
② —Not used.
③ —Not used.
④ —M.T.—950
** —See engine decal.
⑤ —31B—M.T.
⑥ —22B—340 H.P.
⑦ —23B—Police
⑧ —31B—M.T.
⑨ —M.T.-850; A.T.-650
⑩ —Solenoid energized
⑪ —Not used.
⑫ —A.T.-600

WHEEL ALIGNMENT

YEAR	MODEL	CASTER		CAMBER		TOE-IN (In.)	KING-PIN INCLINATION (Deg.)	WHEEL PIVOT RATIO	
		Range (Deg.)	Pref. Setting (Deg.)	Range (Deg.)	Pref. Setting (Deg.)			Inner Wheel	Outer Wheel
1965-68	All Series	1N-2N	1½N	¼N-¾P	¼P	0-⅛	8½	20	18
1969-70	All Series	1N-2N	1½N	0-½P	¼P	0-⅛	8½	20	18
1971-72	Exc. Grand Prix, Catalina, Grandville & Bonneville	1N-2N	1½N	¼P-1¼P	¾P	⅛-¼	8½	20	18
	Grand Prix	1N-2N	1½N	½N-½P	0	1/16-3/16	8½	20	18
	Catalina, Grandville & Bonneville	½P-1½P	1P	¼P-1¼P	¾P	⅛-¼	8½	20	18

N—Negative.
P—Positive.

TUNE-UP SPECIFICATIONS, continued

YEAR	MODEL	SPARK PLUGS Type	Gap (In.)	DISTRIBUTOR Point Dwell (Deg.)	Point Gap (In.)	IGNITION TIMING (Deg.) ▲	CRANKING COMP. PRESSURE (Psi)	VALVES Tappet (Hot) Clearance (In.) Intake	Exhaust	Intake Opens (Deg.)	FUEL PUMP PRESSURE (Psi)	IDLE SPEED (Rpm) *
1970	V8—350, 2-BBL., 255 HP	R46S	.035	30	.019	9B	150-170	Zero	Zero	22B	5-6½	800 ①
	V8—400, 2-BBL. (Low C.)	R46S	.035	30	.019	9B	150-170	Zero	Zero	22B	5-6½	800 ①
	V8—400, 2-BBL., M.T.	R46S	.035	30	.019	9B	185-210	Zero	Zero	30B	5-6½	800
	V8—400, 2-BBL., A.T.	R46S	.035	30	.019	9B	185-210	Zero	Zero	22B	5-6½	650
	V8—400, 4-BBL., M.T.	R45S	.035	30	.019	9B	185-210	Zero	Zero	23B	5-6½	950
	V8—400, 4-BBL., A.T.	R45S	.035	30	.019	9B	185-210	Zero	Zero	30B	5-6½	650
	V8—455, 4-BBL., 360 HP	R45S	.035	30	.019	9B	185-210	Zero	Zero	23B	5-6½	650 ④
	V8—455, 4-BBL., 370 HP	R45S	.035	30	.019	9B	185-210	Zero	Zero	23B ⑧	5-6½	650 ④
1971-72	V8—350, 2-BBL	R47S†	.035	30	.019	12B**	120-160	Zero	Zero	26B	5-6½	800 ⑫
	V8—400, 2-BBL, A.T.	R47S†	.035	30	.019	12B**	120-160	Zero	Zero	26B	5-6½	600
	V8—400, 4-BBL, M.T.	R47S†	.035	30	.019	12B**	120-160	Zero	Zero	23B	5-6½	600
	V8—400, 4-BBL, A.T.	R47S†	.035	30	.019	12B**	120-160	Zero	Zero	23B	5-6½	700
	V8—455, 2-BBL.	R46S†	.035	30	.019	12B**	120-160	Zero	Zero	23B	5-6½	650
	V8—455, 4-BBL.	R46S†	.035	30	.019	12B**	120-160	Zero	Zero	30B	5-6½	650

CAUTION

General adoption of anti-pollution laws has changed the design of almost all car engine production to effectively reduce crankcase emission and terminal exhaust products. It has been necessary to adopt stricter tune-up rules, especially timing and idle speed procedures. Both of these values are peculiar to the engine and to its application, rather than to the engine alone. With this in mind, car manufacturers supply idle speed data for the engine and application involved. This information is clearly displayed in the engine compartment of each vehicle.

CAPACITIES

YEAR	MODEL	ENGINE CRANKCASE ADD 1 Qt. FOR NEW FILTER	TRANSMISSIONS Pts. TO REFILL AFTER DRAINING Manual 3-Speed	4-Speed	Automatic	DRIVE AXLE (Pts.)	GASOLINE TANK (Gals.)	COOLING SYSTEM (Qts.) WITH HEATER
1965-66	Exc. Sta. Wag.	5	2¾	2½	22½ ▲	4½	26½	20
	Sta. Wag.	5	2¾	—	22½ ▲	4½	24	20
1967	Exc. Sta. Wag.	5	2¾	2½	19	4½ ①	26½	18†
	Sta. Wag.	5	2¾	2½	19	4½	24	18
1968	Exc. Sta. Wag.	5	3½	2½	20	4½ ①	26½ ②	18†
	Sta. Wag.	5	3½	2½	20	4½	24	18
1969	Exc. Grand Prix & Sta. Wag.	5	2.8	—	7.5	4.5	26.5	18 ③
	Grand Prix	5	2.8	2.5	7.5	3.0	21.5	18.75 ④
	Sta. Wag.	5	2.8	—	7.5	4.5	24.0	18
1970	Exc. Grand Prix & Sta. Wag.	5	2.75	—	7.5 ⑤	4.5	26.0 ⑥	17.25 ⑦
	Grand Prix	5	4.0	2.5	7.5	3.0	21.5 ④	17.5 ⑧
	Sta. Wag.	5	2.75	—	7.5	4.5	24.0 ⑥	17.25 ⑦
1971-72	Exc. Grand Prix & Sta. Wag.	5	3.5	—	7.5 ⑨	4.25 ⑩	24.5	18.6 ⑪
	Grand Prix	5	2.8	2.5	7.5	3.0 ⑩	24.0	18.6 ⑪
	Sta. Wag.	5	3.5	—	7.5 ⑨	4.25 ⑩	23.0	18.6 ⑪

▲—1966—19 Pts.
†—Grand Prix—18.6 Qts., 428 Cu. In. Opt. Eng. 17.2 Qts.
① 3 pts. with 8.125 in. ring gear; 5 pts. with 8.875 in. ring gear
② 21½ gals. for Grand Prix
③ 428 Cu. In.—17.25
④ With A/C—21.0; 428 Cu. In.—17.5
⑤ 2-speed—6.0; M38—5.0

⑥ With Evaporative Emission Control System: 24.4; Grand Prix—24.0; Sta. Wag.—23.0
⑦ 400 Cu. In. with A/C—18.0; 455 Cu. In.—18.0
⑧ 400 Cu. In. with A/C—18.75; 455 Cu. In.—21.0
⑨ 2-speed—3.0; M38—8.0
⑩ "C" axle—5.5
⑪ 400 Cu. In. with A/C—19.2; 455 Cu. In.—18.0; 455 Cu. In. with A/C—19.0; 350 Cu. In.—20.2; 350 Cu. In. with A/C—21.4

GENERAL ENGINE SPECIFICATIONS

YEAR	CU. IN. DISPLACEMENT	CARBURETOR	ADVERTIZED HORSEPOWER @ RPM	ADVERTIZED TORQUE @ RPM (FT. LBS.)	A.M.A. HORSEPOWER	BORE & STROKE (IN.)	ADVERTIZED COMPRESSION RATIO	VALVE LIFTER TYPE	NORMAL OIL PRESSURE (PSI)
1965–66	389	2-BBL.	256 @ 4600	388 @ 2400	52.8	4.063 x 3.750	8.6:1	Hyd.	30–40
	389	4-BBL.	333 @ 5000	429 @ 3200	52.8	4.063 x 3.750	10.5:1	Hyd.	30–40
	389	2-BBL.	290 @ 4600	418 @ 2400	52.8	4.063 x 3.750	10.5:1	Hyd.	30–40
	389	4-BBL.	325 @ 4800	429 @ 2800	52.8	4.063 x 3.750	10.5:1	Hyd.	30–40
	389	3-2-BBL.	338 @ 4800	433 @ 3600	52.8	4.063 x 3.750	10.75:1	Hyd.	30–40
	421	4-BBL.	338 @ 4600	459 @ 2800	53.6	4.097 x 4.000	10.5:1	Hyd.	30–40
	421	3-2-BBL.	356 @ 4800	459 @ 3200	53.6	4.097 x 4.000	10.75:1	Hyd.	30–40
	421	3-2-BBL.	376 @ 5000	461 @ 3600	53.6	4.097 x 4.000	10.75:1	Hyd.	30–40
1967	400	4-BBL.	265 @ 4600	397 @ 2400	54.3	4.121 x 4.000	8.6:1	Hyd.	30–40
	400	2-BBL.	290 @ 4600	428 @ 2500	54.3	4.121 x 3.750	10.5:1	Hyd.	30–40
	400	4-BBL.	333 @ 5000	445 @ 3000	54.3	4.121 x 3.750	10.5:1	Hyd.	30–40
	400	4-BBL.	350 @ 5000	440 @ 3200	54.3	4.121 x 3.750	10.5:1	Hyd.	30–40
	400	4-BBL.	325 @ 4800	445 @ 2900	54.3	4.121 x 3.750	10.5:1	Hyd.	30–40
	400	4-BBL.	350 @ 4800	440 @ 3000	54.3	4.121 x 3.750	10.5:1	Hyd.	30–40
	428	4-BBL.	360 @ 4600	472 @ 3200	54.3	4.121 x 4.000	10.5:1	Hyd.	30–40
	428	4-BBL.	376 @ 5100	462 @ 3400	54.3	4.121 x 4.000	10.75:1	Hyd.	30–40
1968	400	2-BBL.	265 @ 4400	397 @ 2400	54.3	4.121 x 3.750	8.6:1	Hyd.	30–40
	400	2-BBL.	290 @ 4600	428 @ 2500	54.3	4.121 x 3.750	10.5:1	Hyd.	30–40
	400	4-BBL.	340 @ 4800	445 @ 2900	54.3	4.121 x 3.750	10.5:1	Hyd.	30–40
	400	4-BBL.	350 @ 5000	445 @ 3000	54.3	4.121 x 3.750	10.5:1	Hyd.	30–40
	428	4-BBL.	375 @ 4800	472 @ 3200	54.3	4.121 x 4.000	10.5:1	Hyd.	30–40
	428	4-BBL.	390 @ 5200	465 @ 3400	54.3	4.121 x 4.000	10.75:1	Hyd.	30–40
1969	400	2-BBL.	265 @ 4400	397 @ 2400	54.3	4.121 x 3.750	8.6:1	Hyd.	30–40
	400	2-BBL.	290 @ 4600	428 @ 2500	54.3	4.121 x 3.750	10.5:1	Hyd.	30–40
	400	4-BBL.	340 @ 4800	445 @ 2900	54.3	4.121 x 3.750	10.5:1	Hyd.	30–40
	400	4-BBL.	350 @ 5000	445 @ 3000	54.3	4.121 x 3.750	10.5:1	Hyd.	30–40
	428	4-BBL.	360 @ 4600	472 @ 3400	54.3	4.121 x 4.000	10.5:1	Hyd.	30–40
	428	4-BBL.	370 @ 4800	472 @ 3200	54.3	4.121 x 4.000	10.5:1	Hyd.	30–40
	428	4-BBL.	390 @ 5200	465 @ 3400	54.3	4.121 x 4.000	10.75:1	Hyd.	30–40
1970	350	2-BBL.	255 @ 4600	355 @ 2800	44.3	3.88 x 3.75	8.8:1	Hyd.	35
	400	2-BBL.	265 @ 4600	397 @ 2400	54.3	4.121 x 3.750	8.8:1	Hyd.	30–40
	400	2-BBL.	290 @ 4600	428 @ 2500	54.3	4.121 x 3.750	10.0:1	Hyd.	30–40
	400	4-BBL.	330 @ 4800	445 @ 2900	54.3	4.121 x 3.750	10.0:1	Hyd.	30–40
	400	4-BBL.	350 @ 5000	445 @ 3000	54.3	4.121 x 3.750	10.25:1	Hyd.	30–40
	455	4-BBL.	360 @ 4300	500 @ 2700	55.2	4.15 x 4.21	10.0:1	Hyd.	35
	455	4-BBL.	370 @ 4600	500 @ 3100	55.2	4.15 x 4.21	10.25:1	Hyd.	35
1971	350	2-BBL.	250 @ 4400	350 @ 2400	44.3	3.88 x 3.75	8.0:1	Hyd.	30–40
	400	2-BBL.	265 @ 4400	400 @ 2400	54.3	4.12 x 3.75	8.2:1	Hyd.	30–40
	400	4-BBL.	300 @ 4800	400 @ 3600	54.3	4.12 x 3.75	8.2:1	Hyd.	55–60
	455	2-BBL.	280 @ 4400	455 @ 2000	55.2	4.15 x 4.21	8.2:1	Hyd.	30–40
	455	4-BBL.	325 @ 4400	455 @ 3200	55.2	4.15 x 4.21	8.2:1	Hyd.	55–60
	455	4-BBL.	335 @ 4800	480 @ 3600	55.2	4.15 x 4.21	8.4:1	Hyd.	55–60
1972	400 V8①	2-BBL.	175 @ 4000★	310 @ 2400★	54.3	4.12 x 3.75	8.2:1	Hyd.	30–40
	400 V8②	2-BBL.	200 @ 4000★	325 @ 2400★	54.3	4.12 x 3.75	8.2:1	Hyd.	30–40
	400 V8①	4-BBL.	200 @ 4000★	295 @ 2800★	54.3	4.12 x 3.75	8.2:1	Hyd.	55–60
	400 V8②	4-BBL.	250 @ 4400★	325 @ 3200★	54.3	4.12 x 3.75	8.2:1	Hyd.	55–60
	455 V8①	2-BBL.	185 @ 4000★	350 @ 2000★	55.2	4.15 x 4.21	8.2:1	Hyd.	30–40
	455 V8②	2-BBL.	200 @ 4000★	370 @ 2000★	55.2	4.15 x 4.21	8.2:1	Hyd.	30–40
	455 V8①	4-BBL.	220 @ 3600★	350 @ 2400★	55.2	4.15 x 4.21	8.2:1	Hyd.	55–60
	455 V8②	4-BBL.	250 @ 3600★	375 @ 2400★	55.2	4.15 x 4.21	8.2:1	Hyd.	55–60

★—SAE net rating.
①—Single exhaust.
②—Dual exhaust.

VALVE SPECIFICATIONS

YEAR AND MODEL	SEAT ANGLE (DEG.) IN.	EX.	FACE ANGLE (DEG.)	VALVE LIFT INTAKE (IN.)	VALVE LIFT EXHAUST (IN.)	VALVE SPRING PRESSURE (VALVE OPEN) LBS. @ IN.	VALVE SPRING INSTALLED HEIGHT (IN.)	STEM TO GUIDE CLEARANCE (IN.) Intake	Exhaust	STEM DIAMETER (IN.) Intake	Exhaust
1965 V8—389 (425A) A.T.	30	45	④	.405	.405	109 @ 1.15	1.53	.0021–.0038	.0026–.0043	.3407–.3414	.3402–.3409
V8—389 (425E) A.T.	30	45	④	.370	.370	109 @ 1.15	1.53	.0021–.0038	.0026–.0043	.3407–.3414	.3402–.3409
V8—389 M.T., All	30	45	④	.330	.330	109 @ 1.15	1.53	.0021–.0038	.0026–.0043	.3407–.3414	.3402–.3409
V8—389, 3-2-BBL., 421	30	45	④	.405	.405	114 @ 1.12	1.53	.0021–.0038	.0026–.0043	.3407–.3414	.3402–.3409
1966 V8—389 (Low Comp.)	30	45	④	.370	.406	⑨	1.59	.0021–.0038	.0026–.0043	.3407–.3414	.3402–.3409
V8—389 (High Comp.)	30	45	④	.406	.409	115 @ 1.18	1.59	.0021–.0038	.0026–.0043	.3407–.3414	.3402–.3409
V8—421	30	45	④	.406	.408	⑩	1.59	.0021–.0038	.0026–.0043	.3407–.3414	.3402–.3409
V8—421 H.O.	30	45	④	.409	.409	133 @ 1.18	1.59	.0021–.0038	.0026–.0043	.3407–.3414	.3402–.3409
1967 V8—400, 2-BBL.	30	45	④	.375	.410	⑤	1.59	.0016–.0033	.0021–.0038	.3407–.3414	.3402–.3409
V8—400, 4-BBL.	30	45	④	.407	.411	133 @ 1.17	1.59	.0016–.0033	.0021–.0038	.3407–.3414	.3402–.3409
V8—400, Grand Prix	30	45	④	.410	.413	133 @ 1.17	1.59	.0016–.0033	.0021–.0038	.3407–.3414	.3402–.3409
V8—428, 4-BBL.	30	45	④	.410	.413	133 @ 1.17	1.59	.0016–.0033	.0021–.0038	.3407–.3414	.3402–.3409
V8—428, H.O.	30	45	④	.414	.413	133 @ 1.17	1.59	.0016–.0033	.0021–.0038	.3407–.3414	.3402–.3409
1968 V8—400, 2-BBL.*	30	45	④	.376	.412	⑤	1.59	.0016–.0033	.0021–.0038	.3412–.3419	.3407–.3414
V8—400, 2-BBL., M.T.**	30	45	④	.410	.414	⑥	1.59	.0016–.0033	.0021–.0038	.3412–.3419	.3407–.3414
V8—400, 2-BBL., A.T.**	30	45	④	.376	.412	⑤	1.59	.0016–.0033	.0021–.0038	.3412–.3419	.3407–.3414
V8—400, 4-BBL., M.T.	30	45	④	.410	.413	⑥	1.59	.0016–.0033	.0021–.0038	.3412–.3419	.3407–.3414
V8—400, 4-BBL., A.T.	30	45	④	.410	.414	⑥	1.59	.0016–.0033	.0021–.0038	.3412–.3419	.3407–.3414
V8—428, 4-BBL.	30	45	④	.410	.413	133 @ 1.17	1.59	.0016–.0033	.0021–.0038	.3412–.3419	.3407–.3414
V8—428, H.O., M.T.	30	45	④	.414	.414	133 @ 1.17	1.59	.0016–.0033	.0021–.0038	.3412–.3419	.3407–.3414
V8—428, H.O., A.T.	30	45	④	.410	.413	133 @ 1.17	1.59	.0016–.0033	.0021–.0038	.3412–.3419	.3407–.3414
V8—350, 2-BBL.	30	45	④	.375	.410	127 @ 1.20	1.59	.0016–.0033	.0021–.0038	.3412–.3419	.3407–.3414
V8—350, 4-BBL.	30	45	④	.407	.411	133 @ 1.17	1.59	.0016–.0033	.0021–.0038	.3412–.3419	.3407–.3414
1969 V8—350, 2-BBL.	45	45	④	.375	.410	127 @ 1.20	1.58	.0016–.0033	.0021–.0038	.3407–.3414	.3407–.3414
V8—400, 2-BBL.*	45	45	44	.376	.412	⑤	1.58	.0016–.0033	.0021–.0038	.3407–.3414	.3407–.3414
V8—400, 2-BBL.**	45	45	44	.376	.412	③	1.58	.0016–.0033	.0021–.0038	.3407–.3414	.3407–.3414
V8—400, 4-BBL.	30	45	④	.410	.414	⑥	1.58	.0016–.0033	.0021–.0038	.3407–.3414	.3407–.3414
V8—400, 350 ①	30	45	④	.410	.414	⑦	1.58	.0016–.0033	.0021–.0038	.3407–.3414	.3407–.3414
V8—428, 360 HP	30	45	④	.410	.413	133 @ 1.17	1.58	.0016–.0033	.0021–.0038	.3407–.3414	.3407–.3414
V8—428, 370 HP	30	45	④	.410	.413	133 @ 1.17	1.58	.0016–.0033	.0021–.0038	.3407–.3414	.3407–.3414
V8—428, H.O.	30	45	④	.410 ⑪	.413 ⑪	133 @ 1.17	1.58	.0016–.0033	.0021–.0038	.3407–.3414	.3407–.3414
1970-72 V8—350, 2-BBL.	45	45	44	.376	.412	⑤	1.58	.0016–.0033	.0021–.0038	.3412–.3419	.3407–.3414
V8—400, 2-BBL.*	45	45	44	.376	.412	⑤	1.58	.0016–.0033	.0021–.0038	.3412–.3419	.3407–.3414
V8—400, 2-BBL., M.T.**	45	45	44	.410	.414	⑥	1.58	.0016–.0033	.0021–.0038	.3412–.3419	.3407–.3414
V8—400, 2-BBL., A.T.**	45	45	44	.376	.412	⑤	1.58	.0016–.0033	.0021–.0038	.3412–.3419	.3407–.3414
V8—400, 4-BBL., M.T. ①	30	45	④	.410	.413	⑥	1.58	.0016–.0033	.0021–.0038	.3412–.3419	.3407–.3414
V8—400, 4-BBL., A.T.	45	45	44	.410	.414	⑥	1.58	.0016–.0033	.0021–.0038	.3412–.3419	.3407–.3414
V8—455, 4-BBL., M.T.	45	45	④	.414	.413	⑧	1.58	.0016–.0033	.0021–.0038	.3412–.3419	.3407–.3414
V8—455, 4-BBL., A.T.	45	45	44	.410	.413	⑦	1.56	.0016–.0033	.0021–.0038	.3412–.3419	.3407–.3414
V8—455, 4-BBL., A.T. ②	30	45	④	.410	.413	⑦	1.56	.0016–.0033	.0021–.0038	.3412–.3419	.3407–.3414
V8—400, 350 HP, A.T. ①	30	45	④	.410	.414	⑦	1.56	.0016–.0033	.0021–.0038	.3412–.3419	.3407–.3414

① —Available only in Grand Prix (350 HP)
② —H.O. engine—370 HP (available only with A.T.)
③ —Intake 30°, Exhaust 45°
④ —Intake 29°, Exhaust 44°
⑤ —Intake 127.5 @ 1.21, Exhaust 133.7 @ 1.17
⑥ —Intake 133.4 @ 1.17, Exhaust 131.1 @ 1.16
⑦ —Intake 137.0 @ 1.15, Exhaust 137.7 @ 1.15
⑧ —Intake 134.1 @ 1.17, Exhaust 133.9 @ 1.17
⑨ —Intake 110 @ 1.21, Exhaust 115 @ 1.18
⑩ —Intake 131 @ 1.18, Exhaust 133 @ 1.18
⑪ —M.T. .414, .414
⑫ —"XR"—Intake .410, Exhaust .414

* —Low compression
** —High compression
M.T.—Manual transmission
A.T.—Automatic transmission

CRANKSHAFT BEARING JOURNAL SPECIFICATIONS

YEAR	MODEL	MAIN BEARING JOURNALS (IN.)				CONNECTING ROD BEARING JOURNALS (IN.)		
		Journal Diameter	Oil Clearance	Shaft End-Play	Thrust On No.	Journal Diameter	Oil Clearance	End-Play
1965-66	V8—OHV, Exc. 421 Cu. In.	3.000	.0018▲	.006	4	2.250	.0015	.009
	V8—421 Cu. In.	3.250	.0018▲	.007	4	2.250	.0015	.009
1967-69	V8—400 Cu. In.	3.000	.0018	.006	4	2.250	.0015	.009
	V8—428 Cu. In.	3.250	.0018	.006	4	2.250	.0015	.009
1970	V8—350 Cu. In.	3.000	.0002-.0017	.0035-.0085	4	2.250	.0005-.0025	.012-.017①
	V8—400 Cu. In.	3.000	.0002-.0017	.0035-.0085	4	2.250	.0005-.0025	.012-.017
	V8—455 Cu. In.	3.250	.0005-.0021	.0035-.0085	4	2.250	.0005-.0026	.012-.017
1971-72	V8—350 Cu. In.	3.000	.0002-.0017	.0035-.0085	4	2.250	.0005-.0025	.012-.017
	V8—400 Cu. In.	3.000	.0002-.0017	.0035-.0085	4	2.250	.0005-.0025	.012-.017
	V8—455 Cu. Inc.	3.250	.0005-.0021②	.0035-.0085	4	2.250	.0005-.0026	.012-.017

▲—Bearing No. 1—.0015.
①—Total for two rods.
②—455 Cu. In. with small valve on No. 1 cylinder—.0003-.0019.

GENERAL CHASSIS AND BRAKE SPECIFICATIONS

YEAR	MODEL	CHASSIS		BRAKE CYLINDER BORE			BRAKE DRUM	
		Overall Length (In.)	Tire Size	Master Cylinder (In.) Power	Wheel Cylinder Diameter (In.)		Diameter (In.)	
					Front	Rear	Front	Rear
1965	Catalina, Grand Prix	214.6	8.25 x 14	1.0	1³/₁₆	¹⁵/₁₆	11	11
	Bonneville, Star Chief	221.7	8.25 x 14	1.0	1³/₁₆	¹⁵/₁₆	11	11
	Station Wagon	217.9	8.55 x 14	1.0	1³/₁₆	¹⁵/₁₆	11	11
1966	Catalina, Grand Prix	214.8	8.25 x 14	.875	1³/₁₆	¹⁵/₁₆	11	11
	Bonneville, Star Chief	221.8	8.25 x 14	.875	1³/₁₆	¹⁵/₁₆	11	11
	Station Wagon	218.1	8.55 x 14	.875	1³/₁₆	¹⁵/₁₆	11	11
1967	Catalina	215.6	8.25 x 14	1.0	1³/₁₆	¹⁵/₁₆	11	11
	Executive, Bonneville	222.6	8.55 x 14	1.0	1³/₁₆	¹⁵/₁₆	11	11
	Grand Prix	215.6	8.55 x 14	1.0	1³/₁₆	¹⁵/₁₆	11.8	11
	Station Wagon	218.4	8.55 x 14	1.0	1³/₁₆	¹⁵/₁₆	11	11
1968	Catalina	216.5	8.55 x 14*	1.0	1⅛	¹⁵/₁₆	11	11
	Executive, Bonneville	223.5	8.55 x 14	1.0	1⅛	¹⁵/₁₆	11	11
	Grand Prix	216.3	8.55 x 14	1.0	1⅛	¹⁵/₁₆	11	11
	Station Wagon	218.4	8.55 x 14	1.0	1⅛	¹⁵/₁₆	11	11
	Models w/Disc Brakes	—	—	1.125	2¹/₁₆	¹⁵/₁₆	11.12 (Disc)	11
1969	Catalina	217.5	8.55 x 15	1.0	1⅛	¹⁵/₁₆	11	11
	Executive	223.5	8.55 x 15	1.0	1⅛	¹⁵/₁₆	11	11
	Bonneville	224.0	8.55 x 15	1.0	1⅛	¹⁵/₁₆	11	11
	Grand Prix	210.2	6.78 x 14	1.0	1⅛	¹⁵/₁₆	10.9 (Disc)	11
	Station Wag.	220.5	8.85 x 15	1.0	1⅛	¹⁵/₁₆	11	11
	Models w/Disc Brakes	—	8.85 x 15	1.125	2¹⁵/₁₆	¹⁵/₁₆	11.68 (Disc)	11
1970	Catalina	217.9	H78 x 15	1.0	1⅛	¹⁵/₁₆	11	11
	Executive	223.9	H78 x 15	1.0	1⅛	¹⁵/₁₆	11	11
	Bonneville	224.6	H78 x 15	1.0	1⅛	¹⁵/₁₆	11	11
	Grand Prix	210.2	G78 x 14	1.125	2¹⁵/₁₆	⅞	10.9 (disc)	9.5
	Station Wag.	220.9	L78 x 15	1.0	1⅛	¹⁵/₁₆	11	11
	Models w/Disc Brakes	—	H78 x 15	1.125	2¹⁵/₁₆	¹⁵/₁₆	11.7 (Disc)	11
1971-72	Catalina	219.9	G78 x 15	1.125	2.9375	¹⁵/₁₆	11.68 (Disc)	11
	Grandville	223.9	H78 x 15	1.125	2.9375	¹⁵/₁₆	11.68 (Disc)	11
	Bonneville	223.9	H78 x 15	1.125	2.9375	¹⁵/₁₆	11.6 (Disc)	11
	Grand Prix	210.5	G78 x 14	1.125	2.9375	⅞	11	9.5
	Station Wagon	230.0	L78 x 15	1.125	2.9375	¹⁵/₁₆	11.68 (Disc)	12

*—Sedan—8.25 x 14.

DELCOTRON AND AC REGULATOR SPECIFICATIONS

YEAR	PART NUMBER	ALTERNATOR		Part No.	REGULATOR						
		Field Current Draw @ 12V. Amps.	Output @ 12V. and Engine RPM 5,000		Field Relay			Regulator			
					Air Gap (In.)	Point Gap (In.)	Volts to Close	Air Gap (In.)	Point Gap (In.)	Volts at 125°	
1965–66	1100699	1.9–2.3	42	1119511	.015	.030	2.3–3.7	.057	.015	13.5–14.4	
	1100700	1.9–2.3	55	1119511	.015	.030	2.3–3.7	.057	.015	13.5–14.4	
	1100692	1.9–2.3	55	1119511	.015	.030	2.3–3.7	.057	.015	13.5–14.4	
	1100702	N.A.	60	1119511	.015	.030	2.3–3.7	.057	.015	13.5–14.4	
	1100758	N.A.	66	1119511	.015	.030	2.3–3.7	.057	.015	13.5–14.4	
1967–69	1100699	1.9–2.3	42	1119511	.015	.030	2.3–3.7	.057	.015	13.5–14.4	
	1100700	1.9–2.3	55	1119511	.015	.030	2.3–3.7	.057	.015	13.5–14.4	
	1100800	1.9–2.3	55	1119511	.015	.030	2.3–3.7	.057	.015	13.5–14.4	
	1100801	1.9–2.3	42	1119511	.015	.030	2.3–3.7	.057	.015	13.5–14.4	
1970	1100704	2.2–2.6	37	1119515	.015	.030	2.3–3.7	.057	.015	13.5–14.4	
	1100700	2.2–2.6	55	1119515	.015	.030	2.3–3.7	.057	.015	13.5–14.4	
	1100895	2.2–2.6	61	1119515	.015	.030	2.3–3.7	.057	.015	13.5–14.4	
	1117765	4.1–4.6	62	1116368	TRANSISTORIZED REGULATOR						
1971–72	1100927	4–4.5	37	—	TRANSISTORIZED REGULATOR						
	1100928	4–4.5	55	—	TRANSISTORIZED REGULATOR						
	1101015	4–4.5	80	—	TRANSISTORIZED REGULATOR						

TORQUE SPECIFICATIONS

YEAR	MODEL	CYLINDER HEAD BOLTS (FT. LBS.)	ROD BEARING BOLTS (FT. LBS.)	MAIN BEARING BOLTS (FT. LBS.)	CRANKSHAFT BALANCER BOLT (FT. LBS.)	FLYWHEEL TO CRANKSHAFT BOLTS (FT. LBS.)	MANIFOLD (FT. LBS.)	
							Intake	Exhaust
1965–72	All Series	80–95	35–45	85–95▲①	160	90–95	40	30

▲—Rear Main, 120.
①—1968-72—100.

CYLINDER HEAD BOLT TIGHTENING SEQUENCE

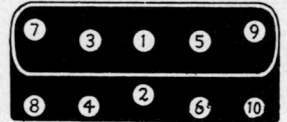

LIGHT BULBS

1965–69

Ash tray	1445; 1 CP
Back-up	1156; 32 CP
Clock, heater controls, radio dial	1895; 2 CP
Cornering lamp	1195; 50 CP
Dome lamp	211; 12 CP
Headlamp (low beam)	4002; 50/37.5 CP
(high beam)	4001; 37.5 CP
License	67; 4 CP
Luggage compt.	1003; 15 CP
Tachometer	194; 2 CP
Underhood	93; 15 CP

1970–72

	Pont.	G.P.
Air cond. controls	1895	1895
Ash tray	1445	1445
Back-up lamp	1156	1157

	Pont.	G.P.
Brake warning	194	194
Clock	1895	1895
Cigar lighter	1445	1445
Console compt.	—	1893
Cornering lamps	1195	1195
Courtesy lamp	550	89
Courtesy (sta. wag. rear compt.)	90	—
Dir. signal ind.	194	194
Dome lamp	211-1	211-1
Head lamp (lower) or (inner)	Type 1	Type 1
Head lamp (upper) or (outer)	Type 2	Type 2
Head lamp beam ind.	194	194
Heater cont.	1895	1895
Inst. panel compt.	1895	1895
License lamp	67	67
Low fuel warning	159	159
Luggage compt.	89	89

	Pont.	G.P.
Oil pressure	194	194
Park & dir. signal	1157 NA	1157 NA
Radio dial	1895	1895
Reading lamp	1004	1004
Rr. seat arm rest (conv.)	68	—
Side marker-front	194 A	1157NA
Side marker-rear	1895 (3)	168
Side marker-rear	194 (4)	—
Shift ind. (exc. console)	1895	1893 (5)
Shift ind. (console)	—	1445
Speedo. ill. (exc. aux. ga.)	194	194
Tail stop & signal	1157	1157
Tachometer (hood)	—	194
Tachometer (i.p. mtg.)	—	1895
Temp. ga. (exc. aux. ga.)	194	194
Under hood or utility	1003	1003

FUSES AND CIRCUIT BREAKERS

1965

Air conditioner controls, clock lamp, instrument
    panel lamps............................ 4 Amp. Fuse
Air conditioner power and blower........ 30 Amp. Fuse
Back-up lamps, cruise control, windshield washer
    and wiper............................ 25 Amp. Fuse
Cigar lighter, clock power, directional signal, stop
    lamp, dome lamp, license lamp, power antenna,
    tail lamps........................... 14 Amp. Fuse
Heater blower .... 20 Amp. Fuse
Radio power .... 2.5 Amp. Fuse

1966

Same as 1965 except the following:
    Power antenna .... 20 Amp. Fuse
    Radio power .... 9 Amp. Fuse

1967–69

Same as 1965 except the following:
    Directional signal & radio power........ 10 Amp. Fuse
    Dome lamp, hazard warning, heater blower,
        power antenna & stop lamps .... 25 Amp. Fuse

1970–72

	Pont.	G.P.
Air cond. controls lamp (custom)	SFE-4	SFE-4①
Air. Cond. master relay	20	—
Air cond. power & blower mtr. (custom)	AGC-30	AGC-30

	Pont.	G.P.
Ash tray lamp	SFE-4	SFE-4
Back up lamp	SFE-20	SFE-20
Cigar lighter......................	SFE-20	SFE-20
Cigar lighter lamp..................	SFE-4	SFE-4
Clock lamp	SFE-4	SFE-4
Clock Power	SFE-20	SFE-20
Console compartment lamp	—	SFE-20
Cornering lamps	SFE-20	SFE-20
Convertible top circuit breaker	40	—
Courtesy lights	20	20
Cruise Control	25	25
Deck lid release	SFE-20	SFE-20
Directional signal & stop lamp.......	SFE-20	SFE-20
Dome, rear qtr. or rear courtesy lamp......................	SFE-20	SFE-20
Electric door lock circuit breaker.....	40	40
Electrocruise & low fuel lamp	AGC-10	AGC-10
Glove box light	20	20
Hazard flasher....................	SFE-20	SFE-20
Headlight telltale light	20	—
Heater cont. lamp	SFE-4	SFE-4
Heater blower motor	AGC-25	AGC-25
Idle Stop Solenoid.................	20	10
Instrument lamps	SFE-4	SFE-4
Instrument panel compartment lamps.........................	SFE-20	SFE-20
Instrument panel courtesy lamp	SFE-20	SFE-20
License lamp	SFE-20	SFE-20

	Pont.	G.P.
Lugg. compt. lamp	SFE-20	SFE-20
Park lights	20	20
P.B. warning lamp..................	AGC-10	AGC-10
Power seat circuit breaker..........	40	40
Power tail gate wind. circuit breaker	40	—
Power window circuit breaker.......	40	40
Power side window circuit breaker...	40	40
Radio dial lamp....................	SFE-4	SFE-4
Radio power......................	AGC-10	AGC-10
Rear seat cigar lighter	20	—
Rear wind. defogger...............	AGC-25	AGC-25
Safeguard speedo	AGC-25	AGC-25
Seat back release circuit breaker	40	40
Seat belt warning telltale	25	25
Shift indicator lamp (column & console)	SFE-4	SFE-4
Side marker lamps frt. & rear.......	SFE-20	SFE-20
Stop lights	20	20
Tachometer lamp	—	SFE-4
TCS System.......................	20	10
Tail lamp	SFE-20	SFE-20
Travel, lamp	25	25
Trunk light.......................	20	20
Under hood or utility	SFE-20	SFE-20
W/S Washer pump..................	AGC-25	AGC-25
W/S wiper or washer motor.........	AGC-25	AGC-25

① 25 Amp—1971–72

Distributor

Distributor Removal

The distributor is located in the back of the block. To remove, disconnect the air cleaner and the distributor cap and wire assembly, mark the position of the rotor relative to the distributor body and the body relative to the block for easy replacement. Do not move the engine after removing the distributor. Detach the vacuum lines and the ignition primary wire from the distributor and remove the bolt which holds the distributor down to the block. The unit can then be lifted up. On V8 models, the drive gear is located on the bottom of the distributor. When replacing it, it will be necessary to index the groove in the bottom of the distributor shaft with the oil pump driveshaft.

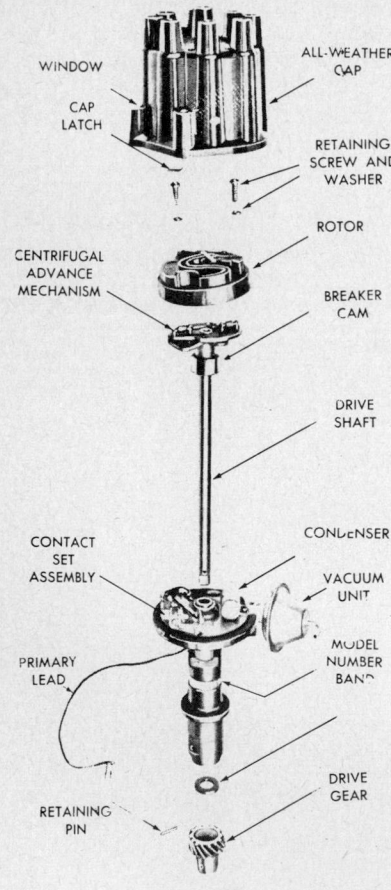

V8 distributor
(© Pontiac Div., G.M. Corp.)

Distributor Operation

An external adjustment distributor is used. The cap has a window for adjusting dwell time (cam angle) with the cap in place.

Adjustment of dwell is made on the car while the engine is operating or while the distributor is being checked on a distributor tester. The

centrifugal advance parts have been relocated above the breaker plate and cam. This plan permits the cam and breaker lever to be located closer to the upper bearing for greater stability.

The breaker plate is one piece, and rotates on the outer diameter of the upper bearing. The plate is held in position by a retainer clip in the upper shaft bushing. The molded rotor serves as a cover for the centrifugal advance mechanism. The vacuum control unit is mounted under the movable breaker plate and is fastened to the distributor housing.

The point set has the breaker lever spring tension and point alignment pre-set and is serviced as an assembly. Only the dwell angle requires adjustment after replacement.

Under part throttle operation, manifold vacuum is enough to actuate the vacuum control diaphragm. This causes the movable plate to advance the spark and aid fuel economy. During acceleration, or on a heavy pull, the vacuum is insufficient to move the plate. The plate is spring-loaded, through the vacuum control diaphragm, and remains in the retarded position.

The centrifugal advance is conventional and operates through two spring-loaded weights.

On 1970-72 Pontiacs, the radios are more sensitive to ignition interference due to the antenna in the windshield. To combat this all distributors have a Radio Frequency Interference Shield covering the circuit breaker plate assembly. Shield must be removed to install points or condenser, but dwell angle may be set through an opening in the shield.

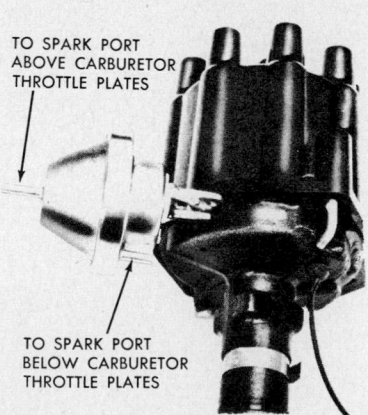

Vacuum advance valve
(© Pontiac Div. G.M. Corp.)

Transistor Ignition

This system consists of a special distributor, an ignition pulse amplifier, and a special ignition coil. The distributor is simlar in external appearance to the standard V8 distributor, but the internal construction bears little resemblance to the contact-point unit. An iron timer core

replaces the breaker cam. This eight-lobed timer rotates inside a magnetic pick-up assembly, which replaces the contact points and condenser. The magnetic pick-up assembly consists of a ceramic permanent magnet, a steel pole piece, and a pick-up coil.

The magnetic pick-up assembly is mounted over the distributor shaft bearing, and is rotated by the vacuum advance unit to provide automatic spark advance. Centrifugal advance is provided by the rotating timer core, which is attached to normal advance weights. Troubleshooting is found in the Unit Repair Section.

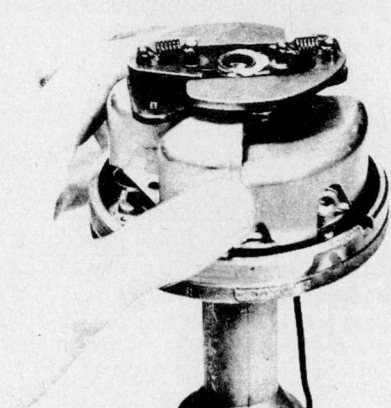

Installing Radio Interference Shield
(© Pontiac Div. G.M. Corp.)

Transistor ignition distributor
(© Pontiac Div. G.M. Corp.)

Removal

1. Disconnect pick-up coil connector.
2. Remove distributor cap.
3. Crank engine so that rotor points to No. 1 cylinder plug tower and timing mark on crankshaft pulley are indexed with pointer.
4. Remove distributor vacuum line.
5. Remove distributor hold-down bolt and clamp, then remove distributor.

Disassembly

1. Remove rotor.
2. Remove centrifugal weight springs.
3. Remove weights.
4. Remove roll pin, drive gear and washer.
5. Remove drive shaft.
6. Remove weight support and timer core from drive shaft.
7. Remove magnetic core assembly.

Unitized Ignition System— 1971-72

A new utilized ignition system is optional on late 1971 and all 1972 Grand Prix SJ, Grand Ville and Grand Safari models having the 455 cu. in. V8 with four-barrel carburetor. This system replaces the ignition coil, distributor, amplifier, wiring and spark plug wires used with previous transistorized systems. The conventional contact points and condenser have been eliminated in this system, thus making it unnecessary to perform any tune-up jobs other than spark plug replacement, ignition timing adjustment and idle speed adjustment.

Delcotron (AC Generator)

1965-72

The Delco-Remy Delcotron is used. The purpose of this unit is to satisfy the increase in electrical loads that have been imposed upon the car battery by modern conditions of traffic and driving patterns.

The Delcotron is covered in the Unit Repair Section under Basic Electrical Diagnosis.

Since the Delcotron and regulator are designed for use on only one polarity system, the following precautions must be observed:

1. The polarity of the battery, generator and regulator must be matched and considered before making any electrical connections to the system.
2. When connecting a booster battery, be sure to connect the negative battery terminals respectively, and the positive battery terminals respectively.
3. When connecting a charger to the battery, connect the charger positive lead to the battery positive terminal. Connect the charger negative lead to the battery negative terminal.
4. Never operate the Delcotron on open circuit. Be sure that all connections in the circuit are clean and tight.
5. Do not short across or ground any of the terminals on the Delcotron regulator.
6. Do not attempt to polarize the Delcotron.
7. Do not use test lamps of more than 12 volts for checking diode

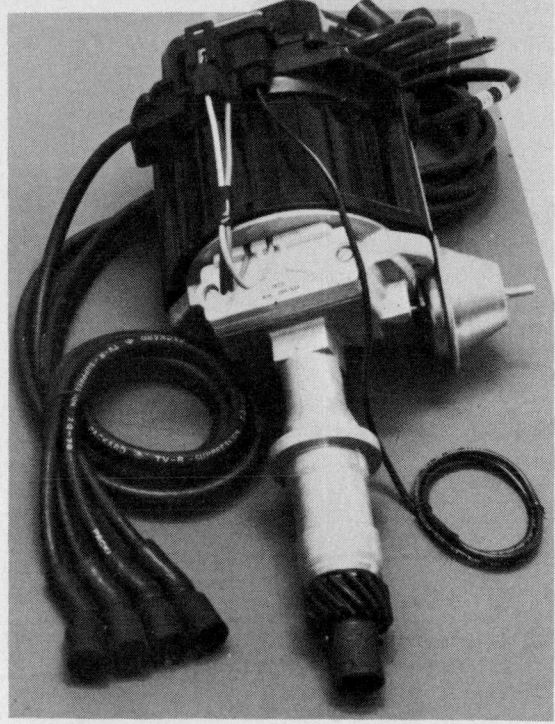

New unitized ignition system used in 1971-72
(© Pontiac Div. G.M. Corp.)

continuity.
8. Avoid long soldering times when replacing diodes or transistors. Prolonged heat is damaging to these units.
9. Disconnect the battery ground terminal when servicing any AC system. This will prevent the possibility of accidental reversal of polarity.

Series 10-S.I. (Integrated Circuit) AC Generator

See Basic Electrical Diagnosis Section in Unit Repair Section for service and test procedures.

Alternator R & R

1. Disconnect positive battery cable.
2. Remove two terminal plug leads from alternator.
3. Loosen adjusting bolts.
4. Remove V-belt and through-bolt.
5. Remove alternator.
6. To install, reverse removal procedure. Tighten all bolts to 30 ft. lbs., except slotted adjuster bolt (20 ft. lbs.).

Battery, Starter

Detailed information on the battery and starter will be found in the Battery and Starter Specifications table of this section.

A more detailed discussion of starters and their troubles can be found in the Unit Repair Section under the heading Basic Electrical Diagnosis.

Starter R & R

1. Disconnect starter motor cable from battery.
2. Raise front of car and support on stands.
3. Pull cable and wire loom down to hang free.
4. Disconnect brace, starting 1971.
5. Remove mounting screws and starter motor with cable and solenoid wires.
6. Remove wires from starter.
7. To reinstall reverse the above, first installing the wires to solenoid.

Instruments

Cluster R & R

1967-68

1. Disconnect battery.
2. Remove instrument panel pad. If car is equipped with front speaker replace speaker wire.
3. Remove two bolts on each end of instrument panel trim plate.
4. On air conditioned cars it is necessary to remove lower duct assembly.
5. Remove bolts connecting instrument panel trim plate and lower instrument panel.

6. If car is equipped with automatic transmission, remove column cover and remove transmission indicator.
7. On Grand Prix models, it may be necessary to disconnect vacuum lines from headlight switch.
8. On models with upper level ventilation system, remove pipes connecting to nozzle assembly.
9. If car is equipped with radio, remove bolt from radio to radio support brace.
10. If car is equipped with Safeguard speedometer, buzzer assembly must be detached.
11. Disconnect feeder of fiber optic system from cigar lighter.
12. If car is equipped with multiplex, disconnect mutiplex unit.
13. Disconnect speedometer.
14. Pull instrument panel plate out. Make sure all wires and routing clips are loose enough to allow panel to move out.
15. Disconnect wires attaching instrument cluster.
16. Remove four nuts that retain instrument cluster to instrument panel trim panel.
17. Remove cluster.
18. Replace by reversing procedure.

1969 Pontiac Except Grand Prix

1. Disconnect battery.
2. Remove lower instrument panel cover.
3. Remove radio.
4. Remove heater or air conditioning control panel.
5. Disconnect speedometer, printed circuit connector, cigar lighter and instrument panel harness from rear of cluster.
6. Remove four cluster retaining screws.
7. Position ground straps so that cluster may be pulled from studs and removed toward center of car.
8. Reverse procedure to install.

1969 Grand Prix

1. Disconnect battery.
2. Remove glove compartment.
3. Disconnect speedometer cable and wire connectors at headlamp switch, windshield wiper, turn signal, ignition switch, printed circuit, and heater or air conditioning control panel.
4. Remove lower column trim and disconnect air control at heater case.
5. Remove three screws at instrument nacelles.
6. Remove two instrument panel to column support.
7. Remove one screw at each outboard lower end of panel.
8. Remove screws retaining right and left side of instrument panel to body. To do this, remove upper vent nozzles by inserting two thin blade screwdrivers on

right and left side of nozzle to disengage metal retaining clip. Pull nozzle towards rear of car to remove.
9. Remove upper instrument panel cover plate. Studs are pushed into retaining clips.
10. Remove two upper panel retaining screws and upper speaker support bracket screw.
11. Remove console to instrument panel retaining screws.
12. Loosen toe plate screws.
13. Remove column to lower instrument panel retaining nuts and drop column.
14. Pull entire instrument panel rearward on left far enough to gain access to cluster.
15. Remove ground strap retaining screws, and two instrument panel harness conduit retaining screws.
16. Remove instrument panel cluster retaining screws and remove cluster.
17. Reverse procedure to install.

1970 Pontiac Except Grand Prix

1. Disconnect battery and remove lower air conditioning duct.
2. Remove lower instrument panel trim at steering column.
3. Remove radio, radio support and ground plate.
4. Remove automatic transmission shift indicator, if so equipped.
5. Disconnect speedometer cable and heater cables at heater case.
6. Lower steering column.
7. Remove instrument panel trim plate screws and place trim plate on steering column.
8. Disconnect printed circuit.
9. Remove wire harness retaining screws and clock.
10. Remove cluster retaining nuts and cluster.
11. Reverse procedure to install.

1970-72 Grand Prix

1. Disconnect battery and remove lower air conditioning duct, if so equipped.
2. Remove pillar post mouldings and filler plate at windshield.
3. Remove lower instrument panel trim at steering column.
4. Disconnect speedometer cable and radio antenna lead.
5. Lower steering column.
6. Remove upper air outlet vents and instrument panel attaching screws at steering column, console, ends and upper center.
7. Remove lower defroster duct screw at heater case.
8. Move instrument pad outward on steering column.
9. Disconnect printed circuit.
10. Remove wire harness retaining screws and cluster ground screw.
11. Remove cluster mounting screws and remove cluster. Reverse

procedure to install.

1971-72 Except Grand Prix

1. Disconnect battery and remove upper instrument panel trim plate.
2. Remove automatic transmission shift indicator and speedometer bezel.
3. Remove cluster retaining screws, pull cluster rearward and disconnect speedometer cable and printed circuit connector.
4. To install, reverse removal procedure.

Ignition Switch Replacement

1965-66

1. Disconnect battery.
2. Remove lock cylinder by placing in off position and insert wire in small hole in cylinder face. While pushing in on wire, continue to turn cylinder counterclockwise and pull cylinder from case.
3. Remove nut from face of switch. (Spanner tool J-7607 will assist.)
4. Pull switch from dash and remove wiring connector. (See illustration).
5. Install in reverse of above.

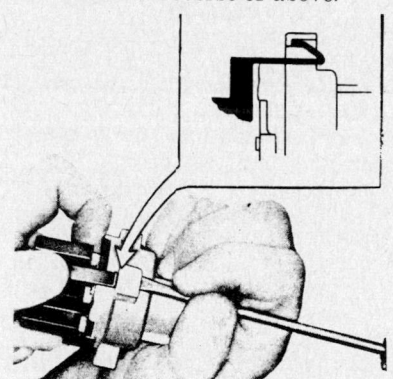

Unlocking ignition switch connector
(© Pontiac Div. G.M. Corp.)

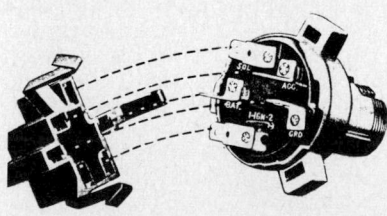

Separated ignition switch and connector
(© Pontiac Div. G.M. Corp.)

1967-68

1. Remove ignition lock.
2. Remove bezel retaining switch to dash. Take care not to destroy fiber optic light.
3. Remove wire connector from ignition switch.
4. Remove switch.
5. Reverse procedure to install.

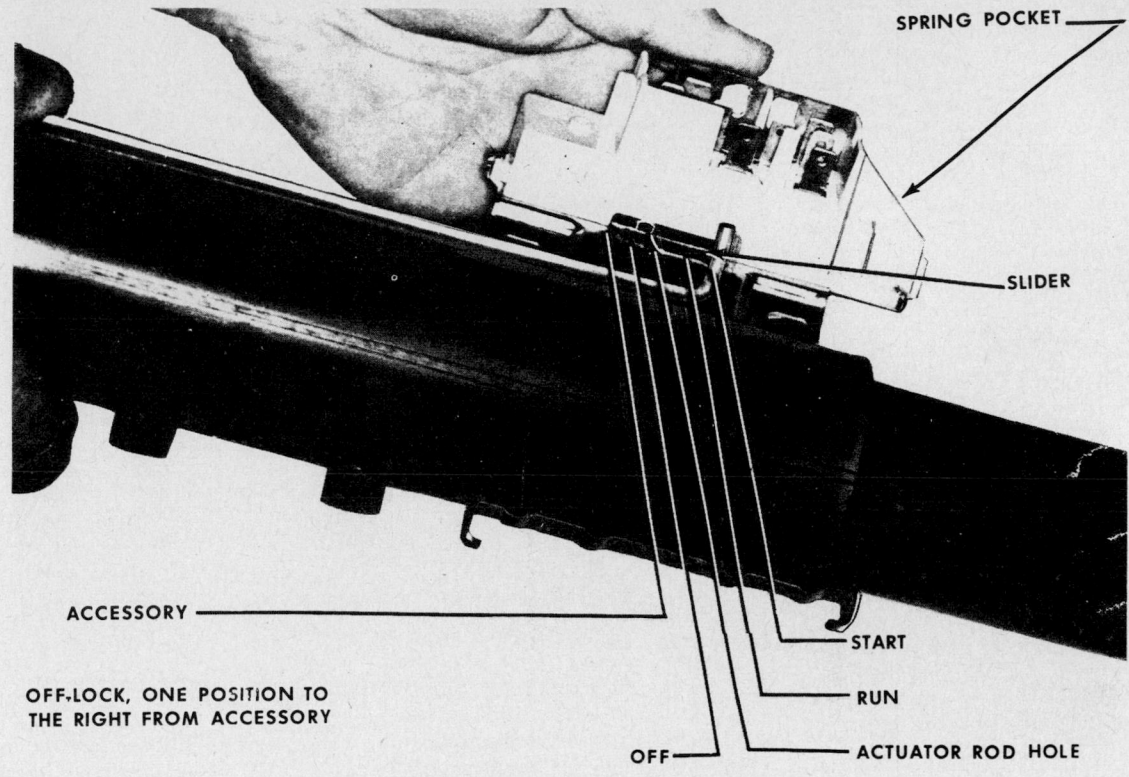

SPRING POCKET

SLIDER

ACCESSORY

OFF-LOCK, ONE POSITION TO
THE RIGHT FROM ACCESSORY

OFF

START

RUN

ACTUATOR ROD HOLE

Installing ignition switch (© Pontiac Div. G.M. Corp.)

1969-72

1. Disconnect battery.
2. Loosen toe pan screws on steering column.
3. Remove column to instrument panel attaching nuts.
4. Lower column and disconnect switch wire connectors.
5. Remove switch attaching screws and remove switch.
6. To replace move key lock to OFF- LOCK position.
7. Move actuator rod hole in switch to OFF-LOCK position.
8. Install switch with rod in hole.
9. Position and reassemble steering column in reverse of disassembly procedure.

Lock Cylinder Replacement —1969-72

1. Remove steering wheel.
2. Pull turn signal switch up far enough to allow access to spring latch slot.
3. Place key in RUN position, insert a thin screwdriver into the slot next to the switch mounting screw boss and depress spring latch.
4. Remove lock from housing. Thin flash of metal over slot is easily broken.
5. To install, first hold lock cylinder sleeve and rotate knob clockwise against stop.
6. Lay a 1/6 in. drill on housing surface next to housing bore.
7. Insert cylinder into housing bore, aligning keyway, and push

in to abutment.
8. Rotate knob counterclockwise, pushing in slightly, until cylinder mates with sector.
9. Push in until spring latch pops into groove, then remove drill.

Caution If lock cylinder is forced beyond its normal latched position, complete disassembly of upper bearing assembly will be necessary to free it.

Headlight Switch Replacement

1965-66

1. Disconnect battery.
2. Pull knob out to ON position.
3. Reach under instrument panel and depress the switch shaft retainer (see illustration), and remove knob and shaft assembly.
4. Remove retaining ferrule nut.
5. Remove switch from instrument panel.
6. Disconnect multi-plug connector from switch.
7. Install in reverse of above. (In checking lights before installation, switch must be grounded to test dome lights on some models.)

1967

1. Disconnect battery.
2. Pull switch knob to ON position, push latch button on side of switch to ON position and pull out switch knob.
3. Unscrew bushing from switch and remove switch.
4. Remove push on connector with leads from light switch and con-

nect to new switch.
5. On Grand Prix models remove vacuum connectors and connect new switch.
6. Position new switch in instrument panel, and start bushing through ferrule into switch. Tighten bushing securely.
7. Insert knob into switch until end of knob engages catch.
8. Connect battery.

1968-72

1. Depress button on switch and remove knob and shaft.
2. Remove retaining nut.
3. Remove wire connector from switch and remove switch.
4. On vacuum operated headlight models, remove vacuum connector.
5. Reverse procedure to install.

Brakes

Specific information on brake cylinder sizes can be found in the General Chassis and Brake Specifications table of this section.

Information on brake adjustment, lining replacement, bleeding procedure, master and wheel cylinder overhaul can be found in the Unit Repair Section.

Information on troubleshooting and overhauling power brakes can be found in the Unit Repair Section.

Information on the grease seals which may need replacement can also be found in the Unit Repair Section.

Standard brakes are of the duo-servo, self-adjusting type. The self-adjusting feature operates only when the brakes are applied with car moving in reverse. When the brakes are applied, friction between the primary shoe and the drum causes the primary shoe to bear against the anchor pin. Hydraulic pressure in the wheel cylinder forces the upper end of the secondary shoe away from the anchor pin. As this moves, the upper end of the adjuster lever is prevented from moving by the actuating link attached to the anchor pin, thus forcing the lower end of the lever against the star wheel. If the linings are worn, the adjuster lever moves the star wheel a predetermined distance to maintain the proper shoe-to-drum clearance.

Metallic brake linings, used on some early high-performance models, never should be installed on cars equipped with standard brake drums unless the drums are radius ground and honed to a special finish. See the Unit Repair Section of this manual for more information on metallic brake linings.

Disc Brakes

From 1967, single-piston, sliding caliper disc brakes have been available as optional equipment on most models (standard with high performance packages). These brakes have a vented, cast-iron rotor with two braking surfaces. For 1971-72, power disc brakes are standard on all Grand Prix and full-size Pontiac models. Drum brakes are no longer available on the front wheels.

Disc brakes need no adjustment because, during operation, the application and release of hydraulic pressure causes the piston and caliper to move only slightly. In the released position, the pads do not move very far from the rotor; thus, as pads wear down, the piston simply moves farther out of the caliper bore and the caliper repositions itself on its mounting bolts to maintain proper pad-to-rotor clearance.

A metering valve in the front brake circuit prevents the discs from operating until about 75 psi exists in the system. This enables the rear drum brakes to operate in synchronization with the front discs and reduces the possibility of unequal brake application and premature lock-up. A proportioning valve in the rear brake circuit of some models accomplishes the same. Starting 1971, all functions of the two separate valves are performed by either a two-or three-element combination valve. The two-function valve is used on all wagons and sedans except Grand Prix, which uses a three-function valve. Disc brake pads should be examined for

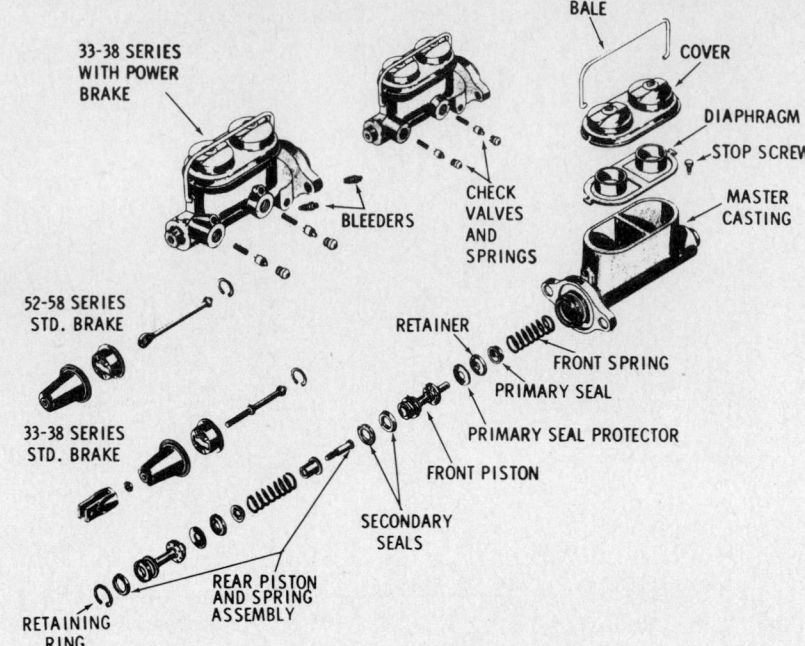

Dual type master cylinder (Delco) (© Pontiac Div. G.M. Corp.)

wear every 12,000 miles. See the Unit Repair Section of this manual for service procedures.

Master Cylinder Removal

The master cylinder is located in the engine compartment just above the steering column.

The master cylinder is a sealed unit. A sealing diaphragm covers the reservoir, hermetically sealing the system from contmination.

From under the dash, disconnect the brake pedal from the master cylinder on Bendix power brakes and non-power brakes. Delco power booster pushrods are not connected to the master cylinder. From under the hood, disconnect the hydraulic line and the stoplight wire.

Remove the bolts which hold the master cylinder to the cowl panel and lift off the master cylinder.

The unit is installed in reverse order of removal.

Parking Brake Adjustment

1. Jack up both rear wheels.
2. Apply parking brake, five notches from full release.
3. Loosen equalizer rear locknut. Adjust forward nut until a light to moderate drag is felt when rear wheels are rotated.
4. Tighten the locknut.
5. Fully release the parking brake and rotate rear wheels; no drag should be felt.

Parking Brake Lever Removal

A foot-operated parking brake is used on these models.

Remove the clevis which holds the cable to the foot-brake lever, then disconnect the bolts that hold the

lever assembly to the bracket. Let the assembly come down sufficiently to get the bolts which hold the cable conduit to the bracket assembly.

Disconnect the release lever at the dash and move the entire assembly out from under the vehicle.

Fuel System

Data on capacity of the gas tank will be found in the Capacities table. Data on correct engine idle speed and fuel pump pressure will be found in the Tune-up Specifications table. Both the above tables can be found at the start of their sections.

Since 1966, a disposable-type fuel pump has been used. When a fuel pump failure is noted, a pump assembly replacement is in order.

Information covering operation and troubles of the fuel gauge will be found in the Unit Repair Section.

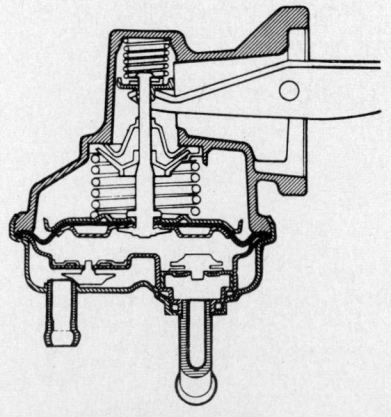

Fuel pump—1966-70
(© Pontiac Div. G.M. Corp.)

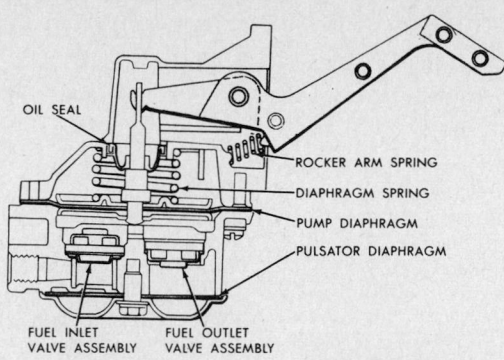

OIL SEAL

ROCKER ARM SPRING

DIAPHRAGM SPRING

PUMP DIAPHRAGM

PULSATOR DIAPHRAGM

FUEL INLET
VALVE ASSEMBLY

FUEL OUTLET
VALVE ASSEMBLY

Fuel pump—1964-65 (© Pontiac Div. G.M. Corp.)

Fuel Pump Removal

1965-72

1. From the left front side of the engine, disconnect the input and output line from the fuel pump.
2. Remove the bolts which hold the fuel pump to the timing case cover and lift off the pump.

NOTE: on models equipped with power steering it is possible, but somewhat difficult, to reach the mounting bolts with the steering pump in place. It may pay to slack off on the power steering pump, remove its mounting bolts and, with it still connected to its lines, lift it up out of the way.

Fuel Filter

Paper and Bronze Types— 1965-72

1. Disconnect fuel line connection at inlet of carburetor.
2. Remove inlet fuel filter nut from carburetor using a box wrench.
3. Remove filter element and spring.
4. If a bronze element, blow through cone end—element should allow air to pass freely.
5. Install element spring and new element into carburetor. Bronze elements are installed with small section of cone facing outward.
6. Install new gasket on fitting nut and install nut.
7. Install fuel line and tighten securely. Start engine and check for leaks.

Idle Speed and Mixture Adjustments

1965-67

Adjust with air cleaner installed.
1. Connect a vacuum gauge to the engine.
2. Set parking brake, place transmission in Neutral, connect a tachometer.
3. Start engine and allow it to warm up to normal operating temperature. Choke must be open and engine off fast idle.
4. Depress hot idle compensator

pin on all V8 with automatic transmission. Place transmission in Neutral for manual, Drive for automatic.
5. Adjust idle speed screw to obtain specified idle speed, making sure hot idle compensator is still depressed.
6. Adjust mixture screws to obtain highest idle speed and vacuum with best quality idle. "Missing" usually means mixture is too lean; "loping", too rich.
7. Reset idle speed screw to obtain specified idle speed.

1968-69

Adjust with air cleaner installed.
1. Turn in idle mixture screws until lightly seated, then back out 4 turns (2-BBL.) or 6 turns (4-BBL.).
2. Connect a tachometer, start engine and allow it to warm up to normal operating temperature. On automatic transmission, A/C cars, turn off A/C.
3. Place automatic in Drive, manual in Neutral. With idle stop solenoid energized, adjust mixture screws for best lean idle speed.
4. Adjust idle stop solenoid screw to obtain specified idle speed for all 1968 models; use idle screw for all 1969 cars.
5. Disconnect idle stop solenoid, then adjust idle speed screw on carburetor to obtain 650 rpm idle for manual transmission 4-BBL., 500 rpm for all others.
NOTE: do not re-adjust mixture screws.
6. Place fast idle lever on top step of cam and adjust fast idle speed.

1970

Adjust with air cleaner installed.
1. On California cars, remove fuel filler cap.
2. Disconnect and plug distributor vacuum advance hose.
3. Plug hot idle compensator on all automatic transmission V8's with Quadrajet (4MV). Also plug compensator on all V8 2-BBL. with automatic and A/C.
4. With automatic in Drive, Man-

ual in Neutral, adjust curb idle speed as follows:
5. Back out mixture screws 3-5 turns from lightly seated positions.
6. Adjust carburetor idle speed screw to obtain 850 rpm for manual 350 and 400 2-BBL., 1,050 rpm for manual 400 and 455 4-BBL., or 675 rpm for all automatic 350, 400, 455 engines.
7. Lean mixture screws equally (turn in) to obtain 800 rpm for manual 350 and 400 2-BBL., 950 rpm for manual 400 and 455 4-BBL., or 650 rpm for all automatic 350, 400, 455 engines.

1971

Adjust with air cleaner installed.

The idle stop solenoid is no longer used, having been replaced by the Combination Emission Control valve. This valve is energized through the transmission to increase idle speed under conditions of high gear deceleration and to provide full vacuum spark advance during high gear operation. The valve is deenergized at curb idle and in the lower gears to provide a retarded spark under these conditions, the result of which is lower hydrocarbon emission. *The valve need not be adjusted unless the solenoid or throttle body is removed, or the carburetor overhauled.*

1. Disconnect carburetor "EVAP" hose from vapor storage canister.
2. Disconnect and plug carburetor-to-vacuum (distributor vacuum) solenoid hose at solenoid. Disconnect throttle solenoid wire on 4-BBL. manual transmission engines.
3. Set dwell and timing (in that order) at specified idle speed.
4. Adjust carburetor speed screw to obtain specified idle speed, automatic in Drive, manual in Neutral.
5. On 4-BBL. manual transmission models, reconnect throttle solenoid wire, manually extend solenoid screw and adjust to specified idle rpm.
6. Place automatic in Park, manual in Neutral and check fast idle speed with screw on top step of cam. Adjust fast idle screw to obtain 1,700 rpm.
NOTE: 2 BBL. carburetors are not adjustable for fast idle.
7. Reconnect distributor, vacuum and vapor storage hoses.

Alternate Procedure

If the carburetor has been overhauled, or the plastic locks removed from the mixture screws, the following procedure must be used to adjust idle speed and mixture. It must be emphasized that the manufacturer does not recommend this procedure as a substitute for the preceding methods, in that exhaust emission quality can be adversely affected unless the proper test equipment is available.

1. Turn in mixture screws until lightly seated, then back out 3½ turns.
2. Start engine and adjust carburetor idle speed screw to obtain a speed 25 rpm above specified idle (automatic), 75 rpm higher for 2-BBL. V8 (manual), or 100 rpm higher for 4-BBL. V8 (manual).
3. Turn mixture screws in equally until specified idle speed is obtained. At this point a CO meter should be employed to adjust mixture. A reading of 1.0% or less must be maintained.
4. Shut off engine and install new limiter caps, with tabs against full rich stops.
5. Adjust fast idle speed, as described previously.

C. E. C. Valve Adjustment

1. With engine running at specified slow idle, manually extend C.E.C. plunger to contact throttle lever.
2. Adjust plunger length to obtain 1,000 rpm for 400 4-BBL. and 455 H.O. 4-BBL. with manual transmission.

1972

The idle circuit is set and sealed at the factory. No adjustment is possible unless the seal is broken.

Exhaust System

All exhaust pipes are retained to the manifold with a flange and two bolts or studs on a ball-type socket. The rest of the pipes, mufflers and resonators are held together with U-bolt clamps. When inspecting the exhaust system, check for holes in the mufflers and resonators and check

that the drain holes are facing down and are not clogged.

The exhaust system is suspended from the frame with rubber dampened hangers. Exhaust system components should have at least ¾ in. clearance from the floor pan to avoid possible overheating.

Tighten exhaust pipe to manifold flange bolts or stud nuts to 25 ft. lbs., U-bolts clamp nuts to 15 ft. lbs. pipe hangers to 10 ft. lbs., and Y-pipe U-bolt nuts to 25-30 ft. lbs.

Engine

1965-72

Only one basic V8 engine has powered Pontiacs since 1955. It is a conventional V8 with wedge-shaped combustion chambers, and a very compact block for its displacement. When it was first introduced, its stud mounted rocker arms and manifold-valley cover unit were very unusual, but today these features have been so widely adopted as to be quite conventional.

At the start of the period, the engine was used in 389 and 421 cu. in. displacements. The 389 version had a 4 1/16 in. bore and a 3¾ in. stroke. The 421 had a 4 3/32 in. bore and a 4 in. stroke as well as ¼ in. larger main bearing journals. Both engines have used four bolt main caps for their most powerful versions.

In 1967, Pontiac increased the bore of both V8s to 4.120 in., increasing the 389 to 400 cu. in. and the 421 to 428 cu. in. At the same time, Pontiac introduced a new cylinder head with larger ports and valves and larger combustion chambers than used previously.

In 1970 Pontiac increased the displacement of its largest engine again by bringing the bore and stroke of its 428 engine out to 4.15 in. by 4.21 in. for 455 cu. in., and they introduced a small bore 350 cu. in. version of their 400 V8 for their base Catalina engine. In 1971, Pontiac retained the 1970 engines, modifying them to operate on low-lead fuel. No premium-fuel

engines are offered by Pontiac in 1972.

Exhaust Emission Control Systems

In compliance with anti-pollution laws involving all of the continental United States, the General Motors Corporation has elected to adopt a special system of terminal exhaust treatment. This plan supersedes (in most cases) the method used to conform to 1966-67 California laws. The new system cancels out (except with stick shift and special purpose engine applications) the use of the A.I.R. method previously used.

The new concept, Combustion Control System (C.C.S.) utilizes engine modification, with emphasis on carburetor and distributor changes. Any of the methods of terminal exhaust treatment require close and frequent attention to tune-up factors of engine maintenance.

Since 1968, all car manufacturers have posted idle speeds, and other pertinent data relative to the specific engine-car application, in a conspicuous place in the engine compartment.

The more stringent 1970 laws require tighter control of emissions. Crankcase emissions are controlled by the Closed Positive Crankcase Ventilation System, and exhaust emissions by the engine Controlled Combustion System (C.C.S.), in conjunction with the new Transmission Controlled Spark System (T.C.S.).

In addition, cars sold in California are equipped with an Evaporation Control System that limits the amount of gasoline vapor discharged into the atmosphere (usually from the carubretor and fuel tank).

The T.C.S. system consists of a transmission switch, a solenoid valve, and a temperature switch. Under normal conditions, the system permits the vacuum distributor (spark) advance to operate only in high gear (both manual and automatic transmissions). When the engine temperature is below 85° F., or above 220° F., however, the system allows the vacuum advance to operate normally.
t For details, consult the Unit Re-
b pair Section.

Manifolds

Exhaust Manifold Removal

Tab locks are used on front and rear pairs of bolts on each exhaust manifold. When removing bolts, straighten tabs from beneath car using long handled screw driver. When installing tab locks, bend tabs against sides of bolt not over top of bolt.

Left-Side Manifold

1. If the car is equipped with power steering, disconnect the power steering pump but leave it at-

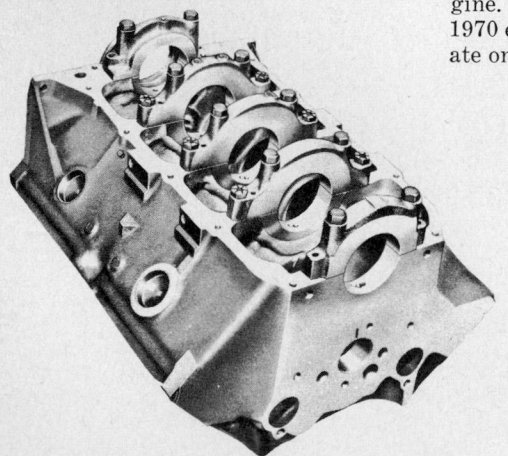

Heavy duty block with four bolt main caps
(© Pontiac Div. G.M. Corp.)

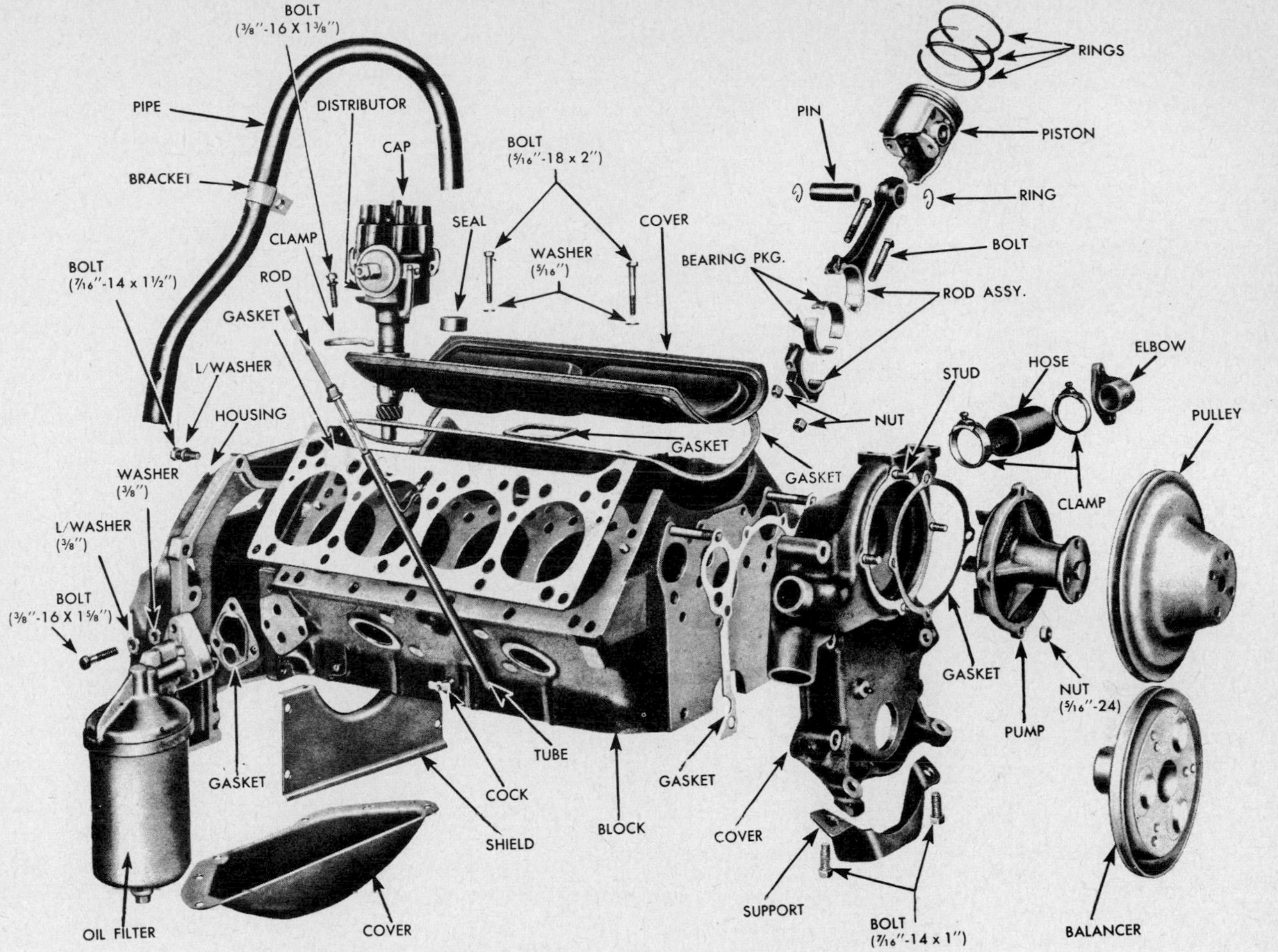

BOLT
(3/8"-16 X 1 3/8")

PIPE

DISTRIBUTOR

CAP

BRACKET

CLAMP

SEAL

BOLT
(5/16"-18 x 2")

WASHER
(5/16")

COVER

RINGS

PIN

PISTON

RING

BEARING PKG.

BOLT

ROD ASSY.

BOLT
(7/16"-14 x 1 1/2")

ROD

GASKET

L/WASHER

HOUSING

WASHER
(3/8")

L/WASHER
(3/8")

BOLT
(3/8"-16 x 1 5/8")

GASKET

GASKET

GASKET

STUD

NUT

HOSE

HOSE

ELBOW

PULLEY

CLAMP

GASKET

NUT
(5/16"-24)

PUMP

OIL FILTER

COVER

TUBE

COCK

SHIELD

BLOCK

GASKET

COVER

SUPPORT

BOLT
(7/16"-14 x 1")

BALANCER

Cylinder block and related external parts (© Pontiac Div. G.M. Corp.)

tached to its hoses and pull it up out of the way.

2. From underneath the vehicle, disconnect the exhaust crossover pipe flange.

3. If the car is equipped with power brakes, the rear bolts of the manifold are difficult to reach but they can be removed with a box wrench.

4. Remove the bolts that hold the manifold to the left cylinder head and take off the manifold.

Right-Side Manifold

From underneath the vehicle, disconnect the upper flange from the right manifold. This is the upper flange where the cross manifold, exhaust pipe and right manifold join.

From underneath the vehicle, remove the bolts that hold the manifold to the head on the back two flanges. The front flange can be removed from the top of the car with a box wrench.

Intake Manifold Removal

All Models

1. Drain coolant from petcocks on radiator and on each side of block.
NOTE: most of the coolant can be

drained from block through radiator drain by raising rear end of car approximately 15-18 in. off floor.

2. Remove air cleaner.

3. Remove water outlet fitting bolts and position fitting out of way, leaving radiator hose attached.

4. Disconnect heater hose from fitting.

5. Disconnect wire from thermogauge unit.

6. Remove spark plug wire brackets from manifold.

7. On cars equipped with power brakes, remove power brake vacuum pipe from carburetor.

8. Disconnect distributor to carburetor vacuum hoses.

9. Disconnect fuel line connecting carburetor and fuel pump.

10. Disconnect crank case vent hose from intake manifold.

11. Disconnect throttle rod from carburetor.

12. Remove screws retaining throttle control bracket assembly.

13. Remove intake manifold retaining bolts and nuts, and remove manifold and gaskets. Make sure that O-ring seal between intake manifold and timing chain cover is retained and installed during assembly.

14. Reverse procedure to install. Use plastic gasket retainers, as shown, to prevent manifold gaskets from slipping out of place.

Engine R & R

1965-72

1. Disconnect battery cables and

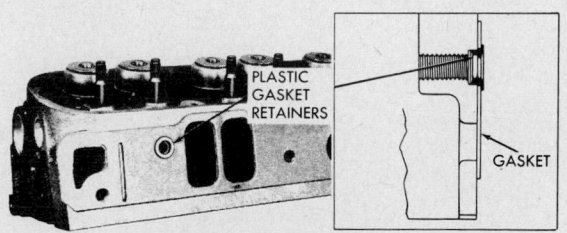

PLASTIC GASKET RETAINERS

GASKET

Plastic manifold retainers
(© Pontiac Div. G.M. Corp.)

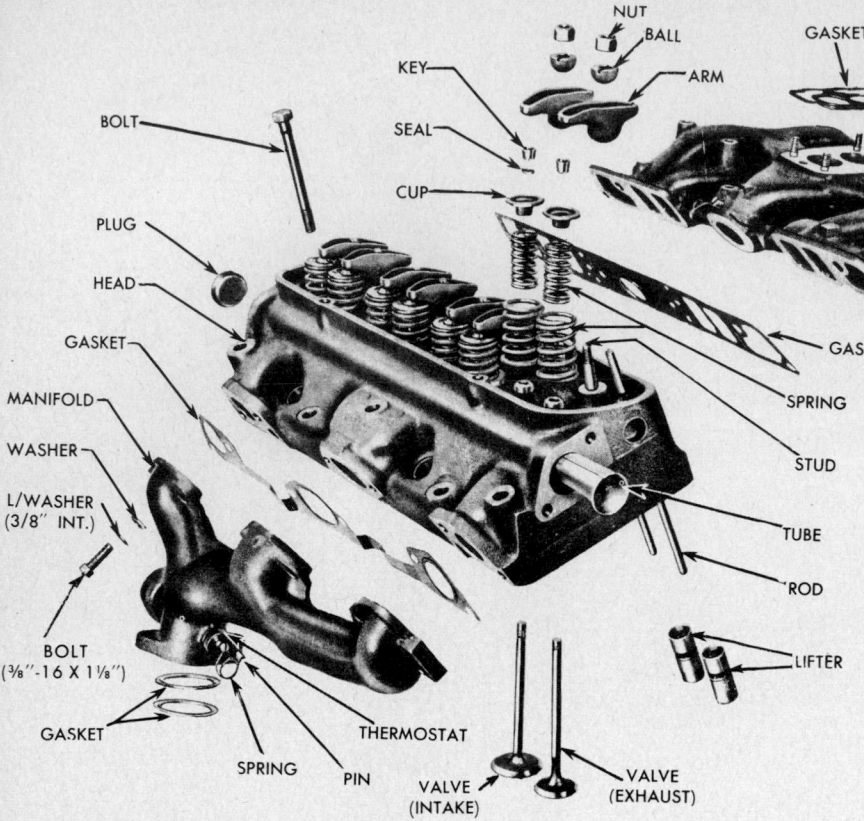

Cylinder head, manifolds and related parts (© Pontiac Div. G.M. Corp.)

remove battery.

2. Drain cooling system.
3. Scribe alignment marks around hood hinges and remove hood.
4. Disconnect engine wiring and all ground straps.
5. Remove air cleaner and fan shroud, then disconnect radiator and heater hoses.
6. If equipped with manual transmission, remove radiator (up to 1969).
7. Remove power steering pump and A/C compressor from brackets and swing units aside without disconnecting hoses.
8. Remove fan and fan pulley.
9. Disconnect accelerator linkage or cable and remove bracket.
10. Disconnect transmission vacuum modulator line (automatic) and power brake vacuum line.
11. Jack up car and support on axle stands.
12. Drain engine oil, disconnect fuel lines at pump and exhaust pipes from maniford.
13. Disconnect starter wires and remove starter motor on manual transmission cars.
14. If equipped with automatic transmission: remove converter cover and three converter retaining bolts. Slide converter rearward.
15. If equipped with manual transmission: disconnect clutch linkage and remove cross-shaft and flywheel housing cover.

16. Remove four lower bellhousing bolts—two per side.
17. Disconnect auto transmission filler tube support and starter wire shield.
18. Remove the two front motor mount bolts, then lower car to floor.
19. Support auto transmission with a wood-padded jack, then remove the two remaining bellhousing bolts from above.
20. Jack up auto transmission slightly, attach a chain hoist and pull engine.
21. To install, reverse removal procedure.

Harmonic Balancer R & R

Drain cooling system. Remove the radiator assembly. Remove fan belt and position fan with wide angle to clear balancer. The harmonic balancer can then be removed from the crankshaft by the use of a special puller. When installing, lock flywheel and tighten bolt to 160 ft. lbs., making sure keyway is aligned with key.

Cylinder Head

Rocker Arm Removal

1. Remove the four bolts that hold the rocker cover to the cylinder head and lift off the rocker cover.
NOTE: it is a good idea to disconnect the spark plug wires and get

them out of the way, although this is not absolutely necessary.
2. On the left side rocker cover, the job is somewhat simplified by taking off the air cleaner.
3. Each rocker is held to a pressed-in stud in the cylinder head and is removed separately.
4. When reinstalling, simply run the rocker pivot nut down until it bottoms, then tighten it to 15-25 ft. lbs.

Cylinder Head Removal

1. Remove intake manifold, valley cover, and rocker arm cover.
2. Loosen all rocker arm retaining nuts and pivot rockers off pushrods.
3. Remove pushrods and place in order.
4. Remove exhaust pipe flange bolts.
5. Remove battery ground strap and engine ground strap on left head; engine ground strap and automatic transmission oil filler tube bracket on right head.
6. Remove cylinder head bolts and head, with exhaust manifold attached.
NOTE: left head must be maneuvered to clear power steering and power brake units.

Cylinder Head Installation

1. Check head surface for straightness, then place a new head gasket on block.
NOTE: bolts are of three different lengths on all V8s. When bolts are properly installed, they will project an equal distance from head.
2. Install all bolts and tighten evenly to specified torque.
3. Install pushrods in original positions.
4. Position rocker arms over pushrods and tighten ball retaining nuts to 20 ft. lbs.
5. Replace rocker arm cover.
6. Replace valley cover.
7. Replace ground straps, oil filler tube bracket, intake manifold.
8. Install exhaust pipe flange nuts.
NOTE: most left and right cylinder heads are interchangeable within a single year. Large and small valve

heads should not be used on the same engine.

Stud Removal

Pressed-in Studs

Caution This procedure can be used *only* on engines with pressed-in rocker studs. GTO and some special high performance engines have screwed-in rocker studs which are easily identified by their hex head lower portion. Another common stud-securing procedure on standard engines is "pinning" pressed-in studs by drilling through the stud boss and stud and inserting an interference-fit roll pin. Make sure any such pins are removed before attempting the following procedure.

1. Disconnect battery and drain cooling system.
2. Remove rocker cover.
3. Pack oily rags around stud holes and engine openings.
4. Remove rocker arm and push-rod, then file two slots 3/32-1/8 in. deep on opposite sides of the stud. The top of the slots should be 1/4-3/8 in. below thread travel.
5. Place a spacer washer (or tool J-8934-3) over the stud, then position stud remover (or tool J-7934-1) on stud and tighten Allen screws.
6. Place a spacer (socket or J-8934-2) over the remover, then thread a 7/8 in. nut on stud remover and turn in until stud pulls from head.
7. If an oversize stud is to be used (0.003 in. oversize studs are available), ream stud hole to the proper size, then clean chips from area.
8. To install, coat press-pit area of stud with axle lube, then press or hammer into place. If possible use Pontiac Tool J-23342. If tool is not available chill stud in dry ice to facilitate installation. Take care as dry ice makes studs very brittle.

Valve System

Cylinder Head Disassembly

1. Remove cylinder heads, as previously described.
2. Compress valve springs, using valve spring compressor.
3. Remove valve locks or keys.
4. Release valve springs.
5. Remove valve springs, retainers, oil seals, and valves.

NOTE: if a valve does not slide out of the guide easily, check end of stem for mushrooming or heading over. If head is mushroomed, file off excess material, remove and discard valve. If valve is not mushroomed, lubricate stem, remove valve and check guide for galling.

Valve Guides

Pontiac engines have integral valve guides. Pontiac offers valves with oversize stems for worn guides (0.001, 0.003 and 0.005 in. being available for most engines). To fit these, enlarge valve guide bores with valve guide reamers to an oversize that cleans up wear. If a large oversize is required, it is best to approach that size in stages by using a series of reamers of increasing diameter. This helps to maintain the concentricity of the guide bores with the valve seats. The correct valve stem to guide clearance is given in the Valve Specifications table at the beginning of this section.

As an alternate procedure, some local automotive machine shops fit replacement guides that use standard stem valves.

Hydraulic Valve Lifter Disassembly

Disassemble lifters for cleaning only; no repairs are permitted.

1. Grasp lock ring with needle nose pliers and remove. (Depress plunger to gain clearance.)
2. Remove pushrod cup, metering valve disc, and upper metering disc (if any). Do not bend metering disc.
3. Remove plunger assembly and plunger spring.
4. Remove spring, check valve retainer and check valve from plunger.
5. Clean all parts in solvent (lacquer thinner) and reassemble.

NOTE: internal parts are *not* interchangeable between lifters.

Valve Springs

All Models

In order to check on the condition of the valve springs, lay all of the springs on a flat surface and carefully measure across the top of the intake springs with a straightedge to see that all are the same height. If all are the same height, it may safely be assumed that they are all in good condition because it is very unlikely that they will all collapse an equal amount. Do the same with exhaust valve springs.

If one or more are found to be a different height from the rest of the springs, it is a good idea to get one new spring and carefully measure all the old springs against the new one. Those which come up to the same height as the new spring may be considered to be in good condition. Those which do not should be replaced.

Where regular spring testing equipment is not available, this is generally considered to be a good, safe way to check the condition of the valve springs.

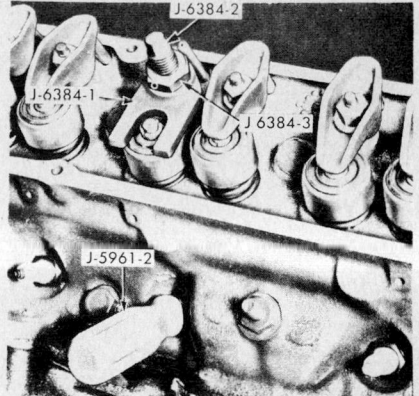

Valve spring compressed
(© Pontiac Div. G.M. Corp.)

Hydraulic Valve Lifter Removal

Remove the rocker cover and the intake manifold, then take off the push-rod cover. Loosen the rocker arm ball nut and lift the rocker arm off the pushrod. The pushrods can be pulled up through the cylinder head and the lifters can then be pulled up out of their bores. The lifters must be returned to the bores from which they were taken.

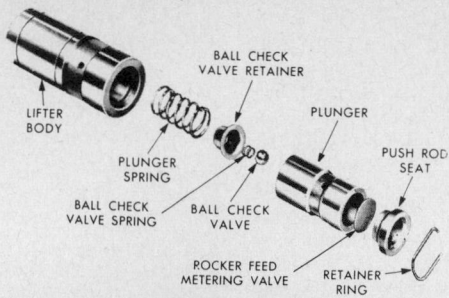

Hydraulic lifter
((C) Pontiac Div. G.M. Corp.)

Caution The hydraulic lifter is a complete assembly, matchmated at the factory, and the bore of one lifter positively cannot be used in the body of another. These parts should not be mixed.

NOTE: the rear-most pushrod on the left bank cannot be lifted out on cars equipped with a defroster unit. However, the pushrod can be lifted up far enough to permit removal of the hydraulic lifter.

Hydraulic Lifter Initial Adjustment

Tighten down on the rocker adjusting nut until it bottoms, then tighten it to 15-25 ft. lbs.

There is a shoulder on the mounting stud which is precision-machined to give the correct operating position when this operation is performed.

Timing Case

Timing Case Cover Removal and Seal Replacement

1. Drain radiator and cylinder block.
2. Loosen alternator adjusting bolts.
3. Remove fan, fan pulley, and accessory drive belts.
4. Disconnect radiator hoses.
5. Remove fuel pump.
6. Remove harmonic balancer bolt and washer.
7. Remove harmonic balancer.

NOTE: do not pry on rubber-mounted balancers. If only seal is to be replaced, proceed to Step 12.

8. Remove front four oil pan to timing cover bolts.
9. Remove timing cover bolts and nuts and cover to intake manifold bolt.
10. Pull cover forward and remove.
11. Remove O-ring from recess in intake manifold, then clean all gasket surfaces.
12. To replace seal, pry it out of the cover using a screwdriver. Install the new seal with lip inwards.

NOTE: seal can be replaced with cover installed.

13. To install, reverse removal procedure, making sure all gaskets are replaced. Tighten four oil pan bolts to 12 ft. lbs., harmonic balancer bolt to 160 ft. lbs., and fan pulley bolts to 20 ft. lbs.

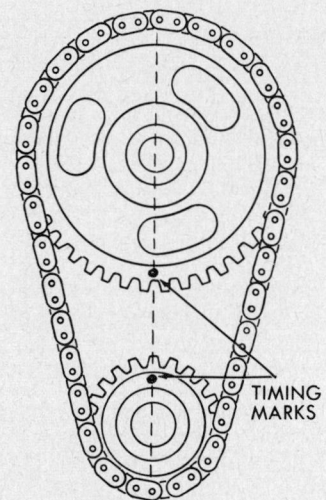

Valve timing marks

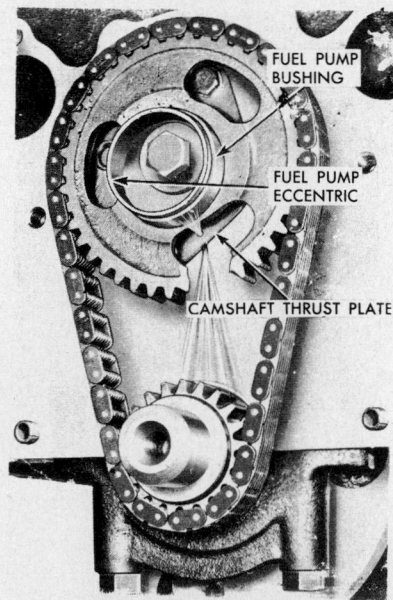

Timing gear assembly, showing oil squirt holes
((C) Pontiac Div. G.M. Corp.)

Timing Chain and Sprocket R & R

1. Remove the timing case cover and fuel pump cam.
2. Turn the crank and camshaft (i the chain is broken) until the two timing marks are in line between the shaft centers.
3. Using a puller, draw the sprocket off the front of the camshaft.
4. Arrange the new chain on the sprocket and set the sprocket up over the camshaft by looping the chain over the crank sprocket. That way, when the cam sprocket engages its key, the timing marks are nearest each other and in line between the shaft centers.
5. Secure the camshaft sprocket in this position, with pump cam in place.

NOTE: when reassembling the timing case cover, extra care should be taken to make sure that the oil seal between the bottom of the timing case cover and the front of the oil pan is still a good one. Plenty of gasket cement should be used, at this point, to prevent oil leaks.

Camshaft R & R

1. Drain cooling system and remove air cleaner.
2. Disconnect all water hoses, vacuum lines and spark plug wires.
3. Disconnect accelerator linkage, temperature gauge wire, and fuel lines.
4. Remove hood latch brace.
5. Remove PCV hose, then remove rocker covers.

NOTE: on air-conditioned models, remove alternator and bracket.

6. Remove distributor, then remove intake manifold.
7. Remove valley cover.
8. Loosen rocker arm nuts and pivot rockers out of the way.
9. Remove pushrods and lifters (keep them in proper order).
10. Remove harmonic balancer, fuel pump, and four oil pan to timing cover bolts.
11. Remove timing cover and gasket, then remove fuel pump eccentric and bushing.
12. Align timing marks, then remove timing chain and sprockets.
13. Remove camshaft thrust plate.
14. Remove camshaft by pulling straight forward, being careful not to damage cam bearings in the process.

NOTE: it may be necessary to jack up the engine slightly to gain clearance, especially if motor mounts are worn.

15. Install new camshaft, with lobes and journals coated with heavy (SAE 50-60) oil, into the engine, being careful not to damage cam bearings.

NOTE: most specialty cams come with a special "break-in" lubricant for the lobes and journals; if such lubricant is available, use it instead of heavy oil.

16. Install camshaft thrust plate and tighten bolts to 20 ft. lbs.

17. To install, reverse Steps 1-12, tightening sprocket bolts to 40 ft. lbs., timing cover bolts and nuts to 30 ft. lbs., oil pan bolts to 12 ft. lbs., and harmonic balancer bolt to 160 ft. lbs.

Engine Lubrication

Oil Pan Removal and Installation

1965-72

1. Disconnect battery cables.
2. Remove fan shroud.

3. On A/C cars up to 1969, and all cars starting 1970, remove fan and pulley.
4. Disconnect engine ground straps. Drain radiator starting 1970.
5. On A/C cars, remove compressor from brackets and swing aside without disconnecting hoses.
6. Check all wiring, fuel lines and water hoses for clearance—engine must be raised some 4½ in. Disconnect radiator hose at water pump starting 1970.
7. Jack up car and drain engine oil.
8. Disconnect steering idler arm from frame on all cars up to 1970. On Grand Prix models starting 1971, both this operation and the removal of the Pitman arm from the steering box are necessary.
9. Remove exhaust crossover pipe on single-exhaust cars; disconnect manifold flanges on dual-exhaust cars. Wire pipes out of the way to gain working room.
10. Remove flywheel housing cover, starter motor, and motor bracket (on 1969 and later models).

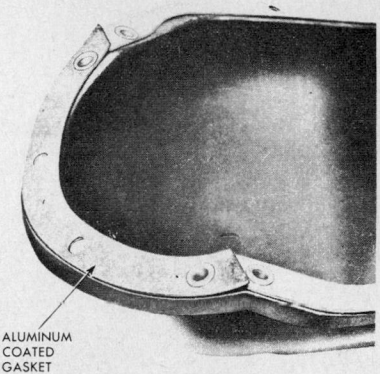

Front oil pan gasket overlapping side gaskets
(© Pontiac Div. G.M. Corp.)

11. Attach a hoist to the front of the engine.
12. Support engine on hoist and remove front motor mount bolts and mounts.
13. Loosen rear motor mount at transmission or, better still, remove it entirely and allow extension housing to rest on crossmember.
14. Remove oil pan bolts, then raise engine straight up about 4½ in. until top of transmission is hitting floor pan. On some 1969 and later models, it also helps to move engine forward about 1½ in.
15. Rotate oil pan forward to clear oil pump, then remove oil pan.
16. Place wood blocks between engine and motor mount brackets for safety.
17. To install, reverse removal procedure.

NOTE: this procedure has been found to work, although it differs slightly from the Pontiac factory procedure. Pontiac uses special engine lifting tools that are not available to independents, the proper use of which often involves loosening the steering box, etc.

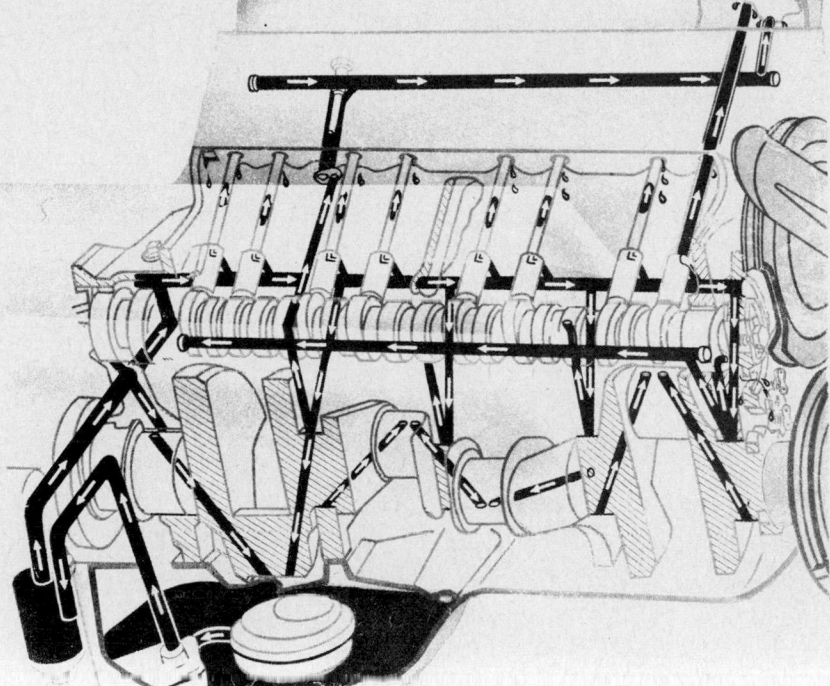

Engine lubrication (© Pontiac Div. G.M. Corp.)

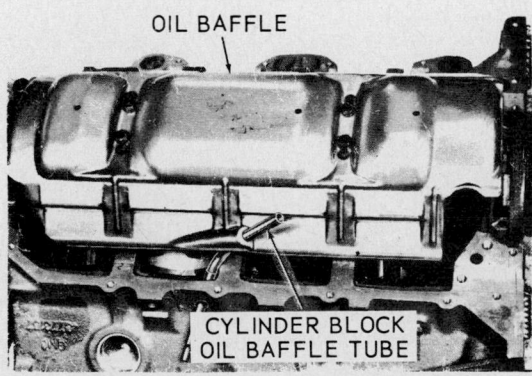

Oil baffle plate for high performance engines
(© Pontiac Div. G.M. Corp.)

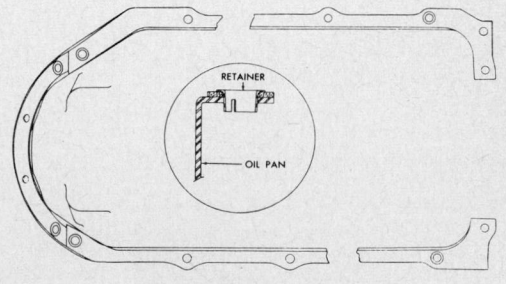

Oil pan gasket retainers
(© Pontiac Div. G.M. Corp.)

5. Inspect regulator spring for distortion, wear, or cracks.
6. Inspect regulator ball for damage.
7. Inspect pump components for wear.
8. To assemble, first install drive and driven gears, then install cover.

NOTE: it is a good idea to pack pump with Vaseline for proper priming.

to replace the upper half. An alternative factory method is to remove the oil pan and transmission, loosen all of the main bearing caps and lower the crankshaft about 3/8 in. This will allow the removal of the old upper half rear bearing seal and the installation of a new one.

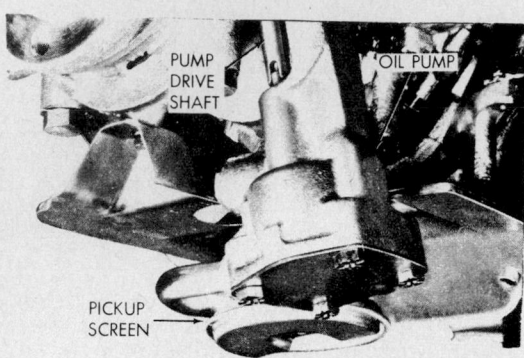

Oil pump and pump drive shaft
(© Pontiac Div. G.M. Corp.)

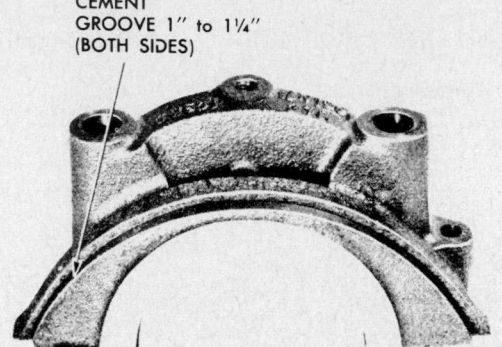

Rear oil pan gasket positioned in bearing cap
(© Pontiac Div. G.M. Corp.)

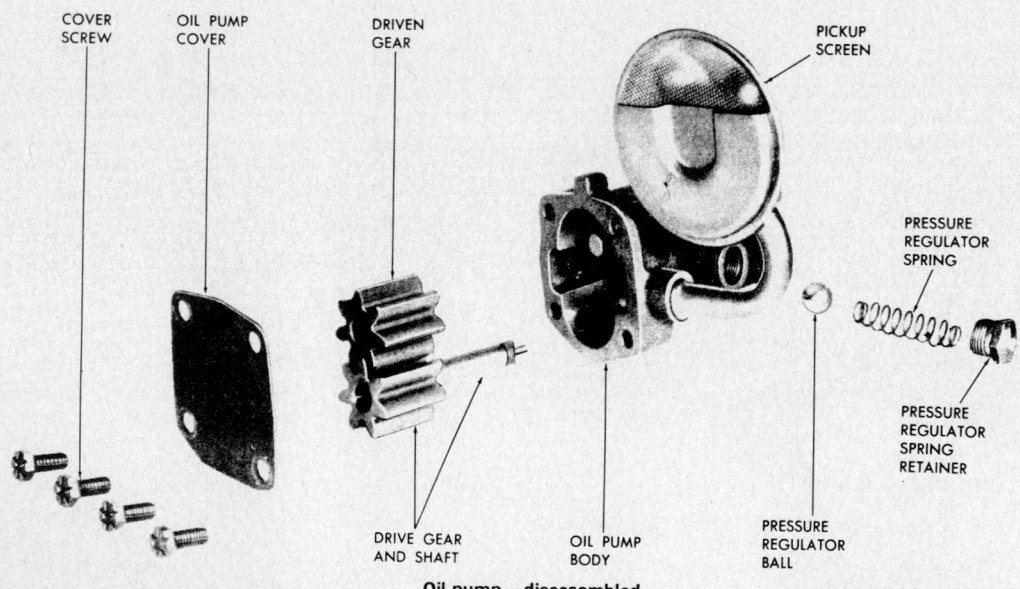

Oil pump—disassembled

Oil Pump Disassembly, Inspection and Assembly

1. Remove pressure regulator spring and ball.
2. Remove cover hold-down bolts and cover.
3. Remove driven gear and drive gear, then remove drive shaft.
4. Clean all parts in solvent, especially pump pickup screen.

CAUTION: do not remove or loosen oil pickup tube or screen.

9. Turn drive shaft by hand to make sure it turns freely.
10. Install regulator ball, spring, and retainer.

Rear Main Bearing Oil Seal

A wick packing is used to seal the rear main bearing. Replacement of the lower half of this seal is simple, however, the factory recommends the removal of the engine and crankshaft

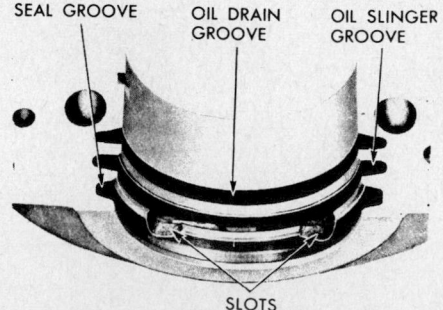

Rear main bearing cap
(© Pontiac Div. G.M. Corp.)

Top Half, Rear Main Bearing Oil Seal Replacement

The following method has proven a distinct advantage in most cases and, if successful, saves many hours of labor.

1. Drain engine oil and remove oil pan.
2. Remove rear main bearing cap.
3. With a 6 in. length of 3/16 in. brazing rod, drive up on either exposed end of the top half oil seal. When the opposite end of the seal starts to protrude, have a helper grasp it with pliers and pull gently while the driven end is being tapped. It is surprising how easily most of these seals can be removed by this method.

Woven Fabric-Type Seal Installation

1. Obtain a 12 in. piece of copper wire (about the same gauge as that used in the strands of an insulated battery cable).
2. Thread one strand of this wire through the new seal, about ½ in. from the end, bend back and make secure.
3. Thoroughly saturate the new seal with engine oil.
4. Push the copper wire up through the oil seal groove until it comes down on the opposite side of the bearing.
5. Pull (with pliers) on the protruding copper wire while the crankshaft is being turned and the new seal is slowly fed into place.
   CAUTION: this snaking operation slightly reduces the diameter of the new seal and care will have to be used to keep the seal from slipping too far through the top half of the bearing.
6. When an equal amount of seal is extending from each side, cut off the copper wire close to the seal and tamp both ends of the seal up into the groove (this will tend to expand the seal again).
   NOTE: don't worry about the copper wire left in the groove, it is too soft to cause damage.
7. Replace the seal in the cap in the usual way and replace the oil pan.

Pistons and Rods

Slipper skirt tin-plated aluminum pistons with steel struts are used.

All three rings are located above the wrist pin. The letter F, or the depression in the edge of the piston, go to the front of the engine in all cases.

Piston Ring Replacement

1. Remove rod and piston assemblies.
2. Remove cylinder head/s.
3. Push connecting rod and piston assemblies up and out of the cylinder bores.
   NOTE: any top ridge on cylinder wall should be removed using a ridge reamer before removing rod and piston assemblies.
4. Using an internal micrometer, measure the cylinder bores both across the thrust faces of the cylinder and parallel to the crankshaft axis.
5. If bore is within tolerance, examine for visible damage. It should be dull silver in color and exhibit a pattern of machining cross hatching. There should be no scratches, tool marks, nicks, or other damage. If any such damage exists, bore cylinder to clean up damage, then bore to next available oversize. Polished or shiny places in the bores cause poor lubrication, high oil consumption and ring damage.
6. If cylinder bore is in satisfactory condition, place each ring in bore, in turn, and square it in bore using a piston top. Measure the ring end gap with feeler gauges. If gap is greater than that specified, get new ring; if gap is less than that specified, file end of ring to bring within tolerance.
7. Clean ring grooves, using a commercial groove cleaner or a broken ring, then install rings. Space ring gaps equally around piston circumference and check ring to groove clearance.

Piston to Cylinder Wall Clearance

Engine	At Skirt Top
1965-66 389 V8	.0005-.0021‡
1967-68 400 V8	.0025-.0031△ (67)
	.0022-.0028△ (68)
1969 400 V8	.0025-.0031△
1967-69 421 V8	.0030-.0036△
1970-72 400 V8	.0025-.0033△
1970-72 455 V8	.0025-.0033◎

△ 1.11 in. below piston top.
‡ 1.18 in. below piston top (.0007-.0013 in. preferred).
◎ 1.08 in. below piston top

Piston Ring Gaps

Year and Engine	Top Compression	Bottom Compression	Oil Control
1965-66 389 V8	0.016-0.026 in.	0.013-0.025 in.	0.015-0.055 in.
1965-66 421 V8	0.016-0.026 in.	0.013-0.025 in.	0.015-0.055 in.
1967-69 All V8s	0.010-0.030 in.	0.010-0.030 in.	0.015-0.055 in.
1970-72 400, 350	0.010-0.030 in.	0.010-0.030 in.	0.015-0.055 in.
1970-72 455	0.010-0.030 in.	0.010-0.030 in.	0.015-0.055 in.

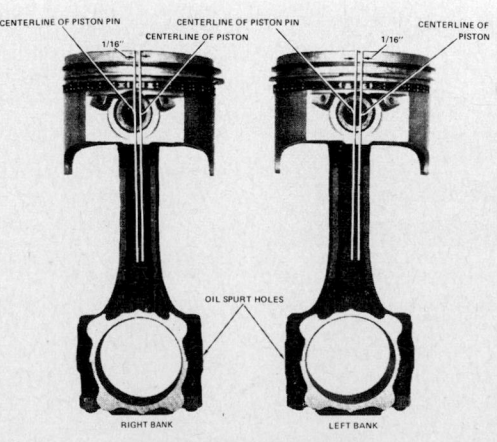

Piston and rod assembly
(© Pontiac Div. G.M. Corp.)

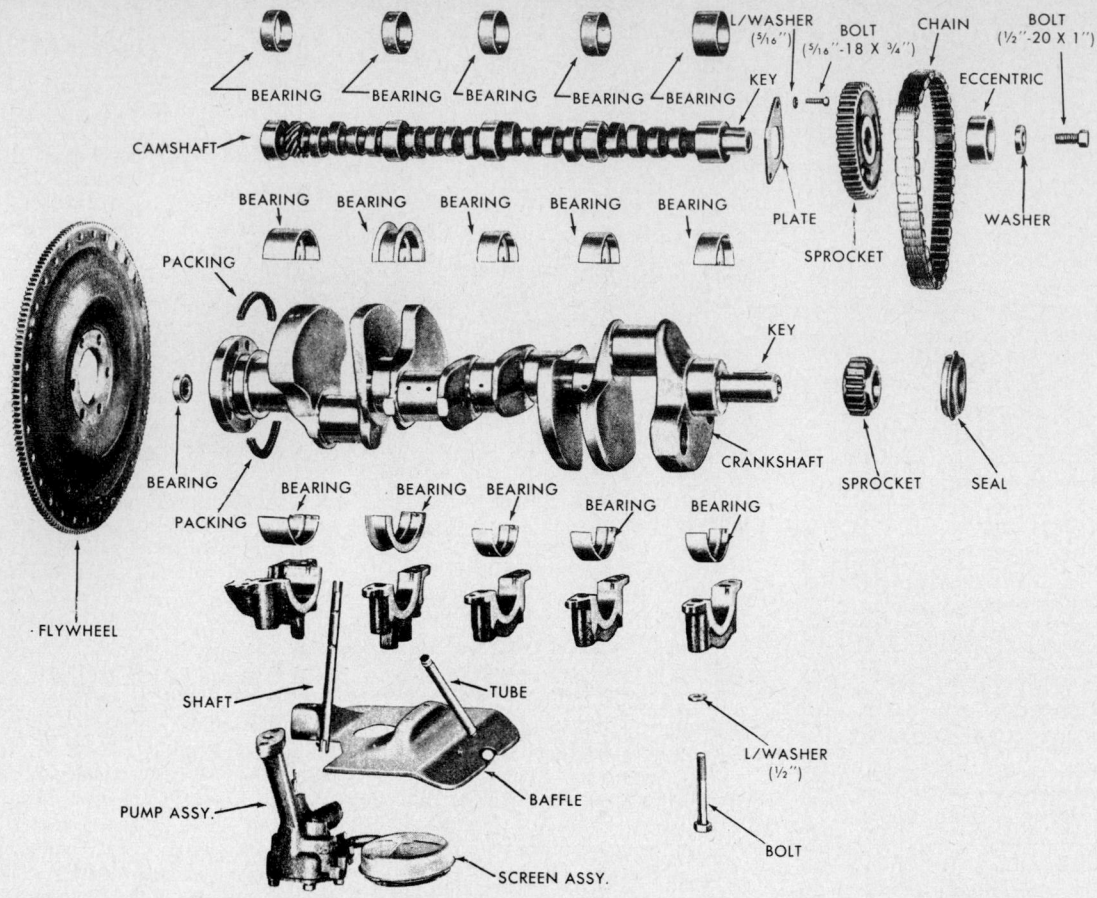

Camshaft, crankshaft and related parts (© Pontiac Div. G.M. Corp.)

Ring Side Clearance

Year and Engine	Top Compression	Bottom Compression	Oil Control
1965-66 V8s	0.0015-0.0030 in.	0.0015-0.0035 in.	0.0005-0.0055 in.
1967-72 V8s	0.0015-0.0050 in.	0.0015-0.0050 in.	0.0015-0.0050 in.

8. Lower rod and piston assemblies, one at a time, into bore until ring compressor contacts block. Using wooden hammer handle, push piston into bore while guiding rod onto journal.
9. Squirt oil on cylinder walls, then install rod bolts and tighten to specification.
10. Install cylinder head.

Front Suspension

Description

Independent, coil-spring front suspension is used on all models. Each wheel is attached to the frame by means of a steering knuckle, upper and lower control arms, and upper and lower ball joints.

Ball joints are of two basic types. Upper ball joints are of the tension type, which normally display no looseness due to their being preloaded by rubber cushions. Lower ball joints on Pontiac models up to 1970 are of the compression type, which normally have a built-in "looseness". An exception to this is the Grand Prix, which has tension type lower joints in 1969-70. In 1971, all lower ball joints were changed to the tension type.

Ball Joint Checking

Upper—Tension Type

1. Disengage the ball stud from the steering knuckle, weight of car being supported by a jack under the spring seat on the side being checked.
2. Install stud nut onto stud and check torque required to rotate ball stud.
3. If torque is less than ½ ft. lb., the joint must be replaced.

Lower—Compression Type

1. Place a jack under lower control arm spring seat and jack up car.
2. Pry wheel and tire up and down (or remove wheel and hub to eliminate wheel bearing play) and measure play in joint using a dial indicator or a standard inspection station ball joint checking device.
3. If play exceeds 0.050 in., the ball joint must be replaced.

Lower—Tension Type

1. Place a jack under the lower control arm spring seat and jack up car.
2. Remove grease fitting from lower ball joint.
3. Remove hub and backing plate, or caliper, assembly.
4. Separate lower ball stud from steering knuckle using a pry bar and hammer.
   NOTE: make sure seal is not damaged.
5. Place probe of dial indicator into grease fitting hole until it touches base of ball joint.
6. Preload and zero indicator, then pull up and down on threaded portion of stud and measure play.

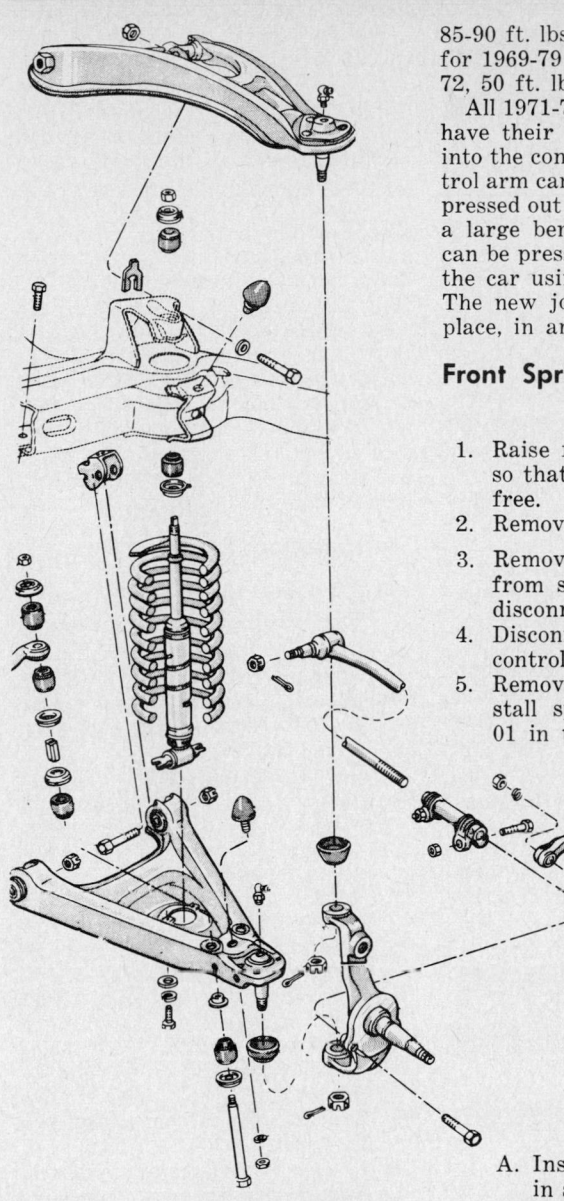

Typical front suspension
(© Pontiac Div. G.M. Corp.)

85-90 ft. lbs. (120 ft. lbs. maximum) for 1969-79 Grand Prix and all 1971-72, 50 ft. lbs. for all others.

All 1971-72 and 1969-70 G.P. models have their lower ball joints pressed into the control arms. The entire control arm can be removed and the joint pressed out using various spacers and a large bench vise, or the old joint can be pressed from the arm while in the car using a screw-type remover. The new joint must be pressed into place, in any case, to avoid damage.

Front Spring R & R

1965-68

1. Raise front end of car; support so that lower control arm hangs free.
2. Remove wheel and brake drum.
3. Remove brake backing plate from steering knuckle. (Do not disconnect brake line.)
4. Disconnect stabilizer from lower control arm.
5. Remove shock absorber, and install spring compressor J-7592-01 in the following manner:

7. If play exceeds 0.050 in., the ball joint must be replaced.

Ball Joint Replacement

Ball joints are riveted to the control arms at the factory except on 1969-70 Grand Prix and all 1971-72 models. To remove, drill or chisel rivet heads away and replace with a service ball joint. The service joint comes with specially hardened bolts and nuts that replace the rivets. It is extremely important that only these special fasteners are installed—standard bolts are not strong enough for this application. Tighten service bolts to 9 ft. lbs. for upper joints, 16 ft. lbs. for lower joints. Upper ball stud nuts must be tightened to a minimum torque of 50 ft. lbs. (80 ft. lbs. is allowable in order to line up cotter pin holes). Lower ball stud nuts must be tightened to a minimum torque of

A. Install one J-7592-7 cast plate in spring with boss down; be sure the angled center hole of the plate is aligned with axis of spring. Rotate the plate upward into highest position in coil.
B. Install another J-7592-7 plate under the third coil from the bottom with the boss up and center hole aligned with axis of spring. This plate should be slanted in the same direction and parallel with the upper plate.
C. Install long bolt up through both plates with thread end down. Install J-7592-4 retainer (cup up) and J-7592-2 locking clip through opening at upper shock bracket to hold bolt to upper plate.
D. Place J-7592-6 (ball up) thrust bearing, and J-7592-3 nut (threads down) on the bolt and screw up snug.
6. While holding upper end of rod, turn nut at lower end to compress spring.

7. Support lower control arm with a jack, then disconnect lower ball stud from steering knuckle with J-6627.
8. Support upper control arm and steering knuckle assembly by inserting a wood block between upper control arm and frame.
9. Carefully lower jack, allowing outer end of lower control arm to swing down until spring is free. Remove the spring.
10. Before replacing spring, assemble compressor J-7592 on the new spring.
11. Install spring by placing one end in the frame seat and the other end in the lower control arm seat. The end of the spring coil must be visible through the drain hole in the lower control arm spring seat.
12. Install spring by reversing removal procedure.

1969-72

1. Jack up car and support on jack stands at frame side rails.
2. Remove shock absorber.
3. Disconnect stabilizer bar at lower control arm.
4. Support lower control arm with

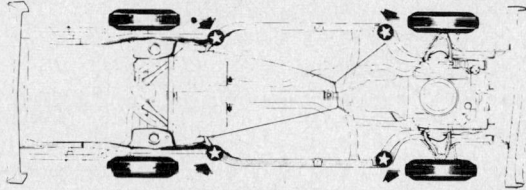

Hoist contact lifting points

a hydraulic floor jack, then remove the two inner control arm to front crossmember bolts.
5. Carefully lower the control arm, allowing the spring to relax.
6. Reach in and remove spring.
NOTE: this is probably the best all-around procedure and it can be used, with slight modification, for all models from 1965.
7. To install, reverse removal procedure. Tighten pivot bolts to 110 ft. lbs., nuts to 80 ft. lbs., with car resting on wheels.

Jacking, Hoisting

Jack car at front spring seats of lower control arms and, at rear, at axle housing.

When using frame lift, use side rails at points shown on diagram. Be sure that adapters are properly supporting these designated areas.

Steering Gear

Manual Steering

Instructions covering the overhaul of the steering gear will be found in the Unit Repair Section.

Manual Steering Gear Removal and Installation

1965-72

1. Disconnect pitman arm.
2. Scribe position of steering shaft on worm shaft flange and disconnect lower flange from shaft.
3. Remove three gear-to-frame bolts and lift out gear.

To replace:

1. Align scribe marks at shaft and flange.
2. Position gear assembly. Install three gear-to-frame bolts and tighten to 70-90 ft. lbs.
3. Install pitman arm. Tighten nut to 110-140 ft. lbs. (185 ft. lbs. for 1971-72).
4. Install two flange nuts and lock washers and tighten to 10-20 ft. lbs.

NOTE: in connecting and aligning shaft and jacket, avoid metal to metal contacts to counteract noise transmission to driver.

Power Steering

Troubleshooting and repair instructions covering power steering gears are given in the Unit Repair Section.

Power Steering Pump Removal

1. Disconnect and cover the two hoses at the back of the pump. Remove the bolt from the tensioner bracket and take off the drive belt.
2. Tilt the pump in toward the engine and remove the bolts that hold its bracket to the cylinder head.

Power Gear Removal

1965-72

1. Scribe alignment mark on shaft and worm shaft flange, then remove two nuts and washers.
2. Disconnect oil lines from valve body.
3. Remove pitman arm.
4. Remove gear to frame bolts and lift out gear.
5. Reverse above procedure to replace. When installing mounting bolts, tighten finger-tight, only, until proper alignment is obtained. See manual gear procedure for bolt torques.

Clutch

Clutch Pedal Adjustment

1. Disconnect return spring.
2. With pedal against stop, loosen locknut to allow adjusting rod to be turned out of swivel until the throwout bearing contacts the release fingers in the pressure plate.
3. Turn adjusting rod into swivel or pushrod 3½ turns; tighten locknut to 8-12 ft. lbs. for 1965-68, 30 ft. lbs. for 1969-72.
4. Install return spring and check pedal lash; it should be approximately 1 in.

Clutch Removal

Remove transmission, making sure that its weight is not allowed to rest on the hub of the clutch disc.

On all models, unhook the clutch pedal, pull back spring, and take out the clutch fork ball support, the clutch fork and the clutch throwout bearing. Remove starter and flywheel housing. Be sure to mark the flywheel and clutch cover so that assembly can be made in the same relative position to preserve the clutch balance. A little at a time, loosen the bolts holding clutch to flywheel and remove clutch.

Transmissions

Standard Transmission

Transmission Information

Transmission refill capacities will be found in the Capacities table of this section.

Step-by-step repair procedures are covered in the Unit Repair Section. Full-sized Pontiacs have used six different manual transmissions: 1. a light duty three speed with synchromesh on second and third only, recognizable by its five bolt side cover, 2. a heavy duty Borg Warner three speed with synchromesh on second and third only, a nine bolt side cover, and a very long extension shaft, 3. a fully synchromesh, Dearborn, top cover, three speed built by Ford, 4. Borg Warner fully synchromesh four speed with a nine bolt side cover, 5. a Muncie fully synchromesh four speed with a seven bolt side cover. 6. a Muncie three speed with seven bolt side cover, used on Grand Prix models from 1970 to 1972.

Transmission Removal

Light Duty Three Speed and Borg Warner Three Speed

1. Drain transmission if it is equipped with a drain plug.
2. Remove U-bolt nuts, lock plates, and U-bolts from rear axle drive pinion flange.
3. Use a suitable rubber band to hold bearing on to journals if tie wire has been removed to prevent loss of needle bearings when rear joint is disconnected.
4. Remove complete drive line assembly by sliding rearward to disengage yoke from splines on transmission main shaft.
5. Disconnect speedometer cable from speedometer driven gear.
6. Disconnect shift rods and remove lever and cross-shaft assembly.
7. Support rear of engine with a floor jack.
8. Remove two transmission brackets to crossmember retaining nuts.
9. Remove upper transmission to

Light duty three speed with non synchromesh low gear
(© Pontiac Div. G.M. Corp.)

FLANGED SIDE

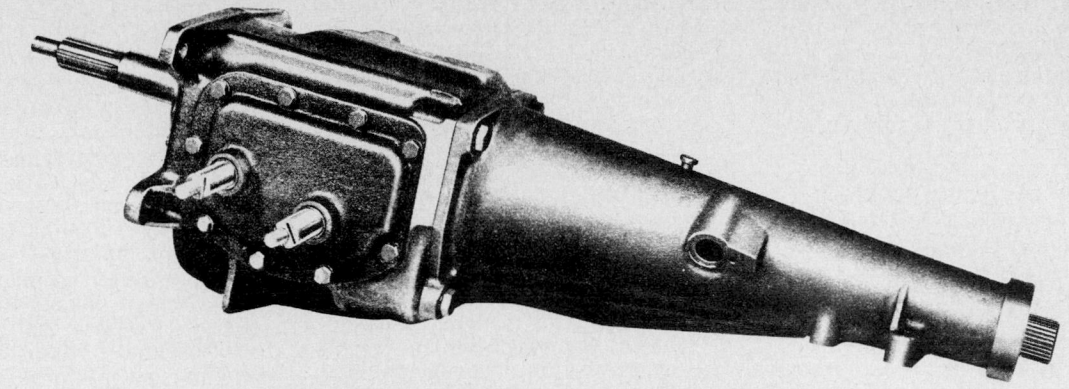

Heavy duty Borg Warner three speed (© Pontiac Div. G.M. Corp.)

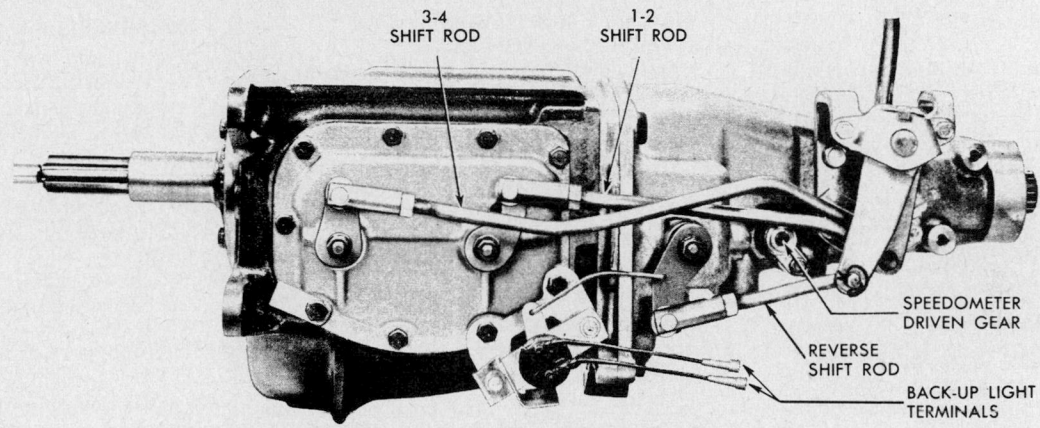

3-4 SHIFT ROD

1-2 SHIFT ROD

SPEEDOMETER DRIVEN GEAR

REVERSE SHIFT ROD

BACK-UP LIGHT TERMINALS

Borg Warner four speed transmission (© Pontiac Div. G.M. Corp.)

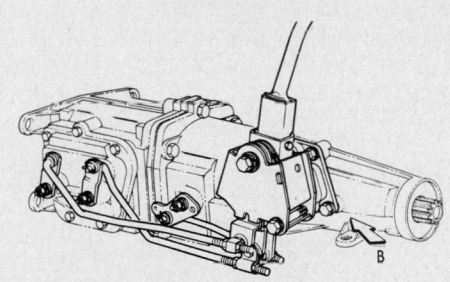

B

Muncie four speed transmission
(© Pontiac Div. G.M. Corp.)

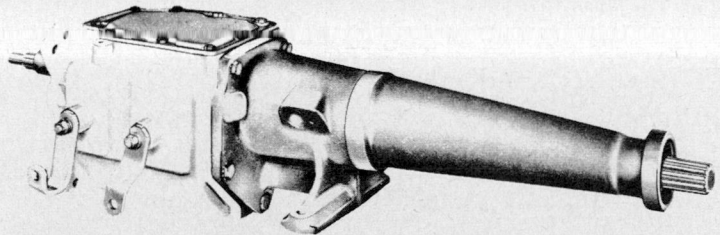

Dearborn three speed fully synchromesh transmission (© Ford Motor Co.)

stall.

Dearborn and Muncie Three Speed

1. Disconnect speedometer cable.
2. Disconnect shift control rods and TCS wires from transmission.
3. Remove driveshaft.
4. Support rear of engine and remove transmission mount.
5. Remove four crossmember bolts and slide member rearward.
6. Remove two upper transmission to flywheel housing bolts and insert guide pins.
7. Remove two lower transmission to flywheel housing attaching bolts.
8. Slide transmission straight back on guide pins until main drive gear splines are free of splines in clutch friction plate.
9. Remove transmission.

Borg Warner Four Speed

1. Remove drain plug and drain transmission.
2. Remove six metal boot retainer attaching screws and slide boot over shift lever.
3. Disconnect speedometer cable from speedometer.
4. Disconnect back up light leads from back up light switch.
5. Disconnect shift control rods from shifter levers.

clutch housing bolts and insert transmission aligning studs.

NOTE: aligning studs are necessary since they support the transmission and prevent distortion of the clutch driven plate hub when the lower transmission bolts are removed.

10. Remove lower transmission to clutch housing bolts, tilt rear of extension upward to engage bracket studs from crossmember support and withdraw transmission from clutch housing.
11. Tilt front downward and remove. Reverse procedure to in-

6. Remove U-bolt nuts, lock plates, and U-bolts from rear axle drive pinion flange.
7. Use suitable rubber band to hold bearing on to journals if wire has been removed to prevent loss of needle bearings.
8. Remove complete drive line assembly by sliding rearward to disengage yoke from splines on main shaft.
9. Support rear of engine and remove two transmission extension bracket retaining nuts.
10. Remove two top transmission to clutch housing bolts and insert two transmission aligning studs.
11. Remove two lower transmission to clutch housing bolts.
12. Tilt rear of extension housing upward to disengage bracket studs from crossmember support and withdraw transmission from clutch housing.

NOTE: on long wheelbase Pontiacs (Star Chiefs and Bonnevilles), remove crossmember before removing transmission because of the additional length of the extension housing.

13. Remove transmission. Reverse procedure to install.

Muncie Four Speed

1. Remove drain plug and drain transmission.
2. Disconnect speedometer cable, back up lights, and TCS.
3. Disconnect shift control rods from shifter levers and remove two levers and bracket screws and remove shift lever and bracket.

---

4. Remove U-bolt nuts, lock plates, and U-bolts from rear axle drive pinion flange.
5. Use rubber band to hold bearing onto journals if wire has been removed to prevent loss of needle bearings.
6. Remove complete driveshaft assembly by sliding rearward to disengage yoke from splines on transmission main shaft.
7. Support rear of engine and remove two transmission extension insulator to crossmember support retaining bolts.
8. Remove two top transmission to clutch housing bolts and insert two transmission aligning studs.
9. Remove two lower transmission to clutch housing bolts.
10. Tilt rear of extension upward to disengage bracket studs from cross member support and withdraw transmission from clutch housing.
11. Remove transmission. Reverse procedure to install.

Three-Speed Transmission Linkage Adjustment

1965-66

1. Put selector lever in neutral.
2. Back off trunnion adjusting nuts several turns.
3. Line up shift levers so that they move freely back and forth.
4. With transmission levers in full neutral detent adjust second and third shifter rod trunnion at cross-shaft lever and first and reverse trunnion at transmission lever. Tighten trunnion nuts to

---

60-120 in. lbs.
5. Move selector lever to first gear and check key at first and reverse shift lever. Key should just clear lower side of opening in steering column.
6. Move selector lever to third gear and check key at second and third shift lever. Key should just clear lower side of opening in steering column.
7. Apply wheel bearing grease to all gear shift linkage joints.
8. Check complete shift pattern movement with engine off, start engine and perform shift pattern.

1967-69 Column Shift

1. Align upper and lower gear shift levers on steering column assembly in neutral position by inserting gauge pin in hole as shown in figure.
2. Loosen clamp screws at transmission gear shift control rods.
3. Position levers on transmission in neutral.
4. Torque clamp screws to 20 ft. lbs. and check shift pattern.

1967-72 Floor or Console Shift

1. Put selector lever in neutral.
2. Loosen trunnion jam nuts on transmission gear shift control rods.
3. Place transmission lever and bracket assembly in neutral and install gauge pin as shown in figure.
4. Put levers on transmission in neutral.

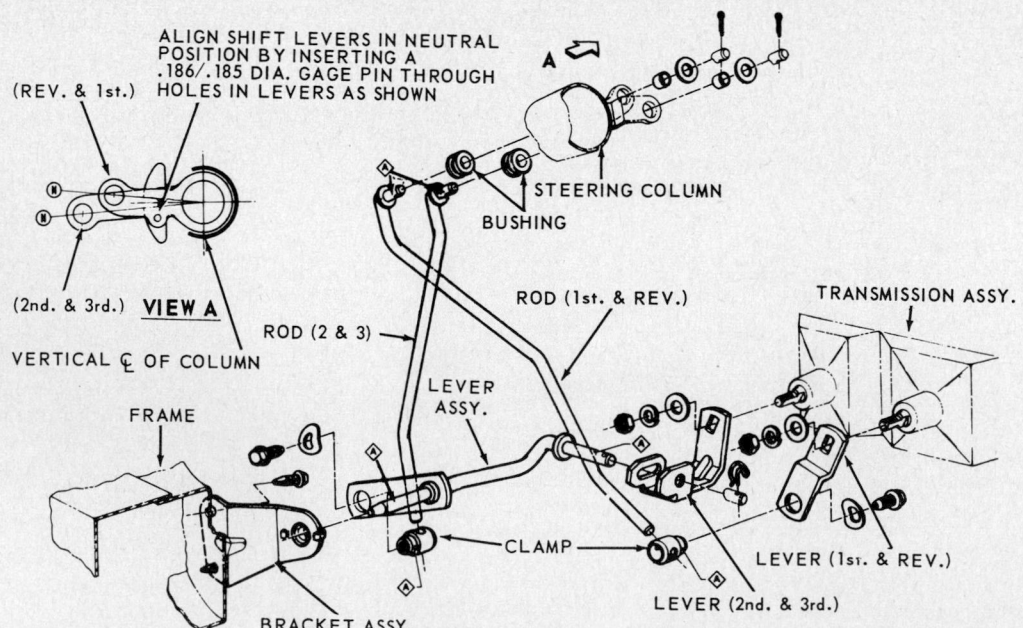

ALIGN SHIFT LEVERS IN NEUTRAL POSITION BY INSERTING A .186/.185 DIA. GAGE PIN THROUGH HOLES IN LEVERS AS SHOWN

(REV. & 1st.)

(2nd. & 3rd.) **VIEW A**

VERTICAL ℄ OF COLUMN

A

STEERING COLUMN

BUSHING

ROD (1st. & REV.)

TRANSMISSION ASSY.

ROD (2 & 3)

LEVER ASSY.

FRAME

CLAMP

LEVER (1st. & REV.)

LEVER (2nd. & 3rd.)

BRACKET ASSY.

◇ LUBRICANT AS INDICATED WITH CHASSIS LUBRICANT

Standard shift controls—1967-69 (© Pontiac Div. G.M. Corp.)

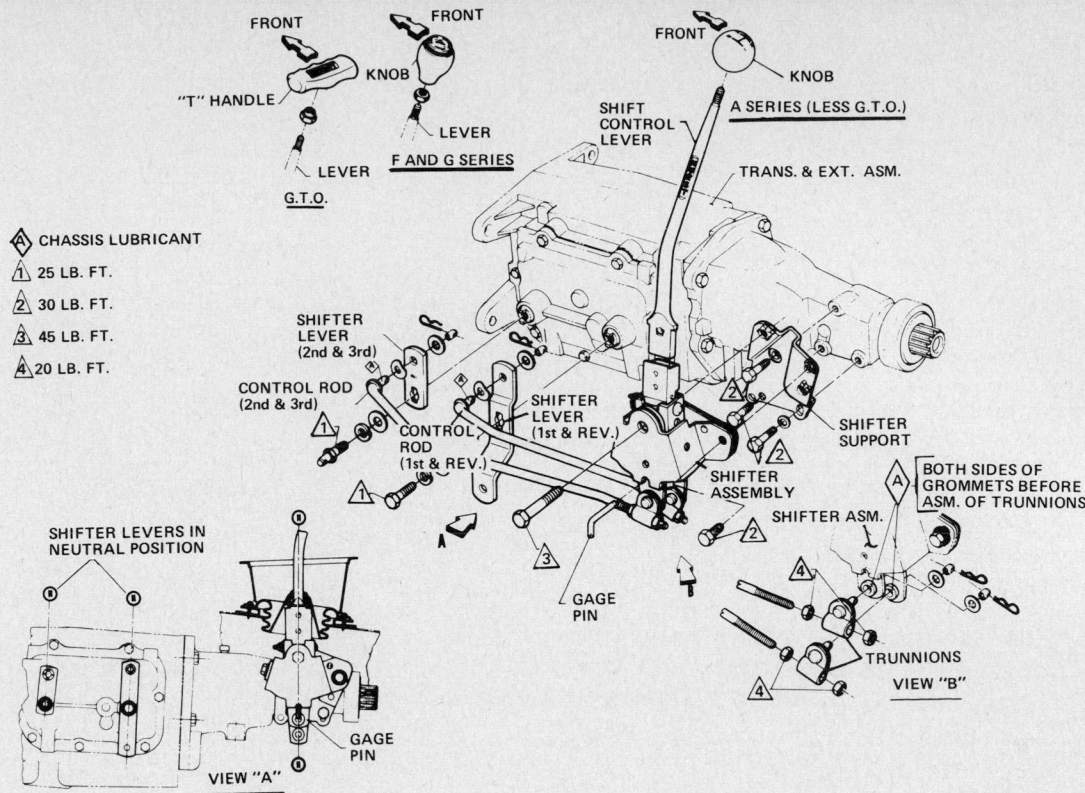

Three-speed Muncie floorshift (Hurst)—1971-72 (ⓒ Pontiac Div. G.M. Corp.)

SHIFT CONTROL ADJUSTMENT

1. POSITION LEVERS ON TRANSMISSION IN NEUTRAL WITH GAGE PIN IN PLACE IN LEVER AND BRACKET ASSEMBLY (AS SHOWN IN VIEW "A") ASSEMBLE SHIFT CONTROL RODS TO LEVER AND BRACKET ASSEMBLY LEVERS AND TIGHTEN NUTS ON SWIVEL AS INDICATED.

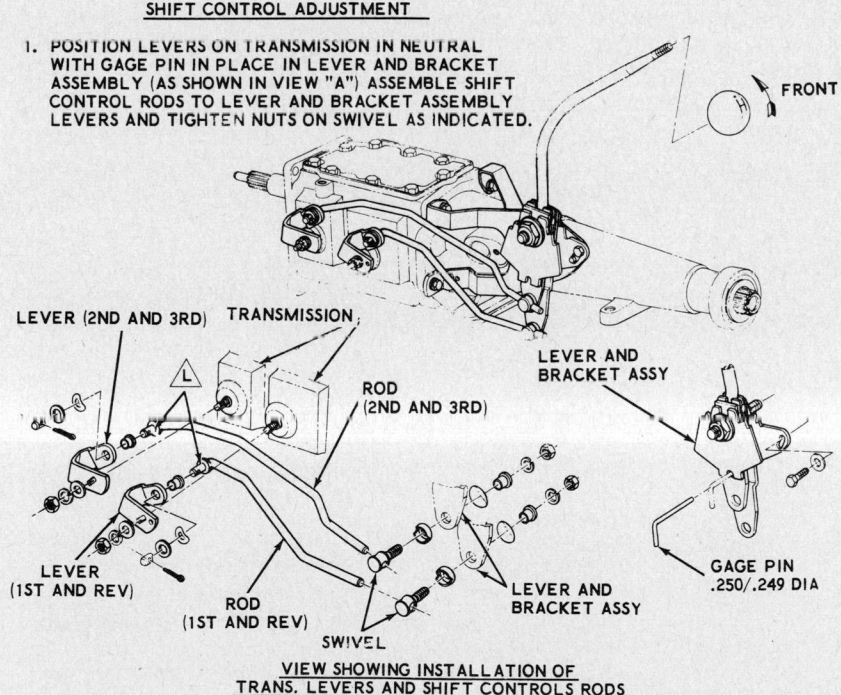

VIEW SHOWING INSTALLATION OF TRANS. LEVERS AND SHIFT CONTROLS RODS

3-speed gearshift linkage—1965-70 (ⓒ Pontiac Div. G.M. Corp.)

5. Torque trunnion jam nuts to 30 (20 for 1971-72) ft. lbs.
6. Remove gauge pin and check complete shift pattern for freeness of operation.

1970-72 Column Shift

Standard shift Pontiacs incorporate a transmission controlled spark switch (TCS) which prevents the distributor vacuum advance from operating when the transmission is in the lower gears.

1. Set gear shift lever in reverse and lock ignition.
2. Loosen swivel clamp screws C at first and reverse lever and D at cross-shaft assembly.
3. Position second and third lever in neutral and first and reverse lever . . . in reverse position.
4. Tighten swivel clamp screw C to 20 ft. lbs., unlock steering column and shift to neutral.
5. Align lower control levers E and F in neutral position and insert 0.185-0.186 in. diameter gauge pin through hole in lower control levers.
6. Tighten swivel clamp screw D to 20 ft. lbs., remove gauge pin and check shift pattern.
7. Shift transmission into high gear and adjust TCS switch so its plunger is fully depressed against second and third lever.

Four-Speed Linkage Adjustment

Borg Warner Four Speed

The four-speed transmission gearshift linkage uses three shift rods and levers. Adjustment can be made with the aid of a simple gauge block, J-9574. An alternative method is to have an assistant hold the manual shifter lever firmly in the neutral position.

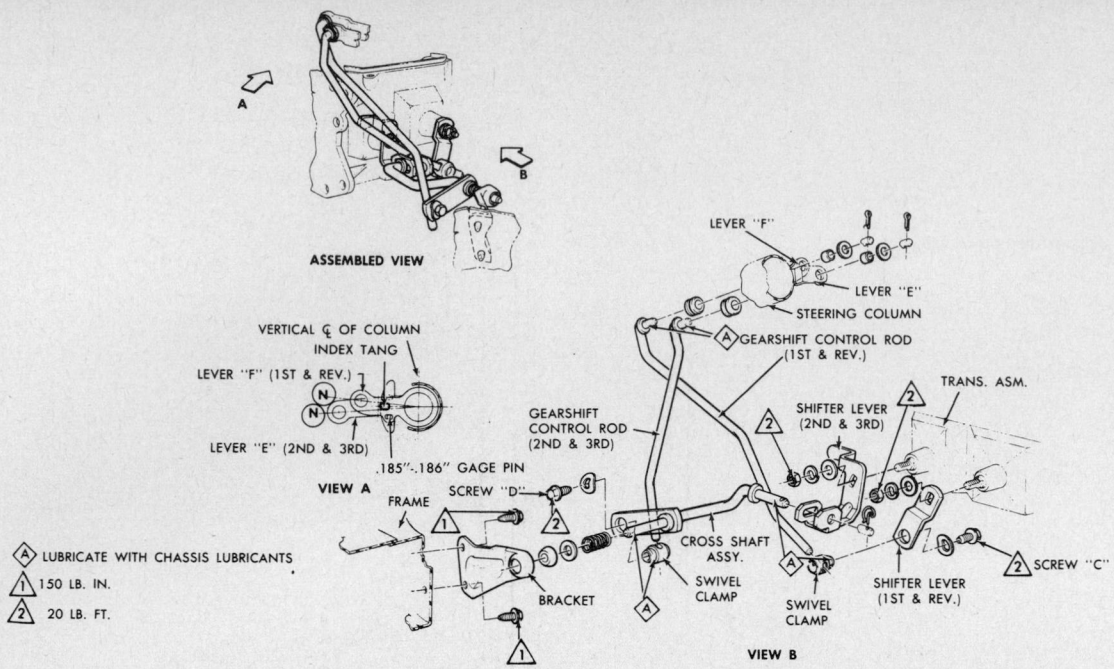

ASSEMBLED VIEW

VERTICAL ₵ OF COLUMN
INDEX TANG
LEVER "F" (1ST & REV.)
LEVER "E" (2ND & 3RD)
.185"-.186" GAGE PIN
VIEW A
FRAME
SCREW "D"

LEVER "F"
LEVER "E"
STEERING COLUMN
GEARSHIFT CONTROL ROD
(1ST & REV.)
GEARSHIFT CONTROL ROD
(2ND & 3RD)
SHIFTER LEVER
(2ND & 3RD)
TRANS. ASM.
CROSS SHAFT ASSY.
SWIVEL CLAMP
SWIVEL CLAMP
SHIFTER LEVER
(1ST & REV.)
SCREW "C"
BRACKET

△A LUBRICATE WITH CHASSIS LUBRICANTS
△1 150 LB. IN.
△2 20 LB. FT.

VIEW B

Standard shift controls—1970 (© Pontiac Div. G.M. Corp.)

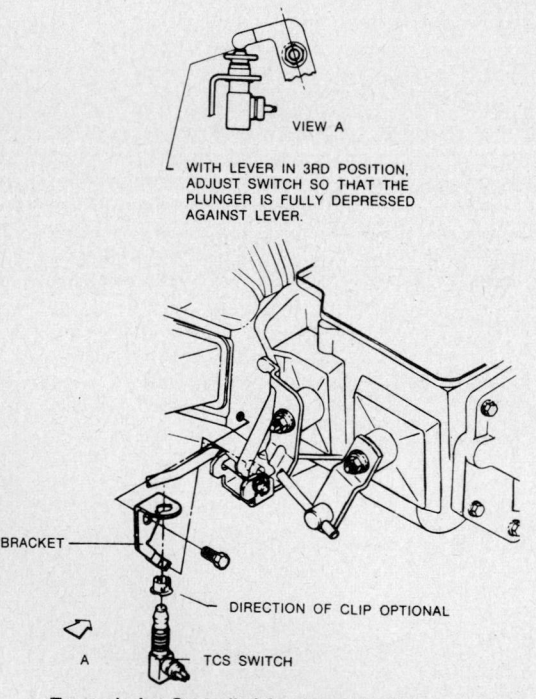

VIEW A

WITH LEVER IN 3RD POSITION,
ADJUST SWITCH SO THAT THE
PLUNGER IS FULLY DEPRESSED
AGAINST LEVER.

BRACKET

DIRECTION OF CLIP OPTIONAL

A

TCS SWITCH

Transmission Controlled Spark switch (TCS)
(© Pontiac Div. G.M. Corp.)

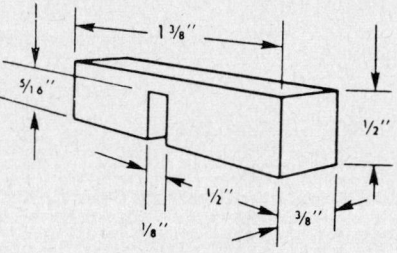

1 3/8"
5/16"
1/2"
1/8"
1/2"
3/8"

4-speed gauge block
(© G.M. Corp.)

1. Remove three screws that hold the chrome ring to the floor pan, then remove ring.
2. Remove three screws that hold the boot and retainer to the floor pan, then slide the boot up the shift rod.
3. Place transmission in neutral and install gauge block (or have assistant hold the manual shift lever in neutral.)
4. Remove the cotter pin, anti-rattle washer, and clevis pin at each of the three shift levers.
5. On each shift rod, adjust the threaded clevis to permit free entry of the clevis pin into the hole in the transmission lever. This adjustment is quite critical.
6. Lubricate shift rod clevis pin and connect clevises to shift levers.
7. Remove gauge block (if used), and check for freedom and ease of shifting. If any one of the shifts is not smooth, one of the clevises may require one-half turn.
8. Position gearshift manual lever boot and chrome ring onto floor pan.

Muncie Four Speed

1. Put selector lever in neutral.
2. Loosen trunnion nuts on transmission gear shift control rods.
3. Put transmission bracket and lever assembly in neutral position and install gauge pin.
4. Put levers on transmission in neutral.
5. Torque trunnion nuts to 30 ft. lbs. (20 ft. lbs.—1971-72).
6. Remove gauge pin and check complete shift pattern.

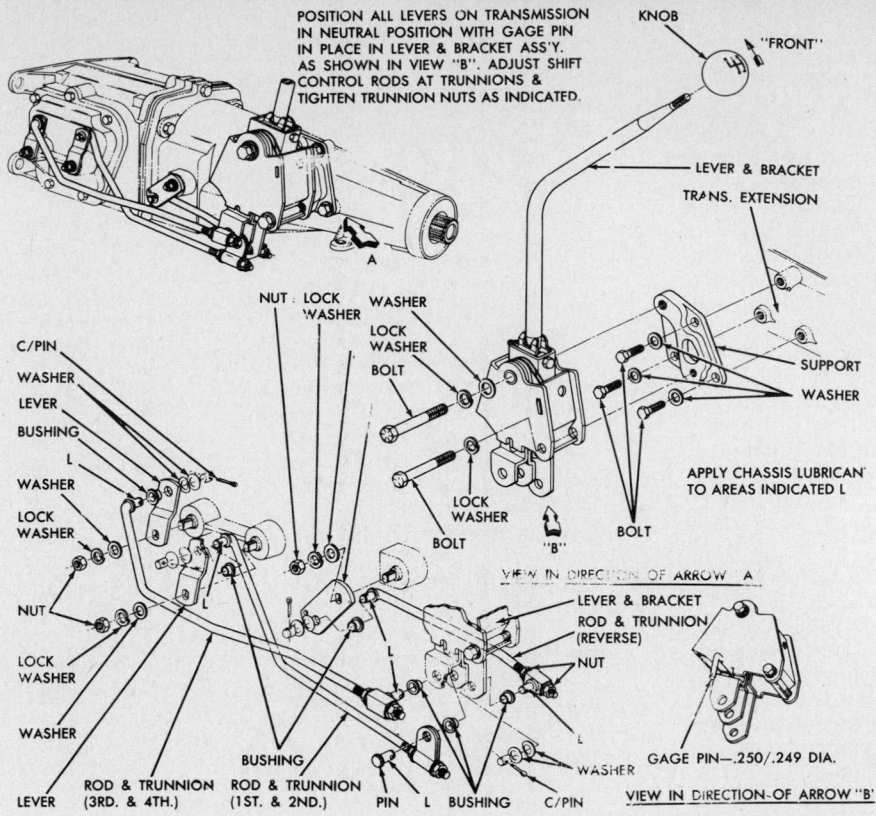

POSITION ALL LEVERS ON TRANSMISSION IN NEUTRAL POSITION WITH GAGE PIN IN PLACE IN LEVER & BRACKET ASS'Y. AS SHOWN IN VIEW "B". ADJUST SHIFT CONTROL RODS AT TRUNNIONS & TIGHTEN TRUNNION NUTS AS INDICATED.

KNOB   "FRONT"

LEVER & BRACKET

TRANS. EXTENSION

NUT LOCK WASHER   WASHER
    LOCK WASHER
    BOLT

C/PIN
WASHER
LEVER
BUSHING
L
WASHER
LOCK WASHER
NUT
LOCK WASHER
WASHER

SUPPORT
WASHER

APPLY CHASSIS LUBRICANT TO AREAS INDICATED L

LOCK WASHER
BOLT

"B"   BOLT

VIEW IN DIRECTION OF ARROW A

LEVER & BRACKET
ROD & TRUNNION (REVERSE)
NUT
L

GAGE PIN—.250/.249 DIA.

VIEW IN DIRECTION OF ARROW "B"

LEVER   ROD & TRUNNION (3RD. & 4TH.)   BUSHING   ROD & TRUNNION (1ST. & 2ND.)   PIN L BUSHING   C/PIN   WASHER

4-speed gearshift linkage—1965 (© Pontiac Div. G.M. Corp.)

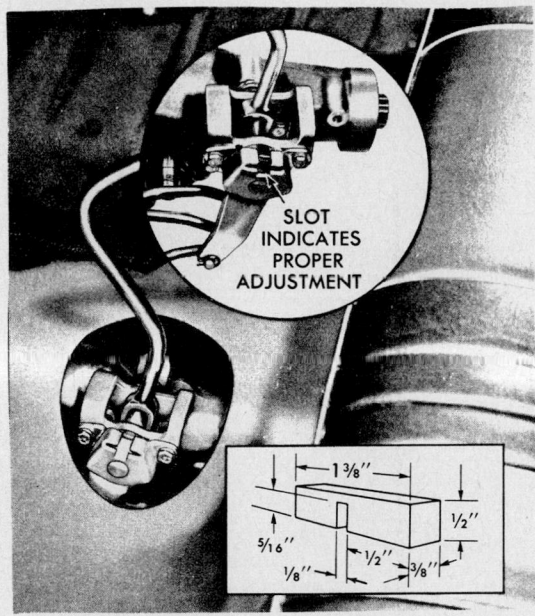

SLOT INDICATES PROPER ADJUSTMENT

1 3/8"
1/2"
5/16"
1/8" 1/2" 3/8"

Borg Warner four speed shift linkage adjustment
(© Pontiac Div. G.M. Corp.)

Automatic Transmission

Full sized Pontiacs use five types of automatic transmission. The Roto-Hydramatic and Super-Hydramatic were used on some 1965 models, and from 1966 to the present two Turbo-Hydramatic transmissions (M-38 and M-40) plus a two-speed automatic (M-35) were used.

Linkage Adjustments

Caution Satisfactory linkage operation can not prevail if binding or excessive wear exists.

Throttle Linkage Adjustment

Roto-Hydramatic and Super-Hydramatic

1. Remove carburetor air cleaner.
2. Loosen locknuts at top of transmission throttle control rod trunnion.
3. With engine at normal operating temperature and selector in drive, adjust idle to 480-500 rpm, (540-560 with air conditioning).
4. Stop the engine and install proper diameter pin through holes in throttle control lever and bracket.

NOTE: four-barrel units have a throttle return check. Before installing the pin on these models, it is advisable to remove the throttle return check to prevent interference with linkage adjustment.

5. With throttle valves fully closed, loosen locknut and adjust length of transmission throttle control rod to carburetor so that the gauge pin is free in the hole. Then, tighten the locknut.

6. Push throttle rod to transmission, (TV rod) downward until the outer throttle lever reaches the end of its travel.

Caution Make sure that, when the lever is in this position, the upper locknut is not interfering with the trunnion.

7. While holding the throttle rod to transmission in this position, tighten upper and lower trunnion locknuts finger-tight. Shorten throttle control rod to transmission by backing off the lower trunnion nut four and one-half turns and tightening upper nut securely. Remove gauge pin.

8. Loosen locknut on carburetor throttle rod. Adjust carburetor throttle rod to obtain 4 29/64 in. from roller end of pedal rod to body toe board or 3¾ in. to carpet.

9. Tighten locknut on carburetor throttle rod.

10. Reinstall the air cleaner.

11. To complete throttle linkage adjustment, road test the car. Modify the adjustment, as required, by shortening or lengthening the throttle control rod to transmis-

sion, (TV rod) one-half turn at a time to obtain the best shift pattern.

1970-72 M-35 Two-Speed (Catalina)

1. Remove air cleaner.
2. Disconnect accelerator linkage at carburetor.
3. Disconnect return spring and T.V. rod return spring.
4. Pull upper T.V. rod forward until through detent. At same time, open throttle at carburetor to W.O.T. position. W.O.T. must be reached at the same time the ball stud contacts end of slot in upper T.V. rod.
5. If necessary, adjust upper swivel. Tolerance is ± 1/32 in.
6. Reconnect return springs and linkage, then install air cleaner.

Selector Lever Linkage Adjustment

Roto-Hydramatic and Super-Hydramatic

1. With upper shift control lever and transmission lever in Park position, and with the trans-

mission outer shift lever trunnion nuts backed clear of the trunnion, pull the shift rod down toward the transmission all the way. While holding the rod in this position, run the trunnion upper nut down to contact the trunnion.

2. Holding the shift rod, shift transmission into Reverse, using shift lever, and observe the position of upper trunnion nut.

3. If the upper nut is short of trunnion, then the transmission will be short of full travel to reverse detent by that same amount. Screw the upper nut down to contact the trunnion and then screw it down two additional turns to assure necessary reserve. Tighten the lower nut.

If the upper nut is contacting the trunnion, count the number of turns the nut can be backed off and still contact the trunnion. If less than two turns, turn nut down two turns against the trunnion from the contact position and lock the lower nut. If more than two turns, turn upper nut down against the trunnion from the contact position to the original

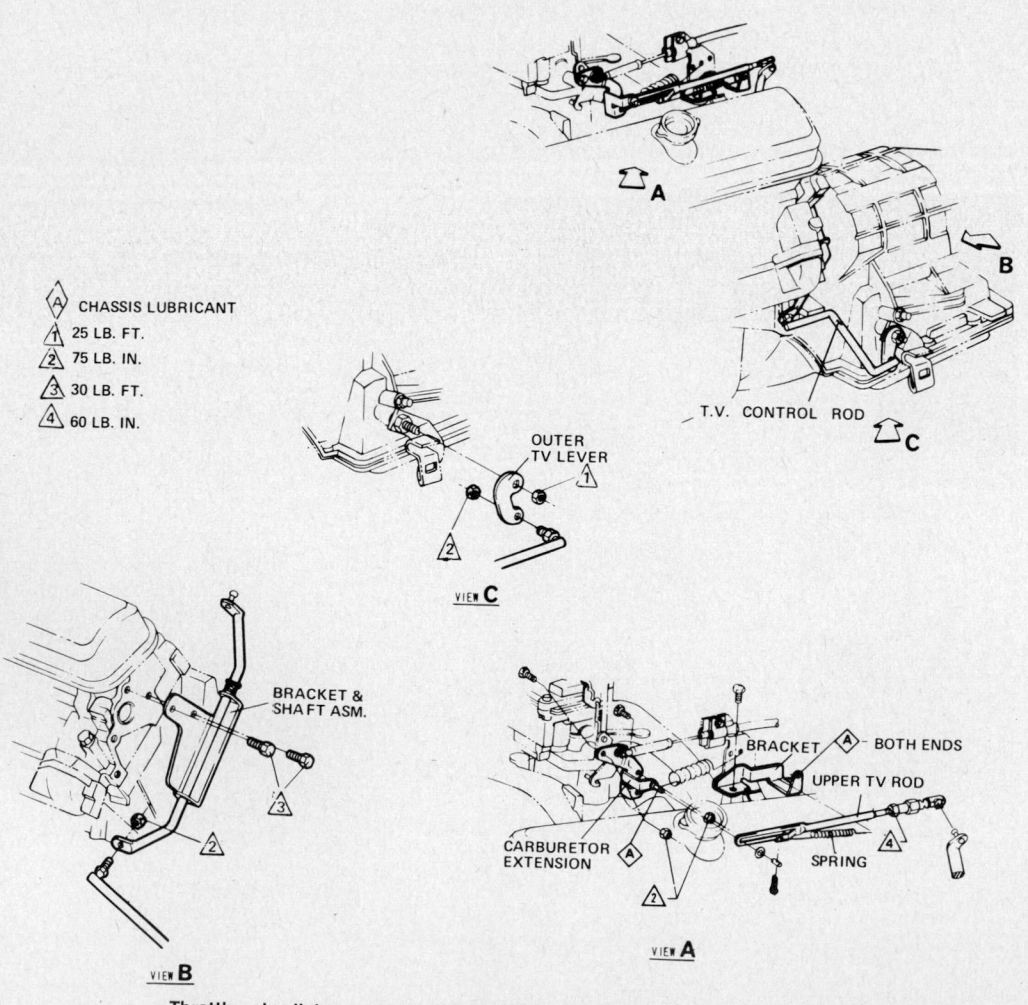

CHASSIS LUBRICANT
△1 25 LB. FT.
△2 75 LB. IN.
△3 30 LB. FT.
△4 60 LB. IN.

OUTER TV LEVER

T.V. CONTROL ROD

VIEW **C**

BRACKET & SHAFT ASM.

BRACKET — BOTH ENDS
UPPER TV ROD
CARBURETOR EXTENSION
SPRING

VIEW **B**

VIEW **A**

Throttle valve linkage adjustment—1970-72 Catalina with M-35 transmission
(ⓒ Pontiac Div. G.M. Corp.)

or starting position and lock the lower nut.

4. After completing above adjustment, check transmission parking lock with car on ramp or grade to insure positive lock.

5. The selector indicator must not be off index register more than 1/16 in. after adjustment is complete.

1967-68 Turbo-Hydramatic

See illustrations.

All Turbo-Hydramatic and M-35 Two-Speed (Catalina) Column— 1969-72

1. Loosen screw on adjusting swivel clamp.

2. Place gearshift lever in Park and lock ignition.

3. Place transmission shift lever in Park detent (rotate clockwise, see illustrations).

4. Push up on gearshift control rod until lash is taken up in steering column lock mechanism, then tighten screw on swivel clamp to 20 ft. lbs.

All Turbo-Hydramatic Console— 1969-72

1. Disconnect shift cable from transmission shift lever by removing nut from pin.

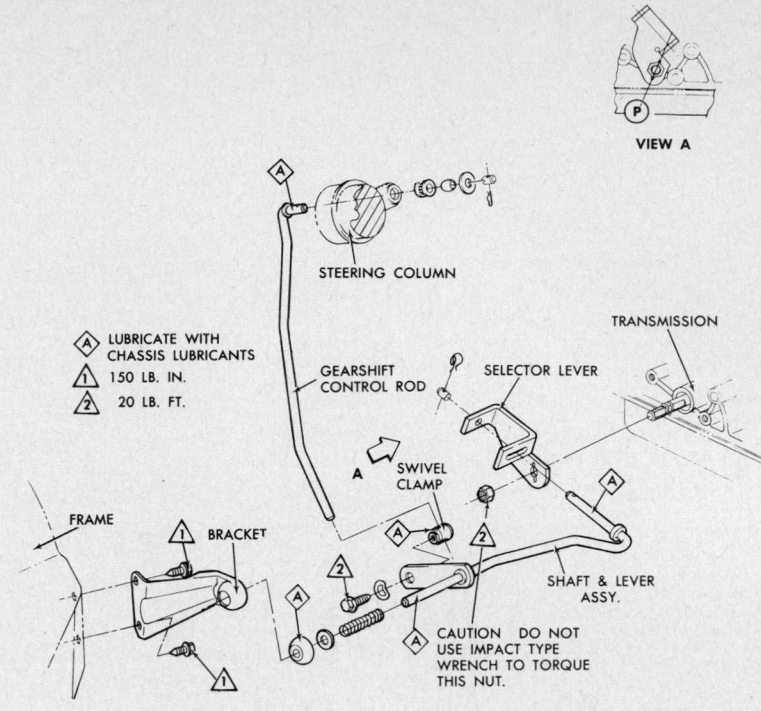

Automatic shift linkage adjustment—1969-70 column shift (© Pontiac Div. G.M. Corp.)

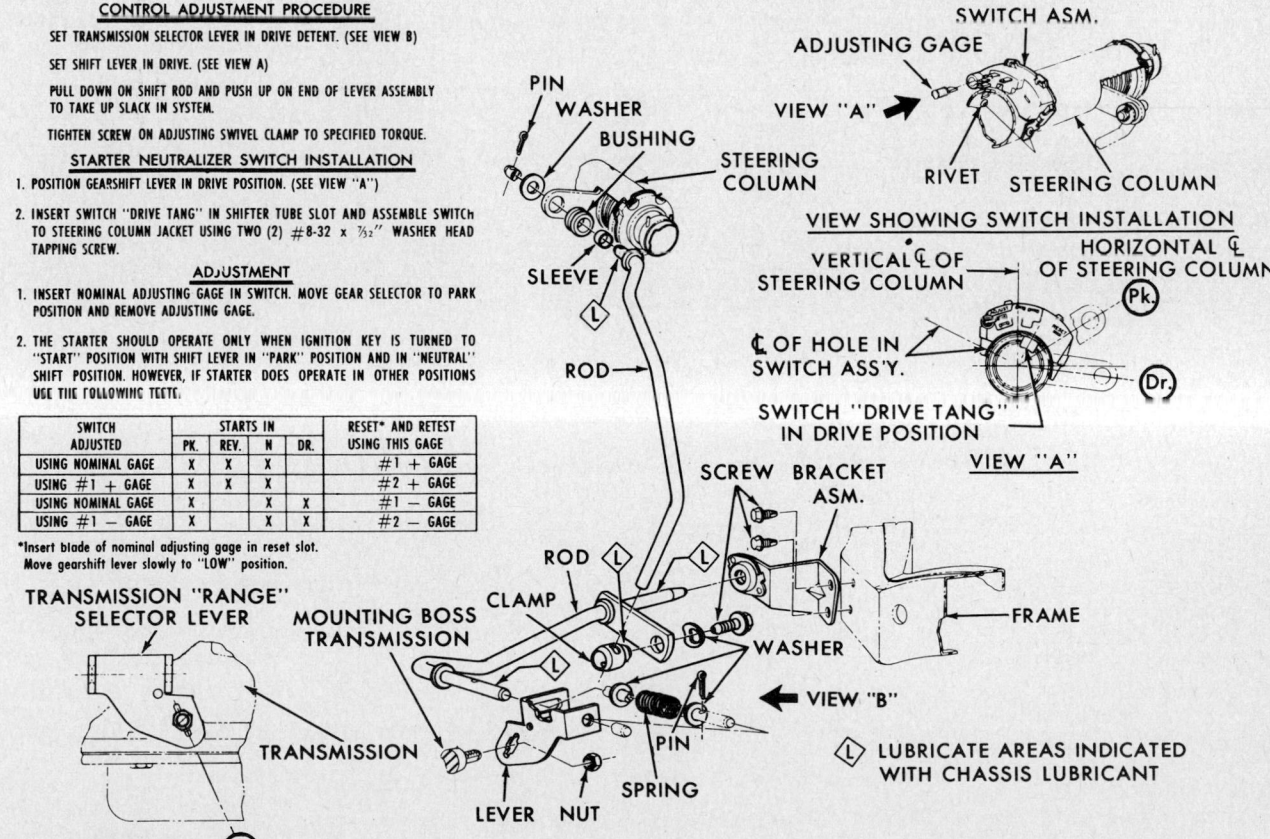

CONTROL ADJUSTMENT PROCEDURE

SET TRANSMISSION SELECTOR LEVER IN DRIVE DETENT. (SEE VIEW B)

SET SHIFT LEVER IN DRIVE. (SEE VIEW A)

PULL DOWN ON SHIFT ROD AND PUSH UP ON END OF LEVER ASSEMBLY TO TAKE UP SLACK IN SYSTEM.

TIGHTEN SCREW ON ADJUSTING SWIVEL CLAMP TO SPECIFIED TORQUE.

STARTER NEUTRALIZER SWITCH INSTALLATION

1. POSITION GEARSHIFT LEVER IN DRIVE POSITION. (SEE VIEW "A")

2. INSERT SWITCH "DRIVE TANG" IN SHIFTER TUBE SLOT AND ASSEMBLE SWITCH TO STEERING COLUMN JACKET USING TWO (2) #8-32 x ⁷⁄₃₂" WASHER HEAD TAPPING SCREW.

ADJUSTMENT

1. INSERT NOMINAL ADJUSTING GAGE IN SWITCH. MOVE GEAR SELECTOR TO PARK POSITION AND REMOVE ADJUSTING GAGE.

2. THE STARTER SHOULD OPERATE ONLY WHEN IGNITION KEY IS TURNED TO "START" POSITION WITH SHIFT LEVER IN "PARK" POSITION AND IN "NEUTRAL" SHIFT POSITION. HOWEVER, IF STARTER DOES OPERATE IN OTHER POSITIONS USE THE FOLLOWING TESTS.

SWITCH ADJUSTED	STARTS IN				RESET* AND RETEST USING THIS GAGE
	PK.	REV.	N	DR.	
USING NOMINAL GAGE	X	X	X		#1 + GAGE
USING #1 + GAGE	X	X	X		#2 + GAGE
USING NOMINAL GAGE			X	X	#1 − GAGE
USING #1 − GAGE	X		X	X	#2 − GAGE

*Insert blade of nominal adjusting gage in reset slot.
Move gearshift lever slowly to "LOW" position.

Automatic shift linkage adjustment—1967-68 column shift (© Pontiac Div. G.M. Corp.)

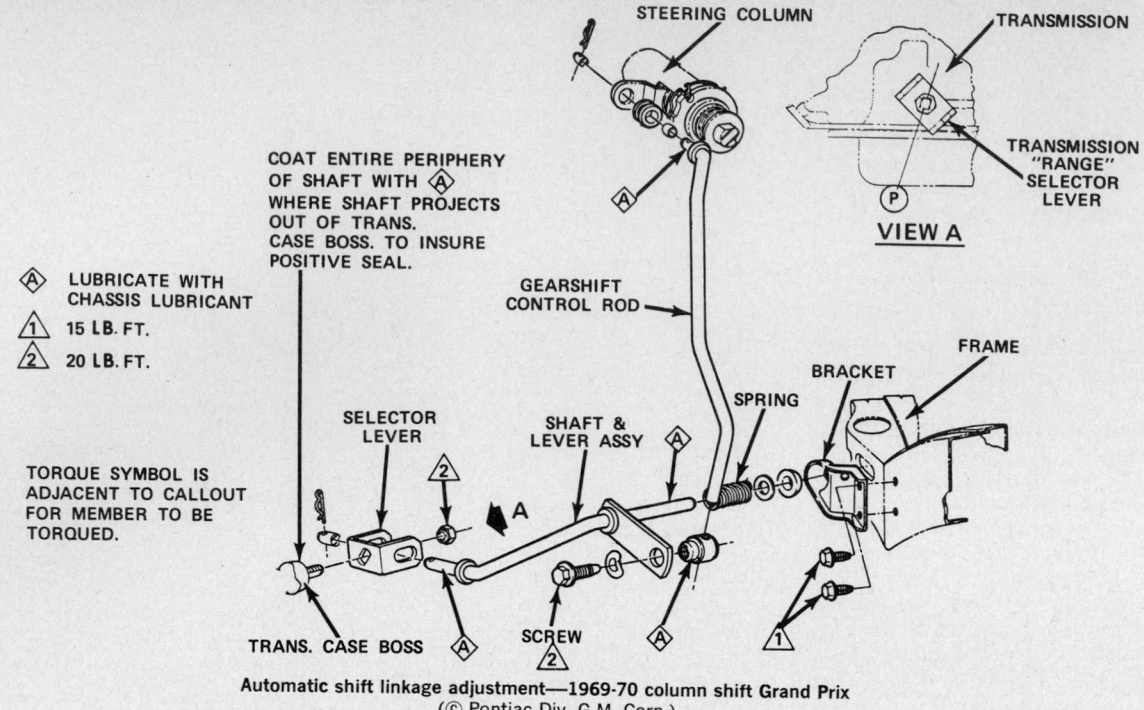

Automatic shift linkage adjustment—1969-70 column shift Grand Prix
(© Pontiac Div. G.M. Corp.)

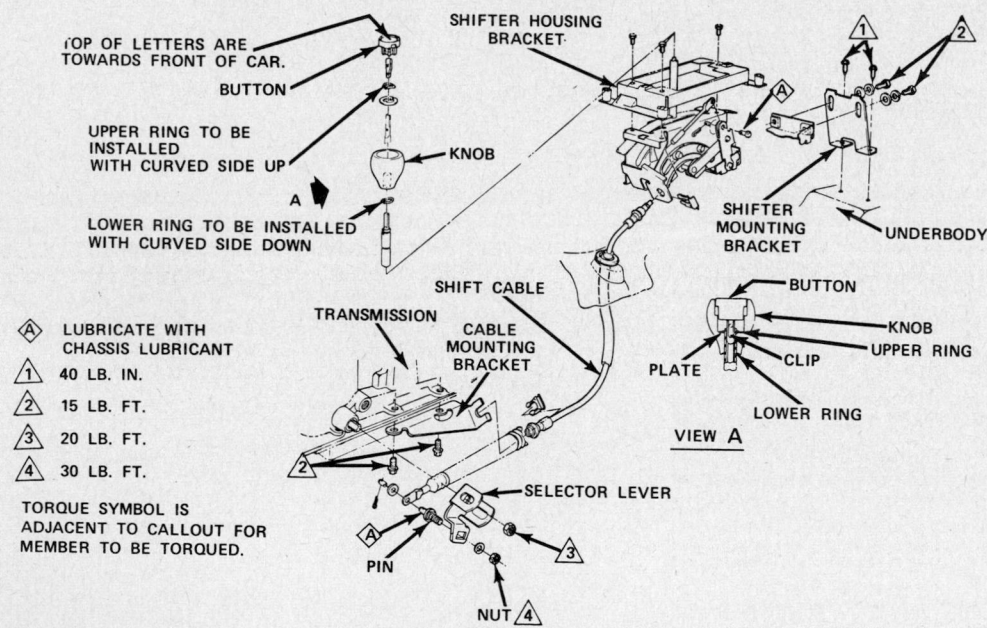

Automatic shift linkage adjustment—1969-70 console shift Grand Prix
(© Pontiac Div. G.M. Corp.)

2. Adjust back drive linkage (as in Step 4, above).
3. Unlock ignition and rotate transmission shift lever counterclockwise two detents.
4. Place console lever in Neutral and move against forward Neutral stop.
5. Assemble shift cable and pin to transmission shift lever so that no binding exists, then tighten nut to 30 ft. lbs. (20 ft. lbs.—1970-72).

Neutral Start Switch Adjustment

1965-66

The neutral start switch on column shift cars is non-adjustable. Adjust console shift neutral start switch by removing the console, loosening two screws, and adjusting it so that car starts only in Park and Neutral.

1967-68

See illustrations.

Transmission Removal

Roto-Hydramatic and Super-Hydramatic

Before raising the car on the lift, remove one cable (either one) from the battery and release the emergency brake.

1. Remove the filler tube and drain the transmission. Push the filler tube up toward its upper bracket out of the way.
2. Disconnect propeller shaft from transmission:

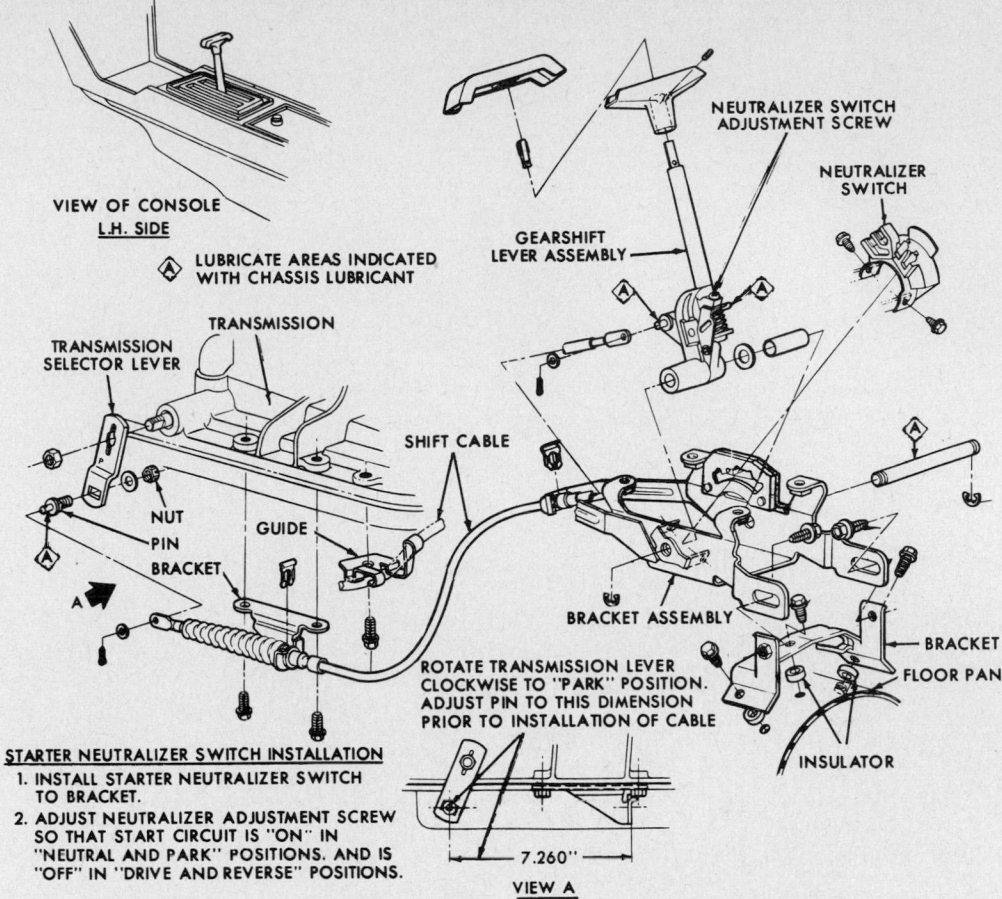

STARTER NEUTRALIZER SWITCH INSTALLATION
1. INSTALL STARTER NEUTRALIZER SWITCH TO BRACKET.
2. ADJUST NEUTRALIZER ADJUSTMENT SCREW SO THAT START CIRCUIT IS "ON" IN "NEUTRAL AND PARK" POSITIONS. AND IS "OFF" IN "DRIVE AND REVERSE" POSITIONS.

Neutral start switch adjustment—1967-68 console shift (© Pontiac Div. G.M. Corp.)

A. Remove U-bolt nuts, lock plates, and U-bolts from rear axle drive pinion flange.

B. Use a suitable rubber band or tape to hold bearings onto U-joint journals if tie-wire is broken.

C. Slide propeller shaft rearwards from transmission output shaft.

3. Disconnect speedometer cable from speedometer-driven gear.

4. Remove gearshift control lower rod.

5. Remove lower end of gearshift control upper rod by removing E-ring.

6. Remove the two cross-shaft bracket-to-frame attaching bolts, then remove the bracket, cross-shaft lever, and bushing from car.

7. Remove lower end of throttle control transmission rod (engine to transmission idler lever.)

8. Remove idler lever to outer throttle lever control rod.

9. Remove throttle control idler lever.

10. Remove parking brake return spring and brake cable guide hook from frame crossmember.

11. Remove oil cooler lines.

12. Loosen exhaust pipe to manifold bolts about ¼ in.

13. Remove both starter cables.

14. Remove the starter and shield by removing the two attaching bolts.

15. Remove bottom cover from bottom of case cover (three attaching bolts).

16. Remove the four bolts which hold the flywheel front cover plate to the transmission case cover.

17. Place special automatic transmission jack under transmission and raise it enough to support the transmission

18. Remove two rear mount support-to-frame crossmember nuts and raise transmission so studs clear the crossmember.

19. Remove the two bolts at each end of the frame crossmember and remove crossmember.

20. Lower the transmission until the jack is barely supporting it.

21. Remove breather pipe clip bolt and remove pipe from transmission.

22. Using a long wrench extension with a U-joint, remove the remaining six transmission case cover-to-engine attaching bolts.

23. Raise transmission to its normal position, slide rearward from the engine and flywheel, and lower it away from the car.

24. Remove rear mount support from rear mount by removing a

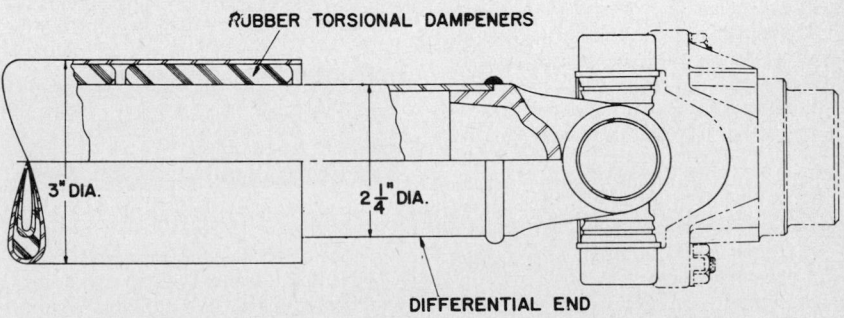

Drive shaft with rubber torsional dampeners (© Pontiac Div. G.M. Corp.)

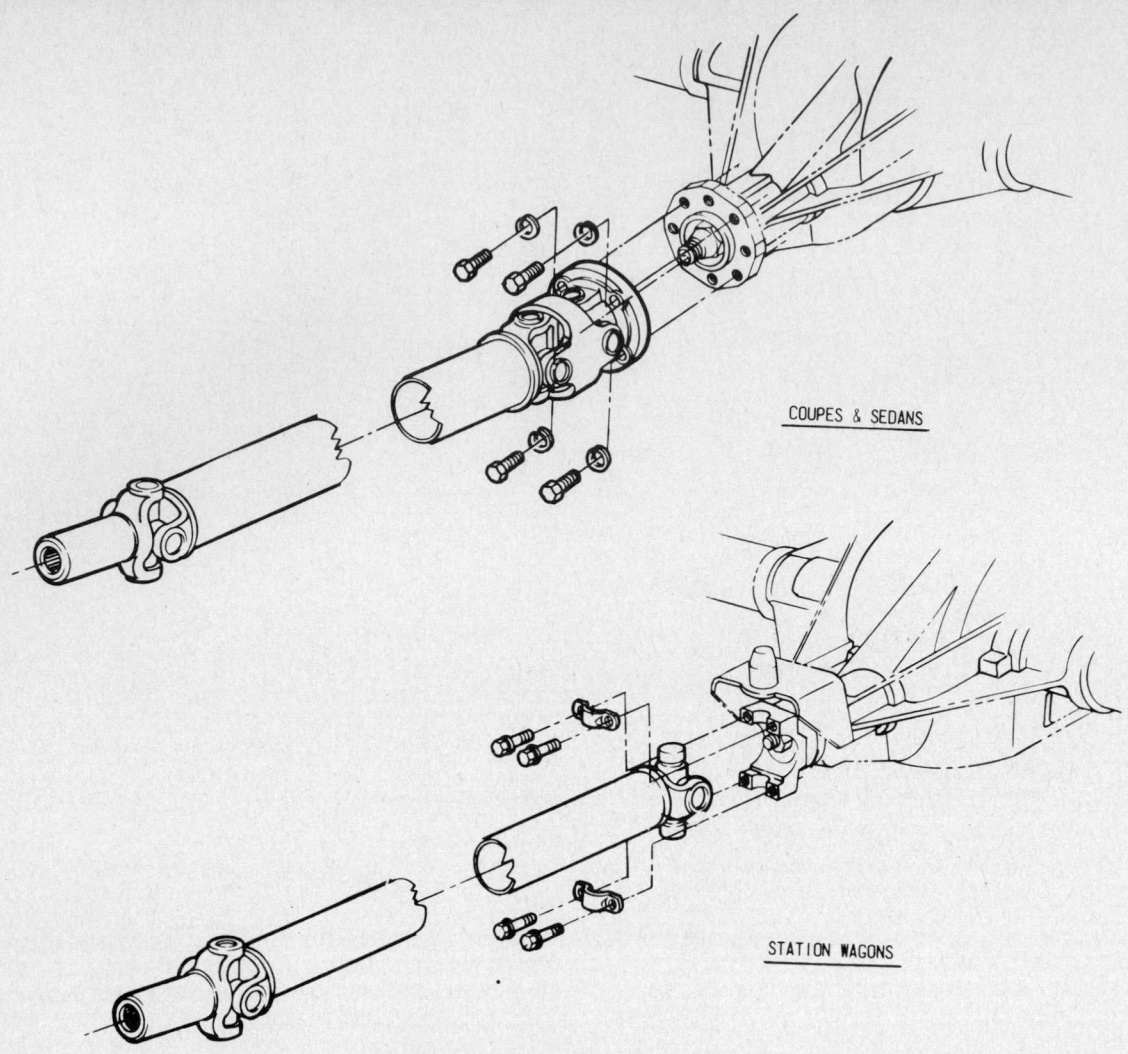

COUPES & SEDANS

STATION WAGONS

1971-72 Pontiac U-joint and driveshaft construction. Grand Prix similar to station wagon. (© Pontiac Div. G.M. Corp.)

nut from each insulator.

25. Remove four rear mount to rear bearing retainer attaching screws.

26. Install by reversing above procedure.

Two-Speed M-35, Turbo-Hydramatic M-38 and M-40

1. Remove driveshaft. Drain oil from M-35.
2. Disconnect speedometer cable, electrical lead to case connector, vacuum line at modulator, and oil cooler pipes (after Step 9 for M-38).
3. Disconnect shift control linkage.
4. Support transmission with jack.
5. Disconnect rear mount from transmission and frame connector.
6. Remove two bolts at each end of frame crossmember and remove crossmember.
7. Remove converter dust shield.
8. Remove converter to flex plate bolts. Disconnect oil filler tube on M-38.

9. Loosen exhaust pipe to manifold bolts approximately ¼ in. and lower transmission until jack is barely supporting it.
10. Remove transmission to engine mounting bolts.
11. Raise transmission to its normal position, slide it rearward from engine, and remove it from car. When lowering tranmission keep rear end lower than front to avoid dropping converter.
12. Reverse procedure to install.

U Joints, Drive Lines

1965-72

Three basic designs are used; one is a typical solid shaft with two joints. One incorporates five rubber torsional dampeners. The accompanying diagram shows the rubber dampeners inserted between the solid and tubular

sections. Starting 1971, a new double-Cardon constant velocity joint is used at the rear on all Pontiac models except the Grand Prix and station wagons.

There are two types of cross-and-bearing U-joints. One type held with a C-shaped lock ring; the other held with a lock plate.

1. From under the car, remove the four bolts which hold the two rear universal joint pillow blocks to the rear axle pinion shaft flange.
2. Tap the pillow blocks until they come off the flange.
3. Lower the rear end of the driveshaft and slide the front end off the splines of the transmission, together with the front universal joint.
4. Take the entire assembly to the bench. If lock-type bearings are used, remove the screws which hold the lock plates over the bearing. If lock ring-types are used, remove the lock rings.

5. Place the back end of the driveshaft in a vise so that the two bearings which remain in the end of the driveshaft are in a horizontal position.

6. With the two bearings in a hori-

Installing snap-ring retainer
(© Pontiac Div. G.M. Corp.)

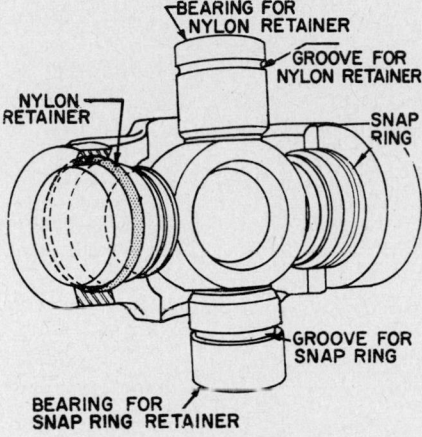

U-joint locking methods
(© Pontiac Div. G.M. Corp.)

zontal position, take a blunt punch and drive the bearing on the right inwards, which will force the bearing on the left out of the yoke.

7. When the left bearing has been taken out, pack a couple of washers under the cross and, driving from the left side, push the cross against the right side bearing, which will drive it out.

8. On reassembling the bearings in the universal joint cross, a press or a very heavy C-clamp should be used to press the bearings into position. They should not be driven into position because this tends to cock the rollers in the pillow blocks, resulting in early failure of the universal joint.

Rear Axles, Suspension

Troubleshooting and Adjustment

A four link pivoted control arm suspension system is used, with the exception of station wagons starting 1971. These models have a leaf-spring

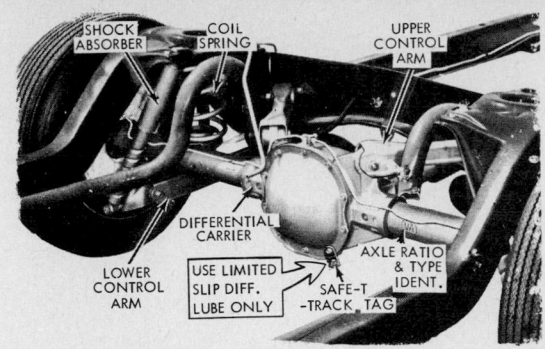

Typical rear suspension—1965-70
(© Pontiac Div. G.M. Corp.)

rear suspension for better side roll stability.

General instructions covering the rear axle, and how to repair and adjust it, together with information on installation of rear axle bearings and grease seals, are given in the Unit Repair Section.

Capacities of the rear axle are given in the Capacities tables of this section.

All 1965 and later rear axles have integral carriers with access plates at the back. It is easier to remove the entire axle from the car to work on these rear ends. 1971 Type C differential can, however, be removed.

Real Axle Removal—1965-72

1. Raise rear of car high enough to permit working underneath. Place floor jack under center of axle housing so it just starts to raise rear axle assembly. Place car stands solidly under frame members on both sides.

2. Disconnect rear universal joint from companion flange by removing two U-bolts. Use rubber band or tape to hold bearings onto journal. Support drive shaft out of the way.

3. Remove wheels, and brake drums. Both right and left wheel studs have right hand threads.

4. Remove nuts holding retaining plates and brake backing plates.

5. Remove axles with suitable puller.

NOTE: before removing axle shafts, remove rear axle carrier cover, and check for C-locks, which retain the axle shafts.

6. Support brake backing plates out of way.

7. Disconnect rear brake hose bracket by removing top cover bolt. Remove brake line from housing by bending back tabs.

8. Loosen remaining cover bolts, break cover loose about 1/8 in. and allow lubricant to drain.

9. Disconnect shock absorbers at axle housing. Lower jack under axle housing until rear springs can be removed. Remove

springs.

10. Disconnect upper and lower control arms from axle housing.

11. Remove housing. Reverse procedure to install.

Rear Leaf Spring Replacement —1971-72 Station Wagon

1. Jack up car at axle housing. Make sure you don't crush exhaust pipe.

2. Support car at both frame side rails, using axle stands.

3. Remove nut and lockwasher from lower shock stud.

4. Move shock out of the way.

5. Remove spring anchor plate nuts, then remove anchor plate and cushion.

6. Jack axle housing up and remove upper cushion.

7. Loosen upper and lower spring shackle nuts.

8. Loosen front spring eye bolt.

9. Remove front eye bolt and carefully lower spring.

10. Support spring and remove lower shackle pin.

11. Remove spring.

12. To install, reverse removal procedure. Tighten front eye bolt to 75 ft. lbs., shackle nuts to 95 ft. lbs., and lower shock nut to 65 ft. lbs.

Rear Coil Spring Replacement

1. Jack up the back of the car and support both sides on stand jacks on the frame, in front of the rear axle. Disconnect shock absorber.

2. Place a jack under the lower trailing arm and remove the bolts which hold the trailing arm to the rear axle housing.

3. Slowly, and very carefully, let the trailing arm come down until the tension is released from the rear coil spring. Then, take off the coil spring.

4. When starting a new coil spring, make certain that the bottom of the coil is properly inserted into the socket in the frame and into the form plate on the trailing arm.

5. Jack the trailing arm into place

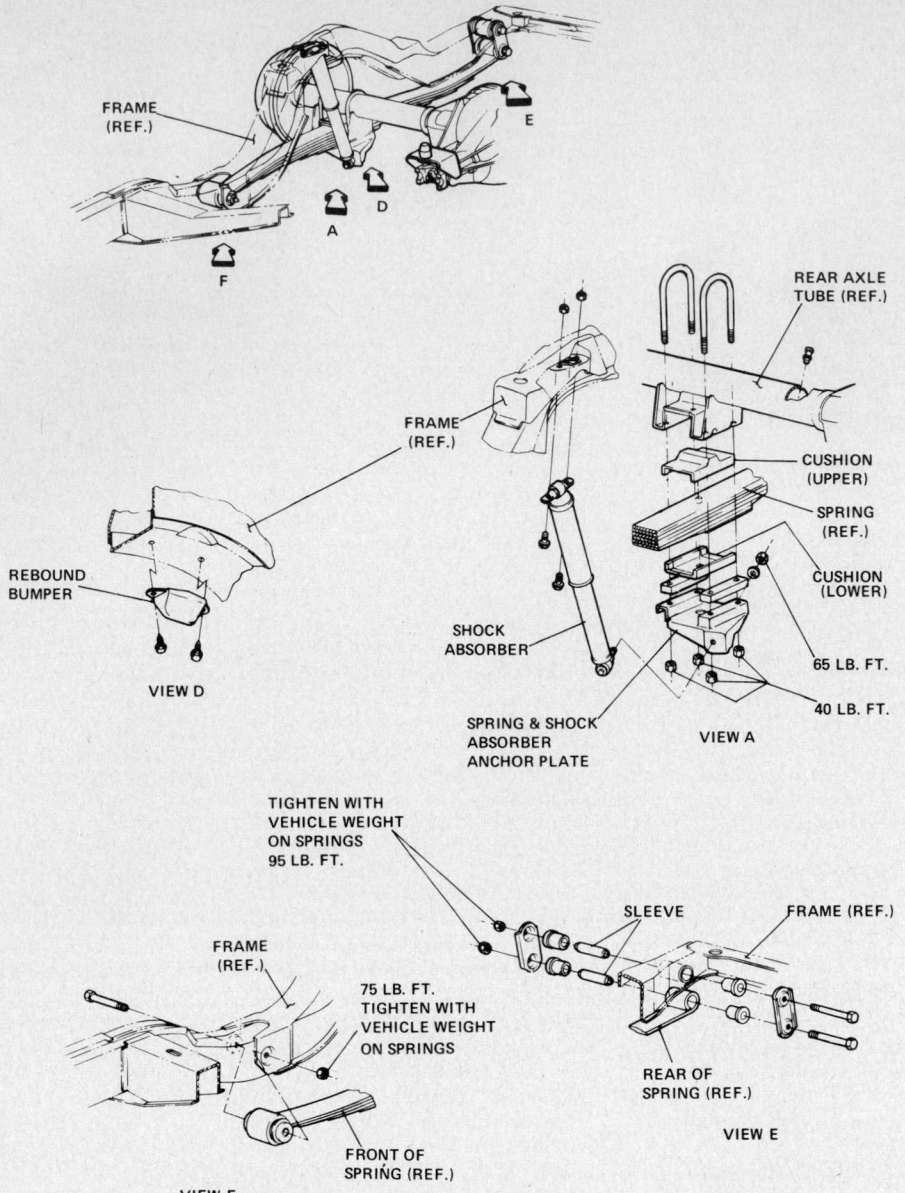

FRAME
(REF.)

E

D

A

F

REAR AXLE
TUBE (REF.)

FRAME
(REF.)

CUSHION
(UPPER)

SPRING
(REF.)

CUSHION
(LOWER)

REBOUND
BUMPER

SHOCK
ABSORBER

65 LB. FT.

40 LB. FT.

VIEW D

SPRING & SHOCK
ABSORBER
ANCHOR PLATE

VIEW A

TIGHTEN WITH
VEHICLE WEIGHT
ON SPRINGS
95 LB. FT.

SLEEVE

FRAME (REF.)

FRAME
(REF.)

75 LB. FT.
TIGHTEN WITH
VEHICLE WEIGHT
ON SPRINGS

REAR OF
SPRING (REF.)

VIEW E

FRONT OF
SPRING (REF.)

VIEW F

1971-72 Pontiac station wagon leaf spring rear suspension
(© Pontiac Div. G.M. Corp.)

and reinstall the trailing arm *rear* bolt.

NOTE: spring can often be removed without disconnecting lower control arm.

Radio

Removal & Installation

1967-68

1. Remove stereo tape player, if so equipped.
2. Remove knobs, springs, nuts, and bezels from control bushings.

3. If car is air conditioned, remove three Phillips cross head screws holding bottom air conditioning air duct and remove duct.
4. Disconnect stereo multiplex plug from radio, if so equipped.
5. Remove antenna lead in and speaker connector.
6. Remove hex head screw holding right side of radio to brace.
7. Disconnect dial light socket and lower radio to floor.
8. Remove multiplex adapter if so equipped.
9. Reverse procedure to install.

1969-70

1. Disconnect battery.
2. Remove lower air conditioning duct if equipped.
3. Remove two radio control knobs

and hex nuts.
4. Remove ash tray and bracket.
5. Remove upper air conditioning duct, if so equipped.
6. Disconnect all radio connections.
7. Remove screws holding radio brace to lower edge of instrument panel and remove radio.
8. Reverse procedure to install.

1971-72 Pontiac

1. Disconnect battery, then remove radio knobs and hex nuts.
2. Remove upper and lower instrument panel trim plates and lower front radio bracket.
3. Remove glove box and disconnect radio connections.
4. Loosen side brace screw and slide radio toward front seat.
5. To install, reverse removal

procedure.

1971-72 Grand Prix

1. Disconnect battery and remove lower A/C duct.
2. Remove control knobs and hex nuts, then remove support bracket bolt.
3. Disconnect electrical leads and remove radio.
4. To install, reverse removal procedure.

Windshield Wipers

Motor R & R

1. Disconnect electrical and hose connections at wiper.
2. Disconnect wiper crank from wiper transmission linkage, through cowl opening.
3. Remove wiper motor mounting screws, then remove the motor from the firewall.
4. Install by reversing removal procedure. Motor must be in park position.

Transmission and Linkage R & R

1. Remove arm and blade assemblies.
2. Remove fresh air intake grille.
3. Remove wiper transmission retaining screws.
4. Loosen retainer holding linkage which connects with wiper motor crank.
5. Remove wiper transmission and linkage.
6. Install by reversing removal procedure. Be sure wiper blades are in park position after they are installed.

Heater System

1965

Heater Blower R & R

1. Drain radiator.
2. Raise front of car, and remove right front wheel.
3. Remove right headlamp assembly.
4. Disconnect right front fender skirt, and move downward and toward rear of car.
5. Disconnect wires at blower.
6. Disconnect vacuum hose at air inlet duct diaphragm.
7. Disconnect heater inlet and outlet water hose at heater.
8. Remove nuts securing air duct and remove assembly.
9. Install in reverse of above.

Heater Core R & R

1. Drain radiator.
2. Remove glove compartment.
3. Disconnect hoses at heater.
4. Disconnect temperature control cable at top of core and air out-

let duct.

5. Disconnect vacuum hose from defroster air valve diaphragm.
6. Remove wire connector from resistor assembly at top left side of heater air outlet duct by prying connector up with flat-bladed screwdriver.
7. Remove nuts attaching heater to air duct and remove heater.
8. Remove core and case assembly.
9. Remove heater core.
10. Install in reverse of above.

1966-67

Heater Blower, Impeller and Inlet Duct R & R

1. Disconnect wires at connector to blower.
2. Disconnect water hoses and plug openings.
3. Disconnect vacuum hose at air inlet duct diaphragm.
4. Remove nuts and screws that hold air inlet and remove assembly.
5. Remove large motor retaining ring from motor.
6. Remove motor and impeller assembly.
7. Install in reverse of above.

Heater Core R & R

1. Drain radiator.
2. Disconnect inlet and outlet hoses at heater.
3. Disconnect temperature control cable at top of heater core and case.
4. Disconnect vacuum hose from defroster and air inlet diaphragms.
5. Remove wire connector from resistor assembly at top of air outlet duct by prying up with flat blade screwdriver.
6. Remove nuts and screws securing heater to air inlet duct assembly.
7. Remove heater core and case assembly.
8. Remove heater core.
9. Install in reverse of above.
10. Adjust temperature control cable.

1968

Heater Blower Motor, Impeller and Duct R&R

1. Remove hood hinge to fender retaining bolts.
2. Prop hood and rest hinge on plenum.
3. Remove blower motor or duct retaining screws as desired.
4. Remove motor electrical lead.
5. Remove motor or duct as desired.
6. Reverse procedure to install.

Heater Core R & R

1. Drain radiator.
2. Disconnect inlet and outlet hoses at heater.
3. Disconnect temperature control cable at top of heater core and case.
4. Disconnect vacuum hose from defroster and air inlet dia-

phragms.

5. Remove wire connector from resistor assembly at top of air outlet duct by prying up with flat blade screwdriver.
6. Remove nuts and screws securing heater to air inlet duct assembly.
7. Remove heater core and case assembly.
8. Remove heater core.
9. Install in reverse of above.
10. Adjust temperature control cable.

1969, Except G.P.

Blower Motor R & R

1. Remove fender skirt.
2. Disconnect power lead.
3. Remove retaining screws.
4. Remove motor.
5. To install, reverse removal procedure.

Heater Core R & R

Same as 1970-72 Pontiac.

1970-72 Except G.P.

Blower Motor and Impeller

1. Jack up front of car and remove right front wheel.
2. Cut access hole along stamped outline on right fender skirt, using an air chisel.
3. Disconnect blower power wire.
4. Remove blower.
5. To install, reverse removal procedure, covering access hole with a metal plate secured with sealer and sheet metal screws.

Heater Core R & R

1. Drain radiator.
2. Disconnect heater hoses at air inlet assembly.

NOTE: the water pump hose goes to right-hand heater core pipe, the other hose (from rear of right cylinder head) goes to the left-hand heater core pipe.

3. Remove nuts from core studs on firewall (under hood).
4. From inside the car, pull the heater assembly from the firewall.
5. Disconnect control cables, vacuum hoses and wires, then remove heater assembly.
6. To remove core, unhook retaining springs.
7. To install, reverse removal procedure, making sure core is properly sealed during installation.

1969-72 Grand Prix

Blower Motor R & R

1. Disconnect power wire.
2. Remove motor retaining screws.
3. Remove motor.
4. To install, reverse removal procedure.

Heater Core R & R

Same as 1970-72 Pontiac.

Rambler, Javelin, AMX, Hornet and Gremlin

Index

YEAR IDENTIFICATION

SERIES 10 AND 20 CLASSIC AND REBEL

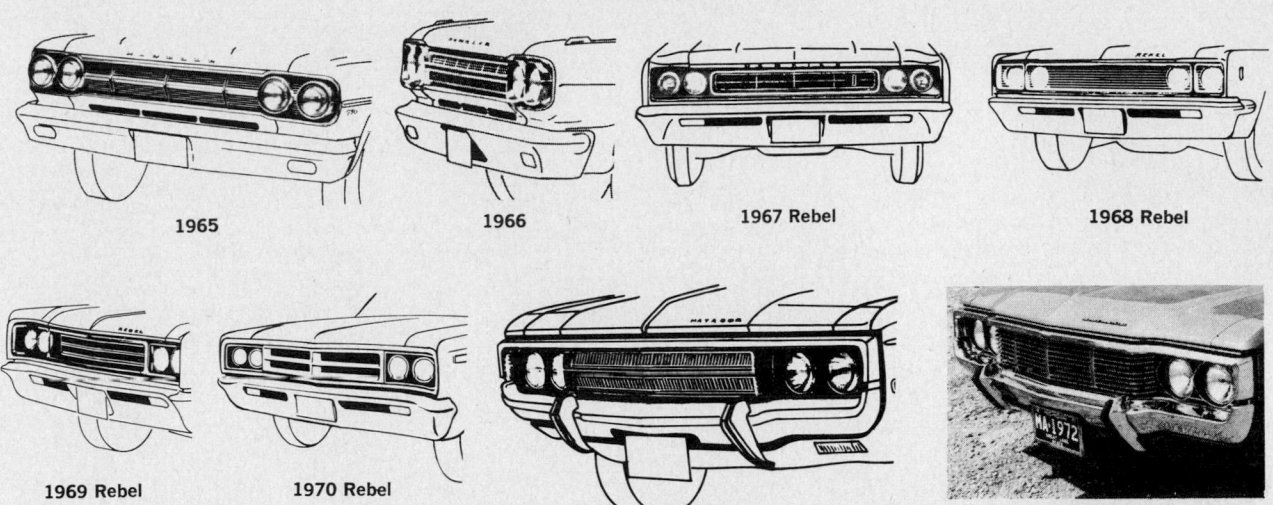

1965   1966   1967 Rebel   1968 Rebel

1969 Rebel   1970 Rebel   1971 Matador   1972 Matador

SERIES 80, AMBASSADOR

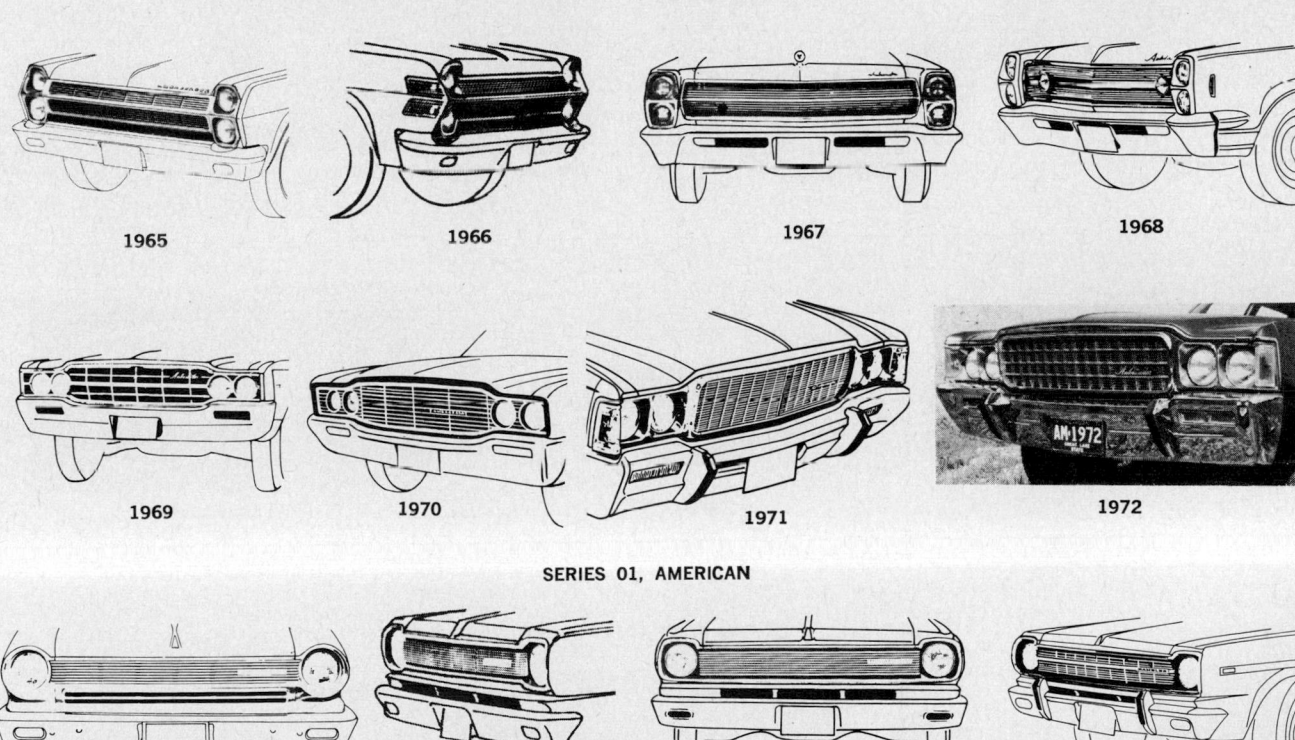

1965   1966   1967   1968

1969   1970   1971   1972

SERIES 01, AMERICAN

1965   1966   1967   1968

1970-72 Hornet   1970 Gremlin   1971-72 Gremlin

YEAR IDENTIFICATION

SERIES 50, MARLIN

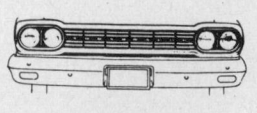

1966

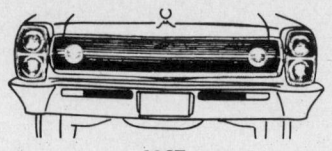

1967

SERIES 70, JAVELIN

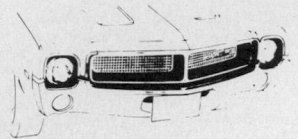

1968

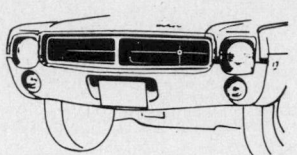

1969

1970

1971 Javelin SST

1972 Javelin SST

SERIES 30, AMX

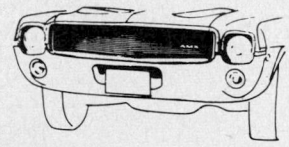

1968-69 AMX

1970 AMX

1972 Javelin AMX

FIRING ORDER

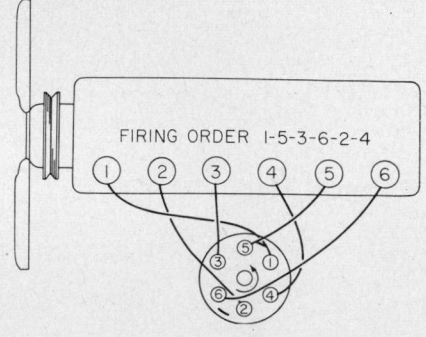

6 cylinder L-head 196

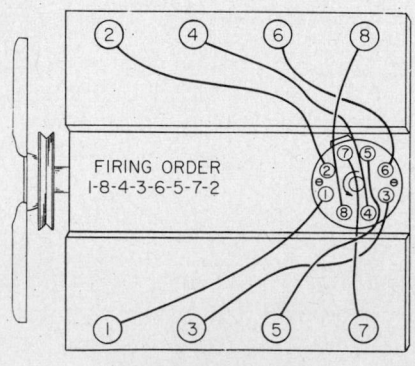

V8 287 and 327—1965-66

FIRING ORDER

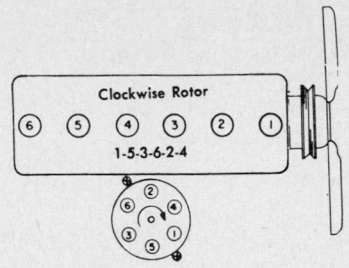

6 cylinder OHV 199, 232 and 258—1965-72

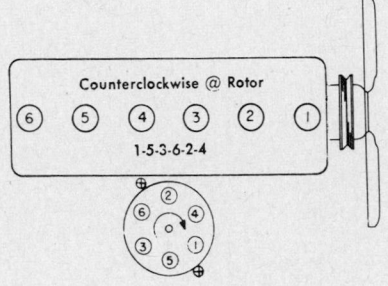

6 cylinder
OHV 196

Ignition timing marks—
199, 232, 258 6 cylinder engines
(© American Motors Corp.)

Timing marks—
all 196 OHV
and L-head
6 cyl.

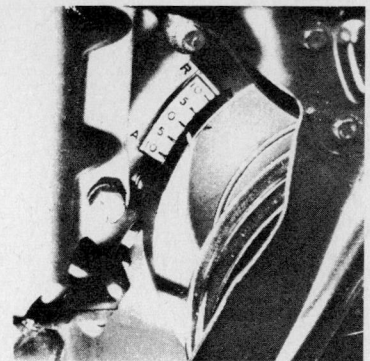

Timing marks— 290, 304,
343, 360, 390, and 401 V8

Timing marks—
287 and 327 V8

809L27

6 cyl. engine code location

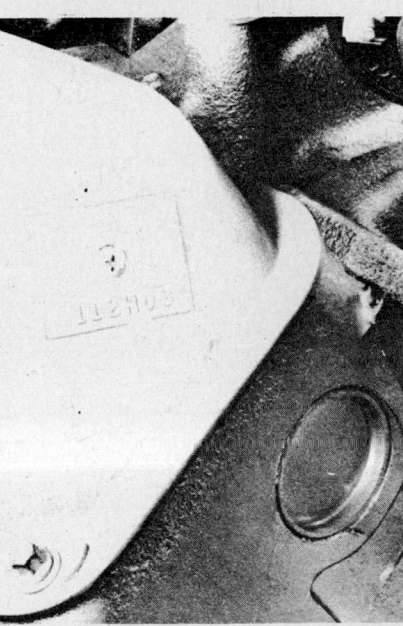

V8 (1967-72) engine code location

CAR SERIAL NUMBER LOCATION

1965-68

The car serial number is found on a plate attached to the right front wheelwell, under the hood.

1969-72

The thirteen digit car serial number is stamped on the left top of the dashboard, visible through the windshield. On 1970-71 vehicles, this number also can be found on a non removable sticker on the front, left-side door pillar.

Engine Identification Code

Six—196—Stamped on machined surface at left front upper corner of cylinder block.

Six—199, 232, 258—Stamped on right upper side of block.

V8—287, 327—Stamped on generator or alternator mounting bracket.

V8—290, 304, 343, 360, 390, 401—Stamped on a tag attached to right-hand front of valve cover. *NOTE: From 1967, all new series V8 engines have their cubic inch displacement cast into block, on both banks, between the first and second core plugs. This is the best way to tell engine displacement, because valve covers are interchangeable between engines.*

VEHICLE IDENTIFICATION

COMPANY
YEAR
TRANSMISSION TYPE
SERIES
BODY TYPE
GROUP
ENGINE TYPE
PLANT
SEQUENTIAL SERIAL NO.

A 9 S 0 5 0 A 1 0 0 0 0 1

Engine Identification Code

No. Cyls	Cu. In. Displ	Type	1965	1966	1967	1968	1969
6	199	American 1 BBL.		A	A		J
6	232	American 2 BBL.		B	B		L
8	290	American 2 BBL.			C		H
8	290	American 4 BBL.			D		N
8	287	Ambassador	E				
6	199	Classic 1 BBL.		E			J
6	232	American 1 BBL.			E		L
6	232	Classic 1 BBL.		F			J
6	232	Rebel 1 BBL.			F		L
6	232	Classic 2 BBL.		G			L
6	232	Rebel 2 BBL.			G		L
8	327	Ambassador	H				
8	287	Classic 2 BBL.		H			
8	290	Rebel 2 BBL.			H		H
6	199	Classic	J				J
8	327	Classic 4 BBL.		J			
8	343	Rebel 2 BBL.			J		S
8	327	Classic 4 BBL.		K			
8	343	Rebel 4 BBL.			K		Z
6	232	Classic	L				L
6	232	Ambassador 2 BBL.		M	M		L
8	287	Ambassador 2 BBL.		N			
8	290	Ambassador 2 BBL.			N		H
6	196	American	P				
8	327	Ambassador 2 BBL.		P			
6	232	Ambassador 2 BBL.			P	L	L
6	199	American	Q			J	J
8	327	Ambassador 4 BBL.		Q			

No. Cyls	Cu. In. Displ	Type	1965	1966	1967	1968	1969	1970	1971
8	343	Ambassador 4 BBL.		Q	Z	Z			
8	343	Ambassador 2 BBL.		R	S	S			
6	232	Ambassador	S			L	L		
6	232	Marlin		S	S				
8	287	Marlin		T					
6	232	Marlin 2 BBL.			T				
8	327	Classic	U						
8	327	Marlin		U					
8	290	Marlin 2 BBL.			U				
6	232	Marlin 1 BBL.		V					
8	343	Marlin 2 BBL.			V				
6	232	American	W			L	L		
8	327	Marlin 2 BBL.		W					
8	343	Marlin 4 BBL.			W	Z			
8	287	Classic	Z						
6	232	Marlin	2						
8	287	Marlin	3						
8	327	Marlin	4						
8	390	4-BBL.					W	X	—
8	360	4-BBL.						P	P
8	360	2-BBL.						N	N
8	304	2-BBL.						H	H
6	232	2-BBL.					L	G	E
6	232	1-BBL.					L	L	—
6	199	1-BBL.					J	E	—
6	258	1-BBL.						A	A
8	390	4-BBL. (Machine)						Y	
8	401	4-BBL.							Z

AC GENERATOR AND REGULATOR SPECIFICATIONS

YEAR	Part No.	ALTERNATOR		Part No.	REGULATOR					
		Field Current Draw @ 12V.	Output @ 15 Volts		Field Relay			Regulator		
					Air Gap (In.)	Point Gap (In.)	Volts to Close	Air Gap (In.)	Point Gap (In.)	Volts at 125°
1965	A-12NAM451	2.0-2.5	33	TUR-12NAM6	(Not adjustable, sealed at factory)					
1966	A-12NAM453	2.0-2.6	35	R2AM1	(Not adjustable, sealed at factory)					
	A-12NAM552	1.8-2.4	40	R2AM1	(Not adjustable, sealed at factory)					
1967-68	ALE6305(6)	2.3-2.4	40	R2AM1	(Not adjustable, sealed at factory)					
	ALK6310	2.4-2.5	35	VSC-62436	(Not adjustable, sealed at factory)					
	A12NAM453	2.0-2.6	35	R2AM1	(Not adjustable, sealed at factory)					
	ALK6309	2.4-2.5	35	VSC-62436	(Not adjustable, sealed at factory)					
	A12NAM552	1.8-2.4	40	R2AM1	(Not adjustable, sealed at factory)					
	A12NAM455	2.0-2.6	35	R2AM1	(Not adjustable, sealed at factory)					
	ALK6311(0)	2.4-2.5	35	VSC-6234L	(Not adjustable, sealed at factory)					
	A12NAM553	1.8-2.4	40	R2AM1	(Not adjustable, sealed at factory)					
1969-70	3195534(5)	2.4-2.5	35*	3195003	(Not adjustable, sealed at factory)					
	A12NAM456(7)	2.0-2.6	35	R2AM4	(Not adjustable, sealed at factory)					
	A12NAM606(2)	1.8-2.4	55	R2AM4	(Not adjustable, sealed at factory)					
1971-72	70D44186C01 (6 Cyl.)①	2.4-2.5	35	8RB2005	(Not adjustable, sealed at factory)					
	70D44187C01 (V8)①	2.0-2.6	35	8RB2005	(Not adjustable, sealed at factory)					
	70D44188C01 (6 Cyl.)② 70D44189C01 (V8)	1.8-2.4	55	8RB2005	(Not adjustable, sealed at factory)					

① . . . C02 for Matador.
② Std. with A/C or rear defogger.
* — At 14.2 volts

GENERAL ENGINE SPECIFICATIONS

YEAR	CU. IN. DISPLACEMENT	CARBURETOR	ADVERTIZED HORSEPOWER @ RPM	ADVERTIZED TORQUE @ RPM (FT. LBS.)	A.M.A. HORSEPOWER	BORE & STROKE (IN.)	ADVERTIZED COMPRESSION RATIO	VALVE LIFTER TYPE	NORMAL OIL PRESSURE (PSI)
1965	195.6 (L-hd.)	1-BBL.	90 @ 3800	160 @ 1600	23.4	3.125 x 4.250	8.0-1	Mech.	50–58
	195.6 (OHV)	1-BBL.	125 @ 4200	180 @ 1600	23.4	3.125 x 4.250	8.7-1	Mech.	50–58
	199	1-BBL.	128 @ 4400	182 @ 1600	33.7	3.750 x 3.000	8.5-1	Hyd.	40–50
	232	1-BBL.	145 @ 4300	215 @ 1600	33.7	3.750 x 3.500	8.5-1	Hyd.	40–50
	232	2-BBL.	155 @ 4400	222 @ 1600	33.7	3.750 x 3.500	8.5-1	Hyd.	40–50
	287	2-BBL.	198 @ 4700	280 @ 2600	45.0	3.750 x 3.250	8.7-1	Hyd.	55–60
	327	2-BBL.	250 @ 4700	340 @ 2600	51.2	4.000 x 3.250	8.7-1	Hyd.	55–60
	327	4-BBL.	270 @ 4700	360 @ 2600	51.2	4.000 x 3.250	9.7-1	Hyd.	55–60
1966	199	1-BBL.	128 @ 4400	182 @ 1600	33.7	3.750 x 3.000	8.5-1	Hyd.	55–60
	232	1-BBL.	145 @ 4300	215 @ 1600	33.7	3.750 x 3.500	8.5-1	Hyd.	55–60
	232	2-BBL.	155 @ 4400	222 @ 1600	33.7	3.750 x 3.500	8.5-1	Hyd.	55–60
	287	2-BBL.	198 @ 4700	280 @ 2600	45.0	3.750 x 3.250	8.7-1	Hyd.	55–60
	327	2-BBL.	250 @ 4700	340 @ 2600	51.2	4.000 x 3.250	9.7-1	Hyd.	55–60
	327	4-BBL.	270 @ 4700	360 @ 2600	51.2	4.000 x 3.250	9.7-1	Hyd.	55–60
1967–69	199	1-BBL.	128 @ 4400	182 @ 1600	33.7	3.750 x 3.000	8.5-1	Hyd.	55–60
	232	1-BBL.	145 @ 4300	215 @ 1600	33.7	3.750 x 3.500	8.5-1	Hyd.	55–60
	232	2-BBL.	155 @ 4400	222 @ 1600	33.7	3.750 x 3.500	8.5-1	Hyd.	55–60
	290	2-BBL.	200 @ 4600	285 @ 2800	45.0	3.750 x 3.280	9.0-1	Hyd.	55–60
	290	4-BBL.	225 @ 4700	300 @ 3200	45.0	3.750 x 3.280	10.0-1	Hyd.	55–60
	343	2-BBL.	235 @ 4400	345 @ 2600	53.3	4.080 x 3.280	9.0-1	Hyd.	55–60
	343	4-BBL.	280 @ 4800	365 @ 3000	53.3	4.080 x 3.280	10.2-1	Hyd.	55–60
	390	4-BBL.	315 @ 4600	425 @ 3200	55.5	4.165 x 3.574	10.2-1	Hyd.	55–60
1970	199	1-BBL.	128 @ 4400	182 @ 1600	33.7	3.750 x 3.000	8.5-1	Hyd.	55–60
	232	1-BBL.	145 @ 4300	215 @ 1600	33.7	3.750 x 3.500	8.5-1	Hyd.	①
	232	2-BBL.	155 @ 4400	222 @ 1600	33.7	3.750 x 3.500	8.5-1	Hyd.	①
	304	2-BBL.	210 @ 4400	305 @ 2800	45.0	3.750 x 3.440	9.0-1	Hyd.	①
	360	2-BBL.	245 @ 4400	365 @ 2400	53.3	4.080 x 3.440	9.0-1	Hyd.	①
	360	4-BBL.	290 @ 4800	395 @ 3200	53.3	4.080 x 3.440	10.0-1	Hyd.	①
	390	4-BBL.	325 @ 5000	420 @ 3200	55.5	4.165 x 3.574	10.0-1	Hyd.	①
	390*	4-BBL.	340 @ 5100	430 @ 3600	55.5	4.165 x 3.574	10.0-1	Hyd.	①
1971	232	1-BBL.	135 @ 4000	210 @ 1600	33.7	3.750 x 3.500	8.0-1 ②	Hyd.	①
	258	1-BBL.	150 @ 3800	240 @ 1800	33.7	3.750 x 3.900	8.0-1 ②	Hyd.	①
	304	2-BBL.	210 @ 4400	300 @ 2600	45.0	3.750 x 3.440	8.4-1 ②	Hyd.	①
	360	2-BBL.	245 @ 4400	365 @ 2600	53.3	4.080 x 3.440	8.5-1 ②	Hyd.	①
	360	4-BBL.	285 @ 4800	390 @ 3200	53.3	4.080 x 3.440	8.5-1 ②	Hyd.	①
	401	4-BBL.	330 @ 5000	430 @ 3400	55.5	4.165 x 3.680	9.5-1 ③	Hyd.	①
1972	232	1-BBL.	100 @ 3600	185 @ 1800	33.7	3.750 x 3.500	8.0-1 ②	Hyd.	①
	258	1-BBL.	110 @ 3500	195 @ 2000	33.7	3.750 x 3.900	8.0-1 ②	Hyd.	①
	304	2-BBL.	150 @ 4200	245 @ 2500	45.0	3.750 x 3.440	8.4-1 ②	Hyd.	①
	360	2-BBL.	175 @ 4000	285 @ 2400	53.3	4.080 x 3.440	8.5-1 ②	Hyd.	①
	360	4-BBL.	195 @ 4400	295 @ 2900	53.3	4.080 x 3.440	8.5-1 ②	Hyd.	①
	360	4-BBL. ④	220 @ 4400	315 @ 3100	53.3	4.080 x 3.440	8.5-1 ②	Hyd.	①
	401	4-BBL. ④	255 @ 4600	345 @ 3300	55.5	4.165 x 3.680		Hyd.	①

*—Rebel Machine.
① —13 psi @ idle; 45–85 psi at 40 mph and above.
② —For unleaded fuel.
③ —Premium fuel.
④ —Dual exhaust.

TUNE-UP SPECIFICATIONS

YEAR	MODEL	SPARK PLUGS		DISTRIBUTOR		IGNITION TIMING (Deg.) ▲	CRANKING COMP. PRESSURE (Psi)	VALVES Tappet (Hot) Clearance (In.)		Intake Opens (Deg.)	FUEL PUMP PRESSURE (Psi)	IDLE SPEED (Rpm) ★
		Type	Gap (In.)	Point Dwell (Deg.)	Point Gap (In.)			Intake	Exhaust			
1965	Ambassador—V8, A.T.	H18Y	.035	30	.020	5B	145	Zero	Zero	12½B	4½	475
	American—L-Hd. 6	H18Y	.035	32	.016	3B	130	.016C	.018C	10B	4½	550
	American—OHV 6, M.T.	H18Y	.035	32	.016	8B	145	.012	.016	12½B	4½	550
	American—OHV 6, A.T.	H18Y	.035	32	.016	10B	145	.012	.016	12½B	4½	500
	Classic (199 Cu. In.)	N14Y	.035	32	.016	5B	145	Zero	Zero	12½B	4½	550
	Classic—OHV 6, Iron Hd.	H18Y	.035	32	.016	5B	145	.012	.016	12½B	4½	550
	Amer. & Classic (232, 1-BBL.)	N14Y	.035	32	.016	5B	145	Zero	Zero	12½B	4½	550
	Amer. & Classic (232, 2-BBL.)	N14Y	.035	32	.016	8B	145	Zero	Zero	12½B	4⅛	550
	Ambassador—V8, M.T.	H18Y	.035	30	.016	TDC	145	Zero	Zero	12½B	4½	550
	Ambassador—V8, A.T.	H18Y	.035	30	.016	5B	145	Zero	Zero	12½B	4½	475
	Classic—V8, M.T.	H18Y	.035	30	.016	TDC	145	Zero	Zero	12½B	4½	550
	Classic—V8, A.T.	H18Y	.035	30	.016	5B	145	Zero	Zero	12½B	4½	475
1966	American—OHV 6	N14Y	.035	32	.016	5B●	145	Zero	Zero	12½B	4½	550
	All—232—OHV 6	N14Y	.035	32	.016	5B●	145	Zero	Zero	12½B	4½	550
	All—287—V8	H14Y	.035	30	.016	5B●	145	Zero	Zero	12½B	4½	550
	All—327—V8	H14Y	.035	30	.016	5B	145	Zero	Zero	12½B	4½	550
1967	All—199—OHV 6 ⑥	N14Y	.035	32①	.016②	10B③	145	Zero	Zero	12½B	4½	525
	All—232—OHV 6 ⑥	N14Y	.035	32①	.016②	5B④	145	Zero	Zero	12½B	4½	600
	290—(200 HP)⑥	N12Y	.035	30	.016	3B	145	Zero	Zero	18½B	5½	600
	290—(225 HP)⑥	N12Y	.035	30	.016	TDC■	145	Zero	Zero	18½B	5½	600
	343—(235 HP)⑥	N12Y	.035	30	.016	TDC■	145	Zero	Zero	18½B	5½	600
	343—(280 HP)⑥	N12Y	.035	30	.016	TDC■	145	Zero	Zero	18½B	5½	600
1968-69	6 Cyl.—199, M.T.	N14Y	.035	32	.016	TDC	145	Zero	Zero	12½B	5	600
	6 Cyl.—199, A.T.	N14Y	.035	32	.016	5B	145	Zero	Zero	12½B	5	525
	6 Cyl.—232 (Rogue) A.T.	N14Y	.035	32	.016	5B	145	Zero	Zero	12½B	5	525
	6 Cyl.—232, A.T.	N14Y	.035	32	.016	TDC	145	Zero	Zero	12½B	5	525
	6 Cyl.—232, M.T.	N14Y	.035	32	.016	TDC	145	Zero	Zero	12½B	5	600
	V8—290, M.T.	N12Y	.035	30	.016	TDC■	145	Zero	Zero	18½B⑤	6	650
	V8—290, A.T.	N12Y	.035	30	.016	TDC■	145	Zero	Zero	18½B⑤	6	550
	V8—343, 390, M.T.	N12Y	.035	30	.016	TDC■	145	Zero	Zero	18½B⑤	6	650
	V8—343, 390, A.T.	N12Y	.035	30	.016	TDC■	145	Zero	Zero	18½B⑤	6	550
1970	6 Cyl.—199, M.T.	N14Y	.033-.037	31-34	.016	3B ± 1	145	Zero	Zero	12½B	4-5½	⑦
	6 Cyl.—199, A.T.	N14Y	.033-.037	31-34	.016	3B ± 1	145	Zero	Zero	12½B	4-5½	⑦
	6 Cyl.—232, A.T.	N14Y	.033-.037	31-34	.016	3B ± 1	145	Zero	Zero	12½B	4-5½	⑦
	6 Cyl.—232, M.T.	N14Y	.033-.037	31-34	.016	3B ± 1	145	Zero	Zero	12½B	4-5½	⑦
	V8—304, M.T.	N12Y	.033-.037	29-31	.016	5B ± 1	145	Zero	Zero	18½B	4-5½	⑧
	V8—360, 2-V.	N12Y	.033-.037	29-31	.016	5B ± 1	145	Zero	Zero	18½B	4-5½	⑧
	V8—360,390, 4-V. ⑨	N12Y	.033-.037	29-31	.016	5B ± 1■	145	Zero	Zero	18½B⑤	4-5½	⑧
	V8—390, 4-V ⑩	N12Y	.033-.037	29-31	.016	TDC ± 1■	145	Zero	Zero	18½B⑤	4-5½	⑧
	V8—390⑥	N10Y	.033-.037	29-31	.016	TDC ± 1■	145	Zero	Zero	46B	4-5½	600
1971-72	6 Cyl.—232, M.T.	N14Y	.033-.037	31-34	.016	3B	145	Zero	Zero	12½B	4-5½	700
	6 Cyl.—232, A.T.	N14Y	.033-.037	31-34	.016	5B	145	Zero	Zero	12½B	4-5½	600
	6 Cyl.—258, M.T., A.T.	N14Y	.033-.037	31-34	.016	5B	145	Zero	Zero	12½B	4-5½	700⑪
	V8—304, 360, 401, M.T.	N12Y	.033-.037	29-31	.016	2½B	145	Zero	Zero	⑫	4-5½	750
	V8—304, 360, 401, A.T.	N12Y	.033-.037	29-31	.016	2½B	145	Zero	Zero	⑫	4-5½	650

VALVE SPECIFICATIONS

YEAR AND MODEL		SEAT ANGLE (DEG.)	FACE ANGLE (DEG.)	VALVE LIFT INTAKE (IN.)	VALVE LIFT EXHAUST (IN.)	VALVE SPRING PRESSURE (VALVE OPEN) LBS. @ IN.	VALVE SPRING INSTALLED HEIGHT (IN.)	STEM TO GUIDE CLEARANCE (IN.)		STEM DIAMETER (IN.)	
								Intake	Exhaust	Intake	Exhaust
1965-66	6 Cyl.—L-hd 195.6* Cu. In.	45	44	.324	.322	79 @ $1^7/_{16}$	$1^3/_4$	.0025-.004	.0025-.004	.3407-.3412	.3407-.3412
	6 Cyl.—OHV 199 Cu. In.	①	②	.375	.375	155 @ $1^7/_{16}$	$1^{13}/_{16}$	.001-.003	.001-.003	.3715-.3725	.3715-.3725
	6 Cyl.—OHV 232 Cu. In.	①	②	.375	.375	155 @ $1^7/_{16}$	$1^{13}/_{16}$	.001-.003	.001-.003	.3715-.3725	.3715-.3725
	V8—287 Cu. In.	①	②	.375	.375	155 @ $1^7/_{16}$	$1^{13}/_{16}$	.001-.003	.001-.003	.3718-.3725	.3718-.3725
	V8—327 Cu. In.	①	②	.375	.375	155 @ $1^7/_{16}$	$1^{13}/_{16}$	.001-.003	.001-.003	.3718-.3725	.3718-.3725
1967-68	6 Cyl.—OHV 199 Cu. In.	①	②	.254†	.254†	195 @ $1^7/_{16}$	$1^{13}/_{16}$	.001-.003	.001-.003	.3715-.3725	.3715-.3725
	6 Cyl.—OHV 232 Cu. In.	①	②	.254†	.254†	195 @ $1^7/_{16}$	$1^{13}/_{16}$	.001-.003	.001-.003	.3715-.3725	.3715-.3725
	V8—290 Cu. In.	①	②	.265†	.265†	194 @ $1^{13}/_{32}$	$1^{13}/_{16}$	.001-.003	.001-.003	.3715-.3725	.3715-.3725
	V8—343 Cu. In.	①	②	.265†	.265†	194 @ $1^{13}/_{32}$	$1^{13}/_{16}$	.001-.003	.001-.003	.3715-.3725	.3715-.3725
	V8—390 Cu. In.	①	②	.265†	.265†	250 @ $1^{21}/_{64}$	$1^{13}/_{16}$	.001-.003	.001-.003	.3715-.3725	.3715-.3725
1969	6 Cyl.—OHV (199)	③	②	.254†	.254†	195 @ $1^7/_{16}$	$1^{13}/_{16}$	.001-.003	.001-.003	.3715-.3725	.3715-.3725
	6 Cyl.—OHV (232)	③	②	.254†	.254†	195 @ $1^7/_{16}$	$1^{13}/_{16}$	.001-.003	.001-.003	.3715-.3725	.3715-.3725
	V8—290 Cu. In.	①	④	.265†	.265†	200 @ $1^{25}/_{64}$	$1^{13}/_{16}$	.001-.003	.001-.003	.3715-.3725	.3715-.3725
	V8—343 Cu. In.	①	④	.265†	.265†	200 @ $1^{25}/_{64}$	$1^{13}/_{16}$	.001-.003	.001-.003	.3715-.3725	.3715-.3725
	V8—390 Cu. In.	①	④	.265†	.265†	200 @ $1^{25}/_{64}$	$1^{13}/_{16}$	.001-.003	.001-.003	.3715-.3725	.3715-.3725
1970	6 Cyl.—199, 232 Cu. In.	①	②	.254†	.254†	195 @ $1^7/_{16}$	$1^{13}/_{16}$	.001-.003	.001-.003	.3715-.3725	.3715-.3725
	V8—304, 360 Cu. In.	①	④	.265†	.265†	195 @ $1^7/_{16}$	$1^{13}/_{16}$	.001-.003	.001-.003	.3715-.3725	.3715-.3725
	V8—390 Cu. In.	①	④	.265†	.265†	200 @ $1^{25}/_{64}$	$1^{13}/_{16}$	.001-.003	.001-.003	.3715-.3725	.3715-.3725
	V8—390 Cu. In.⑤	①	④	.287†	.287†	189 @ $1^{23}/_{64}$	$1^{13}/_{16}$	.001-.003	.001-.003	.3715-.3725	.3715-.3725
1971-72	6 Cyl.—232 Cu. In.	①	②	.381	.381	195 @ .437	$1^{13}/_{16}$	.001-.003	.001-.0027	.3715-.3725	.3718-.3725
	6 Cyl.—258 Cu. In.	①	②	.381	.381	195 @ .365	$1^{13}/_{16}$	.001-.003	.001-.0027	.3715-.3725	.3718-.3725
	V8—304, 360 Cu. In.⑥	①	②	.425	.425	195 @ .365	$1^{13}/_{16}$	.001-.003	.001-.003	.3715-.3725	.3715-.3725
	V8—401 Cu. In.⑥	①	②	.457	.457	189 @ .365	$1^{13}/_{16}$	.001-.003	.001-.003	.3715-.3725	.3715-.3725

*—Not used in 1966.
①—Intake 30°, Exhaust 45°.
②—Intake 29°, Exhaust 44°.
③—Intake 30°, Exhaust 44°.
④—Intake 29°, Exhaust $44^1/_2$°.
⑤—Rebel Machine.

⑥—Dealer hi-perf cam = .477 lift, 302° duration, int. opens 46° BTDC, spring pressure with valve open is 240-260 @ 1.329.
†—Cam lobe lift x rocker arm ratio = valve lift.
   Rocker arm ratio — 1.5 6 cyl., 1.6 all V8.

CAUTION

General adoption of anti-pollution laws has changed the design of almost all car engine production to effectively reduce crankcase emission and terminal exhaust products. It has been necessary to adopt stricter tune-up rules, especially timing and idle speed procedures. Both of these values are peculiar to the engine and to its application, rather than to the engine alone. With this in mind, car manufacturers supply idle speed data for the engine and application involved. This information is clearly displayed in the engine compartment of each vehicle.

▲—With vacuum advance disconnected. Add 50 rpm when equipped with air conditioning. NOTE: These settings are only approximate. Engine design, altitude, temperature, fuel octane rating and the condition of the individual engine are all factors which can influence timing. The limiting advance factor must, therefore, be the "knock point" of the individual engine.
★—With manual transmission in N and automatic in D.
●—With premium fuel 10B.
■—Regular fuel not recommended.
B—Before top dead center.
M.T.—Manual transmission.
A.T.—Automatic transmission.
⊚—Cars with exhaust emission control = timing, TDC.
①—Prestolite = 39°.
②—Prestolite = .019 in.

③—w/Air Guard—3 B.
④—Premium fuel = 8B.
⑤—w/H.L. Cam 46° B.
⑥—Rebel Machine.
⑦—For six cylinder engines—600 rpm M.T.; 550 rpm A.T. with air cond. off, parking brake applied, and A.T. in D1.
⑧—For V8 engines—650 rpm M.T.; 600 rpm A.T. with air cond. off, parking brake applied, and A.T. in D1.
⑨—Prior to 390 engine 209x26 (Type 1 distributor).
⑩—After 390 engine 209x26 (Type 2 distributor).
⑪—600 A.T., in Drive.
⑫—$14^3/_4$° BTDC for 304 and 360; $25^1/_2$° BTDC for 401 (Dealer hi-perf- cam opens 46° BTDC).
**—See engine decal.

GENERAL CHASSIS AND BRAKE SPECIFICATIONS

YEAR	MODEL	CHASSIS		BRAKE CYLINDER BORE			BRAKE DRUM	
		Overall Length (In.)	Tire Size	Master Cylinder (In.)	Wheel Cylinder Diameter (In.)		Diameter (In.)	
					Front	Rear	Front	Rear
1965	American (Series 01)	177.25	6.45 x 14	1.0	1 1/8	15/16	9	9
	Classic, 6 Cyl. (Series 10)	195.0	6.95 x 14	1.0	1 1/8★	15/16●	9	9
	Classic, V8 (Series 10)	195.0	7.75 x 14	1.0	1 1/8★	7/8†	10	10
	Ambassador, 6 Cyl. (Series 80)	200.0	7.35 x 14	1.0	1 3/16★	15/16●	9	9
	Ambassador, V8 (Series 80)	200.0	7.75 x 14	1.0	1 3/16★	15/16●	10	10
1966	American (Series 01)	181.0	6.45 x 14	1.0	1 1/8★	15/16	9	9
	Marlin (Series 50)	195.0	7.35 x 14▲	1.0	1 1/8★	15/16●	10	10
	Classic, 6 Cyl. (Series 10)	195.0	6.95 x 14	1.0	1 1/8★	15/16●	9	9
	Classic, 8 Cyl. (Series 10)	195.0	7.75 x 14	1.0	1 3/16★	15/16●	10	10
	Ambassador, 6 Cyl. (Series 80)	200.0	7.35 x 14	1.0	1 3/16★	15/16●	9	9
	Ambassador, 8 Cyl. (Series 80)	200.0	7.75 x 14	1.0	1 3/16★	15/16●	10	10
	Ambassador, Sta. Wag. (Series 80)	199.0	7.75 x 14	1.0	1 1/8	15/16●	10	10
1967–69	American, Rambler (Series 01)	181.0	6.45 x 14■	1.0	1 1/8 (2)(3)	15/16 (4)	9 (1)(7)	9 (1)
	American (Wagon) (Series 01)	181.0	6.95 x 14★★	1.0	1 1/8 (2)(3)	15/16 (4)	9 (1)(7)	9 (1)
	Rebel (Series 10)	197.0	7.35 x 14☆	1.0	1 1/8 (2)(3)	15/16 (3)	9 (1)(7)	9 (1)
	Rebel (Wagon) (Series 10)	198.0	7.75 x 14☆☆	1.0	1 3/32 (2)(3)	15/16 (3)	10 (7)	10
	Marlin, 6 Cyl. (Series 50)	201.5	7.35 x 14☆	1.0	1 1/8 (3)	15/16 (3)	10 (7)	10
	Marlin, V8 (Series 50)	201.5	7.75 x 14☆☆	1.0	1 3/16 (3)	15/16 (3)	10 (7)	10
	Ambassador (Series 80)	202.5 (9)	7.35 x 14☆	1.0	1 1/8 (2)(3)	15/16 (6)	10 (7)	10
	Ambassador (Wagon) (Series 80)	203.0 (10)	8.25 x 14	1.0	1 3/16 (2)(3)	15/16	10 (7)	10
	Javelin (Series 70)	189.2	6.95 x 14 (8)	1.0	1 3/16 (3)	15/16 (5)	10 (7)	10
	AMX (Series 30)	177.2	7.35 x 14 (14)	1.0	2.0	7/8	(7)	10
1970	Hornet (Series 01)	179.3	B78 x 14 (11)	1.0	1 1/8 (2)(3)	15/16 (4)	9 (1)(7)	9 (1)
	Gremlin (Series 40)	161.3	6.00 x 13 (18)	1.0	1 1/8	7/8	9 (1)(7)	9
	Rebel (Series 10)	199.0	E78 x 14 (12)	1.0	1 1/8 (2)(3)	15/16 (3)	10 (7)	10 (10)
	Rebel (Wagon) (Series 10)	198.0	G78 x 14 (13)	1.0	1 3/32 (2)(3)	15/16 (3)	10 (7)	10
	Ambassador (Series 80)	208.0	F78 x 14 (16)	1.0	1 1/8 (2)(3)	15/16 (4)	10 (7)	10
	Ambassador (Wagon) (Series 80)	207.0	H78 x 14 (17)	1.0	1 3/16 (3)	15/16	10 (7)	10
	Javelin (Series 70)	191.0	C78 x 14 (15)	1.0	1 3/16 (3)	15/16 (5)	10 (7)	10
	AMX (Series 30)	179.0	E78 x 14 (14)	1.0	2.0	7/8	(7)	10
1971–72	Hornet 2-dr. sedan (Series 01)	179.3	6.45 x 14 (21)	1.0 (22)	1.13 (23)	.88 (26)	9-6 Cyl. 10-V8 (19)	9-6 Cyl. 10-V8
	Hornet 4-dr. sedan (Series 01)	179.3	6.95 x 14 (21)	1.0 (22)	1.13 (23)	.88 (26)	9-6 Cyl. 10-V8 (19)	9-6 Cyl. 10-V8
	Hornet Sportabout S/W	179.3	6.95 x 14 (21)	1.0 (22)	1.13 (23)	.88 (26)	9-6 Cyl. 10-V8 (19)	9-6 Cyl. 10-V8
	Hornet SC/360	179.3	D70 x 14	1.0 (22)	1.19 (24)	.88 (26)	10-V8 (19)	10-V8
	Matador 2-dr. h.t. (Series 10)	206.0	E78 x 14 (12)	1.0 (22)	1.09 (24)	.94 (26)	10 (19)	10
	Matador 4-dr sedan (Series 10)	206.0	E78 x 14 (12)	1.0 (22)	1.09 (24)	.94 (26)	10 (19)	10
	Matador (Wagon)(Series 10)	205.0	G78 x 14 (13)	1.0 (22)	1.09 (24)	.94 (23)	10 (19)	10
	Ambassador 2-dr (Series 80)	210.8	F78 x 14 (16)	1.0 (22)	1.09 (24)	.94 (26)	10 (19)	10
	Ambassador 4-dr (Series 80)	210.8	F78 x 14 (16)	1.0 (27)	1.09 (24)	.94 (26)	10 (19)	10
	Ambassador (Wagon)(Series 80)	209.7	H78 x 14	1.0 (22)	1.09 (24)	.94 (23)	10 (19)	10
	Javelin-AMX (Series 70)	191.8	C78 x 14 (15)	1.0 (22)	1.13 (23)	.88 (26)	9-6 Cyl. 10-V8 (19)	9-6 Cyl. 10-V8
	Gremlin 2-pass. sedan (Series 40)	161.3	6.00 x 13 (20)	1.0	1.13 (23)	.88	9	9
	Gremlin 4-pass. sedan (Series 40)	161.3	6.00 x 13 (20)	1.0	1.13 (23)	.88	9	9

CAPACITIES

YEAR	MODEL	ENGINE CRANKCASE ADD 1 Qt. FOR NEW FILTER	TRANSMISSIONS Pts. TO REFILL AFTER DRAINING			DRIVE AXLE (Pts.)	GASOLINE TANK (Gals.)	COOLING SYSTEM (Qts.) WITH HEATER
			Manual		Automatic			
			3-Speed	4-Speed				
1965	195.6—6 Cyl.	4	1½ ①	—	18	3	16	12 ⑥
	199—6 Cyl.	4	1½ ①	—	18	3	16	12 ⑥
	232—6 Cyl.	4	2¼ ①	3½	18	4	19 ⑤	10½
	287—6 Cyl.	4	3½ ⑦	3½	22	4	19 ⑤	19
	327—V8	4	4 ⑧	3½	22	4	19 ⑤	19
1966	199—6 Cyl.	4	1½ ①	—	18	3	16	10½
	232—6 Cyl.	4	2¼ ⑦	—	18	4	19 ⑤	10½
	287, 290—V8	4	2¼ ⑦	3½	22	4	19 ⑤	19
	327—V8	4	4 ⑦	3½	22	4	19 ⑤	19
1967	199—6 Cyl	4	1½ ①	—	18	3	16	10½
	232—6 Cyl.	4	1½ ①	—	18	4	21½ ⑨	10½
	290—V8	4	2½ ⑩	3½	18	4	21½ ⑨	14
	343—V8	4	—	3½	20	4	21½ ⑨	13
1968-69	199—6 Cyl.	4	1½ ①	—	18 ⑭	3	16	10½
	232—6 Cyl.	4	2½ ①	—	18 ⑭	3 ⑪	⑫	10½
	290—V8	4	3 ⑬	3½ ⑮	18 ⑭	4	⑫	14
	343, 390—V8	4	—	3½ ⑮	20	4	⑫	13
1970-71	199—6 Cyl.	4	1½	—	19	3	⑯ ④	10½
	232, 258—6 Cyl.	4	2½ ②	—	19	3	⑯ ③ ④	10½
	304—V8	4	3	—	19	4	⑯ ③ ④	14
	360,390, 401—V8	4	3	2½	20	4	⑯ ③ ④	13
1972	232, 258—6 Cyl.	4	6½	—	17	3	⑰ ③ ④	10½
	304 V8	4	4¾	—	19	4	⑰ ③ ④	14
	360 V8	4	4¾	7½	19	4	⑰ ③ ④	13
	401 V8	4	—	7½	19	4	⑰ ③ ④	13

① Overdrive—2¾.
② 1½ for T96J transmission used with 232 engine.
③ 1971 Ambassador sedans—19.5; wagon—17.0.
1971 Matador sedans—19.5; 2-seat wagon—19.5; 3-seat wagon—17.0.
④ 1970 Hornet—17.0; 1971-72 Hornet—16.0.
1971-72 Javelin—16.0.
⑤ Three-seat sta. wag.—17.
⑥ OHV—11.
⑦ Overdrive—3½.
⑧ Overdrive—4.
⑨ Three-seat sta. wag.—19.
⑩ Overdrive—3¾.
⑪ 01, 70—3; 10, 80—4.
⑫ 30, 70—19; 10, 80—21½
⑬ Overdrive 3.1
⑭ 1969—19.
⑮ 1969—2½.
⑯ —1970-71 Gremlin—21. 1970 Rebel and Ambassador sedans—21½; all other 1970 models except those noted—19.
⑰ —1972 Ambassador sedans—19.5; wagon—20.0.
1972 Matador sedan—19.5; wagons—20.0.
1972 Gremlin—21.

★—With disc brakes—2 in.
●—With disc brakes, sedan, H.T., conv.—1 in., sta. wag.—1⅛ in.
†—With disc brakes, sedan, H.T., conv.—15/16 in., sta. wag.—1 in.
▲—Opt.—7.75 x 14.
■—6.95 x 14 & 6.85 x 15 optional.
★★—6.85 x 15 optional.
☆—7.75 x 14 & 7.35 x 15 optional.
☆☆—8.25 x 14 & 7.75 x 15 optional.
①—10 in. with V8 engine.
②—V8 = 1 3/16 in.
③—Disc brakes 2 in.
④—V8 = 29/32 in.
⑤—6 Cyl. disc brakes 1 in.
⑥—Disc brakes 1⅛ in.
⑦—Disc diam. 11 3/16 in.
⑧—V8—7.35 x 14.
⑨—1969—206.5.
⑩—1969—207.
⑪—V8—C78 x 14 std., D78 x 14 and D70 x 14 optional.
⑫—F78 x 14 optional; Machine—E60 x 15 std.
⑬—H78 x 14 optional.
⑭—E70 x 14 and F70 x 14 optional; E60 x 15 available special order for 1970-71
⑮—6 cyl. size std.; 6 cyl. optional tires: D78 x 14, E78 x 14, E70 x 14. V8 size std.—D78 x 14, with E78 x 14, E70 x 14, F70 x 14 and E60 x 15 optional.
⑯—G78 x 14 and H78 x 14 optional.
⑰—Recommended size; std. size is F78 x 14
⑱—6.45 x 13 and B78 x 14 optional.
⑲—Ventilated disc brakes optional—outer dia. 10.91 in., 1.0 in. wide, 2.75 in. wheel cyl. bore.
⑳—6.45 x 13, B78 x 14, D70 x 14 optional. (std. on Gremlin X).
㉑—6.95 x 14, B78 x 14, C78 x 14 optional—6 cyl. C78 x 14, D78 x 14, D70 x 14 optional—V8
㉒—Optional disc brakes on Hornet, Javelin, Matador, and Ambassador V8: Hornet, Javelin—1.063 man., 1.000 power. Matador, Ambassador—1.125 power only avail.
㉓—6-Cyl. Std. models. Hornet and Javelin V8 use 1.19 in. bores.
㉔—6-Cyl. Std. Models. V8 models use 1.19 in. bores.
㉕—V8 Wagons with disc brakes use 1.00 in. rear bores.
㉖—With front disc brakes; .94 in. rear bores.
S/W—Sedan/wagon configuration.

CYLINDER-HEAD BOLT TIGHTENING SEQUENCE

196 6 cylinder cast-iron OHV

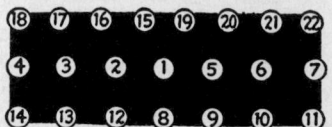

196 6 cylinder L-head

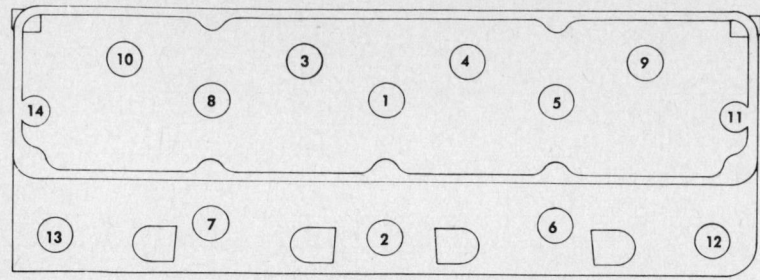

290, 304, 343, 360, 390, and 401 V8

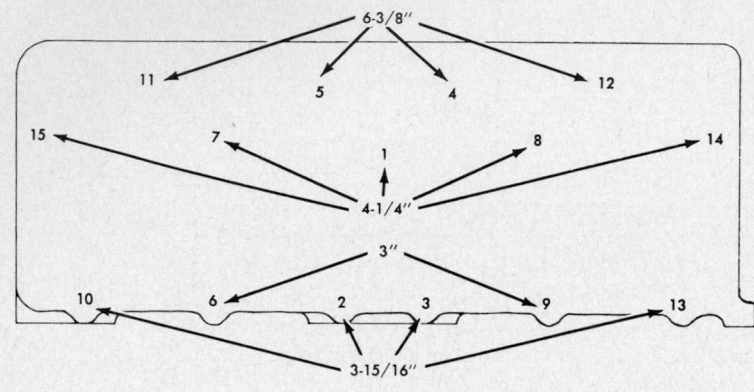

287 and 327 V8

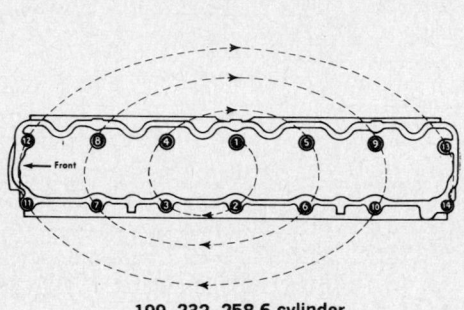

199, 232, 258 6 cylinder

TORQUE SPECIFICATIONS

YEAR	MODEL	CYLINDER HEAD BOLTS (FT. LBS.)	ROD BEARING BOLTS (FT. LBS.)	MAIN BEARING BOLTS (FT. LBS.)	CRANKSHAFT BALANCER BOLT (FT. LBS.)	FLYWHEEL TO CRANKSHAFT BOLTS (FT. LBS.)	MANIFOLD (FT. LBS.)	
							Intake	Exhaust
1965–66	6 Cyl. L-Hd.	60	30	70	80	105	20	25
	6 Cyl. OHV (199 & 232)	85	30	80	80	105	20	25
	All V8	60	50	65▲	80	105	20	25
1967–72	6 Cyl.	80	26–30	75–85	50–60	100–110	20–25	20–25
	All V8	①	②	95–105	20–25③	100–110	40–45	30–35

▲—No. 5 (rear main)—55 ft. lbs.
①—To 1969—90-100; 1970-72—105-115.
②—290, 304, 343, 360—26-30; 390, 401—35-40.
③—Pulley-to-damper bolts.

WHEEL ALIGNMENT

YEAR	MODEL	CASTER		CAMBER		TOE-IN (In.)	KING-PIN INCLINATION (Deg.)	WHEEL PIVOT RATIO	
		Range (Deg.)	Pref. Setting (Deg.)	Range (Deg.)	Pref. Setting (Deg.)			Inner Wheel	Outer Wheel
1965–66	Series 01, W/PS	³/₄P–1¹/₂P	1¹/₂P	¹/₄N–¹/₄P	0	¹/₁₆–³/₁₆	6¹/₂	25	22
	Series 01, WO/PS	0–¹/₂P	¹/₄P	¹/₄N–¹/₄P	0	¹/₁₆–³/₁₆	6¹/₂	25	22
	Series 10, 80, W/PS	³/₄P–1¹/₂P	1¹/₂P	¹/₄N–¹/₄P	0	¹/₁₆–³/₁₆	6¹/₈	25	22
	Series 10, 80, WO/PS	0–¹/₂P	¹/₄P	¹/₄N–¹/₄P	0	¹/₁₆–³/₁₆	6¹/₈	25	22
1967–68	American, Javelin, AMX	¹/₂N to ¹/₂P▲	0	³/₈N–³/₈P	0	¹/₁₆–³/₁₆	6¹/₂	25	25
	Rebel	¹/₂N to ¹/₂P▲	0	³/₈N–³/₈P	0	¹/₁₆–³/₁₆	6¹/₂	25	25
	Marlin	¹/₂N to ¹/₂P▲	0	³/₈N–³/₈P	0	¹/₁₆–³/₁₆	6¹/₈	25	25
	Ambassador	¹/₂N to ¹/₂P▲	0	³/₈N–³/₈P	0	¹/₁₆–³/₁₆	6¹/₈	25	25
1969	Series 01, 30, 70	¹/₂N to ¹/₂P▲	0	³/₈N–³/₈P	0	¹/₁₆–³/₁₆	6¹/₂	25	22
	Series 10, 80	0 to 1N	¹/₂N	³/₈N–³/₈P	0	¹/₁₆–³/₁₆	6¹/₂	25	22
1970–72	All Series	¹/₂P to 1¹/₂P	1P	³/₈N–³/₈P	0	¹/₁₆–³/₁₆	7³/₄	25	22

▲—With power steering ¹/₂P to 1¹/₂P.
N—Negative.
P—Positive.
PS—Power steering.

CRANKSHAFT BEARING JOURNAL SPECIFICATIONS

YEAR	MODEL	MAIN BEARING JOURNALS (IN.)				CONNECTING ROD BEARING JOURNALS (IN.)		
		Journal Diameter	Oil Clearance	Shaft End-Play	Thrust On No.	Journal Diameter	Oil Clearance	End-Play
1965–66	6 Cyl., L-Hd.	2.4794	.0012	.005	1	2.0952	.0012	.010
	6 Cyl., OHV	2.4987	.0012	.005	3	2.0952	.0012	.010
	V8, All	2.4988	.0015	.005	1	2.2486	.0017	.010
1967–69	6 Cyl., OHV	2.4986–2.5001	.001–.002	.0015–.007	3	2.0934–2.0955	.001–.002	.008–.010
	v8, All	①	.001–.002②	.003–.008	3	③	.001–.002	.009–.015
1970–72	6 Cyl., OHV	2.4986–2.5001	.001–.002	.0015–.007	3	2.0934–2.0955	.001–.002	.008–.010
	V8, All	①	.001–.002②	.003–.008	3	④	.001–.002	.009–.015

① —Nos. 1–4—2.7474–2.7489; No. 5—2.7464–2.7479.
② —Rear main—.002–.003.
③ —V8 290, 343 2.0934–2.0955; V8 390—2.2471–2.2492.
④ —1970 390, All 401—2.2471–2.2485; 304, 360—2.0934–2.0955.

LIGHT BULBS

1965

Headlamps (low beam)............... 4002; 50/37.5 W.
Headlamps (high beam) .... 4001; 37.5 W.
Radio .... 1893; 2 CP
Panel switches, overdrive signal .... 1445; 1.5 CP
Turn signals, park, stop, tail .... 1157; 32/4 CP
Back-up .... 1156; 32 CP
Dome, cargo, courtesy .... 1004; 15 CP
Parking brake warning.................. 256; 1.6 CP
Gauge indicators........................ 158; 2 CP
License lamp .... 67; 3 CP
Clock, glove compartment.................. 57; 2 CP
Headlights (Series 01) .... 6012; 50/40 W.
Trunk, convertible courtesy.............. 89; 6 CP
Auto. floorshift indicator .... 1816; 2 CP

1966

Clock .... 57; 2 CP
License............................... 67; 3 CP
Trunk, convertible courtesy............. 89; 6 CP
Instrument, hi beam, turn, charge, oil,
  trans. quadrant with Adjust-O-Tilt lights ... 158; 2 CP
Rear pillar, courtesy .... 211; 12 CP
01-50-80 Series brake warning .... 256; 1.6 CP
10 Series brake warning .... 257; 1.6 CP
Dome, cargo, courtesy .... 1004; 15 CP
Back-up................................ 1156; 32 CP
Park, turn signals, stop, tail .... 1157; 32/4 CP
Auto. trans. quadrant, instrument panel
  switches, emergency flasher lights .... 1445; 1.5 CP
Auto. trans. floorshift light .... 1816; 3 CP
Radio, glove compartment .... 1893; 2 CP
Headlight (inner) 4001
Headlight (outer) 4002
Headlights (Series 01) .... 6012; 50/40 W.
Radio (Series 01)..................... 1892; 2 CP

1967–69

Compass light .... 53; 1 CP
Clock, glove box, tachometer .... 57; 2 CP
License plate.......................... 67; 4 CP
Convertible courtesy, trunk............. 89; 6 CP
Courtesy (panel)........................ 94; 15 CP
Instrument, hi beam, alternator, oil, turn
  indicator, brake warning lights .... 158; 2 CP
Rear shelf light (Marlin-1968–69
  01 hardtop) .... 211; 12 CP
Parking brake warning (on) .... 257; 1.6 CP
Cargo, dome, rear quarter .... 1004; 15 CP
Back-up............................. 1156; 32 CP
Park, turn signals, stop, tail .... 1157; 4/32 CP

Control lights, cigarette lighter, ignition
  switch, light switch, wiper switch, gear
  selector quadrant, A/C thermostat
  lights .... 1445; 1.5 CP
Heater and A/C control lights .... 1881; 1.5 CP
Radio .... 1893; 2 CP
Headlight (inner) 4001
Headlight (outer) 4002
Headlights (Series 01) .... 6012; 50/40 W.
Park and front turn (1968–69
  Series 30) .... 1157A; 3-32 CP
Radio dial (30–70 AM; 10–80 AM/FM; 30–70
  AM/Tape) 1815
Clock (1968–69 Series 10-80) .... 1816; 3 CP
Heater and A/C control (1968–69
  Series 30–70) .... 1881; 1.5 CP
Radio dial (1968–69 Series 01) .... 1892; 1.3 CP
Radio dial (1968–69 Series 30-70 AM/FM) ..... 1893; 2 CP
Tachometer (1968–69 Series 01-10-80) ..... 1895; 2 CP
Headlights (1968–69 Series 01-30-70) .... 6012; 50/40 W.

1970

Back-up .... 1156; 32 CP
Cargo (Series 10) 561
Clock (Series 01-30) .... 1816; 3 CP
Clock (Series 10) .... 57; 2 CP
Control lights........................ 1445; 1.5 CP
Console (Series 30).................... 211; 12 CP
Courtesy (Series 01-10-80) .... 94/561; 15 CP
Courtesy (Series 30-70) .... 211; 12 CP
Dome (Series 01-10-80).................. 562
Gearshift quadrant (LAW) .... 1816; 3 CP
Gearshift quadrant (WAW-WFS) .... 1893; 2 CP
Glove box (Series 01) .... 57; 2 CP
Glove box (Series 10-30-70-80) .... 1891; 2 CP
Indicators and instrument lights........... 158; 2 CP
License plate 2286V
Low fuel warning .... 257; 1.6 CP
Map light (Series 30-70).................. 563; 4 CP
Parking brake warning.................. 257; 1.6 CP
Park and turn (Series 10-70-80) ...... 1157; 4/32 CP
Park and turn (Series 01-30) .... 1157A; 3-32 CP
Rear quarter (Series 10-70-80) 562
Stop, tail .... 1157; 4/32 CP
Side marker (front and rear)........... 194; 2 CP
Side marker (rear Series 01 only) .... 1895; 2 CP
Tachometer (Series 01)................ 1157A; 3-32 CP
Tachometer (Series 10-70-80) .... 158; 2 CP
Tail (Series 80) .... 1095; 4 CP
Radio 1815
Trunk .... 89; 6 CP

Headlights (Series 01-30-70)........... 6012; 50/40 W.
Headlight (inner Series 10-80) 4001
Headlight (outer Series 10-80) 4002

1971–72

Headlights (Series 01-40-70).............. 6014-S
Headlights (Series 10-80)
  Outer (hi-low).................... 4000-S
  Inner (hi) 5001
Hi beam ind. (Series 01-10-40-80) 158
Hi beam ind. (Series 70) 53
Alt. charge light (Series 01-10-40-80) 158
Alt. charge light (Series 70) 1815
Oil press. light (Series 01 10 40 80) 158
Oil press. light (Series 70) 1815
Park and brake warn. (Series 01-10-40-80) 158
Park and brake warn. (Series 70)....... 1815
Low fuel warning (Series 01-10-40-80) 257
Low fuel warning (Series 70) 256
Tail-Stop lights (All Series) 1157
Park-Turn lights (All Series) 1157
Instrument lights (All Series) 158
Headlight-wiper control (All Series) 1445
Heater and A/C control (All Series) 1445
Cigar lighter, heater rear window
  (Series 10-80).................... 1445
Clock (All Series) 1816
License light assy. (All Series) 2286-U
Trans. ind. light (All Series col.) 1816
Trans. ind. light (All Series fl.) 1445
Radio (All Series) 1815
Ashtray (Series 10-80) 1445
Side marker front (Series 01-10-40-70).......... 194
Side marker rear (Series 10-80-70-40) 194
Side marker front (Series 80)........... 94
Side marker rear (Series 01) 1895
Dome lights (Series 01-40-70)......... 562
Dome lights (Series 10-80) 561
Cargo lights (series 10-80) 561
Courtesy lights (All Series) 561
Glove box (All Series) 1891
Trunk (All Series) 89
Turn sig. ind. (Series 01-40-10-80)......... 158
Turn sig. ind. (Series 70) 53
Back-up lights (All Series) 1156
Map light (Series 70) 563
Tach lights (Series 01-40) 1895
Tach lights (Series 70) 1816

BATTERY AND STARTER SPECIFICATIONS

YEAR	MODEL	BATTERY					STARTERS						
		Ampere Hour Capacity	Volts	Group Number	Terminal Grounded	Lock Test			No-Load Test			Brush Spring Tension (Oz.)	
						Amps.	Volts	Torque	Amps.	Volts	RPM		
1965–66	6 Cyl., All	50	12	2-SM	Neg.	285	4.0	6.5	62	10.6	7,850	35	
	V8, Classic & Ambassador	60	12	2-SMH	Neg.	290	4.0	9.0	82	10.6	4,350	48	
1967–69	6 Cyl.	50	12	2-CM50	Neg.	290	4.3	6.5	63	10.6	7,850	35	
	V8	60	12	2-SM60	Neg.	500	4.5	9.0	70	12.0	9,500	40	
	V8 (opt.)	70	12	2-SH70	Neg.	500	4.5	10.0	70	12.0	9,500	40	
1970–72	6 Cyl., 304V8	50	12	2SM-50	Neg.	600①	3.4	—	65	12.0	9,250	40	
	V8 360, 401	60	12	2SM-60	Neg.	600①	3.4	—	65	12.0	9,250	40	
	All (opt.)	70	12	2SH-70	Neg.	600①	3.4	—	65	12.0	9,250	40	

① —1970—500 @ 4.5

FUSES AND CIRCUIT BREAKERS

1965

Dome, courtesy, cargo, trunk, glove box,
clock .... 9 AMP. fuse
Park, tail, instrument, license, clock light,
trans. light .... 9 AMP. fuse
Gauges, alternator and oil lights, park warn,
.... 4 AMP. fuse
Heater motor, twin-stick relay, V8 auto.
trans.............................. 20 AMP. fuse
Air cond., A/C clutch .... 30 AMP. fuse
Stop, turn, back-up lights, flasher .... 9 AMP. fuse
Headlights.................... 20 AMP. CB (on switch)
Wipers........................ 6 AMP. CB (on switch)
Power windows..... 30 AMP. CB; 4-15 AMP. CB (in doors)
Power tail gate,
window ..... 2-30 AMP. CB (Series 01–3-25 AMP. CB)
Overdrive relay .... 15 AMP. fuse (on relay)
Radio.................................. 5 AMP. (inline)

1966

Dome, courtesy, cargo, trunk, glove box,
clock .... 9 AMP. fuse
Park, tail, instrument, license, clock and
trans. lights .... 9 AMP. fuse
Gauges, alternator and oil lights,
brake warn.......................... 4 AMP. fuse
Heater motor, air cond. motor, A/C clutch,
overdrive........... 20 AMP. (30 AMP. with A/C)
Stop, turn, back-up, flasher .... 9 AMP. fuse
Radio.............................. 5 AMP. (inline)
Headlights.................... 20 AMP. CB (on switch)
Wipers........................ 5 AMP. CB (on switch)
Power windows...... 30 AMP. CB; 1-15 AMP. CB for each
door; 2-25 AMP. CB for quarter
windows.
Power tail gate window .... 3-25 AMP. CB
Convertible top .... 30 AMP. CB (under dash)

1967

Dome, courtesy, cargo, clock, glove box,
trunk............................... 9 AMP. fuse
Tail, park, instrument, light switch, wiper switch,
heater control, ignition switch, cigarette lighter,
clock, license, trans. light, cruise command,
A/C thermostat, radio, tachometer, ash tray
lights.............................. 9 AMP. fuse
Stop, turn, emergency flasher.............. 9 AMP. fuse
Turn signals, radio, vibra-tone, cruise command
feed, spotlight, back-up lights .... 9 AMP. fuse
Gauges, alternator and oil lights, brake warn,
park lights .... 4 AMP. fuse

Heater motor, A/C motor, A/C clutch, overdrive,
auto. trans. .... 20 AMP. fuse (30 AMP. with A/C)
Headlights...................... 20 AMP. CB (on switch)
Convertible top .... 30 AMP. CB (under dash)
Power windows.............. 25 AMP. CB (under dash)
Wipers .... 6 AMP. CB (in switch)
Power tail gate window .... 3-25 AMP. CB

1968–70

Dome, cargo, courtesy, clock, glove box,
trunk lights........................... 9 AMP. fuse
Park, tail, instrument, light switch, wiper
switch, heater control, cigarette lighter,
clock, license, auto. trans., cruise command,
A/C thermostat, radio, tachometer, ash tray
lights.............................. 9 AMP. fuse
Stop, turn ind., flasher .... 14 AMP. fuse
Turn signals, back-up, accessories .... 14 AMP. fuse
Indicators, alternator and oil lights, brake warn,
parking brake lights .... 4 AMP. fuse
Heater motor, A/C motor, A/C clutch, overdrive,
auto. trans. .... 20 AMP. fuse (30 AMP. with A/C)
Headlights .... 20 AMP. CB (in switch)
Power windows.............. 20 AMP. CB (under dash)
Wipers .... 6 AMP. CB (in switch)
Power tailgate window.................. 2-20 AMP. CB

1971–72

Dome, cargo, courtesy, clock, glove
box, trunklights .... 9 AMP. fuse
Tail, park, instruments, light switch, wiper
switch, heater controls, cigarette lighter,
clock, license, A/C thermostat, trans. ind.,
radio, tach., ash tray................. 14 AMP. fuse
Stop lights, turn sig. ind., four-way
flashers .... 20 AMP. fuse
Turn signals, back-up lights, all accessories
not listed........................... 20 AMP. fuse
Indicators, charge light, oil pressure and
brake warning lights, park. brake light.... 4 AMP. fuse
Heater motor, A/C clutch, auto. trans.
.... 20 AMP. fuse (30 AMP. with A/C)
Headlights .... 20 AMP. CB (in switch)
Electric windows .... 20 AMP. CB (under dash)
Wiper motor...................... 6 AMP. CB (in switch)
Tailgate window... 2-20 AMP. CB (lower lip of dashboard)

1969–70 Fusible Links

Location	Color	Protects
Battery terminal of starter relay to main wire harness	Red	Complete wiring
Battery terminal of horn relay to main wire harness	Pink	Horn circuit
Accessory terminal of ignition switch to wire harness	Brown	Electric tailgate instrument panel switch, cigarette lighter, all accessories from fuse panel, and electric windshield wiper
Ignition terminal of ignition switch to wire harness	Yellow	Alternator exciter voltage, fuel temperature indicator, park brake warning light.

There are two additional fusible links which protect optional equipment when the car is so equipped:

Location	Color	Protects
Battery terminal of starter relay to air conditioning blower motor relay (10-80 Series)	Red	Blower motor circuit (high speed)
Battery terminal of starter relay to junction block for "Rally Pac" ammeter (30-70 Series)	Black	"Rally Pac" wiring

1971–72 Fusible Links

Location	Color	Protects
Bat. terminal of starter relay to main wiring harness.	Red	Complete wiring
Bat. terminal of horn relay to main wiring harness	Pink	Horn circuit
Acc. terminal of ign. switch to wiring harness.	Brown	Electric Tailgate instr: panel switch, cigarette lighter, all acc. from fuse board, elec. wipers.
Bat. terminal of starter relay to rear window defogger switch on dash.	Red	Rear window defogger

Distributor

Detailed information on cylinder numbering, firing order, point gap, point dwell, timing, spark plugs, and idle speed will be found in the Specifications tables. Rambler uses both Auto-Lite and Delco-Remy Distributors.

Distributor Removal

6-Cylinder Models

The distributor is mounted on the side of the engine. Remove the distributor cap and mark the position of the rotor relative to the distributor body, then mark the distributor body relative to the block. Remove the distributor hold-down screw, disconnect the ignition primary wire and the vacuum advance tube. Lift the distributor out of the block.

V8 Models

1. Remove the distributor cap, mark the position of the rotor relative to the distributor body and mark the body relative to the block. Remove the carburetor air cleaner, the distributor primary wire and the distributor vacuum lines.
2. Remove the hold-down bolt and take the distributor up out of the block.

The rotor and body are marked so that they can be returned to the position from which they were removed. Do not turn the engine after the dis-

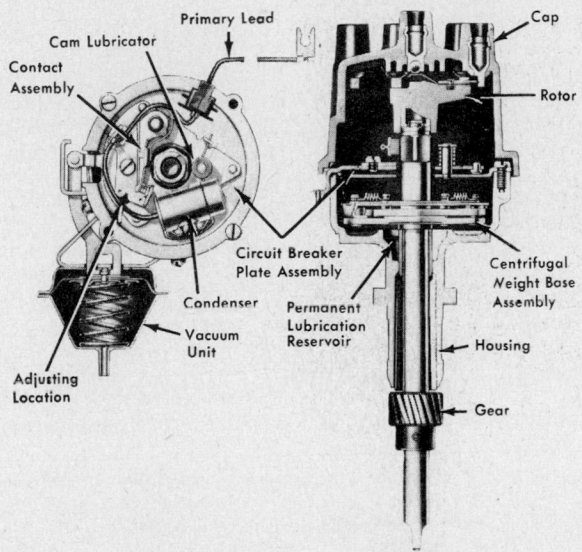

Distributor—199/232/258 6 cylinder
(© American Motors Corp.)

tributor has been taken off.

Ignition Resistor/Fusible Link

The ballast resistor is a white porcelain unit located on the dash panel above and behind the engine.

Late-model engines are equipped with ignition ballast resistance wire in the ignition, primary circuit.

This wire replaces the dash mounted-resistance-unit.

Point Replacement

6-Cylinder Models

The condenser and primary leads are retained by spring tension. Remove the distributor rotor and cap, release the tension and remove the leads. Loosen contact base screw and remove contact point assembly. Install a new condenser, set approximate point gap of new contact set, lubricate cam lobes or reverse lubricator and install rotor and cap. Check dwell and adjust if necessary.

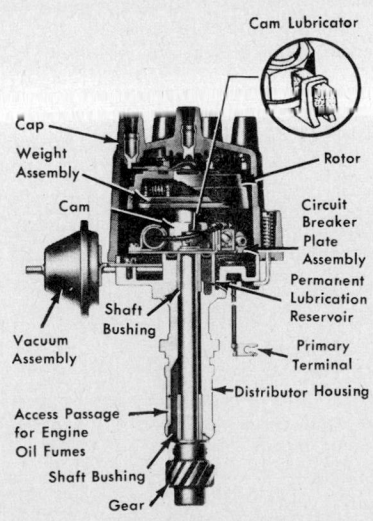

Distributor—all V8
(© American Motors Corp.)

V8 Models

Remove the distributor cap, condenser and primary leads which are attached to the nylon terminal. Loosen the two base screws and remove points. When installing points, make sure pilot hole is properly positioned over hole in breaker plate. Install new condenser, then attach primary and condenser leads to nylon terminal. Reverse lubricator and check that terminal leads will not touch rotor. Install rotor, making sure round and square holes are lined up with their respective dowels. Adjust point dwell to specification by turning Allen screw on point set through window in side of cap.

Generator, Regulator

Detailed facts on the alternator and the regulator can be found in the Alternator and Regulator Specifications table.

General information on generator and regulator repair and troubleshooting can be found in the Unit Repair Section.

Regulator Removal

Disconnect plug to the regulator. Remove the metal screws which hold the regulator to the sheet metal and lift off the regulator.

Alternator R & R

1. Disconnect battery cables.
2. Disconnect alternator wires or plug, then loosen adjusting bolt.
3. Remove V-belt, mounting bolts and alternator.
4. To install, reverse removal procedure. V8 brackets have a hole to use as a tensioner bar fulcrum.

AC Generator

Caution Since the alternator and regulator are designed for use on only one polarity system, the following precautions must be observed:

1. The polarity of the battery, generator and regulator must be matched and considered before making any electrical connections in the system.
2. When connecting a booster battery, be sure to connect the negative battery terminals respectively and the positive battery terminals respectively.
3. When connecting a charger to the battery, connect the charger positive lead to the battery positive terminal. Connect the charger negative lead to the battery negative terminal.
4. Never operate the alternator on open circuit. Be sure that all con-

nections in the circuit are clean and tight.

5. Do not short across or ground any of the terminals on the alternator regulator.

6. Do not attempt to polarize the alternator.

7. Do not use test lamps of more than 12 volts for checking diode continuity.

8. Avoid long soldering times when replacing diodes or transistors. Prolonged heat is damaging to these units.

9. Disconnect the battery ground terminal when servicing any AC system. This will prevent the possibility of accidental reversing of polarity.

Battery, Starter

Detailed information on the battery and starter will be found in the Battery and Starter Specifications table.

Starter repair procedures can be found in the Unit Repair Section.

Starter Removal

6 Cylinder

Remove the oil filler pipe, disconnect the battery lead from the starter and the solenoid lead from the starter. From underneath the vehicle, remove the bolts which hold the starter to the bell housing and lift off the starter.

V8

Disconnect the battery wire and the solenoid wire at the starter. From underneath the vehicle, remove the bolts which hold the starter to the flywheel housing and lift off the starter.

Instruments

Speedometer and/or Instrument Removal

1965 American

1. Disconnect battery.
2. Remove ignition switch, headlight switch, fan temperature control knob and defroster control knobs.
3. Disconnect speedometer cable, harness plug and flasher harness plug.
4. Remove air and defroster control assembly and blower switch.
5. Remove the two screws on top of cluster, then pull unit through opening.

1965-66 Classic

1. Disconnect battery.
2. Remove flasher harness, printed circuit connectors and speedometer cable.
3. Remove the two 5/16 in. hex screws that hold harness.
4. Remove cluster opening molding.
5. Remove the four screws that hold instrument panel bezel to panel.
6. Remove four screws that hold cluster to panel, then remove cluster and bezel.

NOTE: remove air discharge grill on air-conditioned cars.

1965-66 Ambassador and 1966 Marlin

1. Follow Steps 1-4, above.
2. Remove windshield wiper control.
3. Remove two screws that hold bezel to panel.
4. Remove cluster and bezel from front.

NOTE: models with automatic transmission and tilt wheel; remove bracket bolts from column to allow passage of cluster.

1966 American

1. Disconnect battery.
2. Remove ash tray and bracket, radio and overlay panel.
3. Remove Weather Eye console, bulb and socket.
4. If car is air conditioned, remove air discharge grill and glove compartment.

NOTE: remove center air discharge bezel and vent to reach center screw.

5. Disconnect printed circuit plug and speedometer cable; remove harness clips.
6. Detach headlight switch, ignition switch and windshield wiper control and wire them out of the way without detaching their connections.
7. Pull down cluster and remove two upper tabs from slotted rubber brackets.
8. Work the cluster to the rear and out the bottom center of the dashboard. If air conditioned, work the cluster over the evaporator and out through the glove compartment door.

1967 Marlin, 1967-72 Ambassador, 1968-70 Rebel, AMX and Javelin, 1971-72 Matador

1. Disconnect battery.
2. Remove screws from cluster overlay. Remove A/C thermostat control knob starting 1970.
3. Remove overlay, speedometer cable and parking brake warning light.
4. Remove screws that secure cluster to instrument panel; remove harness plug. Remove "low

fuel" warning relay.
5. Remove cluster assembly from the front.

NOTE: grounding clip on clock and tachometer must be replaced when installing into Javelin and AMX.

1967-69 American, 1970-72 Hornet and Gremlin

1. Disconnect battery.
2. Up to 1969, remove cigarette lighter assembly and ignition switch. Ignition switch is removed from rear; hold escutcheon while pressing assembly toward panel and turning counter clockwise.
3. On Hornet, remove package tray if so equipped.
4. Remove wiper control knob, nut, headlight switch knob, shaft assembly and nut.
5. Remove flasher unit, then disconnect speedometer cable.
6. Remove the two screws at the top of cluster overlay; slide cluster away from panel slightly for access to cluster plug.
7. Remove plug and "low fuel" relay screw; pull cluster out.

1971-72 Javelin and AMX

1. Disconnect battery and cover the painted surface of the steering column with a cloth.
2. Remove top, side and lower bezel screws, then remove radio and retaining nuts.
3. Remove instrument panel switch knobs.
4. If equipped with A/C, release speedometer cable clip on wheel-well panel.
5. Move bezel and cluster out of opening as an assembly, then reach behind cluster and disconnect speedometer cable, using harness plug and wires.
6. Remove eight cluster screws and separate cluster from bezel.
7. To install, reverse removal procedure.

Ignition Switch R & R

1965-69

Two types of ignition switch and mountings are used on American Motors products to 1969. Removal and installation of each type follows:

Type I

1. Disconnect battery.
2. Disconnect switch wires.
3. Remove screws at rear of panel and remove switch toward rear of panel.
4. With switch removed, turn key to Acc. position and insert wire (paper clip) in small hole in housing. Depress retainer while turning and pulling out cylinder.
5. Install in reverse of above.

Ignition switch assembly (I)
(© American Motors Corp.)

Type II

1. Disconnect battery.
2. Depress switch and turn counter-clockwise.
3. Remove switch through rear of panel and bevel from front.

Ignition switch assembly (II)
(© American Motors Corp.)

4. Remove wires from switch.
5. Remove cylinder as in Step 4 of **Type 1** above.
6. Install in reverse of above.

1970-72

The ignition switch on all models is mounted on the lower steering column tube and is connected to the lock cylinder via a lock rod.

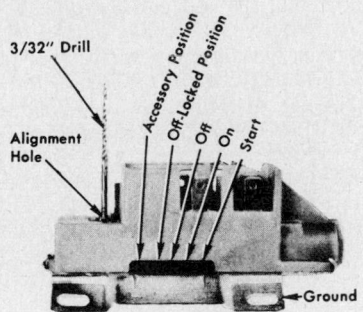

Ignition switch positions—1970-72
(© American Motors Corp.)

1. Place key in "OFF-LOCK".
2. Remove switch mounting screws.
3. Disconnect lock rod, remove harness connector and switch.
4. To install, first place both key and switch slide in "OFF-LOCK" positions.
5. Insert a 3/32 in. drill bit into switch alignment hole.
6. With drill in place, hook up lock rod and remove all slack by sliding switch toward steering wheel.
7. Install mounting bolts and tighten securely. Remove drill and hook up wires.

Lock Cylinder R & R—1970-72

1. Loosen anti-theft cover screws

and remove cover from column. Remove steering wheel.

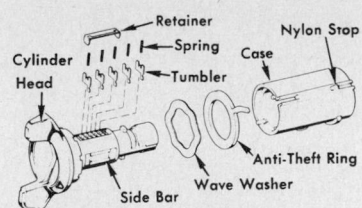

Ignition key lock—1970-72
(© American Motors Corp.)

2. Depress lock plate as far as possible, using a spacer and steering wheel nut.
3. Remove wire snap-ring from shaft groove, then remove compressor tool, snap-ring, lock plate, turn signal cam, upper bearing preload spring and thrust washer.

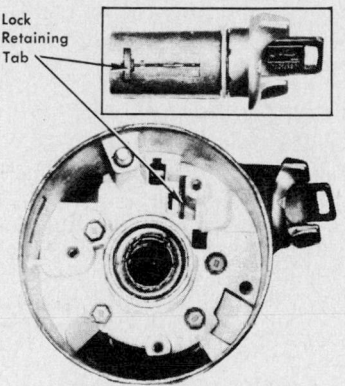

Lock cylinder removal—1970-72
(© American Motors Corp.)

4. Place turn signal lever in "right turn" position and remove lever.
5. Depress hazard warning switch and remove button by turning CCW.
6. Place automatic in Park, manual in Reverse.
7. Drive out shift lever pin with a 1/4 in. punch, then remove shift lever.
8. Remove turn signal wiring block from steering column (lower), then depress shift quadrant light wire lock tab with a paper clip (terminal D) and remove the wire.
9. Remove turn signal switch retaining screws and pull switch and wires out of column.
10. Place key in "IGN" position and lift key warning buzzer switch from housing.

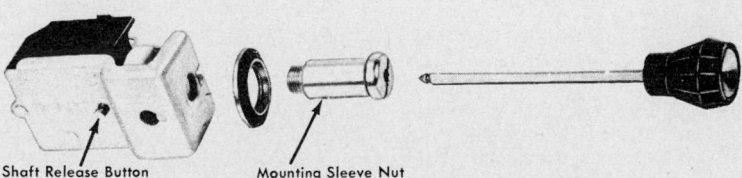

Light switch assembly (© American Motors Corp.)

11. Place key in "LOCK" position, then depress lock cylinder retaining tab and remove cylinder.
12. To install, reverse removal procedure.

Headlight Switch R & R

1965-72

Light switches are similar in all models. Some variation occurs in the shape and position of the nut mounting the switch to dash.

1. Disconnect battery.
2. With switch in "OFF" (up to 1968), "ON" (from 1969), position press the release button and remove the knob and shaft.
3. Remove screws, attaching switch or bracket to panel.
4. Reverse for installation, positioning switch so that the shaft is lined up properly before tightening the bracket screws.

Brakes

Specific information on brake cylinder sizes can be found in the General Chassis and Brake Specifications table.

Information on brake adjustments, lining replacement, bleeding procedure, master and wheel cylinder overhaul can be found in the Unit Repair Section.

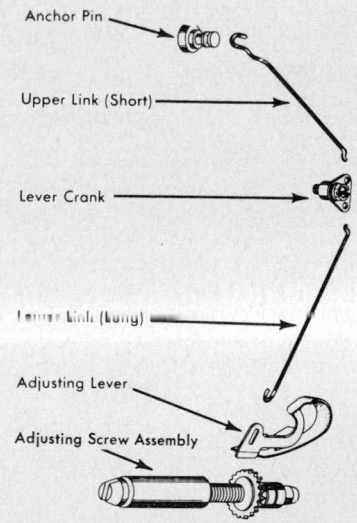

Automatic adjuster brake parts—Wagner
(© American Motors Corp.)

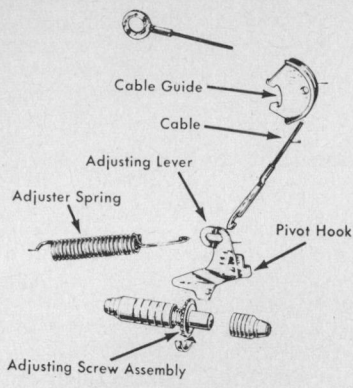

Automatic adjuster brake parts—Bendix
(© American Motors Corp.)

Information on troubleshooting and overhauling power brakes can be found in the Unit Repair Section.

Information on the grease seals which may need replacement can be found in the Unit Repair Section.

Description

American Motors products have used four basic brake types since 1965: Bendix duo-servo, having various diameters and drum designs; Wagner compound brakes, also with different diameters and with different drum configurations; Bendix non-servo brakes, used on the rear of some cars with disc brakes; and both Bendix Series 'E' (solid rotor) and Kelsey-Hayes (vented rotor) disc brakes on the front of some models. See the Unit Repair Section for repair, bleeding and adjustment procedures.

Rear Wheel Hub Installation

1965-72

The rear axle splines cut serrations into the inner diameter of the rear wheel hub. If the hub is to be removed, match mark the hub to the

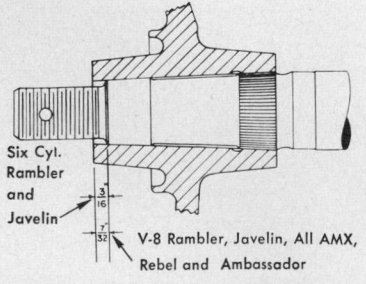

Rear hub installation—1965-69
(© American Motors Corp.)

axle so that the job of aligning the serrations and splines will be easier. If this is not done, the axle will cut new splines which may be so near the old that the hub will move on the axle with resultant damage to the hub, axle and differential gears.

When a new hub is installed, the

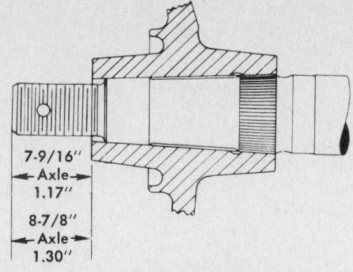

Rear hub installation—1970-72
(© American Motors Corp.)

serrations will be cut in the hub as it is installed on the shaft.

If a new axle shaft is installed, a new hub, without serrations, must be installed. An old shaft with a new hub also is an allowable combination.

Slide the hub onto the axle shaft, aligning the serrations of the hub with those of the shaft. Now, install the nut and tighten the hub onto the shaft until the face of the hub is the specified distance from the outer taper of the shaft. Nut must be torqued to 250 ft. lbs.

Master Cylinder Power Unit Removal

Remove the clevis pin from the power-unit operating rod. Disconnect the vacuum line and the hydraulic lines from the power unit, remove the stop light wires, remove the mounting bolts and lift off the power cylinder.

Parking Brake Lever Removal

Foot-operated Lever

The foot-operated lever is mounted under the left side of the instrument panel. Slack off on the brake cable and remove the clevis which holds the cable to the top part of the lever. Remove the brackets which hold the lever assembly to the side of the body and lift off the lever.

Parking Brake Cable Replacement

All Models

1. Disconnect the lower end of the cable at the cross-shaft or equalizer, disconnect it at the handbrake end.

2. Remove the brackets which retain it to the body and firewall and thread it out of the vehicle. When a new cable is to be installed, it is always a good idea to tie the new one to the end of the old one so that it will thread through in the same route as the old one. This, sometimes, will require the service of a helper to guide it.

Automatic Adjusters

1965-72

All models are available with automatically-adjusted service brakes. This is the Bendix Duo-Servo or the Wagner Compound brake. It automatically adjusts for lining wear, as the case requires. This continuous adjustment maintains a constant pedal height and is a decided safety and economic factor throughout the entire lining life.

The adjuster is operated by the movement of the secondary shoe during reverse brake application. The automatic mechanism is attached to, and works through the standard-type star wheel adjuster. Therefore, care must be used during a reline or major brake job to assure freedom of adjuster parts movement. Care must also be used to eliminate the mixing of right with left-hand parts.

Dual Master Cylinder

The front reservoir supplies rear brakes, and the rear one supplies the front brakes. This allows one pair of brakes to operate, should there be a failure of the opposite pair. If lines have been disconnected, be sure to reinstall in proper place (front to rear cylinder, and rear to front.)

With pressure bleeder, the Bendix system can be bled from front reservoir by covering rear reservoir with

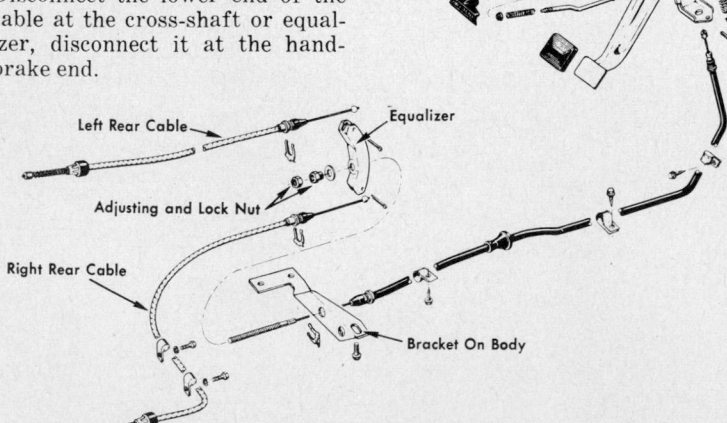

Typical foot pedal type parking brake linkage (© American Motors Corp.)

solid cap. The Moraine type must be bled separately, front and rear.

Without pressure bleeder, keep both reservoirs nearly full.

Fuel System

General

Data on capacity of the gas tank will be found in the Capacities table. Data on correct engine idle speed and fuel pump pressure will be found in the Tune-Up Specifications table.

Information covering operation and diagnosis of the fuel gauge will be found in the Unit Repair Section.

Fuel Pump Removal

Disconnect both gas lines from the fuel pump, disconnect the vacuum line, if it is a vacuum pump. Remove the two bolts which hold it to the block and lift off the pump.

Fuel Pump

A vacuum booster fuel pump is used on some models.

This is a piston-type vacuum pump, capable of much greater volume than some older models. It has been adapted to satisfy the needs of vacuum wiper motors on cars equipped with blades large and heavy enough to cover modern wrap around windshields.

An electric wiper is optional, allowing the use of a single-unit fuel pump.

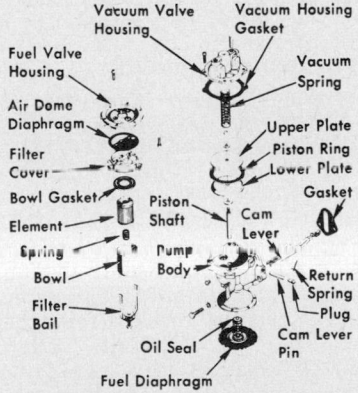

Typical fuel pump—V8 illustrated
(© American Motors Corp.)

Fuel Filter

Up to 1969, fuel filters are located on the fuel pump inside a bowl. The bowl is attached either to the side or the bottom of the pump, and the element can be replaced (12,000 miles) by unscrewing the bail wire and removing the cartridge.

Starting 1969, an inline fuel filter is located in the carburetor inlet. To change these filters (12,000 miles), unscrew the gas line at the carbure-

tor, remove the element and install a new element. Do not try to clean these elements.

Idle Speed and Mixture Adjustments

1965

Adjust with air cleaner removed.

1. Attach a vacuum gauge and tachometer to the engine.
2. Start engine and allow it to warm up to normal operating temperature.
3. Adjust throttle stop screw to obtain specified idle speed.
4. Adjust mixture screw/s to obtain highest steady manifold vacuum *or* maximum smoothest idle speed. (CCW leans mixture, CW richens it.)
5. Reset idle speed screw and adjust mixture again, tending toward the rich adjustment.
6. Initial mixture screw adjustments are as follows:

Carter RBS—1/4 to 1 1/4 turns open
Carter WCD—1/2 to 2 turns open
Holley 1909—0 to 2-3/4 turns open
Holley 1931—1/4 to 2 1/4 turns open (manual)
Holley 1931—3/4 to 1 1/4 turns open (auto)
Holley 2209—1/2 to 1 1/2 turns open
Holley 4150—1/2 to 1 1/2 turns open

1966-67 Except 1967 232 Six

Adjust with air cleaner installed.

1. Connect a tachometer to the engine.
2. On 2-BBL. and 4-BBL. carburetors, gently seat both mixture screws, then back out exactly one turn.

NOTE: all adjustments of dual mixture screws must be made equally.

3. Start engine and allow it to warm up to normal operating temperature.
4. Adjust throttle stop screw to obtain 550 rpm for all 1966, 600 rpm for 1967 (except 1967 232), models, both manual and automatic transmissions in Neutral. On A/C cars, set speed to 500 rpm for 1966, 600 rpm for 1967, with A/C turned *on*.
5. Turn mixture screw/s counterclockwise until engine speed drops off, then slowly turn screw/s (equal amounts) clockwise until speed picks up. Continue past this point until speed begins to fall off again, then back out screw/s to again obtain the fastest idle. This mid-range adjustment is called the "lean best idle" speed.
6. Readjust idle stop screw, if necessary, to obtain specified idle. If idle speed changed more than 50 rpm during the mixture adjustment, readjust the mix-

ture.
7. Disconnect tachometer.

1967 232 Six-Cylinder

Adjust with air cleaner installed.

1. Connect a tachometer to the engine.
2. Turn idle mixture screw/s clockwise until gently seated, then back out 3 turns.
3. Start engine and allow it to warm up to normal operating temperature.
4. With both manual and automatic transmissions in Neutral, A/C on, adjust throttle stop screw to obtain 600 rpm.
5. Turn idle mixture screw/s counterclockwise (out) until no further increase in engine idle speed is obtained, then turn screw/s inward (equally) until a 20 rpm drop is noted.
6. Turn mixture screw/s outward again until original idle speed is just regained.
7. At this point, idle speed should be 600 rpm. If not, reset idle speed screw to achieve this figure, then readjust mixture until 600 rpm is obtained without requiring further mixture adjustment.
8. Disconnect tachometer.

1968 199/232 Six-Cylinder (1-BBL. and 2-BBL.) and 290/343 V8 (4-BBL. Manual)

Adjust with air cleaner installed.

1. Turn in mixture screw/s until gently seated, then back out one turn. Connect a tachometer.
2. Start engine and set idle speed to 550 rpm (manual six), 475 rpm (auto six) with auto transmission in Drive, or 650 rpm V8 4-BBL. (manual).
3. Turn mixture screw/s counterclockwise until engine speed drops off slightly. On 2-BBL. and 4-BBL. carburetors, turn both mixture screws equally unless the engine definitely demands otherwise.
4. Turn mixture screw/s (equally) inwards until speed is regained, then continue inwards until speed just begins to fall off again.
5. Turn mixture screw/s outwards until speed is regained. This is the "lean best idle" setting.
6. Readjust idle speed screw to obtain 600 rpm for manual, 525 rpm for auto.
7. Disconnect tachometer. If any idle speed change over 30 rpm is noticed, readjust idle mixture screws.

1968 290/343 V8 (Automatic 2-BBL. and 4-BBL.) and 290/343 V8 (Manual 2-BBL.)

Adjust with air cleaner installed.

1. Connect a tachometer.

2. Starting from a counterclockwise mixture stop position, turn mixture screws inward ½ turn each.

3. Start engine and adjust idle speed screw to obtain 500 rpm in Drive for auto transmission, 650 rpm in Neutral for manual transmission.

4. Turn mixture screws counterclockwise until engine speed drops off, moving screws equally unless the engine demands otherwise.

5. Turn screws clockwise until speed is regained, then continue turning screws until speed drops off again.

6. Turn both screws equally outward until speed is just regained. This is the "lean best idle" setting. This point may be reached at the maximum full rich stop position.

7. Readjust carburetor idle speed screw to obtain 550 rpm for auto transmission, 650 rpm for manual, then disconnect tachometer. If any idle speed change over 30 rpm is noticed, readjust idle mixture screws.

1969-71

Adjust with air cleaner installed.

1. Start engine and allow it to warm up to operating temperature. Connect a tachometer. *On engine with air pumps, disconnect air bypass hose at valve.*

2. Adjust carburetor idle speed screw to obtain 600 rpm for 6-cylinder manual, 525 rpm for 1969 6-cylinder automatic (in Drive), 550 rpm for 1970 6-cylinder automatic (in Drive), 650 rpm for V8 manual, 550 rpm for 1969 V8 automatic (in Drive), or 600 rpm for 1970 V8 automatic (in Drive).

3. Starting from full rich stop/s (or two turns from seated on 4-BBL. manual V8) turn mixture screw/s clockwise until engine speed drops off.

4. Turn mixture screw/s counterclockwise until engine speed picks up to former level. The highest idle speed obtainable within the range of the limiter caps (or between the rich drop-off and lean drop-off points for 4-BBL. manual V8) is the "lean best idle setting." Both mixture screws should be turned equally unless the engine definitely demands otherwise.

5. If idle speed changes more than 30 rpm during mixture adjustment, reset carburetor idle speed screw and readjust mixture.

6. On cars with air pumps, reconnect air bypass valve hose.

NOTE: if idle quality is poor within the range of the limiter caps, the caps may be removed and the idle speed set using the corrective procedure. Keep in mind that a combustion gas analyzer is necessary to meet the critical federal exhaust emission standards. All cars should have a 14:1 air/fuel ratio except 4-BBL. manual transmission V8's, which should be set up at 13.5:1 (air bypass hose disconnected).

Idle Quality Corrective Procedure

1. Remove idle limiter caps by inserting a sheet metal screw into the center of the cap.

2. Adjust carburetor idle speed screw to obtain 50 rpm less than specified idle speed for all 6-cylinder, and all V8 automatic. Manual transmission V8's should be set to specified idle speed.

3. Adjust mixture as described under *1968 199/232 Six-Cylinder and 290/343 V8 4-BBL. Manual.*

4. Install new service idle limiter caps with ears against full rich stops.

Exhaust System

Exhaust Pipe Removal

1. Disconnect the exhaust pipe at the flange on the manifold. Squirt plenty of penetrating oil between the muffler and the exhaust pipe, or, if it is frozen too solidly, heat it.

2. Remove the clamps which hold the exhaust pipe to the muffler and slide the exhaust pipe out the front of the muffler. It can be threaded out from underneath the car.

3. Reinstall the new exhaust pipe so that the pipe extends past the slots in the muffler connections.

Muffler Installation

1. Squirt a good penetrating or de-rusting oil at the joint between the exhaust pipe and the muffler and the joint between the muffler and the tail pipe.

2. Let this oil work in. Remove the clamps which hold the muffler to the exhaust pipe and the muffler to the tail pipe. Loosen the tail pipe hanger bracket so that tail pipe can be slid backwards slightly, and can be cleared from the muffler.

3. Let the tail pipe clear, bend the muffler downwards and slide it off the back of the exhaust pipe.

4. Reinstall in reverse order and tighten all of the clamps which were loosened to permit removal of the muffler.

Tail Pipe Installation

1. Squirt plenty of penetrating oil where the tail pipe joins the muffler and remove the clamp.

2. Remove the hangers which hold the tail pipe up to the underbody and slide the front of the tail pipe out of the back of the muffler.

3. When the new tail pipe is installed, slide it far enough into the muffler to cover the slots in the muffler joint.

4. Arrange the muffler so that it hangs on each of its hangers approximately equally. Don't leave one hanger carrying all the weight so that it can rattle on the other one.

5. Equality can be accomplished easily by twisting the muffler slightly in order that pressures are reasonably equal on all hangers. This will prevent rattles.

Cooling System

Detailed information on cooling system capacity can be found in the Capacities table.

Information on the water temperature gauge can be found in the Unit Repair Section.

Radiator Core Removal

Raise the hood, drain the radiator, remove the upper and lower radiator hose. Take out the bolts which hold the radiator to its cradle and, if the car is fitted with an oil cooler for the transmission, disconnect the oil cooler lines and lift the core up and out.

Water Pump Removal

The water pump is a centrifugal unit having a non-adjustable packless seal. It is non-serviceable and must be replaced if defective—no maintenance is required.

Slack off and remove the fan belt, take out the bolts which hold the fan pulley to the hub and remove the fan blades and hub assembly. The water pump can then be unbolted from the cylinder head or distribution manifold and lifted off.

Water pump bolts are tightened to 10-15 ft. lbs. for 199, 232, and 258 6-cylinder engines, 45-50 *in. lbs.* for 290, 304, 343, 360, 390 and 401 V8's starting 1968.

Thermostat Removal

The thermostat is located in the water outlet housing at the top of the cylinder head, or on V8 models in front of the manifold.

Disconnect the upper radiator hose and remove the bolts which hold the water outlet neck to the engine. Remove the thermostat.

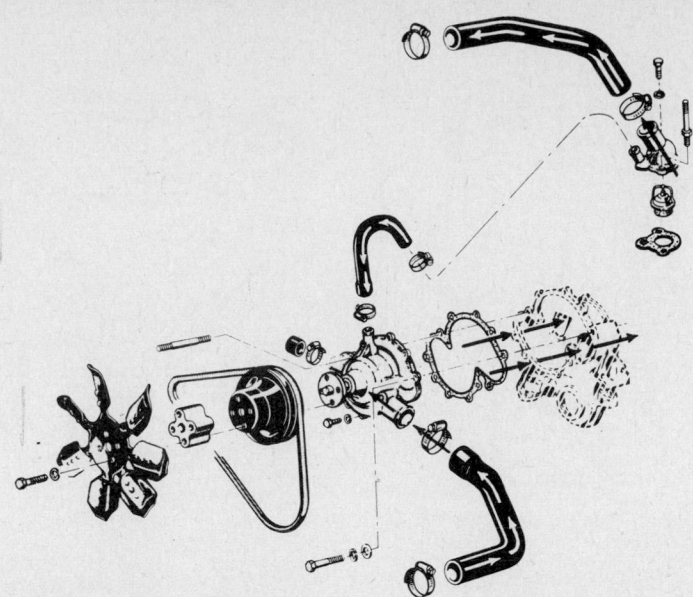

Water pump components and coolant flow—1967-72 V8 (© American Motors Corp.)

Engine

Description

American Motors has used, since 1965, eight V8 engines of various displacement, one six-cylinder L-head engine and three OHV six-cylinder engines. Up to and including mod-year 1966, two 327 cu. in. V8 engines having 250 (two-barrel) and 270 (four-barrel) horsepower and a 198 horsepower 287 cu. in. V8 were available in the large and intermediate models. In 1967, two new 290 cu. in. V8s, one having 200 horsepower and the other 225 (depending on carburetion), replaced these engines. In the same year, two 343 cu. in. engines having 235 and 280 horsepower were available. In 1969, a 390 cu. in. V8, based on the 343, was introduced. This engine had a forged steel crankshaft and was rated at 315 horsepower.

In 1970, the 290 became a 304 and the 343 a 360. Horsepower figures increased by ten, except for the 300 horsepower, four-barrel 360. The 390 power rating was increased to 335 horsepower the same year. In 1971, the 390 engine was replaced by the similar 401 cu. in. unit.

The 196 cu. in. L-head six-cylinder was dropped after model year 1965. The cast iron 196 OHV was used until 1965; it was replaced the next year by the more modern seven-main bearing OHV six, which had been used in conjunction with the older six in 1965, of 199 cu. in. and two 232 cu. in. sixes of 145 and 155 horsepower (depending on whether a single- or two-barrel carburetor was used). These last engines were used up to the 1970, the 199 and the small 232 being available in the Gremlin. In 1971, the 232 became a 258.

Engine crankcase capacities are listed in the Capacities table of this section.

Approved torque wrench readings and head bolt tightening sequences are covered in the Torque Specifications table.

Information on the engine marking code will be found in the Engine Identification table of this section.

Exhaust Emission Control

In compliance with anti-pollution laws involving all of the continental United States, American Motors Corporation has elected to adopt a special system of terminal exhaust treatment.

The new system phases out (except in cases of special purpose engines and applications) the Air Guard (afterburner) type, previously used in California in 1966-67.

American Motor's new approach, the MOD system, utilizes engine modification, with emphasis on carburetor and distributor changes. The new concept employs broader, yet more critical, distributor control. However, any terminal exhaust treatment renders engine adjustments more critical. Therefore, it means that close and frequent attention to tune-up maintenance details are necessary.

Since 1968, all car manufacturers have posted idle speeds, and other

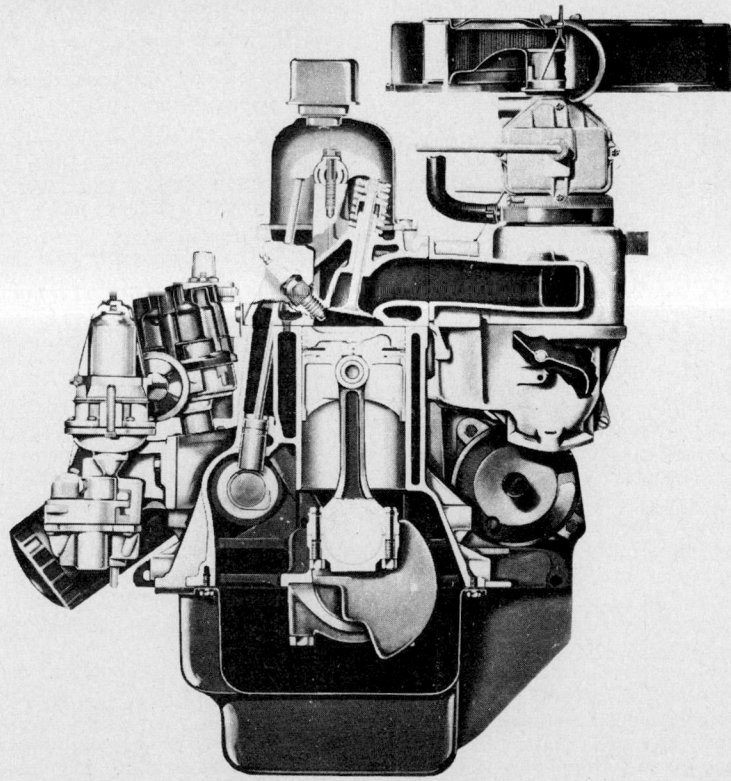

6-cylinder OHV 199/232/258 engine (© American Motors Corp.)

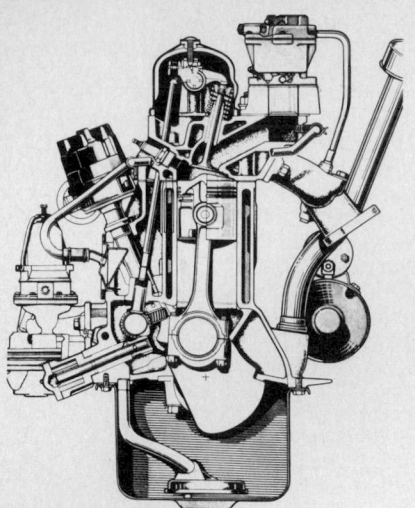

6 cylinder, OHV 196 cast iron engine
(© American Motors Corp.)

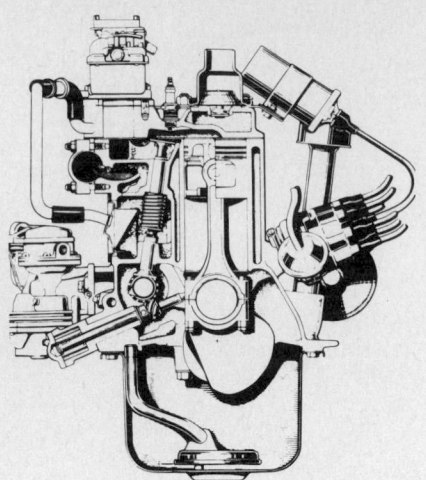

6 cylinder 196 L-head engine
(© American Motors Corp.)

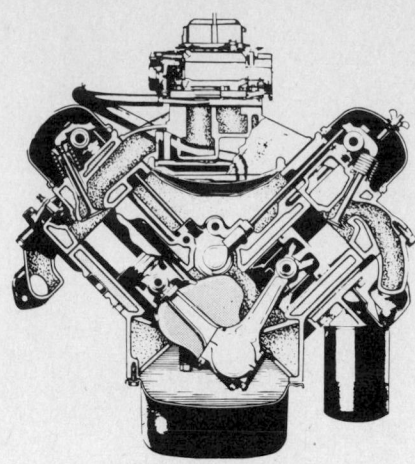

V8 287/327 engine
(© American Motors Corp.)

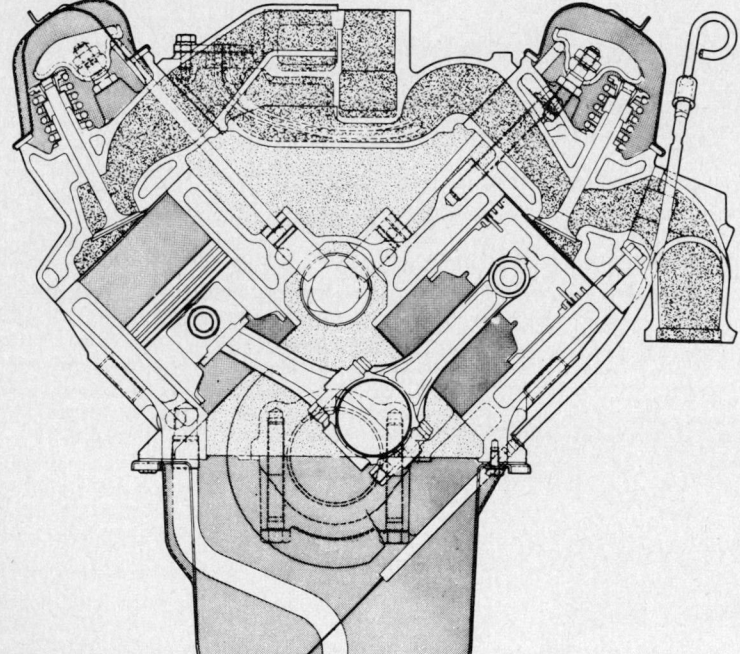

6-cylinder OHV 199/232/258 engine (© American Motors Corp.)

pertinent data relative to the specific engine-car application, in a conspicious place in the engine compartment.

For details, consult the Unit Repair section.

Engine Removal

All 1965-72 6-Cylinder

1. Remove hood; mark hinge position for easy assembly.
2. Remove battery.
3. Drain engine oil and cooling system.
4. On automatic transmission equipped cars: drain transmission oil and remove cooler lines (if so equipped).
5. Remove power steering pump, smog pump and air conditioner compressor and condenser (if so equipped).

Caution do *not* disconnect air conditioner or power steering lines.

6. Disconnect all hoses, tubes and wiring connecting engine and radiator to body and chassis. Remove radiator and starter motor for extra clearance in some models.
7. Disconnect exhaust pipe at manifold.
8. Disconnect speedo cable and shift linkage.
9. Support engine and transmission and remove rear engine crossmember.
10. On torque tube models, disconnect torque tube from extension housing.
11. Either disconnect rear U-joint and pull driveshaft from transmission, or:
12. Disconnect front motor mounts at engine, then lift engine and transmission forward and out through hood opening, while allowing slip joint to pull out of extension housing.

1965-66 Classic, Ambassador and Marlin 287/327 V8

1. Follow Steps 1-6, inclusive, from previous procedure, then continue as follows:
2. Disconnect exhaust pipes from manifold.
3. Support engine with chain hoist.
4. Remove rear engine crossmember.
5. Disconnect brake tube bracket (rear) that is secured to body pan.
6. Disconnect rear shock absorbers at lower brackets, then disconnect torque tube at transmission extension housing.
7. Disconnect parking brake equalizer and brake cable housing at torque tube bracket. Using a chain and body jack, pull the rear axle back far enough to remove front U-joint from transmission.
8. Disconnect speedometer cable and shift rods from transmission.
9. Unbolt front motor mounts, then pull engine forward and upward through hood opening.

1967-72 V8—All Models

1. Follow Steps 1-6, inclusive, of six-cylinder procedure, then continue as follows:
2. Disconnect exhaust pipes from manifolds.
3. Support engine with chain hoist.
4. Remove engine rear crossmember.
5. Disconnect speedometer cable at transmission.
6. Disconnect automatic transmission shift linkage or standard transmission shift rods at transmission. If equipped with American Motors four-speed shifter, remove boot from floor pan and pull the two bolts that hold shift lever to shift mechanism; the mechanism can remain attached. If equipped with Hurst linkage, the shift lever should be removed from transmission for adequate clearance (see illustration).
7. Disconnect front motor mounts and pull engine forward and upward, while supporting driveshaft as slip joint is removed from extension housing.

NOTE: if desirable, remove entire

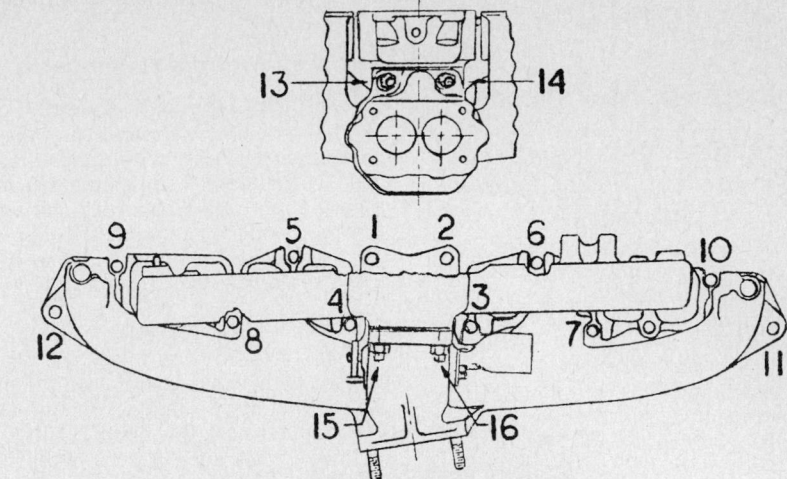

Intake manifold torque sequence—OHV 232 and 258 6-cylinder (ⓒ American Motors Corp.)

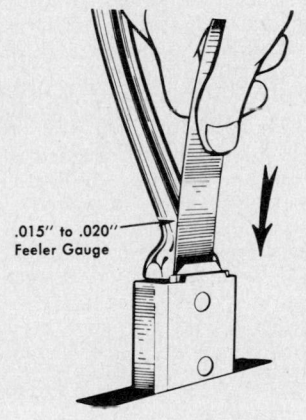

.015″ to .020″ Feeler Gauge

Removing lever from Hurst shifter
(ⓒ American Motors Corp.)

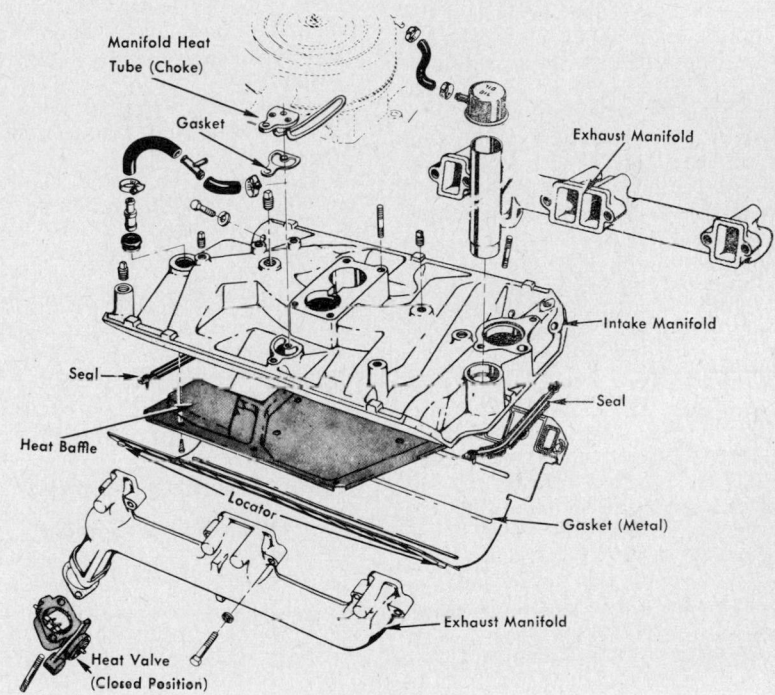

OHV 290/343 two-barrel intake manifold (ⓒ American Motors Corp.)

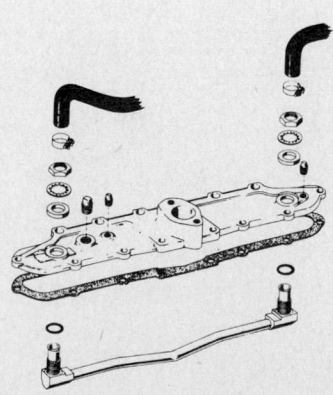

OHV 196 intake manifold
(ⓒ American Motors Corp.)

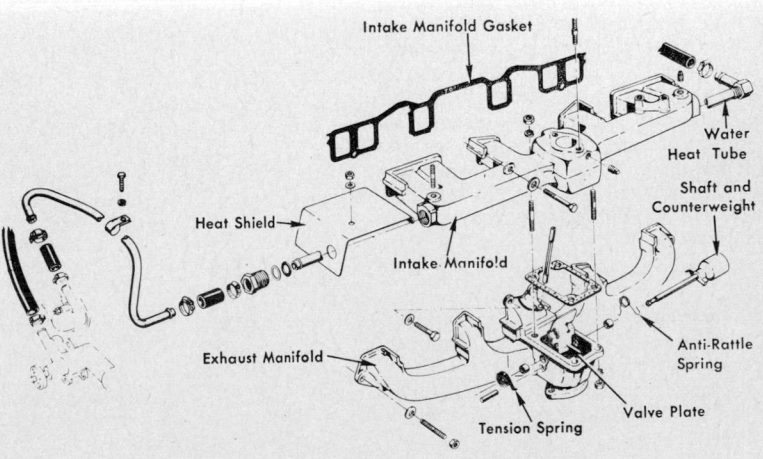

OHV 199/232 6 cylinder intake and exhaust manifold (ⓒ American Motors Corp.)

driveshaft beforehand by splitting rear U-joint.

Engine Manifolds

Intake Manifold

All 196 L-head and OHV 6 Cylinder

On these models, the intake manifold is cast integrally with the cylinder head. To remove top cover on OHV, remove linkage, lines and bolts.

287/327 V8

1. Disconnect the water outlet tube and remove the distributor.
2. Take off the air cleaner.
3. Disconnect all throttle lines across the cylinder head.
4. Disconnect the vacuum lines, the coil and ignition primary leads.
5. Remove the bolts which hold the intake manifold to both cylinder heads and lift off the manifold.

199/232/258 6-Cylinder

The intake manifold is mounted on the left-hand side of the engine and bolted to the cylinder head. A gasket is used between the intake manifold and the head, none is required for the exhaust manifold. The manifold on the Rogue 232 incorporates an internal water tube to supply carburetor heat; it is secured with a tapered fitting.

1. Remove air cleaner, carburetor and linkage.
2. On Rogue 232 engines, remove coolant hoses from intake manifold and plug the ends.
3. Disconnect the exhaust pipe at the manifold flange.
4. Remove manifold hold-down bolts and separate the intake and exhaust manifold from the head as a unit. Always use a new gasket when installing manifolds.

NOTE: manifold bolts and nuts are tightened to 25 ft. lbs.

290/304/343/360/390/401 V8

The cast iron manifold completely encloses and seals the tappet valley between the cylinder heads. The manifold contains water passages, a crankcase vent passage, exhaust crossover and induction passages. A one-piece metal gasket seals the intake manifold to cylinder head joint and also serves as an oil baffle. The left-hand carburetor bores supply cylinders No. 1, 7, 4 and 6; the right-hand bores cylinders No. 3, 5, 2 and 8.

1. Drain the radiator.
2. Disconnect throttle linkage, hoses, wiring and vacuum lines.
3. Remove manifold hold-down bolts and lift manifold straight up.

NOTE: when installing, coat gasket with sealer. Tighten bolts to 45 ft. lbs. evenly.

Exhaust Manifold Removal

All 196 L-head 6 Cylinder

The exhaust manifold on these models is actually the exhaust pipe held at the side of the cylinder head. Remove the caps which hold the pipe to the cylinder head, split the pipe at the flange and remove it from the vehicle. Tighten bolts to 10-15 ft. lbs.

V8 Models

Two exhaust manifolds are used, one on each bank. Disconnect the exhaust pipe at the flange, remove the bolts which hold the manifold to the cylinder head and lift the manifold off.

OHV 196 6 Cylinder

The cast iron exhaust manifold is removed in the following manner;

1. Disconnect exhaust pipe at flange.
2. Loosen the manifold bolts and break manifold away from engine.
3. Remove all bolts and manifold. When installing, tighten end flange bolts to 8-10 ft. lbs., center bolts to 20-25 ft. lbs.

OHV 199/232/258 6 cylinder

Exhaust manifold is removed along with *intake* manifold; see previous instructions.

Cylinder Head

Rocker Assembly Removal

OHV 196 6 Cylinder

The rocker arms and valve assembly are lubricated high pressure oil from an opening in the head through the front rocker support. The rocker shaft is one-piece construction, the rocker arms being retained by a snap-ring, thrust washers and a wave washer on each end of the shaft. The rocker shaft is installed with the oil holes down.

1. Remove the carburetor air cleaner and take off the nuts which hold the rocker cover to the cylinder head. Carefully remove the gasket from both the hood and the cover.
2. Working a few turns at a time, remove the bolts which hold the rocker assembly brackets to the cylinder head until the valve spring tension has been released.
3. Continue to remove the bolts until the rocker assembly is clear.

287/327 V8

The rocker shaft assembly is secured to the head with four cap bolts. The hollow rocker shafts serve as oil galleries for the rocker arms, push rod ends and valve stems. Oil pressure is supplied by the valve tappet main oil gallery and enters the rocker shafts via passages in the block and heads through a special drilled bolt at the rear of each shaft. Although the shaft assemblies are interchangeable between banks, two different rocker arms are used to actuate intake and exhaust valves. Rocker shafts are 0.8580-0.8585 in. diameter; oil clearance is 0.002 in.

290/304/343/360/390/401 V8

Individually mounted, pressed steel rocker arms operate the valves. These rockers are mounted on threaded studs and are held by a pivot ball and locknut. The hollow pushrods conduct oil from each hydraulic tappet to the rockers. There is a metering system in each tappet, consisting of a stepped lower push-

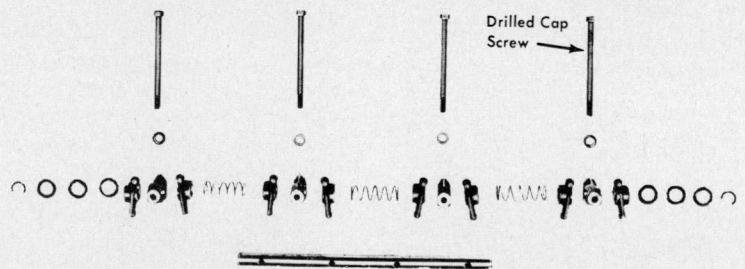

OHV 287/327 V8 rocker arm assembly (© American Motors Corp.)

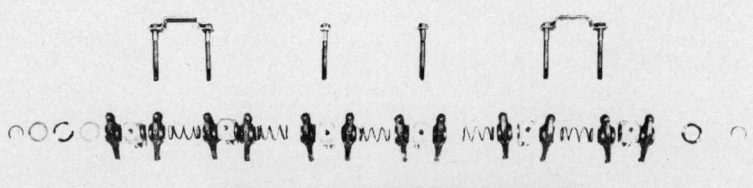

OHV 196 6 cylinder rocker arm assembly (© American Motors Corp.)

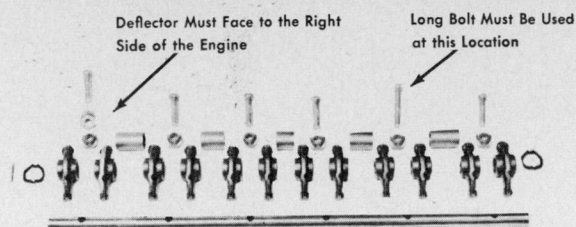

Deflector Must Face to the Right Side of the Engine

Long Bolt Must Be Used at this Location

OHV 199/232/258 6- cylinder rocker arm assembly
(© American Motors Corp.)

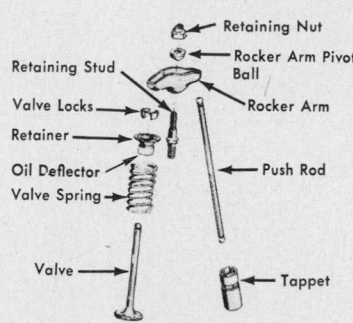

- Retaining Nut
- Rocker Arm Pivot Ball
- Retaining Stud
- Rocker Arm
- Valve Locks
- Retainer
- Oil Deflector
- Valve Spring
- Push Rod
- Valve
- Tappet

OHV new series V8 (1967-72) rocker arm assembly
(© American Motors Corp.)

rod cap surface and a flat plate. Any loss of lubrication to the rockers usually can be traced to failure of this part, or to a blocked pushrod oil passage. The pushrods rub against the cylinder head during operation and serve to maintain the correct rocker to valve stem angle.

1. Remove valve covers, after first removing any accessories and the air cleaner preheat tube.
2. Loosen and remove the retaining locknuts, ball pivots and rocker arms. It is a good idea to lay them out in order, along with their respective pushrods.
   NOTE: when installing new threaded studs, make sure hex nut is fully seated and tightened to 65-70 ft. lbs. Retaining locknuts are tightened to 20-25 ft. lbs.

OHV 199/232/258 6 Cylinder

The rocker shaft assembly is secured to the cylinder head with six cap bolts. Oil pressure for rocker lubrication is supplied via No. 3 camshaft bearing from the main oil gallery to No. 5 rocker support. Rocker shaft is 0.8575-0.8585 in. diameter; oil clearance is 0.003-0.005 in.

1. Remove valve cover.
2. Unbolt cap bolts and remove rockers and shaft.
   NOTE: hold rockers in place using large rubber bands.

Cylinder Head Removal

6 Cylinder 196 L-head and All OHV

1. Disconnect throttle linkage, fuel lines, water hoses, spark plug wires and vacuum line.
2. Loosen all nuts and remove; note position of battery strap.
3. Slide a heavy scraper around the head-to-block joint to free gasket. If necessary, reconnect battery ground and crank engine (coil wire out) to allow compression to free head. CAUTION: Do not hammer on head.
4. Before replacing head, wire brush studs and make sure they are tight. Clean top surface of block and lower head surface; check head for straightness. If head is out of true 0.006 in. over its length (or 0.001 in. every 1 in.) it must be resurfaced on a milling machine.
5. When installing, use sealer on both sides of gasket.

287/327 V8

The cylinder heads have two holes to assist head location. Maximum out of true is 0.006 in. for the entire length of head; 0.001 in every 1 in. Make sure the rear rocker arm bolts are properly installed, otherwise no oil will get to the rockers.

1. Remove oil filler tube, rocker covers, power steering pump, alternator, exhaust manifolds and air conditioner. Swing air conditioner out of the way without disconnecting its hoses.
2. Remove rockers and pushrods.
3. Disconnect water hoses, fuel lines, wiring, vacuum lines; remove distributor and intake manifold.
4. Remove cylinder head bolts and lift off heads carefully, making sure all ground straps, etc. have been disconnected.

290/343/390/304/360/401 V8

Procedure is similar to that for 287/327 cu. in. V8, except that rocker lubrication is accomplished through the pushrods and the distributor does not have to be removed. Cylinder head out of true is 0.006 in. for the full head length, 0.002 in. every 6 in. and 0.001 in. every 1 in. Torque sequence is different as well; see illustrations under Torque Specifications table.

NOTE: second bolt from front, bottom row, *must* have threads coated with sealer to prevent coolant leakage.

Engine Lubrication

Oil Pan Removal

NOTE: it is far easier to remove the engine in most cases.

1965-67 All 6 Cylinder Models

1. Support weight of front of car, and remove front springs.
2. Support front of engine from above the engine compartment, then remove the engine support-cushion attaching nuts at the mounting bracket.
3. Disconnect idler arm.
4. If equipped, remove front stabilizer bar.
5. Remove attaching bolts from front crossmember and pry crossmember down to gain clearance. To assist in holding crossmember down, install wood spacer blocks between the crossmember and body side sill.
6. Remove flywheel dust cover.
7. Drain oil and turn crankshaft so No. 1 piston is on upstroke, and remove pan.
8. To install, reverse the removal procedure.

1968-72 All 6 Cylinder Models

1. Disconnect front cushions from engine bracket and remove right bracket from engine.
2. Disconnect ground strap.
3. Remove valve cover and air cleaner.
4. If equipped, remove fan shroud.
5. Raise engine as far as possible.
6. Disconnect idler arm from side sill.
7. If equipped, disconnect stabilizer bar.
8. Loosen strut rod bolts at lower control arms.
9. Remove bolts retaining crossmember, and, with weight of car on wheels, pry down crossmember and insert wooden blocks to hold it down.
10. Drain oil and remove pan.
11. To install, reverse removal procedure.

1965-67 V8 Engines

1. Remove front springs. (See Front Suspension.) Support weight of front of car.
2. Support front of engine from above, and take away support cushion at engine.
3. Remove idler arm and piston rod from bracket on power steering models.
4. Remove sway bar.
5. Remove front suspension cross member from side sills.
6. Pry crossmember down to get clearance for pan. Use of wooden blocks between crossmember and side sills will aid.
7. Remove flywheel dust cover.
8. Drain oil and remove pan.

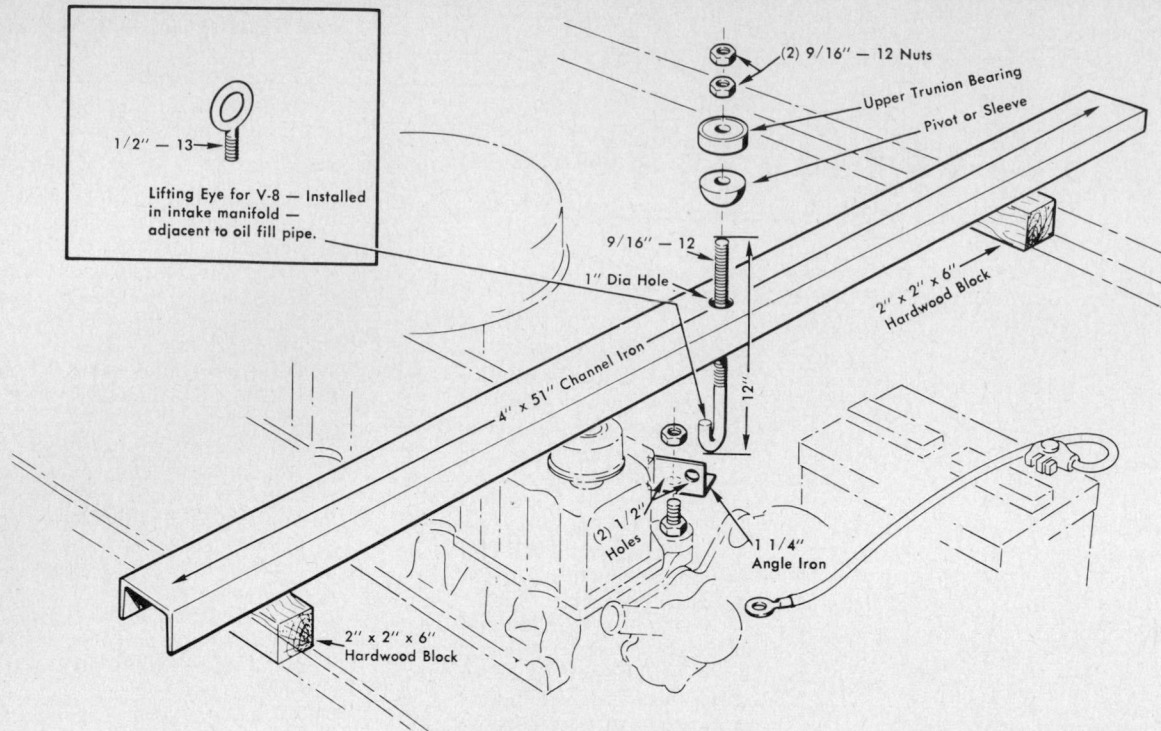

1/2" — 13 →

Lifting Eye for V-8 — Installed in intake manifold — adjacent to oil fill pipe.

(2) 9/16" — 12 Nuts

Upper Trunion Bearing

Pivot or Sleeve

9/16" — 12

1" Dia Hole

12"

2" x 2" x 6" Hardwood Block

4" x 51" Channel Iron

(2) 1/2" Holes

1 1/4" Angle Iron

2" x 2" x 6" Hardwood Block

Lifting fixture can be fabricated as illustrated to facilitate oil pan and motor mount removal
(© American Motors Corp.)

All 1966 Ambassador V8 Engines

1. Drain oil.
2. Remove flywheel dust cover.
3. Disconnect sway bar at rear mounts.
4. Remove oil pan bolts and oil pan.

All 1968-72 V8 Engines

1. Turn crankshaft until mark on damper is 180° from cover marks.
2. Disconnect engine cushion mounts from crossmember; remove fan shroud, if so equipped.
3. Disconnect ground strap; disconnect cushion mount brackets from block on American.
4. Remove starter motor.
5. Remove idler arm, except on 1969 Ambassador.
6. Ambassador sway bar: disconnect at side sills. American, Javelin, AMX, Rebel, Matador, Gremlin, Hornet sway bar: loosen links at lower control arms as far as possible.
7. Disconnect shock absorbers at lower control arms on all 1969 except Ambassador.
8. Attach chain hoist or lifting fixture and raise engine as far as possible.
9. Remove cushion mounts and brackets from American.
10. Loosen strut rod bolts at lower control arms; remove crossmember side sill bolts.
11. With car weight on front wheels, pry crossmember down far enough for clearance. Use wood blocks for support between

crossmember and side sills.
12. Remove oil pan bolts and oil pan.

Rear Main-Bearing Oil Seal

6 Cylinder Engines

Several different kinds of rear main-bearing oil seals are used, such as wood, rubber, felt and packing. Wooden plugs are used to seal the sides of the rear main-bearing caps. Later models use synthetic rubber key strips overlapping the bearing cap and seal the sides as well as the mating surfaces. As an actual oil seal, a slinger, an integral part of the crankshaft, is used to throw the oil into the trough so that it cannot get on the clutch.

To remove and replace the neoprene seal used on 199/232/258 engines:

1. Remove oil pan, as previously described.
2. Scrape clean all gasket surfaces, then remove rear main cap.
3. Discard lower portion of seal; drive out upper portion, using a brass drift, until it can be grasped with pliers.
4. Clean main cap, then *loosen* all remaining main cap bolts.
5. Lightly oil all surfaces, then coat the block-side surface of the new upper seal with soap and the seal lip with SAE 40 engine oil.
6. Install upper seal portion with the lip facing the front.
7. Coat the cap and block-side surface with Permatex No. 2.
8. Coat the back surface of new

lower seal with soap, the lip with SAE 40 engine oil. Install lower seal firmly into main cap.
9. Coat both chamfered edges of rear main cap with Permatex No. 2, install bearing inserts (if removed) and tighten cap bolts to 75-80 ft. lbs.
10. Cement oil pan gasket to block; coat gasket tongues with Permatex No. 2 where they fit into rear main cap, as well as front neoprene seal.
11. Coat rear pan seal with soap and place into proper recess, then install oil pan bolts (1/4 in.—5-8 ft. lbs.; 5/16 in.—10-12 ft. lbs).

287/327 V8 Engines

On these models, a packing-type rear main-bearing seal is used. The upper half can be replaced only after the crankshaft has been removed. The lower half can be replaced any time the rear main-bearing cap is taken down. To replace the lower half, take down the oil pan and remove the rear main-bearing cap. Remove the oil packing and set the new packing into the cap so that it protrudes a little at both ends. Temporarily, bolt it up into place. This will probably cause the upper portion of the oil seal to compress and rivet over just a little bit. Trim off the riveted portion and again insert the cap into position. The reason this is done is that, sometimes, the compression from the new oil seal will cause the upper seal to come down tighter against the crankshaft and prevent leaks, even in the

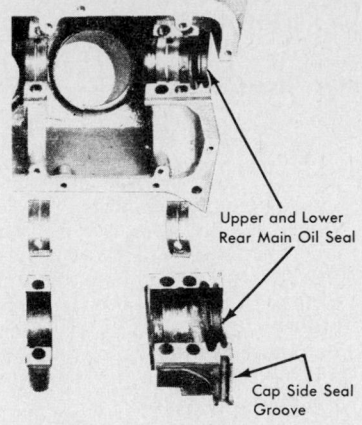

Rear main bearing oil seal, 287/327 V8
(ⓒ American Motors Corp.)

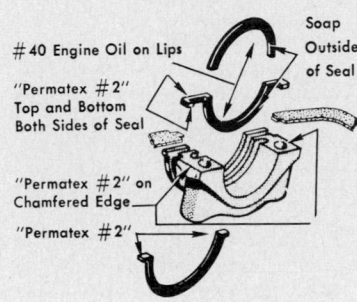

#40 Engine Oil on Lips

Soap Outside of Seal

"Permatex #2" Top and Bottom Both Sides of Seal

"Permatex #2" on Chamfered Edge

"Permatex #2"

**Rear main bearing oil seal—
199/232/258 6-cylinder and all 1967-72 V8**
(ⓒ American Motors Corp.)

upper half which has not been replaced.

290/343/390/304/360/401 V8 Engines

A neoprene seal, consisting of two pieces, is used. Procedure is identical to that used for the 199/232/258 6 cylinder, except that main cap bolts are tightened to 95-105 ft. lbs.

Oil Pump Service

Lubrication, on all American Motors engines, is full pressure except to the wrist pins. Pressure is supplied by a gear-type pump.

L-head 196 and OHV 196 6 Cylinder

The oil pump is mounted on the outside of the cylinder block on the right-hand side.

The engine oil pressure relief valve is found in the cylinder block where oil enters the distribution channel. The valve is not adjustable and is set to 50-58 psi at the factory. Oil pump bolts are tightened to 20-25 ft. lbs.

NOTE: always make sure connection between oil tube and block is tight.

199/232/258 6 Cylinder and 287/327 V8

The oil pump is driven by the distributor drive shaft. Oil pump R&R

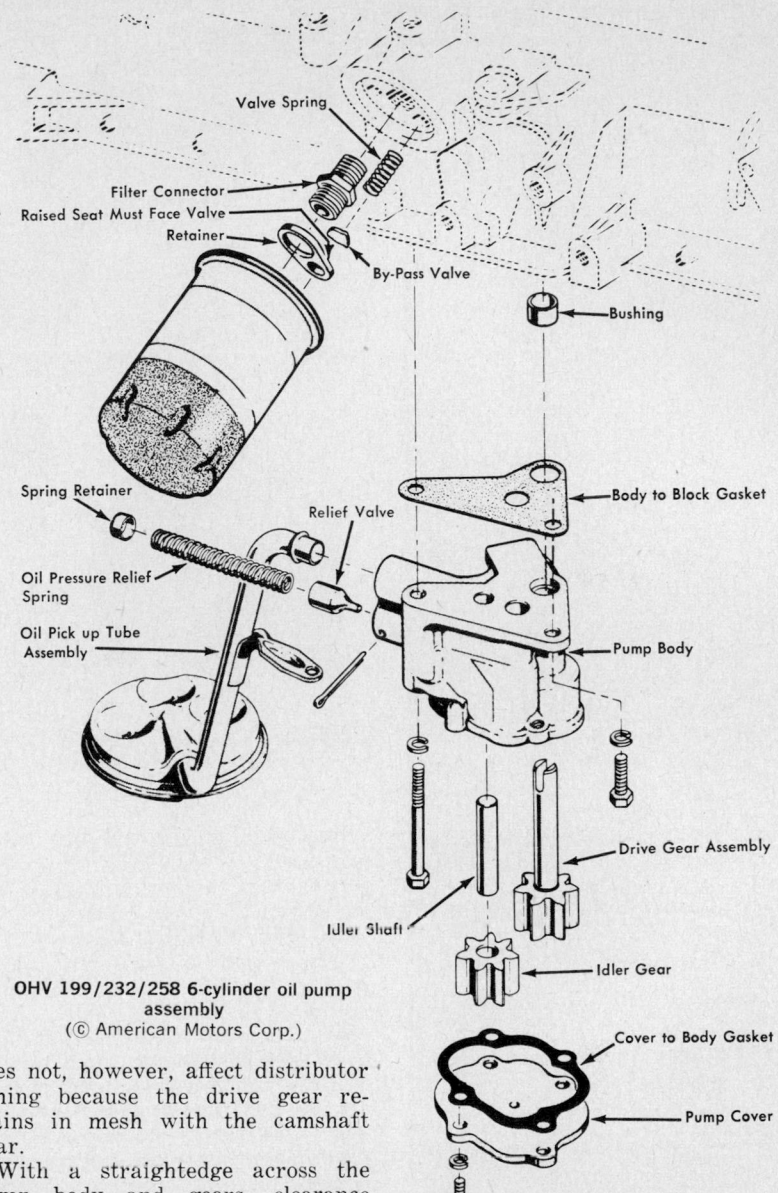

OHV 199/232/258 6-cylinder oil pump assembly
(ⓒ American Motors Corp.)

does not, however, affect distributor timing because the drive gear remains in mesh with the camshaft gear.

With a straightedge across the pump body and gears, clearance should be 0.000-0.004 in. (gears should project above body). Do not disturb location of tube in pump body if possible. Now, measure clearance

between gears and wall of gear cavity opposite point of gear mesh; should be 0.0005-0.0025 in. for

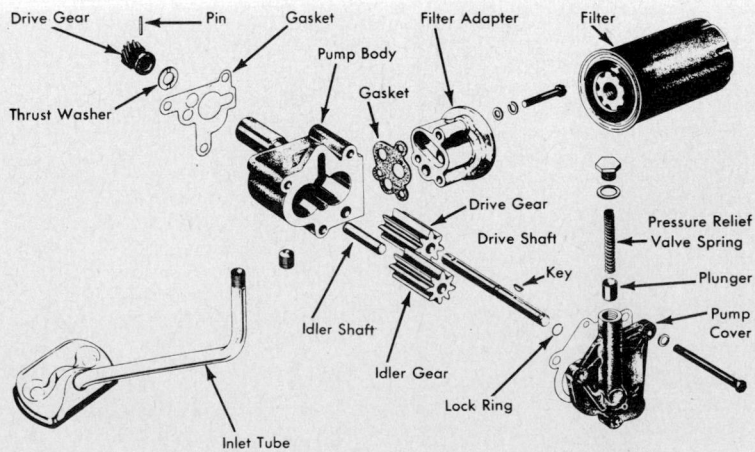

OHV 196 6 cylinder oil pump assembly (ⓒ American Motors Corp.)

⏻ CHILTON TIME-SAVER

Top Half, Rear Main-Bearing Oil Seal Replacement—Wick-Type

The following method has proven a distinct advantage in most cases and, if successful, saves many hours of labor.

1. Drain engine oil and remove oil pan.
2. Remove rear main-bearing cap.
3. With a 6 in. length of 3/16 in. brazing rod, drive up on either exposed end of the top half oil seal. When the opposite end of the seal starts to protrude, have a helper grasp it with pliers and pull gently while the driven end is being tapped.

Wick-Type Seal Installation

1. Obtain a 12 in. piece of copper wire (about the same gauge as that used in the strands of an insulated battery cable.)
2. Thread one strand of this wire through the new seal, about ½ in. from the end, bend back and make secure.
3. Thoroughly saturate the new seal with engine oil.
4. Push the copper wire up through the oil seal groove until it comes down on the opposite side of the baring.
5. Pull (with pliers) on the protruding copper wire while the crank-shaft is being turned and the new seal is slowly fed into place.
NOTE: this snaking operation slightly reduces the diameter of the new seal and care will have to be used to keep the seal from slipping too far through the top half of the bearing.
6. When an equal amount of seal is extending from each side, cut off the copper wire close to the seal and tamp both ends of the seal up into the groove. This will tend to expand the seal again.
NOTE: don't worry about the copper wire left in the groove. It is too soft to cause damage.
7. Replace the seal in the cap in the usual way and replace the oil pan.

Checking oil pump gear end clearance
(ⓒ American Motors Corp.)

Checking oil pump gear to body clearance
(ⓒ American Motors Corp.)

six, 0.008 in. for 287/327 V8. The oil pressure relief value is set at the factory to 60 psi and is not adjustable.

290/343/390/304/360/401 V8

The oil pump is located in, and as part of, the timing cover. The pump is driven by the distributor drive shaft. Oil pump R&R does not, however, affect distributor timing.

Remove pump cover and place a straightedge across pump body and gears. Clearance should be 0.0025-0.0065 in. (gears projecting above body). Measure clearance between gears and wall of gear cavity opposite point of gear mesh; should be 0.002-0.004 in. The oil pressure relief valve is set to 75 psi up to 1969, 85 psi starting 1970, and is not adjustable.

Valve System

Valve Removal

L-head Engines

1. Remove the cylinder head and the valve chamber cover. Using a valve spring compressor, contract the valve spring and remove the keeper. Of course, this is done with the valves in the closed position.
2. Let the valve spring come down, and pull the valve up out of the top of the cylinder.
3. Thoroughly clean up the valve and examine the seat for pits and scratches. If any are found, the valve face should be ground on a facing machine. When refaced, examine carefully to make sure that too much metal was not removed from the valves, since a sharp corner on the head of the valve will not last long in an engine.
4. There should be plenty of metal above the seat.
5. Examine the valve stem for wear and, if necessary, mike the valve stem in two or three places to check the amount of wear.

Overhead Valve Engines

Remove the cylinder head, compress the valve spring and remove the keeper. Release the pressure from the spring and push the valve out.

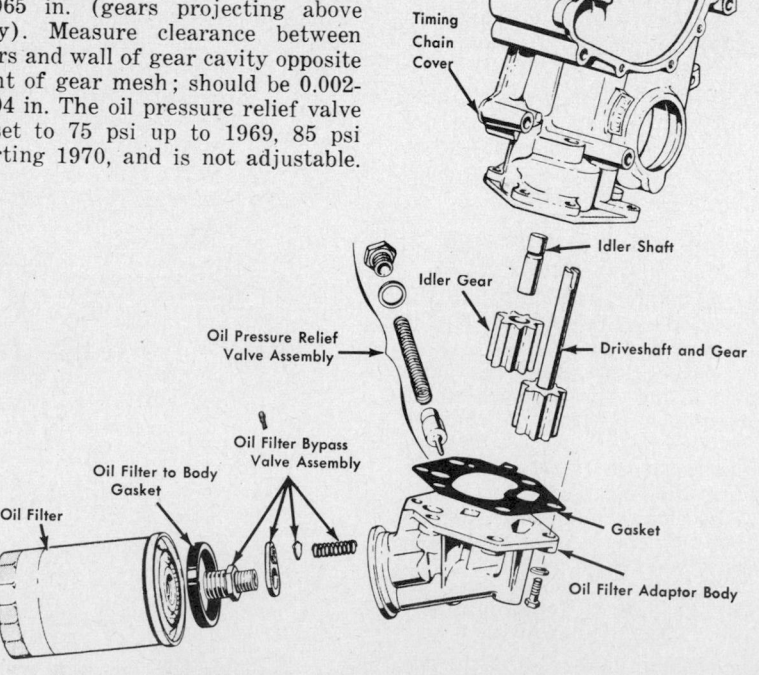

New series V8 (1967-72) oil pump assembly (ⓒ American Motors Corp.)

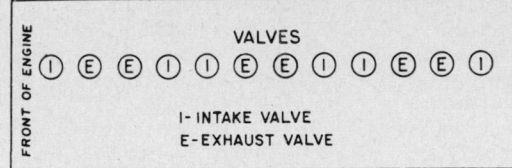

Valve sequence—6-cylinder L-head and OHV 196
(© American Motors Corp.)

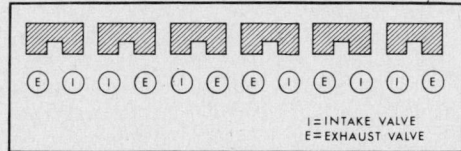

**Valve sequence—OHV 6 199/232/258—
bottom view**
(© American Motors Corp.)

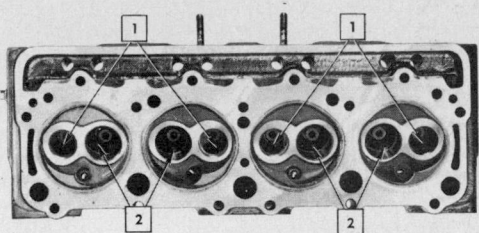

Valve sequence V8
(© American Motors Corp.)

1 Exhaust valves
2 Intake valves

199/232/258 6 Cylinder 1967-72 V8

These engines do not have replaceable valve guides.

Measure the stem to guide clearance in one of two ways. The valve stem can be measured with a micrometer and the guide measured using calibrated pilots, then the difference computed. The best way is to install the valve into the guide, without spring, and measure the lateral movement using a dial indicator. If stem to guide clearance is excessive, guides must be reamed to the proper oversize. Three oversize valves are available with stems 0.003, 0.015 and 0.030 in. larger than standard diameter.

NOTE: the exhaust valve stem is

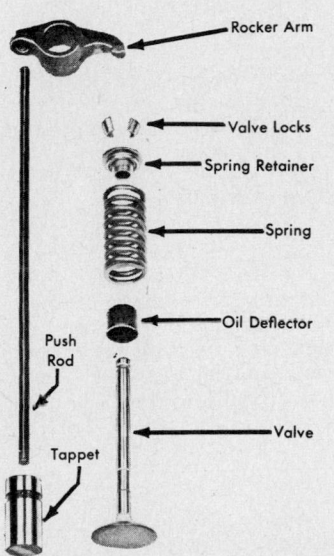

Valve assembly sequence—OHV 6 cylinder
(© American Motors Corp.)

Rocker Arm
Valve Locks
Spring Retainer
Spring
Oil Deflector
Push Rod
Valve
Tappet

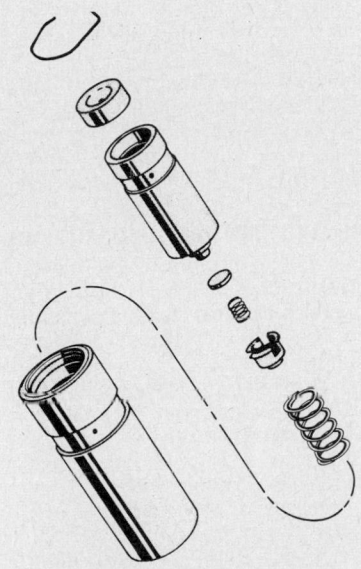

**Sectional view of hydraulic tappet
(metering disc not shown)**
(© American Motors Corp.)

Valve Margin

Correct Valve Facing

Incorrect Valve Facing

(© American Motors Corp.)

Valve Spring Check

Valve spring pressure specifications are given in the Valve Specifications table.

However, a quick check can be made by placing all of the intake springs next to one another on a straight edge. If they all come up to the same height it can be presumed, with a fair degree of accuracy, that all the valve springs are in good condition since it is unlikely that all of them would collapse the same amount.

Valve Guide Removal

L-head 196 6 Cylinder

Remove the valves and, using a draw-type puller, draw the valve guide up through the top of the bore. Before the guide is pulled, the distance from the top of the cylinder head to the top of the guide should be measured and noted so that a new guide can be driven in just that amount. Sometimes, driving a new

guide into the bore disturbs the top of the guide somewhat, making it necessary to ream the guide so that the valve will fit properly. Any time a new valve guide is installed the valve should be reseated to make certain that the seat is concentric with the new guide.

Cast-iron OHV 196 6 Cylinder

With cylinder head off, remove the valves and carefully measure the distance from the top of the cylinder head to the top of the valve guide. Then, drive the guide out into the combustion chamber.

A new guide is driven in from the top towards the combustion chamber the distance noted before the old guide was removed. NOTE: 23/32 in. above head.

Sometimes, driving the guide disturbs it somewhat, making it necessary to ream for a good fit on the valve.

Removing valve spring keepers
(© American Motors Corp.)

tapered 0.0005-0.001 in., smaller diameter toward valve head. Proper stem to guide clearance is 0.001-0.003 in. for both intake and exhaust valves.

No provision is made for adjustment of hydraulic tappet travel. Tappets having various thicknesses of push rod seats are available and can be installed to get a standard center travel position under normal operating conditions.

1965-66 287/327 V8

The valve stem to guide clearance is maintained through replacement of valve guides. The valve guides are an interference fit in their bores in the cylinder head, and can be replaced by driving out the old guides and driving in the new. The new guides are driven to a depth to permit ¾ in. + or — 1/64 in. to remain exposed above the cylinder head.

Tool J-21753, when driven until bottomed, establishes the required ¾ in. guide height.

Valve stem to guide clearance is .001-.003 in. for intake and exhaust.

Timing Case

Vibration Damper Removal

All Models

Remove the radiator core and the fan. Remove the nut from the center of the pulley and, using a puller, remove the pulley from the front of the crankshaft.

Timing Case Cover R&R
199/232/258 OHV 6 Cylinder

The timing chain cover has a seal

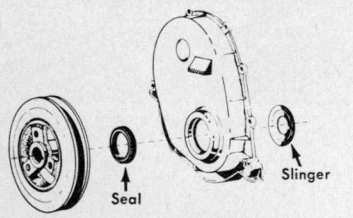

Timing chain cover assembly—
199/232/258 6- cylinder
(© American Motors Corp.)

and oil slinger to prevent oil leakage past the crankshaft pulley hub.

1. Remove all V-belts, fan blades and pulley.
2. Remove vibration damper.
3. Remove oil pan to cover bolts and cover to block bolts.
4. Raise cover and pull oil pan front seal up far enough to extract the tabs from the holes in cover.
5. Remove cover gasket from block; cut off seal tab flush with front face of block.
6. Clean all mating surfaces and remove oil seal.
7. Install new front oil seal, using proper size arbor.
8. Install new neoprene front oil pan seal, cutting off protruding tab to match original.
9. Position cover on block and install bolts. Tighten cover bolts to 4-6 ft. lbs.; four lower bolts to 10-12 ft. lbs.
10. Install vibration damper, tightening bolt to 50-60 ft. lbs.
NOTE: front oil seal can be installed with cover in place only if proper tool or duplicate is available.

290/343/390/304/360/401 V8

The die-cast timing cover incorporates an oil seal at the vibration damper hub. This seal must be installed from the rear; therefore the cover must be removed from engine in every case to replace front seal.

1. Drain coolant and remove hoses from cover.
2. Remove distributor, fuel pump, alternator drive belt, accessory drive belts, fan and hub assembly.
3. Remove the vibration damper bolt, then pull off the damper.
4. Remove air conditioner compressor and power steering pump, if so equipped, and swing them out of the way *without* disconnecting hoses.
5. Remove the two front oil pan bolts from beneath the car, then remove the eight 9/16 in. hex head cover bolts.
6. Remove cover from block, then clean all parts and mating surfaces and remove oil seal.
7. Coat new seal lips with Vaseline

and seal surface with sealer, then drive seal into cover bore until it seats against the outer cover face. Use a proper size arbor for this job.

8. Remove lower dowel pin from cylinder block; this must be replaced when cover is in position but before bolts are installed.
9. Cut the oil pan gasket flush with the block on both sides of the oil pan.
10. Cut corresponding pieces of gasket from another oil pan gasket and cement them to cover. Install neoprene oil pan front seal into cover and align cork gasket tabs with pan seal.
11. Apply Permatex No. 2 to gaskets, then position cover. Install oil pan bolts and tighten evenly until cover lines up with upper dowel pin.
12. Install lower dowel pin, then cover to block bolts; tighten to 20-30 ft. lbs.
13. Install all removed pieces and adjust ignition timing.

Valve Timing

Camshaft (valve) timing is determined by the relationship between the camshaft sprocket and the crankshaft gear. A jumped timing chain can cause any number of problems (backfiring, spitting back, poor performance), not the least of which is a non-starting engine.

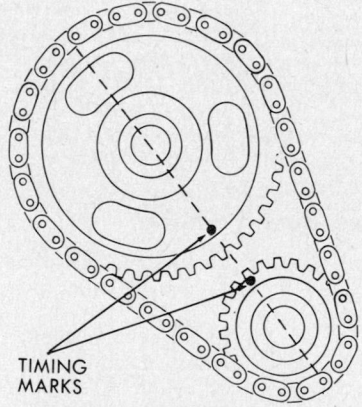

TIMING MARKS

Six-cylinder timing chain and sprockets

Valve Timing Check—all 6 Cylinder

To check valve timing, remove valve cover and spark plugs, then rotate crankshaft until No. 6 piston is at TDC on compression stroke. Compression stroke can be determined by holding a finger in the No. 6 spark plug hole while turning the engine by hand—finger will be forced out by compression pressure. Set the valves of No. 1 cylinder to 0.003 in. clearance and rock the crankshaft back and forth. The exhaust valve should open before the TDC mark on the pulley lines up with the

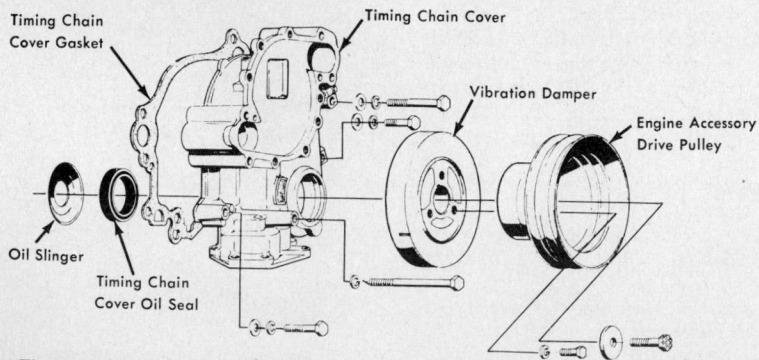

Timing Chain Cover Gasket
Timing Chain Cover
Vibration Damper
Engine Accessory Drive Pulley
Oil Slinger
Timing Chain Cover Oil Seal

Timing chain cover assembly—new series (1967-72) V8 (© American Motors Corp.)

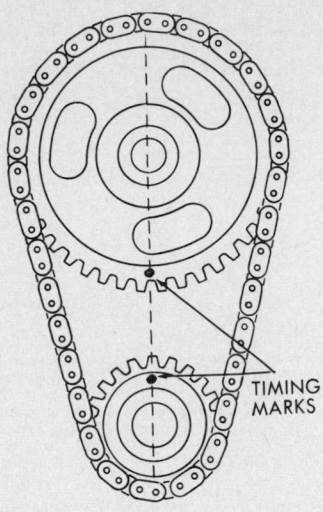

V8 timing chain and sprockets

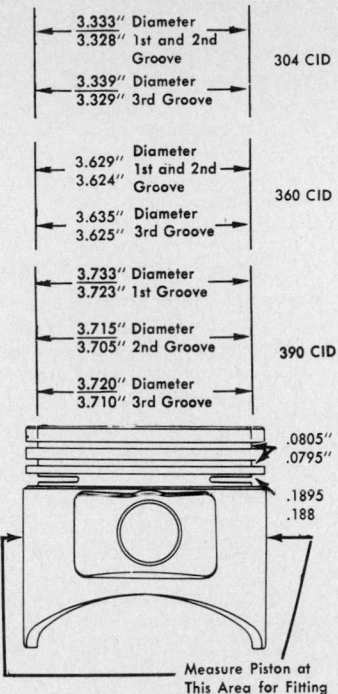

3.333″ Diameter 3.328″ 1st and 2nd Groove	304 CID
3.339″ Diameter 3.329″ 3rd Groove	
3.629″ Diameter 3.624″ 1st and 2nd Groove	360 CID
3.635″ Diameter 3.625″ 3rd Groove	
3.733″ Diameter 3.723″ 1st Groove	
3.715″ Diameter 3.705″ 2nd Groove	390 CID
3.720″ Diameter 3.710″ 3rd Groove	

.0805″ / .0795″
.1895 / .188

Measure Piston at
This Area for Fitting

304/360/390 piston dimensions
(© American Motors Corp.)

pointer—measure the actual distance. The intake valve should open the same distance *past* the pointer—if it varies more than ½ in., remove the timing cover and inspect the chain.

Valve Timing Check—all V8

To check the valve timing, remove the rocker covers and spark plugs, then rotate the crankshaft until No. 6 piston is at TDC on compression stroke. This places No. 1 piston on TDC exhaust overlap. Rotate the crankshaft counterclockwise 90° (¼ turn) and install a dial indicator on No. 1 intake rocker pushrod end. Crank the engine in the normal direction of rotation until the pushrod moves, as indicated on the dial by a ± 0.020 in. pointer movement. In this position, the timing pointer should align with TDC mark on 1967-72 engines; about 25/32 in. before TDC mark on 1965-66 287/327 engines. If this varies more than about ¼ in., remove timing cover for chain inspection.

Camshaft Timing and/or Timing Chain Installation

All Models

1. Remove the timing case cover and turn the engine until the mark on the crankshaft sprocket

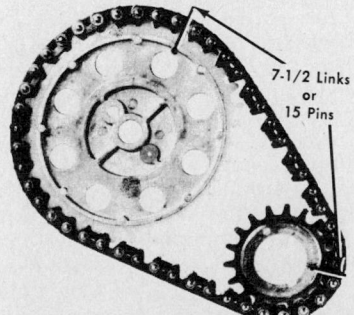

7-1/2 Links
or
15 Pins

Correct timing chain installation—
199/232/258 6-cylinder
(© American Motors Corp.)

points upwards, and the mark on the camshaft sprocket points downwards. Marks should be near each other and in line between the shaft centers.
2. Remove the bolts which hold the camshaft sprocket to the camshaft and start a puller over the crank gear.
3. Pull the crank gear off the front of the crankshaft.

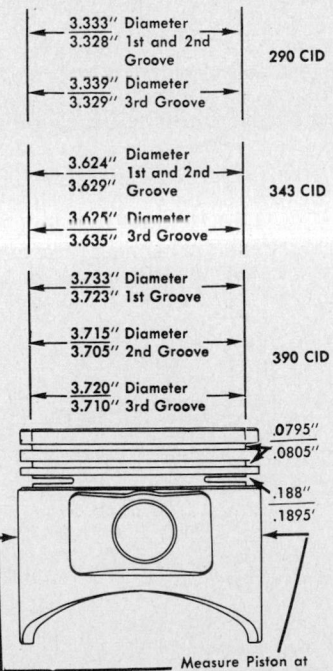

3.333″ Diameter 3.328″ 1st and 2nd Groove	290 CID
3.339″ Diameter 3.329″ 3rd Groove	
3.624″ Diameter 3.629″ 1st and 2nd Groove	343 CID
3.625″ Diameter 3.635″ 3rd Groove	
3.733″ Diameter 3.723″ 1st Groove	
3.715″ Diameter 3.705″ 2nd Groove	390 CID
3.720″ Diameter 3.710″ 3rd Groove	

.0795″ / .0805″
.188″ / .1895′

Measure Piston at
This Area for Fitting

290/343/390 V8 piston dimensions
(© American Motors Corp.)

4. On the bench, arrange the new chain over the sprockets so that the marks are nearest each other and in line between their own centers, then carry this to the engine. Start the crank gear up on its key and arrange the camshaft so that, when the three bolts line up, the marks are between shaft centers.
   NOTE: on 6 cylinder engines, locate the marked cam tooth at one o'clock position; mark on crank should be approximately at point of mesh. Count the number of links between the marks; should be 19 pins or 9½ links for OHV and L-head 196 cast iron engine, 15 pins or 7½ links for OHV 199/232/258 engine.
   On all V8 engines, locate the marked cam tooth on a horizontal line at three or nine o'clock position; mark on crank at point of mesh. Count the number of links between marks; should be 20 pins or 10 links.
5. Secure the cam gear to the camshaft and force the crankshaft gear all the way on the shaft.
6. Reassemble the front of the engine.

Piston Fitting

Rod and Piston Assembly Installation

On engines using split-skirt pistons, the slit in the skirt must be installed opposite the oil squirt hole in the connecting rod. Solid skirt pistons are assembled so that the boss, or dimple, (and, in some instances, the letter F) at the top of the piston is on the same side of the connecting rod as the boss. This will be found on the connecting rod channel about halfway up the rod.

The piston and rod assemblies are united to the engine from the top and the dimple, or dot, on the top of the piston goes toward the front. On those engines having split-skirt pistons, the slit in the skirt of the piston goes to the left side of the engine.

1967-72 V8 Engine

The piston pins are a press fit in the connecting rod, hand fit in piston at 68° F; they must be removed and installed using an arbor press. The connecting rod is centered on the piston pin ± 0.030 in.; piston pin to piston bore clearance is 0.0003-0.0005 in. at room temperature.

Two compression rings and one oil ring are used. Before assembly, ring grooves must be cleaned of all carbon deposits using a broken ring or a commercial groove cleaner. Oil drain holes on pin boss and in grooves must be cleaned at the same time.

Side clearance between land and piston ring should be 0.002-0.004 in. for No. 1 and No. 2 rings, 0.000-0.005

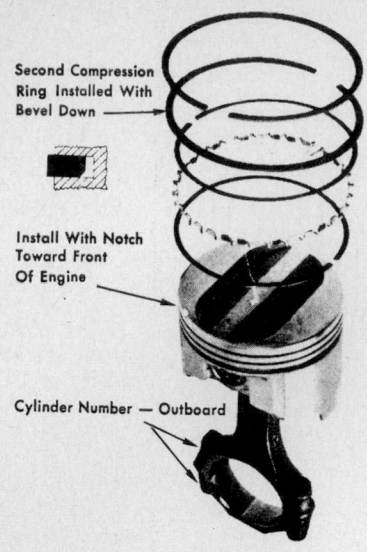

Second Compression Ring Installed With Bevel Down

Install With Notch Toward Front Of Engine

Cylinder Number — Outboard

Squirt Hole — Inboard

390 V8 piston assembly
(© American Motors Corp.)

in. for No. 3 oil control ring.

Ring end gap is measured at the bottom of the cylinder bore near the end of ring travel area; push ring down using an inverted piston and measure gap with feeler gauge. Compression rings—0.010-0.020 in.; oil ring—0.015-0.055 in. (rail gap).

Prior to installing piston and connecting rod assembly into 1967-72 engines, except 1968-69 390, arrange ring gaps with No. 1 180° from No. 2 and No. 3 at least 90° from No. 2. Each rail gap on oil control ring should be 30° apart.

On 1968-69 390 engine, arrange

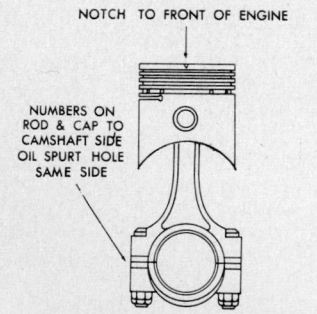

NOTCH TO FRONT OF ENGINE

NUMBERS ON ROD & CAP TO CAMSHAFT SIDE OIL SPURT HOLE SAME SIDE

Piston and rod assembly 6-cylinder engine

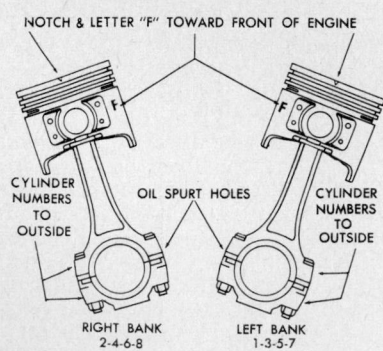

NOTCH & LETTER "F" TOWARD FRONT OF ENGINE

CYLINDER NUMBERS TO OUTSIDE

OIL SPURT HOLES

CYLINDER NUMBERS TO OUTSIDE

RIGHT BANK 2-4-6-8

LEFT BANK 1-3-5-7

Piston and rod assembly—V8 engines

No. 1 gap 180° from No. 2; oil control expander spacer tangs must be installed in drilled holes above piston pin and oil control rails must be 180° apart.

Piston to cylinder bore clearance should be 0.001-0.0018 in. for 290 and 304 engine; 0.0012-0.002 in. for 343 and 360 engine; 0.0010-0.0018 in. for 390 and 401 engine.

1965-66 287/327 V8 Engine

Piston pins are a press fit in connecting rod, hand fit in piston at 68°F. Before assembly, clean ring grooves using broken ring or commercial groove cleaner. Piston to cylinder bore clearance at top land should be 0.028-0.032 in.; at skirt top 0.0009-0.0025 in.; at skirt bottom 0.0009-0.0015 in.

Piston ring groove clearance should be 0.002-0.006 in. for compression rings, 0.0001-0.004 in. for oil ring. Ring end gap, with ring near bottom of cylinder, should be 0.010-0.020 in. for compression rings, 0.015-0.055 in. for oil ring rail.

Piston rings should be arranged with the end gaps 120° apart, with no gap being placed over the pin boss.

199/232/258 6 Cylinder Engine

Pistons of the 199 engine can be identified by their flat head and two notches; 232 and 258 pistons have a concave head with one notch. Specified piston to cylinder bore clearance is 0.0005-0.0013 in.

Ring side clearance on No. 1 and No. 2 ring should be 0.0015-0.0035 in.; 0.0000-0.005 in. on oil ring. End gap on compression rings should be 0.010-0.020; 0.015-0.055 in. on oil control rail. Arrange rings in the same manner as on 290 V8 engine.

196 L-head and OHV 6 Cylinder Engines

Piston ring side clearance in grooves should be 0.002-0.004 in. for compression rings, 0.0001-0.004 in. for oil ring. Piston to cylinder bore clearance 0.0006-0.0012 in. at skirt bottom, 0.017-0.019 in. at top land. Pis-

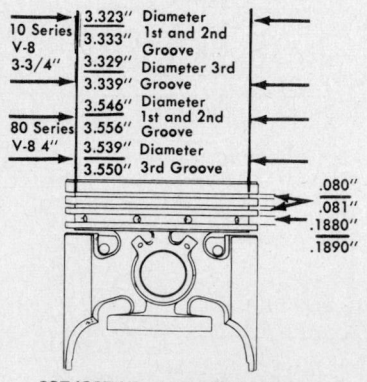

10 Series V-8 3-3/4"
3.323" Diameter 1st and 2nd Groove
3.333"
3.329" Diameter 3rd Groove
3.339"

80 Series V-8 4"
3.546" Diameter 1st and 2nd Groove
3.556"
3.539" Diameter 3rd Groove
3.550"

.080"
.081"
.1880"
.1890"

287/327 V8 piston dimensions
(© American Motors Corp.)

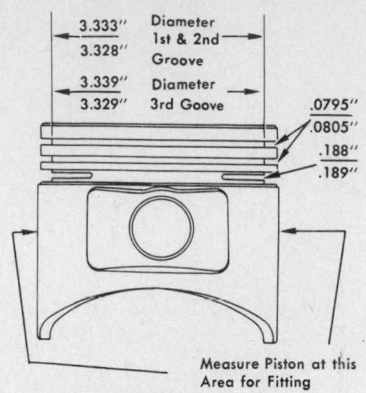

3.333" Diameter 1st & 2nd Groove
3.328"
3.339" Diameter 3rd Groove
3.329"

.0795"
.0805"
.188"
.189"

Measure Piston at this Area for Fitting

199/232 6 cylinder piston dimensions
(© American Motors Corp.)

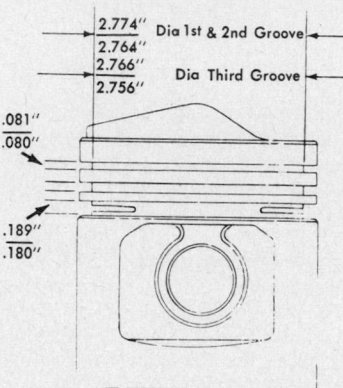

2.774" Dia 1st & 2nd Groove
2.764"
2.766" Dia Third Groove
2.756"

.081"
.080"

.189"
.180"

196 OHV and L-head 6 cylinder piston dimensions
(© American Motors Corp.)

ton ring gap should be 0.010-0.020 in. for compression rings, 0.015-0.055 in. for oil ring.

Arrange piston rings with gaps 120° apart.

Front Suspension

Description

The front suspension on all models is an independent linked type with the coil springs located between seats in the wheelwell panels and seats in the upper control arms. Rubber insulators between the springs and seats reduce noise transmission to the body.

Direct acting, telescopic shock absorbers are located inside the coil springs and the control arms are attached to the body via rubber bushings.

Up to 1969, the lower control arm contained a single ball joint which attached to the steering knuckle, while the upper portion of the knuckle was attached to a trunnion. In 1970, this system was replaced by a double ball joint design, both upper and lower control arms each having one joint.

On all models, strut rods serve to support the lower control arms. Stabilizer bars are used on some models.

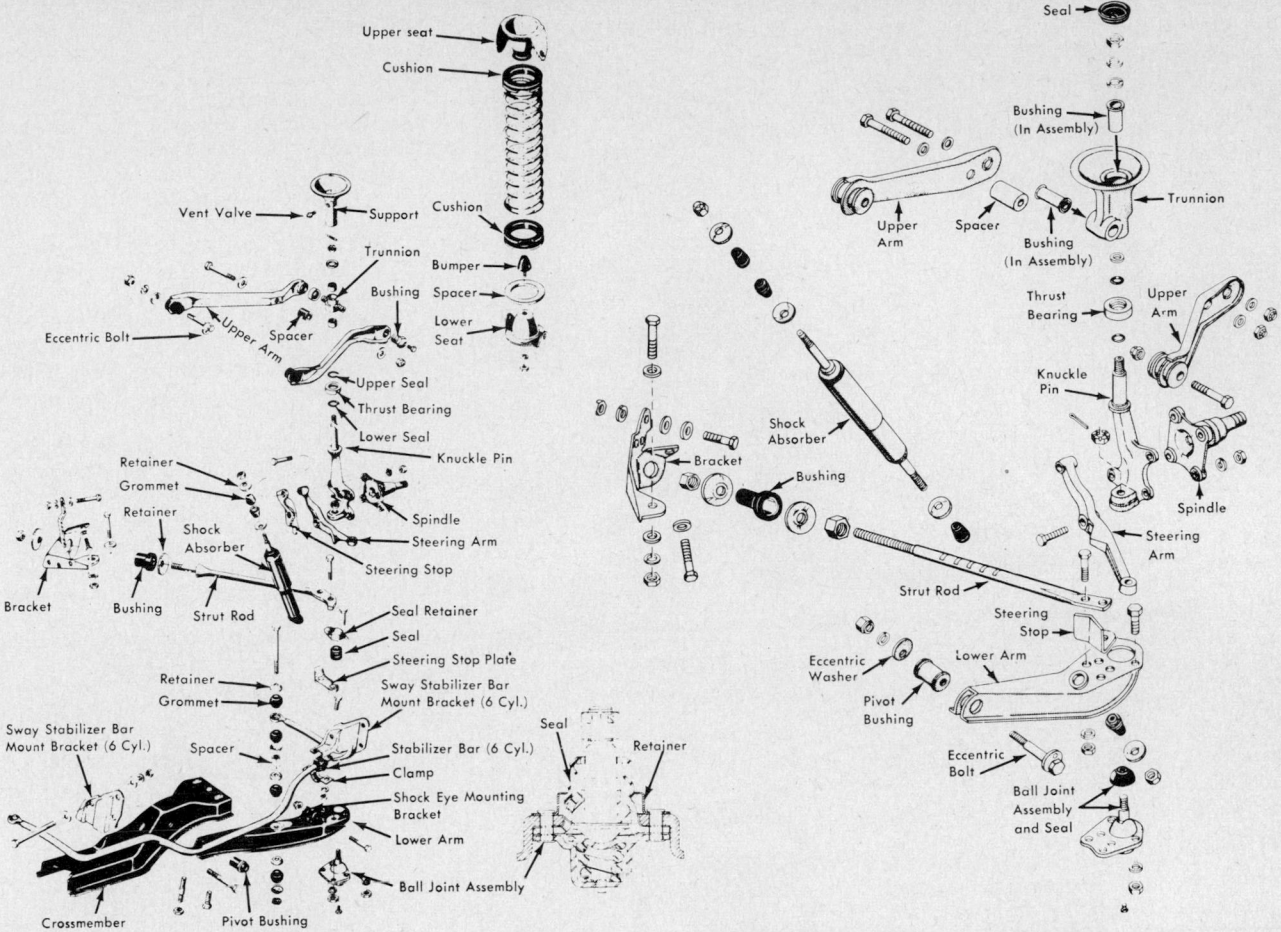

Upper seat
Cushion
Seal
Vent Valve
Support
Cushion
Bushing (In Assembly)
Trunnion
Trunnion
Bumper
Upper Arm
Spacer
Bushing
Bushing (In Assembly)
Spacer
Lower Seat
Eccentric Bolt
Upper Arm
Spacer
Thrust Bearing
Upper Arm
Upper Seal
Thrust Bearing
Knuckle Pin
Lower Seal
Knuckle Pin
Spindle
Retainer
Grommet
Shock Absorber
Steering Arm
Bracket
Shock Absorber
Spindle
Retainer
Shock Absorber
Steering Stop
Bushing
Steering Arm
Bracket
Bushing
Strut Rod
Seal Retainer
Seal
Strut Rod
Steering Stop
Retainer
Steering Stop Plate
Eccentric Washer
Lower Arm
Grommet
Sway Stabilizer Bar Mount Bracket (6 Cyl.)
Pivot Bushing
Sway Stabilizer Bar Mount Bracket (6 Cyl.)
Spacer
Stabilizer Bar (6 Cyl.)
Seal
Retainer
Eccentric Bolt
Clamp
Shock Eye Mounting Bracket
Lower Arm
Ball Joint Assembly and Seal
Crossmember
Pivot Bushing
Ball Joint Assembly

Typical front suspension—1965-69 Ambassador, Rebel, Classic and Marlin
(ⓒ American Motors Corp.)

Typical front suspension—1965-69 American, Javelin and AMX
(ⓒ American Motors Corp.)

Front Spring Removal and Installation

1965-69

Raise rear of car at diagonal corner from front spring to be removed. Install hooks in holes provided in spring seats while compressed. Release load and lower rear corner. This allows spring removal from car.

To install new spring, compress it by means of hydraulic press or jack with seats in place. Be sure holes in seats are aligned. Install hooks to hold spring in compression while placing in position. Reversing the above removal procedures will control position to release hooks when spring is in place.

1970-72

Jack up the car far enough to reach the two lower shock absorber nuts. Remove the nuts, washers and grommets, then remove the upper mounting bracket screws and bolts from the wheelwell. Lift the bracket and shock absorber from the panel.

Lower the car to the floor, then install either spring compressor J-23474 (American Motors part number) or equivalent homemade unit through the upper spring seat opening and bolt it to the lower spring seat using the lower shock absorber mounting holes. Remove the lower spring seat spindle retaining nuts, then tighten the compressor tool to compress the spring about 1 in. Jack up the front of the car and support it on axle stands at the subframe (allowing the control arms to hang free). Remove the front wheel and pull the lower spring seat

1970-72 Hornet, Gremlin, Matador, Javelin, AMX, Rebel and Ambassador front suspension with double ball joints

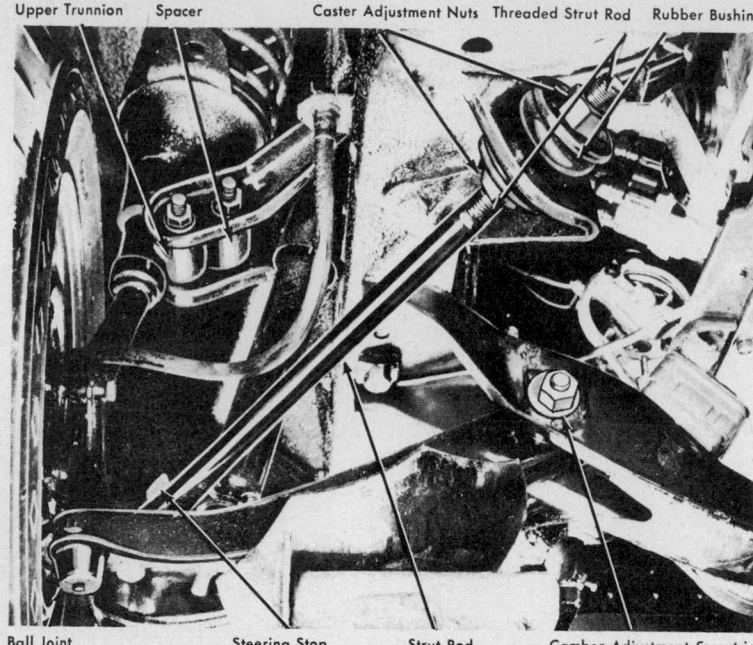

Upper Trunnion   Spacer   Caster Adjustment Nuts   Threaded Strut Rod   Rubber Bushing

Ball Joint   Steering Stop   Strut Rod   Camber Adjustment Eccentric

Rear view of front suspension—models to 1969 (© American Motors Corp.)

compress the coil spring approximately 2 in., using the procedure outlined earlier under Front Spring Removal and Installation—1970-72.

Jack up the front of the car and support the body on jackstands placed under the subframes (allow the control arms to hang free). Remove the wheel and the upper ball joint cotter pin and retaining nut. Separate the ball joint stud from the steering knuckle using two hammers—one as a brace and the other to apply shock to the knuckle. Remove the inner pivot bolts from the panel, then remove the control arm.

To install, reverse the removal procedure. Do not tighten the pivot bolt nuts until the full weight of the car is on the wheels. The ball joint stud nut must be tightened to 45 ft. lbs., the lower spring seat pivot retaining nuts to 35 ft. lbs., and the

out away from the car, then slowly release the spring tension and remove the coil spring and lower spring seat.

To install, place the spring compressor through the coil spring and tape the rubber spring cushion to the small-diameter end of the spring (upper). Place the lower spring seat against the spring with the end of the coil against the formed shoulder in the seat. The shoulder and coil end face inwards, toward the engine, when the spring is installed.

Place the spring up against the upper seat, then align the lower spring seat pivot so that the retaining studs will enter the holes in the upper control arm. Compress the coil spring and install the spring, then install the wheel and tire and lower the car to the floor (to place weight on

Lower Coil End Must Butt Against Formed Shoulder In Spring Seat

Lower spring seat installation—1970-72 front coil springs (© American Motors Corp.)

suspension). Install and tighten lower spring seat spindle retaining nuts and tighten them to 35 ft. lbs. Remove the spring compressor and install the shock absorber.

Control Arm Removal

Upper Control Arm—1965-69

1. Remove front spring as described above.
2. Remove front or rear arm by disconnecting it at the trunnion, at wheelhouse panel mounting bolt, and the control arm spacer. Upon reassembly, torque spacer bolt nut to 80-90 ft. lbs.
3. Both front and rear arms may be removed as an assembly by disconnecting them from the mounting bracket. Remove lower spring seat support, lock pin and nut from the knuckle pin.

NOTE: to facilitate caster and camber adjustments upon reassembly, mark position of eccentric washers before disassembly.

Upper Control Arm—1970-72

Remove the shock absorber and

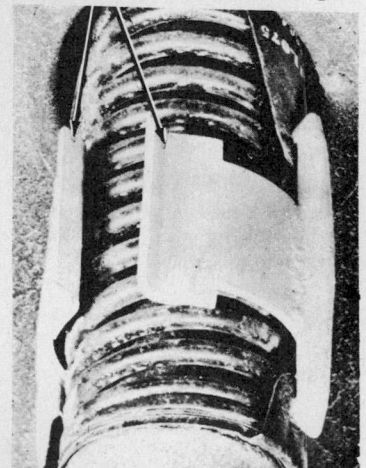

Front coil spring removal tools in place (arrows) (© American Motors Corp.)

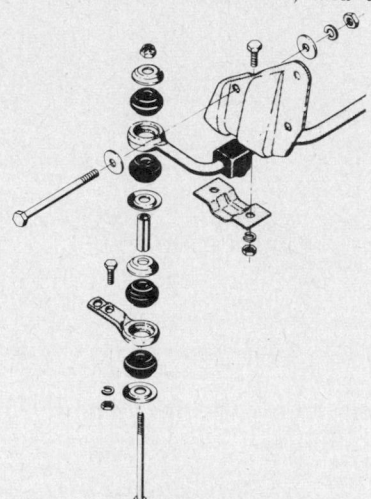

Front stabilizer bar assembly sequence—Series 01, 30 and 70 to 1969 (© American Motors Corp.)

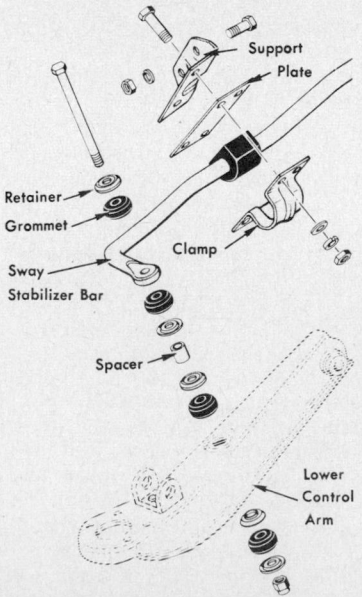

Support
Plate
Retainer
Grommet
Clamp
Sway Stabilizer Bar
Spacer
Lower Control Arm

Front stabilizer bar assembly sequence—Series 10, 50 and 80 to 1969 (© American Motors Corp.)

control arm inner pivot bolts to 60 ft. lbs.

NOTE: it may be necessary to align the front end.

Lower Control Arm—1965-72

The inner end of the lower control arm is attached to a removable cross-member. The outer end is attached to the steering knuckle pin and ball joint assembly.

NOTE: on 1965-69 models, it is recommended that the coil spring be removed.

To remove, jack up the car and support it on axle stands under the subframes. Remove the brake drum or caliper and rotor from the spindle, then disconnect the steering arm from the knuckle pin. Remove the lower ball joint stud cotter pin and nut. Separate the ball joint from the knuckle pin using two hammers—one as a brace and the other to apply shock to the knuckle.

Disconnect the sway bar from the control arm, then unbolt the strut rod. Remove the inner pivot bolt and the control arm.

To install, reverse the removal procedure; do not tighten inner pivot bolt until car weight is on wheels. Tighten ball joint retaining nut to 45 ft. lbs., strut rod bolts to 70 ft. lbs., sway bar bolts to 8 ft. lbs., steering arm bolts to 70 ft. lbs., and control arm inner pivot bolt to 95-100 ft. lbs.

Ball Joint Check and Replacement

Jack up the front of the car under the front crossmember or at the subframe jacking points. The control arms must hang free to get an accurate check. Grasp the wheel and tire and lift up and down and pull in and out while observing the lower ball joint. If there is measurable vertical or lateral free-play, the joint is worn enough to warrant replacement.

To check the upper ball joint on 1970-72 models, where a degree of looseness is normal, use a pry bar under the wheel to move tire vertically. If play is more than 0.080 in., the upper joint must be replaced.

To replace the ball joint, the rivets that hold it to the control arm must be drilled out or chiseled away. Remove the rivets and the strut rod mounting bolts if the lower joint is being worked on. In addition, place a punch of suitable size in the bottom open end of the lower control arm to keep the control arm from distorting while pressing the bushing. Remove the steering arm and stud nut, then separate the ball joint from the knuckle pin using two hammers, one as a brace against the knuckle pin and the other to shock the tapered stud loose.

The new ball joint has special 5/16 in. hardened bolts that replace the rivets. Use only these bolts to secure the joint—standard bolts are not strong enough. Tighten nuts to 25 ft. lbs.

Jacking, Hoisting

1. Jack car, at front, under lower support arms and, at rear, under rear axle housing.
2. To lift, contact car at rear lift pads marked lift just forward of rear wheels. Front lift points are on underbody sill just to the rear of strut rod-to-sill mounting bracket.

Steering Gear

Manual Steering Gear

Instructions covering the overhaul of the steering gear will be found in the Unit Repair Section.

Power Steering Gear

Troubleshooting and repair instructions covering power steering gears are given in the Unit Repair Section.

Steering Gear Removal

1. If power steering, disconnect pressure and return lines from gear box. Raise hoses above pump level and tie with wire to prevent fluid loss.
2. Remove flexible coupling nuts, noting any size differences.
3. Using a puller, remove Pitman arm.
4. Remove steering gear mounting screws, and lower gear to move out bottom.

Caution Starting 1969, a mandatory column alignment procedure must be followed during installation.

Steering Gear Installation

1. Center steering gear and make sure clearance between coupling hub and housing is at least 1/16 in.
2. Index flexible coupling bolts to shaft. Tighten nuts to 20 ft. lbs. and pinch bolt to 30 ft. lbs.
3. Tighten steering gear-to-frame screws to 45 ft. lbs. and Pitman arm nut to 115 ft. lbs.
4. Centerpunch thread near Pitman nut to stake it to the shaft.
5. Align steering column, as described later.
6. Connect pressure and return lines to power steering gears, tighten fittings to 25 ft. lbs.

Check fluid level and bleed air from system.

Steering Column Alignment

1969

Rambler, AMX and Javelin Series

1. Loosen clamp bolt at lower end of jacket tube.
2. Loosen the toeboard two-piece seal cover and remove lower clamp bracket nut and bolt.
3. Remove instrument panel trim plate below jacket tube.
4. Loosen the mounting bracket forward attaching bolt to free the front wedge.
5. Loosen the mounting bracket rear attaching bolts which will allow the column to assume an aligned position with the steering gear.
6. Pull the steering column upward and position the flexible coupling so that it is flat and not distorted. Maintain upward pressure while tightening the mounting bracket rear attaching bolts to 10 ft. lbs.
7. Position the wedge at the mounting bracket front bolt, using light finger pressure to ensure square alignment with the mounting bracket; tighten the bolt to 10 ft. lbs.
8. Position lower jacket tube clamp on the dash panel and tighten to a snug slip fit.
9. Install the lower clamp bracket nut and bolt and tighten securely.
10. Install two-piece seal retainer.
11. Install instrument panel trim plate below jacket tube.
12. Securely tighten clamp bolt at lower jacket tube clamp.
13. Upon completion of steering column alignment, column shift linkage adjustment must be checked to ensure proper operation.

Rebel and Ambassador Series

1. Loosen clamp bolt at lower end of jacket tube.
2. Loosen toe plate by removing all attaching screws, including the insulator cover, insulator, and two-piece seal retainer. Remove lower clamp bracket stud nut.
3. Remove instrument panel trim plate below jacket tube.
4. Loosen the two mounting bracket forward attaching bolts to free the two front wedges.
5. Loosen the mounting bracket rear attaching bolts, which will allow the column to assume an aligned position with the steering gear.
6. Pull the steering column upward

and position the flexible coupling so that it is flat and not distorted. Maintain upward pressure while tightening the mounting bracket rear attaching bolts to 10 ft. lbs.

7. Position the wedges at the mounting bracket front bolts, using light finger pressure to ensure square alignment with the mounting bracket; tighten the bolts to 10 ft. lbs.

8. Position lower jacket tube clamp on the dash panel studs and tighten to a snug slip fit.
9. Install the lower clamp bracket stud nut and tighten securely.
10. Install two-piece seal retainer insulator and insulator cover above seal retainer and tighten securely.
11. Install instrument panel trim plate below jacket tube.
12. Securely tighten clamp bolt at

lower jacket tube clamp.
13. Upon completion of steering column alignment, column shift linkage adjustment must be checked to ensure proper operation.

1970-72

All Series

1. Loosen the toeboard two-piece seal cover and remove lower clamp bracket.

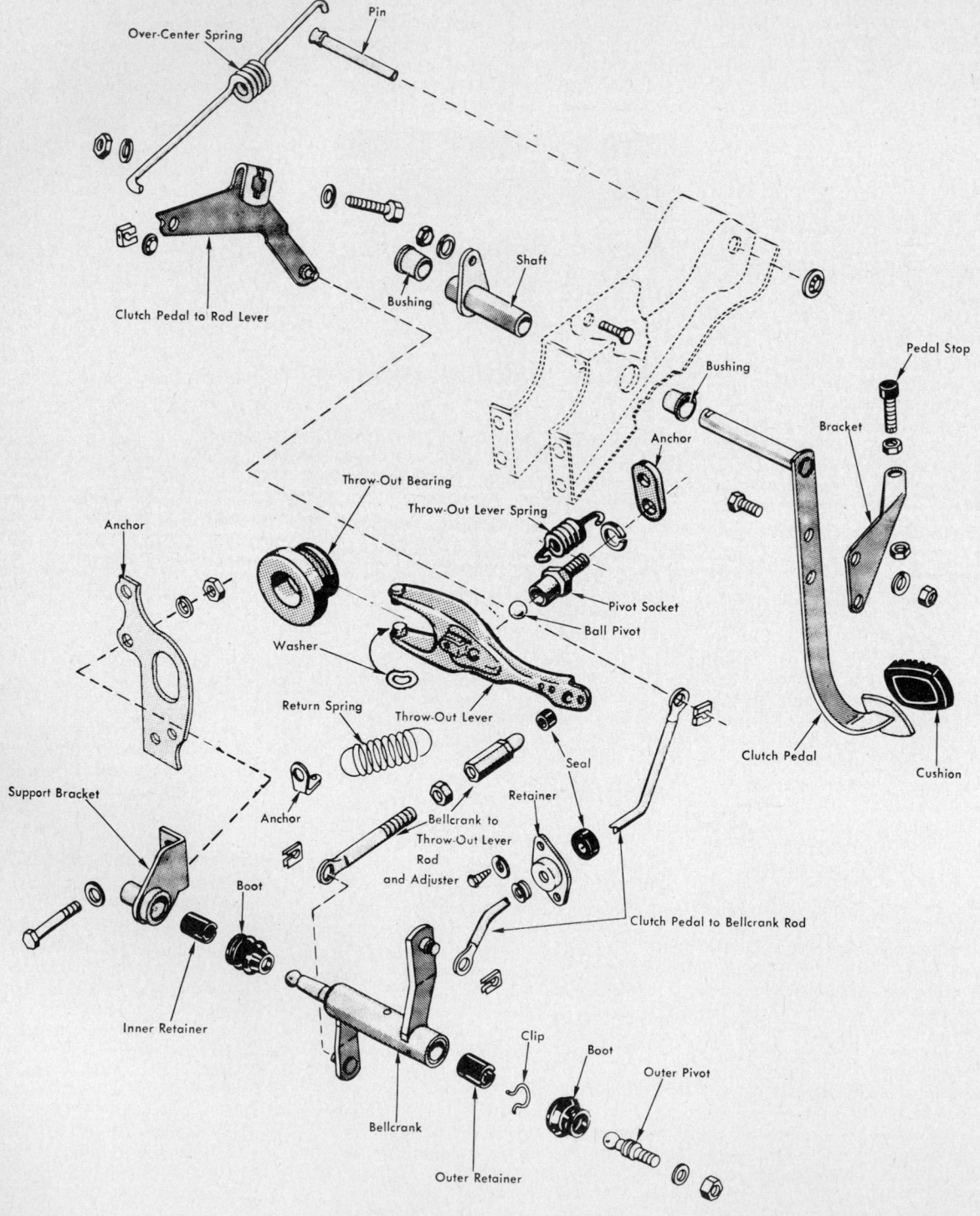

Typical clutch linkage—all except S-type (© American Motors Corp.)

2. Remove instrument panel trim plate below jacket tube.

3. Loosen the mounting bracket attaching bolts which will allow the column to assume an aligned position with the steering gear.

4. Pull the steering column upward and position the flexible coupling so that it is flat and not distorted. Maintain upward pressure while tightening the mounting bracket attaching bolts to 10 ft. lbs.

5. Install two-piece seal retainer.

6. Install instrument panel trim plate below jacket tube.

7. Upon completion of steering column alignment, column shift linkage adjustment must be checked to ensure proper operation.

Clutch

Standard Clutch

The clutch is a single-plate, dry-disc, coil spring type (except for the S-type in 1966-67 Ambassador, Classic, Marlin and Rebel models with the 232 cu. in. six). A semi-centrifugal clutch assembly is used with the 4-speed transmission V8 starting 1966, three rollers (six with 390) being equally spaced between the three clutch levers. These rollers are forced outward by centrifugal force and supply additional force to the pressure plate to prevent clutch slippage. The driven plate is spring-cushioned and has riveted linings. The throwout bearing is a ball bearing, pre-packed with grease at the factory.

No adjustment for wear is provided in the clutch itself, although an adjustment is built into the clutch cover to allow the release lever height to be varied. These adjusting nuts normally are not disturbed unless the clutch pressure plate is removed for overhaul.

Pedal travel decrease due to normal wear of the linings can be compensated for by adjusting the clutch pedal free-play (as described later).

S-type Clutch

In 1966-67, a self-adjusting clutch system was introduced as standard equipment on the Rebel, Ambassador, Marlin and Rambler Classic series. It is smoother in action, needs less pedal pressure, and is self-adjusting throughout its service life.

Linkage design utilizes an enclosed cable to transmit motion between the clutch pedal and the main lever. The lever oscillates on a sealed, oilite bushing, or needle bearings (depending upon engine application) and is supported on a fulcrum pin attached to the engine, or clutch housing. The main lever transmits motion through an automatic wear adjuster to the fork, then to the cover assembly. This engages and releases the clutch. The cable assembly absorbs the effect of engine motion on clutch actuation.

Pressure plate load is obtained from an externally mounted spring, one end of which is attached to the engine and transmission assembly. The other end is attached to the main lever. Spring load acts on the main lever through the wear compensator (adjuster) fork and cover assembly, applying the pressure plate load required to carry the engine torque.

The automatic wear adjuster is located between the main spring and the cover assembly.

The adjuster senses and maintains a specific angular travel of the main lever. As the clutch facing wears, the travel of the main lever increases causing the actuating arm on the lever to contact a spring. The spring acts as a one-way clutch on a threaded push rod. The actuating arm, pushing on the spring when the clutch is released, rotates the rod and increases the overall length of the adjuster. The actuating arm also repositions the spring on the rod when the clutch is engaged. This sequence of events reduces the travel of the main lever to the desired arc and continues throughout clutch life. An annular contact ball bearing is used to carry the load between fork and cover assembly levers. This bearing is under load at all times.

NOTE: crankshaft end-play has an effect on light torque chatter. Therefore, if this type of chatter does exist, it is recommended that crankshaft end-play be held to .006 in. maximum. The light bearing loads (of the type S system) at initial engagement are insufficient to prevent crankshaft end flutter until about 20% of engagement is reached.

Pedal Clearance Adjustment

Adjust the free-play of the clutch pedal to $\frac{1}{2}$-$\frac{3}{4}$ in. up to 1967, $\frac{7}{8}$-$1\frac{1}{8}$ in. thereafter. This is done by changing the length of the link between the throw out lever and the clutch lever.

NOTE: adjust clutch pedal to floor clearance to $6\frac{1}{2}$ in. for models with 199 cu. in. engine. On 232, 258 and all V8 models, adjust clutch pedal height by inserting a 5/16 in. x $4\frac{1}{2}$ in. long pin into the alignment holes in the pedal bracket. Adjust pedal height so that pin slides freely.

Clutch Removal

Remove the transmission as outlined later (place wood-padded jack under oil pan instead of clutch housing), then disconnect the clutch linkage at the release lever and remove the capscrews that hold the bellhousing (clutch housing) to the engine. It may be necessary to move the rear of the engine up or down to gain wrench clearance.

NOTE: any shims between the housing and engine must be replaced in exactly the same place to prevent misalignment.

Matchmark the clutch cover, pressure plate and flywheel before removal to ensure proper balance. Loosen each clutch cover capscrew a few

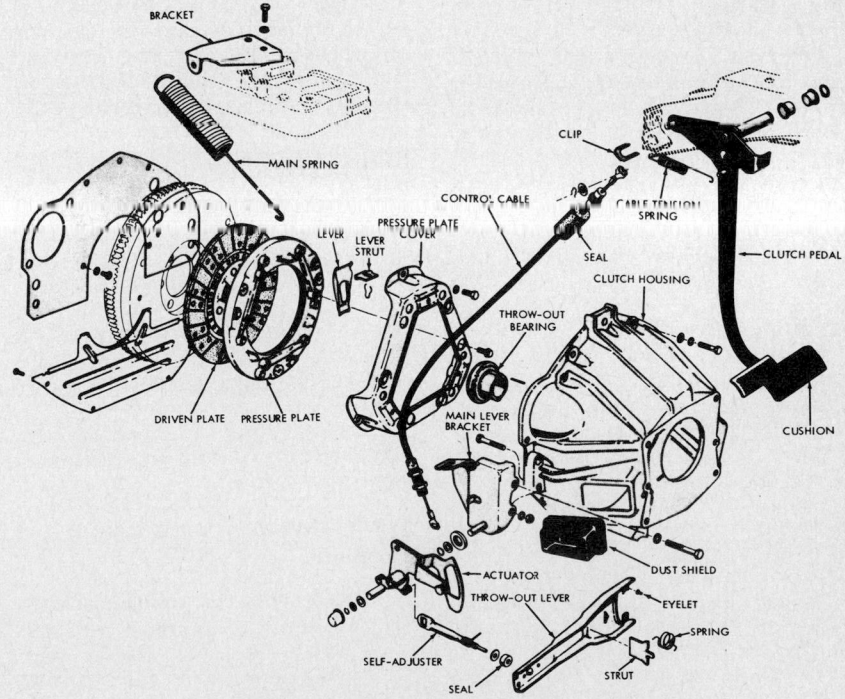

S-type clutch and linkage assembly (© American Motors Corp.)

turns at a time until spring tension is released, then remove the cover, pressure plate, and disc.

Pilot Bushing

Check the pilot bushing in the end of the crankshaft for scoring or looseness. If it is necessary to replace the bushing, use either an expanding-end slidehammer or a suitable tap. Screwing the tap into the bore until it bottoms will force the bushing out.

Lubricate the bushing with wheel bearing grease or Molykote before installing the clutch.

Flywheel

Inspect the flywheel surface for heat cracks, scoring, or blue heat marks. Check the flywheel capscrews for proper torque (105 ft. lbs.). It will be necessary to lock-up the flywheel ring gear with a block or flywheel holding clamp tool before tightening these capscrews.

Throwout Bearing

The throwout (release) linkage consists of a forked, pivoted lever contacting the bearing at one end and the linkage pushrod on the other. A return spring keeps the lever in contact with the ball pivot.

The throwout bearing itself is pre-lubricated and cannot be re-packed if dry. Failure is evidenced by uneven clutch pedal pressure and a grinding, rattling noise when the pedal is depressed. Replace any noisy throwout bearings as soon as is practicable to prevent disintegration and possible transmission or clutch damage.

Clutch Installation

Slide the new clutch disc onto the transmission input shaft to check for binding. Remove any burrs from either the splines or hub using sandpaper, then clean with gasoline and lubricate the splines and hub with Molykote. Place the clutch disc against the flywheel and secure it by inserting a dummy pilot shaft (such shafts, made of wood, are available from automotive jobbers) or an old transmission input shaft.

Place the new pressure plate (it's always good policy to replace the pressure plate when installing a new disc) in position, after first making sure that the clutch disc is facing the proper direction (flywheel side is so marked), and that matchmarks are aligned if old pressure plate is used. Install all the capscrews finger-tight. Tighten the screws a little at a time, working around the pressure plate to avoid distorting it, to 40 ft. lbs. Remove the pilot shaft.

NOTE: do not depress clutch pedal until transmission is installed or throwout bearing will fall out.

Install the clutch housing, throwout bearing and transmission. Hook up clutch linkage and check adjustment.

Clutch Housing Alignment

A misaligned clutch housing can cause improper clutch release, disc failure, front transmission bearing failure, pilot bushing wear, chattering, vibration, and jumping out of gear during deceleration.

Remove the transmission, clutch housing and clutch. Remove one of the flywheel attaching bolts.

Make a dial indicator support from a ½ in.—20 x 4 in. long bolt and a nut. Screw the nut onto the bolt so that five or six threads are exposed, then install the bolt into the crankshaft and tighten the nut to hold it.

Install the clutch housing and tighten capscrews to proper torque. Install and zero a dial indicator on the bolt so that it contacts the rear face of the clutch housing about ⅛ in. from the edge of the round opening (see illustration). Rotate the crankshaft slowly (at the front pulley)—total dial indicator reading should not exceed 0.010 in.

NOTE: crankshaft end-play must be held to "zero" when making check.

To align a housing, shims are installed between the clutch housing and engine-to-housing spacer.

Check bore alignment by locating the dial indicator on the inside diameter of the rear opening in the clutch housing. Rotate crankshaft and check reading at four equally spaced points—total reading should not exceed 0.010 in.

Any change in face alignment will affect bore alignment; therefore bore can be realigned by changing the face alignment slightly. If both face and bore alignment cannot be achieved at the same shim setting, the housing must be replaced or remachined.

Transmissions

Standard Transmission

General Information

Transmission refill capacities can be found in the Capacities table of this section.

Troubleshooting and repair of overdrive units are covered in the Unit Repair Section.

Synchromesh Transmission Removal

Models with Hotchkiss Drive

1. Split the rear universal joint and slide the driveshaft off the back of the transmission. (See Universal Joints and Drive Lines.)
2. Remove shift mechanism linkage

to the transmission, and disconnect the clutch linkage and speedometer cable.

3. Disconnect the overdrive mechanism (if so equipped) and remove the rear mounts.

NOTE: on V8 models with dual exhaust, exhaust pipes must be disconnected from manifolds so that rear crossmember can be removed. On Javelin and AMX models having Hurst shifter, entire shifter should be removed so that transmission can slide back far enough for removal.

4. Take out the transmission support crossmember, remove the two studs which hold the transmission to the bell housing and replace these two studs with two long pilot studs.
5. Take out the two bottom studs and slide the transmission assembly along the pilot studs and out of the car.

Models with Torque Tubes

1. Disconnect the brake lines and brake cables. Jack the car sufficiently high so that the operator can work under it.
2. Remove the bolts that hold the front flange at the torque tube to the back of the transmission, detach the rear end of the springs and the shock absorbers, remove the U-bolts which hold the rear axle assembly to the leaf spring and roll the rear axle assembly back a couple of inches to clear the transmission.
3. Disconnect the shift levers at the transmission speedometer cable, and, if equipped with overdrive, the overdrive wiring.
4. Support the back of the engine and remove the bolts which hold the back of the transmission to the crossmember. Take out the crossmember.
5. Remove the bolts which hold the transmission to the bell housing and replace two of the bolts with long guide studs. Slide the transmission out along the guide studs and down and out of the car.

⏻ CHILTON TIME-SAVER

To facilitate transmission removal, attach a Body Buddy or Come-Along between the axle housing and the rear bumper or frame using lengths of chain. Disconnect front of torque tube and left stabilizer bar mount and jack axle rearward carefully; the axle will pull back far enough to allow the tube to be completely disconnected from the transmission. It may be necessary to disconnect the shock absorbers and brake line to gain sufficient clearance.

Twin-Stick Overdrive Control Disassembly

1. Place the assembly in a vise.
2. Remove the four screws that retain the gearshift pivots to the gearshift lever pivot bracket.
3. Remove the four cap screws that secure the pivot bracket to the gear shift lever housing. After removing the gearshift knob, the pivot bracket can be removed.

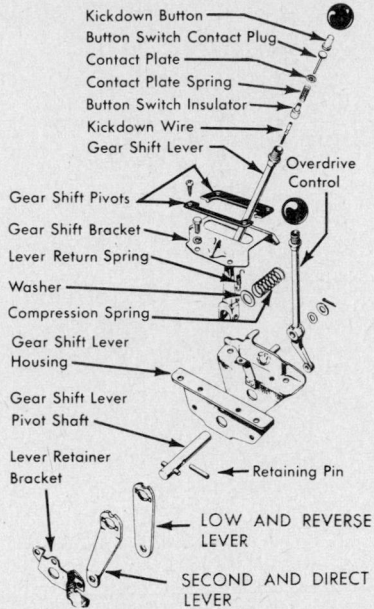

Kickdown Button
Button Switch Contact Plug
Contact Plate
Contact Plate Spring
Button Switch Insulator
Kickdown Wire
Gear Shift Lever
Overdrive Control
Gear Shift Pivots
Gear Shift Bracket
Lever Return Spring
Washer
Compression Spring
Gear Shift Lever Housing
Gear Shift Lever Pivot Shaft
Lever Retainer Bracket
Retaining Pin
LOW AND REVERSE LEVER
SECOND AND DIRECT LEVER

Twin-stick assembly components
(© American Motors Corp.)

4. Remove the two cap screws from the retainer that holds the selector levers on the gearshift lever pivot shaft. Then the levers can be removed.
5. Remove the lever return spring from the gearshift lever.

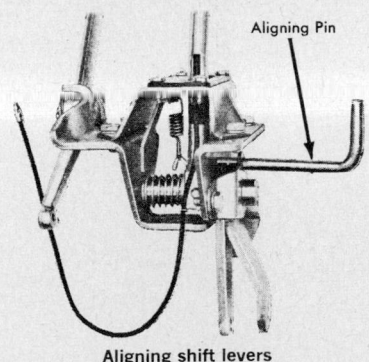

Aligning Pin

Aligning shift levers
(© American Motors Corp.)

6. Use a 3/16 in. punch to remove the pin that secures the gearshift lever to the gearshift lever pivot shaft and remove the shaft.
   NOTE: the gearshift lever pivot shaft and the selector pin are serviced as an assembly.

Twin-Stick Overdrive Control Assembly

1. With the gearshift lever housing held in a vise, install the gear shift lever, washer, and compression spring in the housing.
2. Install the gearshift lever pivot shaft through the housing, and the gearshift lever, washer, compression spring in the housing.
3. Install the pin in the gearshift lever and through the pivot shaft. Use a long-fiber grease as a lubricant for the pivot shaft.
4. Position the low and reverse selector lever on the pivot shaft. Then, place the second and high-selector lever on the pivot shaft and place the lever-retaining-bracket over the shaft. Secure the bracket in place with two cap screws.
5. Install the lever return spring to the gearshift lever.
6. Place the pivot bracket over the gearshift lever and secure it to the gearshift housing bracket with four cap screws.
7. Place the two pivots on the pivot bracket and retain them in place with four screws. Position the gearshift knob on the shift lever. The floor shift assembly can then be installed in the vehicle.
8. Secure the gearshift rods to the operating levers of the floor shift assembly. Secure the gearshift lever housing to the floor pan.
9. Adjust the shift levers. (See illustration)
10. Install the console assembly on the floor pan.
11. Connect the kickdown and overdrive indicator light wires to their respective connectors.
12. Secure the overdrive control cable to the overdrive control lever.
13. Check gearshift lever operation in all positions, and the overdrive control for full engagement.

Shift Lever Adjustment

Column Shift—1965-72

Loosen the trunnion locknuts on the shift rods, then position the two operating levers in the center of the jacket tube cut-out. Insert a 3/16 in. drill through any existing aligning holes in the shift levers, shift gate and bracket. With the levers in neutral, adjust the trunnions for a free fit, without binding, in the levers. Lock the trunnions in this position, then check the shift lever positions for binding.

Three-Speed Floorshift— Through 1969

Place the transmission shift levers in neutral. Loosen the 2-3 transmission lever attaching nut and adjustment bolt. With the 1-R shift rod in neutral position, align the 2-3 rod so the shift notch is exactly aligned with the 1-R shift rod notch.

Aligning shift levers column shift models with gauge hole
(© American Motors Corp.)

Tighten the adjustment bolt and attaching nut. Operate the shift lever to make sure there is no binding in the 1-2 shift.
To adjust the back-up light switch, loosen the two jam nuts and slide the switch forward or backward.

Three-Speed Floorshift—1970-72

Loosen the reverse lock rod trunnion locknuts about 1/2 in. Shift into reverse and lock the steering column. It may be necessary to move the lower column lever upward until it is in the locked position.
Tighten the lower trunnion locknut until it contacts the trunnion. Tighten the upper locknut while holding the trunnion centered in the column lever. Unlock the steering column, shift in neutral, and check that the transmission shift levers are in their neutral positions.
Loosen the 2-3 transmission lever attaching nut and adjustment bolt. With the 1-R shift rod in the neutral position, align the 1-R and 2-3 shift rod notches. Tighten the adjustment bolt and attaching nut.
Shift through the gears, checking for binding in the 1-2 shift in particular. Shift into reverse and lock the column—this operation should be smooth with no binding.

Four-Speed AM Floorshift— Through 1969

Loosen the transmission shift lever nuts (two per lever) and loosen the locknuts on the reverse shift rod at the trunnion.
Install a 1/4 in. drill through the selector lever retainer, through the levers, spacer plate and aligning hole in the mounting bracket (this is the neutral position).
Place all three transmission levers in neutral, then adjust the trunnion on the reverse shift rod so that it en-

ters freely into the reverse lever without binding. Lock the nuts on the reverse rod and install washer and cotter pin.

Tighten the lower nuts on the shift levers, making sure the outer levers stay in position, then tighten the upper nut to approximately 10 ft. lbs.

Caution
Do not overtighten these nuts, otherwise the shift shafts might break.

Remove the ¼ in. drill rod, then lubricate the shift rod ends with chassis grease and check operation of shifter in all gears.

Four-Speed Hurst Floorshift—Starting 1969

Remove the boot assembly or plug and loosen the lower nuts and bolts on the two transmission forward speed shift levers. Loosen the two self-locking nuts at the center of the shift levers. Loosen the two locknuts on the reverse shift rod trunnion.

With the shifter in neutral position, insert a ¼ in. diameter aligning pin into the shifter housing and through the center of the three shifter levers. Make sure that the pin enters the notch in the far side of the housing. Check that the transmission levers are in their neutral positions. Remove and reinsert the aligning pin. The pin should slide in freely. If it does not, the shifter is not correctly aligned in the neutral position.

Tighten the lower bolts and nuts at the transmission forward speed shift levers. Tighten the self-locking nuts to 10 ft. lbs. Make sure the transmission reverse lever is in the neutral position. Tighten the trunnion nuts, being careful not to bind the trunnion in the reverse lever, then remove the aligning pin.

NOTE: on 1970-72 models, loosen the steering column reverse lock-up rod trunnion locknuts about ½ in. each. Shift into reverse and lock the column. It may be necessary to move the lower column lever upward until it is in the locked position. Tighten the lower trunnion locknut until it contacts the trunnion. Tighten the upper locknut while holding the trun-

nion centered in the column lever. Unlock the column and check for proper shifting. The column should lock without binding.

Automatic Transmission

Description

The Borg-Warner automatic transmission is used through model year 1971. The Unit Repair Section details troubleshooting and repair procedures for these units, which are called either Flash-O-Matic or Shift Command, depending on whether the transmission upshifts can be manually controlled or not. Shift-Command transmissions use a modified valve body to enable the driver to manually select a gear and hold the transmission in that gear.

In 1972, American Motors elected to use Chrysler Corporation Torque-flite automatic transmissions in all their cars. These transmissions are the same as the equivalent Chrysler units, and are covered in the Unit Repair Section, the only differences being in case design required by the difference in American Motors' bell-housing configuration and drive-shafts.

Automatic Transmission Removal and Installation

Torque Tube Models

Removal
1. Disconnect the battery.

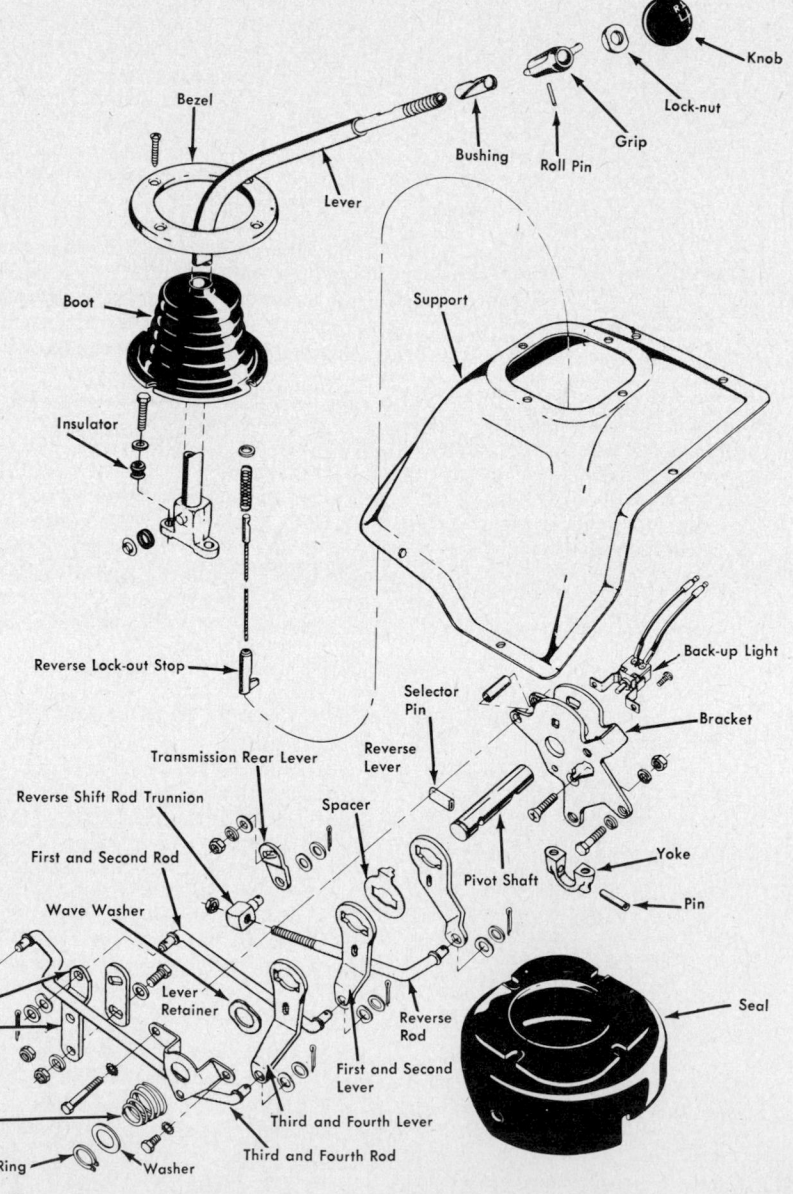

Four-speed American Motors floorshift linkage (© American Motors Corp.)

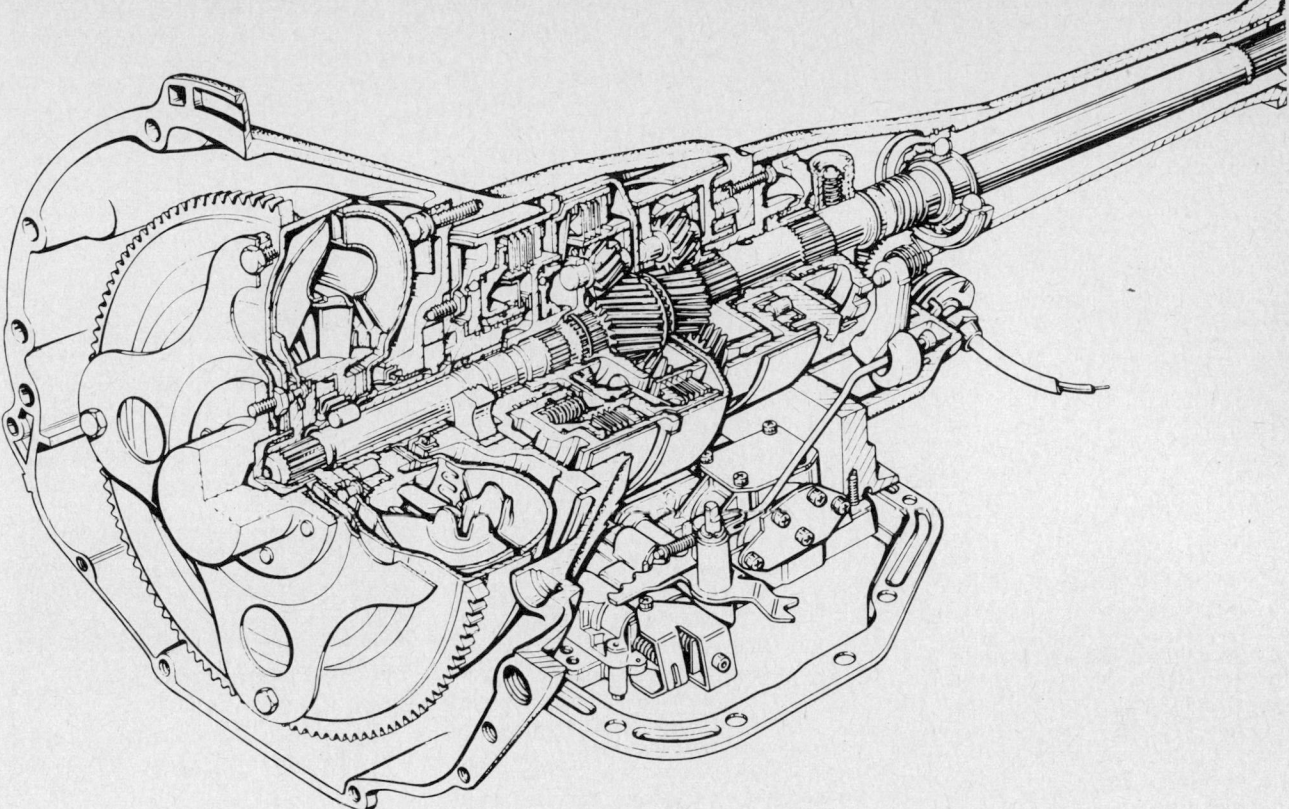

Automatic transmission, beginning 1972 (© American Motors Corp.)

2. Disconnect the throttle valve control cable at the throttle linkage bracket on the engine.
3. Raise the car and support on stands.

NOTE: support car body to remove weight from wheels.

4. Disconnect the following:
   a. The oil filler tube and drain the transmission.
   b. The selector linkage at the transmission outer manual lever.
   c. The speedometer cable from the transmission.
   d. The exhaust pipe from the manifold and remove the exhaust pipe bracket from the converter housing.
5. Position a transmission hoist with suitable cradle under the transmission to support the transmission.
6. Disconnect the rear support crossmember from the body side sill brackets and the transmission.
7. Lower the transmission and the rear of the engine for access to the upper converter housing-to-cylinder block bolts.
8. Remove the converter housing lower cover.
9. Mark the converter and drive plate to ensure original location upon assembly.
10. Remove the converter-to-drive plate capscrews.

11. Remove the starter mounting bolts and the converter housing-to-cylinder block bolts.
12. Push the converter housing and converter to the rear a sufficient distance to clear the crankshaft.

NOTE: the rear of the engine tends to raise when the transmission weight is removed and may bind the converter in the crankshaft pilot bushing. Blocking the engine up at the front will allow separating the converter from the crankshaft.

13. Maintain pressure against the converter housing and lower the transmission, coverter housing and converter as an assembly until the housing is clear of the engine.
14. At this point, the following items may be serviced:
    a. Converter may be replaced.
    b. Converter drive plate replaced.
    c. Front pump oil seal replaced.
15. Disconnect transmission from torque tube and driveshaft for transmission replacement or overhaul.

NOTE: the converter cannot be taken apart and is only serviced as a complete assembly.

16. The converter may be full of oil; therefore, place a drain pan under the converter housing before removing the converter from the front pump.

Installation

1. Place the transmission, with the converter housing and converter attached, on a transmission hoist.
2. Connect transmission to driveshaft and torque tube.
3. Raise transmission assembly and align converter to drive plate. Pull transmission forward to start converter hub in crankshaft. Raise or lower transmission slightly to align converter housing dowel pins with cylinder block aligning holes.
4. Using the two lower converter housing attaching bolts, pull the transmission assembly in place.
5. Insert and tighten the remaining converter housing attaching bolts.
6. Connect the drive plate to the converter and tighten the nuts or capscrews evenly to 23-28 ft. lbs. (V8) or 33 ft. lbs. (6) torque.
7. Install starter motor.
8. Connect cooling tubes, if so equipped. Connect the manual rod shift linkage, speedometer cable, and the fluid filler tube.
9. Raise the transmission assembly until it contacts the floor pan, and connect the rear crossmember to the side sills.
10. Lower the transmission assembly until it rests on the rear crossmember, and attach the transmission to the crossmember with the two attaching bolts.

11. Remove the transmission hoist.
12. Connect the exhaust pipe.
13. Lower vehicle to the floor.
14. Connect transmission throttle valve control cable to bracket and carburetor.
15. Connect battery cable.
16. Pour five quarts of Automatic Transmission fluid into the transmission. Set the hand brake and start the engine. Operate engine with the selector lever in the "N" position. Add three quarts of fluid to the transmission and move selector lever through all drive ranges. Add enough fluid to bring fluid level up to the "F" or full mark on the transmisson fluid level dipstick.
17. Check transmission control pressure, as outlined in the Unit Repair Section. Adjust if necessary.

Open Drive Line Models

Removal

1. Disconnect the battery.
2. Raise the car and support on stands. The car weight must be on the rear springs; therefore, support the rear of the car with stands placed under the rear axle tubes.

Caution Before removing the rear crossmember on Javelin and AMX Series equipped with power steering, it is necessary to open the hood to avoid damage to the hood from the power steering pump reservoir wingnut.

3. Disconnect the following:
    a. The oil filler tube and drain the transmission.
    b. The selector linkage at the transmission outer manual lever.
    c. The speedometer cable from the transmission.
    d. Disconnect vacuum hose and solenoid wire at transmission.
    e. The exhaust pipe from the manifold and remove the exhaust pipe bracket from the converter housing.
4. Positon a hydraulic hoist with suitable cradle under the transmission to support the transmission.
5. Disconnect the rear support crossmember from the body side sill brackets and the transmission.
6. Lower the transmission and the rear of the engine for access to the upper converter housing-to-cylinder block bolts.
7. Remove the converter housing lower cover (6-cylinder). Remove converter access cover (V8).
8. Mark the converter and drive plate to ensure original location upon assembly.

9. Remove the converter to drive plate capscrews. (6-cylinder), stud nuts (V8).
10. Remove the starter mounting bolts and the converter housing-to-engine block bolts.
11. Push the converter housing and converter to the rear a sufficient distance to clear the crankshaft.
    NOTE: the rear of the engine tends to raise when the transmission weight is removed and may bind the converter in the crankshaft pilot bushing. Blocking the engine up at the front will allow separating the converter from the crankshaft.
12. Maintain pressure against the converter housing and lower the transmission, converter housing and converter as an assembly until the housing is clear of the engine.
13. At this point, the following items may be serviced:
    a. Converter may be replaced.
    b. Converter drive plate replaced.
    c. Pump oil seal replaced.
14. Disconnect transmission from driveshaft for transmission replacement or overhaul.
    NOTE: the converter cannot be taken apart and is only serviced as a complete assembly.
15. The converter may be full of oil; therefore, place a drain pan under the converter housing before removing the converter from the pump.

Installation

1. Place the transmission, with the converter housing and converter attached, on a transmission hoist.
2. Connect transmission to driveshaft.
3. Raise transmission assembly and align converter to drive plate. Refer to markings made during removal for proper alignment. Pull transmission forward to start converter hub in crankshaft. Raise or lower transmission slightly to align converter housing dowel pins with engine block aligning holes.
4. With the use of the two lower converter housing attaching bolts, pull the transmission assembly into position.
5. Insert and tighten the remaining converter housing attaching bolts.
6. Connect the drive plate to the converter and tighten the nuts or capscrews evenly to 35 ft. lbs. torque.
7. Install starter motor.
8. Connect the manual rod shift linkage, speedometer cable, and the fluid filler tube.
9. Connect vacuum hose and solenoid kickdown wire.
10. Raise the transmission assembly

until it contacts the floor pan, and connect the rear crossmember to the side sills.
11. Lower the transmission assembly until it rests on the rear crossmember, and attach the transmission to the crossmember with the two attaching bolts.
12. Remove the transmission hoist.
13. Connect the exhaust pipe.
14. Lower vehicle to the floor.
15. Connect battery cable.
16. Fill the transmission to the correct level as outlined in the Unit Repair Section.
17. Adjust transmission pressure as outlined in the Unit Repair Section.
18. Road test for transmission operation and proper shift operation.

U Joints, Drive Lines

1965-66 American Open Drive Line

An open tubular shaft is used with a slip joint at front. The 195

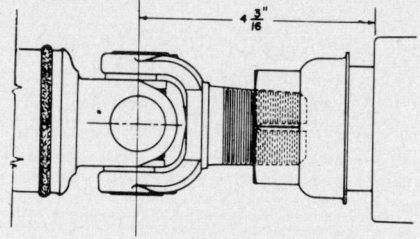

1965-66 Series 01 rear coupling installation
(© American Motors Corp.)

6-cylinder and 199 rear joint uses a coupling nut on the rear axle pinion shaft. Both joints are the cross- and trunnion-type.

Removal

1. To remove assembly, raise and place stands under rear of body and axle.
2. Disconnect parking brake cable.
3. Disconnect rear shock absorbers.
4. Disconnect rear brake line at body bracket.
5. Disconnect rear spring U-bolts.
6. Remove coupling nut (see illustration).
7. Shift rear axle assembly to rear, allowing front joint to slide from transmission shaft and separate at rear coupling.

Installation

1. Place the shaft and coupling on the rear axle pinion shaft until the center of the joint yoke bearing is 4 3/16 in. from the front face of the pinion shaft housing (see illustration).

2. Tighten coupling nut to 300 ft. lbs.
3. Slide the front slip joint onto the transmission output shaft.
4. Reposition rear axle assembly.
5. Reinstall U-bolts.
6. Reconnect brake line, parking brake cable and shock absorbers.
7. Bleed brakes.
8. Lower car to floor.

1965-66 Torque Tube Drive Line

Removal

Two types of drive line are used. Both are torque tube drives, one with a solid shaft and one with a tubular shaft.

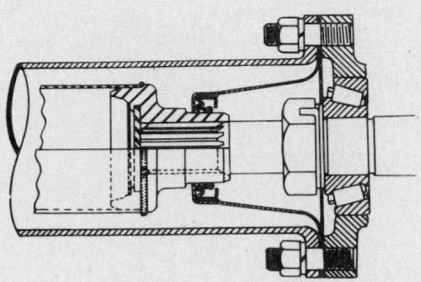

Tubular shaft in torque tube
(© American Motors Corp.)

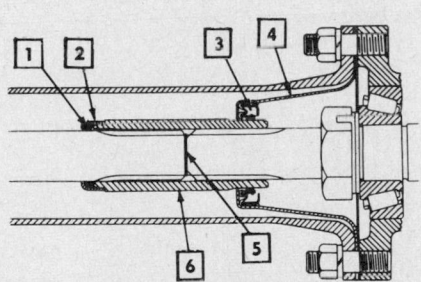

Solid shaft in torque tube
(© American Motors Corp.)

1. To remove assembly, raise and place stands under rear of body.
2. Disconnect parking brake cable.
3. Disconnect rear stabilizer bar.
4. Disconnect lower ends of shock absorbers.
5. Disconnect truss rods at center bracket.
6. On solid shaft types, remove trunnion bracket rear nuts.
7. On tubular shaft types, disconnect torque tube from front adapter.
8. Move the rear axle and drive line assembly to the rear and disconnect the torque tube from the rear axle housing.
9. Move the tube forward to release rear slip joint. On cars using torque tube drive, no rear spring U-bolts are used. The spring is held in place by car weight and shock absorber travel limits.

NOTE: the solid shaft-type uses a slip joint. It also has a center bearing held in place by a snap-ring. The tubular shaft uses a slip joint.

Installation

On both torque tube-types, reverse the removal procedures above. Use care, when inserting at slip joints, not to damage oil seals.

1967-72 Open Drive Line

A one-piece, tubular driveshaft is used on these models. Some rear yokes are held to the pinion shaft by a bolt, others by the pinion nut. Do not loosen this nut.

Removal and Installation

1. Split rear U-joint by removing nuts.
2. Drop rear of driveshaft and slide front yoke out of transmission.
3. To install, reverse removal procedure, tightening U-joint bolts to 18-22 ft. lbs.

Universal Joint Repairs

1. Remove the lock rings from the inner side of two opposite bearings and press on the outer side of one of the bearings, forcing the crossover. This will force the bearing on the opposite side out of its yoke.
2. Remove the bearing which was forced out of the yoke, then press the cross in the opposite direction to force the other bearing out.
3. Repeat this procedure on the third and fourth bearing.

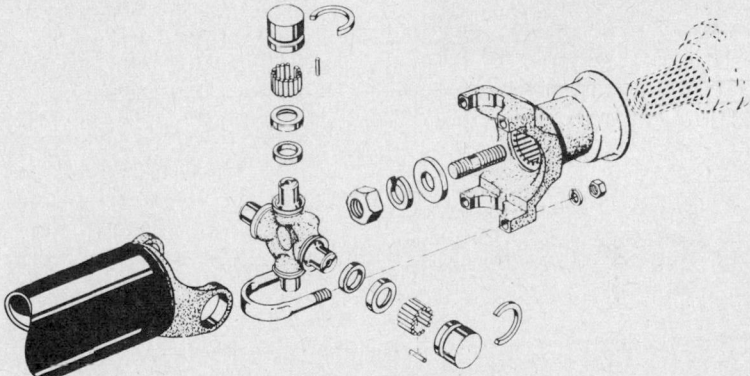

Rear U-joint assembly—1967-72 Series 01 illustrated (© American Motors Corp.)

Typical torque tube drive line (© American Motors Corp.)

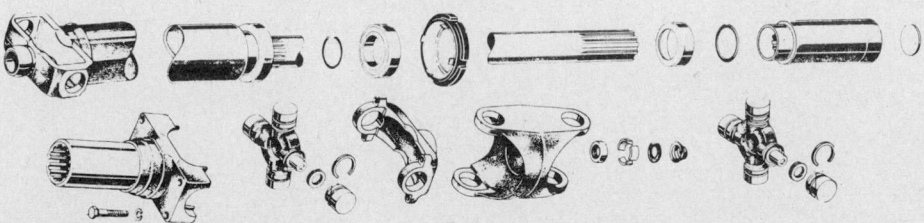

Driveshaft—1965-66 V8 (© American Motors Corp.)

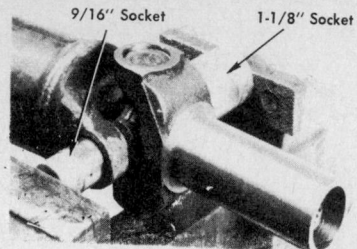

9/16" Socket   1-1/8" Socket

Removing end bearing from the yoke

4. When installing the new bearings in the universal joint yoke, it is possible to put them in with a driver of some type, but it is recommended that this work be done in an arbor press because a heavy jolt on the needle bearings can very easily misalign them, and greatly shorten their life.

9/16" Socket

Installing end bearing

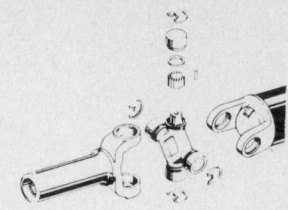

Front universal joint exploded view

Drive Axle, Suspension

Rear Suspension

Description

All 1965 to 1972 American, Javelin, Hornet, Gremlin and AMX models use a four or five-leaf semi-elliptic spring, Hotchkiss drive rear suspension. Shock absorbers are mounted at their lower ends to studs and are bayonet type at their upper ends. Upper shock nuts are accessible by removing cover plates or by removing trunk floormat; except for AMX models. The upper ends of the shocks in the AMX are mounted to bolted-on brackets, which must be removed in order to remove the shocks.

The 1965-66 Classic and Ambassador uses a torque tube rear suspension, with rear track bar and truss rods. The track bar serves to maintain vertical alignment between the axle and body, and coil springs are used to support the vehicle weight. Shock absorbers are bayonet type at their top ends and the upper nuts are accessible by removing cover plates.

The rear suspension on Rebel, Ambassador and Marlin models was changed starting 1967 to a four-trailing arm, coil spring type. The two lower control arms are attached to the outer ends of the axle tubes and to the body side sills, while the two upper control arms are attached to the differential housing and to a rear crossmember. Rubber bushings are used on the lower arms and on the crossmember ends of the upper arms. The lower ends of the upper arms are attached to pressed in bushings in ears on the differential case. Shock absorbers are accessible at their upper ends by removing cover plates in the body or by removing brackets from underneath the car. This suspension was carried over to 1971-72 on the Matador and Ambassador models.

Drive Axle

1965-66 Classic and Ambassador Rear Axle Removal

While it is possible to remove the rear axle assembly leaving the torque tube under the car, this practice is not recommended.

1. Disconnect the brake tubes and brake lines. Disconnect the shock

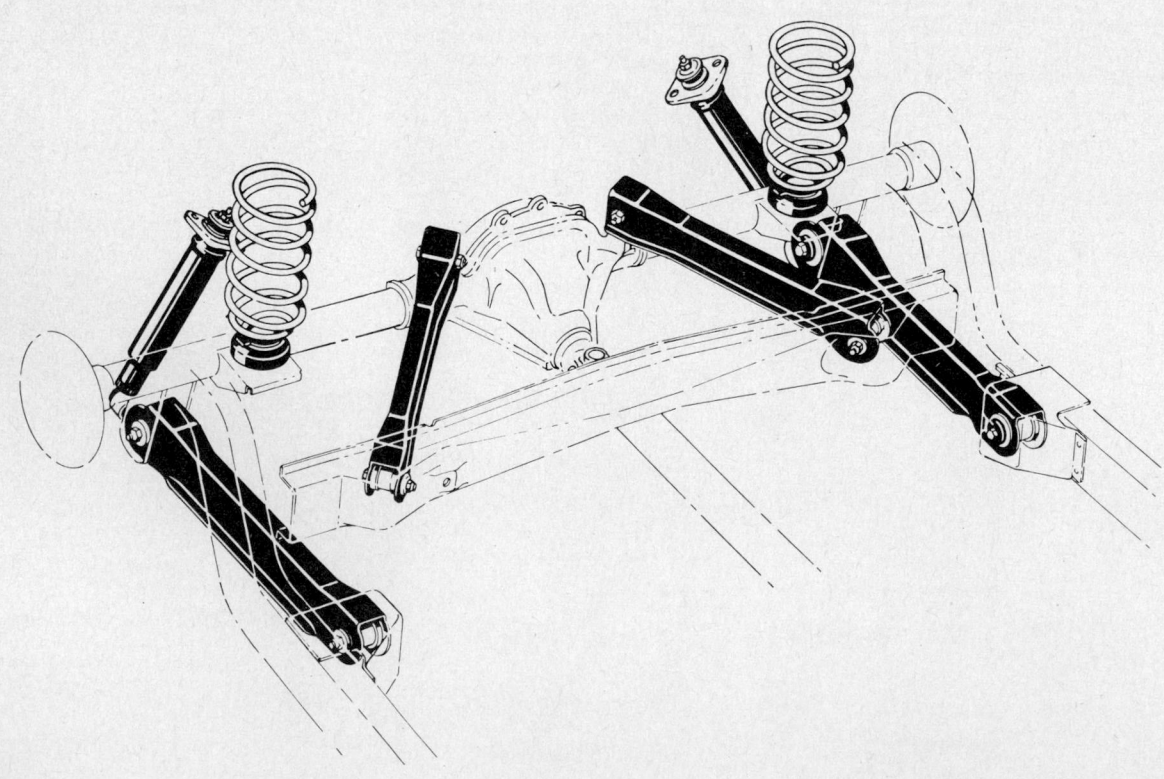

Four-trailing arm, coil spring rear suspension (© American Motors Corp.)

absorber and sway bar.

2. Remove the bolts which hold the front of the torque tube to the back of the transmission. Jack up the car and support the weight of the car on the frame in front of the rear springs.

3. Remove the bolts which hold the rear spring to the rear shackle. Remove the four U-bolts which hold the rear axle housing assembly to the rear spring, let the rear axle assembly come down with the springs and roll it out from under the vehicle. If the vehicle is jacked high enough, it is possible to roll the rear axle out on its own wheels. On cars using torque tube drive, no rear spring U-bolts are used. The spring is held in place by car weight and shock absorber travel limits.

1967-72 Marlin, Ambassador, Rebel and Matador Rear Axle Removal

1. Raise rear of car high enough to permit working under the car. Place a floor jack under center of axle housing so it just starts to raise rear axle assembly. Place car stands solidly under body members on both sides.

2. Mark rear universal joint and pinion flange for proper indexing at the time of installation, then, disconnect rear universal joint at pinion flange. Wire the propeller shaft back out of the way.

3. Disconnect parking brake cables at the sheave. Remove cable connector and two clips. Slide cable back until free of body.

4. Disconnect rear brake hose at floor pan.

5. Disconnect shock absorbers at axle housing. Lower jack under housing until rear springs can be removed.

6. Disconnect upper control arms at axle.

7. Disconnect lower control arms at axle housing and roll rear axle assembly out from under the car.

1965-69 American, 1968-72 Javelin, AMX, Hornet, Gremlin Rear Axle Removal

1. Loosen rear axle nuts, then jack up rear of car and support on stands under sills.

2. Remove axle housing cover to drain lube oil, then remove rear wheels and drums.

3. Disconnect parking brake cables at equalizer, remove backing plates and brakes, and remove axle shafts.

NOTE: save the shims found between left-side backing plate and axle tube.

4. Matchmark U-joint yoke and bearing, then disconnect driveshaft at rear joint.

5. Disconnect lower ends of shocks and brake line at floorpan. Remove axle U-bolts and torque links (if fitted).

6. Remove axle housing and differential assembly from under the car.

Windshield Wipers

Motor R & R

1965-72 Series 01, 30, 40, 70

The wiper motor is mounted on the engine side of the firewall and is easily accessible from under the hood.

1. Remove four screws that hold motor to firewall.

2. Remove hose and control cable, if equipped with vacuum wipers.

3. Unplug harness plug under dash, if equipped with electric wipers.

4. Disconnect motor link and remove motor.

5. To install, reverse removal procedure.

1965-72 Series 10, 20, 80

1. Remove wiper arms and blades and the cowl air intake cover.

2. Slide the link-to-motor retainer clip off of the motor arm stud. Remove the link from the motor.

3. Disconnect control cable and vacuum hose or wiring harness from the motor.

4. Remove the motor and mounting plate-to-dash screws, and the motor assembly.

5. Install by reversing removal procedure.

Transmission R & R

1965-72 Series 01, 30, 40, 70

To remove the pivot shaft body and link assembly after the link has been disconnected from the motor:

1. Remove pivot shaft spacer mounting nut, spacer and gaskets.

2. Disconnect washer hose.

3. Remove cowl ventilator air intake cover fastened to the cowl top by one screw at the front on each side and a retainer pin in the rear center of the cover.

4. The retainer pin is welded to the cover and inserted into a rubber

grommet in the cowl top which serves as a retainer.

5. After the air intake cover is removed, the pivot shaft body retaining nuts are accessible for removal. The pivot shaft body and link assembly can then be removed from inside the body.

1965-72 Series 10, 20, 80

1. Remove the wiper arm and blade assembly and pivot shaft to cowl top nut and spacer.

2. Disconnect the link end from the motor arm, after removing cowl air intake.

3. Close hood and remove two capscrews that hold each pivot shaft body. Remove assembly through cowl opening.

4. Install by reversing removal procedure.

Heater System

Series 10, 20, 80—1965-72

Heater Core R & R

1. Disconnect hoses from core and plug hoses and tubes. It will not be necessary to drain entire cooling system.

2. Remove lower blower housing attaching nuts and washers in engine compartment.

3. Remove glove compartment door and glove compartment.

4. Remove remaining heater housing screws in passenger compartment, and remove core and housing as an assembly.

5. Slide core from housing.

6. Install in reverse of above.

Heater Blower R & R

1. Remove water valve from blower housing. It is not necessary to disconnect hoses and control cable.

2. Remove nuts, washers and screws attaching blower housing to dash panel in engine compartment.

3. Remove motor and fan, then separate fan from motor.

4. Install in reverse of above.

Series 01, 30, 40, 70 —1965-72

Heater Core, Defroster and Blower Housing R & R— 1965-72 Series 01, 30, 70 Except 1970-72 Series 01, 40

1. Drain 1½ qts. (2 qts. beginning

'70) of coolant from system.

2. Disconnect hoses from heater core tubes in engine compartment. Install corks in hoses and tubes.
3. Disconnect blower motor wires.
4. Remove housing attaching nuts at blower motor opening in dash.
5. Remove glove compartment door and glove compartment.

NOTE: on Javelin and AMX, remove glove box hinge bracket.

6. Disconnect air and defroster cables from damper levers.
7. Remove assembly.
8. Install in reverse of above.

Heater Core, Defroster, and Blower Housing R & R— 1970-72 Series 01, 40

1. Open heater valve and drain 2 qts. of coolant.

2. Disconnect heater hoses and plug hoses and core fittings.
3. Disconnect blower wires and remove motor and fan assembly.
4. Remove package shelf, if so equipped.
5. Disconnect wire at resistor, located below glove box.
6. Remove instrument panel center bezel, air outlet and duct.
7. Disconnect air and defroster cables from damper levers.
8. Remove right-side windshield pillar molding, the instrument panel upper sheet metal screws and the capscrew at the right door post.
9. Remove right kick panel and heater housing screws.
10. Pull right side of instrument panel outward slightly and remove housing.
11. To install, reverse removal procedure.

Heater Core R & R

1. Remove core, defroster and blower housing.
2. Remove core from housing.

Heater Blower R & R— 1965-66 Series 01

1. Remove assembly, as described.
2. Remove blower scroll cover above which blower is assembled, and remove blower from motor shaft for access to motor attaching nuts.
3. Install in reverse of above.

Heater Blower R & R—1967-72 Series 01, 30, 40, 70

1. Disconnect blower wires.
2. Remove three retaining nuts for scroll cover and remove motor and fan assembly.
3. To install, reverse removal procedure.

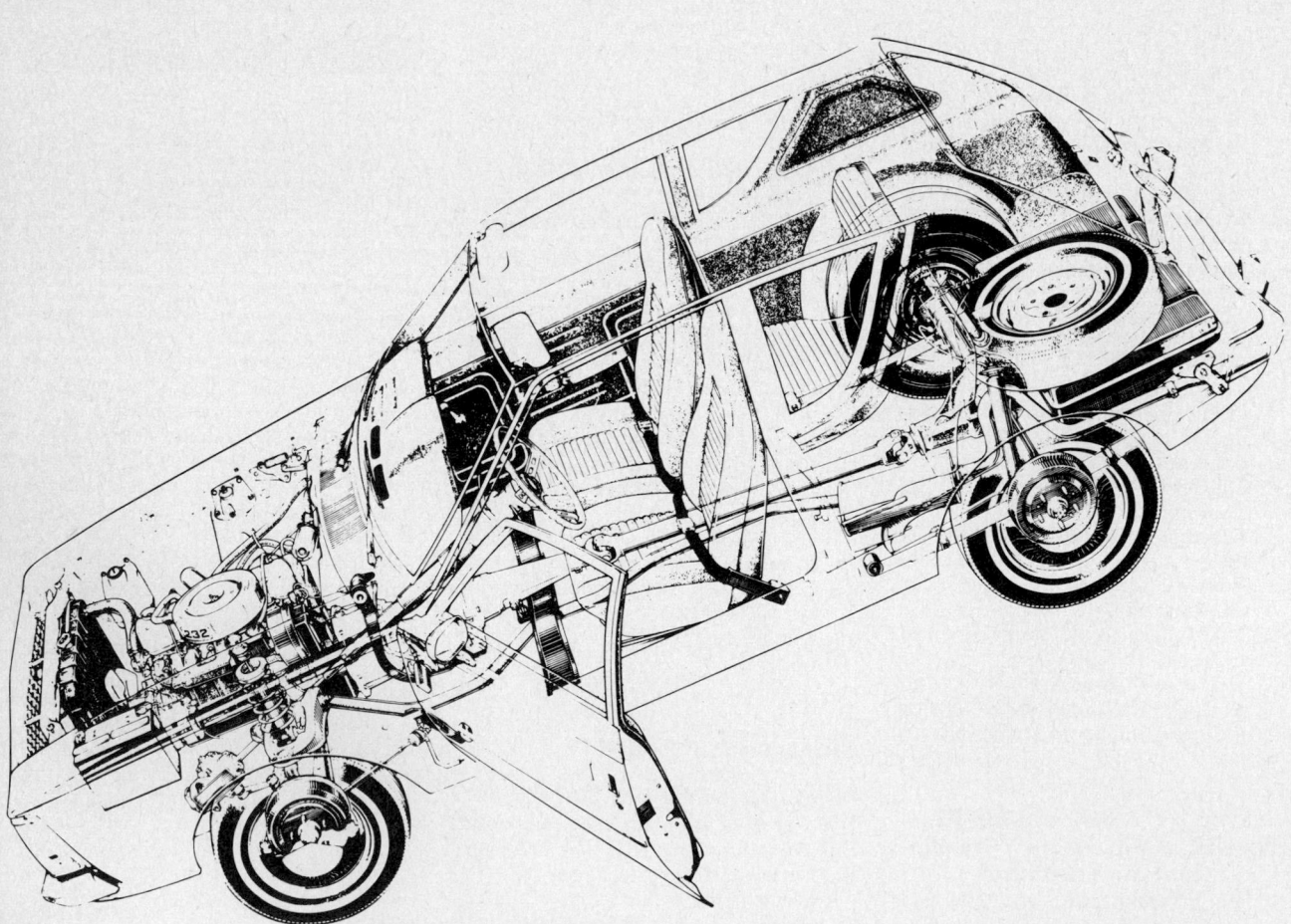

1972 Gremlin cutaway (© American Motors Corp.)

Valiant, Dart, Barracuda, Challenger

Index

YEAR IDENTIFICATION

VALIANT

1964

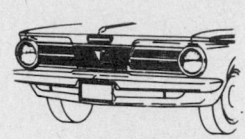

1965

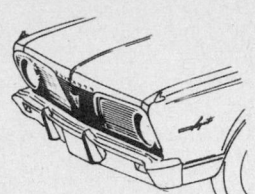

1966

1967

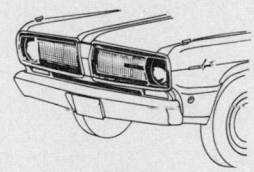

1968

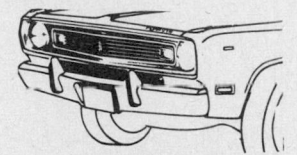

1969

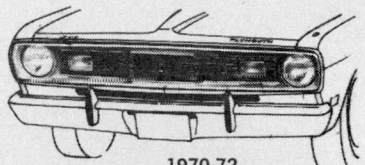

1970-72

1970 Plymouth Cuda

1971 Cuda

1972 Cuda

DART

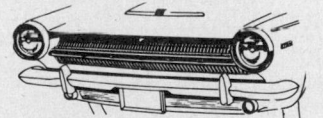

1964

1965

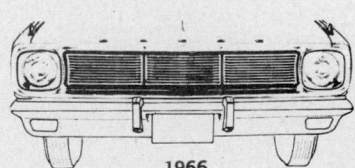

1966

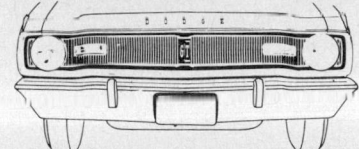

1967

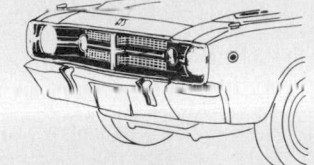

1968

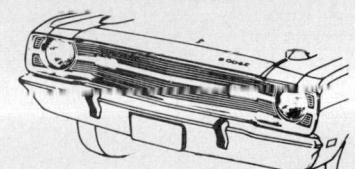

1969

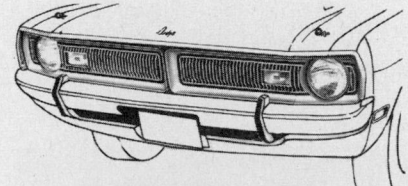

1970 Dart

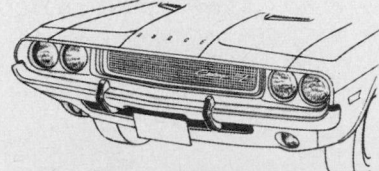

1971 Challenger

1971 Demon

1972 Dart

1972 Demon

1972 Challenger

FIRING ORDER

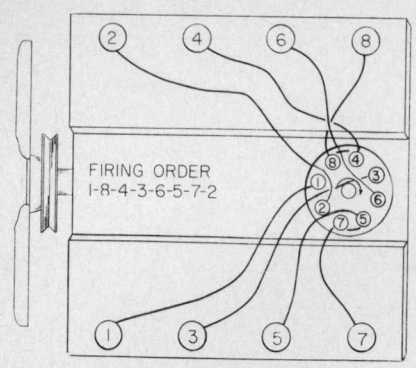

273, 318, 340 cu. in.

FIRING ORDER 1-8-4-3-6-5-7-2

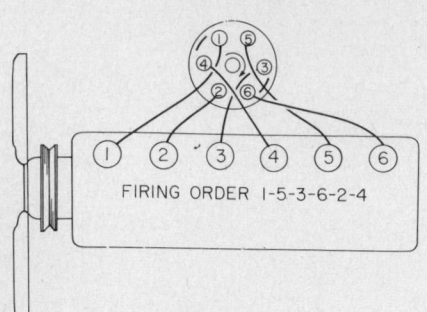

170, 225 cu. in.

FIRING ORDER 1-5-3-6-2-4

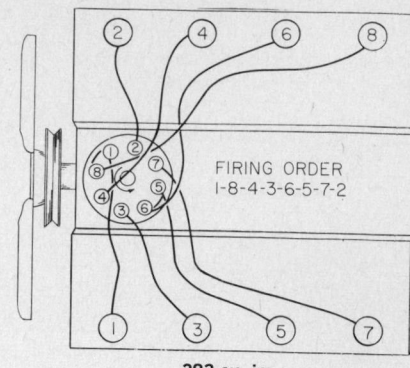

383 cu. in.

FIRING ORDER 1-8-4-3-6-5-7-2

YEAR IDENTIFICATION FIRING ORDER CAR SERIAL NUMBER LOCATION AND ENGINE IDENTIFICATION

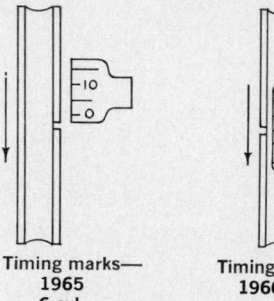

Timing marks— 1965 6 cyl.

Timing marks— 1966 6 cyl.

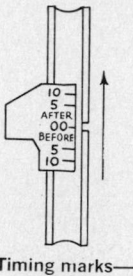

Timing marks— 1967-72 6 cyl.

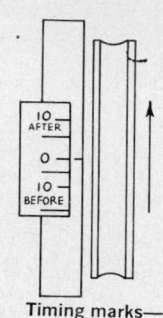

Timing marks— 1966-72 V8

1965

The vehicle serial number is located on a metal plate attached to the left front door hinge pillar. The serial number contains ten digits, interpreted as follows:

First digit
V . . . . Valiant
2 . . . . Dart (six cyl.)
L . . . . Dart (V8)
Second digit
1 . . . . V100 series
3 . . . . V200 series
4 . . . . Signet series
5 . . . . . . V100 station wagon
7 . . . . V200 station wagon
Third digit
5 . . . . 1965 production
Fourth digit
Assembly plant code
Fifth to tenth digits
Series production number

1966

The vehicle serial number is located on a metal plate attached to the left front door hinge pillar. The serial number now consists of thirteen digits, interpreted as follows:

First digit
B . . . . Barracuda
V . . . . Valiant
L . . . . Dart
Second digit (price range)
E . . . . Economy
L . . . . Low
M . . . . Medium
Third and fourth digits
21 . . . . 2-dr. sedan
23 . . . . 2-dr. hardtop
27 . . . . Convt.
41 . . . . 4-dr. sedan
43 . . . . 4-dr. sedan
45 . . . . Station wagon
Fifth digit (engine identification)
A . . . . 170 cu. in. six
B . . . . 225 cu. in. six
D . . . . 273 cu. in. V8
Sixth digit
6 . . . . 1966 production
Seventh digit
Assembly plant code
Eighth to thirteenth digits
Series production number

1967

The vehicle serial number is located on a metal plate attached to the left front door hinge pillar. The serial number contains thirteen digits, interpreted as follows:

First digit
L . . . . Dart
V . . . . Valiant
Second digit (price range)
E . . . . Economy
L . . . . Low
M . . . . Medium
H . . . . High
Third and fourth digits
21 . . . . 2-dr. sedan
23 . . . . 2-dr. hardtop
27 . . . . Convt.
41 . . . . 4-dr. sedan
43 . . . . 4-dr. sedan
45 . . . . 6-pass. station wagon
46 . . . . 9-pass. station wagon
Fifth digit (engine identification)
A . . . . 170 cu. in. six
B . . . . 225 cu. in. six
D . . . . 273 cu. in. V8
Sixth digit
7 . . . . 1967 production
Seventh digit
Assembly plant code
Eighth to thirteenth digits
Series production number

Engine code location—273, 318, 340

Engine code location—383, 440

1968

The vehicle number is located on a plate on the left side of the instrument panel, visible through the windshield. The serial number is interpreted as follows:

First digit
V . . . . Valiant
B . . . . Barracuda
L . . . . Dart

Second digit (price range)
E . . . . Economy
L . . . . Low
M . . . . Medium
H . . . . High
S . . . . Special
K . . . . Police
T . . . . Taxi
O . . . . Superstock

Third and fourth digits
Same as 1967, except the following: 29 . . . . 2-dr. sports hdtp.

Fifth digit (engine identification)
A . . . . 170 cu. in. six
B . . . . 225 cu. in. six
C . . . . Spec. Ord. 6
D . . . . 273 cu. in. V8
E . . . . . 273 cu. in. High Perf. V8
F . . . . 318 cu. in. V8
G . . . . 383 cu. in. V8
H . . . . 383 cu. in. High Perf. V8
N . . . . 340 cu. in. V8
P . . . . . 340 cu. in. High Perf. V8

Sixth digit
8 . . . . 1968 production

Seventh digit
Assembly plant code

Eighth to thirteenth digits
Series production number

1969

The vehicle number is located on a plate on the left side of the instrument panel, visible through the windshield. The serial number is interpreted as follows:

First digit
V . . . . Valiant
B . . . . Barracuda
L . . . . Dart

Second digit (price range)
Same as 1968, with the following exception:
X . . . . Fast Top

Third and fourth digits
Same as 1967-68

Fifth digit (engine identification)
Same as 1968, omitting "E" and "P"

Sixth digit
9 . . . . 1969 production

Seventh digit
Assembly plant code

Eighth to thirteenth digits
Series production number

1970-71

The vehicle number is located on a plate on the left side of the instrument panel, visible through the windshield. The serial number is interpreted as follows:

First digit
V . . . . Valiant
B . . . . Barracuda
L . . . . Dart
J . . . . Challenger

Second digit (price range)
E . . . . Economy
L . . . . Low
M . . . . Medium
H . . . . High
P . . . . Premium
K . . . . Police
T . . . . Taxi
S . . . . Special
O . . . . Super Stock

Third and fourth digits
23 . . . . Two door hardtop
27 . . . . Convertible
29 . . . . Two door special hardtop
41 . . . . Four door sedan

Fifth digit (engine identification)
B . . . . 198 cu. in. six
C . . . . 225 cu. in. six
E . . . . Special six
G . . . . 318 cu. in. V8
H . . . . 340 cu. in. V8
L . . . . 383 cu. in. V8
N . . . . 383 high perf. V8
R . . . . . . 426 cu. in. Hemi V8
T . . . . 440 cu. in. V8
U . . . . 440 high perf. V8
V . . . . 440 six pack V8
Z . . . . Special V8

Sixth digit (model year)

Seventh digit (assembly plant)

Eighth to thirteenth digits
(series production number)

Engine Number Location

170, 198 and 225 cu. in. six engines . . . stamped on joint face of block, next to No. 1 cylinder.

273, 318 and 340 cu. in. V8 engines . . . stamped on front of block, just below left cylinder head.

383, 426 and 440 cu. in. V8 engine . . . stamped on cylinder block pan rail, at left rear corner below starter opening.

BATTERY AND STARTER SPECIFICATIONS

YEAR	MODEL	BATTERY			STARTERS							
		Ampere Hour Capacity	Volts	Terminal Grounded	Lock Test			No-Load Test			Brush Spring Tension (Oz.)
					Amps.	Volts	Torque	Amps.	Volts	RPM	
1965-67	170	38	12	Neg.	380	4	20.0	90	11.0	2,950	32-48
	225	48	12	Neg.	380	4	24.0	85	11.0	1,950	32-48
	V8—273	48	12	Neg.	450	4	24.0	90	11.0	2,400	32-48
1968-69	6—170	38	12	Neg.	380	4	20.0	90	11.0	2,950	32-36
	6—225, 273, 318, 340	48	12	Neg.	425	4	24.0	90	11.0	2,300	32-36
	V8—383	59	12	Neg.	425	4	24.0	90	11.0	2,300	32-36
1970	6 & V8—198, 225, 318, 340	46	12	Neg.	400-450	4	—	90	11.0	1925-2600	32-36
	V8—383	59	12	Neg.	400-450	4	24.0	90	11.0	1925-2600	32-36
	V8—426, 440	70	12	Neg.	400-450	4	24.0	90	11.0	1925-2600	32-36
1971	6 & V8—198, 225, 318	46	12	Neg.	400-450	4	—	90	11.0	1925-2600	32-36
	V8—340, 383	59	12	Neg.	400-450	4	—	90	11.0	1925-2600	32-36
	V8—426, 440	70	12	Neg.	400-450	4	—	90	11.0	1925-2600	32-36
1972	6 & V8—198, 225, 318	46	12	Neg.	400-450	4	—	90	11.0	1925-2600	32-36
	V8—340	46	12	Neg.	400-450	4	—	90	11.0	1925-2600	32-36

TUNE-UP SPECIFICATIONS

| YEAR | MODEL | SPARK PLUGS | | DISTRIBUTOR | | IGNITION TIMING (Deg.) ▲ | CRANKING COMP. PRESSURE (Psi) | VALVES Tappet (Hot) Clearance (In.) | | Intake Opens (Deg.) | FUEL PUMP PRESSURE (Psi) | IDLE SPEED (Rpm) * |
		Type	Gap (In.)	Point Dwell (Deg.)	Point Gap (In.)			Intake	Exhaust			
1965	All Exc. V8 — 273 Cu. In.	N14Y	.035	40–45	.020	2½B	145	.010	.020	8B	3½–5	550
	V8 — 273 Cu. In.; A.T.	N14Y	.035	28–33	.017	10B	145	.013	.021	14B	5–7	550
	V8 — 273 Cu. In.; M.T.	N14Y	.035	28–33	.017	5B	145	.013	.021	14B	5–7	550
1966	170 Cu. In.	N14Y	.035	40–45	.020	5B	125	.010	.020	8B	3½	550
	170 Cu. In.	N14Y	.035	40–45	.020	5A⊙	125	.010	.020	8B	3½	650
	225 Cu. In.	N14Y	.035	40–45	.020	5B	125	.010	.020	10B	3½	550
	225 Cu. In.	N14Y	.035	40–45	.020	5A⊙	125	.010	.020	10B	3½	650
	273 Cu. In. M.T.	N14Y	.035	28–32	.017	5B	135	.013	.021	14B	5–7	600
	273 Cu. In. A.T.	N14Y	.035	28–32	.017	10B	135	.013	.021	14B	5–7	600
	273 Cu. In. M.T.	N14Y	.035	28–32	.017	5A⊙	135	.013	.021	14B	5–7	650
	273 Cu. In. A.T.	N14Y	.035	28–32	.017	5A⊙	135	.013	.021	14B	5–7	650
	273 Cu. In. 4-BBL.	N9Y	.035	27–31*	.017	10B	148	.013	.021	14B	5–7	650
	273 Cu. In. 4-BBL.	N9Y	.035	27–31*	.017	5A⊙	148	.013	.021	14B	5–7	700
1967	170 Cu. In.	N14Y	.035	40–45	.020	5B	125	.010	.020	10B	3½–5	550
	170 Cu. In.	N14Y	.035	40–45	.020	5A⊙	125	.010	.020	10B	3½–5	700
	225 Cu. In.	N14Y	.035	40–45	.020	5B	125	.010	.020	10B	3½–5	550
	225 Cu. In.	N14Y	.035	40–45	.020	TDC⊙	125	.010	.020	10B	3½–5	650
	273 Cu. In. M.T.	N14Y	.035	28–32	.017	5B	135	.013	.021	14B	5–7	650
	273 Cu. In. A.T.	N14Y	.035	28–32	.017	10B	135	.013	.021	14B	5–7	650
	273 Cu. In. 2-BBL.	N14Y	.035	28–32	.017	5A⊙	135	.013	.021	14B	5–7	650
	273 Cu. In. 4-BBL.	N10Y	.035	27–31*	.017	10B	148	.013	.021	14B	5–7	650
	273 Cu. In. 4-BBL.	N10Y	.035	27–31*	.017	5A⊙	148	.013	.021	14B	5–7	700
1968	170 Cu. In., M.T.	N14Y	.035	40–45	.020	5A	125	.010	.020	10B	3½–5	700
	170 Cu. In., A.T.	N14Y	.035	40–45	.020	2½A	125	.010	.020	10B	3½–5	700
	225 Cu. In.	N14Y	.035	40–45	.020	TDC	125	.010	.020	10B	3½–5	650
	273 Cu. In., M.T.	N14Y	.035	28–33	.017	5A	135	Zero	Zero	10B	5–7	700
	273 Cu. In., A.T.	N14Y	.035	28–33	.017	2½A	135	Zero	Zero	10B	5–7	650
	318 Cu. In., M.T.	N14Y	.035	28–33	.017	5A	140	Zero	Zero	10B	5–7	650
	318 Cu. In., A.T.	N14Y	.035	28–33	.017	2½A	140	Zero	Zero	10B	5–7	600
	340 Cu. In., M.T.	N9Y	.035	27–32●	.017	TDC	140	Zero	Zero	26B	5–7	700
	340 Cu. In., A.T.	N9Y	.035	27–32●	.017	5B	140	Zero	Zero	22B	5–7	650
	383 Cu. In., M.T.	J11Y	.035	28–33	.017	TDC	150	Zero	Zero	18B	3½–5	650
	383 Cu. In., A.T.	J11Y	.035	28–33	.017	5B	150	Zero	Zero	18B	3½–5	600
1969	170 Cu. In., 1-BBL. M.T.	N14Y	.035	42–47	.020	5A	125	.010	.020	10B	3½–5	750
	170 Cu. In., 1-BBL. A.T.	N14Y	.035	42–47	.020	2½A	125	.010	.020	10B	3½–5	750
	225 Cu. In., 1-BBL. M.T.	N14Y	.035	42–47	.020	TDC	125	.010	.020	10B	3½–5	700
	225 Cu. In., 1-BBL. A.T.	N14Y	.035	42–47	.020	TDC	125	.010	.020	10B	3½–5	650
	273 Cu. In., 2-BBL. M.T.	N14Y	.035	30–35	.017	2½A	135	Zero	Zero	10B	5–7	700
	273 Cu. In., 2-BBL. A.T.	N14Y	.035	30–35	.017	2½A	135	Zero	Zero	10B	5–7	650
	318 Cu. In., 2-BBL. M.T.	N14Y	.035	30–35	.017	TDC	140	Zero	Zero	10B	5–7	700
	318 Cu. In., 2-BBL. A.T.	N14Y	.035	30–35	.017	TDC	140	Zero	Zero	10B	5–7	650
	340 Cu. In., 4-BBL. M.T.	N9Y	.035	27–32●	.017	TDC	150	Zero	Zero	22B	5–7	750
	340 Cu. In., 4-BBL. A.T.	N9Y	.035	30–35	.017	5B	150	Zero	Zero	22B	5–7	700
	383 Cu. In., 4-BBL. M.T. H.P.	J11Y	.035	30–35	.017	TDC	140	Zero	Zero	18B	3½–5	700
	383 Cu. In., 4-BBL. A.T. H.P.	J11Y	.035	30–35	.017	5B	140	Zero	Zero	18B	3½–5	650
1970	198 Cu. In., 1-BBL.	N14Y	.035	41–46	.017–.023	⑦†	100‡	.010	.020	10B	3½–5	750
	225 Cu. In., 1-BBL. M.T.	N14Y	.035	41–46	.017–.023	TDC†	100‡	.010	.020	10B	3½–5	700
	225 Cu. In., 1-BBL. A.T.	N14Y	.035	41–46	.017–.023	TDC†	100‡	.010	.020	10B	3½–5	650
	318 Cu. In., 2-BBL. M.T.	N14Y	.035	30–34	.014–.019	TDC†	100‡	Zero	Zero	10B	5–7	750
	318 Cu. In., 2-BBL. A.T.	N14Y	.035	30–34	.014–.019	TDC†	100‡	Zero	Zero	10B	5–7	700
	340 Cu. In., 4-BBL. M.T.	N9Y	.035	27–32●	.014–.019	5B†	110‡	Zero	Zero	22B	5–7	900
	340 Cu. In., 4-BBL. A.T.	N9Y	.035	30–34	.014–.019	5B†	110‡	Zero	Zero	22B	5–7	900

TUNE-UP SPECIFICATIONS, continued

| YEAR | MODEL | SPARK PLUGS | | DISTRIBUTOR | | IGNITION TIMING (Deg.) ▲ | CRANKING COMP. PRESSURE (Psi) | VALVES | | | FUEL PUMP PRESSURE (Psi) | IDLE SPEED (Rpm) ★ |
| | | Type | Gap (In.) | Point Dwell (Deg.) | Point Gap (In.) | | | Tappet (Hot) Clearance (In.) | | Intake Opens (Deg.) | | |
								Intake	Exhaust			
	383 Cu. In., 4-BBL. M.T. H.P.	J11Y	.035	28–32	.016–.021	10B†	110‡	Zero	Zero	21B	3½–5	750
	383 Cu. In., 4-BBL. A.T. H.P.	J11Y	.035	28–32	.016–.021	12½B†	110‡	Zero	Zero	21B	3½–5	750
	383 Cu. In. 4-BBL. A.T.	J11Y	.035	28½–32½	.016–.021	12½B	110‡	Zero	Zero	18B	3½–5	700
	383 Cu. In., 2-BBL., M.T.	J14Y	.035	28–32	.016–.021	10B†	100‡	Zero	Zero	18B	3½–5	750
	383 Cu. In., 2-BBL. A.T.	J14Y	.035	28–32	.016–.021	12½B†	100‡	Zero	Zero	18B	3½–5	650
	426 Cu. In., Hemi	N10Y	.035	●	.014–.019	③†	110‡	Zero	Zero	36B	7–8½	900
	440 Cu. In., H.P., M.T.	J11Y	.035	28–32	.016–.021	10B†	110‡	Zero	Zero	21B	3½–5	900
	440 Cu. In., H.P., A.T.	J11Y	.035	28–32	.016–.021	12½B†	110‡	Zero	Zero	21B	3½–5	800
	440 Cu. In., 3-2-BBL.	J11Y	.035	●	.014–.019	12½B†	110‡	Zero	Zero	21B	3½–5	900①
1971	198 Cu. In., 1-BBL.	N114Y	.035	41–46	.017–.023	TDC	100–125	.010	.020	16B	3½–5	800
	225 Cu. In., 1-BBL. M.T.	N114Y	.035	41–46	.017–.023	TDC	100–125	.010	.020	16B	3½–5	750
	225 Cu. In., 1-BBL. A.T.	N114Y	.035	41–46	.017–.023	TDC	100–125	.010	.020	16B	3½–5	750
	318 Cu. In., 2-BBL. M.T.	N114Y	.035	30–34	.014–.019	TDC	100–140	Zero	Zero	10B	5–7	750
	318 Cu. In., 2-BBL. A.T.	N114Y	.035	30–34	.014–.019	TDC	100–140	Zero	Zero	10B	5–7	700
	340 Cu. In., 4-BBL. M.T.	N9Y	.035	●	.014–.019	5B	110–150	Zero	Zero	22B	5–7	900
	340 Cu. In., 4-BBL. A.T.	N9Y	.035	30–34	.014–.019	5B	110–150	Zero	Zero	22B	5–7	900
	340 Cu. In., 3-2-BBL.	N.A.	.035	●	.014–.019	TDC	110–150	Zero	Zero	22B	5–7	④
	383 Cu. In., 4-BBL. M.T.	J11Y	.035	28–32	.016–.021	10B	10–150	Zero	Zero	21B	3½–5	750
	383 Cu. In., 4-BBL. A.T.	J11Y	.035	28–32	.016–.021	12½B	110–150	Zero	Zero	21B	3½–5	700
	383 Cu. In., 2-BBL. A.T.	J14Y	.035	28–32	.016–.021	12½B	100–140	Zero	Zero	18B	3½–5	700
	426 Cu. In., Hemi	N10Y	.035	●	.014–.019	TDC	110–150	Zero	Zero	36B	7–8½	900
	440 Cu. In., 3-2-BBL.	J11Y	.035	●	.014–.019	12½B	110–150	Zero	Zero	21B	3½–5	900
1972	198 Cu. In., 1 BBL.	N14Y	.035	41–46	.017–.023	2.5B	100‡	.010	.020	16B	3½–5	**
	225 Cu. In., 1-BBL.	N14Y	.035	41–46	.017–.023	TDC	100‡	.010	.020	16B	3½–5	**
	318 Cu. In., 2-BBL.	N14Y	.035	30–34	.014–.019	TDC	100‡	Zero	Zero	10B	5–7	**
	340 Cu. In., 4-BBL.	N9Y	.035	⑤	⑤	2.5B	110‡	Zero	Zero	22B	5–7	**

▲—With vacuum advance disconnected and plugged. NOTE: These settings are only approximate. Engine design, altitude, temperature, fuel octane rating and the condition of the individual engine are all factors which can influence timing.

★—With manual transmission in 'N' and automatic in 'D', air conditioning on— if so equipped.

*—Both sets 36°–40°.

Ⓢ—Engines equipped with C.A.P. system.

●—Dual Points: one set of points 27°–32°; both sets of points 37°–42°.

A—After top dead center.

B—Before top dead center.

A.T.—Automatic transmission.

M.T.—Manual transmission.

T.D.C.—Top dead center.

H.P.—High performance.

① —With electric solenoid throttle stop connected.

② —M.T.—2½B; A.T.—TDC.

** —See engine decal.

† — ±2½° with engine at curb idle.

③ —M.T.—TDC†; A.T.—2½B†.

‡ —Minimum.

④ —M.I.—1000; A.T.—950.

⑤ —Transistorized electronic ignition standard or 340 4-BBL.

Caution

General adoption of anti-pollution laws has changed the design of almost all car engine production to effectively reduce crankcase emission and terminal exhaust products. It has been necessary to adopt stricter tune-up rules, especially timing and idle speed procedures. Both of these values are peculiar to the engine and to its application, rather than to the engine alone. With this in mind, car manufacturers supply idle speed data for the engine and application involved. This information is clearly displayed in the engine compartment of each vehicle.

GENERAL ENGINE SPECIFICATIONS

YEAR	CU. IN. DISPLACEMENT	CARBURETOR	ADVERTIZED HORSEPOWER @ RPM	ADVERTIZED TORQUE @ RPM (FT. LBS.)	A.M.A. HORSEPOWER	BORE & STROKE (IN.)	ADVERTIZED COMPRESSION RATIO	VALVE LIFTER TYPE	NORMAL OIL PRESSURE (PSI)
1965	170	1-BBL.	101 @ 4400	155 @ 2400	27.8	3.406 x 3.125	8.2:1	Mech.	45–65
	225	1-BBL.	145 @ 4000	215 @ 2800	27.8	3.406 x 4.125	8.2:1	Mech.	45–65
	273	2-BBL.	180 @ 4200	260 @ 1600	42.0	3.625 x 3.310	8.8:1	Mech.	45–65
	273	4-BBL.	235 @ 5200	280 @ 4000	42.0	3.625 x 3.310	10.5:1	Mech.	45–65
1966	170	1-BBL.	101 @ 4400	155 @ 2400	27.8	3.406 x 3.125	8.5:1	Mech.	45–65
	225	1-BBL.	145 @ 4000	215 @ 2400	27.8	3.406 x 4.125	8.4:1	Mech.	45–65
	273	2-BBL.	180 @ 4200	260 @ 1600	42.0	3.625 x 3.310	8.8:1	Mech.	45–65
	273	4-BBL.	235 @ 5200	280 @ 4000	42.0	3.625 x 3.310	10.5:1	Mech.	45–65
1967	170	1-BBL.	115 @ 4400	155 @ 2400	27.7	3.406 x 3.125	8.5:1	Mech.	45–65
	225	1-BBL.	145 @ 4000	215 @ 2400	27.7	3.406 x 4.125	8.4:1	Mech.	45–65
	273	2-BBL.	180 @ 4200	260 @ 1600	42.2	3.625 x 3.310	8.8:1	Mech.	45–65
	273	4-BBL.	235 @ 5200	280 @ 4000	42.2	3.625 x 3.310	10.5:1	Mech.	45–65
1968	170	1-BBL.	115 @ 4400	155 @ 2400	27.7	3.406 x 3.125	8.5:1	Mech.	45–60
	225	1-BBL.	145 @ 4000	215 @ 2400	27.7	3.406 x 4.125	8.4:1	Mech.	45–60
	273	2-BBL.	190 @ 4400	260 @ 2000	42.2	3.625 x 3.310	9.0:1	Hyd.	45–65
	318	2-BBL.	230 @ 4400	340 @ 2400	48.9	3.910 x 3.310	9.2:1	Hyd.	45–65
	340	4-BBL.	275 @ 5000	340 @ 3200	52.2	4.040 x 3.310	10.5:1	Hyd.	45–65
	383	4-BBL.	300 @ 4400	400 @ 2400	57.8	4.250 x 3.375	10.0:1	Hyd.	45–65
1969	170	1-BBL.	115 @ 4400	155 @ 2400	27.7	3.406 x 3.125	8.5:1	Mech.	45–60
	225	1-BBL.	145 @ 4000	215 @ 2400	27.7	3.406 x 4.125	8.4:1	Mech.	45–60
	273	2-BBL.	190 @ 4400	260 @ 2000	42.2	3.625 x 3.310	9.0:1	Hyd.	45–65
	318	2-BBL.	230 @ 4400	340 @ 2400	48.9	3.910 x 3.310	9.2:1	Hyd.	45–65
	340	4-BBL.	275 @ 5000	340 @ 3200	52.2	4.040 x 3.310	10.5:1	Hyd.	45–65
	383	4-BBL.	330 @ 5200	410 @ 3600	57.8	4.250 x 3.375	10.0:1	Hyd.	45–65
1970	198	1-BBL.	125 @ 4500	180 @ 2000	27.7	3.406 x 3.640	8.4:1	Mech.	45–65
	225	1-BBL.	145 @ 4000	215 @ 2400	27.7	3.406 x 4.125	8.4:1	Mech.	45–65
	318	2-BBL.	230 @ 4400	320 @ 2000	48.9	3.910 x 3.310	8.8:1	Hyd.	45–65
	340	4-BBL.	275 @ 5000	340 @ 3200	52.2	4.040 x 3.310	10.5:1	Hyd.	45–65
	383	2-BBL.	290 @ 4400	390 @ 2800	57.8	4.250 x 3.375	8.7:1	Hyd.	45–65
	383 H.P.	4-BBL.	335 @ 5200	425 @ 3400	57.8	4.250 x 3.375	9.5:1	Hyd.	45–65
	426 Hemi	2-4-BBL.	425 @ 5000	490 @ 4000	57.8	4.250 x 3.750	10.25:1	Hyd.	45–65
	440 H.P.	4-BBL.	375 @ 4600	480 @ 3200	59.7	4.320 x 3.750	9.7:1	Hyd.	45–65
	440 Six Pack	3-2-BBL.	390 @ 4700	490 @ 3200	59.7	4.320 x 3.750	10.50:1	Hyd.	45–65
1971	198	1-BBL.	125 @ 4400	180 @ 2000	27.7	3.406 x 3.640	8.4:1	Mech.	45–65
	225	1-BBL.	145 @ 4000	215 @ 2400	27.7	3.406 x 4.125	8.4:1	Mech.	45–65
	318	2-BBL.	230 @ 4400	320 @ 2000	48.9	3.910 x 3.310	8.6:1	Hyd.	45–65
	340	4-BBL.	275 @ 5000	340 @ 3200	52.2	4.040 x 3.310	10.2:1	Hyd.	45–65
	340	3-2-BBL.	290 @ 5000	340 @ 3200	52.2	4.040 x 3.310	10.2:1	Hyd.	45–65
	383	2-BBL.	275 @ 4400	375 @ 2800	57.8	4.250 x 3.375	8.5:1	Hyd.	45–65
	383 H.P.	4-BBL.	300 @ 4800	410 @ 3400	57.8	4.250 x 3.375	8.5:1	Hyd.	45–65
	426 Hemi	2-4-BBL.	42.5 @ 5000	490 @ 4000	57.8	4.250 x 3.750	10.25:1	Hyd.	45–65
	440 H.P.	4-BBL.	370 @ 4600	480 @ 3200	59.7	4.320 x 3.750	9.7:1	Hyd.	45–65
	440 Six Pack	3-2-BBL.	425 @ 5000	490 @ 3200	59.7	4.320 x 3.750	10.3:1	Hyd.	45–65
1972	198	1-BBL.	100 @ 4400 ①	160 @ 2400 ①	27.7	3.406 x 3.640	8.4:1	Mech.	45–65
	225	1-BBL.	110 @ 4000 ②	185 @ 2000 ②	27.7	3.406 x 4.125	8.4:1	Mech.	45–65
	318	2-BBL.	150 @ 4000	260 @ 1600	48.9	3.910 x 3.310	8.6:1	Hyd.	45–65
	340	4-BBL.	240 @ 4800	290 @ 3600	52.2	4.040 x 3.375	8.5:1	Hyd.	45–65

H.P.—High performance.

①—Calif. emission package 94 HP @ 4400, 158 ft. lbs. @ 2400 RPM.

②—Calif. emission package 97 HP @ 4000, 180 ft. lbs. @ 2000 RPM.

CAPACITIES

| YEAR | MODEL | ENGINE CRANKCASE ADD 1 Qt. FOR NEW FILTER | TRANSMISSIONS Pts. TO REFILL AFTER DRAINING | | | DRIVE AXLE (Pts.) ② | GASOLINE TANK (Gals.) | COOLING SYSTEM (Qts.) WITH HEATER (No A/C) |
| | | | Manual | | Automatic | | | |
			3-Speed	4-Speed				
1965	Valiant—6 Cyl.	4	6	N.A.	17	③	18	12
	Dart—6 Cyl.	4	6	7	17	③	18	12
	V8—All	4	6	7	17	③	18	18
1966	6 Cyl. 170	4	6½	N.A.	16	③	18	12
	6 Cyl. 225	4	6½	N.A.	16	③	18	13
	V8—273	4	6½	8	16	③	18	18
1967	Exc. 170	4	6½	N.A.	16	③	18	12
	6 Cyl. 225	4	6½	N.A.	16	③	18	13
	V8—273	4	6½	8	16	③	18	19
1968	6 Cyl.	4	6½	N.A.	15½	③	18	●
	V8—273	4	6	8	15½	③	18	19
	V8—318	4	6	8	15½	③	18	18
	V8—340, 383	4	N.A.	9	18½	③	18	17
1969	6 Cyl. 170	4	6½	N.A.	15½	③	18	12
	6 Cyl. 225	4	6½	N.A.	15½	③	18	13
	V8—273	4	6½	7	15½	③	18	17
	V8—318	4	6½	7	15½	③	18	16
	V8—340	4	N.A.	7	18½	③	18	16
	V8—383	4	N.A.	7	18½	③	18	16
1970–72	6 Cyl. 225, 198	4	① 6½	N.A.	17	2.0 ③	18 ⑩	13
	V8—318	4	4¾ ①	7½	16 ⑧	③	18 ⑩	16
	V8—340	4	① 4¾	7½ ⑦	16 ⑨	③	18 ⑩	16 ⑤ ⑪
	V8—383	4	N.A.	7½	19 ⑥ ⑨	③	18	16 ⑫
	V8—426	6	N.A.	7½	17.0 ⑨	5½	18	15 ⑬
	V8—440	6	N.A.	7½	19.0	5½	18	15 ⑬

①—All Synchromesh 3-spd., 4.75 pts. Dexron A.T. Fluid.
②—Use only limited slip lube for limited slip drive units.
③—7¼ in. axle, 2.0; 8¾ in. axle, 4.4; 9¾ in. axle, 5.5.

Axle	Filler location	Cover fastening
7¼ in.	Cover	9 bolts
8¼ in.	Carrier, right side	10 bolts
8¾ in.	Carrier, right side	Welded
9¾ in.	Cover	10 bolts

④—Barracuda, 19.

●—170—12, 225—13.
⑤—Valiant and Dart, 15.
⑥—1970 4-BBL. Hi Perf., 16.
⑦—Valiant and Dart—7.0
⑧—1971-72—17
⑨—AH 1971-72 340 Cu. In., 383 Cu. In., 4-BBL, and 426 Cu In.—16.3
⑩—1971-72 Valiant and Dart—17
⑪—1971-72 Challenger and Barracuda—15.5
⑫—1971-72—14.5
⑬—1971-72—15.5; 1971 Challenger with 426 Cu. In.—17.
N.A.—Not applicable.

ALTERNATOR AND AC REGULATOR SPECIFICATIONS

| YEAR | Part Number | ALTERNATOR | | | REGULATOR | | | | | | |
| | | | | | | Field Relay | | | Regulator | | |
		Field Current Draw @ 12V.	Output @ Engine RPM 1250 (AMP.)	Part Number	Air Gap (In.)	Point Gap (In.)	Volts to Close	Air Gap (In.)	Point Gap (In.)	Volts at 140°
1964-67	2098835 ●	2.38-2.75	30	2098300	.050	.014	13.8	.050	.015	13.2-14.2
	2098830 ●	2.38-2.75	35	2098300	.050	.014	13.8	.050	.015	13.2-14.2
	2098850	2.38-2.75	46	2098300	.050	.014	13.8	.050	.015	13.2-14.2
	2444599 ●	2.38-2.75	46	2098300	.050	.014	13.8	.050	.015	13.2-14.2
1968-69	2642538 ●	2.38-2.75	30	2098300	.050	.014	13.8	.050	.015	13.2-14.2
	2642537	2.38-2.75	37	2098300	.050	.014	13.8	.050	.015	13.2-14.2
1970-72	3438171	2.38-2.75	30	3438150	Non-adjustable transistor regulator					13.3-14.0
	3438172	2.38-2.75	37	3438150	Non-adjustable transistor regulator					13.3-14.0
	3438176	2.38-2.75	37	3438150	Non-adjustable transistor regulator					13.3-14.0
	3438389	2.38-2.75	34	3438150	Non-adjustable transistor regulator					13.3-14.0

●Replaced by 2098850

GENERAL CHASSIS AND BRAKE SPECIFICATIONS

YEAR	MODEL	CHASSIS		BRAKE CYLINDER BORE			BRAKE DRUM	
		Overall Length (In.)	Tire Size	Master Cylinder (In.)	Wheel Cylinder Diameter (In.) Front	Rear	Diameter (In.) Front	Rear
1965	Barracuda 6 Cyl.	188.2	6.50 x 13	1	1	$13/16$	9	9
	Barracuda V8	188.2	7.00 x 13	1	1	$13/16$	9	9
	Valiant Pass.	188.2	6.50 x 13 [1]	1	1 [2]	$13/16$	9 [3]	9 [3]
	Valiant Sta. Wag.	188.8	6.50 x 13 [1]	1	1 [2]	$13/16$	9 [3]	9 [3]
	Dart Pass.	196.4	6.50 x 13 [1]	1	1 [2]	$13/16$	9 [3]	9 [3]
	Dart Sta. Wag.	190.2	6.50 x 13 [1]	1	1 [2]	$13/16$	9 [3]	9 [3]
1966	6 Cyl.—All exc. Sta. Wag.	188.3	6.50 x 13	1	1	$13/16$	9 [3]	9 [3]
	6 Cyl.—Station Wagon	189.0	7.00 x 13	1	1	$13/16$	9 [3]	9 [3]
	V8—All exc. Sta. Wag.	188.3	7.00 x 13	1	$1\frac{1}{8}$	$15/16$	10	10
	V8—Station Wagon	189.0	7.00 x 13	1	$1\frac{1}{8}$	$15/16$	10	10
1967	6 Cyl. exc. Conv.	195.4 [4]	6.50 x 13	1	1	$15/16$	9	9
	Conv.	195.4 [4]	7.00 x 13	1	1	$15/16$	9	9
	V8, All	195.4 [4]	7.00 x 13	1	$1\frac{1}{8}$	$15/16$	10	10
	6 & V8—Opt. Disc Brakes	195.4 [4]	6.95 x 14	1	$1\frac{5}{8}$	$15/16$	$10\frac{25}{32}$	10
	Barracuda 6 Cyl.	192.8	6.95 x 14	1	1	$29/32$	9	9
	Barracuda V8	192.8	6.95 x 14	1	$1\frac{1}{8}$ [5]	$29/32$	10 [6]	10
1968	Valiant 6 Cyl.	188.4	6.50 x 13 [8]	1	1	$13/16$	9	9
	Valiant V8	188.4	7.00 x 13	1	$1\frac{1}{8}$	$15/16$	10	10
	Valiant (Disc.)	188.4	6.95 x 14	1 [10]	[11]	$15/16$	[9]	10
	Barracuda 6 Cyl.	192.8	6.95 x 14	1	1	$13/16$	9	9
	Barracuda V8	192.8	6.95 x 14	1	$1\frac{1}{8}$	$15/16$	10	10
	Barracuda (Disc.)	192.8	D70 x 14	1 [10]	[11]	$15/16$	[9]	10
	Dart 6 Cyl.	195.4	6.50 x 13 [8]	1	1	$13/16$	9	9
	Dart V8	195.4	[7]	1	$1\frac{1}{8}$	$15/16$	10	10
	Dart (Disc.)	195.4	6.95 x 14	1	[11]	$15/16$	[9]	10
1969	Valiant 6 Cyl.	188.4	6.50 x 13 [8]	1	1	$13/16$	9	9
	Valiant V8	188.4	7.00 x 13	1	$1\frac{1}{8}$	$15/16$	10	10
	Valiant Disc	188.4	6.95 x 14	[12]	[13]	$15/16$	[14]	10
	Barracuda 6 Cyl.	192.8	6.95 x 14	1	1	$13/16$	9	9
	Barracuda V8	192.8	6.95 x 14	1	$1\frac{1}{8}$	$15/16$	10	10
	Barracuda Disc	192.8	6.95 x 14	[12]	[13]	$15/16$	[14]	10
	Dart 6 Cyl.	195.4	6.50 x 13 [8] ·	1	1	$13/16$	9	9
	Dart V8	195.4	[7]	1	$1\frac{1}{8}$	$15/16$	10	10
	Dart (Disc.)	195.4	6.95 x 14	[12]	[13]	$15/16$	[14]	10
1970	Valiant	188.4	6.95 x 14	1.00	1.187 [16]	.9375	9 [17]	9
	Valiant V8	188.4	[15]	1.00	1.187 [16]	.9375	10 [17]	10
	Baracuda 6 Cyl.	186.7	E78 x 14	1.00 [19]	1.187 [20]	.9375	10 [21]	10
	Barracuda V8	186.7	F70 x 14 [18]	1.00 [19]	1.187 [20]	.9375	11 [21] [22]	11 [22]
	Dart 6 Cyl.	196.2	D78 x 14	1.00	1.187 [16]	.8125	10 [17]	9
	Dart V8	196.2	D78 x 14 [23]	1.00	1.187 [16]	.9375	10 [17]	10
	Challenger 6 Cyl.	191.3	F78 x 14	1.00 [19]	1.187 [20]	.9375	10 [21]	10
	Challenger V8	191.3	F70 x 14 [18]	1.00 [19]	1.187 [20]	.9375	11 [21] [22]	11 [22]
1971–72	Valiant 6 Cyl.	188.4	6.45 x 14 [24]	1.03	1.00 [26]	.8125	9 [17]	9
	Valiant V8	188.4	6.95 x 14 [23]	1.03	1.187 [26]	.9375	10 [17]	10
	Barracuda 6 Cyl.	186.6	7.35 x 14	1.03 [29]	1.187 [20]	.9375	10 [21]	10
	Barracuda V8	186.6	7.35 x 14 [27]	1.03 [29]	1.187 [20]	.9375	11 [21] [22]	11 [22]
	Dart 6 Cyl.	[25]	[28]	1.03	1.00 [26]	.8125	9 [17]	[9]
	Dart V8	[25]	[28]	1.03	1.187 [26]	.9375	10 [17]	10
	Challenger 6 Cyl.	191.3	7.35 x 14	1.03 [29]	1.187 [26]	.9375	10 [21]	10
	Challenger V8	191.3	[30]	1.03 [29]	1.187 [20]	.9375	11 [21] [22]	11 [22]

VALVE SPECIFICATIONS

YEAR AND MODEL		SEAT ANGLE (DEG.)	FACE ANGLE (DEG.)	VALVE LIFT INTAKE (IN.)	VALVE LIFT EXHAUST (IN.)	VALVE SPRING PRESSURE (VALVE OPEN) LBS. @ IN.	VALVE SPRING INSTALLED HEIGHT (IN.)	STEM TO GUIDE CLEARANCE (IN.)		STEM DIAMETER (IN.)	
								Intake	Exhaust	Intake	Exhaust
1965–66	170	45	①	.371	.364	145 @ 1 5/16	1 11/16	.001–.003	.002–.004	.372–.373	.371–.372
	225	45	①	.394	.390	145 @ 1 5/16	1 11/16	.001–.003	.002–.004	.372–.373	.371–.372
	273, 2-BBL.	45	45	.395	.405	145 @ 1 5/16	1 11/16	.001–.003	.002–.004	.372–.373	.371–.372
	273, 4-BBL.	45	45	.415	.425	177 @ 1 5/16	1 11/16	.001–.003	.002–.004	.372–.373	.371–.372
1967	6-Cyl.	45	②	.395	.395	145 @ 1 5/16	1 11/16	.001–.003	.002–.004	.372–.373	.371–.372
	273, 2-BBL.	45	45	.395	.405	145 @ 1 5/16	1 11/16	.001–.003	.002–.004	.372–.373	.371–.372
	273, 4-BBL.	45	45	.415	.425	177 @ 1 5/16	1 11/16	.001–.003	.002–.004	.372–.373	.371–.372
1968	6 Cyl.	45	①	.395	.395	145 @ 1 5/16	1 11/16	.001–.003	.002–.004	.372–.373	.371–.372
	273, 318	45	①	.373	.399	177 @ 1 5/16	1 11/16	.001–.003	.002–.004	.372–.373	.371–.372
	340	45	①	③	④	242 @ 1 7/32	1 11/16	.001–.003	.002–.004	.372–.373	.371–.372
	383, 2-BBL.	45	45	.425	.435	200 @ 1 7/16	1 55/64	.001–.003	.002–.004	.372–.373	.371–.372
	383, 4-BBL.	45	45	.425	.435	230 @ 1 13/32	1 55/64	.001–.003	.002–.004	.372–.373	.371–.372
1969	6 Cyl.	45	①	.395	.395	145 @ 1 5/16	1 11/16	.001–.003	.002–.004	.372–.373	.371–.372
	273, 318	45	①	.373	.399	177 @ 1 5/16	1 11/16	.001–.003	.002–.004	.372–.373	.371–.372
	340	45	①	.429	.444	242 @ 1 7/32	1 11/16	.001–.003	.002–.004	.372–.373	.371–.372
	383, 2-BBL.	45	45	.425	.435	200 @ 1 7/16	1 55/64	.001–.003	.002–.004	.372–.373	.371–.372
	383, 4-BBL.	45	45	.450	.458	246 @ 1 23/64	1 55/64	.001–.003	.002–.004	.372–.373	.371–.372
1970	6 Cyl.	44.5–45.0	45.0–45.5	.397	.393	156 @ 1.26	1.65	.001–.003	.002–.004	.372–.373	.371–.372
	318	44.5–45.0	45.0–45.5	.372	.400	189 @ 1.28	1.65	.001–.003	.002–.004	.372–.373	.371–.372
	340	44.5–45.0	45.0–45.5	.430	.445	242 @ 1.21	1.65	.001–.003	.002–.004	.372–.373	.371–.372
	383, 2-BBL.	44.5–45.0	45.0–45.5	.425	.437	200 @ 1 7/16	1 55/64	.0010–.0027	.0020–.0037*	.372–.373	.371–.372
	383, 4-BBL.	44.5–45.0	45.0–45.5	.425	.437	234 @ 1 4/10	1 55/64	.0010–.0027	.0020–.0037*	.372–.373	.371–.372
	383, Hi Perf.	44.5–45.0	45.0–45.5	.450	465	234 @ 1 4/10	1 55/64	.0010–.0027	.0020–.0037*	.372–.373	.371–.372
	426	44.5–45.0	45.0–45.5	.490	.480	310 @ 1 3/8	1 55/64	.002–.004	.003–.005	.3085–.3095	.3075–.3085*
	440, Hi Perf.	44.5–45.0	45.0–45.5	.450	.465	234 @ 1 4/10	1 55/64	.0010–.0027	.0020–.0037	.372–.373	.371–.372
	440, 3 2 BBL.	44.5 45.0	45.0 45.5	.450	.465	310 @ 1 3/8	1 55/64	.0010–.0027	.0020–.0037	.372–.373	.371–.372
1971	6 Cyl.	44.5–45.0	45.0–45.5	.406	.414	156 @ 1.26	1 11/16	.001–.003	.002–.004	.372–.373	.371–.372
	318	44.5–45.0	45.0–45.5	.372	.400	189 @ 1.28	1 11/16	.001–.003	.002–.004	.372–.373	.371–.372
	340, 4-BBL./6-BBL.	44.5–45.0	45.0–45.5	.430	.445	242 @ 1.21	1 11/16	.0015–.0035	.0025–.0045	.3715–.3725	.3705–.3715
	383, 2-BBL.	44.5–45.0	45.0–45.5	.425	.437	200 @ 1 7/16	1 55/64	.0010–.0027	.0020–.0037*	.3723–.2730	.3713–.3720*
	383	44.5–45.0	45.0–45.5	.450	.465	234 @ 1.40	1 55/64	.0015–.0032	.0020–.0037*	.3718–.3725	.3708–.3715*
	426 Hemi	44.5–45.0	45.0–45.5	.490	.480	310 @ 1 3/8	1 55/64	.002–.004	.003–.005	.3085–.3095	.3075–.3085
	440, 3-2-BBL.	445.–45.0	45.0–45.5	.450	.465	310 @ 1 3/8	1 55/64	.0015–.0032	.0025–.0042*	.3718–.3725	.3708–.3715*
1972	6 Cyl.	44.5–45.0	45.0–45.5	.397	.393	156 @ 1.26	1.65	.001–.003	.002–.004	.372–.373	.371–.372
	318	44.5–45.0	45.0–45.5	.372	.400	189 @ 1.28	1.65	.001–.003	.002–.004	372–.373	.371–.372
	340	44.5–45 0	45.0–45.5	.430	.445	242 @ 1.21	1.65	.001–.003	.002–.004	.372–.373	.371–.372

① —Intake 45; Exhaust 43.
② —Intake 45; Exhaust 47.
③ —Manual trans. 444; Auto trans. 429
④ —Manual trans. .453; Auto trans. .444
* —Hot Eng.

① —All V8 models—7.00 x 13.
② —All V8 models—1 1/8.
③ —Optional and V8 models—10
④ —Valiant—overall length 188.4
⑤ —With disc brakes—front—1 41/64
      rear—15/16
⑥ —With disc brakes—11 7/8
⑦ —273, 318, 7.00 x 383 E70 x 14
⑧ —225 Cu. I. —7.00 x 13
⑨ —Disc od. Kelsey Hayes—11.04
      Bendix—11.19
      Budd—11.88
⑩ —Budd 1 1/8
⑪ —Kelsey Hayes 1.638
      Bendix—2
      Budd—2.375

⑫ —Kelsey Hayes—1
      Bendix—1 7/8
      Kelsey Hayes (Floating)—1–1 1/8
⑬ —Kelsey Hayes—1.636
      Bendix—2
      Kelsey Hayes (Floating)—2 3/4
⑭ —Kelsey Hayes—11.04
      Bendix—11.19
      Kelsey Hayes (Floating)—11.75
⑮ —318 Cu. In. wo/A.C.—6.95 x 14; 318 Cu. In. w/A.C.—D78 x 14; 340 Cu. In.—E70 x 14
⑯ —Disc—1.638
⑰ —Disc—10.79
⑱ —426 Cu. In.—F60 x 15; 318 Cu. In.—E78 x 14
⑲ —Disc—1.125
⑳ —Disc—2.750

㉑ —Disc—10.72
㉒ —318, 340, 383 (not H.P.) Cu. In.—10
㉓ —340 Cu. In.—E70 x 14
㉔ —Scamp and 4-door—6.95 x 14
㉕ —2-door Hardtop and 4-door—196.2; Coupe—192.5
㉖ —Disc—1.625
㉗ —383 Cu. In.—F78 x 14; 'Cuda and AAR 'Cuda with 340 Cu. In. 4-BBL, 383 Cu. In. 4-BBL. or 440 Cu. In.—F70 x 14; 'Cuda and AAR 'Cuda with 426 Hemi—F60 x 15; 'Cuda and AAR 'Cuda with 340 Six Pack—front: E60 x 15, rear: G60 x 15
㉘ —Coupe 6 Cyl.—6.45 x 14; 2-door Hardtop and 4-door 6 Cyl. and V8-318 Cu. In.—6.95 x 14; Demon 340—E70 x 14.
㉙ —426 Hemi, Disc—1.125
㉚ —318 Cu. In.—7.35 x 14; 383 Cu. In.—F78 x 14; 340 Cu. In. R/T 383 Cu. In., 440 Cu. In.—F70 x 14; 426 Hemi—F60 x 15.

CRANKSHAFT BEARING JOURNAL SPECIFICATIONS

YEAR	MODEL	MAIN BEARING JOURNALS (IN.)					CONNECTING ROD BEARING JOURNALS (IN.)		
		Journal Diameter	No. of Main Bearings	Oil Clearance	Shaft End-Play	Thrust On No.	Journal Diameter	Oil Clearance	End-Play
1965-72	6 Cyl.	2.750	4	.0005–.0015	.002–.007	3	2.187	.0005–.0025	.006–.012
	V8—273, 318, 340	2.500	5	.0005–.0015	.002–.007	3	2.125	.0005–.0025	.006–.012
	V8—383	2.625	5	.0005–.0015	.002–.007	3	2.375	.0007–.0032	.009–.017
	V8—440	2.750	5	.0005–.0015	.002–.007	3	2.375	.0007–.0032	.009–.017
	V8—426 Hemi	2.750	5	.0015–.0025	.002–.007	3	2.375	.0010–.0035	.009–.017

TORQUE SPECIFICATIONS

YEAR	MODEL	CYLINDER HEAD BOLTS (FT. LBS.)	ROD BEARING BOLTS (FT. LBS.)	MAIN BEARING BOLTS (FT. LBS.)	CRANKSHAFT BALANCER BOLT (FT. LBS.)	FLYWHEEL TO CRANKSHAFT BOLTS (FT. LBS.)	MANIFOLD (FT. LBS.)	
							Intake	Exhaust
1965-72	6 Cyl.—198, 170, 225	65	45	85	Press Fit	55	10①	10
	V8—273, 318, 340	95⑦	45	85	135④	55	35	30
	V8—383, 440	70	45	85	135	55	35⑤	30
	V8—426 Hemi	70-75②	75	100⑧	135	70	③	24

① —Intake to Exhaust Bolts—20.
② —Bolts and studs same torque.
③ —See text.
④ —1971-72—100
⑤ —1971-72—40
⑥ —1971-72—35
⑦ —1968-70 318 Cu. In.—85
⑧ —Side Bolts—45

CYLINDER HEAD BOLT TIGHTENING SEQUENCE

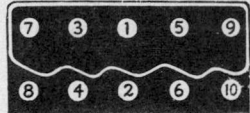

273, 318, 340 cu. in. V8

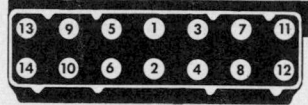

6 cyl.

383, 440 cu. in. V8

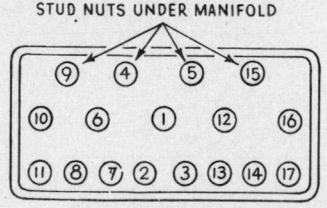

426 cu. in. Hemi V8

DODGE
LIGHT BULBS

1965

	Dart
Sealed beam—single 2 filament	6012
Tail, stop & turn signal	*1034
Tail light	*1095
Park & turn signal	1034
Back up lights	1073
License light	67
Trunk and/or under hood	1004
Glove compartment	1891
Radio	1893
Gear shift indicator	1445
Handbrake indicator	57
Dome lamp	1004
Map lamp	90
Turn signal indicator	57
High beam indicator	57
Oil pressure warning light	57
Instrument cluster illumination	57

*67 on Dart Station Wagon.

1966

	Dart
Back-up lights	1073
Clock	57
Dome lights	1004
Door and/or pocket	90
Emergency flasher	57
Gear selector indicator	1445
Gear selector with console	57
Glove compartment	1891
Handbrake indicator	57
Heater and/or A.C. Control	**
High beam indicator	158
Instrument cluster illumination	158
License light	67
Map light	90
Oil pressure indicator	158
Panel and/or ridge light	90
Park and turn signal	
Radio	1893
Sealed sealed beam—single "7"	6012
Tail stop and turn signal	1034
Trunk and/or under hood light	1004
Turn signal indicator	158

**Not lighted

1967

	Dart
Back-up lights	1141
Brake system warning light	57
Dome and/or "C" pillar light	1004
Door, pocket panel and/or reading light	90
Fender mounted turn signal indicator	1893
Gear selector indicator	1445
Gear selector with console	57
Glove compartment	1891

Handbrake indicator	57
High beam indicator	158
Instrument cluster illumination	158
License light	67
Map light	90
Oil pressure indicator	158
Park and turn signal	1034
Portable reading light	90
Radio	1893
Sealed beam—single "7"	6012
Tachometer	1816
Tail, stop and turn signal	1034
Trunk and/or under hood light	1004
Turn signal indicator (panel)	158

1968

	Dart
Air conditioning indicator	1445
Ash tray	1445
Back-up lights	1073
Brake system warning light	57
Courtesy lamp	89
Dome and/or "C" pillar light	1004
Door, pocket panel and/or reading light	90
Fender mounted turn signal indicator	330
Gear selector indicator	1445
Gear selector with console	57
Glove compartment	1891
High beam indicator	158
Instrument cluster illumination	158
License light	67
Map light	
Oil pressure indicator	158
Park and turn signal	1034A
Radio	1816
Sealed beam—single "7"	6012
Side marker	1895
Tachometer	1816
Tail, stop and turn signal	1034
Trunk and/or under hood light	1004
Turn signal indicator (panel)	158

1969

	Dart
Air conditioning indicator	**1445
Ash tray	**1445
Back-up lights	1156 (2)
Brake system warning light	57
Dome and/or "C" pillar light	1004
Door, pocket panel and/or reading light	90
Fender mounted turn signal indicator	330 (2)
Gear selector indicator	**1445
Gear selector with console	** 57
Glove compartment	1891
High beam indicator	158
Ignition lamp	1445
Instrument cluster illumination	** 158 (4)
License light	67

Map light	89
Oil pressure indicator	158
Park and turn signal	1157 A(2)
Radio	**1816
Reverse 4-speed transmission indicator	53
Sealed beam—single "7"	6012
Tail, stop and turn signal	1157 (2)
Trunk and/or under hood light	1004
Turn signal indicator (panel)	158 (2)

***Headlamp rheostat dimming.

1970–72

	Challenger (Rallye)	Challenger	Dart
Air conditioner control	**1815	**1815	**1445
Ash tray	**1445	**1445	**1445
Back-up lights	1156 (2)	1156 (2)	1156 (2)
Brake system warning	57	57	57
Clock			
Cornering lights	1445	1445	
Dome lamp	550 or 1004	550 or 1004	1004
Door ajar indicator	1892	1892	
Pocket panel lamp	90	90	
Fender mounted turn signal indicator	330 (2)	330 (2)	330 (2)
Gear selector indicator (column)	** 161	** 161	** 161
Gear selector with console	** 57	** 57	** 57
Glove compartment	1891	1891	1891
Headlamp switch rheostat valve	15.5 Ohms	15.5 Ohms	28 Ohms
High beam indicator	57	57	158
Instrument cluster and speedometer illumination	**1893(4)	**1816 (3)	** 158 (4)
Ignition lamp	1445	1445	1445
License light	67	67	67
Low fuel indicator	1892	1892	

DODGE
LIGHT BULBS
1970–72

	Challenger (Rallye)	Challenger	Dart
Map and courtesy lamp	89	89	89
Oil indicator	57	57	158
Park and turn signal	1157 (2)	1157 (2)	1157 (2)
Radio—AM and tape ..	**1816	**1816	**1816
Radio—AM-FM stereo	**1815	**1815	
Reverse 4-speed transmis-			

	Challenger (Rallye)	Challenger	Dart
sion indicator	53	53	53
Sealed beam —hi-beam (No. 1)	4001	4001	
Sealed beam —hi-lo beam (No. 2)	4002 ①	4002 ①	
Sealed beam —single "7"			6012
Seat belts indicator ..	1892 ②	53	53
Side marker	1895(4)	1895(4)	1895(4)

	Challenger (Rallye)	Challenger	Dart
Stereo indicator ..	1445	1445	
Switch lighting ...	*	*	
Tachometer ..	*	*	
Tail, stop and turn signal	1157 (4)	1157 (4)	1157 (2)
Trunk and/or under hood lamp	1004		1004
Turn signal indicator (panel)....	57 (2)	1004 ③	158(2) ⑦

*Included in instrument cluster lighting.
**Headlamp rheostat dimming.

① —1971-72—4000.
② —1971-72 only.
③ —1971-72—57(2).

WHEEL ALIGNMENT

YEAR	MODEL	FRONT END HEIGHT (In.)	CASTER Range (Deg.)	CASTER Pref. Setting (Deg.)	CAMBER Range (Deg.)	CAMBER Pref. Setting (Deg.)	TOE-IN (In.)	KING-PIN INCLINATION (Deg.)	WHEEL PIVOT RATIO Inner Wheel	WHEEL PIVOT RATIO Outer Wheel
1965	Manual	$1^3/_4 \pm 1/_8$	1N to 0	$1/_2$N	▲	▲	$1/_8$	$7^1/_2$	20	17.6
	Power	$1^3/_4 \pm 1/_8$	$1/_4$P to $1^1/_4$P	$3/_4$P	▲	▲	$1/_8$	$7^1/_2$	20	17.6
1966–68	Manual	2 $\pm 1/_8$ ●	1N to 0	$1/_2$N	+	+	$3/_{32}$-$5/_{32}$	$7^1/_2$	20	17.6
	Power	2 $\pm 1/_8$ ●	$1/_4$P to $1^1/_4$P	$3/_4$P	+	+	$3/_{32}$-$5/_{32}$	$7^1/_2$	20	17.6
1969	Manual	2 $\pm 1/_8$ ●	1N to 0*	$1/_2$N	+	+	$3/_{32}$-$5/_{32}$ ☉	$7^1/_2$	20	17.6
	Power	2 $\pm 1/_8$ ●	$1/_4$P to $1^1/_4$P*	$3/_4$P	+	+	$3/_{32}$-$5/_{32}$ ☉	$7^1/_2$	20	17.6
1970	Valiant Manual	$2^1/_8 \pm 1/_8$	$1/_2$N $\pm 1/_2$	$1/_2$N	①	②	$1/_8 \pm 1/_{32}$	$7^1/_2$	20	17.5
	Valiant Power	$2^1/_8 \pm 1/_8$	$3/_4$P $\pm 1/_2$	$3/_4$P	①	②	$1/_8 \pm 1/_{32}$	$7^1/_2$	20	17.5
	Dart Manual	$2^1/_8 \pm 1/_8$	0 to 1N	$1/_2$N	①	②	$1/_8 \pm 1/_{32}$	$7^1/_2$	20	17.6
	Dart Power	$2^1/_8 \pm 1/_8$	$1/_4$ P to $1^1/_4$ P	$3/_4$P	①	②	$1/_8 \pm 1/_{32}$	$7^1/_2$	20	17.6
	Barracuda Manual	$1^3/_{16} \pm 1/_8$	$1^5/_{16}$ N to $15/_{16}$ N	1 N	①	②	$1/_{32}$-$7/_{32}$	$7^1/_2$	20	17.5
	Barracuda Power	$1^3/_{16} \pm 1/_8$	$15/_{16}$ P to $3/_8$ N	$1/_{16}$ N	①	②	$1/_{32}$-$7/_{32}$	$7^1/_2$	20	17.5
	Challenger Manual	$1^3/_{16} \pm 1/_8$	$1^5/_{16}$ N to $15/_{16}$ N	1 N	①	②	$1/_{32}$-$7/_{32}$	$7^1/_2$	20	17.8
	Challenger Power	$1^3/_{16} \pm 1/_8$	$15/_{16}$ P to $3/_8$ N	$1/_{16}$N	①	②	$1/_{32}$-$7/_{32}$	$7^1/_2$	20	17.8
1971–72	Manual	③	1N to 0	$1/_2$ N	①	②	$1/_8 \pm 1/_{32}$	$7^1/_2$	20	17.5
	Power	③	$1/_4$ P to $1^1/_4$ P	$3/_4$ P	①	②	$1/_8 \pm 1/_{32}$	$7^1/_2$	20	17.5

① —Left wheel: $1/_2$P $\pm 1/_4$; Right wheel: $1/_4$P $\pm 1/_4$.
② —Left wheel: $1/_2$P; Right wheel $1/_4$P.
③ —Dart and Valiant 4-DR—$2^1/_8 \pm 1/_8$; Dart and Valiant 2-DR—$1^5/_8 \pm 1/_8$; Barracuda and Challenger—1 $\pm 1/_8$.
▲—Right side, $1/_{16}$N to $3/_8$P; left side, $1/_8$P to $5/_8$P.
+—Right side, 0 to $1/_2$P, $1/_4$P preferred; left side, $1/_4$P to $3/_4$P, $1/_2$P preferred.

N—Negative.
P—Positive.
●—Barracuda—$1^3/_8 \pm 1/_8$.
*—Dart: manual—$1/_{16}$P to $1^1/_{16}$N; power—$3/_{16}$P to $1^5/_{16}$P.
☉—Dart $1/_{16}$-$3/_{16}$.

Plymouth

1965–66

	Valiant, Barracuda
Single beam 2 filament	6012
Tail, stop & turn signal	1034
Park & turn signal	1034
Back-up lamps	1073
License lamp	67
Trunk and/or under hood lamp	1004
Glove compartment	1891
Radio	1893
Transmission gear shift control	1445
Handbrake indicator	57
Dome lamp	1004
Map lamp	90
Turn signal indicator	158
High beam indicator	158
Oil pressure indicator	158
Instrument and speedometer cluster illumination	158
Emergency flasher	57
Gear selector with console	53X

1967

	Valiant
Brake system warning light	57
Dome and/or "C" pillar light	1004
Door, pocket panel and/or reading light	90
Fender mounted turn signal indicator	330
Gear selector indicator	1445
Gear selector with console	57
Glove compartment	1891
Handbrake indicator	57
High beam indicator	158
Instrument cluster illumination	158
License light	67
Map light	90
Oil pressure indicator	57
Park and turn signal	1034A
Radio	1893
Sealed beam—single "7"	6012
Tail, stop and turn signal	1034
Trunk and/or under hood light	1004
Turn signal indicator (panel)	158

1968

	Barracuda	Valiant
Air conditioning indicator	1445*	1445*
Ash receiver	1445*	1445*
Back-up lights	1073	1141 (Sta. Wag.)
Brake system warning light	158	57
Courtesy lamp	89	89
Dome and/or "C" pillar light	211-1	1004
Door, pocket panel and/or reading light	90	90
Fender mounted turn signal indicator	330	330H
Gear selector indicator	1445	1445
Gear selector with console	57	57
Glove compartment	1891	1891
High beam indicator	158	158
Instrument cluster illumination	158	158
License light	67	67
Oil pressure indicator		158
Park and turn signal	1034A	1034
Radio	1816	1816
Sealed beam—single "7"	6012	6012
Side marker	1895	1895
Tachometer	*	1816
Tail, stop and turn signal	1034	1034
Trunk and/or under hood light	1004	1004
Turn signal indicator (panel)	158	158

*Included in instrument cluster.

1969

	Barracuda	Valiant
Air conditioner control and auto-temp	**1445	**1445
Ash receiver	**1445	**1445
Back-up lights	1156 (2)	1156 (2)
Brake system warning indicator	158	158
"C"-pillar light	211-1 (2)	—
Courtesy lamp	89	
Dome lamp	1004	1004
Pocket panel lamp	90	NA
Fender mounted turn signal indicator	330 (2)	330 (2)
Gear selector indicator	**1445	**1445
Gear selector with console	** 57	
Glove compartment	1891	1891
High beam indicator	158	158
Instrument cluster and speedometer illumination	** 158 (4)	** 158 (3)
Ignition lamp	1445	1445
License light	67	67
Map and courtesy lamp	89	89
Oil pressure indicator		158
Park and turn signal	1157A (2)	1157A (2)
Radio	**1816	**1816
Sealed beam—single "7"	6012	6012
Tachometer	*	—
Tail, stop and turn signal	1157 (2)	1157 (2)
Trunk and/or under hood lamp	1004	1004
Turn signal indicator (panel)	158 (2)	158 (2)
Reverse 4-speed transmission indicator	53	53

NA—Not available.
*—Included in instrument cluster lighting.
**—Headlamp rheostat dimming.

1970–72

	Valiant	Barracuda	Barracuda (Rallye)
Air conditioner control and Auto-Temp	1445**	1815**	1815**
Ash tray	1445**①	1445**	—
Back-up lights	1156(2)	1156(2)	1156(2)
Brake system warning indicator	158	57	57
Clock	—	*	*
Courtesy lamp	89	1445②	1445②
Dome lamp	1004	1004③	1004③
Door ajar indicator	—	1892	1892
Fender-mounted turn signal indicator	330(2)	330(2)	330(2)
Front park and turn signal	1157NA(2)	1157NA(2)	1157NA(2)
Gear selector indicator (column)	161**	161**	161**
Gear selector indicator (console)	—	57**	57**
Glove compartment	1891	1891	1891
Headlamp switch rheostat valve	28 Ohms	15.5 Ohms	15.5 Ohms
High beam indicator	158	57	57
Instrument cluster and speedometer	158(3)**	1916(3)**	1816(3)**④
Ignition lamp	1445	1445	1445
License lamp	67	67	67
Low fuel indicator	—	1892	1892
Map and courtesy lamp	89	89	89
Oil indicator	158	57	57
Pocket panel lamp	—	90	90
Radio—AM and tape	1816**	1816**	1816**
Radio—AM/FM and stereo	—	1815**	1815**
Reverse 4-speed indicator	53	53	53
Sealed beam—high beam (No. 1)	—	4001	4001
Sealed beam—hi/lo beam (No. 2)	—	4000	4000
Sealed beam—single "7"	6012	6012	6012
Seat belts indicator	53	53⑤	53⑤
Side marker	1895(4)	1895(4)	1895(4)
Stereo indicator	—	1445	1445
Tachometer	—	⑥	*
Tail, stop and turn signal	1157(2)	1157(2)	1157(2)
Trunk and/or under hood lamp	1004	1004⑦	1004⑦
Turn signal indicator (panel)	158(2)	57(2)	57(2)

① —1971-72—1892**.
② —1971-72—89.
③ —1971-72—or 211-1; 1970—or 550.
④ —1971-72—1893(4)**.
⑤ —or 1892.
⑥ —1971-72—included in instrument cluster lighting.
⑦ —1971-72—1003.
*—Included in instrument cluster lighting.
**—Headlamp rheostat dimming.

FUSES AND CIRCUIT BREAKERS

PLYMOUTH

1965–66

FUSES

Radio	5 AMP
Heater or air conditioning	20 AMP
Accessories	20 AMP
Cigar lighter	20 AMP
Tail, stop, dome	20 AMP
Instrument lamps	*

*AV-1 and AV-2—2 ampere; AR-1 and AR-2—3 ampere; AP-1 and AP-2—4 ampere.

CIRCUIT BREAKERS

Windshield wiper—variable speed (integral with wiper switch)	*
Windshield wiper—single speed (integral with wiper switch)	5 AMP
Lighting system (integral with headlamp switch)	15 AMP
Power windows, power seats, top lift (behind left front kick panel)	30 AMP
Electric door locks (behind left front kick panel)	15 AMP

*AV-1, AV-2, AR-1 and AR-2—6 ampere; AP-1 and AP-2—7½ ampere.

1967

FUSES

Accessories	20 AMP
Cigar lighter (front)	20 AMP
Emergency flasher	20 AMP
Heater or air conditioner	20 AMP
Instrument lights	2 AMP
	—Valiant
Radio	5 AMP
Tail, stop, dome	20 AMP

CIRCUIT BREAKERS

	Valiant
Convertible top (*integral with top lift switch)	30 AMP
Headlights (integral with headlight switch)	15 AMP
Windshield wipers (integral with wiper switch)	6 AMP

1968

FUSES

	Barracuda	Valiant
Accessories	20	20
Cigar lighter (front) and dome light	20	20
Heater or air conditioner	20	20
Instrument lights	2	2
Radio and back-up lamps	5	5
Tail, stop and emergency flasher	20	20

CIRCUIT BREAKERS

	Barracuda (Amps.)	Valiant (Amps.)
Convertible top (integral with top lift switch)	30	30
Headlights (integral with headlight switch)	15	15
Windshield wipers (integral with wiper switch)	6	6

1969–72

FUSES

	Barracuda (Amps.)	Valiant (Amps.)
Accessory	20	20
Console	20	—
Dome/stop lamps	20	20
Emergency	20	20
Headlamp delay (in-line)	20	20
Heater and air conditioner	20	20
Instrument lamps	3	3
Radio and back-up lamps	7.5*	7.5*
Stop and dome lamps	20	20
Tail lamps and cigar lighter	20	20

*—1970-72—20

CIRCUIT BREAKERS

	Barracuda (Amps.)	Valiant (Amps.)
Convertible (integral with switch)	30	—
Headlights (integral with headlamp switch)	15	15*
Windshield wipers (integral with wiper switch)	6**	6**

*—1971-72—20
**—Variable speed—7.5

Dodge

1965

FUSES

Radio	3 AG/AGC; 5 AMP
Heater or air cond.	3 AG/AGC; 20 AMP
Accessories	3 AG/AGC; 20 AMP
Cigar lighter	3 AG/AGC; 20 AMP
Tail, stop, dome	3 AG/AGC; 20 AMP
Instrument lights	3 AG/AGC; 2 AMP Dart

CIRCUIT BREAKERS

Windshield wiper—variable speed (integral with wiper switch)	6 AMP
Windshield wiper—single speed (integral with wiper switch)	5 AMP
Lighting system (integral with headlight switch)	15 AMP Dart
Top lift (behind left front kick panel)	30 AMP

1966–67

FUSES

Accessories	3 AG/AGC; 20 AMP
Cigar lighter	3 AG/AGC; 20 AMP
Heater or air cond.	3 AG/AGC; 20 AMP
Instrument lights	3 AG/AGC; 2 AMP Dart
Radio	3 AG/AGC; 5 AMP
Tail, stop, dome	3 AG/AGC; 20 AMP

CIRCUIT BREAKERS

Lighting system (integral with headlight switch)—Dart	15 AMP
Top lift (behind left front kick panel)	30 AMP

Windshield wiper (integral with wiper switch)	
Single speed	5 AMP
Variable speed	6 AMP

1968

FUSES

	Dart
Accessories	20 AMP
Cigar lighter (front) and dome light	20 AMP
Heater or air conditioner	20 AMP
Instrument lights	2 AMP
Radio and back-up lamps	5 AMP
Tail, stop and emergency flasher	20 AMP

CIRCUIT BREAKERS

	Dart
Convertible top (integral with top lift switch)	30 AMP
Headlights (integral with headlight switch)	15 AMP
Windshield wipers (integral with wiper switch)	6 AMP

1969

FUSES

	Dart
Accessory, tail lamps and cigar lighter	20 AMP
Emergency, stop and dome	20 AMP
Heater and air conditioner	20 AMP
Instrument lamps	3 AMP
Radio and back-up lamps	7.5 AMP

CIRCUIT BREAKERS

	Dart
Convertible top (integral with top lift switch)	30 AMP
Headlights (integral with headlight switch)	15 AMP
Windshield wipers (integral with wiper switch)	6 AMP

1970–72

FUSES

	Challenger (Amps.)	Dart (Amps.)
Accessory	20	20
Emergency flasher	20	—
Heater and air conditioner (blower motor)	20	20
Headlamp delay (in-line)	20	20
Instrument lamps	3*	3*
Radio and back-up lamps	20	20
Stop and dome lamps	20	20
Tail lamps and cigar lighter	20	20

*—1971-72—5

CIRCUIT BREAKERS

	Challenger (Amps.)	Dart (Amps.)
Convertible (on fuse block)	30	—
Headlamps (integral with headlamp switch)	20	15
Windshield wipers (integral with wiper switch)		
2-speed motor	6.0	6.0
3-speed motor (optional)	7.5*	7.5*
Variable speed motor (optional)	7.5*	7.5*

Distributor

Removal

1. Remove distributor cap.
2. Disconnect primary wire.
3. Disconnect vacuum line.
4. Rotate engine crankshaft until distributor rotor is pointing at cylinder block. Scribe mark on block at this point to indicate position of rotor.
5. Remove hold down bolt and remove distributor.

Installation

If engine has not been disturbed, install distributor so that rotor aligns with scribe mark on block. If engine has been disturbed, proceed as follows.

1. Rotate crankshaft until mark on inner edge of crankshaft pulley is in line with the O (TDC) mark on timing chain case cover.
2. With distributor gasket in position, hold distributor over the mounting pad.

3. Turn the rotor to point forward, corresponding to four o'clock.
4. Install distributor so that, with distributor fully seated on the engine, the gear has spiraled to bring rotor to a five o'clock position.
5. Turn the housing until the ignition points are separating and rotor is under No. 1 cap tower.
6. Install hold-down bolt.
7. Adjust timing to specifications, using a timing light.

Alternator, Regulator

Removal

To remove alternator:
1. Disconnect battery ground cable.
2. Disconnect BAT and FLD leads from alternator.
3. Remove alternator by removing two mounting bolts and belt tensioner bracket bolt.
4. To reinstall, reverse above.

NOTE: never attempt to polarize an alternator, nor short the regulator.

Starter

Removal

1. Disconnect negative cable at battery.
2. Disconnect starter cable at starter.
3. Remove starter attaching bolts and remove starter and cylinder block seal from beneath the engine.
4. Reverse above procedure.

Instruments

Thermal type fuel and temperature gauges are used on Valiant and Dart cars.

Both gauges receive a constant voltage supply from a voltage regulator built into the temperature gauge. They are sensitive only to changes in fuel level or temperature

The terminals on the temperature gauge housing the constant voltage regulator, internally, are marked as follows:

A: the output terminal for the controlled voltage from the constant voltage regulator.

I: the 12-volt input voltage terminal to the voltage regulator.

S: the terminal for the connection to the sending unit.

The fuel gauge will have only the controlled voltage terminal A and the terminal S for the connection to the tank sending unit.

The oil pressure indicator lamp is connected between the oil pressure sending unit in the oil pump body and the ignition terminal of the ignition switch. When oil pressure exceeds 8-12 psi, the contacts open and the light goes out.

More detailed information on instruments may be found in the Unit Repair Section.

Cluster R & R

1965 Valiant, Dart, and Barracuda

1. Disconnect battery.
2. Cover steering column jacket tube between steering wheel and instrument panel with masking tape to avoid scratching finish.
3. Loosen steering column clamp screws several turns to lower steering column slightly.
4. Reach up under instrument panel and disconnect speedometer cable at speedometer.
5. Remove four screws visible on face of cluster.
6. Tilt cluster downward and to right and disconnect lead wires

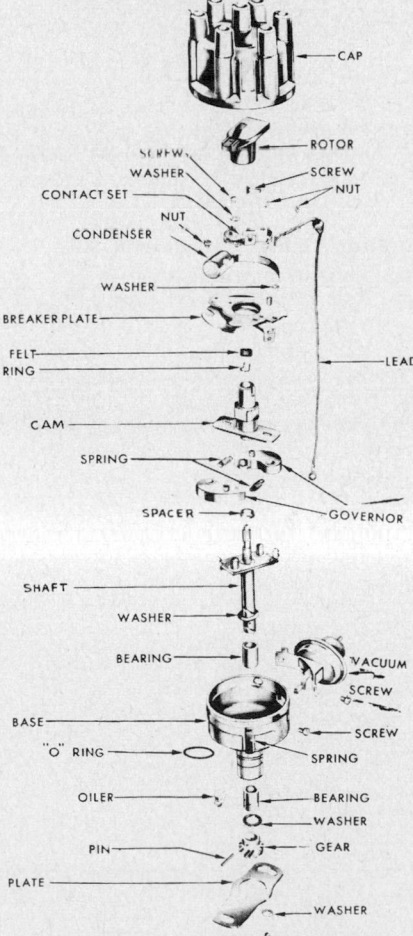

6 cylinder distributor
(© Chrysler Corp.)

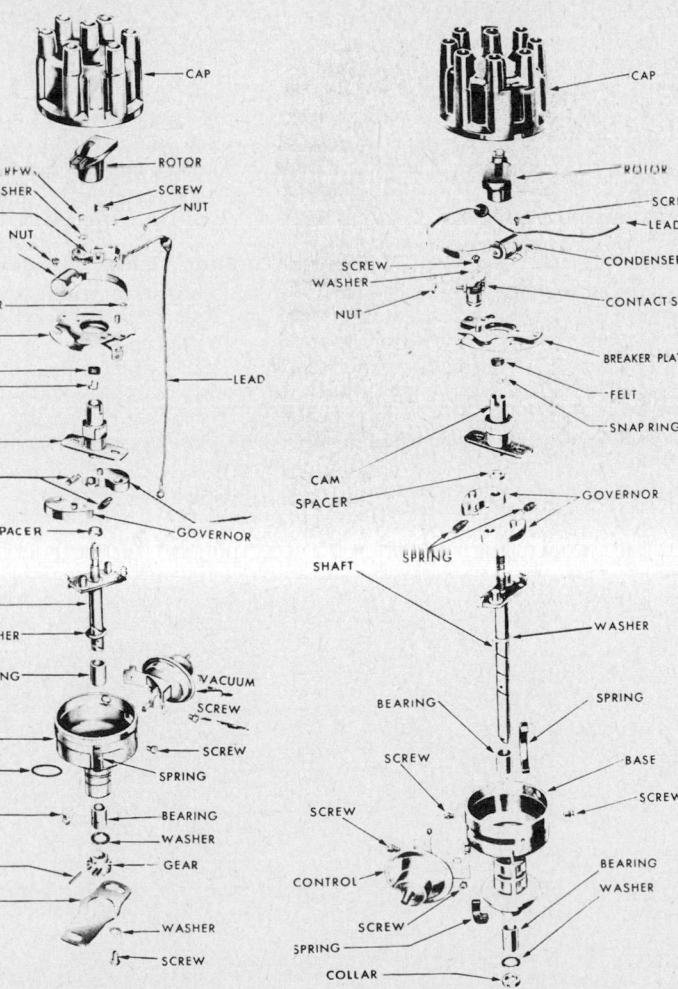

Chrysler distributor
(© Chrysler Corp.)

to ammeter, ignition switch multi-connector, and printed circuit multi-connector.

7. Remove cluster. Reverse procedure to install.

1966 Valiant and Barracuda

1. Disconnect battery. Disconnect speedometer at speedometer head.
2. Remove steering column clamp, and lower the support plate at the firewall.
3. Protect top of steering column jacket against scratches.

NOTE: on the Barracuda, remove ignition switch bezel.

4. Remove four cluster mounting screws and pull cluster out far enough to disconnect printed circuit board and ignition switch multiple connectors.
5. Disconnect wires and remove cluster to work area for service.
6. Install by reversing removal procedure.

1966 Dart

1. Disconnect battery, then tape steering column jacket to protect against scratches.
2. If car is air conditioned, remove left spot cooler duct, hose and fuse block.
3. Disconnect speedometer cable at speedometer head.
4. Remove steering column support bracket and lower the column support plate at firewall.
5. Remove radio control knobs, attaching nuts, ash tray and housing, and the cigar lighter.
6. From under the dash, remove mounting nut next to heater switch.
7. Remove headlight switch knob and bezel by depressing release button on headlight switch and pulling out on headlight switch knob. Remove switch bezel. Do not remove switch from panel.
8. Loosen set screw in wiper switch knob and remove switch bezel. Do not remove switch from panel.
9. Remove four instrument cluster retaining screws and pull cluster out far enough to disconnect printed circuit board and ignition switch multiple connectors. Disconnect two ammeter wires, then remove cluster to work area.
10. Install by reversing removal procedure.

1967-72 Valiant and Dart

1. Disconnect battery.
2. From under instrument panel, disconnect speedometer cable from speedometer. On Dart models, remove the fuse box attaching screw and position the fuse box out of the way.
3. Loosen steering column floor plate attaching screws, remove

steering column upper clamp, and allow steering column to rest in lowered position.

4. Tape top of steering column to prevent damage to finish.
5. Remove six mounting screws from cluster.
6. Reach up behind and above cluster and bend three harness clips out of the way.
7. Roll upper edge of cluster out far enough to disconnect wire connectors.
8. Remove cluster. Reverse procedure to install.

1967-69 Barracuda

1. Disconnect battery.
2. Tape steering column to prevent damage to finish.
3. Reaching up from under panel, disconnect multiple connector from left printed circuit board.
4. Remove four cluster retaining screws from underside of crash pad and four retaining screws from lower front face of cluster.
5. Remove clock reset cable.
6. Disconnect speedometer cable at speedometer.
7. Pull cluster out far enough to reach behind and disconnect right printed circuit board multiple connector, ammeter wires, vacuum gauge hose or tachometer wire, and emergency flasher switch conductor.
8. Loosen air conditioner or heater knobs and remove from slide control. Remove air conditioner or heater control mounting screws and move control out of way.
9. Depress headlight switch knob release button on bottom side of switch and pull knob and shaft out of switch.
10. Pull windshield wiper knob from shaft. Remove wiper switch bezel nut and allow switch to remain connected to wire harness.
11. Roll cluster out from panel open-

ing face down and to the right. Reverse procedure to install.

1970-72 Challenger and Barracuda

1. Disconnect battery.
2. Remove six lamp panel mounting screws.
3. Carefully slide lamp panel out and lay on top of instrument panel. It is not necessary to disconnect wire harness.
4. Remove four switch bezel mounting screws and let bezel hang loose. It is not necessary to disconnect switches.
5. Remove steering column "Duffy" plate mounting screws and two column support clamp retaining nuts. Allow column to rest on seat.
6. From under instrument panel disconnect speedometer cable from speedometer.
7. Remove six cluster bezel mountings screws.
8. Angle bezel out in such a manner as to clear clock reset button.
9. Reach between bezel and panel and disconnect stereo control wiring harness, if so equipped. On Rallye cluster, remove clock reset button and odometer reset button from cluster bezel to remove clock.
10. Remove four cluster to panel mounting screws.
11. Disconnect all wiring harnesses and remove cluster. Reverse procedure to install.

Speedometer Removal

1. Remove instrument cluster.
2. Remove clock reset button, if so equipped.
3. Place cluster assembly on padded surface with cluster face down.
4. Remove screws attaching bezel assembly to cluster base and remove bezel.
5. Remove attaching nuts or screws and remove speedometer.

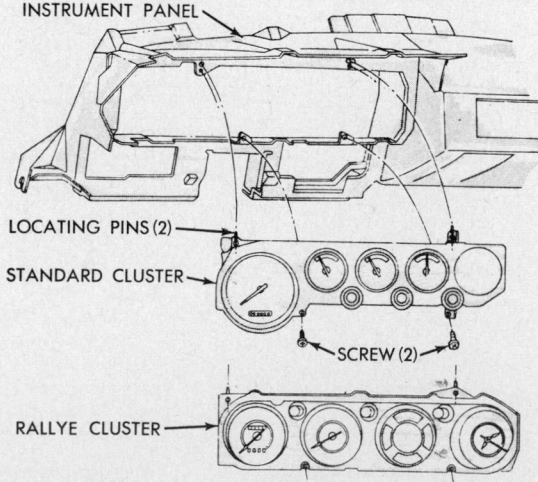

Challenger cluster removal (© Chrysler Corp.)

Headlight Switch

1965-69 All Models and 1970-72 Valiant and Dart

1. Remove the fuse box attaching screw and position the fuse box out of the way.
2. Press the release button on the body of the headlight switch and pull the control knob and shaft from the switch.
3. Disconnect the multiple connector from the rear of the headlight switch.
4. Remove the bezel nut that attaches the headlight switch to the dash and remove the switch.
5. Reverse above procedure to install.

1970-72 Barracuda and Challenger

1. Disconnect the negative battery cable.
2. Remove the six lamp panel mounting screws and carefully slide the lamp panel out of the dash and lay it on top of the instrument panel. It is not necessary to disconnect the wiring harness.
3. Remove the four switch bezel mounting screws. Carefully slide the switch bezel out and to the right, overlapping the center instrument cluster, then lower it until it is free of the instrument panel and disconnect the wiring harness.
4. Remove the two headlight switch mounting screws and remove the switch from the bezel assembly.

Ignition Switch

1965-69 All Models

1. Disconnect the multiple connector from the rear of the switch.
2. Remove the bezel nut that attaches the ignition switch to the dash and remove the switch.

1970-72 All Models

See Chrysler section.

Brakes

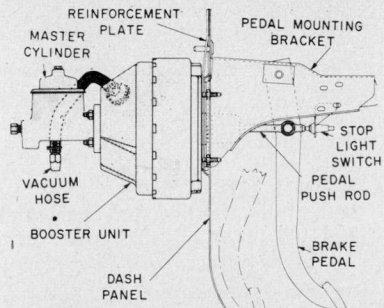

Vacuum-suspended power brake unit
(© Chrysler Corp.)

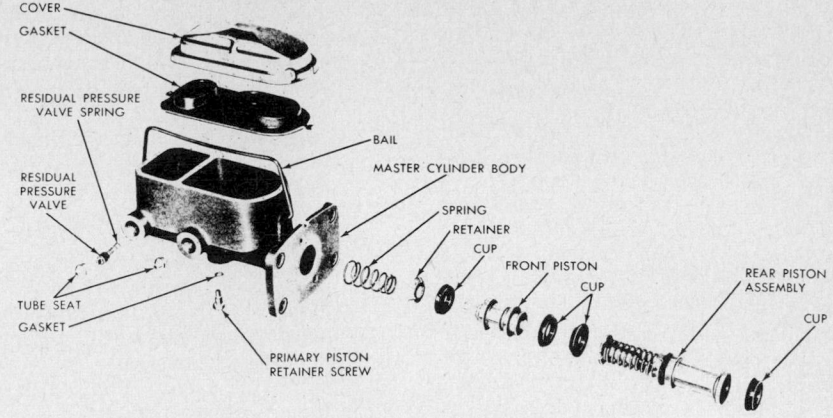

Dual type master cylinder (disc brakes) (© Chrysler Corp.)

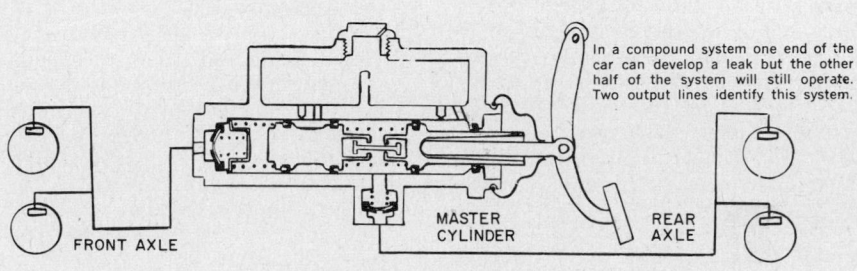

In a compound system one end of the car can develop a leak but the other half of the system will still operate. Two output lines identify this system.

Dual type master cylinder (© Chrysler Corp.)

Master Cylinder R&R

1. Disconnect the brake line/s from the master cylinder.
2. Remove the nuts that attach the master clyinder to the cowl panel or brake booster.
3. On models with standard brakes, disconnect the master cylinder pushrod from the brake pedal.
4. Slide the master cylinder straight out and off the cowl panel or brake booster.
5. Reverse above procedure to install and bleed brake system.

Power Brake Booster R&R

1. Remove the nuts that attach the master cylinder to the brake booster and position the master cylinder out of the way without disconnecting the lines. Use care not to kink the brake lines.
2. Disconnect the vacuum hose from the brake booster.
3. Working under the dash, remove the nut and bolt that attaches the brake booster pushrod to the brake pedal. On linkage type brake boosters, remove the lower pivot retaining bolt.
4. Remove the four brake booster attaching nuts and washers.
5. Remove booster assembly from the vehicle.
6. Reverse above procedure to install.

Parking Brake Adjustment

1. Release the parking brake lever and clean and lubricate the parking brake cable adjusting nut and threads. Loosen the cable adjusting nut.
2. Tighten the cable adjusting nut until a slight drag is felt in the rear wheels when the rear wheels are rotated. Loosen the cable adjusting nut until the rear wheels can be rotated freely. Back off the cable adjusting nut two additional turns.
3. Apply and release the parking brake several times and check to verify that the rear wheels rotate freely, without any brake drag.

Fuel System

Carburetors

Since 1965, Dodge and Plymouth compact and intermediate models have used many different types of carburetors. However, the adjustment procedure for all these carburetors, with a few exceptions, is the same. Some 1966-67 and all 1968 and later carburetors incorporate modifications to reduce engine exhaust emissions. Carburetor modifications for 1966-69 are part of Chrysler's Cleaner Air Package, and 1970 and later models are part of the Cleaner Air System. The only carburetor changes used with the Cleaner Air Package are the installation of carburetor mixture limiter stops on the carburetor idle mixture adjustment screws, and leaner carburetor mixtures. With the Cleaner Air System, in addition to the above mentioned changes, faster acting chokes were added and, on some models, solenoid operated throttle stops and distributor retard mechanisms. The throttle stop raises the engine idle speed to reduce engine emissions, but de-energizes when the ignition is shut off to prevent the engine from dieseling. The distributor retard solenoid is activated when the idle speed adjustment screw returns to the curb idle position and contacts a sensor, mounted on the carburetor, which retards ignition timing while the engine is at idle. These carburetors also incorporate an internally mounted hot idle compensator which opens to induct additional air into the carburetor during low speed-high temperature operation.

The 426 Hemi and the 340 and 440 engines are available with multiple carburetor options. The 426 Hemi is equipped with two Carter AFB carburetors. Both of these carburetors have complete idle systems which must be adjusted and synchronized to obtain a satisfactory engine idle. The 340 and 440 Six-Pack engines are equipped with three Holley 2300 two-venturi carburetors. Only the center carburetor on these engines is equipped with an idle system and the inboard and outboard carburetors contain no idle adjustments

Idle Speed and Mixture Adjustments (See Illustrations in Dodge Section)

NOTE: 1966-67 CAP carburetors can be identified by a green tag attached to the air horn.

1965-67 Without CAP

Adjust with air cleaner removed.
1. Run engine at fast idle to stabilize engine temperature.
2. Make sure the choke plate is fully released.
3. Attach a tachometer of known accuracy to the engine.
4. If equipped with air conditioning, turn the air conditioner ON.
5. On models wth a six cylinder engine, turn the headlights on high beam.
6. Adjust the carburetor idle speed screw to obtain a curb idle speed of 500 rpm (550 if equipped with air conditioner).
7. Turn the idle mixture screws in or out to obtain the highest rpm possible. After obtaining the highest rpm, turn each idle mix-

ture screw clockwise until the engine speed starts to drop, then turn the mixture screw counterclockwise just enough to regain the lost rpm.
8. If the mixture adjustment procedure has changed the curb idle speed, adjust the idle speed.

1966-72 with CAP or CAS Except 426 Hemi

Adjust with air cleaner removed.
NOTE: this is the basic carburetor adjustment procedure, any specific exceptions are listed below.
1. Run engine at fast idle to stabilize engine temperature.
2. Make sure choke plate is fully released.
3. Attach a tachometer of known accuracy to the engine.
4. Connect an exhaust analyzer to the engine and insert the probe as far into the tailpipe as possible. On vehicles with dual exhaust, insert the probe into the left tailpipe as this is the side without the heat riser valve.
5. Check ignition timing and adjust it as required to conform to specification.
6. If equipped with air conditioning, turn the air conditioner OFF.
7. Place the transmission in the Neutral position. Make sure the hot idle compensator valve is fully seated in the closed position.
8. Turn the engine idle speed adjustment screw in or out to adjust idle speed to specification. If equipped with an electric solenoid throttle positioner, turn the solenoid adjusting screw in or out to obtain specified rpm. Then, adjust the curb idle speed screw until it just touches the stop on the carburetor body. Now, back the curb idle speed adjusting screw out one full turn.
9. Turn each idle mixture adjustment screw 1/16 turn richer (counterclockwise). Wait 10 seconds and observe the reading on the exhaust gas analyzer. Continue this procedure until the meter indicates a definite increase in the richness of the mixture.
NOTE: this step is very important. A carburetor that is set too lean will cause the exhaust gas analyzer to give a false reading indicating a rich mixture. Because of this, the carburetor must first be known to have a rich mixture to verify the reading on the exhaust gas analyzer.
10. After verifying the reading obtained on the meter, adjust the mixture screws to get an air /fuel ratio of 14.2. Turn the mixture screws clockwise (lea-

ner) to raise the meter reading or counterclockwise (richer) to lower the meter reading.

1968-69 383 and 440 V8

The carburetors used on these engines (Ball & Ball 2V, Carter 4V or Holley 4V) have lead or cup plugs installed over the idle mixture screws and an additional off idle mixture control screw added to the body of the carburetor. When adjusting the carburetor idle speed and mixture, use the off idle adjustment screw to alter the idle speed air /fuel mixture so it conforms to the 14.2:1 ratio specified. If unable to obtain an acceptable engine idle by adjusting this screw, refer to the procedure to correct rough idle and low speed surge.

Rough Idle and Low Speed Surge

Rough idle and low speed surge can be the result of improper balance of the idle mixture adjustment in the right and left carburetor bores. To correct this condition, perform the following operation.
1. On 1968-69 383 or 440 V8, remove the lead plugs from the two limited screws in the base of the carburetor (Ball & Ball or Carter) or the cup plugs from the sides of the primary metering body (Holley). The best way to remove the lead plugs is with a small drill and easy-out. Use a sharp punch to remove cup plugs from a Holley carburetor.
2. On all other models, remove the plastic limiter caps from the idle mixture adjustment screws.
3. Perform Steps 1-8 of the idle speed and mixture adjustment procedure.
4. On 1968-69 383 or 440 V8, turn the single off idle mixture adjustment screw counterclockwise (richer) until it is seated, then turn it clockwise (lean) 3/4 turn. Do not disturb this adjustment during the remainder of this procedure.
5. Turn both idle mixture adjustment screws clockwise until they are lightly seated. On some models, the idle mixture screws have a prevailing torque feature which causes the screws to become more difficult to turn as they approach the seated position.
6. On Ball & Ball carburetors, turn both idle mixture screws 1½ turns counterclockwise. On Carter and Holley carburetors, turn both idle mixture screws 2-3 turns clockwise.
7. Start the engine and perform Steps 9-11 of the idle speed and mixture adjustment procedure.

NOTE: in order to obtain a smooth idle, it is important that both mixture adjustment screws are adjusted an equal number of turns from the fully seated position.

8. Install lead plugs, cup plugs, or plastic caps on the idle mixture screws.

426 Hemi

Because each carburetor is equipped with a complete idle system, accurate carburetor synchronization is very important. After adjusting the idle speed and mixture, it should be rechecked and rebalanced as required in the outside ambient temperature after a road test.

Adjust with air cleaner removed.

1. Run engine at fast idle to stabilize engine temperature.
2. Make sure the choke plate is fully released.
3. Attach a tachometer of known accuracy to the engine.
4. If equipped with a hot idle compensator valve, make sure it is fully seated in the closed position.
5. Place the transmission in the Neutral position.
6. Turn the idle speed adjustment screws in or out to adjust the engine idle speed to specification. If equipped with an electric solenoid throttle positioner, turn the solenoid adjusting screw in or out to obtain specified engine idle speed. Then, turn the curb idle speed adjusting screw clockwise until it just touches the stop on the carburetor throttle body. Next, back the curb idle speed adjusting screw out one full turn.
7. Adjust each idle mixture screw to obtain the highest rpm possible. Repeat this operation until all four mixture adjustment screws have been properly adjusted and balanced.
8. If the idle mixture adjustment procedure has changed the engine idle speed, adjust the idle speed.

Linkage Adjustment

1965-66 Valiant, Dart, and Barracuda with Six Cylinders and Automatic Transmission

1. Apply thin film of multi-purpose grease on outside surface of carburetor lever isolator (1), torque shaft plastic bushing (2), torque shaft ball stud (3), and bellcrank pin (10).
2. Disconnect transmission intermediate rod ball socket (5) from bellcrank ball end.
3. Disconnect choke at carburetor (4) or block choke valve in full open position. Open throttle slightly to release fast idle cam, then return throttle to curb idle.
4. Loosen locknut (8) in transmission rod, insert 3/16 in. diameter rod (7) approximately four

in. long in holes provided in transmission rod bellcrank bracket and lever assembly.

5. Move transmission lever (9) forward against stop and tighten transmission rod locknut (8).
6. Disconnect top end of accelerator pedal rod (6). Adjust length of rod to provide pedal angle of 111—113 degrees. To increase pedal angle, increase length of rod by means of screw adjustment. Reinstall top end of rod.
7. Remove 3/16 in. diameter rod (7) from transmission rod bracket and lever assembly. Adjust length of transmission bellcrank to torque shaft rod with screw adjustment at top end. The correct rod length will allow ball socket to line up with ball end, when rod is held upward

against transmission stop.

8. Install ball socket on torque shaft level ball end (5).
9. Connect choke rod (4) or remove blocking fixture.

1965-66 Valiant, Dart, and Barracuda with Six Cylinders and Manual Shift

1. Apply thin film of multi-purpose grease on outside of carburetor lever isolator (1), torque shaft plastic bushing (2), and torque shaft ball stud (3).
2. Disconnect choke at carburetor (4), or block choke valve in full open position. Open throttle slightly to release fast idle cam, then return throttle to curb idle.
3. Disconnect top end of accelerator pedal rod (6). Adjust length

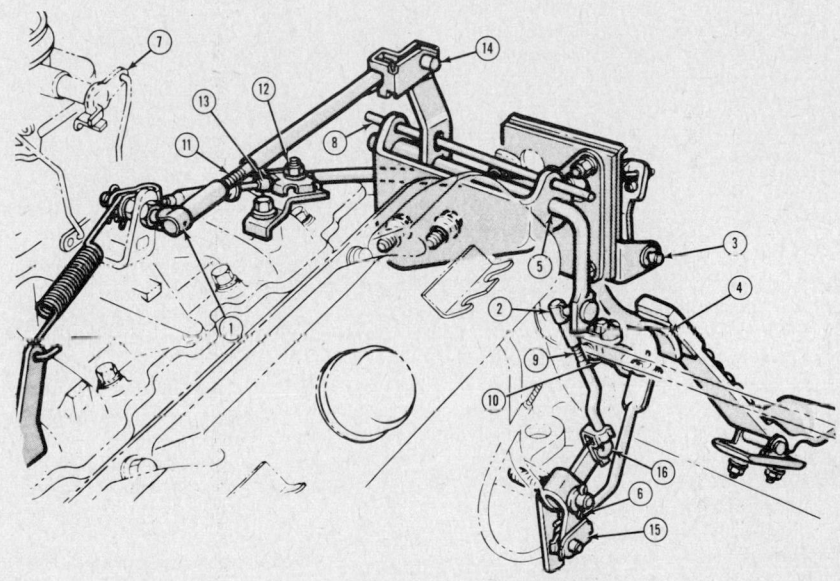

Throttle linkage adjustment—1965-66 Dart and Valiant (© Chrysler Corp.)

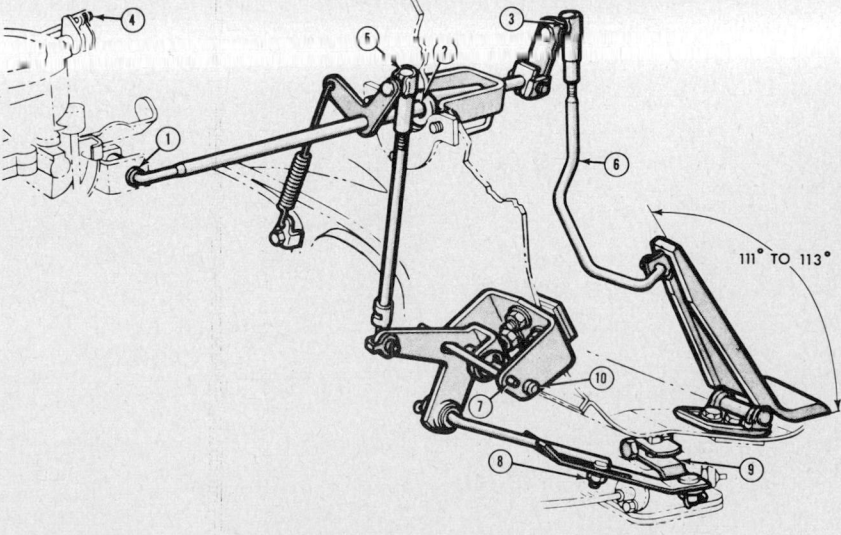

Throttle linkage adjustment—1964-66 Dart, Barracuda and Valiant 170 and 225 cu. in.
(© Chrysler Corp.)

of rod by means of screw adjustment to obtain pedal angle of 111 to 113 degrees. Reinstall top end of rod (6). Connect choke rod (4) or remove blocking fixture.

V8 Valiant with 273 Cu. In. Engine and Automatic Transmission (See Illustration)—1965-66

1. Apply thin coat of grease to shaft (3), bottom of pedal (4) and pivots (5-6), and transmission linkage areas (14, 15, 16).
2. Disconnect transmission intermediate rod ball socket (2).
3. Block choke in open position and be sure throttle is at full curb idle.
4. Insert 3/16 x 6 in. rod in gauge holes (8) at engine-mounted bell-crank. Adjust the rod (9) at upper end. The socket must line up with ball with rod held against stop (10).
5. Assemble the socket (2) and remove the rod (8).
6. Hold throttle rod (11) forward against transmission stop (10) and adjust at threads (11) to gain proper line up with ball (1).
7. Lengthen carburetor rod four turns by turning ball socket (1) counterclockwise.
8. Assemble ball socket and reconnect return spring.
9. Loosen clamp (12) and adjust position of housing ferrule (13) so that all slack is removed from the cable with carburetor at curb idle.
10. Back off ferrule (13) ¼ in. to provide ¼ in. cable slack at idle. Tighten clamp nut (12).
11. Remove block from choke.

V8 Valiant with 273 Cu. In. Engine and Manual Transmission—1965-66

Follow procedures from above automatic transmission, Steps 1, 3, 9, 10 and 11.

Dart and Valiant with 170 or 225 Cu. In. Engine and Automatic Transmission (See Illustration)—1967

1. Apply thin coat of grease to points (1, 2, 3 and 10).
2. Disconnect intermediate rod at ball socket (5).
3. Block choke in open position and be sure that throttle is against curb idle stop.
4. Loosen locknut (8) and insert a 3/16 in. rod into gauge holes (1) provided in bellcrank bracket.
5. Move transmission lever (3) for-

ward against stop and tighten clamp nut (8).
6. Disconnect top of rod (6) and adjust to provide a pedal angle of 111—113°. Reconnect rod (6).
7. Remove the 3/16 in. rod (7) and adjust at ball joint (5) to create a neat connection.
8. Install the ball socket (5).
9. Remove choke block.

Dart and Valiant with 170 or 225 Cu. In. Engine and Manual Transmission—1967

Follow procedures from above automatic transmission, Steps 1, 3, 6 and 9.

1966 Dart and Valiant with 225 Cu. In. Engine, Air Conditioning, and Automatic Transmission

1. Apply thin film of multi-purpose

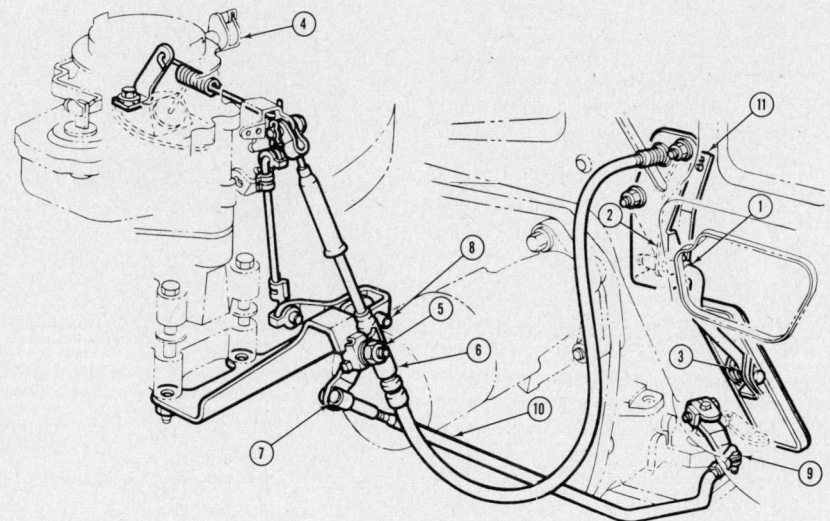

Throttle linkage adjustment—1967 Valiant and Dart 6 cyl. (© Chrysler Corp.)

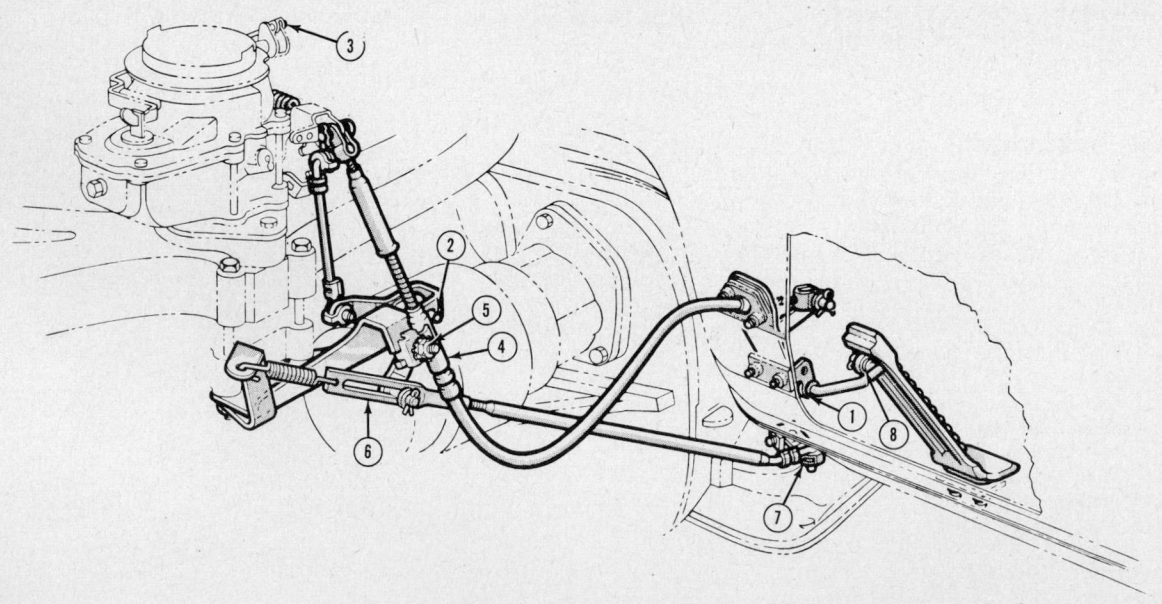

Linkage adjustment—1966 225 six cylinder with air conditioning (© Chrysler Corp.)

grease on the ends of the accelerator shaft (1) where it turns in the bracket, nylon roller (8) at pedal and bellcrank pin (2).

2. Disconnect return spring and slotted transmission rod (6) from the bellcrank lever pin.

3. Block choke in open position. Open throttle to fast idle cam and then return to curb idle position.

4. Hold transmission lever forward (7) against its stop (rod or lever must not be moved vertically) and adjust transmission rod at threaded adjustment (6) at upper end. Rear of slot should contact bellcrank lever pin without exerting any force.

5. Lengthen rod by two full turns.

6. Assemble slotted adjustment (6) to bellcrank pin with washer and retainer pin and reconnect return spring. Check to be sure slotted adjuster link (6) returns to the full forward position.

7. Loosen cable clamp nut (5) and adjust position of cable housing ferrule (4) in clamp so that all slack is removed from the cable with the carburetor at curb idle. To remove slack, move ferrule (4) away from carburetor lever.

8. Back off ferrule (4) ¼ in. to provide ¼ in. cable slack at idle. Tighten clamp nut (5).

9. Remove choke blocking.

1966 Dart and Valiant with 225 Cu. In. Engine, Air Conditioning, and Manual Transmission

1. Apply thin film of multi-purpose grease on the ends of the accelerator shaft (1) where it turns in the bracket and nylon roller at pedal (8).

2. Block choke in open position and operate throttle to be sure throttle returns to curb idle.

3. Follow steps 7, 8, and 9 above, under Automatic Transmission. (See illustration.)

Valiant, Dart, and Barracuda with 273 V8 and Automatic Transmission —1967

1. Apply thin film of multi-purpose grease on accelerator shaft (3) where it turns in bracket, anti-rattle spring (5) where it contacts shaft (4), pivot points of both upper (6) and lower (7) linkage bellcranks, ball end pocket (15) at rear end of throttle cable.

2. Disconnect choke (8) at carburetor or block choke valve in full open position. Open throttle slightly to release fast idle cam, then return carburetor to curb idle.

3. Hold or wire transmission lever (11) firmly forward against its stop while performing adjustments in next four steps. It is important that lever remains firmly against stop during these steps to ensure correct adjustment.

4. With 3/16 in. diameter rod (9) placed in holes provided in upper bellcrank (6) and lever, adjust length of intermediate transmission rod (10) by means of threaded adjustment at upper

end with slight downward effort on rod.

5. Assemble ball socket (2) to ball end and remove 3/16 in. rod (9) from upper bellcrank and lever.

6. Adjust length of carburetor rod (12) by pushing rearward on rod with slight effort and turning threaded adjustment (1) so that ball socket lines up with ball end on carburetor lever.

7. Assemble ball socket (1) to ball end, then remove wire securing transmission lever.

8. Loosen clamp nut (13), adjust position of cable housing ferrule (14) in clamp so that all slack is removed from cable with carburetor at curb idle. To remove slack from cable, move ferrule (14) in clamp in direction away from carburetor lever.

9. Back off ferrule (14) ¼ in. This provides ¼ in. free play between front edge of accelerator shaft lever and dash bracket. Tighten cable to clamp nut to 45 in. lbs.

10. Connect choke rod (8) or remove blocking fixture.

Valiant, Dart, and Barracuda with 273 V8 and Manual Transmission —1967

Follow steps 1, 2, 8, 9, and 10 in automatic transmission procedure.

Valiant, Dart, Barracuda, and Challenger with Six Cylinder and Automatic Transmission—1968-72

1. Appy thin film of multi-purpose grease on accelerator shaft (1)

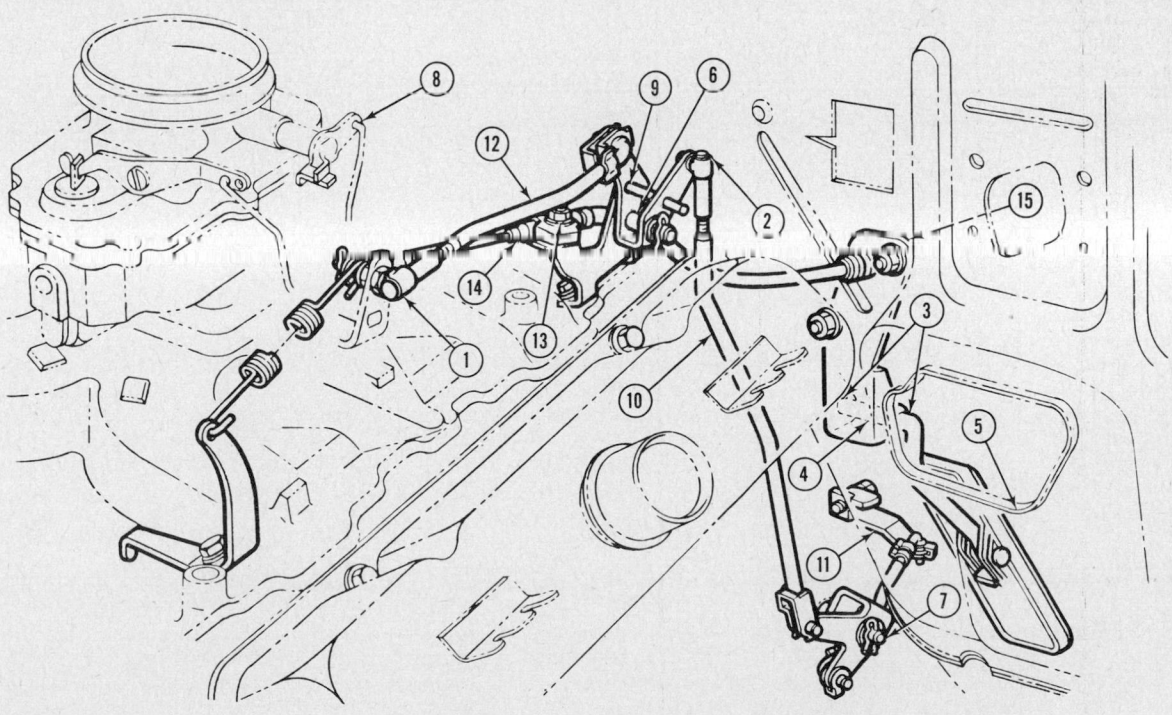

Linkage adjustment—1967 273 V8 (© Chrysler Corp.)

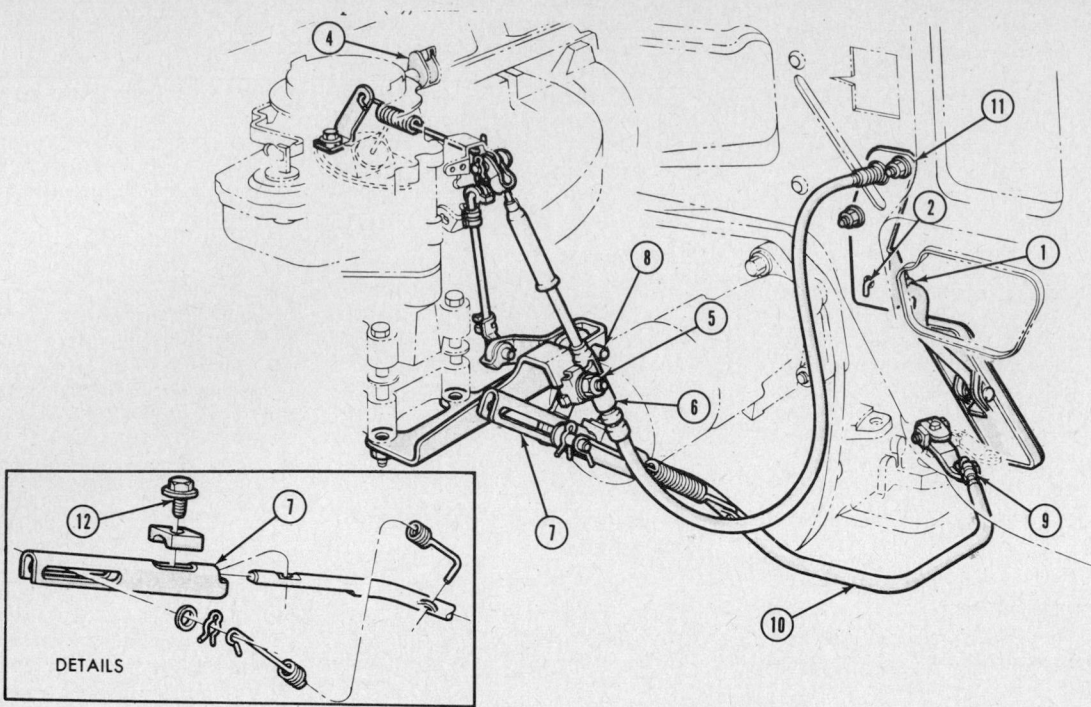

Linkage adjustment—1968-70 six cylinders (© Chrysler Corp.)

where it turns in bracket, anti-rattle spring (8), bellcrank pivot pin (9), and ball end and pocket (11) at rear end of throttle cable.

2. Disconnect choke (4) at carburetor or block choke valve in full open position. Open throttle to release fast idle cam, then return.

3. Hold transmission rod (10) forward with slight pressure so transmission lever (9) is against stop. Hold slotted adjusting link (7) forward against pin. Tighten adjusting link lock screw (5) to 95 in. lbs.

4. Assemble slotted adjuster link (7) to carburetor lever pin and install washer and retaining pin. Assemble transmission linkage return spring in place.

5. Check transmission linkage freedom of operation by moving slotted adjuster link (7) to full rearward position, then allow it to return slowly, making sure it returns to full forward position.

6. On 1968-70 models, loosen cable clamp nut (5) and adjust position of cable housing ferrule (6) in clamp so that all slack is removed from the cable with carburetor at curb idle. To remove slack from cable, move ferrule (6) in clamp in direction away from carburetor lever.

7. Back off ferrule (6) ¼ in. This provides ¼ in. free play between dash mounted accelerator lever and bracket. Tighten cable

clamp nut (5) to 45 in. lbs.

8. Connect choke rod (4) or remove blocking fixture.

1968-72 All V8s with Automatic Transmission

See Dodge-Plymouth section.

Valiant, Dart, and Barracuda with Six Cylinder and Manual Transmission—1968

Follow steps 1, 2, 6, 7, and 8 in automatic transmission procedure.

1. Apply thin film of multi-purpose grease on accelerator shaft (3) where it turns in bracket, pivot points of both upper (6) and lower (7) linkage bellcranks, and ball end and pocket (14) at rear end of throttle cable.

2. Disconnect choke (8) at carburetor or block choke valve in full open position. Open throttle slightly to release fast idle cam, then return carburetor to curb idle.

3. With 3/16 in. diameter rod (9) placed in holes provided in upper bellcrank and lever, adjust length of intermediate transmission rod (10) by means of threaded adjustment at upper end. Ball socket must line up with ball end when rod is held upward and transmission lever is forward against its stop.

4. Assemble ball socket (2) to ball

end and remove 3/16 in. rod (9) from upper bellcrank and lever.

5. Disconnect return spring (13), then adjust length of carburetor rod (12) by pulling forward on rod so transmission lever is against stop and turning threaded adjuster link. Turn link so rear end of slot just contacts carburetor lever pin when link is placed in its normal operating position against lever pin nut. Lengthen rod by two full turns of link.

6. Assemble slotted adjustment (1) to carburetor lever pin and install washer and retainer pin. Assemble transmission linkage return spring (13) in place.

7. Check transmission linkage freedom of operation, by moving slotted adjuster link (1) to full rearward position, then allow it to return slowly, making sure it returns to full forward position.

8. Loosen cable clamp nut (4). Adjust position of cable housing ferrule (5) in clamp so that all slack is removed from cable with carburetor at idle. To remove slack from cable, move ferrule (5) in clamp in direction away from carburetor lever.

9. Back off ferrule (5) ¼ in. This provides ¼ in. free play between front edge of accelerator shaft lever and dash bracket. Tighten cable clamp nut (4) to 45 in. lbs.

10. Connect choke (8) or remove blocking fixture

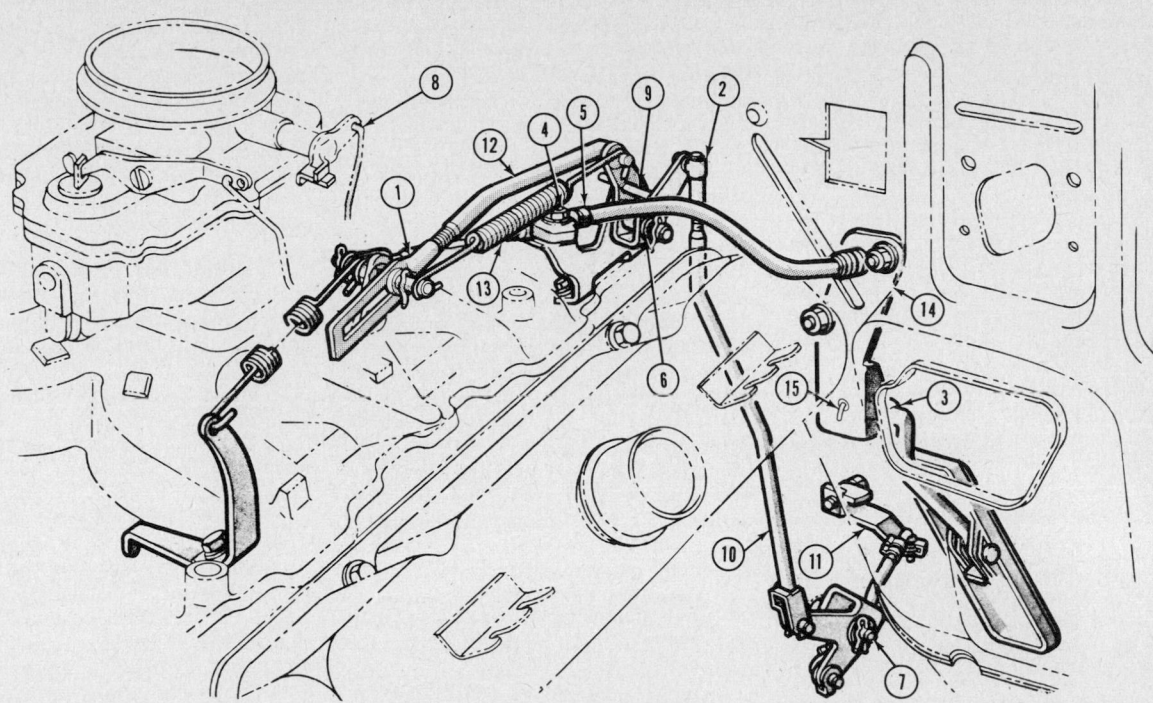

Linkage adjustment—1968-70 273, 318, and 340 V8s (© Chrysler Corp.)

Valiant, Dart, and Barracuda with 273 and 340 V8s and Manual Transmission—1968

Follow steps 1, 2, 8, 9, and 10 in automatic transmission procedure.

Valiant, Dart, Barracuda and Challenger with All Engines and Manual Transmission Except 426 Hemi—1969-72

1. Apply thin film of multi-purpose grease on accelerator shaft where it turns in the bracket, ball end and pocket at rear end of throttle cable.
2. Disconnect choke at carburetor or block choke valve in full open position. Open throttle slightly to release fast idle cam, then return carburetor to curb idle.
3. Loosen cable clamp nut (1) adjust position of cable housing ferrule (2) in the clamp so that all slack is removed from the cable with carburetor at idle. To remove slack from cable, move ferrule (2) in clamp away from carburetor lever.
4. Back off ferrule (2) ¼ in. To provide ¼ in. cable slack at idle. Tighten cable clamp nut to 45 in. lbs.
5. Connect choke rod or remove blocking fixture.

426 Hemi
See Dodge-Plymouth section for Hemi linkages.

Exhaust System

Muffler and Tail Pipe
The exhaust pipe and muffler, as produced at assembly, is a one-piece

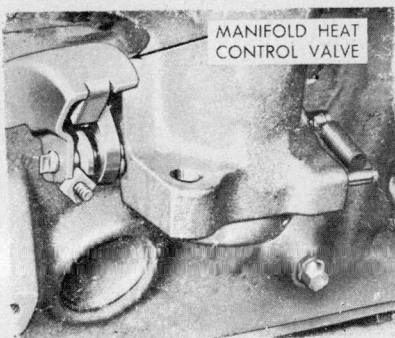

Manifold heat control valve—318 cu. in. (© Chrysler Corp.)

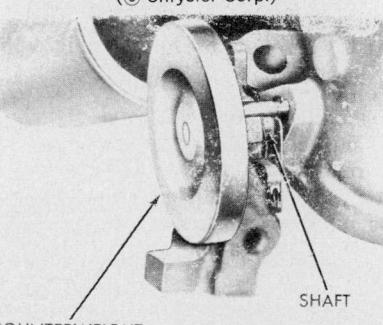

Manifold heat control valve—340 cu. in. (© Chrysler Corp.)

unit. It is handled in the customary manner. Replacement of muffler can be done only by cutting off the exhaust pipe just ahead of the muffler. Connect the new muffler to the exhaust pipe and clamp in place with the present saddle bracket and U-bolt clamp.

Cooling System

The 180° F. thermostat is located in the aluminum housing above the water pump. A 160° F. thermostat is available for use with an alcohol-type solution. The radiator pressure cap is calibrated to maintain 11 psi.

Cooling system capacities can be found in the capacities table of this section.

Water Pump Removal
1. Drain the cooling system.
2. Loosen the drive belt adjusting strap at the alternator and move alternator toward the engine.
3. Remove the fan, spacer, pulley and belt.
   NOTE: if a fluid drive is used in place of spacer, do not set drive unit with shaft pointing downwards or silicone fluid will drain into fan drive bearing and ruin grease.
4. Remove the pump inlet hose and the heater hose.
5. Remove clamp from the by-pass hose, where used.
6. Remove water pump body-to-

housing bolts and push the pump body down, off the by-pass hose where used.

Water Pump Installation

1. Place by-pass hose clamp on the hose, then lift the pump up into the hose.
2. Attach pump body to the housing, using the two long bolts above and below the inlet hose.
3. Attach the inlet and heater hose.
4. Install drive belt, pulley, spacer and fan.
5. Adjust drive belt.
6. Close radiator drain cock, and fill and bleed cooling system.

Engine

Most Darts and Valiants are equipped with the 170 or 225 cu. in. slant six cylinder engines. These engines are very conventional in design, except that the cylinder block is canted 30 degrees to the right.

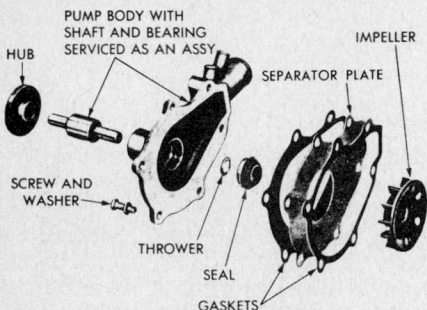

Water pump—6 cyl.
(© Chrysler Corp.)

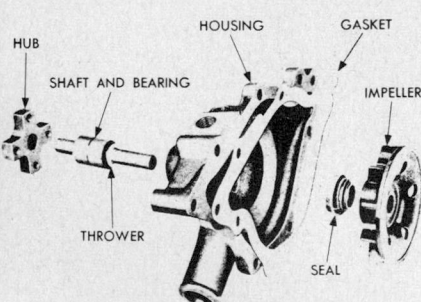

Water pump—273 and 318
(© Chrysler Corp.)

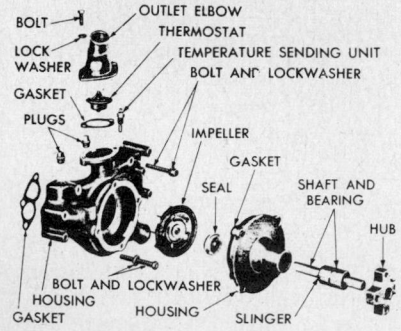

Water pump—383
(© Chrysler Corp.)

Many parts interchange between the two and the main difference between them is that the 225 engine has a one in. longer stroke and correspondingly higher block. Most recently a 198 cu. in. six has replaced the 170 cu. in. six. It is essentially a 170 six with a stroke half way between a 170 engine and a 225 engine.

In 1964 Dart and Valiant introduced a 273 cu. in. V8 which was a redesigned and substantially lightened version of the Dodge and Plymouth 318 V8. The engine is conservative in design and very rugged. It uses a rocker shaft to carry the rockers instead of the currently more popular but more fragile stud mounted rockers. It has had throughout its production, 1964-69, the smallest bore of any contemporary American V8, and until 1968 continued to use mechanical tappets.

In 1968 Dart and Valiant added a 318 and a 340 V8 to their line up. The 318 had been redesigned to the point where it was merely a 273 with a 5/16 in. larger bore. The 340 V8 had still a larger bore in the basic 273 block, but also added heads with big valves.

The 383 and 440 wedge V8s and the 426 Hemi V8 are basically big car power plants and are covered in detail in the Dodge and Plymouth section.

Exhaust Emission Control

Positive Crankcase Ventilation

All models are equipped with a positive crankcase ventilation system which draws air into the engine through the oil filler cap and circulates it through the engine. The air combines with vapors in the crankcase and exits the engine through a metering valve mounted in the rocker arm cover. The air-vapor mixture then re-enters the engine through the carburetor or intake manifold and passes into the combustion chamber where it is burned.

Cleaner Air Package (CAP)

Some 1966-67 and all 1968-69 models use this package to reduce engine exhaust emissions. Changes include the addition of limiters to the carburetor idle mixture screws, leaner carburetor mixtures and vacuum controled ignition timing retard mechanisms.

Cleaner Air System (CAS)

All 1970 and later models are equipped with this type of exhaust emission control. This system consists of: heated carburetor air cleaner intake ducts, carburetor modifications, ignition timing controls, and reduced engine compression ratios.

Engine R & R

6 Cylinder

1. Scribe the hood hinge outlines on the underside of the hood, then remove the hood.
2. Drain the cooling system, remove the battery and carburetor air cleaner.
3. Remove radiator and heater hoses, then the radiator.
4. Remove the outlet vent pipe from the cylinder head cover.
5. Disconnect fuel lines, linkage and

6 cyl. engine
(© Chrysler Corp.)

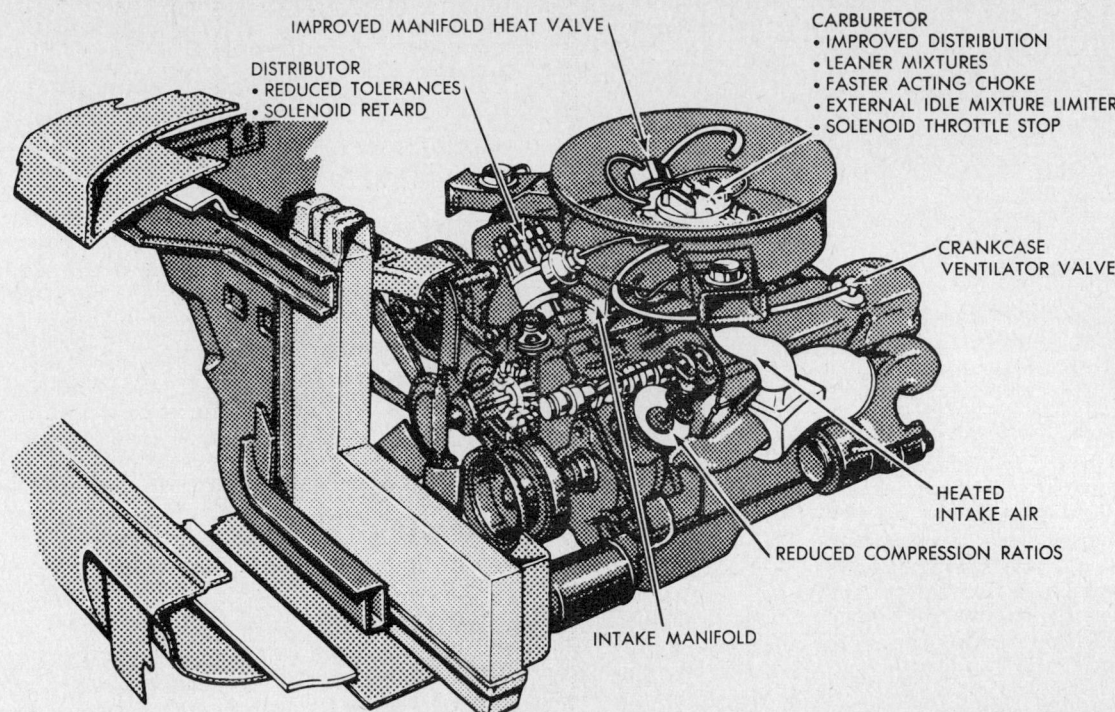

DISTRIBUTOR
• REDUCED TOLERANCES
• SOLENOID RETARD

IMPROVED MANIFOLD HEAT VALVE

CARBURETOR
• IMPROVED DISTRIBUTION
• LEANER MIXTURES
• FASTER ACTING CHOKE
• EXTERNAL IDLE MIXTURE LIMITER
• SOLENOID THROTTLE STOP

CRANKCASE
VENTILATOR VALVE

HEATED
INTAKE AIR

REDUCED COMPRESSION RATIOS

INTAKE MANIFOLD

Cleaner Air System (© Chrysler Corporation)

wiring to the engine.

6. Disconnect exhaust pipe at exhaust manifold.
7. Raise car on hoist.
8. If equipped with automatic transmission, drain the converter and the transmission. Remove the oil cooler lines, filler tube and push button cable.
9. Remove the clutch torque shaft, brake cables and rods.
10. Remove the speedometer cable and gear shift rods.
11. Disconnect propeller shaft and tie out of the way.
12. Install an engine support fixture to the rear of the engine.
13. Remove the engine rear support crossmember.
14. Remove transmission mounting bolts from clutch housing.
15. Remove the transmission.
16. Lower the car.
17. Position engine lifting fixture onto the engine, and attach chain hoist to the fixture eyebolt.
18. Remove the engine support fixture.
19. Remove the engine front mounting bolts.
20. Lift the engine out of the engine compartment and lower it onto a substantial work stand.
21. To install the engine, reverse the above procedure.

V8

1. Scribe the outline of the hood hinge brackets on the bottom of the hood and remove the hood.
2. Drain the cooling system and remove the radiator.
3. Remove the battery.
4. Remove the fuel line from the

⏱ CHILTON TIME-SAVER

It is possible to remove the engine without removing the transmission. If the engine is to be removed from the vehicle without removing the transmission, care must be exercised not to allow the weight of the engine to rest on the torque converter hub (automatic transmission) or transmission input shaft (standard transmission).

To remove the engine without removing the transmission, use the following operation. Perform Steps 1-7 and 10 of the removal operation. If the vehicle is equipped with an automatic transmission, attach a remote starter switch to the engine, remove the inspection plate from the bellhousing, crank the engine to gain access to the torque converter-to-driveplate attaching nuts and remove the nuts. If the vehicle is equipped with a manual transmission, disconnect the clutch torque shaft from the engine block and the clutch linkage from the adjustment rod. Remove the bolt that attaches the transmission filler tube to the engine (automatic transmission). Support the transmission and remove the bolts that attach the trans-

mission to the engine or clutch bell housing. When removing the engine, place a block of wood on the lifting point of a floor jack and position the jack under the transmission. As the engine is removed from the vehicle, raise and lower the jack as required so the angle of the transmission duplicates as nearly as possible the angle of the engine.

When installing the engine into a vehicle with an automatic transmission, keep in mind that the crankshaft flange bolt circle, the inner and outer circle of holes in the driveplate, and the four tapped holes in the front face of the converter all have one hole offset. To insure proper engine-torque converter balance, the torque converter must be mounted to the driveplate in the same location it was originally installed.

When installing the engine into a vehicle with a manual transmission, it may be necessary to disconnect the driveshaft and turn the transmission output shaft, with the transmission in gear, to get the transmission input shaft spline to mesh with the inner hub on the clutch disc.

fuel pump and plug the line.
5. Remove all wires and hoses that attach to the engine.

6. If equipped with air conditioning and/or power steering, remove the unit from the engine

and position it out of the way *without disconnecting the lines.*

7. Attach lifting sling to the engine. On models equipped with a 426 Hemi engine, never attempt to remove the engine with the lifting sling attached to the intake manifold.
8. Raise the vehicle on a hoist and install an engine support fixture to support the rear of the engine.
9. On automatic transmission models, drain the transmission and torque converter. On standard transmission models, disconnect the clutch torque shaft from the engine.
10. Disconnect the exhaust pipe/s from the exhaust manifold/s.
11. Remove the driveshaft.
12. Disconnect the transmission linkage and any wiring or cables that attach to the transmission.
13. Remove the engine rear support crossmember and remove the transmission.
14. Remove the bolts that attach the motor mounts to the chassis.
15. Lower the vehicle and attach a chain hoist or other lifting device to the engine.
16. Raise the engine and carefully remove it from the engine.

6 Cylinder Combination Manifold

Removal

See Dodge-Plymouth section.
1. Remove air cleaner.
2. Remove vacuum control tube at carburetor and distributor.
3. Remove fuel line and carburetor.
4. Remove three bolts that hold the flange.
5. Remove nuts and washers holding the intake and exhaust manifolds to the cylinder head.
6. Remove the assembly from the head.
7. Remove three bolts holding the intake and exhaust manifolds together.
8. Clean manifold mating and attaching surfaces with a straight edge and feeler gauge. All mating surfaces should be flat and plane within .008 in.

Installation

1. Place a new gasket between intake and exhaust manifolds and install three attaching bolts, loosely.
2. With a new gasket in place, position the complete manifold combination on the cylinder head.
3. Install conical washers (cupped side away from the nut) and nuts. Torque alternately to a final 10 ft. lbs.
4. Now, torque the three intake-to-

exhaust manifold nuts to 15 ft. lbs.
5. Connect the exhaust pipe to the manifold flange and torque these two bolts to 30 ft. lbs.
6. Install carburetor and connect line, vacuum line and throttle linkage.
7. Install air cleaner. Start engine and check for intake and exhaust leaks.

V8 Exhaust Manifold

1. Remove exhaust pipe-to-manifold bolts and, on the left side, remove the attaching brace bolt.
2. Remove manifold - to - cylinder head bolts and remove manifold.
3. Reinstall by reversing the above. Be sure mating surfaces are clean, in complete alignment, and that heat control valve is free.

V8 Intake Manifold R&R

All Engines Except 426 Hemi

1. Drain the cooling system. Disconnect the negative battery cable.
2. Remove the air cleaner and disconnect the fuel line from the carburetor.
3. Disconnect all vacuum lines that attach to the carburetor or intake manifold.
4. Disconnect the spark plug wires from the plugs and remove the distributor cap and wires as an assembly.
5. Disconnect the wires from the coil and the temperature sending unit.
6. Disconnect the heater hose and bypass hose from the intake manifold.
7. Remove the intake manifold attaching bolts and remove the manifold, carburetor and coil from the engine as an assembly.
8. Clean all gasket mounting surfaces and firmly cement new gaskets to the engine.
9. Reverse above precedure to install.

426 Hemi

See Dodge-Plymouth section.

Cylinder Head

6 Cylinder Removal

1. Drain the cooling system.
2. Remove carburetor air cleaner and fuel lines.
3. Disconnect accelerator linkage.
4. Remove the vacuum line from carburetor to distributor.
5. Carefully disconnect spark plug wires by pulling straight, in line with plug.
6. Disconnect heater hose and clamp holding the by-pass hose.
7. Disconnect the heat indicator-sending-unit wire.
8. Disconnect exhaust pipe at the exhaust manifold flange.
9. Remove the intake and exhaust manifold and carburetor as an assembly.
10. Remove the outlet vent tube and cylinder head cover.
11. Remove the rocker arms and shaft.
12. Remove the pushrods and place them in order.
13. Remove the head bolts and lift off the cylinder head.
14. Place cylinder head on bench and remove the spark plugs and tubes.

6 Cylinder Installation

1. Clean carbon from the combustion area. Clean all gasket surfaces of both head and cylinder block. Install spark plugs (the aluminum plug shields act as satisfactory gasket material between spark plug body and cylinder head.)
2. If there is any cause to suspect leakage, check all surfaces with a straightedge. If out of flatness exceeds 0.00075 times the span length in any direction, replace head or machine head gasket surface. For example, on a 12 in. span the maximum allowable out of flat is 12 x 0.00075 or 0.009 in.
3. Apply a reliable sealer to the new gasket and install the gasket and cylinder head.
4. Install the 14 cylinder head bolts. Starting at the top center, tighten all cylinder head bolts to 65 ft. lbs.

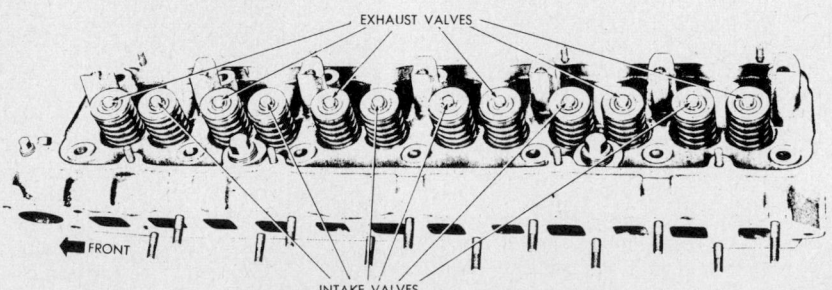

**Cylinder head, showing valve sequence—
170 and 225 cu. in.**
(© Chrysler Corp.)

5. Inspect all push rods for bends or wear. Replace if necessary.
6. Insert the pushrods, small ends down into the tappets.
7. Install rocker arms and shaft assembly with flat on the end of the shaft on top and pointing toward the front of the engine. This is necessary to provide lubrication to the rocker assemblies. Torque the attaching bolts to 30 ft. lbs.
8. Loosen the three bolts that connect the intake and exhaust manifolds. (This is necessary to obtain proper alignment.)
9. Position intake and exhaust manifold and carburetor assembly onto the cylinder head. Put the cup side of the conical washers against the manifolds, install the attaching nuts and torque to 10 ft. lbs.
10. Retighten the three intake-to-exhaust manifold bolts to 15 ft. lbs.
11. Connect the heater hose and by-pass hose clamp.
12. Connect the heat indicator sending-unit wire, the accelerator linkage and the spark plug wires.
13. Install carburetor-to-distributor vacuum line.
14. Connect exhaust pipe to the exhaust manifold.
15. Install the fuel line and carburetor air cleaner.
16. Refill the cooling system.
17. Start the engine and let run until operating temperatures have been reached.
18. Adjust valve tappet clearance to .010 in. (intake) and .020 in. (exhaust.) The adjusting screw in the pushrod end of the rocker arm should have a minimum of 3 ft. lbs. (36 in. lbs.) tension as it is turned. If less, replace the adjusting screw and the rocker arm.
19. Place the new cylinder head cover gasket in position and install cylinder head cover. Torque attaching nuts to 40 in. lbs. (3 1/3 ft. lbs.).
20. Install outlet vent tube.

273, 318, 340, 360 V8

Removal

1. Drain cooling system and disconnect battery.
2. Remove alternator, air cleaner and fuel line.
3. Disconnect accelerator linkage.
4. Remove vacuum hose between carburetor and distributor.
5. Remove distributor cap and wires. If removing heads in vehicle, remove plugs to prevent breaking them.
6. Disconnect coil wires, temperature sending wire, heater hoses, and bypass hose.
7. Remove closed ventilation system (PCV), evaporative control

system if so equipped, and valve covers.
8. Remove intake manifold, ignition coil, and carburetor as an assembly.
9. Remove exhaust manifolds.
10. Remove rocker arm and shaft assemblies. Remove pushrods and identify to ensure installation in original location.
11. Remove 10 head bolts from each cylinder head and lift off heads.
12. Clean all surfaces.
13. Inspect all surfaces with straight edge if there is any reason to suspect leakage. If out of flatness exceeds 0.00075 times span length in any direction, replace head or machine mating surface. For example, if span length is 12 in., maximum out of flatness is 12 x 0.00075 or 0.009 in.
14. Reverse procedure to install.

383 and 440 Wedge V8s and 426 Hemi V8

See Dodge-Plymouth Section.

Disassembly of Cylinder Head

1. Remove cylinder heads.
2. Compress valve springs using valve spring compressor.
3. Remove valve locks or keys.
4. Release valve springs.
5. Remove valve springs, retainers, oil seals, and valves.

NOTE: if a valve does not slide out of the guide easily, check end of stem for mushrooming or heading over. If head is mushroomed, file off excess, remove and discard valve. If valve is not mushroomed, lubricate stem of valve, remove, and check for stem wear or damage.

⏱ CHILTON TIME-SAVER

Frequently valves become bent or warped or their seats become blocked with carbon or other material. Left unattended, this can cause burnt valves, damaged cylinder heads and other expensive troubles. To detect leaking valves early, perform this test whenever the cylinder head is removed.

1. After removing head, replace sparkplugs. Removing sparkplugs before removing heads eliminates breakage.
2. Place head on bench with valves, springs, retainers and keys installed and combustion chambers up.
3. Pour enough gasoline in each combustion chamber to completely cover both valves. Watch combustion chambers for two minutes for any air bubbles that indicate leakage.

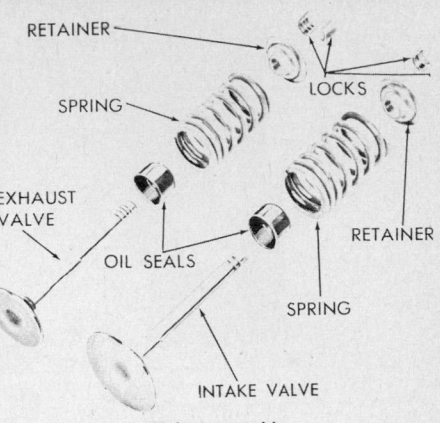

Valve assembly
(© Chrysler Corp.)

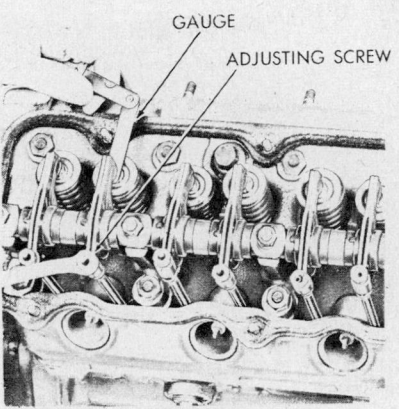

Valve adjustment
(© Chrysler Corp.)

Valve Train

Dodge and Plymouth do not use separate valve guides. They do sell 0.005, 0.015, and 0.030 in. oversize valves. To use these, ream the worn guides to the smallest oversize that will clean up wear. Always start with the smallest reamer and proceed by steps to the larger reamers as this maintains the concentricity of the guide with the valve seat.

As an alternative procedure, some local automotive machine shops bore out the stock guides and replace them with bronze or cast iron guides which use stock valve stem sizes.

Hydraulic Tappets

Removal Except 426 Hemi

NOTE: only 1967-70 V8 engines have hydraulic lifters.

Tappets may be removed without removing manifolds or cylinder heads as follows:

1. Remove rocker covers and rocker shaft assembly.
2. Remove pushrods and identify to ensure installation in original bore.
3. Slide magnetic or claw tool through opening in cylinder head and seat tool firmly in head of tappet.

Measuring timing chain stretch (© Chrysler Corporation)

Removing vibration damper (© Chrysler Corporation)

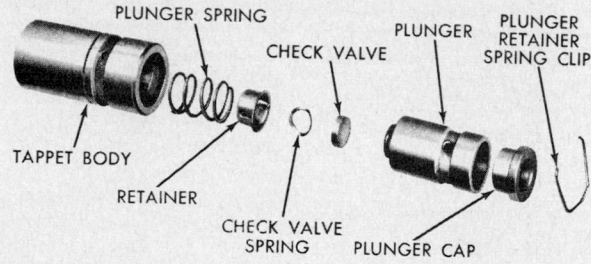

Disassembly of hydraulic tappet (© Chrysler Corp.)

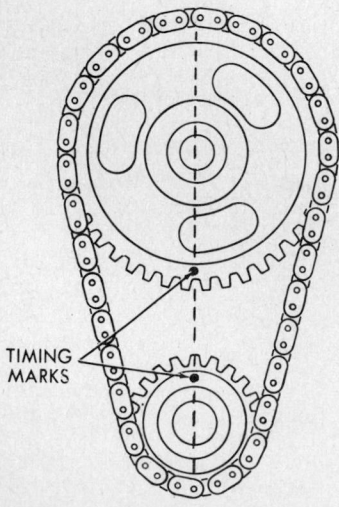

Alignment of timing marks—V8

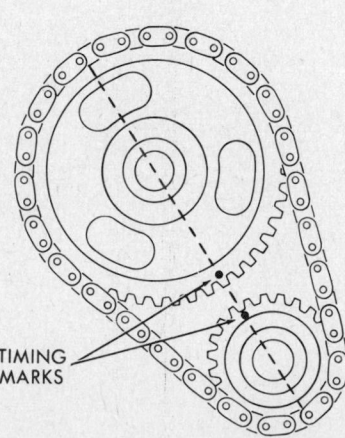

Alignment of timing marks—6 cyl.

4. Pull tappet out of bore with twisting motion.

NOTE: all tappets must be installed in their original bores.

Timing Case

Removal—Six Cylinder

1. Drain cooling system.
2. Remove radiator and fan.
3. With puller, remove vibration damper.
4. Loosen engine oil pan bolts to allow clearance, and remove timing case cover and gasket.
5. Slide crankshaft oil slinger off the front of crankshaft.
6. Remove the camshaft sprocket bolt.
7. Remove the timing chain with camshaft sprocket.

Installation—Six Cylinder

1. Turn crankshaft to line up the timing mark on the crankshaft sprocket with the centerline of camshaft (without the chain.)
2. Remove the camshaft sprocket and reinstall with chain.
3. Torque camshaft sprocket to 35 ft. lbs.
4. Replace oil slinger.
5. Reinstall timing case cover with new gasket and torque to 15 ft. lbs. Retighten engine oil pan to 17 ft. lbs.
6. Replace vibration damper.
7. Replace radiator and hoses.
8. Refill and bleed cooling system.

Removal—273, 318, 340 and 360 V8

1. Drain cooling system and remove radiator, fan belt and water pump assembly.
2. Remove pulley from vibration damper and bolt and washer securing vibration damper on crankshaft.
3. Pull vibration damper from end of crankshaft using suitable puller.
4. Remove fuel lines and fuel pump.
5. Loosen oil pan bolts and remove front bolt at each side.
6. Remove timing cover and gasket taking care not to damage oil pan gasket.
7. Slide crankshaft oil slinger from end of crank.
8. Remove camshaft sprocket attaching cupwasher, and fuel pump eccentric and remove timing chain with sprockets.
9. Reverse procedure to install. Tighten timing cover to 30 ft. lbs. and pan bolts to 15 ft. lbs.

Removal—383, 440 and 426 Hemi

See Dodge-Plymouth section.

Engine Lubrication

Engine Oil Pan Removal

Valiant, Dart and 1965-69 Barracuda —6 Cylinder

1. Raise the vehicle on hoist.
2. Drain oil pan.
3. Remove ball joints from steering linkage center link.
4. Remove dust shield.
5. Remove motor mount stud nuts.
6. Lower vehicle. On 1965-67 models, remove horns and horn brackets. Disconnect battery.
7. Attach an engine life plate and raise engine 1½—2 in.
8. Again, raise vehicle on hoist. Remove pan bolts and pan.

1970-72 Barracuda and Challenger—6 Cylinder

1. Raise vehicle on hoist.
2. Drain oil pan.
3. Remove ball joints from steering linkage center link.
4. Remove dust shield.
5. Remove oil pan bolts, rotate crankshaft to clear counterweights and remove pan.

1970-72 Barracuda and Challenger—V8

1. Disconnect battery. Remove dipstick.
2. Raise vehicle on hoist. Drain oil. Remove engine to converter left housing brace.
3. Remove ball joints from center steering link.
4. Remove crossover pipe from manifolds. On Dart, it can hang. On Valiant, remove completely.
5. Remove oil pan bolts and pan.

Oil Pump

Six Cylinder Removal

1. Drain radiator, disconnect upper and lower hoses, and remove fan shroud.
2. Raise vehicle on hoist, support front of engine with jack stand placed under right front corner

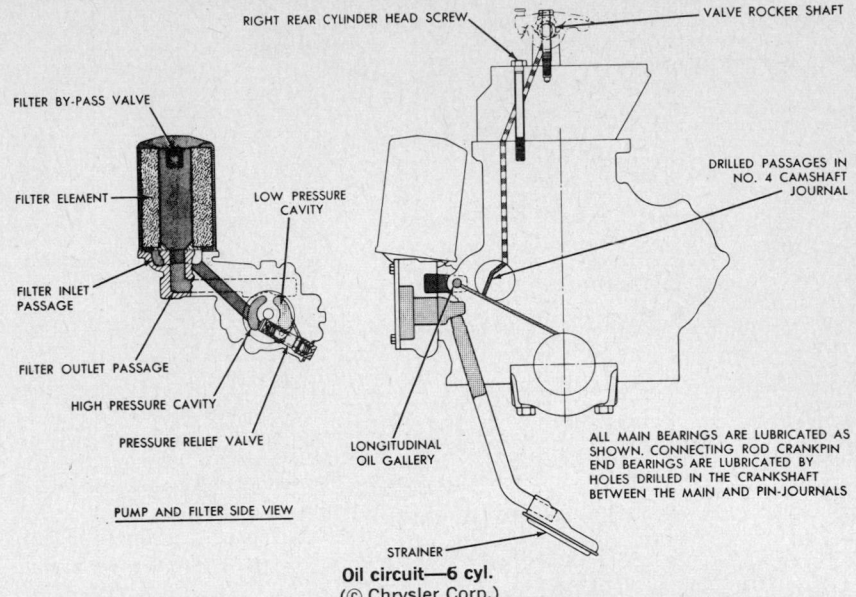

PUMP AND FILTER SIDE VIEW

ALL MAIN BEARINGS ARE LUBRICATED AS SHOWN. CONNECTING ROD CRANKPIN END BEARINGS ARE LUBRICATED BY HOLES DRILLED IN THE CRANKSHAFT BETWEEN THE MAIN AND PIN-JOURNALS

Oil circuit—6 cyl.
(© Chrysler Corp.)

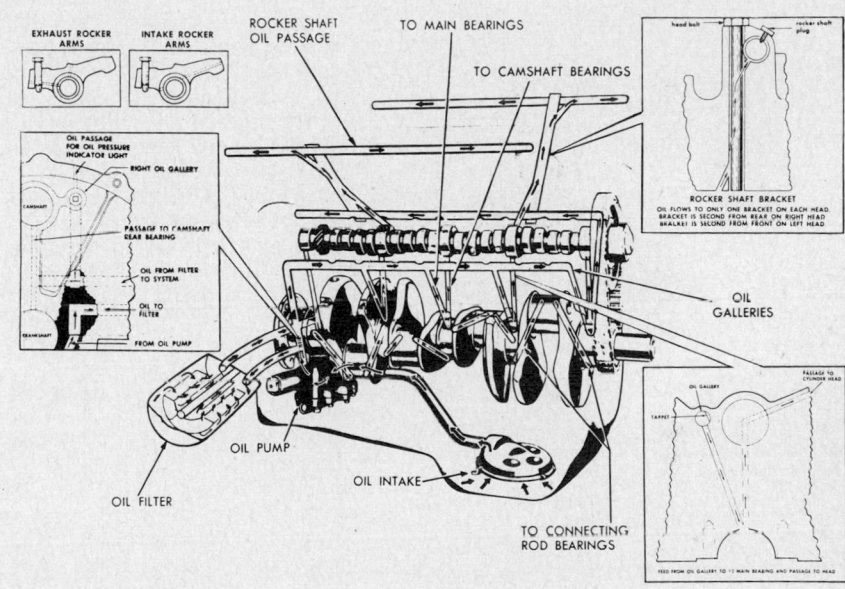

Oil circuit—V8
(© Chrysler Corp.)

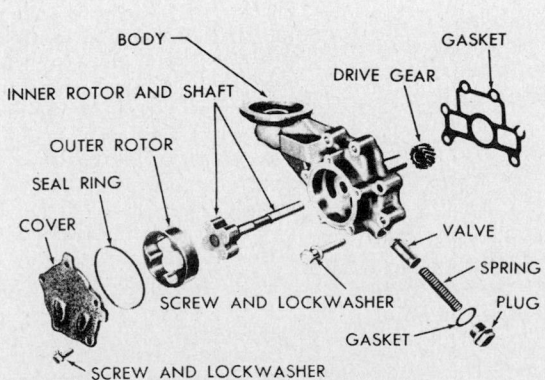

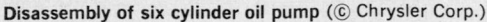

Disassembly of six cylinder oil pump (© Chrysler Corp.)

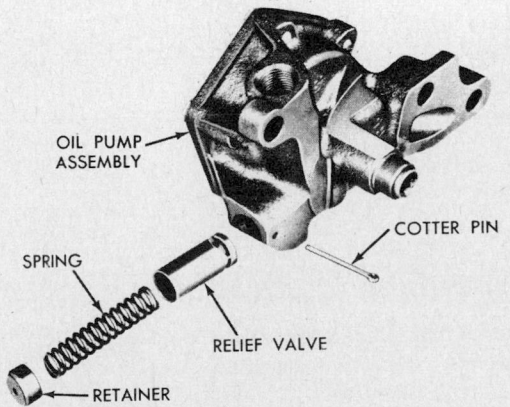

Relief valve—273, 318, and 340 V8s (© Chrysler Corp.)

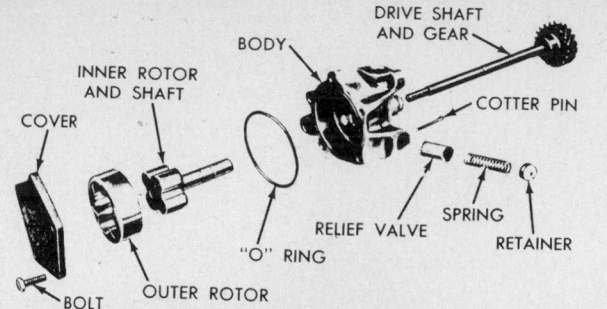

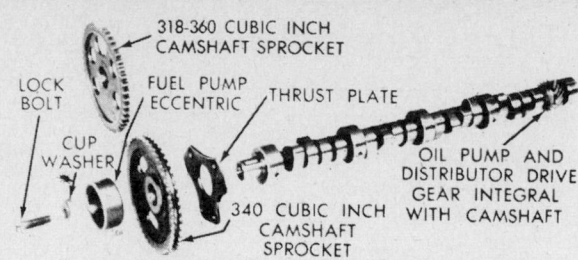

Camshaft and sprocket assembly (© Chrysler Corporation)

Exploded view of oil pump—V8 (© Chrysler Corp.)

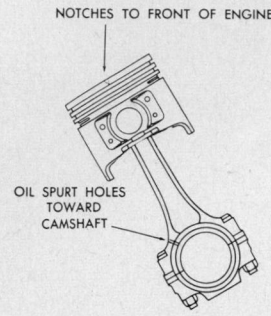

Piston and rod assembly—6 cyl.
(© Chrysler Corp.)

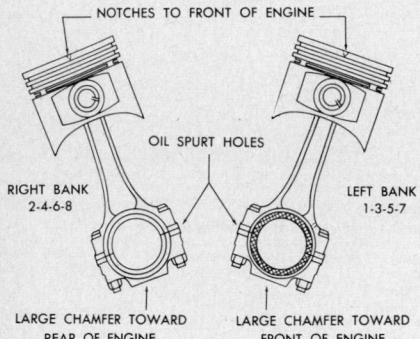

Piston and rod assembly—V8
(© Chrysler Corp.)

of oil pan, and remove engine mount bolts. Do not support engine at crankshaft pulley or vibration damper.

3. Raise engine approximately 1½ —2 in.
4. Remove oil filter, oil pump attaching bolts, and pump assembly.

273, 318, and 340 Engines

1. Remove oil pan.
2. Remove oil pump from rear main bearing cap.

Pistons and Connecting Rods

Piston Ring Replacement

1. Remove the cylinder heads.
2. Remove the oil pan.
3. Turn the crankshaft until the No. 1 piston is at the bottom of its stroke. Place a rag over the top of the piston, and using a ridge reamer, remove the ridge of carbon from the top of the cylinder wall. Repeat this operation on all cylinders.

4. Remove the connecting rod cap from the No. 1 piston connecting rod. Place a block of wood against the bottom of the piston and carefully drive the piston-connecting rod assembly from the cylinder block. Replace the connecting rod cap and bearing half on the connecting rod so they do not become mixed. Repeat this operation until all the pistons have been removed.
5. Using a piston ring removal tool remove the piston rings.
6. If cylinder bore is in satisfactory condition, place each ring in bore in turn and square it in bore with head of piston. Measure ring gap. If ring gap is greater than limit, use new ring. If ring gap is less than limit, file end of ring to obtain correct gap.
7. Check ring side clearance by installing rings on piston, and inserting feeler gauge of correct dimension between ring and lower land. Gauge should slide freely around ring circumference without binding. Any wear will form a step on lower land. Replace any pistons having high steps. Before checking ring side clearance be sure ring grooves are clean and free of carbon, sludge, or grit.
8. Space ring gaps at equidistant intervals around piston circumference. Be sure to install piston in its original bore. Install short lengths of rubber tubing over connecting rod bolts to prevent damage to rod journal. Install ring compressor over rings on piston. Lower piston rod assembly into bore until ring compressor contacts block. Using wooden handle of hammer push piston into bore while guiding rod onto journal.

Rear Main Bearing Oil Seal

Service replacement seals are of split rubber type composition. This type of seal makes it possible to replace the upper half of the rear main oil seal without removing the engine from the car. When installing rubber seals, they must be replaced as a set and can not be combined with the rope type rear main seal. The following procedure is for removing the rope type seal and replacing it with the rubber type seal.

NOTE: on vehicles with a 426 Hemi engine, remove the transmission and vibration damper in addition to the procedure listed below.

Replacement

1. Remove the oil pan.
2. Remove the rear seal retainer and the rear main bearing cap.
3. Remove the lower rope seal by prying from the side with a small screwdriver.
4. To remove the upper rope seal, drive up on either exposed end of the seal with a 6 in. piece of 3/16 in. brazing rod. When the opposite end of the seal starts to protrude from the block, have an assistant grasp it with pliers and gently pull it from the block while the opposite end is being driven.
5. Wipe crankshaft clean and lightly oil crankshaft and new seal before installing seal.
6. Loosen all main bearing caps slightly to lower the crankshaft which will ease installation.

Caution Do not allow the crankshaft to drop enough to perimt the main bearings to become displaced on the crankshaft.

7. Hold the seal tightly against the crankshaft with the thumb (with paint stripe to the rear) and install the seal in the block groove. Rotate the crankshaft if necessary while installing the seal in the groove. *Make sure the sharp edges on the block groove do not cut or nick the rear of the seal.*
8. Install lower half of seal (with paint stripe to the rear) into the lower seal retainer.
9. Install rear main bearing cap.
10. Tighten all main bearing caps to specification.

NOTE: make sure all main bearings are located in their proper position before tightening the main bearing caps.

Ring Gap

Year and Engine	Top Compression	Bottom Compression	Oil Control
65 Six	0.010-0.020 in.	0.010-0.020 in.	0.015-0.062 in.
1966-70 Six	0.010-0.047 in.	0.010-0.047 in.	0.015-0.062 in.
1965-72 273, 318, 340 and 360 V8s	0.010-0.020 in.	0.010-0.020 in.	0.015-0.062 in.

Ring Side Clearance

Year and Engine	Top Compression	Bottom Compression	Oil Control
65 Six	0.0015-0.0040 in.	0.0015-0.0040 in.	0.009 in. max.
65 273 V8	0.0015-0.0030 in.	0.0015-0.0040 in.	0.009 in. max.
1966-70 Six and 273, 318 340 and 360 V8s	0.0015-0.0040 in.	0.0015-0.0040 in.	0.0002-0.0050 in.

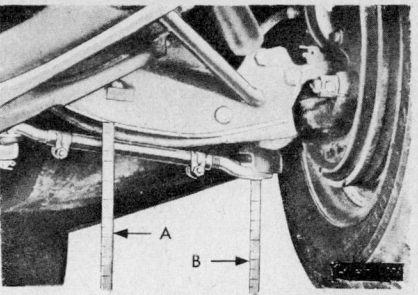

Front suspension height
(© Chrysler Corp.)

Front Suspension

References

Figures covering the caster, camber, toe-in, front end height, and turning radius can be found in the Wheel Alignment table of this section.

Torsion-Aire front suspension is similar in principle to that used on other cars of the Chrysler family. The torsion bars are used in the front, only, and are connected to the lower control arms and anchored to the body under the front floor.

Ball joints are used at the upper and lower ends of the steering knuckles. Cam-type caster and camber adjustment methods are employed. Direct-acting Oriflow shock absorbers are attached between the lower control arms, and stamped steel towers welded into the body-frame unit.

Radius rods are used on the lower control arms and extend forward to attach to the K-shaped engine support member. The upper control arm is angled downward, toward the rear, to reduce nose dive during brake application.

Peculiar to this suspension is a compression-type lower ball joint and a torsion bar adjustment in the lower control arm.

The torsion bar adjustment permits rotating the bar relative to the lower control arm to obtain correct front-end height settings. This adjustment is located at the front end of the bar, and permits easy adjustment during wheel alignment operations.

Lubrication

Balloon-type and semi-permanently lubricated steering linkage and front suspension ball joints are used. Relubrication at these points is required at about 36,000 miles, or three year periods (whichever comes first.) However, the balloon seals should be inspected for leaks, or other damage, two or three times a year.

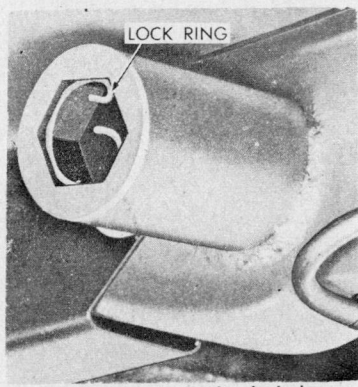

Torsion bar rear anchor lock ring
(© Chrysler Corp.)

When lubricating these points, use only multi-mileage long-life chassis grease. Remove the threaded plug from each joint to be lubricated, and temporarily install lube fittings. Inject lubricant, while feeling the seal with the fingers. Stop just before the seal starts to balloon. Remove lube fittings and reinstall plugs.

Front Height Adjustment (Without Gauge)

1. Jounce the car and measure from the lower ball joint to the floor (measurement A).
2. Measure from the control arm torsion bar spring anchor housing to the floor (measurement B)

3. Subtract A from B.
4. Measure the other side in the same way.
5. Adjust, if necessary, by turning the torsion bar adjusting bolt, in to raise; out to lower.

Torsion Bar Springs

Contrary to appearance, the torsion bars are not interchangeable from right to left. They are marked with an R or an L, according to their location.

Removal

1. Lift the car, by the body, high enough to free the front suspension of all load. If the car is to be raised with jacks, place jack under center of K-member and raise until suspension is free of all load.
2. Release load from torsion bar by backing off anchor adjusting nuts. Remove the adjusting nut and swivel bolt.
3. Remove the lower control arm strut.
4. Remove the lock spring from the rear of torsion bar rear anchor.
5. Install tool or clamp, and remove torsion bar rearward by striking the clamping tool with a hammer.

NOTE: do not apply heat to the front or rear anchors. Do not scratch or otherwise mar the skin of the torsion bar during removal or installation.

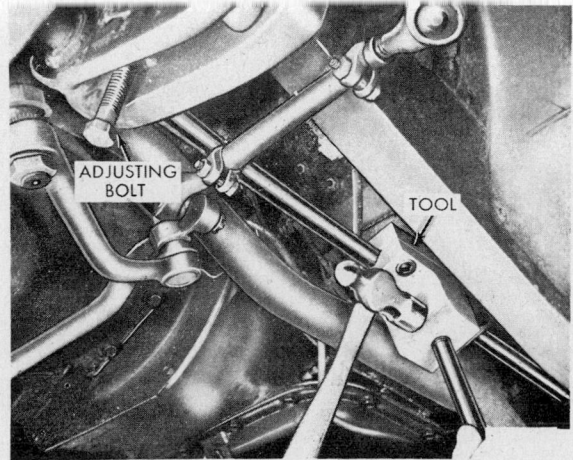

Removing torsion bar (© Chrysler Corporation)

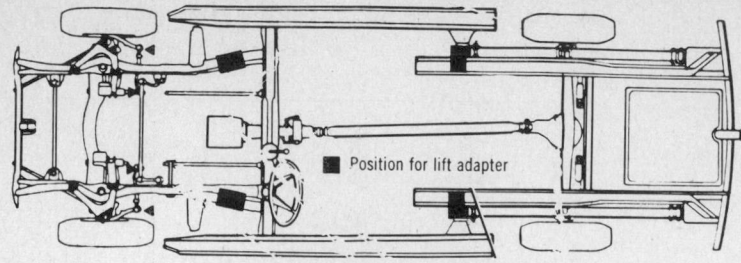

Positioning lift adapter (© Chrysler Corp.)

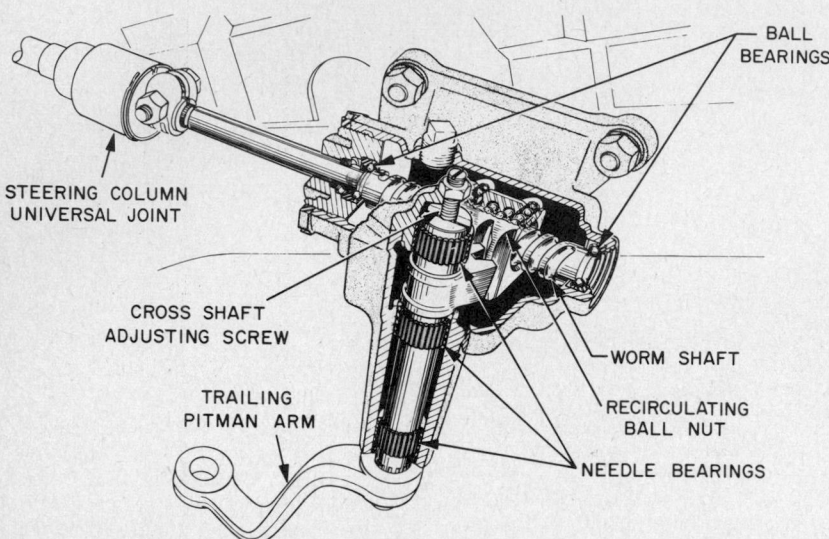

Manual steering gearbox (© Chrysler Corp.)

6. Remove the clamping tool and slide the rear anchor balloon seal off the front end of the bar.
7. Remove torsion bar by sliding the bar rearward and out through the rear anchor.

Installation

1. Clean the hex openings of both front and rear anchors, also clean the male ends of the torsion bar.
2. Feed the torsion bar through the rear anchor.
3. Slide the balloon-type seal over the torsion bar, with the large cupped side of the seal facing the rear.
4. Coat both ends of the torsion bar with multi-purpose grease.
5. When starting the bar into the anchor in the lower control arm, position the adjusting arm about 60° below the horizontal plane. This will permit windup for future adjustment.
6. Position the lock-ring into the rear anchor, then move torsion bar rearward until the bar contacts the lock-ring.
7. Position swivel bolt on the control arm and hold in place while installing the adjusting nut and seat. Tighten the adjustment about ten turns before lowering car to the floor.

8. Pack the annular opening in the rear anchor with multi-purpose grease. Slide the rear anchor balloon type seal into position over the rear anchor until the lip of the seal fits in the groove.
9. Install lower control arm strut.
10. Lower car to the floor and adjust front suspension height.

Upper and Lower Ball Joints

See Dodge-Plymouth section.

Jacking, Hoisting

Jack car at front control arms and at rear under axle housing.

To lift at frame use adapters, so that contact will be made at points shown. Lifting pads must extend beyond sides of supporting structure.

Steering Gear

Instructions for the adjustment of the steering gear will be found in the Unit Repair Section.

Manual Steering

A worm and recirculating ball type steering gear is used with the manual steering system.

The worm shaft is supported at each end by ball-type thrust bearings.

The sector shaft includes an integral sector gear which meshes with helical grooves on the worm shaft ball nut.

The sector shaft is supported, and rotates, in two needle bearings in the housing and one in the housing cover.

Service information may be found in the Unit Repair Section.

Power Steering

Constant-Control power steering is an option on all models. Hydraulic power is provided by a vane-type, belt-driven pump. A double-groove pump pulley is used. The power steering gear and pump are essentially the same as those used on other Chrysler Corporation cars. Service information may be found in the Unit Repair Section.

1965-69

1. Remove the pin or bolt that attaches the coupling on the steering shaft to the steering gear worm gear.
2. Pull back the carpet and remove the screws that attach the steering column mounting plate to the floor pan.
3. Loosen the steering column-to-instrument panel attaching clamp bolts enough to disengage the tap on the clamp from the slot in the steering column jacket.
4. On 1965-66 models equipped with standard transmission and on all 1967-69 models, disconnect the shift linkage from the shift tube.
5. Slide the steering column upward to disengage the steering shaft coupling from the steering gap worm gear.
6. Remove the nut that attaches the Pitman arm to the steering gear and, using a puller, remove the steering arm from the steering gear. On models equipped with a 273 V8, it may be necessary to remove the starter, the left motor mount attaching stud nut and raise the left-side of the engine to gain enough clearance to remove the steering gear.
7. On models equipped with a 426 Hemi engine, remove the battery, the battery tray and the left motor mount attaching stud nut and washer.
8. If equipped with power steering, disconnect the lines from the steering gear and plug them to prevent fluid spillage.

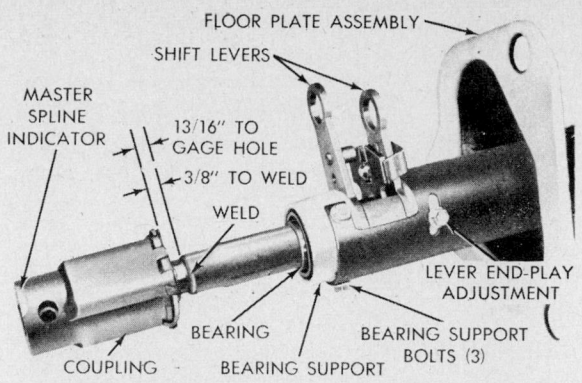

Steering column lower end (© Chrysler Corporation)

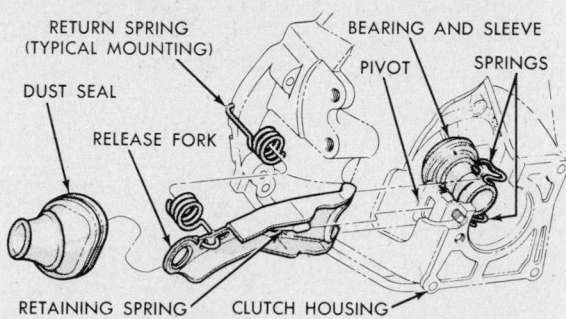

Clutch release fork, bearing and sleeve
(© Chrysler Corp.)

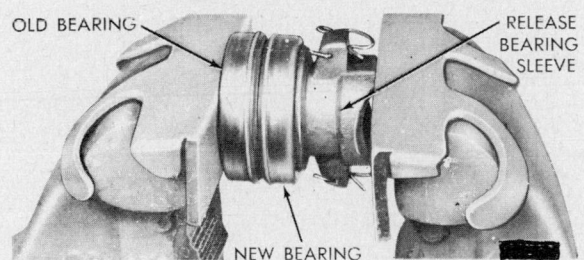

Replacing clutch release bearing
(© Chrysler Corp.)

9. Remove the bolts that attach the steering gear to the chassis and remove the steering gear. On models with a six cylinder engine, remove the steering gear from the engine compartment. On all V8 models except the 246 Hemi, remove the steering gear from under the vehicle. On models with a 426 Hemi, jack the engine up 1½ in. and rotate the steering gear forward and remove it from under the hood through the battery tray opening.

10. To install steering gear, position it on the chassis and install the attaching bolts. Align the master spline on the steering gear-worm gear (12 o'clock position) with the master spline on the steering shaft coupling, making sure the front wheels and the steering wheel are in the straight ahead position.

11. Install the pin or bolt that attaches the coupling to the worm gear.

12. Position the steering column on the instrument panel and loosely install the nuts or bolts that attach the steering column bracket to the dash. Move the column up or down in the instrument panel support until the dimension between the steering shaft coupling and the gauge hole in the steering shaft is 13/16 in. 1968-69 models with power steering do not have a gauge hole in the steering shaft. On these models, move the column up or down until the dimension between the top of the steering shaft coupling and the weld on the steering shaft is ⅜ in.

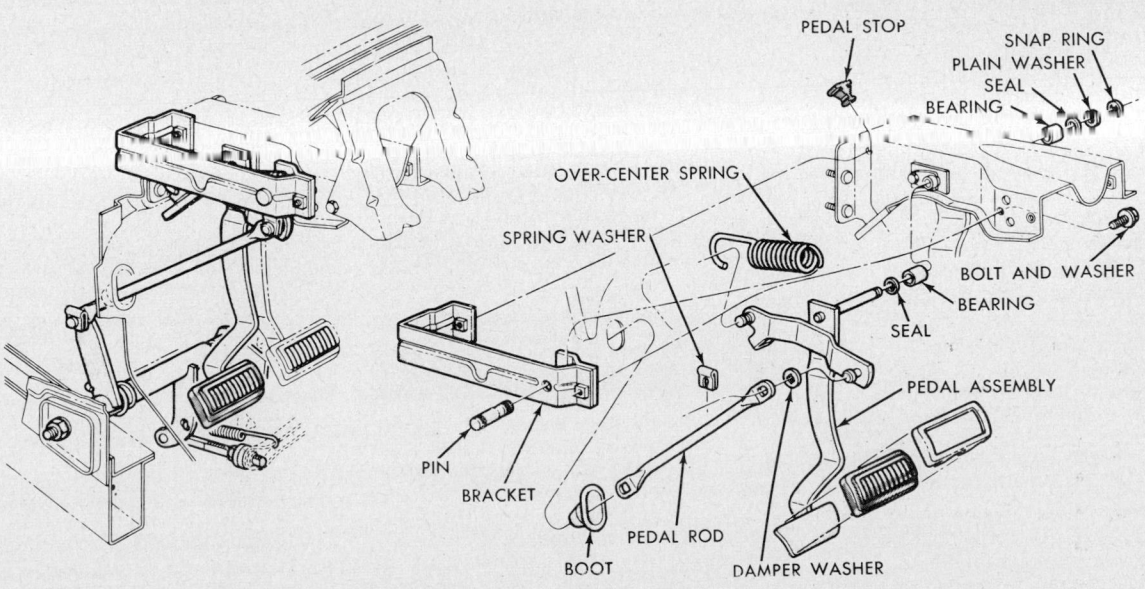

Typical clutch pedal and linkage (© Chrysler Corp.)

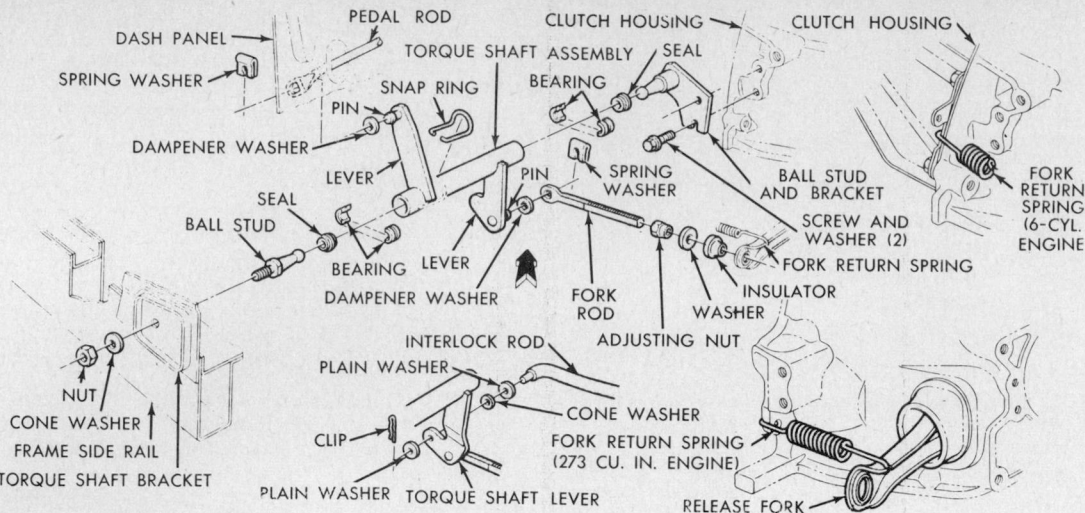

Typical clutch linkage (© Chrysler Corp.)

1970-72

To prevent damage to the energy absorbing steering column, it is necessary to completely detach the column from the floor and the instrument panel before the steering gear is removed.

1. Disconnect the negative battery cable.
2. Disconnect the linkage from the bottom of the steering column.
3. Remove the steering shaft lower coupling-to-worm gear roll pin.
4. Disconnect the wiring connectors at the steering column.
5. Remove the horn ring ornament assembly.
6. Disconnect the wire from the horn switch. Remove the screws that attach the horn ring and switch to the steering wheel and remove the ring and switch.
7. Remove the steering wheel attaching nut and washer and, using a puller, remove the steering wheel from the steering shaft.
8. Remove the turn signal lever.
9. Remove the screws that attach the steering column base plate to the floor pan. Remove the finish plate from under the instrument panel to expose the steering column mounting bracket.
10. On Fury, Polara and Monaco models, remove the automatic transmission shift indicator pointer from the shift tube bracket.
11. Remove the nuts or bolts that attach the steering column bracket to the instrument panel support. If shims are used between the bracket forward leg and the panel support, they must be installed in the same location when the column is installed.
12. Carefully pry steering shaft lower coupling from the steering

gear worm shaft and remove the steering column assembly from the vehicle. Use care not to scratch or damage the column during removal.
13. Remove the nut and washer that attaches the Pitman arm to the steering gear.
14. Using a puller, remove the steering arm from the gear.
15. Remove the bolts that attach the steering gear to the chassis and remove the gear from the vehicle.
16. To install the steering gear, position it on the chassis and install the retaining bolts. Align the master spline on the worm gear (12 o'clock position) with the master spline on the steering shaft coupling, making sure the front wheels and the steering wheel are in the straight ahead positon.
17. Install the pin that attaches the coupling to the worm gear.
18. Position the steering column on the instrument panel and loosely install the nuts or bolts that attach the steering column bracket to the dash. Move the steering column and bracket up or down in the instrument panel support until the dimension between the steering shaft coupling and the gauge hole in the steering shaft is 13/16 in.

Clutch

The clutch is a single dry plate-type operated by a pedal suspended under the dash, and equipped with an assist spring.

Removal

1. Remove transmission.
2. Remove the clutch housing pan.
3. Disconnect clutch linkage and

retracting spring at the release fork.
4. Remove the fork from throwout bearing assembly.
5. Prick punch the clutch cover and flywheel to assure correct relocation when installing.
6. Remove the six clutch-to-flywheel bolts and remove the clutch cover and driven plate.

Installation

Install the clutch in reverse order and adjust clutch linkage.

Linkage Adjustment

Adjust the length of the release fork rod until there is 5/32 in. free-play measured at the outer end of the clutch fork. This will produce the 1 in. free-play required at the pedal.

Standard Transmission

For details on reconditioning, see Unit Repair Section.

Dodge and Plymouth have used four synchromesh manual transmissions in recent years. Six cylinders use a three speed, top cover transmission with synchromesh on second and third. V8s up to 1970 use a similar three speed, top cover transmission with synchromesh on second and third. 1970 V8s use a new fully synchromesh, side cover three speed. All Dodge and Plymouth four speed cars use a fully synchromesh, side cover four speed.

Removal

Top Cover Three Speed

1. Drain transmission.
2. Disconnect driveshaft at rear universal joint. Carefully pull shaft yoke out of transmission.
3. Disconnect speedometer cable and back up light switch.
4. Install engine support fixture or

jack up engine about 1 in. and block in place.

5. Disconnect transmission extension housing from center crossmember.

6. Support transmission with jack and remove crossmember. Remove bolts that attach transmission to clutch housing.

7. Slide transmission rearward until pinion shaft clears clutch disc before lowering transmission.

8. Lower transmission and remove.

Fully Synchromesh, Side Cover Three Speed

1. Remove shift rods from transmission levers.
2. Drain transmission fluid.
3. Disconnect driveshaft at rear universal joint. Mark both parts for reassembly.
4. Carefully pull yoke out of transmission extension.
5. Disconnect speedometer and back-up lights.
6. Remove part of exhaust if it blocks transmission.
7. Raise engine slightly and block in place.
8. Support transmission with jack, and remove crossmember.
9. Remove transmission to clutch housing bolts.
10. Slide transmission to rear until drive pinion shaft clears clutch disc, lower transmission, and remove from vehicle.

Four Speed

1. Raise vehicle on a hoist and drain transmission.
2. Disconnect all shift controls from transmission levers. Remove three bolts securing

shift unit to extension housing.
3. Disconnect driveshaft at rear universal joint. Carefully pull yoke out of transmission extension.
4. Disconnect speedometer cable and back-up light switch leads.
5. Disconnect left exhaust pipe or dual exhausts. Disconnect parking brake cable.
6. Raise engine slightly and block in place.
7. Disconnect transmission extension from crossmember.
8. Remove crossmember.
9. Support transmission with jack. Remove clutch housing to transmission bolts.
10. Slide transmission to rear until drive pinion shaft clears clutch disc.
11. Lower transmission and remove from vehicle.

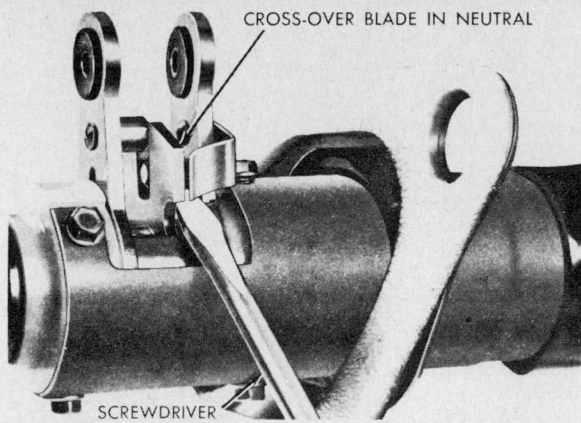

Holding cross-over blades in Neutral (© Chrysler Corporation)

CROSS-OVER BLADE IN NEUTRAL

SCREWDRIVER

Linkage Adjustment

Column Mounted 1965-67

With the second and third control rod disconnected from the lever on the column, and first and reverse control rod disconnected at the transmission, levers in neutral:

1. Check for axial freedom of the shift levers in the column. If the outer end of the levers move up or down along the column axis over 1/16 in., loosen the two upper bushing screws and rotate the plastic bushing, downward, until all of the axial play is eliminated. Retighten bushing screws.
2. Wedge a screwdriver between the crossover blade and the second and third lever, so that the crossover blade is engaged with both lever crossover pins.
3. Adjust the swivel on the end of second and third control rod until the stub shaft of the swivel enters the hole in the column lever. Install washers and clip. Tighten swivel locknut to 70 in. lbs.
4. Slide the clamp and swivel, on the end of the first and reverse control rod, until the swivel stub shaft enters the hole in the transmission lever. Install washers and clip. Tighten the swivel clamp bolt to 100 in. lbs.

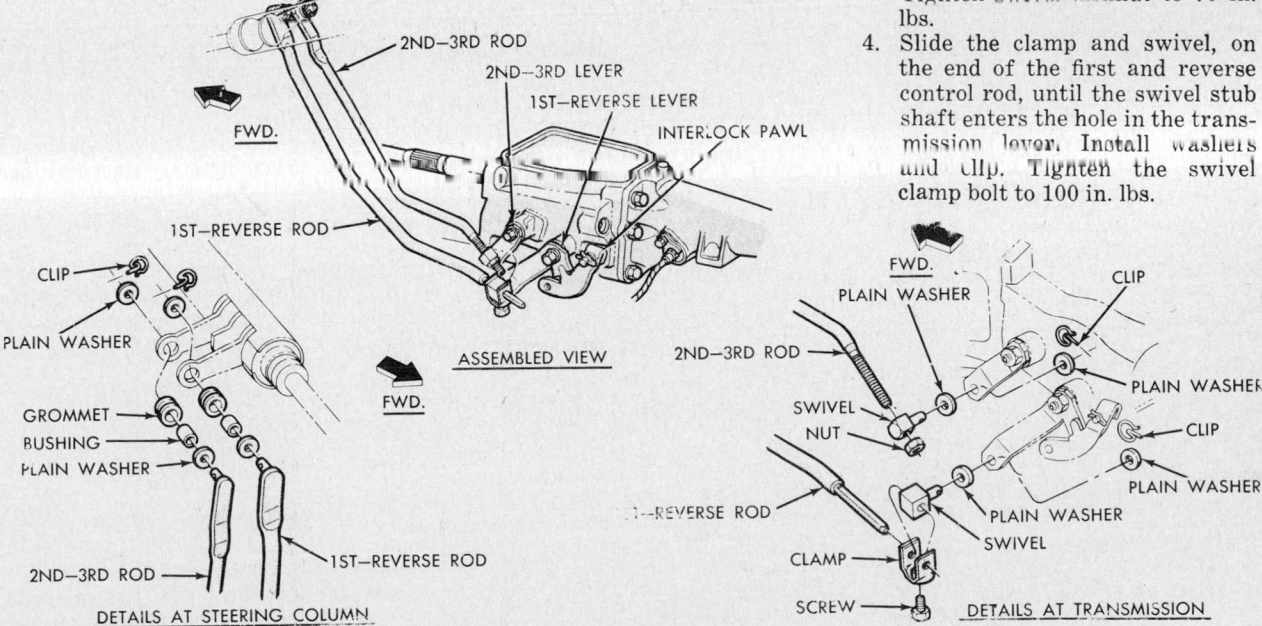

3-speed shift linkage (© Chrysler Corp.)

Column Mounted 1968-69

1. Remove both shift rod lever swivels at the transmission levers.
2. Make sure both transmission levers are in the Neutral (middle) position.
3. Adjust the 2nd-3rd shift rod swivel so it will enter the 2nd-3rd (forward) lever at the transmission while the hand lever on the steering column is held 10° above the horizontal (neutral) position. Position the swivel in the lever and install the washer and clip and tighten the attaching nut to 70 in. lbs.
4. Place a screwdriver or other suitable tool between the cross-over blade and the 2nd-3rd lever at the base of the steering column, so that both lever pins are engaged by the cross-over blade.
5. Adjust the 1st-reverse shift rod swivel so it will freely enter the lever on the transmission. Position the swivel in the transmission lever and install the washer and clip and tighten the attaching nut to 100 in. lbs.
6. Remove the tool from the cross-over blade at the steering column and check linkage operation.

Column Mounted 1970-72

1. Remove both shift rod swivels from the transmission.
2. Make sure the transmission levers are in the Neutral (middle) position.
3. Move the shift lever on the steering column to line up the locating slots in the bottom of the steering column housing and bearing housing. Install a suitable tool in the slots and lock the ignition switch.
4. Place a screwdriver between the cross-over blade and the 2nd-3rd lever at the base of the steering column so that both lever pins are engaged by the cross-over blade.
5. Set the 1st-reverse (rear) lever on the transmission to the Reverse (forward) position.
6. Adjust the 1st-reverse rod swivel so it will freely enter the lever on the transmission. Insert the swivel into the lever on the transmission and install the washer and clip and tighten the attaching nut to 100 in. lbs.
7. Remove the tool from the slots in the steering column, unlock the ignition switch and place the shift lever on the column in the Neutral position.
8. Adjust the 2nd-3rd shift rod swivel so it will freely enter the lever on the transmission. Insert the swivel into the lever and in-

stall the washer and clip and tighen the attaching nut to 100 in. lbs.
9. Remove the tool from the cross-over blades on the steering column and check linkage operation.

Four Speed—1965

1. Remove boot attaching screws and slide boot up shift lever.
2. Disconnect shift rods from levers at adjusting swivels.
3. Slide tool C-3951, or equivalent, over levers to align the three levers in shift control assembly and hold them in neutral position.
4. With shift operating levers in neutral position, adjust the three shift rods by turning swivels until swivel stubs match the lever holes.
5. Remove the aligning tool.

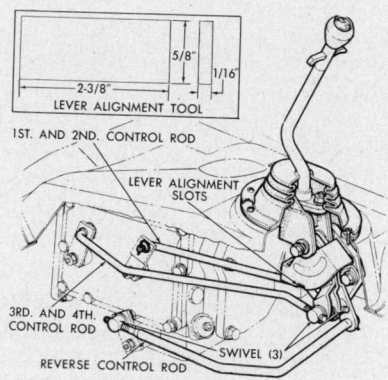

1966-68 4-speed shift linkage
(© Chrysler Corp.)

6. With hand-shift lever in third or fourth position, adjust lever stop screw (front and rear) to provide .020—.040 in. between the lever and the stops.

Caution Because there is no reverse gear interlock, it is very important that the transmission linkage adjustments be correctly performed in order to prevent the possibility of engaging two gears at once.

For cars with cable-type throttle control, and all 1965 models, see notes under Fuel System.

Floor Mounted Three and Four Speed—1966-72

NOTE: this procedure is for Chrysler Corporation linkage only. On models equipped with a Hurst shifter, see the Hurst Shifter section of this manual for adjustment procedure.

1. Make up a lever aligning tool from 1/16 in. thick metal, as illustrated.
2. With transmission in neutral, disconnect all control rods from the transmission levers.

3. Insert lever aligning tool through the slots in the levers, making sure it is through all the levers and against the back plate.
4. Now that all levers are locked in neutral, adjust length of control rods so they enter the transmission levers freely, without any forward or reverse movement.
5. Install control rod flat washers and retaining clips. Then, remove the aligning tool.
6. Check linkage for ease of shifting into all gears and for cross-over smoothness.

Automatic Transmission

1965-72

This three-speed automatic transmission and torque converter are enclosed in a one-piece housing. The transmission extension is separate.

Functionally, this transmission resembles the earlier Torqueflite. It uses the same gear selection and performs about the same. In design detail, however, it is entirely different. It is more compact and the internal parts are engineered to accommodate the torque requirements of the 6 cylinder and V8 engines.

Within the transmission extension, there is a parking pawl operated by a sliding lever. The parking pawl locks the transmission output shaft.

General information, troubleshooting and repairs will be found in the Unit Repair Section.

1965 Steering Column Gearshift

The steering column gear shift sequence is (left to right): P (Park), R (Reverse), N (Neutral), D (Drive), 2 (Second), and 1 (Low). Two cables connect the column with the transmission as in the push button-type shift.

Adjustments at the transmission end are the same as in the push button-type. To adjust the sprag lever and detent plate, hold the lever firmly in the 1 (Low) position.

1. Rotate the sprag lever pivot clockwise until the slot in the sprag lever is tight against the pin, then tighten the three pivot screws.
2. With the pawl spring in place, adjust the detent plate to align the end detent with the pin on the detent pawl. Tighten the plate screws.
3. Move the lever in and out of 1 (Low) several times and inspect the adjustment
4. Install the cable bracket and tighten the retaining screws, if it has been disturbed.

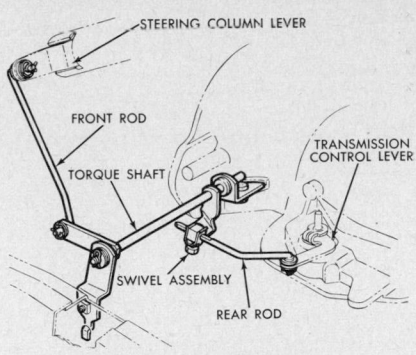

**Automatic column shift linkage—
except 1970 Barracuda and Challenger**
(© Chrysler Corp.)

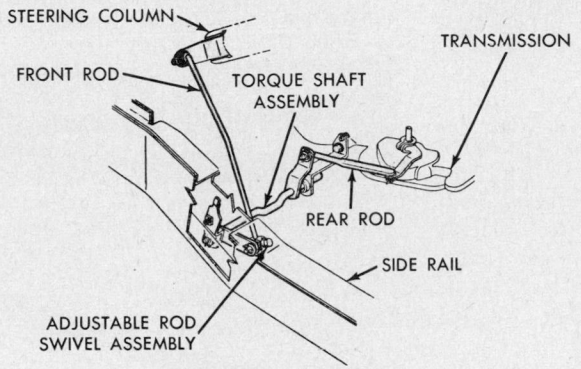

**Column shift linkage—
1970 Barracuda and Challenger**
(© Chrysler Corp.)

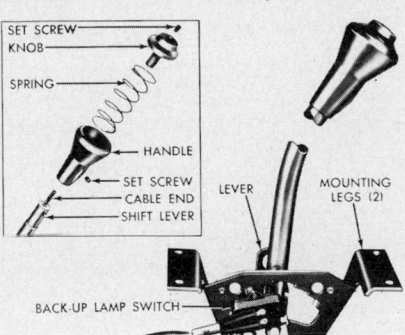
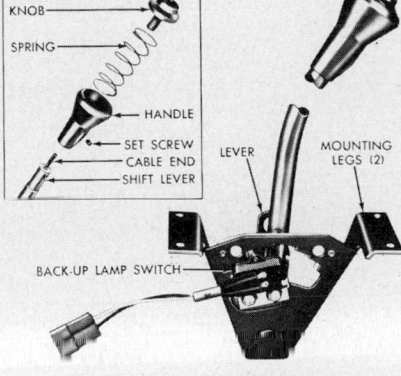

Automatic console shift linkage
(© Chrysler Corp.)

Automatic console shift linkage
(© Chrysler Corp.)

1966-72 Column Mounted and 1969-72 Console Mounted Linkage Adjustment

1. Place the gear shift selector lever in the Park position.
2. Loosen the transmission linkage control rod swivel clamp screw a few turns.
3. Manually move the transmission lever to the Park (rear) position.
4. With the control lever on the transmission in the Park detent and the selector lever in Park, tighten the swivel clamp screw to 100 in. lbs.

tacts the neutral start switch and provides a ground to complete the starter solenoid circuit. On late model compacts and intermediates, the back-up light switch has been incorporated into the neutral switch. The combination neutral and back-up light switch can be identified by the three electrical terminals on the rear of the switch. On this type of switch, the center terminal is for the neutral switch and the two outer terminals are for the back-up lights.

NOTE: in order for the neutral start switch to function properly, the transmission manual linkage must be properly adjusted and the actuator cam in the transmission must be centered in the neutral switch mounting hole in the transmission.

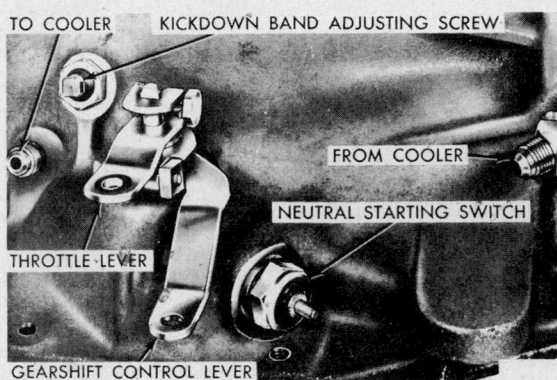

Torqueflite external controls (© Chrysler Corp.)

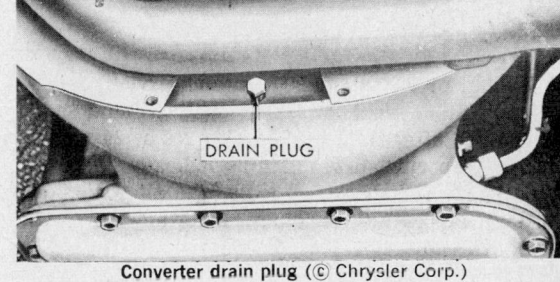

Converter drain plug (© Chrysler Corp.)

Console Gearshift Linkage Adjustment—1965-68

1. With gearshift selector lever in park position, loosen bolt in lower rod adjusting lever.
2. Move transmission control lever all the way to the rear (park detent.)
3. With control lever in transmission in park position detent, and selector lever in park position, tighten the bolt in the lower rod adjusting lever securely.
4. Reconnect the battery.

Neutral Start Switch

The neutral switch is mounted in the transmission case on all models. When the transmission manual lever is placed in either the Park or Neutral position, a cam, which is attached to the transmission throttle lever inside the transmission, con-

Torqueflite Removal and Installation

Remove transmission and torque converter as an assembly or the converter drive plate, pump bushing, and oil seal will be damaged. The drive plate will not support a load; therefore, do not allow weight of transmission to rest on drive plate.

1. Connect remote control starter switch to starter solenoid and position switch so engine can be rotated from under vehicle.
2. Disconnect secondary (High Tension) cable from ignition coil.
3. Remove cover plate from in front of converter to provide access to converter drain plug and mounting bolts.
4. Rotate engine with remote control starter switch to bring drain plug to six o'clock position.

Drain torque converter and transmission.

5. Mark converter and drive plate to aid in reassembly. There is an offset hole in crankshaft flange bolt circle, inner and outer circle of holes in drive plate, and four tapped holes in front face of coverter so these parts will be installed in original position.

6. Rotate engine with remote control switch to locate two converter to drive plate bolts at five and seven o'clock positions. Remove bolts, rotate engine and remove two more bolts. Do not rotate converter by prying as this will distort drive plate. Do not engage starter if drive plate is not attached to converter with at least one bolt or if transmission to block bolts have been loosened.

7. Disconnect battery.

8. Remove starter.

9. Disconnect wire from neutral start switch.

10. Disconnect gear shift rod from transmission lever. Remove gearshift torque shaft from transmission housing and left side rail. On console shifts, remove two bolts securing gearshift torque shaft lower bracket to extension housing. Swing bracket out of way for transmission removal. Disconnect gearshift rod from transmission lever.

11. Disconnect throttle rod from bellcrank at left side of transmission bell housing.

12. Disconnect oil cooler lines at transmission and remove oil filler tube. Disconnect speedometer cable.

13. Disconnect driveshaft at rear universal joint. Carefully pull shaft assembly out of extension housing.

14. Remove transmission mount to extension housing bolts.

15. Raise engine slightly and block in place.

16. Remove crossmember attaching bolts and remove crossmember.

17. Support transmission with jack.

18. Attach a small "C" clamp to edge of converter housing to hold converter in place during removal of transmission.

19. Remove converter housing retaining bolts. Carefully work transmission to rear of engine dowels and disengage converter hub from end of crankshaft.

20. Lower and remove transmission. Remove "C" clamp and remove converter. Reverse procedure to install.

Drive Shaft, U Joints

Six cylinder cars and 1965 eight cylinder cars with manual transmission use a driveshaft with a ball-and-trunnion-type front universal joint and a cross-and-roller-type rear universal joint. 1965 Darts and Valiants with eight cylinder engines and automatic transmission and all subsequent models use crossing-and-roller-type universal joints both front and rear.

Driveshaft R & R

1. Remove both clamps from the pinion yoke and remove the bearings.

2. Remove the front universal joint bolts at the transmission flange.

NOTE: to install, reverse above procedure. Do not overtorque the rear universal bearing clamp nuts, as distortion may result.

Ball and Trunnion Universal Joint Replacement

Remove the boot and slide the housing back to expose the bearings. The ball and needle bearing assemblies can now be removed. If the pin, or housing, is worn, a press should be used on the pin. The pin must be a very tight fit in the driveshaft.

Cross and Roller Universal Joint Replacement

Remove the retainers and push one roller and bushing assembly out by pressing the opposite side in. The remaining one can be pushed out by using the cross to press it.

Drive Axle, Suspension

Darts, Valiants, Barracudas, and Challengers use three types of axles,

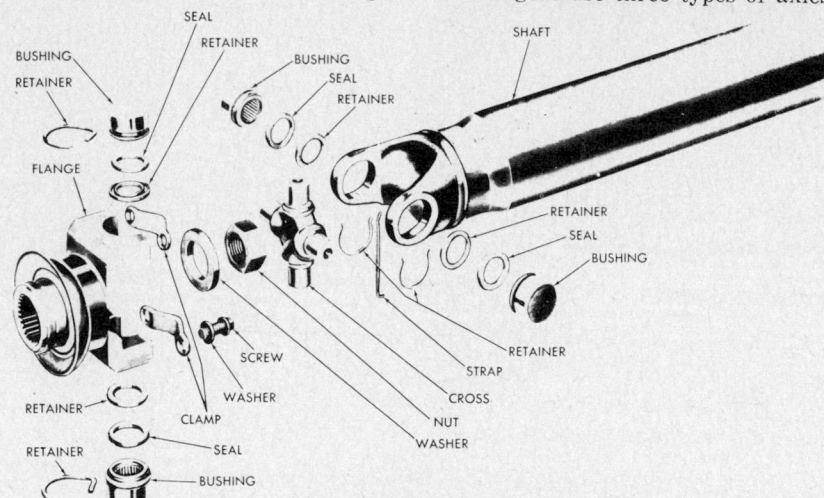

Rear cross and roller universal joint (© Chrysler Corp.)

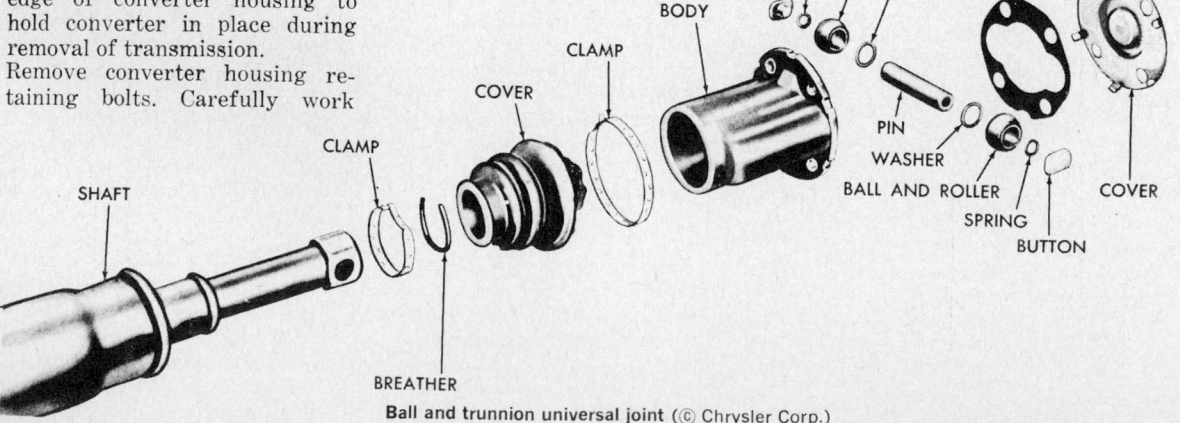

Ball and trunnion universal joint (© Chrysler Corp.)

a 7¼ in. axle ring gear, an 8¾ in. axle ring gear, and a 9¾ in. axle ring gear.

The 7¼ in. axle is a small lightweight axle for use with six cylinder engines. It has a one piece housing with a removable nine bolt cover plate in back.

The 8¾ in. axle is a larger axle for eight cylinder cars. It has a housing with a welded cover and a removable carrier assembly.

The 9¾ in. axle is a husky heavy duty axle for large V8s and high performance applications. It has a one piece housing and a 10 bolt cover plate.

7¼ and 9¾ In. Axles

Due to design, the drive pinion and differential case with drive gear are mounted directly to the center (carrier) section of the rear axle housing assembly. Access to the drive gears and carrier bearings is obtained through the carrier cover opening. Axle shafts and pinion oil seal can be changed without removal of the assembly from the car. However, the unit should be removed for any other operations.

8¾ In. Axles

Since 8¾ in. axles have removable carrier assemblies, it is not necessary to remove the axle housing to perform any axle repairs.

One Piece Axle Housing Assembly Removal

1. Raise the rear of the car to have the wheels clear the floor. Support the body in front of rear springs.
2. Block the brake pedal up.
3. Remove rear wheels.

4. Disconnect hydraulic flex line.
5. Remove the cotter pin and unhook the parking brake rear cable rod from the intermediate arm.
6. Disconnect the driveshaft at the rear end.
7. Remove rear spring U-bolts and shock absorbers.
8. Remove axle assembly from the car.

Axle Housing Installation

1. Position the rear axle housing spring seats over the spring center bolts.
2. Install U-bolts and shock absorbers. Torque U-bolts to 45 ft. lbs.
3. Connect parking brake cable at intermediate arm.
4. Connect driveshaft and torque nuts to 14 ft. lbs.
5. Reconnect the brake line or lines.
6. Install brake drums and retainer clips.
7. Install wheels and torque nuts to 55 ft. lbs.
8. Remove brake pedal block and bleed brake system.
9. Fill differential with two pints of specified compound.
10. Remove support and lower car to the floor.

Axle Assembly Reconditioning

General instructions covering rear axle troubles and how to repair and adjust, and information on installation of seals and bearings, are given in the Unit Repair Section.

Rear Springs

Rear springs are leaf semi-elliptic-type, using rubber bushings in the eye of each end of the main leaf.

Oriflow shock absorbers are mounted in rubber at both ends.

Radio

Removal

1965-67 Valiant and Barracuda and 1965 Dart

1. Disconnect battery.
2. Remove control knobs from front of radio.
3. From under instrument panel disconnect radio feed wire at connector.
4. Remove bottom screw from radio mounting bracket.
5. Remove left defroster tube.
6. Loosen top screw on radio mounting bracket and remove bracket.
7. Disconnect antenna and speaker leads.
8. Remove mounting nuts from front of radio and remove radio bezel.
9. Remove radio from below instrument panel.

1966 Dart

1. Disconnect battery.
2. If air conditioned, remove spot cooler tubes and spot cooler.
3. Disconnect antenna, speaker, and power supply leads.
4. Remove radio control knobs and mounting nuts.
5. Remove radio support bracket. Rotate front edge of radio down and remove from under panel.

1967 Dart and 1968 Valiant and Barracuda

1. Disconnect battery.
2. Remove radio control knobs and

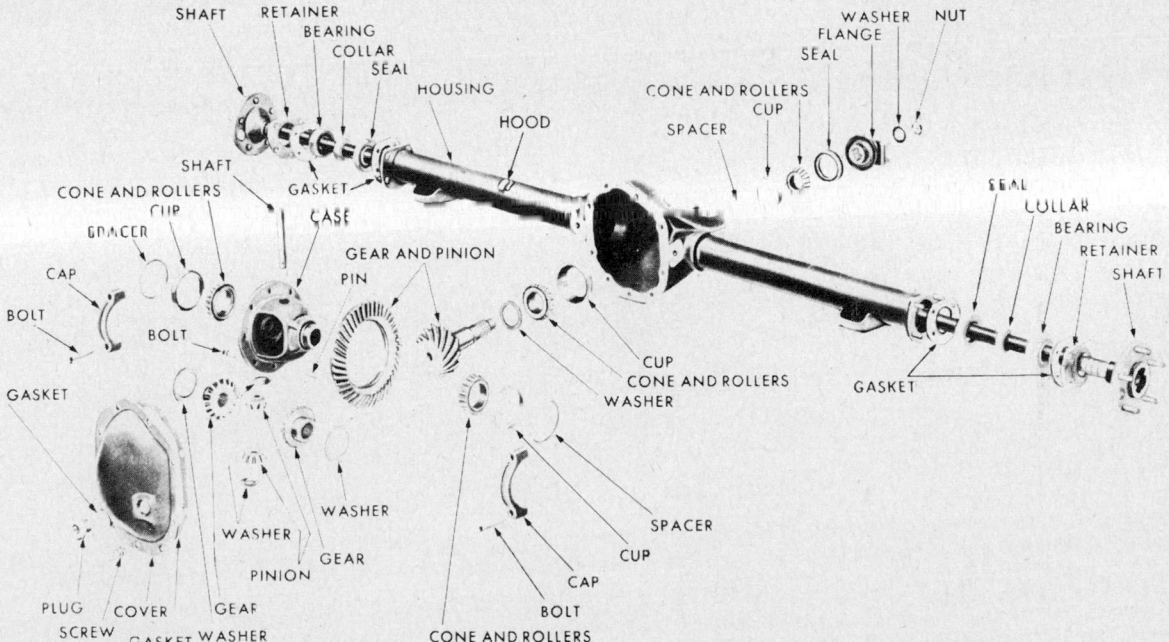

7¼ in. rear axle assembly (© Chrysler Corporation)

mounting nuts.

3. On air conditioned vehicles remove two outlet duct retaining bolts and remove duct. Remove right defroster hose and hose bracket.
4. From under instrument panel, remove radio support bracket lower screw and upper stud nut. Remove bracket.
5. Lower radio to position under panel and disconnect feed and speaker wires and antenna cable.
6. Remove radio.

1968 Dart

1. Disconnect battery.
2. Remove instrument cluster. See front of section.
3. Remove six glove box mounting screws, collapse glove box, and remove box from panel.
4. Remove temperature control knobs.
5. Working through cluster and glove box openings, remove two heater or air conditioning mounting stud nuts and move controls out of way.
6. Remove center bezel seven mounting screws and remove center bezel.
7. Remove radio mounting bracket.
8. Disconnect speaker and antenna leads.
9. Remove ashtray by removing four mounting screws.
10. Remove two radio mounting screws.
11. Remove radio from under instrument panel.

1969 Valiant, Dart, Barracuda, and Challenger

1. Disconnect battery.
2. From under panel disconnect speaker and wiring leads at radio.
3. Remove two radio mounting nuts from radio mounting bracket.
4. Move radio down and out from under instrument panel.

1970-72 Valiant, Dart, Barracuda, and Challenger

1. Disconnect battery.
2. From under panel, disconnect speaker and wiring leads at radio.
3. Remove channel selector shaft and knobs if so equipped.
4. Remove two radio mounting screws from under panel and loosen radio to lower support bracket mounting nut.
5. Move radio rearward, down, and out from under instrument panel.

1970-72 Dart and Valiant with Rallye Dash

1. Disconnect the negative battery cable.
2. Remove the control knobs from the front of the radio.
3. On models equipped with air conditioning, remove the two air conditioner outlet duct retaining nuts and remove the duct. Disconnect the right-side defroster hose and hose bracket and position them out of the way of the radio.
4. Remove the bottom screw from the radio mounting bracket.
5. Remove the left-side defroster hose.
6. Loosen the top screw on the radio mounting bracket and remove the bracket.

7. Disconnect the speaker and antenna leads.
8. Remove the radio mounting nuts from the front of the radio.
9. Remove the radio bezel.
10. Lower the radio and disconnect the radio power lead.
11. Remove the radio from under the instrument panel.

Windshield Wipers

Motor Removal

1965-66 Valiant, Dart, and Barracuda

1. Disconnect the wiper link at the wiper motor. For variable speed motors, note position of follower cam.
2. Disconnect the wiper motor lead wires at the wiper motor.
3. Remove the three nuts attaching the wiper motor and wiper motor bracket assembly to the cowl panel. Pull the motor bracket assembly down from the bracket mounting studs and out from underneath the instrument panel.
4. Install by reversing removal procedure.

1967-72 Valiant and Dart and 1967-69 Barracuda

1. Disconnect battery.
2. Disconnect wiper motor wiring harness.
3. Remove three wiper motor mounting nuts. On vehicles with air conditioning it is easier to remove crank arm nut and crank arm from under instrument panel first and omit steps 4 and 5.

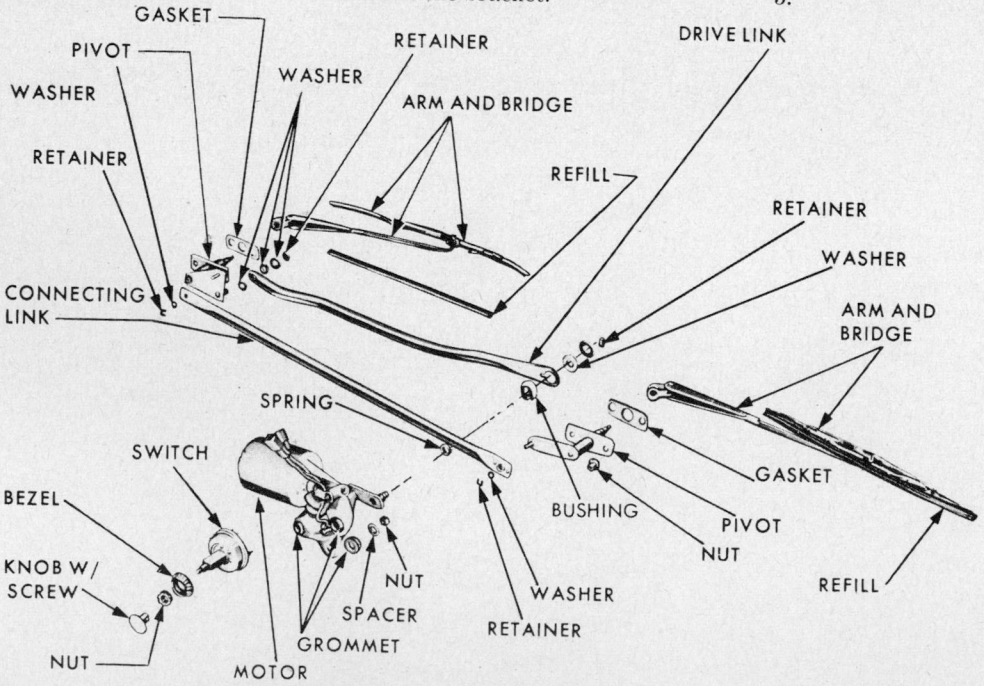

1965-66 single speed windshield wiper (© Chrysler Corp.)

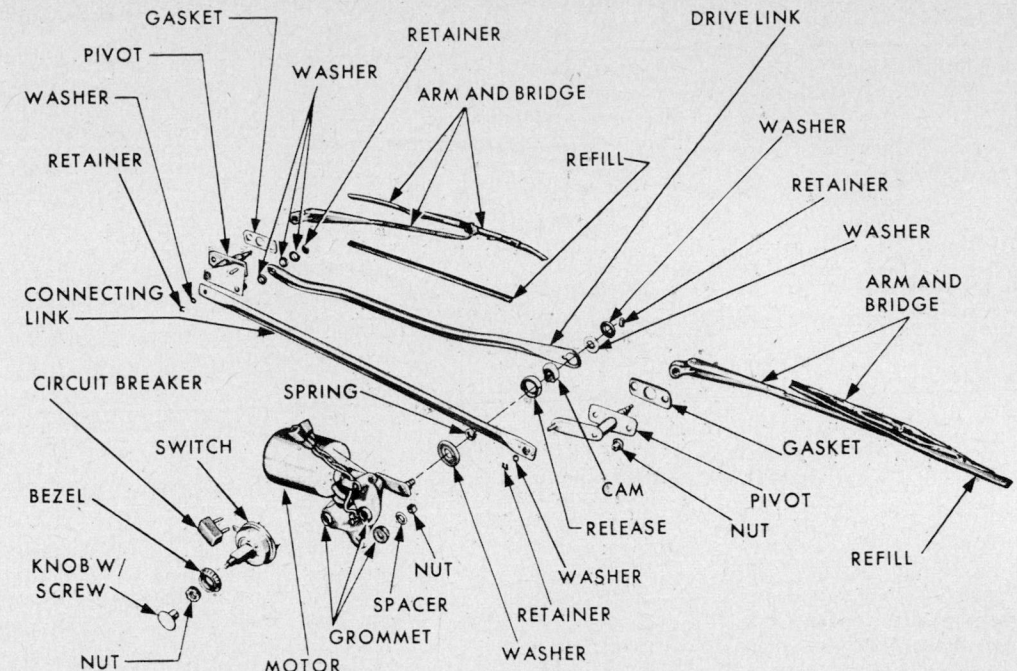

1965-66 variable speed windshield wiper (© Chrysler Corp.)

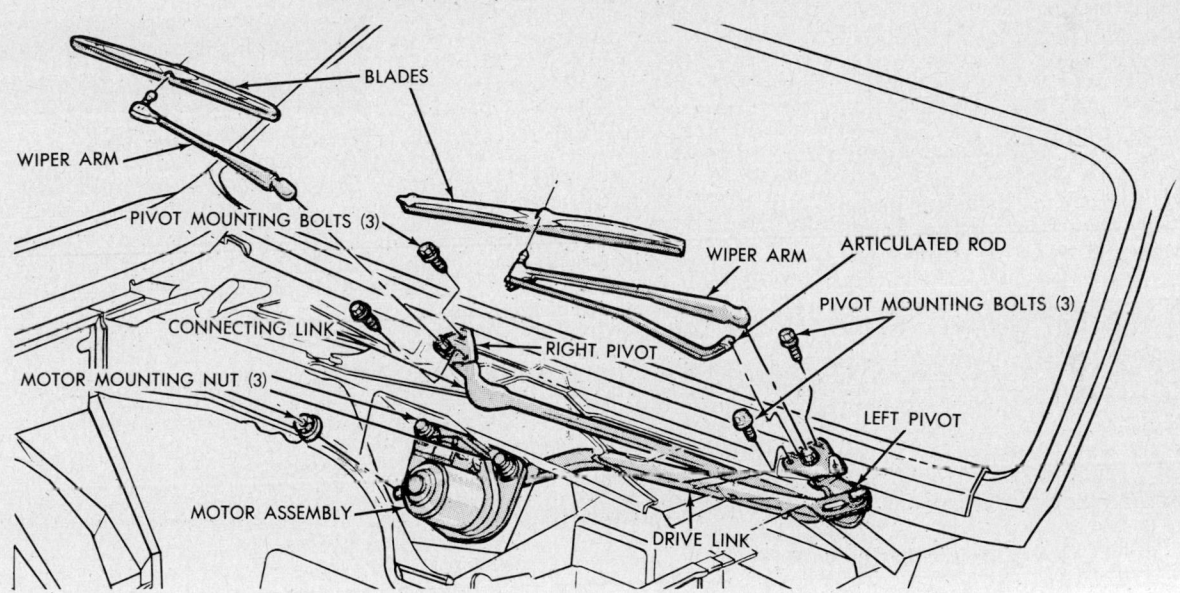

1970 Barracuda and Challenger windshield wiper linkage (© Chrysler Corp.)

4. Work motor off mounting studs far enough to gain access to crank arm mounting nuts.

CAUTION: do not force or pry motor from mounting studs as drive link can be easily distorted.

5. Using ½ in. open end wrench, remove motor crank arm nut. Carefully pry arm off shaft.
6. Remove wiper motor.

1970-72 Barracuda and Challenger

1. Disconnect battery.
2. Carefully remove wiper arm and blade assemblies.
3. Remove left cowl screen.
4. Remove drive crank arm re-
taining nut and drive crank. Disconnect wiring to motor.
5. Remove three wiper motor mounting nuts and remove motor.

Linkage Removal

1965-66 Valiant, Dart, and Barracuda Single Speed

1. From under instrument panel remove retaining clip and core washer from pivot arm pins.
2. Remove link and pin from motor crank.
3. Withdraw assembly from under instrument panel and remove drive link and bushing.

1965-66 Valiant, Dart, and Barracuda Variable Speed

1. Remove connecting link retaining clips and washers from pivot pins.
2. Remove connecting link.
3. Remove drive link retainer clip and washers from left pivot pin.
4. Remove retainer and washer from motor drive crank pin.
5. Remove drive link.
6. Remove cam, release, parking spring, and washer for examination, lubrication, or replacement.

1967-72 Valiant, Dart, and 1967-69 Barracuda

1. Disconnect battery.

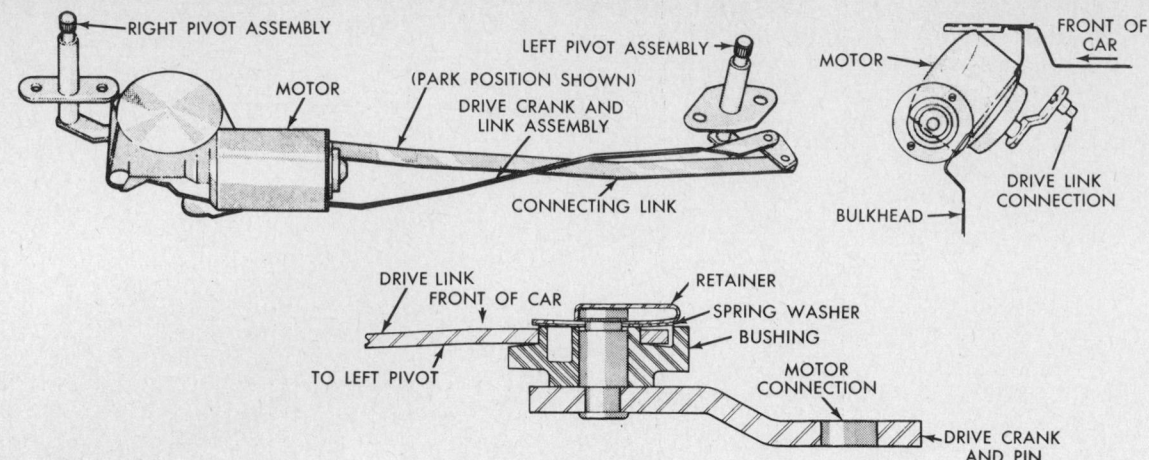

1967-70 Valiant and Dart and 1967-69 Barracuda windshield wiper linkage
(© Chrysler Corp.)

2. If air conditioning equipped, remove duct supplying left spot cooler to provide easier access to left wiper pivot. Insert wide blade screwdriver between plastic link bushing and pivot crank arm. Gently twist screwdriver to force bushing and link from pivot pin. Remove three motor mounting nuts, pull motor away from bulkhead and remove motor crank arm retaining nut. After crank arm is removed from motor shaft, remove drive link assembly from under left side of panel. In heater equipped models, remove motor drive crank arm retaining nut and pry crank arm off of motor shaft. Gently pry drive link and bushing from left pivot crank arm

pin and withdraw assembly from under panel. Remove motor drive crank arm from drive link after removal of assembly from vehicle.
3. To remove connecting link from pivots, remove glove box. Reaching through glove box opening, gently pry bushing and link from right pivot pin. Lift link from pivot crank arm pin and repeat operation at left pivot. Withdraw from under left side of panel.

1970-72 Barracuda and Challenger

1. Remove wiper arm and blade assemblies.
2. Remove left cowl screen for access to linkage.

3. Disconnect battery.
4. Remove crank arm nut and crank from motor shaft.
5. Remove bolts mounting left and right pivots to body.
6. Remove links and pivots through cowl top opening.

Heater System

Heater Assembly R&R

1966-72 Valiant and Dart and 1966-69 Barracuda

1. Drain radiator.
2. Disconnect heater hoses from heater and remove heater hoses to dash retainer plate.
3. Remove heater motor seal retain-

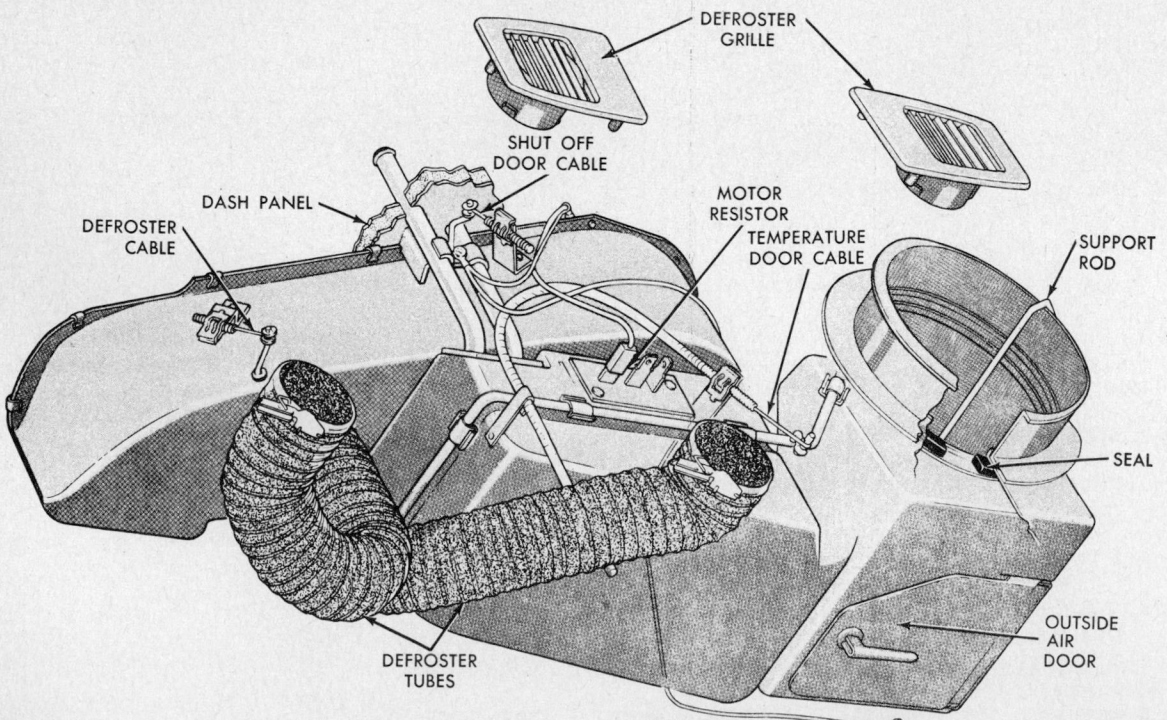

Valiant-Dart heater assembly (© Chrysler Corporation)

er plate from dash panel.

4. Disconnect heater-defroster and temperature control cables from heater assembly.
5. Remove heater motor resistor wire from resistor.
6. Remove defroster tubes from heater assembly.
7. Disconnect heater housing support rod from fresh air duct.
8. Remove heater assembly.

1970-72 Barracuda and Challenger

1. Disconnect battery.
2. Drain coolant.
3. Disconnect heater hoses from core tubes at dash panel. Plug core tubes to prevent spilling coolant on interior of car.
4. Remove three mounting nuts from studs around blower motor and remove flange and air seal.
5. Unplug antenna from radio and place wire to one side.
6. Remove screw from housing to plenum support rod on right side of housing above fresh air opening.
7. Disconnect three air door cables.
8. Disconnect wires from blower motor resistor.
9. Tip unit down and out from under instrument panel.

Heater Blower Motor R&R

1965 Valiant, Dart and Barracuda

1. Disconnect battery.
2. Disconnect heater ground wire.
3. Loosen fresh air intake duct clamp at blower end and remove duct from blower assembly.
4. Remove screw attaching blower to plenum.
5. Remove heater blower assembly from heater housing.
6. From inside heater housing, disconnect blower assembly wires.

1966-72 Valiant and Dart and 1966-69 Barracuda

1. Remove the heater assembly.
2. Remove the seal from around the heater blower motor mounting studs.
3. Remove the spring clips that retain the spacers and the blower motor to the heater housing.
4. Remove the blower motor from the heater housing.

1970-72 Barracuda and Challenger

1. Remove heater assembly from car.
2. Disconnect blower motor lead from resistor block and ground wire from mounting plate.
3. Remove six sheet metal screws and six retaining clips holding blower motor assembly from housing.
4. Remove blower wheel from motor shaft.
5. Remove two retaining nuts and separate motor from mounting plate.

Heater Core R & R

1965 Valiant, Dart and Barracuda

1. Drain coolant as necessary.
2. Disconnect heater hoses at core and temperature control valve.
3. Remove screws that hold temperature control valve cover to heater housing.
4. Carefully withdraw control valve from opening in heater housing and disconnect valve control cable.
5. Disconnect hose connecting water valve to core.
6. Remove water valve and valve cover.
7. Remove screws that attach core housing to cowl panel and remove housing.

8. Insert screwdriver between cowl and heating housing, and carefully pry heater housing from cowl.
9. Remove screws that secure core to housing and remove core.
10. Install in reverse of above.

1966-72 Valiant and Dart and 1966-69 Barracuda

1. Remove the heater assembly and the heater blower motor as outlined above.
2. Remove the fresh air door seal from either the inner or outer heating housing half only.
3. Remove the clips that retain the heater housing halves together.
4. Separate the heater housing halves.
5. Remove the screw that attaches the seal retainer and seal around the heater core tubes.
6. Remove the heater core tube support clamp.
7. Remove the screws that attach the heater core to the heater housing and remove the heater core.
8. Reverse above procedure to install.

1970-72 Barracuda and Challenger

1. Remove the heater assembly.
2. Remove the nine spring clips and four screws that hold the front cover to the heater housing.
3. Cut the sponge rubber plenum-to-heater housing air seal in two places where the front cover separates the cover from the housing.
4. Remove the core tube retaining screw from behind the housing, between the core tubes.
5. Remove the two sponge rubber gaskets from the heater core tubes and remove the core from the heater housing.

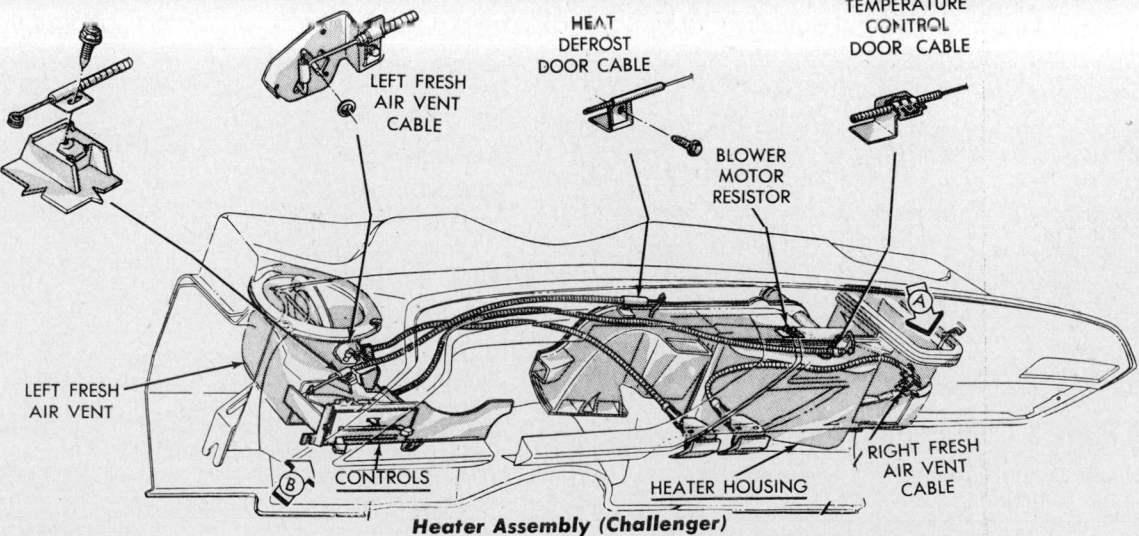

Heater Assembly (Challenger)

(c) Chrysler Corp.

Vega

Index

YEAR IDENTIFICATION

1971 Vega Coupe

1971 Vega Sedan

1971 Vega Kammback Wagon

1971 Vega Sedan Delivery

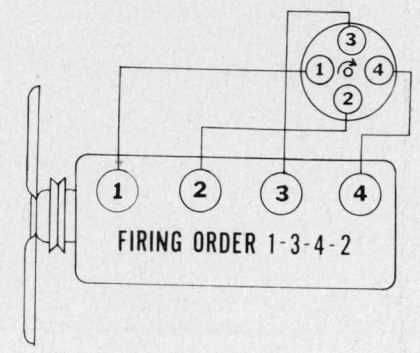

1972 Vega Coupe

Serial Number Location

14111 . . . . 2 dr., 4 passenger, pillar sedan
14177 . . . . 2 dr., 4 passenger pillar coupe (hatchback)
14115 . . . . 2 dr., 4 passenger, station wagon
14105 . . . . 2 dr. panel delivery

Model Identification

The vehicle serial number plate is found on top of the instrument panel and is visible through the left side of the windshield. The body number, trim code and paint number are located on the upper right side of the dash panel. Interpretation of the serial number is as follows:

FIRING ORDER

FIRING ORDER 1-3-4-2

1971-72 Vega firing order

Manufacturer Identity ①	Body Style ②	Model Year ③	Assembly Plant ④	Unit Number ⑤
1	4111	1	U	100025

①—Manufacturer's identity number assigned to all Chevrolet vehicles
②—See Model Identification
③—Last digit of model year (1971)
④—Lordstown
⑤—Unit numbering to begin with 100001

ENGINE IDENTIFICATION NUMBER

The engine identification number is located on a machined pad, on the right side of the cylinder block, above the starter motor.

GENERAL ENGINE SPECIFICATIONS

YEAR	CU. IN. DISPLACEMENT	CARBURETOR	ADVERTIZED HORSEPOWER @ RPM	ADVERTIZED TORQUE @ RPM (FT. LBS.)	A.M.A. HORSEPOWER	BORE & STROKE (IN.)	ADVERTIZED COMPRESSION RATIO	VALVE LIFTER TYPE	NORMAL OIL PRESSURE (PSI)
1971	140	1-V	90 @ 4800	136 @ 2400	19.6	3.501 x 3.625	8.0:1	Mech.	40
	140	2-V	110 @ 4800	138 @ 3200	19.6	3.501 x 3.625	8.0:1	Mech.	40
1972	140	1-V	80 @ 4800	121 @ 2400	19.6	3.501 x 3.625	8.0:1	Mech.	40
	140	2-V	98 @ 4800	121 @ 2400	19.6	3.501 x 3.625	8.0:1	Mech.	40

VALVE SPECIFICATIONS

YEAR AND MODEL	SEAT ANGLE (DEG.)	FACE ANGLE (DEG.)	VALVE LIFT INTAKE (IN.)	VALVE LIFT EXHAUST (IN.)	VALVE SPRING PRESSURE (VALVE OPEN) LBS. @ IN.	VALVE SPRING INSTALLED HEIGHT (IN.)	STEM TO GUIDE CLEARANCE (IN.) Intake	STEM TO GUIDE CLEARANCE (IN.) Exhaust	STEM DIAMETER (IN.) Intake	STEM DIAMETER (IN.) Exhaust
1971-72 1-BBL	46	45	.4199	.4302	183–197 @ 1.31	1.75 ①	.001–.0027	.001–.0027	.341–.3417 ②	.341–.3417 ②
2-BBL	46	45	.4366	.4366	183–197 @ 1.31	1.75 ①	.001–.0027	.001–.0027	.341–.3417 ②	.341–.3417 ②

①—Free length = 2.03 in.
Damper free length = 1.84 in.

②—Service limit = .0037 in. intake, .0047 in. exhaust.

TUNE-UP SPECIFICATIONS

YEAR	MODEL	SPARK PLUGS		DISTRIBUTOR		IGNITION TIMING (Deg.) ▲	CRANKING COMP. PRESSURE (Psi)	VALVES		Intake Opens (Deg.)	FUEL PUMP PRESSURE (Psi)	IDLE SPEED (Rpm) ★
		Type	Gap (In.)	Point Dwell (Deg.)	Point Gap (In.)			Tappet (Cold) Clearance (In.)				
								Intake	Exhaust			
1971-72	90 H.P.	R42TS①	.035	31-34	.019②	6B③	140	.015	.030	22	3-4½	④
1971-72	110 H.P.	R42TS①	.035	31-34	.019②	6B (Man.) 10B (Auto.)	140	.015	.030	25	3-4½	④

① Cold plug—AC R41TS.
② —.016 in. (used).
③ —Manual and Automatic.

④—Automatic—650.
 3-speed manual—850.
 4-speed manual—1200.
▲—With vacuum advance disconnnected and plugged.

CAUTION

General adoption of anti-pollution laws has changed the design of almost all car engine production to effectively reduce crankcase emission and terminal exhaust products. It has been necessary to adopt stricter tune-up rules, especially timing and idle speed procedures. Both of these values are peculiar to the engine and to its application, rather than to the engine alone. With this in mind, car manufacturers supply idle speed data for the engine and application involved. This information is clearly displayed in the engine compartment of each vehicle.

CRANKSHAFT BEARING JOURNAL SPECIFICATIONS

YEAR	MODEL	MAIN BEARING JOURNALS (IN.)				CONNECTING ROD BEARING JOURNALS (IN.)		
		Journal Diameter	Oil Clearance	Shaft End-Play	Thrust On No.	Journal Diameter	Oil Clearance	End-Play
1971-72	All	2.2983-2.2993	.0029-.003	.002-.008	4	1.999-2.000	.0007-.0027 ①	.0009-.0014

① —Maximum service clearance = .004 in.

BATTERY AND STARTER SPECIFICATIONS

YEAR	MODEL	BATTERY				STARTERS						Brush Spring Tension (Oz.)
		Ampere Hour Capacity	Volts	Group Number	Terminal Grounded	Lock Test			No-Load Test			
						Amps.	Volts	Torque	Amps.	Volts	RPM	
1971-72	All	45	12	Y-86①	Neg.	Not Recommended			50-75	9	6,500-10,000	N.A.

① —Y-86A used on Verti-Pak.

CAPACITIES

YEAR	MODEL	ENGINE CRANKCASE ADD 1 Qt. FOR NEW FILTER	TRANSMISSIONS Pts. TO REFILL AFTER DRAINING			DRIVE AXLE (Pts.)	GASOLINE TANK (Gals.)	COOLING SYSTEM (Qts.) WITH HEATER
			Manual		Automatic			
			3-Speed	4-Speed				
1971-72	All	3	2.4	2.4	18.0	2.0	11.0	7①

①—Add ½ qt. for air conditioning.

AC GENERATOR AND REGULATOR SPECIFICATIONS

YEAR	Part No.	ALTERNATOR			REGULATOR					
		Field Current Draw @ 12V.	Output @ Generator RPM		Field Relay			Regulator		
			1100	5000	Air Gap (In.)	Point Gap (In.)	Volts to Close	Air Gap (In.)	Point Gap (In.)	Volts at 85°
1971-72	1100545 1100559	4-4.5	—	31	Integral					
					—	—	None	—	—	13.8-14.8
	1100546 1100560	4-4.5	—	50						

GENERAL CHASSIS AND BRAKE SPECIFICATIONS

| YEAR | MODEL | CHASSIS | | BRAKE CYLINDER BORE | | | BRAKE DRUM | |
| | | Overall Length (In.) | Tire Size | Master Cylinder (In.) | Wheel Cylinder Diameter (In.) | | Diameter (In.) | |
					Front	Rear	Front	Rear
1971-72	All	169.7	6.00 x 13①	.75	1.875	.75	9.64②	9.0

①—Optional: A78 x 13, A70 x 13.
②—Front disc diameter.

WHEEL ALIGNMENT

| YEAR | MODEL | CASTER | | CAMBER | | TOE-IN (In.) | KING-PIN INCLINATION (Deg.) | WHEEL PIVOT RATIO | |
		Range (Deg.)	Pref. Setting (Deg.)	Range (Deg.)	Pref. Setting (Deg.)			Inner Wheel	Outer Wheel
1971-72	All	1 & $^3/_4$N-$^1/_4$P	$^3/_4$N	1 & $^1/_4$P-$^3/_4$N	$^1/_4$P	$^3/_{16}$-$^5/_{16}$	—	N.A.	N.A.

TORQUE SPECIFICATIONS

| YEAR | MODEL | CYLINDER HEAD BOLTS FT. LBS. | ROD BEARING BOLTS FT. LBS. | MAIN BEARING BOLTS FT. LBS. | CRANKSHAFT BALANCER BOLT FT. LBS. | FLYWHEEL TO CRANKSHAFT BOLTS FT. LBS. | MANIFOLD (FT. LBS.) | |
							Intake	Exhaust
1971-72	All	60	35	65	80	60	30	30

CYLINDER HEAD BOLT TIGHTENING SEQUENCE

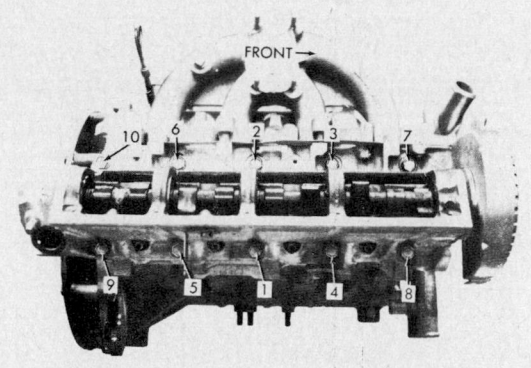

1971-72 Vega (all engines)

LIGHT BULBS

1971-72

Light Bulb	Bulb Number	Candlepower
Headlights—High beam....	6014	60
Low beam....	Sealed beam	55W
Front parking and turn signals..............	1157	32
Side markers, rear window defog lamp, indicator lamps	194	2
License plate light	67	4
Back-up lights............	1156	32
Courtesy light............	631	6
Dome light	211	12
Instrument illumination....	168	3
Heater or A/C control panel light, glove compartment light	1895	2
Radio light.............	1816	2

FUSES AND CIRCUIT BREAKERS

1971-72

TCS, idle stop solenoid (gauges) .... 10 amp.
Turn signal, fuel gauge, instrument panel warning
    lights, back-up lights, heat gauge, tachometer. 20 amp.
Radio .... 10 amp.
Wiper .... 25 amp.
Heater or A/C............................. 25 amp.
Instrument panel lights, radio light .... 4 amp.
Warning lights (flashers) .... 20 amp.
Tail lights, side markers, parking lights........ 20 amp.
Clock, dome light, cigarette lighter .... 20 amp.
Electric fuel pump........................ 20 amp.

Distributor

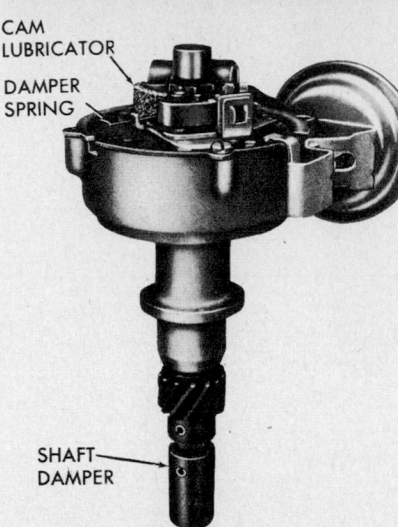

CAM
LUBRICATOR

DAMPER
SPRING

SHAFT
DAMPER

Distributor assembly
(© Chevrolet Division, G.M. Corp.)

The distributor is mounted in the cylinder head at the rear of the engine and is driven by the camshaft. An unusual feature of this unit is a cup, mounted at the lower end of the driveshaft. This cup is under full engine oil pressure when the engine is running, acting as a vibration damper to reduce driveshaft oscillations. If this cup is not installed, engine oil pressure will be lost.

A replaceable cam lubricator is installed, which should be changed each time the points are replaced.

Distributor Removal

1. Release the cap hold-down screws and remove the cap.
2. Disconnect the vacuum line and the primary lead.
3. Matchmark the distributor housing and the engine in line with the rotor centerline.
4. Remove the hold-down clamp and distributor.

NOTE: avoid turning the engine while the distributor is removed.

Installation

1. Turn the rotor approximately ⅛ turn clockwise past the matchmark.
2. Push the distributor into position, moving the rotor to mesh the gears.
3. Install the clamp bolt.
4. Connect the vacuum line and the primary lead.
5. Install the cap and, if necessary, adjust the timing.

Installation—Engine Disturbed

1. Remove No. 1 spark plug and place a finger over the plug hole. Remove the center coil wire and crank the engine until compression is felt in No. 1 cylinder. Rotate the engine until the timing pointer is aligned with the 8° ATDC mark.
2. Install the distributor with the vacuum advance pointing toward the front of the engine and the punchmarks on the drive gear in line with the No. 1 cap tower.
3. Install the hold-down clamp and rotate the distributor slightly so that the points are just open. Tighten the clamp bolt.
4. Install the rotor, cap and vacuum line.
5. Connect the primary lead.
6. Check and adjust the ignition timing.

Ignition Timing

The timing marks are on a plate mounted on the front of the block and the timing notch is on the crankshaft pulley.

The ignition timing is set with the engine at normal operating temperature, with the air conditioner on, E.E.C. vapor canister FUEL TANK line disconnected, the distributor vacuum line disconnected at the distributor and plugged, and the anti-dieseling solenoid disconnected.

Point Adjustment

Inspect the points for alignment and pitting. If necessary, clean the points with a points files. All the roughness need not be removed. To set the gap, rotate the crankshaft until one of the distributor cam lobes is directly opposite the rubbing block of the point arm (gap at maximum separation). Measure the gap. If it is not 0.016 in., loosen the contact point assembly attaching screw and move the assembly to obtain the specified gap. New points are set at 0.019 in. and used points at 0.016 in. Tighten the attaching screw.

If a dwell meter is available, check the dwell angle. It should be 31-34°. If the dwell angle is less than 31°, check for defective or misaligned points or worn distributor cam lobes. When the engine speed is increased from idle to 1750 rpm, the dwell angle should not vary over 3° either way.

Check the ignition timing, adjusting if necessary.

Alternator

A 10-SI Series Delcotron alternator is used. This unit features a non-adjustable, integral solid-state regulator mounted inside the slip-ring end frame. Testing and overhaul procedures for the integrated charging system are found in the Unit Repair Section.

Delcotron R & R

1. Disconnect the battery.
2. Disconnect the alternator wiring.
3. Remove the alternator brace bolt and V-belt.
4. Remove the pivot mount bolt and the alternator.
5. Installation is the reverse of the removal procedure. Adjust the belt tension.

Battery, Starter

A 45 amp./hr., 54 plate battery is standard equipment on all Vega models. Vehicles being shipped by the Vert-Pak method (on end in railway cars) use a special RPO VK5 battery having side terminals and filler caps along the edge. These batteries require special terminal adapters to facilitate charging.

The starter is a solenoid actuated Delco-Remy unit similar to other Chevrolet starters used in the past. See the Unit Repair Section for testing and overhaul procedures.

Starter R & R

1. Disconnect the battery ground cable and all wiring at the solenoid terminals. Install each nut on the terminal from which it was removed, as these nuts are not interchangeable.
2. Loosen the front starter bracket and remove the two mounting bolts.
3. Remove the front bracket bolt and rotate the bracket out of the way.
4. Remove the starter from the car, lowering the front end first.
5. To install, reverse the removal procedure.

Instruments

There are two basic instrument panel designs used on Vega models. The standard cluster consists of a full-panel-width speedometer with fuel gauge, clock and indicator lights. The optional GT model has a sep-

Starter motor installation
(© Chevrolet Division, G.M. Corp.)

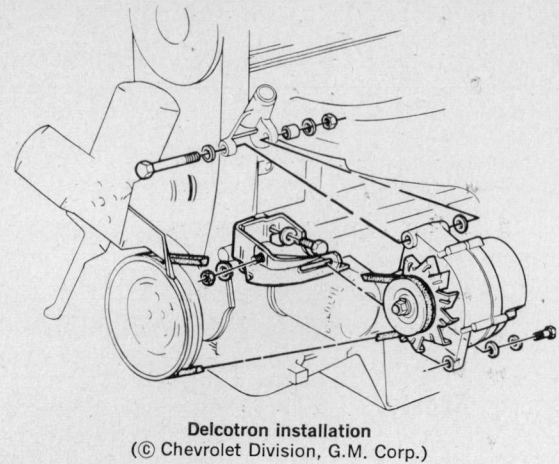

Delcotron installation
(© Chevrolet Division, G.M. Corp.)

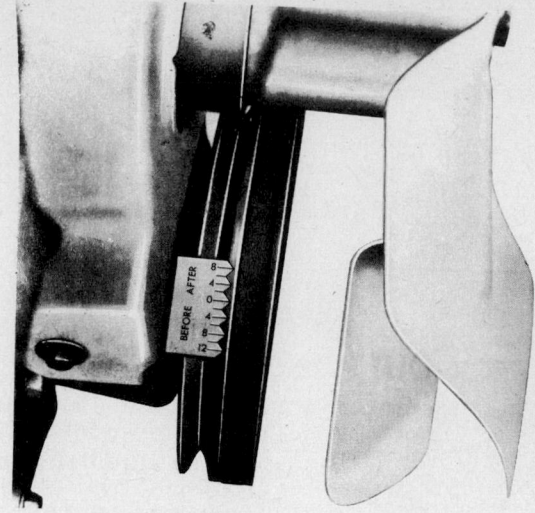

Timing mark location
(© Chevrolet Division, G.M. Corp.)

arate 7,000 rpm tachometer and 130 mph speedometer units, surrounded by a fuel gauge, clock, water temperature gauge and ammeter.

The speedometer cable and instruments are removed from the front of the panel. All indicator bulbs are ¼ turn twist-in type and are removed from the rear.

Instrument Cluster R & R

1. Disconnect the battery ground cable.
2. Remove the nine screws that secure the cluster bezel and remove the bezel.
3. Remove the instrument cluster lens-light shield combination (there are two screws at the top and two screws at the bottom of the lens). Tip the lens out at the top, then lift it clear. Clock stem must be removed first, if so equipped.

4. Any of the GT cluster instruments or standard speedometer and fuel gauge may be removed at this time.
5. Install in the reverse order of removal.

Ignition Switch R & R

The ignition switch is mounted on top of the column jacket under the dashboard, completely inaccessible unless the steering column is lowered. The energy-absorbing column is fragile when disconnected and should not be subjected to any shock or excess pressure. Since the column will distort under its own weight, make sure that it is fully supported along its entire length while it is disconnected from the dashboard.

1. Disconnect the battery ground cable.
2. Remove the steering wheel.

3. On manual steering columns, remove the pot joint coupling clamp bolt.
4. On power steering columns, remove the flexible coupling pinch bolt.
5. Move the front seat back out of the way.
6. Remove the three floor pan bracket screws.
7. Remove the two column-to-instrument panel nuts and carefully lower the column far enough to allow the harness plugs to be disconnected.
8. Disconnect the turn signal and ignition switch harnesses.
9. Place the ignition switch in LOCK position.
10. Remove the two switch screws and the switch assembly.
11. When installing, make sure that the switch is in LOCK position.

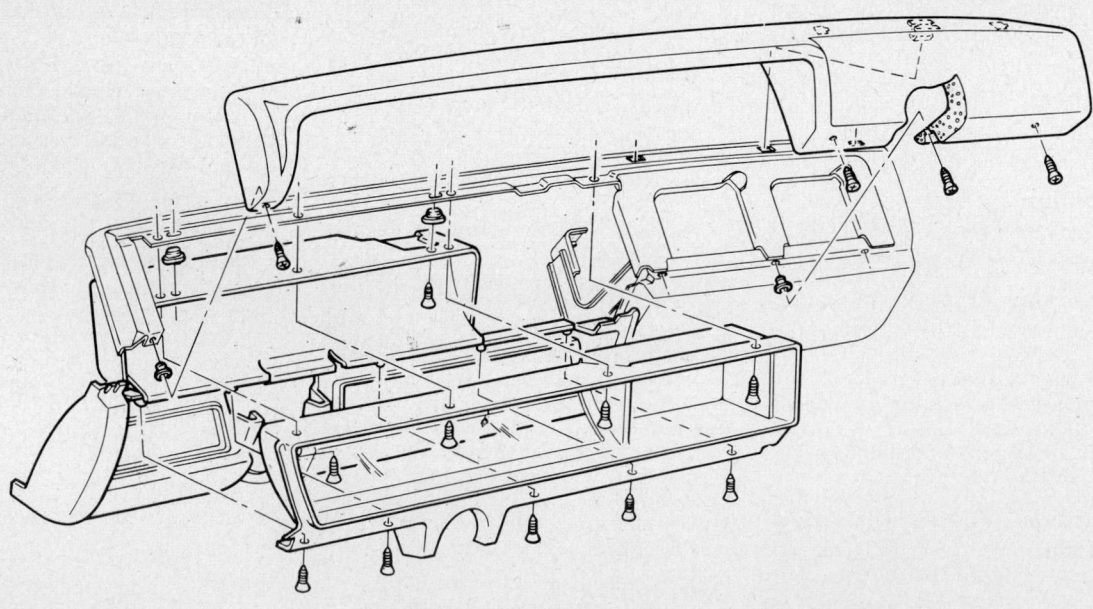

Standard instrument panel (© Chevrolet Division, G.M. Corp.)

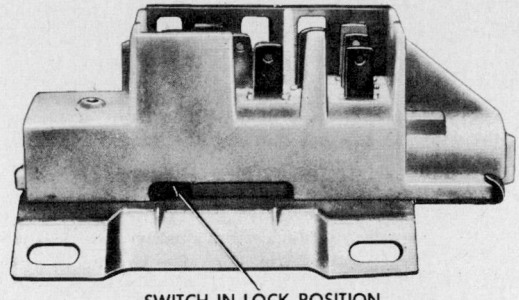

SWITCH IN LOCK POSITION

Ignition switch in Lock
(©Chevrolet Division, G.M. Corp.)

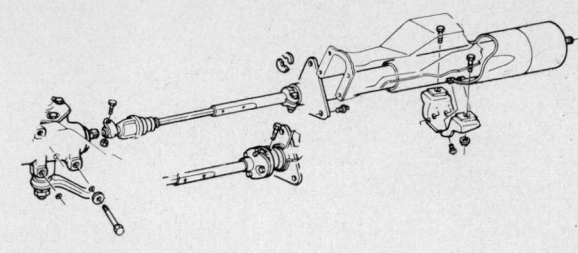

Steering column installation
(©Chevrolet Division, G.M. Corp.)

**Removing lockplate retaining ring
from steering column assembly**
(©Chevrolet Division, G.M. Corp.)

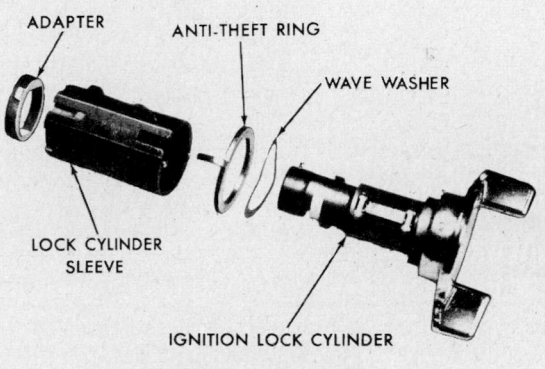

ADAPTER   ANTI-THEFT RING   WAVE WASHER

LOCK CYLINDER
SLEEVE

IGNITION LOCK CYLINDER

Ignition lock assembly
(©Chevrolet Division, G.M. Corp.)

12. Install the rod to the switch and the switch to the column. Do not use mounting screws longer than the original ones because they could interfere with the ability of the column to collapse.

NOTE: the following is a mandatory column installation procedure, and must be followed exactly to prevent severe column damage.

13. On power steering models, place the pot joint clamp (H) over the lower end of the pot joint (J) and assemble the intermediate shaft assembly (pot joint, intermediate shaft and flex coupling) to the steering gear stub shaft, aligning the flat on the stub shaft (K) with the flat in the pot joint.

14. Position the column in the vehicle.

15. On manual steering models, place the pot joint clamp (H) over the lower end of the pot joint (J) and assemble the pot joint to the steering gear wormshaft (K) with the flat in the pot joint. On power steering models, align the steering shaft flat with the flat in the flex coupling. When the shaft is bot-

tomed against the coupling reinforcement, install and tighten bolt (G) to 30 ft. lbs.

16. Connect the turn signal and ignition switch wiring harnesses.

17. Loosely install the steering column bracket to instrument panel stud nuts (E).

18. Align the pot joint clamp (H) with the groove across the end of the pot joint (J). Install bolt (N) and nut (O), tightening nut (O) to 55 ft. lbs.

NOTE: bolt (N) must pass through the shaft undercut.

19. With the vehicle on the ground, tighten nuts (E) to 19 ft. lbs.

20. Slide the toe plate (P) down the column to the floorboard and install the three screws (Q).

NOTE: on power steering models, alignment flange (R) on the toe plate must be engage with the front of the toe pan before driving screws (Q). On manual steering models, no side load is allowed during installation of the attaching screws (Q). A side load could cause misalignment.

21. On manual steering models: remove the alignment spacers (S). The minimum allowable clearance between the O.D. of

the steering shaft and the I.D. of the column jacket lower plastic bushing after installation is 0.18 in.

22. Install the steering wheel.

23. Connect the battery ground cable.

Lock Cylinder R & R

1. Remove the steering wheel.

2. Loosen the three cover screws and remove the cover.

3. Depress the lockplate using a U-shaped piece of stock and the steering wheel nut. Pry out the wire snap-ring, remove the tool the lockplate.

4. Remove the cancelling cam, upper bearing preload spring, thrust washer, turn signal lever screw and lever.

5. Push in the hazard warning knob and unscrew it.

6. Disconnect the turn signal wire harness as described under *Ignition Switch R&R*.

7. Wrap the harness connector and wires with tape to prevent snagging.

8. Remove the three turn signal switch screws and pull the switch up and out, guiding the

Front disc brake
(© Chevrolet Division, G.M. Corp.)

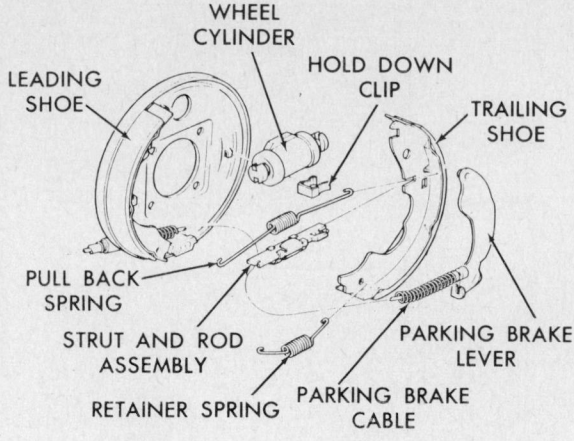

WHEEL CYLINDER
HOLD DOWN CLIP
LEADING SHOE
TRAILING SHOE
PULL BACK SPRING
STRUT AND ROD ASSEMBLY
RETAINER SPRING
PARKING BRAKE LEVER
PARKING BRAKE CABLE

Rear brake assembly
(© Chevrolet Division, G.M. Corp.)

harness up through the column.

9. Insert a small screw driver into the turn signal housing slot, break the flashing away and depress the spring latch at the lower end of the lock cylinder.

10. With the latch depressed, remove the cylinder. Lock cylinders cannot be disassembled, therefore a new cylinder, coded to the existing key, must be obtained if the cylinder is defective.

11. To install, reverse the removal procedure, following the *Mandatory Column Installation Procedure.*

Headlight Switch R & R

1. Disconnect the battery ground cable.
2. Pull the light switch to ON position.
3. Reach up under the instrument panel and depress the switch retainer button while pulling on the knob.
4. Remove the knob and shaft, then remove the ferrule nut with a large screwdriver.
5. Disconnect the multi-contact connector, prying gently with a small screwdriver.

Brakes

Front disc brakes are standard equipment on all models. The disc is 10 in. in diameter and 0.5 in. thick. Hub and disc are one-piece and the assembly is mounted to a one-piece steering knuckle and steering arm. The disc caliper design is similar to the single-piston Delco-Moraine disc brake used on other Chevrolet vehicles.

Rear brakes are drum-type, 9 in. in diameter. Unlike most other brake designs, the rear brakes are not automatically adjusted when the brakes are applied, but are adjusted when the parking brake is applied. For this reason, consistent parking in gear without using the parking brake is not recommended.

The tandem master cylinder pushrod is not adjustable, thus eliminating a pedal free travel adjustment.

Both front and rear hydraulic systems are routed to and from a distribution valve. Any significant change in the pressure difference between the front and rear systems moves a piston which activates a warning light switch, indicating pressure failure in one of the systems.

Master Cylinder R & R

1. Disconnect the master cylinder from the brake pedal.
2. Disconnect the two hydraulic lines at the master cylinder, plugging or covering the ends of the lines.
3. Remove master cylinder attaching nuts and remove the master cylinder.

4. Reverse the removal procedure to install.
5. Bleed the hydraulic system.

Front Disc Brake

Caliper R & R

1. Raise the front of the vehicle and remove the front wheel.
2. Remove and discard the two mounting pin stamped nuts.

NOTE: it is not necessary to disconnect the hydraulic line when removing the caliper. Do not let the weight of the caliper assembly hang on the hydraulic line.

3. Remove the two caliper mounting pins.
4. Lift the caliper off the disc.
5. Remove the shoes (pads) by sliding them to the mounting sleeve opening.
6. The mounting sleeves and bushing assemblies may be removed for inspection.
7. To install, position the sleeves with bushings into the caliper grooves with the shouldered end toward the outside.
8. Install the inner shoe and slide the shoe ears over the sleeve, then install the outer shoe in the same manner.
9. Position the caliper on the vehicle.

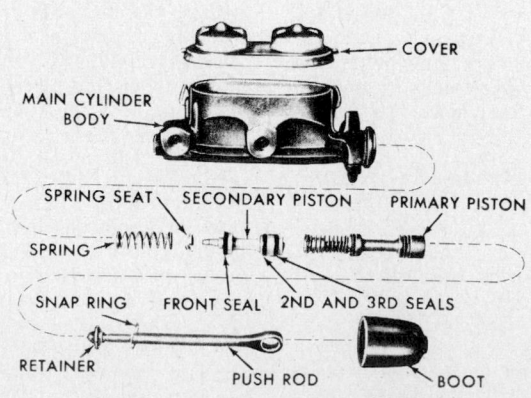

COVER
MAIN CYLINDER BODY
SPRING SEAT
SECONDARY PISTON
PRIMARY PISTON
SPRING
SNAP RING
FRONT SEAL
2ND AND 3RD SEALS
RETAINER
PUSH ROD
BOOT

Brake master cylinder
(© Chevrolet Division, G.M. Corp.)

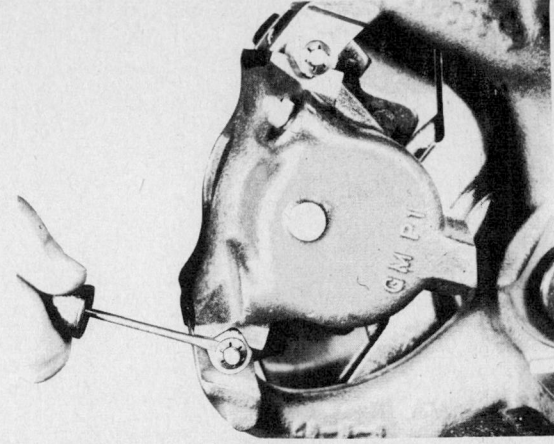

Removing disc brake caliper retainers
(© Chevrolet Division, G.M. Corp.)

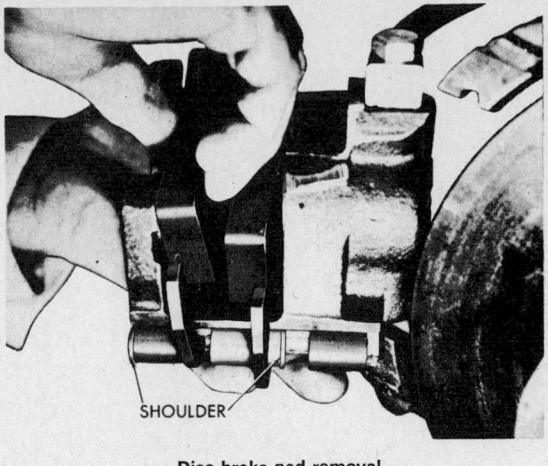

SHOULDER

Disc brake pad removal
(© Chevrolet Division, G.M. Corp.)

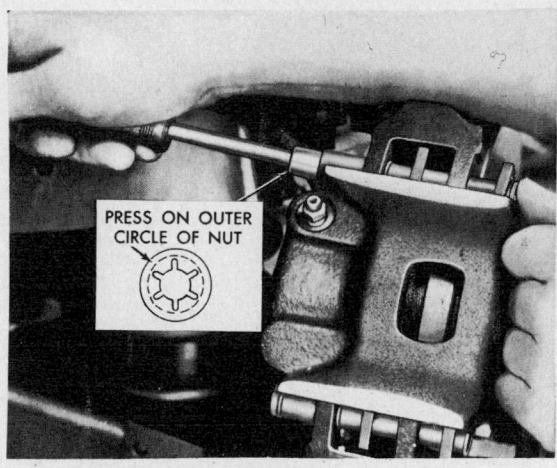

PRESS ON OUTER
CIRCLE OF NUT

Installing disc brake retaining nut
(© Chevrolet Division, G.M. Corp.)

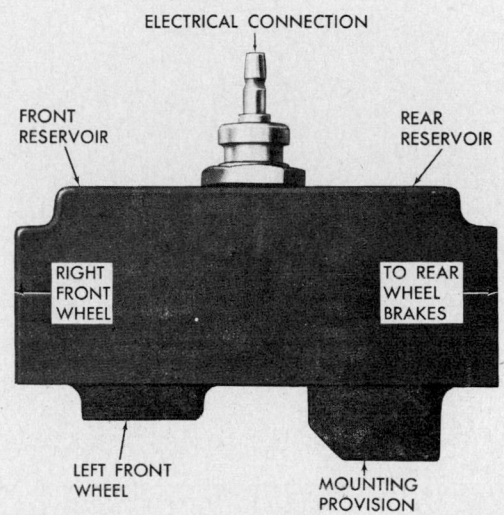

ELECTRICAL CONNECTION

FRONT
RESERVOIR

REAR
RESERVOIR

RIGHT
FRONT
WHEEL

TO REAR
WHEEL
BRAKES

LEFT FRONT
WHEEL

MOUNTING
PROVISION

Brake distributor and switch assembly
(© Chevrolet Division, G.M. Corp.)

NOTE: if new shoes have been installed, there may be too much fluid in the master cylinder reservoir. Remove about ½ of the fluid.

10. Install the mounting pins, head end to the outside.
11. Install new stamped retaining nuts with a socket that just seats on the outer edge of the nut.
12. Install the front wheels and lower the vehicle.

Disc R & R

1. Raise the vehicle and remove the wheel and caliper as described above.
2. Remove the dust cap with pliers.
3. Remove the cotter pin and nut from the spindle.
4. Pull on the disc to loosen the outer bearing, then remove the outer bearing.
5. Remove the disc and clean the spindle.
6. The inner bearing may be knocked out (use a brass drift or wooden hammer handle) for inspection or replacement.

7. If the disc is to be machined for refinishing, the following specifications must be met:
  a. Must be flat within 0.002 in. T.I.R. (Total Indicated Runout).
  b. Sides must be parallel (when checked radially) within 0.003 in. T.I.R.
  c. Thickness variation must not exceed 0.0005 in.
  d. Surfaces must be square with bearing cup centerline within 0.003 in. T.I.R.
  e. Original thickness is 0.500 in.; minimum thickness after refinishing is 0.470 in.; and absolute minimum thickness is 0.440 in.
8. Clean the bearings and bearing surfaces, then install the inner bearing.
9. Pack the inner bearing with grease, then install the hub onto the spindle.
10. Grease the outer bearing and install the bearing and washer.
11. Tighten the nut while rotating the disc until the rotation be-

comes difficult. This seats the bearings. If a torque wrench is available, tighten the nut to 12 ft. lbs.
12. Back off the nut enough to install the cotter pin and install the pin.

NOTE: this procedure should result in zero bearing preload and 0.001 to 0.008 in. end movement.

13. Install the dust cap, tapping it into place around the circumference of the cap.
14. Make sure that no grease or dirt has contaminated the disc. It must be completely clean.
15. Install the brake caliper as described above.
16. Install the wheel and lower the vehicle.

Brake Distribution and Switch Assembly

R & R

1. Disconnect the battery cable and the lead from the switch.
2. Disconnect the four hydraulic

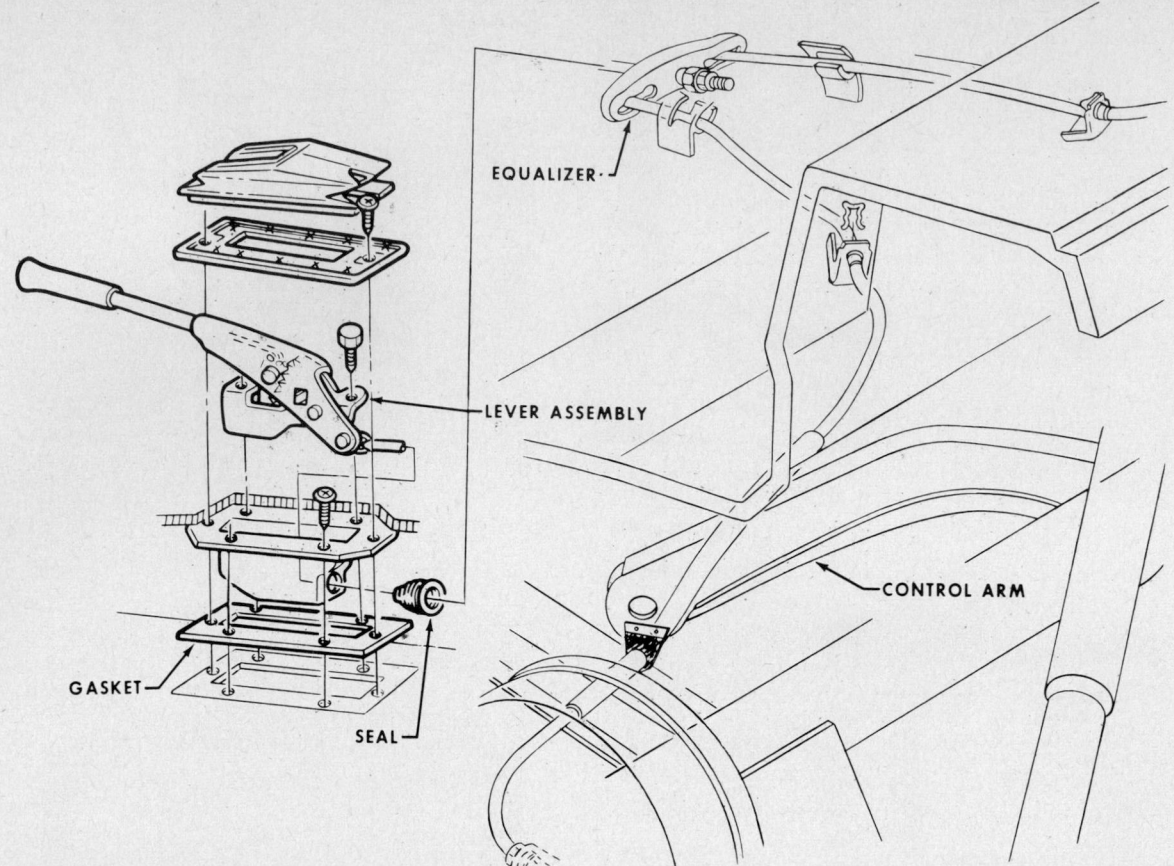

EQUALIZER

LEVER ASSEMBLY

CONTROL ARM

GASKET

SEAL

Parking brake assembly (© Chevrolet Division, G.M. Corp.)

lines from the switch and cover the ends of the lines.
3. Remove the mounting screw and the switch assembly.
4. The switch assembly may be cleaned with denatured alcohol.
5. The switch assembly is non-serviceable and must be replaced as a unit if defective.
6. Install the switch with the mounting screw.
7. Connect the hydraulic lines to the switch.
8. Connect the electrical lead to the switch and the battery cable.
9. Bleed the hydraulic system.

Checking the Warning Light

1. Disconnect the wire from the switch and use a jumper to make a good ground.
2. Turn the ignition to ON. The warning light should come on. If it does not, check the circuit or change the bulb as required.
3. Turn the ignition off and connect the wire to the switch.
4. To check the switch mechanism turn the ignition to ON, remove a rear wheel, install a bleeder hose and momentarily open the bleeder valve while heavy pressure is being applied to the brake pedal. Close the bleeder valve before the pedal is released.

5. The warning light should have come on.
6. Repeat Step 4 above for one of the front brakes.
7. If the warning light did not come on during either Step 4 or Step 6, replace the defective switch as a unit.

Parking Brake

Adjustment

1. Raise the vehicle on a hoist.
2. Apply the parking brake one notch from the fully released position.
3. Loosen the adjusting locknut and tighten the adjusting nut until a slight drag is felt when the rear wheels are rotated.
4. Tighten the locknut securely.
5. The rear wheels should rotate freely when the parking brake is fully released.
6. Lower the vehicle.

Cable R & R

1. Raise the car on a hoist.
2. Disconnect the equalizer from the cables.
3. Free the cable from the underbody tabs and remove the cable retainers (two per cable).
4. Remove the rear wheels and drums.
5. Remove the parking brake cable

from the parking brake lever.
NOTE: do not let the lever swing forward, causing the brakes to self-adjust.
6. Remove the pull-back spring and remove the brake shoes with the strut and adjuster assembly attached.
7. Compress the conduit locking fingers at the backing plate entry hole and withdraw the cable.
8. To install, push the cable through the hole in the backing plate and make sure the locking fingers are fully expanded.
9. Connect the cable end to the parking brake lever.
10. Install both shoes on the backing plate with the lower spring under the shoe anchor, guiding the adjusting lever and assembly into position.
11. Engage the leading and trailing shoes with the wheel cylinder links and the parking brake lever with the leading shoe.
12. Install the pull back spring on the leading shoe.
13. Install the drums and wheels.
14. Route the cable through the underbody retainers and tabs, bending the tabs to secure the cable in position.
15. Install the equalizer to the cables and to the parking brake lever rod. Install the adjusting nut

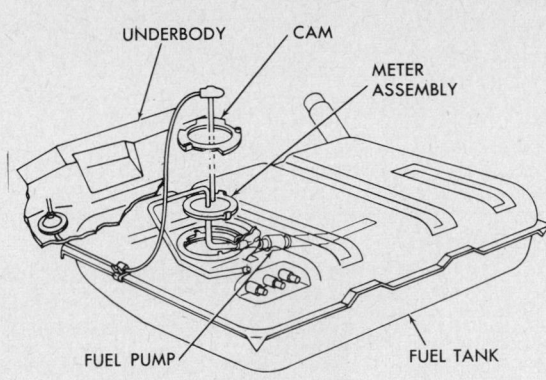

Fuel pump installation
(© Chevrolet Division, G.M. Corp.)

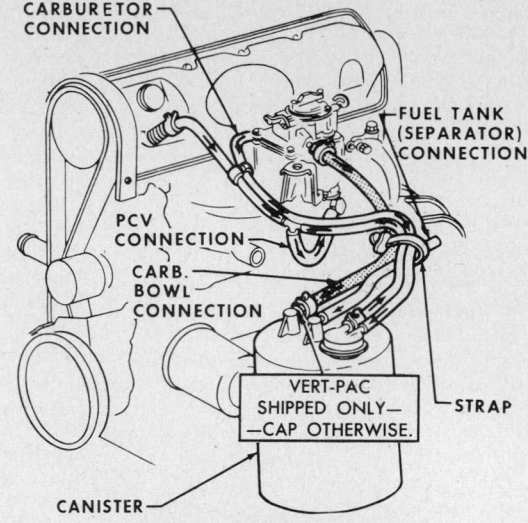

**Evaporation Control System canister
and hoses**
(© Chevrolet Division, G.M. Corp.)

and locknut.

16. Adjust the parking brake as described above.

17. Lower the vehicle.

Fuel System

The Vega may be equipped with one of four different carburetors. The 90 H.P. engine has a single-barrel Rochester Monojet and the 110 H.P. engine is equipped with the two-barrel Rochester 2GV. There are variations of each carburetor for manual and automatic transmission applications. Each has in integral fuel filter.

The Evaporative Control System is standard equipment on all Vegas. This system is designed to reduce the emission of gasoline vapors from the fuel tank into the atmosphere.

The electrical fuel pump is an integral part of the fuel tank unit assembly, which includes the fuel gauge metering unit. The fuel is energized by the ignition switch when the key is in start (cranking) position. After the engine starts, the pump receives current through the oil pressure safety switch as long as there is approximately 2 psi oil pressure.

Evaporation Control Canister

The evaporative emsion control canister is located in the engine compartment to the right front of the engine. The canister filter should be serviced every 12,000 miles or 12 months, whichever comes first.

Canister Filter Removal

1. Note the positions of the hoses and identify them as they are disconnected.

2. Loosen the clamps and remove the canister.

3. Remove the filter through the bottom of the canister.

Inspection

1. Check all the hose openings to make sure that they are open.

2. Check the operation of the purge by valve by applying vacuum to the small hose which leads to the cap on the valve. The valve should hold vacuum. The valve cap may be removed and defective parts replaced.

Installation

1. Install a new filter element in the canister.

2. Install the canister and tighten the clamp bolts.

3. Connect the hoses to the canister, making sure they are all in their original positions.

Electric Fuel Pump

Removal

1. Disconnect the wiring for the gauge and pump at the rear harness connector.

2. Raise the vehicle on a hoist.

3. Drain the fuel tank.

4. Disconnect the fuel line hose at the gauge unit pickup line and the tank vent lines to the vapor separator.

5. Remove the gauge ground wire screw at the underbody floorpan.

6. Unscrew the retaining cam ring with a large spanner wrench and remove the fuel pump-tank unit assembly.

Fuel Pump Replacement

1. Remove the flat wire conductor from the plastic clip on the fuel tube.

2. Squeeze the clamp and pull the pump straight back about ½ in.

3. Remove the conductor wires and nuts from the pump terminals.

4. Squeeze the clamp and pull the pump straight back to remove it from the tank unit. Be careful not to bend the circular support bracket.

5. Slide the new pump into position, until it rests against the rubber coupling. Make sure the pump has the rubber isolator and the saran strainer attached.

6. Connect the two wires to the pump terminals with the lockwashers and nuts. The flat conductor is attached to the terminal farthest from the float arm.

7. Squeeze the clamp and push the pump into the rubber coupling.

8. Replace the flat wire conductor in the plastic clip on the fuel pick-up tube.

Installation

1. Install the fuel pump assembly in the fuel tank.

2. Install the retaining cam ring, preferably using a spanner.

3. Connect the wires and complete installation by reversing Steps 1 through 4 of the removal procedure above.

4. Lower the vehicle, start the engine and check for leaks.

Fuel Filter R & R

1. Disconnect the fuel line at the intake fuel filter nut on the carburetor.

2. Remove the intake fuel filter nut.

3. Remove the filter element and spring.

4. Replace the filter element every 12,000 miles or 12 months, whichever comes first. Inspect the filter element to determine its serviceability.

5. Install the element spring and element. Bronze filters (2-barrel)

are installed with the conical section facing out and with a gasket between the filter element and the fuel intake nut.

6. Install the nut using a new gasket and tightening securely.
7. Install fuel line and tighten the connector.

Carburetor Mixture and Idle Speed Adjustment

Due to the delicate balance of tuning factors required to maintain low exhaust pollutant emission, the mixture adjustment should only be made when all other possible causes of poor idle condition have been thoroughly checked and eliminated. Normally, the idle mixture is adjusted only after carburetor overhaul, throttle body part replacement, mixture needle part replacement, or limiter cap and needle removal. Idle mixture adjustment screw limiter caps are installed at the factory to discourage nonessential tuning of the mixture.

Idle speed and mixture adjustment must be made according to the following procedure:

NOTE: this adjustment is made with the air cleaner installed.

1. Follow all the instructions on the vehicle tune-up sticker (this decal is conspicuously placed on the underside of the hood). The procedures and conditions apply:
   a. All adjustments are made with the engine at normal operating temperature and the air conditioning on, with the choke valve and air cleaner damper door fully open, and with automatic transmission in Drive or manual transmission in Neutral.
   b. The ignition timing and the dwell are according to specifications.
   c. Disconnect the Fuel Tank line from the vapor canister.
   d. Disconnect vacuum advance hose from the distributor and plug the hose.
   e. Disconnect the wire from the anti-dieseling solenoid.
   f. Adjust the idle speed to the specified rpm (Column 2 in chart).
   g. Reconnect the wire to the anti-dieseling solenoid and adjust the solenoid screw to obtain the specified rpm (Column 4 in chart).
2. Leave the distributor vacuum hose and the fuel tank vapor hose disconnected while performing the remainder of the adjustments.
3. If not already removed, remove the idle mixture screw limiter cap(s).
4. Turn the idle mixture screw(s) in until there is light contact

with the seat, then back out four full turns.

5. Adjust the idle speed screw to obtain Initial Idle Speed (Column 1 in the chart below).
6. Adjust the mixture screw(s) in (equally if there two) to obtain the specified CO percentage in the exhaust gas. This measurement can only be made with an exhaust gas analyzer. If this CO analyzer is unavailable, adjust the screw (s) to obtain the Final Idle Speed specified in Column 2 of the chart below.
7. If an exhaust analyzer was used, adjust the idle speed screw again to obtain the Final Idle Speed specified in Column 2 of the chart below.
8. Install service idle limiter cap(s) on the mixture screw(s).
9. Connect the distributor vacuum hose and the fuel tank vapor hose.

Throttle Solenoid Adjustment

NOTE: this adjustment is made with the air cleaner installed.

1. With the engine warmed, the choke fully open and the air conditioning on, disconnect:
   a. Fuel tank hose from the vapor canister.
   b. Distributor vacuum hose at the carburetor (plug the hose).
   c. Electrical connection at the solenoid.
2. Adjust the ignition timing and dwell angle.
3. Adjust the carburetor idle speed screw to obtain the Final Idle Speed specified in Column 2 of the Carburetor Adjustment Specifications chart.
4. Connect the wire to the solenoid.
5. Open the throttle momentarily and adjust the solenoid screw to the speed specified in Column 4 of the Carburetor Adjustment Specifications chart.
6. Connect the distributor vacuum hose and the fuel vapor hose.

Exhaust System

The exhaust system consists of a single exhaust pipe, a transverse mounted muffler and a short tail pipe.

The exhaust pipe is clamped to the muffler and the tail pipe and muffler are integral.

When replacing the muffler, it is recommended that the tailpipe be replaced at the same time. The exhaust pipe is suspended only by its connections to the exhaust manifold and muffler. When installing the exhaust pipe, loosely clamp it to the muffler, then install it securely to the exhaust manifold before tightening the clamp bolt.

Cooling System

Vega engine cooling is of conventional design incorporating a centrifugal vane impeller type water pump which circulates the coolant in a cycle from engine to radiator. The system operates under pressure to increase cooling efficiency and utilizes a thermostat to maintain operating temperature.

There are two radiators: a standard type and a larger heavy duty radiator equipped with a fan shroud.

Radiator R & R

1. Drain the radiator.
2. On models with the heavy duty radiator, remove the fan shroud as described below.
3. Disconnect the intake and outlet hoses.
4. Remove the two screws which secure the fan guard to the radiator support, then remove the support and the two radiator pads.
   NOTE: on vehicles with the heavy duty radiator, remove the two upper brackets (instead of the single support).
5. Lift the radiator up and out of the lower brackets.
6. To install, reverse the removal procedure.

Fan Shroud R & R

1. Remove the two screws which secure the shroud to the upper radiator brackets.
2. Remove the screw which holds the two halves of the shroud together at the lower left-hand corner.
3. Remove the left and right sections of the shroud from the

Carburetor Adjustment Specifications

Transmission	Engine	Column 1 Initial Idle Speed (rpm)	Column 2 Final Idle Speed (rpm)	Column 3 % CO @ Idle	Column 4 Solenoid Adjustment (rpm)
Manual in Neutral	90 H.P.	730	700	2.0	850
	110 H.P.	730	700	2.0	1200
Automatic in Drive	90 H.P.	570	550	2.0	650
	110 H.P.	570	550	2.0	700

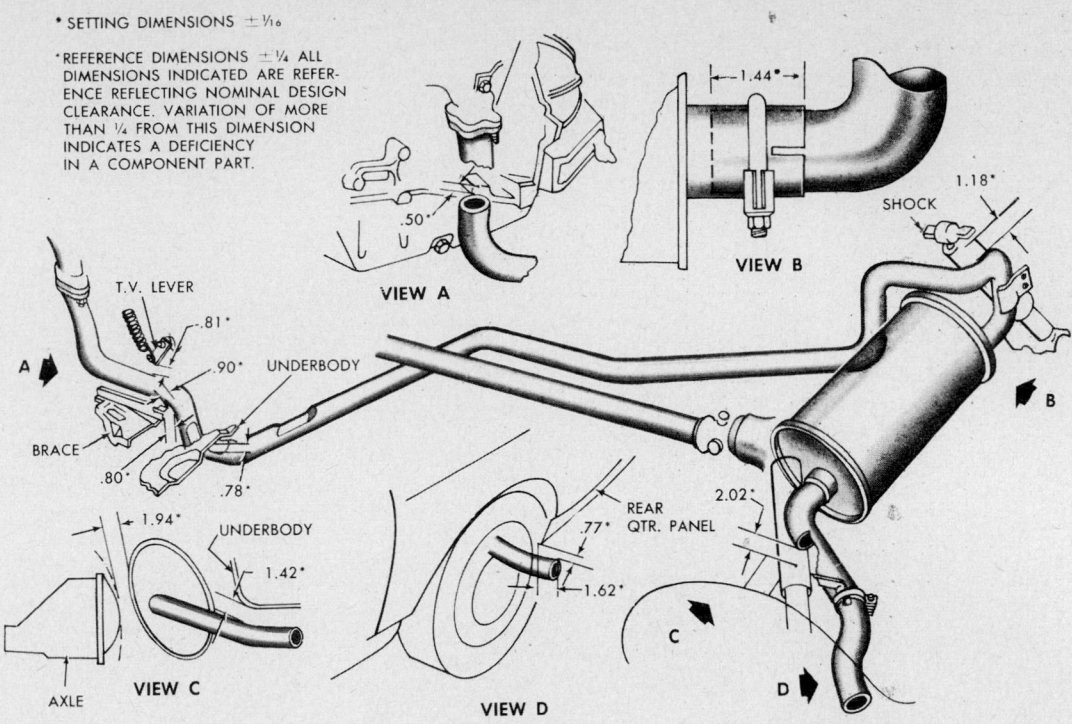

* SETTING DIMENSIONS ±1/10

*REFERENCE DIMENSIONS ±1/4 ALL
DIMENSIONS INDICATED ARE REFER-
ENCE REFLECTING NOMINAL DESIGN
CLEARANCE. VARIATION OF MORE
THAN 1/4 FROM THIS DIMENSION
INDICATES A DEFICIENCY
IN A COMPONENT PART.

VIEW A

VIEW B

T.V. LEVER

.81*

A

.90* UNDERBODY

BRACE

.80* .78*

.50*

SHOCK

1.18*

B

1.94* UNDERBODY

1.42*

REAR
QTR. PANEL

.77*

1.62*

2.02*

C

D

AXLE

VIEW C

VIEW D

Exhaust system (© Chevrolet Division, G.M. Corp.)

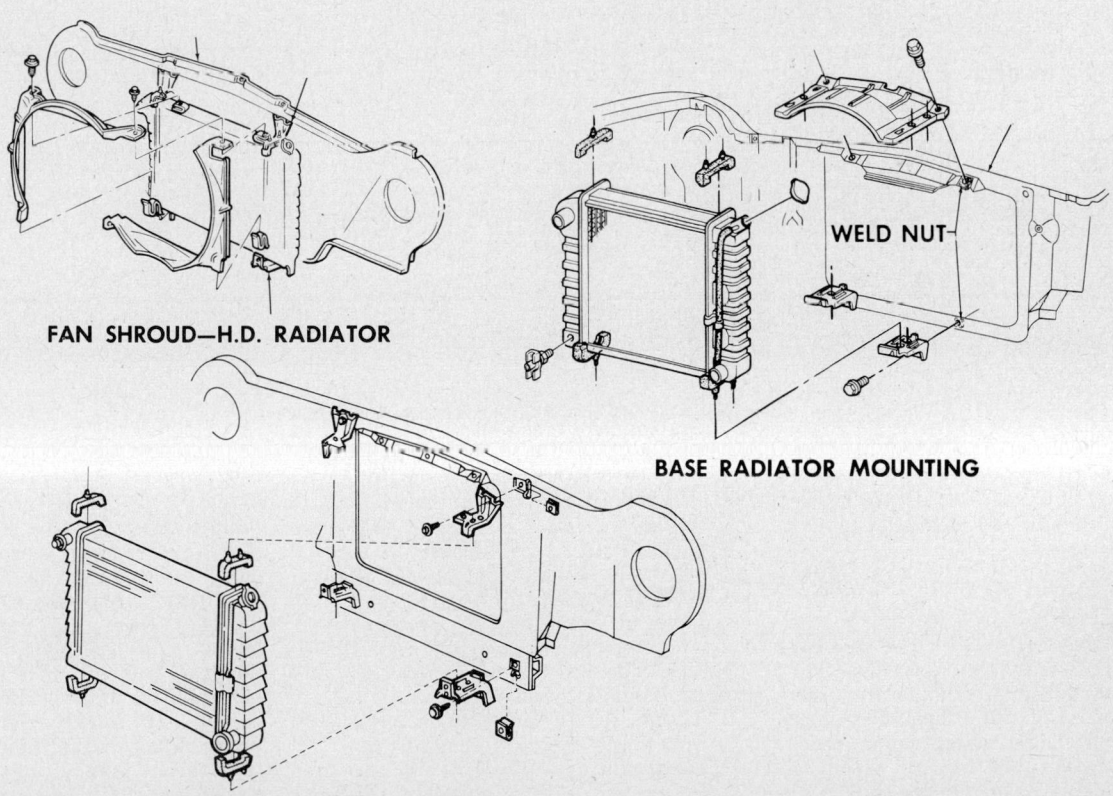

FAN SHROUD—H.D. RADIATOR

WELD NUT

BASE RADIATOR MOUNTING

H.D. RADIATOR MOUNTING

Radiator installation (© Chevrolet Division, G.M. Corp.)

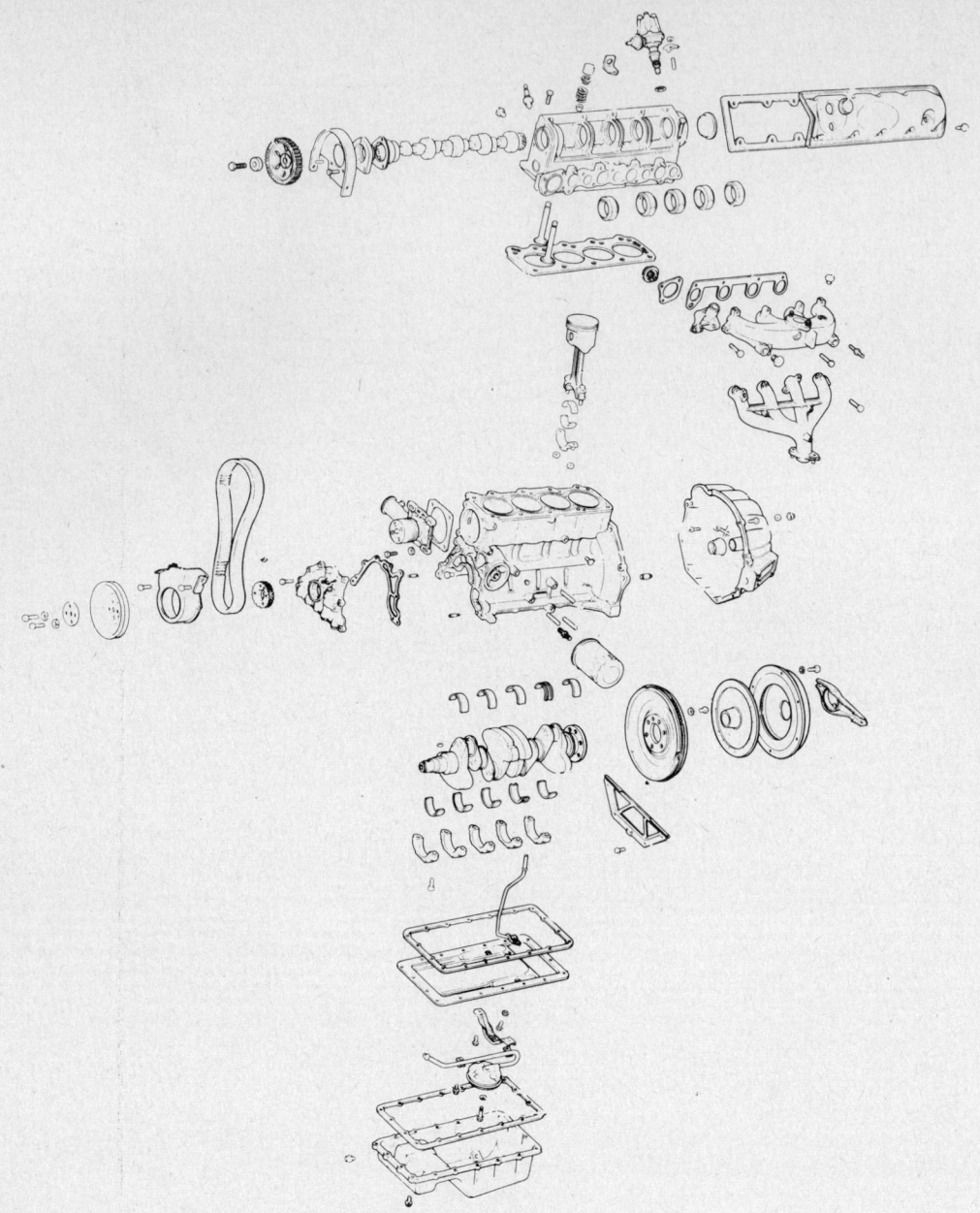

Vega 140 cu. in. OHC engine (© Chevrolet Division, G.M. Corp.)

clips at the bottom of the radiator.

4. To install, reverse the above procedure.

Water Pump R & R

The water pump is located on the front of the engine block immediately above the crankshaft pulley. The pump bearings are permanently lubricated during manufacture and do not require periodic maintenance other than keeping the air vent (top of housing) and drain holes (bottom of housing) free of dirt and grease.

The pump components cannot be serviced separately and, in the event of pump failure, the complete assembly must be replaced as a unit, as follows:

1. Raise the hood and install a bolt through the hood hold-open link.

2. Disconnect the battery negative cable.

3. Remove the fan and spacer.

Caution   No attempt should be made to repair a bent or damaged fan. The fan assembly must be in proper balance and an improperly balanced fan may cause extensive damage.

4. Loosen, but do not remove, the two lower timing belt cover retaining screws. The holes in the cover are slotted so that the cover is easily removed.

5. Remove the two upper timing belt cover retaining screws and remove the cover.

6. Drain the coolant.

7. Loosen the water pump bolts to relieve the tension on the timing belt.

8. Remove the hoses from the water pump.

9. Remove the water pump bolts, pump and gasket.

10. Thoroughly clean the old gasket material from the pump and block.

11. To install, position the water pump on the block using a new gasket and loosely install the water pump bolts. Make sure that the V grooves of the belt are aligned with the grooves in the water pump.

NOTE: use an anti-seize compound on the water pump bolt threads.

12. Using tool J-23564 inserted in the gauge hole to the right of the pump, apply 15 ft. lbs. torque to

the water pump while tightening the water pump bolts to 15 ft. lbs.

13. Install the radiator and heater hoses to the pump.

14. Install the timing belt cover, lowering the cover lower screw slots over the screws. Loosely tighten the screws against the cover.

15. Install the two upper timing cover screws, then tighten the upper and lower screws to 50 in. lbs.

16. Install the fan spacer and fan, tightening the bolts to 20 ft. lbs.

17. Fill the cooling system, connect the battery negative cable, start the engine and check for leaks

18. Remove the bolt from the hood hold-open link and close the hood.

Engine

The Vega engine is a single overhead camshaft, four-cylinder design using a die cast aluminum cylinder block and a cast iron cylinder head. The iron-plated aluminum pistons ride directly on honed and electrochemically treated aluminum bores. The cylinder block is cast of an alloy containing silicon which, after suitable etching, provides a proper bore surface for the pistons and rings.

The valve train is completely contained in the head, with a straight-line vertical valve configuration. The camshaft is driven by a timing belt which in turn is driven from a front crankshaft pulley.

The 140 cu. in. engine is available in the base 90 H.P. single-barrel and an optional 110 H.P. two-barrel version.

Emission Control

All Vega models are equipped with exhaust emission control systems to reduce the amount of pollution each vehicle contributes to the atmosphere. Crankcase vapors are drawn off by manifold vacuum, metered through the PCV valve and are finally burned during combustion.

The Controlled Combustion System increases combustion efficiency by means of leaner carburetor adjustments and revised distributor advance. Most models will be equipped with an air intake heater to maintain hotter intake air (100°F or above) in order to support the leaner carburetor mixture.

The Transmission Controlled Spark (TCS) System allows for the regulation of vacuum distributor advance by the transmission. Distributor vacuum advance is eliminated in low range on vehicles equipped with automatic transmissions, in first and second gear on vehicles equipped

with three and four speed manual transmissions, and in reverse on all vehicles. A transmission switch energizes a solenoid which functions as a valve in the vacuum line. When the solenoid is de-energized, the distributor vacuum line is vented to the atmosphere through the air cleaner. There is a thermostatic override switch which allows for full vacuum in all gears when the engine is cold.

The emission of fuel vapors into the atmosphere is controlled by using manifold vacuum, to draw fuel tank vapors from the carburetor bowl into a carbon canister, where they are condensed and later drawn into the intake manifold for combustion.

A more complete discussion of emission control systems may be found in the Unit Repair Section.

Engine Removal

1. Raise the hood and install a bolt in the hold-open link.

2. Disconnect the battery positive cable at the battery and the negative cable at the engine block (except on air conditioned vehicles).

3. Drain the cooling system and disconnect the hoses at the radiator.

4. Disconnect the heater hoses at the water pump and at the heater inlet (bottom hose).

5. Disconnect the following emission hoses:
   a. PCV at the cam cover.
   b. The canister vacuum hose at the carburetor.
   c. PCV vacuum hose at the intake manifold.
   d. Bowl vent at the carburetor.

6. Remove the radiator, fan, fan spacer and air cleaner.

7. Disconnect the following electrical leads:
   a. Alternator.
   b. Ignition coil.
   c. Starter solenoid.
   d. Oil pressure sending unit.
   e. Temperature sending unit.
   f. TCS switch at the transmission.
   g. TCS solenoid.
   h. Ground strap at the firewall.

8. Disconnect:
   a. Automatic transmission throttle valve linkage at the manifold mounted bellcrank.
   b. Fuel line at the rubber hose, rearward of the carburetor.
   c. Transmission vacuum modulator and air conditioning vacuum line at the intake manifold.
   d. Throttle cable at the manifold bellcrank.

9. On cars with air conditioning, disconnect the compressor at the front support, rear support, rear lower bracket and remove the drive belt from the compressor.

10. Being careful not to crimp or bend the hoses, and move the compressor slightly forward, allowing the front of the compressor to rest on the frame forward brace. Secure the rear of the compressor to the engine compartment so that it does not interfere with the engine removal.

11. If so equipped, disconnect the power steering pump and position it out of the way.

12. Raise the car on a hoist.

13. Disconnect the exhaust pipe at the exhaust manifold.

14. Remove the engine flywheel dust cover or the converter underpan.

15. On vehicles equipped with automatic transmission:
   a. Remove the convertor to flywheel retaining bolts and install a converter safety strap.
   b. Remove the converter housing to engine retaining bolts.
   c. Loosen the engine front mount retaining bolts at the frame attachment and lower the vehicle on the hoist.
   d. Install a floor jack under the transmission and an engine lifting adapter to raise the engine slightly from its mounts.
   e. Remove the engine front mount retaining bolts.
   f. Remove the engine from the vehicle. Pull the engine forward enough to clear the transmission while slowly lifting the engine.

16. On vehicles with manual transmission:
   a. Remove the flywheel housing to engine retaining bolts.
   b. Proceed with Step 15 above, parts c, d, e and f.

Manifolds

Intake Manifold R & R

1. Raise the hood and install a bolt through the hold-open link.

2. Disconnect the negative battery cable.

3. Drain the cooling system.

4. Disconnect the heater hose at the fitting on the intake manifold.

5. Disconnect the vent tube at the base of the air cleaner, then remove the air cleaner.

6. Remove the air cleaner silencer.

7. Disconnect:
   a. The choke rod at the carburetor.
   b. PCV valve at the cam cover.
   c. Fuel line at the carburetor.
   d. The carburetor bowl vent line at the carburetor.
   e. Throttle linkage and the transmission throttle valve linkage.
   f. Power steering pump brace at the manifold.

8. Remove the alternator to thermostat housing through-bolt and loosen the alternator swivel bolt. Move the alternator aside to gain access to the manifold bolt.
9. Remove the four intake manifold bolts and remove the manifold.
10. Remove from the manifold:
    a. The carburetor and carburetor linkage.
    b. Pipe plug.
    c. Vacuum fittings.
    d. Hot water nipple.
11. Install the items removed in Step 10 above to the new manifold.
12. Clean the gasket surfaces on the manifold and the cylinder head.
13. Position a new gasket over the dowels on the cylinder head, then carefully install the manifold. Make sure that the gasket remains in place.
14. Install the manifold bolts, tightening to 30 ft. lbs. The stud goes in the hole nearest No. 3 intake port.
15. Connect the power steering pump brace to the manifold.
16. Install the alternator to thermostat housing through bolt and adjust the belt tension.
17. Connect:
    a. The choke rod at the carburetor.
    b. The PCV valve at the cam cover.
    c. Fuel line at the carburetor.
    d. Carburetor bowl vent line at the carburetor.
    e. The throttle and transmission throttle valve linkage.
    f. Vacuum connections at the carburetor.
18. Install the air cleaner silencer and secure it to the heat stove tube.
19. Install the air cleaner. Connect the vent tube at the base of the air cleaner.
20. Connect the heater hose to the intake manifold fitting and fill the cooling system.
21. Connect the negative battery cable and start the engine. Check for leaks and adjust the carburetor.
22. Check and adjust the ignition timing and dwell.
23. Remove the safety bolt from the hood hold-open link and close the hood.

Exhaust Manifold R & R

1. Raise the car on a hoist and disconnect the exhaust pipe from the manifold. Lower the vehicle.
2. Remove the intake manifold as described above.
3. Disconnect the oil dipstick bracket at the exhaust manifold.
4. Remove the exhaust manifold bolts, then remove the manifold

and carburetor heater assembly.
5. Install the carburetor heater assembly on the new manifold.
6. Install the exhaust manifold and manifold bolts (loosely). The upper manifold bolts are 1-1/2 in. and the lower bolts are 2-1/4 in.
7. Tighten the manifold bolts to 30 ft. lbs.
8. Raise the vehicle on a hoist and connect the exhaust pipe to the manifold.
9. Connect the oil dipstick bracket to the exhaust manifold.
10. Install the intake manifold as described above.

Cylinder Head

Removal

1. Remove the engine front cover and camshaft cover.
2. Remove the timing belt and camshaft sprocket.
3. Remove the intake and exhaust manifolds.
4. Disconnect the water hose at the thermostat housing (outlet).
5. Remove the cylinder head bolts, then the head and gasket.

Disassembly

1. Remove the camshaft retainer and the timing belt upper cover
2. Remove the camshaft, tappets, valve springs, stem seals and valves.
3. Remove the spark plugs and thermostat housing.

Assembly

1. Clean and inspect the valve train components.
2. Install the valves, stem seals, valve springs and tappets.
3. Install the camshaft and timing belt upper cover (use a new gasket), camshaft retainer (use a new seal) and camshaft sprocket.
4. Check and adjust the camshaft end-play.

5. Install the spark plugs.
6. Clean the thermostat housing gasket surface and install the housing, using a new gasket.
7. Clean the top of the pistons and the gasket surface of the block.

Installation

1. Using a new gasket (smooth side up), carefully position the cylinder head on the block.
2. Install the cylinder head bolts finger-tight. Use an anti-seize compound on the threads. Install the lifting bracket under the second head bolt from the front on the spark plug side. The 6-3/8 in. bolts are installed on the manifold side and the 5-5/8 in. bolts are installed on the spark plug side.
3. Tighten the head bolts to 60 ft. lbs. (in steps), using the illustration.
4. Connect the water hose to the thermostat housing.
5. Install the intake and exhaust manifolds.
6. Install the timing belt and sprocket.
7. Install the front cover and camshaft cover.

Front Cover R & R

1. Raise the hood and install a bolt in the hood hold-open link.
2. Disconnect the negative battery cable.
3. Remove the fan and spacer.
4. Loosen the two lower cover retaining screws.
5. Remove the two top cover retaining screws and remove the cover, lifting it until the slots clear the lower screws.
6. To install, position the cover, lowering it until the slots are over the lower screws. Loosely tighten the lower screws.
7. Install the upper screws, then tighten all four screws to 50 in. lbs.

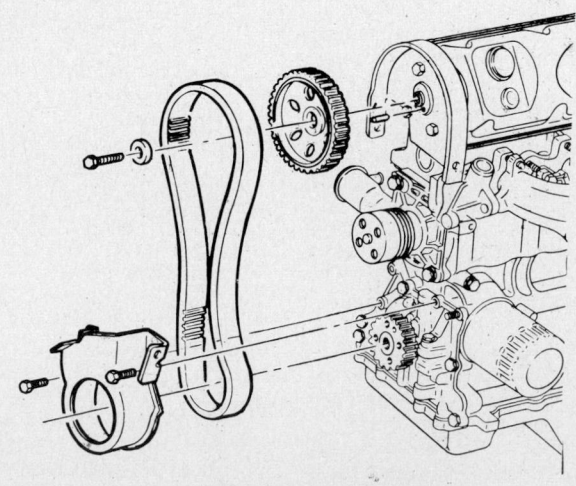

Timing belt and sprockets
(© Chevrolet Division, G.M. Corp.)

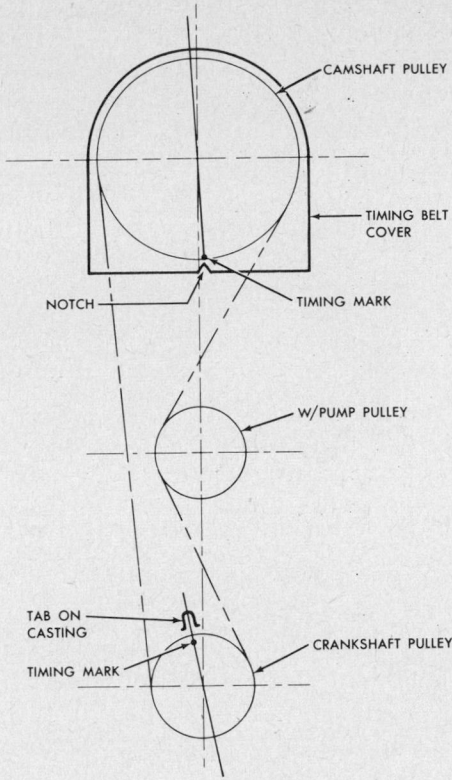

CAMSHAFT PULLEY

TIMING BELT COVER

NOTCH

TIMING MARK

W/PUMP PULLEY

TAB ON CASTING

TIMING MARK

CRANKSHAFT PULLEY

Timing sprocket alignment marks
(© Chevrolet Division, G.M. Corp.)

J-23591

Installing camshaft removing tool
(© Chevrolet Division, G.M. Corp.)

with the keyway on the crankshaft. Install the damper locating dowel in the locating hole of the sprocket.

20. Loosely install the four sprocket bolts, then install the crankshaft (center) bolt. Tighten the crankshaft bolt to 80 ft. lbs. and the four sprocket bolts to 15 ft. lbs.

21. Install the alternater and air conditioning compressor as applicable and adjust the belts.

22. Install the engine front cover, fan and fan spacer.

23. Connect the battery cable and remove the bolt from the hood hold-open link.

Camshaft Cover R & R

1. Raise the hood and install a bolt in the hood hold-open link.
2. Disconnect the negative battery cable.
3. Remove the air cleaner and the vent tube (at cam cover).
4. Remove the PCV valve from the cam cover.
5. Remove the cam cover screws and the cover.
6. To install, reverse the above procedure. The gasket is reusable. The oil filler cap is at the forward end of the cover. Tighten the cam cover screws to 35 in. lbs.

Camshaft Removal

1. Remove the hood.
2. Remove the camshaft timing sprocket.
3. Remove the three screws securing the camshaft seal and retainer assembly and timing cover to the cylinder head.
4. Inspect the seal, prying it out and replacing it if necessary.
5. Remove the camshaft cover.
6. Disconnect the fuel line at the carburetor.
7. Remove:
   a. Idle solenoid from its bracket.
   b. The choke coil, cover and rod assembly.
   c. Ignition distributor.

8. Install the spacer and fan, tightening the bolts to 20 ft. lbs.
9. Connect the battery cable and remove the bolt from the hood hold-open link.

Timing Belt and Sprocket R & R

1. Raise the hood and install a bolt in the hood hold-open link.
2. Disconnect the negative battery cable.
3. Loosen the air conditioner and alternator as necessary and remove the drive belts.
4. Remove the crankshaft pulley and four pulley-to-sprocket bolts Remove the pulley and damper or washer as applicable.
   NOTE: it is not necessary to remove the pulley if only the camshaft sprocket is being removed.
5. Drain the engine coolant and loosen the water pump bolts to relieve the tension on the timing belt.
6. Remove the timing belt lower cover.
7. Remove the timing belt.
8. Align one of the holes in the camshaft timing sprocket with the head bolt behind the sprocket. Using a socket on the head bolt to keep the sprocket from rotating, remove the sprocket retaining bolt and washer.

9. Remove the camshaft sprocket.
10. The crankshaft sprocket may be removed.
11. To install the crankshaft sprocket, use tool J-23523. Make sure that the timing mark is facing out and that the key is installed.
12. To install the camshaft sprocket, align the dowel in the camshaft with the locating hole in the end of the camshaft.
13. Install the sprocket retaining bolt, tightening to 80 ft. lbs.
14. Align the timing mark on the cam sprocket with the notch on the timing belt upper cover and the crankshaft sprocket timing mark with the cast rib on the oil pump cover.
15. Install the timing belt on the crankshaft sprocket, then with the back of the belt position in the water pump track, install the belt on the camshaft sprocket. Make sure that both sprockets maintain their indexed positions.
16. Install the lower timing belt cover, using anti-sieze compound on the threads of the bolts and tightening them to 50 in. lbs.
17. Adjust the timing belt tension as described under Water Pump R&R above, Steps 11 and 12.
18. Fill the cooling system.
19. Install the accessory drive pulley to the crankshaft sprocket, aligning the tang on the pulley

Camshaft bearing alignment
(© Chevrolet Division, G.M. Corp.)

Valve tappet and adjusting screw assembly
(© Chevrolet Division, G.M. Corp.)

8. Raise the vehicle on a hoist, disconnect the front engine mounts at the body attachment, raise the front of the engine and install wood blocks, about 1-½ in. thick, between the engine mounts and the body.
9. Install camshaft removal tool J-23591 on the cylinder head to hold down the lifters so that the camshaft may be removed.
   a. Position the tool J-23591 so that the attaching holes are aligned with the lower cam cover bolt holes and the tappet levers of the tool are aligned to depress both valves of each cylinder.
   b. Back off the bolts in the bottom of the tool so that they are not contacting the bosses beneath the tool.
   c. Install the tool attaching bolts, tightening them securely.
   d. Tighten the bolts in the bottom of the tool until they just touch the bosses of the cylinder head.
   e. Grease the ball end of the lever depressing bolts and tighten the bolts to depress the tappets.

NOTE: torque the lever bolts to 10 ft. lbs. If more tightening is required, check to see that the tool is properly installed, then proceed cautiously to prevent damaging the depressing lever.
10. Slide the camshaft forward until it clears the head.

NOTE: the camshaft bearings may be removed. It is not necessary to remove the camshaft end plug. Gently tap out the bearings, starting at the forward end. Tap out the rear bearing slowly into the distributor housing, being careful not to unseat the end plug. Crush the rear bearing to remove it from the distributor housing. Install, starting with the rear bearing. The oil holes in the bearings must align with the oil holes in the case. On the first two bearings the oil holes are in the 11 o'clock (as seen from the front of the engine) and the oil groove in the number one

bearing toward the front of the engine.

Camshaft Installation

1. Install the camshaft with the journals seated in the bores.
2. With the car up on a hoist, raise the front of the engine and remove the wood blocks from the engine mounts.
3. Install the front engine mounts, then lower the vehicle.
4. Using a new gasket, install the timing belt upper cover and retainer plate and seal assembly. Tighten the retaining bolts to 15 ft. lbs.
5. Using a dial indicator, measure the camshaft end-play. If it is not 0.004-0.012 in., select a camshaft retainer (according to cam locator thickness) which will provide more or less end-play as required.
6. Remove the tappet depressing tool J-23591 by first releasing the tappet depressing lever bolts then removing the tool attaching bolts.
7. Install:
   a. Camshaft timing sprocket.
   b. The timing belt.
   c. Front engine cover.
   d. Distributor.
   e. Vehicle hood.
8. Adjust the valve tappets.
9. Install the camshaft cover.

10. Install and adjust the carburetor choke coil, cover and rod assembly.
11. Connect the carburetor fuel line.
12. Install the idle solenoid to the bracket.
13. Check and adjust the ignition timing.

Valve Tappet Removal

NOTE: the tappet adjusting screw may be replaced without removing the tappet from the engine.

1. Remove the camshaft as described above.
2. Release the tension on the tappet depressing levers and slide the levers to one side.
3. Remove the tappet and adjusting screw assembly. Identify each tappet so that it may be installed in its original position.
4. Remove the adjusting screw from the tappet.

NOTE: identify each adjusting screw and the tappet from which it was removed. Tappet adjusting screws may be standard, or one of two undersizes.

Valve Tappet Installation

1. Install the adjusting screw in the tappet (hole nearer the top of the tappet).
2. With the flat side of the adjusting screw facing down, install the tappet in its original bore.
3. Depress the tappet with tool J-23591 and install the camshaft as described above.
4. Adjust the valve lash as described below.

Valve Lash Adjustment

1. Valve lash is adjusted with the tappet on the base circle of the camshaft lobe.
2. Rotate the camshaft until the timing mark on the sprocket is aligned with the inverted V notch on the timing belt upper cover. The following valves may be adjusted:
   a. No. 1 cylinder—intake and exhaust.
   b. No. 2 cylinder—intake.
   c. No. 3 cylinder—exhaust.
3. Measuring the clearance between the tappet and the cam lobe with a feeler gauge, turn the adjusting screw to obtain 0.014-0.016 in. cold lash on the intake and 0.029-0.031 in. cold lash on the exhaust. Use an Allen (hex) wrench to turn the

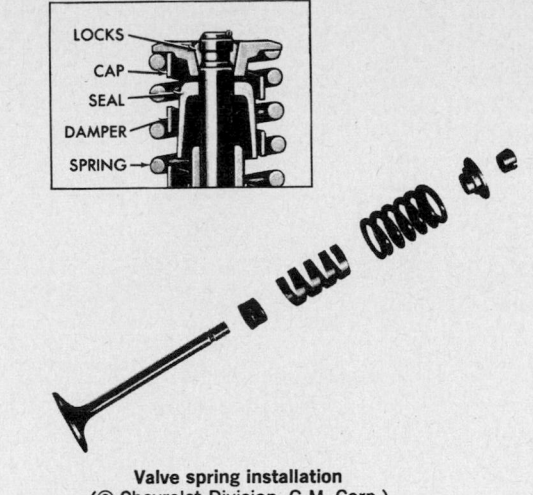

Valve spring installation
(© Chevrolet Division, G.M. Corp.)

Compressing valve springs
(© Chevrolet Division, G.M. Corp.)

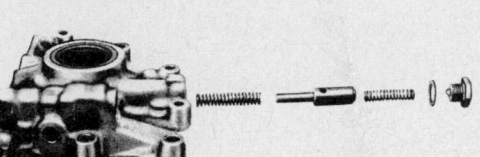

Oil pump pressure regulator
(© Chevrolet Division, G.M. Corp.)

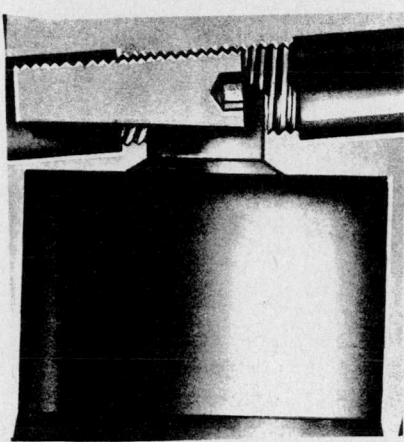

Adjusting valve lash
(© Chevrolet Division, G.M. Corp.)

adjusting screw.

NOTE: the adjusting screw is threaded on all areas except the valve stem contact surface. The flat surface must always be down. Adjustment is made in increments of one complete revolution only, always resulting in the flat side of the adjusting screw facing directly downward. Each complete revolution of the adjusting screw will result in a 0.003 in. change of valve lash.

4. Rotate the camshaft sprocket 180° so that the timing mark is at 12 o'clock position and aligned with the notch on the timing belt cover. The following valves may be adjusted:
   a. No. 2 cylinder—exhaust.
   b. No. 3 cylinder—intake.
   c. No. 4 cylinder—intake and exhaust.

Valve Stem Oil Seal Replacement

1. Remove the valve tappet, and leave the tappet compressing tool in place.
2. Remove the spark plug at the cylinder to be serviced.
3. With the crankshaft position 90° from top dead center, install an air line adapter in the spark plug hole and apply air pressure to hold the valves in place.

4. Use tool J-23592 to compress the valve spring, then remove the valve keepers.
5. Remove the valve cap, valve spring and damper assembly and the valve stem oil seal.
6. Install a new valve stem oil seal over the valve guide.
7. Install the valve spring and damper assembly and the valve cap over the valve stem.
8. Compress the valve spring and install the keepers.
9. Remove the air line adaptor too and install the spark plug.
10. Install the valve tappet.
11. Adjust the tappets.
12. Install all of the components which were removed. See Camshaft Installation above.

Valve Guides

Valves with oversize stems are available in three sizes: 0.003 in. o/s, 0.015 in. o/s and 0.030 in. o/s. Remove the cylinder head and remove the camshaft from the head. Remove the valves. Ream the valve guides with an appropriate oversize reamer.

Engine Lubrication

The oil pump is crankshaft driven, externally mounted on the front of the engine, and is an eccentric gear

type. Oil flow from the pump is at 40-45 psi and leads directly to the oil filter. There are two main oil galleys: the crankcase main galley and the cylinder head main galley. The main and rod bearings are lubricated from the crankcase galley. The cylinder head galley is supplied with oil from the front main bearing, which acts as a metering device, through a vertical passage in the block. The head galley has five passages to the cam bearings, from which all valve train components are lubricated. At the rear end of the head galley there is a short passage which supplies oil pressure for the distributor damper.

Oil Pan and Baffle R & R

1. Raise the vehicle on a hoist and drain the engine oil.
2. Support the engine with a jack and remove the frame crossmember and both front crossmember braces.
3. Disconnect the steering idler arm at the frame side rail. On vehicles with air conditioning, disconnect the idler arm at the relay rod.
4. Mark the position of the steering linkage pitman arm to the steering gear pitman shaft and remove the pitman arm.

NOTE: do not rotate the steering gear pitman shaft while the linkage

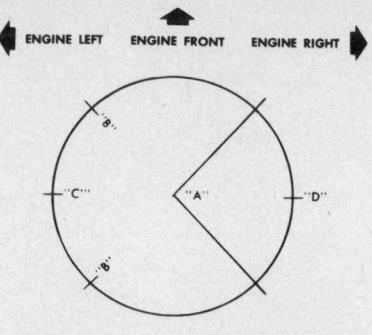

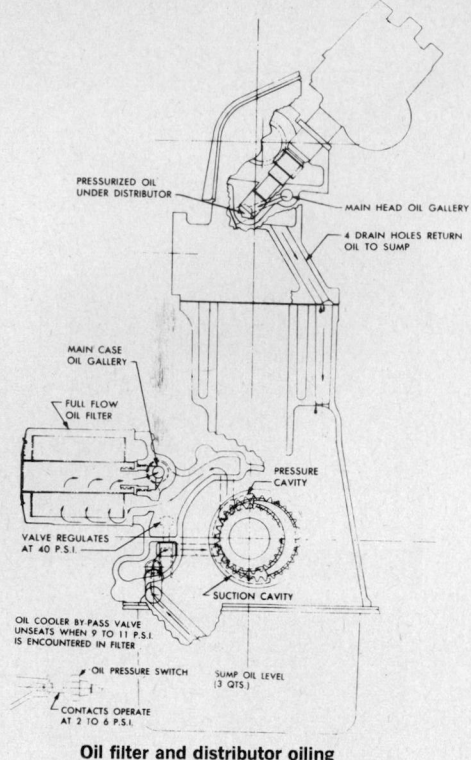

"A" OIL RING SPACER GAP   "C" 2ND COMPRESSION RING GAP
"B" OIL RING RAIL GAPS   "D" TOP COMPRESSION RING GAP

Ring gap locations
(© Chevrolet Division, G.M. Corp.)

Oil filter and distributor oiling
(© Chevrolet Division, G.M. Corp.)

is disconnected, because the steering wheel alignment will be changed.

5. Remove the flywheel cover or converter underpan.
6. Remove the oil pan bolts, tap the oil pan to break the seal, then remove the pan.
7. Remove the pick-up screen-to-support retaining bolt and the pick-up screen-to-baffle support bolts, then remove the support from the baffle.
8. Remove the bolt which secures the oil drain back tube to the baffle, then rotate the baffle 90° toward the left side of the car and remove the baffle from the pick-up screen.
9. The oil pump screen and pick up tube may be removed as follows:
   a. Remove the two self-locking mounting bolts (in block).
   b. Lightly tap on the U section of the pick-up tube to remove the tube from the casting.
   c. If damaged, the tube and screen assembly are replaced as a unit.
   d. Apply sealing compound to the pick-up tube sealing surface.
   e. Install the tube into its bore, using an open end wrench on the tube boss, tapping the wrench with a mallet. Make sure that the retaining brackets are aligned with the bolt holes.
   f. Using anti-seize compound on the threads, install the re-

taining bolts. Tighten the bolts to 25 ft. lbs.

10. Install the oil pan and baffle in the reverse order of removal. Use sealing compound on the oil pump gasket surface. Tighten the oil pan bolts to 15 ft. lbs. See Steering Linkage R&R for correct pitman arm and idler arm installation procedure. Tighten frame crossmember and brace bolts to 35 ft. lbs.

Oil Pump R & R

1. Remove:
   a. Front engine cover.
   b. Accessory drive pulley.
   c. Timing belt.
   d. Timing belt lower cover.
   e. Crankshaft sprocket.
2. Raise the vehicle on a hoist and drain the engine oil.
3. Remove the oil pan and baffle.
4. Remove the oil pump bolts and the pump.
5. Inspect the oil pump for wear. The pump gears and body are not serviced separately. Replacement of the entire oil pump is required. Check the pressure regulator for free operation.
6. When installing, clean all gasket surfaces. Be sure that the pump drive key is installed properly. Use anti-seize compound to the threads of the pump mounting bolts, tightening them to 15 ft. lbs. The stud is installed in the upper right (facing pump) and tightened to 30 ft. lbs. Install the

oil pan before tightening the timing cover bolts.

Oil Pump (Front Cover) Seal R & R

1. Remove the following:
   a. Engine front cover.
   b. Accessory drive pulley.
   c. Timing belt.
   d. Timing belt lower cover.
   e. Crankshaft timing sprocket.
2. Pry out the old seal, being careful not to damage the housing seal surfaces.
3. Coat the lips of the new seal with oil and apply sealing compound to the outside diameter of the seal.
4. Install the seal with the closed end outward.
5. Install all components removed in Step 1 above.

Crankshaft, Piston & Rod Assembly

Piston & Rod R & R

1. Remove the intake and exhaust manifolds, cylinder head, oil pan and baffle.
2. Check the connecting rods and caps for cylinder number identification and, if necessary, mark them.
3. Using a ridge reamer, remove any ridge or deposits from the upper end of the cylinder bore.
4. Remove the connecting rod cap and install protective tubes on the studs. Push the piston and connecting rod assembly out the top of the block.
5. The piston and wrist pin are a matched set and not serviced separately. Oversize pistons are not available since bore reconditioning is not recommended. Production pistons are available in four size ranges, for selected fit to each cylinder bore: 3.4977-3.4982 in., 3.4982-3.4987 in., 3.4987-3.4992 in. and 3.4992-3.4997 in. To fit the pis-

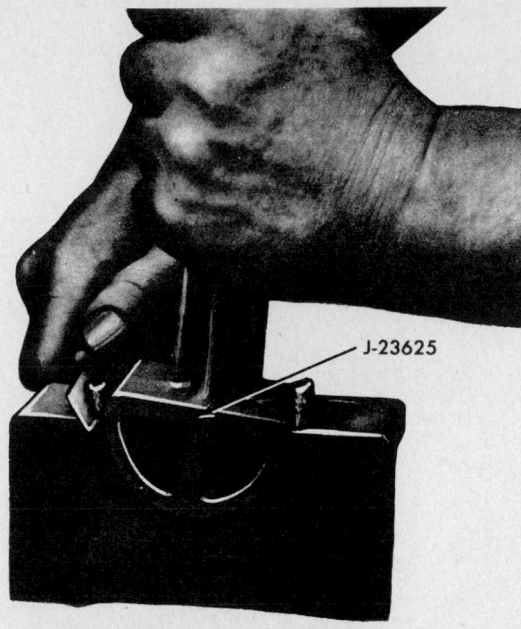

J-23625

Cutting bearing cap rope seal
(© Chevrolet Division, G.M. Corp.)

tons, subtract the measured piston diameter from the measured cylinder bore to obtain the piston clearance. Piston clearance must be less than 0.0050 in.

6. Select the piston rings comparable in size to the piston being used. Measure the ring gap with the ring squarely in the cylinder bore. If the gap is not within specifications, select the ring to fit. Install the rings on the piston in the following order, making sure that the gaps are positioned as illustrated:
   a. Install the oil spacer.
   b. Holding the oil spacer ends butted, install the lower oil ring rail.
   c. Install the upper steel oil ring rail.
   d. Install the second compression ring.
   e. Install the first compression ring.
   Check the ring side clearance, dressing the groove with a cut file if necessary.
7. Clean the cylinder bores thoroughly and wipe with a light engine oil.
8. If required, install new bearing inserts in the rod and cap. Maximum rod bearing clearance is 0.004 in. Maximum crankpin out-of-round is 0.001 in. If the crankpin is out-of-round, fit the bearing to the maximum value. Be sure that the pistons and rods are installed in their original locations. Tighten the bearing cap bolts to 35 ft. lbs.
9. Measure the connecting rod side clearance. Maximum allowable side clearance is 0.0135 in.

Main Bearings

Main bearing inserts are replaced only in pairs. No shims are used to remove excessive clearance. Bearings are available in standard size and 0.001 in., 0.002 in., 0.010 in. and 0.020 in. undersize. During production, bearings may be selectively fitted, resulting in occassional 0.001 in. undersize bearings. If main bearing caps are replaced, shimming may be necessary to increase clearance (0.001 in. minimum).

Maximum main journal taper is 0.0002 in. (production) or 0.001 in. (service). Maximum journal out-of-round is 0.0002 in. (production) or 0.001 in. (service).

Main Bearing R & R

1. Remove the cap on the main bearing which requires replacement.
2. Use a rollpin in the journal oil hole and rotate the crankshaft clockwise (from front of engine), rolling the upper bearing out.
3. Oil the new selected upper bearing and insert the plain (unnotched) end between the crankshaft and the indented or notched side of the block.

4. Rotate the bearing into place and remove the rollpin from the oil hole in the journal.
5. Oil the lower bearing and install it in the bearing cap.
6. Install the bearing cap with the F toward the front of the engine and install the bearing cap bolts, tightening to 65 ft. lbs.

Rear Main Oil Seal R & R

1. Remove the oil pan and baffle.
2. Remove the rear main bearing cap and discard the lower seal.
3. Loosen the remaining bearing caps to allow the crankshaft to be lowered.
4. Push the upper seal on one end enough so that the other end can be grasped with pliers. Pull out the upper seal.
5. Cut and form a new braided fabric upper seal in the bearing cap. Taper the end of the seal and insert a piece of soft wire through the seal about 1/4 in. from the end. Wrap the wire around the seal to form a secure attachment.
6. Thread the wire through the upper seal groove, then start the seal and pull it into position.
7. Tighten all the bearing caps except the rear cap to 65 ft. lbs.
8. Cut the seal flush to 1/64 in. below the bearing edge, making a clean cut and leaving no raveled edges.
9. Install and cut a seal in the rear main bearing cap.
10. Install the rear main bearing cap and measure the clearance with Plastigage, tightening the cap bolts to 65 ft. lbs. If the bearing clearance is within specifications, the seal is properly seated.
11. Install the bearing cap, tightening to 65 ft. lbs.
12. Install rear main bearing cap side sealant. Force the compound firmly into place to ensure that there are no air bubbles.
13. Install the oil pan and baffle.

Piston Ring Specifications
(Inches)

		Top Compression	2nd Compression	Oil
Side Clearance	Original	.0012-.0027	.0012-.0027	.000-.005
	Service	.0012-.0037	.0012-.0037	.000-.006
Gap	Original	.009-.020	.009-.019	.010-.030
	Service	.009-.020	.009-.020	.010-.031

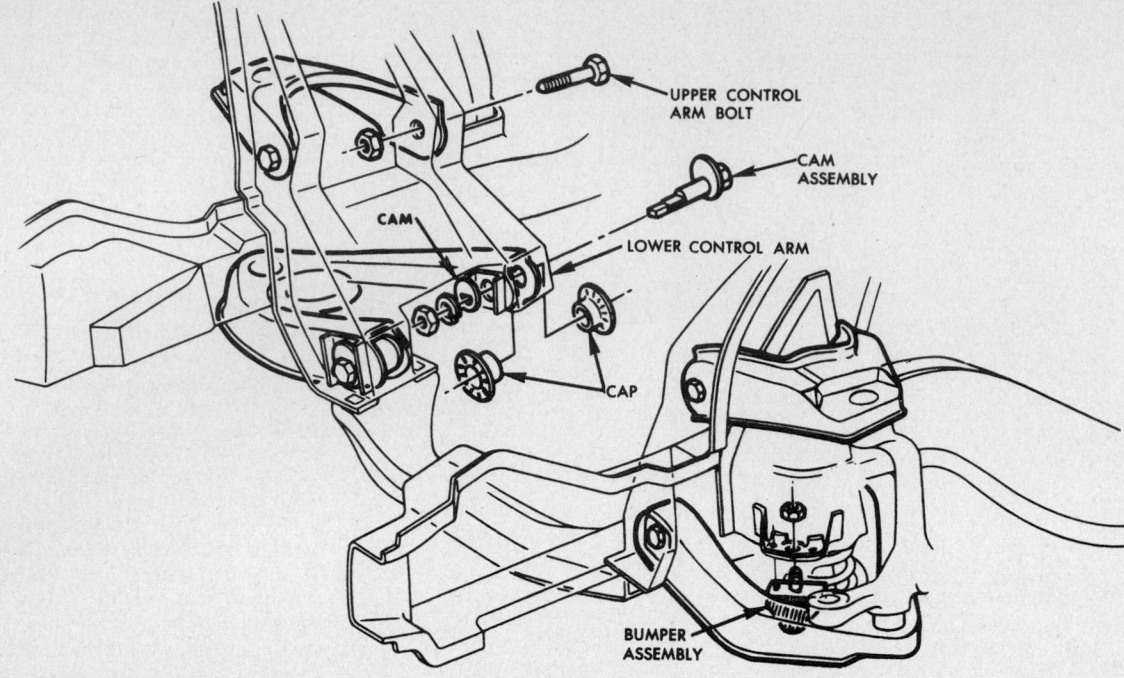

Front suspension (© Chevrolet Division, G.M. Corp.)

Front Suspension

Vega front suspension utilizes unequal length A-arms. The lower control arm bolts to the front end sheet metal with cam bolts which adjust the camber and caster. The upper ball joint is riveted to the upper control arm and the lower ball joint is pressed into the lower control arm. The steering knuckle is nodular iron with an integral steering arm.

Coil Spring

Removal

1. With shock absorber removed and stabilizer bar removed (if equipped) raise the vehicle and place jackstands under front braces.
2. Remove the wheels.
3. Place a hydraulic floor jack under the lower control arm and support the arm. Use a block of wood between the control arm and the jack.
4. Remove the lower ball stud from the steering knuckle.
5. Remove the tie rod end from the steering knuckle.
6. Lower the control arm by slowly releasing jack until the spring can be removed.

Installation

1. Properly position spring in spring tower and on control arm and lift control arm with hydraulic jack.
2. Guide the lower control arm ball stud into the steering knuckle and install nut. Torque to 60 ft. lbs.
3. Install the tie rod end to the steering arm.
4. Install the shock absorber and stabilizer bar (if removed).
5. Remove the vehicle from the jackstands and lower to the floor and install the upper end of the shock absorber.

Lower Control Arm

Removal

1. Raise vehicle on a hoist.
2. Remove shock absorber.
3. Remove ball stud from steering knuckle.
4. Remove coil spring.
5. Remove the inner pivot cam nuts and bolts.
   NOTE: mark the position of the cam bolts before loosening nuts. This step will aid in assembly.
6. Remove the control arm.

Installation

1. Install the control arm.
   NOTE: be sure that the control arm bushings have the metal caps installed.
2. Install the cam bolts through the control arm bushings.
   NOTE: the front cam bolt (camber) must be installed with the head toward the front of the vehicle and the rear cam bolt (caster) must be installed with the head toward the rear of the vehicle.
3. Install the inner cams to the cam bolt.
4. Install the lockwasher and nut.
5. Align the cam bolts with the marks made before removal.
6. Install the coil spring.
7. Install the shock absorber.
8. Lower vehicle to the floor.
9. Check front alignment.

Upper Control Arm

Removal

1. Raise vehicle on a hoist and remove the wheel.
2. Support the lower control arm with a floor jack.
3. Remove upper ball stud nut and remove ball stud from steering knuckle.
4. Remove control arm pivot bolts and remove control arm from vehicle.

Installation

1. Install upper control arm to vehicle at inner pivot.
   NOTE: the inner pivot bolts must be installed with the bolt heads to the front (on the front bushing) and to the rear, (on the rear bushing).
2. Install the inner pivot nuts.
3. Position the control arm in a horizontal plane and tighten the inner pivot nuts.
4. Install ball stud to steering knuckle. Tighten nut and install cotter pin.
5. Install tire and wheel assembly and lower vehicle.

Upper Ball Joint

Removal

1. Raise the vehicle on a hoist and remove the wheels.
2. Support the lower control arm with a floor jack.

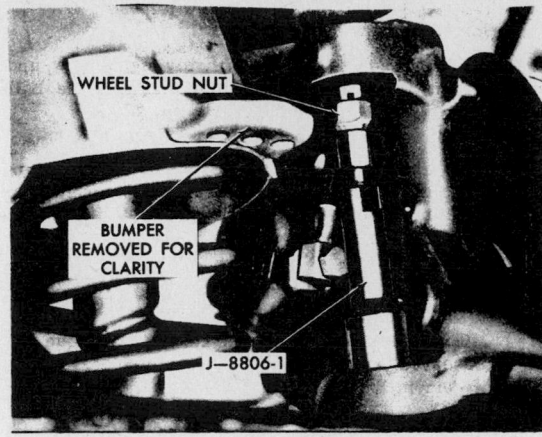

Removing ball joint stud from steering knuckle
(© Chevrolet Division, G.M. Corp.)

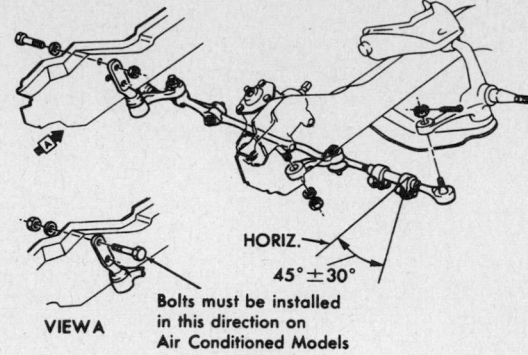

Steering linkage
(© Chevrolet Division, G.M. Corp.)

3. Remove cotter pin from upper ball stud and loosen the ball stud nut but do not remove.
4. Install a wheel stud nut.
5. Using a suitable puller, pull the ball stud free of the steering knuckle and remove both nuts from ball stud.

Installation

1. Mate the upper control arm to the steering knuckle.
2. Install the stud to the steering knuckle.
3. Install the ball stud nut and cotter pin.
4. Install the wheels and lower the vehicle.

Lower Ball Joint R & R

1. Lower ball joint removal and installation is identical to that for upper ball joint.

Steering Knuckle

Removal

1. Raise vehicle on a hoist and support the lower control arm with a jackstand.
NOTE: this keeps the coil spring compressed.
2. Remove the tire and wheel assembly.
3. Remove the disc brake caliper.
NOTE: secure the caliper to the suspension using wire. Do not allow the caliper to hang by the brake hose. Insert a piece of wood (about the same thickness as a brake disc) between the shoes to hold the piston in the caliper bore.
4. Remove the hub and disc.
5. Remove the splash shield.
6. Remove the tie rod end from the steering knuckle.
7. Remove upper cotter pins and lower ball stud and loosen the ball stud nuts.
8. Install a spare wheel stud nut on either the upper or lower ball stud and press the ball stud from the steering knuckle.

9. Using a spare nut as in Step 8 press the other ball stud from the steering knuckle.
10. Remove ball stud nuts and remove the steering knuckle.

Installation

1. Place steering knuckle in position and insert the upper and lower ball studs into knuckle bosses.
2. Install ball stud nuts and tighten to 60 ft. lbs. Install cotter pin.
NOTE: if necessary, tighten to the next slot to insert cotter pin. Never back off on a ball stud nut to align cotter pin.
3. Install splash shield to the steering knuckle.
4. Install the tie rod end to the steering knuckle. Torque to 35 ft. lbs.
5. Install the hub and disc, bearings and nut. Install cotter pin.
6. Install the brake caliper.
7. Install the wheels, remove the jackstand and lower the car.

Jacking, Hoisting

Using bumper jack, floor jack or hoist at positions indicated in the illustration.

Steering Gear

Removal

1. Remove the pot joint coupling clamp bolt at the steering gear wormshaft.
2. Remove pitman arm nut and washer from pitman shaft and mark relation of arm position to shaft.
3. Remove pitman arm.
4. Remove the bolts securing the steering gear to the frame and remove the gear from the vehicle.

Installation

1. Place the steering gear in position in the vehicle, aligning the groove across the end of the pot joint with the flat on the wormshaft. Push the gear onto the coupling until the wormshaft bottoms in the coupling.
2. Secure the gear to the frame with bolts and washers and torque to 70 ft. lbs.
3. Align pot joint clamp with groove across end of pot joint, install and torque clamp bolt to 55 ft. lbs.
4. Install pitman arm, aligning marks made during removal, and secure with washer and retaining nut.

Tie Rod Removal

1. Place vehicle on hoist.
2. Remove cotter pins from ball studs and remove special nuts.
3. To remove outer ball stud, tap on steering arm at tie rod end with a hammer while using a heavy hammer or similar tool as a backing.
4. Remove inner ball stud from relay rod using same procedure as described in Step 3.
5. To remove tie rod ends from tie rod, loosen clamp bolts and unscrew end assemblies.

Tie Rod Installation

1. If the tie rod ends were removed, lubricate the tie rod threads with chassis lube and install ends on tie rod making sure both ends are threaded an equal distance from the tie rod.
2. Make sure that threads on ball studs and in ball stud nuts are perfectly clean and smooth. Check condition of ball stud seals; replace if necessary.
NOTE: if threads are not clean and smooth, ball studs may turn in tie rod ends when attempting to tighten nut.
3. Install ball studs in steering arms and relay rod.

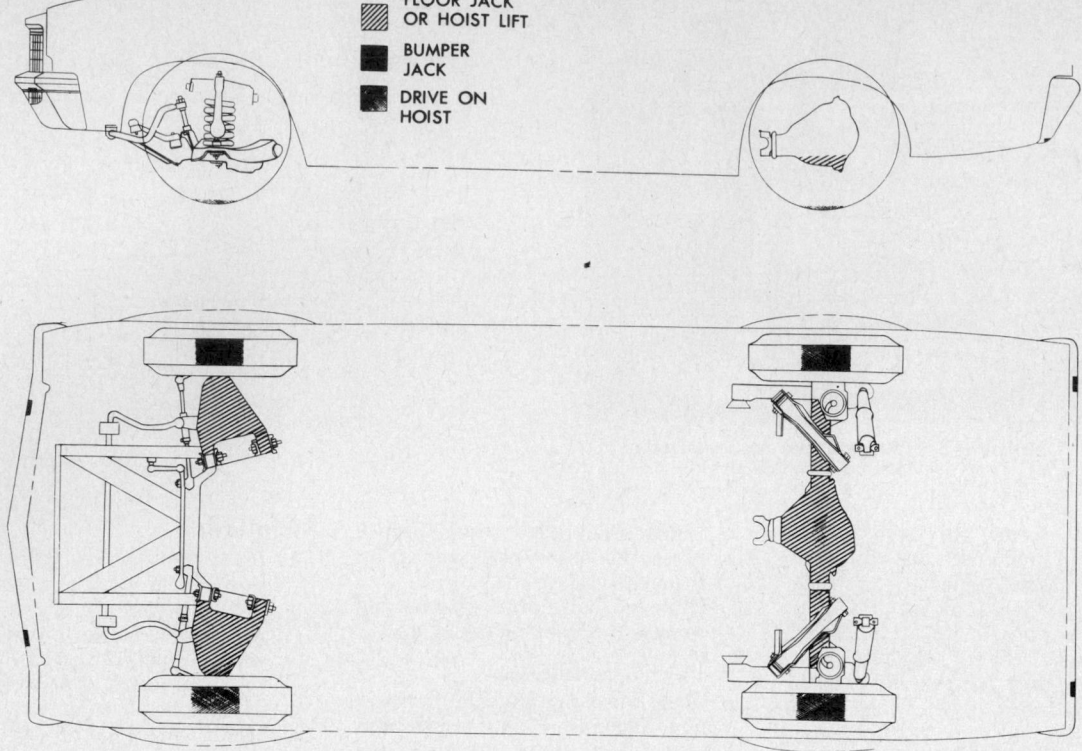

FLOOR JACK
OR HOIST LIFT

BUMPER
JACK

DRIVE ON
HOIST

Vega lift points (© Chevrolet Division, G.M. Corp.)

4. Install ball stud nut, tighten and install new cotter pins. Lubricate tie rod ends.
5. Remove vehicle from hoist.
6. Adjust toe-in.

Caution Before tightening the tie rod adjusting sleeve clamp bolts, be sure that the following conditions have been met:

a. The sleeve clamps must be positioned between the locating dimples at either end of the sleeve.
b. The clamps must be positioned within the angular travel as illustrated.
c. The relationship of the clamp slot with the slit in the sleeve should be maintained as shown.
d. Both inner and outer tie rod ends must rotate for full travel in the same direction. The position of each tie rod end must be maintained as the clamps are tightened to ensure free movement of each joint.
e. All procedures for alignment, adjustment and assembly of tie rods applies to each side.

Relay Rod Removal
1. Place vehicle on hoist.
2. Remove inner ends of the tie rods from relay rod.
3. Remove the cotter pins from the pitman and idler arm ball studs at the relay rod. Remove the special nuts.

4. Remove the relay rod from the pitman and idler arms by tapping on the relay rod ball stud bosses with a hammer, while using a heavy hammer as a backing.
5. Remove the relay rod from the vehicle.

Relay Rod Installation
1. Make sure that threads on the ball studs and in the ball stud nuts are perfectly clean and smooth. Check condition of ball stud seals; replace if necessary.
   NOTE: if threads are not clean and smooth, ball studs may turn in sockets when attempting to tighten nut.
2. Install the relay rod to the idler arm and pitman arm ball studs, making certain the seals are in place. Install and torque the nut and then install the cotter pin. Tighten nut to 35 ft. lbs.
3. Install the tie rods to the relay rod. Lubricate the tie rod ends.
4. Remove the vehicle from the hoist.
5. Adjust toe-in and align steering wheel.

Idler Arm Removal
1. Place vehicle on a hoist.
2. Remove the cotter pin and special nut from ball stud at the relay rod. Remove the ball stud from the relay rod by tapping on the relay rod boss with a hammer, while using a heavy hammer as a backing.

3. Remove the idler arm to frame bolts and remove the idler arm assembly.

Idler Arm Installation
1. Position the idler arm on the frame and install the mounting bolts (special plain washers under bolt heads). Torque the nuts to 30 ft. lbs.
2. Make sure that the threads on the ball stud and in the ball stud nut are perfectly clean and smooth. Check condition of ball stud seal; replace if necessary.
   NOTE: if threads are not clean and smooth, ball stud may turn in the socket when attempting to tighten nut.
3. Install the idler arm ball stud in the realy rod, making certain the seal is positioned properly; install the nut and cotter pin, tightening to 35 ft. lbs.
4. Remove the vehicle from the hoist.

Pitman Arm Removal
1. Place vehicle on a hoist.
2. Remove the cotter pin and special nut from ball stud at the relay rod. Remove the ball stud from the relay rod by tapping on the relay rod boss with a hammer, while using a heavy hammer as a backing.
3. Remove the pitman arm to pitman shaft nut. Mark relationship of the arm to the shaft and then remove the pitman arm.

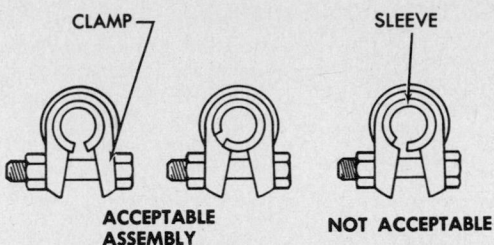

CLAMP   SLEEVE

ACCEPTABLE ASSEMBLY   NOT ACCEPTABLE

Tie rod clamp installation
(© Chevrolet Division, G.M. Corp.)

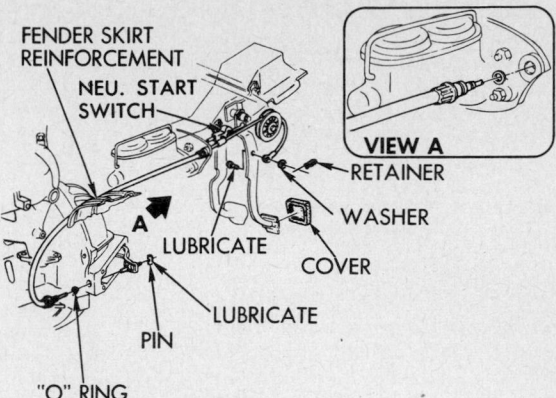

FENDER SKIRT REINFORCEMENT
NEU. START SWITCH
VIEW A
RETAINER
WASHER
A
LUBRICATE   COVER
LUBRICATE
PIN
"O" RING

Clutch control cable
(© Chevrolet Division, G.M. Corp.)

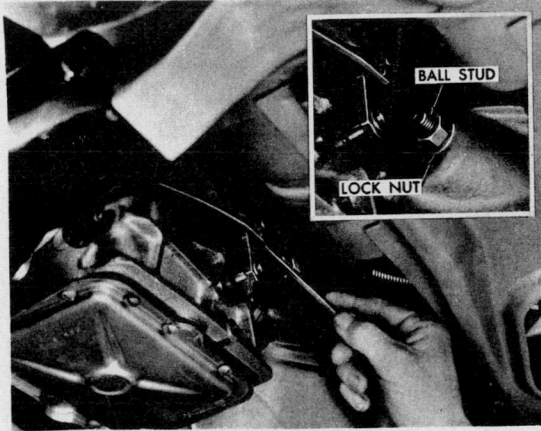
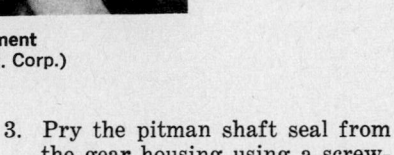

BALL STUD

LOCK NUT

Clutch ball stud adjustment
(© Chevrolet Division, G.M. Corp.)

Pitman Arm Installation

1. Install the pitman arm on the pitman shaft, aligning the marks made during removal. Install and torque the nut.
2. Make sure that the threads on the ball stud and in the ball stud are perfectly clean and smooth. Check condition of ball stud seal; replace if necessary.
   NOTE: if threads are not clean and smooth, ball stud may turn in the socket when attempting to tighten nut.
3. Install the pitman arm ball stud to the relay rod, making certain the seal is positioned properly. Install the nut and cotter pin.
4. Remove the vehicle from the hoist.

Pitman Shaft Seal Replacement

A faulty seal may be replaced without removal of steering gear from car by removing pitman arm and proceeding as follows:
1. Rotate the steering wheel from stop to stop, counting the total number of turns. Then turn back exactly half-way, placing the gear on center (the wormshaft flat should be at the 12 o'clock position).
2. Remove the three self-locking bolts attaching side cover to the housing and lift the pitman shaft and side cover assembly from the housing.

3. Pry the pitman shaft seal from the gear housing using a screwdriver and being careful not to damage the housing bore.

Caution Inspect the lubricant in the gear for contamination. If the lubricant is contaminated in any way, the gear must be removed from the vehicle and completely overhauled as outlined in the Unit Repair Section of this manual.

4. Coat the new pitman shaft seal with steering gear lubricant. Position the seal in the pitman shaft bore and tap into position using a suitable size socket.
5. Remove the lash adjuster locknut. Remove the side cover from the pitman shaft assembly by turning the lash adjuster screw clockwise.
6. Place the pitman shaft in the steering gear such that the center tooth of the pitman shaft sector enters the center tooth space of the ball nut.
7. Fill the steering gear housing with 9 oz. of steering gear lubricant.
8. Install a new side cover gasket on the gear housing.
9. Install the side cover onto the lash adjuster screw by reaching through the threaded hole in the side cover with a small screwdriver and turning the lash adjuster screw counter-clockwise.
10. Install the side cover bolts and torque to 18 ft. lbs.

11. Install the lash adjuster screw locknut, perform steering gear adjustment and install the pitman arm.

Clutch

The Vega clutch is of conventional design. The clutch disc is pressed against the flywheel by the spring-loaded clutch cover. The clutch release fingers are depressed by a ball bearing type release bearing. The release fork pivots on an adjustable ball stud which is located on the right side of the bell housing. Control from the pedal is by means of a cable.

Clutch Adjustment

The initial adjustment is made after clutch or control cable replacement at the ball stud and at the lower end of the cable as described below.

Initial Ball Stud Adjustment

1. Prior to attachment of cable, place gauge J-23644 so flat end is against front face of the clutch housing and the hooked end is located at point of cable attachment on fork.
2. Turn ball stud inward by hand until clutch release bearing makes contact with clutch spring.
3. Install locknut and tighten (25 ft. lbs.) being careful not the change ball stud adjustment.
4. Install ball stud cap.
5. Remove gauge by pulling outward at housing end.

Clutch Cable Attachment and Adjustment (Lower End)

1. Place cable through hole in clutch fork.
2. Pull cable until clutch pedal is firmly against rubber bumper.
3. Push clutch fork forward until throw out bearing contacts clutch spring fingers.

4. Screw pin on cable until it bottoms out on fork.
5. Turn ¼ additional revolution clockwise and drop pin down into groove in fork.
6. Attach return spring. This procedure will produce a .90 ± .25 in. lash at clutch pedal.
7. Install clutch fork cover. Tighten retaining screws to 80 in. lbs.

Clutch Pedal Free Travel

Adjustment for normal clutch wear is accomplished by turning the clutch fork ball stud counterclockwise to give .90 ± .25 in. lash at clutch pedal.

1. Remove ball stud cap and loosen locknut on ball stud end located to the right of the transmission on the clutch housing (fig. 5).
2. Adjust ball stud to obtain .90 ± .25 in. free travel.
3. Tighten locknut (25 ft. lbs.) being careful not to change adjustment and install ball stud cap.
4. Check operation of clutch.

Clutch Cable Replacement

1. Remove clutch fork cover at side of housing.
2. Disconnect return spring and clutch cable at clutch shift fork.
3. Remove clip and pin retaining cable to pedal arm.
4. Pull cable assembly through reinforcement and disengage from fender skirt reinforcement.
5. Push new cable through body reinforcement and around pulley. Secure cable end to pedal arm with pin, washer and clip.
NOTE: lubricate retaining pin with graphite type grease.

6. Route cable over fender skirt reinforcement and down to the clutch fork lever. Install cable end in fork lever as previously outlined under adjustment procedures.
7. Install clutch fork cover and tighten retaining screws to 80 in. lbs.

Clutch Removal

1. Raise vehicle on hoist.
2. Remove transmission as outlined in this section.
3. Remove clutch fork cover then disconnect clutch return spring and control cable from clutch fork.
4. Remove main drive gear oil seal from clutch release bearing sleeve.
5. Remove flywheel housing lower cover.
6. Remove flywheel housing from engine.
7. To remove, release bearing from clutch fork and sleeve, slide lever off ball stud against spring action. If necessary to replace ball stud, remove cap, locknut and stud from housing.
8. If assembly marks on clutch assembly and flywheel are not distinguishable, remark with paint or center-punch.
9. Loosen clutch cover to flywheel, attaching bolts one turn at a time until spring pressure is released, to avoid bending clutch cover flange.
10. Support the pressure plate and cover assembly then remove the bolts and clutch assembly.

Caution Do not disassemble the clutch cover, spring and pressure plate for repair. If defective replace complete assembly.

Installation

1. Index alignment marks on clutch assembly and flywheel. Place driven plate on pressure plate with long end of splined end facing forward, damper springs inside pressure plate, and insert a dummy clutch gear shaft through the cover and driven plate.
2. Position the complete assembly against the flywheel and insert the dummy shaft into the pilot bearing in the crankshaft.
3. Index the alignment marks and install clutch cover to flywheel bolts finger-tight.

Caution Tighten all bolts evenly and gradually until tight to avoid possible clutch distortion. Torque bolts 18 ft. lbs. and remove dummy shaft.

4. Lubricate the clutch fork ball socket and the fingers at the release bearing with a high melting point grease such as graphite grease.
5. Lubricate the recess on the inside of the throwout bearing collar and the fork groove with a light coat of graphite grease. Install fork in housing but not on stud.
6. Install bearing on sleeve, then position clutch fork over bearing in housing and slide fork onto ball stud.
7. Install flywheel housing and lower cover. Tighten bolts to 25 ft. lbs.
8. Install transmission as outlined previously.
9. Adjust clutch as previously outlined.
10. Lower and remove vehicle from hoist.

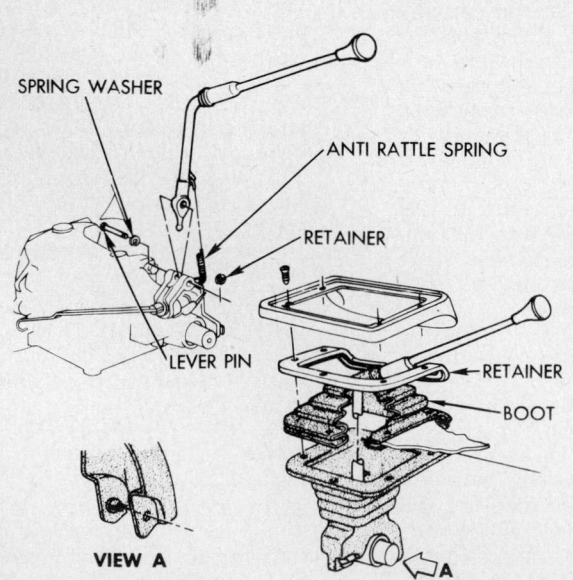

SPRING WASHER

ANTI RATTLE SPRING

RETAINER

LEVER PIN

RETAINER

BOOT

VIEW A

Shift control lever installation
(© Chevrolet Division, G.M. Corp.)

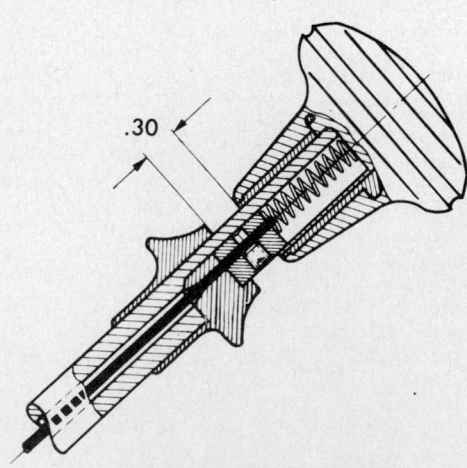

.30

4-speed gearshift lever knob
(© Chevrolet Division, G.M. Corp.)

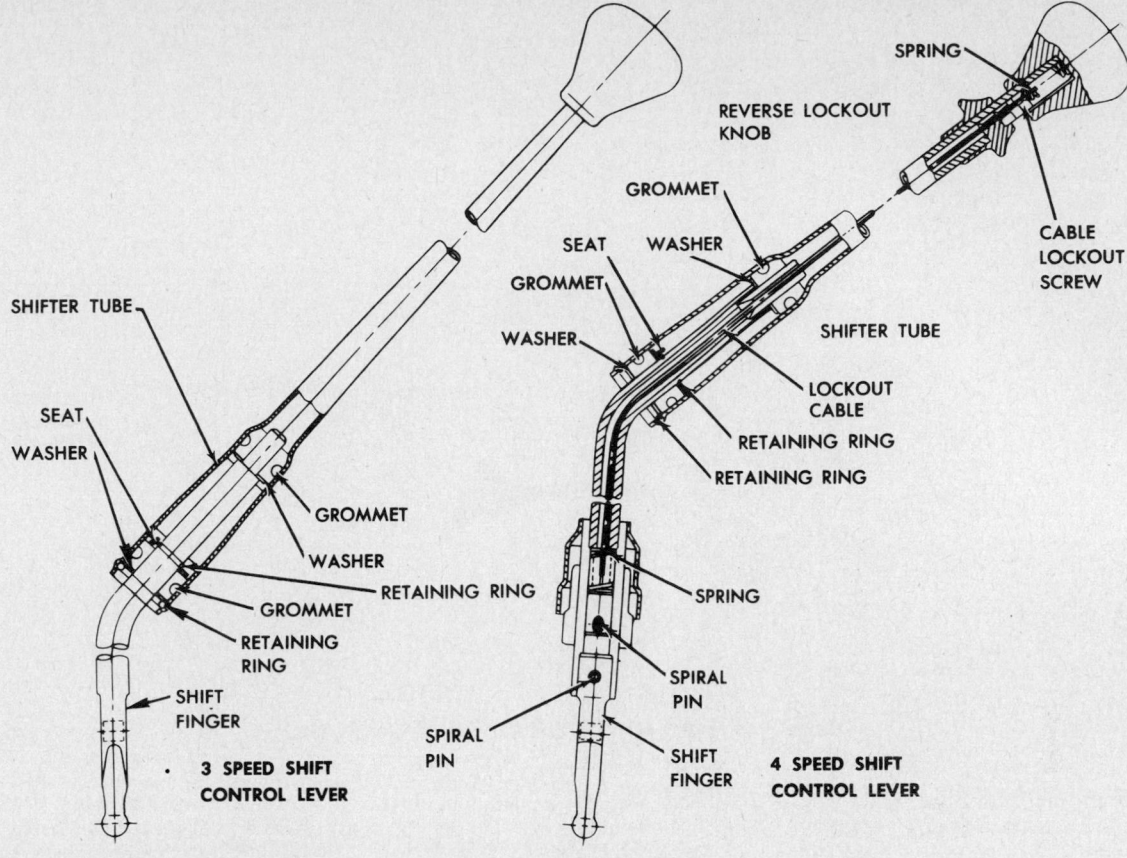

Shift control lever (© Chevrolet Division, G.M. Corp.)

Manual Transmission

The Vega may be equipped with either of two manual transmissions. Both units are fully synchronized in all forward gears and have floor mounted shift controls.

The three-speed transmission is constant mesh in first and second and direct drive in third. The first-reverse synchronizer sleeve has gear teeth on the outside diameter which enables it to function as a reverse gear when engaged with the reverse idler gear.

The reverse gear on the four-speed transmission is similar to that of the three-speed except that the reverse teeth are on the first-second synchronizer. The control lever on this transmission has a reverse lockout feature.

Gearshift Lever Control Wire Replacement, 4-Speed

1. Remove gearshift lever from vehicle.
2. Carefully remove gearshift lever knob (by pulling) and loosen set screw.
3. Drive out spiral pins.
4. Take off shift finger and pull Bowden control wire out of gearshift lever. Thrust spring may also be removed at this time.
   NOTE: before installation, oil sliding surface of stop sleeve on shift finger tube.
5. Install new control wire through gearshift lever and fasten new control wire with clamp sleeve so that the cutout of the stop sleeve shows toward the left. Insert spiral pin (long pin).
   NOTE: spiral pin must not protrude on either side.
6. With set screw, clamp Bowden control wire tight so that pull ring is positioned on gearshift lever tube and clamping block on pull ring.
   NOTE: do not put tension on Bowden cable. Pull knob should have approximately 1/16 in. free travel.
7. With short spiral pin, attach shift finger.
8. Install gearshift lever knob and adhere to a distance of .30 in.

Transmission Removal

1. Place transmission shift lever in neutral and remove the shift lever from the transmission.
2. Raise vehicle on hoist and drain lubricant from transmission.
3. Remove driveshaft assembly.
4. Disconnect the speedometer cable, TCS switch and back-up lamp switch.
5. Remove crossmember-to-transmission mount bolts.
6. Support engine with an appropriate jack stand and remove crossmember-to-frame bolts. Recrossmember from vehicle.
7. Remove transmission to clutch housing upper retaining bolts and install guide pins in holes.
8. Remove lower bolts, then slide move crossmember from vehicle. transmission rearward and remove from vehicle.
   NOTE: inspect throwout bearing support gasket located beneath lip of support. If defective, replace gasket before installing transmission.

Installation

1. Lightly lubricate inside diameter of clutch drive gear seal and install seal on drive gear.
2. Position new gasket to face of clutch housing.
3. Position transmission to clutch housing and slide forward, piloting clutch gear in to pilot bearing.
   NOTE: make certain main drive gear splines are clean and dry.
4. Install transmission-to-clutch housing retaining bolts and lockwashers.
5. Position crossmember to frame and loosely install retaining bolts. Install crossmember-to-transmission mount bolts.

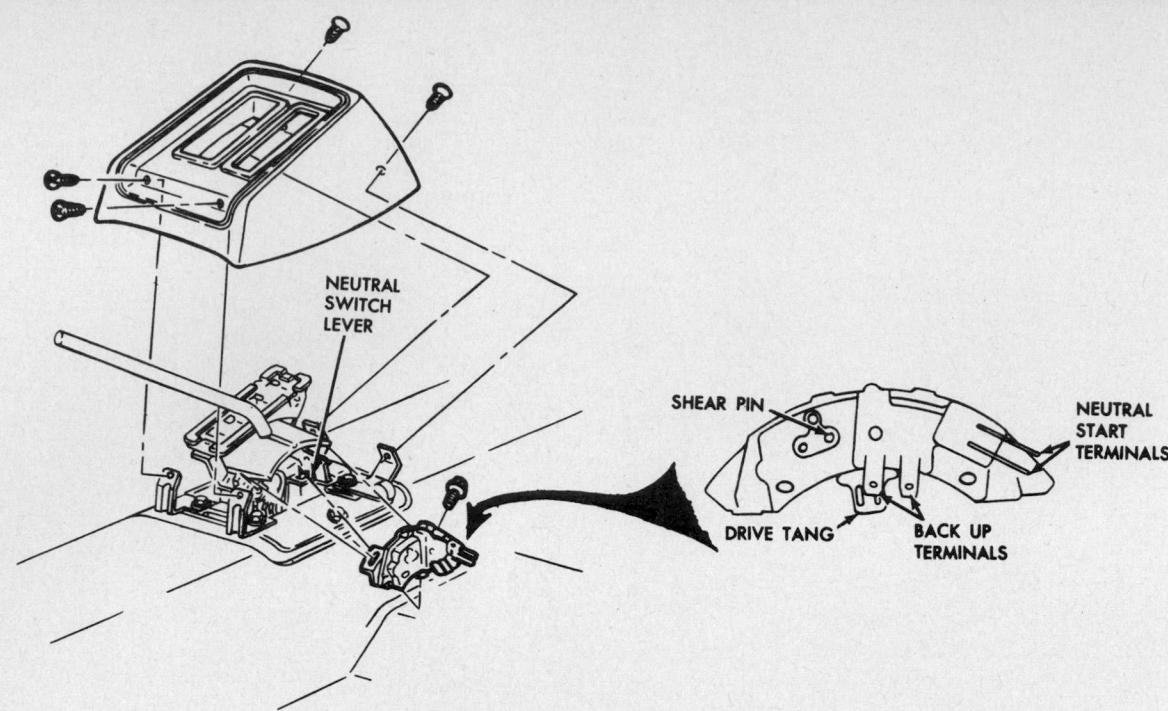

NEUTRAL
SWITCH
LEVER

SHEAR PIN

NEUTRAL
START
TERMINALS

DRIVE TANG

BACK UP
TERMINALS

Neutral safety switch adjustment (© Chevrolet Division, G.M. Corp.)

Tighten all retaining bolts to specifications. Remove engine support.

Caution Check position of engine in front mounts and align as required.

6. Connect speedometer cable, back-up lamp switch and TCS switch.
7. Install driveshaft assembly.
8. Fill transmission to proper level. Lower vehicle and remove from hoist after installing shift lever.
9. Lubricate shift finger bolt and spherical end of shaft. Install shift lever in shift housing and install bolt. Secure with retaining clip.
10. Install shift lever spring. Position shift lever boot and bezel to floor pan. Install retaining screws.
11. Check operation of transmission.

Automatic Transmission

There are two automatic transmissions available. The aluminum Powerglide consists of a three-element torque converter which drives through a two-speed planetary gearset. The Torque Drive transmission is essentially a Powerglide without the automatic shifting mechanisms. For overhaul procedures, see the Unit Repair Section.

Transmission Removal

1. Raise vehicle on hoist and remove oil pan drain plug to drain oil.

2. Disconnect the vacuum modulator line (Powerglide) and the speedometer drive cable fitting at the transmission. Tie lines out of the way.
3. Disconnect manual and TV (Powerglide) control lever rods from transmission.
4. Disconnect driveshaft from transmission.
5. Install suitable transmission lift equipment to jack or other lifting device and attach on transmission.
6. Disconnect engine rear mount on transmission extension, then disconnect the transmission support crossmember at the frame and remove.
7. Remove converter underpan, scribe flywheel-converter relationship for assembly, then remove the flywheel-to-converter attaching bolts.
8. Support engine at the oil pan rail with a jack or other suitable brace capable of supporting the engine weight when the transmission is removed.
9. Lowert he rear of the transmission slightly so that the upper transmission housing-to-engine attaching bolts can be reached using a universal socket and a long extension. Remove upper bots.
10. Remove remainder of transmission housing-to-engine attaching bolts.
11. Remove the transmission by moving it slightly to the rear and downward, then remove from beneath the car and trans-

fer to a work bench.
NOTE: observe converter when moving the transmission rearward. If it does not move with the transmission, pry it free of flywheel before proceeding.

Caution Keep front of transmission upward to prevent the converter from falling out.

Installation

1. Mount transmission on transmission lifting equipment installed on jack or other lifting device.
2. Raise transmission into place at rear of engine and install transmission case to engine upper mounting bolts, then install remainder of the mounting bolts. Torque bolts to 35 ft. lbs.
3. Remove support from beneath engine, then raise rear of transmission to final position.
4. Align scribe marks on flywheel and converter cover. Install converter to flywheel attaching bolts. Torque bolts to 30-35 ft. lbs.
5. Install converter underpan.
6. Install transmission support crossmember to transmission and frame.
7. Remove transmission lift equipment.
8. Connect driveshaft to transmission.
9. Connect manual and TV control lever rods to transmission.
10. Connect oil cooler lines (if so equipped), vacuum modulator line, and speedometer drive cable to transmission.

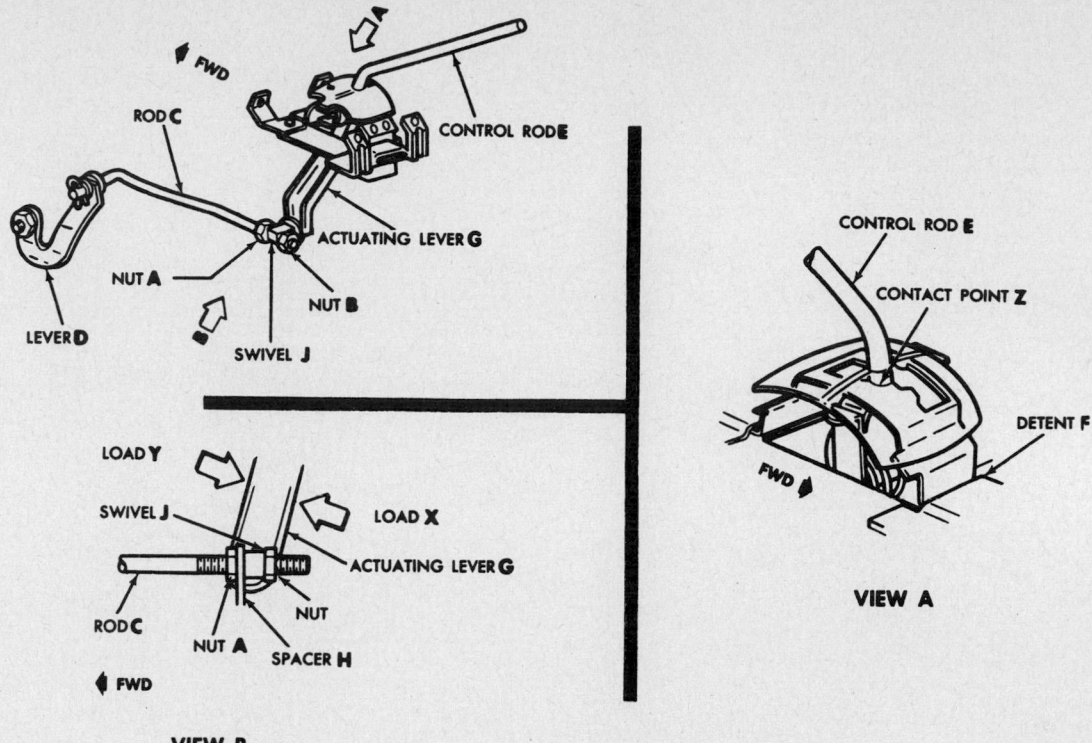

VIEW A

VIEW B

Transmission control linkage adjustment (© Chevrolet Division, G.M. Corp.)

11. Fill transmission with approved transmission fluid.
12. Check transmission for proper operation and for leakage. Check and, if necessary, adjust linkage.
13. Lower vehicle and remove from hoist.

Neutral Safety Switch Adjustment

1. Remove four screws securing floor console.
2. Disconnect electrical plugs on back-up contacts and neutral start contacts of neutral start switch assembly.
3. Place shift lever in Neutral.
4. Remove two screws securing shift indicator plate.
5. Remove two screws securing shift lever curved cover.
6. Remove two screws securing neutral start switch to lever assembly.
NOTE: screws are hidden beneath lever cover.
7. Tilt switch assembly to right as you lift switch out of lever hole.
8. Make sure shift lever is in Neutral before installing switch assembly.
9. Assemble switch assembly to control lever bracket by inserting drive tang into hole in neutral start switch lever.
10. Tighten two mounting screws securing switch assembly to lever bracket.
11. Install curved shift lever cover

and secure with two screws.
12. Install shift indicator plate and attach with two screws.
13. Moving control lever out of Neutral will shear the switch plastic locating pin.
14. Plug electrical connectors into switch assembly; apply parking

brake and start vehicle—check for starting in Neutral and Park only. Also check for back-up lamps on in reverse.
15. Turn off ignition and install console cover securing with four screws.

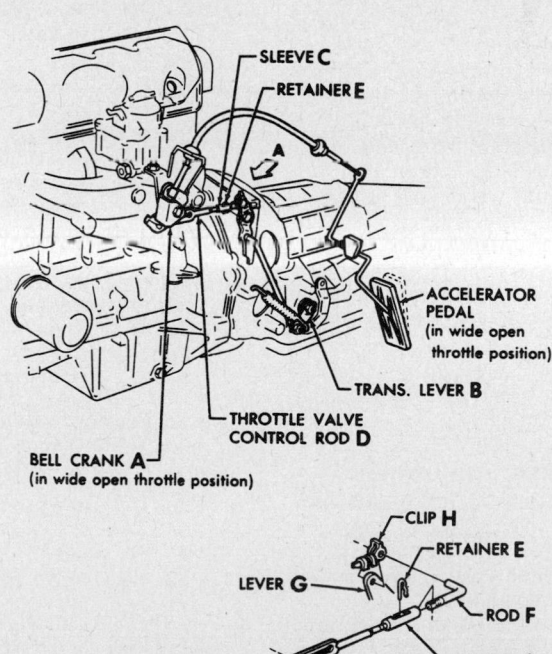

VIEW A
Throttle valve linkage adjustment
(© Chevrolet Division, G.M. Corp.)

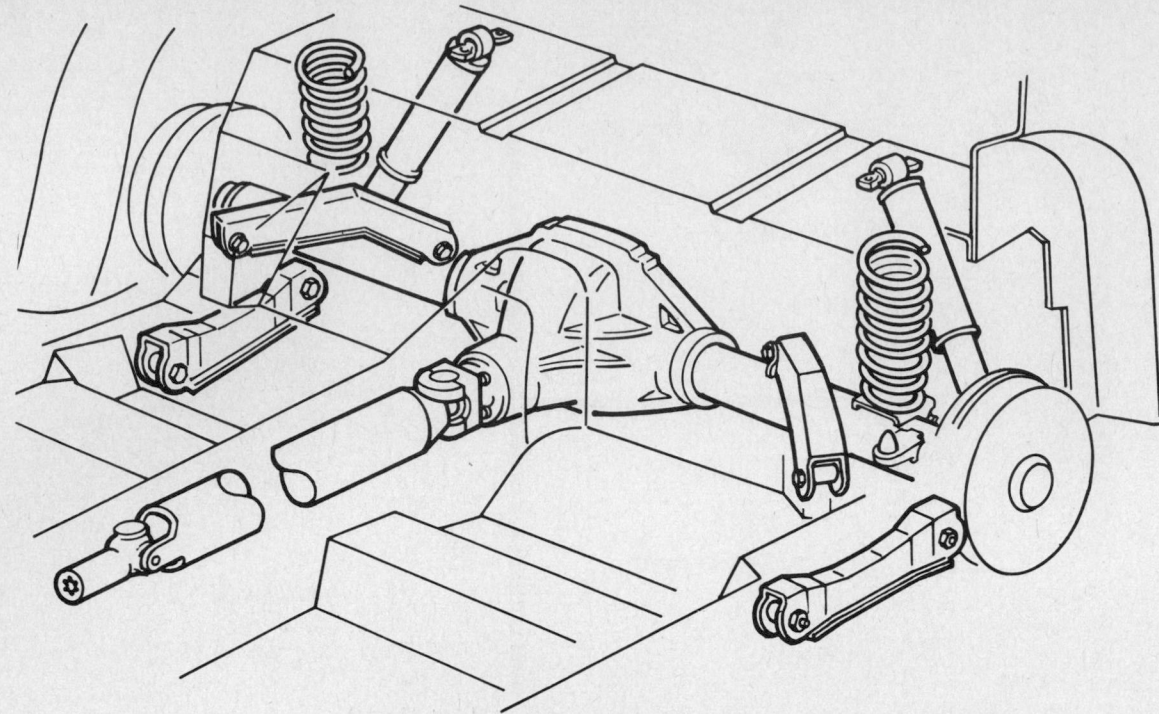

Rear suspension (© Chevrolet Division, G.M. Corp.)

Transmission Control Linkage Adjustment

1. Loosely assemble nut (A), swivel (J) and nut (B) on rod (C).
2. Set transmission lever (D) in Neutral.
   NOTE: obtain Neutral by moving transmission lever (D) clockwise to Park detent, then counterclockwise two detent positions to Neutral.
3. Set control rod (E) in Neutral notch of detent (F).
4. Apply load in direction of arrow (Y) on actuating lever (G) until rod comes in contact with detent at contact point (Z).
5. Place a .073 in. spacer (H) between nut (A) and against swivel (J) and tighten nut (A) against spacer (H).
6. Remove spacer (H), apply load in direction of arrow (X) on actuating lever (G). Tighten nut (B).

The foregoing procedure will provide a .05 in. overtravel gap in the notches of detent (F).

Throttle Valve Adjustment

1. With accelerator pedal depressed, bellcrank (A) must be in wide open throttle position.
2. Transmission lever (B) must be against internal stop.
3. Attach rod (D) to bellcrank lever stud (A) and adjust sleeve (C) to align rod (F) with Lever (G) hole, ± one turn. Insert retainer (E) through sleeve (C) and rod (F). Attach clip (H) to lever (G) and rod (F).

Drive Shaft

Driveshaft R & R

1. Raise vehicle on hoist. Mark relationship of shaft to companion flange and disconnect the rear universal joint by removing trunnion bearing U bolts. Tape bearing cups to trunnion to prevent dropping and loss of bearing roller.

2. Withdraw driveshaft front yoke from transmission by moving shaft rearward and passing it under the axle housing. Watch for oil leakage from transmission output shaft housing.

3. Inspect yoke seal in the transmission extension, replace if necessary.

4. Insert driveshaft front yoke into transmission extention, making sure that output shaft splines mate with driveshaft yoke splines.

5. Align driveshaft with companion flange using reference marks established in removal procedure. Remove tape used to retain trunnion bearing caps. Connect exposed bearing caps to companion flange.

Rear Axles, Suspension

Rear Spring

Removal

1. Raise vehicle on hoist and support the rear axle.
2. Disconnect both shock absorbers from lower brackets.
3. Lower axle and remove springs and spring insulators.
   NOTE: one or both springs may be removed at this point.

Caution When lowering axle do not stretch brake hose running from frame to axle.

Installation

1. Install insulators on top and bottom of springs and position on axle.
2. Raise axle and reconnect shock absorbers.
3. Lower vehicle and remove from hoist.

Upper Control Arm

Removal

Caution If both control arms are to be replaced, remove and replace one control arm at a time to prevent the axle from rolling or slipping sideways.

1. Raise vehicle on hoist and support the rear axle.
2. Remove control arm front and rear bolts and remove arm.

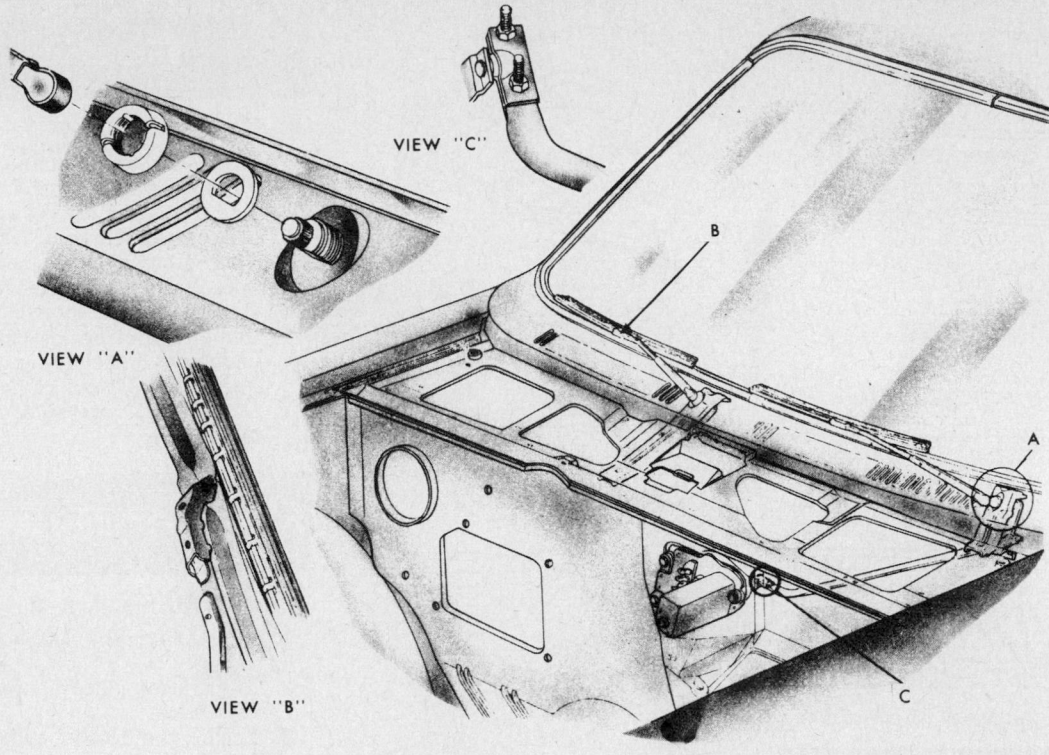

VIEW "C"

VIEW "A"

VIEW "B"

B

A

C

Windshield wiper installation (© Chevrolet Division, G.M. Corp.)

Replacement

1. Using suitable tools, press out the bushing.
2. Before bushing installation, observe that holes in control arm have different diameters.
3. Install small end of bushing in largest hole.
4. Press bushing into control arm until bushing flange seats on control arm.

Installation

1. Install control arm front and rear attaching bolts. Torque to 60 ft. lbs.
   NOTE: car must be at curb height when tightening pivot bolts.
2. Remove support from axle.
3. Lower vehicle and remove from hoist.

Lower Control Arm Removal

Caution If both control arms are to be replaced, remove and replace one control arm at a time to prevent the axle from rolling or slipping sideways.

1. Raise vehicle on hoist.
2. Support rear axle.
3. Disconnect stabilizer bar if so equipped.
4. Remove control arm front and rear attaching bolts and remove control arm.

Lower Control Arm Bushing Replacement

Replacement of these bushings is the same procedure as that described for the Upper Control Arm above.

Lower Control Arm Installation

1. Place control arm into position and install front and rear bolts. Torque to 80 ft. lbs.
2. Attach stabilizer bar if so equipped.
3. Remove support from axle.
4. Lower vehicle and remove from hoist.

Rear Shock Absorber

Removal

1. Raise vehicle on hoist and support the rear axle.

2. Remove upper attaching bolts and lower attaching nut, retainer, and cushion.
3. Remove shock absorber.

Installation

1. Install retainer and rubber grommet onto shock.
2. Place shock absorber into installed position and install upper retaining bolts. Torque to 18 ft. lbs.
3. Install cushion, retainer and nut onto lower shock absorber attachment. Torque to 80 ft. lbs.
4. Lower vehicle and remove from hoist.

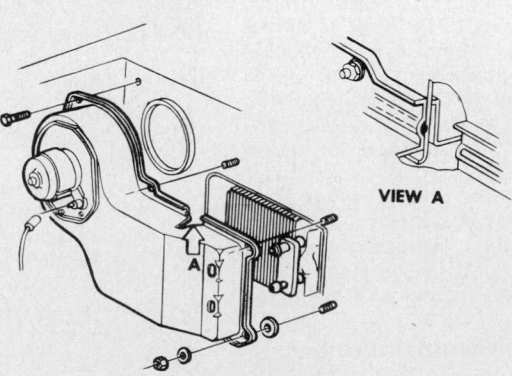

VIEW A

Heater installation
(© Chevrolet Division, G.M. Corp.)

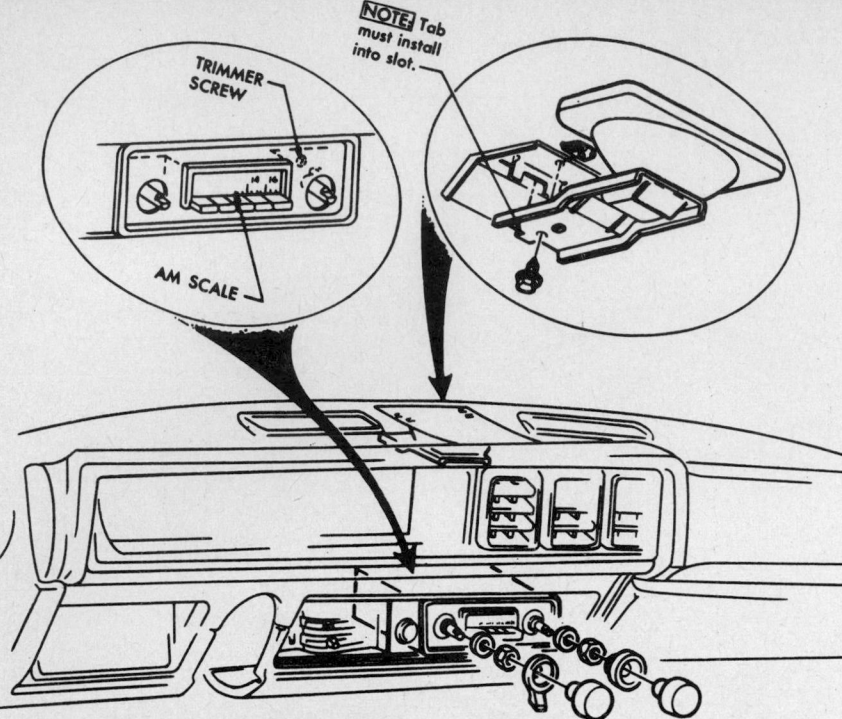

NOTE: Tab must install into slot.

TRIMMER SCREW

AM SCALE

Radio installation (© Chevrolet Division, G.M. Corp.)

Drive Axles

Axle Assembly Removal

1. Raise vehicle on hoist.
2. Place adjustable lifting device under axle.
3. Disconnect right and left shock absorbers from axle.
4. Remove driveshaft.
5. Disconnect upper control arms from axle.
6. Remove right and left wheels.
7. Remove right and left brake drums.
8. Disconnect brake lines from clips on axle tubes.
9. Remove differential cover and gasket, draining lubricant.
10. Unscrew differential pinion lockscrew, remove pinion shaft and axle shaft C locks. Install pinion shaft and tighten lockscrew to retain differential gears.
11. Remove both axle shafts.
12. Remove brake backing plate retaining nuts (both sides). Remove backing plates (with shoes and brake lines attached) and wire to frame. Exercise caution not to damage or bend brake lines.
13. Remove right and left lower control arm pivot bolts at axle.
14. Lower axle assembly slowly until coil spring tension is released then remove axle from vehicle.

Axle Assembly Installation

1. Raise axle into position.
2. Install right and left lower and upper control arms pivot bolts.
3. Install brake backing plates to axle. Exercise caution not to damage or bend brake lines.
4. Install both axle shafts.
5. Install axle shaft C locks, differential pinion and pinion lockscrew.
6. Install differential cover and gasket.
7. Fill differential with lubricant.
8. Connect brake lines to clips on axle tube.
9. Install right and left brake drums.
10. Install right and left wheels.
11. Connect driveshaft.
12. Connect right and left shock absorbers to axle.
13. Remove adjustable lifting device from under axle.
14. Lower vehicle and remove from hoist.

Windshield Wipers

Wiper Motor R & R

1. Raise hood.
2. Reaching through cowl opening, loosen the two transmission drive link attaching nuts to motor crankarm.
3. Remove transmission drive link from motor crankarm.
4. Disconnect wiring.
5. Remove three motor attaching screws.
6. Remove motor while guiding crankarm through hole.
7. To install, reverse the removal procedure.

Radio

Radio R & R

1. Remove battery ground cable.
2. Remove knobs, controls, washers and nuts from radio bushings.
3. Disconnect antenna lead, power connector, and speaker connectors from rear of receiver.
4. Remove two screws securing radio mounting bracket to instrument panel lower reinforcement and lift out radio receiver.
5. To install, reverse the removal procedure.

Heater System

Blower Motor R & R

1. Disconnect the battery ground cable.
2. Disconnect the blower motor lead wire.
3. Scribe the blower motor flange to case position.
4. Remove the blower to case attaching screws and remove the blower wheel and motor assembly. Pry the flange gently if the sealer acts as an adhesive.
5. Remove the blower wheel retaining nut and separate the motor and wheel.
6. To install, reverse Steps 1-5, lining up the match-marks on the motor flange and case which were made at removal.

NOTE: assemble the blower wheel to the motor with the open end of the blower away fro mthe motor. Replace sealer at the motor flange if necessary.

Heater Core R & R

1. Disconnect the battery ground cable.
2. Disconnect the blower motor lead wire.
3. Place a pan under the vehicle. Disconnect the heater hoses at the core connections and secure the ends of the hoses in a raised position.
4. Remove the coil bracket to dash panel stud nut and move the coil out of the way.
5. Remove the blower intake to dash panel screws and nuts and remove the blower intake, blower motor and wheel as an assembly.
6. Remove the core retaining strap screws and remove the core from the vehicle.
7. To install, reverse Steps 1-6.

NOTE: be sure that the blower intake sealer is intact, replace if necessary.

Unit Repair Section

Model	American Motors — Flash-O Matic Shift-Command	Chrysler Corp. — Torque flite Torque-③ Command	Ford Motor Company — FMX Select-Shift (3-Speed)	Multi-drive	Twin Range Turbo-Drive	Cruise-O-Matic (3-Speed)	C4 (3-Speed) C4S	C6 (3-Speed)
Page Number	**882**	**903**	**928**	**928**	**928**	**928**	**947**	**975**
Ambassador	1965-71	1972						
American	1965-71							
AMX	1965-71	1972						
Buick								
Buick Special								
Cadillac								
Cadillac Eldorado								
Camaro								
Challenger		1970-72						
Chevelle								
Chevrolet								
Chevy II, Nova								
Chrysler		1965-72						
Comet				1965		1968	1965-68 1971-72	1966-67
Corvette								
Cougar			1969-72				1967-72	1966-67
Dart		1965-72						
Dodge		1965-72						
Fairlane			1969-70			1965-68	1965-70	1966-70
Falcon						1965-68	1965-70	
Firebird								
Ford			1969-72			1965-68	1965-72	1966-72
F-85, Cutlass								
Gremlin	1970-71	1972						
GTO								
Hornet	1970-71	1972						
Imperial		1965-72						
Javelin	1970-71	1972						
Lincoln Cont.					1965			1966-72
Mark III								1967-72
Matador	1971	1972						
Maverick							1970-72②	
Mercury							1965-72	1966-72
Monte Carlo								
Montego			1969-70			1968	1968-72	1966-72
Mustang			1969-72			1965-68	1965-72	1966-72
Oldsmobile①								
Olds. Toronado								
Pinto							1971-72	
Plymouth		1965-72						
Pontiac①								
Rambler	1965-71							
Rebel	1965-71							
Tempest								
Thunderbird						1970		1966-72
Torino			1969-70				1971-72	1971-72
Valiant, Demon, Duster, Barracuda		1965-72						
Vega								
Ventura II								

① Dual-coupling Hydra-Matic and Roto-Hydra-Matic were used on some 1965 models. These transmissions are not covered in this manual.
② Maverick equipped with C4S in 1970, in addition to C4.
③ American Motors designation.

Identification Chart

Power glide	Type C Torque Drive	Turbo-Hydra-matic M-40	Turbo-Hydra-matic M-38	M-35	M-31	Jet-away	2-Speed Automatic	Super Turbine 300	Super Turbine 400	Turbo-Hydra-matic 350	Turbo-Hydra-matic 400	Model
984	997	1033	1013	984	984	999	999	999	1033	1013	1033	Page Number
												Ambassador
												American
												AMX
								1965-69	1965-68	1971-72	1965-72	Buick
								1965-69	1965-68	1969-72	1965-72	Buick Special
											1965-72	Cadillac
											1965-72	Cadillac Eldorado
1967-72	1969-70									1969-72	1968-72	Camaro
												Challenger
1965-72										1969-72	1966-72	Chevelle
1965-72										1969-72	1966-72	Chevrolet
1965-72	1969-72									1969-72	1969-72	Chevy II, Nova
												Chrysler
												Comet
1965-67											1968-72	Corvette
												Cougar
												Dart
												Dodge
												Fairlane
												Falcon
		1968-72	1969-72	1970-72	1970-72		1967-69			1969-72		Firebird
												Ford
						1965-69				1971-72	1965-72	F-85, Cutlass
												Gremlin
		1967-72	1971-72				1965			1971-72		GTO
												Hornet
												Imperial
												Javelin
												Lincoln Cont.
												Mark III
												Matador
												Maverick
												Mercury
1970-72										1970-72	1970-72	Monte Carlo
												Montego
												Mustang
						1965-69				1965-72		Oldsmobile①
										1966-72		Olds. Toronado
												Pinto
												Plymouth
		1966-72					1965					Pontiac①
												Rambler
												Rebel
		1969-72	1969-72	1970-72	1970-72		1965-69			1969-72		Tempest
												Thunderbird
												Torino
												Valiant, Demon Duster, Barracuda
1971-72	1971-72											Vega
1971-72			1971-72	1971-72						1971-72		Ventura II

Automatic Transmissions

American Motors Corporation

Flash-O-Matic • Shift-Command

Application

All American Motors products, 1965-71

Diagnosis

This diagnosis guide covers the most common symptoms and is an aid to careful diagnosis. The items to check are listed in the sequence to be followed for quickest results. Thus, follow the checks in the order given for the particular transmission type.

Flash-O-Matic

	CONDITIONS	Corrections		
		Group 1	**Group 2**	**Group 3**
Engage-ments	Harsh	BCD	LS	cf
	Delayed forward	ABCD	KLS	a
	Delayed reverse	ACDF	KLS	a
	None	ABCJ	KLS	aklmo
	No forward D-1	AC	KLS	abi
	No forward D-2	ABC	KLS	ab
	No reverse	ABCFE	OKS	aeh
	No neutral	C	LS	c
Upshifts	No 1-2	ACE	MKLNS	ay
	No 2-3	ACE	LNS	aety
	Shift points too high	ABCE	LS	a
	Shift points too low	ABE	LS	a
Upshift Quality	1-2 Delayed followed close by 2-3 shift	ABCE	MKLNS	abg
	2-3 slips	ABCE	KLNS	aegt
	1-2 harsh	ABCE	MLS	b
	2-3 harsh	ABCE	MLS	f
	1-2 ties up	AF	LS	fj
	2-3 ties up	AC	MN	
Downshifts	No 2-1 in D-1	ABCE	LS	iy
	No 2-1 in L-range	ABCE	LOS	hy
	No 3-2	ABE	LNS	gy
	Shift points too high	ABCE	LS	a
	Shift points too low	ABCE	LS	a
Forced Downshifts	2-1 slips	ABC	S	bi
	3-2 slips	ABC	MKLNS	aegt
	3-1 shifts above—mph.	CE	KLNS	ag
	2-1 harsh			abi
	3-2 harsh	ABC	MLNS	ef

Reverse	Slips or chatters	ABCF	OKLS	aceht
	Tie up	A	MNLS	ac
Line Pressure	Low idle pressure	ACDE	KLS	am
	High idle pressure	AB	LS	
	Low stall pressure	ABE	KLS	amy
	High stall pressure	AB	LS	
Stall Speed	Too low (200 rpm or more)	H		o
	Too high D-1	ABCJ	KLS	uvabiko
	Reverse too high	ABCFJ	KLOS	uvheko
Others	No push starts	A		n
	Poor acceleration	H		yo
	Noisy in neutral		S	fpdo
	Noisy in park		S	pdo
	Noisy in all gears		S	pro
	Noisy in 1st & 2nd gear only			prw
	Park brake does not hold	C	Q	q
	Oil out breather	AGE	KL	anx
	Oil out fill tube	AGI	K	anx
	Ties up in low, 1st gear		MKLNS	fa
	Ties up in D-1, 1st gear		MKLNS	fa
	Ties up in D-1 or D-2, 2nd gear	FC	LOS	faj
	Ties up in D-1 or D-2, 3rd gear	FC	MKLNOS	taj

Correction Code Key

Group 1
On The Car Without Draining or Removing Oil Pan

A. Check oil level
B. Check oil pressure (gauges)
C. Manual linkage adjustment
D. Engine idle speed
E. Governor inspection
F. Rear band adjustment
G. Check dip stick length
H. Engine tune-up
I. Breather restricted
J. Broken propeller shaft or axle shaft

Group 2
On The Car After Draining and Removing Oil Pan

K. Oil tubes missing or damaged
L. Valve body attaching bolts loose or missing
M. Front band adjustment
N. Front servo, remove, disassemble and inspect
O. Rear servo, remove, disassemble and inspect .
P. Tube or servo seal rings missing, broken, leaking
Q. Parking linkage inspection
R. Pressure regulator (V8)
S. 1. Remove control valve assembly and inspect for loose screws.
   2. Replace control valve if no defects in Step 1.
   NOTE: Road test car after Step 1 if defect is corrected.
   Road test car after control valve replacement.

Group 3
Bench Overhaul

a. Sealing rings missing or broken
b. Front clutch slipping, worn plates or faulty parts
c. Front clutch seized or distorted plates
d. Front clutch hub thrust washer missing (detectable in N, P, R only)
e. Rear clutch slipping, worn or faulty parts
f. Rear clutch seized or distorted plates
g. Front band worn or broken
h. Rear band worn or broken
i. One-way (sprag) clutch slipping or incorrectly installed
j. One-way (sprag) clutch seized

k. Broken input shaft
l. Front pump drive tangs or converter hub broken
m. Front pump worn
n. Rear pump
o. Converter
p. Front pump
q. Parking linkage
r. Planetary assembly
s. Fluid distributor sleeve in output shaft (V8)
t. Rear clutch piston ball check leaks
u. Broken output shaft
v. Broken gears
w. Forward sun gear thrust washer missing
x. Breather baffle missing
y. Output shaft plug missing (6 cyl.)

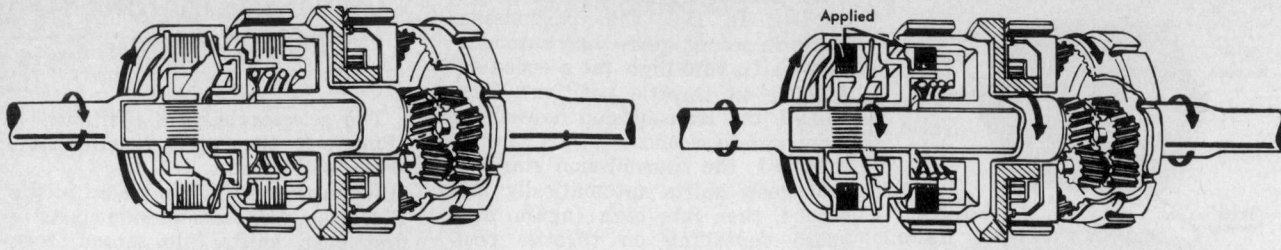

Power flow in neutral
(© American Motors)

Power flow in high (direct)
(© American Motors)

In the 2 position, the transmission starts in second gear and remains in that gear until the lever is shifted to another range. If the lever is moved to the 2 position from D, at a speed below the second-third shift point, the transmission drops down into second gear.

In the 1 position, the transmission starts in first gear and remains in that gear until the lever is shifted to another range. If the lever is moved to the 1 position at a vehicle speed below the automatic first-second shift point, the transmission drops down two gears into first, and remains in first until the selector lever is moved to another range. If, however, vehicle speed is greater than the first-second shift point, the transmission drops down only one gear, into second, and remains in second until either vehicle speed is reduced or the lever is moved to another position.

Towing

The car may be towed with the rear wheels on the road if the selector lever is in Neutral, tow speed does not exceed 35 mph, and tow distance does not exceed 50 miles. Do not tow with wheels on ground if transmission malfunction is known or suspected.

Transmission Tune-up

The transmission tune-up consists of five checks and adjustments:
1. Fluid level.
2. Selector linkage inspection and adjustment.
3. Front band check and adjustment.
4. Rear band check and adjustment.
5. Oil pressure check and adjustment.

Because the transmission pressures are controlled by intake manifold vacuum, the engine must be in good running condition for satisfactory transmission performance. A poor-running engine, with attendant low intake manifold vacuum, usually causes harsh or delayed shifting.

To test intake manifold vacuum, connect a T-fitting into the line at the transmission vacuum control unit, then connect a vacuum test gauge to

the T-fitting. Set the parking brake and start the engine. With the brakes applied and the transmission in D or D-1, accelerate to 1,000 rpm and note vacuum reading. Do not, under any circumstances, maintain stall speed for more than 10 seconds—the transmission fluid will boil. Any vacuum leaks must be corrected before further transmission testing can continue.

Fluid Level

The "full" (F) mark on the dipstick is calibrated for normal operating temperature. If the transmission is filled to the 'F' mark when cool, the fluid may froth and be forced out the vent or filler tube.

To check fluid cold, position car on the level, set the parking brake, and start the engine. Move the selector lever through all gear positions and check the fluid—it should be at the level indicated in the chart.

Fluid Level

Model	Level
36	¼ in. below L
37, 42, 43	¼ in. below L
40, 44	5/16 in. above L
11, 11B	L
12	L

Selector Linkage

1965
1. Disconnect gearshift rod trunnion from operating shaft lever.
2. Make sure transmission lever is in rear position.
3. Adjust trunnion for free pin fit.
4. Check linkage action, then test drive car.

Column Shift—1966-67
1. Turn off ignition switch.
2. Place selector in Neutral.
3. Disconnect manual lever from transmission outer lever.
4. Move outer lever to extreme rear notch (Low).
5. Move lever forward three notches to Neutral.
6. With lever linkage held against Neutral stop, adjust for free pin fit.

NOTE: 1966 287/327—free pin fit, then shorten linkage three full turns.

7. Connect linkage and check action, then test drive car.

Floorshift (Shift-Command)— 1966-67
1. Place selector in Neutral.
2. Disconnect linkage rod from shift lever.
3. Move transmission outer lever to extreme forward notch (1).
4. Move lever three notches to rear (Neutral).
5. Adjust for free pin fit.
6. Connect linkage and check action, then test drive car.

1968-71
1. Place selector in Neutral.
   NOTE: range 1 for American series.
2. Push shift rod against Neutral stop on shift gate.
3. Push selector lever forward to remove free play, then adjust clevis for free pin fit.
4. Connect linkage and check action, then test drive car.
5. On 1970 and 1971 models, place selector in Park and check column lock operation.

Console Shift—1970-71
1. Loosen park lockup rod trunnion locknuts.
2. Place console lever in Neutral.
3. Place transmission shift lever in neutral position.
4. Adjust shift rod for a free pin fit.
5. Place console lever in Park. Lock the steering column. It may be necessary to move the lower column lever upward until it is in the locked position.
6. Tighten the lower trunnion locknut until it contacts the trunnion. Tighten the upper locknut while holding the trunnion centered in the column lever.

Front Band
1. Drain transmission fluid and remove oil pan.
2. Check for debris, "scorched" smelling fluid, and loose parts.
3. Check pick up screen for clogging, then check that all valve body cap screws and servo bolts are tight (do not overtighten).
4. Check that oil delivery tubes

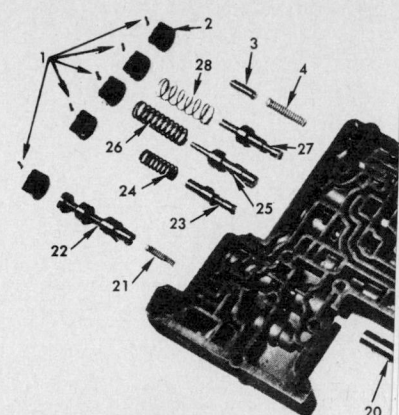

1 Retainer plug pins
2 Retainer plugs
3 2-3 shift valve plunger
4 2-3 shift valve spring (inner)
5 Main valve body
6 2-3 shift valve spring (outer)
8 Main valve body end plate
9 End plate retainer screws
10 1-2 shift valve
11 Cutback valve
12 Throttle modulator valve
13 Throttle modulator valve spring
14 Primary regulator spring retainer
15 Primary regulator spring (outer)
16 Primary regulator spring seat
17 Primary regulator valve spacer
18 Primary regulator valve plug
19 Primary regulator spring (inner)

20
21
22
23
24
25
26
27
28

1970-71 M11B, M12 main valve body

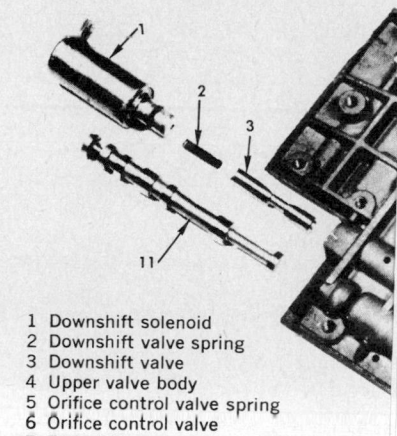

1 Downshift solenoid
2 Downshift valve spring
3 Downshift valve
4 Upper valve body
5 Orifice control valve spring
6 Orifice control valve
7 End plate screws
8 Upper valve body end plate
9 Servo regulator time valve
10 Throttle valve
11 Manual valve

1970-71 M11B, M12 upper valve bod

lockwashers.
NOTE: on torque tube models
remove torque tube adapter bolts.
7. Rotate extension housing clock
wise until parking brake ancho
pin clears extension housing
then remove anchor pin witl
pliers or a magnet.
8. Remove parking brake toggl
link and pawl assembly.
9. To install, reverse remova
procedure, using a new O-rin
on toggle pin.

Front servo comp

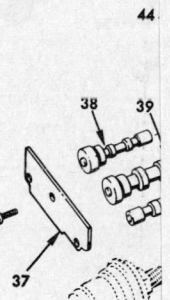

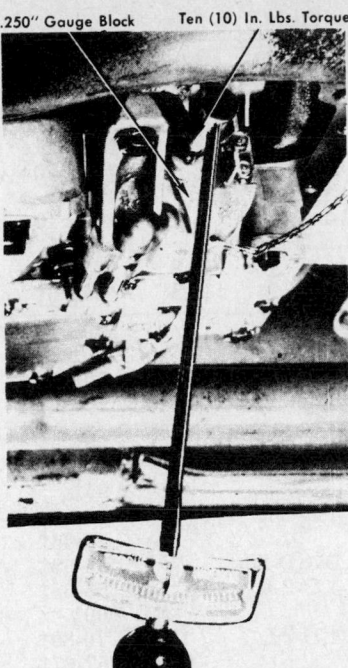

.250" Gauge Block   Ten (10) In. Lbs. Torque

Adjusting front servo—1967-70
(© American Motors)

are in place and snug.
5. To adjust, insert a ¼ in. gauge
block between the front servo
adjusting screw and the piston
rod, then tighten adjusting screw
to 9 in. lbs. for 1965-67 transmissions, 10 in. lbs. for 1968-71
transmissions.

Caution the adjusting screw on
M11, M11B and M12
transmissions has a left-hand thread.
6. For 1969-71 only: inspect the
adjuster wire for proper clearance—one screw thread must be
exposed between the wire and the
servo actuating lever.
7. Clean and install the oil pan,
using a new gasket, then install
proper quantity of approved
fluid.

Rear Band
1. Place a hydraulic jack under the
transmission, then remove the
four crossmember fasteners and
the crossmember.
NOTE: not necessary to remove
crossmember on most Ambassador
models. On AMX and Javelin equipped with power steering, lift the hood
before lowering transmission to keep
the power steering fluid reservoir
wingnut from hitting the hood.
2. Lower the transmission, then
loosen the rear band adjusting
screw locknut and tighten the
adjusting screw to 10 ft. lbs. for
1965 and later transmissions.
3. Back off adjusting screw ¾ turn
for M36, M37, M40, M43, and
M44 transmissions, 1¼ turns
for M11, M11B, and M12 trans-

missions. Tighten locknut to 28
ft. lbs.
NOTE: 1966 287/327 transmission
—1½ turns, then tighten locknut to
35-40 ft. lbs.
4. Raise transmission and replace
crossmember.

Control Pressure
Remove the pipe plug on the left-
hand side of the transmission case,
then install a pressure gauge (0-400
psi). Connect a T-fitting and vacuum
gauge into the line to the vacuum
control unit, chock the wheels, set the
parking brake, and bring the engine
to normal operating temperature.
Place selector lever in Reverse and,
with brakes locked, accelerate engine
to obtain vacuum in chart. Make sure
the pressure is the same as that listed
for the appropriate vacuum and rpm.
Do not exceed 10 seconds at stall
speed.
If pressure is too low, remove the
vacuum control unit line and turn the
adjusting screw clockwise. If pressure is too high, turn adjusting screw
counterclockwise. For M36, M37,
M40, M43, and M44 transmission,
one turn of the adjusting screw

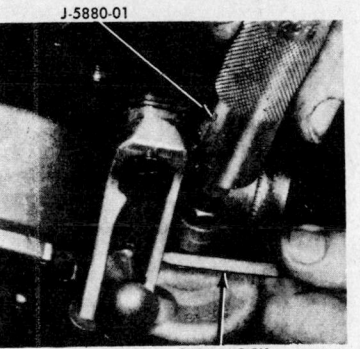

.250" BLOCK

**Adjusting front servo—1964-66 V8,
1967 343 V8**
(© American Motors)

J-9639
.250" Block

Adjusting front servo—1964-66 6 cylinder
(© American Motors)

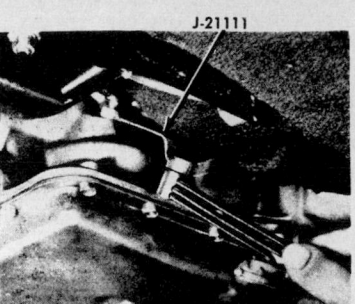

J-21111

Adjusting rear band—1964-66 6 cylinder
(© American Motors)

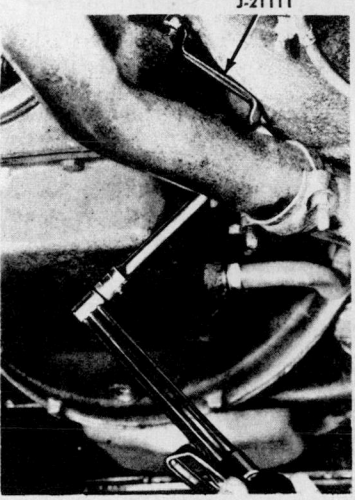

J-21111

Adjusting rear band—1964-66 V8
(© American Motors)

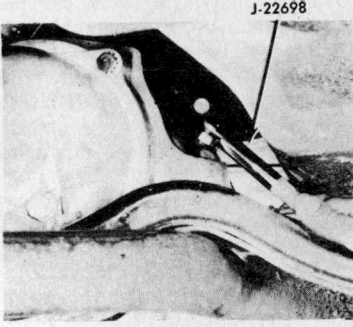

J-22698

Adjusting rear band—1967-70
(© American Motors)

equals approximately 18 psi pressure
change; for M11, M11B, and M12
transmissions prior to 1971, 10 psi
pressure change. Starting 1971, one
turn produces 18 psi change for all
models.
If correct pressure cannot be obtained, check the vacuum control
unit. The pushrod on the M11, M11B,
and M12 transmissions prior to 1971
should be 3.439 in. long (with altitude correction type control unit).
The pushrod on the M36, M37, M40,
M43, and M44 transmissions should
be 4.116 ± .005 in. long (diaphragm
type control unit). Starting 1971, the
M11B and M12 pushrod length is
2.940 ± .005 in.
If pressure is O.K. in Reverse,
check the pressure in the forward

ranges. Do not, h...
just the pressure...
ranges. If pressure...
ward ranges, but...
remove and inspect...
sticking or loose s...
is correct in all ran...
mission does not...
cally when in Driv...
governor is not stu...

Service—Tra...
in C...

Oil Pan and Scr...
1965-71 All

1. Jack up the ca...
   the oil filler tu...
   mission, then...
   mission oil.
2. Remove oil pan...
   washers, then...
   and gasket.
3. Remove Alnico r...
   head of the rear...
   bolt, then rem...
   screen.
   NOTE: do not use...
   any solvents other...
   clean.
4. To install, rev...
   procedure, tight...
   screws to 15 ft. lb...

Downshift Solenoi...
1967-71

1. Drain oil and re...
   then disconnect...
   from transmission...
2. Push in on the s...
   twisting, to detac...
   control valve.
   CAUTION: do not...
   valve spring.
3. To install, reve...
   procedure, using...

Control Valve R&R—
M36, M37, M40, M...

1. Disconnect filler tu...
   transmission oil.
2. Remove oil pan.
3. Disconnect vacuum...
   control unit.
4. Remove vacuum co...
   pushrod.
5. Remove rear servo...
   clutch oil tube, fro...
   lease tube, and fron...
   tube.
6. Disconnect solenoid...
   minal, then remov...
   control valve-to-cas...
   screws.
7. Remove control valv...
8. To install, begin wit...
   pressure and convert...
   "out" tubes, then in...
   O-ring on the pump...
   and install the tub...
   pump.
9. Engage the manual l...

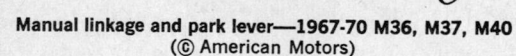

1970-71 M42, M43, M44 front clutch or...
valve body section
(© American Motors)

1 Front clutch orifice control valve bod...
2 Front clutch orifice control valve
3 Front clutch orifice control valve spri...
4 Front clutch orifice control valve stop...

procedure, tightening screws...
17-22 ft. lbs.

Control Shaft Inner Levers...
Manual Control Shaft Seals...
R&R—1965-71

1. Disconnect filler tube and d...
   transmission oil.
2. Remove oil pan and gasket.
   NOTE: and throttle control ca...
   if so equipped.
3. Remove control valve assem...
4. Remove the shift rod from...
   outer manual lever.
5. Remove the hex nut, and in...
   lever, from the shaft.
6. Using diagonal cutters and...
   screwdriver, remove the tape...
   lockpin from the case.
7. Remove the manual valve le...
   shaft from the case.
8. To install, reverse rem...
   procedure, using a new O-r...
   NOTE: if manual control shaf...
   inserted past the tapered pin gro...
   the O-ring will be damaged.

Parking Brake Control Tog...
Hub Shaft R&R—1965-71

1. Follow Steps 1-3, above.
2. Remove the retaining spring...
   washer from the inner end...
   the toggle hub, then remov...
   park lever assembly.
3. Remove the toggle lift asse...
   from the shaft, then remove...
   tapered lockpin, using diag...
   cutters, and pull the shaft f...
   the case.
4. To install, reverse rem...
   procedure, using a new O-...
   on the shaft.

Parking Pawl Assembly R...
—1965-71

1. Place a jack under the rea...
   the engine; support torque...
   if so equipped.
2. Remove the speedometer...
   and exhaust pipe clamp.
3. Remove the two rear crossm...
   ber bolts from the engine...
   support, then disconnect...
   crossmember from the side...
   NOTE: on Javelin and AMX...
   power steering, lift hood.
4. Remove the crossmember...
   pulling down on exhaust pi...
   gain clearance.

Sub-Assembly Removal

Front Pump—1965-71

1. Remove oil pressure tube, suction tube, and O-ring, then
   remove converter "in" and "out"
   tubes from pump.
2. Remove the oil seal from the
   pump body.
3. Remove pump cap screws, pump,
   and selective thrust washer.

Front Clutch, Rear Clutch, and
Primary Sun Gear Assemblies—
1965-71

1. Remove front and rear clutch assemblies and sun gear assembly
   by inserting a screwdriver between rear clutch drum and center support. Keep parts together
   as a unit.
2. Remove front band through

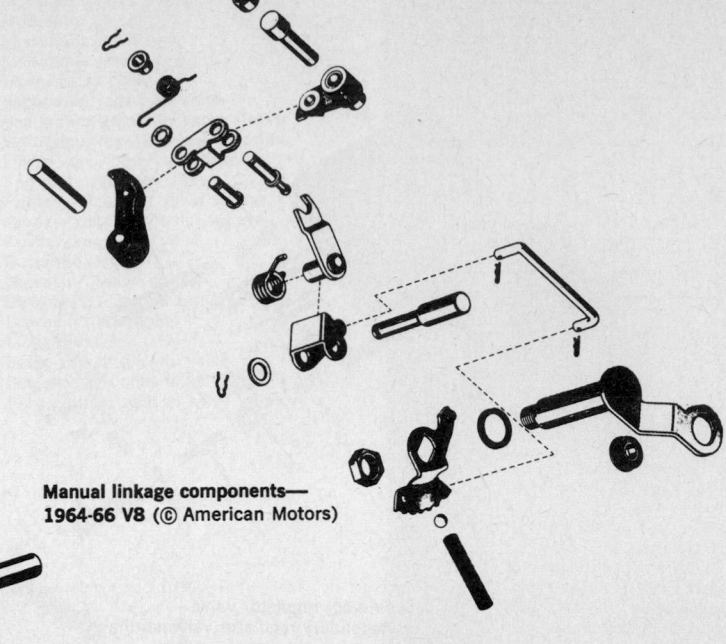

Manual linkage components—
1964-66 V8 (© American Motors)

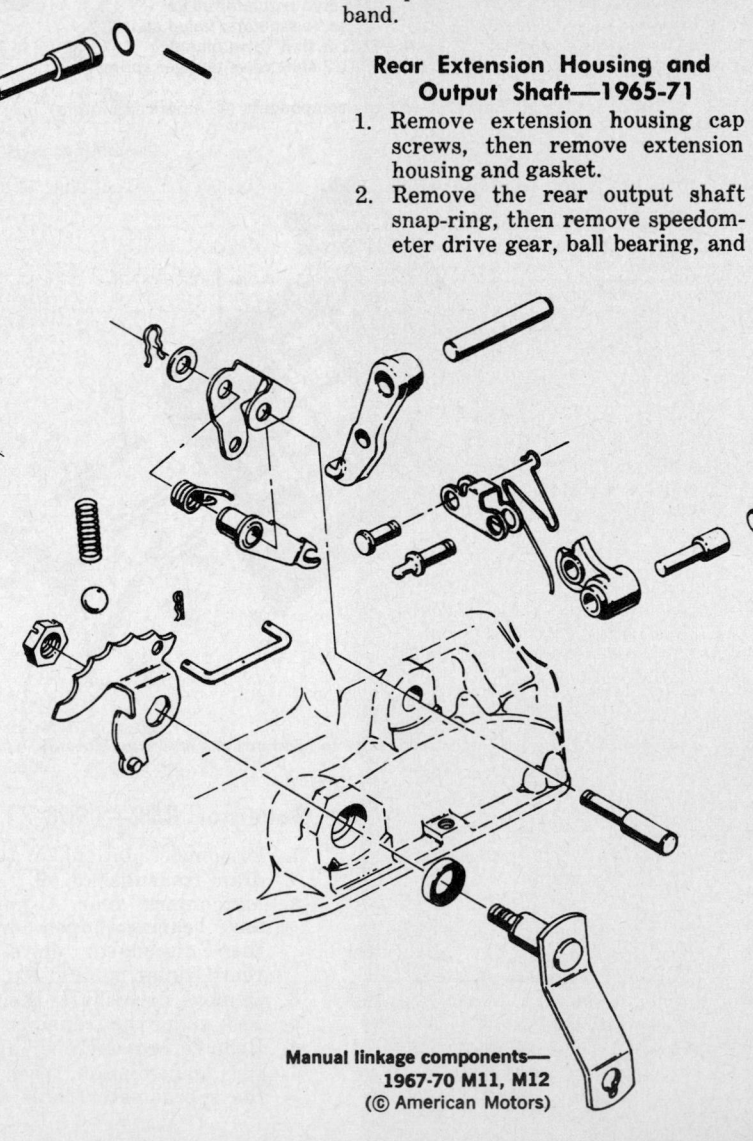

Manual linkage and park lever—1967-70 M36, M37, M40
(© American Motors)

front of case. (Remove from
bottom of case on 1965-66 V8
and 1967-71 M11, M11B, and
M12.

Center Support and Planet
Carrier Assemblies—1965-71

1. Remove two cap screws from
   sides of case, then remove center
   support, sprag clutch, and planet
   carrier.
2. Remove rear band through front
   of case. (Remove through rear
   of case on 1965-66 V8 and
   1967-71 M11, M11B, and M12.
   NOTE: bands do not interchange
   and can be identified on 1965-66
   6-cylinder models by the red lining
   on front band, brown lining on rear
   band. From 1967-71, the bands can
   be identified by the one-piece con-

struction of the front band and
three-piece construction of the rear
band.

Rear Extension Housing and
Output Shaft—1965-71

1. Remove extension housing cap
   screws, then remove extension
   housing and gasket.
2. Remove the rear output shaft
   snap-ring, then remove speedometer drive gear, ball bearing, and

Manual linkage components—
1967-70 M11, M12
(© American Motors)

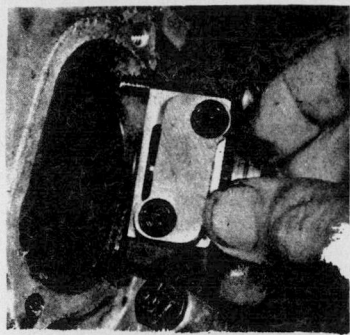

Governor removal
(© American Motors)

front snap-ring.

3. Remove governor snap-ring, governor assembly, and ball bearing from output shaft.
4. Remove the six large screws from the rear case adapter, then remove adapter.
5. Remove the three oil rings from the output shaft, then remove output shaft and rear thrust washer through the front end of the case.

Rear Pump—1965-66

1. Remove the six large Fillister

Checking transmission end-play
(© American Motors)

Front sun gear and shaft—1964-69 typical
(1970 has thrust washer in place of Torrington bearing)
(© American Motors)

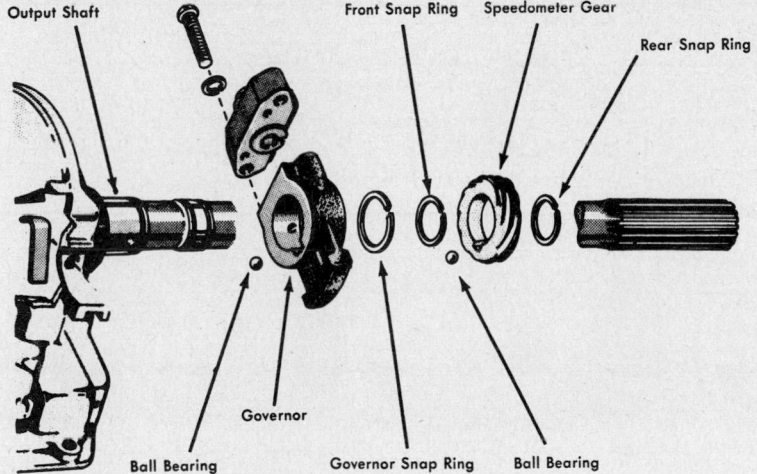

Output Shaft   Front Snap Ring   Speedometer Gear   Rear Snap Ring

Governor

Ball Bearing   Governor Snap Ring   Ball Bearing

Speedometer drive gear and governor—1964-66 6 cylinder, 1967-70 M36, M37, M40
(© American Motors)

head screws and the small Fillister head screw from the rear pump body.

2. Remove rear pump body and driven gear.
3. Remove the three oil rings from the output shaft, then the rear pump drive gear, drive gear key, and rear pump body plate.
4. Remove the output shaft and rear thrust washer through the front end of the case.

Component Reconditioning

Front Clutch Disassembly and Assembly—1965-66 V8; 1967-71 M11, M11B, M12

1. Remove cover snap-ring, then

input shaft and fiber washer from hub.

2. Remove the four driven and three drive plates, pressure plate, and hub from the drum.
3. Using spring compressor on release spring, remove snap-ring and release spring.
   NOTE: front cover snap-ring and release spring snap-ring are not the same—the thicker snap-ring goes against the release spring.
4. Force the piston from drum bore by applying air pressure to the clutch apply hole.
5. The outer seal and inner O-ring may now be removed.
6. Check all parts and replace as needed. The lined plates should be replaced when the grooves in the lining are no longer visible or the plates are warped.
7. Lubricate all parts in reassembly with transmission fluid. Replace the outer seal and O-ring and reassemble in reverse of disassembly procedure.

Front Clutch Disassembly and Assembly—1965-66 6 Cyl.; 1967-71 M36, M37, M40, M42, M43, M44

1. With front and rear clutch and planet carrier on bench, lift front clutch and input shaft from rear clutch.
2. Remove input shaft snap-ring, then input shaft.
3. Remove hub and fiber thrust washer, drive and driven plates and pressure plate from front clutch cylinder.
4. Remove snap-ring from return spring, then remove spring.
5. Using air pressure at oil apply hole, blow annular piston from cylinder.
6. Inspect all parts and replace seal and O-ring, together with any other required parts.
7. Reverse above sequences in reinstallation.

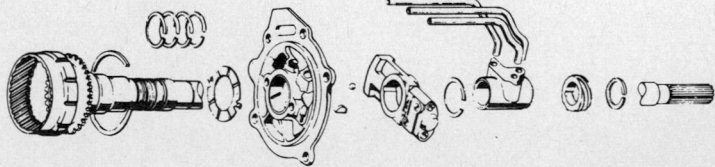

Output shaft assembly sequence—1964-70 heavy duty transmission (© American Motors)

Front clutch—1964-70 typical
(© American Motors)

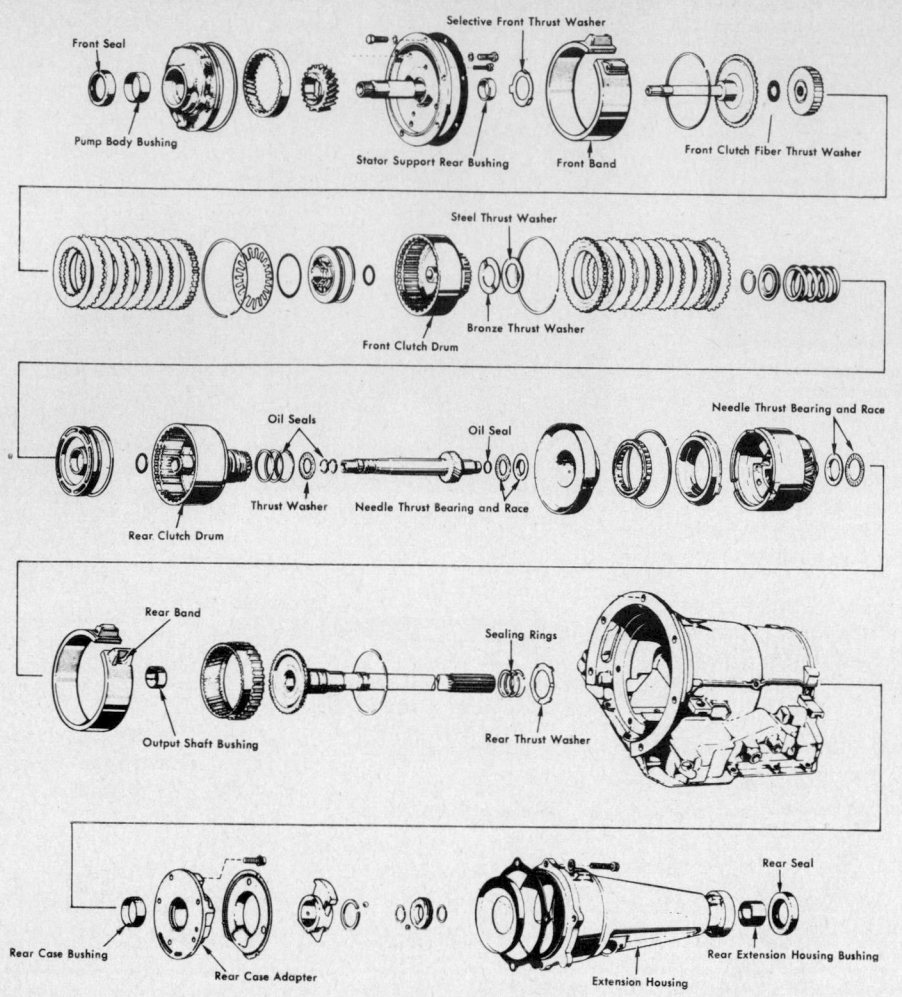

Front Seal

Pump Body Bushing

Selective Front Thrust Washer

Stator Support Rear Bushing

Front Band

Front Clutch Fiber Thrust Washer

Steel Thrust Washer

Front Clutch Drum

Bronze Thrust Washer

Oil Seals

Oil Seal

Needle Thrust Bearing and Race

Rear Clutch Drum

Thrust Washer

Needle Thrust Bearing and Race

Rear Band

Output Shaft Bushing

Sealing Rings

Rear Thrust Washer

Rear Seal

Rear Case Bushing

Rear Case Adapter

Extension Housing

Rear Extension Housing Bushing

M42, M43, M44 transmission components (© American Motors)

Rear clutch components—1964-70 (© American Motors)

Sprag clutch and planet carrier—typical 1964-70
(© American Motors)

"O" Ring

Seal

Pump Suction

Convertor In-Out Tubes

Pump Pressure

Front pump components—1964-70 (© American Motors)

Rear Pump—1964-66 V8
(© American Motors)

Rear Clutch Disassembly—All

1. Remove thrust washers and seal rings from sun gear shaft and lift from shaft. Remove rear clutch drum.

2. Remove sun gear from planet carrier.

3. Remove snap-ring from **rear**

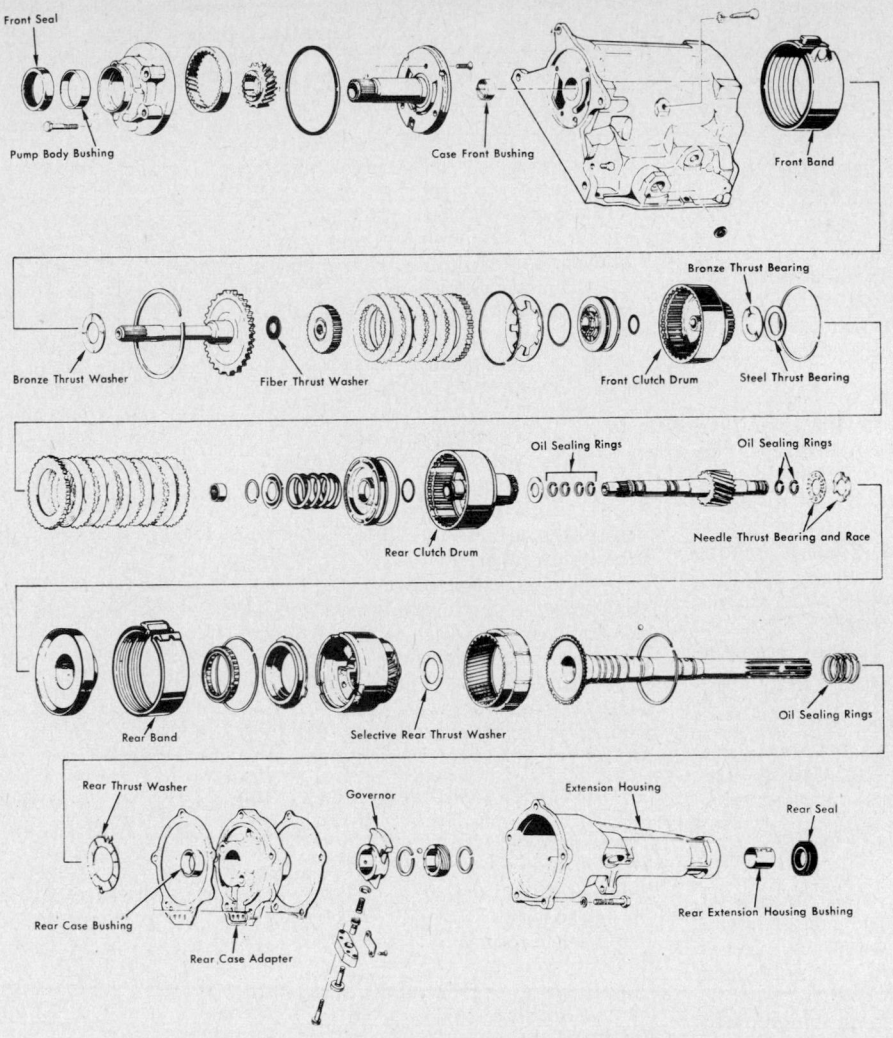

Front Seal

Pump Body Bushing

Case Front Bushing

Front Band

Bronze Thrust Bearing

Bronze Thrust Washer

Fiber Thrust Washer

Front Clutch Drum

Steel Thrust Bearing

Oil Sealing Rings

Oil Sealing Rings

Rear Clutch Drum

Needle Thrust Bearing and Race

Rear Band

Selective Rear Thrust Washer

Oil Sealing Rings

Rear Thrust Washer

Governor

Extension Housing

Rear Seal

Rear Case Bushing

Rear Case Adapter

Rear Extension Housing Bushing

M11B, M12 transmission components (© American Motors)

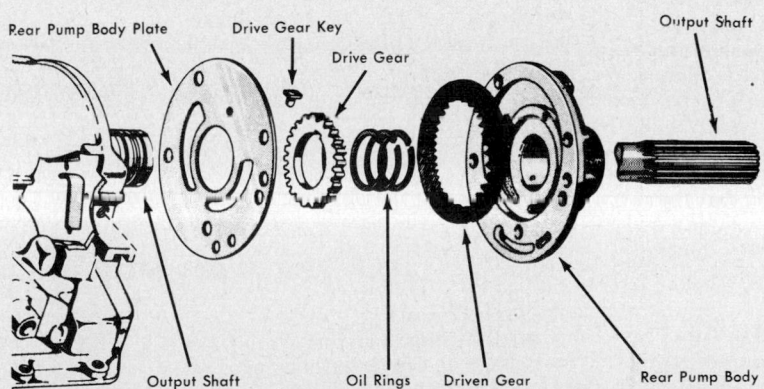

Rear Pump Body Plate

Drive Gear Key

Drive Gear

Output Shaft

Output Shaft

Oil Rings

Driven Gear

Rear Pump Body

Rear pump components—1964-66 (1965-66 has no plate) (© American Motors)

drum and remove drive, driven, and pressure plates.

4. Using spring compressor on release spring, remove snap-ring and release spring.

5. Apply air pressure and remove piston from drum.

6. Remove piston seal and O-ring.

7. Inspect all parts and replace as required. Always renew oil seal and O-ring.

Rear Clutch Assembly—1965-66 V8; 1967-71 M11, M11B, M12

1. Lubricate all rear clutch parts with transmission oil before reassembly.

2. Check the steel plates for proper dish. This dish should be .010-.020 in., when measured on a flat plate.

3. Install piston. Press spring and retainer into position and install snap-ring.

4. Install the drive and driven plates and the pressure plate, then install the snap-ring. (Note: the dished plates are installed with the dished side up and the pressure plate with the smooth side down.)

5. Follow the assembly procedure

in reverse of the removal procedure.

NOTE: side clearance between grooves and new cast-iron rings must be less than 0.005 in. to prevent pressure loss.

Rear Clutch Assembly 1965-66 6 Cyl.; 1967-71 M36, M37, M40, M42, M43, M44

1. Lubricate all parts with transmission oil before reassembly.
2. Check the steel plates for proper dish. This dish should be .010-.015 in., when measured on a flat surface.
3. Be sure that the 30 needle bearings are properly installed into the drum. Use petrolatum to hold in place during assembly.
4. Place small O-ring on cylinder hub and seal ring on the annular piston, then place in piston installing tool.
5. Place tool in rear clutch drum, then drive into drum.
6. Install return spring, retainer and snap-ring into drum and compress spring. Then, install snap-ring.
7. Install drive and driven plates and pressure plate. (Note: the dished plates are installed with the dished side up.)
8. Install pressure plate and snap-ring.
9. Place sun gear shaft in planet carrier, with one Torrington bearing on top side of sun gear, and install clutch assembly onto shaft.
10. Install two oil seal rings onto sun gear shaft.
11. Install steel and bronze thrust washers, using petrolatum to hold them in place.
12. Install front clutch cylinder onto shaft, aligning it with plates in rear drum.
13. Install front clutch hub and fiber thrust washer.
14. Install front clutch pressure plate, with smooth side up, then install drive and driven plates.
15. Install input shaft and snap-ring.

Sprag Clutch—1965-72 All

1. A sprag clutch is incorporated in the pinion carrier. Twenty-four sprags are installed into the clutch assembly.
2. Fit the outer race into the pinion carrier assembly.

NOTE: planet carrier should freewheel in counterclockwise rotation, and lock-up clockwise, when viewed from rear.

Front and Rear Pumps

Normal disassembly and inspections are required for scratches, scores and excessive wear. See illustrations for reassembly sequences.

Torque Specifications

V8 up to and incl. 1966

	Foot-Pounds	Inch-Pounds
Converter to drive plate stud nuts	23-28	
Transmission case to converter housing	40-45	
Front pump to transmission case	17-22	
Front servo to transmission case	30-35	
Rear servo to transmission case	40-45	
Planetary center support to transmission case	20-25	
Upper to lower valve body	4-6	
Control valve body to transmission case	8-10	
Pressure regulator to transmission case	17-22	
Extension to transmission case	28-38	
Oil pan to transmission case	10-20	
Case assembly—gauge hole plug	10-15	
Rear servo adjusting screw locknut	35-40	
Front servo adjusting screw locknut	20-25	
Detent lever attaching nut	35-40	
Front pump cover screws		25-35
Rear pump cover (1/4—20)		80-90
Rear pump cover (10—24)		25-35
Governor inspection cover		50-60
Transmission vent assembly	7-10	
Governor valve body to counterweight		50-60
Governor valve body cover		20-30
Pressure regulator cover screws		20-30
Control valve body plug	10-14	
Control valve lower body plug	7-15	

M36, M37, M40, M42, M43, M44, and 6 Cyl. up to and incl. 1966

	Foot-Pounds
Converter to drive plate	30-35
Transmission case to converter housing	17-22
Rear extension to case	30-40
Oil pan to case	10-20
Front servo to case	9-12
Rear servo to case	20
Pump adapter to front pump housing	17-22
Pump adapter to case	10-18
Rear pump to case	6.2*
Rear oil screen	6.2
Governor valve body to counter weight	6.2
Governor valve body cover to governor	2-3
Case line pressure plug	6-10
Rear case adapter to case	6.2★
Center support to case	20
Valve body to case (1/4—20)	6.2
Valve body screws (10—24)	2-3

* Up to and including 1966 only.
★ After 1967.

1967-71 M11, M11B, M12

	Foot-Pounds	Inch-Pounds
Converter to flex plate	35	
Converter housing to engine	28	
Transmission to converter housing	55	
Case line pressure plug	15	
Front pump assembly to pump body	20	
Front pump assembly to transmission case	20	
Manual control lever to shaft	45	
Center support to case	25	
Front servo adjusting screw locknut	20	
Front servo to case	35	
Extension housing to case	35	
Valve body screws		30
Upper, lower valve body and cover bolts	10	
Valve body to transmission	10	
Oil screen to valve body		30
Governor body to counterweight		75
Vacuum control unit to case	15	
Oil pan to case	15	

Chrysler Corporation
Torqueflite

Application

American Motors, 1972	**Challenger, 1970-72**	**Barracuda, 1965-72**
Chrysler, 1965-72	**Dart, 1965-72**	**Valiant, 1965-72**
	Dodge, 1965-72	**Plymouth, 1965-72**

NOTE: Torqueflite Transmissions have no rear pump starting with 1966 Models.

Diagnosis

This guide covers the most common symptoms and is an aid to careful diagnosis. The items to check are listed in sequence to be followed for quickest results. Follow the checks in the order given for the particular transmission type.

TROUBLE SYMPTOMS	Items to Check	
	In Car	Out of Car
Harsh N to D or N to R shift	CDEFGIJ	ab
Delayed Shift—N to D	ACIHKJ	ca
Runaway on upshift and 3-2 kickdown	ABCDLIHK	b
Harsh upshift and 3-2 kickdown	BCDLIHJ	b
No upshift	ABCDLIHKM	b
No kickdown on normal downshift	ABNCDLIHKM	d
Erratic shifts	ABNCFOPQ IKMJ	c
Slips in forward drive positions	ACIHK	abd
Slips in reverse only	CEGIK	
Slips in all positions	ACOIK	e
No drive in any position	ACOQIKJ	ca
No drive in forward positions	CDOLIHK	abd
No drive in reverse	CEGKMI	b
Drives in neutral	NIJ	a
Drags or locks	DELG	abfd
Noises	AORPMIJ	a
Hard to fill or blows out	AORSTQI	
Transmission overheats	ADEORTMI	abe
Unable to push-start car (No rear pump after 1965)	ACEGI	g

Key to Checks

A. Oil level	H. Accumulator	O. Regulator valve and/or spring	a. Front-kickdown clutch
B. Control linkage	I. Valve body assembly	P. Output shaft bushing	b. Rear clutch
C. Oil pressure check	J. Manual valve lever	Q. Strainer	c. Front pump and/or sleeve
D. Kickdown band	K. Air pressure check	R. Converter control valve	d. Overrunning clutch
E. Low-reverse band	L. K-D servo link	S. Breather clogged	e. Converter
F. Improper engine idle	M. Governor	T. Cooler or lines	f. Planetary
G. Servo linkage	N. Gear shift cable		g. Rear pump (not after 1965)

Torqueflite Specifications

	A-904	A-727
Type—three speed with torque converter	Yes	Yes
Torque converter dia. std.	10¾ in.	11¾ in.
1968-70 High Perf.		10¾ in.
Converter oil capacity		
1965	17 pts.	19½ pts.
1966-67	16 pts.	18½ pts.
1968-69 std.	15½ pts.	18½ pts.
1968-69 High Perf.		15½ pts.
1970-72 std.	17 pts.	19 pts.
1970 High Perf.		16½ pts.
Cooling method	Water	Water
Lubrication pump	Rotor type	Rotor type
Clutches (No. of Plates and Discs)		
Front plates 1965-72 170/198/225 six	3	
Front discs 1965-72 170/198/225 six	3	
Rear plates 1965-72 170/198/225 six	2	
Rear discs 1965-72 170/198/225 six	3	
Front plates 1965-69 273 V8	4	
Front discs 1965-69 273/V8	4	
Rear plates 1965-69 273/V8	3	
Rear discs 1965-69 273/V8	4	
Front plates 1965 police and taxi six		4
Front discs 1965 police and taxi six		4
Rear plates 1965 police and taxi six		2
Rear discs 1965 police and taxi six		3
Front plates 1965 318 V8		4
Front discs 1965 318 V8		4
Rear plates 1965 318 V8		2
Rear discs 1965 318 V8		3
Front plates 1965-66 large V8s		4
Front discs 1965-66 large V8s		4
Rear plates 1965-66 large V8s		3
Rear discs 1965-66 large V8		4
Front plates 1966 318 and police and taxi six		4
Front discs 1966 318 and police and taxi six		4
Rear plates 1966 318 and police and taxi six		3
Rear discs 1966 318 and police and taxi six		4
Front plates 1967-72 318 V8, 1971-72 340, 360, 383-2 V8's and police and taxi six		3
Front discs 1967-72 318 V8, 1971-72 340, 360, 383-2 V8's and police and taxi six		3
Rear plates 1967-72 318 V8, 1971-72 340, 360, 383-2 V8's and police and taxi six		3
Rear discs 1967-72 318 V8, 1971-72 340, 360, 383-2 V8's and police and taxi six		4
Front plates 1968-69 318 V8	4	
Front discs 1968-69 318 V8	4	
Rear plates 1968-69 318 V8	3	
Rear discs 1968-69 318 V8	4	
Front plates 1967-72 340, 383, 440 V8		4
Front discs 1967-72 340. 383, 440 V8		4
Rear plates 1967-72 340, 383, 440 V8		3
Rear discs 1967-72 340, 383, 440 V8		4
Front plates 1967-72 426 Hemi, 440-6		5
Front discs 1967-72 426 Hemi, 440-6		5
Rear plates 1967-72 426 Hemi, 440-6		3
Rear discs 1967-72 426 Hemi, 440-6		4
Pump Clearances		
End clearance 1965 front pump	0.001-.0025 in.	0.001-0.0025 in.
End clearance 1965 rear pump	0.0015-0.003 in.	0.0015-0.003 in.
End clearance 1966	0.001-0.0025 in.	0.001-0.0025 in.

NOTE: after 1965, Torqueflites do not have rear pumps

	A-904	A-727
End clearance 1967-72	0.0015-0.003 in.	0.0015-0.003 in.
Outer rotor to case bore 1969-72	0.004-0.008 in.	0.004-0.008 in.
Outer rotor tip to inner rotor tip measured diametrically 1969-72	0.005-0.010 in.	0.005-0.010 in.
Planetary assembly end play 1969-72	0.006-0.033 in.	0.010-0.037 in.
Drive train end play		
1964	0.023-0.068 in.	0.030-0.069 in.
1965	0.023-0.089 in.	0.036-0.084 in.
1966-67	0.022-0.091 in.	0.036-0.084 in.
1968	0.030-0.089 in.	0.036-0.084 in.
1969-70	0.030-0.089 in.	0.037-0.084 in.
Clutch Plate Clearance		
1965 front 3 disc	0.042-0.087 in.	
1965 front 4 disc	0.056-0.104 in.	
1965 rear 3 disc	0.018-0.036 in.	0.022-0.042 in.
1965 rear 4 disc	0.024-0.049 in.	0.026-0.054 in.
1965-66 front		0.024-0.123 in.
1966-70 front 3 disc	0.042-0.087 in.	
1966-70 front 4 disc	0.056-0.104 in.	
1966 rear 3 disc	0.026-0.055 in.	
1966 rear 4 disc	0.032-0.055 in.	
1966-67 rear		0.037-0.060 in.
1967-70 rear	0.032-0.055 in.	
1967-70 front 3 disc		0.036-0.086 in.
1967-70 front 4 disc		0.024-0.125 in.
1968-70 front, 4 disc, high perf.		0.066-0.123 in.
1967 front, 5 disc, Hemi		0.029-0.151 in.
1968-70 front, 5 disc, Hemi		0.022-0.079 in.
1968-70 rear		0.025-0.045 in.
1971-72 front 3 disc	0.036-0.087 in.	0.035-0.088 in.
1971-72 front 4 disc	0.048-0.109 in.	0.047-0.110 in.
1971-72 front 5 disc		0.033-0.075 in.
1971-72 rear 3 disc	0.026-0.055 in.	
1971-72 rear 4 disc	0.032-0.056 in.	0.025-0.045 in.
Snap Rings, Front and Rear Clutches		
Rear (selective)	0.060-0.062 in.	0.060-0.062 in.
	0.068-0.070 in.	0.074-0.076 in.
	0.076-0.78 in.	0.088-0.090 in.
Output shaft (forward end) 1965-70	0.040-0.044 in.	0.048-0.052 in.
	0.048-0.052 in.	0.055-0.059 in.
	0.059-0.065 in.	0.062-0.066 in.
Output shaft bearing 1965	0.061-0.063 in.	
Thrust Washers		
Output shaft to input shaft (selective)	0.052-0.054 in. (natural) 0.068-0.070 in. (red) 0.083-0.085 in. (black)	

	A-904	A-727
Reaction shaft support to front clutch retainer (selective)		(green) 0.084-0.086 in. (red) 0.102-0.104 in. (yellow)
Reaction shaft support to front clutch retainer (1971-72)	0.061-0.063 in.	0.061-0.63 in. (natural) 0.084-0.086 in. (red) 0.102-0.104 in. (yellow)
Front planetary gear to driving shell	0.060-0.062 in.	
Driving shell (steel) (2)	0.034-0.036 in.	
Rear planetary gear to driving shell	0.060-0.062 in.	
Front annulus gear support	0.121-0.125 in.	
Front clutch to rear clutch	0.043-0.045 in.	
Front clutch to reaction shaft support	0.043-0.045 in.	
Driving shell thrust plate		0.034-0.036 in.
Rear planetary gear to driving shell		0.062-0.064 in.
Output shaft to input shaft		0.062-0.064 in.
Front planetary gear to annulus gear		0.062-0.064 in.
Front annulus gear to driving shell		0.062-0.064 in.
Front clutch piston retainer to rear Clutch piston retainer		0.061-0.063 in.
Rear planetary gear to annulus gear 1967-72		0.034-0.036 in.
Front clutch to rear clutch 1971-72	0.061-0.063 in. (selective)	0.061-0.063 in.
Input shaft to output shaft 1971-72	0.052-0.054 in. (natural) 0.068-0.070 in. (red) 0.083-0.085 in. (black)	
Front annulus support to front carrier 1971-72		0.060-0.062 in.
Front annulus support to front driving shell 1971-72		0.060-0.062 in.
Rear carrier to driving shell 1971-72		0.060-0.062 in.
Rear annulus thrust plate	0.034-0.036 in.	0.034-0.036 in.

Transmission Applications

Model	Year and Engines
A 904 G	1965-72 170, 198 and 225 sixes
A 904 LA	1965-68 273 V8 and 1969-72 318 V8
A 904 A	1969 273 V8
A 727 A	1965-72 318 V8, 1968-72 340 V8, 1971-72 360 V8 and 1965-68 225 police and taxi six
A 727 RG	1969-72 225 police and taxi six
A 727 B	1965-72 all B block engines, 361, 383, 400, 413, 426, 426 Hemi, and 440 V8's

General

The Torqueflite transmission combines a torque converter with a fully automatic three-speed gear system. The converter housing and transmission case are combined into one aluminum casting. The transmission consists of two multiple-disc clutches, an overrunning clutch, two servos and bands, and two planetary gear sets. This provides three forward speeds and one reverse.

The torque converter is driven by the crankshaft, through a bolted-on, flexible driving plate. Cooling of the converter-transmission assembly is controlled by circulating the transmission fluid through a cooler core, located in the radiator lower tank. The torque converter assembly is a sealed unit, impractical to service in the field, except for cleaning.

For information relative to application, such as linkage adjustments, and unit removal and replacement, refer to the car section.

Starting in 1966, the rear pump has been eliminated from the Torqueflite transmission assembly.

Operating differences are essentially, that the governor receives oil from the manual control valve rather than from the rear pump, then distributes it to the shift valves, according to the pressures applied to the governor.

Band Adjustments
Kickdown Band

The kickdown band adjusting screw is located on the left-hand side of the transmission case near the throttle lever shaft.

1. Loosen the locknut and back off about five turns. Be sure the adjusting screw is free in the case.
2. Using wrench, tool C-3380 with adapter C-3790, or similar tools, torque the adjusting screw to 47-50 in. lbs. If adapter is not used, tighten adjusting screw to 72 in. lbs. which is the true torque.
3. Back off the adjusting screw, exactly to specification. Keep the screw from turning, and torque the locknut to specification.

Kickdown Band Adjustments

A-904	
1965-70 170 six	2⅝ turns
1965-70 198 and 225 six	2 turns
1965-69 273 V8	2 turns
1968-72 318 V8	2 turns
A-727	
1965-70 sixes and V8 except Hemi	2 turns
1968-72 Hemi V8 and 440-6	1½ turns
1971-72 225 six, 318, 340, 360, 383, 400, 440 V8s	2½ turns
1971-72 440 w/dual exhaust	2 turns
A-904 kickdown adjusting screw torque	25 ft. lbs.
A-727 kickdown adjusting screw torque	29 ft. lbs.
A-904 (1971-72) kickdown adjusting screw torque	29 ft. lbs.

Low and Reverse Band

Access to the low and reverse band requires oil pan removal.

1. Raise the car, drain transmission and remove the transmission oil pan.
2. Loosen the band adjusting screw locknut and back off the nut about five turns. Be sure the adjusting screw turns freely in the lever.
3. With the same tools as used on the kickdown band adjustment (C-3380 and C-3790), tighten the adjusting screw to 47-50 in. lbs. If adapter is not used, torque to 72 in. lbs., the true torque.
4. Back off the adjusting screw exactly to specification. Keep the screw from turning and torque the locknut to specification.
5. Reinstall oil pan, using new gasket, and torque the pan bolts to 150 in. lbs.
6. Refill transmission to prescribed level.

Low and Reverse Band Screw Adjustment

A-904	
1965-66	5¼ turns
1967-72 except 318 V8	3¼ turns
1968-72 318 V8	4 turns
Adjustment screw torque	20 ft. lbs.
Adjustment screw torque (1971-72)	35 ft. lbs.
A-727	
1965-66	3 turns
1967-72	2 turns
Adjustment screw torque	35 ft. lbs.

A-904 type Torqueflite transmission (© Chrysler Corp.)

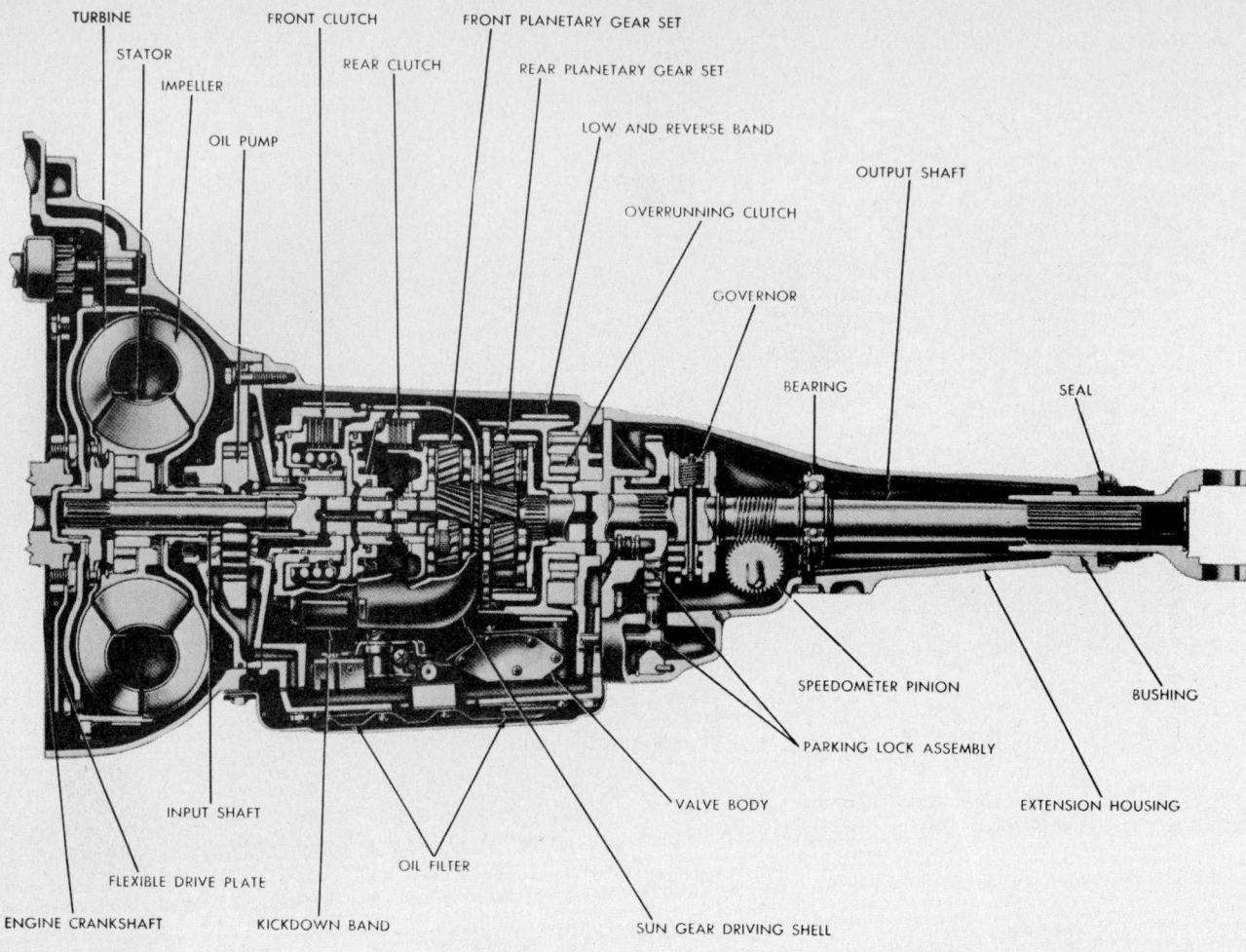

Fluid Leaks

Some leaks that can normally be corrected without transmission removal are:

1. Transmission output shaft oil seal.
2. Extension housing gasket.
3. Speedometer pinion seal and cable seal.
4. Oil filler tube seal.
5. Oil pan gasket and drain plug.
6. Gearshift control cable seal.
7. Throttle shaft seal.
8. Neutral starting switch seal.
9. Oil cooler line fittings and pressure take-off plugs.

Oil found inside the converter housing should be positively identified as transmission oil before any major transmission work is performed.

Leaks Requiring Transmission Removal

1. Fractures or sand holes in transmission case.
2. Sand hole or fracture in front oil pump.
3. Front pump housing retaining screws or damaged sealing washers.
4. Front oil pump housing seal (on outside diameter of pump housing).
5. Converter assembly and impeller shaft oil seal (located in front pump housing).

Tests

Air Pressure Tests

The front clutch, rear clutch, kickdown servo and low and reverse servo may be checked with air pressure, after the valve body assembly has been removed.

To make air pressure tests, proceed as follows:

Caution Compressed air must be free of dirt and moisture. Use pressure of 30-100 psi.

Front Clutch

Apply air pressure to the front clutch apply passage and listen for a dull thud. This will indicate operation of the front clutch. Hold the air pressure at this point for a few seconds and check for excessive oil leaks.

NOTE: if a dull thud cannot be heard in the clutch, place finger tips on clutch housing and again apply air pressure. Movement of piston can be felt as clutch is applied.

Rear Clutch

Apply air pressure to the rear clutch apply passage and proceed in an identical manner as that described in the previous paragraph.

Kickdown Servo

Air pressure applied to the kickdown servo apply passage should tighten the front band. Spring tension should be sufficient to release the band.

Low and Reverse Servo

Direct air pressure into the low and reverse servo apply passage. Response of the servo will result in a tightening of the rear band. Spring tension should be enough to release the band.

If clutches and servos operate properly, no upshift or erratic shift conditions existing, trouble exists in the control valve body assembly.

Governor

Governor troubles can usually be found during a road or pressure test.

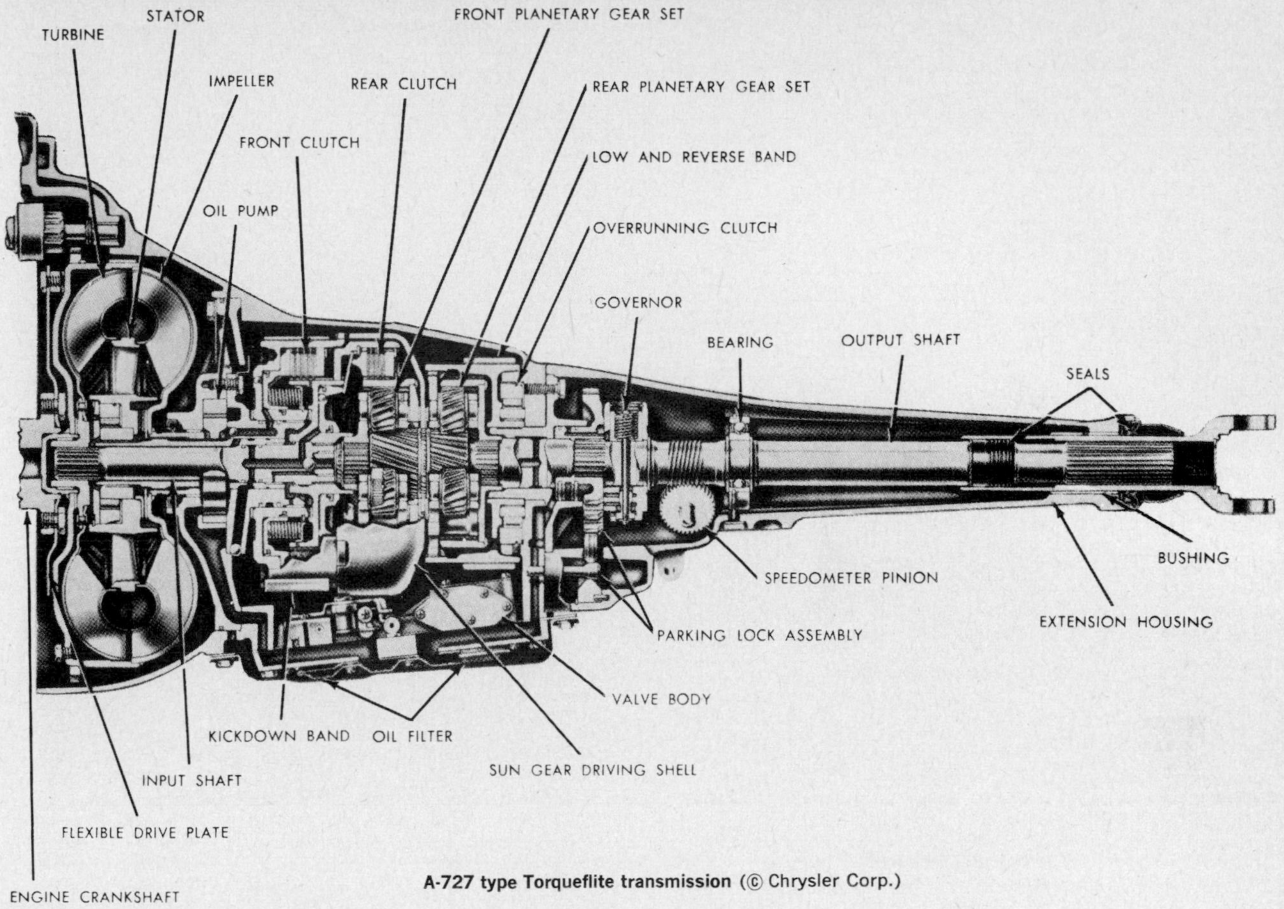

TURBINE
STATOR
IMPELLER
FRONT CLUTCH
OIL PUMP
FRONT PLANETARY GEAR SET
REAR CLUTCH
REAR PLANETARY GEAR SET
LOW AND REVERSE BAND
OVERRUNNING CLUTCH
GOVERNOR
BEARING
OUTPUT SHAFT
SEALS
BUSHING
SPEEDOMETER PINION
EXTENSION HOUSING
PARKING LOCK ASSEMBLY
VALVE BODY
KICKDOWN BAND   OIL FILTER
SUN GEAR DRIVING SHELL
INPUT SHAFT
FLEXIBLE DRIVE PLATE
ENGINE CRANKSHAFT

A-727 type Torqueflite transmission (© Chrysler Corp.)

Hydraulic Control Pressure Checks

Line Pressure and Front Servo Release Pressure

NOTE: these pressure checks must be made in the D position with the rear wheels free to turn. The transmission fluid must be at operating temperature (150°-200° F).

1. Install an engine tachometer, then, raise the car on a hoist and locate the tachometer so it can be read from under the car.
2. Connect two 0-100 psi pressure gauges (tool C-3292 or other good gauges) to pressure take-off points at the top of the accumulator and at the front servo release.
3. With the selector in D position, increase engine speed gradually until the transmission shifts into High. Reduce engine speed slowly to 1000 rpm. The line pressure must be 54-60 psi with front servo release having no more than a 3 psi drop.
4. Disconnect throttle linkage from transmission throttle lever and move throttle lever gradually to full throttle position. Line pressure must rise to maximum of 90-96 psi just before or at kickdown into low gear. Front servo release pressure must follow line

pressure up to kickdown point and should not be more than 3 psi below line pressure. If pressure is not 54-60 psi at 1000 rpm, adjust line pressure.

If line pressure is not as above, adjust the pressure as outlined under the heading: Hydraulic Control Pressure Adjustments—"Line Pressure."

If front servo release pressures are less than specified, and line pressures are within limits, there is excessive leakage in the front clutch and/or front servo circuits.

Lubrication Pressures

A lubrication pressure check

should be made when line pressure and front servo release pressures are checked.

1. Install a T fitting between the cooler return line fitting and the fitting hole in the transmission case at the rear left side of the transmission. Connect a 0-100 psi pressure gauge to the T-fitting.
2. At 1000 engine rpm, with throttle closed and transmission in High, lubrication pressure should be 5-15 psi. Lubrication pressure will approximately double as throttle is opened to maximum line pressure.

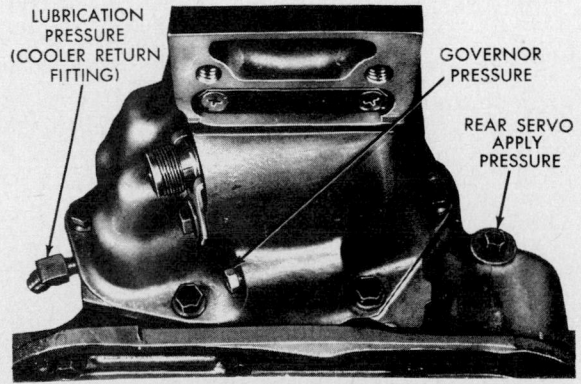

LUBRICATION PRESSURE (COOLER RETURN FITTING)

GOVERNOR PRESSURE

REAR SERVO APPLY PRESSURE

Torqueflite pressure test locations (rear end of case)—1970-72 (© Chrysler Corp.)

Governor Pressure Chart

Axle Ratio to Vehicle Speed

1965-66 ALL MODELS

6.50x13 Tires		6.95x14 Tires		7.35x14 Tires			Pressure Limits (PSI)
3.23	3.55	2.93	3.55	2.93	3.23	3.55	
16-17	14-16	17-19	14-16	17-19	15-17	14-16	15
36-45	33-41	35-46	30-37	36-47	33-42	30-38	50
59-67	53-61	61-70	50-58	62-71	56-65	51-59	75

1967

Valiant and Dart		Belvedere, Fury, and Coronet		Pressure Limits (PSI)
2.76	2.93	2.93	3.23	
17-20	16-19	17-19	15-17	15
44-52	36-44	37-45	33-41	50
70-77	61-67	62-69	56-62	75

1968-69

170			198 and 225			Pressure Limits (PSI)
2.76	2.93	3.23	2.76	2.93	3.23	
18-20	17-19	15-17	18-20	17-20	16-18	15
44-57	41-48	37-48	38-46	36-46	34-41	50
69-76	65-72	59-65	64-70	60-70	57-62	75

1970-72 VALIANT AND DART

198	225	Pressure Limits (PSI)
2.76	2.76	
19-20	19-20	15
49-55	49-55	50
72-79	72-79	75

EIGHT CYLINDERS

1965-66 BELVEDERE, FURY, CORONET, AND DART

7.00x13		7.35x14		7.75x14		Pressure Limits (PSI)
2.93	3.23	2.93	3.23	2.93	3.23	
18-19	16-17	17-19	15-17	18-20	16-18	15
40-51	37-46	36-47	33-42	38-47	35-42	50
66-75	60-68	62-71	56-65	65-72	59-65	75

1965-66 POLARA, MONACO, AND 880

8.25x14	8.55x14	8.25x14	8.55x14	Pressure Limits (PSI)
2.76	2.76	3.23	3.23	
19-22	20-22	16-19	17-19	15
45-51	45-52	35-43	36-44	50
70-78	71-79	60-66	61-88	75

1965-66 CHRYSLER AND IMPERIAL

Newport	300	New Yorker	Imperial	Pressure Limits (PSI)
2.76	3.23	3.23	2.93	
19-22	17-19	17-19	19-22	15
42-51	36-44	36-44	43-51	50
70-78	61-68	61-68	71-78	75

1967 DART, VALIANT, AND BARRACUDA

2.93	3.23	Pressure Limits (PSI)
17-19	15-17	15
42-50	43-49	50
67-74	64-67	75

1967 CORONET, CHARGER, AND BELVEDERE

2.94	3.23	Pressure Limits (PSI)
17-19	15-18	15
43-51	39-46	50
69-76	63-69	75

1967 FURY, POLARA, AND MONACO

Polara and Fury	Fury	Polara and Monaco	Pressure Limits (PSI)
2.94	3.23	2.76	
18-20	16-18	19-22	15
44-52	40-48	48-57	50
70-76	64-71	76-84	75

1967 CHRYSLER AND IMPERIAL

Newport	300 and New Yorker	Imperial	Pressure Limits (PSI)
2.76	2.76	2.94	
19-22	19-22	19-22	15
48-57	49-58	48-57	50
76-84	78-86	77-85	75

1968-69 BELVEDERE, FURY, CORONET, CHARGER, VALIANT, DART AND BARRACUDA

273 and 318 V8s			340, 383, and 440 V8s			Pressure Limits (PSI)
2.76	2.93	3.23	2.76	3.23	3.55	
18-20	17-19	15-17	19-21	14-16	15-17	15
45-53	42-50	38-44	46-55	39-46	44-50	50
71-78	67-74	60-66	74-82	58-65	64-71	75

1968-69 POLARA AND MONACO

2.76	2.94	3.23	Pressure Limits (PSI)
19-22	18-20	16-18	15
48-57	44-52	40-48	50
76-84	71-78	64-71	75

1968-70 CHRYSLER AND IMPERIAL

Chrysler		Imperial	Pressure Limits (PSI)
2.76	3.23	2.94	
20-22	17-19	19-22	15
48-57	41-49	48-57	50
77-85	66-73	77-85	75

1970 DODGE AND PLYMOUTH

318, 383, and 440 V8s			Pressure Limits (PSI)
2.76	3.23	3.55	
19-21	15-17	14-17	15
46-55	44-50	39-51	50
74-82	64-71	58-71	75

1971-72

Satellite Coronet Charger 318	Barracuda Challenger 340	Fury Polara Monaco 360	Fury Chrysler Polara Monaco 383	Imperial Polara Monaco 440	Pressure Limits (PSI)
2.71	3.23	2.71	2.76	2.94	
20-22	17-18	20-22	21-22	20-22	15
56-64	49-53	54-63	55-64	54-62	50
80-88	66-71	78-86	80-87	78-85	75

Rear Servo Apply Pressure

1. Connect a 0-300 psi pressure gauge, tool C-3293 or its equivalent, to the apply pressure take-off point at the rear servo.
2. With the control in the R position, and the engine running at 1600 rpm, the reverse servo apply pressure should be 230-300 psi.

Governor Pressure

1. Connect a 0-100 psi gauge (same as the one used for line pressure and front servo release pressure) to the governor pressure take-off point. This location is at the lower left rear corner of the extension mounting flange.
2. Governor pressure should fall within limits in chart.

Pressure should change smoothly with car speeds.

Bottom view of transmission—pan removed (© Chrysler Corp.)

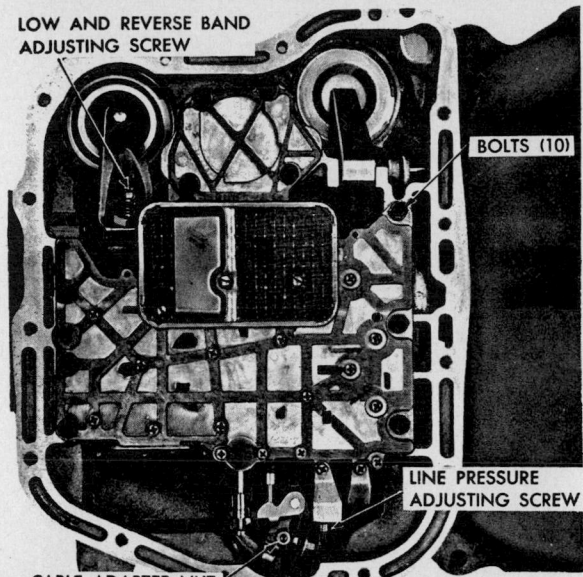

Torqueflite air pressure checks—1970-72 (© Chrysler Corp.)

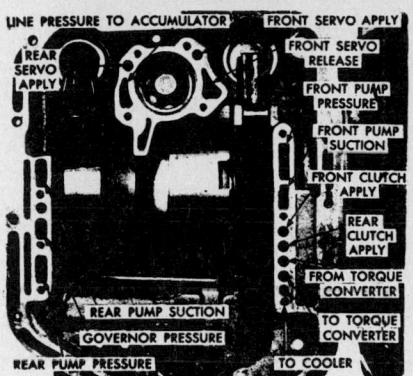

Air pressure checks
(© Chrysler Corp.)

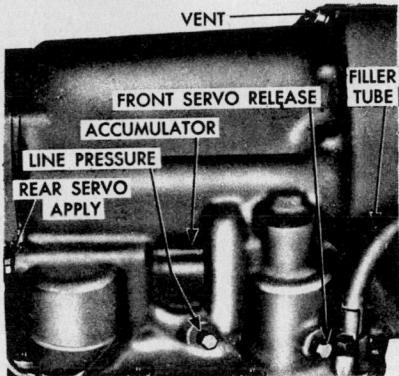

Pressure test locations (right side of case)
(© Chrysler Corp.)

If governor pressures are incorrect at the prescribed speeds, the governor valve and/or weights are probably sticking.

Hydraulic Control Pressure Adjustments

Line Pressure

An incorrect throttle pressure setting will cause incorrect line pressure even though line pressure adjustment is correct. Always inspect and correct throttle pressure adjustment before adjusting line pressure.

NOTE: before adjusting line pressure, measure distance between manual valve (valve in 1-low position) and line pressure adjusting screw. This measurement must be 1⅞ in. Correct by loosening spring retainer screws and repositioning spring retainer. The regulator valve may cock and hang up in its bore if spring retainer is out of position.

If line pressure is not correct remove valve body assembly to adjust. The correct adjustment is 1-5/16 in. measured from valve body to inner edge of adjusting nut. Vary adjustment slightly to obtain specified line pressure.

One complete turn of the adjusting screw (Allen head) changes closed throttle line pressure about 1.66 psi. Turning the screw counterclockwise increases pressure, clockwise decreases pressure.

Throttle Pressure

Because throttle pressures cannot be checked, exact adjustments should be checked and made correct whenever the valve body is disturbed.

1. Remove the valve body assembly, as outlined in a succeeding coverage entitled, Valve Body Assembly and Accumulator Piston.
2. Loosen throttle lever stop screw

HIGH PERFORMANCE V8s
1965 DODGE AND PLYMOUTH 426 WEDGE

3.23	3.91	Pressure Limit (PSI)
16-18	13-15	15
45-51	37-42	50
67-73	55-60	75

1967 DODGE AND PLYMOUTH

426 Hemi	Pressure Limit (PSI)
3.23	
19-22	15
54-61	50
79-87	75

1968-70 DODGE AND PLYMOUTH

426 Hemi	383 High Perf., 440 High Perf. and 440 Six Pack	Pressure Limit (PSI)
3.23	3.23	
20-23	16-19	15
55-64	46-52	50
82-90	68-73	75

1971-72

Fury Chrysler Polara Monaco 383	Fury Chrysler Polara Monaco 440 Hi-perf.	Pressure Limits (PSI)
3.23	3.23	
18-19	18-19	15
53-58	53-58	50
71-77	71-77	75

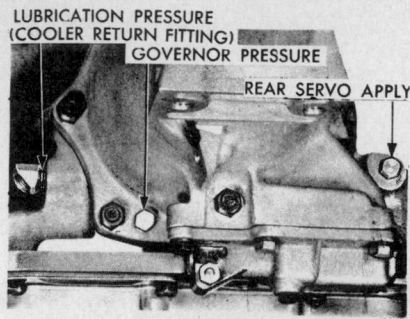

Pressure test locations (rear of case)
(© Chrysler Corp.)

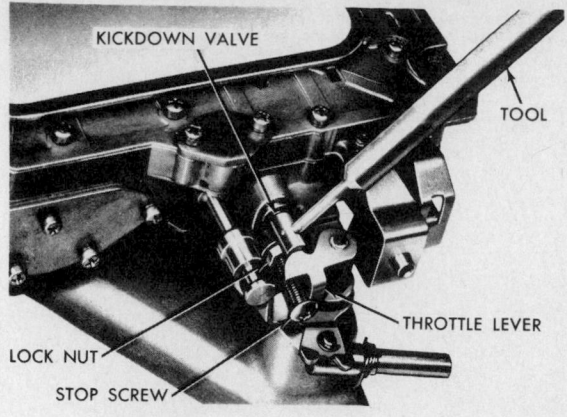

Throttle pressure adjustment (© Chrysler Corp.)

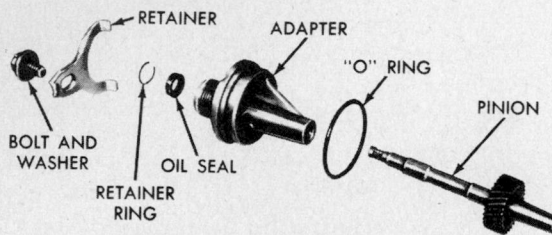

Speedometer drive (© Chrysler Corp.)

Measuring distance between manual valve
and line pressure adjusting screw
(© Chrysler Corp.)

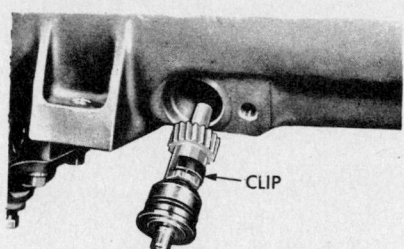

Removing or installing speedometer pinion
(© Chrysler Corp.)

Line pressure adjustment (© Chrysler Corp.)

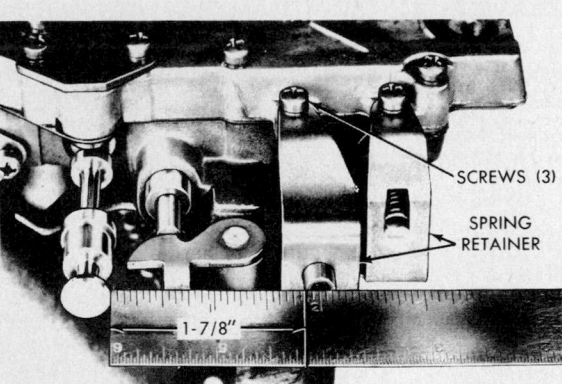

locknut and back off the screw about five turns.

3. Insert gauge pin of tool C-3763 between the throttle lever cam and the kickdown valve.

4. Push on the tool and compress the kickdown valve against its spring, so that the throttle valve is completely bottomed inside the valve body.

5. As the spring is being compressed, finger tighten the throttle lever stop screw against the throttle lever tang, with the lever cam touching the tool and the throttle valve bottomed. (Be sure the adjustment is made with the spring fully compressed and the valve bottomed in the valve body.)

6. Remove the tool and secure the stop screw locknut.

Service Operations in Car

Some sub-assemblies can be removed for repairs without removing the transmission from the car. Detailed reconditioning of sub-assemblies is covered further in the text.

Speedometer Pinion

Removal and Installation 1965

1. Remove screw and retainer which holds the cable to the extension housing. Carefully work the pinion and sleeve out of the housing.

2. Replace the pinion and/or oil seal by prying the clip off the pinion and sliding the pinion and seal assembly from the cable.

3. If transmission fluid is found in the cable housing, replace the seal inside the pinion bore, then, slide the pinion over the end of the cable and secure it with the spring clip.

4. To install, push the pinion and sleeve into the extension housing as far as possible, then install the retainer screw. Tighten to 150 in. lbs.

Removal and Installation 1966-72

Rear axle gear ratio and tire size determine pinion gear size.

1. Remove bolt and retainer securing speedometer pinion adapter in extension housing.

2. With cable housing connected, carefully work adapter and pinion out of extension housing.

3. If transmission fluid is found in

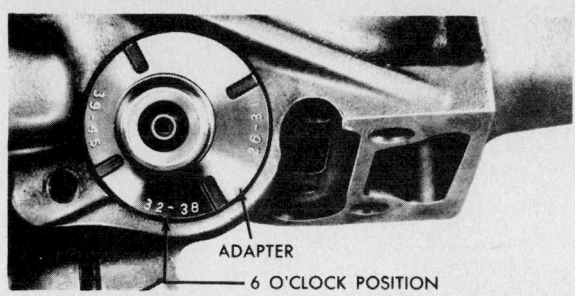

Speedometer pinion and adapter installed (© Chrysler Corp.)

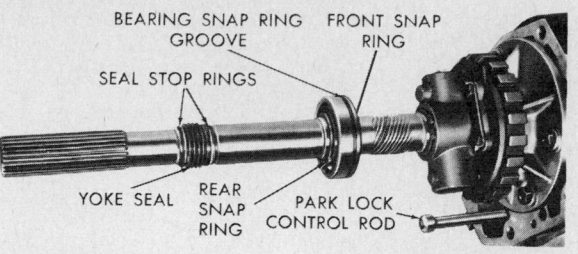

Output shaft bearing and yoke seal (© Chrysler Corp.)

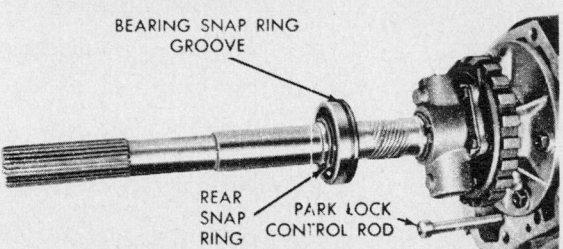

Output shaft bearing—1970-72 (© Chrysler Corp.)

Removing or installing extension housing (© Chrysler Corp.)

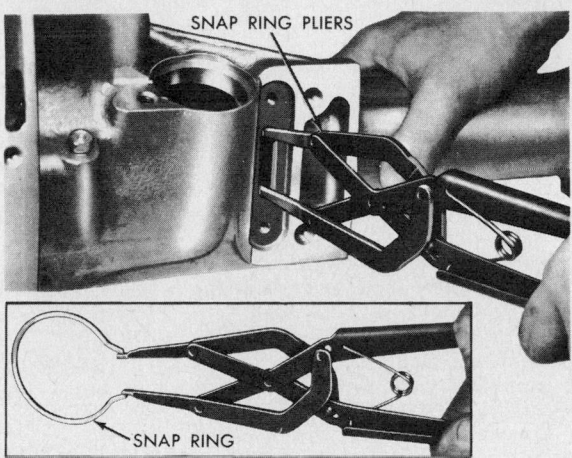

cable housing, replace seal in adapter. Start seal and retainer ring in adapter, then push them into adapter with Tool C4004 or equivalent until tool bottoms.

CAUTION: before installing pinion and adapter assembly make sure adapter flange and mating area on extension housing are perfectly clean. Dirt or sand will cause misalignment and speedometer pinion gear noise.

4. Note number of gear teeth and install pinion gear into adapter.
5. Rotate pinion gear and adapter assembly so that number on adapter corresponding to number of teeth on gear is in six o'clock position as assembly is installed.
6. Install retainer and bolt with retainer tangs in adapter positioning slots. Tap adapter firmly into extension housing and tighten retainer bolt to 100 in. lbs.

Output Shaft Oil Seal

Replacement—1965 A-904

1. Disconnect drive shaft at transmission flange.
2. Hold transmission flange with Tool C-3281 or equivalent and remove retaining nut and washer. Slide flange off output shaft.
3. Screw taper threaded end of Tool C-748 or equivalent into seal, and tighten screw of tool to remove seal. If tool is not available, remove by gently tapping out around circumference of seal with slide hammer. Take care not to engage slide hammer on tail shaft bearing.
4. To install new seal, place seal in opening of extension housing

with lip of seal facing inward. Drive seal into housing with Tool C-3837 or suitable drift.
5. Install transmission output shaft flange. Install washer with three projections toward flange and nut with its convoluted surface contacting washer. Hold flange with Tool C-3281 or equivalent to prevent flange from turning and torque nut to 175 ft. lbs.
6. Connect drive shaft to flange.

Replacement—1965 A-727

1. Disconnect driveshaft at rear universal joint. Carefully pull shaft out of transmission extension housing. Be careful not to scratch or nick ground surface on sliding spline yoke.
2. Cut boot end off seal, then screw taper threaded end of Tool C-748 or equivalent into seal. Tighten screw of tool to remove seal. If tool is not available, remove by gently tapping out around circumference of seal with slide hammer. Take care not to engage slide hammer or tail shaft bearing.
3. To install new seal, place seal in opening of extension and drive it into housing with Tool C-3972 or suitable drift.
4. Carefully guide front universal joint into extension housing and onto output shaft splines. Connect driveshaft to rear axle pinion shaft yoke.

Replacement—1966-72 All

1. Mark parts for reassembly. Dis-

connect driveshaft at rear universal joint. Carefully pull shaft yoke out of transmission extension housing. Be careful not to scratch or nick ground surface of sliding spline yoke.
2. Remove extension housing yoke seal with Tool C-3994 or C-3985 or equivalent. If tools are not available, remove by gently tapping out around circumference of seal with slide hammer.
3. To install new seal, place seal in opening of extension housing and drive it into housing with Tool C-3995 or C-3972 or suitable drift.
4. Carefully guide front universal joint yoke into extension housing and onto the mainshaft splines. Align marks made at removal and connect driveshaft to pinion shaft yoke.

Extension Housing Removal 1965

1. Remove the speedometer drive pinion and sleeve assembly.
2. Disconnect front universal joint at companion flange.
3. Drain about two quarts of fluid from the transmission.
4. Loosen parking lock cable clamp bolt where cable enters housing cover. Tap end of clamp bolt lightly to release its hold on the cable. Remove housing cover lower plug. Insert screwdriver through hole. While exerting pressure against projecting por-

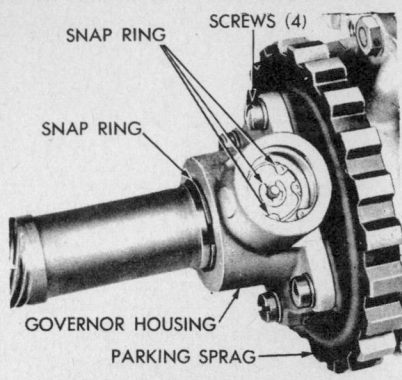

Governor shaft and weight snap-rings
(© Chrysler Corp.)

Removing or installing rear oil pump
inner rotor—1965
(© Chrysler Corp.)

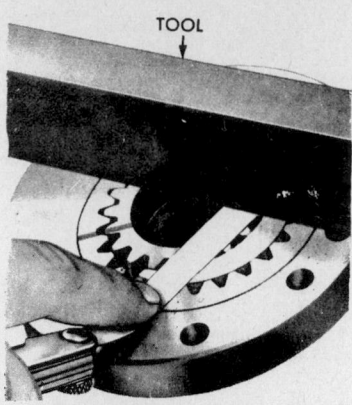

Checking oil pump rotor clearance
(© Chrysler Corp.)

tion of cable lock-spring, with-draw lock cable.

5. Remove two bolts securing extension housing to crossmember insulator.
6. Raise transmission slightly with service jack to clear crossmember. Remove crossmember attaching bolts and remove crossmember, insulator, and spring assembly.
7. Remove extension housing to transmission bolts, tap housing lightly with soft mallet to break it loose from transmission, and remove housing.

1966-72

1. Mark parts for reassembly. Disconnect driveshaft at rear universal joint. Carefully pull shaft out of extension housing.
2. Remove speedometer pinion and adapter assembly. Drain approximately two quarts of fluid from transmission.
3. Remove bolts securing extension housing to crossmember. Raise transmission slightly with service jack and remove center crossmember and support assembly.
4. Remove extension housing to transmission bolts. On console shifts, remove two bolts securing gearshift torque shaft lower bracket to extension housing. Swing bracket out of way.
NOTE: gearshift lever must be in 1-low position so that parking lock control rod can be engaged or disengaged with parking lock sprag.
5. Remove two screws, plate, and gasket from bottom of extension housing mounting pad.
6. Spread large snap ring from output shaft bearing with Tool C-3301 or equivalent.
7. With snap-ring spread as far as possible tap extension housing gently off output shaft bearing.
8. Carefully pull extension housing rearward to bring parking lock control rod knob past parking sprag and remove housing.

Governor

Removal

1. Remove extension housing.
NOTE: remove output shaft support bearing if so equipped.
2. With a screwdriver, carefully pry the snap-ring from the weight end of governor valve shaft. Slide the valve and shaft assembly out of the governor housing.
3. Remove the large snap-ring from the weight end of the governor housing and lift out the governor weight assembly.
4. Remove snap-ring from inside governor weight, remove inner weight and spring from the outer weight.
5. Remove the snap-ring from behind the governor housing, then slide the governor housing and support assembly from the output shaft. If necessary, remove the four screws and separate the governor housing from the support.

Cleaning and Inspection

The primary cause of governor operating trouble is sticking of the valve or weights, brought about by dirt or rough surfaces. Thoroughly clean and blow dry all of the governor parts. Remove any burrs or rough bearing surfaces with crocus cloth and clean again. If all moving parts are clean and operating freely, the governor may be reassembled.

Installation

1. Assemble the governor housing to the support, then finger tighten the screws. Be sure the oil passage of the governor housing aligns with the passage in the support.
2. Align the master spline of the support with the master spline on the output shaft, slide the assembly into place. Install the snap-ring behind the governor housing. Torque bolts to 100 in. lbs.

3. Assemble the governor weights and spring, and fasten with snap-ring inside of large governor weight. Place the weight assembly in the governor housing shafts retaining snap-ring. Install output shaft support bearing if so equipped.
4. Place the governor valve on the valve shaft, insert the assembly into the housing and through the governor weights. Install the shaft retaining snap-ring. Install output shaft support bearing if so equipped.
5. Install the extension housing. Connect the driveshaft.

Rear Oil Pump, 1965 Only

Removal

1. Remove extension housing.
2. Remove governor and support.
3. Unscrew the rear oil pump cover retaining bolts and remove the pump cover.
4. Draw a line across the face of the inner and outer pump rotors (with dye) so that they may be reinstalled in the same position.
5. Slide off the inner rotor, (don't drop the small driving ball). Remove the outer rotor from the pump body.
NOTE: if replacement of the pump body is necessary, the transmission must be dismantled to allow driving the pump body out (rearward) with a wood block.

Inspection

Clean and blow dry all pump parts and examine contacting surfaces for evidence of wear, burrs or other damage. With the parts cleaned and reassembled, place a straightedge across the face of the rotors and pump body. With a feeler gauge, check clearance between the straightedge and the face of the rotors. Clearance limits are at front of section.

Installation

1. Place the outer rotor in the pump body.
2. Rotate the output shaft so that the inner rotor driving ball (or ball key) pocket is up. Drop the ball into the pocket and slide the inner rotor onto the output shaft, in alignment with the ball.
3. Position the outer rotor to align its dye mark with the mark on the inner rotor.
4. Install the pump cover with the attaching bolts turned in a few threads. Slide the aligning fixture, tool C-3762 all the way in until it bottoms against the rotor. Tighten the cover bolts evenly to 140 in. lbs., then remove the tool.
5. Install the governor and support.
6. Install extension housing, brake assembly and connect the driveshaft.
7. Connect the parking brake cable (drum-type).

Neutral Starting Switch

Removal

1. Drain about two quarts of transmission fluid.
2. Disconnect wire from switch and unscrew from transmission case.

Installation and Test

1. With the proper control cable adjustment assured, and the N selector depressed, make sure the switch operating lever is aligned in the center of the switch opening in the case.
2. Place the cupped washer and O ring over the threads of the switch. Screw the switch into the transmission case a few turns.
3. Connect one lead of a test lamp to battery current and the other lead to the switch terminal. Screw into the transmission case until the lamp lights. Now, tighten the switch an additional one-third to one-half turn.
   NOTE: the switch must be tight enough to prevent oil leaks. If not, add a thin washer and readjust the switch.
4. Remove test lamp and attach the regular wire to the switch.
5. Fill transmission to correct level.

Valve Body Assembly and Accumulator Piston

Removal 1965

1. Loosen pan bolts and drain all of the fluid from the transmission.
2. Remove the oil pan and gasket.
3. Loosen the clamp bolt and lift the throttle lever, washer and seal from the transmission throttle lever shaft.
4. Shift the manual control into 1 (Low) position to expose the nut holding the cable adapter to the

manual lever. Remove the nut and disengage the adapter from the lever.
5. With a drain pan under the transmission, remove the ten hex-head valve body to transmission case bolts. Hold the valve body in position while removing bolts.
6. Lower the valve body assembly. Be careful not to cock the throttle lever shaft in the case hole or lose the accumulator spring.
7. Insert tool C-434 inside the accumulator piston and remove the piston from the transmission case. Inspect the piston assembly for scoring, broken rings and wear. Replace as required.
   NOTE: servicing the valve body is outlined later in the text.

Installation 1965

1. All mating surfaces must be clean and free of burrs.

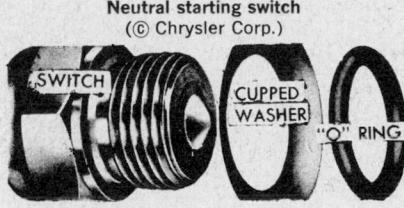

Neutral starting switch
(© Chrysler Corp.)

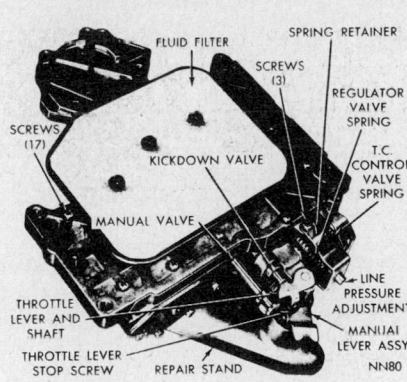

Regulator and converter control valves—
assembled view
(© Chrysler Corp.)

2. Install accumulator piston into the transmission case.
3. Position accumulator spring on the valve body.
4. Position the valve body assembly in place in the transmission and start all the retaining bolts.
5. Snug the bolts down evenly then torque to 100 in. lbs.
6. Connect the control cable adapter to the manual lever and install retaining nut.
7. Install seal, flat washer and throttle lever onto the throttle shaft. Tighten the clamp bolt.
8. Install clean oil pan with new gasket.
9. Add fluid to correct level.

Removal 1966-72

1. Raise vehicle on hoist and loosen oil pan bolts, tap pan to break it loose, allowing fluid to drain.
2. Remove pan and gasket.
3. Disconnect throttle and gearshift linkage from levers on transmission. Loosen clamp bolts and remove levers.
4. Remove E clip securing parking lock rod to valve body manual lever.
5. Remove backup light and neutral start switch.
6. Place drain pan under transmission, remove ten hex head valve body to transmission case bolts. Hold valve body in position while removing bolts.
7. While lowering valve body down out of transmission case, disconnect parking lock rod from lever. To remove rod pull it forward out of case. If necessary rotate driveshaft to align parking gear and sprag to permit knob on end of control rod to pass sprag.
8. Withdraw accumulator piston from transmission case. Inspect piston for scoring, and rings for wear or breakage.
9. If valve body manual lever shaft seal requires replacement, drive it out of case with punch.
10. Drive new seal into case with 15/16 in. socket and hammer.

Installation 1966-72

1. If parking lock rod was removed, insert it through opening in rear of case with knob positioned against plug and sprag. Move front end of rod toward center of transmission while exerting rearward pressure on rod to force it past sprag. Rotate driveshaft if necessary.
2. Install accumulator piston in transmission case.
3. Place accumulator spring on valve body.
4. Place valve body manual lever in low position. Lift valve body into its approximate position, connect parking lock rod to manual lever and secure with E clip. Place valve body in case, install retaining bolts finger tight.
5. With neutral start switch installed, place manual lever in neutral position. Shift valve body if necessary to center neutral finger over neutral switch plunger. Snug bolts down evenly. Torque to 100 in. lbs.
6. Install gearshift lever and tighten clamp bolt. Check lever shaft for binding by moving lever through all detents. If lever binds, loosen valve body bolts and re-align.
7. Make sure throttle shaft seal is in place, install flat washer and lever and tighten clamp bolt.

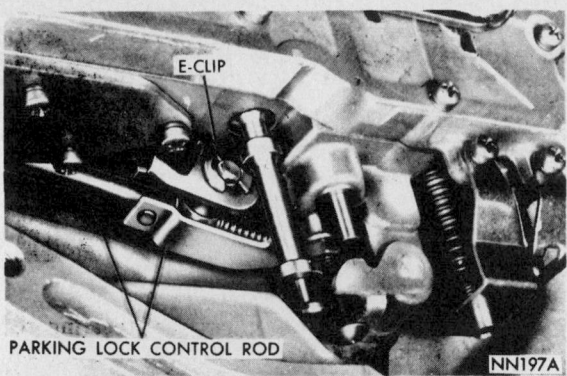

Parking lock control rod (© Chrysler Corp.)

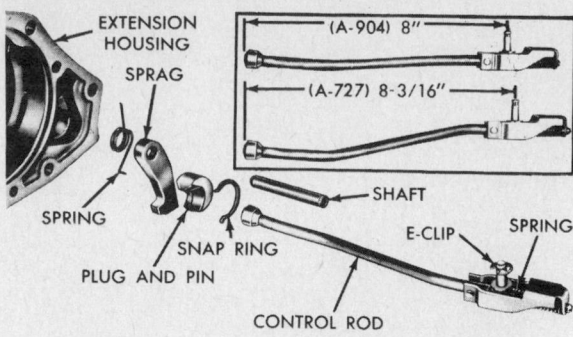

Parking lock components (© Chrysler Corp.)

Installing valve body manual lever shaft oil seal
(© Chrysler Corp.)

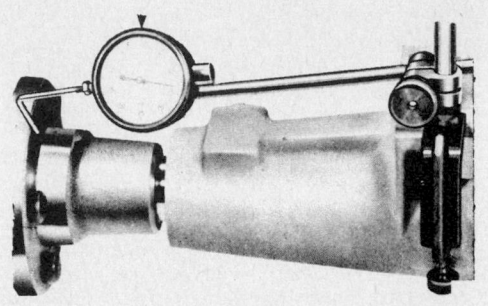

Checking drive end-play
(© Chrysler Corp.)

Connect throttle and gearshift linkage and adjust as required.

8. Install oil pan using new gasket. Add transmission fluid to proper level.

Detailed Unit Reconditioning

The following reconditioning data covers the removal, disassembly, inspection, repair, assembly and installation procedures for each sub-assembly in detail.

NOTE: should any transmission component fail, the converter should be thoroughly flushed to insure the removal of fine particles that may cause damage to the reconditioned transmission.

Oil Pan Removal

1. Secure transmission in a repair stand.
2. Unscrew attaching bolts and remove oil pan and gasket.

Valve Body Removal

1965

1. Unscrew nut and remove control cable adapter from valve body manual lever.
2. Remove (ten) hex-head valve body-to-transmission case bolts. (Hold the valve body in position while removing bolts.)
3. Lift the valve body out of the

transmission case, don't cock the throttle lever shaft.

1966-72

1. Loosen clamp bolts and remove throttle and gearshift levers from transmission.
2. Remove backup light and neutral start switch.
3. Remove ten hex head valve body to transmission bolts. Remove E clip securing parking lock rod to valve body manual lever.
4. While lifting valve body upward out of transmission case, disconnect parking lock rod from lever.

Accumulator Piston and Spring

Removal

1. Lift the spring from the accumulator piston and withdraw the piston from the case. Spring will be on the small end of the piston on 440 dual exhaust engines.

Checking Drive Train End-Play

1965-70

1. Attach a dial indicator to the extension housing and seat the plunger on the end of the output shaft.
2. Pry the output shaft out and tap it in to register the extreme shaft end-play.
3. Record this reading for possible

future use. Correct end play is found at front of section.

1970-72

1. Mount dial indicator on the transmission bell housing with the plunger seated against the end of the input shaft.
2. Move the input shaft in and out to obtain the end-play reading.
3. Record this reading for future use when assembling the transmission. Correct end-play is found at the front of the section.

Extension Housing Removal

1. See Service Operations in Car.

Governor and Support Removal

1. Remove the snap-ring from the weight end of the governor valve shaft. Slide the valve and shaft assembly from the governor housing.
2. Remove the snap-ring from behind the governor housing, then slide the governor housing and support from the output shaft.

Rear Oil Pump 1965

Removal

1. See Service Operations in Car.

Front Oil Pump and Reaction Shaft Support

Removal

1. Tighten the front band adjusting screw until the front band is tight on the front clutch retainer. This prevents the front clutch from coming out with the

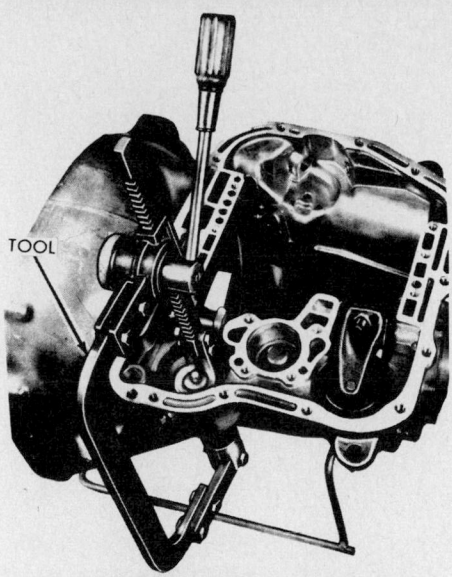

Compressing kickdown servo spring
(© Chrysler Corp.)

pump and damaging the clutches.
2. Remove the front pump housing retaining bolts.
3. Attach tool C-3752 to the pump housing flange, using the eleven and four o'clock hole locations.
4. Bump out evenly, with the tool, to withdraw the oil pump and reaction shaft support assembly from the case.

Front Band and Front Clutch
Removal
1. Loosen the front band adjuster, remove the head strut and slide the band from the case.
2. Slide the front clutch assembly from the case.

Input Shaft and Rear Clutch
Removal
1. Grasp the input shaft and slide the shaft and rear clutch assembly out of the case.
NOTE: don't lose the thrust washer located between the rear end of the input shaft and the front end of the output shaft.

Planetary Gear Assemblies, Sun Gear, Driving Shell, Low and Reverse Drum Removal
1. While hand-supporting the output shaft and driving shell, carefully slide the assembly forward and out of the case.

Rear Band and Low-Reverse Drum Removal
Remove low-reverse drum, loosen rear band adjuster, remove band strut and link, and remove band from case. On 1968-72 A-904LA transmissions with double wrap band, loosen band adjusting screw and remove band and low-reverse drum.

Overrunning Clutch Removal
1. Notice the established position of the overrunning clutch rollers and springs before disassembly.
2. Slide out the clutch hub and remove rollers and springs.
3. Remove low and reverse drum thrust washer from inside the overrunning clutch case on 1965 transmissions.

Kickdown Servo Removal
1. Compress kickdown servo spring using engine valve spring compressor. Then remove snap ring.
2. Remove the rod guide, spring and piston rod from the case. Don't damage the piston rod or guide during removal.
3. Withdraw piston from the transmission case.
4. If equipped, disassemble the "Controlled Load" servo piston by removing the small snap-ring and washer from the piston. Remove the spring and piston rod.

Low and Reverse Servo Removal
1. Using a suitable tool, depress the piston spring retainer and remove the snap ring.

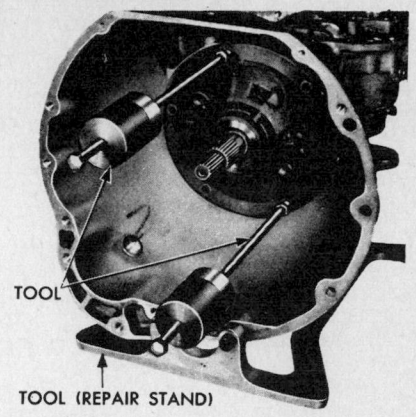

TOOL (REPAIR STAND)

Removing or installing front oil pump and reaction shaft support assembly
(© Chrysler Corp.)

2. Remove the spring retainer, spring, servo piston and plug assembly from the case.

Flushing the Torque Converter

1965-72
1. The torque converter must be removed in order to flush it.
2. Place the converter in a horizontal position and pour two quarts of new clean solvent into the converter through the impeller hub.
3. Turn and shake the converter, swirling the solvent through the internal parts. Turn the turbine and stator with the input and reaction shafts to dislodge foreign material.
4. Position the converter in its normal position with the drain plug at its lowest point. Drain the solvent. At the same time, rotate the turbine and stator and shake the converter, to prevent dirt particles from settling.
5. Repeat the flushing operation at least once, until the solvent or kerosene is clear.

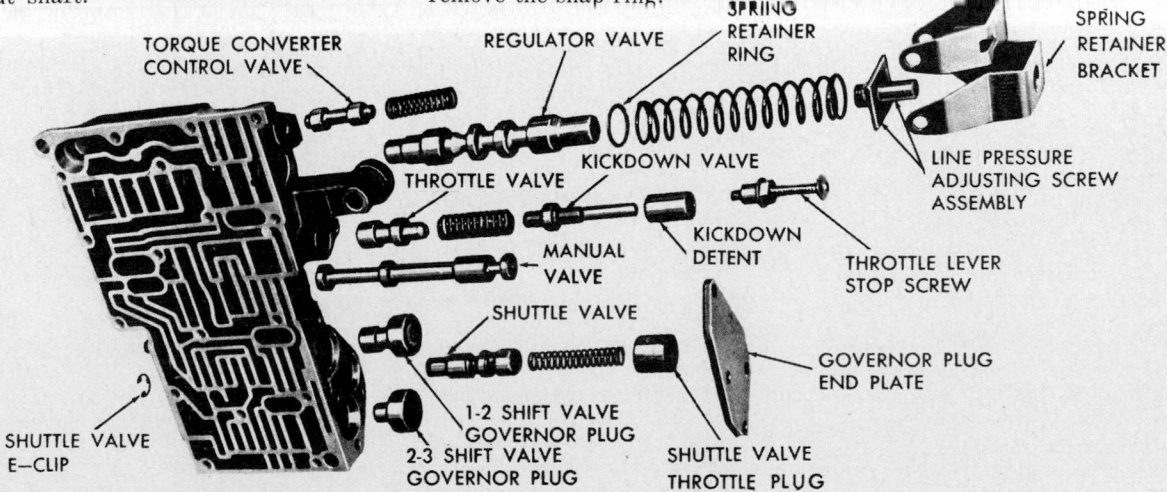

Valve body—lever side—1965 (© Chrysler Corp.)

6. After flushing, shake and rotate the converter several times, with the drain plug removed, to drain out any residual solvent or dirt.

7. Flush any remaining solvent or dirt with two quarts of new transmission fluid. Tighten the drain plug to 110 in. lbs.

8. Flush and blow out the oil cooler and lines.

Before removing any of the transmission sub-assemblies, thoroughly clean the exterior of the unit, preferably by steam. When disassembling, each part should be washed in a suitable solvent, and either set aside to drain or dried with compressed air. Do not wipe with shop towels. All of the transmission parts require extremely careful handling to avoid nicks and other damage to the accurately machined surfaces.

Sub-Assembly Reconditioning

The following procedures cover the disassembly, inspection, repair and assembly of each sub-assembly as removed from the transmission.

The use of crocus cloth is permissible but not encouraged as extreme care must be used to avoid rounding off sharp edges of valves. The edge portion of valve body and valves is very important to proper functioning.

NOTE: use all new seals and gaskets, and coat each part with automatic transmission fluid, type A, suffix A, during assembly.

Valve Body

Disassembly 1965-70

NOTE: this area is extremely critical, and sensitive to distortion. Never clamp any portion of the valve body or transfer plate in a vise. Clean with new solvent and dry with compressed air. Start all valves into their respective chambers with a twisting motion, seeing that they are well lubricated with automatic transmission fluid.

1. With the valve body on a clean repair stand, remove three attaching screws and the oil screen.

2. Hold the spring retainer bracket against spring tension, remove the three bracket retaining screws.

3. Remove spring bracket, torque converter valve spring, and the regulator valve spring with line pressure adjusting screw assembly.

NOTE: do not alter the setting of the line pressure adjusting screw and nut. The nut has an interference thread and does not turn easily on the screw.

4. Slide the regulator valve and spring retainer ring from the valve body. Slide torque con-

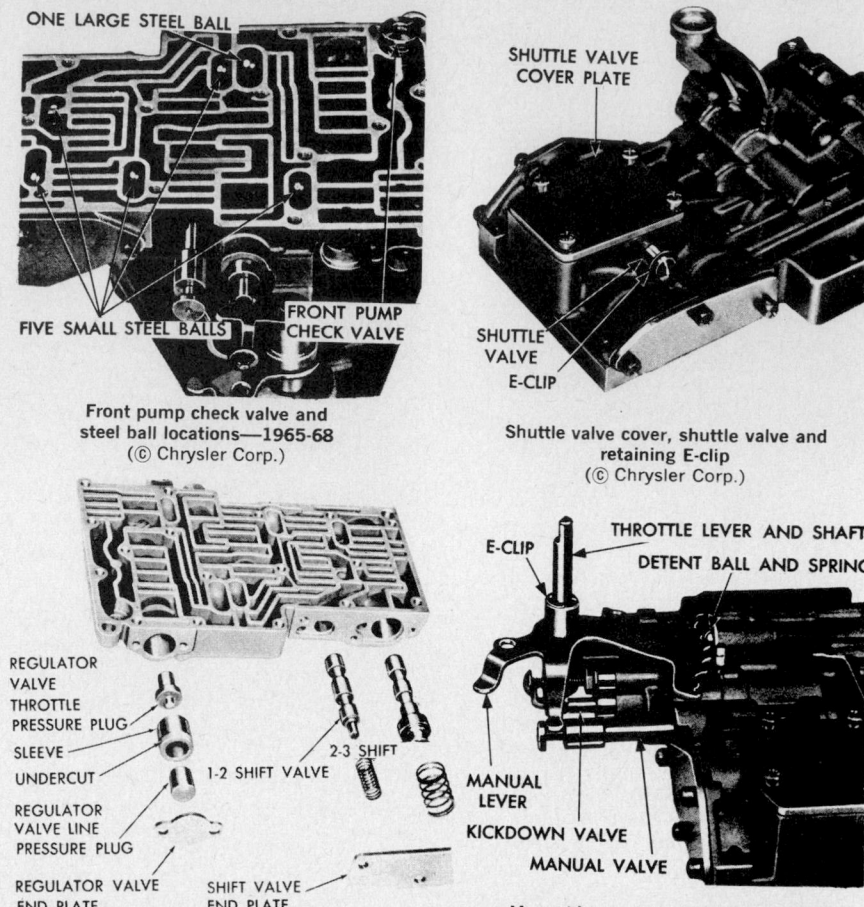

Front pump check valve and steel ball locations—1965-68
(© Chrysler Corp.)

Shuttle valve cover, shuttle valve and retaining E-clip
(© Chrysler Corp.)

Valve body—shift valve side
(© Chrysler Corp.)

Manual lever, detent ball and spring, throttle lever and shaft, manual valve, and kickdown valve
(© Chrysler Corp.)

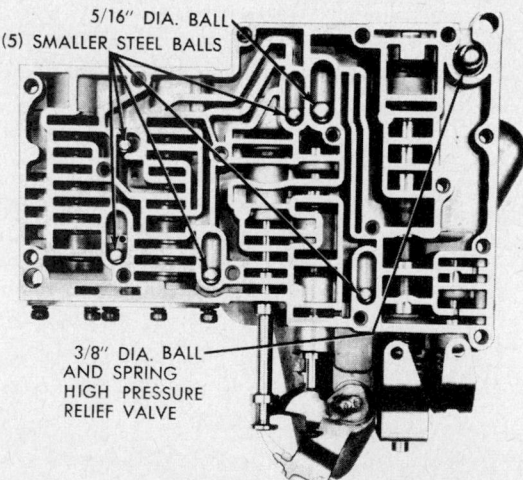

Steel ball location, 1969-72 (© Chrysler Corp.)

verter control valve from the valve body.

5. Remove the (14) transfer plate retaining screws. Lift the transfer plate and steel plate assembly off the valve body.

6. Invert the transfer plate assembly and remove the stiffener plate. Remove the remaining screws securing the steel plate to the transfer plate, and lift off the steel plate.

Remove rear pump check valve and spring on 1965 transmissions.

7. On 1965 transmissions, remove reverse blocker valve cover and lift out spring and valve.

8. On 1965 transmissions, note location of six steel balls in valve body. On 1969-70, note location of seven steel balls. (two of them are larger than the others and are in larger chambers. Remove

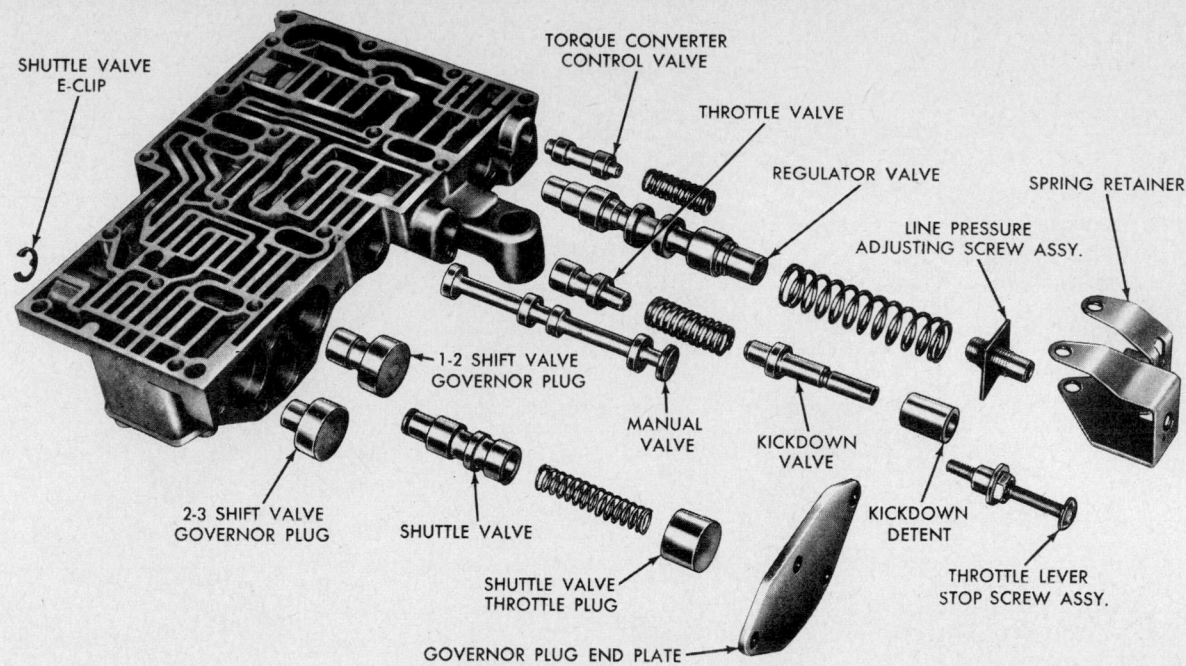

SHUTTLE VALVE
E-CLIP

TORQUE CONVERTER
CONTROL VALVE

THROTTLE VALVE

REGULATOR VALVE

SPRING RETAINER

LINE PRESSURE
ADJUSTING SCREW ASSY.

1-2 SHIFT VALVE
GOVERNOR PLUG

2-3 SHIFT VALVE
GOVERNOR PLUG

MANUAL
VALVE

KICKDOWN
VALVE

SHUTTLE VALVE

SHUTTLE VALVE
THROTTLE PLUG

KICKDOWN
DETENT

THROTTLE LEVER
STOP SCREW ASSY.

GOVERNOR PLUG END PLATE

Valve body—lever side, 1966-72 (©) Chrysler Corp.)

the steel balls, front pump check valve and spring.

9. On 1965 transmissions, invert valve body and lay it on clean paper. Remove E-clip from the throttle lever shaft. While holding manual lever detent ball and spring in their bore with tool C-3765, or similar tool, slide manual lever from the throttle shaft. Remove detent ball and spring.

10. Remove manual valve from valve body.

11. Remove throttle lever and shaft from body.

12. Remove shuttle valve cover plate. Remove E-clip from the exposed end of shuttle valve.

13. Remove throttle lever stop screw, being careful not to disturb the setting.

14. Remove kickdown detent, kickdown valve, throttle valve spring and throttle valve.

15. Remove governor plug and end plate. Tip up the valve body to allow the shuttle valve throttle plug, spring, shuttle valve and the shift valve governor plugs to slide out.

NOTE: the first-second valve plug has a longer stem.

16. Remove the shift valve end plate and slide out the two springs and valves.

17. Remove the regulator valve end plate. Slide the regulator valve line pressure plug, sleeve, and the regulator valve throttle pressure plug from the body.

Disassembly 1971-72

1. Place the valve body on a clean repair stand. Never place any part of the valve body or transfer plate in a vise, since distortion can cause sticking valves and excessive leakage.

2. Remove the three screws from the fluid filter and remove the filter.

3. Remove the 17 transfer plate retaining screws and 2 of the spring retainer mounting screws.

4. Lift off the transfer plate assembly. Separate the stiffener and separator plate for cleaning.

5. Remove the seven balls and spring from the valve body. Tag all springs as they are removed, for identification.

6. Turn the valve body over and remove the shuttle valve cover plate.

7. Remove the governor plug end plate and slide out the shuttle valve throttle valve and spring, 1-2 shift valve governor plug and the 2-3 shift valve governor plug.

8. Remove the shuttle valve E-clip and remove the shuttle valve.

9. Hold the spring retainer firmly against the spring and remove the last screw from the valve body.

10. Remove the spring retainer, line pressure adjusting screw (do not disturb the setting), and the line pressure and torque converter regulator springs.

11. Slide the torque converter and line pressure valves out of their bores.

12. Remove the E-clip and washer from the throttle lever shaft. Remove any burrs from the shaft, and, while holding the manual lever detent ball and spring in their bore with tool C-3765, or similar tool, slide the

manual lever from the throttle shaft. Remove detent ball and spring.

13. Slide the manual valve from its bore.

14. Remove the throttle lever stop screw assembly from the valve body and slide out the kickdown detent, kickdown valve, throttle valve spring and throttle valve.

15. Remove the line pressure regulator valve end plate and slide out the regulator valve sleeve, line pressure plug and throttle pressure plug.

16. Remove the throttle plug housing and slide the throttle plug out.

17. Remove the shift valve springs and slide both shift valves from their bores.

Cleaning and Inspection

Inspect all components for scores, loose or bent levers, burrs and warping. Don't straighten bent levers; renew them. Loose levers may be silver soldered at the shaft. Burrs and minor nicks may be carefully removed with crocus cloth. Check for valve body warping or distortion with a surface plate (plate glass will do) and a feeler gauge. Do not attempt to service a distorted plate or valve body, since this is a very critical area. Check all springs for distortion or fatigue. Check valves for scores and freedom of movement in the bores, they should fall of their own weight, in and out of the bore. The front and rear pump check valves are provided with a controlled leakage path. This keeps the rear pump primed (1965 only).

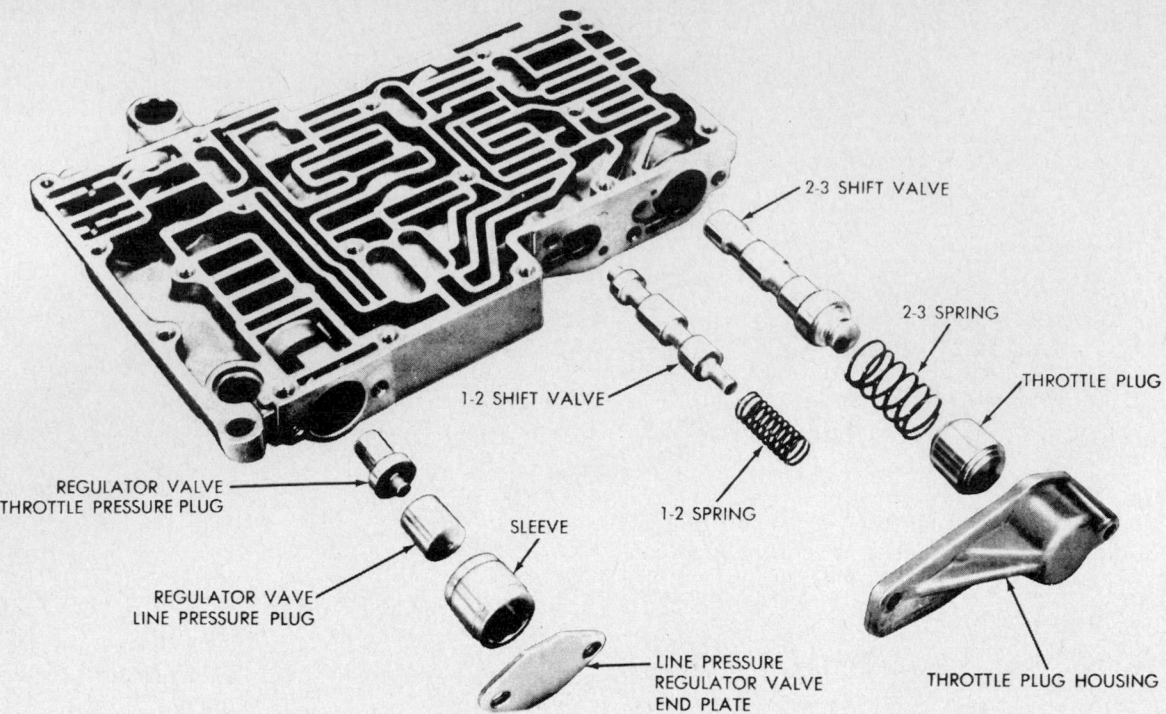

A-904 shift valves and pressure regulator valve plugs—1970-72 (© Chrysler Corp.)

2-3 SHIFT VALVE
2-3 SPRING
THROTTLE PLUG
1-2 SHIFT VALVE
REGULATOR VALVE THROTTLE PRESSURE PLUG
SLEEVE
1-2 SPRING
REGULATOR VAVE LINE PRESSURE PLUG
LINE PRESSURE REGULATOR VALVE END PLATE
THROTTLE PLUG HOUSING

Assembly 1965-70

1. On 1965 transmissions, insert the rear pump check valve and springs into the transfer plate. Position the steel plate on pump check valve in its bore with a thin steel scale and install four steel plate to transfer plate retaining screws. Torque these screws evenly to 28 in. lbs. Check rear pump check valve for free movement in the transfer plate. Install stiffener plate and tighten retaining screw to 28 in. lbs.

2. On 1965 transmissions, turn transfer plate over and install reverse blocker valve spring and valve. Rotate valve until it seats through the steel plate. Hold the valve down and install blocker valve cover plate Torque the two retaining screws to 28 in. lbs. On 1966-70 transmissions, place separator plate on transfer plate. Install stiffener plate and retaining screws exactly as shown. Make sure all bolt holes are aligned. Tighten stiffener plate screws to 28 in. lbs.

3. Insert the first-second and second-third shift valve governor plugs into their respective bores. Install shuttle valve, valve spring and shuttle valve throttle plug. Install governor plug end plate and torque the four retaining screws to 28 in. lbs.

4. Install E-clip onto end of shuttle valve. Install shuttle valve cover plate and torque the four retaining screws to 28 in. lbs.

5. Install the first-second and sec-

ond-third shift valves and springs. Install shift valve and plate and torque the three retaining screws to 28 in. lbs.

6. Insert regulator valve throttle pressure plug, sleeve (with the undercut on the sleeve toward the end plate), and the line pressure plug. Install regulator valve end plate and torque the two retaining screws to 28 in. lbs.

7. Insert throttle valve and spring. Slide the kickdown detent onto kickdown valve (with counterbore side of detent toward valve), then insert the assembly in the valve body.

8. Install throttle lever stop screw and tighten locknut finger tight.

9. Insert manual valve into the valve body.

10. Install throttle lever and shaft on the valve body. Insert detent spring and ball into its bore in the valve body. Depress ball and spring and slide manual lever over throttle shaft so that it engages manual valve and detent ball. Install the retaining E-clip onto the throttle shaft.

11. Position the valve body assembly on the bench or holding stand.

12. Place six steel balls in the valve body chambers (with large ball in the large chamber). Place the front pump check valve and spring in the valve body. On 1969-70 transmissions, install spring and 3/8 in. high pressure relief valve ball.

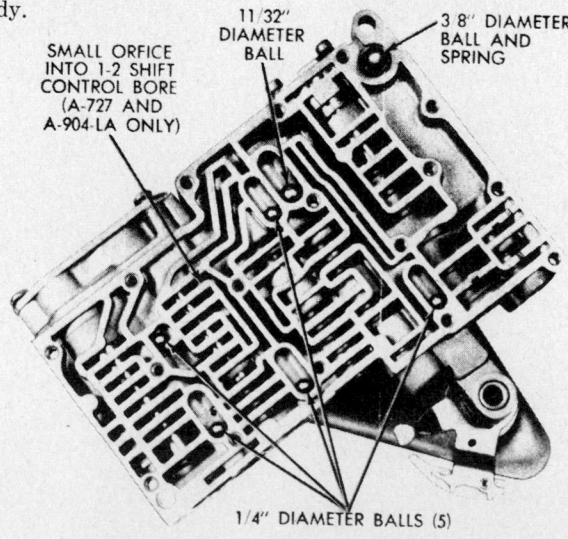

SMALL ORFICE INTO 1-2 SHIFT CONTROL BORE (A-727 AND A-904-LA ONLY)
11/32" DIAMETER BALL
3 8" DIAMETER BALL AND SPRING
1/4" DIAMETER BALLS (5)

Steel ball locations—1970-72 (© Chrysler Corp.)

13. Position transfer plate assembly on the valve body. Hold front pump check valve in its bore with a thin steel scale. Install the (14) retaining screws, starting at the center and working outward. Torque screws to 28 in. lbs.

14. Install the torque converter valve, regulator valve and spring retainer ring.

15. Place the torque converter valve spring and the regulator valve spring over the ends of their respective valves. Place line pressure adjusting screw assembly on the end of the regulator valve spring, with the long dimension of the nut at right angles to the valve body.

16. Install spring retainer bracket (make sure the converter valve spring is engaged on the tang in the bracket). Torque the three bracket retaining screws to 28 in. lbs.

17. Install oil strainer and torque the three retaining screws to 28 in. lbs.

NOTE: after reconditioning the valve body, adjust the throttle and line pressure. However, if line pressure was satisfactory before disassembly, do not change this adjustment.

Assembly 1970-72

1. Slide the shift valves and springs into the proper valve body bores.

2. If so equipped, assemble the downshifts housing. Insert the limit valve and spring into the housing. Slide the spring retainer into the groove.

3. Insert the throttle into the housing bore and install the housing on the valve body. Torque the screws to 28 in. lbs.

4. Install the throttle pressure plug, line pressure plug and sleeve, fastening the end plate. Torque to 28 in. lbs.

5. Install the throttle valve, throttle valve spring, kickdown valve, kickdown detent and throttle lever stop screw with the locknut (do not adjust yet).

6. Slide the manual valve into its bore.

7. Install the throttle lever and shaft on the valve body. Insert the detent ball and spring into its bore in the valve body. Depress the ball and spring and slide the manual lever over the throttle shaft. Be sure that it engages the manual valve and detent ball. Install the seal, retaining washer and E-clip on the throttle shaft.

8. Insert the torque converter control valve and spring into the valve body.

9. Insert the line pressure regulator and spring into the valve body.

10. Install the line pressure adjusting screw assembly and spring retainer on the springs and temporarily with one screw.

11. Place the 1-2 and 2-3 shift valve governor plugs in their proper bores.

12. Install the shuttle valve spring, shuttle valve and shuttle valve throttle plug.

13. Install the governor plug end plate and torque the screws to 28 in. lbs.

14. Install the E-clip on the end of the shuttle valve.

15. Install the shuttle valve cover plate and torque screws to 28 in. lbs.

16. Install the spring and seven balls in the valve body.

17. Place the separator plate on the transfer plate. Make sure all bolt holes are aligned and torque the two transfer plate screws and two stiffener plate screws to 28 in. lbs.

18. Place the transfer plate assembly on the valve body. Align the spring loaded ball as the 17 shorter screws are installed. Start at the center and work outward, tightening the screws to 35 in. lbs.

19. Install the oil filter and torque to 35 in. lbs.

20. Check spring engagement with the tang and adjusting nut. Install the remaining spring retainer screws. Check alignment and torque to 28 in. lbs.

21. After valve body has been serviced and completely assembled, adjust throttle and line pressures. If pressures were satisfactory prior to disassembly, use the original settings.

Accumulator Piston and Spring

Inspect both seal rings for wear and freedom in the piston grooves. Check the piston for scores, burrs, nicks and wear. Check the piston bore for corresponding damage and check piston spring for distortion and fatigue. Replace parts as required.

Governor

Disassembly

1. Remove the large snap-ring from the weight end of governor housing and lift out the governor weight assembly.

2. Remove the snap-ring from inside the governor weight, remove the inner weight and spring from the outer weight.

NOTE: thoroughly clean all parts in a suitable and clean solvent. Check for damage and free movement before assembly.

3. If lugs on support gear are damaged, remove four bolts and sep-

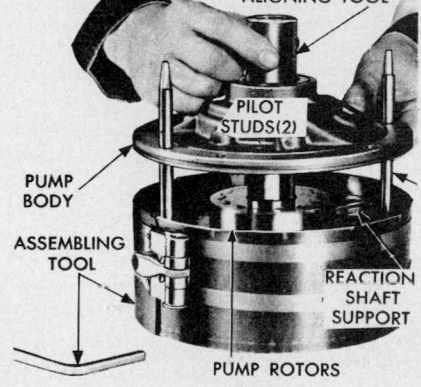

Assembling front pump and reaction shaft support
(© Chrysler Corp.)

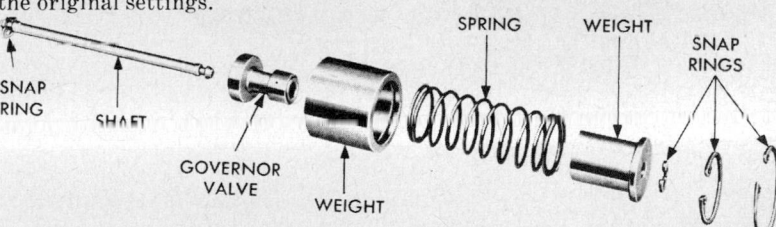

Governor valve, weights, spring and shaft (© Chrysler Corp.)

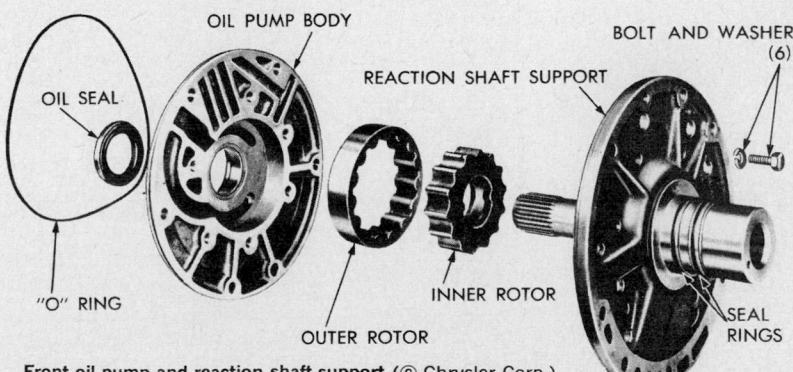

Front oil pump and reaction shaft support (© Chrysler Corp.)

arate support from governor body.

Assembly

1. If support was separated from governor body, assemble and tighten bolts finger tight.
2. Assemble the governor weights and spring, then secure with snap-ring inside large governor weight.
3. Place the weight assembly in the governor housing and install snap-ring.

Rear Oil Pump, 1965
Inspection

Clean and inspect oil pump body and cover for wear, gouging or any other type of damage. Inspect rotors for scoring or pitting. With rotors cleaned and assembled in the pump body, apply a straightedge across the face of rotors and pump body. With a feeler gauge, check clearance between straightedge and face of ro-

tors. Clearance limits are at front of section.

Front Pump and Reaction Shaft Support
Disassembly

The illustration shows the front oil pump and reaction shaft support disassembled.

1. Remove bolts from rear side of reaction shaft support and lift support from the pump.
2. Dye-spot the face of the inner and outer rotors so they may be reinstalled in their original relationship, then remove the rotors.
3. Remove the rubber seal ring from front pump body flange.
4. Drive out the oil seal with blunt punch.

Inspection

Clean and inspect interlocking seal rings on the reaction shaft support for wear or broken interlocks, be sure

they turn freely in their grooves. Check all machined surfaces of pump body and reaction shaft support for scuff marks and burrs. Inspect pump rotors for scores and pits. With rotors clean and installed into the pump body, apply a straightedge across the face of the rotors and pump body. With a feeler gauge, check straightedge to rotor face clearance. Limits are in front of section.

Assembly

1. Place reaction shaft support in assembling tool C-3759 and place it on the bench, with the support hub resting on the bench. Screw two pilot studs, tool C-3283, or satisfactory substitutes, into threaded holes of reaction shaft support flange.
2. Assemble rotors with dye marks aligned, place rotors in center of the support. The two driving lugs inside rotor must be next to the face of the reaction shaft

A-727 oil pump and reaction shaft support—1970-72 (© Chrysler Corp.)

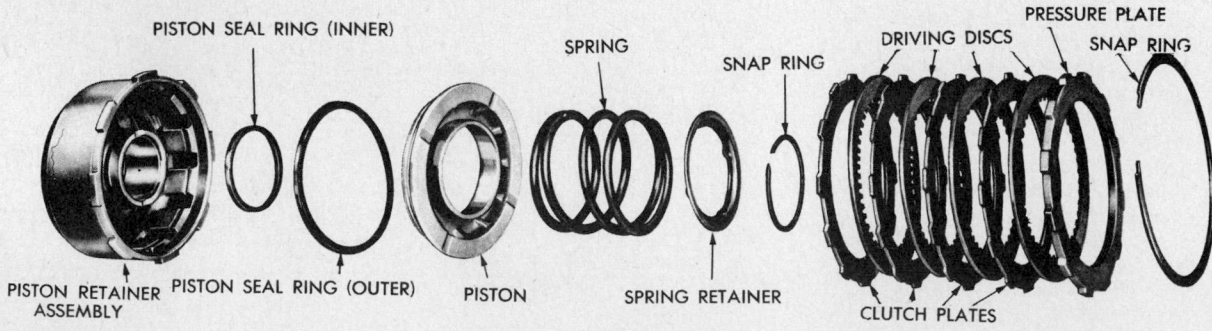

Front clutch assembly—A-904
(© Chrysler Corp.)

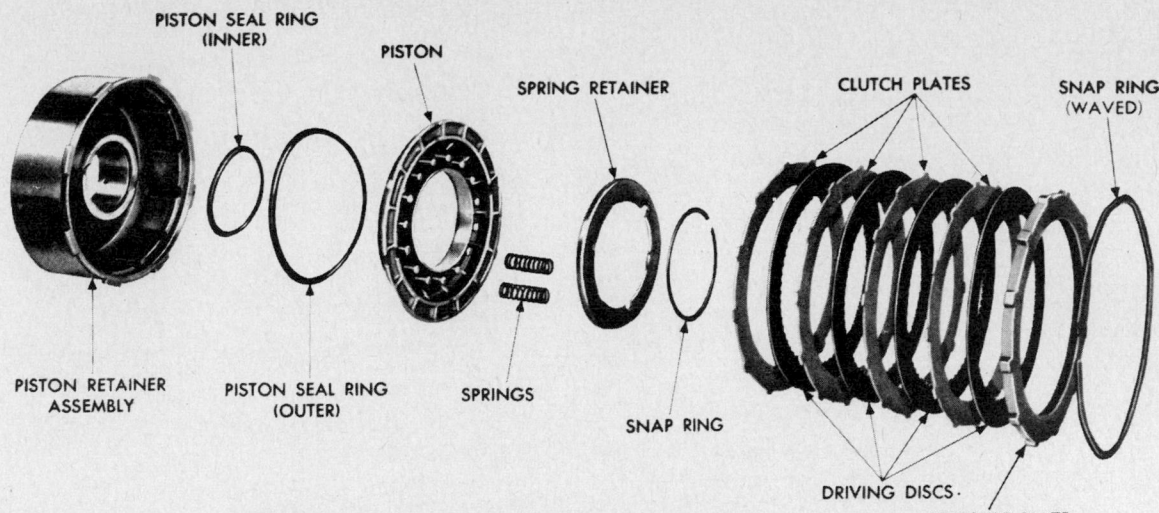

A-727 front clutch disassembled—1970-72 (© Chrysler Corp.)

support.

3. Lower pump body over pilot studs, insert tool C-3756 or substitute through pump body and engage pump inner rotor. Turn the rotors, with the tool, to enter them into pump body. With the pump body firmly against the reaction shaft support, tighten ring squeezer or clamping tool securely.

4. Invert the front pump and reaction shaft support assembly, with the clamping tool intact. Install support to pump body bolts. Remove clamping tool, pilot studs and rotor aligning studs.

5. Insert new oil seal into opening of front oil pump housing (with lip of seal facing inward). Drive seal into housing.

Front Clutch

Disassembly

Exploded view of front clutch assembly is shown.

1. With screwdriver or pick, remove large snap-ring, which holds the pressure plate in the clutch piston retainer. Lift pressure plate and clutch plates out of the retainer.

2. Install compressor, tool C-3575 for A-904 transmissions, or C-3863 for A-727 transmissions, or similar tool, over piston spring retainer. Compress spring and remove snap-ring, then, slowly release tool until the spring retainer is free of the hub. Remove the compressor, retainer and spring.

3. Turn the clutch retainer upside down and bump on a wooden block to remove the piston. Remove seal rings from the piston and clutch retainer hub.

Inspection

Inspect clutch discs for evidence of burning, glazing and flaking. A general method of determining clutch plate breakdown is to scratch the lined surface of the plate with a finger nail. If material collects under the nail, replace all driving discs. Check driving splines for wear or burrs. Inspect steel plates and pressure plate surfaces for discoloration, scuffing or damaged driving lugs. Replace if necessary.

Check steel plate lug grooves in clutch retainer for smooth surfaces. Plate travel must be free. Inspect band contacting surface of clutch retainer, being sure the ball moves freely. Check seal ring surfaces in clutch retainer for scratches or nicks, light annular scratches will not interfere with the sealing of neoprene rings.

Inspect inside bore of piston for score marks. If light marks exist, polish with crocus cloth. Check seal ring grooves for nicks and burrs. Inspect neoprene seal rings for deterioration, wear and hardness. Check piston spring, retainer, and snap-ring for distortion and fatigue.

Assembly

1. Lubricate and install inner seal ring onto hub of clutch retainer. Be sure that lip of seal faces down and is properly seated in the groove.

2. Lubricate and install outer seal ring onto clutch piston, with lip of seal toward the bottom of the clutch retainer. Place piston assembly in retainer and, with a twisting motion, seat the piston in the bottom of the retainer.

3. Place spring on the piston hub and position spring retainer and snap-ring on spring. Compress spring with tool, or suitable ring compressor, and seat snap-ring in the hub groove. Remove compressor.

4. Lubricate all clutch plates, then, install a steel plate, followed by a lined plate, until all plates are installed. Install the pressure plate and snap-ring. Be sure the snap-ring is correctly seated.

5. With front clutch assembled, insert a feeler gauge between the pressure plate and snap-ring. The clearance should be to specification. If not, install a snap-ring of proper thickness.

Rear Clutch

Disassembly

1. With a small screwdriver or pick, remove the large snap-ring that secures the pressure plate in the clutch piston retainer. Lift the pressure plate, clutch plates, and inner pressure plate from the retainer.

2. On 1965 A-904 transmissions, install compressor Tool C-3760 or equivalent over piston spring. Compress spring just enough to clear snap ring and remove snap ring. On 1965 A-727 transmissions, remove piston ring snap ring and remove spring. On 1966-72 transmissions, carefully pry one end of wave spring out of its groove in clutch retainer and remove wave spring, spacer ring and clutch piston spring.

3. Remove compressor tool and piston spring. Turn clutch retainer assembly upside down and bump

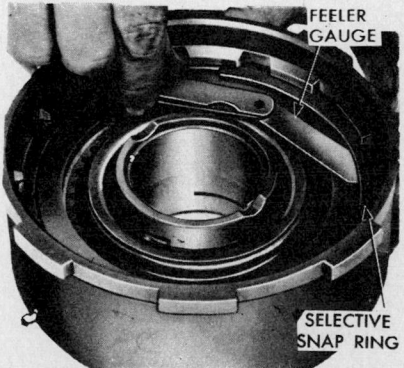

Checking front clutch plate clearance (© Chrysler Corp.)

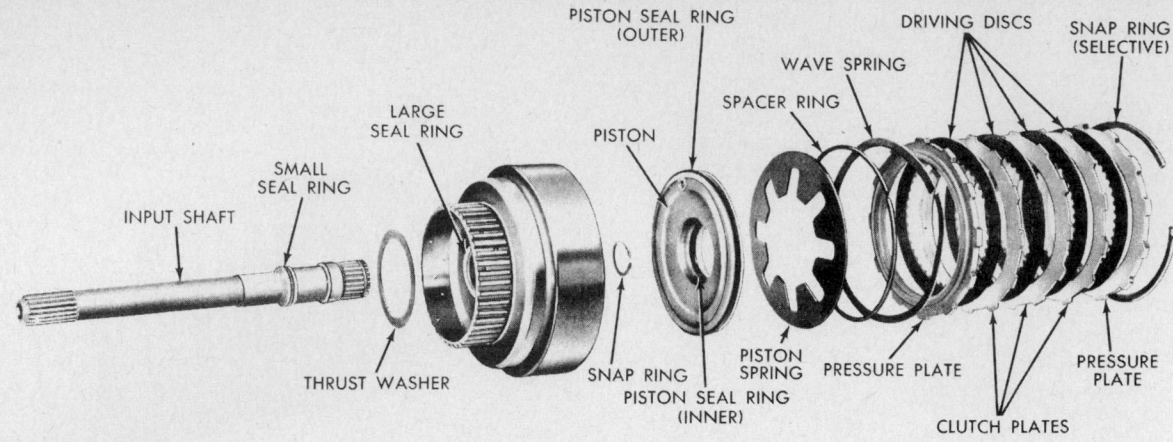

A-904 rear clutch disassembled—1970-72 (© Chrysler Corp.)

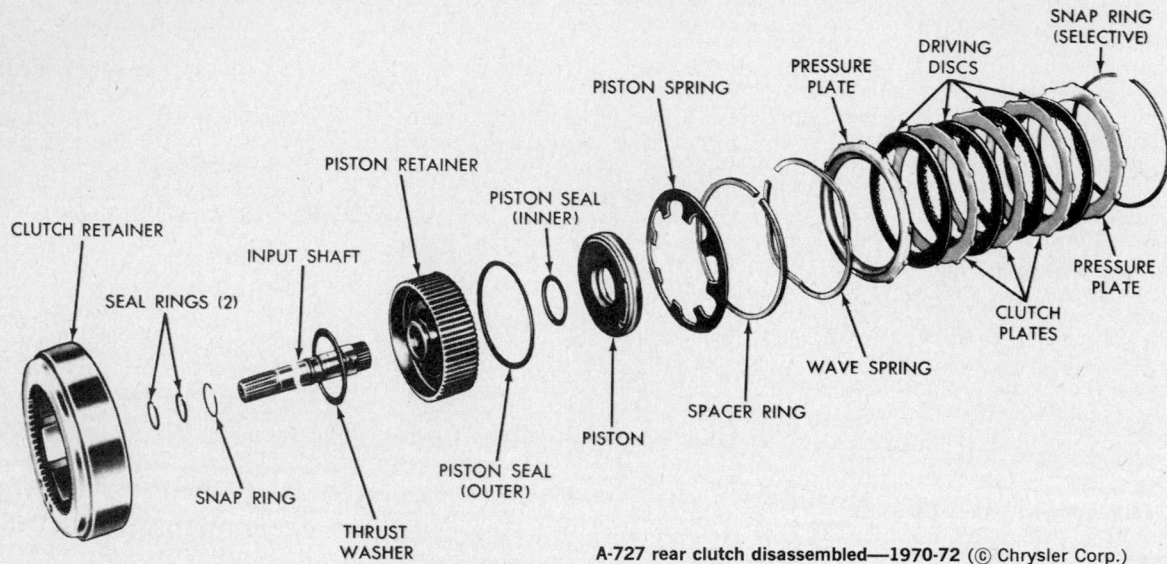

A-727 rear clutch disassembled—1970-72 (© Chrysler Corp.)

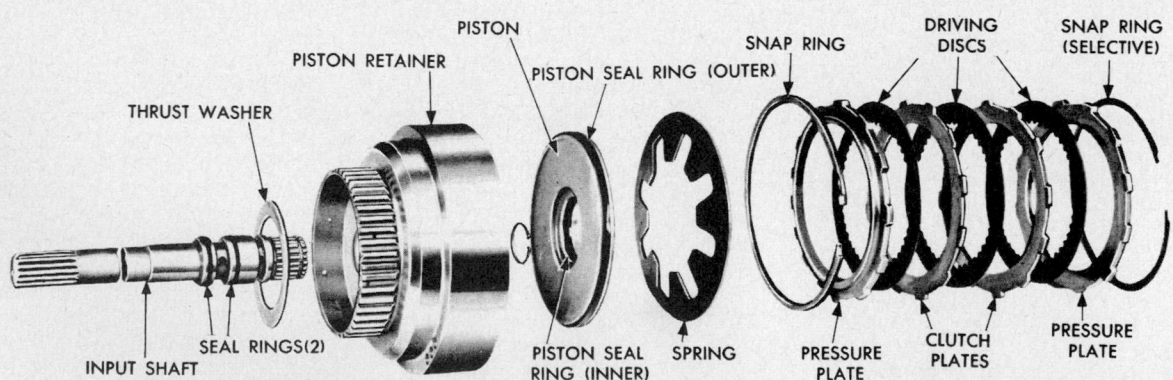

Rear clutch assembly—A-904
(© Chrysler Corp.)

on a wood block to remove the piston. Remove seal rings from the piston.

4. If necessary, remove the snapring and press input shaft from the piston retainer.

Inspection

Inspect driving discs for indication of damage; handle as previously outlined under front clutch inspection.

Assembly

1. If removed, press input shaft into the piston retainer and install the snap-ring.
2. Lubricate, then install inner and outer seal rings onto the clutch piston. Be sure the seal lips face toward the head of the clutch retainer and seals are properly seated in the piston grooves.

3. Place piston assembly in retainer and, with a twisting motion, seat piston in bottom of retainer.
4. On 1965 A-904 transmissions, place spring over piston with outer edge of spring positioned below snap ring groove. Install compressor Tool C-3760 or equivalent over spring. Compress spring just enough to install snap ring. Remove tool. On 1965

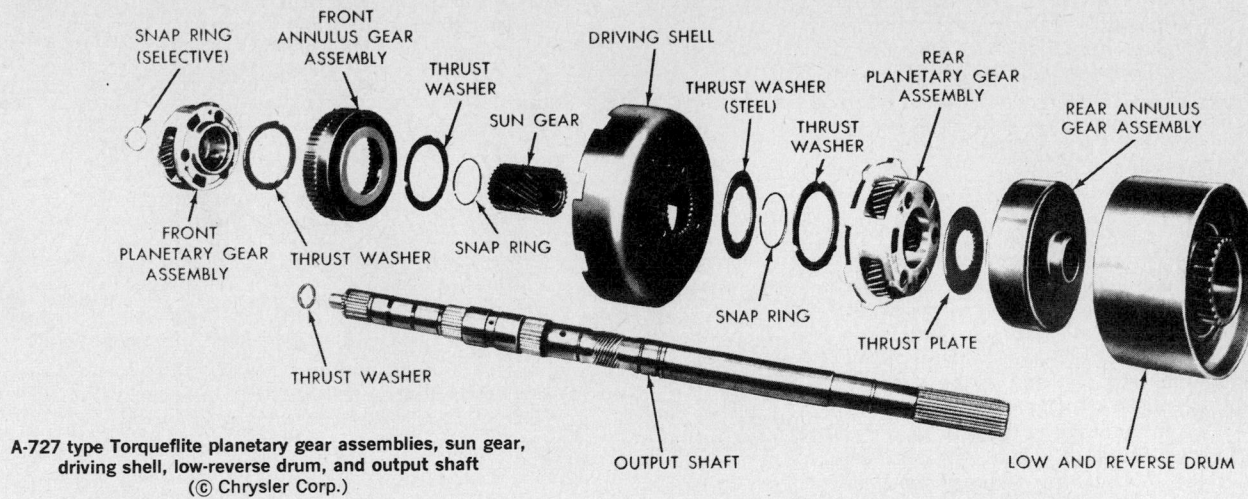

A-727 type Torqueflite planetary gear assemblies, sun gear, driving shell, low-reverse drum, and output shaft
(© Chrysler Corp.)

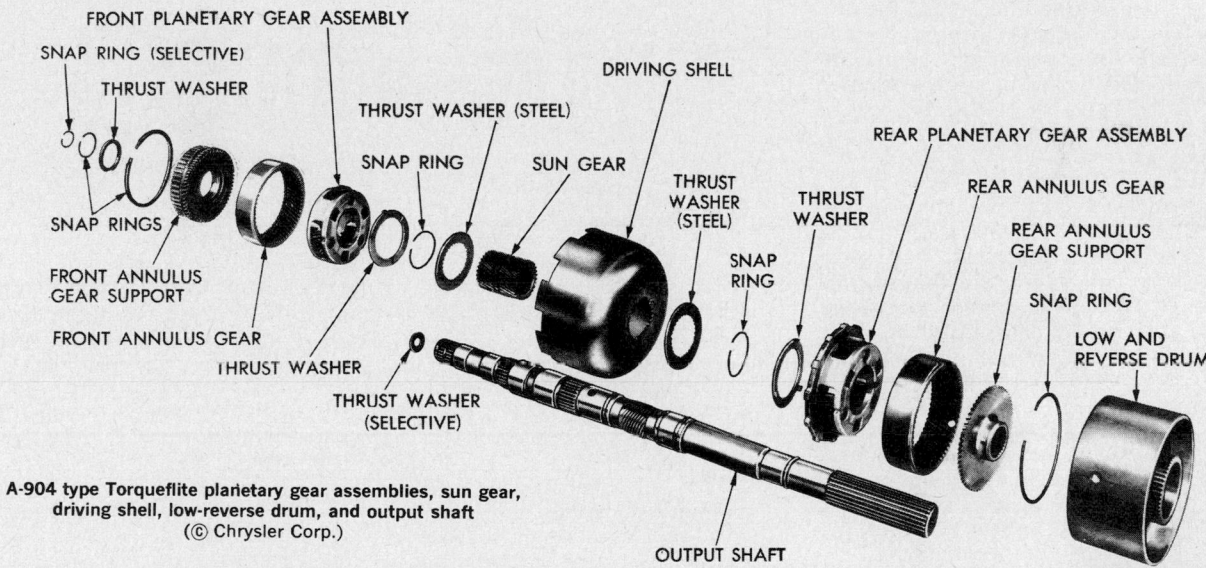

A-904 type Torqueflite planetary gear assemblies, sun gear, driving shell, low-reverse drum, and output shaft
(© Chrysler Corp.)

A-727 transmissions, place spring over piston with outer edge of spring positioned below snap ring groove. Start one end of snap ring in groove. Make sure spring is exactly centered on piston. Progressively tap snap ring into groove. Be sure snap ring is fully seated in groove. On 1966-72 transmissions, place clutch piston spring and spacer ring on top of piston in clutch retainer. Make sure spring and spacer ring are placed in retainer recess. Start one end of wave spring in retainer groove. Progressively push or tap spring into place making sure it is fully seated in groove.

5. Install inner pressure plate into clutch retainer, with raised portion of plate resting on the spring.

6. Lubricate all clutch plates, then install one lined plate, followed by a steel plate, until all plates are installed. Install outer pressure plate and snap-ring.

7. With rear clutch completely assembled, insert a feeler gauge between the pressure plate and snap-ring. The clearance should be to specification. If not, install snap-ring of proper thickness to obtain the required clearance.

NOTE: rear clutch plate clearance is very important to obtaining satisfactory clutch performance. Clearance is influenced by the use of various thickness outer snap-rings.

Planetary Gear Train
Disassembly

Refer to illustrations for assembly and disassembly of these units.

1. Remove thrust washer from forward end of output shaft.

2. Remove snap-ring from forward end of output shaft, then, slide front planetary assembly from the shaft.

3. On A-904 transmissions, remove snap ring and thrust washer from forward hub of planetary gear assembly. Slide front annulus gear and support off plane-

tary gear set. Remove thrust washer from rear side of planetary gear set. If necessary, remove snap ring from front of annulus gear to separate support from annulus gear. On A-727 transmissions, slide front annulus gear off planetary gear set. Remove thrust washer from rear side of planetary gear set.

4. Slide the sun gear, driving shell, and rear planetary assembly, with low and reverse drum, from the output shaft.

5. Remove sun gear and driving shell from the rear planetary assembly. On A-727 transmissions, remove thrust washer from inside driving shell. On all transmissions, remove snap-ring and steel washer from sun gear (rear side of driving shell). Slide sun gear out of driving shell, then remove snap-ring and steel washer from opposite end of sun gear, if necessary.

6. Remove thrust washer from forward side of rear planetary as-

sembly. Remove snap-ring from front side of low and reverse drum, then slide rear planetary assembly out of drum. If necessary, remove snap-ring from rear of annulus gear in order to separate the support from the annulus gear.

Inspection

Inspect output shaft bearing surfaces for burrs or other damage. Light scratches or burrs may be polished out with crocus cloth or a fine stone. Check speedometer drive gear for damage, and make sure all oil passages are clear.

Check bushings in the sun gear for wear or scores. Replace sun gear assembly if bushings show wear or other damage. Inspect all thrust washers for wear and scores. Replace if necessary. Check lockrings for distortion and fatigue. Inspect annulus gear and driving gear teeth for damage. Inspect planetary gear carrier for cracks and the pinions for broken or worn gear teeth.

Assembly—A-904

1. Locate the rear annulus gear support in the annulus gear and install snap-ring. Install the rear annulus gear on the output shaft. Lightly, grease the thrust washer and place it on the shaft and in the annulus gear, making sure the teeth are over the shaft splines.
2. Position the rear planetary gear assembly in the rear annulus gear, then slide the assembly into low and reverse drum. Put thrust washer on the front side of the planetary gear assembly.
3. Insert output shaft into the rear opening of the drum. Carefully work the shaft through the annulus gear support and planetary gear assembly. Make sure the shaft splines are fully engaged in the splines of the annulus gear support.
4. Install steel washer and snap-ring onto the shortest end of the sun gear. Insert sun gear through front side of the driving shell, then install rear steel washer and snap-ring. (The longer end of the sun gear must be toward the rear, extending from the driving shell).
5. Carefully slide the driving shell and sun gear assembly onto the output shaft, engaging the sun gear teeth with the planetary pinion teeth.
6. Place front annulus gear support in annulus gear and install snap-ring.
7. Position front planetary gear assembly in front annulus gear, place thrust washer over planetary gear assembly hub and in-

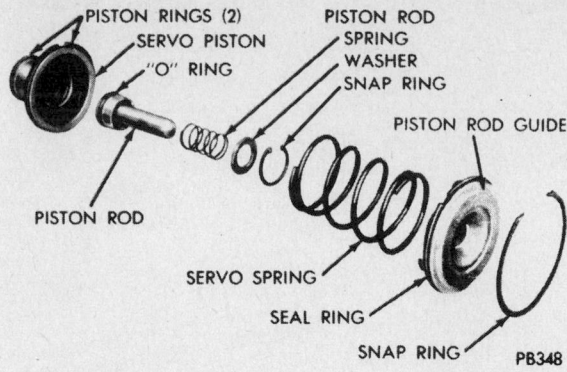

Controlled load kickdown servo—1970-72 (© Chrysler Corp.)

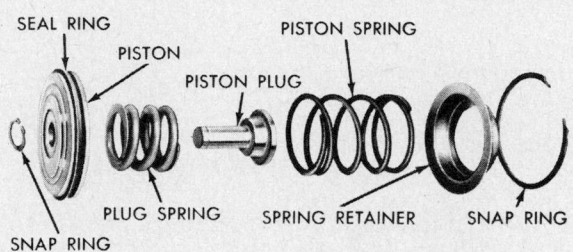

Low and reverse servo—1970-72 (© Chrysler Corp.)

stall snap-ring. Position thrust washer on rear side of planetary gear assembly.
8. Carefully work the front planetary and annulus gear assembly onto the output shaft, meshing the planetary pinions with the sun gear teeth.
9. With all components properly assembled, install snap-ring onto the front end of the output shaft. Clearance can be adjusted through the use of various thickness snap-rings, listed at front of section.

Assembly—A-727

1. On 1965 transmissions, place rear planetary gear assembly in rear annulus gear. Place thrust washer on front side of planetary gear assembly. Insert output shaft in rear opening of rear annulus gear. Carefully, work shaft through annulus gear and planetary gear assembly. Make sure shaft splines are fully engaged in splines of annulus gear.
2. On 1966-72 transmissions, install rear annulus gear on output shaft. Apply thin coat of grease on thrust plate, place it on shaft, and in annulus gear making sure teeth are over shaft slines. Position rear planetary gear assembly in rear annulus gear. Place thrust washer on front side of planetary gear assembly.
3. Install snap-ring in front groove of sun gear (long end of gear). Insert sun gear through front

side of driving shell. Install rear steel washer and snap-ring.
4. Carefully slide driving shell and sun gear assembly on output shaft, engaging sun gear teeth with rear planetary pinion teeth. Place thrust washer inside front driving shell.
5. Place thrust washer on rear hub of front planetary gear set. Slide assembly into front annulus gear.
6. Carefully work front planetary and annulus gear assembly on output shaft, meshing planetary pinions with sun gear teeth.
7. With all components properly positioned, install selective snapring on front end of output shaft. Measure end-play of assembly. Adjust end-play with selective snap rings.

Overrunning Clutch Inspection

Inspect clutch rollers for smooth round surfaces, they must be free of flat spots, chipped edges and flaking. Inspect roller contacting surfaces on both cam and race for pock marks and roller wear-marks. Check springs for distortion and fatigue and inspect low and reverse drum thrust. On 1966-72 A-727 transmissions, inpect cam set screw for tightness. If loose, tighten and restake the case.

Kickdown Servo and Band
Inspection

Inspect piston and guide seal rings for wear, and be sure of their free-

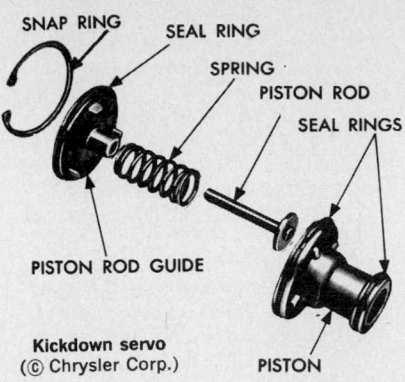

Kickdown servo
(© Chrysler Corp.)

dom in grooves. It is not necessary to remove seal rings, unless circumstances warrant. Inspect piston for scores, burrs or other damage. Check fit of guide on piston rod. Check piston for distortion and fatigue. Inspect band lining for wear and fit of lining material to the metal band. This lining is grooved; if grooves are not still visible at the ends or any part of the band, replace the band. Inspect band for distortion or cracked ends.

Low and Reverse Servo and Band

Disassembly

Remove snap-ring from piston and remove the piston plug and spring.

Inspection

Inspect neoprene seal ring for damage, rot, or hardness. Check piston and piston plug for nicks, burrs, scores and wear. The piston plug must operate freely in the piston. Check the piston bore in the case for scores or other damage. Examine springs for distortion and fatigue.

Check band lining for wear and the fit of the lining to the metal band. This lining has a grooved surface; if the grooves are worn away at the ends or at any part of the band, replace the band. Inspect the band for distortion or cracked ends.

Assembly

Lubricate and insert the piston plug and spring into the piston, and secure with the snap-ring.

Sub-Assemblies Installation

The following assembly procedures include the installation of sub-assemblies into the transmission case and adjustment of the drive train end-play. Do not use force to assemble any of the mating parts. Always use new gaskets during the assembly operations.

NOTE: use only automatic transmission fluid, type A, suffix A, or fluid of equivalent chemical structure, to lubricate automatic transmission parts during, or after, assembly.

Rear Oil Pump Body

1965

The following procedures should be followed closely when installing a new rear pump body, or reinstalling the original pump body, in order to prevent pump body distortion.

1. Cut a piece of .002-.003 in. thick wrapping paper, slightly smaller than the outside diameter of the outer rotor, to use as a shim during installation.
2. Chill the pump body to approximately 0°F. in a deep freeze, or with dry ice.
3. Quickly place pump body in the case, and install inner and outer rotors. Smear a daub of grease on the face of the rotors, center the paper shim on face of rotors, then install pump cover and tighten retaining bolts firmly.
4. After the pump body has warmed to room temperature, remove the pump cover, paper shim and rotors.

Overrunning Clutch

1965

1. With the transmission case positioned upright, place low and reverse drum thrust washer in overrunning clutch housing, then, place the clutch hub (race) on the thrust washer.
2. Install springs and rollers, as shown in illustration.

1966-72

With transmission case in upright position, insert clutch hub inside cam. Install overrunning clutch rollers and springs as shown in figure.

Low and Reverse Servo and Band

1. Carefully work servo piston assembly into the case with a twisting motion. Place spring, retainer and snap-ring over the piston.
2. Using the screw portion of tool C-3322, or suitable substitute, depress the spring and install the snap-ring.
3. Position rear band in the case, install the short strut, then connect the long lever and strut to the band. Screw in band adjuster just enough to hold struts in place. Install low-reverse drum. On 1966-72 A-727 transmissions, be sure long link and anchor assembly is installed to provide running clearance for low-reverse drum.

Low-Reverse Band A-904-LA 1968-72 318 V8 Only

This transmission has a double wrap band supported at two points by a band reaction pin in case and acted upon at one point by a servo lever adjusting screw.

1. Push band reaction pin with new O-ring into case flush with gasket surface.
2. Place band in case resting two lugs against band reaction pin.

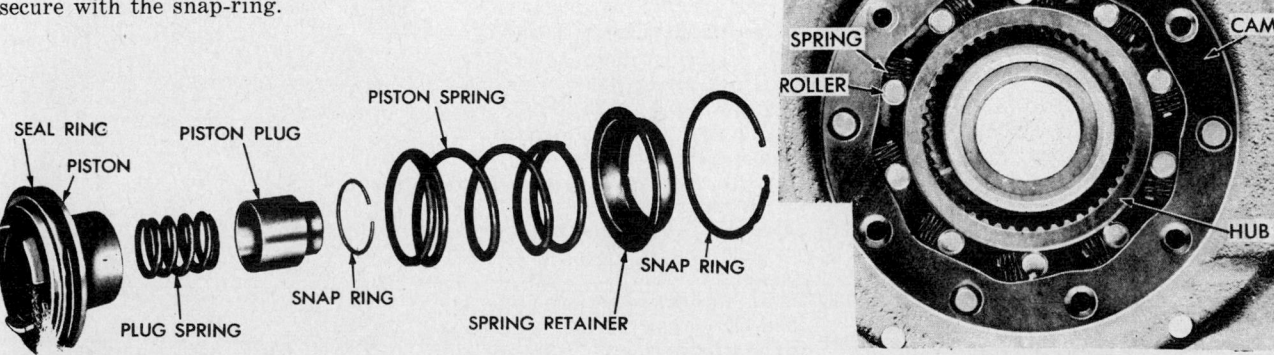

Low and reverse servo
(© Chrysler Corp.)

Overrunning clutch
(© Chrysler Corp.)

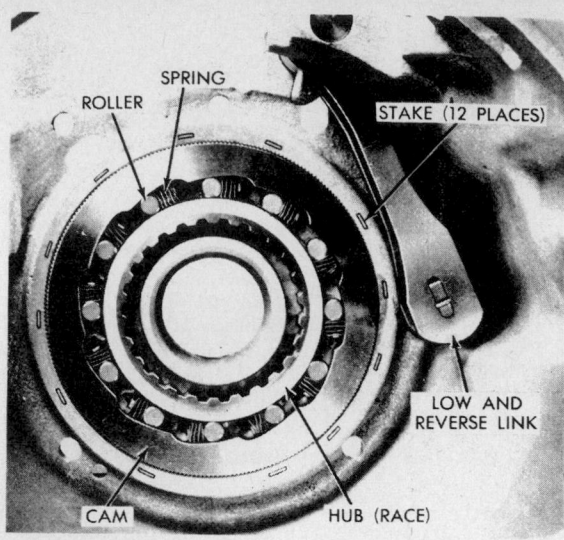

Overrunning clutch—1970-72 (© Chrysler Corp.)

3. Install low-reverse drum into overrunning clutch and band.
4. Install operating lever with pivot pin flush in case and adjusting screw touching center lug on band.

Kickdown Servo

1. If equipped with a controlled load servo piston, sub-assemble the unit as follows: grease the O ring and install on the piston rod; install the piston rod into the servo piston; install the spring, flat washer and snapring.
2. Carefully insert servo piston into case bore. Install piston rod, two springs and guide. Depress guide and install snap-ring.
NOTE: A-904 transmissions and maximum performance A-727 transmissions use only one small spring.

Planetary Gear Assemblies, Sun Gear, Driving Shell, Low and Reverse Drum

1. While supporting the assembly in the case, insert output shaft through the overrunning clutch hub. Carefully work the assembly rearward, engaging the drum splines with splines of the overrunning clutch hub.

Caution   Be careful not to damage the ground surfaces of the output shaft during installation.

2. Apply a daub of grease to the selective thrust washer and install washer on the front end of the output shaft.
NOTE: if the drive train end-play was not within specifications when checked (Checking Drive Train End-Play), replace the thrust washer with one of proper thickness.

Input Shaft and Rear Clutch 1965-69

1. Turn transmission in an upright position, with the output shaft pointing downward.
2. Align the rear clutch plate inner splines, then lower the input shaft and clutch assembly into position in the case.
3. Carefully work the clutch assembly, in a circular motion, to engage the clutch splines with the splines of the kickdown annulus gear support.
4. Daub one side of the fiber thrust washer with heavy grease, then position washer in the recess on the front face of the rear clutch retainer.

Front Clutch

1. Align the front clutch plate inner splines, then lower the clutch assembly into position in the case.
2. Carefully work the clutch assembly, in a circular motion, to engage clutch splines with splines of the rear clutch piston retainer. Be sure the front clutch driving lugs are fully engaged in the slots of the driving shell.

Front and Rear Clutch 1970-72

1. The following method may be used to support the transmission; cut a 3½" hole in a bench, small drum or box, strong enough to support the transmission; file notches at the edge so the output shaft support will lie flat; insert the output shaft into the hole and support the transmission upright.
2. On A-904 transmissions, apply a coat of grease to the selective thrust washer and install the washer on the front end of the output shaft. If drive train

end-play was not correct before disassembly, replace the thrust washer with one of suitable thickness.
3. On A-727 transmissions, apply a coat of grease to the input shaft to output shaft thrust washer and install the thrust washer on the front end of the output shaft.
4. Align the front clutch plate inner splines, and place the assembly in position on the rear clutch. Be sure the clutch plate splines are fully engaged.
5. Align the rear clutch plate inner splines and lower the two clutch assemblies in to the case.
6. Carefully, work the clutch assemblies in a circular motion to engage the rear clutch splines over the front annulus gear splines. Make sure the front clutch drive lugs are fully engaged in the driving shell.

Front Band

1. Slide the band over the front clutch assembly.
2. Install band strut, screw in the adjuster just enough to hold the band in place.

Front Oil Pump and Reaction Shaft Support

1. On A-904 transmissions, install the thrst washer on the reaction shaft support hub. On A-727 transmissions, if drive train end-play was not within specifications, replace the thrust washer on the reaction shaft support hub, with one of proper thickness (see specifications).
2. Screw (two) pilot studs into front pump opening in the case.
3. Place a new rubber seal ring in groove on outer flange of pump. Be sure the seal ring is not twisted.
4. Install the assembly into the case, tap lightly with a soft mallet if necessary. Install four bolts, remove pilot studs, install remaining bolts and pull down evenly, then, torque the bolts to specification.

Aligning front pump rotors
(© Chrysler Corp.)

5. Rotate the pump rotors until the two small holes in the handle of the tool are vertical. This is to locate the inner rotor so the converter impeller shaft will engage the inner rotor lugs during installation.

Rear Oil Pump 1965

1. Place outer rotor in pump body.
2. Turn output shaft so the inner rotor driving ball pocket is facing up. Install the ball and slide the inner rotor onto the output shaft, in alignment with the ball.
3. Position the outer rotor so the dye marks will be aligned, then push the inner rotor into mesh with the outer rotor. (see illustration).
4. Install the pump cover, with the retaining bolts threaded a few turns. Slide aligning sleeve, tool C-3762, all the way in, until it bottoms against the rotors. Tighten the cover bolts to 140 in. lbs., then remove the tool.

Governor

1. Align the master spline of the governor support with the master spline on the output shaft, then slide the assembly into place. Install snap-ring behind the governor housing. Torque housing-to-support screws to specification.
2. Place the governor valve on the valve shaft, insert the assembly into the housing and through the governor weights. Install the valve shaft retaining snap-ring.

Extension Housing

1965

1. Using new gasket, slide extension housing into place. Install retaining bolts and washers, and tighten bolts to 25 ft. lbs.
2. Install transmission output shaft flange. Install washer with its three projections toward flange and install nut with its convofront. Press or tap bearing tight against front snap ring.
3. Install rear snap ring.

luted surface contacting washer. Hold flange so that it does not move and torque nut to 175 ft. lbs. Torque reading must be taken as nut passes over hump.

1966-72

1. Install snap ring in front groove on output shaft.
2. Install bearing on shaft with its outer race ring groove toward
4. Place new extension housing gasket on transmission case.
5. Place output shaft bearing retaining snap-ring in extension housing. Spread ring as far as possible, then carefully tap extension housing into place. Make sure snap-ring is fully seated in bearing groove.
6. Install and torque extension housing bolts to specification.
7. Install gasket, plate, and two screws on bottom of extension housing mounting pad.
8. Install speedometer pinion and adapter assembly.

Torque Reference

	Foot-Pounds	Inch-Pounds
Kickdown band adjusting screw locknut (eight cylinder cars)	29	—
Kickdown band adjusting screw locknut (six cylinder cars)	—	—
Kickdown lever shaft plug	25	150
Reverse band adjusting screw locknut (eight cylinder cars)	35	—
Reverse band adjusting locknut (six cylinder cars)	20	—
Cooler line fitting 1965-68	—	75
1969-72		110
Control cable adjusting wheel bolt		
Converter drive plate to crankshaft bolt	55	40
Converter drive plate to torque converter bolt	—	
1970-72		270
Extension housing to transmission case bolt	—	270
Extension housing to insulator mounting bolt		
1965-67	35	
1968-72	40	—
Extension housing—crossmember to frame bolt	75	—
Front oil pump housing to transmission case bolt	—	150
1970-72		175
Governor body to parking sprag bolt	—	100
Neutral starter switch	25-30	—
Oil pan bolt	—	150
Output shaft flange nut 1965 only	175	—
Overrunning clutch cam set screw	—	40
Reaction shaft support to front oil pump bolt		
1965-67 all and 1968-69 A-727	—	150
1968-69 A-904	—	125
1970-72	—	160
Rear oil pump cover bolt 1965 only	—	140
Transmission to engine bolt	25-30	—
Valve body screw 1965-67	—	28
1968-72		35
Valve body to transmission case bolt	—	100

Ford Motor Company

3-Speed Automatic (FMX)

Application

The FMX 3-speed automatic transmission has been used in Ford Motor Company cars under various titles, such as, Cruise-O-Matic, Merc-O-Matic, Select Shift, Multi-Drive, and Twin Range Turbo-Drive. The basic transmission has remained the same since the beginning, except for small modifications. The various models of this transmission and the cars in which they are used are listed below:

FMX SELECT SHIFT: Ford—1969-72; Meteor—1969-72; Cougar—1969-72; Fairlane—1969-70; Montego—1969-70; Mustang—1969-72.

CRUISE-O-MATIC: Ford—1965-68; Fairlane—1965-68; Falcon—1965 (Fordomatic), 1965-68; Mustang—1965-68; Comet—1968; Montego—1968; Cyclone—1968; Maverick—1970; Thunderbird—1970.

MERC-O-MATIC: Mercury Cyclone & GT—1967; Mercury Comet 202—1967; Mercury Capri—1967; Mercury Caliente—1967; Mercury Cougar—1967-68; Mercury Comet—1965 (Multi-Drive) and 1966.

TWIN RANGE TURBO-DRIVE: Lincoln Continental—1965.

Diagnosis

This diagnosis guide covers the most common symptoms and is an aid to careful diagnosis. The items to check are listed in the sequence to be followed for quickest results. Thus, follow the checks in the order given for the particular transmission type.

TROUBLE SYMPTOMS	Items to Check	
	In Car	Out of Car
Rough initial engagement in D1 or D2	KBWFEG	
1-2 or 2-3 shift points incorrect or erratic	ABCDWEL	
Rough 2-3 shifts	BGFEJ	
Engine overspeeds on 2-3 shift	BGEF	m
No 1-2 or 2-3 upshift	DECJG	bcf
No 3-1 shift	KBE	
No forced downshift	LWE	
Runaway engine on forced downshift	GFEJB	c
Rough 3-2 or 3-1 shift at closed throttle	KBE	
Creeps excessively	KZ	
Slips or chatters in first gear, D1	ABWFE	acfi
Slips or chatters in second gear	ABGWFEJ	ac
Slips or chatters in R	AHWFEIB	bcf
No drive in D1	CE	i
No drive in D2	ERC	acf
No drive in L	CER	acf
No drive in R	HIERC	bef
No drive in any selector position	ACWFER	cd
Lockup in D1	CIJ	bgc
Lockup in D2	CHI	bgci
Lockup in L	GJE	bjc
Lockup in R	GJ	agc
Parking lock binds or does not hold	C	g
Transmission overheats	OFG	l
Engine will not push-start	ACFE	ec
Maximum speed too low, poor acceleration	Y	l
Transmission noisy in N and P	F	ad
Noisy transmission during coast 30-20 mph with engine stopped		e
Transmission noisy in any drive position	F	hbad
Fluid leaks	MNOPQSTUX	jkl

Key to Checks

A. Fluid level
B. Vacuum diaphragm unit or tubes
C. Manual linkage
D. Governor
E. Valve body
F. Pressure regulator
G. Front band
H. Rear band
I. Rear servo
J. Front servo
K. Engine idle speed
L. Downshift linkage
M. Converter drain plug
N. Oil pan, filler tube and/or seals

O. Oil cooler and/or connections
P. Manual or throttle shaft seals
Q. Pipe plug, side of case
R. Perform air pressure checks
S. Extension housing-to-case gasket or washer
T. Center support bolt lock washer
U. Extension housing rear oil seal
W. Make control pressure check
X. Speedometer drive gear adaptor seal
Y. Engine performance
Z. Vehicle brakes

a. Front clutch
b. Rear clutch
c. Hydraulic system leakage
d. Front pump
e. Rear pump
f. Fluid distributor sleeve—output shaft
g. Parking linkage
h. Planetary assembly
i. Planetary oneway clutch
j. Engine rear oil seal
k. Front oil pump seal
l. Front pump-to-case seal or gasket
m. Rear clutch piston air bleed valve

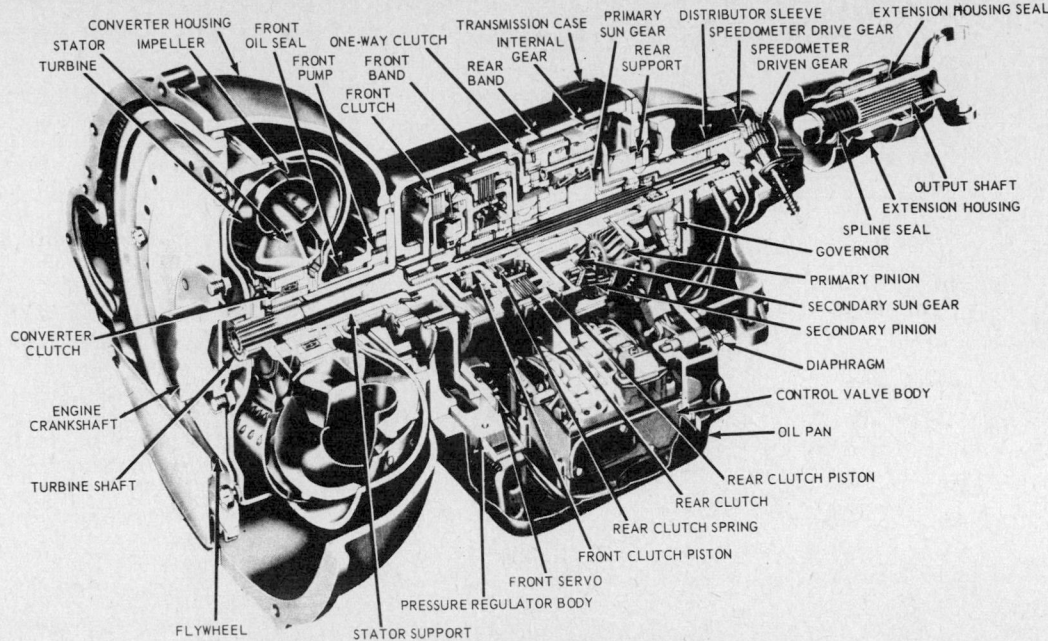

Typical FMX automatic tranmission. Three-speed Ford Cruise-O-Matic,
Mercury Merc-O-Matic, Mercury Multi-Drive, Lincoln Continental Twin Range Turbo Drive
(© Ford Motor Co.)

General Information

This section provides procedures for testing, inspecting, adjusting, and repairing the FMX 3-speed automatic transmission. Where there are differences in procedures or specifications for various models, these differences will be outlined.

The Ford FMX 3-speed automatic transmission (see illustration) is a three-speed unit that provides automatic upshifts and downshifts through three forward gear ratios and also provides manual selection of first and second gears. The transmission consists of a torque converter, planetary gear assembly, two multiple disc clutches, and a hydraulic control system.

The FMX transmission cools its transmission fluid through a cooler core in the radiator lower tank when a steel converter is used. If an aluminum converter is used, the transmission fluid is air-cooled.

Towing

A disabled car may be towed up to 15 miles, at a maximum of 30 mph, with the selector lever in Neutral. If the vehicle must be towed in excess of 15 miles, or it is impossible to put the selector lever in Neutral, raise the rear wheels and tow the car backwards.

Transmission Checks

Before performing any of the tests and adjustments given in this section, the following preliminary check should be performed:

Transmission Fluid Level Check

1. Position the car on a level surface.
2. Run the engine at fast idle speed to bring the transmission fluid to operating temperature, then decrease engine speed to normal idle.
3. Hold the service brake, and shift the selector lever through the quadrant slowly, returning to Park.
4. Locate the dipstick, and check the fluid level with the engine running. The dipstick is located either at the right rear of the engine compartment or under the front floormat to the right of center. Add fluid to bring the level between the ADD and FULL marks on the dipstick. Do not overfill the transmission.

If the transmission is overfilled, the fluid will be foamy or aerated. This condition will cause low control pressure and the fluid may be forced out of the vent or through ruptured seals.

Check the transmission fluid level for low level conditions that may indicate fluid leaks or, at the very least, poor operation.

Transmission Fluid Leakage Checks

Make the following checks if a leakage is suspected from the transmission case:

1. Clean all dirt and grease from the transmission case.
2. Inspect the speedometer cable connection at the extension housing of the transmission. If fluid is leaking here, disconnect the cable and replace the rubber seal.
3. Inspect the oil pan gasket and attaching bolts for leaks. Tighten any bolts that appear loose to the proper torque (10-13 ft. lbs.). Recheck for signs of leakage. If necessary, remove the pan attaching bolts and old pan gasket and install new gasket. Reinstall the pan and its attaching bolts.
4. Check filler tube connection at the transmission for signs of leakage. If tube is leaking, tighten the connection to stop the leak. If necessary, disconnect the filler tube, replace the O-ring, and reinstall the filler tube.
5. Inspect all fluid lines between the transmission and the cooler core in the lower radiator tank. Replace any lines or fittings that appear to be worn or damaged. Tighten all fittings to the proper torque.
6. Inspect the engine coolant for signs of transmission fluid in the radiator. If there is transmission fluid in the engine coolant, the oil cooler core is probably leaking.

NOTE: the oil cooler core may be tested further by disconnecting all lines to it and applying 50-75 psi air pressure through the fittings. Remove the radiator cap to relieve any pressure build-up outside the cooler core. If air bubbles appear in the coolant or if the cooler core will not hold pressure, the oil cooler core is leaking and must be replaced.

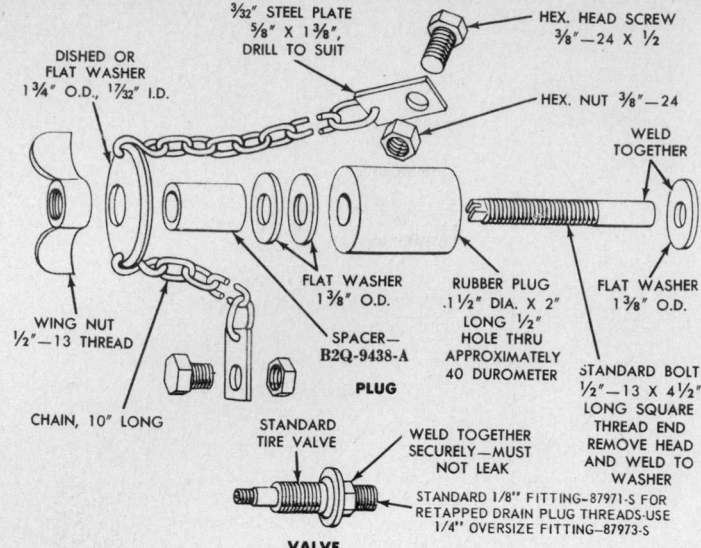

¾₂" STEEL PLATE
⅝" X 1⅜",
DRILL TO SUIT

HEX. HEAD SCREW
⅜"—24 X ½

DISHED OR
FLAT WASHER
1¾" O.D., 1⁷⁄₃₂" I.D.

HEX. NUT ⅜"—24

WELD
TOGETHER

WING NUT
½"—13 THREAD

FLAT WASHER
1⅜" O.D.

RUBBER PLUG
.1½" DIA. X 2"
LONG ½"
HOLE THRU
APPROXIMATELY
40 DUROMETER

FLAT WASHER
1⅜" O.D.

STANDARD BOLT
½"—13 X 4½"
LONG SQUARE
THREAD END
REMOVE HEAD
AND WELD TO
WASHER

CHAIN, 10" LONG

SPACER—
B2Q-9438-A

PLUG

STANDARD
TIRE VALVE

WELD TOGETHER
SECURELY—MUST
NOT LEAK

STANDARD ⅛" FITTING—87971-S FOR
RETAPPED DRAIN PLUG THREADS-USE
¼" OVERSIZE FITTING—87973-S

VALVE

Converter leak checking tool (© Ford Motor Co.)

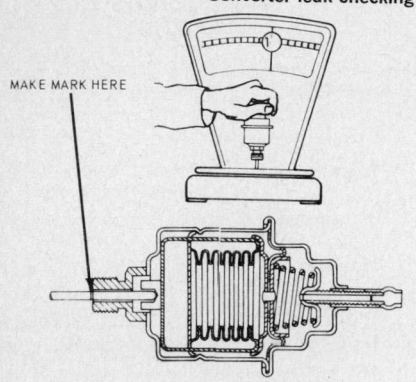

MAKE MARK HERE

BELLOWS INTACT

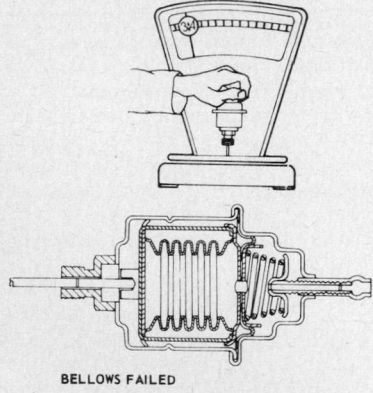

BELLOWS FAILED

Checking vacuum unit bellows-altitude
compensating type
(© Ford Motor Co.)

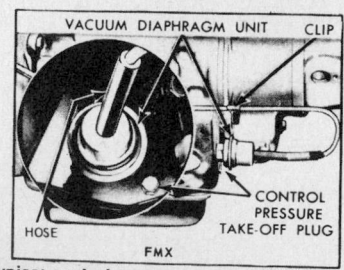

VACUUM DIAPHRAGM UNIT   CLIP

HOSE

CONTROL
PRESSURE
TAKE-OFF PLUG

FMX

Typical control pressure connecting points
(© Ford Motor Co.)

7. Inspect the openings in the case where the downshift control lever shaft and the manual lever shaft are located. If necessary, replace the defective seal.

8. Inspect all plugs or cable connections in the transmission for signs of leakage. Tighten any loose plugs or connectors to the proper torque according to the specifications.

9. Remove the lower cover from the front of the bellhousing and inspect the converter drainplugs for signs of leakage. If there is a leak around the drainplugs, loosen the plug and coat the threads with sealing compound. Tighten the plug to the proper torque.

NOTE: fluid leaks from around the converter drainplug may be caused by engine oil leaking past the rear main bearing or from the oil gallery plugs. To determine the exact cause of the leak before beginning repair procedures, an oil-soluble aniline or fluorescent dye may be added to the transmission fluid to find the source of the leak and whether the transmission is leaking. If a fluorescent dye is used, a black light must be used to detect the dye.

If further converter checks are necessary, remove the transmission from the car and the converter from the transmission. The converter cannot be disassembled for cleaning or repair. If the converter is leaking, it must be replaced with a new unit. To check the converter for leaks, assemble and install the converter leak checking tool shown and fill the converter with 20 psi air pressure. Then, place the converter in a tank of water and watch for air bubbles. If no air bubbles are seen, the converter is not leaking.

Engine Idle Speed Check

Check the idle speed of the engine and adjust it at the carburetor using the procedure given in the Car Section. Too slow an idle speed will cause the engine to run roughly; and too fast an idle speed will cause the car to creep while the transmission is in a Drive position, shift harshly, and downshift roughly.

Manual Linkage Checks

Correct manual linkage is necessary for the proper operation of the manual valve which helps control fluid pressure to various transmission components. Improperly adjusted manual linkage may cause fluid leaks if not corrected. See the section on linkage adjustments in the Car Section.

Control Pressure Check

When the vacuum diaphragm unit operates properly and the downshift linkage is adjusted correctly, all transmission shifts (automatic and kickdown) should occur within the specified road speed limits. If these shifts do not occur within the limits or if the transmission slips during a shift point, perform the following procedure to locate the problem:

1. Connect the Automatic Transmission Tester (see illustration) as follows:

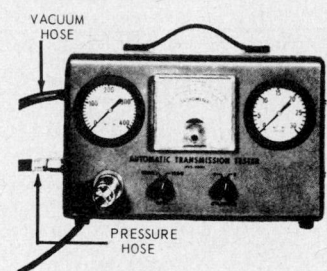

VACUUM
HOSE

PRESSURE
HOSE

Rotunda ARE-2905 automatic
transmission tester
(© Ford Motor Co.)

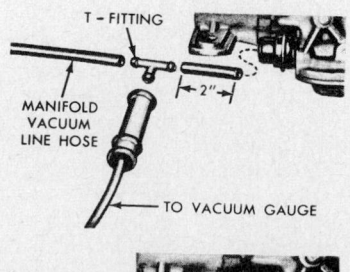

T - FITTING

MANIFOLD
VACUUM
LINE HOSE

TO VACUUM GAUGE

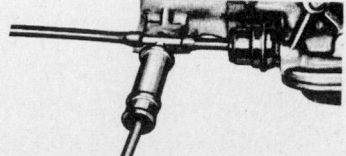

Typical vacuum test line connections
(© Ford Motor Co.)

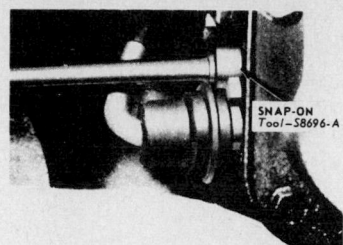

Removing or installing vacuum diaphragm
(© Ford Motor Co.)

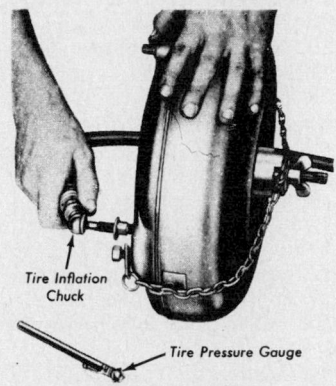

Tire Inflation Chuck

Tire Pressure Gauge

Converter leak tool installation
(© Ford Motor Co.)

a. Tachometer cable to engine.
b. Vacuum gauge hose with a T-fitting between the vacuum hose and vacuum diaphragm (see illustration).
c. Pressure gauge to the control pressure outlet on the transmission (see illustration).
2. Apply the parking brake and start the engine. On a car equipped with a vacuum brake release, use the service brakes since the parking brake will release automatically when the transmission is put in any Drive position.
3. Check engine idle speed and throttle and downshift linkage for correct operation. Check the transmission diaphragm unit for leaks (see below).
4. Check control pressure in all selector lever positions at specified manifold vacuum (see specifications). Record readings and compare to specifications.

Vacuum Diaphragm Unit Check

Non-Altitude Compensating Type
1. Remove the vacuum diaphragm unit from the transmission after disconnecting the vacuum hose. See illustration.
2. Adjust a vacuum pump until the vacuum gauge shows 18 in/Hg. with the vacuum hose blocked.
3. Connect the vacuum hose to the vacuum diaphragm unit and note the reading on the vacuum

gauge. If the reading is 18 inches of vacuum, the vacuum diaphragm unit is good. While removing the vacuum hose from the vacuum diaphragm unit, hold a finger over the end of the control rod. As the vacuum is released, the internal spring of the vacuum diaphragm unit will push the control rod out.

Altitude-Compensating Type
The vacuum diaphragm unit may be checked for damaged or ruptured bellows by using the procedure below:
1. Remove the diaphragm and the throttle valve rod from the transmission.
2. Insert a rod into the diaphragm unit until it is seated in the hole. Make a reference mark on the rod where it enters the diaphragm (see illustration).
3. Place the diaphragm unit on a weighing scale with the end of the rod resting on the weighing pan and gradually press down on the diaphragm unit.
4. Note the force (in pounds) at which the reference mark on the rod moves into the diaphragm. If the reference mark is still visible at 12 pounds, the diaphragm bellows are satisfactory.

Shift Point Checks for Automatic Transmissions

To determine if the transmission is shifting at the proper road speeds, use the following procedure:
1. Check the minimum throttle upshifts by placing the transmission selector lever in the Drive position and noting the road speeds at which the transmission shifts from first gear to second gear to third gear. All shifts should occur within the specified limits.
2. While driving in third gear, depress the accelerator pedal past the detent (to the floor). Depending on vehicle speed, the transmission should downshift from third gear to second gear or from second gear to first gear.
3. Check the closed-throttle down-

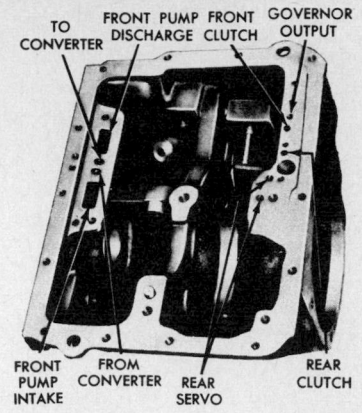

Case fluid hole identification—FMX automatic
(© Ford Motor Co.)

shift from third gear to first gear by coasting down from about 30 mph in third gear. This downshift should occur at the specified road speed.

NOTE: when the transmission selector lever is at 2, the transmission will operate only in second gear. Move the selector lever to Drive to shift gears automatically.

4. With the transmission in third gear and the car moving at a road speed of 35 mph, the transmission should downshift to second gear when the selector lever is moved from D to 2 to 1. This check will determine if the governor pressure and shift control valves are operating properly. If the transmission does not shift within the specified limits or certain gears cannot be obtained, refer to the Trouble Diagnosis chart at the beginning of this section.

Air Pressure Checks

If the car will not move in one or more ranges, or, if it shifts erratically, the items at fault can be determined by using air pressure at the indicated passages.

Drain the transmission and remove the oil pan and the control valve assembly.

Front Clutch
Apply sufficient air pressure to the front clutch input passage. (See illustration.) A dull thud can be heard

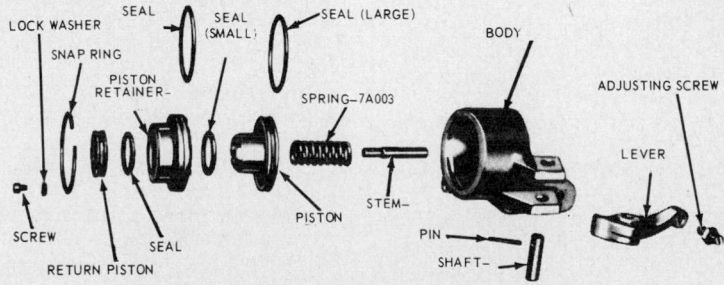

Front servo disassembled (© Ford Motor Co.)

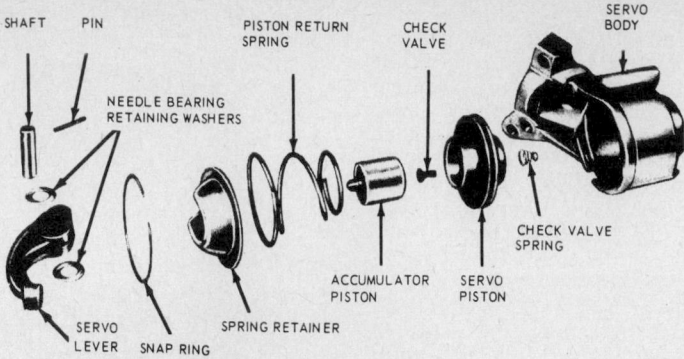

SHAFT PIN PISTON RETURN SPRING CHECK VALVE SERVO BODY

NEEDLE BEARING RETAINING WASHERS

CHECK VALVE SPRING

ACCUMULATOR PISTON SERVO PISTON

SERVO LEVER SNAP RING SPRING RETAINER

Rear servo disassembled (© Ford Motor Co.)

when the clutch piston moves.

Governor

Remove the governor inspection cover from the extension housing. Apply air to the front clutch input passage. (See illustration). Listen for a sharp click and watch to see if the governor valve snaps inward as it should.

Rear Clutch

Apply air to the rear clutch passage (see illustration) and listen for the dull thud that will indicate that the rear clutch piston has moved. Listen for leaks.

Front Servo

Apply air pressure to the front servo apply tube and note if front band tightens. Shift the air to the front servo release tube, which is next to the apply tube, and watch band release.

Rear Servo

Apply air, pressure to the rear servo apply passage. The rear band should tighten around the drum.

Conclusions

If the operation of the servos and clutch is normal with air pressure, the no-drive condition is due to the control valve and pressure regulator valve assemblies, which should be disassembled, cleaned and inspected.

If operation of the clutches is not normal; (e.g., both clutches apply from one passage or one fails to move), the aluminum sleeve (bushing) in the output shaft is out of position or badly worn.

Use air pressure to check the passages in the sleeve, shaft, and primary sun gear shaft.

If the passages in the two shafts and the sleeve are clean, remove the clutch assemblies, clean and inspect the parts.

Erratic operation can also be caused by loose valve body screws. When re-installing the valve body be careful to tighten the pressure regulator valve to case bolts to 17-22 ft. lbs.,

the pressure regulator valve cover screws to 20-30 in. lbs., the control valve body screws to 20-30 in. lbs., the 1/4-20 capscrew (lower to upper valve body) to 4-6 ft. lbs., and the control valve body to case bolts to 8-10 ft. lbs.

In-Vehicle Adjustments and Repairs

The adjustments and repairs presented in this part of the section on FMX transmissions may be done without removing the entire transmission from the car. Some of these procedures will require the use of special tools and instruments.

Transmission Fluid Drain and Refill

Normal maintenance and lubrication requirements do not include periodic changes of transmission fluid. Only when it is necessary to remove the pan for major repairs or adjustments will it be necessary to replace the transmission fluid. At this time the converter, oil cooler core, and cooler lines should be thoroughly flushed out to remove any dirt or deposits that might clog these units later.

When filling a completely dry (no fluid) transmission and converter, install five quarts of transmission fluid and then start the engine. Shift the selector lever through all positions briefly and set at Park position. Check the fluid level and add enough fluid to raise the level to between the ADD and FULL marks on the dipstick. *Do not overfill the transmission.*

The procedure for a partial drain and refill of the transmission fluid is as follows:

1. Raise the car on a hoist or jack stands.
2. Place a drain pan under the transmission pan.
3. Loosen the pan attaching bolts to allow the fluid to drain.

NOTE: on FMX Transmissions

(also called Cruise-O-Matic and Merc-O-Matic) used in 1968 and earlier models, the transmission fluid is drained by disconnecting the fluid filler tube from the transmission fluid pan.

4. When the fluid has stopped draining to level of the pan flange, remove the pan bolts starting at the rear and along both sides of the pan, allowing the pan to drop and drain gradually.
5. When all the transmission fluid has drained, remove the pan and the fluid filter and clean them.
6. After completing the transmission repairs or adjustments, install the fluid filter screen, a new pan gasket, and the pan on the transmission. Tighten the pan attaching bolts to the proper torque (10-13 ft. lbs.).
7. Install three quarts of transmission fluid through the filler tube. If the filler tube was removed to drain the transmission, install the filler tube using a new O-ring.
8. Start and run the engine for a few minutes at low idle speed and then at the fast idle speed (about 1200 rpm) until the normal operating temperature is reached. *Do not race the engine.*
9. Move the selector lever through all positions and place it at the Park position. Check the fluid level, and add fluid until the level is between the ADD and FULL marks on the dipstick. *Do not overfill the transmission.*

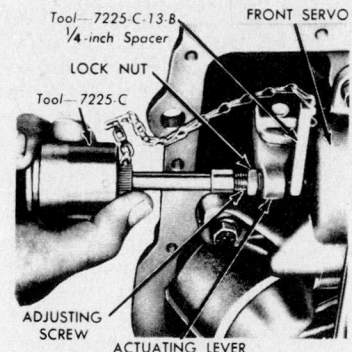

Tool—7225-C-13-B FRONT SERVO
1/4-inch Spacer
LOCK NUT
Tool—7225-C
ADJUSTING SCREW ACTUATING LEVER

Adjusting front band—Typical
(© Ford Motor Co.)

Band Adjustments

Front Band Adjustment

When it is necessary to adjust the front band of the transmission, perform the following procedure:

1. Drain the transmission fluid and remove the oil pan, fluid filter screen, and clip. The same transmission fluid may be reused if it is filtered through a 100-mesh screen before being installed. Only transmission fluid in good condition should be used.

2. Clean the pan and filter screen and remove the old gasket.

3. Loosen the front servo adjusting screw locknut. See illustration.
NOTE: special band adjusting wrenches are recommended to do this operation correctly and quickly.

4. Pull back the actuating rod and insert a ¼ in. spacer bar between the adjusting screw and the servo piston stem. Tighten the adjusting screw to 10 in. lbs. torque. Remove the spacer bar and tighten the adjusting screw an additional ¾ turn. Hold the adjusting screw fast and tighten the locknut securely (20-25 ft. lbs.).
NOTE: on 1965 Lincoln transmissions, the procedure is slightly different. The locknut should be loosened and the adjusting screw backed off. Retighten the adjusting screw to 10 ft. lbs. torque, then back it off exactly three full turns. Tighten the locknut securely. *Severe damage to the transmission may result if the adjusting screw is not backed off exactly three full turns.*

5. Install the transmission fluid filter screen and clip. Install the pan with a new pan gasket.

6. Refill the transmission to the FULL mark on the Dipstick. Start the engine, run for a few minutes, shift the selector lever through all positions, and place it in Park. Recheck the fluid level again and add fluid to proper level if necessary.

Rear Band Adjustments

The rear band of the FMX transmission may be adjusted by any of the methods given below. On most cars the basic external band adjustment is satisfactory. The internal band adjustment procedure may be done when the external adjustment procedure cannot be done correctly. On certain cars with a console floor shift, the entire console, shift lever and linkage will have to be removed to gain access to the rear band external adjusting screw.

Rear Band External Adjustment

The procedure for adjusting the rear band externally is as follows:

1. Locate the external rear band adjusting screw on the transmission case, clean all dirt from the threads, and coat the threads with light oil.
NOTE: the adjusting screw is located on the upper right side of the transmission case. Access is often through a hole in the front floor to the right of center under the carpet.

2. Loosen the locknut on the rear band external adjusting screw. On 1970-72 Cougar and Mustang cars, use the special tool illustrated to loosen the locknut.

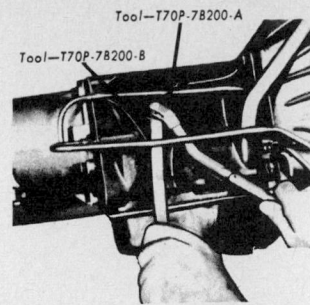

Adjusting rear band externally 1970-72 Mustang and Cougar
(© Ford Motor Co.)

Adjusting rear band externally—1970-72 Ford, Meteor, 1970 Fairlane and Montego
(© Ford Motor Co.)

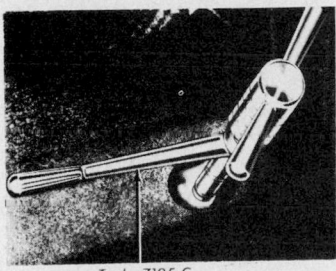

Adjusting rear band externally—1965 to 1969 Ford and Meteor
(© Ford Motor Co.)

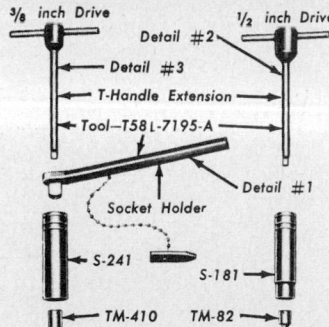

Front and rear band adjusting tools
(© Ford Motor Co.)

3. Using the special preset torque wrench shown, tighten the adjusting screw until the handle clicks at 10 ft. lbs. torque. If the adjusting screw is tighter than 10 ft. lbs. torque, loosen the adjusting screw and retighten to the proper torque.

4. Back off the adjusting screw 1½

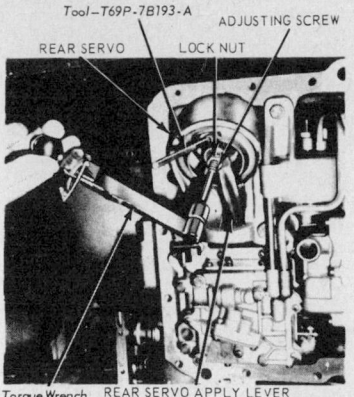

Adjusting rear band internally—1969-70 Fairlane, Montego, 1970-72 Mustang, and Cougar
(© Ford Motor Co.)

turns. Hold the adjusting screw steady while tightening the locknut to the proper torque (35-40 ft. lbs.). *Severe damage may result if adjusting screw is not backed off exactly 1½ turns.*

Rear Band Internal Adjustment

The rear band is adjusted internally as follows:

1. Drain the transmission fluid. If it is to be reused, pour the fluid through a 100-mesh screen as it drains from the transmission. Reuse the transmission fluid only if it is in good condition.

2. Remove and clean the pan, fluid filter, and clip.

3. Loosen the rear servo adjusting locknut.

4. Pull the adjusting screw end of the actuating lever away from the servo body and insert the spacer tool (see illustration) between the servo accumulator piston and the adjusting screw. *Be sure the flat surfaces of the tool are placed squarely between the adjusting screw and the accumulator piston. Tool must not touch servo piston and the handle must not touch the servo piston spring retainer.*

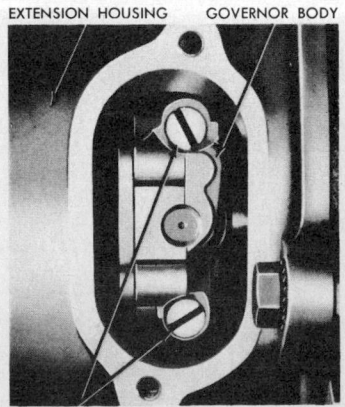

Removing governor inspection plate on extension housing—1965 to 1967
(© Ford Motor Co.)

5. Using a torque wrench with an Allen head socket, tighten the adjusting screw to 24 in. lbs. torque.

6. Back off the adjusting screw exactly 1½ turns. Hold adjusting screw steady and tighten the locknut securely. Remove the spacer tool.

7. Install the fluid filter, clip, and pan with a new gasket.

8. Fill the transmission with the correct amount of fluid.

Transmission Component Removal and Installation

Various components of the FMX transmission may be removed while the transmission is in the car. Installation is often the reverse of the removal instructions except for adjustment and alignment. Repair of the individual components is given in the overhaul section.

Governor Assembly Removal and Installation

The governor assembly may be removed from transmissions built before 1968 through an extension housing access or inspection plate. On 1968 and later models of the FMX transmission, the extension housing must be removed to remove the governor assembly from the output shaft. It may be necessary to remove the entire transmission from the car to do this.

1968 and Earlier

1. Remove the governor inspection plate from the right side of the extension housing (see illustration), and rotate the driveshaft until the governor appears in the opening.

2. Remove the two screws holding the governor body to the counter weight sleeve. Be careful not to drop the screws or the valve into the extension housing.

3. Disassemble the governor by removing the two screws holding the side plate. Inspect the governor valve for scoring and free movement in its bore. Be sure the spring, sleeve, and plug are not damaged. Blow valve body passages clear of obstructions.

4. Reassemble the governor assembly (see illustration), aligning the passages in the sleeve and body. Tighten the valve body cover screws with 20-30 in. lbs. torque.

5. Install the governor assembly on the counterweight sleeve, tightening the mounting screws with 50-60 in. lbs. torque. Replace the governor inspection plate on the extension housing.

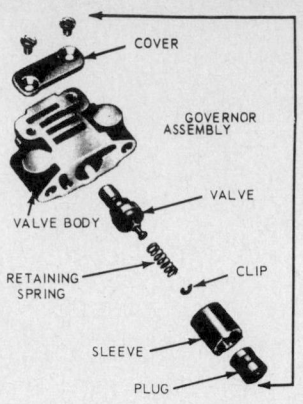

Governor disassembled
(© Ford Motor Co.)

Extension Housing Removal and Installation

1. Raise the car high enough for easy access to the extension housing.

2. Drain the transmission.

3. Disconnect the driveshaft from the rear axle and slide the front yoke from the extension housing.

4. Disconnect the speedometer cable from the extension housing.

5. Remove the rear engine support nuts. Place a transmission jack under the transmission and raise it enough to clear the crossmember.

6. Remove the bolts and nuts securing the crossmember to the side rails of the frame. Move the crossmember out of the way.

7. Remove the attaching bolts holding the engine rear support to the extension housing and remove the rear support from the extension housing.

8. Remove all the extension housing attaching bolts, slide the housing off the output shaft, and discard the gasket.

9. Installation is the reverse of the removal procedures. Tighten the housing attaching bolts to 30-40 ft. lbs. torque. Check that the output shaft rotates freely by hand. If it binds or feels tight, check the needle bearing and race for correct position.

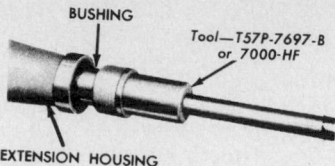

Installing extension housing bushing
(© Ford Motor Co.)

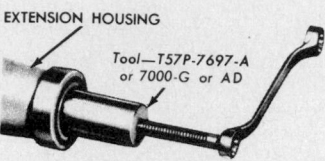

Removing extension housing bushing
(© Ford Motor Co.)

Extension Housing Bushing and Rear Seal Removal and Installation

1. Disconnect the driveshaft from the extension housing.

2. Carefully remove the rear seal from the housing using the special tools shown in the illustration.

3. Remove the extension housing bushing using the bushing remover tool (see illustration). *Be careful not to damage the spline seal.*

4. Install new bushing in the extension housing using the special tool (see illustration).

5. Inspect the universal joint yoke sealing surface for scoring or gouges. Replace the yoke if damaged.

6. Inspect the housing counterbore for burrs and, if necessary, smooth with crocus cloth.

7. Using the special tool shown, install the new rear seal into the end of the extension housing. Check that the seal is firmly seated.

Control Valve Body and Oil Pan Removal and Installation

1. Raise the car on a hoist or jackstands and place a drain pan under the transmission.

2. Drain the transmission.

3. Remove the oil pan, fluid filter screen, and clip and clean them thoroughly. Discard the old pan gasket.

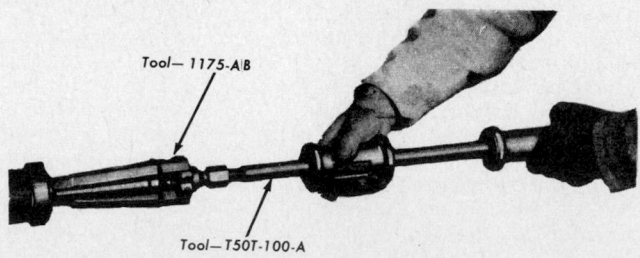

Removing extension housing seal (© Ford Motor Co.)

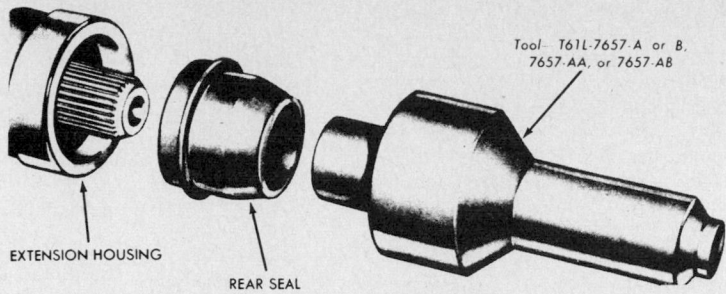

EXTENSION HOUSING

REAR SEAL

Tool T61L-7657-A or B,
7657-AA, or 7657-AB

Installing extension housing seal (© Ford Motor Co.)

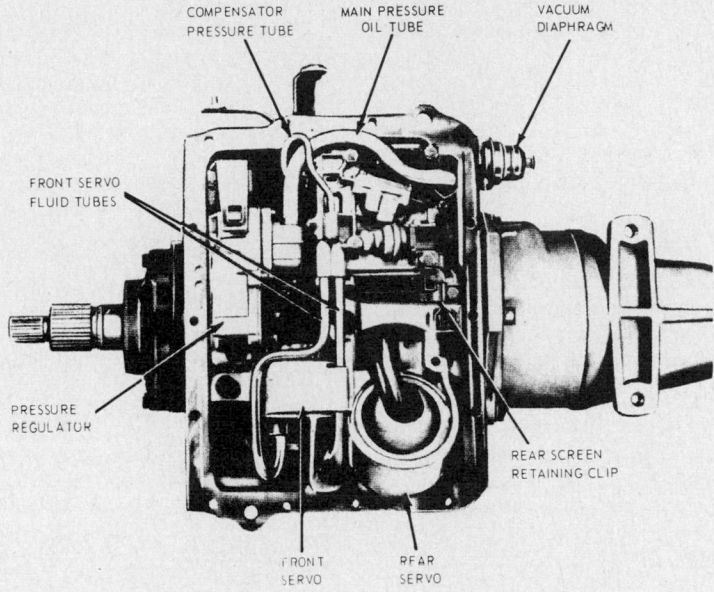

COMPENSATOR PRESSURE TUBE

MAIN PRESSURE OIL TUBE

VACUUM DIAPHRAGM

FRONT SERVO FLUID TUBES

PRESSURE REGULATOR

REAR SCREEN RETAINING CLIP

FRONT SERVO

REAR SERVO

Typical hydraulic control system (© Ford Motor Co.)

4. Remove the vacuum diaphragm assembly using the special tool required (Snap-On tool S8696-A or FCO-24). *Do not use pliers, pipe wrenches, etc. to remove the vacuum diaphragm unit. Do not let any solvents enter the vacuum diaphragm unit.* Remove the push rod, the fluid screen and its retaining clip.

5. Remove the small compensator pressure tube. See illustration.

6. Disconnect the main pressure oil tube by carefully loosening the end connected to the control valve body first and then removing the tube from the pressure regulator unit.

CAUTION: be sure to remove the tube in this manner. Otherwise, the tube could be kinked or bent causing improper fluid pressures and possible damage to the transmission.

7. Loosen the front servo attaching bolts about three turns.

8. Remove the three control valve body attaching bolts and carefully lower the valve body, sliding it off the front servo tubes. *Do not damage the valve body or the tubes.*

9. Disassemble the control valve body into the various parts as shown in the illustration in the major repair section.

10. When installing the control valve body, align the front servo tubes with the holes in the valve body. Shift the manual lever to the 1 detent and place the inner downshift lever between the downshift lever stop and the downshift valve. Be sure the manual lever engages the actuating pin in the manual detent lever.

11. Loosely install the control valve body attaching bolts and move the control valve body toward the center of the transmission case until there is a clearance of 0.050 in. between the manual valve and the actuating pin on the manual detent lever.

12. Tighten the attaching bolts to 8-10 ft. lbs. torque. Ensure that the rear fluid filter retaining clip is installed under the valve body.

13. Install the main pressure oil tube, connecting the end to the pressure regulator unit first and then connecting the other end to the main control valve assembly

by gently tapping it with a soft-faced hammer.

14. Install the compensator pressure tube on the pressure regulator and control valve body.

15. Check the manual lever for free motion in each detent position by rotating it one full turn. If the manual lever binds in any detent position, loosen the valve body attaching bolts and move the valve body away from the center of the transmission case until the binding is relieved. Retighten the attaching bolts according to step 12.

16. Place the pushrod in the bore of the vacuum diaphragm unit and insert the other end of the pushrod into the threaded opening in the case. Install the vacuum diaphragm unit and tighten it to 20-30 ft. lbs. torque.

17. Tighten the front servo attaching bolts to 30-35 ft. lbs. torque.

18. Adjust the front band.

19. Install the fluid filter and its retaining clip.

20. Adjust the rear band.

21. Install the oil pan with a new pan gasket, tightening the pan attaching bolts to 10-13 ft. lbs. torque.

22. Fill transmission with fluid. Start and run engine for a few minutes and check the fluid level after shifting the transmission through all positions. *Do not overfill the transmission.*

23. Check the adjustment of the transmission control linkage.

Pressure Regulator Removal and Installation

1. Drain the transmission of fluid and remove the pan, fluid filter screen, and its retaining clip. Discard the used pan gasket.

2. Remove the compensator pressure tube from between the control valve body and the pressure regulator. See illustration for location of components.

3. Remove the main pressure oil tube by gently prying off the end connected to the control valve first and then disconnect the other end from the pressure regulator. *Be sure to remove the tube in this order to prevent kinking or bending it.*

4. Loosen the spring retainer clip and carefully release the spring tension on the pressure springs. Remove the valve springs, retainer and valve stop, and the valves from the pressure regulator body.

5. Remove the pressure regulator attaching bolts and washers and take the regulator body out of the transmission case.

6. After cleaning, inspection, and reassembly, install the pressure

regulator unit in the transmission by reversing the procedures in steps 1 through 5.

Front Servo Removal and Installation

1. Drain the transmission fluid from the transmission and remove the pan, fluid filter screen, and its retaining clip.
2. Remove the vacuum diaphragm unit.
3. Loosen the three control valve body attaching bolts.
4. Remove the front servo attaching bolts, hold the band strut steady, and remove the front servo unit.
5. After repairing the front servo unit, install it by first positioning the front band forward in the transmission case with the end of the band facing downward. Be sure the front servo anchor pin is placed in the case web. Align the large end of the servo strut with the servo actuating lever, and align the small end with the band end.
6. Rotate the band, strut, and servo to align the anchor end of the band with the anchor in the case. Push the servo unit onto the control valve body tubes.
7. Install the attaching bolts and tighten them to 30-35 ft. lbs. torque.
8. Tighten the control valve body attaching bolts to 8-10 ft. lbs. torque. Check the clearance (0.050 in.) between the manual valve and the manual lever actuating pin.
9. Adjust the front band.
10. Install the vacuum diaphragm unit and its pushrod.
11. Install the fluid filter screen, its retaining clip, and the pan with a new pan gasket.
12. Fill the transmission with fluid.
13. Adjust the downshift and manual shift linkage.

Rear Servo Removal and Installation

1. Drain the transmission fluid from the transmission, and remove the pan, fluid filter screen, and its retaining clip.
2. Remove the vacuum diaphragm unit.
3. Remove the control valve body and the two front servo tubes.
4. Remove the rear servo attaching bolts, hold the actuating and anchor struts, and remove the rear servo unit.
5. Before installing the rear servo unit, position the servo anchor strut on the servo band and rotate the band to engage the strut.
6. While holding the servo anchor strut in place, position the ac-

tuating lever strut and install the rear servo unit in place.
7. Loosely install the rear servo attaching bolts, with the longer bolt in the inner bolt hole.
8. Move the rear servo unit toward the center of the transmission case against the attaching bolts. While holding the servo in this position, tighten the attaching bolts to 40-45 ft. lbs. torque.
9. Install the two front servo tubes and the control valve body. Check for proper clearance (0.050 in.) between the manual valve and the manual actuating pin.
10. Adjust the rear band.
11. Install the fluid filter screen, its retaining clip, and the oil pan with a new gasket. Fill the transmission with fluid.

Parking Pawl Removal and Installation

1. Raise the car and drain the fluid from the transmission.
2. Place the special engine support bar (T65E-6000J) under the converter housing.
3. Remove the driveshaft from the rear axle and slide the front yoke out of the extension housing.
4. Remove the two nuts securing the engine rear support to the crossmember.
5. Place a transmission jack under the transmission and raise the engine and transmission enough to take the weight off the crossmember.
6. Remove the bolts and nuts securing the crossmember to the frame side rails and slide the crossmember out of the way. Lower the jack slowly until the engine and transmission are resting on the special engine support bar.
7. Remove the two rear support-to-extension housing bolts and remove the rear support.
8. Disconnect the speedometer cable from the extension housing.
9. Remove the oil pan, fluid filter screen, and its retaining clip.
10. Loosen the rear band adjusting screw locknut and tighten the adjusting screw to 24 in. lbs. torque.

NOTE: the rear band will tighten around the planet carrier and hold the planet carrier and clutch assemblies in position during repair operations on the parking pawl.
11. Remove the small compensator pressure tube from the pressure regulator and control valve body.
12. Remove the main pressure oil tube from between the main control valve body and the pressure

regulator. Be sure to disconnect the end of the tube connected to the control valve body first to avoid kinking or bending the tube.
13. Disconnect the vacuum diaphragm unit after removing the vacuum hose.
14. Loosen the front servo attaching bolts.
15. Remove the three control valve body attaching bolts and lower the valve body while carefully pulling it off the front servo tubes.
16. Remove the rear servo attaching bolts and the rear servo unit.
17. Remove the extension housing attaching bolts and housing.
18. Remove the output shaft and rear support assembly.
19. Remove the parking pawl pin from the case with a magnet.
20. Working from inside the case, tap the shoulder of the toggle lever pin to move the retaining plug part way out of the case. Remove the plug with pliers.
21. Loosen and remove the toggle lever pin by alternately sliding the toggle lever from side to side and pushing outward at the same time. Lift the pawl and toggle from the case as an assembly.
22. After replacing worn or damaged parts, reinstall the new parking pawl assembly with the toggle lever pin and plug.
23. Secure the pawl to the case with the pawl pin.
24. Ensure that the thrust washer is in place, and install the rear support and output shaft after putting a new gasket on the rear support. Make sure the pressure tubes are positioned properly in the case.
25. Position a new gasket on the extension housing and secure the extension housing to the transmission case.
26. Install the rear servo and struts.
27. Install the main control valve body assembly.
28. Tighten the front servo attaching bolts to 30-35 ft. lbs. torque.
29. Install the main pressure oil tube and the small compensator pressure tube to the control valve body and the pressure regulator.
30. Adjust the front band.
31. Adjust the rear band.
32. Install the vacuum control rod, the vacuum diaphragm unit, and attach the vacuum hose.
33. Install the fluid filter screen, retaining clip, and pan with a new gasket.
34. Connect the speedometer cable to the extension housing.
35. Secure the engine rear support to the extension housing with

the two attaching bolts.

36. Place transmission jack under the transmission and raise the transmission and engine high enough to position and secure the rear support crossmember to the frame side rails. Tighten the attaching bolts and nuts to the specified torque.

37. Lower the transmission jack till the transmission and engine are resting on the rear support crossmember. Install and tighten to specified torque the nuts securing the rear support to the crossmember. Remove the transmission jack and the engine support bar.

38. Adjust the transmission control linkage.

39. Install the driveshaft and lower the car.

40. Fill the transmission with correct amount of fluid.

Transmission Overhaul Procedures

The transmission overhaul procedures presented here are the checks and repairs that must be done with the transmission out of the car. Each transmission subassembly is illustrated by exploded views of the subassembly showing how the individual parts fit together. Assembly is often the reverse of the disassembly procedure except for alignment, special tolerances, etc.

Procedures for removing and installing the transmission are given in the Car Section.

During all repairs to the transmission subassemblies, the following instructions must be followed:

1. Be sure that no dirt or grease gets in the transmission. All parts must be clean. *Remember—a little dirt can disable a transmission completely if it gets in a fluid passage.*

2. Handle all transmission parts carefully to avoid burring or nicking bearing or mating surfaces.

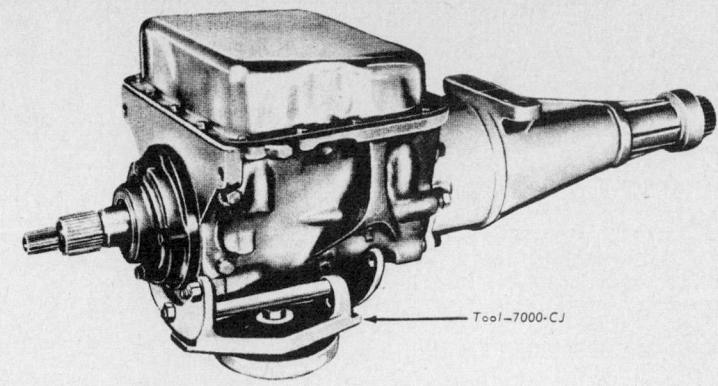

Transmission mounted in holding fixture (© Ford Motor Co.)

3. Lubricate all internal parts of the transmission with clean transmission fluid before assembling. *Do not use any other lubricants except on gaskets or thrust washers which may be coated lightly with vaseline to ease assembly.*

4. Always use new gaskets when assembling the transmission.

5. Tighten all bolts and screws to the recommended torque limits using a torque wrench.

Transmission Disassembly

1. Thoroughly clean the outside of the transmission to prevent dirt or grease from getting inside. *Do this before removing any subassembly.*

2. Place the transmission in the transmission holder. See illustration.

3. Remove the transmission oil pan, gasket, and fluid filter retaining clip.

4. Lift the fluid filter screen off the forward tube, and then off the rear tube.

5. Remove the spring seat from the pressure regulator. *Maintain constant pressure on the spring seat and release slowly to prevent spring distortion and personal injury.*

6. Remove the pressure regulator springs and pilots, but do not remove the valves yet.

7. Loosen but do not remove the pressure regulator attaching bolts.

8. Remove the small compensator pressure tube from the pressure regulator and the control valve body.

9. Remove the main pressure oil tube from the pressure regulator and the main control valve body assembly. Gently pry off the end connected to the main control valve body first and then remove the tube from the pressure regulator. *Failure to do this may kink or bend the tube causing damage to the transmission.*

10. Loosen the front and rear band adjusting screws five turns. Loosen the front servo attaching bolts three turns.

11. Remove the vacuum diaphragm unit and pushrod.

12. Remove the control valve body attaching bolts and align the levers to allow removal of the valve body. Lift the valve body up and pull it off the servo tubes. Place the valve body on a clean surface.

13. Remove the pressure regulator from the case. Keep the control pressure valve and the converter pressure valve in the regulator

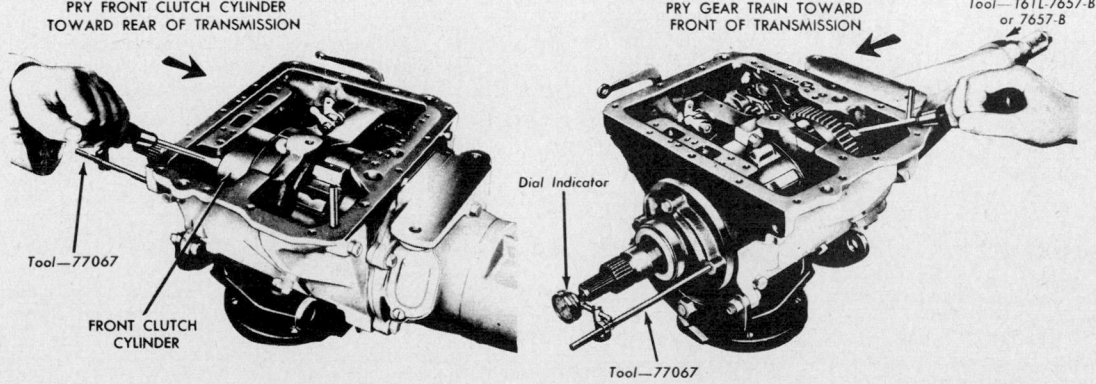

PRY FRONT CLUTCH CYLINDER TOWARD REAR OF TRANSMISSION

Tool—77067

FRONT CLUTCH CYLINDER

PRY GEAR TRAIN TOWARD FRONT OF TRANSMISSION

Tool—T61L-7657-B or 7657-B

Dial Indicator

Tool—77067

Transmission end play check (© Ford Motor Co.)

body to avoid damaging the valves.

14. Remove the front servo supply and release tubes by twisting and pulling at the same time. Remove the front servo attaching bolts. While holding the front servo strut, lift the front servo from the case.

15. Remove the rear servo attaching bolts. While holding the actuating and anchor struts, lift the rear servo from the case.

Transmission End-Play Check

The transmission end-play is checked as follows:

1. Remove one of the front pump attaching bolts and mount the dial indicator support tool in the hole. Mount a dial indicator on the support so that the stem rests on the end of the turbine shaft. See illustration.

2. Install the extension housing seal replacer on the output shaft to provide support for the shaft.

3. Using a screwdriver, move the front clutch cylinder to the rear of the transmission case as far as possible. Set the dial indicator to zero while holding a slight pressure on the screwdriver.

4. Remove the screwdriver. Insert it between the large internal gear and the case and move the front clutch cylinder to the front of the case.

5. Record the indicator reading for later use during transmission reassembly. The end-play reading should be between 0.010-0.029 in. If the reading is not within these limits, a new selective thrust washer must be used when reassembling the transmission.

Case and Extension Housing Parts Removal

1. Remove the remaining front pump attaching bolts and the front pump assembly from the case. If necessary, tap the cap screw bosses to loosen the front pump.

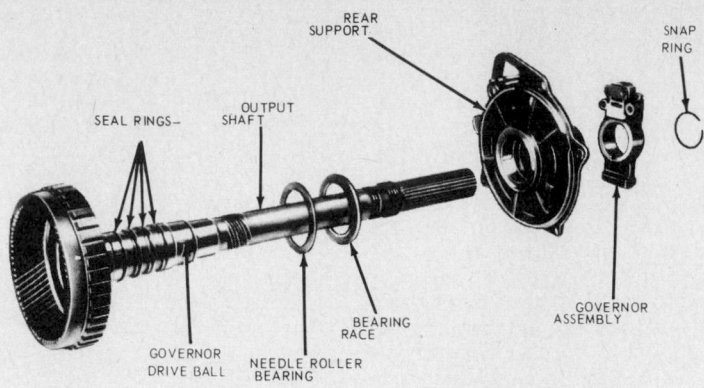

Output shaft disassembled (© Ford Motor Co.)

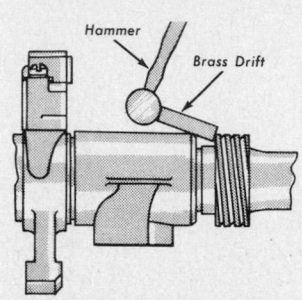

Removing speedometer drive gear— 1965-66 FMX transmission (© Ford Motor Co.)

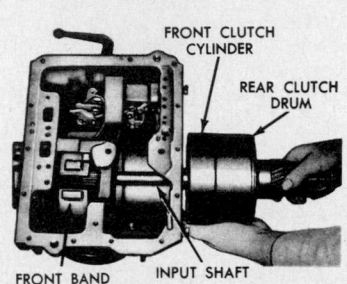

Removing or installing input shaft and clutch (© Ford Motor Co.)

2. Remove the five case-to-extension housing attaching bolts. These bolts also hold the rear pump in the case. While holding the rear pump in position remove the housing carefully.

3. Remove the output shaft assembly (see illustration). To aid in removing the assembly, insert a screwdriver between the output shaft ring gear and the pinion carrier and move the assembly rearward. Be careful not to bend the pressure tubes between the rear support or distributor sleeve and the case as they are removed.

NOTE: on output shaft assemblies used in 1965 and 1966 transmissions, the speedometer drive gear is removable. The nylon speedometer drive gear may be replaced by removing

the snap-ring securing it on the shaft, prying the oil distributor sleeve both rearward and forward on the shaft, and then, tapping the drive gear loose from the output shaft with a hammer and a small drift.

4. Remove the four seal rings from the output shaft.

5. Remove the governor snap-ring from the output shaft. Tap the governor assembly off the output shaft with a hard rubber hammer. Remove the governor drive ball (see illustration).

6. Pull the rear support and gasket from the output shaft. Take the needle bearings and race from the rear support.

7. Remove the selective thrust washer from the rear of the pinion carrier and then remove the pinion carrier.

8. Remove the primary sun gear rear thrust bearing and races from the pinion carrier.

9. Note the position of the band for later reference during assembly. Use the depression in the band end next to the adjusting screw for a reference. Squeeze the ends of the rear band together, tilt the band to the rear, and remove the band from the case.

10. Remove the two center support outer bolts (one on each side) from the case.

11. Hold the end of the input shaft in tight enough to hold the clutch units together and pull the center support and the front

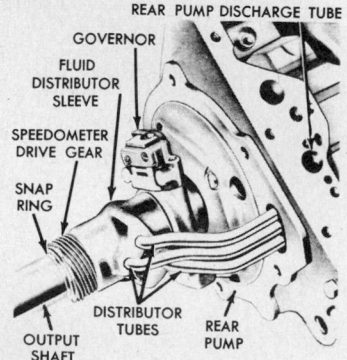

Rear pump and output shaft installed— 1965-67 FMX transmission (© Ford Motor Co.)

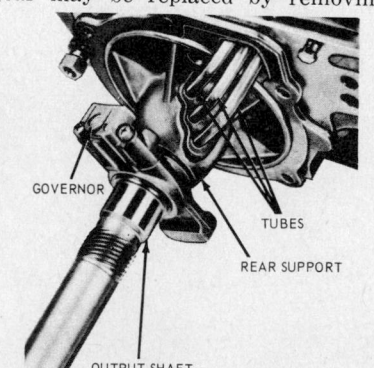

Rear support and output shaft installed— 1968-72 FMX transmission (© Ford Motor Co.)

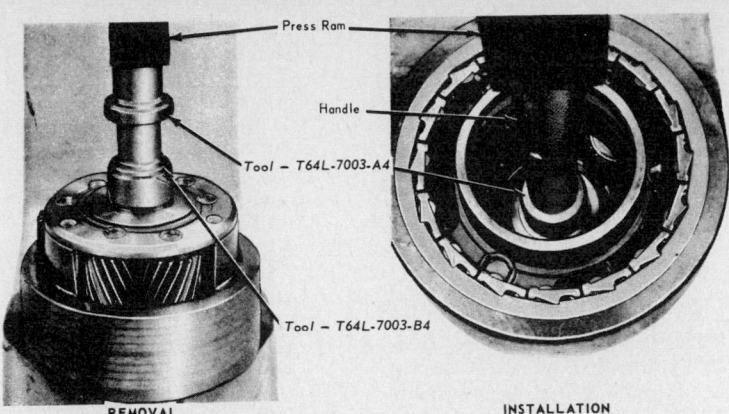

REMOVAL   INSTALLATION

Replacing rear brake drum support bushing (© Ford Motor Co.)

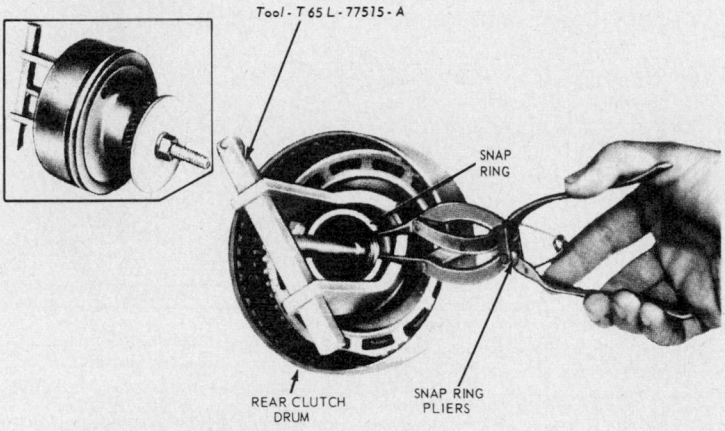

Removing rear clutch spring snap ring (© Ford Motor Co.)

and rear clutch assemblies from the case as one unit (see illustration).

12. Install the clutch assemblies in the bench fixture as shown.
13. Remove the thrust washer from the front of the input shaft.
14. To remove the front band, position the band ends between the case webbing and tilt the bottom of the band rearward. Then, squeeze the ends of the band together and remove from the rear of the case.
15. Lift the front clutch assembly from the primary sun gear shaft.
16. Remove the bronze and the steel thrust washers from the rear clutch assembly. Wire the thrust washers together to assure correct installation.
17. Remove the front clutch seal rings from the primary sun gear shaft.
18. Lift the rear clutch assembly from the primary sun gear shaft.
19. Remove the rear clutch seal rings from the primary sun gear shaft. *Do not break the seal rings.*
20. Remove the primary sun gear shaft front thrust washer.

Rear Brake Drum Support Bushing Removal and Installation

If the rear brake drum support bushing is to be replaced, press the bushing from the support as shown in the illustration. Then, press a new bushing into the brake drum support with the tool shown.

Output Shaft Bushing Removal and Installation

1. Remove the worn bushing by using a cape chisel to break through the bushing wall.
2. Pry the loose ends of the bushing up with an awl and remove the bushing.
3. Install a new bushing on the output shaft hub by pressing it on with the installation tool as shown in the illustration.

Primary Sun Gear Shaft Seal Ring Replacement

1. Place the primary sun gear shaft in the clutch bench fixture.
2. Check the fit of the seal rings in their respective bores. If equipped with cast iron seal rings, there should be a clearance of 0.002-0.009 in. between the ends. If equipped with teflon

seals that are worn or damaged, cut the seals from the shaft with a sharp knife. Do not score the ring grooves.
3. Replace the teflon seals with cast iron seal rings, and check for free movement in the groove.

Rear Clutch Disassembly and Assembly

1. Remove the clutch pressure plate snap-ring and the pressure plate from the drum. Also, remove the waved cushion spring and the composition and steel plates.

NOTE: in 1967-70 transmissions, composition plates replaced bronze plates and a waved cushion spring was added.

2. Compress the spring with the tool shown and remove the snap-ring with snap-ring pliers.
3. Carefully guide the spring retainer while releasing spring pressure so that the retainer does not lock in the snap-ring grooves.
4. Position the primary sun gear shaft in the rear clutch. Place an air hose nozzle in one of the holes in the shaft and block the other hole to force the clutch piston out of the clutch drum. *Hold the piston to prevent damaging it.*
5. Remove the inner and outer seal rings from the clutch piston.
6. Remove the rear clutch sun gear bushing if it is worn or damaged by cutting it out with a cape chisel. See illustration. When the

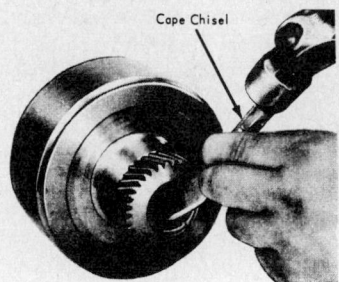

Removing rear clutch sun gear bushing (© Ford Motor Co.)

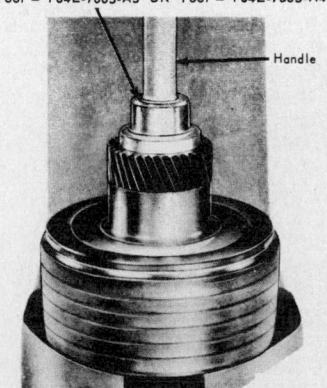

Installing rear clutch sun gear bushing (© Ford Motor Co.)

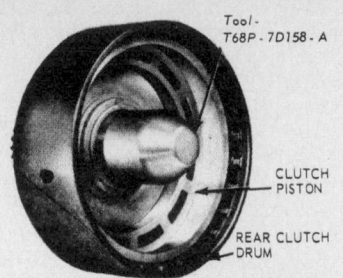

Installing rear clutch piston
(© Ford Motor Co.)

bushing is cut through, pry the ends up with an awl and remove the bushing.

7. Install a new rear clutch sun gear bushing using the tool shown in the illustration.
8. Install new inner and outer seal rings on the piston.
9. When installing the piston in the clutch drum, lubricate the piston seals and the tools with clean transmission fluid.
10. Push the small fixture down over the cylinder hub.
11. Insert the piston into the large fixture with the seal toward the thin-walled end. See illustration.
12. Hold the piston and large fixture and insert as one unit into the cylinder. Push down over the small fixture until the large tool stops against the shoulder in the cylinder; then push the piston down, out of the tool, until it bottoms in the cylinder. Remove the tools.
13. Install the clutch release spring and position the retainer on the spring.
14. Install the spring compressor retainer and install the snap-ring. *While compressing the spring, guide the retainer to avoid catching on the snap-ring groove. Be sure the snap-ring is fully seated in the groove.*
15. If new composition plates are installed, soak them in clean transmission fluid for 15 minutes before assembling them.
16. Install a steel clutch plate and the waved cushion spring. Then, install steel and composition friction plates alternately starting with a steel plate.
17. Install the clutch pressure plate with the bearing surface down. Then install the snap-ring, being sure the snap ring is fully seated in its groove.
18. Check the free pack clearance between the pressure plate and the snap-ring with a feeler gauge. The clearance should be 0.030-0.055 in. If the clearance is not within this range, install a selective snap-ring with one of the following thicknesses: 0.060-0.064, 0.074-0.078, 0.088-0.092, 0.102-0.106 in. Insert the correct

snap-ring and recheck the clearance.
19. Install the thrust washer on the primary sun gear shaft. Lubricate all parts with transmission fluid and install the two center seal rings.
20. Install the rear clutch on the primary sun gear shaft. *Be sure all loose needle bearings are in the hub correctly if so equipped.* Install the seal rings in the front grooves.
21. Install the steel and the bronze thrust washers on the front of the secondary sun gear assembly. If the steel washer is chamfered, place the chamfered side down.

Front Clutch Disassembly and Assembly

1. Remove the clutch cover snap-ring by prying it up with a screwdriver, and remove the input shaft from the clutch drum.
2. Remove the thrust washer from the thrust surface of the clutch hub. Lift the clutch hub straight up to remove it from the clutch drum.
3. Remove the composition and the steel clutch plates and the pressure plate from the clutch drum.
4. Place the front clutch spring compressor on the release spring, position the clutch drum on the bed of an arbor press, and compress the release spring with the arbor press until the release spring snap-ring can be removed (see illustration).
5. Remove the clutch release spring from the clutch drum.
6. Using the special air nozzle shown in the illustration, force the piston out of the housing.
7. Remove the piston inner seal from the clutch housing and remove the piston outer seal from the groove in the piston.
8. Remove the input shaft bushing if it is worn or damaged. Use a cape chisel and cut along the bushing seam until the chisel breaks through the bushing wall.

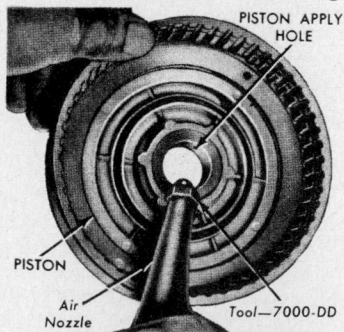

Removing front clutch piston
(© Ford Motor Co.)

Pry up the loose ends of the bushing with an awl and remove the bushing.

9. Put a new bushing over the end of the installation tool and position the tool and bushing over the bushing hole. Then, press the bushing into the input shaft (see illustration).
10. Install a new piston inner seal ring in the clutch cylinder and a new piston outer seal in the groove in the piston. Lubricate all parts with transmission fluid before installation.
11. Install the piston in the clutch housing. *Be sure the steel bearing ring is in place on the piston.*

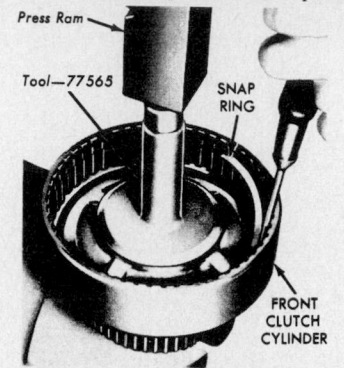

Removing or installing front clutch snap ring
(© Ford Motor Co.)

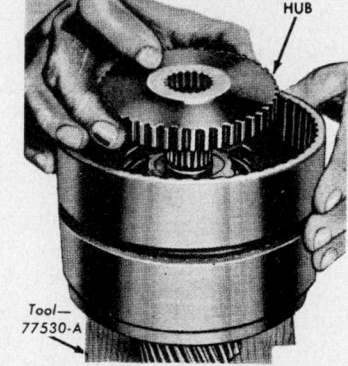

Installing clutch hub
(© Ford Motor Co.)

12. Place the release spring in the clutch cylinder with the concave side up. Put the release spring compressor on the spring and compress the spring with an arbor press. Then, install the snap-ring in the groove in the piston.
13. Install the front clutch housing on the primary sun gear shaft by rotating the clutch units to mesh the rear clutch plates with the serrations on the clutch hub. *Do not break the seal rings.*
14. Install the clutch hub in the clutch cylinder with the deep counterbore down. Install the thrust washer on the clutch hub. See illustration.
15. Install the pressure plate in the clutch cylinder with the bearing

Installing pressure plate
(© Ford Motor Co.)

Installing clutch plates
(© Ford Motor Co.)

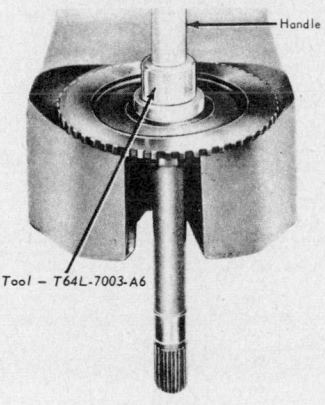

Installing input shaft bushing
(© Ford Motor Co.)

Front Pump Disassembly and Assembly

1. Remove the stator support attaching screws and remove the stator support. Mark the top surface of the pump driven gear with Prussian blue to assure correct assembly. *Do not scratch the pump gears.*
2. Remove the drive and driven gears from the pump body (see illustration). Inspect the pump body housing, gear pockets and crescent for scoring and burrs.
3. If the pump housing bushing needs replacing, press it from the front housing as shown in the illustration. Press a new bushing into the pump housing with the tools shown.
4. If any parts other than the stator support or bushings are defective, replace the pump as a unit. Minor burrs and scores may be removed with crocus cloth. The stator support is serviced separately.
5. Bolt the front pump to the transmission case with capscrews. Install the oil seal remover and pull the front seal from the pump body. See illustration.
6. Clean and inspect the counterbore, smoothing any rough spots with crocus cloth.
7. Remove the pump body from the transmission case.
8. Coat the new seal with sealing compound. Drive the seal into the pump body with the tool shown in the illustration. The tool may be reworked to install the latest type of seal if necessary (see illustration).
9. Place the pump driven gear in the pump body as it was originally installed. Install the drive gear in the pump body with the chamfered side of the flats facing down.
10. Install the stator support and attaching screws. Check the pump gears for free rotation.

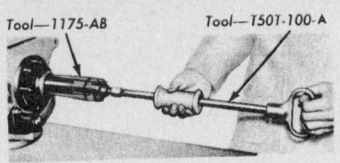

Removing front pump seal
(© Ford Motor Co.)

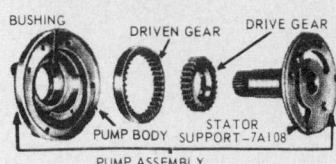

Front pump disassembled
(© Ford Motor Co.)

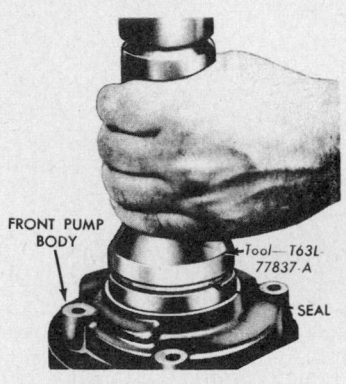

Installing front pump seal
(© Ford Motor Co.)

Rear Pump Disassembly and Assembly

A rear pump was used in 1967 and earlier transmissions.

1. When the rear pump has been removed from the output shaft, remove the screws and lockwashers holding the pump cover to the pump body. Remove the pump cover.
2. Mark the top faces of the pump drive and the pump driven gears with Prussian blue for realignment during assembly. *Do not scratch or gouge the pump gears.*

surface up (see illustration). Install the composition and the steel clutch plates alternately, starting with a composition plate (see illustration). Lubricate all the plates with transmission fluid before installing. The last friction plate is selective in thickness. Select the thickest plate that will be a minimum of 0.010 in. below the input shaft shoulder in the cylinder. All other plates should be the thinnest available.

16. Install the turbine shaft in the clutch cylinder, and then install the snap-ring in the groove.
17. Install the thrust washer on the turbine shaft.

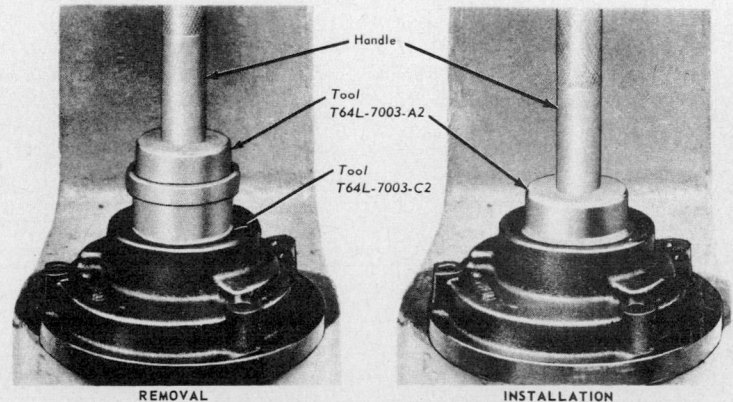

Replacing front pump housing bushing (© Ford Motor Co.)

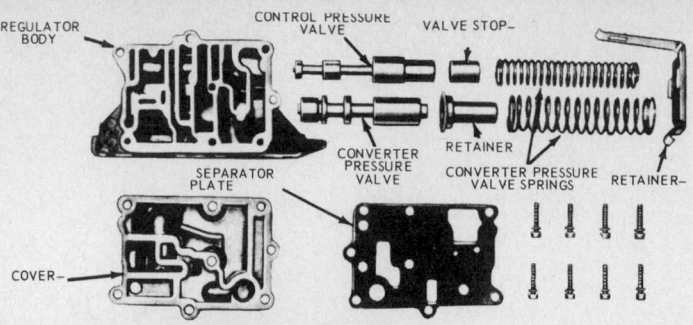

Pressure regulator disassembled (© Ford Motor Co.)

3. Remove the drive and driven gears from the pump body.
4. After cleaning and inspection, place the pump drive gear in the body with the mark facing up. Place the pump driven gear in the body with its mark facing up and in line with the drive gear mark. Install the pump cover, attaching screws and lockwashers. Tighten the screws to proper torque.
5. Check the pump for free rotation.

Rear Support Bushing Removal and Installation

1. Remove the three pressure tubes from the support housing.
2. Remove the rear support bushing if worn or damaged by cutting it with a cape chisel along the bushing seam until it breaks. Pry up the loose ends and

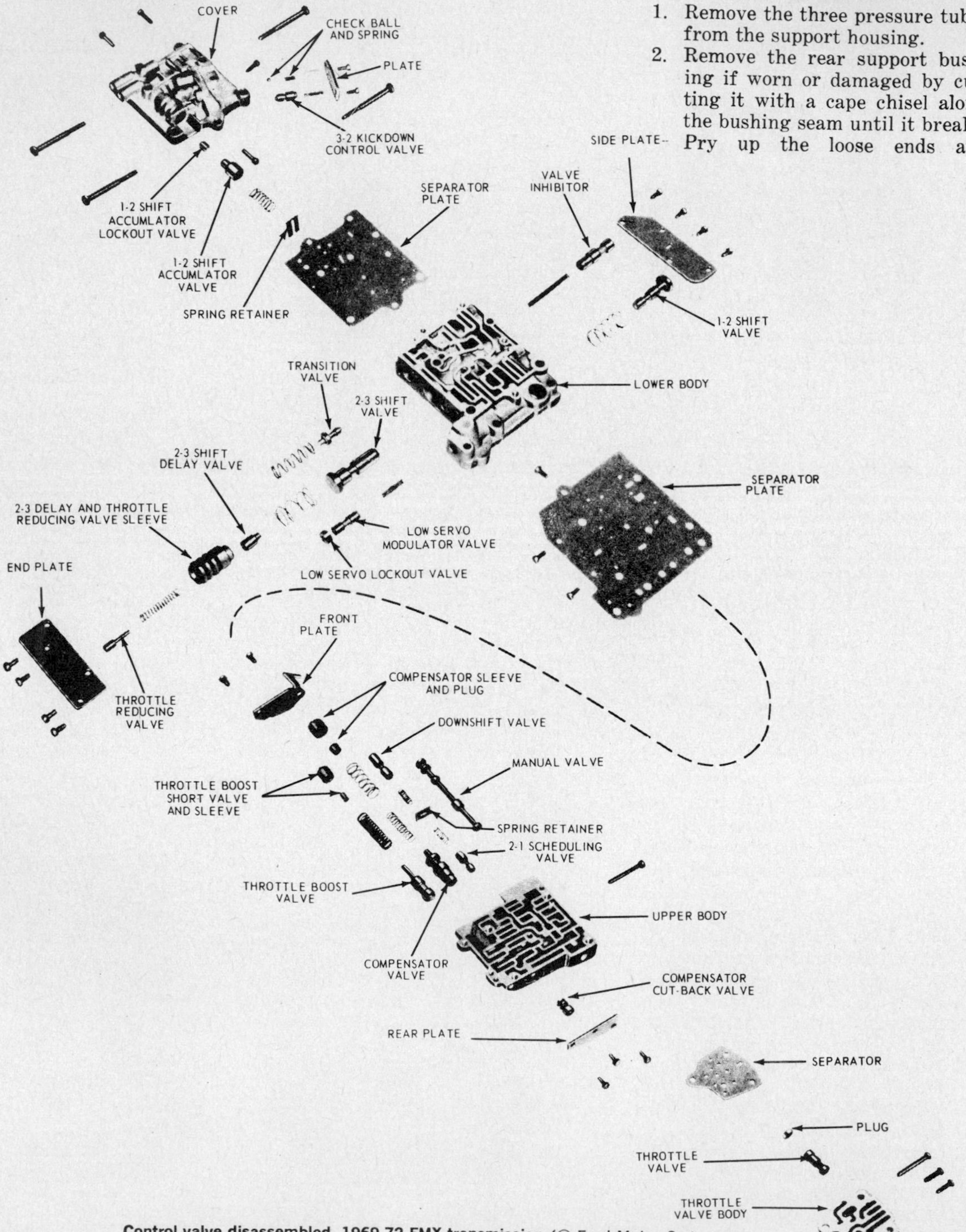

Control valve disassembled, 1969-72 FMX transmission (© Ford Motor Co.)

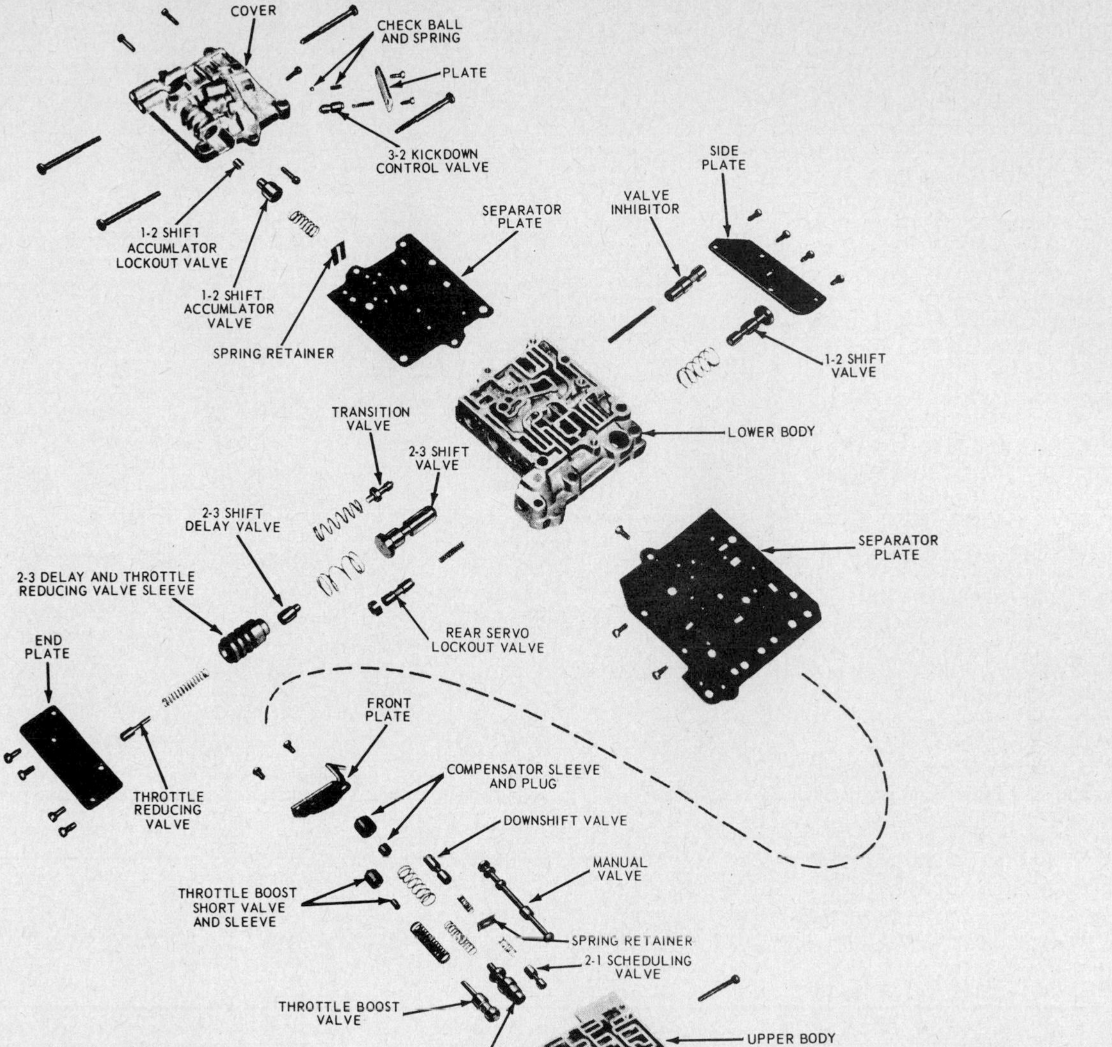

COVER

CHECK BALL
AND SPRING

PLATE

3-2 KICKDOWN
CONTROL VALVE

1-2 SHIFT
ACCUMLATOR
LOCKOUT VALVE

1-2 SHIFT
ACCUMLATOR
VALVE

SPRING RETAINER

SEPARATOR
PLATE

VALVE
INHIBITOR

SIDE
PLATE

1-2 SHIFT
VALVE

TRANSITION
VALVE

2-3 SHIFT
VALVE

2-3 SHIFT
DELAY VALVE

2-3 DELAY AND THROTTLE
REDUCING VALVE SLEEVE

END
PLATE

THROTTLE
REDUCING
VALVE

LOWER BODY

SEPARATOR
PLATE

REAR SERVO
LOCKOUT VALVE

FRONT
PLATE

COMPENSATOR SLEEVE
AND PLUG

DOWNSHIFT VALVE

THROTTLE BOOST
SHORT VALVE
AND SLEEVE

MANUAL
VALVE

SPRING RETAINER

2-1 SCHEDULING
VALVE

THROTTLE BOOST
VALVE

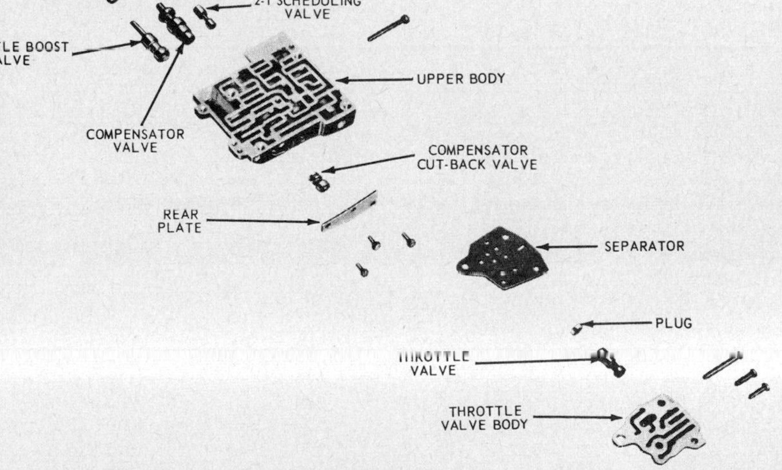

COMPENSATOR
VALVE

UPPER BODY

COMPENSATOR
CUT-BACK VALVE

REAR
PLATE

SEPARATOR

PLUG

THROTTLE
VALVE

THROTTLE
VALVE BODY

Control valve disassembled, 1967-68 FMX transmission (© Ford Motor Co.)

remove the bushing.

3. Press a new bushing into the support housing with the tool shown in the illustration.

4. Install the pressure tubes.

Pressure Regulator Disassembly and Assembly

1. Remove the valves from the regulator body.

2. Remove the regulator body cover attaching screws, and remove the cover (see illustration).

3. Remove the separator plate.

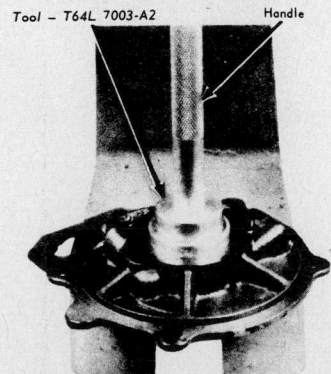

Tool — T64L 7003-A2   Handle

Installing rear support housing seal
(© Ford Motor Co.)

4. Clean all parts in solvent and dry with compressed air.

5. Inspect the regulator body and cover mating surfaces for burrs. Check the fluid passages for obstructions. Inspect the control pressure and converter pressure valves and their bores for burrs and scoring. Remove all burrs carefully with crocus cloth. Be sure the valves move freely in their bores when dry. Inspect the valve springs for distortion.

6. Reassemble the pressure regula-

tor by placing the separator plate and the regulator cover on the regulator body and installing the attaching screws. Tighten the screws to 20-30 in. lbs. torque. Insert the valves in the regulator body.

Control Valve Body Disassembly and Assembly

The control valve body is disassembled according to the procedure given below. The reassembly is basically the reverse of the disassembly procedure but careful reference should be made to the accompanying illustration showing the entire control valve body disassembled. During the disassembly of the control valve body assembly, be careful not to damage the valves. Place the valve body on a clean surface while disassembling it. *Do not separate the upper and lower valve bodies and cover until the valves have been removed.*

1. Remove the manual valve (see illustration).
2. Remove the throttle valve body and the separator plate. Do not lose the check valve when removing the separator plate from the valve body. Remove the throttle valve and plug.
3. Remove one attaching screw from the separator plate holding it to the lower valve body. Remove the upper body front plate. *Since the plate is spring-loaded, hold the plate steady while removing the attaching screws.*
4. Remove the compensator sleeve and plug, the compensator valve springs and the compensator valve.
5. Remove the throttle boost short valve and sleeve. Remove the throttle boost valve spring and valve.
6. Remove the downshift valve and spring. Remove the 2-1 scheduling valve retainer from the valve body and remove the spring and valve.
7. Remove the upper valve body rear plate.
8. Remove the compensator cut-back valve.
9. Remove the lower body side plate. *This plate is spring-loaded and must be held steady while removing the attaching screws.*
10. Remove the 1-2 shift valve and spring. Remove the inhibitor valve and spring.
11. Remove the two screws attaching the separator plate to the cover. Remove the lower body end plate. *The end plate is spring-loaded and must be held steady while removing the attaching screws.*
12. Remove the low servo lockout valve, low servo modulator valve and spring.
13. Remove the 2-3 delay and throttle reducing valve sleeve, the throttle reducing valve, spring, and the 2-3 shift delay valve. Also, remove the 2-3 shift valve spring and valve.
14. Remove the transition valve spring and valve.
15. Remove the plate from the valve body cover. Remove the check ball spring and the check ball. Remove the 3-2 kickdown control valve spring and valve.

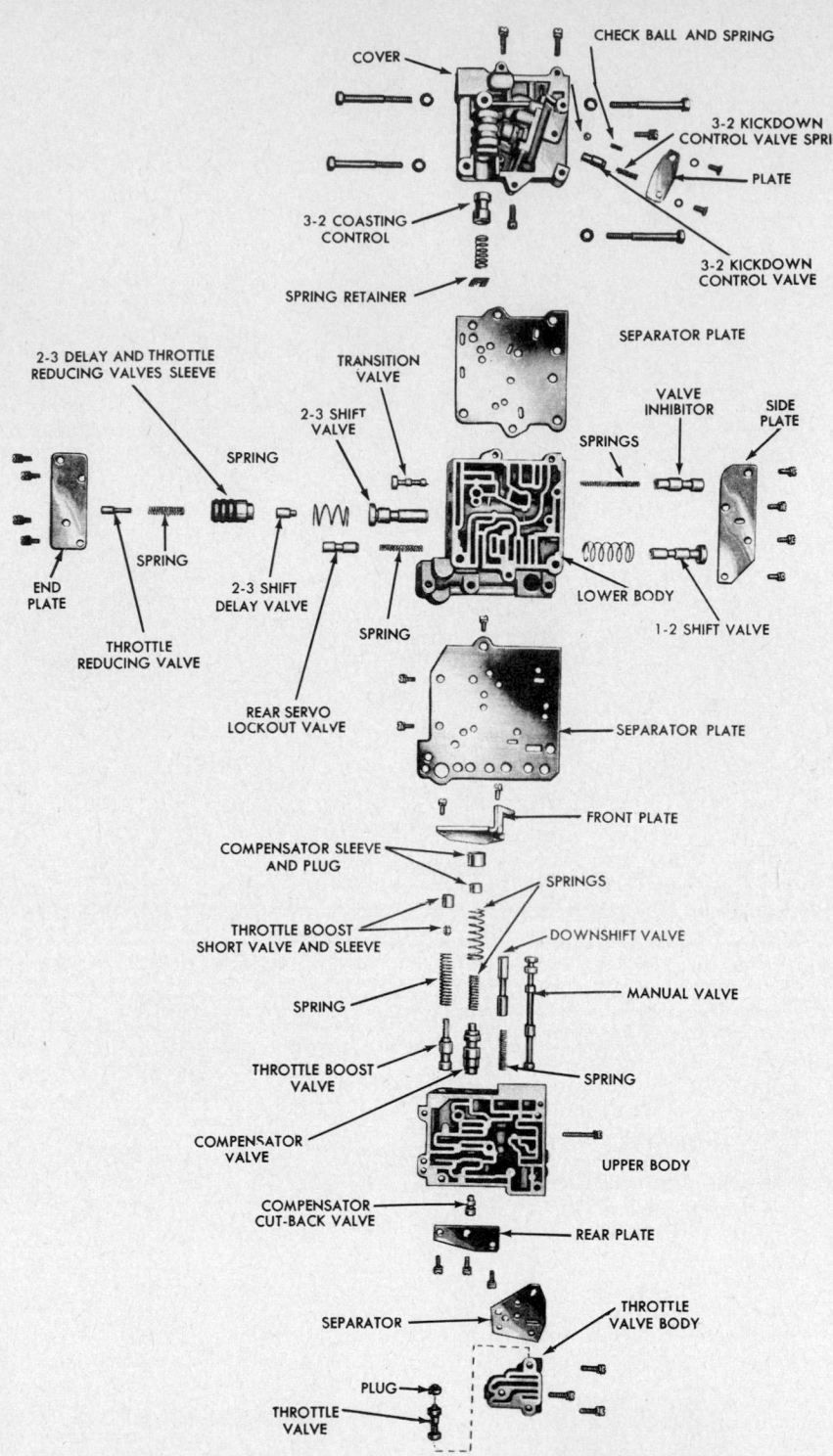

Control valve disassembled, 1965-66 FMX transmission (ⓒ Ford Motor Co.)

16. Remove the 1-2 shift accumulator valve spring retainer from the cover. Remove the spring, 1-2 shift accumulator valve and 1-2 shift accumulator lockout valve.
17. Remove the long through-bolts and screws and separate the upper and lower valve bodies. Remove the separator plates from the valve bodies and cover.

Do not lose the check valves.

After cleaning and inspecting the parts of the disassembled control valve body assembly, reassemble the control valve body as follows:

1. Arrange all the parts in their correct positions according to the illustration. When inserting the valves and plugs, rotate them in their bores to avoid damaging the soft body castings.

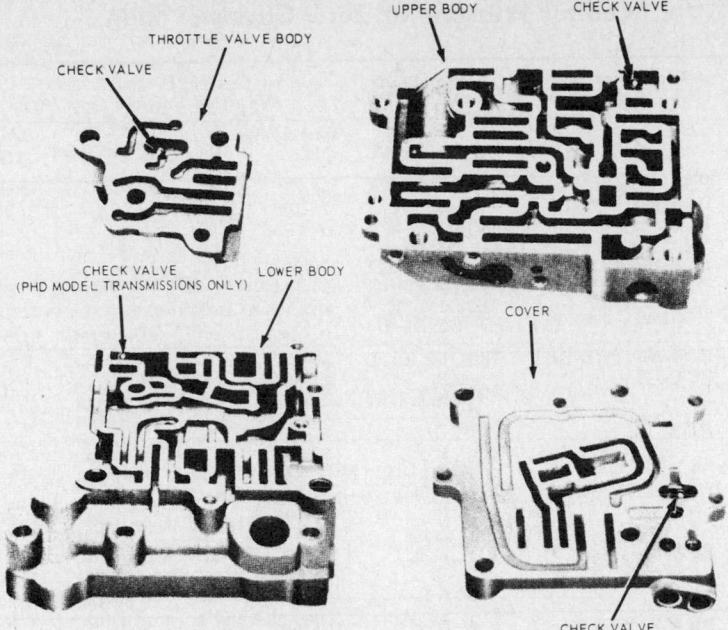

UPPER BODY   CHECK VALVE

THROTTLE VALVE BODY

CHECK VALVE

CHECK VALVE
(PHD MODEL TRANSMISSIONS ONLY)   LOWER BODY

COVER

CHECK VALVE

Check valve locations (© Ford Motor Co.)

2. Place the check valve in the upper body (see illustration) and then position the separator plate on the body.

3. Position the lower body on the upper body and loosely install the attaching screws.

4. Put the check valve in the cover and position the cover and separator plate on the lower body. Install, but do not tighten, the four long through-bolts.

5. Align the separator with the upper and lower valve body attaching bolt holes and install the attaching bolts, tightening them to 48-72 in. lbs. torque. *Excessive tightening of the bolts may distort the valve bodies, causing valves or plugs to stick.*

6. Install the 3-2 kickdown control valve and spring and the check ball and spring in the cover. Install the plate.

7. Insert the 1-2 shift accumulator lockout valve, the 1-2 accumulator valve, and the spring in the cover. Install the valve spring retainer.

8. Install the transition valve and spring in the lower body. Also install the 2-3 shift valve and spring, the 2-3 shift delay valve, and the spring and throttle reducing valve in the sleeve. Slide the valve and sleeve into the lower body.

9. Install the low servo lockout valve spring, the low servo modulator, and low servo lockout valves. Install the lower body end plate.

10. Install the inhibitor valve spring and valve in the lower body. Install the 1-2 shift valve spring and valve. Install the lower body

side plate.

11. Install the compensator cut-back valve in the upper body and install the upper body rear plate.

12. Install the 2-1 scheduling valve, spring, and spring retainer in the body. Install the downshift valve spring and valve.

13. Install the throttle boost valve and spring and the throttle boost short valve and sleeve.

14. Install the compensator valve, inner and outer compensator springs and the compensator sleeve and plug.

15. Position the front plate correctly and press it against the upper body while installing the attaching screws.

16. Install the throttle valve, plug and check valve in the throttle valve body. Position the separator on the upper body and install the throttle valve body with the three attaching screws.

17. Install the four screws attaching the cover to the lower body, the two screws attaching the separator plate to the upper body, and one screw attaching the separator plate to the lower body. Tighten the cover and body screws to the proper torque.

18. Install the manual valve.

Front Servo Disassembly and Assembly

1. Remove the servo piston retainer snap-ring. Since the servo piston is spring-loaded, hold the piston steady while removing the snap-ring and release the spring pressure gradually.

2. Remove the servo piston retainer, servo piston, and the return

piston from the servo body. It may be necessary to tap the piston stem lightly with a soft-faced hammer to separate the piston retainer from the servo body.

3. On PHD models, remove the screw and washer from the end of the piston stem and separate the piston retainer, return piston, and the servo piston.

4. Remove all seal rings and the spring from the servo body.

5. Inspect the servo body for cracks and the piston bore and the servo piston stem for scores. Check all fluid passages for obstructions.

6. Check the actuating lever for free movement and wear. If it is necessary to replace the actuating lever shaft, remove the retaining pin and push the shaft out of the bracket. If the shaft is not held in place by a retaining pin, it is press-fit. To remove this type of shaft, press on the end opposite the serrations. Inspect the adjusting screw threads and the threads in the lever.

7. Check the servo spring and servo band strut for distortion.

8. Inspect the servo band lining for excessive wear and bonding to the metal. Replace the lining if it is worn so much that the grooves are not clearly seen. Inspect the band ends for cracks and check the band for distortion.

9. Lubricate all parts of the front servo by soaking in transmission fluid to ease assembly.

10. Install the inner and outer seal rings on the piston retainer. Install new O-rings on the return piston and the servo piston.

11. On PHD models, tap the piston stem into the servo piston. Insert the servo piston in the piston retainer. Tap the return piston onto the piston stem and into the piston retainer. Be sure the dished side of the return piston is toward the servo piston. Fasten the return piston to the stem with a screw and plain washer.

12. Place the servo piston release spring in the servo body. Install the servo piston, retainer, and return piston in the servo body as an assembly. Compress this assembly into the body and secure it with the snap-ring. *Be sure the snap-ring is fully seated in the groove.*

13. Install the adjusting screw and locknut in the actuating lever, and install the lever if it was removed.

Rear Servo Disassembly and Assembly

1. Remove the servo actuating lever

3. Back off the adjusting screw *exactly 3 full turns*.
4. Hold the adjusting screw steady and tighten the locknut to the proper torque.

Transmission Component Removal and Installation

Prior to the removal of components, the transmission fluid must be drained, and the oil pan and filter screen removed.

Control Valve Removal and Installation 1970-72 All Models Except 1970 Falcon

1. Perform the preliminary operations indicated above.
2. On 1970 model C4 transmissions only, shift the transmission to Park position and remove the two bolts holding the manual detent spring to the control valve body and case.
3. Remove all the valve body-to-case attaching bolts. Hold the manual valve in place and remove the valve body from the case. If the manual valve is not held in place, it could be bent or damaged.
4. Refer to the Component Disassembly and repair section for control valve body repair procedures.
5. Thoroughly clean the old gasket material from the case and remove the nylon shipping plug from the oil filler tube hole. This nylon plug is installed before shipment and should be discarded when the transmission oil pan is removed.
6. Be sure the transmission is in the Park position (manual detent lever is in P detent position). Install the valve body in the case. Position the inner downshift lever between the downshift lever stop and the downshift valve. Be sure the two lands on the end of the manual valve engage the actuating pin on the manual detent lever.
7. Install seven valve body attaching bolts but do not tighten them.
8. Place the detent spring on the lower valve body and install the spring-to-case bolt finger tight.
9. While holding the detent spring roller in the center of the manual detent lever, install the detent spring-to-lower valve body bolt and tighten it to 80-120 in-lbs. torque.
10. Tighten the remainder of the control valve body attaching bolts to 80-120 in-lbs. torque.
11. Put a new gasket on the oil pan,

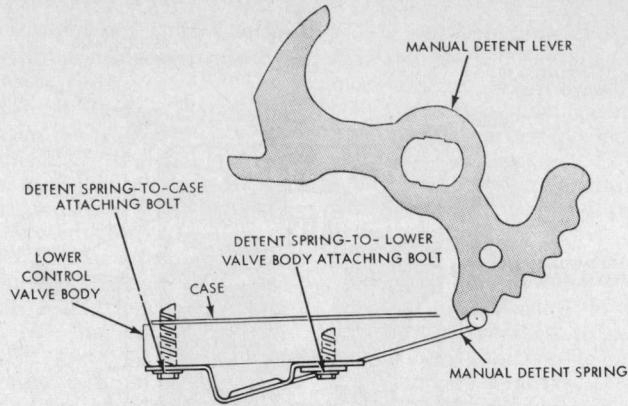

Control valve body with detent spring installed (© Ford Motor Co.)

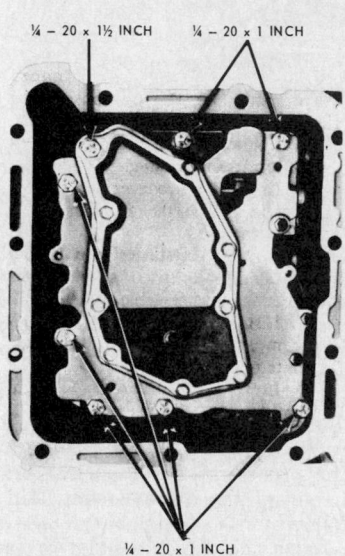

¼ – 20 x 1½ INCH   ¼ – 20 x 1 INCH

¼ – 20 x 1 INCH

Control valve body attaching bolts
(© Ford Motor Co.)

install pan in place, and install and tighten all the pan attaching bolts to the proper torque.
12. If the filler tube was removed, reinstall it and tighten securely. If necessary, replace the oil seal around the filler tube to prevent leakage.
13. Lower the car and fill the transmission with enough fluid to bring the level up to the FULL mark on the dipstick.

Control Valve Removal and Installation 1965-69 All Models, 1970 Falcon

1. Perform the preliminary operations indicated above.
2. Remove the valve body attaching bolts. Remove the valve body from the case and the transmission inner control levers.
3. Refer to the Component Disassembly and Repair section for control valve body repair operations.
4. Thoroughly clean and remove all traces of old gasket material and dirt from the case. Remove and

discard the nylon shipping plug from the filler tube if present. Install the valve body to the case, engaging the transmission inner control levers with the valve body manual and downshift valves.
5. Install the valve body attaching bolts, tightening them to the proper torque. Operate the external manual and downshift levers to check for proper travel of the valve body manual and downshift valves.
6. Place a new gasket on the oil pan and install the oil pan and the attaching bolts. Tighten the bolts to the proper torque.
7. Lower the car and fill the transmission with enough fluid to raise the fluid level to the FULL mark on the dipstick. Check for leaks.

Intermediate Servo Removal and Installation

1. Raise the car and remove the four servo cover attaching bolts (right-hand side of case). Remove the cover and identification tag (*do not lose tag*).
   NOTE: to gain access to the servo on a six-cylinder Maverick or 1971-72 Comet, the crossmember must be removed.
2. Remove the gasket, piston, and piston return spring.
3. Install the piston return spring in the case. Place a new gasket on the cover. Install new seals on the piston, lubricate the seals with transmission fluid, and install the piston in the servo cover. Install the piston and cover in the transmission case, using two 5/16-18 x 1¼ bolts 180 degrees apart to align the cover against the case.
   NOTE: on eight-cylinder 1971-72 Comets and Mavericks, hold the servo cover in position with a pry bar between the floor pan and the cover while installing the retaining bolts and the identification tag.
4. Install the transmission identifi-

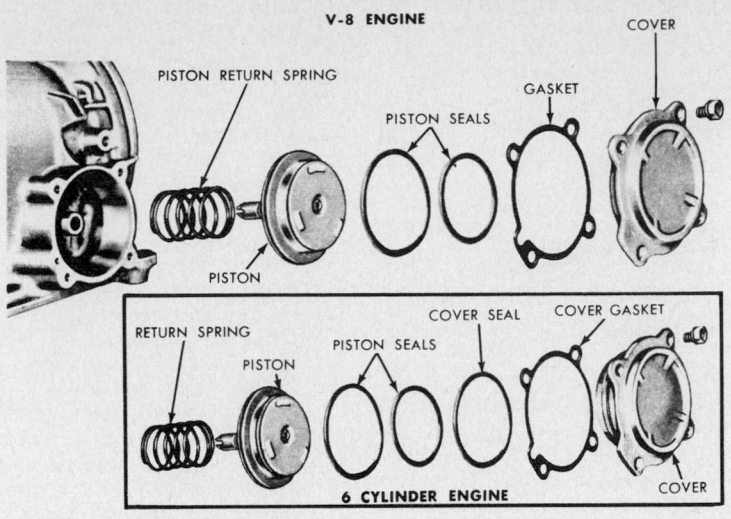

V-8 ENGINE

PISTON RETURN SPRING — GASKET — COVER — PISTON SEALS — PISTON

RETURN SPRING — PISTON — PISTON SEALS — COVER SEAL — COVER GASKET — COVER

6 CYLINDER ENGINE

Intermediate servo disassembled (© Ford Motor Co.)

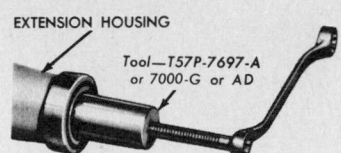

EXTENSION HOUSING — Tool—T57P-7697-A or 7000-G or AD

Removing extension housing bushing
(© Ford Motor Co.)

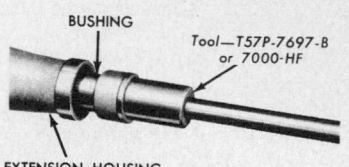

BUSHING — Tool—T57P-7697-B or 7000-HF — EXTENSION HOUSING

Installing extension housing bushing
(© Ford Motor Co.)

cation tag and two attaching bolts. Remove the two 1¼ bolts and install the other two cover attaching bolts. Tighten all cover attaching bolts to the proper torque.

5　On a Maverick or Comet, position the crossmember and install the attaching bolts, tightening them to the proper torque.

6　Adjust the intermediate band. If the intermediate band cannot be adjusted correctly, remove the control valve body and see that the struts are installed correctly. Adjust the struts and reinstall the control valve body. Install the oil pan with a new gasket.

7.　Lower the car and fill the transmission with enough fluid to raise the fluid level to the FULL mark on the dipstick.

Low-Reverse Servo Piston Removal and Installation

1.　Raise the car on a hoist.

2.　Loosen the reverse band adjusting screw locknut and tighten the adjusting screw to 10 ft lbs torque. This operation will hold the band strut against the case and prevent it from falling when the reverse servo piston is removed.

3.　Remove the four servo cover attaching bolts and remove the servo cover and seal from the case.

4.　Remove the servo piston from the case. *The piston and piston seal are bonded together and must be replaced together.*

NOTE: to remove the piston from the shaft for replacement, insert a small screwdriver through the hole in the shaft to hold the shaft, and remove the retaining nut. Install a new piston, and torque the nut to specifications.

5.　Install the servo piston assembly

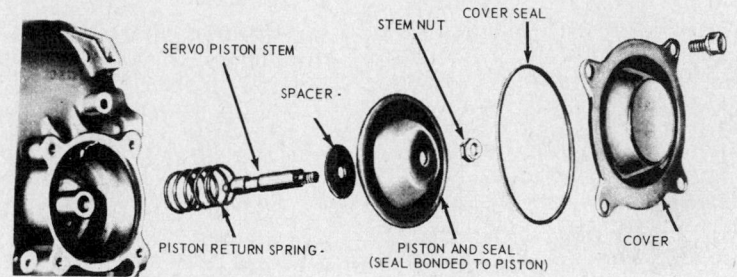

SERVO PISTON STEM — STEM NUT — COVER SEAL — SPACER — PISTON RETURN SPRING — PISTON AND SEAL (SEAL BONDED TO PISTON) — COVER

Low-reverse servo disassembled (© Ford Motor Co.)

LOW-REVERSE PISTON

Removing or installing low-reverse servo piston
(© Ford Motor Co.)

into the case. Place a new cover seal on the cover and position it on the case using two 5/16-18 bolts, 1¼ in. long, 180° apart. Install two cover attaching bolts with the identification tag.

6.　Remove the two positioning

bolts and install the other two cover bolts. Tighten all the cover attaching bolts to the proper torque.

7.　Adjust the low-reverse band. If the low-reverse band cannot be adjusted properly, remove the control valve body and check the alignment of the band struts. Reinstall the valve body and the oil pan with a new gasket.

8.　Lower the car and fill the transmission with enough fluid to raise the fluid level to the FULL mark on the dipstick.

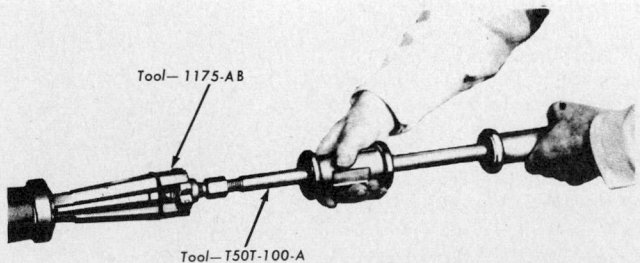

Tool— 1175-AB — Tool—T50T-100-A

Removing extension housing seal (© Ford Motor Co.)

Extension Housing Bushing and Rear Seal Removal and Installation

1.　Disconnect the drive shaft from the transmission.

2.　If only the rear seal needs re-

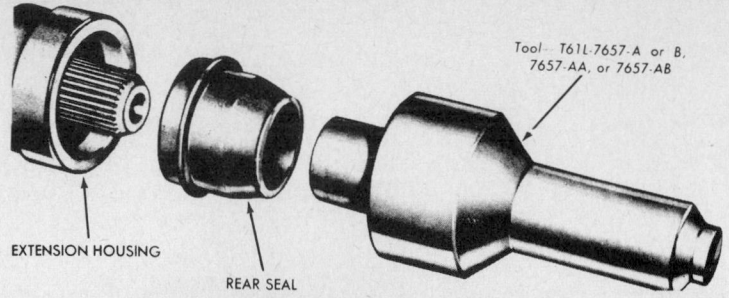

EXTENSION HOUSING

REAR SEAL

Tool T61L-7657-A or B, 7657-AA, or 7657-AB

Installing extension housing seal (© Ford Motor Co.)

placing, carefully remove it with a tapered chisel or use the tools shown in the illustration. Remove the bushing as shown. Be careful not to damage the spline seal with the bushing remover.

3. Install the new bushing, using the special tool shown.
4. Before installing a new rear seal, inspect the sealing surface of the universal joint yoke for scores. If the universal joint yoke is scored, replace the yoke.
5. Inspect the housing counterbore for burrs and remove them with crocus cloth if necessary.
6. Install the new rear seal into the housing, using the tool shown in the illustration. The seal should be firmly seated in the housing. Coat the inside diameter of the fiber portion of the seal with chassis lubricant.
7. Coat the front universal joint spline with chassis lubricant and install the drive shaft.

Extension Housing Removal and Installation

1. Raise the car on a hoist.
2. Remove the drive shaft. Place a transmission jack under the transmission for support.
3. Remove the speedometer cable from the extension housing.
4. Remove the extension housing-to-crossmember mount attaching bolts. Raise the transmission and remove the mounting pad between the extension housing and the crossmember.
NOTE: on 1971-72 eight-cylinder Comets and Mavericks it is necessary to disconnect the exhaust pipe from the exhaust manifolds and remove the crossmember in order to remove the engine rear support from the extension housing.
5. Loosen the extension housing attaching bolts to drain the transmission fluid.
6. Remove the six extension housing attaching bolts and remove the extension housing.
7. To install the extension housing, reverse the above removal instructions. Install a new extension housing gasket. When the

extension housing has been installed and all parts have been secured, lower the car and fill the transmission with the correct amount of fluid. Check for fluid leaks around the extension housing area.

Governor Removal and Installation (C4 Automatic Only)

1. After removing the extension housing according to the instructions above, remove the governor housing-to-governor distributor attaching bolts. Remove the governor housing from the distributor.
2. Refer to the Component Disassembly and Repair section for instructions on repairing the governor assembly.
3. Install the governor housing on the governor distributor and tighten the attaching bolts to the proper torque.
4. Install the extension housing with a new gasket according to the instructions above.
5. When the extension housing has been installed and all bolts have

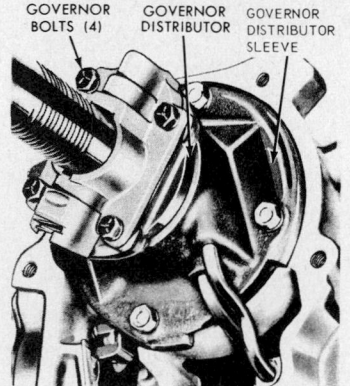

GOVERNOR BOLTS (4) GOVERNOR DISTRIBUTOR GOVERNOR DISTRIBUTOR SLEEVE

Governor assembly installed
(© Ford Motor Co.)

been tightened to the proper torque, lower the car and fill the transmission with fluid to the proper level. Check around the extension housing area for leaks.

Transmission Overhaul Procedures

The following procedures must be performed with the transmission removed from the car. Assembly is often the reverse of the disassembly procedure except for alignment, special tolerances, etc.

Procedures for removing and installing the transmission are given in the Car Section.

During the transmission overhaul operation, ten thrust washers that are installed between the subassemblies of the gear train must be removed and reinstalled correctly. Since it is very important that these thrust washers be installed correctly, they are shown in their positions and they are numbered for further identification. The No. 1 thrust washer is located at the front pump, and the No. 10 thrust washer is located at the parking pawl ring gear.

During all repairs to the transmission subassemblies, the following instructions must be followed:

1. Be sure that no dirt or grease gets in the transmission. All parts must be clean. *Remember—a little dirt can disable a transmission completely if it gets in a fluid passage.*
2. Handle all transmission parts carefully to avoid burring or nicking bearing or mating surfaces.
3. Lubricate all internal parts of the transmission with clean transmission fluid before assembling. *Do not use any other lubricants except on gaskets or thrust washers which may be coated lightly with vaseline to ease assembly.*
4. Always use new gaskets when assembling the parts of the transmission.
5. Tighten all bolts and screws to the recommended torque limits using a torque wrench.

Transmission Disassembly

1. Thoroughly clean the outside of the transmission to prevent dirt or grease from getting inside.
2. Place the transmission in the transmission holder. See illustration.
3. Remove the converter from the transmission front pump and converter housing.
4. Remove the transmission vacuum unit with the tool shown in the illustration. Remove the vacuum unit gasket and the control rod (C4 only).
5. Remove the primary throttle valve from the opening at the rear of the case (C4 only).
6. Remove the transmission pan attaching bolts, oil pan, and gas-

Transmission mounted in holding fixture
(© Ford Motor Co.)

Tool—T57L-500-A
or 6005-M or 6005-MS

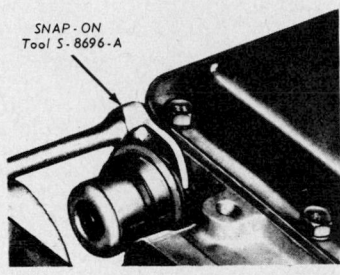

Removing vacuum diaphragm unit
(© Ford Motor Co.)

SNAP-ON
Tool S-8696-A

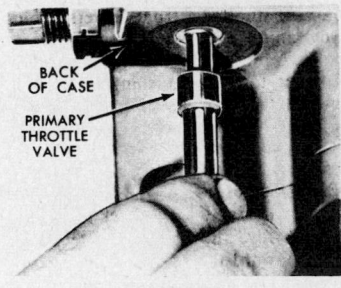

BACK
OF CASE

PRIMARY
THROTTLE
VALVE

Removing or installing primary throttle valve
(© Ford Motor Co.)

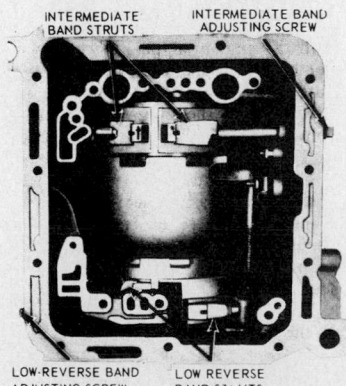

INTERMEDIATE
BAND STRUTS

INTERMEDIATE BAND
ADJUSTING SCREW

LOW-REVERSE BAND
ADJUSTING SCREW

LOW REVERSE
BAND STRUTS

Band adjusting screws and struts
(© Ford Motor Co.)

ket.

7. Remove the control valve body attaching bolts and then lift the control valve body from the case.
8. Loosen the intermediate band adjusting screw and remove the intermediate band struts from the case. Loosen the low-reverse band adjusting screw and remove the low-reverse band struts.

Transmission End-Play Check

1. Remove one of the converter housing attaching bolts and mount a dial indicator support tool in the hole. Mount a dial indicator on the support so that the stem rests on the end of the input shaft. See illustration.

GEAR TRAIN
END PLAY
LIMITS
0.008-0.042
INCH

Tool—4201-C

Checking transmission end-play
(© Ford Motor Co.)

2. Install the extension housing seal replacer tool on the output shaft to provide support and alignment for the shaft.
3. Using a screwdriver, move the input shaft and the gear train to the rear of the case as far as possible. Set the dial indicator at zero while holding a slight pressure on the screwdriver.
4. Remove the screwdriver and insert it behind the input shell. Move the input shell and the front part of the gear train forward.
5. Record the dial reading for later reference during transmission reassembly. The end play reading should be from 0.008 to 0.042 in. If the end play reading is not within this range, selective thrust washers must be used to obtain the proper reading. The selective thrust washers to be used are listed in the table in the rear of this section.
6. Remove the dial indicator, its support bar, and the extension housing seal replacer tool.

Removal of Case and Extension Parts

1. Rotate the transmission in the

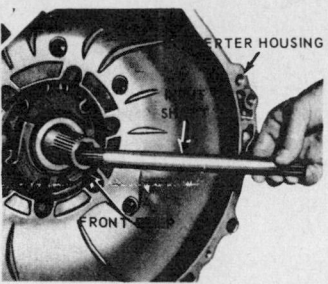

Removing or installing input shaft
(© Ford Motor Co.)

PRY
INPUT SHELL
FORWARD

Removing front pump (© Ford Motor Co.)

holding fixture until it is in a vertical position with the converter housing up.

2. Remove the five converter housing attaching bolts and remove the converter housing from the transmission case.
3. Remove the seven front pump attaching bolts. Remove the front pump by inserting a screwdriver behind the input shell and pushing it forward until the front pump seal is above the edge of the case. Remove the front pump and gasket from the case. If the selective thrust washer No. 1 did not come out with the front pump, lift it from the top of the reverse-high clutch.
4. Remove the intermediate and low-reverse band adjusting screws from the case. Rotate the intermediate band to align the band ends with the clearance hole in the case. Remove the intermediate band from the case.
5. Using a screwdriver between the input shell and the rear planet carrier (see illustration), lift

INTERMEDIATE BAND CLEARANCE
HOLE IN CASE

Position of intermediate band for removal or installation
(© Ford Motor Co.)

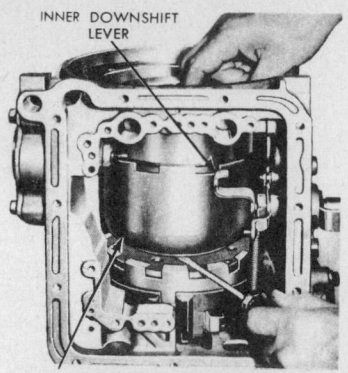

Lifting input shell and gear train
(© Ford Motor Co.)

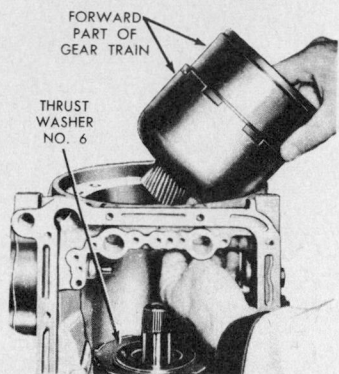

Removing or installing forward part of gear train
(© Ford Motor Co.)

Holding Fixture Tool - 77530-A

Forward part of gear train positioned in holding fixture
(© Ford Motor Co.)

the input shell upward and remove the forward part of the gear train as an assembly.

6. Place the forward part of the gear train in the holding fixture shown.

7. With the gear train in the holding fixture, remove the reverse-high clutch and drum from the forward clutch. If thrust washer No. 2 did not come out with the front pump, remove the thrust washer from the forward clutch cylinder. If a selective spacer was used, remove the spacer. Remove the forward clutch from the forward clutch hub and ring gear.

8. If the thrust washer No. 3 did not come out with the forward clutch, remove the thrust washer from the forward clutch hub and lift the forward clutch hub and ring gear from the front planet carrier.

9. Remove thrust washer No. 4 and the front planet carrier from the input shell.

10. Remove the input shell, sun gear and thrust washer No. 5 from the holding fixture.

11. From inside the transmission case, remove thrust washer No. 6 from the top of the reverse planet carrier. Remove the reverse planet carrier and thrust washer No. 7 from the reverse ring gear and hub.

12. Move the output shaft forward and, with the tool shown in the illustration, remove the reverse ring gear hub-to-output shaft retaining ring. Remove the reverse ring gear and hub from the output shaft. Remove the thrust washer No. 8 from the low and reverse drum.

13. Remove the low-reverse band from the case. Remove the low-reverse drum from the one-way clutch inner race. Remove the one-way clutch inner race by rotating the race clockwise as it is removed.

14. Remove the 12 one-way clutch rollers, springs and the spring retainer from the outer race. *Do not lose or damage any of the 12 springs or rollers. The outer*

Removing or installing reverse ring gear hub retaining ring
(© Ford Motor Co.)

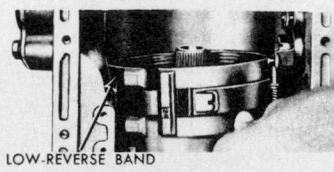

Removing or installing low-reverse band
(© Ford Motor Co.)

Removing or installing output shaft and governor distributor
(© Ford Motor Co.)

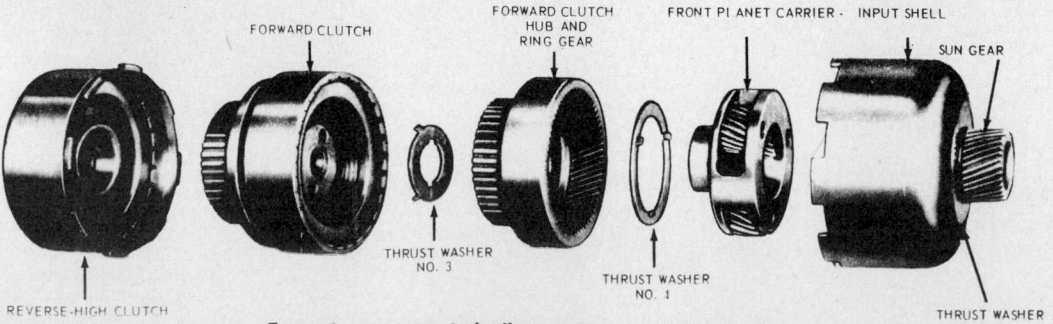

Forward part of gear train disassembled (© Ford Motor Co.)

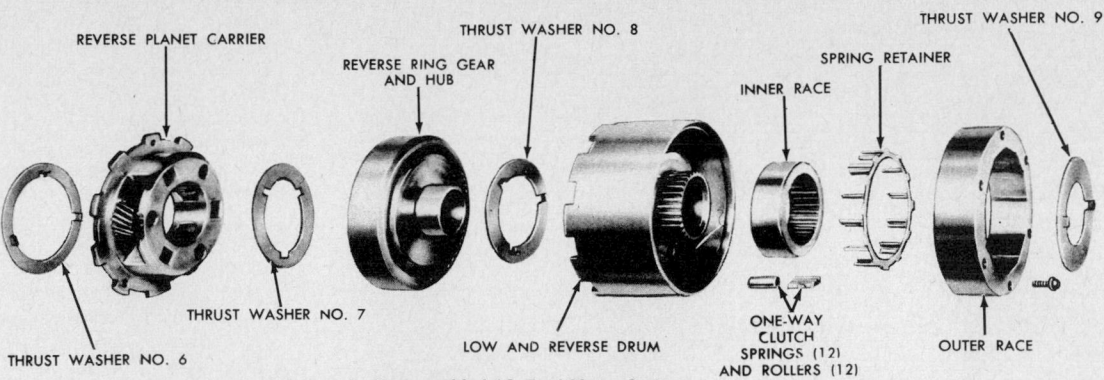

Lower part of gear train disassembled (© Ford Motor Co.)

race of the one-way clutch cannot be removed from the case until the extension housing, output shaft and governor distributor sleeve are removed.

15. Remove the transmission from the holding fixture. Place the transmission on the bench in a vertical position with the extension housing up. Remove the four extension housing attaching bolts, the extension housing, and the gasket from the case.

16. Pull outward on the output shaft and remove the output shaft and governor distributor assembly (if so equipped) from the governor distributor sleeve.

17. Remove the governor distributor lock ring from the output shaft. Remove the governor distributor from the output shaft (C4 only).

18. Remove the four distributor sleeve attaching bolts and the distributor sleeve from the case. *Do not bend or distort the fluid tubes as the tubes are removed from the case with the distributor sleeve.*

19. Remove the parking pawl return spring, pawl, and pawl retaining pin from the case.

20. Remove the parking gear and thrust washer No. 10 from the case.

21. Remove the six one-way clutch

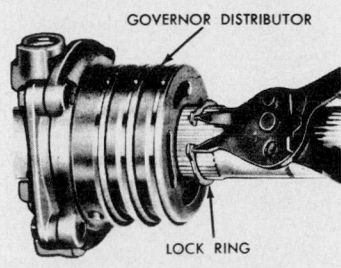

Removing or installing governor distributor snap-ring (© Ford Motor Co.)

outer race attaching bolts with the tool shown. As the bolts are removed, hold the outer race that is located inside the case in position. Then, remove the outer race and thrust washer No. 9 from the case.

Component Disassembly and Assembly

Downshift and Manual Linkage

1. Loosen the outer downshift lever nut with penetrating oil. Remove the nut and the inner and outer downshift levers.
   From inside the case, remove the upper retaining ring and the flat washer from the manual lever link. Remove the upper end of the lever link from the case retain-

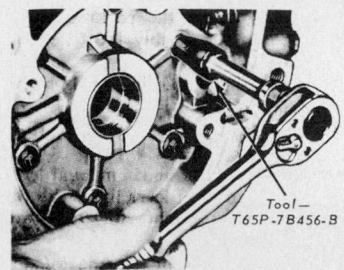

Tool—T65P-7B456-B

Removing one-way clutch outer race attaching bolts (© Ford Motor Co.)

ing pin.

2. From the back of the transmission case, remove the upper retaining ring and flat washer from the parking pawl link. Remove the pawl link and spacer from the case retaining pin.

3. From the back of the transmission case, remove the parking pawl link, toggle rod, and the manual lever link as an assembly.

4. Remove the inner manual lever retaining nut and lever. Remove the outer manual lever from the case. Remove manual lever seal, and drive a new seal into the case with an appropriate driver.

5. Install outer manual lever into the case. Install inner manual lever and retaining nut. Torque nut to specifications.

6. From back of the transmission case, install parking toggle rod and link into the case. Install parking pawl link spacer onto the case retaining pin. Dimpled side of the spacer should be facing the link.

7. Install the parking pawl link onto the case retaining pin. Install flat washer and retaining ring.

8. Position inner manual lever behind the manual lever link, with the cam on the lever contacting the lower link pin.

9. Install the upper end of the manual lever link onto the case retaining pin. Install flat washer and retaining ring.

10. Operate the manual lever and check for correct linkage operation.

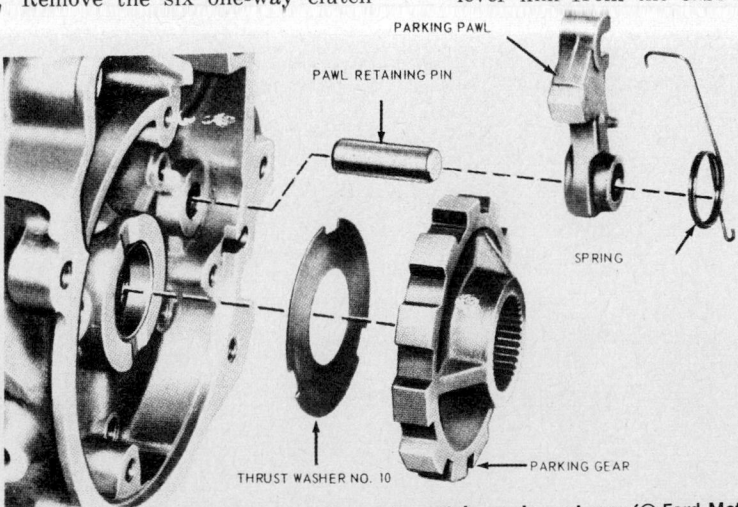

Parking pawl, return spring, retaining pin, and gear (© Ford Motor Co.)

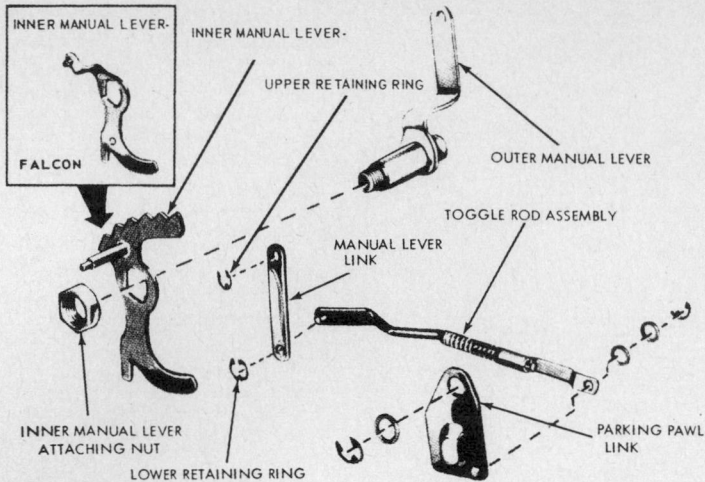

Transmission case internal linkage (© Ford Motor Co.)

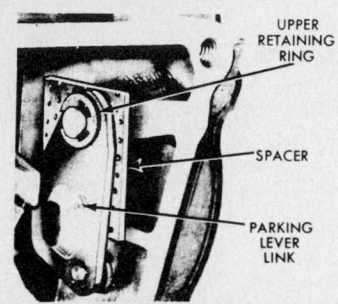

Parking pawl link (© Ford Motor Co.)

Control Valve Body Disassembly and Assembly

1970-72 C4 Automatic (Except 1970 Falcon)

1. Remove the screws attaching the oil screen to the valve body and remove the oil screen. Be careful not to lose the throttle pressure limit valve and spring when separating the oil screen from the valve body.
2. Remove the attaching screws from the lower valve body and separate the upper and lower valve bodies, the gasket, separator plate and the hold-down plate. Be careful not to lose the upper valve body shuttle valve and check valve when separating the upper and lower valve bodies.
3. Slide the manual valve out of the body.
4. Pry the low servo modulator valve retainer from the body and remove the retainer plug, spring, and valve from the valve body. Pry the retainer, spring, and the downshift valve from the same bore (see illustration).
5. Depress the throttle booster plug and remove the retaining pin. Then, remove the plug, valve, and spring from the valve body.
6. Remove the cover over the cut-back valve and the transition valve from the valve body.
7. Remove the cut-back valve and the transition valve spring, transition valve, 2-3 back-out valve, and spring from the valve body.
8. Remove the cover from over the 1-2 shift valve and the 2-3 shift valve. Remove the 2-3 shift valve, spring, and the throttle modulator valve from the valve body. Remove the 1-2 shift valve, D-2 valve, and spring from the valve body.
9. Remove the retaining pin from the retainer after depressing the intermediate servo accumulator valve. Remove the retainer, intermediate servo accumulator valve, and spring from the valve body
10. Depress the main oil pressure booster valve and remove the retaining pin. Remove the main oil pressure booster valve, sleeve, springs, retainer, and main oil pressure regulator valve from the valve body.
11. Remove the line coasting boost valve retaining clip, the spring, and line coasting boost valve from the valve body.

Assembly procedures are the reverse of the disassembly procedures given above. The shuttle valves should be installed in the lower valve body and the separator plate fastened securely before proceeding with the upper valve body. All valves should move freely in the bores and any burrs or scoring should be carefully removed with crocus cloth. Tighten all screws to the proper torque.

1965-69 All Models, 1970 Falcon C4 Automatic

NOTE: basic rebuilding procedures for the above valve bodies are identical; however, minor differences exist in the valve body from year to year. Consult illustrations to determine the specific configuration for each model year.

1. Remove the screws attaching the oil screen to the lower valve body and remove the oil screen.
2. Remove the attaching screws from the bottom of the lower valve body and separate the valve body, gasket, separator plate, and hold-down plate from the upper valve body. Be careful not to lose the upper valve body rubber ball shuttle valve and spring when separating the upper and lower valve bodies.
3. Depress the manual valve detent spring and remove the retaining pin. Then, remove the spring and manual valve detent plug from the valve body (see illustration).
4. Slide the manual valve from the valve body.
5. Remove the retainer clip, spring, and the downshift valve from the valve body.
6. Remove the stop pin after depressing the throttle booster valve and plug. Then, remove the plug, throttle booster valve, and spring from the valve body.
7. Remove the cover over the cut-back valve and the 2-3 back-out and manual low valves. Remove the cut-back valve and the 2-3 back-out valve, spring, and the manual low valve from the valve body.
8. Remove the cover over the 2-3

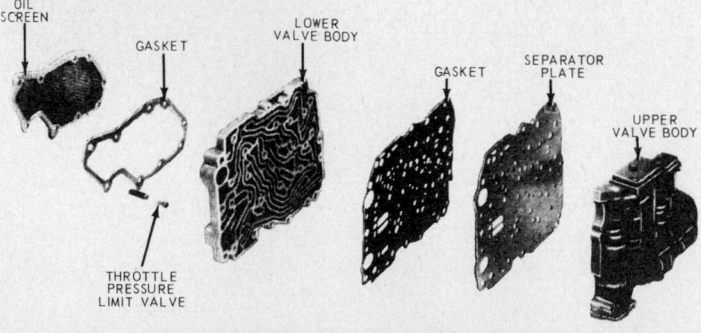

Upper and lower control valve bodies disassembled—
1970-2 C4 transmissions except Falcon
(© Ford Motor Co.)

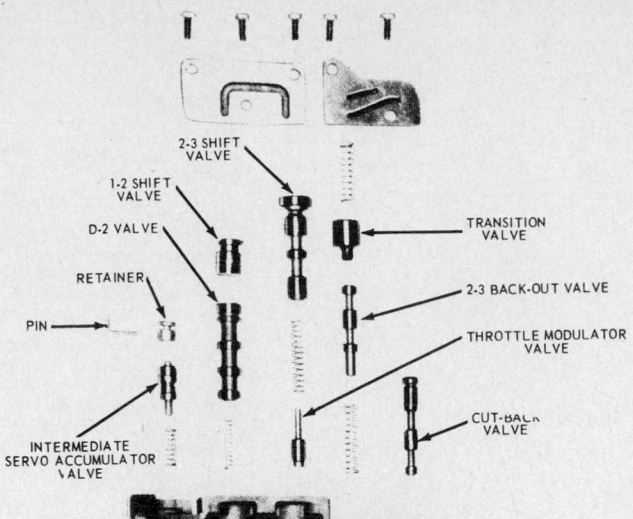

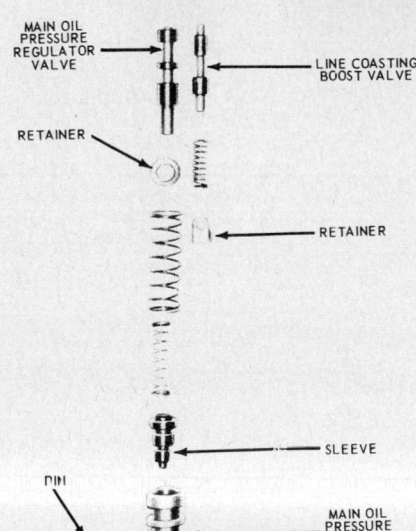

coasting boost valve and spring from the valve body.

Assembly procedures are the reverse of the disassembly procedures given above. The rubber ball shuttle valve should be placed in the lower valve body as shown and the separator plate, hold-down plates, and attaching screws installed on the lower valve body (see illustrations). All valves should move freely in their bores and any burrs or scoring should be removed with crocus cloth. Tighten all attaching screws to the proper torque.

1970 C4S Semi-Automatic

1. Remove the attaching screws from the oil screen on the lower valve body and remove the oil

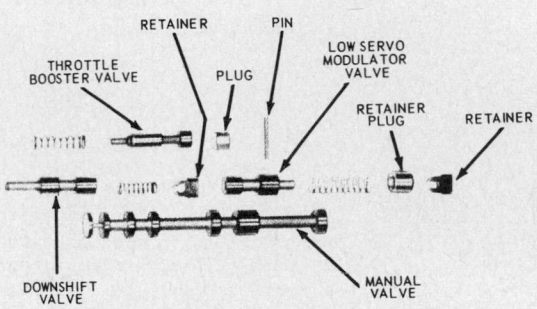

Upper control valve body disassembled—1970-72 C4 transmissions except 1970 Falcon (© Ford Motor Co.)

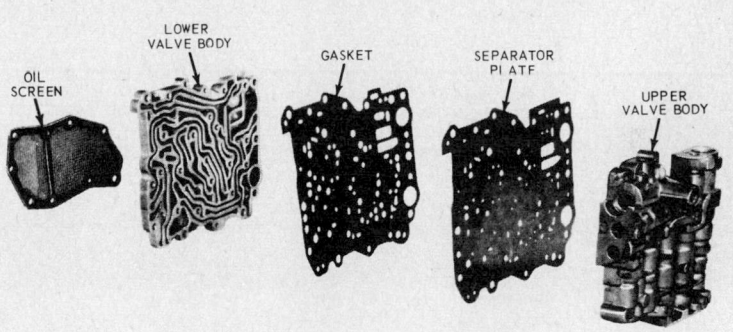

Upper and lower control valve bodies disassembled—1970 Falcon C4 transmissions (© Ford Motor Co.)

shift valve, throttle modulator valve, 1-2 shift valve, and the D2 valve and remove these valves and their springs from the valve body.

9. Remove the cover over the 3-2 control valve and the accumulator valve. Remove the sleeve, 3-2 control valve, and the accumulator valve from the valve body.

10. Remove the cover over the control pressure booster valve and sleeve and the line coasting boost valve. Remove the control pressure booster valve and sleeve, springs, and main regulator valve. Also, remove the line

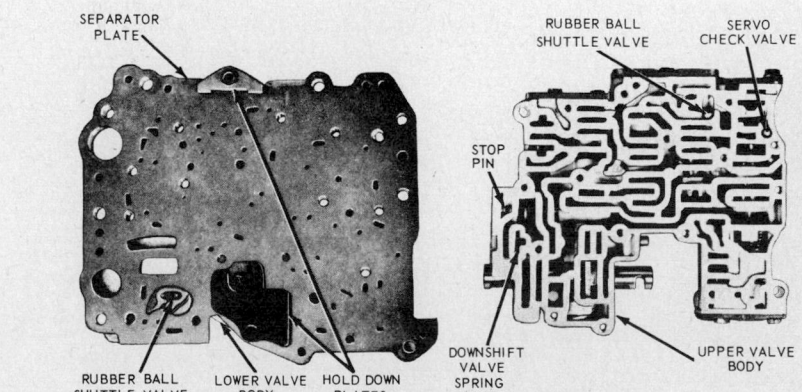

Separating upper and lower control valve bodies— all 1970 Falcon transmissions (© Ford Motor Co.)

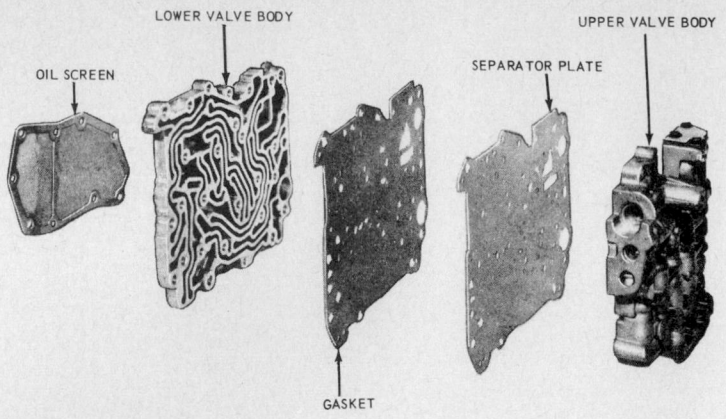

Upper and lower control valve bodies disassembled—1966 C4 automatic
(© Ford Motor Co.)

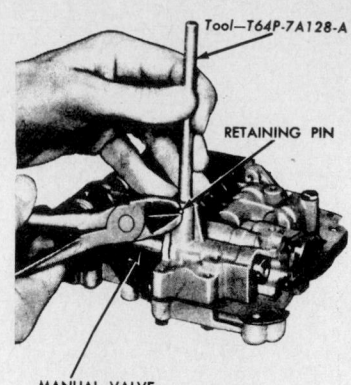

Removing manual valve—
1970 Falcon C4 transmissions
(© Ford Motor Co.)

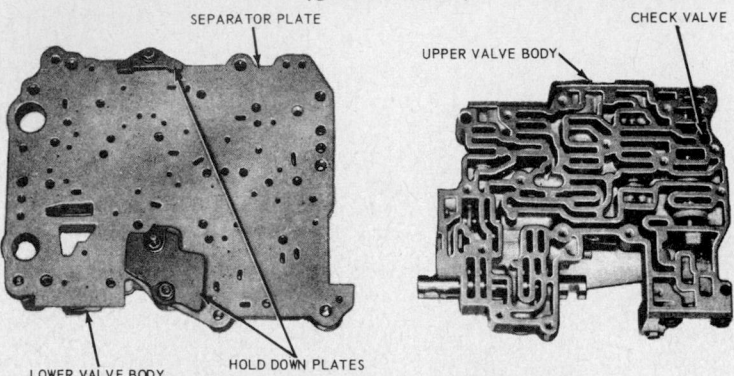

Separating upper and lower control valve bodies—
1965 and 1966 C4 automatic
(© Ford Motor Co.)

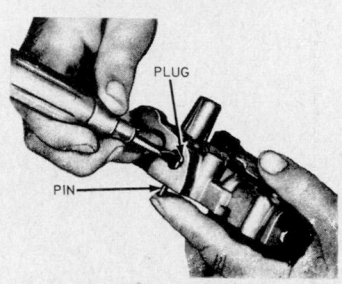

Removing or installing throttle booster valve
—1970 Falcon C4 transmission
(© Ford Motor Co.)

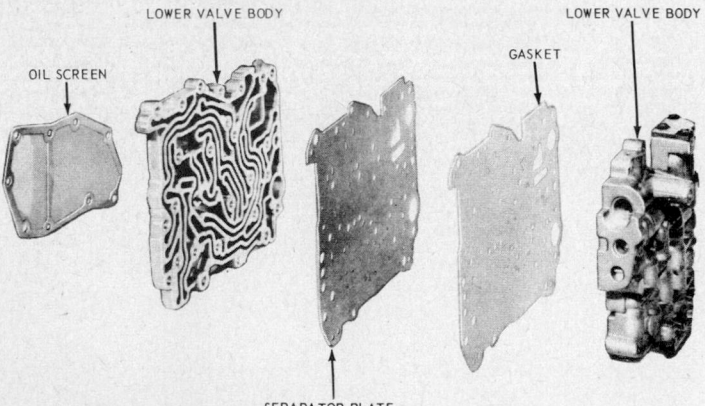

Upper and lower control valve bodies disassembled—1965 C4 automatic
(© Ford Motor Co.)

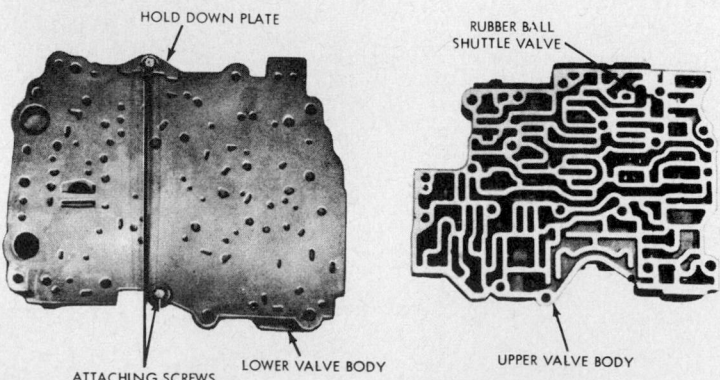

Separating upper and lower control valve bodies—
1970 C4S semi-automatic transmission
(© Ford Motor Co.)

screen.

2. Remove the attaching screws from the underside of the lower valve body and the two attaching screws from the top side of the upper valve body and separate the valve bodies. Be careful not to lose the rubber ball shuttle valve when separating the upper and lower valve bodies.

3. Slide the manual valve from the valve body. Remove the retainer clip, plug, spring, low servo modulator valve, and plug from the valve body.

4. Remove the cover over the cutback, 1-2 transition, and 2-3 back-out valves. Remove the cutback valve and the 1-2 transition and the 2-3 back-out valves and the spring from the valve body.

5. Remove the cover plate from over the 2-3 shift valve, throttle pressure modulator valve, 1-2 shift valve, and drive 2 valve. Remove the 2-3 shift valve, spring, and the throttle pressure modulator valve. Then, remove the 1-2 shift valve, Drive 2 valve, and spring from the valve body.

6. Depress the main oil pressure booster valve inward and remove the retaining pin. Then, remove the main oil pressure booster valve, sleeve, spring, retainer, and main oil pressure regulator valve from the valve body.

Assembly procedures are the reverse of the disassembly procedures

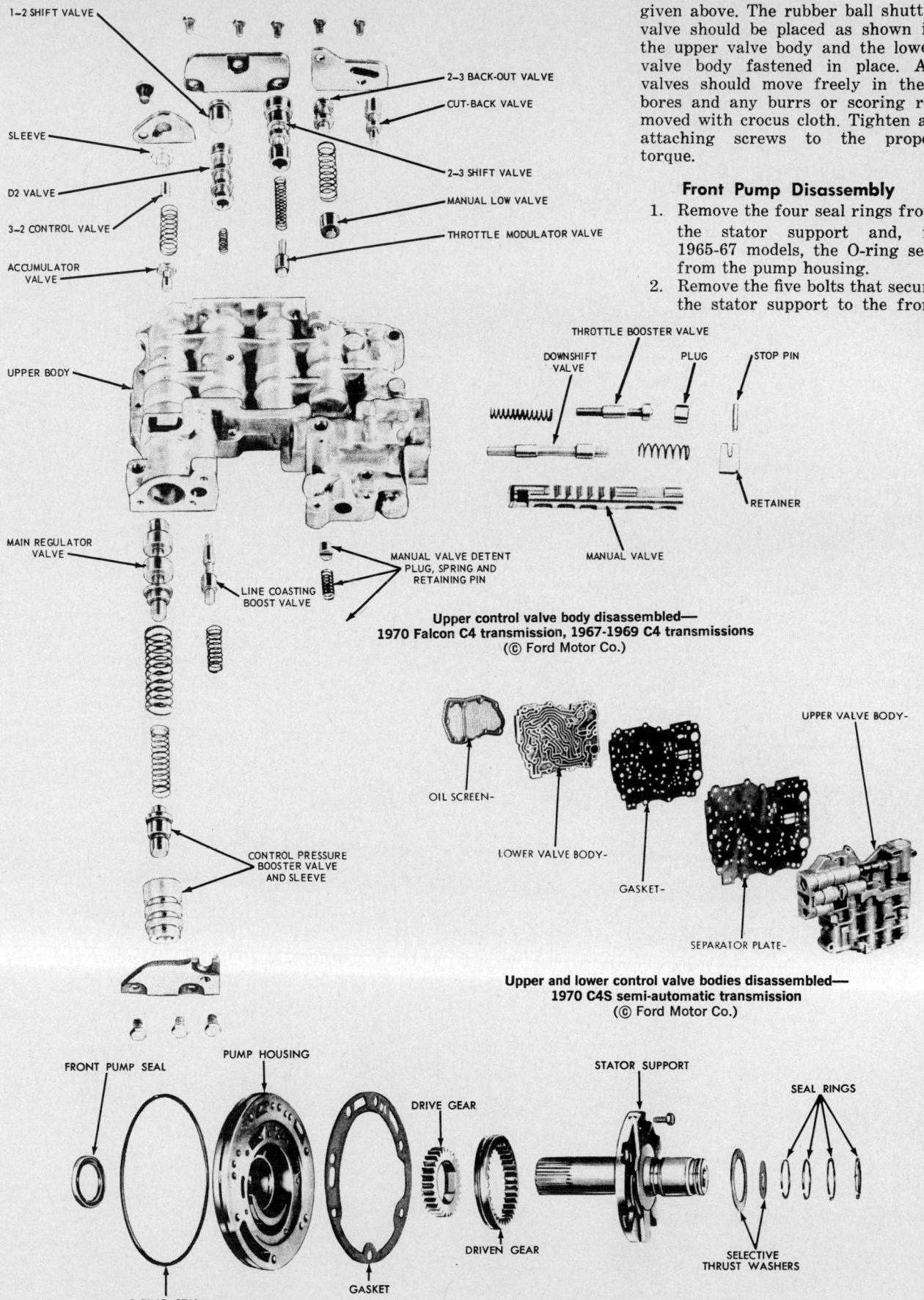

given above. The rubber ball shuttle valve should be placed as shown in the upper valve body and the lower valve body fastened in place. All valves should move freely in their bores and any burrs or scoring removed with crocus cloth. Tighten all attaching screws to the proper torque.

Front Pump Disassembly

1. Remove the four seal rings from the stator support and, in 1965-67 models, the O-ring seal from the pump housing.
2. Remove the five bolts that secure the stator support to the front

1-2 SHIFT VALVE

2-3 BACK-OUT VALVE

CUT-BACK VALVE

SLEEVE

D2 VALVE

2-3 SHIFT VALVE

MANUAL LOW VALVE

3-2 CONTROL VALVE

THROTTLE MODULATOR VALVE

ACCUMULATOR VALVE

UPPER BODY

THROTTLE BOOSTER VALVE

DOWNSHIFT VALVE

PLUG

STOP PIN

RETAINER

MAIN REGULATOR VALVE

MANUAL VALVE

MANUAL VALVE DETENT PLUG, SPRING AND RETAINING PIN

LINE COASTING BOOST VALVE

Upper control valve body disassembled—1970 Falcon C4 transmission, 1967-1969 C4 transmissions
(© Ford Motor Co.)

CONTROL PRESSURE BOOSTER VALVE AND SLEEVE

OIL SCREEN-

UPPER VALVE BODY-

LOWER VALVE BODY-

GASKET-

SEPARATOR PLATE-

Upper and lower control valve bodies disassembled—1970 C4S semi-automatic transmission
(© Ford Motor Co.)

FRONT PUMP SEAL

PUMP HOUSING

DRIVE GEAR

STATOR SUPPORT

SEAL RINGS

O-RING SEAL

GASKET

DRIVEN GEAR

SELECTIVE THRUST WASHERS

Front pump and stator support disassembled—1965-67 C4 automatic (© Ford Motor Co.)

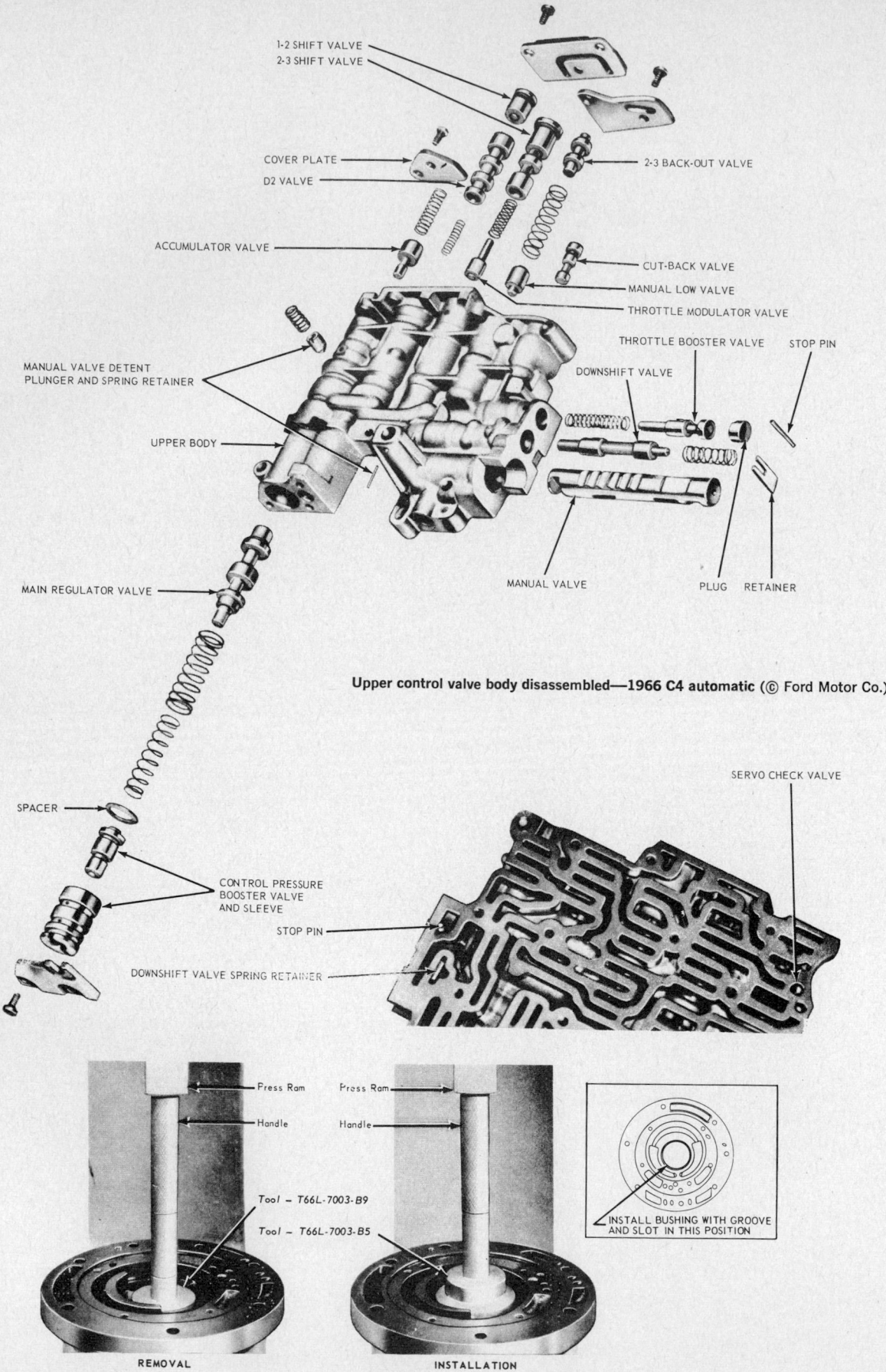

1-2 SHIFT VALVE
2-3 SHIFT VALVE
2-3 BACK-OUT VALVE
COVER PLATE
D2 VALVE
CUT-BACK VALVE
MANUAL LOW VALVE
THROTTLE MODULATOR VALVE
ACCUMULATOR VALVE
THROTTLE BOOSTER VALVE
STOP PIN
MANUAL VALVE DETENT PLUNGER AND SPRING RETAINER
DOWNSHIFT VALVE
UPPER BODY
MAIN REGULATOR VALVE
MANUAL VALVE
PLUG   RETAINER

Upper control valve body disassembled—1966 C4 automatic (© Ford Motor Co.)

SERVO CHECK VALVE
SPACER
CONTROL PRESSURE BOOSTER VALVE AND SLEEVE
STOP PIN
DOWNSHIFT VALVE SPRING RETAINER

Press Ram
Handle
Press Ram
Handle
Tool – T66L-7003-B9
Tool – T66L-7003-B5
INSTALL BUSHING WITH GROOVE AND SLOT IN THIS POSITION
REMOVAL
INSTALLATION

Replacing front pump housing bushing (© Ford Motor Co.)

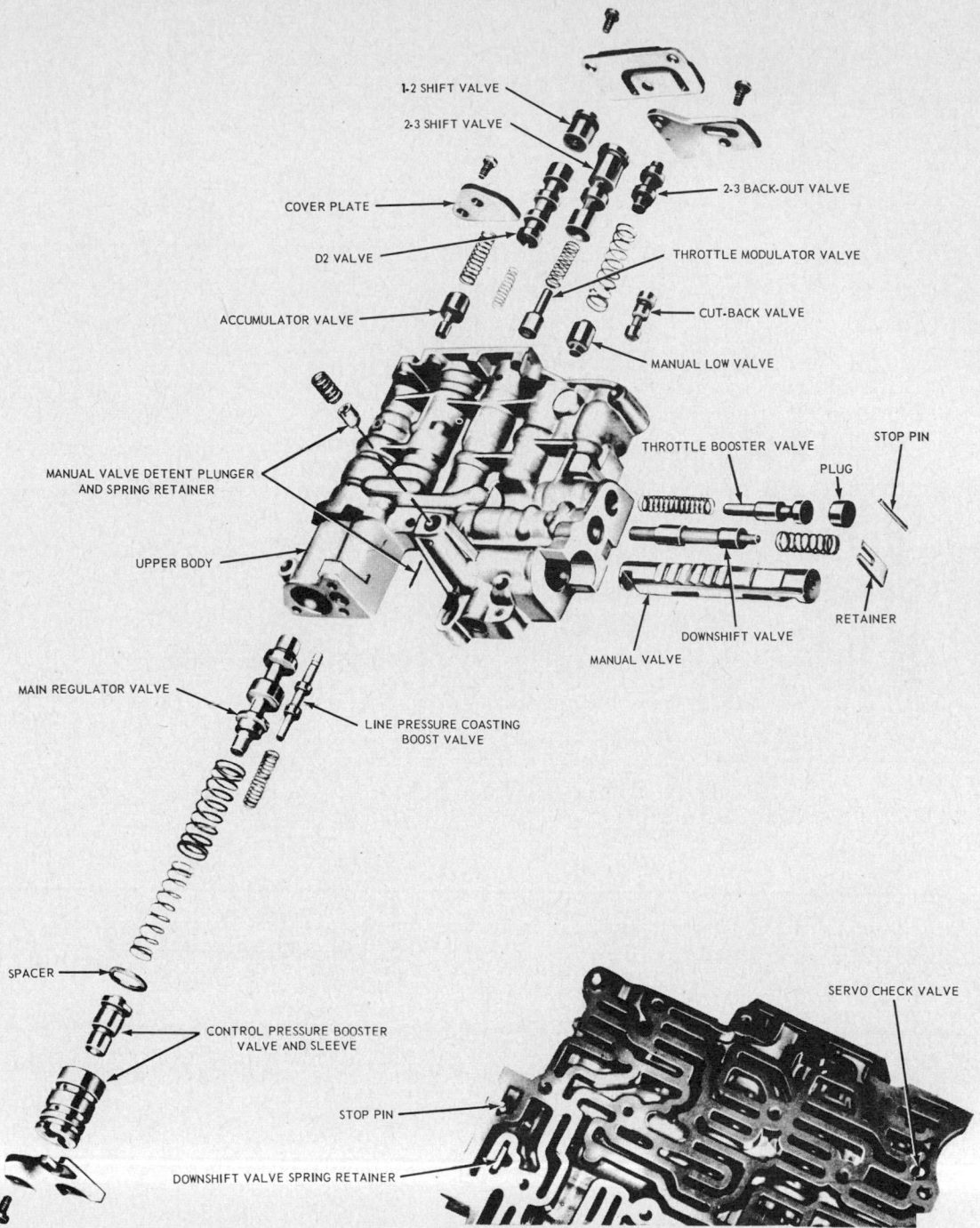

1-2 SHIFT VALVE

2-3 SHIFT VALVE

2-3 BACK-OUT VALVE

COVER PLATE

THROTTLE MODULATOR VALVE

D2 VALVE

CUT-BACK VALVE

ACCUMULATOR VALVE

MANUAL LOW VALVE

MANUAL VALVE DETENT PLUNGER AND SPRING RETAINER

THROTTLE BOOSTER VALVE

STOP PIN

PLUG

UPPER BODY

RETAINER

DOWNSHIFT VALVE

MANUAL VALVE

MAIN REGULATOR VALVE

LINE PRESSURE COASTING BOOST VALVE

SPACER

SERVO CHECK VALVE

CONTROL PRESSURE BOOSTER VALVE AND SLEEVE

STOP PIN

DOWNSHIFT VALVE SPRING RETAINER

Upper control valve body disassembled—1965 C4 automatic (© Ford Motor Co.)

pump housing. Remove stator support from pump housing.

3. Replace the stator bushings if they are worn or damaged. Use a cape chisel to cut the bushing through. Then, pry up the loose ends of the bushing with an awl and remove the bushing. Press a new bushing into the stator support.

NOTE: ensure that the oil hole in the bushing lines up with the hole in the stator support.

4. Remove drive and driven gears from the front pump housing.

5. Replace the bushing in the pump housing with the tools shown, making sure the slot and groove are toward the rear of the body and 60° below the centerline.

6. Install the drive and driven gears in the pump housing. The chamfered side of each gear has an identification mark that must be positioned downward, against the face of the pump housing.

7. Place stator support in pump housing. Install and torque the five retaining bolts.

8. Install four seal rings onto the

stator support. The two large oil rings are assembled first, in the oil ring grooves toward the front of the stator support. Install the O-ring seal onto the pump housing.

9. Check pump gears for free rotation by placing pump on the converter drive hub and turning pump housing.

10. If the front pump seal must be replaced, mount the pump in the transmission case and remove the seal with a seal removing tool.

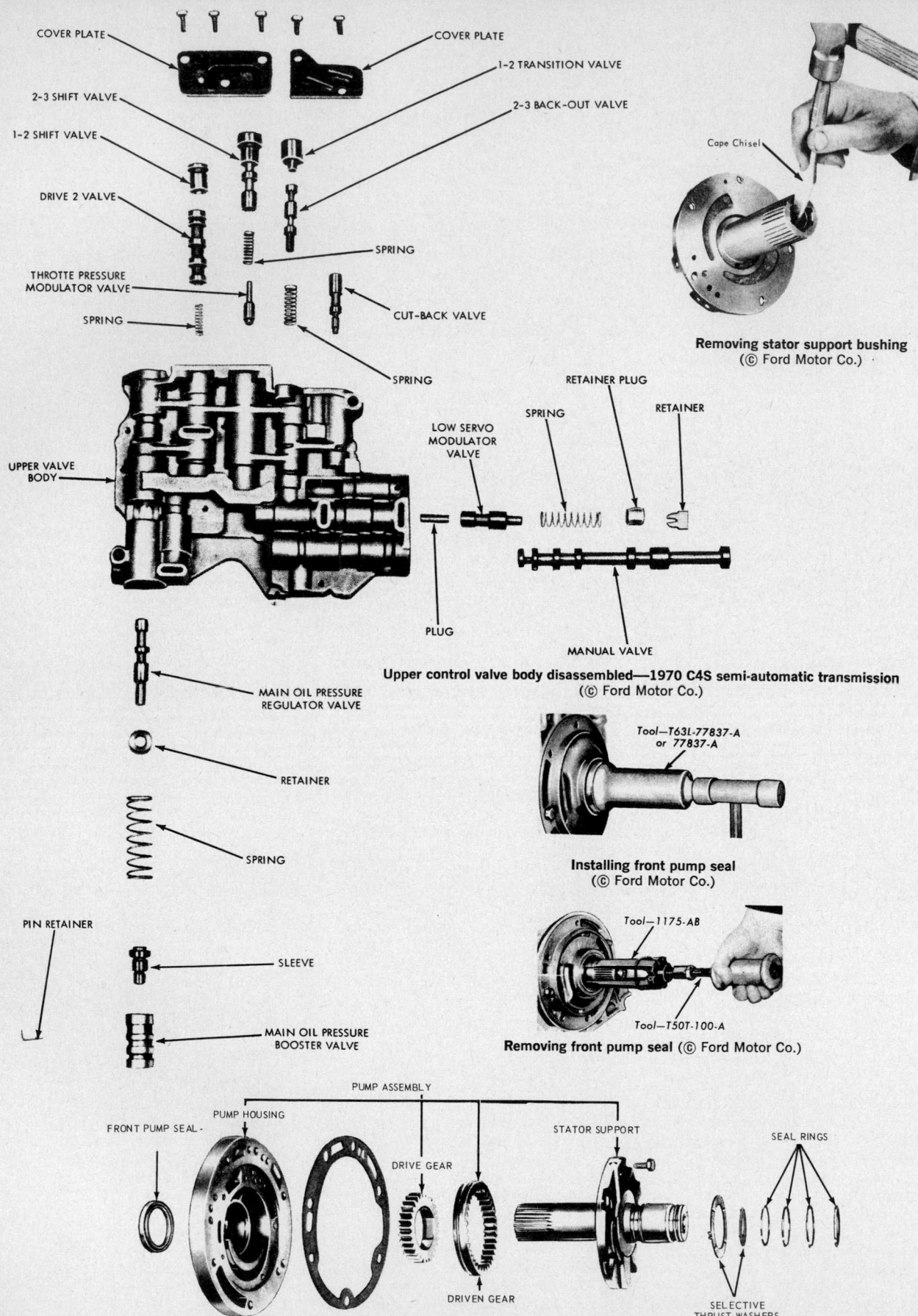

COVER PLATE

COVER PLATE

1-2 TRANSITION VALVE

2-3 SHIFT VALVE

2-3 BACK-OUT VALVE

1-2 SHIFT VALVE

DRIVE 2 VALVE

SPRING

Cape Chisel

THROTTE PRESSURE
MODULATOR VALVE

SPRING

CUT-BACK VALVE

SPRING

Removing stator support bushing
(© Ford Motor Co.)

UPPER VALVE
BODY

LOW SERVO
MODULATOR
VALVE

RETAINER PLUG

SPRING

RETAINER

PLUG

MANUAL VALVE

Upper control valve body disassembled—1970 C4S semi-automatic transmission
(© Ford Motor Co.)

MAIN OIL PRESSURE
REGULATOR VALVE

RETAINER

Tool—T63L-77837-A
or 77837-A

SPRING

Installing front pump seal
(© Ford Motor Co.)

PIN RETAINER

SLEEVE

Tool—1175-AB

MAIN OIL PRESSURE
BOOSTER VALVE

Tool—T50T-100-A

Removing front pump seal (© Ford Motor Co.)

PUMP ASSEMBLY

PUMP HOUSING

FRONT PUMP SEAL

STATOR SUPPORT

SEAL RINGS

DRIVE GEAR

DRIVEN GEAR

SELECTIVE
THRUST WASHERS

Front pump and stator support disassembled—1968-72 C4 automatic (© Ford Motor Co.)

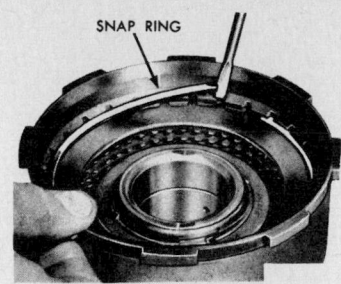

**Removing or installing
reverse-high clutch pressure plate snap-ring**
(© Ford Motor Co.)

Removing reverse-high clutch piston
(© Ford Motor Co.)

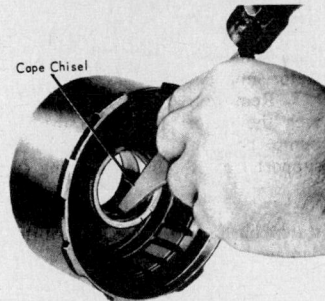

Removing reverse-high clutch bushing
(© Ford Motor Co.)

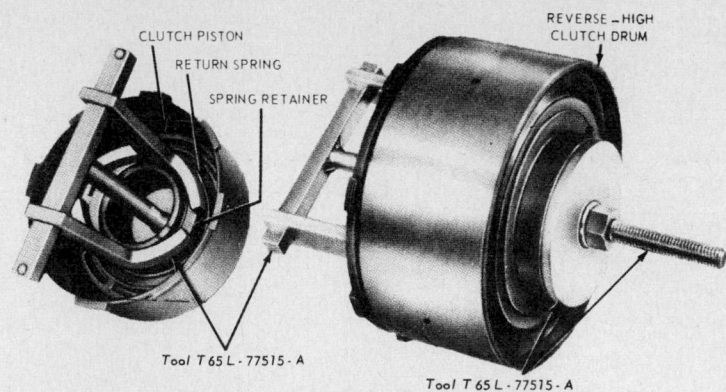

Removing or installing reverse-high clutch piston spring retainer—1970-72 C4 automatic
(© Ford Motor Co.)

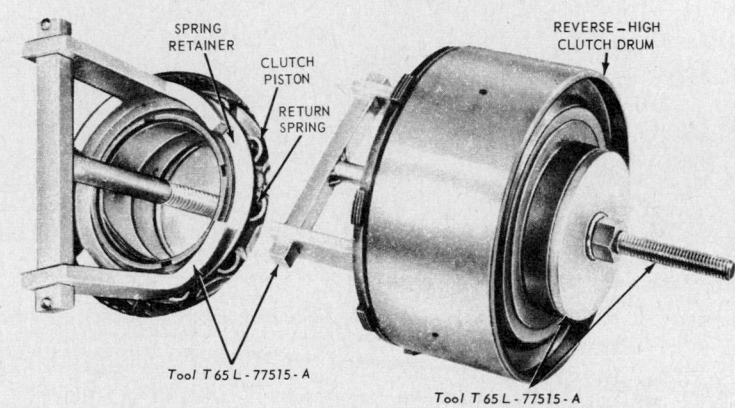

**Removing or installing reverse-high clutch piston spring snap-ring—
1965-69 C4 automatic** (© Ford Motor Co.)

Reverse-High Clutch Disassembly and Assembly

1. Remove pressure plate retaining snap-ring.
2. Remove the pressure plate, and the drive and driven clutch plates.

Caution Use no detergent or other cleaning solution on the lined clutch plates. Wipe the plates with a lint-free cloth.

3. Remove piston spring retainer by applying pressure to the clutch hub. Compress piston return springs, and remove the retainer.
4. Remove the ten piston return springs.
5. Remove the piston by applying air pressure to the piston apply hole of the clutch hub.
6. Remove piston outer seal from the piston and the piston inner seal from the clutch drum.
7. Remove the drum bushing if it is worn or damaged. Use a cape chisel to cut the bushing seam until it is broken. Pry up the loose ends of the bushing with an awl and remove the bushing. *To prevent leakage at the stator*

support O-rings, do not nick or damage the hub surface with the chisel.

8. Position the drum and a new bushing in a press and install the bushing with the tool shown.
9. Install a new inner seal into the clutch drum and a new outer seal onto the clutch piston. Lubricate and install the piston into the clutch drum.
10. Locate the ten piston return springs on the piston. Place retainer on top of the springs. Compress the assembly with a press, and install the retainer snap-ring.
11. Soak new composition plates in transmission fluid before installation. Install clutch plates, alternately, starting with a steel plate. The last plate installed is the pressure plate with the internally-chamfered side up.
12. Install the pressure plate retaining snap-ring.
13. Using feeler gauges, check the clearance between the pressure plate and the snap-ring while applying pressure to the plate. If clearance is not within specifica-

tions, selective thickness snap-rings are available.

Forward Clutch Disassembly and Assembly

1. Remove the clutch pressure plate retaining snap ring.
2. Remove the pressure plate, drive and driven plates from the hub.
3. Remove the disc spring retaining snap-ring.
4. Apply air pressure to the clutch

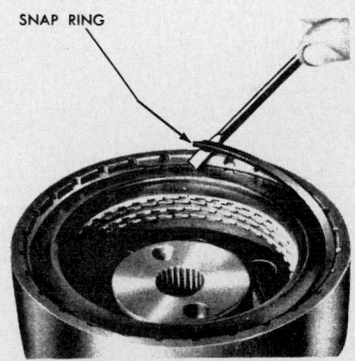

**Removing or installing
forward clutch pressure plate snap ring**
(© Ford Motor Co.)

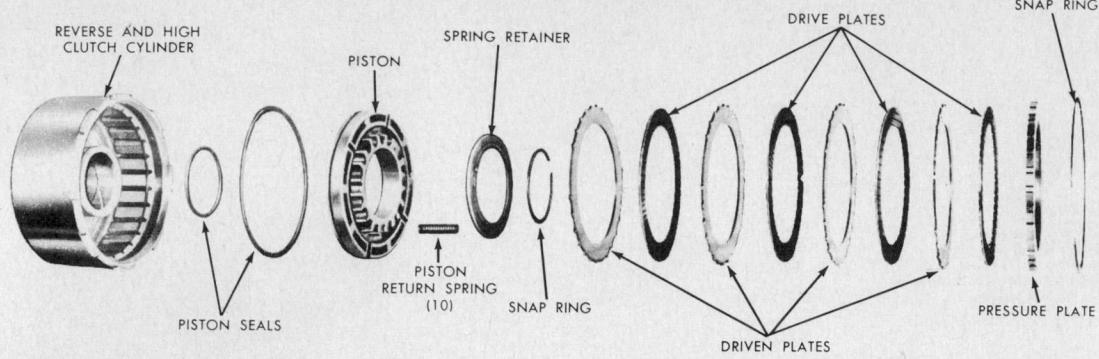

Reverse-high clutch disassembled—1965-69 C4 automatic (© Ford Motor Co.)

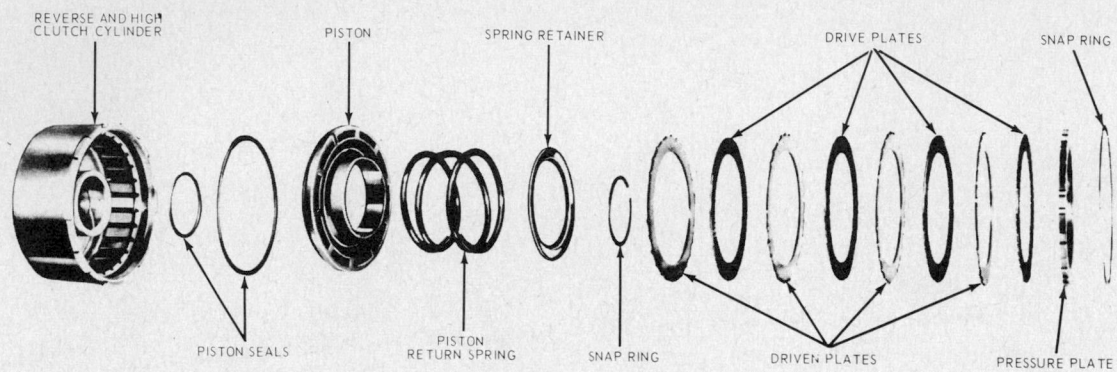

Reverse-high clutch disassembled—1970-72 C4 automatic (© Ford Motor Co.)

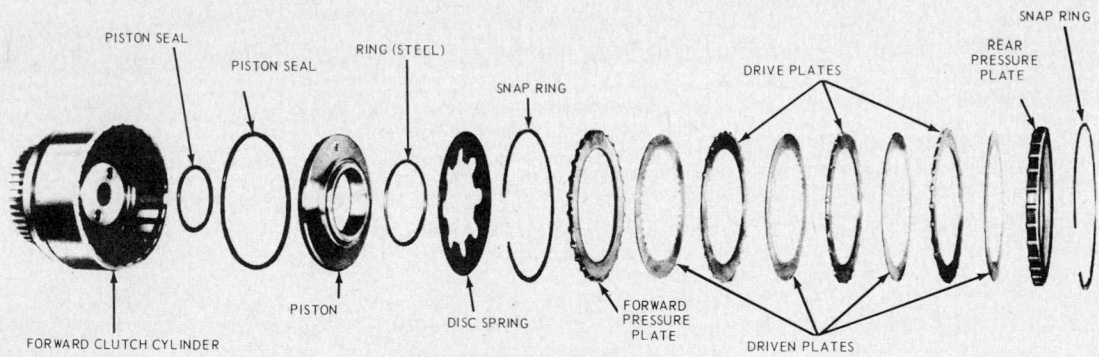

Forward clutch disassembled (© Ford Motor Co.)

piston pressure hole to remove the piston from the hub.

5. Remove piston outer seal and the inner seal from the clutch hub.

6. Install new piston seals onto the clutch piston and drum.

7. Lubricate and insert the piston into the clutch hub. Install the disc spring and retaining snapring.

8. Install the lower pressure plate, with the flat side up and the radiused side downward. Install one composition clutch plate and alternately install the drive and driven plates. Install the pressure plate with the internally chamfered side up.

9. Install pressure plate retaining snap-ring.

10. With a feeler gauge, check clearance between the snap ring and the pressure plate. Downward pressure on the plate should be used when making this check. If clearance is not within specifications, selective snap-rings are available.

Forward Clutch Hub and Ring Gear Disassembly and Assembly

1. Remove forward clutch hub retaining snap-ring.

2. Separate clutch hub from ring gear.

3. Press the bushing from the clutch hub.

4. Install a new bushing into the clutch hub as shown.

5. Install clutch hub into ring gear.

6. Install hub retaining snap-ring.

Input Shell and Sun Gear Disassembly and Assembly

1. Remove external snap-ring from sun gear.

2. Remove thrust washer No. 5 from input shell and sun gear.

3. From inside the shell, remove the sun gear. Remove internal snapring from sun gear.

4. If the sun gear bushings are to be replaced, use the tool shown in the illustration and press both bushings through the gear.

5. Press a new bushing into each end of the sun gear.

6. Install internal snap-ring onto sun gear. Install sun gear into the input shell.

7. Install thrust washer No. 5 onto sun gear and input shell.

8. Install external snap-ring onto sun gear.

Reverse Ring Gear and Hub Disassembly and Assembly

1. Remove hub retaining snap-ring

REMOVAL

INSTALLATION

Replacing forward clutch hub bushing
(© Ford Motor Co.)

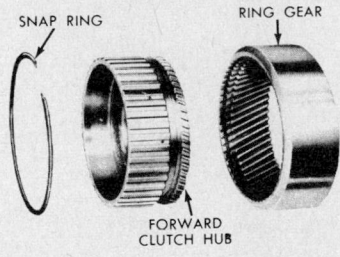

Forward clutch hub and ring gear disassembled
(© Ford Motor Co.)

from reverse ring gear.
2. Remove the hub from reverse ring gear.
3. Install hub into reverse ring gear.
4. Install snap-ring into reverse ring gear.

Governor and Oil Distributor Disassembly (C4 Automatic Only)

1. Remove the oil rings from the governor oil distributor.
2. Remove the governor housing attaching bolts and remove the governor assembly from the distributor. Remove the governor oil screen.
3. Remove the primary governor valve retaining ring. Remove the washer, spring, and primary governor valve from the housing.
4. Remove the secondary governor

valve retaining clip, spring, and governor valve from the housing.
5. After cleaning and inspecting all governor parts, install the secondary governor valve in its housing. Install the spring and spring retaining clip with its small concave area facing downward.
6. Install the primary governor valve in the housing. Install the spring, washer, and retaining clip. Be sure the washer is centered in the housing on the spring and the retaining ring is fully seated in the ring groove in the housing.
7. Install the oil rings on the governor distributor. Install the governor oil screen and mount the governor assembly on the distributor, tightening the attaching bolts to the proper torque.

Transmission Assembly

1. Install thrust washer No. 9 inside the transmission case.
2. Place the one-way clutch outer race inside the case. From the rear of the case, install the six outer race-to-case retaining bolts. Torque to specifications.

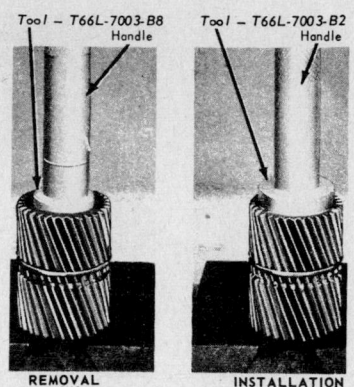

REMOVAL   INSTALLATION

Replacing sun gear bushing
(© Ford Motor Co.)

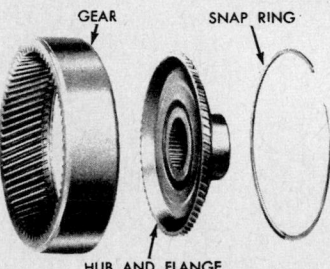

Reverse ring gear and hub disassembled
(© Ford Motor Co.)

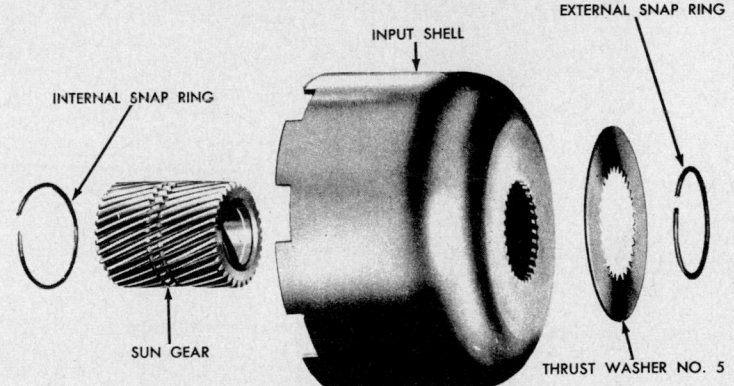

Input shell and sun gear disassembled (© Ford Motor Co.)

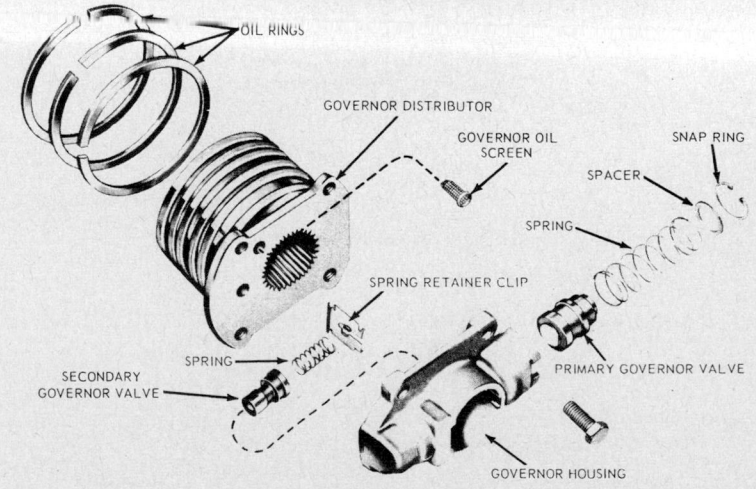

Governor and oil distributor disassembled—1965-72 C4 automatic (© Ford Motor Co.)

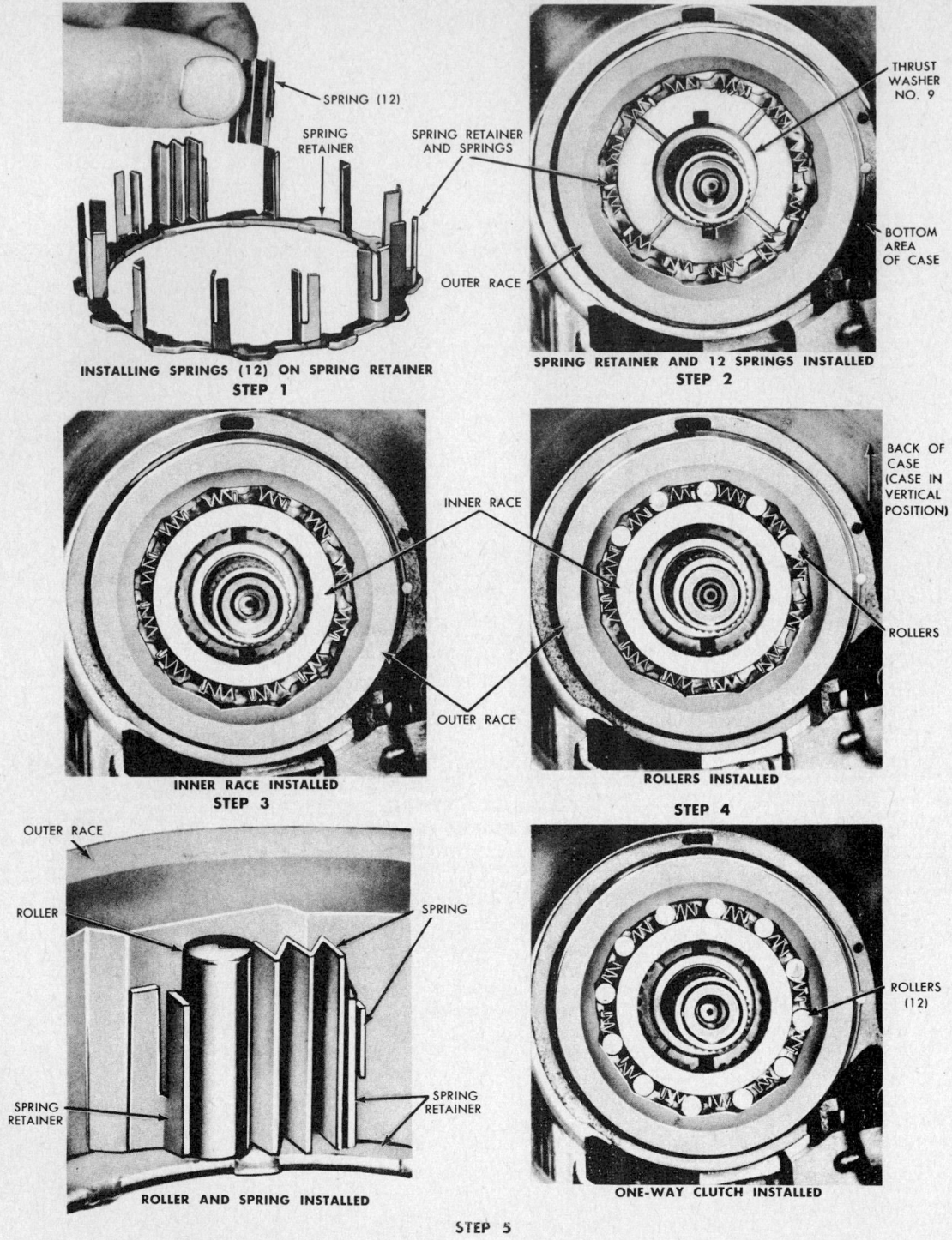

One-way clutch assembly and installation (© Ford Motor Co.)

3. Stand the transmission case on end (rear end up). Install parking pawl retaining pin.
4. Install parking pawl on the case retaining pin. Install pawl return spring.
5. Install thrust washer No. 10 onto the parking pawl gear. Place gear and thrust washer on back face of case.
6. Place two oil distributor tubes in the governor distributor sleeve. Install the sleeve onto the case.

As the distributor sleeve is installed, the oil tubes have to be inserted into the two holes in the case and the parking pawl retaining pin has to be inserted in the alignment hole in the distributor.
7. Install the four governor distributor sleeve-to-case retaining bolts and torque to specifications.
8. Install governor distributor assembly onto the output shaft. Install the distributor retaining snap-ring.

9. Check oil rings in the governor distributor for free rotation. Install the output shaft and governor distributor into the distributor sleeve.
10. With a new gasket in place on the extension housing, install the extension housing, vacuum tube clip and the extension housing to case retaining bolts. Torque bolts to specifications.
11. Rotate transmission case so that front end is up, making sure that

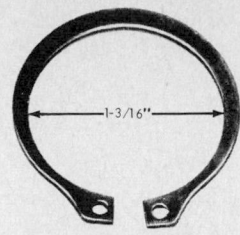

RETAINS REVERSE RING GEAR AND
HUB TO OUTPUT SHAFT

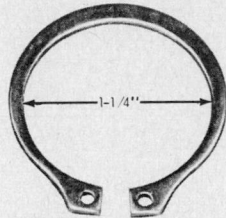

RETAINS GOVERNOR DISTRIBUTOR
TO OUTPUT SHAFT

**Governor and reverse ring hub
retaining snap-ring identification**
(ⓒ Ford Motor Co.)

thrust washer No. 9 is in position at the bottom of the case.

12. Install the 12 one-way clutch springs onto the spring retainer.

13. Place the one-way clutch spring retainer, with springs installed, into the outer race, located inside the transmission.

14. Install the inner race inside the spring retainer and 12 springs.

15. Starting at the back of the one-way clutch outer race, install the 12 clutch rollers.

16. After the clutch has been assembled, rotate the inner race clockwise to center the rollers and springs. Install low and reverse drum. The splines of the drum must engage the splines of the one-way clutch inner race. Check the clutch operation by rotating the low and reverse drum. The drum should rotate clockwise but not counterclockwise.

17. Install thrust washer No. 8 on top of the low and reverse drum. Install the low and reverse band into the case, with the small strut end facing the low-reverse servo.

18. Install the reverse ring gear and hub onto the output shaft.

19. Move the output shaft forward and install the reverse ring gear hub-to-output shaft retaining ring.

20. Place thrust washers Nos. 6 and 7 on the reverse planet carrier. Install planet carrier into the reverse ring gear and engage the tabs of the carrier with the slots in the low-reverse drum.

21. From inside the transmission case, install the inner downshift lever.

22. Install the forward clutch into the reverse-high clutch by meshing the reverse-high clutch plates with the splines of the forward clutch. Using the end-play check reading obtained during the transmission disassembly, determine which No. 2 thrust washer is necessary to get the proper end-play reading and proceed as follows:

  a. Place the stator support vertically on the bench and install the correct No. 2 thrust washer or washer and saucer as required to bring the end-play within the correct range.

  b. Install the reverse-high clutch and the forward clutch on the stator support.

  c. Invere the complete assembly making sure the intermediate brake drum bushing is seated on the forward clutch mating surface. Select the thickest fiber washer (No. 1) that can be inserted between the stator support and the intermediate brake drum thrust surfaces and still maintain a slight clearance. Do not select a washer that must be forced between the stator support and the intermediate brake drum.

  d. Remove the intermediate brake drum and forward clutch unit from the stator support.

  e. Install the selected No. 1 and No. 2 thrust washers on the front pump stator support using vaseline to hold the thrust washers in place while installing the front pump.

23. Install thrust washer No. 3 onto the forward clutch.

24. Install forward clutch hub and ring in the forward clutch by rotating the units to mesh the forward clutch plates with the splines on the forward clutch hub.

25. Install thrust washer No. 4 on the front planet carrier, and install the planet carrier into the forward clutch hub and ring gear.

26. Install input shell and sun gear onto the gear train. Rotate the input shell to engage the drive lugs of the reverse-high clutch. If the drive lugs will not engage, the outer race inside the forward planet carrier is not centered in the end of the sun gear inside the input shell. Center the thrust bearing race and install the input shell.

27. Hold the gear train together and install the forward part of the gear train assembly into the case. The input shell sun gear must

mesh with the reverse pinion gears. The front planet carrier internal splines must mesh with the splines of the output shaft.

28. Install intermediate band through front of case. The side of the band with the anchor tabs faces the back of the transmission. If using a new band, soak it in transmission fluid prior to installation.

29. Install a new front pump gasket onto the case. Install selective thrust washers Nos. 1 and 2 onto the front pump stator support. Use vaseline to hold the washers in place.

30. Lubricate the front pump O-ring with transmission fluid, and install the front pump stator support into the reverse-high clutch.

31. Install the converter housing onto the front pump and case. Install the six converter housing to case retaining bolts. Torque bolts to specifications.
Align the pump to the case and install the front pump to case retaining bolts.

32. Install input shaft. Place transmission in horizontal position, then check transmission end play. If end-play is not within limits, either the wrong selective thrust washers were used, or one of the 10 thrust washers is improperly positioned.

33. Remove the dial indicator used for checking end play and install the one converter housing to case retaining bolt. Torque the bolt to specifications.

34. Install the intermediate and low-reverse band adjusting screws into the case. Install the struts for each band.

35. Adjust intermediate and low-reverse band.

36. Install a universal joint yoke onto the output shaft. Rotate the input and output shafts in both directions to check for free rotation of the gear train.

37. Install control valve body. As the valve body is installed, engage the manual and down-shift valves with the inner control levers. Torque the eight control valve body-to-case bolts to specifications.

38. With a new oil pan gasket in place, install the oil pan and torque the bolts to specifications.

39. Install primary throttle valve into the transmission case.

40. Install vacuum unit, gasket and control rod into the case.

41. Make sure the input shaft is properly installed in the front pump, stator support and gear train. Install the converter into the front pump and the converter housing.

Specifications

Control Pressure at Zero Output Shaft Speed—1965, 1966, 1967

Engine Speed	Throttle	Manifold Vac. Ins. Hg.	Selector Lever Position	Control Pressure (P.S.I.)
Idle	Closed	*Above 18	P, N, D1, D2, L	55-62
			R	55-100
As required	As required	17 Approx.	D1, D2, L	Pressure starts to increase
As required	As required	10	D1, D2, L	96-105
As required	As required	3	D1, D2, L	138-148
			R	215-227

*Vehicles checked at high altitudes

Control Pressure at Zero Output Shaft Speed
C4 Transmission—1968, 1969

Engine Speed	Throttle	Manifold Vac. Ins. Hg	Range	P.S.I.
Idle	Closed	Above 18①	P, N, D, 2, 1	55-61 102
				55-102
			R	55-182
As required	As required	10	D, 2, 1	93-101
As required	Wide open	Below 1.0	D, 2, 1	142-150
			R	254-268

Control Pressure at Zero Output Shaft Speed—1970

Engine Speed	Throttle	Manifold Vac. Ins. Hg.	Range	P.S.I.
Idle	Closed	① Above 18	P. N. D.	52-69
			2, 1	80-110
			R	100-180
As required	As required	10	D, 2, 1	96-110
As required	As required	3.0	D, 2, 1	135-155
			R	220-250

Control Pressure at Zero Output Shaft Speed—1971-72

Engine Speed	Throttle	Manifold Vac. Ins. Hg	Range	P.S.I.
As required	As required	15 and Above	P, N, D	52-85
			2, 1	52-115
			R	52-180
As required	As required	10	P, N, D	96-110
Stall	As required	Below 1.0	D, 2, 1	143-160
			R	230-260

At altitudes above sea level it may not be possible to obtain 18" of vacuum at idle. For idle vacuums of less than 18" refer to following table to determine idle speed pressure specification in forward driving ranges (D1, D2, or L).

Engine Vacuum	Control Pressure (PSI)
17	55-62
16	55-68
15	55-74
14	55-80
13	55-87
12	55-93
11	55-99

① At altitudes above sea level, it may not be possible to obtain 18 inches of engine vacuum at idle. For idle vacuums of less than 18 inches, refer to the following table to determine idle speed pressure specifications in D driving range.

Engine Vacuum	Line Pressure
17 inches	55-66
16 inches	55-71
15 inches	55-76
14 inches	55-81
13 inches	55-86
12 inches	55-91
11 inches	55-96

① At altitudes above sea level, it may not be possible to obtain 18 inches of engine vacuum at idle. For idle vacuums of less than 18 inches, refer to the following table to determine idle speed pressure specification in D driving range.

Engine Vacuum	Line Pressure
17 inches	52-74
16 inches	52-78
15 inches	52-84
14 inches	52-90
13 inches	52-95
12 inches	52-100
11 inches	52-106

Control Pressure at Zero Output Shaft Speed—C4S Semi-Automatic—1970

Engine Speed	Throttle	Range	P.S.I.
Idle	Closed	P, N, H1, 2, 1	70-130
		R	70-260
1400 rpm	As required	H1, 2, 1	110-130
1400 rpm	As required	R	210-260

Checks and Adjustments—1965

Operation	Specification
Transmission end play check	0.008-0.042 inch Selective thrust washers available
Turbine and stator end play check	0.060 inch (maximum)
Intermediate band adjustment	Adjust screw to 10-foot-pounds torque, and back off 1¾ turns
Low-reverse band adjustment	Adjust screw to 10-foot-pounds torque, and back off 3 turns
Forward clutch pressure plate to snap ring clearance	0.022 to 0.042 inch Selective snap ring thicknesses 0.092-0.088 0.078-0.074 0.064-0.060
Reverse-high clutch pressure plate to snap ring clearance	0.060-0.080 inch Selective snap ring thicknesses 0.102-0.106 0.092-0.088 0.078-0.074 0.064-0.060

Selective Thrust Washers (No. 1 and 2)

Thrust Washer No. 1		Thrust Washer No. 2	
Composition Thrust Washer	Color of Washer	No. stamped on Washer	Metal Thrust Washer
.138-.142	Purple		
.121-.125	Red		
.108-.104	Blue	5	.109-.107
.091-.087	Yellow	4	.092-.090
.074-.070	Black	3	.075-.073
.057-.053	Tan	2	.058-.056
.042-.038	Green	1	.043-.041

Checks and Adjustments— 1966, 67

Operation	Specification
Transmission end play	0.008-0.042 inch Selective thrust washers available
Turbine and stator end play check	0.060 inch (maximum)
Intermediate band adjustment	Adjust screw to 10 ft-lbs torque, then back off 1¾ turns and tighten locknut to spec.
Low-reverse band adjustment	Adjust screw to 10 ft-lbs torque, then back off 3 turns and tighten locknut to spec.
Forward clutch pressure plate-to-snap ring clearance	No. of Composition Plates in Clutch / Clearance Specification 4 0.020-0.036 in. 5 0.026-0.042 in. Selective snap ring thicknesses 0.102-0.106 0.088-0.092 0.074-0.078 0.060-0.064

Reverse-high clutch pressure plate-to-snap ring clearance	0.050-0.066 inch Selective snap ring thicknesses 0.102-0.106 0.088-0.092 0.074-0.078 0.060-0.064

Selective Thrust Washers (No. 1 and 2)

Thrust Washer No. 1		Thrust Washer No. 2	
Composition Thrust Washer	Color of Washer	No. Stamped on Washer	Metal Thrust Washer
.138-.142	Purple		
.121-.125	Red		
.108-.104	Blue	5	.109-.107
.091-.087	Yellow	4	.092-.090
.074-.070	Black	3	.075-.073
.057-.053	Tan	2	.058-.056
.042-.038	Green	1	.043-.041

Checks and Adjustments C4 Transmission—1968

Operation	Specification
Transmission end play	0.008-0.042 inch (selective thrust washers available)
Turbine and stator end play	New or rebuilt 0.023 max. Used 0.040 max.
Intermediate band adjustment	Adjust screw to 10 ft-lbs torque, then back off 1¾ turns.
Low-reverse band Adjustment	Adjust screw to 10 ft-lbs torque, then back off 3 turns.
Forward clutch pressure plate to snap ring clearance	0.028-0.050 Selective snap ring thicknesses 0.106-0.102, 0.092-0.088, 0.078-0.074, 0.064-0.060
Reverse-high clutch pressure plate to snap ring clearance	0.050-0.066 selective snap ring thicknesses 0.106-0.102, 0.092-0.088, 0.078-0.074, 0.064-0.060

Selective Thrust Washers

Nylon Thrust Washer W/Tangs	Color of Washer	No. Stamped On Washer	Metal Thrust Washer
.053-.0575	Red		
.070-.074	Green	5	.109-.107
.087-.091	Natural	4	.092-.090
.104-.108	Black	3	.075-.073
.121-.125	Yellow	2	.058-.056
.138-.142	Blue	1	.043-.041

Checks and Adjustments C4 Transmission—1969

Operation	Specification
Transmission end play	0.008-0.042 inch (selective thrust washers available)

Turbine and stator end play	Model PEB—New or rebuilt 0.044 max., used 0.060 max. Model PEE, PEA new or rebuilt 0.023 max., used 0.040 max.
Intermediate band adjustment	Remove and discard lock nut. Adjust screw to 10 ft-lbs torque, then back off 1¾ turns. Install new lock nut and torque to specification.
Low-reverse band adjustment	Remove and discard lock nut. Adjust screw to 10 ft-lbs torque, then back off 3 turns. Install new locknut and torque to specification.
Forward clutch pressure plate to snap ring clearance	Model PEB 0.020-0.036 Models PEA, PEE 0.026-0.042 Selective snap ring thicknesses 0.106-0.102, 0.092-0.088, 0.078-0.074, 0.064-0.060
Reverse-high clutch pressure plate to snap ring clearance	0.050-0.066 Selective snap ring thicknesses 0.106-0.102, 0.092-0.088, 0.078-0.074, 0.064-0.060

Selective Thrust Washers

Thrust Washer No. 1		Thrust Washer No. 2	
Nylon Thrust Washer W/Tangs	Color of Washer	No. Stamped On Washer	Metal Thrust Washer
.053-.0575	Red	1	.041-.043
.070-.074	Green	2	.056-.058
.087-.091	Natural (White)	3	.073-.075
.104-.108	Black	4	.090-.092
.121-.125	Yellow	5	.107-.109

Checks and Adjustments C4—1970-2

Operation	Specification
Transmission end play	0.008-0.042 inch (selective thrust washers available)
Turbine and stator end play	Model PEB, PEG—new or rebuilt 0.044 max. Used 0.060 max. Model PEE, PEA, PEF—New or rebuilt 0.023 max. Used 0.040 max.
Intermediate band adjustment	Remove and discard lock nut. Adjust screw to 10 ft-lbs torque, then back off 1¾ turns. Install new lock nut and torque to specification.

Operation	Specification
Low-reverse band adjustment	Remove and discard lock nut. Adjust screw to 10 ft-lbs torque, then back off 3 turns. Install new lock nut and torque to specification.
Forward clutch pressure plate to snap ring clearance	0.025-0.050 Selective snap ring thicknesses 0.082-0.078, 0.068-0.064, 0.054-0.050
Reverse-high clutch pressure plate to snap ring clearance	0.050-0.071 Selective snap ring thicknesses 0.096-0.092, 0.082-0.078, 0.068-0.064, 0.054-0.050

Selective Thrust Washers

Thrust washer No. 1		Thrust Washer No. 2	
Nylon Thrust Washer W/Tangs	Color of Washer	No. Stamped On Washer	Metal Thrust Washer
.053-.0575	Red	1	.041-.043
.070-.074	Green	2	.056-.058
.087-.091	Natural (White)	3	.073-.075
.104-.108	Black		
.121-.125	Yellow	Spacer	.032-.036①

① This is a selective spacer. The spacer must be installed next to the stator support to obtain correct end play.

Control Valve Body Spring Identification—1965

Spring	Total Coils	Free Length	O.D.	Wire Diameter	Lbs. Load	Length
Manual valve detent	9	.74	.295	.045	7.5	.601
Line pressure coasting boost	15	1.12	.287	.032	3.5	.620
2-3 backout control valve	11½	1.26	.45	.032	1.47	.580
Main oil pressure regulator valve	9.75	1.86	.615	.047	6.2	.208
Throttle pressure modulator valve	15	1.513	.292	.0286	3.573	.620
Control 1-2 shift valve	13	.95	.230	.019	1.0	.450
Throttle downshift valve	9	1.042	.360	.031	3.0	.476
Throttle pressure booster valve	15	.458	.243	.036	5.25	.84
Line pressure boost (inner)	12.5	2.055	.450	.032	2.98	.564
Intermediate band accumulator valve	12.5	1.107	.325	.025	1.10	.551

Control Valve Body Spring Identification— 1966, 1967

Spring	Total Coils	Free Length	O.D.	Wire Diameter	Lbs. Load	Length
Manual valve detent	9	.74	.295	.045	7.5	.601
2-3 backout control valve	10	1.515	.450	.026	1.353	.580
Main oil pressure regulator valve	9.75	1.86	.615	.047	6.200	.608
Throttle pressure modulator	15	1.513	.292	.286	3.675	.620
Control 1-2 shift valve	13	.950	.230	.019	1.00	.450
Throttle downshift valve	9	1.042	.360	.031	3.0	.476
Throttle pressure booster valve	15	1.421	.326	.036	5.250	.730
Control pressure booster valve	23.5	.965	.290	.032	1.00	.715
Intermediate band accumulator valve	12.5	1.107	.325	.025	1.100	.551

Control Valve Body Spring Identification C4 Transmission—1968

Spring	Total Coils	Free Length	O.D.	Wire Dia.	Lbs. Load	Length	Color Code
Manual valve detent	9	0.74	0.295	0.045	7.5	0.601	None
2-3 backout control valve	10	1.515	0.450	0.026	1.353	0.580	White
Main oil press. reg. valve	12	2.53	0.615	0.047	7.24	0.716	Pink
Throttle press. modulator	15	1.513	0.292	0.028	3.675	0.620	Yellow
Drive 2 valve	10	0.735	0.230	0.019	0.80	0.450	Gray
Throttle downshift valve	9	0.962	0.380	0.034	3.44	0.440	Dk. Green
Throttle press. booster valve	15	1.39	0.249 I.D.	0.036	5.250	0.730	Purple
Control press. booster valve	12.8	1.66	0.350	0.028	1.63	0.696	None
Inter. band accumulator valve	11	1.38	0.375 I.D.	0.024	1.00	0.400	White
Line coasting boost valve	10	1.03	0.346	0.034	4.42	0.464	White

Control Valve Body Spring Identification C4 Transmission—1969

Spring	Total Coils	Free Length	O.D.	Wire Dia.	Lbs. Load	Length	Color Code
Manual valve detent all except PEC-EI	10	.764	.295		.44	6.5	White
Model PEC-EI	9	.74	.295	.045	7.5	.601	None
2-3 backout control valve	10	1.515	.450	.026	1.353	.580	White
Main oil press. reg. valve	12	2.53	.615	.047	7.24	.716	Pink
Throttle press. modulator	15	1.513	.292	.028	3.675	.620	Yellow
Drive 2 valve	10	.735	.230	.019	.80	.450	Gray
Throttle downshift valve	9	.962	.380	.034	3.44	.440	Dk. Green
Throttle press. booster valve	15	1.39	.249 I. D.	.036	5.250	.730	Purple
Control press. booster valve	12.8	1.66	.350 I. D.	.028	1.63	.696	None
Inter. band accumulator valve ①	11	1.38	.375 I. D.	.024	1.0	.400	Purple
Inter. band accumulator valve ②	10	1.293	.375 I. D.	.0258	1.25	.400	None
Line press coasting boost valve	10	1.03	.346	.034	4.42	.464	White
Main oil pressure reg., valve inner	11	1.40	.407	.0286	1.49	.739	None
Main oil pressure reg. valve outer	9	1.667	.668	.0507	7.30	.586	Pink

① Used on models PEA-A2, MI, NI,
② Used on models PEB-B2, C2, PEE

Control Valve Body Spring Identification C4 Automatic—1970

Spring	Total Coils	Free Length	O.D.	Wire Dia.	Lbs. Load	Length	Color Code
Manual valve detent		Leaf Type			7.25	.542	None
2-3 backout valve	13	1.345	.345	.0258	1.45	.620	Gray
1-2 transition valve:	12	1.150	.330	.023	.95	.480	Dk. Green
Throttle downshift valve	10	0.816	.280	.0301	3.00	.500	None
Low servo modulator valve	12	1.270	.380	.0268	1.54	.553	Orange
Throttle pressure booster valve all except PEE-AC1, AH1, M1, V1, PEF	15	1.109	.281	.0332	4.50	.620	None
model PEE-AC1, AH1, M1, V1, PEF	15	1.39	.285	.036	5.25	.730	Purple
Throttle pressure limit valve	14	1.192	.295	.0379	6.25	.770	Brown
Throttle pressure modulator valve	15	1.513	.292	.0286	3.575	.620	Yellow
Line pressure coast boost valve	10	1.023	.340	.0332	4.10	.494	Dk. Blue
Drive 2 valve	13	.950	.230	.019	1.00	.450	Violet
Int. servo accumulator valve Model PEE-AC1, AH1, M1, V1, AG1	9	.680	.300	.0244	1.00	.390	Orange
model PEA-A3, PEE-AD1, AE1, AF1, PEB, PEF	8	.680	.300	.0258	1.50	.390	Lt. Green
model PEA-M2, N2	9	.845	.300	.258	2.00	.390	None

Control Valve Body Spring Identification C4 Automatic—1971-72

Spring	Total Coils	Free Length	O.D.	Wire Dia.	Lbs. Load	Length	Color Code
Manual valve detent		Leaf Type			7.25	.542	None
2-3 backout valve	13	1.345	.345	.0258	1.45	.620	Gray
1-2 transition valve:	12	1.150	.330	.023	.95	.480	Dk. Green
Throttle downshift valve	10	0.816	.280	.0301	3.00	.500	None
Low servo modulator valve Model PEA, PEE-AE1, AK, AM, PEF	12	1.335	.380	.0286	1.72	.553	Purple
Model PEB, PEE-AG1, AD1, AE1, AF1, AH1, AL, M1, V1	12	1.158	.380	.0286	1.35	.553	Yellow
Throttle pressure booster valve Model PEA, PEB, PEE-AD1, AE1, AF1, AK, AM	15	1.109	.281	.0332	4.50	.620	White
Model PEE-AC1, AG1, AH1, AL, M1, V1, PEF	15	1.191	.281	.0332	5.25	.620	Dk. Green
Throttle pressure limit valve	14	1.192	.295	.0379	6.25	.770	Brown
Throttle pressure modulator valve	15	1.513	.292	.0286	3.575	.620	Yellow
Line pressure coast boost valve	10	1.023	.340	.0332	4.10	.494	Dk. Blue
Main oil pressure boost valve	11	1.400	.350	.0286	1.49	.739	None
Int. servo accumulator valve Model PEB	9	.680	.300	.0244	1.00	.390	White
Model PEE-AC1, AD1, AE1, AF1, AK, AL, AM, M1, V1	8	.680	.300	.0258	1.50	.390	Lt. Green
Model PEA-M2, N2, PEF	9.5	.853	.300	.0272	2.50	.390	Orange
Main oil pressure reg. valve	9	1.667	.668	.0507	7.30	.586	None
1-2 shift valve	11	.730	.265	.0258	.80	.580	Violet

Control Valve Body Spring Identification C4S Semi-Automatic—1970

Spring	Total	Free Length	O.D.	Wire Dia.	Lbs. Load	Length
2-3 backout control valve	10	1.031	.356	.034	4.44	.464
Main oil press reg. valve	9	1.667	.671	.0507	7.30	.586
Throttle press modulator	15	1.24	.297	.034	4.50	.740
Drive 2 valve	9.3	.594	.230	.030	3.0	.450
Low servo modulator valve	12	1.412	.380	.028	1.89	.553

Torque Limits—C4 and C4S Automatic Transmissions—Ft. Lbs.

Item	Ft-lbs							
	1965	1966	1967	1968	1969	1970	1971	1972
Converter to flywheel	20-30	20-30	20-30	20-30	23-28	23-28	23-28	23-28
Converter hsg. to trans.	28-40	28-40	28-40	28-40	28-40	28-40	28-40	28-40
Front pump to trans. case	28-40	28-40	28-40	28-40	28-40	28-40	28-40	28-40
Outer race to case	13-20	13-20	13-20	13-20	13-20	13-20	13-20	13-20
Oil pan to case	12-16	12-16	12-16	12-16	12-16	12-16	12-16	12-16
Rear servo cover to case	12-20	12-20	12-20	12-20	12-20	12-20	12-20	12-20
Stator support to pump	12-20	12-20	12-20	12-20	12-20	12-20	12-20	12-20
Converter cover to converter hsg.	10-13	10-13	10-13	12-16	12-16	12-16	12-16	12-16
Intermediate servo cover to case	12-20	12-20	12-20	16-22	16-22	16-22	16-22	16-22
Extension hsg. to case	28-40	28-40	28-40	28-40	28-40	28-40	28-40	28-40
Converter drain plug	20-30	20-30	20-30	20-30	20-30	20-30	20-30	20-30
Pressure gauge tap	9-15	9-15	9-15	9-15	9-15	9-15	9-15	9-15
Manual control lever nut	35-45	30-40	30-40	30-40	8-12	8-12	8-12	8-12
Downshift lever to shaft	12-20	12-16	12-16	12-16	12-16	12-16	12-16	12-16
Filler tube to engine	20-25	20-25	20-25	20-25	20-25	20-25	20-25	20-25
Filler tube to pan					32-42	32-42	32-42	32-42
Diaphragm assy to case	15-23	15-23	15-23	15-23	15-23	15-23	15-23	15-23
Distributor sleeve to case	12-20	12-20	12-20	12-20	12-20	12-20	12-20	12-20
Reverse servo piston to rod	12-20	12-20	12-20	*	*	*	12-20	12-20
Transmission to engine		40-50	40-50	40-50	40-50	40-50	23-33	23-33
Transmission to engine: Falcon and Mustang					23-33	23-33	23-33	23-33
Cooler bracket & oil pan to case		12-16	12-16					
Band adjust stop to case	35-45	35-40	35-40	35-45	35-45	35-45	35-45	35-45
Yoke to output shaft					60-80	60-80	60-120	60-120

* Tighten to 10 ft-lbs and back off ⅝ turn.

Torque Limits—C4 and C4S Automatic Transmissions—In. Lbs.

Item	1965	1966	1967	1968	1969	1970	1971	1972
End plate to valve body screw	20-35	20-35	20-35	20-35	20-35	20-35	20-35	20-35
Lower to upper valve body bolts	20-35	40-55	40-55	40-50	40-55	40-55	40-55	40-55
Screen to valve body screws	20-35	40-55	40-55	40-55	40-55	40-55	40-55	40-55
Neutral switch to case screws	30-45	55-75	55-75		55-75 *	55-75 *	55-75	55-75
Neutral switch to column					20	20		
Screen & valve body to case bolts	80-120	80-120	80-120	80-120	80-120	80-120	80-120	80-120
Screen to valve body bolts		80-120	80-120	80-120	80-120	80-120	40-55	40-55
Governor body to distributor (collector) body bolts		80-120	80-120	80-120	80-120	80-120	80-120	80-120
Cooler line fittings		80-120	80-120	80-120	80-120	80-120	80-120	80-120
Reinforcement plate to body				40-55	40-55	40-55	40-55	40-55
Accumulator plate to body				80-120	50-90	50-90		
Inner downshift lever stop				40-55	40-55	40-55		

* Mustang and Cougar only

3-Speed Automatic (C6)

Application
Comet, 1966-67
Cougar, 1966-72
Fairlane, 1966-70

Ford & T-Bird, 1966-72
Lincoln, 1966-72
Mercury, 1966-72

Montego, 1966-72
Mustang, 1966-72
Torino, 1971-72

Diagnosis

This diagnosis guide covers the most common symptoms and is an aid to careful diagnosis. The items to check are listed in the sequence to be followed for quickest results. Thus, follow the checks in the order given for the particular transmission type.

TROUBLE SYMPTOMS	Items to Check In Car	Out of Car
No drive in D, 2 and 1	CWER	ac
Rough initial engagement in D or 2	KBWFE	a
1-2 or 2-3 shift points incorrect or erratic	ABLCDWER	
Rough 1-2 upshifts	BJGWEF	
Rough 2-3 shifts	BJWFGER	br
Dragged out 1-2 shift	ABJWGEFR	c
Engine overspeeds on 2-3 shift	CABJWEFG	br
No 1-2 or 2-3 shift	CLBDWEGJ	bc
No 3-1 shift in D	DE	
No forced downshifts	LEB	
Runaway engine on forced 3-2 downshift	WJGFEB	c
Rough 3-2 or 3-1 shift at closed throttle	KBJEF	
Shifts 1-3 in D	GJBEDR	
No engine braking in first gear—1 range	CHEDR	
Creeps excessively	K	
Slips or chatters in first gear, D	ABWFE	aci
Slips or chatters in second gear	ABJGWFER	ac
Slips or chatters in R	ABHWFER	bcr
No drive in D only	CWE	i
No drive in 2 only	ACWJER	c
No drive in 1 only	ACWER	c
No drive in R only	ACHWER	bcr
No drive in any selector lever position	ACWFER	cd
Lockup in D only		gc
Lockup in 2 only	H	bgci
Lockup in 1 only		gc
Lockup in R only		agc
Parking lock binds or does not hold	C	g
Transmission overheats	OFBW	ns
Maximum speed too low, poor acceleration	YZ	n
Transmission noisy in N and P	AF	d
Transmission noisy in first, second, third or reverse gear	AF	hadi
Fluid leak	AMNOPQS UXBJ	jmp
Car moves forward in N	C	a

Key to Checks

A. Fluid level
B. Vacuum diaphragm unit or tubes restricted—leaking—adjustment
C. Manual linkage
D. Governor
E. Valve body
F. Pressure regulator
G. Intermediate band
H. Low-reverse clutch
J. Intermediate servo
K. Engine idle speed
L. Downshift linkage—including inner level position
M. Converter drain plugs

N. Oil pan gasket, filler tube or seal
O. Oil cooler and connections
P. Manual or downshift lever shaft seal
Q. ⅛ inch pipe plugs in case
R. Perform air pressure check
S. Extension housing-to-case gasket
U. Extension housing rear oil seal
W. Perform control pressure check
X. Speedometer driven gear adapter seal
Y. Engine performance
Z. Vehicle brakes
a. Forward clutch

b. Reverse-high clutch
c. Leakage in hydraulic system
d. Front pump
g. Parking linkage
h. Planetary assembly
i. Planetary one-way clutch
j. Engine rear oil seal
m. Front pump oil seal
n. Converter one-way clutch
p. Front pump to case gasket or seal
r. Reverse-high clutch piston air bleed valve
s. Converter pressure check valves

General Information

The C6 automatic transmission is a three-speed unit that provides automatic upshifts and downshifts through the three forward gear ratios and also provides manual selection of first and second gears. The converter housing and the fixed splines which engage the splined OD of the low-reverse clutch steel plates are both cast integrally into the case.

Only one band (intermediate) is used in the C6 transmission. This band, along with the forward clutch, is used to obtain intermediate gear. Only the adjustment of the intermediate band can be done without major disassembly.

The C6 automatic transmission is very similar to the C4 automatic transmission, and most of the maintenance and overhaul procedures given for the C4 transmission will apply to the C6 transmission. One

important difference between the C6 and the C4 transmissions is that the C6 transmission uses a low-reverse clutch in place of the low-reverse band. Otherwise, the gear trains are the same, as are the clutch combinations. The hydraulic control systems are very similar, except for minor differences in design. All components which are different from the C4 components are illustrated and the procedures to repair them are given.

There is no drain plug in the transmission pan. To drain the transmission oil, remove all of the oil pan attaching bolts, except the two at the front; loosen these, and let the pan tilt and drain.

Intermediate Band Adjustment

1. Raise the car on a hoist or place it on jack stands.
2. Clean threads of the intermediate band adjusting screw.
3. Loosen adjustment screw lock-

nut.
4. Tighten the adjusting screw to 10 ft. lbs., and back the screw off exactly 1 turn (1971-72 models, 1½ turns). Tighten the adjusting screw locknut.

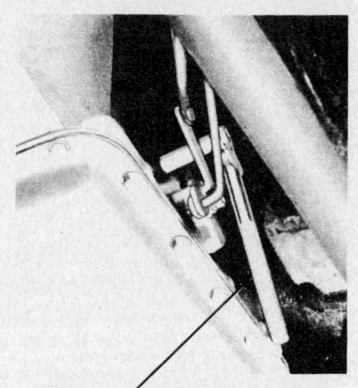

TOOL - T 59 P - 77370 - B

Adjusting intermediate band
(© Ford Motor Co.)

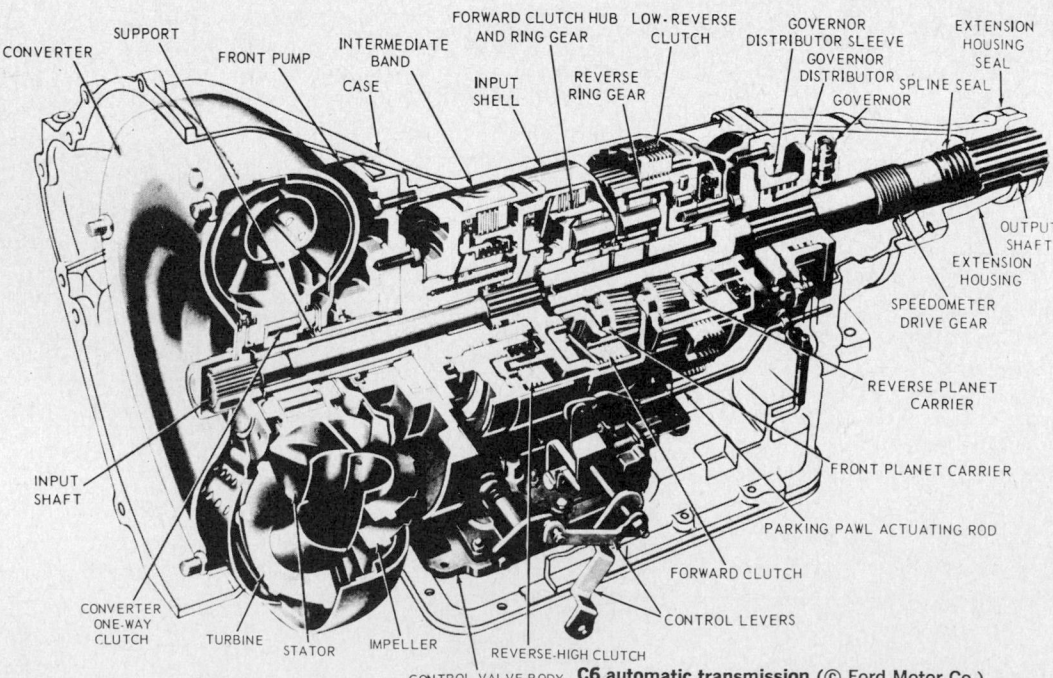

C6 automatic transmission (© Ford Motor Co.)

Transmission Disassembly

1. Thoroughly clean outside of transmission.
2. Secure the unit in a repair stand, and drain the oil.

9. Remove the forward part of the gear train as an assembly.
Remove the large snap-ring that holds the reverse planet carrier in the low-reverse clutch hub. Lift the planet carrier from the drum.

10. Remove the snap-ring that holds the reverse ring gear and hub on the output shaft. Slide the ring gear and hub from the shaft.
11. Rotate the low-reverse clutch hub clockwise, and withdraw it from the case.

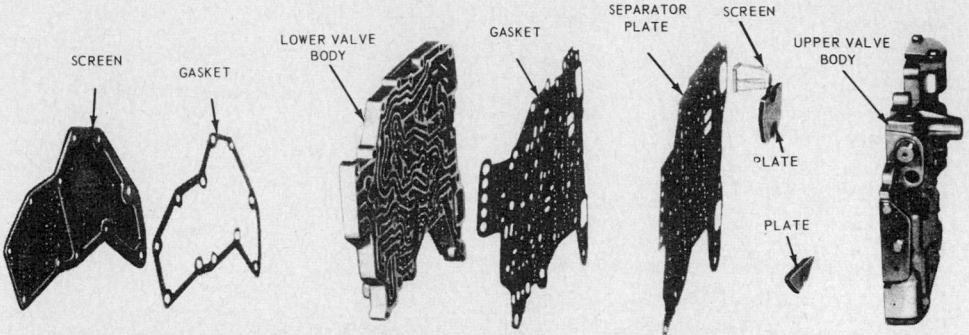

Upper and lower control valve bodies disassembled—1966, 1968-72 C6 automatic
(© Ford Motor Co.)

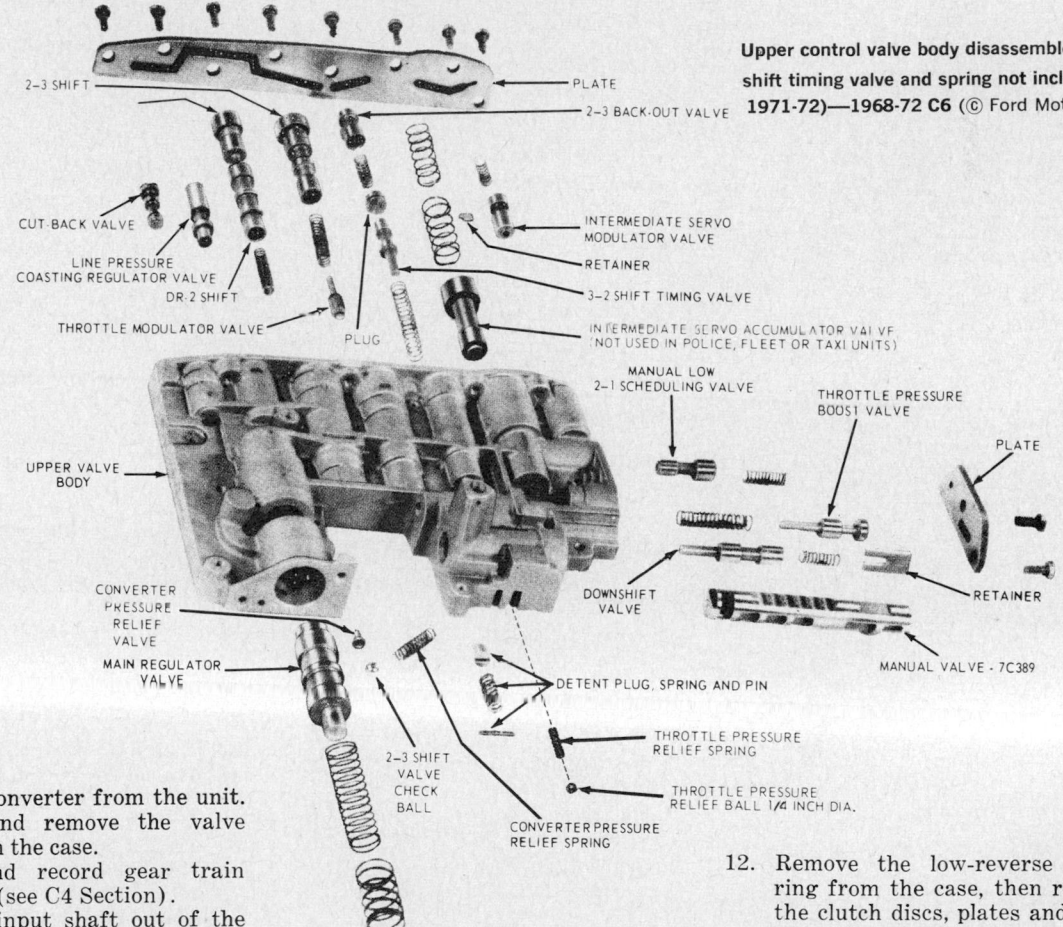

Upper control valve body disassembled (3-2 shift timing valve and spring not included in 1971-72)—1968-72 C6 (© Ford Motor Co.)

3. Remove converter from the unit.
4. Unbolt and remove the valve body from the case.
5. Check and record gear train end-play (see C4 Section).
6. Slip the input shaft out of the front pump. Remove the vacuum diaphragm, rod and primary throttle valve from the case.
7. Remove the front pump attaching bolts. Pry the gear train forward to remove the pump.
8. Loosen the band adjusting screw and remove the two struts. Rotate the band 90° counterclockwise, to align the ends with the slot in the case. Slide the band off the reverse-high clutch drum.

12. Remove the low-reverse snapring from the case, then remove the clutch discs, plates and pressure plate from the case.
13. Remove the extension housing bolts and vent tube from the case. Remove the extension housing and gasket.
14. Slide the output shaft assembly from the transmission case.
15. Remove the distributor sleeve attaching bolts and remove the sleeve parking gear and the thrust washer.
16. Compress the low-reverse clutch piston release spring. Remove

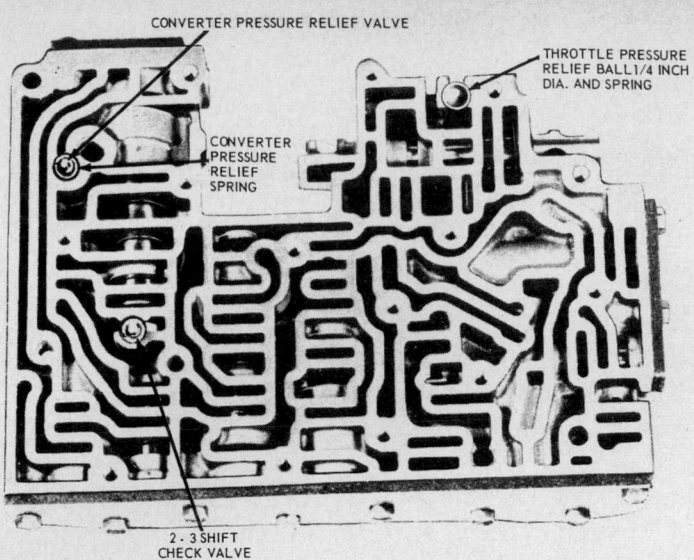

Converter pressure relief valve, throttle pressure relief valve, and 2-3 shift check valve locations—1968-72 C6 automatic (© Ford Motor Co.)

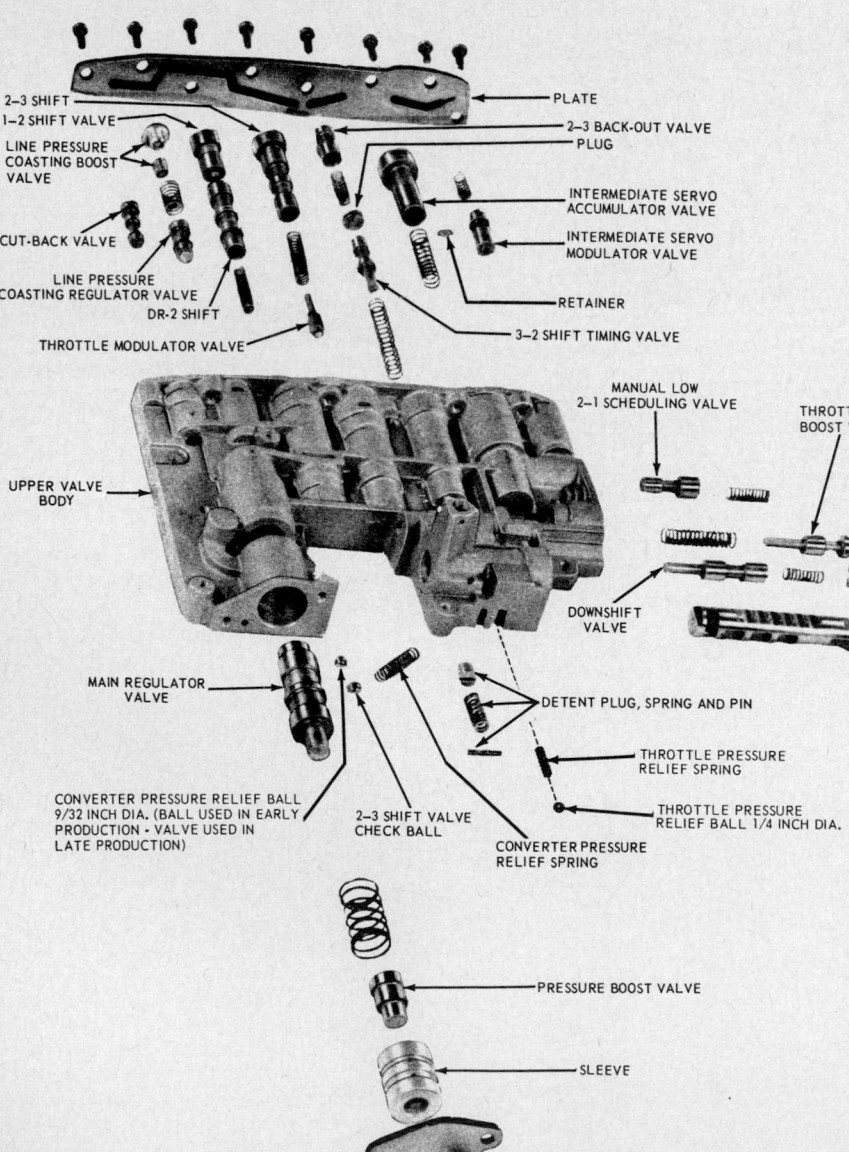

Upper control valve body disassembled—1967 C6 automatic (© Ford Motor Co.)

the snap-ring. Remove the tool and spring retainer.

17. Remove the one-way clutch inner race attaching bolts from the rear of the case. Remove the inner race from the inside of the case.

18. Remove the low-reverse clutch piston from the case.

Component Disassembly and Assembly

NOTE: For most component services, see Component Disassembly and Assembly, in the C4 Section. The exceptions are as follows.

Output Shaft Hub and Ring Gear

1. Remove the hub retaining snap-ring from the ring gear.
2. Lift hub from ring gear.
3. Position the hub in the ring gear.
4. Secure the hub with the retaining snap-ring. Make sure the snap-ring is fully engaged with the groove.

One-Way Clutch

1. Remove the snap-ring and rear bushing from the rear of the low-reverse clutch hub.
2. Remove the springs and rollers from the spring retainer and lift the spring retainer from the hub.
3. Remove the remaining bushing and snap-ring from the hub.

4. Install the snap-ring in the forward snap-ring groove of the low-reverse clutch hub.
5. Place the forward clutch bushing against the snap-ring with the flat side up. Install the one-way clutch spring retainer on top of the bushing. Install the retainer in the hub so that the springs load the rollers in a counterclockwise direction.
6. Install a spring and roller into each of the spring retainer compartments by slightly compressing each spring and placing the roller between the spring and the spring retainer.

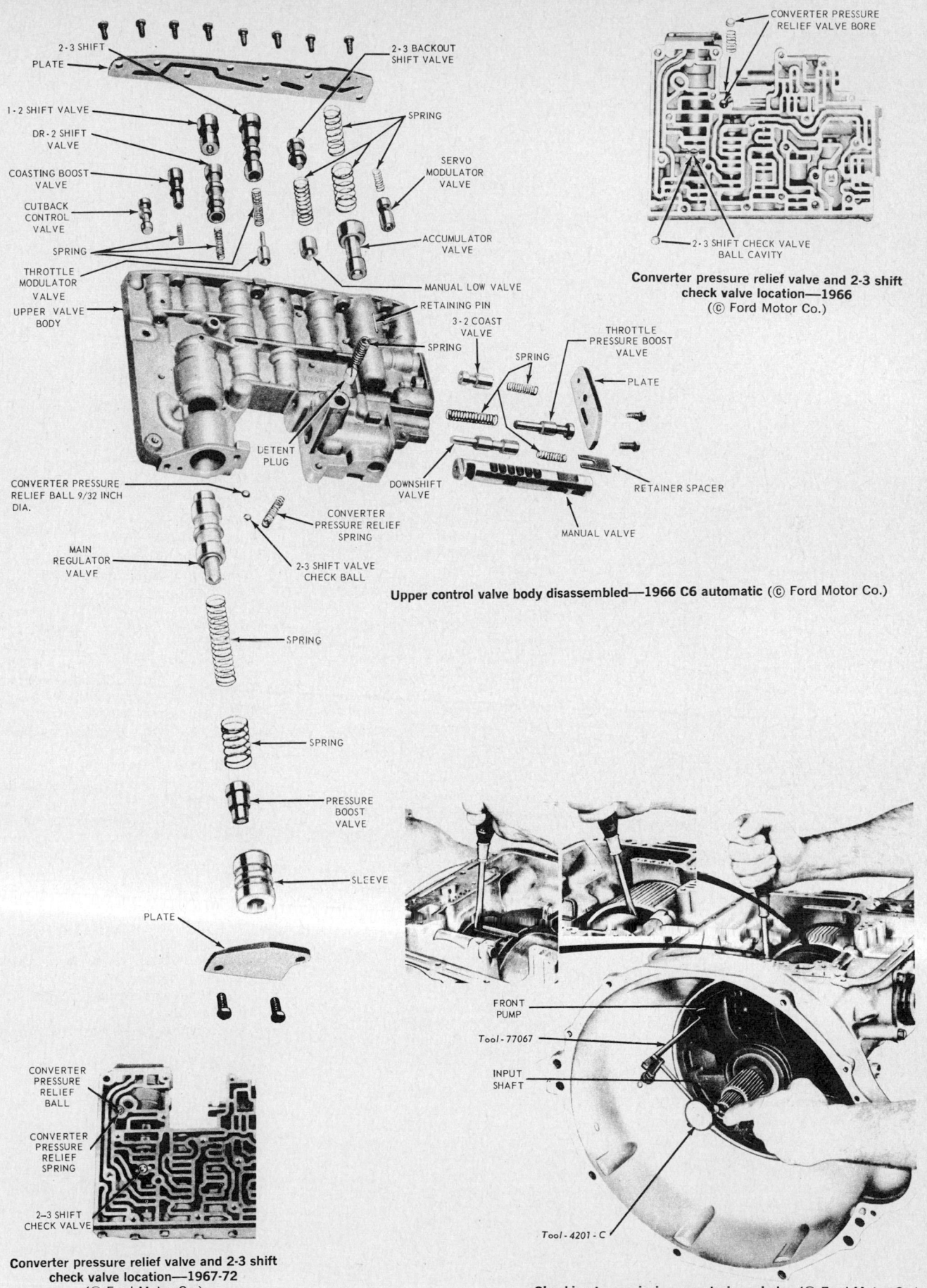

2-3 SHIFT
PLATE

2-3 BACKOUT
SHIFT VALVE

1-2 SHIFT VALVE

DR-2 SHIFT
VALVE

COASTING BOOST
VALVE

CUTBACK
CONTROL
VALVE

SPRING

THROTTLE
MODULATOR
VALVE

UPPER VALVE
BODY

SPRING

SERVO
MODULATOR
VALVE

ACCUMULATOR
VALVE

MANUAL LOW VALVE

RETAINING PIN

3-2 COAST
VALVE

SPRING

SPRING

THROTTLE
PRESSURE BOOST
VALVE

PLATE

DETENT
PLUG

DOWNSHIFT
VALVE

CONVERTER PRESSURE
RELIEF SPRING

RETAINER SPACER

MANUAL VALVE

CONVERTER PRESSURE
RELIEF BALL 9/32 INCH
DIA.

MAIN
REGULATOR
VALVE

2-3 SHIFT VALVE
CHECK BALL

CONVERTER PRESSURE
RELIEF VALVE BORE

2-3 SHIFT CHECK VALVE
BALL CAVITY

**Converter pressure relief valve and 2-3 shift
check valve location—1966**
(© Ford Motor Co.)

Upper control valve body disassembled—1966 C6 automatic (© Ford Motor Co.)

SPRING

SPRING

PRESSURE
BOOST
VALVE

SLEEVE

PLATE

CONVERTER
PRESSURE
RELIEF
BALL

CONVERTER
PRESSURE
RELIEF
SPRING

2-3 SHIFT
CHECK VALVE

**Converter pressure relief valve and 2-3 shift
check valve location—1967-72**
(© Ford Motor Co.)

FRONT
PUMP

Tool-77067

INPUT
SHAFT

Tool-4201-C

Checking transmission gear train end-play (© Ford Motor Co.)

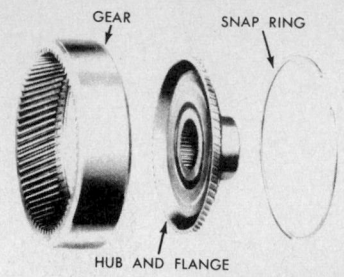

Output shaft hub and ring gear disassembled
((C) Ford Motor Co.)

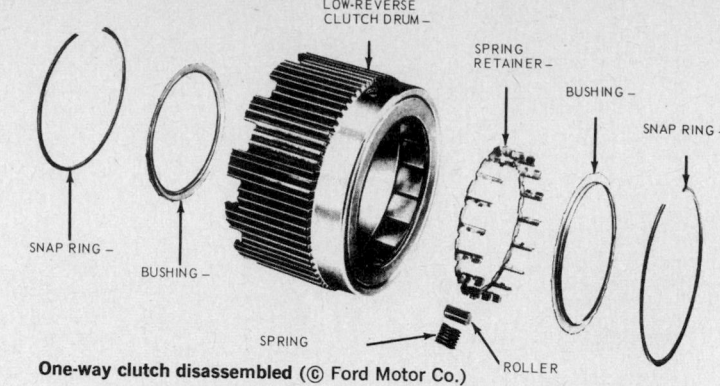

One-way clutch disassembled ((C) Ford Motor Co.)

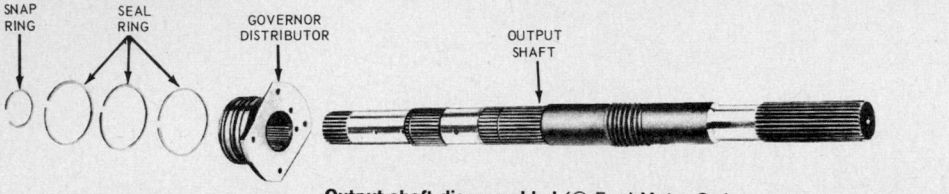

Output shaft disassembled ((C) Ford Motor Co.)

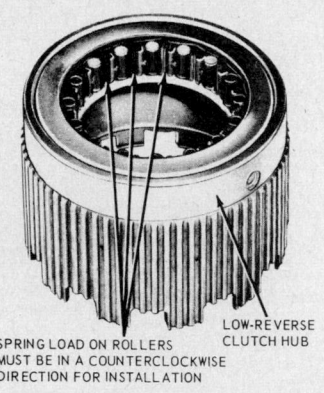

SPRING LOAD ON ROLLERS
MUST BE IN A COUNTERCLOCKWISE
DIRECTION FOR INSTALLATION

Installing one-way clutch ((C) Ford Motor Co.)

7. Install the rear bushing on top of the retainer with the flat side down.
8. Install the remaining snap-ring at the rear of the low-reverse clutch hub.

Servo

1. Apply air pressure to the port in the servo cover in order to remove the piston and stem.
2. Remove the seals from the piston.
NOTE: on Lincoln Continental and Continental Mark III models, replace the complete piston and rod assembly if the piston or piston sealing lips are damaged or unserviceable.
3. Dip the new seals in transmission fluid.
4. Install the new seals onto the piston and cover.
5. Dip the piston in transmission fluid and install it into the cover.

Output Shaft Disassembly

1. Remove the governor attaching bolts and the governor.
2. Remove the snap-ring that se-

cures the governor distributor onto the output shaft and slide it off of the shaft.
3. Remove the seal rings from the distributor.
4. Carefully install new seal rings onto the distributor.
5. Slide the governor distributor into place on the shaft, and install the snap-ring to secure it. Make sure the snap-ring is seated in the groove.
6. Position the governor on the distributor and secure with attaching screws.

Parking Pawl Linkage

1. Unbolt and remove the parking pawl guide plate from the case.
2. Remove the spring, parking pawl, and shaft from the case.
3. Drill a 1/8 in. hole in the park plate shaft retainer plug, and pull the plug out with a wire hook. Unhook the spring from the park plate.
4. Thread a bolt into the park plate shaft, and pull the shaft from the case. Remove the park plate and spring.
5. Position the spring and park plate in the case and install the shaft. Hook the spring on the park plate.
6. Install a new retainer plug.
7. Install the parking pawl shaft in the case, and slip the parking pawls and spring onto the shaft.
8. Bolt the guide plate to the case, making sure that the actuating rod is seated in the slot of the plate.

Transmission Assembly

1. Place transmission case in a holding fixture.

2. Tap the reverse clutch piston into place with a rubber hammer.
3. Hold the one-way clutch inner race in position, install and torque attaching bolts.
4. Install a low-reverse clutch return spring into each pocket of the reverse clutch piston. Press the springs firmly into the piston to prevent their falling out.
5. Position the spring retainer over the springs and position the retainer snap-ring in place on the one-way inner race.
6. Install the compressing tool and compress the springs just enough to install the low-reverse clutch piston retainer snap-ring.
7. Place the transmission case on the bench, bellhousing facing downward.
8. Position the parking gear thrust washer and gear on the case.
9. Position the oil distributor sleeve and tubes in place on the rear of the case. Install and torque the attaching bolts.
10. Install the output shaft and as an assembly.
11. Place a new gasket on the rear of the transmission case. Position the extension housing on the case and install attaching bolts. Return the case to the holding fixture.
12. Align the low-reverse clutch hub and one-way clutch with the inner race at the rear of the case. Rotate the low-reverse clutch hub clockwise, while applying pressure to seat it.
13. Install the low-reverse clutch plates. Start with a steel plate and follow with friction and steel plates, alternately. If new

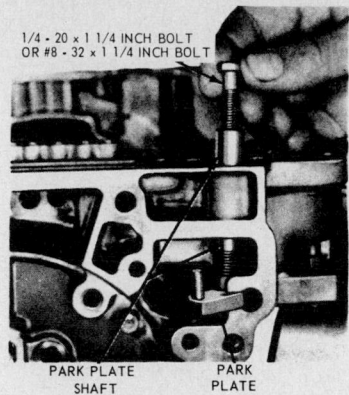

1/4 - 20 x 1 1/4 INCH BOLT
OR #8 - 32 x 1 1/4 INCH BOLT

PARK PLATE   PARK
SHAFT   PLATE

Removing park plate shaft
(© Ford Motor Co.)

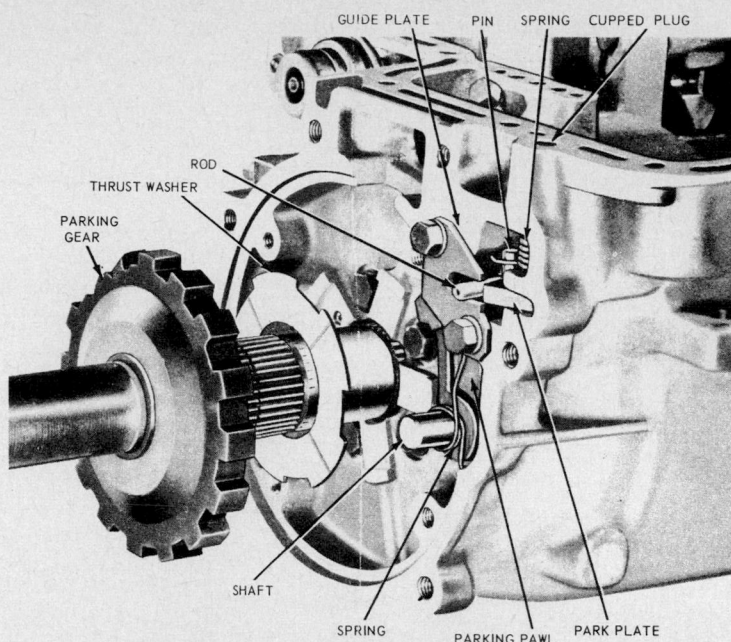

GUIDE PLATE   PIN   SPRING   CUPPED PLUG

ROD

THRUST WASHER

PARKING GEAR

SHAFT

SPRING   PARKING PAWL   PARK PLATE

Parking pawl mechanism (© Ford Motor Co.)

composition (friction) plates are being used, soak them in transmission fluid for 15 mniutes before installation. Install the pressure plate and snap-ring. Test the operation of the low-reverse clutch by applying air pressure at the clutch pressure apply hole in the case.

14. Install the reverse planets ring gear thrust washer, ring gear and hub assembly. Insert the snap-ring into its groove in the output shaft.

15. Assemble the front and rear thrust washers onto the reverse planet assembly. Retain them with vaseline, then insert the assembly into the ring gear. Install the snap-ring into the ring gear.

16. Install the thrust washer onto the rear end of the reverse-high clutch assembly. Retain the thrust washer with vaseline and insert the splined end of the forward clutch into the open end of the reverse-high clutch so that the splines engage the reverse-high clutch friction plates.

17. Install the thrust washer onto the front end of the planet ring gear and hub. Insert the ring gear into the forward clutch.

18. Install the thrust washer onto the front end of the forward planet assembly. Retain the washer with vaseline and insert the assembly into the ring gear. Install the input shell and sun gear assembly.

19. Install the reverse-high clutch, forward clutch, forward planet assembly and input shell and sun gear, as an assembly, into the transmission case.

20. Insert the intermediate band into the case around the reverse and high clutch cylinder, with the narrow band end facing the servo apply lever. Install the struts and tighten the band adjusting screw just enough to retain the band.

21. Place a selective thickness bronze thrust washer on the rear

shoulder of the stator support and retain it with vaseline. Lay a new gasket on the rear mounting face of the pump and position it on the case, being careful not to damage the O-ring. Install six of the seven mounting bolts. Adjust the intermediate band as previously described. Then, install the input shaft.

22. Install a dial indicator stand in the seventh mounting bolt and

check the transmission end-play. Remove the tool, then install the remaining bolt.

23. Install the control valve into the case, making sure that the levers engage the valves properly.

24. Install the primary throttle valve, rod, and the vacuum diaphragm into the case.

25. Install a new oil pan gasket, and the oil pan.

26. Install the converter assembly.

Approximate Refill Capacities

Lincoln Continental—1968-72	13 qt.
All other models—1968-72	12¾ qt.
All models—1966-67	13.3 qt.

Checks and Adjustments—1966-67

Operation	Specification
Transmission end play	0.008-0.044 inch selective thrust washers available
Turbine and stator end play	0.060 in.
Intermediate band adjustment	Adjust screw to 10 ft-lbs torque, then back off one full turn and tighten lock nut to specification.
Forward clutch pressure plate-to-snap ring clearance	0.048-0.061 in.
Selective snap ring thicknesses	0.065-0.069 in. 0.083-0.087 in. 0.074-0.078 in.

Reverse-high clutch pressure plate-to-snap ring clearance	*Transmission Models*	
	PDD—B, C, K, T, U, S and W	PDD—D, L, F, H and N
	0.022-0.036 Inch	0.027-0.043 Inch

Selective snap ring clearances		
	0.065-0.069 in. 0.083-0.087 in. 0.074-0.078 in.	

Checks and Adjustments—1968-72

Operation	Specification
Transmission end play	0.008-0.044 (selective thrust washers available)
Turbine and stator end play	New or rebuilt 0.021 in. max. Used 0.030 in. max. ①
Intermediate band adjustment	Remove and discard locknut. Adjust screw to 10 ft-lbs torque, then back off 1 turn, install new lock nut and tighten locknut to specification. ②
Forward clutch pressure plate-to-snap ring clearance	0.031-0.044
Selective snap ring thicknesses	0.056-0.060 in., 0.065-0.069 in., 0.074-0.078 in., 0.083-0.087 in., 0.092-0.096 in.

Operation	Specification
Reverse-high clutch pressure plate-to-snap ring clearance	*Transmission Models*
	PGA, PJA 0.022-0.036 in.
	PGB-AF2, F3, G3, PJB, PJC-A, B, E, F, PJD 0.027-0.043 in.
Selective snap ring thicknesses	0.065-0.069 in., 0.074-0.078 in, 0.083-0.087 in.

① To check end play, exert force on checking tool to compress turbine to cover thrust washer wear plate. Set indicator at zero.

② 1971-72 models: back off adjusting screw 1½ turns.

Selective Thrust Washers—1966-72

Identification No.	Thrust Washer Thickness— Inch	Identification No.	Thrust Washer Thickness— Inch
1	0.056-0.058	4	0.103-0.105
2	0.073-0.075	5	0.118-0.120
3	0.088-0.090		

Control Pressure at Zero Governor RPM—1968-72

Engine speed			Idle			As required		As required		
Throttle			Closed			As required		As required		
Manifold vacuum (inches Hg)			Above 18 ①			10		Below 1.0		
Range			Control Pressure (psi) P, N, D, 2, 1	R	TV Pressure (psi)	Control Pressure (psi) D, 2, 1	TV Pressure (psi)	Control Pressure (psi) D, 2, 1	R	TV Pressure (psi)
	Barometric Pressure in Inches HG	Nominal Altitude (Feet)								
psi @ Barometric Pressure ②	29.5	Sea Level	56-62	71-86	7-10	100-115	40-44	160-190	240-300	77-84
psi @ barometric pressure ③	28.5	1000	49-59	65-80	4-7	99-114	37-41	158-176	233-290	74-80
	27.5	2000	49-56	60-75	2-5	96-111	35-39	156-174	228-284	72-78
	26.5	3000	49-56	56-71	0-3	91-106	32-36	151-169	222-277	69-75
	25.5	4000	49-56	56-65	0	88-103	30-34	146-164	215-269	66-72
	24.5	5000	49-56	56-65	0	84-98	27-31	143-161	211-264	64-70
	23.5	6000	49-56	56-65	0	80-95	25-29	138-156	204-256	61-67

Manifold Vacuum	Barometric Pressure at 29.5 Inches ② T.V.	Barometric Pressure at 29.5 Inches ② Cont.	Barometric Pressure at 24.5 Inches ④ T.V.	Barometric Pressure at 24.5 Inches ④ Cont.
17	11-14	56-69	0-1	49-56
16	15-18	56-75	2-5	49-56
15	20-22	56-84	7-9	49-61
14	23-26	56-92	10-13	56-67
13	28-31	56-98	15-18	56-75
12	32-35	56-105	19-22	56-84
11	36-40	56-111	23-27	56-92

① It may not be possible to obtain 18 inches of engine vacuum at idle. For idle vacuums of less than 18 inches the following table provides idle speed pressure specifications in D range:

② These specifications (with altitude compensating diaphragm) apply at observed barometric pressure of 29.5 inches (nominal sea level).

③ Specifications for barometric pressures of less than 29.5 inches.

④ At barometric pressures between 29.5 inches and 24.5 inches idle, pressures should fall between the values shown.

Control Pressure at Zero Output Shaft Speed— Altitude Compensating Type Vacuum Diaphragm—1966-67

Engine speed		Idle			As required		As required		As required		
Throttle		Closed			As required		As required		Open through detent		
Manifold vacuum (inches Hg)		Above 17			15		10		Below 1.0		
Range		Control Pressure (psi) P, N, D1, D2, L	R	TV Pressure (psi)	Control Pressure (psi) D1, D2, L	TV Pressure (psi)	Control Pressure (psi) D1, D2, L	TV pressure (psi)	Control Pressure (psi) D1, D2, L	R	TV Pressure (psi)
	Barometric pressure in inches HG	Nominal altitude (feet)									
psi @ barometric pressure	29.5	Sea Level	51-66	72-108	0-13	70-78	20-22	98-109	40-44	157-172	230-252	80-84
	28.5	1000	51-59	72-104	0-11	67-75	18-20	94-105	38-41	149-163	220-242	77-81
	27.5	2000	51-59	72-99	0-8	63-71	15-17	91-101	36-38	145-159	215-236	74-78
	26.5	3000	51-59	72-99	0-5	59-67	12-14	87-97	33-36	142-157	211-231	72-76
	25.5	4000	51-59	72-92	0-3	57-64	10-12	85-94	31-33	139-154	207-227	70-74
	24.5	5000	51-59	72-83	0	51-60	7-9	81-90	28-31	136-151	202-222	67-72
	23.5	6000	51-59	72-83	0	51-60	5-7	78-87	26-28	132-147	198-217	64-68

Torque Limits—1968-72

	Ft-Lbs
Converter to flywheel	20-30
Front pump to trans. case	12-20
Overrunning clutch race to case	18-25
Oil pan to case	12-16
Stator support to pump	12-16
Converter cover to converter hsg.	12-16
Guide plate to case	12-16
Intermediate servo cover to case	10-14
Diaphragm assy. to case	15-23
Distributor sleeve to case	12-16
Extension assy. to trans. case	25-30
Pressure gauge tap	9-15
Band adj. screw locknut to case	35-45
Cooler tube connector lock	25-35
Converter drain plug	14-28
Manual valve inner lever to shaft	30-40 ①
Downshift lever to shaft	12-16
Filler tube to engine	20-25
Transmission to engine	40-50
Steering col. lock rod adj. nut	10-20
Neutral start switch actuator lever bolt	6-10

	In-Lbs
End plates to body	20-30
Inner downshift lever stop	20-30
Reinforcement plate to body	20-30
Screen and lower to upper valve body	50-60 ②
Neutral switch to case	55-75
Neutral switch-to column	20
Control assy. to case	90-125 ③
Gov. body to collector body	80-120 ④
Oil tube connector	80-145

① 1969 torque limits— 8-12 ft.-lbs.
② 1968 torque limits— 40-50 ft.-lbs.
③ 1968 torque limits—100-120 ft.-lbs.
④ 1968 torque limits—100-120 ft.-lbs.

Torque Limits—1966-67

	Ft-Lbs
Pressure gauge tap	9-15
Servo cover to case	10-14
Parking rod guide plate to case	12-16
Outer downshift lever to shaft	12-16
Distributor sleeve to case	12-16
Support assy. to pump body	12-16
Oil pump to case	12-16
Oil pan to case	12-16
Conv. hsg. lower cover to trans.	12-16
Converter drain plugs	14-28
Diaphragm assy. to case	15-23
One-way clutch race to case	18-25
Flywheel to converter	20-30
Extension hsg. to case	25-30
Connector assy. to case	25-35
Manual lever to shaft	30-40
Band adj stop to case	35-45
Transmission to engine	40-50

	In-Lbs
Plate to control assy.	20-30
Lower to upper valve body	40-50
Upper to lower valve body	40-50
Screen & lwr v.b. to upper v.b.	40-50
Neutral switch assy. to case	55-75
Control assy. to case	100-120
Governor to collector	100-120

General Motors Corporation

Powerglide

Application

Camaro, 1967-69, 1971-72	Firebird (M-35), 1970-72	Ventura II (M-35), 1971-72
Chevelle, 1965-72	Monte Carlo, 1970-72	Catalina (M-35), 1970-72
Chevrolet, 1965-72	Nova, 1969-72	
Chevy II, 1965-68	Tempest (M-35), 1970-72	
Corvette, 1965-67	Vega, 1971-72	

Diagnosis

This diagnosis guide covers the most common symptoms and is an aid to careful diagnosis. The items to check are listed in the sequence to be followed for quickest results. Thus, follow the checks in the order given for the particular transmission type.

TROUBLE SYMPTOMS	Items to Check	
	In Car	Out of Car
Car will not move in any selector position	ABC	cab
Engine speed flares, as slipping clutch	ABDFE	def
Engine speed flares on upshift	ADBG	ghi
Transmission will not upshift	HIJ	klm
Harsh upshift	JDGK	
Harsh deceleration downshift	DLMNG	
No downshift	MHI	
Clutch failure, burnt plates	DAHO	hi
Excessive creep in drive	JL	
Car creeps in neutral	J	hd
No drive in reverse	J	jng
Improper shift points	JIH	l
Unable to push-start car		m
Oil leaks	PQG	oa
Oil forced out at filler tube	AQ	p

Key to Checks

A. Oil level
B. Oil screen
C. Pressure regulator valve
D. Band adjustment
E. Servo seal
F. Servo blocked
G. Vacuum modulator or line
H. Governor
I. Throttle valve

J. Throttle linkage
K. Hydraulic modulator valve
L. Too high idle speed
M. Valves malfunctioning
N. Make pressure tests
O. Driving too fast in low
P. Oil leaks at external points
Q. Oil cooler or lines

a. Front pump
b. Input shaft
c. Front pump priming valve
d. Low band
e. Low band linkage
f. Converter stator
g. Clutch feed blocked
h. High clutch

i. Front clutch relief valve
j. Reverse clutch relief valve
k. Low clutch valve stuck
l. Rear pump priming valve
m. Rear pump or drive
n. Low clutch
o. Front pump attaching bolts
p. Pump circuit leakage

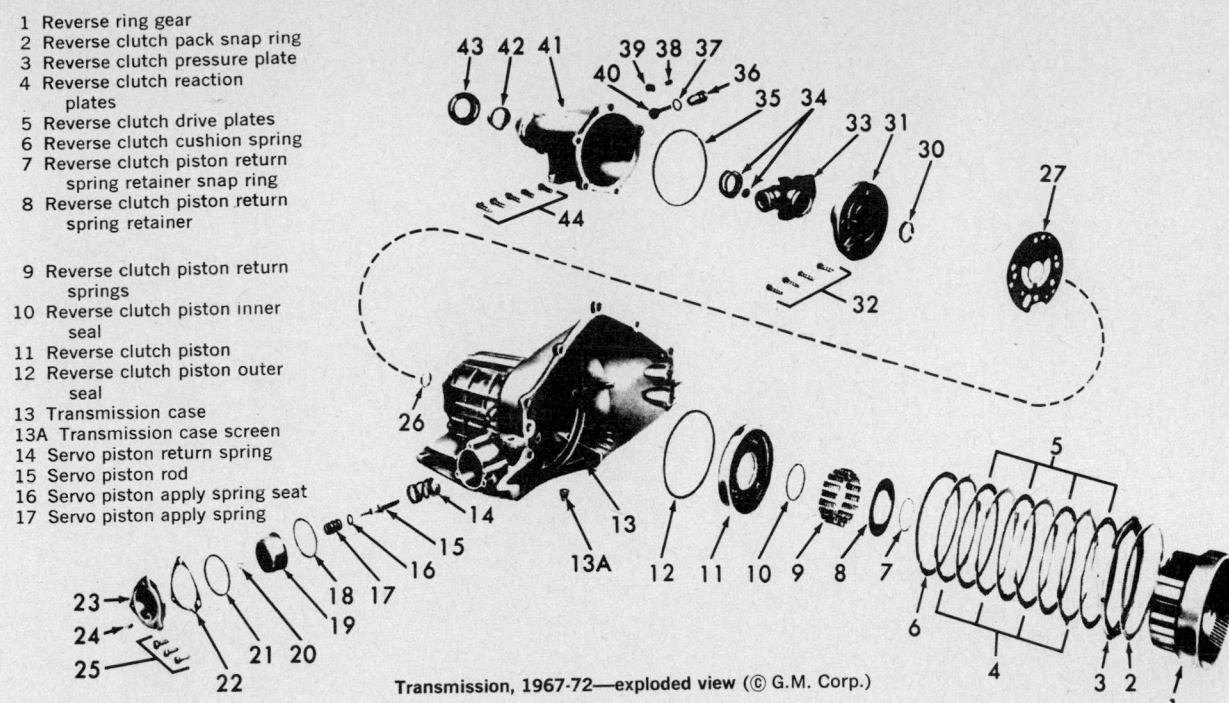

1 Reverse ring gear
2 Reverse clutch pack snap ring
3 Reverse clutch pressure plate
4 Reverse clutch reaction plates
5 Reverse clutch drive plates
6 Reverse clutch cushion spring
7 Reverse clutch piston return spring retainer snap ring
8 Reverse clutch piston return spring retainer
9 Reverse clutch piston return springs
10 Reverse clutch piston inner seal
11 Reverse clutch piston
12 Reverse clutch piston outer seal
13 Transmission case
13A Transmission case screen
14 Servo piston return spring
15 Servo piston rod
16 Servo piston apply spring seat
17 Servo piston apply spring

18 Servo piston seal ring
19 Servo piston
20 Servo piston rod spring retainer
21 Servo cover seal
22 Servo cover gasket
23 Servo cover
24 Servo cover plug
25 Servo cover bolts
26 Transmission case bushing
27 Gasket
30 Governor support bushing
31 Governor support
32 Governor support to case attaching bolts

33 Governor assembly
34 Speedometer drive gear and clip
35 Seal
36 Speedometer shaft fitting
37 Speedometer shaft fitting oil seal
38 Lock plate attaching screw
39 Lock plate
40 Speedometer driven gear
41 Transmission extension
42 Extension bushing
43 Extension oil seal
44 Extension to case attaching screws

Transmission, 1967-72—exploded view (© G.M. Corp.)

General Description

The Powerglide transmission is a two speed unit with a one piece aluminum case and an aluminum case extension.

Driving ranges are low, high and reverse, with a throttle controlled downshift to low range available for sudden acceleration.

The gear type oil pump is used integrally as the front bulkhead of the transmission. The torque converter is a three element welded unit bolted to the engine flywheel, driveing through a two speed planetary gearset. Low range uses a band clutch; drive and reverse ranges use disc clutches. The valve body assembly is bolted to the bottom of the transmission case and is accessible for service when the oil pan is removed. The vacuum modulator is located on the left rear face of the transmission case and the modulator valve bore is in the upper part of the valve body assembly. The governor is mounted to the output shaft, inside the case extension.

Transmission removal and installation, shift linkage adjustment, neutral safety switches, and transmission downshift linkages are covered in the car sections.

Fluid Change Schedule

On 1965-66 models, it is not necessary to change the oil unless the transmission is removed. On 1967 models, the manufacturer recommends draining the transmission every 12,000 miles. On 1968-72 models, drain the transmission every 24,000 miles (12,000 miles if a taxi or used heavily in city traffic). All transmissions should be checked for proper fluid level every 6,000 miles at least. The Camaro, Chevy II, Nova, Vega and Pontiac models require 1½ quarts fluid to refill; all others, 2 quarts. Check the fluid level with the engine idling, transmission in Neutral and engine at operating temperature.

Transmission Disassembly

Extension, Governor and Rear Oil Pump—1965-66

1. Place transmission in a holding fixture, if possible.
2. Remove converter holding tool, then lift off the converter.
3. If replacement is necessary, remove speedometer driven gear. Loosen cap screw and retainer clip and remove gear from extension.
4. Remove transmission extension by removing five attaching bolts. Note seal ring on rear pump body.
5. Remove speedometer drive gear from output shaft.
6. Remove C-clip from governor shaft of the weight side of governor, then remove the shaft and governor valve from the opposite side of the governor assembly and the two belleville springs.
7. Loosen the governor drive screw and slide the governor over the end of the output shaft.
8. Remove four bolts holding the rear oil pump to the transmission case and remove the pump body, drain back baffle, extension seal ring, drive and driven gears.
9. Remove oil pump drive pin. (This is of extreme importance.)
10. Remove the rear pump wear plate.

Extension, Governor and Governor Support—1967-72

1. Proceed with Steps 1-7 from the procedure for 1965-66 models given above.

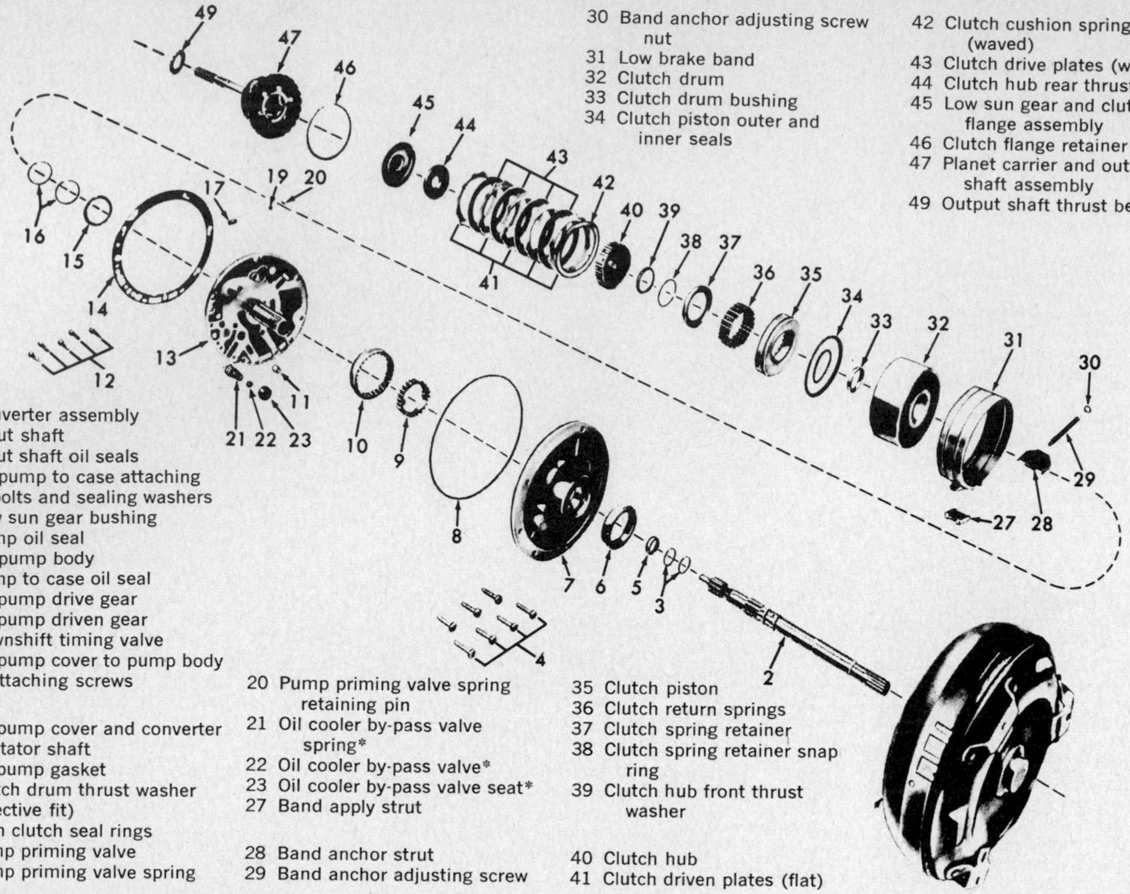

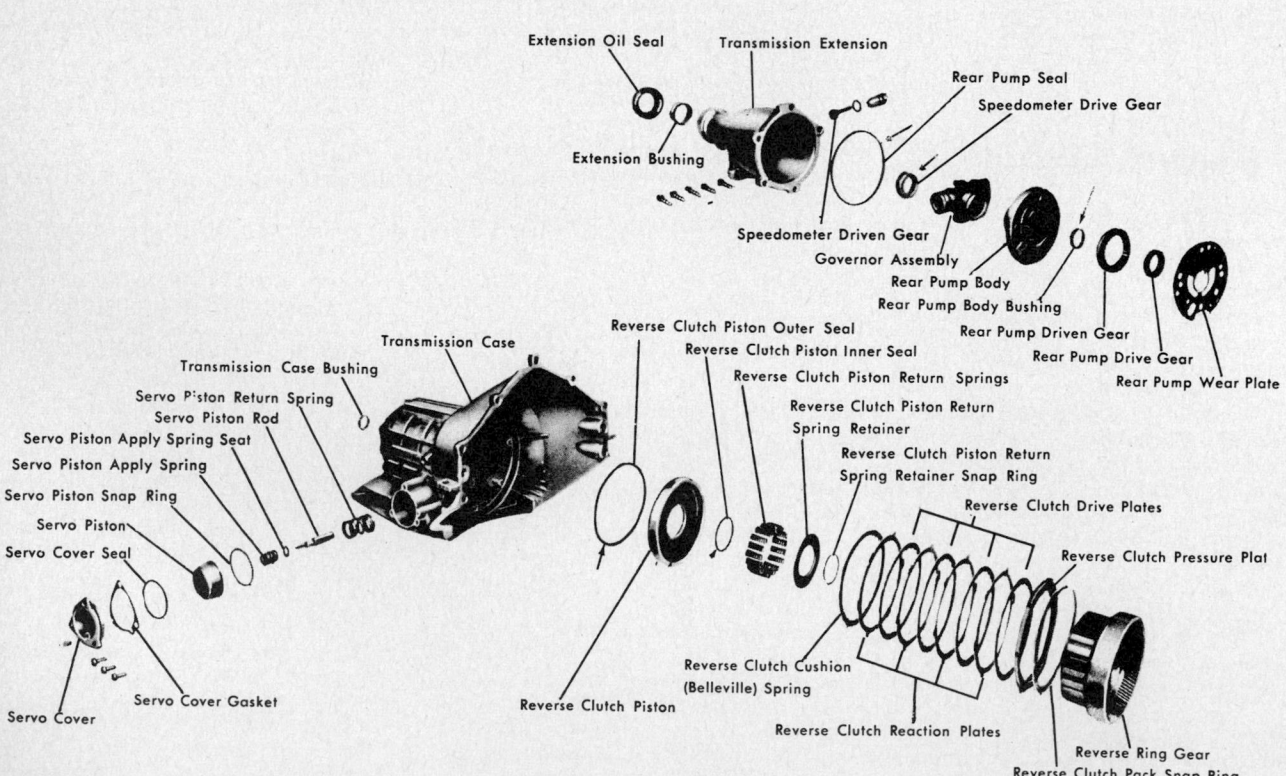

30 Band anchor adjusting screw
    nut
31 Low brake band
32 Clutch drum
33 Clutch drum bushing
34 Clutch piston outer and
    inner seals

42 Clutch cushion spring
    (waved)
43 Clutch drive plates (waved)
44 Clutch hub rear thrust washer
45 Low sun gear and clutch
    flange assembly
46 Clutch flange retainer ring
47 Planet carrier and output
    shaft assembly
49 Output shaft thrust bearing

1 Converter assembly
2 Input shaft
3 Input shaft oil seals
4 Oil pump to case attaching
    bolts and sealing washers
5 Low sun gear bushing
6 Pump oil seal
7 Oil pump body
8 Pump to case oil seal
9 Oil pump drive gear
10 Oil pump driven gear
11 Downshift timing valve
12 Oil pump cover to pump body
    attaching screws

13 Oil pump cover and converter
    stator shaft
14 Oil pump gasket
15 Clutch drum thrust washer
    (selective fit)
16 High clutch seal rings
17 Pump priming valve
18 Pump priming valve spring

20 Pump priming valve spring
    retaining pin
21 Oil cooler by-pass valve
    spring*
22 Oil cooler by-pass valve*
23 Oil cooler by-pass valve seat*
27 Band apply strut

28 Band anchor strut
29 Band anchor adjusting screw

35 Clutch piston
36 Clutch return springs
37 Clutch spring retainer
38 Clutch spring retainer snap
    ring
39 Clutch hub front thrust
    washer

40 Clutch hub
41 Clutch driven plates (flat)

*Except air cooled and 11" converter models.

Internal mechanism, 1967-72—exploded view (© G.M. Corp.)

Transmission—1965-66 (© G.M. Corp.)

Removing governor valve and shaft
(© G.M. Corp.)

REAR PUMP DRIVE PIN

Removing rear oil pump drive pin
(© G.M. Corp.)

2. Remove four bolts holding the governor support to the transmission case and remove the support body, gasket, and extension seal ring.
3. Go on to Step 11.

Transmission Internal Components

11. Rotate holding fixture, or turn the transmission, until the front end is pointing up. Then remove the seven front oil pump bolts. (The bolt holes are of unequal spacing to prevent incorrect location upon installation.)
12. Remove the front oil pump and stator shaft assembly and the selective fit thrust washer using an inertia puller or substitute.

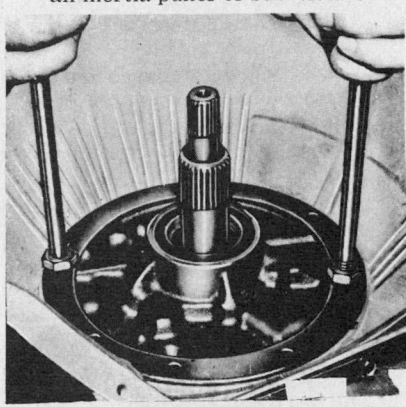

Removing front pump
(© G.M. Corp.)

LOW SUN GEAR THRUST WASHER

LOW SUN GEAR BUSHING

Removing clutch drum and input shaft
(© G.M. Corp.)

13. Release tension on the low band adjustment, then with transmission horizontal, grasp the transmission input shaft and carefully work it and the clutch drum out of the case. Be careful not to lose the low sun gear bushing from the input shaft. The low sun gear thrust washer will probably remain in the planet carrier.
14. The low brake band and struts may now be removed.
15. Remove the planet carrier and the output shaft thrust caged bearing from the front of the transmission.
16. Remove reverse ring gear if it did not come out with the planet carrier.
17. With a large screwdriver, remove the reverse clutch pack retainer ring and lift out the reverse clutch plates and the cushion spring.

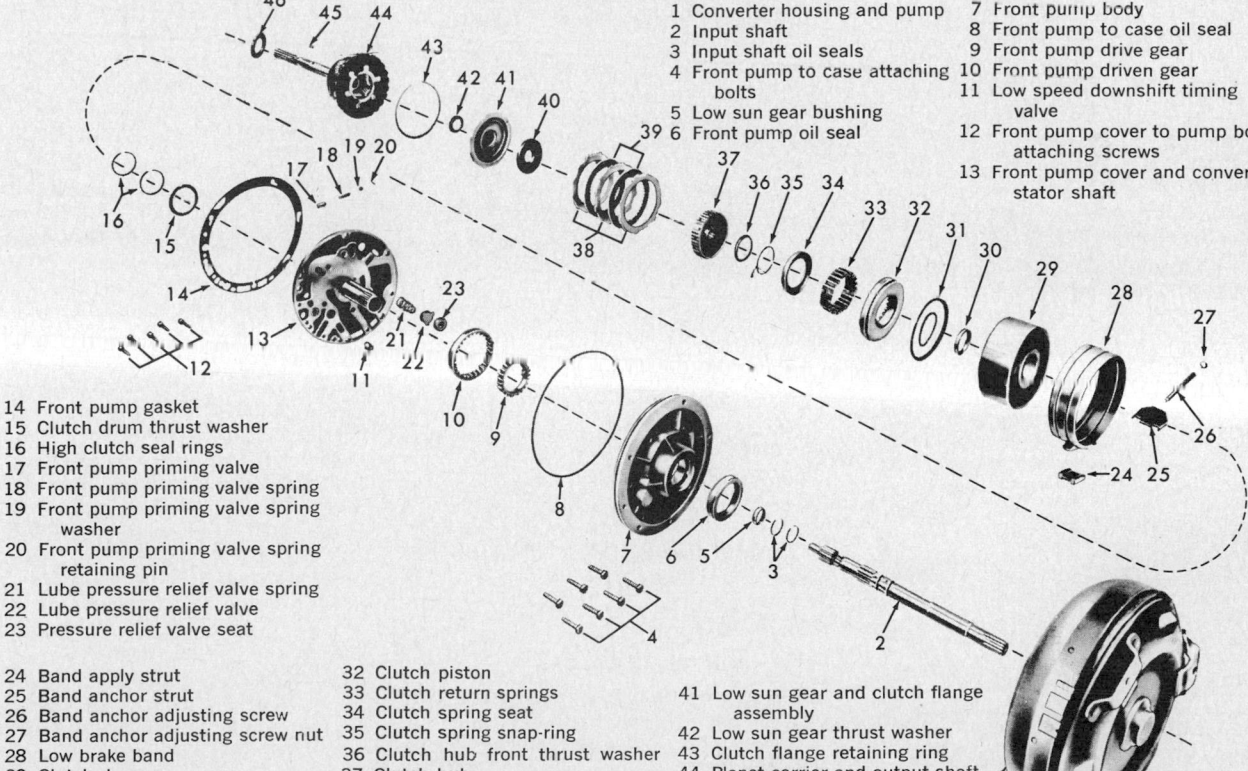

1 Converter housing and pump
2 Input shaft
3 Input shaft oil seals
4 Front pump to case attaching bolts
5 Low sun gear bushing
6 Front pump oil seal
7 Front pump body
8 Front pump to case oil seal
9 Front pump drive gear
10 Front pump driven gear
11 Low speed downshift timing valve
12 Front pump cover to pump body attaching screws
13 Front pump cover and converter stator shaft

14 Front pump gasket
15 Clutch drum thrust washer
16 High clutch seal rings
17 Front pump priming valve
18 Front pump priming valve spring
19 Front pump priming valve spring washer
20 Front pump priming valve spring retaining pin
21 Lube pressure relief valve spring
22 Lube pressure relief valve
23 Pressure relief valve seat

24 Band apply strut
25 Band anchor strut
26 Band anchor adjusting screw
27 Band anchor adjusting screw nut
28 Low brake band
29 Clutch drum
30 Clutch drum bushing
31 Clutch piston outer and inner seals

32 Clutch piston
33 Clutch return springs
34 Clutch spring seat
35 Clutch spring snap-ring
36 Clutch hub front thrust washer
37 Clutch hub
38 Clutch driven plates (flat)
39 Clutch drive plates (waved) (2)
40 Clutch hub rear thrust washer

41 Low sun gear and clutch flange assembly
42 Low sun gear thrust washer
43 Clutch flange retaining ring
44 Planet carrier and output shaft assembly
45 Rear pump drive pin
46 Output shaft thrust bearing

Internal mechanism—1965-66 (© G.M. Corp.)

18. Install reverse piston spring compressor through rear bore of the case, with the flat plate on the rear face of the case, and turn down wing nut to compress the rear piston spring retainer and springs. Then remove the snap ring. A spring compressor may be made up from a suitable length bolt and large flat washers.
19. Remove the compression tool, the reverse piston spring retainer, and the 17 piston return springs.
20. Remove the rear piston by applying air pressure to the reverse port in the rear of the transmission case. Remove inner and outer seals.
21. Remove the three servo cover bolts, servo cover, piston and spring.

Oil Pan and Valve Body

NOTE: the oil pan and valve body may be serviced without removing the extension, and internal components, covered in the preceding steps.
22. Rotate the transmission until the unit is upside down (oil pan on top). Remove oil pan attaching bolts, oil pan, and gasket. Remove the screen. Replace at assembly, using a new case screen.
23. Remove vacuum modulator and gasket, and vacuum modulator plunger, dampening spring, and valve.
24. Remove two bolts holding the detent guide plate to the valve body and the transmission case. Remove the guide plate and the range selector detent roller spring.
25. Remove the remaining valve body-to-transmission case attaching bolts and lift out the valve body and gasket. Disengage the servo apply tube from the transmission case as the valve body is removed. On Pontiac applica-

Applying air pressure to remove rear piston
(© G.M. Corp.)

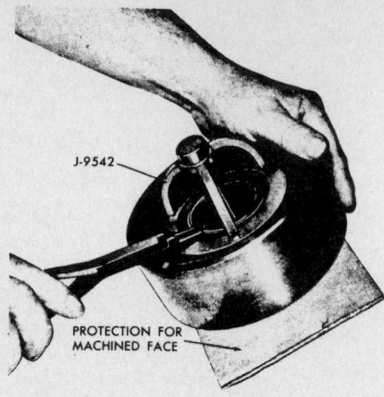

Removing clutch spring retainer snap-ring
(© G.M. Corp.)

J-9542

PROTECTION FOR MACHINED FACE

tions, remove the manual control valve from the valve body.
26. If necessary, the throttle valve, shift and parking actuator levers and the parking pawl and bracket may be removed, as follows:
   a. Loosen the allen head screw on the inner TV lever and remove the inner TV lever and shaft from the outer TV lever. Remove the O-ring seal and special washer from the outer TV shaft and remove the inner TV shaft from the case.
   b. Remove the selector outer lever and shaft from the selector inner lever. Remove the inner selector lever parking pawl actuator from the case. Separate the actuator from the inner lever.
   c. Remove the parking pawl bracket from the case. Remove the parking pawl spring and E-clip and drive the pawl shaft forward out of the case. Remove the parking pawl.

Unit Assembly Overhaul

Converter and Stator

The converter is a welded assembly and no internal repairs are possible. Check the seams for stress or breaks and replace the converter if necessary.

Front Pump

Seal Replacement

If the front pump seal requires replacement, remove the pump from the transmission, pry out and replace the seal. Drive new seal into place. Then, if no further work is needed on the front pump, install it in the case. (The outer edge of the seal should be coated with non-hardening sealer before installation.)

Disassembly

1. Remove pump cover-to-body attaching bolts and the cover.
2. On Pontiac models, remove the 2 oil seal rings from the hub of the pump cover. Remove the downshift timing valve from the pump cover.
3. Remove the oil seal ring, match-

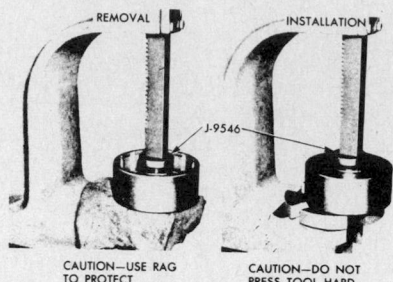

REMOVAL   INSTALLATION

J-9546

CAUTION—USE RAG TO PROTECT MACHINED FACE

CAUTION—DO NOT PRESS TOOL HARD AGAINST MACHINED FACE

Removing and installing clutch drum bushing
(© G.M. Corp.)

mark the gears for assembly, and remove the gears from the body.

Caution Do not drop or nick the gears. They are not heat treated.

Inspection

1. Wash all parts in solvent. Blow out all oil passages.
2. Inspect pump gears for nicks or damage.
3. Inspect body and cover faces for nicks or scoring. Inspect cover hub outside diameter for nicks or burrs.
4. Check for free operation of priming valve. Replace if necessary.
5. Inspect body bushing for galling or scoring. Check clearance between body bushing and converter pump hub. Maximum clearance is .005 in. If the bushing is damaged, replace the pump body.
6. Inspect converter housing hub outside diameter for nicks or burrs. Repair or replace.
7. If oil seal is damaged or leaking, pry out and drive in a new seal.
8. Check condition of oil cooler bypass valve. Replace if leaking. An "Easy-Out" type remover may be used to remove the valve. Tap new valve seat into place with a soft hammer or brass drift so that it is flush or up to .010 in. below the surface.
9. With all parts clean and dry, install pump gears and check:
   a. clearance between outside diameter of driven gear and body should be .0035-.0065 in.
   b. clearance between inside diameter of driven gear and crescent should be .003-.009 in.
   c. gear end clearance should be .0005-.0015 in.

Assembly

1. Remove the input shaft, clutch drum, low band and struts as outlined under "Transmission Disassembly."
2. Install downshift timing valve, conical end out, into place in the pump cover to a height of 17/32 in. measured from shoulder of valve assembly to face of pump cover.
3. Oil the drive and driven gears and install them into the pump body.
4. Set pump cover in place over the body and loosely install two attaching bolts. Assemble drive gear with recessed side of drive lug facing the converter.
5. Place pump assembly, less the rubber seal ring, upside down into the pump bore of the case. Install remaining attaching bolts and torque to 20 ft. lbs.
6. Remove pump assembly from case bore. On Pontiac models, install 2 high clutch oil seal rings. Replace the clutch drum and input shaft, low band and struts as described under "Transmission Assembly."
7. Renew rubber seal ring in its groove in the pump body and install the pump assembly in place in the case bore, using a new gasket. Be sure that the selective fit thrust washer is in place.
8. Install attaching bolts. (Use new bolt sealing washers if necessary.)

Rear Pump—1965-66 Models

The rear pump is removed as described in the "Transmission Disassembly" procedures earlier in this section. Inspection procedures are the same as for the front pump. Assembly of the rear pump is described in the "Transmission Assembly" procedures later in this section.

Clutch Drum

Disassembly

Caution When working with the clutch drum, use extreme care that the machined face on the front of the drum not be scratched, scored, nicked, or otherwise damaged. This machined face must be protected whenever it is brought to bear on a press or tool of any sort.

1. Remove retainer ring, low sun gear and clutch flange assembly from the clutch drum.
2. Remove the hub rear thrust washer.
3. Lift out clutch hub, then remove clutch pack and hub front thrust washer. Note the number and sequence of plates.

4. Remove spring retainer. Compress the springs with a spring compressor or an arbor press enough to permit removal of the retainer snap-ring. Then, releasing pressure on the springs, remove retainer and the 24 springs.
5. Lift up on the piston with a twisting motion to remove it from the drum, then remove inner and outer seals.

Inspection

1. Wash all parts in solvent, blow out all passages, and air dry. Do not use rags to dry parts.
2. Check drum bushing for scoring or excessive wear.
3. Check steel ball relief valve in clutch drum. Be sure that it is free to move and that orifice in front face of drum is open. If ball is loose enough to come out, or not loose enough to rattle, replace drum. Do not attempt replacement or restaking of ball.
4. Check fit of low sun gear and clutch flange assembly in clutch drum slots. There should be no appreciable radial play.
5. Check low sun gear for nicks or burrs. Check gear bore for wear.
6. Check clutch plates for burring, wear, pitting, or metal pick-up. Faced plates should be a free fit over clutch hub; steel plates should be a free fit in clutch drum slots.
7. Check condition of clutch hub splines and mating splines of clutch faced plates.
8. Check clutch pistons for cracks or distortion.

Clutch Drum Bushing Replacement

If replacing drum bushing, carefully press out the old bushing. Then press (don't hammer) the new bushing into place from the machined face side of the drum. Press only far enough to bring the bushing flush with the clutch drum. Do not force the tool against the clutch drum machined face.

Assembly

1. Install new piston inner seal into hub of clutch drum with seal lip toward front of transmission.
2. Install new piston seal into clutch piston. Seal lips must be pointed toward the clutch drum, (front of transmission). Lubricate the seals and install piston into clutch drum with a twisting motion.
3. Place 24 springs in position on the piston, then place the retainer on the springs.

4. Depress the retainer plate and springs far enough to permit installation of the spring retainer snap-ring into its groove on the clutch drum hub.
5. Install the hub front washer with its lip toward the clutch drum, then install the clutch hub.
6. Install the cushion spring if used. On Pontiac V8 and Chevrolet 350 V8 applications, the first steel drive plate to the rear of the cushion spring is a selective fit. To correctly install the clutch pack proceed as follows.

   a. Before installing the clutch pack into the drum, stack the 5 steel driven plates (except selective fit) and 5 faced drive plates. Measure this stack height.
   b. Using the measurement obtained, select the proper selective fit drive plate from the chart and install it on top of the cushion spring. Then install the faced drive plates and steel drive plates (see chart) alternately, beginning with a steel driven plate, for Chevrolet applications. On Pontiac applications, install the faced drive plates and steel driven plates, alternately, beginning with a faced drive plate.
   c. On all six-cylinder models, install the drive plates and driven plates (see chart) alternately, beginning with a steel driven plate.

NOTE: the number and sequence of plates varies with the power and torque requirements of the car model involved. On some models, the first driven plate is a selective fit. See the clutch assemblies chart for details.

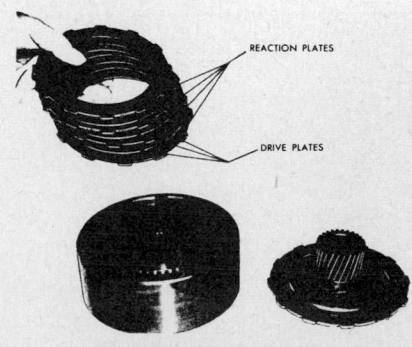

Installing clutch plates
(© G.M. Corp.)

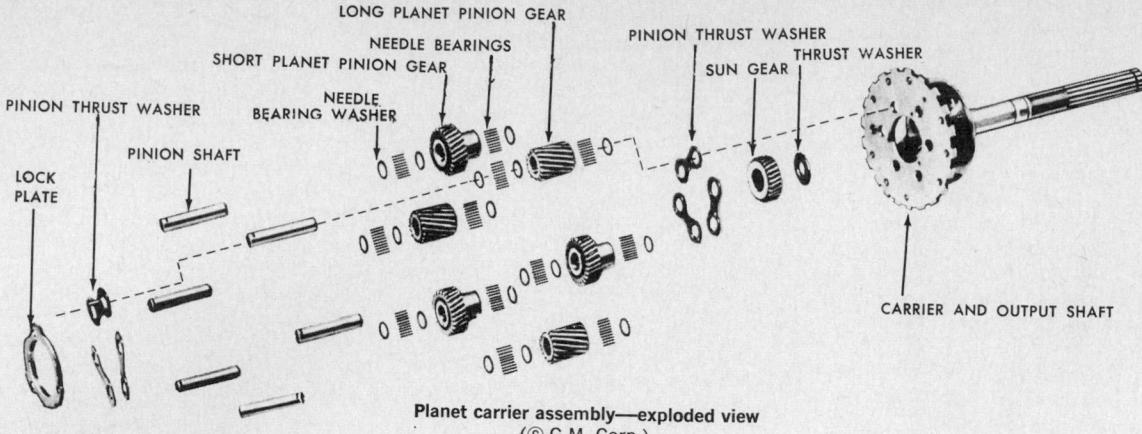

PINION THRUST WASHER — PINION SHAFT — LOCK PLATE — NEEDLE BEARING WASHER — SHORT PLANET PINION GEAR — NEEDLE BEARINGS — LONG PLANET PINION GEAR — SUN GEAR — PINION THRUST WASHER — THRUST WASHER — CARRIER AND OUTPUT SHAFT

Planet carrier assembly—exploded view
(© G.M. Corp.)

Clutch Assemblies

Up to 1968 Models	L-4 & 230 L-6 Pass. Cars.	307 V-8; Pass. Car; 250L-6 Pass. Cars (exc. Taxi & Hvy. Duty Chassis) 327V-8 Pass. Cars	250L-6 Taxi & Hvy. Duty Chassis; 396V-8 Pass. Cars.	350V-8 396V-8
Drive Plate	3	4	5	5
Driven Plate	4	5	6	6
Cushion Spring	1	1	None	1

1969-72 Models	L-4 & 230 L-6 Pass. Cars	307V-8; 230 L-6 Truck; 250-L-6 Exc. Taxi & Hvy. Duty Chassis 292 L-6 Truck	250L-6 Taxi & Hvy. Duty Chassis; 350 V-8 Truck	350V-8
Drive Plate	3	4	5	5
Driven Plate	4	5	6	6
Cushion Spring	1	1	None	1

TORQUE DRIVE

1969-72 Models	L-4, L-6
Drive Plate	5
Driven Plate	6
Cushion Spring	1

350 and 396 V8 Selective Driven Plate Chart

Plate Stack Height (Less Selective Plate)	Plate Part Number	Color Code	Plate Thickness
.903-.872	3883903	Orange	.060±.0025
.872-.798	3883904	Blue	.090±.0025

7. Install the rear hub thrust washer with its flange toward the low sun gear, then install the low sun gear and flange assembly and secure with retaining ring. When installed, the openings in the retainer ring should be adjacent to one of the lands of the clutch drum.
8. Check assembly for freedom of movement by turning the clutch hub.

Low Band

Due to band design and transmission characteristics, this band should require very little attention. However, while the transmission is disassembled, the band should be thoroughly cleaned, then replaced if any trace of scoring, burning, cracks, or excessive wear or damage is found.

Planet Assembly and Input Shaft

Inspection

1. Wash planet carrier and input shaft in cleaning solvent, blow out all passages, and air dry. Do not use rags to dry parts.
2. Inspect planet pinions for nicks or other tooth damage.
3. Check end clearance of planet gears. The clearance should be .006-.030 in.
4. Check input sun gear for tooth damage. Check thrust washer for damage.
5. Inspect output shaft bearing surface and input pilot bushing for nicks or scoring.
6. Inspect input shaft splines for nicks or damage. Check fit in clutch hub, input sun gear, and turbine hub.
7. Check oil seal rings for damage; rings must be free in input shaft ring grooves. Remove rings and insert in stator support bore. Check to see that hooked ring ends have clearance. Replace rings on shaft.

Repairs

NOTE: all large planet carrier assemblies from 1970-72, and some large planet carriers before 1970, have pinion shafts flared at each end for retention in the carrier. Do not attempt to overhaul this type of carrier assembly. If excessive wear or damage is evident, replace the entire carrier assembly. For those carriers without flared pinion shafts, the following procedure may be used for overhaul.

1. Place the planet carrier assembly in a padded vise so that the front (parking lock gear end) of the assembly is up.
2. Using a prick punch, mark each pinion shaft and the carrier assembly so that, when reassembling, each shaft will be returned to its original location.
3. Remove pinion shaft lockplate screws and rotate plate counterclockwise far enough to remove it.
4. Starting with a short planet pinion, drive the lower end of the pinion shaft up until the shaft is above the press fit area of the output shaft flange. Feed a dummy shaft into the short planet pinion from the lower end, pushing the planet pinion shaft ahead of it until the tool is centered in the pinion and the pinion shaft is removed.
5. Remove short planet pinion.
6. Remove dummy shaft, needle and bearing spacers from short pinion.

NOTE: twenty needle bearings are used in each end of each gear and are separated by a bearing spacer in the center.

7. By following Steps 4, 5, and 6, remove the adjacent long planet pinion that was paired, by thrust washers, to the short pinion now removed.
8. Remove upper and lower thrust washers.
9. Remove and disassemble remaining planet pinions, in pairs, as above.
10. Remove low sun gear needle thrust bearing, input sun gear, and thrust washer.
11. Wash all parts in solvent and blow dry, then inspect.
12. Inspect input shaft bushing in base of output shaft. If damaged, it may be removed by using a slide hammer. New bearing can be installed by using pilot end of input shaft as press tool.
13. Using dummy shaft, assemble needle bearings and spacer (20

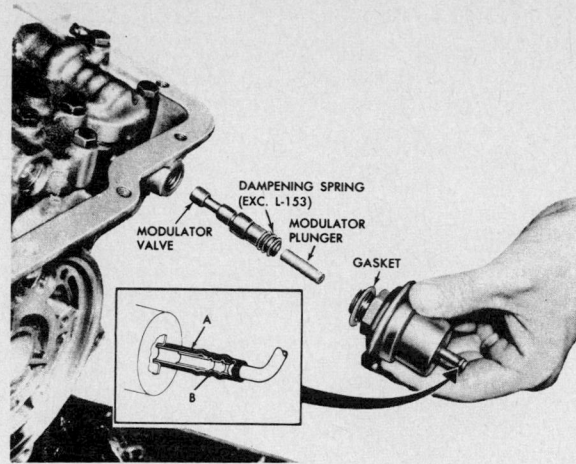

Vacuum modulator, dampening spring, plunger, and valve
(© G.M. Corp.)

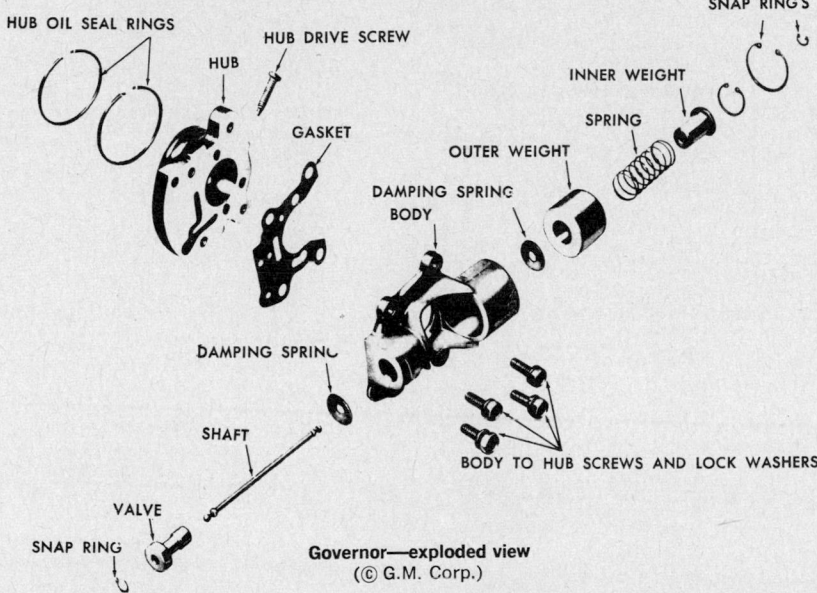

Governor—exploded view
(© G.M. Corp.)

HUB OIL SEAL RINGS
HUB DRIVE SCREW
HUB
GASKET
SNAP RINGS
INNER WEIGHT
SPRING
OUTER WEIGHT
DAMPING SPRING
BODY
DAMPING SPRING
SHAFT
VALVE
SNAP RING
BODY TO HUB SCREWS AND LOCK WASHERS

22. Check end clearance of planet gears. This clearance should be .006-.030 in.
23. Place the shaft lockplate in position. Then, with the extended portions of the lockplate aligned with slots in the planet pinion shafts, rotate the lockplate clockwise until the three attaching screw holes are accessible.
24. Install lock plate attaching screws and torque to 2½ ft. lbs.

Governor

The governor assembly is a factory balanced unit. If body replacement is needed, the two sections must be replaced as a unit.

Disassembly

NOTE: the governor valve and shaft were removed in Step 6 of "Transmission Disassembly" procedures.
1. Remove the outer weight by sliding toward center of body.
2. Remove smaller inner weight retaining snap-ring and remove inner weight and spring.
3. Remove the four body assembly bolts and separate the body, hub and gasket. Remove the two seal rings.

Inspection

1. Clean all parts in solvent and air dry.
2. Check all parts. Replace all bent, scored, or otherwise damaged parts. Body and hub must be replaced as a unit.

Assembly

1. Reassemble governor weights and install into body bore. Replace seal rings on hub.
2. Slide hub into place on output shaft and lock into place with drive screw. Install gasket and governor body over output shaft, install governor shaft, line up properly with output shaft and install body attaching bolts. Torque bolts to 6-8 ft. lbs. While tightening these bolts, engage the transmission selector lever in Park, to prevent the shaft from turning.
3. Check governor weight for free fit in body after the four attaching bolts are torqued. If the weight sticks or binds, loosen the bolts and retorque.

Valve Body

Removal

Remove valve body, as described under "Transmission Disassembly". If performing the operation on the car, the vacuum modulator valve, oil pan and gasket, guide detent plate and range selector detent roller spring must be removed in order to remove the valve from the transmission.

rollers in each end) in one of the long planet pinions. Use petroleum jelly to aid in holding the rollers in position.
14. Position long planet gear, with dummy shaft centered in the pinion and with thrust washers at each end, in the planet carrier. Oil grooves on thrust washers must be toward the gears.
NOTE: long pinions are located opposite the closed portions of the carrier and short pinions are located in the openings.
15. Feed a second dummy shaft in from the top, picking up the upper thrust washer and the pinion and pushing the already installed dummy shaft out the lower end. As the first dummy is pushed down, be sure that it picks up the lower thrust washer.
16. Select the correct pinion shaft, as marked in Step 2, lubricate the shaft and install it from the

top, pushing the assembling tools (dummy) ahead of it.
17. Turn the pinion shaft so that the slot or groove at the upper end faces the center of the assembly.
18. With a brass drift, drive the shaft in until the lower end is flush with the lower face of the planet carrier.
19. Following the same procedure as outlined in Steps 13 through 18, assemble and install a short planet pinion into the planet carrier adjacent to the long pinion now installed.
NOTE: the thrust washers, already installed with the long planet pinion, also serve for this short planet pinion, because the two pinions are paired together on one set of thrust washers.
20. Install the input sun gear thrust washer, input sun gear, and low sun gear needle thrust bearing.
21. Assemble and install the remaining planet pinions, in pairs, as previously explained.

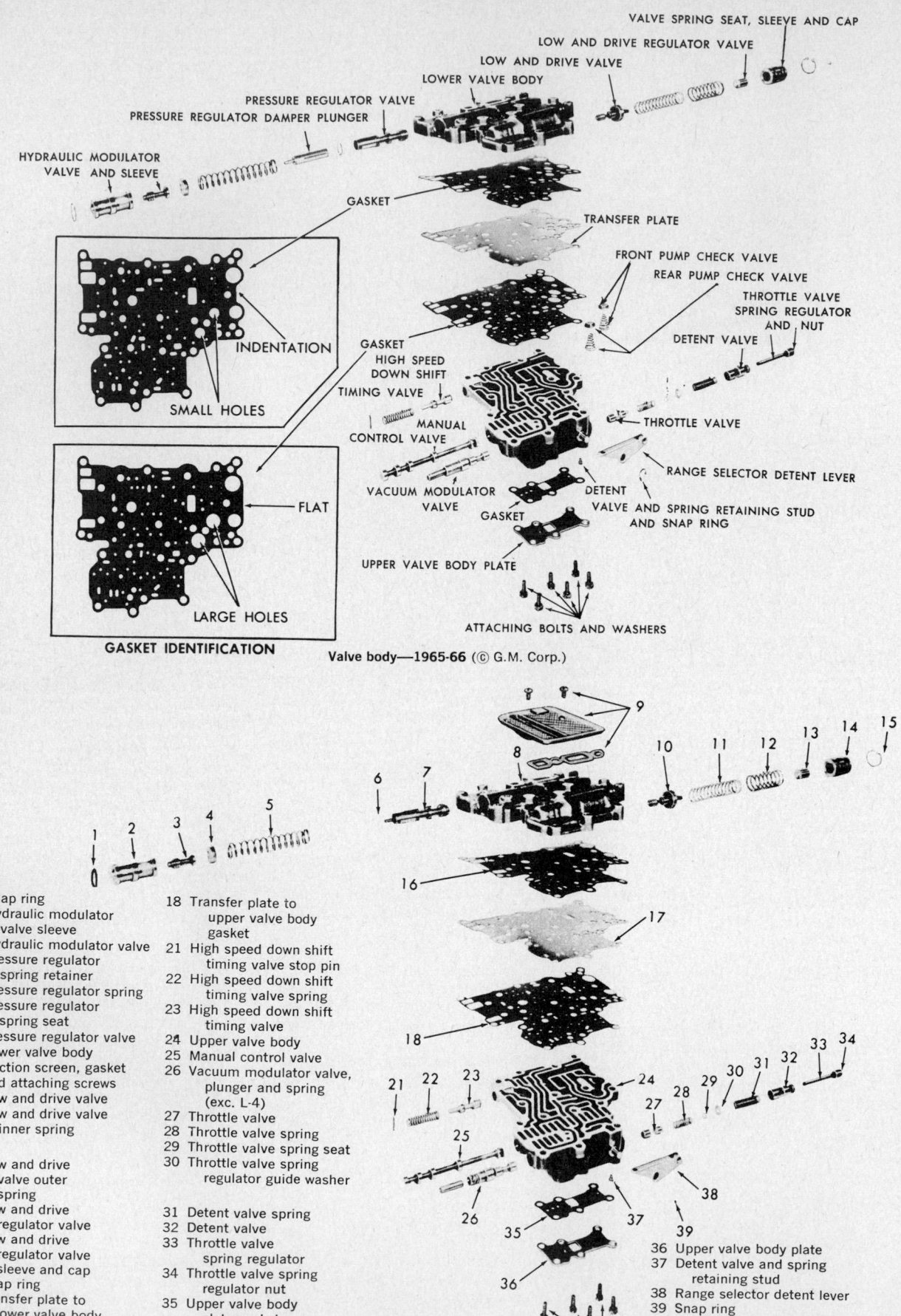

VALVE SPRING SEAT, SLEEVE AND CAP
LOW AND DRIVE REGULATOR VALVE
LOW AND DRIVE VALVE
LOWER VALVE BODY
PRESSURE REGULATOR VALVE
PRESSURE REGULATOR DAMPER PLUNGER
HYDRAULIC MODULATOR VALVE AND SLEEVE
GASKET
TRANSFER PLATE
FRONT PUMP CHECK VALVE
REAR PUMP CHECK VALVE
THROTTLE VALVE SPRING REGULATOR AND NUT
DETENT VALVE
INDENTATION
GASKET
HIGH SPEED DOWN SHIFT TIMING VALVE
THROTTLE VALVE
SMALL HOLES
MANUAL CONTROL VALVE
VACUUM MODULATOR VALVE
DETENT
RANGE SELECTOR DETENT LEVER
VALVE AND SPRING RETAINING STUD AND SNAP RING
GASKET
FLAT
UPPER VALVE BODY PLATE
LARGE HOLES
ATTACHING BOLTS AND WASHERS
GASKET IDENTIFICATION

Valve body—1965-66 (©) G.M. Corp.)

1 Snap ring
2 Hydraulic modulator valve sleeve
3 Hydraulic modulator valve
4 Pressure regulator spring retainer
5 Pressure regulator spring
6 Pressure regulator spring seat
7 Pressure regulator valve
8 Lower valve body
9 Suction screen, gasket and attaching screws
10 Low and drive valve
11 Low and drive valve inner spring
12 Low and drive valve outer spring
13 Low and drive regulator valve
14 Low and drive regulator valve sleeve and cap
15 Snap ring
16 Transfer plate to lower valve body gasket
17 Transfer plate

18 Transfer plate to upper valve body gasket
21 High speed down shift timing valve stop pin
22 High speed down shift timing valve spring
23 High speed down shift timing valve
24 Upper valve body
25 Manual control valve
26 Vacuum modulator valve, plunger and spring (exc. L-4)
27 Throttle valve
28 Throttle valve spring
29 Throttle valve spring seat
30 Throttle valve spring regulator guide washer
31 Detent valve spring
32 Detent valve
33 Throttle valve spring regulator
34 Throttle valve spring regulator nut
35 Upper valve body plate gasket

36 Upper valve body plate
37 Detent valve and spring retaining stud
38 Range selector detent lever
39 Snap ring
40 Upper valve body plate to upper valve body attaching bolts and washers

Valve body, 1967-72—exploded view (©) G.M. Corp.)

Disassembly

1. Remove manual valve, suction screen and gasket. On Pontiac applications, remove the roller spring and E-clip from the range selector detent lever and remove the detent lever from side of valve body.
2. Remove cover bolts, then remove lower valve body and transfer plate from upper valve body. Discard gaskets.
3. Remove the front and rear pump check valves and springs from 1965-66 models.
4. From the upper valve body, remove the throttle valve and detent valve and the downshift timing valve as follows:
   a. Throttle Valve and Detent Valve—Remove the retaining pin by wedging a thin screwdriver between its head and the valve body, then removing the detent valve assembly and throttle spring. Tilt valve body to allow the throttle valve to fall out. If necessary, remove the C-clip and disassemble the detent valve assembly.
   NOTE: do not change adjustment of hex nut on the detent valve assembly. This is a factory setting and should not normally be changed. However, some adjustment is possible if desired. See "Throttle Valve Adjustment," in later text.
   b. Downshift Timing Valve — Drive out the roll pin, remove valve spring and downshift timing valve.
5. From the lower valve body, remove the low-drive shift valve and the pressure regulator valve as follows:
   a. Low-Drive Shift Valve—Remove the snap-ring and tilt valve body to remove low-drive regulator valve sleeve and valve assembly, valve spring seat, valve springs and the shifter valve.
   b. Pressure Regulator Valve—Remove the snap-ring, then tilt valve body to remove the hydraulic modulator valve sleeve and valve, pressure regulator valve spring seat, spring, damper valve, spring seat and valve.

Inspection

1. Clean all parts in solvent. Air dry; use no rags.
2. Check all valves and valve bores for burrs or other deformities which could cause valve hang-up.

Assembly

NOTE: see the valve body illustration for identification of upper and lower valve body gaskets for 1965-66 models. For 1967-72 models, the gaskets are identical.

1. Replace valve components in proper bores, reversing the steps of disassembly outlined above.
2. Place front and rear pump check valves and springs into place in upper valve body on 1965-66 models only. Install the gasket and transfer plate.
3. Install lower valve body and gasket and install attaching bolts. Torque to 15 ft. lbs.
4. Install valve body onto transmission, as outlined under "Transmission, Assembly" in later text.

Vacuum Modulator

The vacuum modulator is mounted on the left rear of the transmission and can be serviced from beneath the car.

Removal

1. Remove vacuum line at the modulator.
2. Unscrew the modulator from the transmission with a thin 1 in. tappet-type wrench.
3. Remove vacuum modulator valve.

Inspection

1. Check the vacuum modulator plunger and valve for nicks and burrs. If such damage cannot be repaired with a stone, replace the part.
2. Check the vacuum modulator for leakage with a vacuum source. If the modulator leaks, replace the assembly.

Installation

Reverse removal procedure.

Transmission Assembly

NOTE: if removed, assemble manual linkage to case, as described in Steps 1-7.

1. Install parking lock pawl and shaft and insert a new E-ring retainer.
2. Install parking lock pawl pullback spring over its boss at rear of pawl. The short leg of the spring should locate in the hole in the pawl.
3. Install parking pawl reaction bracket with its two bolts.
4. Fit the actuator assembly between the parking pawl and the bracket.
5. Insert outer shift lever into the case. Pick up inner shift lever and parking lock assembly. Tighten Allen-head lock.
6. Insert outer throttle valve lever and shaft, special washer, and O-ring into case and pick up inner throttle valve lever. Tighten Allen-head lock.
7. Thread low band adjusting screw into case.

NOTE: to prevent possible binding between throttle lever and range selector controls, allow .010-.020 in. clearance between inner throttle valve lever and inner shift lever.

Transmission Internal Components

8. Install inner and outer rear piston seals onto reverse piston and, (with lubrication) install piston into the case.
9. With transmission case facing up, install the 17 reverse piston springs and their retainer ring.
10. Install spring compressing tool. Compress the return springs, allowing the retaining ring snapring to be installed. Remove the compressor.
11. Install the cushion spring.
12. Lubricate and install reverse clutch pack, beginning with a reaction spacer plate and alternating with the faced plates until all plates are installed.

NOTE: the number and sequence of plates varies with the power and torque requirements of the car model involved.

The notched lug on each reaction plate is installed in the groove at the seven o'clock position in the case. Then, install the thick pressure plate

Installing gearset
(© G.M. Corp.)

Installing reverse piston
(© G.M. Corp.)

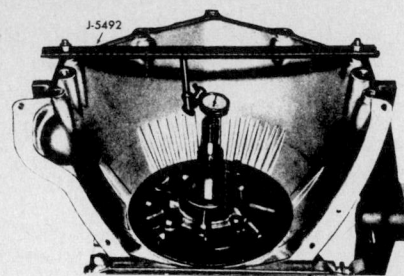

Checking end-play for proper thrust washer selection
(© G.M. Corp.)

SLIDE HAMMER BOLT

DIAL INDICATOR SET

Checking gear end-play

which has a dimple in one lug to align with the same slot in the case as the notched lugs on the other reaction plates.

13. Install clutch plate retainer ring.
14. Turn rear of transmission case down.
15. Align the internal lands and grooves of the reverse clutch pack faced plates, then engage the reverse ring gear with these plates. This engagement must be made by feel while turning the ring gear.
16. Place output shaft thrust bearing over the output shaft and install the planetary carrier and output shaft into the transmission case.
17. Move transmission to horizontal position.
18. The two input shaft seal rings should be in place on the shaft. Install clutch drum (machined face first) onto the input shaft and install the low sun gear bushing against shoulder.
19. Install clutch drum and input shaft assembly into case, aligning thrust washer on input shaft and indexing low sun gear with the short pinions on the planet carrier.
20. Remove rubber seal ring from the front pump body and install front pump, gasket and selective fit thrust washer into case. Install pump-to-case bolts.
21. To check for correct thickness of the selective fit thrust washer, move transmission so that output shaft points down and proceed as follows:
    a. Mount a dial indicator so that the indicator plunger is resting on the end of the input shaft. Zero the indicator.
    b. Push up on the output shaft and watch the total dial movement.
    c. The indicator should read .028-.059 in. If reading is not within specifications, remove front pump, change to a thicker or thinner selective thrust washer. Repeat above checking procedure.

NOTE: washers are available in thicknesses of .061, .078, .092 in. and .106 in.

22. Install servo piston, piston ring, and spring into the servo bore. Then, using a new gasket and O-ring, install the servo cover.
23. Remove front pump and selective fit washer from the case, and install the low brake band, anchor and apply struts into the case. Tighten the low band adjusting screw enough to prevent struts from falling out of case.
24. Place the seal ring in the groove around front pump body and the two seal rings on the pump cover extension. Install the pump, gasket and thrust washer into the case. Install all pump bolts. Torque bolts to 15 ft. lbs.

Extension, Governor and Rear Oil Pump—1965-66 Models

25. Turn transmission so that output shaft points upward. Install rear pump wear plate, drive pin, and drive gear, indexing gear to drive pin.
26. Install rear pump body and driven gear, drain back baffle and pump-to-case attaching bolts.
27. Install governor over output shaft. Install governor shaft and valve, two Belleville washers, and retaining C-clips. Center shaft in output shaft bore and tighten governor drive screw.
28. Install speedometer drive gear onto output shaft.
29. Place extension seal ring over rear pump body and install transmission extension and five retaining bolts.
30. If removed, replace speedometer driven gear.

Extension, Governor and Governor Support—1967-72 Models

25. Turn transmission so that output shaft points upward.
26. Install governor support and gasket, drain back baffle, and support to case attaching bolts.

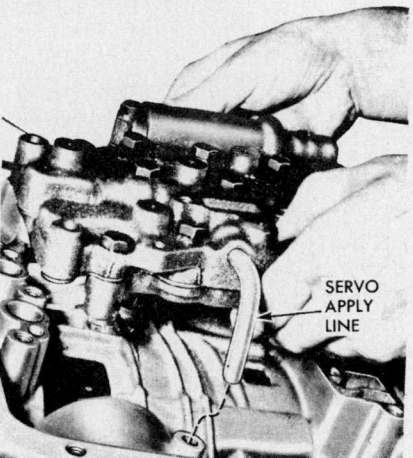

SERVO APPLY LINE

Installing valve body
(© G.M. Corp.)

Installing detent guide plate
(© G.M. Corp.)

27. Install governor over output shaft. Install governor shaft and valve, urethane washer, and retaining C clips. Center shaft in output shaft bore and tighten governor hub drive screw.
28. Install speedometer gear to output shaft.
29. Place extension seal ring over governor support. Install transmission extension and five retaining bolts.
30. Replace speedometer driven gear.

Oil Pan and Valve Body

31. With transmission upside down, the manual linkage and the se-

Checking pump body bushing to converter pump hub clearance
(© G.M. Corp.)

Checking driven gear to crescent clearance
(© G.M. Corp.)

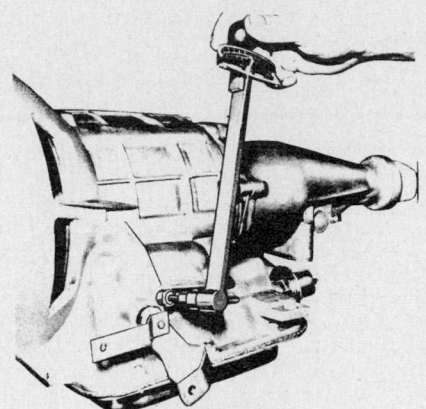

Low band adjustment
(© G.M. Corp.)

Checking drive gear to pump body clearance
(© G.M. Corp.)

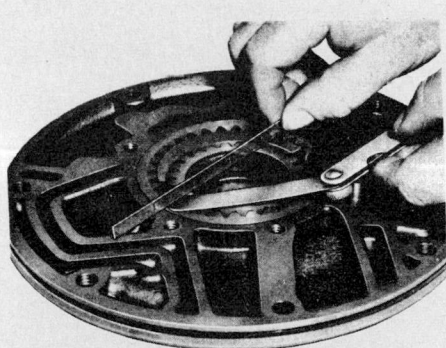

Checking gear end-play
(© G.M. Corp.)

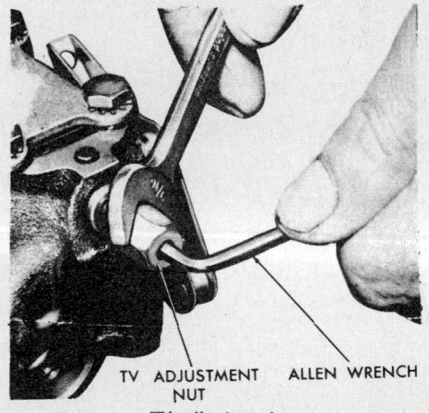

TV ADJUSTMENT NUT   ALLEN WRENCH
TV adjustment
(© G.M. Corp.)

lector lever detent roller installed, install the valve body with a new gasket. (Carefully guide the servo apply line into its boss in the case as the valve body is set in place.) Position the manual valve actuating lever fully forward to more easily pick up the manual valve. Install six mounting bolts and the range se-

lector detent roller spring. On 1967-72 models, install new gasket and suction screen to valve body.
32. Install the guide plate. Install attaching bolts.
33. Install vacuum modulator valve, the vacuum modulator and the gasket.
34. Install oil pan, using a new gas-

ket, then the pan attaching bolts.
35. Install the converter and safety holding strap.

Low Band Adjustment

Tighten the low servo adjusting screw to 40 in. lbs. for 1965-66 models; 70 in. lbs. for 1967-70 models. The input and output shaft must be rotated simultaneously to properly center the low band on the clutch drum. Then, back off four complete turns for a band which has been in use for 6,000 miles or more, or three turns for one in use less than 6,000 miles, and tighten the locknut.

Caution   The amount of back-off is very critical. Back off exactly three or four turns.

Throttle Valve TV Adjustment

No provision is made for checking TV pressures. However, if operation of the transmission is such that some adjustment of the TV is indicated, pressures may be raised or lowered by adjusting the position of the jam nut on the throttle valve assembly. To raise TV pressure 3 psi, back off the jam nut one full turn.

Conversely, tightening the jam nut one full turn, lowers TV pressure 3 psi. A difference of 3 psi in TV pressure will cause a change of about 2-3 mph in the wide open throttle upshift point. The end of the TV adjusting screw has an Allen head so the screw may be held stationary while the jam nut is locked.

NOTE: use care in changing this adjustment, as no pressure tap is provided to check TV pressure.

Torque References

	Foot-Pounds	
	1965-66 Models	1967-72 Models
Transmission case to engine	25-30	35
Oil pan to case	7-10	7-10
Extension to case	20-30	20-30
Servo cover to case	15-20	20
Front pump to case	13-17	13-17
Front pump cover to body attaching bolts	15-20	20
Pinion shaft lock plate attaching screws	2-3	2-3
Governor body to hub	6-8	6-8
Governor hub drive screw	6-8	6-8
Rear pump or governor support to case	8-11	8-11
Valve body to case	8-11	15
Suction screen attaching screws	2-3	2-3
Upper valve body plate	3-5	5
Lower to upper valve body	13-15	15
Inner control lever allen head locks	6-8	2½
Low band adjusting locknut	13-17	13-17
Converter to engine	15-20	35

Torque Drive

Application
Camaro with 6 Cylinder Engine, 1969-70
Nova with 4 or 6 Cylinder Engine, 1969-70

General Description

A new manual shift Torque Drive transmission is available for the Nova 4 and 6 and for the Camaro 6. This Torque Drive transmission is a modified version of the Powerglide transmission, with the automatic shifting aspects removed.

The new transmission has five con-trol positions: Park, Reverse, Neutral, High, and First. Forward motion is accomplished by placing the selector in first position. After gradual acceleration to about 20 mph, the selector should be manually shifted into high. Operation of the transmission in high range at car speeds less than 20 mph is not recommended, because this may lead to overheating of the transmission oil.

Operation of the car in first at speeds above 55 mph will cause undue strain on engine components, due to the high engine rpm associated with these speeds.

The selector lever may be moved freely between High and First, but

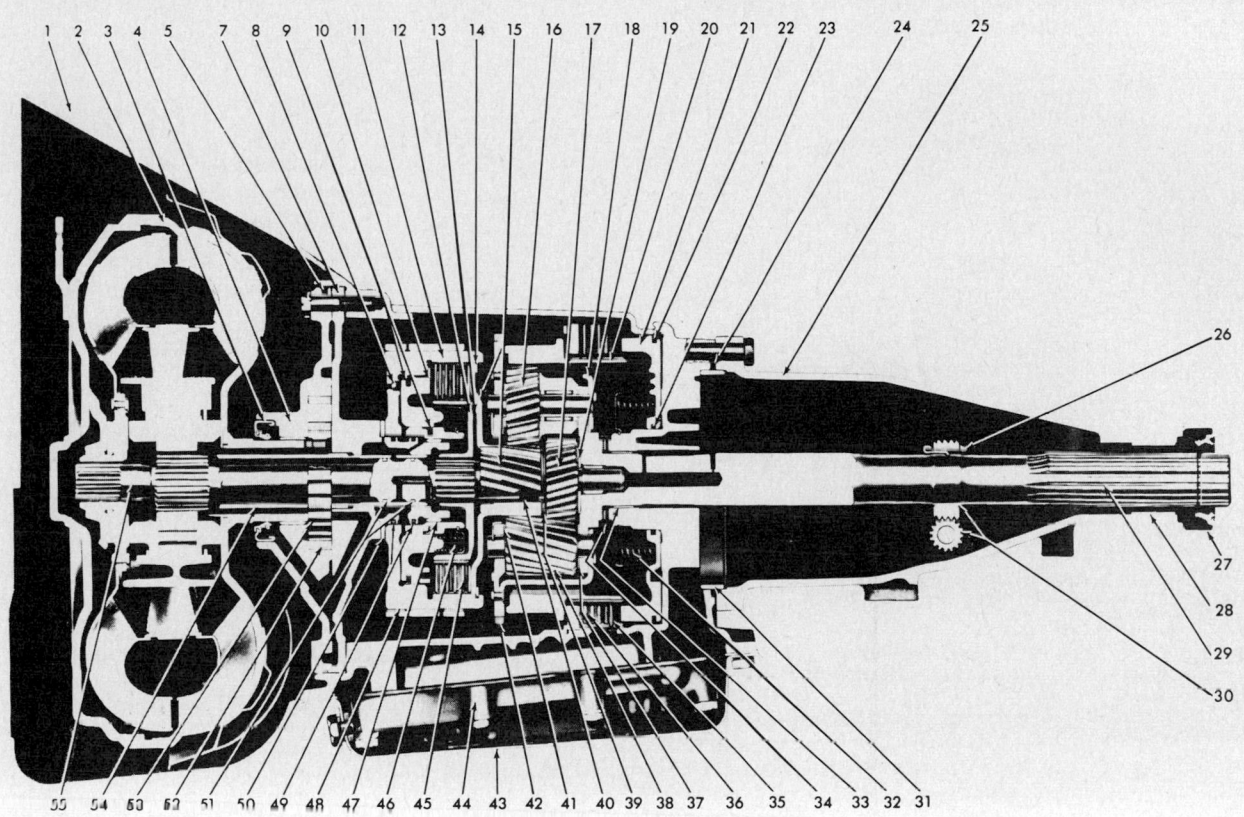

Torque drive transmission—sectional view

1 Transmission case
2 Welded converter
3 Oil pump seal assembly
4 Oil pump body
5 Oil pump body square ring seal
6 Not given
7 Oil pump cover
8 Clutch relief valve ball
9 Clutch piston inner and outer seal
10 Clutch piston
11 Clutch drum
12 Clutch hub
13 Clutch hub thrust washer
14 Clutch flange retainer ring
15 Low sun gear and clutch flange assembly
16 Planet short pinion
17 Planet input sun gear
18 Planet carrier
19 Planet input sun gear thrust washer
20 Ring gear

21 Reverse piston
22 Reverse piston outer seal
23 Reverse piston inner seal
24 Extension seal ring
25 Extension
26 Speedometer driven gear
27 Extension rear oil seal
28 Extension rear bushing
29 Output shaft
30 Speedometer drive and driven gear
31 Pilot ring
32 Reverse piston return springs, retainer and retainer ring
33 Transmission rear case bushing
34 Output shaft thrust bearing
35 Reverse clutch cushion spring (waved)
36 Reverse clutch pack
37 Pinion thrust washer
38 Planet long pinion

39 Low sun gear needle thrust bearing
40 Low sun gear bushing (splined)
41 Pinion thrust washer
42 Parking lock gear
43 Transmission oil pan
44 Valve body
45 High clutch pack
46 Clutch piston return spring, retainer and retainer ring
47 Clutch drum bushing
48 Low brake band
49 High clutch seal rings
50 Clutch drum thrust washer (selective)
51 Turbine shaft seal rings
52 Oil pump driven gear
53 Oil pump drive gear
54 Stator shaft
55 Input shaft

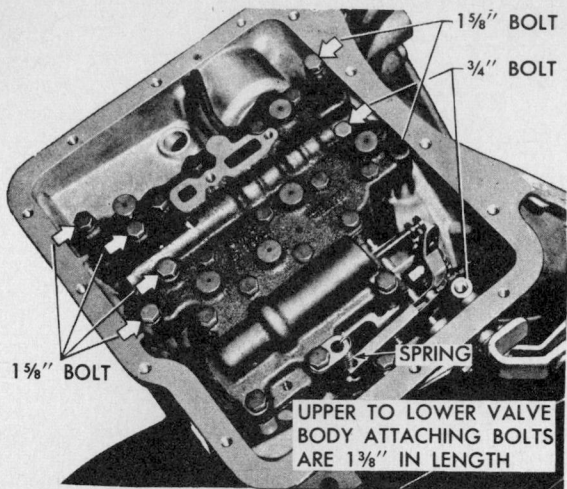

1⅝″ BOLT
¾″ BOLT
1⅝″ BOLT
SPRING

UPPER TO LOWER VALVE BODY ATTACHING BOLTS ARE 1⅜″ IN LENGTH

Valve body removal

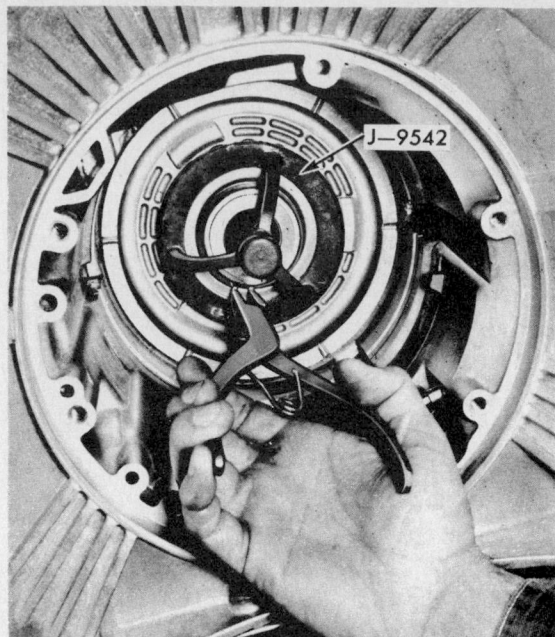

J—9542

Removing rear piston spring
retainer snap-ring

Suggested pinion shaft markings

Checking planet gear end-play

must be raised in order to shift from High to Neutral or Reverse. The lever must also be raised in order to shift into, or out of, Park.

Service Procedures

The Torque Drive transmission is a Powerglide transmission with the automatic shifting provisions omitted. Lubrication, maintenance and service information is the same as that for Powerglide. Some internal differences are as follows:

Transmission Case

The Torque Drive transmission does not use a vacuum modulator or governor. Therefore, the Powerglide case has been modified to remove the vacuum modulator tapped hole and the governor feed passage. Machining of the case, in the governor support area, has also been eliminated, since the governor and governor support are not used. Due to the elimination of the governor support, which also

performed the function of extension-to-case alignment, a pilot ring has been added to perform this function.

Park Lock and Range Selector Lever

The Torque Drive transmission does not use a throttle valve, therefore, the park lock and range selector lever is different from that used in the Powerglide, in that it does not incorporate the throttle valve lever hole.

Low Servo

The Torque Drive transmission uses higher rated return and apply springs and a longer piston rod to achieve the shifting characteristics needed for manual shift application.

Front Pump

The front pump has a new downshift timing valve, stator shaft, and pump cover. The stator shaft and cover incorporate larger orifices for

lubrication and converter feed. The pump body is the same as Powerglide.

Input Shaft

The input shaft is new only to the extent that it has larger feed orifices.

Carrier Assembly

The Torque Drive carrier is different from Powerglide in that the output shaft has a lube orifice extending to the former Powerglide rear pump drive pin hole. Oil is agitated at this point to lubricate the extension housing bushing and the speedometer gears.

Valve Body

All valves except the pressure regulator, hydraulic modulator, and manual shift have been eliminated from the valve body. The valve body has the raised letters T. D. in the center of the casting of the upper and lower portions.

Type 300

Application

Super Turbine 300—Buick, 1965-69
Buick Special, 1965-69

Two-Speed Automatic—Pontiac and GTO, 1965-66
Tempest, 1965-69
Firebird, 1967-69

Jetaway—Oldsmobile, 1965-69
Olds F-85, 1965-69

Diagnosis

This diagnosis guide covers the most common symptoms and is an aid to careful diagnosis. The items to check are listed in the sequence to be followed for quickest results. Thus, follow the checks in the order given for the particular transmission type.

TROUBLE SYMPTOMS*	Items to Check In Car	Out of Car
No drive in any selector position	ABCDE	a
Erratic operation and slippage—light acceleration	FAG	
Slippage or flare coasting to stop or cornering	HFIGJ	
Sluggish standing start	K	b
No reverse	L	cd
Slips in any range	FAGLA	
Harsh N to drive shift at idle	GH	
No upshift	MGNL	
Long shift time—not positive engagement	GL	e
Engine flares on upshift	L	fae
Late upshift	GLMNOP	
Erratic up- or down-shifts	NFAGQ	
No wide open throttle downshift	MQP	
Engine flares on wide open throttle downshift	IBGLPA	
Delayed engagement in manual low	G	
No stator action	KQP	gh
Oil surges out breather	AR	ij
Drive clutch plates burned—low band and reverse clutch ok	L	fdae
Drive clutch and reverse clutch burned, low band burned	GLA	

* Items referring to Stator Control refer to Variable Pitch Converter Models only.

Key to Checks

A. Oil level
B. Make pressure check
C. Linkage adjustment (external)
D. Linkage adjustment (internal)
E. Pressure regulator
F. Clogged filter or suction pipe leaks
G. Modulator and/or line

H. Engine idle
I. Low band adjustment
J. Low servo
K. Stator switch and/or valve
L. Valves, body and/or leaks
M. Detent solenoid or valve
N. Governor

O. Governor roll pin
P. Valve body bolt torque
Q. Crossed solenoid wires
R. Cooler or line leaks
a. Front pump
b. Stator valve or solenoid
c. Reverse clutch and/or seals

d. Reverse clutch feed
e. Front clutch and/or seals
f. Front clutch check ball
g. Reactor shaft bushing
h. Input shaft seals
i. Front pump line leaks
j. Front pump cover leaks

Maximum Line Pressure Checks①
Buick, 1965-69

Year	Engine and Vacuum Modulator Identification	Sea Level @ 29.92 D and L ± 4 psi	Sea Level @ 29.92 R ± 6 psi	2,000 @ 27.82 D and L ± 4 psi	2,000 @ 27.82 R ± 6 psi	5,000 @ 24.89 D and L ± 4 psi	5,000 @ 24.89 R ± 6 psi	10,000 @ 20.58 D and L ± 4 psi	10,000 @ 20.58 R ± 6 psi
1965	225 V6 # 1365186 # 1365187	137	213	130	202	120	186	105	163
	225 V6 # 1367031 # 1367032	141	219	134	207	124	192	109	168
	300 V8 # 8623364 # 8623365	149	230	142	219	131	203	117	183
1966- 1967	225 V6 # 1367032	152	218	144	206	131	189	114	164
	340 V8 # 8623365 # 8623947	161	231	153	218	140	201	123	177
	300 V8 # 1377046	156	224	148	213	136	195	118	177
	Skylark GS (1966) # 1361577	166	237	157	225	145	208	127	183
1968	250 L6 # 1367032	160	243	152	230	138	210	119	180
1969	350 V8 # 8623947	170	258	161	244	148	224	129	195

Oldsmobile, 1965-69

Year	Engine and Vacuum Modulator Identification	Sea Level @ 29.92 D and L ± 4 psi	Sea Level @ 29.92 R ± 6 psi	2,000 @ 27.82 D and L ± 4 psi	2,000 @ 27.82 R ± 6 psi	5,000 @ 24.89 D and L ± 4 psi	5,000 @ 24.89 R ± 6 psi	10,000 @ 20.58 D and L ± 4 psi	10,000 @ 20.58 R ± 6 psi
1965	225 V6	135-143②	207-219③	N.A.	N.A.	N.A.	N.A.	N.A.	N.A.
	330 V8 (regular fuel)	142-150②	223-235③	N.A.	N.A.	N.A.	N.A.	N.A.	N.A.
	330 V8 (premium fuel)	146-154②	226-238③	N.A.	N.A.	N.A.	N.A.	N.A.	N.A.
1966- 1967	250 L6 # 1367032	152	218	144	206	131	189	114	164
	330 V8 # 8623365	161	231	153	218	140	201	123	177
	400 V8 (1966) # 8623365	166	237	157	225	145	208	127	183
1968- 1969	250 L6 # 1367032	160	243	152	230	138	210	119	180
	350 V8 # 8623365	161	257	153	243	140	224	123	186

Pontiac, 1965-69

Year	Engine and Vacuum Modulator Identification	Sea Level @ 29.92 D and L ± 4 psi	Sea Level @ 29.92 R ± 6 psi	2,000 @ 27.82 D and L ± 4 psi	2,000 @ 27.82 R ± 6 psi	5,000 @ 24.89 D and L ± 4 psi	5,000 @ 24.89 R ± 6 psi	10,000 @ 20.58 D and L ± 4 psi	10,000 @ 20.58 R ± 6 psi
1965	215 L6	140-160	N.A.	N.A.	N.A.	N.A.	N.A.	N.A.	N.A.
	350 V8	150-160	N.A.	N.A.	N.A.	N.A.	N.A.	N.A.	N.A.
1966- 1967	215 L6, 326 V8	N.A.	N.A.	N.A.	N.A.	N.A.	N.A.	N.A.	N.A.
	215 L6	152	218	144	206	131	189	114	164
	215 L6 (4-BBL.) 326 V8 (A.I.R.)	156	224	148	213	136	195	118	171
	326 V8 (w/o A.I.R.)	161	231	153	218	140	201	123	177
1968- 1969	215 L6 (w/o A.C.)	155	④	147	④	134	④	N.A.	N.A.
	215 L6 (w/ A.C.)	147	④	140	④	128	④	N.A.	N.A.
	350 V8 (w/o A.C.)	165	④	157	④	144	④	N.A.	N.A.
	350 V8 (w/ A.C.)	163	④	155	④	144	④	N.A.	N.A.

①—Engine speed at 1,000 rpm with vacuum modulator line disconnected and plugged.

②—@ 750 rpm.

③—@ 1,000 rpm.

④—Reverse line pressure should exceed drive pressure by at least 60 psi.

General Information

The illustration is typical. While design and repair procedures are similar, components vary with car application and should not be considered interchangeable.

This transmission consists of a torque converter and a two-speed planetary transmission.

A variable pitch stator, with different valve body design was used on some 1965 models.

In either case, the torque converter is not serviceable, and must be replaced as a unit.

Minor Maintenance
Fluid Checking

The transmission must be at normal operating temperature, approximately 180° F., before the fluid level is checked. Normal operating temperature is reached after about fifteen miles of highway driving. Check the fluid level with the vehicle level, the engine idling, and the transmission in Park. The fluid level on the dipstick should be at the full mark.

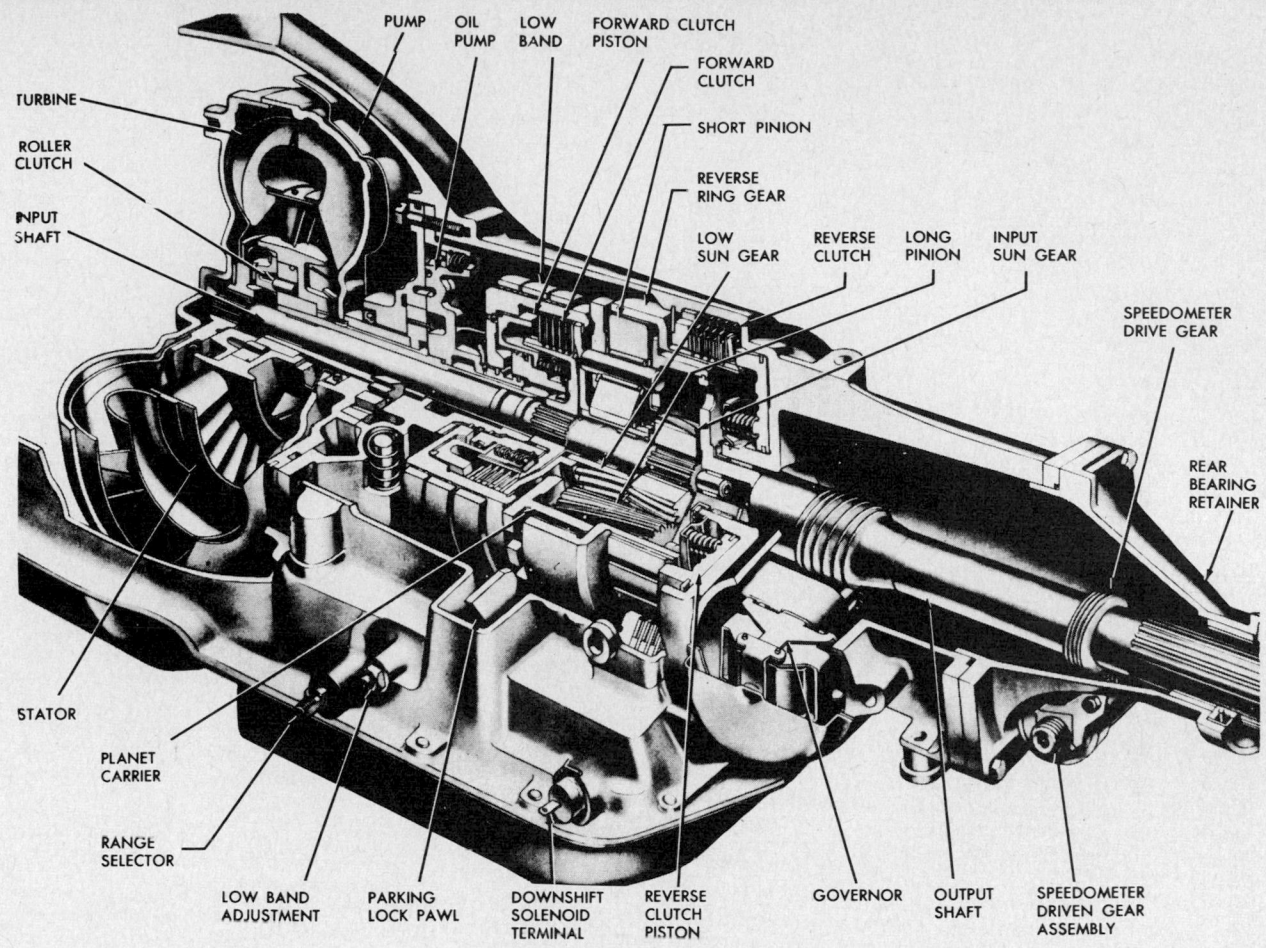

PUMP · OIL PUMP · LOW BAND · FORWARD CLUTCH PISTON · FORWARD CLUTCH · SHORT PINION · REVERSE RING GEAR · LOW SUN GEAR · REVERSE CLUTCH · LONG PINION · INPUT SUN GEAR · SPEEDOMETER DRIVE GEAR · REAR BEARING RETAINER

TURBINE · ROLLER CLUTCH · INPUT SHAFT · STATOR · PLANET CARRIER · RANGE SELECTOR · LOW BAND ADJUSTMENT · PARKING LOCK PAWL · DOWNSHIFT SOLENOID TERMINAL · REVERSE CLUTCH PISTON · GOVERNOR · OUTPUT SHAFT · SPEEDOMETER DRIVEN GEAR ASSEMBLY

Cross-section of Type 300 transmission
(© G.M. Corp.)

Minimum Line Pressure Checks[1]

Buick, 1965-69

Year	Model	Pressure (psi) @ Gear and Speed		
		Drive, 20-40 mph coast, foot off throttle	Low, 20-40 mph coast, foot off throttle	Reverse, coast, foot off throttle
1965	all	60±2	90±4	93±4
1966-67	all	56±2	92±4	84±4
1968-69	all	56±2	99±4	85±4

Oldsmobile, 1965-69

1965-67[2]	all	60±2	90±4	93±4
1968-69	all	56±2	92±4	89±4

Pontiac, 1965-69

1965	all	N.A.	90	90
1966	N.A.	N.A.	N.A.	N.A.
1967-68	all	56	92	84

[1]—To be checked while road testing car; pressure is not affected by altitude or barometric pressure.
Park and neutral may be tested at 1,000 rpm.

[2]—1965 only—check pressures at 750 rpm

Capacity

See the Capacities table of the car section for quantity of fluid required to refill transmission after overhaul. The amount given is for both transmission and torque converter. To avoid overfilling and resultant damage, check the fluid level after adding about two-thirds of the required amount. To check fluid level after overhaul:

1. Start engine, operate shift lever through all ranges slowly. Do not race engine.
2. Place shift lever in Park with engine idling

3. Fluid level should be no higher than ½-¾ in. below Add mark on dipstick. Correct level is determined by the relation of the fluid level to the mark on the dipstick, rather than by the amount added. Do not fill a transmission at normal operating temperature above the full mark, or a cold transmission above ½-¾ in. below the Add mark.

Draining and Refilling

The transmission should be drained and refilled at 24,000 mile intervals. The oil pan and strainer should be removed and thoroughly cleaned at the same time.

Transmission Disassembly

Clean outside of transmission thoroughly to prevent dirt from entering the unit.

Oil Pan and Strainer Removal

1. Place transmission on clean work bench or in special holding fixture if available.
2. If oil has not been drained, drain

Location of serial and model number (© G.M. Corp.)

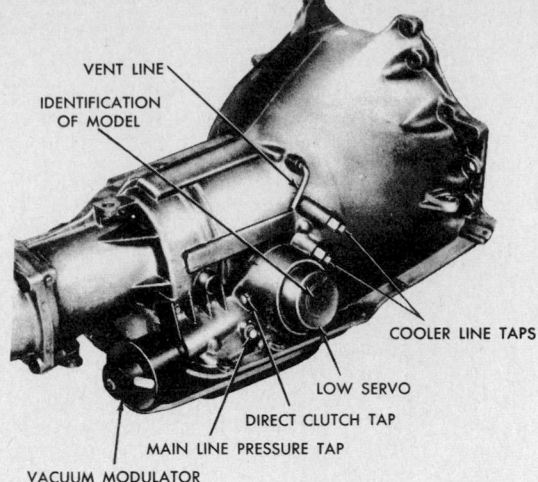

VENT LINE

IDENTIFICATION OF MODEL

COOLER LINE TAPS

LOW SERVO

DIRECT CLUTCH TAP

MAIN LINE PRESSURE TAP

VACUUM MODULATOR

External features of Type 300 (© G.M. Corp.)

oil and pull converter from the case.

3. Remove the oil pan and strainer.

Valve Body Removal

1965 Oldsmobile and F-85, Buick and Buick Special

1. Disconnect solenoid connector from solenoid switch, then remove switch from case.
2. With permanent marking agent, mark stator control solenoid with letter S for future reference.
3. Remove the two attaching bolts and the solenoid.
4. Remove spring detent assembly bolt and spring detent assembly from valve body.
5. Remove 7 bolts holding the stator control valve body to the transmission case and remove stator control valve body.
6. Remove stator control valve body plate.
7. Remove 11 valve body-to-case attaching bolts. (Do not remove valve body).
8. Remove manual control valve link by rotating the valve body, counterclockwise. This will detach the link from park lock and range selector inner valve.
9. Remove manual control valve and link from valve body assembly. Remove the valve body.
10. Remove valve body plate and plate gasket.

1966-69 Oldsmobile, F-85, Buick, and Buick Special, 1965-69 Tempest, 1967-69 Firebird

1. Disconnect detent solenoid wire from case connector.
2. Remove case connector from case. Replace O-ring as necessary.
3. Remove spring detent assembly from valve body.
4. Remove oil channel support plate.
5. Remove eleven body to case bolts. Do not remove valve body.
6. Remove manual control valve link from inner park lock and range selector lever.
7. Remove manual control valve and link from valve body assem-

bly. Remove valve body.

8. Remove valve body plate and gasket.

Low Servo Piston Removal

1. Release tension on low band by turning adjusting screw counterclockwise. (This requires a 7/32 in. Allen wrench.)
2. Press in on servo cover with suitable tool, and remove the cover snap-ring.
3. Release pressure tool from cover, remove cover, then remove servo piston assembly from case.

Pump, Forward Clutch and Low Band Removal

1. With transmission front end up, remove eight pump attaching bolts, then, with slide hammers, remove the front pump and gasket.

1/2" SOCKET

SPRING DETENT ASSEMBLY

Removing spring detent assembly (© G.M. Corp.)

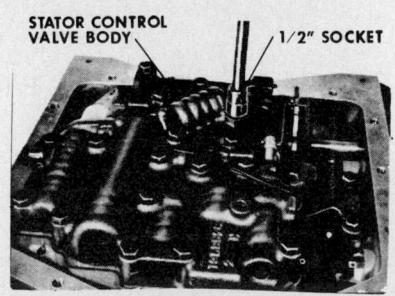

STATOR CONTROL VALVE BODY　1/2" SOCKET

Removing stator control valve body bolts (© G.M. Corp.)

2. Remove input shaft from forward clutch drum.
3. Remove forward clutch assembly by lifting straight out of case. (Be sure low band has first been released.)
4. Remove low band and struts from case, then remove the band adjusting screw.

Rear Bearing Retainer and Component Removal

1. With transmission horizontal, remove speedometer driven gear sleeve retainer with 1/2 in. wrench. Remove sleeve and gear.
2. Remove four attaching bolts and remove rear bearing retainer and retainer to case oil seal.
3. Pry out retainer rear oil seal.
4. Remove rear bearing retainer bushing by collapsing the bushing with a screwdriver.
5. On 1965 models, with transmission in Park, pull speedometer drive gear with suitable puller. On 1966-69 models, depress the retainer clip and slide the drive gear off the output shaft.

Governor and Vacuum Modulator Removal

1. Remove three attaching bolts, then remove governor cover and gasket.
2. With a twisting motion, slide the governor assembly out of its bore.

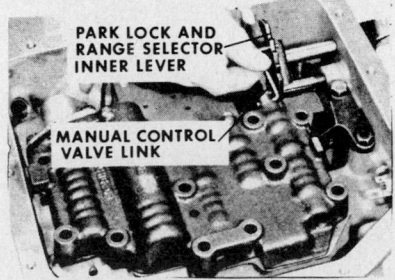

PARK LOCK AND RANGE SELECTOR INNER LEVER

MANUAL CONTROL VALVE LINK

Detaching manual control valve link (© G.M. Corp.)

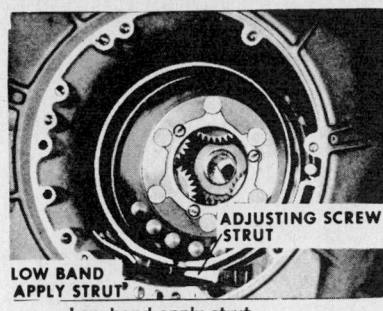

Low band apply strut
(© G.M. Corp.)

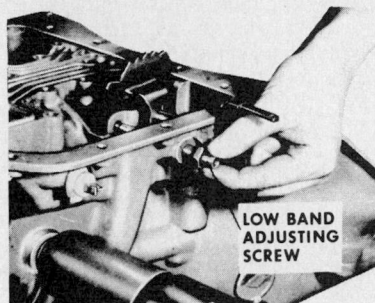

Removing low band adjusting screw
(© G.M. Corp.)

3. With a ½ in. socket, remove vacuum modulator retainer bolt. Then, remove the retainer and the vacuum modulator valve assembly.

Planetary Gear Set, Reverse Clutch and Parking Lock Mechanism Removal

1. Carefully remove planet carrier assembly.
2. Lift reverse ring gear from case.

Removing speedometer driven gear sleeve retainer
(© G.M. Corp.)

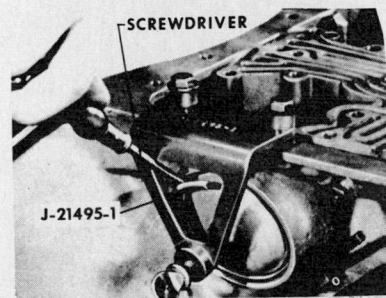

Removing low servo cover snap-ring
(© G.M. Corp.)

3. Remove needle thrust bearing and two races from rear of planet carrier.
4. With transmission in vertical position, remove reverse clutch pack snap-ring, then lift reverse clutch pressure plate from transmission case.
5. Remove reverse clutch pack, then the cushion spring, if installed.
6. To remove reverse piston, install spring compressor onto reverse piston return seat. Install flat plate over threaded shaft at rear of case. Apply pressure to compressor, then remove piston snap-ring.
7. Remove compression tool and lift off piston seat and 17 return springs.
8. With transmission in horizontal position, remove reverse clutch piston with compressed air applied to valve body.

Removing governor assembly
(© G.M. Corp.)

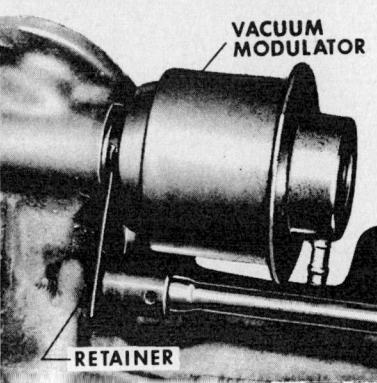

Removing vacuum modulator valve assembly
(© G.M. Corp.)

Oil pump removal
(© G.M. Corp.)

9. Remove two parking lock bracket bolts with ½ in. socket, then remove the lock bracket.
10. Remove range selector shaft retainer.
11. With a 9/16 in. wrench, loosen the nut that holds the outer range selector lever to inner park lock and range selector lever.
12. Slide outer range selector lever out of case. Remove nut, inner park lock, and range selector lever.
13. Remove retainer ring which holds inner park lock and range selector to park lock assembly.
14. Slide parking lock pawl shaft from parking lock pawl. Remove parking lock pawl and spring.

Component Disassembly and Assembly

Valve Body Disassembly

1. Remove two bolts which hold

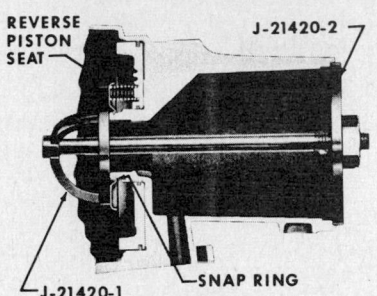

Details of spring compressor
(© G.M. Corp.)

Location of reverse piston return springs
(© G.M. Corp.)

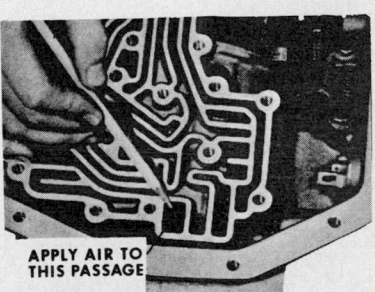

Reverse piston air passage
(© G.M. Corp.)

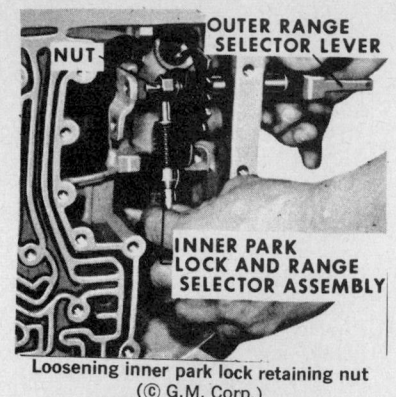

NUT

OUTER RANGE SELECTOR LEVER

INNER PARK LOCK AND RANGE SELECTOR ASSEMBLY

Loosening inner park lock retaining nut
(© G.M. Corp.)

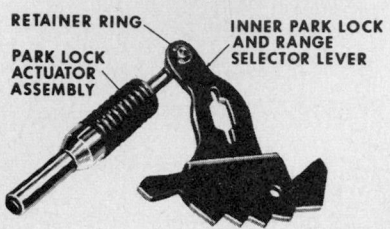

RETAINER RING

PARK LOCK ACTUATOR ASSEMBLY

INNER PARK LOCK AND RANGE SELECTOR LEVER

Park lock actuator assembly
(© G.M. Corp.)

the stator, where installed, and detent solenoid valves. Remove solenoid valve, gasket, spring, stator and detent valve. (Note cutout notch on solenoid valve gasket on models with stator solenoid.)

2. Depress shift control valve sleeve and remove retaining pin. Remove shift control valve sleeve, shift control valve, spring, and shift valve.

3. Depress modulator limit spring. NOTE: modulator limit valve spring is under moderate pressure. Use care during removal.

Invert valve body so retaining pin will fall free. Remove spring and valve from body.

4. Depress high speed downshift timing valve plug and remove pin by inverting valve body. Remove valve assembly. There may be one or two springs in the assembly. Some assemblies have no plug.

5. Clean all valves and valve body in solvent and blow dry with air. Inspect and test each valve in its bore. All valves must move freely of their own weight.

Valve Body Assembly

1. Install high speed downshift tim-

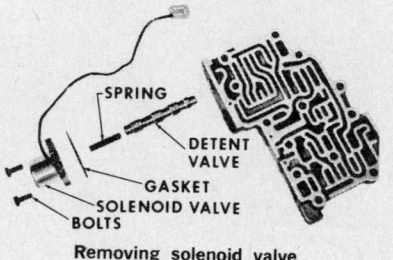

SPRING

DETENT VALVE

GASKET

SOLENOID VALVE

BOLTS

Removing solenoid valve
(© G.M. Corp.)

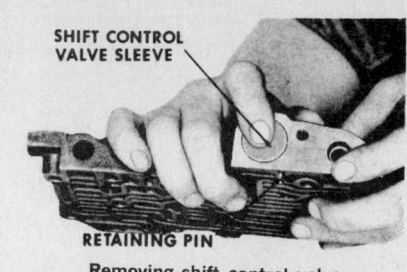

SHIFT CONTROL VALVE SLEEVE

RETAINING PIN

Removing shift control valve
(© G.M. Corp.)

ing valve assembly. Install retaining pin.

2. Install modulator limit valve and spring into bore of valve body. Compress spring and install retaining pin.

3. Install the spring and shift control valve into the sleeve. Depress the spring and valve and insert the retainer. Install the shift valve assembly and retaining pin.

4. Install detent valve and spring. Install gasket to solenoid, with notch facing bottom of valve body.

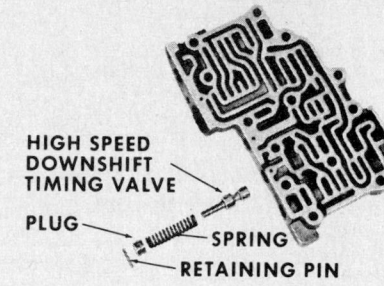

HIGH SPEED DOWNSHIFT TIMING VALVE

PLUG

SPRING

RETAINING PIN

Removing high speed downshift timing valve
(© G.M. Corp.)

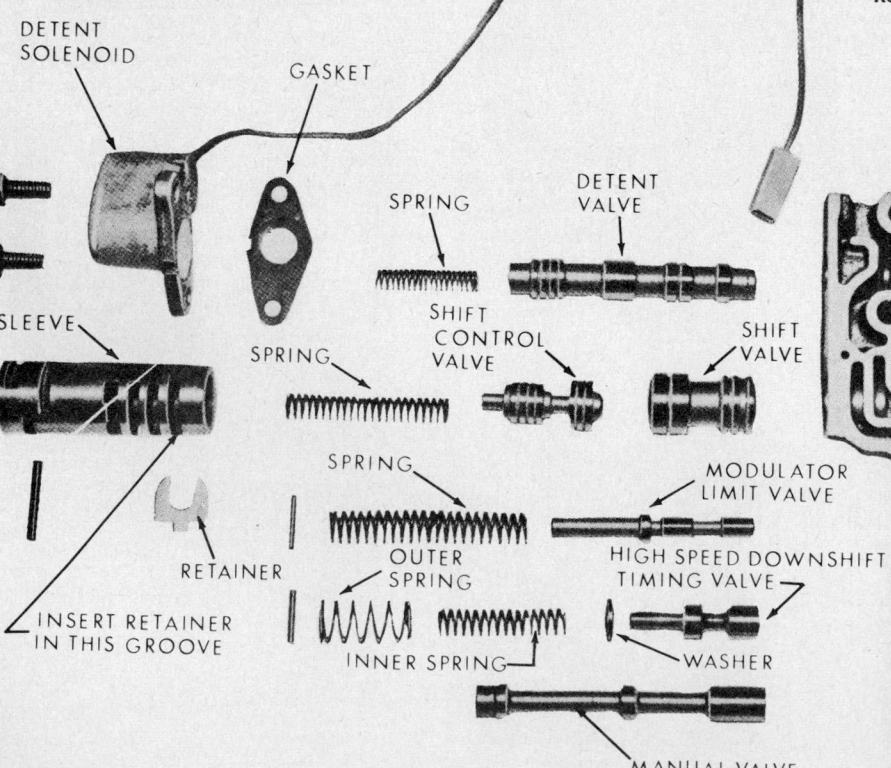

DETENT SOLENOID

GASKET

SPRING

DETENT VALVE

SLEEVE

SPRING

SHIFT CONTROL VALVE

SHIFT VALVE

RETAINER

INSERT RETAINER IN THIS GROOVE

SPRING

OUTER SPRING

INNER SPRING

MODULATOR LIMIT VALVE

HIGH SPEED DOWNSHIFT TIMING VALVE

WASHER

MANUAL VALVE

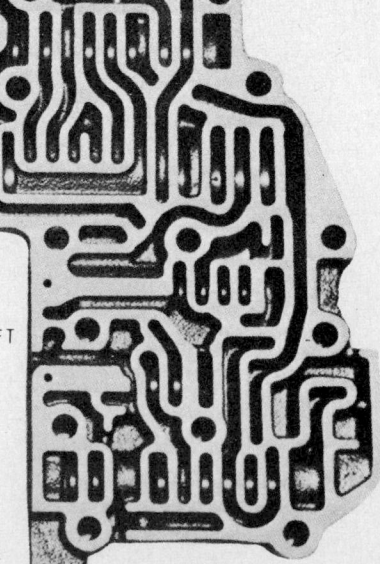

Valve assemblies, 1966-69 models (© G.M. Corp)

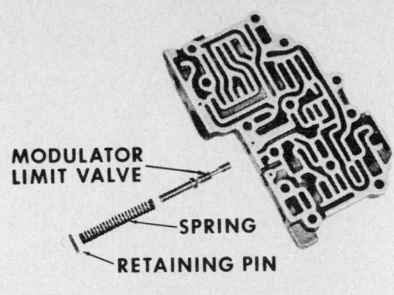

MODULATOR LIMIT VALVE

SPRING

RETAINING PIN

Installing modulator limit valve
(© G.M. Corp.)

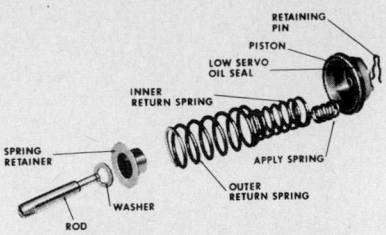

RETAINING PIN
PISTON
LOW SERVO OIL SEAL
INNER RETURN SPRING
SPRING RETAINER
WASHER
ROD
APPLY SPRING
OUTER RETURN SPRING

Low servo piston assembly, 1964-65
(© G.M. Corp.)

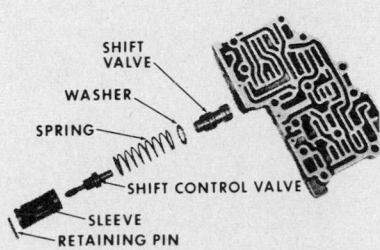

SHIFT VALVE

WASHER

SPRING

SHIFT CONTROL VALVE

SLEEVE
RETAINING PIN

Installing shift valve assemblies
(© G.M. Corp.)

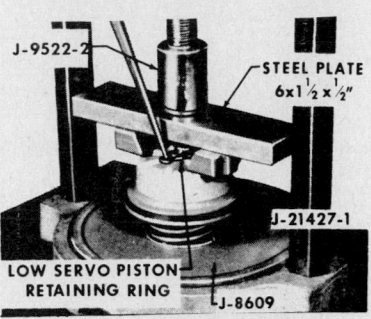

J-9522-2

STEEL PLATE 6x1½x½"

J-21427-1

LOW SERVO PISTON RETAINING RING

J-8609

Compressing low servo piston
(© G.M. Corp.)

Install solenoid to valve body with two ¼ in. bolts.

Stator Control Valve Body Disassembly

1965 Buick and Buick Special, Oldsmobile and F-85

1. Compress stator control valve plug. Invert valve body to release retaining pin. Remove plug, spring and valve from body.

Stator Control Valve Body Assembly

1965 Buick and Buick Special, Oldsmobile and F-85

1. Install stator control valve, spring, and plug into bore of valve body. Compress plug and install retaining pin.

Low Servo Disassembly

1965

1. Remove low servo piston seal.
2. Compress low servo piston in an

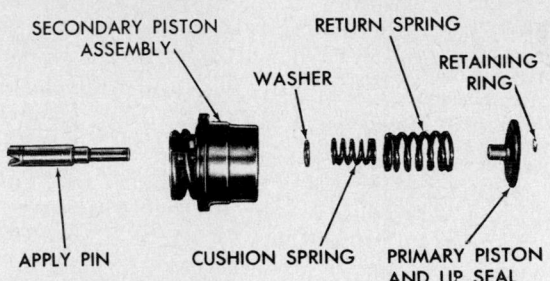

SECONDARY PISTON ASSEMBLY

WASHER

RETURN SPRING

RETAINING RING

APPLY PIN

CUSHION SPRING

PRIMARY PISTON AND LIP SEAL

Low servo piston assembly, 1966-69 (© G.M. Corp)

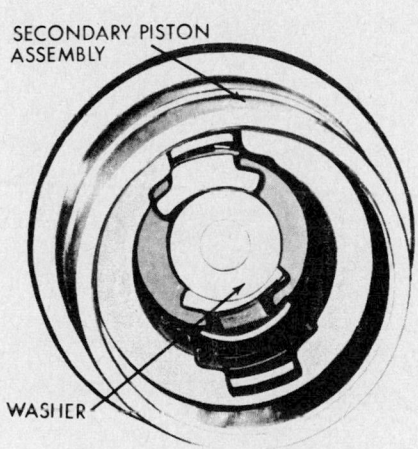

SECONDARY PISTON ASSEMBLY

WASHER

Installing washer into secondary piston
(© G.M. Corp)

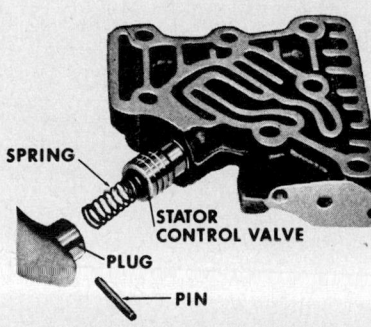

SPRING

STATOR CONTROL VALVE

PLUG

PIN

Removing stator control valve
(© G.M. Corp.)

arbor press. Exercise extreme caution in compressing this piston so as to avoid damage.

3. Compress low servo enough to relieve pressure on retaining ring. Remove retaining ring and gradually relieve tension on the servo assembly.

4. With tension relieved, remove piston low servo, inner apply spring, the outer return springs, spring retainer, washer, and piston apply rod.

5. With tension relieved, remove piston low servo, inner apply spring, the outer return springs, spring retainer, washer, and piston apply rod.

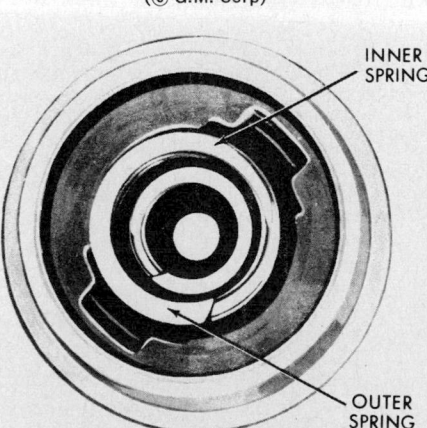

INNER SPRING

OUTER SPRING

Installing cushion and return springs into secondary piston
(© G.M. Corp.)

J-2619

J-21361

Coast downshift timing valve
(© G.M. Corp.)

1966-69

1. Remove secondary piston seal.
2. Compress primary piston in arbor press and remove retaining snap-ring.
3. Remove primary piston, cushion spring, return spring, apply pin, and washer.
4. Inspect primary piston lip seal. If nicked, torn, or worn, replace piston.

Removing low sun gear and flange assembly retaining snap-ring
(© G.M. Corp.)

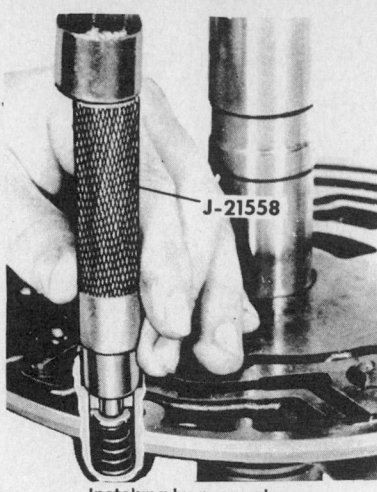

Installing by-pass valve
(© G.M. Corp.)

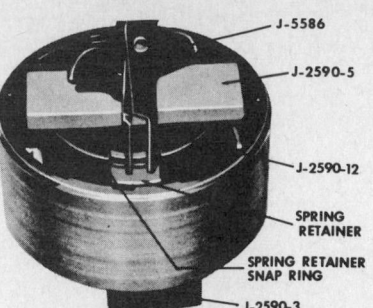

Compressing forward clutch unit spring retainer
(© G.M. Corp.)

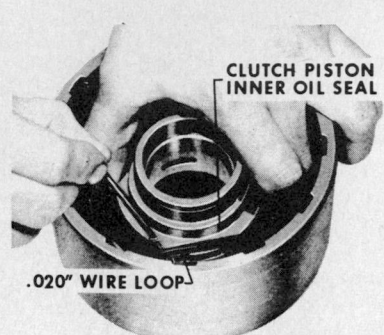

Removing clutch piston inner oil seal
(© G.M. Corp.)

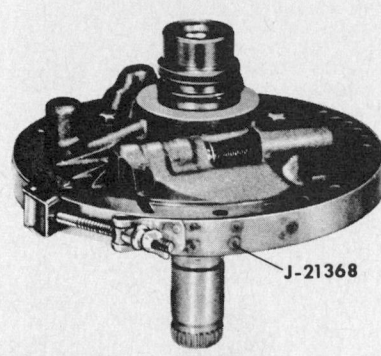

Use of clamp to obtain pump alignment
(© G.M. Corp.)

Removing spring retainer
(© G.M. Corp.)

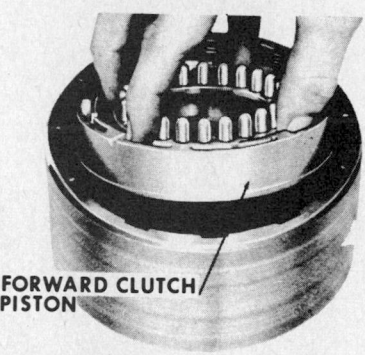

Removing forward clutch piston
(© G.M. Corp.)

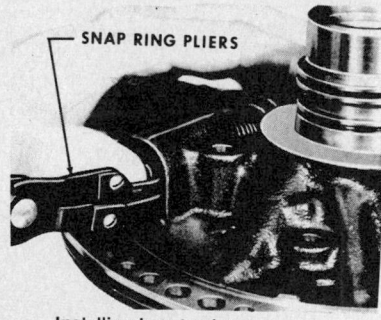

Installing boost valve snap-ring
(© G.M. Corp.)

Checking pump end clearance
(© G.M. Corp.)

Low Servo Assembly

1965
1. Assemble inner and outer return springs into the servo. Install spring retainer.
2. Place this assembly in an arbor press.
3. Install piston apply rod and washer through hole in press plate, compress assembly, then install retainer pin.
4. Install low servo piston seal.

1966-69
1. Install washer into secondary piston assembly.
2. Install cushion and return springs into secondary piston assembly.
3. Install primary piston. Compress piston. Install new retaining snap-ring.

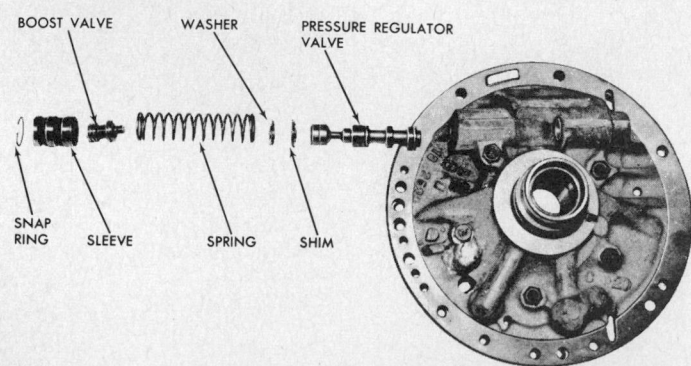

Pressure regulator valve (© G.M. Corp.)

Oil Pump Disassembly

1. Remove the two hook-type oil sealing rings (metal) from the pump hub.
2. Remove pump cover to forward clutch drum thrust washer.
3. Remove oil pump to case seal and discard.
4. Remove five pump cover bolts with a ½ in. socket. Remove pump cover.
5. Match mark the gear faces, so gears can be assembled in their original position.
6. Remove oil pump drive gear and oil pump driven gear.
7. Remove seat, valve and spring from cooler by-pass valve.
8. Remove coast downshift timing valve from the pump cover and inspect for damage.
9. Depress the converter pressure relief valve spring. Remove the retaining pin, spring and relief ball.
10. Compress reverse and modulator boost valve with thumb and remove retaining snap-ring. Use caution, since the boost valve sleeve is under strong spring pressure. Be careful after removing snap-ring.
11. After snap-ring is removed, remove reverse and modulator boost valve sleeve and valve, spring, washer, and pressure regulator valve.
12. If oil pump seal needs replacement, pry out the old seal with screwdriver.
13. If oil pump bushing needs replacement, press bushing out of pump body. If stator shaft bushing needs replacement, drive out bushing.

Oil Pump Inspection

1. Wash all parts in solvent. Air dry.
2. Inspect pump gears for nicks or damage.
3. Inspect pump body for nicks or damage.
4. Install pump gears, aligning marks previously made on gears.
5. Install pump body on converter hub. Check gear end clearance in housing using a straight edge and a feeler gauge or a dial indicator. Allowable end clearance is .0005-.0015 in. for 1965 Buick and 1965-68 Pontiac; .0008-.0018 in. for 1965-66 Oldsmobile; and .0005-.0035 in. for 1965-69 Buick, 1967-69 Oldsmobile, and 1969 Pontiac.

Oil Pump Assembly

1. If oil pump bushing is being replaced, press the new bushing into the pump body until it is flush or up to .010 in. below opposite face (front pump seal side).
2. Press stator shaft bushing into shaft until tool J-24124-7 is flush with top of shaft.
3. Install new oil seal into pump housing.
4. Install new oil pump-to-case seal.
5. Assemble pressure regulator valve, shim, washer, spring, boost valve, and sleeve.

NOTE: when installing spring and shim make certain that the same color spring and the original number of shims are installed.

6. Compress boost valve sleeve with thumb, then install retaining snap-ring.
7. Install the converter pressure relief ball, spring and retaining pin.
8. Install coast downshift timing valve, bottom end up, into the cover.
9. Install spring, valve, and seat into cooler by-pass valve. Press seat into bore of pump body until tool bottoms on face of pump.
10. Install pump cover to pump body. Install five retaining bolts, do not tighten. Tighten clamping band around pump to get proper alignment.

Forward Clutch Disassembly

1. Remove low sun gear and flange assembly retaining snap-ring.
2. Remove low sun gear and flange.
3. Remove clutch hub rear thrust washer.
4. Lift forward clutch hub from pack and remove clutch hub front thrust washer.
5. Remove the clutch pack.
6. Compress the spring retainer. Remove the snap-ring. Then, remove the compression tool and lift out the spring retainer and 24 coil springs.
7. Lift out the piston, with a twisting motion, and remove piston seal.
8. Remove piston inner seal.
9. If clutch drum bushing is to be replaced, press bushing from clutch drum.
10. If low sun gear and flange bushings are to be replaced, press out the bushing.

Forward Clutch Unit Inspection

1. Wash all parts in solvent. Air dry.
2. Check steel ball in forward clutch drum. Make certain that ball is free to move in hole. Check that orifice leading to front of clutch drum is open.
3. Check clutch lined plates and steel driven plates.

Forward Clutch Assembly

1. Install bushing in forward clutch drum. Press bushing into bore until tool J-24124-5 bottoms on the hub.

Installing forward clutch piston into clutch drum
(© G.M. Corp.)

Installing clutch hub
(© G.M. Corp.)

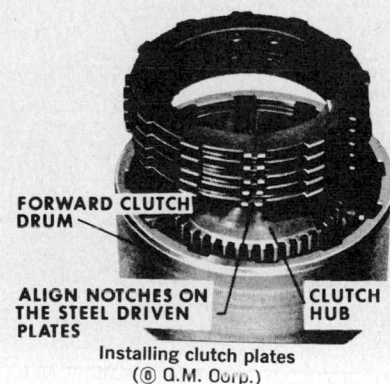

Installing clutch plates
(© G.M. Corp.)

Installing clutch hub rear thrust washer
(© G.M. Corp.)

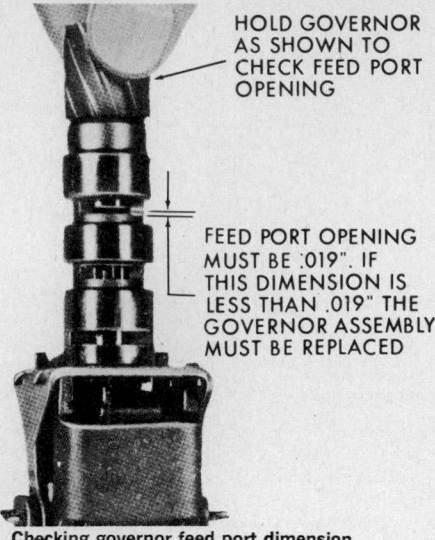

HOLD GOVERNOR AS SHOWN TO CHECK FEED PORT OPENING

FEED PORT OPENING MUST BE .019". IF THIS DIMENSION IS LESS THAN .019" THE GOVERNOR ASSEMBLY MUST BE REPLACED

Checking governor feed port dimension (© G.M. Corp.)

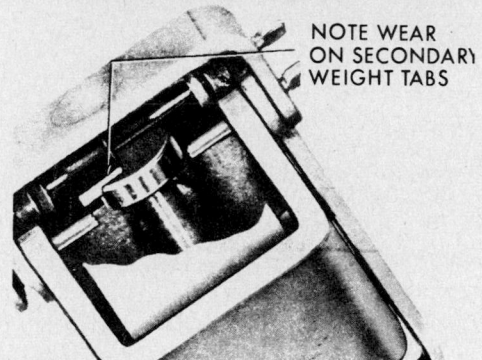

MAKE CERTAIN GEAR IS SEATED AGAINST SLEEVE

SHIM

SHIM SUPPORTS

NO ATTEMPT SHOULD BE MADE TO SUPPORT GOVERNOR OTHER THAN SHOWN, OR VALVE WILL BE DAMAGED

Pressing on governor gear (© G.M. Corp.)

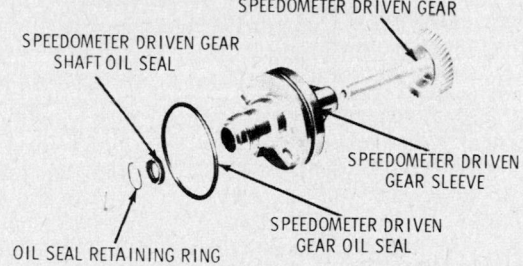

NOTE WEAR ON SECONDARY WEIGHT TABS

Checking governor weight tab wear (© G.M. Corp.)

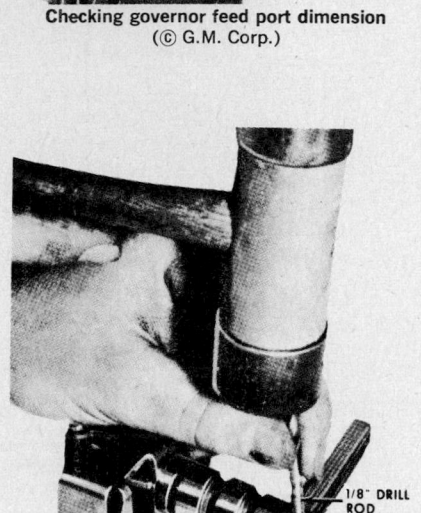
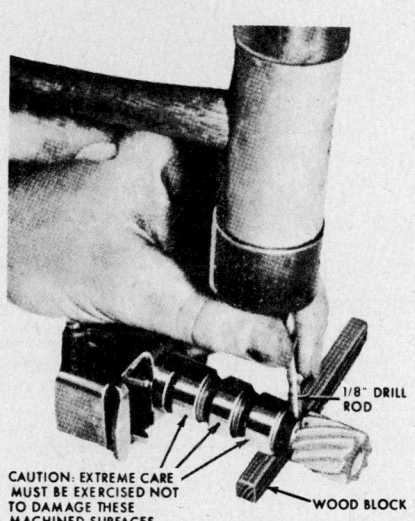

CAUTION: EXTREME CARE MUST BE EXERCISED NOT TO DAMAGE THESE MACHINED SURFACES

1/8" DRILL ROD

WOOD BLOCK

Driving out governor gear pin (© G.M. Corp.)

SPEEDOMETER DRIVEN GEAR

SPEEDOMETER DRIVEN GEAR SHAFT OIL SEAL

SPEEDOMETER DRIVEN GEAR SLEEVE

SPEEDOMETER DRIVEN GEAR OIL SEAL

OIL SEAL RETAINING RING

Speedometer driven gear (© G.M. Corp.)

2. Press new bushing into low sun gear until tool is flush with top of low sun gear.
3. Lubricate with transmission fluid then install new forward clutch piston inner seal with seal lip pointing downward.
4. Lubricate with transmission oil and install new forward clutch piston outer seal into clutch piston, seal lip down.
5. Install forward clutch piston into clutch drum by using a loop of wire to start lip of seal into drum bore.
6. Reassemble return springs, retainer and snap-ring.
7. With spring retainer in place, compress spring retainer with the same tools used to disassemble the unit, then install the snap-ring. Remove compression tool.
8. Install the cushion ring in the piston groove and fit the clutch hub front thrust washer to front

Clutch Plates

Year	Model	Reverse Clutch		Forward Clutch	
		Driven Plates	Drive Plates	Driven Plates	Drive Plates
1965	Buick 225 V6, Oldsmobile 225 V6, Pontiac 215 L6	4	4	5	4
	Buick 300 V8, Oldsmobile 330 V8, Pontiac 326 V8	5	5	6	5
	Pontiac GTO 389 V8	6	6	7	6
1966	Buick 225 V6, Oldsmobile 250 L6, Pontiac 215 L6	4	4	5	4
	Buick 300, 340 V8, Oldsmobile 330 V8, Pontiac 326 V8	5	5	6	5
	Buick Skylark Gran Sport, Oldsmobile 400 V8	6	6	7	6
1967	Buick 225 V6, Oldsmobile 250 L6, Pontiac 230 L6	4	4	5	4
	Buick 300, 340 V8, Oldsmobile 330 V8, Pontiac 326 V8	5	5	6	5
1968-1969	Buick, Oldsmobile, Pontiac 250 L6	4	4	5	4
	Buick, Oldsmobile, Pontiac 350 V8	5	5	6	5

Marking pinion shafts and planet carrier
(© G.M. Corp.)

PLANET PINION
SHAFT LOCK
PLATE SCREW
& LOCKWASHER
ASSEMBLY

Removing pinion shaft lock plate screws
(© G.M. Corp.)

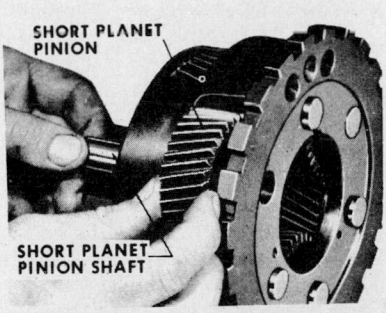

SHORT PLANET
PINION

SHORT PLANET
PINION SHAFT

Removing a short planet pinion and shaft
(© G.M. Corp.)

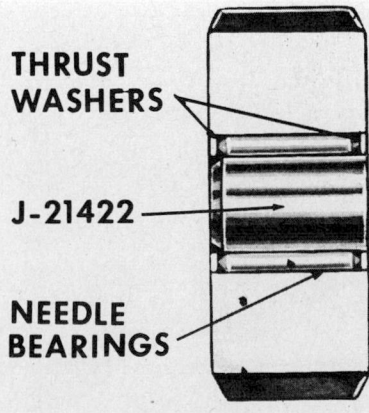

THRUST
WASHERS

J-21422

NEEDLE
BEARINGS

Short pinion gear
(© G.M. Corp.)

clutch hub (retain with petroleum jelly). Install clutch hub.

9. Align notches on steel driven plates. Install steel plates and lined drive plates alternately, beginning with a steel plate.

10. Install clutch hub rear thrust washer with its flange toward low sun gear and flange assembly.

11. Install low sun gear and flange assembly.

12. Install snap-ring. Position so gap in ring is located between slots in drum.

Speedometer Driven Gear Disassembly

1. Remove speedometer driven gear and oil seal (large O-ring).
2. Remove speedometer driven gear shaft oil seal (small seal).

Speedometer Driven Gear Assembly

1. Install speedometer driven gear shaft oil seal, lip of seal toward rear of gear sleeve. Install seal retaining ring.
2. Install speedometer driven gear oil seal.
3. Install speedometer driven gear.

Governor Inspection

1. Check for secondary governor weight tab wear. If tab shows wear, replace governor assembly.
2. Check governor feed port opening. If opening is less than .019 in., replace governor assembly.

Governor Driven Gear Removal

1. Support governor sleeve on wood block. Drive out roll pin with 1/8 in. drill rod.
   NOTE: do not place block under nylon gear. This would result in breaking the gear inside the governor sleeve. Be careful not to damage machined surfaces of governor sleeve.
2. Remove driven gear. Remove chips or burrs from inside governor sleeve.

Governor Driven Gear Installation

1. Place shims supplied in replacement gear kit between second and third lands of governor sleeve. Support governor in press by shim. Do not support or hammer on rear of governor.
2. Press new gear into sleeve until seated against sleeve.
3. Drill out existing hole in governor sleeve to 1/8 in. Drill half-way through from each end.
4. Support end of governor sleeve (not gear) on wooden block. Install new roll pin, staking both ends.

5. Check for burrs on sleeve. Check that valve is free in its bore.

Planet Carrier Disassembly

1. Scribe a mark on each pinion shaft and on the planet carrier assembly in order to facilitate reassembly.
2. Remove three pinion shaft lock plate screws and lockwashers.
3. Slightly rotate, then remove lock plate.
4. Start with the short planet pinion, insert brass drift into front of carrier.
5. Remove pinion shaft and pinion gear from carrier.
6. Remove the other two short planet pinions in the same way.
7. Remove brass drift, needle bearings, and two thrust washers from each of the short planet pinion gears.

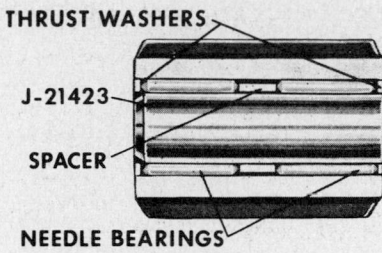

THRUST WASHERS

J-21423

SPACER

NEEDLE BEARINGS

Long pinion gear
(© G.M. Corp.)

FRONT PLANET PINION
THRUST WASHER

LONG PLANET
PINION GEAR

Removing front planet pinion thrust washer
(© G.M. Corp.)

LOW SUN GEAR
NEEDLE
THRUST BEARING

Removing low sun gear needle
thrust bearing
(© G.M. Corp.)

8. Remove low sun gear needle thrust bearing.

9. Remove input sun gear and sun gear thrust washer.

10. Insert brass drift through long planet pinion, then remove the long planet pinion.

11. Remove front planet pinion thrust washer and long planet pinion gear.

12. Remove brass drift, needle bearings, spacer, and two thrust washers from long planet pinion.

13. Repeat Steps 10-12 to remove remaining long planet pinions.

14. If cleaning and inspection reveals worn or damaged parts, rebuild the unit.

Planet Carrier Assembly

1. Press in a new bushing, until tool J-21424-3 touches the machined surface of the planet carrier assembly.

2. Begin with the long planet pinion gears and install a long planet pinion rear thrust washer. The oil groove must face the pinion gear. Retain the thrust washer with petroleum jelly.

3. Install the front planet pinion thrust washer. Retain in position (oil grooves facing pinion) with petroleum jelly.

4. Coat the inside of the pinion gear with petroleum jelly and install the pinion shaft into the long planet pinion gear. Install 20 needle bearings, spacer, 20 more needle bearings and two thrust washers. Carefully, remove the pinion shaft and with a twisting motion, lock both sets of needle rollers in place.

5. Position the long planet pinion assembly, with thrust washers at each end, in the planet carrier. As the shaft is inserted, be sure that it picks up the thrust washer. Turn the pinion shaft so that the groove faces the center of the planet carrier.

NOTE: install the other (2) long planet gears as described in Steps 2, 3, 4 and 5.

6. Install the input sun gear thrust washer with the oil groove facing the input sun gear.

7. Install the input sun gear into the planet carrier.

8. Install the low sun gear needle thrust bearing.

9. Install the rear planet pinion thrust washer and retain in place (oil groove toward the pinion gear) with petroleum jelly.

NOTE: the front thrust washers already installed, act as thrust washers for the short planet pinions, since the two pinions are paired together on one set of thrust washers.

10. Install 20 needle bearings and one thrust washer in the pinion gear. With a twisting motion, lock the rollers in place.

11. Position the short planet pinion assembly and thrust washers at each end of the planet carrier. Install the pinion shaft from the front of the planet carrier. As the pinion shaft is inserted, be sure that it picks up the thrust washer. Turn the pinion shaft so that the lockplate groove faces the center of the planet carrier.

12. Install the planet pinion lockplate. Rotate the plate to align the extended portions with the slots in the planet pinion shafts.

13. Install the three screws and lockwashers.

Transmission Assembly

Range Selector and Parking Lock Actuator Installation

1. Hold locking pawl and spring in the case with parking lock pawl shaft.

2. Install outer shift lever shaft seal, lip pointing inward.

3. Lubricate, then insert outer range selector lever and shaft assembly into the case.

4. Assemble parking lock actuator assembly to inner parking lock and range selector.

5. Install inner park lock and range selector onto outer range selector lever. Install nut onto range selector lever. Long end of selector lever goes toward bottom of transmission.

6. Slide outer range selector lever into case and tighten the attaching nut.

7. Install range selector shaft retainer.

8. Install parking lock bracket to transmission case.

Reverse Clutch Installation

1. Lubricate with transmission fluid, then install outer and inner piston seals.

2. With transmission case vertical, install the reverse clutch piston into the case.

3. Install 17 piston return springs.

4. Position piston spring seat on the return springs and lay the retainer ring in place.

5. Compress return spring seat far enough to seat the snap-ring. Seat the snap-ring, then remove compressor.

6. Install reverse clutch cushion spring, if used, with the dish down.

7. Align notches on the steel driven plates. Install steel plates and lined drive plates alternately, starting with a steel plate. The notched lugs on the driven plates should all be aligned and in the five o'clock groove in the case.

NOTE: steel plates are dished and should all face in the same direction.

8. Install reverse clutch pressure plate, with identification mark installed in the five o'clock groove.

9. Install clutch pack snap-ring.

10. For 1965 models only: insert feeler gauge between any reaction plate and adjacent lined plate.

When the dimension between the reaction plate and its adjacent plate is within .058-.021 in. use the reaction plate with one identification mark. If the dimension is from .095-.058 in. use a plate with two marks. If the dimension is .133-.095 in. use a plate with three identification marks.

Planetary Gear Set Installation

1. Assemble thrust bearing race with lip, needle bearing, and a second plain thrust bearing race to the rear face of the planetary gear set. Retain with grease.

2. Install reverse ring gear into the case.

3. Install planetary gear set into the case.

Low Servo and Band, and Forward Clutch Installation

1. Install low servo piston assembly into case.

2. Install servo cover oil seal, then

Installing thrust bearing races
(© G.M. Corp.)

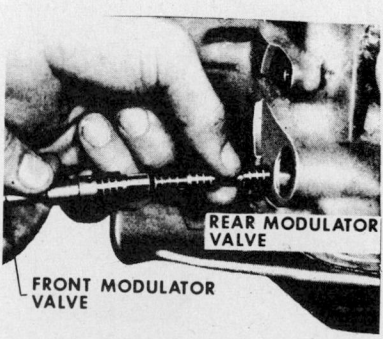

Installing modulator valve
(© G.M. Corp.)

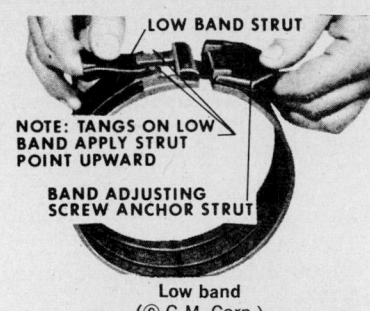

Low band
(© G.M. Corp.)

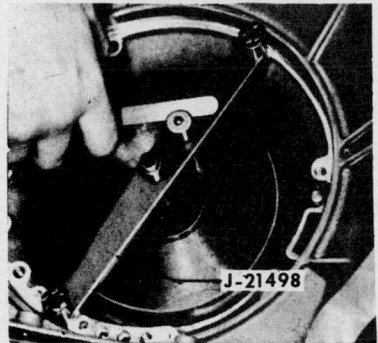

J-21498

Checking oil pump end-play with feeler gauge
(© G.M. Corp.)

J-8001

J-21371-3

Making converter end-play check
(© G.M. Corp.)

install the cover.

3. Compress the cover and install retainer snap-ring.

4. With transmission case vertical, install band adjusting screw into case.

5. Install low band. Install apply strut and band adjusting screw strut. Tighten band adjustment enough to prevent struts from falling out.

6. Install forward clutch assembly by turning slightly to engage low sun gear with planet pinions. Install pump into case. Install pump to case bolts.

7. Check forward clutch to oil pump clearance by installing a shim selector gauge, then check end-play with a feeler gauge. The measurement taken with the gauge determines the thickness of the thrust washer to be used. End-play can also be measured with a feeler gauge.
   If it is not possible to insert a feeler gauge, use a .099-.095 in. thrust washer. If a .001-.020 in. feeler is acceptable, use a .081-

.077 in. thrust washer. If a .021-.040 in. feeler is acceptable, use a .063-.059 in. thrust washer. Select washer so the clearance will be .022-.054 in.
On Pontiac applications the following chart applies.

End-play	Correct Thrust Washer Thickness
.008-.038 in.	.061 in.
.039-.079 in.	.079 in.
.061-.085 in.	.097 in.

8. Install selective fit washer to pump cover hub.

9. Install two pump cover to clutch drum oil sealing hook-type rings.

Oil Pump Assembly Installation

1. Install oil pump to case outer seal (chamfers on corners of seal to the outside) then a new pump gasket and guide pins.

2. Install input shaft oil rings, then install the shaft into the oil pump.

3. Apply transmission fluid to edge of pump, and install pump into the case.

4. Remove pump guide pins, then install eight retaining bolts with new O-rings or washer type seals under their heads. Torque pump bolts to 16-24 ft. lbs.

5. Check forward clutch to oil pump clearance.

Low Band Adjustment

1. Tighten adjusting screw to 40 in. lbs. (about 3½ ft. lbs.). Now back off adjustment four turns, then lock with locknut. Install adjusting screw cap.

Speedometer Drive Gear Installation

1965

1. With transmission in horizontal position, install speedometer driving gear.

2. Place control in Park. Drive speedometer driving gear (worm) onto the output shaft. Drive gear on until the tool bottoms on the end of the output shaft.

1966-69

1. Place retainer in hole in output shaft.

2. Align slot in speedometer drive gear with retainer clip. Slide gear onto shaft.

Rear Bearing Retainer Bushing, Oil Seal, Bearing Retainer and Speedometer Driven Gear Installation

1. Press in rear retainer bushing until flush with the bore.

2. Install output shaft-to-rear bearing retainer oil seal, then install the retainer-to-transmission case oil seal.

3. Place rear bearing retainer against the case and install four retaining bolts.

4. Install speedometer driven gear assembly into the rear bearing retainer.

5. Install driven gear sleeve retainer.

Valve Body Installation

1965

1. With transmission upside down, install valve body to plate gasket, then the valve body plate.

2. Install manual control valve and link into valve body assembly.

3. Install manual control valve link into park lock and range selector inner lever.

4. Install eleven valve body-to-case attaching bolts. Torque to 8-11 ft. lbs.

5. Install stator control valve plate.

6. Install stator control solenoid and gasket to stator control valve body.

7. Install spring detent assembly. Torque bolt to 8-12 ft. lbs.

8. Install solenoid switch, then install the solenoid connector.

9. Install oil strainer pipe to case seal onto the pipe, lubricate the seal, then install the pipe into the transmission case.

10. Install oil strainer.

11. Install strainer attaching bolt or clip.

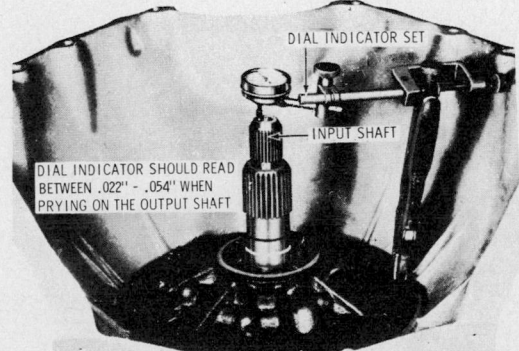

DIAL INDICATOR SET

INPUT SHAFT

DIAL INDICATOR SHOULD READ BETWEEN .022" - .054" WHEN PRYING ON THE OUTPUT SHAFT

Checking oil pump end-play with a dial indicator
(© G.M. Corp.)

12. With a new gasket on the oil pan, install pan and attach pan to case. Torque all fourteen bolts to 10-12 ft. lbs.

1966-69

This valve body installation procedure is the same as that given for 1965 models, with the substitution of the following steps:

5. Install oil channel support plate. Torque bolts to 8-12 ft. lbs.
6. Delete Step 6.
12. With a new gasket on the oil pan, install pan and attach pan to case. Torque fourteen bolts to 10-16 ft. lbs.

Governor and Vacuum Modulator Installation

1. Slide the governor into its bore in the case. Turn the governor assembly so teeth on governor gear engage teeth on output shaft.
2. Install governor gasket and cover to case. Torque bolts to 8-12 ft. lbs.
3. Slide rear modulator valve into front modulator valve, then install into bore in case.
4. Install case-to-modulator oil seal, then install modulator into the case.
5. Install vacuum modulator retainer so the retainer tang points toward the vacuum modulator. Torque bolts to 8-12 ft. lbs.

Checking the Converter

NOTE: the converter is a welded unit, therefore, it is not serviceable. If the converter is bad, renew the unit.

1. Install converter pressure check fixture and tighten.
2. Fill converter with 80 psi air.
3. Submerge in water and check for bubbles.
4. Then, check for end-play with a dial indicator.
5. Tighten the hex nut.
6. Install dial indicator and set at zero.
7. Loosen hex nut. When nut is fully loosened, the reading obtained on the dial indicator will be converter end-play. If clearance is .050 in. or more, or the oil has the appearance of containing aluminum particles (aluminum paint), replace the converter.

Torque References

	Foot-Pounds
Case to cylinder block	30-40
Converter cover pan to transmission case	8-12
Cooler pipes to case	25-35
Low band adjusting screw nut	20-30
Pump cover to body	16-24
Transmission case bolt	8-12
Valve body to case	8-12
Solenoid valve to valve body	8-12
Vacuum modulator to case	8-12
Pump assembly to case	16-24
Rear bearing retainer to case	25-35
Oil pan to case	10-16
Governor cover to case	8-12
Speedometer sleeve retainer to bearing retainer	5-10

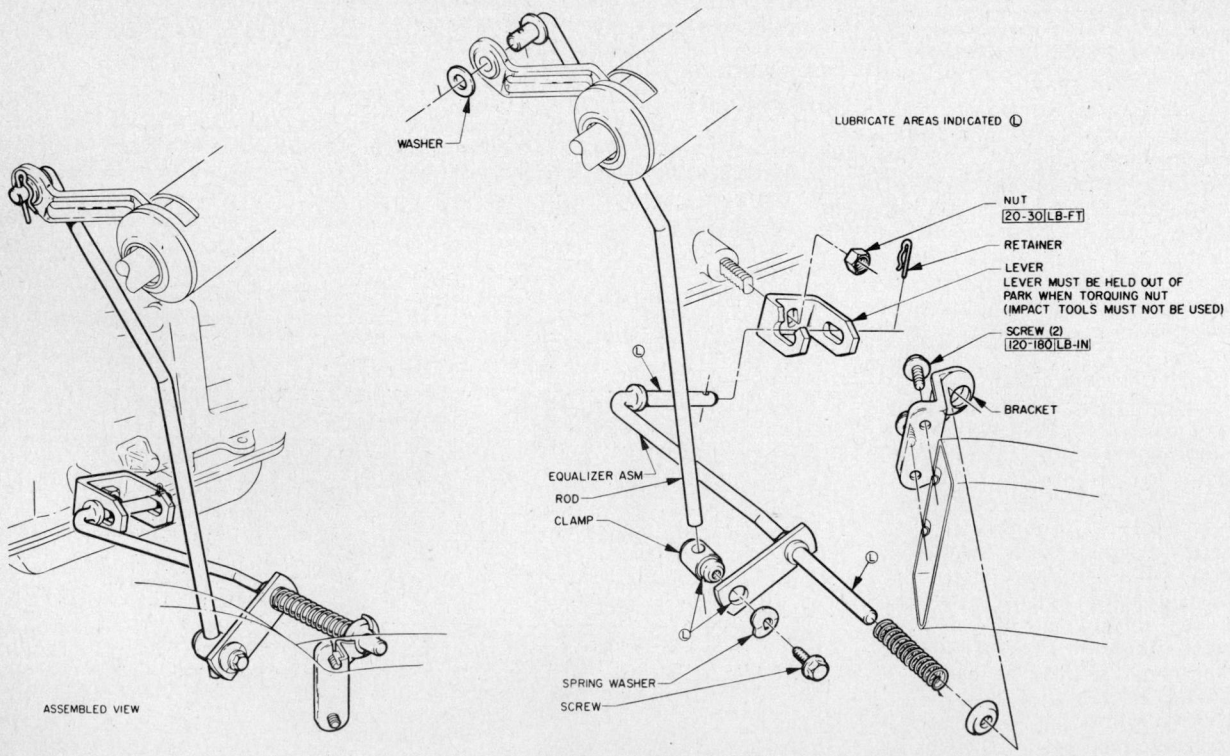

SHIFT LINKAGE ADJUSTMENTS ALL SERIES

Type 350

Application

Turbo Hydra-Matic 350—Buick Special, 1969-72
    Buick Skylark and LeSabre (350), 1971-72
Turbo Hydra-Matic 350—Chevrolet, Nova, Camaro, Chevelle, 1969-72
    Monte Carlo, 1970-72
Turbo Hydra-Matic 350—Oldsmobile F-85, 1969-72
    Oldsmobile Cutlass, 1971-72
Turbo Hydra-Matic M-38—Pontiac Tempest and Firebird, 1969-72
    Pontiac LeMans and GTO, 1971-72
    Ventura II, 1971-72

Diagnosis

This diagnosis guide is a list of the most common troubles and their causes. The items to check are listed in the sequence to be followed.

TROUBLE SYMPTOMS	Items to Check	
	In Car	Out of Car
Slips in all ranges	ACDFGMO	N
Drive slips—no 1st gear	ACDFGMO	NQV
No 1-2 upshift	BEFGH	SU
1-2 upshift, early or late	BEFH	
Slips, 1-2 upshift	ACFGHL	NSU
Harsh 1-2 upshift	BCG	
No 2-3 upshift	FI	R
2-3 upshift, early/late	BCEFIK	
Slips, 2-3 upshift	ACFGI	NR
Harsh 2-3 upshift	BCGIL	
No full throttle downshift	K	
2-3 upshift, wide open throttle only	BK	
L₁ gear—no engine braking	GHJM	PQU
Car drives in neutral	K	Q
Slips in reverse	ACDFGHMO	RT
1-2, 2-3 shift noisy	A	RSY
Noisy in all ranges	ADFO	NXYW
Spews oil out of breather	AD	

Key to Checks

A. Low oil level/water in oil
B. Vacuum leak
C. Modulator and/or valve
D. Strainer and/or gasket leak
E. Governor valve/screen
F. Valve body gasket/plate
G. Pressure regulator and/or boost valve
H. 1-2 shift valve

I. 2-3 shift valve
J. Manual low control valve
K. Detent valve and linkage
L. 2-3 accumulator
M. Manual valve linkage
N. Pump gears
O. Gasket screen-pressure
P. Band—intermediate overrun roller clutch

Q. Forward clutch assembly
R. Direct clutch assembly
S. Intermediate clutch assembly
T. Low & reverse clutch assembly
U. Intermediate roller clutch
V. Low & reverse roller clutch
W. Parking pawl/linkage
X. Converter assembly
Y. Gear set and bearings

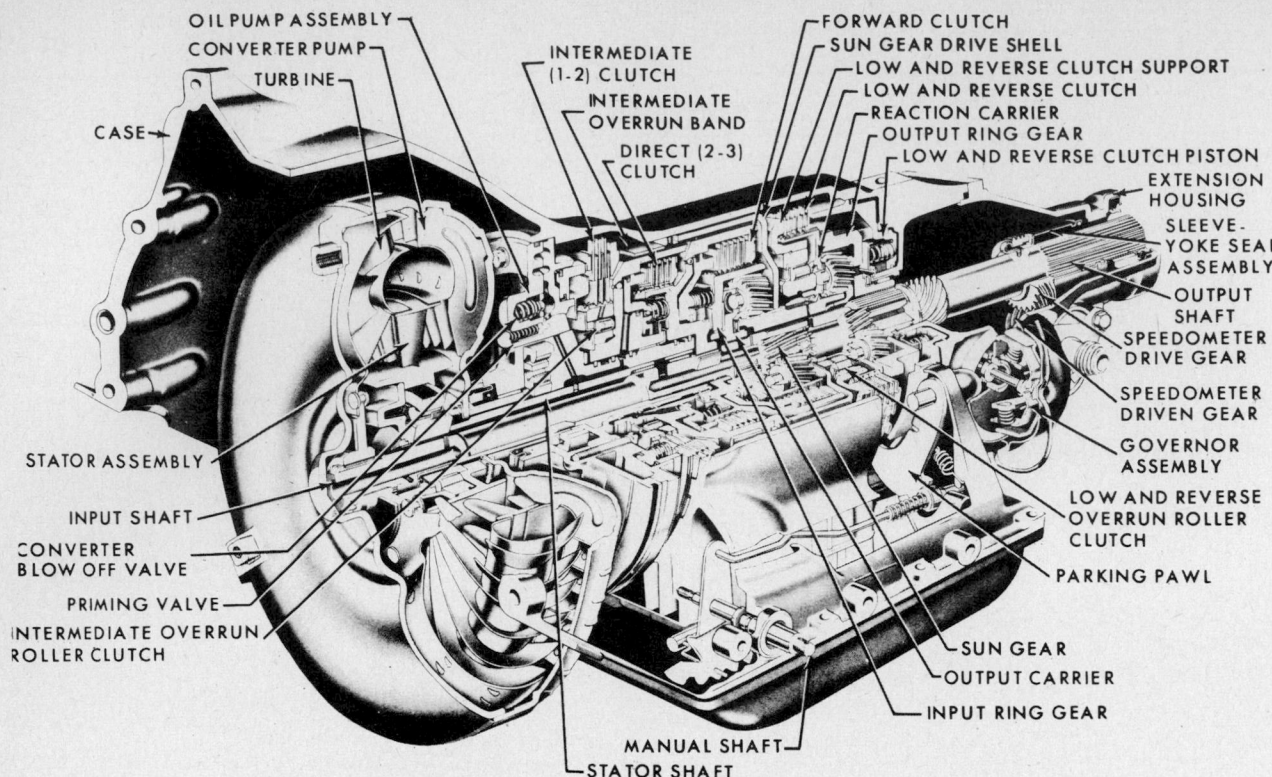

OIL PUMP ASSEMBLY
CONVERTER PUMP
TURBINE
CASE
INTERMEDIATE (1-2) CLUTCH
INTERMEDIATE OVERRUN BAND
DIRECT (2-3) CLUTCH
FORWARD CLUTCH
SUN GEAR DRIVE SHELL
LOW AND REVERSE CLUTCH SUPPORT
LOW AND REVERSE CLUTCH
REACTION CARRIER
OUTPUT RING GEAR
LOW AND REVERSE CLUTCH PISTON
EXTENSION HOUSING
SLEEVE-YOKE SEAL ASSEMBLY
OUTPUT SHAFT
SPEEDOMETER DRIVE GEAR
SPEEDOMETER DRIVEN GEAR
GOVERNOR ASSEMBLY
LOW AND REVERSE OVERRUN ROLLER CLUTCH
PARKING PAWL
STATOR ASSEMBLY
INPUT SHAFT
CONVERTER BLOW OFF VALVE
PRIMING VALVE
INTERMEDIATE OVERRUN ROLLER CLUTCH
SUN GEAR
OUTPUT CARRIER
INPUT RING GEAR
MANUAL SHAFT
STATOR SHAFT

General Motors, 3-speed, Type 350 transmission (© G.M. Corp.)

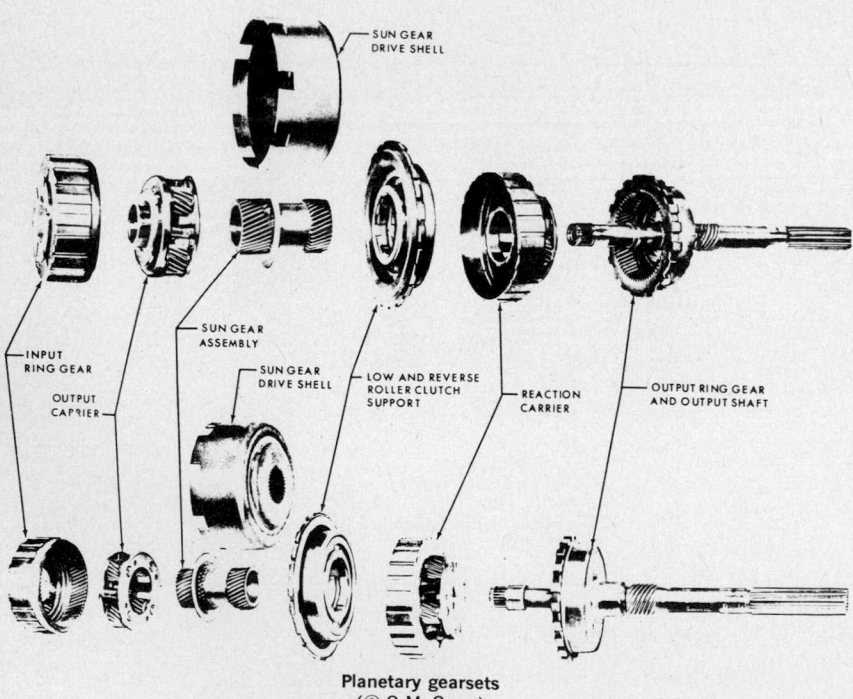

SUN GEAR DRIVE SHELL
INPUT RING GEAR
OUTPUT CARRIER
SUN GEAR ASSEMBLY
SUN GEAR DRIVE SHELL
LOW AND REVERSE ROLLER CLUTCH SUPPORT
REACTION CARRIER
OUTPUT RING GEAR AND OUTPUT SHAFT

Planetary gearsets
(© G.M. Corp.)

The illustration is typical. While design and repair procedures are similar, R & R methods and components may vary with car application. Therefore, some differences may exist.

General Information

The "350" three-speed transmission is a fully automatic unit, consisting of a three-element hydraulic torque converter and two planetary gear sets. Four multiple-disc clutches, two roller clutches, and an intermediate overrun band provide the friction elements needed to obtain the desired function of the two planetary gear sets.

The torque converter couples the engine to the planetary gears through oil and hydraulically provides added torque multiplication when required. The two planetary gear sets give three forward ratios and one reverse. The torque converter consists of three basic elements:

1. Converter pump—driving member
2. Turbine—driven member
3. Stator—reaction member

Changing of the gear ratios is fully automatic and relative to car speed and engine torque input. Car speed and engine torque signals are constantly fed to the transmission to provide the proper gear ratio for maximum efficiency and performance.

The shift quadrant has six positions, marked as follows:

$$P, R, N, D, L_2, L_1$$

Shift positions of the type 350 and type 400 are identical.

Capacity and General Specifications

Oil Capacity (dry) .... 20 Pints
Cooling .... Water
Oil Filter Type
.... Bottom Suction Screen
Clutches 4
Roller Clutches 2
Band (non-adjustable) 1

Draining and Refilling

The transmission should be drained of fluid and refilled at 24,000 mile intervals. To do this:

1. Drain transmission oil.
2. Remove oil pan attaching screws.
3. Remove oil pan and gasket.

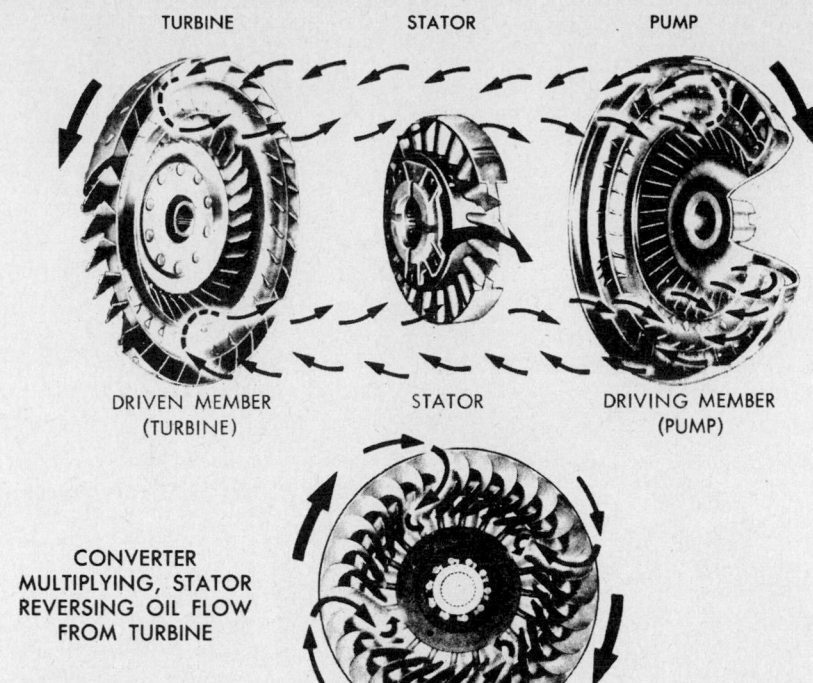

TURBINE   STATOR   PUMP

DRIVEN MEMBER   STATOR   DRIVING MEMBER
(TURBINE)   (PUMP)

CONVERTER
MULTIPLYING, STATOR
REVERSING OIL FLOW
FROM TURBINE

(© G.M. Corp.)

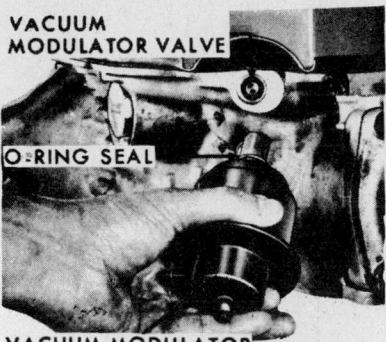

VACUUM
MODULATOR VALVE

O-RING SEAL

VACUUM MODULATOR

Removing vacuum modulator
(© G.M. Corp.)

EXTENSION
HOUSING
TO CASE
OIL SEAL

Removing extension housing O-ring
(© G.M. Corp.)

4. Remove oil strainer screws and strainer.
5. Thoroughly clean oil strainer and oil pan in solvent. Blow dry with air.
6. Renew oil strainer gasket and oil pan gasket.
7. Install oil strainer.
8. Install oil pan. Torque attaching screws to 10-12 ft. lbs.
9. Add about 5 pints of transmission fluid.
10. Start engine. Do not race engine. Move selector lever slowly through each range. Check fluid level with transmission in Park.
11. With transmission cold, add enough fluid to bring level to ¼ in. below the Add mark. With the transmission hot, add enough fluid to bring level to Full mark.
12. In case of transmission overhaul, proceed as in steps 9-11. Start with 5 pints of fluid if converter has not been replaced; 8 pints if it has been replaced. Total capacity is about 20 pints, but correct level is determined by the mark on the dipstick rather than by amount added.

Transmission Disassembly

Clean ouside of transmission thoroughly to prevent dirt from entering the unit.
1. With transmission in a holding fixture, lift off torque converter assembly.

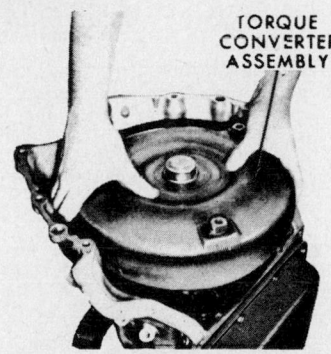

TORQUE
CONVERTER
ASSEMBLY

Removal of torque converter
(© G.M. Corp.)

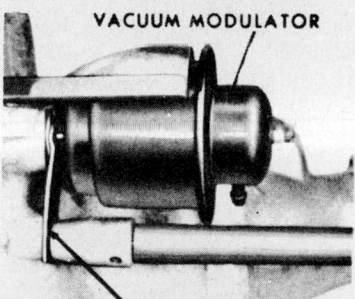

VACUUM MODULATOR

VACUUM MODULATOR RETAINER

Unbolting vacuum modulator
(© G.M. Corp.)

2. Remove vacuum modulator assembly attaching bolt and retainer.
3. Remove vacuum modulator assembly, O-ring seal and modulator valve from the case.
4. Remove four extension housing-to-case attaching bolts.
5. Remove extension housing and the square cut O-ring seal.

6. Remove extension housing lip seal from output end of housing, using a screwdriver.
7. Remove extension housing bushing, using chisel to collapse bushing.
8. Drive in new extension housing bushing.
9. Install extension housing lip seal.
10. Depress speedometer drive gear retaining clip, then slide speedometer drive gear off output shaft.
11. Remove governor cover retainer wire with a screwdriver.
12. Remove governor cover and O-ring seal from case, then remove O-ring seal from governor cover.
13. Remove governor assembly from case.
NOTE: check governor bore and sleeve for scoring.
14. Remove oil pan attaching screws, pan, and gasket.
15. Remove two oil pump suction screen (strainer) to valve body attaching screws.
16. Remove oil pump screen (strainer) and gasket from valve body.
17. Remove detent roller and spring assembly from valve body. Remove valve body-to-case attaching bolts.
18. Remove manual control valve link from range selector inner lever. Remove valve body. Remove detent control valve link from detent actuating lever.
NOTE: refer to later text for valve body disassembly and passage identification.

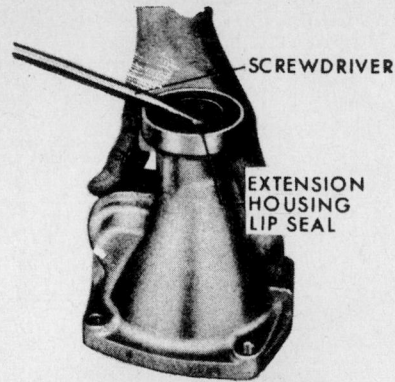

Removing extension housing lip seal
(© G.M. Corp.)

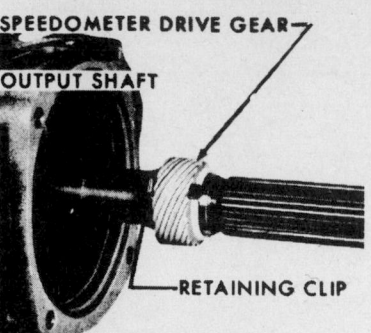

Speedometer drive gear
(© G.M. Corp.)

Removing oil pan
(© G.M. Corp.)

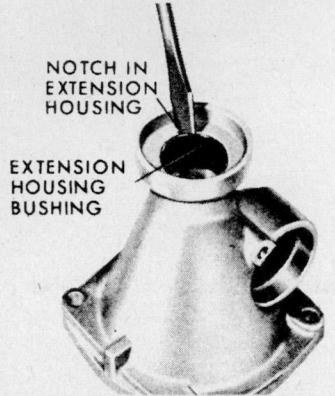

Removing extension housing bushing
(© G.M. Corp.)

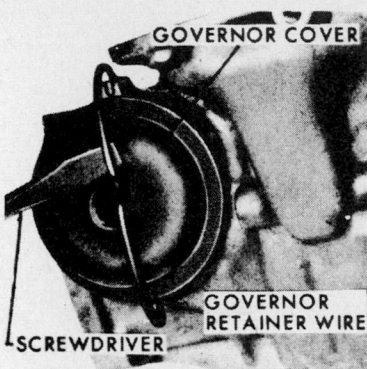

Releasing governor retainer wire
(© G.M. Corp.)

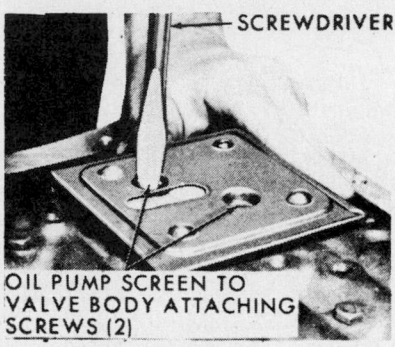

Detaching oil screen
(© G.M. Corp.)

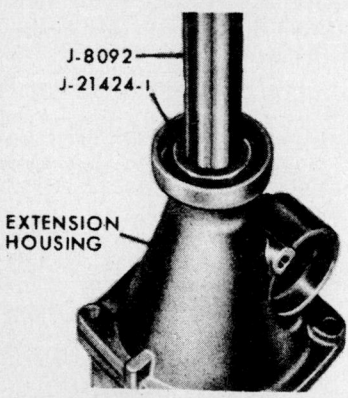

Driving in extension housing bushing
(© G.M. Corp.)

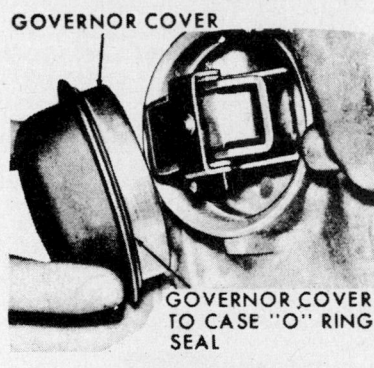

Removing governor cover
(© G.M. Corp.)

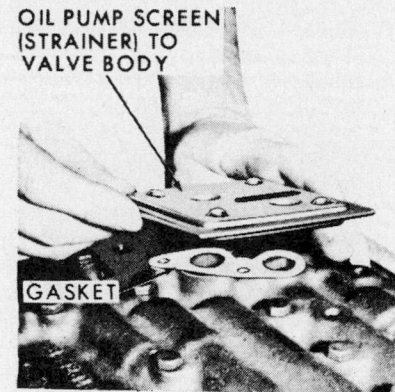

Oil screen gasket
(© G.M. Corp.)

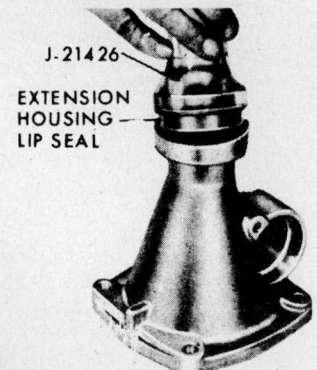

Installing new extension housing lip seal
(© G.M. Corp.)

Removing governor assembly
(© G.M. Corp.)

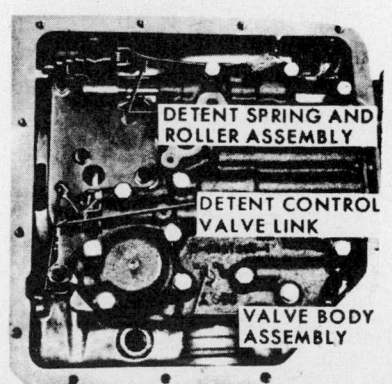

Detent roller and spring
(© G.M. Corp.)

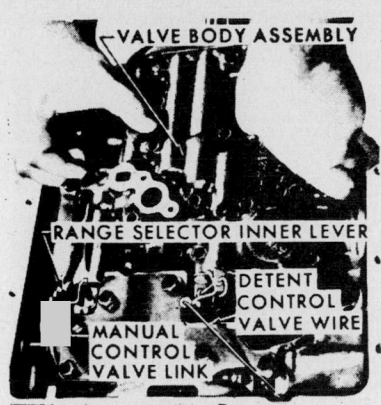

Manual control valve link
(© G.M. Corp.)

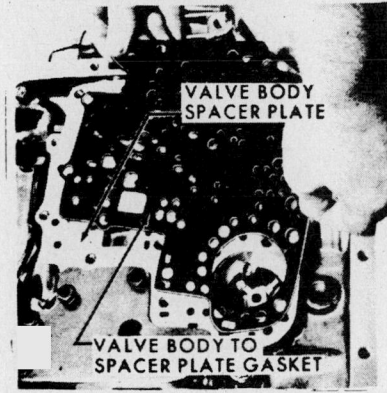

Removing valve body to spacer plate gasket
(© G.M. Corp.)

NOTE: at this time, when handling valve body assembly, do not touch sleeves, because retaining pins may fall into the transmission.

19. Remove valve body-to-spacer plate gasket.
20. Remove spacer support plate gasket. Remove spacer support plate.
21. Remove valve body spacer plate and plate-to-case gasket.
22. Remove four check balls from passages, as illustrated, in case face.

NOTE: if, during assembly, any of the balls are omitted or installed in the wrong locations, transmission failure will result.

23. Remove oil pump pressure screen from oil pump pressure hole in the case.
24. Remove governor feed screen from governor feed passage in case.
25. Remove manual shaft to case retainer with a screwdriver.
26. Remove jam nut holding range selector inner lever to manual shaft. Remove manual shaft.
27. Disconnect parking pawl actuating rod from range selector inner lever. Remove both from case.
28. Remove manual shaft to case lip oil seal, using a screwdriver.
29. Remove parking lock bracket.

30. Disconnect and remove parking pawl disengaging spring.
31. Remove parking pawl shaft retaining plug with a bolt extractor. Cock parking pawl on shaft. Using drift and hammer, tap on drift to force the parking pawl shaft from the case. Remove the parking pawl.
32. Remove intermediate servo piston and metal oil seal ring. Remove washer, spring seat, and apply pin.
33. On Buick applications, check the band apply pin. Using band apply pin selection tool J-23071, and a straightedge, exert firm downward pressure on the selection pin. If the tool is below the

Removing spacer support plate
(© G.M. Corp.)

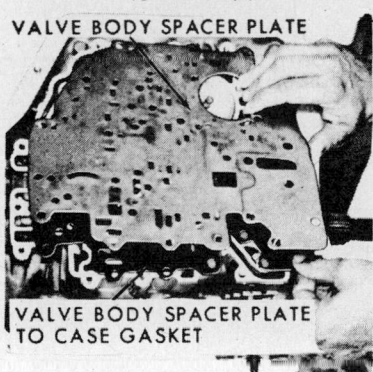

Removing valve body spacer plate and gasket
(© G.M. Corp.)

Check ball locations
(© G.M. Corp.)

Intermediate servo
(© G.M. Corp.)

Removing oil pump pressure screen
(© G.M. Corp.)

Removing governor screen
(© G.M. Corp.)

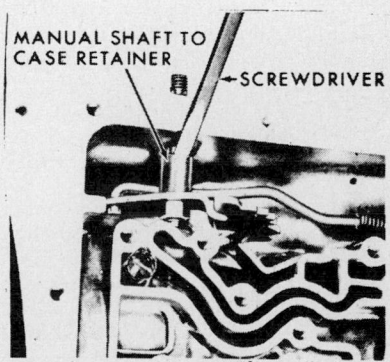

Removing manual shaft to case retainer
(© G.M. Corp.)

RANGE SELECTOR INNER
LEVER TO MANUAL SHAFT
NUT TORQUE TO 30 LB.FT

Loosening range selector inner lever jam nut
(© G.M. Corp.)

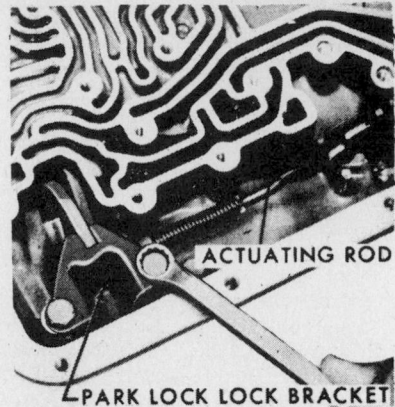

ACTUATING ROD

PARK LOCK LOCK BRACKET

Unbolting parking lock bracket
(© G.M. Corp.)

PRESS DOWN ON TOOL J-23071 UNTIL IT BOTTOMS:
IF TOOL IS ABOVE SCALE EDGE - USE SHORT PIN
(2.830", PLAIN END)
IF TOOL IS BELOW SCALE EDGE - USE LONG PIN
(2.945", GROOVED 3/8"
BACK FROM BAND END
OF PIN)

J-23071

PLATE OR STRAIGHT
EDGE ACROSS OPENING

Checking band apply pin length
(© G.M. Corp.)

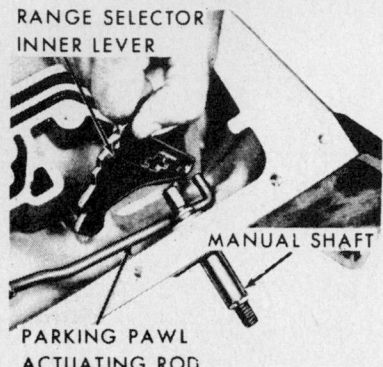

RANGE SELECTOR
INNER LEVER

MANUAL SHAFT

PARKING PAWL
ACTUATING ROD

Removing range selector inner lever
(© G.M. Corp.)

PARKING PAWL

PARKING PAWL
DISENGAGING SPRING

Disconnecting parking pawl spring
(© G.M. Corp.)

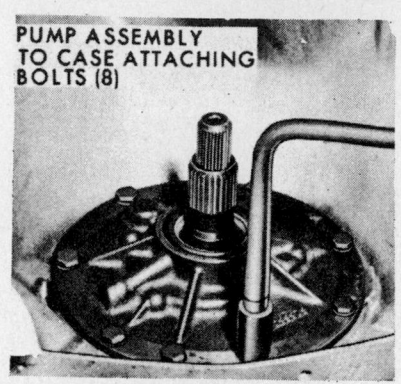

PUMP ASSEMBLY
TO CASE ATTACHING
BOLTS (8)

Oil pump
(© G.M. Corp.)

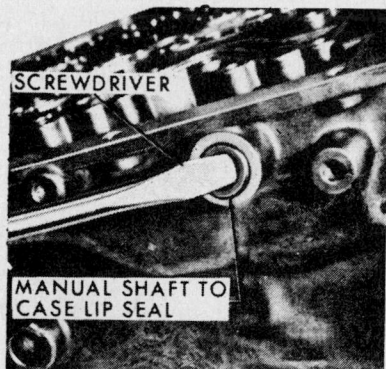

SCREWDRIVER

MANUAL SHAFT TO
CASE LIP SEAL

Removing manual shaft to case lip seal
(© G.M. Corp.)

PARK PAWL

PARK PAWL
SHAFT

PARKING PAWL SHAFT
RETAINING PLUG

Parking pawl shaft details
(© G.M. Corp.)

SLIDE
HAMMERS
J-7004

TIGHTEN JAM NUTS

Removing oil pump
(© G.M. Corp.)

straightedge surface, a long apply pin must be used. If the tool is above the straightedge surface, a short pin should be used. The long apply pin is identified by a groove, while the short pin has no groove. If a new pin is required, make note of the pin size and remove the selection tool. Selecting the proper pin is the equivalent of adjusting the band.

34. Remove eight pump attaching bolts with washer-type seals. Discard seals.
35. Install two threaded slide hammers into threaded holes in pump body. Tighten jam nuts and remove pump assembly from the case.
36. Remove pump assembly to case gasket and discard.
37. Remove intermediate clutch cushion spring. Refer to exploded view of intermediate clutch.
38. Remove intermediate clutch faced plates and steel separator plates. Inspect lined plates for pitting, flaking, wear, glazing, cracking and chips or metal particles imbedded in lining. Re-

place any lined plates showing any of these conditions. Inspect steel plates for heat spot discoloration or surface scuffing. If the surface is smooth and has an even color smear, the steel plates may be re-used.
39. Remove intermediate clutch pressure plate.
40. Remove intermediate overrun brake band.
41. Remove direct and forward clutch assemblies.
42. Remove forward clutch housing-to-input ring gear front

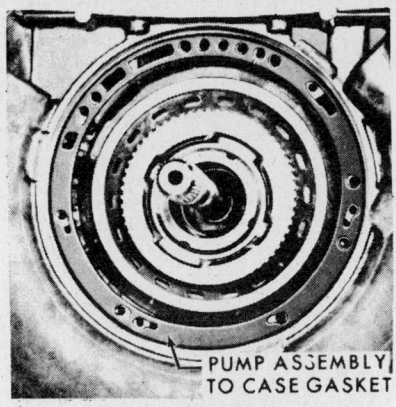

Pump to case gasket
(© G.M. Corp.)

Removing intermediate clutch cushion spring
(© G.M. Corp.)

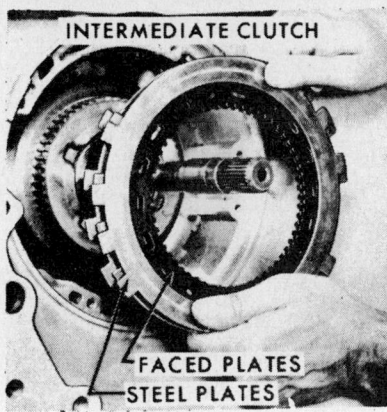

Removing intermediate clutch plates
(© G.M. Corp.)

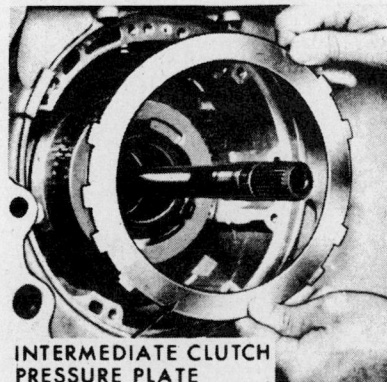

Removing intermediate clutch pressure plate
(© G.M. Corp.)

thrust washer.

NOTE: washer has three tangs.

43. Remove output carrier-to-output shaft snap-ring.
44. Remove input ring gear.
45. Remove input ring gear to output carrier thrust washer.
46. Remove output carrier assembly.
47. Remove sun gear drive shell assembly.
48. Remove low and reverse roller clutch support to case retaining ring.
49. Remove low and reverse roller clutch, support assembly, and retaining spring.
50. Remove low and reverse clutch faced plates and steel separator plates.
51. Remove reaction carrier assembly from output ring gear and shaft assembly.
52. Remove output ring gear and shaft assembly from case.
53. Remove reaction carrier to output ring gear tanged thrust washer.
54. On Oldsmobile applications, remove output ring gear to output shaft snap-ring. Remove output ring gear from output shaft.

NOTE: do not over-stress snapring upon reassembly. Use new snapring.

55. Remove output ring gear-to-case needle bearing assembly.

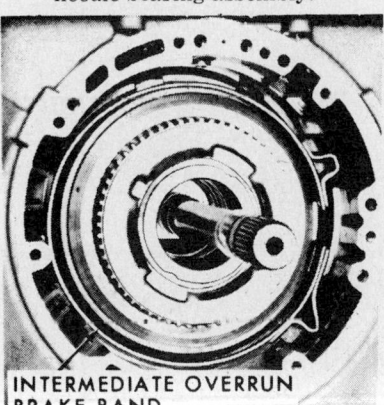

Intermediate overrun brake band
(© G.M. Corp.)

Removing forward and direct clutch assemblies
(© G.M. Corp.)

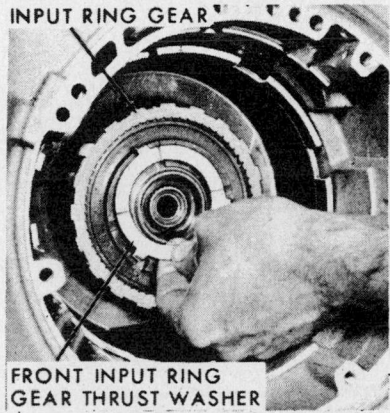

Removing forward clutch housing to input ring gear front thrust washer
(© G.M. Corp.)

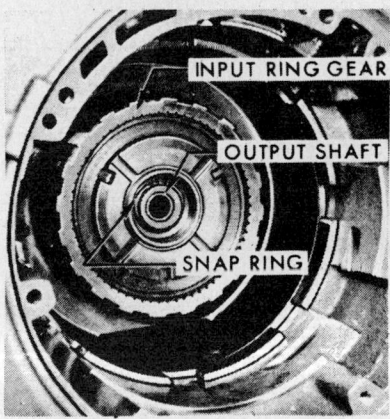

Output carrier to output shaft snap ring
(© G.M. Corp.)

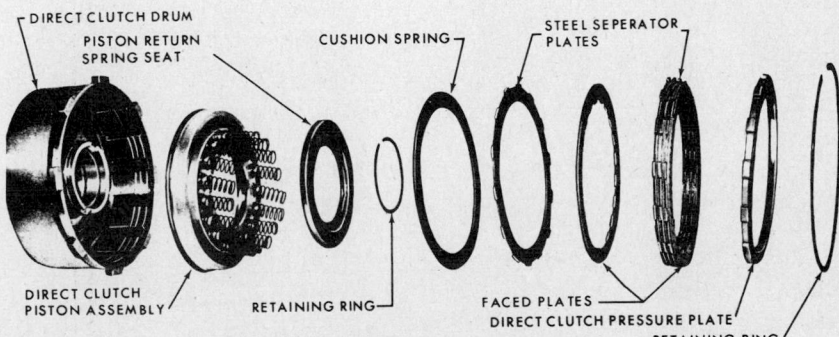

Direct clutch assembly
(© G.M. Corp.)

56. Compress low and reverse clutch piston spring retainer and remove piston retaining ring and spring retainer.

57. Remove 17 piston return coil springs from piston.

58. Remove low and reverse clutch piston by application of air pressure.

59. Remove low and reverse clutch piston outer seal.

60. Remove low and reverse clutch piston center and inner seal.

61. Install suitable tool to compress intermediate clutch accumulator cover and remove retaining ring.

62. Remove intermediate clutch accumulator piston cover. Remove cover O-ring seal from case.

63. Remove intermediate clutch accumulator piston spring.

64. Remove intermediate clutch accumulator piston assembly. Remove inner and outer hook-type oil seal rings if required.

Removing output carrier assembly
(© G.M. Corp.)

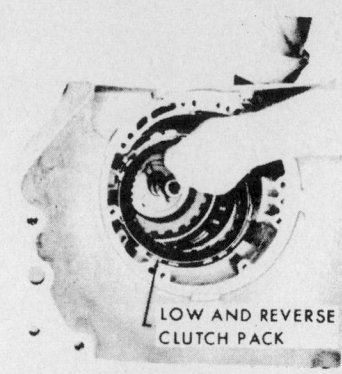

Removing low and reverse clutch pack
(© G.M. Corp.)

Removing sun gear drive shell assembly
(© G.M. Corp.)

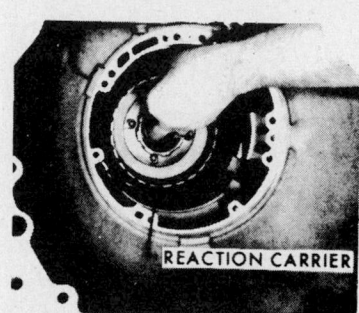

Removing reaction carrier assembly
(© G.M. Corp.)

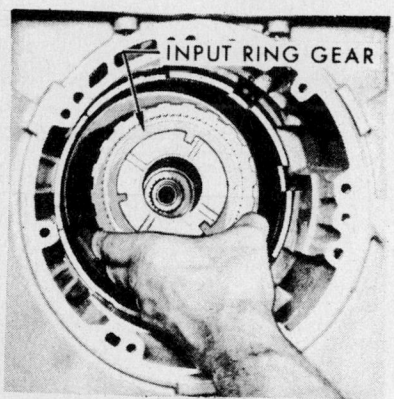

Removing input ring gear
(© G.M. Corp.)

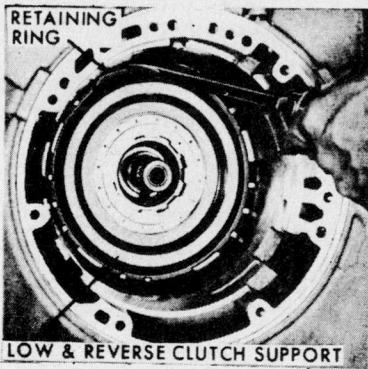

Removing low and reverse roller clutch support to case retaining ring
(© G.M. Corp.)

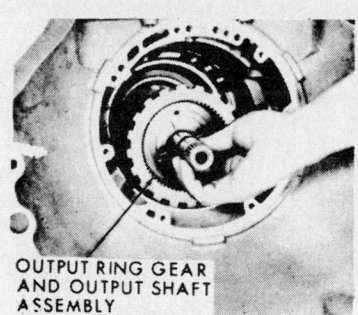

Removing output ring gear and shaft assembly
(© G.M. Corp.)

Removing input ring gear to output carrier thrust washer
(© G.M. Corp.)

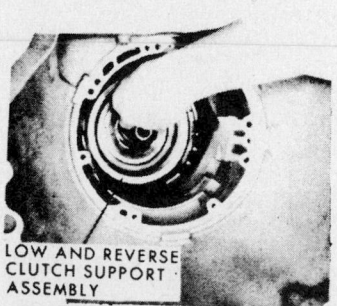

Removing low and reverse clutch support assembly
(© G.M. Corp.)

Removing reaction carrier to output ring gear thrust washer
(© G.M. Corp.)

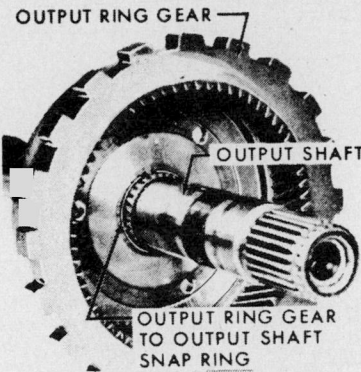

Output ring gear to output shaft snap-ring
(© G.M. Corp.)

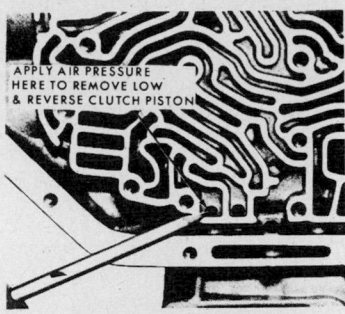

Air pressure application
to remove low and reverse clutch piston
(© G.M. Corp.)

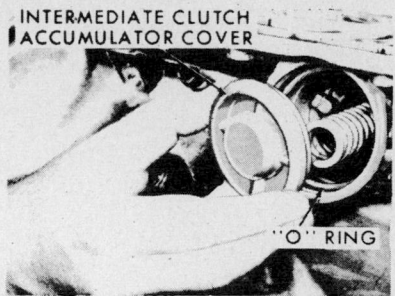

Removing intermediate clutch accumulator
piston cover
(© G.M. Corp.)

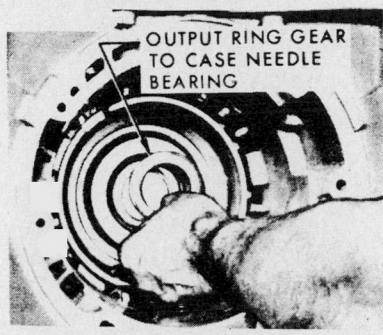

Removing output ring gear to case
needle bearing
(© G.M. Corp.)

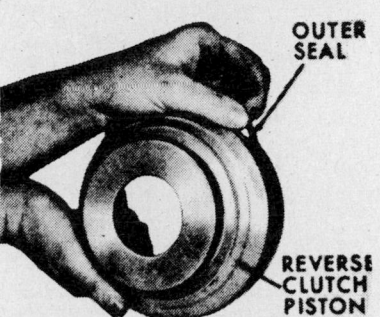

Removing low and reverse clutch piston
outer seal
(© G.M. Corp.)

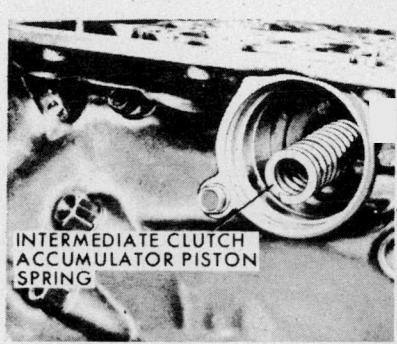

Location of accumulator piston spring
(© G.M. Corp.)

Using spring compressor to remove low
and reverse clutch piston retaining ring
(© G.M. Corp.)

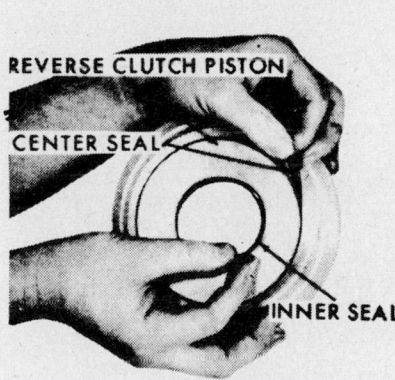

Removing low and reverse clutch piston
inner and center seals
(© G.M. Corp.)

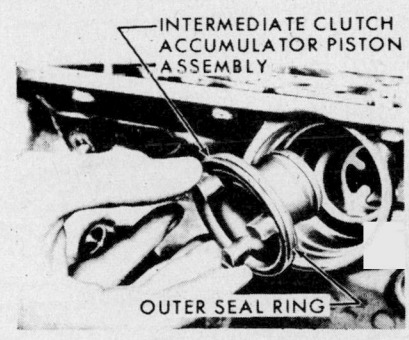

(© G.M. Corp.)

Component Disassembly

Valve Body

Disassembly

1. Position valve body assembly with cored face up and direct clutch accumulator piston pocket located as illustrated in valve body assembly illustration.
2. Remove manual valve from lower left-hand bore, A.
3. From lower right-hand bore, B, remove the pressure regulator valve train retaining pin, boost valve sleeve, intermediate boost valve, reverse and modulator boost valve, pressure regulator valve spring, and the pressure regulator valve.

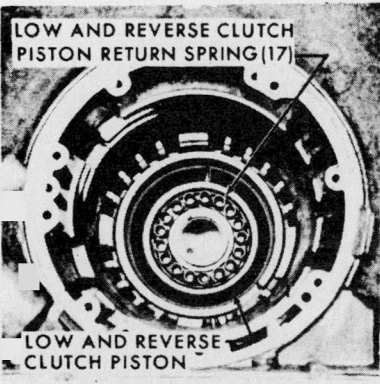

Location of low and reverse piston
return springs
(© G.M. Corp.)

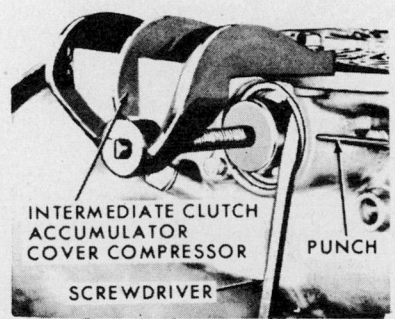

Compressing intermediate clutch
accumulator cover
(© G.M. Corp.)

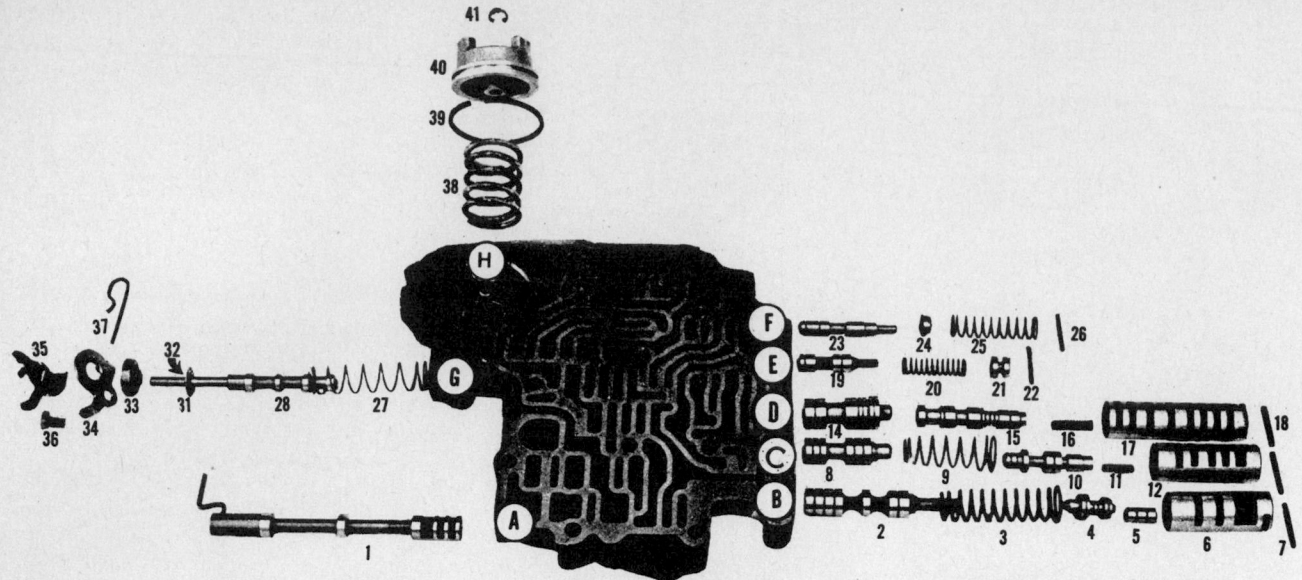

	1. MANUAL VALVE AND LINK ASSEMBLY		14. 1-2 SHIFT VALVE		27. DETENT VALVE OUTER SPRING

A
1. MANUAL VALVE AND LINK ASSEMBLY
2. PRESSURE REGULATOR VALVE
B
3. PRESSURE REGULATOR VALVE SPRING
4. REVERSE AND MODULATOR BOOST VALVE
5. INTERMEDIATE BOOST VALVE
6. BOOST VALVE SLEEVE
7. RETAINING PIN
8. 2-3 SHIFT VALVE
9. 2-3 SHIFT VALVE SPRING
C
10. 2-3 SHIFT CONTROL VALVE
11. 2-3 SHIFT CONTROL VALVE SPRING
12. 2-3 SHIFT CONTROL VALVE SLEEVE
13. RETAINING PIN

D
14. 1-2 SHIFT VALVE
15. 1-2 SHIFT CONTROL VALVE
16. 1-2 SHIFT CONTROL SPRING
17. 1-2 SHIFT CONTROL SLEEVE
18. RETAINING PIN
E
19. MANUAL LOW CONTROL VALVE
20. MANUAL LOW CONTROL SPRING
21. PLUG
22. RETAINING PIN
F
23. DETENT REGULATOR VALVE
24. DETENT REGULATOR SPRING SEAT
25. DETENT REGULATOR SPRING
26. RETAINING PIN

27. DETENT VALVE OUTER SPRING
28. DETENT VALVE

G
31. DETENT VALVE OUTER SPRING SEAT
32. DETENT VALVE SPRING RETAINER
33. DETENT VALVE STOP
34. DETENT VALVE BRACKET
35. DETENT VALVE ACTUATING LEVER
36. RETAINING BOLT
37. RETAINING PIN
H
38. DIRECT CLUTCH ACCUMULATOR SPRING
39. OIL SEAL RING
40. DIRECT CLUTCH ACCUMULATOR PISTON
41. RETAINER RING

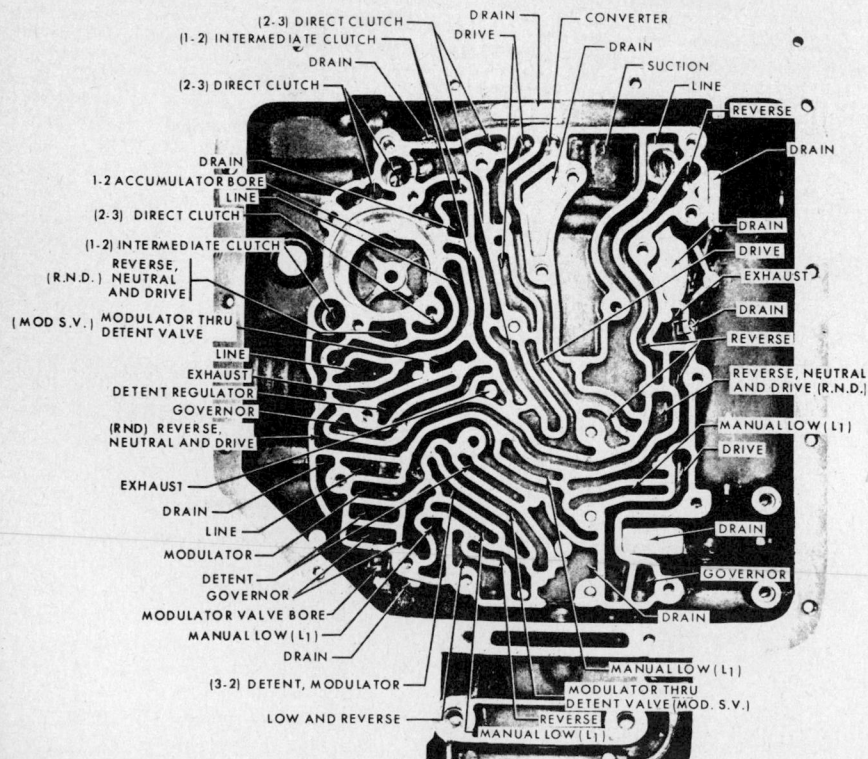

4. From the next bore, C, remove the second-third shift valve train retaining pin, sleeve, control valve spring, second-third shift control valve, shift valve spring, and the second-third shift valve.

5. From the next bore, D, remove the first-second shift valve train retaining pin, sleeve, shift control valve spring, first-second shift control valve, and the first-second shift control valve.

6. From the next bore, E, remove retaining pin, plug, manual low control valve spring, and the manual low control valve.

7. From the next bore, F, remove retaining pin, spring, seat and the detent regulator valve.

8. Install spring compressor onto direct clutch accumulator piston and remove retaining E-ring at H.

9. At location H, remove direct clutch accumulator piston, then metal oil seal ring and spring.

10. From the upper left hand bore, G, remove the detent actuating lever bracket bolt, bracket, actuating lever and retaining pin, stop, spring retainer, seat, outer spring, and the detent valve.

Inspection

1. Wash all parts in solvent. Air dry. Blow out all passages.
2. Inspect all valves for scoring, cracks, and free movement in their bores.

3. Inspect sleeves for cracks, scratches, or distortion.
4. Inspect valve body for cracks, scored bores, interconnected oil passages, and flatness of mounting face.
5. Check all springs for distortion or collapsed coils.

Assembly

1. Reverse disassembly procedures for assembly. Refer to Valve Body Springs chart for identification of springs.

Valve Body Springs

Valve	Free Length of Spring (in.)	Diameter (in.)
Detent regulator	1 ⅞	9/16
Manual low control valve	1 ½	7/16
1-2 shift control valve	1 15/16	¼
2-3 shift valve	2 1/16	⅞
2-3 shift control valve	11/16	3/16
Pressure regulator valve	1 11/16	17/32
Direct clutch accumulator	1 ¾	1 ½
Detent valve	1 ⅞	¾

Oil Pump

Disassembly

1. Remove five pump cover-to-body attaching bolts. Remove spring seat retainer.
2. Remove the intermediate clutch spring seat retainer, 30 intermediate clutch return springs (20 on Buick applications) and the intermediate clutch piston assembly.
3. Remove intermediate clutch piston inner and outer seals.
4. Remove two forward clutch-to-pump hub hook-type oil seal rings. Remove three direct clutch-to-pump hub hook type oil rings.
5. Remove pump cover-to-direct clutch drum selective thrust washer.
6. Remove pump cover and stator shaft assembly from pump body.
7. Remove pump drive gear and driven gear from pump body.
8. Remove pump outside diameter-to-case square cut O-ring seal.
9. Pry out pump body to converter hub lip seal, using a screwdriver. Place pump on wood blocks to prevent damage to surface finish.
10. Install pump-to-converter hub lip seal, using seal driver. Examine

after installation to be sure the sealing surface is not damaged.
11. Remove oil pump priming valve and spring.
12. Remove cooler by-pass valve seat. Pack cooler by-pass passage with grease. Insert 5/16 in. dia. rod and tap with hammer to lift seat. Remove check ball and spring.

Inspection

1. Wash all parts in solvent. Air dry. Blow out all passages.
2. Inspect drive and driven gears, gear pocket, and crescent for nicks, galling or other damage.
3. Inspect pump body and cover for nicks or scoring.
4. Check pump cover outer diameter for nicks or burrs.
5. Inspect pump body bushing for galling or scoring. Check clearance between pump body bushing and converter hub. It must be no more than .005 in. If bushing is damaged, replace pump body.
6. Install pump gears in body and check pump body face to gear face clearance. It should be from .0008-.0035 in. (.0005-.0015 in. for Chevrolet).

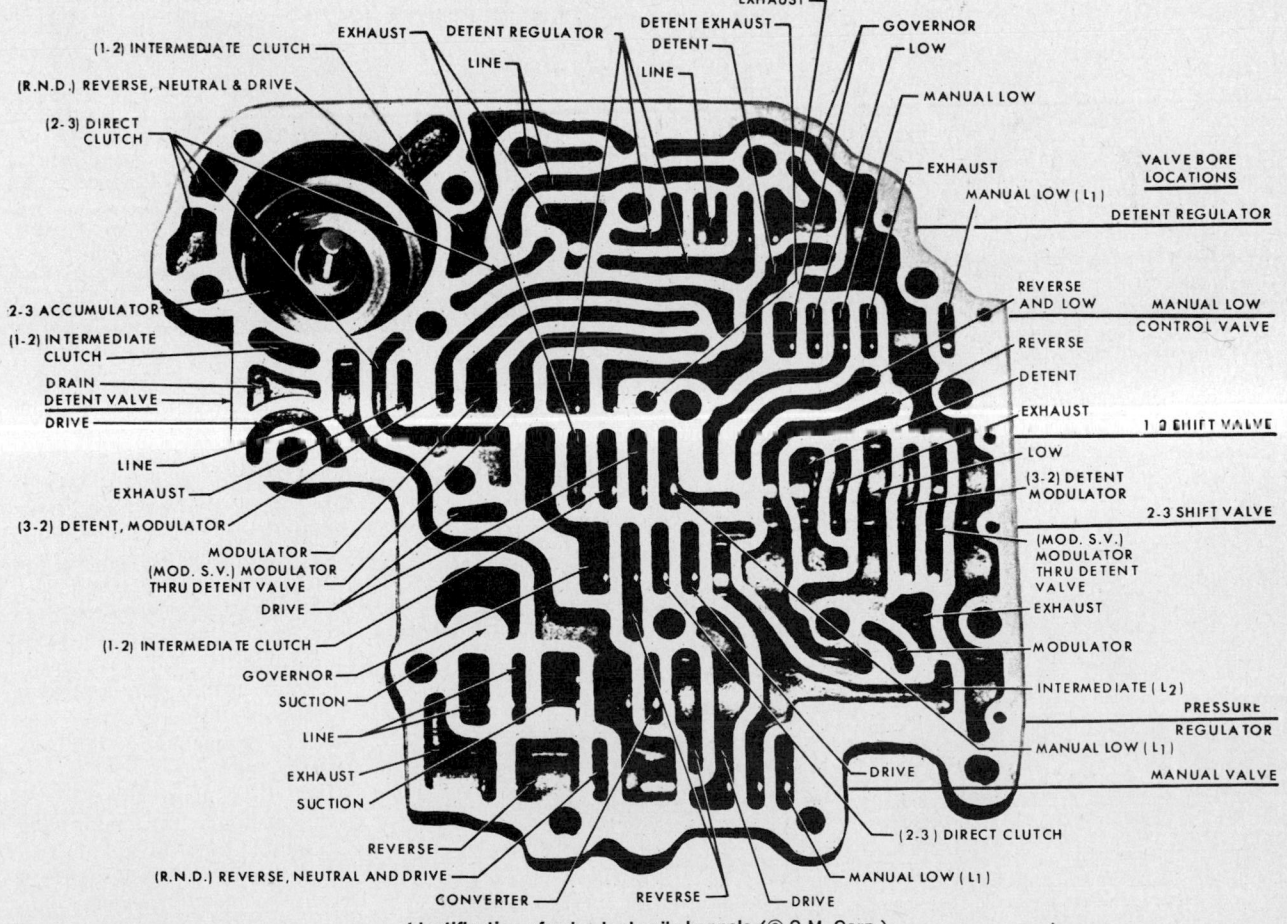

Identification of valve body oil channels (© G.M. Corp.)

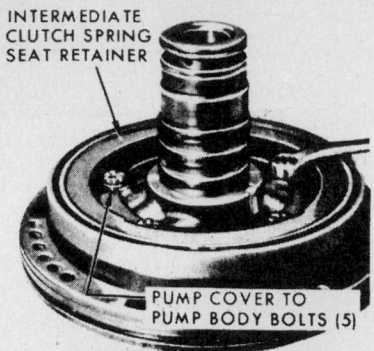

Removing oil pump cover bolts
(© G.M. Corp.)

Labels: INTERMEDIATE CLUTCH SPRING SEAT RETAINER; PUMP COVER TO PUMP BODY BOLTS (5)

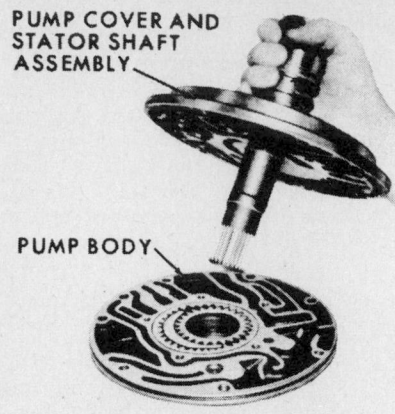

Removing pump cover and stator shaft
(© G.M. Corp.)

Labels: PUMP COVER AND STATOR SHAFT ASSEMBLY; PUMP BODY

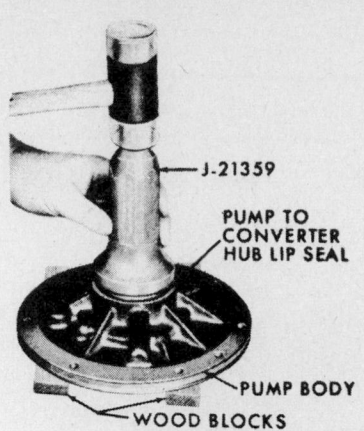

Driving in lip seal
(© G.M. Corp.)

Labels: J-21359; PUMP TO CONVERTER HUB LIP SEAL; PUMP BODY; WOOD BLOCKS

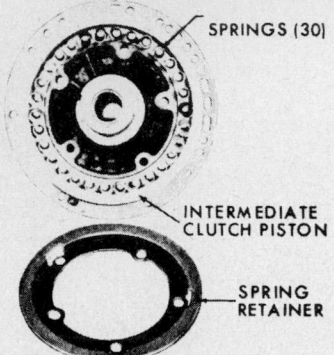

Details of intermediate clutch return springs
(© G.M. Corp.)

Labels: SPRINGS (30); INTERMEDIATE CLUTCH PISTON; SPRING RETAINER

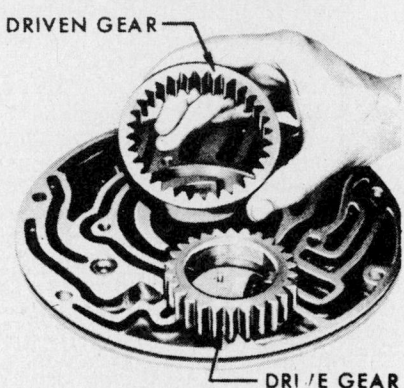

Removal of pump gears
(© G.M. Corp.)

Labels: DRIVEN GEAR; DRIVE GEAR

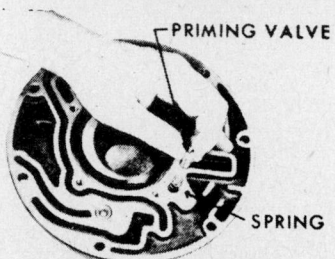

Removal of priming valve
(© G.M. Corp.)

Labels: PRIMING VALVE; SPRING

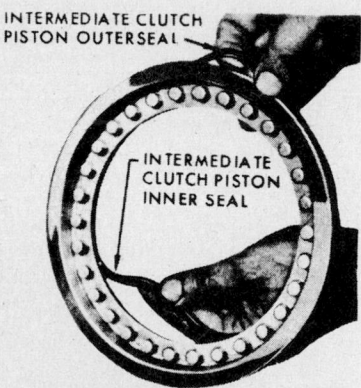

Removal of intermediate clutch piston seal
(© G.M. Corp.)

Labels: INTERMEDIATE CLUTCH PISTON OUTERSEAL; INTERMEDIATE CLUTCH PISTON INNER SEAL

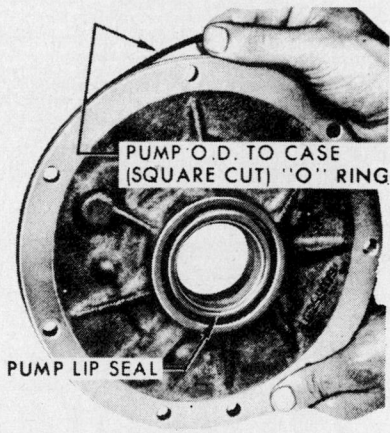

Removal of pump to case O-ring
(© G.M. Corp.)

Labels: PUMP O.D. TO CASE (SQUARE CUT) "O" RING; PUMP LIP SEAL

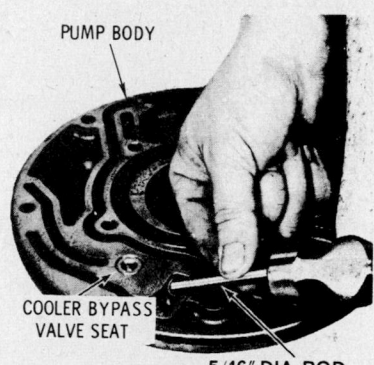

Removing cooler by-pass valve seat
(© G.M. Corp.)

Labels: PUMP BODY; COOLER BYPASS VALVE SEAT; 5/16" DIA. ROD

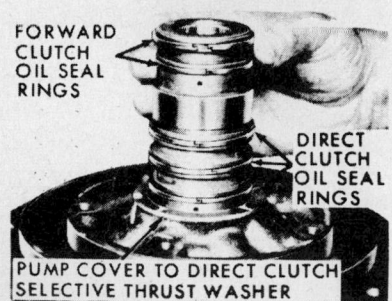

Removal of oil seal rings and selective thrust washer
(© G.M. Corp.)

Labels: FORWARD CLUTCH OIL SEAL RINGS; DIRECT CLUTCH OIL SEAL RINGS; PUMP COVER TO DIRECT CLUTCH SELECTIVE THRUST WASHER

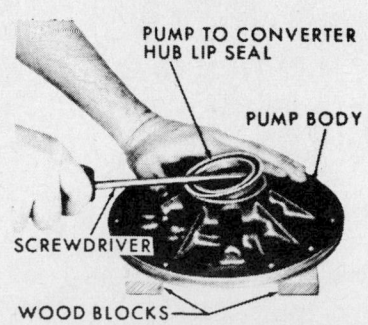

Prying out pump to converter hub lip seal
(© G.M. Corp.)

Labels: PUMP TO CONVERTER HUB LIP SEAL; PUMP BODY; SCREWDRIVER; WOOD BLOCKS

7. Inspect pump body to converter hub lip oil seal. Inspect converter hub for nicks or burrs which might have damaged pump lip oil seal or pump body bushing.

8. Check priming valve for free operation. Replace if necessary.

9. Check condition of cooler bypass valve. Replace valve if it leaks excessively.

10. Check all springs for distortion or collapsed coils.

11. Check oil passages in pump body and in pump cover.

12. Inspect three pump cover stator shaft bushings for galling or scoring. If they are damaged, remove using a slide hammer. Drive the new bushings into place. The front stator shaft

bushing must be .250 in. below the front face of the pump body. The center bushing should be 11/32 in. below the face of the pump cover hub. The rear bushing should be flush or up to .010 in. below the face of the pump cover hub.

13. Check three pump cover and hub lubrication holes to make certain they are not restricted.

7. Install pump cover on pump body.

8. Install intermediate clutch piston and clutch return springs.

9. Install spring retainer and pump cover bolts. Position aligning strap over pump body and cover. Tighten strap. Torque pump bolts to 18 ft. lbs.

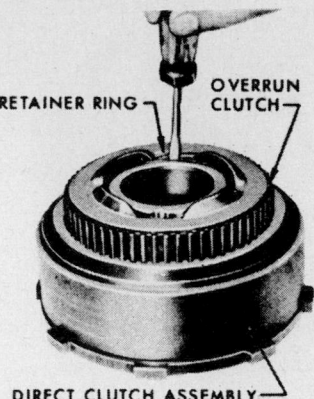

Removing intermediate overrun clutch front retainer ring
(© G.M. Corp.)

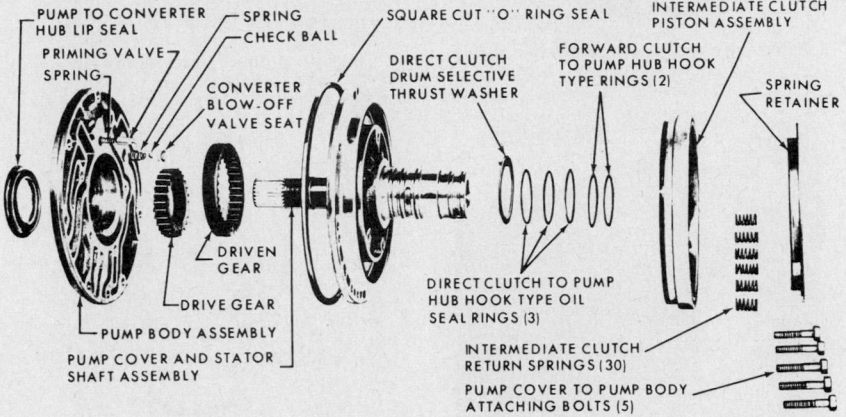

Components—oil pump assembly (© G.M. Corp.)

Assembly

1. Install cooler by-pass valve spring, check ball and seat. Press seat into bore until top of seat is flush to .010 in. with face of pump body.
2. Install oil pump priming valve and spring. The priming valve is used on all pump bodies having a reamed hole in the priming valve area and on all replacement pump assemblies.
3. Install new pump outside diameter to case square cut O-ring seal.
4. Install pump drive and driven gears. If drive gear has offset tangs, assemble with tangs face up to prevent damage by converter.
5. Install selective thrust washer and five oil seal rings on pump cover hub.
6. Install intermediate clutch piston inner and outer seals.

Location of pump cover lube holes
(© G.M. Corp.)

Direct Clutch and Intermediate Overrun Roller Clutch

Disassembly

1. Remove intermediate overrun clutch front retainer ring and retainer.
2. Remove intermediate overrun clutch outer race.

  Note: before removal, check for correct assembly. The outer race should free wheel counterclockwise only.
3. Remove intermediate overrun roller clutch assembly.
4. Remove intermediate overrun roller clutch cam (Oldsmobile).
5. Remove direct clutch drum to forward clutch housing special thrust washer.
6. Remove direct clutch pressure plate to clutch drum retaining ring and pressure plate.
7. Remove direct clutch lined and steel plates.
8. Remove direct clutch piston return spring seat retaining ring and spring seat.
9. Remove 17 clutch return coil springs and piston.
10. Remove direct clutch piston inner and outer seals.
11. Remove direct clutch piston center seal.

Inspection

1. Wash all parts in solvent. Blow out all passages. Air dry.

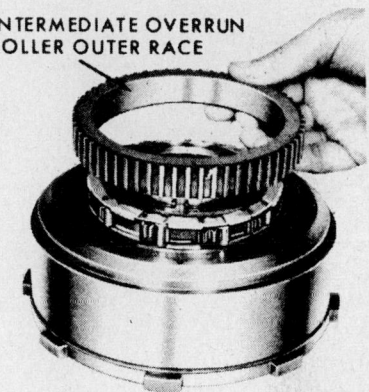

Removing intermediate overrun clutch outer race
(© G.M. Corp.)

2. Inspect clutch plates for burning, scoring, or wear.
3. Check all springs for collapsed coils or distortion.
4. Inspect piston for cracks and free operation of ball check. Ball should be loose enough to rattle but not to fall out.
5. Check overrun clutch inner cam and outer race for scratches, wear, or indentations.
6. Inspect overrun roller clutch assembly rollers for wear. Check springs for distortion.
7. Inspect clutch drum for wear, scoring, cracks, proper opening of oil passages, wear on clutch plate drive lugs, and free operation of ball check.
8. Check direct clutch drum bushing for galling or scoring. When replacing bushing, drive the new bushing 9/32 in. below clutch plate side of hub face and .010 in. below slot in hub face.

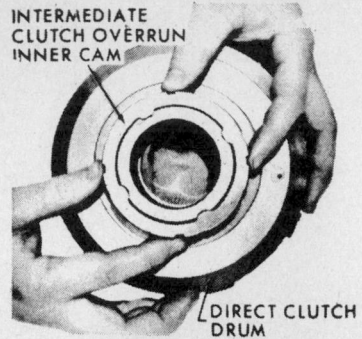

Removing roller clutch cam
(© G.M. Corp.)

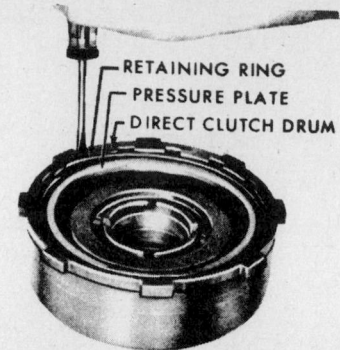

Removing direct clutch retaining ring
(© G.M. Corp.)

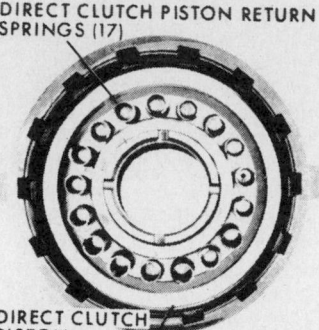

Location of direct clutch return springs
(© G.M. Corp.)

Removing intermediate overrun roller
clutch assembly
(© G.M. Corp.)

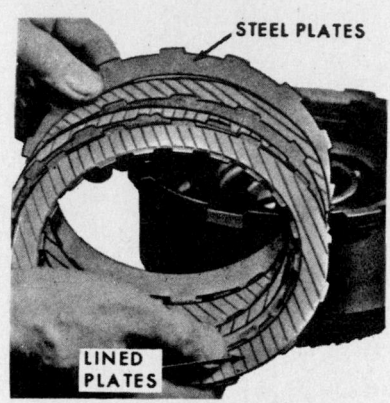

Direct clutch plates (© G.M. Corp.)

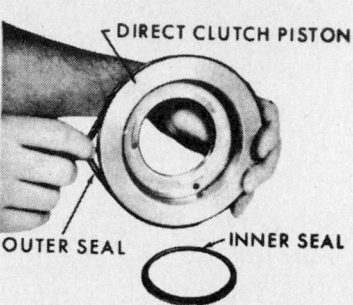

Removing direct clutch piston seals
(© G.M. Corp.)

CAUTION: IF ROLLER FALLS OUT DURING ASSEMBLY OPERATION—REINSTALL ROLLER
FROM INSIDE TO OUTSIDE CAGE DIRECTION TO AVOID BENDING SPRING

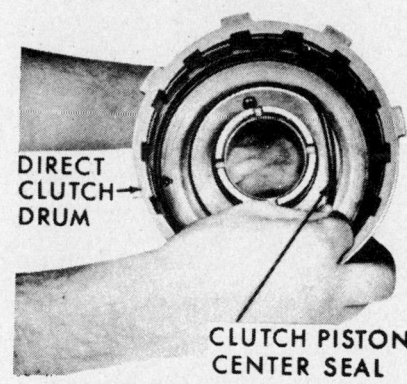

Removing direct clutch drum center seal
(© G.M. Corp.)

Intermediate overrunning roller clutch assembly (© G.M. Corp.)

Assembly

NOTE: Buick model MA transmissions require a pressure relief ball in the direct clutch piston. Clutch pack failure will result if this is not observed.

1. Install direct clutch drum center seal.
2. Install direct clutch piston inner and outer seals.
3. Install direct clutch piston into housing with a loop of .020 in. wire crimped into a length of copper tubing.
4. Install 17 clutch return springs on piston.
5. Install direct clutch piston return spring seat and retaining ring using snap-ring pliers and spring compressor.
6. Install direct clutch housing. In-

Removing thrust washer
(© G.M. Corp.)

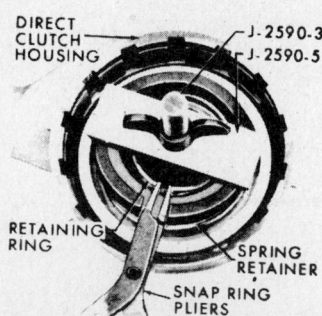

Removing spring seat retaining ring
(© G.M. Corp.)

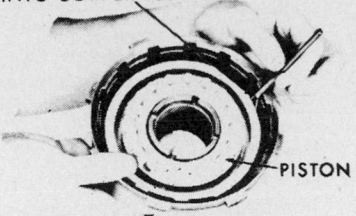

.020" MUSIC WIRE CRIMPED
INTO COPPER TUBING

PISTON

DIRECT CLUTCH HOUSING

Installing clutch piston into housing
(© G.M. Corp.)

stall steel and faced plates alternately, beginning with a steel plate.

7. Install direct clutch pressure plate in clutch drum. Install retaining ring.

8. Install intermediate overrun roller clutch inner cam on hub of direct clutch drum.

9. Replace intermediate overrun roller clutch assembly.

10. Install intermediate overrun clutch outer race. The outer race must free-wheel in the counterclockwise direction only.

11. Replace intermediate overrun clutch retainer and retainer ring. If the retainer ring is dished, install the ring so that it compresses the retainer.

12. Install direct clutch drum to forward clutch housing needle thrust washer on hub of roller clutch inner race.

Forward Clutch

Disassembly

1. Remove forward clutch drum to pressure plate retaining ring.

2. Remove forward clutch pressure plate.

3. Remove forward clutch housing faced plates, steel plates and cushion spring.

4. Compress springs. Remove forward clutch piston return spring seat retaining ring and spring seat.

5. Remove 21 clutch return springs.

6. Remove forward clutch piston assembly.

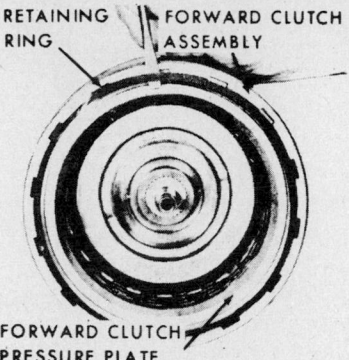

RETAINING RING — FORWARD CLUTCH ASSEMBLY

FORWARD CLUTCH PRESSURE PLATE

Removing forward clutch pressure plate retaining ring
(© G.M. Corp.)

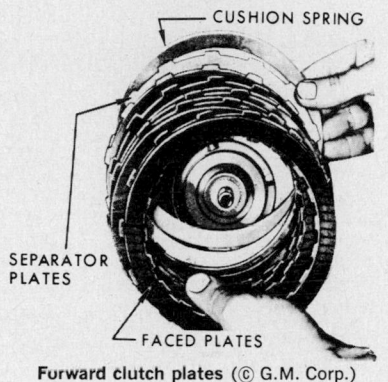

CUSHION SPRING

SEPARATOR PLATES

FACED PLATES

Forward clutch plates (© G.M. Corp.)

7. Remove forward clutch piston inner and outer seals.

8. Be sure the ball check exhaust in the drum is operable and free of dirt.

Inspection

1. Wash all parts in solvent. Blow out all passages. Air dry.

2. Inspect clutch plates for burning, scoring, or wear.

3. Check all springs for distortion or collapsed coils.

4. Inspect piston for cracks.

5. Inspect clutch drum for wear, scoring, cracks, proper opening of oil passages, and free operation of ball check.

FORWARD CLUTCH PISTON SPRING SEAT

RETAINING RING

Forward clutch piston retaining ring and spring seat
(© G.M. Corp.)

Clutch Plates

Year	Model	Intermediate Clutch		Direct Clutch		Forward Clutch		Low-Reverse Clutch	
		Driven Plates	Drive Plates	Driven Plates	Drive Plates	Driven Plates	Drive Plates	Driven Plates	Drive Plates
1969-72	Chevrolet L6, 307 V8 Oldsmobile L6 Pontiac L6	2	2	3	3	4	4	4	4
1969-72	Chevrolet 350, 400 V8① Oldsmobile V8 Pontiac V8 Buick 350 V8	3	3	4	4	5	5	5	5
1970-72	Buick L6	2	2	3	3	4	4	4	4

①—Forward and direct clutches on models CF, CR, CS and CY use 6 driven and 6 drive plates.

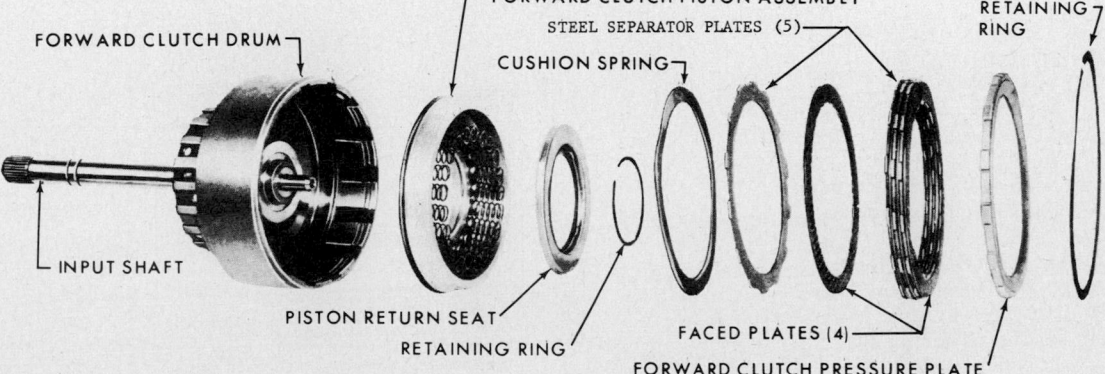

FORWARD CLUTCH DRUM

FORWARD CLUTCH PISTON ASSEMBLY

STEEL SEPARATOR PLATES (5)

CUSHION SPRING

RETAINING RING

INPUT SHAFT

PISTON RETURN SEAT

RETAINING RING

FACED PLATES (4)

FORWARD CLUTCH PRESSURE PLATE

Forward clutch assembly (© G.M. Corp.)

6. Check input shaft for:
   a. Open lubrication passages at each end.
   b. Damage to splines or shaft.
   c. Damage to ground bushing journals.
   d. Cracks or distortion of shaft.

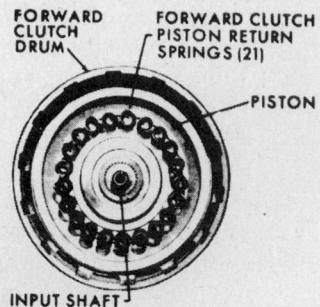

Forward clutch springs
(© G.M. Corp.)

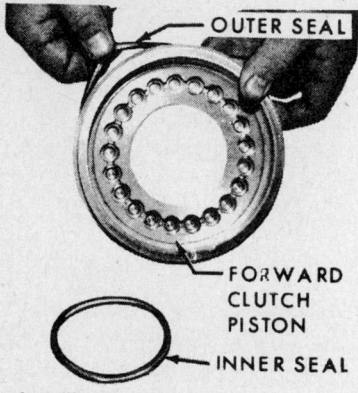

Installing forward clutch piston seals
(© G.M. Corp.)

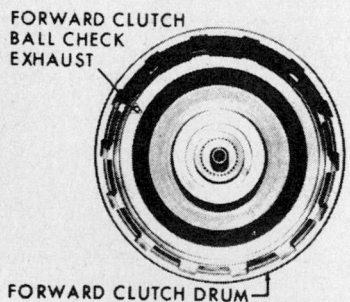

Forward clutch ball check
(© G.M. Corp.)

Assembly

1. Install forward clutch piston inner and outer seals.
2. Install forward clutch piston with a loop of .020 in. wire crimped into a length of copper tubing.
3. Install the 21 forward clutch return springs. These springs are identical to those used in the direct clutch. Install spring seat.
4. Compress springs and replace spring seat retaining ring.

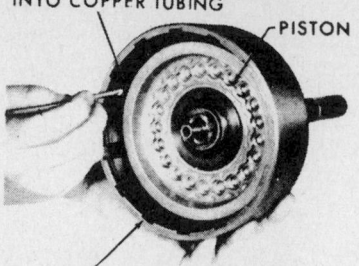

Installing forward clutch piston
(© G.M. Corp.)

5. Replace forward clutch housing cushion spring. Replace steel and faced plates alternately, starting with a steel plate.
6. Install forward clutch pressure plate and retaining ring.
7. Use a feeler gauge to check the clearance between the top faced plate and the pressure plate. The clearance should be .010-.080 in. for Oldsmobile, Buick and Pontiac applications. Selective pressure plates for Oldsmobile applications are available in .200 in., .230 in. and .260 in. thicknesses. Pontiac and Buick applications use selective pressure plates in .245-.255 in., .275-.285 in. and .306-.316 in. thicknesses. Use the following chart to determine the proper plate for Chevrolet applications.

Subtract dim. B from C
to obtain dim. A

When dim. A is:	use plate number
.016-.052 in.	6261072
.052-.083 in.	6261349
.083-.122 in.	6261350

8. Install direct clutch drum on input shaft and align faced plates with splines on forward clutch housing.

WHEN DIM. C IS		USE
.0160—	.0520	6261072
.0520—	.0830	6261349
.0830—	.1218	6261350

Sun Gear and Sun Gear Drive Shell

Disassembly

1. Remove sun gear to sun gear drive shell rear retaining ring.
2. Remove sun gear to drive shell flat rear thrust washer.
3. Remove sun gear and front retaining ring from drive shell.
4. Remove front retaining ring from sun gear.

Inspection

1. Wash all parts in solvent. Air dry.

Removing sun gear retaining ring
(© G.M. Corp.)

2. Inspect sun gear and sun gear drive shell for wear or damage.
3. Inspect sun gear bushings for galling or scoring. Drive out damaged bushings. Install new bushings flush to .010 in. below surface of counterbore.

Assembly

1. Install new front retaining ring on sun gear. Be careful not to over-stress this ring.
2. Install sun gear and retaining

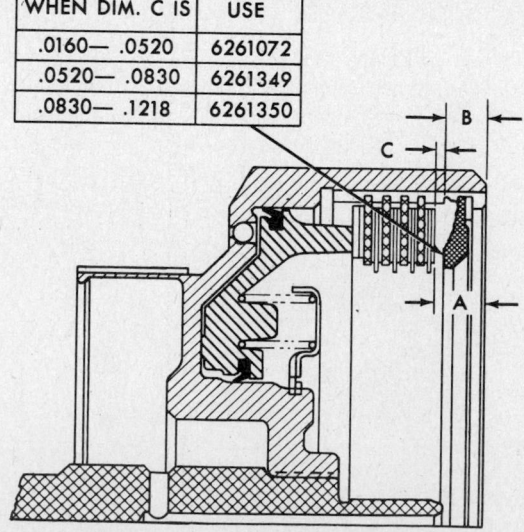

Determining selective fit forward clutch pressure plate on Chevrolet applications
(© G.M. Corp.)

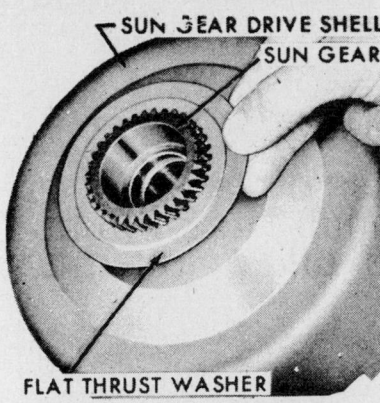

Removing sun gear rear thrust washer
(© G.M. Corp.)

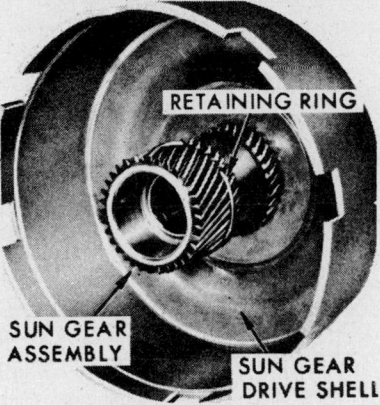

Sun gear front retaining ring
(© G.M. Corp.)

ring in drive shell.

3. Install sun gear to drive shell flat rear thrust washer.
4. Install new sun gear to sun gear drive shell retaining ring.

Low and Reverse Roller Clutch Support

Disassembly

1. Remove low and reverse clutch to sun gear shell thrust washer.
2. Remove low and reverse overrun clutch inner race.
3. Remove low and reverse roller clutch retaining ring.
4. Remove low and reverse roller clutch assembly.

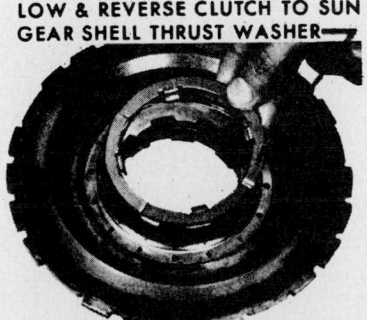

Removing low and reverse clutch thrust washer
(© G.M. Corp.)

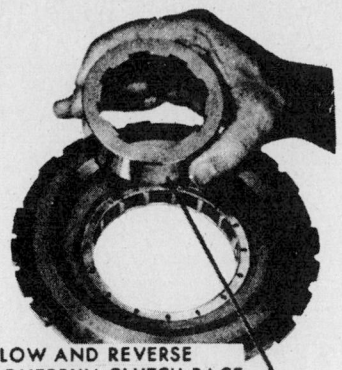

Removing low and reverse overrun clutch inner race
(© G.M. Corp.)

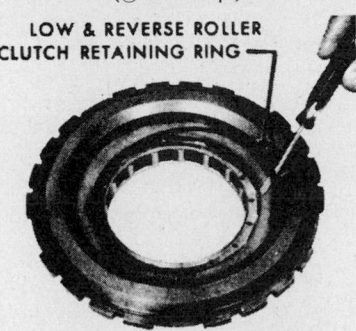

Removing low and reverse roller clutch retaining ring
(© G.M. Corp.)

Removing low and reverse roller clutch
(© G.M. Corp.)

Inspection

1. Wash all parts in solvent. Air dry.
2. Inspect roller clutch inner and outer races for scratches, wear, or indentations.
3. Inspect roller clutch assembly rollers for wear and roller springs for distortion. If rollers are removed from assembly, install rollers from outside in to avoid bending springs.

Assembly

1. Install low and reverse roller clutch assembly.
2. Install low and reverse roller clutch retaining ring.
3. Install low and reverse overrun clutch inner race. Inner race must free-wheel in the clockwise direction only.

Transmission Assembly

1. Install inner and outer hook type oil seal rings on accumulator piston. Install intermediate clutch accumulator piston assembly. Install O-ring seal against shoulder in case. Install accumulator piston spring and piston cover. Compress spring and cover as in disassembly and install retaining ring.
2. Install low and reverse clutch piston center, outer, and inner seal on piston. Install piston assembly. Notch in low and reverse clutch piston must be installed adjacent to parking pawl. Install 17 return springs in piston. Place spring seat on return springs. Compress springs as in disassembly and install retaining ring.

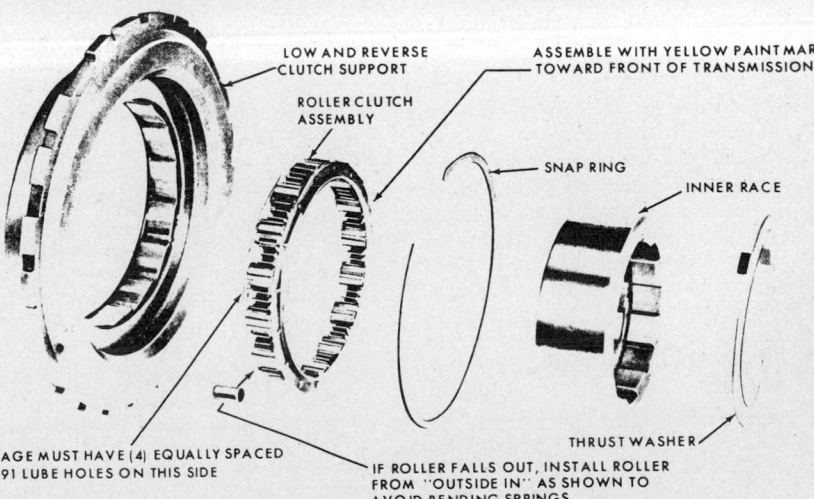

Low and reverse roller clutch assembly
(© G.M. Corp.)

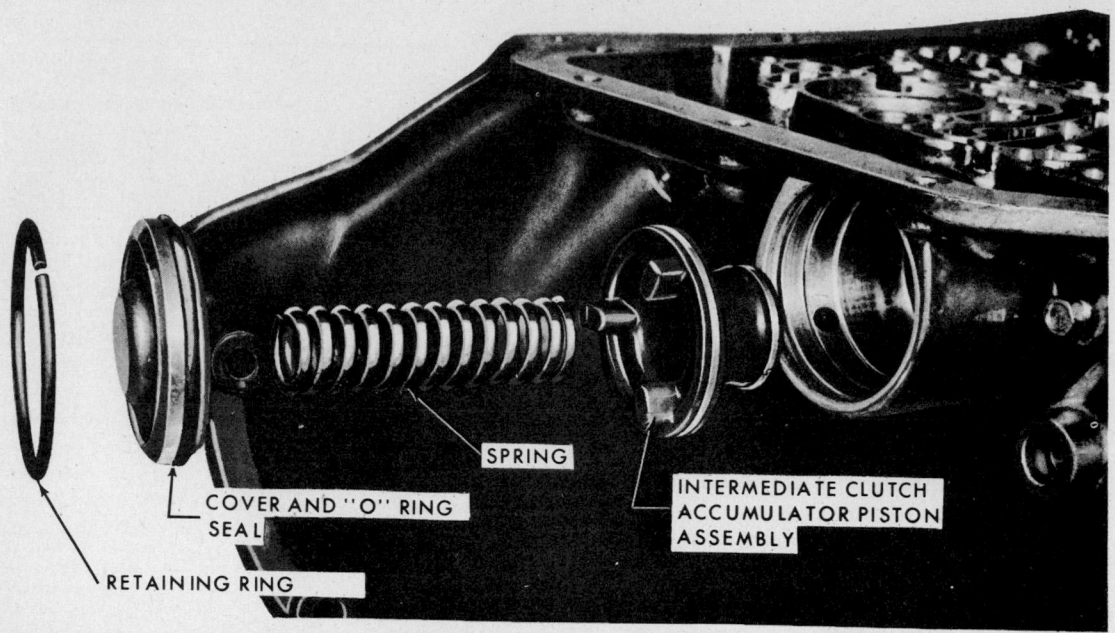

SPRING

COVER AND "O" RING SEAL

INTERMEDIATE CLUTCH ACCUMULATOR PISTON ASSEMBLY

RETAINING RING

Intermediate clutch accumulator (© G.M. Corp.)

3. Install output ring gear to case needle bearing assembly, shoulder down. Assemble output ring gear on output shaft. Use new snap-ring on shaft. Install reaction carrier to output ring gear tanged thrust washer. This washer has three narrow tangs on the outside circumference. Install output ring rear and shaft assembly in case.

4. Install reaction carrier assembly on output ring gear and shaft assembly.

5. Install low and reverse clutch plates. Start with a steel plate and alternate steel and faced plates. The notch in the steel plates must be toward the bottom of the case.

6. Install low and reverse roller clutch support retaining spring, then support assembly. Align tangs on inner race with slots in reaction carrier. Install retaining ring.

7. Install sun gear to roller clutch thrust washer on the roller clutch inner race. This washer has four tangs on the inside circumference. Install sun gear drive shell assembly.

8. Install output carrier assembly. Install new output carrier to output shaft snap-ring.

9. Install input ring gear to output carrier thrust washer. Install forward clutch housing to input ring gear front thrust washer. This washer has three wide tangs on the outside circumference.

10. Install direct and forward clutch assemblies in case. Align plates with splines and insert until tangs are 1/8 in. below notches in drive shell.

11. Install intermediate overrun brake band, intermediate clutch pressure plate, and steel and faced clutch plates. Insert a steel plate first, then alternate faced and steel plates. Install intermediate clutch cushion spring.

12. Lubricate case bore, then install new pump to case gasket in bore. Install the proper selective thrust washer to obtain .033-.064 in. shaft end-play with pump installed. Selective thrust washers are available in .066, .083 and .100 in. thicknesses.

13. Install pump into case. Drive in until seated. Install new washer type seals on pump attaching bolts. Torque to 15-25 ft. lbs. If the input shaft cannot be rotated clockwise as the pump is being bolted into place, the direct clutch and forward clutch housing has not been properly installed to index the faced plates with their respective parts. This condition must be corrected before the pump is bolted into place.

14. Invert transmission and install intermediate servo spring, spring seat, apply pin, washer, and piston assembly.

15. Install parking pawl tooth toward the inside of case. Install parking pawl shaft into case

through disengaging spring. Install disengaging spring on parking pawl and slide shaft through pawl. Drive in pawl shaft retainer plug using a 3/8 in. drift. Drive plug flush to .010 in. below face of case. Stake plug in three places. Install park lock bracket. Torque bolts to 29 ft. lbs.

16. Install range selector inner lever to parking pawl actuating rod. Install actuating rod under the park lock bracket and parking pawl.

17. Drive in new manual shaft lip seal using a 7/8 in. drift. Insert manual shaft through case and range selector inner lever. Torque manual shaft jam nut to 30 ft. lbs. Install manual shaft retainer.

18. Replace governor screens in case. Replace oil pump pressure screen in oil pump pressure hole in case. Ring end of screen goes in first. Replace four check balls in correct passages in case face. Replace valve body spacer plate to case gasket, spacer plate, spacer support plate, and seven bolts. Do not tighten bolts yet. Install valve body to spacer plate gasket.

19. Install detent control valve link in detent actuating lever. Install valve body while installing manual control valve link in range selector inner lever. When handling valve body, be careful not

to depress sleeves as retaining pins may fall out into the transmission.

20. Torque valve body attaching bolts to 13 ft. lbs. Install detent roller and spring to valve body.
21. Replace oil pump screen and gasket to valve body. Replace oil pump screen attaching screws.
22. Install pan and gasket. Torque bolts to 12 ft. lbs.
23. Check governor bore and sleeve for scoring. Install governor assembly into case. Install new O-ring on governor cover and install governor cover. Use a brass drift on the flange of the cover, but do not hammer on the cover. Replace governor cover retainer.
24. Place retainer clip on output shaft. Slide speedometer drive gear over output shaft until secured by clip.
25. Position yoke seal on output shaft. Tap seal into place with a suitable tool.
26. Install extension housing lip seal if not replaced on disassembly. Install extension housing square cut O-ring seal. Replace extension housing. Torque bolts to 35 ft. lbs.
27. Lubricate new modulator O-ring, then install on modulator. Replace vacuum modulator valve in case, bolting down retainer.
28. Install torque converter to transmission, engaging lugs, and install a holding tool to prevent converter from dropping off.

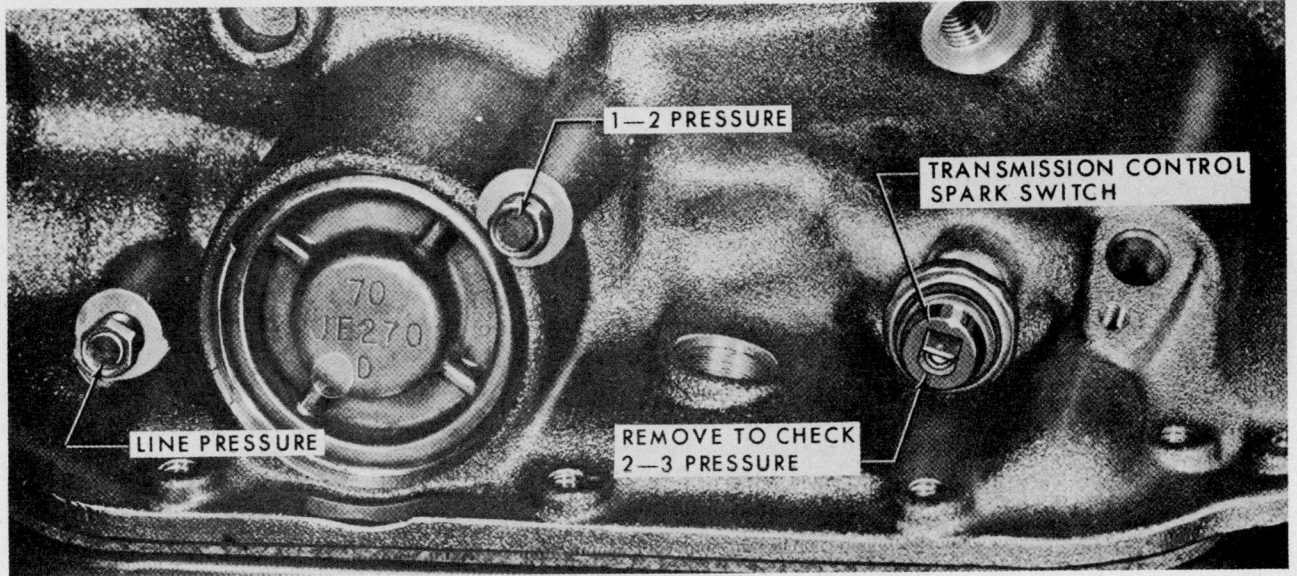

Side view of transmission (© G.M. Corp.)

Oil Pressure Checks

Year	Model	Oil Pressure (psi) @ Altitude (± 5 psi) ①								
		Sea Level			2,000 Ft.			10,000 ft.		
		D, N, P	S, L	R	D, N, P	S, L	R	D, N, P	S, L	R
1969	All Pontiac and Buick applications	176	175	251	164	166	234	137	146	195
1970-72	All Pontiac and Buick applications	153	153	239	153	153	221	110	123	164
1971-72	Chevrolet 307	168	167	254	159	160	240	126	136	191
	Chevrolet 350	174	171	262	164	164	248	132	140	199

① Pressures are at 0 output speed, 1,200 engine rpm and vacuum line disconnected and plugged.

Year	Model	Pressure (psi), with vehicle coasting @ 25 mph vacuum line connected, foot off throttle				
		Neutral ± 5 psi	Drive ± 5 psi	Super ± 5 psi	Low ± 5 psi	Reverse ± 5 psi
1969	All Pontiac applications	67	67	90	90	90
1970-72	All Pontiac applications	60	60	85	85	N.A.
1969	All Buick applications	67	67	95	95	96
1970-72	All Buick applications	60	60	85	85	86

Oldsmobile, 1969-72

Range	Normal Pressure (psi)
Drive—Brakes applied, engine @ 1,000 rpm	60-90
Super-low—Brakes applied, engine @ 1,000 rpm	85-110
Reverse—Brakes applied, engine @ 1,000 rpm	85-150
Neutral—Brakes applied, engine @ 1,000 rpm	55-70
Drive—Idle set to engine specifications	60-85
Drive—30 mph coast (closed throttle) *	55-70

*—Can be performed by running engine on lift at 2,000 rpm. Release throttle and read pressure before rpm drops below 1,200.

Torque Specifications

Oil pan to transmission case	13 ft. lbs.
Pump assembly to transmission case	20 ft. lbs.
Vacuum modulator retainer to case	12 ft. lbs.
Valve body assembly to case	13 ft. lbs.
Oil channel support plate to case	13 ft. lbs.
Pump body to pump cover	15-18 ft. lbs.
Parking lock bracket to case	29 ft. lbs.
Extension housing to case	35 ft. lbs.
Inside shift nut	30 ft. lbs.
External test plugs to case	8 ft. lbs.
Cooler fitting to case	30 ft. lbs.
Oil pickup screen to valve body	36 in. lbs.
Detent valve actuating lever bracket to valve body	48 in. lbs.
Detent valve actuating lever bracket to valve body	48-52 in. lbs.

GENERAL MOTORS TYPE 350 TRANSMISSION

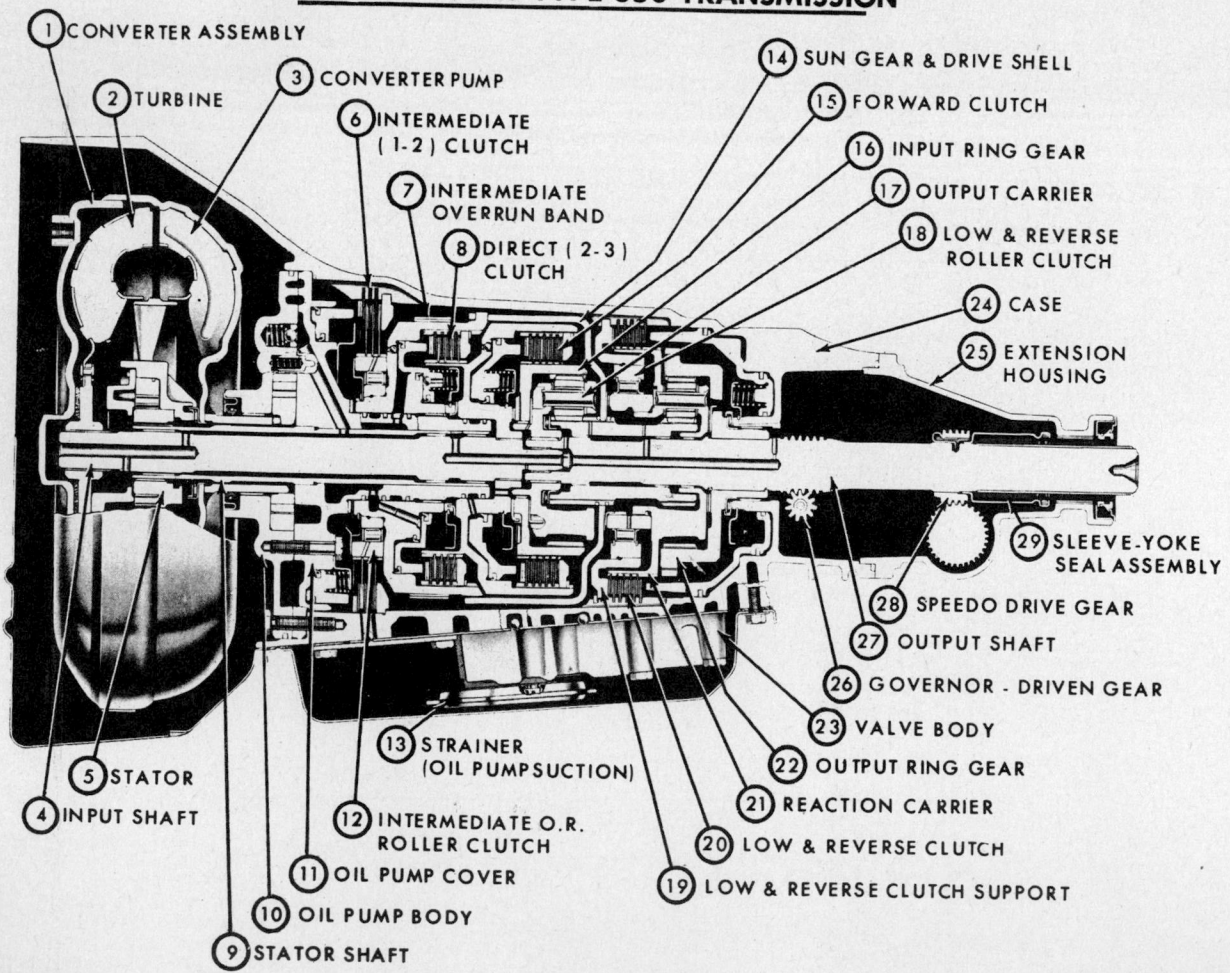

1 CONVERTER ASSEMBLY
2 TURBINE
3 CONVERTER PUMP
6 INTERMEDIATE (1-2) CLUTCH
7 INTERMEDIATE OVERRUN BAND
8 DIRECT (2-3) CLUTCH
14 SUN GEAR & DRIVE SHELL
15 FORWARD CLUTCH
16 INPUT RING GEAR
17 OUTPUT CARRIER
18 LOW & REVERSE ROLLER CLUTCH
24 CASE
25 EXTENSION HOUSING
29 SLEEVE-YOKE SEAL ASSEMBLY
28 SPEEDO DRIVE GEAR
27 OUTPUT SHAFT
26 GOVERNOR - DRIVEN GEAR
23 VALVE BODY
22 OUTPUT RING GEAR
21 REACTION CARRIER
20 LOW & REVERSE CLUTCH
19 LOW & REVERSE CLUTCH SUPPORT
5 STATOR
4 INPUT SHAFT
13 STRAINER (OIL PUMP SUCTION)
12 INTERMEDIATE O.R. ROLLER CLUTCH
11 OIL PUMP COVER
10 OIL PUMP BODY
9 STATOR SHAFT

Type 400

Application

Super Turbine 400,

Turbo Hydra-Matic 400—Buick, 1965-72

        Buick Special, GS 400, 455, 1967-72

Turbo Hydra-Matic 400—Cadillac and Eldorado, 1965-72

Turbo Hydra-Matic 400—Chevrolet and Chevelle, 1966-72,

        Camaro and Corvette, 1968-72,

        Nova, 1969-72,

        Monte Carlo, 1970-72

Turbo Hydra-Matic M-40—Pontiac, 1966-72,

        GTO, 1967-72,

        Firebird, 1968-72,

        Tempest, 1969-72

Turbo Hydra-Matic 400—Oldsmobile, 1965-72,

        F-85, 1966-70

        Toronado, 1966-72

        Cutlass Supreme, 1970-72

Diagnosis

This diagnosis guide covers the most common symptoms and is an aid to careful diagnosis. The items to check are listed in the sequence to be followed for quickest results. Thus, follow the checks in the order given for the particular transmission type.

TROUBLE SYMPTOMS	Items to check	
	In Car	Out of Car
No drive in D range	ABCD	abc
No drive in R or slips in reverse	ABCEGHIJL	efa
Drive in neutral	B	a
First speed only—no 1-2 shift	KG	g
1-2 shift at full throttle only	MNG	
First and second speeds only—no 2-3 shift	MNG	f
Slips in all ranges	ACEFG	dfahc
Slips—1-2 shift	ACELGO	gh
Rough 1-2 shift	CELGJOGJ	hi
Slips 2-3 shift	ACELG	fh
Rough 2-3 shift	CELO	
Shifts occur—too high or too low car speed	CKEMGL	
No detent downshifts	NMG	
No part throttle downshift	CEG	
No engine braking—super range—second speed	O	j
No engine braking—low range—first speed	GJ	ik
Park will not hold	BPQ	
Poor performance or rough idle—stator not functioning	RS	lo
Noisy transmission	TF	dafgn

Key to Checks

A. Oil level
B. Manual linkage (external)
C. Check oil pressure
D. Manual control disconnected inside
E. Modulator and/or lines
F. Clogged strainer or intake leaks
G. Valves, body and/or leaks
H. Reverse feed passages

I. Valve check balls
J. Rear servo and accumulator
K. Governor and/or feed line seals
L. Pump regulator and boost valve
M. Detent solenoid
N. Detent switch
O. Front servo and accumulator
P. Internal linkage

Q. Parking pawl and/or link
R. Stator switch
S. Valve body-stator section
T. Cooler or lines
a. Front clutch
b. Clutch feed seals and gaskets
c. Low sprags
d. Front pump
e. Rear band
f. Direct clutch

g. Intermediate clutch
h. Pump-to-case gasket
i. Intermediate check valve ball in case
j. Front band
k. Rear band
l. Turbine shaft
m. Converter assembly
n. Planetary assembly

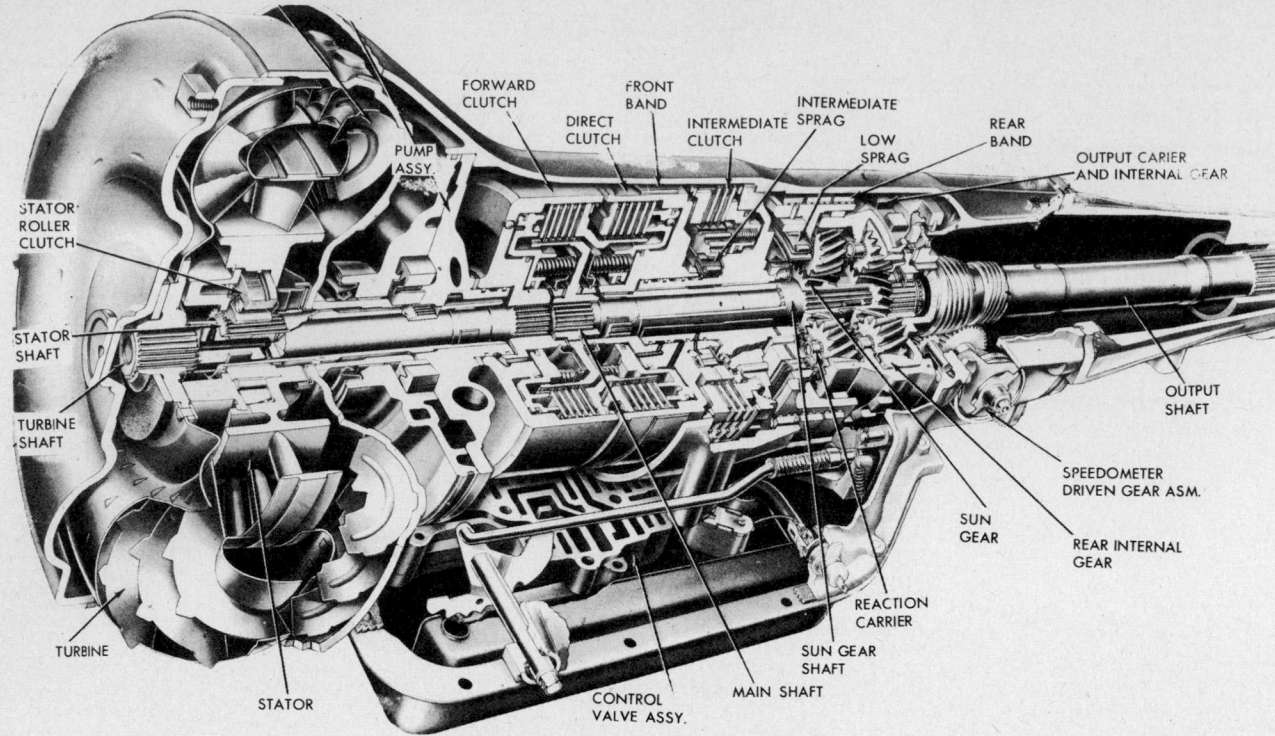

STATOR ROLLER CLUTCH

STATOR SHAFT

TURBINE SHAFT

PUMP ASSY.

FORWARD CLUTCH

DIRECT CLUTCH

FRONT BAND

INTERMEDIATE CLUTCH

INTERMEDIATE SPRAG

LOW SPRAG

REAR BAND

OUTPUT CARIER AND INTERNAL GEAR

OUTPUT SHAFT

SPEEDOMETER DRIVEN GEAR ASM.

SUN GEAR

REAR INTERNAL GEAR

REACTION CARRIER

SUN GEAR SHAFT

MAIN SHAFT

CONTROL VALVE ASSY.

TURBINE

STATOR

General Motors, Type 400 transmission
(© G.M. Corp.)

The illustrations are typical. While design and repair procedures are similar, components vary with car application and should not be considered interchangeable.

General Information

The General Motors type 400 transmission is a fully automatic unit consisting of a three element torque converter and a three speed and reverse planetary gear set. Three multiple disc clutches, one sprag, one roller clutch, and two bands control the planetary gear set operation.

The torque converter consists of a driving member, a driven member, and a stator assembly. The stator has a roller clutch which allows it to turn in one direction only. As the speed of the driving member increases, the roller clutch allows the stator to free-wheel on its shaft. This causes the torque converter to cease its torque multiplication function and to operate as a fluid coupling with a drive ratio of approximately one to one.

Fluid Specifications

Oil capacity, transmission
  and converter
    Approx. 22 pints
Capacity between marks
  on dip stick
    1 pint
Type of oil
  Automatic transmission fluid
    Type A
Drain and refill
  24,000 miles

Draining and Refilling

The transmission fluid should be drained and refilled at 24,000 mile intervals. To do this:
1. Drain transmission oil.
2. Remove oil pan attaching screws.
3. Remove oil pan and gasket.
4. Remove strainer or filter.
5. Thoroughly clean oil strainer or filter and oil pan in solvent. Blow dry with air.
6. Renew oil strainer gasket and oil pan gasket.
7. Install oil strainer or filter.
8. Install oil pan. Torque attaching screws to 10-12 ft. lbs.
9. Add about five pints of transmission fluid.
10. Start engine. Do not race engine. Move selector lever slowly through each range. Check fluid level.
11. With transmission cold, add enough fluid to bring level to 1/4 in. below the Add mark. With the transmission at normal temperature, add enough fluid to bring the level to the Full mark. About fifteen miles of highway driving is required to bring the transmission to normal temperature.
12. In case of transmission overhaul, proceed as in Steps 9-11. Start with five pints of fluid if converter has not been replaced; eight pints if it has been replaced. Total capacity is about 22 pints, but correct level is determined by the mark on the dipstick rather than by amount of fluid added.

Transmission Disassembly

Clean outside of the unit thoroughly to prevent dirt from entering the unit.
1. With transmission in a work cradle or on a clean bench, lift the converter straight off the transmission input shaft.
2. With transmission bottom-up, remove modulator assembly attaching screw and retainer, then remove the modulator assembly and O-ring seal.

Governor, Speedometer Driven Gear, Oil Pan, Strainer and Intake Pipe Removal

1. Remove attaching screws, governor cover and gasket, then withdraw governor from the case.
2. Remove speedometer driven gear attaching screw and retainer, then withdraw the driven gear assembly.
3. Remove oil pan attaching screws, then the oil pan. Discard gasket.
4. Remove pump intake pipe and strainer assembly, then the pipe-to-case O-ring seal.

Control Valve Assembly, Governor Pipes and Detent Spring Assembly Removal

1. Disconnect the lead wire from the pressure switch assembly. Remove the switch assembly from the valve body, if necessary. This switch is installed on 1970-72 models only. Pontiac

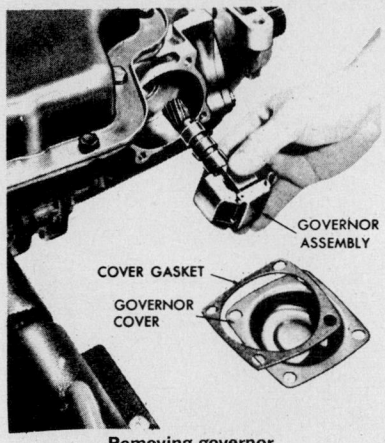

Removing governor
(© G.M. Corp.)

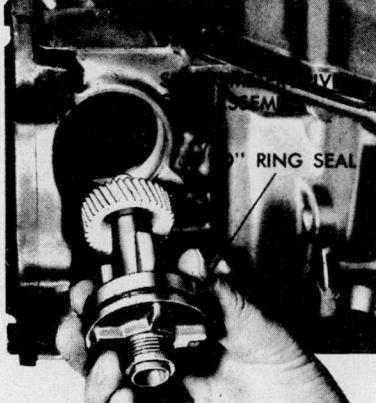

Removing speedometer driven gear
(© G.M. Corp.)

model PQ and Chevrolet model CM are not equipped with a pressure switch assembly.
2. Remove control valve body attaching screws and detent roller and spring assembly.
NOTE: do not remove solenoid attaching screws.
Remove control valve body and governor pipes.
3. Remove the governor pipes from valve body. Then remove valve body-to-spacer gasket.

Rear Servo, Solenoid, Valve Body Spacer, Front Servo, Manual Detent and Parking Linkage Removal

1. Remove rear servo cover attaching screws, the cover and gasket, then the rear servo assembly from the case.
2. Remove servo accumulator springs.
3. Disconnect the solenoid leads from connector terminal. Withdraw connector and O-ring seal.
4. Remove solenoid attaching screws, solenoid and gasket.
5. Remove valve body spacer plate and gasket.
6. Remove six check balls from cored passages in transmission case. There are seven check balls on Toronado and Eldorado transmissions. An eighth, held in place, should not be removed, unless defective.
7. Remove the front servo assembly.
8. Loosen the jam nut which holds the detent lever to the manual shaft. Then remove detent lever from manual shaft. The manual shaft should not be removed from the case unless replacement is necessary.
9. Remove parking actuator rod and detent lever assembly. Then remove detent lever E-ring and the detent lever.
10. Remove attaching screws and park bracket; then the parking pawl return spring.
11. Remove parking pawl shaft retainer, then the parking pawl shaft, O-ring and pawl.

Rear Oil Seal and Extension Housing Removal

1. Pry rear oil seal from extension housing.
2. Remove housing attaching bolts, then remove extension housing and housing-to-case oil seal.

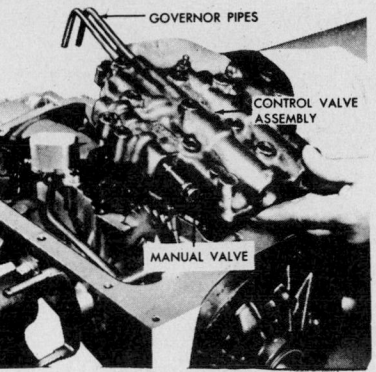

Removing control valve assembly
(© G.M. Corp.)

Removing rear servo from case
(© G.M. Corp.)

Removing case connector
(© G.M. Corp.)

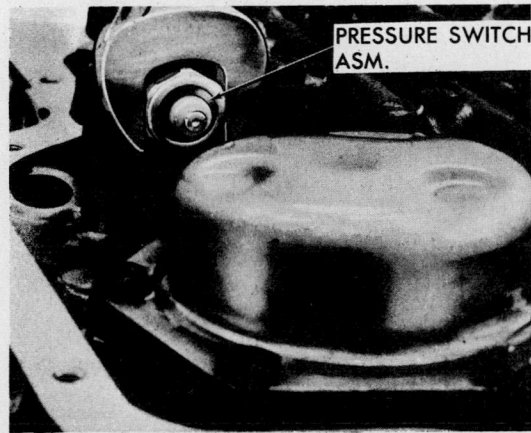

Removing pressure switch assembly (© G.M. Corp.)

Removing detent roller and spring assembly (© G.M. Corp.)

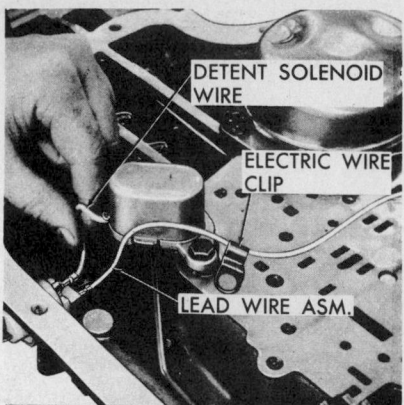

Disconnecting solenoid leads (© G.M. Corp.)

Location of check balls (© G.M. Corp.)

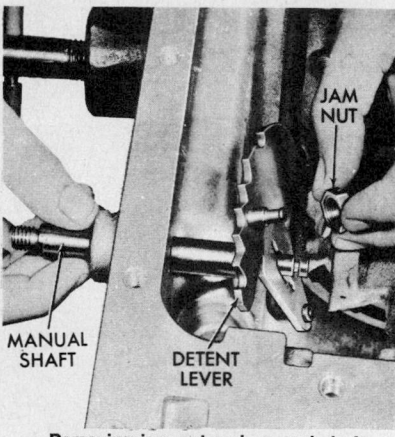

Removing jam nut and manual shaft
(© G.M. Corp.)

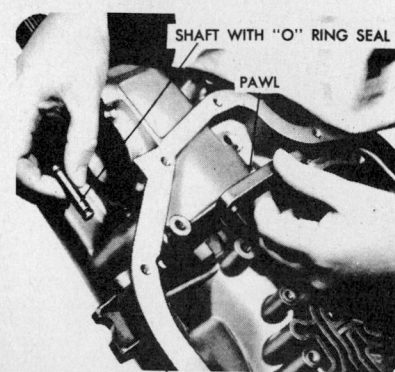

Removing parking pawl shaft shaft and O-ring
(© G.M. Corp.)

Sprocket Cover, Link Assembly, Drive and Driven Sprocket Removal— Eldorado and Toronado

1. Remove the sprocket cover attaching screws, cover and gasket. Discard the gasket.
2. Remove the snap-rings (as illustrated) from beneath the drive and driven sprockets. Leave the snap-rings in a loose position.
3. Remove the drive and driven sprockets, link assembly, bearings and shafts simultaneously, by alternately pulling up on the drive and driven sprockets until the bearings and shafts are free of the housings.
4. Remove the link assembly from the sprockets.
5. Remove the hook type oil seal ring from the turbine shaft.
6. Be sure that the drive and driven sprocket bearings are not damaged.
7. Inspect the drive sprocket teeth for nicks, burrs, scoring, galling or excessive wear. Inspect the drive sprocket ball bearings for wear or damage.
8. Be sure that the turbine shaft lubrication openings are clear and free.
9. Inspect the splines and ground bushing journals for damage.
10. Inspect the turbine shaft for cracks or distortion.
11. Inpect the link assembly for damage or loose links.

Oil Pump, Forward Clutch and Gear Unit Removal

1. Pry front seal from the pump. Then remove pump attaching bolts.
2. With slide hammers attached, remove pump from transmission case. Discard pump-to-case seal ring. Discard pump-to-case gasket.
3. Remove turbine shaft from transmission.
4. Remove forward clutch assembly. Be sure that the bronze thrust washer came out with the clutch housing assembly.
5. Remove the direct clutch assembly. Remove front band and sun gear shaft.
6. Remove the case center support-to-case bolt and center support locating screw. 1969-70 models have no locating screw.
7. Remove intermediate clutch backing plate-to-case snap-ring. Then remove the backing plate, three composition, and three steel clutch plates.
8. Remove the center support-to-case retaining snap-ring.
9. Remove the entire gear unit assembly.
10. Remove the output shaft-to-case

Removing drive sprocket snap-ring— Toronado and Eldorado
(© G.M. Corp.)

thrust washer from the rear of the output shaft, or from inside the case.
11. Remove rear unit selective washer from transmission case.
12. Remove rear band assembly.
13. Remove support to case spacer from inside case.
14. Remove the reaction carrier and roller clutch assembly from the output carrier. Remove the roller clutch assembly from the reaction carrier.

Removing gear assembly
(© G.M. Corp.)

Removing pump body with slide hammers
(© G.M. Corp.)

Removing center support bolt (© G.M. Corp.)

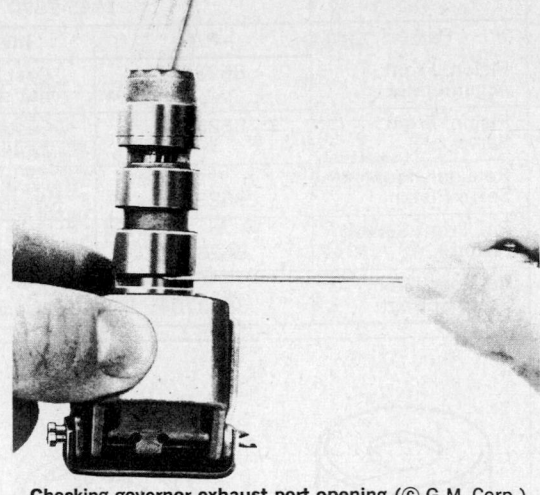

Checking governor exhaust port opening (© G.M. Corp.)

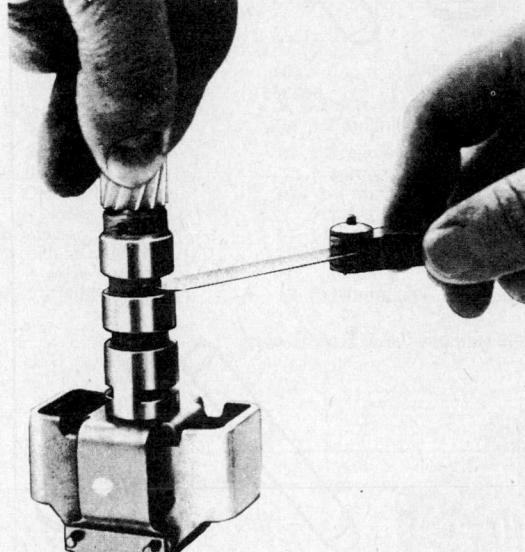

Checking governor feed port opening (© G.M. Corp.)

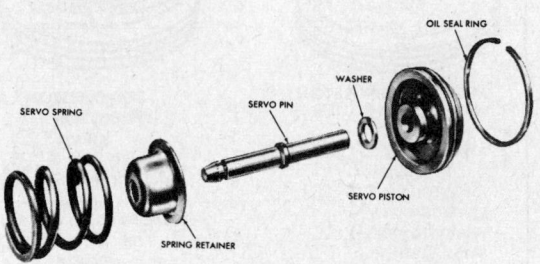

Front servo components (© G.M. Corp.)

Component Disassembly, Inspection, and Assembly

Governor

All components of the governor, except the driven gear, are a select fit and so calibrated. Therefore, service this unit as an assembly.

Clean and inspect all parts for wear or other damage. Check valve opening at feed port with a feeler gauge, holding the governor with the weights extended completely outward. Check valve opening at exhaust port, holding governor with weights completely inward. If either opening is less than .020 in., replace governor assembly.

If a new governor drive gear is installed, a new pin hole must be drilled 90 degrees from the original hole.

Front Servo Inspection

1. Inspect servo pin for damage.
2. Inspect servo piston for damaged oil ring groove, cracks, or porosity. Check freedom of oil seal ring in groove.
3. Check fit of servo pin in piston.
   NOTE: The front servo assembly is new for 1971. Pre-1971 parts are not interchangeable.

Rear Servo Disassembly

1. Remove rear accumulator piston from rear servo piston.
2. Remove E-ring which holds the servo piston to band apply pin.
3. Remove servo piston and seal from band apply pin. Remove second washer from band apply pin.
4. Remove washer, spring, and retainer.

Rear Servo Inspection

1. Check freedom of accumulator rings in piston.
2. Check fit of band apply pin in servo piston. Inspect pin for scores or cracks.
3. Inspect accumulator and servo pistons for cracks or porosity.

Rear Servo Assembly

1. Install spring retainer cup side down, spring, and washer on band apply pin.
2. Install band apply pin, retainer, spring, and washer into bore of servo piston and secure with E-ring.
3. Install oil seal on servo piston. Install outer and inner oil seal rings on accumulator piston and assembly into bore of servo piston.

Control Valve Body Disassembly

When disassembling control valve body, identify all springs so that they can be replaced in their proper locations.

1. Position valve assembly with cored face up and accumulator pocket on bottom.
2. Remove manual valve from upper bore.
3. Compress accumulator piston spring and remove E-ring retainer. Remove accumulator piston and spring.

Manual Transmissions

Applicability Chart

Type Numbers Refer to Sections in Text

Make	Model	3-Spd. Type	4-Spd. Type
American Motors	1965–70 199–232 Six; 1971 232 Six	21	
	1965–67 232, 287, 290	20	
	1966–67 Six HD		
	1966 327 V8	19	
	1968–71 232, 258, 290, 304, 360	17	
	1966 287, 327 1967–69 290, 343 1967–70 390 1970 360; 1971 401		22
	1972 232, 258 Six	3	
	1972 304, 340, 360	1	
	1972 401		4
Barracuda	1965–72		4
	1966–72 Six	3	
	1966–69	2	
	1970–72	1	
Buick	LeSabre, 1970–72	6	
	Wildcat, 1966–70	6	22
	LeSabre, 1966–68	12	
	LeSabre, 1965	10	
	Wildcat, 1965	19	22
Buick Special	1966–72	12	
	1971–72 GS	12	13
	1965–69 GS, 1966–69 V8	6	
	1965 except Skyroof wagon and GS	10	
	1965, 1966 GS		22
Camaro	1967–72	12	13, 14
	1969–72	11	
	1967–68	18	
Challenger	1970–72 Six	3	
	1970–72	1	4
Charger	1967–72 Six	3	
	1966–72		4
	1967–69	2	
	1970–72	1	
Chevelle	1966–72	12	14
	1969–72	11	
	1965–72		13
	1966 396, 1967–68	18	
	1965	10	
Chevrolet	1969–72	11	
	1966–72	12	14
	1965–72		13
	1965–67 396, 427, 1968	18	
	1965	10	

Make	Model	3-Spd. Type	4-Spd. Type
Chevy II, Nova	1969–72	11	
	1966–72	12	14
	1965–72		13
	1968	18	
	1965	10	
Chrysler	1970–72	1	
	1965–69	2	
	1965–67		4
Comet	1965–70 V8		9
	1965–66 Six	5	7
	1965–66 V8, 1967 All, 1971–72	6	
Corvette	1967–72		14
	1965–72		13
	1966–69	12	
	1966–68	18	
	1965	10	
Cougar	1967–72	6	9
Dart	1970–72	1	
	1965–72 Six	3	
	1965–72		4
	1965–69	2	
Dodge	1970–72	1	
	1965–72		4
	1965–72 Six	3	
	1965–69	2	
Fairlane	1965–72 V8		9
	1965–66 V8, 1967–72 All	6	
	1965–66 Six	5	7
Falcon	1967–70 All, 1965–66 V8	6	
	1965–70 V8		9
	1965–67 Six	5	
	1965–66 Six		7
Firebird	1970–72	11	
	1967–72	12	13
	1968–69 V8	6	
	1969 Six		14
	1967 V8	18	
Ford	1965–72	6	9
Maverick	1970–72	6	8
Mercury	1965–70	6	9
Monte Carlo	1970–72		13
	1971–72	11	
Montego	1968–72	6	9

Make	Model	3-Spd.	4-Spd. Type
Mustang	1965-72		9
	1965-66 V8, 1967-72 All	6	
	1965-66 Six	5	7
	1965 V8		22
Oldsmobile	1971-72 Delta 88	12	
	1966-70	6	
	1965 Jetstar 88	10	
	1965		13
Oldsmobile F-85	1971-72 Cutlass, F-85, 4-4-2	12	14
	1970 F-85, 4-4-2	11	
	1966-72	12	
	1965-72		13
	1965-69 V8	6	
	1965	10	
Pinto	1971-72		8

Make	Model	3-Spd.	4-Spd. Type
Plymouth	1970-72	1	•
	1965-72		4
	1965-72 Six	3	
	1965-69	2	
Pontiac	1970-72 GP	11	
	1968-72 GP		13
	1966-72	6	
Tempest	1970-72 Tempest, 1970 GTO	11	
	1966-72	12	
	1965-72		13
	1965-69 V8	6	
	1967-68 Six		14
	1965	10	
Torino	1971-72	6	
Valiant	1970-72	1	
	1965-72		4
	1965-72 Six	3	
	1966-69	2	
Vega	1971-72	15	16
Ventura II	1971-72	12	

Manual Transmission Index

Transmission	Type	Page No.
Chrysler Corporation		
A-230 Fully Synchronized Chrysler 3-Speed	1	1056
A-745 Chrysler 3-Speed	2	1060
A-903 Chrysler 3-Speed	3	1063
A-833 Chrysler 4-Speed	4	1065
Ford Motor Company		
2.77 Ford 3-Speed	5	1067
3.03 Fully Synchronized Ford 3-Speed	6	1069
Ford (Dagenham) 4-Speed	7	1071
Ford (Pinto) 4-Speed	8	1074
Ford 4-Speed	9	1077
General Motors Corporation		
Muncie 3-Speed	10	1081

Transmission	Type	Page No.
Muncie Fully Synchronized 3-Speed	11	1083
Saginaw Fully Synchronized 3-Speed	12	1083
Muncie 4-Speed	13	1087
Saginaw 4-Speed	14	1089
Vega 3-Speed	15	1091
Vega 4-Speed	16	1093
Warner Gear		
Warner T-14, T-15 Fully Synchronized 3-Speed	17	1095
Warner T-16 Fully Synchronized 3-Speed	18	1096
Warner T-85 3-Speed	19	1098
Warner T-90, T-86 3-Speed	20	1099
Warner T-96 3-Speed	21	1101
Warner T-10 4-Speed	22	1102

Diagnosis Chart—1056

Manual Transmissions

Diagnosis

Jumping out of High Gear

1. Misalignment of transmission case or clutch housing.
2. Worn pilot bearing in crankshaft.
3. Bent transmission shaft.
4. Worn high speed sliding gear.
5. Worn teeth in clutch shaft.
6. Insufficient spring tension on shifter rail plunger.
7. Bent or loose shifter fork.
8. End-play in clutch shaft.
9. Gears not engaging completely.
10. Loose or worn bearings on clutch shaft or mainshaft.

Sticking in High Gear

1. Clutch not releasing fully.
2. Burred or battered teeth on clutch shaft.
3. Burred or battered transmission main-shaft.
4. Frozen synchronizing clutch.
5. Stuck shifter rail plunger.
6. Gearshift lever twisting and binding shifter rail.
7. Battered teeth on high speed sliding gear or on sleeve.
8. Lack of lubrication.
9. Improper lubrication.
10. Corroded transmission parts.
11. Defective mainshaft pilot bearing.

Jumping out of Second Gear

1. Insufficient spring tension on shifter rail plunger.
2. Bent or loose shifter fork.
3. Gears not engaging completely.
4. End-play in transmission main-shaft.
5. Loose transmission gear bearing.
6. Defective mainshaft pilot bearing.
7. Bent transmission shaft.
8. Worn teeth on second speed sliding gear or sleeve.
9. Loose or worn bearings on transmission mainshaft.
10. End-play in countershaft.

Sticking in Second Gear

1. Clutch not releasing fully.
2. Burred or battered teeth on sliding sleeve.
3. Burred or battered transmission main-shaft.
4. Frozen synchronizing clutch.
5. Stuck shifter rail plunger.
6. Gearshift lever twisting and binding shifter rail.
7. Lack of lubrication.
8. Second speed transmission gear bearings locked will give same effect as gears stuck in second.
9. Improper lubrication.
10. Corroded transmission parts.

Jumping out of Low Gear

1. Gears not engaging completely.
2. Bent or loose shifter fork.
3. End-play in transmission main-shaft.
4. End-play in countershaft.
5. Loose or worn bearings on transmission mainshaft.
6. Loose or worn bearings in countershaft.
7. Defective mainshaft pilot bearing.

Sticking in Low Gear

1. Clutch not releasing fully.
2. Burred or battered transmission main-shaft.
3. Stuck shifter rail plunger.
4. Gearshift lever twisting and binding shifter rail.
5. Lack of lubrication.
6. Improper lubrication.
7. Corroded transmission parts.

Jumping out of Reverse Gear

1. Insufficient spring tension on shifter rail plunger.
2. Bent or loose shifter fork.
3. Badly worn gear teeth.
4. Gears not engaging completely.

5. End-play in transmission main-shaft.
6. Idler gear bushings loose or worn.
7. Loose or worn bearings on transmission mainshaft.
8. Defective mainshaft pilot bearing.

Sticking in Reverse Gear

1. Clutch not releasing fully.
2. Burred or battered transmission main-shaft.
3. Stuck shifter rail plunger.
4. Gearshift lever twisting and binding shifter rail.
5. Lack of lubrication.
6. Improper lubrication.
7. Corroded transmission parts.

Failure of Gears to Synchronize

1. Binding pilot bearing on mainshaft, will synchronize in high gear only.
2. Clutch not releasing fully.
3. Detent springs weak or broken.
4. Weak or broken springs under balls in sliding gear sleeve.
5. Binding bearing on clutch shaft.
6. Binding countershaft.
7. Binding pilot bearing in crankshaft.
8. Badly worn gear teeth.
9. Scored or worn cones.
10. Improper lubrication.
11. Constant mesh gear not turning freely on transmission mainshaft. Will synchronize in that gear only.

Gears Spinning When Shifting into Gear from Neutral

1. Clutch not releasing fully.
2. In some cases an extremely light lubricant in transmission will cause gears to continue to spin for a short time after clutch is released.
3. Binding pilot bearing in crankshaft.

Type-1
A-230 Fully Synchronized Chrysler 3-Speed

Application

American Motors, 1972
Barracuda, 1970-72
Challenger, 1970-72

Charger, 1970-72
Chrysler, 1970-72
Dart, 1970-72

Dodge, 1970-72
Plymouth, 1970-72
Valiant, 1970-72

Disassembly
Shift Housing and Mechanism

1. Shift to second gear.
2. Unbolt and remove side cover with shift mechanism.

If shaft O-ring seals need replacement:

3. Pull shift forks out of shafts.
4. Remove nuts and operating levers from shafts.
5. Deburr shafts. Remove shafts.

Drive Pinion Retainer and Extension Housing

1. Unbolt pinion bearing retainer

from front of transmission case. Remove retainer and gasket. Pry off retainer oil seal.

For clearance:

2. With a brass drift, tap drive pinion as far forward as possible. Rotate cut away part of second gear next to countershaft gear.

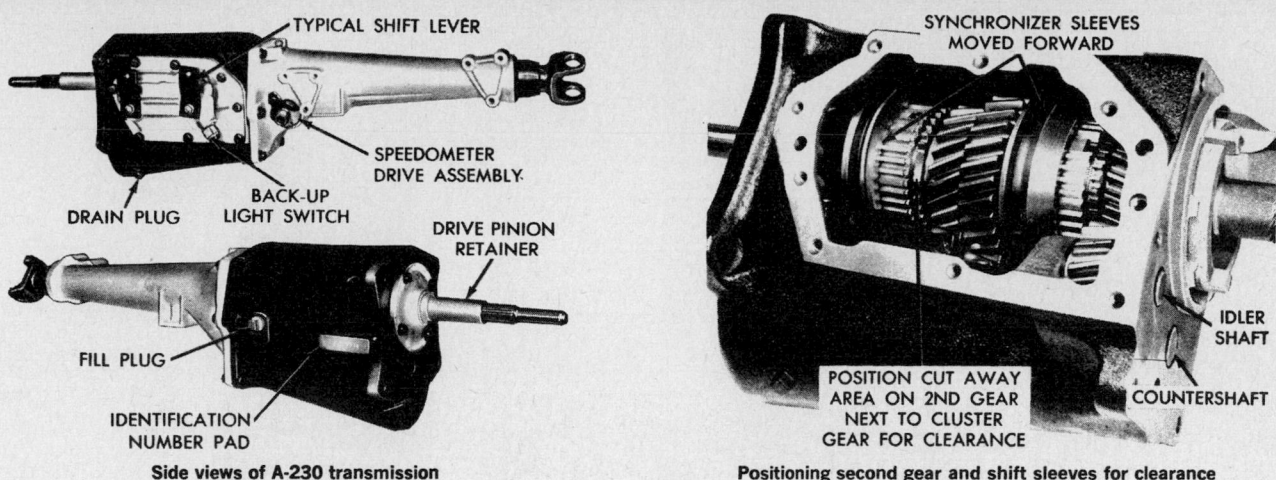

Side views of A-230 transmission
(© Chrysler Corp.)

TYPICAL SHIFT LEVER
SPEEDOMETER DRIVE ASSEMBLY
BACK-UP LIGHT SWITCH
DRAIN PLUG
DRIVE PINION RETAINER
FILL PLUG
IDENTIFICATION NUMBER PAD

SYNCHRONIZER SLEEVES MOVED FORWARD
IDLER SHAFT
COUNTERSHAFT
POSITION CUT AWAY AREA ON 2ND GEAR NEXT TO CLUSTER GEAR FOR CLEARANCE

Positioning second gear and shift sleeves for clearance
(© Chrysler Corp.)

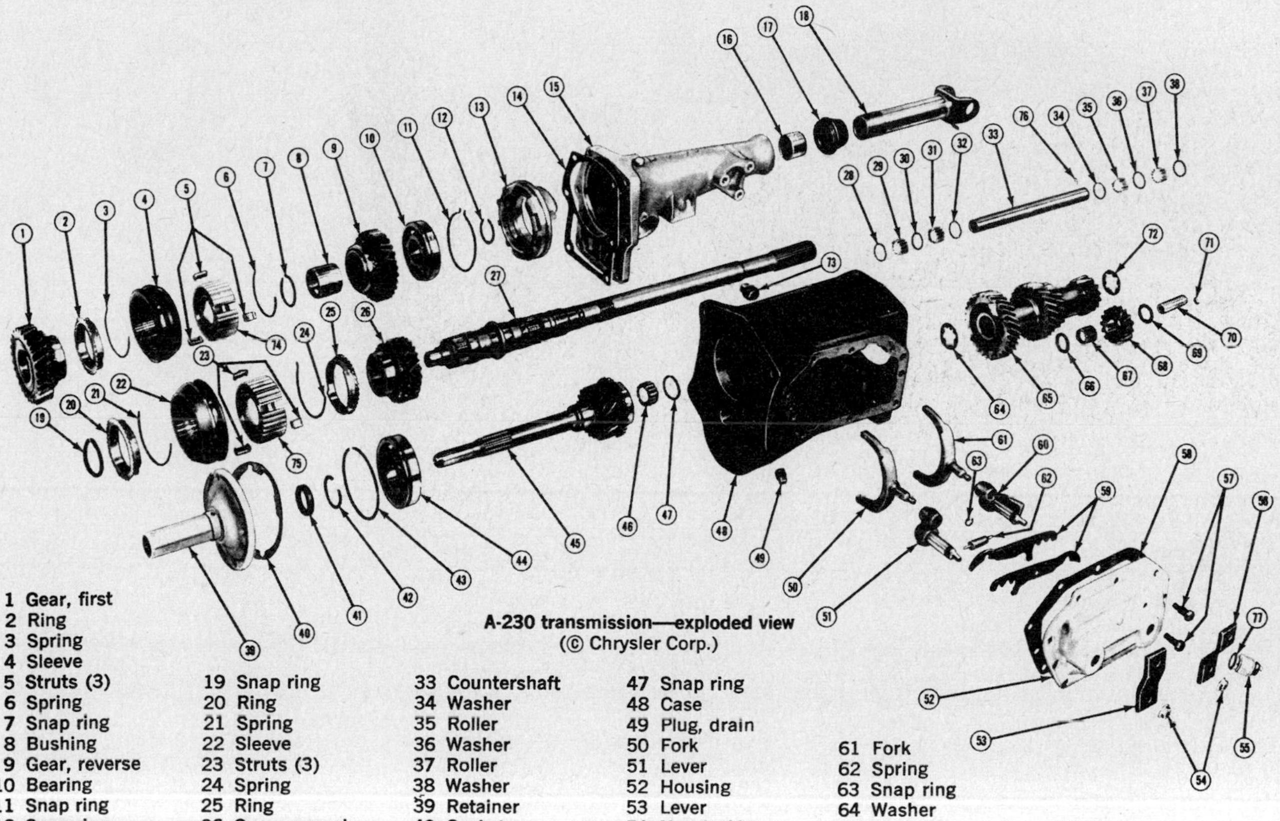

A-230 transmission—exploded view
(© Chrysler Corp.)

1 Gear, first	19 Snap ring	33 Countershaft	47 Snap ring
2 Ring	20 Ring	34 Washer	48 Case
3 Spring	21 Spring	35 Roller	49 Plug, drain
4 Sleeve	22 Sleeve	36 Washer	50 Fork
5 Struts (3)	23 Struts (3)	37 Roller	51 Lever
6 Spring	24 Spring	38 Washer	52 Housing
7 Snap ring	25 Ring	39 Retainer	53 Lever
8 Bushing	26 Gear, second	40 Gasket	54 Nut, locking
9 Gear, reverse	27 Shaft, output	41 Seal	55 Switch
10 Bearing	28 Washer	42 Snap ring	56 Lever
11 Snap ring	29 Roller	43 Snap ring	57 Bolt
12 Snap ring	30 Washer	44 Bearing	58 Gasket
13 Retainer	31 Roller	45 Pinion, drive	59 Lever, interlock
14 Gasket	32 Washer	46 Roller	60 Lever
15 Extension			
16 Bushing			61 Fork
17 Seal			62 Spring
18 Yoke			63 Snap ring

64 Washer		
65 Gear, countershaft	71 Key	
66 Washer	72 Washer	
67 Roller	73 Plug, filler	
68 Gear, idler	74 Gear, clutch	
69 Washer	75 Gear, clutch	
70 Shaft	76 Key	
	77 Gasket	

Shift second-third synchronizer sleeve forward.

3. Remove speedometer pinion adapter retainer. Work adapter and pinion out of extension housing.

4. Unbolt extension housing. Break housing loose with plastic hammer and carefully remove.

Idler Gear and Mainshaft

1. Insert dummy shaft in case to push reverse idler shaft and key

out of case.

2. Remove dummy shaft and idler gear together to prevent losing rollers.

3. Remove both tanged idler gear thrust washers.

4. Remove mainshaft assembly through rear of case.

Countershaft Gear and Drive Pinion

1. Using a mallet and dummy shaft, tap the countershaft rear-

ward enough to remove key. Drive countershaft out of case, maintaining contact between countershaft and dummy shaft so that washers will not drop out.

2. Lower countershaft gear to bottom of case.

3. Remove snap-ring from pinion bearing outer race (outside front of case).

4. Drive pinion shaft into case with plastic hammer. Remove assem-

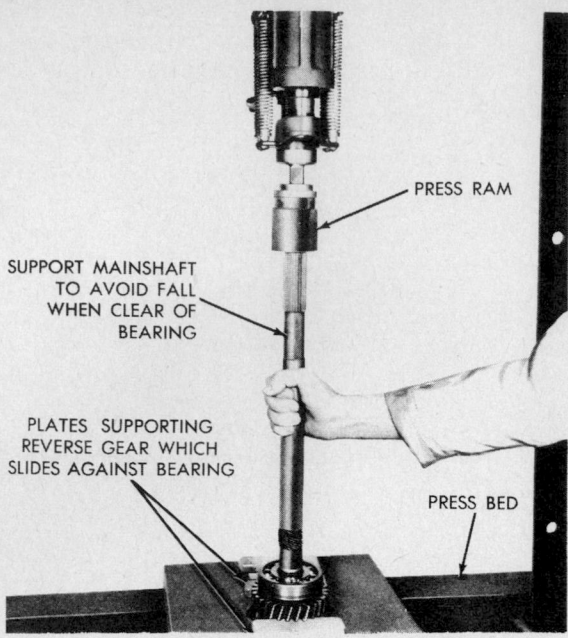

PRESS RAM

SUPPORT MAINSHAFT
TO AVOID FALL
WHEN CLEAR OF
BEARING

PLATES SUPPORTING
REVERSE GEAR WHICH
SLIDES AGAINST BEARING

PRESS BED

Pressing off mainshaft bearing
(© Chrysler Corp.)

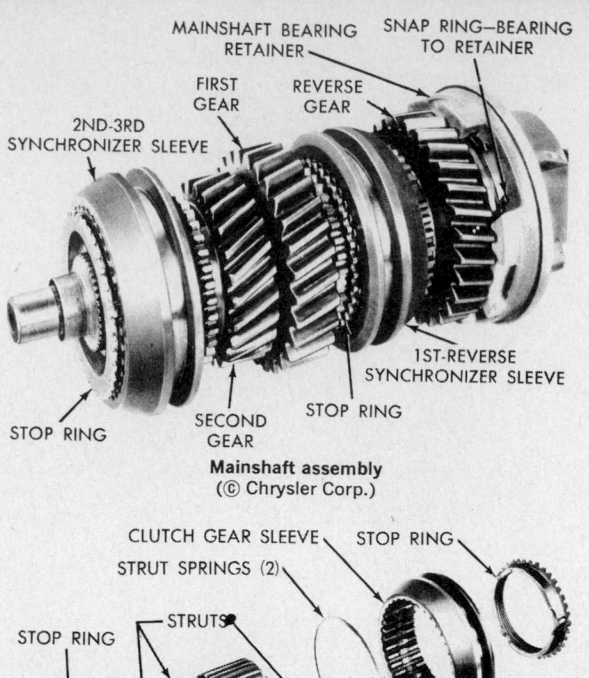

MAINSHAFT BEARING
RETAINER

SNAP RING—BEARING
TO RETAINER

FIRST
GEAR

REVERSE
GEAR

2ND-3RD
SYNCHRONIZER SLEEVE

1ST-REVERSE
SYNCHRONIZER SLEEVE

STOP RING

STOP RING

SECOND
GEAR

STOP RING

Mainshaft assembly
(© Chrysler Corp.)

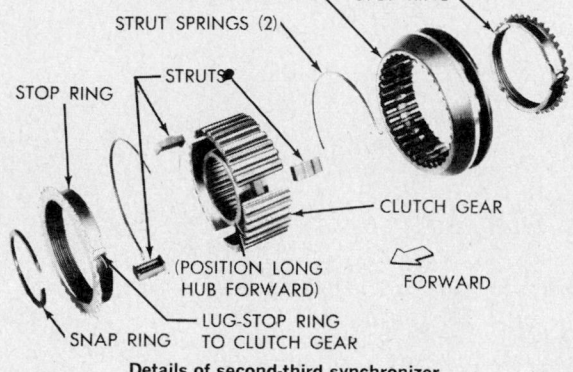

CLUTCH GEAR SLEEVE

STOP RING

STRUT SPRINGS (2)

STOP RING

STRUTS

CLUTCH GEAR

(POSITION LONG
HUB FORWARD)

FORWARD

SNAP RING

LUG-STOP RING
TO CLUTCH GEAR

Details of second-third synchronizer
(© Chrysler Corp.)

bly through rear of case.

5. If bearing is to be replaced, remove snap-ring and press off bearing.

6. Lift countershaft gear and dummy shaft out through rear of case.

Mainshaft

1. Remove snap-ring from front end of mainshaft along with second gear stop ring. Remove second gear from mainshaft.

2. Spread snap-ring in mainshaft bearing retainer. Slide retainer back off the bearing race.

3. Remove snap-ring at rear of mainshaft. Support front side of reverse gear. Press bearing off mainshaft. Be careful not to let parts drop when bearing clears shaft.

4. Remove from press. Remove mainshaft bearing and reverse gear from shaft.

5. Remove snap-ring from rear of shaft. Slide first-reverse synchronizer assembly off splines and remove rearward. Remove stop-ring and first gear through the rear.

Inspection

1. Clean all parts with solvent.
2. Dry with compressed air.

Case

1. Check for cracks, stripped threads, and burrs or nicks on machined surfaces. Dress off any burrs with a fine file. Stripped threads may be repaired by use of Helicoil inserts.

Ball Bearings

1. Do not spin bearings with air pressure; turn slowly by hand to avoid damage.
2. Lubricate with light engine oil.
3. Check for pitting.
4. Check fit on shafts.

Needle Bearings

1. Check rollers for flats or brinelling.
2. Check roller spacers for wear or galling.

Gears

1. Check gear splines on synchronizer clutch gears and stop-rings for chipping or worn teeth.
2. Be sure the clutch sleeve slides easily on clutch gear.
3. Check countershaft gear and all gear teeth for chipping, broken teeth, or excessive wear. Stone off small nicks or burrs.
4. If oil seal contact area on drive pinion shaft is pitted, rusted, or scratched, replace the pinion.

Synchronizer Stop Rings

1. Check for cracks or wear.
2. Check new rings for good fit on gear cones with minimum wobble.

Mainshaft

1. Check mainshaft gear and bearing mating surfaces for galling or excessive wear.
2. Check snap-rings for burred edges. Remove burrs with a fine file.
3. Check synchronizer clutch gear splines on shaft for burrs.

Assembly

Countershaft Gear

1. Slide dummy shaft into countershaft gear.
2. Slide one roller thrust washer over dummy shaft and into gear, followed by 22 greased rollers.
3. Repeat Step 2, adding one roller thrust washer on end.
4. Repeat steps 2 and 3 at other end of countershaft gear. There is a total of 88 rollers and 6 thrust washers.
5. Place greased front thrust washer on dummy shaft against gear with tangs forward.
6. Grease rear thrust washer and stick it in place in the case, with tangs rearward. Place countershaft gear assembly in bottom of transmission case until drive pinion is installed.

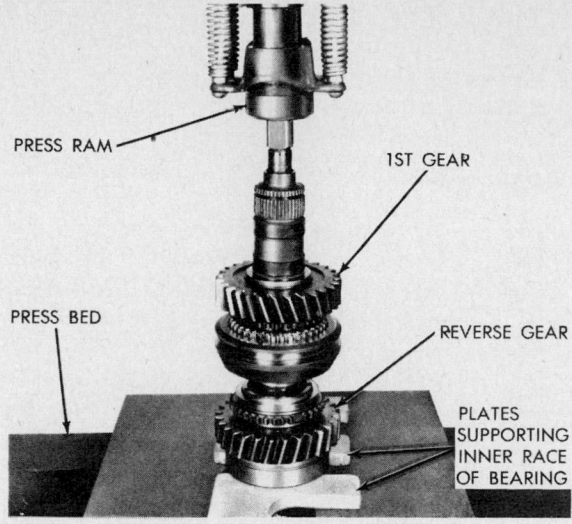

PRESS RAM

1ST GEAR

PRESS BED

REVERSE GEAR

PLATES
SUPPORTING
INNER RACE
OF BEARING

Pressing on mainshaft bearing
(© Chrysler Corp.)

2. Align oil hole in bushing with oil slot in housing. Drive bushing into place. Drive new seal into housing.
3. Install extension housing and gasket to hold mainshaft and bearing retainer in place.

Drive Pinion Bearing Retainer

1. Install outer snap-ring on drive pinion bearing. Tap assembly back until snap-ring contacts case.
2. Install a new seal in retainer bore.
3. Position main drive pinion bearing retainer and gasket on front of case. Coat threads with sealing compound, install bolts, torque to 30 ft. lbs.

Pinion Gear

1. Press new bearing on pinion shaft with snap-ring groove forward. Install new snap-ring.
2. Install 15 rollers and retaining ring in drive pinion gear.
3. Install drive pinion and bearing assembly into case.
4. Install the countershaft gear assembly by positioning it and thrust washers so countershaft can be tapped into position. Be careful to keep the countershaft against the dummy shaft to keep parts from falling between them. Install key in countershaft.
5. Tap drive pinion forward for clearance.

Mainshaft

1. Place a stop-ring flat on the bench. Place a clutch gear and a sleeve on top. Drop the struts in their slots and snap in a strut spring placing the tang inside one strut. Turn the assembly over and install second strut spring, tang in a different strut.
2. Slide first gear and stop-ring over rear of mainshaft and against thrust flange between first and second gears on shaft.
3. Slide first-reverse synchronizer assembly over rear of mainshaft, indexing hub slots to first gear stop-ring lugs.
4. Install first-reverse synchronizer clutch gear snap-ring on mainshaft.
5. Slide reverse gear and mainshaft bearing into place. Press bearing on shaft, supporting inner race of bearing. Be sure snap-ring groove on outer race is forward.
6. Install bearing retaining snap-ring on mainshaft. Spread snap-ring in retainer groove and slide it over the bearing. Seat ring in groove.
7. Place second gear over front of mainshaft with thrust surface against flange.
8. Install stop-ring and second-third synchronizer assembly against second gear. Install second-third synchronizer clutch gear snap-ring on shaft.
9. Move second-third synchronizer sleeve forward as far as possible. Install front stop-ring, inside the sleeve with lugs indexed to struts. Coat the stop-ring with grease to hold it in position.
10. Rotate cut-out on second gear toward countershaft gear to provide clearance.
11. Insert mainshaft assembly into case. Tilt assembly to clear cluster gears and insert pilot rollers in drive pinion gear. If assembly is correct, the bearing retainer will bottom to the case without force. If not, check for a misplaced strut, pinion roller, or stop-ring.

Reverse Idler Gear

1. Place dummy shaft into idler gear. Insert 22 greased rollers.
2. Position reverse idler thrust washers in case with grease.
3. Position idler gear and dummy shaft in case. Install idler shaft and key.

Extension Housing

1. Remove extension housing yoke seal. Drive bushing out from inside housing.

Gearshift Mechanism and Housing

1. If removed, place two interlock levers on pivot pin with spring hangers offset toward each other, so that spring installs in a straight line. Place E-clip on pivot pin.
2. Grease and install new O-ring seals on both shift shafts. Grease housing bores. Push each shaft into its bore.
3. Install spring on interlock lever hangers.
4. Rotate each shift shaft fork bore to vertical position. Install shift forks through bores and under both interlock levers.
5. Position second-third synchronizer sleeve to rear, in second gear position. Position first-reverse synchronizer sleeve to middle of travel, in neutral position. Place shift forks in the same positions.
6. Install gasket and gearshift mechanism. The bolt with the extra long shoulder must be installed at the center rear of the case. Torque bolts to 15 ft. lbs.
7. Install speedometer drive pinion gear and adapter. Range number on adapter, which represents the number of teeth on the gear, should be in 6 o'clock position.

Exhaust Emission Control System Switch

Some models have a switch in the shift cover, adjacent to the 2-3 shift lever. It is actuated by a flat on the 2-3 shift lever, when in third gear. If vehicle is not equipped with Emission System, a plug is installed in the mounting hole. Torque the switch or plug to 15 ft. lbs.

Type-2
A-745 Chrysler
3-Speed

Application

Barracuda, 1966-69
Charger, 1967-69
Chrysler, 1965-69

Dart, 1965-69
Dodge, 1965-69

Plymouth, 1965-69
Valiant, 1966-69

Disassembly

1. Remove output flange nut, then the drum and flange assembly, if so equipped. Remove parking brake assembly, if so equipped.
2. Remove case cover. Measure synchronizer float with feeler gauges. This measurement is taken between the end of a synchronizer pin and the opposite synchronizer outer ring. A measurement from .050-.090 in. is acceptable for 1965-68 models. The measurement should be .060-.117 in. for 1969 models.
3. Remove five bolts and one nut attaching the extension housing to the transmission case.
4. Remove the extension housing.
5. Remove the mainshaft rear bearing, if it did not come off with the extension housing.

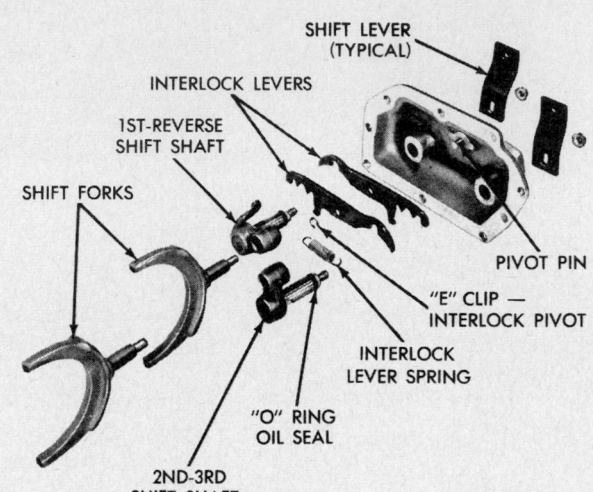

Details of side cover and shift mechanism
(© Chrysler Corp.)

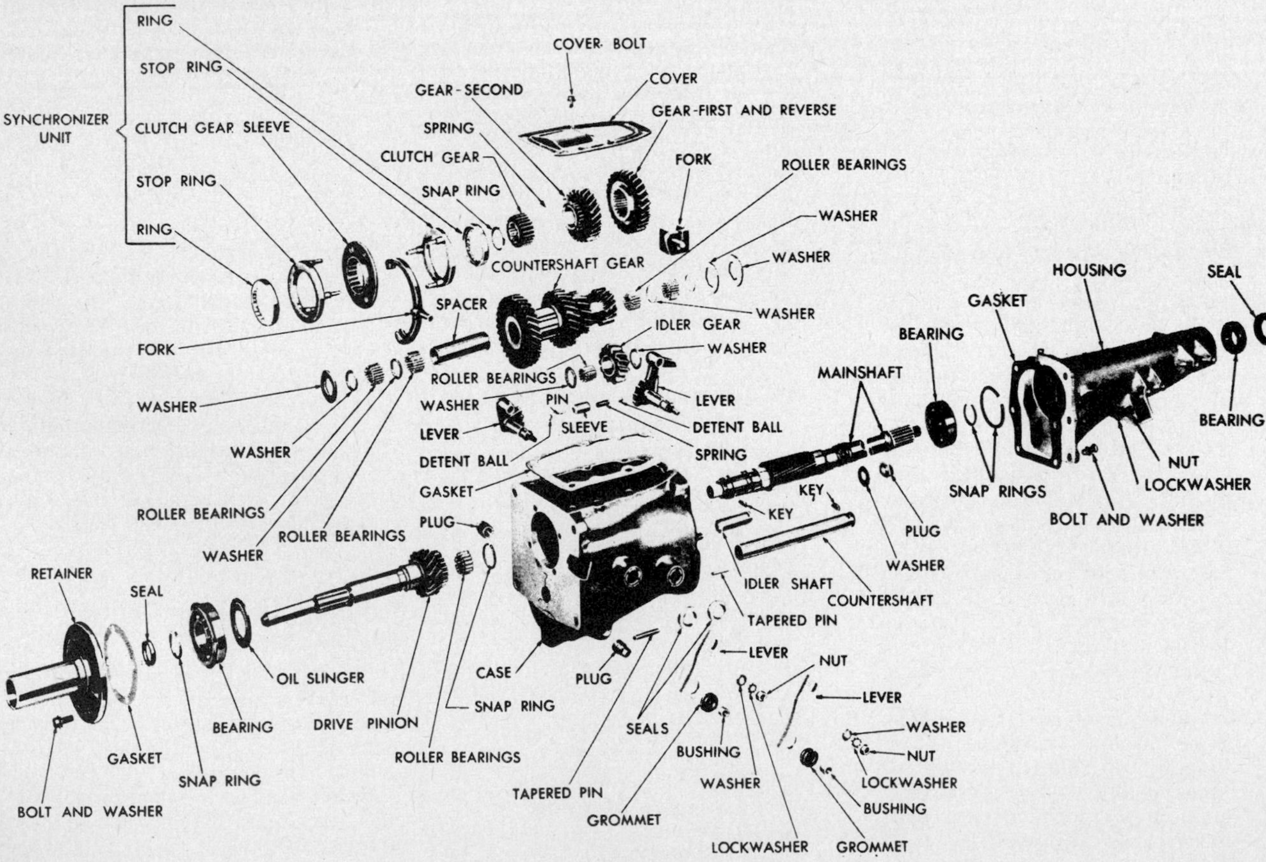

A-745 Chrysler

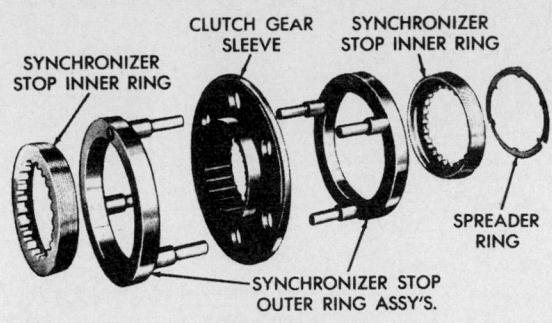

Synchromesh assembly

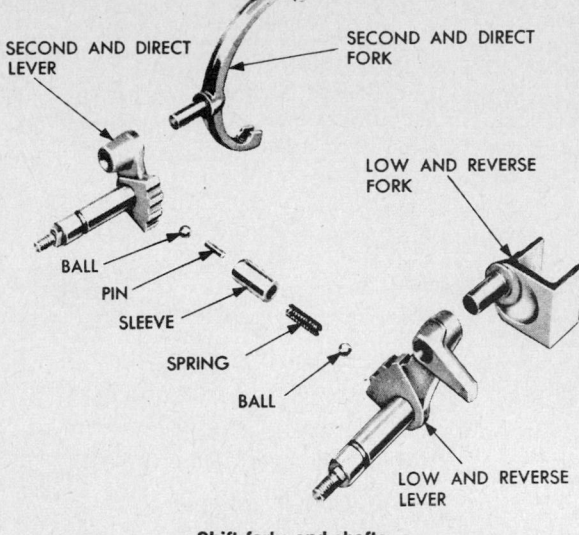

Shift forks and shafts

6. Remove transmission case cover and gasket.
7. Remove four bolts from the drive pinion bearing retainer, then remove the retainer.
8. When removing the drive pinion and bearing assembly from the transmission case, slide the front inner stop-ring from the short splines on the pinion as the assembly is being removed from the case.
9. Remove the snap-ring that holds the main drive pinion bearing onto the shaft.
10. Press bearing off pinion shaft and remove oil slinger.
11. Remove mainshaft pilot bearing snap-ring from the cavity of the pinion gear.
12. Remove the 15 pilot roller bearings.
13. Remove seal from pinion retainer.
14. Remove mainshaft rear bearing snap-ring from groove in mainshaft rear bearing bore in the case.
15. Slide the mainshaft and rear bearing assembly to the rear, until the rear bearing is out of the case.
16. Remove synchronizer assembly from case.
17. Remove second and third-speed shift fork.
18. Remove synchronizer clutch gear snap-ring.
19. Remove synchronizer clutch gear, second-speed gear, and first and reverse sliding gear from the mainshaft.
20. Withdraw mainshaft and bearing out through the rear of the case.
21. Remove the synchronizer clutch gear, second-speed gear, low and reverse sliding gear, and low and reverse shift fork from the case.
22. With a dummy shaft, drive the countershaft toward the rear of the case until the small key can be removed from the countershaft.
23. Drive the countershaft the remaining way out of the case.
24. Lift the cluster gear, the thrust washers and the dummy shaft assembly out of the case.
25. Remove the cluster gear (88 rol-

lers, four spacer rings) and the center spacer from the cluster.
26. With a blunt drift, drive the reverse idler shaft toward the rear of the case far enough to remove the key from the shaft.
27. Completely remove the shaft from the case, then remove the idler gear.
28. Remove the thrust washers and 22 rollers.
29. With a small punch, remove low and reverse gear lever shaft tapered lockpin by driving it toward the top of the transmission case.
30. Remove the second and third gear lever shaft in the same manner.
31. Remove the lever shafts from the transmission case. Don't lose the spring-loaded detent balls.
32. Remove the interlock sleeve, spring, pin and detent balls.
33. Remove both lever shaft seals and discard same.

Assembly

1. Place oil slinger on the main drive pinion with the offset outer portion next to the drive pinion teeth.
2. Place the main drive pinion bearing on the pinion shaft with the outer snap-ring away from the pinion gear.
3. Press the bearing into position so it is seated firmly against the oil slinger and pinion gear.
4. Install the bearing retaining snap-ring on the pinion shaft. Be sure the snap-ring is seated in its groove.
5. Coat the 15 pilot bearing rollers with heavy grease and install them in the cavity at the rear of the main drive pinion.
6. Install the snap-ring.
7. Place the bearing spacer in the center of the bore in the cluster gear and use the dummy shaft to assist in assembling the roller bearings.

8. Install a row of 22 rollers next to one end of the spacer, using heavy grease to hold them.
9. Place one of the four bearing spacer rings next to the row of rollers, and install another row of 22 rollers next to the spacer ring.
10. Install another spacer ring at the outside end of the second row of bearing rollers.
11. At the opposite end of the cluster gear bore, install the remaining spacer rings and bearing rollers in the same sequence as listed in Steps 8, 9, and 10.
12. With a small amount of grease, install the front thrust washer on the dummy shaft at the front end of the cluster gear, with the tabs outward.
13. Install the tabbed rear thrust washer onto the dummy shaft against the rear of the cluster gear with the tabs positioned in the grooves provided in the cluster gear.
14. Install the remaining rear thrust washer plate onto the rear of the gear and dummy shaft with the step in the washer facing upward, as viewed from the rear.
15. Align tabs of the front thrust washer vertically to index with notches in the transmission case and with the step in the rear thrust washer positioned upward. Insert the cluster gear and dummy shaft in the transmission case.
16. Using the countershaft, drive the dummy shaft forward, out of case. Countershaft end-play should be .0045-.028 in.
17. Position a dummy shaft in the reverse idler gear and, using heavy grease, install the 22 roller bearings into the gear.
18. Place the thrust washers at each end of the reverse idler gear, then position the assembly in the transmission case with the cham-

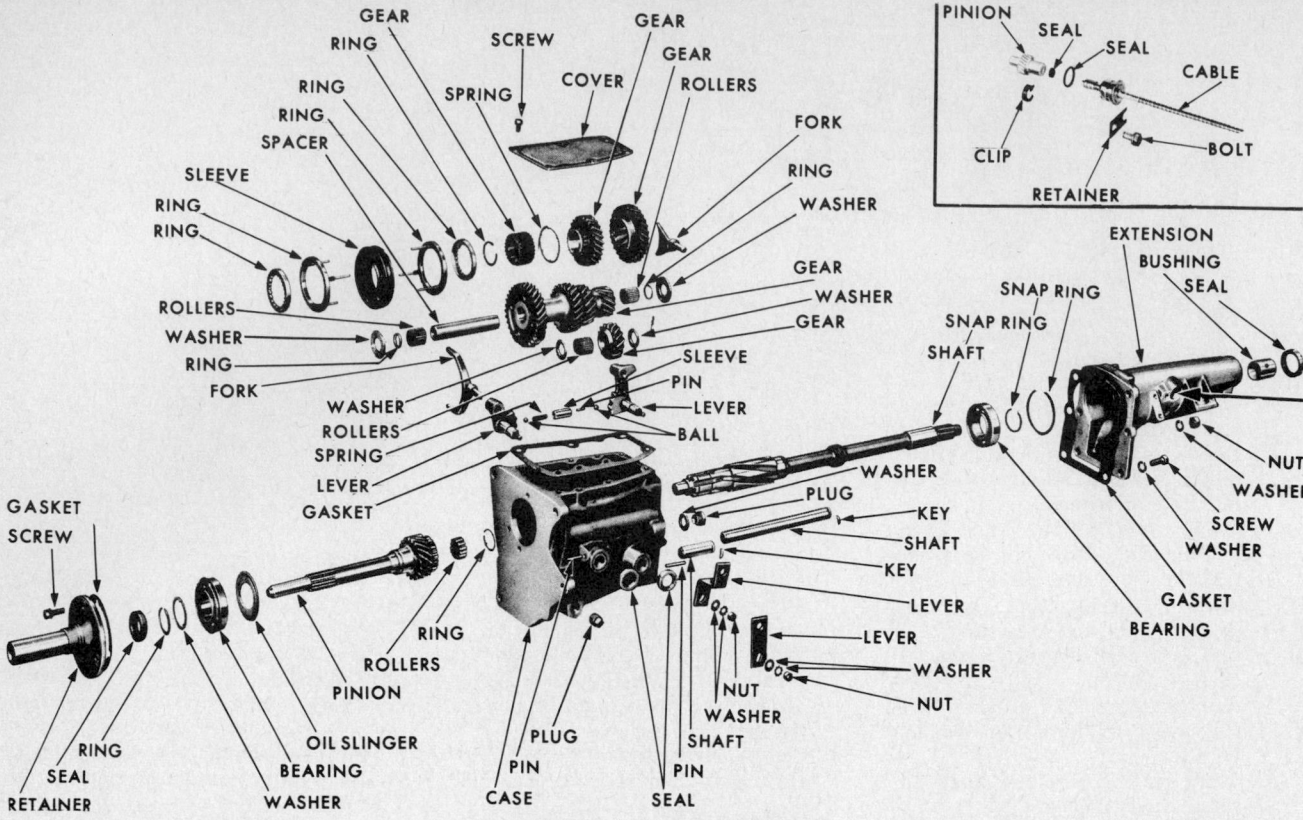

A-903 Chrysler transmission

fered end of the gear teeth toward the front.

19. Insert the reverse idler shaft into the bore at the rear of the case, with the keyway to the rear, pushing the dummy shaft forward and out of the front of the transmission.

20. With the keyway in proper alignment, insert the key and continue driving the shaft forward until the key seats in the recess.

21. Install two new lever shaft seals in the transmission case.

22. Lubricate and install second and third-speed lever shaft in the bores of the case.

23. Install the second and third speed lever shaft lockpin in the hole in the case. Drive it in firmly, in a downward direction.

24. Place interlock parts in the case in the following order: ball, sleeve, spring, pin and ball.

25. Enter low and reverse lever shaft in the case bore, depress the detent ball against spring tension and push the lever shaft firmly into position, in order to prevent the ball from escaping.

26. Install low and reverse lever shaft lockpin in the case by driving it downward.

27. Place low and reverse fork in the lever shaft, with the offset toward the rear.

28. While holding the low and reverse sliding gear in position in the fork, with the hub extension to

the rear, insert the mainshaft with the rear bearing through the rear of the case and into the sliding gear.

29. Place synchronizer stop-ring spring, then the rear stop-ring, on the synchronizer splines of the second-speed gear. Install the second-speed gear onto the mainshaft. Synchronizer shims must be added if synchronizer float is more than the maximum in Step 2, disassembly. If float was less than minimum, the six pins must be shortened.

30. Install the synchronizer clutch gear on the mainshaft with the shoulder to the front.

31. Select the thickest synchronizer clutch gear snap-ring that can be used, and install it in the mainshaft groove.

32. Check clearance between clutch gear and second-speed gear. Clearance should be .004-.014 in.

33. Hold the synchronizer clutch gear sleeve and two outer rings together with pins properly entered into the holes in the clutch gear sleeve. The clutch gear sleeve should engage in the groove of the second- and third-speed shift fork. Position the fork in the second and third-speed lever shaft.

34. While holding the synchronizer parts and fork in position, slide the mainshaft forward, entering the synchronizer clutch gear into

the clutch gear sleeve. At the same time, enter the mainshaft rear bearing in the case bore.

35. While still holding the synchronizer parts in position, tap the mainshaft forward until the rear bearing bottoms in the case bore.

36. Install the mainshaft rear bearing snap-ring into place in the case bore.

37. Install a new seal in the drive pinion retainer.

38. Place the synchronizer front inner ring in position in the front outer ring, and enter the main drive pinion through the case bore.

39. Engage the splines on the rear of the pinion with the inner stop ring, and tap the drive pinion into the case until the outer snap-ring on the pinion bearing is against the transmission case.

40. Place the drive pinion bearing retainer over the pinion shaft and against the transmission case. While holding the retainer against the transmission case, measure the clearance between the retainer and case.

41. Select a gasket .003-.005 in. thicker than the clearance found.

42. Install and tighten the front bearing retainer bolts to 30 ft. lbs. torque.

43. Install a new seal in the extension housing.

44. Install extension housing. Torque the attaching bolts and nuts to 50 ft. lbs.

45. Install the parking brake assembly, on vehicles so equipped.
46. Install the parking brake drum (if so equipped) and flange assembly. Install the washer and nut

and torque to 175 ft. lbs.
47. Install the drain plug in the transmission case.
48. Install the gearshift operating levers, and torque to 12 ft. lbs.

49. Install the back-up light switch.
50. Install the speedometer cable and drive gear. Fill with transmission lubricant to the proper level.

Type-3
A-903 Chrysler
3-Speed

Application

Charger (6 Cyl.), 1967-72
Challenger (6 Cyl.), 1970-72
Chrysler (6 Cyl.), 1971-72

Barracuda (6 Cyl.), 1966-72
Dart (6 Cyl.), 1965-72
Dodge (6 Cyl.), 1965-72

Gremlin, Hornet, 232 (6 Cyl.), 1972
Plymouth (6 Cyl.), 1965-72
Valiant (6 Cyl.), 1965-72

Disassembly

1. Remove output shaft yoke.
2. Remove the bolts that attach the extension housing to the transmission case. Remove the housing.
3. Remove extension housing oil seal.
4. Remove the transmission case cover. Measure synchronizer float with feeler gauges. This measurement is taken between the end of a synchronizer pin and the opposite synchronizer outer ring. A measurement from .050-.090 in. is acceptable for 1965-68 models. This measurement should be .060-.117 in. for 1969-72 models.
5. Remove the attaching bolts and remove the main drive pinion bearing retainer. Then grasp the pinion shaft and pull the assembly out of the case.

Caution Be careful not to bind the inner synchronizer ring on the drive pinion clutch teeth.

6. Remove the snap-ring that locks the main drive pinion bearing onto the pinion shaft. Remove the bearing washer, press the shaft out of the bearing and remove the oil slinger.
7. Remove the snap-ring from the pilot bearing in the end of the drive pinion and remove the 14 rollers.
8. With the transmission in reverse, remove the outer center bearing snap-ring, then partially remove the mainshaft.
9. Cock the mainshaft, then remove the clutch sleeve, the outer synchronizer rings, the front inner ring and the second-third shift box.
10. Remove clutch gear retaining snap ring and slide the clutch gear off the end of the mainshaft.

11. Slide the second-speed gear, stop-ring and synchronizer spring off the mainshaft.
12. Remove the low and reverse sliding gear and shift fork, as the mainshaft is completely withdrawn from the case.
13. Check cluster gear end-play. End-play should be .005-.022 in. This measurement will determine thrust washer value at reassembly.
14. Drive the countershaft rearward, removing key, and out of the case.
15. Lift the gear cluster and thrust washers out of the case. Remove the needle bearings, (22 each end) and spacer from the cluster.
16. Drive the reverse idler shaft toward the rear and out of the case. Remove key.
17. Lift the reverse idler gear, thrust washers and 22 needle bearings out of the case.
18. Remove gearshift operating levers from their respective shafts.
19. Drive out tapered retaining pin from either of the two lever shafts, then withdraw the shaft from inside the transmission case.

(The detent balls are spring-loaded, as the shaft is being withdrawn, the balls will fall to the bottom of the case.)
20. Remove the interlock sleeve, spring, pin and both balls from the case. Drive out the remaining tapered pin, then slide the lever shaft out of the transmission.
21. Remove the lever shaft seals and discard them.

Assembly

1. Install two new shift lever shaft seals in the case.
2. Carefully insert low and reverse lever shaft into the rear of the case, through the seal and into position. Lock with a tapered pin. Turn lever until the center detent is in line with the interlock bore.
3. Slide the interlock sleeve in its bore in the case, followed by one of the interlock balls. Then, install interlock spring and pin.
4. Place the remaining interlock ball on top of the interlock spring.
5. Depress the interlock ball and at the same time install the second

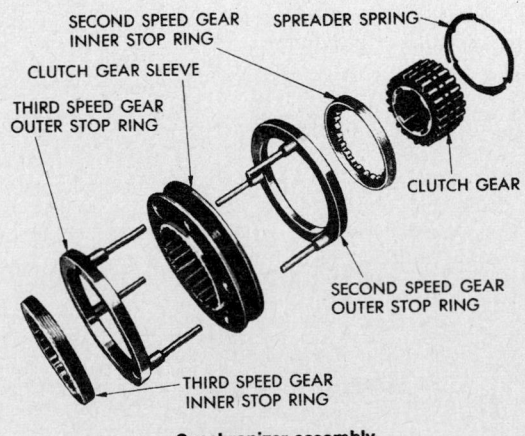

SECOND SPEED GEAR INNER STOP RING
SPREADER SPRING
CLUTCH GEAR SLEEVE
THIRD SPEED GEAR OUTER STOP RING
CLUTCH GEAR
SECOND SPEED GEAR OUTER STOP RING
THIRD SPEED GEAR INNER STOP RING

Synchronizer assembly

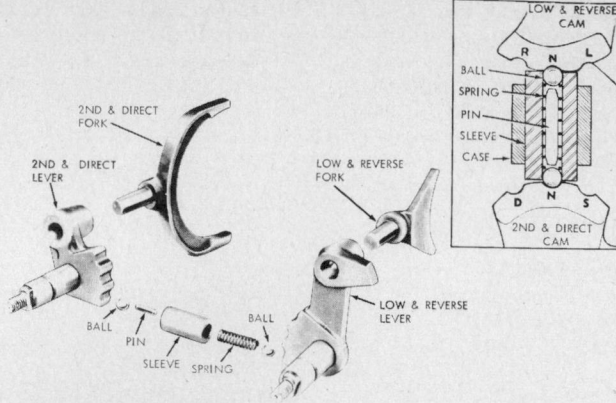

Shift forks and levers

and high lever shaft into the fully seated position, with the center detent aligned with the detent ball. Secure the shaft with the remaining tapered pin.

6. Install the operating levers and secure to the shafts with nuts. Torque the nuts to 18 ft. lbs.

Countershaft (Cluster) Gear

1. Slide the dummy shaft and tubular spacer into the bore of the countergear.
2. Grease and install 22 bearing rollers into each end of the countergear bore in the area around the arbor. Install the bearing retaining rings at each end of the gear, covering the bearings. If countershaft gear end-play measured over .022 in. at disassembly, install new thrust washers.
3. Install a thrust washer at each end of the countergear and over the arbor. Install the countergear assembly in the case, making sure the tabs on the thrust washers slide into the grooves in the case.

Reverse Idler Gear

1. Coat the bore of the reverse idler gear with grease, then slide dummy shaft into the bore, then install 22 bearing rollers in the bore and around the dummy shaft.
2. Install a new thrust washer at each end of the gear and over the arbor.
3. With the beveled end of the teeth forward, slide the gear into position in the case. Install the reverse idler shaft in its bore in the rear of the case. Install Woodruff key and align with the keyway in the case.
4. Align the idler gear with the shaft, then drive the shaft into the case and gear until the key seats in recess.

Mainshaft

1. Install rear bearing on mainshaft and install selective fit snap-ring.
2. Hold low and reverse sliding gear in position with shift fork. Insert mainshaft with rear bearing through rear of case and into the sliding gear. Both shift forks are offset toward rear of the case.
3. Place synchronizer spreader ring, and then rear stop ring, on synchronizer splines of second speed gear. Install second speed gear on mainshaft, with shims if required. Shims should be installed to correct excessive synchronizer float. If synchronizer float is below minimum, as measured on disassembly, shorten all six synchronizer pins.
4. Install synchronizer clutch gear on mainshaft. Install snap-ring.
5. Install second and direct fork in lever shaft with offset toward rear of transmission. Hold synchronizer clutch gear sleeve and two outer rings together, with pins in holes in clutch gear sleeve. Engage second and direct fork with clutch gear sleeve.
6. While holding synchronizer parts and fork in position, slide mainshaft forward, starting synchronizer clutch gear into clutch gear sleeve and mainshaft rear bearing into the case bore. Synchronizer parts must be correctly positioned before mainshaft is positioned.
7. While holding synchronizer parts in position, tap mainshaft forward until rear bearing bottoms in the case bore.
8. Install mainshaft rear bearing selective fit snap-ring into groove in case bore.

Drive Pinion (Clutch Shaft)

1. Slide the oil slinger over the pinion shaft and down against the gear.

2. Slide the bearing over the pinion shaft (ring groove away from the gear), then press to a firm seat against the oil slinger and gear.

3. Install the keyed washer, then the snap-ring. Four thicknesses of snap-ring are available to eliminate end-play. Install the large snap-ring onto the race of the ball bearing.
4. Install 14 greased bearing rollers in the bore of the pinion shaft gear. Install bearing roller retaining ring in the pinion gear bore.

5. Install third gear outer stop-ring and third gear inner stop-ring onto the mainshaft. Guide the drive pinion through the front of the case and engage the inner stop-ring with the clutch teeth, then seat the bearing so the large snap-ring is hard against the case.

6. Install a new seal in the pinion bearing retainer.
7. Install the gasket on the retainer and install with attaching bolts torqued to 30 ft. lbs.

Extension Housing

1. Install a new rear mainshaft bushing, and a new oil seal.
2. Protect the oil seal with thimble-type seal protector, and with gasket attached, slide the extension housing over the mainshaft and down against the case. Attach with bolts torqued to 50 ft. lbs.
3. Install flange assembly and secure with new washer and nut. Torque the nut to 140 ft. lbs.
4. Grease the cover gasket, and install gasket on cover. Torque attaching bolts to 12 ft. lbs.
5. Install drain plug and back-up light switch (if so equipped) and tighten securely. Refill transmission to proper level.

Exhaust Emission Control Switch

Some models have a switch mounted above the 2-3 shift lever, for emission control. In the absence of a switch a plug is substituted. Torque the plug or switch to 15 ft. lbs.

NOTE: cou[...]
not exceed .02[...]

20. Install a.[...]
    verse gea[...]
21. Lubricate[...]
    the lever[...]
    the case.[...]
    the lever.[...]
22. Install r[...]
    and sprin[...]
    tainer. Ti[...]
23. Start re[...]
    into the[...]
    press in[...]
    the rever[...]
    truding e[...]
    same tir[...]
    groove v[...]
    fork.
24. With rev[...]
    positione[...]
    into the[...]
    finish se[...]
    flush wit[...]
25. Grease, t[...]
    ket on tl[...]
    housing.
26. Center re[...]
    shaft, th[...]
    mainshaf[...]
    (Be sure[...]
    and four[...]
    shifter pl[...]
27. Move th[...]
    clutch sle[...]

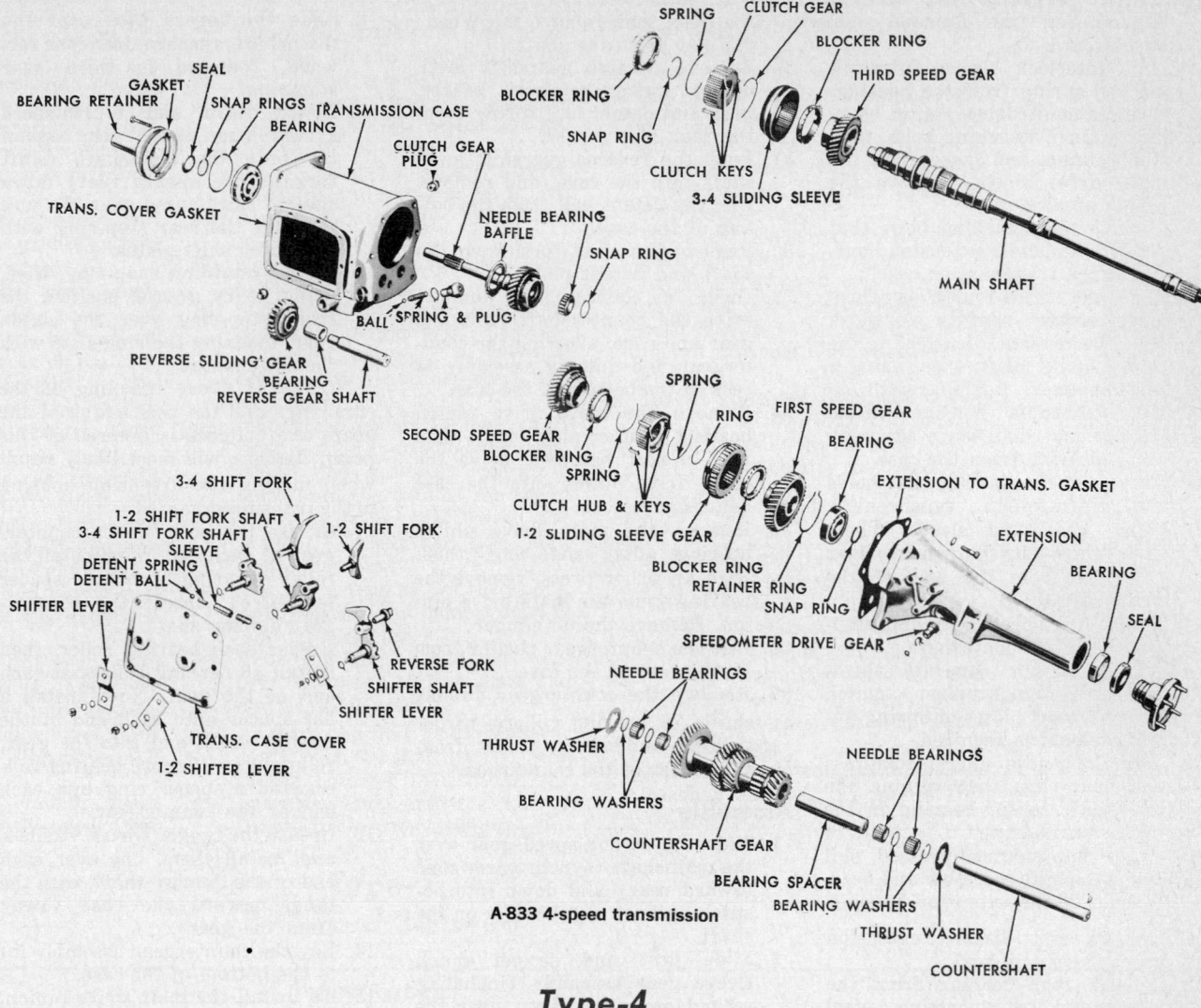

A-833 4-speed transmission

Type-4
A-833 Chrysler
4-Speed

Application

Barracuda, 1965-72	Chrysler, 1965-67	Javelin (360V8—4-BBL., 401
Challenger, 1970-72	Dart, 1965-72	V8), 1972
Charger, 1966-72	Dodge, 1965-72	Plymouth, 1965-72
		Valiant, 1965-72

Fairlane (6[...]

Disassembl[...]
1. Drain the[...]
   mission c[...]
2. Remove[...]
   the interl[...]
3. Remove[...]
   taching b[...]
   gine rea[...]
   the exten[...]
   Tap the[...]
   with a s[...]
   draw ext[...]
4. Remove[...]
   snap-ring[...]
   gear and[...]
   put shaft[...]
5. Remove[...]
   retainer.
6. With a c[...]
   shaft out[...]
   case. Lea[...]
   the cluste[...]
   of the ca[...]
7. Remove[...]
   tainer an[...]

This unit is used by Chrysler Corporation cars and varies somewhat with car application. However, illustrations and repair procedures may be considered as typical.

Disassembly
1. If available, mount transmission in a repair stand.
2. Disconnect gearshift control rods from the shift control levers and the transmission operating levers.
3. Remove the two gearshift control housing mounting bolts.
4. Remove gearshift control housing from the transmission extension housing or mounting bracket (if so equipped).
5. Remove the gearshift control housing mounting bracket bolts, then remove the bracket (if so equipped).
6. Remove back-up light switch (if so equipped).
7. Remove output companion flange nut and washer, then pull the flange from the mainshaft (output shaft).
8. Remove gearshift housing-to-transmission case attaching bolts.
9. With all levers in the neutral de-tent position, pull housing out and away from the case.
   NOTE: if first and second, or third and fourth shift forks remain in engagement with the synchronizer sleeves, work the sleeves and remove forks from the case.
10. Remove nuts, lock washers and flat washers that hold first-second, and third-fourth-speed shift operating levers to the shafts.
11. Disengage shift levers from the flats on the shafts and remove levers.
12. Remove gearshift lever shafts out of the housing, allowing detent

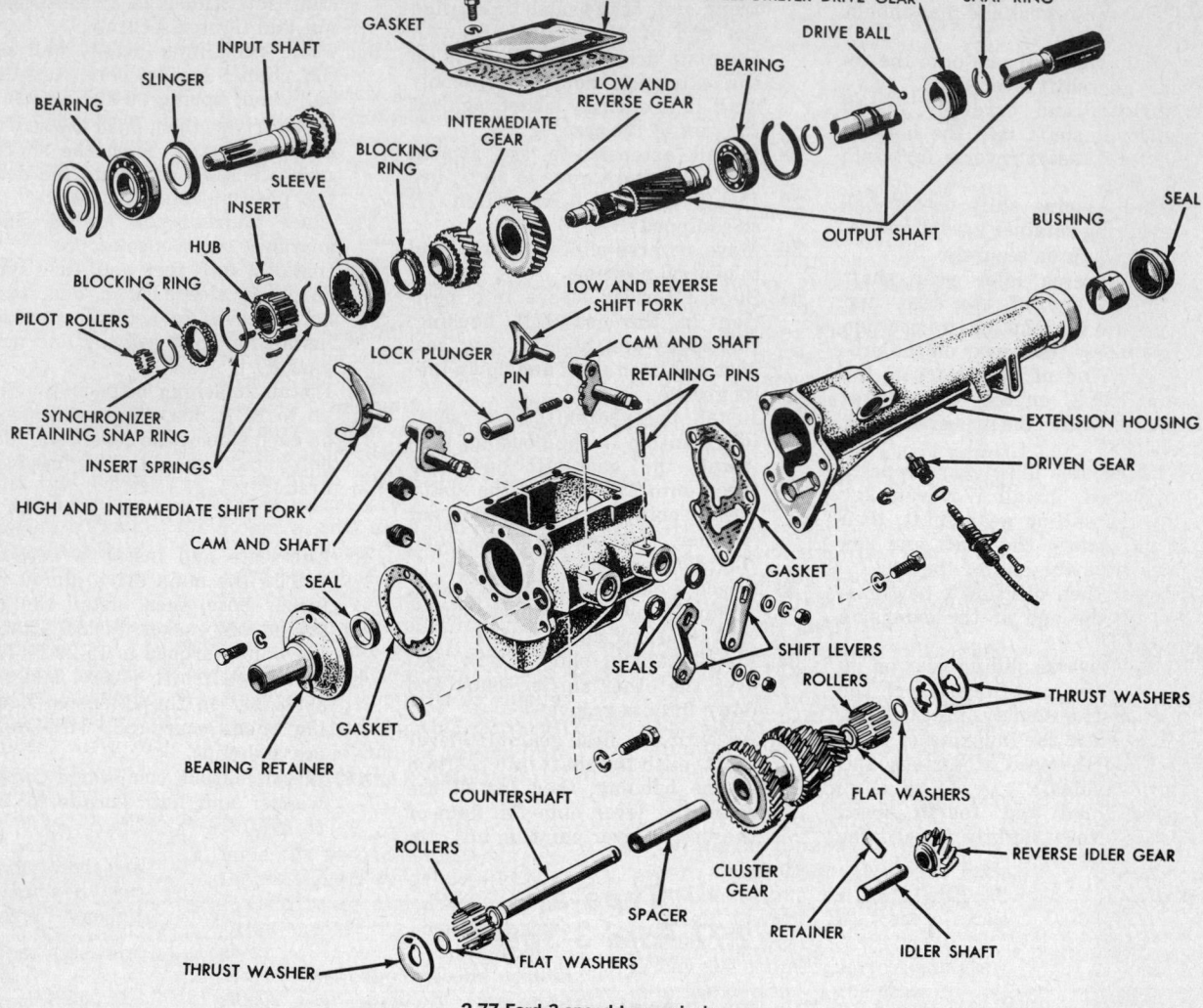

2.77 Ford 3-speed transmission
(© Ford Motor Co.)

3. Insert the tubular spacer and dummy shaft into the cluster gear assembly. Position one flat washer at each end of the spacer. Apply grease to the needle bearings and assemble the needle rollers around the dummy shaft at each end of the gear. Apply grease to the other two flat washers and thrust washers and assemble at each end of the cluster gear. Position the gear cluster assembly in the bottom of the transmission case.

4. Install reverse and low shift cam and shaft through the case opening. Assemble the spacer and spring in the plunger. Apply grease to each ball and position in each end of the plunger. Hold the plunger assembly in position and install the intermediate and high cam and shaft into the case opening, allowing the balls to register in the cam detents.

5. Align the cam and shaft grooves with the openings in the shaft bosses, then install the retaining pins. Check the cam action.

6. Position the reverse idler gear, and insert the shaft (from the rear) through the case far enough to hold the gear.

7. Assemble the synchronizer hub and insert the hub assembly into the intermediate and high sleeve. Install one of the blocking rings into the rear side of the hub. Coat the blocking rings with grease.

8. Using grease, assemble the needle bearings in the input shaft and install the front synchronizer blocking ring on the input shaft.

9. Install the shift forks in the shift lever shaft assemblies, with the large fork in the intermediate and high shaft assembly. The web of the low and reverse fork must be to the rear of the shaft center.

10. Start the output shaft through the rear opening of the transmission case. Place the low and reverse gear on the shaft, followed by the intermediate gear. Tilt the output shaft enough to allow the rear shift fork to engage the sliding gear groove.

11. With the longer hub forward,

slide the synchronizer assembly onto the output shaft and engage the synchronizer sleeve in the intermediate and high shift fork.

12. Install the synchronizer hub snap ring.

13. Position the input shaft and front synchronizer blocking ring.

14. Place a new gasket on the input shaft bearing retainer. Install bearing retainer oil seal, then install the bearing retainer. Line up the drain groove in the retainer with the oil hole in the case, then with sealer on the retainer attaching screws, torque them to 12-15 ft. lbs.

15. Raise the cluster gear and align the dummy shaft with the countershaft hole in the case. Tap the countershaft into the case and countershaft gear until the countershaft is entirely in position and the dummy shaft is out of the case. Cluster gear end-play should be .004-.018 in. Adjust by replacing thrust washers.

16. Install the idler gear shaft and install the retainer.

17. Secure the speedometer gear and **drive ball** with the snap-ring.
18. If necessary, install new bushing and seal in extension housing.
19. Using sealer on the attaching bolts, install extension housing. Torque the attaching bolts to 37 to 42 ft. lbs. for 7/16 in. x 14 bolts or 28 to 38 ft. lbs. for 3/8 in. x 16 bolts.
20. Lubricate and install new seal on each cam and shaft.
21. Install the shift levers.
22. Check transmission operation through all shift positions.
23. Fill transmission to level and install case cover and gasket. Torque attaching bolts to 10-13 ft. lbs.

Type-6
3.03 Fully Synchronized Ford 3-Speed

Application

Buick LeSabre, 1972
Buick Wildcat, 1966-70
Buick Special, 1965-69 (GS), 1966-69 (V8)
Comet, 1965-66 (V8), 1967 (All), 1971-72
Cougar, 1967-72

Fairlane, 1965-66 (V8), 1967-72 (All)
Firebird (V8), 1968-69
Ford, 1965-72
Maverick, 1970-72
Mercury, 1965-70
Montego, 1968-72

Mustang, 1965-66 (V8), 1967-72 (All)
Oldsmobile, 1966-70
Olds F-85 (V8), 1965-69
Tempest (V8), 1965-69
Torino, 1971-72
Pontiac, 1966-72
Pontiac GP, 1969

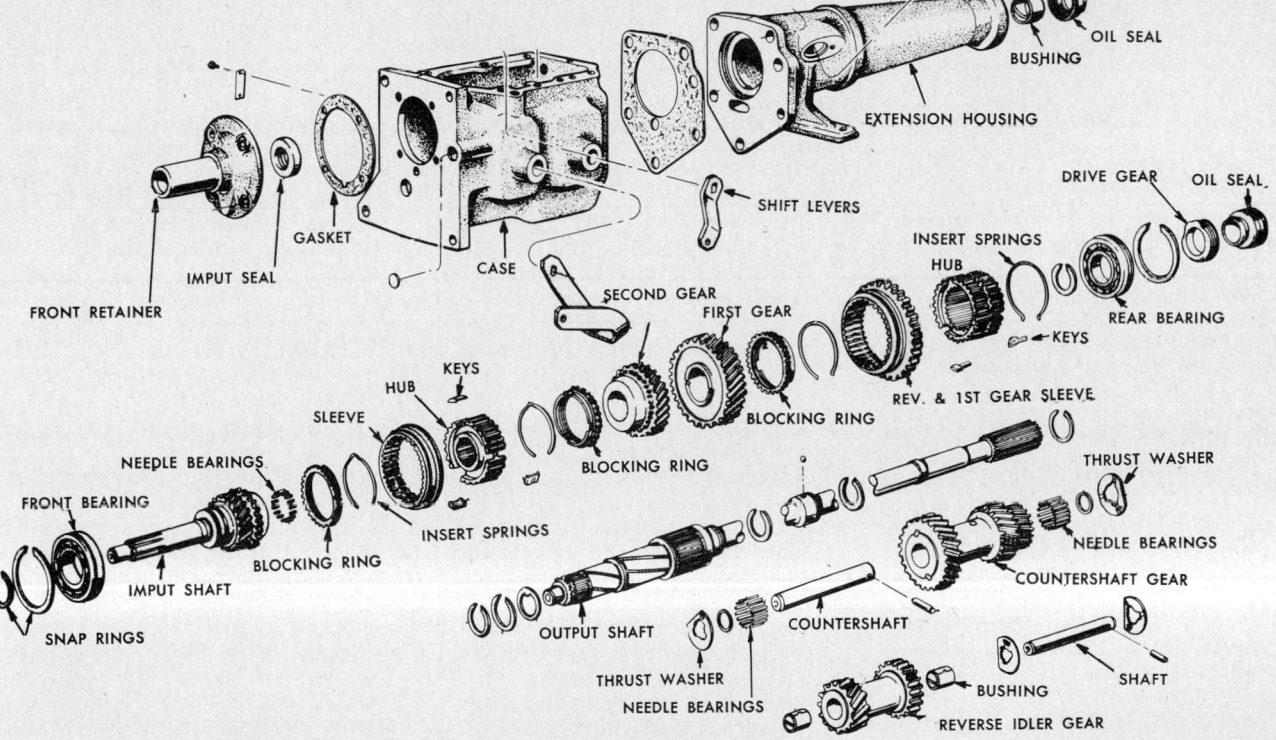

3.03 Ford 3-speed transmission (© Ford Motor Co.)

Disassembly

1. Drain the lubricant, then remove the cover bolts and the case cover.
2. Remove the five attaching screws, then remove the extension housing from the transmission case. Remove a long spring which retains the detent plug in the case. Remove the detent plug with a small magnet.
3. Remove the four attaching screws, then remove the front bearing retainer from the case.
4. Remove the filler plug. Working through the filler plug hole, drive the roll pin out of the case and countershaft with a small punch.
5. With a dummy shaft, push the countershaft out of the rear of the case until the countershaft cluster gear can be lowered to the bottom of the case. Remove the countershaft from the rear of the case.
6. Remove the snap-ring. Lift the input gear and shaft from the front of the case. Press the shaft out of the bearing.
7. Remove the snap-ring that holds the speedometer gear onto the shaft. Slide the speedometer gear off the output shaft. Remove the speedometer gear lockball.
8. Remove the snap-ring that holds the output shaft bearing on the shaft. With a puller, remove the

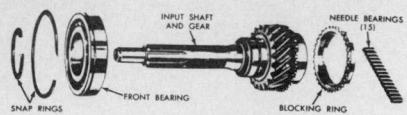

Input shaft and bearing
(© Ford Motor Co.)

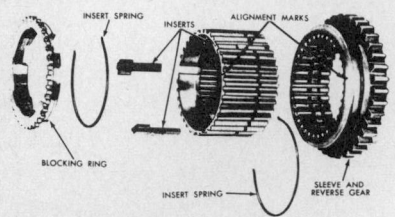

First and reverse synchronizer
(© Ford Motor Co.)

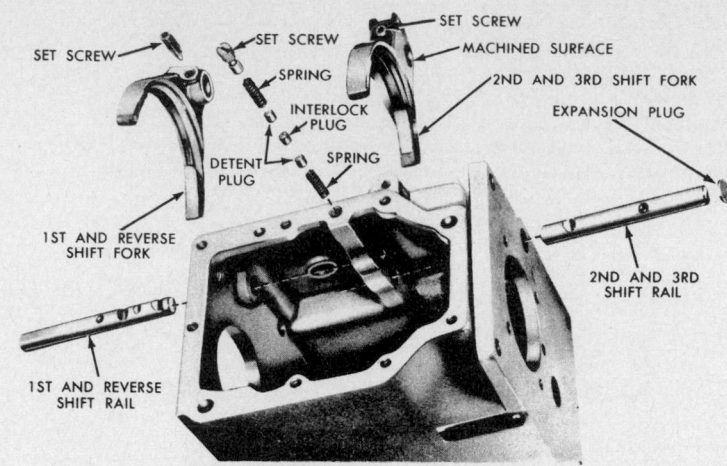

Shift rail and forks (© Ford Motor Co.)

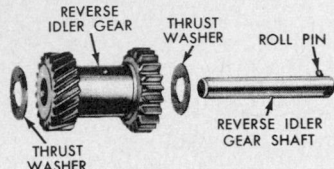

Reverse idler shaft
(© Ford Motor Co.)

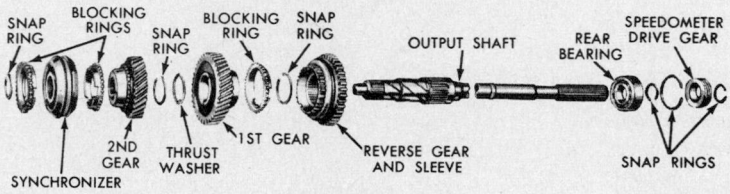

Output shaft
(© Ford Motor Co.)

bearing from both the case and shaft.

9. Place both shaft levers in the neutral position.
10. Remove the set screw that holds the detent springs and plugs in the case. Remove a detent spring and plug from the case.
11. Remove the set screw that holds the first and reverse shift fork to the shift rail. Slide first and reverse shift rail out through the rear of the case.
12. Rotate the first and reverse shift fork upward, then lift it from the case.
13. Remove the set screw that holds the second and third shift fork to the shift rail. Rotate the shift rail 90°.
14. With a magnet, lift the interlock plug from the case.
15. Tap on the inner end of the second and third shift rail to remove the expansion plug from the front of the case. Remove the shift rail.
16. Remove second and third detent plug and spring from the detent bore.

NOTE: on 1971-72 RAT model transmissions, pull the input gear and shaft forward until the gear contacts the case. On all other models, remove the input gear and shaft through the front of the case.

17. Rotate the second and third shift fork upward, then lift it from the case.
18. Lift the output shaft out through the top of the case.

19. Working through the front bearing opening, drive the reverse idler shaft out through the rear of the case.
20. Lift the reverse idler gear and two thrust washers from the case.
21. Lift the countershaft gear and thrust washers from the case.
22. Remove the countershaft-to-case retaining pin and any needle bearings which may have fallen into the case.
23. Remove the shift levers and shafts from the case. Discard the O-rings.
24. Remove the snap-ring from the front of the output shaft, then slide the synchronizer and the second-speed gear from the shaft.
25. Remove the next snap-ring and thrust washer from the output shaft, then slide the first gear and blocking ring off the shaft.
26. Remove the next snap-ring from the output shaft, then press off the first-reverse synchronizer hub from the shaft.
27. Remove the dummy shaft, 50 bearing rollers and the two retainer washers from the countershaft gear.
28. Disassemble the synchronizers.

Assembly

1. Coat the bore in each end of the countershaft gear with grease. Hold the dummy shaft in the gear and install 25 bearing rollers and a retainer washer in each end of the gear. Install the countershaft

gear, thrust washers and dummy shaft in the case. End-play is controlled with variable thickness thrust washers to .004-.018 in. Let the gear cluster assembly lie in the bottom of the case.
2. Install the idler gear, thrust washers and shaft in the case. Make sure that the thrust washer with the flat side, is at the web end and that the spur gear is toward the rear of the case. Idler gear end-play should be .004-.018 in.
3. Install an insert spring into the groove of the first and reverse synchronizer hub. Be sure that the spring covers all insert grooves. Start the hub in the sleeve, being sure the alignment marks are properly indexed. Position the three inserts in the hub and be sure the small end is over the spring and that the shoulder is on the inside of the hub. Slide the sleeve and reverse gear onto the hub until the detent is engaged. Install the other insert spring in the front of the hub to hold the inserts against it.
4. Install one insert spring into a groove of the second-third synchronizer hub. With the alignment marks on the hub and sleeve aligned, start the hub into the sleeve. Place the three inserts on top of the retaining spring and push the assembly together. Install the remaining insert spring, so that the spring

ends cover the same slots as do the other spring. Do not stagger the springs. Place a synchronizer blocking ring in each end of the synchronizer sleeve.

5. Lubricate the output shaft splines and machined surfaces with transmission lubricant.
6. Press the first and reverse synchronizer hub onto the output shaft, with the teeth end of the gear facing toward the rear end of the shaft. Secure it with the snap-ring.
7. Place the blocking ring on the tapered machined surface of the first gear.
8. Slide the first gear onto the output shaft, with the blocking ring toward the rear of the shaft. Rotate the gear to engage the three notches in the blocking ring with the synchronizer inserts. Secure the first gear with the thrust washer and snap-ring.
9. Slide the blocking ring onto the tapered, machined surface of the second gear. Slide the second gear, with blocking ring and the second and third gear synchronizer, onto the mainshaft. The tapered machined surface of the second gear must be toward the front of the shaft. Secure the synchronizer with a snap-ring.
10. Install new O-rings onto the two shift lever shafts. Lubricate the shafts with transmission fluid and install them into the case. Secure each shift lever onto its shaft.
11. Coat the bore of the input shaft with a light coat of grease. Install the 15 bearing rollers into the bore.
   NOTE: on RAT models (1971-72) install the input gear and bearing

through the top of the case. On other models the input shaft is installed through the front of the transmission.

12. Position the output shaft assembly in the case.
13. Place a detent plug spring and a plug in the case. Place a second and third-speed shift fork in the synchronizer groove. Rotate the fork into position and install the second and third-speed shift rail. Move the rail inward until the detent plug engages the forward notch (second). Secure the fork to the shaft with a set screw. Move the synchronizer to the neutral position.
14. Install the interlock plug in the case.
15. Place first and reverse shift fork in the groove of the first and reverse synchronizer. Rotate the fork into position and install the first and reverse shift rail. Move the rail inward until the center notch is aligned with the detent bore. Secure the fork to the shaft with a set screw. Install the remaining detent plug and spring. Secure the detent spring with the slotted head set screw. Tighten set screw until the head is flush with the case.
16. Install a new expansion plug in the case front.
17. Install the input shaft and gear in the front of the case.
18. Place front bearing retainer (with new gasket in place) on the case with the oil return groove at the bottom. Torque attaching screws to 30 ft. lbs.
19. Install the large snap-ring on the rear bearing. Place the bearing on the output shaft, with the snap-

ring end toward the rear of the shaft. Press bearing into place and secure with a snap-ring.

20. Hold the speedometer drive gear lock ball in the detent and slide the speedometer gear into place. Secure the gear with a snap-ring.
21. Lift the countershaft gear cluster up into place, and, by entering the countershaft at the rear of the case, push the dummy shaft out of the gear and transmission case. Before the countershaft is completely in place, align the roll pin hole in the shaft with the hole in the case.
   NOTE: on all eight-cylinder vehicles and Ford six-cylinder models the countershaft is a press fit in the case. On Ford six-cylinder models with RAN transmissions, there is a radial clearance of .020 in. at front bore and .010 in. at rear.
22. Working through the filler hole, install a roll pin into the case and countershaft.
23. Install filler and drain plugs in the case.
24. Coat a new extension housing gasket with sealer and install it on the case.
25. Apply sealer to attaching screws and secure extension housing to the case by torqueing the screws to 42 to 50 ft. lbs.
26. With transmission in gear, pour lubricant over the entire gear train while rotating the input or output shaft.
27. Install the transmission cover, with a new sealer-coated gasket in place, and torque the nine attaching screws to 14-19 ft. lbs.
28. Check operation of transmission in all of the gear positions.

Type-7

Comet (6 Cyl.), 1965-66
Falcon, 1965-66

Ford (Dagenham) 4-Speed

Application

Fairlane (6 Cyl.), 1965-66
Mustang (6 Cyl.), 1965-66

Disassembly

1. Disconnect the three shift rods from the shift levers.
2. Remove the three bolts that hold the shift selector assembly to the extension housing.
3. Insert a reworked screwdriver through the clutch release lever and unhook the retainer that holds the clutch release lever to the retainer bracket.
4. Remove the four bolts that hold the flywheel housing to the transmission.
5. Remove the eight attaching bolts and the shift cover from the transmission.
6. Remove the three bolts and the

input bearing retainer from the front of the transmission.

7. Remove the four bolts that hold the extension housing and output bearing adapter to the transmission case. Remove the extension housing.
8. Working from the front of the case, drive the countershaft toward the rear, until it is clear of the front wall of the case. Using a dummy shaft, push the countershaft out until the dummy shaft and gear cluster drop out of position.
9. Remove the output shaft assembly from the rear of the case.

10. Remove the input gear and bearing from the front of the case.
11. Lift the countershaft gear assembly out through the cover opening. Note that the smallest diameter thrust washer is between the rear of the countershaft gear and the case and that the larger diameter steel and bronze washers are at the front.

12. Thread a 5/16 in. x 24 bolt into the rear end of the reverse idler gear shaft and pull the shaft out with a puller. Remove the idler gear.

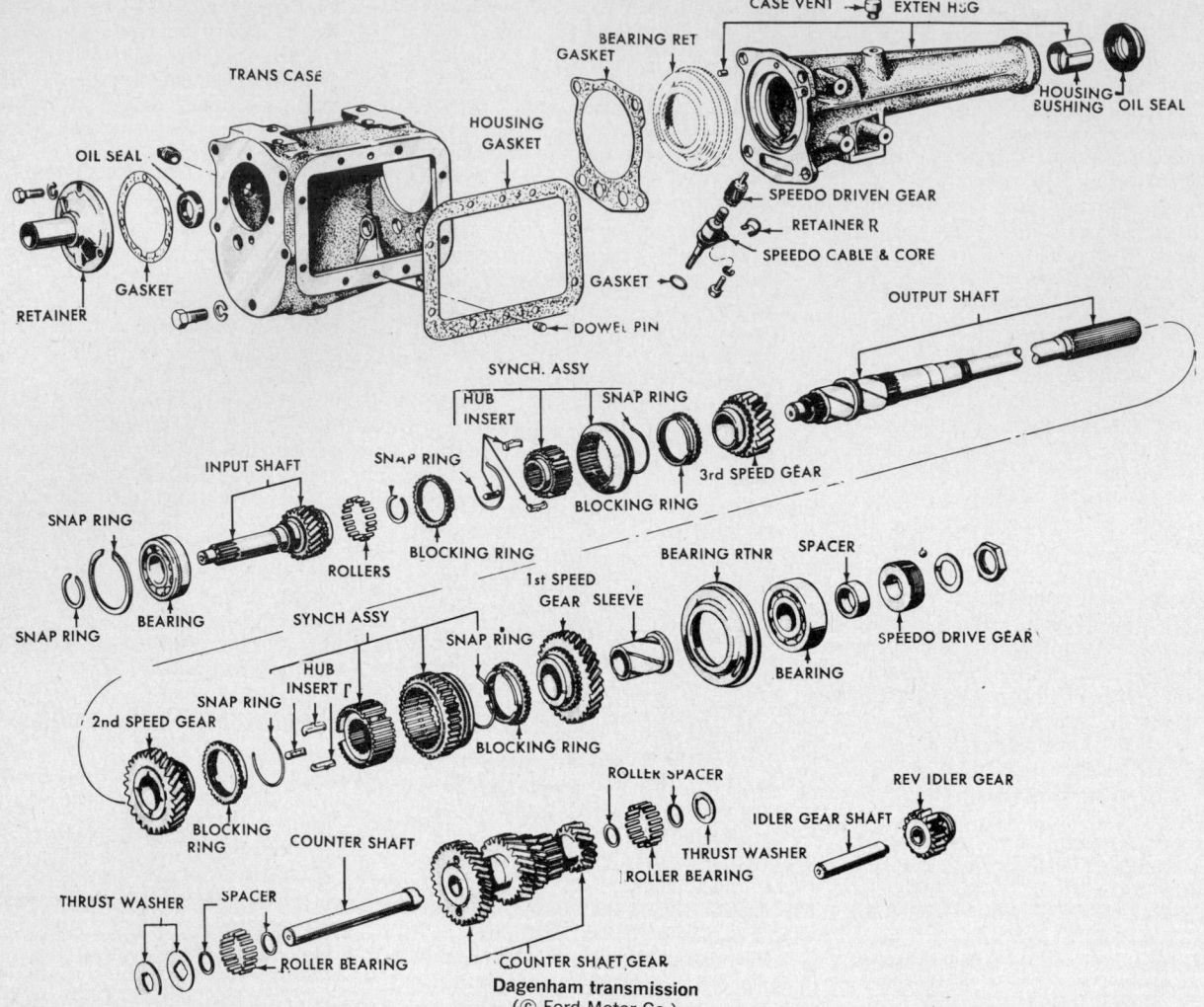

Dagenham transmission
(© Ford Motor Co.)

13. Remove the snap-ring from the input shaft and pull the input shaft bearing.
14. Straighten the output shaft lock-nut tab and remove the nut and lock.
15. Remove the speedometer gear, drive ball, and gear spacer.
16. With the output shaft in a press, remove the bearing, adapter, first gear, first and second synchronizer assembly and second gear from the shaft.
17. Remove the snap-ring from the front of the third-fourth synchronizer on the output shaft. Press the third gear and the third-fourth synchronizer from the shaft. Before disassembling the synchronizers, scribe an alignment mark across the hub and sleeve. These marks will furnish identification at the time of assembly. Remove the front and rear insert springs from both synchronizer assemblies. Slide the sleeves off the hubs. Remove hub inserts.
18. Remove snap-ring from the end of the selector shaft.
19. Remove the flat washer and spring.

20. Remove two bolts, then pull the retainer, selector levers and bracket from the shaft.
21. Drive the short selector lever pin from the shaft.
22. Drive the long trunnion pin from the shaft and remove the trunnion and shaft.
23. Remove the shifter levers from the cam and shafts.
24. Remove the roll pin from the upper fork shaft and remove the shaft and forks.
25. Remove the reverse cam and shaft.
26. Rotate the reverse fork and shaft assembly to disengage the detent ball, then remove the fork and shaft.
27. Remove the first-second and third-fourth shift cam assemblies.
28. Push the interlock sleeve, spring and remaining ball out of the cover.
29. Remove first-second and third-fourth to reverse interlock pins from the reverse fork and shaft bosses in the cover.

Assembly

1. Place the first-second and third-fourth-to-reverse interlock pins in

the holes in the reverse fork and shaft bosses.
2. Install the third-fourth shift cam into the cover.
3. Install the parts of the first-second to third-fourth cam interlock, sleeve, ball, spring and another ball, in that order.
4. Hold the third-fourth ball in neutral and the first-second ball depressed while the first-second cam is installed in the cover.
5. Install the first-second and the third-fourth levers, washers, and nuts.
6. Check clearance between the interlock, detent sleeve and the first-second and third-fourth shift cams in, and between, all shift positions. Sleeve to cam clearance must be 0.0005 to 0.010 in. Various length service sleeves are available.
7. With the first-second and third-fourth shift cams in neutral and the third-fourth-to-reverse interlock pin resting on the cams, install the reverse shaft detent spring and ball and the reverse fork and shaft.
8. Install the reverse shift cam through the cover and into the

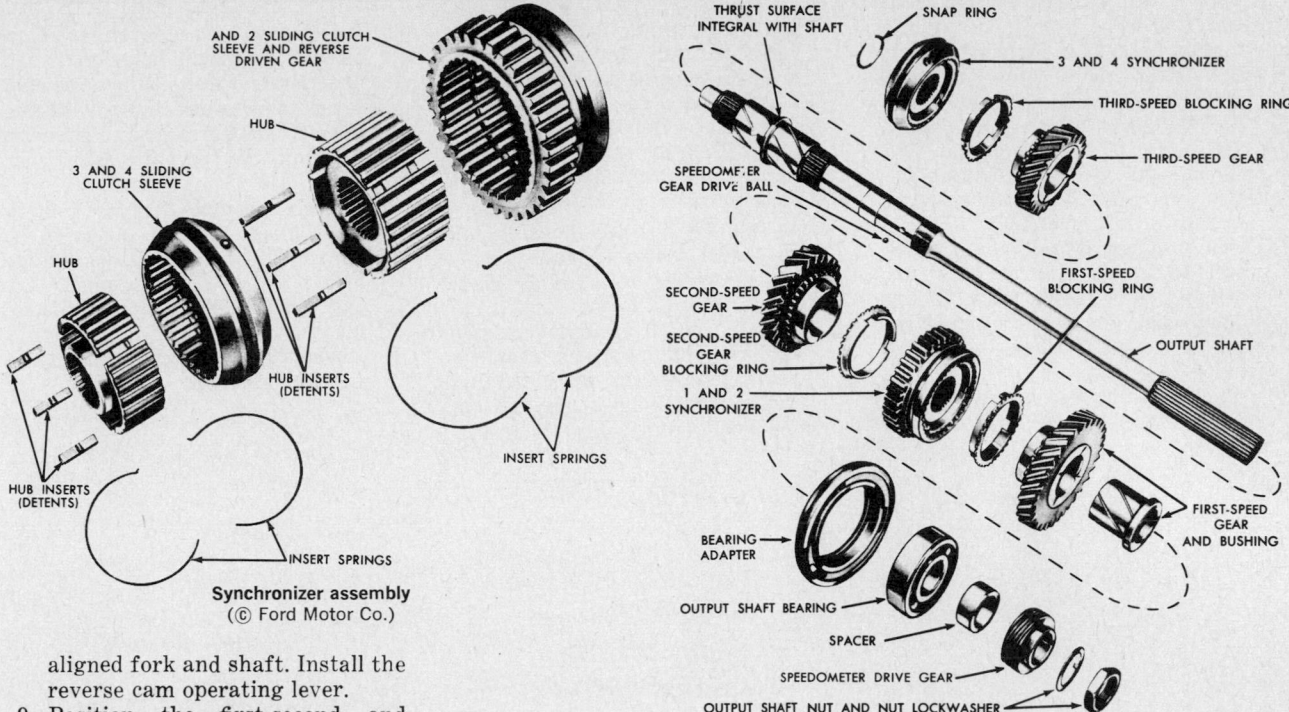

Synchronizer assembly
(© Ford Motor Co.)

Output shaft
(© Ford Motor Co.)

aligned fork and shaft. Install the reverse cam operating lever.

9. Position the first-second and third-fourth forks onto the shift cams and install the fork shaft. Align the shaft hole with the one in the cover and install the lock-pin.

10. Check all positions for freedom of operation and detent action.

11. In assembling the transmission, place the long detent inserts into the slots in the first-second synchronizer hub and slide the combination sleeve and reverse gear over it, being sure that the scribe marks are aligned. Snap the insert springs into place. The tab on each spring must set into the under-side of an insert.

12. Position the short inserts into the slots in the third-fourth synchronizer hub and slide the clutch sleeve over it, being sure that the scribe marks are aligned. Install the insert springs in the same way as with the first-second synchronizer.

13. Place the second gear on the rear of the output shaft with the clutch teeth and tapered synchronizer end toward the rear. Install a blocking ring with the clutch teeth toward the front.

14. Install the first and second synchronizer and reverse gear assembly on the rear of the output shaft with the shift fork groove to the rear.

15. Install the first-speed blocking ring with the clutch teeth to the rear and the slots engaging the synchronizer inserts.

16. Slide the first gear and sleeve onto the output shaft, taper and clutch teeth to the front, and the sleeve shoulder to the rear.

17. Assemble the output shaft ball

bearing into the recess in the bearing adapter. Position the adapter and bearing on the rear of the output shaft, with the adapter forward. Hold the first gear and sleeve (bushing) forward and place the assembly in a press with the tool applied to the bearing inner race. Press the bearing on until it is firmly against the first gear sleeve.

18. Place the spacer, speedometer gear drive ball, speedometer gear, lock and nut on the output shaft. Torque nut to 80 ft. lbs., then loosen. Torque the nut to 20-25 ft. lbs. and bend over the flat lockwasher.

19. Set the third-speed gear on the front of the output shaft, with the clutch teeth toward the front. Place a blocking ring on the rear.

20. Install the third-fourth synchronizer with the wide thrust surface of the hub toward the rear. Align the blocking ring slots with the synchronizer inserts.

21. Install the snap-ring into its groove on the front of the output shaft.

22. Place a dummy shaft in the countershaft gear cluster. Starting at either end, drop a steel washer over the shaft and into the gear. Grease each bearing roller and install 22 of them into the gear. Lay another steel washer on the ends of the needles and the thrust washers.

23. Repeat the above operation for the other end of the gear.

24. Position the cluster gear in the case with the two thrust washers

at the front. Allow the gear assembly to lie in the bottom of the case. Check gear end-play. It must be .004-.018 in. Correct by replacing thrust washers.

25. Press the input bearing onto the input shaft, with the outer race ring groove toward the front.

26. Install snap-rings onto the bearing outer race and the gear shaft.

27. Using grease, install 17 bearing rollers into the bore of the input gear.

28. Install input gear assembly. Place the fourth gear blocking ring on the rear of the input gear, with the clutch teeth forward.

29. Enter the output shaft assembly through the rear of the case and guide the output shaft front pilot into the input gear bore and bearings. Be sure that the fourth gear synchronizer blocking ring slots index with the inserts on the third-fourth synchronizer assembly.

30. Raise the countershaft gear until the countershaft can be inserted from the rear of the case into the gear and bearings. Push on the shaft until it contacts the front of the case. Position the flat on the rear of the countershaft on a horizontal plane so it will align with the slot in the extension housing; tap the shaft into place.

31. Install the reverse idler gear with the fork groove toward the rear and the idler shaft flat horizontal and parallel with the countershaft flat.

32. Position a new gasket to the rear of the case using non-drying-

33. Install extension housing. Align the dowel and be sure that the housing is seated squarely on the case before tightening the attaching bolts. If two long and two short bolts are used, install the two long bolts in the upper right and lower left holes.
34. Using sealer, install new gasket on the input shaft bearing retainer. With drain slot facing downward, install the bearing retainer. Seal and torque the bolts to 12-15 ft. lb.
35. Place the first-second and third-fourth synchronizer in neutral

and the reverse idler gear in reverse position. Set reverse shift lever in reverse position. Install a new shift cover gasket onto the case with sealer. Install the shift cover. With sealer-coated threads, torque the shift cover attaching bolts to 12-15 ft. lbs.
36. Install the flywheel housing and with seal coated threads, torque the attaching bolts to 40-45 ft. lbs.
37. Install clutch release bearing onto the clutch release lever. Position the release lever through the housing from inside and clip the lever retainer onto its hook.

38. Install the shift selector assembly on the extension housing.
39. Insert the shift rods into the cam levers and secure them with the spring washers and fasteners. Tighten the reverse cam lever nut.
40. Loosely assemble the shift rods to the linkage levers. Insert a ¼ in. rod through the three linkage levers and into the support. Adjust linkage, then remove the ¼ in. rod.
41. Assemble the shield over the shift selector assembly.

Type-8
Ford (Pinto) 4-Speed

Application

Pinto, 1971-72
Maverick, 1970-72

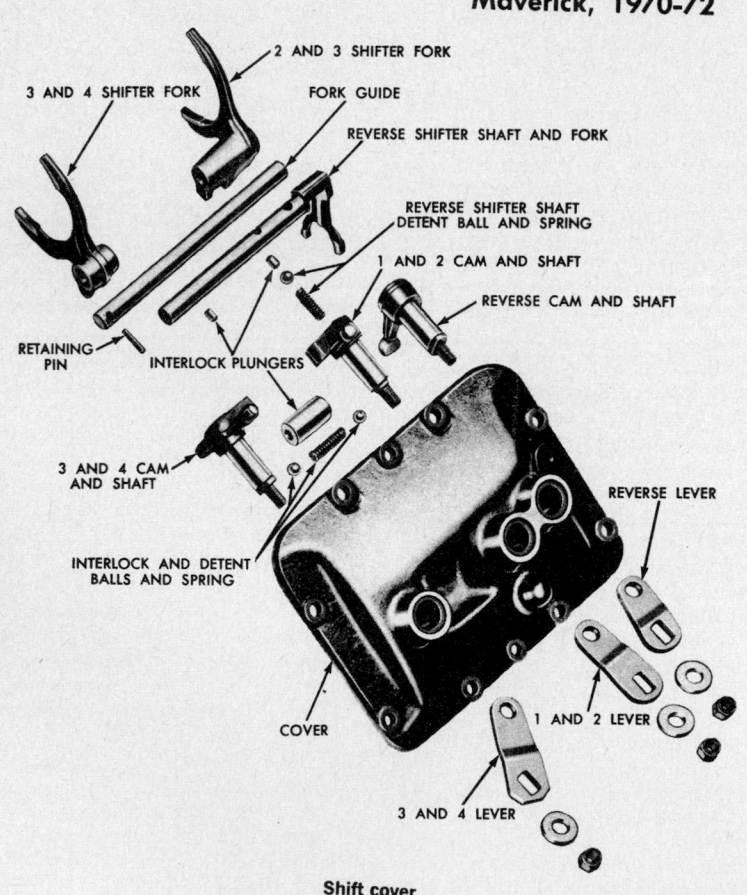

Shift cover
(© Ford Motor Co.)

Transmission Disassembly

1. Remove the clutch release bearing and detach the clutch or converter housing.
2. Drain the lubricant and remove the cover and gasket from the case.
3. Remove the threaded plug,

spring and shift rail detent plunger from the front of the case.
4. Drive the access plug from the rear of the case. Drive the interlock retaining pin from the case and remove the interlock plate.
5. Remove the roll pin from the selector lever arm.

6. Tap the front end of the shift rail, to displace the plug at the rear of the extension housing.
7. Remove the selector arm and shift fork from the case.
8. Loosen the extension housing and rotate the housing to align the countershaft with the cutaway in the extension housing flange.
9. Drive the countershaft rearward until the shaft clears the front of the case. Install a dummy shaft in the case and gear until the countershaft gear can be lowered to the bottom of the case. Remove the countershaft.
10. Lift the extension housing and mainshaft from the case as an assembly.
11. Remove the input shaft and bearing retainer from the case as an assembly.
12. Remove the reverse idler gear and shaft from the rear of the case.
13. Remove the bearing retainers, bearings (19 each end), dummy shaft and spacer from the countershaft gear.
14. Remove the pilot bearing and bearing retainer from the input shaft gear.
15. Do not remove the ball bearing from the input shaft unless replacement is necessary.
16. Pry the input shaft seal out of the bearing retainer.
17. Lift the fourth gear blocker ring from the front of the output shaft.
18. Remove the snap-ring from the forward end of the output shaft.
19. Support third gear on press plates and place the output shaft and extension housing in a press. Press the output shaft out

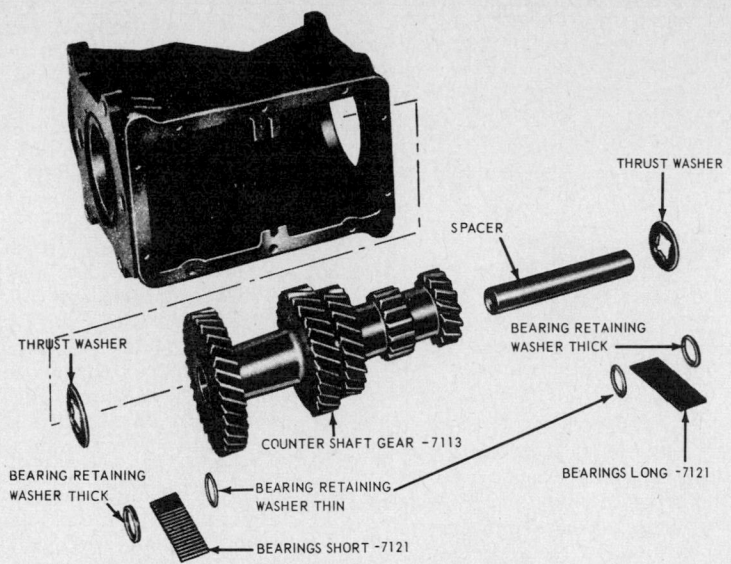

Installing speedometer driven gear
(© Ford Motor Co.)

Countershaft gear disassembled (© Ford Motor Co.)

of the third-fourth speed synchronizer and third gear, while supporting the extension housing and output shaft from beneath. Remove the snap-ring and washer and remove second gear and the blocker ring from the output shaft.

20. Disassemble the synchronizer assembly by pulling the sleeve from the hub and removing the inserts and spring.

21. Remove the snap-ring which retains the output shaft bearing to the extension housing.

22. Use a plastic hammer and tap the output shaft assembly from the extension housing.

23. Position press plates behind first gear and place the assembly in a press. The first and second speed synchronizer are serviced as an assembly. No attempt should be made to separate the hub from the shaft. The only serviceable parts are the springs and inserts. If the hub or sleeve is worn, the shaft and synchronizer must be replaced as an assembly.

24. Drive the shift rail bushing from the rear of the extension

housing, using a 9/16 in. socket. Do not remove serviceable bushings.

25. Pry the shift rail seal from the rear of the case.

26. Remove the remaining shaft linkage from the case.

Transmission Assembly

1. Install a new shift rail seal in the rear of the case.

2. If the shift rail bushing was removed, drive a new one into position with a 9/16 in. socket.

3. Slide the synchronizer hub over the shaft, making sure that the shift fork groove is toward the front of the shaft. The sleeve and hub are select fit and must be assembled with the etch marks in the same relative locations. Locate an insert in each of three slots in the hub. Oil all parts, and install an insert spring inside the sleeve. The spring tab must locate in a section of an insert. Fit the other spring to the opposite face, making sure that the tab locates in the same insert. Both springs should be in the same rotational direction. The tab end of one

spring should be aligned with the tab of the spring on the opposite side.

4. Assemble a blocker ring on the first gear side of the first-second synchronizer. Lubricate the cone surface of first gear and slide the cone onto the output shaft, so that the cone surface engages the blocker ring.

5. Position the spacer on the output shaft, larger diameter rearward.

6. Install a snap-ring (selected from the chart) which will come closest to removing all end-play from the output shaft bearing. Position the output shaft bearing on the shaft and press the bearing into place. Secure the bearing with the thickest snapring that will fit the groove.

Part No.	Thickness Identification
D1FZ-7030-A	0.0679- Color Coded—Copper
D1FZ-7030-B	0.0689- Letter—W
D1FZ-7030-C	0.0699- Letter-V
D1FZ-7030-D	0.0709- Letter—U
D1FZ-7030-E	0.0719- None
D1FZ-7030-F	0.0728- Color Coded—Blue
D1FZ-7030-G	0.0738- Color Coded—Black
D1FZ-7030-H	0.0748- Color Coded—Brown

7. Slide the synchronizer over the hub and locate an insert in each of three slots in the sleeve. The sleeve and hub must be assembled with the etch marks in the

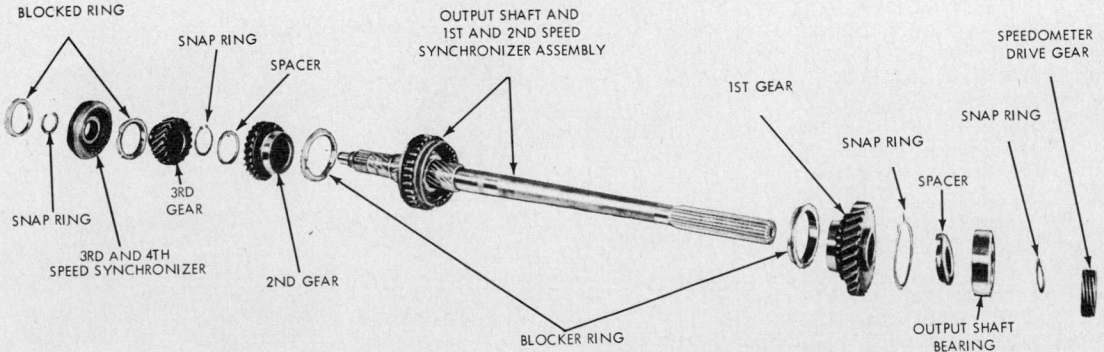

Output shaft disassembled (© Ford Motor Co.)

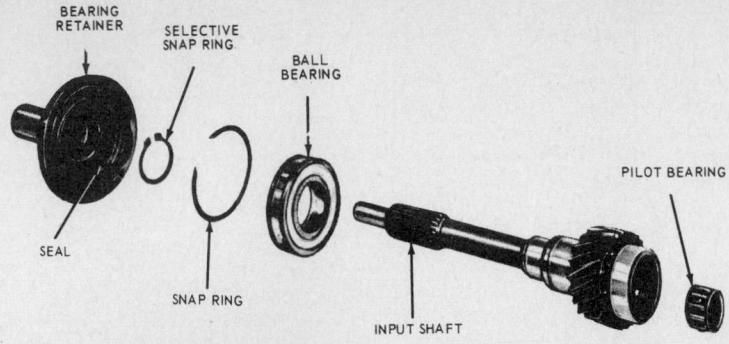

BEARING RETAINER / SELECTIVE SNAP RING / BALL BEARING / SEAL / SNAP RING / INPUT SHAFT / PILOT BEARING

Input shaft disassembled (© Ford Motor Co.)

same relative locations. Lightly oil all parts. Complete assembly of the synchronizer by following directions in previous Step 3.

8. Position second gear and the blocker ring on the output shaft, dog teeth facing rearward. Install the washer and snap-ring. Position third gear on the output shaft, dog teeth forward. Lubricate the gear cones and assemble a blocker ring on third gear cone.

9. Position the third-fourth synchronizer assembly on the output shaft, hub boss facing forward.

10. Install press plates against the boss on the synchronizer hub.

11. Place the entire unit in a press, extension end up, and press the synchronizer assembly onto the output shaft as far as possible.

12. Retain the third-fourth synchronizer assembly to the output shaft with a snap-ring. Pull up on the synchronizer so that the snap-ring is tight in the groove.

13. Lubricate the gear cone and place the blocker ring on the input shaft gear cone.

14. Using Tool T71P-17271-A, press the speedometer drive gear onto the shaft until the dowels of the tool just contact the bearing outer race.

15. Lubricate the bearing bore of the extension housing. Install the output shaft in the housing. It may be necessary to tap the shaft while holding the synchronizer sleeves firmly. Secure the shaft to the housing with the snap-ring previously installed.

16. Press the bearing on the input shaft. The snap-ring groove must be toward the front of the shaft. Use the thickest snap-ring that will fit.

17. Slide the spacer and dummy shaft into the countershaft gear. Position a thin bearing retaining washer on each end of the dummy shaft. Lubricate the roller bearings and load 19 long bearings in the small end of the gear and 19 short bearings in

the long end of the gear. Place a thick retaining washer over each end of the dummy shaft. Grease the thrust washers and place one on each end of the dummy shaft. The tabs must be in the same relative position to engage the slots in the case when the gear is lowered. Loop a piece of rope around each end of the gear and carefully install the gear and rope through the rear of the case. Lower the gear in place.

18. Lubricate the reverse idler gear shaft. Position the selector lever relay on the pivot pin. Secure with a spring clip. Hold the gear in the lever, long hub toward the rear of the case, and slide the reverse idler shaft into place. Seat the shaft in the case with a brass hammer.

19. Install a new seal in the bearing retainer.

20. Carefully slide third-fourth synchronizer sleeve into fourth speed position.

21. Place a new gasket on the extension housing.

22. Lubricate and install the input shaft pilot bearing on the shaft. Slide the extension housing and output shaft into place, being careful not to disturb the fourth speed synchronizer.

23. Align the cutaway in the extension housing flange with the countershaft bore in the rear of the case.

24. Lift the countershaft gear into place and install the countershaft, making sure that the thrust washers remain in place. The flat on the countershaft should be parallel to the top of the case. Tap the shaft with a brass hammer until the front of the shaft is flush with the case.

25. Place the shift forks in the synchronizer sleeves. Install the interlock lever and new retaining pin. Lubricate the shift rail oil seal and slide the shift rail through the extension housing, case and second and first speed shift forks. Position the selector arm on the rail and slide the rail through third and fourth speed shift fork. Slide the shift rail through the front of the case until the center detent bore is aligned with the detent plunger bore. Install a new retaining pin in the selector arm.

26. Install the detent plunger, spring and plug.

27. Install a new access plug in the rear of the case.

28. Align the extension housing and install the bolts finger-tight. Be sure the shift rail slides freely. Tighten the bolts.

29. Position a new oil seal with tension spring and lip facing in the direction of the case.

30. Drive the seal in until it bottoms.

31. Position a new O-ring in the groove in the case. Position the input shaft bearing retainer with the groove in the retainer aligned with the oil passage in the case. Install the retaining bolts finger-tight.

32. Install the flywheel housing and tighten the retaining bolts and the front bearing retainer attaching bolts.

33. Install the clutch release arm and bearing.

34. Install a new extension housing plug.

35. Install a new cover gasket and cover.

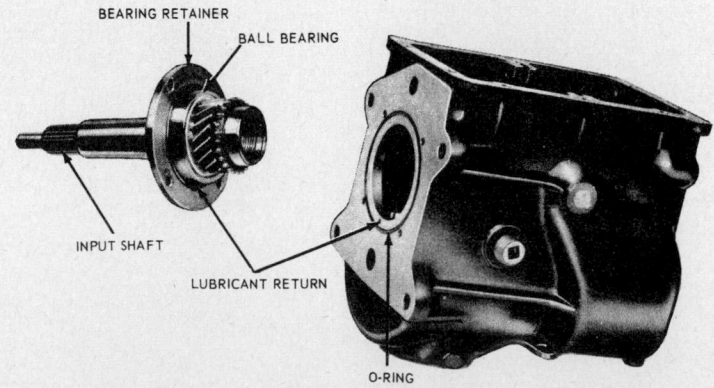

BEARING RETAINER / BALL BEARING / INPUT SHAFT / LUBRICANT RETURN / O-RING

Installing input shaft gear (© Ford Motor Co.)

Type-9
Ford 4-Speed

Application

Comet V8, 1965-70
Cougar, 1967-72
Fairlane V8, 1965-72

Falcon V8, 1965-70
Ford, 1965-72
Mercury, 1965-70

Montego, 1968-72
Mustang V8, 1965-72

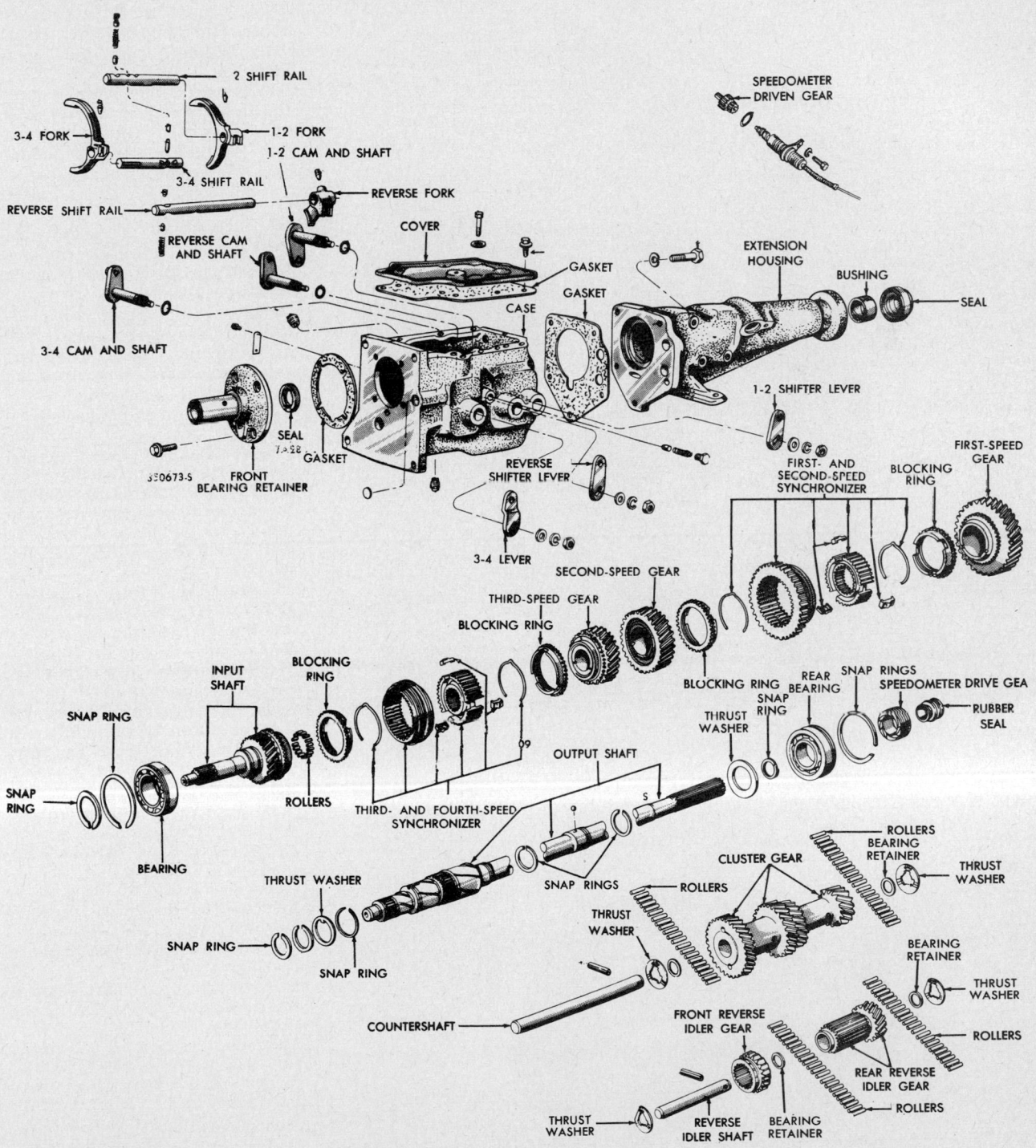

Ford 4-speed transmission (© Ford Motor Co.)

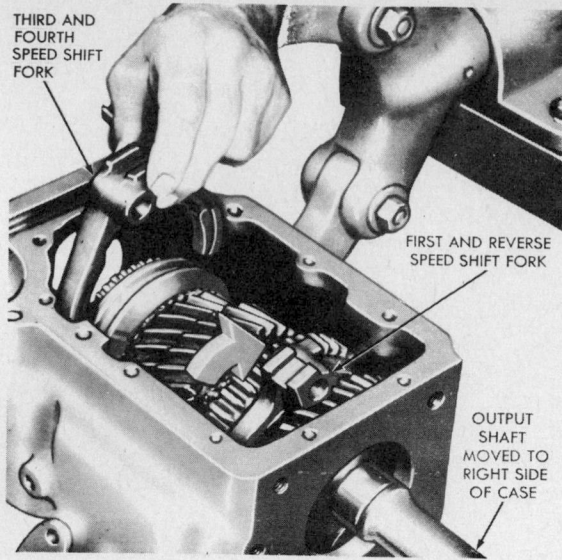

THIRD AND FOURTH SPEED SHIFT FORK

FIRST AND REVERSE SPEED SHIFT FORK

OUTPUT SHAFT MOVED TO RIGHT SIDE OF CASE

Removing shift forks (© Ford Motor Co.)

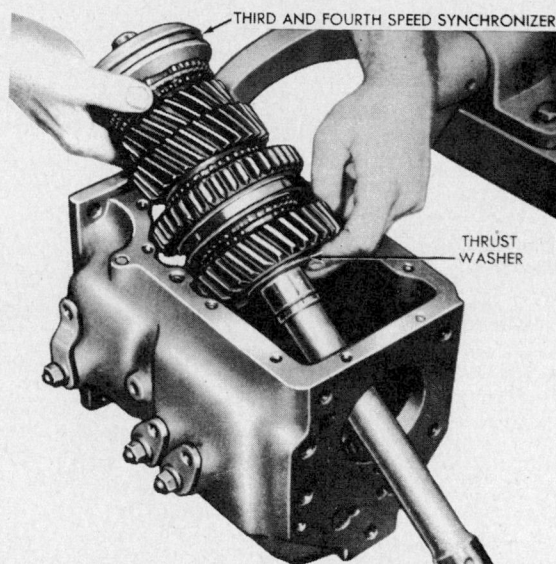

THIRD AND FOURTH SPEED SYNCHRONIZER

THRUST WASHER

Removing output shaft (© Ford Motor Co.)

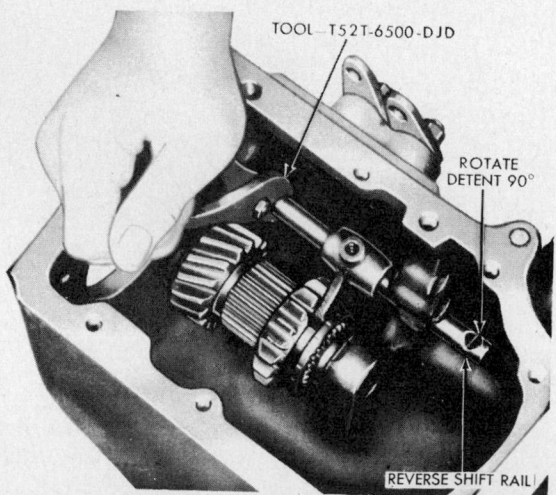

TOOL T52T-6500-DJD

ROTATE DETENT 90°

REVERSE SHIFT RAIL

Rotating the reverse shift rail (© Ford Motor Co.)

Disassembly

1. Remove retaining clips and flat washers from the shift rods at the levers.
2. Remove shift linkage control bracket attaching screws and remove shift linkage and control bracket.
3. Remove cover attaching screws. Then lift cover and gasket from the case.
4. Remove extension housing attaching screws. Then, remove extension housing and gasket.
5. Remove input shaft bearing retainer attaching screws. Then, slide retainer from the input shaft.
6. Working a dummy shaft in from the front of the case, drive the countershaft out the rear of the case. Let the countergear assembly lie in the bottom of the case.

7. Locate first - second - speed gear shift lever in neutral. Locate third fourth-speed gear shift lever in third-speed position.
8. Remove the lockbolt that holds the third-fourth-speed shift rail detent spring and plug the left side of the case. Remove spring and plug with a magnet.
9. Remove the detent mechanism set screw from top of case. Then, remove the detent spring and plug with a small magnet.
10. Remove attaching screw from the third-fourth-speed shift fork. Tap lightly on the inner end of the shift rail to remove the expansion plug from front of case. Then, withdraw the third-fourth-speed shift rail from the front. (Do not lose the interlock pin from rail.)
11. Remove attaching screw from the first and second-speed shift fork. Slide the first-second shift rail from the rear of case.
12. Remove the interlock and detent plugs from the top of the case with a magnet.
13. Remove the snap-ring or disengage retainer that holds the speedometer drive gear to the output shaft. Slide the gear from the shaft, then remove speedometer gear drive ball.
14. Remove the snap-ring used to hold the output shaft bearing to the shaft. Remove output shaft bearing.
15. Remove the input shaft bearing and blocking ring from the front of the case.
16. Move output shaft to the right side of case. Then, maneuver the forks to permit lifting them from the case.
17. Support first-speed gear to prevent it sliding from the shaft, then lift output shaft from the case.

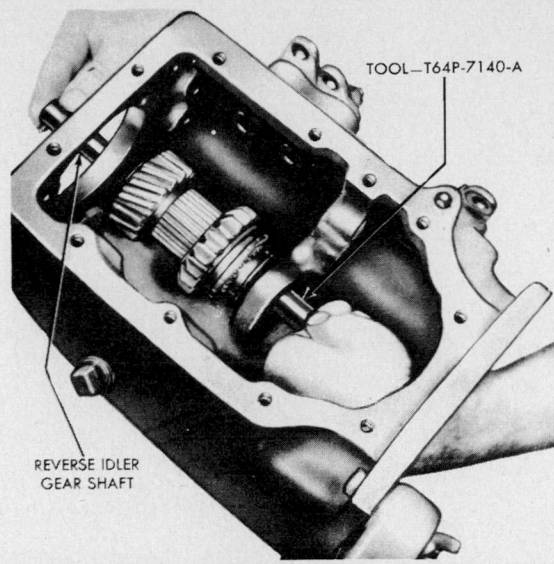

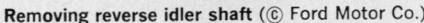

REVERSE IDLER
GEAR SHAFT

TOOL—T64P-7140-A

Removing reverse idler shaft (© Ford Motor Co.)

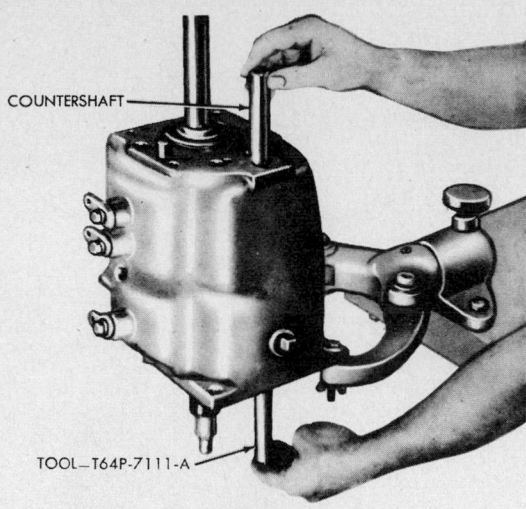

COUNTERSHAFT

TOOL—T64P-7111-A

Installing countershaft (© Ford Motor Co.)

18. Remove reverse gear shift fork attaching screw. Rotate the reverse shift rail 90°, then, slide the shift rail out the rear of the case. Lift out the reverse shift fork.

19. Remove the reverse detent plug and spring from the case with a magnet.

20. Using a dummy shaft, remove the reverse idler shaft from the case.

21. Lift reverse idler gear and thrust washers from the case. Be careful not to drop the bearing rollers or the dummy from the gear.

22. Lift the countergear, thrust washers, rollers and dummy shaft assembly from the case.

23. Remove the snap-ring from the front of the output shaft. Then, slide the third-fourth synchronizer blocking ring and the third-speed gear from the shaft.

24. Remove the next snap-ring and the second-speed gear thrust washer from the shaft. Slide the second-speed gear and the blocking ring from the shaft.

25. Remove the snap-ring, then slide the first-second synchronizer, blocking ring and the first-speed gear from the shaft.

26. Remove the thrust washer from rear of the shaft.

Unit Repairs

Cam and Shaft Seals

1. Remove attaching nut and washers from each shift lever, then remove the three levers.

2. Remove the three cams and shafts from inside the case.

3. Replace the old O-rings with new ones that have been well-lubricated.

4. Slide each cam and shaft into its respective bore in the transmission.

5. Install the levers and secure them with their respective washers and nuts.

Input Shaft Bearing

1. Remove the snap-ring that holds the bearing to the shaft.

2. Press the shaft gear from the bearing.

3. Press a new bearing onto the input shaft.

4. Secure the bearing with a snap-ring.

Synchronizers

1. Push the synchronizer hub from each synchronizer sleeve.

2. Separate the inserts and springs from the hubs. Do not mix parts of the first-second with parts of third-fourth synchronizers.

3. To assemble, position the hub in the sleeve. Be sure the alignment marks are properly indexed.

4. Place the three inserts into place on the hub. Install the insert springs so that the irregular surface (hump) is seated in one of the inserts. Do not stagger the springs.

Countershaft Gear

1. Dismantle the countershaft gear assembly.

2. Assemble the gear by coating each end of the countershaft gear bore with grease.

3. Install dummy shaft in the gear. Then install 21 bearing rollers and a retainer washer in each end of the gear.

Reverse Idler Gear

1. Dismantle reverse idler gear.

2. Assemble reverse idler gear by coating the bore in each end of reverse idler gear with grease.

3. Hold the dummy shaft in the gear and install the 22 bearing rollers and the retainer washer into each end of the gear.

4. Install the reverse idler sliding gear on the splines of the reverse idler gear. Be sure the shift fork groove is toward the front.

Input Shaft Seal

1. Remove the seal from the input shaft bearing retainer.

2. Coat the sealing surface of a new seal with lubricant, then press the new seal into the input shaft bearing retainer.

Assembly

1. Grease the countershaft gear thrust surfaces in the case. Then, position a thrust washer at each end of the case.

2. Position the countershaft gear, dummy shaft, and roller bearings in the case.

3. Align the gear bore and thrust washers with the bores in the case. Install the countershaft.

4. With the case in a horizontal position, countershaft gear end-play should be from .004-.018 in. Use thrust washers to obtain play within these limits.

5. After establishing correct end-play, place the dummy shaft in the countershaft gear and allow the gear assembly to remain on the bottom of the case.

6. Grease the reverse idler gear thrust surfaces in the case, and position the two thrust washers.

7. Position the reverse idler gear, sliding gear, dummy, etc. in place. Make sure that the shift fork groove in the sliding gear is toward the front.

8. Align the gear bore and thrust washers with the case bores and install the reverse idler shaft.

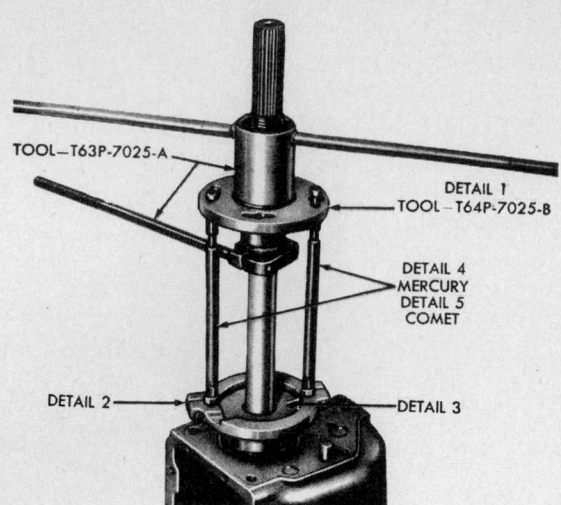

TOOL—T63P-7025-A

DETAIL 1
TOOL—T64P-7025-B

DETAIL 4
MERCURY
DETAIL 5
COMET

DETAIL 2

DETAIL 3

Installing output shaft bearing (© Ford Motor Co.)

9. Reverse idler gear end - play should be .004-.018 in. Use selective thrust washers to obtain play within these limits.

10. Position reverse gear shift rail detent spring and detent plug in the case. Hold the reverse shift fork in place on the reverse idler sliding gear and install the shift rail from the rear of the case. Lock the fork to the rail with the Allen head set screws.

11. Install the first-second synchronizer onto the output shaft. The first and reverse synchronizer hub are a press fit and should be installed with gear teeth facing the rear of the shaft.

12. Slide second-speed gear onto the front of the shaft with the synchronizer coned surface toward the rear.

13. Install the second-speed gear thrust washer and snap-ring.

14. Slide the third-speed gear onto the shaft with the synchronizer coned surface front.

15. Coat the cone of third-speed gear with grease. Place a blocking ring on the third-speed gear.

16. Slide the third-fourth speed gear synchronizer onto the shaft. Be sure that the inserts in the synchronizer engage the notches in the blocking ring. Install the snap-ring onto the front of the output shaft.

17. Coat the cone of second-speed gear with grease and position the blocking ring on the gear.

18. Slide the first-second speed synchronizer onto the rear of the output shaft. Be sure that the inserts engage the notches in the blocking ring and that the shift fork groove is toward the rear.

19. Coat the coned surface of first-speed gear with grease and position the blocking ring on it.

20. Slide the first-speed gear onto the rear of the output shaft. Be sure that the notches in the blocker ring engage the synchronizer inserts.

21. Install heavy thrust washer onto the rear of the output shaft.

22. Lower the output shaft assembly into the case.

23. Position the first-second speed shift fork and the third-fourth-speed shift fork in place on their respective gears. Rotate them into place.

24. Place a detent plug in the detent bore. Place the reverse shift rail into neutral position.

25. Coat the third-fourth-speed shift rail interlock pin with grease, then position it in the shift rail.

26. Align the third-fourth-speed shift fork with the shift rail bores and slide the shift rail into place. Be sure that the three detents are

facing the outside of the case. Place the front synchronizer into third-fourth-speed position and install the set screw into the third - fourth - speed shift fork. Move the synchronizer to neutral position. Install the third-fourth-speed shift rail detent plug, spring and bolt into the left side of the transmission case. Place the interlock plug (tapered ends) in the detent bore.

27. Align first-second-speed shift fork with the case bores and slide the shift rail into place. Lock the fork with the set screw. Install the detent plug and spring into the detent bore. Thread the set screw into the case until the head is flush with the case.

28. Coat the input gear bore with a small amount of grease. Then install the 15 bearing rollers.

29. Place the input shaft gear in the case. Be sure that the output shaft pilot enters the roller bearing of the input shaft gear.

30. With a new gasket on the input bearing retainer, dip attaching bolts in sealer, install bolts and torque to 30-36 ft. lbs.

31. Install the output shaft bearing, then install the snap-ring to hold the bearing.

32. Position the speedometer gear drive ball in the output shaft and slide the speedometer drive gear into place. Secure gear with snapring.

33. Align the countershaft gear bore and thrust washers with the bore in the case. Install the countershaft.

34. With a new gasket in place, install and secure the extension housing. Dip the extension housing screws in sealer, then torque screws to 42-50 ft. lbs.

35. Install the filler plug (torque 10-20 ft. lbs.) and the drain plug (torque 20-30 ft. lbs.), the drain plug is magnetic.

36. Pour in four pints of mild E.P. gear oil over the entire gear train while rotating the input shaft.

37. Place each shift fork in all positions to make sure they function properly.

38. With a new cover gasket in place, install the cover. Dip attaching screws in sealer, then torque screws to 14-19 ft. lbs.

39. Coat the third-fourth speed shift rail plug bore with sealer. Install a new plug.

40. Secure each shift rod to its respective lever with a spring washer, flat washer and retaining pin.

41. Position the shift linkage control bracket to the extension housing. Install and torque the attaching screws to 12-15 ft. lbs.

Type-10
Muncie 3-Speed

Application

Buick Le Sabre, 1965
Buick Special, 1965
   (Except Skyroof Wagon and G.S.)

Chevrolet, 1965
Chevelle, 1965
Chevy II, 1965

Corvette, 1965
Oldsmobile Jetstar 88, 1965
Olds F-85, 1965
Tempest, 1965

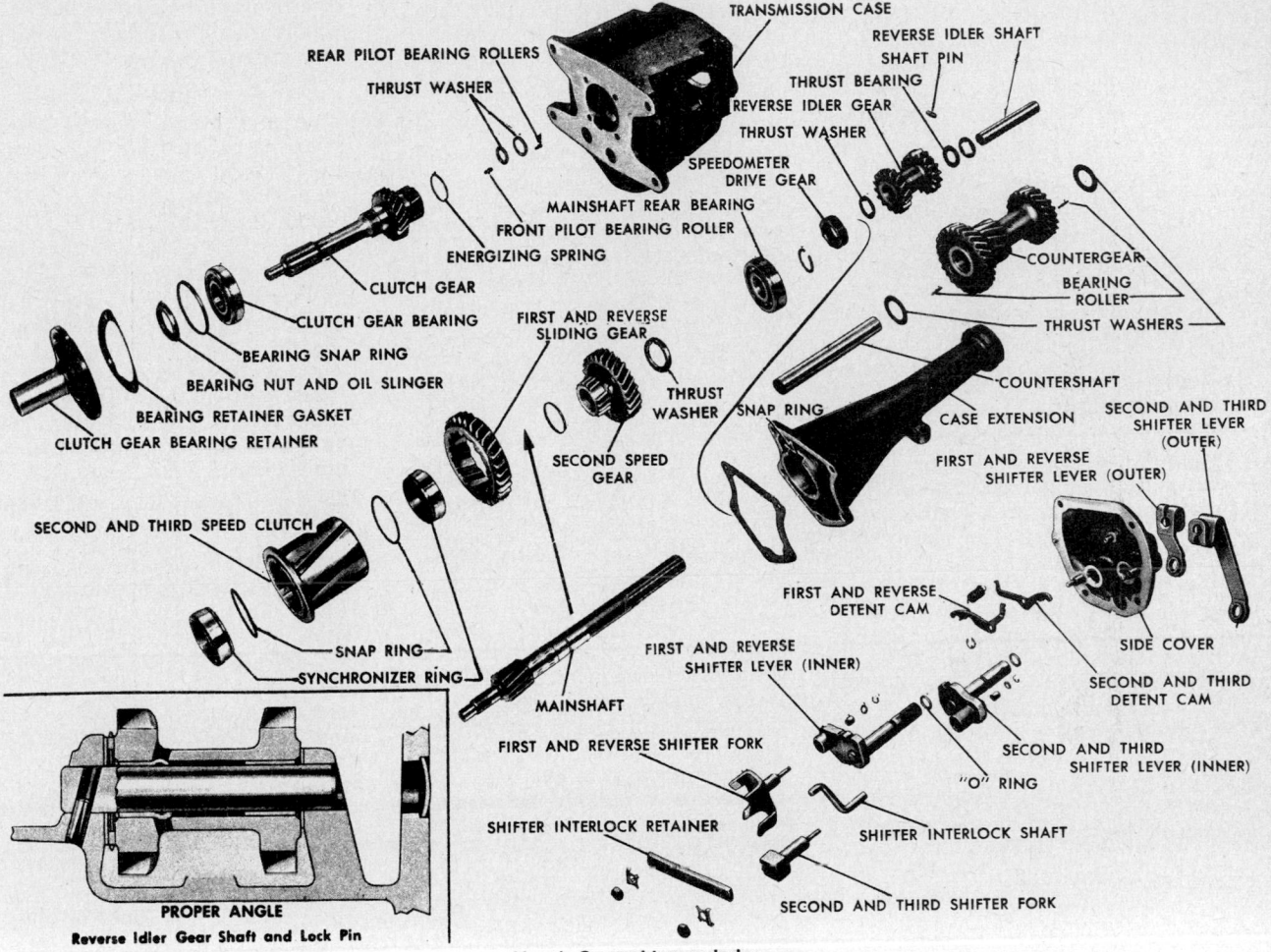

Muncie 3-speed transmission
(© G.M. Corp.)

Disassembly

1. Remove bolts from the transmission side cover and remove the cover and gasket.
2. Remove rear extension attaching bolts and pull extension and mainshaft assembly out of the transmission case, leaving second- and third-speed clutch and first and reverse sliding gear in the case.
3. Slide first and reverse gear from synchronizing clutch sleeve, then remove them separately through side opening in transmission case.
4. Remove 24 rear and 14 larger front pilot bearing rollers from inside the main drive (clutch) gear.

5. Remove four clutch gear bearing retainer bolts and washers and remove the retainer.
6. Remove the countershaft by driving it from front to rear, using a dummy shaft. Lower the countergear to the bottom of the case.
7. Remove the clutch gear bearing snap-ring. Tap end of shaft to move gear and bearing assembly into case and remove through side of case.
8. Remove the counter gear with dummy, 50 rollers, and washers intact, from the case.
9. Drive the reverse idler shaft lock-pin into the shaft. The pin is shorter than the diameter of the

shaft.
10. With a drift, tap rear of reverse idler shaft to drive out plug ahead of the shaft.
11. Remove reverse idler gear, front thrust washer, radial roller thrust bearing and the rear thrust washer.
12. To remove the mainshaft from the extension, remove the speedometer driven gear from side of extension. Expand and remove bearing snap-ring. Tap rear of shaft with a soft hammer to bring shaft, speedometer drive gear, second-speed gear and bearing as an assembly, forward and out of the extension.

Servicing the Mainshaft

1. Press speedometer drive gear off the main shaft.
2. Remove rear bearing - to - main shaft snap-ring and press bearing off shaft.
3. Remove second-speed gear thrust washer and second-speed gear.
4. Replace necessary parts and reassemble as follows.
   a. Slide second-speed gear on the shaft and install thrust washer with oil grooves toward the gear.
   b. Install new rear bearing, groove in outside of bearing toward second-speed gear.
   c. Select one of four available snap-rings so that end-play of bearing on shaft does not exceed .004 in.
   d. Start the speedometer drive gear on shaft with chamfered inside diameter of gear toward the bearing. Press the gear on the shaft until forward face of gear is 53/64 in. from the rear face of bearing.

Servicing the Clutch Gear

1. With clutch gear in a soft-jawed vise, remove bearing retaining nut and oil slinger. The nut and oil slinger is a one piece steel casting with a left-hand thread and is staked in place on the clutch gear shaft.
2. To remove the bearing from the clutch gear, up-end the front of the transmission case on the bench. Install the gear and bearing in the front of the case with the snap-ring on the bearing.
3. Press the shaft out of the bearing and into the case.
4. Tap the bearing out of the case.
5. Press clutch gear bearing onto the clutch gear. Be sure the bearing locating ring groove is toward the front of the shaft.
6. Install clutch bearing retaining nut, tighten and stake securely.

Servicing the Synchronizer

1. Turn one synchronizer ring in the clutch (sleeve) until the ends of the ring retainer can be seen through the slot in the clutch sleeve.
2. Using a snap-ring expander, spread the retainer in the counterbore in the clutch sleeve, then withdraw the synchronizer ring.
3. Remove the other synchronizer ring in the same manner.
4. Lightly grease both synchronizer rings.
5. Install a synchronizer ring retainer in the counterbore at one end of the clutch sleeve.

6. Insert ring expander through slot in clutch sleeve and expand retainer in counterbore. Install ring in clutch sleeve.
7. Install other synchronizer ring in the same manner.

Assembly

Transmission

1. Coat thrust washers and needle roller thrust bearing with grease.
2. Position the needle bearing against the rear of the gear (end with chamfered teeth) and position the large thrust washer against the bearing. Position small thrust washer at opposite end of gear.
3. From the rear of the case, install idler shaft, aligning lock pin hole in shaft with hole in case.
4. Position reverse idler gear in the case so the radial roller thrust bearing is toward the rear of the case and the gear is lined up with the shaft. Tap shaft from rear until lockpin holes are lined up.
5. Coat new idler shaft pin with sealer and drive it in about 1/16 in. Peen the hole slightly.
6. Install new idler shaft expansion plug in front of case.
7. Grease both ends of the counter-gear bore and insert the dummy shaft.
8. Install 25 bearing rollers at each end of countergear.
9. Grease the bearing thrust washers and countergear thrust washers and place bearing thrust washers, followed by countergear thrust washers, at both ends of the countergear, making sure that the tangs on the countergear thrust washers face out.
10. Let the gear, dummy shaft and washer assembly lie in the bottom of the case.
11. From inside the case, push clutch gear assembly through opening in front face of case and tap clutch gear assembly until clutch gear bearing locating ring groove is outside front of case.
12. Install snap-ring in bearing groove and tap clutch gear toward the rear until snap-ring is firm against the face of the case.
13. Install clutch gear bearing retainer and gasket.
14. Apply sealer to threads of bearing retainer bolts and torque to 12—15 ft. lbs.
15. Lift the countershaft into place and alignment with the countershaft bore. Be sure that the thrust washers are in place.
16. Lubricate and start the countershaft into the case from the rear. Be sure the flat on the face of the shaft is horizontal and at the bottom to permit installation of case

extension.
17. Push countershaft in and dummy shaft out until the flat on the end of the countershaft is flush with the rear face of the case.
18. Grease and install 14 large rollers in the pilot hole of the main drive gear, then install small I.D. spacer.
19. Insert the large I.D. front spacer, followed by the 24 small rollers.
20. Insert the large I.D. rear spacer with chamfered side out.
21. Insert synchronizing clutch assembly, shoulder to front, through rear opening in case.
22. Line up two inner lugs of clutch sleeve synchronizing ring with two wide grooves in main drive gear and slide clutch assembly onto main drive gear.
23. Through side opening in the case, insert first and reverse sliding gear, with wide inner bevel and small round depression toward the rear. Pilot the first and reverse sliding gear onto the clutch.
24. Insert mainshaft assembly in the transmission case extension, and by spreading the mainshaft bearing snap-ring, tap front end of mainshaft until snap-ring seats in mainshaft bearing groove.
25. Install new extension housing gasket to transmission case.
26. Align clutch splines on the mainshaft with clutch splines on second-speed gear so that they will receive the two inner lugs of the synchronizer ring of second and third-speed clutch. Mark for identification.
27. Insert mainshaft assembly through opening at rear of transmission case. Be sure the two inner lugs of the synchronizing ring engage the previously marked grooves of mainshaft and second speed gear.
28. Rotate extension housing to line up with case and insert five extension housing bolts with sealer on them. Leave them finger-tight.
29. Set transmission assembly top side up. Maneuver second and third speed clutch until extension housing fits flush against transmission case. Torque attaching bolts to 40 to 45 ft. lbs.
30. Install speedometer driven gear, and side cover assembly.

Type-11
Muncie Fully Synchro-nized 3-Speed

Application

Camaro, 1969-72
Chevelle, 1969-72
Chevrolet, 1969-72
Chevy II, 1969-72

Firebird, 1970-72
GTO, 1970
Monte Carlo, 1971-72

Olds F-85, 4-4-2, 1970
Pontiac Grand Prix, 1970-72
Tempest, 1970-72

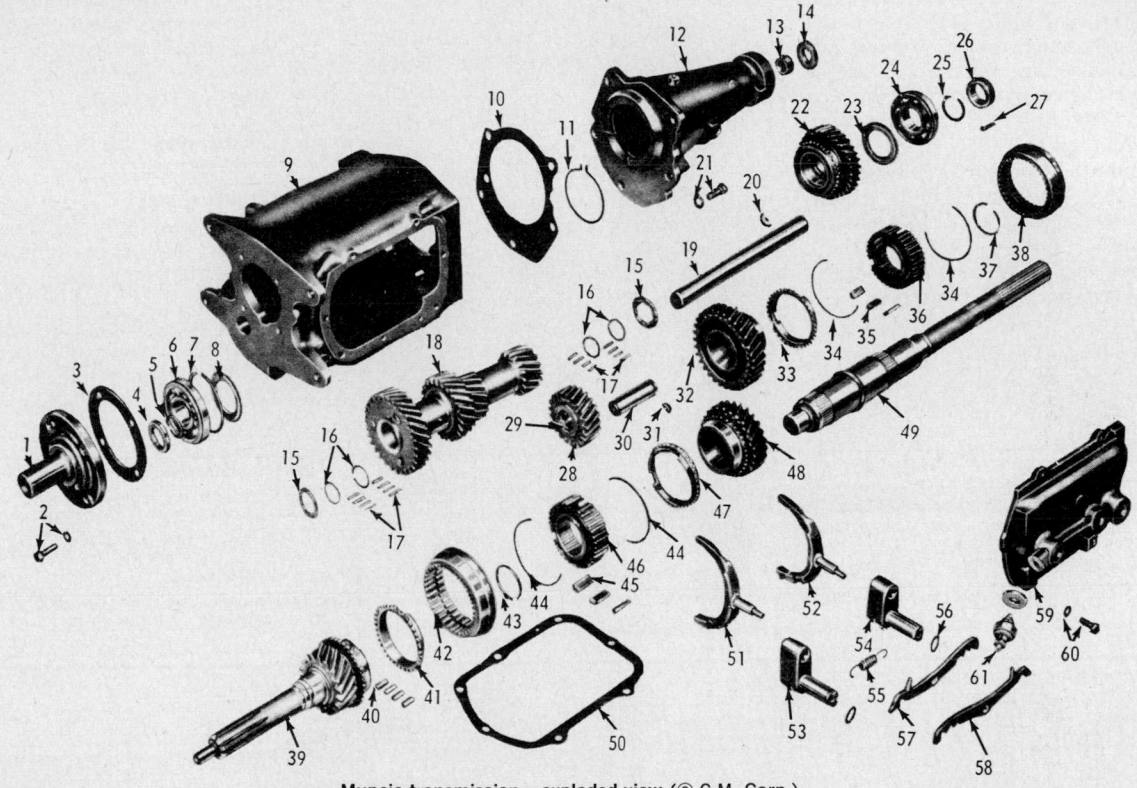

Muncie transmission—exploded view (© G.M. Corp.)

1 Bearing retainer	17 Needle bearings	35 Synchronizer keys	49 Mainshaft
2 Bolt and lock washer	18 Countergear	36 1st and reverse synchronizer	50 Gasket
3 Gasket	19 Countershaft	hub assembly	51 2nd and 3rd shifter fork
4 Oil seal	20 Woodruff key	37 Snap ring	52 1st and reverse shifter fork
5 Snap ring (bearing-to-main	21 Bolt (extension-to-case)	38 1st and reverse synchronizer	53 2-3 shifter shaft assembly
drive gear)	22 Reverse gear	collar	54 1st and reverse shifter
6 Main drive gear bearing	23 Thrust washer	39 Main drive gear	shaft assembly
7 Snap ring bearing	24 Rear bearing	40 Pilot bearings	55 Spring
8 Oil slinger	25 Snap ring	41 3rd speed blocker ring	56 O-ring seal
9 Case	26 Speedometer drive gear	42 2nd and 3rd synchronizer	57 1st and reverse detent cam
10 Gasket	27 Retainer clip	collar	58 2nd and 3rd detent cam
11 Snap ring (rear bearing-to-	28 Reverse idler gear	43 Snap ring	59 Side cover
extension)	29 Reverse idler bushing	44 Synchronizer key spring	60 Bolt and lock washer
12 Extension	30 Reverse idler shaft	45 Synchronizer keys	
13 Extension bushing	31 Woodruff key	46 2nd and 3rd synchronizer	
14 Oil seal	32 1st speed gear	hub	
15 Thrust washer	33 1st speed blocker ring	47 2nd speed blocker ring	
16 Bearing washer	34 Synchronizer key spring	48 2nd speed gear	

Transmission Disassembly

1. Remove side cover and shift forks.
2. Unbolt extension. Rotate extension to line up groove in extension flange with reverse idler shaft. Drive reverse idler shaft and key out of case with a brass drift.
3. Move second-third synchronizer sleeve forward. Remove extension housing and mainshaft assembly.
4. Remove reverse idler gear from case.
5. Remove third speed blocker ring from clutch gear.
6. Expand snap-ring which retains mainshaft rear bearing. Tap gently on end of mainshaft to remove extension.
7. Remove clutch gear bearing retainer and gasket.
8. Remove snap-ring. Remove clutch gear from inside case by gently tapping on end of clutch gear.
9. Remove oil slinger. Remove 16 mainshaft pilot bearings from clutch gear cavity.
10. Slip clutch gear bearing out front of case. Aid removal with

a screwdriver between case and bearing outer snap-ring.

11. Drive countershaft and key out to rear.

12. Remove countergear and two tanged thrust washers.

Mainshaft Disassembly

1. Depress speedometer drive gear retaining clip. Slide off gear. Some speedometer drive gears, made of metal, must be pulled off.
2. Remove rear bearing snap-ring.
3. Support reverse gear and press on rear of mainshaft to remove reverse gear, thrust washer, and rear bearing. Be careful not to cock the bearing on the shaft.
4. Remove first and reverse sliding clutch hub snap-ring.
5. Support first gear. Press on rear of mainshaft to remove clutch assembly, blocker ring, and first gear.
6. Remove second and third speed sliding clutch hub snap-ring.

2. Check faces for burrs. Remove with a fine file.
3. Check bearing bores for damage. If they are damaged, replace case.

Front and Rear Bearings

1. Do not spin bearings with air pressure; turn them slowly by hand.
2. Lubricate bearings with light oil. Turn slowly to check for roughness.

Bearing Rollers

1. Check for wear; replace if worn.
2. Check countershaft and reverse idler shaft.
3. Replace all worn washers.

Gears

1. Check for wear, chips, or cracks.
2. If reverse gear bushing is worn or damaged, replace entire gear.
3. Check to see that both clutch sleeves slide freely on their hubs.

Repair

Clutch Keys and Springs

Keys and springs may be replaced if worn or broken, but the hubs and sleeves must be kept together as originally assembled.

1. Mark hub and sleeve for reassembly.
2. Push hub from sleeve. Remove keys and springs.
3. Place three keys and two springs, one on each side of hub, so all three keys are engaged by both springs. The tanged end of the springs should not be installed into the same key.
4. Slide the sleeve onto the hub, aligning the marks.

Extension Oil Seal and Bushing

1. Remove seal.
2. Using bushing remover and installer, or other suitable tool, drive bushing into extension housing.
3. Drive new bushing in from rear. Lubricate inside of bushing and seal. Install new oil seal with extension seal installer or suitable tool.

Clutch Bearing Retainer Oil Seal

1. Pry old seal out.
2. Install new seal using seal installer or suitable tool. Seat seal in bore.

Mainshaft Assembly

1. Turn front of mainshaft up.

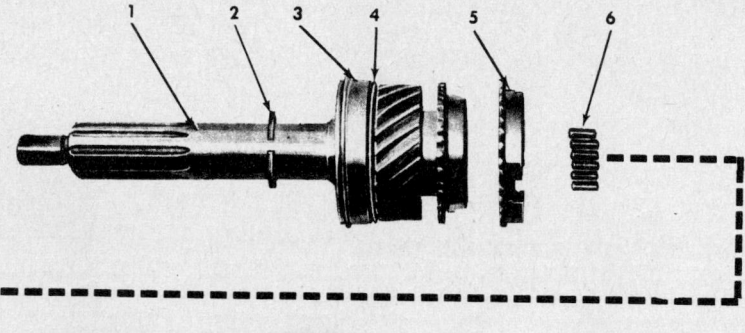

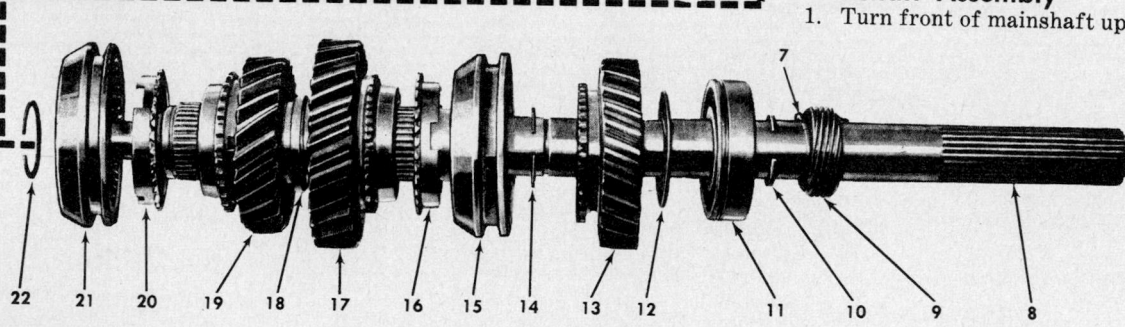

Clutch gear and mainshaft assembly (© G.M. Corp.)

1 Clutch gear	7 Retaining clip	13 Reverse gear	18 Shoulder (part of mainshaft)
2 Snap ring	8 Mainshaft	14 Snap ring	19 2nd speed gear
3 Clutch gear bearing	9 Speedo drive gear	15 1st speed synchronizer assembly	20 2nd speed blocker ring
4 Oil slinger	10 Snap ring		21 2-3 synchronizer assembly
5 3rd speed blocker ring	11 Rear bearing	16 1st speed blocker ring	22 Snap ring
6 Mainshaft pilot bearings (16)	12 Reverse gear thrust washer	17 1st speed gear	

7. Support second gear. Press on front of mainshaft to remove clutch assembly, second speed blocker ring, and second gear from shaft.

Inspection

1. Wash all parts in solvent.
2. Air dry.

Case

1. Check for cracks.

Reverse Idler Gear Bushing

This bushing may not be serviced separately. If the bushing requires replacement, replace the gear.

Countergear Anti-Lash Plate

1. Check the plate teeth for wear or damage.
2. Do not disassemble.

2. Install second gear with clutching teeth up; the rear face of the gear butts against the flange on the mainshaft.
3. Install a blocking ring with clutching teeth downward. All three blocking rings are the same.
4. Install second and third synchronizer assembly with fork slot down. Press it onto mainshaft splines. Both synchronizer

assemblies are identical but are assembled differently. The second-third speed hub and sleeve is assembled with the sleeve fork slot toward the thrust face of the hub; the first-reverse hub and sleeve, with the fork slot opposite the thrust face. Be sure that the blocker ring notches align with the synchronizer assembly keys.

5. Install synchronizer snap-ring. Both synchronizer snap-rings are the same.
6. Turn rear of shaft up.
7. Install first gear with clutching teeth upward; the front face of the gear butts against the flange on the mainshaft.
8. Install a blocker ring with clutching teeth down.
9. Install first and reverse synchronizer assembly with fork slot up. Press it onto mainshaft splines. Be sure blocker ring notches align with synchronizer assembly keys and both synchronizer sleeves face front of mainshaft.
10. Install snap-ring.
11. Install reverse gear with clutching teeth down.
12. Install steel reverse gear thrust washer with flats aligned.

13. Press rear ball bearing onto shaft with snap-ring slot down.
14. Install snap-ring.
15. Install speedometer drive gear and retaining clip.

Transmission Assembly

1. Place a row of 29 roller bearings, a bearing washer, a second row of 29 bearings, and a second bearing washer at each end of the countergear. Hold in place with grease.
2. Place countergear assembly through rear case opening with a tanged thrust washer, tang away from gear, at each end. Install countershaft and key from rear of case. Be sure that thrust washer tangs are aligned with notches in case.
3. Place reverse idler gear in case. Do not install reverse idler shaft yet.
4. Expand snap-ring in extension. Assemble extension over mainshaft and onto rear bearing. Seat snap-ring.
5. Load 16 mainshaft pilot bearings into clutch gear cavity. Assemble third speed blocker ring onto clutch gear clutching sur-

face with teeth toward gear.
6. Place clutch gear assembly, without front bearing, over front of mainshaft. Make sure that blocker ring notches align with keys in second-third synchronizer assembly.
7. Stick gasket onto extension housing with grease. Assemble clutch gear, mainshaft, and extension to case together. Make sure that clutch gear teeth engage teeth of countergear anti-lash plate.
8. Rotate extension housing. Install reverse idler shaft and key.
9. Torque extension bolts to 45 ft. lbs.
10. Install oil slinger with inner lip facing forward. Install front bearing outer snap-ring to bearing. Slide bearing into case bore.
11. Install snap-ring to clutch gear stem. Install bearing retainer and gasket. Torque bolts to 20 ft. lbs. Retainer oil return hole must be at 6 o'clock.
12. Shift both synchronizer sleeves to neutral positions. Install side cover, aligning shifter forks with synchronizer sleeve grooves.
13. Torque side cover bolts to 20 ft. lbs.

Type-12
Saginaw Fully Synchro-
nized 3-Speed

Application

Buick LeSabre, 1966-68
Buick Special, 1966-72
Camaro, 1967-72
Chevelle, 1966-72

Chevrolet, 1966-72
Chevy II, 1966-72
Corvette, 1966-69
Firebird, 1967-72
GTO, 1971-72

Olds F-85, 1966-72
Olds 442, Delta 88, 1971-72
Tempest, 1966-72
Ventura II, 1971-72

Transmission Disassembly

1. Remove side cover assembly and shift forks.
2. Remove clutch gear bearing retainer.
3. Remove clutch gear bearing to gear stem snap-ring. Pull clutch gear outward until a screwdriver can be inserted between bearing and case. Remove clutch gear bearing.
4. Remove speedometer driven gear and extension bolts.
5. Remove reverse idler shaft snap-ring. Slide reverse idler gear forward on shaft.
6. Remove mainshaft and extension assembly.
7. Remove clutch gear and third speed blocker ring from inside case. Remove 14 roller bearings from clutch gear.
8. Expand the snap-ring which re-

tains the mainshaft rear bearing. Remove the extension.
9. Using a dummy shaft, drive the countershaft and key out the rear of the case. Remove the gear, two tanged thrust washers, and dummy shaft. Remove bearing washer and 27 roller bearings from each end of countergear.
10. Use a long drift to drive the reverse idler shaft and key through the rear of the case.
11. Remove reverse idler gear and tanged steel thrust washer.

Mainshaft Disassembly

1. Remove second and third speed sliding clutch hub snap-ring from mainshaft. Remove clutch assembly, second speed blocker ring, and second gear from front of mainshaft.

2. Depress speedometer drive gear retaining clip. Remove gear. Some units have a metal speedometer drive gear which must be pulled off.
3. Remove rear bearing snap-ring.
4. Support reverse gear. Press on rear of mainshaft. Remove reverse gear, thrust washer, spring washer, rear bearing, and snap-ring. When pressing off the rear bearing, be careful not to cock the bearing on the shaft.
5. Remove first and reverse sliding clutch hub snap-ring. Remove clutch assembly, first speed blocker ring, and first gear.

Inspection

1. Wash all parts in solvent.
2. Air dry.

Case

1. Check for cracks.

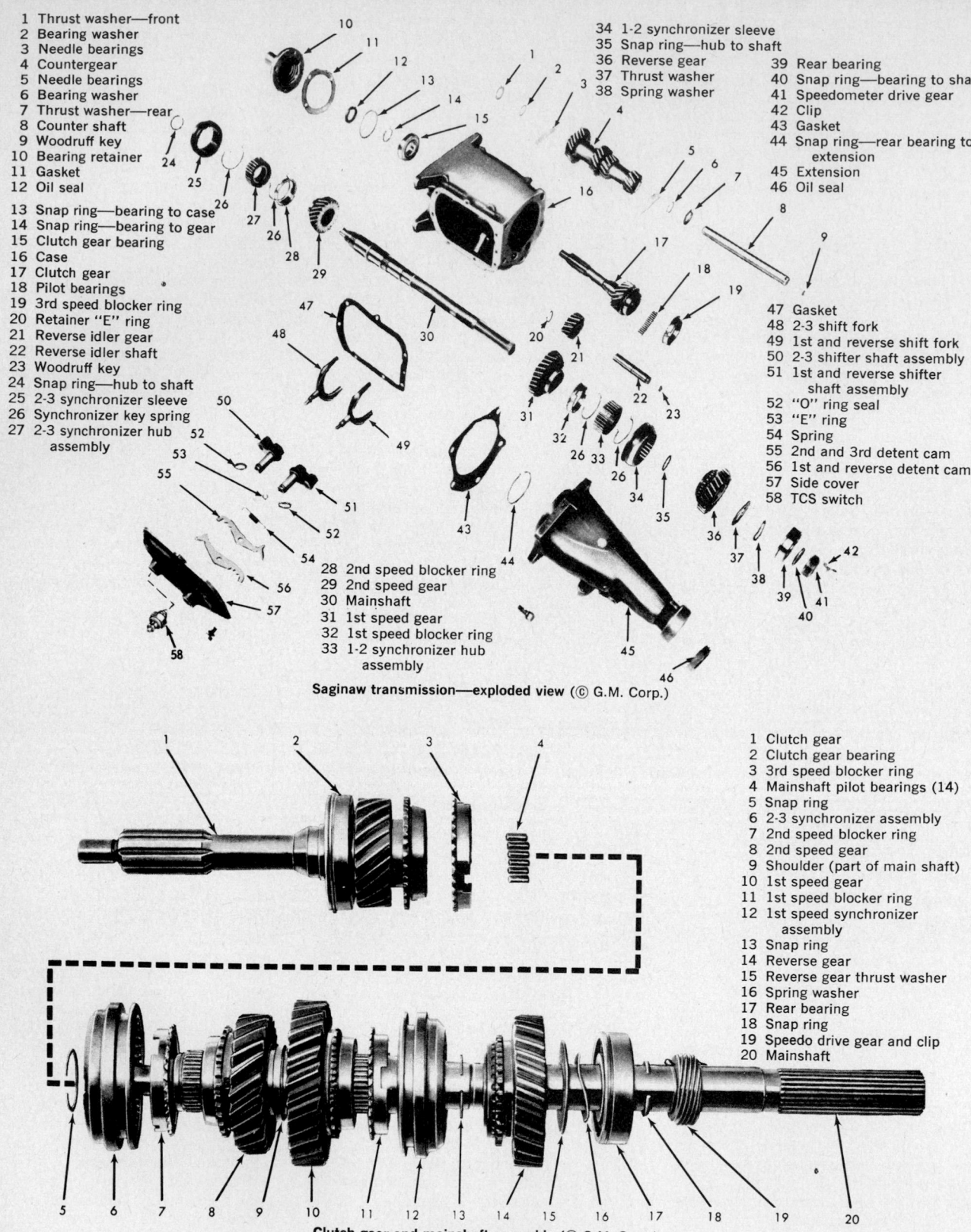

1 Thrust washer—front
2 Bearing washer
3 Needle bearings
4 Countergear
5 Needle bearings
6 Bearing washer
7 Thrust washer—rear
8 Counter shaft
9 Woodruff key
10 Bearing retainer
11 Gasket
12 Oil seal
13 Snap ring—bearing to case
14 Snap ring—bearing to gear
15 Clutch gear bearing
16 Case
17 Clutch gear
18 Pilot bearings
19 3rd speed blocker ring
20 Retainer "E" ring
21 Reverse idler gear
22 Reverse idler shaft
23 Woodruff key
24 Snap ring—hub to shaft
25 2-3 synchronizer sleeve
26 Synchronizer key spring
27 2-3 synchronizer hub
   assembly

28 2nd speed blocker ring
29 2nd speed gear
30 Mainshaft
31 1st speed gear
32 1st speed blocker ring
33 1-2 synchronizer hub
   assembly

34 1-2 synchronizer sleeve
35 Snap ring—hub to shaft
36 Reverse gear
37 Thrust washer
38 Spring washer

39 Rear bearing
40 Snap ring—bearing to shaft
41 Speedometer drive gear
42 Clip
43 Gasket
44 Snap ring—rear bearing to
   extension
45 Extension
46 Oil seal

47 Gasket
48 2-3 shift fork
49 1st and reverse shift fork
50 2-3 shifter shaft assembly
51 1st and reverse shifter
   shaft assembly
52 "O" ring seal
53 "E" ring
54 Spring
55 2nd and 3rd detent cam
56 1st and reverse detent cam
57 Side cover
58 TCS switch

Saginaw transmission—exploded view (© G.M. Corp.)

1 Clutch gear
2 Clutch gear bearing
3 3rd speed blocker ring
4 Mainshaft pilot bearings (14)
5 Snap ring
6 2-3 synchronizer assembly
7 2nd speed blocker ring
8 2nd speed gear
9 Shoulder (part of main shaft)
10 1st speed gear
11 1st speed blocker ring
12 1st speed synchronizer
   assembly
13 Snap ring
14 Reverse gear
15 Reverse gear thrust washer
16 Spring washer
17 Rear bearing
18 Snap ring
19 Speedo drive gear and clip
20 Mainshaft

Clutch gear and mainshaft assembly (© G.M. Corp.)

2. Check faces for burrs. Remove with a fine file.
3. Check bearing bores for damage. If they are damaged, replace case.

Front and Rear Bearings

1. Do not spin bearings with air

pressure; turn them slowly by hand.
2. Lubricate bearings with light oil. Turn slowly to check for roughness.

Bearing Rollers

1. Check for wear; replace if worn.

2. Check countershaft and reverse idler shaft for wear or damage.
3. Replace all worn washers.

Gears

1. Check for wear, chips, or cracks.
2. If reverse gear bushing is worn or damaged, replace entire gear.

3. Check that both clutch sleeves slide freely on their hubs.

Reverse Idler Gear Bushing

This bushing may not be serviced separately. If the bushing requires replacement, replace the gear.

Countergear Anti-Lash Plate

1. Check the plate teeth for wear or damage.
2. Do not disassemble unit.

Repair

Clutch Keys and Springs

Keys and springs may be replaced if worn or broken, but the hubs and sleeves are matched pairs and must be kept together.

1. Mark hub and sleeve for reassembly.
2. Push hub from sleeve. Remove keys and springs.
3. Place three keys and two springs, one on each side of hub, in position, so all three keys are engaged by both springs. The tanged end of the springs should not be installed into the same key.
4. Slide the sleeve onto the hub, aligning the marks.

NOTE: a groove around the outside of the synchronizer hub marks the end that must be opposite the fork slot in the sleeve when assembled.

Extension Oil Seal and Bushing

1. Remove seal.
2. Using bushing remover and installer tool, or other suitable tool, drive bushing into extension housing.
3. Drive new bushing in from the rear. Lubricate inside of bushing and seal. Install new oil seal with extension seal installer tool or other suitable tool.

Clutch Bearing Retainer Oil Seal

1. Pry old seal out.

2. Install new seal using seal installer or suitable tool. Seat seal in bore.

Mainshaft Assembly

1. Turn front of mainshaft up.
2. Install second gear with clutching teeth up; the rear face of the gear butts against the flange on the mainshaft.
3. Install a blocker ring with clutching teeth down. All three blocker rings are the same.
4. Install second and third speed synchronizer assembly with fork slot down. Press it onto mainshaft splines. Both synchronizer assemblies are the same. Be sure that blocker ring notches align with synchronizer assembly keys.
5. Install synchronizer snap-ring. Both synchronizer snap-rings are the same.
6. Turn rear of shaft up.
7. Install first gear with clutching teeth up; the front face of the gear butts against the flange on the mainshaft.
8. Install a blocker ring with clutching teeth down.
9. Install first and reverse synchronizer assembly with fork slot down. Press it onto mainshaft splines. Be sure blocker ring notches align with synchronizer assembly keys.
10. Install snap-ring.
11. Install reverse gear with clutching teeth down.
12. Install steel reverse gear thrust washer and spring washer.
13. Press rear ball bearing onto shaft with snap-ring slot down.
14. Install snap-ring.
15. Install speedometer drive gear and retaining clip. Press on metal speedometer drive gear.

Transmission Assembly

1. Using dummy shaft, load a row of 27 roller bearings and a thrust washer at each end of countergear. Hold in place with grease.

2. Place countergear assembly into case through rear. Place a tanged thrust washer, tang away from gear, at each end. Install countershaft and key, making sure that tangs align with notches in case.
3. Install reverse idler gear thrust washer, gear, and shaft with key from rear of case. Be sure thrust washer is between gear and rear of case with tang toward notch in case.
4. Expand snap-ring in extension. Assemble extension over rear of mainshaft and onto rear bearing. Seat snap-ring in rear bearing groove.
5. Install 14 mainshaft pilot bearings into clutch gear cavity. Assemble third speed blocker ring onto clutch gear clutching surface with teeth toward gear.
6. Place clutch gear, pilot bearings, and third speed blocker ring assembly over front of mainshaft assembly. Be sure blocker rings align with keys in second-third synchronizer assembly.
7. Stick extension gasket to case with grease. Install clutch gear, mainshaft, and extension together. Be sure clutch gear engages teeth of countergear anti-lash plate. Torque extension bolts to 45 ft. lbs.
8. Place bearing over stem of clutch gear and into front case bore. Install front bearing to clutch gear snap-ring.
9. Install clutch gear bearing retainer and gasket. The retainer oil return hole must be at the bottom. Torque retainer bolts to 10 ft. lbs.
10. Install reverse idler gear shaft E-ring.
11. Shift synchronizer sleeves to neutral positions. Install cover, gasket, and forks, aligning forks with synchronizer sleeve grooves. Torque side cover bolts to 10 ft. lbs.
12. Install speedometer driven gear.

Type-13

Muncie 4-Speed

Application

Buick Special (GS), 1967-72	Corvette, 1965-72	Olds F-85, 1965-72
Camaro, 1967-72	Firebird, 1967-72	Olds Cutlass, 442, 1971-72
Chevelle, 1965-72	GTO, 1971-72	Pontiac, 1968-70
Chevrolet, 1965-72	Monte Carlo, 1970-72	Pontiac (GP), 1968-72
Chevy II, 1965-72	Oldsmobile, 1965	Tempest, 1965-72

Disassembly

1. Remove side cover and shift controls after draining.
2. Remove bolts and bolt lock strips

from front bearing retainer and remove retainer and gasket.
3. Lock up transmission by shifting into two gears and remove main drive gear retaining nut.

NOTE: this nut may have left-hand threads.

4. Return gears to neutral and remove lock pin from reverse shifter lever boss and pull shaft out

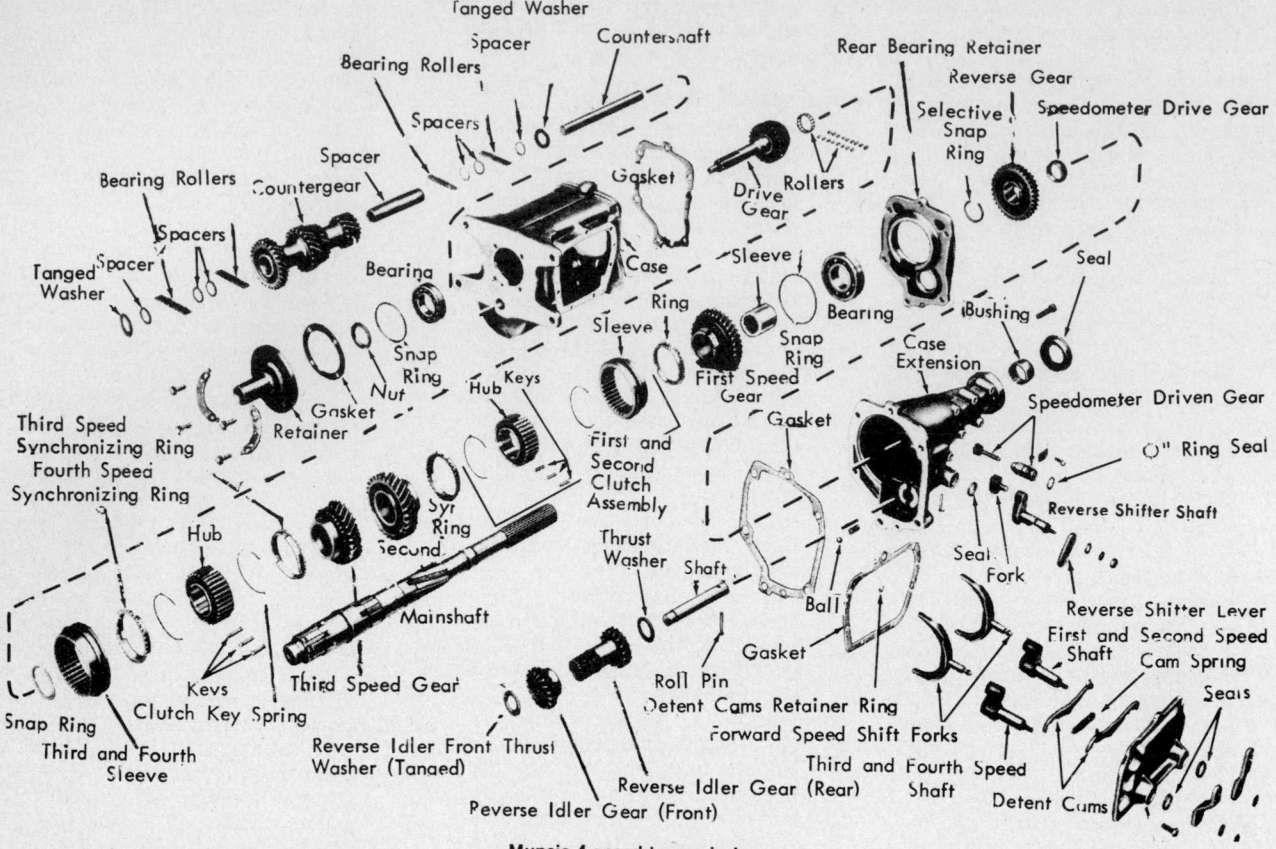

Muncie 4-speed transmission

about ⅛ in. This will disengage reverse shift fork from reverse gear.

5. Remove extension case attaching bolts. Tap extension with soft hammer toward rear. When idler shaft is out as far as it will go, move extension to left so reverse fork clears gear and remove extension and gasket.

6. Remove reverse idler gear, flat washer, shaft and roll spring pin.

7. Remove speedometer and reverse gears.

NOTE: slide third-fourth synchronizer clutch sleeve to fourth-speed gear position (forward) before trying to remove mainshaft assembly from case.

8. Remove rear bearing retainer and mainshaft assembly from case by tapping bearing retainer with soft hammer.

9. Unload bearing rollers from main drive gear and remove fourth-speed synchronizer blocking ring.

10. Lift front half of reverse idler gear with tanged thrust washer from case.

11. Press main drive gear down from bearing.

12. Tap front bearing and snap-ring from case.

13. From front of case, press out countershaft. Then, remove the countershaft gear and both tanged washers.

14. Remove the rollers (112), six

spacers and roller spacer from countergear.

15. Remove mainshaft front snap-ring and slide third and fourth-speed clutch and third-speed gear and synchronizer ring from front of mainshaft.

16. Spread rear bearing retainer snap-ring and press mainshaft out of retainer.

17. Remove mainshaft snap-ring. Support second-speed gear and press on rear of mainshaft to remove rear bearing, first-speed gear and sleeve, first-speed synchronizing ring, first-second-speed synchronizer clutch, second-speed synchronizer ring and second-speed gear.

After thoroughly cleaning case and all parts, make thorough inspection and replace required parts. In checking bearings do not spin at high speeds, but rather clean and rotate by hand to detect roughness and unevenness. Spinning can damage balls and races.

Assembly

Mainshaft

1. From rear of shaft, assemble second-speed gear (hub of gear toward rear of shaft).

2. Install first-second synchronizer clutch assembly onto mainshaft (sleeve taper toward rear, hub to front); together with a synchro-

nizer ring on each side of clutch assembly so that keyways line up with clutch keys.

3. Press first-speed sleeve onto mainshaft. (A 1¾ in. or 1⅝ in. ID pipe cut to convenient length makes a suitable tool).

4. Install first-speed gear (hub toward front) and press onto the rear bearing with snap-ring grooves toward front of transmission. Be sure bearing is firmly seated.

5. Choose selective fit snap-ring (.087, .090, .093 or .096 in.) and install it into groove in mainshaft behind rear bearing. Maximum clearance of snap-ring and rear face should be between zero and .005 in.

NOTE: always use new snap-ring.

6. Install third-speed gear (hub to front of transmission) and third-speed gear synchronizing ring (notches to front).

7. Install third and fourth-speed gear clutch assembly with both sleeve taper and hub toward front.

8. Install snap-ring onto mainshaft in front of third and fourth-speed clutch, with ends of snap-ring seated behind spline teeth.

9. Install rear bearing retainer. Spread snap-ring in plate, to allow ring to drop around rear bearing, and press on the end of mainshaft until snap-ring en-

gages the groove in rear bearing.

10. Install reverse gear (shift collar to rear).
11. Install speedometer drive gear.

Countergear

1. Install roller spacer into counter gear.
2. With heavy grease to assist, install a spacer in either end of countergear, 28 roller bearings, then a spacer and 28 more rollers. Then, install another spacer. In the other end of the countergear, do the same.
3. Insert dummy shaft into counter gear.

Transmission

1. Rest case on side with cover opening toward mechanic. Install countergear tanged thrust washers in place, holding with heavy grease. Make sure tangs are in proper notches.
2. Set countergear in place. Use care not to disturb tanged washers.
3. Position transmission case so that it rests on front face.
4. Lubricate and insert countershaft in rear. Turn countershaft so flat on end of shaft is horizontal and facing bottom of case.
   NOTE: the flat of shaft must be horizontal and toward bottom to mate with rear bearing retainer when installed.
5. Align countergear with shaft in rear and hole in front of case (pushing dummy shaft out front of case) until flat of shaft is flush with rear of case. Be sure thrust washers remain in place.
6. Check end-play in countergear (dial indicator should be used). If end-play is more than .025 in. install new thrust washer.

7. Install cage and 17 roller bearings into main drive gear. Use heavy grease to hold bearings.
8. Install main drive gear with bearings through side opening of case and into position in front bore.
9. Place gasket in position on rear bearing retainer.
10. Install fourth-speed synchronizing ring onto main drive gear (notches toward rear).
11. Position tanged thrust washer for reverse idler on machined face. Position front reverse idler gear next to thrust washer (hub facing toward rear of case).

Caution Before attempting to install mainshaft to case, slide the third-fourth synchronizer clutch sleeve forward into fourth-speed detent position.

12. Lower mainshaft assembly into case. Be sure notches on fourth-speed synchronizer ring correspond to keys in clutch assembly.
13. With guide pin in rear bearing retainer aligned with hole in rear of case, tap rear bearing retainer into position with soft hammer.
14. From rear of case, insert reverse idler gear, engaging splines with portion of front gear in case.
15. Place gasket in position on rear face of bearing retainer.
16. Install remaining flat washer on reverse idler shaft.
17. Install reverse idler shaft, roll pin, and thrust washer into gears and front boss of case. Make sure to pick up front tanged thrust washer.
18. Pull reverse shifter shaft to left side of extension and rotate shaft to bring reverse shift fork forward in extension (reverse detent position). Start extension onto transmission case, while slowly

pushing in on shifter shaft to engage the shift fork with the reverse gear shift collar. Then, pilot the reverse idler shaft into the extension housing, permitting the extension to slide into the transmission case.

19. Install extension and retainer-to-case attaching bolts.
20. Push or pull reverse shifter shaft to line up grooves in the shaft with the holes in the boss and drive in the lockpin. Install shift lever.
21. Press bearing onto main drive gear (snap-ring groove in front), and into case until several main drive gear retaining nut threads are exposed.
22. Lock transmission by shifting into two gears. Install main drive gear retaining nut onto the gear shaft and draw it up tight. Be sure bearing is completely seated against shoulder. Torque retaining nut to 40 ft. lbs. and lock in place by staking into main drive gear shaft hole with punch. Do not damage shaft threads.
23. Install main drive gear bearing retainer, gasket attaching bolts and boltlock retainers. Use a suitable seal on bolts. Tighten to 20 ft. lbs.
24. Shift mainshaft third-fourth sliding clutch sleeve into neutral position and first-second sliding clutch into second gear (forward) detent position. Shift side cover third-fourth shift lever into neutral detent and first-second shift lever into second gear detent position.
25. Install side cover, with gasket, and carefully position in place. A dowel pin provides proper alignment position. Install bolts and tighten evenly to avoid distortion. Torque to 20 ft. lbs.

Type-14
Saginaw 4-Speed

Application

Camaro, 1967-72
Chevy II, 1966-72
Chevelle, 1966-72

Chevrolet, 1966-72
Corvette, 1967-72

Olds Cutlass, 442, 1971-72
Tempest, 1967-68 (6 Cyl.)
Firebird, 1969 (6 Cyl.)

NOTE: repair procedures on the Saginaw four-speed transmission are typical of the Muncie four-speed. Parts, however, are not interchangeable.

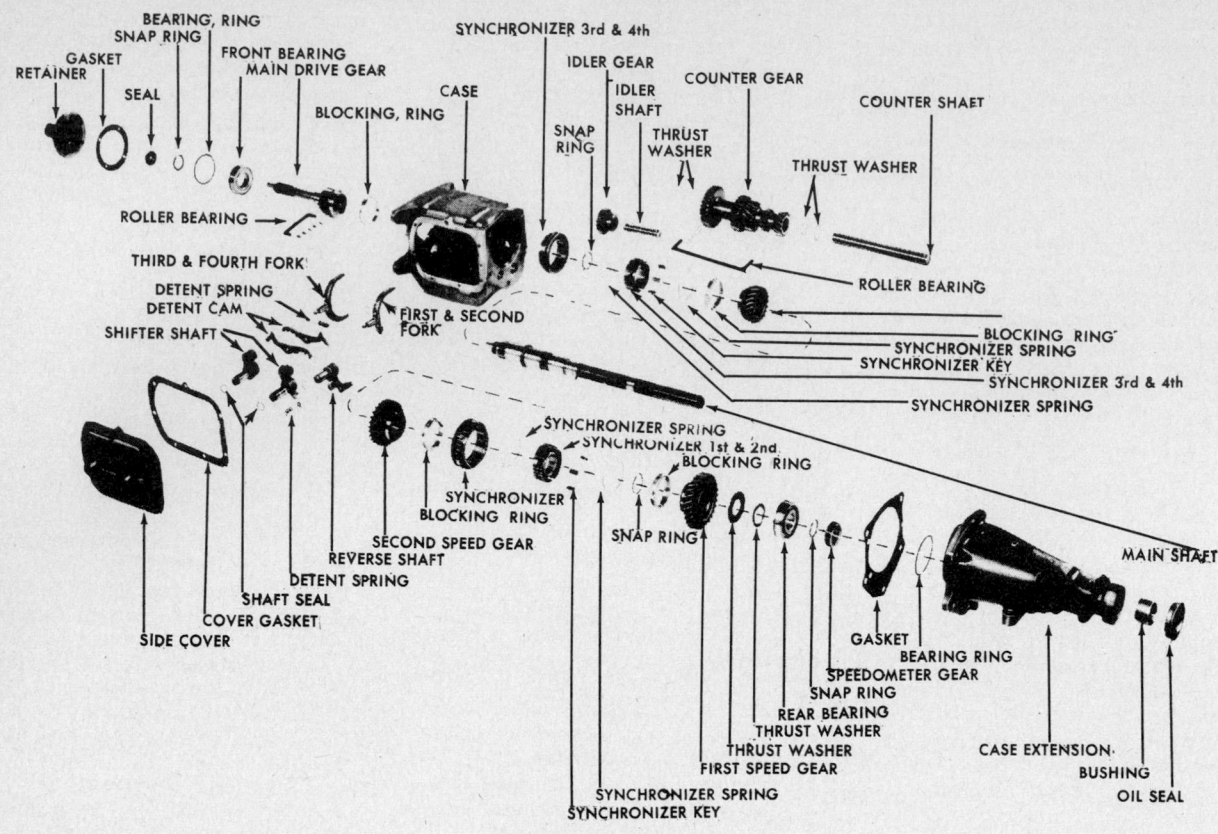

Saginaw 4-speed transmission

Type-15
Vega 3-Speed
Application
Vega, 1971-72

Transmission Disassembly

1. Remove the shift lever boot. Remove the TCS switch and back-up light switch.
2. Remove the cotter pins from each end of the shift control rod. Remove washers and shift control rod.
3. Remove retaining rings, wave rings, and selector ring from selector shaft. Slide the selector lever and shift idler lever shaft from the intermediate shift lever assembly while simultaneously removing the selector ring.
4. Remove the transmission case cover and gasket.
5. Invert the transmission to drain the oil.
6. Remove the rear extension attaching bolts and rotate the extension until the countergear shaft is exposed.
7. From the front of the transmission, remove the countergear shaft. Lift the countergear from the case. Do not lose the lockball.
8. Engage second gear to prevent the second-third fork pin from

binding against the case. Use a ⅛ in. pin punch to remove all lockpins.

9. Drive the lockpins from both shifter forks. Place the transmission in third gear and be sure that the second-third intermediate lever engages the shifter shaft. This will allow the intermediate levers to pivot as the shifter shaft is removed.
10. Insert a long narrow drift through the bolt hole at the rear of the case and drive the second-third shifter shaft from the case. Remove the fork.
11. Drive the first-reverse shifter shaft from the front of the case and remove the fork from the case.
12. Remove the selector shaft intermediate lever lockpins. Remove the shaft and levers from the case.
13. Remove the snap-ring from the rear bearing retainer groove and slide the rear extension from the mainshaft assembly.
14. Remove the clutch drive gear

from the case.
15. Position first-reverse sliding gear to the rear of the hub shaft and remove the mainshaft assembly from the case. Remove the lockpins and detent balls from the bottom of the case.
16. Drive the plugs and springs from the shift rail detent holes.
17. Remove the reverse idler gear and shaft from the case.

Mainshaft Disassembly

NOTE: the synchronizer hubs and sliding sleeves are a select assembly and kept together as originally assembled. Keys and springs may be replaced.

1. Remove the snap-ring from in front of the clutch hub.
2. Depress the retaining clip and slide the speedometer drive gear from the shaft.
3. Remove the snap-ring, spacer and Belleville washer from the shaft.
4. Support first gear and press the mainshaft until the bearing and

1 Rear extension to case bolts
2 Back-up lamp switch
   and seal ring
3 Shift idler lever spring.
4 Intermediate lever bushing
   snap-ring
5 Intermediate lever bushing
6 Shift idler lever
7 Rear extension
8 Rear extension gasket
9 Reverse idler gear
   shaft and lockball
10 Reverse idler gear
   and bushing assembly
11 2-3 speed shifter shaft
12 2-3 speed shift fork
   and spiral pin
13 Cotter pin
14 Waved washer

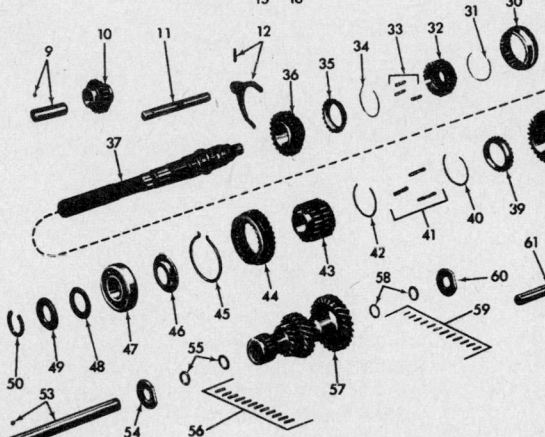

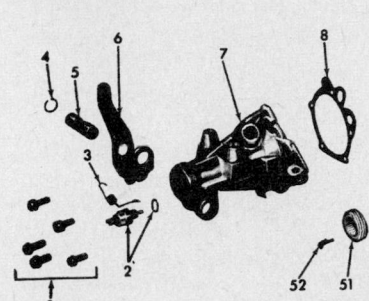

15 Shift selector rod	28 Transmission case	43 1st-reverse synchronizer hub
16 Washer	29 2-3 speed synchronizer	44 1st-reverse synchronizer
17 Selector shaft	assembly retaining ring	sleeve
18 Selector shaft seal	30 2-3 speed synchronizer sleeve	45 Rear bearing to extension
19 2-3 intermediate shift lever	31 Synchronizer spring	locking ring
and spiral pin	32 2-3 synchronizer hub	46 1st-reverse key stop-ring
20 1st-reverse intermediate	33 2-3 synchronizer keys	47 Mainshaft rear bearing
shift lever and spiral pin	34 Synchronizer spring	48 Rear bearing spacer
21 Cover gasket	35 2nd gear synchronizer ring	49 Belleville washer
22 Cover assembly	36 2nd speed gear	50 Rear bearing retaining ring
23 Cover-to-case screws	37 Mainshaft	51 Speedo drive gear
23a Clutch drive gear seal	38 1st speed gear	52 Speedo drive clip
24 Clutch drive gear assembly	39 1st speed gear	53 Countergear shaft and
25 Mainshaft pilot bearing	synchronizer ring	lockball
assembly	40. Synchronizer spring	54 Countergear thrust washer
26 Pilot bearing spacer ring	41 1st-reverse synchronizer keys	55 Countergear bearing washer
27 3rd gear synchronizer ring	42 Synchronizer spring	56 Countergear roller bearings
		(24)

57 Countergear
58 Countergear bearing
   washer
59 Countergear roller bearings
   (24)
60 Countergear thrust washers
61 1st-reverse shift shaft
62 1st-reverse shift fork and
   spiral pin
63 Intermediate lever shaft
   and pin
64 TCS switch and gasket
65 2-3 shift detent ball, spring
   and hole plug
66 1st-reverse shift detent ball,
   spring and hole plug
67 Pivot pin lockring
68 Shift selector rod
69 Selector lever pivot pin
70 Oil filler plug
71 Selector shaft oil seal
72 Selector shaft lockring
73 Selector shaft ring
74 Belleville washer
75 Selector shaft lockring

Exploded view of Vega 3-speed transmission (© Chevrolet Division, G.M. Corp.)

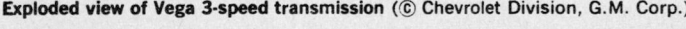

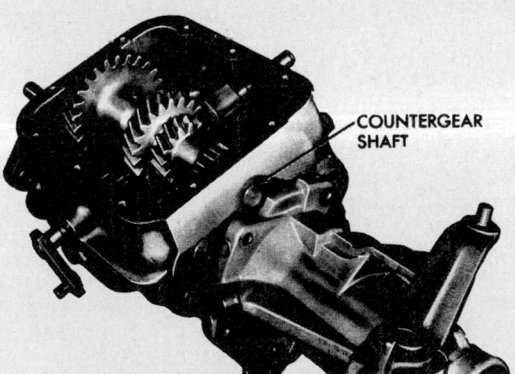

COUNTERGEAR
SHAFT

Countergear shaft exposed for removal
(© Chevrolet Division, G.M. Corp.)

synchronizers are free on the shaft. Remove all loose parts from the shaft.
5. Support second speed gear and press and shaft until second-third synchronizer assembly and second speed gear are free.

Inspection
1. Examine the shaft, bearing gear and hubs for excessive wear. Examine for chips, nicking or scoring. Wash ball bearings in solvent and blow dry. Re-

place worn synchronizer rings, clutch keys an dhubs. Oil all parts with SAE 90 transmission fluid during assembly.

Mainshaft Assembly
1. From the front of the mainshaft, install the second speed gear. The gear must turn freely on the shaft.
2. Install the second-third synchronizer onto second speed gear cone.
3. Install front and rear synchronizer key springs into second-third speed synchronizer hubs, so that hooked spring ends are in the same slot and raised ends are against the blocker rings.
4. Install sliding sleeve and keys on clutch hub. Arrows must point to front of shaft.
5. Press second-third speed synchronizer hub onto the mainshaft. Secure with a snap-ring.
6. Install both clutch key springs

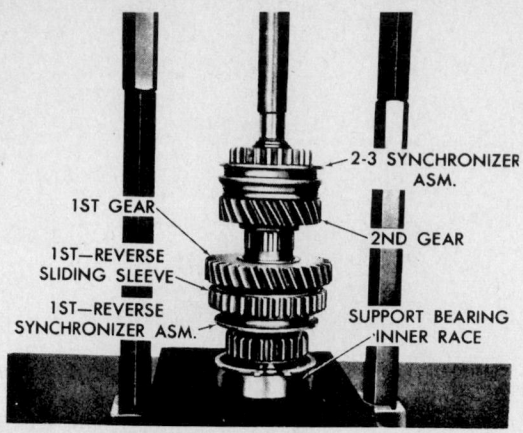

Assembling mainshaft components
((C) Chevrolet Division, G.M. Corp.)

Labels: 2-3 SYNCHRONIZER ASM., 1ST GEAR, 1ST—REVERSE SLIDING SLEEVE, 1ST—REVERSE SYNCHRONIZER ASM., 2ND GEAR, SUPPORT BEARING INNER RACE

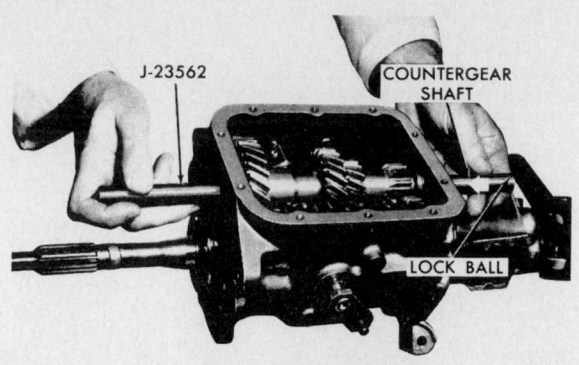

Installing countergear shaft
((C) Chevrolet Division, G.M. Corp.)

Labels: J-23562, COUNTERGEAR SHAFT, LOCK BALL

into first-reverse speed synchronizer hub. Hooks of both springs must rest in the same hub slot and raised spring ends should be positioned opposite each other against the blocker rings.

7. Assemble the sliding gear and keys on hub assembly with longer key flat and fork groove on gear toward the rear of the shaft.

8. From the rear of the mainshaft, slide on first gear. Gear must turn freely.

9. Place first-reverse speed synchronizer ring onto first speed gear cone.

10. Slide the first-reverse synchronizer assembly onto the mainshaft. Slide the stop-ring, rear extension retaining ring and rear bearing onto the shaft. Support the rear bearing inner race and press the components together.

Caution Align slots with synchronizer keys. The clutch drive bearing is used to service the mainshaft rear bearing. Install replacement bearing with shield side toward rear of shaft.

11. Place spacer and Belleville washer on the mainshaft. Secure with a snap-ring.

12. Position the speedometer drive gear retaining clip on shaft and install the speedometer drive gear.

13. Install the mainshaft into the extension housing up to the stop. Secure with a retaining ring.

Transmission Assembly

1. Install a new gasket on the rear extension and slide mainshaft assembly into the case. Install one or two bolts to keep the extension from rotating.

2. Coat the pilot roller bearing with grease. From the front, slide the lockring and pilot roller bearing onto the mainshaft.

3. Install the blocker ring on clutch drive gear, and install the gear into the transmission case, up to the snap-ring stop.

4. Insert the first-reverse speed shifter shaft at the front of the case with the notches down, pushing it through the shifter fork. Position the fork shoulder toward the front of the case. Drive the lockpin in place.
NOTE: all lockpins should be installed protruding 1/16 in. to 5/16 in. above the fork or lever.

5. Insert the second-third speed shifter shaft, from the front of the case, with the notches down, pushing it through the shifter fork shoulder toward the front. Install the lockpin.

6. Install the selector shaft in the case. Push it through the second-third speed intermediate lever and the first-reverse lever. Install lockpins.

7. Install both lockballs and springs into the bores in the case and drive in the plugs.

8. Remove the rear extension bolt(s), pull back on the extension and rotate the extension until the bore for the reverse idler gear is exposed.

9. Install the lockball into the shaft from the rear of the case and install the shaft into the gear. Drive the shaft into place.

10. Using a dummy shaft, install a spacer at each end of the countergear. Hold them in place with heavy grease.

11. Coat the thrust washer with grease and stick it to the case. The lugs of the thrust washers must the slots in the case.

12. Turn the case extension until the countergear bore is exposed.

13. Place the lockball in the shaft. From the rear of the transmission, insert the shaft so that the thrust washer is held in position. Hold the opposite thrust washer in position with a short drift.

14. Insert the countergear into the case.

15. Insert the shaft into the countergear and push out the dummy shaft. Align the lockball with the groove in the case and tap the shaft into the case.

16. Align the rear bearing retainer and tighten the bolts.

17. Install the case cover gasket, cover and screws.

18. Install the gearshift linkages in reverse sequence to removal.
NOTE: start the idler lever shaft into the shift control simultaneously when installing selector ring.

Type-16

Vega 4-Speed

Application

Vega, 1971-72

1 Intermediate lever bushing
   snap-ring
2 Cotter pin
3 Shift idler lever and spring
4 Intermediate lever bushing
5 Rear extension and
   retaining bolts
6 Rear extension gasket
7 Reverse idler gear shaft
   and lockball
8 Reverse idler gear and
   bushing assembly

9 Reverse idler gear shift fork and spiral pin	26 Transmission case	45 1st-2nd synchronizer hub	63 Countergear bearing washers
10 Reverse idler gear shifter shaft	27 Cover gasket, cover, and screws	46 1st-2nd synchronizer keys	64 Countergear roller bearings (24)
11 3-4 speed shifter shaft	28 Clutch drive gear to housing seal	47 Synchronizer spring	65 Countergear
12 3-4 speed shift fork and spiral pin	29 Clutch drive gear assembly	48 1st-2nd synchronizer sleeve	66 Countergear bearing washer
13 Washers	30 4th gear synchronizer ring	49 1st speed synchronizer ring	67 Countergear roller bearings (24)
14 Shift control rod	31 Mainshaft pilot bearing assembly	50 1st speed gear bushing	68 Countergear bearing washer
15 Washers	32 Pilot bearing spacer ring	51 1st gear needle bearing assembly	69 Countergear thrust washer
16 Cotter pin	33 3-4 speed synchronizer assembly retaining ring	52 1st speed gear	70 1st-2nd shift fork and spiral pin
17 Selector shaft	34 3-4 speed synchronizer sleeve	53 Rear bearing to extension locking ring	71 1st-2nd shift shaft
18 Spiral pins	35 Synchronizer spring	54 Rear bearing spacer ring (front)	72 1st-2nd selector lever cam and spiral pin
19 Back-up lamp switch and seal ring	36 3-4 synchronizer hub	55 Mainshaft rear bearing	73 Intermediate lever shaft and pin
20 Selector shaft oil seal	37 3-4 synchronizer keys	56 Rear bearing spacer (rear)	74 Shift selector rod, pivot pin and lock ring
21 3rd-4th speed intermediate shifter lever	38 Synchronizer spring	57 Belleville washer	75 TCS switch and gasket
22 1st-2nd intermediate shift lever	39 3rd speed gear synchronizer ring	58 Rear bearing retaining ring (brg.-to-mainshaft)	76 Shifter shaft detent balls, springs and hole plugs
23 Reverse intermediate lever	40 3rd speed gear	59 Speedo drive gear	77 Oil filler plug
24 Reverse intermediate lever pin	41 Mainshaft	60 Speedo drive clip	78 Selector shaft oil seal
25 Reverse shifter shaft detent ball, spring and cap	42 2nd speed gear	61 Countergear shaft and lockball	79 Selector shaft adjusting ring
	43 2nd speed synchronizer ring	62 Countergear thrust washer	80 Selector shaft locknut
	44 Synchronizer spring		

Exploded view of Vega 4-speed transmission (© Chevrolet Division, G.M. Corp.)

Transmission Disassembly

1. Follow Steps 1-7 under Vega 3-Speed (Type-15) for removal of gearshift linkage, case cover and countergear shaft and countergear.
2. Drive out intermediate shift lever pin and remove intermediate lever. Use a 1/8 in. pin punch to drive out all pins.
3. Slide the reverse shaft to rear of the case so that the scallop in the selector shaft will clear the reverse shaft.
4. Shift transmission to neutral. Push in on the selector shaft and turn so that the lockpins are in the vertical position. Drive the lockpin out of the third-fourth speed intermediate lever cam and then from the first-second speed intermediate lever cam. Remove the selector shaft.
5. Pry the selector shaft seal rings out of the case.
6. Remove the lockball plugs with a slide hammer. Remove the thrust springs and balls.
7. Place the transmission in first gear and drive the lockpins out of the shifter forks and selector levers. Remove the first-second lever pin first.
8. From the rear of the transmission drive out the first-second shifter shaft with a brass drift. Remove the fork from the sliding sleeve.
9. Tap the third-fourth shifter shaft rearward until the fork can be removed from the shaft, then drive out the third-fourth shifter shaft through the front of the case.
10. Remove the clutch drive gear from the case.
11. Remove the rear extension and mainshaft from the case.
12. Push the reverse idler gear shaft toward the rear. Be sure that the lockball is not lost, and remove the reverse idler gear and shaft from the case.
13. From the front of the transmission, drive out the reverse shifter shaft with a brass drift. Remove the shifter fork from the case.

Mainshaft Disassembly

1. Remove the snap-ring from the rear bearing retainer groove and

remove the mainshaft assembly from the rear bearing retainer.

2. Depress the retaining clip and remove the speedometer driven gear.

3. Remove needle bearing, spacer ring and synchronizer ring. The sliding sleeve, keys and clutch keys can also be removed.

NOTE: the synchronizer hubs and sliding sleeves are a select assembly and should be kept together as originally assembled.

4. Remove the snap-ring from in front of the synchronizer hub.

5. Remove the snap-ring, spacer and Belleville washer from the shaft.

6. Support second gear and press the mainshaft until the bearing and synchronizers are free on the shaft. Remove all loose parts.

7. Remove third speed synchronizer hub snap-ring. Support third gear and press the mainshaft until the synchronizer and third gear are free.

Inspection

1. See inspection of components under Vega 3-Speed (Type-15) transmission.

Mainshaft Assembly

1. From the front of the mainshaft, install the third speed gear. Gear must turn freely.

2. Install the third speed synchronizer ring onto the third speed gear cone.

3. Install the rear clutch key spring into the third-fourth speed synchronizer hub so that the hooked spring rests in one of the slots and the raised end is toward the blocker ring.

4. Press the third-fourth speed clutch hub onto the mainshaft.

5. Secure the third-fourth synchronizer hub with a snap-ring.

6. From the rear of the mainshaft slide on the second speed gear. Gear must turn freely.

7. Place the second speed synchronizer ring on the second speed gear cone.

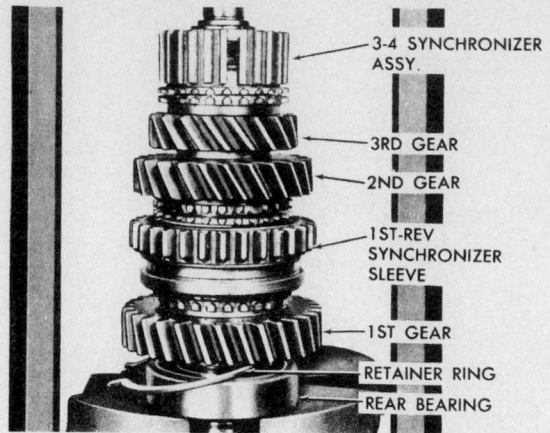

Assembling mainshaft components
(© Chevrolet Division, G.M. Corp.)

8. Install both synchronizer key springs into the first-second speed synchronizer hub, so that the spring hooks rest in the same hub slot and the other spring ends are positioned opposite each other and toward the blocker rings. Install the sliding gear and keys on the hub.

9. Slide the first-second speed synchronizer hub, needle bearing and inner sleeve onto the mainshaft. Slide the spacer, rear extension retaining ring and rear bearing onto the shaft.

10. Support the rear bearing inner race and press the components together.

NOTE: align the slots in the synchronizer rings with the synchronizer keys.

11. Install the spacer and Belleville washer on the mainshaft and secure with snap-ring.

NOTE: the concave side of the Belleville washer should face the bearing.

12. Position the speedometer gear retaining clip on the shaft and install the gear.

13. Place the mainshaft assembly into the rear bearing retainer up to the stop. Secure with a snap-ring.

14. Assemble the third-fourth speed synchronizer assembly on hub

with the raised end of the key springs toward the blocker ring.

NOTE: arrows on the keys point toward the shifter fork groove.

Transmission Assembly

1. Install a new gasket onto the rear extension.

2. Slide the mainshaft assembly into the transmission case.

3. From the front, slide the spacer ring and needle bearing onto the mainshaft. Coat the needle bearing and roller with grease.

4. Install the synchronizer blocker ring on the clutch drive gear and install the gear into the case up to the stop.

5. Insert the first-second shifter shaft at the front of the case with the notches down, pushing it first through the L shaped selector dog. Push the first-second speed selector shaft through the shifter fork, positioning the shoulder toward the front of the case. Drive the lockpins in. Install selector dog pin first.

NOTE: all lockpins should protrude 1/16 in. to 5/64 in.

6. Insert the third-fourth speed shifter shaft from the front of the case. The notches should be down and it is pushed through the third-fourth speed shifter fork, positioning the shoulder to-

Installing synchronizer key springs
(© Chevrolet Division, G.M. Corp.)

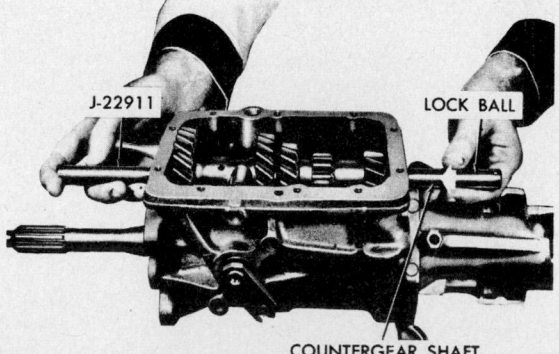

Installing countergear shaft
(© Chevrolet Division, G.M. Corp.)

ward the front. Install lockpin.

7. Install the reverse shifter shaft from the rear of the case with the notches up. Push it through the reverse shifter fork and install the lockpin. Position the shoulder of the shift fork toward the front of the case.

8. Insert the selector shaft into the case, through the third-fourth speed intermediate lever and through the first-second speed intermediate lever. Install lockpins.

9. Place the transmission in neutral and rotate the selector shaft to engage the levers with the shifter shafts.

10. Engage reverse speed intermediate levers with third-fourth speed intermediate lever and install pivot pin. Reverse speed intermediate lever end-play on the pin should be .004-.012 in.

11. Insert both lockballs and springs into their bores. Drive in plugs.

12. Turn the transmission case extension until the bore for the re-

verse idler gear shaft is exposed.

13. Place the lockball into the shaft and from the rear of the case, install the shaft into the gear.

14. Simultaneously, position the reverse idler gear and reverse shifter fork. The shifter fork groove of the reverse idler gear and the shoulder of the shifter fork should be toward the front of the mainshaft.

15. Follow Steps 10-18 under Transmission Assembly for Vega 3-Speed (Type-15).

Type-17
Warner T-14, T-15 Fully Synchronized 3-Speed

T-14 Application

American Motors (232), 1968- 72

American Motors, (258), 1971-72

T-15 Application

American Motors (232, 290, 304, 360), 1968-70

American Motors, (304, 360), 1971-72

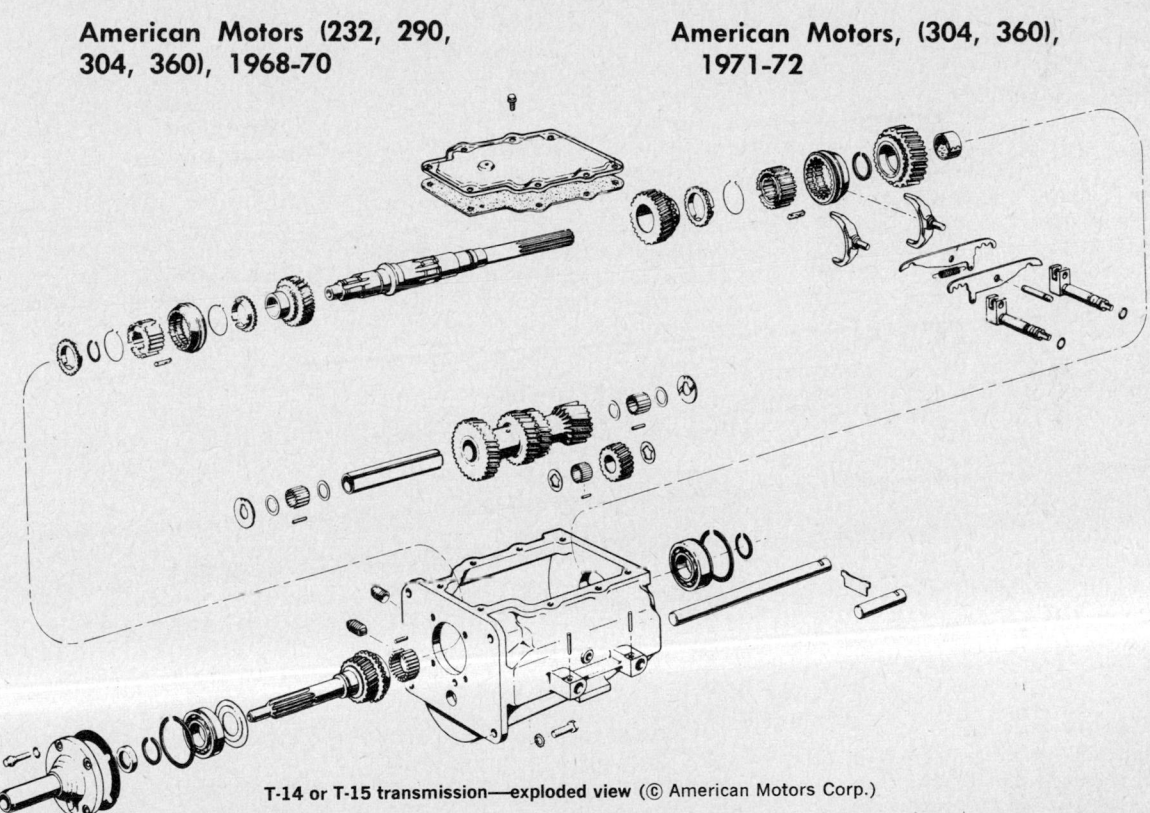

T-14 or T-15 transmission—exploded view (© American Motors Corp.)

Transmission Disassembly

1. Remove cover, front bearing cap, gasket, and two front bearing snap rings.

2. Align notch in clutch shaft third gear with countergear. Remove clutch shaft and front bearing. A puller may be needed.

3. Pull off front bearing.

4. Remove extension housing and

gasket. Using oil seal remover and slide hammer, remove extension housing oil seal. Remove extension housing bushing. Install new bushing, aligning oil groove with housing slot.

5. Remove snap-ring, speedometer drive gear, and locating ball.

6. Remove two rear bearing snap-rings and pull off rear bearing.

7. Move mainshaft aside. Remove

both shift forks.

8. Push front synchronizer toward rear. Tilt front of mainshaft up and out through top of case.

9. If necessary, remove the transmission controlled spark switch assembly.

10. Drive out roll pins. Push shift shafts into case. Remove shift shafts and detent assembly.

11. Tap reverse idler shaft and coun-

tershaft rearward. Remove shaft lockplate. Drive reverse idler shaft from case. Use dummy shaft to drive out countershaft.

Mainshaft Disassembly

1. From front of shaft, remove front snap-ring, second-third synchro-clutch assembly, and second gear.
2. From rear of shaft, remove reverse gear, rear snap-ring, rear synchro-clutch assembly, and low gear.

Inspection

1. Check gears for worn, chipped, or cracked teeth. Check fit to mainshaft.
2. Check bearings for smoothness and excessive play.
3. Check roller bearings for wear or damage.
4. Slide synchro-clutch and friction rings on gear cones and clutch shaft. Replace rings if taper is worn or pitted. There should be no play between hub and shaft splines. .
5. Check case for cracks or damaged bearing bores.

Mainshaft Assembly

1. Install low gear and friction ring; friction ring hub to the rear.
2. Install low synchro-gear into synchro-collar so deep end of gear faces low gear. Install synchro-plates (dogs) and retainer ring with large end of plates toward low gear.

3. Place synchro-clutch assembly on mainshaft with synchro-collar groove toward low gear. Install the thickest snap-ring that will fit in groove.
4. Measure clearance between first gear and collar on mainshaft. The clearance should be .003-.012 in. for the T-14; .003-.014 in. for the T-15.
5. Place second gear and the friction ring on the front of the mainshaft with the gear hub and ring forward. Place second synchro-gear into synchro-collar with deep end of gear facing rear of shaft.
6. Hold synchro-clutch assembly with one synchro-plate, or dog, in 12 o'clock position. Install tang of retainer ring into the dog at 12 o'clock and install ring clockwise. On opposite side, start with the same dog and install ring clockwise.
7. Place second synchro assembly on shaft with deep end to rear. Install the thickest snap-ring that will fit into the groove.
8. Measure clearance between second gear and collar on mainshaft. It must be .003-.018 in.
9. Install reverse gear on rear of mainshaft.

Transmission Assembly

1. Install dummy shaft in countergear. Install spacer washers and roller bearings.
2. Place countergear in case. Align thrust washers at each end. Insert countershaft.
3. Install rollers in reverse idler

gear. Hold rollers with petroleum jelly. Place gear in case. Position thrust washers. Insert shaft. Install shaft lockplate.
4. Insert shifter shafts in case. Position low-reverse lever to inside of case. Locate notches on top of levers to rear of case stud. Align shift detent assembly with shifter shafts and case stud. Push detent assembly and shifter shafts into place. Install shaft roll pins.
5. If removed, install the transmission controlled spark switch.
6. Place front synchronizer in second shift position. Place mainshaft assembly in case to one side.
7. Pull detent levers up. Place shift forks in shifting assembly.
8. Install mainshaft pilot end support in case. Install front bearing cap. Drive rear bearing on thickest rear bearing snap-ring with a 1¼ x 17 in. pipe. Install support and bearing cap.
9. Install locating ball, speedometer drive gear, and snap-ring.
10. Press front bearing onto clutch shaft.
11. Place rollers in clutch shaft. Hold with petroleum jelly.
12. Place friction ring on mainshaft. Slide clutch shaft into position from front.
13. Install thickest front bearing snap-ring that will fit in groove, gasket and cap. Align cap lubrication hole with hole in case.
14. Install extension housing. Install oil seal. Install shift lever, gaskets, and cover.

Type-18
Warner T-16 Fully Synchronized 3-Speed

Application

Camaro, 1967-68
Chevelle, 1966 (396), 1967-68

Chevrolet, 1965-67 (396-427), 1968
Chevy II, 1968

Corvette, 1966-68
Firebird, 1967 (V8)

Disassembly of Unit

1. Clean outside of transmission to keep foreign matter from entering the case and to improve working conditions.
2. Remove side cover assembly and shift forks.
3. Remove extension housing attaching screws. Rotate extension clockwise to expose reverse idler gear shaft.
4. With a long drift through the side cover opening, drive the reverse idler shaft and Woodruff key through the rear of the case.
5. Rotate the extension counter-

clockwise to expose countergear shaft and, with a brass drift, drive shaft and Woodruff key out the rear of case.
6. With the countergear dropped to the bottom of case, remove the mainshaft and extension assembly through the rear of the case, remove the mainshaft pilot roller bearings from the clutch gear.
7. Remove snap-ring which retains mainshaft rear bearing and remove the extension from the rear bearing and mainshaft by tapping on end.
8. Remove the clutch gear bearing

retainer and clutch gear bearing snap-ring and washer from the mainshaft.
9. Drive the clutch gear through its bearing into the case and remove the bearing by tapping from inside the case.
10. Remove countergear and roller bearings, both countergear thrust washers, reverse idler gear and 25 roller bearings, and both idler gear thrust washers from the case.

Mainshaft Disassembly

1. With snap-ring pliers, remove

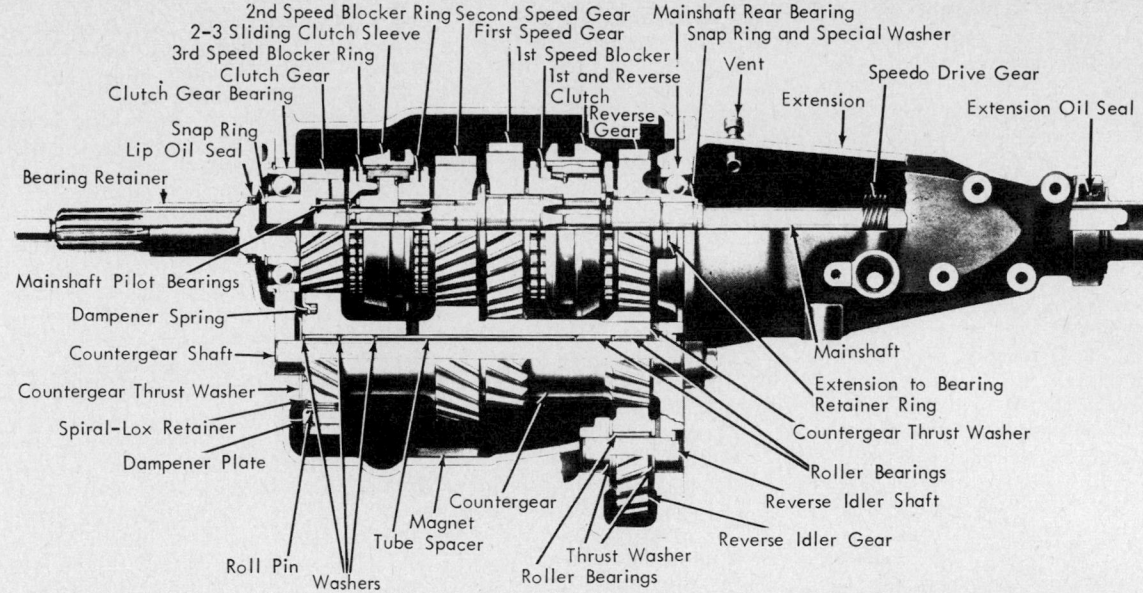

2nd Speed Blocker Ring
2-3 Sliding Clutch Sleeve
3rd Speed Blocker Ring
Clutch Gear
Clutch Gear Bearing
Snap Ring
Lip Oil Seal
Bearing Retainer
Second Speed Gear
First Speed Gear
1st Speed Blocker
1st and Reverse Clutch
Reverse Gear
Mainshaft Rear Bearing
Snap Ring and Special Washer
Vent
Extension
Speedo Drive Gear
Extension Oil Seal

Mainshaft Pilot Bearings
Dampener Spring
Countergear Shaft
Countergear Thrust Washer
Spiral-Lox Retainer
Dampener Plate
Roll Pin
Washers
Magnet
Tube Spacer
Countergear
Thrust Washer
Roller Bearings
Mainshaft
Extension to Bearing Retainer Ring
Countergear Thrust Washer
Roller Bearings
Reverse Idler Shaft
Reverse Idler Gear

Warner T-16 transmission

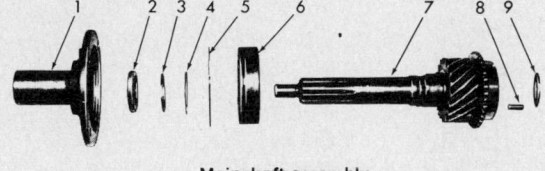

Mainshaft assembly
(© G.M. Corp.)

1 Retainer
2 Lip seal
3 Snap ring
4 Special washer
5 Snap ring
6 Clutch gear bearing
7 Clutch gear
8 Mainshaft pilot bearings
9 Bearing spacer

second and third-speed sliding clutch hub snap-ring from mainshaft. Then remove clutch assembly, second-speed blocker ring and second-speed gear from front of mainshaft.

2. Remove rear bearing snap-ring from mainshaft groove.

3. With reverse gear supported on press plates, apply pressure to the rear of the mainshaft to remove reverse gear, rear bearing, special washer, snap-ring and the speedometer drive gear from rear of mainshaft.

4. Remove first and reverse sliding clutch hub snap-ring from the mainshaft and remove clutch assembly, first-speed blocker ring and first-speed gear from rear of mainshaft.

Cleaning and Inspection

Clean and inspect all parts for wear or other damage. Replace if necessary.

The countergear anti-rattle plate is spring-loaded. If weak or broken, remove plate and/or spring. Replace as necessary.

Synchronizer clutch hubs and sliding sleeves are selected assemblies and should be kept together as in the original assembly. The keys and springs, however, may be replaced if worn or broken.

If bushing in rear of extension housing needs replacement, remove the seal. Then, drive bushing into extension housing. Drive new bushing into the case from the rear. Lubricate inside diameter of bushing and seal, then install new oil seal with driver.

If the lip seal in the clutch bearing retainer needs replacing, pry out the old seal. Then, drive a new seal into place until seal bottoms in its bore.

Mainshaft Assembly

1. Install first-speed gear onto rear

of mainshaft, with gear clutching teeth to the rear.

2. Install first-speed gear blocker ring over the first-speed gear tapered cone end (clutch key notches toward the rear).

3. Install first and reverse sliding clutch assembly over rear of mainshaft (be careful to engage the three keys with the notches of first-speed blocker ring). If properly installed, the straightest side of the clutch hub and the taper of the sliding sleeve will both be toward the rear of the mainshaft.

4. Install the first and reverse clutch hub snap-ring into the mainshaft groove.

NOTE: snap-rings are available in

three thicknesses. Use thickest snapring that will assemble with all parts stacked tightly, endwise.

5. Install reverse gear over rear of mainshaft, with the gear clutching teeth toward the front.

6. Press mainshaft rear bearing over rear of mainshaft, with its outer race snap-ring groove closest to reverse gear.

7. Install rear bearing special washer and snap-ring onto mainshaft.

8. Press the speedometer gear onto the rear of mainshaft until centered on the shaft boss.

9. Install the second-speed gear over the front of the mainshaft, with the gear clutching teeth toward the front.

10. Install the second-speed gear

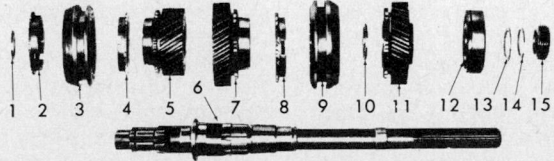

Clutch gear components
(© G.M. Corp.)

1 Snap ring
2 3rd speed blocker ring
3 2-3 clutch assembly
4 2nd speed blocker ring
5 2nd speed gear
6 Mainshaft
7 1st speed gear
8 1st speed blocker ring
9 1st reverse clutch assembly
10 Snap ring
11 Reverse gear
12 Rear bearing
13 Special washer
14 Snap ring
15 Speedo drive gear

blocker ring over the second-speed gear tapered cone end (clutch key notches toward the front).

11. Install the second and third sliding clutch assembly over the front of the mainshaft, engaging the clutch keys with the notches of the second-speed blocker ring. If properly installed, the straightest side of the clutch hub should be toward the rear. The clutch sliding sleeve taper should be toward the front of the mainshaft.

12. Install the second and third-speed clutch hub retainer snap-ring onto the mainshaft.

NOTE: snap-rings are available in four thicknesses. Use thickest snap-ring that will assemble with all parts stacked tightly, endwise.

Assembly of Unit

1. Insert tube spacer in counter-gear. Install a spacer, 20 rollers, another spacer, 20 more rollers, then another spacer at each end of countergear. Use heavy grease and the dummy shaft to hold them in place.

2. Insert countergear assembly through case rear opening along with a tanged countergear thrust washer (tang away from the gear) at each end (large washer at front) and install countergear shaft and Woodruff key from the rear of the case.

NOTE: attach a dial indicator to the case and measure the countergear end-play. If end-play greater than 0.025 in. is shown, new thrust washer

must be installed.

3. With heavy grease, insert the 25 reverse idler gear bearing rollers into position in the bore of the reverse gear. Place gear and bearing assembly, along with a thrust washer on each end, into position inside the case. The beveled edge of the gear teeth face toward the front of the case.

4. Load the pilot bearing rollers into clutch gear, using grease to hold them in place, and position gear in case. Do not install clutch gear ball bearing at this time.

5. Stand case on end with clutch gear down through hole in bench. Place third-speed blocker ring over clutch gear.

6. Install mainshaft assembly from the rear of the case, picking up the spacers, pilot bearing and third-speed blocker rings.

7. Install reverse idler shaft and Woodruff key.

8. Install extension housing gasket to rear of case. Then, using snap-ring pliers, expand the extension-to-bearing snap-ring and install extension over mainshaft and rear bearing. Be sure the snap-ring has started over the rear bearing. Install and tighten extension attaching bolts to 35-45 ft. lbs. Use graphite sealer on the two lower attaching bolts.

9. Tap on the front of clutch gear shaft to force rear bearing-to-extension snap-ring to seat in its groove.

10. With driving sleeve, drive the

clutch gear ball bearing onto the clutch gear and into the case. Install washer and snap-ring onto input shaft.

NOTE: this snap-ring is available in five thicknesses. Use thickest snap-ring that will assemble with all parts stacked tightly, endwise.

Install snap-ring to outer race of clutch gear bearing. If bearing snap-ring groove is partially inside case opening, tap on inside bearing outer race with a long drift through side cover opening.

NOTE: if mainshaft does not turn freely, check clutch sliding sleeves for neutral positions and that the blocker rings are free on their gear cone surfaces.

11. Install gaskets, clutch gear bearing retainer and lip seal assembly with oil drain passages at bottom. Then, tighten attaching screws to 15-20 ft. lbs. Use graphite sealer on threads of retainer bolts.

NOTE: install two retainer-to-case gaskets (.010 and .015 in. thick) instead of the one .025 in. production gasket removed.

12. Place the shift forks in the clutch sleeve grooves with the first and reverse fork hump toward the bottom.

13. Install side cover and gasket. Torque retaining bolts to 15-20 ft. lbs.

NOTE: the two side cover-to-case retaining bolts have special oil sealing splines and must be used at these two through locations.

Type-19
Warner T-85 3-Speed

Application

American Motors, 1966   (327 V8)   **1965 Wildcat**

Disassembly

1. With transmission drained and mounted in an adequate stand, remove the cap screws, washers, and side cover assembly of transmission.

2. Remove four cap screws and washers holding the mainshaft rear bearing retainer extension to case and move the extension away from the case about ½ in. Then rotate retainer to expose countershaft end and lock key.

3. From front of transmission, drive countershaft to rear, using countershaft dummy.

4. Work countershaft all the way out of cluster, end spacers, rollers and roller bearing spacer.

5. Leave dummy shaft in place in the countershaft gear cluster to keep the bearings and spacers in location.

6. Lower countergear cluster down into bottom of case, then remove rear bearing retainer extension, gasket, and mainshaft assembly from transmission case.

7. Remove mainshaft front bearing rollers from inside the main drive gear.

8. Remove bearing spacing washer from front end of mainshaft.

9. Remove attaching cap screws and washers, then the main drive gear bearing retainer from front of case.

10. Remove main drive gear bearing snap ring from front side of main drive gear bearing.

11. With transmission case up-ended (front up) press main drive gear out of bearing.

12. Remove oil retainer from main drive gear.

13. Tap main drive gear bearing out

through front of case and remove mian drive gear bearing snap-ring from shaft.

14. Using brass drift, drive reverse idler shaft to rear of case to clear lock key.

15. Remove lock key and, from rear of case, drive idler gear shaft into case, then remove idler gear and shaft from case.

16. Lift out countergear, dummy shaft, and washers from case.

17. Remove synchronizing ring from front side of second and third-speed clutch. Remove clutch hub retaining snap-ring from front end of mainshaft.

18. Remove second- and third-speed clutch sleeve from clutch hub, then remove clutch hub from mainshaft.

19. Remove two clutch key springs and three clutch keys from clutch

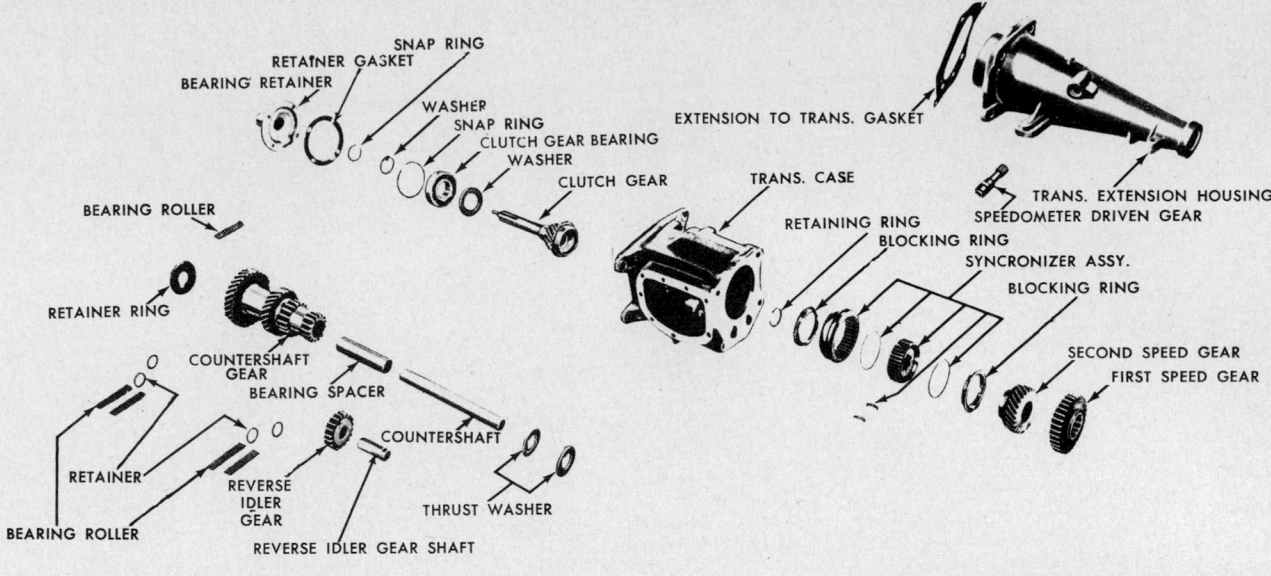

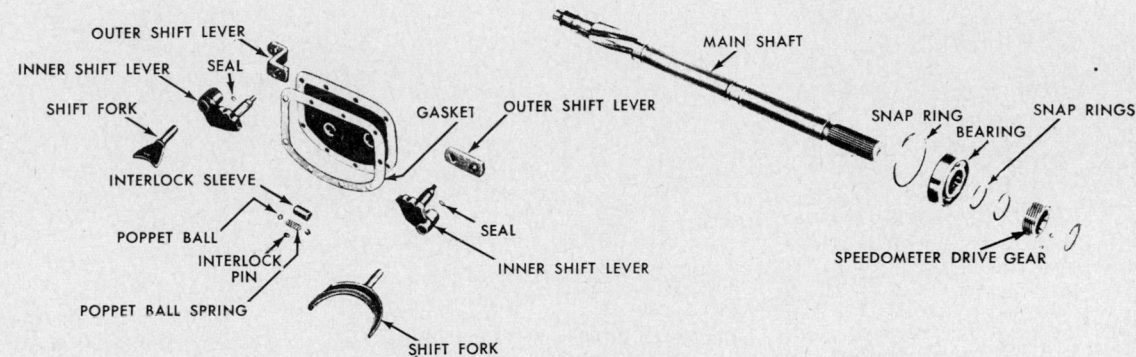

Warner T-85 transmission (Ⓒ Buick Div., G.M. Corp.)

hub.

20. Remove rear synchronizer ring and second-speed gear from the mainshaft.
21. Remove first and reverse sliding gear from the mainshaft.
22. Remove speedometer driven gear lock plate to extension bolt and lock washer, then remove lock plate.
23. Insert screwdriver in lockplate slot in fitting and pry fitting, and shaft from extension.
24. Remove mainshaft rear bearing front snap-ring from rear bearing retainer extension and tap mainshaft and rear bearing out of retainer extension.
25. Remove snap-ring from rear of speedometer drive gear.
26. Remove speedometer drive gear. detent ball and speedometer gear front snap-ring.
27. Remove mainshaft rear bearing rear snap-ring.
28. Using a press, press mainshaft rear bearing toward rear of shaft until loose and remove.
29. Remove seal from rear bearing retainer.

Assembly
1. Assemble by reversing the above procedure.

Type-20
Warner T-90, T-86
3-Speed

T-90 Application

American Motors (6 Cyl. HD), 1966-67

Disassembly
1. Remove cover.
2. Remove front bearing cap, clutch shaft snap-ring and bearing lock-ring.
3. Remove the front bearing, using a bearing puller and a thrust yoke to prevent damaging synchronizer clutches.
4. Remove extension housing. Drive out seal from inside housing with oil seal remover and installer tool. Use bushing remover and installer tool to replace bushing.
5. Move mainshaft assembly back about ¾ in. Lower front end of clutch shaft, move mainshaft as-

T-86 Application

American Motors (232, 287, 290), 1965-67

sembly over countergear and out of shift forks. Remove clutch shaft from front of case.
6. Check roller bearings inside rear of clutch shaft for wear or damage.
7. Remove snap-ring, speedometer drive gear, and key.
8. Remove snap-ring, synchro-

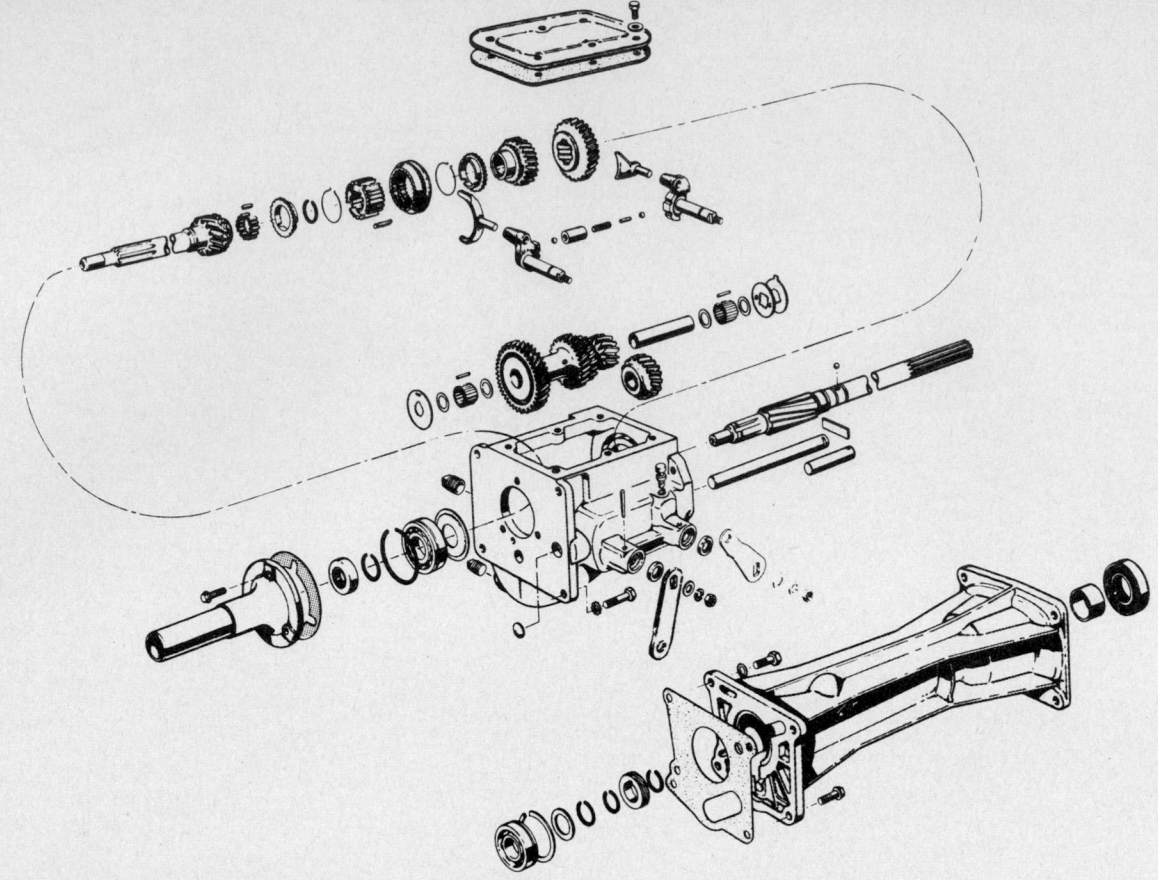

T-90 or T-86 transmission—exploded view (© American Motors Corp.)

clutch assembly, second gear, friction ring, and low-reverse sliding gear. Press off rear bearing.
9. Remove shifter forks.
10. Remove shaft lockplate from rear of case.
11. Drive countershaft out to rear, using dummy shaft. Lower countergear to bottom of case.
12. Drive out reverse idler shaft. Remove reverse idler gear and countergear.
13. Remove outer shift levers and shifter shaft lockpins. Remove shifter shafts and two interlock ball bearings. Remove interlock sleeve and spring. Remove shaft oil seals from case.

Inspection
1. Wash all parts in solvent.
2. Air dry.
3. Check gears for worn, cracked, or chipped teeth. Check fit to shaft. Gears should fit smoothly without excessive play between splines.
4. Check bearings for cracked races, and worn or scored balls.
5. Slide synchronizer rings on cones of second gear and clutch shaft. Replace rings if there is excessive wear or pits on the taper.
6. Check case bearing recesses for

wear or scoring. Check case for cracks.

Assembly
1. Install new shift shaft oil seals.
2. Install low-reverse shift shaft, interlock sleeve, ball bearing, pin, and spring. Install second-third shift shaft and second ball bearing.
3. Shift mechanism into any gear position. With one end of interlock sleeve against shift shaft quadrant, clearance between opposite end of sleeve and quadrant on other shaft should be .001-.007 in. Interlock sleeves are available in several sizes for adjustment.
4. Install lockpins and shift levers.
5. Install dummy shaft and bearings in countergear. Install thrust washers; the bronze front

washer must index with the case.
6. Place countergear and dummy shaft in bottom of case.
7. Install reverse idler gear with chamfered side of teeth to front of case. Drive in shaft from rear.
8. Align slots in countershaft and reverse idler shaft. Position countergear and drive in countershaft. Install lockplate.
9. Install shifter forks.
10. Press rear bearing onto mainshaft. Install key, speedometer drive gear, and snap-ring.
11. Install low-reverse sliding gear on mainshaft with sliding collar to front. Gear should slide easily. Install second gear with tapered cone to front.
12. Install rear bearing snap-ring. Install the thickest mainshaft

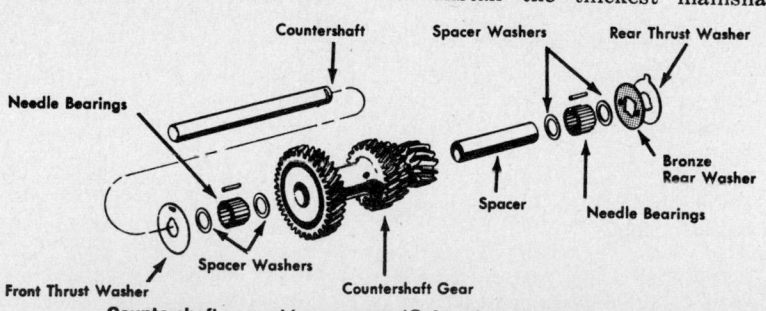

Countershaft assembly sequence (© American Motors Corp.)

rear snap-ring that will fit into groove.

13. Install synchro-clutch assembly and thickest mainshaft front snap-ring that will fit in groove.

14. When synchro-clutch hub is pressed against snap-ring, there should be .003-.010 in. clearance between second gear and shoulder on mainshaft.

15. Install 14 rollers in clutch shaft. Retain with light grease.

16. Install front friction ring on clutch shaft. Insert clutch shaft through top of case. Install mainshaft assembly through rear of case, moving to right to engage shifter forks in synchro-clutch collar and low-reverse sliding gear. Guide clutch shaft onto mainshaft.

17. Install a new oil seal in extension housing.

18. Install extension housing.

19. Install oil slinger, concave side to rear. Drive in front bearing using thrust yoke to prevent synchronizer damage.

20. Install thickest clutch shaft snap-ring that will fit in groove.

21. Install front bearing cap with new gasket. Choose thickness of gasket to give zero clutch shaft end-play.

22. Check clearance of friction rings. The clearance should be .056-.145 in.

23. Install cover and gasket.

Type-21
Warner T-96 3-Speed

Application

American Motors, 1965-72 (199, 232 6 Cyl.)

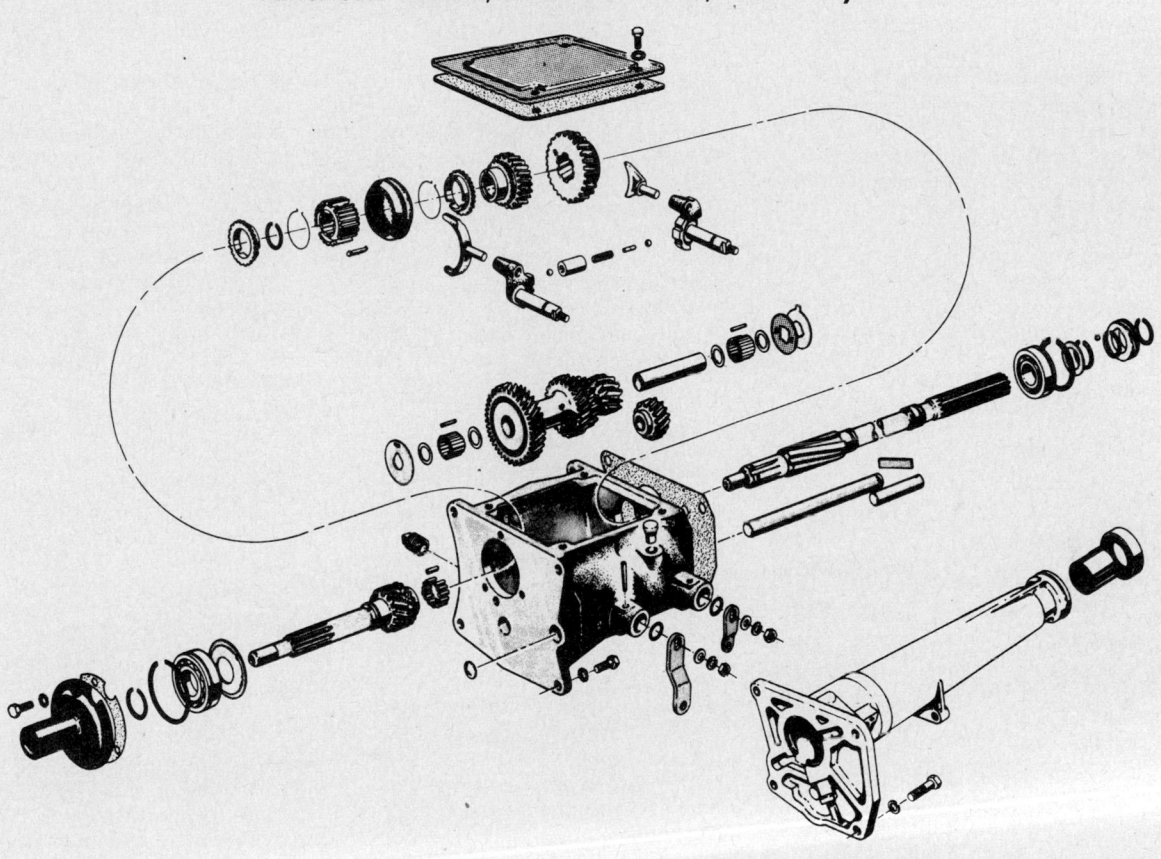

T-96 transmission—exploded view (© American Motors Corp.)

Disassembly

1. Remove top cover.
2. Remove front bearing cap, clutch shaft snap-ring, and bearing lockring.
3. Use a bearing puller and a thrust yoke to remove front bearing.
4. Remove oil slinger.
5. Remove extension housing. Replace rear bearing oil seal and extension housing bushing if necessary.
6. Remove speedometer drive gear snap-ring, drive gear, and retaining ball.
7. Move mainshaft assembly to rear ½ in. Lower front of clutch shaft and raise rear of countergear. Remove clutch shaft.
8. Check 21 roller bearings inside rear of clutch shaft for wear, pitting, or scoring.
9. Remove second-third shifter fork. Tilt mainshaft to remove synchro-clutch snap-ring.
10. Remove synchro-clutch. second gear, and low and reverse gear.
11. Remove low-reverse shifter fork.
12. Remove mainshaft and rear bearing from rear of case. Press rear bearing from shaft.
13. Remove reverse idler shaft and countershaft lockplate.
14. Drive countershaft out to rear with a dummy shaft. Lower dummy shaft and countergear to bottom of case.
15. Drive reverse idler shaft out to rear. Remove gear. Remove countergear.
16. Note position of reverse idler shaft thrust washers; check for wear or damage.
17. Remove outer shift levers and

shifter shaft lockpin. Remove shifter shafts from inside case. Remove two interlock ball bearings. Remove interlock sleeve, pin, and spring. Remove shifter shaft O-rings.

Inspection

1. Wash all parts in solvent.
2. Air dry.

Gears and Mainshaft

1. Check for worn, cracked, or chipped teeth.
2. Check fit of gears to mainshaft. If gears are replaced, also replace the gear with which they mesh.

Bearings

1. Check for cracked races.
2. Check for worn or scored balls.

Synchro-Clutch and Friction Rings

1. Slide rings on cones of second gear and clutch shaft.
2. Replace rings if there is excessive wear or a pitted condition on the taper.

Case

1. Check for evidence of bearings turning in their bores.
2. Check for cracks.

Assembly

1. Install new shift shaft O-rings.
2. Install low-reverse shift shaft interlock sleeve, ball bearing, and spring.
3. Install second-third shift shaft. Place second ball bearing in position.
4. Place shifter mechanism in any gear. With one end of interlock sleeve against shifter shaft quadrant, measure clearance between opposite end of sleeve and the other quadrant. Clearance should be .001-.007 in. Selective lengths of interlock sleeves are available for adjustment. Install lockpins and shift levers.
5. Install dummy shaft in countergear. Install needle bearings, spacer, and washers. Install thrust washers. The bronze front washer must index with the case. Install countergear assembly in bottom of case.
6. Install reverse idler gear with chamfered side of teeth to front. Drive reverse idler shaft in from rear.
7. Drive countershaft into place. Install lockplate.
8. Press rear bearing on mainshaft. Install snap-rings. Place mainshaft in case.
9. Install shifter forks. Install first-reverse sliding gear, second

gear, and synchro-clutch assembly, hub forward.
10. Install thickest mainshaft front snap-ring that will fit in groove.
11. There should be .003-.010 in. clearance between second gear and the mainshaft shoulder, with the synchro-clutch hub pressed against the snap-ring.
12. Hold the 21 clutch shaft bearings in place with petroleum jelly. Install front friction ring and clutch shaft on mainshaft.
13. Simultaneously install the mainshaft rear bearing, align the shifter forks and gears, and guide the mainshaft into the clutch shaft.
14. Install the thickest rear mainshaft snap-ring that will fit in the groove.
15. Install retaining ball, speedometer drive gear, and snap-ring.
16. Install extension housing with a new oil seal.
17. Place oil slinger on clutch shaft with concave side to rear. Install front bearing using thrust yoke. Install thickest snap-ring that will fit in the groove.
18. Install bearing cap and a new gasket.
19. Check clearance of synchro-clutch friction rings. Both clearances should be .036-.100 in.
20. Check transmission operation in all gears; then install the case cover and gasket.

Type-22
Warner T-10 4-Speed

Application

American Motors, 1966 (287, 327), 1967-69 (290, 343), 1967-70 (390), 1970 (360), 1971-72 (401)

Wildcat, 1965
Buick Special, 1965
1966 (GS)
Mustang, 1965 (V8)

Disassembly

1. Drain transmission, mount in adequate stand. Then remove the side cover and shift controls.
2. Remove four bolts from front bearing retainer, then remove retainer and gasket.
3. Remove output shaft companion flange.
4. Drive lockpin up from reverse shifter lever boss, then pull shift-shaft out about ⅛ in. to disengage shifter fork from reverse gear.
5. Remove five bolts from the case extension and tap the extension (with soft hammer) rearward. When idler gear shaft is out as far as it will go, move extension to the left so the reverse fork clears the reverse gear. Remove extension and gasket.
6. Remove rear bearing snap-ring

from mainshaft.
7. Remove case extension oil seal.
8. Remove speedometer drive gear with puller.
9. Remove the reverse gear, reverse idler gear and tanged thrust washer.
10. Remove self-locking bolt holding the rear bearing retainer to transmission case.
11. Remove the entire mainshaft assembly.
12. Unload bearing rollers from main drive gear and remove fourth-speed synchronizer blocking ring.
13. Lift the front half of reverse idler gear and its thrust washer from the case.
14. Remove the main drive gear snap-ring and remove spacer washer.
15. With soft hammer, tap main

drive gear toward rear and out of front bearing.
16. From inside the case, tap out front bearing and snap-ring.
17. From the front of the case, tap out the countershaft, using dummy shaft.
18. Then lift out the countergear assembly with both tanged washers.
19. Dismantle the countergear, consisting of 80 rollers, six .050 in. spacers and a roller tubular spacer.
20. Remove mainshaft front snapring and slide third and fourth-speed clutch assembly, third-speed gear and synchronizer ring, second and third-speed gear thrust bearing, second-speed gear and second-speed synchronizer ring from front of mainshaft.
21. Spread rear bearing retainer

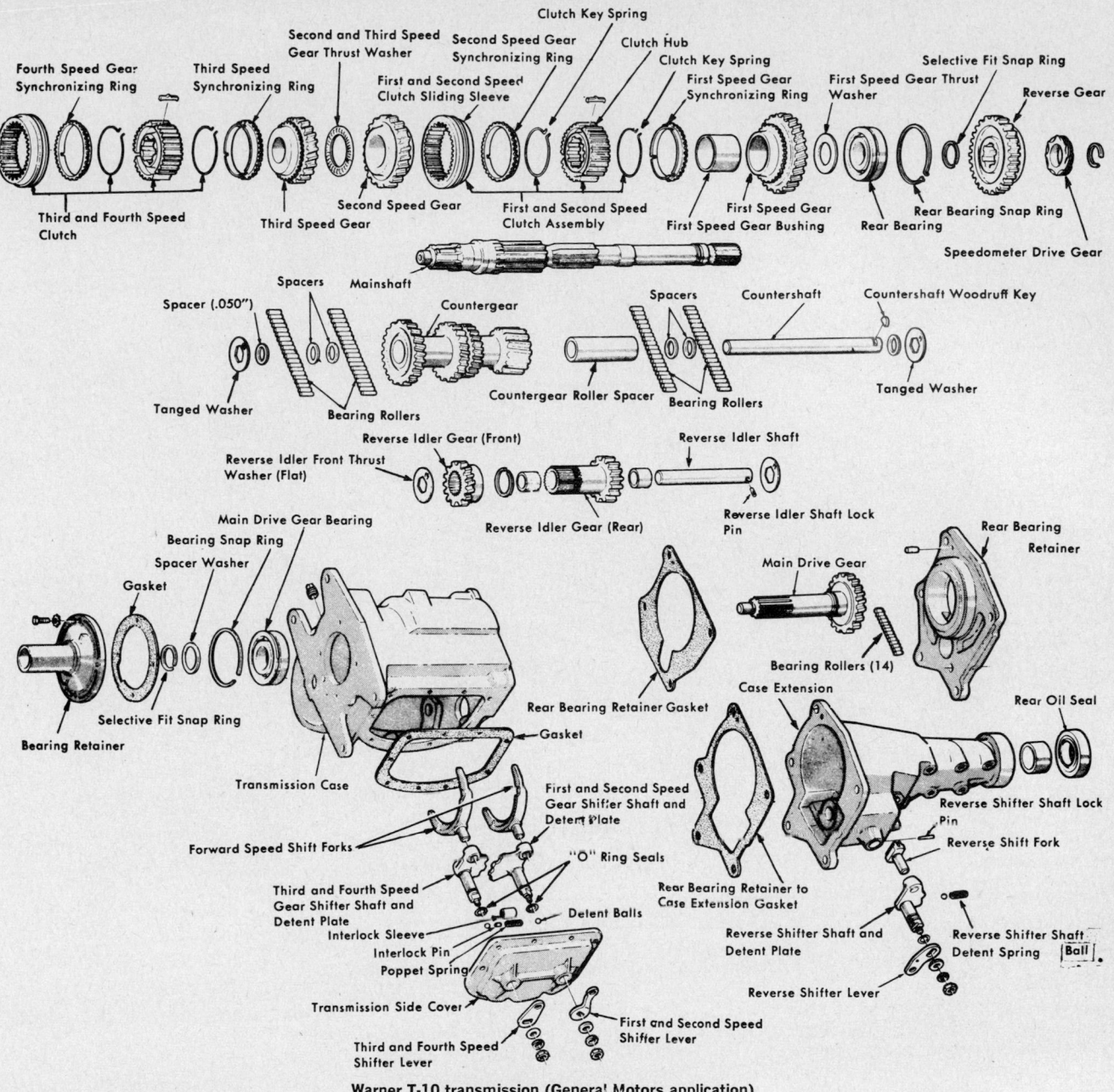

Warner T-10 transmission (General Motors application)
(© Buick Div., G.M. Corp.)

snap-ring and press mainshaft out of retainer.

22. Remove the mainshaft rear snapring.

23. Support first and second-speed clutch assembly and press on rear of mainshaft to remove shaft from rear bearing, first-speed gear, and synchromesh ring, first and second-speed clutch sliding sleeve and first-speed gear bushing.

Assembly

Mainshaft

1. From the rear of the mainshaft, assemble first and second-speed clutch assembly to mainshaft (sliding clutch sleeve taper toward the rear, hub to the front) and press the first-speed gear bushing onto the shaft.

2. Install first-speed gear synchronizing ring so notches in ring align with keys in hub.

3. Install first-speed gear (hub toward front) and the first-speed gear thrust washer. Be sure the grooves in the washer are facing first-speed gear.

4. Press on the rear bearing, with the snap-ring groove toward the front of the transmission. Be sure the bearing is firmly seated against the shoulder on the mainshaft.

5. Install the selective fit snap-ring onto the mainshaft behind the rear bearing. Use the thickest ring that will fit between the rear face of the bearing and the front face of the snap-ring.

6. From the front of the mainshaft, install the second-speed gear synchronizing ring so that notches in the ring correspond with the keys in the hub.

7. Install the second-speed gear (hub toward the back) and install the second and third-speed gear thrust bearing.

8. Install third-speed gear (hub to front) and third-speed gear synchronizing ring (notches front).

9. Install third and fourth-speed gear clutch assembly (hub and sliding sleeve) with taper front, being sure keys in the hub correspond with notches in third-

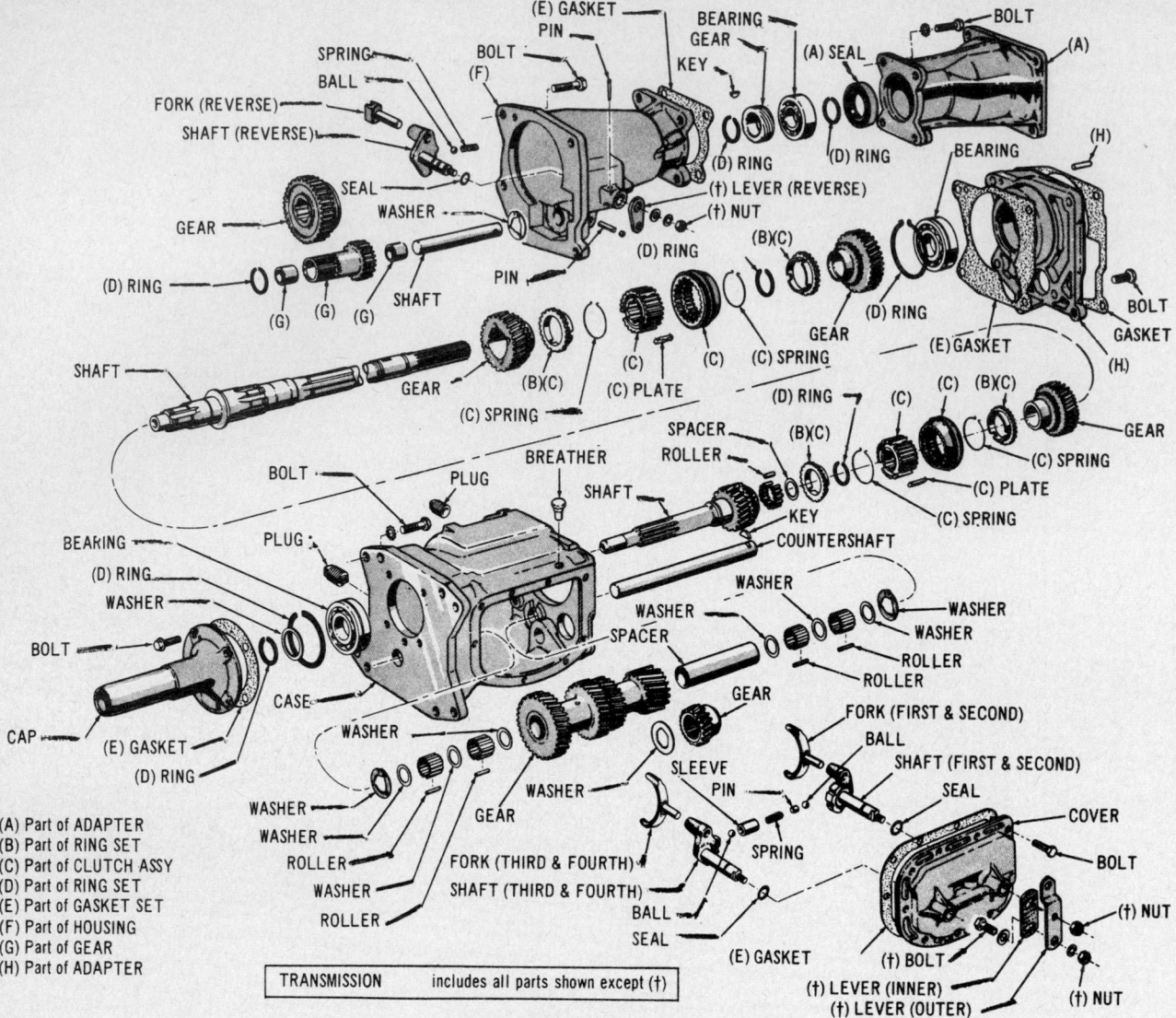

(A) Part of ADAPTER
(B) Part of RING SET
(C) Part of CLUTCH ASSY
(D) Part of RING SET
(E) Part of GASKET SET
(F) Part of HOUSING
(G) Part of GEAR
(H) Part of ADAPTER

| TRANSMISSION | includes all parts shown except (†) |

Warner T-10 transmission (American Motors application)

speed gear synchronizing ring.

10. Install snap-ring (.086-.088 in. thickness) into groove in main-shaft, in front of the third and fourth-speed clutch assembly.

11. Install rear bearing retainer plate. Spread the snap-ring on the plate to allow the snap-ring to drop around the rear bearing and press on the end of the main-shaft until the snap-ring engages the groove in the rear bearing.

12. Install reverse gear (shift collar to the rear).

13. Press speedometer drive gear onto the mainshaft. Position the speedometer gear to get a measurement of 4½ in. from the center of the gear to the flat surface of the rear bearing retainer.

14. Install special snap-ring into the groove at the rear of the main-shaft.

Countergear

1. Install countergear dummy and tubular roller bearing spacer into the countergear.

2. Using heavy grease to hold the rollers, install 20 bearing rollers in either end of the countergear, two spacers, 20 more rollers, then one spacer. Install the same combination of rollers and spacers in the other end of the countergear.

3. Set the countergear assembly in the bottom of the transmission case, be sure the tanged thrust washers are in their proper position.

Main Drive Gear

1. Press bearing (snap-ring groove front) onto main drive gear until the bearing fully seats against the shoulder on the gear.

2. Install spacer washer and selective fit snap-ring in the groove in the main drive gear shaft.

NOTE: variable thickness snap-rings are available to obtain a prescribed clearance of .000-.005 in. between the rear face of the snap ring and the front face of the spacer washer.

Transmission

1. Install main drive gear and bearing assembly through the side cover opening and into position in the transmission front bore. After assembly is in place, install snap-ring into groove in front bearing.

2. Lift countergear and thrust washers into place. Install Woodruff key into end of countershaft, then from the rear of the case, press the countershaft in until the end of the shaft is flush with rear of transmission case and the dummy shaft is displaced. End-play in the countergear must not exceed .025 in.

3. Install the 14 bearing rollers into the grease-coated end of the main drive gear.

4. Using heavy grease, position gasket on front face of rear bearing retainer. Install the fourth-speed

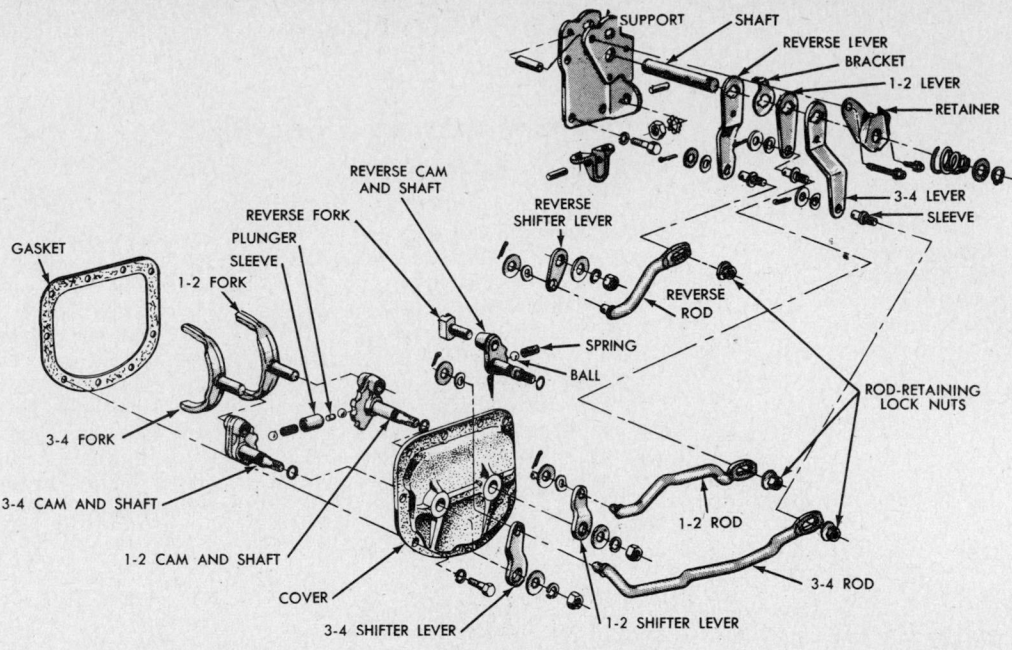

Linkage and cover

synchronizing ring onto main drive gear with clutch key notches toward rear of transmission.

5. Position the reverse idler gear thrust washer on the machined face of the ear cast in the case for the reverse idler shaft. Position the front reverse idler gear on top of the thrust washer, hub facing toward rear of case.

6. Lower the mainshaft assembly into the case, with the notches of the fourth-speed synchronizing ring corresponding to the keys in the clutch assembly.

7. Install self-locking bolt, holding the rear bearing retainer to the transmission case. Torque to 20-30 ft. lbs.

8. From the rear of the case, insert the rear reverse idler gear, engaging the splines with the portion of the gear within the case.

9. Grease gasket, and place in position on the rear face of the rear bearing retainer.

10. Install remaining tanged thrust washer into place on reverse idler shaft, being sure the tang on the thrust washer is in the notch in the idler thrust face of the extension.

11. Place the two clutches in neutral position.

12. Pull reverse shifter shaft to left side of extension and rotate shaft to bring reverse fork to extreme forward position in extension. Line up forward and reverse idler gears.

13. Start the extension onto the transmission case by inserting reverse idler shaft through reverse idler gears. Push in on shifter until shift fork engages reverse gear shift collar. When the fork engages, rotate the shifter shaft to move reverse gear rearward. This will allow the extension to slide onto the transmission case.

14. Install three extension and retainer to case attaching bolts and torque to 35-45 ft. lbs. Install two extension to retainer attaching bolts and torque to 20-30 ft. lbs. Use sealer on the lower, right attaching bolt.

15. Adjust reverse shift shaft so that groove in shaft lines up with hole in boss. Drive in lockpin from top of boss.

16. Install the main drive gear bearing retainer and gasket, being sure the oil well lines up with the oil outlet hole. Install four sealer-coated attaching bolts and torque to 15-20 ft. lbs.

17. Install a shift fork into each clutch sleeve.

18. With both clutches in neutral, install side cover gasket and lower side cover into place.

19. Install attaching bolts and torque to 10-20 ft. lbs. Use sealer on the lower right bolt.

20. Install first and second, and third and fourth shift levers, lockwashers and nuts.

NOTE: when used in American Motors cars equipped with torque tube drive, the tailshaft extension housing is peculiar to torque tube design. Both torque tube and open driveshaft designs are shown in the accompanying illustration.

Hurst Shift Linkage

Three-Speed Transmission Floor Shift Linkage Adjustment

The floor-mounted three-speed transmission linkage uses two shift rods and levers. Adjustment can be made with the aid of a neutral alignment rod, supplied with the floor shift linkage kit, or a 1/4 in. diameter rod.

Adjustment Procedure

1. Place shifter unit in the neutral position.
2. Back both shifter stop bolts out of shifter frame until only a few threads remain engaged.
3. Remove both shifting rods and rod adjusting buttons from the shifter unit.
4. Place neutral alignment rod through alignment holes in shifter unit and levers.
5. Making doubly sure that both transmission levers are in the neutral position, adjust the rod adjusting buttons to permit easy slip-in fit of button into nylon bushing in proper lever.
6. Fasten buttons in lever with spring clips and remove neutral alignment rod.
7. Push stick firmly into second gear and hold. Screw second gear stop bolt in until contact is felt. Back bolt out one full turn and tighten locknut. Pull stick firmly back into third gear, screw third gear stop bolt in until contact is made, then back stop bolt out one full turn and tighten locknut.

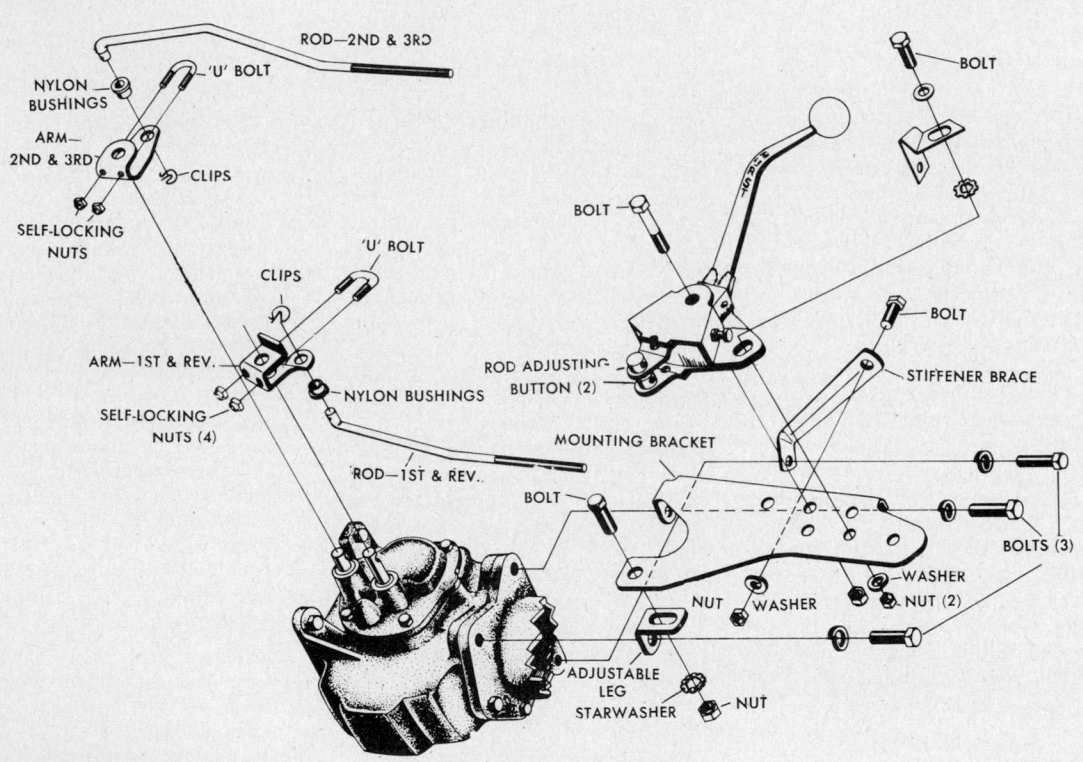

ROD—2ND & 3RD
NYLON BUSHINGS
'U' BOLT
ARM—2ND & 3RD
CLIPS
SELF-LOCKING NUTS
CLIPS
'U' BOLT
ARM—1ST & REV.
NYLON BUSHINGS
SELF-LOCKING NUTS (4)
ROD ADJUSTING BUTTON (2)
ROD—1ST & REV.
MOUNTING BRACKET
BOLT
BOLT
BOLT
BOLT
STIFFENER BRACE
BOLTS (3)
WASHER
NUT
WASHER
NUT (2)
ADJUSTABLE LEG
STARWASHER
NUT

Typical 3-speed floorshift linkage
(© Hurst Perf. Inc.)

Four-Speed Transmission Linkage Adjustment

The four-speed transmission gearshift linkage uses three shift rods and levers. The adjustment can be made with the aid of a neutral alignment rod, supplied with the floor shift linkage kit, or a 1/4 in. diameter rod.

Adjustment Procedure

1. Place shifter unit in the neutral position.
2. Back both shifter stop bolts out of shifter frame until only a few threads remain engaged.
3. Remove shifting rods and rod adjusting buttons from the shifter unit.
4. Align levers with shifter frame and insert neutral alignment rod through notches in frame and holes in levers.
5. Rotate transmission arms backward and forward. The neutral position for each arm can be felt at the mid-position of full travel. Reverse arm must be moved to the end of its travel toward the front (disengaged position).
6. Adjust positions of buttons on each rod to permit easy slip-in fit of button into nylon bushing in proper lever.
NOTE: transmission arms must remain in neutral positions while alignment is accomplished. Fasten buttons in levers with spring clips.
7. Remove neutral alignment rod. Test shifter. Stick should move freely from side to side in neutral. If shifter functions properly,

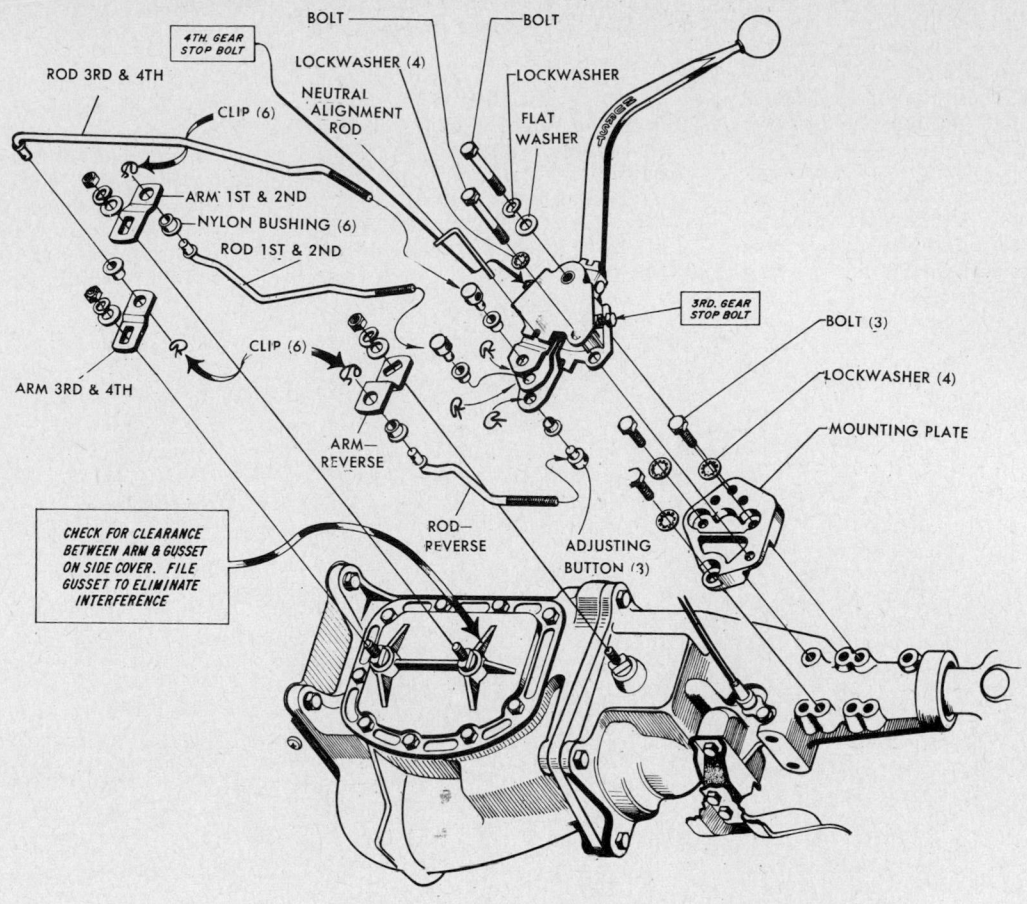

Borg-Warner 4-speed shift linkage
(© Hurst Perf. Inc.)

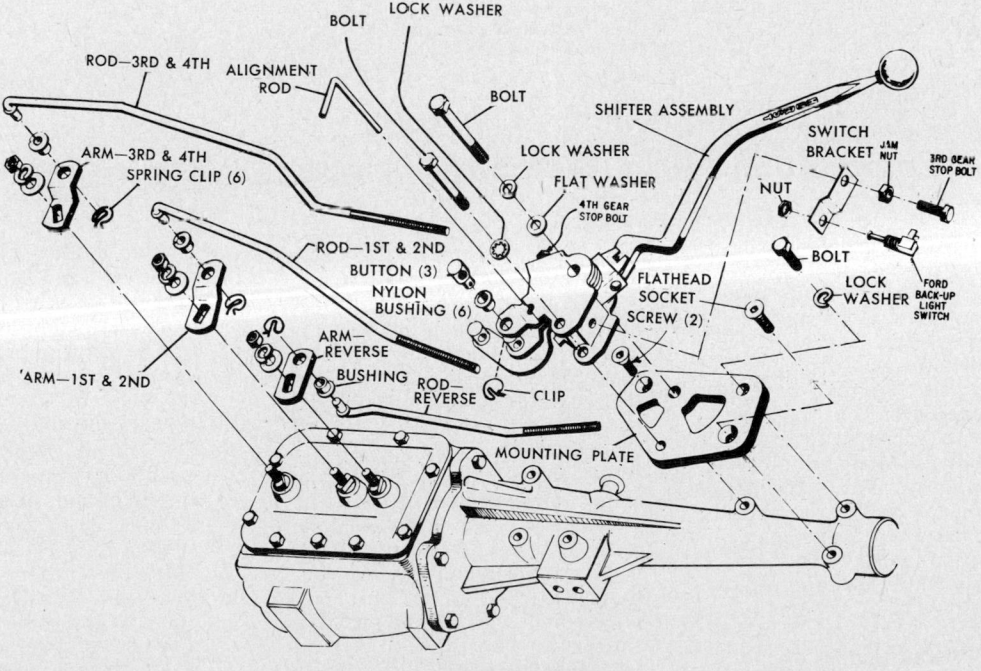

Dagenham 4-speed shift linkage
(© Hurst Perf. Inc.)

8. If the stick cannot be moved freely between first-second, third-fourth or reverse path, one or more of the rod button adjustments must be corrected. Move stick forward to third gear, then back to fourth, then into neutral. Insert neutral alignment rod. If rod cannot be inserted freely, the third-fourth rod button is incorrectly adjusted. Similar testing

of first-second shift will prove alignment of first-second adjustment.

9. To check reverse rod button adjustment, place stick at neutral. Disconnect reverse rod adjusting button from reverse lever. Grasp rod and push toward front of car. (Reverse arm is disengaged when at end of forward travel). Adjust rod button for easy slip-in fit in

bushing. Reassemble and fasten with spring clip.

10. Push stick firmly into third gear and hold. Screw third gear stop bolt in until contact is felt. Back bolt out one full turn and tighten locknut. Pull stick firmly back into fourth gear, screw fourth gear stop bolt in until contact is felt, then back stop bolt out one full turn and tighten locknut.

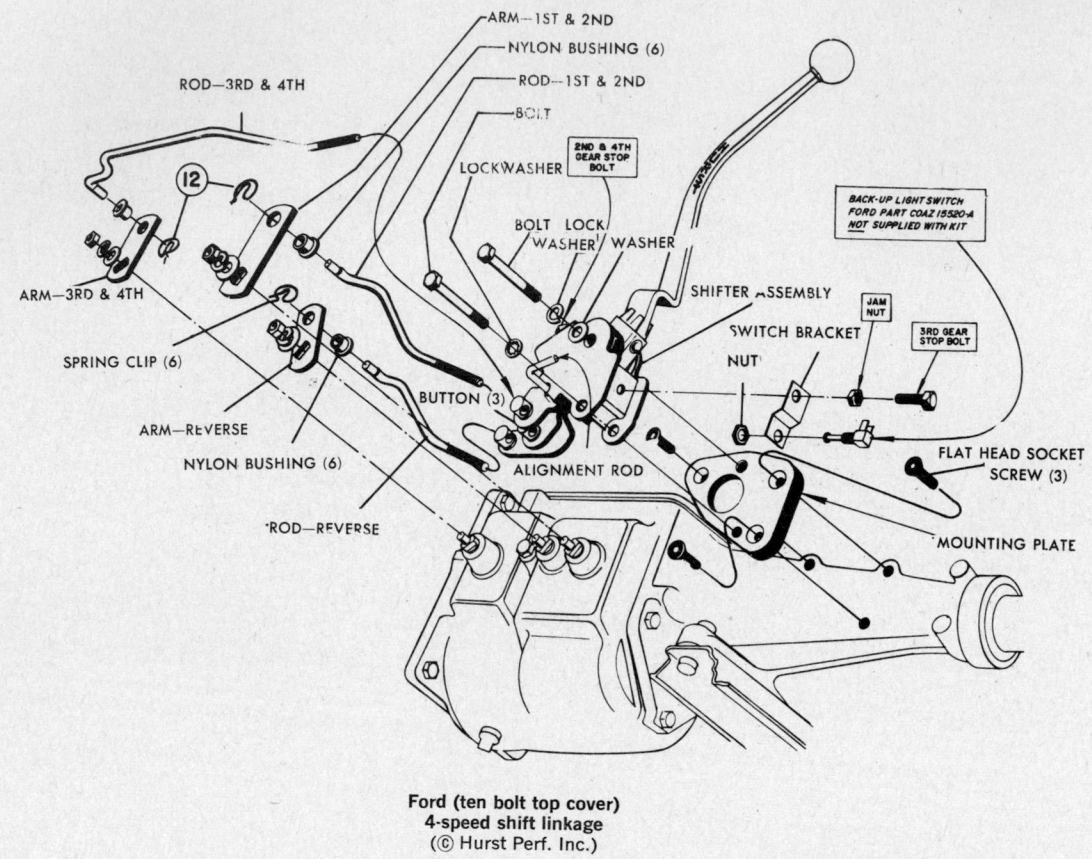

Ford (ten bolt top cover)
4-speed shift linkage
(ⓒ Hurst Perf. Inc.)

Competition Plus® Transmission Linkage Adjustment

The Competition Plus® shift linkage uses three shift rods and levers. The shift lever on the transmission rear housing operates the transmission reverse gear and the reverse lockup mechanism (on cars so equipped). The lever on the rear of the transmission side cover controls first and second gears. The front transmision lever controls third and fourth gears. A spring load of 21-28 lbs. must be overcome to move the shift lever to the extreme left for a shift into reverse. Adjustment of the shifter can be made with the aid of a neutral alignment rod or a short ¼ in. diameter pin.

Adjustment Procedure

1. Place the transmission shift levers into their neutral positions

and check for neutral by rotating the drive shaft.

2. Loosen the lower nuts and bolts on the transmission shift levers and the two upper "hug nuts" at the center of the shift levers. Loosen the two locknuts on the reverse shift rod at each end of the trunnion.

3. Insert the aligning pin into the shifter housing and through the three rear shift levers. Make sure that the pins enters the notch in the mounting bracket.

4. Remove the aligning pin completely and reinsert the pin. The shifter is aligned correctly in neutral if the aligning pin freely enters the housing and the holes in the levers.

5. Tighten the lower bolts and nuts at the forward shift levers, then tighten the upper "hug nuts" to 10 ft. lbs. Tighten the trunnion nuts to lock the trunnion in position, taking care not to bind the trunnion in the reverse lever. Remove the aligning pin.

6. On cars equipped with a reverse lockup mechanism the lockup rod trunnion locknuts must be loosened ½ in. to permit adjustment of the lock.

7. Shift the transmission into reverse and lock the steering column. It may be necessary to move the lower column shift lever upward until it is in the locked position.

8. Tighten the lower trunnion lock-

nut while holding the trunnion centered in the column lever.

9. Unlock the steering column and check for proper engagement of all gears, including reverse. The steering must lock without any binding when reverse is engaged.

10. On cars equipped with a backup light switch actuated by the shift linkage check for correct operation of lights.

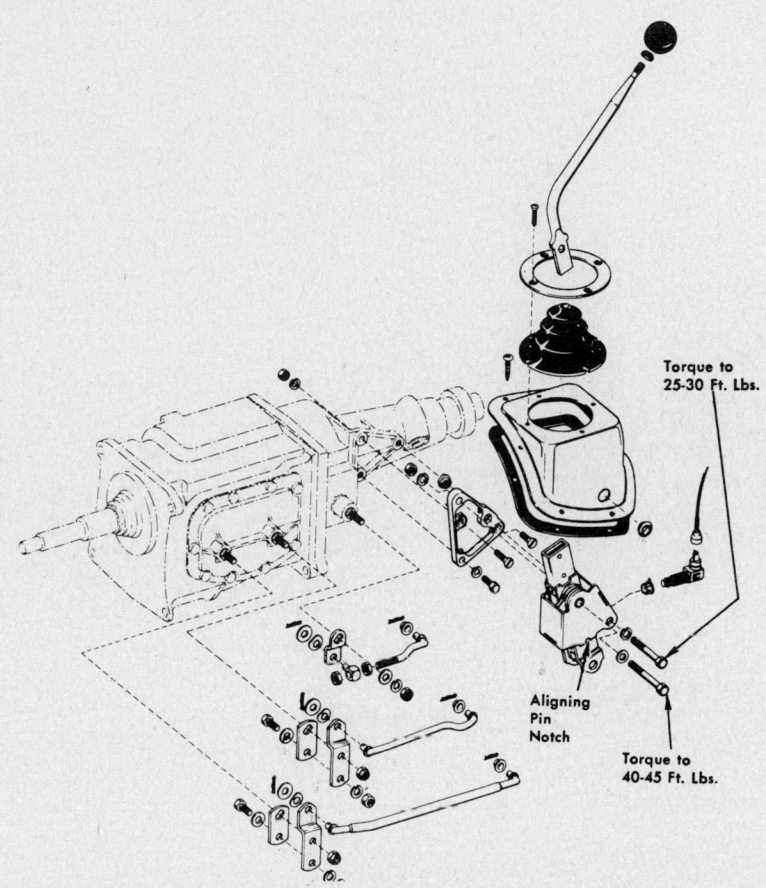

Torque to 25-30 Ft. Lbs.

Aligning Pin Notch

Torque to 40-45 Ft. Lbs.

Competition Plus® linkage as used on Borg Warner T10 (© American Motors Corp.)

OVERDRIVE TRANSMISSION AVAILABILITY

Make and Model (No. cyl./cu. in. displ.)	1965	1966	1967	1968	1969	Make and Model (No. cyl./cu. in. displ.)	1965	1966	1967	1968	1969
American Motors						Galaxie (8/292)					
Ambassador (6/232)	X	X	X	X	X	Galaxie (8/352)					
Ambassador (8/287)	X	X				Galaxie (8/390)					
Ambassador (8/290)			X	X		Galaxie 500 (6/223)					
Ambassador (8/327)	X					Galaxie 500 (8/292)					
American (6/195)	X					Galaxie 500 (8/352)					
American (6/199)		X	X	X	X	Galaxie 500 (8/390)					
American (6/232)					X	500 XL (8/352)					
AMX (8/290)				X		500 XL (8/390)					
Classic (6/199)	X					Mercury (8/390)	X				
Classic (6/232)	X	X				Meteor (8/221)					
Classic (8/287)	X	X				Meteor (8/260)					
Classic (8/327)	X					**General Motors Corporation**					
Javelin (6/23?)				X	X	Bel Air (6/250)				X	
Marlin (6/232)		X	X			Bel Air (8/307)				X	
Marlin (8/287)		X				Biscayne (6/250)				X	
Rebel (6/232)			X	X	X	Biscayne (8/307)				X	
Rebel (8/290)				X		Caprice (8/307)				X	
Rogue (6/232)				X		Chevelle (6/194)	X	X			
Ford Motor Company						Chevelle (6/230)	X	X	X	X	
Fairlane (8/221)						Chevelle (8/283)	X	X	X		
Fairlane (8/260)						Chevelle (8/307)				X	
Fairlane (8/289)	X	X	X			Chevrolet (6/230)	X				
Falcon (6/144)						Chevrolet (6/250)		X	X		
Falcon (6/170)						Chevrolet (8/283)	X	X	X		
Ford 300 (6/223)						Concours (6/230)				X	
Ford 300 (8/292)						Concours (8/307)				X	
Ford 300 (8/352)						Impala (6/250)				X	
Ford 300 (8/390)						Impala (8/307)				X	
Ford (6/240)	X	X	X			Malibu (6/230)				X	
Ford (8/289)	X	X	X			Malibu (8/307)				X	
Ford (8/352)						Nomad (6/230)				X	
Ford (8/390)	X					Nomad (8/307)				X	
Galaxie (6/223)											

Overdrive Transmissions

Operation of the Overdrive

Mechanical Controls

An overdrive is designed so that when the instrument panel control knob is in the in position (overdrive functioning) the final drive is through a free-wheeling clutch, so that any time the car speed is greater than that of the engine free-wheeling takes place. However, if the car speed is greater than about 27 mph, the solenoid will act to lock the sun gear so that free-wheeling cannot occur.

Locking the sun gear causes the planetary pinions of the overdrive to rotate the internal ring gear at a greater speed than that of the input shaft. The increase of output over input speed is approximately 7:10. That is, for every 0.7 of a revolution of the input shaft, the output makes a complete revolution.

When the dash control is pulled out, the shift rail is moved to the rear position. This causes the shifter fork to move the sun gear into engagement with the planet carrier, thus locking the two together. As a result, the planetary gear set is locked and the output shaft rotates with the input shaft.

If the dash control is in, and the manual gear shift lever is moved to reverse, the shift rail of the overdrive is moved to the rear by a cam on the transmission reverse gear fork. Thus the overdrive is automatically locked out when in reverse.

When the overdrive is operative, but not engaged, the car will free-wheel. However, once it moves up into overdrive it will no longer free-wheel. This is a normal condition.

Where an overdrive is known to be in good condition mechanically, but does not function properly, it is a good idea to check the solenoid, using battery.

Electrical Controls

When the speed of the car reaches approximately 27 mph (the cut-in point of the governor) the governor contacts close, completing a control circuit to ground. This causes a current to flow through the relay coil, causing the relay contacts to close. The power circuit to the solenoid is completed at the relay, and current flows through the solenoid windings causing the solenoid armature to move to the in position.

The armature of the solenoid is moved by two coils, a holding coil and a traction coil. When the armature moves in, it automatically disconnects the traction coil and re-

mains in position due to the holding coil, which is lighter and takes less current.

The movement of the armature is conveyed to the pawl, which blocks the sun gear with a spring so that the pawl is not forced into engagement. When the driver eases up on the accelerator momentarily, the pawl is permitted to nudge the balk ring out of its way and engage the control plate. As soon as the pawl has engaged the plate the car is in overdrive.

The overdrive shifts down automatically when the vehicle speed drops to the cut-out speed of the governor (about 21 mph). At this point, the governor contacts open, interrupting the control circuit and so causing the relay points to open. This releases the solenoid armature and it returns to the out position. This, of course, pulls the pawl from engagement with the control ring, and the car is out of overdrive.

Downshift from overdrive to direct

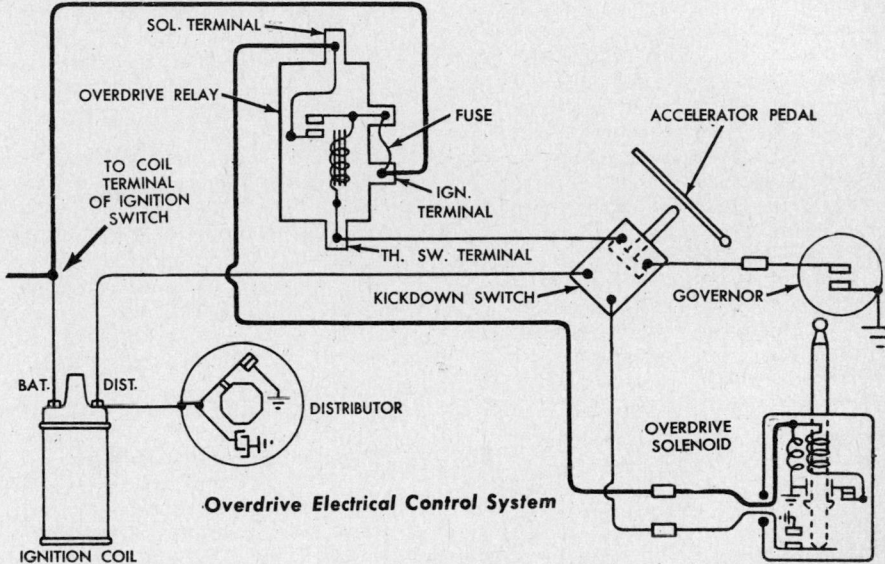

Overdrive Electrical Control System

Schematic wiring diagram of typical overdrive installation (© Ford Motor Co.)

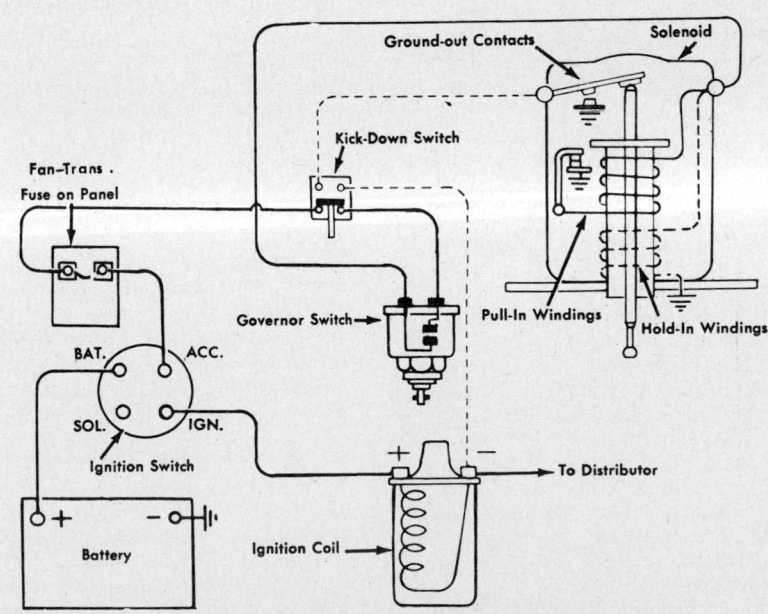

Schematic wiring diagram, American Motors. Solid line is governor solenoid circuit. Dotted line is kick-down circuit.
(© American Motors Corp.)

drive, even though the governor is calling for overdrive, is accomplished by a switch under the accelerator pedal called the kickdown switch. The switch has two functions in the circuit:

First, it opens the circuit to release the solenoid. However, the pawl cannot release itself from the control plate until the driving torque is removed.

Second, it momentarily grounds out the engine ignition circuit. This shorting out lasts only about one-half of a revolution of the crankshaft, but it is enough to release the torque on the pawl so that it can retract and so drop the car into direct drive for faster acceleration.

This ability of the kickdown switch to ground out the ignition is controlled by another set of contacts in the solenoid, which restore the ignition as soon as the solenoid armature has returned to the out position.

On some early models, there is a rail switch (reverse lock-out switch) which locks out the governor circuit when the dash control is in the out position. This rail switch is actuated by the shift rail. On later models, the movement of the shift rail accomplishes the same thing, mechanically, by moving the control plate so that the pawl cannot engage it.

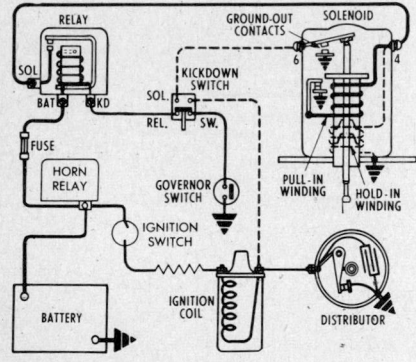

Schematic wiring diagram, Chevrolet
(© G.M. Corp.)

Troubleshooting Chart

Overdrive Does Not Engage

1. Check that the control lever on the unit moves as far, in each direction, as it should and that hand control on dash has ¼ in. free travel before lever moves.
2. Be sure that fuse on relay has not burnt out.
3. With ignition on, connect test lamp from fuse clip to ground. If lamp does not light, replace wire from switch to relay.
4. Connect test lamp between kickdown switch terminal on relay and ground. If relay does not click, replace it.

5. Disconnect wire from solenoid terminal on relay. Connect test lamp between this solenoid terminal and ground. Ground kickdown switch terminal on relay. If lamp does not light, replace the relay.
6. Disconnect the wire from the relay at the solenoid. Connect test lamp between end of wire and ground. Ground the kickdown switch terminal on the relay. If lamp does not light, replace the wire from relay to solenoid.
7. Ground kickdown switch terminal on the relay. Solenoid should click. If it does not, replace the solenoid.
8. Operate kickdown switch several times to be sure it is not sticking. Ground each terminal on the switch in turn. Solenoid should click when one terminal is grounded. If it does not, replace kickdown switch.

Overdrive Does Not Release

1. With control pushed in turn ignition key on. If a click is heard in the overdrive relay, the trouble is electrical. If no click, the trouble is mechanical and unit must be removed and overhauled.
2. Disconnect wire at governor. If overdrive then releases, replace governor.
3. Disconnect wire from governor at kickdown switch. If overdrive then releases, the wire is grounded.
4. Disconnect wire from relay and wire from governor, at the kickdown switch. If the overdrive then releases, replace the kickdown switch.
5. Disconnect wire from kickdown switch at the relay. If overdrive then releases, replace the wire; it is grounded.
6. Disconnect wire from solenoid at the relay. If overdrive then releases, replace the relay.
7. Loosen the screws holding the solenoid to the case. If the solenoid can be pulled out, without turning it, the pin which normally prevents the solenoid plunger from turning has been sheared or omitted. It will be necessary to assemble the solenoid correctly. If it can be withdrawn ½ in., without being turned, the solenoid is defective and should be replaced.

Overdrive Does Not Kick Down

1. With engine running, ground the kickdown switch terminal on the solenoid. If engine stops, replace solenoid.
2. With engine running, depress the kickdown switch and ground each of the terminals, in turn. If engine dies, all is well. If engine does not die when one terminal

is grounded, replace the kickdown switch. If engine does not die at any time, replace the wire from the switch to the coil.
3. Ground the governor terminal at the governor. This should cause the solenoid to click on. Now, operate the kickdown switch. This should cause a second click as the solenoid releases. If there is no second click, the kickdown switch is defective.

Engine Stops When Kickdown Switch is Depressed

1. With engine running disconnect wire from kickdown switch at solenoid. Operate kickdown switch. If engine does not stop, replace the solenoid. If engine does stop, replace the wire.

Car Will Not Move Unless Overdrive Is Locked Out, Acts like Slipping Clutch

1. Remove unit and overhaul freewheel mechanism.

Stays in Overdrive When Hand Control Is Positioned to Lock Out of Overdrive

1. Check hand control. Lever on unit must move from stop to stop. If all is well there, the shift rail is binding. Remove and overhaul.

Does Not Reverse Unless Locked Out

1. Check operation of gear-shift mechanism on transmission. The shift rail in the overdrive is not being moved by reverse fork.

Servicing the Overdrive

The overdrive gets its oil supply from the regular transmission. Therefore the standard transmission of a car equipped with an overdrive requires an extra pint of lubricant. The overdrive has its own drain plug.

Some models also have a separate fill plug, through which the extra pint should be installed when transmission, plus overdrive assembly, has been drained. One must remove the transmission and overdrive assembly from the car in order to be able to do any mechanical work on the overdrive.

Overdrive Disassembly— GM Type

First, remove the lock-out switch, if present. (The lock-out switch is located toward the rear of the overdrive on the left side.) Then, turn over the assembly to permit the two steel balls under the switch to drop out.

Remove the governor assembly and the overdrive housing bolts (which hold the overdrive housing to the

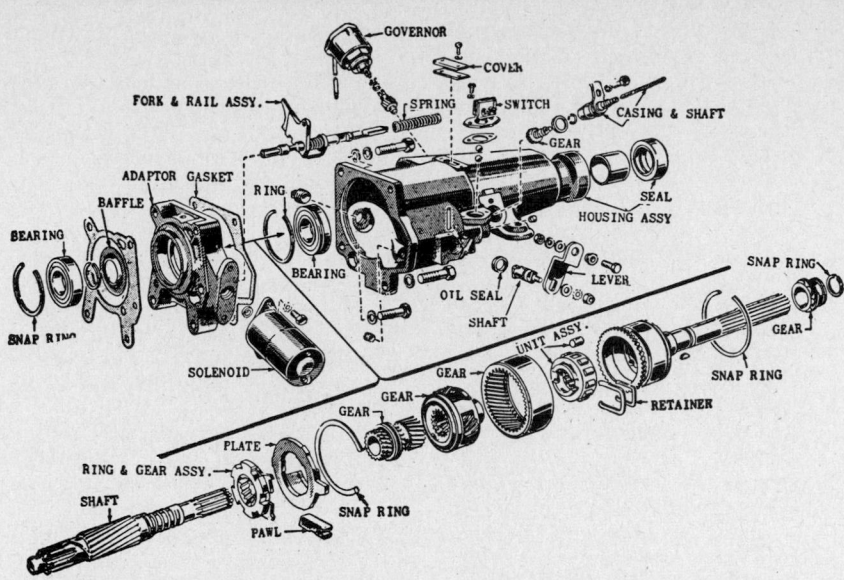

Overdrive assembly, Ford installation shown (© Ford Motor Co.)

transmission housing). Remove the shift rail pin and the cover, which is located on top of overdrive housing.

NOTE: do not remove the bolt holding the adapter to the transmission case at this time.

Pull the shift rail lever and shaft out as far as it will go. Reach down through the hole in the top of the overdrive housing and spread the snap-ring, then tap with a soft hammer on the end of the overdrive mainshaft, while pulling the housing toward the rear. This will separate the overdrive housing from the internal parts.

Now, remove the overdrive mainshaft from the assembly. Remove the clutch assembly retainers, the clutch and planetary gear assemblies and the sun gear and shift rail. These will come off as a unit, after the retainer is raised to permit their removal from the shaft.

Inspection After Disassembly

If the overdrive has a history of noisy gears, examine the sun gear, ring gear, and planetary pinions for scratches, nicks, burrs or roughness. If any are found, it will be necessary to replace the defective gears.

If the overdrive has a history of slipping in normal drive (not overdrive), examine the free-wheeling rollers and the roller cage for roughness or pits.

If the free-wheeling rollers have little depressions worn in the free-wheeling cam, it will be necessary to replace both the cam and the free-wheeling rollers.

American Motors Overdrive Units

Overdrive Shift Shaft

1. Drive out the shift shaft lock pin, then remove the shift shaft out of the case.

Governor and Solenoid

1. With a 1⅜ in. thin, open-end wrench, remove the governor from the overdrive case.
2. Remove solenoid attaching screws, then rotate solenoid one-quarter turn clockwise to release the plunger from the overdrive locking pawl.

Overdrive Case

1. Remove rear bearing snap ring and spacer washer from overdrive mainshaft.
2. Remove the four cap screws, then remove the overdrive case from the transmission case adapter housing.

NOTE: while withdrawing the overdrive case, keep tapping the end of the overdrive mainshaft to prevent the overdrive rollers from dropping out of position.

Overdrive Disassembly

1. Slide the speedometer gear and the governor drive gear from their Woodruff drive key and the overdrive mainshaft. Remove the Woodruff key.
2. Slide off the mainshaft ring-gear assembly, while holding one hand underneath the unit to catch the loose overdrive clutch rollers as they spill.

Typical overdrive transmission unit,

American Motors (© American Motors Corp.)

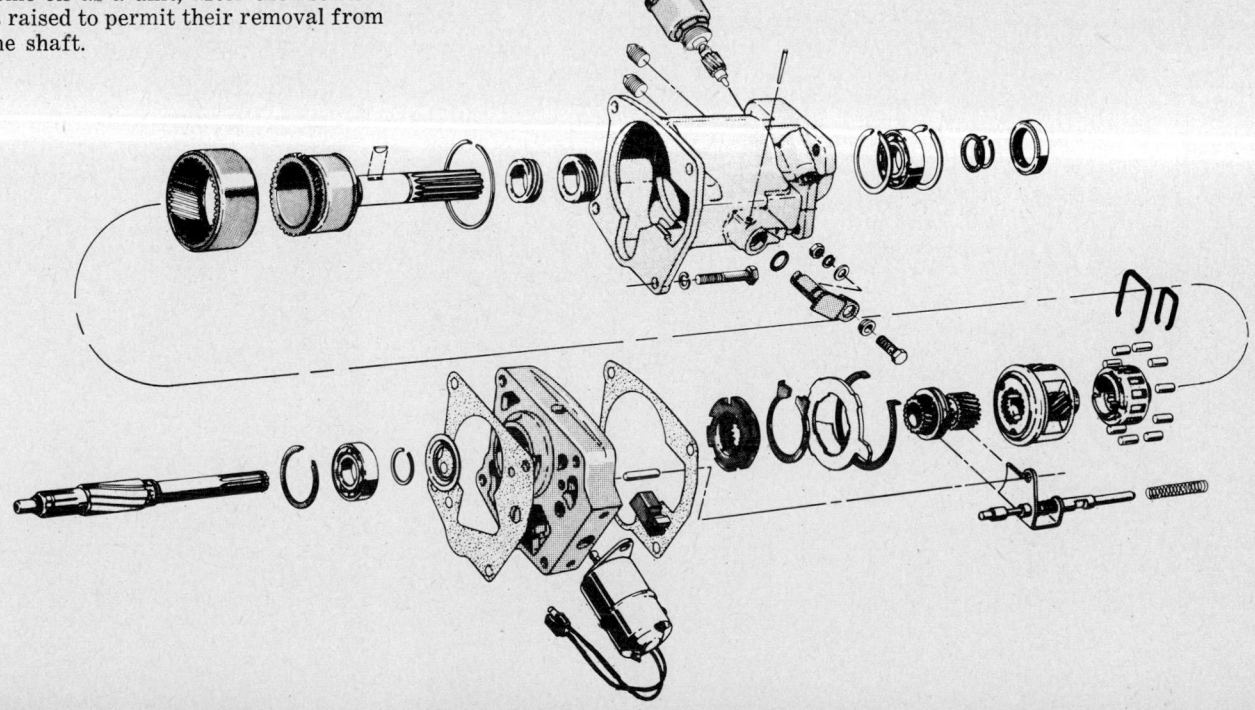

3. To separate the ring gear from the mainshaft, remove the large ring gear snap-ring.

4. To remove overdrive clutch cam, remove the cam snap-ring.

5. Remove the remaining lock ring on the mainshaft, then remove the pinion cage.

6. Remove the overdrive shifter rail and sun gear and collar from the mainshaft as a unit. When the sun gear is free of the sun gear hub, the shifter rail assembly can be separated from the sun gear shifting collar.

7. Remove the large snap-ring that holds the sun gear cover plate, hub and overdrive balk ring in place. Remove the cover plate and trough assembly and the sun gear hub assembly. The overdrive locking pawl can now be lifted out.

8. The control lever and shaft may be removed from the overdrive case, also remove the retracting spring from the overdrive case.

Overdrive Unit Assembly and Installation

1. Install the hub and balk ring assembly, chamfered side of the ring against the sun gear hub.

2. Install the locking pawl, positioning the pawl and balk ring in the locked out position, with the pawl on the step of the ring for correct installation of the solenoid.

3. Install the cover plate and trough in position and lock it in place with the large snap-ring. The snap-ring is available in various thicknesses from .0625—.0705 in. Use the thickest ring that will fit the groove.

4. Install the fork of the shifter rod into the sun gear shift collar. Then hold them together as you slide the sun gear onto the mainshaft and the shifter rod into the opening in the bearing adapter.

5. Install the pinion cage lock ring onto the mainshaft, then install the pinion cage assembly onto the mainshaft. The pinion cage pinions will mesh with the sun gear and the cage will butt up against the lock ring previously installed.

6. Position the free-wheeling cam onto the mainshaft so the counterbore of the cam slides over the machined surface of the pinion cage.

7. Install the free-wheeling cam snap-ring onto the mainshaft. This ring is available in thicknesses of .063—.073 in. Use the thickest ring which will fit the groove.

8. Replace the ring gear on the overdrive mainshaft and lock it in place with a snap-ring. This ring is available in various thicknesses from .055—.059 in. Use the thickest ring which will fit the groove.

9. Replace the free-wheeling rollers in the free-wheeling cage. A rubber band wound around the roller and cage assembly, just tight enough to hold the rollers in their retracted position, will simplify the installation of the ring gear.

10. Rotate the roller and cage assembly counterclockwise so that the rollers are at the bottom of their cams. The rubber band should hold the cage and rollers in this position. This will permit installing the overdrive mainshaft and ring gear.

11. Insert the Woodruff key into the mainshaft, then slide on the governor drive gear and the speedometer drive gear. The governor gear (small one) goes on first.

12. Install the shift shaft oil seal, then the retractor spring in the overdrive case.

13. Holding the bearing adapter to the transmission case, work the overdrive case onto the overdrive assembly. Secure the assembly with the four attaching cap screws.

14. Push the shift shaft into the case so that the operating cam will engage with the slot in the shift rod. Then install the lock pin to hold the shaft in position.

15. Insert the solenoid plunger in the opening in the bearing adapter and engage it with the notch in the locking pawl. Rotate the solenoid one-quarter turn counter-

clockwise to lock the pawl and plunger together.

16. Pull the solenoid to make sure the plunger is locked with the pawl, then install and tighten the two solenoid attaching screws.

17. Thread the governor into the overdrive case, then tighten just enough to prevent oil seepage.

18. Drive rear bearing on the overdrive mainshaft. Install rear spacer and snap-ring. This snap-ring is available in various thicknesses, from .087-.102 in. Use the thickest snap-ring that will fit the groove.

19. Install a new oil seal in the torque tube adapter, then attach the adapter to the overdrive case with the four cap screws.

20. Place the oil slinger on the clutch shaft, concave side toward the rear.

21. Install the large lock ring onto the clutch shaft bearing and place the bearing on the clutch shaft.

22. With the use of tool J-2995 and a thrust yoke J-6652, install the bearing onto the clutch shaft and into the transmission case. These are special tools. In the absence of special tools, be sure to have a helper to back-up the clutch gear with a substantial brass support (a drift or bar) to remove the possibility of damaging the synchronizer rings while driving the clutch bearing into place.

23. When the bearing is properly seated, install the spacer washer and install the clutch shaft bearing snap ring. This ring is available in various thicknesses, from .087-.102 in. Use the thickest ring which fits the groove.

24. Install the clutch shaft bearing cap, without a gasket. Then check the clearance between the bearing cap and case with a feeler gauge. Clutch shaft end-play should be zero in. Therefore, the clearance between the bearing cap and case must be accomplished by the installation of a gasket of a select thickness.

25. Install the bearing cap and new gasket then attach with four cap screws.

Service Procedure Index

Drive Axles and Differential

Number in Columns Refer to Section Numbers in Text

Make and Model		Adjust Axle Shaft End-Play	REPLACEMENT: Axle Shaft and/or Bearing	REPLACEMENT: Axle Outer Oil Seal	REPLACEMENT: Axle Inner Oil Seal	REPLACEMENT: Pinion & Ring Gear and/or Pinion Bearing
American Motors	1965–72	5	5	5	8	11
Buick	1965–72	2	3	none	8	9
Cadillac	1965–72	2	3	6	8	9*
Cadillac Eldorado	1967–72	See Car Section				
Chevrolet	1965–72	2	3	none	8	11
Chevelle, Chevy Nova, Camaro	1965–72	2	3	none	8	11
Chrysler, Imperial	1965–72	①	①	①	①	①
Continental	1965–72	2	3	none	8	12
Corvette	1965–72	none	13	13	13	13
Dodge, Challenger	1965–72	①	①	①	①	①
Fairlane, Meteor	1965–72	2	3	none	8	12
Falcon, Comet-6 cyl.	1965–72	2	3	none	8	12
Mustang, Cougar-8 cyl.	1965–72	2	3	none	8	12
Firebird	1967–72	2	3	none	8	11
Ford	1965–72	2	3	none	8	12
Maverick	1970–72	2	3	none	8	12
Mercury	1965–72	2	3	none	8	12
Oldsmobile	1965–72	2	3	none	8	11
F-85, Cutlass, 442	1965–67, 1970–72	2	3	none	8	11
	1968–69	none	3	none	8	11
Toronado	1966–72	See Car Section				
Pinto	1971–72	2	3	none	8	11
Plymouth	1965–72	①	①	①	①	①
Pontiac	1965–72	2	3	none	8	11
Tempest	1965–72	2	3	none	8	11
Valiant, Dart, Barracuda	1965–72	①	①	①	①	①
Vega	1971–72	2	3	none	8	11
Ventura II	1971–72	2	3	none	8	11

*—1970–72 only

①—All Chrysler Corporation cars are serviced according to axle type which is identified by use of the chart:

Axle	Filler Location	Cover Fastening
7¼ in.	Cover	9 Bolts
8¼ in.	Carrier, Right Side	10 Bolts
8¾ in.	Carrier, Right Side	Welded
9¼ in.		
9¾ in.	Cover	10 Bolts

Service on the 9¼ in. and 9¾ in. axles is identical.

Axle	End-play Adjustment	Axle Shaft and/or Bearing Replacement	Outer oil Seal Replacement	Inner Oil Seal Replacement	Ring & Pinion Gear and/or Pinion Bearing Replacement
7¼ in.	2	3	none	8	10
8¼ in.	2	3	none	8	10
8¾ in.	1	4	4	7	10
9¼ in.		4	4	7	10
9¾ in.	1	4	4	7	10

Section Page Numbers

Section	Page	Section	Page
1	1116	6	1119
2	1116	7	1119
3	1117	8	1120
4	1118	9	1120
5	1119	10	1121

Section	Page	Section	Page
11	1124	16	1135
12	1128	17	1136
13	1132	18	1136
14	1134	19	1137
15	1135		

Drive Axles, Differential
Diagnosis

Noises
1. Wheels loose on drums.
2. Worn drum or axle shaft keyways (key-type axles).
3. Hub bolts loose.
4. Burned or scored wheel bearings, carrier bearings or pinion bearings.
5. Insufficient or improper lubricant.
6. Bent axle shaft, wheel or hub.
7. Improperly adjusted wheel bearings, carrier bearings or pinion bearings.
8. Excessive gear lash between drive gear and pinion.
9. Loose pinion driving flange.
10. Damaged gears.

Overheating of Unit
1. Insufficient or improper lubricant.
2. Bearing adjusted too tightly.
3. Excessively worn gears.

Loss of Lubricant
1. Lubricant level too high.
2. Improper type lubricant.
3. Clogged breather.
4. Worn oil seals, pinion or wheel bearing areas.

Excessive Backlash
1. Excessive gear wear.
2. Excessive spline wear.

3. Worn or improperly adjusted gears.
4. Loose pinion driving flange.

Limited Slip Differential— Only One Wheel Spins
1. Improper type of lubricant.
2. Clutch plates improperly assembled.
3. Clutch plates burnt.

Limited Slip Differential— Chatter on Turns
1. Improper type lubricant, not penetrating between plates, causing plates to stick together.

Section 1
Axle Shaft End-Play Adjustment

Chrysler—1965-1972
Dodge—1965-1972

Plymouth—1965-1972
Valiant, Dart, 1965-72

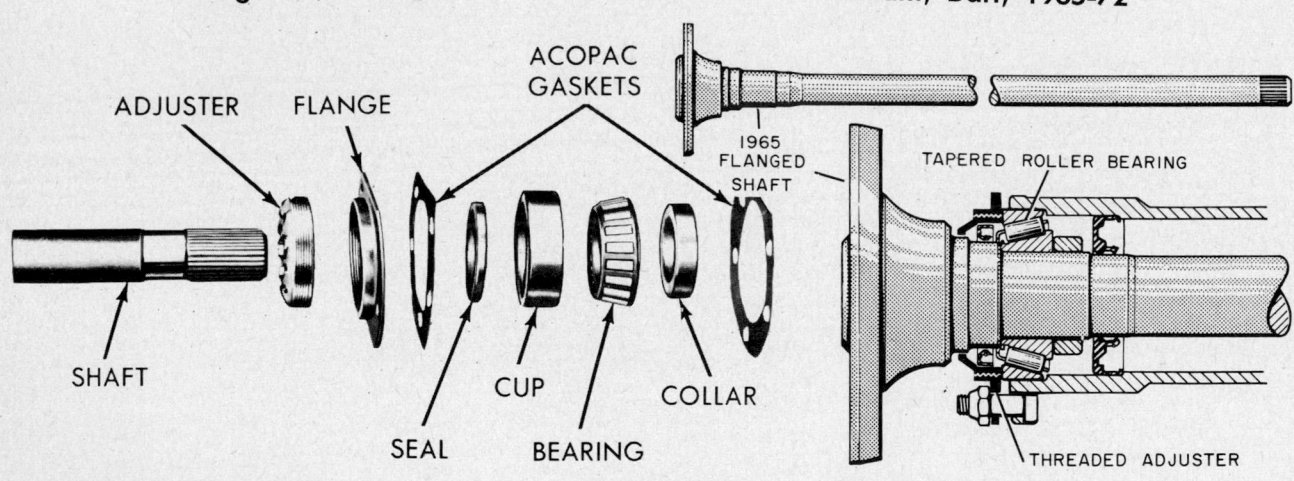

1965—Chrysler-Dodge-Plymouth axle shaft and bearing

1. To adjust the axle shaft end-play on these cars, consult Steps 5-10, Section 6, Axle Shaft and/or Bearing Replacement.

NOTE: axle shaft end-play on the 1971 8¼ in. axle is no longer adjustable.

Section 2
Axle Shaft End-Play Adjustment

Ford Motor Company, 1965-72

On this construction, the axle bearing is held in place by pressure from the backing plate. Drive bearing, a radial ball bearing, is held to the axle shaft by a ring, which has been

General Motors, 1965-72 (Except Cadillac)

shrunken on. If excessive end-play exists in this construction, either the bearing is loose on the shaft, the bearing retainer has moved on the shaft, or the backing plate is bent

Cadillac, 1970-72 Valiant, Dart, 1965-69

where it retains the bearing in the housing.

To correct this condition, consult the reference chart for the appropriate section.

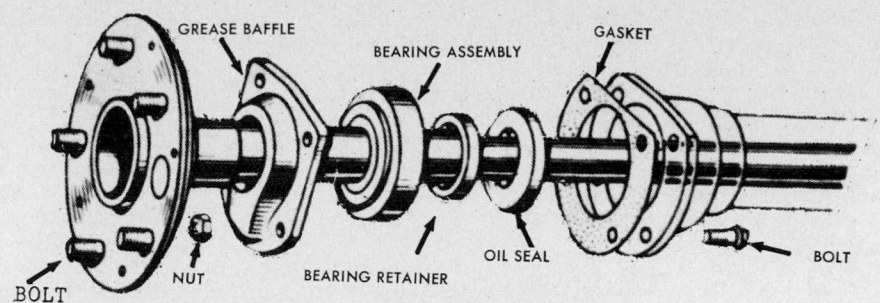

GREASE BAFFLE   BEARING ASSEMBLY   GASKET

BOLT   NUT   BEARING RETAINER   OIL SEAL   BOLT

Axle shaft, bearing and oil seals

Section 3
Axle Shaft and/or Bearing Replacement

Cadillac, 1970-72
Ford Motor Company, 1965-72

General Motors Corp., 1965-72 (Except Cadillac)

Plymouth, 1965-72
Valiant, Dart, 1965-72

Axle shaft lock arrangement

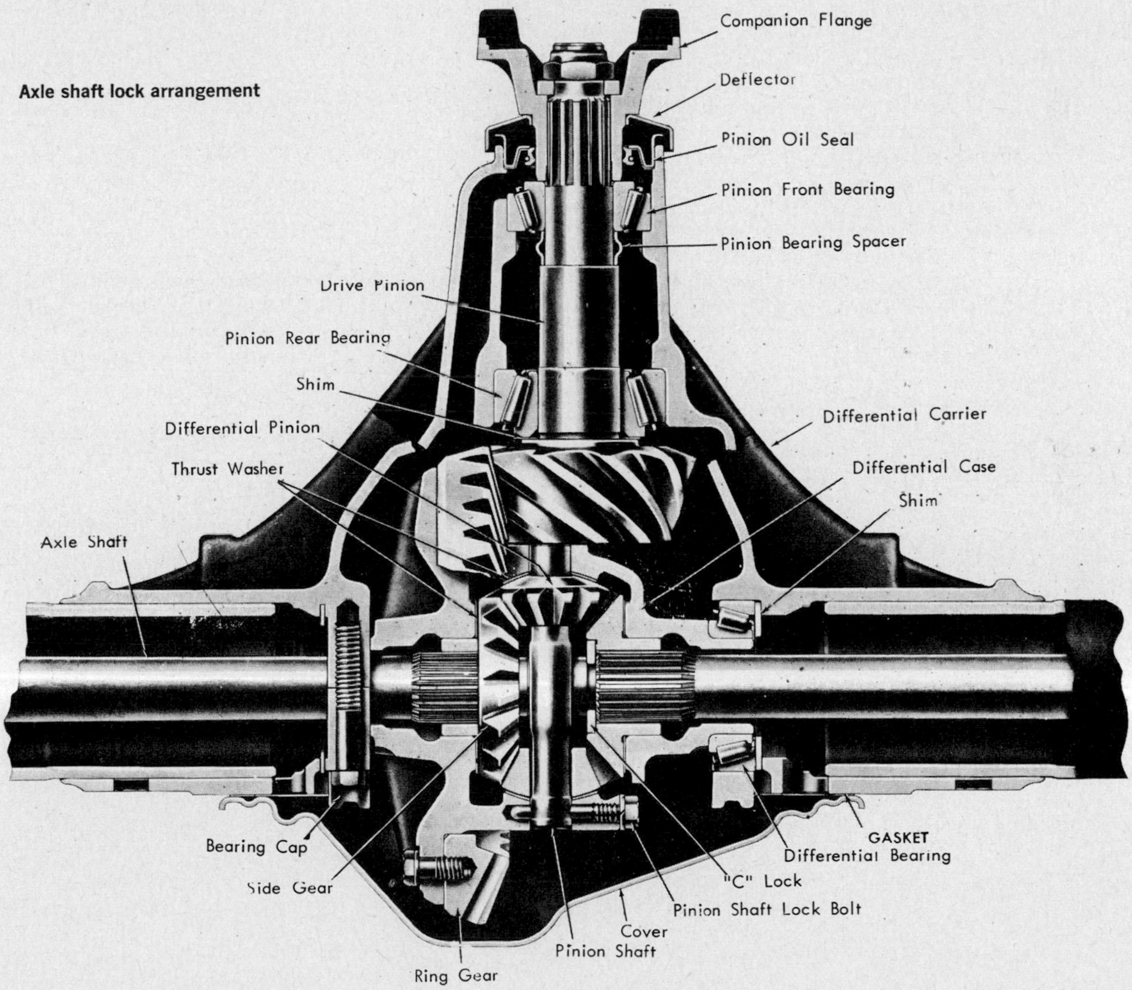

Companion Flange

Deflector

Pinion Oil Seal

Pinion Front Bearing

Pinion Bearing Spacer

Drive Pinion

Pinion Rear Bearing

Shim

Differential Pinion

Thrust Washer

Axle Shaft

Differential Carrier

Differential Case

Shim

Bearing Cap

Side Gear

Ring Gear

Cover

Pinion Shaft

Pinion Shaft Lock Bolt

"C" Lock

GASKET
Differential Bearing

The above car applications use, basically, two different types of drive axle, the "C" and the non "C" type. Axle shafts in the "C" type are retained by C-shaped locks, which fit grooves at the inner end of the shaft. Axle shafts in the non "C" type are retained by the brake backing plate, which is bolted to the axle housing. Bearings in the "C" type axle consist of an outer race, bearing rollers and a roller cage, retained by snap-rings. The non "C" type axle uses a unit roller bearing (inner race, rollers and outer race), which is pressed onto the shaft, up to a shoulder. When servicing "C" or non "C" type axles, it is imperative to determine the axle type before attempting any service.

Non "C" Type

Caution   Before attempting any service to the drive axle or axle shafts, remove the axle carrier cover and visually determine if the axle shafts are retained by C-shaped locks at the inner end, or by the brake backing plate at the outer end. If the shafts are not retained by "C" locks, proceed as follows.

If end-play is found to be excessive, the bearing should be replaced. Shimming the bearing is not recommended as this ignores end-play of the bearing itself and could result in improper seating of the bearing.

1. Remove the wheel, tire and brake drum.
2. Remove the nuts holding the retainer plate to the backing plate. Disconnect the brake line.
3. Remove the retainer and install nuts, fingertight, to prevent the brake backing plate from being dislodged.
4. Pull out the axle shaft and bearing assembly, using a slide hammer.
5. Using a chisel, nick the bearing retainer in three or four places. The retainer does not have to be cut, merely collapsed sufficiently, to allow the bearing retainer to be slid from the shaft.
6. Press off the bearing and install the new one by pressing it into position.
7. Press on the new retainer.

NOTE: do not attempt to press the bearing and the retainer on at the same time.

8. Assemble the shaft and bearing in the housing, being sure that the bearing is seated properly in the housing.
9. Install the retainer, drum, wheel and tire. Bleed the brakes.

"C" Type

Caution   Before attempting any service to the drive axle or axle shafts, remove the carrier cover and visually determine if the axle shaft(s) are retained by C-shaped locks at the inner ends or by a brake backing plate at the outer end. If they *are* retained by C-shaped locks, proceed as follows.

1. Raise the vehicle and remove the wheels.
2. The differential cover has already been removed (see Caution note above). Remove the differential pinion shaft lockscrew and the differential pinion shaft.
3. Push the flanged end of the axle shaft toward the center of the vehicle and remove the "C" lock from the end of the shaft.
4. Remove the axle shaft from the housing, being careful not to damage the oil seal.
5. Remove the oil seal by inserting the button end of the axle shaft behind the steel case of the oil seal. Pry the seal loose from the bore.
6. Seat the legs of the bearing

puller behind the bearing. Seat a washer against the bearing and hold it in place with a nut. Use a slide hammer to pull the bearing.

7. Pack the cavity between the seal lips with wheel bearing lubricant and lubricate a new wheel bearing with same.
8. Use a suitable driver and install the bearing until it bottoms against the tube. Install the oil seal.
9. Slide the axle shaft into place. Be sure that the splines on the shaft do not damage the oil seal. Make sure that the splines engage the differential side gear.
10. Install the axle shaft "C" lock on the inner end of the axle shaft and push the shaft outward so that the "C" lock seats in the differential side gear counterbore.
11. Position the differential pinion shaft through the case and pinions, aligning the hole in the case with the hole for the lockscrew.
12. Install the pinion shaft lockscrew.
13. Use a new gasket and install the carrier cover. Be sure that the gasket surfaces are clean before installing the gasket and cover.
14. Fill the axle with lubricant to the bottom of the filler hole.
15. Install the brake drum and wheels and lower the car. Check for leaks and road test the car.

Section 4
Axle Shaft and/or Bearing Replacement

Chrysler—1965-72
Dodge—1965-72

Plymouth—1965-72
Valiant, Dart—1965-72

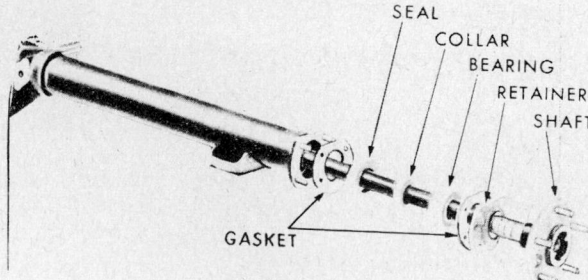

SEAL
COLLAR
BEARING
RETAINER
SHAFT

GASKET

Typical rear axle shaft bearing assembly

Removal

1. Remove wheel and brake drum. If necessary, disconnect the brakeline at the wheel cylinder.
2. Through hole in flange, remove five nuts from the retainer plate. The right-hand shaft, with the adjuster in the retainer plate, will

also have a lock on one of the studs that will be removed at this time.
3. Pull the assembly with a slide hammer.
4. Remove Dinner seal, using tool C-637. Install new seal, using tool C-839 or equivalent.

Disassembly

1. Install the shaft in vise and notch the collar with a chisel.
2. Remove the roller retainer by cutting it off at the lower edge with a chisel.

Caution   To prevent the possibility of nicking the shaft or damaging the sealing surface, slide protective sleeve SP5041 over the shaft.

3. Grind a section from the flange of the inner bearing cone.
4. Remove rollers from the section of flange which was ground away.
5. Pull retainer down as far as possible and remove by using side cutters.
6. Remove cup from axle shaft.
7. Using tool C-3971 or equivalent, remove cone.
8. Replace seal in plate.

Assembly
1. Install retainer plate onto shaft.
2. Install new bearing cone, cup, and collar, using tool C-3971 or equivalent.

Installation
1. Install new gasket (Chrysler part 2467173) on left end of housing and add the backing plate with gasket (Chrysler part 2404191).
2. Slide left axle shaft assembly into position. Use care not to damage seal.

3. Install retainer plate nuts and torque to 30-35 ft. lbs.
4. Repeat Step 1 on right side of housing.
5. Back off adjuster on right axle shaft assembly until inner face of adjuster is flush with inner face of retainer. Slide right assembly into housing, being careful not to damage seal, and install five retaining nuts. Torque to 30-35 ft. lbs.
6. With dial indicator mounted on brake support, tighten adjuster

until there is zero end-play. Back off approximately four notches to get end-play of .013-.023 in.
7. Tap end of left axle with non-metallic mallet to seat right wheel bearing against adjuster, in order to get true end-play reading.
8. Install the adjuster lock under one of the nuts.
9. Recheck end-play and repeat adjustment procedure, if needed.
10. Remove indicator and reinstall drum, drum retaining clips and wheel.

Section 5
Axle Shaft and/or Bearing Replacement

American Motors 1965-72

Axle shaft detail showing serrated axle (© American Motors)

On this construction, with tapered roller bearings, end-play adjustment is accomplished by adding or removing shims from behind the backing plate. The hub and axle shaft are serrated to fit together on the taper.

1. Remove rear wheels, drums, and hubs. Rear Hub Puller J-1644 or J-736 should be used to remove the hub. The use of a "knock-out" may cause damage to the rear wheel bearings or the

thrust block. The hub is held to the drum by three cap screws.
2. Remove brake support plate assembly, oil seal, and axle shims from axle shaft.
3. Use Axle Shaft Bearing Puller Tool J-2498 to pull the axle shaft and bearing from the axle tube. Remove inner oil seal.
4. Press off bearing.
   NOTE: the axle shaft bearings have no provision for lubrication

after assembly. They should be packed with a good quality grease prior to assembly.
5. Press on new bearing.
6. Apply sealer to outer surface of oil seal and install.
7. Install axle shafts, outer bearing cup, shims, oil seal retainer plate, and brake support plate. Tighten to 30-35 ft. lbs.
8. From this point on, refer to the car section for further assembly.

Section 6
Axle Outer Oil Seal Replacement

Cadillac—1965-1972

Rear axle shaft, showing arrangement of oil seals
(© G.M. Corp.)

On these models, an outer oil seal is included in the bearing. There is a drain plate which tends to drain away whatever lubricant gets past the bearing to the inside of the backing

plate. Cadillac however, uses a synthetic O-ring seal recessed into the outer diameter of the axle bearing race.

Section 7
Axle Outer Oil Seal Replacement

Dodge—1965-72

1965-1972—See also Section 4.
These outer oil seals are pressed into backing plates.
1. Remove wheel, tire, hub and

Chrysler—1965-1972

drum (using puller). Do not use knock-off puller.
2. Disconnect brake line and remove backing plate.

Plymouth, 1965-72

3. Press out the old seal and install a new one.
4. Replace parts in reverse order of above and bleed brakes.

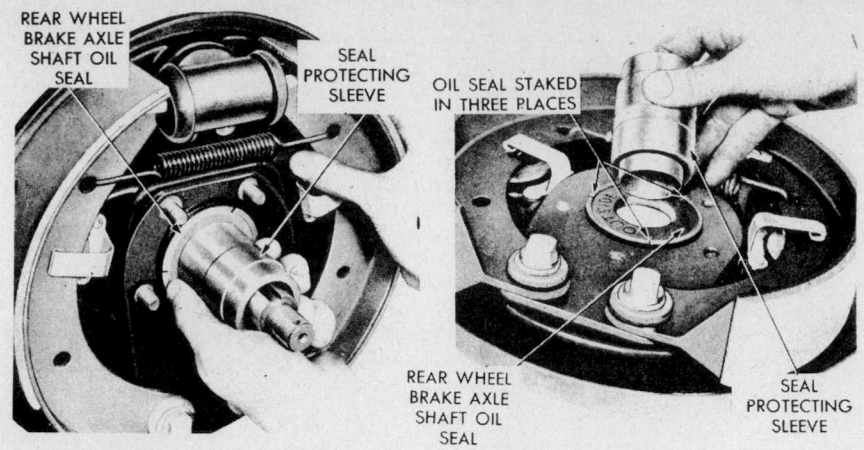

REAR WHEEL BRAKE AXLE SHAFT OIL SEAL

SEAL PROTECTING SLEEVE

OIL SEAL STAKED IN THREE PLACES

REAR WHEEL BRAKE AXLE SHAFT OIL SEAL

SEAL PROTECTING SLEEVE

Removing or installing rear brake support plate, using seal protecting sleeve

Section 8
Axle Inner Oil Seal Replacement

All Makes—All Models
(See Index For Exceptions)

The inner oil seal is seated in the inside of the bearing, in the **axle tube** on all American cars except those noted in index.

Remove the axle shaft as outlined in the paragraphs devoted to axle shafts for the car on which you are working. After the axle shaft, bearing and outer oil seal have been removed, reach into the housing with an inertia-type puller and pull out the inner oil seal.

The new oil seal is driven, by its rim, into the housing. Install the bearing, outer oil seal and axle shaft, replace the hub and drum assemblies and the wheels.

Section 9
Ring and Pinion Gear and/or Pinion Bearing Replacement

Cadillac—1970-72

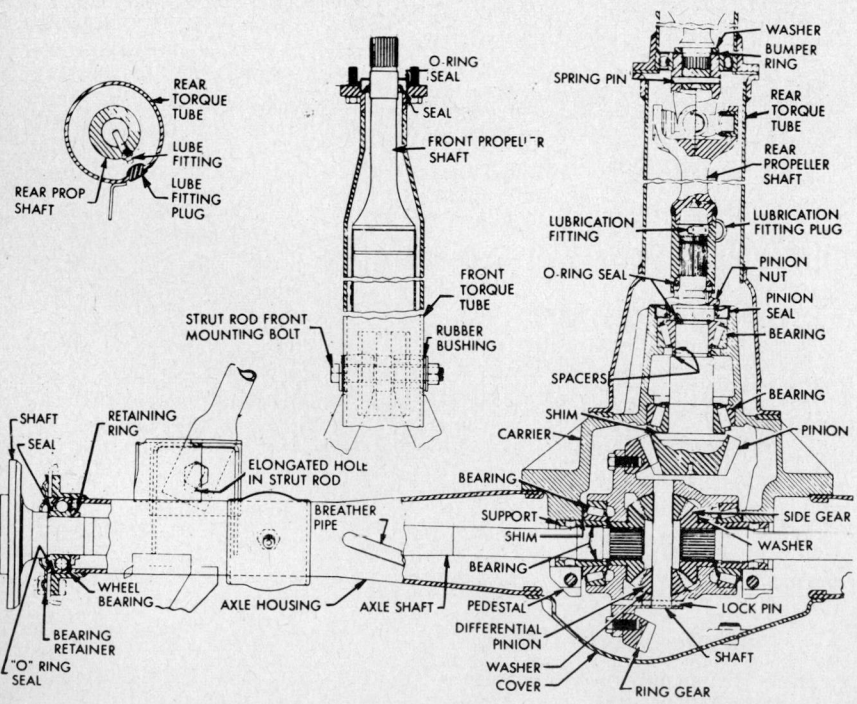

REAR TORQUE TUBE
LUBE FITTING
REAR PROP SHAFT
LUBE FITTING PLUG

O-RING SEAL
SEAL
FRONT PROPELLER SHAFT
FRONT TORQUE TUBE
RUBBER BUSHING

STRUT ROD FRONT MOUNTING BOLT

SHAFT
SEAL
RETAINING RING
ELONGATED HOLE IN STRUT ROD
BREATHER PIPE
"O" RING SEAL
WHEEL BEARING
BEARING RETAINER
AXLE HOUSING
AXLE SHAFT

SPRING PIN
WASHER
BUMPER RING
REAR TORQUE TUBE
REAR PROPELLER SHAFT
LUBRICATION FITTING
LUBRICATION FITTING PLUG
O-RING SEAL
PINION NUT
PINION SEAL
BEARING
SPACERS
BEARING
SHIM
PINION
CARRIER
BEARING
SUPPORT
SIDE GEAR
SHIM
WASHER
BEARING
PEDESTAL
DIFFERENTIAL PINION
WASHER
COVER
LOCK PIN
SHAFT
RING GEAR

Rear axle assembly

Differential Carrier Removal
1. Support car on rear axle housing and remove wheels, drums, and axle shafts.
2. Remove two attaching bolts and lockwashers that secure differential carrier nose bumper arm.
3. Disconnect driveshaft and support out of way, loosen cover bolts and drain case, remove cover and gasket.
4. Remove bearing caps, differential adjuster nut-lock and nut, differential shim, differential gear case.

Differential Carrier Installation
1. Install pinion and original pinion shims, install bolts and tighten to 30 ft. lbs.
2. Install bearing cups on side bearings. Wide bearing cup goes on left-side bearing.
3. Install differential case in housing. Install differential case adjuster nut.
4. Install right-side bearing cap and two cap bolts. Do not tighten bolts. Align bearing cap threads with adjuster nut threads by pulling cap straight

back on bolts and gently pushing cap into position. Tighten bolts to 50 ft. lbs.

5. Slide differential case to extreme right, tighten adjuster nut until it makes contact with right-side bearing.

6. Slide left-side bearing and cup to right, install the original shim between carrier and left-side bearing cup.

7. Position dial indicator on carrier, with feeler against plate as shown in picture. Using spanner wrench or pin wrench, tighten adjuster nut until a reading of 0.003-0.004 in. is obtained. Rotate gear case to check for steady reading.

8. Position dial indicator gauge against heel of ring gear tooth. Correct reading is 0.005-0.010 in. If reading is too high, increase shim, if reading is too low, de-

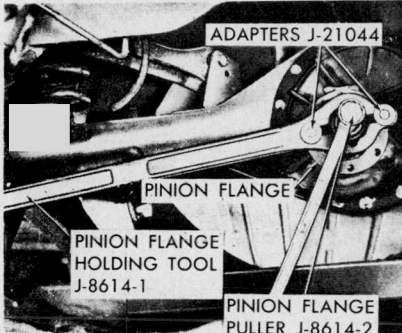

Removing pinion flange

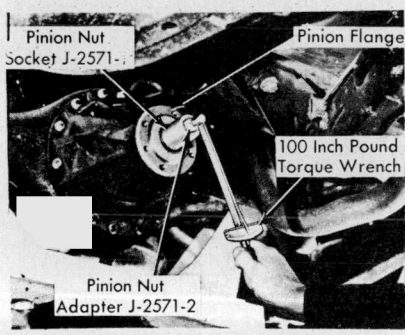

Checking preload—Cadillac pinion seal replacement
(© Cadillac Div., G.M. Corp.)

creases shim. A .002 in. shim change will alter backlash by about .001 in. Recheck backlash, if it cannot be obtained, reset the spread and repeat Steps 5-7.

9. Final check backlash with the method described in *Pinion Mesh Markings*.

10. If it is necessary to change pinion shim, backlash must be rechecked again.

11. Install lock tab on adjuster nut and tighten bolt to 18 ft. lbs.

12. Install new differential carrier cover gasket, install differential cover, tighten bolts to 30 ft. lbs.

13. Install axle shafts. Install two attaching bolts and lockwashers that secure differential carrier nose bumper arm and tighten to 50 ft. lbs.

14. Install driveshaft, fill axle to proper level, then mount wheels.

Pinion Disassembly

NOTE: differential ring gear and pinion are serviced as a matched set. If one is replaced, both must be replaced.

1. Remove and discard pinion O-ring.

2. Using pinion flange holder, remove pinion nut. A torque multiplier is recommended because it will require 200+ ft. lbs. to remove the nut.

3. Remove pinion flange. Pry oil seal out of pinion retainer and discard.

4. Remove pinion outer bearing. Press outer bearing outer cup from retainer. Press out inner bearing outer cup. Remove pinion bearing collapsible spacer from pinion shaft and discard.

5. Remove pinion inner bearing.

Pinion Assembly

1. Install inner bearing on pinion shaft. Install inner bearing cup.

2. Install outer bearing, outer bearing cup.

3. Install new collapsible spacer on pinion shaft.

4. Position pinion retainer on pinion, lubricate pinion outer bearing and install outer bearing in retainer.

5. Position oil seal on retainer, be sure it is lubricated. Install a new pinion nut, washer and oil seal and installer and press oil seal into retainer by tightening pinion nut. When properly installed, oil seal will protrude 1/16 in. from machined face of retainer.

6. Remove pinion nut, washer and oil seal installer from pinion.

7. Position pinion flange on pinion shaft using marks made during disassembly, install pinion nut until end-play is removed.

8. With a dial indicator, measure the radial run-out of the pinion flange (.005 in. or less). If run-out, exceeds .005 in. re-index pinion flange 90° or 180° until run-out is acceptable.

9. Using care, preload pinion nut to 22-30 in. lbs. with a new bearing and 15-20 in. lbs. with an old bearing. If the preload is exceeded, the unit will have to be disassembled and assembled using a new collapsible spacer. Never back off pinion nut to obtain proper preload.

Differential Case Disassembly

1. Remove side bearings on differential case using puller.

2. With differential case in holder mark alignment of differential case and ring gear, loosen ring gear-to-case bolts.

3. Remove three bolts and insert pilots, remove remaining bolts, tap pilots to loosen and remove ring gear.

4. Remove differential cross-shaft, pinion gears and side gears.

Differential Case Assembly

1. Install side gears and thrust washers.

2. Install pinion gears and thrust washers.

3. Insert cross-shaft and roll pin.

4. Using guide pins and alignment marks, position ring gear on case. Tap the ring gear on to the gear case. Torque the bolts, alternately, to 85 ft. lb.

5. Install side bearings.

Section 10
Ring and Pinion Gear and/or Pinion Bearing Replacement

Chrysler—1965-72
Dodge—1965-72

Plymouth—1965-72
Valiant, Dart—1965-72

NOTE: beginning December 1, 1970, the 7 1/4 in. axle uses a collapsible spacer to control pinion bearing preload.

Differential Removal

NOTE: Chrysler Corporation uses

several different design axle housing for the above years. While some differentials may be removed from the case in a slightly different manner, service procedures are typical for all Chrysler axles and differentials.

1. Raise and support car under rear axle housing.

2. Remove wheels, hubs and drums and rear axle shafts, as described in appropriate section. Drain lubricant.

3. Disconnect rear universal joint

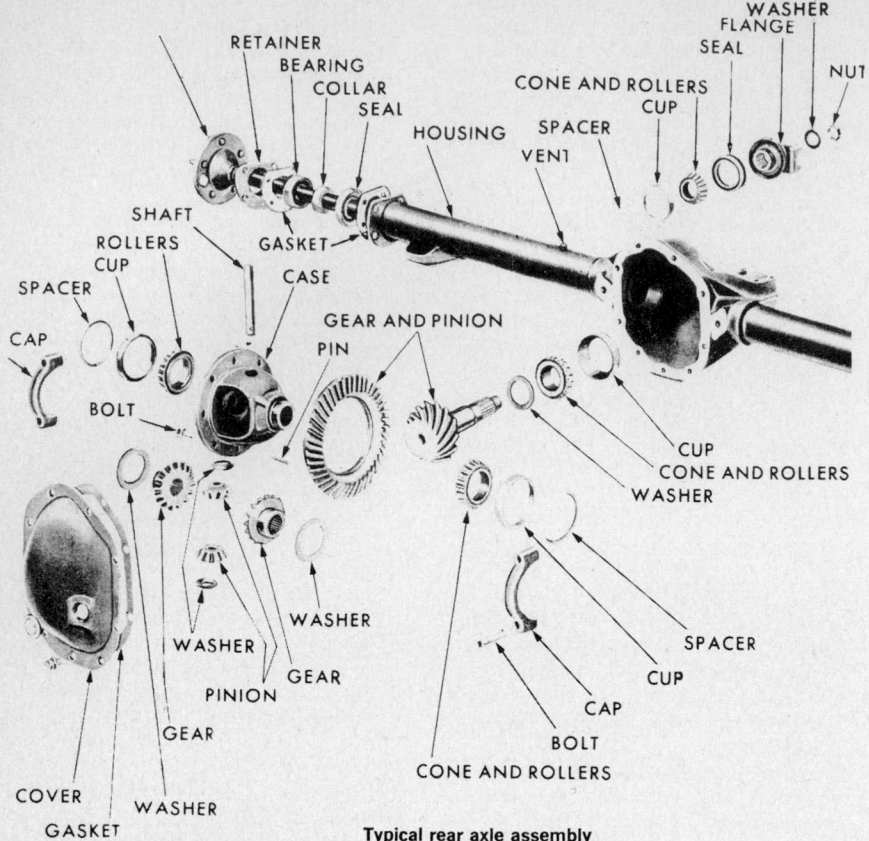

Typical rear axle assembly

slightly.

8. **Remove the differential assembly,** being sure to keep each bearing **cup** with the proper bearing.

9. **Remove the pinion and rear bearing cone from the carrier.**

10. **The bearing cone and pinion locating washer may now be removed from the shaft.**

11. **Remove the bearing cups from the carrier housing.**

Differential Case Disassembly

1. Mount the differential case and ring gear in vise with soft jaws. Remove the ring gear bolts.
   NOTE: the ring gear bolts have left-hand threads.

2. Tap the ring gear loose, using a non-metallic hammer.

3. If the ring gear runout exceeds .005 in., when previously measured, recheck the case as follows:
   a. Install the cap bolts, bearing caps and bearing adjusters.
   b. Tighten the cap bolts sufficiently to prevent any side-play in the bearings.
   c. Mount a dial indicator so that the pointer contacts the ring gear surface of the differential case flange. Measure the runout, which should not exceed .003 in. If the runout exceeds .003 in., the case must be replaced.

4. With a hammer and drift, remove the differential pinion shaft lockpin from the rear side of the ring gear flange. The hole is reamed only part way through, making it necessary to remove the pin from the proper side.

5. Remove the pinion shaft and thrust block.

6. Rotate differential side gears until the pinions and thrust washers can be removed.

7. Remove both differential side gears and thrust washers.

and place out of way.

4. **Remove attaching bolts and remove carrier assembly to bench.**

Differential Installation

1. Using new gasket, insert carrier in housing, and tighten nuts. Torque nuts to 45 ft. lbs. Install rear universal joint.

2. Fill with lubricant. Install axle shafts, hubs, drums, wheels and tires. Lower car to floor.

Differential Reconditioning

1. Mount carrier in holding tool, with pinion flange up.

2. Remove pinion shaft nut and washer. Remove flange with suitable puller.

3. With proper puller screwed into oil seal, pull seal from housing.

4. Rotate assembly with holding tool to allow oil slinger, shim pack and spacer (where used), to drop from the carrier.

5. Matchmark the differential pedestals, adjusting nuts, and bearing caps for reassembly identification.

6. Remove the bearing lockscrews and locks.

7. Remove the cap bolts, caps and back off bearing adjusting nuts

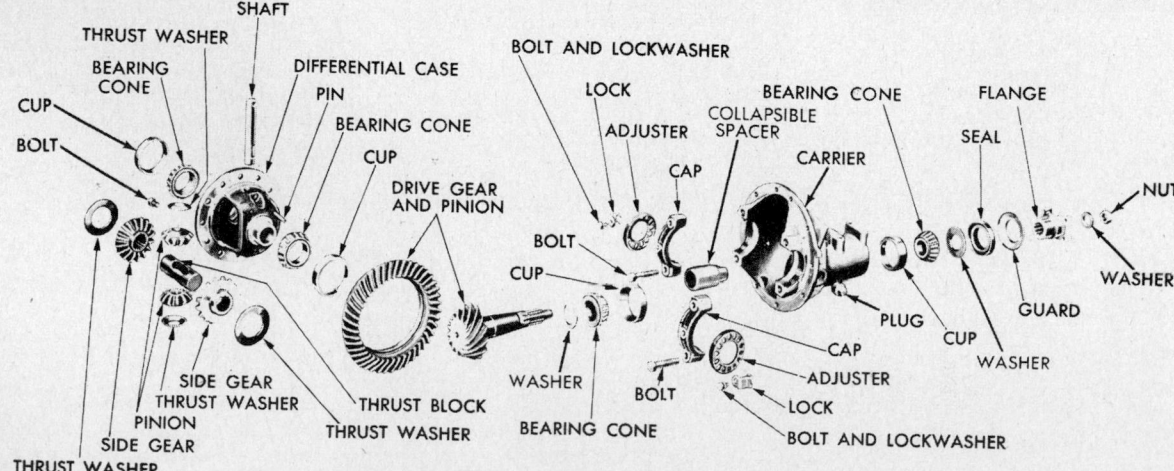

Typical Chrysler differential with collapsible spacer (© Chrysler Corp.)

Differential Case Assembly

1. Lubricate all parts before assembly, with rear axle lubricant.
2. Install the thrust washers on the differential side gears and install the side gears into the case.
3. Place thrust washers on both differential pinions and, working through the large access window, mesh the pinion gears with the side gears. The pinions should be exactly 180° apart.
4. Rotate the side gears 90° to align the pinions and thrust washers with the pinion shaft holes.
5. From the pinion shaft lockpin hole side of the case, insert the slotted end of the pinion shaft through the case, conical thrust washer and just through one of the pinion gear.
6. Install a thrust block through the side gear hub, so that the slot is centered between the side gears.
7. Hold all these parts in alignment, and align the lockpin holes in the pinion shaft and case. Install the lockpin from the pinion shaft side of the ring gear flange.
8. With an Arkansas stone, relieve the edge of the chamfer on the inside diameter of the ring gear.
9. Heat the ring gear (fluid bath or heat lamp) to a temperature not exceeding 300° F.
   NOTE: do not heat ring gear with a torch.
10. Align the ring gear with the case. Insert the ring gear screws through the case flange and into the ring gear.
11. Alternately tighten each cap screw to 55 ft. lbs.
12. Position each differential bearing cone on the hub of the differential case (taper away from ring gear) and install the bearing cones. An arbor press may be helpful.

Differential Assembly, Pinion Bearing Preload and Depth of Mesh

This type axle uses two types of pinions. Pinion depth of mesh and bearing preload are determined in the same manner for small and large stem pinions; only the sequence of adjustments varies. Small stem pinion require bearing preload adjustment first, while large stem pinions require pinion depth of mesh adjustment first. The position of the drive pinion, relative to the position of the ring gear (depth of mesh) is determined by the location of the bearing cup shoulders in the carrier and by the portion of the pinion behind the rear bearing.

NOTE: factory service procedures recommend the use of very specialized tools to assure proper adjustment of the rear axle without duplicating labor. However, the special tools are not readily available. The following procedures are substituted in place of special factory tools.

Differential Assembly

1. Assembly procedures, excluding adjustments and selection of shims, are the reverse of disassembly.
   NOTE: some rear axles of this type, use a collapsible spacer. Once this spacer has been collapsed or the pinion bearing preload exceeded, the collapsible spacer must be replaced with a new one. Before assembly, gather together shims of several sizes and several spacers in case the assembly is not properly adjusted the first time.

If the differential assembly was satisfactory when disassembled, the drive pinion may be assembled with the original components, excepting the pinion front bearing and collapsible spacer (if used). If any replacement parts are installed, a complete adjustment willl be necessary. Ring gears and pinions are available in matched sets only, and the adjustment position for best tooth contact is marked on the end of the pinion head.

Proper pinion setting, relative to the ring gear is determined by a shim, selected before the pinion is installed in the carrier. Pinion bearing shims are available in .002 in. increments from .084-.100 in. (small stem) and in .001 in. increments from .020-.038 in. (large stem with collapsible spacer).

Depth of Mesh

The head of the pinion is marked with a (+) or (−) followed by a number ranging from 0 to 4. If the old and new pinion have the same marking and the old bearing is being installed, use a shim of the original thickness. But, if the old pinion is marked (0), for example, and the new pinion is marked +2, try a .002 in. thinner shim. If the new pinion is marked −2, try a .002 in. thicker shim.

Pinion Bearing Preload (Small Stem)

1. If the bearings are being replaced, place the bearings in the carrier and drive into place with a drift.
2. Assemble the pinion shim (chamfered side toward the gear) onto the pinion stem. Install the tubular spacer if equipped, and the preload shims on the pinion stem.
3. Insert the pinion assembly into the carrier.
4. Install the front pinion bearing cone, U joint flange, Belleville washer (convex side up) and nut. Do not install the oil seal.
5. Tighten the flange nut to 240 ft. lbs. Rotate the pinion to properly seat the bearing rollers. The preload torque required to turn the pinion with the bearings oiled, should be 20-30 in. lbs. with new bearings and 0-15 in. lbs. for used bearings. Use a thinner shim pack to increase preload and a thicker shim pack to decrease preload.
6. After the correct pinion depth has been established and the preload obtained, remove the drive pinion flange.
7. Lubricate and install the drive pinion oil seal.
8. Install the pinion flange, washer and nut. Torque the nut to 240 ft. lbs.

Pinion Bearing Preload (Large Stem)

1. Place the rear pinion bearing cone on the pinion stem (small side away from pinion head).
2. Lubricate front and rear bearing cones and install the rear pinion bearing cone onto the pinion stem with an arbor press.
3. Insert the pinion bearing and collapsible spacer assembly through the carrier and install the front bearing cone. Install the companion flange.
   NOTE: during installation of pinion bearing, do not collapse the spacer.
4. Install the drive pinion oil seal into the carrier. Use tool C-3890 to insure proper seal depth.
5. Support the pinion in the carrier and install the anti-clang washer.
6. Install the Belleville washer (convex side up) and pinion nut.
7. Hold the companion flange and tighten the pinion nut to remove all end-play, while rotating the pinion to insure proper bearing seating. Remove the tools and rotate the pinion several revolutions.
8. Torque the pinion nut to 170 ft. lbs. With an in. lbs. torque wrench, measure the pinion bearing preload, which should be 20-30 in. lbs. for new bearings or 10 in. lbs. over the original figure if the old pinion bearing is used.

NOTE: the correct preload reading can only be obtained with the carrier nose upright. The final assembly is incorrect if the final pinion nut torque is below 170 ft. lbs. or if the pinion bearing preload is not within specifications. Under no circumstances should the pinion nut be backed off to reduce the pinion bearing preload. If this is done, a new collapsible spacer will have to be installed and the unit adjusted again until proper preload is obtained.

9. Make a gear tooth contact pattern. Refer to the section of *Pinion Mesh Markings*.

Carrier Installation

1. Install the differential bearing cups onto their respective bearings and position assembly in the carrier.
2. Install the caps and bolts and tighten bolts finger tight. Be sure all identification markings are properly aligned and positioned.
3. Tighten the adjusters enough to square the bearing cups with the bearings and eliminate end-play.

Allow some backlash to remain.

4. Tighten one corresponding bolt on each cap to 85-90 ft. lbs.
5. Set dial gauge to contact outer end of ring gear tooth and take readings at 90° intervals to find the spot with the least clearance. Do not rotate ring gear after this position is found.
6. Turn both adjusters equally until backlash is between .0005 and .0015 in.
7. Install adjuster lock into adjuster at rear face of ring gear. If holes do not align, tighten to next hole. Never back off to meet hole.
8. Turn the adjuster, on tooth side of ring gear, a notch at a time

until the backlash is a minimum of .006 in. and a maximum of .008 in. This will establish proper bearing preload and correct backlash.

9. Install the remaining adjuster lock and tighten cap screws to 15-20 ft. lbs.
10. Using a new gasket, install carrier assembly into housing. Tighten mounting nuts to 45 ft. lbs.
11. Install axle shafts, backing plates, hubs and drums, bleed brakes and install wheels.
12. Fill differential to proper level with approved lubricant. Lower car to floor. Road test the car.

Section 11
Ring and Pinion Gear and/or Pinion Bearing Replacement

Buick—1965-72	Camaro—1967-72	Rambler—1965-72
Buick Special—1965-72	Firebird—1967-72	Tempest—1965-72
Chevrolet—1965-72	Oldsmobile F-85—1965-72	Valiant-Dart—1965-72
Chevelle—1965-72	Oldsmobile 88—1965-72	Vega—1971-72
Chevy II—1965-72	Pontiac—1965-72	Ventura II—1971-72

The above-captioned models are all equipped with an integral housing-type rear axle assembly. On this type axle all adjustments—pinion depth, pinion bearing preload, differential bearing preload, ring and pinion backlash—are controlled and adjusted by means of shims. There are no screw adjusters.

Differential Removal

1. Raise car under frame, allowing axle housing to hang by shock absorbers.
2. Remove wheels, brake drums and axle shafts, as described in cor-

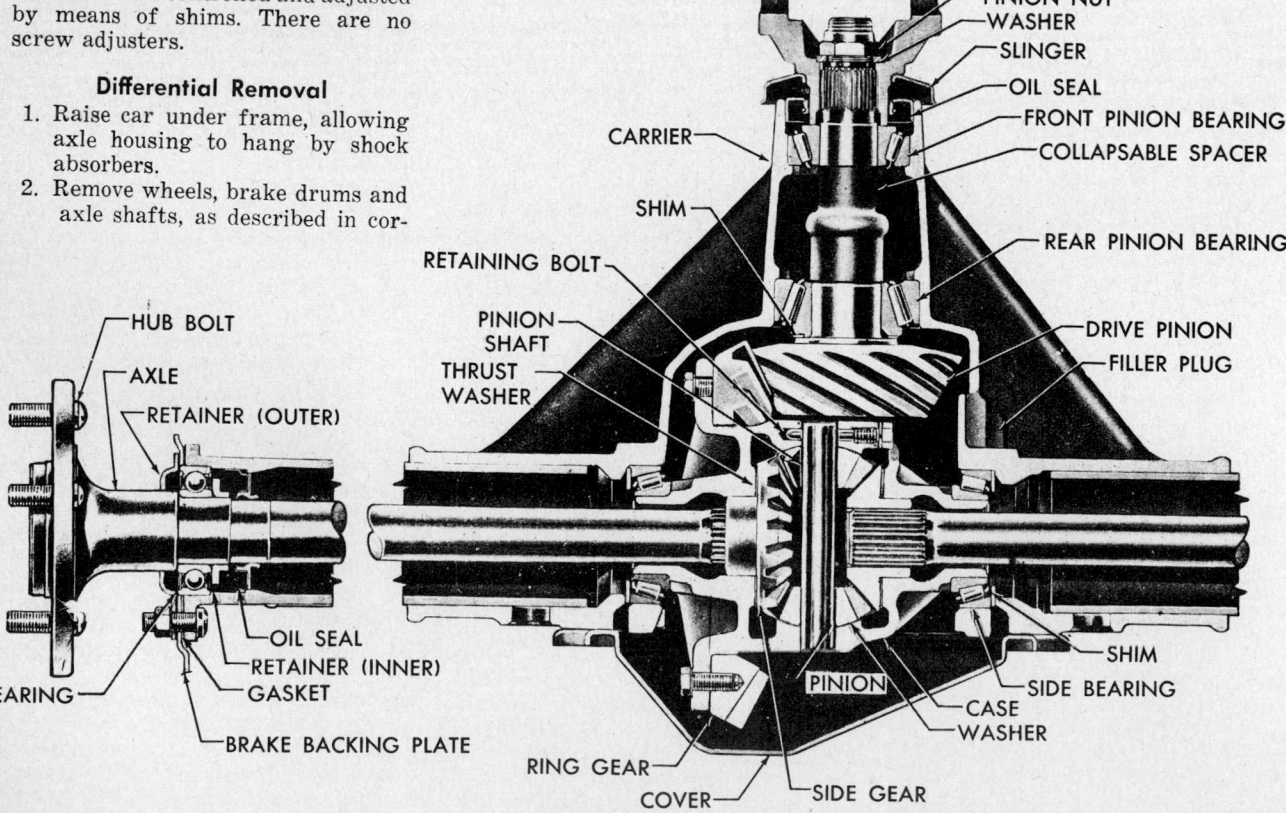

Typical General Motors rear axle (non-C type) (© Oldsmobile Div., G.M. Corp.)

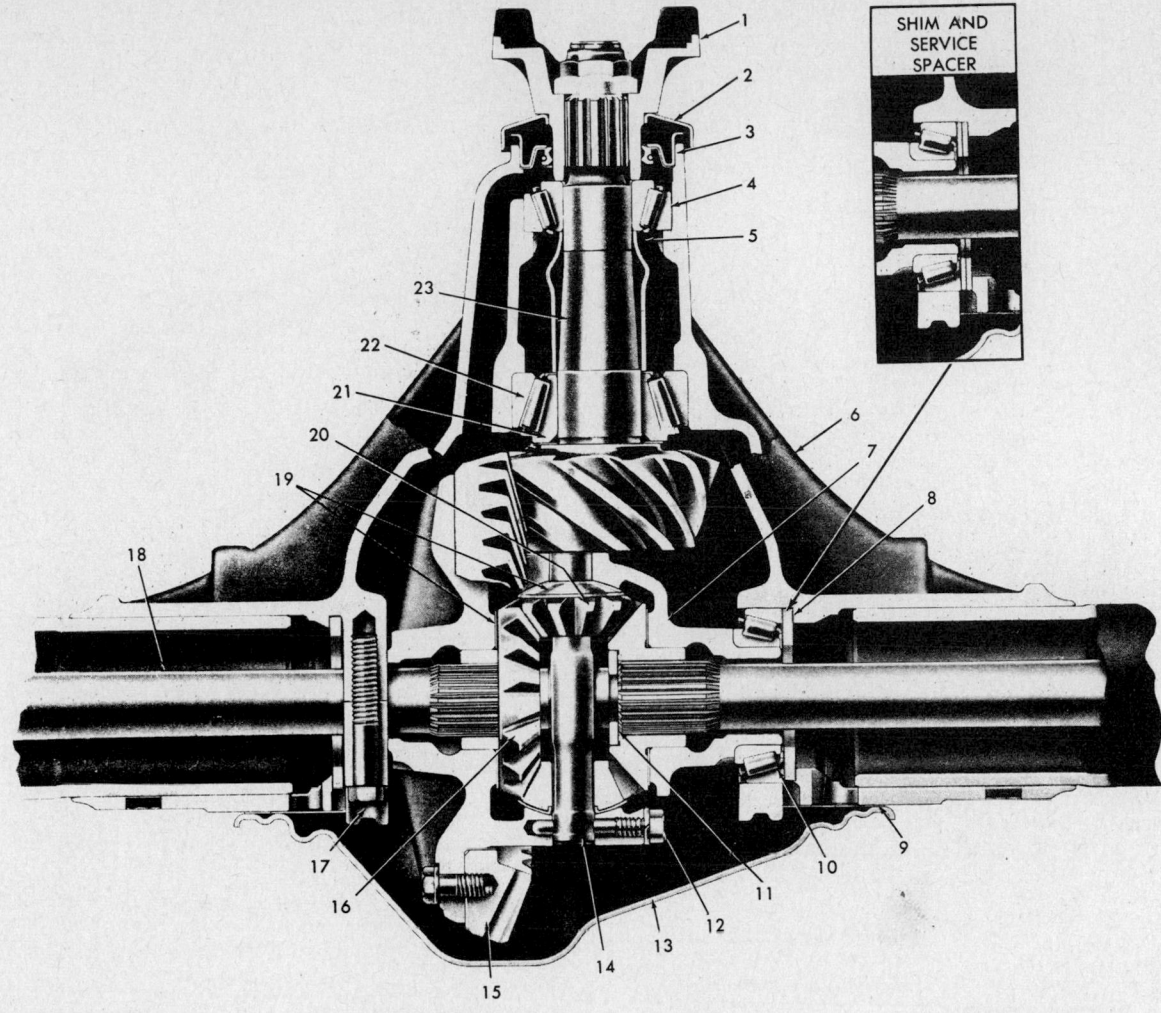

SHIM AND SERVICE SPACER

1 Companion flange	7 Differential case	13 Cover	19 Thrust washer
2 Deflector	8 Shim	14 Pinion shaft	20 Differential pinion
3 Pinion oil seal	9 Gasket	15 Ring gear	21 Shim
4 Pinion front bearing	10 Differential bearing	16 Slide gear	22 Pinion rear bearing
5 Pinion bearing spacer	11 C lock	17 Bearing cap	23 Drive pinion
6 Differential carrier	12 Pinion shaft lockbolt	18 Axle shaft	

Typical General Motors rear axle (C type) (Ⓒ Chevrolet Div., G.M. Corp.)

rect section.

3. Drain lubricant. Remove rear cover from housing.
   (It would be well, at this point, to check and record backlash as an aid in assembly).
4. Disconnect rear universal joint and wire propeller shaft to exhaust line to hold away from working area.
5. Remove companion flange nut, washer and companion flange.
6. Remove the four bearing cap bolts.
   NOTE: caps must be marked for proper reassembly.
7. Install the bearing caps using four 7/16-14 x 4½ in. cylinder head bolts, finger tight, as safety bolts.
8. Remove differential assembly by using two pry bars behind the differential case. After removing past a point, the assembly will fall free onto the two safety

bolts. These can now be removed and the unit taken to the bench.

9. Pinion assembly can now be tapped out, using a soft hammer. Guide assembly with hand to avoid damaging bearing outer races.

Differential Disassembly

1. Inspect the differential side bearings for visible damage.
2. Inspect the fit of the inner races on the case hubs. Bearing inner races must be tight.
3. If bearing inspection warrants replacement of the differential side bearings, mount the case in a soft jawed vise and pull the bearings.
4. Remove the pinion shaft lockscrew.
5. Drive the pinion shaft from the case with a brass drift.
6. Remove the differential pinion

gears thrust washers and side gears. Place these parts in sets so they may be installed in their original location.

7. Clamp the case in a vise with the jaws 90° to the pinion shaft holes. Remove the ring gear retaining bolts. Partially install two of the bolts in opposing holes in the ring gear.
   NOTE: ring gear bolts have left-hand threads.
8. Tap the ring gear lightly using the two bolts previously installed. Do not pry on the ring gear.
9. Remove the ring gear bolts and ring gear.

Differential Assembly

1. After making sure that all mating surfaces are free of dirt and burrs, position the ring gear on the case and align the bolt holes.

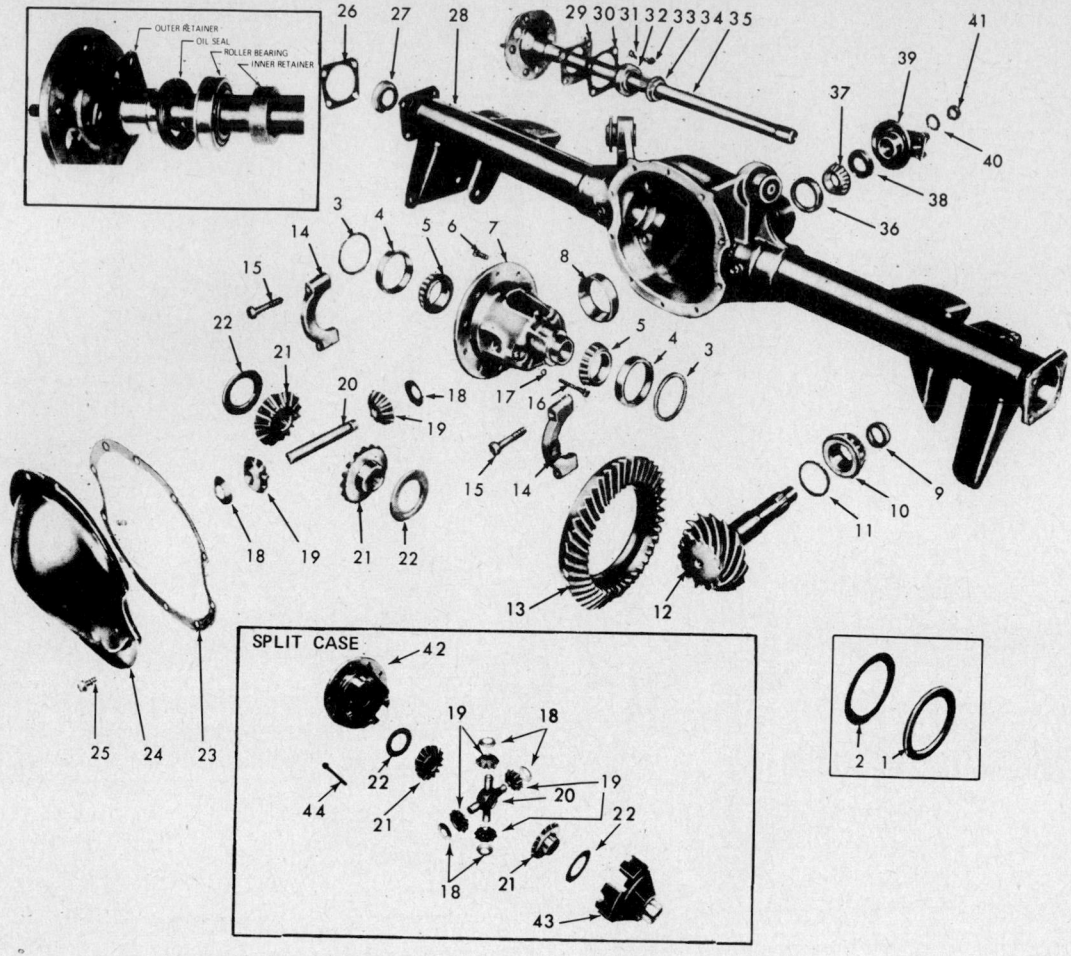

Exploded view of typical General Motors rear axle (© Pontiac Div., G.M. Corp.)

1 Spacer
2 Differential side bearing shim (service)
3 Side bearing shim (production)
4 Side bearing race
5 Differential side bearing
6 Ring gear to differential case bolt
7 Differential case
8 Rear pinion bearing outer race

9 Bearing spacer
10 Drive pinion bearing
11 Bearing shim
12 Drive pinion gear
13 Ring gear
14 Differential side bearing cap
15 Cap bolt
16 Pinion shaft lockbolt
17 Washer
18 Pinion gear thrust washer
19 Differential pinion gear
20 Differential pinion shaft

21 Differential side gear
22 Side gear thrust washer
23 Cover gasket
24 Cover
25 Cover bolt
26 Inner retainer gasket
27 Axle shaft oil seal
28 Carrier & tube assy.
29 Outer retainer
30 Outer retainer gasket
31 Nut
32 Axle shaft bearing

33 Brake assy. to housing bolt
34 Inner retainer
35 Axle shaft
36 Front pinion bearing outer race
37 Front pinion bearing
38 Pinion oil seal
39 Companion flange
40 Washer
41 Pinion nut
42 Flange half of case
43 Cap half of case
44 Case half-bolts

2. Lubricate the attaching bolts with clean engine oil and install. Do not force the ring gear onto the case. Pull the ring gear down by alternately tightening the bolts around the case.

3. Place the side gear thrust washers over the side gear hubs and install the side gears into the case.

4. Position one pinion without washer, between the side gears and rotate the side gears until the pinion is directly opposite the loading opening in the case. Place the other pinion between

the side gears with the pinion shaft holes aligned.

5. Rotate the pinions back just far enough to permit installation of the pinion thrust washers.

6. Install the pinion shaft and pinion shaft lockbolt.

7. Install the side bearings with an arbor press. Lubricate the outer bearing surfaces.

Differential Parts Replacement

1. Examine pinion shaft bearing outer races and bearings. If replacement is indicated, the outer races can be removed and re-

placed and the bearings pulled from the shaft with proper pullers.

2. Front pinion oil seal can now be replaced. Use proper driver to avoid damage.

3. Before proceeding, the pinion shim which determines pinion depth, must be selected. If the original ring gear, pinion and rear pinion bearing are being installed, use the original shim. If any of the above parts are installed new, the shim must be selected.

NOTE: never install rear gear or

pinion separately. Each ring gear and pinion has been matched by the manufacturer and should only be installed as matched pair.

It will be wise to assemble several spacers and shims of various thicknesses, in order to satisfy all conditions. By comparing the markings on the new pinion with those on the old pinion, a reasonable determination of shim thickness can be made. For instance, on Oldsmobile rear axles, production pinions are coded 45 (see chart). This means that they are .000 in. (nominal) relative to the ring gear. If the new pinion is marked 43 (see chart) try a shim .002 in. thicker than the original. If the new pinion is marked 47 (see chart) try a shim .002 in. thinner than the original.

Drive Pinion Code Chart (Typical)

40 .005 in. Minus	46 .001 in. Plus
41 .004 in. Minus	47 .002 in. Plus
42 .003 in. Minus	48 .003 in. Plus
43 .002 in. Minus	49 .004 in. Plus
44 .001 in. Minus	50 .005 in. Plus
45 .000 in.	

This method of determining the shim thickness does not guarantee proper shim selection the first time. The unit must be assembled, adjusted and checked. If the preload, backlash or gear tooth pattern test are not satisfactory, the pinion must be removed, a new collapsible spacer installed and another shim selected accordingly. Assemble the unit again and retest.

4. Position the selected shim on the pinion stem and install the rear bearing.
5. Install a new collapsible spacer (if used) on the pinion stem and install the pinion. Position the front bearing and press to contact the spacer.
6. Install companion flange, washer and nut and tighten to very slight pressure. Check preload. Preload should be according to specifications.
7. Continue to tighten pinion nut in very small increments. Less than one-eighth turn is advisable. Repeatedly test for proper preload, and frequently turn the shaft in bearings to be sure proper seating is obtained.

(In differential case installation, bearing preload and side spacing must be considered. Do not use original production shims, as they are cast iron and may be damaged when being tapped into place. Service spacers are furnished in .170 in. thickness, with shims available in .002 in. increments. Make sure all bearing surfaces and shim surfaces are absolutely clean before starting assembly).

8. Place differential case, with bearing outer races, in position in carrier.
9. Install .170 in. thick service spacer between each race and housing.
10. If new bearings are being used, add shims to both spacers to produce a total thickness on each side to correspond to the original shim thickness. If original bearings are used, increase this thickness .002 in. on each side.
11. Slip left shim between bearing and spacer, then tap right shim carefully into place.
12. As a safety precaution, install the 7/16-14 x 4½ in. head bolts into the caps.
13. Rotate differential several times to be sure bearings are properly seated. With torque wrench on ring gear attaching bolt, check bearing preload. It should be according to specifications (see preceding chart). In some cases, specifications are not given for differential bearing preload. It is necessary to check preload by means of gear backlash (see next step).
14. Mount dial gauge to read gear lash at outer edge of ring gear. Check lash at three or four positions to be sure that there is not more than .002 in. runout. If more than this is found, corrections should be made to such items as burrs, uneven bearing seating, distorted differential case, etc.
15. Gear lash at the minimum point should be .003-.010 in. for all new gears. If original gears are reinstalled, the measurement of backlash taken before disassembly should be maintained within ±.001 in. If lash is not within specifications, addition or removal of shims must be done to obtain desired measurements. Always keep the total shim measurement the same as when started, simply moving from one side to the other. This will maintain the bearing preload. Each .004 in. shim moved will change backlash approximately .002 in.
16. After proper backlash is obtained, remove the four safety head bolts and install the regular cap bolts. Tighten to 60-75 ft. lbs.
NOTE: at this point, it is best to make a red lead test to check contact pattern. If proper pattern is not obtained, it may be necessary to change shim on pinion shaft, thus changing pinion depth. See section on *Pinion Mesh Markings*.
17. Install axle shafts, drums, hubs and wheels, install proper lubricant and lower car to floor.

Bearing Preload Chart

Year	Model	Pinion Bearing Preload (in. lbs.) New Bearing	Pinion Bearing Preload (in. lbs.) Old Bearing	Differential Bearing Preload (in. lbs.) New Bearing	Differential Bearing Preload (in. lbs.) Old Bearing
1965-66	Buick (Std.)	20-30	15-20	30-40	15-25
1967	Buick (Std.)	20-30	15-20	35-40	20-25
1968-70	Buick (Std.)	25-30	10-15	35-40	20-25
1969-72	Buick (C type)	20-25	10-15	35-40	20-25
1965-69	American Motors	17-28①			
1970-72	American Motors (7–9/16 in.)	15-25	N.A.	N.A.	N.A.
1970-72	American Motors (8–7/8 in.)	17-28			
1965-66	Oldsmobile (Std.)	20-30	12-20	30-40	20-30
1967-72	Oldsmobile (Std.)	24-32	8-12		
1969-72	Oldsmobile (C type)	20-30	5-15	N.A.	N.A.
1965-68	Chevrolet	20-30	5-15		
1969	Chevrolet	N.A.	N.A.	N.A.	N.A.
1970-72	Chevrolet	20-25	5-10		
1965-72	Pontiac	25	17	N.A.	N.A.
1965-72	Valiant, Dart	15-25	N.A.	N.A.	N.A.

①—15-25 in. lbs. on 199 six cylinder engine

Section 12
Ring and Pinion Gear and/or Pinion Bearing Replacement

**All Ford, Lincoln, Mercury
and Continental Applications—
1965-72**

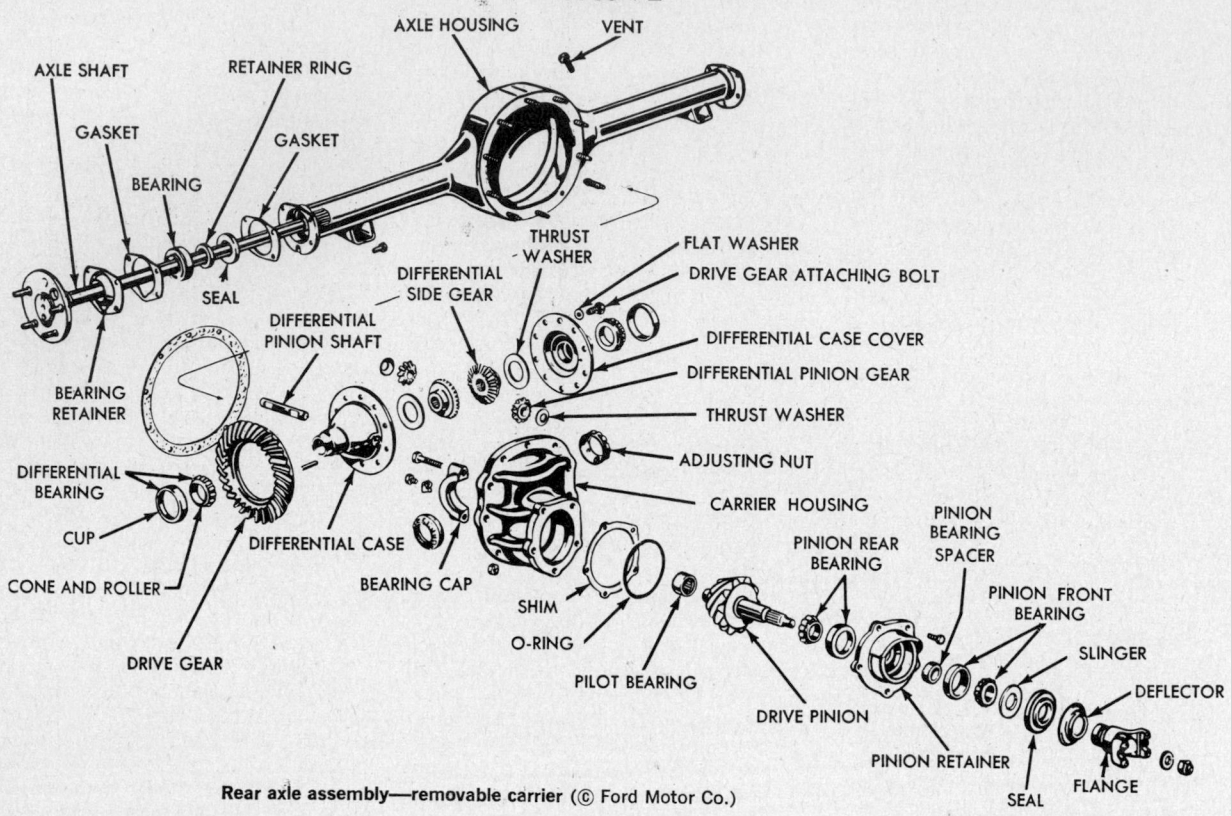

AXLE HOUSING   VENT

AXLE SHAFT   RETAINER RING

GASKET   GASKET

BEARING   THRUST WASHER   FLAT WASHER

SEAL   DIFFERENTIAL SIDE GEAR   DRIVE GEAR ATTACHING BOLT

BEARING RETAINER   DIFFERENTIAL PINION SHAFT   DIFFERENTIAL CASE COVER

DIFFERENTIAL PINION GEAR

THRUST WASHER

DIFFERENTIAL BEARING   ADJUSTING NUT

CUP   CARRIER HOUSING   PINION BEARING SPACER

CONE AND ROLLER   DIFFERENTIAL CASE   PINION REAR BEARING   PINION FRONT BEARING

DRIVE GEAR   BEARING CAP   SHIM   SLINGER

O-RING   DEFLECTOR

PILOT BEARING

DRIVE PINION   SEAL   FLANGE

PINION RETAINER

Rear axle assembly—removable carrier (© Ford Motor Co.)

Two types of differentials are used on the above cars. An integral carrier type axle, using a differential carrier integral with the axle housing, and a removal carrier type, in which the differential carrier is bolted to the axle housing. Several sizes of ring gears are available, and a locking differential is available as an option.

NOTE: before attempting any service to the differential, determine which type is being serviced and proceed according to type.

Removable Axle Carrier Type

This type of axle uses a removable pinion bearing housing, in addition to a removable carrier. Pinion depth is controlled by shims between the carrier housing and pinion bearing housing.

Differential Carrier Removal

1. Remove filler plug and drain lubricant.
2. Matchmark the rear universal joint; disconnect it from companion flange and tie it to one side, out of work area.
3. Remove wheels, drums and axle shafts.

4. Remove the nuts holding carrier to axle housing.
5. Remove carrier assembly and mount in holding fixture.

Differential Carrier Installation

1. Install carrier into housing and install nuts. Tighten to 30-40 ft. lbs.
2. Assemble rear universal to companion flange. Torque U-bolt nuts to 12-15 ft. lbs.
3. Install backing plates, axle shafts, drums and wheels. Where axle shafts of different lengths are used the longer shaft goes to the right side.
4. Fill the differential to the bottom of filler plug hole with approved lubricant.

Differential Carrier Reconditioning

Before disassembling, check for gear runout, parts chipping or other damage. Check and note amount of backlash.

1. Mark bearing supports and caps for aid in proper assembly.
2. Remove locks, caps and adjusting rings, then remove differential from carrier.
3. Necessary replacements can now

be made.

4. Turn the carrier with pinion shaft upright and remove the bolts securing the pinion retainer assembly. Remove the O-ring.
5. Remove the pinion locating shim; measure and record its thickness.
6. Remove the pinion pilot bearing. Use proper tool to avoid damaging housing or bearing. When replacing pilot, use caution so as not to crack the bearing support.
7. With pinion retainer assembly mounted in holding tool, remove the pinion nut and washer. Then, remove the companion flange.
8. Remove the oil slinger and seal.
9. Press the pinion shaft out of the retainer and front bearing cone. Discard the collapsible spacer.
10. Remove the rear bearing cone.
11. Bearing cups may now be removed and replaced.
12. Remove the differential bearings, using a puller.
13. Remove the ring gear bolts and tap the ring gear from the case, using a soft faced hammer.
14. Drive out the differential pinion shaft lockpin.
15. Drive out the pinion shaft and remove the gears and thrust

washers.

16. Proceed as follows to assemble the differential case. Lubricate all the differential parts prior to assembly.
17. Install the side gears and thrust washers into the case.
18. Install the two pinion gears and thrust washers exactly opposite each other in the case opening. Mesh the pinion gears with the side gears.
19. Align the holes in the pinion gears with the pinion shaft holes in the case.
20. Align the pinion shaft lockpin hole and install the pinion shaft. Drive in the lockpin.
21. Place the ring gear on the case and install the bolts.
22. Press in the differential bearings.
23. In reassembling the pinion shaft and bearings, install the rear bearing cone onto the pinion shaft first.
24. Place a new collapsible spacer on the pinion shaft.
25. Place the pinion gear and rear bearing cone in the retainer.
26. Install the front pinion bearing in cone onto the shaft.
27. Place oil slinger on shaft.
28. Place new pre-soaked oil seal in position, coating outer edges with oil resistant sealer.
29. Place companion flange on shaft and start nut with washer.
30. Tighten the pinion shaft nut to a maximum of 175 ft. lbs. While tightening, continually rotate the shaft to be sure the bearings are properly seated and rollers aligned.
31. Check the bearing preload. With used bearings and seal, preload should be 8 in. lbs. With new bearings, preload should be 5-8 in. lbs. If the torque on the pinion shaft nut is less than 175 ft. lbs., after proper preload is obtained, a new collapsible spacer must be used. Never back the nut off to reduce preload. Install a new spacer and torque to obtain the preload.

If new gears are being used, check the mating numbers on the pinion and ring gear. The proper shim must be selected for the drive pinion retainer. The number on the pilot end of the pinion indicates the shim thickness to be used; —1 indicates that a shim .001 in. thinner than standard is required. +1 indicates that a shim .001 in. thicker than standard is required. Markings are based on a standard shim thickness of .020 in. When replacing gear sets, these numbers should be compared with the old ones so the shims can be selected allowing for the difference between markings of the different gear sets.

If there are painted timing (index) marks on either the old or new gears, line up the matching marks when the ring gear is meshed with the pinion.

32. Lubricate the O-ring with axle lubricant and snap it into place on the pinion retainer. Do not roll into place.
33. Place the pinion gear and retainer in the carrier, with the proper shim. Be careful not to disturb the O-ring in groove. Torque bolts to 30-40 ft. lbs.
34. Coat the differential pedestal bores with lubricant so that bearing cups will move easily, and place the differential, with bearings, in the carrier. Slide along the bores until a slight backlash can be felt. Set the adjusting nuts until they just contact the bearing cups.
35. Position the caps on the carrier, checking the match marks formerly made to be sure of proper assembly. Also, check that threads are not crossed. Install the bolts and torque to 55-65 ft. lbs.
36. Loosen the cap bolts and torque to 20 ft. lbs.
37. Loosen right-side nut, tooth side of ring gear, until it is away from the cup. Tighten left-side nut until the ring gear mates with the pinion, with no backlash, being sure the right-side nut is still loose. Tighten right-side nut two notches beyond point where it contacts the bearing. Rotate ring gear several times to be sure the bearings are properly seated.
38. Loosen the right-side nut to release preload. If there is any backlash, tighten left-side nut just enough to remove. Tighten right-side nut to obtain proper preload. This will be two and one-half to three notches tight. The backlash should be .008-.012 in. Torque the cap bolts to 55-65 ft. lbs. Always be sure that, in adjusting the nuts, final rotation is in a tightening direction. Do not back off.

At this point, it is well to check the pinion lash markings in the section on *Pinion Mesh Markings*. If no corrections are required, install assembly into axle housing, as described above.

Ring and Pinion Gear and/or Pinion Bearing Replacement

All Ford, Lincoln, Mercury and Continental Applications— 1965-72

Integral Axle Carrier Type

There are four different axle housings and three types of differential case used in this rear end construction. The design change depends upon car model and engine size, therefore, the model-year identification plate should be used to identify correct model and gear ratio when ordering replacement parts.

The rear axle assembly uses an integra-type housing. The differential assembly is mounted on two opposed tapered roller bearings. The bearings support and position the differential between two pedestals and spanner adjustable caps. Differential bearing preload and drive gear backlash is controlled by the thrust of these large pedestal nuts against the differential side bearing cups.

The drive pinion assembly is mounted on two opposed tapered roller bearings. Pinion bearing preload is adjusted by a collapsible spacer on the pinion shaft. Pinion and ring gear tooth contact is adjusted by shims between the rear bearing cone and pinion gear. Gear ratio is stamped on a metal tag attached to the differential case inspection cover. This axle is not equipped with a lubricant drain.

Rear Axle Housing Assembly Removal

1. Raise car and support on the underbody.
2. Loosen the differential carrier inspection cover, drain and discard lubricant.
3. Disconnect driveshaft at rear U-joint.
4. Disconnect rear shock absorbers at axle.
5. Remove both rear axle shafts.
6. Separate brake T from rear axle housing and separate hydraulic brake line from its retaining clip.
7. Disconnect both rear brake backing plates from the axle housing and wire them out of the way.
8. Support the axle housing on a jack, then remove spring U-bolts and plates.
9. Lower axle housing and remove it from underneath the car.

Rear Axle Housing Assembly Installation

1. Raise the axle housing into posi-

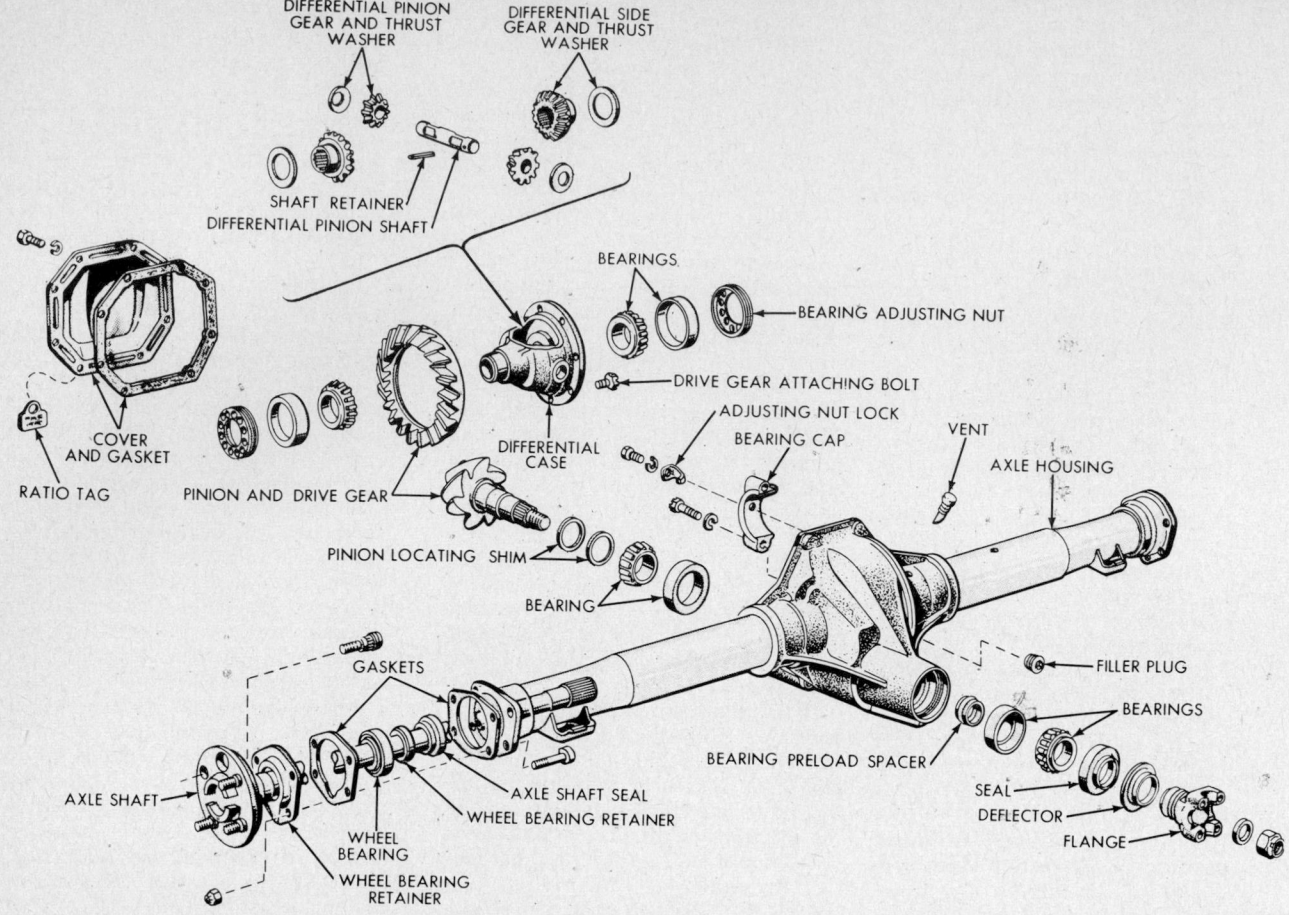

DIFFERENTIAL PINION
GEAR AND THRUST
WASHER

DIFFERENTIAL SIDE
GEAR AND THRUST
WASHER

SHAFT RETAINER
DIFFERENTIAL PINION SHAFT

BEARINGS

BEARING ADJUSTING NUT

DRIVE GEAR ATTACHING BOLT

ADJUSTING NUT LOCK

BEARING CAP

VENT

AXLE HOUSING

COVER
AND GASKET

RATIO TAG

PINION AND DRIVE GEAR

DIFFERENTIAL
CASE

PINION LOCATING SHIM

BEARING

FILLER PLUG

BEARINGS

GASKETS

AXLE SHAFT

WHEEL
BEARING

WHEEL BEARING
RETAINER

AXLE SHAFT SEAL
WHEEL BEARING RETAINER

BEARING PRELOAD SPACER

SEAL

DEFLECTOR

FLANGE

Rear axle assembly—integral carrier (© Ford Motor Co.)

tion and install spring U-bolts and plates. Torque spring U-bolt nuts to 13-20 ft. lbs.

2. Install brake backing plates. Use new gaskets on each side of the backing plates.

3. Install axle shafts, brake drums and wheels.

4. Attach brake line T-fitting to the axle housing, and fasten the hydraulic brake line to its retainer on the housing.

5. Raise the axle housing and connect the shock absorbers.

6. Connect driveshaft at rear U-joint.

7. Clean inspection cover and axle housing. Apply sealer to both sides of inspection cover gasket. Daub cover attaching screw threads with anti-seize compound. Attach inspection cover and torque screws to 15-20 ft. lbs.

8. Fill axle to level with proper lubricant.

Differential Case and Drive Pinion Removal and Disassembly

With the axle assembly out of the car and the inspection cover removed:

1. Remove the differential side bearing adjusting nutlocks.

2. Mark the differential bearing caps, adjusting nuts and case for relative identity during reassem-

bly.

3. Remove differential bearing pedestal cap bolts and caps.

4. Remove differential case and bearing cups.

5. Remove ring gear attaching bolts. Separate ring gear from differential case with a soft-faced hammer.

6. Drive out the differential pinion shaft retaining pin with a punch.

7. Use a drift to drive out the differential pinion shaft. Remove the gears and thrust washers.

8. Hold the drive pinion flange and remove pinion nut and flat washer.

9. With a soft-faced hammer, drive the pinion out of the front bearing cone and remove it through the rear of the carrier casting.

10. Remove and replace damaged bearings and bearing cups as required. Special pullers are needed, except for the differential side bearing cups.

Drive Pinion Shim Selection

Pinion bore dimension tolerances, and operating positions of the gears, present the need for various shim thicknesses between the pinion rear bearing cone and the pinion gear. When the shim thickness is decreased, the pinion is moved away

from the ring gear. When shim thickness is increased, the pinion is moved closer to the ring gear. Shims are available in thicknesses of 0.008 in. through 0.024 in. in increments of 0.001 in.

If a new ring gear and pinion set is to be installed, refer to the pinion gear end marking for plus (+) or minus (−) signs, followed by a number.

To select the correct shim thickness required for proper installation of a new pinion gear, perform the following steps:

1. Measure the thickness of the original shim pack.

2. Refer to Shim Thickness Table. Note the shim adjustment number on both the old and new pinion. Observe the amount of change shown in the table under New Pinion Marking, in line with Old Pinion Marking. Note the reading. Add or subtract the reading obtained from that of the original shim pack and note the result.

3. To the above result, add or subtract the shim thickness correction indicated during the gear tooth contact pattern check. This final result is the shim thickness required for installation of the new drive pinion.

Old Pinion Marking	New Pinion Marking								
	−4	−3	−2	−1	0	+1	+2	+3	+4
+4	+0.008	+0.007	+0.006	+0.005	+0.004	+0.003	+0.002	+0.001	0
+3	+0.007	+0.006	+0.005	+0.004	+0.003	+0.002	+0.001	0	−0.001
+2	+0.006	+0.005	+0.004	+0.003	+0.002	+0.001	0	−0.001	−0.002
+1	+0.005	+0.004	+0.003	+0.002	+0.001	0	−0.001	−0.002	−0.003
0	+0.004	+0.003	+0.002	+0.001	0	−0.001	−0.002	−0.003	−0.004
−1	+0.003	+0.002	+0.001	0	−0.001	−0.002	−0.003	−0.004	−0.005
−2	+0.002	+0.001	0	−0.001	−0.002	−0.003	−0.004	−0.005	−0.006
−3	+0.001	0	−0.001	−0.002	−0.003	−0.004	−0.005	−0.006	−0.007
−4	0	−0.001	−0.002	−0.003	−0.004	−0.005	−0.006	−0.007	−0.008

Drive Pinion Assembly and Installation

1. Place the shim and pinion bearing cone on the pinion shaft. Press the bearing and shim firmly against the pinion shaft shoulder.
2. Install a new pinion bearing preload spacer onto the pinion shaft. If the unit uses a long spacer, be sure the large diameter end of the spacer is against the pinion rear bearing inner race.
3. Lubricate the pinion rear bearing with axle lubricant.
4. Lubricate the pinion front bearing and cone and place cone in the housing.
5. Coat the outer edge of a new oil seal with oil resistant sealer and install it into the carrier casting.
6. Insert the drive pinion shaft flange into the oil seal and hold it firmly against the pinion front bearing cone. From the rear of the carrier casting, insert the pinion shaft into the flange.
7. Place the flat washer and nut on the pinion shaft. Use a holding tool on the flange and tighten the shaft nut. As the nut is tightened the pinion shaft is pulled into the front bearing cone and into the flange. Continue tightening, reducing end-play, until the bearing cone and flange have bottomed on the collapsible spacer (no end-play). From this point on, tighten the nut slowly as the preload sleeve is being collapsed. A minimum torque of 140 ft. lbs. is required.

Caution If the nut is over-torqued, the pinion shaft must be removed and a new collapsible sleeve installed. Do not decrease the preload by loosening the pinion shaft nut.

8. As soon as there is preload on the bearings, turn the pinion shaft in both directions a few times to seat them.
9. Adjust pinion preload to specifications.

Differential Case Assembly and Installation

1. Lubricate all differential parts with axle lubricant before they are installed.
2. Place side gears and thrust washers in case.
3. Place the two pinion gears and thrust washers exactly opposite each other in the case opening. Make sure they mesh with the side gears.
4. Turn the pinions and thrust washers until the holes in the pinion gears align with the pinion shaft holes in the case.
5. Start the pinion shaft into the differential case. Align the shaft retaining pin hole with the pin hole in the case. Drive the shaft into place and install the retaining pin.
6. Place the drive gear on the differential case and install attaching bolts. Torque the bolts to 40-50 ft. lbs.
7. Press differential bearing cones onto the differential assembly.
8. Lubricate the bearing bores of the pedestals, place the cups on the bearings and set the case assembly in the carrier casting.
9. Position the differential case in the bores until a slight amount of backlash is felt between the gear teeth. Hold differential in place.
10. Set adjusting nuts in the bores so that they just contact the bearing cups.
11. Match the bearing caps and place on their respective pedestals.
12. Install bearing cap bolts. While tightening the bolts, turn the adjusting nut with a spanner wrench.
13. If the adjusting nuts bind as the pedestal caps are tightened, remove the caps and inspect for cross-threading or other damage. When satisfied that the nuts are correctly seated in the pedestals and caps, tighten the cap bolts. Now, loosen the cap bolts, then torque them to 5 ft. lbs.
14. Loosen the right-hand adjusting nut until it is away from the cup. Tighten the left-hand nut until the ring gear is just fully meshed.
15. Loosen the left-hand adjusting nut one to one and one-half notches. Tighten the right-hand adjusting nut to the specified two and one-half to three notches beyond the point where it first contacts the bearing cup. As preload is applied from the right-hand side, the ring gear is moved away from the pinion. This usually results in correct backlash. Backlash should be 0.008-0.012 in.
16. Torque differential cap bolts to 40-50 ft. lbs. Measure pinion-to-ring gear backlash at several points around the ring gear in order to check runout. Runout should not exceed 0.002 in.
17. Run a gear tooth contact pattern check. See section on *Pinion Mesh Markings*.

Bearing Preload

Year	Pinion Bearing Preload (in. lbs.)				Differential Bearing Preload④			
	Integral Carrier		Removable Carrier		Integral Carrier		Removable Carrier	
	New Bearings	Old Bearings	New Bearings	Old Bearings	New Bearings	Old Bearings	New Bearings	Old Bearings
1971	20-30	8-14	22-32	8-14	.006-.010	.008-.012	.006-.010	.008-.012
1970	20-30	8-14①	22-32	8-14	.005-.008	.008-.012	.006-.010	.008-.012
1967-69	22-32	8-14	22-32	8-14	②	.008-.012	②	.008-.012
1966	22-32	10-14	22-32	10-14	.012	.005-.008	.012	.005-.008
1965	17-27	6-12	22-32	10-14	③	③	③	③

①—13-33 in. lbs. with solid spacer
②—Differential bearing preload (Old bearings):
    7.25 in. ring gear   .003-.005 in.
    8.75 in. ring gear   .005-.008 in.
    8.5 in. ring gear   .006-.010 in.
③—2-3 notches tight
④—Differential case spread

Section 13
Corvette Three-Link Rear Suspension

Rear Wheel Bearing, Spindles and Oil Seal Adjustment and/or Replacement

To measure roller bearing end-play on spindle. (Should be .001-.007 in.):

1. Raise rear of car until wheels clear ground.
2. Remove outboard axle driveshaft flange from spindle.
3. Mark camber cam and bolt in relation to bracket.
4. Loosen and turn camber bolt to force strut rods outward. This will give clearance to drop axle driveshaft.
5. Mount dial indicator on inboard surface of torque arm with pointer contacting spindle end.
6. Measure and record in and out movement of spindle.

To remove wheel spindle and support:

1. Remove wheel and tire assembly.
2. Remove spindle cotter pin, nut and washer and pull drive flange from spindle.
3. Remove brake drum or caliper and disc and pull spindle from support.
4. Pry out inner and outer seals. Remove races and rollers. Remove shims and spacers.

NOTE: bearing cups may be removed while spindle support is mounted to torque arm.

5. Disconnect brake line and remove nuts holding backing plate and spindle. Hang backing plate on frame.
6. Disconnect lower end of shock absorber. Support end of spring if necessary.
7. Remove cotter pin and nut from strut rod mounting shaft and

drop strut rod. Support may now be removed.

To assemble spindle and support:

1. If using original bearings, pack with lubricant and place in support with spacer and original shims.
2. Replace both seals. Be sure they are well seated.
3. Proceed to assemble spindle and support in sequence opposite to removal steps.
4. If using new wheel bearings, assemble with a .145 in. shim and check end-play as in Steps 1 through 6.

NOTE: shims are furnished in thicknesses from .097-.145 in. in increments of .006 in. If the .145 in. shim allows excess play, use thinner shim.

5. Now, select proper shims needed to bring the play to the specified .001-.007 in. tolerance.

Axle Driveshaft Replacement

1. Remove U-bolt clamps from inboard side gear yoke.
2. Remove bolts securing outboard flange to spindle flange.
3. Pry driveshaft out at outboard end.
4. Joints may now be repaired or replaced as in the conventional cross and trunnion-type universal joint.
5. Assemble inboard trunnions into side gear yokes and install U-bolts. Torque to 14-18 ft. lbs.
6. Install outboard flange to spindle bolts and torque to 70-90 ft. lbs.

Differential Removal and/or Ring and Pinion Gear and Bearing Replacement

1. Raise rear of car and support on frame, slightly forward of control arm pivots.
2. Remove wheels and tires.
3. Place jack under spring at link bolt and raise spring until nearly flat.
4. With chain around crossmember,

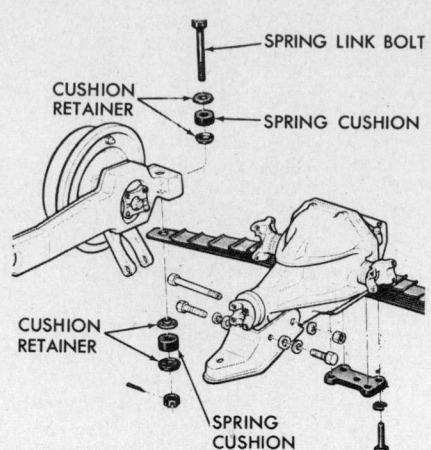

Spring mounting with link bolt
(© Chevrolet Div., G.M. Corp.)

secure spring in this flattened position. A C-clamp should be used to prevent chain from slipping on spring.

5. Lower jack and remove link bolt.
6. Repeat Steps 3, 4 and 5 on opposite side.
7. Disconnect axle driveshafts at carrier yokes.
8. Disconnect carrier front support bracket at crossmember. Remove bolts, then remove the bracket.
9. Disconnect driveshaft at transmission and companion flange.
10. Slide transmission yoke forward. Drop driveshaft down and out toward rear.
11. Mark camber cam and bolt relative location on strut rod bracket and loosen cam bolts.
12. Remove bolts securing bracket to carrier. Then, drop bracket.
13. Remove camber cam bolts and swing strut rods up and out of way.
14. Remove carrier - to - cover bolts. Loosen slowly to allow lubricant to drain.
15. With bolts out, pull carrier slightly out of cover and drop nose to clear crossmember. Work carrier down and out.

NOTE: use care not to damage gasket mounting surface in order to avoid any possible oil-leak condition.

Differential Case Removal

1. Mount the case in a holding fixture and remove the snap-rings that secure the side gear yokes and remove the side gear yokes from the case.
2. Matchmark the differential bearing caps and remove them.
3. Pull the differential assembly from the carrier and remove the differential bearing shims. Mark these for future reference.

SPINDLE SUPPORT
BEARING SPACER
BEARING PRE-LOAD SPACER
CONTROL ARM
SPINDLE
DRIVE FLANGE
INNER BEARING
OUTER BEARING
DRIVE SPINDLE
DEFLECTOR

Spindle and support cross-section
(© Chevrolet Div., G.M. Corp.)

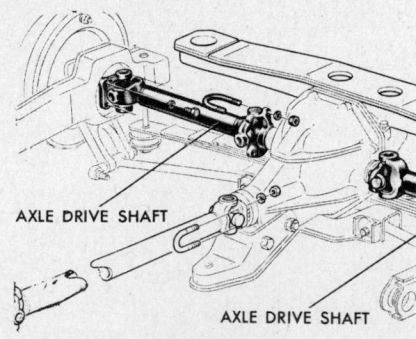

AXLE DRIVE SHAFT

AXLE DRIVE SHAFT

Axle driveshaft

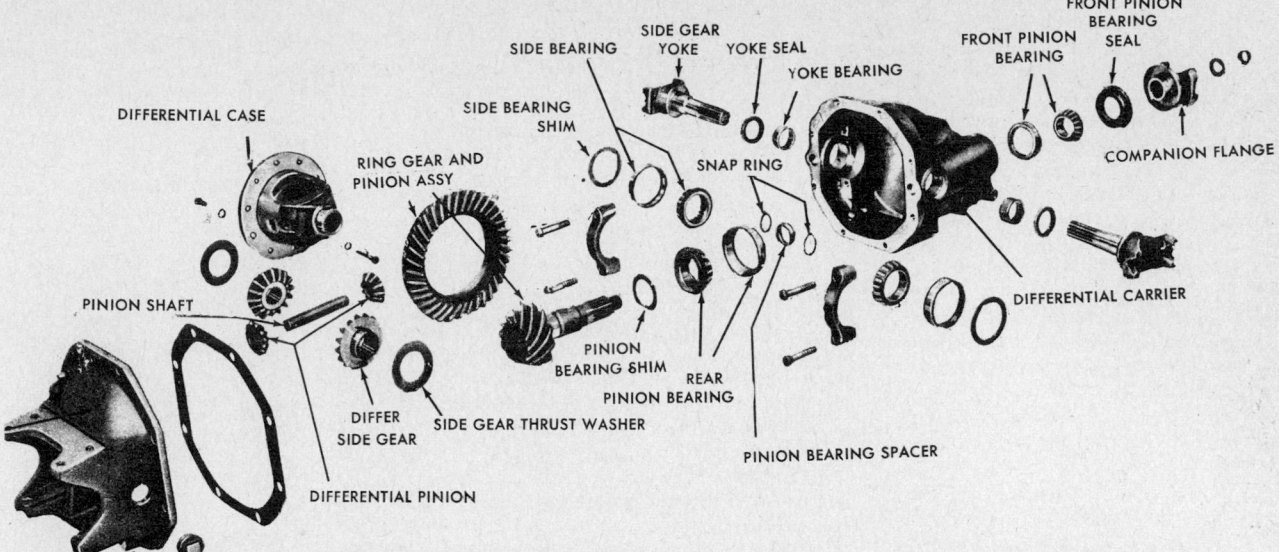

Corvette differential—exploded view (© Chevrolet Div., G.M. Corp.)

Marking camber cam and bracket
(© Chevrolet Div., G.M. Corp.)

4. Disassemble the differential by removing the pinion lockscrew, pinion shaft, differential pinions, pinion thrust washers, side gears and side gear thrust washers. Do not remove the ring gear unless replacement of the ring gear or case is necessary.

Differential Bearing Replacement

1. Remove the differential bearings from the side gear bores.
2. Install new side gear bearings into the side gear bores.

Ring Gear or Differential Case Replacement

1. Remove the ring gear bolts and tap the ring gear from the differential case.
2. Install guide pins fabricated from 3/8-24 x 1½ in. bolts with heads removed and ends slotted.
3. Install the ring gear and every other ring gear bolt. Draw the bolts up evenly, until the ring gear is seated against the flange.
4. Remove the guide pins and in-

stall the remaining ring gear bolts.
5. Install the side gears and thrust washers into the case. Position the pinions and thrust washers through the loading hole in the case, 180° apart. Engage the pinion gears with the side gears. Rotate the gears to align the bores in the case and pinion shaft. Install the pinion shaft and lockscrew.

Side Gear Yoke Bearing and/or Seal Replacement

1. Place new yoke bearings in the carrier bores and drive in until fully seated.
2. Install a new seal into the seal bore outboard of the bearing.

Drive Pinion Removal

1. Remove the differential case.
2. Remove the companion flange nut and pull the companion flange from the carrier.
3. Remove the pinion and rear bearing from the carrier.
4. Pry the companion flange seal from the carrier and remove the front pinion bearing.
5. Pry the differential side gear yoke seals from the carrier and discard the seals. Use a piece of 1.75 in. O.D. pipe to drive the yoke bearings from the bore.
6. If necessary to replace the pinion bearings, tap the old cups out of the carrier using a brass drift. Select front and rear pinion bearings and drive the cups into the carrier. Seat the cups squarely against the shoulders.
7. Using a press and press plates, remove the rear pinion bearing inner race and roller assembly.

Pinion Installation

1. If the original parts are to be installed, the original pinion shim should be suitable, provided the differential operated satisfactorily prior to disassembly. However, if any parts are being replaced (ring gear and pinion should only be replaced as a matched set) a new pinion shim will have to be used.
2. By comparing the pinion markings on the old and new pinion, a reasonable determination of shim thickness can be made. If the original pinion is zero (no marking) and the old pinion is marked +2 use a .002 in. thinner shim. If the new pinion is marked −2, use a shim .002 in. thinner than the original. This is not an absolute determination of shim thickness, but is a reasonable starting point. Gather several pinion spacers and shims, in order to provide a large number of adjustment combinations.

NOTE: after the unit is assembled, if the shim thickness is found to be incorrect, the unit will have to be disassembled and the shim changed in accordance with test results. The spacer cannot be used over again.

3. Position the pinion shim selected on the head of the pinion and press the rear bearing on the pinion.
4. Lubricate the pinion bearings and install the pinion gear in the carrier.
5. Place a new pinion bearing spacer over the pinion stem so that it seats on the inner race of the rear bearing.
6. Slide the pinion front bearing cone and roller over the pinion stem so that it seats against the spacer.

7. Pack the cavity between the seal lips of the pinion and the flange oil seal with a lithium base grease and position the seal in the bore. Press the seal into the carrier so that is seats squarely in the bore and properly against the pinion flange.
8. Install the companion flange.
9. Pack the cavity between the end of the pinion splines and the pinion flange with a non-hardening sealer.
10. Install a new nut on the pinion shaft. Tighten the nut to remove end-play. Continue alternately tightening, in small increments, and checking preload with a torque wrench. Rotating torque should be 20-30 in. lbs. for new bearings and 5-15 in. lbs. for old bearings. Do not exceed preload or a new collapsible spacer must be installed. Never back off the pinion nut to achieve preload.

Differential Bearing Preload and Ring Gear Adjustment

1. Check the condition of the bearing cups and cup seats in the carrier. Lubricate the bearings with axle lubricant. Position the cups on the proper bearings and install the differential assembly in the carrier. Install the right bearing cap and tighten to a snug fit.
2. Service shims are available in .160 in. thickness only. Consult the accompanying chart to determine which shims to use in addition to the service spacer. Under no circumstances should the cast iron production shim be installed, once it has been removed.
3. Tighten the left bearing bolts alternately and evenly to a snug fit.
4. With the ring gear tight against the pinion gear (.000-.001 in. backlash) insert a combination

of gauge block and feeler gauges (both available locally) until a noticeable drag is felt.
5. The thickness of the service shim is determined by subtracting the thickness of the service spacer from the reading of the gauge block and feeler gauges.

Example:

Gauge thickness	.254 in.
Service spacer	(-) .160 in.
Service shim size (left side)	.094 in.

6. Install the selected shim between the service spacer and bearing.
7. Install the left bearing cap and tighten to a snug fit.
8. Remove the right bearing cap and tighten the left cap snugly.
9. Repeat Step 4.
10. The thickness of the service shim is determined as in Step 5, however, an additional .008 in. must be added for preload.
11. Install the selected shim between the service spacer and the bearing.
12. Install the right bearing cap and tighten both caps.
13. Mount a dial indicator on the carrier and check the backlash between ring gear and pinion. Backlash should be .003-.010 in. Variation should not exceed .002 in.
14. If gear lash is not within limits, correct by decreasing shim thickness on one side and increasing on the other side. Always increase and decrease by the same amount. Total shim thickness must be maintained.
15. Make a gear tooth contact test. See Pinion Mesh Markings. Adjustments must be made by decreasing shim thickness by .002 in. at a time. Check the contact pattern after each adjustment. Backlash must remain within limits.

Installation

1. Carefully clean inside of cover and gasket surface. Install new gasket on cover with liberal amount of grease.

Shim Identification

Shim	Notches I.D.	Notches O.D.
.064	None	2
.066	None	3
.068	None	4
.070	1	None
.072	1	1
.074	1	2
.076	1	3
.078	1	4
.080	2	None
.082	2	1
.084	2	2
.086	2	3
.088	2	4
.090	3	None
.092	3	1
.094	3	2
.096	3	3
.098	3	4
.100	4	None

2. Make two guide pins by cutting heads from two ¼-13 x 1¼ in. bolts up to 1966 cars, two ½-13 x 1¼ in. bolts for 1967 to 1972 cars, and slotting unthreaded end.
3. Install these guide bolts into two holes below center, one on each side of carrier.
4. Carefully raise carrier into position, aligning the guide studs in cover.
5. Install cover bolts and tighten evenly.
6. Starting with Step 13 of previous procedure, Differential Removal, reverse sequence until Step 2 is reached. Be sure to return camber cam and bolt positions to their proper positions (Step 11).
7. Fill to plug level with hypoid lubricant and reinstall plug.

Section 14
Shim Pack Selection By Pinion Code Markings

There are several marks on most pinions, usually the part number, the number indicating a matched gear set, and the pinion depth code mark. The pinion depth code mark can be identified easily because it is usually etched rather than stamped and it is almost always etched on the rear face of the tooth itself rather than on the body or hub of the gear. In almost all cases, a plus or minus symbol is etched on one gear tooth and the number is etched on the next tooth. If neither a plus or minus sign nor a number is found, the marking is presumed to be zero.

A plus sign indicates there is too

much metal on the pinion (uses less shims.) A minus sign indicates too little metal on the gear (uses more shims.) The number states how many thousandths too much or too little.

Using the chart, start at the number between the old markings and no change in shims will be necessary to compensate for pinion depth.

For a pinion having different markings from the old one, refer to the chart. The chart shows that if you count toward the bottom, the shim pack is decreased; toward the top increases the shim pack.

For example, an old pinion has —5 etched on the tooth. The new pinion

has +3 etched on the tooth. The shim pack has .038 in. total thickness. On the chart starting with —5 (the old pinion mark), count to +3 (the mark on the new pinion). This equals —8 blocks or .008 in. to be subtracted from the shim pack. The original pack had .038 in. Subtracting .008 in., new pack will have .030 in. shim thickness.

It may be necessary, however, to adjust the shim pack thickness to compensate for new bearings.

Example:

Old bearing meas.	1.495 in.	across
Parallel measures	.500	the parallel
Old bearing is	.995 in.	
New bearing meas.	1.499 in.	across
Parallel measures	.500	the parallel
New bearing is	.999 in.	wide
New bearing	.999	
Old bearing	.995	
Difference	.004 in.	

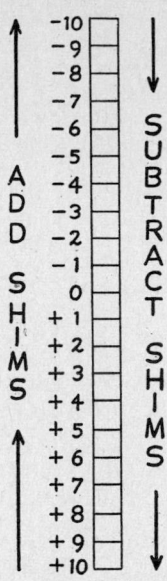

ADD SHIMS ↑

```
 -10
 -9
 -8
 -7
 -6
 -5
 -4
 -3
 -2
 -1
  0
 +1
 +2
 +3
 +4
 +5
 +6
 +7
 +8
 +9
+10
```

↓ SUBTRACT SHIMS ↓

Section 15
Shim Pack Selection for New Bearings

The standard manufacturing tolerance on the total width of a tapered roller bearing can be as much as .008 in. Therefore, in order to make proper allowances for possible differences between the old and new bearings, it is necessary to know the total width of both the old and the new bearing.

On the old bearing, remove the cone from the pinion and the outer race from the housing. Assemble the bearing on the bench and place a machinist parallel bar across the outer race. Then, using micrometers, measure from the face of the inner cone to the face of the parallel bar. Subtract the thickness of the parallel bar. The difference will be the total width of the bearing. Make a note of this figure. Do the same with the new bearing and make a note of the figure. The difference between the width of the old and new bearing will be the amount of shims which will have to be changed to accommodate the new bearing.

Remove .004 in. from the shim pack if the new bearing is thicker than the old bearing.

If the new bearing is thinner, add shims to the pack.

Section 16
Differential Side Bearing Shim Selection

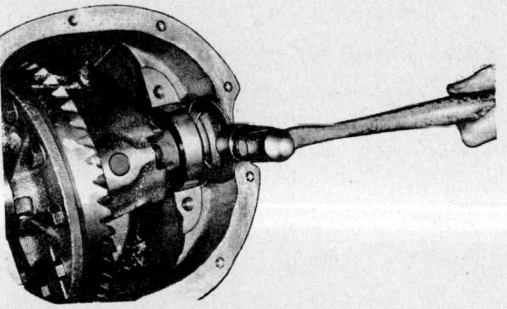

Installing differential side bearing adjusting shims

When selecting shim pack thickness for differential side bearings, keep in mind that the bearings are preloaded a sufficient amount to spread the pedestals approximately .010 in. This means that the final shim packs make the differential .010 in. wider than the space where it must fit. Remove both differential side bearings and carefully measure, with a micrometer, the shim packs found behind each bearing. Make a note of the thickness of each pack and also the total thickness of both packs. Refer to section Shim Pack Selection for New Bearings and alter the total shim pack to compensate for the new bearings.

In the above example .085 in. shim thickness will be required to set the differential up with proper preload. It remains, then, to decide how many on the ring gear side, how many on the side opposite the ring gear.

Press the bearing cones onto the differential without any shims. Make sure the bearing cones are seated firmly against the shoulder.

Slip the races over the bearing cones and install the differential into the carrier. Do not install the pedestal caps. Using two screwdrivers or

Example:

Shim pack on ring gear side	.038 in.
Shim pack opposite ring gear	.045 in.
Total	.083 in.
Required adjustment for bearings	
Ring gear side	.005 added
Side opposite ring gear	.003 removed
Net difference	.002 in.
Old shim pack	.083 in.
Add for new bearings	.002 added
New shim pack total	.085

putty knives, pry against the outer race of the bearing on the ring side, forcing the ring gear into mesh with the pinion. Pry until there is zero lash between the ring gear and pinion.

Caution Be sure the bearing on the side opposite the ring gear is fully entered into its race, otherwise the differential may tend to cock slightly, giving a false reading. To insure that the bearing is firmly seated, some shops install the pedestal cap finger tight on the side opposite the ring gear. This offers some resistance to the pry bars and keeps the bearing firmly seated.

With the differential pried over until there is zero lash in the gears, select, from the shim pack, a combination of shims which will just take up the space between the outer race and the shoulder in the carrier on the ring gear side. The shims are too small, of course, to fit around the race at the same time, but the selection can be rolled around in the space to be sure they fit tightly all the way around.

This group of shims will be just right for the ring gear side of the differential.

Remove the differential, pull off the bearing cone on the ring gear side and install the group of shims just selected onto the differential. Reinstall the bearing, pressing it firmly against the shim pack.

The balance of the shims go behind the bearing cone on the side opposite the ring gear. Remove that bearing, install the shims and reinstall the bearing, seating it firmly.

As stated in the first section, the differential assembly is now .010 in. wider than the space into which it must fit. If a spreader is available, spread the carrier just barely enough to slip the differential into place. If a spreader is not available, start the assembly into the carrier by cocking the outer races slightly, so that their edges will enter the carrier bearing seat. Then, press the differential into the carrier. Quite a bit of force is needed, since pressing the differential spreads the carrier something more than .010 in.

Install the pedestal caps and secure.

Section 17
Shim Combination Chart

Most bearing manufacturers supply, for each of their bearings, shims in .005 in., .007 in. and .020 in. thickness. Using combinations of the above three shims the following shim packs can be obtained:

Required thickness	Shim combinations	
.005	(1) .005	
.007	(1) .007	
.010	(2) .005	
.012	(1) .005	(1) .007
.014	(2) .007	

Required thickness	Shim combinations	
.015	(3) .005	
.017	(2) .005	(1) .007
.019	(1) .005	(2) .007
.020	(1) .020	
.021	(3) .007	
.022	(3) .005	(1) .007
.024	(2) .005	(2) .007
.025	(1) .005	(1) .020
.026	(1) .005	(3) .007
.027	(1) .007	(1) .020
.028	(4) .007	

Required thickness	Shim combinations		
.029	(3) .005	(2) .007	
.030	(2) .005	(1) .020	
.031	(2) .005	(3) .007	
.032	(1) .020	(1) .007	(1) .005
.003	(1) .005	(4) .007	
.034	(1) .020	(2) .007	
.035	(1) .020	(3) .005	

The above sample list can be continued in increments of .001 in. to any desired pack thickness.

Section 18
Pinion Mesh Markings

DRIVE SIDE
MOVE PINION TOWARDS REAR OF CAR

COAST SIDE   DRIVE SIDE

MOVE RING GEAR CLOSER TO PINION

COAST SIDE

MOVE PINION TOWARDS FRONT OF CAR

CORRECT MESH MARKINGS

TOE END OF TOOTH

MOVE RING GEAR AWAY FROM PINION

HEEL END OF TOOTH

Proper tooth contact

The following method of determining the relative position of the ring gear and pinion, and whether or not they are in proper mesh, will prove satisfactory for all pinion and ring gears. This should be followed by a final check, even when the pinion depth has been determined by special micrometers. Assemble the pinion in the housing, without preload, and tighten the pinion nut until a preload of about 10 in. lbs. is developed on the bearings to insure that they are completely free of end-play.

This, of course, is not the final bearing preload setting, but is a good one for checking the pinion mesh markings. .

Install the differential assembly and adjust it to provide from .004-.008 in. backlash of the ring gear, measured at the rim of the gear.

Paint five or six of the ring gear teeth with red or white lead and, while the helper brakes the ring gear with a piece of wood, slowly turn the pinion until the ring gear makes at least one full revolution. The mesh of the pinion with the ring gear will be indicated as a mark in the red lead on the ring gear teeth. Compare this mark with the accompanying photographs. The caption on each photograph explains whether the mark indicates the pinion is too deep or too shallow, the ring gear too close or too far away.

When the marking is found to be improper, it is customary to make trial changes in increments of .005 or .007 in. If changing the shim .005-.007 in. throws the marking from too deep to too shallow, the proper distance is about half-way between.

If, after changing this increment of shims, the mark still indicates that more must be changed, it is advisable to continue changing in the same increments, that is .005-.007 in.

While considerable time is generally required to disassemble the rear, press off the bearings, change the shims, press the bearing back on and assemble the rear; this is still the only positive method of determining if the rear will operate quietly after it is finally installed in the vehicle.

Section 19
Improved Traction Differentials

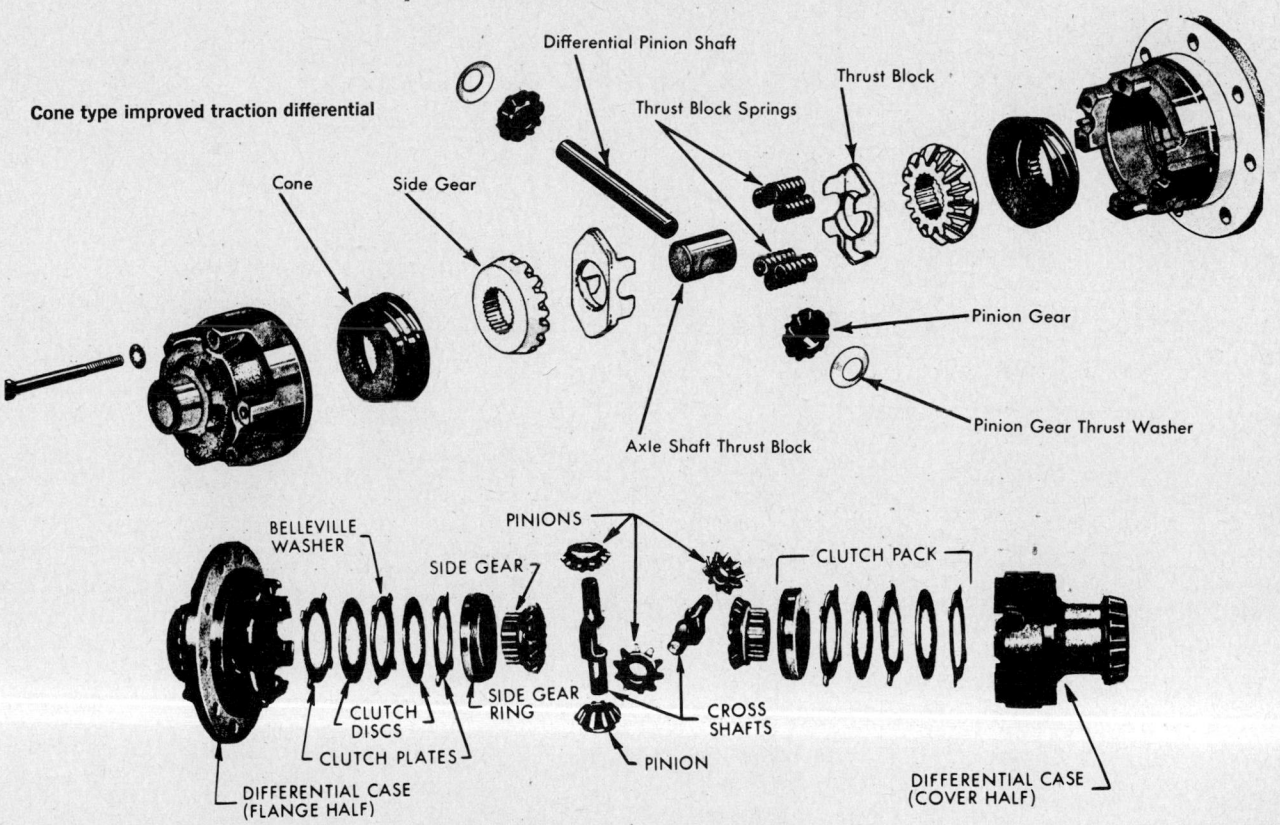

Cone type improved traction differential

Disc type improved traction differential

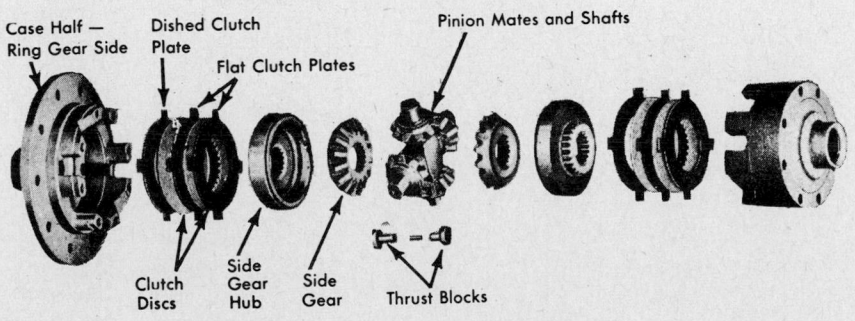

Disc type improved traction differential

Two general types of improved traction differentials are used. Either type accomplishes the same purpose. The direction of extra pulling power is to the rear wheel with the most traction.

The cone clutch-type drives the axle shaft through side gear, seating in the cone, the cone seating in the case. The pressure actuating these clutches is obtained either through cross pins riding up ramps in the case or through thrust springs exerting pressure on thrust blocks.

The disc-type drives the axle shaft through a series of Bellville and fric-tion plates. The pressure is obtained by the cross pins riding up ramps in the case. In this type differential, the number of plates used will vary from car to car.

In servicing these assemblies, the general procedures for pinion gears, shafts and bearings, and for ring gears, bearings and cases are followed.

For servicing the improved traction part of differential, proceed as follows:

1. Clamp case assembly in brass-protected vise and mark the case halves for proper reassembly.

2. Separate the case halves and remove the internal actuating parts.
3. Replace the required parts and reassemble in reverse of above.
4. Also, be sure to use the manufacturer's specified lubricant.

Caution   Dynamic wheel balancers should not be used unless the wheel opposite the one being balanced is completely removed. With this type differential, only one driving wheel has to be in contact with the ground for the vehicle to move.

Hydraulic Brakes

Hydraulic Brakes

Brake Diagnosis Chart

Condition	Mechanical	Hydraulic	Vacuum (Power Unit)
Low pedal (Excessive pedal travel to apply brakes)	FGIMfg	T	k
Spongy Pedal (A springy sensation of pedal upon application)	I	PQU	
Hard Pedal (Excessive pedal pressure needed to stop vehicle)	AFGKVaf	RTUW	cehk
Fading Pedal (A falling away of pedal under steady foot pressure)	I	PQSTW	
Grabbing or Pulling	ADEGHIKL NVXYZa	RW	k
Noise (Squealing, clicking or scraping noise)	FGHILMN		
Chatter or Shudder (May be accompanied by brake roughness or pedal pumping)	DGILNO		
Dragging Brakes (Slow or incomplete release of brakes)	ABCFGHK LVafg	RUTW	k

A. Pedal linkage binding. (Check by bleeding one wheel cylinder using light pedal effort.
   Observe for smooth full travel of pedal)
B. Parking brake cables and linkage sticking, dirty or corroded.

C. Parking brake improperly adjusted (too loose or too tight).
D. Wheel bearings loose.
E. Front wheel alignment or uneven tire tread.
F. Brake shoes improperly adjusted. Automatic adjuster parts corroded, distorted or broken.
G. Brake linings or disc pads worn, contaminated or distorted.
H. Shoe return spring weak, broken, improperly installed.
I. Drums cracked, thin (beyond 0.060" of original specifications), scored, hard spotted, or out of round.
K. Brake support plate ledges rusted or grooved.
L. Support plate loose, worn, or distorted.
M. Disc brake pad "knock back" (loose or worn wheel bearings or steering parts).
N. Caliper not aligned with disc or loose.
O. Disc has excessive lateral runout. Excessively out of parallel.
P. Hydraulic system fluid has air in it, improper quality (low boiling point).
Q. Hoses and lines soft or weak (expanding under pressure).
R. Hose sand lines kinked, collapsed, dented, or clogged.
S. Hoses and lines loosely connected, ruptured, or damaged (causing leakage).
T. Master cylinder primary cup worn or damaged, bore worn, rough, corroded.
U. Master cylinder check valve faulty, or compensator port blocked.
V. Wheel or caliper cylinder pistons frozen or seized.
W. Wheel or caliper cylinder cups swollen, worn or damaged seals; bores rough or corroded.
X. Wheel or caliper cylinders mismatched (size).
Y. Check tire pressure.
Z. Rear wheels (both) grabbing. Rear brake line proportioning valve defective—replace.
a. Power unit valve rod linkage binding.
c. Vacuum lines loose, broken, collapsed. Engine vacuum low.
e. Vacuum check valve defective or sticking.
f. Power unit hydraulic pushrod improperly adjusted.
g. Air trapped in hub cavity of master cylinder.
   Inspect and remove master cylinder boot if installed.
h. Air filter dirty, clogged.
k. Corrosion or lack of lubrication in power cylinder. Control valve, power cylinder, piston or diaphragm defective.

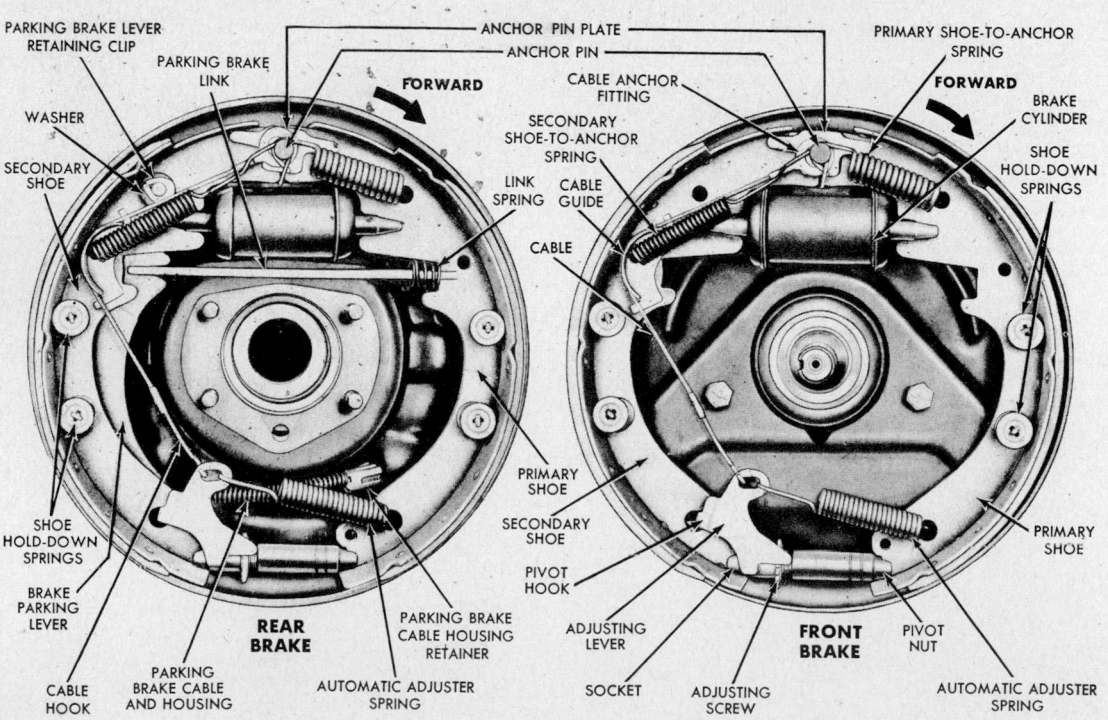

Bendix Duo-Servo self-adjusting brake

Servicing Self-Adjusting Drum Brakes

Bendix Duo-Servo Brake

Star and Screw Type

The Bendix duo-servo brake with star and screw type self-adjusters is by far the most common brake used on late model American cars. The same basic brake unit is used on all cars from 1970, and on most cars from 1965. General Motors cars use a rod-operated lever to turn the star-wheel, while all others use a cable-operated lever. This is only difference, other than size, between units used on different models. To adjust this brake manually (to facilitate drum removal or after lining replacement):

1. Remove the access slot plug from the backing plate.
2. Using a brake adjusting spoon or screwdriver pry downward on the end of the tool (starwheel teeth moving up) to tighten the brakes, or upward on the end of the tool (starwheel teeth moving down) to loosen the brakes.

NOTE: it may be necessary to use a small screwdriver to hold the adjusting lever away from the star wheel. Be careful not to bend the adjusting lever.

3. When the brakes are tight almost to the point of being locked, back off on the starwheel (usually 10-15 notches) until the wheel is able to rotate freely.
4. When all four brakes are adjusted, check brake pedal travel and then make several stops while backing the car up to equalize all the wheels.

To test automatic adjuster operation:

1. Raise the vehicle on a hoist with a helper in it to apply the brakes.
2. Loosen the brakes by holding the adjuster lever away from the starwheel and backing the starwheel off approximately 30 notches.
3. Spin the wheel and brake drum in reverse and apply the brakes. The movement of the secondary shoe should pull the adjuster lever up, and when the brakes are released the lever should snap down and turn the starwheel.
4. If the automatic adjuster doesn't work the drum must be removed and the adjuster components inspected carefully for breakage, wear, or improper installation.

To replace brake shoes:

1. Remove wheels and brake drums.
2. Remove primary and secondary shoe return springs using flanged end of brake spring pliers.
3. Remove the adjuster actuating rod or cable.
4. On the rear brakes remove the parking brake strut and spring and disconnect the parking brake cable from the lever.
5. Remove the brake shoe hold-down springs (a small screwdriver may be used to push in center of spring on cars with cable operated adjusters). Remove the adjuster mechanism and the shoes. Keep left and right adjuster screw assemblies

and levers separate; they are not interchangeable.

6. Inspect the linings for scoring, wear, rivet condition, cracking, and signs of oil or brake fluid. Replace riveted shoe assemblies or linings when they have less than 40% of original thickness left, and bonded shoe assemblies or linings when they have less than 25% of original thickness left.
7. Inspect brake drums for scoring and distortion. If a drum must be turned down do not remove more than 0.030 in. (increasing diameter by 0.060 in.) If standard size linings will be used remove no more than 0.015 in.
8. Inspect front wheel bearings and seals, and check wheel cylinders for leakage.
9. Clean brake backing plate and lubricate shoe contact points.
10. Install shoes in reverse order of removal.
11. Lightly sand linings, replace drums and wheels. Adjust brakes.

Expanding Strut Type

Bendix duo-servo brakes with expanding strut adjusters are used exclusively on the Vega. Adjustment is made simply by setting and releasing the parking brake several times. To replace the brakes:

1. If the drum does not slip off easily it will be necessary to knock out the metal plug in the drum and push in on the adjuster rod to retract the shoes.
2. Remove the drum. Remove the parking brake cable from the lever.

Adjuster Brake Type	Bendix Duo-Servo		Wagner Compound Shoe		Bendix Non-Servo	
Star & screw self-adjusting	General Motors (exc. Vega)	1965-72	American Motors Rebel OHV 6 (ex. wagon)	1969		
	Ford Motor Co.	1965-72	Models with OHV 6 (ex. American)	1965-68		
	Chrysler Corp.	1965-72	American with 232 C.I.D. engine	1965-66		
	American Motors	1970-72				
	American Motors (exc. Rebel Sedan with OHV 6)	1969				
	American Motors V8 models (exc. American)	1965-68				
	American	1967-68				
	American (with 195 & 199 C.I.D. engines)	1965-66				
Expanding strut self-adjusting	Vega (rear only)	1971-72			American Motors Models with front disc brakes	1965-68

Disc Brake Specifications

Manufacturer/Model/Year	Fixed Caliper Four Piston	Floating Caliper Single Piston	Mounting Bolts Torque ft. lbs.	Bridge Bolts Torque ft. lbs.	Proportioning Valve	Metering Valve	Original Thickness	Resurfacing Min. Thickness	Parallel Variation	Runout Maximum
AMERICAN MOTORS										
All 1971-72	Bendix	Kelsey-Hayes	upper: 105/lower: 85	35	yes	yes	1.000 in.	.940 in.	.0005 in.	.005 in.
All 1965-70			85	100-110	yes 68-70	no	.500 in.	.450 in.	.0005 in.	.005 in.
CHRYSLER CORPORATION										
Imperial 1970-72		Kelsey-Hayes	50-80	35	no	yes	1.250 in.	1.200 in.	.0005 in.	.0025 in.
Full Size Models 1969-72 ▲										
Intermediates 1970-72		Kelsey-Hayes	50-80	35	yes	yes	1.000-1.010 in.	.980 in.	.0005 in.	.0025 in.
Barracuda 1970-72 ▲										
Valiant, Dart 1965-72	Kelsey-Hayes		50-80	70-80	yes	no	.810 in.	.780 in.	.0005 in.	.0025 in.
Barracuda 1965-69										
Imperial 1967-69	Budd		70-80	7/16 in. 50-60 5/8 in. 140-160	no	yes	.8725-.8775 in.	.829 in.	.0005 in.	.005 in.
Full Size Models 1965-68 ▲										
Intermediates 1966-69	Bendix		85-90	120-140	yes	no	.886-.898 in.	.816 in.	.0005 in.	.005 in.
FORD MOTOR COMPANY										
Lincoln 1970-72		Kelsey-Hayes	upper: 115/lower: 100	25-35	yes	yes	1.180 in.	1.120 in.	.0007 in.	.003 in.
Full Size Models 1968-72 ▲										
All but Full Size 1968-72		Kelsey-Hayes	upper: 120/lower: 70	25-35	yes	no	.935 in.	.875 in.	.0007 in.	.002 in.
Lincoln 1965-69	Kelsey-Hayes		1965-66: 100 1967-on: 125	1965-66: 70 1967-on: 90	yes	no (Lincoln yes)	1.250 in.	1.215 in.	.0007 in.	.002 in.
All but Full Size 1965-67 ▲							.810 in.	.780 in.		
Pinto 1971-72		yes	45-60	75-105	yes	no	.652 in.		.0007 in.	.002 in.
GENERAL MOTORS										
Buick (Full Size) 1970-72		Delco-Moraine	125	35	yes (no 1970)	yes	1.290 in.	1.230 in.	.0005 in.	.005 in.
Buick Special 1969-72		Delco-Moraine	70	35	no	yes	1.040 in.	.965 in.	.0005 in.	.004 in.
Buick (Full Size) 1967-69	Bendix	Delco-Moraine	75	125	no	yes	1.000 in.	.965 in.	.0005 in.	.004 in.
Buick Special 1967-68		Delco-Moraine	95	130	no	yes	1.000 in.	.965 in.	.0005 in.	.004 in.
Cadillac Eldorado 1969-72		Delco-Moraine		30	yes	yes	1.210 in.	1.195 in.	.0005 in.	.008 in. (on hub)
Cadillac 1968-72		Delco-Moraine	95	35	yes (68-70 no)	yes	1.250 in.	1.230 in.	.0005 in.	.002 in.
Cadillac Eldorado 1967-68	Kelsey-Hayes	Delco-Moraine	60-90	75-105	yes (69-70 no)	yes	1.250 in.	1.215 in.	.0007 in.	.002 in.
Chevrolet (Full Size) 1969-72		Delco-Moraine	60-90	35	yes (HD)	no	1.250 in. (69-70) 1.285 in. (71-72)	1.215 in. (69-70) 1.285 in. (71-72)	.0005 in.	.002 in.
Corvette 1965-72	Delco-Moraine		60-90	F/130 R/60 1969-70: 35 1971-72: 85	yes	yes	1.250 in.	1969-70: .965 in. 1971-72: .980 in.	.0005 in.	.002 in.
Chevelle, Nova, Camaro 1969-72		Delco-Moraine	125	130	no	yes	1969-70: 1.00 in. 1971-72: 1.035 in.	1.215 in.	.0005 in.	.002 in.
Chev. (Full Size) 1967-68	Delco-Moraine		60-90	130	yes	yes	1.250 in.	.965 in.	.0005 in.	.002 in.
Chevelle, Camaro 1967-68	Delco-Moraine		60-90	130	yes	yes	1.000 in.	1.215 in. (69-70) 1.20 in. (71-72)	.0005 in.	.002 in.
Chevy II										
Olds Toronado 1969-72		Delco-Moraine	55	40	yes	yes	1.205 in.	.980 in.	.0005 in.	.002 in.
Olds 88 & 98 1969-72		Delco-Moraine		40	yes	yes	1.250 in. (69-70) 1.280 in. (71-72)	1.215 in. (69-70) 1.20 in. (71-72)	.0005 in.	.002 in.
Olds F85 1969-72	Kelsey-Hayes		70	35	no	yes	1.035 in.	.980 in.	.0005 in.	.004 in.
Olds Toronado 1967-68	Delco-Moraine		54	85	yes	yes	1.250 in.	1.215 in.	.0007 in.	.004 in.
Olds 88 & 98 1967-68	Delco-Moraine		70	130	yes	yes	1.250 in.	1.215 in.	.0005 in.	.004 in.
Olds F85 1967-68			70	130	no	yes	1.000 in.	.965 in.	.0005 in.	.004 in.
Pontiac (Full Size) 1969-72	Delco-Moraine		60	35	yes (no 69-70)	yes	1.250 in. (71-72) 1.230 in. (69-70)	1.230 in. (71-72) 1.195 in. (69-70)	.0005 in.	.004 in.
Tempest, LeMans, Firebird, G.P. 1969-72	Delco-Moraine		60	35	yes	yes	1.005 in.	.960 in.	.0007 in.	.004 in.
Pontiac (Full Size) 1967-68	Delco-Moraine			130	no	yes	1.250 in.	1.215 in.	.0005 in.	.004 in.
Tempest, LeMans, Firebird, G.P. 1967-68	Delco-Moraine			130	yes	yes	1.000 in.	.965 in.	.0005 in.	.004 in.
Vega 1971-72		Delco-Moraine			yes	no	.500 in.	.470 in.	.0005 in.	.005 in.
Ventura II 1971-72 (see Pontiac)										

▲ = specifications same as above

---

3. Remove the spring, then remove the shoes with the strut and adjuster as a unit.

4. Follow steps 6-10 as given for star and screw adjusted Bendix brakes.

Wagner Compound Shoe Brake

This brake unit is very similar to the Bendix duo-servo type with star and screw self-adjusters. Servicing and adjusting procedures are virtually the same, with these exceptions:

1. Do not lift the adjusting lever off of the starwheel when adjusting the brakes manually.

2. The lower brake spring should be installed with the long hook end in the secondary shoe with the hook facing out.

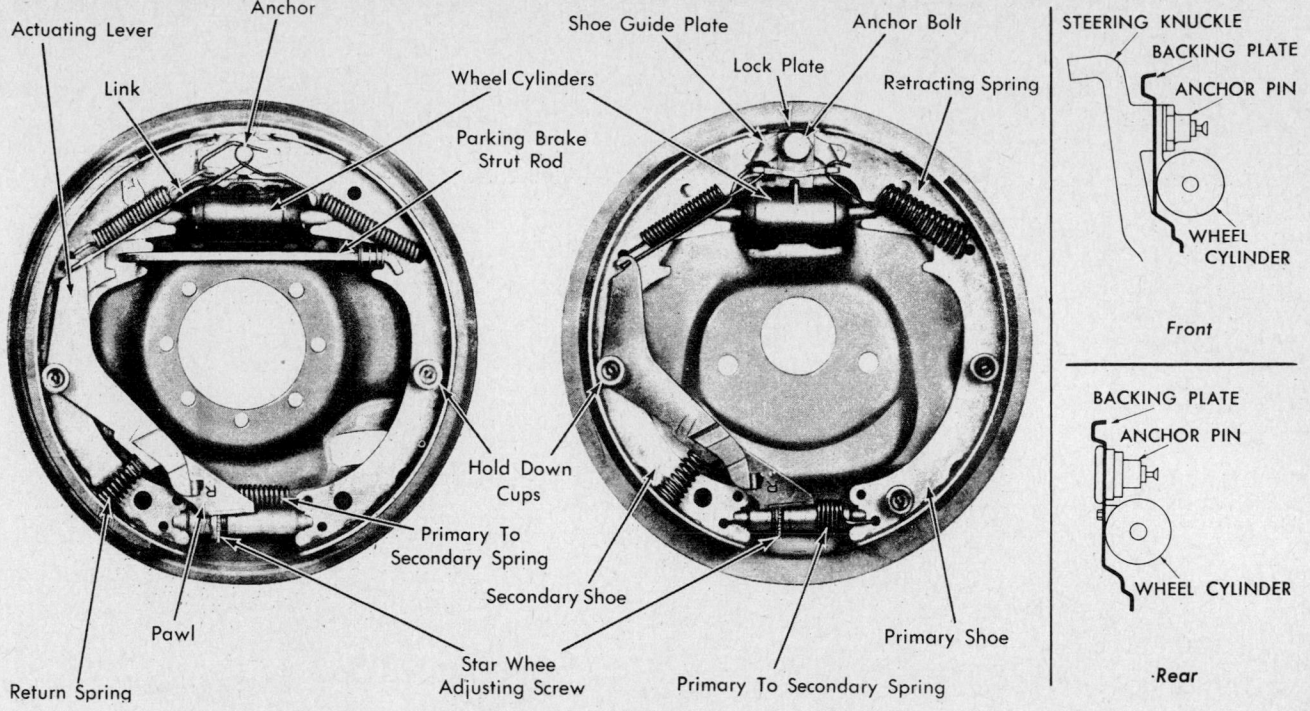

Bendix Duo-Servo self-adjusting brake (G.M. type)

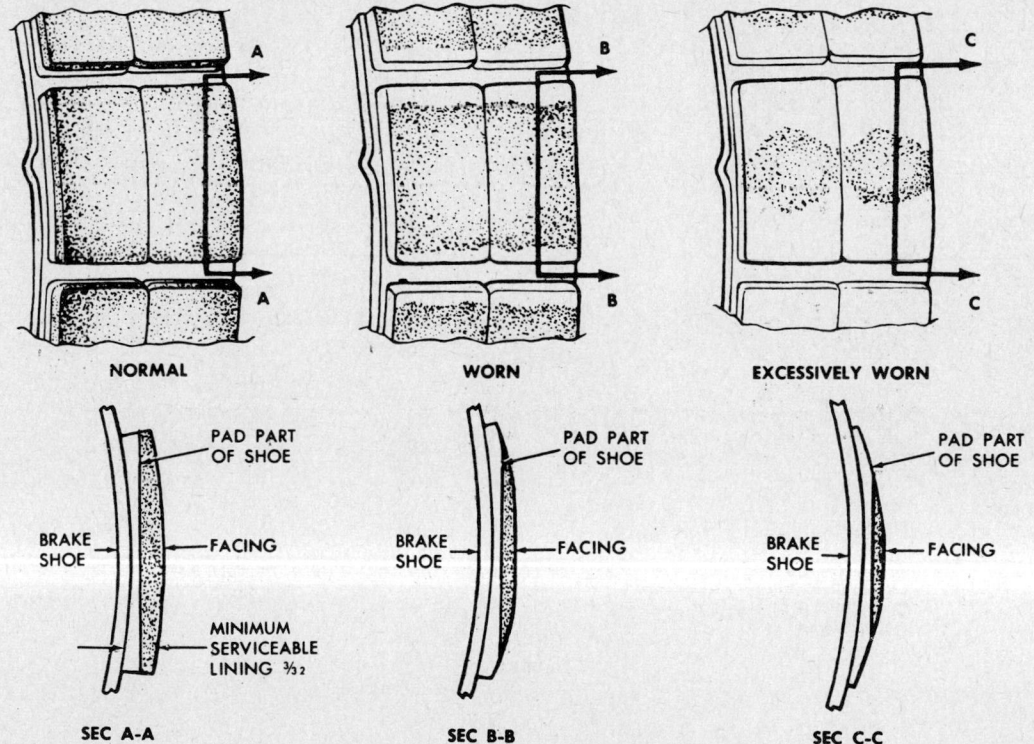

Metallic brake linings (Pontiac and Chevrolet)

3. If the shoes have been removed for any reason, an initial adjustment must be made before drum installation. Adjust the screw assemblies so that approximately ¼ in. of threads are exposed.

4. The anchor block must be installed with the arrow pointing in the direction of forward rotation.

Bendix Non-Servo Brake

This brake is used only on the rear of 1965-68 American Motors models equipped with front disc brakes. Adjustment is automatically made through brake applications. To remove and replace brakes:

1. Insert a screwdriver through the access hole in the backing plate and push down on the adjuster latch to allow the shoes to retract.

2. Remove the adjuster spring from the strut. Remove the upper and lower brake springs.

3. Unhook the parking brake cable from the actuation lever and slide the shoes out from under the hold down springs.

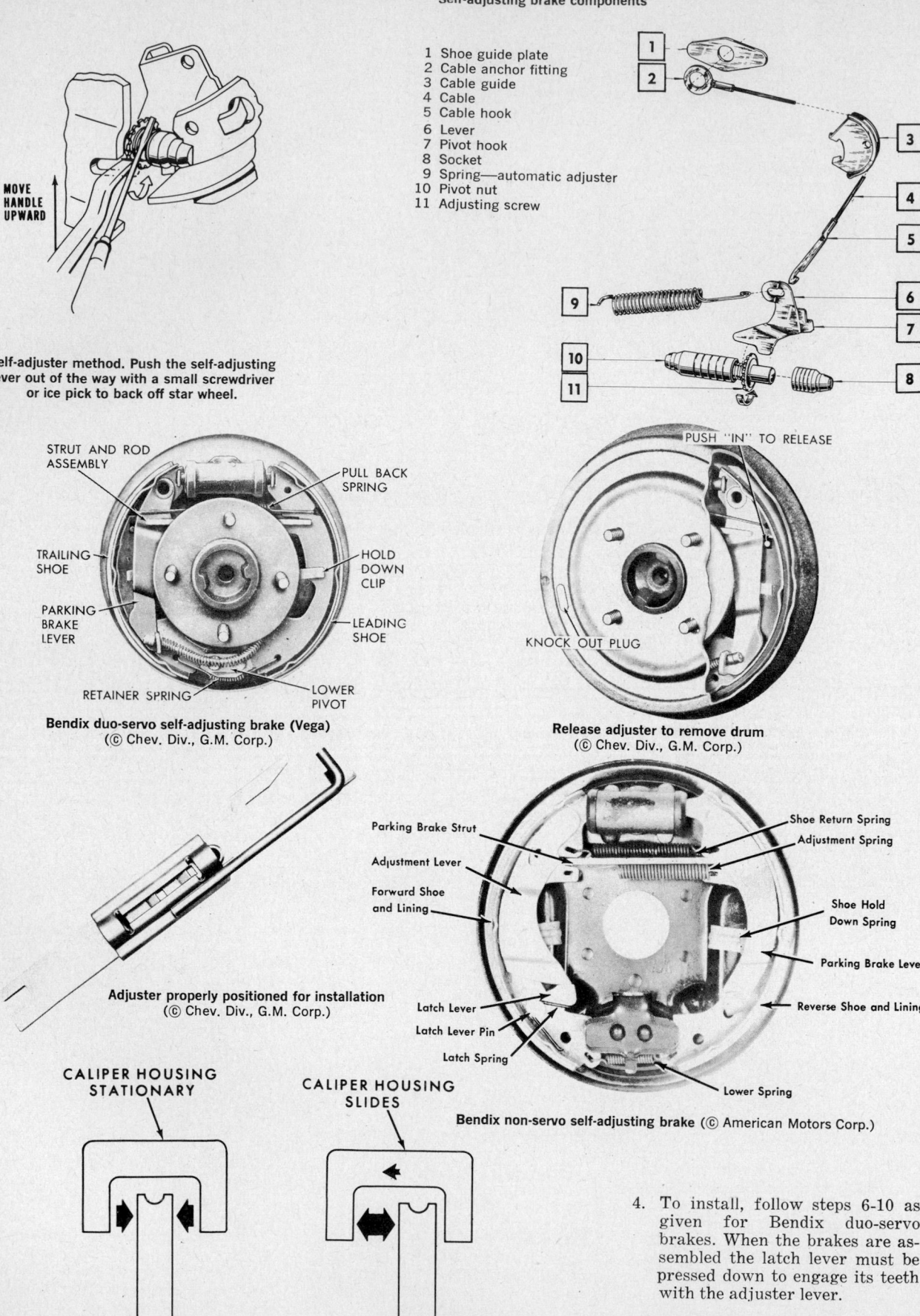

Self-adjusting brake components

1 Shoe guide plate
2 Cable anchor fitting
3 Cable guide
4 Cable
5 Cable hook
6 Lever
7 Pivot hook
8 Socket
9 Spring—automatic adjuster
10 Pivot nut
11 Adjusting screw

MOVE HANDLE UPWARD

Self-adjuster method. Push the self-adjusting lever out of the way with a small screwdriver or ice pick to back off star wheel.

STRUT AND ROD ASSEMBLY

PULL BACK SPRING

TRAILING SHOE

HOLD DOWN CLIP

PARKING BRAKE LEVER

LEADING SHOE

RETAINER SPRING

LOWER PIVOT

Bendix duo-servo self-adjusting brake (Vega)
(© Chev. Div., G.M. Corp.)

PUSH "IN" TO RELEASE

KNOCK OUT PLUG

Release adjuster to remove drum
(© Chev. Div., G.M. Corp.)

Adjuster properly positioned for installation
(© Chev. Div., G.M. Corp.)

Parking Brake Strut

Shoe Return Spring

Adjustment Spring

Adjustment Lever

Forward Shoe and Lining

Shoe Hold Down Spring

Parking Brake Lever

Reverse Shoe and Lining

Latch Lever

Latch Lever Pin

Latch Spring

Lower Spring

Bendix non-servo self-adjusting brake (© American Motors Corp.)

CALIPER HOUSING STATIONARY

CALIPER HOUSING SLIDES

4. To install, follow steps 6-10 as given for Bendix duo-servo brakes. When the brakes are assembled the latch lever must be pressed down to engage its teeth with the adjuster lever.

Fixed caliper disc brake operation

Floating caliper disc brake operation

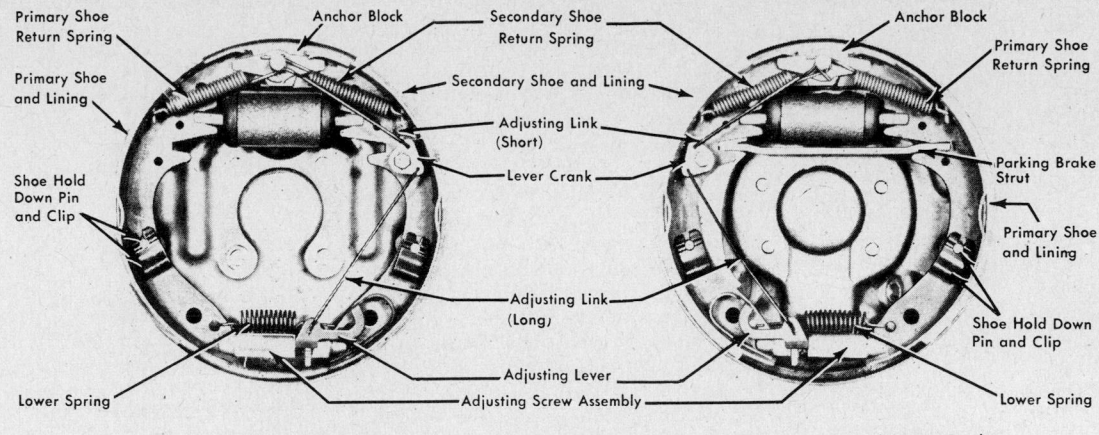

Wagner compound shoe self-adjusting brake (© American Motors Corp.)

Servicing Disc Brakes

General Description and Inspection

Caliper disc brakes were first used on American production cars in 1965. Most of the cars equipped with disc brakes prior to 1969 use the four piston fixed caliper design, while most later cars use the single piston floating caliper design. Except for the Corvette and a limited number of Camaros, disc brakes are used only on the front.

In the four piston type (two in each side of the caliper) braking effect is achieved by hydraulically pushing both shoes against the disc sides. With the single piston type the inboard shoe is pushed hydraulically into contact with the disc, while the reaction force thus generated is used to pull the outboard shoe into frictional contact (made possible by letting the caliper move slightly along the axle centerline).

To properly inspect disc pad wear it is necessary to remove the pads. On all but the Kelsey-Hayes and Delco-Moraine four piston (fixed caliper) brakes it is necessary to remove the caliper to accomplish this. Disc pads (lining and shoe assemblies) should be replaced in axle sets when the lining on any pad is worn to 1/8 in. at any point. *If lining is allowed to wear past 1/16 in. minimum thickness severe damage to disc may result.* Note that disc pads in floating caliper type brakes may wear at an angle, and measurement should be made at the narrow end of the taper. Tapered linings should be replaced if the taper exceeds 1/8 in. from end to end (the difference between the thickest and thinest points).

When replacing disc pads on any system it is a good idea to remove some brake fluid from the master cylinder reservoir so that it won't overflow when the piston is pushed into the caliper. When the caliper is unbolted from the hub do not let it dangle by the brake hose; it can be rested on a suspension member or wired on to the frame. Wheel lug nuts on disc-braked cars should be torqued to approximately 70 ft. lbs. (Eldorado and Toronado 100 ft. lbs.). All disc brake systems are inherently self-adjusting and have no provision for manual adjustment.

Bendix 4 Piston Brake

Disc Pad Replacement

1. Raise the vehicle on a hoist and remove the front wheels.
2. Working on one side at a time only, remove the caliper mounting bolts and slide the caliper off of the disc.
NOTE: on American Motors cars the shims under the mounting bolts must be replaced exactly as removed.
3. Remove the disc pads and inspect the caliper for damaged or leaking seals and casting cracks.
4. To install new pads insert the curved edge first (tabs, if any, should be up) and position the steel plate against the pistons.
5. Spread the pads apart until the pistons are bottomed in their bores and slide the caliper assembly over the disc.
6. Align the mounting holes and install shims (if used) and mounting bolts. Torque to specifications.
7. Check brake fluid level and pump the brake pedal to seat the linings against the disc. Replace the wheels and road test the vehicle.

Servicing the Caliper Assembly

1. Raise the vehicle on a hoist and remove the front wheels.
2. Working on one side at a time only, disconnect the hydraulic inlet line from the caliper and plug the end. Remove the caliper mounting bolts and shims (if used) and slide the caliper off of the disc.
3. Remove the disc pads from the caliper. If the old ones are to be reused, mark them so that they can be reinstalled in their original positions.

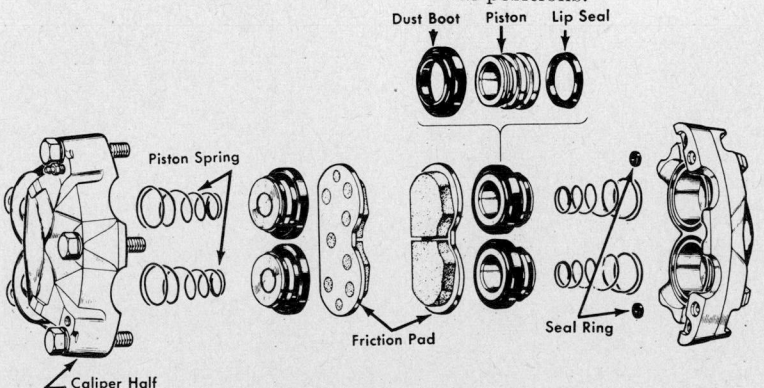

Bendix 4 piston disc brake (© American Motors Corp.)

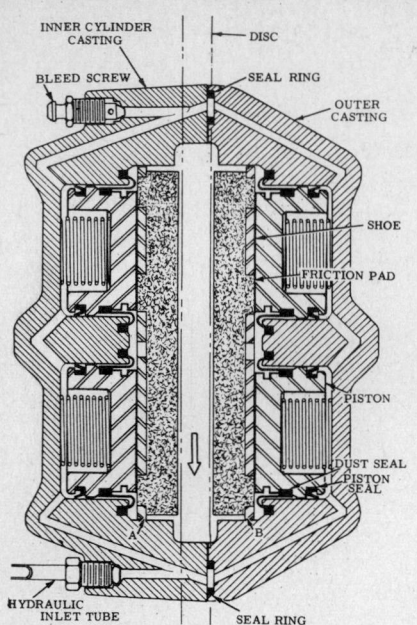

Cross-section, caliper and passages

sary, air pressure may be used to force the pistons out of the bores, using care to prevent them from popping out of control.

7. Remove the boots and seals from the pistons and clean the pistons in brake fluid. Blow out the caliper passages with an air hose.

8. Inspect the cylinder bores for scoring, pitting, or corrosion. Light rough spots may be removed by rotating crocus cloth, using finger pressure, in the bores. Do not polish with an in and out motion or use any other abrasive.

9. If the pistons are pitted, scored, or worn, they must be replaced. A corroded or deeply scored caliper should also be replaced.

10. Check the clearance of the pistons in the bores using a feeler gauge. Clearance should be 0.002-0.006 in. If there is excessive clearance the caliper must be replaced.

11. Lubricate all new rubber parts with brake fluid. Install the seals and boots in the grooves in each piston. The seal should be installed in the groove closest to the closed end of the piston with the seal lips facing the closed end. The lip on the boot should be facing the seal.

12. Lubricate the piston and bore with brake fluid. Position the piston return spring, large coil first, in the piston bore.

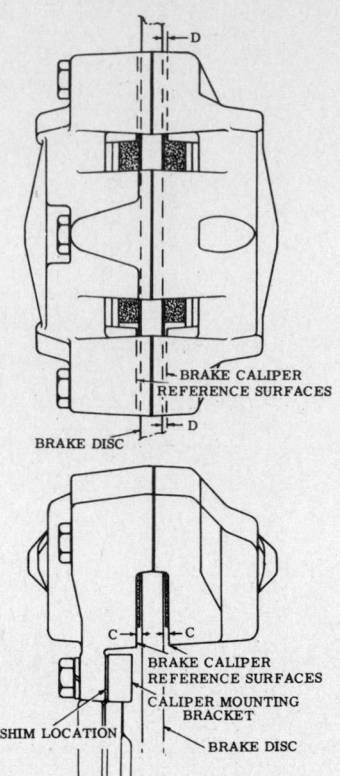

Alignment of caliper to disc (American Motors cars)

4. Open the caliper bleed screw and drain the fluid. Clean the outside of the caliper and mount it in a vise with padded jaws.

5. Remove the bridge bolts, separate the caliper halves, and remove the two O-ring seals from the transfer holes.

6. Pry the lip on each piston dust boot from its groove and remove the piston assemblies and springs from the bores. If neces-

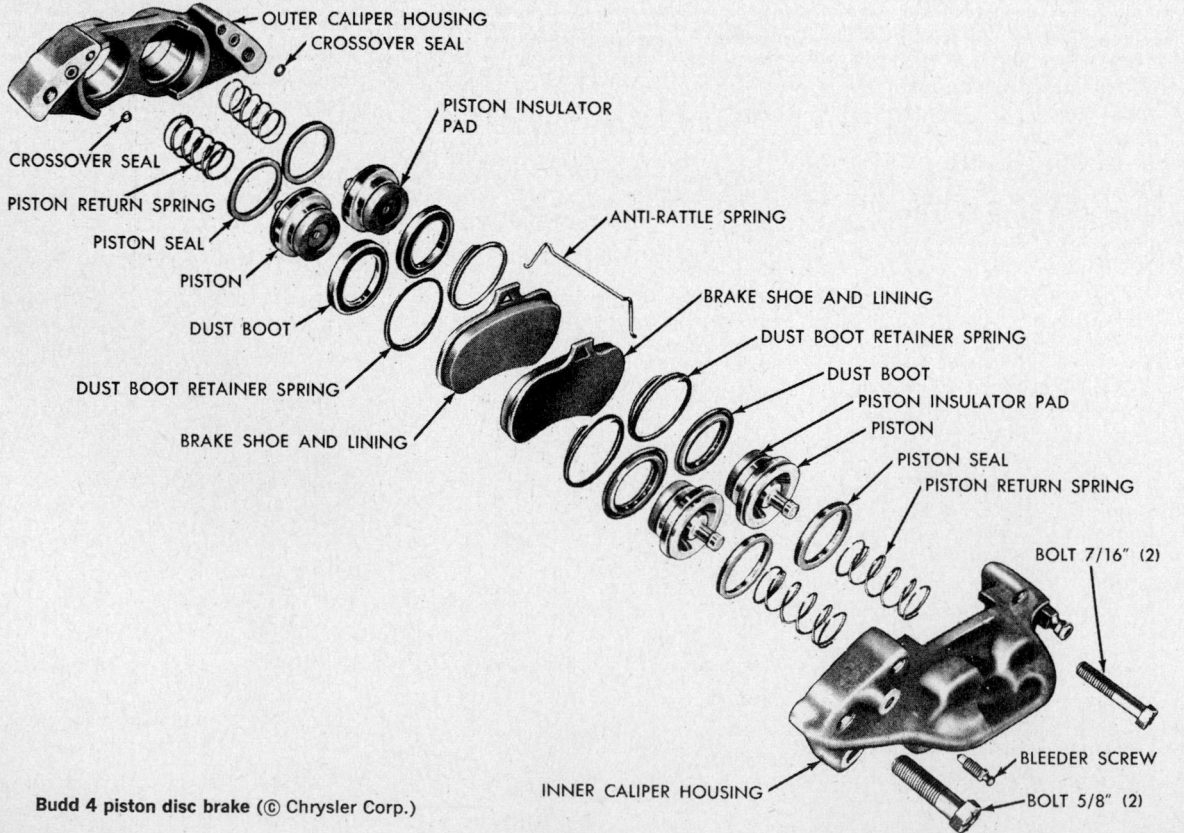

Budd 4 piston disc brake (© Chrysler Corp.)

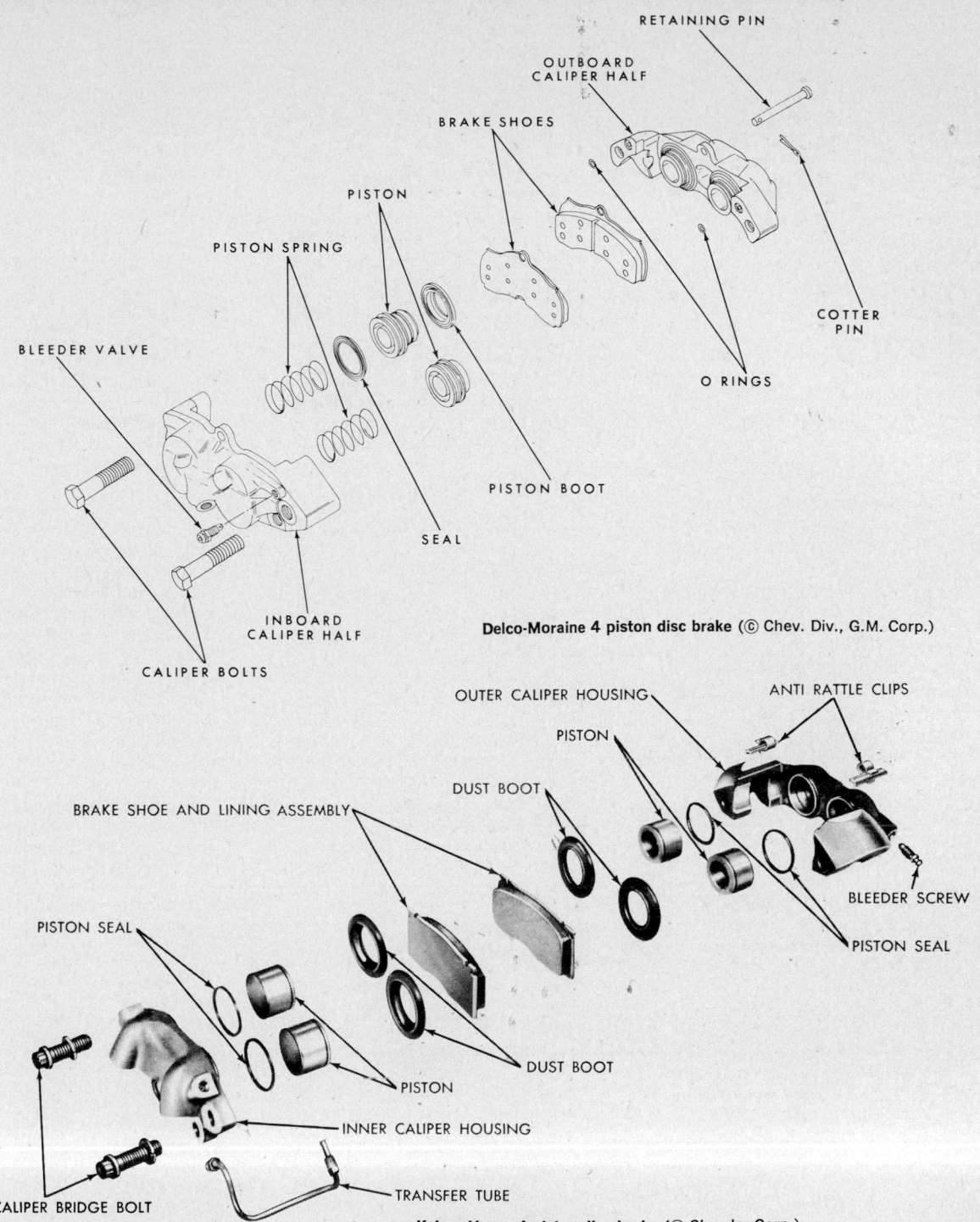

RETAINING PIN

OUTBOARD
CALIPER HALF

BRAKE SHOES

PISTON

PISTON SPRING

BLEEDER VALVE

COTTER
PIN

O RINGS

PISTON BOOT

SEAL

INBOARD
CALIPER HALF

CALIPER BOLTS

Delco-Moraine 4 piston disc brake (© Chev. Div., G.M. Corp.)

OUTER CALIPER HOUSING

ANTI RATTLE CLIPS

PISTON

DUST BOOT

BRAKE SHOE AND LINING ASSEMBLY

BLEEDER SCREW

PISTON SEAL

PISTON SEAL

DUST BOOT

PISTON

INNER CALIPER HOUSING

CALIPER BRIDGE BOLT

TRANSFER TUBE

Kelsey-Hayes 4 piston disc brake (© Chrysler Corp.)

13. Install the piston in the bore, taking great care to avoid damaging the seal lip as it passes the edge of the cylinder bore.

14. Compress the lip on the dust boot into the groove in the caliper. Be sure the boot is fully seated in the groove, as poor sealing will allow contaminants to ruin the bore.

15. Position the O-rings in the cavities around the caliper transfer holes, and fit the caliper halves together. Install the bridge bolts and torque to specification.

16. Install the disc pads in the caliper and remount the caliper on the hub (see Disc Pad Replacement). Connect the brake line to the caliper and bleed the brakes (see Brake Bleeding). Replace the wheels. Recheck the brake fluid level, check the brake pedal travel, and road test the vehicle.

Caliper Alignment Procedure for American Motors Cars

1. Check dimension "C" on either side of the disc (rotor). Both measurements should be within 0.010 in. of each other.

2. Check dimension "D" at both ends of the caliper. The measurements between the caliper reference surface and disc at both ends of the caliper should be within 0.005 in. of each other.

3. Add or remove shims as required to bring the dimensions to within the tolerance limits.

Budd 4 Piston Brake

Disc Pad Replacement

See Bendix 4 Piston Brake—Disc Pad Replacement. Procedure is identical except that the Budd brake has a retainer spring that must be unhooked to release the disc pads.

Servicing the Caliper Assembly

See Bendix 4 Piston Brake—Servicing the Caliper Assembly. Prodecure is identical except that:

1. The piston boot has a retaining spring. It can be removed and installed with a small screwdriver, and should be fully seated in its groove upon assembly of the caliper.
2. The piston dust boot should be installed so that the lip of the boot is toward the piston insulator pad.
3. The piston seal does not need to be installed in its groove in any special manner.

Delco-Moraine 4 Piston Brake

Disc Pad Replacement

1. Raise the car and remove the front wheels.
2. Remove and discard the cotter pin from the end of the pad retaining pin. Remove the retaining pin.
3. Push one pad back so that it is as far away from the disc as possible. Remove that pad and replace it with a new one. Replace the second pad in the same manner.

NOTE: pads are interchangeable from inboard to outboard and right to left on all cars except the Corvette. Disc pads for the Corvette have more metal showing (in relation to the lining centerline) at one end of the pad, and this end must be towards the front of the car. To remove Corvette pads lift straight out, to remove all others swivel one end up and lift out.

Shims (if any) between the pads and pistons should be replaced in the exact position as removed.

4. With new pads in place install the retaining pin and lock it in place with a new cotter pin.
5. Replace the wheels, check the brake fluid level, check brake pedal travel, and road test the car.

Servicing the Caliper Assembly

See Bendix 4 Piston Brake—Servicing the Caliper Assembly. Procedure is identical except that:

1. To free the end of the brake hose at the bracket the U-shaped bracket must be removed.
2. Corvette rear disc brakes have

only one transfer hole and O-ring.

3. Each piston boot has a retaining ring. It can be pried out using the piston as a fulcrum. When installing the ring in the piston bore make sure it is seated evenly flush or below the machined face of the caliper.
4. Piston to bore clearance should be from 0.0045-0.010 in. (except Corvette rear which is 0.0035-0.009 in.
5. The piston seal lip faces toward the spring end of the piston, and the fold in the piston boot faces toward the seal.
6. Ehen the brake hose is connected it should not be twisted or touch other parts at any time during suspension or steering travel.

Kelsey-Hayes 4 Piston Brake

Disc Pad Replacement

1. Raise the car and remove the front wheels.
2. Remove the retainer bolts and the retainer(s).
3. Using two pairs of pliers, grasp the outer ends of one of the pads and pull straight out. Push the two pistons into their bores using a flat metal bar and install a new disc pad. Repeat for the second pad.
4. Install the retainer(s) and bolts.
5. Replace the wheels, check the brake fluid level, check brake pedal travel, and road test the car.

Servicing the Caliper Assembly

See Bendix 4 Piston Brake—Servicing the Caliper Assembly. Procedure is identical except that:

1. This unit does not use internal transfer passages with O-rings, an external crossover line is used instead. It must be removed before the caliper is disassembled.
2. The piston seal is not installed on the piston, but is installed in the groove in the piston bore.
3. This unit does not use piston return springs.

Delco-Moraine Single Piston Brake

Disc Pad Replacement

1. Raise the vehicle on a hoist and remove the front wheels.
2. Place a "C" clamp on the caliper so that the solid side of the clamp rests against the back of the caliper and the screw end rests against the metal part of the outboard shoe. Tighten the clamp until the caliper moves en-

ough to bottom the piston in the bore. Remove the clamp.

3. Remove the caliper mounting bolts and lift the caliper away from the disc.
4. Remove the disc pads and inspect the caliper for fluid leaks and damage.
5. Place the inboard pad in the caliper so that the bottom edge contacts the piston and the two spring ends, and press the pad flat against the piston. When properly seated, the ends of the spring should not extend more than 0.10 in. beyond the metal part of the pad.

NOTE: most 1969 and later cars use a clip instead of a spring to locate the pad. The clip must be assembled onto the pad before the pad is placed over the piston.

6. Place the outboard pad in the caliper so that the two ears on the pad fit over the ears on the caliper. Squeeze the ears on the pad tight around the caliper ears with a pair of pliers.
7. Position the caliper assembly onto the disc, align the mounting holes, and make sure that the brake line isn't twisted.
8. Install the mounting bolts (making sure that they pass under the retaining ears on the inboard shoe) and torque to specification.
9. Check the brake fluid level and pump the brake pedal to seat the linings against the disc. Replace the wheels and road test the car.

Servicing the Caliper Assembly

1. Raise the vehicle on a hoist and remove the front wheels.
2. Working on one side at a time only, disconnect the brake hose from the steel brake line and cap the fittings. Remove the U-shaped retainer from the hose fitting (if applicable).
3. Remove the caliper mounting bolts (locating pins) and lift the caliper away from the disc.
4. Clean the holes and the bushing grooves in the caliper ears, and wipe all dirt from the mounting bolts. If the bolts are corroded or damaged they should be replaced.
5. Remove the shoe support springs (if applicable) from the piston.
6. Remove the sleeves from the ears of the caliper with a suitable drift pin. Remove the rubber bushings from the grooves in the caliper ears.
7. Remove the brake hose, drain the brake fluid, and clean the outside of the caliper.
8. Pad the inside of the caliper with towels and direct compressed air into the brake fluid

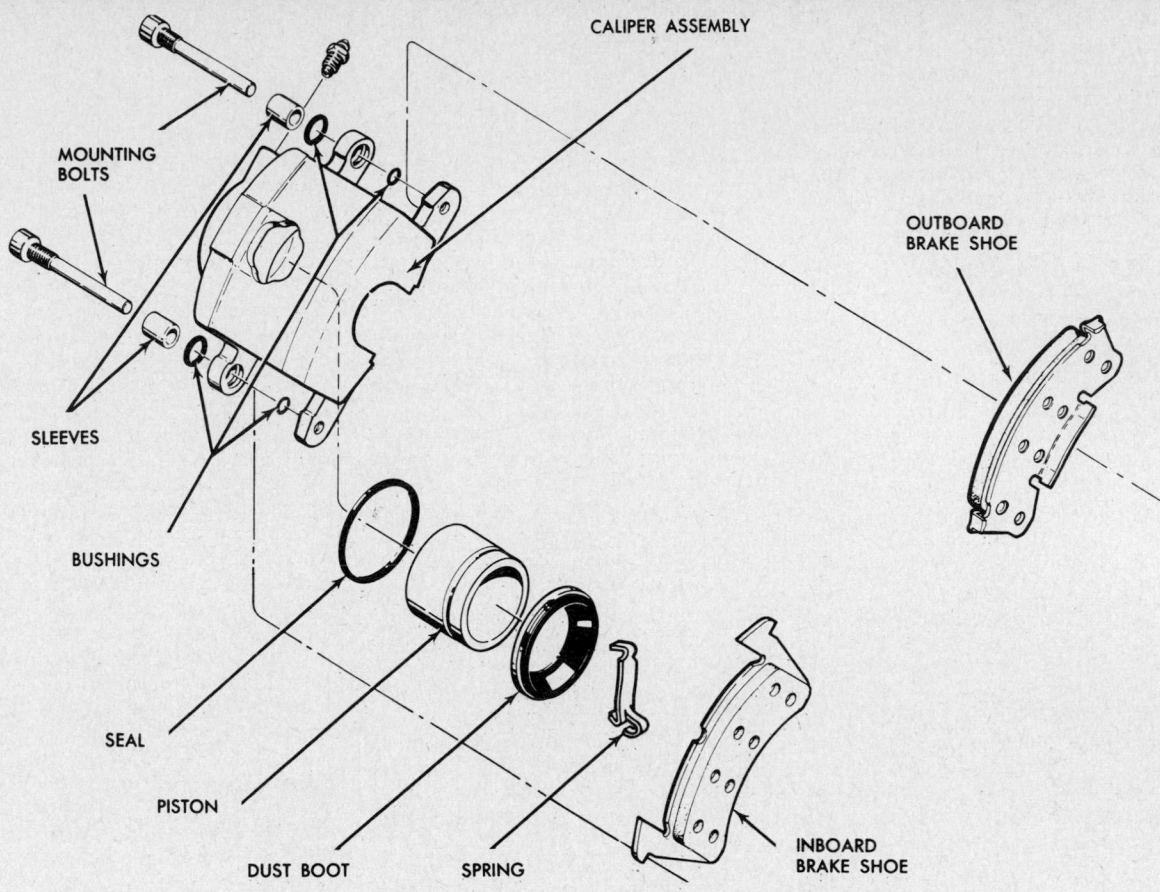

Delco-Moraine single piston disc brake (© Chev. Div., G.M. Corp.)

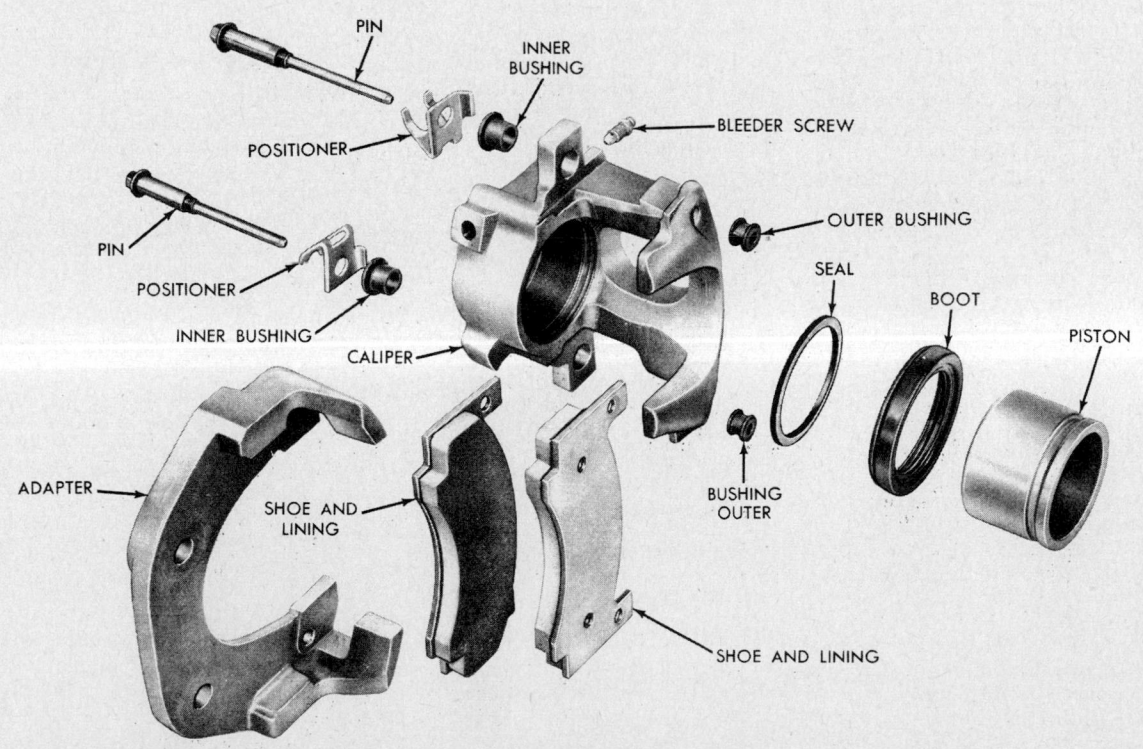

Kelsey-Hayes single piston disc brake (Chrysler) (© Chrysler Corp.)

inlet hole to remove the piston.

Caution To prevent damage to the piston use just enough air pressure to ease it out of the bore. Do not attempt to catch or protect the piston with the hand.

9. Use a screwdriver to pry the boot out of the caliper. Avoid scratching the bore.
10. Remove the piston seal from its groove in the caliper bore. *Do not use a metal tool of any type for this operation.*
11. Blow out all passages in the caliper and bleeder valve. Clean the piston and piston bore with fresh brake fluid.
12. Examine the piston for scoring, scratches, or corrosion. If any of these conditions exist the piston must be replaced, as it is plated and cannot be refinished.
13. Examine the bore for the same defects. Light rough spots may be removed by rotating crocus cloth, using finger pressure, in the bore. Do not polish with an in and out motion or use any other abrasive.
14. Lubricate the piston bore and the new rubber parts with fresh brake fluid. Position the seal in the piston bore groove.
15. Lubricate the piston with brake fluid and assemble the boot into the piston groove so that the fold faces the open end of the piston.
16. Insert the piston into the bore, taking care not to unseat the seal.

17. Force the piston to the bottom of the bore. (This will require a force of 50-100 lbs.). Seat the boot lip around the caliper counterbore. Proper seating of the boot is very important for sealing out contaminants.
18. Install the brake hose into the caliper using a new copper gasket.
19. Lubricate the new sleeves and rubber bushings. Install the bushings in the caliper ears. Install the sleeves so that the end toward the disc pad is flush with the machined surface.
NOTE: lubrication of the sleeves and bushings is essential to ensure the proper operation of the sliding caliper design.
20. Install the shoe support spring (if applicable) in the piston.
21. Install the disc pads in the caliper and remount the caliper on the hub (see Disc Pad Replacement).
22. Reconnect the brake hose to the steel brake line. Install the retainer clip. Bleed the brakes (see Brake Bleeding).
23. Replace the wheels, check the brake fluid level, check the brake pedal travel, and road test the vehicle.

Kelsey-Hayes Single Piston Brake (Chrysler)

Disc Pad Replacement

1. Raise the vehicle on a hoist and remove front wheels.
2. Working on only one brake at a time, remove the caliper guide pins and positioners which attach caliper to adapter. Lift the caliper away from the disc.
3. Remove (and discard) the positioners and inner bushings from the guide pins, and the outboard bushings from the caliper.
4. Slide the disc pads out of the caliper, and carefully push the piston back into the bore.
5. Lubricate the outboard bushings and work them into position from the outboard side of the caliper.
6. Slide the new disc pads into position (outboard pad in the retaining spring) and carefully slide the caliper assembly over the rotor.
7. Lubricate and install the inner bushings in the caliper. Install new positioners on the guide pins with the open ends toward the outside.
8. Install the assembled guide pins from the inboard side and press in while threading pin into adapter. *Use extreme care to avoid crossing threads.* Tighten to specifications. Be sure the tabs of the positioners are over the machined surfaces of the caliper.
9. Check the brake fluid level and pump the brake pedal to seat the linings against the disc. Replace the wheels and road test the car.

Servicing the Caliper Assembly

See Delco-Moraine Single Piston Brake—Servicing the Caliper Assembly. Procedure is identical, except that:

1. The Kelsey-Hayes brake has no removable sleeves in the guide pin holes.
2. The retaining (support) springs are of a different shape.
3. Piston to bore clearance should be 0.002-0.006 in.
4. The guide pin positioners must be correctly installed on the guide pins (see Disc Pad Replacement).

Kelsey-Hayes Single Piston Brake (Ford)

Disc Pad Replacement

1. Raise the vehicle on a hoist and remove the front wheels.
2. Remove the lockwires from the two mounting bolts and lift the caliper away from the rotor.

3. Remove the retaining clips with a screwdriver and slide the outboard pad and retaining pins out of the caliper. Remove the inboard pad.
4. Slide the new inboard pad into the caliper so that the tabs are between the retaining clips and anchor plate and the backing plate lies flush against the piston.
5. Insert the outboard pad retaining pins into the outboard pad and position in caliper.
NOTE: stabilizer, insulators, pad clips and pins should always be replaced when disc pads are replaced.
6. Hold the retaining pins in place (one at a time) with a short drift pin or dowel and install the retaining clips.
7. Slide the caliper assembly over the disc and align the mounting bolt holes.
8. Install the lower bolt finger-tight. Install the upper bolt and torque to specification. Torque the lower bolt to specification. Safety wire both bolts.

Caution Do not deviate from this procedure. The alignment of the anchor plate depends on the proper sequence of bolt installation.

9. Check the brake fluid level and pump the brake pedal to seat the linings against the disc. Replace the wheels and road test the car.

Servicing the Caliper Assembly

1. Raise the vehicle on a hoist and remove the front wheels.
2. Disconnect and plug the brake line.
3. Remove the lockwires from the two caliper mounting bolts and remove the bolt. Lift the caliper off the disc.
4. Remove and discard the locating pin insulators. Replace all rubber parts at reassembly.
5. Remove the retaining clips with a screwdriver and slide the outboard pad and retaining pins out of the caliper. Remove the inboard pad. Loosen the bleed screw and drain the brake fluid.
6. Remove the two small bolts and caliper stabilizers.
7. Remove the inboard pad retaining clips and bolts.
8. Clean and inspect all parts, and reinstall on anchor plate. Do not tighten stabilizer bolts at this time.
9. Remove the piston by applying compressed air to the fluid inlet hole. Use care to prevent the piston from popping out of control.

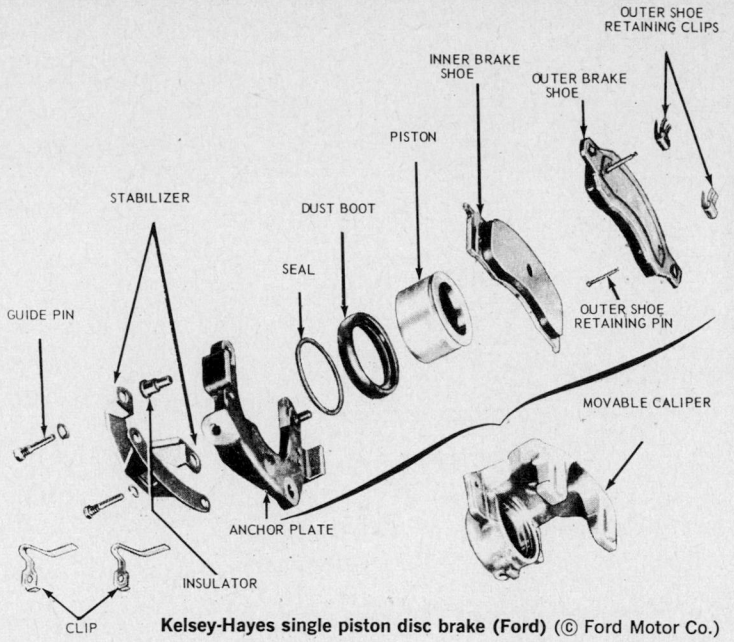

Kelsey-Hayes single piston disc brake (Ford) (© Ford Motor Co.)

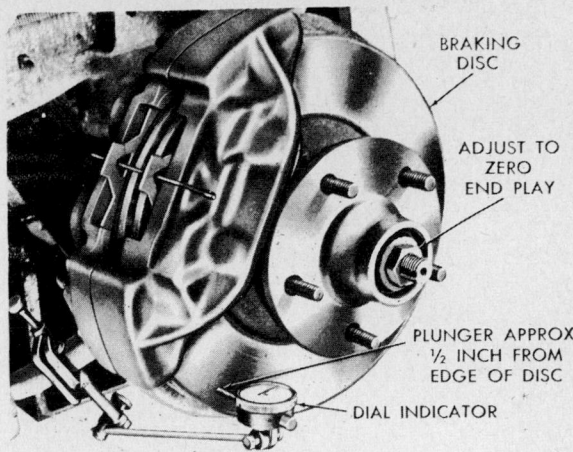

Checking disc runout (© Chrysler Corp.)

Caution Do not attempt to catch the piston with the hand. Use folded towels to cushion it.

10. Remove the piston boot. Inspect the piston for scoring, pitting, or corrosion. The piston must be replaced if there is any visible damage or wear.

11. Remove the piston seal from the cylinder bore. *Do not use any metal tools for this operation.*

12. Clean the caliper with fresh brake fluid. Inspect the cylinder bore for damage or wear. Light defects can be removed by rotating crocus cloth around the bore. Do not use any other type of abrasive.)

13. Lubricate all new rubber parts in brake fluid. Install the piston seal in the cylinder groove. Install the boot into its piston groove.

14. Install the piston, open end out, into the bore while working the boot around the outside of the piston. Make sure boot lip is seated in the piston groove.

15. Slide the anchor plate assembly onto the caliper housing and reinstall the locating pins. Tighten pins to specification. Tighten stabilizer anchor plate bolts.

16. Slide the inboard pad into the caliper that the tabs are between the retaining clips and anchor plate and the backing plate lies flush against the piston.

17. Insert the outboard pad retaining pins into the outboard pad and position in caliper.

18. Hold the retaining pins in place (one at a time) with a short drift pin or dowel and install the retaining clips.

19. Slide the caliper assembly over the disc and align the mounting bolt holes.

20. Install the lower bolt finger-tight. Install the upper bolt and torque to specification. Torque the lower bolt to specification. Safety wire both bolts.

Caution Do not deviate from this procedure. The alignment of the anchor plate depends on the proper sequence of bolt installation.

21. Connect the brake line and bleed the brakes (see Brake Bleeding).

22. Install the front wheels, recheck the brake fluid level, and road test the car.

Servicing the Disc

Disc Replacement

1. Raise the vehicle on a hoist and remove the wheel.

2. Remove the caliper mounting bolts. Slide the caliper away from the disc and suspend it using a wire loop.

3. Remove the wheel bearing nut from the spindle and remove the outer wheel bearing roller assembly from the hub.

4. Remove the hub and disc assembly from the spindle.

5. Installation of hub and disc is in reverse order of removal.

Caution Alignment of the caliper assembly depends on proper sequence of bolt installations on some cars. Check caliper installation procedure under Disc Pad Replacement of proper brake type.

NOTE: the disc is removable from the hub on the Eldorado, Toronado, and Corvette (rear only).

Lateral Runout

Lateral runout is the movement of the disc from side to side (wobble) as it rotates. Excessive runout will result in brake chatter, pedal pumping, excessive pedal travel, or vibration during braking.

To check lateral runout:

1. Tighten the spindle nut until there is no end-play in the bearings.

2. Fasten a dial indicator to the suspension so that the point contacts the disc face about ½ in. from the outer edge.

3. Set the dial to zero. Turn the disc through one complete revolution and check the indicator as the disc moves.

If the runout is more than the allowable maximum the disc and hub assembly should be replaced. Be sure to readjust the spindle nut if its setting was changed while checking the disc.

Parallelism

Parallelism refers to the variations in thickness of the disc. Excessive variation can cause pedal vibration and front end vibration during braking. Parallelism can be checked by measuring thickness at four or more equally spaced points around the braking surface of the disc. All measurements must be made at the same distance from the outer edge of the disc. The disc and hub should be replaced if variations in thickness exceed specification. Do not forget to adjust the spindle nut to specification if its setting was changed while checking the disc.

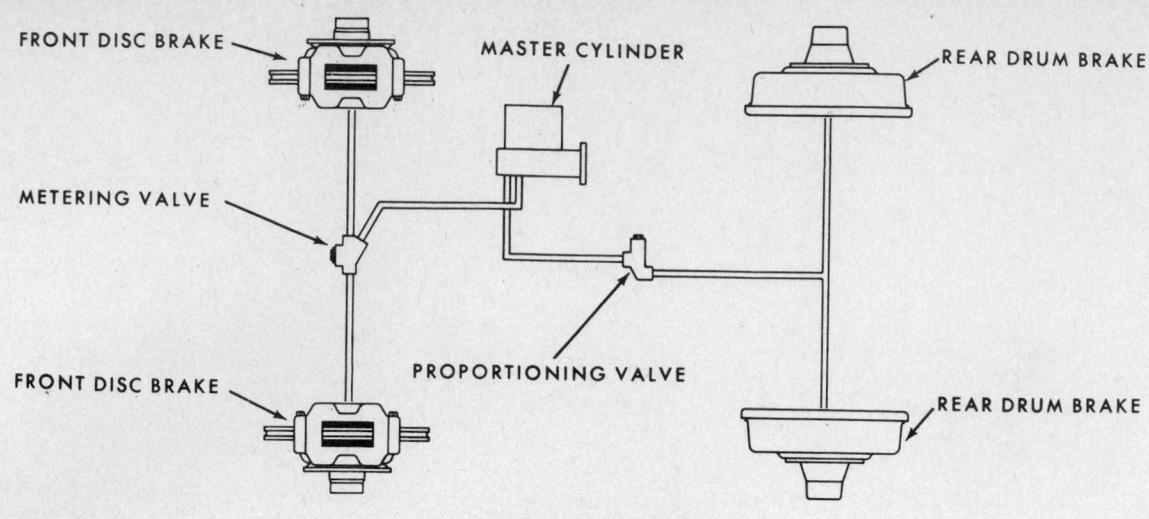

Disc brake hydraulic system

Hydraulic Cylinders and Valves

Master Cylinders

Dual master cylinders, commonly in use since 1967, are actually two single master cylinders operating in the same bore. They are designed so that the front and rear brakes have separate hydraulic systems. Malfunction in either system has no effect on the other system but is immediately evident to the driver because of the additional pedal travel required actuate the remaining half of the brake system. Service procedure for single master cylinders is identical, except that there is only one piston assembly and no stop screw. Some master cylinders have bleed screws on the outlet flanges and may be bled without disturbing the wheel cylinders.

Servicing Master Cylinders

1. Remove the cylinder from the car and drain the brake fluid.
2. Mount the cylinder in a vise so that the outlets are up and remove the seal from the hub.
3. Remove the stop screw from the bottom of the front reservoir.
4. Remove the snap-ring from the front of the bore and remove the rear piston assembly.
5. Remove the front piston assembly using compressed air. Cover the bore opening with a cloth to prevent damage to the piston.
6. Clean metal parts in brake fluid and discard rubber parts.
7. Inspect the bore for damage or wear, and check pistons for damage and proper clearance in the bore.
8. If the bore is only slightly scored or pitted it may be honed. Always use hones that are in good condition and completely clean

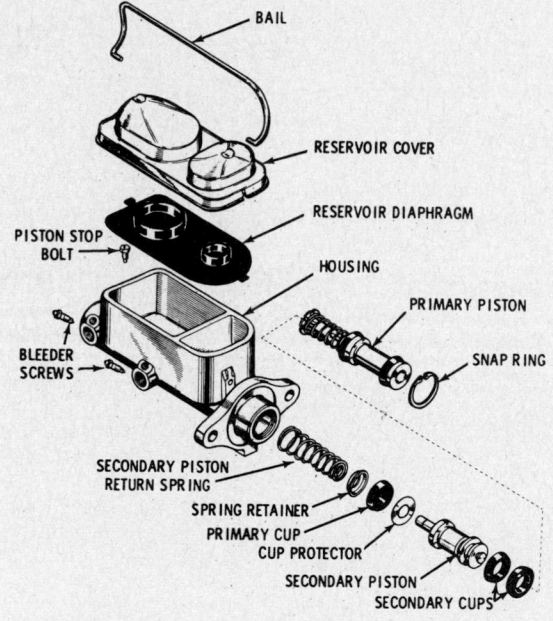

Bendix dual master cylinder (© Olds. Div., G.M. Corp.)

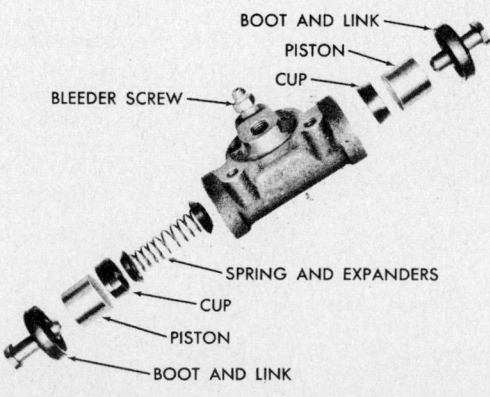

Wheel cylinder (© Chev. Div., G.M. Corp.)

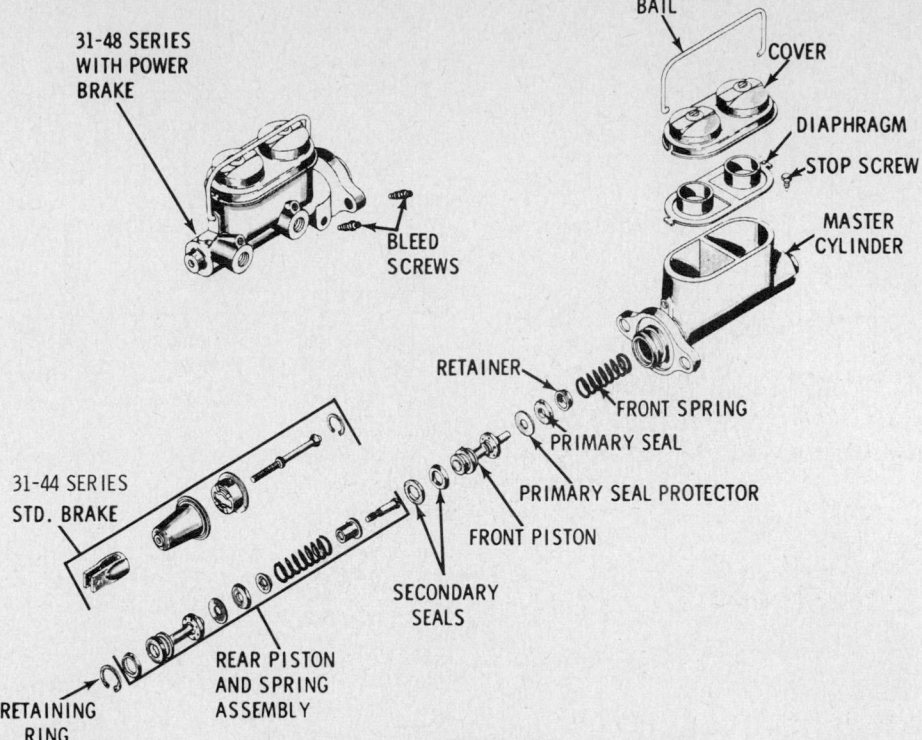

Moraine dual master cylinder (© Olds. Div., G.M. Corp.)

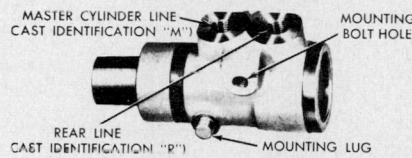

Proportioning valve

the cylinder with brake fluid when honing is completed. If any evidence of contamination exists in the master cylinder the entire hydraulic system should be flushed and refilled with clean brake fluid. Blow out passages with compressed air.

9. Install new secondary seals in the two grooves in the flat end of the front piston. The lips of the seals will be facing away from each other.
10. Install a new primary seal and the seal protector on opposite end of the front piston with the lips of the seal facing outward.
11. Coat the seals with brake fluid. Install the spring on the front piston with the spring retainer in the primary seal.
12. Insert the piston assembly, spring end first, into the bore and use a wooden rod to seat it.
13. Coat the rear piston seals with brake fluid and install them into the piston grooves with the lips facing the spring end.
14. Assemble the spring onto the piston and install the assembly into the bore spring first. Install the snap-ring.
15. Hold the piston train at the bottom of the bore and install the stop screw. Install a new seal on

the hub. Bench-bleed the cylinder or install and bleed the cylinder on the car.

Wheel Cylinders

Servicing Wheel Cylinders

1. Raise the vehicle on a hoist and remove the wheel and drum from the brake to be serviced.
2. Remove the brake shoes and clean the backing plate and wheel cylinder.
3. Disconnect the brake line from the brake hose. Remove the brake hose retainer clip at the frame bracket and remove the hose from the wheel cylinder. (On rear brakes it will only be necessary to remove the line from the wheel cylinder.)
4. Remove the cylinder mounting bolts and remove the cylinder.
5. Remove the boots from the cylinder ends and discard. Remove the pistons, remove and discard the seal cups, and remove the expanders and spring.
6. Inspect the bore and pistons for damage or wear. Damaged pistons should be discarded, as they cannot be reconditioned. Slight bore roughness can be removed using a brake cylinder hone or crocus cloth. (Cloth should be rotated in the bore under finger pressure. Do not slide lengthwise.)
7. Clean the cylinder and internal parts with brake fluid.
8. Insert the spring expander assembly. Lubricate all rubber parts with fresh brake fluid.

9. Install new cups with the seal lips facing inwards.
10. Install the pistons and rubber boots. Install the cylinder on the car in reverse order of removal. Bleed the cylinder (see Brake Bleeding).

Proportioning Valves

On vehicles equipped with front disc and rear drum brakes a proportioning valve is an important part of the system. It is installed in the hydraulic line to the rear brakes. Its function is to maintain the correct proportion between line pressures to the front and rear brakes. *No attempt at adjustment of this valve should be made, as adjustment is pre-set and tampering will result in uneven braking action.*

To assure correct installation when replacing the valve, the outlet to the rear brakes is stamped with the letter "R".

Metering Valves

On some vehicles equipped with front disc brakes a metering valve is used. This valve is installed in the hydraulic line to the front brakes, and functions to delay pressure buildup to the front brakes on application. Its purpose is to reduce front brake pressure until rear brake pressure builds up adequately to overcome the rear brake shoe return springs. In this way disc brake pad life is extended because it prevents the front disc brakes from carrying all or most of the braking load at low operating line pressures.

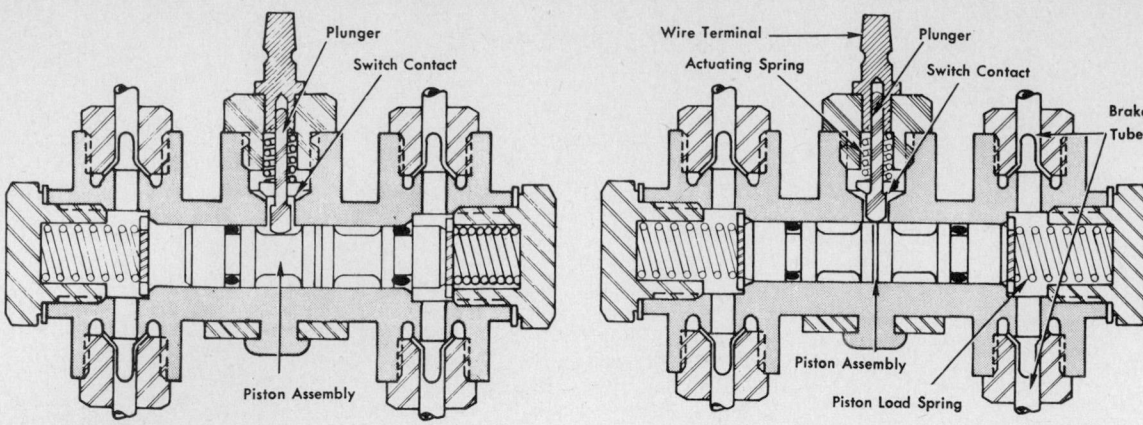

Pressure differential warning valve, "on" position

Pressure differential warning valve, "off" position

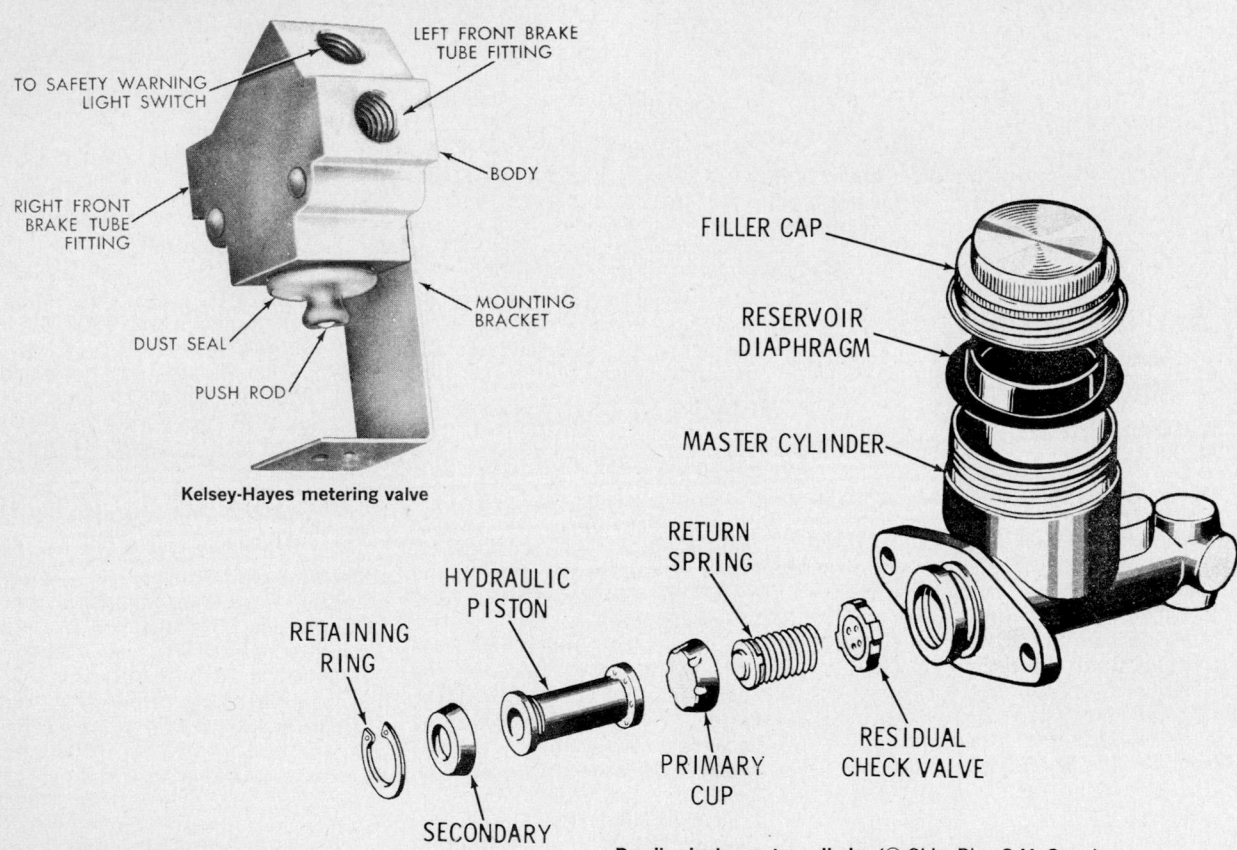

Kelsey-Hayes metering valve

Bendix single master cylinder (© Olds. Div., G.M. Corp.)

The metering valve can be checked very simply. With the car stopped, gently apply the brakes. At about one inch of travel a very small change in pedal effort (like a small bump) will be felt if the valve is operating properly. Metering valves are not serviceable, and must be replaced if defective.

Pressure Differential Warning Valves

Since the introduction of dual master cylinders to the hydraulic brake system, a pressure differential warning signal has been added. This sig-nal consists of a warning light on the dashboard activated by a differential pressure switch located below the master cylinder. The signal indicates a hydraulic pressure differential between the front and rear brakes of 80-150 psi, and should warn the driver that a hydraulic failure has occurred.

After repairing and bleeding any part of the hydraulic system the warning light may remain on due to the pressure differential valve remaining in the off-center position. To centralize the valve a pressure difference must be created in the opposite branch of the hydraulic system that was repaired or bled last.

NOTE: front wheel balancing of cars equipped with disc brakes may also cause a pressure differential in the front branch of the system.

To centralize the valve:
1. Switch the ignition on.
2. Loosen the differential valve brake tube nut at the opposite side of the brake system that was affected or repaired last.
3. Press the brake pedal slowly until the valve is centralized and the light goes out. Retighten the brake tube nut at the outlet port.
4. Check brake fluid level and brake pedal height and firmness. Road test the car.

Brake Bleeding

The purpose of bleeding brakes is to expel air trapped in the hydraulic system, and there are two methods of accomplishing this. The quickest and easiest of the two is pressure bleeding, but special pressure equipment is needed to externally pressurize the hydraulic system. The other, more commonly used method is gravity bleeding.

Gravity Bleeding Procedure

1. Clean the bleed screw at each wheel.
2. Attach a small rubber hose to one of the bleed screws and place the end in a container of brake fluid.
3. Top up the master cylinder with brake fluid. (Check often during bleeding.)
4. Open the bleed screw about one-quarter turn, press the brake pedal to the floor and slowly release it. Continue until no more air bubbles are forced from the cylinder on application of the brake pedal.
5. Repeat procedure on remaining wheel cylinders.

Master cylinders equipped with bleed screws may be bled independently. When bleeding the Bendix-type dual master cylinder it is necessary to solidly cap one reservoir section while bleeding the other to prevent pressure loss through the cap vent hole.

Disc brakes may be bled in the same manner as drum brakes, except that:
1. Brakes should be bled in this order: right rear, left rear, right front, left front.
2. It usually requires a longer time to bleed a disc brake thoroughly.
3. The disc should be rotated to make sure that the piston has returned to the unapplied position when bleeding is completed and the bleed screw closed.

Pressure Bleeding Disc Brakes

Pressure bleeding disc brakes will close the metering valve and the front brakes will not bleed. For this reason it is necessary to manually hold the metering valve open during pressure bleeding. Never use a block or clamp to hold the valve open, and never force the valve stem beyond its normal position. Two different types of valves are used. The most common type requires the valve stem to be held in while bleeding the brakes, while the second type requires the valve stem to be held out (.060 in. minimum travel). Determine the type by visual inspection.

POWER BRAKE IDENTIFICATION CHART

Car	Bendix Treadle Vac Section 1	Bendix Master Vac Section 2	Bendix Dual Diaphragm Section 3	Bendix Single Diaphragm Section 4	Moraine Diaphragm Section 5	Moraine Diaphragm Section 6	Moraine Diaphragm Section 7	Midland-Ross Diaphragm Section 8	Kelsey-Hayes Bellows Section 9	Kelsey-Hayes Diaphragm Section 10	Bendix Single Diaphragm Hydrovac Section 11	Bendix Dual Diaphragm Hydrovac Section 12	Delco Moraine Tandem Diaphragm Section 13	Midland-Ross Tandem Diaphragm Section 14
American Motors			1968-72	1965-72										
Buick				1965-72			1965-72						1970-72	
Buick Special							1965-72							
Cadillac				1965-72			1965-72							
Camaro and Chevy II				1965-72				1970-72						
Chevrolet			1970-72	1965-72				1970-72			1970-72	1970-72		
Chevelle							1965-72	1970-72						
Chrysler			1965-72	1967-72				1965-72		1965-66				
Continental		1965-72	1968-72					1965-67						
Corvette				1965-72			1965-72	1970-72						
Cougar				1967-72				1965-72		1965-66				1967-69
Dodge, Dart, Challenger, Demon	1965-72	1965-72	1967-72											
Fairlane, Falcon				1965-72										
Firebird, Tempest, GTO							1965-72							
Ford			1966-72	1966-72				1968-72	1965-72					
Mercury, Montego			1970-72	1967-72					1965-72					
Mustang, Comet				1965-72										
Plymouth			1967-72	1965-72		1965-72		1965-72		1965				1967-69
Pontiac		1965-72	1967-72		1965-72		1965-72							
Thunderbird				1967-72				1965-72						
Oldsmobile			1967-72	1965-68	1966-72		1965						1970-72	
F-85 and Cutlass			1967-72	1965-68	1966-72		1965			1965				
Ventura II				1971-72			1971-72							

Section Page Numbers

Section	Page	Section	Page	Section	Page
1	1157	6	1162	10	1168
2	1158	7	1164	11	1170
3	1160	8	1165	12	1172
4	1160	9	1166	13	1173
5	1161			14	1175

Power Brakes

The following items are in addition to those listed under non-power brakes. Check those items first.

Dragging Brakes

(Refer to non-power brakes first)

1. Excessive hydraulic seal friction or binding.
2. Compensator port plugged.
3. Sticking valve plunger.

4. Improper booster pushrod length.
5. Fluid return lines blocked.
6. Valve sleeve not properly positioned or staked.

Grabbing Brakes

(Refer to non-power brakes first)

1. Sticking actuating valve.
2. Broken plunger stem.

Hard Pedal

(Refer to non-power brakes first)

1. Faulty vacuum check valve.

2. Collapsed or leaking vacuum hose.
3. Plugged vacuum fittings.
4. Leaking vacuum chamber.
5. Diaphragm assembly out of place.
6. Vacuum leak in forward vacuum housing.

Pedal Goes to Floor (or Excessively Low)

(Refer to non-power brakes first)

1. Shoe (s) hanging at backing plate.
2. Broken plunger stem.
3. Self-adjusters not operating.

Section 1
Bendix Treadle-Vac Power Brakes

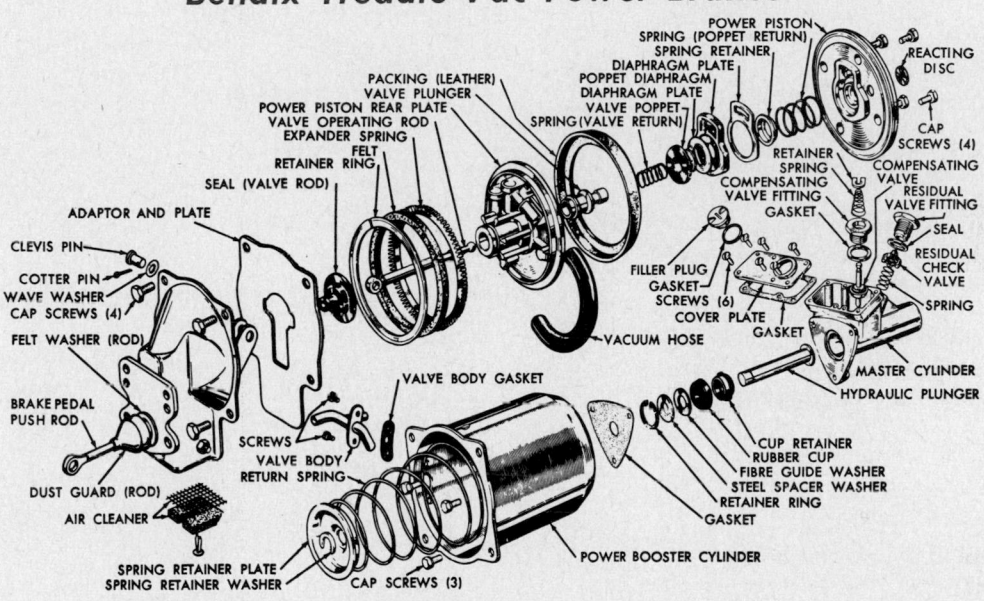

Exploded view of Treadle-Vac unit (hydraulic reaction type) (© Oldsmobile Div., G.M. Corp.)

The Treadle-Vac is a self-contained unit in which the master cylinder of the regular hydraulic system is part of the unit. It is therefore called an adjacent-type unit. It is worthy to note that this is an atmospherically balanced unit in which, when the brakes are not applied, there is atmospheric pressure on both sides of the piston.

Removal

1. Disconnect the hydraulic line at the hydraulic cylinder, and cap so that all the fluid does not run out. Disconnect the vacuum line at the unit. Remove the brake pedal pivot pin and tip the upper end of the pedal back to expose the pushrod pivot pin under the pedal pad.
2. Remove the brake pedal and the accelerator pedal. Fold back the carpet. Unfasten the steering column grommet and slide it up the column.

3. Remove steering column cover plate-to-toe pan screws and remove the cover plate and power brake unit as an assembly.
4. Remove four bolts to release the unit from the plate.
5. Reverse the procedure to reinstall.

NOTE: be careful not to pull pushrod out of the plunger.

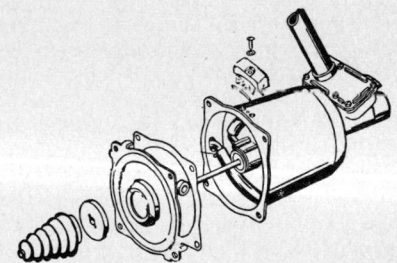

End plate removal
(© Oldsmobile Div., G.M. Corp.)

Sleeve valve and vacuum hose removal
(© Oldsmobile Div., G.M. Corp.)

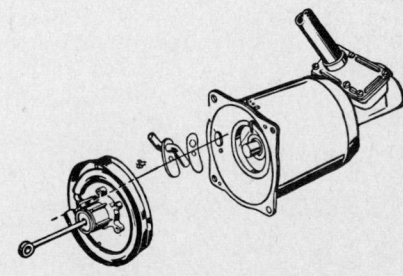

Vacuum piston and valve removal
(© Oldsmobile Div., G.M. Corp.)

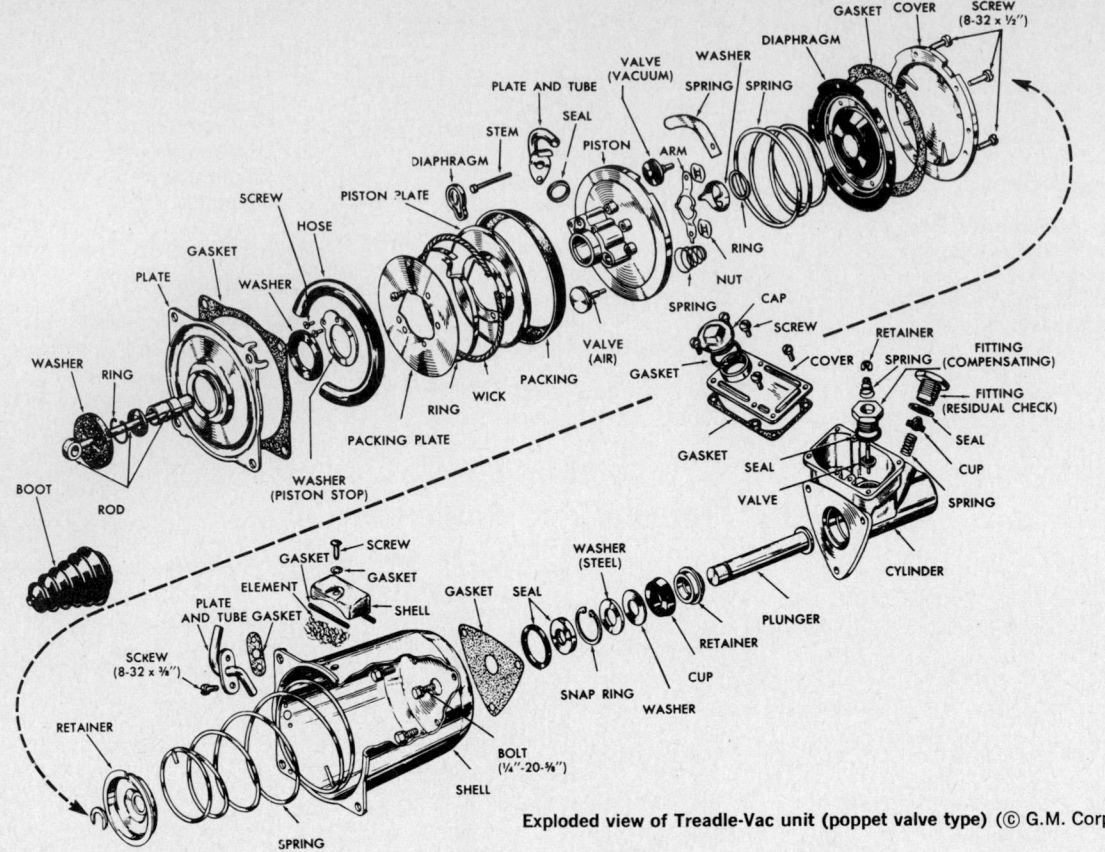

Exploded view of Treadle-Vac unit (poppet valve type) (© G.M. Corp.)

Bleeding the Treadle-Vac

Bleed the brakes in the normal manner. This unit does not have any bleed-screws. Fill to within ¼ in. of top.

Overhaul

Repair parts for the unit come in kits. Always install all the parts supplied in the kit, regardless of whether it appears necessary.

Be sure to keep the parts clean, as any sign of grease will interfere with the operation of the rubber seals. Be sure to scribe across the vacuum cylinder and the hydraulic cylinder to facilitate assembly to the same position. Do the same thing to show assembly position of the cover and the hydraulic cylinder. Use alcohol to clean the parts and be sure that no fluid gets on the valve assembly. Inspect all parts for damage and excessive wear. If the inside of the vacuum cylinder is rusted or corroded, it can be cleaned with steel wool or emery cloth, but be sure to remove all traces of the abrasive. If it is scored it must be replaced. Replace the hydraulic plunger if it is rusted or scored.

Section 2
Bendix Master-Vac

Removal

1. Disconnect clevis at brake pedal to pushrod.

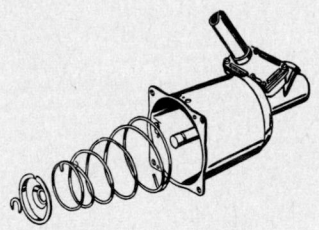

Vacuum piston return spring and retainer removal (© Oldsmobile Div., G.M. Corp.)

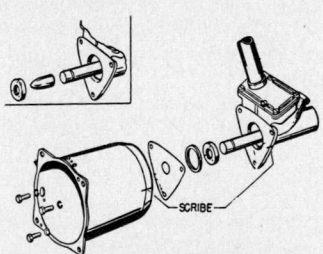

Vacuum cylinder and leather seal removal (© Oldsmobile Div., G.M. Corp.)

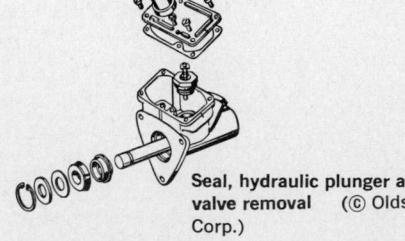

Seal, hydraulic plunger and compensating valve removal (© Oldsmobile Div., G.M. Corp.)

Residual check valve removal (© Oldsmobile Div., G.M. Corp.)

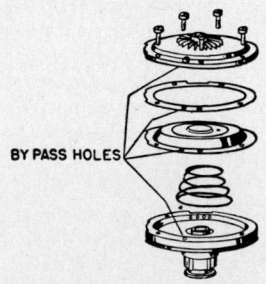

Diaphragm cover and valve spring removal (© Oldsmobile Div., G.M. Corp.)

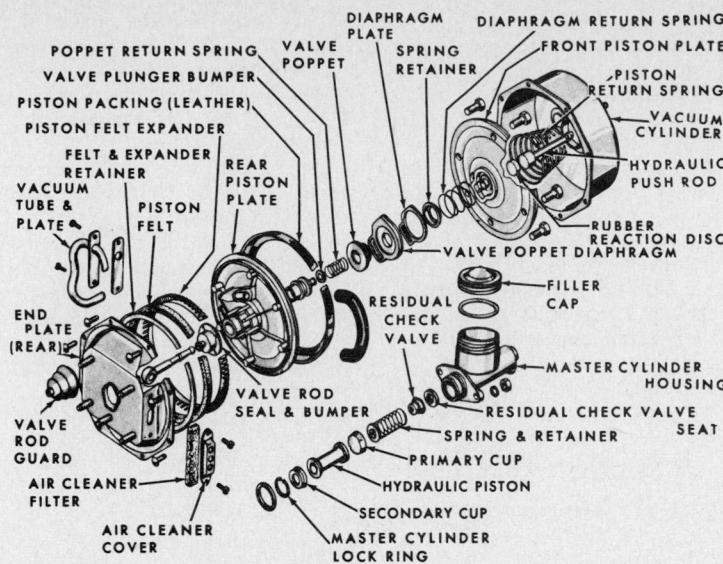

POPPET RETURN SPRING
VALVE PLUNGER BUMPER
PISTON PACKING (LEATHER)
PISTON FELT EXPANDER
FELT & EXPANDER RETAINER
VACUUM TUBE & PLATE
PISTON FELT
REAR PISTON PLATE
VALVE POPPET
DIAPHRAGM PLATE
SPRING RETAINER
DIAPHRAGM RETURN SPRING
FRONT PISTON PLATE
PISTON RETURN SPRING
VACUUM CYLINDER
HYDRAULIC PUSH ROD
RUBBER REACTION DISC
VALVE POPPET DIAPHRAGM
FILLER CAP
END PLATE (REAR)
VALVE ROD GUARD
AIR CLEANER FILTER
AIR CLEANER COVER
VALVE ROD SEAL & BUMPER
RESIDUAL CHECK VALVE
MASTER CYLINDER HOUSING
RESIDUAL CHECK VALVE SEAT
SPRING & RETAINER
PRIMARY CUP
HYDRAULIC PISTON
SECONDARY CUP
MASTER CYLINDER LOCK RING

Bendix Master-Vac (© Ford Motor Co.)

2. Remove vacuum hoses from power cylinder.
3. Disconnect hydraulic line from master cylinder.
4. Remove the four attaching nuts and lock washers that hold the unit to the firewall. Remove the power brake unit.

Disassembly

1. Remove four master cylinder-to-vacuum cylinder attaching nuts and washers.
2. Separate master cylinder from vacuum cylinder, then remove rubber seal from outer groove at end of master cylinder.
3. Remove pushrod from power section. (Do not disturb adjusting screw.)
4. Remove pushrod boot and valve operating rod.
5. Scribe alignment marks across rear shell and vacuum cylinder. Remove all but two of the end plate attaching screws (opposite each other). Hold down on rear shell while removing two remaining screws to prevent the piston return spring from expanding.
6. Scribe a mark across face of piston, to index the mark on rear shell, and remove rear shell with vacuum piston and piston return spring.
7. Remove vacuum hose from vacuum piston and from vacuum tube on inside of rear shell. Separate rear shell from vacuum piston.
8. Remove air cleaner and vacuum tube assembly, and air filter from the rear shell.
9. Spring the felt retaining ring enough to disengage ring from grooves in bosses on rear piston plate.
10. Remove piston felt and expander ring from piston assembly.

11. Remove six piston plate attaching screws and separate front piston plate and packing from piston plate.
12. Remove valve return spring, floating control valve and diaphragm assembly, valve spring and diaphragm plate. Separate floating control valve spring retainer and diaphragm plate from control valve.
13. Remove rubber reaction disc and shim (if present) from front piston plate.
    NOTE: do not remove valve operating rod plunger from rear piston plate unless it is necessary to replace defective parts. Normally, the next two steps can be omitted.
14. When it is necessary to replace valve operating rod or valve plunger, remove valve rod seal from groove in piston plate and pull seal over end of rod.
15. Hold piston with valve plunger side down and inject alcohol into valve plunger through opening around valve rod. This will wet the rubber lock in the plunger. Then drive valve plunger off the valve rod.
    NOTE: if master cylinder is not to be rebuilt, omit Steps 16-19.
16. Remove snap-ring from groove in base at end of master cylinder.
17. Remove piston assembly, primary cup, retainer spring, and check-valve from master cylinder.
18. Remove filler cap and gasket from master cylinder body.
19. Remove secondary cup from master cylinder piston.

Cleaning Note

After disassembly, cleaning of all metal parts in Bendix Metalclene or satisfactory commercial cleaner solvent is recommended. Use only alcohol or Declene on rubber parts or parts containing rubber. After cleaning and drying, metal parts should be rewashed in clean alcohol or Declene before assembly.

Assembly

Steps 1-5 apply to a completely disassembled master cylinder. Otherwise, omit these steps (1-5).

1. Coat bore of master cylinder with brake fluid.
2. Dip secondary cup in brake fluid and install on master cylinder piston.
3. Dip other piston parts in brake fluid and assemble the piston. Install piston.
4. Install snap-ring into groove of cylinder.
5. Use new gasket and install filler cap.
6. Assemble valve rod seal on rod and insert valve rod through the piston. Dip valve plunger in alcohol and assemble to ball end of valve rod. Be sure ball end of rod is locked in place in plunger.
7. Assemble floating control valve diaphragm over end of floating control valve. Be sure diaphragm is in recess of floating control valve. Press control valve spring retainer over end of control valve and diaphragm.
8. Clamp valve operating rod in a vise with rear piston plate up. Lay leather piston packing on rear piston plate with lip of leather over edge of piston plate.
9. Install floating control valve return spring over end of valve plunger.
10. Assemble diaphragm plate to diaphragm and assemble floating control valve with diaphragm in recess of rear piston plate.
11. Install floating control valve spring over retainer. Align and assemble front piston plate with rear piston plate. Center the floating control valve spring on front piston plate and center valve plunger stem in hole of piston.
12. Holding front and rear piston plates together, loosely install six piston plate cap screws.
13. Install shim and rubber reaction disc in recess at center of front piston plate.
    NOTE: a piston assembling ring (tool J-7780) is handy in assembling the piston.
14. Place the assembling tool over piston packing, turn piston assembly upside down and assemble the expander ring against inside lip of leather packing. Saturate felt with Bendix Vacuum Cylinder Oil or Delco shock absorber fluid—type A, then assemble in expander ring. Assemble retainer ring over bosses on rear piston plate. Be sure retainer is anchored in grooves of piston plate.

15. Assemble air cleaner filter over vacuum tube of air cleaner and attach air cleaner shell in position with screws.

16. Slide vacuum hose onto vacuum inlet tube of piston and align hose to lay flat against piston.

17. Wipe a coat of vacuum cylinder oil on bore of cylinder. Remove assembling ring from vacuum piston and coat leather piston packing with vacuum cylinder oil.

18. Install rear shell over end of valve operating rod and attach vacuum hose to tube end on each side of end plate.

19. Center small end of piston return spring in vacuum cylinder. Center large diameter of spring on piston. Check alignment mark on piston with marks on vacuum cylinder and rear shell, compress spring and install two attaching screws at opposite sides to hold rear shell and cylinder together. Now, install balance of screws and tighten evenly.

20. Dip small end of pushrod boot in alcohol and assemble guard over end of valve operating rod and over flange of shell.

21. Insert large end of pushrod through hole in end of vacuum cylinder and guide into hole of front piston plate.

NOTE: before going on with assembly, check the distance from the outer end of the pushrod to the master cylinder mounting surface on the vacuum cylinder. This measurement should be 1.195-1.200 in.

22. After pushrod adjustment is correct, replace rubber seal in groove on master cylinder body.

23. Assemble master cylinder to the vacuum cylinder at four studs. Replace lock washers and nut and securely tighten.

Section 3
Bendix Dual Diaphragm Type

The Bendix Dual Diaphragm booster features direct pedal connection to a vacuum unit mounted on the firewall, with the master cylinder directly mounted to booster.

The booster chamber contains two diaphragms and is under constant engine vacuum. When brakes are applied, the control valve is opened to allow atmospheric pressure behind both diaphragms. This provides the power boost to the master cylinder.

This vacuum-suspended system provides reserve against fade. Pedal linkages are eliminated, no additional vacuum storage tanks are needed.

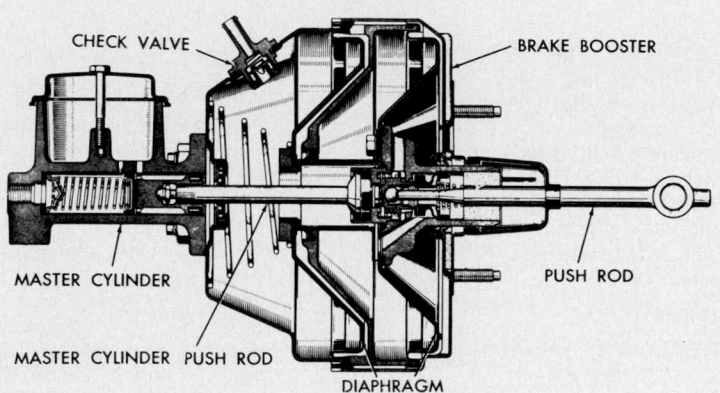

Cutaway view of brake booster and master cylinder

Removal

1. Remove bolt attaching pedal to pushrod.
2. Disconnect fluid line from master cylinder.
3. Disconnect vacuum line from check valve.
4. Remove four attaching nuts and washers under dash.
5. Pull booster and cylinder assembly forward from support bracket.
6. Remove four nuts and washers holding master cylinder to booster and remove cylinder.

Installation

Reverse the above procedure.

NOTE: do not attempt to disassemble the booster. It is serviced only by the dealer.

Section 4
Bendix Single Diaphragm

Disassembly

1. After emptying unit and thoroughly cleaning outside, mount in vise with pushrod up. Clamp on sides of master cylinder.
2. Remove rear retainer and boot and install nuts on rear shell studs. Scribe line between two shells for reassembly. With pry bar behind nuts, rotate rear shell so that cutouts in shell line up with tangs of front shell.

Caution Loosen carefully, as it is spring loaded.

3. Lift rear shell and plate, and valve rod and plunger assembly from unit. Remove return spring.
4. Remove plate and valve body, valve rod and plunger assembly

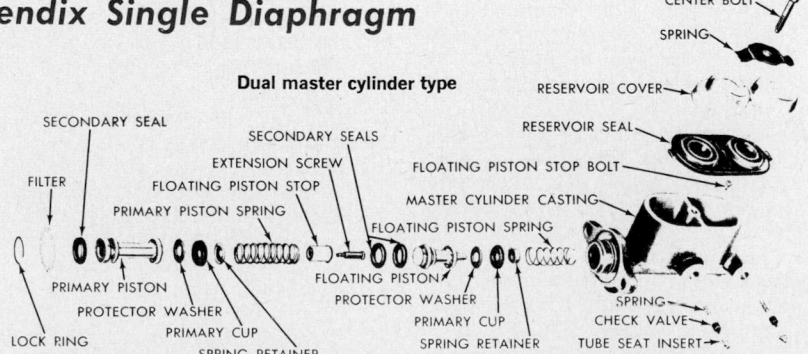

Dual master cylinder type

from unit. Do not remove rear shell bearing seal unless defective and new seal is on hand for replacement.

5. Remove master cylinder pushrod. Remove master cylinder attaching nuts and separate cylinder from shell.

6. Remove seal and vacuum check valve from front shell.

7. Pry off filter retainer and remove air silencer and filter from body. Do not chip plastic. Remove diaphragm from plate and valve

body, then remove valve retainer key, valve rod and plunger. Press reaction disc from diaphragm plate.

8. If required, recondition master cylinder in conventional manner.

Inspect all parts thoroughly, replacing any parts with scuffing, nicks, or scratches that cannot be cleaned with crocus cloth. Diaphragms that show deterioration or cracking also should be replaced.

9. Reassemble in reverse of above procedures.

Gauging is only necessary when major structural parts have been replaced. To gauge, remove master cylinder so that pushrod is exposed.

Place gauge over piston rod so that it fits between the two studs on front of housing. The gap between the cut-out of gauge and piston rod should not be more than .010 in. Proper clearance may be obtained by adjusting screw to meet the requirements.

Bendix power brake

Section 5
Moraine Diaphragm Type

Disassembly

1. Empty system and thoroughly clean outside of assembly. Be sure no oils or greases contact diaphragm units.
2. Clamp assembly in vise with operating rod up.
3. Scribe an alignment mark on end plate and vacuum cylinder. Separate by rotating end plate counterclockwise.
4. Remove end plate and vacuum piston assembly from vacuum cylinder.
5. Remove boot, silencer, air filter and spacer from operating rod. Pull end plate away from vacuum piston, remove vacuum hose and separate end plate.
6. Remove vacuum inlet attaching screws. Then remove vacuum inlet and gasket from end plate.
7. Remove rubber bearing from end plate.
8. Remove vacuum piston return spring from cylinder.
9. Remove vacuum cylinder.
10. Remove support plate and dia-

phragm from vacuum piston assembly and separate diaphragm from support plate.
11. Remove master cylinder pushrod from plate.
12. Remove O-ring and reaction levers from vacuum piston.
13. Push air valve and operating rod from floating valve side of vacuum piston. This will dislodge floating valve from seat.
14. Rotate air valve extension and unlock it from air valve. Remove air valve return spring, floating valve return spring and floating valve.
15. Remove air valve O-rings.
16. Remove vacuum hose. Disassem-

ble floating valve.

Thoroughly clean and inspect all parts. Check for scoring and pitting, dents and nicks. Inspect the diaphragm for nicks, deterioration and abrasion.

17. Check master cylinder parts and replace as in normal master cylinder repairs.
18. Assemble in reverse of the disassembly procedure. Keep all diaphragm parts clean and free of oil and grease. Lubricate other parts with clean hydraulic brake fluid.
19. Check pushrod adjustment.
   A. With vacuum unit assembled and master cylinder removed, position gauge over pushrod end, with legs of gauge over pushrod and resting on vacuum cylinder. Adjustment is correct if screw contacts gauge or legs of gauge are .020 in. from vacuum cylinder.
   B. If necessary rotate screw until this adjustment is attained.

Major parts of power brake unit

Exploded view of power piston assembly

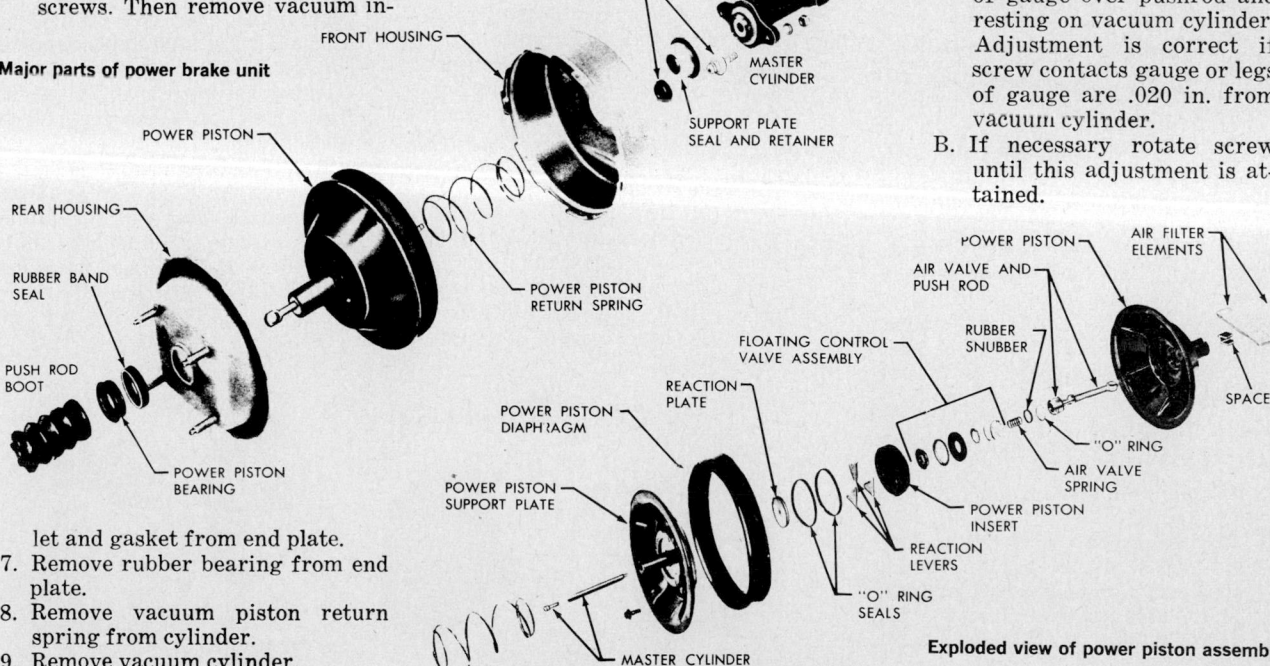

Section 6
Moraine Diaphragm Type

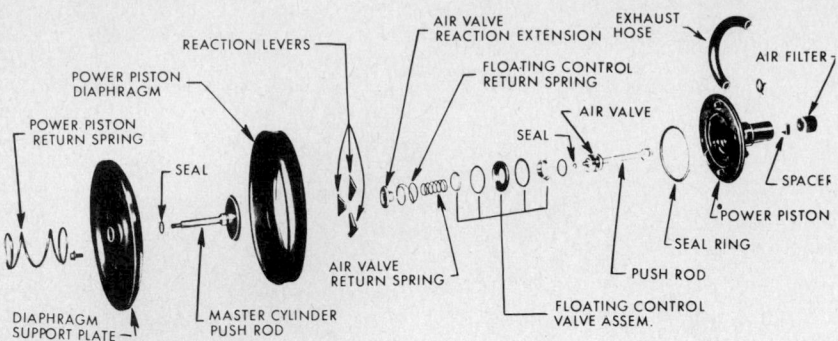

Exploded view of power piston assembly

Cleaning Note

Use Declene or fresh brake fluid to clean all parts thoroughly. Soak in the fluid and use hair brush to dislodge all foreign matter. Use compressed air on all orifices and valve holes, then air dry.

Gasoline, kerosene or any other mineral cleaner will react with rubber parts. *Lubricate with brake fluid only.*

Assembly

1. Position filter element and air filter cover over two holes in the rear housing.
2. Inspect exhaust tube assembly for damage. Insert tube (with new gasket) into rear housing and install two screws.
3. Insert small rubber bumper into counterbore of master cylinder piston. Place two secondary seals in grooves of master cylinder piston, with lips toward the small drilled holes in end of piston.
4. Install O-ring into second groove from the counterbored end of master cylinder piston. Lubricate with silicone grease and insert piston into piston diaphragm plate, from flange side. install snap-ring into groove.
5. Place reaction lever plate (with raised rim away from piston diaphragm plate) over piston and
6. Set the assembly aside for the moment.
7. Place reaction diaphragm support plate over hub of floating control valve. Assemble reaction diaphragm over flanged hub of control valve so that flange fits into groove on inside diameter of diaphragm.
8. Insert diaphragm retainer under lip of diaphragm and place floating control valve spring retainer over reaction diaphragm hub. The six small rubber bumpers

Removal

1. Disconnect clevis at brake pedal assembly.
2. Remove vacuum hoses from power brake unit.
3. Disconnect hydraulic line from master cylinder.
4. Remove nuts and lockwashers holding unit to firewall. Lift out the unit.
5. Remove cotter pin, clevis pin and washer from end of brake pedal pushrod.
6. Remove the cotter pin, clevis pin and washers from end of power brake operating rod.
7. Remove cotter pin, then tap out pivot pin. Remove two operating levers and the pivot collar.

Disassembly

1. Place unit in vise with pushrod up. Clamp firmly on side of master cylinder reservoir.
2. Place long wooden hammer handle in position to bear against two studs. Rotate counterclockwise to separate housings.
3. Lift rear housing and power piston assembly from unit.
4. Remove hose from rear housing tube and remove pushrod boot.
5. Remove power piston return spring from front housing.
   NOTE: unless front housing or master cylinder assembly is damaged and must be replaced there is no need to remove front housing from master cylinder assembly.

Caution Protect all parts from nicks or cuts. Keep grease, oils and foreign matter from diaphragm.

6. Remove screws and lift master cylinder piston, rolling diaphragm from piston with support plate and reaction plate from power piston. Thoroughly inspect for any damage.
7. Remove retaining ring from mas-

ter cylinder piston and remove reaction plate.
8. Push master cylinder piston through support plate. Then remove O-ring, secondary seals and rubber bumper from inside piston.
9. Remove power piston assembly from reaction disc, reaction levers, air valve reaction plate, floating control valve return spring and power piston seal ring.
10. Turn power piston over and inspect hose. Replace hose if damaged.
11. Remove air valve boot. Force pushrod air valve assembly through power piston, dislodging floating control valve and diaphragm assembly. If pushrod air-valve assembly is bad, replace with complete new assembly.
12. Remove floating control valve spring retainer from floating control valve and diaphragm. Remove reaction diaphragm retainer. Then remove reaction diaphragm and support plate from hub of floating control valve.
13. Check master cylinder parts and replace as required.
14. Carefully inspect all parts and replace as needed, reassembling in reverse of disassembly procedure. Coat all parts with clean brake fluid during assembly. *This does not apply to diaphragm.*

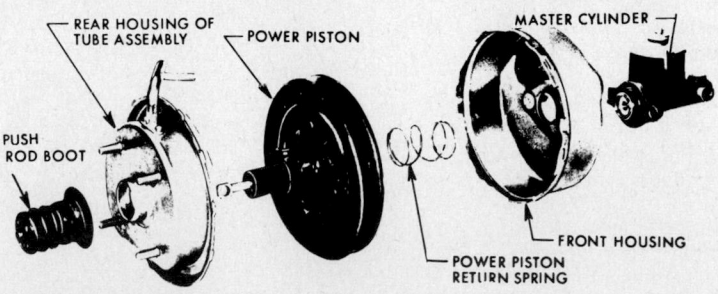

Major parts of Moraine diaphragm unit

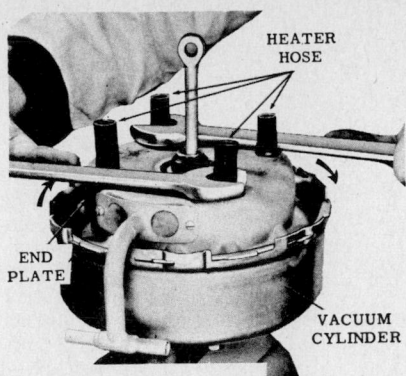

HEATER HOSE

END PLATE

VACUUM CYLINDER

Installing end plate (© Oldsmobile Div., G.M. Corp.)

must be positioned in the spring retainer.

9. Place power piston in vise with flat surface up. (Do not clamp.)

10. Insert pushrod end of air valve pushrod into piston and press down into piston to seat.

11. Wipe a light film of silicone grease on the outer diameter of reaction liaphragm.

12. Place floating control valve and diaphragm assembly down over air valve and press outer edge of reaction diaphragm into position in the power piston.

13. Place air valve return spring inside floating control valve to seat on the air valve. Place floating control valve spring to seat on flange of spring retainer. Position air valve reaction plate over air valve so low center portion rests on inner spring (air valve return spring). The outer spring (floating control valve spring) will also be in position to engage the reacion lever plate.

14. Position ears of the reaction levers in machined locations in power piston and rest the small ends on reaction lever plate. Insert seal-ring into inner groove on flat surface of power piston face.

15. Pull skirt of power piston diaphragm down over piston and place the bead on inner diameter of diaphragm in the outer groove of power piston face, so bumpers are toward piston.

16. The master cylinder piston and piston diaphragm plate are positioned over power piston diaphragm, and the lugs are aligned with the depressions in the power piston.

17. The snap-ring on the master cylinder piston must be rotated to position lobes between reaction levers. The ears of reaction le-

vers must stay in place in machined seats on power piston as the diaphragm plate contacts power piston face. The position of the bead and levers must be correct as support plate is finally positioned and the ¼ in. screws tightened through the support plate and into power piston. Torque to 65-85 in. lbs.

18. Turn power piston assembly upside down to assemble air valve boot. Position large lip of boot in groove of power piston. Then place small diameter lip in groove in air valve.

19. Coat outside diameter of the tube-like boss on power piston with rubber trim cement and allow a minute or two to air dry. Then slip exhaust hose fully onto boss so hose is parallel to power piston.

20. Place gasket on front shell. Place the seal, master cylinder-to-housing, in groove on master cylinder body.

21. Place front shell on a flat surface with studs up. Insert and position master cylinder body on studs and press into front shell. Install lockwashers and nut, and torque to 15-20 ft. lbs.

22. Turn assembly upside down in a vise (so that the master cylinder bore is now accessible). Insert valve seat washer into bore. Press check valve into open end of spring and retainer assembly, and position in bore with check valve against valve seat washer. Dip the primary cup into clean brake fluid and place in bore with lips over the spring and retainer.

23. Work groove of pushrod boot into position in the center hole or the rear shell.

24. Place return spring over flange in center of front shell. Place power piston over front shell and insert master cylinder piston through return spring into master cylinder bore.

25. Press power piston assembly down and hold it in poisition while placing the bead of the power piston diaphragm into the recess in rim of front shell.

26. Place exhaust hose onto exhaust tube of rear shell assembly. Force pushrod through boot on rearshell. Press shell down and align the locking lugs.

NOTE: the following gauging operation is necessary only after structural parts have been replaced. It is also necessary if the exact number of shims removed at disassembly are not known.

With the brake cylinder in the released position, force air into the hydraulic outlet of the master cylinder. If air passes freely through the compensating port (the smaller of the two holes in the bottom of the master cylinder reservoir), shimming can be considered satisfactory. If air does not flow, remove the master cylinder and add shims until it does flow freely.

When the correct number of shims is in position, the master cylinder is assembled to the housing. After inserting the master cylinder piston into the bore and positioning the cylinder on the studs, the four attaching nuts should be torqued to 15-20 ft. lbs.

Installation

If linkage was removed, proceed as follows:

1. Place one operating lever on the collar. Tap in place until it seats against shoulder. Install second operating lever.

2. Place lever and collar in position and install pivot pin and cotter key.

3. Place one wave washer on inner side of outer operating lever (over the upper hole) and install clevis pin, flat washer and cotter pin to the power brake assembly operating rod.

4. Place the remaining wave washer on the inner side of the outer operating lever (over the middle hole) and install the clevis pin, flat washer and cotter key to the brake pedal pushrod.

5. Install the power brake assembly with the four attaching nuts and lockwashers.

6. Hook hydraulic line to master cylinder.

7. Attach vacuum lines.

8. Attach pushrod clevis to brake pedal assembly. Adjust pedal height by means of clevis on brake pedal pushrod at pedal.

Section 7
Moraine Diaphragm Type

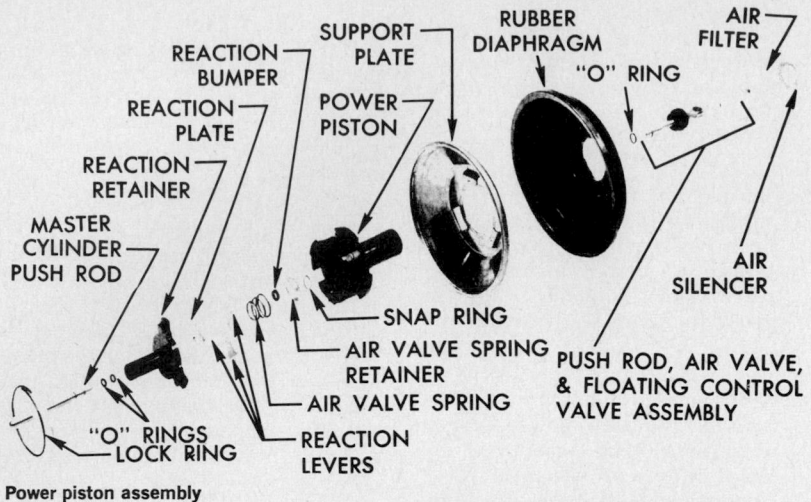

Power piston assembly

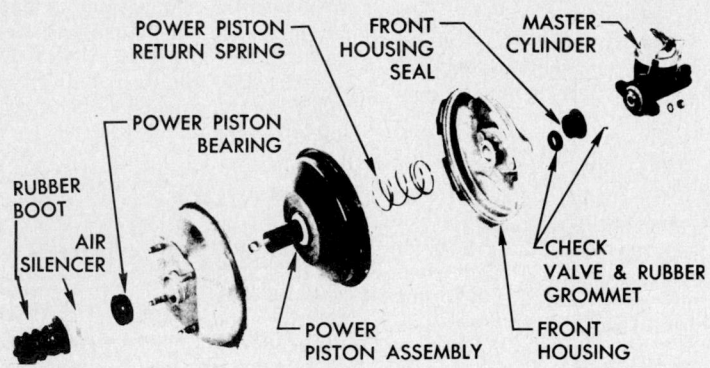

Power brake unit

17. Remove rolling diaphragm from support plate.
18. Place power piston, tube down, in vise. Do not clamp tube.
19. Remove snap-ring on air valve.
20. Using power ram, press and remove air valve assembly, using 3/8 in. drive extension as a remover.

21. Removal of air valve pushrod disassembles the floating control valve, floating valve retainer, pushrod limiter washer and air filters from the power piston.

22. Remove floating control valve assembly from pushrod, as it must be replaced by new floating control valve assembly.

23. Master cylinder pushrod can now be pushed from the center of reaction retainer. Remove O-rings from groove in master cylinder piston rod.

24. Carefully clean and inspect all parts, replace all seals, clean up any corrosion. Where corrosion is present, the entire system should be completely flushed and all new fluid used. Minor cleaning may be done with crocus cloth.

25. Reassemble in reverse of the above procedures.

Gauging is only necessary when major structural parts such as front or rear housing, power piston assembly, master cylinder piston or master cylinder assembly is replaced. To gauge, remove master cylinder so that master cylinder pushrod is exposed. Place gauge over piston rod so that it fits between the two studs on front of housing. The gap between the cutout of gauge and piston rod should be not more than .010 in. If corrections must be made a service adjustable piston rod and adjusting screw should be used.

Disassembly

1. Empty assembly and thoroughly clean outside surfaces.
2. Scribe mark on top center of front and rear housings and in line with the master cylinder reservoir cover.
3. Separate the housings by rotating counterclockwise.
4. Lift power piston and rear housing assembly from unit.
5. Remove clevis from pushrod, then jam nut. Remove boot from rear housing. Remove retaining ring on pushrod that holds silencer in place and remove silencer.
6. Remove power piston return spring from front housing.
7. While holding master cylinder in vise, remove front housing from master cylinder.
8. Remove nuts, lockwashers, and master cylinder. Master cylinder reconditioning is in the conventional manner.
9. Remove front housing seal, then the vacuum check valve and grommet from front housing.

10. Remove silencer from neck of power piston tube.
11. Remove lockring from power piston by prying one end from under large divided locking lug, then pull it from under the two small locking lugs on power piston.
12. Remove reaction retainer, piston rod, reaction plate, reaction levers and air valve spring.
13. Remove reaction bumper and air valve spring retainer from air valve.
14. Place power piston tool (J-21524) with square shank in vise. Hold support plate and power piston with tube of piston up.
15. Pull diaphragm edges away from support plate so that steel support plate can be gripped by hand. Position assembly so that the three lugs on tool fit into three notches in piston.
16. Press down on support plate and rotate counterclockwise until support plate separates from power piston.

Section 8
Midland-Ross Diaphragm Type

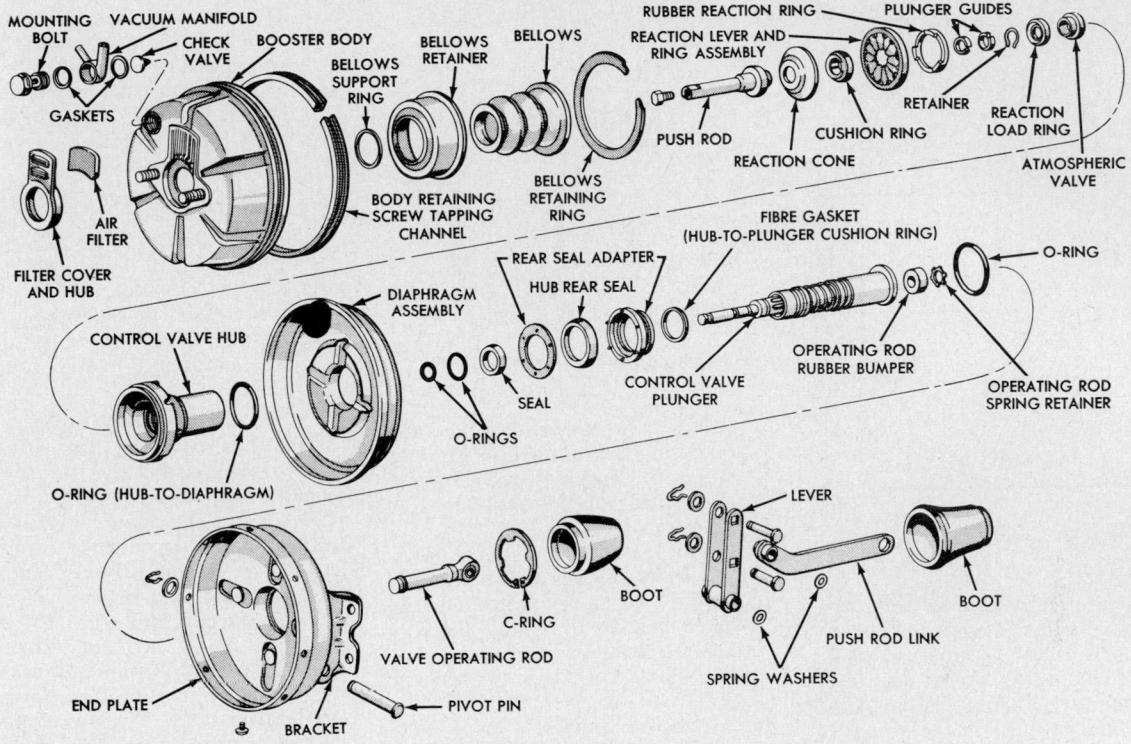

Disassembled view of booster

The self-contained booster assembly is mounted on the engine side of the firewall. It is connected directly to the brake pedal. This booster is not equipped with a separate vacuum tank.

The master cylinder is attached to the forward side of the booster. The balance of the hydraulic brake system is identical to other standard service brakes.

Booster Removal

1. Detach booster pushrod link from brake pedal.
2. Disconnect wires from the stoplight switch.
3. Disconnect hydraulic line at master cylinder.
4. Disconnect manifold vacuum hose from the booster. Remove transmission vacuum throttle valve hose.
5. Pull booster and bracket assembly from firewall.

Booster Repairs

1. Separate master cylinder from booster body.
2. Remove air filter cover, hub and filter from booster body.
3. Remove vacuum manifold mounting bolt, manifold, gaskets and vacuum check valve from the booster body.

4. Disconnect valve operating rod from lever.
5. Disconnect lever from end plate brackets.
6. Remove two brackets from end plate.
7. Remove rubber boot from valve operating rod.
8. To remove the bellows, control valve, and diaphragm assemblies, remove large C-ring that holds the rear seal adapter assembly to the booster end plate.
9. Scribe matching lines on booster body and end plate. Remove retaining screws. Tap the outside of the plate with a soft hammer and separate plate from booster body.
10. Push bellows assembly into vacuum chamber and remove bellows, control valve, and diaphragm as an assembly.
11. Remove outer O-ring from control valve hub.
12. To disassemble bellows, pushrod, and control valve assemblies, remove large bellows retaining ring, bellows, bellows retainer, and support ring from diaphragm and valve assembly.
13. Remove retainer and support ring from bellows.
14. Remove pushrod assembly, reaction lever and ring assembly,

and rubber reaction ring from control valve hub.
15. Remove reaction cone and cushion ring from pushrod assembly. Then remove reaction levers from ring.
16. Remove two plastic plunger guides from control valve plunger. Then remove retainer that holds the reaction load ring and atmospheric valve on control valve hub.
17. Slide reaction load ring and atmospheric valve from control valve hub.
18. Separate control valve hub and plunger assembly from diaphragm by sliding the plunger and rear seal adapter from rear of hub. Then remove hub outer O-ring from front side of diaphragm.
19. To disassemble control valve plunger, remove hub rear seal adapter from valve plunger assembly, and remove seal from adapter.
20. Remove O-rings, seal, and fiber gaskets from plunger.
21. If plunger assembly needs replacement, hold plunger and pull out valve operating rod with pliers. Do not separate operating rod and plunger unless plunger is to be replaced.

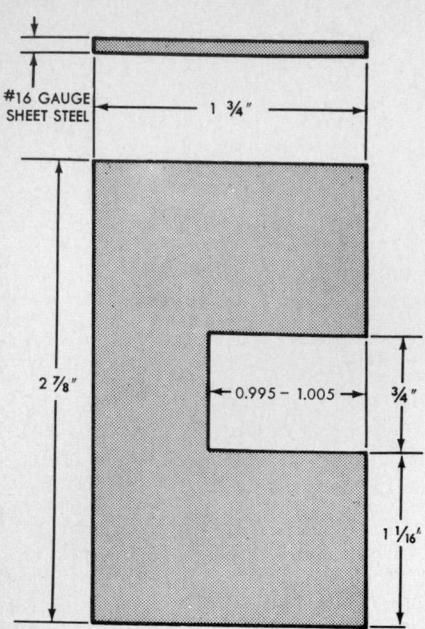

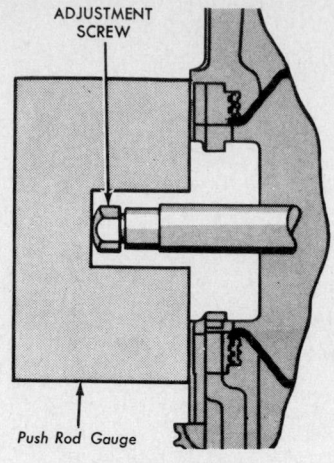

ADJUSTMENT SCREW

Push Rod Gauge

Checking pushrod screw with gauge

Pushrod gauge

Assembly

1. If valve operating rod was removed, install new rubber bumper spring retainer on rod before installing it on the replacement plunger. Then push rod firmly until it bottoms in plunger.
2. Install fiber gaskets, plunger seal, and two O-rings on the plunger assembly.
3. Install valve hub rear seal in adapter assembly with the sealing lip toward the rear. Then slide adapter assembly onto plunger with small end of the hub toward rear.
4. To assemble control valve, pushrod, and bellows, install hub outer O-ring. Then install plunger with seal adapter and hub on diaphragm. Hold hub on front side of the diaphragm and insert plunger assembly in hub from rear side of diaphragm.

5. Install atmospheric valve and reaction load ring onto plunger and hub. Compress valve spring, and install load ring retainer in groove of plunger.
6. Install two plastic plunger guides into their grooves on the plunger.
7. Install rubber reaction ring into valve hub so that ring locating knob indexes in the notch in the hub, with ring tips toward the front.
8. Assemble reaction lever and ring assembly, and install assembly into valve hub.
9. Install reaction cone and cushion ring on pushrod. Then install pushrod assembly on valve hub so that the plunger indexes in rod.
10. Assemble bellows, retainer, and support ring. The ring should be positioned on middle fold of bellows.
11. Position bellows assembly on diaphragm, and secure it with the retaining ring. Make sure retaining ring is fully seated.
12. Install bellows, control valve and diaphragm assemblies with a screwdriver, moving the booster

body retaining screw channel just enough to prove a new surface for the self-tapping screws.
13. Install diaphragm, control valve components, and bellows as an assembly into booster body. (Be sure lip of diaphragm is evenly positioned on the retaining radius of booster body). Pull front lip of bellows through booster body, and position it around outer groove of body.
14. Install O-ring in front side of end plate, and locate plate on booster body. Align the scribed lines, compress the two assemblies with a clamp. Then install alll ten self-tapping screws.
15. Install large C-ring onto rear seal adapter at rear side of end plate.

Pushrod Adjustment

The pushrod has an adjusting screw to maintain the correct relationship between the control valve plunger and the master cylinder piston after the booster is completely assembled. If this screw is not properly adjusted, the brakes may drag.

To check adjustment of the screw, make a gauge to the dimensions shown. Place this gauge against the master cylinder mounting surface of the booster body. The pushrod screw should be adjusted so that the end of the screw just touches the inner edge of the slot in the gauge.

Installation

1. Install rubber boot on valve operating rod.
2. Position the two mounting brackets on end plate, and install retaining nuts.
3. Connect lever assembly to lower end of mounting brackets. Then install spring washer and retaining clip.
4. Connect valve operating rod to upper end of lever.
5. Install vacuum check valve, vacuum manifold, two gaskets, and mounting bolt. Torque mounting bolt to 8-10 ft. lbs.

Section 9
Kelsey-Hayes Bellows Type

Removal

1. Use a pedal depressor. Depress pedal to prevent trigger arm from extending beyond bracket limits. If pedal linkage is permitted to extend through hole in firewall, the trigger arm may be damaged.
2. Disconnect vacuum hose at power vent.
3. Remove master cylinder power unit and bracket assembly, nuts and lock washers.
4. Withdraw unit from firewall. Don't lose the nylon bushing at pedal linkage crosspin.

Disassembly

1. Remove mounting plate-to-unit attaching nuts.
2. Slide plate off and away from unit.
3. Remove mounting plate O-ring.
4. With an Allen wrench, back out two set screws enough to permit removal of yoke.
5. Slide yoke from end of guide and away from unit.
6. Remove rubber stop seal washer.
7. Lift valve operating rod out of unit; remove, and discard valve operating rod button seal.
8. Remove outer mounting plate nuts.

9. Gently pry and lift the plate straight up and away from the unit.
10. Compress bellows by hand to expose the guide bearing. Slide bearing off end of guide.
11. Remove and discard bearing seal from outside bearing.
12. Peel outer lip of bellows from around inner mounting plate.
13. Remove plate and lift out return spring and retainer.
14. Remove bolts and lockwashers that attach valve cover to valve. Lift off cover.
15. Remove and discard O-ring from valve cover.

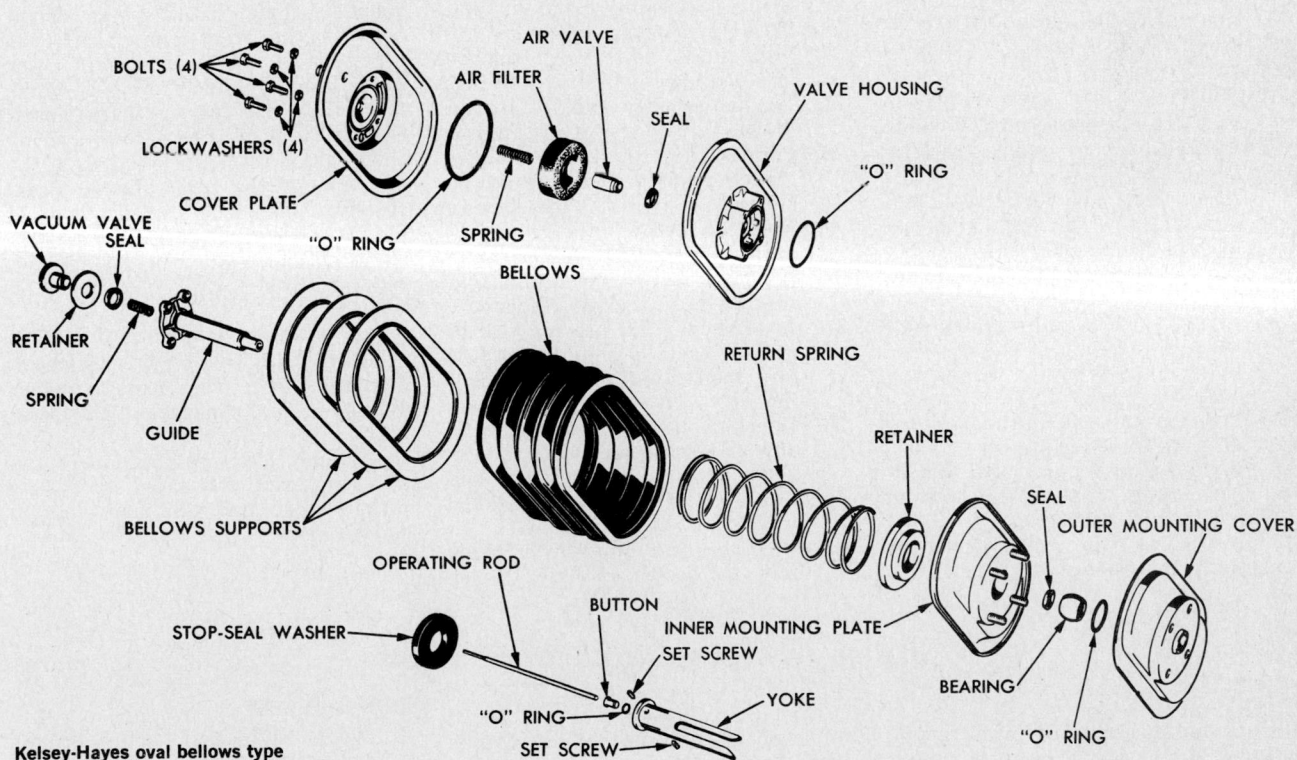

Kelsey-Hayes round bellows type

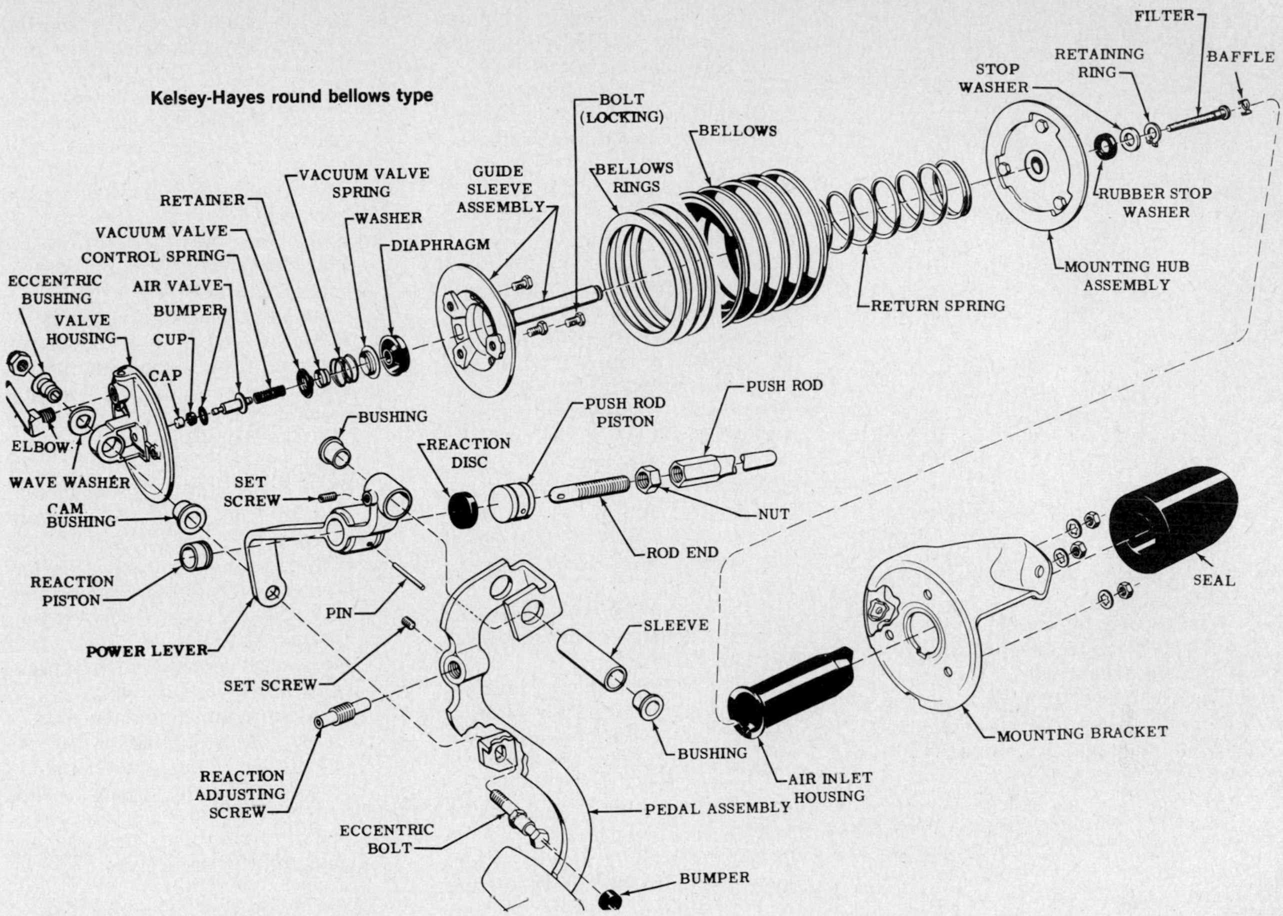

BOLT (LOCKING)
BELLOWS
BELLOWS RINGS
GUIDE SLEEVE ASSEMBLY
VACUUM VALVE SPRING
WASHER
DIAPHRAGM
RETAINER
VACUUM VALVE
CONTROL SPRING
AIR VALVE
BUMPER
CUP
CAP
ECCENTRIC BUSHING
VALVE HOUSING
ELBOW
WAVE WASHER
CAM BUSHING
REACTION PISTON
SET SCREW
REACTION DISC
PUSH ROD PISTON
PUSH ROD
NUT
ROD END
SLEEVE
BUSHING
POWER LEVER
PIN
SET SCREW
REACTION ADJUSTING SCREW
ECCENTRIC BOLT
PEDAL ASSEMBLY
AIR INLET HOUSING
BUMPER
SEAL
MOUNTING BRACKET
FILTER
RETAINING RING
BAFFLE
STOP WASHER
RUBBER STOP WASHER
MOUNTING HUB ASSEMBLY
RETURN SPRING

BOLTS (4)
AIR VALVE
AIR FILTER
SEAL
VALVE HOUSING
LOCKWASHERS (4)
COVER PLATE
"O" RING
SPRING
"O" RING
VACUUM VALVE SEAL
RETAINER
SPRING
GUIDE
BELLOWS
BELLOWS SUPPORTS
RETURN SPRING
RETAINER
SEAL
OUTER MOUNTING COVER
OPERATING ROD
STOP-SEAL WASHER
BUTTON
INNER MOUNTING PLATE
SET SCREW
BEARING
"O" RING
YOKE
"O" RING
SET SCREW

Kelsey-Hayes oval bellows type

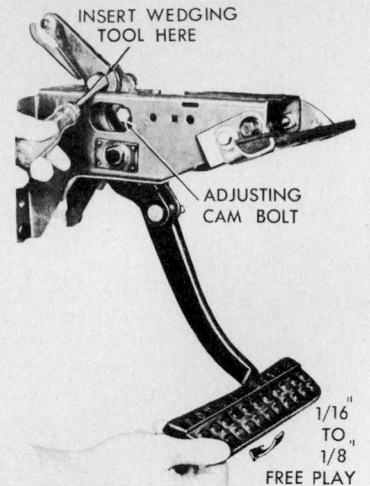

INSERT WEDGING TOOL HERE

ADJUSTING CAM BOLT

1/16" TO 1/8" FREE PLAY

Pedal play adjustment (© Ford Motor Co.)

16. Remove air valve spring from center of valve.
17. Remove air filter and pull the air valve out of the housing using a small bent wire.
18. Place valve housing on bench. Remove bellows from valve by peeling back outer lip of bellows.
19. Lift bellows up, away from valve.
20. Remove guide-to-valve body bolts and lift off guide to expose vacuum valve, valve spring and seals.
21. Remove seals, then lift out vacuum valve and retainer.
22. Remove valve housing-to-guide seal.
23. Insert valve housing and remove air valve seal from groove in valve body.

Assembly

Lubricate all seals and O-rings with silicone grease before installation.

1. Insert new air valve seal into bore of valve housing (with lips of seal facing out).
2. Position new vacuum valve in retainer.
3. Invert valve housing and install vacuum valve and retainer.
4. Press down firmly on retainer to snap it in place.
5. Position new valve housing-to-guide seal in groove.
6. Install new vacuum valve seal in bore guide, (lip of seal toward bottom of bore).
7. Install vacuum valve spring in center of valve.

8. Position guide over vacuum valve, lining up bolt in guide with bolt holes in valve body.
9. Lower guide down against valve body. Be certain that the tapered portion of valve enters seal evenly.
10. Press down on guide to seal and install bolts and lock washers. Tighten bolts evenly.
11. If new bellows is being installed, position supports in bellows.
12. Using holding fixture (made from 3 in. length of 4 in. diameter pipe) to support guide and valve assembly in upright position, install the bellows. Be sure arrows on edge of bellows and housing are aligned.
13. With assembly in holding fixture, wipe outer surface of air valve with silicone grease and insert the small end into bore of housing.
14. Use finger pressure to test for free movement of valve against vacuum valve spring.
15. Install air valve spring into recess in air valve and air filter.
16. Install new valve housing cover O-ring on shoulder provided on valve body hub.
17. Position valve body cover over valve housing, with notch in edge of cover matching arrow on bellows. Be sure air valve spring rests on dimple in center of cover.
18. Press cover down evenly over valve housing to seat over O-ring, install bolts, then tighten securely.
19. Remove assembly from holding fixture and invert unit.
20. Wipe guide lightly with silicone grease and install return spring.
21. Position spring evenly around hub of valve housing and guide.
22. Place spring retainer and inner mounting plate over spring, (be sure arrow marks on plate are in line with arrow on edge of bellows).
23. Compress return spring and fold bellows lip over edge of plate.
24. Install new guide bearing seal in groove inside bearing bore.
25. Seat the seal snugly in the bearing.
26. Lubricate inside of bearing with silicone grease and slide it over guide, while compressing bellows. (Bearing to be installed with lip of seal facing out.)
27. Push bearing down over guide and into pocket of plate.

28. Release bellows and the bearing will ride up guide with plate into position.
29. Install bearing-to-mounting plate O-ring and lower outer mounting plate down on assembly.
30. Install nuts and draw down finger tight.
31. Slide new valve operating rod seal ring over nylon bumper on end of rod and into groove.
32. Install rod in center of guide.
33. Press on end of rod to test for free operation or movement of air and vacuum vanes. A two-step movement should be felt when rod is depressed and released fully.
34. Place new stop seal washer in position and install yoke on end of guide.
35. Compress bellows slightly and alternately tighten set screws. Hub of yoke must be down snug against shoulder of guide, with set screws aligned with tapered holes in guide.
36. Tighten mounting plate nuts.
37. Place mounting bracket in position, with long centerline of bracket at right angle to long centerline of unit section.
38. Install nuts and lockwashers, then tighten securely.

Pedal Free-Play (On the Car)

A pedal free-play check should be made with no vacuum in the system. Apply the brakes several times (engine not running) to exhaust the vacuum supply. Insert a screwdriver between the trigger pivot and the rear side of the hole in the power brake lever. This will force the brake pedal and the power lever apart. Check free-play with screwdriver in this position by pressing lightly at the pad end of the brake pedal. Pedal free-play should be 1/16 in.-1/8 in. If play is not correct, adjust by lengthening or shortening the master cylinder pushrod.

Trigger Adjustment

After pedal free-play is adjusted, final check should be made to insure maximum performance of the booster.

A slight clockwise rotation of the adjusting cam will speed up a slow pedal return and eliminate lag on sudden stops.

Section 10
Kelsey-Hayes Diaphragm Type

Identification

This power brake unit was incorporated in Chrysler Corporation cars during the first part of 1964.

The Kelsey-Hayes power brake unit can be identified by the twist-lock housing and cover, plus the white-colored vacuum check valve assembly.

Removal

1. With engine off, apply brakes several times to equalize internal brake pressure.
2. Disconnect hydraulic line from

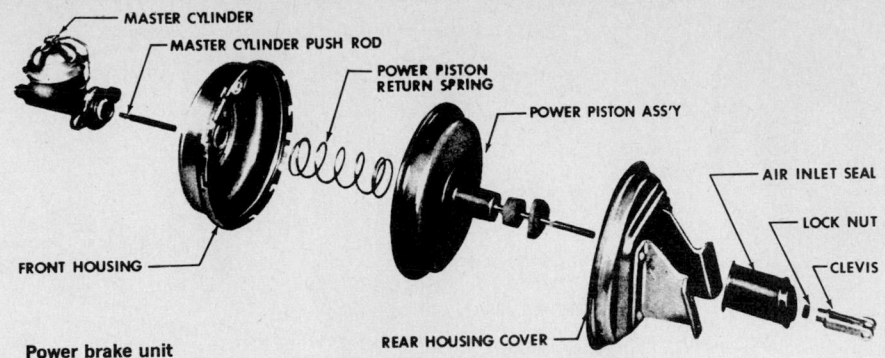

MASTER CYLINDER
MASTER CYLINDER PUSH ROD
POWER PISTON RETURN SPRING
POWER PISTON ASS'Y
AIR INLET SEAL
LOCK NUT
CLEVIS
FRONT HOUSING
REAR HOUSING COVER

Power brake unit

master cylinder.

3. Disconnect vacuum hose from power brake check valve.
4. Disconnect power brake from brake pedal (under instrument panel).
5. Disconnect power brake unit from firewall and remove.

Disassembly

1. Separate master cylinder from power brake unit.
2. Remove master cylinder pushrod and air cleaner plate.
3. Mount the power unit in a vise with master cylinder studs up. (A handy mounting bracket is the engine lifting fixture tool C-3804.)
4. Scribe an index line across the housing and cover for reassembly reference.
5. Pry out the housing lock. Do not damage lock, as it must be used at assembly.
6. Remove check valve from cover by prying out of rubber grommet.
7. Place parking brake flange holding tool C-3281 over the master cylinder mounting studs.
8. Rotate tool and cover counterclockwise. Then, separate the cover from the housing. This will expose the power piston return spring and diaphragm.
9. Lift out power piston return spring. Remove brake unit from vise.
10. Remove power piston by slowly lifting the piston straight up.
11. Remove air cleaner, guide seal and seal retainer from cover.
12. Remove block seal from center hole of housing, using a blunt drift. (Do not scratch the bore of the housing; it could cause a vacuum leak.)

Power Piston Disassembly

1. Remove power piston diaphragm from piston. Keep it clean.
2. Remove screws that attach plastic guide to power piston. Remove guide and place to one side.
3. Remove the power piston square seal ring, reaction ring insert, re-

action ring and reaction plate.

4. Depress operating rod slightly, then remove the Truarc snapring.
5. Remove control piston by pulling the operating rod.
6. Remove O-ring seal from end of control piston.
7. Remove filter elements and felt from control piston rod.

Cleaning and Inspection

Thoroughly wash all metal parts in a suitable solvent and dry with compessed air. *The power diaphragm, plastic power piston and guide should be washed in a mild soap and water solution.* Blow dust and all cleaning material out of internal passages. All rubber parts should be replaced, regardless of condition. Install new air filters at assembly. Inspect all parts for scoring, pits, dents or nicks. Small imperfections can be smoothed out with crocus cloth. Replace all badly damaged parts.

Assembly

When assembling, be sure that all rubber parts, except the diaphragm and the reaction ring, are lubricated with silicone grease.

1. Install control piston O-ring onto piston.
2. Lubricate and install control piston into power piston. Install Truarc snap-ring into groove. Wipe all lubricant off the end of control piston.
3. Install air filter elements and felt seal over the pushrod and down past retaining shoulder on the rod. Install power piston square seal ring into its groove.
4. Install reaction plate in power piston. Align the three holes with those in the power piston.
5. Install rubber reaction ring in reaction plate. *Do not lubricate this ring.*
6. Lubricate outer diameter of reaction insert and install in reaction ring.
7. Install reaction insert bumper into guide.
8. Place guide on power piston, align holes wih aligning points on the power piston. Install re-

taining screws and torque to 80-100 in. lbs.

9. Install diaphragm on power piston; be sure that the diaphragm is correctly seated in the power piston groove.
10. With the housing blocked to prevent damage, install block seal in housing, using tool C-3205 or suitable substitute.
11. Install a new cover seal on the retainer and lubricate thoroughly, inside and out, with silicone grease, then install in the cover bore. Install new air filter.
12. Lubricate check valve grommet and install vacuum check valve.
13. Mount the power unit in a vise, with master cylinder attaching studs up. (Use the same engine lifting fixture, tool C-3804, if available.)
14. Apply a light coating of silicone grease to the bead, *outer edge only,* of the power piston diaphragm.
15. Install power piston assembly in housing with the operating rod down.
16. Install power piston return spring into flange of guide.
17. Place cover over return spring and press down. At the same time, pilot the guide through the seal.
18. Rotate cover to lock it to the housing. Be sure scribe lines are in correct index and that the diaphragm is not pinched during assembly.
19. Install housing lock on one of the long tangs of the housing.
20. Remove power unit from vise and remove mounting bracket, if used.
21. Install master cylinder push-rod and air cleaner plate, then install master cylinder on studs. Install attaching nuts and washers. Torque to 200 in. lbs.

Installation

1. Install firewall-to-power brake seal.
2. Install power brake unit onto firewall and troque the attaching nuts to 200 in. lbs.

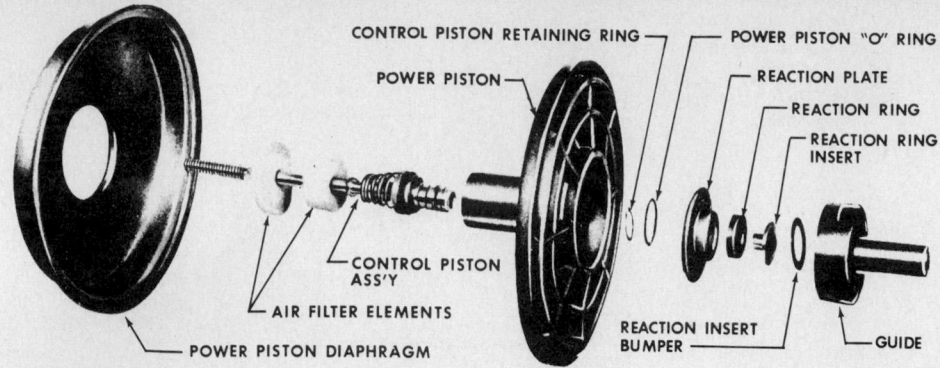

CONTROL PISTON RETAINING RING — POWER PISTON "O" RING
POWER PISTON — REACTION PLATE
REACTION RING
REACTION RING INSERT
CONTROL PISTON ASS'Y
AIR FILTER ELEMENTS
POWER PISTON DIAPHRAGM
REACTION INSERT BUMPER — GUIDE

Power piston assembly

3. Install pushrod-to-brake pedal attaching bolt. Torque to 30 ft. lbs.
4. Install vacuum hose onto power brake unit.
5. Attach hydraulic tube and fill master cylinder. Bleed hydraulic system.
6. Adjust stop-light switch if necessary.

Testing Operations

Vacuum Leak, Released Position

With transmission in Neutral or Park, stop the engine and wait one minute. Apply the brake several times. Each application should provide less and less assist, as a result of normal depletion of reserve vacuum.

The number of applications on reserve vacuum assist will depend on how hard the pedal is applied and how far the pedal travels. If vacuum assist is not present, an air leak is indicated.

Unit Operation

After depleting the reserve vacuum, apply light foot pressure to the pedal, then start the engine. If the power system is working properly, the pedal will fall away slightly, as vacuum is restored.

Vacuum Leak, Holding Position

With transmission in neutral or park, stop the engine while holding a moderately heavy load on the brake pedal. After one minute, release and apply the pedal several times. If there is no vacuum assist during this test, but the system was normal during test No. 1, there is an air leak wihin the unit. Some units will leak air internally if the pedal load is light. This is a normal condition.

Hydraulic Leak Test

Depress the brake pedal lightly while engine is running, maintaining constant pressure. If the pedal falls noticeably in one minute, the hy-draulic system is probably leaking.

If the pedal has a spongy feel, air may be present in the hydraulic system.

Road test the car, making a brake application at about 40 mph to determine if the car stops evenly and quickly.

If system tests are satisfactory and the pedal travels to within 1 in. of the floor pan, the brake shoes probably need adjustment or replacement.

General Inspection

1. Check for free operation and return of the brake pedal. If binding exists, check all pivot points and lubricate as required.
2. Check stop-light switch for operation and possible adjustment.
3. Inspect master cylinder for proper fluid level.
4. Inspect vacuum line and connections for leaks.

Section 11
Bendix Single Diaphragm Hydrovac

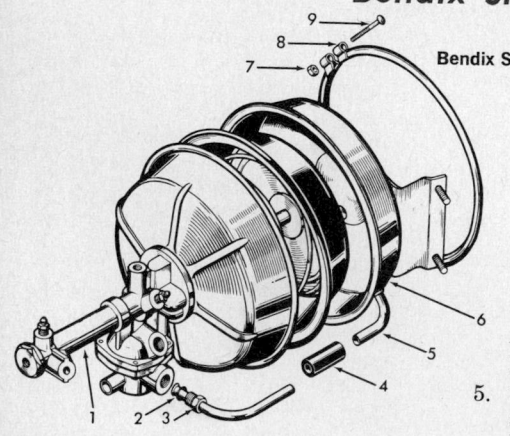

Bendix Single Diaphragm Hydrovac Power Brake
(© Chevrolet Div., G.M. Corp.)

1 Hydraulic cylinder
2 Control tube seal
3 Control tube nut
4 Vacuum hose
5 Rear shell control tube
6 Rear shell
7 Nut
8 Clamp band
9 Clamp bolt

Removal

1. Empty system and thoroughly clean outside of assembly.
2. Scribe across front and rear shells. Clamp hydraulic cylinder in vise in horizontal position.
3. Remove clamp and separate shells.
4. Turn rim of diaphragm back and

press support plate to compress diaphragm return spring.
5. Using snap-ring pliers, remove snap-ring from groove inside bore of hydraulic cylinder.
6. Pull diaphragm assembly straight out of cylinder. Parts may be removed from assembly by removing nut from diaphragm end.

Pushrod and Piston Disassembly

1. Piston rod parts are removed

from the pushrod at the piston end of the pushrod.
2. Slide retainer ring out of groove in piston and separate piston from pushrod by removing retainer pin.
3. With thin-bladed screw driver remove piston cap from piston. Slide off seal retainer, pushrod seal cup, pushrod bearing, stop washer and snap ring.
4. Remove O-ring seal from bearing groove.
5. If necessary, remove pushrod seal from end of pushrod with pliers and discard.

Control Valve Disassembly

1. Scribe across flanges of control valve body and hydraulic cylinder housing.
2. Remove four cap screws and lift off valve body and spring.
3. Remove washer, diaphragm, washer and cup from valve piston.

1 End cap
2 Gasket
3 Hydraulic cylinder housing
4 Cup
5 Valve piston
6 Washer
7 Diaphragm
8 Washer
9 Valve body spring
10 Vacuum poppet and stem
11 Poppet spring
12 Control valve body
13 Capscrews
14 Poppet
15 Retainer
16 Valve body cover
A Pressure check valve
B Spring
C Snap-ring retainer
D Snap-ring

Control valve (© Chevrolet Div., G.M. Corp.)

Control Valve Assembly

1. Assemble cup facing up on control valve piston. If two cups are used install them on piston back to back. Then assemble piston, washer, and diaphragm, seating inner bed of diaphragm in piston groove.
2. Lay piston and diaphragm assembly aside. Assemble poppet return spring, vacuum poppet, and atmospheric poppet in valve body from opposite sides.
3. Snap poppet retainer over end of vacuum poppet stem.
4. Assemble cover securely in groove of valve body. Assemble spring retainer washer and spring on end of control valve piston. Insert control valve piston, diaphragm and spring assembly in valve body with spring around bosses.
5. Press outer bead of diaphragm onto valve body groove and, while holding spring compressed, dip piston and cup in clean brake fluid.
6. Align valve body to scribe marks and assemble control valve piston carefully in its bore below hydraulic cylinder bore. Secure valve body with four capscrews.
7. Tighten screws to 40-60 in. lbs. Install check valve, spring, retainer and snap ring in end fitting. Install fitting and gasket

4. Using screw driver, pry off plastic valve body cover.
5. Pry off plastic retainer, lift off atmospheric poppet and then remove vacuum poppet and stem and poppet spring from valve body.
6. Using 1⅜ in. wrench, remove end cap and gasket.
7. If residual pressure check valve is used, lift snap-ring from groove inside the cap. Remove spring retainer, spring and residual pressure check valve.

Piston and Pushrod Assembly

1. To install a new pushrod seal in pushrod, place the new seal (rubber side down) on a clean block of wood. Hold pushrod vertically with drilled end of rod resting on shaft end of seal and strike upper end with a soft mallet to seat.
2. Dip cup in brake fluid and assemble cup on piston.
3. Slide snap-ring, stop washer, bearing (with O-ring installed in groove), pushrod seal cup, seal retainer, retainer ring and piston assembly on pushrod, in that order.
4. Assemble retainer pin through holes in piston and rod. Secure pin in place with retainer ring, making sure ring is seated in groove on piston.

Front Shell Assembly

1. Place new gasket in groove on flange of hydraulic cylinder.
2. Assemble front shell to cylinder, aligning cutout in shell with porting in cylinder flange.
3. Assemble capscrew; tighten to 130-230 in. lbs.
4. If diaphragm plate and return spring were disassembled, install nut and tighten to 160-200 in. lbs.; then washer, diaphragm plate, (concave side first) on threaded end of pushrod.
5. Install diaphragm, washer, and

nut on pushrod, and tighten nuts to 160-200 in. lbs.
6. Coat hydraulic cylinder bore with clean brake fluid. Dip piston and bearing parts in brake fluid. Slide diaphragm return spring onto pushrod, large diameter first.
7. Seat spring against concave surface of diaphragm plate and align entire assembly with hydraulic cylinder bore.
8. Carefully insert hydraulic piston assembly, retainer, seal and bearing into cylinder bore. Press against diaphragm and plate to compress return spring, seat stop-washer against bearing inside bore, and install snap-ring groove in cylinder bore.

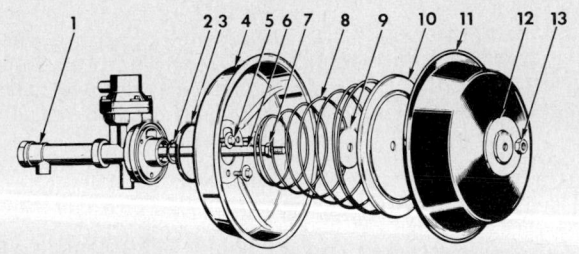

Diaphragm and front shell assembly (© Chevrolet Div., G.M. Corp.)

1 Hydraulic cylinder
2 Snap-ring
3 Gasket
4 Front shell
5 Capscrews
6 Pushrod
7 Nut
8 Return spring
9 Washer
10 Diaphragm plate
11 Diaphragm
12 Washer
13 Nut

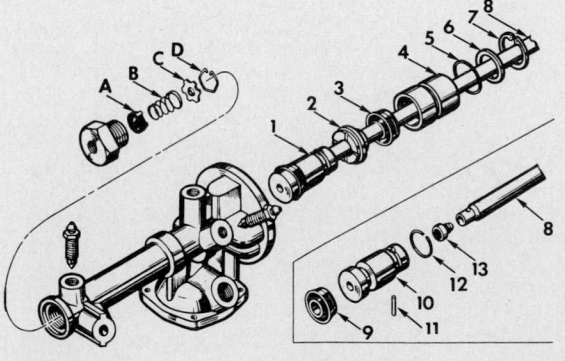

Pushrod and piston (© Chevrolet Div., G.M. Corp.)

1 Piston
2 Seal retainer
3 Pushrod seal cup
4 Pushrod bearing
5 O-ring seal
6 Stop washer
7 Snap-ring
8 Pushrod
9 Piston cup
10 Piston (same as item 1)
11 Retainer pin
12 Retainer ring
13 Pushrod seal

on end of hydraulic cylinder and tighten fitting to 50-85 ft. lbs. If removed, install bleed screws; tighten to 10-15 ft. lbs.

Rear Shell, Control Tube, Hose Assembly

1. Coat bead of diaphragm or flanges of front and rear shells with talcum powder or equival-

ent and place rear shell on diaphragm.
2. Align scribe marks on both shells. Make certain bead of diaphragm is seated in outer flanges of both shells and hold rear shell in position while assembling clamp band over flanges. Position opening of clamp band 45 degrees off vertical center line

away from mounting bracket.
3. Squeeze ends of band together and tighten nut and bolt.
4. Place new seal on control tube, and assemble hose to tube on rear shell and to control tube. Attach tube and nut to control valve body port.

Section 12
Bendix Tandem Diaphragm Hydrovac

Control Tube, Rear Shell, Center Shell Disassembly

1. Empty system and thoroughly clean outside of assembly.
2. Scribe across shells and clamp bands. Clamp hydraulic cylinder in vise in horizontal position.
3. Remove hose clamps, hose tee. Disconnect control tube from control valve housing.
4. Remove rear clamp band and rear shell. Remove front clamp band, center shell, and diaphragm assembly.

Diaphragm Return Spring, Hydraulic Parts Disassembly

1. Use a ¾ in. diameter hose tee or a block of wood with a ¾ in. hole over the end of the pushrod and press to compress return spring. Using snap-ring pliers, remove snap-ring from groove inside bore of end plate.
2. Using both hands, carefully pull assembly straight out of cylinder. Parts may be removed from assembly by removing retainer ring and spring retainer from pushrod. To remove front shell, remove three capscrews and lift front shell and support plate off flange of cylinder.

Pushrod and Piston Disassembly

1. Piston parts are removed from the pushrod from the piston end.
2. Slide retainer ring out of groove in piston and separate piston from pushrod by removing retainer pin.
3. With thin-bladed screw driver remove piston cap from piston. Slide off seal retainer, pushrod seal, pushrod bearing, stop washer and snap-ring.

Control Valve and Check Valve Disassembly

1. Scribe across flanges of control valve body and hydraulic cylinder housing.
2. Remove four cap screws and lift off valve body and spring.
3. Remove washer, diaphragm,

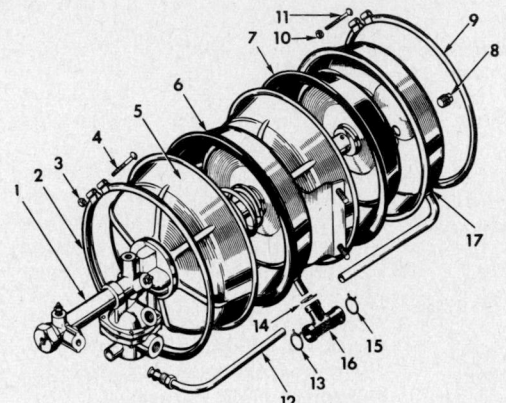

Bendix Tandem Diaphragm Type Power Brake (© Dodge Div., Chrysler Corp.)

1 Hydraulic cylinder
2 Clamp ring
3 Nut
4 Bolt
5 Front shell
6 Center shell
7 Diaphragm
8 Pipe plug
9 Clamp ring
10 Nut
11 Bolt
12 Control tube
13 Hose clamp
14 Hose clamp
15 Hose clamp
16 Hose tee
17 Rear shell

washer and cup from valve piston.
4. Using screw driver, pry off plastic valve body cover.
5. Pry off plastic retainer, lift off atmospheric poppet and then remove vacuum poppet and stem and poppet spring from valve body.
6. Using 1⅜ in. wrench, remove end cap and gasket.
7. To disassemble pressure check valve, lift snap-ring from groove inside end cap. Remove spring retainer, spring and residual pressure check valve.

Diaphragm and Center Shell Disassembly

1. Clamp nut on end of shaft in vise and remove nut, diaphragm, and washer from shaft. *Carefully* slide center shell assembly off shaft and remove seal from groove inside brass bearing hub with ice pick.
2. Remove shaft and diaphragm assembly from vise and insert drift punch through holes in shaft next to diaphragm. Use 1¾ in. wrench to remove nut from end of shaft.
3. Slide washer, diaphragm, diaphragm plate and washer off end of shaft. *No further disassembly is possible without damage to parts.*

Cleaning and Inspection Note

Thoroughly clean all metal parts

in denatured alcohol or suitable cleaner. Inspect all parts not included in repair pack for excessive wear. Replace any that are worn or damaged. Inspect control valve body atmospheric valve seat. If damaged, replace housing.

Diaphragm and Center Shell Assembly

1. Slide washer, diaphragm plate, diaphragm, washer on shaft and thread nut until tight.
2. Insert drift punch through holes in shaft next to diaphragm and use 1¾ in. wrench to tighten nut securely. Stake nut to washer in two places. Press new O-ring seal into groove inside brass bearing hub of center shell. Clamp nut on end of shaft in vise and lubricate shaft with Lubriplate.
3. Lubricate inside of brass bearing hub and seal in center shell assembly and slide center shell carefully on shaft, seal side of hub last.
4. Install washer on pushrod end of shaft, followed by diaphragm, diaphragm plate, and nut. With nut securely held by vise, tighten nut to 160-200 in. lbs. and stake nut in place.

Control Valve and Check Valve Assembly

1. Assemble poppet return spring, vacuum poppet and stem and atmospheric poppet in valve body

from opposite sides. Snap poppet retainer over end of vacuum poppet stem.

2. Assemble valve body cover securely in groove of body. Dip cups in clean brake fluid and assemble back-to-back on valve piston.

3. Align valve body to scribe mark, seat outer edge of diaphragm in groove in valve body and assemble four capscrews.

4. To assemble residual pressure check valve, install check valve in end cap, followed by spring and spring retainer, concave center diameter centered on spring. Compress spring and install snap-ring in groove inside end cap. Place new gasket on end cap and install end cap in cylinder.

Piston and Pushrod Assembly

1. To install a new pushrod seal in pushrod, place new seal (rubber side down) on a clean block of wood. Hold pushrod vertically with drilled end of rod resting on shaft end of seal and strike upper end with a soft mallet to seat.

2. Dip cup in clean brake fluid and assemble cup to piston.

3. Slide snap-ring, stop washer, bearing with O-ring installed in groove, pushrod seal cup, seal retainer, retainer ring and piston assembly on pushrod, in that order.

4. Assemble retainer pin through holes in piston and rod. Secure pin in place with retainer ring, making sure ring is seated in groove on piston.

Front Shell, Return Spring and Hydraulic Parts Assembly

1. Place new gasket in groove on flange of hydraulic cylinder.

2. Assemble front shell and support plate to cylinder, aligning cutouts in shell and plate with porting in cylinder flange, and assemble capscrews securely.

3. Coat hydraulic cylinder bore with clean brake fluid. If removed, install spring retainer and snap-ring on end of pushrod.

4. Dip hydraulic piston and bearing parts in brake fluid. Slide diaphragm return spring on pushrod, small end first, over hydraulic piston end. Seat spring against concave surface of spring retainer and then align entire assembly.

5. Carefully insert piston, bearing and seals in bore.

6. Slide hose tee (or block of wood with hole) on end of pushrod and press against it to compress return spring. Using both hands seat stop washer against bearing inside bore and install snap-ring in groove in cylinder bore.

Shell and Diaphragm Assembly

1. With hydraulic cylinder held in vise with bleed screws up, guide center shell and diaphragm assembly onto end of pushrod, seating rod in end of rear shaft.

2. Align scribe marks on center shell and front shell and press together to seat bead of front diaphragm in flanges of shells. Dust diaphragm and flanges with talcum powder.

3. Assemble clamp band over shell flanges, (opening 45 degrees from vertical center line on side away from bracket.)

4. Tighten nut and bolt of band.

5. Assemble rear shell to scribe marks and seat bead of rear diaphragm in shell flanges.

6. Assemble rear clamp band over shell flanges in line with front clamp.

7. Place new seal on control tube, and assemble hose tee to tubes on rear shell, center shell, and control tube.

8. Attach control tube and nut to control valve body port. Tighten tube nut. If removed, install pipe plug in port in rear shell.

Section 13
Delco-Moraine Tandem-Diaphragm Type

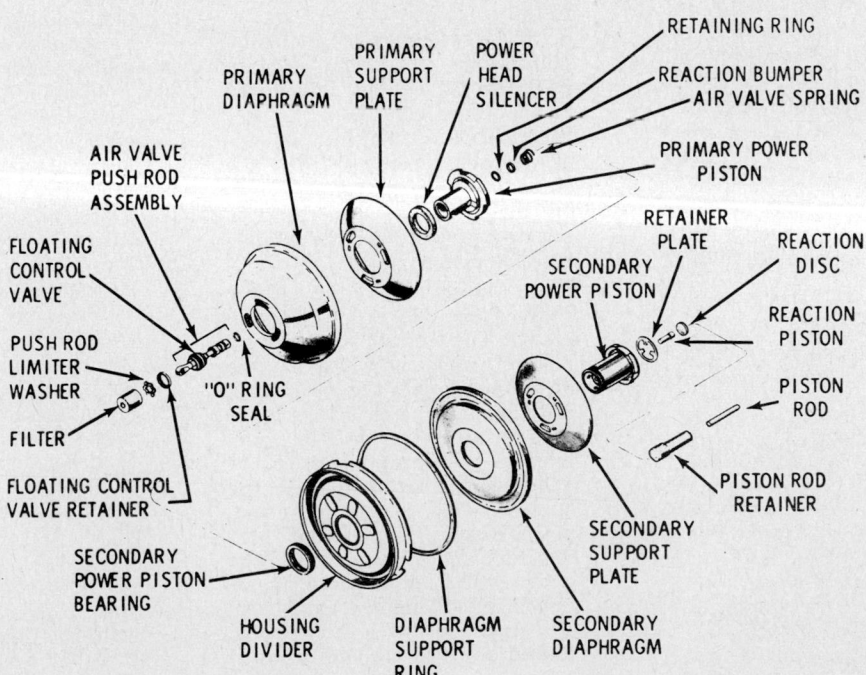

Delco-Moraine Tandem Diaphragm Power Brake (© Oldsmobile Div., G.M. Corp.)

Disassembly

1. Empty system and clean outside throughly. Be sure no oil or grease contacts the diaphragm unit.
2. Scribe front and rear housings for alignment. Remove front housing seal and master cylinder pin.
3. Using Tool J-23456, separate shells. Remove front shell, return spring retainer plate and piston rod retainer.
4. Remove dust boot retainer, boot and pushrod from rear housing. Remove felt silencers.
5. Remove power piston assembly from rear shell and primary power piston bearing from center opening.
6. Lift bead of secondary diaphragm and remove diaphragm
7. Mount Tool J-23101 in vise and position secondary power piston on tool.
8. Fold back primary diaphragm and unscrew primary power piston from secondary power piston.
9. Remove the housing divider from the secondary power piston and the bearing from the housing divider.
10. Fold back secondary diaphragm and unscrew secondary support plate from secondary power piston. Remove diaphragm from support plate.
11. Push down on end of reaction piston of secondary power piston to remove the reaction piston.
12. Remove air valve spring from end of air valve.
13. Position primary power piston on small jaws of Tool J-23101. Fold back primary diaphragm and primary support plate from primary power piston.
14. Remove primary diaphragm from primary support plate.
15. Remove air filter and pushrod limiter washer from primary power piston.
16. Remove power head silencer from neck of power piston tube.
17. Remove rubber reaction bumper from air valve.
18. Remove snap ring from air valve.
19. Pull primary power piston to remove air valve pushrod assembly.
20. Remove O-ring seal from air valve.

Assembly

1. Discard all old rubber parts except the power diaphragms. Lubricate O-ring with silicone lubricant and place on air valve.
2. If floating control valve needs replacement, replace complete air valve pushrod assembly.
3. Lubricate floating control valve with silicone lubricant and place air valve end into tube of primary power piston. Push air valve

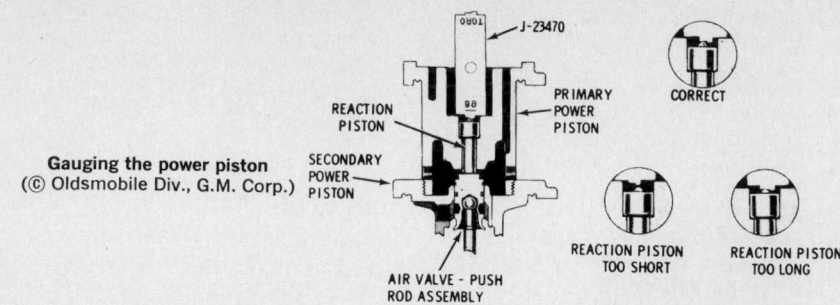

Gauging the power piston
(© Oldsmobile Div., G.M. Corp.)

pushrod assembly so floating control valve bottoms on tube section of primary power piston.
4. Press retainer into primary power piston with Tool J-23175.
5. Place pushrod limiter washer over pushrod and position on the floating control valve.
6. Install filter element over the pushrod eye and press into primary power piston tube.
7. Place snap-ring into groove in air valve.
8. Install rubber reaction bumper on air valve.
9. If either power piston has been replaced, proceed to step 10, otherwise proceed to step 17.
10. To maintain correct power output, the power piston assembly must be gauged for selective fit of the reaction piston if either power piston is replaced.
11. Hand tighten the secondary power piston to the primary power piston without the air valve spring.
12. Insert reaction piston into its cavity in the secondary power piston.
13. With the secondary power piston pointing up, push on the reaction piston to insure that it is seated on the air valve.
14. Insert Tool J-23470 into secondary power piston so that the outer edge of the gauge rests on the bottom, with the two gauging levels within the smaller reaction piston cavity.
15. Move the gauge to the left or right of the nose of the reaction piston. The correct size reaction piston is indicated when the nose of the piston hits the lower level of the gauge and clears the higher level of the gauge while permitting the outer edges of the gauge to remain seated on the larger cavity of the secondary power piston. If the reaction piston is too short, both levels of the gauge will clear the nose. If the piston is too long, the gauge will not seat.
16. Repeat steps 12 through 15 until a correct size piston is found. Selective fit reaction pistons are available as follows:

98 SERIES

Color	Size
Red	1.148 in.–1.154 in.
Yellow	1.161 in.–1.167 in.
Blue	1.174 in.–1.180 in.

TORONADO SERIES

Color	Size
Red	1.178 in.–1.184 in.
Yellow	1.191 in.–1.197 in.
Blue	1.204 in.–1.210 in.
White	1.217 in.–1.223 in.

17. Lubricate and seat rubber reaction disc in large cavity of secondary power piston on reaction piston.
18. Unlock the two power pistons.
19. Assemble the primary diaphragm to the primary support plate from the side of the support plate opposite the locking tangs. Press the raised flange on the I.D. of the diaphragm through the center hole of the support plate. Be sure that the edge of the support plate center hole fits into the groove in the raised flange of the diaphragm. Lubricate diaphragm I.D. and the raised surface of the flange with silicone lubricant.
20. Fold diaphragm away from support plate. Place primary support plate and diaphragm assembly over tube of primary power piston. Screw on.
21. Place power head silencer on tube of primary power piston.
22. Assemble secondary diaphragm, support plate and power piston as described in paragraphs 19 and 20.
23. Place secondary diaphragm support ring on secondary power piston assembly so it rests on edge of diaphragm.
24. Hold housing divider with formed lip facing down and insert the secondary bearing so the extended lip of the bearing faces up.
25. Position Tool J-23188 on threaded end of secondary power piston. Hold the housing divider with the formed lip up and press it down over the tool and onto the secondary power piston till it rests on the supporting ring. Remove Tool J-23188.

26. Pick up primary power piston assembly and position small end of air valve return spring on air valve so it contacts air valve retaining ring.

27. Position the primary power piston on the tubular portion of the secondary power piston. Seat air valve return spring on raised center of secondary piston.

28. Screw secondary power piston securely onto primary power piston.

29. Fold primary diaphragm onto support plate and pull bead over formed lip of housing divider.

30. Lubricate O.D. of piston rod retainer. Insert master cylinder piston rod retainer into the cavity in the secondary power piston so flat end bottoms against rubber reaction disc.

31. Place primary power piston bearing in rear housing center hole so the thin lip of the bearing protrudes to the outside of the housing.

32. Coat inside of power piston bearing with silicone lubricant and assemble primary power piston to rear shell by pressing the tube through the bearing. Press down until housing seats against shell.

33. Mount Tool J-23456 in vise and position rear shell in tool.

34. Place piston rod retainer plate on the end of the power piston and install power piston return spring.

35. Lower front shell over rear shell and position bar on front shell bearing.

36. Tighten down front shell and fit the tangs in the appropriate slots on rear shell.

37. Rotate bar until locked and remove power head.

38. Place the filter in the power head boot. Stretch boot over flange of rear housing and install boot retainer.

39. Place the power head assembly in a vise with the front shell facing up. Insert the flat end of the piston rod retainer.

40. Press on the master cylinder piston rod to check the seat.

41. Place gauge J-22647 over the piston rod in a position that allows it to be moved left and right without contacting the studs. *Correct adjustment allows the lower step to contact the piston rod and the upper step to miss.*

42. Lubricate the I.D. of the front housing seal and insert seal.

43. Position master cylinder on housing, install nuts and torque to 20 ft. lbs.

Section 14
Midland Ross Tandem Diaphragm

Removal

1. With engine turned off, apply brakes several times to equalize pressures.

2. Disconnect hydraulic brake lines from master cylinder and vacuum hose from check valve.

3. Under instrument panel, remove bolt connecting brake pedal link to pedal.

4. Remove unit from car.

Disassembly

1. Remove master cylinders from unit.

2. Remove filter cover and retainer, separate and remove filter.

3. Disconnect valve operating rod from power lever assembly.

4. Remove lower pivot and power lever, pedal link, boot retaining plate and boot.

5. Remove rear bracket and rubber boot from valve operating rod.

6. Scribe a mark on covers and clamp band, remove clamp band.

7. Push bellows retaining lip into front cover chamber and separate bellows, control hub and diaphragm assemblies from covers.

8. Remove vacuum check valve rubber grommet from body. Remove rear seal from rear cover.

Cover and Diaphragms Disassembly

1. Remove the bellows clamp with a screw driver, and remove the bellows from the control hub. Remove the two bellows support rings.

2. Remove pushrod and reaction cone assembly and the reaction lever assembly from control hub.

3. Remove plastic pushrod guide, retainer and reaction cone from pushrod assembly.

4. Remove operating rod from valve plunger. Pull pushrod firmly until plastic retainer shears. Remove all pieces from groove in pushrod and plunger.

5. Fold back bead of rear diaphragm, turn diaphragm plate and remove.

6. Remove O-ring from center assembly.

7. Roll ribbed bead of front diaphragm from center plate assembly retaining ring and remove center assembly.

8. Remove center seal from center plate assembly.

9. Using tool C-3984, turn control hub clockwise 1/4 turn while holding retaining plate. Separate diaphragm, retaining plate, tail stock extension, tail stock and two O-rings.

Control Hub Disassembly

1. Remove snap-ring retainer which holds plunger to control hub and separate. It may be necessary to file away the small burr from the end of the plunger before they can be separated.

2. Compress spring of plunger assembly toward rubber valve and remove spring retainer. Separate spring, washer, and rubber valve from spring end, and O-ring and fibre washer from other end of plunger.

Cleaning Note

Clean all metal parts in suitable solvent, and dry with compressed air. Plastic parts should be cleaned with soap and water. Replace all rubber parts and filters. Inspect and replace all parts showing wear. Lubricate all rubber parts except diaphragms and reactor ring with silicone lubricant.

Control Hub Assembly

1. Assemble O-ring and fibre washer on plunger. Insert plunger into hub and install snap-ring.

2. Assemble rubber valve onto control hub so that the two round holes in the valve index with the two projections on the hub. Assemble washer into hub so the flat edge indexes with the flat projection of the hub.

3. Install spring and spring retaining clip over plunger by compressing spring.

Diaphragm Assembly

1. Install tail stock over plunger with flat indexing on flat on control hub.

2. Insert large O-ring in groove between tail stock and control hub. Insert small O-ring in sealing ring on rear of tail stock, install tail stock extension over tail stock and O-rings.

3. Install ribbed diaphragm-to-control hub retainer plate and place over tail stock extension.

4. Using tool C-3984, turn control hub assembly 1/4 turn counterclockwise to the stop.

5. Insert center seal into center plate assembly and install over

Bellows assembly (© Dodge Div., Chrysler Corp.)

tail stock extension. Roll ribbed diaphragm bead over center plate retaining ring.

6. Insert O-ring into sealing groove of rear diaphragm plate assembly and install over tail stock extension.

7. Rotate rear diaphragm plate assembly ¼ turn counterclockwise to the stop.

8. Place groove of rear diaphragm sealing bead over mating lip of center plate assembly.

9. Install lever assembly in control hub with rubber protrusions toward hub. Be sure the levers are evenly spaced within the hub.

10. Assemble the reaction cone, retainer, and plastic pushrod guide on pushrod. Install pushrod assembly in control hub so that pushrod indexes in valve plunger.

11. Install two bellows support rings on bellows. Install bellows on control hub so the lip on bellows indexes in groove on hub.

12. Secure bellows to hub with large bellows clamp.

13. Assemble rear seal into rear cover. Position diaphragms, bellows, and control hub as assembled into rear cover. Make sure lip of seal fits over rear flange.

14. Install rubber grommet in front cover with larger diameter on outside of unit. Install vacuum manifold assembly through grommet.

15. Install front cover to rear cover, making sure that scribe lines are aligned. Pull front lip of bellows through front cover and position it evenly around hole in front cover.

16. Install clamp band over lips of front and rear cover, aligning scribe marks. It is necessary to force the covers together, requiring about 300 lbs. Engine vacuum or a vise may be used.

Tighten the band.

17. Install rubber boot on valve operating rod and assemble plastic retainer to end of rod. Insert rod into plunger so that the retainer engages groove in plunger. Install lip of boot in groove of rear seal.

18. Install brackets on rear cover.

19. Install pedal link, power lever, clevis pin, boot retaining plate and boot. Attach assembly to brackets.

20. Connect power lever to operating rod.

21. Position air filter in metal retainer and snap plastic cover on. Install assembly onto mounting studs of front cover.

22. Install master cylinders and torque to 100 ft. lbs.

23. Install dash panel-to-power brake seal.

24. Position unit on dash, tighten nuts to 200 ft. lbs.

25. Lubricate the bearing surface of the bolt to connect the pedal link with the pedal linkage. Tighten to 30 ft. lbs.

26. Connect vacuum hoses and hydraulic brake lines.

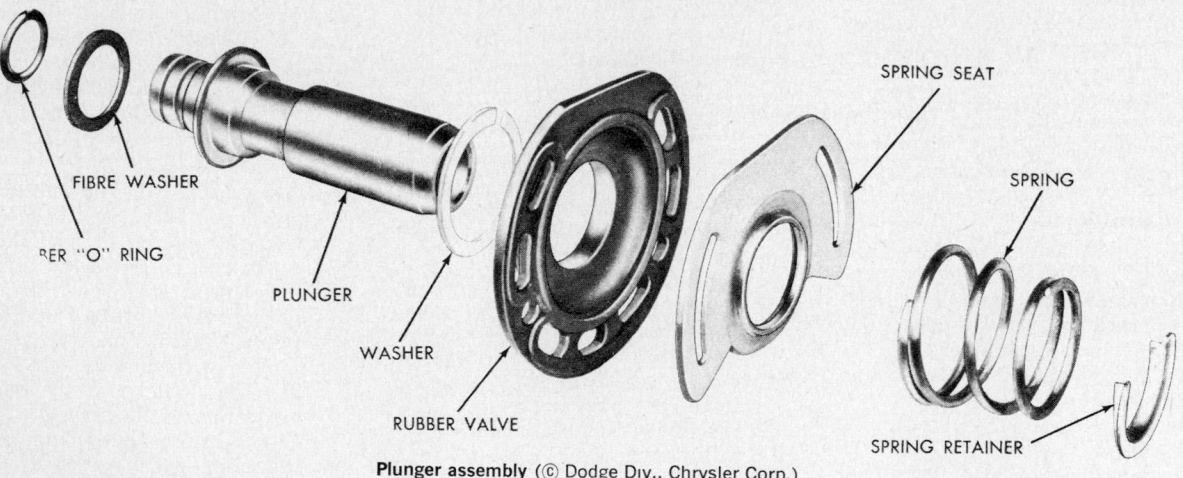

Plunger assembly (© Dodge Div., Chrysler Corp.)

Application Index

Manual Steering

There are five different types of steering gears used. Each type of steering gear and the make of car it is installed in is listed below. The section numbers refer to the sections in the text that cover that particular type of steering gear.

Gear Type	Section	Make	Year
A	2	American Motors Corp. Series 01	1965–67
B	3	Ford Motor Co. and Lincoln-Mercury Division All models except Pinto, Lincoln Continental, Continental Mark III, Thunderbird.	1965–72
C	4	General Motors Corp. All models	1965–72
		American Motors Corp. All models except Series 01 to 1967	1965–72
D	5	Chrysler Corp. All models	1965–72
E	6	Ford Motor Co. Pinto	1971–72

Gear Types

A   Gemmer worm and double roller tooth with screw adjusted mesh
B   Ford steering gear, recirculating ball
C   Saginaw steering gear, recirculating ball
D   Chrysler steering gear, recirculating ball
E   Rack and pinion steering gear

Section Page Numbers

Section	Page
1	1178
2	1178
3	1179
4	1182
5	1185
6	1188

Manual Steering

Manual Steering Diagnosis

Condition	Possible Cause	Correction
Hard steering	(a) Low or uneven tire pressure.	(a) Inflate tires to recommended pressures.
	(b) Insufficient lubricant in the steering gear housing or in steering linkage.	(b) Lubricate as necessary.
	(c) Steering gear shaft adjusted too tight.	(c) Adjust according to instructions.
	(d) Front wheels out of line.	(d) Align the wheels. See the Front Suspension Section.
	(e) Steering column misaligned.	(e) See the Car Section for alignment procedures.
Excessive play or looseness in the steering wheel	(a) Steering gear shaft adjusted too loose or badly worn.	(a) Replace worn parts and adjust according to instructions.
	(b) Steering linkage loose or worn.	(b) Replace worn parts. See the Front Wheel Alignment Section.
	(c) Front wheel bearings improperly adjusted.	(c) Adjust according to instructions.
	(d) Steering arm loose on steering gear shaft.	(d) Inspect for damage to the gear shaft and steering arm, replace parts as necessary.
	(e) Steering gear housing attaching bolts loose.	(e) Tighten attaching bolts to specifications.
	(f) Steering arms loose at steering knuckles.	(f) Tighten according to specifications.
	(g) Worn ball joints.	(g) Replace the ball joints as necessary. See the Front Suspension Section.
	(h) Worm shaft bearing adjustment too loose.	(h) Adjust worm bearing preload according to instructions.

Section 1
Steering Gear Alignment

Before any steering gear adjustments are made, it is recommended that the front end of the car be raised and a thorough inspection be made for stiffness or lost motion in the steering gear, steering linkage and front suspension. Worn or damaged parts should be replaced, since a satisfactory adjustment of the steering gear cannot be obtained if bent or badly worn parts exist.

It is also very important that the steering gear be properly aligned in the car. Misalignment of the gear places a stress on the steering worm shaft, therefore a proper adjustment is impossible. To align the steering gear, loosen the mounting bolts to permit the gear to align itself. Check the steering gear mounting seat, and if there is a gap at any of the mounting bolts, proper alignment may be obtained by placing shims where excessive gap appears. Tighten the steering gear bolts. Alignment of the gear in the car is very important and should be done carefully so that a satisfactory, trouble-free gear adjustment may be obtained.

Section 2
Gemmer Worm and Double Roller Tooth Type
With Screw Adjusted Mesh

The steering gear is of the worm and roller type with a 24 to 1 gear ratio. The cross-shaft is straddle mounted with a bearing surface at the top and bottom points of the shaft mounting areas. The three tooth cross-shaft roller is mounted on ball bearings. The proper lubricant used in the gear box is S.A.E. 90 Extreme Pressure Lubricant.

The external adjustments given below will remove all play from the steering gear. Before doing these adjustments, refer to Section 1 to insure that the steering gear requires adjustment.

Worm Bearing Adjustment

1. Turn the steering wheel about one full turn from straight ahead and secure it so it doesn't move.
2. Determine if there is any worm gear end-play by shaking the front wheel sideways and noting if there is any end movement that may be felt between the steering wheel hub and the steering jacket tube. *Be sure any movement noted is not looseness in the steering jacket tube.*
3. If end-play is present, adjust the worm bearings by loosening the four cover cap screws about 1/8 in. Separate the top shim, using a knife blade, and remove it. Do not damage the remaining shims or gaskets.
4. Replace the cover and recheck the end-play again. If necessary, repeat steps 2 and 3 until the end-play movement is as small possible without tightening the steering gear too much.

NOTE: adjustment may be done with the pitman arm disconnected. With the steering wheel turned about one full turn from straight ahead, using the Spring Scale Tool J-544, adjust with the shims as given above until the spring scale pull is between 1/4 and 5/8 lbs.

NOTE: torque wrench calibrated in in. lbs. may be used instead of spring scale.

Cross-Shaft Roller and Worm Mesh Adjustment

1. Turn the steering wheel to the middle of its turning limits with

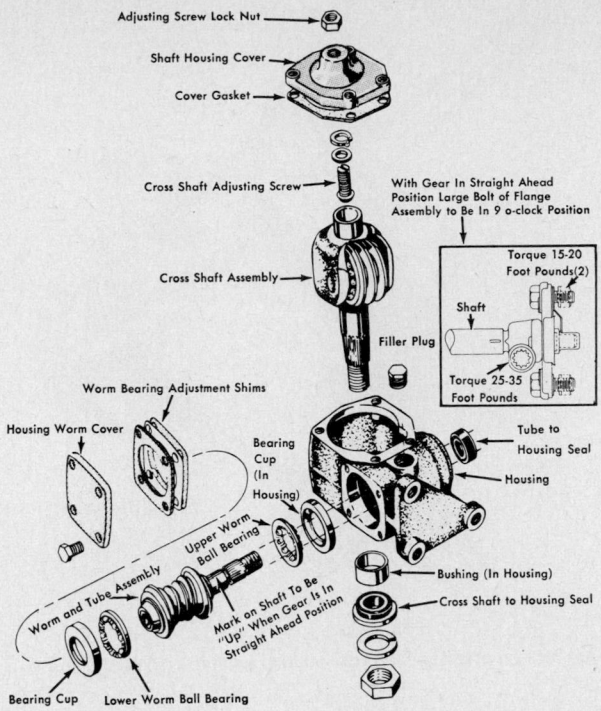

Gemmer worm and double roller tooth type steering gear
(© American Motors Corp.)

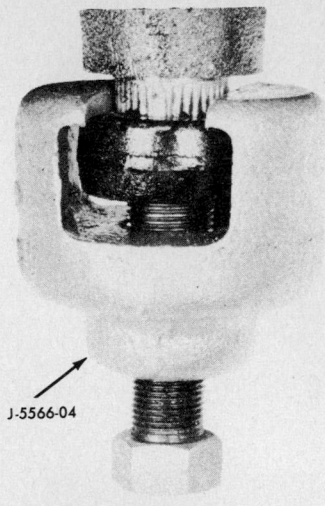

J-5566-04

Removing Pitman arm
(© American Motors Corp.)

the pitman arm disconnected. The steering gear roller should be on the worm high spot.

2. Shake the pitman arm sideways to determine the amount of clearance between the worm cross-shaft roller. Movement of more than 1/32 in. indicates the roller and worm mesh must be adjusted.

3. Loosen the adjusting screw lock nut and tighten the external cross-shaft adjusting screw a small amount. Recheck the clearance by shaking the pitman arm. Repeat until the clearance is correct. *Do not overtighten.*
NOTE: the cross-shaft roller and

worm mesh adjustment may be done, using Spring Scale Tool J-544, by measuring the amount of wheel pull as the external cross-shaft adjusting screw is tightened. When the spring scale pull is between 7/8 and 1 1/8 lbs. through the high spot the adjustment is correct.

4. Tighten the pitman arm attaching nut to 100-125 ft. lbs. and center punch at threads to insure retention. The steering wheel nut (if loosened) should be tightened to 15-20 ft. lbs.

Steering Gear Removal and Installation

1. Disconnect the horn wire.

Remove the horn button or ring by pressing down and twisting counterclockwise.

2. Remove the steering wheel, using Puller Tool J-21232. Note the line up of dash marks on steering shaft and steering wheel.

3. Remove pitman arm with Puller Tool J-5566-04.

4. Loosen the steering jacket tube assembly at the support plate and at the instrument panel mounting bracket. Remove the steering gear attaching bolts, and remove the steering gear from the car. On some cars, two flexible couplings are used in the steering shaft assembly.

5. To install the steering gear, reverse the above procedure and torque mounting bolts to 40 ft. lbs. Adjust worm and roller gears and worm bearing.

Section 3
Ford Steering Gear—Recirculating Ball Type

Steering Worm and Sector Gear Adjustments

The ball nut assembly and the sector gear must be adjusted properly to maintain a minimum amount of steering shaft end-play and a minimum amount of backlash between the sector gear and the ball nut. There are only two adjustments that may be done on this steering gear and they should be done as given below:

1. Disconnect the pitman arm from the steering pitman-to-idler arm rod.

2. Loosen the locknut on the sector shaft adjustment screw and turn the adjusting screw counterclockwise.

3. Measure the worm bearing preload by attaching an in. lbs. torque wrench to the steering wheel nut. With the steering wheel off center, note the reading required to rotate input shaft about 1 1/2 turns either side of center. If the torque reading is not about 4-5 in. lbs., adjust the gear as given in the next step.

4. Loosen the steering shaft bearing adjuster locknut and tighten or back off the bearing adjusting screw until the preload is within the specified limits.

5. Tighten the steering shaft bearing adjuster locknut, and recheck the preload torque.

6. Turn the steering wheel slowly to either stop. Turn *gently* against the stop to avoid possible damage to the ball return guides. Then rotate the wheel 2 3/4 turns to center the ball nut.

7. Turn the sector adjusting screw clockwise until the proper torque (9-10 in. lbs.) is obtained that is necessary to rotate the worm gear past its center (high spot).

8. While holding the sector adjusting screw, tighten the sector screw adjusting locknut to 32-40 ft. lbs. and recheck the backlash adjustment.

9. Connect the pitman arm to the steering arm-to-idler arm rod.

Within the exploded diagram:

Adjusting Screw Lock Nut
Shaft Housing Cover
Cover Gasket
Cross Shaft Adjusting Screw
Cross Shaft Assembly
With Gear In Straight Ahead Position Large Bolt of Flange Assembly to Be In 9 o-clock Position
Torque 15-20 Foot Pounds(2)
Shaft
Filler Plug
Torque 25-35 Foot Pounds
Worm Bearing Adjustment Shims
Housing Worm Cover
Bearing Cup (In Housing)
Tube to Housing Seal
Housing
Upper Worm Ball Bearing
Worm and Tube Assembly
Mark on Shaft To Be "Up" When Gear Is In Straight Ahead Position
Bushing (In Housing)
Cross Shaft to Housing Seal
Bearing Cup
Lower Worm Ball Bearing

Line-up Dash Marks on Steering Shaft and Wheel

J-544

Checking pull at steering wheel rim
(© American Motors Corp.)

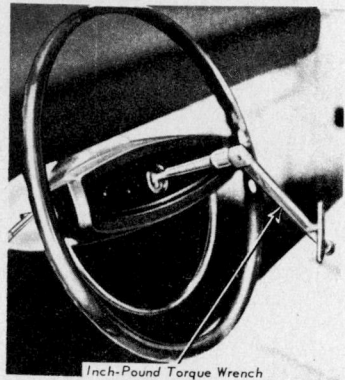

Inch-Pound Torque Wrench

Checking steering gear pre-load
(© Ford Motor Co.)

Steering Gear Removal and Installation

1. Remove the bolt(s) that holds the flex coupling to the steering shaft.
2. Remove the nut and lock-washer that secures the pitman arm to the sector shaft using a suitable gear puller or Tool T64P-3590-F.

Caution Do not hammer on the end of the puller as this can damage the steering gear.

3. To gain enough clearance on some cars with standard transmissions, it may be necessary to disconnect the clutch linkage. On some cars with V8 engines, it may be necessary to lower the exhaust system.
4. Remove the steering gear-to-side rail bolts and remove the steering gear.
5. To install the steering gear, position the steering gear and flex coupling in place and install and torque the steering gear-to-side rail bolts to 50-65 ft. lbs.
6. If clutch linkage has been disconnected, reposition and adjust it. If the exhaust system has been lowered, reinstall it to its proper position.

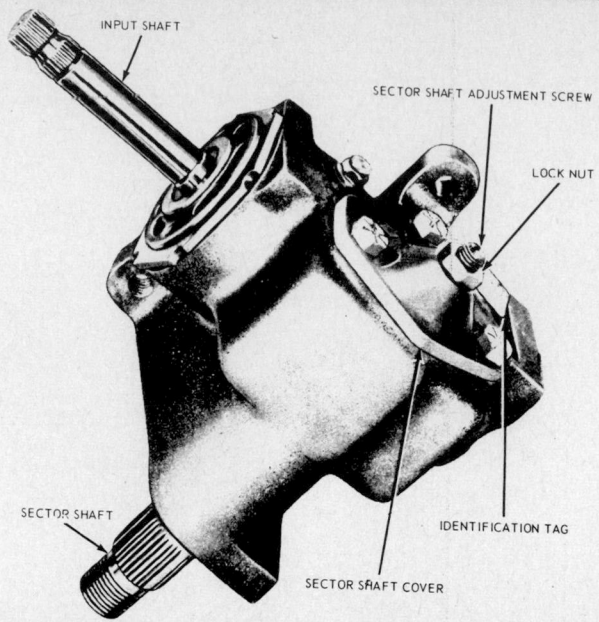

INPUT SHAFT

SECTOR SHAFT ADJUSTMENT SCREW

LOCK NUT

SECTOR SHAFT

IDENTIFICATION TAG

SECTOR SHAFT COVER

Ford manual steering gear, recirculating ball type (© Ford Motor Co.)

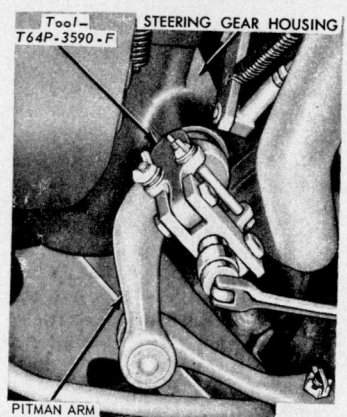

Tool-T64P-3590-F   STEERING GEAR HOUSING

PITMAN ARM

Removing Pitman arm (© Ford Motor Co.)

ADJUSTER LOCK NUT

FILLER PLUG

SECTOR SHAFT ADJUSTING SCREW

Steering gear adjustments (© Ford Motor Co.)

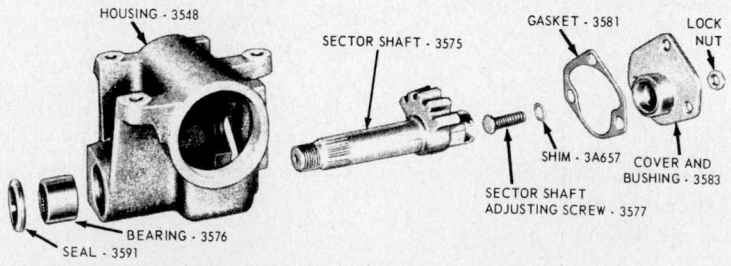

HOUSING - 3548

SECTOR SHAFT - 3575

GASKET - 3581

LOCK NUT

SHIM - 3A657

SECTOR SHAFT ADJUSTING SCREW - 3577

COVER AND BUSHING - 3583

BEARING - 3576

SEAL - 3591

Sector shaft and housing disassembled (© Ford Motor Co.)

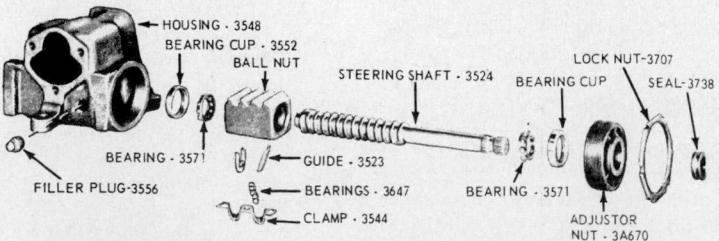

HOUSING - 3548

BEARING CUP - 3552

BALL NUT

STEERING SHAFT - 3524

BEARING CUP

LOCK NUT-3707

SEAL-3738

BEARING - 3571

FILLER PLUG-3556

GUIDE - 3523

BEARINGS - 3647

CLAMP - 3544

BEARING - 3571

ADJUSTOR NUT - 3A670

Steering shaft, ball nut, and bearings disassembled (© Ford Motor Co.)

7. Position the pitman arm and the sector shaft and install the attaching nut and lock washer. Tighten the nut to 150-225 ft. lbs.

8. Install the flex coupling attaching nut(s) and tighten to specification (tilt steering column, one bolt—20-37 ft. lbs.; fixed column, two bolts—10-22 ft. lbs.)

Steering Gear Disassembly and Assembly

1. Rotate the steering shaft three turns from either stop.

2. Remove the sector shaft adjusting screw locknut and the housing cover bolts and remove the sector shaft with the cover. Remove the cover from the shaft by turning the screw clockwise. *Keep the shim with the screw.*

3. Loosen the worm bearing adjuster nut and remove the adjuster assembly and the steering shaft upper bearing.

4. Carefully pull the steering shaft and ball nut from the housing, and remove the steering shaft lower bearing. *Do not run the ball nut to either end of the worm gear to prevent damaging the ball return guides. Disassemble the ball nut only if there are signs of binding or tightness.*

5. To disassemble the ball nut, remove the ball return guide clamp and the ball return guides from the ball nut. *Keep ball nut clamp side up until ready to remove the ball bearings.*

6. Turn the ball nut over and rotate the worm shaft from side to side until all the balls have dropped out into a clean pan. With all balls removed, the ball

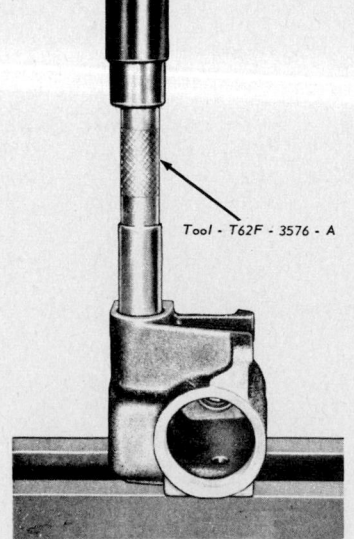

Removing oil seal and bearing
(© Ford Motor Co.)

Tool - T62F - 3576 - A

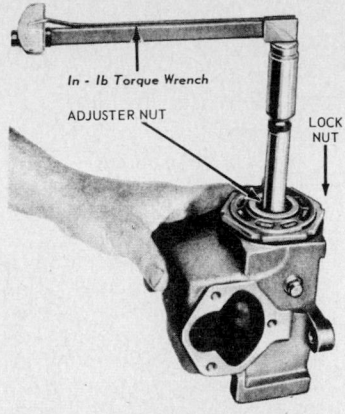

In - lb Torque Wrench
ADJUSTER NUT
LOCK NUT

Checking steering shaft bearing pre-load
(© Ford Motor Co.)

nut will slide off the wormshaft.

7. Remove the upper bearing cup from the bearing adjuster and the lower cup from the housing. It may be necessary to tap the housing or the adjuster on a wooden block to jar the bearing cups loose.

8. If the inspection shows bearing damage, the sector shaft bearing and the oil seal should be pressed out.

9. If the sector shaft bearing and oil seal have been removed, press a new bearing and oil seal into the housing. Do not clean, wash, or soak seals in cleaning solvent. Apply the recommended steering gear lubricant to the housing and seals.

10. Install a bearing cup in the lower end of the housing and in the adjuster.

11. Install a new seal in the bearing adjuster if the old seal was removed.

12. Insert the ball guides into the holes in the ball nut, lightly tapping them if necessary to seat them.

13. Insert half of the balls into the hole in the top of each ball guide. If necessary, rotate the shaft slightly to distribute the balls evenly in the circuit.

14. Install the ball guide clamp, tightening the screws to 42 in. lbs. Check that the worm shaft rotates freely.

15. Coat the threads of the steering shaft bearing adjuster, the housing cover bolts, and the sector adjusting screw with a suitable oil-resistant sealing compound. Do not apply sealer to female threads. *Do not get sealer on the steering shaft bearings.*

16. Coat the worm bearings, sector shaft bearings, and gear teeth with steering gear lubricant.

17. Clamp the housing in a vise, with the sector shaft axis horizontal, and place the steering shaft lower bearing in its cup.

Place the steering shaft and ball nut assemblies in the housing.

18. Position the steering shaft upper bearing on top of the worm gear and install the steering shaft bearing adjuster, adjuster nut, and the bearing cup. Leave the nut loose.

19. Adjust the worm bearing preload according to the instructions given earlier.

20. Position the sector adjusting screw and adjuster shim, and check for a clearance of not more than 0.002 in. between the screw head and the end of the sector shaft. If the clearance exceeds 0.002 in., add enough shims to reduce the clearance to under 0.002 in. clearance.

21. Start the sector shaft adjusting screw into the housing cover. Install a new gasket on the cover.

22. Rotate the steering shaft until the ball nut teeth mesh with the sector gear teeth, tilting the housing so the ball will tip toward the housing cover opening.

23. Lubricate the sector shaft journal and install the sector shaft and cover. With the cover moved to one side, fill the gear with steering gear lubricant (0.90 lb.). Push the cover and the sector shaft into place, and install the two top housing bolts. Do not tighten the bolts until checking to see that there is some lash between the ball nut and the sector gear teeth. Hold or push the cover away from the ball nut and tighten the bolts to 30-40 ft-lbs.

24. Loosely install the sector shaft adjusting screw locknut and adjust the sector shaft mesh load as given earlier. Tighten the adjusting screw locknut.

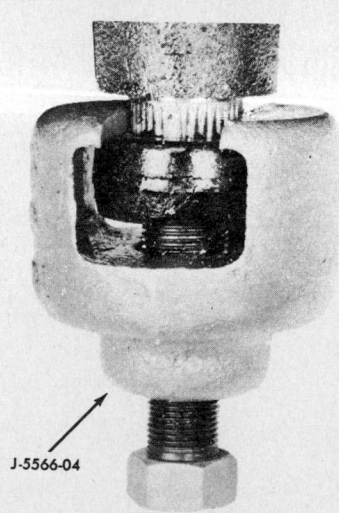

J-5566-04

Removing Pitman arm
(© American Motors Corp.)

Section 4
Saginaw Recirculating Ball Type

The steering gear is of the recirculating ball nut type. The ball nut, mounted on the worm gear, is driven by means of steel balls which circulate in helical grooves in both the worm and nut. Ball return guides attached to the nut serve to recirculate the two sets of balls in the grooves. As the steering wheel is turned to the right, the ball nut moves upward. When the wheel is turned to the left, the ball nut moves downward.

The sector teeth on the pinion shaft and the ball nut are designed so that they fit the tightest when the steering wheel is straight ahead. This mesh action is adjusted by an adjusting screw which moves the pinion shaft endwise until the teeth mesh properly. The worm bearing adjuster provides proper preloading of the upper and lower bearings.

Before doing the adjustment procedures given below, refer to Section 1 to ensure that the steering problem is not caused by faulty suspension components, bad front end alignment, etc. Then, proceed with the following adjustments.

Worm Bearing Preload Adjustment

Caution Do not turn steering wheel hard against stops as damage to ball nut assembly may result.

1. Disconnect the ball stud from the pitman arm, and retighten the pitman arm nut.
2. Loosen the pitman shaft adjusting screw locknut and back off adjusting screw a few turns.
3. Attach Spring Scale Tool J-544 to the steering wheel and measure the pull needed to move the steering wheel when off the high point. The pull should be between 1/8 and 3/8 lb.
4. To adjust the worm bearing, loosen the worm bearing adjuster locknut with a brass drift and turn the adjuster screw until the proper pull is obtained. When adjustment is correct, tighten the adjuster locknut, and recheck with the spring scale again.

Sector and Ball Nut Backlash Adjustment

1. After the worm bearing preload has been adjusted correctly, loosen the pitman shaft adjusting screw locknut and turn the pitman shaft adjusting screw clockwise until a pull of 3/4 to 1 1/8 lbs. is shown on the spring scale. When the adjustment is correct, tighten the pitman shaft adjusting screw locknut and recheck the adjustment.

NOTE: a torque wrench calibrated in in. lbs. may be substituted for the spring scale in adjusting steering gear.

2. Turn the steering wheel to the center of its turning limits (pitman arm disconnected). If the steering wheel is removed, the mark on the steering shaft should be at top center.
3. Connect the ball stud to the pitman arm, tightening the attaching nut to 115 ft. lbs.

Steering Gear Removal and Installation

1. Remove the flexible coupling bolts.
2. Remove the pitman arm, using Puller Tool J-5566-04 or suitable gear puller.

Caution Do not hammer on end of puller or gear may be damaged.

3. Remove the steering gear mounting screws and lower the

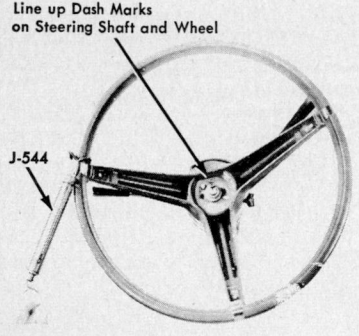

Line up Dash Marks on Steering Shaft and Wheel

J-544

Checking pull at steering wheel rim
(© American Motors Corp.)

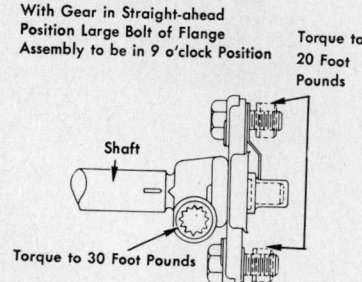

With Gear in Straight-ahead Position Large Bolt of Flange Assembly to be in 9 o'clock Position

Torque to 20 Foot Pounds

Shaft

Torque to 30 Foot Pounds

Shaft and flange alignment
(© American Motors Corp.)

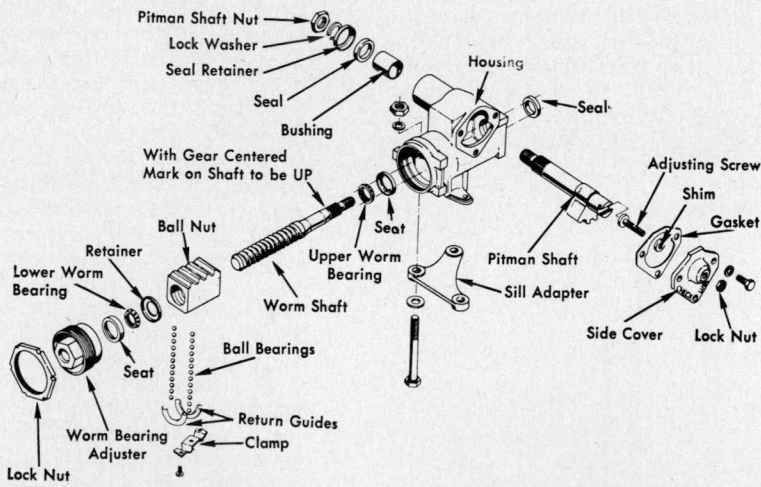

Pitman Shaft Nut
Lock Washer
Seal Retainer
Seal
Bushing
Housing
Seal
With Gear Centered Mark on Shaft to be UP
Ball Nut
Retainer
Lower Worm Bearing
Seat
Upper Worm Bearing
Worm Shaft
Seat
Ball Bearings
Worm Bearing Adjuster
Return Guides
Clamp
Lock Nut
Adjusting Screw
Shim
Gasket
Pitman Shaft
Sill Adapter
Side Cover
Lock Nut

Saginaw steering gear, recirculating ball type (© American Motors Corp.)

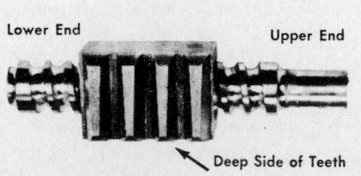

Lower End   Upper End

Deep Side of Teeth

Ball nut properly installed on worm shaft
(© American Motors Corp.)

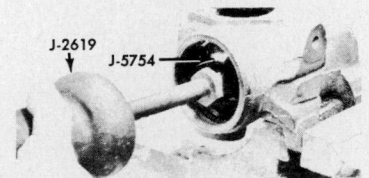

J-2619   J-5754

Removing bearing cup from steering gear housing
(© American Motors Corp.)

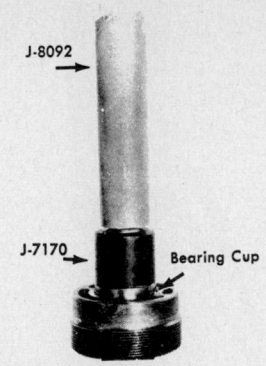

Installing bearing cup in worm adjuster
(© American Motors Corp.)

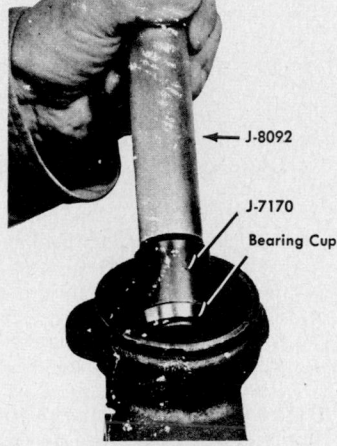

**Installing bearing cup
in steering gear housing**
(© American Motors Corp.)

**Positioning the Pitman shaft
and ball nut in housing**
(© American Motors Corp.)

Installing Pitman shaft seal
(© American Motors Corp.)

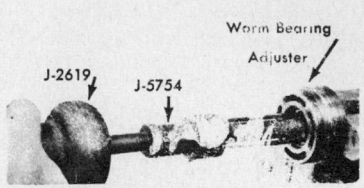

**Removing bearing cup
from worm bearing adjuster**
(© American Motors Corp.)

steering gear.

4. Center the steering gear with the index mark up. Mark on shaft on flange must be aligned at assembly.

5. Insert the flexible coupling bolts to the shaft and tighten to 20 ft. lbs. Tighten the pinch bolt to 30 ft. lbs. Tighten the steering gear mounting screws to 45 ft. lbs., and the pitman arm nut to 115 ft. lbs. *Stake pitman arm nut with a center punch to insure nut retention.*

NOTE: whenever the steering gear is removed for replacement or overhaul, or the mounting bolts are loosened for any reason, the steering column *must* be realigned to the gear assembly. Slight misalignment of the steering column may cause increased steering effort and extra wear to the steering components. Refer to the Car Section for alignment procedures.

Steering Gear Disassembly and Assembly

1. After removing the steering gear from the car, place the steering gear assembly in a bench vise.

NOTE: worm seal may be replaced without disassembling gear. Be careful not to damage shaft or housing when removing seal.

2. Rotate the worm shaft until it is centered with the mark facing upward. Remove three cover attaching screws and the adjusting screw locknut. Remove the cover and gasket by turning adjusting screw clockwise through the cover.

3. Remove the adjusting screw with its shim from the slot in the end of the pitman shaft. Remove the pitman shaft from the housing being careful not to damage the seal in the housing.

4. Loosen the worm bearing adjuster locknut with a brass drift and remove the adjuster and bearing. Remove the bearing retainer with a screwdriver.

5. Remove the worm and shaft assembly with the ball nut assembly and bearing. Remove the ball nut return guide clamp by removing screws. Remove the guides, turn ball nut over, and remove the steel balls by rotating the shaft from side to side. After all 50 steel balls have been removed, take the ball nut off the worm shaft.

6. Clean all parts in solvent. Inspect all bearings, bearing cups, bushings, seals, worm groove, and gear teeth for signs of wear, scoring, pitting, etc. If the pitman shaft bushings or seal, steering shaft seal, or upper and lower bearing cups need replacement, see the replacement procedures given below.

7. Remove the pitman shaft seal with a screwdriver or punch. If there is leakage around the threads of the bearing adjuster, apply a non-hardening sealer.

8. Remove faulty bushings from the pitman shaft with Puller J-5754 and Slide Hammer J-2619. Install new bushings with Tool J-7133, seating the

inner end of the bushing flush with the inside surface of the housing.

9. Remove the steering shaft seal with a punch or screwdriver. Tap new seal in place, using a section of tubing to seat the seal.

10. Remove the upper or lower bearing cup from the worm bearing adjuster or steering gear housing using Puller J-5754 and Slide Hammer J-2619. Install the new bearing cups with the Installer Tool J-7170 and Handle J-8092 or J-8592.

11. Lubricate all seals, bushings, and bearings before installing into the steering gear assembly.

12. Position the ball nut on the worm shaft. Install the steel balls in the return guides and the ball nut, placing an equal number in each circuit of the ball nut. Install the return guide clamp and screws.

Caution do not rotate the worm shaft while installing the steel balls since the balls may enter the crossover passage between the circuits, causing incorrect operation of the ball nut.

13. Place bearing on shaft above the worm gear, center ball nut on worm gear; then, slide the steering shaft, bearing, and ball nut into the housing. *Do not damage the steering shaft seal in the housing.*

14. Place the bearing in the worm adjuster, install the bearing retainer, and install the adjuster and locknut on the housing, tightening it just enough to hold the bearing in place.

15. Install the pitman shaft adjusting screw and selective shim in the pitman shaft. Be sure there is no more than 0.002 in. of end play of the screw in the slot. If

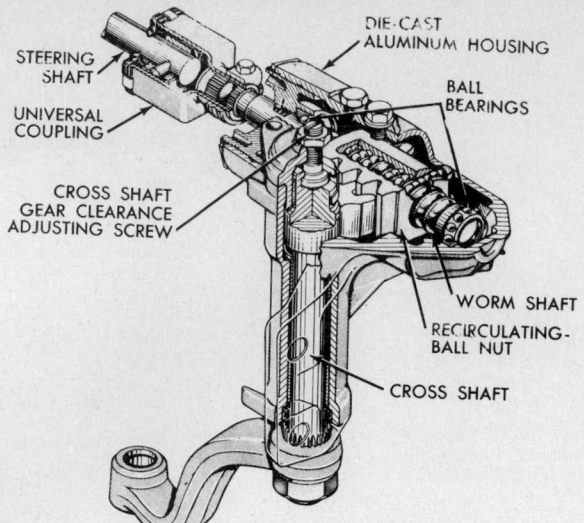

Chrysler steering gear, recirculating ball type
(© Chrysler Corp.)

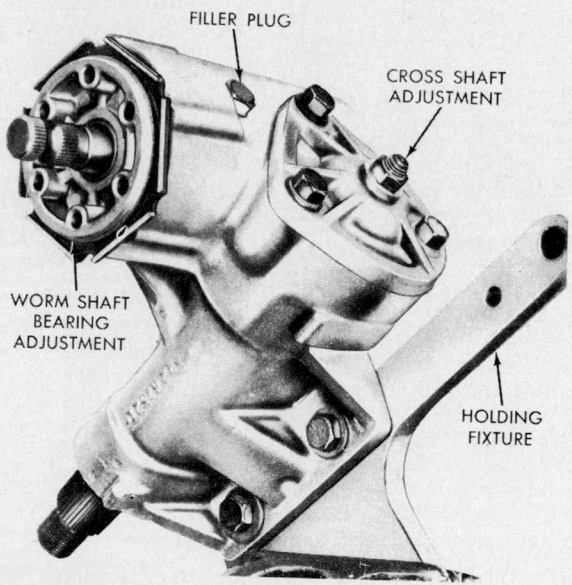

Steering gear adjustment locations (© Chrysler Corp.)

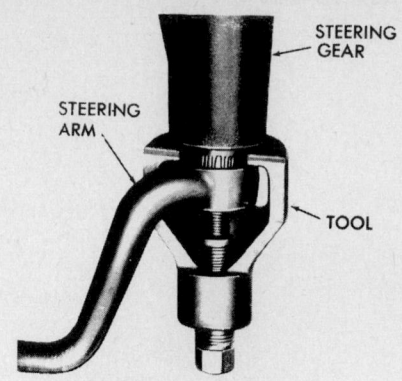

Removing steering gear arm
(© Chrysler Corp.)

the end-play is more than 0.002 in., install a new selective shim to get the proper clearance. Shims are available in four thicknesses: 0.063 in., 0.065 in., 0.067 in., and 0.069 in.

16. Install the pitman shaft and adjusting screw with the sector and ball nut positioned as shown.

17. Install the cover and gasket on the adjusting screw, turning screw counterclockwise until it extends through the cover from 5/8 to 3/4 in. Install the cover attaching screws and torque to 35 ft. lbs.

18. Tighten the pitman shaft adjusting screw so that the teeth on the shaft and the ball nut engage but do not bind. Final adjustment must be made later.

19. Wrap the pitman shaft splines with tape to protect the seal and install the seal using Tool J-7171.

20. Fill steering gear with a good quality steering gear lubricant. Turn the steering gear from one extreme to the other to make sure it does not bind. *Do not allow the ball nut to strike the ends of the ball races on the worm gear to avoid damaging the ball return guides.*

21. Install the steering gear as described previously. Perform the final adjustments on the worm bearing preload and the sector and ball nut backlash adjustments.

Section 5
Chrysler Recirculating Ball Type Steering Gear

This steering gear is quite similar to the Saginaw recirculating ball design. The main differences are adjustment and torque specifications. Refer to the introduction to Section 4 before proceeding with the adjustments below.

Worm Bearing Pre-load Adjustment

1. Remove the steering gear arm

and lockwasher, using a suitable gear puller or Tool C-3646.

2. Remove the horn button or horn ring.

3. Loosen the cross-shaft adjusting screw locknut, and back out the adjusting screw about two turns.

4. Turn the steering wheel two complete turns from the straight ahead position, and place torque

wrench Tool C-3380 on the steering shaft nut.

5. Rotate the steering shaft at least one turn toward the straight ahead position while measuring the torque on the torque wrench. The torque should be between 1½ and 4½ in. lbs. to move the steering wheel. If torque is not within these limits, loosen the worm shaft bearing adjuster

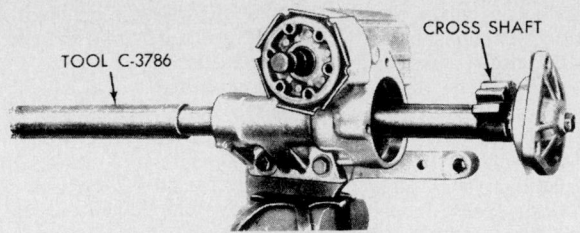

TOOL C-3786 / CROSS SHAFT

Removing the cross shaft (© Chrysler Corp.)

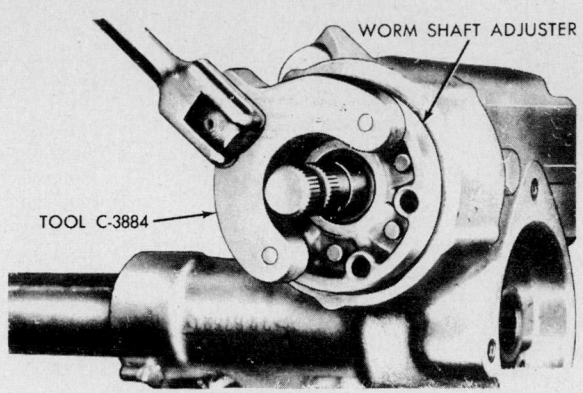

WORM SHAFT ADJUSTER / TOOL C-3884

Removing the worm shaft adjuster (© Chrysler Corp.)

locknut and turn the adjuster clockwise to increase the preload or counterclockwise to decrease the preload. Use the adjuster wrench Tool C-3884 to do the adjustment. When the preload is correct, hold the adjuster screw steady and tighten the locknut. Recheck preload.

Ball Nut Rack and Sector Mesh Adjustment

NOTE: this adjustment can be accurately made only after proper preloading of worm bearing.

1. Turn steering wheel gently from one stop to the other, counting the number of turns. Turn the steering wheel back exactly half way, to the center position.
2. Turn the cross-shaft adjusting screw clockwise to remove all lash between ball nut rack and the sector gear teeth, then tighten adjusting screw locknut to 35 ft. lbs.
3. Turn the steering wheel about 1/4 turn away from the center or high spot position. With the torque wrench Tool C-3380 on the steering wheel nut measure the torque required to turn the steering wheel through the high spot at the center position. The reading should be between 8 and 11 in. lbs. This is the total of the worm shaft bearing preload and the ball nut rack and sector gear mesh load. Readjust the cross-shaft adjustment screw if necessary to obtain a correct torque reading.
4. After completing the adjustments, place the front wheels in a straight ahead position, and with the steering wheel and steering gear centered, install the steering arm on cross-shaft. Tighten the steering arm retaining nut to 180 ft. lbs.

Steering Gear Removal and Installation

To avoid damaging the steering column, it may be necessary to remove it before taking the steering gear out of the car. This is very important on cars equipped with energy-absorbing type steering columns. See the Car Section for proper removal,

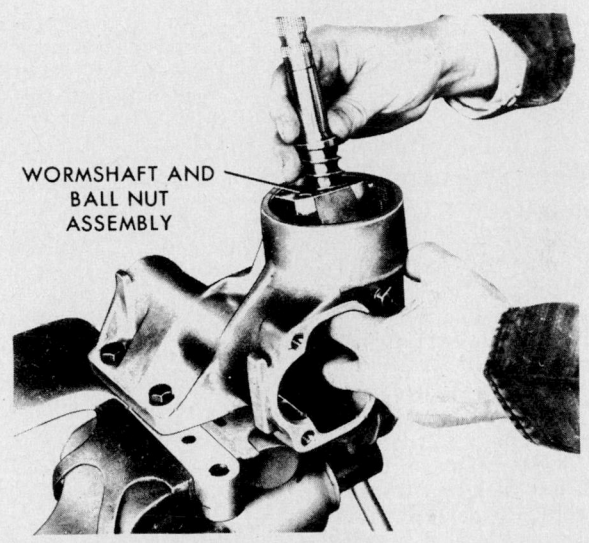

WORMSHAFT AND BALL NUT ASSEMBLY

Removing the worm shaft and ball nut assembly
(© Chrysler Corp.)

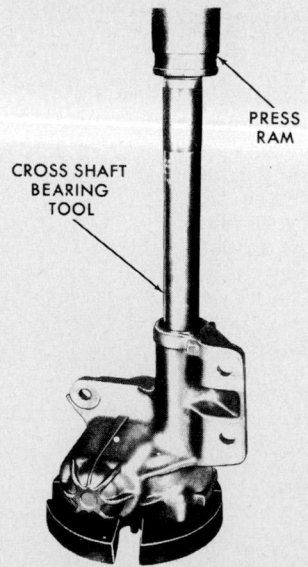

PRESS RAM / CROSS SHAFT BEARING TOOL

Removing the cross shaft inner and outer bearings
(© Chrysler Corp.)

installation, and alignment procedures.

1. After removing the steering column, remove the steering arm retaining nut and lockwasher. Remove the steering arm with a small gear puller or Tool C-3646.
2. Remove the steering gear attaching bolts, and remove the steering gear from the car.
3. To install the steering gear, position the gear assembly on the frame and install the attaching bolts and lockwashers. Tighten the bolts to 100 ft. lbs.
4. Rotate the worm shaft by hand and center the cross-shaft to the middle of its travel. Align the master serration on the cross-shaft with the splines in the steering arm. Install the steering arm with its lockwasher and nut, tightening it to 180 ft. lbs.
5. Install and align the steering column as given in the Car Section.

Steering Gear Disassembly and Assembly

1. Attach the steering gear assembly to a holding fixture (Tool C-3323) and put the holding fixture in a bench vise. Thoroughly clean the outside surface before disassembly.
2. Loosen the cross-shaft adjusting screw locknut, and back out the adjusting screw about two turns to relieve the mesh load between the ball nut rack and the sector gear teeth. Remove the cross-shaft seal as given in the procedure for cross-shaft seal replacement.
3. Position the steering gear worm shaft in a straight ahead position.
4. Remove the attaching bolts from the cross-shaft cover and slowly remove the cross-shaft while sliding arbor Tool C-3786 (1¼ in. shaft) or Tool C-3875 (1⅛ in. shaft) into the housing. Remove the locknut from the adjusting screw and remove the screw from the cover by turning it clockwise. Slide the adjustment screw and its shim out of the slot in the end of the cross-shaft.
5. Loosen the worm shaft bearing adjuster locknut with a brass drift (punch) and remove the locknut. Hold the worm shaft steady while unscrewing the adjuster, using the wrench from Tool Set C-3884. Slide the worm adjuster off the shaft.

Caution Handle the adjuster carefully to avoid damaging the aluminum threads. Also, do not run the ball nut down to either end of the worm shaft to avoid damaging the ball guides.

6. Carefully remove the worm and ball nut assembly. This assembly is serviced as a complete assembly only and is not to be disassembled or the ball return guides removed or disturbed.
7. Remove the cross-shaft needle bearing by placing the gear housing in an arbor press; insert Tool C-3786 or Tool C-3875 in the lower end of the housing and press both bearings through the housing.

Caution The adaptor ring must be used with Tool C-3875 or bearings will be crushed.

The cross-shaft cover assembly, including a needle bearing or bushing, is serviced as an assembly.

8. Remove the worm shaft oil seal from the worm shaft bearing adjuster by inserting a blunt punch behind the seal and tapping alternately on each side of the seal until it is driven out of the adjuster.
9. Remove the worm shaft in the same manner as that given in step 8. *Be careful not to cock the bearing cup and distort the adjuster counter bore.*
10. Remove the lower cup if necessary by placing the locking head jaws of remover tool C-3868 behind the bearing cup and expanding the remover head by pressing down on the center plunger of the tool. Pull the bearing cup out by turning the remover screw clockwise while holding the center screw steady.
11. Wash all parts in clean solvent and dry thoroughly. Inspect all parts for wear, scoring, pitting, etc. Test operation of the worm shaft and ball nut assembly. If ball nut does not travel smoothly

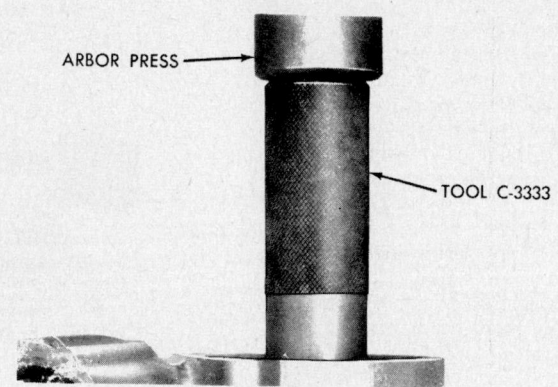

Installing the inner bearing (© Chrysler Corp.)

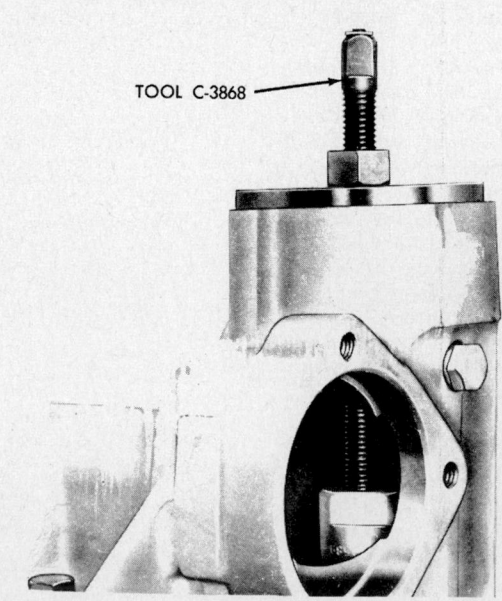

Removing the lower bearing cup
(© Chrysler Corp.)

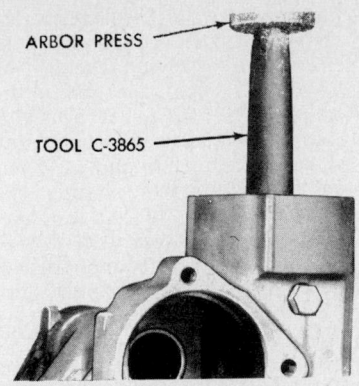

Installing the worm shaft lower bearing cup
(© Chrysler Corp.)

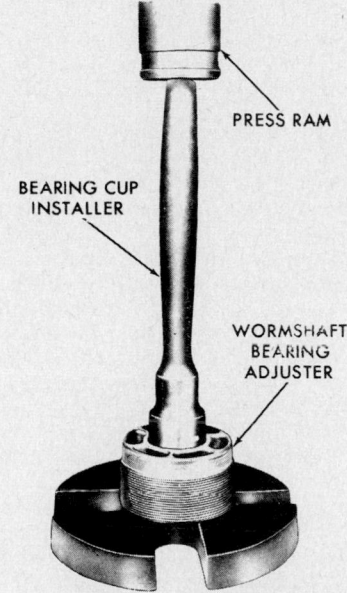

Installing the worm shaft upper bearing cup
(© Chrysler Corp.)

and freely on the worm shaft or if there is binding, replace the assembly.

NOTE: extreme care must be taken when handling the aluminum worm bearing adjuster to avoid thread damage. Also, be careful not to damage the threads in the gear housing. Always lubricate the worm bearing adjuster before screwing it into the housing.

12. Inspect the cross-shaft for wear and check the fit of the shaft in the housing bearings. Inspect the fit of the shaft pilot bearing in the housing. Be sure the worm shaft is not bent or damaged.
13. Install the cross-shaft outer needle bearing by placing the bearing on the end of Tool C-3875 or Tool C-3786 *with an adapter ring*. Press the bearing into the housing about ½ in. below the end of the bore to leave space for the new oil seal.
14. Install the inner needle bearing in the same manner and press it into the inside end of the hous-

TOOL C-3880   HOUSING

Removing the cross shaft oil seal
(© Chrysler Corp.)

ing bore flush with the inside end of the bore surface.
15. Install the worm shaft bearing cups (upper and lower) by placing them and their spacers in the adjuster nut and pressing them in place with Tool C-3865.
16. Install the worm shaft oil seal by placing the seal in the worm shaft adjuster with the metal seal retainer up. Drive the seal into place with a suitable sleeve until it is just below the end of the bore in the adjuster.

NOTE: apply a coating of steering gear lubricant to all moving parts during assembly. Also, put lubricant on and around oil seal lips.

17. Clamp the holding fixture and housing in a bench vise with the bearing adjuster opening upward. Place a thrust bearing in the lower cup in the housing.
18. Hold the ball nut from turning and insert the worm shaft and ball nut assembly into the housing with the end of the worm shaft resting in the thrust bearing. Place the upper thrust bearing on the worm shaft. Thoroughly lubricate the threads on the adjuster and the threads in the housing.
19. Place a protective sleeve of tape over the splines on the worm shaft to avoid damaging the seal. Slide the adjuster assembly over the shaft.
20. Thread the adjuster into the housing and, with Tool wrench C-3884 and the splined nut set,

tighten the adjuster to 50 ft. lbs. while rotating the worm shaft to seat the bearings.

21. Loosen the adjuster so no bearing preload exists. Tighten the adjuster for a worm shaft bearing preload of 1⅛ to 4½ in. lbs. Tighten the bearing adjuster locknut and recheck the preload.
22. Before installing the cross-shaft, pack the worm shaft cavities in the housing above and below the ball nut with steering gear lubricant. A good grade of multi-purpose lubricant may be used if steering gear lubricant is not available. *Do not use gear oil.* Pack enough lubricant into the worm cavities to cover the worm.
23. Slide the cross-shaft adjusting screw and shim into the slot in the end of the shaft. Check the end clearance for no more than 0.004 in. clearance. If the clearance is not within the limit, remove old shim and install a new shim, available in three different thicknesses, to get the proper clearance.
24. Start the cross-shaft and adjuster screw into the bearing in the housing cover. Using a screwdriver through the hole in the cover, turn the screw counterclockwise to pull the shaft into the cover. Install the adjusting screw locknut, but do not tighten at this time.
25. Rotate the worm shaft to center the ball nut.
26. Place a new gasket on the housing cover and install the cross-shaft and cover assembly into the steering gear housing. *Be sure to coat the cross-shaft and sector teeth with steering gear lubricant before installing the cross-shaft in the housing.* Allow some lash between the cross-shaft sector teeth and the ball nut rack. Install and tighten the cover bolts to 25 ft. lbs.
27. Place the cross-shaft seal on the cross-shaft with the lip of the seal facing the housing. Place the installing adapter SP-3828 from Tool C-3880 against the seal with short step toward the seal. Place the nut from Tool C-3880 on the

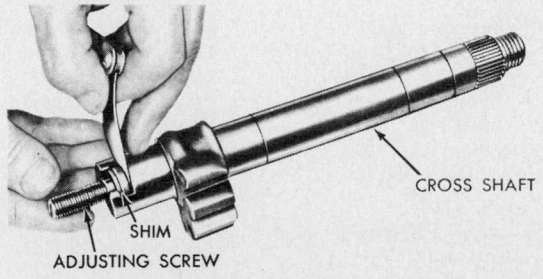

SHIM
ADJUSTING SCREW
CROSS SHAFT

Measuring cross shaft adjusting screw end clearance
(© Chrysler Corp.)

cross-shaft and turn it down against the adapter, pressing the seal into the housing until the step on the adapter touches the housing. Remove the tool.

28. Turn the worm shaft about ¼ turn away from the center of the high spot position. Using a torque wrench and a ¾ in. socket on the worm shaft spline, check the torque needed to rotate the shaft through the high spot. The reading should be between 8 and 11 in. lbs. Readjust the cross-shaft adjusting screw until the proper reading is obtained. Tighten the locknut to 35 ft. lbs. and recheck cross-shaft torque.

Cross-Shaft Oil Seal Replacement

1. Remove the steering gear arm

retaining nut and lockwasher. Remove the steering gear arm using Tool C-3646. Use Tool C-3880 to service seal.

NOTE: Tool C-3880 consists of three pieces: adapter SP3056; half rings SP-1932; and nut SP-3610.

2. Slide the threaded adapter over the end of the cross-shaft and install the nut portion of the tool on the shaft. Maintain pressure on the adapter with the tool nut while turning the adapter into the oil seal until the adapter grips the seal firmly. Place two half rings and the retainer over both portions of the tool. Turn the tool nut counterclockwise to pull the seal from the housing.

3. Place a new oil seal onto the splines of the cross-shaft with the lip of the seal facing the housing. Place the installing adapter SP-3052 from Tool C-3880 against the seal and press it in until a gap of ¼ in. exists between the adapter and the housing.

4. Place the nut from Tool C-3880 on the cross-shaft and turn it down against the adapter until the seal is pressed into the housing.

5. Remove the tool, and install the steering gear arm, lockwasher, and retaining nut. Tighten the nut to 180 ft. lbs. torque.

Section 6
Rack and Pinion Gear Type

The rack and pinion steering gear is mounted in rubber insulators on brackets attached to the front crossmember. Movement of the steering wheel is passed by the steering shaft through a universal joint and flexible coupling to the helically-toothed pinion. Rotation of the pinion causes the rack to move sideways and the connecting rods, attached to the ends of the rack, transmit this movement to the spindle arms and thus cause the road wheels to turn. The steering mechanism provides for about 3½ turns of the steering wheel from lock to lock (approximately 4.92 inches of travel of the rack).

The steering gear has three tenths (0.3) U.S. pint of S.A.E. 90 Hypoid installed during manufacture and normally requires no more lubrication. But if it should be necessary to add or refill the steering gear, *do not fill completely with oil.* Leave some space to prevent a pressure buildup during use.

Due to the design and construction of the rack and pinion gear, there are only two adjustments required: rack damper adjustment, and pinion bearing preload adjustments. Both adjustments are done by varying the thickness of a shim pack under a cover plate. It is necessary to remove the assembly from the car to do any adjustment.

Caution

When car is jacked up so the front wheels are off the ground, do not turn the steering quickly from lock to lock. This will cause hydraulic pressure to build up in the steering gear and may burst or blow off the bellows.

Rack Damper and Pinion Preload Adjustments

1. After removing the steering gear assembly from the car, carefully mount the steering

gear in a vise (with protected jaws) so that the pinion is horizontal and the rack damper cover is facing up.

2. Remove the two cover attaching screws from the housing.

3. Lift off the cover plate, shim pack and gasket, and remove the spring and slider.

4. Remove the two screws holding the pinion bearing preload cover plate to the housing and lift off the cover plate, shim pack, and gasket.

5. Replace the pinion cover plate and loosely install the attaching screws. Do not install the shim pack and gasket.

6. Tighten the attaching screws on the cover plate until the cover plate just touches the pinion bearing. Using a feeler gauge, measure the gap between the cover plate and the housing and note the reading. Check that the screws are evenly tightened by measuring the fit between the plate and housing next to each screw.

7. Make up a shim pack (including the gasket) that is 0.002 to 0.004 in. *smaller* than the measured gap. This shim pack will provide the proper preload on the pinion bearing when installed.

8. Remove the cover plate and the attaching screws and install the assembled shim pack. Reinstall the cover plate and the attaching screws, coating the threads with sealing compound, and tighten them to 6-8 ft. lbs.

9. To adjust the rack damper (also called a "slipper"), it is necessary that the distance between the cover plate and the top of the rack damper be 0.0005-0.0035 in.

10. Place the rack damper on the rack bar and seat it firmly.

Measure the distance from the top of the rack damper to the cover plate mounting surface of the housing and note the reading.

11. Make up a shim pack (including two gaskets that sandwich the shim pack) that is 0.0005 to 0.0035 in. *greater* than the measurement just made. *It is extremely important that this measurement be accurate to ensure correct steering. Otherwise excessive wear and possible failures will result.*

12. Install the spring into the recess in the rack damper, and position the shim pack, gaskets, and cover plate over the spring. Install the attaching screws, using sealing compound on the threads, and tighten them to 6-8 ft. lbs.

13. Using an in. lb. torque wrench, check the torque required to start the pinion rotating. The torque reading should be 10-18 in. lbs. If the reading is not within these limits, the adjustment is incorrect and must be redone. Check the shimming again, and inspect the gear assembly for tight bearings, broken gear teeth, lack of lubricant, etc.

Steering Gear Removal and Installation

1. With the steering wheel set straight ahead, raise the car and place jack stands under the front frame.

2. Remove the nut and bolt holding the flexible coupling to the pinion splines. Bend back the locktabs and remove the attaching screws holding the steering gear to the mounting brackets on the crossmember. Remove the screws, locking plates, and U-clamps.

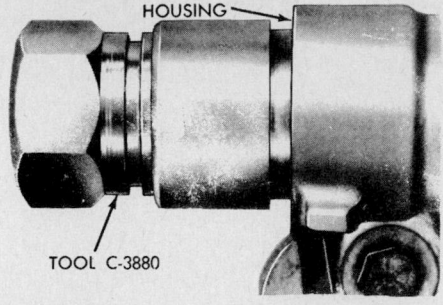

Installing the cross shaft oil seal
(© Chrysler Corp.)

 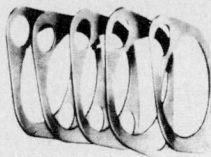 

Rack damper and shims disassembled (© Ford Motor Co.)

3. Remove the cotter pins and the castellated nuts holding the connecting rod ends to the spindle arms. Using the steering ball joint separator Tool 3290-C, separate the connecting rod ends from the spindle arms. Remove the castellated nuts and pull the steering gear from the car.

4. Remove the connecting rod ends and the locknuts, noting the number of turns it takes to unscrew them.

5. When installing the steering gear, replace the locknuts and the connecting rod ends by turning them the exact number of turns it took to remove them.

6. With the steering wheel in the straight ahead position, locate the steering gear and align the mating splines on the flexible coupling and pinion shaft. Check the condition of the rubber mounting insulators and replace them if necessary.

7. Fasten the steering gear assembly to the mounting brackets on the crossmember and tighten to 50 ft. lbs.

8. Place the connecting rods on the spindle arms. Install the castellated nuts, tighten to 20-30 ft. lbs., and install new cotter pins.

9. Tighten the flexible coupling to the pinion shaft attaching bolt to 12-15 ft. lbs. torque.

10. Raise the car enough to remove the jack stands and lower the car to the ground.

11. Check the front wheel toe-in and lock angles. Check position of steering wheel spokes.

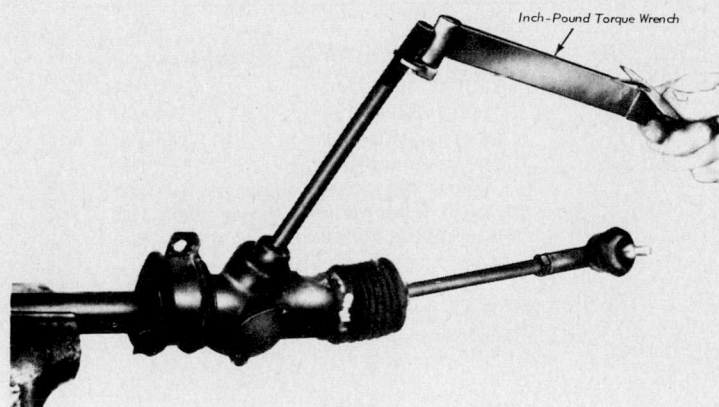

Measuring pinion turning torque (© Ford Motor Co.)

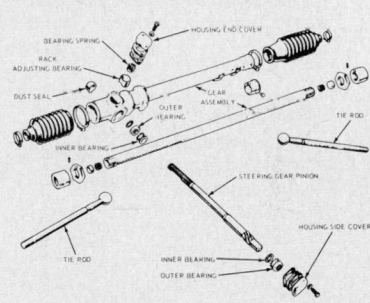

Rack and pinion steering gear disassembled
(© Ford Motor Co.)

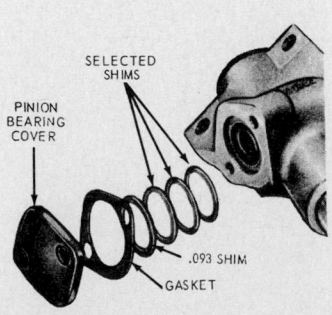

Pinion bearing preload cover and shims (© Ford Motor Co.)

Power Steering

Application Index

Section Numbers Refer to Sections in Text

Make	Year	Gear Type	Sections
American Motors			
All	1965–72	D	2,6
Chrysler Corporation			
All	1965–72	C	2,7
Ford Motor Company			
Maverick-Comet	1970–72	A	2,4
Falcon	1965–70	A	2,4
Mustang-Cougar	1965–70	A	2,4
	1971–72	D	2,6
Fairlane-Comet	1965–67	A	2,4
Torino-Montego	1968–72	A	2,4
Ford-Mercury	1965–72	E	2,8
Ford	1965–70	D	2,6
Thunderbird	1965–72	E	2,8
Lincoln, Mark III	1965–72	E	2,8

Make	Year	Gear Type	Sections
General Motors			
Chevrolet	1965–72	D	2,6
Chevelle	1965–72	D	2,6
Chevy II	1965–67	B	2,5
Nova	1968–72	D	2,6
Camaro	1967–72	D	2,6
Corvette	1965–72	B	2,5
Vega	1971–72	D	2,6
Pontiac	1965–72	D	2,6
Oldsmobile	1965–72	D	2,6
Buick	1965–72	D	2,6
Cadillac	1965–72	D	2,6

Gear Type

A—Bendix linkage
B—Saginaw linkage
C—Chrysler constant control
D—Saginaw rotary
E—Ford torsion bar

Section Page Numbers

Power Steering
Preliminary

Before investigating any power steering system, first be sure of the general condition of the systems around it. Simple items such as tire pressure, loose belts, or faulty front end parts can have great effect on the function of the power steering system. After a common-sense general inspection has been made, consult Section 1 and proceed from there.

Specific listings of make, model and year will be found in the Application Index.

Section 1
General Diagnosis

Hard Steering
1. Improper tire pressure.
2. Loose pump drive belt.
3. Low or incorrect hydraulic fluid.
4. Loose, bent or poorly lubricated front end parts.
5. Improper front end alignment, especially caster.
6. Bind in steering column or mechanism.
7. Air in hydraulic system.
8. Low pump output or leaks in system.
9. Obstruction in lines.
10. Pump valves sticking or out of adjustment.

Loose Steering
1. Loose wheel bearings.
2. Faulty shocks.
3. Worn Pitman arm or front end components.
4. Loose steering gear mountings or linkage points.
5. Steering mechanism worn or improperly adjusted.
6. Valve spool improperly adjusted.

Veer or Wander
1. Improper tire pressure.
2. Improper front end alignment.
3. Dragging brakes.
4. Bent frame.
5. Improper rear end alignment.
6. Faulty shocks or springs.
7. Loose or bent front end components.
8. Play in Pitman arm.
9. Loose wheel bearings.
10. Binding Pitman arm.
11. Spool valve sticking or improperly adjusted.

Wheel Oscillation
1. Improper tire pressure.
2. Loose wheel bearings.
3. Improper front end alignment.
4. Bent spindle.
5. Worn, bent or broken front end components.
6. Tires out of round or imbalanced.

Noises
1. Loose belts.
2. Low fluid, air in system.
3. Foreign matter in system.
4. Improper lubrication.
5. Interference or chafing in front end.
6. Steering gear mountings loose.
7. Incorrect adjustment or wear in mechanism.
8. Faulty valves or wear in pump.

Section 2
Preliminary Tests

Lubrication
Proper lubrication of the steering linkage and the front suspension is very important for the proper operation of power steering systems. Check the steering gear box for sufficient lubricant by removing the filler plug and checking the level. Add enough fluid gear oil S.A.E. 90 to bring the oil level to the filler plug hole if necessary.

Caution   Do not use a pressure gun to add fluid gear oil since the pressure will force the oil out of the steering gear box.

NOTE: the Chrysler power steering systems use the same lubricant in the steering gear box and in the power steering pump reservoir.

Air Bleeding
Air bubbles in the power steering system must be removed from the fluid. Be sure the reservoir is filled to the proper level and the fluid is warmed up to the operating temperature. Then, turn the steering wheel through its full travel three or four times until all the air bubbles are removed. *Do not hold the steering wheel against its stops.* Recheck the fluid level.

Fluid Level Check
1. Run the engine until the fluid is at the normal operating temperature. Then, turn the steering wheel through its full travel three or four times, and shut off the engine.
2. Check the fluid level in the steering reservoir. On cars built before 1968, the fluid level is checked by removing the reservoir cap and looking in the filler tube for the fluid level. On 1968 and later cars, a dipstick is provided in the filler tube that shows the proper fluid level. If the fluid level is low, add enough fluid to raise the level to the Full mark on the dipstick or filler tube. Use automatic transmission fluid, type A.

Pump Belt Check
1. Inspect the pump belt for cracks, glazing, or worn places. Using a belt tension gauge, check the belt

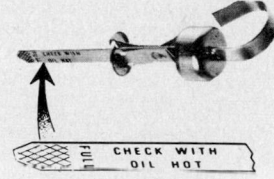
Power steering pump dipstick
(© Ford Motor Co.)

adjustment. The amount of tension varies with the make of car and the condition of the belt. New belts (those belts used less than 15 minutes) require a higher figure. The belt deflection method of adjustment may be used only if a belt tension gauge is not available. The belt should be adjusted for a deflection of $3/8$ to $1/2$ in.

Fluid Leaks
Check all possible leakage points (hoses, power steering pump, or steering gear) for loss of fluid. Start engine and rotate the steering wheel from lock to lock several times. Tighten all loose fittings and replace any defective lines or valve seats.

Turning Effort

Check the effort required to turn the steering wheel after aligning the front wheels and inflating the tires to the proper pressure.

1. With the vehicle on dry pavement and the front wheels straight ahead, set the parking brake and turn the engine on.
2. After a short warm-up period turn the steering wheel back and forth several times to warm the steering fluid.
3. Attach a spring scale to the steering wheel rim and measure the pull required to turn the steering wheel one complete revolution in each direction. The effort needed to turn the steering wheel should not exceed the limits given in the specifications.

NOTE: this test may be done with torque wrench on the steering wheel nut. See the section on Manual Steering for a discussion of this test.

Power Steering Pump Flow

Since the power steering pump provides all the power assist in a power steering system, the pump must operate properly at all times. After performing all the checks given above, the power steering pump may be tested for proper flow by the following procedure:

1. Disconnect the pressure and return lines at the power steering pump and connect the test pressure and return lines to the pump. The test pressure and return lines are connected to a pressure gauge and two manual valves.
2. Open the two manual valves, connect a tachometer to the engine, and start the engine. Run the engine at idle speed until the reservoir fluid temperature reaches 165-175°F. *This temperature must be maintained during the test.* Manual valve B may be partially closed to create a back pressure of no more than 350 psi to aid the temperature rise. Reservoir fluid must be at the proper level.
3. After the engine and the reservoir fluid are sufficiently warmed up, close valve B. Note the pressure gauge reading. It must be a minimum of 620 psi.
4. If the pressure reading is below

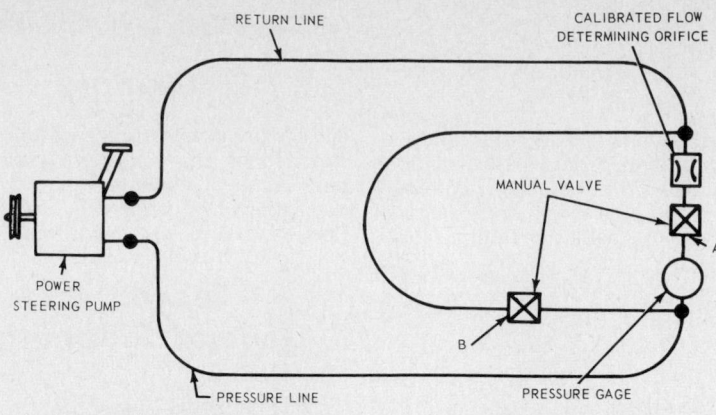

Power steering pump test circuit diagram (© Ford Motor Co.)

the minimum acceptable pressure, the pump is defective and must be repaired. If the pressure reading is at or above the minimum value, the pump is normal. Open manual valve B and proceed to the pump fluid pressure test.

Power Steering Pump Fluid Pressure Test

1. Keep the lines and pressure gauge connected as in the Pump Flow Test.
2. With manual valves A and B opened fully, run the engine at the proper idle speed. Then, close valve A and valve B, in that order. *Do not keep both valves closed for more than 5 seconds since the fluid temperature will increase causing severe pump wear.*
3. With both manual valves closed, the pressure reading should be as given in the specifications. If the pressure reading is below the minimum reading, the pump is defective and must be repaired. If the pressure reading is at or above the minimum reading, the pump is normal and the power steering gear or power assist control valve must be checked.

Power Steering Hose Inspection

1. Inspect both the input and output hoses of the power steering pump for worn spots, cracks, or signs of leakage. Replace hose if defective, being sure to recon-

nect the replacement hose properly. Many power steering hoses are identified as to where they are to be connected by special means, such as, fittings that will only fit on the correct pump fitting, or hoses of special lengths.

Checking the Oil Flow and Pressure Relief Valve in the Pump Assembly

When the wheels are turned hard right or hard left, against the stops, the oil flow and pressure relief valves come into action. If these valves are working, there should be a slight buzzing noise. Do not hold the wheels in the extreme position for over three or four seconds because, if the pressure relief valve is not working, the pressure could get high enough to damage the system.

Test Driving Car to Check the Power Steering

When test driving to check power steering, drive at a speed between 15 and 20 mph. Make several turns in each direction. When a turn is completed, the front wheels should return to the straight ahead position with very little help from the driver.

If the front wheels fail to return as they should and yet the steering linkage is free and properly adjusted, the trouble is probably due to misalignment of the power cylinder or improper adjustment of the spool valve.

Section 3
Power Steering
Oil Pumps

The power steering oil pump supplies all the power assist used in power steering systems of all designs. There are various designs of oil pumps used by the automobile

manufacturers but all pumps supply power to operate the steering systems with the least effort. All power steering pumps have a reservoir tank built onto the oil pump. These pumps

are driven by belts turned by pulleys on the front of the crankshaft.

With the engine at idle speed, the pump supplies high fluid pressure. When the car is moving straight ahead, less pressure is needed and the excess is relieved through a pressure relief and flow control valve. The pressure relief part of the valve is inside the flow control part and is basically the same for all pumps. The flow control valve regulates the constant flow of fluid from the pump to meet the demands of the steering gear. The pressure relief valve limits the hydraulic pressure built up when the steering gear is turned against its stops.

During all pump disassembly work, make sure all work is done on a clean work surface. Clean the outside of the pump thoroughly and do not allow dirt of any kind to get inside the pump. Do not immerse the shaft oil seal in solvent.

When replacing the rotor shaft seal, be extremely careful not to scratch sealing surfaces.

Vane Type Power Steering Pump Overhaul

The vane type power steering pump is used in Saginaw steering systems. The operation is basically the same as that of the roller type pumps. Centrifugal force moves a number of vanes outward against the pump ring, pumping the fluid to the control valve.

Removal and Installation

1. Place drain pan under pump.
2. Disconnect hoses at the pump, securing them in a raised position to prevent oil drainage. Cap or cover the ends of the hoses to keep dirt out.
3. Loosen the bracket-to-pump mounting nuts, move pump toward engine slightly, and remove the pump drive belt.
4. Remove the pump from the car.
5. While holding the drive pulley steady, loosen and remove the

Removing end plate ring
(© Chevrolet Motor Div., G.M. Corp.)

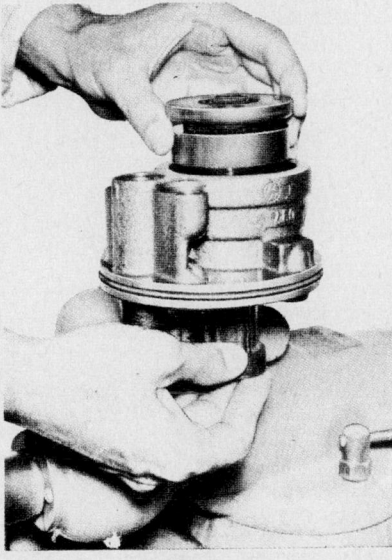

Removing impeller unit
(© Chevrolet Motor Div., G.M. Corp.)

Power steering pump mounting
(© Chevrolet Motor Div., G.M. Corp.)

pulley attaching nut. Slide the pulley off the shaft. *Do not hammer the pulley off the shaft because the pump will be damaged.*
6. To install the pump on the car, reverse the removal procedure. Always use a new pulley nut, tightening it to 35-45 ft. lbs.
7. After reconnecting the hoses to the pump, fill the reservoir with fluid and bleed the pump of air by turning the drive pulley counterclockwise (as viewed from the front) until air bubbles disappear.
8. Install the pump drive belt over the pulley, move the pump against the belt until tight enough, and tighten the mounting bolts and nuts.
9. Bleed the air from the system as noted above.

Disassembly

1. Clean the outside of the pump in a non-toxic solvent before disassembling.
2. Mount the pump in a vise, being careful not to distort the front hub of the pump.
3. Remove the union and seal.
4. Remove the reservoir retaining studs and separate the reservoir from the housing.
5. Remove the mounting bolt O-rings and the union O-rings.
6. Remove the filter and filter cage; discard the filter element.
7. Remove the end plate retaining ring by compressing the retaining ring and then prying it out with a screwdriver. The retaining ring may be compressed by inserting a small punch in the 1/8 in. diameter hole in the housing and pushing in until the ring clears the groove.
8. Remove the end plate. The end plate is spring-loaded and should rise above the housing level. If it is stuck inside the housing, gentle tapping should free the plate.
9. Remove the shaft Woodruff key and tap the end of the shaft gently to free the pressure plate, pump ring, rotor assembly, and thrust plate. Remove these parts as one unit.
10. Remove the end plate O-ring. Separate the pressure plate, pump ring, rotor assembly, and thrust plate.

Inspection

Clean all metal parts in a non-toxic solvent and inspect them as noted below:

1. Check the flow control valve for free movement in the housing bore. If the valve is sticking, see if there is dirt or roughness in the bore.
2. Check the cap screw in the end of the flow control valve for

looseness. Tighten if necessary, being careful not to damage the machined surfaces.

3. Inspect the pressure plate and pump plate surfaces for flatness, cracks, or scores. Do not mistake the normal wear marks for scoring.

4. Check the vanes in the rotor assembly for free movement. See that they were installed with the radiused edge toward the pump ring.

5. If the flow control valve plunger is defective, install a new part. It is factory calibrated and supplied as a unit.

6. Check the driveshaft for worn splines, cracks, bushing material pick-up, etc.

7. Check the reservoir, studs, casting, etc. for burrs and other defects that would impair operation.

8. Use new O-rings when assembling.

the splines. Countersunk side must be toward the pulley.

4. Install the shaft retaining ring. Install the pump ring on the dowel pins with the direction of rotation arrow to the rear of the pump housing. Rotation is clockwise as seen from the pulley.

5. Install the vanes in the rotor slots with the radius edge towards the outside.

6. Lubricate the outside diameter and chamfer of the pressure plate with petroleum jelly so as not to damage the O-ring and install the plate on the dowel pins with the ported face toward the pump ring. Seat the pressure plate by placing a large socket on top of the plate and pushing down with hand.

7. Install the pressure plate spring in the center groove of the plate.

8. Install the end plate O-ring. Lubricate the outside diameter and chamfer of the end plate

Installing thrust plate
(© Chevrolet Motor Div., G.M. Corp.)

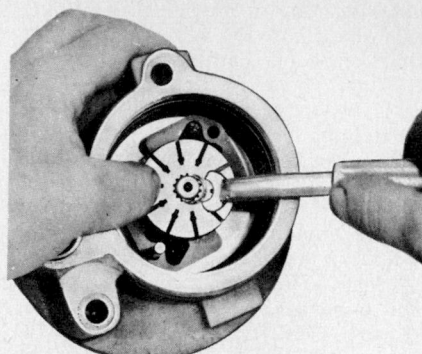

Installing shaft snap ring
(© Chevrolet Motor Div., G.M. Corp.)

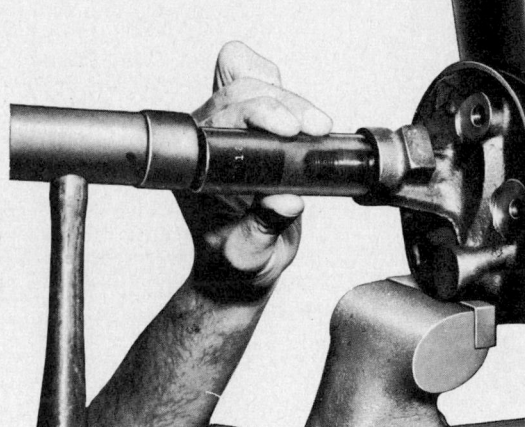

Installing shaft seal
(© Chevrolet Motor Div., G.M. Corp.)

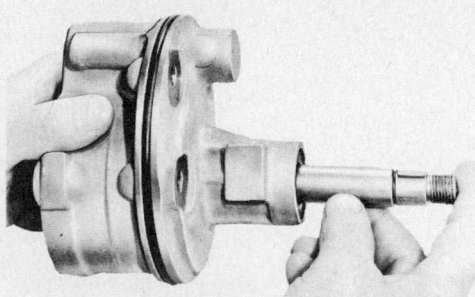

Shaft installation
(© Chevrolet Motor Div., G.M. Corp.)

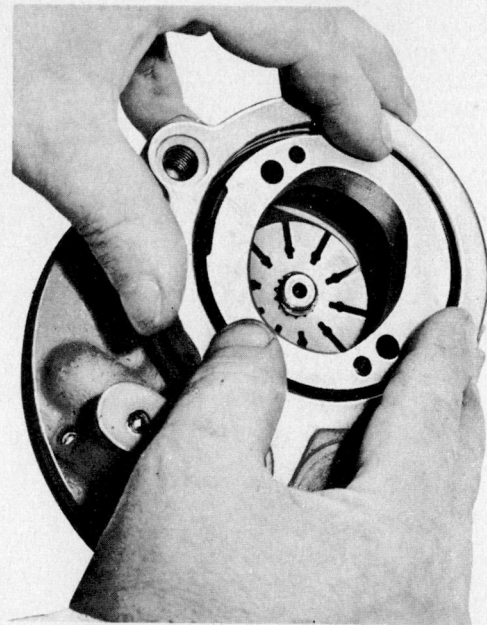

Installing pump ring
(© Chevrolet Motor Div., G.M. Corp.)

Assembly

1. Install a new shaft seal in the housing and insert the shaft at the hub end of housing, splined end entering mounting face side.

2. Install the thrust plate on the dowel pins with the ported side facing the rear of the pump housing.

3. Install the rotor on the shaft, making sure it moves freely on

with petroleum jelly so as not to damage the O-ring and install the end plate in the housing using an arbor press. Install the end plate retaining ring while pump is in the arbor press. Be sure the ring is in the groove and the ring gap is positioned properly.

9. Install the flow control spring and plunger, hex head screw end

in bore first. Install the filter cage, new filter stud seals and union seal.

10. Place the reservoir in the normal position and press down until the reservoir seats on the hous-stud seals and the union seal.

11. Install the studs, union, and driveshaft Woodruff key. Support the shaft on the opposite side of the key when tapping the

Installing vanes
(© Chevrolet Motor Div., G.M. Corp.)

Installing pressure plate spring
(© Chevrolet Motor Div., G.M. Corp.)

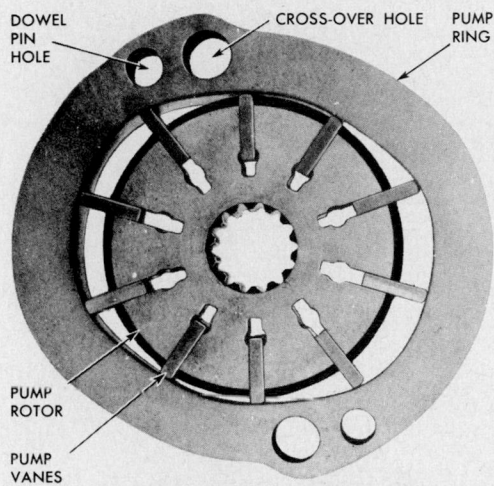

DOWEL PIN HOLE — CROSS-OVER HOLE — PUMP RING — PUMP ROTOR — PUMP VANES

Correct vane assembly
(© Chevrolet Motor Div., G.M. Corp.)

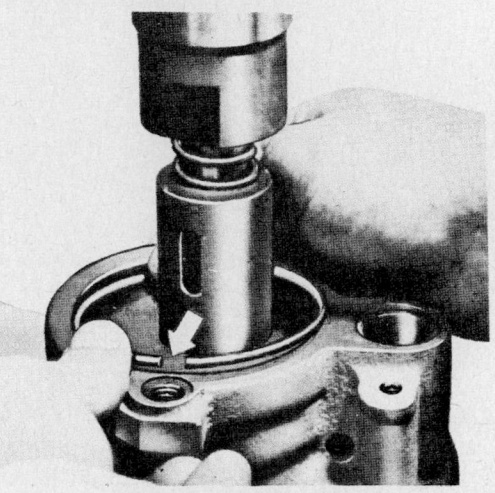

Installing end plate retaining ring
(© Chevrolet Motor Div., G.M. Corp.)

key into place.

Roller Type Power Steering Pump Overhaul

The roller type power steering pump is similar to other constant flow centrifugal force pumps. A star-shaped rotor forces 12 steel rollers against the inside surface of a cam ring. As the rollers follow the eccentric pattern of the cam ring, oil is drawn into the inlet ports and exhausted through the discharge ports while the rollers are forced into vee shaped cavities of the rotor, forcing oil into the high pressure circuit. A flow control valve permits a regulated amount of oil to return to the intake side of the pump when excess output is produced during high speed operation. This reduces the power needed to drive the pump and minimizes temperature build-up.

Under high pressure demand (such as turning the wheels against the stops), the pressure built up in the steering gear exerts force on the spring end of the flow control valve. This end of the valve contains the

pressure relief valve. High pressure lifts the relief valve ball from its seat, allowing oil to flow through a trigger orifice located in the front land of the flow control valve. This reduces pressure on the spring end of the valve which then opens and allows the oil to return to the intake

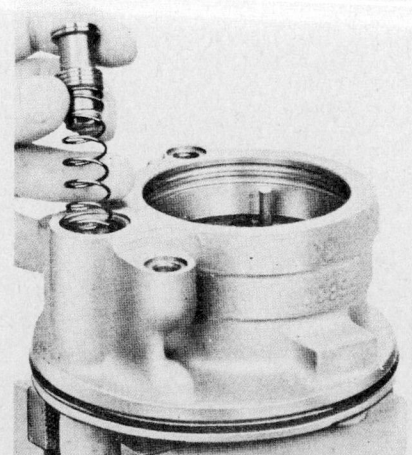

Installing flow control valve
(© Chevrolet Motor Div., G.M. Corp.)

side of the pump. This action limits the maximum pressure output of the pump to a safe level. Normally, the pressure needs of the pump are below the maximum pressure output of the pressure relief ball and the flow control valve to remain closed.

Removal

1. Loosen the pump mounting and locking bolts and remove the belt.
2. Disconnect both hoses at the pump. Cap and tie the hoses out of the way. Cap the hose fittings on the pump.
3. Remove the mounting and locking bolts and remove the pump and brackets from the car.

Installation

1. Install the brackets and pump on the engine.
2. Install the drive belt and adjust for the proper tension.
3. Connect the pressure and return hoses, using a new pressure hose O-ring.
4. Fill the pump reservoir to the

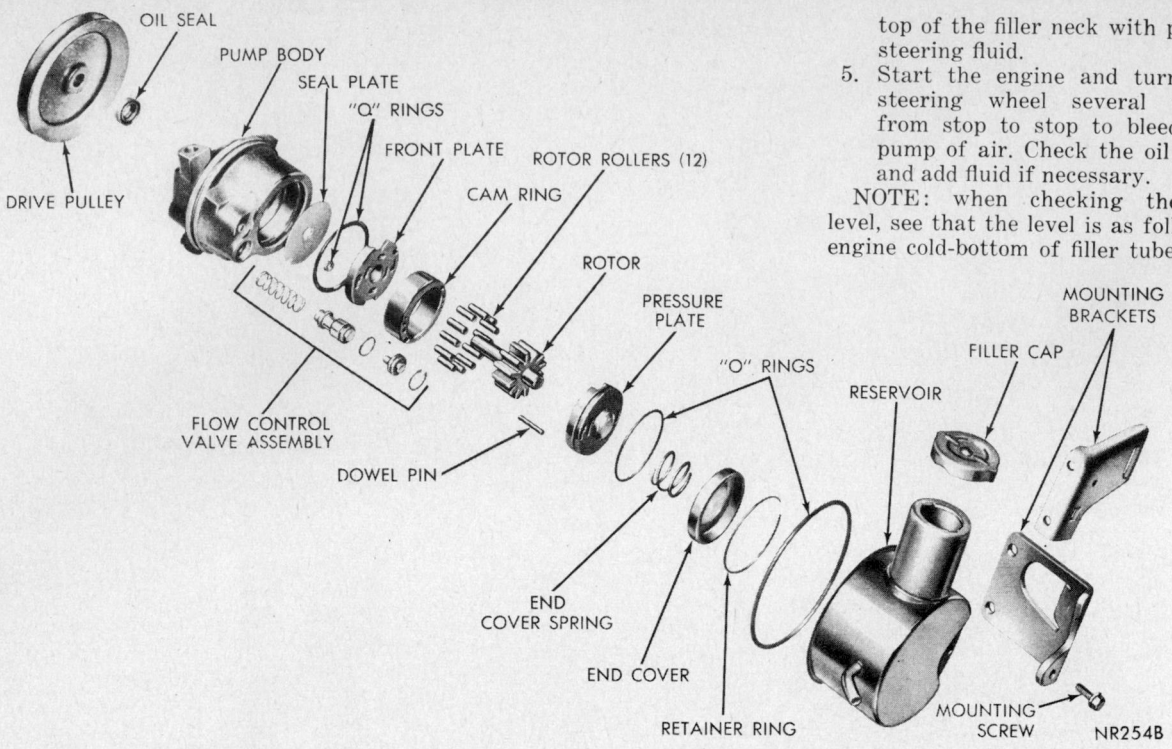

top of the filler neck with power steering fluid.

5. Start the engine and turn the steering wheel several times from stop to stop to bleed the pump of air. Check the oil level and add fluid if necessary.

NOTE: when checking the oil level, see that the level is as follows: engine cold-bottom of filler tube; en-

Chrysler 1.06 power steering pump, disassembled view (© Chrysler Corp.)

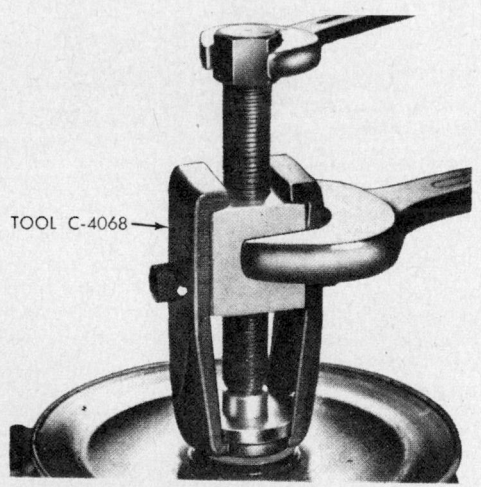

Removing drive pulley (© Chrysler Corp.)

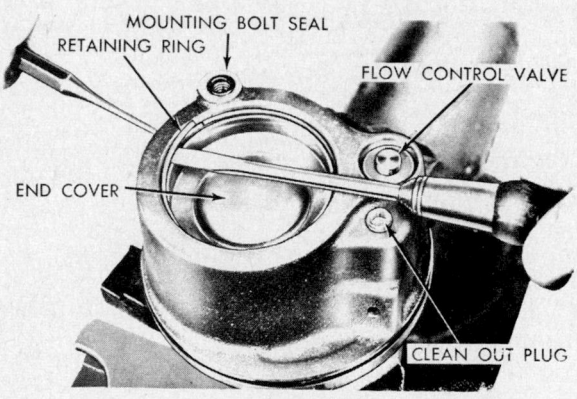

Removing end cover retaining ring (© Chrysler Corp.)

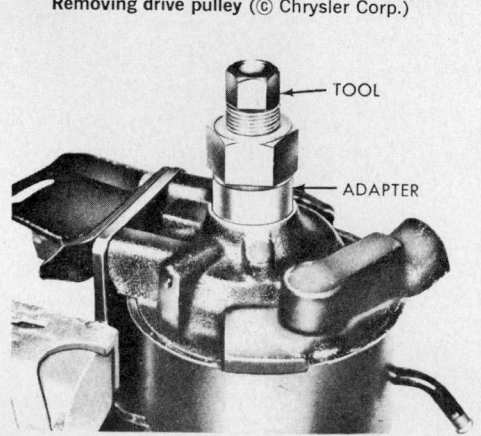

Removing shaft seal (© Chrysler Corp.)

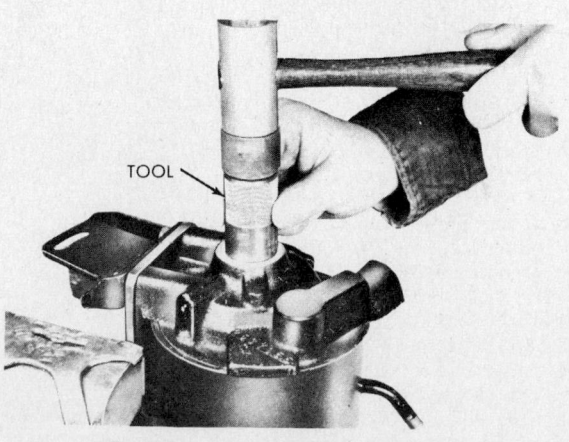

Installing shaft seal (© Chrysler Corp.)

gine hot-half way up filler tube.

Disassembly

1. Remove pump from engine, drain reservoir, and clean outside of pump. Clamp the pump in a vise at the mounting bracket.
2. Remove the drive pulley.
3. Remove the shaft seal by installing the seal remover adapter over the end of the driveshaft with the large end toward the pump. Place the seal remover tool over the shaft and through the adapter. Then, screw the tapered thread well into the metal portion of the seal. Tighten the large drive nut and remove the seal.
4. Remove the pump from the vise and remove the bracket mounting bolts. Remove the bracket.
5. Remove the reservoir and place the pump in a soft-faced vise with the shaft down. Discard the mounting bolt and the reservoir O-rings.
6. Move the end cover retaining ring around until one end of the ring lines up with the hole in the pump body. Insert a small punch in the hole and push it in far enough to bend the ring so a screwdriver can be inserted to pry the ring loose.
7. Remove the end cover and spring from the housing. It may be necessary to tap the cover gently to loosen it.
8. Remove the pump from the vise and turn the pump over so the rotating group may come out of the housing. Tap the end of the driveshaft to loosen these parts. Lift the pump body off the rotating group. Check that the seal plate is removed from the bottom of the housing bore.
9. Discard the O-rings from the pressure plate and end cover.
10. Remove the snap ring, bore plug, flow control valve and spring from the housing. Discard the O-ring. If necessary to disassemble the flow control valve for cleaning, see the procedure for disassembly.

Inspection

1. Remove the clean out plug with an Allen wrench.
2. Wash all metal parts in clean, non-toxic solvent. Blow out all passages with compressed air and air dry all cleaned parts.
3. Inspect the driveshaft for excessive wear and the seal area for nicks or scoring. Replace if necessary.
4. Inspect the end plates, rollers, rotor and cam ring for nicks, burrs, or scratches. If any of the components are damaged enough

to cause poor operation of the pump, all the internal parts may have to be replaced to prevent later failures.
5. Inspect the pump body drive shaft bushing for excessive wear. Replace the pump body and bushing as one assembly.

Assembly

1. Install the ⅛ in. pipe clean out plug, tightening it to 80 in. lbs.
2. Place the pump body on a clean flat surface and drive a new shaft seal into the bore.
3. Install a new lubricated end cover O-ring into the groove in the pump bore.
4. Lubricate and install a new O-ring on the pump body to reservoir joint.
5. Install a new fiber gasket and brass seal plate on bottom of housing floor, taking care to align correctly. Align the notch in the seal plate with the dowel pin hole in the housing.
6. Carefully install the front plate with the chamfered edge down in the pump bore. Align the index notch in the plate with the dowel pin hole in the housing.

Caution Be extremely careful to align the dowel pin properly. Pump can be completely assembled with the dowel pin improperly seated in the housing and positioned improperly in the end plates.

7. Place the dowel pin in the cam ring and position the cam ring inside the pump bore. Notch in the cam ring must be facing up (away from the pulley end of pump housing). If the cam ring has two notches, one machined

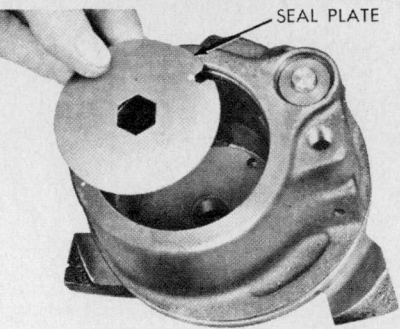

Installing seal plate (© Chrysler Corp.)

and one cast, install with machined notch up. If dowel pin protrudes above cam ring surface by more than 3/16 in., the dowel pin is not seated in the index hole in the housing.
8. Install the rotor and shaft in the cam ring and carefully install the 12 steel rollers in the rotor. Lubricate the rotor, rollers, and the inside surface of the cam ring with power steering fluid. Rotate the shaft by hand to be sure all the rollers are seated and are not sticking or binding.
9. Position the pressure plate by carefully aligning the index notch on the plate with the dowel pin and inserting a clean drill (number 13 to 16) in the cam ring oil hole next to the dowel pin notch until it bottoms on the housing floor.
10. Lubricate and install a new O-ring on the pressure plate. Position the pressure plate in the pump bore so that the dowel pin is in the index notch on the plate and the drill extends through the

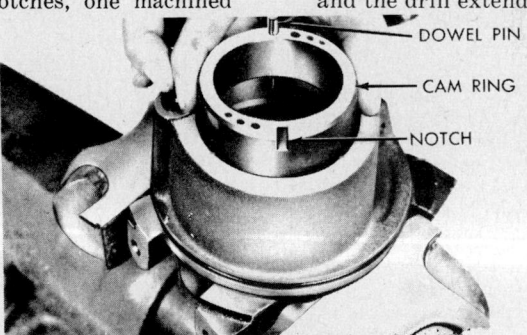

Installing cam ring (© Chrysler Corp.)

Installing rotor (© Chrysler Corp.)

Installing rollers in rotor
(© Chrysler Corp.)

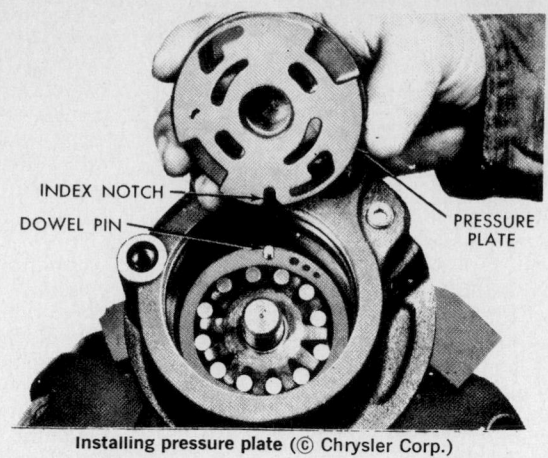

Installing pressure plate (© Chrysler Corp.)

INDEX NOTCH
DOWEL PIN
PRESSURE PLATE

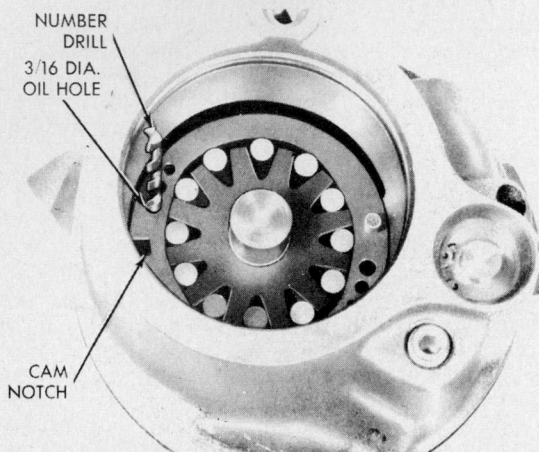

NUMBER DRILL
3/16 DIA. OIL HOLE
CAM NOTCH

Aligning oil holes (© Chrysler Corp.)

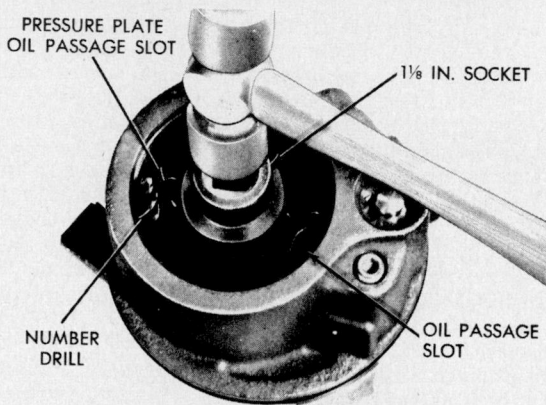

PRESSURE PLATE OIL PASSAGE SLOT
1⅛ IN. SOCKET
NUMBER DRILL
OIL PASSAGE SLOT

Seating pressure plate (© Chrysler Corp.)

oil passage in the pressure plate. Seat the pressure plate on the cam ring using a clean 1⅛ in. socket and a soft-faced hammer to tap it gently. Remove the drill and inspect the plate at both oil passage slots to be sure that the plate is squarely seated on the cam ring.

11. Place the large coil spring over the raised portion of the installed pressure plate.

12. Place the end cover, lip edge facing up, over the spring. Press the end cover down below the retaining ring groove. Install the retaining ring in the groove. Be sure the end cover chamfer is squarely seated against the snap-ring.

13. Replace the reservoir mounting bolt seal.

14. Lubricate the flow control valve assembly with power steering fluid and insert the valve spring and valve in the bore. Install a new O-ring on the bore plug, lubricate with fluid, and carefully install in the bore. Install the snap ring with the sharp edge up. *Do not depress the bore plug more than 1/16 in. below the snap-ring groove.*

15. Place the reservoir on the pump body and visually align the mounting bolt hole. Tap the res-

ervoir down on the pump with a plastic-faced hammer.

16. Remove the pump from the vise and install the mounting brackets on the pump. Tighten to 18 ft. lbs.

17. Install the drive pulley by using the installer tool as follows. Place the pulley on the end of the shaft and thread the installer tool into the ⅜ in. threaded hole in the end of the shaft. Put the installer shaft in a vise and tighten the drive nut against the thrust bearing, pressing the pulley on the shaft until it is flush with the end of the shaft. *Do not try to press the pulley on the shaft without the special installer tool since the pump will be damaged by any other installation procedure.* A small amount of driveshaft end-play will be seen when the pulley

is installed. This end-play is necessary and will be minimized by a thin coat of oil between the rotor and the end plates when the pump is operating.

18. Install the pump assembly on the engine, install the drive belt and hoses (use new O-ring on pressure hose), and check for leaks.

Flow Control Valve Disassembly

1. After removing the pump from the engine and the reservoir from the pump, remove the snap-ring and plug from the flow bore. Discard the O-ring.

2. Depress the control valve against the spring pressure and allow the valve to spring out of the bore. If the valve is stuck in the bore or it did not come out far enough, it may be necessary to tap the housing lightly.

3. If the valve has dirt or foreign

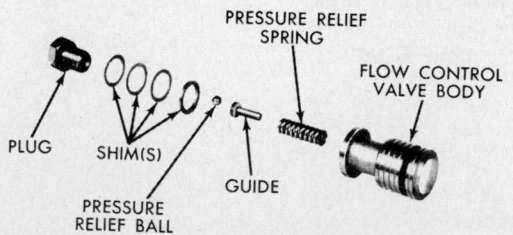

PLUG
SHIM(S)
PRESSURE RELIEF BALL
GUIDE
PRESSURE RELIEF SPRING
FLOW CONTROL VALVE BODY

Flow control valve, disassembled view
(© Chrysler Corp.)

particles on it or in its bore, the rest of the pump needs cleaning. The hoses should be flushed and the steering gear valve body reconditioned. If the valve bore is badly scored, replace the pump body and the flow control valve.

4. Remove any nicks or burrs by gently rubbing the valve with crocus cloth. Clamp the valve land in a soft-jawed vise and remove the hex head ball seat and shims. Note the number and gauge (thickness) of the shims on the ball seat. They must be re-installed at the same shim thickness to keep the same value of relief pressure.

5. Remove the valve from the vise and remove the pressure relief ball, guide, and spring.

Flow Control Valve Assembly

1. Insert the spring, guide and pressure relief ball in the end of the flow control valve.

2. Install the hex head plug using the same number and thickness shims that were removed. Tighten the plug to 80 in. lbs.

3. Lubricate the valve with power steering fluid and insert the flow control valve spring and valve in the housing bore. Install a new O-ring on the bore plug, lubricate with fluid and carefully install into the bore. Install the snap ring. *Do not depress the bore plug more than 1/16 in. beyond the snap-ring groove.*

Slipper Type Power Steering Pump Overhaul

The slipper type power steering pump is a belt-driven constant displacement unit that uses a number of spring-loaded slippers in the pump rotor to force oil from the inlet side to the flow control valve. Openings in the metering pin allow a flow of about two gpm. of fluid to the steering gear before the flow control valve directs the excess fluid to the inlet side of the pump again. Maximum pressure in the pump is limited by the pressure relief valve which opens when the oil pressure exceeds the

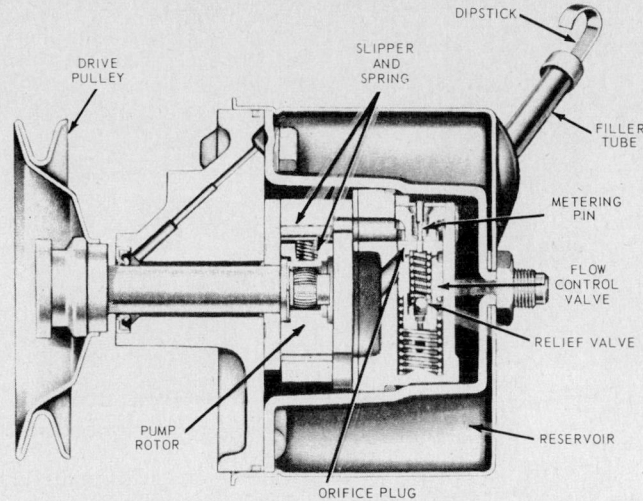

Ford-Thompson power steering pump, sectional view (© Ford Motor Co.)

maximum pressure limits.

The slipper type power steering pump discussed in this section is used in Ford cars except the Lincoln Continental and Continental Mark III and is called the Ford-Thompson power steering pump. It is also used in Chrysler cars, such as the Imperial, and called the 1.2 pump.

Removal and Installation

1. Drain the fluid from the pump reservoir by disconnecting the fluid return hose at the pump. Then, disconnect the pressure hose from the pump.

2. Remove the mounting bolts from the front of the pump. On eight cylinder engines, there is a nut on the rear of the pump that must be removed. After removal, move the pump inward to loosen the belt tension and

remove the belt from the pulley. Then, remove the pump from the car.

3. To reinstall the pump, position on mounting bracket and loosely install the mounting bolts and nuts. Put the drive belt over the pulley and move the pump outward against the belt until the proper belt tension is obtained. Measure the belt tension with a belt tension gauge for the proper adjustment. Only in cases where a belt tension gauge is not available should the belt deflection method be used. If the belt deflection method is used, be sure to check with a belt tension gauge as soon as possible, since deflection method is not accurate.

4. Tighten the mounting bolts and nuts to the specified torque.

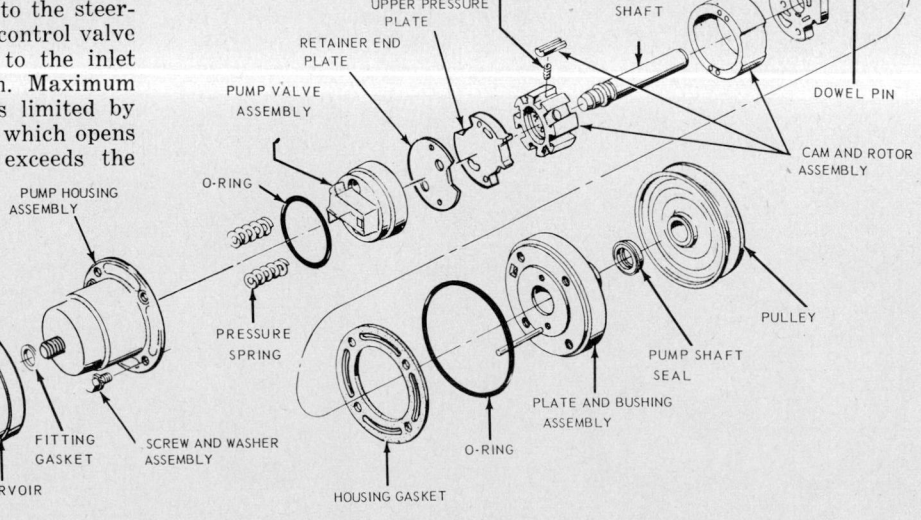

Ford-Thompson power steering pump, disassembled view (© Ford Motor Co.)

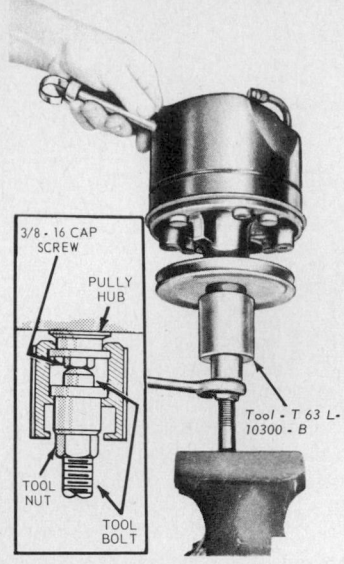

Removing drive pulley (© Ford Motor Co.)

Removing pump reservoir (© Ford Motor Co.)

Pump gasket locations (© Ford Motor Co.)

5. Tighten the pressure hose fitting hex nut to the proper torque. Then, connect the pressure hose to the pump and tighten the hose nut to the proper torque.
6. Connect the fluid return hose to the pump and tighten the clamp.
7. Fill the pump reservoir with power steering fluid, and bleed the air bubbles from the system.

8. Check for leaks and recheck the fluid level. If necessary, add fluid to the proper level.

Disassembly

1. Drain as much fluid from the pump as possible after removing the pump from the car.
2. Install a ⅜-16 in. capscrew in the end of the pump shaft to avoid damaging the shaft. Install the pulley remover tool on the pulley hub and place the pump and remover tool in a vise as shown. Hold the pump steady and turn the tool nut counterclockwise to draw the pulley off the shaft. *The pulley must be removed without in and out pressure on the pump shaft to avoid damaging the internal thrust washers.*
3. Remove the pump reservoir by installing the pump in a holding fixture in a vise with the reservoir facing up.
4. Remove the outlet fitting hex nut and any other attaching parts from the reservoir case.
5. Invert the pump so the reservoir is now facing down. Using a wooden block, remove the reservoir by tapping around the flange until the reservoir is loose. Remove the reservoir O-ring seal and the outlet fitting

gasket from the pump.
6. Again invert the pump assembly in the vise, remove the pump housing holding bolts, and the pump housing.
7. Remove the housing cover, the O-ring seal, and the pressure springs from inside the pump housing. Remove the pump cover gasket and discard it.
8. Remove the retainer end plate and upper pressure plate. In some pumps, the end plate and the upper pressure plate are one unit.
9. Remove the loose-fitting dowel pin. Be careful not to bend the fixed dowel pin which remains in the housing plate assembly.
10. Remove the rotor assembly, being careful not to let the slippers and springs fall out of the rotor. It may not be necessary to disassemble the rotor assembly unless the lower pressure plate, housing plate, rotor shaft and/or seal is to be replaced. However, the rotor assembly may be disassembled by removing the slippers and springs from the cam ring.
11. Clean any rust, dirt, burrs, or scoring from the pulley end of the rotor shaft before removing the shaft from the housing plate. The shaft must come out without restrictions to avoid scoring or damaging the bushing. Remove the pump rotor shaft.
12. Remove the lower pressure plate.
13. Remove the rotor shaft seal after first wrapping a piece of 0.005 in. shim stock around the shaft and pushing it into the inside of the seal until it touches the bushing. With a sharp tool, pierce the seal body and pry the seal out. *Do not damage the bushing, housing, or the shaft.* Install a new seal using the tool shown and a soft-faced hammer.
14. If the pump has a flow control valve, disassemble according to instructions given in the section

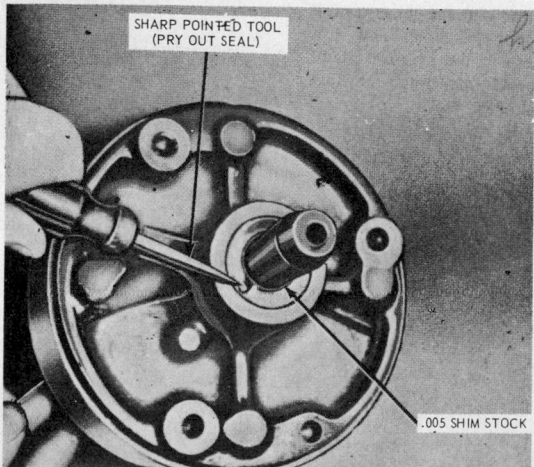

Rotor shaft seal removal (© Ford Motor Co.)

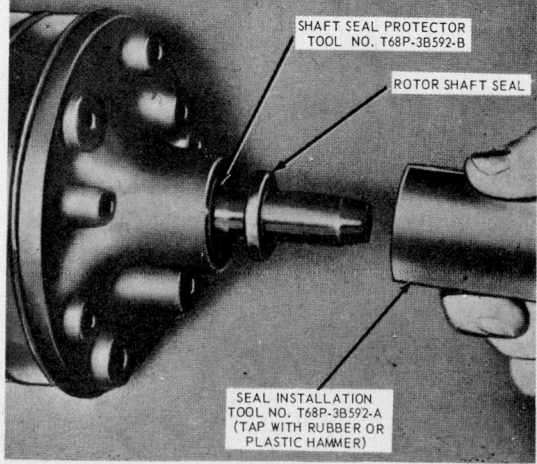

Rotor shaft seal installation (© Ford Motor Co.)

on the roller type power steering pump.

Inspection

1. Wash all metal parts in clean, non-toxic solvent. Blow out all oil passages with compressed air and air dry all cleaned parts.
2. Inspect the driveshaft for excessive wear and the seal area for nicks or scoring. Replace if necessary.
3. Inspect the pressure plates, slippers, rotor, and cam ring for nicks, burrs, or scratches. If any of the parts are damaged enough to cause poor operation or binding of the pump, replace the defective part.
4. Inspect the driveshaft bushing in the pump body for excessive wear. Replace if necessary.

Assembly

1. With the pump assembly in the holding fixture, install the lower pressure plate on the anchor pin with the chamfered slots at the center hole facing up.
2. Lubricate the rotor shaft with power steering fluid and insert the shaft into the lower pressure plate and housing plate.
3. Assemble the rotor, slippers, and springs by wrapping a piece of wire around the rotor, installing the springs, and sliding a slipper into each groove of the rotor over the springs. Then, insert the assembly into the cam ring. Be sure the flat side of the slippers are toward the left side as shown. (Ford-Thompson power steering pump). The Chrysler power steering pump slippers

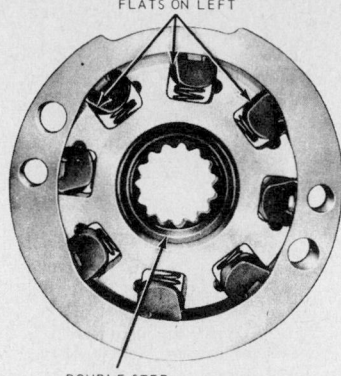

FLATS ON LEFT

DOUBLE STEP

Correct slipper installation, Ford-Thompson power steering pump
(© Ford Motor Co.)

FIXED DOWEL   DOUBLE STEP

ARROW POINTING DOWN

Cam and rotor installation
(© Ford Motor Co.)

are installed as shown. Be sure that the springs are installed straight and are not cocked to one side under the slippers.

4. Install the cam ring and rotor assembly on the driveshaft with the fixed dowel passing through the first hole to the left of the cam notch when the arrow on the cam outside diameter is pointing toward the lower pres-

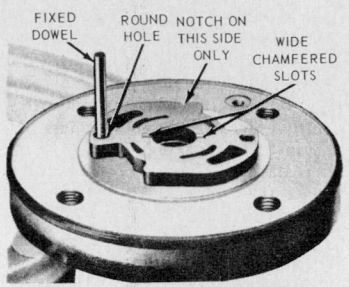

FIXED DOWEL   ROUND HOLE   NOTCH ON THIS SIDE ONLY   WIDE CHAMFERED SLOTS

Lower pressure plate installed
(© Ford Motor Co.)

sure plate. If the cam and rotor assembly does not seat properly, turn the rotor shaft slightly until the spline teeth mesh, allowing the cam and rotor to drop into position.

5. Insert the loose-fitting dowel through the cam insert and lower pressure plate into the hole in the housing plate assembly. When both dowels are installed properly, they will be the same height.
6. Install the upper pressure plate so the tapered notch is facing down against the cam insert. The fixed dowel should pass through the round dowel hole and the loose dowel through the long hole. The slot between the ears on the outside of the pressure plate should match the notch on the cam insert.
7. Install the retainer end plate so the slot on the end plate matches the notches on the upper pressure plate and the cam insert.
8. Install the pump valve assembly O-ring seal on the pump valve assembly. *Do not twist the seal.*
9. Place the pump valve assembly on top of the retainer end plate with the large exhaust slot on the pump valve in line with the outside notches of the cam, upper pressure plate, and retainer end plate. All parts must be fully seated. If correctly in-

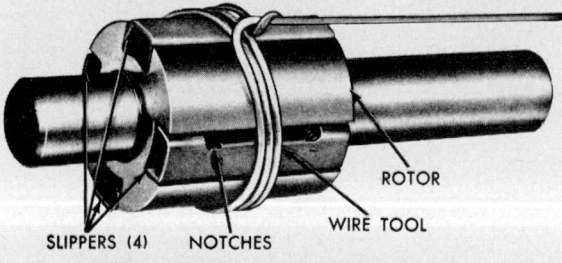

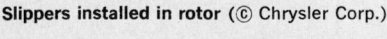

SLIPPERS (4)   NOTCHES   ROTOR   WIRE TOOL

Slippers installed in rotor (© Chrysler Corp.)

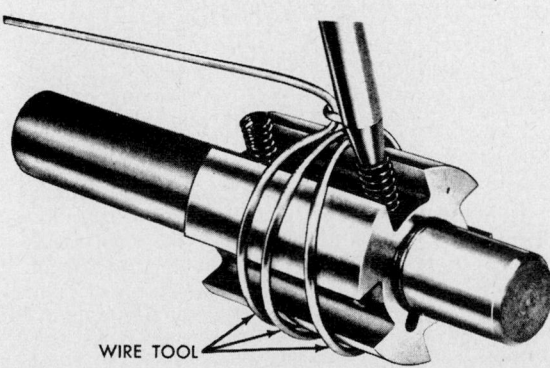

WIRE TOOL

Installing slipper springs (© Chrysler Corp.)

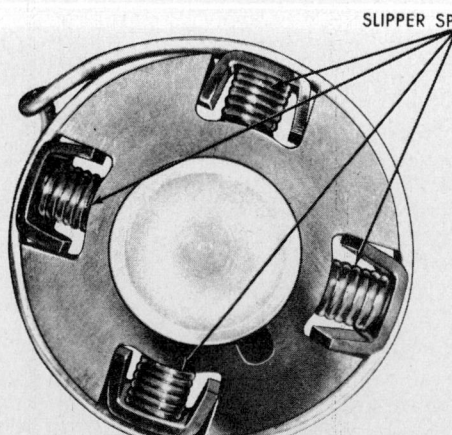

SLIPPER SPRINGS (8)

Correct slipper installation, Chrysler 1.2 power steering pump
(© Chrysler Corp.)

stalled, the relief valve stem will be in line with the lube return hole in the pump housing plate.

10. Put small amounts of vaseline on the pump housing plate to hold the cover gasket in place. Install the cover gasket.

11. Insert the pressure plate springs into the pockets in the pump valve assembly.

12. Block the intake hole in the housing.

13. Lubricate the inside of the housing and the housing cover seal with power steering fluid. Make and install two studs for use as positioning guides, one in the bolt hole nearest the drain hole and the other in the bolt hole on the opposite side of the housing plate.

14. Align the small lube hole in the housing rim and the lube hole in the housing plate. Install the housing, using a steady, even, downward pressure. *Do not jar the pressure spring out of position.* Remove the guide studs and loosely install the housing retaining bolts finger tight. Remove the block from the intake hole.

15. Tighten the retaining bolts evenly to 28-32 ft. lbs. until the housing flange contacts the gasket.

16. Install a 3/8-16 hex head screw into the end of the rotor shaft. Check the amount of torque

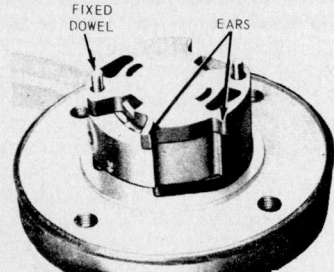

Upper pressure plate installation
(© Ford Motor Co.)

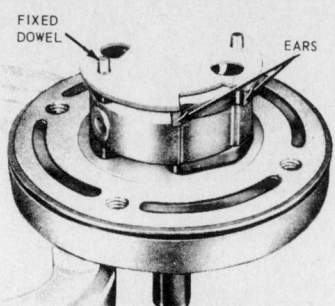

Retainer end plate installation
(© Ford Motor Co.)

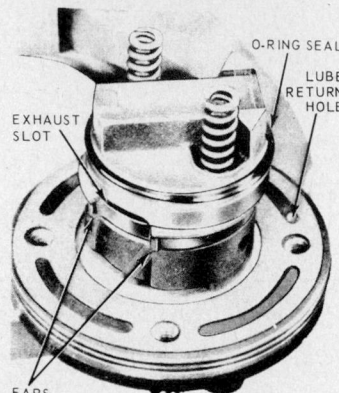

Valve and pressure spring installation
(© Ford Motor Co.)

Tool T69P-3B586-A

Pump housing installation
(© Ford Motor Co.)

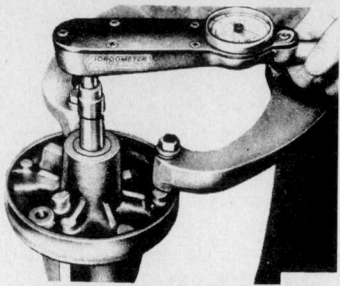

Checking pump rotational torque
(© Ford Motor Co.)

needed to rotate the shaft. If the torque is more than 15 in. lbs., loosen the retaining bolts slightly and rotate the rotor shaft. Then, retighten the retaining bolts evenly. *Do not use the pump if the shaft torque exceeds 15 in. lbs.*

17. Remove pump from the bench holding fixture and shake the assembly back and forth. If there is a rattle, the pressure springs have fallen out of their seats and must be reinstalled.

18. Install the reservoir O-ring seal on the housing plate without twisting it. Lubricate the seal and install the reservoir, aligning the notch in the reservoir flange with the notch in the outside edge of the pump housing plate and bushing assembly. Using a soft-faced hammer, tap at the rear outer corners of the reservoir. Inspect the assembly to be sure the reservoir is fully seated on the housing plate.

19. Install the identification tag (if any) on the outlet valve fitting. Install the outlet valve fitting nut and tighten to 43-45 ft. lbs.

20. Turn the pump assembly over and install the pulley with the tool used to remove it. Draw the pulley onto the shaft until it is flush with the shaft end. *Do not exert inward and outward pressures on the shaft to avoid damaging the internal thrust areas.*

Section 4
Bendix Linkage-Type Power Steering System

The Bendix linkage-type power steering system is a hydraulically controlled linkage-type system composed of an integral pump and fluid reservoir, a control valve, a power cylinder, connecting fluid lines, and the steering linkage. The hydraulic pump, which is driven by a belt turned by the engine, draws fluid from the reservoir and provides fluid pressure through hoses to the control valve and the power cylinder. There is a pressure relief valve to limit the pressures within the steering system to a safe level. After the fluid has

passed from the pump to the control valve and the power cylinder, it returns to the reservoir.

The Bendix linkage-type steering system when used in Ford-built cars is called the Ford Non-Integral Power Steering System.

In-Car Adjustments

Control Valve Centering Spring Adjustment

1. Raise the car and remove the spring cap attaching screws and

the spring cap.

Caution Be very careful not to position the hoist adapters of two-post hoists under the suspension and/or steering components. Place the hoist adapters under the front suspension lower arms.

2. Tighten the adjusting nut snugly (about 90-100 in. lbs.); then loosen the nut 1/4 turn (90 degrees) Do not tighten the adjusting nut too tight.

3. Place the spring cap on the valve housing. Lubricate and install the attaching screws and wash-

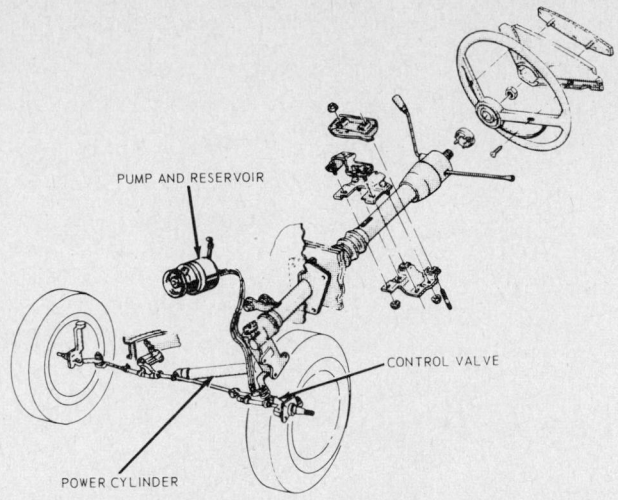

Bendix linkage-type power steering system (© Ford Motor Co.)

ers. Tighten the screws to 72-100 in. lbs.

4. Lower the car and start the engine. Check the steering effort using a spring scale attached to the steering wheel rim for a torque of no more than 12 lbs.

Power Steering Control Valve Removal and Installation

1. Raise the car on a hoist. If a post hoist is used, be sure to place the hoist adapters under the front suspension steering arms. *Do not allow the hoist adapters to contact the steering linkage.*
2. Disconnect the four fluid line

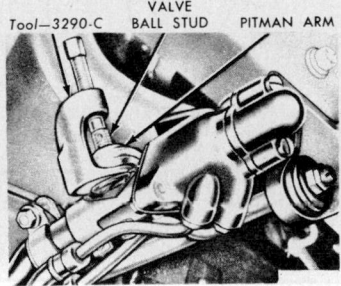

Removing control valve ball stud
(© Ford Motor Co.)

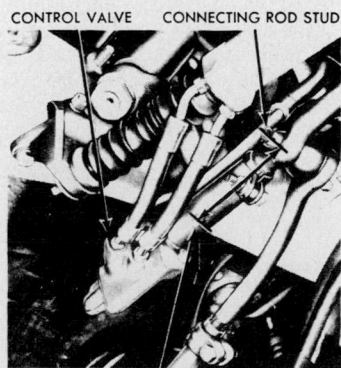

Control valve installation measurements
(© Ford Motor Co.)

fittings at the control valve and drain the fluid from the lines. Turn the front wheels back and forth to force all the fluid from the system.

3. Loosen the clamping nut and bolt at the right end of the sleeve.
4. Remove the roll pin from the steering arm-to-idler arm rod through the slot in the sleeve.
5. Remove the control valve ball stud nut.
6. Remove the ball stud from the sector shaft arm using puller.
7. After turning the front wheels fully to the left, unthread the control valve from the center link steering arm-to-idler arm rod.
8. To install the control valve, thread the valve on the center link until about four threads are still visible.
9. Position the ball stud in the sector shaft arm.
10. Measure the distance between the grease plug in the sleeve and the stud at the inner end of the left spindle connecting rod. For Ford Mustang and Cougar cars, the distance should be 4⅞ in. For Montego, Falcon and Fairlane cars, the distance should be 5⅜ in. 1970 and later Maverick and Comet are 5⅞ in. If the distance is not correct, disconnect the ball stud from the sector shaft arm and turn the valve on the center link until the correct distance is obtained.
11. When the distance is correct and the ballstud is positioned in the sector shaft arm, align the hole in the steering arm-to-idler arm rod with the slot near the end of the valve sleeve. Install the roll pin in the rod hole to lock the valve in place on the rod.
12. Tighten the valve sleeve clamp bolt to the proper torque: 18-42

in. lbs. for all Ford Motor Co. applications.

13. Install the ball stud nut and tighten to the proper torque. Install a new cotter pin.
14. Connect all fluid lines to the control valve and tighten all fittings securely. Do not over-tighten.
15. Fill the fluid reservoir with power steering fluid to the full mark on the dipstick.
16. Start the engine and run it for a few minutes to warm the fluid in the power steering system. Turn the steering wheel back and forth to the stops and check the system for leaks.
17. Increase the engine speed to about 1000 rpm, turn the steering wheel back and forth several times, and stop the engine. Check the control valve and hose connections for leaks.
18. Recheck the fluid level and add fluid if necessary.
19. Start the engine again, and check the position of the steering wheel when the front wheels are straight ahead. *Do not make any adjustments until toe-in is checked.*
20. With engine running, check toe-in (see Front Wheel Alignment section).
21. Check steering wheel turning effort which should be equal in both directions.

Power Steering Power Cylinder Removal and Installation

1. Disconnect the two fluid lines from the power cylinder and drain the fluid.
2. Remove the pal nut, attaching nut, washer and the insulator from the end of the power cylinder rod. Remove the cotter pin and castellated nut holding the power cylinder stud to the center link.
3. Disconnect the power cylinder stud from the center link as shown.
4. Remove the insulator sleeve and washer from the end of the power cylinder.
5. Inspect the tube fittings and seats in the power cylinder for nicks, burrs, or other damage.

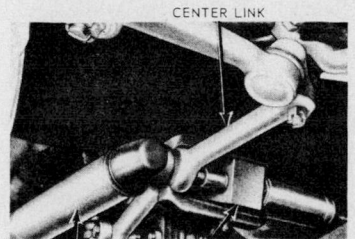

Disconnecting power cylinder stud
(© Ford Motor Co.)

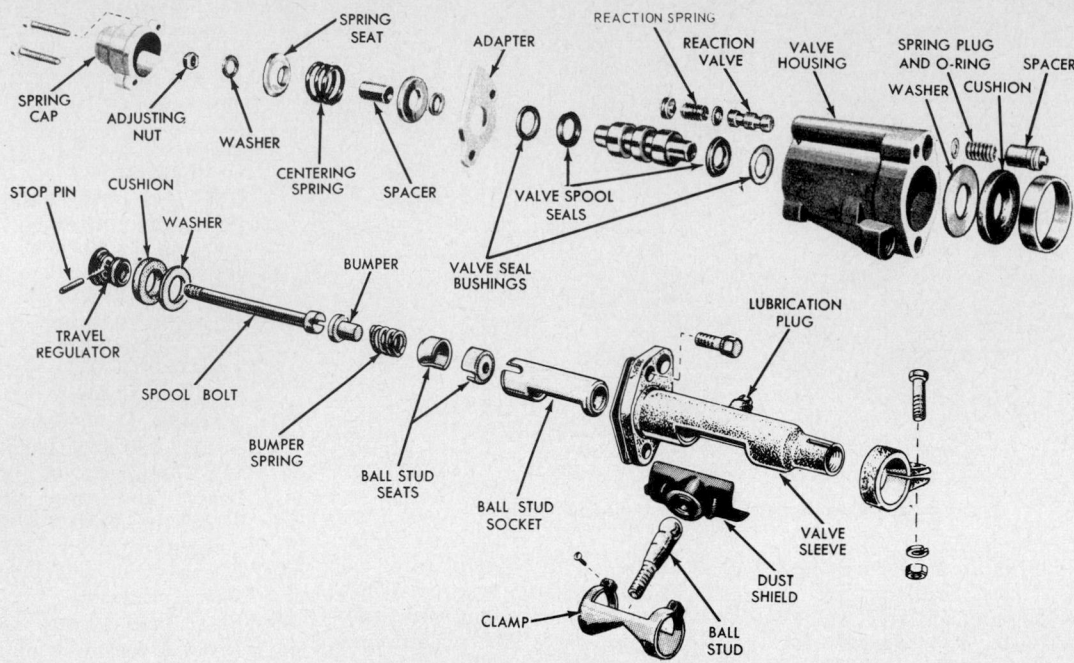

Control valve, disassembled view (© Ford Motor Co.)

Replace the seats or tubes if damaged.

6. Install the washer, sleeve and the insulator on the end of the power cylinder rod.

7. Extend the rod as far as possible, insert the rod in the bracket on the frame and compress the rod so the stud may be inserted in the center link. Secure the stud with the castellated nut and a new cotter pin.

8. Install the insulator, washer, nut, and a pal nut on the power cylinder rod.

9. Connect the two fluid lines to their proper ports on the power cylinder.

10. Fill the reservoir with power steering fluid to the full mark on the dipstick. Start the engine and run for a few minutes to warm the fluid. Turn the steering wheel back and forth to the stops to fill the system. Stop the engine.

11. Recheck the fluid level and add fluid if necessary. Check for fluid leaks.

12. Start the engine again, turn the steering wheel back and forth, and check for leaks while the engine is running.

Control Valve Disassembly and Assembly

1. Clean the outside of the control valve of dirt and fluid.

2. Remove the centering spring cap from the valve housing. The control valve should be put in a soft-faced bench vise during disassembly. Clamp the control valve around the sleeve flange only, to avoid damaging the housing, spool, or sleeve.

3. Remove the nut from the end of the valve spool bolt. Remove the washers, spacer, centering spring, adapter, and the bushing from the bolt and valve housing.

4. Remove the two bolts holding the valve housing and the sleeve together. Separate the valve housing and the sleeve.

5. Remove the plug from the sleeve. Push the valve spool out of the centering spring end of the valve housing, and remove the seal from the spool.

6. Remove the spacer, bushing, and seal from the sleeve end.

7. Drive the stop-pin out of the travel regulator stop with a punch and hammer. *Pull the head of the valve spool bolt tightly against the travel regulator stop before driving out the pin.*

8. Turn the travel regulator stop counterclockwise in the valve sleeve to remove the stop from the sleeve.

9. Remove the valve spool bolt, spacer, and rubber washer from the stop.

10. Remove the rubber boot and clamp from the valve sleeve. Slide the bumper, spring, and ball stud seat out of the valve sleeve, and remove the ball stud socket from the sleeve.

11. Remove the return port hose seat and the return port relief valve.

12. Remove the spring plug and O-ring. Then, remove the reaction limiting valve.

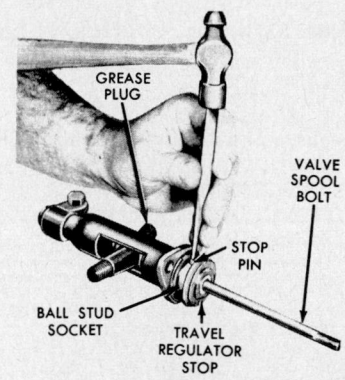

Removing the stop pin (© Ford Motor Co.)

13. Replace all worn or damaged hose seats by using an Easy-Out screw extractor or a bolt of proper size as a puller. Tap the existing hole in the hose seat, using a starting tap of the correct size. *Remove all metal chips from the hose seat after tapping.* Place a nut and washer on a bolt of the same size as the tapped hole. The washer must be large enough to cover the hose seat port. Insert the bolt in the

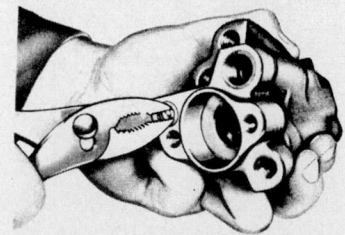

Removing the reaction valve plug (© Ford Motor Co.)

tapped hole and remove the hose seat by turning the nut clockwise and drawing the bolt out. Install a new hose seal in the port, and thread a bolt of the correct size in the port. Tighten the bolt enough to bottom the seal in the port.

14. Coat all parts of the control valve assembly with power steering fluid. Seals should be the ball stud socket, travel regu-installing.

15. Install the reaction limiting valve, spring, and plug. Install the return port relief valve and the hose seat.

16. Insert one of the ball stud seats (flat end first) into the ball stud socket, and insert the threaded end of the ball stud into the socket.

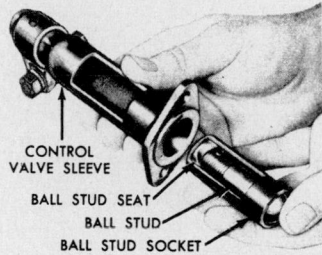

Installing ball socket, seal, and bracket
(© Ford Motor Co.)

CONTROL VALVE SLEEVE
BALL STUD SEAT
BALL STUD
BALL STUD SOCKET

17. Place the socket in the control valve sleeve so that the threaded end of the ball stud can be pulled out through the slot in the sleeve.

18. Place the other ball stud seat, spring, and bumper in the socket. Install and securely tighten the travel regulator stop.

19. Loosen the stop just enough to align the nearest hole in the stop with the slot in the ball stud socket, and install the stop pin in the ball stud socket, travel regulator stop, and valve spool bolt.

20. Install the rubber boot, clamp, and the plug on the control valve sleeve. Be sure the lubrication fitting is turned on tightly and does not bind on the ball stud socket.

21. Insert the valve spool in the valve housing, rotating it while

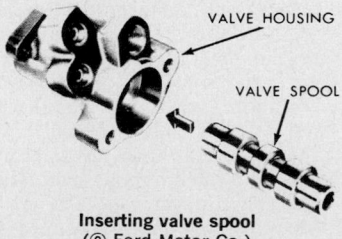

VALVE HOUSING

VALVE SPOOL

Inserting valve spool
(© Ford Motor Co.)

installing.

22. Move the spool toward the centering spring end of the housing, and place the small seal, bush-

ing, and spacer in the sleeve end of the housing.

23. Press the valve spool against the inner lip of the seal and, at the same time, guide the lip of the seal over the spool with a small screwdriver. *Do not nick or scratch the seal or spool during installation.*

24. Place the sleeve end of the housing on a flat surface so that the seal, bushing, and spacer are at the bottom end, and push down the valve spool until it stops.

25. Carefully install the spool seal and bushing in the centering spring end of the housing. Press the seal against the end of the spool, guiding the seal over the spool with a small screwdriver. *Do not nick or scratch the seal or the spool during installation.*

26. Pick up the housing, and slide the spool back and forth to check for free movement.

27. Place the body gasket and valve sleeve on the housing so that the ball stud is on the same side of the housing as the ports for the two power cylinder lines. Install the two bolts in the sleeve, and torque them to the proper specification.

28. Place the adapter on the centering spring end of the housing, and install the bushing, washers, spacers, and centering spring on the valve spool bolt.

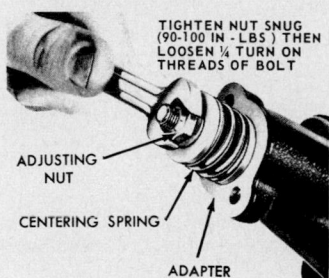

TIGHTEN NUT SNUG (90-100 IN-LBS) THEN LOOSEN ¼ TURN ON THREADS OF BOLT

ADJUSTING NUT

CENTERING SPRING

ADAPTER

Adjusting centering spring
(© Ford Motor Co.)

29. Compress the centering spring, and install the nut on the bolt. Tighten the nut snug (90-100 in. lbs.) ; then, loosen it not more than ¼ turn. *Do not overtighten, to avoid breaking the stop-pin at the travel regulator stop.*

30. Move the ball stud back and forth to check for free movement.

31. Lubricate the two cap attaching bolts. Install the centering spring cap on the valve housing, and tighten the two cap bolts to the proper torque.

32. Install the nut on the ball stud so that the valve can be put in a vise. Then, push forward on the cap end of the valve to check the valve spool for free movement.

33. Turn the valve around in the

vise, and push forward on the sleeve end to check for free movement.

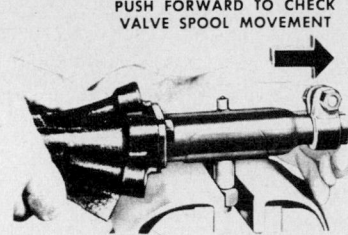

PUSH FORWARD TO CHECK VALVE SPOOL MOVEMENT

Inspecting valve spool movement
(© Ford Motor Co.)

Power Cylinder Seal Removal and Installation

1. Clamp the power cylinder in a vise, and remove the snap-ring from the end of the cylinder. *Do not distort or crack the cylinder in the vise.*

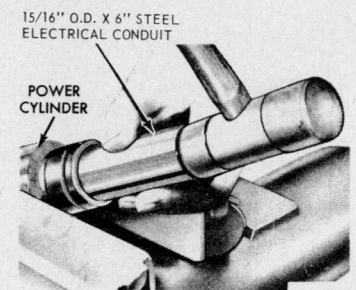

15/16" O.D. X 6" STEEL ELECTRICAL CONDUIT

POWER CYLINDER

Installing power cylinder seals
(© Ford Motor Co.)

2. Pull the piston rod out all the way to remove the scraper, bushing, and seals. If the seals cannot be removed in this manner, remove them by carefully prying them out of the cylinder with a sharp pick. *Do not damage the shaft or seal seat.*

3. Coat the new seals with power steering fluid and place the parts on the piston rod, which should be lubricated.

4. Push the rod in all the way, and install the parts in the cylinder with a deep socket slightly smaller than the cylinder opening.

Power Steering Pump Removal and Replacement

To remove or replace the power steering pump, see the section on the slipper type pump for instructions.

Power Steering Gear Removal and Replacement

To remove and replace the steering gear, see the section on Manual Steering for instructions.

Section 5
Saginaw Linkage-Type Power Steering System

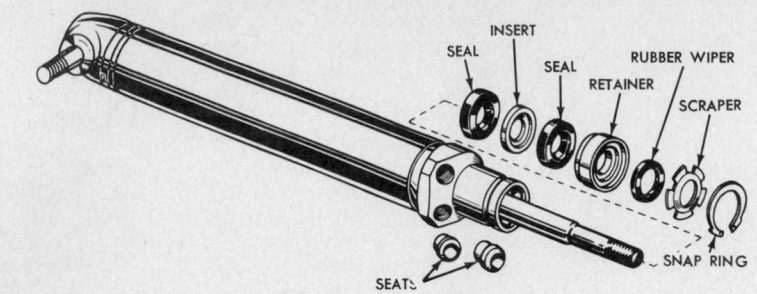

Power cylinder, disassembled view (© Ford Motor Co.)

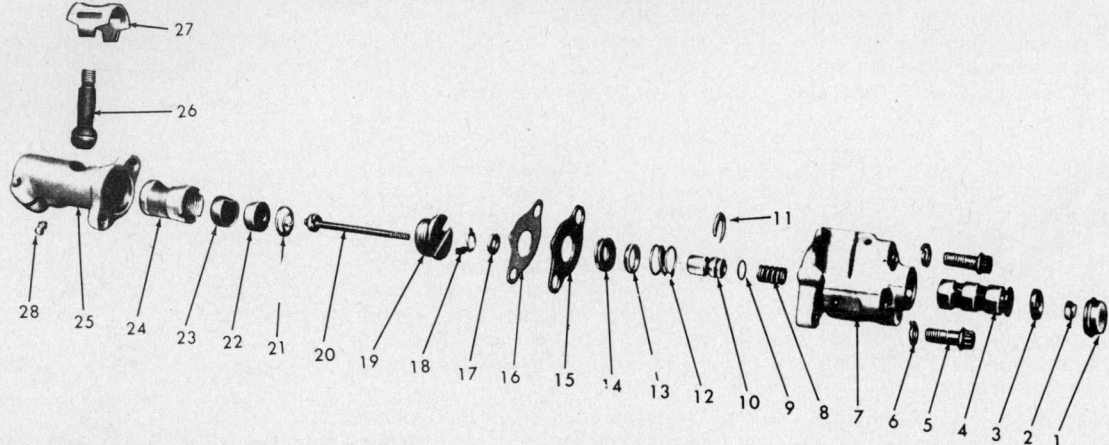

Control valve, disassembled view (© Chevrolet Motor Div., G.M. Corp.)

1 Dust cover	9 "O" ring seal	15 Annulus spacer	20 Valve shaft
2 Adjusting nut	10 Valve reaction	16 Gasket	21 Ball seat spring
3 Vee block seal	spool	17 Valve shaft	22 Ball seat
4 Valve spool	11 Spring thrust	washer	23 Ball seat
5 Valve mounting	washer	18 Plug to sleeve	24 Sleeve bearing
bolts	12 Valve spring	key	25 Adapter housing
6 Lock washer	13 Spring retainer	19 Ball adjuster	26 Ball stud
7 Valve housing	14 Annulus seal	nut	27 Dust shield
8 Valve adjustment			28 Lubrication fitting
spring			

Control Valve

Removal

1. Raise front of vehicle and place on stands.
2. Remove relay rod-to-control clamp bolt.
3. Disconnect pump-to-control valve hose connections and drain fluid, then disconnect the valve-to-power cylinder hoses.
4. Remove ball stud-to-pitman arm retaining nut and disconnect control valve from pitman arm.
5. Turn steering gear so that pitman arm is away from valve, to allow working room, and unscrew control valve from relay rod.
6. Remove control valve from vehicle.

Disassembly

1. Place valve assembly in vise with dust cap end up and remove dust cap.
2. Remove adjusting nut.
3. Remove valve-to-adapter bolts and remove valve housing and

spool from adapter.
4. Remove spool from housing.
5. Remove spring, reaction spool,

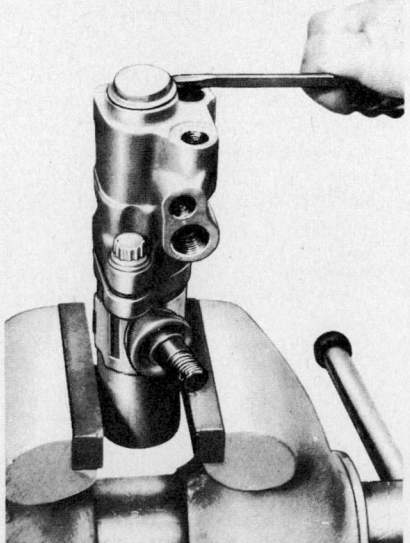

Dust cap removal
(© Chevrolet Motor Div., G.M. Corp.)

washer, reaction spring, and seal. O-ring may now be removed from reaction spool.
6. Remove annulus spacer, valve shaft washer and plug-to-sleeve key.
7. Carefully turn adjuster plug out of sleeve. Use care not to nick the top surface.
8. If necessary to replace a connector seat, tap threads in center hole using a 5/16-18 tap. Thread a bolt with a nut and a flat washer into the tapped hole so the washer is against the face of the port boss and the nut is against the washer. Hold the bolt from turning while backing the nut off the bolt. This will force the washer against the port boss face and back out the bolt, drawing the connector seat from the top cover housing. Discard the old connector seat and clean the housing out thoroughly to remove any metal chips. Drive a new connector seat against the housing seat, being careful not

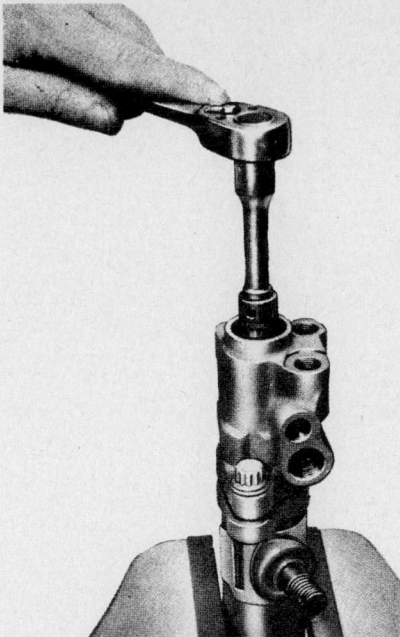

Removing adjusting nut
(© Chevrolet Motor Div., G.M. Corp.)

Removing spool from housing
(© Chevrolet Motor Div., G.M. Corp.)

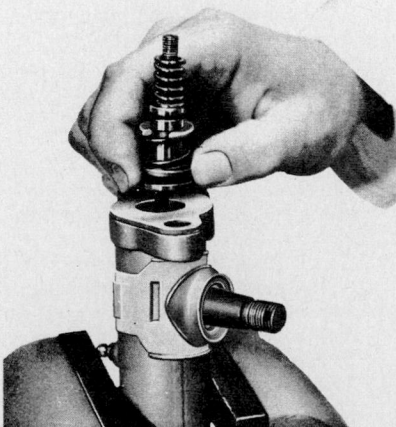

Removing valve parts from shaft
(© Chevrolet Motor Div., G.M. Corp.)

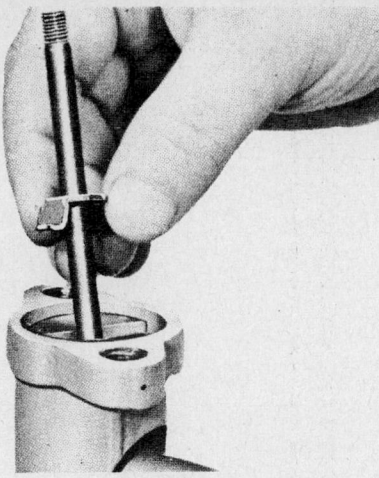

Removing plug-to-sleeve key
(© Chevrolet Motor Div.. G.M. Corp.)

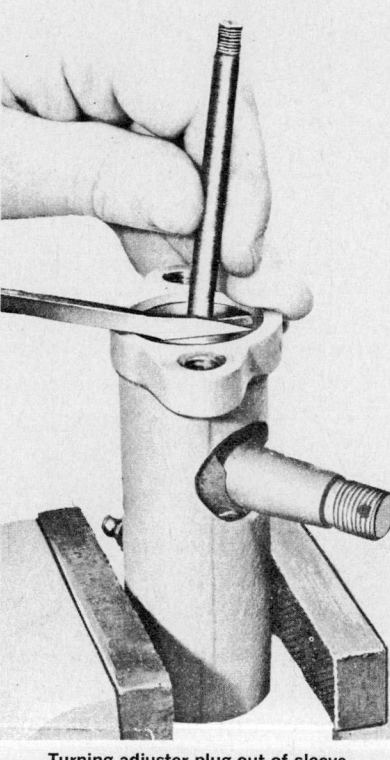

Turning adjuster plug out of sleeve
(© Chevrolet Motor Div., G.M. Corp.)

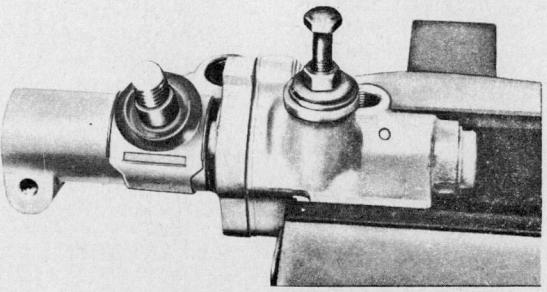

Removing connector seat
(© Chevrolet Motor Div., G.M. Corp.)

to damage either the connector seat or the housing seat.

9. Remove adapter from vise and turn over to allow spring and one of the two ball seats to drop out.
10. Remove ball stud with other ball seat and allow sleeve to fall free.

Inspection

1. Wash all parts in clean, non-toxic solvent and blow dry with air.
2. Inspect all parts for scratches, burrs, distortion, or excessive wear and replace worn or damaged parts.
3. Replace all seals and gaskets.

NOTE: Corvette valves incorporate a 55 pound centering spring which might be interchanged with Chevrolet, Chevelle and Chevy II springs. They should not be interchanged as the other springs are only 30 pounds. Corvette valves ar stamped with an X on the dust cover.

Assembly

1. Replace sleeve and ball seat in adapter, then the ball stud and then the other ball seat and spring. (small end down)
2. Place adapter in vise. Put the shaft through the seat in the adjuster plug and screw adjuster plug into sleeve.
3. Turn plug in until tight, then back off until slot lines up with notches in sleeve.
4. Insert key. Be sure small tangs on end of key fit into notches in sleeve.
5. Install valve shaft washer, annulus spacer, and reaction seal (lip up), spring retainer, reaction spring and spool, then washer and adjustment spring. Install O-ring seal on reaction spool before installing spool on shaft. Install washer with chamfer up.
6. Install seal on valve spool with lip down. Then install spool, being careful not to jam spool in housing.
7. Install housing with spool onto adapter. The side ports should be on the same side as the ball stud. Bolt the housing to the adapter.
8. Depress the valve spool and turn the locknut into the shaft about four turns. Use a clean wrench

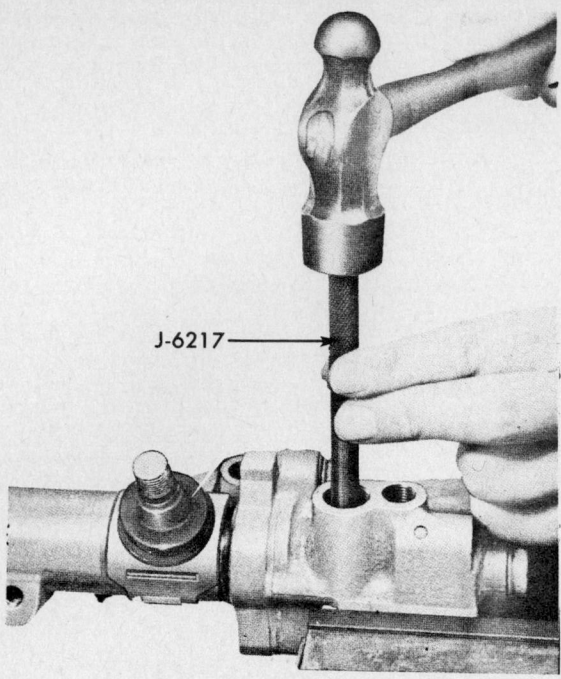

J-6217 —

Installing connector seat
(© Chevrolet Motor Div., G.M. Corp.)

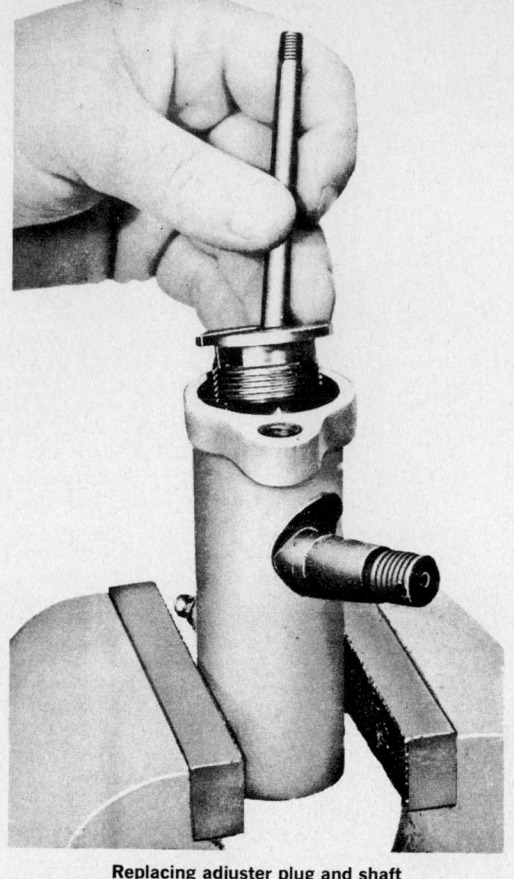

Replacing adjuster plug and shaft
(© Chevrolet Motor Div., G.M. Corp.)

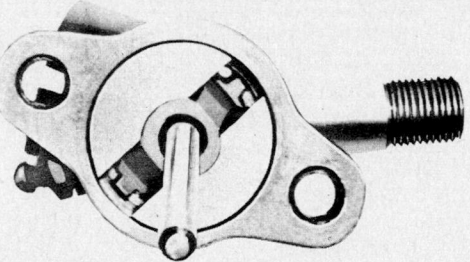

Proper key installation
(© Chevrolet Motor Div., G.M. Corp.)

or socket.

NOTE: always use a new nut.

Installation and Balancing

1. Install the control valve on the relay rod so that control valve bottoms, then back off enough (if necessary) to install the clamp bolt. Do not back off more than two turns. There will be approximately 1/16-1/8 in. gap.
2. Tighten control valve clamping bolt and install ball stud to Pitman arm.
3. Reconnect the four hoses to the valve.
4. Fill system with type A fluid and bleed air by running engine, then slowly turning wheels from lock to lock with engine idling. Be sure to keep reservoir full during this process. Do not replace dust cover before the following balancing procedure is completed.
5. Disconnect the piston rod from frame bracket if not already separated.
6. If piston rod is retracted, turn adjusting nut clockwise until rod begins to move out. Then, turn nut counterclockwise until rod just begins to move in. Now, turn the nut clockwise just exactly half the rotation needed to change the direction of piston rod movement. If piston rod is extended before starting, reverse the above to get the mid-point in piston movement.

Caution Do not turn the nut back and forth more

than is absolutely necessary to balance the valve.

7. With valve properly balanced it should be possible to move the rod in and out manually.
8. Shut off engine and connect piston rod to frame bracket.
9. Restart engine with front wheels still off ground. If the wheels do not turn in either direction from center, the valve has been properly balanced. Correct the condition by rebalancing the valve if necessary.
10. After proper adjustment, grease the end of valve and install dust cap.

Power Cylinder

Removal

1. Remove the two hoses which are

connected to the cylinder and drain fluid.

2. Remove power cylinder from frame bracket.
3. Remove cotter pin and nut and pull stud out of relay rod.
4. Remove cylinder from vehicle.

Inspection

1. Check seals for leaks around cylinder rod. If leaks are found, replace seals.
2. Check hose connection seats for damage and replace if necessary.
3. For service other than seat or seal replacement, it is necessary to replace the power cylinder.
4. The ball stud may be replaced by removing snap-ring.

Disassembly and Reassembly

1. To remove piston rod seal, re-

move snap-ring and pull out on rod. Remove back-up washer, piston rod scraper, and piston rod seal from rod.

2. To remove the ball stud, depress the end plug and remove the snap ring. Push on the end of the ball stud and the end plug, spring, spring seat, and ball stud and seal may be removed. If the

ball seat is to be replaced, it must be pressed out.

3. Reverse disassembly procedure. Be sure snap-ring is properly seated.

Installation

1. Install power cylinder on vehicle by reversing the removal procedure.

2. Reconnect the hydraulic lines, fill system and bleed out air as described in the control valve section.

Power Steering Hoses

Carefully inspect the hoses. When installing hoses be sure to install in such a position as to avoid all chafing or other abuse when making sharp turns.

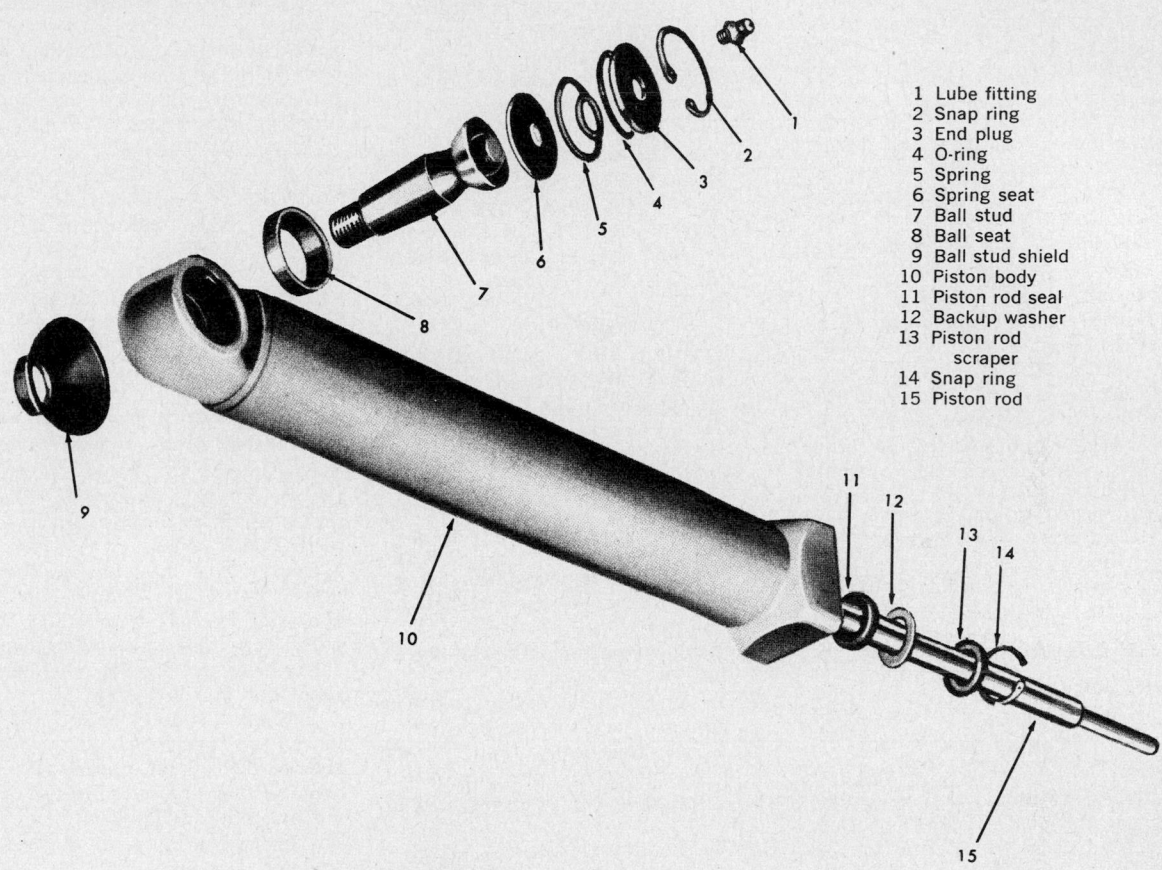

1 Lube fitting
2 Snap ring
3 End plug
4 O-ring
5 Spring
6 Spring seat
7 Ball stud
8 Ball seat
9 Ball stud shield
10 Piston body
11 Piston rod seal
12 Backup washer
13 Piston rod scraper
14 Snap ring
15 Piston rod

Power cylinder, disassembled view (© Chevrolet Motor Div., G.M. Corp.)

Removing ball cup
(© Chevrolet Motor Div., G.M. Corp.)

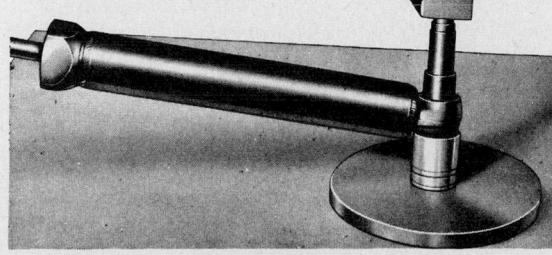

Installing ball cup
(© Chevrolet Motor Div., G.M. Corp.)

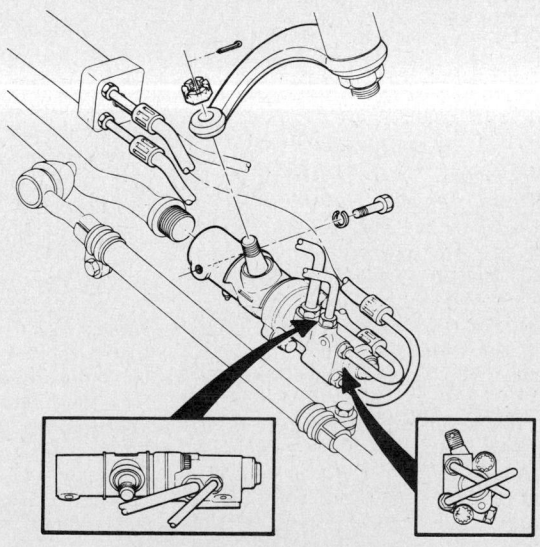

Power steering hose installation
(© Chevrolet Motor Div., G.M. Corp.)

Section 6
Saginaw Rotary-Type Power Steering

The rotary type power steering gear is designed with all components in one housing.

The power cylinder is an integral part of the gear housing. A double-acting piston allows oil pressure to be applied to either side of the piston. The one-piece piston and power rack is meshed to the sector shaft.

The hydraulic control valve is composed of a sleeve and valve spool. The spool is held in the neutral position by the torsion bar and spool actuator. Twisting of the torsion bar moves the valve spool, allowing oil pressure to be directed to either side of the power piston, depending on the directional rotation of the steering wheel, to give power assist.

On many General Motors cars a modified version of the system provides variable ratio steering for easier and safer control. The steering gear ratio will vary from a high ratio of about 16:1 while steering straight ahead to a lower gear ratio of about 12.4:1 while making a full turn to either side. See the specifications for the exact gear ratios.

Roller Pump Removal and Installation

Removal

Remove the reservoir cover and use a suction gun to empty the reservoir. Disconnect the hoses from the pump and tie them in a raised position to prevent oil spillage. Loosen the pump adjusting screw and remove the pump belt, then take out the retaining bolts and remove the pump and reservoir.

NOTE: on cars equipped with air conditioning, the pump is removed from underneath the vehicle.

Installation

Position the pump assembly and install the retaining bolts. Be sure there is clearance between the pump bracket and the engine front support bracket. Install the hoses and place the pump belt on the pulley. Adjust the belt to ½ in. deflection, then tighten the adjusting screw.

Connect the hoses to the pump assembly.

Fill the reservoir to within ½ in. of the top with automatic transmission fluid type A.

Start the engine and rotate the steering wheel several times to the right and left to expel air from the system, then recheck the oil level and install the reservoir cover.

Rotary Steering Unit Removal and Installation

Removal

1. Remove the lines from the steering gear and tie them in a raised position to prevent oil drainage.
2. Remove the power brake assembly, if necessary.
3. Using a puller, remove the pitman arm from the sector shaft.
4. Take out the nuts and bolts that hold the steering shaft coupling to the steering gear.
5. Remove the bolts that secure the gear assembly to the frame side rail and remove the gear assembly from the vehicle.

Installation

1. Position the gear assembly against the frame side rail and install the retaining bolts.
2. Install the pitman arm, aligning the large spline on the sector shaft with the large groove in the arm.

Caution Do not drive the pitman arm onto the sector shaft. Draw the arm into position with the nut.

3. Replace the power brake assembly.
4. Assemble the steering shaft coupling to the steering gear.
5. Install the hoses, then fill and bleed the power steering system.
6. Fill and bleed the brake system.

Power Steering Unit

Fluid Used

This unit uses automatic transmission fluid type A.

Bleeding the System

Fill the pump reservoir to within ½ in. of the top. Start and run the engine to attain normal operating temperatures. Now, turn the steering wheel through its entire travel three or four times to expel air from the system, then recheck the fluid level.

Checking Steering Effort

Run the engine to attain normal operating temperatures. With the wheels on a dry floor, hook a pull scale to the spoke of the steering wheel at the outer edge. The effort required to turn the steering wheel should be 3½-5 lbs. If the pull is not within these limits, check the hydraulic pressure.

Pressure Test

To check the hydraulic pressure, disconnect the pressure hose from the gear. Now connect the pressure gauge between the pressure hose from the pump and the steering gear housing. Run the engine to attain normal operating temperatures, then turn the wheel to a full right and a full left turn to the wheel stops.

Hold the wheel in this position only long enough to obtain an accurate reading.

The pressure gauge reading should be within the limits specified. If the pressure reading is less than the minimum pressure needed for proper operation, close the valve at the gauge and see if the reading increases. If the pressure is still low, the pump is defective and needs repair. If the pressure reading is at or near the minimum reading, the pump is normal and needs only an adjustment of the power steering gear or power assist control valve.

Worm Bearing Preload and Sector Mesh Adjustments

Disconnect the Pitman arm from the sector shaft, then back off on the sector shaft adjusting screw on the sector shaft cover.

Center the steering on the high point, then attach a pull scale to the spoke of the steering wheel at the outer edge. The pull required to keep the wheel moving for one complete turn should be ½-⅔ lbs.

If the pull is not within these limits, loosen the thrust bearing locknut and tighten or back off on the valve sleeve adjuster locknut to bring the preload within limits. Tighten the thrust bearing locknut and recheck the preload.

Slowly rotate the steering wheel several times, then center the steering on the high point. Now, turn the sector shaft adjusting screw until a steering wheel pull of 1-1½ lbs. is required to move the worm through the center point. Tighten the sector shaft adjusting screw locknut and recheck the sector mesh adjustment.

Install the pitman arm and draw the arm into position with the nut.

Repair Operations

Adjuster Plug and Rotary Valve Removal

1. Thoroughly clean exterior of gear assembly. Drain by holding valve ports down and rotating worm back and forth through entire travel.
2. Place gear in vise.
3. Loosen adjuster plug locknut with punch. Remove adjuster plug.
4. Remove rotary valve assembly by grasping stub shaft and pulling it out.

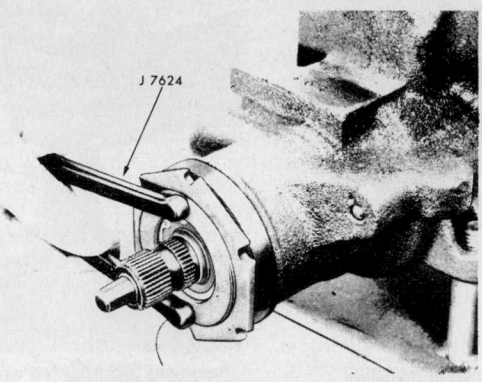

Removing adjuster plug assembly
(© Pontiac Div., G.M. Corp.)

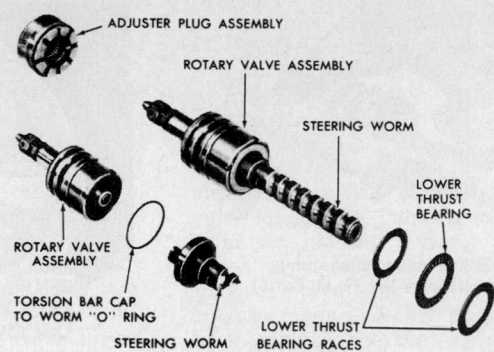

Adjuster plug and O-ring removal
(© Pontiac Div., G.M. Corp.)

Adjuster Plug Disassembly

1. Remove upper thrust bearing retainer with screwdriver. Be careful not to damage bearing bore. Discard retainer. Remove spacer, upper bearing and races.
2. Remove and discard adjuster plug O-ring.
3. Remove stub shaft seal retaining ring (Truarc pliers will help) and remove and discard dust seal.
4. Remove stub shaft seal by prying out with screwdriver and discard.
5. Examine needle bearing and, if required, remove same by pressing from thrust bearing end.
6. Inspect thrust bearing spacer, bearing rollers and races.
7. Reassemble in reverse of above.

Rotary Valve Disassembly

Repairs are seldom needed. Do not disassemble unless absolutely necessary. If the O-ring seal on valve spool dampener needs replacement, perform this portion of operation only.

wood rod through opening in valve body cap and push spool until it is out far enough to be removed. In this procedure, rotate to prevent jamming. If spool becomes jammed it may be necessary to remove stub shaft, torsion bar and cap assembly.

Rotary Valve Reassembly

Caution   All parts must be free of dirt, chips, etc., before assembly and must be protected after assembly.

1. Lubricate three new back-up O-ring seals with automatic transmission oil and reassemble in the ring grooves of valve body. Assemble three new valve body rings in the grooves over the O-ring seals by carefully slipping over the valve body.
   NOTE: if the valve body rings seem loose or twisted in the grooves, the heat of the oil during operation will cause them to straighten.
2. Lubricate a new dampener O-ring

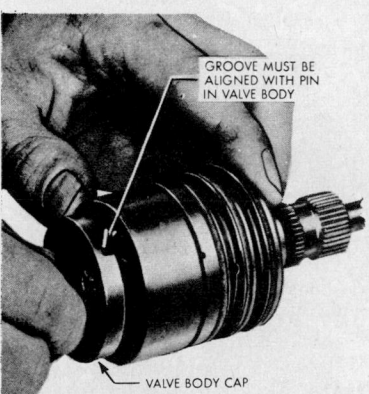

Assembling stub shaft, torsion bar, and cap assembly
(© Buick Motor Div., G.M. Corp.)

parts together during the remainder of assembly.

4. Lubricate spool. With notch in spool toward valve body, slide the spool over the stub shaft. Align the notch on the spool with

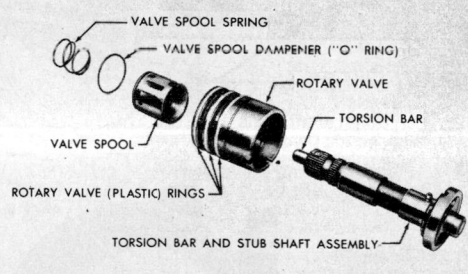

Rotary valve, disassembled view
(© Pontiac Div., G.M. Corp.)

1. Remove cap-to-worm O-ring seal and discard.
2. Remove valve spool spring by prying on small coil with small screwdriver to work spring onto bearing surface of stub shaft. Slide spring off shaft. Be careful not to damage shaft surface.
3. Remove valve spool by holding the valve assembly in one hand with the stub shaft pointing down. Insert the end of pencil or

with automatic transmission oil and install in valve spool groove.
3. Assemble stub shaft torsion bar and cap assembly in the valve body, aligning the groove in the valve cap with the pin in the valve body. Tap lightly with soft hammer until cap is against valve body shoulder. Valve body pin must be in the cap groove. Hold

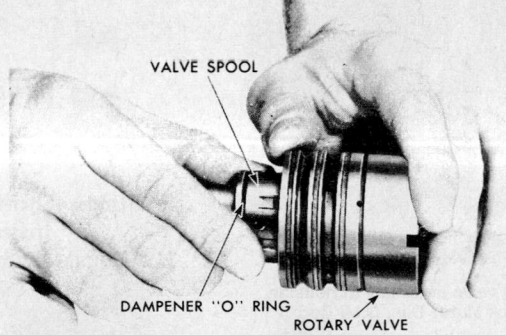

Removing valve spool from rotary valve
(© Pontiac Div., G.M. Corp.)

the spool drive pin on stub shaft and carefully engage spool in valve body bore. Push spool evenly and with slight rotating motion until spool reaches drive pin. Rotate spool slowly, with some pressure, until notch engages pin. Be sure dampener O-ring seal is evenly distributed in the spool groove.

4. If spool is not free, check for burrs and remove with a hard stone.
5. Check valve for burrs and if burrs are found, stone valve in a radial direction only. Be sure valve is entirely free.
6. Remove spool from housing.
7. Slide spool into actuator, making sure groove in spool annulus is toward worm.
8. Install snap-ring to retain spool.
9. Check clearance between spool and snap-ring. It should be 0.0005-0.0035 in. If not within these limits, select snap-ring that will produce 0.002 in clearance.

Piston and Ball Nut R & R

1. Remove the Teflon ring and O-ring from piston and ball nut.
2. Dip new O-ring in gear lubricant and install on piston and ball nut.
3. Install new Teflon ring, using care not to stretch more than necessary.

Gear Housing R & R

1. Remove snap-ring and spacer washer from lower end of housing.
2. Remove outer seal from housing. Lift out spacer washer.
3. Remove upper seal in same manner as lower seal.
4. Press upper and lower bushings from housing if worn or defective.
5. Press new bushings into place.
6. Dip both sector shaft seals in gear lubricant.
7. Apply lubricant to sector shaft seal bore of housing and position sector shaft inner seal in housing with lip facing inward. Press into place.
8. Place a 0.090 in. thick spacer washer on top of seal and apply more lubricant to housing bore.
9. Place outer seal in housing with lip facing inward and press into place. Then place a 0.090 in. thick spacer washer on top of seal.

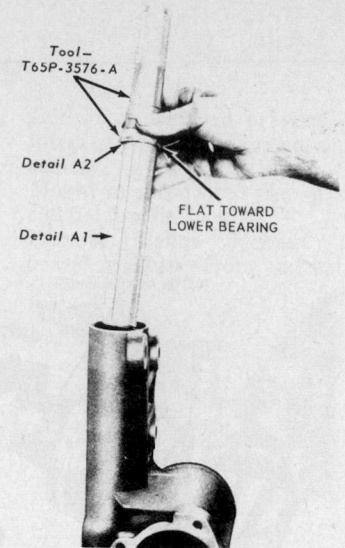

Installing lower bushing
in steering gear housing
(© Lincoln-Mercury Div., Ford Motor Co.)

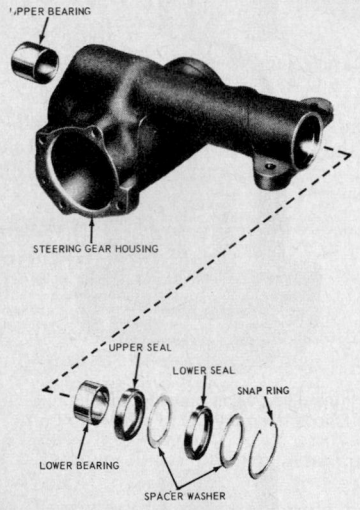

Steering gear housing, disassembled view
(© Lincoln-Mercury Div., Ford Motor Co.)

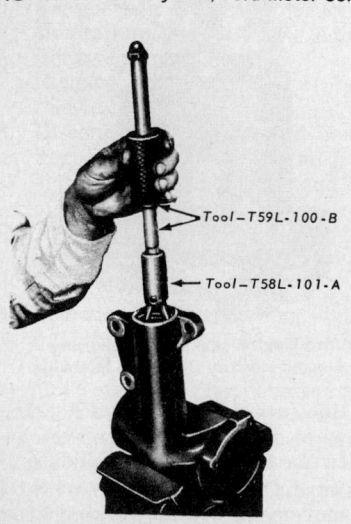

Removing outer seal
(© Lincoln-Mercury Div., Ford Motor Co.)

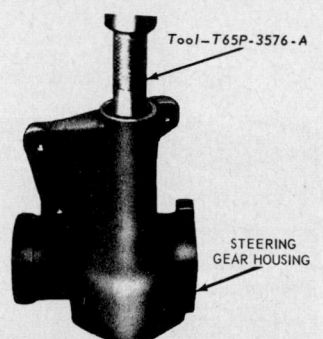

Removing steering gear housing upper
and lower bushings
(© Lincoln-Mercury Div., Ford Motor Co.)

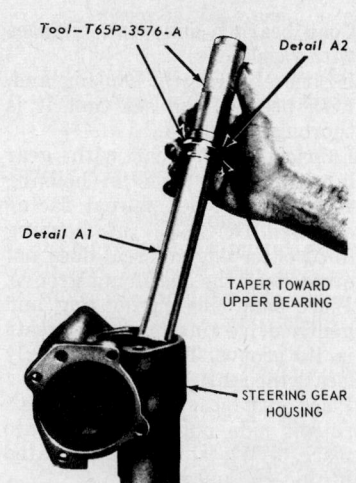

Installing upper bushing
in steering gear housing
(© Lincoln-Mercury Div., Ford Motor Co.)

10. Place snap-ring in housing and press into position to locate seals and engage the snap-ring in groove.

FIG. 30—Installing Sector Shaft Inner Seal

Installing sector shaft inner seal
(© Lincoln-Mercury Div., Ford Motor Co.)

Gear Assembly

1. Mount valve housing in fixture with flanged end up.
2. Place the same thickness valve spool centering shim in the housing as was removed. Use only one shim.
3. Install worm and valve in housing.
4. Install retaining nut in housing and torque to 55-65 ft. lbs.
5. Install locknut and tighten to 20-30 ft. lbs.
6. Place piston on bench with ball guide holes facing up. Insert worm shaft into piston so that first groove is in alignment with hole nearest to center of piston.
7. Place ball guide in position and feed balls (27) into guide, turning worm clockwise. If all balls have not been fed into guide upon reaching stop, rotate shaft back

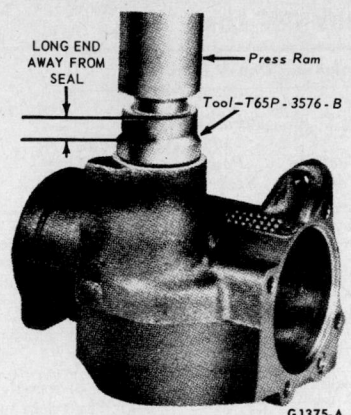

FIG. 31—Installing Sector Shaft Outer Seal

Installing sector shaft outer seal
(© Lincoln-Mercury Div., Ford Motor Co.)

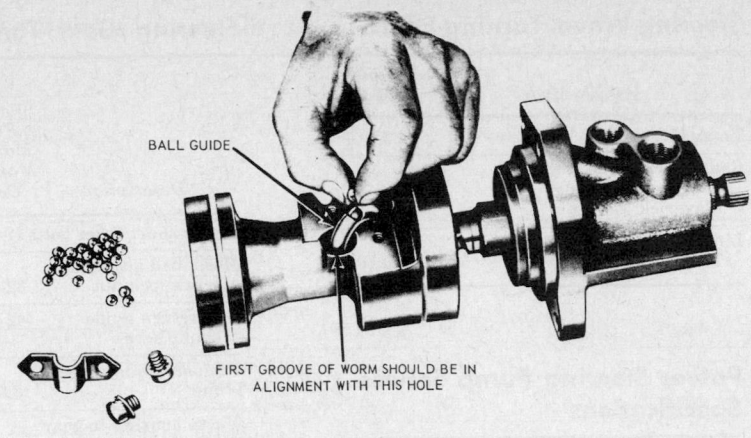

Assembling piston on wormshaft (© Lincoln-Mercury Div., Ford Motor Co.)

and forth while installing balance of balls.

8. Secure guides in ball nut with the clamp.
9. Position new lube passage O-ring in counterbore of housing.
10. Apply vaseline to Teflon seal on piston.
11. Place new O-ring on valve housing.
12. Position housing spacer ring in housing and slide piston and valve into gear housing. Do not damage Teflon seal.
13. Align lube passage in valve housing with one in gear housing. Install, but do not tighten, attaching bolts.
14. Rotate ball nut so that teeth are in same plane as sector teeth. Tighten valve housing attaching bolts.
15. Position sector shaft cover O-ring in gear housing. Turn input shaft to center the piston.
16. Position sector shaft and cover in gear housing. Install identification tag and shaft cover attaching bolts and tighten. Make adjustments as described under "Adjustments."

Adjustments

Valve Spool Centering

1. Install a 0-2000 psi pressure gauge into the pressure line from pump to gear inlet.
2. Be sure valve of gauge is entirely open.
3. Fill reservoir to proper level.
4. With engine idling, cycle steering from side to side through full travel. Check and keep system full of proper oil.
5. After the above bleeding, with engine at approximately 1000 rpm and the steering wheel centered, attach an in. lb. torque wrench to steering wheel nut. Apply pressure to torque wrench in either direction to produce gauge reading of 250 psi.
6. The torque reading should be similar in both directions. If more than 4 in. lbs. difference in either direction is recorded, the gear must be removed. The valve centering shim must be replaced by either a thicker or thinner shim. Use only one shim. To make this adjustment out of car use the same procedure, but the pressure reading must be made at the right and left stops, instead of either side of center.

Over Center Position Load

1. With no fluid in gear and torque wrench on steering wheel nut, or on input shaft of gear if out of car, rotate the gear slowly through the high point of sector shaft mesh.
2. With no load required to turn through this position and with adjuster locknut loose, gradually turn the adjuster screw to produce 11-12 in. lbs. more than required to turn when mesh is at no contact. Tighten locknut and recheck the torque.

Ford—Thompson Power Steering Pump Attaching Torque Limits (Ft. Lbs.)

Vehicle Application	Ford, Mercury		Falcon, Maverick, Comet		Thunderbird, Lincoln, Mk. III	Fairlane-Torino, Comet-Montego, Mustang-Cougar	
Engine	Six	V8	Six	V8	All	Six	V8
Pump to Front Bracket	30-40	30-45	30-45	30-45	30-40	30-40	30-45
Pump Pivot	30-40	30-40	30-40	25-40	30-40	30-40	30-40
Pump Bracket to Engine (Front)	15-20	30-45	7-10	30-45	30-45	7-10	30-45
Pump Bracket to Engine (Side)	45-65	-	19-25	-	-	30-45	-
Pump to Rear Bracket Nut	-	20-30	20-30	20-30	20-30	20-30	20-30
Pressure Hose to Pump Nut	28-37	28-37	28-37	25-34	28-37	28-37	28-37
Belt Adj. Bolt	30-40	30-40	30-40	30-40		30-40	30-40

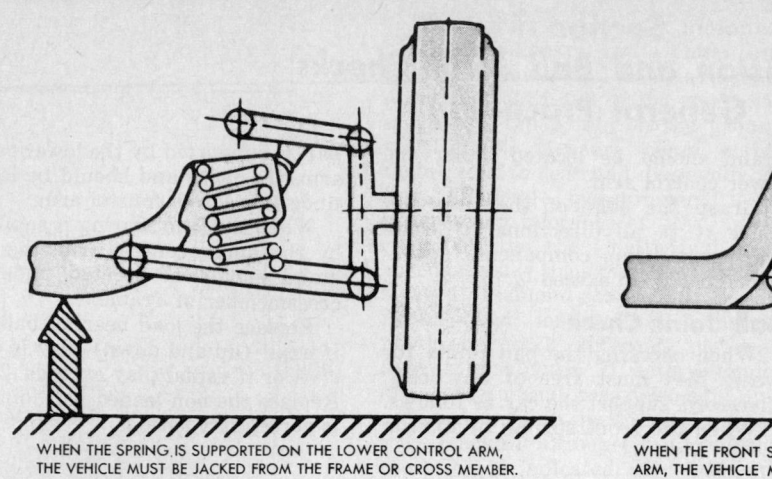

WHEN THE SPRING IS SUPPORTED ON THE LOWER CONTROL ARM, THE VEHICLE MUST BE JACKED FROM THE FRAME OR CROSS MEMBER.

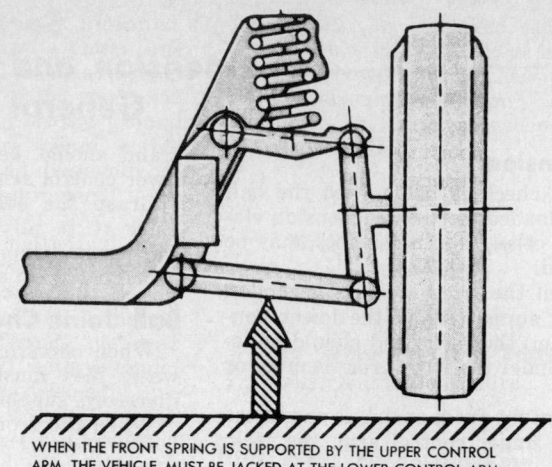

WHEN THE FRONT SPRING IS SUPPORTED BY THE UPPER CONTROL ARM, THE VEHICLE MUST BE JACKED AT THE LOWER CONTROL ARM.

Steering and suspension jacking procedure

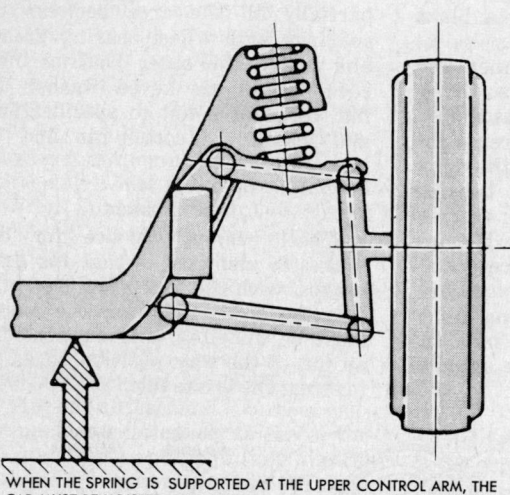

WHEN THE SPRING IS SUPPORTED AT THE UPPER CONTROL ARM, THE CAR MUST BE HOISTED AT THE FRAME.
REJECT IF LOWER JOINT IS PERCEPTIBLY LOOSE.

WHEN THE SPRING IS SUPPORTED AT THE LOWER CONTROL ARM, THE CAR MUST BE HOISTED AT THE ARM
REJECT IF UPPER JOINT IS PERCEPTIBLY LOOSE.

Ball joint inspection jacking procedure

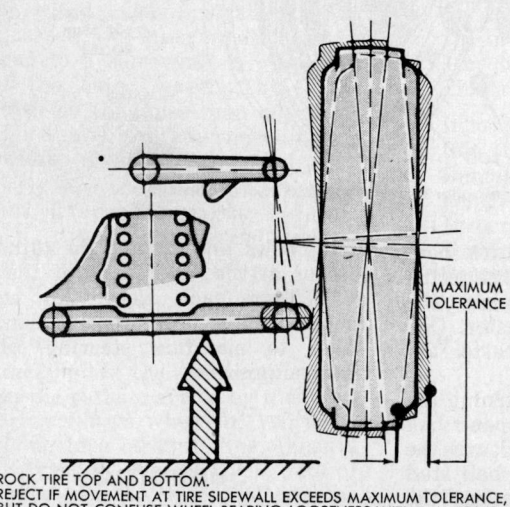

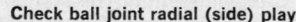

ROCK TIRE TOP AND BOTTOM.
REJECT IF MOVEMENT AT TIRE SIDEWALL EXCEEDS MAXIMUM TOLERANCE, BUT DO NOT CONFUSE WHEEL BEARING LOOSENESS WITH BALL JOINT WEAR.

Check ball joint radial (side) play

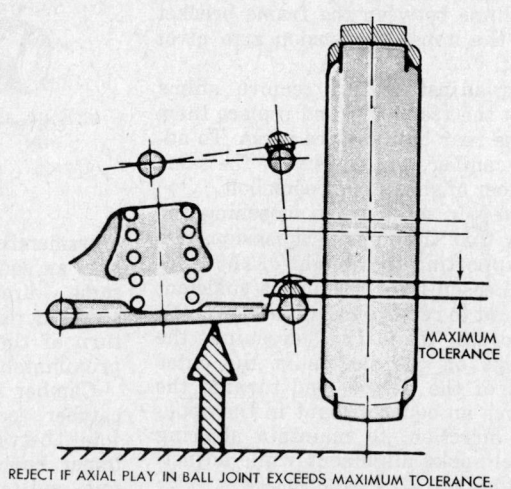

REJECT IF AXIAL PLAY IN BALL JOINT EXCEEDS MAXIMUM TOLERANCE.

Check ball joint axial (up-and-down) play

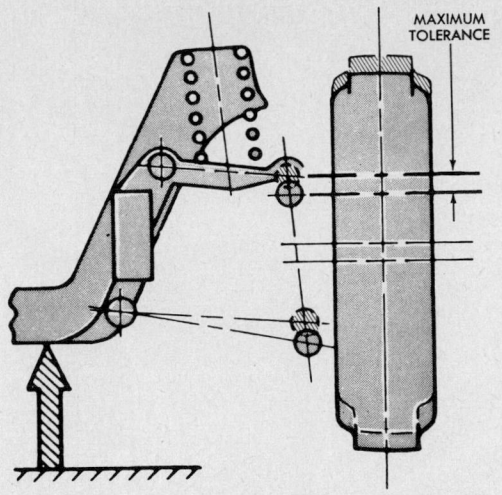

REJECT IF AXIAL PLAY IN BALL JOINT EXCEEDS MAXIMUM TOLERANCE.

Check ball joint axial (up-and-down) play

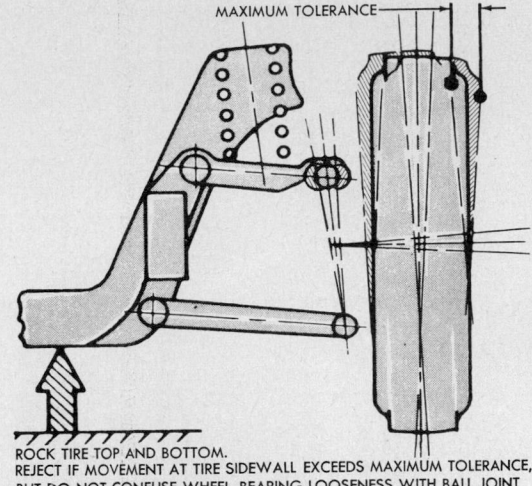

ROCK TIRE TOP AND BOTTOM.
REJECT IF MOVEMENT AT TIRE SIDEWALL EXCEEDS MAXIMUM TOLERANCE, BUT DO NOT CONFUSE WHEEL BEARING LOOSENESS WITH BALL JOINT WEAR.

Check ball joint radial (side) play

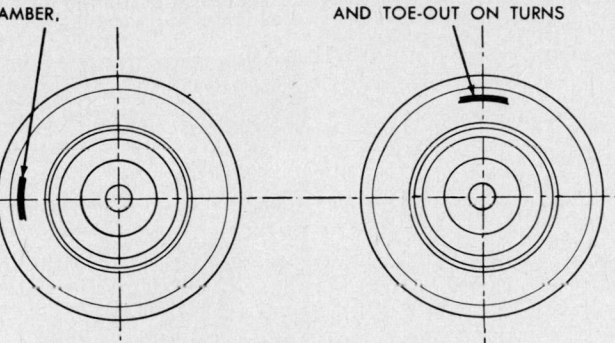

CHALK MARK IN THIS POSITION WHEN CHECKING CASTER AND CAMBER.

CHALK MARK IN THIS POSITION WHEN CHECKING TOE-IN AND TOE-OUT ON TURNS

LOCATION OF POINT OF GREATEST LATERAL RUN-OUT ON FRONT WHEELS WHEN CHECKING ALIGNMENT FACTORS

Wheel position for checking alignment

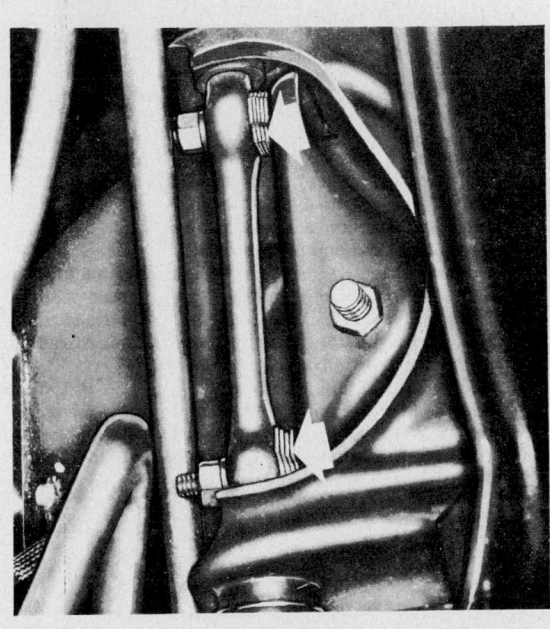

Caster and camber adjusting shim installation (© Chevrolet Div., G.M. Corp.)

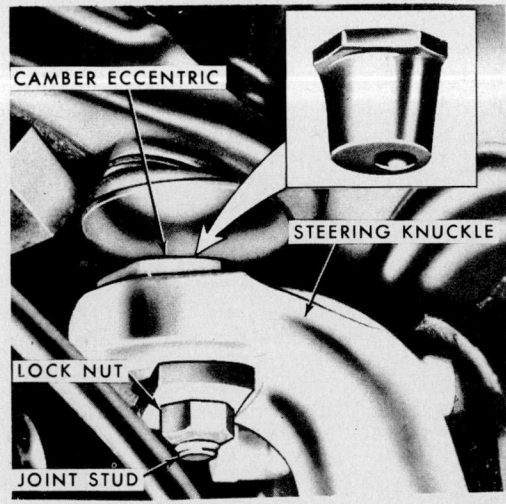

CAMBER ECCENTRIC

STEERING KNUCKLE

LOCK NUT

JOINT STUD

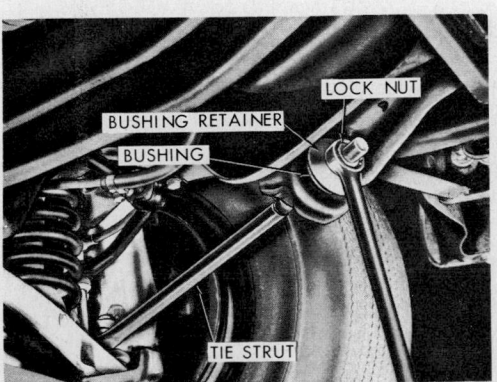

LOCK NUT

BUSHING RETAINER

BUSHING

TIE STRUT

Caster and camber adjustments (© Cadillac Div., G.M. Corp.)

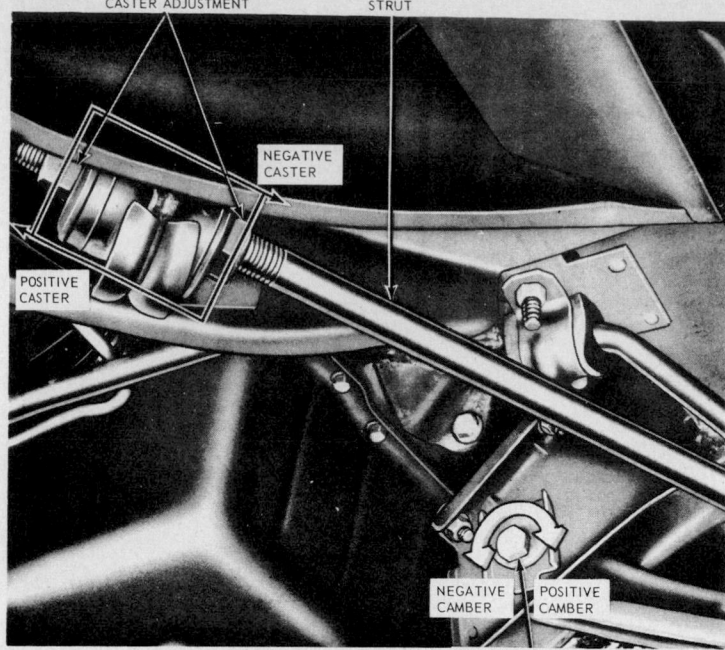

Caster and camber adjustment

Tool – T65P-3000-A

Caster and camber adjustment using pry bar
(© Ford Motor Co.)

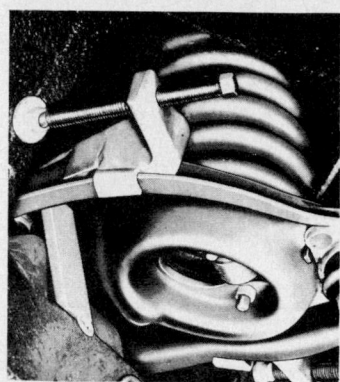

Caster and camber adjusting tool installation
(© Ford Motor Co.)

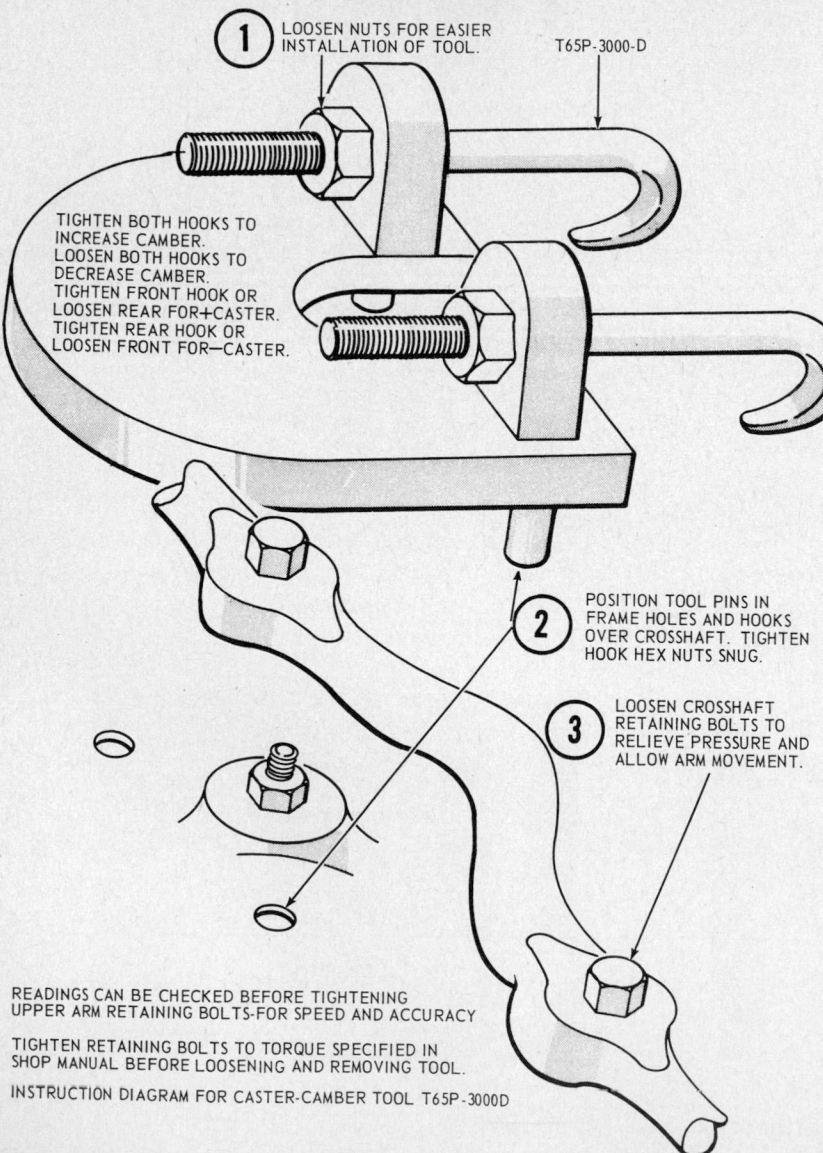

① LOOSEN NUTS FOR EASIER INSTALLATION OF TOOL.   T65P-3000-D

TIGHTEN BOTH HOOKS TO INCREASE CAMBER. LOOSEN BOTH HOOKS TO DECREASE CAMBER. TIGHTEN FRONT HOOK OR LOOSEN REAR FOR +CASTER. TIGHTEN REAR HOOK OR LOOSEN FRONT FOR −CASTER.

② POSITION TOOL PINS IN FRAME HOLES AND HOOKS OVER CROSSHAFT. TIGHTEN HOOK HEX NUTS SNUG.

③ LOOSEN CROSSHAFT RETAINING BOLTS TO RELIEVE PRESSURE AND ALLOW ARM MOVEMENT.

READINGS CAN BE CHECKED BEFORE TIGHTENING UPPER ARM RETAINING BOLTS-FOR SPEED AND ACCURACY

TIGHTEN RETAINING BOLTS TO TORQUE SPECIFIED IN SHOP MANUAL BEFORE LOOSENING AND REMOVING TOOL.

INSTRUCTION DIAGRAM FOR CASTER-CAMBER TOOL T65P-3000D

should be within 1/4° of the opposing side of the car.

To adjust camber, loosen the lower control arm pivot bolt and rotate the eccentrics.

Adjust toe-in by loosening the clamp bolts, and turning the adjuster sleeves at the outer ends of the tie rod. Turn each sleeve an equal amount in the opposite direction, in order to maintain steering wheel spoke alignment.

Section 6

Caster and camber are controlled by eccentrics fixed to the upper control arm mounting bolts. To adjust caster, loosen the nut on the mounting bolt, and turn either eccentric. Camber is adjusted by turning both eccentrics an equal amount. Recheck caster after setting camber, and torque the nuts to 65 ft. lbs.

To adjust toe-in, loosen the clamp bolts, and turn the adjuster sleeves at the outer ends of the tie rod an equal amount in the opposite direction, to maintain steering wheel spoke alignment.

Section 7

With the car positioned to adjust alignment, mark the position of the upper control arm pivot shaft, and loosen the pivot shaft retaining bolts. Lift the front end of the car and allow it to drop, to break the shaft loose from the frame. Using a pry bar, return the shaft to the index marks, and tighten the retaining bolts only enough to hold the shaft in position (loose enough to permit movement with the pry bar).

To adjust caster, move either end of the pivot shaft in or out, using the pry bar. A movement of 3/32 in. at either bolt location will change caster approximately ½°. Camber is adjusted in a similar manner, by moving both ends of the shaft an equal distance. Moving the entire shaft 3/32 in. will change camber approximately ½°. After adjusting camber, tighten the retaining bolts to specifications and recheck caster.

To adjust toe-in, loosen the sleeve clamp bolts, and turn the adjuster sleeves at the outer ends of the tie-rod an equal amount in the opposite direction, to maintain steering wheel spoke alignment.

Section 8

Install Ford tool T65P-3000D or its equivalent on the frame rail, position the hooks around the upper control arm pivot shaft, and tighten the adjusting nuts slightly. Loosen the pivot shaft retaining bolts to permit adjustment.

To adjust caster, loosen or tighten either the front or rear adjusting nut. After adjusting caster, adjust camber by loosening or tightening both nuts an equal amount. Tighten the shaft retaining bolts to specifications, remove the tool, and recheck the adjustments.

Adjust toe-in by loosening the clamp bolts, and turning the adjuster sleeves at the outer ends of the tie-rod. Turn the sleeves an equal amount in the opposite direction, to maintain steering wheel spoke alignment.

Section 9

Caster and camber are controlled by the mounting of the upper control arm pivot shaft on the frame. Slots are provided to permit adjustment of the mounting point. Ford tool 62F3000A or its equivalent, installed on the upper control arm, will ease adjustment.

Loosen the pivot shaft mounting bolts three or four turns, and hit the

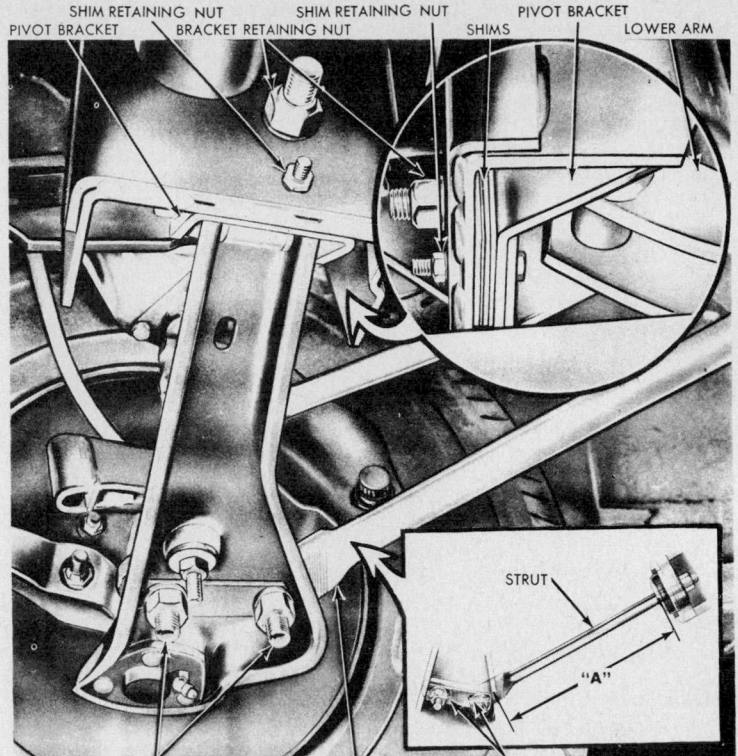

Caster and camber adjustments (© Ford Motor Co.)

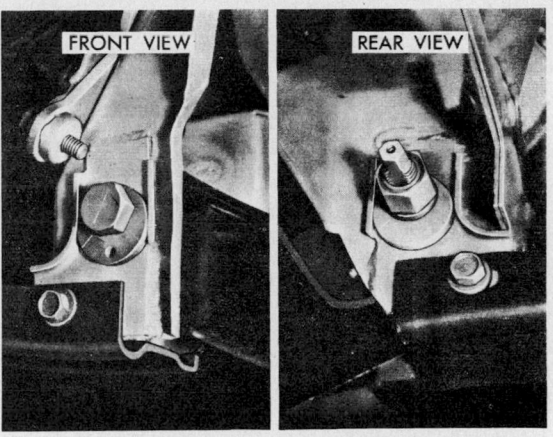

Camber (left) and caster adjustments
(© Chevrolet Div., G.M. Corp.)

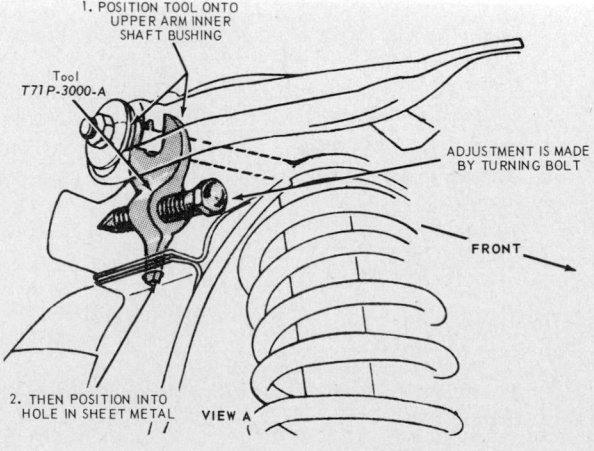

Caster and camber adjusting tool installation (© Ford Motor Co.)

head of the bolt to free the nut from the serations. To adjust caster, alternately loosen and tighten the front and rear adjusting screws. If either screw backs away from the panel while adjusting caster, the shaft mounting bolts are not free of the serations. Camber is adjusted by alternately loosening or tightening both screws an equal amount.

NOTE: do not turn either screw in excess of two turns at a time (before adjusting other screw), to prevent collapsing the inner fender well sheet metal.

Following the above adjustments, tighten the pivot shaft mounting bolts to specifications, remove the adjusting tool and recheck caster and camber. To adjust toe-in, loosen the clamp bolts, and turn the adjusting sleeves at the outer ends of the tie-rod an equal amount in the opposite direction, to maintain steering wheel spoke alignment.

Section 10

Caster is determined by the position of the strut on the lower control arm, which is controlled by bolts and serations on the arm and strut. To adjust caster, loosen the strut retaining bolts enough to free the serations, and reposition the strut on the arm. Tighten the retaining bolts, and recheck caster.

Camber is adjusted by altering the number of shims between the lower control arm pivot bracket and the frame. A 1/16 in. change in shim thickness will alter camber 1/3°. Loosen both the bracket and shim retaining nuts, and add or remove shims as required.

NOTE: total shim stack thickness should not exceed 11/16 in.

Tighten the bracket and shim retaining nuts, and recheck caster and camber. Toe-in is adjusted by loosening the clamp bolts, and turning each adjuster sleeve at the outer end of the tie-rod an equal amount in the equal direction, to maintain steering wheel alignment.

Section 11

Position one Ford tool T71P-3000-A at each end of the upper control arm, pivot shaft with the leg of the tools through the holes in the sheet metal (see illustration). Turn the adjusting bolts until they are solidly contacting sheet metal, and loosen the pivot shaft retaining bolts.

Caster is adjusted by turning the front and rear adjusting bolts in the opposite direction. Camber is adjusted by turning both bolts an equal amount in the same direction. Following the adjustments, tighten the pivot shaft retaining bolts, remove the adjusting tools, and recheck caster and camber.

Prior to adjusting toe-in, align the straight ahead marks at the base of the steering wheel and the head of the steering column. Loosen both the clamp at the outer end of the rack bellows and the tie rod jam nuts. Using suitable pliers (i.e. Vise-Grips), turn the inner tie rod shafts to adjust toe-in. Turn the shafts an equal amount in the opposite direction, to maintain steering wheel spoke alignment. Following the adjustment, hold the inner shafts with pliers, and tighten the jam nuts.

Section 12

Camber and caster are adjusted using eccentrics on the lower control arm pivot bolts. Camber is adjusted first, by loosening the front pivot nut and rotating the eccentric. Tighten the front, and loosen the rear pivot nuts. Adjust caster by rotating the rear eccentric, and tighten the rear pivot nut while holding the bolt in position. Recheck camber and caster.

To adjust toe-in, loosen the clamps on the adjusting sleeves at the outer ends of the tie rod, and turn each sleeve an equal amount in the opposite direction, to maintain steering wheel spoke alignment while adjusting toe-in.

Wheel Bearing Torque Specifications

Make	Year	Torque ①
American Motors (all models)	1965–67	20 ft. lbs., back off 2 lock nut slots.
	1968–72	20 ft. lbs., back off 1/3 turn, retorque to 12 in. lbs.
Buick (all models)	1965–70	19 ft. lbs., back off completely, retorque to 11 ft. lbs.
	1971–72	② 30 ft. lbs., back off 1/2 turn, finger tighten lightly.
Cadillac	1965–72	③ 30 ft. lbs., back off 1/2 turn.
		④ 30 ft. lbs., back off completely, retorque to 6 ft. lbs.
Cadillac Eldorado	1967–72	Front Wheel Drive
Chevrolet (all models except Chevy II)	1965	15 ft. lbs., back off one flat.
	1966–72	12 ft. lbs., back off one flat.
Chevy II, Nova	1965	9 ft. lbs., back off one flat.
	1966–72	12 ft. lbs., back off one flat.
Chrysler Corporation (all models except Dart, Valiant, Duster, Demon)	1965–72	90 in. lbs., back off one slot.
Dart, Valiant, Duster, Demon	1965–72	70 in. lbs., back off one slot.
Ford, Mercury, Lincoln (all models)	1965–72	17–25 ft. lbs., back off 1/2 turn, retorque to 10–15 in. lbs.
Oldsmobile (all models except Toronado)	1965–72	30 ft. lbs. back off 1/2 turn, finger tighten.
Oldsmobile Toronado	1966–72	Front Wheel Drive
Pontiac (all models)	1965–68	② 10–16 ft. lbs., back off completely, retorque to 20–25 in. lbs., back off until slot in nut aligns with hole in spindle.
	1969–72	② 30 ft. lbs., back off 1/2 turn, retorque finger tight, back off until slot in nut aligns with hole in spindle.

①—Rotate the wheel while torquing.

②—.002–.006 in. play is necessary to ensure proper operation of the bearings. The bearings must not be preloaded when in use.

③—Drum brakes

④—Disc brakes

Basic Electrical Diagnosis

Index

Basic Electrical Diagnosis

Testing the Battery

Selection of Battery

The modern car battery (with very few exceptions) is a 12-volt lead-acid unit having a particular ampere hours capacity, depending upon the required work load (radio, air conditioning, electric windows, tail gate, telephone, etc.).

Batteries come in different forms as specified and designed by the car manufacturer and are matched to the car's electrical needs.

The prime purpose of the battery is to supply a source of energy for cranking the car engine. It also provides the necessary power for the ignition system. A battery can, for a limited time, supply adequate current to satisfy electrical demands during periods when requirements exceed generator output.

Replacing a Battery

The most convenient and popular way to store new batteries is in a dry state. They are charged (with special equipment) at the time of manufacture. A dry charged unit will hold this charge almost indefinitely, in the absence of moisture.

Before deciding on a particular battery, consider some of the essentials that may put the replacement battery in a different category from that of the unit originally supplied with the vehicle. When the original battery wears out, resistance in the wiring circuits is probably much increased, and the starter may be less efficient, along with the ignition system. There is also the likelihood that electrical accessories have been added.

All of the above reasons are justification for choosing a battery of greater capacity than the one supplied by the manufacturer.

Preparation

After the electrical needs have been considered, and a selection made, place the new battery on a bench or work table. Never activate a battery installed in the car. Remove vent caps from all the cells.

Fill each cell carefully, using sulfuric acid and distilled water (electrolyte) at a strength of 1.250-1.265 specific gravity to about 3/8 in. above the top of the separators, or to indicated level mark.

Place a battery type thermometer in one of the center cells. Check specific gravity of the electrolyte with a battery hydrometer. The battery temperature must be above 80°F. and specific gravity must be above 1.250 prior to installing the battery.

In charging 12-volt batteries, set charging rate at 35 amperes (6-volt batteries at 70 amperes) until electrolyte has reached 80° F. and electrolyte gravity is 1.250 or higher. Lower charging rates also may be used to obtain 80° F. and 1.250 specific gravity. When charging, do not allow electrolyte temperature to exceed 125° F. Normally, 10-15 minutes charging will be sufficient; however, in colder climates a little longer is O.K.

When the battery is removed from the charger, top up if necessary, with electrolyte, and replace the vent plugs.

When installing, make sure that both ends of the battery cables are clean and securely tightened, observing correct polarity.

Start engine and make sure that the generator is charging with lights and all accessories on.

Caution Be careful not to install or charge the battery with cables reversed. Damage to battery and generator can result, especially if the car is equipped with an alternator or transistorized radio.

Caution Because electrolyte is extremely corrosive to metals and many other materials, do not pour into sinks or drains. If battery acid is spilled on battery during filling or charging, or on bench or clothing, immediately flush it off with generous amounts of water and baking soda or ammonia.

Battery Troubles—Causes

1. Battery too small for the job (accessories, etc.).
2. Tired battery (worn out).
3. Corroded battery connections.
4. Generator not charging.
5. Generator charging rate too low.
6. Regulator defective.
7. Regulator out of adjustment.
8. Regulator has poor ground.
9. Alternator inoperative.
10. Loose generator or alternator drive belt.
11. Constant drain of current due to short circuit.

Battery Troubles—Corrections

1. Battery capacity may be less than requirements demand. Additional accessories, too frequent use of starter, low operational speeds, require a greater source of electrical supply. Install a larger capacity battery.
2. Either age or abuse is the usual cause of a tired battery. No amount of charging will offer more than temporary relief. Install a new battery of proper capacity if plates are sulfated.
3. Corroded battery posts and connections result from the chemical reaction between dissimilar metals and battery electrolyte. Excessive corrosion at a battery post is usually an indication of the failure of a seal between the post and the battery cover. Clean post and cable clamp, seal post-to-battery cover with rubber cement or other plastic material, then coat post with petroleum jelly, install cable clamp and tighten.
4. Generator not charging can be caused by a defective generator or other system component. Check entire charging system and correct the fault.
5. Low generator charging rate may be caused by a loose drive belt, loose or poor battery post connections, high resistance in charging circuit or a poor or improperly adjusted regulator.
6. Regulator may be defective because of burned points in the regulator or any open circuit in the control system.
7. Regulator out of adjustment.
8. A possible cause of trouble in DC systems is a poor regulator ground in any of the externally grounded (Type A) field circuit or, in heavy-duty (Type B) circuits, the internally grounded field within the generator.
9. The alternator may be inoperative because of damaged diodes, poor internal connections, open, grounded, or shorted field circuit, grounded or shorted stator windings.
10. A loose generator drive belt will cause low, or partial charging. Correct by adjusting drive belt.
11. A constant drain of current from the battery may be caused by frayed insulation on any live wire in the electrical system.

This can cause a short circuit. There is also the possibility of a light (in the trunk, glove box, under the hood. etc.) or other electric accessory remaining on after the ignition is turned off. To correct the situation:

First, with a sensitive ammeter, determine whether or not there is a current drain by opening the circuit at either battery post connection, hooking the ammeter in series, and checking for current drain.

Second, if the meter registers a drain, isolate the leak by reconnecting the battery, then, one by one, check each circuit at the fuse block. This is a tedious but unavoidable procedure and consists of removing each fuse and testing that circuit with the prods of an ammeter (in series). The circuit which activates the meter is the guilty one; identify the trouble spot by elimination. Correct the trouble by correcting the short or replacing the switch or other electrical component.

In the event that the fuse block test does not indicate the trouble, check the circuits which are protected with circuit breakers, (headlamps, parking lamps, seat and window controls, etc.).

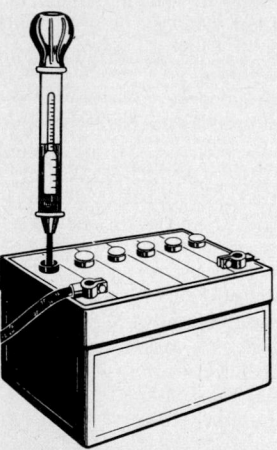

Testing battery specific gravity

Specific Gravity Test— Hydrometer

Before attempting any electrical checks, it is important to check the condition of the battery.

While not technically exact, a practical measurement of the chemical condition of the battery is indicated by measuring the specific gravity of the acid (electrolyte) contained in each cell. The electrolyte in a fully charged battery is usually between 1.260 and 1.280 times as heavy as pure water at the same temperature (80°F.). Variations in the specific gravity readings for a fully charged

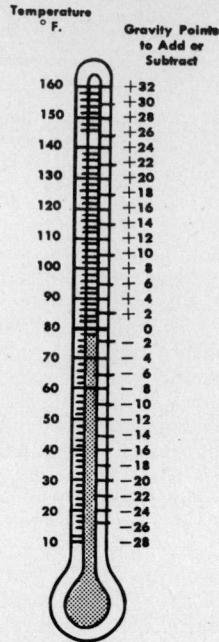

Hydrometer temperature correction chart
(© Chrysler Corp.)

battery may differ. Therefore, it is most important that all battery cells produce an equal reading.

As a battery discharges, a chemical change takes place within each cell. The sulfate factor of the electrolyte combines chemically with the battery plates, reducing the weight of the electrolyte. A reading of the specific gravity of the acid, or electrolyte, of any partially charged battery, will therefore be less than that taken in a fully charged one.

The hydrometer is the instrument

in general use for determining the specific gravity of liquids. The battery hydrometer is readily available from many sources, including local auto replacement parts stores. The following chart gives an indication of specific gravity value, related to battery charge condition. If, after charging, the specific gravity between any two cells varies more than 50 points (.050), the battery is probably bad.

Specific Gravity Reading	Charged Condition
1.260-1.280	Fully charged
1.230-1.250	Three-quarter charged
1.200-1.220	One-half charged
1.170-1.190	One-quarter charged
1.140-1.160	Just about flat
1.110-1.130	All the way down

Testing Battery Polarity

Battery polarity is very important, especially since the introduction of AC generators. Permanent damage to the diodes of alternators (AC generators) will result from reversing polarity.

To determine battery polarity, turn the voltmeter selector to the high reading scale. Connect voltmeter leads to the battery posts. If the gauge needle moves in the correct direction, the positive lead of the meter is on the positive (+) post of the battery. If the gauge needle moves in the wrong direction, polarity is reversed.

Know Your Instruments
Ohmmeter

An ohmmeter is used to measure

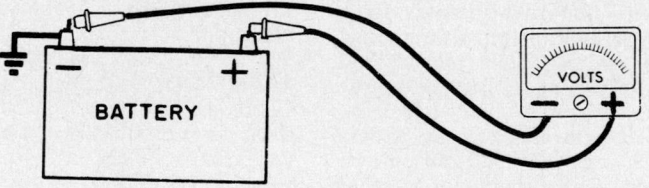

Battery polarity test

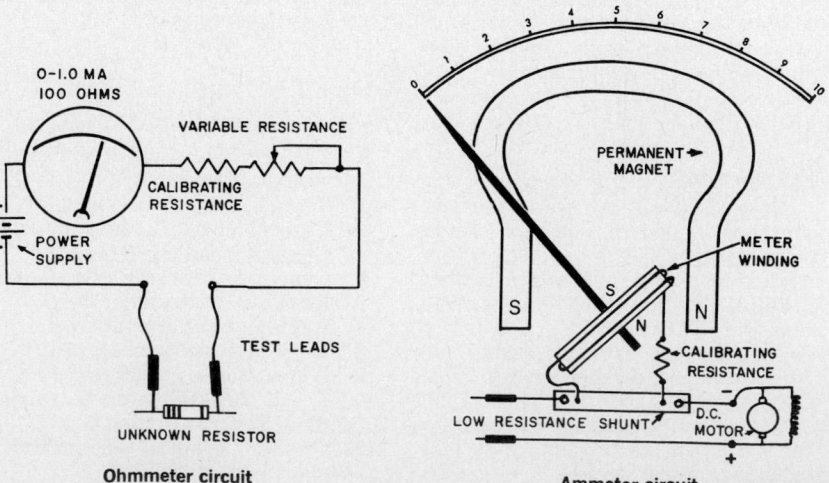

Ohmmeter circuit

Ammeter circuit

electrical resistance in a unit or circuit. The ohmmeter has a self-contained power supply. In use, it is connected across (or in parallel with) the terminals of the unit being tested.

Ammeter

An ammeter is used to measure current (amount of electricity) flowing through a unit, or circuit. Ammeters are always connected in the line (in series) with the unit or circuit being tested.

Voltmeter

A voltmeter is used to measure voltage (electrical pressure) pushing the current through a unit, or circuit. The meter is connected across the terminals of the unit being tested. The meter reading will be the difference in pressure (voltage drop) between the two sides of the unit.

Open Circuit Voltage Tests

An Open Circuit Voltage tester measures the state of charge of a battery cell by measuring its voltage output. Testers of this type are made by a number of manufacturers, and the instructions that come with each type always should be followed. The most common tester contains a fixed resistance, which allows the voltage of each cell to be measured under a

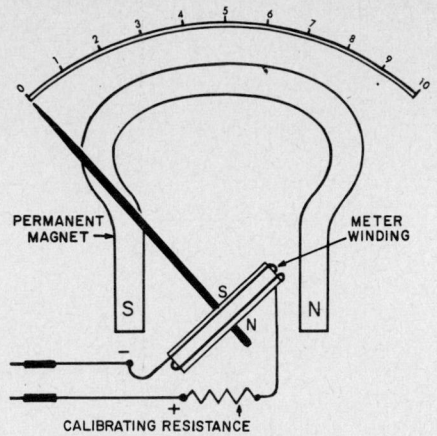

Voltmeter circuit

fixed load. Usually, however, this type of tester is not quite accurate enough to determine battery condition—the voltmeter scale is not expanded.

In general, three battery conditions can be checked using the O.C.V. tester:

1. Battery charged: (all cells greater than 1.95 volts, with a tolerance of .05 volts).
2. Battery discharged: (cells above *and* below 1.95 volts, and high-low readings not greater than .05 volts).

NOTE: if all cells are below 1.95 volts, the battery should be boost-charged in order to obtain an accurate reading, and the surface charge removed.

3. Battery defective: this would be the case if high-low readings were more than .05 volts apart, and any or all cells read 1.95 volts or more.

Two disadvantages of this type of tester somewhat reduce its usefulness:

1. The newer one-piece battery cases do not have connecting straps between cells that are easily accessible without destroying the case.
2. The battery cannot be accurately tested if the state of charge is too low, and the tester will not operate properly if the battery has just been boost-charged. In other words, the surface charge first must be dissipated and a light load (e.g., headlight) must be maintained after charging, (or carbon pile, on testers so equipped, must be adjusted to achieve the same results).

Boost Charging Rates

12-volt Battery: 1,000 ampere/ minutes (50 amps. x 20 min.)
6-volt Battery: 1,800 ampere/ minutes (60 amps. x 30 min.)

Testing the Starting Motor

Testing the Starter Circuit

The starter circuit should be divided and tested in four separate phases:

1. Cranking voltage check.
2. Amperage draw.
3. Voltage drop—grounded side.
4. Voltage drop—battery side.

Cranking Voltage

Turn voltmeter selector to 8-10 volt scale for cars equipped with 6-volt systems, and to the 16-20 volt scale

Starter current indicator

for cars equipped with 12-volt systems.

Connect voltmeter leads to prods tapped into the battery posts (observe polarity and reverse meter leads if necessary). Remove the high tension wire from the distributor cap and ground it to prevent starting. Now, turn the key. Observe both voltmeter reading and cranking speed. The cranking speed should be even, and at a satisfactory rate of speed, with a voltmeter reading of 4.8 volts or more for 6-volt systems, and at least 9.6 volts for 12-volt systems.

Compare this voltage reading with

the reading obtained in the battery capacity test. There should be no more than a difference of 0.3 volt for 6-volt systems or 0.6 volt for 12-volt systems between the two readings. If this reading is satisfactory and the starting motor cranks the engine with sufficient speed, the starting circuit is in good condition.

Amperage Draw

The amount of current the starter motor draws is usually (but not always) associated with the mechanical problems involved in cranking the mechanical aspects of cranking the engine. (Mechanical trouble in the engine, frozen or worn starter parts, misaligned starter or starter components, etc.) Because starter motor amperage draw is directly influenced by **anything** restricting the free turning of the engine, or starter, it is important that the engine and all components be at operating temperatures.

To measure starter current draw, remove the high tension wire from the center of the distributor cap and ground it. A very simple and inexpensive starter current indicator is available at auto stores. This indica-

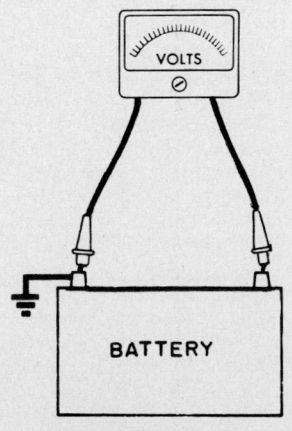

Cranking voltage test

tor is an induction type gauge and shows, without disconnecting any wires, starter current draw.

Place the yoke of the meter directly over the insulated starter supply cable (cable must be straight for a minimum of 2 in.). Close the starter switch for about 20 seconds, watch the meter dial and record the average reading. If the indicator swings in the wrong direction, reverse the position of the meter. On 6-volt systems, normal draw for small to medium size engines is 150 to 225 amperes. Larger and high compression engines may draw as much as 400 amperes. On 12-volt systems, the current draw should be about one-half the amount registered for the 6-volt system.

More accurate but complex, equipment is available from many name brand manufacturers. This equipment consists of a combination voltmeter, ammeter, and carbon pile rheostat. When using this equipment, follow the equipment manufacturer's procedures and recommendations.

High amperage and lazy performance would suggest an excessively tight engine, friction in the starter or starter drive, grounded starter field or armature.

Normal amperage and lazy performance suggest high resistance, or possibly poor connections somewhere in the starter circuit.

Low amperage and lazy or no performance suggest battery condition poor, bad cables or connections along the line.

Voltage Drop—Grounded Side

With a voltmeter on the 3-volt scale, without disconnecting any wires, connect negative test lead of the voltmeter to a prod secured in the grounded battery post. The positive test lead is connected to a cleaned, bare metal portion of the starter motor housing. Close the starter switch and note the voltmeter reading. If the reading is the same as battery reading, the ground circuit is open somewhere between the battery and the starter. In many cases the reading will be very small. The reading shown will indicate voltage drop (loss) between battery ground post and starter housing. The drop should not exceed 0.2 volt. If the voltage drop is above the specified amount, the next step is to isolate and correct the cause. It can be a bad cable or connection anywhere in the battery-to-starter ground circuit. A check of this type should progress along the various points of possible trouble, between the battery ground post and the starter motor housing, until the trouble spot has been located.

NOTE: due to the design of the Chrysler reduction gear starter, testing is limited to measuring voltage

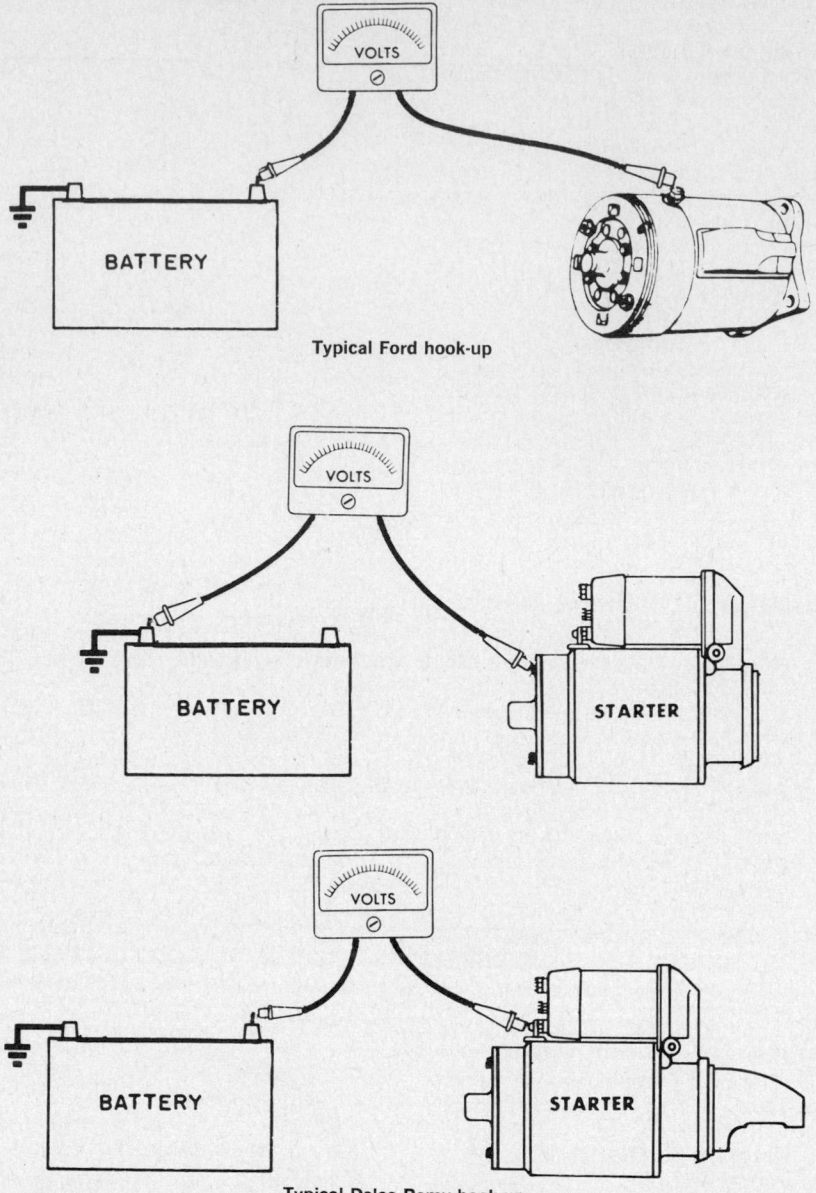

Typical Ford hook-up

Typical Delco-Remy hook-up

drop to starter cable connection.

Voltage Drop—Battery Side

Bad starter cranking may result from poor connections or faulty components of the battery or hot phase of the starter motor circuit. To check this phase of the circuit, without disconnecting any wires, connect one lead of a voltmeter to a prod secured in the hot post of the battery and the other voltmeter lead to the field terminal of the starting motor. The meter should be set to the 16-20 volt scale. Before closing the starter switch, the voltmeter reading will be that of the battery. After closing the starter switch, change the selector on the voltmeter to the 3-volt scale. With a jumper wire between the relay battery terminal and the relay starter switch terminal, crank the engine. If the starting motor cranks the engine, the relay (solenoid) is operating.

While the engine is being cranked, watch the voltmeter. It should not register more than 0.5 volt. If more than this, check each part of the circuit for voltage drop to isolate the trouble, (high resistance).

Without disturbing the voltmeter-to-battery hook-up, move the free voltmeter lead to the battery terminal of the relay (solenoid), and crank the engine. The voltmeter should show no more than 0.1 volt.

If this reading is correct, move the same voltmeter lead to the starting motor terminal of the relay (solenoid). While the engine is being cranked, the voltmeter should show no more than 0.3 volt. If it does, the trouble lies in the relay.

If the reading is correct, the trouble is in the cable or connections between the relay and the starting motor.

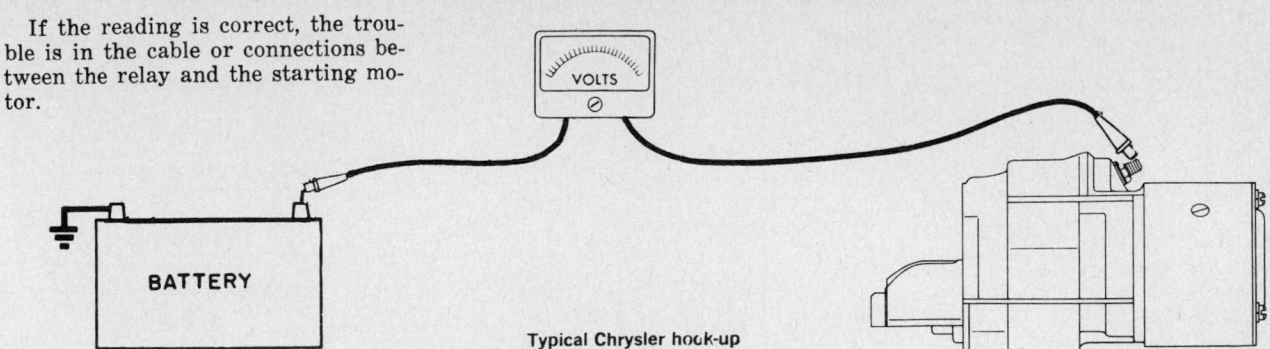

Typical Chrysler hook-up

Starter Motor Service

Diagnosis

Starter Won't Crank the Engine

1. Dead battery.
2. Open starter circuit, such as:
   A. Broken or loose battery cables.
   B. Inoperative starter motor solenoid.
   C. Broken or loose wire from starter switch to solenoid.
   D. Poor solenoid or starter ground.
   E. Bad starter switch, (ignition, dash button or carburetor).
3. Defective starter internal circuit, such as:
   A. Dirty or burnt commutator.
   B. Stuck, worn or broken brushes.
   C. Open or shorted armature.
   D. Open or grounded fields.
4. Starter motor mechanical faults, such as:
   A. Jammed armature end bearings.
   B. Bad bearing, allowing armature to rub fields.
   C. Bent shaft.
   D. Broken starter housing.
   E. Bad starter worm or drive mechanism.
   F. Bad starter drive or flywheel driven gear.
5. Engine hard or impossible to crank, such as:
   A. Hydrostatic lock, water in combustion chamber.
   B. Crankshaft seizing in bearings.
   C. Piston or ring seizing.
   D. Bent or broken connecting rod.
   E. Seizing of connecting rod bearing.
   F. Flywheel jammed or broken.
   G. In some remote cases, an incandescent particle in the combustion chamber of a hot engine will prevent starting. This condition acts like a low battery or ignition timing so far advanced that the engine kicks back. The piston refuses to pass over top center. A two or three minute wait is generally enough to cool the troubled spot and temporarily clear the fault.

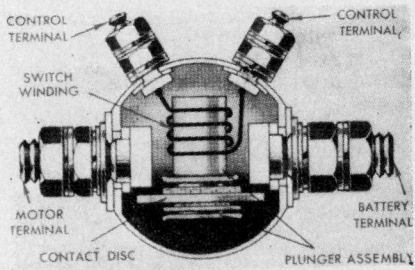

Schematic diagram of a magnetic switch with two control terminals

Starter Spins Free, Won't Engage

1. Sticking or broken drive mechanism.

Magnetic Switches

Magnetic switches serve only to make contact for the starter motor. Usually, such switches are located on the inner fender panel, although they are found mounted on the starter in a few cases.

Magnetic Switches with Two Control Terminals

On this type of magnetic switch current is supplied from the ignition switch or transmission neutral button to one of the magnetic switch control terminals. The other control terminal is connected to the transmission neutral safety switch (on the transmission) where it is grounded.

Magnetic Switches with Ignition Resistor By-Pass Terminals

Used with 12-volt systems. All normally use a magnetic switch with a single control terminal. The second terminal is an ignition resistor by-pass terminal.

Solenoids Without Relays

This type of starter solenoid is always mounted on the starter. Makes electrical contact for the starter and pulls the starter and drive clutch into mesh with the flywheel. The Chrysler reduction gear starter has this solenoid embodied in the starter housing. (See illustration.)

There is only one control terminal oon the solenoid.

The ignition by-pass terminal is usually marked R or IGN, if it is used.

Solenoids With Separate Relays

The solenoid itself is always mounted on the starter. In addition to making contact for the starter, it also pulls the starter drive clutch gear into mesh with the flywheel. A single control terminal is used on the solenoid itself. The relay is usually found mounted to the inner fender panel or on the firewall.

Solenoids With Built-In Relays

These units are always mounted on

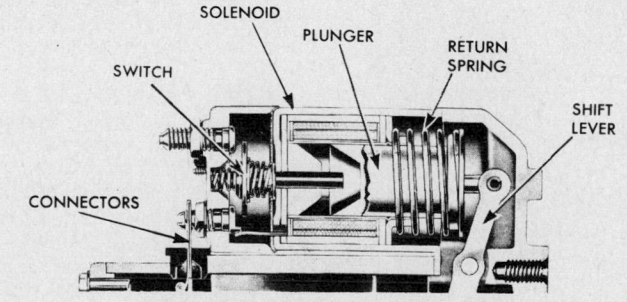

Starter solenoid mounted on starter motor

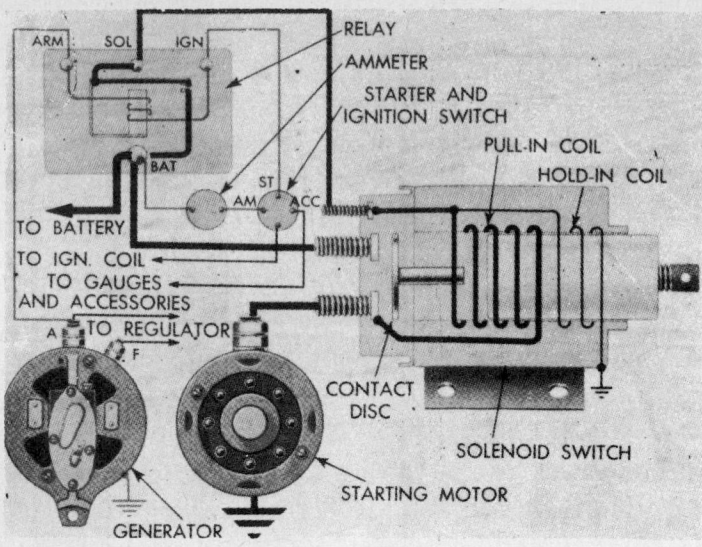

Solenoid with a separate relay

the starter and are connected, through linkage, to the starter drive clutch. The relay portion is a square box built into and integral with the front end of the solenoid assembly.

Neutral Safety Switches

The purpose of the neutral safety switch is to prevent the starter from cranking the engine except when the transmission is in neutral or park.

On some cars, the neutral safety switch is located on the transmission. It serves to ground the solenoid or magnetic switch, whichever is used.

On other cars the neutral safety switch is located either at the bottom of the steering column, where it contacts the shift mechanism, on the steering column, underneath the dash, or on the shift linkage (console).

On most cars, the neutral safety switch and the back-up light switch are combined into a single switch mechanism.

See the car sections and/or the automatic transmission section for specific details.

Troubleshooting Neutral Safety Switches—Quick Test

If the starter fails to function and

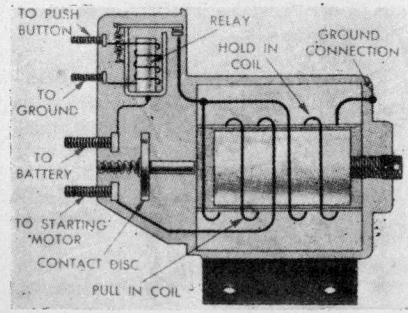

Solenoid with a built-in relay

the neutral safety switch is to be checked, a jumper can be placed across its terminals. If the starter then functions the safety switch is defective.

In the case neutral safety switches with one wire, this wire must be grounded for testing purposes. If the starter works with the wire grounded, the switch is defective.

Neutral Safety Switch— Back-Up Light Switch

When the neutral safety switch is built in combination with the back-up light switch, the easiest way to tell which terminals are for the back-up lights is to take a jumper and cross every pair of wires. The pair of wires which light the back-up lamps should be ignored when testing the neutral safety switch. Once the back-up light wires have been located, jump the other pair of wires to test the neutral safety switch. If the starter functions only when the jumper is placed across these two wires, the neutral safety switch is defective or requires adjustment.

Reduction-Gear Starter Motor

(Chrysler Corporation)

The housing is die-cast aluminum. A 3.5 to 1 reduction, combined with the starter to ring gear ratio, results in a total gear reduction of about 45 to 1.

NOTE: the high-pitched sound is caused by the higher starter speed.

The positive shift solenoid is enclosed in the starter housing and is energized through the ignition switch. When ignition switch is turned to start, the solenoid plunger engages drive gear through a shifting fork. At the completion of travel, the plunger closes a switch to revolve the starter.

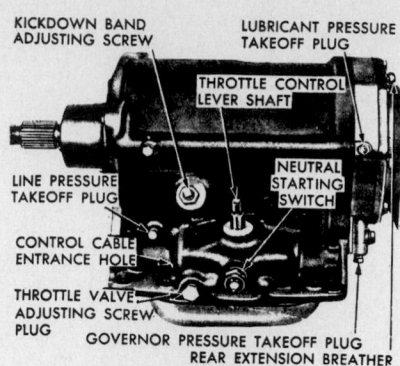

Location of the neutral safety switch on transmission

The tension of the spring-type shifting prevents a butt-tooth lock up and motor will not start before total shift.

An overrunning clutch prevents motor damage if key is held on after engine starts.

No lubrication is required due to Oilite bearings.

Disassembly

1. Support assembly in a vise equipped with soft jaws. Do not clamp. Care must be used not to distort or damage the die cast aluminum.
2. Remove the thru-bolts and the end housing.
3. Carefully pull the armature up and out of the gear housing, and the starter frame and field assembly. Remove the steel and fiber thrust washer.

NOTE: on eight cylinder engines the starting motors have the wire of the shunt field coil soldered to the brush terminal. Six cylinder engines have the four coils in series and do not have a wire soldered to the brush terminal. One pair of brushes is connected to this terminal. The other pair of brushes is attached to the series field coils by means of a terminal screw. Carefully pull the frame and field assembly up just enough to expose the terminal screw and the solder connection of the shunt field at the brush terminal. Place two wood blocks between the starter frame and starter gear housing to facilitate removal of the terminal screw and unsoldering of the shunt field wire at the brush terminal.

4. Support the brush terminal with a finger behind terminal and remove screw.
5. On eight cylinder engine starters unsolder the shunt field coil lead from the brush terminal and housing.
6. The brush holder plate with terminal, contact and brushes is serviced as an assembly.
7. Clean all old sealer from around plate and housing.
8. Remove the brush holder attach-

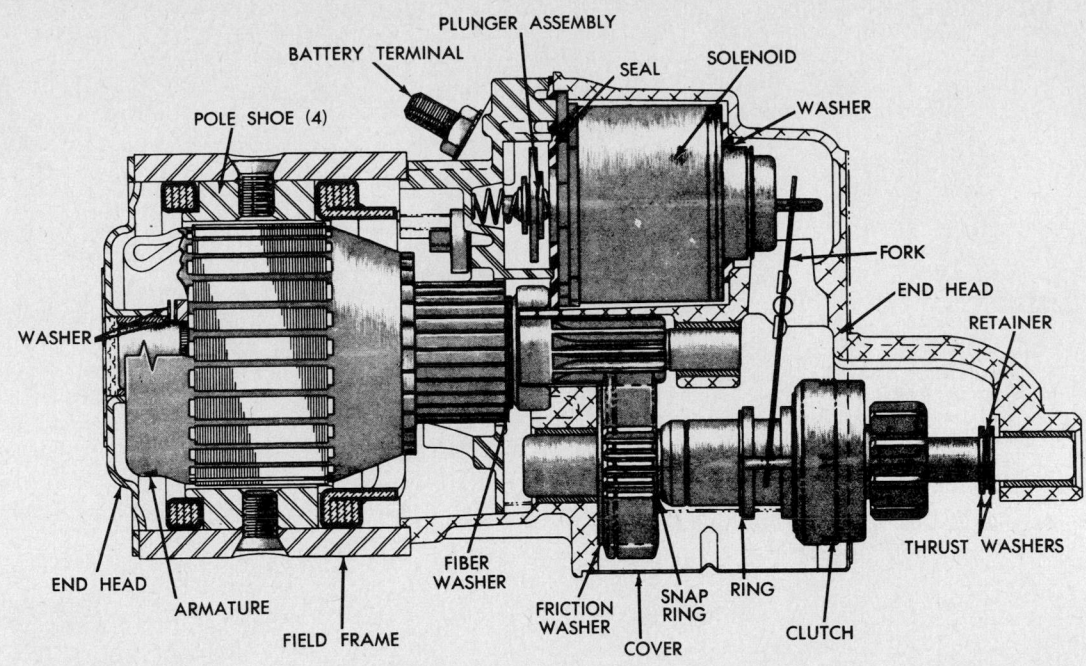

Reduction gear starter motor (© Chrysler Corp.)

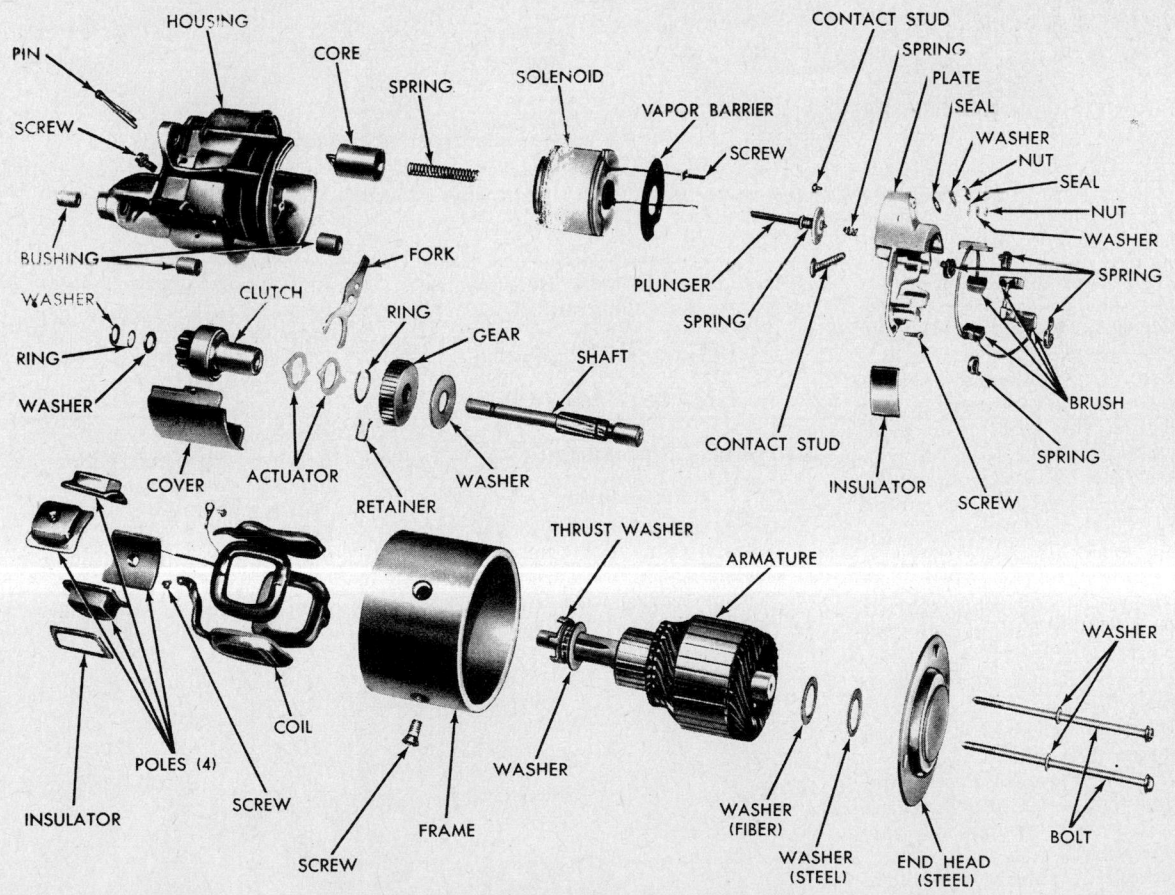

Reduction gear motor—exploded view (© Chrysler Corp.)

ing screw.
9. On the shunt type, unsolder the solenoid winding from the brush terminal.
10. Remove 11/32 in. nut, washer and insulator from solenoid terminal.
11. Remove brush holder plate with brushes as an assembly.
12. Remove gear housing ground screw.
13. The solenoid assembly can be removed from the well.
14. Remove nut, washer and seal from starter battery terminal and

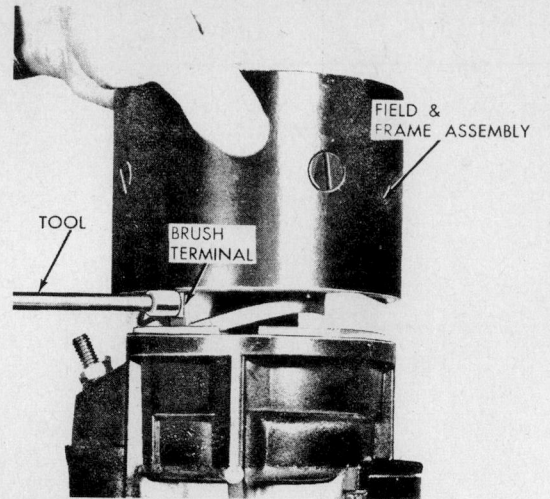

Removing terminal screw—reduction gear motor
(© Chrysler Corp.)

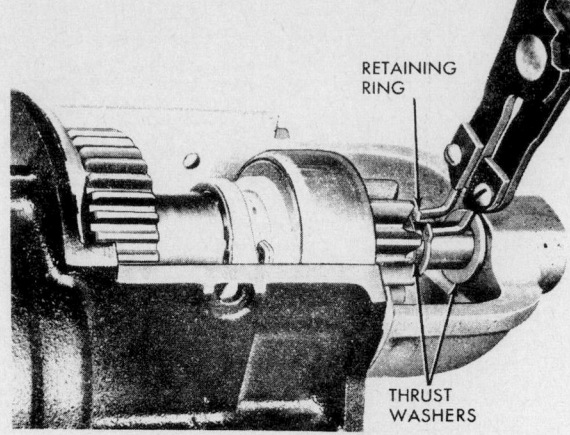

Removing retainer ring—reduction gear motor
(© Chrysler Corp.)

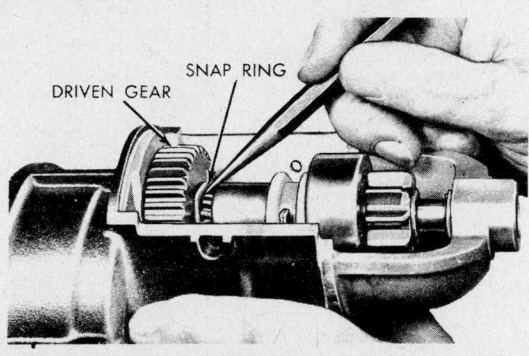

Removing drive gear snap-ring—reduction gear motor
(© Chrysler Corp.)

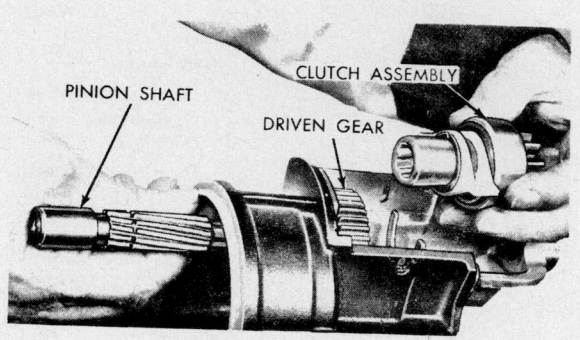

Removing clutch assembly—reduction gear motor
(© Chrysler Corp.)

remove terminal from plate.

15. Remove solenoid contact and plunger from solenoid and remove the coil sleeve.
16. Remove the solenoid return spring, coil retaining washer, retainer and the dust cover from the gear housing.
17. Release the snap-ring that locates the driven gear on pinion shaft.
18. Release front retaining ring.
19. Push pinion shaft toward the rear and remove snap-ring, thrust washers, clutch and pinion, and two shift fork nylon actuators.
20. Remove driven gear and friction washer.
21. Pull shifting fork forward and remove moving core.
22. Remove fork retainer pin and shifting fork assembly. The gear housing with bushings is serviced as an assembly.

To Reassemble: reverse the above procedures. At last portion of assembly, after gear housing ground screw has been securely tightened, clean area at joint between brush holder plate to field frame and housing mating joint. Apply a bead of brush plate sealer around four sides of joint. (A sealer such as MoPar

2421847 is suggested.) Be sure the joints are thoroughly sealed.

Direct Drive Starter Motor

(Chrysler Corporation)

Disassembly

1. Remove through bolts and tap commutator end head from frame.
2. Remove thrust washers from armature shaft.

3. Lift brush holder springs and remove brushes from holders.
4. Remove brush holder plate.
5. Disconnect field coil wires at solenoid connector.
6. Remove solenoid and boot.
7. Drive out shift fork pivot pin.
8. Remove drive end pinion housing and spacer washer.
9. Remove shift fork from starter drive.
10. Slide overrunning clutch pinion gear toward commutator, drive stop retainer toward clutch pinion gear and remove the now-

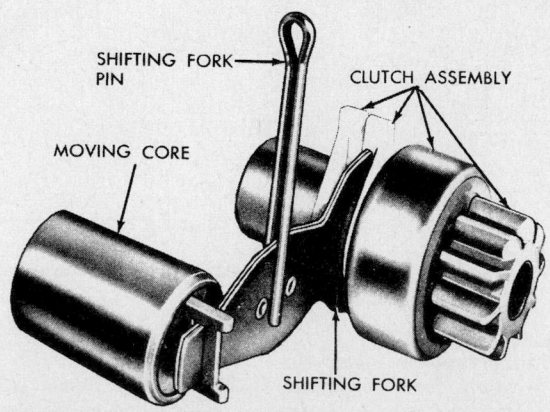

Shift fork and clutch arrangement—reduction gear motor
(© Chrysler Corp.)

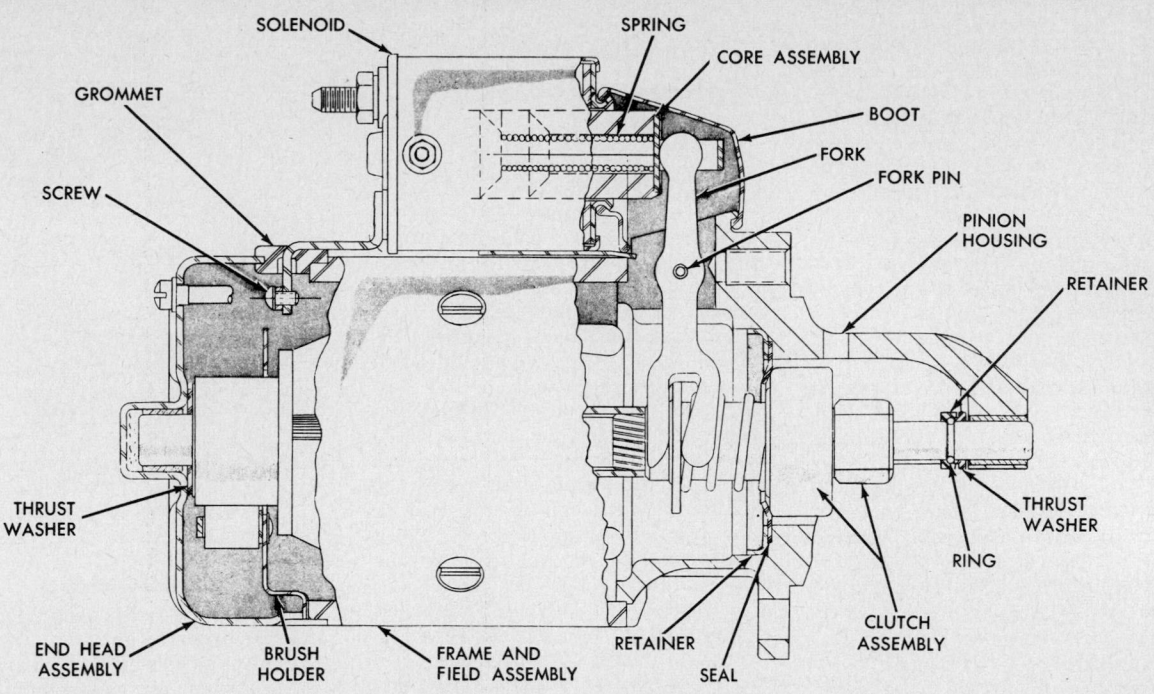

Chrysler direct drive starter motor (© Chrysler Corp.)

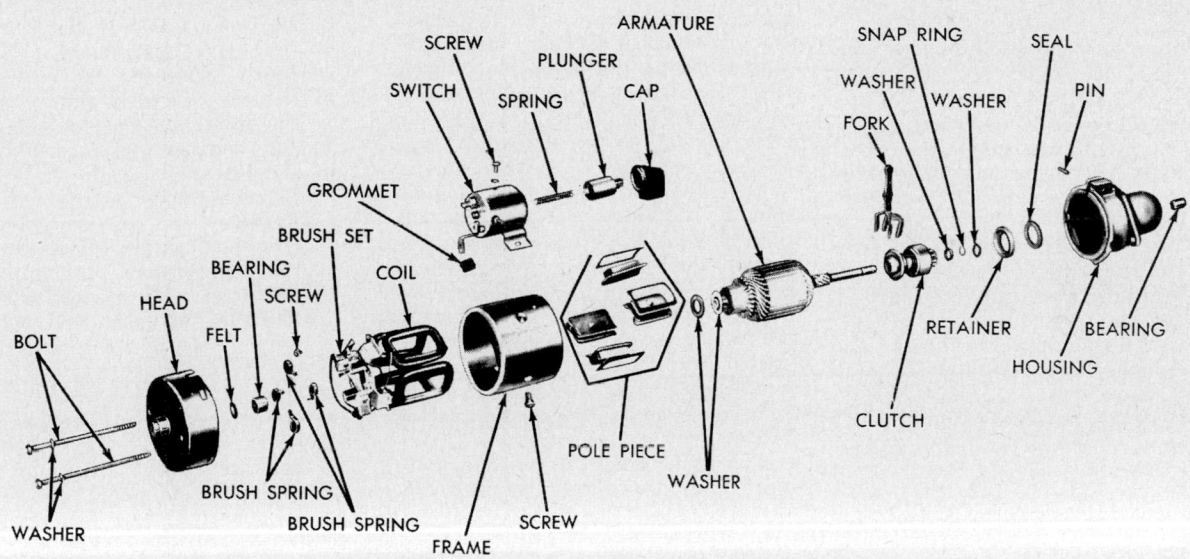

Chrysler direct drive motor—exploded view (© Chrysler Corp.)

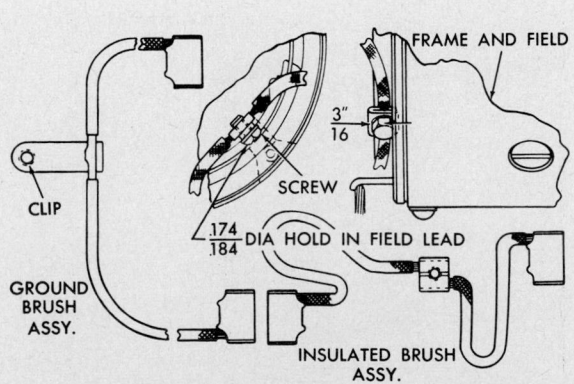

Brush lead arrangement—Chrysler direct drive motor
(© Chrysler Corp.)

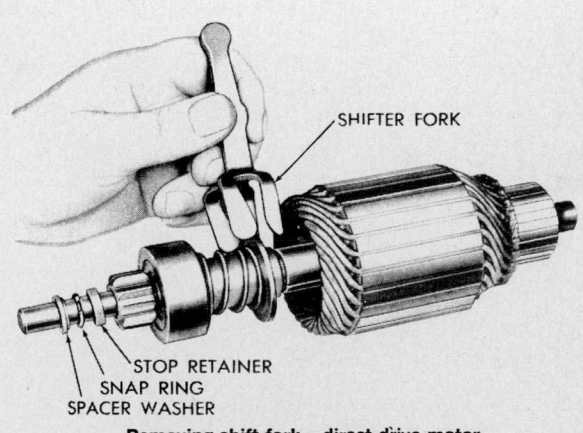

Removing shift fork—direct drive motor
(© Chrysler Corp.)

exposed snap-ring.
11. Remove overrunning clutch drive from armature shaft.
12. If field coils are good, stop disassembly at this point. If field coils must be replaced, remove ground brushes terminal screw and remove brushes, terminal and shunt wire. Remove pole shoe screws, using a ratchet-type impact driver and special wide screwdriver blade, then remove field coils.

Assembly

1. Install field coils into frame, if removed.
2. Lubricate armature shaft and splines with engine oil.
3. Install starter drive, stop retainer, lock ring and spacer washer.
4. Install shift fork, with *narrow* leg of fork toward commutator.
5. Install pinion housing onto armature shaft, indexing shift fork with slot in housing.
6. Install shift fork pivot pin.
7. With clutch drive, shift fork, and pinion housing assembled onto the armature, slide armature into frame until pinion housing indexes with slot.
8. Install solenoid and boot, tightening bolts to 60-70 in. lbs.
9. Connect field coil wires to solenoid connector, making sure they do not touch frame.
10. Install brush holder plate, indexing tang in frame hole.
11. Place brushes in holders, making sure field coil wires do not interfere.
12. Install thrust washers on commutator end of armature shaft to obtain a maximum of 0.010 in. end-play.
13. Install commutator end head and through bolts. Tighten bolts to 40-50 in. lbs.
14. Measure drive gear pinion clearance; it should be ⅛ in. Adjust by moving solenoid fore and aft as required.

Autolite Positive Engagement Starter Motor

(Ford Motor Co.)

This starting motor is a series-parallel wound, four pole, four brush unit. It is equipped with an over-running clutch drive pinion, which is engaged with the flywheel ring gear by an actuating lever, operated by a movable pole piece. This pole piece is hinged to the starter frame and can drop into position through an opening in the frame.

Three conventional field coils are located at three pole piece positions. The fourth field coil is designed to serve also as an engaging coil and a hold-in coil for the operation of the drive pinion.

When the ignition switch is turned to the start position, the starter relay is energized and current flows from the battery to the starter motor terminal. This prime surge of current first flows through the starter engaging coil, creating a very strong magnetic field. This magnetism draws the movable pole piece down toward the starter frame, which then causes the lever attached to it to move the starter pinion into engagement with the flywheel ring gear.

When the movable pole shoe is fully seated, it opens the field coil, grounding contacts, and the starter is then in normal operation. A holding coil is used to hold the movable pole shoe in the fully seated position during the engine cranking operation.

Cars equipped with automatic transmissions have a starter neutral switch circuit control. This is to prevent operation of the starter if the selector lever is not in Neutral or Park.

This type starter is used on both Ford and late-model American Motors products.

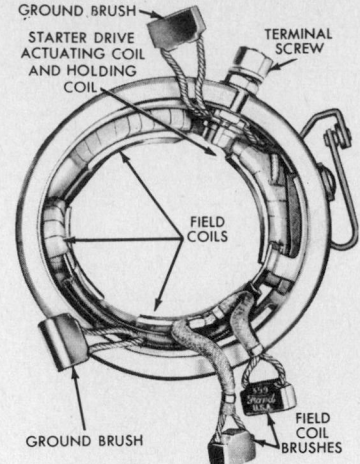

Autolite field coil assembly

Disassembly

1. Remove brush cover band and starter drive gear actuating lever cover. Observe the brush lead locations for reassembly, then remove the brushes from their holders.

NOTE: factory brush length is ½ in.; wear limit is ¼ in.
2. Remove the through bolts, starter drive gear housing and the drive gear actuating lever return spring.
3. Remove the pivot pin retaining the starter gear actuating lever and remove the lever and the armature.
4. Remove the stop ring retainer. Remove and discard the stop ring holding the drive gear to the armature shaft; then remove the drive gear assembly.
5. Remove the brush end plate.
6. Remove the two screws holding the ground brushes to the frame.
7. On the field coil that operates the starter drive gear actuating lever, bend the tab up on the field retainer and remove the field coil retainer.
8. Remove the three coil retaining

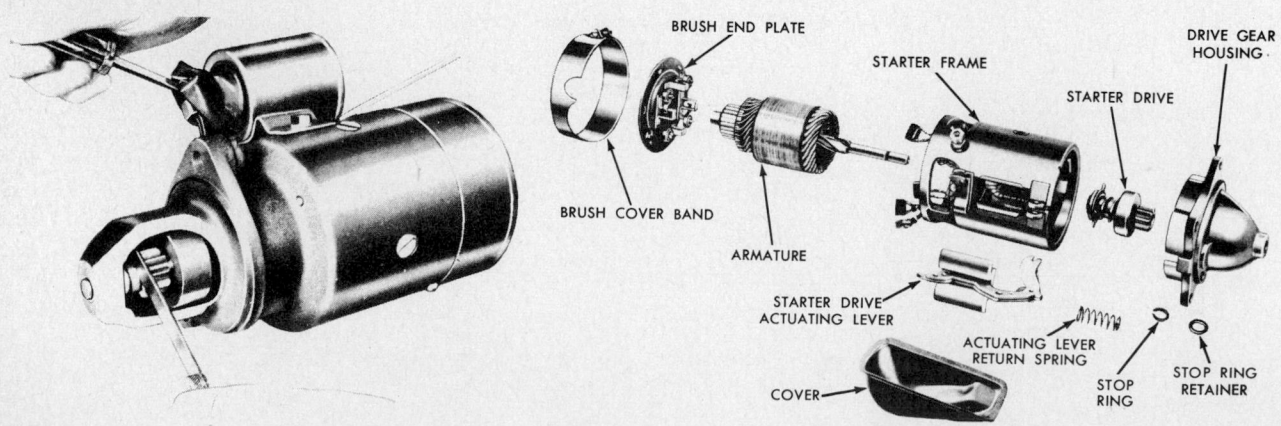

Checking drive pinion clearance—direct drive motor
(© Chrysler Corp.)

Autolite starter motor

screws. Unsolder the field coil leads from the terminal screw, then remove the pole shoes and coils from the frame (use a 300 watt iron).

9. Remove the starter terminal nut, washer, insulator and terminal from the starter frame.

Assembly

1. Install starter terminal, insulator, washers and retaining nut in the frame. (Be sure to position the slot in the screw perpendicular to the frame end surface.)

2. Position coils and pole pieces, with the coil leads in the terminal screw slot, then install the retaining screws. As the pole screws are tightened, strike the frame several sharp hammer blows to align the pole shoes. Tighten, then stake the screws.

3. Install solenoid coil and retainer and bend the tabs to hold the coils to the frame.

4. Solder the field coils and solenoid wire to the starter terminal, using rosin-core solder and a 300 watt iron.

5. Check for continuity and ground connections in the assembled coils.

6. Position the solenoid coil ground terminal over the nearest ground screw hole.

7. Position the ground brushes to the starter frame and install retaining screws.

8. Position the brush end plate to the frame, with the end plate boss in the frame slot.

9. Lightly Lubriplate the armature shaft splines and install the starter drive gear assembly on the shaft. Install a new retaining stop ring and stop ring retainer.

10. Position the fiber thrust washer on the commutator end of the armature shaft, then position the armature in the starter frame.

11. Position the starter drive gear actuating lever to the frame and starter drive assembly, and install the pivot pin.

   NOTE: fill drive gear housing bore $\frac{1}{4}$ full of grease.

12. Position the drive actuating lever return spring and the drive gear housing to the frame, then install and tighten the through bolts. Do not pinch brush leads between brush plate and frame. Be sure that the stop ring retainer is properly seated in the drive housing.

13. Install the brushes in the brush holders and center the brush springs on the brushes.

14. Position the drive gear actuating lever cover on the starter and install the brush cover band with a new gasket.

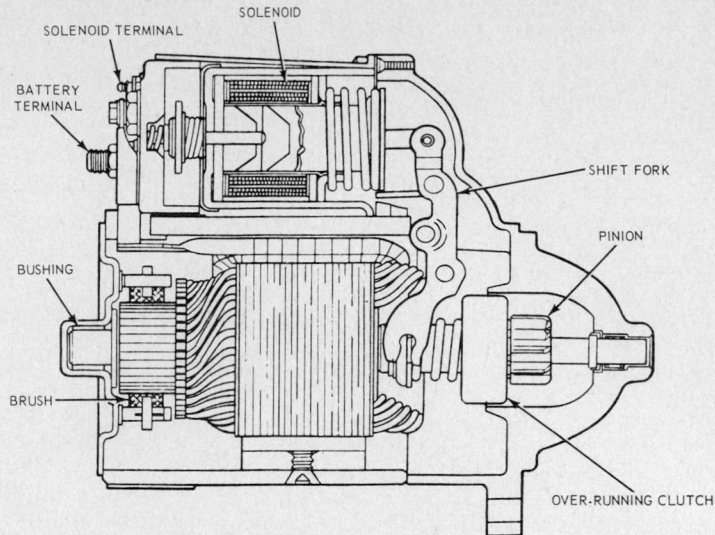

Ford solenoid actuated starter motor (© Ford Motor Co.)

Labels: SOLENOID TERMINAL, SOLENOID, BATTERY TERMINAL, SHIFT FORK, PINION, BUSHING, BRUSH, OVER-RUNNING CLUTCH

15. Check starter no-load amperage draw.

Autolite Solenoid Actuated Starter Motor

(Ford Motor Co.)

This starter motor, usually used with late-model 400, 429 and 460 engines, is a four-brush, four-field, four-pole wound unit. The frame encloses a wound armature, which is supported at the drive end by caged needle bearings and at the commutator end by a sintered copper bushing. The four pole shoes are retained to the frame by one pole screw apiece, and on each pole shoe is wound a ribbon-type field coil conected in series-parallel.

The solenoid is mounted to a flange on the starter drive housing, which encloses the entire shift mechanism and solenoid plunger. The solenoid, following standard industry practice, utilizes two windings—a pull-in winding and a hold-in winding.

Disassembly

1. Disconnect the copper strap from the solenoid starter terminal, remove the remaining screws and remove the solenoid.

2. Loosen the retaining screw and slide the brush cover band back far enough to gain access to the brushes.

3. Remove the brushes from their holders, then remove the through bolts and separate the drive end housing from the frame and brush end plate.

   NOTE: factory brush length is $\frac{1}{2}$ in., wear limit $\frac{1}{4}$ in.

4. Remove the solenoid plunger and shift fork. These two items can be separated from each other by removing the roll pin.

5. Remove the armature and drive assembly from the frame. Remove the drive stop ring and slide the drive off the armature shaft.

6. Remove the drive stop ring retainer from the drive housing.

Assembly

1. Lubricate the armature shaft splines with Lubriplate, then install drive assembly and a new stop ring.

2. Lubricate shift lever pivot pin with Lubriplate, then position solenoid plunger and shift lever assembly in the drive housing.

3. Place a new retainer in the drive housing. Apply a small amount of Lubriplate to the drive end of the armature shaft, then place armature and drive assembly into the drive housing, indexing the shift lever tangs with the drive assembly.

4. Apply a small amount of Lubriplate to the commutator end of the armature shaft, then position the frame and field assembly to the drive housing.

5. Position the brush plate assembly to the frame, making sure it properly indexes. Install through bolts and tighten to 45-85 in. lbs.

6. Install brushes into their holders and make sure leads are not touching any interior starter components.

7. Place the rubber gasket between the solenoid mount and the frame surface.

8. Place the starter solenoid in position with metal gasket and spring, install heat shield (if so equipped) and install solenoid screws.

9. Connect copper strap and install cover band.

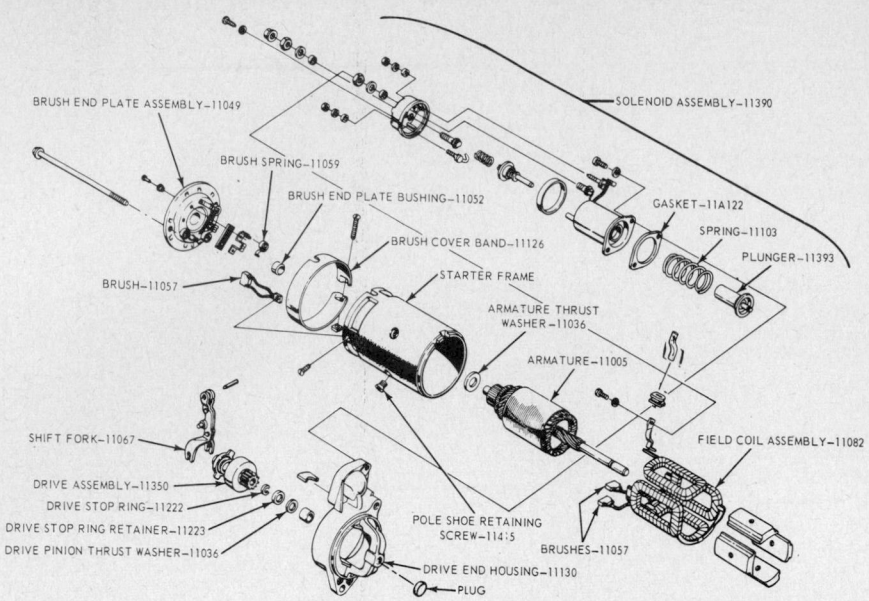

BRUSH END PLATE ASSEMBLY—11049
BRUSH SPRING—11059
BRUSH END PLATE BUSHING—11052
BRUSH COVER BAND—11126
BRUSH—11057
STARTER FRAME
SOLENOID ASSEMBLY—11390
GASKET—11A122
SPRING—11103
PLUNGER—11393
ARMATURE THRUST WASHER—11036
ARMATURE—11005
SHIFT FORK—11067
DRIVE ASSEMBLY—11350
DRIVE STOP RING—11222
DRIVE STOP RING RETAINER—11223
DRIVE PINION THRUST WASHER—11036
POLE SHOE RETAINING SCREW—11415
BRUSHES—11057
FIELD COIL ASSEMBLY—11082
DRIVE END HOUSING—11130
PLUG

Ford solenoid actuated starter motor (© Ford Motor Co.)

Delco-Remy Starter Motor

(General Motors Corp.)

There are many different versions of the Delco-Remy starter, depending upon application. In general, six-cylinder engines use a unit having four field coils in series between the terminal and armature. Standard V8 engines use, depending on displacement, one of three types: one has two field coils in series with the armature and parallel to each other; another has two field coils in parallel between the field terminal and ground, and

another has three field coils in series with the armature and one field connected between the motor terminal and ground. Heavy-duty starter motors, such as used on some of the largest G.M. high-output engines (over 400 cu. in.) have series compound windings.

In spite of these differences, all Delco-Remy starters are disassembled and assembled in essentially the same manner.

Disassembly

1. Disconnect the field coil connectors from the motor solenoid terminal.

NOTE: on models so equipped, remove solenoid mounting screws.
2. Remove the through bolts.
3. Remove commutator end frame, field frame and armature assembly from drive housing.
4. Remove the overrunning clutch from the armature shaft as follows:
   a. Slide the two-piece thrust collar off the end of the armature shaft.
   b. Slide a standard ½ in. pipe coupling or other spacer onto the shaft so that the end of the coupling butts against the edge of the retainer.

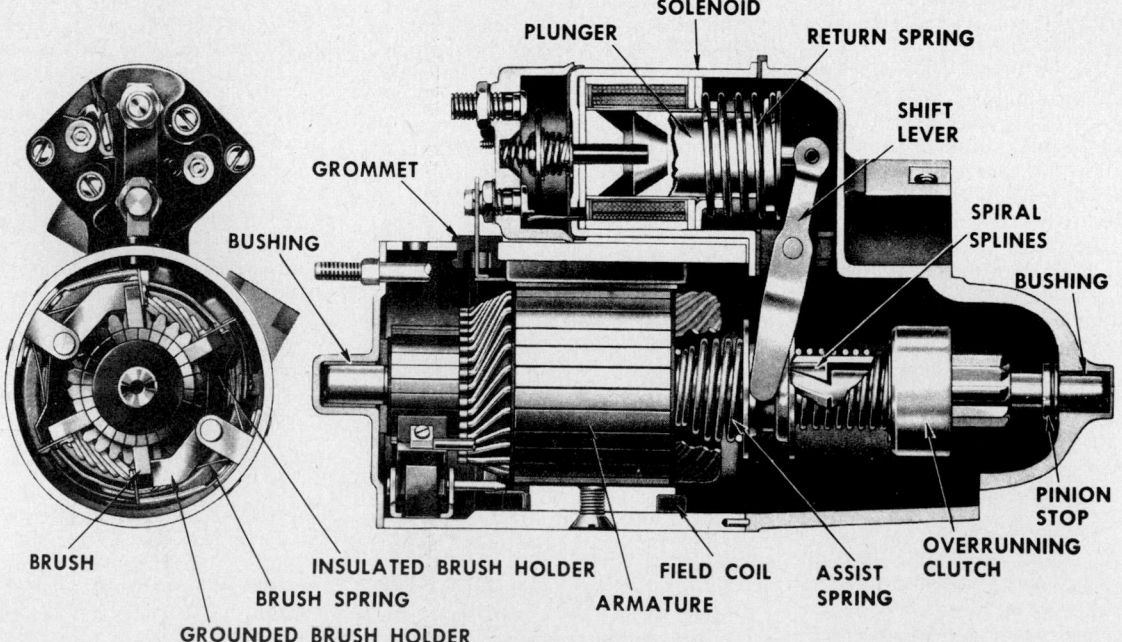

SOLENOID
PLUNGER
RETURN SPRING
SHIFT LEVER
GROMMET
SPIRAL SPLINES
BUSHING
BUSHING
PINION STOP
OVERRUNNING CLUTCH
BRUSH
INSULATED BRUSH HOLDER
BRUSH SPRING
FIELD COIL
ARMATURE
ASSIST SPRING
GROUNDED BRUSH HOLDER

Typical Delco-Remy starter motor using an assist spring—light-duty Chevrolet illustrated
(© Chev. Div., G.M. Corp.)

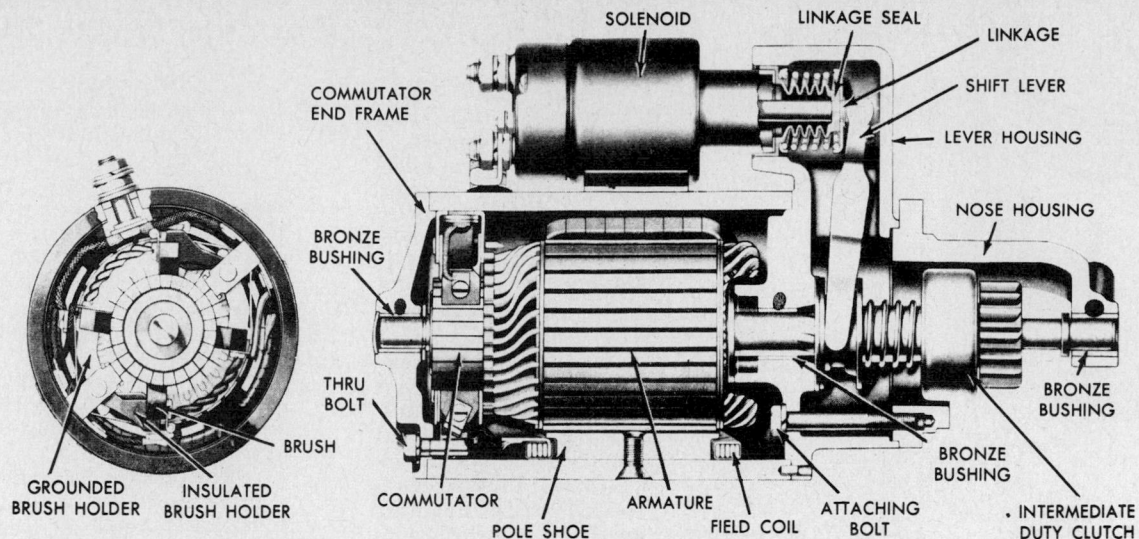

Typical Delco-Remy starter motor as used on intermediate models—
Chevrolet application illustrated
(© Chev. Div., G.M. Corp.)

c. Tap the end of the coupling with a hammer, driving retainer towards armature end of snap-ring.

d. Remove snap-ring from its groove in the shaft using pliers. Slide retainer and clutch from armature shaft.

5. Disassemble brush assembly from field frame by releasing the V-spring and removing the support pin. The brush holders, brushes and springs now can be pulled out as a unit and the leads disconnected.

6. On models so equipped, separate solenoid from lever housing.

Assembly

1. Install brushes into holders. Install solenoid, if so equipped.

2. Assemble insulated and grounded brush holder together using the V-spring and position the assembled unit on the support pin. Push holders and spring to bottom of support and rotate spring to engage the slot in support. Attach ground wire to grounded brush and field lead wire to insulated brush, then repeat for other brush sets.

3. Assemble overrunning clutch to armature shaft as follows:

a. Lubricate drive end of shaft with silicone lubricant.

b. Slide clutch assembly onto shaft with pinion outward.

c. Slide retainer onto shaft with cupped surface facing away from pinion.

d. Stand armature up on a wood surface, commutator downwards. Position snapring on upper end of shaft and drive it onto shaft with a small block of wood and a hammer. Slide snap-ring into groove.

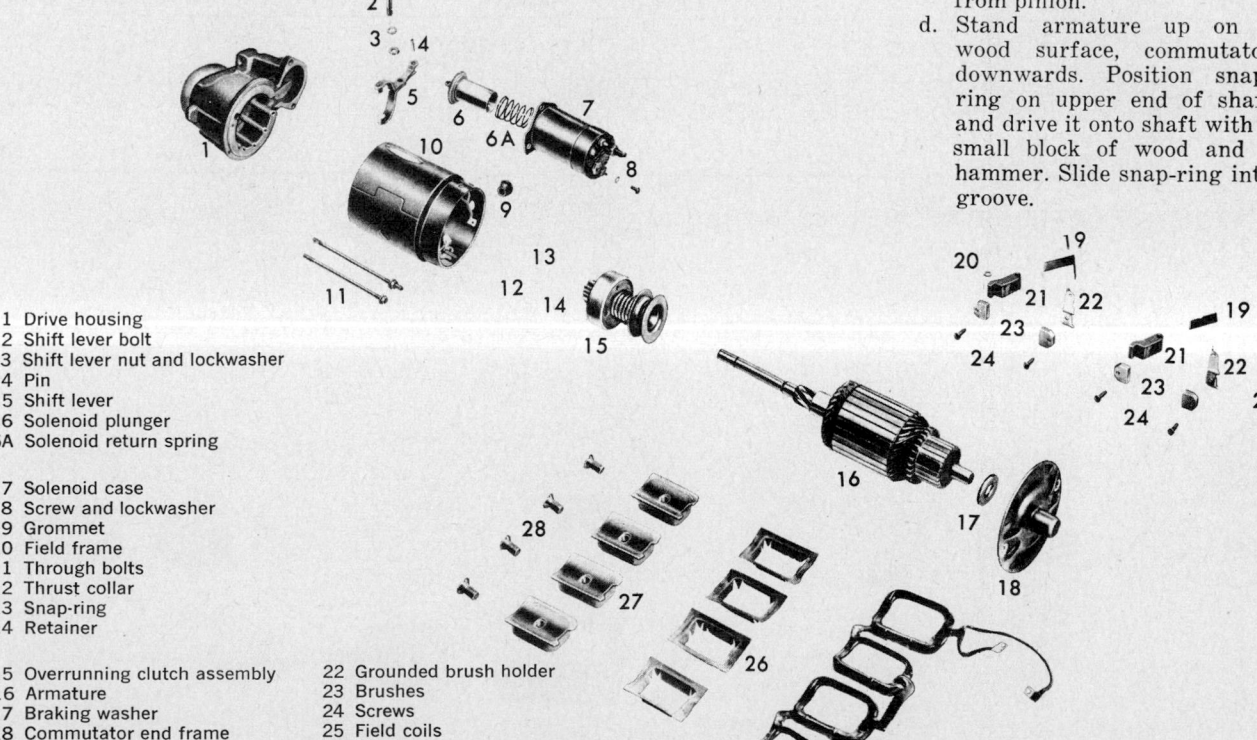

1 Drive housing
2 Shift lever bolt
3 Shift lever nut and lockwasher
4 Pin
5 Shift lever
6 Solenoid plunger
6A Solenoid return spring

7 Solenoid case
8 Screw and lockwasher
9 Grommet
10 Field frame
11 Through bolts
12 Thrust collar
13 Snap-ring
14 Retainer

15 Overrunning clutch assembly
16 Armature
17 Braking washer
18 Commutator end frame
19 Brush springs
20 Washer
21 Insulated brush holders

22 Grounded brush holder
23 Brushes
24 Screws
25 Field coils
26 Insulators
27 Pole shoes
28 Screws

Typical Delco-Remy starter motor exploded view—light-duty Chevrolet illustrated
(© Chev. Div., G.M. Corp.)

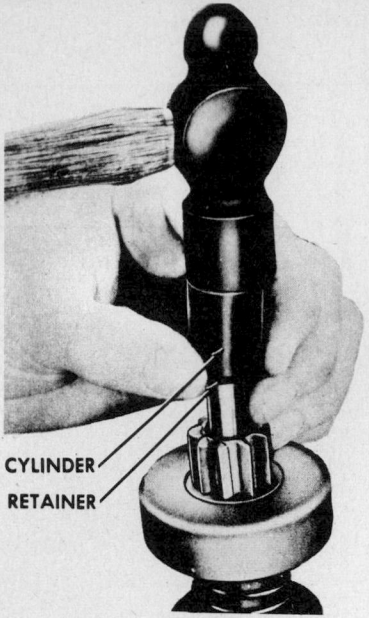

CYLINDER

RETAINER

Driving retainer off snap-ring—
Delco-Remy motor
(© Chev. Div., G.M. Corp.)

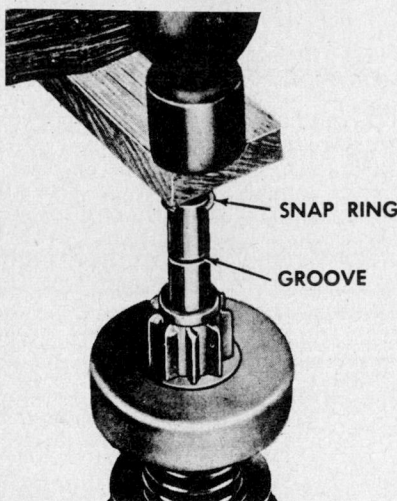

SNAP RING

GROOVE

Forcing snap-ring over armature shaft—
Delco-Remy motor
(© Chev. Div., G.M. Corp.)

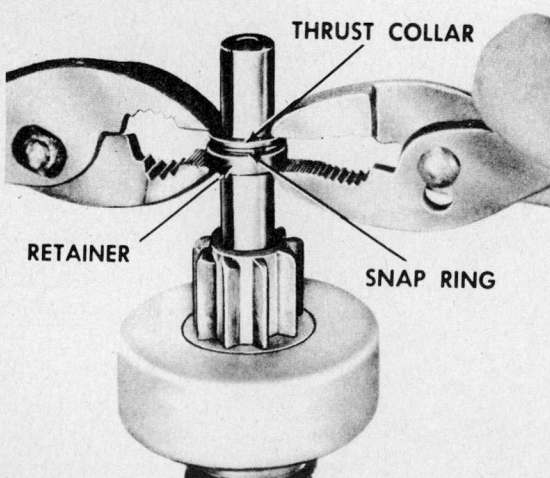

THRUST COLLAR

RETAINER

SNAP RING

Forcing snap-ring into retainer—Delco-Remy motor
(© Chev. Div., G.M. Corp.)

e. Install thrust collar onto shaft with shoulder next to snap-ring.

f. With retainer on one side of snap-ring and thrust collar on the other side, squeeze together with two sets of pliers until ring seats in retainer. On models without thrust collar, use a washer. Remember to remove washer before continuing.

4. Lubricate drive end bushing with silicone lubricant, then slide armature and clutch assembly into place, at the same time engaging shift lever with clutch.

5. Position field frame over armature and apply sealer (silicone) between frame and solenoid case. Position frame against drive housing, making sure brushes are not damaged in the process.

6. Lubricate commutator end bushing with silicone lubricant, place a leather brake washer on the armature shaft and slide commutator end frame onto shaft. Install through bolts and tighten to 65 in. lbs.

7. Reconnect field coil connector/s to the solenoid motor terminal. Install solenoid mounting screws, if so equipped.

8. Check pinion clearance; it should be 0.010-0.140 in. on all models.

Prestolite Starter Motor

Disassembly

1. Disconnect solenoid by removing motor terminal nut and lock-washer and the two retaining bolts.
2. Remove link cover boot and solenoid.
3. Remove starter through bolts, then remove commutator end head and frame.
4. Remove shift lever pin retainer, boot and pivot pin.
5. Remove armature, drive and shift lever from pinion housing.
6. Remove drive assembly as follows:
   a. Slide thrust collar off armature shaft.
   b. Using a standard ½ in. pipe connector, drive snap-ring retainer off shaft.
   c. Remove snap-ring from groove, then remove drive assembly.

Assembly

1. Assemble overrunning clutch to armature shaft as follows:
   a. Lubricate drive end and splines with Lubriplate.
   b. Install clutch assembly onto shaft.
   c. Install snap-ring retainer, cupped surface facing end of shaft.

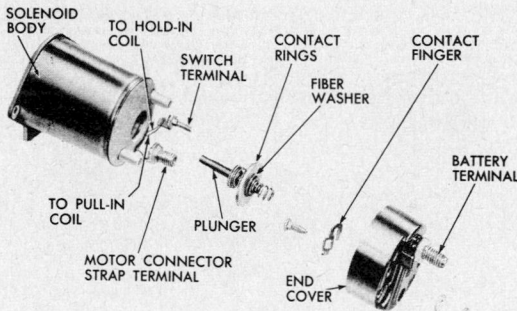

SOLENOID BODY · TO HOLD-IN COIL · SWITCH TERMINAL · CONTACT RINGS · CONTACT FINGER · FIBER WASHER · BATTERY TERMINAL · TO PULL-IN COIL · PLUNGER · MOTOR CONNECTOR STRAP TERMINAL · END COVER

Delco-Remy starter solenoid (© Chev. Div., G.M. Corp.)

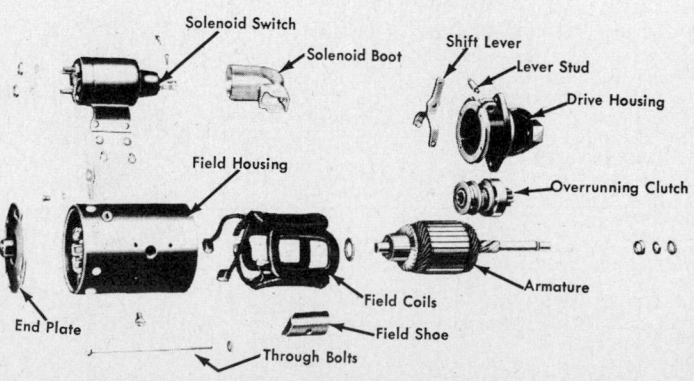

Solenoid Switch · Solenoid Boot · Shift Lever · Lever Stud · Drive Housing · Field Housing · Overrunning Clutch · Armature · Field Coils · End Plate · Field Shoe · Through Bolts

Prestolite starter motor—exploded view (© American Motors Corp.)

d. Install snap-ring into groove. Use a new snap-ring if necessary.

e. Install thrust collar onto shaft, shoulder against snap-ring.

f. Force retainer over snap-ring in the same manner as for Delco-Remy starters.

2. Lubricate overrunning clutch shift collar and drive end bush-ing with engine oil.

3. Hold shift lever in position on collar and assemble armature, drive and shift lever into housing.

4. Install shift lever pivot pin, boot and retainer.

5. Install frame and field coil assembly, making sure brushes are not damaged in the process.

6. Saturate felt washer (commuta-tor head) with engine oil, drain excess and install washer.

7. Install through bolts and tighten to 65 in. lbs.

8. Check armature end-play; it should be 0.005-0.030 in. Adjust, if necessary, by adding or removing thrust washers at commutator end of shaft.

9. Check pinion clearance; it should be 0.010-0.140 in.

AC Generators

Is It the Alternator or the Voltage Regulator?

The first step in diagnosing troubles of the charging system, is to identify the source of failure. Does the fault lie in the alternator or the regulator? The next move depends upon preference or necessity; either repair or replace the offending unit.

It is just as easy to separate an alternator, electrically, from the AC regulator as it is to separate its counterpart, the DC generator from its regulator.

AC generator output is controlled by the amount of current supplied to the field circuit of the system.

Unlike the DC generator, an AC generator is capable of producing substantial current at idle speed. Higher maximum output is also a possibility. This presents a potential danger when testing. As a precaution, a field rheostat should be used in the field circuit when making the following isolation test. The field rheostat permits positive control of the amount of current allowed to pass through the field circuit during the isolation test. Unregulated alternator capacity could ruin the unit.

NOTE: most manufacturers of precision gauges offer special test connectors, in sets, that will adapt to the leads and connections of any AC charging system.

CAUTION: before attempting the isolation test, disconnect the field wire from the regulator. Failure to take this precaution can cause instant burning and permanent damage to the regulator.

Isolation Test

(By-passing the Regulator)

1. Connect voltmeter leads to two prods driven into the battery posts.

2. Disconnect field wire from the FLD terminal of the voltage regulator.

3. Connect one lead of a field rheostat to the undisturbed IGN terminal of the regulator, and the other field rheostat lead to the wire that was removed from the FLD terminal of the regulator.

4. With field rheostat turned to the low side of the scale, (high resistance) start the engine and adjust throttle to about 2,000 rpm.

5. Slowly move field rheostat control knob to decrease resistance, (allowing more current to flow through the field circuit) until voltmeter reading slightly exceeds manufacturers' specifications.

NOTE: under load conditions, observe the alternator for arcing or any other evidence of malfunction.

6. If alternator performs satisfactorily, repair or replace the regulator. Conversely, if the voltmeter reading is zero, or below specifications, repair or replace the alternator.

Alternator Test Plans

The following is a procedure pattern for testing the various alternators and their control systems.

There are certain precautionary measures that apply to alternator tests in general. These items are listed in detail to avoid repetition when testing each make of alternator, and to encourage a habit of good test procedure.

1. Check alternator drive belt for condition and tension.

2. Disconnect battery cables, check physical, chemical, and electrical condition of battery.

3. Be absolutely sure of polarity before connecting any battery in the circuit. Reversed polarity will ruin the diodes.

4. Never use a battery charger to

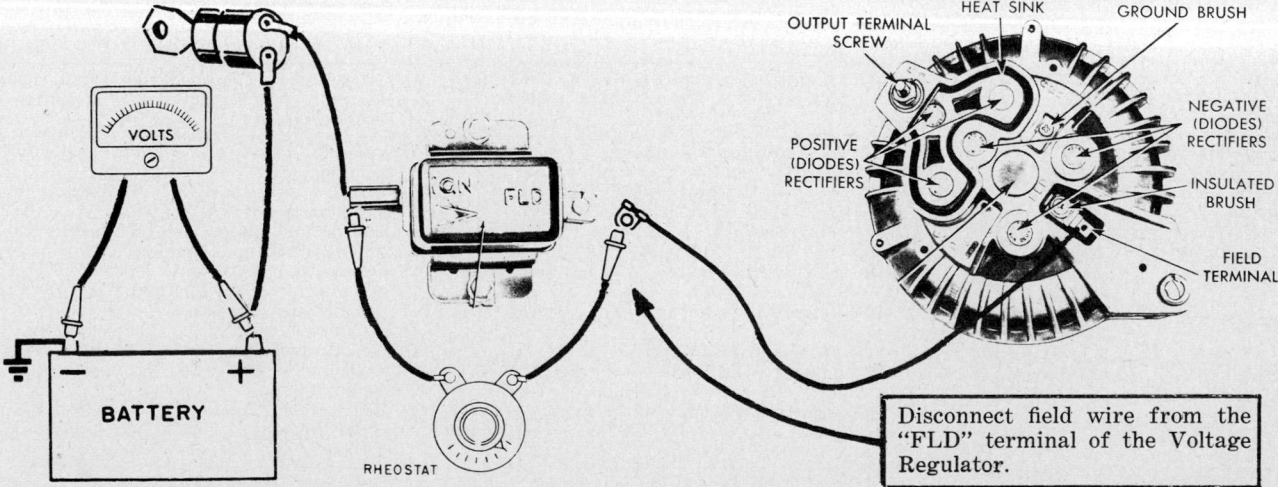

OUTPUT TERMINAL SCREW — HEAT SINK — GROUND BRUSH — NEGATIVE (DIODES) RECTIFIERS — POSITIVE (DIODES) RECTIFIERS — INSULATED BRUSH — FIELD TERMINAL — VOLTS — BATTERY — RHEOSTAT

Disconnect field wire from the "FLD" terminal of the Voltage Regulator.

Typical Chrysler type to 1969

start the engine.

5. Disconnect both battery cables when making a battery recharge hook-up.
6. Be sure of polarity hook-up when using a booster battery for starting.
7. Never ground the alternator output or battery terminal.
8. Never ground the field circuit between alternator and regulator.
9. Never run any alternator on an open circuit with the field energized.

10. Never try to polarize an alternator.
11. Do not attempt to motor an alternator.
12. The regulator cover must be in place when taking voltage limiter readings.
13. The ignition switch must be in off position when removing or installing the regulator cover.
14. Use insulated tools only to make adjustments to the regulator.

15. When making engine idle speed adjustments, always consider potential load factors that influence engine rpm. To compensate for electrical load, switch on the lights, radio, heater, air conditioner, etc.
16. Never electric weld any frame or suspension components unless both battery cables are disconnected.

Condition	Possible Cause	Correction
Alternator Fails To Charge (No Output)	(a) Blown fusible wire in voltage regulator.	(a) Locate and correct cause of the fuse blow-blowing. Install new fuse wire. Solder both ends of new fusible wire securely.
	(b) Alternator drive belt loose.	(b) Adjust drive belt to specifications.
	(c) Worn brushes and/or slip rings.	(c) Install new brushes and/or slip rings.
	(d) Sticking brushes.	(d) Clean slip rings and brush holders. Install new brushes if necessary.
	(e) Open field circuit.	(e) Test all the field circuit connections, and correct as required.
	(f) Open charging circuit.	(f) Inspect all connections in charging circuit, and correct as required.
	(g) Open circuit in stator windings.	(g) Remove alternator and disassemble. Test stator windings. Install new stator if necessary.
	(h) Open rectifiers.	(h) Remove alternator and disassemble. Test the rectifiers. Install new rectifiers if necessary.
Low, Unsteady Charging Rate	(a) Alternator drive belt loose.	(a) Adjust alternator drive belt.
	(b) High resistance at battery terminals.	(b) Clean and tighten battery terminals.
	(c) High resistance in charging circuit.	(c) Test charging circuit resistance. Correct as required.
	(d) High resistance in body-to-engine ground lead.	(d) Tighten ground lead connections. Install new ground lead if necessary.
	(e) Open stator winding.	(e) Remove and disassemble alternator. Test stator windings. Install new stator if necessary.
Low Output and Low Battery	(a) High resistance in charging circuit.	(a) Test charging circuit resistance and correct as required.
	(b) Low regulator setting.	(b) Reset voltage regulator to specifications, if possible. Replace regulator if not.
	(c) Shorted rectifier. Open rectifier.	(c) Perform current output test. Test the rectifiers and install new rectifiers as required. Remove and disassemble the alternator.
	(d) Grounded stator windings.	(d) Remove and disassemble alternator. Test Test stator windings. Install new stator if necessary.
Excessive Charging Rate to Fully Charged Battery	(a) Regulator set too high.	(a) Reset voltage regulator to specifications, or install new regulator.
	(b) Regulator contacts stuck.	(b) Install new voltage regulator.
	(c) Regulator voltage winding open.	(c) Install new voltage regulator.
	(d) Regulator base improperly grounded.	(d) Connect regulator base to a good ground.
Regulator Contacts Burned	(a) High regulator setting.	(a) Reset voltage regulator to specifications, if possible, Replace regulator if not.
	(b) Shorted rotor field coil windings.	(b) Test rotor field coil current draw. If excessive, install new rotor.
Regulator Contact Points Stuck	(a) Poor ground connection between alternator and regulator. Open resistor element.	(a) Correct ground connection. Install new regulator. Test regulator setting, and re-set if necessary.
Noisy Alternator	(a) Alternator mounting loose.	(a) Properly install and tighten alternator mounting.
	(b) Worn or frayed drive belt.	(b) Install a new drive belt and adjust to specifications.
	(c) Worn bearings.	(c) Remove and disassamble alternator. Install new bearing as required.
	(d) Interference between rotor fan and stator leads or rectifiers.	(d) Remove and disassemble alternator. Correct interference as required.
	(e) Rotor or rotor fan damaged.	(e) Remove and disassemble alternator. Install new rotor.
	(f) Open or shorted rectifier.	(f) Remove and disassemble alternator. Test rectifiers. Install new rectifiers as required.
	(g) Open or shorted winding in stator.	(g) Remove and disassemble alternator. Test stator windings. Install new stator if necessary.
Excessive Ammeter Fluctuation	(a) High resistance in the field circuit to the alternator or an improperly set voltage regulator.	(a) Clean and tighten all connections as necessary. Adjust voltage regulator as necessary.

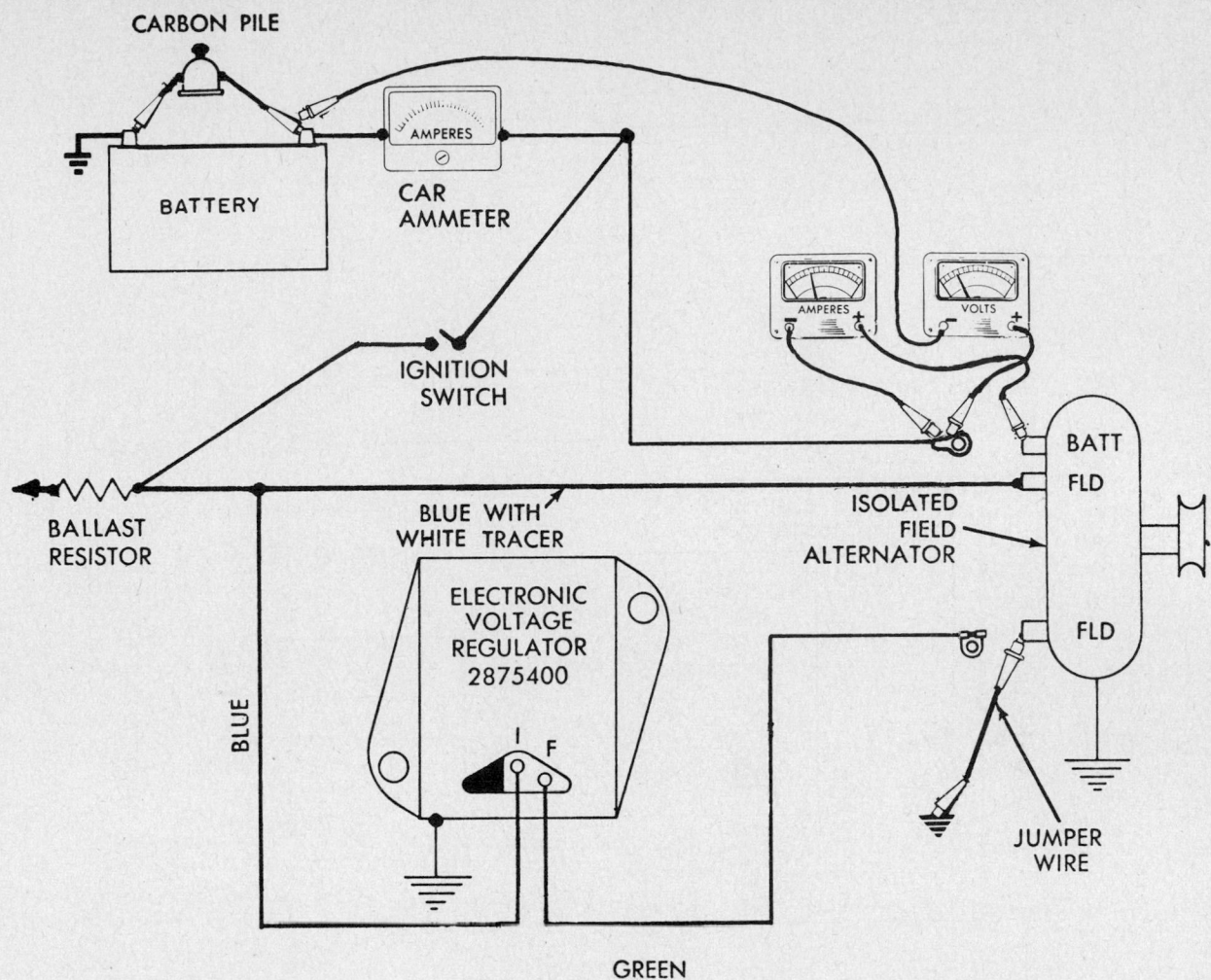

Charging circuit resistance test hook-up—Chrysler isolated field alternator

Chrysler Isolated Field Alternator (Electronic Regulator)

Charging Circuit Resistance Test—1970-72

1. Disconnect battery ground cable.
2. Disconnect the lead from the alternator output (BATT.) terminal.
3. Hook up an ammeter as follows:
   a. Connect the positive lead to the alternator output terminal.
   b. Connect the negative lead to the lead just disconnected from the alternator output terminal.
4. Hook up voltmeter as follows:
   a. Connect the positive voltmeter lead to the lead just disconnected from the alternator output terminal.
   b. Connect the negative voltmeter lead to the positive battery post.
5. Disconnect the lead from the alternator field (FLD.) terminal.

6. Connect a jumper wire between alternator field terminal and ground.
7. Hook up a tachometer to the engine.
8. Connect the battery ground cable, then connect carbon pile to battery terminals.
9. Start the engine and allow to idle.
10. Slowly adjust the engine speed and carbon pile until the ammeter registers 20 amps.
11. The voltmeter reading will now show the voltage drop in the charging circuit. There should not be more than 0.7 volt drop.
12. If the voltage drop exceeds 0.7 volt, stop the engine, clean and tighten all circuit connections, then repeat the test.

Current Output Test—1970-72

1. The ammeter and carbon pile hookup should remain the same as for the circuit resistance test.
2. Connect the voltmeter negative lead to the battery negative post.
3. Move the positive voltmeter lead to the alternator "BATT" post.

4. Start the engine and adjust speed to 1250 rpm.
5. Note voltmeter and ammeter readings. Maintain a 15 volt reading by adjusting the carbon pile control.
6. Compare ammeter reading with manufacturer's specifications. The reading should be no less than specified, 3 amps.
7. If below specifications:
   a. Check drive belt tension, adjust if necessary, then repeat the test.
   b. If results are still below specifications, internal trouble is indicated. Remove alternator for further testing.

Electronic Voltage Regulator Test—1970-72

1. Make sure battery terminals are clean and battery is charged.
2. Connect the positive lead of a test voltmeter to ignition Terminal No. 1 of the ballast resistor.
3. Connect the negative voltmeter lead to a good *body* ground.
4. Start engine and allow it to idle at 1250 rpm, all lights and acces-

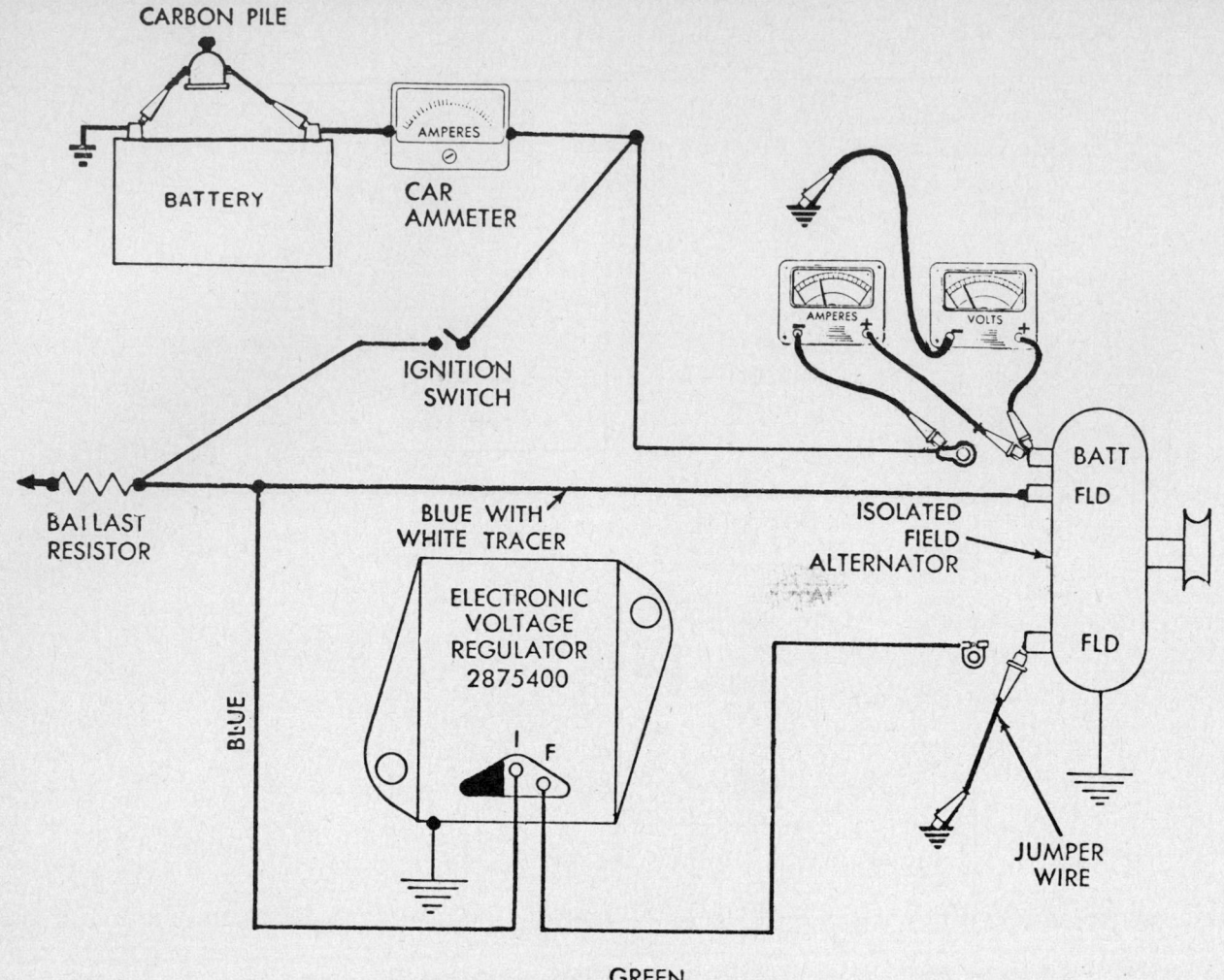

CARBON PILE

BATTERY

CAR AMMETER

IGNITION SWITCH

BALLAST RESISTOR

BLUE

BLUE WITH WHITE TRACER

ELECTRONIC VOLTAGE REGULATOR 2875400

I F

GREEN

AMPERES

VOLTS

BATT FLD

ISOLATED FIELD ALTERNATOR

FLD

JUMPER WIRE

Current output test hook-up—Chrysler isolated field alternator

sories turned off. Voltage should be as follows:

Ambient Temp. ¼ in. from Regulator	Voltage
-20°F.	14.3-15.3
80°F.	13.8-14.4
140°F.	13.3-14.0

5. If the voltage is *below* specifications, check the following:
   a. Voltage regulator ground—check voltage drop between regulator cover and ground.
   b. Harness wiring—disconnect regulator plug (ign. switch off), then turn on ign. switch and check for battery voltage at the terminal having the blue and green leads. *Wiring harness must be disconnected from the regulator when checking individual leads.* If no voltage is present in either lead, the problem is in the car wiring or alternator field.
6. If Step 5 tests showed no malfunctions, install a new regulator and repeat Step 4.
7. If voltage is *above* specifications

(Step 4), or fluctuates, check the following:
   a. Ground between regulator and body, and between body and engine.
   b. Ignition switch circuit between switch and regulator.
8. If voltage is still more than ½ volt above specifications, install a new regulator and repeat Step 4.

Alternator Bench Tests

Field Coil Draw

1. Connect a jumper between one FLD. terminal and the positive terminal of a fully charged 12-volt battery.
2. Connect the positive lead of a test ammeter to the other field (FLD.) terminal and the negative test lead to the negative battery terminal.
3. Slowly rotate the rotor by hand and observe the ammeter. The proper field coil draw is 2.3-2.7 amps. at 12 volts.

Field Circuit Ground Test

1. Touch one test lead of a 110-volt AC test bulb to one of the alter-

nator brush (field) terminals and the other test lead to the end shield.
2. If lamp lights, remove field brush assemblies and separate the end housings by removing the three through bolts.
3. Place one test lead on a slip ring and the other on the end shield.
4. If lamp lights, rotor assembly is grounded internally and must be replaced.
5. If the lamp does not light, the cause of the problem was a grounded brush.

NOTE: examine the illustrations for proper brush assembly sequence.

Chrysler Alternator (Electro-Mechanical Regulator)

Field Circuit Resistance Test—1965-69

1. Disconnect the ignition wire at the coil side of the ballast resistor.
2. Connect the positive lead of a test voltmeter to the positive battery post.

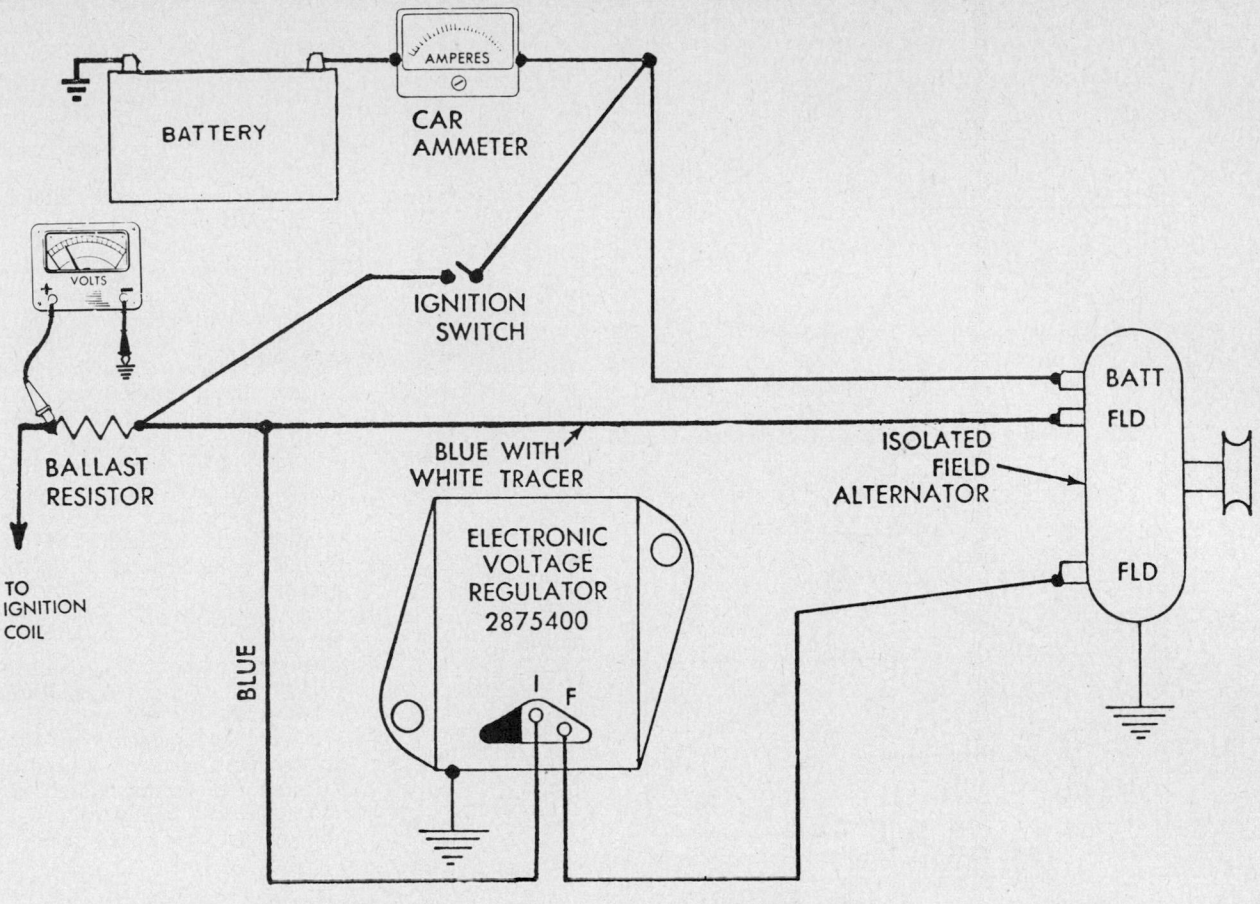

GREEN

Voltage regulator test hook-up—Chrysler isolated field alternator

3. Connect the negative lead of the test voltmeter to the regulator FLD. terminal.

4. Turn on ignition switch, turn off all accessories and lights. Test meter should indicate not more than 0.55 volt. More than this indicates high resistance (loose connections) in the field circuit between battery and regulator FLD. terminal.

Charging Circuit Resistance Test—1965-69

1. Disconnect the battery negative ground cable.

2. Disconnect the lead at the alternator BATT. terminal.

3. Connect a test ammeter in series between the BATT. terminal and the lead just disconnected from it.

4. Connect the positive lead of a test voltmeter to the BATT. lead, and connect the negative test lead to the battery positive post.

5. Disconnect the FLD. lead at the alternator FLD. terminal and the ignition lead at the regulator ignition terminal.

6. Connect a jumper wire between the alternator FLD. terminal and the alternator BATT. terminal to isolate the regulator.

7. Reconnect the battery ground cable.

8. Connect a carbon pile rheostat between the two battery terminals.

9. Start the engine and adjust engine speed to obtain a 10 amp. flow in the circuit. The voltmeter should not exceed 0.3 volt. If a higher voltage drop is indicated, clean and tighten all charging circuit connections.

10. Turn off ignition switch and restore all connections to original positions.

Current Output Test—1965-69

1. Disconnect battery ground cable.

2. Disconnect the BATT. lead from the alternator BATT. terminal.

3. Connect a test ammeter in series between the alternator BATT. terminal and the lead just disconnected from it.

4. Connect the positive lead of a test voltmeter to the BATT. lead and the negative voltmeter test lead to ground.

5. Disconnect the FLD. lead from the alternator and the ignition lead from the regulator IGN. terminal.

6. Connect a jumper wire between the alternator FLD. terminal

and the alternator BATT. terminal.

7. Connect a tachometer to the engine and reconnect the negative battery cable.

8. Connect a carbon pile rheostat between the two battery terminals.

9. Start engine and allow it to idle. Adjust carbon pile and engine speed until 1250 rpm and 15 volts are attained. *Do not exceed* 16 volts.

10. The ammeter should now read specified output for the particular alternator. A reading 5-7 amps. less than specified may indicate an open rectifier; a considerably less than normal reading could mean a shorted rectifier.

11. If reading is within limits, remove test gear and reconnect all leads to original terminals. If reading is outside of limits, remove alternator for bench tests.

Voltage Regulator Test

Upper Contacts

1. With the battery ground cable disconnected at the battery and the BATT. lead disconnected from the alternator output ter-

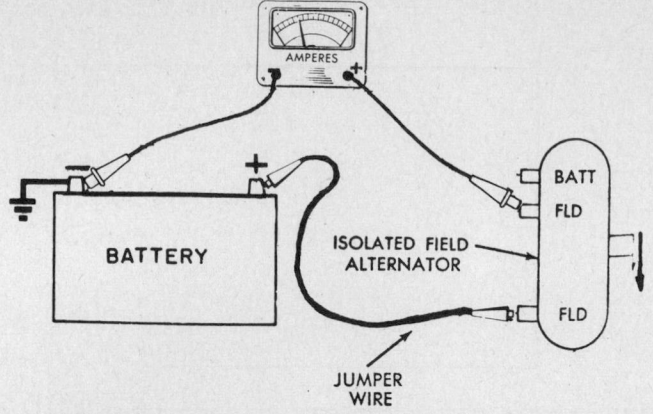

Field coil draw test hook-up—Chrysler isolated field alternator

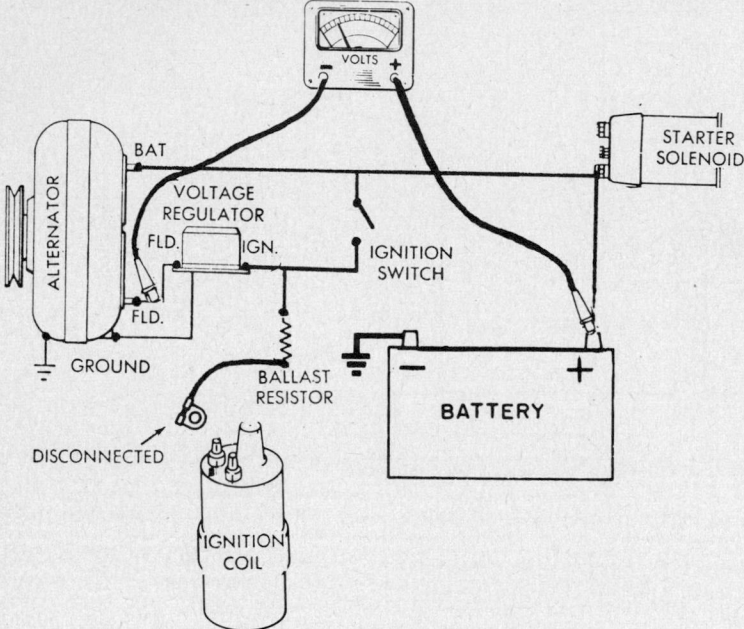

Field circuit resistance test hook-up—1965-69 Chrysler design

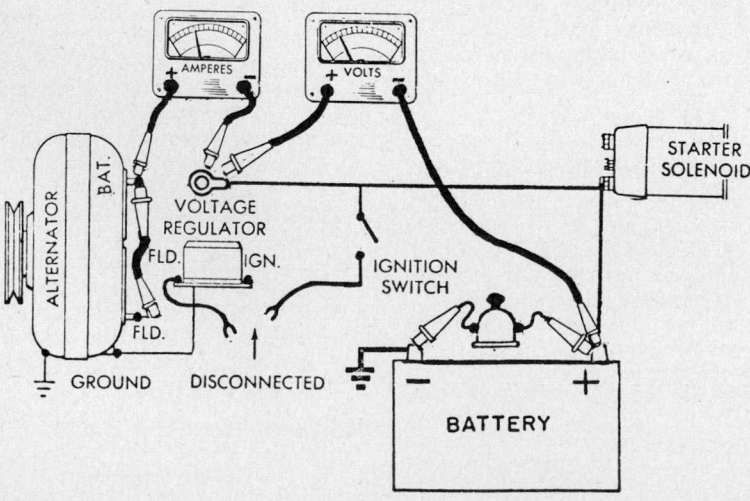

Charging circuit resistance test hook-up—1965-69 Chrysler design

minal, hook up an ammeter as follows:

   a. Connect the ammeter positive lead to the alternator output terminal.

   b. Connect the ammeter negative lead to the lead just disconnected from the alternator output terminal.

2. Hook up a voltmeter as follows:

   a. Disconnect the ignition wire at the IGN. terminal of the regulator. Install a pushbutton switch in series with the IGN. terminal and the wire just disconnected.

   b. Connect the negative voltmeter lead to ground.

   c. Connect the positive voltmeter lead to the IGN. terminal of the regulator or to the regulator side of the test switch.

3. Connect a tachometer to the engine.

4. Hook up the ground cable to the battery.

5. Hook up a carbon pile (load control turned to the off position) between the battery posts.

6. With engine operating at 1250 rpm, adjust carbon pile and/or turn on headlights; watch the voltmeter and ammeter. A 15 amp. output must be obtained.

Caution   Voltmeter reading must not exceed 15 volts. Continue to run the engine at this setting until the regulator has reached operating temperature (15 min.)

7. No current output indicates a low set regulator or a blown fuse wire inside regulator (between upper stationary contact and IGN. terminal).

8. If output is O.K. after 15 minutes, adjust engine rpm to 1250 again and adjust carbon pile to obtain 15 amps.

9. Measure and record temperature of regulator about 1/4 in. from cover.

10. Momentarily open and close the test switch several times and observe the voltmeter; it now reads the upper contact setting (see chart).

11. If regulator is within specifications, proceed to the *Lower Contacts* test. If not, remove regulator cover and adjust upper contacts (see *Regulator Adjustments*).

Lower Contacts

1. Keep the same hook-up as used for upper contact test.

2. Increase engine speed to 2200 rpm, then turn off all lights and accessories and/or adjust carbon pile to decrease output to 7 amps.

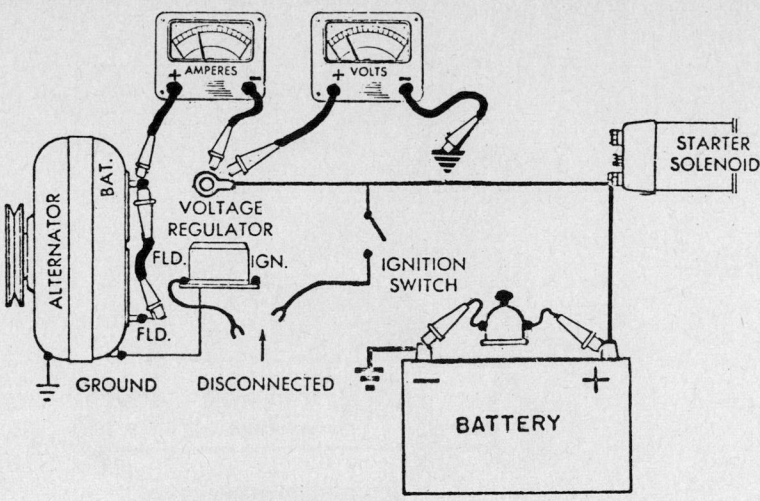

Current output test hook-up—1965-69 Chrysler design

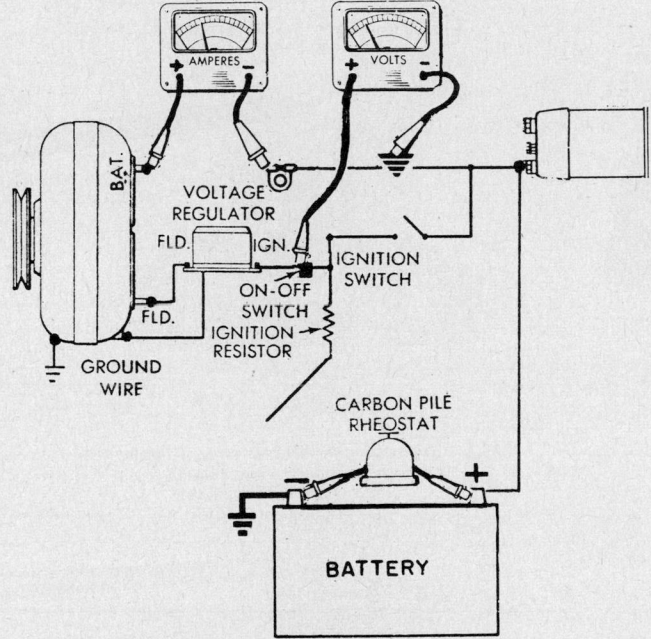

**Voltage regulator test hook-up—
1965-69 Chrysler electro-mechanical regulator**

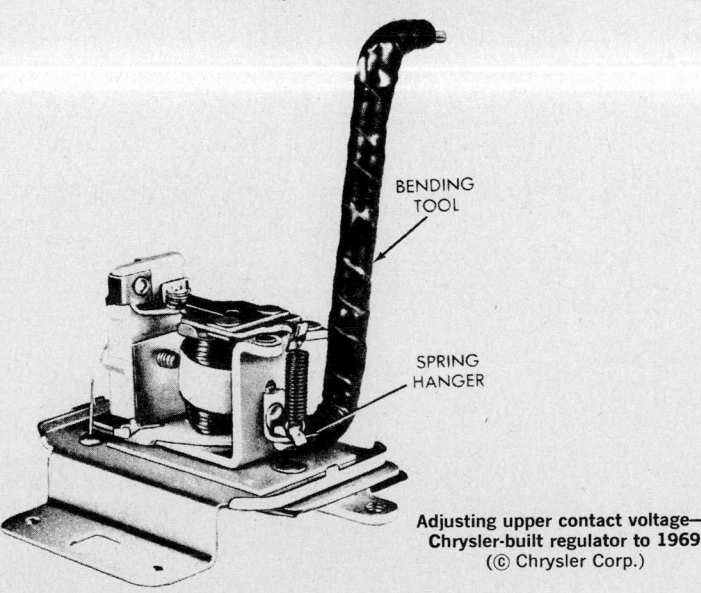

**Adjusting upper contact voltage—
Chrysler-built regulator to 1969**
(© Chrysler Corp.)

3. Again take a regulator temperature reading and turn the test switch on and off a few times.

4. The test voltmeter now will register an increase in voltage over that recorded for the upper contacts. This increase should not be less than 0.2 volt, or greater than 0.7 volt. If the voltage increase is not within these limits, it indicates that the air gap/contact clearance must be adjusted (see *Regulator Adjustments*). If the reading is less than 0.2 volt greater than upper contact voltage, charge the battery and retest.

5. Reduce engine speed to idle, stop engine and reconnect all terminal leads to their original positions.

Regulator Adjustments— 1965-69

Upper Contact Voltage— Chrysler Regulator

Upper contact voltage is set by bending the regulator lower spring hanger *down* to increase voltage, *up* to decrease voltage. The bending tool must be insulated properly in order to prevent grounding and regulator damage. The regulator must be installed, correctly connected and retested after each adjustment of the lower spring hanger. *Cover must be on.*

Lower Contact Voltage— Chrysler Regulator

If the adjustment of the upper contact voltage does not bring the regulator within specifications, measure the lower contact point gap. Gap should be 0.014 in. ± 0.002. This gap is adjusted by bending the lower *stationary* contact bracket, making sure points remain in alignment. If the lower contact gap is correct, and voltage still is out of specification, adjust the air gap, as follows:

1. Connect a 1½-volt test light (with battery) in series between the IGN. and FLD terminals of the regulator.

2. Insert a 0.048 in. wire gauge between the regulator armature and the core of the voltage coil. (see illustration).

3. Press down on the armature, not the contact reed, until the armature hits the wire gauge. At this point, the upper contacts should just open and the test light should be dim.

4. Insert a 0.052 in. wire gauge between the armature and voltage coil coil, next to the armature stop pin. (After removing 0.048 in. gauge).

5. Press down on the armature until it hits the wire gauge. The upper contacts should remain

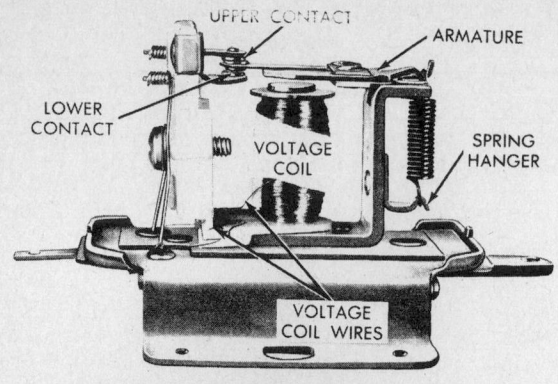

Chrysler voltage regulator to 1969—cover removed
(© Chrysler Corp.)

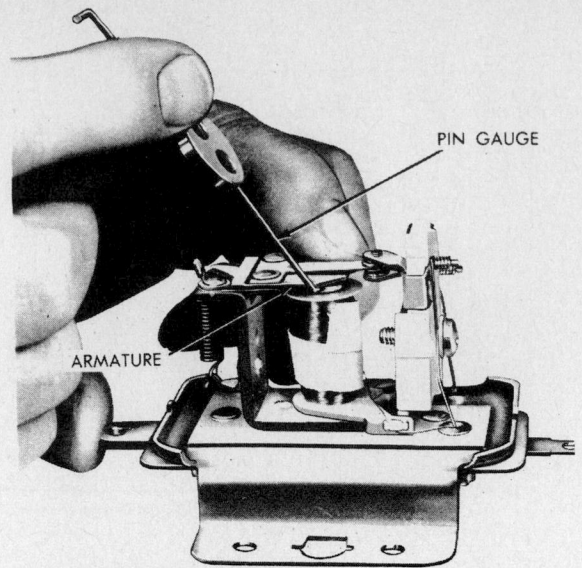

Checking air gap on Chrysler regulator to 1969
(© Chrysler Corp.)

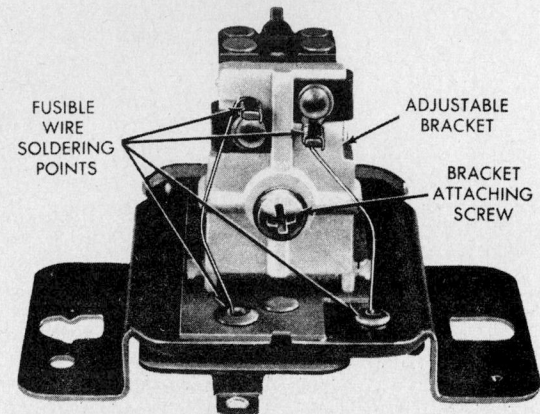

Chrysler voltage regulator to 1969,
showing fusible wires and bracket adjusting screw
(© Chrysler Corp.)

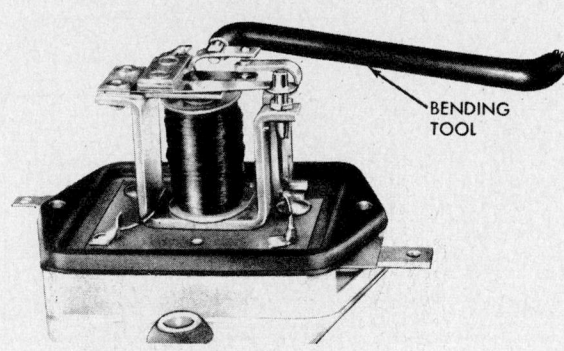

Bending upper contact arm to obtain
upper contact point gap of 0.014 in.—
Essex Wire-built regulator
(© Chrysler Corp.)

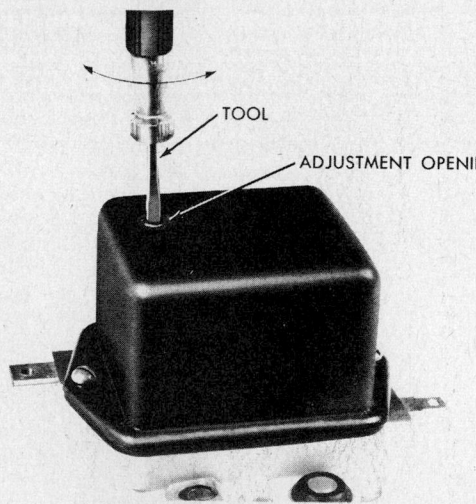

Lower contact voltage adjustment—
Essex Wire-built regulator
(© Chrysler Corp.)

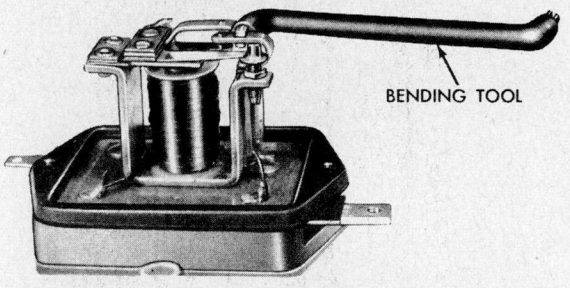

Bending stationary contact arm to obtain proper air gap—
Essex Wire-built regulator
(© Chrysler Corp.)

closed and the test light should be bright.

6. If an adjustment is required, loosen the stationary contact bracket screw and move bracket up and down as necessary to obtain the proper air gap. Following are guidelines for this adjustment:

Voltage Difference	Air. Gap Min.*	Air Gap Max.#
0.7 volt	0.045	0.048
0.2 volt	0.052	0.055

* Contacts open, test light dim.
\# Contacts closed, test light bright.

Lower Contact Voltage— Essex Wire Regulator

Lower contact voltage is adjusted by turning the adjustment screw, accessible through the cover opening. Turning clockwise increases voltage, turning counterclockwise decreases voltage.

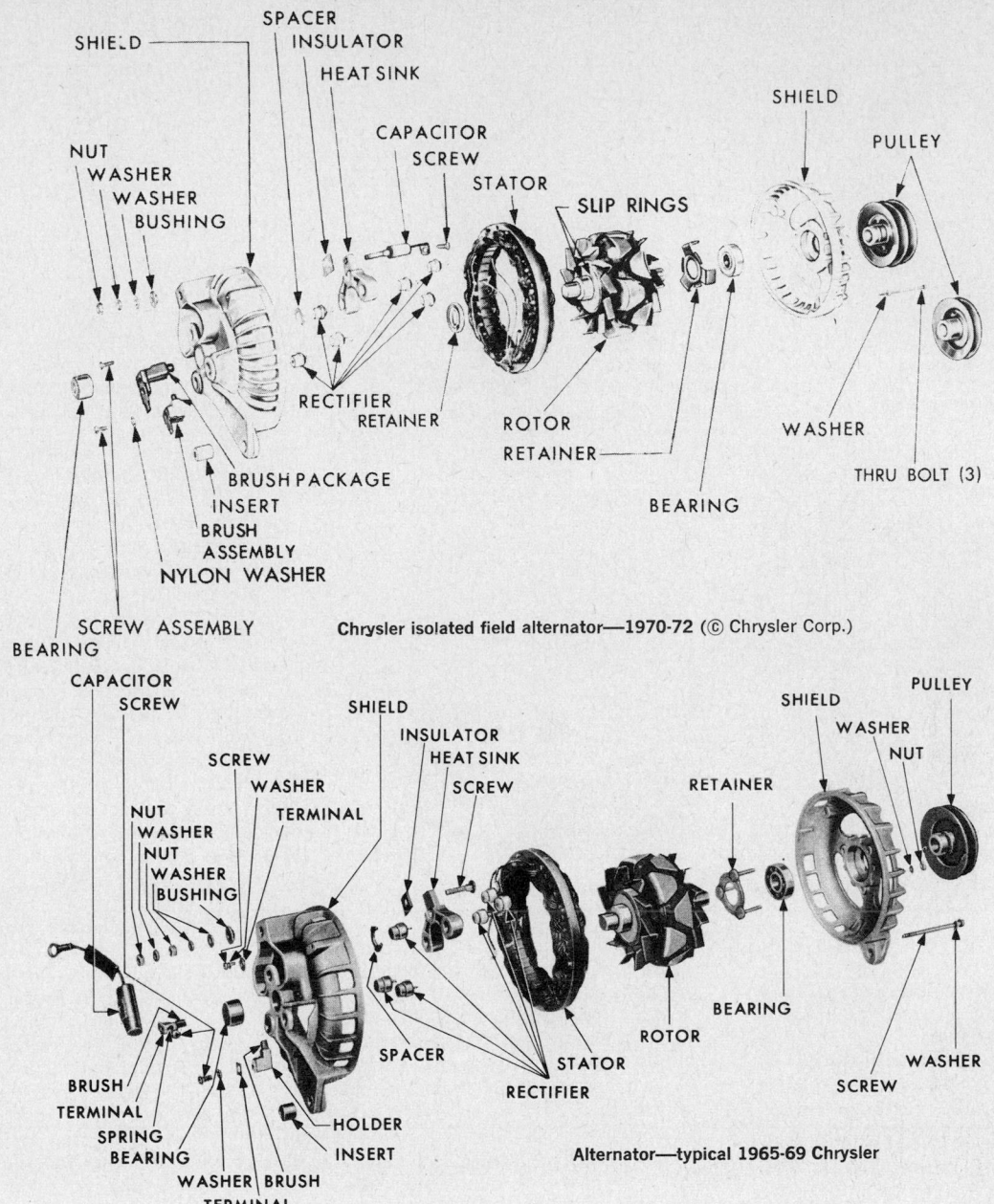

SHIELD
SPACER
INSULATOR
HEAT SINK
NUT
WASHER
WASHER
BUSHING
CAPACITOR
SCREW
STATOR
SLIP RINGS
SHIELD
PULLEY

RECTIFIER
RETAINER
ROTOR
RETAINER
BEARING
WASHER
THRU BOLT (3)

BRUSH PACKAGE
INSERT
BRUSH
ASSEMBLY
NYLON WASHER
SCREW ASSEMBLY
BEARING

Chrysler isolated field alternator—1970-72 (© Chrysler Corp.)

CAPACITOR
SCREW
SHIELD
INSULATOR
HEAT SINK
SCREW
SHIELD
PULLEY
WASHER
NUT
SCREW
WASHER
TERMINAL
NUT
WASHER
NUT
WASHER
BUSHING
RETAINER
BEARING
WASHER
SCREW
SPACER
STATOR
RECTIFIER
ROTOR

BRUSH
TERMINAL
SPRING
BEARING
HOLDER
INSERT
WASHER BRUSH
TERMINAL

Alternator—typical 1965-69 Chrysler

BRUSH ASSEMBLY

Insulator brush
(© Chrysler Corp.)

TOOL
PULLEY

Removing the pulley
(© Chrysler Corp.)

Upper Contact Point Gap— Essex Wire Regulator

Measure the upper contact point gap; it should be 0.014 in. ± 0.004. Adjust gap by bending armature upper contact bracket with an insulated tool, making sure contacts remain in alignment. If upper contact gap is correct, and voltage still is out of specifications, adjust air gap, as follows:

1. Connect a 1½-volt test light (with battery) in series between the IGN. and FLD. terminals of the regulator.
2. Insert a 0.032 in. wire gauge between the regulator armature and voltage core coil.
3. Press down on armature until it hits the gauge. At this point, lower contacts should just open and test light should be dim.

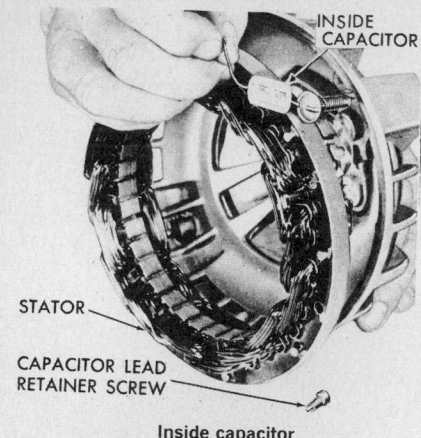

Inside capacitor
(© Chrysler Corp.)

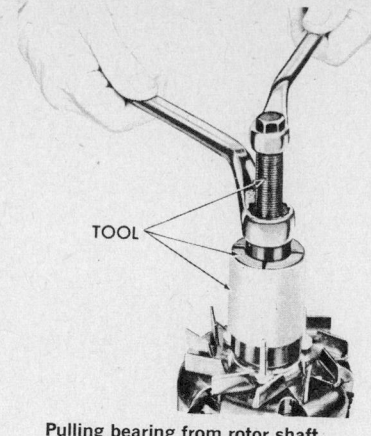

Pulling bearing from rotor shaft
(© Chrysler Corp.)

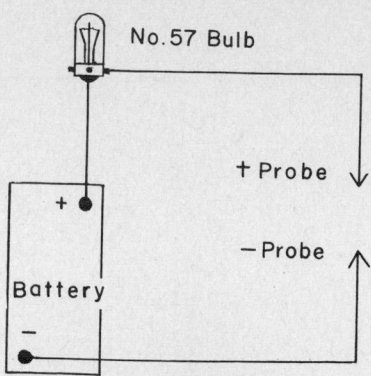

The test light method of testing diodes
(© Chrysler Corp.)

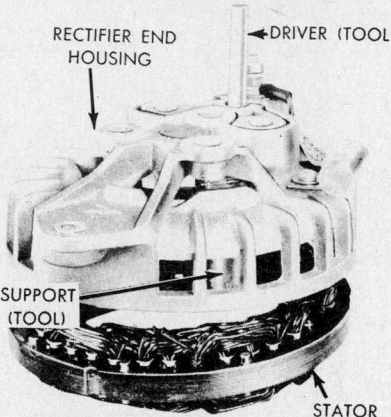

Removing a rectifier
(© Chrysler Corp.)

4. Check that a 0.042 in. gauge cannot be inserted between the armature and voltage core. This must not be possible, or air gap must be readjusted.
   NOTE: if voltage difference is greater than 0.7 volt, reduce air gap; if less than 0.2 volt, increase air gap.

Alternator disassembly, repair and assembly procedures are basically the same for all Chrysler alternators, including the Isolated Field type used for the first time in 1970. Certain variations in design, or in-production modifications, could require slightly different procedures that should be obvious upon inspection of the unit being serviced. An example of this is the new isolated field alternator, which has two FLD. terminals.

Disassembly

To prevent damage to the brush assemblies they should be removed before proceeding with the disassembly of the alternator. The insulated brush is mounted in a plastic holder that positions the brush vertically against one of the slip rings.

1. Remove the retaining screw, flat washer, nylon washer and field terminal and carefully lift the plastic holder containing the spring and brush assembly from the end housing.

2. The ground brush is positioned horizontally against the remaining slip ring and is retained in the holder that is integral with the end housing. Remove the retaining screw and lift the clip, spring and brush assembly from the end housing.

Caution The stator is laminated, don't burr the stator or end housings.

3. Remove the through bolts and pry between the stator and drive end housing with a thin blade screwdriver. Carefully separate the drive end housing, pulley and rotor assembly from the stator and rectifier housing assembly.

4. The pulley is an interference fit on the rotor shaft. Remove with a puller and special adapters.

5. Remove the three nuts and washers and, while supporting the end frame, tap the rotor shaft with a plastic hammer and separate the rotor and end housing.

6. The drive end ball bearing is an interference fit with the rotor shaft. Remove the bearing with puller and adapters.
   NOTE: further dismantling of the rotor is not advisable, as the remainder of the rotor assembly is not serviced separately.

7. Remove the DC output terminal nuts and washers and remove terminal screw and inside capacitor (on units so equipped).
   NOTE: the heat sink is also held in place by the terminal screw.

8. Remove the insulator.
   NOTE: three positive rectifiers are pressed into the heat sink and three negative rectifiers in the end housing. When removing the rectifiers, it is necessary to support the end housing and/or heat sink to prevent damage to these castings. Another caution is in order relative to the diode rectifiers. Don't subject them to unnecessary jolting. Heavy vibration or shock may ruin them.
   A. Cut rectifier wire at point of crimp.
   B. Support rectifier housing.
   NOTE: the factory tool is cut away and slotted to fit over the wires and around the bosses in the housing. Be sure that the bore of the tool completely surrounds the rectifier, then press the rectifier out of the housing.
   NOTE: the roller bearing in the rectifier end frame is a press fit. To protect the end housing it is necessary to support the housing with a tool when pressing out the bearing.

Bench Tests

Testing Silicon Diode Rectifiers With Ohmmeter

Preferred method—rectifiers open in all three phases.

Disassemble the alternator and separate the wires at the Y-connection of the stator.

There are six diode rectifiers mounted in the back of the alternator. Three of them are marked with a plus (+), and three are marked with a minus (—). These marks indicate diode case polarity.

To test, set ohmmeter to its lowest range. If case is marked positive (+), place positive meter probe to case and negative probe to the diode lead. Meter should read between 4 and 10 ohms. Now, reverse leads of ohmmeter, connecting negative meter probe to positive case and positive meter probe to wire of rectifier. Set meter on a high range. Meter needle should move very little, if any (infinite reading). Do this to all three positive diode rectifiers.

The three with minus (—) marks on their cases are checked the same way as above. Only now the negative ohmmeter probe is connected to the case for a reading of 4 to 10 ohms. Reverse leads as above for the other part to test.

If a reading of 4 to 10 ohms is obtained in one direction and no reading (infinity) is read on the ohmmeter in the other direction, diode rectifiers are good. If either infinity or a low resistance is obtained in both directions on a rectifier, it must be replaced.

If meter reads more than 10 ohms when ohmmeter positive probe is connected to positive on diode, and negative probe to negative, replace diode rectifier.

NOTE: with this test, it is necessary to determine the polarity of the ohmmeter probes. This can be done by connecting the ohmmeter to a DC voltmeter. The voltmeter will read up-scale when the positive probe of the ohmmeter is connected to the positive side of the voltmeter and the negative probe of the ohmmeter is connected to the negative side of the voltmeter.

Alternate method—test light.

Make up a tester as shown in sketch. Refer to first paragraph of the preferred method. Be sure lead from center of the diode rectifiers is disconnected.

To test rectifiers with plus (+) case, touch positive probe of tester to case and minus (—) probe to lead wire of rectifier. Bulb should light if rectifier is good. If bulb does not light, replace rectifier.

Now reverse tester probe connections to rectifier. Bulb should not light. If bulb does light, replace rectifier.

For testing minus (—) marked cases, follow above procedure, except that now bulb should light with negative probe of tester touching rectifier case and positive probe touching lead wire.

Rectifier is good if the bulb lights when tester probes are connected one way, and does not light when tester connections are reversed.

Rectifier must be replaced if the bulb does not light either way. Also, replace rectifier if bulb lights both ways.

NOTE: the usual cause of an open or blown diode or rectifier is a defective capacitor or a battery that has been installed in reverse polarity. If the battery is installed properly and the diodes are open, test the capacitor.

Capacitor capacity:
(int. installed)
. . . . .158 microfarad, min.
(ext. installed) . . . . .5 microfarad

Grounded Stator

1. Disconnect the diode rectifiers from the stator leads.
2. Test from stator leads to stator core, using a 110-volt test lamp. Test lamp should not light. If it does, stator is grounded and must be replaced.

Low Output

(About 50% output accompanied with a growl-hum caused by a shorted phase or a shorted rectifier.)

Perform Steps 1, 2 and 3 (rectifier open in all three phases). If the rectifiers are found to be within specifications, replace the stator assembly.

Current Output Too High (No Control) Caused by Open Rectifier or Open Phase

Perform Steps 1, 2 and 3 (rectifier open in all three phases). If the rectifier tests satisfactorily, inspect the stator connections before replacing the stator.

Assembly

1. Support the heat sink or rectifier end housing on circular plate.
2. Check rectifier identification to be sure the correct rectifier is being used. The part numbers are stamped on the case of the rectifier. They are also marked, red for positive and black for negative.
3. Start the new rectifier into the casting and press it in squarely. Do not start rectifier with a hammer or it will be ruined.

Caution

4. Crimp the new rectifier wire to the wires disconnected at removal, or solder (using a heat sink with rosin core solder).
5. Support the end housing on tool so that the notch in the support tool will clear the raised section of the heat sink, then press the bearing into position with tool SP-3381, or equivalent.

NOTE: new bearings are pre-lubricated, additional lubrication is not required.

6. Insert the drive end bearing in the drive end housing and install the bearing plate, washers and nuts to hold the bearing in place.
7. Position the bearing and drive end housing on the rotor shaft and, while supporting the base of the rotor shaft, press the bearing and housing in position on the rotor shaft with an arbor press and arbor tool.

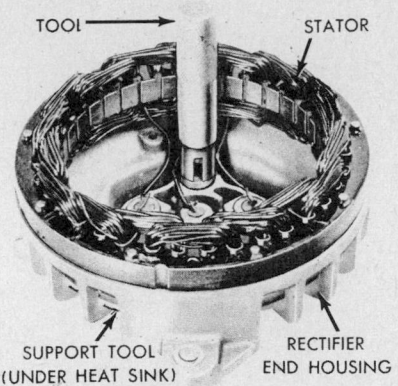

Installing diode rectifier
(© Chrysler Corp.)

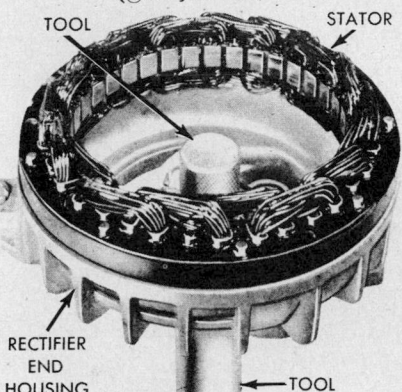

Installing end frame bearing
(© Chrysler Corp.)

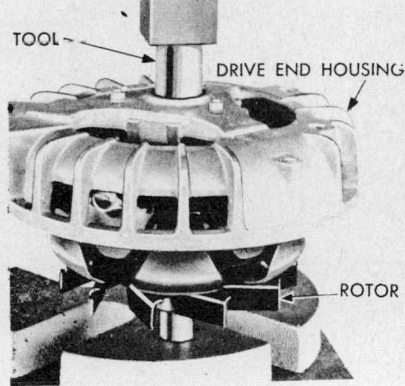

Installing drive end frame and bearing on rotor shaft
(© Chrysler Corp.)

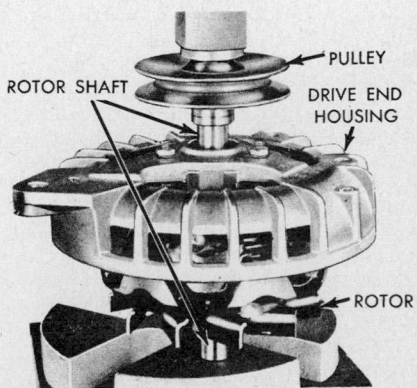

Installing the pulley
(© Chrysler Corp.)

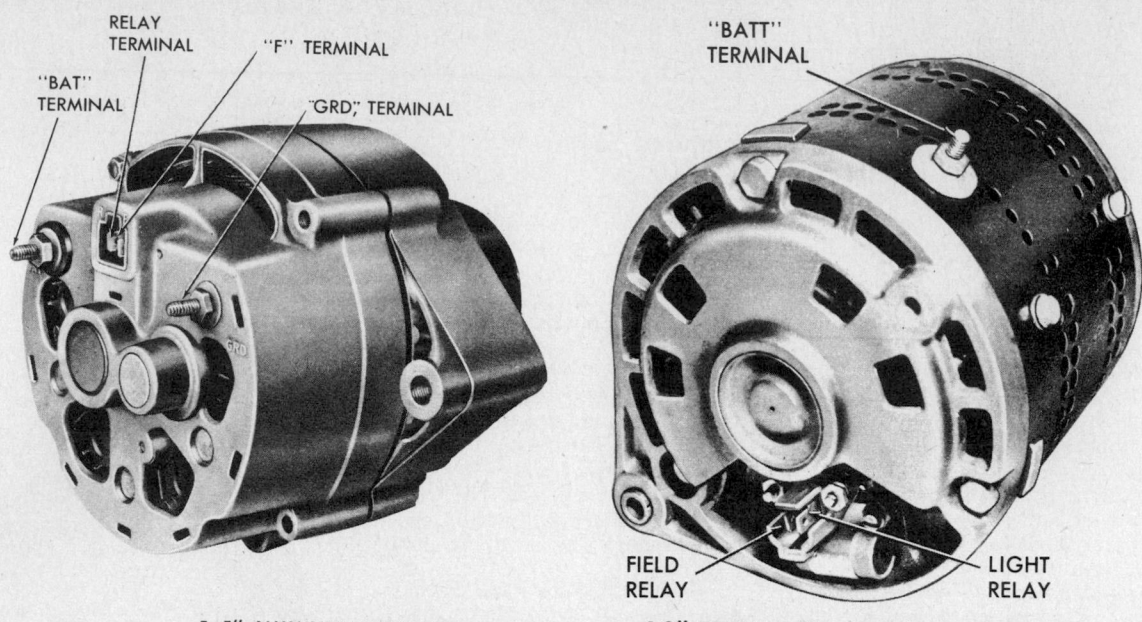

5.5" ALUMINUM DELCOTRON

6.2" PERFORATED STATOR DELCOTRON

5.5 and 6.2 Delcotron models (© Chev. Div., G.M. Corp.)

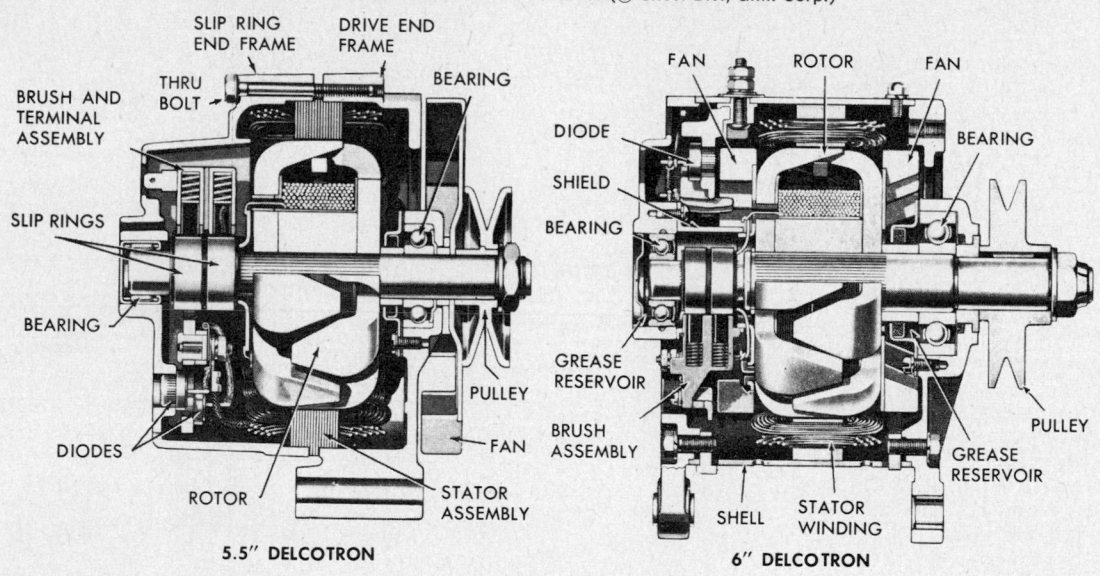

5.5" DELCOTRON

6" DELCOTRON

5.5 and 6.2 Delcotron models—cross-sectional views (© Chev. Div., G.M. Corp.)

Caution Be careful that there is no cocking of the bearing at installation; or damage will result. Press the bearing on the rotor shaft until the bearing contacts the shoulder on the rotor shaft.

8. Install pulley on rotor shaft. Shaft of rotor must be supported so that all pressing force is on the pulley hub and rotor shaft.

NOTE: Do not exceed 6,800 lbs. pressure. Pulley hub should just contact bearing inner race.

9. Some alternators will be found to have the capacitor mounted internally. Be sure the heat sink insulator is in place.

10. Install the output terminal screw with the capacitor attached through the heat sink and end housing.

11. Install insulating washers, lock-washers and locknuts.

12. Make sure the heat sink and insulator are in place and tighten the locknut.

13. Position the stator on the rectifier end housing. Be sure that all of the rectifier connectors and phase leads are free of interference with the rotor fan blades and that the capacitor (internally mounted) lead has clearance.

14. Position the rotor assembly in the rectifier end housing. Align the through bolt holes in the stator with both end housings.

15. Enter stator shaft in the rectifier end housing bearing, compress stator and both end housings manually and install through bolts, washers and nuts.

Delcotron rated output is stamped on the case
(© Olds. Div., G.M. Corp.)

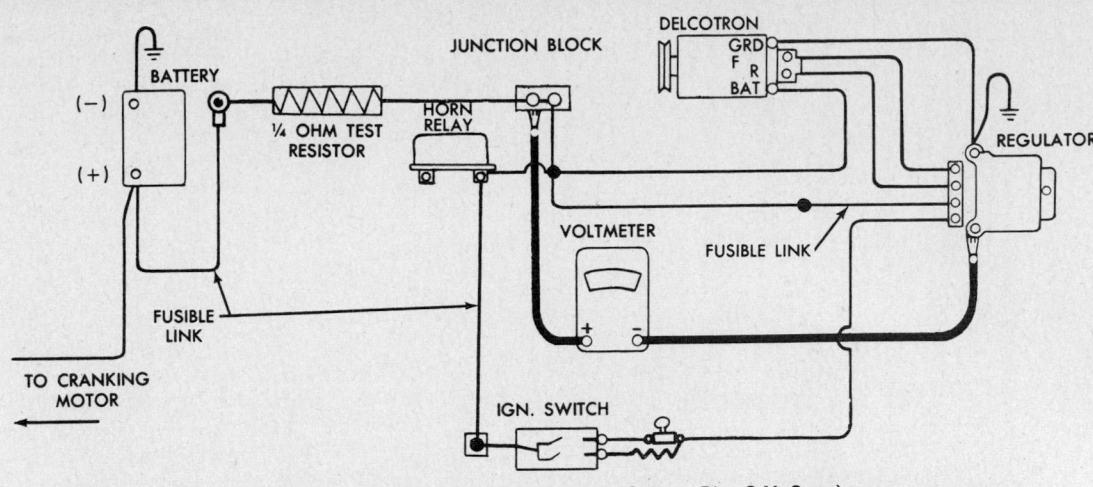

Delcotron regulator setting test hook-up (© Chev. Div., G.M. Corp.)

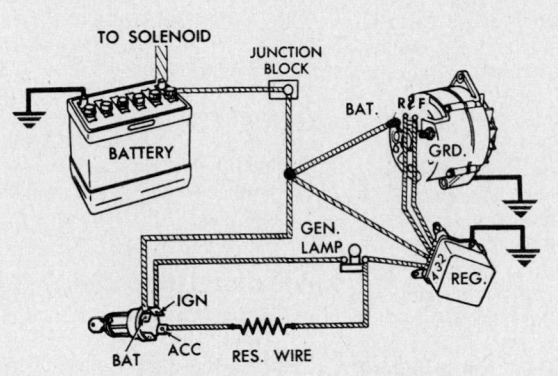

Typical Delcotron circuit diagram
(© Chev. Div., G.M. Corp.)

Adjusting voltage setting—mechanical regulator
(© Chev. Div., G.M. Corp.)

16. Install the insulated brush and terminal attaching screw.
17. Install the ground screw and attaching screw.
18. Rotate pulley slowly to be sure the rotor fan blades do not hit the rectifier and stator connectors.

Delcotron 5.5 Series 1D and 6.2 Series 2D (General Motors Corporation)

Description

The Delcotron continuous output AC generator consists of two major parts—the stator and the rotor. The stator is composed of many turns of wire on the inside of a laminated core that is attached to the generator frame. The rotor is mounted on bearings at each end. Two brushes carry current through slip rings to the field coils, which are wound on the rotor shaft.

The 5.5 Series 1D Delcotron is similar in operation to the 6.2 Series 2D perforated Stator Delcotron. Where differences exist, the two units are mentioned separately.

Six diodes, mounted on internal heat sinks, change the AC current output into DC current. This current is controlled by the regulator. The regulator is a double-contact unit combined with a field relay or a triple-contact unit containing an indicator lamp relay as well as the field relay and voltage relay. Transistor regulators were also used in production intermittently.

On high-output Delcotron units, the regulator incorporates a field discharge diode.

Inspection

Frequency of inspection is determined by exposure to adverse operating conditions. High speed operation, high temperatures, dust and dirt all increase wear on brushes, slip rings and bearings.

At regular periods, inspect terminals for corrosion and loose connections, and the wiring for frayed insulation. Check mounting bolts for tightness, and the belt for alignment, proper tension and wear. Because of higher load capacity and the higher inertia of the heavy rotor used in AC generators, belt tension is more critical. Tension should be adjusted according to the vehicle manufacturer's recommendations. In most cases

this will be slightly greater than for DC generators.

Troubleshooting

Problems in the AC charging system usually are indicated by one of the following conditions:
1. Faulty indicator light operation.
2. Undercharged battery; low cranking speed.
3. Overcharged battery; excessive battery water loss.
4. Excessive generator noise and/or vibration.

Before proceeding with further troubleshooting checks, check for a loose or broken belt, defective battery and loose connections in the system (especially at the push-on Delcotron connectors).

Checking Regulator Setting and Circuit Wiring

1. Place transmission in Neutral and set the parking brake.
2. Connect a voltmeter between junction block at horn relay and regulator ground (base).
3. Connect a tachometer between distributor to coil primary wire and ground.
4. On models having an indicator bulb, turn on ignition switch and look at indicator light; if it does

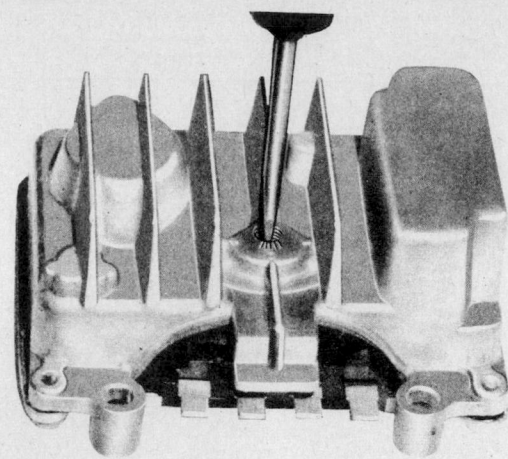

Adjusting voltage setting—transistor regulator
(© Chev. Div., G.M. Corp.)

not light, check circuit and the bulb itself. If it does light, start the engine and run at 1,500 rpm +. If light goes out, field circuit is O.K. and any trouble is in generator or regulator.

5. On models having an ammeter, turn ignition switch to ACC. position and note meter reading. If it fails to read a discharge, check ammeter circuit before continuing. Start engine and run at 1,500 rpm +. If meter still shows discharge, check field circuit.

6. Turn on headlights (highbeam) and heater motor blower (high), run engine at 1,500 rpm + and read voltage on the meter.
   a. If reading is 12.5 volts or greater, turn off electrical accessories and shut off engine. Proceed to Step 7.
   b. If reading is less than 12.5 volts, test Delcotron output as described later in this section. If Deleotron tests "bad," repair unit; if Delcotron tests "good," disconnect regulator plug, remove regulator cover and reconect plug. Repeat Step 6 and turn voltage adjusting screw to raise setting

to 12.5 volts. If 12.5 volts is beyond the adjustment range, remove and replace regulator and repeat test.
   c. On transistor regulators, remove pipe plug and turn screw clockwise to increase setting, counterclockwise to decrease. One notch equals about 0.3 volt.

7. Connect a ¼-ohm, 25-watt test resistor to the junction block at horn relay, as illustrated.

8. Start engine and run at 1,500 rpm+ for at least 15 minutes, then quickly disconnect and reconnect regulator plug (to cycle voltage control) and read the voltage. Voltage should be 13.5-15.2 volts, indicating a good regulator. If voltage is not correct, leave engine running at 1,500 rpm and follow the procedure below:
   a. Disconnect the four-terminal plug and remove regulator cover. Reconnect plug and adjust voltage to 14.2-14.6 volts.
   b. Disconnect plug and install cover, then plug.
   c. Run engine at 1,500 rpm+ for 10 minutes to bring in-

ternal regulator temperature up to par, recycle regulator as previously described and check voltage.

Ambient Temperature	Voltage Setting
65	13.9 to 15.0
85	13.8 to 14.8
105	13.7 to 14.6
125	13.5 to 14.4
145	13.4 to 14.2
165	13.2 to 14.0
185	13.1 to 13.9
205	13.0 to 13.8

Indicator or Ammeter

There are two types of mechanical regulators used with this system.
A. A three-unit regulator, containing a voltage regulator, a field relay, and an indicator lamp relay.
B. A two-unit regulator, containing a voltage regulator, and a field relay. In this instance, the indicator lamp relay is omitted. The two-unit regulator is used in circuits equipped with an ammeter.

Except for the indicator lamp relay test, all other tests are conducted in the same way.

Indicator Lamp Relay Test

1. Turn ignition switch on; do not start the engine. If indicator does not light, check for burned out bulb.
2. If light goes on, but stays on after the engine is started and the generator is in operation:
   A. Connect voltmeter leads to the R terminal and a ground on the regulator.
   B. If voltmeter reading is more than 5 volts, the indicator lamp relay is defective.
   C. If voltmeter reading is 5 volts or less, trouble lies elsewhere in the system.
3. If indicator is on with engine off and ignition switch off, check alternator diodes.

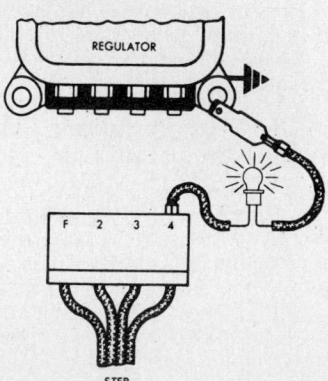

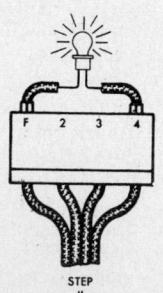

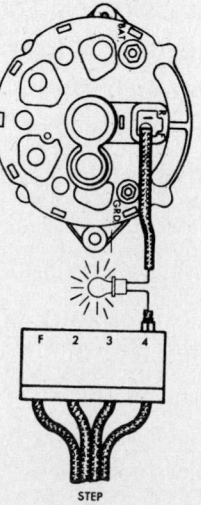

Initial field excitation circuit test hook-ups (© Chev. Div., G.M. Corp.)

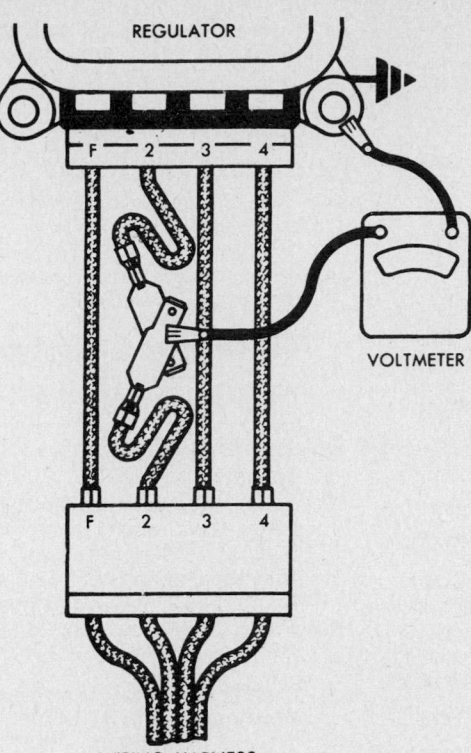

WIRING HARNESS CONNECTOR
Testing field relay (© Chev. Div., G.M. Corp.)

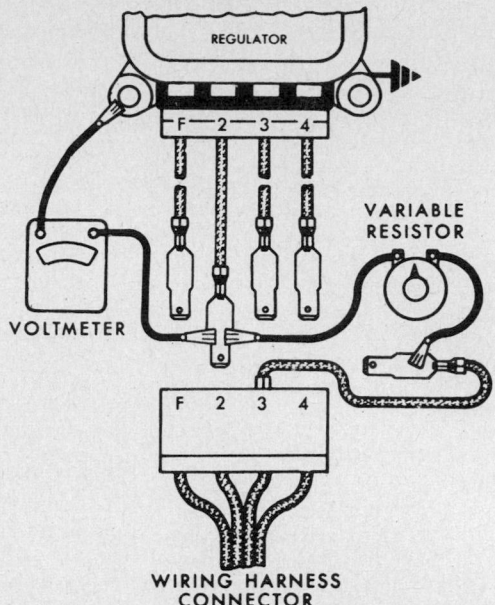

Testing field relay closing voltage
(© Chev. Div., G.M. Corp.)

Adjusting field relay closing voltage
(© Chev. Div., G.M. Corp.)

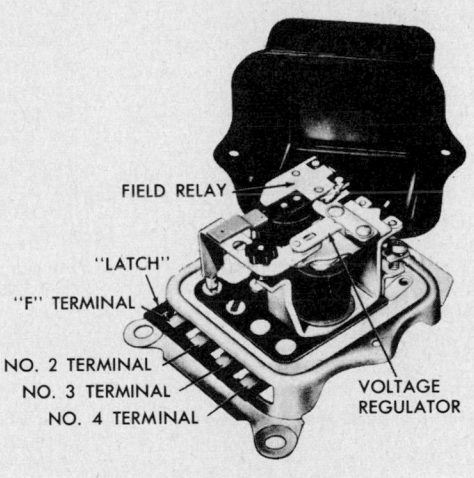

Mechanical voltage regulator
(© Chev. Div., G.M. Corp.)

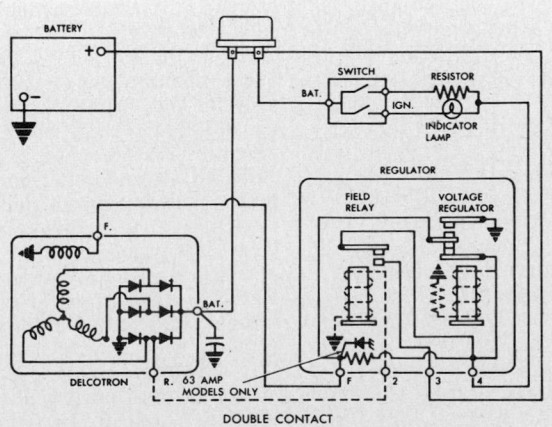

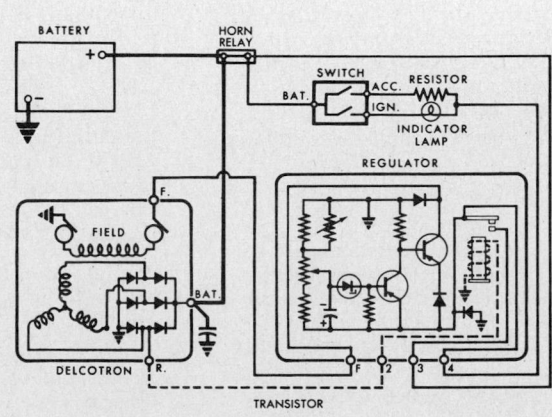

Voltage regulator circuit diagrams (© Chev Div., G.M. Corp.)

Indicator Lamp Relay Opening Voltage Test

1. With a 50-75 ohm field rheostat connected to the R and V terminal of the regulator, turn rheostat control to the open position.
2. Connect a voltmeter to the R and ground terminal on the regulator.
3. Turn the field rheostat control slowly, to reduce resistance, then note voltage the instant the relay opens.
4. Compare this reading with car manufacturers, or Delcotron, specifications.

Indicator Light Testing

The indicator light is important in AC charging systems, for it provides initial field excitation current to the alternator. The light goes out when the field relay closes, which applies battery current to both sides of the bulb. If the light does not go on when key is turned, the bulb could be faulty, there could be an open circuit in the wiring or a positive diode in the alternator could be shorted to ground.

1. Disconnect plug from regulator and connect a test light between terminal No. 4 (in plug) and ground. Turn on ignition switch and observe the light. If light does not go on, check bulb, socket or wiring between switch and regulator plug. If light goes on, check regulator, wiring between regulator F terminal and alternator, or Delcotron itself.
2. Disconnect jumper wire at ground end and reconnect to F terminal in plug. Turn on ignition for a second and note light. If light goes on, problem is in regulator. If light does not go on, problem is in wire between F terminals (regulator and alternator).
3. Disconnect light at plug F terminal and reconnect the free end to F terminal at alternator. Turn on ignition switch for a second and note light. If light goes on, the problem is an open circuit in the wire connecting the regulator and alternator F terminals. If light does not go on, the alternator field windings are defective.

If the indicator light does not extinguish when engine is started, check for a loose drive belt, faulty field relay, faulty alternator, open parallel resistance wire (usually shows up at idle). If the light stays on with the key turned off, an alternator positive diode is shorted to ground.

Field Relay Test

1. Connect a voltmeter between the No. 2 terminal and the ground on the regulator.
2. Turn ignition switch on; do not start the engine. Voltmeter should read battery voltage.
3. If voltmeter reads zero, check circuit connecting regulator terminal No. 2 and Delcotron R terminal.
4. Start engine and run at 1,500-2,000 rpm. If voltage exceeds closing voltage (field relay), and light remains on, field relay is faulty and must be checked.

Field Relay Adjustment

1. Connect a voltmeter between No. 2 regulator terminal and ground.
2. To adjust, connect a 50 ohm rheostat between wiring harness terminal No. 3 and regulator terminal No. 2, after disconnecting the spade lug on the end of the No. 2 regulator terminal wire. Connect a voltmeter between regulator terminal No. 2 and ground, then turn the resistor to "open" position, turn off ignition switch and slowly decrease resistance until relay closes (noting voltage at this point). Voltage can be adjusted by bending heel iron as illustrated.

Field Circuit Resistance Testing

The resistance wire is an integral part of the ignition wiring harness. The wire cannot be soldered; any connections must be made using crimp-type connectors. Resistance is 10 ohms, $6\frac{1}{4}$ watts.

1. Connect a voltmeter between the wiring harness terminal No. 4 and ground.
2. Turn on ignition switch, needle must indicate or resistor is open.

Delcotron Current Output Test

NOTE: disconnect battery ground cable while making test connections, then reconnect cable after completing Step 5. Disconnect battery ground cable again before removing test set-up.

1. Disconnect lead from BAT. terminal of Delcotron.
2. Hook an ammeter to the lead just disconnected, and to the BAT. terminal of the Delcotron.
3. Hook up the voltmeter leads to the BAT. terminal and a good ground on the alternator.
4. Disconnect the lead from the FR. terminal of the Delcotron.
5. Hook up a jumper wire between BAT. and F terminals of the Delcotron.
6. With a carbon pile load control hooked up to the battery posts,

start the engine and set engine to 1,500 rpm, while adjusting carbon pile to obtain 14 volts. With a 6.2 in. alternator, only 600-800 rpm is required.

Caution Be careful not to exceed the recommended regulator voltage setting. This is controlled by the carbon pile load.

7. Ammeter should read within 10% of rated output, as stamped on frame of each unit.

Alternator Overhaul (5.5 and 6.2 Delcotron

Disassembly—5.5 Series 1D

1. Remove four bolts.
2. Separate drive end frame and rotor from stator assembly by prying with screwdriver. Note that separation is between stator frame and drive end frame.
3. Place tape over slip ring end frame bearing to seal dirt.
4. Lightly clamp rotor in vise to remove shaft nut.

Caution Do not distort rotor by overtightening vise.

5. After nut removal, take off washer, pulley, fan and collar.
6. Separate drive end frame from rotor shaft.
7. Remove three stator lead attaching nuts and separate stator from end frame.
8. Remove screws, brushes and holder assembly.
9. Remove BAT., GND., and attaching screw terminals, then remove heat sink.

Disassembly—6.2 Series 2D

1. Clamp drive end mounting flange in a vise, remove the two screws that secure the cover to the brush holder and remove the cover.
2. Remove the nut that holds the indicator light wire to the blade connector post; disconnect wire lead from post.
3. Remove the two screws that hold the condenser and brush holder to rear end frame, then remove brush holder. Allow condenser to remain with alternator.
4. Remove three slip ring end frame bolts and tab nuts, then carefully pry end frame and case apart, working evenly around the circumference.
5. Remove the three drive end frame bolts and tab nuts, then remove end frame, rotor and pulley as an assembly.
6. Remove shaft nut, washer, pulley and Woodruff key from rotor shaft, then slide rotor from end frame.

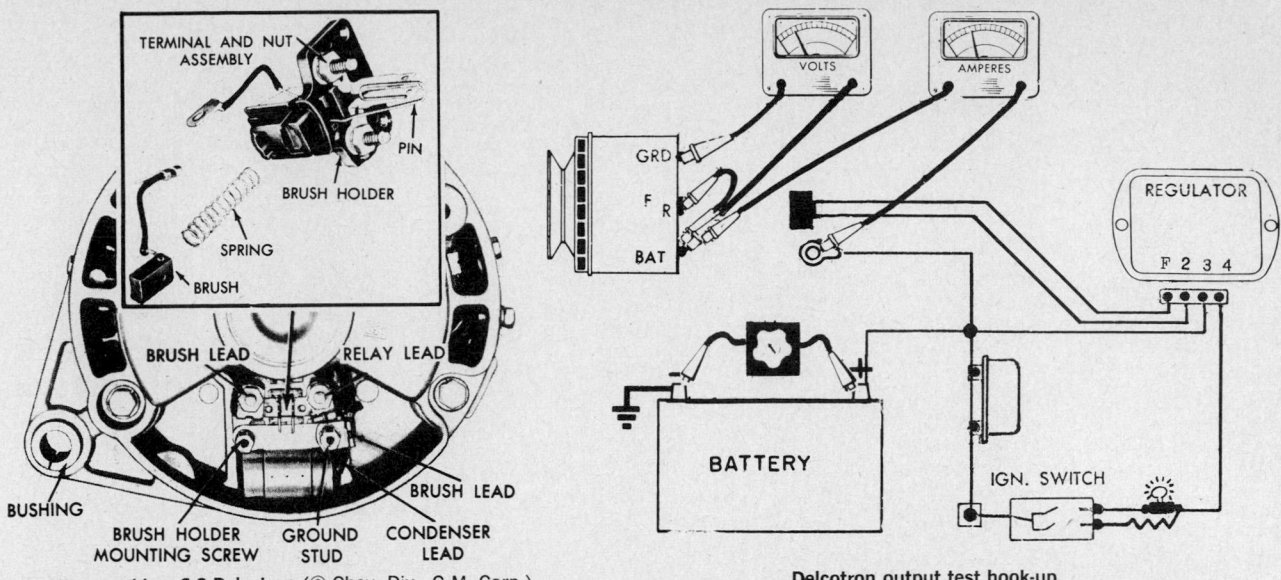

Brush assembly—6.2 Delcotron (© Chev. Div., G.M. Corp.)

Delcotron output test hook-up

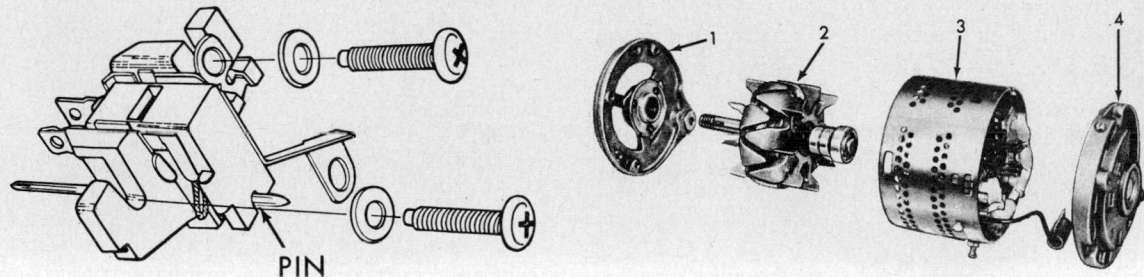

Heat sink assembly—5.5 Delcotron (© Chev. Div., G.M. Corp.)

Brush assembly—5.5 Delcotron (© Chev. Div., G.M. Corp.)

6.2 Delcotron assembly sequence.
1) drive end frame; 2) rotor; 3) stator; 4) end frame.
(© Chev. Div., G.M. Corp.)

7. Remove drive end frame bearing retainer plate and bearing from end frame.
8. Bearing can be removed, if necessary, at this time. Use puller to prevent damage.
9. Disconnect the three stator leads by cutting between coils and diodes.

NOTE: diode leads can be cleaned and unsoldered, *if* proper heat sinks are used to prevent diode damage.

10. Remove heat sink-to-case retaining screws, then remove heat sinks. Insulated heat sink (BATT. terminal) holds positive diode.

Diode Tests

All diodes are marked with either a + or — on the head or are marked with *red* paint for + diodes, *black* paint for — diodes to identify the polarity of the case. On a generator to be used with a negative ground system, the negative case diodes are mounted into the slip ring end frame and the positive case diodes are mounted into the insulated heat sink. Diodes with a negative case have positive polarity leads, whereas positive case diodes have negative polarity leads.

Diodes can be checked for shorts or opens with an ohmmeter.

With the stator leads disconnected, connect one ohmmeter test prod to the diode lead and the other test prod to the heat sink. Reverse the test prods and note the ohmmeter readings. The meter should read high ohms in one direction, low ohms in the other. If both readings are the same, either both high or both low, the diode is faulty and must be replaced. A 1½ volt test light also will indicate a faulty diode. It will light in one direction and not in the other if the diode is good. If it lights in both directions, or in neither direction, the diode is bad.

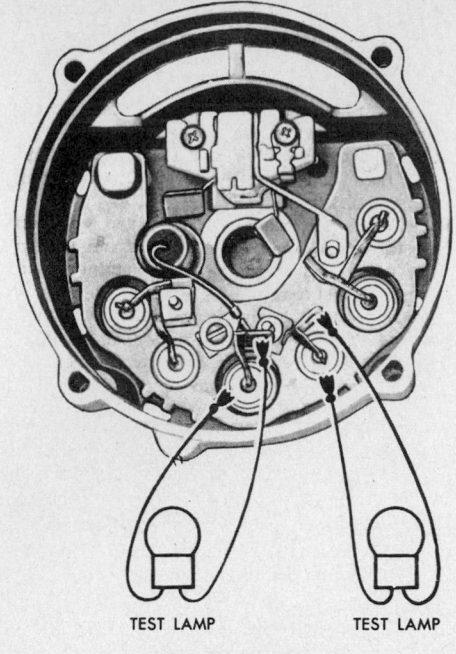

TEST LAMP   TEST LAMP

5.5" DELCOTRON

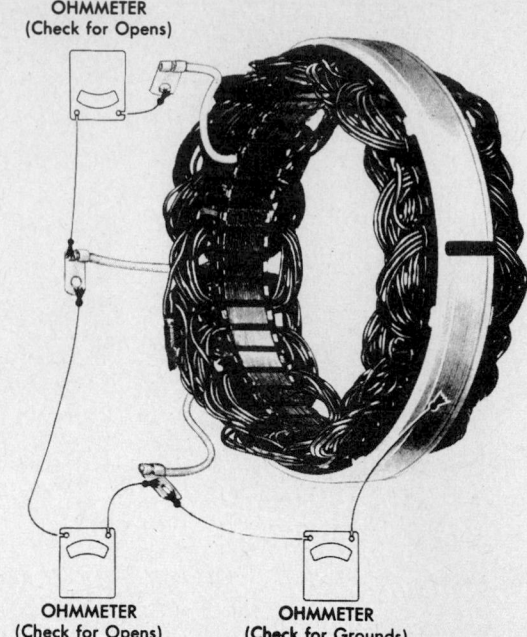

OHMMETER (Check for Opens)

OHMMETER (Check for Opens)   OHMMETER (Check for Grounds)

5.5" STATOR

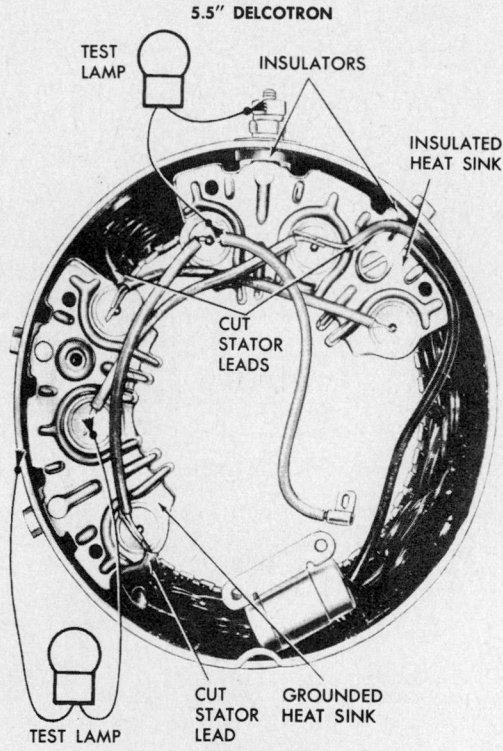

TEST LAMP   INSULATORS   INSULATED HEAT SINK

CUT STATOR LEADS

CUT STATOR LEAD   GROUNDED HEAT SINK

TEST LAMP

6" DELCOTRON

Testing diodes (© Chev. Div., G.M. Corp.)

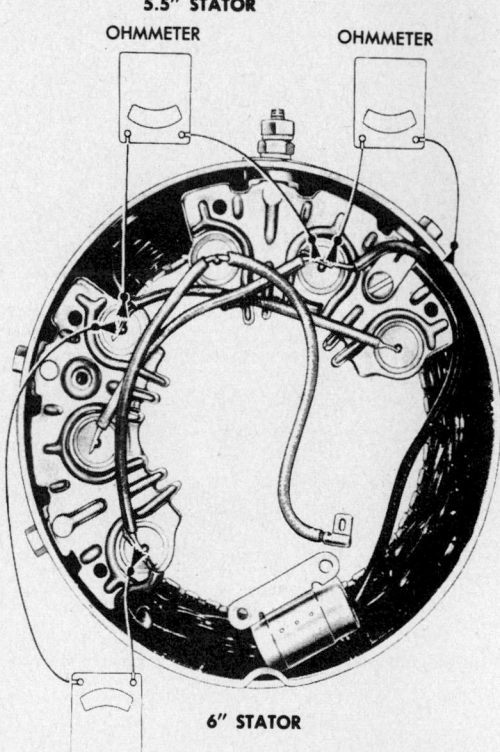

OHMMETER   OHMMETER

6" STATOR

Checking stator for grounds or opens
(© Chev. Div., G.M. Corp.)

Diode Replacement

Early Delcotrons had screwed-in diodes, as does the extremely heavy-duty 6.6 Series 4D Delcotron. Models covered here use pressed-in diodes exclusively. If there is any doubt about the year and model of the Delcotron being serviced, note the diode construction—screwed-in diodes have hexagonal heads and the later, pressed-in, units have straight sides with no hex head. Old-style, screwed-in diodes have both right-hand and left-hand threads. Plus (+) diodes have left-hand and minus (−) have right-hand threads.

5.5 Series 1D

1. Support end frame on a deep socket with a larger inside diameter than the diode outside diameter.
2. Carefully *press* out the diode with a brass drift and an arbor press, or a large bench vise. Be extremely careful so as not to distort the end frame.
3. Select a new diode (red or black), noting that the red (+) diodes go into the heat sink and the black (−) diodes into the end frame.
4. Support end frame on a flat, smooth surface around diode hole and carefully *press* the new diode into position. Diode must be square when starting or both diode and frame will be ruined.

6.2 Series 2D

1. Cut leads connected to diode stem as close as possible to stem, then support end frame as for 5.5 Delcotron and press out diode.
2. Select diode with proper color marking (same as for 5.5 Delcotron), then press new diode into position.
3. Scrape enough insulation from diode stem and leads to ensure good contact, then install a sleeve over diode and place the T-clip from diode package over diode stem.
4. Place the flexible lead and stator lead (if applicable) into the T-clip, crimp clip and solder with rosin core solder only, using heat sinks (pliers) to avoid destroying diode.
5. Tape the leads together to prevent vibration damage.

Rotor Checks—All Models

The rotor may be checked electrically for grounded, open, or shorted field coils.

To check for grounds, connect a 100-volt test light from either slip ring to the rotor shaft or to the laminations. If the lamp lights, the field windings are grounded.

To check for opens, connect the leads of a 110-volt test light to each slip ring. If the lamp fails to light, the windings are open.

The windings are checked for short-circuits by connecting a battery and ammeter in series with the two slip rings. Note the ammeter reading and refer to the chart.

An ammeter reading greater than that specified in the charts preceding each car section of this manual indicates shorted windings.

Since the field windings are not serviced separately, the rotor assembly must be replaced if the windings are defective.

Stator Checks—All Models

Stator windings may be checked for grounded, open, or shorted windings. If a 110-volt test lamp lights when connected from any stator lead to the stator frame, the windings are grounded. If the lamp fails to light when successively connected between each pair of stator leads, the windings are open.

A short circuit in the stator windings is difficult to locate without laboratory equipment, due to the low resistance of the windings. However, if all other electrical checks are normal and the generator fails to supply the rated output, shorted stator windings are indicated.

Slip Ring Servicing and Replacement—All Models

Slip rings which are rough or out of round should be trued in a lathe to .001 in. maximum indicator reading. Remove only enough material to make the rings smooth and round. Finish with 400 grit or finer polishing cloth and blow away all dust.

Slip rings which must be replaced can be removed from the shaft with a gear puller, after the leads have been unsoldered. The new assembly should be pressed on with a sleeve which just fits over the shaft; this will apply all the pressure to the inner slip ring collar and prevent damage to the outer slip ring. Only pure tin solder should be used when reconnecting field leads.

Brush Replacement— All Models

The extent of brush wear can be determined by comparison with a new brush. If brushes are one-half worn, they should be replaced.

1. Remove brush holder assembly from end frame by removing two holder assembly screws.
2. Place springs and brushes in the holder and insert straight wire or pin into holes at bottom of holder to retain brushes.
3. Attach holder assembly onto end frame.

Assembly—5.5 Series 1D

1. Install stator assembly into slip ring end frame and locate diode connectors over the relay, diode and stator leads. Tighten terminal nuts.
2. Install rotor into drive end frame.
3. Install fan, spacer, pulley washer and nut.
4. Install Allen wrench (5/16 in.) into end of shaft to hold drive shaft, then tighten pulley nut to 40-50 ft. lbs. using a crowsfoot wrench (15/16 in.) and torque wrench.
5. Assemble slip ring end frame and stator assembly to drive end frame and rotor.
6. Install four through bolts and tighten securely.

Assembly—6.2 Series 2D

1. Install stator assembly into slip ring end frame and locate diode connectors over the relay, diode and stator leads. Tighten terminal nuts.
2. Install the front frame over the rotor.
3. Install fan, spacer, Woodruff key, pulley, washer and nut.
4. Clamp pulley in a padded-jaw vise and tighten shaft nut to 50-60 ft. lbs.

Caution Do not clamp rotor, or segments will be distorted.

5. Position rotor and drive end frame assembly into slip ring end frame and stator. Install through bolts and tighten securely.
6. Push brushes into holder and secure leads as illustrated.

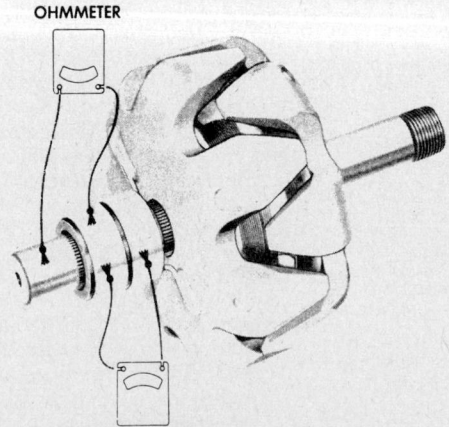

(CHECK FOR GROUNDS)
OHMMETER

OHMMETER
(CHECK FOR SHORTS AND OPENS)

Checking rotor for grounds or opens— all Delcotron models
(© Chev. Div., G.M. Corp.)

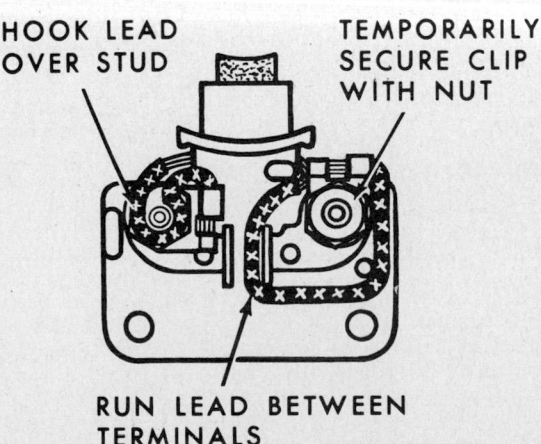

HOOK LEAD OVER STUD

TEMPORARILY SECURE CLIP WITH NUT

RUN LEAD BETWEEN TERMINALS

Brush lead arrangement during assembly—6.2 Delcotron
(© Chev. Div., G.M. Corp.)

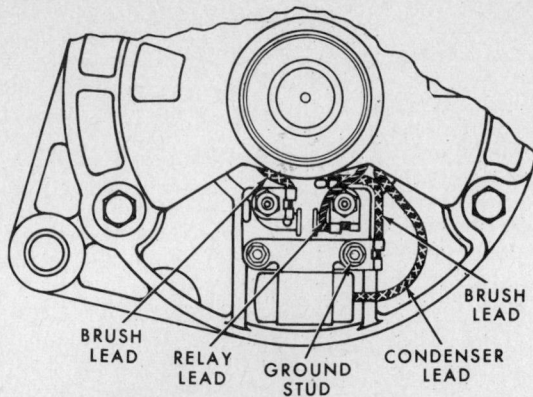

Brush lead arrangement after assembly—6.2 Delcotron
(© Chev. Div., G.M. Corp.)

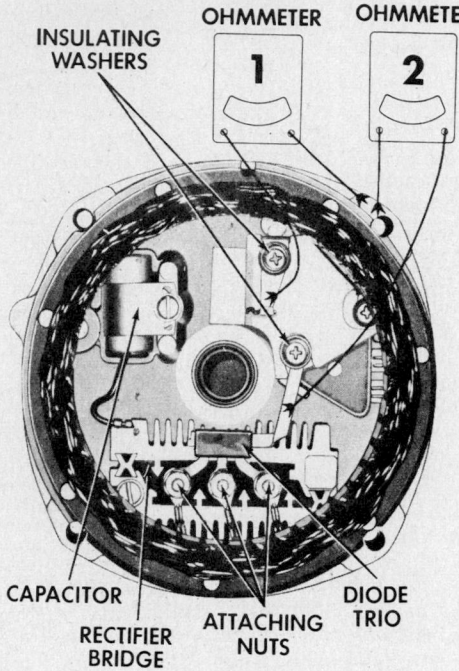

Brush lead clip ground test—10-SI Delcotron
(© Chev. Div., G.M. Corp.)

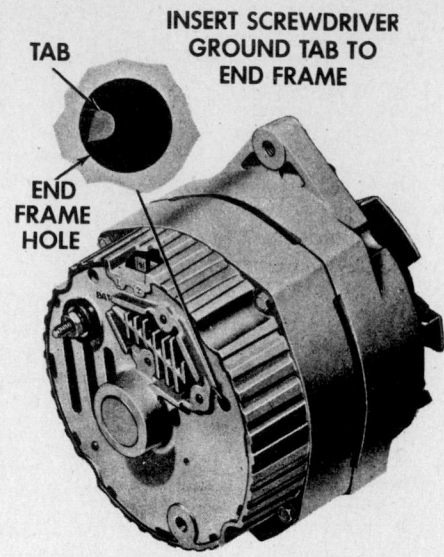

10-SI Delcotron end view
(© Chev. Div., G.M. Corp.)

7. Attach brush assembly and condenser to the end frame with left-hand hex stud only.
8. Arrange leads as illustrated, with right-hand brush lead connected under right-hand hex stud.
9. Attach terminal cover with two screws, making sure not to pinch the leads.

Delcotron 10-SI Series 100 (General Motors Corp.)

This system is an integrated AC generating system containing a built-in voltage regulator. Removal and replacement is essentially the same as for the standard AC generator.

The regulator is mounted inside the slip ring end frame. All regulator components are enclosed in an epoxy molding, and the regulator cannot be adjusted. Rotor and stator tests are the same as for the 5.5 Delcotron, covered previously.

Charging System Test— Low Charging Rate

1. After battery condition, drive belt tension, and wiring terminals and connections have been checked, charge the battery fully and perform the following test:
2. Connect a test voltmeter between the alternator BAT. terminal and ground, ignition switch on. Connect the voltmeter in turn to alternator terminals No. 1 and No. 2, the other voltmeter lead being grounded as before. A zero reading indicates and open circuit between the battery and each connection at the alternator. If this test discloses no faults in the wiring, proceed to Step 3.

3. Connect the test voltmeter to the alternator BAT. terminal (the other test lead to ground), start the engine and run at 1,500-2,000 rpm with all lights and electrical accessories turned on. If the voltmeter reads 12.8 volts or greater, the alternator is good and no further checks need be made. If the voltmeter reads less than 12.8 volts, ground the field winding by inserting a screwdriver into the test hole in the end frame.

Caution Do not force tab more than 1 in. into end frame.

a. If voltage increases to 13 volts or more, the regulator unit is defective.
b. If voltage does not increase significantly, generator is defective.

Charging System Test— High Charging Rate

1. With battery fully charged, connect a voltmeter between alternator terminal No. 2 and ground. If reading is zero, No. 2 circuit from battery is open.
2. If No. 2 circuit is O.K., but an obvious overcharging condition still exists, proceed as follows:
   a. Remove alternator and separate end frames.
   b. Connect a low-range ohmmeter between brush lead clip and end frame, as illustrated (Test #1), then reverse lead connections. If both readings are zero, either the brush lead clip is grounded or the regulator is defective. **A grounded brush lead clip can be due to a damaged insulating sleeve or omission of insulating washer.**

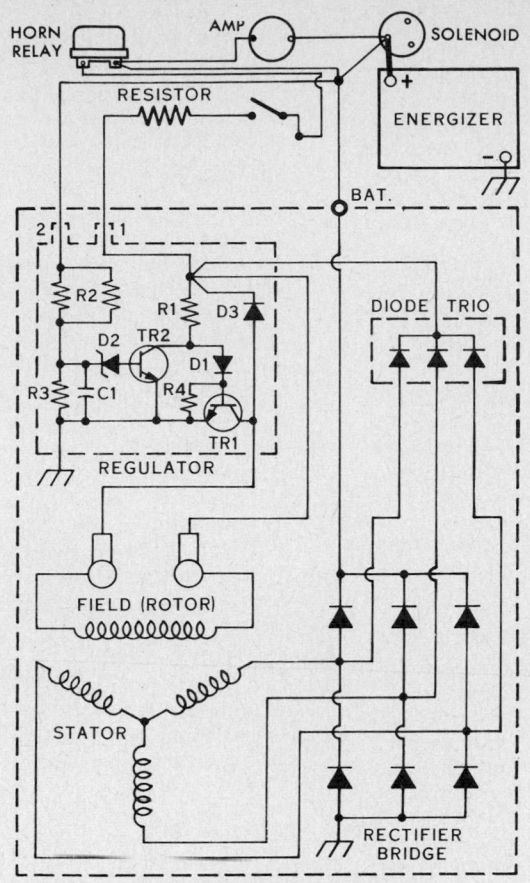

10-SI charging circuit schematic
(© Chev. Div., G.M. Corp.)

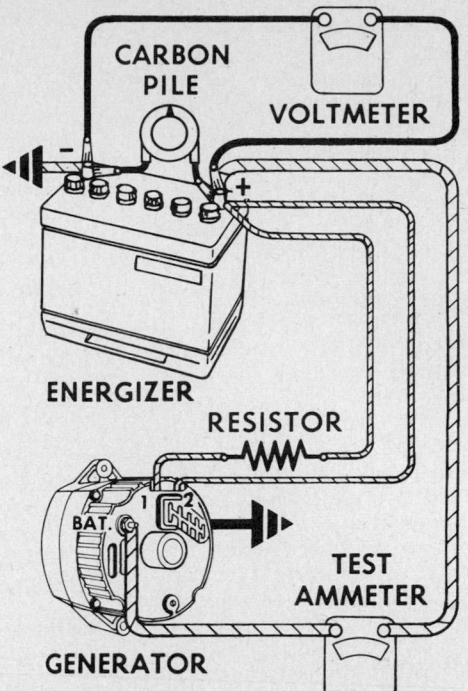

10-SI Delcotron output test hook-up
(© Chev. Div., G.M. Corp.)

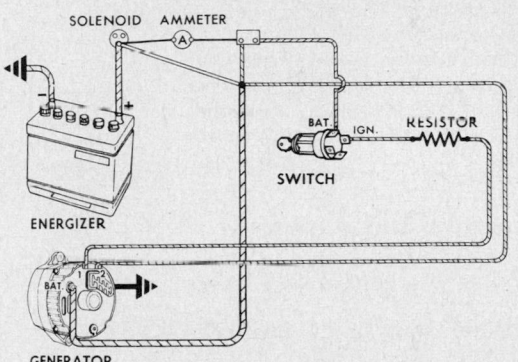

10-SI basic wiring diagram
(© Chev. Div., G.M. Corp.)

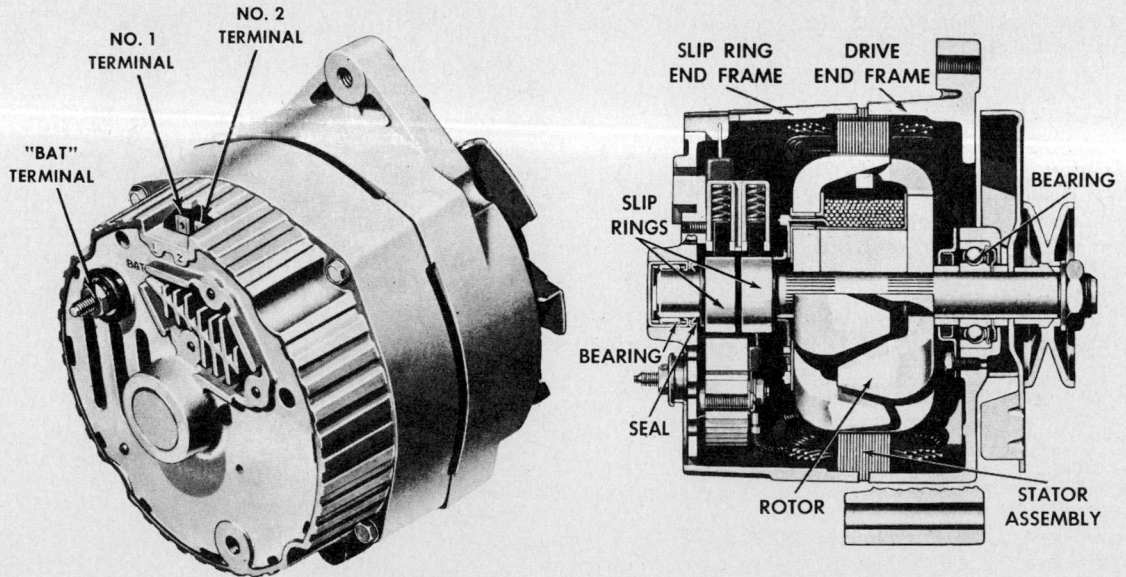

10-SI Delcotron (© Chev. Div., G.M. Corp.)

Alternator Output Test

1. Connect a test voltmeter, ammeter and 10 ohm 6-watt resistor into the charging circuit as illustrated. Do not connect the carbon pile to the battery posts at this time.
2. Increase alternator speed and observe voltmeter—if voltage is uncontrolled with speed and increases to 16 volts or more, check for a grounded brush lead clip as covered previously. If brush lead clip is not grounded, the voltage regulator is faulty and must be replaced.
3. Connect the carbon pile load to the battery terminals.
4. Operate the alternator at moderate speed and adjust the carbon pile to obtain maximum alternator output as indicated on the ammeter. If output is within 10% of rated output as stamped on the alternator frame, alternator is O.K. If output is not within specifications, ground the alternator field by inserting a screwdriver into the test hole in the end frame. If output now is within 10% of rating, replace the voltage regulator; if still not within specifications, check field winding, diode trio, rectifier bridge and stator, as described later. Dissassembly of alternator up to and including Step 6 is necessary.

Disassembly and Assembly

1. Place alternator in a vise, clamped by the mounting flange only.
2. Remove the four through bolts and separate the slip ring end frame and stator assembly from the drive end and rotor assembly, using a screwdriver to pry the two sections apart. Use the slots provided for the purpose.
3. Place a piece of tape over the slip ring end frame bearing to prevent entry of dirt; also tape shaft at slip ring end to prevent scratches.
4. Clean brushes, if they are to be reused, with trichloroethylene or carbon tetrachloride solvent. Use these solvents only in an adequately ventilated area.
5. Remove the stator lead nuts and separate the stator from the end frame.
6. Remove the screw that secures the diode trio and remove diode trio.
NOTE: at this point, test the rotor, rectifier bridge, stator and diode trio if these tests are necessary.
7. Remove the rectifier bridge hold-down screw and the BAT. terminal screw, then disconnect condenser lead. Remove rectifier bridge from end frame.

8. Remove the two securing screws and brush holder and regulator assemblies. Note the insulating sleeves over the screws.
9. Remove the retaining screw and condenser from the end frame.
10. Remove the slip ring end frame bearing, if it is to be replaced, using the procedure given later in this section.
11. Remove the pulley nut, washer, pulley, fan and spacer from the rotor shaft, using a 5/16 in. Allen key to hold the shaft while loosening the nut.
12. Remove rotor and spacers from drive end frame assembly.
13. Remove drive end frame bearing retainer plate, screws, plate, bearing, and slinger from end frame, if necessary.
14. To assemble, reverse order of disassembly. Pulley nut must be tightened to 40-50 ft. lbs.

Cleaning and Inspection

1. Clean all metal parts, except stator and rotor assemblies, in solvent.
2. Wipe off bearings and inspect them for pitting or roughness.
3. Inspect rotor slip rings for scoring. They may be cleaned with 400 grit sandpaper (not emery), rotating the rotor to make the rings concentric. Maximum out-of-true is 0.001 in. If slip rings are deeply scored, the entire rotor must be replaced as a unit.
4. Inspect brushes for wear; minimum length is 1/4 in.

Diode Trio Initial Testing

1. Before removing this unit, easily identified in the illustration, connect an ohmmeter between the brush lead clip and the end frame. The lowest reading scale should be used for this test.
2. After taking a reading, reverse the lead connections. If the meter reads zero, the brush lead clip is probably grounded, due to omission of the insulating sleeve or insulating washer.

Diode Trio Removal

1. Remove the three nuts which secure the stator.
2. Remove stator.
3. Remove the screw which secures the diode trio lead clip, then remove diode trio.
NOTE: The position of the insulating washer on the screw is critical; make sure it is returned to the same position on reassembly.

Diode Trio Testing

1. Connect an ohmmeter, on lowest range, between the single brush connector and one stator lead connector (see illustration).
2. Observe the reading, then reverse the meter leads. Repeat this test with each of the other two stator lead connectors. The readings on each of these tests should NOT be identical, there should be one low and one high reading for each test. If this is not the case, replace the diode trio.
CAUTION: Do not use high voltage on the diode trio.

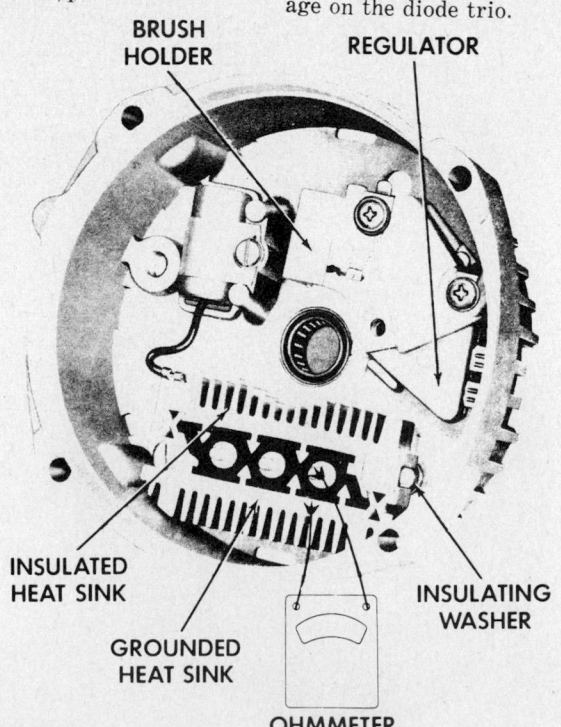

Rectifier bridge testing—10-SI Delcotron
(© Chev. Div., G.M. Corp.)

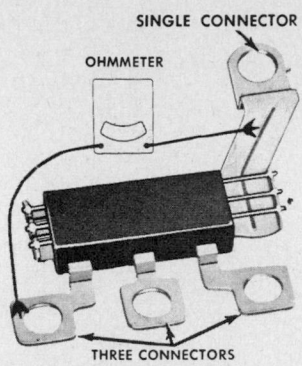

Testing diode trio—10-SI AC generator
(© Pontiac Motor Div., G.M. Corp.)

Brush holder—10-SI generator
(© Pontiac Motor Div., G.M. Corp.)

Grounding tab for voltage regulator test—
10-SI AC generator
(© Pontiac Motor Div., G.M. Corp.)

Rectifier Bridge Testing

1. Connect an ohmmeter between the heat sink (ground) and the base of one of the three terminals (see illustration). Then, reverse the meter leads and take a reading. If both readings are identical, the bridge is defective and must be replaced.
2. Repeat this test with the remaining two terminals, then between the INSULATED heat sink (as opposed to the GROUNDED heat sink in previous test) and each of the three terminals. As before, if any two readings are identical, on reversing the meter leads, the rectifier bridge must be replaced.

Rectifier Bridge Removal

1. Remove the attaching screw and the BAT. terminal screw.
2. Disconnect the condenser lead.
3. Remove the rectifier bridge.

NOTE: The insulator between the insulated heat sink and the end frame is extremely important to the operation of the unit. It must be replaced in exactly the same position on reassembly.

Brush and/or Voltage Regulator R & R

1. Remove two brush holder screws and stator lead to strap nut and washer, brush holder screws and one of the diode trio lead strap attaching screws.
   NOTE: The insulating washers must be replaced in the same position on reassembly.
2. Remove brush holder and brushes. The voltage regulator may also be removed at this time, if desired.
3. Brushes and brush springs must be free of corrosion and must be undamaged and completely free of oil or grease.
4. Insert spring and brushes into holder, noting whether they slide freely without binding. Insert wooden or plastic toothpick into

bottom hole in holder to retain brushes.
NOTE: The brush holder is serviced as a unit; individual parts are not available.
5. Reassemble in reverse order of disassembly.

Slip Ring End Frame Bearing and Seal R & R

1. With stator removed, press out bearing and seal, using a socket or similar tool that fits inside the end frame housing. Press from outside to inside, supporting the frame inside with a hollow cylinder (large, deep socket) to allow the seal and bearing to pass.
2. The bearings are sealed for life and permanently lubricated. If a bearing is dry, do not attempt to repack it, as it will throw off the grease and contaminate the inside of the generator.
3. Using a flat plate, press the new bearing from the outside toward the inside. A large vise is a handy press, but care must be exercised so that end frame is not distorted or cracked. Again, use a deep socket to support the inside of the end frame.
4. From inside the end frame, insert seal and press flush with housing.
5. Install stator and reconnect leads.

Ford-Autolite
(Ford Motor Co.)

To Make All Following Tests

In addition to the regular precautionary measures:
1. Disconnect both battery cables, clean the terminal posts and clamps, then reconnect the ground cable only.
2. Install a special battery make-and-break adapter switch between battery, positive (+) post, and battery cable. Close the adapter switch.

Alternator Output on the Car

1. Connect test ammeter leads to the battery adapter switch. Open and close switch, and check polarity.

NOTE: when the battery adapter switch is opened, current will flow through the test ammeter. Never operate the alternator with an open circuit.
2. Withdraw main connector from the regulator. Connect the field rheostat leads to the A+ and F terminals of the main connector. Set field rheostat to off position.
3. Connect carbon pile load control leads to the battery posts.
4. Connect voltmeter leads to their polar respective battery posts.
5. Throw the battery adapter switch to the closed position, then start the engine.
6. Open the battery adapter switch. Current being generated will now flow through the test ammeter.
7. Increase engine speed to 2,000 rpm, then adjust the field rheostat until the voltmeter registers exactly 15 volts.
8. Read the ammeter, then add to this reading 2 amps for standard ignition, 6 amps for transistor ignition, to determine the total alternator output. This is to compensate for the current used by the ignition, and the alternator field circuits.
NOTE: maximum current output may not be possible if the battery is fully charged. When this situation exists, turn the field rheostat toward the resistance out position, holding the voltage at 15 volts by applying a load with the carbon pile load control.
9. If output is 2-5 amps. below specifications, an open diode is indicated. If 10 amps. below, a shorted diode is indicated.

Stator Neutral Voltage Test (Field Relay Closing Voltage)

The alternator STA terminal is connected to the stator neutral point, as indicated in the wiring diagrams. The voltage generated at this point is utilized to close the field relay in the charging indicator system.
1. Disconnect the regulator plug from the voltage regulator.

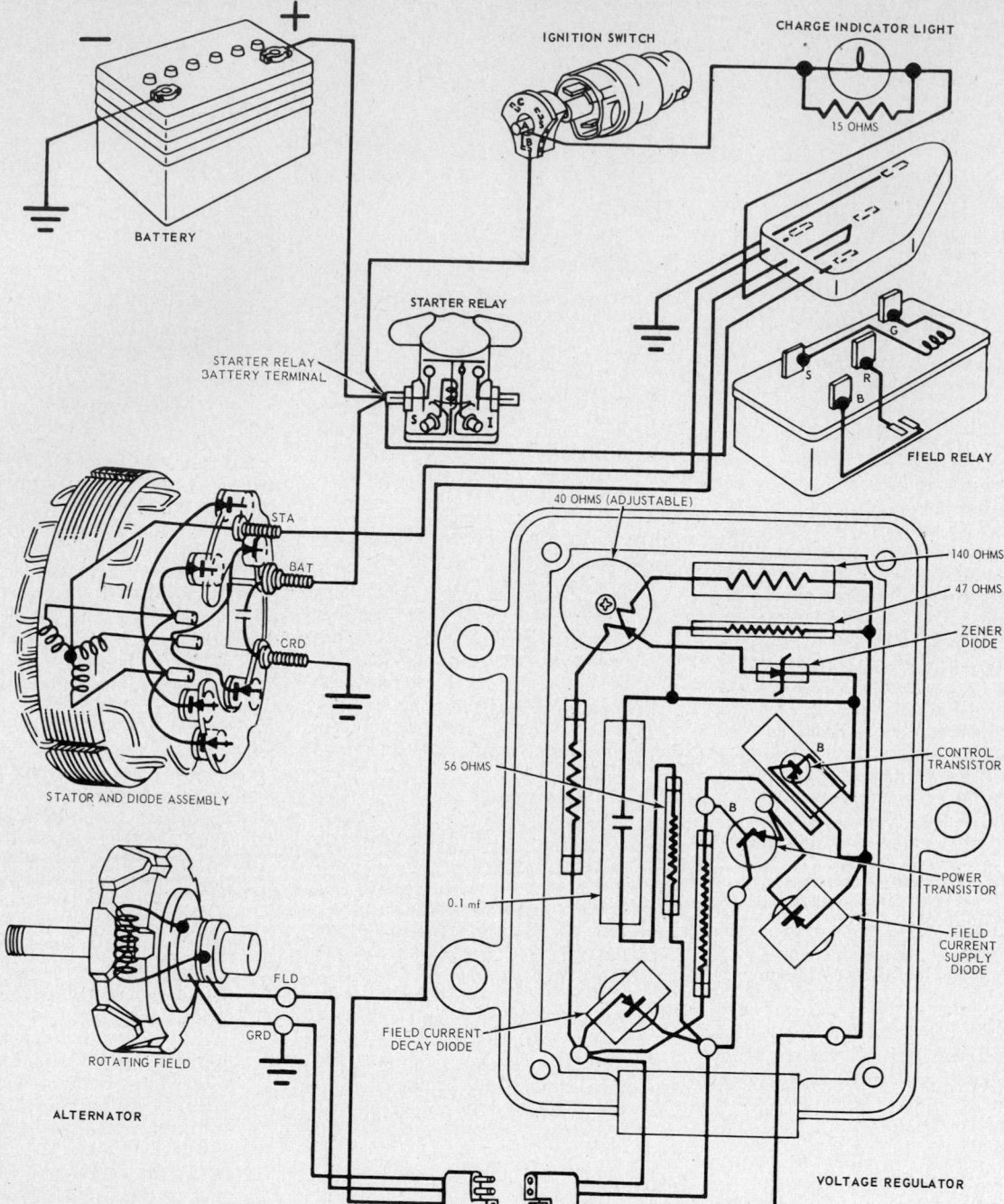

Charging system schematic with transistor regulator and charging light (© Ford Motor Co.)

2. Connect a field rheostat to the A+ and F terminals of the harness plug.
3. Connect a test voltmeter (0-20 volts) between the harness plug S terminal and the negative battery post.
4. Start engine and run at 1,000 rpm, all lights and accessories off.
5. Adjust the field rheostat to obtain at least 6 volts. If this figure cannot be obtained at any field rheostat setting, remove the alternator for diode and stator testing.

Field Current Draw Test

NOTE: alternator must be removed from the car.
1. Connect a test ammeter between the alternator frame and the positive post of a 12-volt test battery.
2. Connect a jumper wire between the negative test battery post and the alternator field terminal.
3. Observe the ammeter:
   a. Little or no current flow indicates high brush resistance, open field windings, or high winding resistance.

b. Current in excess of specifications (approximately 2.9 amps. for most models) indicates shorted or grounded field windings, or brush leads touching.

Diode Tests

Disassemble the alternator, as described later in this section, disconnect diode assembly from stator and make tests as illustrated. To test one set of diodes, contact one ohmmeter probe to the diode plate and contact each of the three stator lead terminals with the other probe. Reverse

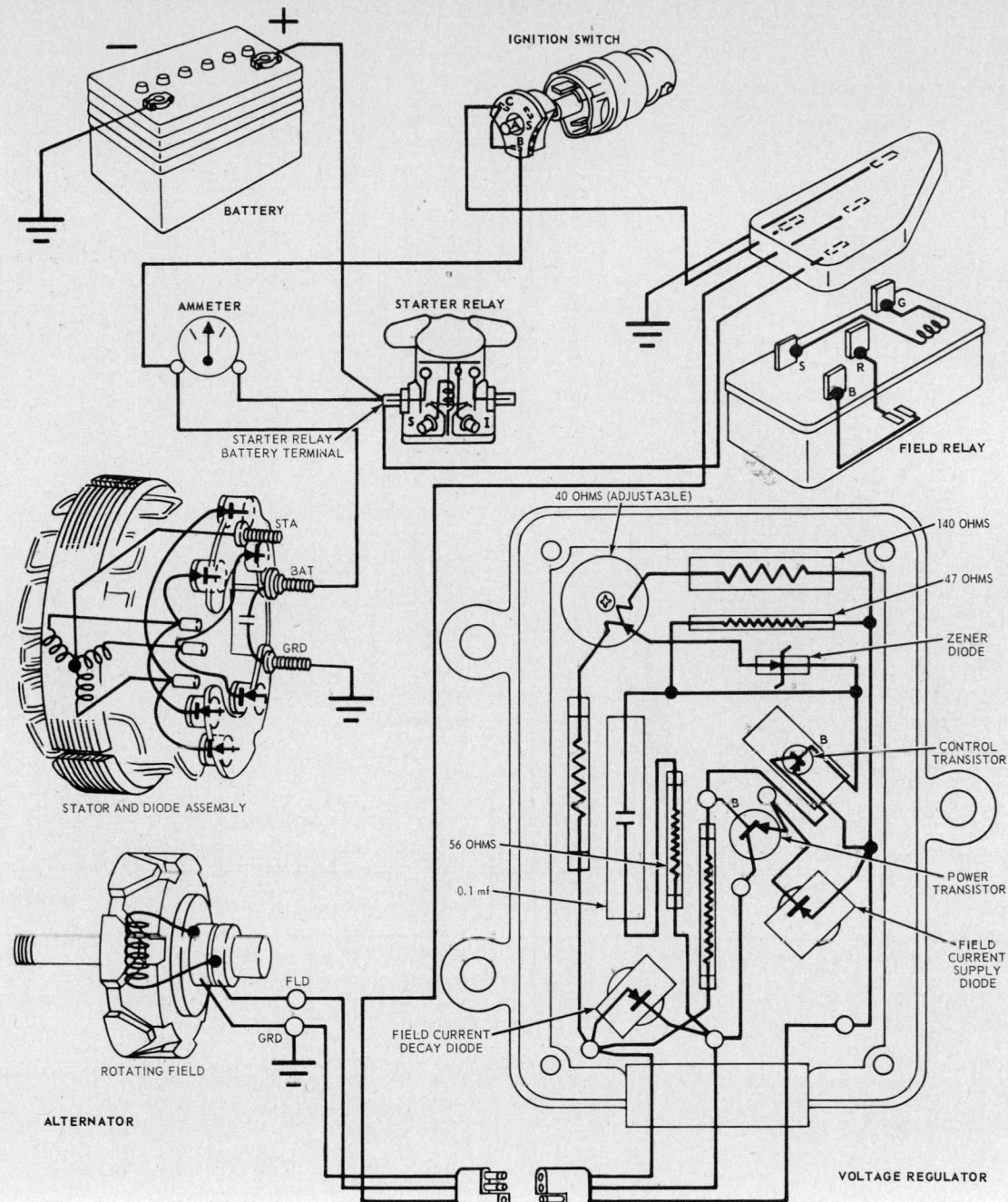

Charging system schematic with transistor regulator and ammeter (© Ford Motor Co.)

the probes and repeat the test. All six tests (eight for 1971-72 61 amp. Autolite eight-diode models) should show a reading of about 60 ohms in one direction and infinite ohms in the other. If two high readings, or two low readings, are obtained after reversing probes the diode is faulty and must be replaced.

Stator Tests

Disassemble the stator from the alternator assembly and rectifiers. Connect test ohmmeter probes between each pair of stator leads. If the ohmmeter does not indicate equally between each pair of leads, the stator coil is open and must be replaced.

Connect test ohmmeter probes between one of the stator leads and the stator core. The ohmmeter should not show any reading. If it does show continuity, the stator winding is grounded and must be replaced.

Voltage Limiter Test

Voltage limiter tests must be made with the regulator cover on and the regulator at normal operating temperature. Also, *no* accessory loads should be in the circuit—battery and ignition loads only. This includes

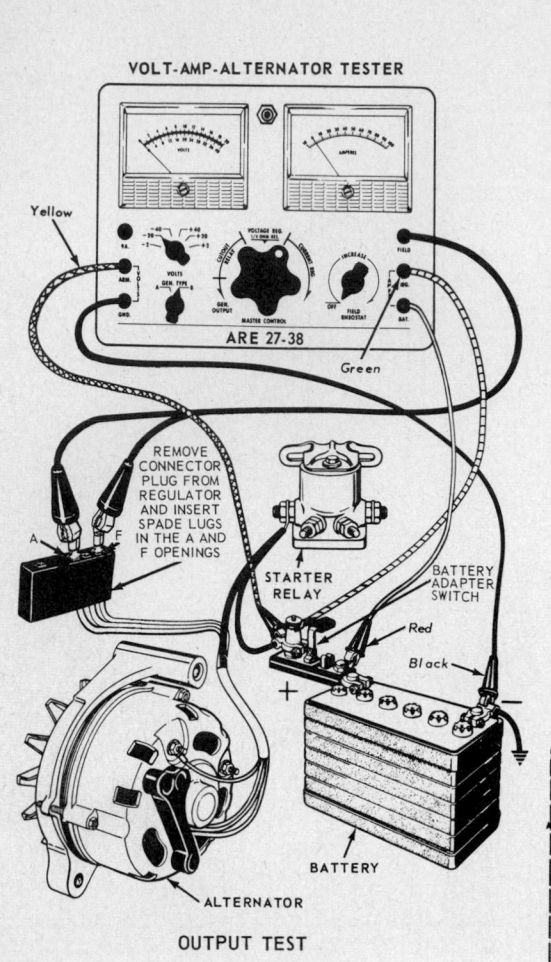

OUTPUT TEST

Alternator stator test hook-up (© Ford Motor Co.)

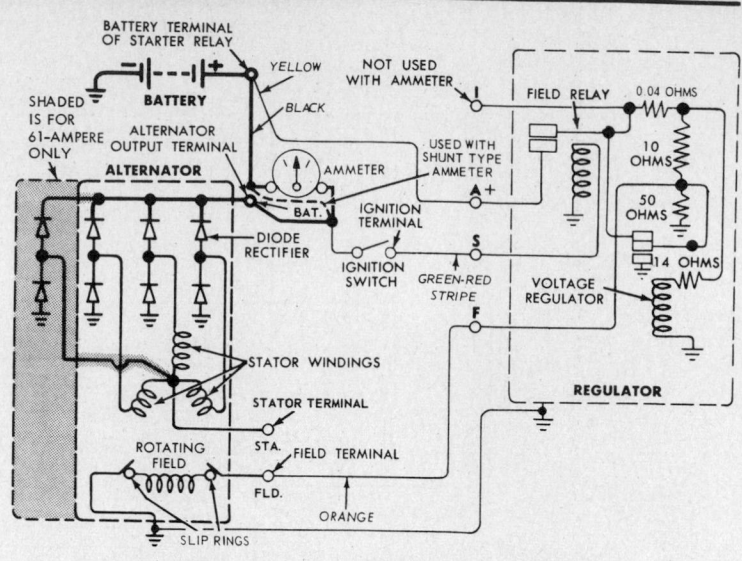

Charging system schematic with electro-mechanical regulator and ammeter
(© Ford Motor Co.)

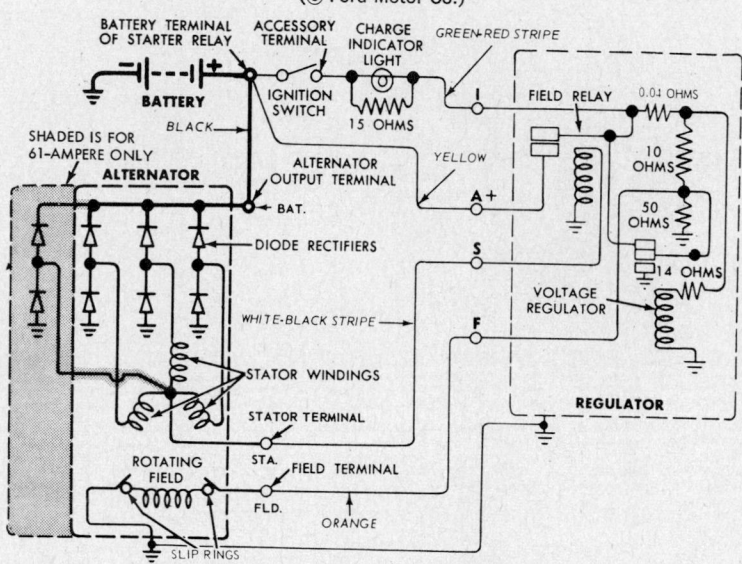

Charging system schematic with electro-mechanical regulator and charging light
(© Ford Motor Co.)

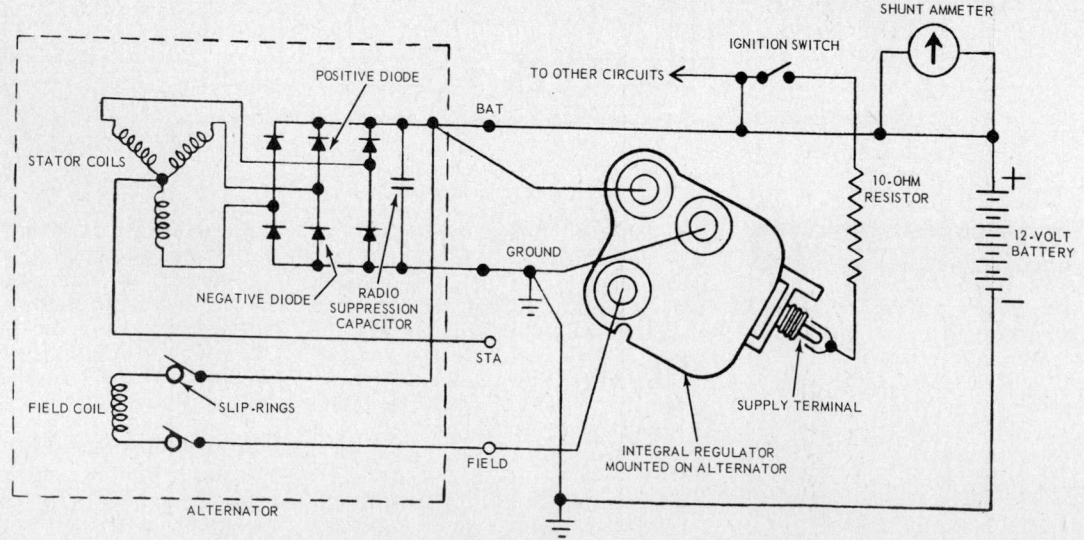

Charging system schematic with integral regulator (© Ford Motor Co.)

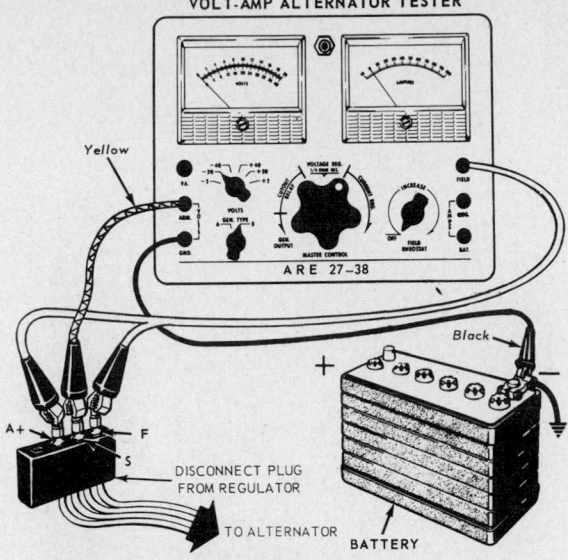

Alternator stator neutral voltage hook-up
(© Ford Motor Co.)

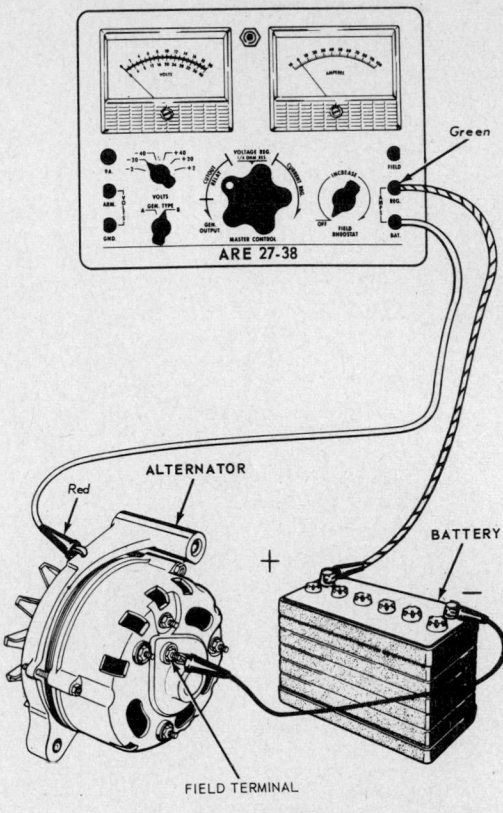

FIELD OPEN OR SHORT CIRCUIT TEST

Alternator field circuit test hook-up
(© Ford Motor Co.)

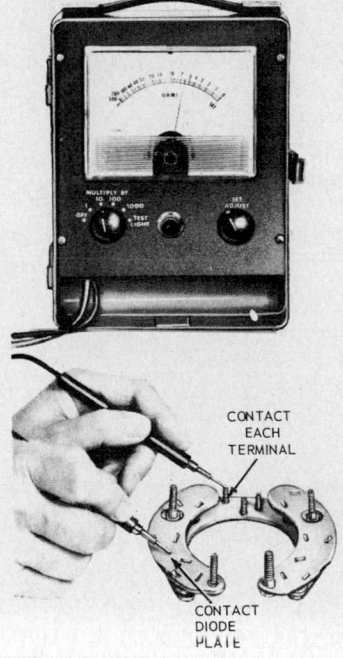

Testing diodes—all except 65 amp. Autolite
(© Ford Motor Co.)

such items as dome and radio lights, as well as the air conditioner, heater blower motor and headlights. Also, the battery specific gravity reading should be at least 1.230 to get accurate test results. If this is not the case, either charge the battery or substitute a fully charged battery while conducting the test.

1. With the regulator connected to its harness plug, attach test voltmeter leads between the battery negative terminal and the circuit side of a battery adapter switch installed on the positive battery terminal. A ¼ ohm test resistor also should be inserted into the circuit.

2. Connect a test ammeter to each side of the battery adapter switch.

3. Close the battery adapter switch, start the engine, then open the adapter switch.

4. Operate engine at 2,000 rpm for approximately five minutes; the ammeter should indicate less than 10 amps.

5. Cycle the regulator as follows:
   a. Turn ignition key to OFF, close adapter switch.
   b. Start engine, open adapter switch.
   c. Increase engine speed to 2,000 rpm and hold for one minute.
   d. Read voltmeter. It should be 13.5-15.3 volts at an air temperature of 50-125° F. If not, replace regulator.

Field Relay Test

1. Remove regulator from car.
2. Connect a jumper wire between the grounded regulator base and the negative terminal of a 12-volt test battery.
3. Connect a 12-volt test light between the positive terminal of the test battery and the A+ terminal of the regulator.
4. Connect one end of a jumper wire to the regulator S terminal. The other end of this jumper should go to a tie point—a bolt will do.

5. Connect a field rheostat between the positive test battery terminal and the tie point that terminates the jumper wire from the S terminal.

6. Connect one lead of a test voltmeter to the grounded regulator base and the other voltmeter lead to the tie point. Three wires now are attached to this tie point.

7. Slowly adjust the field rheostat until the test light just comes on, observing the voltmeter reading at this point. This is the relay closing voltage; if it is not to specifications, the regulator must be replaced.

Regulator Adjustments—1965-67

Field Relay

Remove regulator from car and remove cover. Using a chemically clean feeler gauge, 0.010-0.018 in., placed on the top of the coil core closest to the contact points, press the armature down on the gauge and bend the contact post arm until the bottom

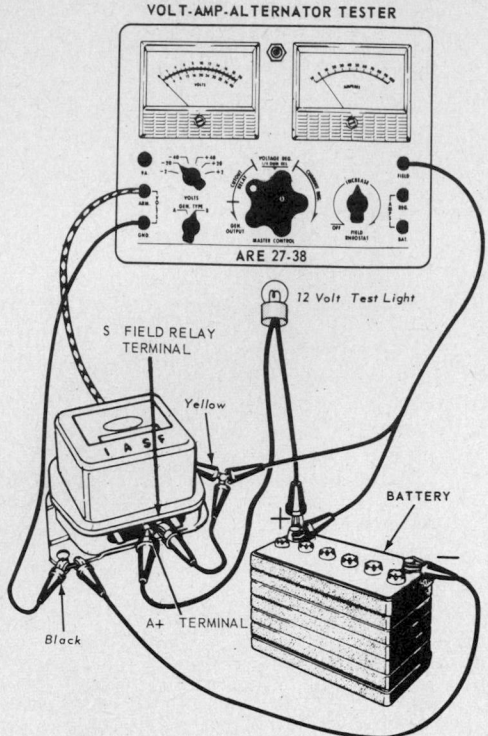

Field relay test hook-up (© Ford Motor Co.)

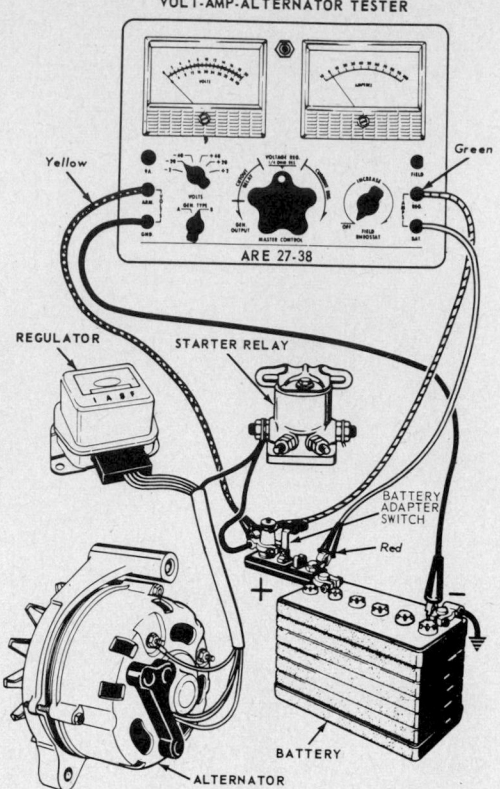

VOLTAGE LIMITER TEST

Voltage limiter test hook-up (© Ford Motor Co.)

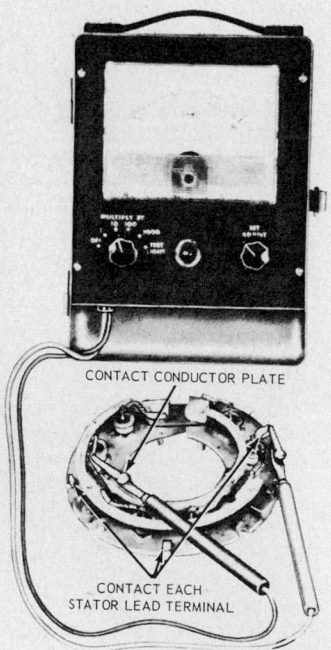

Testing diodes—65 amp. Autolite
(© Ford Motor Co.)

contact just touches the upper contact. This adjusts the air gap. Make sure the spring arm is not bent in the process.

To adjust closing voltage, the armature frame must be bent. To increase closing voltage, bend the armature frame downward; to decrease, bend upward.

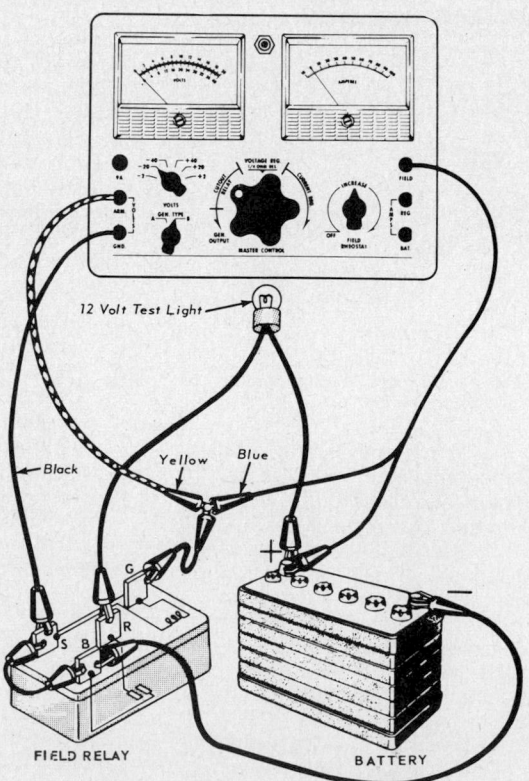

Field relay test hook-up—transistor regulator
(© Ford Motor Co.)

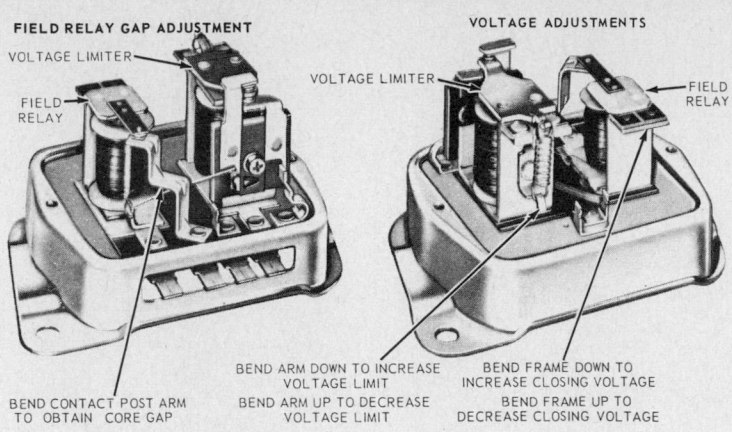

FIELD RELAY GAP ADJUSTMENT

VOLTAGE ADJUSTMENTS

VOLTAGE LIMITER

FIELD RELAY

VOLTAGE LIMITER

FIELD RELAY

BEND CONTACT POST ARM TO OBTAIN CORE GAP

BEND ARM DOWN TO INCREASE VOLTAGE LIMIT
BEND ARM UP TO DECREASE VOLTAGE LIMIT

BEND FRAME DOWN TO INCREASE CLOSING VOLTAGE
BEND FRAME UP TO DECREASE CLOSING VOLTAGE

Electro-mechanical regulator adjustments (© Ford Motor Co.)

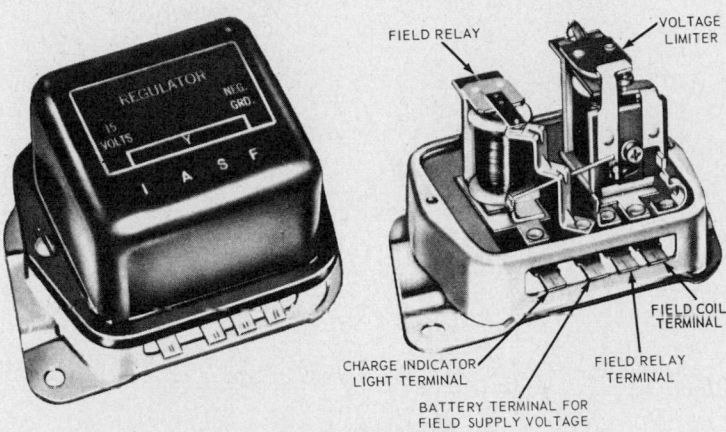

FIELD RELAY

VOLTAGE LIMITER

REGULATOR

NEG. GRD.

15 VOLTS

Y

I A S F

CHARGE INDICATOR LIGHT TERMINAL

BATTERY TERMINAL FOR FIELD SUPPLY VOLTAGE

FIELD COIL TERMINAL

FIELD RELAY TERMINAL

External electro-mechanical regulator (© Ford Motor Co.)

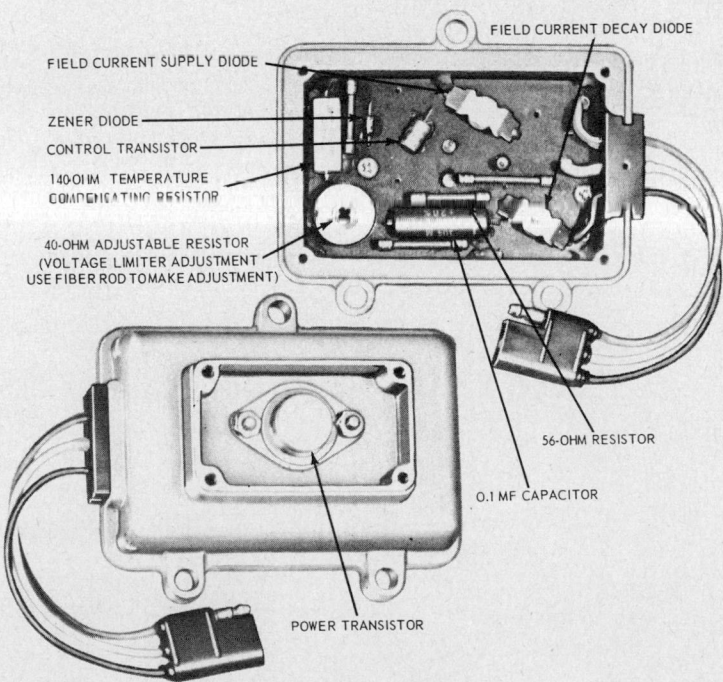

FIELD CURRENT DECAY DIODE

FIELD CURRENT SUPPLY DIODE

ZENER DIODE

CONTROL TRANSISTOR

140-OHM TEMPERATURE COMPENSATING RESISTOR

40-OHM ADJUSTABLE RESISTOR (VOLTAGE LIMITER ADJUSTMENT USE FIBER ROD TO MAKE ADJUSTMENT)

56-OHM RESISTOR

0.1 MF CAPACITOR

POWER TRANSISTOR

External transistor regulator (© Ford Motor Co.)

Voltage Limiter

On electro-mechanical regulators, the voltage limiter is adjusted by bending the voltage limiter spring arm. Voltage setting is increased by bending downward; decreased by bending upward. This adjustment should be made with the regulator removed and mounted on a test stand. If a stand is not available, the regulator must at least be removed, adjusted and reinstalled. Then it must be cycled and retested. If the voltage limiter is not set correctly, the regulator must be removed and adjusted again. Quite often, vehicle design does not allow enough clearance for adjustments to be made in-car.

The transistor regulator is so designed that the voltage limiter is the only portion of the unit that can be adjusted. The adjustment is accomplished by removing the regulator and the bottom cover, then adjusting the round 40-ohm rheostat with a *fiber* screwdriver. See the illustration for the location of the resistor.

Regulator Adjustments— 1968-72

Not adjustable—sealed at factory.

Overhaul—Autolite

Disassembly—Except 65 AMP Autolite

1. Mark both end housings with a scribe mark for assembly.
2. Remove the three housing through bolts.
3. Separate the front housing and rotor from the stator and rear housing.
4. Remove the nuts from the rectifier to rear housing mounting studs, and remove the rear housing.
5. If replacement is necessary, press the bearing from the rear end housing, supporting housing on inner boss.
6. Remove the brush holder mounting screws and remove holder, brushes, springs, insulator and

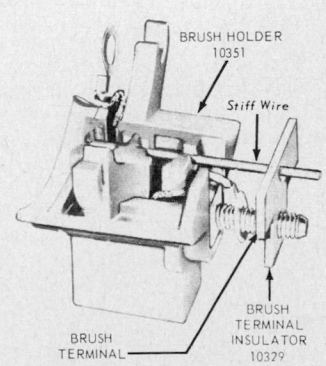

BRUSH HOLDER 10351

Stiff Wire

BRUSH TERMINAL

BRUSH TERMINAL INSULATOR 10329

Autolite brush holder assembly (© Ford Motor Co.)

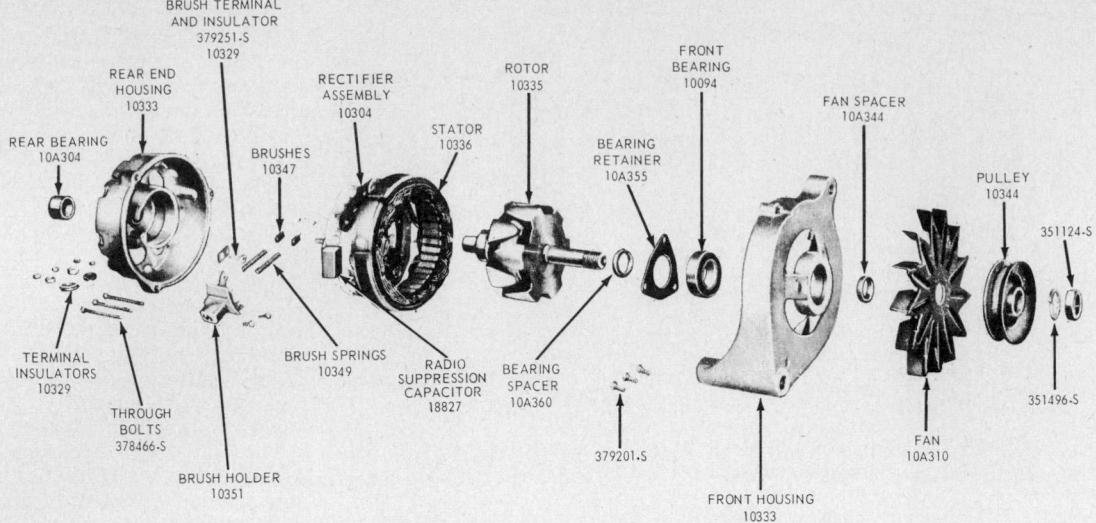

Typical disassembled Autolite alternator—except 65 amp. unit (© Ford Motor Co.)

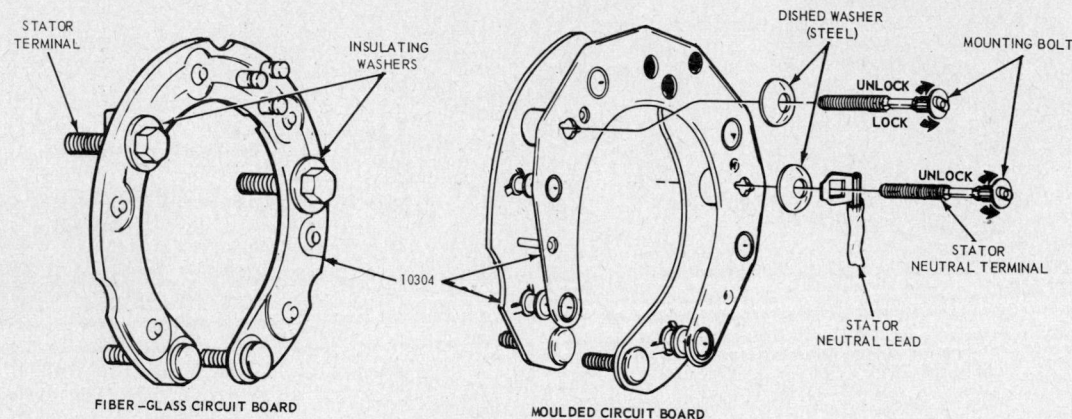

FIBER-GLASS CIRCUIT BOARD

MOULDED CIRCUIT BOARD

Rectifier assembly (© Ford Motor Co.)

terminal.

7. If rectifiers are to be replaced, carefully unsolder the leads from the terminals.

Caution Use only a 100-watt soldering iron. Leave the soldering iron in contact with the diode terminals only long enough to remove the wires. Use pliers as temporary heat sinks in order to protect the diodes.

8. There are various types of rectifier assembly circuit boards installed in production. One type has the circuit board spaced away from the diode plates and the diodes are exposed. Another type consists of a single circuit board with integral diodes; and still another has integral diodes with an additional booster diode plate containing two diodes. This last type is used only on the eight-diode, 61-amp. 1971-72 Autolite alternator. To disassemble, use the following procedures:

a. Exposed Diodes—remove the screws from the rectifier by rotating bolt heads ¼ turn clockwise to unlock, then unscrewing.

b. Integral Diodes—press out the stator terminal screw, making sure not to twist it while doing this. Do not remove grounded screw.

c. Booster Diodes—press out the stator terminal screw about ¼ in., then remove the nut from the end of the screw and lift screw from circuit board, making sure not to twist it as it comes out.

9. Remove the drive pulley and fan.

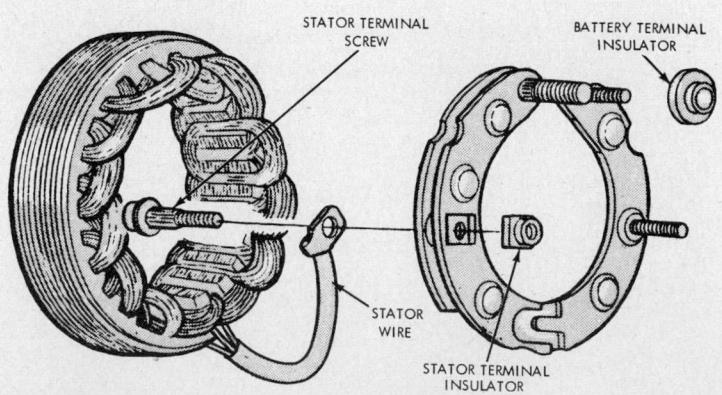

Stator and rectifier assembly—61 amp. booster diode model (© Ford Motor Co.)

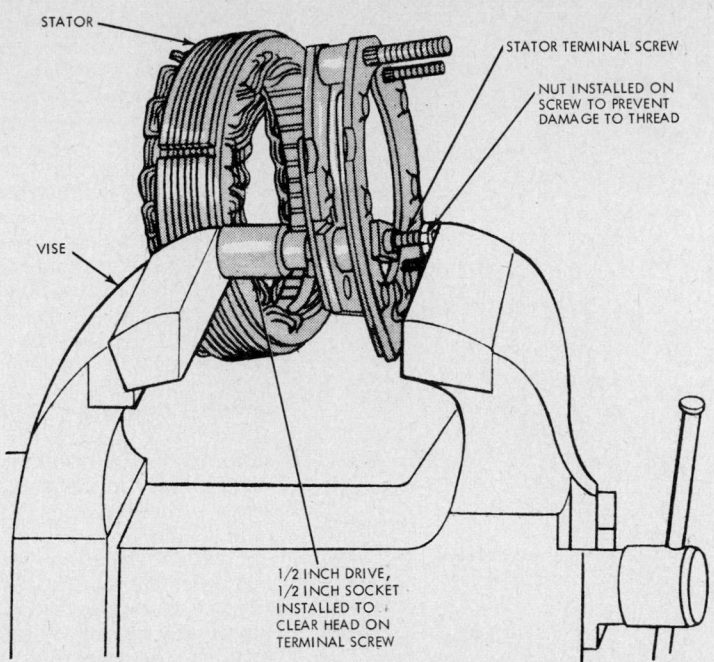

Stator terminal screw removal—61 amp. booster diode model (© Ford Motor Co.)

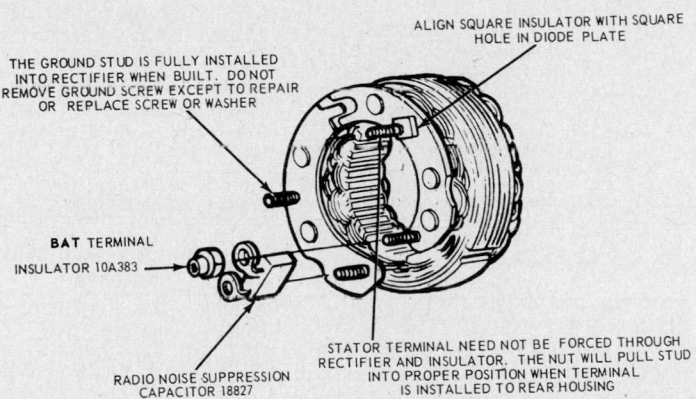

Terminal insulators—fiber circuit board (© Ford Motor Co.)

On alternator pulleys with threaded holes in the outer end of the pulley, use a standard puller for removal.

10. Remove the three screws that hold the front bearing retainer, and remove the front housing.

11. If the bearing is to be replaced, press from housing.

Cleaning and Inspection

1. The rotor, stator, diode rectifier assemblies, and bearings are not to be cleaned with solvent. These parts are to be wiped off with a clean cloth. Cleaning solvent may cause damage to the electrical parts or contaminate the bearing internal lubricant. Wash all other parts in solvent and dry them.

2. Rotate the front bearing on the driveshaft. Check for any scraping noise, looseness or roughness that indicates that the bearing is excessively worn. As the bearing is being rotated, look for excessive lubricant leakage. If any of these conditions exist, replace the bearing. Check rear bearing and rotor shaft.

3. Place the rear end housing on the slip ring end of the shaft and rotate the bearing on the shaft. Make a similar check for noise, looseness or roughness. Inspect the rollers and cage for damage. Replace the bearing if these conditions exist, or if the lubricant is missing or contaminated.

4. Check both the front and rear housings for cracks. Check the front housing for stripped threads in the mounting holes. Replace defective housings.

5. Pulleys that have been removed and installed several times may have to be replaced because of increased bore diameter. A pulley is not suitable for reuse if more than one-quarter of the shaft length will enter the pul-ley bore with light pressure. Replace any pulley that is bent.

6. Check all wire leads on both the stator and rotor assemblies for loose soldered connections, and for burned insulation. Solder all poor connections. Replace parts that show burned insulation.

7. Check the slip rings for damaged insulation and runout. If the slip rings are more than 0.0005 in. out of round, take a light cut (minimum diameter limit 1.22 in.) from the face of the rings to true them. If the slip rings are badly damaged, the entire rotor will have to be replaced, as they are serviced as a complete assembly.

8. Replace any parts that are burned or cracked. Replace brushes that are worn to less than 5/16 in. in length. Replace the brush spring if it has less than 7-12 oz. tension.

Assembly—Except 65 AMP Autolite

1. Press the front bearing into the front housing boss, putting pressure on outer race only. Install bearing retainer.

2. If the stop ring on the drive-shaft was damaged, install a new stop ring. Push the new ring onto the shaft and into the groove.

3. Position the front bearing spacer on the driveshaft against the stop ring.

4. Place the front housing over the shaft, with the bearing positioned in the front housing cavity.

5. Install fan spacer, fan, pulley, lockwasher and retaining nut and tighten nut to 60-100 ft. lbs. holding the drive shaft with an Allen key.

6. If rear bearing was removed, press a new one into rear housing.

7. Assemble brushes, springs, terminal and insulator in the brush holder, retract the brushes and insert a short length of 1/8 in. rod or stiff wire through the hole in the holder to hold the brushes in the retracted position.

8. Position the brush holder assembly in the rear housing and install mounting screws. Position brush leads as illustrated to

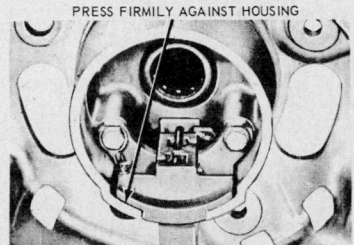

Brush lead positioning (© Ford Motor Co.)

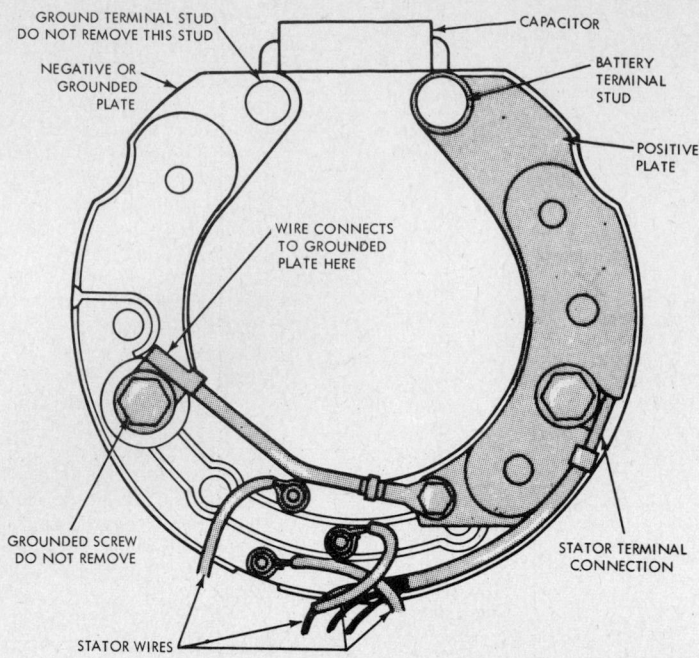

Rectifier terminal locations—61 amp. booster diode model
(© Ford Motor Co.)

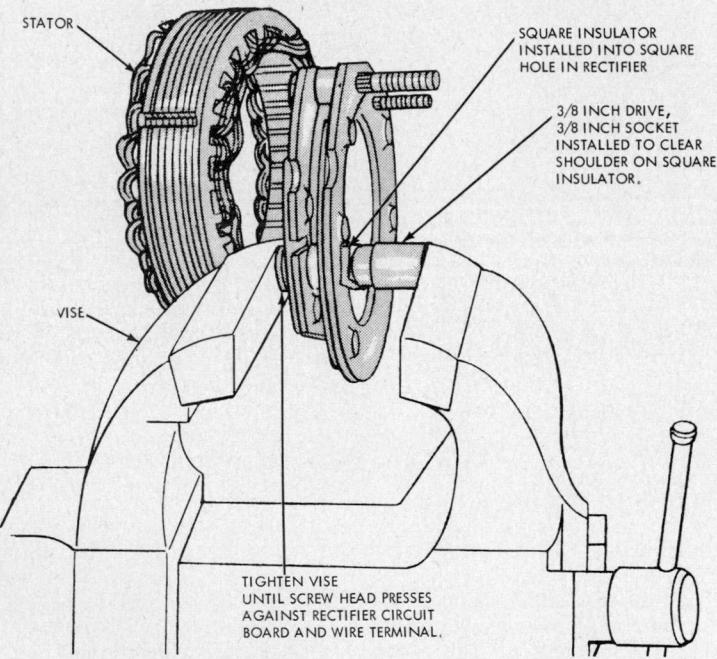

Stator terminal screw installation—61 amp. booster diode model
(© Ford Motor Co.)

prevent shorting.

9. Wrap the three stator winding leads around the circuit board terminals and solder them using only rosin core solder and a 100-watt iron. Position the stator neutral lead eyelet on the stator terminal screw and install the screw in the rectifier assembly.

10. A. Exposed Diodes—insert the special screws through the wire lug, dished washers and circuit board. Turn ¼ turn counterclockwise to lock in place.

   B. Integral Diodes—insert the screws straight through the holes.

NOTE: the dished washers are to be used on *molded* circuit boards only. Using these washers on a *fiber* board will result in a serious short circuit, as only a flat insulating washer between the stator terminal and the board is used on fiber circuit boards.

   C. Booster Diodes—position the stator wire terminal on the stator terminal screw, then

position screw on rectifier. Position square insulator over the screw and into the square hole in the rectifier, rotate terminal screw until it locks, then press it in finger-tight. Referring to the accompanying illustration, position the stator wire, then press the terminal screw into the rectifier and insulator with a vise (also illustrated).

11. Place the radio noise suppression condenser on the rectifier terminals. With molded circuit board, install the STA and BAT terminal insulators. With fiber circuit board, place the square stator terminal insulator in the square hole in the sectifier assembly, then position BAT terminal insulator.

   Position the stator and rectifier assembly in the rear housing, making sure that all terminal insulators are seated properly in the recesses. Position STA, BAT and FLD insulators on terminal bolts; install nuts.

12. Clean the rear bearing surface of the rotor shaft with a rag, then position rear housing and stator assembly over rotor. Align matchmarks made during disassembly and install through bolts. *Remove brush retracting wire and place a dab of silicone sealer over the hole.*

Disassembly—65 AMP. Autolite

1. Remove the brush holder and cover assembly from the rear housing.
2. Mark both end housings and the stator.
3. Remove the three housing through bolts.
4. Separate the front housing and rotor from the stator and rear housing.
5. Remove the drive pulley nut, lockwasher, flat washer, pulley, fan, fan spacer and rotor from the front housing.
6. Remove the three screws that hold the front bearing retainer

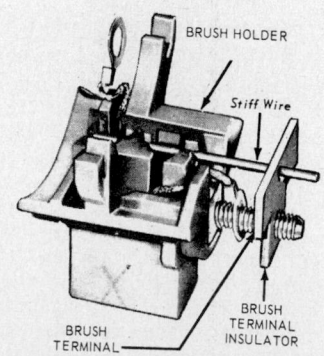

Brush holder assembly (© Ford Motor Co.)

Disassembled view of 65 amp. Autolite alternator (© Ford Motor Co.)

and remove the retainer. If the bearing is damaged or has lost its lubricant, support the housing close to the bearing boss and press out the bearing.

7. Remove all the nut and washer assemblies and insulators from the rear housing and remove the rear housing from the stator and rectifier assembly.

8. If necessary, press the rear bearing from the housing, supporting the housing on the inner boss.

9. Unsolder the three stator leads from the rectifier assembly, and separate the stator from the assembly. Use a 200-watt soldering iron.

10. Perform a diode test and an open and grounded stator coil test.

Cleaning and Inspection

Nicks and scratches may be removed from the rotor slip rings by turning down the slip rings. Do not go beyond the minimum diameter limit of 1.22 in. If the slip rings are badly damaged, the entire rotor must be replaced. The rectifier also is serviced as an assembly.

Assembly—65 AMP. Autolite

1. If the front bearing is being replaced, press the new bearing into the bearing boss, putting pressure on the outer race only. Install the bearing retainer and tighten the retainer screws until the tips of the retainer touch the housing.

2. Position the rectifier assembly to the stator, wrap the three stator leads around the diode plate terminals and solder them using a 200-watt soldering iron.

3. If the rear housing bearing was removed, press in a new bearing from the inside of the housing, putting pressure on the outer race only.

4. Install the BAT-GRD insulator, and position the stator and rectifier assembly in the rear housing.

5. Install the STA (purple) and BAT (red) terminal insulators on the terminal bolts and install the nut and washer assemblies. *Make certain that the shoulders on all insulators, both inside and outside of the housing, are seated properly before tightening the nuts.*

6. Position the front housing over the rotor and install the fan spacer, fan, pulley, flat and lockwashers and nut on the rotor shaft.

7. Wipe the rear bearing surface of the rotor shaft with a clean rag.

8. Position the rotor with the front housing into the stator and rear housing assembly, and align the matchmarks made during disassembly. Seat the machined portion of the stator core into the step in both housings and install the through bolts.

9. If the field brushes have worn to less than 3/8 in., replace both brushes. Hold the brushes in position by inserting a stiff wire into the brush holder.

10. Position the brush holder assembly into the rear housing and install the three mounting screws. Remove the brush retracting wire and put a dab of silicone cement over the hole.

Brush Replacement—65 AMP Autolite

1. Remove the brush holder and cover assembly from the rear housing.

2. Remove the terminal bolts from the brush holder and cover assembly, then remove the brush assemblies.

3. Position the new brush terminals on the terminal bolts and assemble the terminals, bolts, brush holder washers and nuts. The insulating washer mounts under the FLD terminal nut. The entire brush and cover assembly also is available for service.

4. Depress the brush springs in the brush holder cavities and insert the brushes on top of the springs. Hold the brushes in position by inserting a stiff wire in the brush holder as shown. Position the brush leads as shown.

5. Install the brush holder and cover assembly into the rear housing. Remove the brush re-

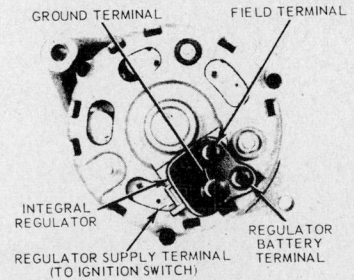

Alternator with integral regulator (© Ford Motor Co.)

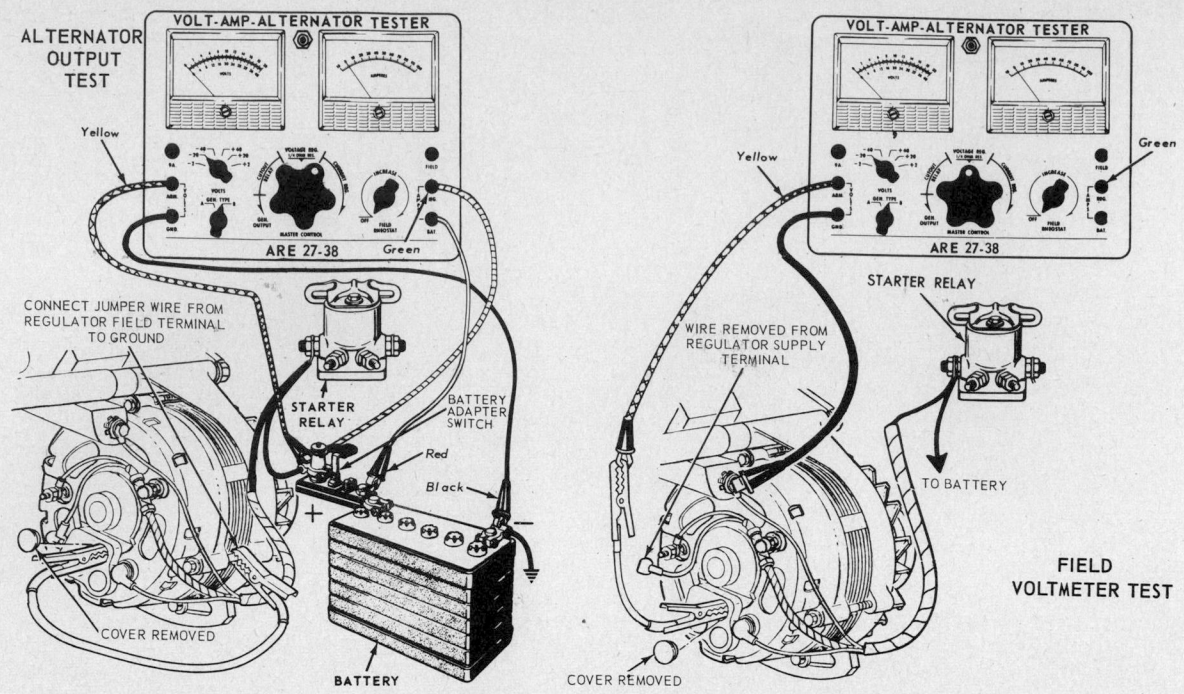

Output test hook-up—integral regulator alternator
(© Ford Motor Co.)

Field voltmeter test hook-up—integral regulator alternator
(© Ford Motor Co.)

tracing wire and put a dab of silicone cement over the hole.

Autolite Alternator with Integral Regulator

Description

Starting in 1969, some vehicles are equipped with an Autolite alternator having an integral regulator mounted to the rear end housing. The regulator is a hybrid unit featuring use of solid state integrated circuits.

These circuits may consist of transistors, diodes and resistors. The unusual feature of this type of micro-electronic circuit is that the entire circuit is within a silicone crystal approximately 1/8 in. square. Because of the small size of the circuit, it is not repairable or adjustable and must be replaced as a unit if found to be defective. It should be noted that the size of the regulator housing is dictated only by the fact that some means of connecting the regulator to the alternator is necessary. Overhaul

is the same as for other Autolite alternators.

Output Test

1. Place transmission in Neutral or Park.
2. Remove the positive battery cable and install a battery adapter switch in the line.
3. Attach one lead of a test voltmeter to the negative battery post and the other test lead to the circuit side of the adapter switch.
4. Connect a test ammeter to each

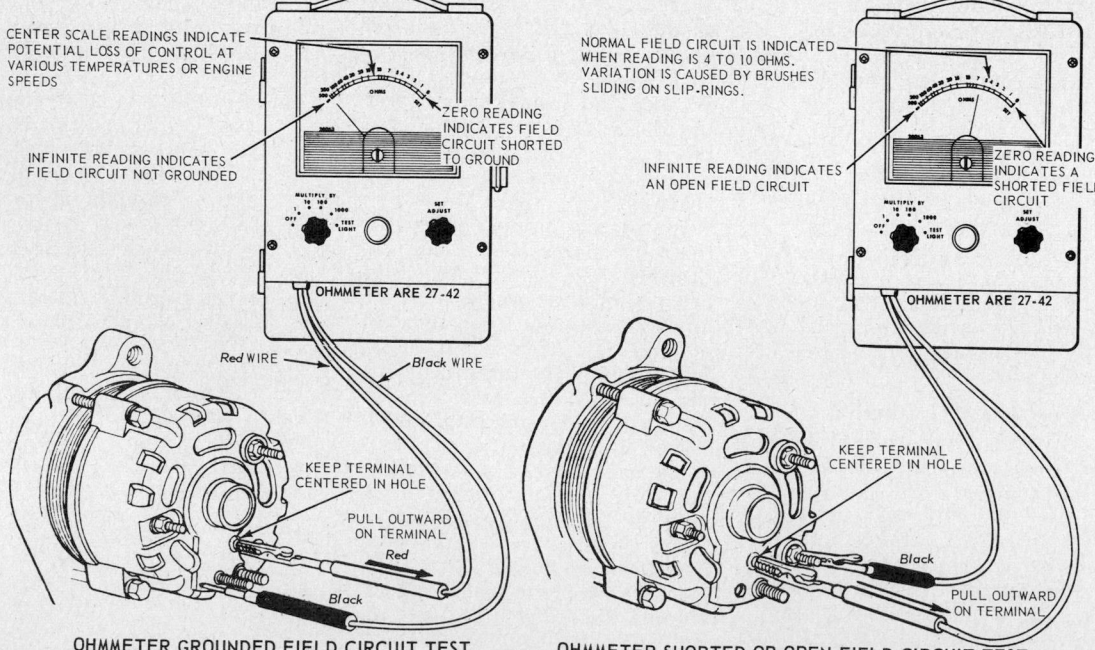

OHMMETER GROUNDED FIELD CIRCUIT TEST

OHMMETER SHORTED OR OPEN FIELD CIRCUIT TEST

Field circuit test hook-ups with ohmmeter—integral regulator alternator (© Ford Motor Co.)

side of the adapter switch, so that charging current will go through the ammeter when the switch is opened.

5. Connect a jumper wire between the alternator frame and the integral regulator field terminal (cover plug removed).
6. Close adapter switch, start engine and open adapter switch.
7. Running engine at 2,000 rpm, observe voltmeter and ammeter. At 15 volts indicated, the ammeter should read 50-57 amps. If so, and there is still a no-charge condition, the regulator is probably faulty and must be replaced. An output 2-8 amps. below 50 amps. usually indicates an open diode rectifier, while an output 10-15 amps. below minimum specifications usually indicates a shorted diode. An alternator with a shorted diode usually will whine at idle speed.

Field Test (Voltmeter)

1. Turn ignition switch to OFF position.
2. Remove wire from regulator supply terminal.
3. Remove cover plug from regulator field terminal and connect one test voltmeter lead to this terminal. A ¼ ohm resistor should be in the circuit.
4. Connect the other test voltmeter lead to a good engine ground.
5. The voltmeter should read 12 volts. If *no* voltage is present, the field circuit is open or grounded.
6. If voltmeter reads more than 1 volt, but still less than battery voltage, there is probably a par-

tial ground in the alternator field circuit and the circuit should be checked with an ohmmeter.

Field Test (Ohmmeter)

1. Disconnect battery ground cable; remove alternator from car.
2. Remove the regulator from the alternator (covered later).
3. Make the ohmmeter tests as illustrated. If any of the tests indicates a field circuit problem, disassemble the alternator to further isolate the trouble.
   a. Contact each ohmmeter probe to a slip ring. Resistance should be 4-5 ohms. A higher reading indicates a damaged slip ring soldered connection or a broken wire. A lower reading indicates a shorted wire or slip ring assembly.
   b. Contact one ohmmeter probe to a slip ring and the other probe to the rotor shaft. Any reading other than infinite ohms indicates a short to ground. If neither of these tests (A and B) isolates the trouble, the brushes or brush assembly are the probable cause.

Voltage Limiter Test

1. Check the battery specific gravity. If it is not at least 1.230, charge the battery or install a charged battery for the test.
2. Make sure all lights and accessories are turned off, including such items as dome lights and radio.

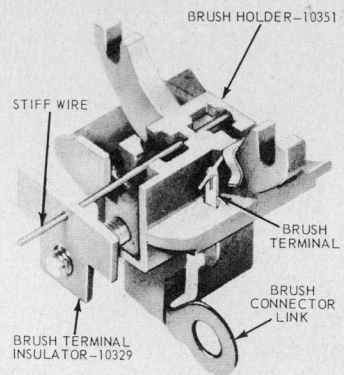

**Brush holder assembly—
integral regulator alternator**
(© Ford Motor Co.)

3. Make the test connections as illustrated.
4. Place transmission in Neutral or Park, close battery adapter switch and start the engine.
5. Open the battery adapter switch and operate engine at 2,000 rpm for 5 minutes. The voltmeter should read 13.3-15.3 volts.
6. If voltage does not rise above 12 volts, perform a regulator supply voltage test to determine whether or not the regulator is getting voltage from the battery. Before replacing a regulator, check the wiring of the entire charging system for shorts, opens, or high resistance connections.

Regulator Supply Voltage Test

The regulator is "turned on" by the application of battery voltage

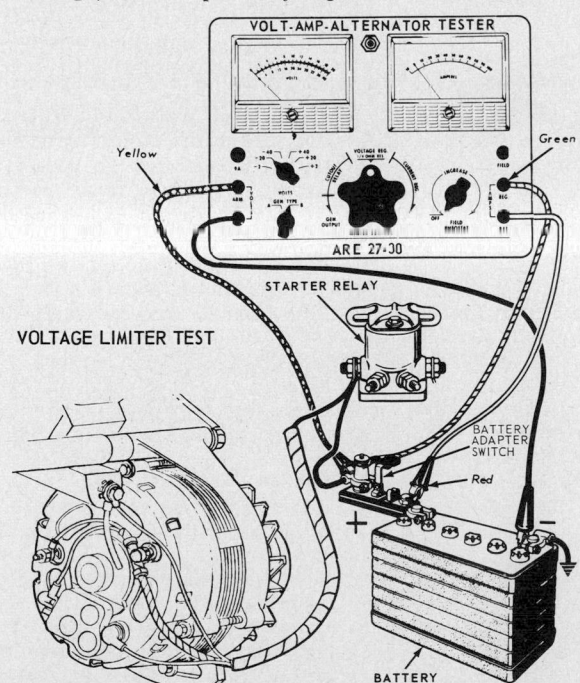

Voltage limiter test hook-up—integral regulator alternator
(© Ford Motor Co.)

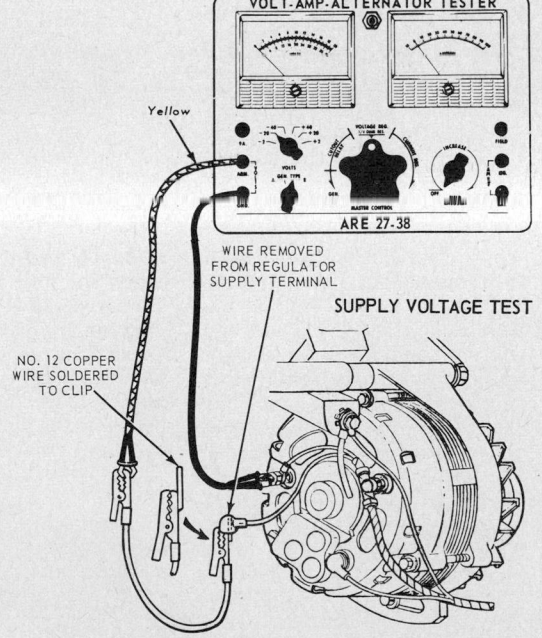

Supply voltage test hook-up—integral regulator alternator
(© Ford Motor Co.)

through a 10 ohm resistor wire. If the supply circuit is defective, the regulator will not function and the alternator will not put out current.

1. Connect a 12-volt test light or voltmeter between the regulator supply lead and ground.
2. Turn ignition switch to ON position. The test light should glow or the voltmeter indicate. If not, the supply circuit should be checked back to the battery, especially the resistance wire.

Regulator R&R

1. Disconnect battery ground cable, loosen alternator bolts, remove V-belt and swing alternator down so that regulator will clear the engine.
2. Remove the terminal cover plugs from the regulator, then remove nuts from alternator studs.
3. Remove regulator from alternator, press on sides of plastic retainer clip and remove voltage supply wire from regulator. Do not pull on wire!
4. To install, first connect voltage supply wire and secure retainer clip.
5. Place regulator in position on alternator and install nuts onto studs. Tighten the nuts to 15-25 in. lbs. for Ground and Field, 10-15 in. lbs. for Battery terminals. *Do not overtighten.*
6. Install terminal cover plugs and reseal brush retracting wire hole.
7. Install belt and adjust, then connect battery cable.

The Motorola System

The Motorola alternator is designed to pass all the DC current through an isolation diode, or diodes, mounted in an external aluminum heat sink. This has three advantages.
  A. It prevents battery discharge through the regulator and alternator without the use of relays or switches.
  B. It renders a way of operating a signal lamp to indicate whether or not the generator is in operation. The signal is connected across the isolation diode. Under normal operating conditions, alternator voltage output is nearly the same as battery voltage. This creates approximately 1 volt across the isolation diode. The voltage value is not enough to cause the signal light to burn, indicating the alternator is in operation.
  C. It connects the alternator and battery to the voltage regulator, automatically, when the alternator begins to operate.

Due to the nature of the alternator,

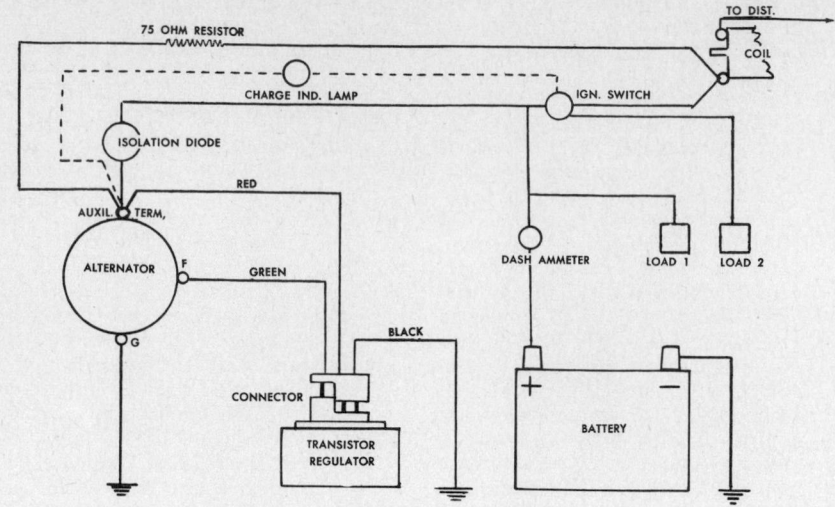

Typical Motorola alternator system charging circuit

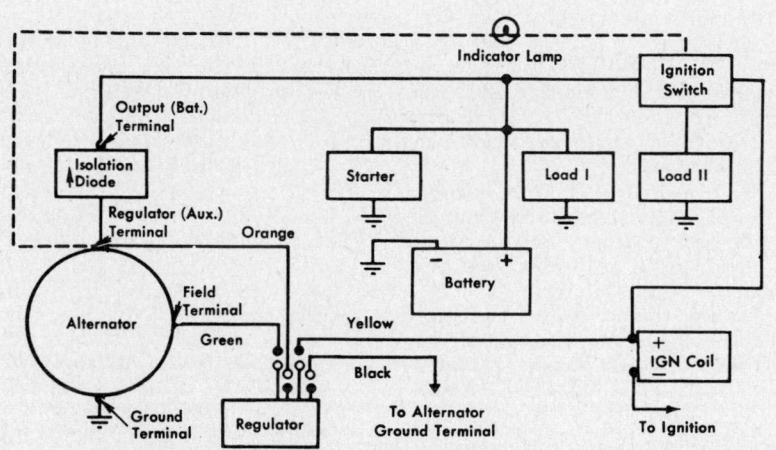

Motorola circuit diagram—1970 American Motors illustrated
(© American Motors Corp.)

Isolation diode—35 amp. models
(© American Motors Corp.)

residual magnetism is at near zero when the unit is at rest. It is, therefore, necessary to provide some small current to excite the field prior to generating current. With Motorola, this priming current is supplied by means of a 75 ohm resistance unit between the ignition coil and the alternator (inside the regulator). It is quite important that this resistance

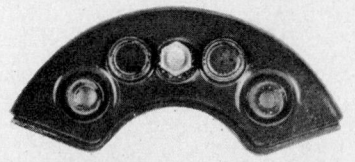

Isolation diodes—55 amp. models
(© American Motors Corp.)

unit be checked and found satisfactory before proceeding with subsequent tests.

The charge indicator light on some cars operates in the same way as this resistor by furnishing the necessary initial field starting current. If this resistor circuit is open (a burned out indicator lamp) on some models, the alternator will not function. On later models, a resistor is placed in parallel with the bulb to provide excitation current if the bulb burns out.

The regulator is a sealed unit and should require no adjustment. It is therefore, recommended that non-functioning regulators be replaced.

Alternator System Test

1. Be sure that the battery is disconnected and the ignition switch is off.
2. Disconnect the wire from the alternator output terminal.
3. Connect the positive lead of a test ammeter to the alternator output terminal and the negative lead of the test ammeter to the wire that was just disconnected

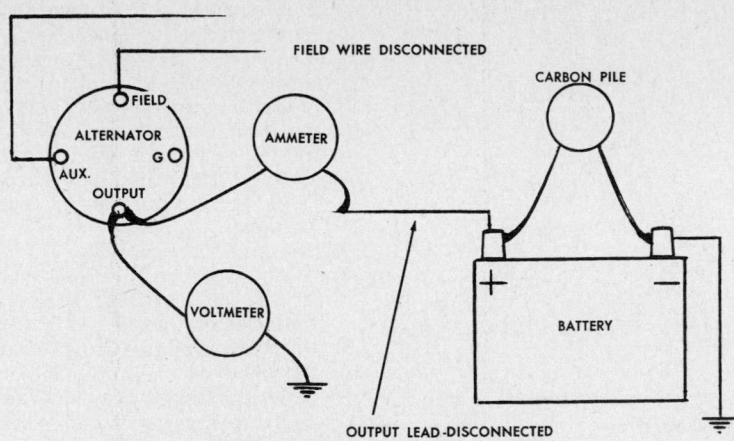

FIELD WIRE DISCONNECTED

OUTPUT LEAD-DISCONNECTED

Plan for making alternator system checks

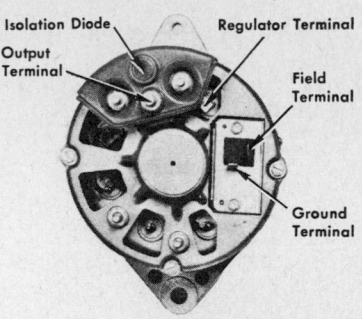

35 amp. alternator—Motorola
(© American Motors Corp.)

from this terminal.

4. Connect the positive lead of a voltmeter to the alternator output terminal and the negative lead of the voltmeter to ground.
5. Reconnect the battery.
6. Connect a carbon pile load control unit (control in off position) to both battery posts.
7. Start engine and run at fast idle for as long as is required to bring it to normal operating temperature.
8. Gradually increase rpm and adjust carbon pile control until current output is reached.
9. Operation is normal if the system develops within 5 amps. of the rated output and voltage registers 14 ± 1 volts.
10. If voltmeter registers over 15 volts, at rated output, replace the regulator.
11. If system is satisfactory at low engine rpm but output is not enough at higher rpm, check for slipping of the drive belt.
12. If current output is low and the output terminal voltage is more than 13 volts, check the isolation diode.
13. If the current output and the output terminal voltage are both low, check the alternator rated output.
14. If current output at specified terminal voltage is produced, check resistance of the charging circuit.

Alternator Output Test

This check is of the alternator only.

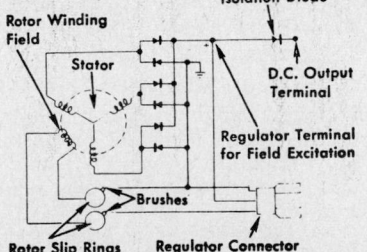

Alternator circuit—35 amp. models
(© American Motors Corp.)

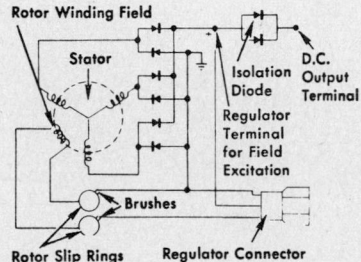

Alternator circuit—40 and 55 amp. models
(© American Motors Corp.)

1. The ammeter, voltmeter and carbon pile test instruments remain connected into the circuit as with the last check.
2. Disconnect the battery, also the wire from the alternator field terminal.
3. With a field rheostat, adjusted to open position, connect its leads to the alternator field terminal and to the alternator output terminal.
4. Reconnect the battery.

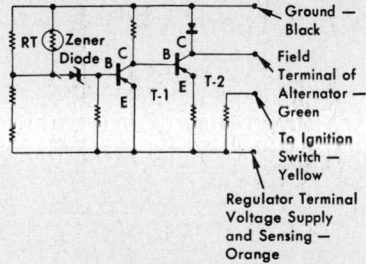

Voltage regulator circuit.
RT is a thermistor that regulates voltage according to temperature.
(© American Motors Corp.)

5. Start and run the engine at 1,750-2,000 rpm.
6. Gradually adjust field rheostat toward the closed position while watching the voltmeter and ammeter (do not exceed 15 volts). Control this voltage with the carbon pile load adjustment. When field rheostat has reached the closed position, note ammeter reading.

7. Adjust field rheostat to the open position and the carbon pile load control off.
8. Compare notes taken in Step 6 with manufacturers' specifications.
9. If readings are low, check drive belt for proper tension.

Field Current Draw Test

1. With battery disconnected, disconnect the wires from the alternator output terminal and the alternator field terminal.
2. With a field rheostat in the

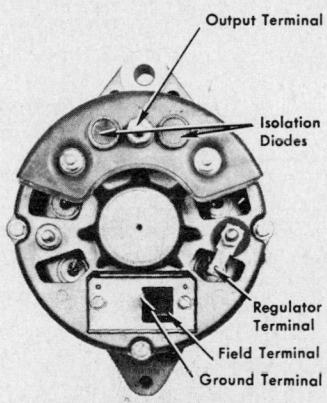

55 amp. alternator—Motorola
(© American Motors Corp.)

open position, connect its leads to the disconnected alternator output wire and to the positive lead of the test ammeter.
3. Connect the negative ammeter lead to the alternator field terminal.
4. Connect the positive voltmeter lead to the alternator field terminal.
5. Connect the negative voltmeter lead to the alternator ground terminal.
6. Reconnect the battery.
7. Start and run the engine at fast idle.
8. Adjust field rheostat to closed position, then note the voltmeter and ammeter readings.
9. Adjust field rheostat control to the open position.
10. Compare the readings obtained in Step 8 with manufacturers'

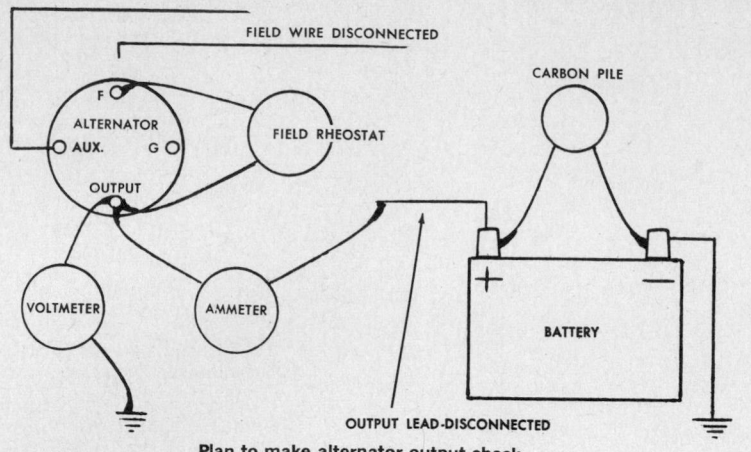

Plan to make alternator output check

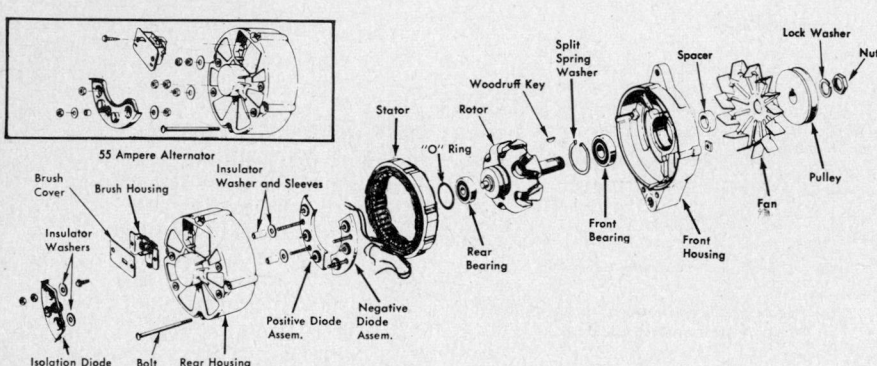

Motorola alternator exploded view (© American Motors Corp.)

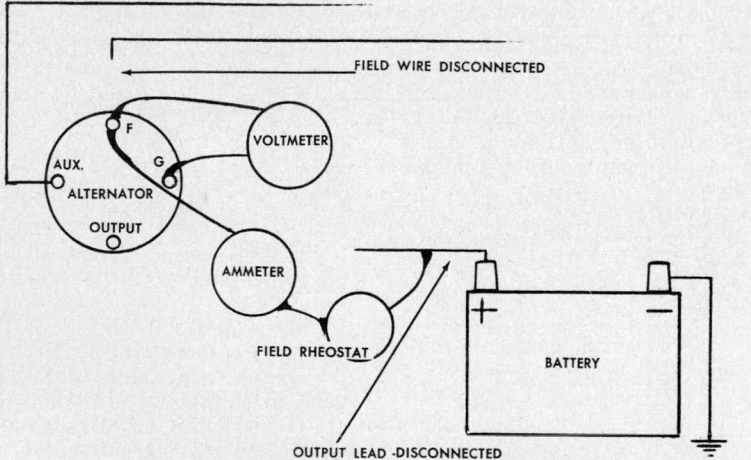

Plan to make field current draw check

specifications.

11. If readings are zero, there is an indication of trouble in the field coil, or the connections between field coil and slip ring.
12. If readings are low, there is probable trouble in the slip rings or brushes.
13. If readings are high, the field coil is probably shorted.
14. If readings are normal, on an alternator which failed to produce its rated output, the probable cause lies in the stator or diodes. Replace the alternator in this case.

Charging Circuit Resistance Test

1. With battery disconnected and the ignition switch off, disconnect the wire from the alternator output terminal.
2. Connect the positive lead of a test ammeter to the alternator output terminal.
3. Connect the negative lead of the ammeter to the wire just discon-

nected from the alternator output terminal.
4. Disconnect the wire from the alternator field terminal.
5. With a field rheostat in open position, connect one of its leads to the alternator field terminal.
6. Connect the other field rheostat lead to the alternator output terminal.
7. Reconnect the battery.
8. With a carbon pile load control in the off position, hook it to both battery posts.
9. Start and set to 1500-1700 rpm.
10. Adjust field rheostat control toward the closed position enough to get a charging rate of 10 amps. Use the carbon pile load control to prevent exceeding 15 volts. Hold at 15 volts.
11. Disconnect voltmeter from the alternator output terminal and the ground.
12. Reconnect voltmeter positive lead to the disconnected alternator output wire.
13. Connect voltmeter negative lead to the battery positive post.
14. Note reading on voltmeter. This is the voltage drop in the hot circuit. It should not exceed 0.3 volt.
15. Disconnect voltmeter from alternator output wire and the battery post.
16. Reconnect voltmeter positive lead to the battery negative post.
17. Connect voltmeter negative lead to the alternator ground terminal.
18. Note voltmeter reading. This is the voltage drop in the ground circuit. This reading should not exceed 0.15 volt.

Bench Tests

Alternator System

1. Mount alternator to be tested according to typical plan. (See illustration.) Alternator must turn clockwise as viewed from pulley end.
2. Connect regulator to alternator and mount regulator solidly on heat sink.
3. Connect ammeter, voltmeter, indicator lamp, battery and carbon pile load.

NOTE: the No. 57X lamp is used to excite field of alternator to develop an output. The resistor wire, or any 75 ohm, 3 watt resistor may be used.

Optional Alternator Test

This test excludes the regulator from the circuit and can be conducted if the regulator is suspected and a known good regulator is not available.

1. Use the same procedure as described in previous paragraph with the exception of the next two steps.

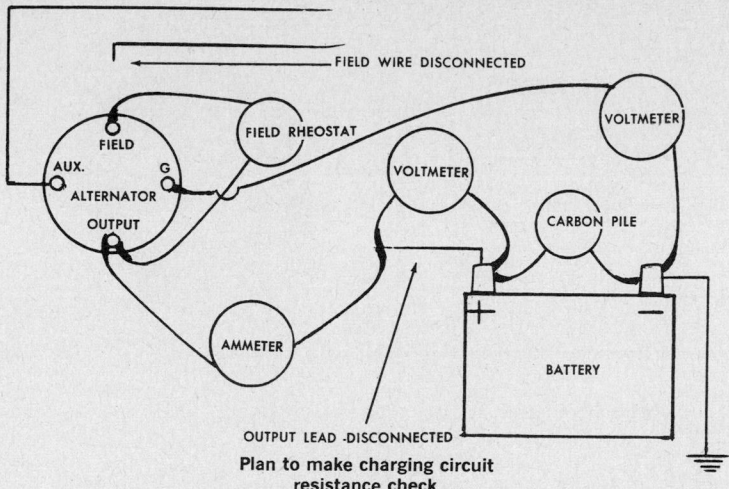

Plan to make charging circuit resistance check

operate the alternator.

2. Measure the voltage from auxiliary terminal F to ground terminal G. The voltage appearing at the auxiliary terminal should not exceed 0.1 volt. Voltage greater than this indicates leakage through the isolation diode. Check the isolation diode with a commercial diode tester, or with a 12-volt DC test lamp.

Alternator Components Test

Rotor (Field Coil) Test

This test checks the condition of the field coil for open or shorted field coil turns, badly worn or sticky brushes and open connections.

1. Construct a field current test circuit. (See illustration).

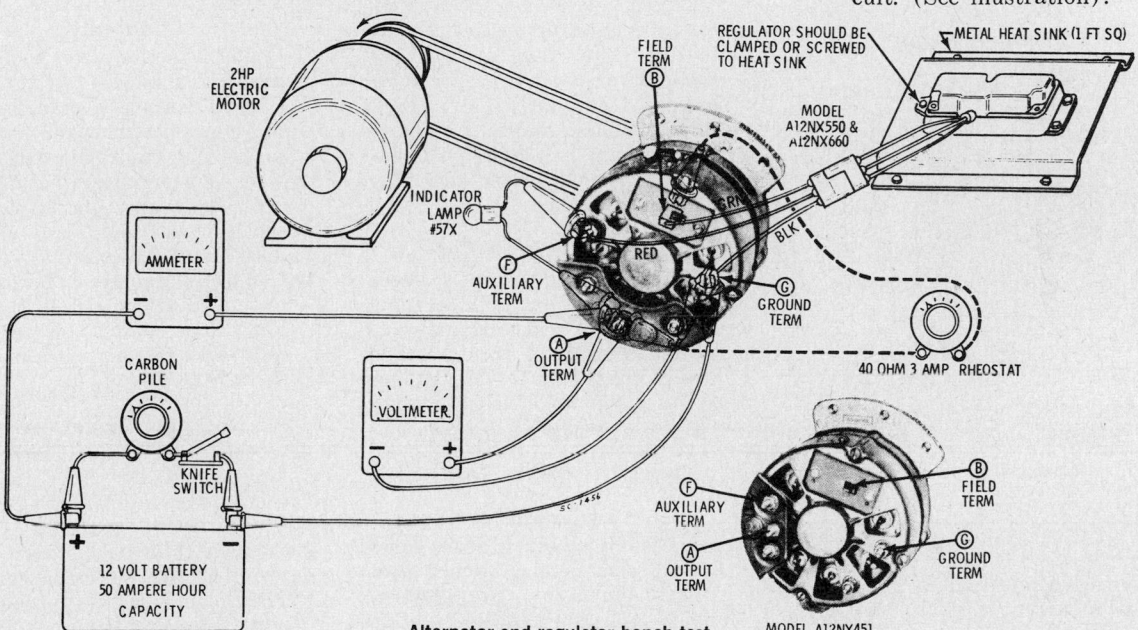

Alternator and regulator bench test

2. Disconnect voltage regulator plug and the field terminal wire.
3. Connect a 40 ohm (3 amp.) rheostat from alternator field terminal to output terminal. Set rheostat to maximum resistance.
4. Start electric drive motor. Increase load with carbon pile and at the same time increase field current by reduction of rheostat resistance.

Caution Do not allow output terminal voltage to exceed 15 volts.

5. Continue to increase the load and decrease rheostat resistance while holding output voltage below 15 volts until rheostat resistance is zero. At this point, maximum field current is being applied.

Alternator is working if the rated output is available. If rated current output is not available, check alternator.

Regulator Test

This test should be made with a

known good alternator and a fully charged battery.

1. Set carbon pile for minimum load (maximum resistance) to prevent discharging the battery when alternator is not running.
2. Start electric drive motor (alternator rpm should be 3000 to 4000).
3. Increase load with carbon pile until a 10 amp. output is reached. Allow a 15 minute temperature stabilization period. Regulator is working properly if the voltage at output terminal is according to specifications and the alternator is supplying a 10 amp. load.

Isolation Diode Circuit Test

Excessive leakage through the isolation diode will discharge the battery. The rate of discharge depends upon the degree of leakage. Normal and tolerable leakage is less than .001 amperes.

1. To check isolation diode leakage, connect the regulator to the battery. (See illustration.) Do not

2. Connect test circuit to field terminal and ground terminal (test point B and G).

NOTE: set rheostat to maximum resistance (40 ohms) before making connections.

3. Slowly reduce resistance of rheostat to zero. With full battery voltage applied to field coil (battery must be fully charged), the field current should be 1.2 to 1.7 amps. Turn rotor by hand while taking reading to indicate value of brush contact. However, a slight fluctuation of current (.2 amps.) is normal.

4. If current is not within limits, inspect brushes and slip rings for dirt, bad brushes and connections. Check brush assemblies for shorts and continuity.

Reinstall repaired or known good brush assembly and repeat the test. If field current is above the maximum value, it indicates that the field coil is shorted or rotor-to-field coil has shorted

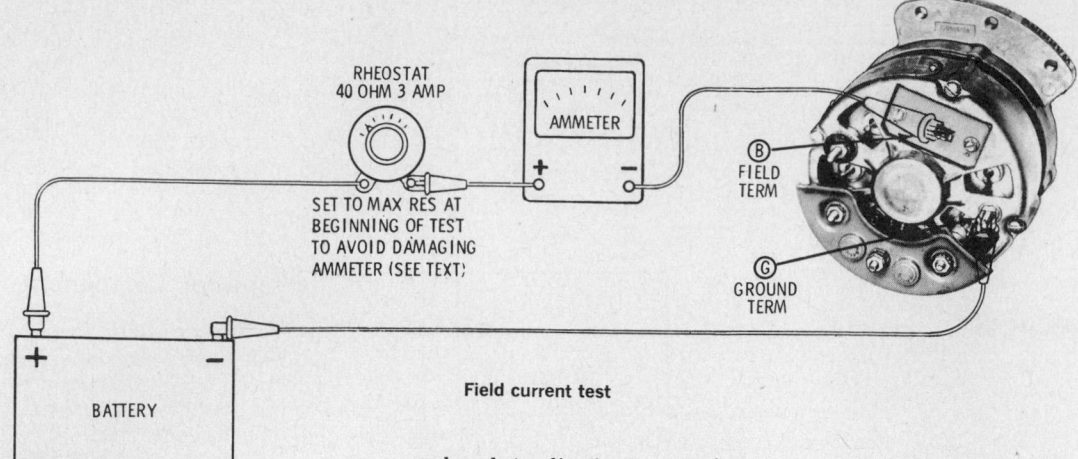

Field current test

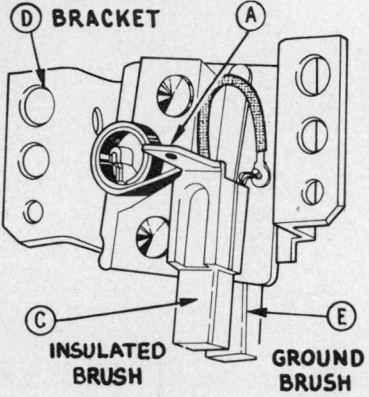

Brush test points

turns.

If field current is zero, it indicates that the field coil or coil-to-slip ring connection is open. If the field current is much less than the value specified, it indicates a poor coil-to-slip ring connection or poor brush-to-slip ring connection. Repeat field current test on rotor by connecting the test circuit to rotor slip rings to ascertain findings after rotor has been removed from alternator. Field current will be about 0.2 amperes higher than the maximum value, due to normal brush slip ring contact resistance.

Rotor Open Circuit Test

An ohmmeter may be used to check continuity of the rotor. Connect ohmmeter probes to field terminal and ground terminal (test points B and G. See illustration). Resistance should be about 6 ohms. If resistance is high, field coil is open.

Brush Assembly Test

Insulation

1. Connect ohmmeter or a test lamp to field terminal and bracket (test points A and D). (See illustration.) Resistance should be high, or the test lamp should not light. If results are contrary, brush as-sembly is shorted.

Continuity

2. Connect an ohmmeter to field terminal and brush (points A and C). Resistance should be zero. Move brush and brush lead wire to make sure that the brush lead wire connections are not intermittent. Resistance should not vary when brush and lead wire are being moved around.

3. Connect ohmmeter to bracket and grounded brush, points E and D. Resistance should be zero. Repeat same test on brush lead wire as in Step 2.

Isolation Diode Test

If a commercial diode tester is not available, use a 12-volt DC test lamp only, otherwise diodes can be damaged.

1. Connect the test lamp to output terminal and auxiliary terminal. Then reverse the test probes. Test lamp should light in one direction only. If test light lights in both directions, the isolation diode is shorted. If lamp won't light in either direction, the diode is open.

In-Circuit Rectifier Diode Test

Any commercial in-circuit diode tester will suffice to make the check.

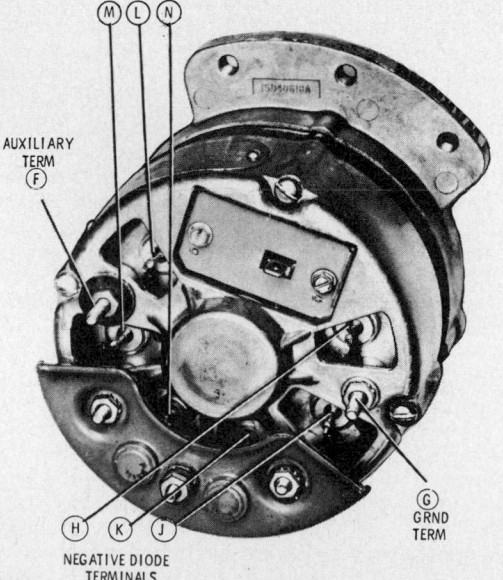

In-circuit diode test points

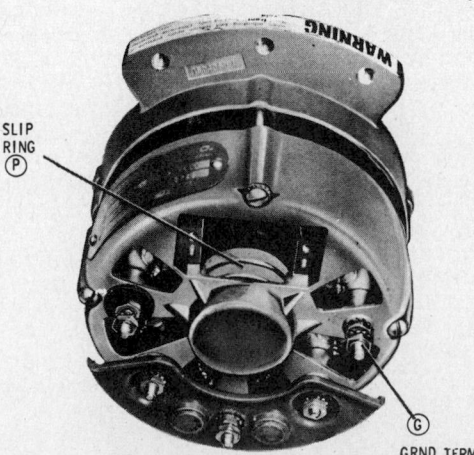

Rotor leakage test points

If the test indicates the diodes to be bad, recheck diodes individually after the diode assemblies have been disconnected from the stator assembly. Shorted stator coil or shorted insulating washers or sleeves on positive diode assembly would make diodes appear to be shorted.

1. To check negative diode assembly, connect tester to test points G and H. (See illustration.) Then, successively check between test points G and J and G and K.
2. To check positive diode assembly, connect tester to test points F and L. Then successively check between test points F and M and F and N.

Rectifier Diode Test, With Lamp

When an in-circuit diode tester is not available, a 12-volt DC test lamp may be used to indicate a shorted diode. The lamp, however, will not show an open condition unless all three diodes of either assembly are open.

1. Connect test light probes to points G and H, then reverse test probes. The lamp should light in one direction but not in the other. If the test lamp lights in both directions, one or more of the rectifier diodes is shorted. If the test lamp does not light in either direction, all three diodes in the assembly are open. Recheck diodes individually after disassembly to pinpoint results.
NOTE: a shorted stator coil to core would appear as a shorted negative rectifier diode assembly. Also check stator for shorts after disassembly.
2. To check positive diode assembly, connect test probes to points F and L. Then reverse test probes. The same procedure and results apply as in Step 1.

Rotor Leakage Test

This is a check of the field coil for leakage or shorts to rotor poles. An ohmmeter or test lamp (12V or 120V)

may be used.

1. Remove the brush assembly to gain access to rotor slip rings.
2. Connect ohmmeter or test lamp probes to one of the slip rings and the ground terminal, points G and P. (See illustration.)
Ohmmeter resistance should be infinite or test lamp should not light. If condition is contrary, leakage or a short exists between field coil and rotor.
Repeat test after rotor has been removed from the alternator to pinpoint findings.

In-Circuit Stator Leak Test

When making this test, consideration must be given to the rectifier diodes that are connected to the stator winding. The negative diode assembly will conduct in one direction when properly polarized. A shorted diode in the negative rectifier-diode assembly will make the stator appear to be shorted. Therefore, the rectifier-diode plate assembly and stator must be checked individually after the alternator has been disassembled if the problem has been narrowed down to the stator.

1. Connect a 12-volt DC test lamp to a diode terminal of the negative diode assembly and ground terminal, points G and H. (See illustration.)
2. Reverse test probes. The test lamp should light in one direction but not in the other direction. If lamp does not light in either direction, it indicates that all three rectifiers in the negative diode assembly are open. If the lamp lights in both directions, the stator winding is shorted to stator or one of the negative rectifier diodes is shorted.

Out-of-Circuit Stator Leak Test

Disassemble alternator and remove the rectifier-diode plates and stator as an assembly. (See illustration.)
An ohmmeter or 12-volt DC test lamp may be used.

1. Connect ohmmeter or test lamp probes to one of the rectifier diode terminals and to the stator test points N and Q.
Resistance reading should be infinite (or the test light should not light). If result is contrary, high leakage or a short exists between stator winding and stator. In either case, stator should be replaced.

Stator Coil Leak and Continuity Test

This check is for shorts or leakage between stator coil windings. The 30 and 40 amp. alternators use a Wye-Type winding. (See illustration.) 45 ampere models use a Delta type winding. (See illustration.)

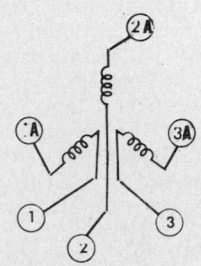

Wye-type stator winding

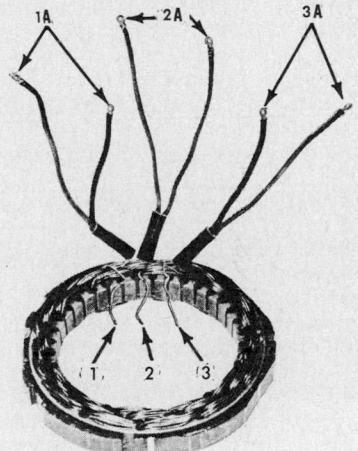

Stator coil test points (Wye-type)

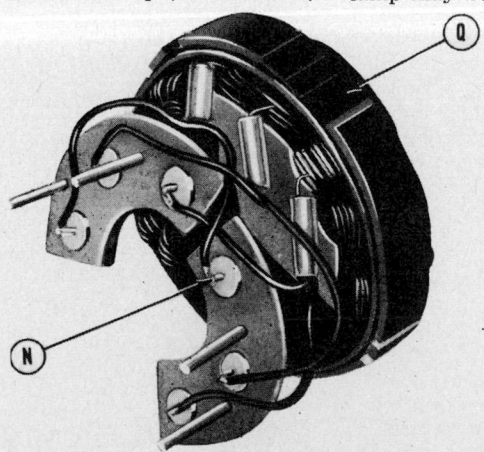

Stator leakage test points

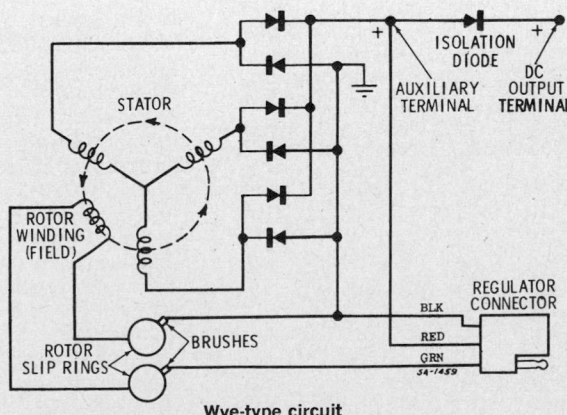

Wye-type circuit

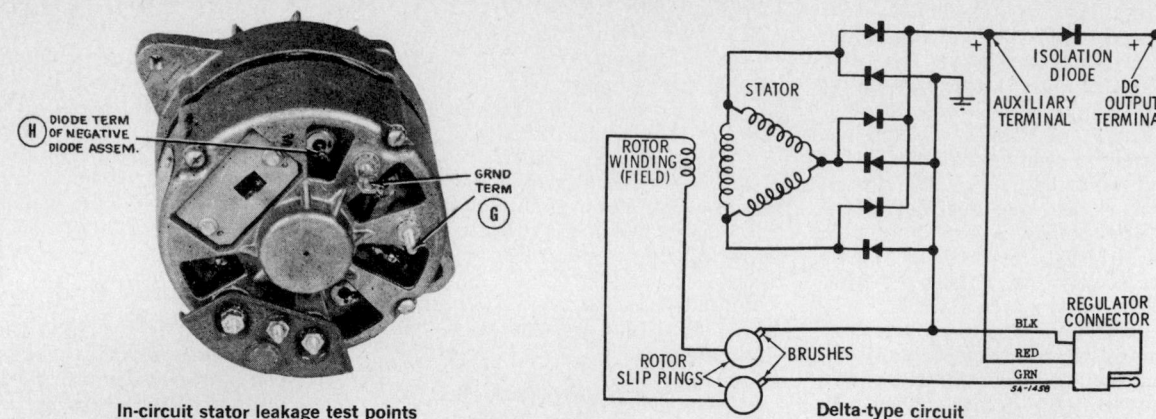

In-circuit stator leakage test points

Delta-type circuit

Wye Type (30 and 40 Amp. Models)

1. Separate winding ends (See illustration.) An ohmmeter or 12-volt DC test lamp may be used.
2. Connect one lead of the ohmmeter or test lamp to point 1. Connect the other test lead to point 2 and then to point 3. Ohmmeter reading should be infinite or the test lamp should not light.
3. Connect test leads to points 2 and 3. Ohmmeter reading should be infinite, or the test lamp should not light.

In test 2 or test 3, if the test results are contrary, excess leakage or a short exists between stator windings; replace the stator.

4. Check continuity by measuring the resistance of each winding in the stator with an ohmmeter, between test points (See illustration.), 1 to 1A, 2 to 2A and 3 to 3A. Resistance should be very low (about 0.1 ohm).

Never replace stator until all other components have been checked and proven satisfactory.

Delta Type (45 Amp. Models)

1. Separate stator winding ends. (See illustration.) An ohmmeter or 12-volt DC test lamp may be used.
2. Connect one lead of the ohmmeter or test lamp to point 4. Connect the other test lead to point 5 and then to point 6. Ohmmeter reading should be infinite or the test lamp should not light.
3. Connect test leads to test points 5 and 6. Ohmmeter reading

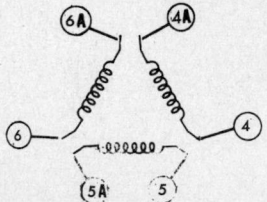

Delta-type stator winding

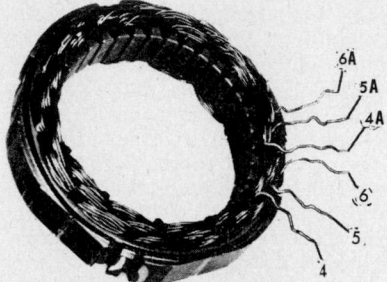

Stator coil test points (Delta-type)

should be infinite, or the test lamp should not light.

In test 2 or test 3, if the test results are contrary, excess leakage or a short exists between stator windings; replace the stator.

4. Check continuity by measuring the resistance of each winding in the stator with an ohmmeter placed between test points 4 to 4A, 5 to 5A and 6 to 6A. (See illustration.) Resistance should be very low (about 0.1 ohm).

Never replace stator until all other components have been checked and proven satisfactory.

Voltage Regulator Test

If previous checks did not prove the regulator bad, but some question still exists as to reliability, the system can be checked while installed and operating in the car. A volt-ampere tester can be used. The system should be first tested by taking a reading of output current and the voltage at the output terminal. With a carbon pile rheostat connected across the output terminal or battery, rated current of the alternator should be available with at least 13 volts.

If this is not obtainable, shut down the engine and disconnect the regulator from the system. Insert a variable resistance in series between the output terminal and the field terminal of the alternator. Start the engine, with maximum resistance in the circuit. Then slowly decrease field resistance while increasing the load on the output of the alternator.

Caution Observe voltage at output terminal and be sure to decrease the field resistance and increase the output load without exceeding 15 volts at the output terminal.

Continue to decrease field resistance and increase output load until there is no resistance in the field circuit. If rated current output is now obtained with 13 volts at the output terminal, the voltage regulator is bad. If rated current is not available under these conditions, the alternator is bad and must be removed for repairs or replacement.

Out-of-Circuit Rectifier Diode Test

If a commercial diode tester is not available, check the diodes with a 12-volt DC test lamp only.

Caution When unsoldering the stator wires from the rectifier diode assembly, provide a heat sink to the diode terminal with a pair of longnosed pliers.

1. Connect test lamp probes to diode terminal and diode plate stud (see illustration), then reverse test lamp probes. The test light should light in one direction but not in the other.

If the test lamp lights in both

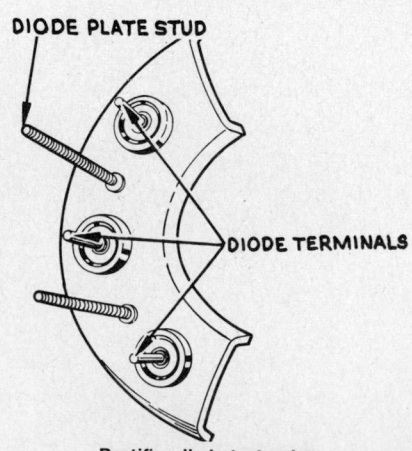

Rectifier diode test points (positive or negative)

directions, the diode is shorted. If test lamp does not light in either direction, the diode is open.

Test the remaining diodes of the assembly in the same manner. Replace entire assembly if one of the diodes is found to be bad.

Alternator Disassembly

1. Remove the two self-tapping screws and cover. Pull the brush assembly straight up to clear the locating pins, then lift out the brush assembly.
2. Remove the two locknuts and remove the isolation diode assembly from the rear housing.
3. Scribe a matchmark across the front housing, stator, and rear housing. Remove the four through bolts and nuts, then carefully separate the rear housing and stator from the front housing using two screwdrivers in the slots provided.

Caution Do not insert screwdrivers deeper than 1/16 in. to avoid damaging stator winding.

4. Remove the four locknuts and insulating washers that hold the stator and diode assembly, then separate the assembly from the rear housing. Avoid bending the stator wires—do not unsolder the wires without using pliers as a heat sink.
5. There is no reason to remove the rotor from the front housing unless there is a defect n the field coil or front bearing. Front and rear bearings are lubricated for life and sealed and, as a rule, do not go bad unless the drive belt has been adjusted with too much tension. If the rotor must be removed, first use a puller to remove the front drive pulley, then unseat the split-ring

Separating Motorola alternator housings
(© American Motors Corp.)

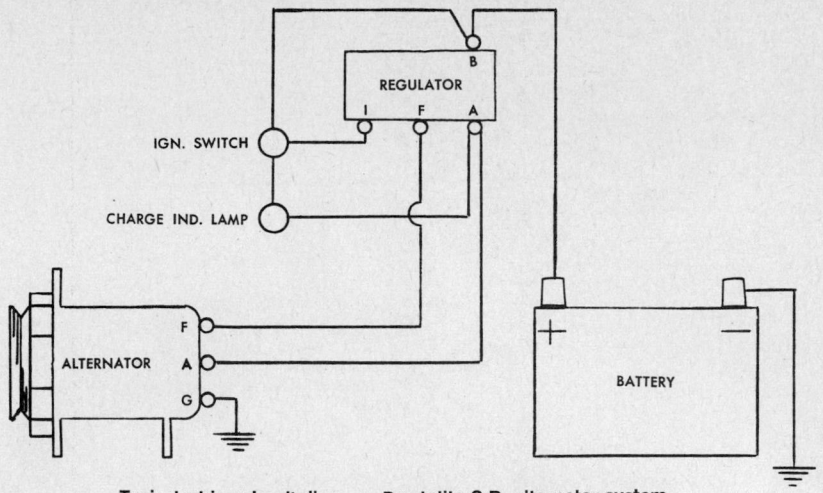

Typical wiring circuit diagram, Prestolite C.B. alternator system

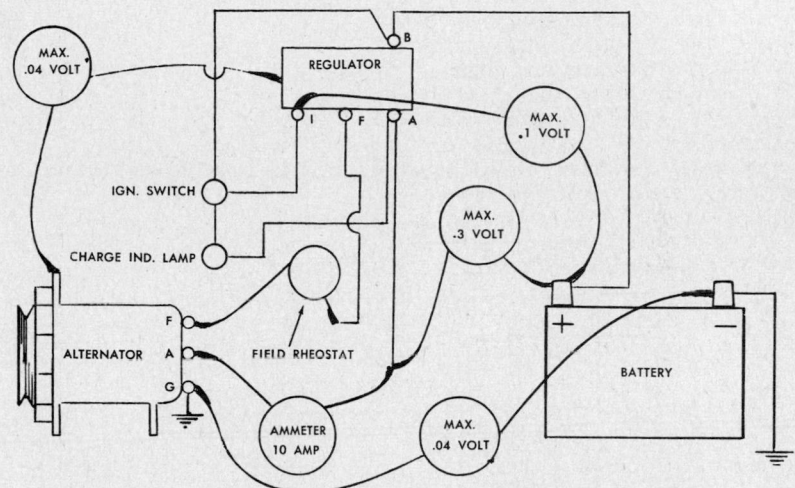

Plan to make charging circuit resistance check—C.B. type

washer using long nose pliers through the front housing to compress the washer while pulling on the rotor. Tap the rotor shaft lightly to remove the rotor and front bearing, then reach in and remove the split-ring washer. Bearings must be removed using a puller and new bearings must be pressed into place.

Alternator Assembly

1. Clean the bearing and the inside of the bearing hub in the front housing, then gently seat the bearing using a socket of appropriate size and a small hammer.
2. Insert the split-ring washer into the hub of the front housing and seat the washer in its groove. Be extremely careful doing this, because the bearing seal is easily damaged.
3. The front bearing now must be seated against the shoulder on the rotor shaft. This job is normally accomplished using a spe-

cial tool (AM J-21156), but a little ingenuity and care will allow use of substitute tools. Install the fan and pulley spacer, then the Woodruff key, fan and pulley. Using a 7/16 in. socket or equivalent tool to fit inside the rear bearing race, apply pressure to drive the bearing against the shoulder of the rotor shaft.
4. Assemble the front and rear housing assemblies by hand, making certain that the rear bearing is properly seated in the rear housing hub and that the diode wires are not touching the rotor at any point.
5. Align the matchmarks made during disassembly, then spin the rotor to make sure sufficient clearance exists between it and the diode wires. Install the through bolts and tighten them evenly, using only a hand wrench. Continue assembly in reverse of disassembly.

The Prestolite System

The Prestolite AC generator reg-

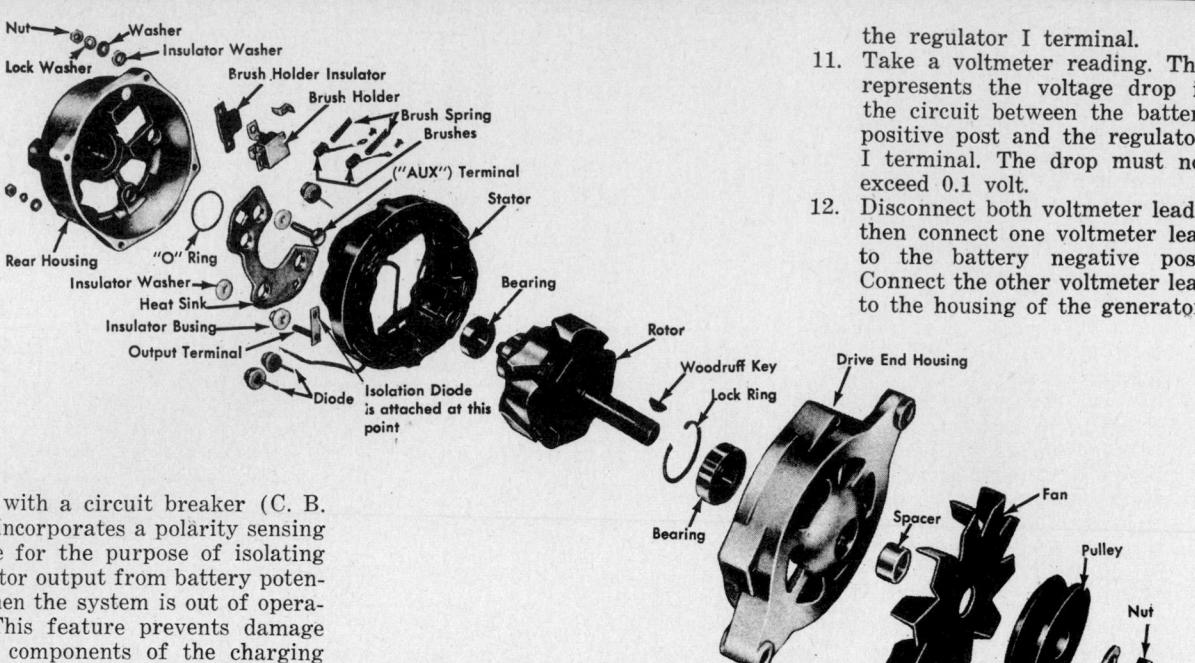

Diode type Prestolite alternator (© American Motors Corp.)

ulator with a circuit breaker (C. B. type) incorporates a polarity sensing feature for the purpose of isolating generator output from battery potential when the system is out of operation. This feature prevents damage to the components of the charging system in the event of battery polarity reversal.

Late model Prestolite alternators incorporate an *isolation diode,*

the regulator I terminal.

11. Take a voltmeter reading. This represents the voltage drop in the circuit between the battery positive post and the regulator, I terminal. The drop must not exceed 0.1 volt.

12. Disconnect both voltmeter leads, then connect one voltmeter lead to the battery negative post. Connect the other voltmeter lead to the housing of the generator.

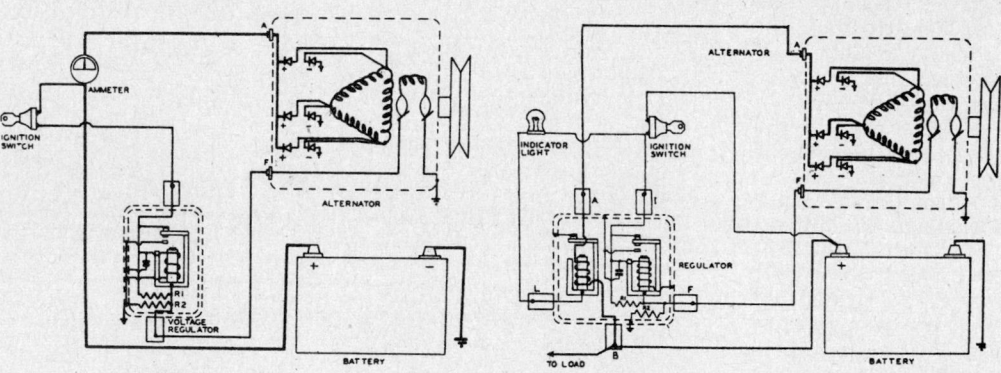

Single and two-unit Prestolite C.B. circuits

Circuit Resistance Test— C. B. Type

1. With the battery ground cable disconnected at the battery, and the lead disconnected from the generator output A terminal, hook up an ammeter as follows:
   A. Connect an ammeter, positive lead to the generator output A terminal.
   B. Connect the ammeter negative lead to the lead that was just removed from the generator A terminal.
2. Disconnect the lead from the generator, field F terminal.
3. With a field rheostat control turned to open position, connect

one lead of this rheostat to the generator F terminal and the other lead to the lead which was just disconnected from this F terminal.
4. Hook up an engine tachometer.
5. Connect battery ground cable.
6. Start engine and set speed to 850 rpm.
7. Adjust field rheostat toward closed position enough to effect a 10 amp. charging rate.
8. Connect a voltmeter to the battery positive post and to the lead which was disconnected from the generator output A terminal.
9. Take a voltmeter reading. This represents the voltage drop in the circuit between the battery positive post and the regulator A terminal. The drop must not exceed 0.3 volt.
10. Disconnect the voltmeter lead from the regulator A lead, then connect this voltmeter lead to

13. Take a voltmeter reading. This represents voltage drop in the ground circuit between the battery negative post and the generator. The drop must not exceed 0.04 volt.
14. Disconnect the voltmeter lead from the battery negative post

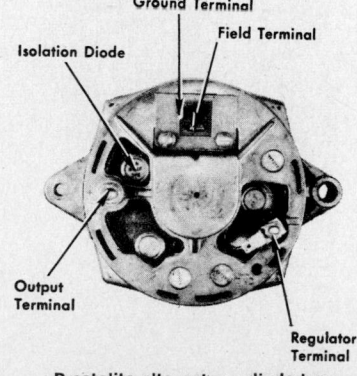

Prestolite alternator—diode type
(© American Motors Corp.)

and connect this same voltmeter lead to a good ground on the regulator.

15. Take a voltmeter reading. This represents voltage drop in the ground circuit between generator and regulator. The drop must not exceed 0.04 volt.

16. Turn field rheostat control to open position, then stop the engine.

Alternator Output Test— C. B. Type

With the battery ground cable disconnected at the battery, and the ignition switch in off position, proceed as follows:

1. Disconnect the leads from regulator terminals A, F and B. Then connect the leads all together and temporarily insulate them.

2. Hook up a voltmeter to the generator output A terminal and the generator frame.

3. Connect an ammeter between the generator output A terminal and spliced connection of the leads removed from the regulator A, F and B terminals.

4. Reconnect the battery ground cable.

5. With a carbon pile adjusted to the open position, connect it to both battery posts. Then start the engine and adjust the speed to 1750 rpm.

6. With a field rheostat connected to the generator F terminal and spliced connection of the leads removed from the regulator A, F and B terminals, adjust the rheostat toward closed position.

7. Hold a voltage of 14.2 with the carbon pile load control.

8. When the field rheostat control is all the way closed, the ammeter reading should agree with manufacturers' specifications, with a tolerance of ± 2 amps.

9. If the generator output has checked out as good, proceed to the voltage regulator check.

10. If the generator output is not OK, make a field current draw check.

11. Adjust field rheostat to open, turn carbon pile to off position, then stop the engine.

12. Disconnect the battery ground cable at the battery.

13. Break the splice, then reconnect all of the leads to their original locations on the regulator and generator.

14. Disconnect the test instruments.

Field Current Draw Test— C. B. Type

1. Disconnect the generator F terminal and insulate the lead to prevent accidental grounding.

2. Connect an ammeter and a field

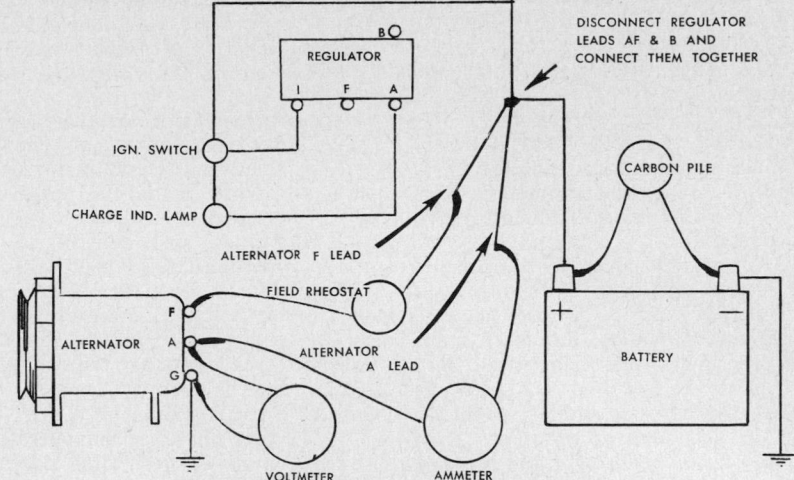

Plan to make alternator output test—C.B. type

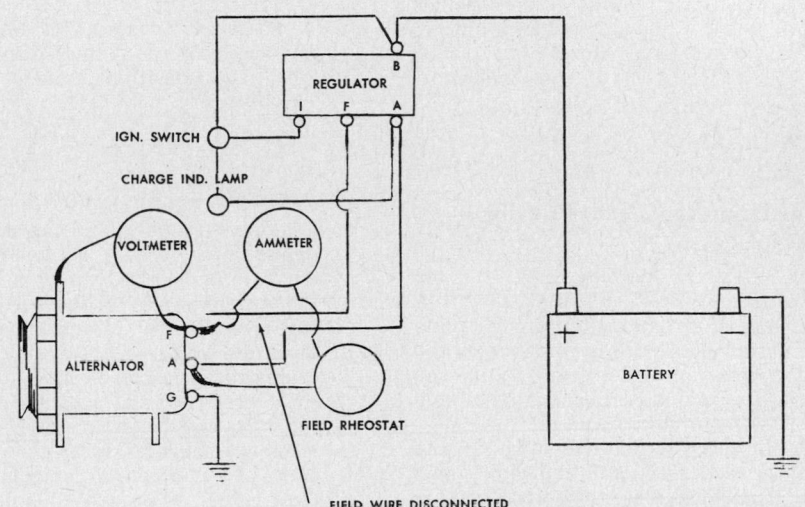

Plan to make field current draw test—C.B. type

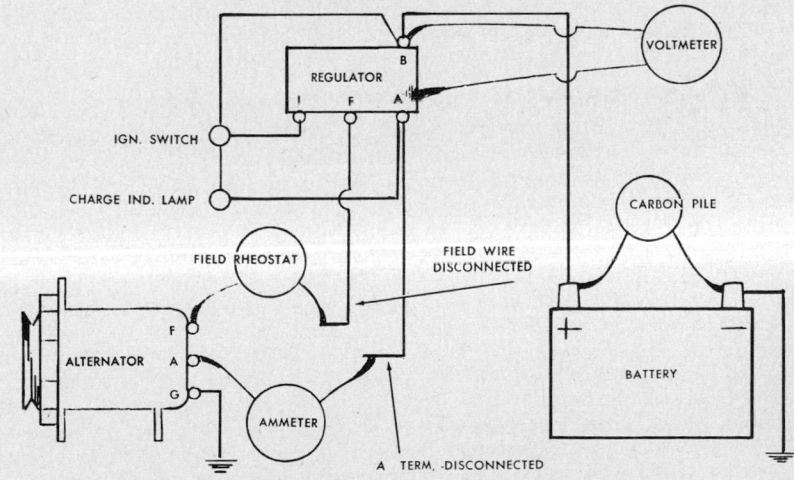

Plan to make voltage regular check—C.B. type

rheostat in series, between the generator F terminal and the generator A terminal in the following manner:

A. With a field rheostat set in the open position, connect one of its leads to the gener-

ator A terminal and the other lead to the test ammeter.

B. Connect the other test ammeter lead to the generator F terminal.

3. Hook up a voltmeter by connecting one voltmeter lead to the

generator F terminal and the other lead to the generator frame.

4. Reconnect the battery ground cable.
5. Turn ignition switch on.
6. Adjust the field rheostat to obtain recommended voltage.
7. Now, read the ammeter. This represents the rotor field current draw.
8. Adjust field rheostat to open position, and turn ignition switch off.
9. Compare the reading with manufacturers' specifications.
   A. If the reading is too low, it indicates trouble, probably slip rings or brushes.
   B. If the reading is too high, it indicates a short in the field winding.
   C. If the reading is as specified on a generator which did not deliver its rated output, look for trouble in the diodes.

Voltage Regulator Setting—C. B. Type

1. With the battery ground cable disconnected at the battery and the ignition switch in off position, hook up an ammeter to the generator A terminal and to the lead just disconnected from this A terminal.
2. Connect a field rheostat to the generator F terminal and to the lead just disconnected from this F terminal. Adjust rheostat to open position.
3. Connect a voltmeter to the regulator B terminal and a good ground on the frame of the regulator.
4. Connect the battery ground cable.
5. Hook up a carbon pile (load control turned to the off position) between the battery posts.
6. Start the engine and while operating at 850 rpm, adjust the field rheostat to obtain a 10 amp. charge. Be careful not to exceed factory voltage recommendation. Run engine long enough to develop normal regulator operating temperature.
7. Open, then fully close the field rheostat to cycle the system.
8. Adjust the carbon pile load to obtain a 10 amp. generator output while reading the voltmeter. This reading is on the upper contacts.
9. Turn carbon pile to off position and increase engine rpm to 1750, then read the voltmeter. This voltage should increase and the amperage decrease if the regulator lower point set is working.

This is known as spread.

10. If the battery is in fully charged condition, the spread may be checked in the following manner.
    A. Adjust load control to produce 15 amps. of charge, then read the voltmeter. This reading is on the upper set of points.
    B. Adjust load control to off position, wait about one-half minute, then read the voltmeter. This reading is on the lower set of points. The difference between the two readings is spread.
    C. Spread should be 0.2 to 0.5 volts higher when operating on lower grounding contact. Operation on lower contacts must not exceed 14.7 volts. If necessary, adjust regulator so as not to exceed 14.7 volts.
11. If regulator does not operate within specifications, renew the regulator.

Disassembly—C.B. Type

1. Remove thru bolts and tap ends lightly with plastic hammer to separate ends from rotor.
2. Remove nuts and washers from negative rectifier brackets, and the nuts, washers and insulator bushings from the positive rectifier brackets, and separate the slip ring end head.
3. Remove insulated brush, gripping brass terminal on brush head with pliers and pulling from field terminal insulator.
4. Remove screw that attaches ground brush. Do not lose brush springs.
5. To remove pulley nut, grip pulley with fan belt and vise to hold while breaking nut loose. Then remove pulley with suitable puller.
6. To remove drive end head, remove key, fan and spacer. Then, using suitable puller remove head.
7. Remove retaining plate and press out drive end head bearing.
8. The slip end head bearing can be removed with a puller.
9. The rectifiers can now be pressed out and in. In cutting and crimping leads keep as close to the sleeve as possible.

Alternator Disassembly—Diode Type

1. Remove the two brush mounting screws and cover, then tip the brush assembly away from the

alternator and remove.

2. Matchmark the rear housing, stator and drive end housing, then remove the four retaining screws. The stator and rear housing are removed as a unit by tapping lightly with a fiber hammer to separate them from the front housing.
3. The rotor should not be removed unless it or the front bearing is defective. To remove the rotor under these conditions, first remove the pulley nut and pulley (using a two-jaw puller), then remove the fan, Woodruff key and spacer. The rotor is removed from the front housing using a three-jaw puller. (Such a puller is made by Snap-On Tool Corp. — part No. CG 253).
4. The front bearing is easily removed, after taking out the retaining ring, by pressing it out in a large vise using sockets to support the housing from the rear.

Stator Coil Test—Diode Type

1. Using a No. 57 bulb, connected in series with a 12-volt battery, as a test light, touch one test lead to the connection of the three stator windings and the other test lead to each stator lead that is connected to the diodes. If the bulb does not light, the winding is open.
2. To test for a grounded stator, use a 110-volt test lamp. First disconnect the diodes from the stator leads, then touch one test lead to the stator core and the other test lead to each of the three stator leads. If the test lamp lights, the winding is grounded.

Removing rotor from front end housing—Prestolite
(© American Motors Corp.)

NOTE: if all other components are O.K. and alternator still does not work, it can be assumed that the stator windings are internally shorted. This type of short is impossible to detect by using the previous test. Diode tests are the same as for the Motorola alternator.

Alternator Assembly— Diode Type

1. Press the front bearing into the front housing, making sure the dust seal faces the rotor. Install the bearing retaining snap-ring, then press the shoulder of the shaft against the inner bearing race using a tool that fits over the shaft and against the race. Install the spacer, Woodruff key, fan and pulley, then install lockwasher and pulley nut.

2. Install the diode heat sink, negative diodes and stator. Solder any stator to diode connections that were unsoldered, using pliers as a heat sink to prevent overheating.

3. Install the rotor and front drive housing to stator and rear housing, aligning matchmarks made during disassembly. Install the four retaining screws, then the brush holder assembly and retaining screws.

4. Make sure the stator leads and brush holder assembly clear the rotor and that the rotor can be spun by hand without binding.

Electronic Ignition Systems

Introduction

In the conventional ignition system, current flows through the coil primary winding to create a magnetic field when the distributor points close. When the points open, the magnetic field collapses rapidly to induce high voltage in the coil secondary windings, which reaches the capacity associated with the high voltage circuit and fires the spark plugs. The amount of energy stored in the magnetic field of the coil during the time the points are closed, determines the output voltage of the coil secondary. The amount of energy stored depends on the primary current value at point break and the inductance of the primary winding. This relationship is expressed as $E = \frac{1}{2} Li^2$, where E is the energy in joules, L is the induct-

ance (in henries) and i is the current (in amps.). Thus, in order to increase the voltage output of the coil, the primary inductance and the current also must be increased. Two factors complicate this, however—contact point erosion and time (Helmholtz Law).

Conventional contact points can carry only about 5.0 amps. before their life is reduced due to arcing and metal transfer. The time factor comes into play at higher engine speeds. Although point dwell in degrees of rotation can be assumed constant at all engine speeds, dwell time in seconds becomes shorter as the rotational speed increases, thus reducing the primary current at point break in proportion. Also, the higher the inductance, the greater the current decrease with speed. By the above formula, it can be seen that the current

value has more effect on the energy stored (because it is squared) than does the inductance. It is more important, then, to have a low inductance and a high break current rather than the reverse. The current limitation of conventional points (5.0 amps.) imposes a restriction to the stored energy value, however, unless a different method of switching the primary current is used. Semiconductors (transistors, diodes) provide such a method, and it is for this basic reason that transistor ignition systems have been developed to meet the needs of high-performance engines. Previous methods used, such as increasing inductance by switching to a 12-volt system and increasing circuit resistance; and increasing dwell time by use of dual points, were made obsolete with the development of economi-

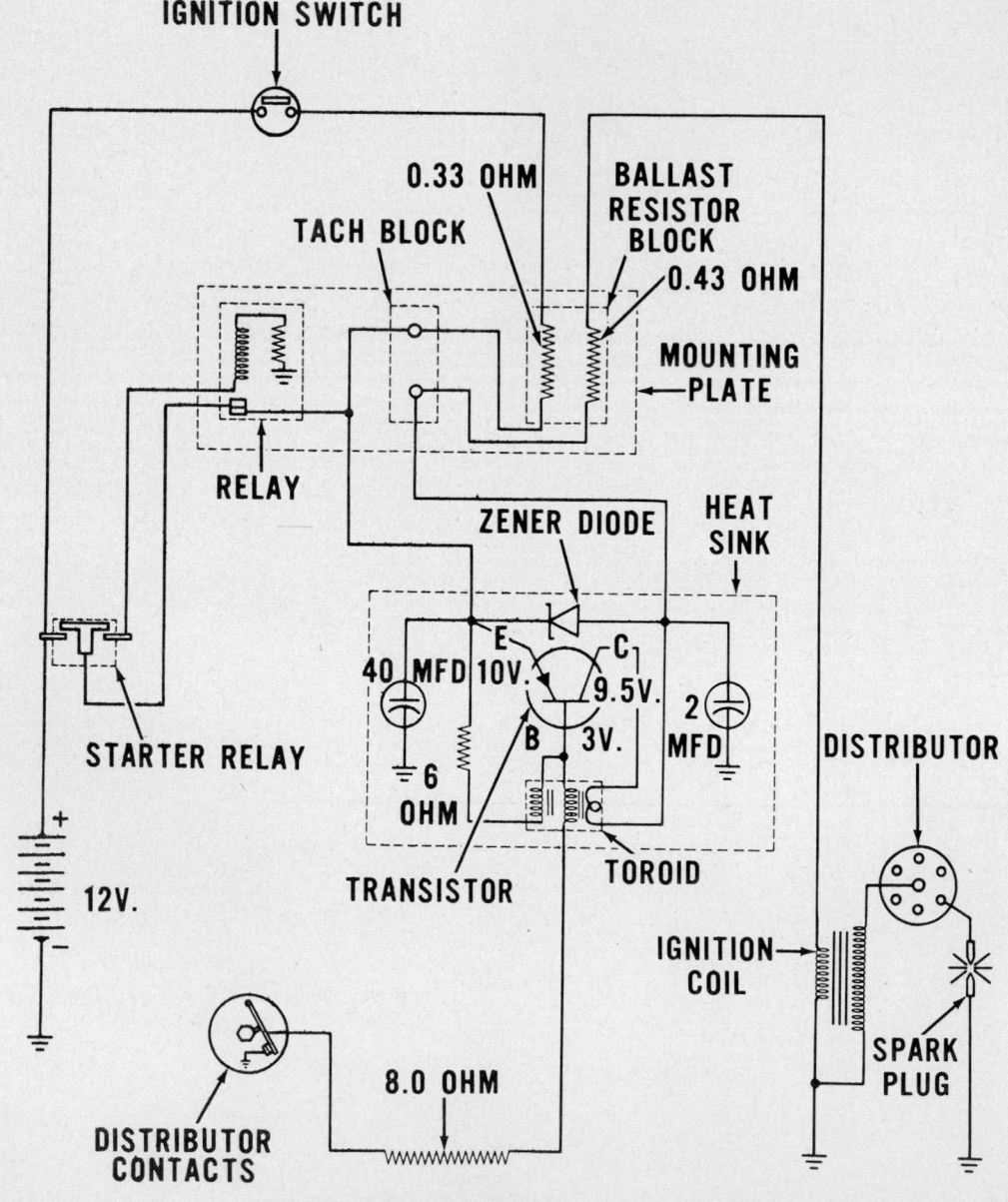

Ford-Autolite transistor ignition schematic (© Ford Motor Co.)

cal semiconductor devices.

Basically, there are two types of transistorized ignition systems in use on production cars—breaker point types and breakerless types. The Ford-Autolite system is of the breaker point type, while the Delco-Remy magnetic pulse and 1971 Chrysler units are breakerless. In 1971, General Motors introduced a variation of their breakerless system on certain Pontiac models equipped with the L-75 engine. This is a Unit Ignition System, which combines the distributor, pulse amplifier, coil and timer into one unit. Another variation is The Delcotronic capacitor discharge system.

Most aftermarket transistor systems will be found to be quite similar to the Ford-Autolite system, with the exception of the Mallory photocell unit and some sophisticated capacitor discharge types.

Ford-Autolite Breaker Point System

The transistor circuit would not be considered reliable by itself and also could give poor secondary performance. Other elements must be used to make the system function in a desirable manner. These elements include a condenser, a zener diode, a toroid (or donut shaped coil), a base-to-emitter resistor and a capacitor, which are combined with the transistor into a unit called the heat sink. Other elements which are necessary but are located elsewhere in the system are an emitter resistor, a base resistor, and a collector resistor. The function, location, and description of these components are as follows:

1. The heat sink of cast aluminum is finned for rapid heat dissipation. It serves as the housing, or base, in which to mount the transistor, the diode, the toroid, the base-emitter resistor and the condensers. The heat sink generally will be located under the dashboard for protection from the weather. The exact location varies with the particular car model.

2. The condenser, located in the heat sink, is a paper dielectric, solid impregnate, hermetically seated unit with an electrostatic capacity of 1.8 to 2.2 microfarads, a power factor of .010 and an insulation resistance (dielec-

tric strength) of 3,000 megohms when measured at 75°-80° F. It serves the same purpose as the condenser in the conventional ignition system; that is, the absorption of the high inductive energy in the coil primary during initial opening of the ignition contacts. It is exposed to a greater current than in the conventional ignition system, and for that reason possesses greater electrostatic capacity and dielectric strength. Also, because it is in the collector circuit it has no effect on the ignition contacts, which are in the base circuit.

3. The zener diode, also located in the heat sink, is a single anode, continuous duty, stud-mounted zener diode intended for transistor over-voltage protection. It acts as a voltage actuated relay that provides a shunt circuit whenever the voltage to the transistor reaches a predetermined value. The intrinsic properties of the zener diode allow it to pass current freely in one direction (forward bias) but prevent the flow of current in the opposite direction (reverse bias). However, sufficient voltage potential forces it to "break down" and pass reverse bias current, producing the same effect as a voltage relay but with far greater efficiency and speed. In the transistorized ignition system, the zener diode is designed to break down at 91 volts $\pm$ 10%, whereas the transistor breakdown voltage is 120 volts. This provides the over-voltage protection for the transistor. The presence of this diode is responsible for the lack of oscillation in the primary circuit.

4. The transistor itself, located in the heat sink, is a continuous duty, PNP, germanium-base power transistor which is designed for long life with a maximum base current of 1 amp., a maximum collector current of 12.0 amps., a base-to-emitter potential of 1.0 volt maximum, and a collector-to-emitter potential of 0.75 volt maximum at 75°-80° F. Although the transistor is very rugged and shock resistant, it is *temperature sensitive*. For this reason, any transistor selected for this application must conform to severe temperature requirements. Certain mounting positions can subject the transistor to rather high ambient temperature, and the heat generated by the transistor in operation, and subsequently dissipated by the heat sink, contributes to the problem. The transistor must operate efficient-

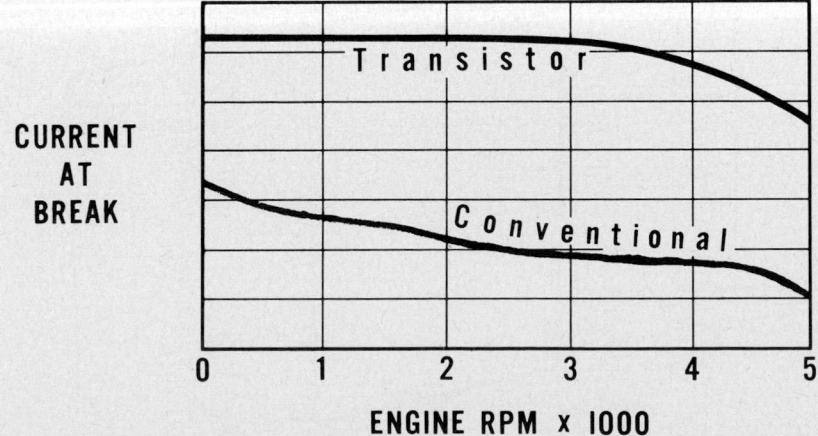

Comparison of conventional and transistor ignition system coil output and break current
(© Ford Motor Co.)

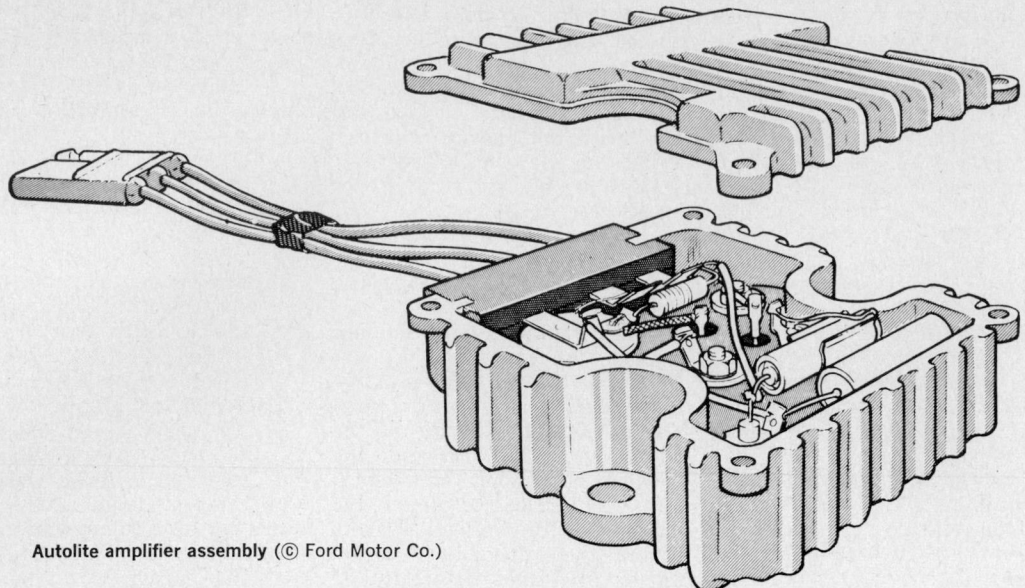

Autolite amplifier assembly (© Ford Motor Co.)

ly within a temperature range of -40°-160°F. The "runaway" tendency of transistors is not exhibited within this system because of the intermittent type of operation and the fact that the unit is already operating at maximum current value.

5. The block and coil assembly (toroid), located in the heat sink, is shaped like a donut with windings, and is encased in plastic. It is shown in the schematic as a double coil with three windings and serves only to stop the base current (and consequently the collector current) at the instant of the initial opening of the ignition contacts. This is accomplished in the toroid by the collapse of the magnetic field sending a reverse pulse through the base circuit. Because transistor characteristics vary in production, the toroid action serves as a means of providing a positive stopping of collector current regardless of the particular characteristics of an individual transistor.

6. The resistor in the base-to-emitter toroid circuit serves to control the path of current in the base-emitter circuit. It acts as a bias resistor to prevent current from flowing through the toroid shunt, thereby shorting the base to emitter section of the transistor.

7. The 40 mfd. condenser is a safety device to prevent transistor damage in the event that the battery circuit is broken with the engine running or high resistance develops at the battery terminals. Disconnecting the battery with the engine running would permit the alternator to produce voltage in excess of transistor capacity.

Without the battery to absorb the voltage it would surge into the ignition system, causing transistor damage.

The base resistor is similar to the conventional ignition resistor wire and is located between the distributor and the transistor (heat sink). It provides an 8.0 ohm resistance which is necessary for current limitation and it should not be replaced with any other wire, resistance or otherwise. To do so would result in immediate transistor destruction.

The collector and emitter resistors both are located in a ballast resistor block made of white ceramic for electrical and thermal insulation. Both resistors serve the same purpose—limiting system current and control of voltages within their respective circuits. The two resistors are in series in the collector-emitter circuit, together with the ignition coil, toroid and transistor. The emitter resistor also is in series with the base resistor, the toroid, and the transistor, in the base-emitter circuit. The transistor and emitter resistance therefore are common to both circuits. The combined resistances in each circuit permit a base current of approximately 1.0 amp. and a collector current of approximately 12 amps.

A tach block is included in the circuit for attaching tachometer and dwellmeter leads. In the conventional system, these leads are connected to the distributor primary lead and ground, but in the transistorized circuit, the connection of the leads in this manner would jump the contact gap, contributing to a current buildup in the base circuit and in the

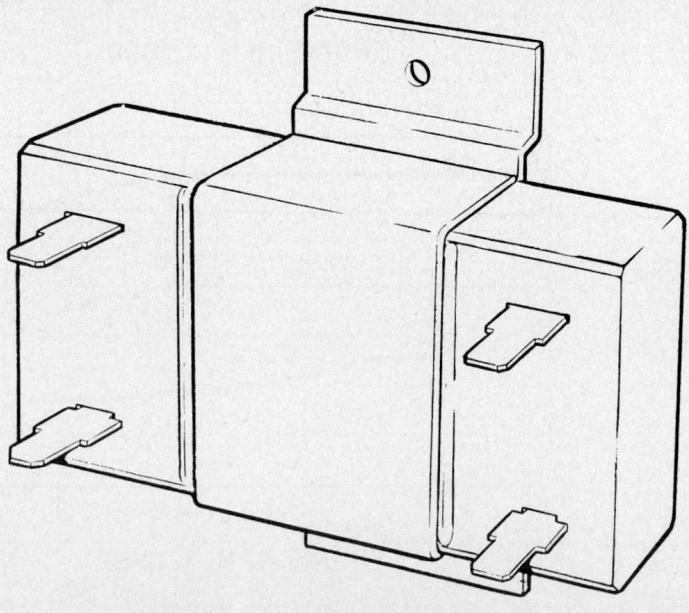

Autolite resistor block (© Ford Motor Co.)

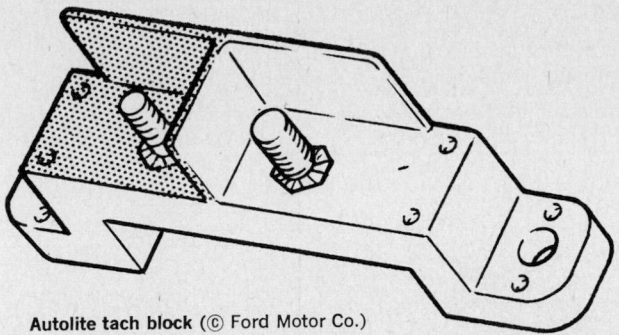

Autolite tach block (© Ford Motor Co.)

collector circuit which would overheat and burn out the transistor. The area surrounding the collector terminal is colored *red* for the meter red lead while the area surrounding the emitter terminal is colored *black* for the meter black lead.

A cold start relay is incorporated into the circuit at the starter relay, interrupting the conventional battery-to-coil lead. The purpose of this is to furnish additional current to the coil primary windings during situations when the starter draw is excessive. The cold start relay contacts normally are closed; only opening during the cranking cycle. However, when the available battery voltage drops below a predetermined value during the cranking cycle, they again close, bypassing the ignition resistor and furnishing full battery current to the system.

The distributor differs from the conventional distributor only in the absence of the condenser and in the highly polished breaker cam. Because

O.H.T. grease used for cam lubrication.

When testing the transistor ignition distributor in a test machin, incorporate a condenser into the primary-to-ground circuit using a jumper wire. This will prevent point pitting or oxidation during testing.

Caution When connecting an in-car tachometer to the Ford System, always shunt the tachometer leads that go to the coil IGN terminal and ignition switch with a 10 in. length of Ford ignition resistor wire, part No. COLF-12250-A, to prevent tachometer damage. The higher current draw of the transistor system can ruin a tach if this precaution is not taken.

Troubleshooting

Ignition problems are caused by a failure in the primary or secondary circuit, or incorrect ignition timing. Isolate the trouble as follows:
1. Remove the coil high tension lead from the distributor cap.

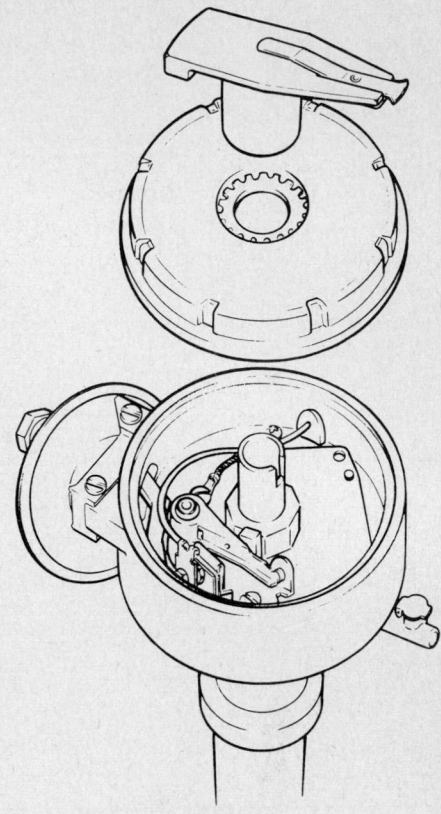

Autolite transistor distributor
(© Ford Motor Co.)

"S" and battery terminals.

If the spark is good, the trouble lies in the secondary (high voltage) circuit. If there is no spark or a weak spark, the trouble is in the primary (low voltage) circuit.

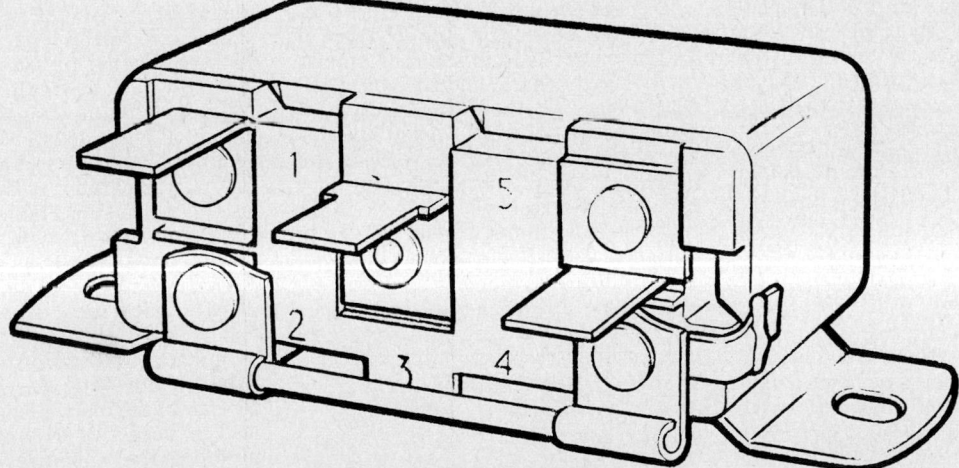

Autolite cold-start relay (© Ford Motor Co.)

one of the big advantages of the transistor ignition is long breaker point life, wear on the rubbing block must be reduced to a minimum. Because the current at the breaker points is so small, the amount of pitting that occurs during normal operation is hardly measurable and point life should be indefinite. The points should be set to .020" gap and Chevron

2. Disconnect the brown wire from the starter relay "I" terminal and the red and blue wire from the starter relay "S" terminal.
3. Turn the ignition switch on.
4. While holding the high tension lead approximately ¼ in. from the engine block, crank the engine by using remote starter switch between the starter relay

A breakdown or energy loss in the primary circuit can be caused by:
1. Defective primary wiring.
2. Improperly adjusted, contaminated or defective distributor points.
3. Defective amplifier assembly.

The trouble can be isolated by performing a primary circuit test.

A breakdown or energy loss in the secondary circuit can be caused by:
1. Fouled or improperly adjusted spark plugs.
2. Defective high voltage wiring.
3. High voltage leakage across the coil distributor cap or rotor.

taminated or are not closing.
2. An open circuit in the distributor lead to the amplifier.

To determine which item listed is causing the trouble, proceed as follows:

Disconnect the distributor lead at the bullet connector, and crank the engine. If the dwellmeter indicates 0° dwell, the distributor points are not opening. If 45° dwell is indicated, the amplifier is malfunctioning or there is no power from the igni-

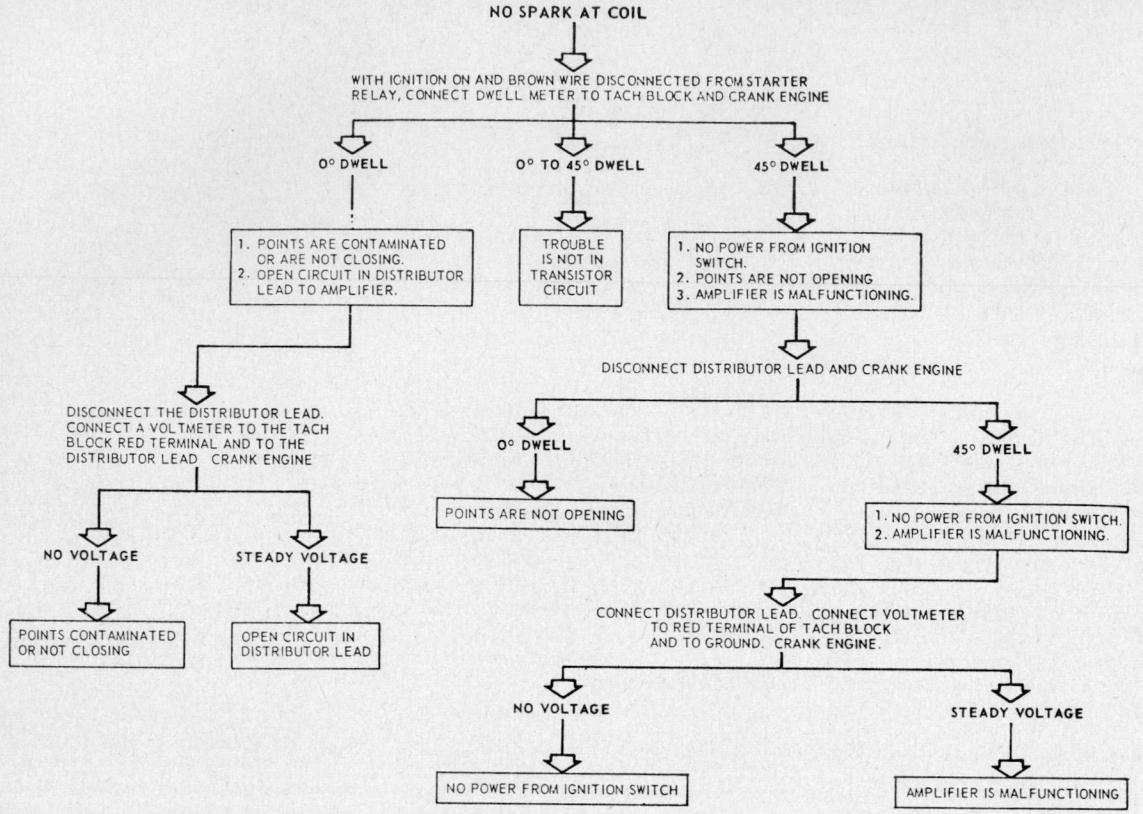

Autolite transistor ignition troubleshooting chart (© Ford Motor Co.)

To isolate a problem in the secondary circuit, turn the ignition switch off, remove the remote starter switch from the starter relay, install the coil high tension lead in the distributor cap, the red and blue wire to the starter relay (this goes on the "S" terminal) and the brown wire to the starter relay (this goes on the "I" terminal) and perform a secondarp circuit test.

Primary Circuit Tests

Caution Do not use any other procedure, conventional short-cut, or connect test equipment in any other manner than described, or extensive damage can be caused to the transistor ignition system.

Connect a dwell meter to the tachometer block. Connect the black lead to the black (large) terminal and the red lead to the red (small) terminal.

With the remote starter switch installed and the ignition switch on, ground the coil high tension wire and crank the engine and observe the dwell reading.

0° Dwell
1. The distributor points are con-

Disconnect the distributor lead at the bullet connector and connect a voltmeter red lead to the red (small) tach block terminal and the voltmeter black lead to the distributor lead from the distributor. *Do not connect the voltmeter to the lead from the amplifier.* Crank the engine and note the voltmeter reading.

If a steady indication of voltage is obtained, the trouble is in the distributor lead to the amplifier. Absence of any voltage indication on the voltmeter shows that there is an open circuit between the distributor lead and the breaker point ground.

0-45° Dwell
1. The transistor and the primary circuit are functioning properly.
2. The trouble could be in the secondary circuit.

45° Dwell
1. No power from the ignition switch.
2. The distributor points are closed and not opening.
3. Defective amplifier assembly.

To determine which of the three items listed is causing the trouble, proceed as follows:

tion switch.

Use a voltmeter or test light to determine if the transistor (amplifier assembly) is at fault. Connect the voltmeter to the red-green lead terminal of the ballast resistor and to ground. Crank the engine.

Absence of any voltage indication on the voltmeter shows there is an open circuit, or no power between the ignition switch and the amplifier. The ballast resistor could be defective. Replace it with a good ballast resistor, and repeat the test.

A steady indication of voltage on the voltmeter indicates either a defective amplifier or the coil to amplifier lead is defective or improperly connected to the ballast resistor. Proceed as follows:
1. Disconnect the amplifier at the quick disconnect.
2. Connect an ohmmeter across the outside terminals of the amplifier side of the quick disconnect.
3. Reverse the ohmmeter leads.

If a very high resistance is obtained one way and a very low or *zero* resistance is obtained the other way, the amplifier is not defective. Check the coil to amplifier wiring for a loose connection or defective wiring.

After a repair has been made, run through the test again to check for any other malfunctions.

Secondary Circuit Tests

Use conventional system test procedures.

Delco-Remy Magnetic Pulse System

The Delco-Remy magnetic pulse, fully transistorized ignition system uses a magnetic pulse distributor having no breaker points. This system switches power electronically rather than with ignition contact points. Instead of the familiar cam and breaker plate assembly, this distributor uses a rotating iron timer core and a magnetic pickup assembly. The magnetic pickup assembly consists of a bearing plate on which are sandwiched a ceramic ring-type permanent magnet, two pole pieces and a pick-up coil. The pole pieces are doughnut shaped steel plates with accurately spaced internal teeth, one tooth for each cylinder of the engine.

A critically important part is the iron timer core. It has a number of equally spaced projections or vanes and is attached to, and rotates with, the distributor shaft.

The transistor control unit, the switchbox of the system, is mounted in an aluminum case and contains three transistors, a zener diode, a condenser and five small resistors. The zener diode is a circuit protection device. Remaining components control and switch ignition-coil current electronically; there are no moving parts in the control unit.

The ignition coil is of standard design except for a special winding. The external primary resistor is a ceramic type, similar to those used on various conventional systems.

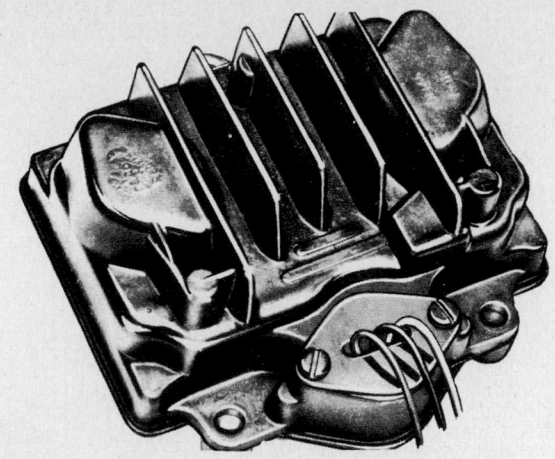

Delco-Remy amplifier unit (© Chev. Div., G.M. Corp.)

The magnetic pulse distributor provides a triggering pulse or signal for the transistor control unit. Within the distributor, a magnetic field is produced through the internal teeth of the upper and lower pole pieces by the permanent magnet between them. As the vanes of the iron timer core on the distributor shaft pass near the pole teeth as the shaft rotates, the magnetic field alternately builds up and collapses. Thus, a voltage pulse is induced in the pick up coil each time a vane of the iron core passes a tooth on the pole pieces.

Each voltage pulse is conducted to the transistor control unit where it turns on the triggering transistor, causing it to turn off the switching transistor. This action interrupts the current flow through the ignition coil primary winding, causing the coil to fire the spark plug. The switching transistor then automatically returns to an on condition, permitting coil current to build up for the next firing.

Troubleshooting

This diagnosis guide has been taken from material furnished by Pontiac Division, General Motors Corporation. It can be applied, however, to other G.M. transistorized ignition systems of the same basic type.

Cautions

1. Don't use 18 volts or 24 volts for emergency starting.
2. Never crank engine with coil high-tension lead or more than three spark plug leads disconnected.
3. Don't short circuit between coil positive terminal and ground.
4. On any repair that necessitates replacement of control unit or ignition resistor, perform complete charging system check before releasing the unit. Basic cause of trouble may be high or uncontrolled charging rate.

Intermittent Miss

1. Check pick-up coil connector to make sure that wire harness leads and pick-up coil leads are tight in connector bodies.
2. Check for loose connections throughout the system.
3. Engine roughness or miss indicates a short or open in the distributor pick-up coil. Connect an ohmmeter between two distributor pick-up coil terminals in connector body. Resistance should read 300-400 ohms. If resistance is infinite, coil is open; if resistance is low, coil is shorted. In either case, the pick-up coil must be replaced.
4. Connect an ohmmeter from either of the terminals to the distributor housing. The reading should be infinite. If not, the wiring is grounded.

Diagnosis

Hard or No Start 75°

Disconnect any one spark plug lead

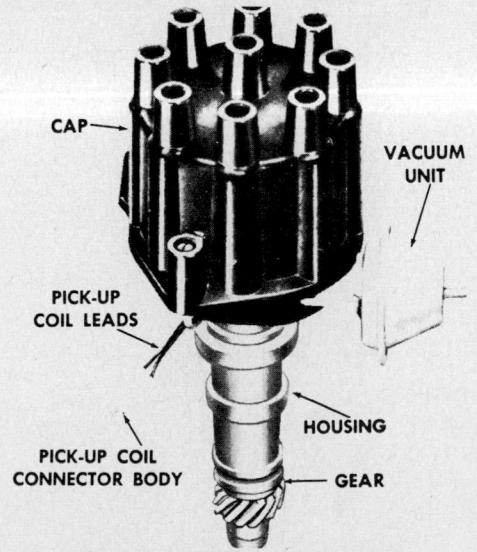

CAP →

VACUUM UNIT →

PICK-UP COIL LEADS →

PICK-UP COIL CONNECTOR BODY →

HOUSING

GEAR

Delco-Remy magnetic pulse distributor
(© Chev. Div., G.M. Corp.)

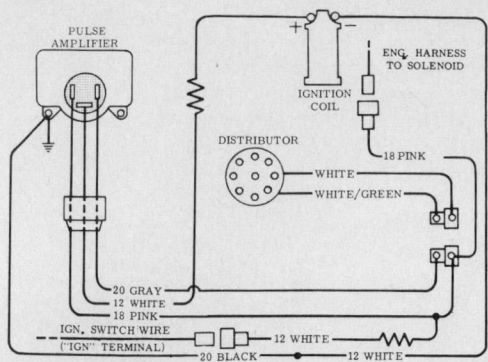

Delco-Remy circuit diagram (© Chev. Div., G.M. Corp.)

and crank the engine while holding the lead about ¼ in. from ground. Do not perform this test by using the coil or distributor secondary wire—damage to the system will result.

IF SPARKS OCCUR

Reconnect spark plug. Problem is not in ignition system.

IF NO SPARK OCCURS

1. Reconnect spark plug.
2. Check ignition coil primary by connecting an ohmmeter between the two terminals. An infinite reading indicates an open primary.
3. Check ignition coil secondary by connecting an ohmmeter between high-voltage center tower and either primary terminal. If the reading is infinite, the secondary is open.
4. Check ground resistor with a low-range ohmmeter. Turn ignition switch off and connect leads across resister terminals. The reading should be .43 ohms.
5. Check by-pass resistor with a low-range ohmmeter. Reading should be .68 ohms with ignition switch off.
6. Check continuity of system as a whole, using a low-range (0-20 volt) voltmeter, in the following manner:

STEP 1

A. Connect the voltmeter between ignition coil positive terminal and ground.
B. Turn on ignition switch and observe reading. Voltage should be 7-9 volts.
C. If reading is 11-12 volts, there is an open circuit between this point and ground. The circuit includes the coil primary winding, ballast resistor and connecting wiring.
D. If reading is zero, there is an open circuit between this point and battery. Go on to Step 2.

STEP 2

A. Connect voltmeter between other ballast resistor and ground. Observe reading with ignition switch on.
B. If the reading is 11-12 volts, there is an open circuit between this ballast resistor and the ignition

coil. The circuit consists of the control unit and associated wiring. If wiring is OK, the control unit must be replaced.

Ignition Coil Check

The ignition coil primary can be checked for an open condition by connecting an ohmmeter across the two primary terminals with the battery disconnected. Primary resistance at 75° F. *should be between .35 and .55 ohm.* An infinite reading indicates the primary is open. For the engine to run but miss at times, the pri-

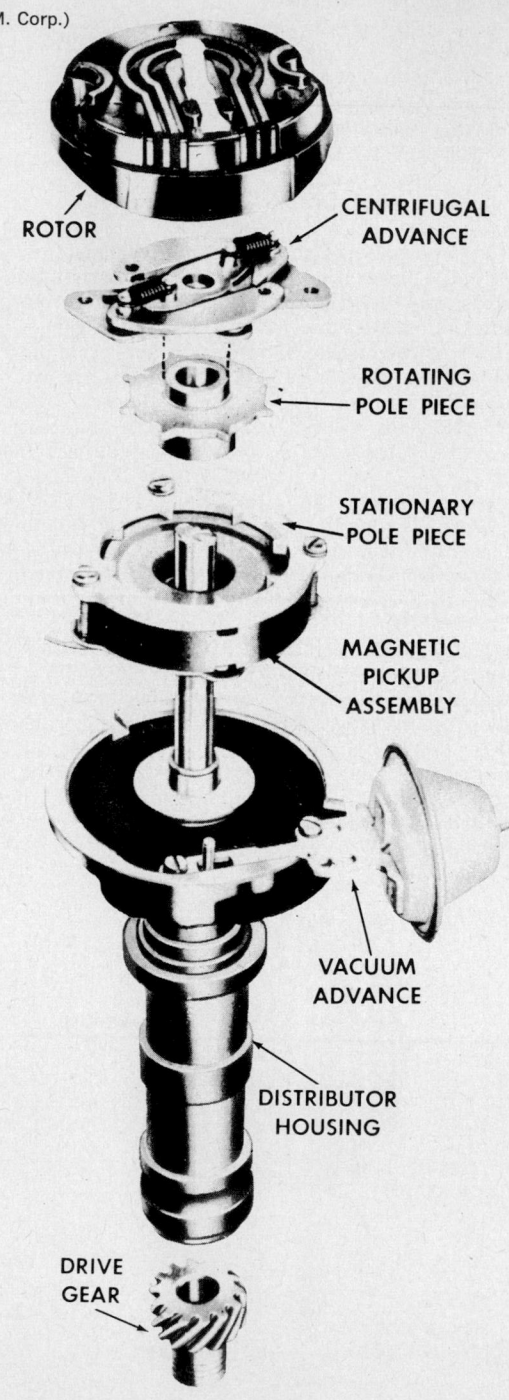

Delco-Remy pulse distributor exploded view
(© Chev. Div., G.M. Corp.)

mary open may be of the intermittent type.

The coil secondary can be checked for an open by connecting either primary terminal. To obtain a reliable reading, a scale on the ohmmeter having the 20,000 ohm value within, or nearly within, the middle third of the scale should be used. *Secondary resistance at 75° F. should be between*

MOUNTING SCREW
RESISTOR R5
DIODE D1
TRANSISTOR TR2 (UNDERNEATH)
TRANSISTOR TR1 (UNDERNEATH)
RESISTOR R2
RESISTOR R4
RESISTOR R3
MOUNTING SCREW
CAPACITOR C1
MOUNTING SCREW
RESISTOR R6
RESISTOR R1
CAPACITOR C3
CAPACITOR C2
TRANSISTOR TR3

Delco-Remy amplifier panel board components
(© Chev. Div., G.M. Corp.)

8,000 and 12,500 ohms. If the reading is infinite, the coil secondary winding is open.

A number of different types of coil test equipment are available from various manufacturers. When using these testers, follow the procedure recommended by the manufacturer.

NOTE: make sure the tester will properly check this special coil.

Ignition Pulse Amplifier

Disassembly

To check the amplifier for defective components, proceed as follows:

1. Remove the bottom plate from the amplifier.
2. To aid in assembly, note the locations of the lead connections to the panel board.
3. Remove the three panel board attaching screws, and lift the assembly from the housing.
4. To aid in assembly, note any transistors and their respective locations on the panel board and heat sink assembly.
5. Note the insulators between the transistors and the heat sink, and the insulators separating the heat sink from the panel board.
6. Remove the transistor attaching screws, and separate the two transistors and heat sink from the panel board.
7. Carefully examine the panel

board for evidence of damage.

Component Checks

With the two transistors separated from the assembly, an ohmmeter may be used to check the transistors and components on the panel board for defects. An ohmmeter having a 1½ volt cell, which is the type usually found in service stations, is recom-

mended. The low range scale on the ohmmeter should be used except where otherwise specified.

A 25-watt soldering gun is recommended, and a 60% tin—40% lead solder should be used when re-soldering. Avoid excessive heat which may damage the panel board. Clip away any epoxy involved, and apply new epoxy.

In order to check the panel board assembly, it is necessary to unsolder at the locations indicated in the illustration (the two capacitors C2 and C3). In all of the following checks, connect the ohmmeter as shown and then reverse the ohmmeter leads to obtain two readings. The amplifier circuitry is illustrated.

1. Transistors TR1 and TR2: Check each transistor by referring to the illustration. If both readings in Step 1 are zero, the transistor is shorted. If both readings in Step 2 are zero, the transistor is shorted; and if both readings are infinite, the transistor is open. Interpret Step 3 the same as Step 2.
2. Trigger Transistor TR3: If both readings in Step 1 are zero, the transistor is shorted. If both readings in Step 2 are zero, the transistor is shorted; and if both readings are infinite, the transistor is open. Interpret Step 3 the same as Step 2.
3. Diode D1: If both readings are zero, the diode is shorted; and if both readings are infinite, the diode is open.
4. Capacitor C1: If both readings are zero, the capacitor is shorted.
5. Capacitors C2 and C3: Connect the ohmmeter across each capacitor (not illustrated). The capacitor is shorted if both readings

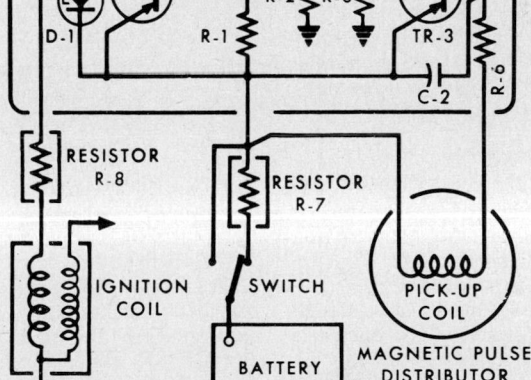

IGNITION PULSE AMPLIFIER
R-5
TR-2
C-1
C-3
R-4
TR-1
R-2
R-3
D-1
R-1
TR-3
C-2
R-6
RESISTOR R-8
RESISTOR R-7
IGNITION COIL
SWITCH
PICK-UP COIL
BATTERY
MAGNETIC PULSE DISTRIBUTOR

Delco-Remy amplifier schematic
(© Chev. Div., G.M. Corp.)

are zero.

6. Resistor R1: The resistor is open if both readings are infinite.
7. Resistor R2: Use an ohmmeter scale on which the 1800 ohm value is within, or nearly within, the middle third of the scale. If both readings are infinite, the resistor is open.
8. Resistor R3: Use an ohmmeter

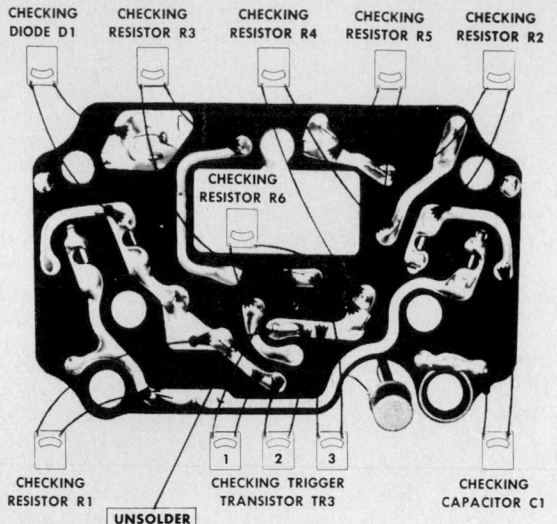

CHECKING DIODE D1   CHECKING RESISTOR R3   CHECKING RESISTOR R4   CHECKING RESISTOR R5   CHECKING RESISTOR R2

CHECKING RESISTOR R6

CHECKING RESISTOR R1   UNSOLDER   CHECKING TRIGGER TRANSISTOR TR3   1 2 3   CHECKING CAPACITOR C1

Delco-Remy amplifier component checks
(© Chev. Div., G.M. Corp.)

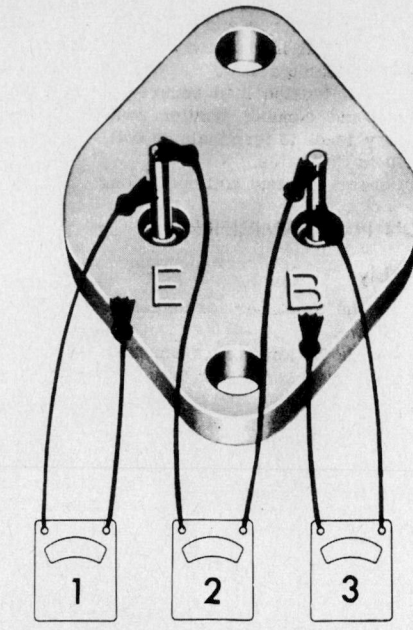

E B

1 2 3

Delco-Remy transistor checks (ohmmeter)
(© Chev. Div., G.M. Corp.)

scale on which the 680 ohm value is within, or nearly within, the middle third of the scale. If both readings are infinite, the resistor is open.

9. Resistor R4: Select an ohmmeter scale on which the 15000 ohm value is within, or nearly within, the middle third of the scale. If *either* reading is infinite, the resistor is open.

10. Resistor R5: Use the lowest range ohmmeter scale. The resistor is open if *either* reading is infinite.

NOTE: this resistor on some applications may be located in the vehicle wiring harness, and not on the panel board.

11. Resistor R6: An ohmmeter scale on which the 150 ohm value is within or nearly within, the middle third of the scale should be used. If both readings are infinite, the resistor is open.

Assembly

During assembly, coat, with silicone grease, both sides of the flat insulators used between the transistors and heat sink, and also the heat sink on the side on which the transistors are mounted. The silicone grease, which is available commercially, conducts heat and provides better cooling.

Delcotronic Capacitor Discharge System

The Delcotronic C-D system consists of a magnetic pulse distributor (virtually identical to the one used with the Delco-Remy Magnetic Pulse System), an ignition pulse amplifier and a special ignition coil. This system charges a capacitor to high voltage (300 volts), then discharges it on a signal from the distributor through the ignition coil primary, including a

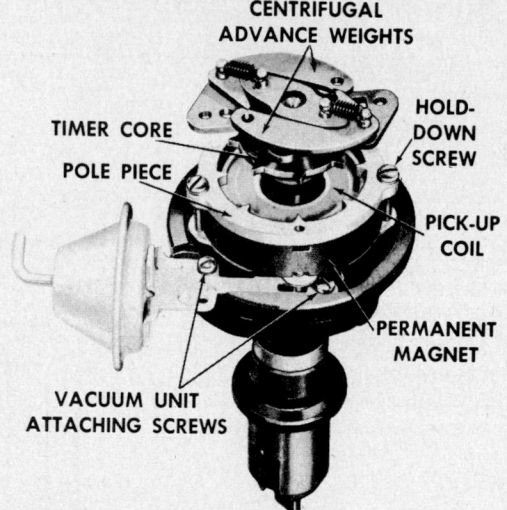

CENTRIFUGAL ADVANCE WEIGHTS

TIMER CORE   HOLD-DOWN SCREW

POLE PIECE   PICK-UP COIL

PERMANENT MAGNET

VACUUM UNIT ATTACHING SCREWS

C-D distributor—Delcotronic System
(© Olds. Div., G.M. Corp.)

high tension secondary voltage pulse to fire each spark plug.

Operation

Transistor Q2 and accompanying circuitry momentarily supplies voltage through the primary of transformer T1. This voltage is increased through transformer action and a much higher voltage is induced in the secondary. The four diodes, CR3, 4, 5 and 6 form a full wave rectifier which has the capability of delivering maximum DC voltage from the transformer T1 secondary. It is this voltage that charges the capacitor C1.

The following is a list of the parts, and their function, used in the amplifier as illustrated in the schematic.

Transistor

Q1	Initiates turn-on and turn-off of Q5.
Q2	Turns T1 primary on and off.
Q3	Turns Q2 on and off with engine running.
Q4	Triggers Thyristor THY.
Q5	When on, it turns off Q3 and Q4.

Diode

CR1	Blocks 3 line current through CR2.
CR2 (Zener)	Clips T1 primary voltage to limit secondary output to approximately 300 volts across C1.
CR3,CR4 CR5,CR6	Provide full wave rectification of T1 secondary voltage.
CR7	Provides proper bias to Q2.
CR8	Clips FB voltage of T1 to limit reverse voltage acros E-B of Q2.
CR9	Provides proper biasing of THY.

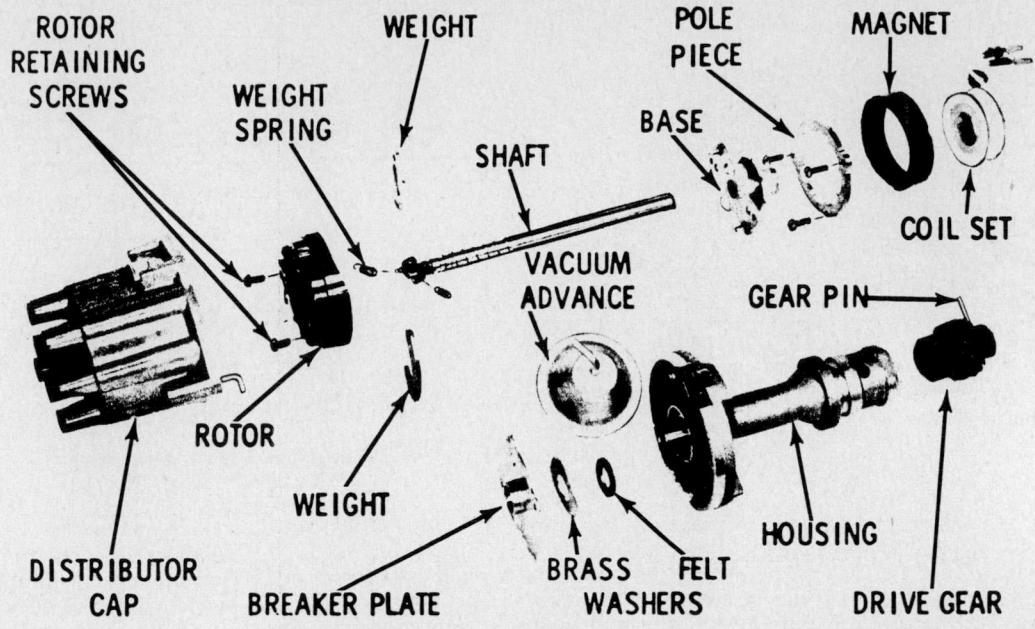

Delcotronic distributor exploded view (© Olds. Div., G.M. Corp.)

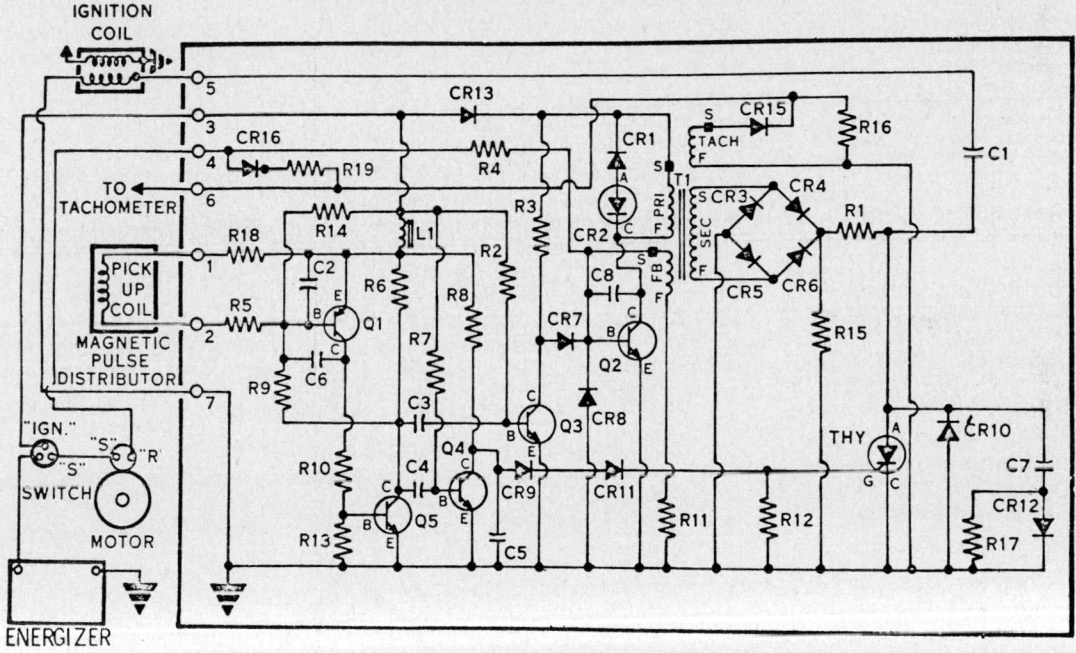

Delcotronic System schematic (© Olds. Div., G.M. Corp.)

CR10	Eliminates reverse voltage across THY, allows ignition coil primary to partially recharge C1.
CR12	Provides proper biasing of THY.
CR13	With C7 and R17 reduces rate of voltage increases across THY. Protects amplifier in case of battery reverse polarity, or lead reversal.
CR15	Half wave rectified T1 tachometer winding voltages for proper tachometer operation.
CR16	With R19 prevents erroneous tachometer reading during cranking.

Resistor

R1	Prevents T1 secondary rectified voltage from being shorted to ground when THY is on.
R2	Provides proper biasing of Q3.
R3	Limits current through Q3.
R4	Provides proper biasing of Q2.
R5	Prevents damage to amplifier if #2 lead is grounded.
R6	Limits current through Q5.
R7	Provides proper biasing of Q4.
R8	Limits current through Q4.
R9	Provides feed back for Q1, holds Q1 on after pick up coil voltage has ceased.
R10	Provides signal to Q5 when Q1 turns on.
R11	Limits current through Q2 from winding of T1.
R12	Provides bias to THY.
R13	Biases B-E of Q5.
R14	Biases E-B of Q1.
R15	Allows C1 to bleed off during shut-down.
R16	Provides proper voltage to tachometer.
R17	Reduces rate of voltage change imposed on THY when C7 discharges.

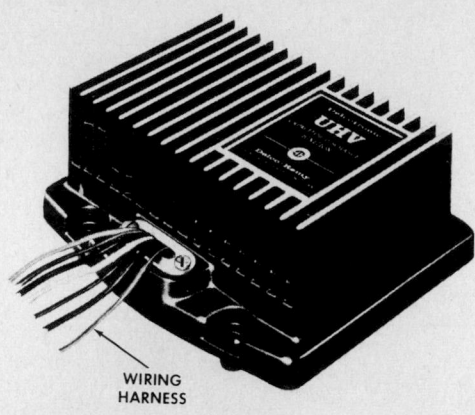

WIRING HARNESS

Delcotronic amplifier unit (© Olds. Div., G.M. Corp.)

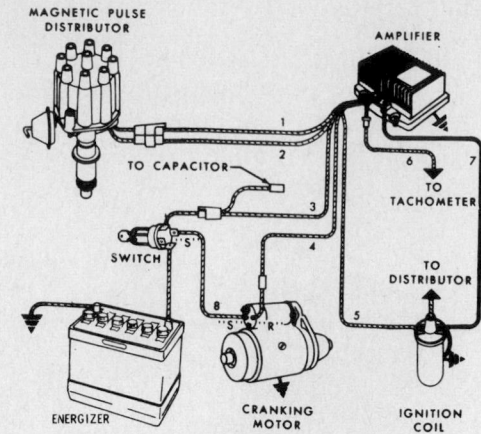

MAGNETIC PULSE DISTRIBUTOR

AMPLIFIER

TO CAPACITOR

TO TACHOMETER

SWITCH

TO DISTRIBUTOR

ENERGIZER

CRANKING MOTOR

IGNITION COIL

Delcotronic System wiring diagram
(© Olds. Div., G.M. Corp.)

R18   Prevents damage to amplifier if #1 lead is grounded.

R19   With CR16 prevents erroneous tachometer reading during cranking.

Capacitor

C1   Stores charge from T1 to energize ignition coil primary.

C2   Protects Q1 from transient voltages.

C3   Turns Q3 off.

C4   Turns Q4 off.

C5   Protects Q4 from transient voltages.

C6   Protects Q1 from transient voltages.

C7   With CR12 and R17 reduces rate of voltage increase across THY.

C8   Reduces radio noise.

Transformer

T1   Steps up voltage to charge C1; provides voltage to operate tachometer; provides feed back voltage to operate Q2.

Thyristor

THY   Discharges C1 through primary of ignition coil.

Troubleshooting

Faulty engine performance will be evidenced by one of the following conditions:

   a. Engine will not run.
   b. Engine will start but not run.
   c. Engine will miss or surge.

When troubleshooting the system, use care to avoid accidental shorts and grounds, which may cause instant damage to the amplifier and wiring.

NOTE: the special coil used in this system cannot be tested with a conventional coil tester.

Engine Will Not Run

To determine if the ignition system is operating, hold one spark plug lead about ¼ in. from the engine block and crank the engine. If sparking occurs, the trouble most likely is not ignition. If sparking does not occur, and the vehicle fuel system is satisfactory, check the ignition system. The spark plugs, wiring, distributor cap and rotor can be checked in the conventional manner. Only the coil requires a different procedure. The ignition coil can be checked for primary and secondary winding continuity with an ohmmeter as follows: with leads disconnected from coil, connect ohmmeter across primary terminals. If reading is infinite, winding is open. To check secondary, connect ohmmeter to high voltage (center tower) and coil case. An infinite reading means coil secondary is open.

NOTE: when checking secondary, use middle or high resistance range on ohmmeter.

Amplifier

1. Temporarily connect a jumper lead between the amplifier housing to a good ground. If the engine will now start and run, the amplifier is not properly grounded. Correct as required.

2. Connect a 12-volt, 2-candlepower bulb to the primary terminals of the ignition coil.

3. Crank the engine.
   a. If the bulb flickers on and off, the amplifier is operating properly. In this case, recheck the secondary system for the cause of the "no run" condition.
   b. If the bulb does not flicker on and off, proceed to next test.

Distributor

1. Insure that the two distributor leads are connected to the dis-

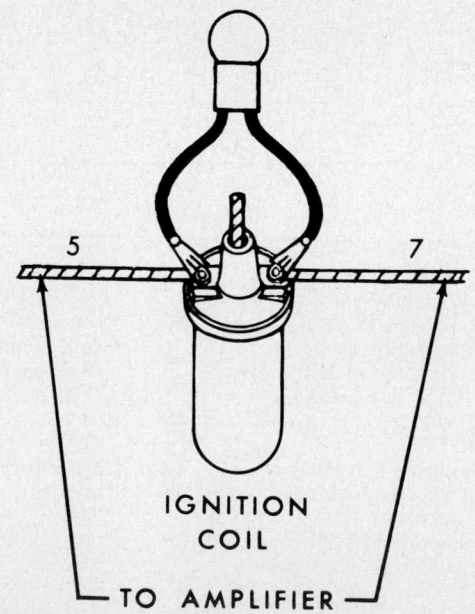

BULB - 12 VOLT 2 CANDLE POWER

5   7

IGNITION COIL

— TO AMPLIFIER —

Amplifier test hook-up
(© Olds. Div., G.M. Corp.)

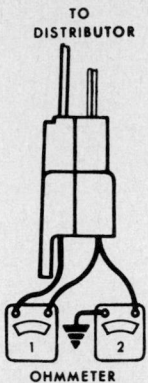

TO
DISTRIBUTOR

OHMMETER

Distributor test hook-up
(© Olds. Div., G.M. Corp.)

tributor connector body as illustrated.

2. With the distributor connector disconnected from the harness connector, connect an ohmmeter (1) to the two terminals of the distributor connector as shown.
3. Connect a vacuum source to the distributor, and observe the ohmmeter reading throughout the vacuum range. (The distributor need not be removed from the engine.)
4. Any reading outside the 550-750 ohm range indicates a defective pickup coil in the distributor.
5. Remove one ohmmeter (2) lead from the connector body and connect to ground.
6. Observe the ohmmeter reading throughout the vacuum range.
7. Any reading less than infinite indicates a defective pickup coil.
8. Reconnect the harness connector to the distributor connector.

Continuity

Carefully inspect all wiring connections to ensure that they are clean and tight. If satisfactory, disconnect the amplifier No. 3 and No. 4 leads from the two connectors. Proceed as follows:

1. Connect a voltmeter from ground to the No. 4 connector lead.
2. Turn switch to "Start" position.
3. If reading is zero, circuit is open between connector body and battery.
4. If reading is obtained, connect voltmeter from ground to the No. 3 connector lead.
5. Turn switch to the run position.
6. If reading is zero, circuit is open between connector body and switch.
7. If reading is obtained, replace amplifier.

Engine Will Start But Not Run

If the engine starts, but then stops when the switch is returned to the run position, check as follows:
1. Ensure that the leads are pro-

perly connected in the No. 3 lead connector body.
2. If satisfactory, connect a voltmeter from ground to the terminal connection inside the connector.
3. Turn switch to run position.
4. If reading is zero, lead between connector and ignition switch is open.
5. If reading is obtained, replace amplifier.

Engine Miss or Surge

The vehicle fuel system should be checked in the usual manner. If satisfactory, check the ignition system as follows:

Timing, Spark Plugs, Wiring, Distributor Cap and Ignition Coil

Checks in these areas should be made in the same manner as for a conventional ignition system. In particular, the spark plugs should be checked in the usual manner. Plugs should be gapped to 0.045 in. Also the timing, the high-voltage wiring, the ignition coil tower, and the distributor cap inside and out should be inspected for evidence of arcing or leakage to ground. The ignition coil can be checked for primary and secondary winding continuity with an ohmmeter, as follows: disconnect coil leads and connect ohmmeter across primary terminals. If reading is infinite (no reading) winding is open. To check secondary, connect ohmmeter to high voltage (center tower) and coil case. An infinite reading means coil secondary is open.
NOTE: when checking secondary, use middle or high resistance range on ohmmeter.

Amplifier

A poorly grounded amplifier can cause an engine miss or surge. To check, temporarily connect a jumper lead from the amplifier housing to a good ground. If the engine performance improves, the amplifier is poorly grounded. Correct as required.

If no defects up to this point have been found, and the secondary system (plugs, wiring, distributor cap and coil) have been thoroughly checked, the most likely cause of the engine condition is a defective amplifier.

C-D Distributor Removal

1. Disconnect the harness connector.
2. Remove distributor cap.
NOTE: if necessary to remove secondary wires from cap, mark position on cap tower for lead to No. 1 cylinder. This will aid in reinstalling of leads.
3. Remove vacuum hose line from vacuum advance unit.
4. Remove distributor clamp.
5. Note position of rotor, then pull distributor up until rotor just

stops turning counterclockwise and again note position of rotor.
6. To install, reverse removal procedure.
NOTE: to ensure correct timing of the distributor, the distributor must be installed with the rotor correctly positioned as noted in Step 5.
7. If the engine has been turned after the distributor was removed, it will be necessary to install a jumper wire and crank engine until the slot on the harmonic balancer indexes with the 0° timing mark on the engine front cover. If both valves of the No. 1 cylinder are closed, the piston will be on top dead center of the firing stroke.

Distributor Disassembly

1. Remove screws securing rotor; remove rotor.
2. Remove centrifugal weight springs, if necessary.
3. Remove centrifugal weights.
4. Remove roll pin.
5. Remove drive gear and washer.
6. Remove drive shaft.
7. Remove weight support and timer core from drive shaft.
8. Remove screws securing magnetic core assembly; remove assembly.
9. Remove connector from primary lead by disengaging leads from connector.
10. Remove coil assembly.
11. Remove retaining ring which secures magnetic core support plate and remove plate.
12. Remove brass washer and felt.
13. Remove vacuum advance unit.
14. To assemble, reverse disassembly procedure.

C-D Amplifier Removal

1. Disconnect negative battery cable.
2. Disconnect the following leads from the amplifier harness assembly:
   a. Tachometer pickup
   b. Harness ground
   c. Coil wires
   d. Distributor connector
   e. Connectors at fuse panel
   f. Connector at junction block
3. Remove three retaining nuts from amplifier assembly and remove amplifier.
4. To install, reverse removal procedure.

No adjustments can be made to the C-D ignition system, and no periodic maintenance is required.

Chrysler Magnetic Pulse System

Installed on 340 cu. in., manual transmission models beginning in mid-1971, this Chrysler system is quite similar to the Delco-Remy Mag-

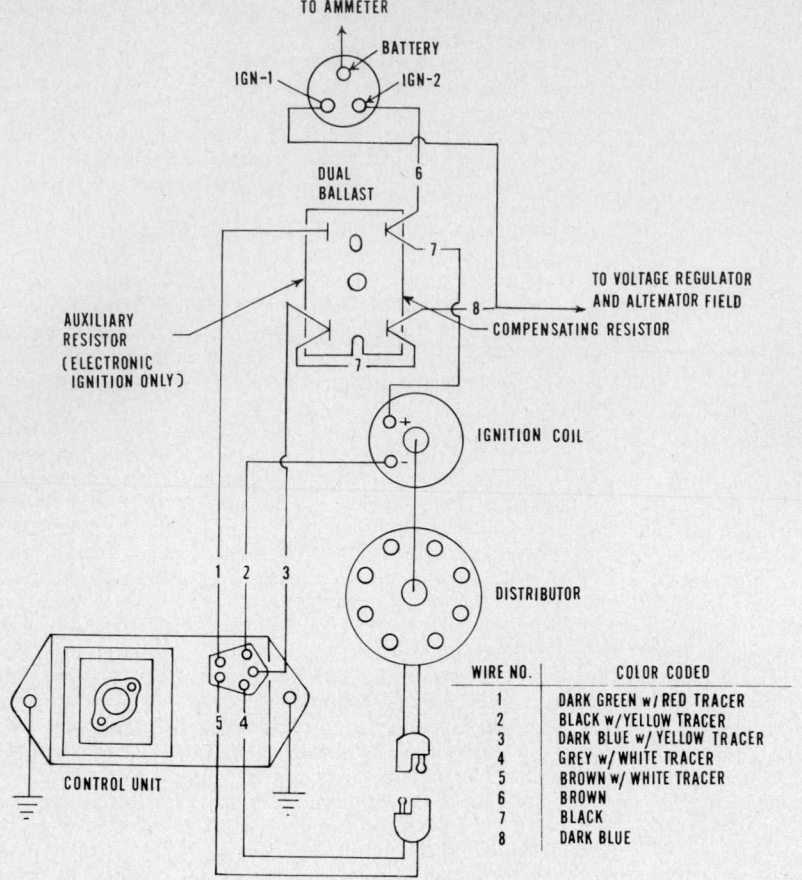

Chrysler System schematic

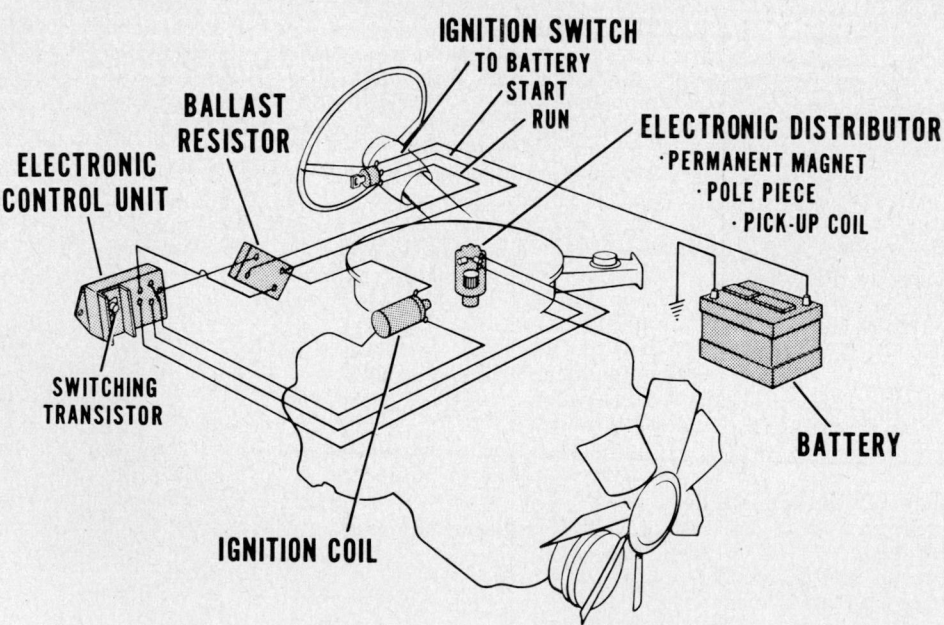

Chrysler system wiring diagram (© Chrysler Corp.)

netic Pulse System described previously. The system is readily recognized by the dual distributor primary wire, dual ballast resistor, and control unit (mounted on firewall or fender well).

The distributor is similar in appearance to the standard Chrysler distributor, but internally there are differences. The contact points have been replaced by a pickup coil and the breaker cam by a reluctor. This system eliminates the need for adjusting dwell.

Troubleshooting

Condition	Possible Cause	Correction
ENGINE WILL NOT START (Fuel and Carburetion Known to be OK)	a) Dual Ballast	Check resistance of each section: Compensating resistance: .50-.60 ohms @ 70°-80°F Auxiliary Ballast: 4.75-5.75 ohms Replace if faulty. Check wire positions.
	b) Faulty Ignition Coil	Check for carbonized tower. Check primary and secondary resistances: Primary: 1.41-1.79 ohms @ 70°-80°F Secondary: 9,200-11,700 ohms @ 70°-80°F Check in coil tester.
	c) Faulty Pickup or Improper Pickup Air Gap	Check pickup coil resistance: 400-600 ohms Check pickup gap: .010 in. feeler gauge should not slip between pickup coil core and an aligned reluctor blade. No evidence of pickup core striking reluctor blades should be visible. To reset gap, tighten pickup adjustment screw with a .008 in. feeler gauge held between pickup core and an aligned reluctor blade. After resetting gap, run distributor on test stand and apply vacuum advance, making sure that the pickup core does not strike the reluctor blades.
	d) Faulty Wiring	Visually inspect wiring for brittle insulation. Inspect connectors. Molded connectors should be inspected for rubber inside female terminals.
	e) Faulty Control Unit	Replace if all of the above checks are negative. Whenever the control unit or dual ballast is replaced, make sure the dual ballast wires are correctly inserted in the keyed molded connector.
ENGINE SURGES SEVERELY (Not Lean Carburetor)	a) Wiring	Inspect for loose connection and/or broken conductors in harness.
	b) Faulty Pickup Leads	Disconnect vacuum advance. If surging stops, replace pickup.
	c) Ignition Coil	Check for intermittent primary.
ENGINE MISSES (Carburetion OK)	a) Spark Plugs	Check plugs. Clean and regap if necessary.
	b) Secondary Cable	Check cables with an ohmmeter, or observe secondary circuit performance with an oscilloscope.
	c) Ignition Coil	Check for carbonized tower. Check in coil tester.
	d) Wiring	Check for loose or dirty connections.
	e) Control Unit	Replace if the above checks are negative.

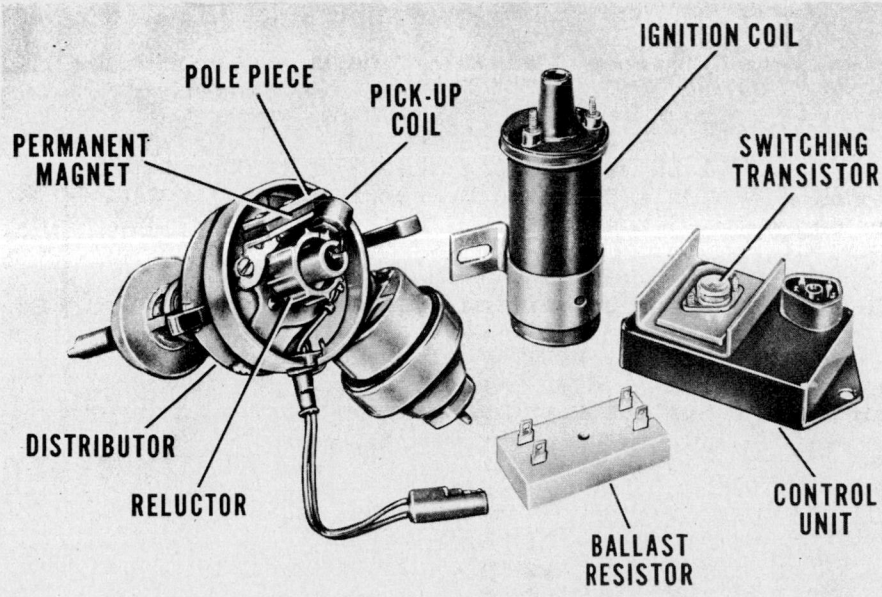

Chrysler system components (© Chrysler Corp.)

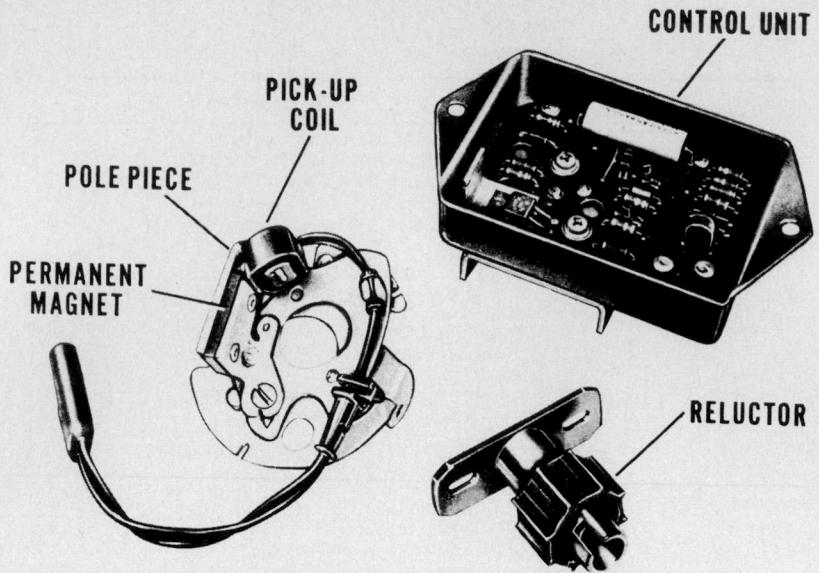

POLE PIECE

PICK-UP COIL

CONTROL UNIT

PERMANENT MAGNET

RELUCTOR

Distributor pickup and control unit components (© Chrysler Corp.)

Delco-Remy Unit Ignition System

This system, introduced in mid-1971 on Pontiac Grand Ville, Grand Prix and Safari models with the L-75 engine, is a Unitized electronic ignition system consisting of a magnetic pulse distributor, pulse amplifier module, distributor cap and wires, and coil. A magnetic pickup assembly located over the shaft contains a permanent magnet, a pole piece with internal teeth, and a pickup coil. When the teeth of the rotating timer core inside the pole piece line up wth the teeth of the pole piece, an induced voltage pulse in the pickup coil signals the amplifier module to open the coil primary circuit. This voltage induces the coil high-voltage secondary to fire the spark plugs.

Vacuum advance is provided by the magnetic pickup assembly, which is mounted over the main bearing on the distributor housing and is made to rotate by the vacuum control unit. The timer core is connected to conventional centrifugal advance weights to provide mechanical spark advance. No periodic lubrication is required, the job being done by engine oil.

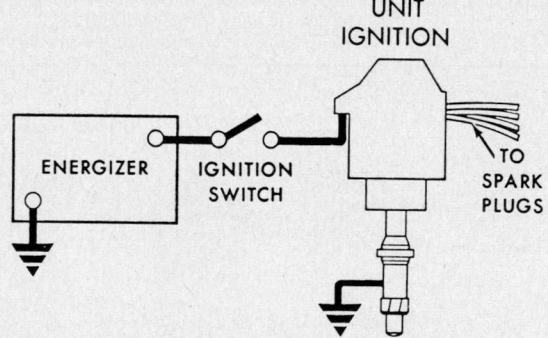

UNIT IGNITION

ENERGIZER

IGNITION SWITCH

TO SPARK PLUGS

Unit Ignition System wiring diagram
(© Pontiac Div., G.M. Corp.)

TROUBLESHOOTING

Insure that black and pink leads are connected as shown in Fig. 1. Tighten both bolts, Fig. 1. Loose bolts may cause poor performance and radio interference.

ON THE VEHICLE

ON THE BENCH

1. Disassemble unit (Fig. 2).
2. Inspect coil, eight inserts, shell and rotor for arc-over or leakage.

ENGINE WILL NOT RUN

1. Check ignition switch connector, Fig. 1.
2. Connect voltmeter from ignition switch connector to ground.
3. Turn on ignition switch.
4. If reading is zero, circuit is open between connector and ignition switch. Repair if needed.
5. If reading is battery voltage, hold one spark lead with insulating pliers about ¼ in. from dry area of engine block while cranking engine.

ENGINE WILL START BUT NOT RUN, AND ENGINE MISS OR SURGE.

1. Insure that fuel system is satisfactory.
2. Check spark plug leads for arcing or leakage to ground.
3. Check spark plugs.

If no defects are found, follow procedure under "On the Bench" with Unit Ignition System initially either on or off the vehicle.

1. Connect ohmmeter, Fig. 3.
2. Parts A and B each should be practically zero. If infinite on either reading, replace coil.
3. Part C should be 6000-9000 ohms. If outside range, replace coil.
4. Part D should be infinite. If not, replace coil.

1. Connect test stand vacuum source to vacuum unit.
2. Connect ohmmeter Parts A and B. Fig. 4.
3. Observe ohmmeter throughout vacuum range.
4. If Part A reads less than 650 ohms, or more than 850 ohms at any time, replace pickup coil, per Step 7 below.
5. If Part B reads other than infinite at any time, replace pickup coil, per step 7 below.
6. If vacuum unit is inoperative, replace per Step 7 below.
7. Remove unit from engine, drive pin from gear, remove rotor and shaft assembly from housing, remove shim and then "C" washer to replace pickup coil or vacuum unit (Fig. 5).

If sparking occurs, trouble most likely is not ignition. Check fuel system.

If no spark, follow procedure under "On the Bench," with Unit Ignition System initially either on or off the engine.

If no defects have been found, remove two attaching screws and replace module.

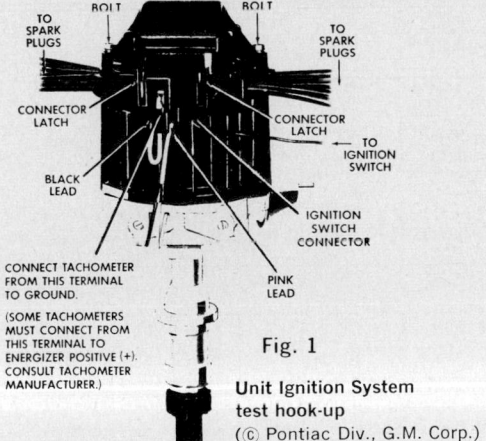

Fig. 1

Unit Ignition System test hook-up
(© Pontiac Div., G.M. Corp.)

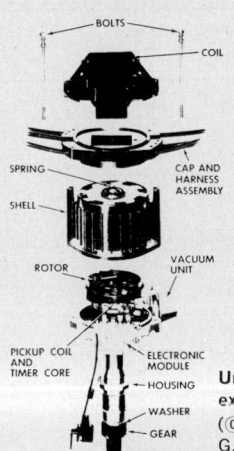

Fig. 2

Unit Ignition System exploded view
(© Pontiac Div., G.M. Corp.)

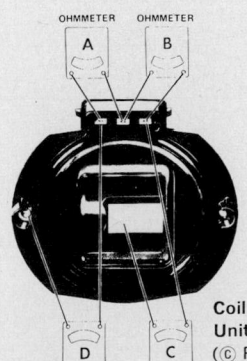

Fig. 3

Coil test hook-up— Unit Ignition System
(© Pontiac Div., G.M. Corp.)

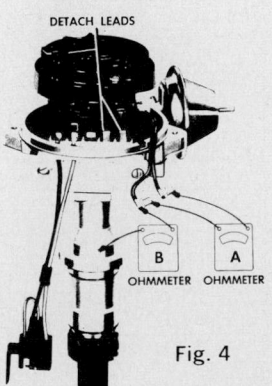

Fig. 4

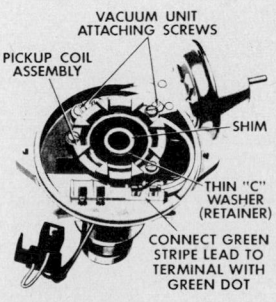

Fig. 5

Carburetors

Carter, Ball and Ball Carburetors

YEAR	MODEL OR TYPE	FLOAT LEVEL (IN.) Prim.	Sec.	FLOAT DROP (IN.) Prim.	Sec.	Pump Travel Travel Setting (IN.)	CHOKE SETTING Unloader (IN.)	Housing	Secondary Lockout Adj.	Throttle Bore Diam. Prim.	Sec.	Venturi Diam. Prim.	Sec.
Buick—Buick Special													
1965	AFB-3921S, 22S, 23S	$7/32$	$7/32$	$3/4$	$3/4$	$7/16$	$7/32$	INDEX	...	$1\,9/16$	$1\,11/16$	$1\,3/16$	$1\,9/16$
1965	AFB-3924S, Rear Syn.	$7/32$	$7/32$	$3/4$	$3/4$	$1/2$	$7/32$	INDEX	...	$1\,9/16$	$1\,11/16$	$1\,3/16$	$1\,9/16$
1965	AFB-3925S, Rear Aut.	$9/32$	$9/32$	$3/4$	$3/4$	$1/2$	$7/32$	INDEX	...	$1\,9/16$	$1\,11/16$	$1\,3/16$	$1\,9/16$
1965	AFB-3645S, Front	$7/32$	$7/32$	$3/4$	$3/4$	$1/2$	...	...	...	$1\,9/16$	$1\,11/16$	$1\,3/16$	$1\,9/16$
1965	AFB-3826S	$3/16$	$3/16$	$3/4$	$3/4$	$7/16$	$1/8$	INDEX	...	$1\,7/16$	$1\,7/16$	$1\,1/8$	$1\,1/4$
1965	AFB-3827S	$3/16$	$3/16$	$3/4$	$3/4$	$7/16$	$1/8$	INDEX	...	$1\,7/16$	$1\,7/16$	$1\,1/8$	$1\,1/4$
1966	AFB-4053S, 4054S	$7/32$	$7/32$	$3/4$	$3/4$	$7/16$	.215	INDEX	...	$1\,9/16$	$1\,11/16$	$1\,3/16$	$1\,9/16$
1966	AFB-4055S	$7/32$	$7/32$	$3/4$	$3/4$	$7/16$	.160	1-RICH	...	$1\,7/16$	$1\,7/16$	$1\,1/8$	$1\,1/4$
1966	AFB-4056S	$7/32$	$7/32$	$3/4$	$3/4$	$7/16$	.160	INDEX	...	$1\,7/16$	$1\,7/16$	$1\,1/8$	$1\,1/4$
1966	AFB-4059S	$7/32$	$7/32$	$3/4$	$3/4$	$7/16$	.215	INDEX	...	$1\,9/16$	$1\,11/16$	$1\,1/2$	$1\,9/16$
1966	AFB-4060S	$7/32$	$7/32$	$3/4$	$3/4$	$7/16$	.215	INDEX	...	$1\,9/16$	$1\,11/16$	$1\,1/2$	$1\,9/16$
1966	AFB-4061S	$7/32$	$7/32$	$3/4$	$3/4$	$7/16$	.160	1-RICH	...	$1\,7/16$	$1\,7/16$	1	$1\,1/4$
1966	AFB-4179S, 80S	$7/32$	$7/32$	$3/4$	$3/4$	$1/2$	.215	INDEX	...	$1\,9/16$	$1\,11/16$	$1\,3/16$	$1\,9/16$
1966	AFB-4181S	$7/32$	$7/32$	$3/4$	$3/4$	$1/2$	.215	INDEX	...	$1\,9/16$	$1\,11/16$	$1\,1/16$	$1\,9/16$
1967	AFB-4331S, Aut.	$1\,13/32$	$1\,13/32$	$3/4$	$3/4$	$7/16$	.160	1-RICH	...	$1\,7/16$	$1\,7/16$	$1\,1/8$	$1\,1/4$
1967	AFB-4332S, Man.	$1\,13/32$	$1\,13/32$	$3/4$	$3/4$	$7/16$	.160	INDEX	...	$1\,7/16$	$1\,7/16$	$1\,1/8$	$1\,1/4$
1967	AFB-4344S, A.I.R.	$1\,13/32$	$1\,13/32$	$3/4$	$3/4$	$17/32$	.160	2-RICH	...	$1\,7/16$	$1\,7/16$	1	$1\,1/4$
Cadillac													
1965	AFB-3903S	$3/8$	$3/8$	$15/16$	$15/16$	$15/32$	$9/32$	INDEX	...	$1\,7/16$	$1\,11/16$	$1\,3/16$	$1\,9/16$
1966	AFB-4168S, 4169S, 4171S	$3/8$	$3/8$	$15/16$	$15/16$	$5/16$	$9/32$	INDEX	...	$1\,7/16$	$1\,11/16$	$1\,3/16$	$1\,9/16$
Chevelle													
1965	AFB-ALL	$7/32$	$7/32$	$3/4$	$3/4$	$1/2$	$1/4$	1-LEAN	.020	$1\,9/16$	$1\,11/16$	$1\,1/4$	$1\,9/16$
1965	WCFB—ALL	$7/32$	$1/4$	$3/4$	$3/4$	$1/2$	$3/16$	INDEX	...	$1\,7/16$	$1\,7/16$	$1\,1/8$	$1\,1/4$
1966	6 Cyl.—YF-4079S, 4080S	$1/2$	...	$1\,3/16$	...	...	.260	...	...	$1\,11/16$	...	...	...
1966	V8-AVS-4027S, 4028S	$1\,15/32$	...	2	...	$11/32$	.170	...	...	$1\,9/16$	$1\,11/16$	...	...
1967	6 Cyl.—YF	$7/32$	...	$1\,3/16$	...	...	.250	...	...	$1\,11/16$	...	...	...
Chevrolet													
1965	WCFB	$7/32$	$1/4$	$3/4$	$3/4$	$1/2$	$3/16$	INDEX	.020	$1\,7/16$	$1\,7/16$	$1\,1/16$	$1\,1/4$
1965	AFB-3720SA-215A	$7/32$	$7/32$	$3/4$	$3/4$	$1/2$	$1/4$	1-LEAN	.020	$1\,9/16$	$1\,11/16$	$1\,1/4$	$1\,9/16$
1965	AFB-3499S	$7/32$	$7/32$	$3/4$	$3/4$	$1/2$	$1/4$	2-RICH	.020	$1\,5/8$	$1\,11/16$	$1\,11/32$	$1\,9/16$
1966	6 Cyl.-YF-4079S, 4080S	$1/2$	...	$1\,3/16$	...	...	.260	...	...	$1\,11/16$	...	...	...
1966	V8-AVS-4027S, 4028S	$1\,15/32$	...	2	...	$11/32$	.170	...	...	$1\,9/16$	$1\,11/16$	...	...
1967	6 Cyl.-YF	$7/32$	...	$1\,3/16$	...	...	.250	...	...	$1\,11/16$	...	...	...
Chevy II													
1965	YF	$7/16$	...	$1\,3/16$	...	...	...	...	...	$1\,11/16$	...	$1\,5/16$	...
1965	AFB	$7/32$	$7/32$	$3/4$	$3/4$	$1/2$	$1/4$	1-LEAN	.020	$1\,9/16$	$1\,11/16$	$1\,1/4$	$1\,9/16$
1966	4 Cyl.-YF-3379S, 3402S	$1/2$	...	$1\,3/16$	...	...	...	...	...	$1\,11/16$	...	...	...
1966	6 Cyl.-YF-4079S, 4080S	$1/2$	...	$1\,3/16$	...	...	.260	...	...	$1\,11/16$	...	...	...
1966	V8-AVS-4027S, 4028S	$1\,15/32$	...	2	...	$11/32$	.170	...	...	$1\,9/16$	$1\,11/16$	...	...
1967	4 Cyl.-YF	$7/32$	...	$1\,3/16$	...	...	.250	...	...	$1\,11/16$	...	...	...
1967	6 Cyl.-YF	$7/32$	...	$1\,3/16$	...	...	.260	...	...	$1\,11/16$	...	...	...

YEAR	MODEL OR TYPE	FLOAT LEVEL (IN.)		FLOAT DROP (IN.)		Pump Travel Setting (IN.)	CHOKE SETTING		Secondary Lockout Adj.	Throttle Bore Diam.		Venturi Diam.	
		Prim.	Sec.	Prim.	Sec.		Unloader (IN.)	Housing		Prim.	Sec.	Prim.	Sec.
Chrysler—Imperial													
1965	AFB-3855S, 56S	7/32	7/32	3/4	3/4	7/16	3/8	2-RICH	.020	1 7/16	1 9/16	1 3/16	1 5/16
1965	AFB-3858S	7/32	7/32	3/4	3/4	7/16	3/8	2-RICH	.020	1 7/16	1 9/16	1 3/16	1 5/16
1965	AFB-3859S, 60S	7/32	7/32	3/4	3/4	7/16	3/8	INDEX	.020	1 7/16	1 9/16	1 3/16	1 5/16
1965	AFB-3871S	7/32	7/32	3/4	3/4	7/16	3/8	2-RICH	.020	1 7/16	1 9/16	1 3/16	1 5/16
1965	BBD-3849S, 50S	5/16	...	...	...	①	1/4	2-RICH	...	1 9/16	...	1 5/16	...
1966	AFB-4130S, 4131S	7/32	7/32	3/4	3/4	7/16	3/8	2-RICH	.020	1 7/16	1 9/16	1 3/16	1 5/16
1966	AFB-4132S, 33S, 4136S, 37S	7/32	7/32	3/4	3/4	7/16	3/8	INDEX	.020	1 7/16	1 9/16	1 1/16	1 1/4
1966	BBD-4125S	5/16	...	...	...	①	1/4	2-RICH	...	1 9/16	...	1 5/16	...
1966	BBD-4126S	5/16	...	...	...	①	1/4	2-RICH	...	1 9/16	...	1 5/16	...
1967	AFB-4298S, 99S	7/32	7/32	3/4	3/4	7/16	3/8	2-RICH	.020	1 7/16	1 9/16	1 3/16	1 5/16
1967	AFB-4309S, 10S, 2/cap	5/16	5/16	3/4	3/4	7/16	5/16	INDEX	.020	1 7/16	1 9/16	1 7/16	1 9/16
1967	AFB-4326S, 27S	7/32	7/32	3/4	3/4	7/16	3/8	INDEX	.020	1 11/16	1 11/16	1 3/16	1 9/16
1967	AFB-4311S, 12S, w/cap	5/16	5/16	3/4	3/4	7/16	5/16	INDEX	.020	1 7/16	1 11/16	1 3/16	1 9/16
1967	AFB-4328S, 29S, w/cap	5/16	5/16	3/4	3/4	7/16	3/8	INDEX	.020	1 11/16	1 11/16	1 7/16	1 9/16
1967	BBD-4296S, 97S	5/16	...	...	...	...	1/4	2-RICH	...	1 9/16	...	1 1/8	...
1968	BBD-4422S-Std. Tr.	5/16	...	...	...	29/32	1/4	2-RICH	...	1 9/16	...	1 5/16	...
1968	BBD-4423S-Aut. Tr.	5/16	...	...	...	29/32	1/4	2-RICH	...	1 9/16	...	1 5/16	...
1968	AVS-4426S-Std. 383	5/16	...	1/2	...	7/16	1/4	INDEX	.020	1 7/16	1 11/16	1 3/16	1 7/16
1968	AVS-4429S-Auto. 440	5/16	...	1/2	...	7/16	1/4	INDEX	.020	1 11/16	1 11/16	1 7/16	...
1969	AVS-4616S-383-Aut.	5/16	...	1/2	...	7/16	1/4	INDEX	.020	1 7/16	1 11/16	1 3/16	...
1969	AVS-4711S-383 Std.	5/16	...	1/2	...	7/16	1/4	INDEX	.020	1 7/16	1 11/16	1 3/16	...
1969	AVS-4638S-Aut. AC	5/16	...	1/2	...	7/16	1/4	INDEX	.020	1 7/16	1 11/16	1 3/16	...
1969	AVS-4617S-4618S-440	7/32	...	1/2	...	7/16	1/4	INDEX	.020	1 11/16	1 11/16	1 7/16	...
1969	AVS-4640S-440-Aut. AC	7/32	...	1/2	...	7/16	1/4	INDEX	.020	1 11/16	1 11/16	1 7/16	...
1969	BBD-4613S-383 Std.	5/16	...	...	...	1	1/4	2-RICH	...	1 9/16	...	1 5/16	...
1969	BBD-4614S-383-Aut.	5/16	...	...	...	1	1/4	2-RICH	...	1 9/16	...	1 5/16	...
1970	BBD-4725S-383, Std. w. CAS	5/16	...	...	...	1	1/4	2-RICH	...	1 9/16	...	1 5/16	...
1970	BBD-4726S-383, Auto. w. CAS, w/o AC	5/16	...	...	...	1	1/4	2-RICH	...	1 9/16	...	1 5/16	...
1970	BBD-4894S-383, Auto. w. CAS, w. AC	5/16	...	...	...	1	1/4	2-RICH	...	1 9/16	...	1 5/16	...
1970	BBD-4727S-383, Std. w. ECS	5/16	...	...	...	1	1/4	2-RICH	...	1 9/16	...	1 5/16	...
1970	BBD-4728S-383, Auto. w. ECS	5/16	...	...	...	1	1/4	2-RICH	...	1 9/16	...	1 5/16	...
1970	AVS-4736S-383, Auto. w/o AC, w. CAS	5/16	...	1/2	...	7/16	1/4	2-RICH	.020	1 7/16	1 11/16	1 3/16	...
1970	AVS-4732S-383, Auto. w. AC, w. CAS	5/16	...	1/2	...	7/16	1/4	2-RICH	.020	1 7/16	1 11/16	1 3/16	...
1970	AVS-4734S-383, Auto. w. ECS	5/16	...	1/2	...	7/16	1/4	2-RICH	.020	1 7/16	1 11/16	1 3/16	...
1970	AVS-4737S-440, Std. w. CAS	7/32	...	1/2	...	7/16	1/4	2-RICH	.020	1 11/16	1 11/16	1 7/16	...
1970	AVS-4738S-440, Auto. w. CAS, w/o AC	7/32	...	1/2	...	7/16	1/4	2-RICH	.020	1 11/16	1 11/16	1 7/16	...
1970	AVS-4741S-440, Auto w. AC, w. CAS	7/32	...	1/2	...	7/16	1/4	2-RICH	.020	1 11/16	1 11/16	1 7/16	...
1970	AVS-4739S-440, Std. w. ECS	7/32	...	1/2	...	7/16	1/4	2-RICH	.020	1 11/16	1 11/16	1 7/16	...
1970	AVS-4740S-440, Auto. w. ECS	7/32	...	1/2	...	7/16	1/4	2-RICH	.020	1 11/16	1 11/16	1 7/16	...
1971	BBD-4961S, 62S	5/16	...	...	...	1	1/4	2-RICH	...	1 9/16	...	1 5/16	...
1971	AVS-6125S	7/32	...	1/2	...	7/16	1/4	2-RICH	.020	1 7/16	1 11/16	1 3/16	...
1971	AVS-4966S	7/32	...	1/2	...	7/16	1/4	2-RICH	.020	1 7/16	1 11/16	1 3/16	...
1971	AVS-4968S	7/32	...	1/2	...	7/16	1/4	2-RICH	.020	1 11/16	1 11/16	1 7/16	...

①—Set pump arm parallel.   CAS—Cleaner Air System   ECS—Evaporation Control System   CAP—Cleaner Air Package

YEAR	MODEL OR TYPE	FLOAT LEVEL (IN.)		FLOAT DROP (IN.)		Pump Travel Setting (IN.)	CHOKE SETTING		Secondary Lockout Adj.	Throttle Bore Diam.		Venturi Diam.	
		Prim.	Sec.	Prim.	Sec.		Unloader (IN.)	Housing		Prim.	Sec.	Prim.	Sec.
Dodge-Plymouth													
1965	BBD-3843S, 44S	1/4	...	...	...	...	1/4	INDEX	...	1 7/16	...	1 1/16	...
1965	BBD-3847S, 48S	1/4	...	...	...	...	1/4	INDEX	...	1 7/16	...	1 3/16	...
1965	BBD-3849S	5/16	...	...	...	Ⓐ	1/4	2-RICH	...	1 9/16	...	1 3/16	...
1965	BBD-3850S	5/16	...	...	...	Ⓐ	1/4	2-RICH	...	1 9/16	...	1 3/16	...
1965	BBS-3833S, 34S, 35S, 36S	1/4	...	...	...	1/16	3/16	2-RICH	...	1 9/16	...	1 1/4	...
1965	BBS-3837S, 38S, 39S, 40S	1/4	...	...	...	1/16	3/16	2-RICH	...	1 11/16	...	1 11/32	...
1965	AFB-3853S, 54S	7/32	7/32	3/4	3/4	7/16	7/32	2-RICH	.020	1 7/16	1 9/16	1 1/16	1 1/4
1965	AFB-3855S, 56S	7/32	7/32	3/4	3/4	7/16	3/8	2-RICH	.020	1 7/16	1 9/16	1 3/16	1 5/16
1965	AFB-3859S, 60S-HP	7/32	7/32	3/4	3/4	7/16	3/8	INDEX	.020	1 7/16	1 9/16	1 3/16	1 5/16

Dodge-Plymouth, continued

YEAR	MODEL OR TYPE	FLOAT LEVEL (IN.) Prim.	Sec.	FLOAT DROP (IN.) Prim.	Sec.	Pump Travel Setting (IN.)	CHOKE SETTING Unloader (IN.)	Housing	Secondary Lockout Adj.	Throttle Bore Diam. Prim.	Sec.	Venturi Diam. Prim.	Sec.
1966	BBD-4125S, 4127S	5/16	...	...	...	Ⓐ	1/4	2-RICH	...	1 9/16	...	1 5/16	...
1966	BBD-4113S, 4114S	1/4	...	...	...	.060	1/4	2-RICH	...	1 7/16	...	1 1/16	...
1966	AFB-4119S	7/32	7/32	3/4	3/4	7/16	7/32	2-RICH	.020	1 7/16	1 9/16	1 1/16	1 1/4
1966	AFB-4130S, 4131S	7/32	7/32	3/4	3/4	7/16	3/8	2-RICH	.020	1 7/16	1 9/16	1 3/16	1 5/16
1966	BBD-4115S	1/4	...	...	...	...	1/4	INDEX	...	1 7/16	...	1 1/16	...
1966	BBD-4116S	1/4	...	...	...	...	1/4	INDEX	...	1 7/16	...	1 1/16	...
1966	BBD-4126S, 4128S	5/16	...	...	...	Ⓐ	1/4	2-RICH	...	1 9/16	...	1 5/16	...
1966	BBS-4099S, 4101S, 4103S, 05S	1/4	...	...	...	.060	3/16	2-RICH	...	1 9/16	...	1 1/4	...
1966	BBS-4100S, 02S, 4104S, 06S	1/4	...	...	...	.060	3/16	2-RICH	...	1 11/16	...	1 11/32	...
1966	AFB-4132S, 33S, 4136S, 37S	7/32	7/32	3/4	3/4	7/16	3/8	INDEX	.020	1 7/16	1 9/16	1 1/16	1 1/4
1966	AFB-4120S	7/32	7/32	3/4	3/4	7/16	3/8	2-RICH	.020	1 7/16	1 9/16	1 1/16	1 1/4
1966	AFB-4121S, 4122S	7/32	7/32	3/4	3/4	7/16	7/32	INDEX	.020	1 7/16	1 9/16	1 1/16	1 1/4
1967	BBS-4286S, 87S	1/4	...	...	...	.060	3/16	2-RICH	...	1 9/16	...	1 1/4	...
1967	BBS-4302S, CAP	1/4	...	...	...	.060	3/16	2-RICH	...	1 9/16	...	1 1/4	...
1967	BBD-4113SA, 4114SA	1/4	...	...	...	.060	1/4	2-RICH	...	1 7/16	...	1 1/16	...
1967	BBD-4115SA, 16SA, CAP	1/4	...	...	...	...	1/4	INDEX	...	1 7/16	...	1 1/16	...
1967	BBD-4296S, 97S	5/16	...	...	...	29/32	1/4	2-RICH	...	1 9/16	...	1 1/8	...
1967	BBD-4306S, 07S, CAP	5/16	...	...	...	Ⓐ	1/4	2-RICH	...	1 9/16	...	1 1/8	...
1967	AFB-4298S, 99S	7/32	7/32	3/4	3/4	7/16	3/8	2-RICH	.020	1 7/16	1 9/16	1 3/16	1 5/16
1967	AFB-4309S, 10S, CAP	5/16	5/16	3/4	3/4	7/16	3/8	INDEX	.020	1 7/16	1 9/16	1 1/16	1 5/16
1967	AFB-4326S, 27S	7/32	7/32	3/4	3/4	7/16	3/8	INDEX	.020	1 11/16	1 11/16	1 7/16	1 9/16
1967	AFB-4311S, 12S	5/16	5/16	3/4	3/4	7/16	5/16	INDEX	.020	1 7/16	1 9/16	1 1/16	1 5/16
1968	BBS-4414S-Std. Tr.	1/4	...	...	...	.060	3/16	2-RICH	...	1 9/16	...	1 1/4	...
1968	BBS-4415S-Aut. Tr.	1/4	...	...	...	.060	3/16	2-RICH	...	1 9/16	...	1 1/4	...
1968	BBD-4416S-Std. Tr.	1/4	...	...	...	...	1/4	2-RICH	...	1 7/16	...	1 1/16	...
1968	BBD-4417S-Aut. Tr.	1/4	...	...	...	...	1/4	2-RICH	...	1 7/16	...	1 1/16	...
1968	BBD-4420S-Std. Tr.	1/4	...	...	...	...	1/4	2-RICH	...	1 7/16	...	1 3/16	...
1968	BBD-4422S, 23S	5/16	...	...	...	29/32	1/4	2-RICH	...	1 9/16	...	1 5/16	...
1968	AFB-4430S	7/32	7/32	3/4	3/4	7/16	...	...	.020	1 7/16	1 11/16	1 3/16	1 9/16
1968	AFB-4431S, 32S	7/32	7/32	3/4	3/4	7/16	1/4	2-RICH	.020	1 7/16	1 11/16	1 3/16	1 9/16
1968	AVS-4424S, 25S	5/16	...	1/2	...	7/16	1/4	INDEX	.020	1 7/16	1 11/16	1 3/16	...
1968	AVS-4426S, 4401S	5/16	...	1/2	...	7/16	1/4	INDEX	.020	1 7/16	1 11/16	1 3/16	...
1968	AVS-4429S	5/16	...	1/2	...	7/16	1/4	INDEX	.020	1 11/16	1 11/16	1 7/16	...
1969	AVS-4615S-383-Std.	5/16	...	1/2	...	7/16	1/4	INDEX	.020	1 7/16	1 11/16	1 3/16	...
1969	AVS-4616S-4638S-383-A.T.	5/16	...	1/2	...	7/16	1/4	INDEX	.020	1 7/16	1 11/16	1 3/16	...
1969	AVS-4711S-383-Std.	5/16	...	1/2	...	7/16	1/4	INDEX	.020	1 7/16	1 11/16	1 3/16	...
1969	AVS-4611S-340-Std.	7/32	...	1/2	...	7/16	1/4	INDEX	.020	1 7/16	1 11/16	1 3/16	...
1969	AVS-4612S, 4639S, 340-Aut.	7/32	...	1/2	...	7/16	1/4	INDEX	.020	1 7/16	1 11/16	1 3/16	...
1969	AVS-4617S-440-Std.	7/32	...	1/2	...	7/16	1/4	INDEX	.020	1 11/16	1 11/16	1 7/16	...
1969	AVS-4618S, 4640S-440-A.T.	7/32	...	1/2	...	7/16	1/4	INDEX	.020	1 11/16	1 11/16	1 7/16	...
1969	AFB-4619S	7/32	7/32	3/4	3/4	7/16	...	...	.020	1 7/16	1 11/16	1 3/16	1 9/16
1969	AFB-4620S, 21S	7/32	7/32	3/4	3/4	7/16	1/4	2-RICH	.020	1 7/16	1 11/16	1 3/16	1 9/16
1969	BBD-4613S, 14S, 4774S	5/16	...	...	...	1	1/4	2-RICH	...	1 9/16	...	1 5/16	...
1969	BBS-4601S-170-M.T.	1/4	...	...	...	...	3/16	2-RICH	...	1 9/16	...	1 1/4	...
1969	BBS-4602S-170-Aut.	1/4	...	...	...	...	3/16	2-RICH	...	1 11/16	...	1 11/32	...
1969	BBD-4605S-273-Std.	1/4	...	...	...	...	1/4	INDEX	...	1 7/16	...	1 1/16	...
1969	BBD-4606S-273-A.T.	1/4	...	...	...	...	1/4	INDEX	...	1 7/16	...	1 1/16	...
1969	BBD-4607S-318-Std.	1/4	...	...	...	...	1/4	INDEX	...	1 7/16	...	1 3/16	...
1969	BBD-4608S-318-A.T.	1/4	...	...	...	...	1/4	INDEX	...	1 7/16	...	1 3/16	...
1970	BBS-4715S-198, Std. w. CAS	1/4	...	...	...	...	3/16	2-RICH	...	1 11/16	...	1 11/32	...
1970	BBS-4716S-198, Auto. w. CAS	1/4	...	...	...	...	3/16	2-RICH	...	1 11/16	...	1 11/32	...
1970	BBS-4717S-198, man. w. ECS	1/4	...	...	...	...	3/16	2-RICH	...	1 11/16	...	1 11/32	...
1970	BBS-4718S-198, Auto. w. ECS	1/4	...	...	...	...	3/16	2-RICH	...	1 11/16	...	1 11/32	...
1970	BBD-4721S-318, Std. w. CAS	1/4	...	...	...	...	1/4	INDEX	...	1 7/16	...	1 3/16	...
1970	BBD-4722-318, Auto. w/o AC, w. CAS	1/4	...	...	...	...	1/4	INDEX	...	1 7/16	...	1 3/16	...
1970	BBD-4895S-318, Auto. w. AC, w. CAS	1/4	...	...	...	...	1/4	INDEX	...	1 7/16	...	1 3/16	...
1970	BBD-4723S-318, Std. w. ECS	1/4	...	...	...	...	1/4	INDEX	...	1 7/16	...	1 3/16	...
1970	BBD-4724S-318, Auto. w. ECS	1/4	...	...	...	...	1/4	INDEX	...	1 7/16	...	1 3/16	...
1970	BBD-4725S-383, Std. w. CAS	5/16	...	...	...	1	1/4	2-RICH	...	1 7/16	...	1 5/16	...
1970	BBD-4726S-383, Auto. w. CAS, w/o AC	5/16	...	...	...	1	1/4	2-RICH	...	1 7/16	...	1 5/16	...

YEAR	MODEL OR TYPE	FLOAT LEVEL (IN.) Prim.	Sec.	FLOAT DROP (IN.) Prim.	Sec.	Pump Travel Setting (IN.)	CHOKE SETTING Unloader (IN.)	Housing	Secondary Lockout Adj.	Throttle Bore Diam. Prim.	Sec.	Venturi Diam. Prim.	Sec.

Dodge—Plymouth, continued

YEAR	MODEL OR TYPE	Prim.	Sec.	Prim.	Sec.	Pump	Unloader	Housing	Lockout	Prim.	Sec.	Prim.	Sec.
1970	BBD-4894S-383, Auto. w. AC, w. CAS	$5/16$	...	...	...	1	$1/4$	2-RICH	...	$1^9/16$	...	$1^5/16$	...
1970	BBD-4725S-383, Std. w. ECS	$5/16$	...	...	...	1	$1/4$	2-RICH	...	$1^9/16$	...	$1^5/16$	...
1970	BBD-4728S-383, Auto. w. ECS	$5/16$	...	...	...	1	$1/4$	2-RICH	...	$1^9/16$	...	$1^5/16$	...
1970	AVS-4933S-340, Std. w. CAS	$7/32$	...	$1/2$	...	$7/16$	$1/4$	INDEX	.020	$1^7/16$	$1^{11}/16$	$1^3/16$	...
1970	AVS-4934S-340, Auto. w/o AC, w. CAS	$7/32$	...	$1/2$	...	$7/16$	$1/4$	INDEX	.020	$1^7/16$	$1^{11}/16$	$1^3/16$	...
1970	AVS-4935S-340, Auto. w. AC, w. CAS	$7/32$	...	$1/2$	...	$7/16$	$1/4$	INDEX	.020	$1^7/16$	$1^{11}/16$	$1^3/16$	...
1970	AVS-4936S-340, Std. w. ECS	$7/32$	...	$1/2$	...	$7/16$	$1/4$	INDEX	.020	$1^7/16$	$1^{11}/16$	$1^3/16$	...
1970	AVS-4937S-340, Auto. w. ECS	$7/32$	...	$1/2$	...	$7/16$	$1/4$	INDEX	.020	$1^7/16$	$1^{11}/16$	$1^3/16$	...
1970	AVS-4736S-383, Auto. w/o AC, w. CAS	$5/16$	...	$1/2$	...	$7/16$	$1/4$	2-RICH	.020	$1^7/16$	$1^{11}/16$	$1^3/16$	...
1970	AVS-4732S-383, Auto. w. AC, w. CAS	$5/16$	...	$1/2$	...	$7/16$	$1/4$	2-RICH	.020	$1^7/16$	$1^{11}/16$	$1^3/16$	...
1970	AVS-4734S-383, Auto. w. ECS	$5/16$	...	$1/2$	...	$7/16$	$1/4$	2-RICH	.020	$1^7/16$	$1^{11}/16$	$1^3/16$	...
1970	AVS-4737S-440, Std. w. CAS	$7/32$	...	$1/2$	...	$7/16$	$1/4$	2-RICH	.020	$1^{11}/16$	$1^{11}/16$	$1^7/16$	...
1970	AVS-4738S-440, Auto. w/o AC, w. CAS	$7/32$	...	$1/2$	...	$7/16$	$1/4$	INDEX	.020	$1^{11}/16$	$1^{11}/16$	$1^7/16$	...
1970	AVS-4741S-440, Auto. w. AC, w. CAS	$7/32$	...	$1/2$	...	$7/16$	$1/4$	INDEX	.020	$1^7/16$	$1^{11}/16$	$1^7/16$	...
1970	AVS-4739S-440, Std. w. ECS	$7/32$	...	$1/2$	...	$7/16$	$1/4$	INDEX	.020	$1^7/16$	$1^{11}/16$	$1^7/16$	...
1970	AVS-4740S-440, Auto. w. ECS	$7/32$	...	$1/2$	...	$7/16$	$1/4$	INDEX	.020	$1^7/16$	$1^{11}/16$	$1^7/16$	...
1970	AFB-4742S-426, Hemi Std. or Auto.	$7/32$	...	$1/2$	...	$7/16$	...	...	.020	$1^7/16$	$1^{11}/16$	$1^3/16$	$1^9/16$
1970	AFB-4745S-426, Hemi Std.	$7/32$	...	$3/4$	...	$7/16$	$1/4$	2-RICH	.020	$1^7/16$	$1^{11}/16$	$1^3/16$	$1^9/16$
1970	AFB-4746S-426, Hemi Auto.	$7/32$	...	$3/4$	...	$7/16$	$1/4$	2-RICH	.020	$1^7/16$	$1^{11}/16$	$1^3/16$	$1^9/16$
1971	BBS-4955S, 56S	$1/4$	...	...	...	...	$3/16$	2-RICH	...	$1^{11}/16$	...	$1^{11}/32$	...
1971	BBD-4957S, 58S	$1/4$	...	...	...	...	$1/4$	INDEX	...	$1^7/16$	...	$1^5/16$	...
1971	BBD-4961S, 62S	$5/16$	...	...	...	...	$1/4$	2-RICH	...	$1^9/16$	...	$1^5/16$	...
1971	TQ-4972S, 73S	1	...	...	...	$31/64$	.190	2-RICH	.020	$1^3/8$	$2^1/4$	$1^7/16$	...
1971	AVS-6125S, 4966S	$7/32$	...	$1/2$	...	$7/16$	$1/4$	2-RICH	.020	$1^7/16$	$1^{11}/16$	$1^7/16$	...
1971	AVS-4967S, 68S	$7/32$	...	$1/2$	...	$7/16$	$1/4$	2-RICH	.020	$1^{11}/16$	$1^{11}/16$	$1^7/16$	...
1971	AFB-4971S	$7/32$	...	$3/4$	...	$31/64$	...	...	.020	$1^7/16$	$1^{11}/16$	$1^3/16$	$1^9/16$
1971	AFB-4969S, 70S	$7/32$	...	$3/4$	...	$31/64$	...	...	.020	$1^7/16$	$1^{11}/16$	$1^3/16$	$1^9/16$
1972	BBD-6149S, 50S	$1/4$	...	...	...	...	$1/4$	INDEX	...	$1^7/16$	...	$1^3/16$	...
1972	BBD-5151S, 52S, Calif.	$1/4$	...	...	...	...	$1/4$	INDEX	...	$1^7/16$	...	$1^3/16$	...
1972	TQ-6138S, 39S	1	...	...	...	$31/64$	.190	2-RICH	...	$1^3/8$	$2^1/4$	$1^7/16$	...
1972	TQ-6090, 6140, 65, 66	1	...	...	...	$31/64$	.190	2-RICH	...	$1^1/2$	$2^1/4$	$1^3/16$	...

Ⓐ—Set pump arm parallel CAP—Cleaner Air Package CAS—Cleaner Air System ECS—Evaporation Control System

Ford-Mercury

YEAR	MODEL OR TYPE	Prim.	Sec.	Prim.	Sec.	Pump	Unloader	Housing	Lockout	Prim.	Sec.	Prim.	Sec.
1967	YF, 170–200 A.T.	.218	...	...	...	...	$1/4$	1-RICH	...	$1^7/16$	...	$1^1/4$	...
1968	YF, 170 A.T.	.218	...	...	...	...	.280	INDEX	...	$1^7/16$	...	$1^3/16$	...
1968	YF, 170 S.T.	.218	...	...	...	...	.280	1-LEAN	...	$1^7/16$	...	$1^1/18$	...
1968	YF, 240 S.T.	$7/32$	...	...	...	...	.280	INDEX	...	$1^{11}/16$	...	$1^5/16$	...
1969	YF, 170 A.T.	$7/32$	...	...	...	...	.280	INDEX	...	$1^7/16$	...	$1^3/16$	...
1969	YF, 170 S.T.	$7/32$	...	...	...	...	.280	1-LEAN	...	$1^7/16$	...	$1^3/16$	...
1969	YF, 240, S.T.	$7/32$	...	...	...	...	.280	INDEX	...	$1^{11}/16$	...	$1^5/16$	...
1970	YF, DODF-N₁R₁S₁U	$7/32$	...	...	...	...	.280	1-RICH	...	$1^7/16$	...	$1^3/16$	...
1970	YF, All others	$3/8$	...	...	...	...	$1/4$	INDEX	...	$1^{11}/16$	...	$1^5/16$	...
1970	RBS, 250	$9/16$	...	...	...	...	$1/4$	INDEX	...	$1^9/16$	...	$1^7/16$	...
1971	YF, D1DF-EA	$3/8$	...	$1^1/4$	...	...	.280	INDEX	...	$1^7/16$	...	$1^3/16$	...
1971	YF, All others	$3/8$	...	$1^1/4$	...	...	$1/4$	INDEX	...	$1^{11}/16$	...	$1^5/16$	...
1971	RBS	$9/16$	...	$1^1/4$	...	...	$1/4$	INDEX	...	$1^9/16$	...	$1^7/16$	...

Lincoln-Continental

YEAR	MODEL OR TYPE	Prim.	Sec.	Prim.	Sec.	Pump	Unloader	Housing	Lockout	Prim.	Sec.	Prim.	Sec.
1965	AFB	$3/16$	$3/16$	$23/32$	$23/32$	$17/32$	$1/8$	1-RICH	.020	$1^9/16$	$1^{11}/16$	$1^3/16$	$1^9/16$
1967-68	C7VF-A w. AC, Auto, w Emission control	$3/16$	...	$23/32$	...	①	.096	1-RICH	.020	$1^9/16$	$1^{11}/16$	$1^3/16$	$1^9/16$
1967-68	C7VF-B w/o AC, Auto, w. Emission control	$3/16$	...	$23/32$	...	①	.096	1-RICH	.020	$1^9/16$	$1^{11}/16$	$1^3/16$	$1^9/16$
1967-68	C7VF-C w. AC, Auto., w/o Emission control	$3/16$	...	$23/32$	...	①	.096	1-RICH	.020	$1^9/16$	$1^{11}/16$	$1^3/16$	$1^9/16$
1967-68	C7VF-D w/o AC, Auto., w/o Emission control	$3/16$	...	$23/32$	...	①	.096	1-RICH	.020	$1^9/16$	$1^{11}/16$	$1^3/16$	$1^9/16$

①—Accelerator pump position—inner hole.

YEAR	MODEL OR TYPE	FLOAT LEVEL (IN.)		FLOAT DROP (IN.)		Pump Travel Setting (IN.)	CHOKE SETTING		Secondary Lockout Adj.	Throttle Bore Diam.		Venturi Diam.	
		Prim.	Sec.	Prim.	Sec.		Unloader (IN.)	Housing		Prim.	Sec.	Prim.	Sec.
Pontiac													
1965	AFB-3896S	5/16	5/16	23/32	23/32	...	5/32	1-RICH	.020	1 7/16	1 11/16	...	...
1965	AFB-3895S, 3898S	3/8	3/8	23/32	23/32	...	5/32	1-RICH	.020	1 7/16	1 11/16	...	...
1966	AFB-4030S	1/4	1/4	23/32	23/32	5/16	5/32	1-RICH	.020	1 7/16	1 11/16		
1966	AFB-4033S, 4041S	5/16	5/16	23/32	23/32	5/16	5/32	1-RICH	.020	1 7/16	1 11/16		
1966	AFB-4034S	1/4	1/4	23/32	23/32	5/16	5/32	1-RICH	.020	1 7/16	1 11/16		
1966	AFB-4035S	3/8	3/8	23/32	23/32	5/16	5/32	1-RICH	.020	1 7/16	1 11/16		
1967	AFB-4242S	5/16	5/16	23/32	23/32	3/8	5/32	1-RICH	.020	1 7/16	1 11/16		
1967	AFB-4243S	3/8	3/8	23/32	23/32	3/8	5/32	1-RICH	.020	1 7/16	1 11/16		
1967	AFB-4244S	1/4	1/4	23/32	23/32	3/8	5/32	1-RICH	.020	1 7/16	1 11/16		
1967	AFB-4245S	5/16	5/16	23/32	23/32	3/8	5/32	1-RICH	.020	1 7/16	1 11/16		
Rambler—American Motors													
1965	RBS-3708S, 3766S	15/32	...	...	...	...	7/64	INDEX	...	1 7/16	...	1 1/4	...
1965	WCD-3706S	1/8	...	5/8	...	...	3/16	INDEX	...	1 5/16	...	1 1/16	...
1966-67	RBS-3882S	15/32	...	...	...	...	1/8	1-RICH	...	1 9/16	...	1 3/8	...
1966	WCD-4191S	1/4	...	5/8	...	...	3/16	INDEX	...	1 7/16	...	1 3/16	...
1966	WCD-3888S	1/4	...	5/8	...	...	3/16	INDEX	...	1 7/16	...	1 3/16	...
1966	AFB-4250S	5/16	...	2	...	3/8	5/32	INDEX	.020	1 7/16	1 11/16	1 3/16	1 9/16
1967	AFB-4216S, 4354S	5/16	...	2	...	3/8	9/32	2-RICH	.020	1 7/16	1 11/16	1 3/16	1 9/16
1967	AFB-4258S, 4358S	5/16	...	2	...	3/8	5/32	INDEX	.020	1 7/16	1 11/16	1 3/16	1 9/16
1967	WCD-3888S	1/4	...				3/16	INDEX	...	1 7/16	...	1 3/16	...
1967	WCD-4365S, Aut.	7/32	...			...	5/16	2-RICH		1 7/16	...	1 3/16	...
1968	RBS	9/16				...	1/8	1-RICH		1 9/16	...	1 3/8	...
1968	WCD	1/4	...			(1)	3/16	INDEX	...	1 7/16	...	1 3/16	
1968	WCD, Aut. Tr.	7/32	...			(1)	5/16	2-RICH	...	1 7/16	...	1 3/16	
1968	AFB-4467S	5/16	...	2		15/64	5/32	2-RICH	.020	1 7/16	1 11/16	1 3/16	1 9/16
1968	AFB-4468S	5/16	...	2		17/64	5/32	INDEX	.020	1 7/16	1 11/16	1 3/16	1 9/16
1968	AFB-4469S	5/16	...	2		17/64	5/32	2-RICH	.020	1 7/16	1 11/16	1 3/16	1 9/16
1969	AFB-4660S	11/32		2		21/64	5/32	2-RICH	.020	1 7/16	1 11/16	1 1/16	1 9/16
1969	AFB-4661S	11/32		2		21/64	5/32	INDEX	.020	1 7/16	1 11/16	1 1/16	1 9/16
1969	AFB-4662S	11/32		2		21/64	5/32	INDEX	.020	1 7/16	1 11/16	1 3/16	1 9/16
1969	AFB-4663S	11/32		2		21/64	5/32	INDEX	.020	1 7/16	1 11/16	1 3/16	1 9/16
1969	AFB-4664S	11/32		2		21/64	5/32	INDEX	.020	1 7/16	1 11/16	1 3/16	1 9/16
1969	AFB-4665S	11/32		2		21/64	5/32	INDEX	.020	1 7/16	1 11/16	1 3/16	1 9/16
1969	WCD-4667S, 68S	7/32	...	...	...	...	3/16	INDEX	...	1 7/16	...	1 3/16	...
1969	RBS-4631S, 33S	9/16	...	...	...	1/64	3/16	INDEX	...	1 9/16	...	1 3/8	...
1969	RBS-4634S, 66S	9/16	...	...	...	1/64	3/16	2-RICH	...	1 9/16	...	1 3/8	
1970	YF-4768S-199, 232, Std.	29/64	...	1 1/4	...	...	21/64	INDEX	...	1 11/16	...	1 5/16	...
1970	YF-4767S, Aut.-199, 232 (2)	29/64	...	1 1/4	...	...	19/64	INDEX	...	1 11/16	...	1 5/16	...
1970	YF-4978S-232, Auto. (3)	29/64	...	1 1/4	...	...	19/64	1-RICH	...	1 11/16	...	1 5/16	...
1970	YF-4770S-232, Std.	29/64	...	1 1/4	...	...	19/64	INDEX	...	1 11/16	...	1 5/16	...
1970	YF-4769S-232, Auto.	29/64	...	1 1/4	...	...	19/64	INDEX	...	1 11/16	...	1 5/16	...
1970	WCD-4950S-232, Std.	7/32	...	...	...	...	3/16	INDEX	...	1 7/16	...	1 3/16	...
1970	WCD-4816S-232, Auto.	7/32	...	...	...	...	3/16	INDEX	...	1 7/16	...	1 3/16	...
1970	WCD-4817S-232, Std.-Auto.	7/32	...	...	...	...	3/16	INDEX	...	1 7/16	...	1 3/16	...
1971	YF-6038S	29/64	...	1 1/4	...	...	.300	INDEX	...	1 11/16	...	1 19/32	...
1971	YF-All others	29/64	...	1 1/4	...	...	.300	INDEX	...	1 11/16	...	1 5/16	...

(1) —Set pump arm parallel. (2) —Prior to engine code 209E22. (3) —Effective with engine code 209E22.

Tempest

YEAR	MODEL OR TYPE	FLOAT LEVEL (IN.)		FLOAT DROP (IN.)		Pump Travel Setting (IN.)	CHOKE SETTING		Secondary Lockout Adj.	Throttle Bore Diam.		Venturi Diam.	
		Prim.	Sec.	Prim.	Sec.		Unloader (IN.)	Housing		Prim.	Sec.	Prim.	Sec.
1965	AFB-3895S, 3899S	3/8	3/8	23/32	23/32	.300	.150	1-RICH	.020	1 7/16	1 11/16	...	...
1965	AFB-3896S, 3900S	5/16	5/16	23/32	23/32	.300	.150	1-RICH	.020	1 7/16	1 11/16	...	...
1966	AFB-4030S	1/4	1/4	23/32	23/32	.375	5/32	1-RICH	.020	1 7/16	1 11/16		
1966	AFB-4031S, 4033S	5/16	5/16	23/32	23/32	.375	5/32	1-RICH	.020	1 7/16	1 11/16		
1966	AFB-4034S, 4041S	5/16	5/16	23/32	23/32	.375	5/32	1-RICH	.020	1 7/16	1 11/16		
1966	AFB-4035S	3/8	3/8	23/32	23/32	.375	5/32	1-RICH	.020	1 7/16	1 11/16		
1966	AFB-4036S	1/4	1/4	23/32	23/32	.375	5/32	1-RICH	.020	1 7/16	1 11/16		
1967	AFB-4242S	5/16	5/16	23/32	23/32	.375	5/32	1-RICH	.020	1 7/16	1 11/16		
1967	AFB-4243S	3/8	3/8	23/32	23/32	.375	5/32	1-RICH	.020	1 7/16	1 11/16		

SINGLE BARREL—BBS TYPE

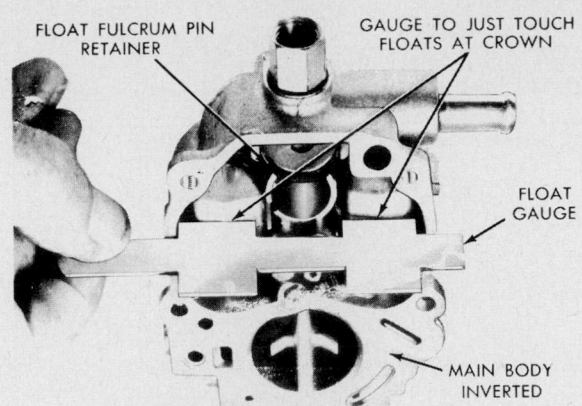

FLOAT FULCRUM PIN RETAINER

GAUGE TO JUST TOUCH FLOATS AT CROWN

FLOAT GAUGE

MAIN BODY INVERTED

Float Adjustment
(© Dodge Division, Chrysler Corp.)

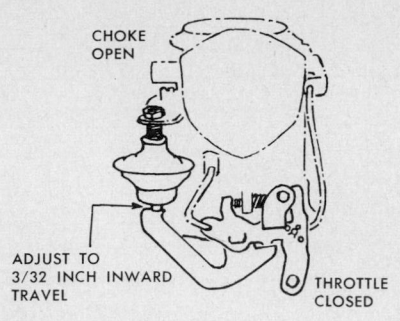

CHOKE OPEN

ADJUST TO 3/32 INCH INWARD TRAVEL

THROTTLE CLOSED

BBS dashpot adjustment

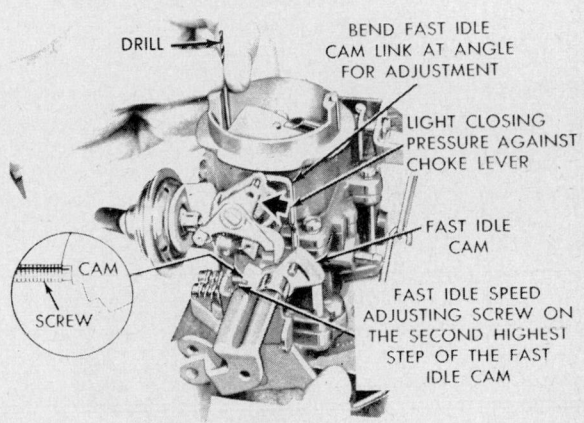

DRILL

BEND FAST IDLE CAM LINK AT ANGLE FOR ADJUSTMENT

LIGHT CLOSING PRESSURE AGAINST CHOKE LEVER

FAST IDLE CAM

FAST IDLE SPEED ADJUSTING SCREW ON THE SECOND HIGHEST STEP OF THE FAST IDLE CAM

CAM SCREW

Fast Idle Cam Setting
(© Dodge Division, Chrysler Corp.)

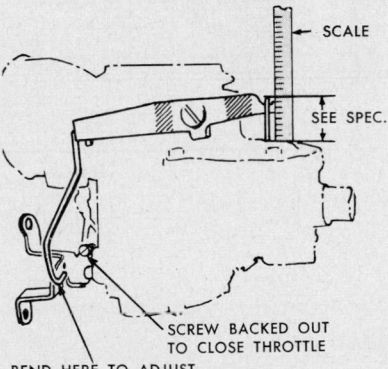

SCALE

SEE SPEC.

SCREW BACKED OUT TO CLOSE THROTTLE

BEND HERE TO ADJUST

BBS pump adjustment

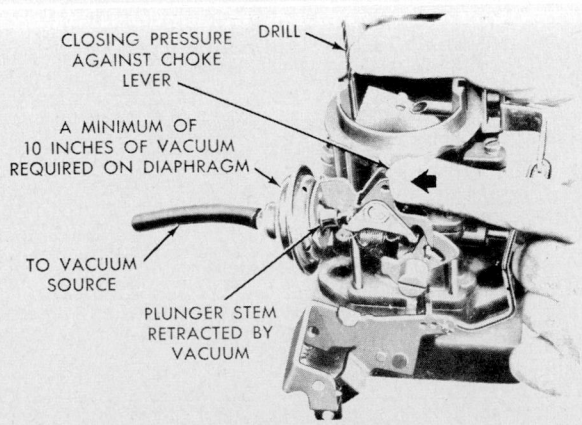

CLOSING PRESSURE AGAINST CHOKE LEVER

DRILL

A MINIMUM OF 10 INCHES OF VACUUM REQUIRED ON DIAPHRAGM

TO VACUUM SOURCE

PLUNGER STEM RETRACTED BY VACUUM

Vacuum Kick Adjustment
(© Dodge Division, Chrysler Corp.)

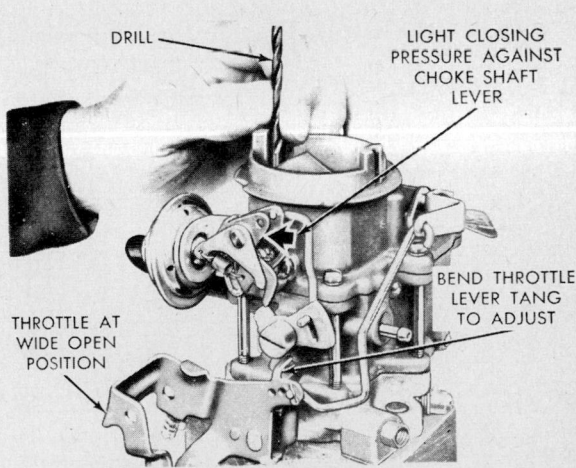

DRILL

LIGHT CLOSING PRESSURE AGAINST CHOKE SHAFT LEVER

THROTTLE AT WIDE OPEN POSITION

BEND THROTTLE LEVER TANG TO ADJUST

Unloader Setting
(© Dodge Division, Chrysler Corp.)

SINGLE BARREL—YF TYPE

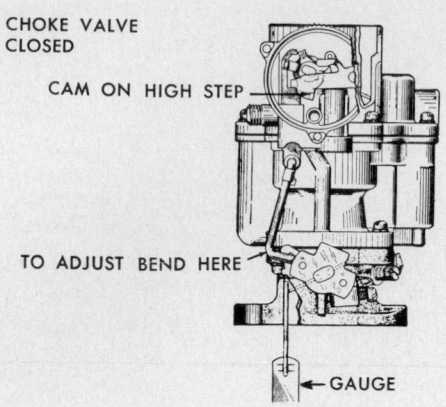

CHOKE VALVE
CLOSED

CAM ON HIGH STEP

TO ADJUST BEND HERE

GAUGE

YF fast idle adjustment

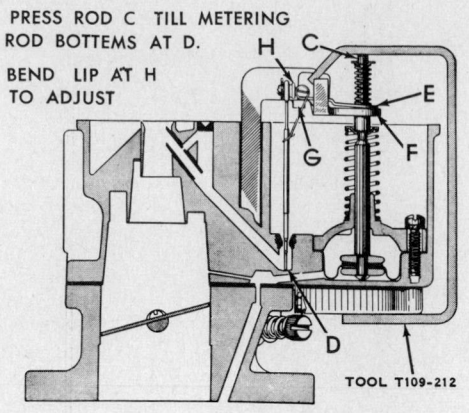

PRESS ROD C TILL METERING
ROD BOTTOMS AT D.

BEND LIP AT H
TO ADJUST

H   C

E

G   F

D

TOOL T109-212

YF metering rod adjustment

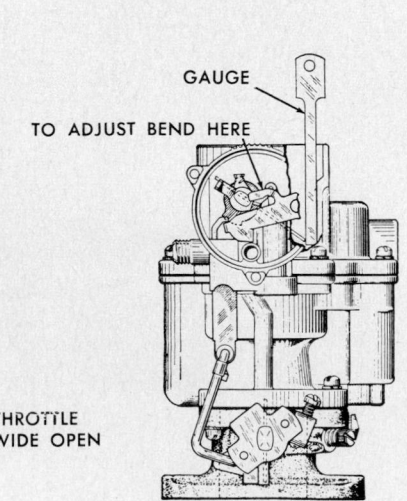

GASKET REMOVED   A

GAUGE

YF float level adjustment

GAUGE

TO ADJUST BEND HERE

THROTTLE
WIDE OPEN

YF unloader adjustment

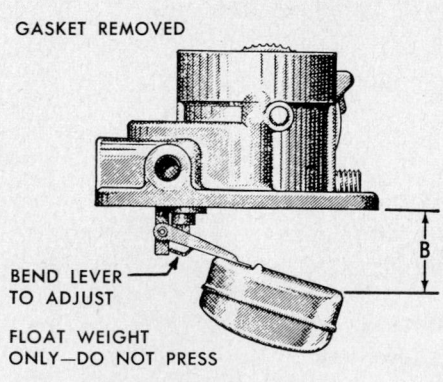

GASKET REMOVED

B

BEND LEVER
TO ADJUST

FLOAT WEIGHT
ONLY—DO NOT PRESS

YF float drop adjustment

SINGLE BARREL RBS TYPE

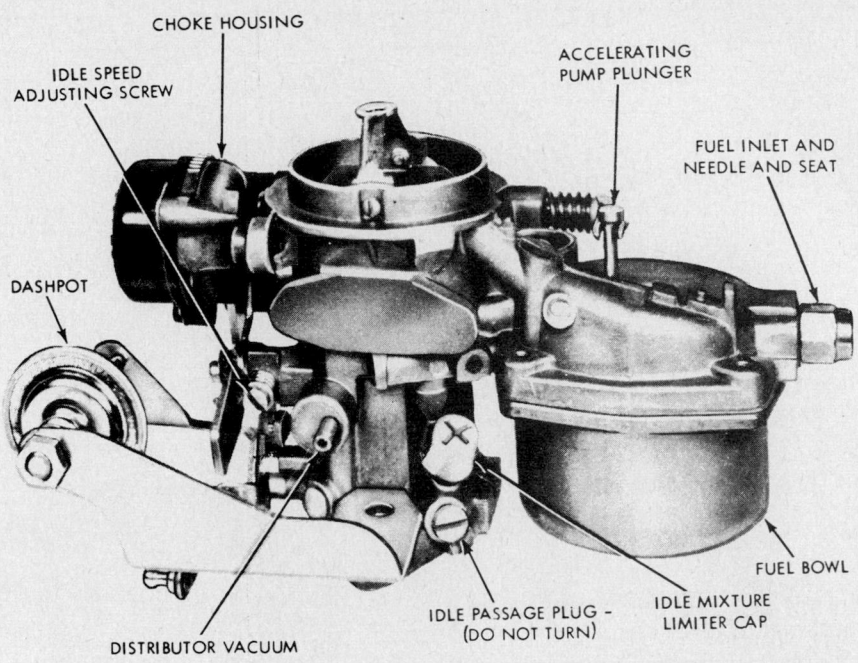

CHOKE HOUSING

IDLE SPEED
ADJUSTING SCREW

ACCELERATING
PUMP PLUNGER

FUEL INLET AND
NEEDLE AND SEAT

DASHPOT

FUEL BOWL

DISTRIBUTOR VACUUM

IDLE PASSAGE PLUG -
(DO NOT TURN)

IDLE MIXTURE
LIMITER CAP

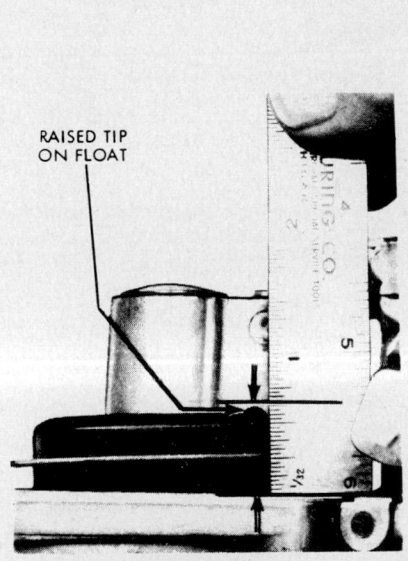

RAISED TIP
ON FLOAT

Float Setting
(© Ford Motor Co.)

PUMP
STROKE

Accelerator Pump Adjustment
(© Ford Motor Co.)

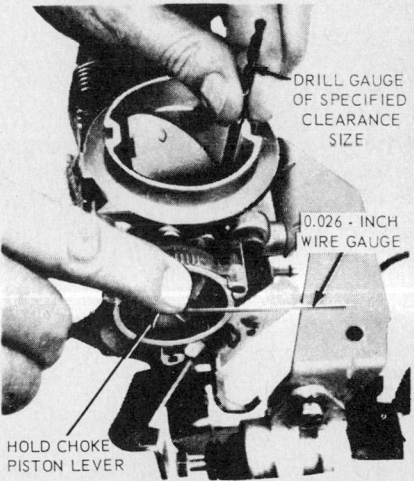

DRILL GAUGE
OF SPECIFIED
CLEARANCE
SIZE

0.026 - INCH
WIRE GAUGE

HOLD CHOKE
PISTON LEVER

Choke Plate Pulldown Setting
(© Ford Motor Co.)

TWO BARREL—BBD TYPE

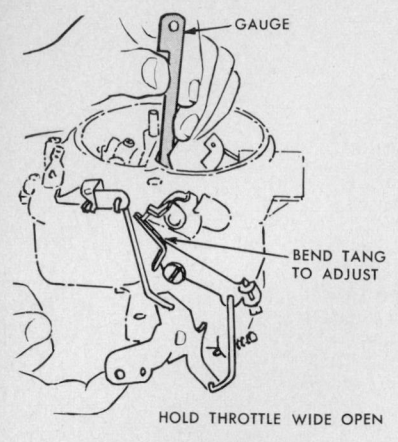

GAUGE

BEND TANG
TO ADJUST

HOLD THROTTLE WIDE OPEN

BBD unloader adjustment

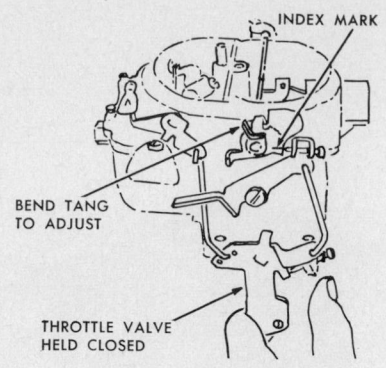

INDEX MARK

BEND TANG
TO ADJUST

THROTTLE VALVE
HELD CLOSED

BBD fast idle index alignment

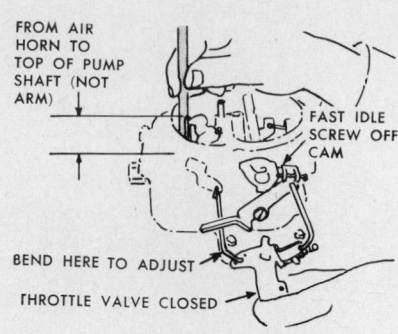

FROM AIR
HORN TO
TOP OF PUMP
SHAFT (NOT
ARM)

FAST IDLE
SCREW OFF
CAM

BEND HERE TO ADJUST

THROTTLE VALVE CLOSED

BBD pump adjustment

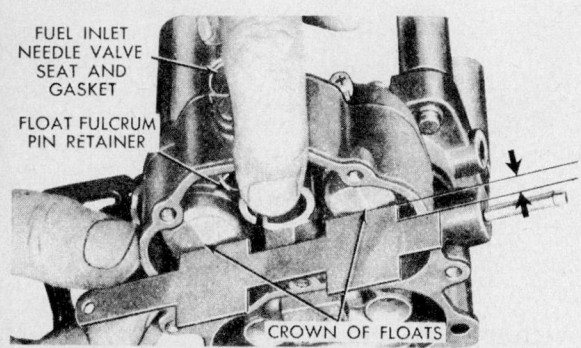

FUEL INLET
NEEDLE VALVE
SEAT AND
GASKET

FLOAT FULCRUM
PIN RETAINER

CROWN OF FLOATS

Float Level Adjustment
(© Dodge Division, Chrysler Corp.)

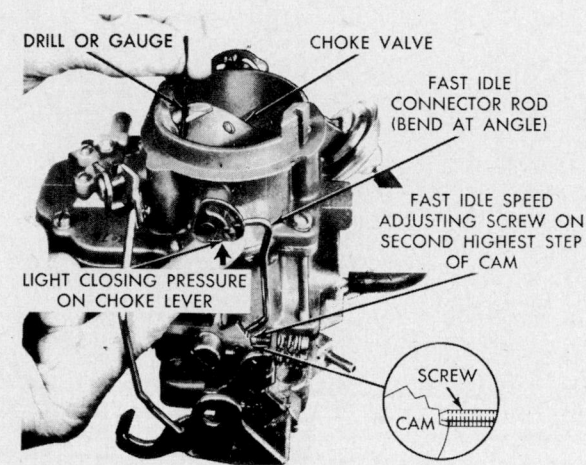

DRILL OR GAUGE

CHOKE VALVE

FAST IDLE
CONNECTOR ROD
(BEND AT ANGLE)

FAST IDLE SPEED
ADJUSTING SCREW ON
SECOND HIGHEST STEP
OF CAM

LIGHT CLOSING PRESSURE
ON CHOKE LEVER

SCREW

CAM

Fast Idle Cam Adjustment
(© Dodge Division, Chrysler Corp.)

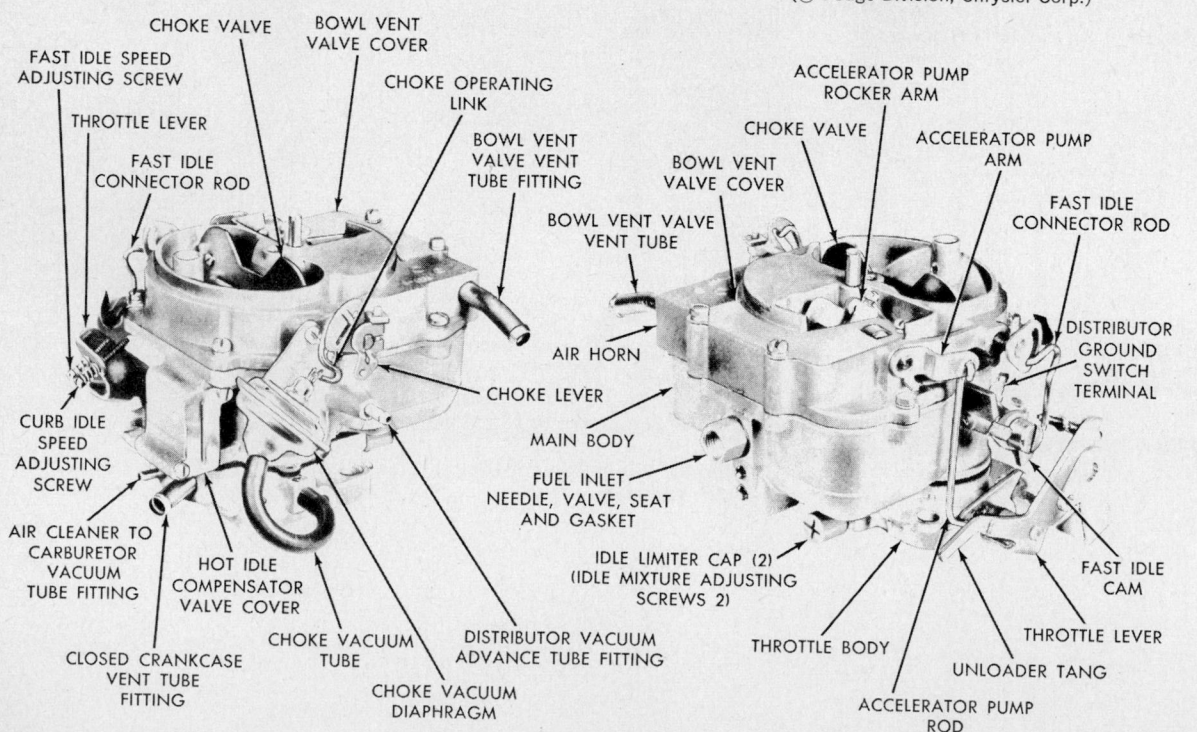

CHOKE VALVE

BOWL VENT
VALVE COVER

FAST IDLE SPEED
ADJUSTING SCREW

CHOKE OPERATING
LINK

THROTTLE LEVER

FAST IDLE
CONNECTOR ROD

BOWL VENT
VALVE VENT
TUBE FITTING

BOWL VENT VALVE
VENT TUBE

AIR HORN

CHOKE LEVER

MAIN BODY

CURB IDLE
SPEED
ADJUSTING
SCREW

FUEL INLET
NEEDLE, VALVE, SEAT
AND GASKET

AIR CLEANER TO
CARBURETOR VACUUM
TUBE FITTING

HOT IDLE
COMPENSATOR
VALVE COVER

CHOKE VACUUM
TUBE

DISTRIBUTOR VACUUM
ADVANCE TUBE FITTING

IDLE LIMITER CAP (2)
(IDLE MIXTURE ADJUSTING
SCREWS 2)

CLOSED CRANKCASE
VENT TUBE
FITTING

CHOKE VACUUM
DIAPHRAGM

ACCELERATOR PUMP
ROCKER ARM

CHOKE VALVE

ACCELERATOR PUMP
ARM

BOWL VENT
VALVE COVER

FAST IDLE
CONNECTOR ROD

DISTRIBUTOR
GROUND
SWITCH
TERMINAL

FAST IDLE
CAM

THROTTLE LEVER

THROTTLE BODY

UNLOADER TANG

ACCELERATOR PUMP
ROD

FOUR BARREL—WCFB TYPE

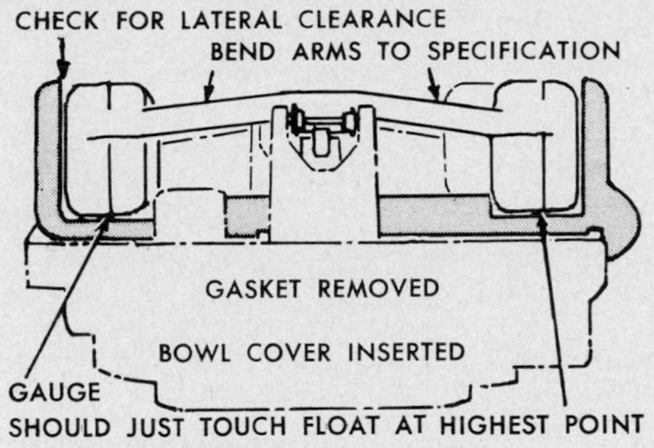

CHECK FOR LATERAL CLEARANCE
BEND ARMS TO SPECIFICATION

GASKET REMOVED

BOWL COVER INSERTED

GAUGE
SHOULD JUST TOUCH FLOAT AT HIGHEST POINT

WCFB float level adjustment

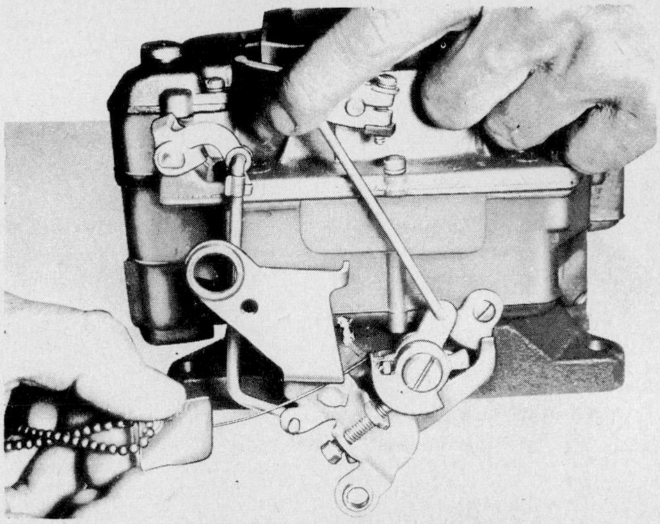

Choke Rod (Fast Idle) Adjustment
(© Chevrolet Division, GM Corp.)

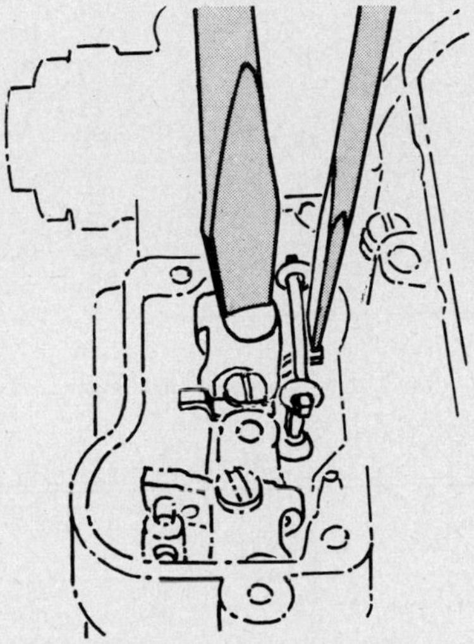

WCFB metering rod adjustment

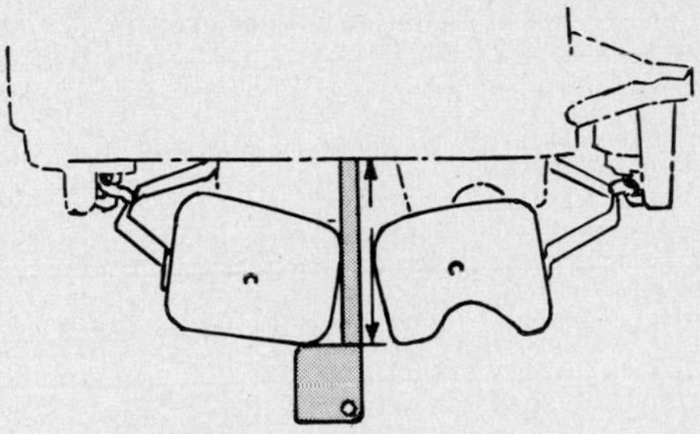

WCFB float drop adjustment

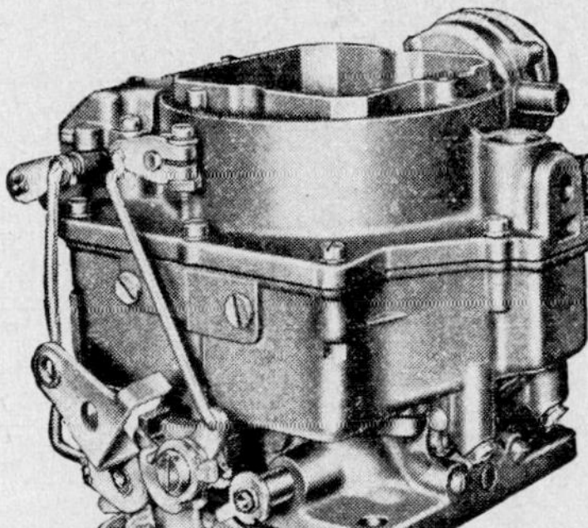

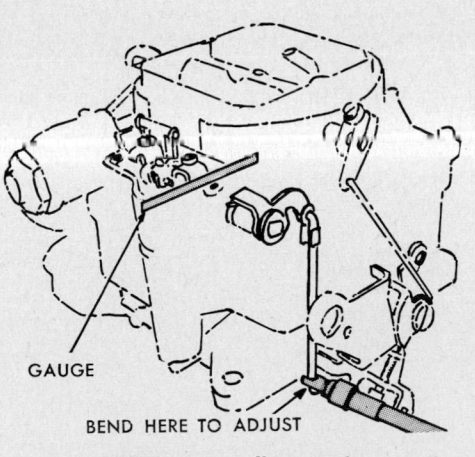

GAUGE

BEND HERE TO ADJUST

WCFB pump adjustment

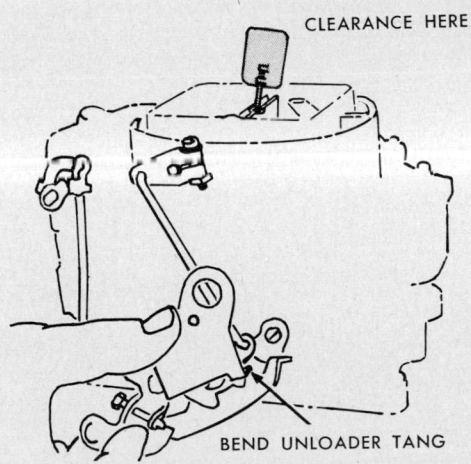

CLEARANCE HERE

BEND UNLOADER TANG

WCFB unloader adjustment

FOUR BARREL—AFB TYPE

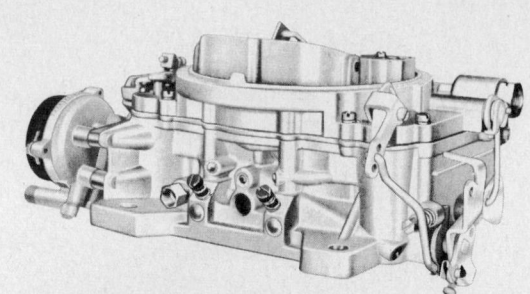

AFB fast idle throttle adjustment

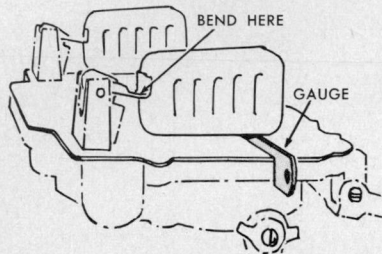

BEND HERE

GAUGE

AFB float level adjustment

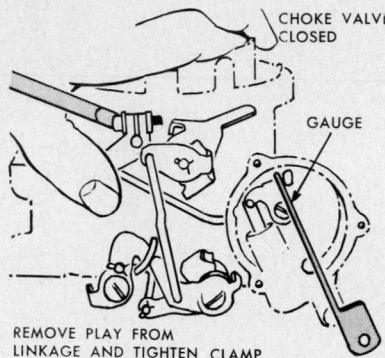

CHOKE VALVE CLOSED

GAUGE

REMOVE PLAY FROM LINKAGE AND TIGHTEN CLAMP

AFB choke piston lever adjustment

BEND HERE TO ADJUST

AFB dashpot adjustment

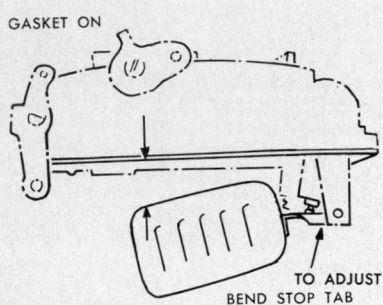

GASKET ON

TO ADJUST BEND STOP TAB

AFB float drop adjustment

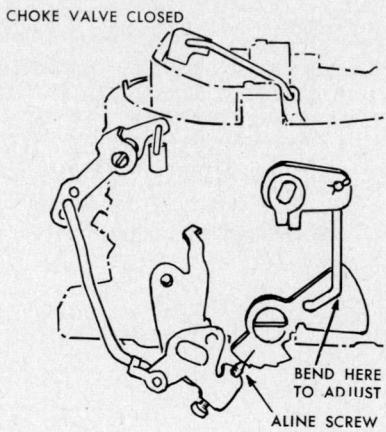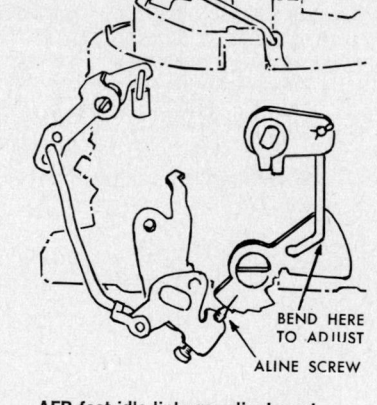

CHOKE VALVE CLOSED

BEND HERE TO ADJUST

ALINE SCREW

AFB fast idle linkage adjustment

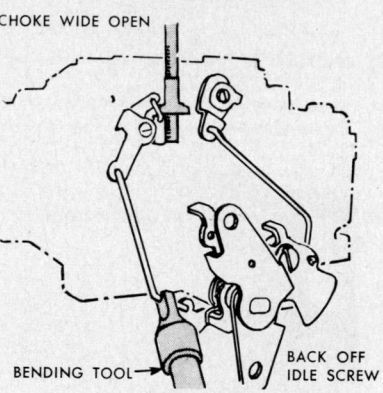

CHOKE WIDE OPEN

BENDING TOOL

BACK OFF IDLE SCREW

AFB pump adjustment

WITH THROTTLE VALVE CLOSED

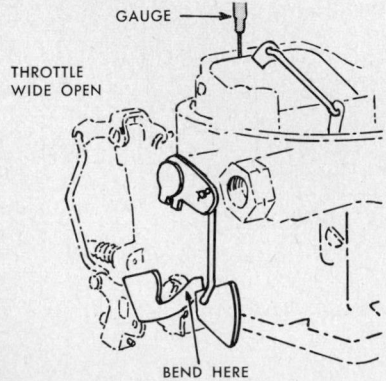

GAUGE

THROTTLE WIDE OPEN

BEND HERE

AFB unloader adjustment

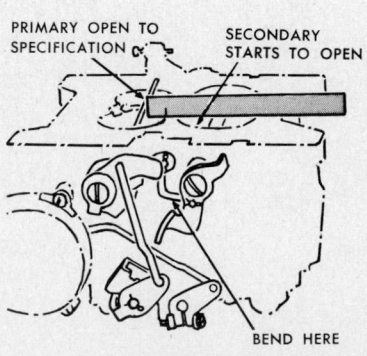

PRIMARY OPEN TO SPECIFICATION

SECONDARY STARTS TO OPEN

BEND HERE

AFB secondary throttle adjustment

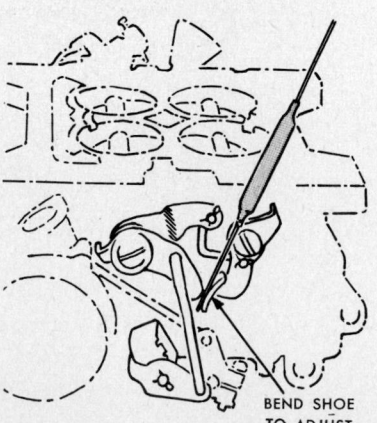

BEND SHOE TO ADJUST

FOUR BARREL — AVS TYPE

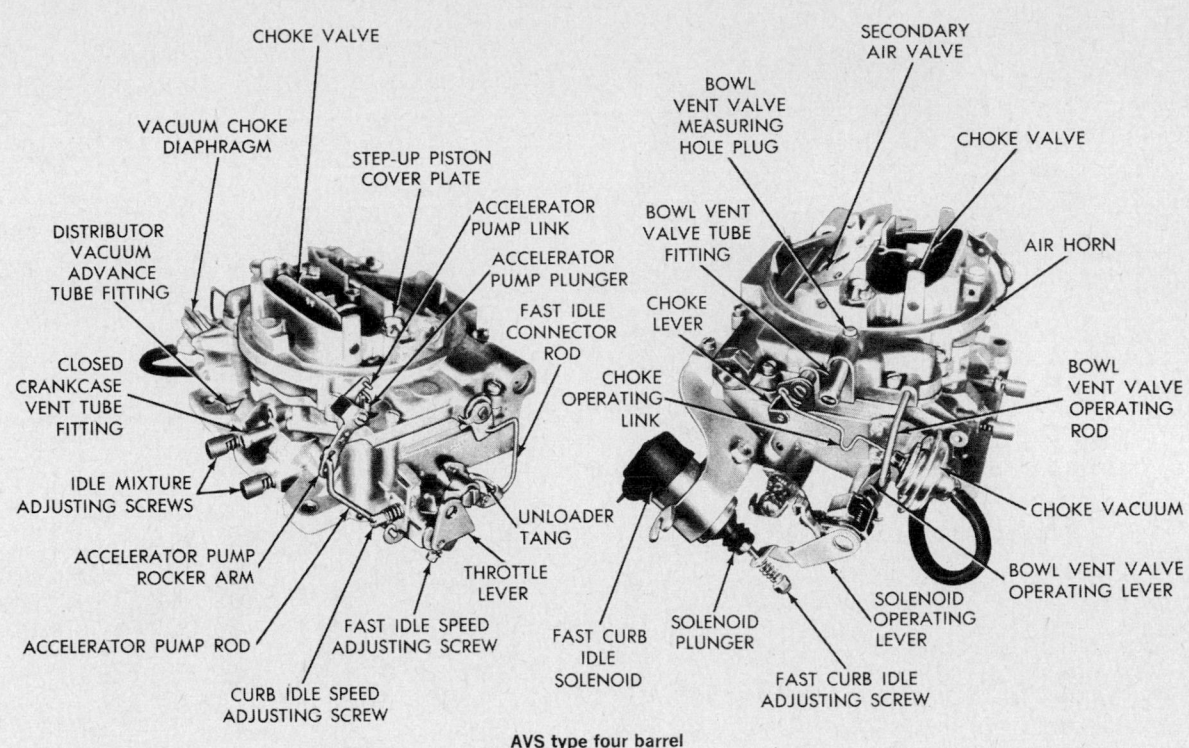

CHOKE VALVE

VACUUM CHOKE DIAPHRAGM

STEP-UP PISTON COVER PLATE

DISTRIBUTOR VACUUM ADVANCE TUBE FITTING

ACCELERATOR PUMP LINK

ACCELERATOR PUMP PLUNGER

FAST IDLE CONNECTOR ROD

CLOSED CRANKCASE VENT TUBE FITTING

IDLE MIXTURE ADJUSTING SCREWS

ACCELERATOR PUMP ROCKER ARM

ACCELERATOR PUMP ROD

UNLOADER TANG

THROTTLE LEVER

FAST IDLE SPEED ADJUSTING SCREW

CURB IDLE SPEED ADJUSTING SCREW

SECONDARY AIR VALVE

BOWL VENT VALVE MEASURING HOLE PLUG

CHOKE VALVE

BOWL VENT VALVE TUBE FITTING

CHOKE LEVER

CHOKE OPERATING LINK

AIR HORN

BOWL VENT VALVE OPERATING ROD

CHOKE VACUUM

BOWL VENT VALVE OPERATING LEVER

SOLENOID OPERATING LEVER

FAST CURB IDLE SOLENOID

SOLENOID PLUNGER

FAST CURB IDLE ADJUSTING SCREW

AVS type four barrel

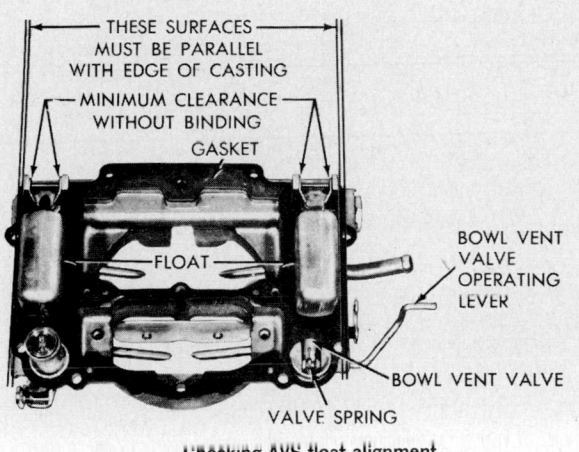

THESE SURFACES MUST BE PARALLEL WITH EDGE OF CASTING

MINIMUM CLEARANCE WITHOUT BINDING

GASKET

FLOAT

BOWL VENT VALVE OPERATING LEVER

BOWL VENT VALVE

VALVE SPRING

Checking AVS float alignment

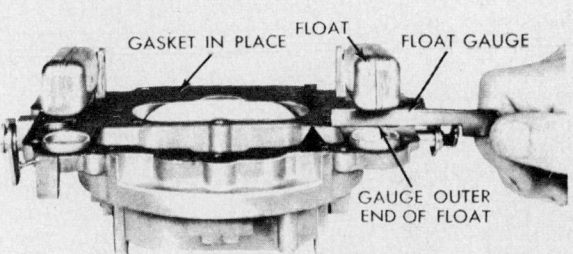

GASKET IN PLACE

FLOAT

FLOAT GAUGE

GAUGE OUTER END OF FLOAT

Checking AVS float height

LEVEL FLOAT POSITION

BEND STOP TABS EACH FLOAT

Checking AVS float drop

FOUR BARREL— AVS TYPE

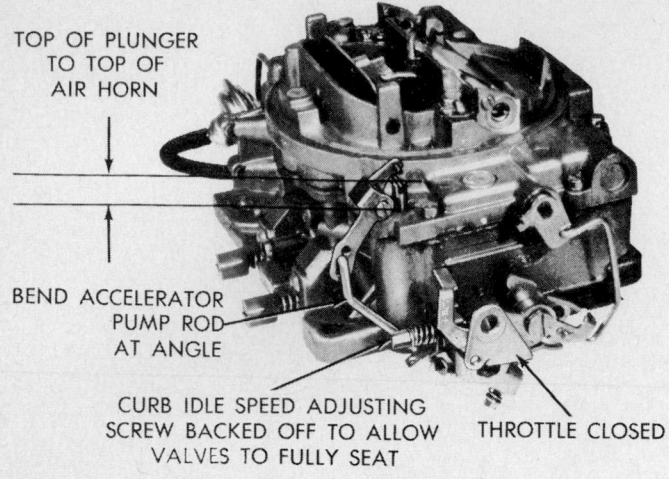

TOP OF PLUNGER
TO TOP OF
AIR HORN

BEND ACCELERATOR
PUMP ROD
AT ANGLE

CURB IDLE SPEED ADJUSTING
SCREW BACKED OFF TO ALLOW
VALVES TO FULLY SEAT

THROTTLE CLOSED

AVS accelerator pump adjustment

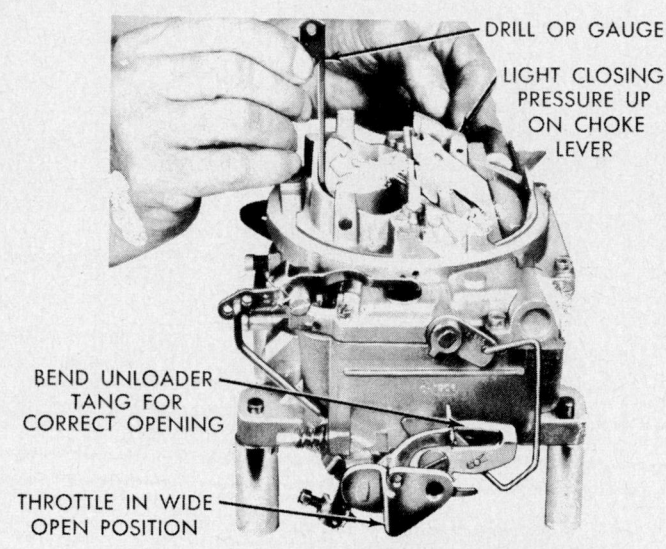

DRILL OR GAUGE

LIGHT CLOSING
PRESSURE UP
ON CHOKE
LEVER

BEND UNLOADER
TANG FOR
CORRECT OPENING

THROTTLE IN WIDE
OPEN POSITION

AVS choke unloader adjustment

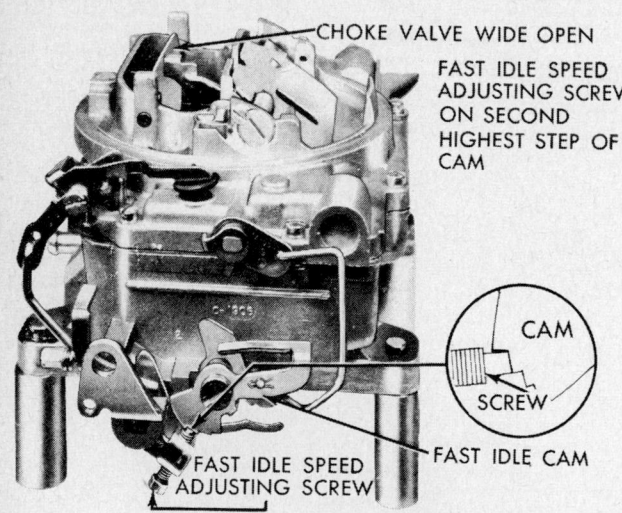

CHOKE VALVE WIDE OPEN

FAST IDLE SPEED
ADJUSTING SCREW
ON SECOND
HIGHEST STEP OF
CAM

CAM

SCREW

FAST IDLE CAM

FAST IDLE SPEED
ADJUSTING SCREW

AVS fast idle adjustment

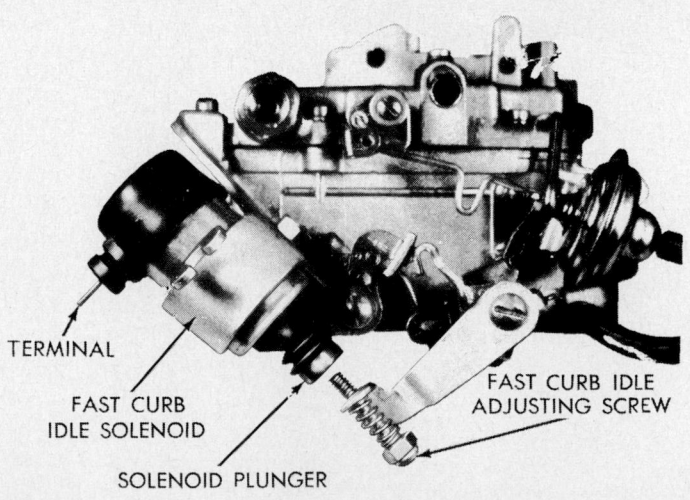

TERMINAL

FAST CURB
IDLE SOLENOID

SOLENOID PLUNGER

FAST CURB IDLE
ADJUSTING SCREW

AVS idle speed solenoid adjustment

TWO BARREL—WGD TYPE

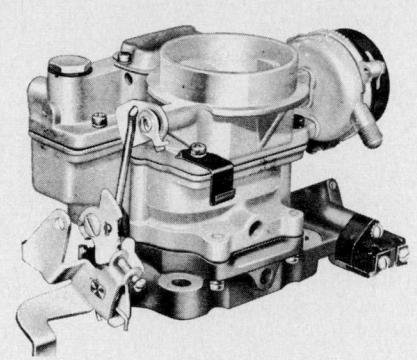

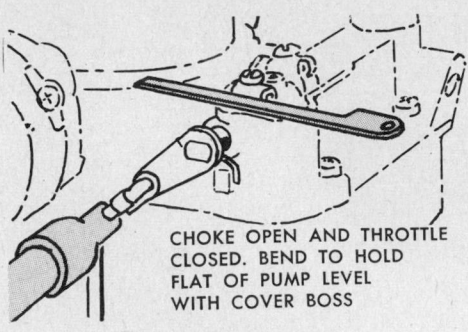

CHOKE OPEN AND THROTTLE CLOSED. BEND TO HOLD FLAT OF PUMP LEVEL WITH COVER BOSS

WGD pump adjustment

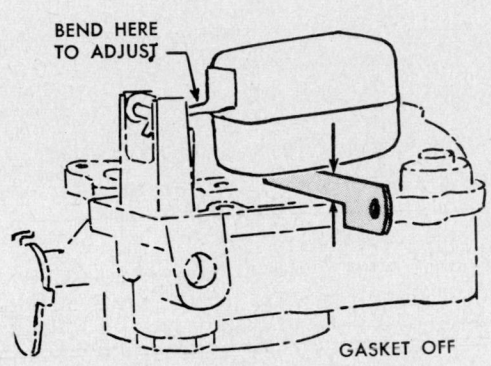

BEND HERE TO ADJUST

GASKET OFF

WGD float adjustment

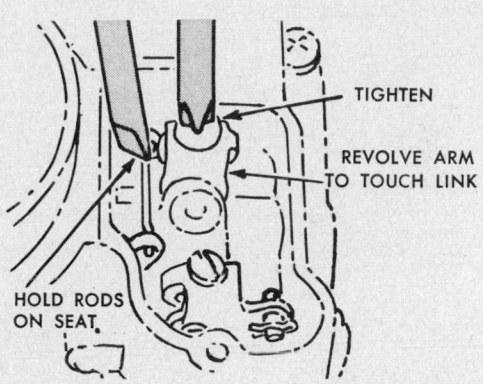

TIGHTEN

REVOLVE ARM TO TOUCH LINK

HOLD RODS ON SEAT.

WGD metering rod adjustment

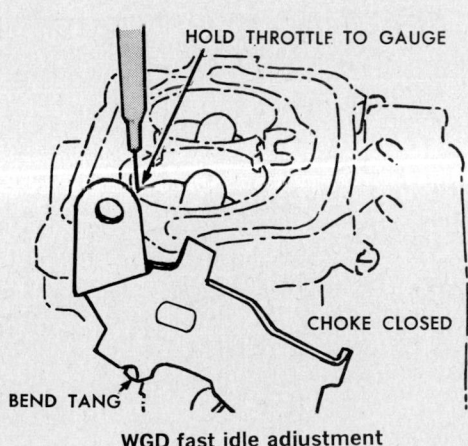

HOLD THROTTLE TO GAUGE

CHOKE CLOSED

BEND TANG

WGD fast idle adjustment

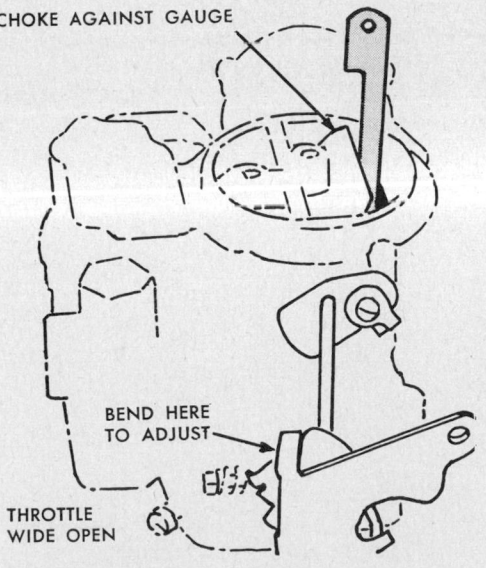

CHOKE AGAINST GAUGE

BEND HERE TO ADJUST

THROTTLE WIDE OPEN

WGD unloader adjustment

TWO BARREL—WCD TYPE

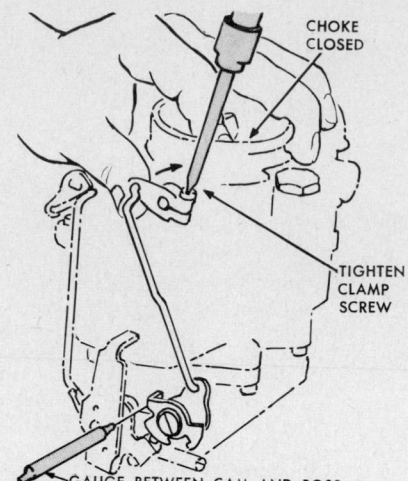

CHOKE CLOSED

TIGHTEN CLAMP SCREW

GAUGE BETWEEN CAM AND BOSS

WCD fast idle adjustment (step 1)

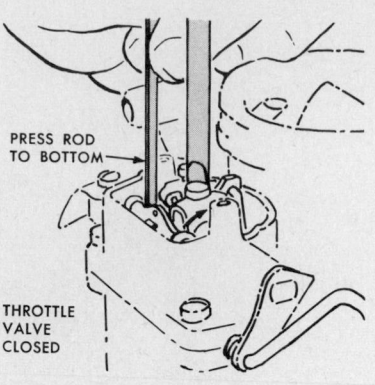

PRESS ROD TO BOTTOM

THROTTLE VALVE CLOSED

WCD metering rod adjustment

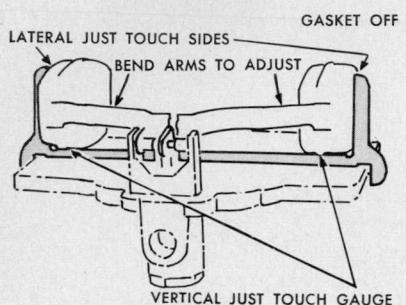

GASKET OFF

LATERAL JUST TOUCH SIDES

BEND ARMS TO ADJUST

VERTICAL JUST TOUCH GAUGE

WCD float adjustment

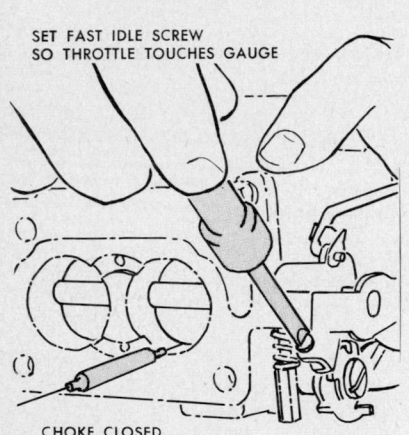

SET FAST IDLE SCREW SO THROTTLE TOUCHES GAUGE

CHOKE CLOSED

WCD fast idle adjustment (step 2)

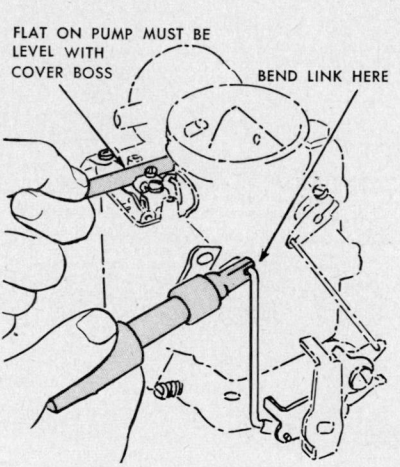

FLAT ON PUMP MUST BE LEVEL WITH COVER BOSS

BEND LINK HERE

WCD pump adjustment

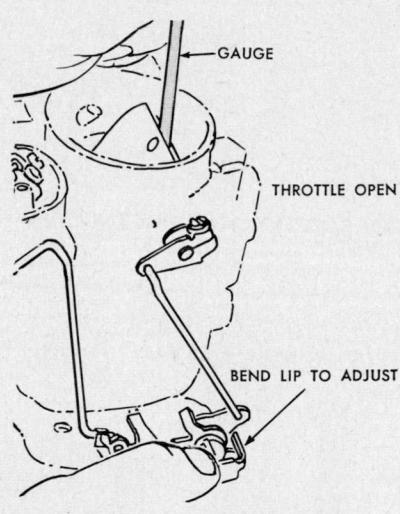

GAUGE

THROTTLE OPEN

BEND LIP TO ADJUST

WCD unloader adjustment

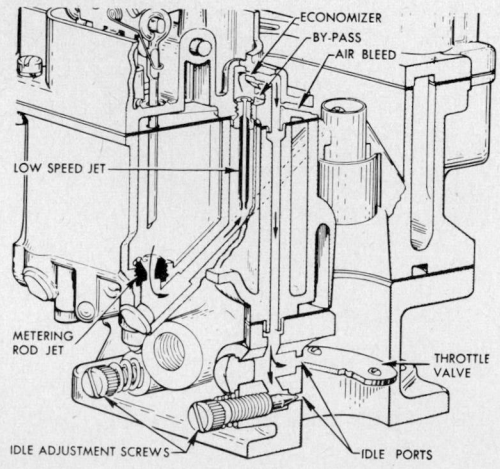

ECONOMIZER
BY-PASS
AIR BLEED

LOW SPEED JET

METERING ROD JET

IDLE ADJUSTMENT SCREWS

IDLE PORTS

THROTTLE VALVE

Low speed system

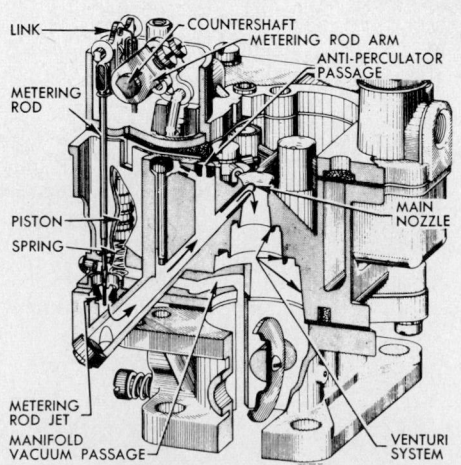

LINK
COUNTERSHAFT
METERING ROD ARM
ANTI-PERCULATOR PASSAGE

METERING ROD

PISTON
SPRING

MAIN NOZZLE

METERING ROD JET
MANIFOLD VACUUM PASSAGE

VENTURI SYSTEM

High speed and power systems

FOUR BARREL THERMO-QUAD TYPE

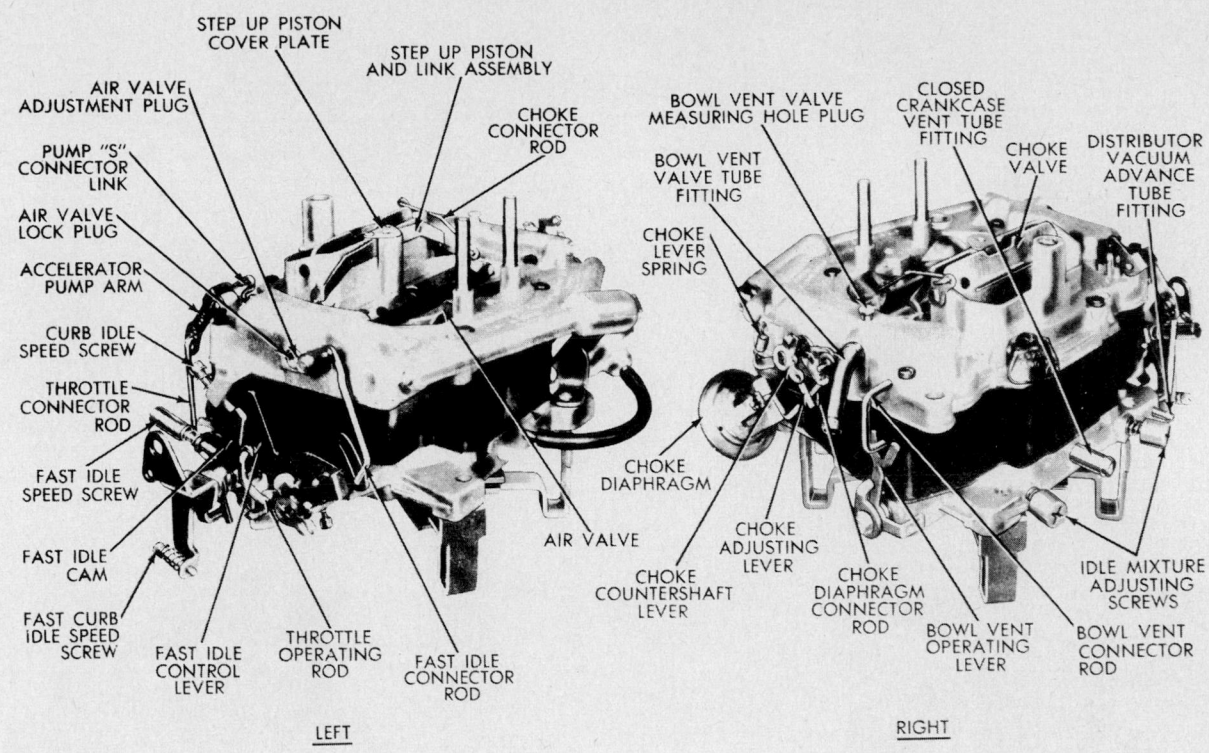

AIR VALVE ADJUSTMENT PLUG

PUMP "S" CONNECTOR LINK

AIR VALVE LOCK PLUG

ACCELERATOR PUMP ARM

CURB IDLE SPEED SCREW

THROTTLE CONNECTOR ROD

FAST IDLE SPEED SCREW

FAST IDLE CAM

FAST CURB IDLE SPEED SCREW

STEP UP PISTON COVER PLATE

STEP UP PISTON AND LINK ASSEMBLY

CHOKE CONNECTOR ROD

AIR VALVE

FAST IDLE CONTROL LEVER

THROTTLE OPERATING ROD

FAST IDLE CONNECTOR ROD

LEFT

BOWL VENT VALVE MEASURING HOLE PLUG

BOWL VENT VALVE TUBE FITTING

CHOKE LEVER SPRING

CHOKE DIAPHRAGM

CHOKE COUNTERSHAFT LEVER

CHOKE ADJUSTING LEVER

CLOSED CRANKCASE VENT TUBE FITTING

CHOKE VALVE

DISTRIBUTOR VACUUM ADVANCE TUBE FITTING

CHOKE DIAPHRAGM CONNECTOR ROD

BOWL VENT OPERATING LEVER

BOWL VENT CONNECTOR ROD

IDLE MIXTURE ADJUSTING SCREWS

RIGHT

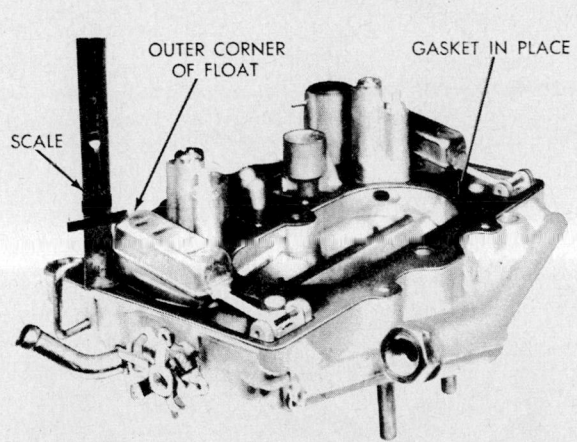

SCALE

OUTER CORNER OF FLOAT

GASKET IN PLACE

Float Setting
(© Dodge Division, Chrysler Corp.)

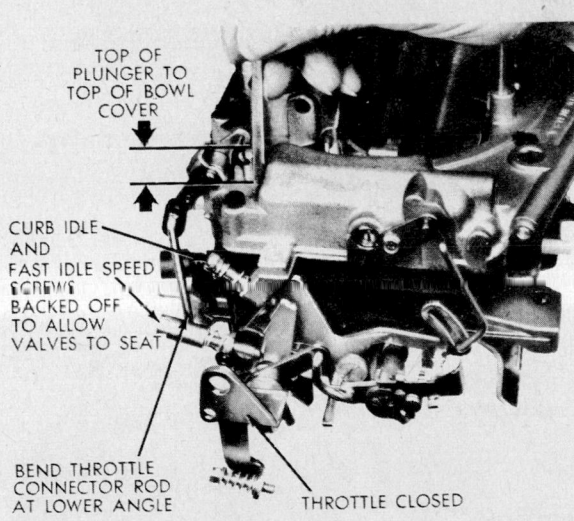

TOP OF PLUNGER TO TOP OF BOWL COVER

CURB IDLE AND FAST IDLE SPEED SCREWS BACKED OFF TO ALLOW VALVES TO SEAT

BEND THROTTLE CONNECTOR ROD AT LOWER ANGLE

THROTTLE CLOSED

Accelerator Pump Adjustment
(© Dodge Division, Chrysler Corp.)

FOUR BARREL THERMO-QUAD TYPE

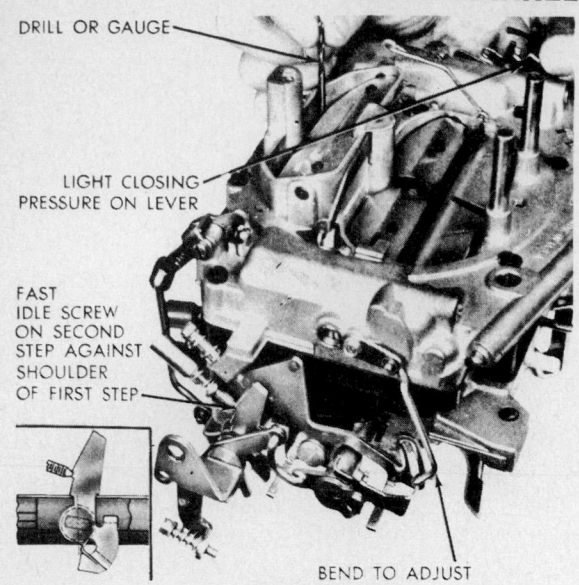

DRILL OR GAUGE

LIGHT CLOSING
PRESSURE ON LEVER

FAST
IDLE SCREW
ON SECOND
STEP AGAINST
SHOULDER
OF FIRST STEP

BEND TO ADJUST

Fast Idle Setting
(© Dodge Division, Chrysler Corp.)

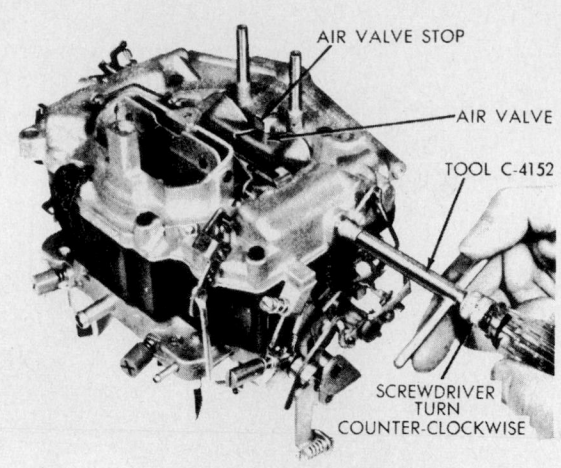

AIR VALVE STOP

AIR VALVE

TOOL C-4152

SCREWDRIVER
TURN
COUNTER-CLOCKWISE

Air Valve Tension Adjustment
(© Dodge Division, Chrysler Corp.)

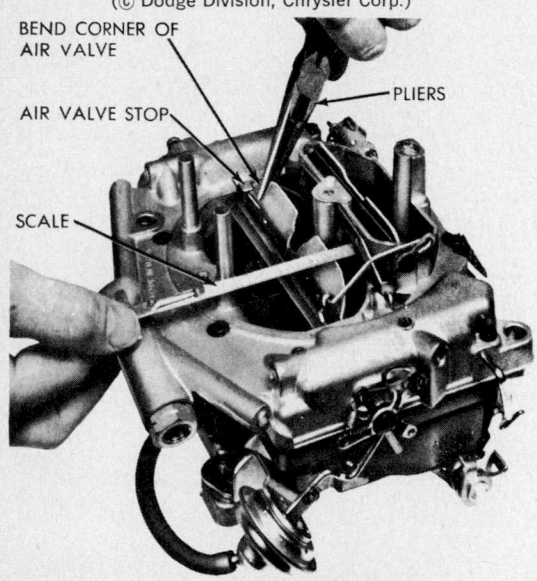

BEND CORNER OF
AIR VALVE

PLIERS

AIR VALVE STOP

SCALE

Secondary Air Valve Opening Adjustment
(© Dodge Division, Chrysler Corp.)

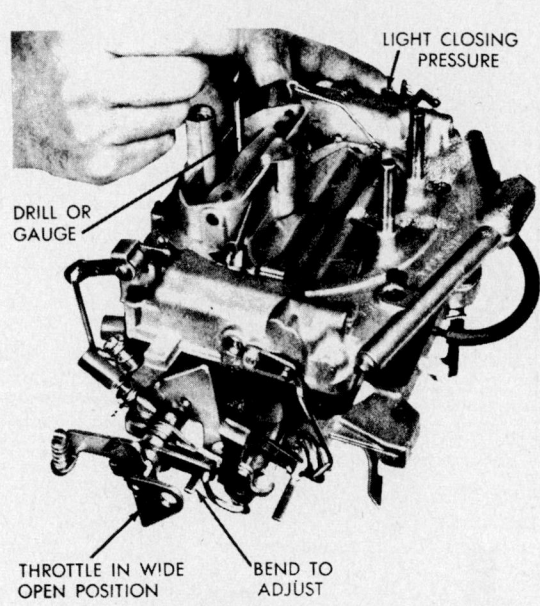

LIGHT CLOSING
PRESSURE

DRILL OR
GAUGE

THROTTLE IN WIDE
OPEN POSITION

BEND TO
ADJUST

Unloader Adjustment
(© Dodge Division, Chrysler Corp.)

SCALE

SECONDARY
THROTTLE VALVES
SHOULD JUST
START TO OPEN

BEND LINK
HERE

Secondary Throttle Adjustment
(© Dodge Division, Chrysler Corp.)

WRONG

CORRECT

Pump Rod "S" Link Installation
(© Dodge Division, Chrysler Corp.)

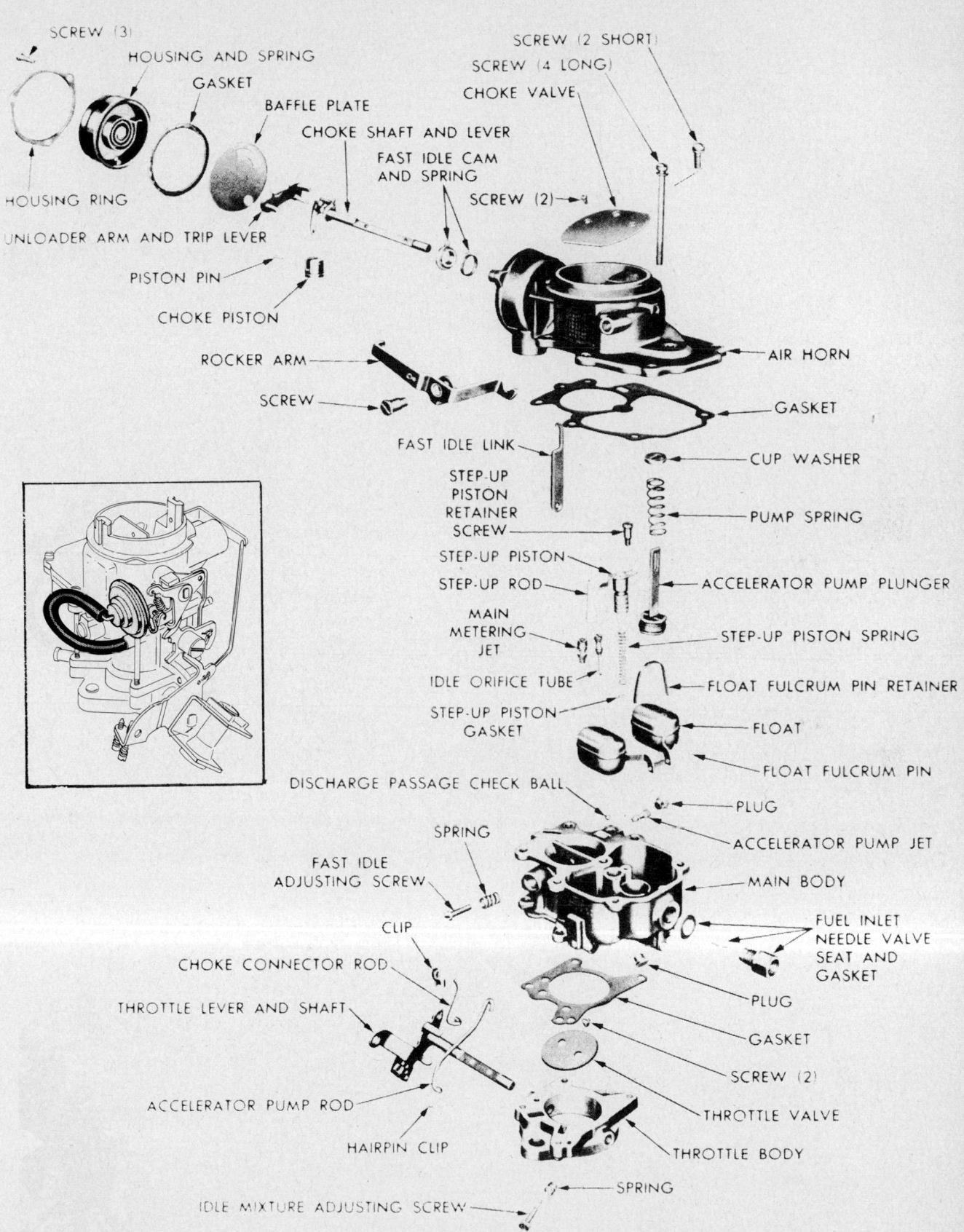

SCREW (3)

HOUSING AND SPRING

GASKET

BAFFLE PLATE

CHOKE SHAFT AND LEVER

FAST IDLE CAM AND SPRING

SCREW (2 SHORT)

SCREW (4 LONG)

CHOKE VALVE

SCREW (2)

HOUSING RING

UNLOADER ARM AND TRIP LEVER

PISTON PIN

CHOKE PISTON

ROCKER ARM

SCREW

FAST IDLE LINK

STEP-UP PISTON RETAINER SCREW

STEP-UP PISTON

STEP-UP ROD

MAIN METERING JET

IDLE ORIFICE TUBE

STEP-UP PISTON GASKET

DISCHARGE PASSAGE CHECK BALL

SPRING

FAST IDLE ADJUSTING SCREW

CLIP

CHOKE CONNECTOR ROD

THROTTLE LEVER AND SHAFT

ACCELERATOR PUMP ROD

HAIRPIN CLIP

IDLE MIXTURE ADJUSTING SCREW

AIR HORN

GASKET

CUP WASHER

PUMP SPRING

ACCELERATOR PUMP PLUNGER

STEP-UP PISTON SPRING

FLOAT FULCRUM PIN RETAINER

FLOAT

FLOAT FULCRUM PIN

PLUG

ACCELERATOR PUMP JET

MAIN BODY

FUEL INLET NEEDLE VALVE SEAT AND GASKET

PLUG

GASKET

SCREW (2)

THROTTLE VALVE

THROTTLE BODY

SPRING

Carter BBS single barrel (typical)

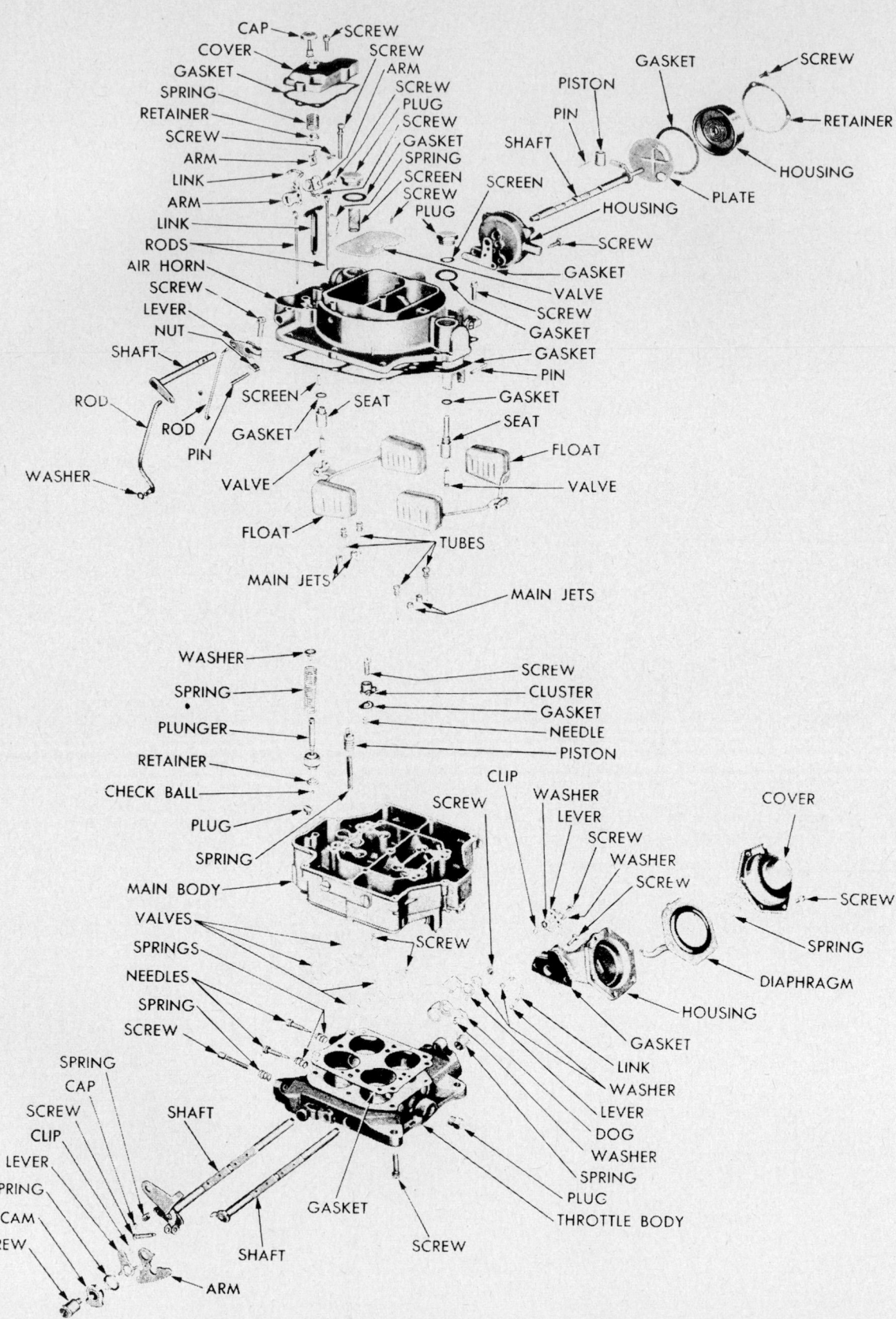

Carter WCFB four-barrel (typical)

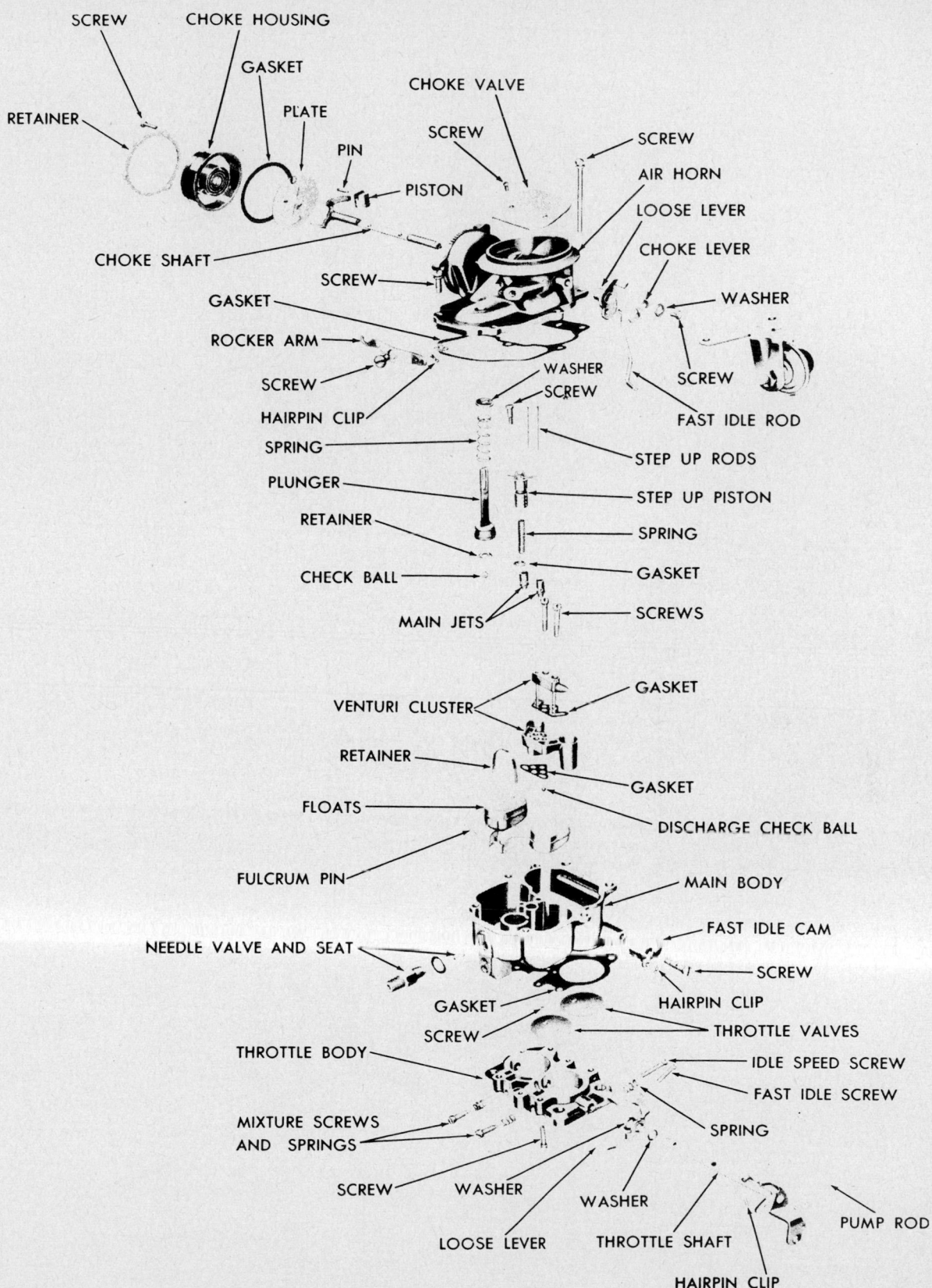

SCREW CHOKE HOUSING
GASKET
RETAINER
PLATE
CHOKE VALVE
PIN
SCREW
PISTON
SCREW
AIR HORN
LOOSE LEVER
CHOKE LEVER
CHOKE SHAFT
SCREW
WASHER
GASKET
ROCKER ARM
SCREW
SCREW
FAST IDLE ROD
WASHER
SCREW
HAIRPIN CLIP
SPRING
STEP UP RODS
PLUNGER
STEP UP PISTON
RETAINER
SPRING
CHECK BALL
GASKET
MAIN JETS
SCREWS
VENTURI CLUSTER
GASKET
RETAINER
GASKET
FLOATS
DISCHARGE CHECK BALL
FULCRUM PIN
MAIN BODY
FAST IDLE CAM
NEEDLE VALVE AND SEAT
SCREW
HAIRPIN CLIP
GASKET
THROTTLE VALVES
SCREW
IDLE SPEED SCREW
THROTTLE BODY
FAST IDLE SCREW
MIXTURE SCREWS
AND SPRINGS
SPRING
SCREW WASHER
WASHER
PUMP ROD
LOOSE LEVER
THROTTLE SHAFT
HAIRPIN CLIP

Carter BBD two-barrel (typical)

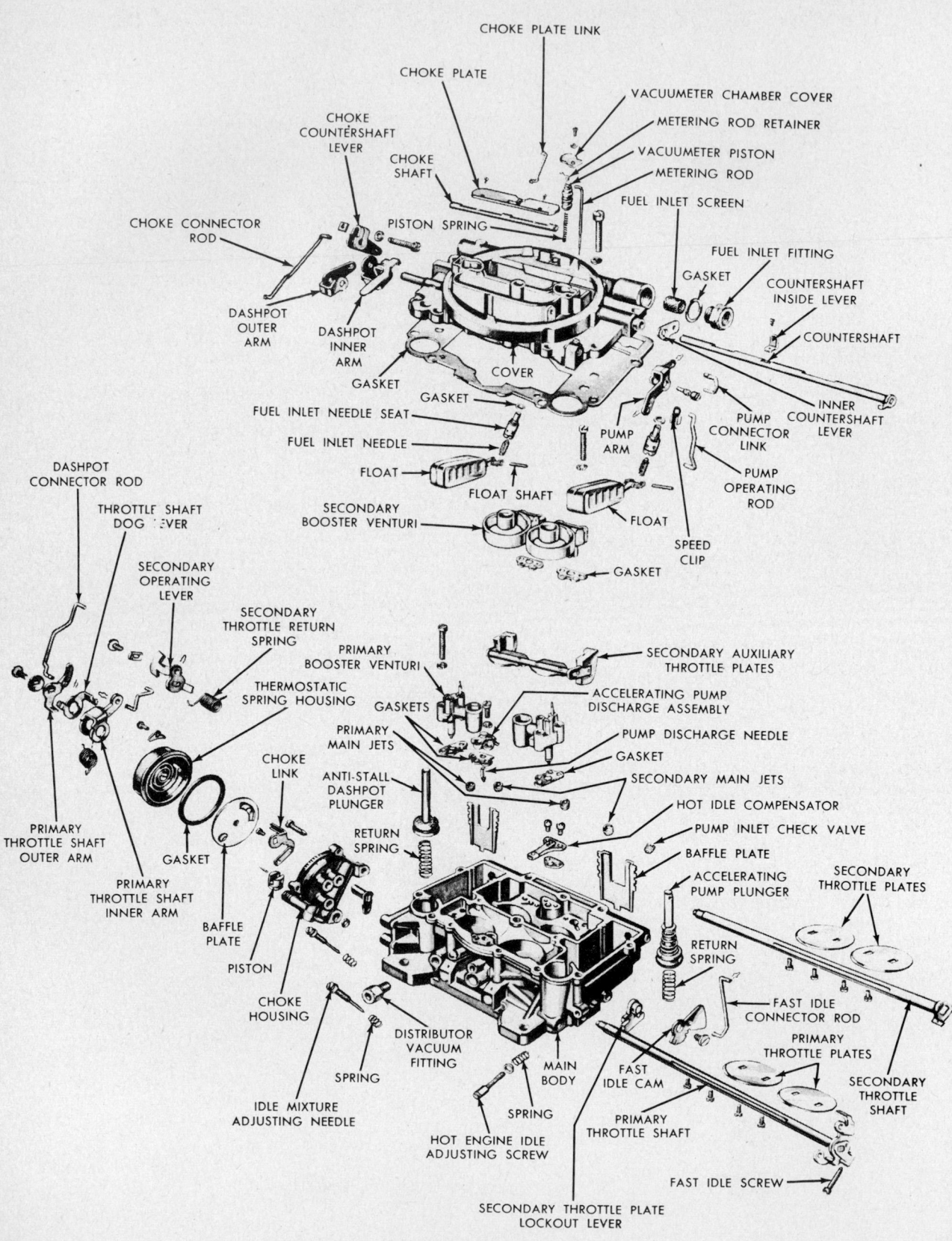

CHOKE PLATE LINK

CHOKE PLATE

VACUUMETER CHAMBER COVER

METERING ROD RETAINER

VACUUMETER PISTON

METERING ROD

FUEL INLET SCREEN

CHOKE COUNTERSHAFT LEVER

CHOKE SHAFT

FUEL INLET FITTING

CHOKE CONNECTOR ROD

PISTON SPRING

GASKET

COUNTERSHAFT INSIDE LEVER

COUNTERSHAFT

DASHPOT OUTER ARM

DASHPOT INNER ARM

COVER

INNER COUNTERSHAFT LEVER

GASKET

PUMP COUNTERSHAFT CONNECTOR LINK

GASKET

FUEL INLET NEEDLE SEAT

PUMP ARM

FUEL INLET NEEDLE

PUMP OPERATING ROD

DASHPOT CONNECTOR ROD

FLOAT

FLOAT SHAFT

FLOAT

THROTTLE SHAFT DOG LEVER

SECONDARY BOOSTER VENTURI

SPEED CLIP

SECONDARY OPERATING LEVER

GASKET

SECONDARY THROTTLE RETURN SPRING

PRIMARY BOOSTER VENTURI

SECONDARY AUXILIARY THROTTLE PLATES

THERMOSTATIC SPRING HOUSING

GASKETS

ACCELERATING PUMP DISCHARGE ASSEMBLY

PRIMARY MAIN JETS

PUMP DISCHARGE NEEDLE

GASKET

CHOKE LINK

SECONDARY MAIN JETS

ANTI-STALL DASHPOT PLUNGER

HOT IDLE COMPENSATOR

PRIMARY THROTTLE SHAFT OUTER ARM

RETURN SPRING

PUMP INLET CHECK VALVE

BAFFLE PLATE

GASKET

ACCELERATING PUMP PLUNGER

SECONDARY THROTTLE PLATES

PRIMARY THROTTLE SHAFT INNER ARM

BAFFLE PLATE

RETURN SPRING

PISTON

FAST IDLE CONNECTOR ROD

CHOKE HOUSING

DISTRIBUTOR VACUUM FITTING

MAIN BODY

PRIMARY THROTTLE PLATES

SPRING

FAST IDLE CAM

SECONDARY THROTTLE SHAFT

IDLE MIXTURE ADJUSTING NEEDLE

SPRING

PRIMARY THROTTLE SHAFT

HOT ENGINE IDLE ADJUSTING SCREW

FAST IDLE SCREW

SECONDARY THROTTLE PLATE LOCKOUT LEVER

Carter AFB four-barrel (typical)

Ford, Autolite Carburetors

YEAR	MODEL OR TYPE	Float Level (IN.)	Fuel Level (IN.)	Fast Idle Cam (IN.)	Pump Travel Setting	Choke Setting	Secondary Lockout Adj.	Throttle Bore Diam. Prim.	Sec.	Venturi Diam. Prim.	Sec.
American Motors											
1968	6200-8HA2-290, Auto.	3/8	...	#3 hole ①	5/64	INDEX	...	1 9/16	...	1 5/64	...
1968	6200-8HM2-290, Std.	3/8	...	#3 hole ①	5/64	INDEX	...	1 9/16	...	1 5/64	...
1968	6200-8ZA2-343, Auto.	3/8	...	#3 hole ①	5/64	INDEX	...	1 9/16	...	1 5/64	...
1969	6200-9HM2-290, Std.	1/2	13/16	#3 hole ①	5/64	INDEX	...	1 9/16	...	1 5/64	...
1969	6200-9HA2-290, Auto.	1/2	13/16	#3 hole ①	5/64	INDEX	...	1 9/16	...	1 5/64	...
1969	6200-9ZA2-343, Auto.	1/2	13/16	#3 hole ①	5/64	INDEX	...	1 9/16	...	1 5/64	...
1970	2100-0DM2-304, Std.	3/8	13/16	#3 hole ①	13/64	INDEX	...	1 9/16	...	1 5/64	...
1970	2100-0DA2-304, Auto.	3/8	13/16	#3 hole ①	13/64	2-RICH	...	1 9/16	...	1 5/64	...
1970	2100-0RA2-360, Auto.	3/8	13/16	#3 hole ①	13/64	1-RICH	...	1 11/16	...	1 15/64	...
1970	4300-0WM4-360, 390 Std.	13/16	...	center hole	19/64	2-RICH	...	1 9/16	1 11/16	1 1/4	...
1970	4300-0WA4-360, 390, Auto.	13/16	...	center hole	19/64	2-RICH	...	1 9/16	1 11/16	1 1/4	...
1971	2100-1DM2	3/8	13/16	.170	13/64	1-RICH	...	1 9/16	...	1 5/64	...
1971	2100-1DA2	3/8	13/16	.170	13/64	2-RICH	...	1 9/16	...	1 5/64	...
1971	2100-1RA2	3/8	13/16	.170	13/64	2-RICH	...	1 11/16	...	1 15/64	...
1971	4300-1TM4	13/16	...	.190	CENTER	INDEX	...	1 9/16	1 11/16	1 1/4	...
1971	4300-1TA4	13/16	...	.190	CENTER	INDEX	...	1 9/16	1 11/16	1 1/4	...

① —Inboard hole on pump lever.

YEAR	MODEL OR TYPE	Float Level (IN.)	Fuel Level (IN.)	Fast Idle Cam (IN.)	Pump Travel Setting	Choke Setting	Secondary Lockout Adj.	Throttle Bore Diam. Prim.	Sec.	Venturi Diam. Prim.	Sec.
Fairlane & Montego											
1965	200-6 Cyl.-Aut.-1 Bbl.	1 3/32	...	...	3/16	INDEX	...	1 7/16	...	1.10	...
1965	289-V8-Std.-2 Bbl.	15/32	7/8	.130②	①	INDEX	...	1 7/16	...	1.145	...
1965	289-V8-Aut.-2 Bbl.	15/32	7/8	.120②	①	2-RICH	...	1 7/16	...	1.145	...
1965	289-V8-Std.-4 Bbl.	29/64	29/32	.125②	①	INDEX	...	1 7/16	1 7/16	1 1/8	1 3/16
1965	289-V8-Aut.-4 Bbl.	29/64	29/32	.109②	①	2-RICH	...	1 7/16	1 7/16	1 1/8	1 3/16
1966	200-6 Cyl.-Std.-1 Bbl.	1 3/32	...	...	3/16	1-LEAN	...	1 7/16	...	1.145	...
1966	200-6 Cyl.-Aut.-1 Bbl.	1 3/32	...	...	7/16	INDEX	...	1 7/16	...	1.145	...
1966	289-V8-Aut.-2 Bbl.	31/64	7/8	.130②	①	2-RICH	...	1 7/16	...	1.145	...
1966	289-V8-Std.-4 Bbl.	17/32	29/32	.120②	①	2-RICH	...	1 7/16	1 7/16	1.08	1.19
1966	289-V8-Aut-4 Bbl.	9/16	15/16	.109②	①	2-RICH	...	1 7/16	1 7/16	1.08	1.19
1966	390-V8-Std.-2 Bbl.	31/64	7/8	.200②	①	INDEX	...	1 9/16	...	1.23	...
1966	390-V8-Aut.-2 Bbl.	31/64	7/8	.180②	①	INDEX	...	1 11/16	...	1.33	...
1966	390-V8-Std.-4 Bbl.	17/32	29/32	.160②	①	2-RICH	...	1 7/16	1 7/16	1.08	1.19
1966	390-V8-Aut.-4 Bbl.	17/32	29/32	.140②	①	1-RICH	...	1 7/16	1 7/16	1.08	1.19
1967	200-6 Cyl.-Std.-1 Bbl.	1 3/32	...	...	3/16	1-LEAN	...	1 7/16	...	1.20	...
1967	200-6 Cyl.-Aut.-1 Bbl.	1 3/32	...	...	3/16	INDEX	...	1 7/16	...	1.20	...
1967	200-6 Cyl.-Std.-1 Bbl.-Ex. Em.	1 3/32	...	...	3/16	2-LEAN	...	1 7/16	...	1.10	...
1967	200-6 Cyl.-Aut.-1 Bbl.-Ex. Em.	1 3/32	...	...	3/16	INDEX	...	1 7/16	...	1.10	...
1967	289-V8-Std.-2 Bbl.	3/8	3/4	7/64	①	INDEX	...	1 7/16	...	1.03	...
1967	289-V8-Std.-2 Bbl.-Ex. Em.	17/32	29/32	7/64	③	INDEX	...	1 7/16	...	1.03	...
1967	289-V8-Aut.-2 Bbl.	17/32	29/32	7/64	①	2-RICH	...	1 7/16	...	1.03	...
1967	289-V8-Aut.-2 Bbl.-Ex. Em.	17/32	29/32	7/64	③	2-RICH	...	1 7/16	...	1.145	...
1967	289-V8-Std.-4 Bbl.	25/32	...	.100	#1	INDEX	...	1 7/16	1 9/16	1	...
1967	289-V8-Std.-4 Bbl.	25/32	...	.100	#1	INDEX	...	1 7/16	1 9/16	1	...
1967	289-V8-Aut.-4 Bbl.	25/32	...	.100	#1	INDEX	...	1 7/16	1 9/16	1	...
1967	289-V8-Aut.-4 Bbl.-Ex. Em.	25/32	...	.100	#1	INDEX	...	1 7/16	1 9/16	1	...
1967	390-V8-Std.-2 Bbl.	31/64	7/8	.160	①	INDEX	...	1 11/16	...	1.23	...
1967	390-V8-Std.-2 Bbl.-Ex. Em.	17/32	29/32	.170	③	INDEX	...	1 9/16	...	1.23	...
1967	390-V8-Aut.-2 Bbl.	3/8	3/4	.150	①	2-RICH	...	1 11/16	...	1.23	...
1967	390-V8-Aut.-2 Bbl.-Ex. Em.	17/32	29/32	.150	③	INDEX	...	1 9/16	...	1.23	...
1967	390-V8-Std.-4 Bbl.	25/32	...	.100	#1	INDEX	...	1 7/16	1 9/16	1	...
1967	390-V8-Std.-4 Bbl.-Ex. Em.	25/32	...	.100	#1	INDEX	...	1 7/16	1 9/16	1	...

YEAR	MODEL OR TYPE	Float Level (IN.)	Fuel Level (IN.)	Fast Idle Cam (IN.)	Pump Travel Setting	Choke Setting	Secondary Lockout Adj.	Throttle Bore Diam.		Venturi Diam.	
								Prim.	Sec.	Prim.	Sec.
Fairlane & Montego—continued											
1968	200-6 Cyl.-Std.-1 Bbl.-Therm	1 3/32	...	...	⑤	2-LEAN	...	1 7/16	...	1.10	...
1968	200-6 Cyl.-Aut.-1 Bbl.-Imco	1 3/32	...	...	⑤	1-LEAN	...	1 7/16	...	1.10	...
1968	289-V8-Std.-2 Bbl.-Therm	3/8	3/4	.110	④	INDEX	...	1 9/16	...	1.08	...
1968	289-V8-Aut.2 Bbl. Imco	3/8	3/4	.120	④	1-LEAN	...	1 9/16	...	1.08	...
1968	302-V8-Std.-2 Bbl.-Therm	3/8	3/4	...	④	INDEX	...	1 9/16	...	1.08	...
1968	302-V8-Aut.-2 Bbl.-Imco	3/8	3/4	.120	④	1-LEAN	...	1 9/16	...	1.08	...
1968	390-V8-Std.-2 Bbl.-therm	...	7/8	.170	①	INDEX	...	1 11/16	...	1.23	...
1968	390-V8-Aut.-2 Bbl.-Imco	31/64	7/8	...	①	INDEX	...	1 11/16	...	1.23	...
1969	250-6 Cyl. Aut. 1 Bbl. C90F-A	1 3/32	...	...	.190	3-LEAN	...	1 11/16	...	1.29	...
1969	250-6 Cyl. Std. 1 Bbl. C90F-B	1 3/32	...	...	.190	1-LEAN	...	1 11/16	...	1.29	...
1969	250-6 Cyl. Aut. 1 Bbl. C90F-K	1 3/32	...	...	.90	3-LEAN	...	1 11/16	...	1.29	...
1969	250-6 Cyl. Std. 1 Bbl. C90F-J	1 3/32	...	...	.190	1-LEAN	...	1 11/16	...	1.29	...
1969	302-V8-Std.-2 Bbl.-C8HF-BD	3/8	3/4	.110	①	2-RICH	...	1 9/16	...	1.08	...
1969	302-V8-Aut.-2 Bbl.-C9ZF-G	3/8	3/4	.110	①	INDEX	...	1 9/16	...	1.08	...
1969	351-V8-Std.-2 Bbl.-C9ZF-A	9/16	15/16	.130	①	1-RICH	...	1 9/16	...	1.23	...
1969	351-V8-Aut.-2 Bbl.-C90F-C	31/64	7/8	.100	①	2-RICH	...	1 9/16	...	1.23	...
1969	351-V8-Std.-4 Bbl.-C9ZF-C	13/16	...	.130	#2	2-LEAN	...	1 7/16	1 9/16	1	...
1969	351-V8-Aut.-4 Bbl.-C90F-D	13/16	...	.100	#2	1-LEAN	...	1 7/16	1 9/16	1	...
1969	390-V8-Std.-4 Bbl.-C9ZF-E	13/16	...	.210	#3	INDEX	...	1 9/16	1 11/16	1 1/4	...
1969	390-V8-Aut.-4 Bbl.-C90F-E	13/16	...	.230	#3	1-LEAN	...	1 9/16	1 11/16	1 1/4	...
1970	2100-DOAFC-302, Std.	7/16	13/16	.130	#3⑥	1-RICH	...	1 9/16	...	1.08	...
1970	2100-DOAFD-302, Auto.	7/16	13/16	.130	#2⑥	1-RICH	...	1 9/16	...	1.08	...
1970	2100-DOAFV-302, Auto w. AC	7/16	13/16	.130	#2⑥	1-RICH	...	1 9/16	...	1.08	...
1970	2100-DOOFK-351C, Std.	7/16	13/16	.190	#4⑥	INDEX	...	1 11/16	...	1.23	...
1970	2100-DOOFL-351C, Auto.	7/16	13/16	.130	#3⑥	1-RICH	...	1 11/16	...	1.23	...
1970	2100-DOOFM-351C, Auto. w. AC	7/16	13/16	.130	#3⑥	1-RICH	...	1 11/16	...	1.23	...
1970	4300-DOOF7., AB-351C, Std.	.79-.85	...	.160	#2	INDEX	...	1 9/16	1 11/16	1 1/4	...
1970	4300-DOOFY, AC-351C, Auto.	.79-.85	...	.180	#2	INDEX	...	1 9/16	1 11/16	1 1/4	...
1970	4300-DOOFAA, AD-351C, Auto. w. AC	.79-.85	...	.180	#2	INDEX	...	1 9/16	1 11/16	1 1/4	...
1970	4300-DOAFL, AB, AL-429, St.	25/32	...	.220	#2	INDEX	...	1 9/16	1 11/16	1 1/4	...
1970	4300-DOAF, AG, AM-429, Auto	25/32	...	.170	#2	INDEX	...	1 9/16	1 11/16	1 1/4	...
1971	2100-D1AF-BA, 302 S.T.	7/16	13/16	.130	#2⑥	INDEX	...	1 9/16	...	1.08	...
1971	2100-D1AF-DA, 302 A.T.	7/16	13/16	.150	#3⑥	1-RICH	...	1 9/16	...	1.08	...
1971	2100-D1ZF-AA, 302 w.AC	7/16	13/16	.130	#2⑥	INDEX	...	1 9/16	...	1.08	...
1971	2100-D1OF-PA, 351 C S.T.	7/16	13/16	.190	#3⑥	INDEX	...	1 11/16	...	1.23	...
1971	2100-D1ZF-SA, 351C A.T.	7/16	13/16	.170	#3⑥	1-RICH	...	1 11/16	...	1.23	...
1971	2100-D1OF-RA, 351C Cal.	7/16	13/16	.170	#3⑥	1-RICH	...	1 11/16	...	1.23	...
1971	4300-D1OF-EA, 351 S.T.	13/16	...	.160	#2⑥	INDEX	...	1 9/16	1 11/16	1 1/4	...
1971	4300-D1OF-AAA, 351 A.T.	13/16	...	.180	#2⑥	INDEX	...	1 9/16	...	1 1/4	...
1971	4300-D1AF-MA, 429 A.T.	49/64	...	.170	#2⑥	INDEX	...	1 9/16	1 11/16	1 1/4	...

①—Install pump operating rod in the inside hole in pump link and no. 3 hole in pump over travel lever for climatic conditions.

②—Clearance between choke plate and air horn.

③—Install pump operating rod in the outside hole in pump link and no. 3 hole.

④—Install pump operating rod in the inside hole in pump link and no. 2 hole in pump over travel lever.

⑤—With throttle plate closed, install 3/32 in. diam. pin in Hi position, .090 clearance between pin and pump cover.

⑥—Rod position—overtravel lever.

Falcon—Comet—Maverick—Mustang—Cougar

YEAR	MODEL OR TYPE	Float Level (IN.)	Fuel Level (IN.)	Fast Idle Cam (IN.)	Pump Travel Setting	Choke Setting	Secondary Lockout Adj.	Throttle Bore Diam.		Venturi Diam.	
								Prim.	Sec.	Prim.	Sec.
1965	170-6 Cyl.-1 Bbl.-Std.	1 3/32	...	①	3/16	INDEX	...	1 7/16	...	1.10	...
1965	170-6 Cyl.-1 Bbl.-Aut.	1 3/32	...	①	3/16	INDEX	...	1 7/16	...	1.10	...
1965	170-6 Cyl.-1 Bbl.-Std.	1 3/32	...	①	3/16	2-LEAN	...	1 7/16	...	1.10	...
1965	170-6 Cyl.-1 Bbl.-Aut.	1 3/32	...	①	3/16	INDEX	...	1 7/16	...	1.10	...
1965	200-6 Cyl.-1 Bbl.-Std.	1 3/32	...	①	3/16	1-LEAN	...	1 7/16	...	1.20	...
1965	200-6 Cyl.-1 Bbl.-Aut.	1 3/32	...	①	3/16	INDEX	...	1 7/16	...	1.20	...
1965	289-V8-2 Bbl.-Std.	15/32	7/8	.130②	#4	INDEX	...	1 9/16	...	1.145	...
1965	289-V8-2 Bbl.-Aut.	15/32	7/8	.120②	#3	2-RICH	...	1 9/16	...	1.145	...
1965	289-V8-225 Hp.-4 Bbl.-Std.	29/64	29/32	.125②	#3	INDEX	...	1 7/16	1 7/16	1.08	1.19
1965	289-V8-225 Hp.-4 Bbl.-Aut.	29/64	29/32	.120②	#3	2-RICH	...	1 7/16	1 7/16	1.08	1.19
1965	289-V8-271 Hp.-4 Bbl.-Std.	29/64	7/8	.200②	#3	INDEX	...	1 9/16	1 9/16	1.13	1.19
1965	289-V8-271 Hp.-4 Bbl.-Std.	15/32	7/8	.160②	#3	...	...	1 9/16	1 9/16	1.13	1.19
1965	289-V8-271 Hp.-4 Bbl.-Aut.	29/64	7/8	.140②	...	INDEX	...	1 9/16	1 9/16	1.13	1.19

Falcon—Comet—Maverick—Mustang—Cougar, continued

YEAR	MODEL OR TYPE	Float Level (IN.)	Fuel Level (IN.)	Fast Idle Cam (IN.)	Pump Travel Setting	Choke Setting	Secondary Lockout Adj.	Throttle Bore Diam. Prim.	Sec.	Venturi Diam. Prim.	Sec.
1966	170-6 Cyl.-Std.-1 Bbl.	1³/₃₂	...	...	³/₁₆	2-LEAN	...	1⁷/₁₆	...	1.10	...
1966	170-6 Cyl.-Aut.-1 Bbl.	1³/₃₂	...	...	³/₁₆	INDEX	...	1⁷/₁₆	...	1.10	...
1966	200-6 Cyl.-Std.-1 Bbl.	1³/₃₂	...	...	³/₁₆	1-LEAN	...	1⁷/₁₆	...	1.20	...
1966	200-6 Cyl.-Aut.-1 Bbl.	1³/₃₂	...	...	³/₁₆	INDEX	...	1⁷/₁₆	...	1.20	...
1966	289-V8-Aut.-2 Bbl.	³¹/₆₄	⁷/₈	.130②	#3	2-RICH	...	1⁷/₁₆	...	1.145	...
1966	289-V8-Std.-4 Bbl.	¹⁷/₃₂	²⁹/₃₂	.120②	#3	2-RICH	...	1⁷/₁₆	1⁷/₁₆	1.08	1.19
1966	289-V8-Aut.-4 Bbl.	⁹/₁₆	¹⁵/₁₆	.120②	#3	2-RICH	...	1⁷/₁₆	1⁷/₁₆	1.08	1.19
1966	390-V8-Std.-2 Bbl.	³¹/₆₄	⁷/₈	.200②	#3	INDEX	...	1⁹/₁₆	...	1.23	...
1966	390-V8-Aut.-2 Bbl.	³¹/₆₄	⁷/₈	.180②	#3	INDEX	...	1¹¹/₁₆	...	1.33	...
1966	390-V8-Std.-4 Bbl.	¹⁷/₃₂	²⁹/₃₂	.160②	#3	2-RICH	...	1⁹/₁₆	1⁷/₁₆	1.08	1.19
1966	390-V8-Aut.-4 Bbl.	¹⁷/₃₂	²⁹/₃₂	.140②	#3	1-RICH	...	1⁹/₁₆	1⁹/₁₆	1.08	1.19
1967	170-6 Cyl.-Std.-1 Bbl.	1³/₃₂	...	...	.190	2-LEAN	...	1⁷/₁₆	...	1.10	...
1967	170-6 Cyl.-Std.-1 Bbl.-Ex. Em.	1³/₃₂	...	...	.190	2-LEAN	...	1⁷/₁₆	...	1.10	...
1967	170-6 Cyl.-Aut.-1 Bbl.	1³/₃₂	...	...	.190	INDEX	...	1⁷/₁₆	...	1.10	...
1967	170-6 Cyl.-Aut.-1 Bbl.-Ex. Em.	1³/₃₂	...	...	.190	INDEX	...	1⁷/₁₆	...	1.10	...
1967	200-6 Cyl.-Std.-1 Bbl.	1³/₃₂	...	...	.190	1-LEAN	...	1⁷/₁₆	...	1.20	...
1967	200-6 Cyl.-Std.-1 Bbl.-Ex. Em.	1³/₃₂	...	...	.190	2-LEAN	...	1⁷/₁₆	...	1.10	...
1967	200-6 Cyl.-Aut.-1 Bbl.	1³/₃₂	...	...	.190	INDEX	...	1⁷/₁₆	...	1.20	...
1967	200-6 Cyl.-Aut.-1-Bbl.-Ex. Em.	1³/₃₂	...	...	.190	INDEX	...	1⁷/₁₆	...	1.10	...
1967	289-V8-Std.-2 Bbl.	³/₈	³/₈	.110	#3	INDEX	...	1⁷/₁₆	...	1.03	...
1967	289-V8-Std.-2 Bbl.-Ex. Em.	¹⁷/₃₂	²⁹/₃₂	.110	#3	INDEX	...	1⁷/₁₆	...	1.03	...
1967	289-V8-Aut.-2 Bbl.	¹⁷/₃₂	²⁹/₃₂	.110	#3	2-RICH	...	1⁷/₁₆	...	1.03	...
1967	289-V8-2 Bbl.-Ex. Em.	¹⁷/₃₂	²⁹/₃₂	.110	#3	2-RICH	...	1⁷/₁₆	...	1.15	...
1967	289-V8-Std.-4 Bbl.	²⁵/₃₂	...	.100	...	INDEX	...	1⁷/₁₆	1⁹/₁₆	1	...
1967	289-V8-Std.-4 Bbl.-Ex. Em.	²⁵/₃₂	...	.100	#1	INDEX	...	1⁷/₁₆	1⁹/₁₆	1	...
1967	289-V8-Aut.-4 Bbl.	²⁵/₃₂	...	.100	#1	INDEX	...	1⁷/₁₆	1⁹/₁₆	1	...
1967	289-V8-Aut.-4 Bbl.-Ex. Em.	²⁵/₃₂	...	.100	#1	INDEX	...	1⁷/₁₆	1⁹/₁₆	1	...
1967	390-V8-Std.-2 Bbl.	³¹/₆₄	⁷/₈	.160	#3	INDEX	...	1¹¹/₁₆	...	1.23	...
1967	390-V8-Std.-2 Bbl.-Ex. Em.	¹⁷/₃₂	²⁹/₃₂	.170	#4	INDEX	...	1⁹/₁₆	...	1.23	...
1967	390-V8-Aut.-2 Bbl.	³/₈	³/₄	.150	#3	2-RICH	...	1¹¹/₁₆	...	1.23	...
1967	390-V8-Aut.-2 Bbl.-Ex. Em.	¹⁷/₃₂	²⁹/₃₂	.150	#4	INDEX	...	1⁹/₁₆	...	1.23	...
1967	390-V8-Std.-4 Bbl.	²⁵/₃₂	...	.100	#1	INDEX	...	1⁷/₁₆	1⁹/₁₆	1	...
1967	390-Vi-Std.-4 Bbl.-Ex. Em.	²⁵/₃₂	...	.100	#1	INDEX	...	1⁷/₁₆	1⁹/₁₆	1	...
1967	390-V8-Aut-4 Bbl.	²⁵/₃₂	...	.100	#1	INDEX	...	1⁷/₁₆	1⁹/₁₆	1	...
1967	390-V8-Aut-4 Bbl.-Ex. Em.	²⁵/₃₂	...	.100	#1	INDEX	...	1⁷/₁₆	1⁹/₁₆	1	...
1968	200-6 Cyl.-Std.-1 Bbl.-Therm.	1³/₃₂	...	...	③	2-LEAN	...	1⁷/₁₆	...	1.10	...
1968	200-6 Cyl.-Aut.-1 Bbl.-Imco	1³/₃₂	...	...	③	1-LEAN	...	1⁷/₁₆	...	1.10	...
1968	289-V8-Std.-2 Bbl.-Therm.	³/₈	³/₄	.110	...	INDEX	...	1⁹/₁₆	...	1.09	...
1968	289-V8-Aut.-2 Bbl.-Imco.	³/₈	³/₄	.120	...	1-LEAN	...	1⁹/₁₆	...	1.08	...
1968	302-V8-Std.-4 Bbl.-Therm.	¹³/₁₆	...	.090	⁷/₁₆	INDEX	...	1⁷/₁₆	1⁹/₁₆	1	...
1968	302-V8-Aut.-4 Bbl.-Imco.	¹³/₁₆	...	.100	⁷/₁₆	2-RICH	...	1⁷/₁₆	1⁹/₁₆	1	...
1969	200-6 Cyl.-Std.-1 Bbl., C8DF-B	1³/₃₂	...	...	.150	3-LEAN	...	1⁷/₁₆	...	1.10	...
1969	200-6 Cyl.-Aut.-1 Bbl., C8OF-B	1³/₃₂	...	...	.190	1-LEAN	...	1⁷/₁₆	...	1.10	...
1969	250-6 Cyl.-Std.-1 Bbl., C9OF-A	1³/₃₂	...	...	.190	3-LEAN	...	1¹¹/₁₆	...	1.29	...
1969	250-6 Cyl.-Aut.-1 Bbl., C9OF-K	1³/₃₂	...	...	.190	3-LEAN	...	1¹¹/₁₆	...	1.29	...
1969	250-6 Cyl.-Std.-1 Bbl., C9OF-B	1³/₃₂	...	...	.190	1-LEAN	...	1¹¹/₁₆	...	1.29	...
1969	250-6 Cyl.-Std.-1 Bbl., C9OF-J	1³/₃₂	...	...	.190	1-LEAN	...	1¹¹/₁₆	...	1.29	...
1969	302-V8-Std.-2 Bbl., C8AF-BD	³/₈	³/₄	.110	①	2-RICH	...	1⁹/₁₆	...	1.08	...
1969	302-V8-Aut.-2 Bbl., C9AF-A	³/₈	³/₄	.110	④	INDEX	...	1⁹/₁₆	...	1.08	...
1969	302-V8-Aut.-2 Bbl., C9ZF-G	³/₈	³/₄	.110	④	INDEX	...	1⁹/₁₆	...	1.08	...
1969	351-V8-Std.-2 Bbl., C9ZF-A	⁹/₁₆	¹⁵/₁₆	.130	①	1-RICH	...	1¹¹/₁₆	...	1.23	...
1969	351-V8-Aut.-2 Bbl., C9ZF-B	³¹/₆₄	⁷/₈	.100	①	2-RICH	...	1¹¹/₁₆	...	1.23	...
1969	351-V8-Std.-4 Bbl., C9ZF-C	¹³/₁₆	...	.130	#2	2-LEAN	...	1⁷/₁₆	1⁹/₁₆	1	...
1969	351-V8-Aut.-4 Bbl., C9ZF-D	¹³/₁₆	...	.100	#2	1-LEAN	...	1⁷/₁₆	1⁹/₁₆	1	...
1969	390-V8-Std.-4 Bbl., C9ZF-E	¹³/₁₆	...	.210	#3	INDEX	...	1⁹/₁₆	1¹¹/₁₆	1¹/₄	...
1969	390-V8-Aut.-4 Bbl., C9ZF-F	¹³/₁₆	...	.230	#3	1-LEAN	...	1⁹/₁₆	1¹¹/₁₆	1¹/₄	...
1969	170-6 Cyl.-1 Bbl., C8DF-G	⁷/₃₂	...	...	...	INDEX	...	1⁷/₁₆	...	1.10	...
1969	170-6 Cyl.-1 Bbl., C8DF-H	⁷/₃₂	...	...	...	1-LEAN	...	1⁷/₁₆	...	1.10	...
1970	2100—D0AFC-302, Std.	⁷/₁₆	¹³/₁₆	.130	#3⑤	1-RICH	...	1⁹/₁₆	...	1.08	...
1970	2100—D0AFD-302, Auto.	⁷/₁₆	¹³/₁₆	.130	#2⑤	1-RICH	...	1⁹/₁₆	...	1.08	...

YEAR	MODEL OR TYPE	Float Level (IN.)	Fuel Level (IN.)	Fast Idle Cam (IN.)	Pump Travel Setting	Choke Setting	Secondary Lockout Adj.	Throttle Bore Diam. Prim.	Throttle Bore Diam. Sec.	Venturi Diam. Prim.	Venturi Diam. Sec.
Falcon—Comet—Maverick—Mustang—Cougar, continued											
1970	2100—D0AFU-302, Auto. w. AC	7/16	13/16	.130	#2⑤	1-RICH	...	1 9/16	...	1.08	...
1970	2100—D0AFE-351W, Std.	7/16	13/16	.190	#3⑤	2-LEAN	...	1 11/16	...	1.23	...
1970	2100—D0AFF-351W, Auto.	7/16	13/16	.170	#4⑤	2-LEAN	...	1 11/16	...	1.23	...
1970	2100—D0AFV-351W Auto. w. AC	7/16	13/16	.170	#4⑤	2-LEAN	...	1 11/16	...	1.23	...
1970	4300—D0OFZ, AB-351C, Std.	.79-.85	...	.160	#2	INDEX	...	1 9/16	1 11/16	1 1/4	...
1970	4300—D0OFY, AC-351C, Auto.	.79-.85	...	.180	#2	INDEX	...	1 9/16	1 11/16	1 1/4	...
1970	4300—D0OFAA, AD-351C, Auto. w. AC	.79-.85	...	.180	#2	INDEX	...	1 9/16	1 11/16	1 1/4	...
1971	2100—D1AF-BA, 302 S.T.	7/16	13/16	.130	#2	INDEX	...	1 9/16	...	1.08	...
1971	2100—D1AF-DA, 302 A.T.	7/16	13/16	.150	#3	1-RICH	...	1 9/16	...	1.08	...
1971	2100—D1ZF-AA, 302 w/AC	7/16	13/16	.130	#2	INDEX	...	1 9/16	...	1.08	...
1971	2100—D1OF-PA, 351C, S.T.	7/16	13/16	.190	#3	INDEX	...	1 11/16	...	1.23	...
1971	2100—D1ZF-SA, 351C, A.T.	7/16	13/16	.170	#3	1-RICH	...	1 11/16	...	1.23	...
1971	2100—D1OF-RA, 351C, CAL	7/16	13/16	.170	#3	1-RICH	...	1 11/16	...	1.23	...
1971	4300—D1OF-EA, 351C, S.T.	13/16	...	.160	#2	INDEX	...	1 9/16	1 11/16	1 1/4	...
1971	4300—D1OF-AAA, 351C, A.T.	13/16	...	.180	#2	INDEX	...	1 9/16	1 11/16	1 1/4	...

① —Set fast idle screw on high step of cam. Adjust screw to recommended rpm.
② —Clearance between choke plate and air horn wall.
③ —Install 3/32 diam. roll pin in Hi position.
④ —Install pump operating rod in the inside hole in pump link and #2 hole in pump over-travel lever.
⑤ —Rod position—overtravel lever.

Ford—Thunderbird-Mercury

YEAR	MODEL OR TYPE	Float Level (IN.)	Fuel Level (IN.)	Fast Idle Cam (IN.)	Pump Travel Setting	Choke Setting	Secondary Lockout Adj.	Throttle Bore Diam. Prim.	Throttle Bore Diam. Sec.	Venturi Diam. Prim.	Venturi Diam. Sec.
1965	1-Bbl. 240-6 Cyl.-Std.	1/32	...	...	③	INDEX	...	1 11/16	...	1.29	...
1965	1-Bbl. 240-6 Cyl.-Aut.	1/32	...	...	③	INDEX	...	1 11/16	...	1.29	...
1965	2-Bbl. 289-V8 Std.	15/32	7/8	.130②	③	INDEX	...	1 7/16	...	1.145	...
1965	2-Bbl. 289-V8-Aut.	15/32	7/8	.120②	③	2-RICH	...	1 7/16	...	1.145	...
1965	4-Bbl. 352-V8-Std.	15/32	7/8	.130②	③	INDEX	...	1 9/16	1 9/16	1 1/8	1 3/16
1965	4-Bbl. 352-V8-Aut.	15/32	7/8	.120②	③	INDEX	...	1 9/16	1 9/16	1 1/8	1 3/16
1965	2-Bbl. 390-V8-Std.	15/32	7/8	.140②	③	2-RICH	...	1 9/16	...	1.23	...
1965	2-Bbl. 390-V8-Aut.	15/32	7/8	.150②	③	2-RICH	...	1 9/16	...	1.23	...
1965	4-Bbl. 390-V8-Std.	15/32	7/8	.130②	③	INDEX	...	1 9/16	1 9/16	1 1/8	1 3/16
1965	4-Bbl. 390-V8-Aut.	15/32	7/8	.120②	③	INDEX	...	1 9/16	1 9/16	1 1/8	1 3/16
1965	4-Bbl. 390-V8-T Bird	15/32	7/8	.125②	...	INDEX	...	1 7/16	1 7/16	1.08	1.19
1966	240-6 Cyl.-Std.-1 Bbl.	1 3/32	...	.200②	③	INDEX	...	1 11/16	...	1.29	...
1966	240-6 Cyl.-Aut.-1 Bbl.	1 3/32	...	.200②	③	INDEX	...	1 11/16	...	1.29	...
1966	289-V8-Std.-2 Bbl.	31/64	7/8	.140②	③	INDEX	...	1 7/16	...	1.145	...
1966	289-V8-Aut.-2 Bbl.	31/64	7/8	.130②	③	2-RICH	...	1 7/16	...	1.145	...
1966	352-V8-Aut.-4 Bbl.	1/2	29/32	.140②	③	INDEX	...	1 9/16	1 9/16	1 1/8	1 3/16
1966	390-V8-Std.-2 Bbl.	31/64	7/8	.200②	③	INDEX	...	1 9/16	...	1.23	...
1966	390-V8-Aut.-2 Bbl.	31/64	7/8	.180②	③	INDEX	...	1 11/16	...	1.33	...
1966	390-V8-Std.-4 Bbl.	17/32	29/32	.160②	③	2-RICH	...	1 7/16	1 7/16	1.08	1.19
1966	390-V8-Aut.-4 Bbl.	17/32	29/32	.140②	③	1-RICH	...	1 7/16	1 7/16	1.08	1.19
1966	428-V8-Std.-4 Bbl.	17/32	29/32	.160②	③	2-RICH	...	1 7/16	1 7/16	1.08	1.19
1966	428-V8-Aut.-4 Bbl.	17/32	29/32	.140②	③	1-RICH	...	1 7/16	1 7/16	1.08	1.19
1967	240-6 Cyl.-Std.-1 Bbl.	1 3/32	...	...	③	INDEX	...	1 11/16	...	1.29	...
1967	240-6 Cyl.-Aut.-1 Bbl.	1 3/32	...	...	③	INDEX	...	1 11/16	...	1.29	...
1967	240-6 Cyl.-Std.-1 Bbl.-Ex. Em.	1 3/32	...	...	③	INDEX	...	1 11/16	...	1.29	...
1967	240-6 Cyl.-Aut.-1 Bbl.-Ex. Em.	1 3/32	...	...	③	1-LEAN	...	1 11/16	...	1.29	...
1967	289-V8-Std.-2 Bbl.	31/64	7/8	.130	③	INDEX	...	1 7/16	...	1.145	...
1967	289-V8-Aut.-2 Bbl.	31/64	7/8	.110	③	2-RICH	...	1 7/16	...	1.145	...
1967	289-V8-Std.-2 Bbl.-Ex. Em.	17/32	29/32	.110	③	INDEX	...	1 7/16	...	1.03	...
1967	289-V8-Aut.-2 Bbl.-Ex. Em.	17/32	29/32	.110	③	2-RICH	...	1 7/16	...	1.03	...
1967	390-V8-Std.-2 Bbl.	31/64	7/8	.160	③	INDEX	...	1 11/16	...	1.23	...
1967	390-V8-Aut.-2 Bbl.	3/8	3/4	.150	③	2-RICH	...	1 11/16	...	1.23	...
1967	390-V8-Std.-2 Bbl.-Ex. Em.	17/32	29/32	.170	③	INDEX	...	1 9/16	...	1.23	...
1967	390-V8-Aut.-2 Bbl.-Ex. Em.	17/32	29/32	.150	③	INDEX	...	1 11/16	...	1.23	...
1967	390-V8-Std.-4 Bbl.	25/32	...	.100	#1 hole	INDEX	...	1 7/16	1 7/16	1	...
1967	390-V8-Aut.-4 Bbl.	25/32	...	.100	#1 hole	INDEX	...	1 7/16	1 7/16	1	...
1967	390-V8-Std.-4 Bbl.-Ex. Em.	25/32	...	.100	#1 hole	INDEX	...	1 7/16	1 7/16	1	...
1967	390-V8-Aut.-4 Bbl.-Ex. Em.	25/32	...	.100	#1 hole	INDEX	...	1 7/16	1 7/16	1	...
1967	428-V8-Std.-4 Bbl.	25/32	...	.100	#2 hole	INDEX	...	1 7/16	1 7/16	1	...
1967	428-V8-Aut.-4 Bbl.	25/32	...	.090	#2 hole	INDEX	...	1 7/16	1 7/16	1	...

Ford—Thunderbird—Mercury, continued

YEAR	MODEL OR TYPE	Float Level (IN.)	Fuel Level (IN.)	Fast Idle Cam (IN.)	Pump Travel Setting	Choke Setting	Secondary Lockout Adj.	Throttle Bore Diam. Prim.	Sec.	Venturi Diam. Prim.	Sec.
1967	428-V8-Std.-4 Bbl.-Ex. Em.	25/32	...	.090	#2 hole	INDEX	...	1 7/16	1 9/16	1	...
1967	428-V8-Aut.-4 Bbl.-Ex. Em.	25/32	...	.100	#1 hole	INDEX	...	1 7/16	1 9/16	1	...
1968	240-6 Cyl.-Aut.-1 Bbl.-Imco	1 3/32	...	...	④	3-LEAN	...	1 11/16	...	1.29	...
1968	302-V8-Std.-2 Bbl.-Therm.	3/8	3/4	...	③	INDEX	...	1 9/16	...	1.08	...
1968	302-V8-Aut.-2 Bbl.-Imco	3/8	3/4	.120	③	1-LEAN	...	1 9/16	...	1.08	...
1968	390-V8-Std.-2 Bbl.-Therm.	31/64	7/8	.170	③	INDEX	...	1 11/16	...	1.23	...
1968	390-V8-Aut.-2 Bbl.-Imco	3/8	3/4	.170	③	INDEX	...	1 11/16	...	1.23	...
1968	390-V8-Std.-4 Bbl.-Therm.	25/32	...	.100	#3 hole	1-RICH	...	1 7/16	1 9/16	1	...
1969	390-V8-Aut.-4 Bbl.-Imco	25/32	...	.100	#3 hole	2-RICH	...	1 7/16	1 9/16	1	...
1968	428-V8-Std.-4 Bbl.-Therm.	25/32	...	.100	#3 hole	1-RICH	...	1 7/16	1 9/16	1	...
1968	428-V8-Aut.-4 Bbl.-Imco	25/32	...	.100	#3 hole	2-RICH	...	1 7/16	1 9/16	1	...
1969	240-6 cyl.-Aut.-1 Bbl.-C8AF-E	1 3/32	...	...	.190	3-LEAN	...	1 11/16	...	1.29	...
1969	302-V8-Std.-2 Bbl.-C8AF-BD	3/8	3/4	.110	①	2-RICH	...	1 9/16	...	1.08	...
1969	302-V8-Aut.-2 Bbl.-C9AF-A	3/8	3/4	.110	④	INDEX	...	1 9/16	...	1.08	...
1969	390-V8-Std.-2 Bbl.-C9AF-B	3/64	7/8	.170	①	1-RICH	...	1 11/16	...	1.23	...
1969	390-V8-Aut.-2 Bbl.-C9AF-C	31/64	7/8	.100	①	2-RICH	...	1 11/16	...	1.23	...
1969	429-V8-Aut.-2 Bbl.-C9AF-J	31/64	7/8	.100	①	2-RICH	...	1 11/16	...	1.23	...
1969	429-V8-Std.-4 Bbl.-C9AF-G	25/32	...	.220	#2	INDEX	...	1 9/16	1 11/16	1 1/4	...
1969	429-V8-Aut.-4 Bbl.-C9AF-r	25/32	...	.160	#2	1-RICH	...	1 9/16	1 11/16	1 1/4	...
1969	429-V8-Aut.-4 Bbl.-C8SF-H	25/32	...	.160	#2	1-RICH	...	1 9/16	1 11/16	1 1/4	...
1970	2100—DOAFC-302, Std.	7/16	13/16	.130	#3 ⑤	1-RICH	...	1 9/16	...	1.08	...
1970	2100—DOAFD-302, Auto.	7/16	13/16	.130	#2 ⑤	1-RICH	...	1 9/16	...	1.08	...
1970	2100—DOAFV-302, Auto. w. AC	7/16	13/16	.130	#2 ⑤	1-RICH	...	1 9/16	...	1.08	...
1970	2100—DOAFE-351W, Std.	7/16	13/16	.190	#3 ⑤	2-LEAN	...	1 11/16	...	1.23	...
1970	2100—DOAFF-35TW, Auto.	7/16	13/16	.170	#4 ⑤	2-LEAN	...	1 11/16	...	1.23	...
1970	2100—DOAFV-351W Auto. w. AC	7/16	13/16	.170	#4 ⑤	2-LEAN	...	1 11/16	...	1.23	...
1970	2100—DOAFY-390, Std.	7/16	13/16	.170	#3 ⑤	1-RICH	...	1 11/16	...	1.23	...
1970	2100—DOAFZ-390, Auto.	7/16	13/16	.170	#3 ⑤	...	...	1 11/16	...	1.23	...
1970	2100—DOAFAA-390, Auto.	7/16	13/16	.160	#3 ⑤	...	...	1 11/16	...	1.23	...
1970	2100—DOAFJ-429, Auto.	7/16	13/16	.160	#3 ⑤	...	...	1 11/16	...	1.23	...
1970	2100—DOAFT-429, Auto. w. AC	7/16	13/16	.160	#3 ⑤	...	...	1 11/16	...	1.23	...
1970	4300—DOAFM, AD, AJ-428, Auto.	1.00	...	.120	#3	2-RICH	...	1 9/16	1 11/16	1 1/4	...
1970	4300—DOAFR, AE, AK— 428 Auto. w AC	1.00	...	.120	#3	2-RICH	...	1 9/16	1 11/16	1 1/4	...
1970	4300—DOAFL, AB, AL-429, Std.	25/32	...	.220	#2	INDEX	...	1 9/16	1 11/16	1 1/4	...
1970	4300—DOAF, AG, AM-429, Auto.	25/32	...	.170	#2	INDEX	...	1 9/16	1 11/16	1 1/4	...
1970	4300—DOSF, A, D, E-429, Auto.	25/32	...	.170	#2	INDEX	...	1 9/16	1 11/16	1 1/4	...
1971	2100—D1AF-BA, 302 S.T.	7/16	13/16	.130	#2	INDEX	...	1 9/16	...	1.08	...
1971	2100—D1AF-DA, 302, A.T.	7/16	13/16	.150	#3	1-RICH	...	1 9/16	...	1.08	...
1971	2100—D1ZF-AA, 302 w/AC	7/16	13/16	.130	#3	INDEX	...	1 9/16	...	1.08	...
1971	2100—D1AF-FA, 351 w S.T.	7/16	13/16	.190	#3	1-RICH	...	1 11/16	...	1.23	...
1971	2100—D1AF-JA, 351W A.T.	7/16	13/16	.130	#3	INDEX	...	1 11/16	...	1.23	...
1971	2100—D1AF-KA, 351W w/AC	7/16	13/16	.130	#3	INDEX	...	1 11/16	...	1.23	...
1971	2100—D1YF-DA, 390 A.T.	7/16	13/16	.160	#3	INDEX	...	1 11/16	...	1.23	...
1971	2100—D1MF-JA, 400 A.T.	7/16	13/16	.160	#3	1-RICH	...	1 11/16	...	1.23	...
1971	2100—D1MF-FA, 429 A.T.	7/16	13/16	.160	#3	1 RICH	...	1 11/16	...	1.23	...
1971	4300—D1AF-MA, 429 A.T.	49/64	...	.170	#2	INDEX	...	1 9/16	1 11/16	1 1/4	...

①—Clearance between top side of fast idle cam and cast stop on back of choke housing.

②—Clearance between choke plate and air horn wall.

③—With link in inboard hole in pump lever, place overtravel lever in long stroke hole. For extremely cold weather intermediate for moderate, and short stroke for warm weather.

④—Install pump operating rod in the inside hole in pump link and No. 2 hole in pump overtravel lever.

⑤—Rod position—overtravel lever.

⑥—Install 3/32 diam. Roll pin in Hi position.

Lincoln-Continental

YEAR	MODEL OR TYPE	Float Level (IN.)	Fuel Level (IN.)	Fast Idle Cam (IN.)	Pump Travel Setting	Choke Setting	Secondary Lockout Adj.	Throttle Bore Diam. Prim.	Sec.	Venturi Diam. Prim.	Sec.
1968	4300—C8VF, 460	25/32	...	.160	#1	1-RICH	...	1 9/16	1 11/16	1 1/4	...
1969	4300—C8VF-J, 460	25/32	...	.160	#2	1-RICH	...	1 9/16	1 11/16	1 1/4	...
1970	4300—DOVF-A, B, C	25/32	...	.170	#2	1-RICH	...	1 9/16	1 11/16	1 1/4	...
1971	4300—D1VF-AA	49/64	...	.170	#2	1-RICH	...	1 9/16	1 11/16	1 1/4	...

Pinto

YEAR	MODEL OR TYPE	Float Level (IN.)	Fuel Level (IN.)	Fast Idle Cam (IN.)	Pump Travel Setting	Choke Setting	Secondary Lockout Adj.	Throttle Bore Diam. Prim.	Sec.	Venturi Diam. Prim.	Sec.
1971	1V, 1600	1.35 DOWN	...	...	.08-.09	...	...	1.42	...	1.10	...
	5200, 2000 S.T.	31/64	...	.010-.030	#2	...	...	1.260	1.417	1.02	1.06
	5200, 2000 A.T.	31/64	...	.010-.030	#2	...	...	1.260	1.417	1.02	1.06

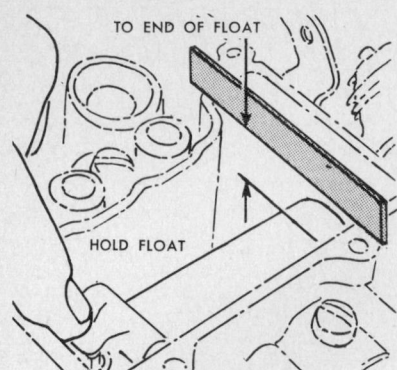

Ford two- and four-barrel float setting

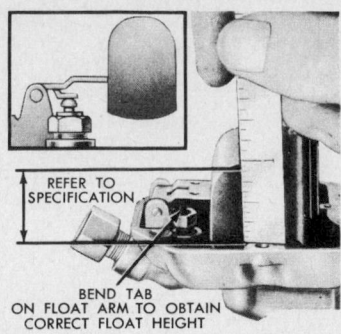

Ford single-barrel float adjustment

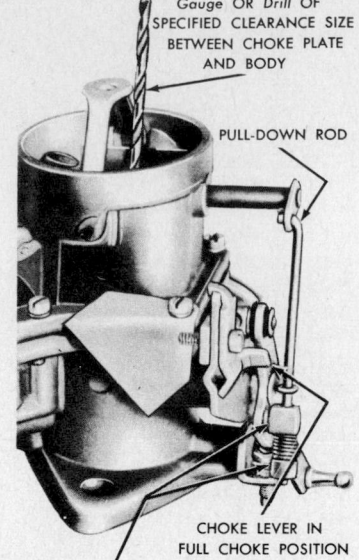

Ford single-barrel manual choke pull-down adjustment

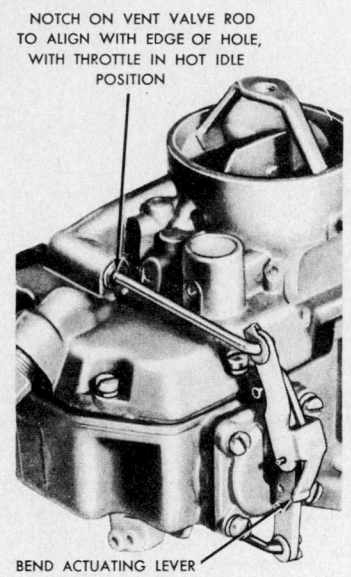

Ford single-barrel float bowl vent valve adjustment

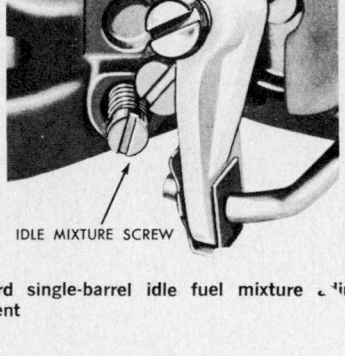

Ford single-barrel idle fuel mixture adjustment

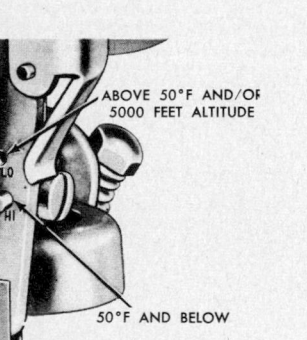

Ford single-barrel accelerating pump lever adjustment

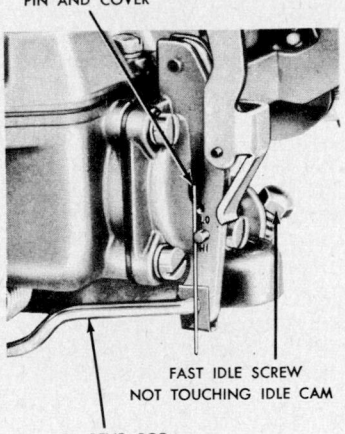

Ford single-barrel accelerating pump adjustment

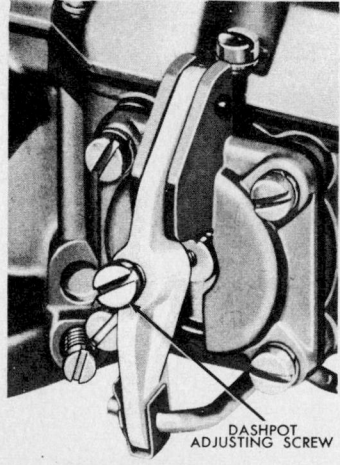

Anti-stall dashpot adjustment

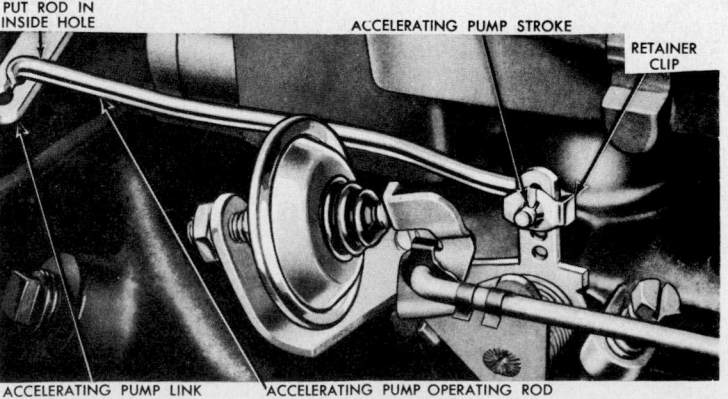

Accelerating pump adjustment

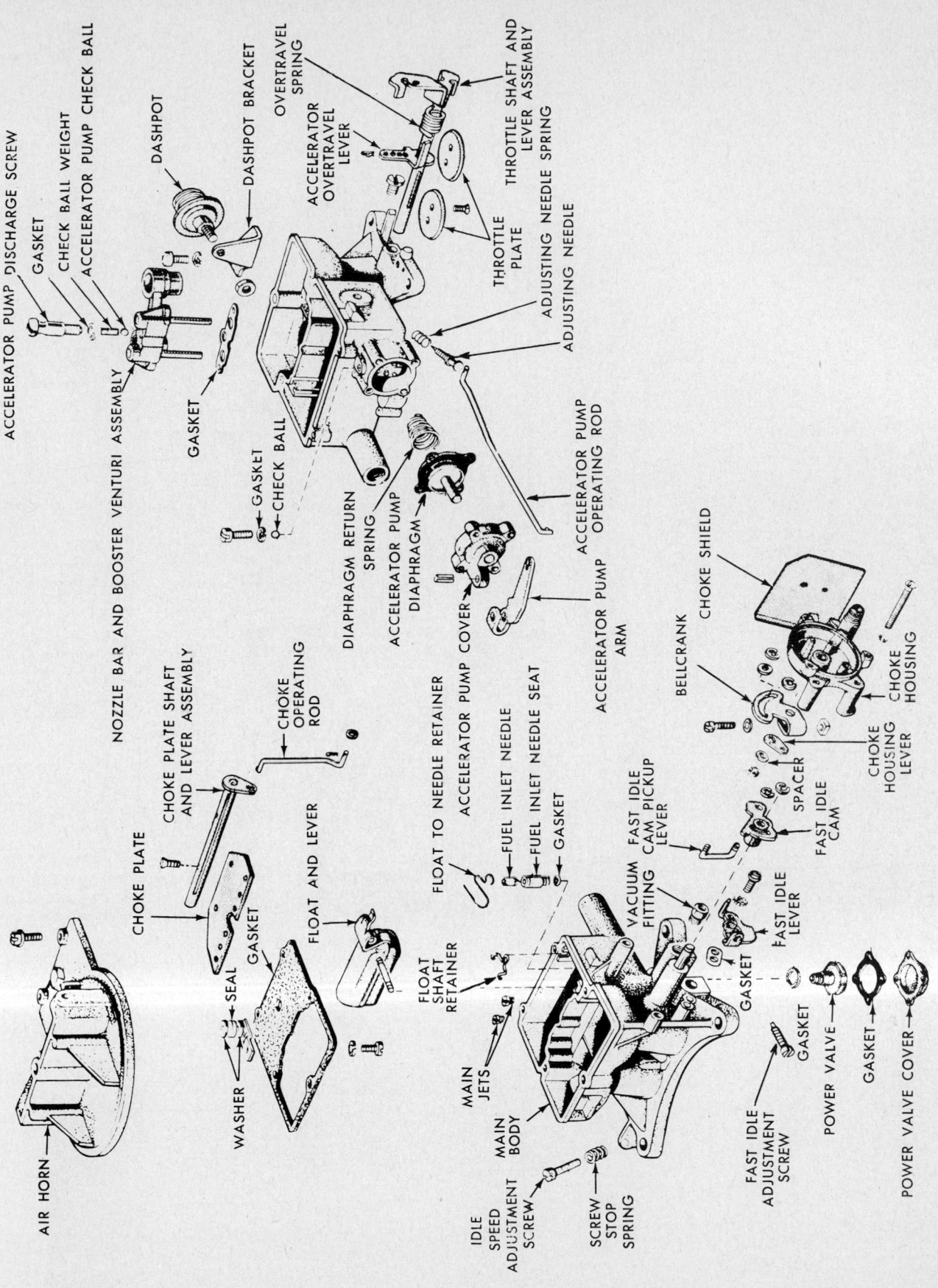

ACCELERATOR PUMP DISCHARGE SCREW
GASKET
CHECK BALL WEIGHT
ACCELERATOR PUMP CHECK BALL
DASHPOT
DASHPOT BRACKET
OVERTRAVEL SPRING
ACCELERATOR OVERTRAVEL LEVER
THROTTLE SHAFT AND LEVER ASSEMBLY
THROTTLE PLATE
ADJUSTING NEEDLE SPRING
ADJUSTING NEEDLE

NOZZLE BAR AND BOOSTER VENTURI ASSEMBLY
GASKET
GASKET
CHECK BALL
DIAPHRAGM RETURN SPRING
ACCELERATOR PUMP DIAPHRAGM
ACCELERATOR PUMP COVER
ACCELERATOR PUMP OPERATING ROD
ACCELERATOR PUMP ARM

CHOKE PLATE SHAFT AND LEVER ASSEMBLY
CHOKE OPERATING ROD
CHOKE PLATE

CHOKE SHIELD
BELLCRANK
CHOKE HOUSING
CHOKE HOUSING LEVER
VACUUM FAST IDLE CAM PICKUP LEVER
SPACER
FAST IDLE CAM
FAST IDLE LEVER

Ford two-barrel (typical)

AIR HORN
WASHER
SEAL
GASKET
FLOAT AND LEVER
FLOAT SHAFT RETAINER
FLOAT TO NEEDLE RETAINER
FUEL INLET NEEDLE
FUEL INLET NEEDLE SEAT
GASKET
VACUUM FAST IDLE FITTING
GASKET
FAST IDLE ADJUSTMENT SCREW
GASKET

MAIN JETS
MAIN BODY
IDLE SPEED ADJUSTMENT SCREW
SCREW STOP SPRING

POWER VALVE
GASKET
POWER VALVE COVER

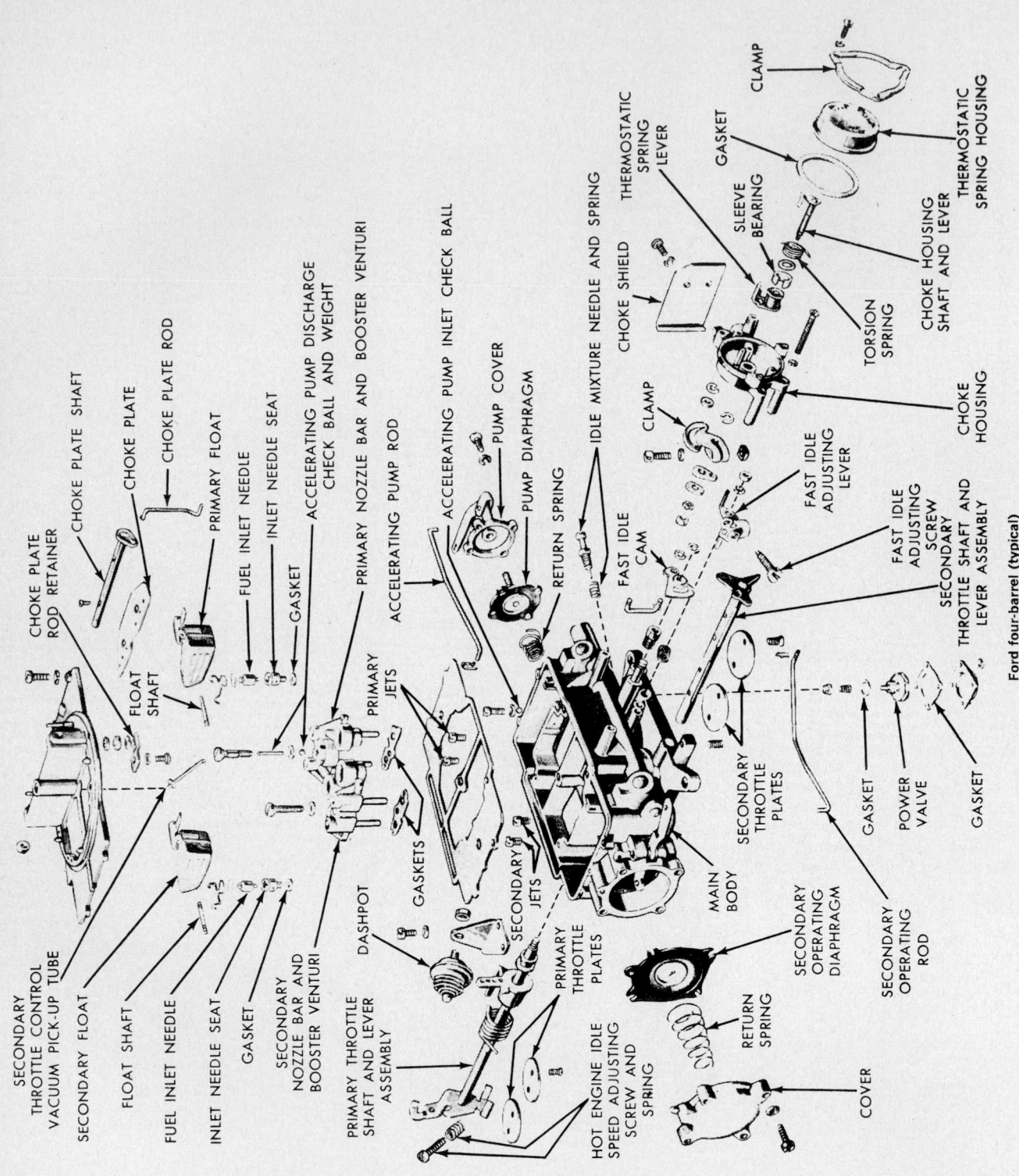

SECONDARY THROTTLE CONTROL VACUUM PICK-UP TUBE

SECONDARY FLOAT

FLOAT SHAFT

FUEL INLET NEEDLE

INLET NEEDLE SEAT

GASKET

SECONDARY NOZZLE BAR AND BOOSTER VENTURI

PRIMARY THROTTLE SHAFT AND LEVER ASSEMBLY

DASHPOT

GASKETS

SECONDARY JETS

PRIMARY THROTTLE PLATES

HOT ENGINE IDLE SPEED ADJUSTING SCREW AND SPRING

COVER

RETURN SPRING

SECONDARY OPERATING DIAPHRAGM

SECONDARY OPERATING ROD

MAIN BODY

SECONDARY THROTTLE PLATES

GASKET

POWER VALVE

GASKET

SECONDARY THROTTLE SHAFT AND LEVER ASSEMBLY

FAST IDLE ADJUSTING SCREW

FAST IDLE ADJUSTING LEVER

CHOKE HOUSING

CHOKE HOUSING SHAFT AND LEVER

TORSION SPRING

THERMOSTATIC SPRING HOUSING

CHOKE HOUSING

CLAMP

SLEEVE BEARING

GASKET

THERMOSTATIC SPRING LEVER

CHOKE SHIELD

IDLE MIXTURE NEEDLE AND SPRING

FAST IDLE CAM

CLAMP

RETURN SPRING

PUMP DIAPHRAGM

PUMP COVER

ACCELERATING PUMP INLET CHECK BALL

ACCELERATING PUMP ROD

PRIMARY NOZZLE BAR AND BOOSTER VENTURI

ACCELERATING PUMP DISCHARGE CHECK BALL AND WEIGHT

GASKET

INLET NEEDLE SEAT

FUEL INLET NEEDLE

PRIMARY FLOAT

CHOKE PLATE ROD

CHOKE PLATE

CHOKE PLATE SHAFT

CHOKE PLATE ROD RETAINER

FLOAT SHAFT

PRIMARY JETS

Ford four-barrel (typical)

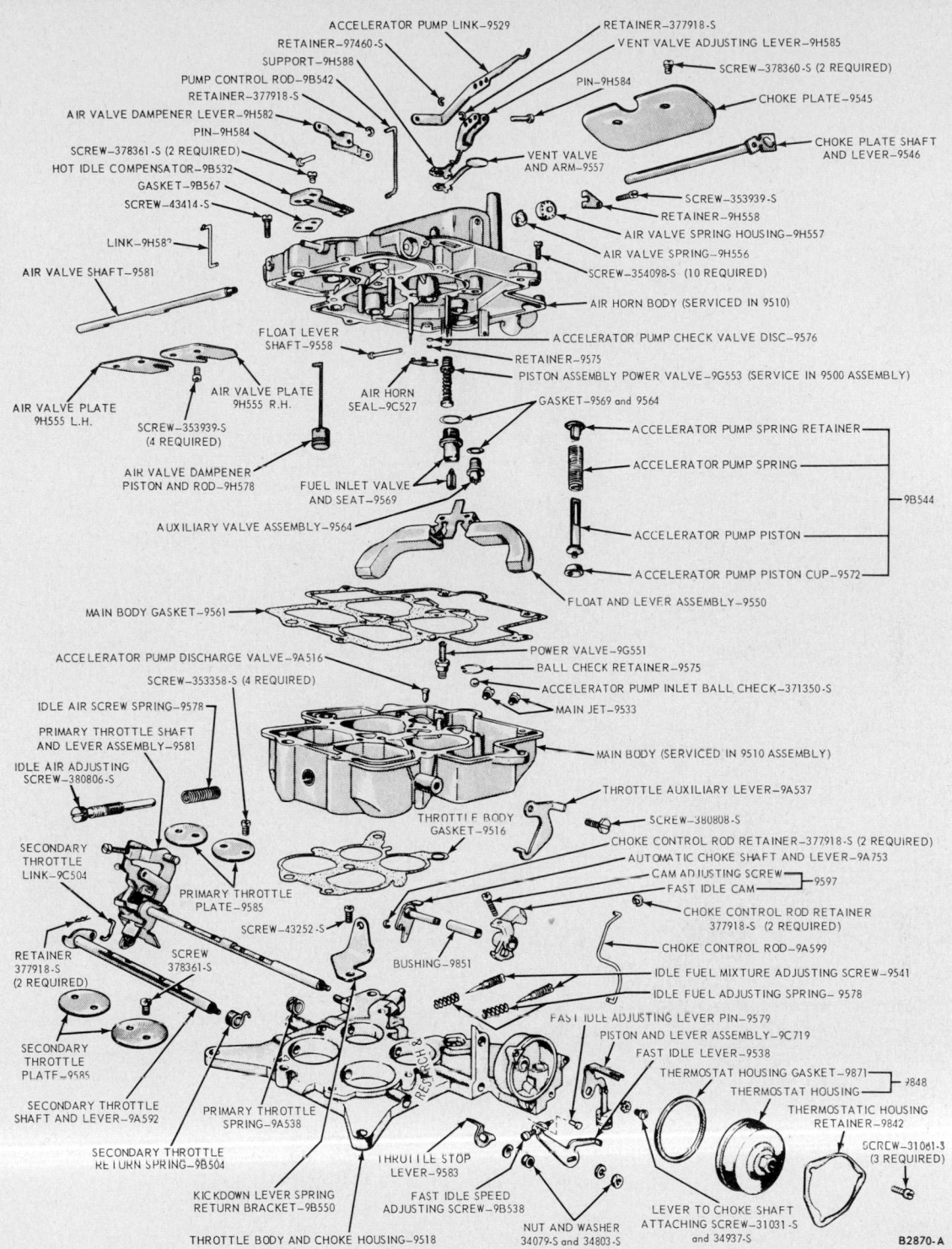

ACCELERATOR PUMP LINK—9529
RETAINER—97460-S
SUPPORT—9H588
PUMP CONTROL ROD—9B542
RETAINER—377918-S
AIR VALVE DAMPENER LEVER—9H582
PIN—9H584
SCREW—378361-S (2 REQUIRED)
HOT IDLE COMPENSATOR—9B532
GASKET—9B567
SCREW—43414-S

LINK—9H582
AIR VALVE SHAFT—9581

FLOAT LEVER SHAFT—9558
AIR VALVE PLATE 9H555 R.H.
AIR VALVE PLATE 9H555 L.H.
SCREW—353939-S (4 REQUIRED)
AIR VALVE DAMPENER PISTON AND ROD—9H578
AIR HORN SEAL—9C527
FUEL INLET VALVE AND SEAT—9569
AUXILIARY VALVE ASSEMBLY—9564

RETAINER—377918-S
VENT VALVE ADJUSTING LEVER—9H585
SCREW—378360-S (2 REQUIRED)
PIN—9H584
CHOKE PLATE—9545
CHOKE PLATE SHAFT AND LEVER—9546
VENT VALVE AND ARM—9557
SCREW—353939-S
RETAINER—9H558
AIR VALVE SPRING HOUSING—9H557
AIR VALVE SPRING—9H556
SCREW—354098-S (10 REQUIRED)
AIR HORN BODY (SERVICED IN 9510)
ACCELERATOR PUMP CHECK VALVE DISC—9576
RETAINER—9575
PISTON ASSEMBLY POWER VALVE—9G553 (SERVICE IN 9500 ASSEMBLY)
GASKET—9569 and 9564

ACCELERATOR PUMP SPRING RETAINER
ACCELERATOR PUMP SPRING
ACCELERATOR PUMP PISTON
ACCELERATOR PUMP PISTON CUP—9572
FLOAT AND LEVER ASSEMBLY—9550
9B544

MAIN BODY GASKET—9561
ACCELERATOR PUMP DISCHARGE VALVE—9A516
SCREW—353358-S (4 REQUIRED)
IDLE AIR SCREW SPRING—9578
PRIMARY THROTTLE SHAFT AND LEVER ASSEMBLY—9581
IDLE AIR ADJUSTING SCREW—380806-S

POWER VALVE—9G551
BALL CHECK RETAINER—9575
ACCELERATOR PUMP INLET BALL CHECK—371350-S
MAIN JET—9533
MAIN BODY (SERVICED IN 9510 ASSEMBLY)

SECONDARY THROTTLE LINK—9C504
PRIMARY THROTTLE PLATE—9585
SCREW—43252-S
RETAINER 377918-S (2 REQUIRED)
SCREW 378361-S
SECONDARY THROTTLE PLATE—9585
SECONDARY THROTTLE SHAFT AND LEVER—9A592
PRIMARY THROTTLE SPRING—9A538
SECONDARY THROTTLE RETURN SPRING—9B504
KICKDOWN LEVER SPRING RETURN BRACKET—9B550
THROTTLE BODY AND CHOKE HOUSING—9518

THROTTLE BODY GASKET—9516
THROTTLE AUXILIARY LEVER—9A537
SCREW—380808-S
CHOKE CONTROL ROD RETAINER—377918-S (2 REQUIRED)
AUTOMATIC CHOKE SHAFT AND LEVER—9A753
CAM ADJUSTING SCREW
FAST IDLE CAM 9597
CHOKE CONTROL ROD RETAINER 377918-S (2 REQUIRED)
CHOKE CONTROL ROD—9A599
BUSHING—9851
IDLE FUEL MIXTURE ADJUSTING SCREW—9541
IDLE FUEL ADJUSTING SPRING—9578
FAST IDLE ADJUSTING LEVER PIN—9579
PISTON AND LEVER ASSEMBLY—9C719
FAST IDLE LEVER—9538
THERMOSTAT HOUSING GASKET—9871
THERMOSTAT HOUSING 9848
THERMOSTATIC HOUSING RETAINER—9842
SCREW—31061-3 (3 REQUIRED)
THROTTLE STOP LEVER—9583
FAST IDLE SPEED ADJUSTING SCREW—9B538
NUT AND WASHER 34079-S and 34803-S
LEVER TO CHOKE SHAFT ATTACHING SCREW—31031-S and 34937-S

B2870-A

Carburetor assembly, four-barrel 4300

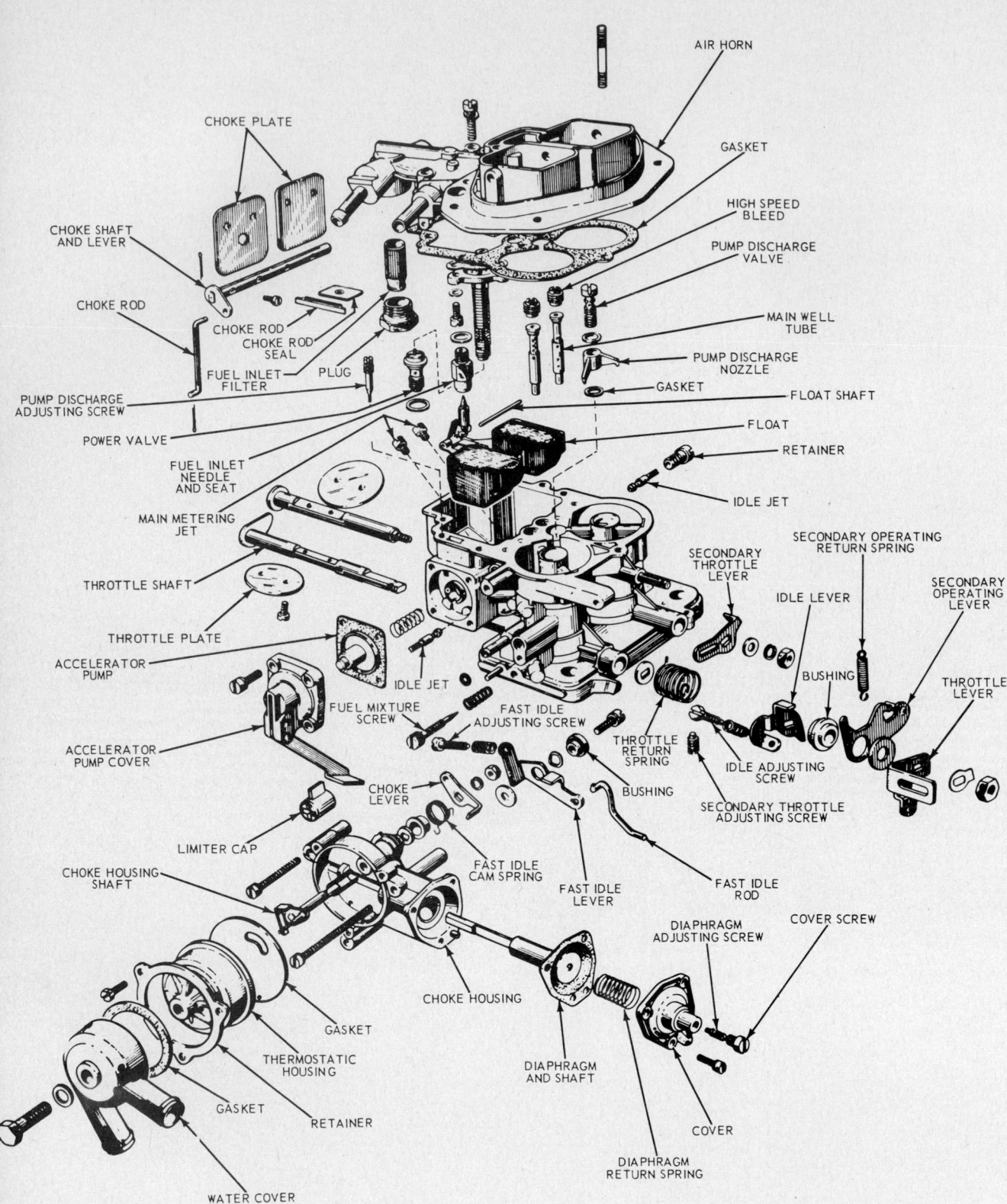

Exploded View, Model 5200-C (© Ford Motor Co.)

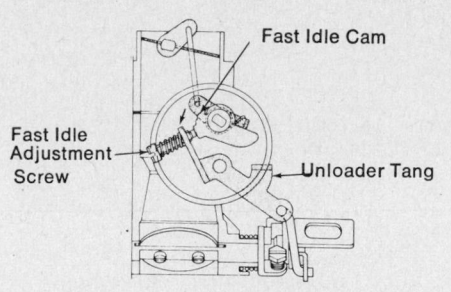

**Fast Idle and Choke Unloader Linkage,
Model 5200-C**
(© Ford Motor Co.)

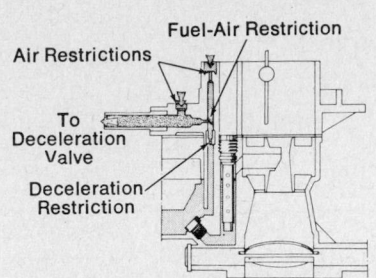

Deceleration System, Model 5200-C
(© Ford Motor Co.)

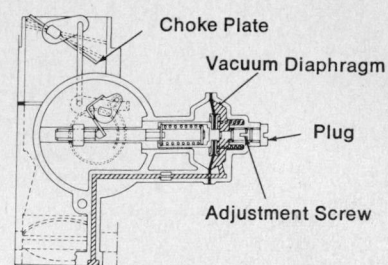

Choke Vacuum Pulldown, Model 5200-C
(© Ford Motor Co.)

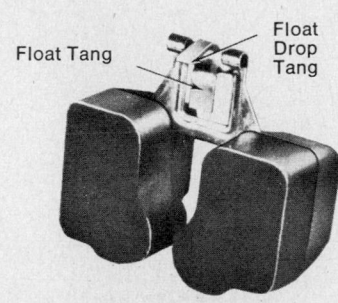

Float Assembly, Model 5200-C
(© Ford Motor Co.)

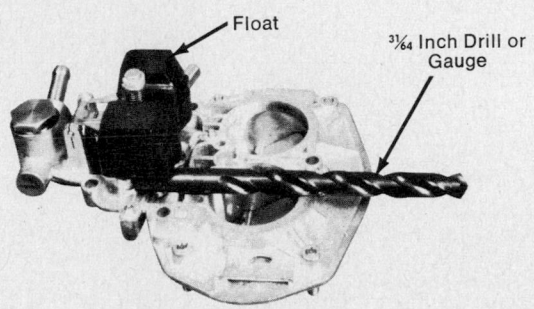

Dry Float Setting, Model 5200-C
(© Ford Motor Co.)

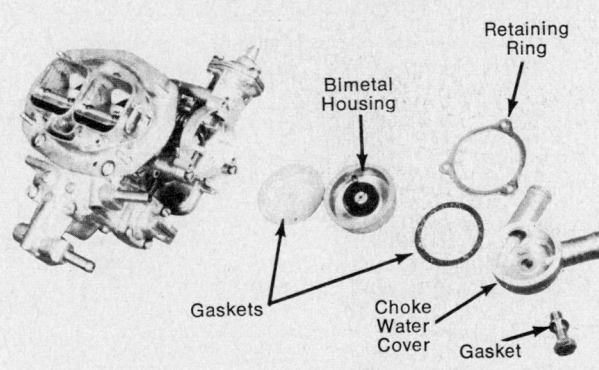

Removal of Choke Thermostat, Model 5200-C
(© Ford Motor Co.)

Dechoke Clearance Adjustment, Model 5200-C
(© Ford Motor Co.)

Bumper Spring Setting, Model 5200-C
(© Ford Motor Co.)

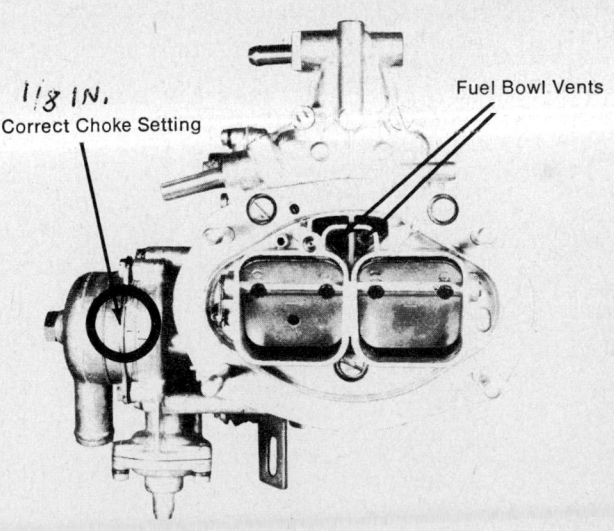

Choke Bimetal Setting, Model 5200-C
(© Ford Motor Co.)

Holley Carburetors

YEAR	MODEL	Float Level (In.)	Fuel Level In.	Bowl Vent Valve (In.)	Pump Travel Setting (In.)	CHOKE SETTING Unloader (In.)	Housing	Secondary Lockout Adj.	Throttle Bore Diam. Prim.	Sec.	Venturi Diam. Prim.	Sec.
Chevrolet												
1965	327 (4150)	①	①	...	.015	.375	...	...	$1\frac{9}{16}$	$1\frac{9}{16}$	$1\frac{1}{4}$	$1\frac{5}{16}$
1965	396	①	①	.065	.015	.275	...	...	$1\frac{11}{16}$	$1\frac{11}{16}$	$1\frac{3}{8}$	$1\frac{7}{16}$
1966	327-350 Hp (4150)	①	①	.065	.015	.260	...	...	$1\frac{9}{16}$	$1\frac{9}{16}$	$1\frac{1}{4}$	$1\frac{5}{16}$
1966	327 (4160)	①	①	.065	.015	.260	...	...	$1\frac{9}{16}$	$1\frac{9}{16}$	$1\frac{1}{4}$	$1\frac{5}{16}$
1966	396 (4160)	①	①	.065	.015	.260	...	...	$1\frac{9}{16}$	$1\frac{9}{16}$	$1\frac{1}{4}$	$1\frac{5}{16}$
1966	427-425 Hp (4150)	①	①	.065	.015	.350	...	...	$1\frac{11}{16}$	$1\frac{11}{16}$	$1\frac{3}{8}$	$1\frac{7}{16}$
1966	427-390 Hp (4160)	①	①	.065	.015	.260	...	...	$1\frac{9}{16}$	$1\frac{9}{16}$	$1\frac{1}{4}$	$1\frac{5}{16}$
1967	427-2 Bbl. (2100)	①	①	...	.015	.275	...	...	$1\frac{1}{2}$	...	$1\frac{3}{16}$	...
1967	327-325 Hp-4 Bbl. (4150)	A①	A①	.065	.015	.265	...	...	$1\frac{9}{16}$	$1\frac{9}{16}$	$1\frac{1}{4}$	$1\frac{5}{16}$
1967	427-425 Hp-4 Bbl. (4150)	A①	A①	.065	.015	.350	...	...	$1\frac{11}{16}$	$1\frac{11}{16}$	$1\frac{3}{8}$	$1\frac{7}{16}$
1967	327, 396, 427-4 Bbl. (4160)	A①	A①	.065	.015	.265	...	...	$1\frac{9}{16}$	$1\frac{9}{16}$	$1\frac{1}{4}$	$1\frac{3}{16}$
1968-69	V8-302, 396, 427 (4150)	B①	B①	.065	.015	.350	...	...	$1\frac{11}{16}$	$1\frac{11}{16}$	$1\frac{3}{8}$	$1\frac{7}{16}$
1968-69	V8-CORVETTE-427-430 Hp (4150)	B①	B①	.065	.015	.350	...	...	$1\frac{3}{4}$	$1\frac{3}{4}$	$1\frac{9}{16}$	$1\frac{9}{16}$
1970	4150—350, 396, 454	.350	...	...	.015	.350	...	...	$1\frac{11}{16}$	$1\frac{11}{16}$	$1\frac{3}{8}$	$1\frac{7}{16}$
1971	4150—350, 454	②	①	...	.015	.350	...	...	$1\frac{11}{16}$	$1\frac{11}{16}$	$1\frac{3}{8}$	$1\frac{7}{16}$
1972	4150—350 (LT-1, Z-28)	②	①	...	.015	.350	...	...	$1\frac{11}{16}$	$1\frac{11}{16}$	$1\frac{3}{8}$	$1\frac{7}{16}$

A—Primary .170, Secondary .300.
B—Primary .350, Secondary .500.
①—Float adjustment: Fuel level should be plus or minus $\frac{1}{32}$ in. with threads at bottom of sight holes. To adjust turn adjusting nut on top of bowl clockwise, to lower, counterclockwise to raise.
②—Float centered in bowl.

YEAR	MODEL	Float Level (In.)	Fuel Level In.	Bowl Vent Valve (In.)	Pump Travel Setting (In.)	CHOKE SETTING Unloader (In.)	Housing	Secondary Lockout Adj.	Throttle Bore Diam. Prim.	Sec.	Venturi Diam. Prim.	Sec.
Chrysler Corp.												
1965	1920	①	$\frac{27}{32}$	$\frac{1}{16}$	...	...	2-RICH	...	$1\frac{11}{16}$	...	$1\frac{5}{16}$	...
1966	1920-Single	①	$\frac{27}{32}$	$\frac{3}{32}$	...	...	2-RICH	...	$1\frac{11}{16}$	...	$1\frac{5}{16}$	...
1967	1920-Single	①	$\frac{27}{32}$	$\frac{3}{32}$	...	...	2-RICH	...	$1\frac{11}{16}$	...	$1\frac{5}{16}$	...
1967	4160, 440	$\frac{1}{8}$	$\frac{9}{16}$	$\frac{3}{32}$	.015	$\frac{5}{32}$	2-RICH	...	$1\frac{9}{16}$	$1\frac{9}{16}$	$1\frac{1}{4}$	$1\frac{5}{16}$
1968	1920, 225	①	$\frac{27}{32}$	$\frac{3}{32}$	...	...	2-RICH	...	$1\frac{11}{16}$	...	$1\frac{5}{16}$	...
1968	4160, 440	$\frac{1}{8}$	$\frac{9}{16}$	$\frac{3}{32}$	.015	$\frac{5}{32}$	2-RICH	...	$1\frac{9}{16}$	$1\frac{9}{16}$	$1\frac{1}{4}$	$1\frac{5}{16}$
1969	1920, 225	①	$\frac{27}{32}$	$\frac{3}{32}$	...	$\frac{9}{32}$	2-RICH	...	$1\frac{11}{16}$	...	$1\frac{5}{16}$	...
1969	4160, 440	$\frac{1}{4}$	$\frac{9}{16}$	$\frac{5}{64}$	.015	$\frac{5}{32}$	2-RICH	...	$1\frac{9}{16}$	$1\frac{9}{16}$	$1\frac{1}{4}$	$1\frac{5}{16}$
1969	2300-6V, center	③	②	.101	.015	$\frac{5}{32}$	2-RICH	...	$1\frac{1}{2}$	...	$1\frac{3}{16}$	...
1969	2300-6V, front, rear	③	②	...	...	...	...	...	$1\frac{3}{4}$	...	$1\frac{9}{16}$	...
1970	1920-R4355A-225, Std. Taxi w. CAS	$\frac{27}{32}$	...	$\frac{3}{32}$	...	$\frac{9}{32}$	2-RICH	...	$1\frac{9}{16}$	...	$1\frac{1}{4}$	...
1970	1920-R4363A-225, Std. Taxi w. CAS	$\frac{27}{32}$	...	$\frac{3}{32}$	...	$\frac{9}{32}$	2-RICH	...	$1\frac{9}{16}$	...	$1\frac{1}{4}$	...
1970	1920-R4351A-225, Std. w. CAS	$\frac{27}{32}$	...	$\frac{3}{32}$	...	$\frac{9}{32}$	2-RICH	...	$1\frac{11}{16}$	...	$1\frac{5}{16}$	...
1970	1920-R4352A-225, Auto. w. CAS	$\frac{27}{32}$	...	$\frac{3}{32}$	...	$\frac{9}{32}$	2-RICH	...	$1\frac{11}{16}$	...	$1\frac{5}{16}$	...
1970	1920-R4353A-225, Std. w. ECS	$\frac{27}{32}$	...	$\frac{3}{32}$	...	$\frac{9}{32}$	2-RICH	...	$1\frac{11}{16}$	...	$1\frac{5}{16}$	...
1970	1920-R4354A-225, Auto. w. ECS	$\frac{27}{32}$	...	$\frac{3}{32}$	...	$\frac{9}{32}$	2-RICH	...	$1\frac{11}{16}$	...	$1\frac{3}{16}$	...
1970	2210-R4371A-383, Auto.	.200	...	$\frac{5}{64}$	...	$\frac{11}{64}$	2-RICH	...	$1\frac{9}{16}$	...	$1\frac{13}{32}$	...
1970	4160-R4367A-383, Std. w. CAS	$\frac{15}{64}$	...	$\frac{5}{64}$	...	#25 Drill	2-RICH	...	$1\frac{9}{16}$	$1\frac{3}{4}$	$1\frac{1}{4}$	$1\frac{9}{16}$
1970	4160-R4368A-383 Auto. w/o AC, w. CAS	$\frac{15}{64}$	...	$\frac{5}{64}$	...	#25 Drill	2-RICH	...	$1\frac{9}{16}$	$1\frac{3}{4}$	$1\frac{1}{4}$	$1\frac{9}{16}$
1970	4160-R4369A-383, Auto. w. AC, w. CAS	$\frac{15}{64}$	...	$\frac{5}{64}$	...	#25 Drill	2-RICH	...	$1\frac{9}{16}$	$1\frac{3}{4}$	$1\frac{1}{4}$	$1\frac{9}{16}$
1970	4160-R4217A-383, Std. w. ECS	$\frac{15}{64}$	...	.025	...	#25 Drill	2-RICH	...	$1\frac{9}{16}$	$1\frac{3}{4}$	$1\frac{1}{4}$	$1\frac{9}{16}$
1970	4160-R4218A-383, Auto. w. ECS	$\frac{15}{64}$	...	.025	...	#25 Drill	2-RICH	...	$1\frac{9}{16}$	$1\frac{3}{4}$	$1\frac{1}{4}$	$1\frac{9}{16}$
1970	2300-R4375A-440, Std. w. CAS, center carburetor—6V	②	...	.101	.015	$\frac{5}{32}$	2-RICH	...	$1\frac{1}{2}$	...	$1\frac{3}{16}$	...
1970	2300-R4376A-440, Auto. w. CAS, center carburetor—6V	②	...	.101	.015	$\frac{5}{32}$	2-RICH	...	$1\frac{1}{2}$	...	$1\frac{3}{16}$	...
1970	2300-R4382AF-440, front carburetor—6V	②	...	...	...	...	...	...	$1\frac{3}{4}$	...	$1\frac{9}{16}$	...
1970	2300-R4383AR-440, rear carburetor—6V	②	...	...	...	...	...	...	$1\frac{3}{4}$	...	$1\frac{9}{16}$	...

Chrysler Corp., continued

YEAR	MODEL	Float Level (In.)	Fuel Level (In.)	Bowl Vent Valve (In.)	Pump Travel Setting (In.)	CHOKE SETTING Unloader (In.)	Housing	Secondary Lockout Adj.	Throttle Bore Diam. Prim.	Sec.	Venturi Diam. Prim.	Sec.
1970	2300—R4374A-440, Std. w. ECS, center carburetor—6V	②	...	.101	.015	5/32	2-RICH	...	1 1/2	...	1 3/16	...
1970	2300—R4144A-440, Auto. w. ECS, center carburetor—6V	②	...	.101	.015	5/32	2-RICH	...	1 1/2	...	1 3/16	...
1970	2300—R4175AF-440, front carburetor—6V	②	...	...	...	...	...	...	1 3/4	...	1 9/16	...
1970	2300—R4365AR-440, rear carburetor—6V	②	...	...	...	...	...	...	1 3/4	...	1 9/16	...
1970	4160—R4366A-440, Auto. w. CAS	15/64	...	5/64	.015	#25 Drill	2-RICH	...	1 9/16	1 9/16	1 1/4	1 5/16
1970	4160—R4360A-440, Auto. w. ECS	15/64	...	5/64	.015	#25 Drill	2-RICH	...	1 9/16	1 9/16	1 1/4	1 5/16
1971	1920—R-4659A, 225 Taxi	27/32	...	1/32	...	9/32	2-RICH	...	1 9/16	...	1 1/4	...
1971	1920—R-4655A, 225 S.T.	27/32	...	1/32	...	9/32	2-RICH	...	1 11/16	...	1 5/16	...
1971	1920—R-4656A, 225 A.T.	27/32	...	1/32	...	9/32	2-RICH	...	1 11/16	...	1 5/16	...
1971	2210—R-4665A, 360 S.T.	.200	...	.015	9/16	11/64	2-RICH	...	1 9/16	...	1 7/16	...
1971	2210—R-4666A, 360 A.T.	.200	...	.015	9/16	11/64	2-RICH	...	1 9/16	...	1 7/16	...
1971	4160—R-6191A, 383 S.T.	15/64	9/16	.015	.015	#25 Drill	2-RICH	...	1 9/16	1 3/4	1 1/4	1 9/16
1971	4160—R-4668A, 383 A.T.	15/64	9/16	.015	.015	#25 Drill	2-RICH	...	1 9/16	1 3/4	1 1/4	1 9/16
1971	4160—R-6193, 383 S.T.	15/64	9/16	.015	.015	#25 Drill	2-RICH	...	1 9/16	1 3/4	1 1/4	1 9/16
1971	4160—R-4735, 383 A.T.	15/64	9/16	.015	.015	#25 Drill	2-RICH	...	1 9/16	1 3/4	1 1/4	1 9/16
1971	2300—R-4791A, 92A, 340 center	③	②	.101	.015	5/32	INDEX	...	1 1/2	...	1 3/16	...
1971	2300—R-4789A, 90A, 340	③	②	...	...	...	...	...	1 3/4	...	1 9/16	...
1971	2300—R-4669A, 70A, 440 center	③	②	101	.015	5/32	2-RICH	...	1 1/2	...	1 3/16	...
1971	2300—R-4671A, 72A, 440	③	②	...	...	...	...	...	1 3/4	...	1 9/16	...
1972	R-6363A, 64A, 198	27/32	...	1/32	...	9/32	2-RICH	...	1 9/16	...	1 1/4	...
1972	R-6365A, 66A, Calif.	27/32	...	1/32	...	9/32	2-RICH	...	1 9/16	...	1 1/4	...
1972	R-6155A, 56A, 225	27/32	...	1/32	...	9/32	2-RICH	...	1 11/16	...	1 5/16	...
1972	R-6153A, 54A, Calif.	27/32	...	1/32	...	9/32	2-RICH	...	1 11/16	...	1 5/16	...
1972	R-6164A, 360	.200	...	.015	9/16	11/64	2-RICH	...	1 9/16	...	1 7/16	...
1972	R-6162A, 360 Calif.	.200	...	.015	9/16	11/64	2-RICH	...	1 9/16	...	1 7/16	...
1972	R-6252A, 53A, 54A, 55A, 440	15/64	9/16	.015	.015	#25 DRILL	2-RICH	...	1 9/16	1 3/4	1 1/4	1 9/16
1972	R-6256A, 57A, 58A, 59A, 440 Calif.	15/64	9/16	.015	.015	#25 DRILL	2-RICH	...	1 9/16	1 3/4	1 1/4	1 9/16
1972	R-6403A, 04A, 440 Center	③	②	.101	.015	5/32	2-RICH	...	1 1/2	...	1 3/16	...
1972	R-6405A, 06A, 440 F & R	③	②	...	...	...	...	...	1 3/4	...	1 9/16	...
1972	R-6160A, 440 Std.	15/64	...	.015	.015	#25 DRILL	2-RICH	...	1 9/16	1 9/16	1 1/4	1 5/16
1972	R-6290A, 440 Std. Calif.	15/64	...	.015	.015	#25 DRILL	2-RICH	...	1 9/16	1 9/16	1 1/4	1 5/16

① —Use gauge C-3903.
② —Fuel level should be at bottom edge of sight plug hole.
③ —Float centered in bowl with bowl inverted.

CAS—Cleaner Air System
ECS—Evaporation control system

Ford—Mercury

YEAR	MODEL	Float Level (In.)	Fuel Level (In.)	Bowl Vent Valve (In.)	Pump Travel Setting (In.)	CHOKE SETTING Unloader (In.)	Housing	Secondary Lockout Adj.	Throttle Bore Diam. Prim.	Sec.	Venturi Diam. Prim.	Sec.
1965	4-Barrel (Single)	Ⓐ	①	...	.013	...	INDEX	...	1 11/16	1 11/16	1 5/16	1 3/8
1965	4-Barrel-Frt.	Ⓐ	①	...	...	...	INDEX	...	1 11/16	1 11/16	1 5/16	1 5/16
1965	4-Barrel-Rear	Ⓐ	①	...	...	...	...	...	1 9/16	1 9/16	1 5/16	1 5/16
1966	4-Barrel (Single)	Ⓐ	①	...	.013	...	INDEX	...	1 11/16	1 11/16	1 5/16	1 3/8
1966	4-Barrel-Frt.	Ⓐ	①	...	...	...	3-LEAN	...	1 9/16	1 9/16	1 5/16	1 5/16
1966	4-Barrel-Rear	Ⓐ	①	...	...	...	...	...	1 9/16	1 9/16	1 5/16	1 5/16
1967	V8-Frt.	Ⓐ	①	...	...	...	INDEX	...	1 11/16	1 11/16	1 5/16	1 3/8
1967	V8-Rear	Ⓐ	①	...	...	...	...	...	1 11/16	1 11/16	1 5/16	1 3/8
1967	V8-Single 4-Barrel	Ⓐ	①	...	...	...	INDEX	...	1 11/16	1 11/16	1 3/8	1 7/16
1968	390 GT	Ⓐ	①	...	...	...	3-RICH	...	1 9/16	1 9/16	1 1/4	1 5/16
1968	427, 428 CJ	Ⓐ	①	.060-.090	.015②	...	2-RICH	...	1 11/16	1 11/16	1 3/8	1 7/16
1969	302 Boss	Ⓐ	①	.070	.015②	...	...	...	1 11/16	1 11/16	1 3/8	1 7/16
1969	4150C-428 CJ Std.	Ⓐ	①	.070	...	...	1-RICH	...	1 11/16	1 11/16	1 3/8	1 7/16
1969	4150C-428 CJ Auto.	Ⓐ	①	.070	...	...	2-RICH	...	1 11/16	1 11/16	1 3/8	1 7/16
1970	4150C-302 Boss	Ⓐ	①	...	...	...	...	...	1 11/16	1 11/16	1 3/8	1 7/16
1970	4150C-428 CJ Std.	Ⓐ	①	...	.015②	...	...	...	1 11/16	1 11/16	1 3/8	1 7/16
1970	4150C-428 CJ Auto.	Ⓐ	①	...	.015②	...	...	...	1 11/16	1 11/16	1 3/8	1 7/16
1970	4150C-429 SCJ, Auto.	Ⓐ	①	...	...	...	2-RICH	...	1 11/16	1 11/16	1 3/8	1 7/16
1970	4150C-429 SCJ Std.	Ⓐ	①	...	...	...	2-RICH	...	1 11/16	1 11/16	1 3/8	1 7/16
1970	4150C-429 Boss	Ⓐ	①	...	...	...	...	...	1 11/16	1 11/16	1 3/8	1 7/16
1971	4150C-429 SCJ ST	Ⓐ	①	...	.013	19/64	2-RICH	...	1 11/16	1 11/16	1 3/8	1 7/16
1971	4150C-429 SCJ, A.T.	Ⓐ	①	...	.015	19/64	2-RICH	...	1 11/16	1 11/16	1 3/8	1 7/16

① —Bottom of sight plug.
② —Min. spring adjustment.
③ —Invert fuel bowl, turn adjusting nut until base of float is parallel with floor of bowl.

Holley Carburetors

Rambler—American Motors

YEAR	MODEL	Float Level (In.)	Fuel Level In.)	Bowl Vent Valve (In.)	Pump Travel Setting (In.)	CHOKE SETTING Unloader (In.)	Housing	Secondary Lockout Adj.	Throttle Bore Diam. Prim.	Sec.	Venturi Diam. Prim.	Sec.
1965	Single-1909	$7/16$	①	.060	...	$9/32$	INDEX	...	$1\,11/16$	...	$1\,1/2$	...
1965	2-Bbl.-2300	$11/32$ ③	$1/2$ ⑤	.060	②	.180	INDEX	...	$1\,5/16$	...	$1\,1/32$	...
1965	4-Bbl.-4150	④	①	.060	②	.180	1-LEAN	...	$1\,7/16$	$1\,7/16$	$1\,1/16$	$1\,3/16$
1966	6 Cyl.-199-1 Bbl.-Std.	$5/16$	...	$1/16$	...	$15/64$	1-RICH	...	$1\,9/16$	...	$1\,1/4$	...
1966	6 Cyl.-199-1 Bbl.-Aut.	$5/16$	...	$1/16$	...	$15/64$	INDEX	...	$1\,9/16$	...	$1\,1/4$	...
1966	6 Cyl.-232-1 Bbl.-Std.	$5/16$	...	$1/16$	...	$15/64$	1-RICH	...	$1\,11/16$	...	$1\,1/2$	...
1966	6 Cyl.-232-1 Bbl.-Aut.	$5/16$	...	$1/16$	...	$15/64$	INDEX	...	$1\,11/16$	...	$1\,1/2$	...
1966	V8-287-2 Bbl.	$11/32$ ③	$1/2$ ⑤	$5/64$	②	$3/16$	INDEX	...	$1\,5/16$	...	$1\,1/32$	...
1966	V8-327-4 Bbl.	④	①	.060	②	.180	1-LEAN	...	$1\,7/16$	$1\,7/16$	$1\,1/16$	$1\,3/16$
1966	V8-290-2 Bbl.	$11/32$	...	$5/64$	#1 Hole	$3/16$	INDEX	...	$1\,5/16$	...	$1\,1/8$	...
1967	6 Cyl.-Std.	$5/16$	...	$1/16$	...	$15/64$	⑥	...	$1\,11/16$	...	$1\,1/2$	...
1967	V8-2 Bbl.	$11/32$ ③	$1/2$ ⑤	$5/64$	②	$3/16$	1-LEAN	...	$1\,5/16$	...	$1\,1/8$	...
1968	6 Cyl.-Std.	$5/16$	...	$1/16$	...	$15/64$	1-RICH	...	$1\,11/16$	...	$1\,1/2$	...
1968	6 Cyl.-Aut.	$5/16$	...	$1/16$	...	$15/64$	1-RICH	...	$1\,11/16$	...	$1\,1/2$	...
1969	6-Cyl.-Aut.	$5/16$	...	$1/16$	#1 Hole	$15/64$	1-RICH	...	$1\,11/16$	...	$1\,1/2$	...

① —To bottom of sight hole.
② —Tighten screw $1/4$ turn beyond touch point.
③ —With bowl cover inverted, measure distance between float and bowl cover.
④ —Parallel with floor of bowl.
⑤ —Measure from fuel level to top of bowl.
⑥ 199—INDEX, 232—1-LEAN.

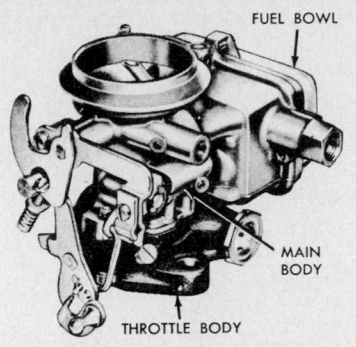

Holley single-barrel carburetor (© Ford Motor Co.)

FUEL BOWL

MAIN BODY

THROTTLE BODY

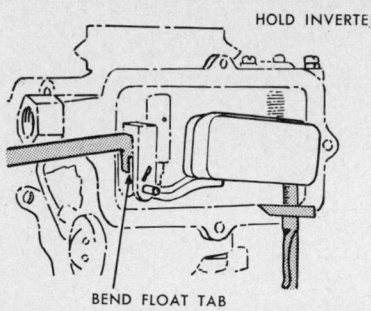

HOLD INVERTED

BEND FLOAT TAB

Holley single-barrel float drop (© Ford Motor Co.)

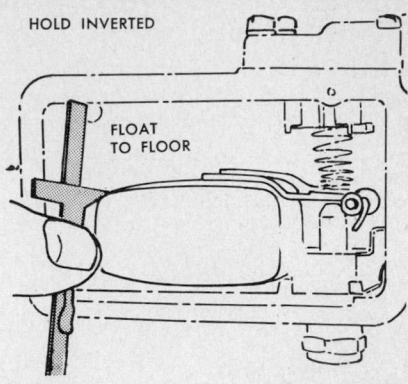

HOLD INVERTED

FLOAT TO FLOOR

Holley two- and four-barrel float adjustment (© Ford Motor Co.)

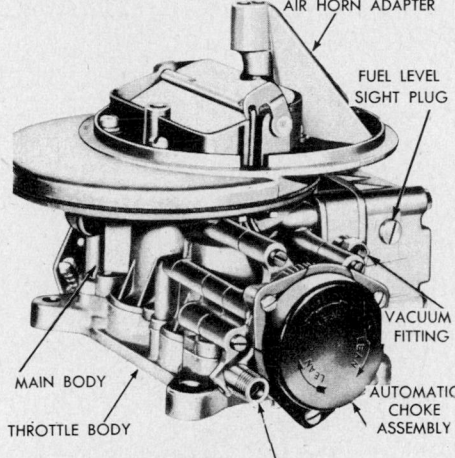

AIR HORN ADAPTER

FUEL LEVEL SIGHT PLUG

VACUUM FITTING

AUTOMATIC CHOKE ASSEMBLY

MAIN BODY

THROTTLE BODY

HEAT TUBE TO AUTOMATIC CHOKE

Holley two-barrel carburetor

ADJUST HERE

SIGHT PLUG FOR FUEL LEVEL

Holley two- and four-barrel fuel level adjustment (© Ford Motor Co.)

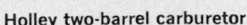

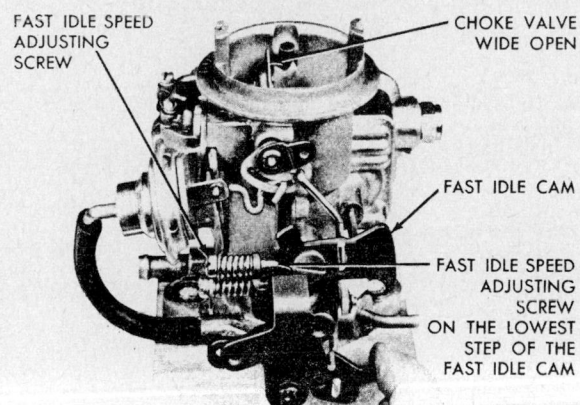

FAST IDLE SPEED ADJUSTING SCREW

CHOKE VALVE WIDE OPEN

FAST IDLE CAM

FAST IDLE SPEED ADJUSTING SCREW ON THE LOWEST STEP OF THE FAST IDLE CAM

Holley single-barrel fast idle speed adjustment (on the car)

SCALE

SURFACE OF CARBURETOR

SURFACE OF FUEL

Holley single-barrel wet fuel level measurement

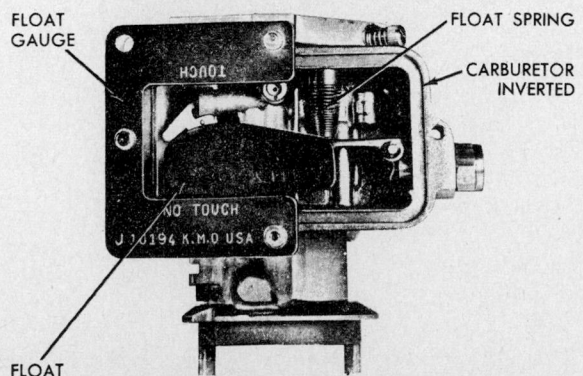

FLOAT GAUGE

FLOAT SPRING

CARBURETOR INVERTED

FLOAT

Holley single-barrel float setting

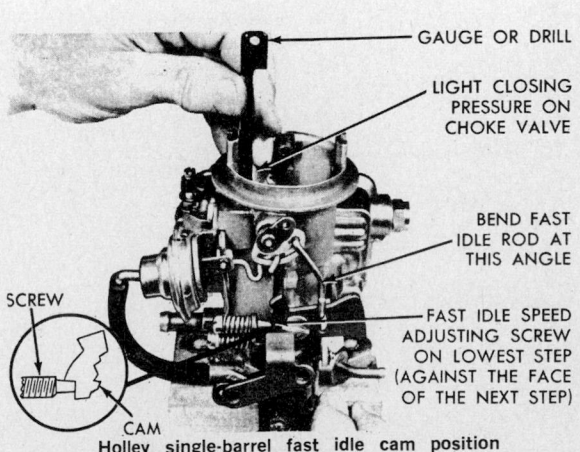

GAUGE OR DRILL

LIGHT CLOSING PRESSURE ON CHOKE VALVE

BEND FAST IDLE ROD AT THIS ANGLE

FAST IDLE SPEED ADJUSTING SCREW ON LOWEST STEP (AGAINST THE FACE OF THE NEXT STEP)

SCREW

CAM

Holley single-barrel fast idle cam position adjustment

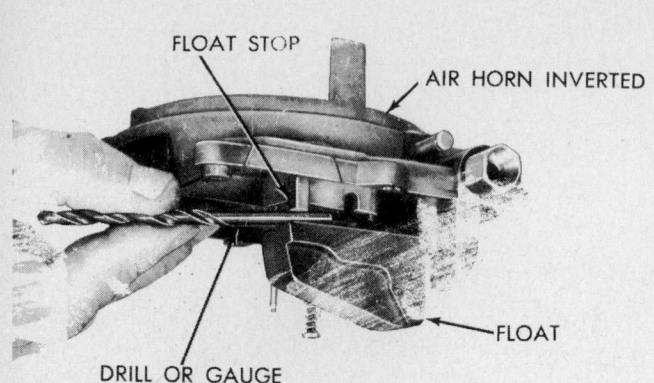

FLOAT STOP

AIR HORN INVERTED

DRILL OR GAUGE

FLOAT

Float Setting, Holley 2200
(© Dodge Division, Chrysler Corp.)

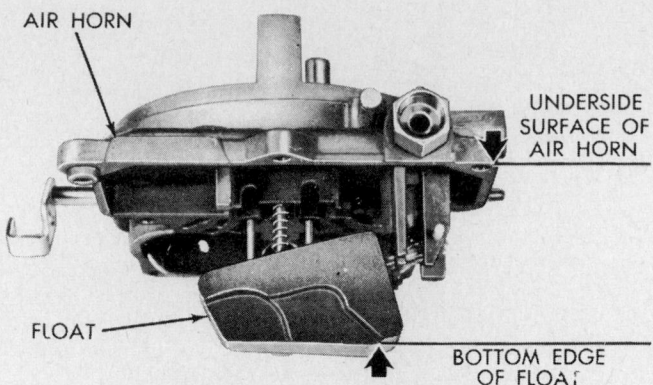

AIR HORN

UNDERSIDE SURFACE OF AIR HORN

FLOAT

BOTTOM EDGE OF FLOAT

FLOAT SHOULD BE PARALLED

Float Drop, Holley 2200
(© Dodge Division, Chrysler Corp.)

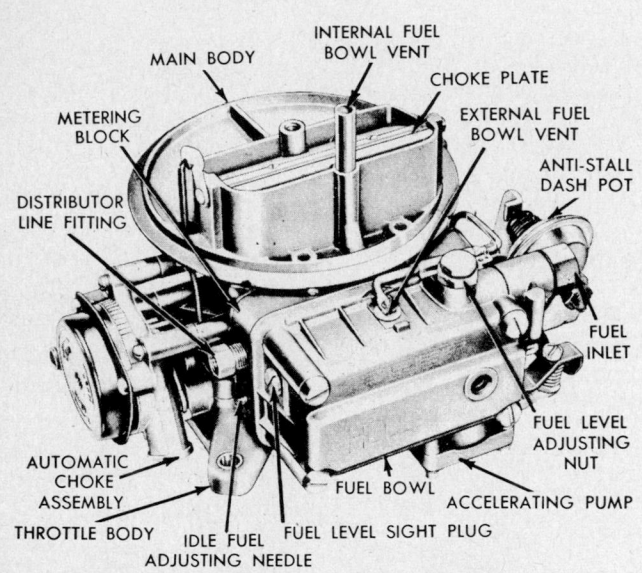

MAIN BODY

INTERNAL FUEL BOWL VENT

CHOKE PLATE

METERING BLOCK

EXTERNAL FUEL BOWL VENT

ANTI-STALL DASH POT

DISTRIBUTOR LINE FITTING

FUEL INLET

AUTOMATIC CHOKE ASSEMBLY

FUEL LEVEL ADJUSTING NUT

THROTTLE BODY

IDLE FUEL ADJUSTING NEEDLE

FUEL BOWL

FUEL LEVEL SIGHT PLUG

ACCELERATING PUMP

Holley dual carburetor (© Ford Motor Co.)

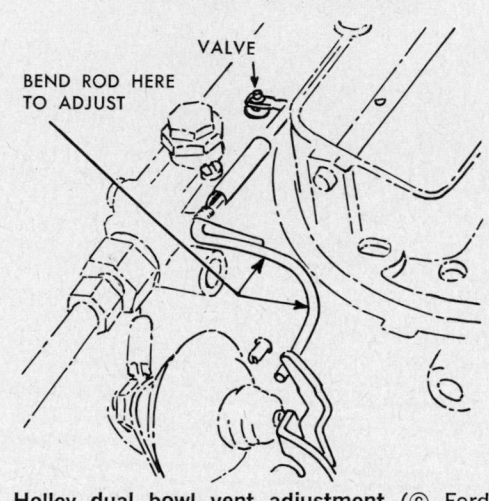

VALVE

BEND ROD HERE TO ADJUST

Holley dual bowl vent adjustment (© Ford Motor Co.)

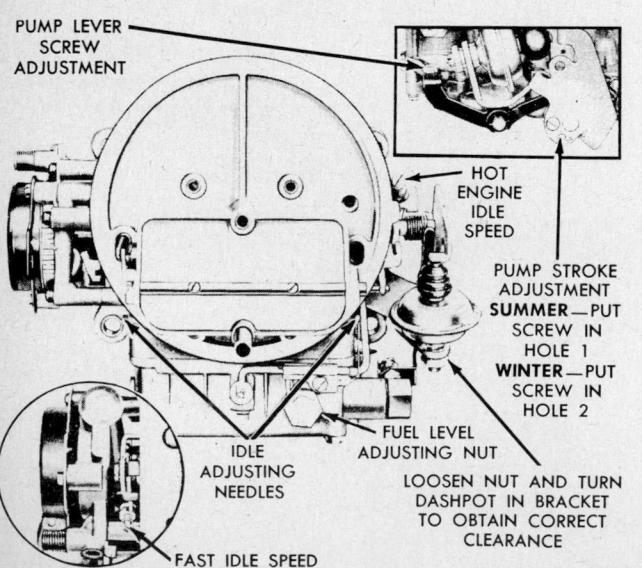

PUMP LEVER SCREW ADJUSTMENT

HOT ENGINE IDLE SPEED

PUMP STROKE ADJUSTMENT
SUMMER—PUT SCREW IN HOLE 1
WINTER—PUT SCREW IN HOLE 2

IDLE ADJUSTING NEEDLES

FUEL LEVEL ADJUSTING NUT

LOOSEN NUT AND TURN DASHPOT IN BRACKET TO OBTAIN CORRECT CLEARANCE

FAST IDLE SPEED

Holley dual carburetor idle adjustment (© Ford Motor Co.)

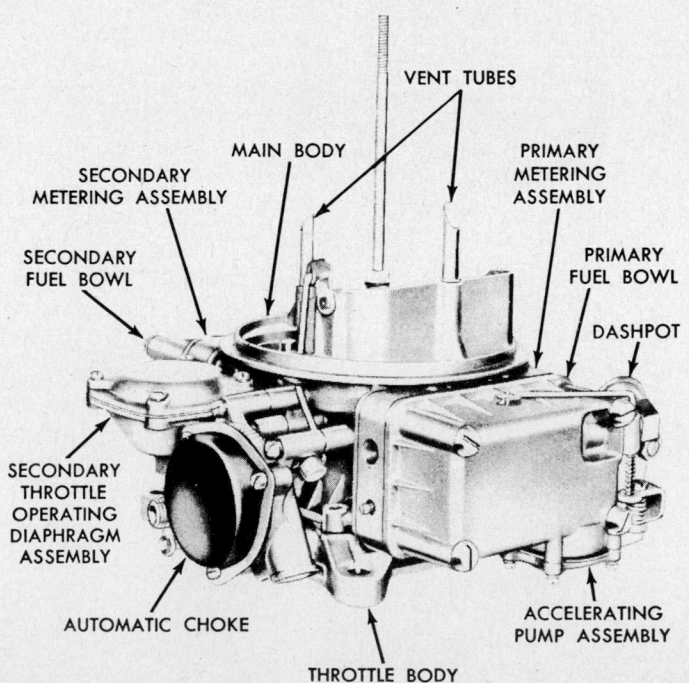

VENT TUBES

SECONDARY METERING ASSEMBLY

MAIN BODY

PRIMARY METERING ASSEMBLY

SECONDARY FUEL BOWL

PRIMARY FUEL BOWL

DASHPOT

SECONDARY THROTTLE OPERATING DIAPHRAGM ASSEMBLY

AUTOMATIC CHOKE

ACCELERATING PUMP ASSEMBLY

THROTTLE BODY

Holley four-barrel carburetor (© Ford Motor Co.)

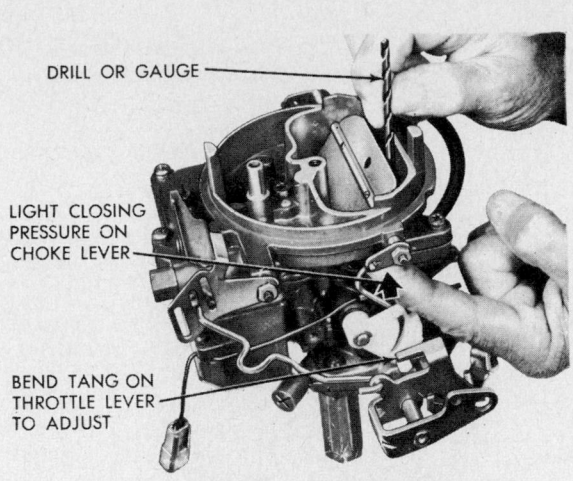

Unloader Adjustment, Holley 2200
(© Dodge Division, Chrysler Corp.)

DRILL OR GAUGE

LIGHT CLOSING PRESSURE ON CHOKE LEVER

BEND TANG ON THROTTLE LEVER TO ADJUST

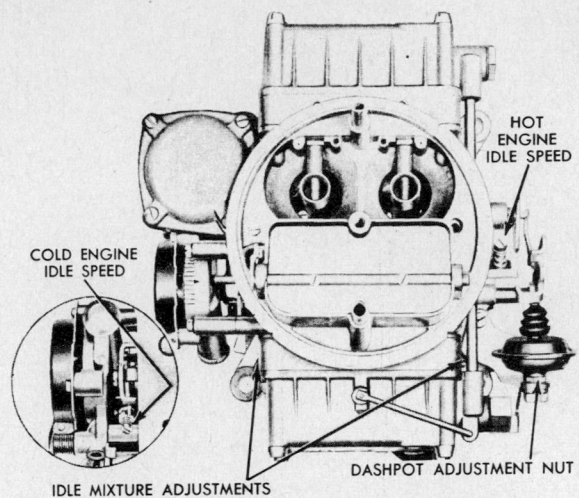

Holley four-barrel idle adjustment (© Ford Motor Co.)

HOT ENGINE IDLE SPEED

COLD ENGINE IDLE SPEED

IDLE MIXTURE ADJUSTMENTS

DASHPOT ADJUSTMENT NUT

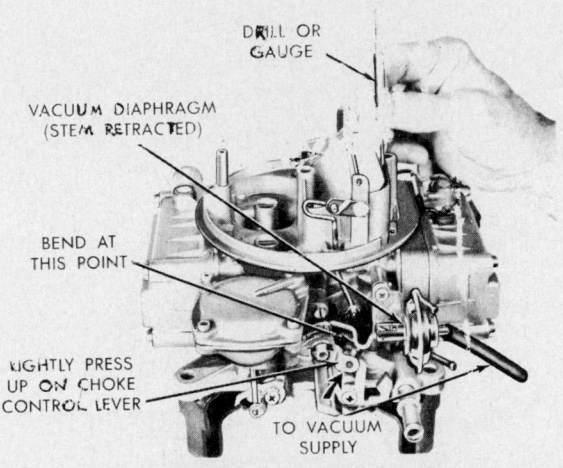

Vacuum Kick Setting, 4 Bbl. (Typical)
(© Dodge Division, Chrysler Corp.)

DRILL OR GAUGE

VACUUM DIAPHRAGM (STEM RETRACTED)

BEND AT THIS POINT

LIGHTLY PRESS UP ON CHOKE CONTROL LEVER

TO VACUUM SUPPLY

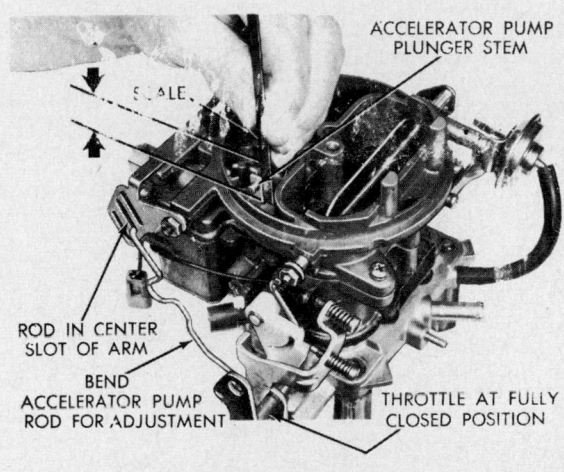

Accelerator Pump Setting, Holley 2200
(© Dodge Division, Chrysler Corp.)

ACCELERATOR PUMP PLUNGER STEM

SCALE

ROD IN CENTER SLOT OF ARM

BEND ACCELERATOR PUMP ROD FOR ADJUSTMENT

THROTTLE AT FULLY CLOSED POSITION

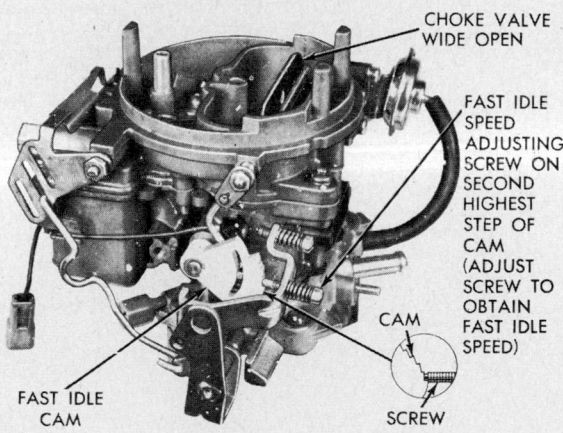

Fast Idle Setting on Car, Holley 2200
(© Dodge Division, Chrysler Corp.)

CHOKE VALVE WIDE OPEN

FAST IDLE SPEED ADJUSTING SCREW ON SECOND HIGHEST STEP OF CAM (ADJUST SCREW TO OBTAIN FAST IDLE SPEED)

FAST IDLE CAM

CAM

SCREW

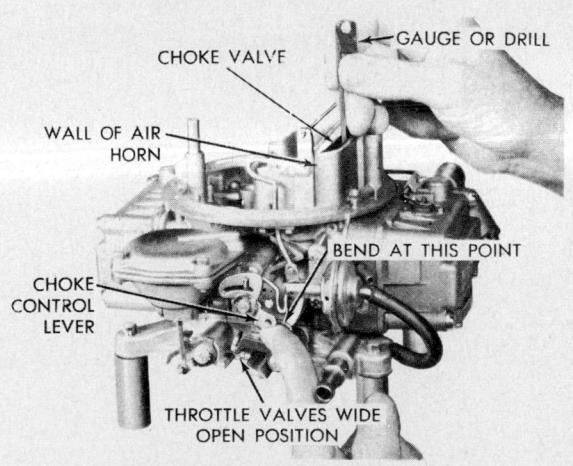

Unloader Adjustment, 4 Bbl.
(© Dodge Division, Chrysler Corp.)

GAUGE OR DRILL

CHOKE VALVE

WALL OF AIR HORN

BEND AT THIS POINT

CHOKE CONTROL LEVER

THROTTLE VALVES WIDE OPEN POSITION

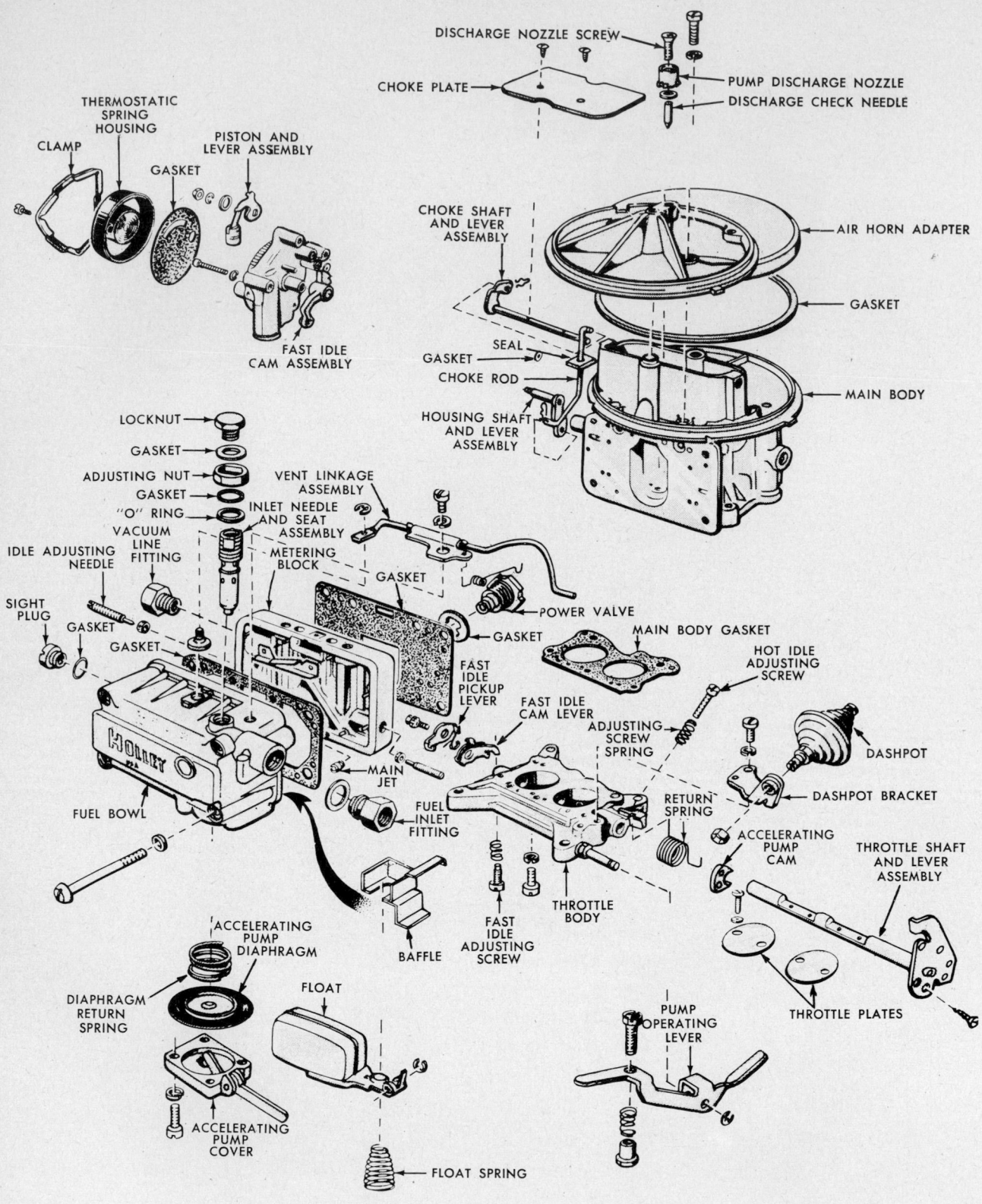

DISCHARGE NOZZLE SCREW

CHOKE PLATE

PUMP DISCHARGE NOZZLE

DISCHARGE CHECK NEEDLE

THERMOSTATIC SPRING HOUSING

CLAMP

GASKET

PISTON AND LEVER ASSEMBLY

FAST IDLE CAM ASSEMBLY

CHOKE SHAFT AND LEVER ASSEMBLY

AIR HORN ADAPTER

GASKET

SEAL

GASKET

CHOKE ROD

MAIN BODY

HOUSING SHAFT AND LEVER ASSEMBLY

LOCKNUT

GASKET

ADJUSTING NUT

GASKET

VENT LINKAGE ASSEMBLY

"O" RING

INLET NEEDLE AND SEAT ASSEMBLY

VACUUM LINE FITTING

METERING BLOCK

GASKET

IDLE ADJUSTING NEEDLE

POWER VALVE

MAIN BODY GASKET

SIGHT PLUG

GASKET

GASKET

HOT IDLE ADJUSTING SCREW

GASKET

FAST IDLE PICKUP LEVER

FAST IDLE CAM LEVER

ADJUSTING SCREW SPRING

DASHPOT

MAIN JET

RETURN SPRING

DASHPOT BRACKET

FUEL BOWL

ACCELERATING PUMP CAM

THROTTLE SHAFT AND LEVER ASSEMBLY

FUEL INLET FITTING

ACCELERATING PUMP DIAPHRAGM

BAFFLE

FAST IDLE ADJUSTING SCREW

THROTTLE BODY

THROTTLE PLATES

DIAPHRAGM RETURN SPRING

FLOAT

PUMP OPERATING LEVER

ACCELERATING PUMP COVER

FLOAT SPRING

Holley two-barrel (typical) (© Ford Motor Co.)

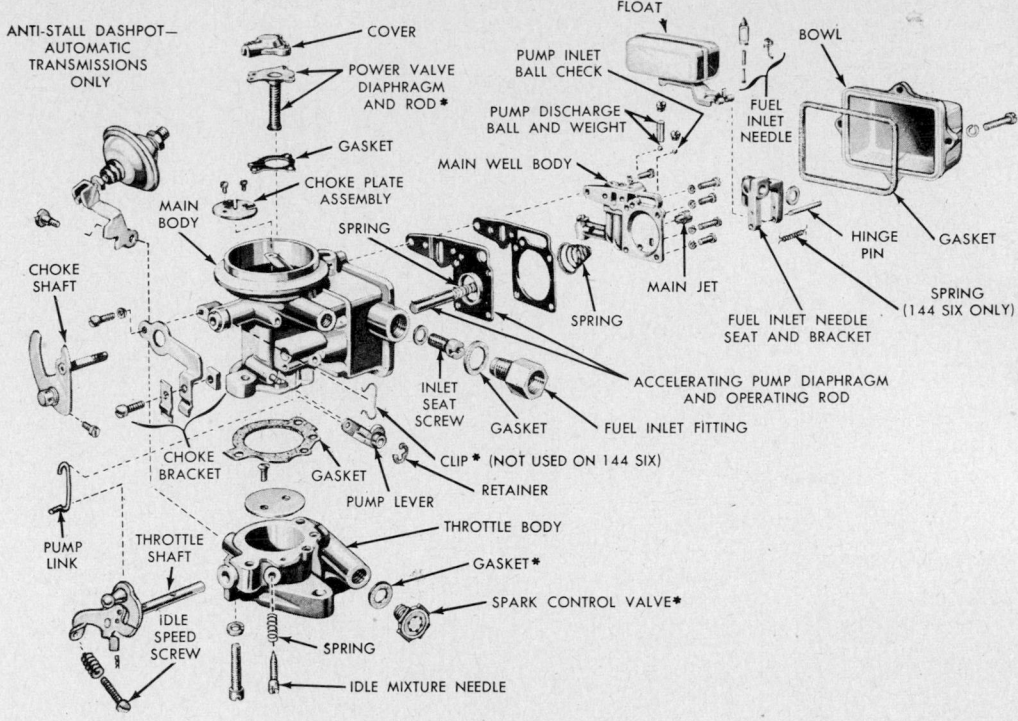

Holley single-barrel (typical) (© Ford Motor Co.)

ANTI-STALL DASHPOT—
AUTOMATIC
TRANSMISSIONS
ONLY

COVER
POWER VALVE
DIAPHRAGM
AND ROD *
GASKET
CHOKE PLATE
ASSEMBLY
MAIN BODY
CHOKE SHAFT
SPRING
CHOKE BRACKET
GASKET
PUMP LEVER
RETAINER
CLIP * (NOT USED ON 144 SIX)
PUMP LINK
THROTTLE SHAFT
IDLE SPEED SCREW
SPRING
IDLE MIXTURE NEEDLE
INLET SEAT SCREW
GASKET
THROTTLE BODY
GASKET *
SPARK CONTROL VALVE *

FLOAT
PUMP INLET BALL CHECK
PUMP DISCHARGE BALL AND WEIGHT
MAIN WELL BODY
FUEL INLET NEEDLE
BOWL
MAIN JET
HINGE PIN
GASKET
SPRING (144 SIX ONLY)
FUEL INLET NEEDLE SEAT AND BRACKET
ACCELERATING PUMP DIAPHRAGM AND OPERATING ROD
FUEL INLET FITTING

DIAPHRAGM SPRING
DIAPHRAGM ASSEMBLY
SECONDARY VACUUM CHECK BALL
SECONDARY HOUSING
THERMOSTAT COVER CLAMP
CHOKE SHAFT
THERMOSTAT COVER AND SPRING
CHOKE THERMOSTAT HOUSING GASKET
THERMOSTAT LEVER LINK AND PISTON ASSEMBLY
CHOKE HOUSING
FAST IDLE CAM ASSEMBLY
CHOKE HOUSING SHAFT AND LEVER
CHOKE PLATE
CHOKE ROD SEAL
CHOKE ROD
PRIMARY METERING BLOCK GASKET
POWER VALVE
LOCK SCREW
GASKET
FUEL LEVEL ADJUSTING NUT
GASKET
FUEL INLET NEEDLE AND SEAT
AIR VENT
O-RING
FUEL LEVEL SIGHT PLUG AND GASKET
PRIMARY FUEL BOWL
PRIMARY FUEL BOWL GASKET
FLOAT
MAIN JETS
PRIMARY METERING BLOCK
FLOAT SPRING
BAFFLE PLATE
FILTER SCREEN
FUEL INLET FITTING
DIAPHRAGM SPRING
DIAPHRAGM ASSEMBLY
ACCELERATING PUMP COVER
BAFFLE PLATE
POWER VALVE GASKET
IDLE ADJUSTING NEEDLE
DIAPHRAGM LEVER ASSEMBLY
FAST IDLE CAM LEVER
THROTTLE BODY
ACCELERATING PUMP OPERATING LEVER
PRIMARY THROTTLE SHAFT ASSEMBLY
PRIMARY THROTTLE PLATES
ACCELERATING PUMP CAM
ACCELERATING PUMP DISCHARGE NOZZLE
ACCELERATING PUMP DISCHARGE NEEDLE
SECONDARY PLATE
SECONDARY FUEL BOWL
SECONDARY METERING BODY
METERING BODY GASKET
FUEL LINE
BALANCE TUBE
O-RING SEALS
GASKET
GASKET
MAIN BODY
THROTTLE BODY-TO-MAIN BODY GASKET
DASHPOT ASSEMBLY
DASHPOT BRACKET
SECONDARY THROTTLE PLATES
SHAFT BUSHINGS
SECONDARY THROTTLE SHAFT
THROTTLE CONNECTING ROD

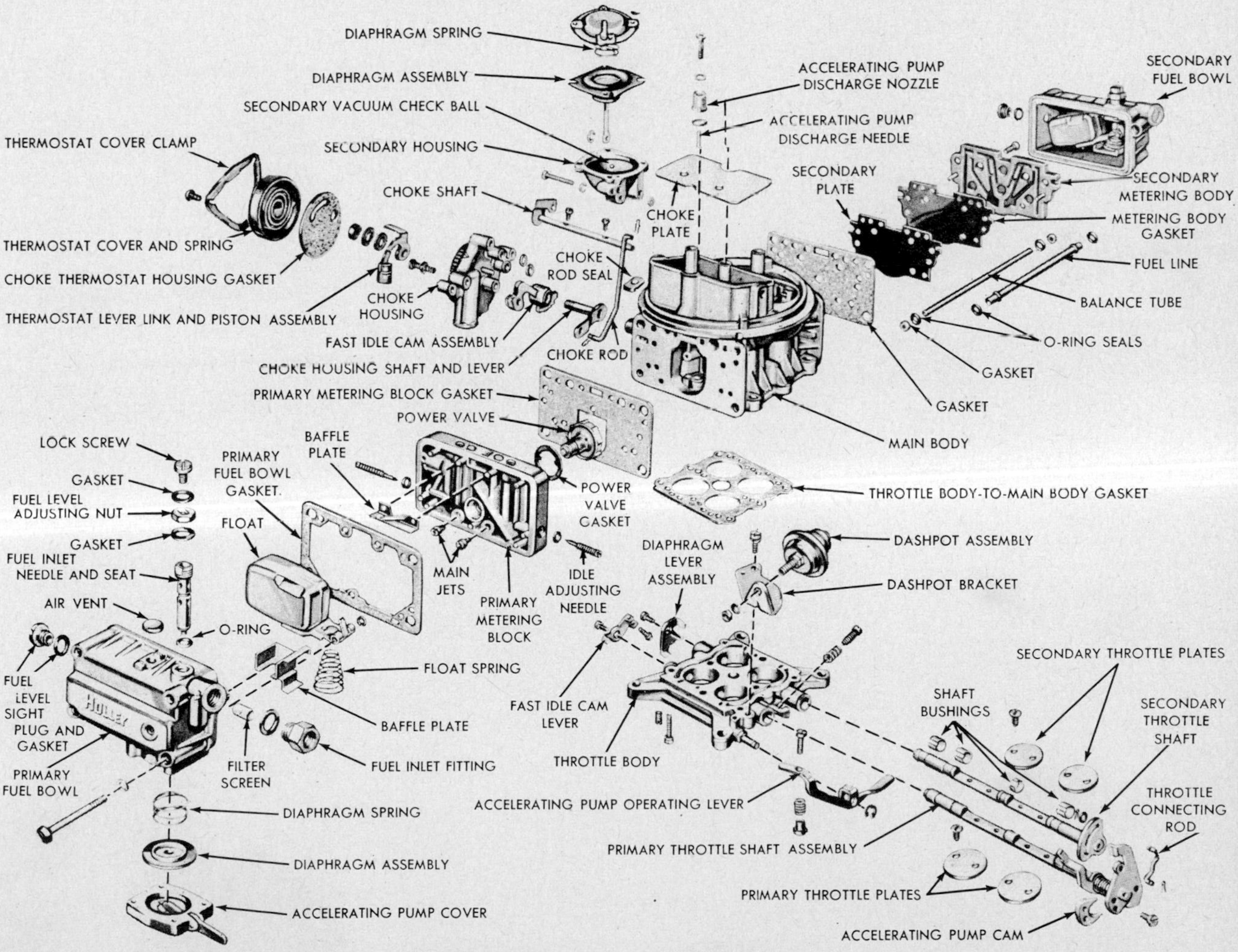

Holley four-barrel (typical) (© Ford Motor Co.)

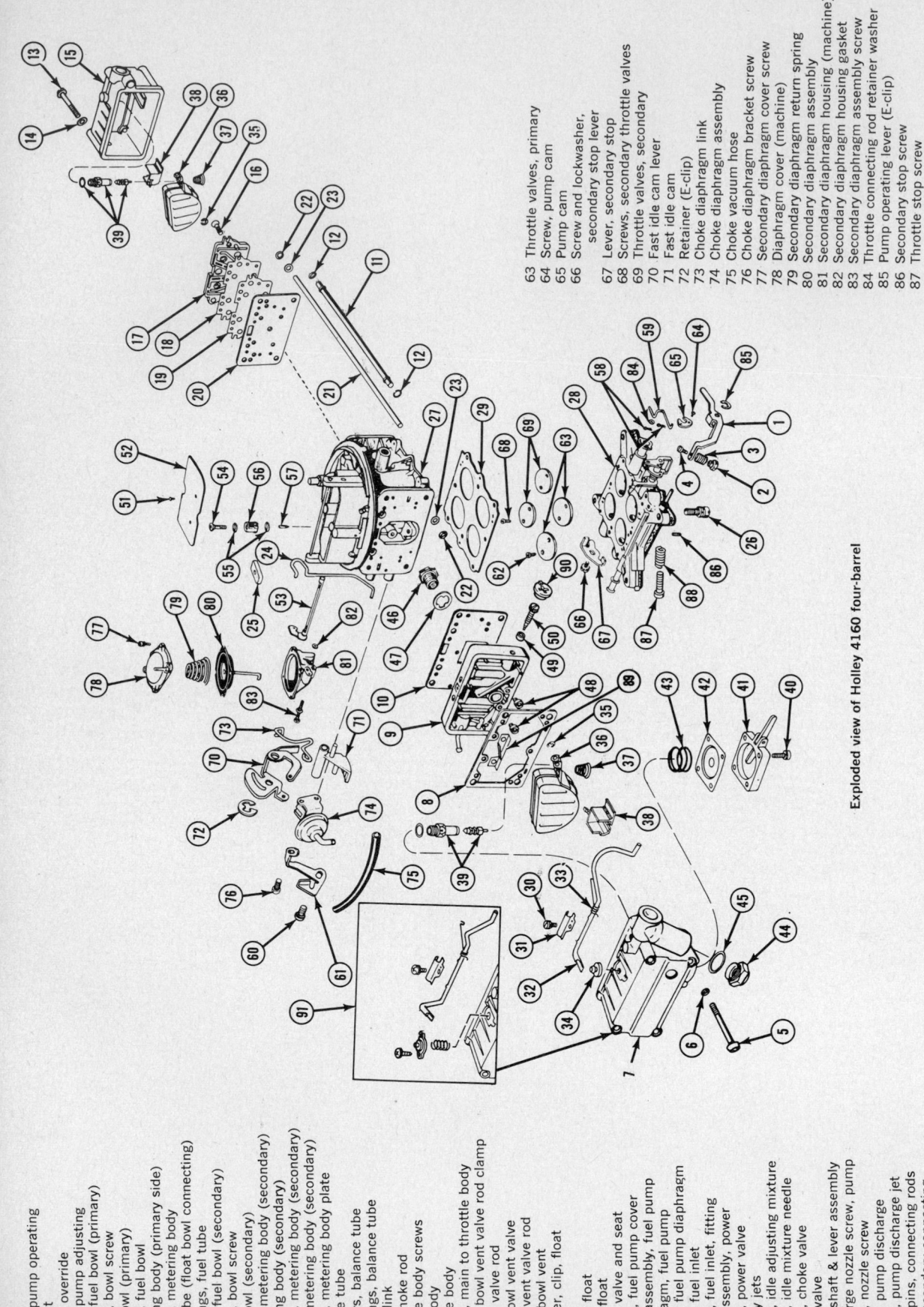

Exploded view of Holley 4160 four-barrel

1 Lever, pump operating
2 Locknut
3 Spring, override
4 Screw, pump adjusting
5 Screw, fuel bowl (primary)
6 Gasket, bowl screw
7 Fuel bowl (primary)
8 Gasket, fuel bowl
9 Metering body (primary side)
10 Gasket, metering body
11 Fuel tube (float bowl connecting)
12 "O" rings, fuel tube
13 Screw, fuel bowl (secondary)
14 Gasket, bowl screw
15 Fuel bowl (secondary)
16 Screw, metering body (secondary)
17 Metering body (secondary)
18 Gasket, metering body (secondary)
19 Plate, metering body (secondary)
20 Gasket, metering body plate
21 Balance tube
22 Washers, balance tube
23 "O" rings, balance tube
24 Choke link
25 Seal, choke rod
26 Throttle body screws
27 Main body
28 Throttle body
29 Gasket, main to throttle body
30 Screw, bowl vent valve rod clamp
31 Clamp, valve rod
32 Rod, bowl vent valve
33 Spring vent valve rod
34 Valve, bowl vent
35 Retainer, clip, float
36 Float
37 Spring, float
38 Baffle, float
39 Needle valve and seat
40 Screws, fuel pump cover
41 Cover assembly, fuel pump
42 Diaphragm, fuel pump
43 Spring, fuel pump diaphragm
44 Fitting, fuel inlet
45 Gasket, fuel inlet, fitting
46 Valve assembly, power
47 Gasket, power valve
48 Primary jets
49 Needle, idle adjusting mixture
50 Gasket, idle mixture needle
51 Screws, choke valve
52 Choke valve
53 Choke shaft & lever assembly
54 Discharge nozzle screw, pump
55 Gasket, nozzle screw
56 Nozzle, pump discharge
57 Needle, pump discharge jet
58 Cotter pins, connecting rods
59 Rod, secondary connecting
60 Screw and lockwasher, fast idle cam lever
61 Lever, fast idle cam
62 Screws, primary throttle valve

63 Throttle valves, primary
64 Screw, pump cam
65 Pump cam
66 Screw and lockwasher, secondary stop lever
67 Lever, secondary stop
68 Screws, secondary throttle valves
69 Throttle valves, secondary
70 Fast idle cam lever
71 Fast idle cam
72 Retainer (E-clip)
73 Choke diaphragm link
74 Choke diaphragm assembly
75 Choke vacuum hose
76 Choke diaphragm bracket screw
77 Secondary diaphragm cover screw
78 Diaphragm cover (machine)
79 Secondary diaphragm return spring
80 Secondary diaphragm assembly
81 Secondary diaphragm housing (machine)
82 Secondary diaphragm housing gasket
83 Secondary diaphragm assembly screw
84 Throttle connecting rod retainer washer
85 Pump operating lever (E-clip)
86 Secondary stop screw
87 Throttle stop screw
88 Throttle stop screw spring
89 Baffle
90 Limiter cap
91 Bowl vent valve assy. (E.C.S.)

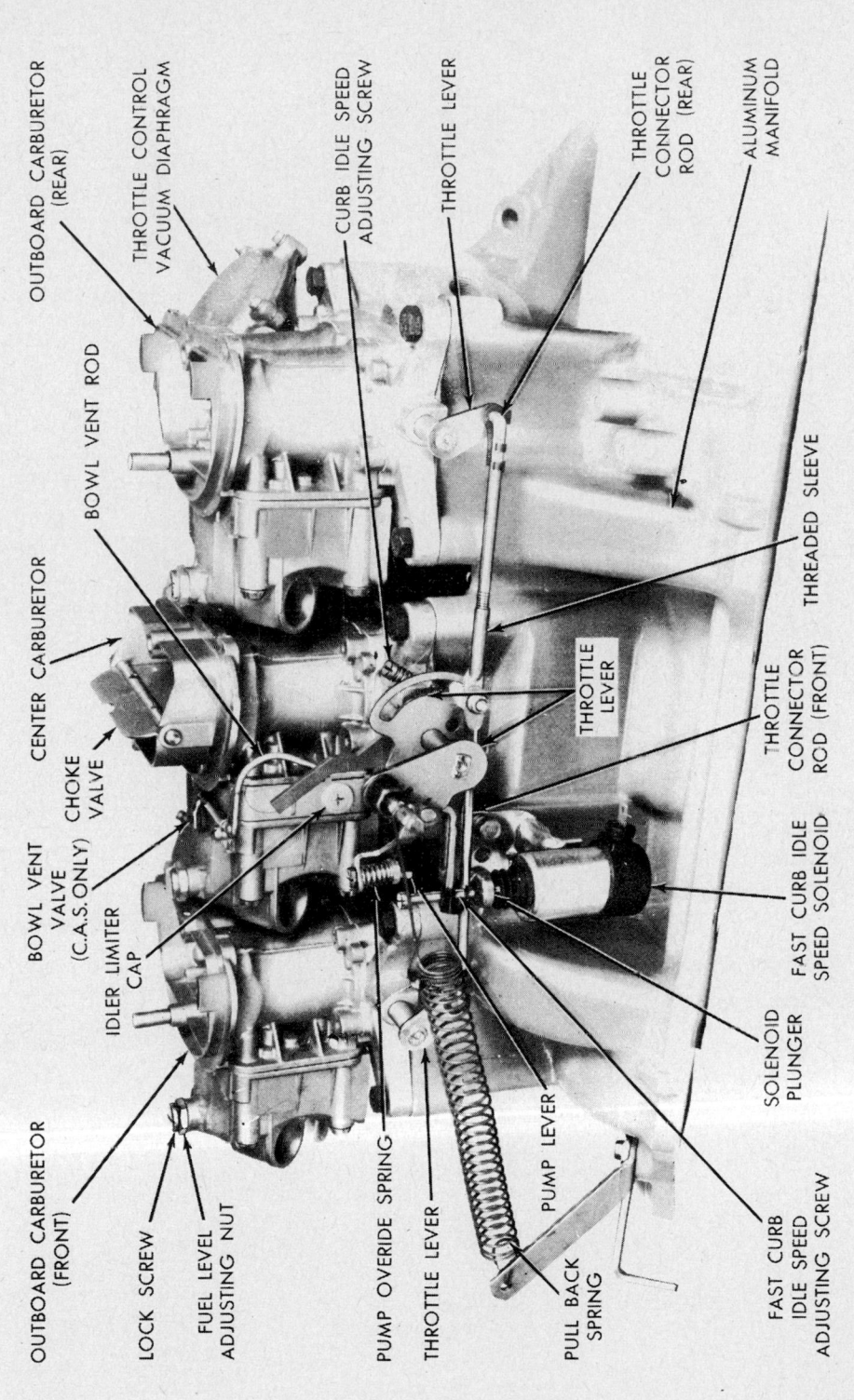

Triple installation of Holley 2300 two-barrel carburetors (Dodge 440 Six-Pack)

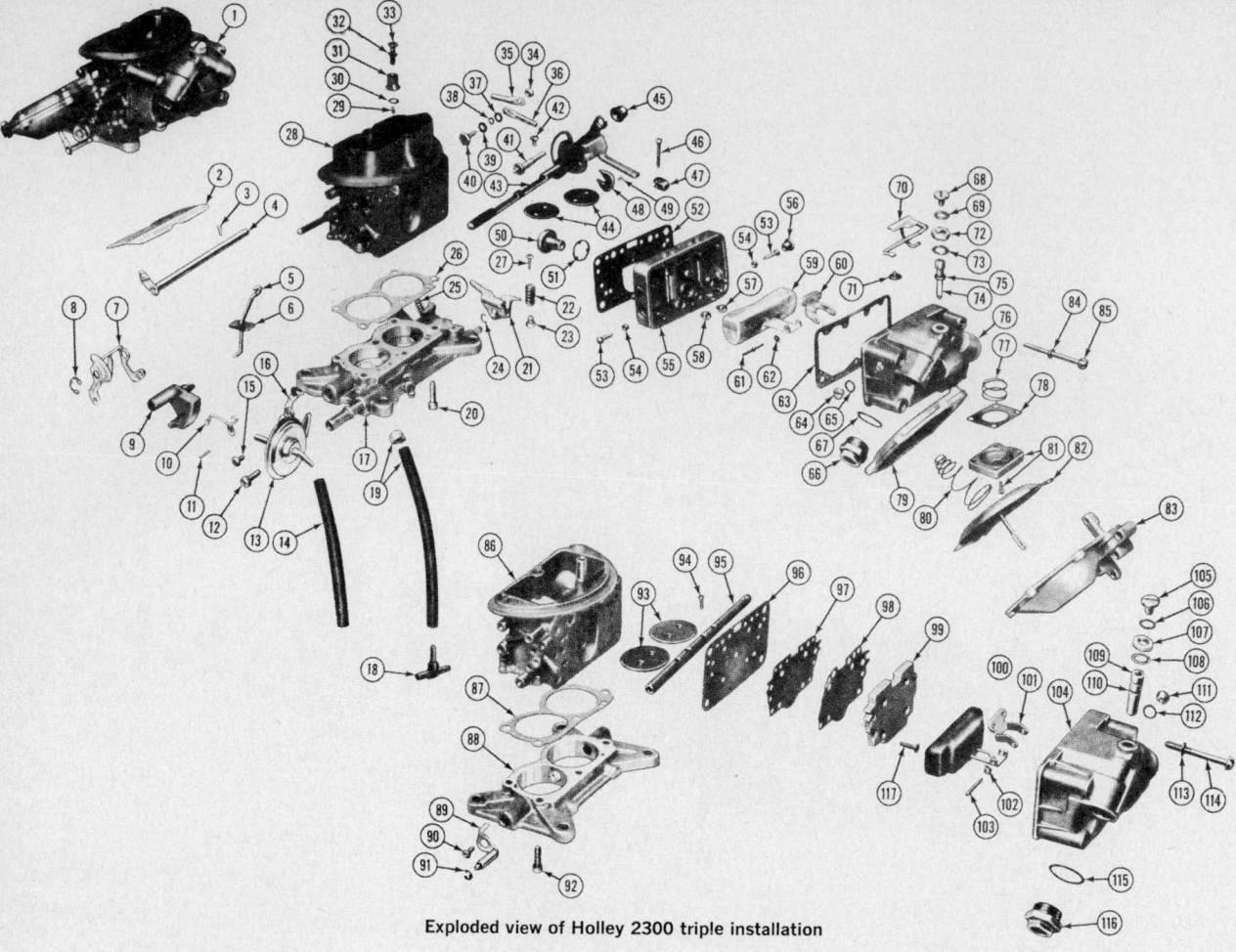

Exploded view of Holley 2300 triple installation

1 Carburetor assembly
   (front or rear)
2 Choke valve
3 Valve screw
4 Choke shaft
5 Operating rod
6 Seal
7 Choke control lever
8 "E" clip
9 Fast idle cam
10 Link
11 Link pin
12 Screw, diaphragm bracket
13 Choke diaphragm
14 Vacuum tube
15 Screw
16 Fast idle cam lever
17 Throttle body (center carb.)
18 Plastic "T"
19 Tube and clamp
20 Screw, throttle body
21 Lever
22 Spring
23 Nut, adjusting
24 Spacer
25 Curb idle screw and spring
26 Gasket
27 Screw Accelerator Pump Adj.
28 Main body (center carb.)
29 Discharge check needle
30 Gasket
31 Cluster, discharge
32 Gasket
33 Cluster screw
34 Nut
35 Sleeve (rear)
36 Sleeve (front)
37 Washer, throttle rod sleeve
38 Spacer, throttle rod sleeve
39 Washer, throttle rod sleeve

40 Screw (throttle rod)
41 Pivot (throttle rod)
42 Throttle valve screw
43 Throttle shaft
44 Throttle valves
45 Insulator
46 Adjusting screw (solenoid)
47 Nut (adjusting screw)
48 Cam, pump
49 Pump cam screw
50 Power valve
51 Power valve gasket
52 Gasket
53 Idle mixture screw
54 Idle mixture screw gasket
55 Metering body
56 Limiter cap (plastic)
57 Metering jet
58 Metering jet
59 Float
60 Float hinge bracket
61 Fulcrum pin
62 Float spring
63 Gasket
64 Sight plug
65 Sight plug gasket
66 Fuel inlet fitting
67 Fuel inlet fitting gasket
68 Lock screw
69 Gasket
70 Bowl vent rod
71 Bowl vent valve
72 Adjusting nut
73 Gasket, nut
74 Fuel inlet needle seat
75 Seat "O" ring
76 Fuel bowl
77 Spring, pump
78 Diaphragm, pump
79 Diaphragm cover

80 Diaphragm spring
81 Pump cover and screw
82 Diaphragm
83 Diaphragm housing
84 Seal (bowl screw)
85 Bowl screw
86 Main body (front or rear)
87 Gasket
88 Throttle body
89 Lever
90 Screw
91 "E" clip
92 Screw, throttle body
93 Throttle valves
94 Valve screw
95 Throttle shaft
96 Gasket
97 Plate
98 Gasket
99 Metering body
100 Float
101 Float hinge bracket
102 Float spring
103 Fulcrum pin
104 Fuel bowl
105 Lock screw
106 Gasket
107 Adjusting nut
108 Gasket
109 Inlet needle seat
110 Seat "O" ring
111 Sight plug
112 Gasket
113 Seal (bowl screw)
114 Bowl screw
115 Gasket
116 Fuel inlet fitting
117 Clutch head screw
   (metering body)

Rochester Carburetors

YEAR	MODEL OR TYPE	FLOAT LEVEL (IN.)		FLOAT DROP (IN.)		Pump Travel Setting (IN.)	CHOKE SETTING		Secondary Lockout Adj.	Throttle Bore Diam.		Venturi Diam.	
		Prim.	Sec.	Prim.	Sec.		Unloader (IN.)	Housing		Prim.	Sec.	Prim.	Sec.
Buick													
1965	2GC—7025046/7	19/32	...	1 29/32	...	1 11/32	.136	INDEX	...	1 7/16	...	1 1/8	...
1965	4GC—7025040	1 13/32	1 13/32	1 1/16	1 1/16	1 1/64	.120	INDEX	.015	1 9/16	1 11/16	1 1/8	1 15/32
1966	2GC—7026046	1/2	...	1 27/32	...	1 5/32	.140	INDEX	...	1 7/16	...	1 1/8	
1966	2GC—7026047	1/2	...	1 27/32	...	1 11/32	.140	INDEX	...	1 7/16	...	1 1/8	
1966	2GC—7036048	1/2	...	1 27/32	...	1 11/32	.140	INDEX	...	1 7/16	...	1 1/8	
1966	4GC—7026040	1 7/16	1 7/16	1 1/16	1 1/16	1	.120	INDEX	.015	1 9/16	1 11/16	1 1/8	1 15/32
1966	4MC—7026240/1	1/4	...	...	...	9/32	.325	INDEX	...	1 3/8	2 1/4	1 3/32	
1966	4MC—7036240/1	1/4	...	...	...	9/32	.325	INDEX	...	1 3/8	2 1/4	1 3/32	
1967	2GC—7027044,46	15/32	...	1 9/16	...	31/32	.140	INDEX	...	1 7/16	...	1 1/8	
1967	2GC—7027045,49,Calif.	15/37	...	1 9/16	...	31/32	.140	INDEX	...	1 7/16	...	1 1/8	
1967	4MV—7027146,48	7/32	...	...	...	9/32	.325	...	.015	1 3/8	2 1/4	1 3/32	
1967	4MV—7027147,49,Calif.	7/32	...	...	...	9/32	.325	...	.015	1 3/8	2 1/4	1 3/32	
1967	4MV—7027240	9/32	...	...	...	9/32	.325	...	.045	1 3/8	2 1/4	1 3/32	
1967	4MV—7027241,Calif.	9/32	...	...	...	13/32	.325	...	.045	1 3/8	2 1/4	1 3/32	
1968	2GV—7028140,41	15/32	...	1 7/32	...	1 11/32	.140	Ⓐ	...	1 7/16	...	1 1/8	
1968	4MV—7028244,45	5/16	...	...	...	9/32	.325	Ⓐ	.015	1 3/8	2 1/4	1 3/32	
1968	4MV—7028240,242	13/32	...	...	...	9/32	.325	Ⓐ	.045	1 3/8	2 1/4	1 3/32	
1968	4MV—7028243	15/32	...	...	...	9/32	.325	Ⓐ	.015	1 3/8	2 1/4	1 3/32	
1969	2GV—7029140,41	15/32	...	1 7/32	...	1 11/32	.140	...	...	1 7/16	...	1 1/8	
1969	4MV—7029244,45	5/16	...	...	...	13/32	.325	...	.015	1 3/8	2 1/4	1 3/32	
1969	4MV—7029240,42	3/8	...	...	...	13/37	.325	...	.045	1 3/8	2 1/4	1 3/32	
1969	4MV—7029243	3/8	...	...	...	13/32	.325	...	.015	1 3/8	2 1/4	1 3/32	
1970	2GV-7040143-350,Std.	15/32	...	1 7/8	...	1 15/32	.200	...	...	1 11/16	...	1 1/4	
1970	2GV-7040142-350,Auto	15/32	...	1 7/8	...	1 13/32	.180	...	...	1 11/16	...	1 1/4	
1970	2GV-7040446-350 Auto,CAL	15/32	...	1 7/8	...	1 13/32	.180	...	...	1 11/16	...	1 1/4	
1970	4MV-7040245-350 Std.	5/16	...	...	...	13/32	.335	...	.015	1 3/8	2 1/4	1 3/32	
1970	4MV-7040244-350 Auto	5/16	...	...	...	13/32	.335	...	.045	1 3/8	2 1/4	1 3/32	
1970	4MV-7040243-455 Std.	3/8	...	...	...	9/32	.335	...	.015	1 3/8	2 1/4	1 3/32	
1970	4MV-7040240-455 Auto	3/8	...	...	...	9/32	.335	...	.015	1 3/8	2 1/4	1 3/32	
1970	4MV-7040247-455 Riviera	3/8	...	...	...	9/32	.325	...	.015	1 3/8	2 1/4	1 3/32	
1971	2GV-7040143-350 Std.	15/32	...	1 7/8	...	1 15/32	.180	...	...	1 11/16	...	1 1/4	
1971	2GV-7041442-350 Auto.	15/32	...	1 7/8	...	1 15/32	.180	...	...	1 11/16	...	1 1/4	
1971	4MV-7041245-350 Std.	15/32	...	...	...	9/32	.335	...	.015	1 3/0	2 1/4	1 3/32	
1971	4MV-7041544-350 Auto.	15/32	...	...	...	9/32	.335	...	.015	1 3/8	2 1/4	1 3/32	
1971	4MV-7041243-455 Std.	13/32	...	...	...	1/4	.335	...	.015	1 3/8	2 1/4	1 7/32	
1971	4MV-7041540-455 Auto.	3/8	...	...	...	1/4	.335	...	.015	1 3/3	2 1/4	1 7/32	

Ⓐ—Remove upper end of choke rod, close choke valve, place rod in notch. Bend rod to adjust. Place rod in std. hole.   CAL—California

Buick Special

YEAR	MODEL OR TYPE	Prim.	Sec.	Prim.	Sec.	Pump	Unloader	Housing	Sec. Lockout	Prim.	Sec.	Prim.	Sec.
1965	BC—7025148/9	1 9/32	...	1 3/4	...	...	.230	INDEX	...	1 9/16	...	1 11/32	...
1965	2GC—7025046/7	19/32	...	1 29/32	...	1 11/32	.136	INDEX	...	1 7/16	...	1 1/8	...
1966	2GC—7026144	1/2	...	1 27/32	...	1 5/32	.140	INDEX	...	1 7/16	...	1 1/8	
1966	2GC—7026145	1/2	...	1 27/32	...	1 11/32	.140	INDEX	...	1 7/16	...	1 1/8	
1966	2GC—7036144, Calif.	1/2	...	1 27/32	...	1 1/16	.140	INDEX	...	1 7/16	...	1 1/8	
1966	2GC—7026046	1/2	...	1 27/32	...	1 5/32	.140	INDEX	...	1 7/16	...	1 1/8	

YEAR	MODEL OR TYPE	FLOAT LEVEL (IN.)		FLOAT DROP (IN.)		Pump Travel Setting (IN.)	CHOKE SETTING		Secondary Lockout Adj.	Throttle Bore Diam.		Venturi Diam.	
		Prim.	Sec.	Prim.	Sec.		Unloader (IN.)	Housing		Prim.	Sec.	Prim.	Sec.
Buick Special, continued													
1966	2GC—7026047	1/2	...	1 27/32	...	1 11/32	.140	INDEX	...	1 7/16	...	1 1/8	...
1966	2GC—7036046, Calif.	1/2	...	1 27/32	...	1 5/32	.140	INDEX	...	1 7/16	...	1 1/8	...
1966	2GC—7036048, Calif.	1/2	...	1 27/32	...	1 5/32	.140	INDEX	...	1 7/16	...	1 1/8	...
1966	4GC—7026040	1 7/16	1 7/16	1 1/16	1 1/16	1	.120	INDEX	.015	1 9/16	1 11/16	1 1/8	1 15/32
1967	2GC—7027040	1/2	...	1 9/32	...	1 1/16	.140	INDEX	...	1 7/16	...	1 1/8	...
1967	2GC—7027042	1/2	...	1 9/32	...	1 5/32	.140	INDEX	...	1 7/16	...	1 1/8	...
1967	2GC—7027041, Calif.	1/2	...	1 9/32	...	1 1/16	.140	INDEX	...	1 7/16	...	1 1/8	...
1967	2GC—7027044/46	15/32	...	1 9/16	...	1 3/32	.140	INDEX	...	1 7/16	...	1 1/8	...
1967	2GC—7027045/49, Calif.	15/32	...	1 9/16	...	1 3/32	.140	INDEX	...	1 7/16	...	1 1/8	...
1967	4MV—7027148/49	7/32	...	...	...	9/32	.325	INDEX	.015	1 3/8	2 1/4	1 3/32	...
1967	4MV—7027146/47	7/32	...	...	...	13/32	.325	INDEX	.045	1 3/8	2 1/4	1 3/32	...
1968	MV—7028014	5/16	...	...	...	...	.350	...	...	1 11/16	...	...	...
1968	MV—7028047	5/16	...	...	...	...	.325	...	...	1 11/16	...	...	...
1968	2GV—7028140/41	13/32	...	1 9/32	...	1 11/32	.140	...	...	1 7/16	...	1 1/8	...
1968	4MV—7028244/45	5/16	...	...	...	9/32	.325	...	.015	1 3/8	2 1/4	1 3/32	...
1968	4MV—7028242	3/8	...	...	...	9/32	.325	...	.045	1 3/8	2 1/4	1 3/32	...
1968	4MV—7028243	7/16	...	...	...	9/32	.325	...	.015	1 3/8	2 1/4	1 3/32	...
1969	MV—7029014, A.T.	1/4	...	...	...	...	.170	...	...	1 11/16	...	...	...
1969	MV—7029047, M.T.	9/32	...	...	...	...	.190	...	...	1 11/16	...	...	...
1969	2GV—7029140/41	15/32	...	1 7/32	...	1 11/32	.140	...	...	1 7/16	...	1 1/8	...
1969	4MV—7029244/45	5/16	...	...	...	13/32	.325	...	.015	1 3/8	2 1/4	1 3/32	...
1969	4MV—7029242/43	3/8	...	...	...	13/32	.325	...	.015	1 3/8	2 1/4	1 3/32	...
1970	2GV-7040143-350, Std.	15/32	...	1 7/8	...	1 15/32	.200	...	...	1 11/16	...	1 1/4	...
1970	2GV-7040142-350, Auto.	15/32	...	1 7/8	...	1 13/32	.180	...	...	1 11/16	...	1 1/4	...
1970	2GV-7040446-350 Auto., CAL	15/32	...	1 7/8	...	1 13/32	.180	...	...	1 11/16	...	1 1/4	...
1970	4MV-7040245-350 Std.	5/16	...	...	...	13/32	.335	...	.015	1 3/8	2 1/4	1 3/32	...
1970	4MV-7040244-350, Auto.	5/16	...	...	...	13/32	.335	...	.045	1 3/8	2 1/4	1 3/32	...
1970	4MV-7040243-455, Std.	3/8	...	...	...	9/32	.335	...	.015	1 3/8	2 1/4	1 3/32	...
1970	4MV-7040240-455, Auto.	3/8	...	...	...	9/32	.335	...	.045	1 3/8	2 1/4	1 7/32	...
1970	4MV-7040246-455, Stage 1	5/16	...	...	...	9/32	.335	...	.015	1 3/8	2 1/4	1 7/32	...
1970	MV-7040015-250, Std.	1/4	...	...	...	...	.350	...	...	1 11/16	...	...	...
1970	MV-7040014-250, Auto.	1/4	...	...	...	...	.350	...	...	1 11/16	...	...	...
1971	2GV-7040143-350 Std.	15/32	...	1 7/8	...	1 15/32	.180			1 11/16	...	1 1/4	...
1971	2GV-7041142-350 Auto.	15/32	...	1 7/8	...	1 15/32	.180			1 11/16	...	1 1/4	...
1971	4MV-7041245-350 Std.	15/32	...	...	...	9/32	.335		.015	1 3/8	2 1/4	1 3/32	...
1971	4MV-7041544-350 Auto.	15/32	...	...	...	9/32	.335		.015	1 3/8	2 1/4	1 3/32	...
1971	4MV-7041243-455 Std.	13/32	...	...	...	1/4	.335		.015	1 3/8	2 1/4	1 7/32	...
1971	4MV-7041540-455 Auto.	3/8	...	...	...	1/4	.335		.015	1 3/8	2 1/4	1 7/32	...
1971	4MV-7041242-Stage I	3/8	...	...	...	1/4	.335		.015	1 3/8	2 1/4	1 7/32	...
1971	MV-7041017-250 Std.	1/4	...	...	...	...	.350			1 11/16	...	...	...
1971	MV-7041014-250 Auto.	1/4	...	...	...	...	.500			1 11/16	...	...	...

CAL—California

Cadillac

YEAR	MODEL OR TYPE	FLOAT LEVEL (IN.)		FLOAT DROP (IN.)		Pump Travel Setting (IN.)	CHOKE SETTING		Secondary Lockout Adj.	Throttle Bore Diam.		Venturi Diam.	
		Prim.	Sec.	Prim.	Sec.		Unloader (IN.)	Housing		Prim.	Sec.	Prim.	Sec.
1965	4GC	1 7/16	1 3/8	1 1/2	1 1/16	13/16	.125	INDEX	.015	1 7/16	1 11/16	1 1/8	1 15/32
1966	4GC	1 7/16	1 3/8	1 1/2	1 1/16	13/16	.125	INDEX	.015	1 7/16	1 11/16	1 1/8	1 15/32
1967	4MV	7/32	...	...	...	.295	.312	...	.015	1 3/8	2 1/4	1 3/32	...
1967	4MV, Calif.	7/32	...	...	...	.296	.300	...	.015	1 3/8	2 1/4	1 3/32	...
1968	4MV-Std.	1/4	...	...	...	11/32	.312	①	.015	1 3/8	2 1/4	1 3/32	...
1968	4MV-Eldorado	11/32	...	...	...	11/32	.312	①	.015	1 3/8	2 1/4	1 3/32	...
1969	4MV-Std.	1/4	...	...	...	11/32	.300	①	.015	1 3/8	2 1/4	1 3/32	...
1969	4MV-Eldorado	3/8	...	...	...	11/32	.300	①	.015	1 3/8	2 1/4	1 3/32	...
1970	4MV	.240	...	...	...	.344	.300	INDEX	.015	1 3/8	2 1/4	1 3/32	...
1971	4MV	.240	...	...	...	.344	.310	INDEX	.015	1 3/8	2 1/4	1 3/32	...
1971	4MV Eldorado	.360	...	...	...	.344	.310	INDEX	.015	1 3/8	2 1/4	1 3/32	...

① —Remove upper end of choke rod, close choke valve, place rod in notch.
Bend rod to adjust, place rod in std. hole.

Chevelle—Camaro—Monte Carlo—Corvette

YEAR	MODEL OR TYPE	FLOAT LEVEL (IN.)		FLOAT DROP (IN.)		Pump Travel Setting (IN.)	CHOKE SETTING		Secondary Lockout Adj.	Throttle Bore Diam.		Venturi Diam.	
		Prim.	Sec.	Prim.	Sec.		Unloader (IN.)	Housing		Prim.	Sec.	Prim.	Sec.
1965	BV	1 9/32	...	1 3/4	...	...	.350	...	...	1 9/16	...	1 11/32	...
1965	2GV	1 23/64	...	1 29/32	...	57/64	13/64	...	...	1 7/16	...	1 3/32	...
1965	4GC	1 33/64	1 37/64	2 1/4	2 1/4	1 1/16	.235	INDEX	...	1 7/16	1 7/16	1 1/8	1 1/4

Chevelle—Camaro—Monte Carlo—Corvette, continued

YEAR	MODEL OR TYPE	FLOAT LEVEL (IN.) Prim.	Sec.	FLOAT DROP (IN.) Prim.	Sec.	Pump Travel Setting (IN.)	CHOKE SETTING Unloader (IN.)	Housing	Secondary Lockout Adj.	Throttle Bore Diam. Prim.	Sec.	Venturi Diam. Prim.	Sec.
1966	BV	1 9/32	...	1 3/4	...	...	.350	...	...	1 9/16	...	1 11/32	...
1966	2GV	3/4	...	1 3/4	...	1 1/8	.215	...	...	1 7/16	...	1 3/32	...
1966	4GC	1 17/32	1 19/32	2 1/4	2 1/4	1 1/16	.250	INDEX	...	1 7/16	1 7/16	1 1/8	1 1/4
1967	BV	1 9/32	...	1 3/4	...	...	.350	...	...	1 9/16	...	1 11/32	...
1967	2GV	3/4	...	1 3/4	...	1 1/8	.215	...	...	1 7/16	...	1 3/32	...
1967	4MV	9/32	...	...	...	13/32	.260	...	.015	1 3/8	2 1/4	1 3/32	...
1967	4MV	9/32	...	...	...	13/32	.300	...	.015	1 3/8	2 1/4	1 3/32	...
1968	MV-Aut.	9/32	...	...	...	...	.350	...	...	1 11/16	...	...	...
1968	MV-Std.	9/32	...	...	...	...	.350	...	...	1 11/16	...	...	...
1968	2GV	3/4	...	1 3/4	...	1 1/8	.200	...	...	1 7/16	...	1 3/32	...
1968	4MV-Aut.	3/16	...	...	...	9/32	.300	...	.010	1 3/8	2 1/4	1 3/32	...
1968	4MV-Std.	3/16	...	...	...	9/32	.300	...	.010	1 3/8	2 1/4	1 3/32	...
1969	MV-Aut.	1/4	...	...	...	...	.350	...	...	1 11/16	...	...	...
1969	MV-Std.	1/4	...	...	...	...	.350	...	...	1 11/16	...	...	...
1969	MV-Aut. w/AC	1/4	...	...	...	...	.350	...	...	1 11/16	...	...	...
1969	2GV-Std.	27/32	...	1 3/4	...	1 1/8	.215	...	...	1 7/16	...	1 3/16	...
1969	2GV-Std. w/AC	27/32	...	1 3/4	...	1 1/8	.215	...	...	1 7/16	...	1 3/16	...
1969	2GV-Aut.	27/32	...	1 3/4	...	1 1/8	.215	...	...	1 7/16	...	1 3/16	...
1969	2GV-Aut. w/AC	27/32	...	1 3/4	...	1 1/8	.215	...	...	1 7/16	...	1 3/16	...
1969	4MV-Aut.	7/32	...	...	...	5/16	.450	...	.015	1 3/8	2 1/4	1 3/32	...
1969	4MV-Std.	7/32	...	...	...	5/16	.450	...	.015	1 3/8	2 1/4	1 3/32	...
1969	4MV-Aut.	1/4	...	...	...	5/16	.450	...	.015	1 3/8	2 1/4	1 3/32	...
1969	4MV-Std.	1/4	...	...	...	5/16	.450	...	.015	1 3/8	2 1/4	1 3/32	...
1970	MV-250, Auto.	1/4	...	...	...	...	.350	...	...	1 11/16	...	...	...
1970	MV-250, Std.	1/4	...	...	...	...	.350	...	...	1 11/16	...	...	...
1970	2GV-1.25-3.05, Auto.	27/32	...	1 3/4	...	1 1/8	.215	...	...	1 7/16	...	1 3/16	...
1970	2GV-1.25-3.07, Auto. w. AC	27/32	...	1 3/4	...	1 1/8	.215	...	...	1 7/16	...	1 3/16	...
1970	2GV-1.25-307, Std.	27/32	...	1 3/4	...	1 1/8	.160	...	...	1 7/16	...	1 3/16	...
1970	2GV-1.25-307, Std. w. AC	27/32	...	1 3/4	...	1 1/8	.225	...	...	1 7/16	...	1 3/16	...
1970	2GV-1.50-350, Auto.	23/32	...	1 3/8	...	1 17/32	.325	...	...	1 11/16	...	1 1/4	...
1970	2GV-1.50-350, Aut. w. AC	23/32	...	1 3/8	...	1 17/32	.325	...	...	1 11/16	...	1 1/4	...
1970	2GV-1.50-350, Std.	23/32	...	1 3/8	...	1 17/32	.275	...	...	1 11/16	...	1 1/4	...
1970	2GV-1.50-350, Std. w. AC	23/32	...	1 3/8	...	1 17/32	.275	...	...	1 11/16	...	1 1/4	...
1970	2GV-1.50-400, Auto.	23/32	...	1 3/8	...	1 17/32	.325	...	...	1 11/16	...	1 1/4	...
1970	2GV-1.50-400, Auto. w. AC	23/32	...	1 3/8	...	1 17/32	.325	...	...	1 11/16	...	1 1/4	...
1970	2GV-1.50-400, Std.	23/32	...	1 3/8	...	1 17/32	.325	...	...	1 11/16	...	1 1/4	...
1970	2GV-1.50-400, Std. w. AC	23/32	...	1 3/8	...	1 17/32	.325	...	...	1 11/16	...	1 1/4	...
1970	4MV-350, Auto., 300 hp.	1/4	...	...	...	5/16	.450	...	...	1 3/8	2 1/4	1 3/32	...
1970	4MV-350, Std., 300 hp.	1/4	...	...	...	5/16	.450	...	...	1 3/8	2 1/4	1 3/32	...
1970	4MV-350, Std., 325 hp.	1/4	...	...	...	5/16	.450	...	...	1 3/8	2 1/4	1 3/32	...
1970	4MV-396, 325 hp., 400, 330 hp., Auto.	1/4	...	...	...	5/16	.450	...	...	1 3/8	2 1/4	1 3/32	...
1970	4MV-396, 325 hp., 400, 330 hp., Std.	1/4	...	...	...	5/16	.450	...	...	1 3/8	2 1/4	1 3/32	...
1970	4MV-396, 350 hp., Auto.	1/4	...	...	...	5/16	.450	...	...	1 3/8	2 1/4	1 3/32	...
1970	4MV-396, 350 hp., Std.	1/4	...	...	...	5/16	.450	...	...	1 3/8	2 1/4	1 3/32	...
1970	4MV-454, 345-360-390 hp., Auto.	1/4	...	...	...	5/16	.450	...	...	1 3/8	2 1/4	1 3/32	...
1970	4MV-454, 360-390 hp., Auto.	1/4	...	...	...	5/16	.450	...	...	1 3/8	2 1/4	1 3/32	...
1970	4MV-454, 360-390 hp., Std.	1/4	...	...	...	5/16	.450	...	...	1 3/8	2 1/4	1 3/32	...
1971	MV-250, Auto.	1/4	...	...	...	...	.350	...	...	1 11/16	...	...	...
1971	MV-250, Std.	1/4	...	...	...	...	.350	...	...	1 11/16	...	...	...
1971	2GV-307, Auto.	13/16	...	1 3/4	...	1 5/16	.215	...	...	1 7/16	...	1 3/16	...
1971	2GV-307, Std.	13/16	...	1 3/4	...	1 5/16	.215	...	...	1 7/16	...	1 3/16	...
1971	2GV-350, Auto.	25/32	...	1 3/8	...	1 17/32	.170	...	...	1 11/16	...	1 1/4	...
1971	2GV-350, Std.	23/32	...	1 3/8	...	1 17/32	.180	...	...	1 11/16	...	1 1/4	...
1971	4MV-350, Std.	1/4	...	...	...	...	.100	...	...	1 3/8	2 1/4	1 7/32	...
1971	4MV-350, Auto.	1/4	...	...	...	...	.100	...	...	1 3/8	2 1/4	1 7/32	...
1971	4MV-402, Std.	1/4	...	...	...	...	.100	...	...	1 3/8	2 1/4	1 7/32	...
1971	4MV-402, Auto.	1/4	...	...	...	...	.100	...	...	1 3/8	2 1/4	1 7/32	...
1971	4MV-454, Std.	1/4	...	...	...	...	.100	...	...	1 3/8	2 1/4	1 7/32	...
1971	4MV-454, Auto.	1/4	...	...	...	...	.100	...	...	1 3/8	2 1/4	1 7/32	...
1972	MV-250	1/4	...	...	...	...	.350	...	...	1 11/16	...	...	...
1972	2GV-307 Std.	13/16	...	1 3/4	...	1 5/16	.215	...	...	1 7/16	...	1 3/16	...
1972	2GV-307 Auto.	13/16	...	1 3/4	...	1 5/16	.215	...	...	1 7/16	...	1 3/16	...
1972	2GV-350 Std.	23/32	...	1 3/8	...	1 17/32	.180	...	...	1 11/16	...	1 1/4	...
1972	2GV-350 Auto.	25/32	...	1 3/8	...	1 17/32	.170	...	...	1 11/16	...	1 1/4	...
1972	4MV-350	1/4	...	...	...	...	.100	...	...	1 3/8	2 1/4	1 7/32	...
1972	4MV-402	1/4	...	...	...	...	.100	...	...	1 3/8	2 1/4	1 7/32	...
1972	4MV-454	1/4	...	...	...	...	.100	...	...	1 3/8	2 1/4	1 7/32	...

YEAR	MODEL OR TYPE	FLOAT LEVEL (IN.)		FLOAT DROP (IN.)		Pump Travel Setting (IN.)	CHOKE SETTING		Secondary Lockout Adj.	Throttle Bore Diam.		Venturi Diam.	
		Prim.	Sec.	Prim.	Sec.		Unloader (IN.)	Housing		Prim.	Sec.	Prim.	Sec.
Chevrolet													
1965	BV	1 9/32	...	1 3/4	...	...	.350	...	...	1 9/16	...	1 11/32	...
1965	2GV	1 23/64	...	1 29/32	...	57/64	.208	...	...	1 7/16	...	1 3/32	...
1965	4GC—327 cu. in.	1 33/64	1 37/64	2 1/4	2 1/4	1 1/16	.235	INDEX	...	1 7/16	1 7/16	1 1/8	1 1/4
1965	4GC-409 cu. in.	13/16	1/2	1 1/2	1 1/8	1 1/32	.130	INDEX	...	1 9/16	1 11/16	1 5/16	1 15/32
1965	4MV-396 cu. in.	1/8	...	...	...	7/32	.325	INDEX	.015	1 3/8	2 1/4	1 3/32	...
1966	BV	1 9/32	...	1 3/4	...	...	.350	...	...	1 9/16	...	1 11/32	...
1966	2GV	3/4	...	1 3/4	...	1 1/8	.215	...	...	1 7/16	...	1 3/32	...
1966	4GC	1 17/32	1 19/32	2 1/4	2 1/4	1 1/16	.250	INDEX	.015	1 7/16	1 7/16	1 1/8	1 1/4
1966	4MV	9/32	...	...	...	13/32	.260	...	.015	1 3/8	2 1/4	1 3/32	...
1966	4MV	9/32	...	...	...	13/32	.300	...	.015	1 3/8	2 1/4	1 3/32	...
1967	BV	1 9/32	...	1 3/4	...	...	.350	...	...	1 9/16	...	1 11/32	...
1967	2GV	3/4	...	1 3/4	...	1 1/8	.215	...	...	1 7/16	...	1 3/32	...
1967	4MV	9/32	...	...	...	13/32	.260	...	...	1 3/8	2 1/4	1 3/32	...
1967	4MV	9/32	...	...	...	13/32	.300	...	.010	1 3/8	2 1/4	1 3/32	...
1968	MV—Aut.	9/32	...	...	...	...	.350	...	...	1 11/16	...	...	...
1968	MV—Std.	9/32	...	...	...	...	.350	...	...	1 11/16	...	...	...
1968	2GV	3/4	...	1 3/4	...	1 1/8	.200	...	...	1 7/16	...	1 3/32	...
1968	4MV—Aut.	9/32	...	...	...	9/32	.260	...	.010	1 3/8	2 1/4	1 3/32	...
1968	4MV—Std.	9/32	...	...	...	9/32	.300	...	.010	1 3/8	2 1/4	1 3/32	...
1968	4MV—Aut.	3/16	...	...	...	9/32	.300	...	.010	1 3/8	2 1/4	1 3/32	...
1968	4MV—Std.	3/16	...	...	...	9/32	.300	...	.010	1 3/8	2 1/4	1 3/32	...
1969	MV—Aut.	1/4	...	...	...	...	.350	...	...	1 11/16	...	...	...
1969	MV—Std.	1/4	...	...	...	...	.350	...	...	1 11/16	...	...	...
1969	2GV—Aut. 327	3/4	...	1 3/4	...	1 13/32	.275	...	...	1 11/16	...	1 1/4	...
1969	2GV—Std. 327	3/4	...	1 3/4	...	1 13/32	.275	...	...	1 11/16	...	1 1/4	...
1969	2GV—Aut. 396	3/4	...	1 3/4	...	1 13/32	.275	...	...	1 11/16	...	1 1/4	...
1969	2GV—Std. 396	3/4	...	1 3/4	...	1 13/32	.275	...	...	1 11/16	...	1 1/4	...
1969	4MV—Aut. 350	7/32	...	...	...	5/16	.450	...	...	1 3/8	2 1/4	1 3/32	...
1969	4MV—Std. 350	7/32	...	...	...	5/16	.450	...	...	1 3/8	2 1/4	1 3/32	...
1969	4MV—Aut. 427	1/4	...	...	...	5/16	.450	...	...	1 3/8	2 1/4	1 3/32	...
1969	4MV—Std. 427	1/4	...	...	...	5/16	.450	...	...	1 3/8	2 1/4	1 3/32	...
1970	MV—250, Auto.	1/4	...	...	...	...	.350	...	...	1 11/16	...	...	...
1970	MV—250, Std.	1/4	...	...	...	...	.350	...	...	1 11/16	...	...	...
1970	2GV-1.50-350, Auto.	23/32	...	1 3/8	...	1 17/32	.325	...	...	1 11/16	...	1 1/4	...
1970	2GV-1.50-350, Auto. w. AC	23/32	...	1 3/8	...	1 17/32	.325	...	...	1 11/16	...	1 1/4	...
1970	2GV-1.50-350, Std.	23/32	...	1 3/8	...	1 17/32	.275	...	...	1 11/16	...	1 1/4	...
1970	2GV-1.50-350, Std. w. AC	23/32	...	1 3/8	...	1 17/32	.275	...	...	1 11/16	...	1 1/4	...
1970	2GV-1.50-400, Auto.	23/32	...	1 3/8	...	1 17/32	.325	...	...	1 11/16	...	1 1/4	...
1970	2GV-1.50-400, Auto. w. AC	23/32	...	1 3/8	...	1 17/32	.325	...	...	1 11/16	...	1 1/4	...
1970	2GV-1.50-400, Std.	23/32	...	1 3/8	...	1 17/32	.325	...	...	1 11/16	...	1 1/4	...
1970	2GV-1.50-400, Std. w. AC	23/32	...	1 3/8	...	1 17/32	.325	...	...	1 11/16	...	1 1/4	...
1970	4MV—350, Auto., 300 h.p.	1/4	...	...	...	5/16	.450	...	...	1 3/8	2 1/4	1 3/32	...
1970	4MV—350, Std., 300 h.p.	1/4	...	...	...	5/16	.450	...	...	1 3/8	2 1/4	1 3/32	...
1970	4MV—454, 345-360-390 h.p., Auto.	1/4	...	...	...	5/16	.450	...	...	1 3/8	2 1/4	1 3/32	...
1970	4MV—454, 360-390, h.p., Auto.	1/4	...	...	...	5/16	.450	...	...	1 3/8	2 1/4	1 3/32	...
1970	4MV—454, 360-390 h.p., Std.	1/4	...	...	...	5/16	.450	...	...	1 3/8	2 1/4	1 3/32	...
1971	MV—250, Auto.	1/4	...	...	...	...	.350	...	...	1 11/16	...	...	...
1971	MV—250, Std.	1/4	...	...	...	...	.350	...	...	1 11/16	...	...	...
1971	2GV—350, Auto.	25/32	...	1 3/8	...	1 17/32	.325	...	...	1 11/16	...	1 1/4	...
1971	2GV—350, Std.	23/32	...	1 3/8	...	1 17/32	.325	...	...	1 11/16	...	1 1/4	...
1971	2GV—400, Auto.	23/32	...	1 3/8	...	1 17/32	.325	...	...	1 11/16	...	1 1/4	...
1971	4MV—350, Auto.	1/4	...	...	...	...	.100	...	...	1 3/8	2 1/4	1 7/32	...
1971	4MV—350, Std.	1/4	...	...	...	...	.100	...	...	1 3/8	2 1/4	1 7/32	...
1971	4MV—402, Auto.	1/4	...	...	...	...	.100	...	...	1 3/8	2 1/4	1 7/32	...
1971	4MV—402, Std.	1/4	...	...	...	...	.100	...	...	1 3/8	2 1/4	1 7/32	...
1971	4MV—454, Auto.	1/4	...	...	...	...	.100	...	...	1 3/8	2 1/4	1 7/32	...
1971	4MV—454, Std.	1/4	...	...	...	...	.100	...	...	1 3/8	2 1/4	1 7/32	...
1972	MV, 250	1/4	...	...	...	...	.350	...	...	1 11/16	...	...	...
1972	2GV, 350	25/32	...	1 3/8	...	1 17/32	.325	...	...	1 11/16	...	1 1/4	...
1972	2GV, 400	23/32	...	1 3/8	...	1 17/32	.325	...	...	1 11/16	...	1 1/4	...
1972	4MV, 402, 454	1/4	...	...	...	...	.100	...	...	1 3/8	2 1/4	1 7/32	...
Chevy II—Vega													
1965	6 Cyl.-BV	1 9/32	...	1 3/4	...	...	.350	...	...	1 9/16	...	1 11/32	...
1965	V8-2GV	1 23/64	...	1 29/32	...	57/64	.203	...	...	1 7/16	...	1 3/32	...
1965	V8-4GC	1 33/64	1 37/64	2 1/4	2 1/4	1 1/16	.235	INDEX	...	1 7/16	1 7/16	1 1/8	1 1/4

YEAR	MODEL OR TYPE	FLOAT LEVEL (IN.) Prim.	Sec.	FLOAT DROP (IN.) Prim.	Sec.	Pump Travel Setting (IN.)	CHOKE SETTING Unloader (IN.)	Housing	Secondary Lockout Adj.	Throttle Bore Diam. Prim.	Sec.	Venturi Diam. Prim.	Sec.
Chevy II-Vega, continued													
1966	6 Cyl.-BV	1 9/32	...	1 3/4	...	...	.350	...	...	1 9/16	...	1 11/32	...
1966	V8-2GV	3/4	...	1 3/4	...	1 1/8	.215	...	...	1 7/16	...	1 3/32	...
1966	V8-4GC	1 17/32	1 19/32	2 1/4	2 1/4	1 1/16	.250	INDEX	.015	1 7/16	1 7/16	1 1/8	1 1/4
1967	BV	1 9/32	...	1 3/4	...	...	.350	...	...	1 9/16	...	1 11/32	...
1967	2GV	3/4	...	1 3/4	...	1 1/8	.215	...	...	1 7/16	...	1 3/32	...
1967	4MV—Aut.	9/32	...	...	...	13/32	.260	...	.010	1 3/8	2 1/4	1 3/32	...
1967	4MV—Std.	9/32	...	...	...	13/32	.300	...	.010	1 3/8	2 1/4	1 3/32	...
1968	M	9/32	...	...	...	...	...	...	...	1 11/16	...	...	...
1968	MV-Aut.	9/32	...	...	...	...	.350	...	...	1 11/16	...	...	...
1968	MV-Std.	9/32	...	...	...	...	.350	...	...	1 11/16	...	...	...
1968	2GV	3/4	...	1 3/4	...	1 1/8	.200	...	...	1 7/16	...	1 3/32	...
1968	4MV	9/32	...	...	...	9/32	.300	...	.010	1 3/8	2 1/4	1 3/32	...
1969	M	1/4	...	...	...	...	...	...	...	1 11/16	...	...	...
1969	MV-Aut.	1/4	...	...	...	.350	...	...	...	1 11/16	...	...	...
1969	MV Std.	1/4	...	...	...	.350	...	...	...	1 11/16	...	...	...
1969	2GV-Std.	27/32	...	1 3/4	...	1 1/8	.215	...	...	1 7/16	...	1 3/16	...
1969	2GV-Aut.	27/32	...	1 3/4	...	1 1/8	.215	...	...	1 7/16	...	1 3/16	...
1969	4MV-Std. 350	7/32	...	...	...	5/16	.450	...	.015	1 3/8	2 1/4	1 3/32	...
1969	4MV-Aut. 350	7/32	...	...	...	5/16	.450	...	.015	1 3/8	2 1/4	1 3/32	...
1969	4MV-Std. 396	1/4	...	...	...	5/16	.450	...	.015	1 3/8	2 1/4	1 3/32	...
1969	4MV-Aut. 396	1/4	...	...	...	5/16	.450	...	.015	1 3/8	2 1/4	1 3/32	...
1970	M-153, (4 Cyl.)	1/4	...	...	...	...	...	...	...	1 11/16	...	...	...
1970	MV-230, Auto	1/4	...	...	...	...	.350	...	...	1 11/16	...	...	...
1970	MV-230, Std.	1/4	...	...	...	...	.350	...	...	1 11/16	...	...	...
1970	MV-250, Auto.	1/4	...	...	...	...	.350	...	...	1 11/16	...	...	...
1970	MV-250, Std.	1/4	...	...	...	...	.350	...	...	1 11/16	...	...	...
1970	2GV-1.25-307, Auto.	27/32	...	1 3/4	...	1 1/8	.215	...	...	1 7/16	...	1 3/16	...
1970	2GV-1.25-307, Auto. w. AC	27/32	...	1 3/4	...	1 1/8	.215	...	...	1 7/16	...	1 3/16	...
1970	2GV-1.25-307, Std.	27/32	...	1 3/4	...	1 1/8	.160	...	...	1 7/16	...	1 3/16	...
1970	2GV-1.25-307, Std. w. AC	27/32	...	1 3/4	...	1 1/8	.225	...	...	1 7/16	...	1 3/16	...
1970	2GV-1.50-350, Auto.	23/32	...	1 3/8	...	1 17/32	.325	...	...	1 11/16	...	1 1/4	...
1970	2GV-1.50-350, Auto. w. AC	23/32	...	1 3/8	...	1 17/32	.325	...	...	1 11/16	...	1 1/4	...
1970	2GV-1.50-350, Std.	23/32	...	1 3/8	...	1 17/32	.275	...	...	1 11/16	...	1 1/4	...
1970	2GV-1.50-350, Std. w. AC	23/32	...	1 3/8	...	1 17/32	.275	...	...	1 11/16	...	1 1/4	...
1970	4MV-All	1/4	...	...	...	5/16	.450	...	...	1 3/8	2 1/4	1 3/32	...
1971	MV-250 Auto	1/4	...	...	...	...	.350	...	...	1 11/16	...	...	...
1971	MV-250 Std.	1/4	...	...	...	...	.350	...	...	1 11/16	...	...	...
1971	2GV-307 Auto	27/32	...	1 3/4	...	1 5/16	.215	...	...	1 7/16	...	1 3/16	...
1971	2GV-307 Std.	27/32	...	1 3/4	...	1 5/16	.215	...	...	1 7/16	...	1 3/16	...
1971	2GV-350 Auto	25/32	...	1 3/8	...	1 17/32	.325	...	...	1 11/16	...	1 1/4	...
1971	2GV-350 Std.	23/32	...	1 3/8	...	1 17/32	.325	...	...	1 11/16	...	1 1/4	...
1971	4MV-All	1/4	...	...	...	...	.100	...	...	1 3/8	2 1/4	1 3/32	...
1971	MV-Vega	1/16	...	...	...	...	.350	...	...	1 11/16	...	...	...
1971	2GV-Vega	3/8	...	1 3/4	...	1 3/8	.180	...	...	1 7/16	...	1 3/32	...
1972	MV, 250	1/4	...	...	...	...	.350	...	...	1 11/16	...	...	...
1972	2GV, 307	27/32	...	1 3/4	...	1 5/16	.215	...	...	1 7/16	...	1 3/16	...
1972	2GV, 350	25/32	...	1 3/8	...	1 17/32	.325	...	...	1 11/16	...	1 1/4	...
1972	4MV, 350	1/4	...	...	...	...	.100	...	...	1 3/8	2 1/4	1 3/32	...
1972	MV, Vega	1/16	...	...	...	...	.350	...	...	1 7/16	...	...	...
1972	2GV, Vega	5/8	...	1 3/4	...	1 3/8	.180	...	...	1 7/16	...	1 3/32	...
Dodge-Plymouth													
1971	318 Auto	21/32	...	1 3/4	...	1 5/64	#29 DRILL	...	...	1 7/16	...	1 3/16	...

YEAR	MODEL OR TYPE	FLOAT LEVEL (IN.)		FLOAT DROP (IN.)		Pump Travel Setting (IN.)	CHOKE SETTING		Secondary Lockout Adj.	Throttle Bore Diam.		Venturi Diam.	
		Prim.	Sec.	Prim.	Sec.		Unloader (IN.)	Housing		Prim.	Sec.	Prim.	Sec.
Ford-Mercury													
1970	DOOF-A, F-429 CJ S.T.	5/8	...	...	...	Outboard	.300	...	.015	1 3/8	2 1/4	1 3/32	...
1970	DOOF-B, E-429 CJ A.T.	5/8	...	...	...	Outboard	.300	...	.015	1 3/8	2 1/4	1 3/32	...
1971	DOOF-A, E-429 CJ A11/T.	11/32	...	...	...	Outboard	.300	...	.015	1 3/8	2 1/4	1 3/32	...
Oldsmobile													
1965	2GC—330 Eng. Syn.	3/4	...	1 7/8	...	1 1/16	.160	INDEX	...	1 7/16	...	1 3/16	...
1965	2GC—330 Eng. Aut.	19/32	...	1 7/8	...	1 1/16	.160	INDEX	...	1 7/16	...	1 3/16	...
1965	4GC—425 Eng.	1 15/32	1 3/8	1 1/2	1 9/32	1	.120	1-RICH	...	1 9/16	1 11/16	1 1/8	1 15/32
1965	4GC—425 Eng.	1 15/32	1 3/8	1 1/16	1 1/16	1	.120	1-RICH	...	1 9/16	1 11/16	1 1/8	1 15/32
1966	2GC—7036159	3/4	...	1 7/8	...	1 7/16	.160	INDEX	...	1 11/16	...	1 1/4	...
1966	2GC—7036053	19/32	...	1 7/8	...	1 7/16	.160	INDEX	...	1 11/16	...	1 3/8	...
1966	4MV—7036254	11/32	...	...	...	9/32	.300	Up-Notch	.015	1 3/8	2 1/4	1 3/32	...
1966	4MV—7036250	...	...	...	...	...	...	...	.015	1 3/8	2 1/4	1 3/32	...
1967	2GC	19/32	...	1 9/16	...	1 7/16	.160	INDEX	...	1 11/16	...	1 1/4	...
1967	2GC	1/2	...	1 9/16	...	1 7/16	.160	INDEX	...	1 11/16	...	1 1/4	...
1967	4MV	1/4	...	...	...	5/16	.325	R-Notch	.015	1 3/8	2 1/4	1 3/32	...
1968	2GC	9/16	...	1 3/8	...	1 7/16	.160	1-LEAN	...	1 11/16	...	1 1/4	...
1968	2GC	9/16	...	1 3/8	...	1 7/16	.160	INDEX	...	1 11/16	...	1 3/8	...
1968	4MV	1/4	...	...	...	5/16	.200	CENTER	.020	1 3/8	2 1/4	1 3/32	...
1969	2GC	9/16	...	1 3/8	...	1 7/16	.170	INDEX	...	1 11/16	...	1 3/8	...
1969	2GC—350	9/16	...	1 3/8	...	1 7/16	.170	1-LEAN	...	1 11/16	...	1 5/16	...
1969	4MV	1/4	...	...	...	5/16	.200	CENTER	.020	1 3/8	2 1/4	1 3/32	...
1970	2GC-7040154-455 (L-33), Auto.	9/16	...	1 3/8	...	1 3/8	.140	INDEX	...	1 11/16	...	1 3/8	...
1970	2GC-7040155-350, 455, Std.	9/16	...	1 3/8	...	1 3/8	.140	1-LEAN	...	1 11/16	...	1 3/8	...
1970	2GC-7040156-350, Auto.	9/16	...	1 3/8	...	1 3/8	.140	INDEX	...	1 11/16	...	1 1/4	...
1970	2GC-7040159-455, Auto.	9/16	...	1 3/8	...	1 3/8	.140	INDEX	...	1 11/16	...	1 3/8	...
1970	4MC-7040250-350	1/4	...	...	...	INNER HOLE	.200	INDEX	.020	1 3/8	2 1/4	1 3/32	...
1970	4MC-7040251-455	1/4	...	...	...	INNER HOLE	.200	INDEX	.020	1 3/8	2 1/4	1 3/32	...
1970	4MC-7040252-455 Toronado.	1/4	...	...	...	INNER HOLE	.200	1-RICH	.020	1 3/8	2 1/4	1 3/32	...
1971	2GC-All, Auto.	9/16	...	1 3/8	...	1 3/8	.170	INDEX	...	1 11/16	...	1 3/8	...
1971	2GC-All, Std.	17/32	...	1 3/8	...	1 3/8	.170	1-LEAN	...	1 11/16	...	1 3/8	...
1971	4MC-455, Auto.	1/4	...	...	...	INNER HOLE	.200	INDEX	.035	1 3/8	2 1/4	1 7/32	...
Oldsmobile F-85													
1965	BC—V-6	1 9/32	...	1 3/4	...	...	.300	INDEX	...	1 9/16	...	1 11/32	...
1965	2GC	3/4	...	1 7/8	...	1 7/16	.160	INDEX	...	1 7/16	...	1 3/16	...
1965	4GC	1 15/32	1 3/8	1 1/2	1 3/16	1	.120	1-RICH	...	1 9/16	1 11/16	1 1/8	1 15/32
1966	BV	1 9/32	...	1 3/4	...	...	.350	...	...	1 9/16	...	1 11/32	...
1966	2GC—7036159	3/4	...	1 7/8	...	1 7/16	.160	INDEX	...	1 11/16	...	1 1/4	...
1966	4MV	11/32	...	...	...	9/32	.300	Up-Notch	.015	1 3/8	2 1/4	1 3/32	...
1967	BV	1 9/32	...	1 3/4	...	...	.350	...	...	1 9/16	...	1 11/32	...
1967	2GC	19/32	...	1 9/16	...	1 7/16	.160	INDEX	...	1 11/16	...	1 1/4	...
1967	2GC	1/2	...	1 9/16	...	1 7/16	.160	INDEX	...	1 11/16	...	1 1/4	...
1967	2GC	19/32	...	1 9/16	...	1 7/16	.160	1-LEAN	...	1 11/16	...	1 3/8	...
1967	4MV	1/4	...	...	...	5/16	.325	R-Notch	.015	1 3/8	2 1/4	1 3/32	...
1968	MV	11/32	...	...	...	...	.350	...	...	1 11/16	...	...	...
1968	2GC	9/16	...	1 3/8	...	1 7/16	.160	1-LEAN	...	1 11/16	...	1 1/4	...
1968	2GC	9/16	...	1 3/8	...	1 7/16	.160	INDEX	...	1 11/16	...	1 1/4	...
1968	4MV	1/4	...	...	...	5/16	.200	CENTER	.020	1 3/8	2 1/4	1 3/32	...
1969	MV	5/16	...	...	...	...	.350	...	...	1 11/16	...	...	...
1969	2GC	9/16	...	1 3/8	...	1 7/16	.170	INDEX	...	1 11/16	...	1 1/4	...
1969	2GC, 350	9/16	...	1 3/8	...	1 7/16	1-LEAN	1-LEAN	...	1 11/16	...	1 1/4	...
1969	4MV	1/4	...	...	...	5/16	.200	CENTER	.020	1 3/8	2 1/4	1 3/32	...

YEAR	MODEL OR TYPE	FLOAT LEVEL (IN.)		FLOAT DROP (IN.)		Pump Travel Setting (IN.)	CHOKE SETTING		Secondary Lockout Adj.	Throttle Bore Diam.		Venturi Diam.	
		Prim.	Sec.	Prim.	Sec.		Unloader (IN.)	Housing		Prim.	Sec.	Prim.	Sec.
Oldsmobile F-85, continued													
1970	MV-7040014-250, Auto.	1/4	...	...	...	...	.350	...	...	1 11/16	...	...	...
1970	MV-7040017-250, Std.	1/4	...	...	...	...	.350	...	...	1 11/16	...	...	...
1970	2GC-7040154-455 (L-33), Auto.	9/16	...	1 3/8	...	1 3/8	.140	INDEX	...	1 11/16	...	1 3/8	...
1970	2GC-7040155-350, 455, Std.	9/16	...	1 3/8	...	1 3/8	.140	1-LEAN	...	1 11/16	...	1 3/8	
1970	2GC-7040156-350, Auto.	9/16	...	1 3/8	...	1 3/8	.140	INDEX		1 11/16	...	1 1/4	
1970	2GC-7040159-455, Auto.	9/16	...	1 3/8	...	1 3/8	.140	INDEX		1 11/16		1 3/8	
1970	4MC-7040250-350	1/4	...	...	...	INNER HOLE	.200	INDEX	.020	1 3/8	2 1/4	1 3/32	
1970	4MC-7040251-455	1/4	...	...	...	INNER HOLE	.200	INDEX	.020	1 3/8	2 1/4	1 3/32	
1970	4MC-7040253-442 Model, Std.	1/4		...	...	INNER HOLE	.200	INDEX	.020	1 3/8	2 1/4	1 3/32	
1970	4MC-7040255-350 W-31	1/4		...	...	INNER HOLE	.200	INDEX	.020	1 3/8	2 1/4	1 3/32	
1970	4MC-7040256-W-30, 442, St.	1/4				INNER HOLE	.200	INDEX	.020	1 3/8	2 1/4	1 3/32	
1970	4MC-7040257-442 Model, Auto	1/4				INNER HOLE	.200	INDEX	.020	1 3/8	2 1/4	1 3/32	...
1970	4MC-7040257-442 Model, Auto	1/4				INNER HOLE	.200	INDEX	.020	1 3/8	2 1/4	1 3/32	
1970	4MC-7040257-455 W-33, Auto	1/4				INNER HOLE	.200	INDEX	.020	1 3/8	2 1/4	1 3/32	
1970	4MC-7040258-442 W-30, Auto	1/4				INNER HOLE	.200	INDEX	.020	1 3/8	2 1/4	1 3/32	
1971	MV-250	1/4	...	1 3/8	...	...	.350	...	...	1 11/16	...	...	...
1971	2GC-All, Auto	9/16	...	1 3/8	...	1 3/8	.170	INDEX	...	1 11/16	...	1 3/8	
1971	2GC-All, Std.	9/16	...	1 3/8	...	1 3/8	.170	1-LEAN	...	1 11/16	...	1 3/8	
1971	4MC-All	1/4	...	...	...	INNER HOLE	.200	INDEX	.035	1 3/8	2 1/4	1 7/32	...
Pontiac													
1965	2GC	19/32	...	1 3/4	...	1 11/32	.160	INDEX		1 11/16	...	1 1/4	...
1965	2GC—Frt. & Rear	21/32	...	1 3/4	...	27/32	...	...		1 11/16	...	1 5/16	...
1965	2GC—Center	11/16	...	1 3/4	...	1 1/8	.160	INDEX		1 7/16	...	1 3/16	
1966	2GC	19/32	...	1 3/4	...	1 21/64	.160	INDEX		1 11/16	...	1 1/4	
1966	2GC—Frt. & Rear	23/32	...	1 3/4	...	27/32	...	...		1 11/16	...	1 5/16	
1966	2GC—Center	23/32	...	1 3/4	...	1 21/64	.160	INDEX		1 7/16	...	1 3/16	
1967	2GC-7027066—M.T.	9/16	...	1 9/16	...	1 11/32	.160	INDEX		1 11/16	...	1 1/4	
1967	2GC-7027060—A.T.	9/16	...	1 9/16	...	1 11/32	.160	INDEX	...	1 11/16	...	1 1/4	
1967	4MV-7027263—M.T.	3/16	...	...	...	9/32	.325	Cent-Notch	.020	1 3/8	2 1/4	1 3/32	
1967	4MV-7027262—A.T.	3/16	...	...	...	9/32	.325	Cent-Notch	.020	1 3/8	2 1/4	1 3/32	
1968	2GC-7028060 A.T.	9/16	...	1 3/4	...	1 11/32	.180	...	...	1 11/16	...	1 1/4	
1968	2GV-7028066 M.T.	9/16	...	1 3/4	...	1 11/32	.180	...	...	1 11/16	...	1 1/4	
1968	4MV-7028262-64	1/4	...	...	...	9/32	.300	...	.015	1 3/8	2 1/4	1 3/32	
1968	4MV-7028263-65	1/4	...	...	...	9/32	.300	...	.015	1 3/8	2 1/4	1 3/32	
1969	2GV-7029060 A.T.	9/16	...	1 3/4	...	1 11/32	.180	...	...	1 11/16	...	1 3/8	
1969	2GV-7028066 M.T.	9/16	...	1 3/4	...	1 11/32	.180	...	...	1 11/16	...	1 3/8	
1969	4MV-7029262	9/32	...	...	...	9/32	.300	Cent-Notch	.015	1 3/8	2 1/4	1 3/32	
1969	4MV-7029263 M.T.	9/32	...	...	...	9/32	.300	Cent-Notch	.015	1 3/8	2 1/4	1 3/32	
1969	4MV-7029268 A.T.	9/32	...	...	...	9/32	.300	Cent-Notch	.015	1 3/8	2 1/4	1 3/32	
1970	2GV—7040060-400, Auto.	11/16	...	1 3/4	...	1 11/32	.180	...	...	1 11/16	...	1 3/8	
1970	2GV—7040460-400, Auto.-CAL.	11/16	...	1 3/4	...	1 11/32	.180	...	...	1 11/16	...	1 3/8	
1970	2GV—7040461-400, Auto. w/AC-CAL.	11/16	...	1 3/4	...	1 11/32	.180	...	...	1 11/16	...	1 3/8	
1970	2GV—7040062-350, Auto.	9/16	...	1 3/4	...	1 11/32	.180	...	...	1 11/16	...	1 3/8	
1970	2GV—7040462-350, Auto.-CAL.	9/16	...	1 3/4	...	1 11/32	.180			1 11/16	...	1 3/8	
1970	2GV—7040462-350, Auto. w/AC-CAL.	9/16	...	1 3/4	...	1 11/32	.180			1 11/16	...	1 3/8	
1970	2GV—7040064-400 Altitude, Auto.	11/16	...	1 3/4	...	1 11/32	.180			1 11/16	...	1 3/8	...

YEAR	MODEL OR TYPE	FLOAT LEVEL (IN.)		FLOAT DROP (IN.)		Pump Travel Setting (IN.)	CHOKE SETTING		Secondary Lockout Adj.	Throttle Bore Diam.		Venturi Diam.	
		Prim.	Sec.	Prim.	Sec.		Unloader (IN.)	Housing		Prim.	Sec.	Prim.	Sec.
Pontiac, continued													
1970	2GV—7040066-400, Std.	11/16	...	1 3/4	...	1 11/32	.180	...	...	1 11/16	...	1 3/8	...
1970	2GV—7040466-400, Std.-CAL	11/16	...	1 3/4	...	1 11/32	.180	...	...	1 11/16	...	1 3/8	...
1970	2GV—7040071-350, Std.	9/16	...	1 3/4	...	1 11/32	.180	...	...	1 11/16	...	1 3/8	...
1970	2GV—7040471-350, Std.-CAL	9/16	...	1 3/4	...	1 11/32	.180	...	...	1 11/16	...	1 3/8	...
1970	2GV—7040072-350 Altitude, Std.	9/16	...	1 3/4	...	1 11/32	.180	...	...	1 11/16	...	1 3/8	...
1970	4MV—7040262-455, Auto-Bonnev. sm. valve......................	9/32	...	...	...	...	...	CENTER NOTCH	.015	1 3/8	2 1/4	1 3/32	...
1970	4MV—7040562-455, Auto-Bonnev. sm. valve-cal.	9/32	...	...	...	...	...	CENTER NOTCH	.015	1 3/8	2 1/4	1 3/32	...
1970	4MV—7040263-400 Std. exc. Ram-Air	9/32	...	...	...	...	...	CENTER NOTCH	.015	1 3/8	2 1/4	1 3/32	...
1970	4MV—7040563-400, Std.-Exc. Ram-Air-cal.	9/32	...	...	...	...	...	CENTER NOTCH	.015	1 3/8	2 1/4	1 3/32	...
1970	4MV—7040264-400, Auto-Exc. Ram-Air	9/32	...	...	...	...	...	CENTER NOTCH	.015	1 3/8	2 1/4	1 3/32	...
1970	4MV—7040564-400, Auto-Exc. Ram-Air-cai	9/32	...	...	...	...	...	CENTER NOTCH	.015	1 3/8	2 1/4	1 3/32	...
1970	4MV—7040267-455, Std.	9/32	...	...	...	...	...	CENTER NOTCH	.015	1 3/8	2 1/4	1 3/32	...
1970	4MV-7040567-455, Std.-CAL.	9/32	...	...	...	...	...	CENTER NOTCH	.015	1 3/8	2 1/4	1 3/32	...
1970	4MV—7040268-455, Auto.............	9/32	...	...	...	...	...	CENTER NOTCH	.015	1 3/8	2 1/4	1 3/32	...
1970	4MV—7040568-455, Auto-CAL.	9/32	...	...	...	...	...	CENTER NOTCH	.015	1 3/8	2 1/4	1 3/32	...
1970	4MV—7040274-455, Altitude, Auto......	9/32	...	...	...	...	...	CENTER NOTCH	.015	1 3/8	2 1/4	1 3/32	...
1971	2GV—7041060-400 A.T. w/AC..........	11/16	...	1 3/4	...	1 11/32	.180	...	...	1 11/16	...	1 3/8	...
1971	2GV—7041062-350 A.T. w/AC	9/16	...	1 3/4	...	1 11/32	.180	...	...	1 11/16	...	1 3/8	...
1971	2GV—7041064-455 A.T.	11/16	...	1 3/4	...	1 11/32	.180	...	...	1 11/16	...	1 3/8	...
1971	2GV—7041070-400 A.T.(ALT.)	11/16	...	1 3/4	...	1 11/32	.180	...	...	1 11/16	...	1 3/8	...
1971	2GV—7041071-350 M.T.	9/16	...	1 3/4	...	1 11/32	.180	...	...	1 11/16	...	1 3/8	...
1971	2GV—7041072-350 A.T. (ALT.)	9/16	...	1 3/4	...	1 11/32	.180	...	...	1 11/16	...	1 3/8	...
1971	2GV—7041074-455 A.T. (ALT.)	11/16	...	1 3/4	...	1 11/32	.180	...	...	1 11/16	...	1 3/8	...
1971	4MV—All	9/32	...	...	...	...	...	CENTER NOTCH	...	1 3/8	2 1/4	1 3/32	...

CAL—California
ALT—Altitude

Tempest—Firebird—Ventura II

YEAR	MODEL OR TYPE	FLOAT LEVEL (IN.)		FLOAT DROP (IN.)		Pump Travel Setting (IN.)	CHOKE SETTING		Secondary Lockout Adj.	Throttle Bore Diam.		Venturi Diam.	
		Prim.	Sec.	Prim.	Sec.		Unloader (IN.)	Housing		Prim.	Sec.	Prim.	Sec.
1965	BV—7025167.......................	1 9/32	...	1 7/8	...	.040	.230	...	...	1 9/16	...	1 11/32	...
1965	2GC-7025062, 326 Eng.	5/8	...	1 3/4	...	1 11/32	.160	INDEX	...	1 11/16	...	1 1/4	...
1965	2GC—389 Eng., Frt.	23/32	...	1 3/4	...	...	...	...	...	1 11/16	...	1 5/16	...
1965	2GC—389 Eng., Cent.	23/32	...	1 3/4	...	1 11/32	...	INDEX	...	1 7/16	...	1 5/16	...
1965	2GC—389 Eng., Rear	23/32	...	1 3/4	...	...	...	...	...	1 11/16	...	1 5/16	...
1966	BV	1 9/32	...	1 7/8	...	.040	.230	...	...	1 9/16	...	1 11/32	...
1966	2GC	3/4	...	1 7/8	...	1 11/32	.160	INDEX	...	1 11/16	...	1 1/4	...
1966	BV—6 Cyl., 230 Eng.	1 5/16	...	1 7/8	...	.040	.230	...	...	1 9/16	...	1 11/32	...
1966	4MV—6 Cyl.	7/32	...	...	...	9/32	.300	...	.020	1 3/8	2 1/4	1 3/32	...
1966	2GC—389 Eng., Frt.	21/32	...	1 3/4	...	27/32	...	...	...	1 11/16	...	1 5/16	...
1966	2GC—389 Eng., Cent.	19/32	...	1 3/4	...	1 21/64	.160	...	...	1 7/16	...	1 5/16	...
1966	2GC—389 Eng., Rear.	21/32	...	1 3/4	...	21/32	...	...	...	1 11/16	...	1 5/16	...
1966	2GC—326 Eng..	19/32	...	1 3/4	...	1 21/64	.160	INDEX	...	1 11/16	...	1 1/4	...
1967	BV—6 Cyl., 230 Eng.	1 9/32	...	1 7/8	...	.040	.230	...	...	1 9/16	...	1 11/32	...
1967	2GC—7027062, 071	9/16	...	1 9/16	...	1 11/32	.160	INDEX	...	1 11/16	...	1 1/4	...
1967	2GC	9/16	...	1 9/16	...	1 11/32	.160	INDEX	...	1 11/16	...	1 1/4	...
1967	4MV—7027260-261, M.T.	7/32	...	...	...	9/32	.325	Cent-Notch	.020	1 3/8	2 1/4	1 3/32	...
1967	4MV—7027260-261, A.T.	7/32	...	...	...	9/32	.325	Cent-Notch	.020	1 3/8	2 1/4	1 3/32	...
1967	4MV—7027262-263	3/16	...	...	...	9/32	.325	Cent-Notch	.020	1 3/8	2 1/4	1 3/32	...

Tempest—Firebird—Ventura II, continued

YEAR	MODEL OR TYPE	FLOAT LEVEL (IN.) Prim.	Sec.	FLOAT DROP (IN.) Prim.	Sec.	Pump Travel Setting (IN.)	CHOKE SETTING Unloader (IN.)	Housing	Secondary Lockout Adj.	Throttle Bore Diam. Prim.	Sec.	Venturi Diam. Prim.	Sec.
1968	MV—7028075-067	5/16	…	…	…	…	.245	…	…	1 11/16	…	1 1/4	…
1968	2BV—All	9/16	…	1 3/4	…	1 11/32	.180	…	…	1 11/16	…	1 3/32	…
1968	4MV—6 Cyl.	5/16	…	…	…	9/32	.300	…	.015	1 3/8	2 1/4	1 3/32	…
1968	4MV—All others	1/4	…	…	…	9/32	.300	…	.015	1 3/8	2 1/4	1 3/32	…
1968	BV—7028168	1 19/32	…	1 3/4	…	…	.230	…	…	1 9/16	…	1 11/32	…
1969	MV—7029165-67, M.T.	9/32	…	…	…	…	.450	…	…	1 11/16	…	…	…
1969	MV—7029166-68, A.T.	9/32	…	…	…	…	.450	…	…	1 11/16	…	…	…
1969	2GV—7029062, A.T.	9/16	…	1 3/4	…	1 11/32	.180	…	…	1 11/16	…	1 1/4	…
1969	4MV	9/32	…	…	…	9/32	.300	Cent-Notch	.015	1 3/8	2 1/4	1 3/32	…
1969	4MV—Ram Air	9/32	…	…	…	1/4	.300	Cent-Notch	.015	1 3/8	2 1/4	1 3/32	…
1970	MV—7040014—250, Auto	1/4	…	…	…	…	.350	…	…	1 11/16	…	…	…
1970	MV—7040017—250, Std.	1/4	…	…	…	…	.350	…	…	1 11/16	…	…	…
1970	2GV—7040060—400, Auto.	11/16	…	1 3/4	…	1 11/32	.180	…	…	1 11/16	…	1 3/8	…
1970	2GV—7040460—400, Auto.-cal.	11/16	…	1 3/4	…	1 11/32	.180	…	…	1 11/16	…	1 3/8	…
1970	2GV—7040461—400, Auto. w/AC-cal.	11/16	…	1 3/4	…	1 11/32	.180	…	…	1 11/16	…	1 3/8	…
1970	2GV—7040062—350, Auto.	9/16	…	1 3/4	…	1 11/32	.180	…	…	1 11/16	…	1 3/8	…
1970	2GV—7040462—350, Auto.-cal.	9/16	…	1 3/4	…	1 11/32	.180	…	…	1 11/16	…	1 3/8	…
1970	2GV—7040063—350, Auto. w/ac-cal.	9/16	…	1 3/4	…	1 11/32	.180	…	…	1 11/16	…	1 3/8	…
1970	2GV—7040064—400 Altitude, Auto	11/16	…	1 3/4	…	1 11/32	.180	…	…	1 11/16	…	1 3/8	…
1970	2GV—7040066—400, Std.	11/16	…	1 3/4	…	1 11/32	.180	…	…	1 11/16	…	1 3/8	…
1970	2GV—7040466—400, Std.-cal.	11/16	…	1 3/4	…	1 11/32	.180	…	…	1 11/16	…	1 3/8	…
1970	2GV—7040071—350, Std.	9/16	…	1 3/4	…	1 11/32	.180	…	…	1 11/16	…	1 3/8	…
1970	2GV—7040471—350, Std.-cal.	9/16	…	1 3/4	…	1 11/32	.180	…	…	1 11/16	…	1 3/8	…
1970	2GV—7040072—350 Altitude, std.	9/16	…	1 3/4	…	1 11/32	.180	…	…	1 11/16	…	1 3/8	…
1970	4MV—7040263—400 Std.-exc. Ram Air	9/32	…	…	…	…	…	Cent-Notch	.015	1 3/8	2 1/4	1 3/32	…
1970	4MV—7040263—400 Std. exc. Ram-Air-cal.	9/32	…	…	…	…	…	Cent-Notch	.015	1 3/8	2 1/4	1 3/32	…
1970	4MV—7040264—400, Auto.-exc Ram-Air	9/32	…	…	…	…	…	Cent-Notch	.015	1 3/8	2 1/4	1 3/32	…
1970	4MV—7040564—400, Auto.-exc. Ram-Air-cal.	9/32	…	…	…	…	…	Cent-Notch	.015	1 3/8	2 1/4	1 3/32	…
1970	4MV—7040267—455, Std.	9/32	…	…	…	…	…	Cent-Notch	.015	1 3/8	2 1/4	1 3/32	…
1970	4MV—7040567—455, Std.-cal.	9/32	…	…	…	…	…	Cent-Notch	.015	1 3/8	2 1/4	1 3/32	…
1970	4MV—7040268—455, Auto.	9/32	…	…	…	…	…	Cent-Notch	.015	1 3/8	2 1/4	1 3/32	…
1970	4MV—7040568—455, Auto-cal.	9/32	…	…	…	…	…	Cent-Notch	.015	1 3/8	2 1/4	1 3/32	…
1970	4MV—7040270—400, Auto, Ram Air III, IV	9/32	…	…	…	…	…	Cent-Notch	.015	1 3/8	2 1/4	1 3/32	…
1970	4MV—7040570—400, Auto, Ram-Air III, IV-cal.	9/32	…	…	…	…	…	Cent-Notch	.015	1 3/8	2 1/4	1 3/32	…
1970	4MV—7040273—400, Std. Ram-Air III, IV	9/32	…	…	…	…	…	Cent-Notch	.015	1 3/8	2 1/4	1 3/32	…
1970	4MV—7040274—455 Altitude, Auto.	9/32	…	…	…	…	…	Cent-Notch	.015	1 3/8	2 1/4	1 3/32	…
1971	MV—250	1/4	…	…	…	…	.350	…	…	1 11/16	…	…	…
1971	2GV—350, All	9/16	…	1 3/4	…	1 11/32	.180	…	…	1 11/16	…	1 3/8	…
1971	2GV—400, All	11/16	…	1 3/4	…	1 11/32	.180	…	…	1 11/16	…	1 3/8	…
1971	4MV—All	9/32	…	…	…	…	…	Cent-Notch	.015	1 3/8	2 1/4	1 7/32	…
1971	MV—Ventura II	1/4	…	…	…	…	.350	…	…	1 11/16	…	…	…
1971	2GV—Ventura II	27/32	…	1 3/4	…	1 13/32	.200	…	…	1 7/16	…	1 3/16	…

SINGLE BARREL—BC TYPE

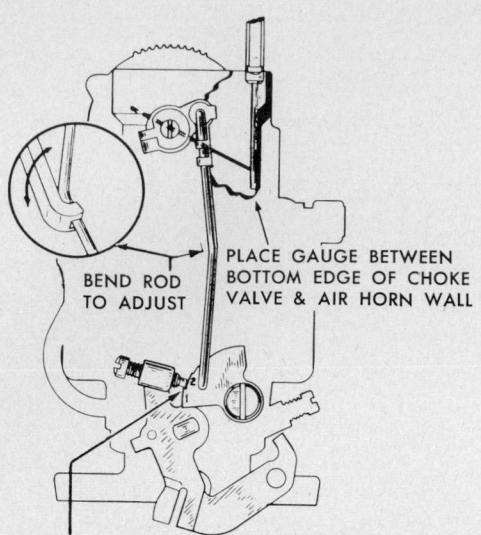

BEND ROD TO ADJUST

PLACE GAUGE BETWEEN BOTTOM EDGE OF CHOKE VALVE & AIR HORN WALL

SCREW ON SECOND STEP AGAINST HIGH STEP

BC choke rod setting

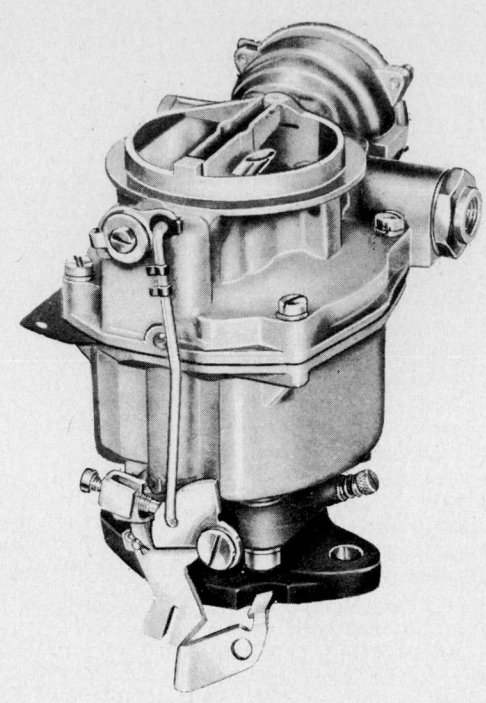

(© G.M. Corp.)

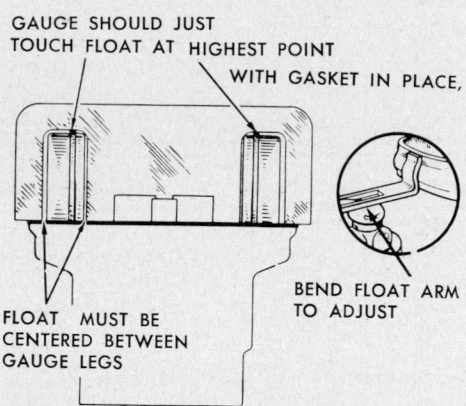

GAUGE SHOULD JUST TOUCH FLOAT AT HIGHEST POINT WITH GASKET IN PLACE,

BEND FLOAT ARM TO ADJUST

FLOAT MUST BE CENTERED BETWEEN GAUGE LEGS

BC float level adjustment (© G.M. Corp.)

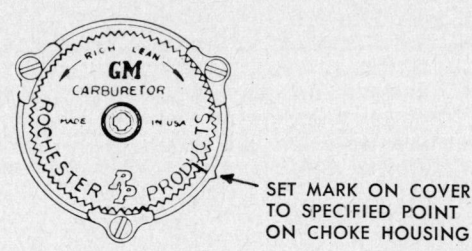

SET MARK ON COVER TO SPECIFIED POINT ON CHOKE HOUSING

BC automatic choke adjustment

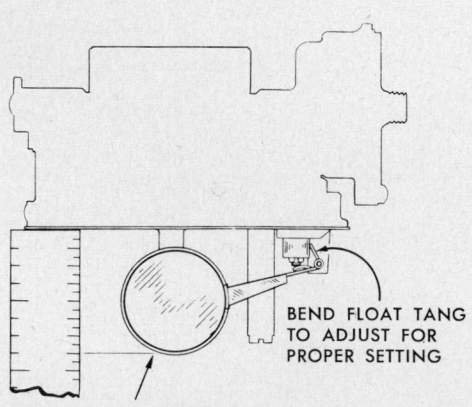

BEND FLOAT TANG TO ADJUST FOR PROPER SETTING

MEASURE FROM GASKET SURFACE TO BOTTOM OF FLOAT

BC float drop adjustment (© G.M. Corp.)

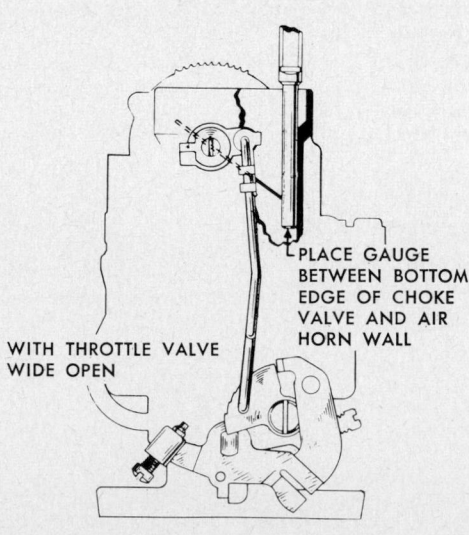

PLACE GAUGE BETWEEN BOTTOM EDGE OF CHOKE VALVE AND AIR HORN WALL

WITH THROTTLE VALVE WIDE OPEN

BC unloader setting (© G.M. Corp.)

FOUR BARREL—4GC TYPE

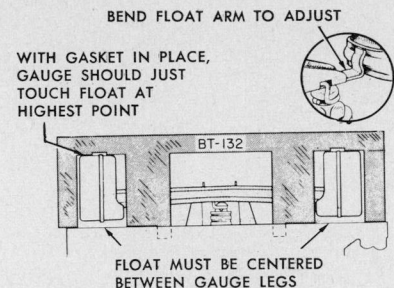

BEND FLOAT ARM TO ADJUST

WITH GASKET IN PLACE, GAUGE SHOULD JUST TOUCH FLOAT AT HIGHEST POINT

BT-132

FLOAT MUST BE CENTERED BETWEEN GAUGE LEGS

4GC float level adjustment

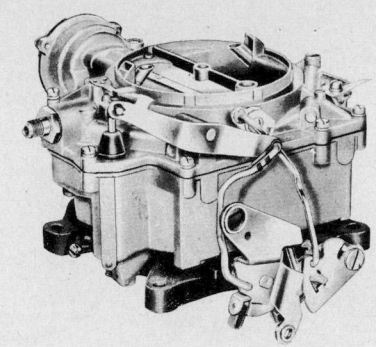

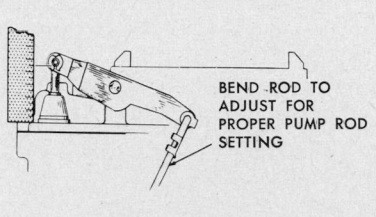

BEND FLOAT TANG TO ADJUST FOR PROPER SETTING

MEASURE FROM GASKET SURFACE TO BOTTOM OF FLOAT

4GC float drop adjustment

BEND FLOAT TANG TO ADJUST FOR PROPER SETTING

MEASURE FROM GASKET SURFACE TO BOTTOM OF FLOAT

4GC float drop adjustment

BEND ROD TO ADJUST FOR PROPER PUMP ROD SETTING

THROTTLE VALVES FULLY CLOSED

4GC pump rod setting

CHOKE VALVE FULLY CLOSED

INSERT FEELER GAUGE BETWEEN LOCKOUT LEVER AND FAST IDLE CAM

BEND TANG TO ADJUST FOR PROPER SETTING

4GC secondary lockout adjustment

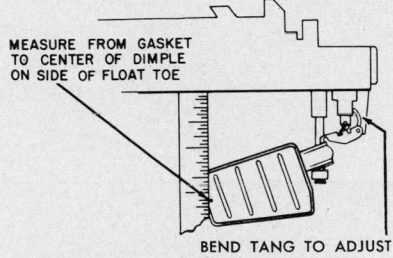

MEASURE FROM GASKET TO CENTER OF DIMPLE ON SIDE OF FLOAT TOE

BEND TANG TO ADJUST

4GC float adjustment

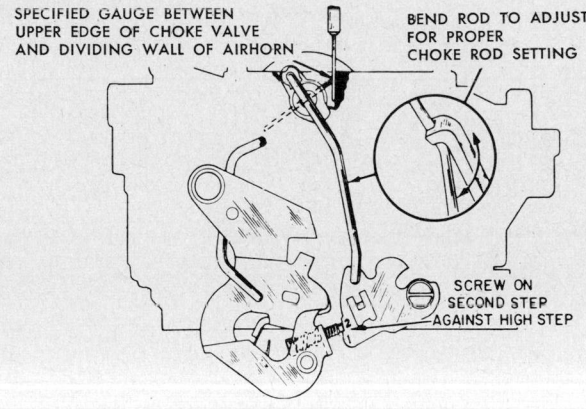

SPECIFIED GAUGE BETWEEN UPPER EDGE OF CHOKE VALVE AND DIVIDING WALL OF AIRHORN

BEND ROD TO ADJUST FOR PROPER CHOKE ROD SETTING

SCREW ON SECOND STEP AGAINST HIGH STEP

4GC choke rod adjustment

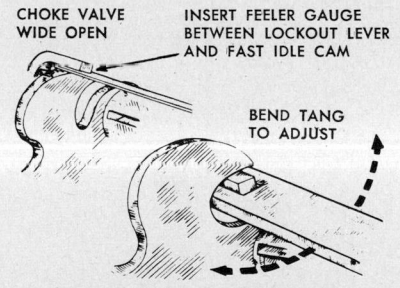

CHOKE VALVE WIDE OPEN

INSERT FEELER GAUGE BETWEEN LOCKOUT LEVER AND FAST IDLE CAM

BEND TANG TO ADJUST

4GC secondary contour adjustment

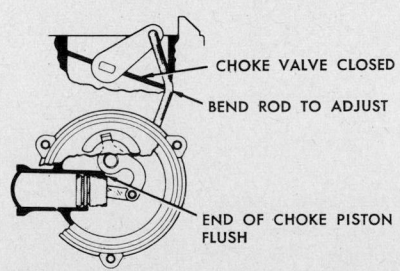

CHOKE VALVE CLOSED

BEND ROD TO ADJUST

END OF CHOKE PISTON FLUSH

4GC intermediate choke rod adjustment

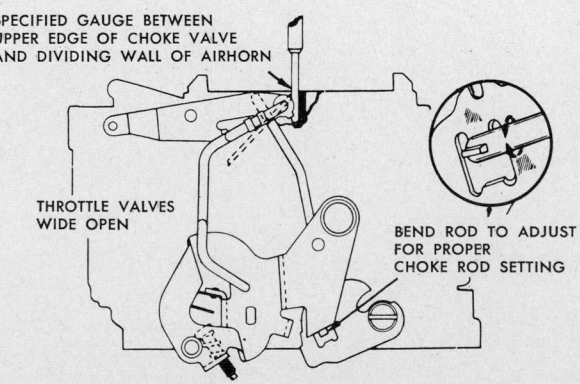

SPECIFIED GAUGE BETWEEN UPPER EDGE OF CHOKE VALVE AND DIVIDING WALL OF AIRHORN

THROTTLE VALVES WIDE OPEN

BEND ROD TO ADJUST FOR PROPER CHOKE ROD SETTING

4GC unloader adjustment

TWO BARREL 2GC-2GV

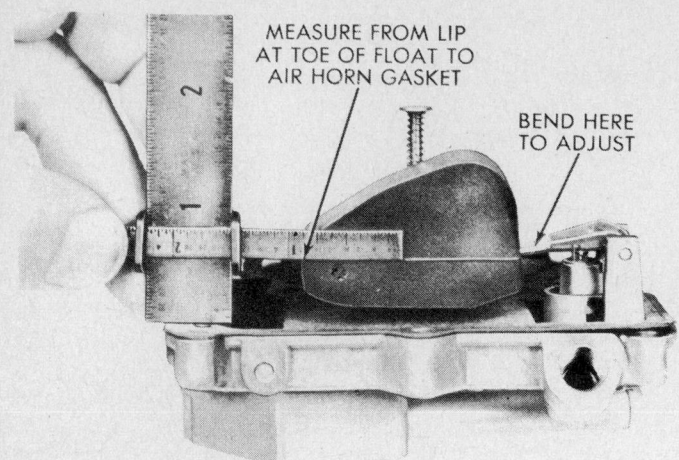

MEASURE FROM LIP AT TOE OF FLOAT TO AIR HORN GASKET

BEND HERE TO ADJUST

Float Setting, 2 Bbl. (Typical)
(© Dodge Division, Chrysler Corp.)

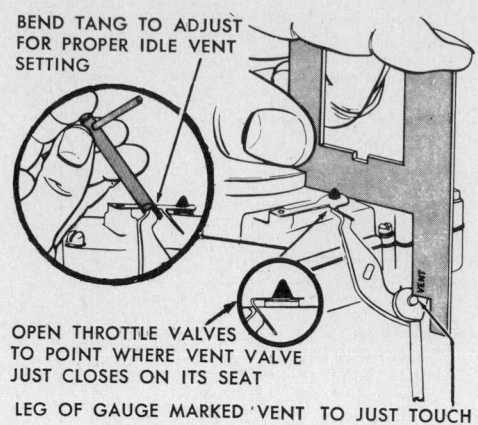

BEND TANG TO ADJUST FOR PROPER IDLE VENT SETTING

OPEN THROTTLE VALVES TO POINT WHERE VENT VALVE JUST CLOSES ON ITS SEAT

LEG OF GAUGE MARKED 'VENT' TO JUST TOUCH

2GC idle vent adjustment

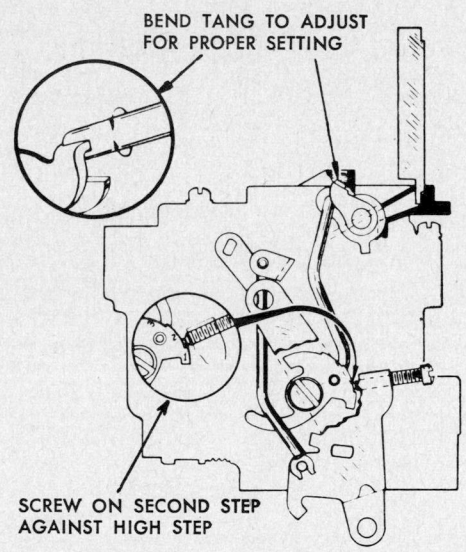

BEND TANG TO ADJUST FOR PROPER SETTING

SCREW ON SECOND STEP AGAINST HIGH STEP

2GC choke rod adjustment

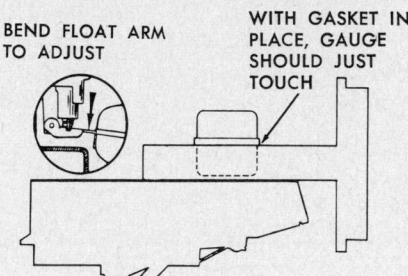

BEND FLOAT ARM TO ADJUST

WITH GASKET IN PLACE, GAUGE SHOULD JUST TOUCH

2GC float level adjustment

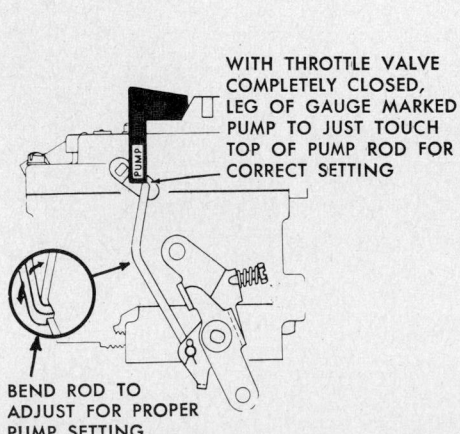

WITH THROTTLE VALVE COMPLETELY CLOSED, LEG OF GAUGE MARKED PUMP TO JUST TOUCH TOP OF PUMP ROD FOR CORRECT SETTING

BEND ROD TO ADJUST FOR PROPER PUMP SETTING

2GC pump rod adjustment

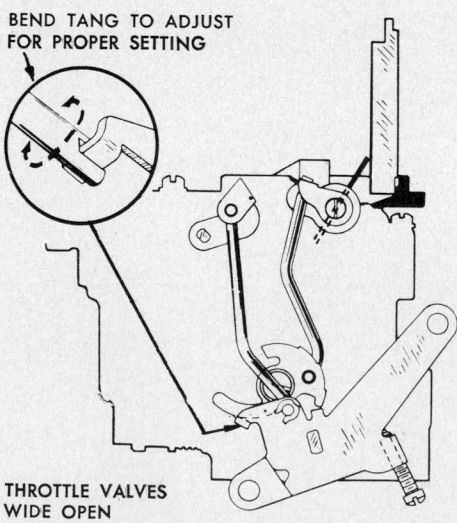

BEND TANG TO ADJUST FOR PROPER SETTING

THROTTLE VALVES WIDE OPEN

2GC unloader adjustment

TWO BARREL 2GC-2GV

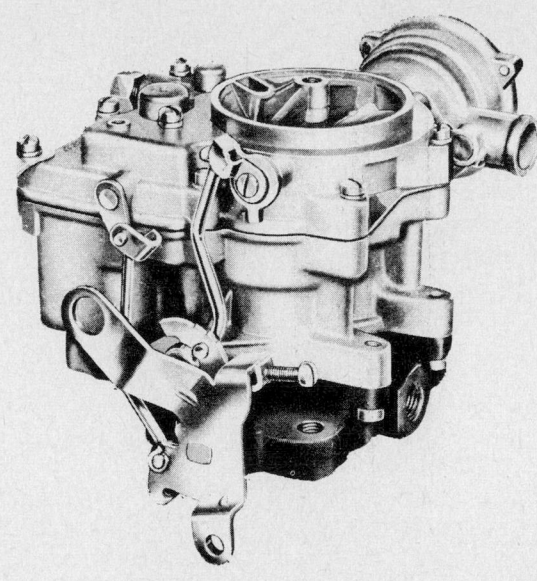

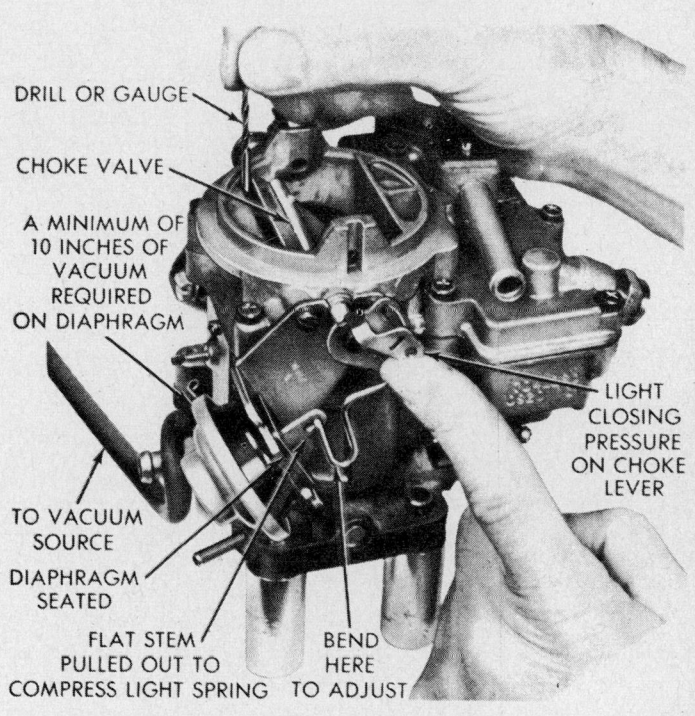

DRILL OR GAUGE

CHOKE VALVE

A MINIMUM OF 10 INCHES OF VACUUM REQUIRED ON DIAPHRAGM

LIGHT CLOSING PRESSURE ON CHOKE LEVER

TO VACUUM SOURCE

DIAPHRAGM SEATED

FLAT STEM PULLED OUT TO COMPRESS LIGHT SPRING

BEND HERE TO ADJUST

Vacuum Kick Setting, 2 Bbl. (Typical)
(© Dodge Division, Chrysler Corp.)

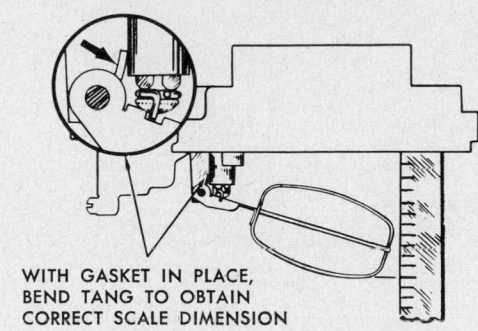

WITH GASKET IN PLACE, BEND TANG TO OBTAIN CORRECT SCALE DIMENSION

2GC float drop adjustment

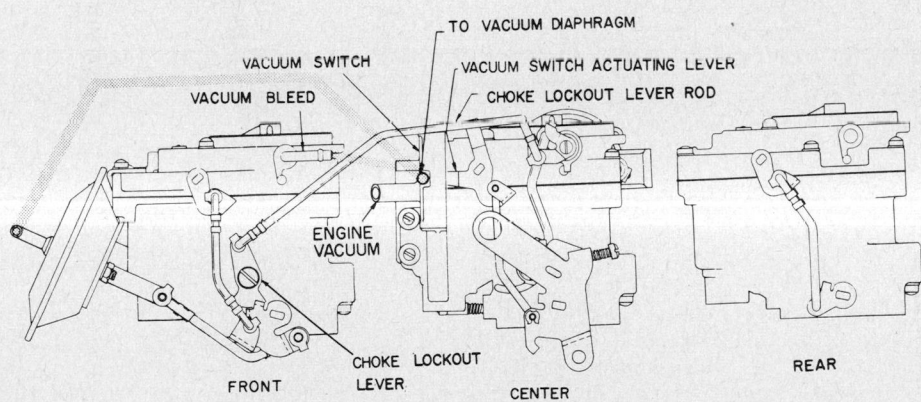

VACUUM SWITCH

VACUUM BLEED

TO VACUUM DIAPHRAGM

VACUUM SWITCH ACTUATING LEVER

CHOKE LOCKOUT LEVER ROD

ENGINE VACUUM

CHOKE LOCKOUT LEVER

FRONT

CENTER

REAR

Typical three two-barrel carburetor installation

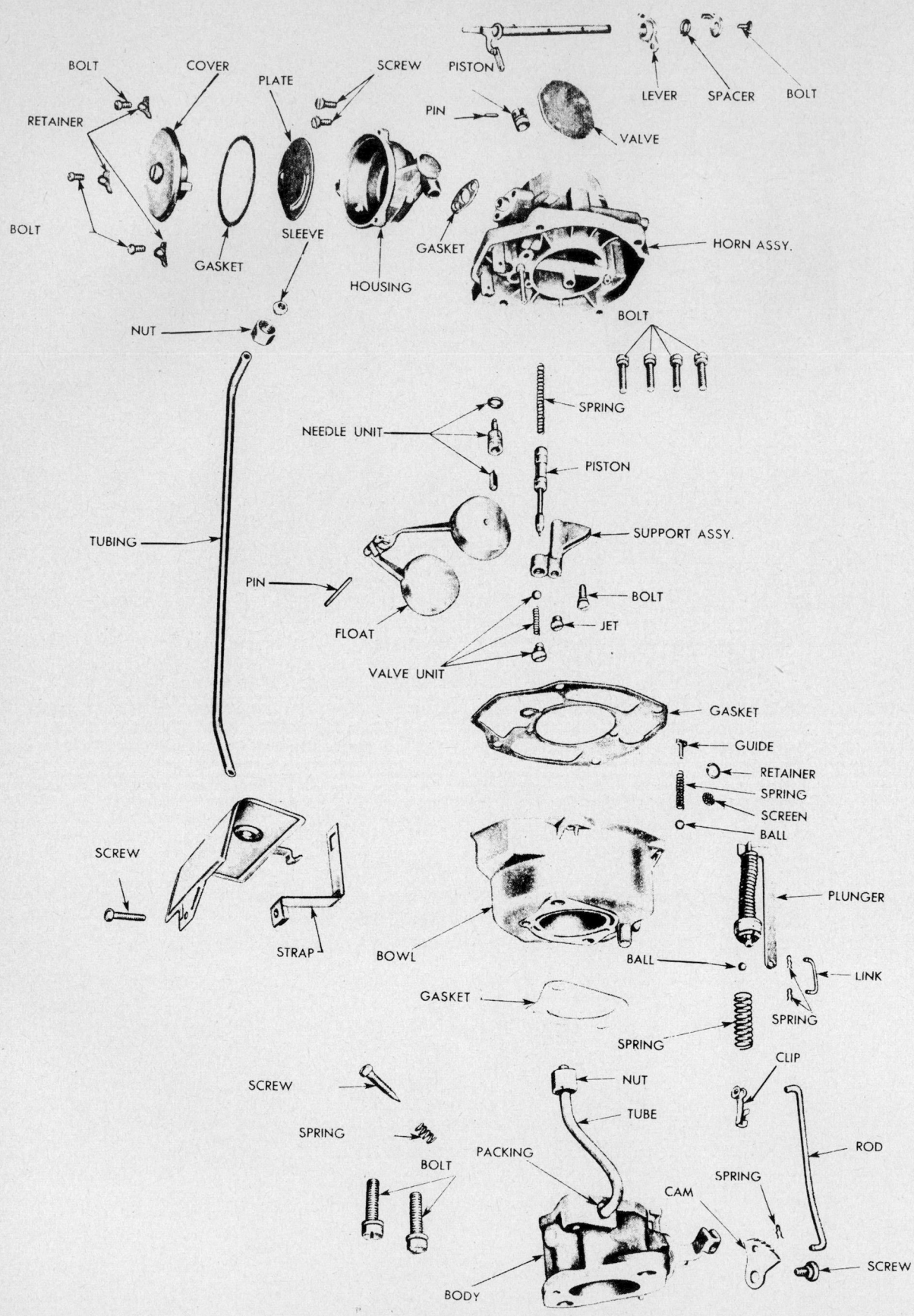

Rochester BC single-barrel (© Chevrolet Div., G.M. Corp.)

SINGLE BARREL MV

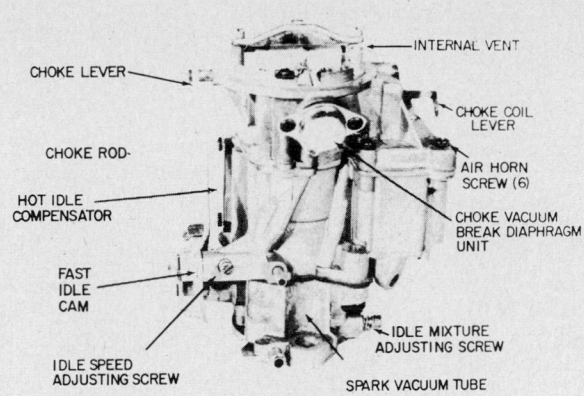

MV Carburetor
((C) Pontiac Division, GM Corp.)

- INTERNAL VENT
- CHOKE LEVER
- CHOKE COIL LEVER
- CHOKE ROD
- AIR HORN SCREW (6)
- HOT IDLE COMPENSATOR
- CHOKE VACUUM BREAK DIAPHRAGM UNIT
- FAST IDLE CAM
- IDLE MIXTURE ADJUSTING SCREW
- IDLE SPEED ADJUSTING SCREW
- SPARK VACUUM TUBE

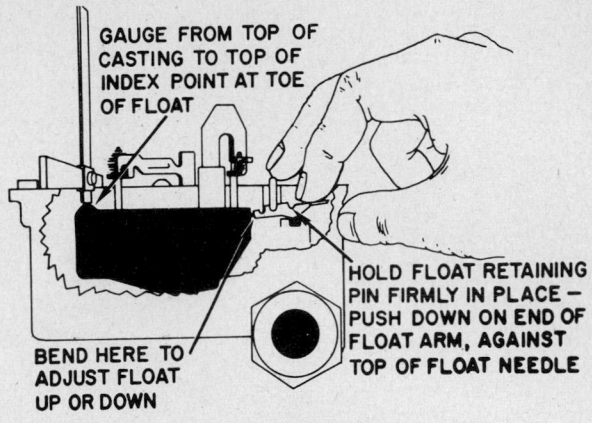

Float Level Setting
((C) Pontiac Division, GM Corp.)

- GAUGE FROM TOP OF CASTING TO TOP OF INDEX POINT AT TOE OF FLOAT
- HOLD FLOAT RETAINING PIN FIRMLY IN PLACE — PUSH DOWN ON END OF FLOAT ARM, AGAINST TOP OF FLOAT NEEDLE
- BEND HERE TO ADJUST FLOAT UP OR DOWN

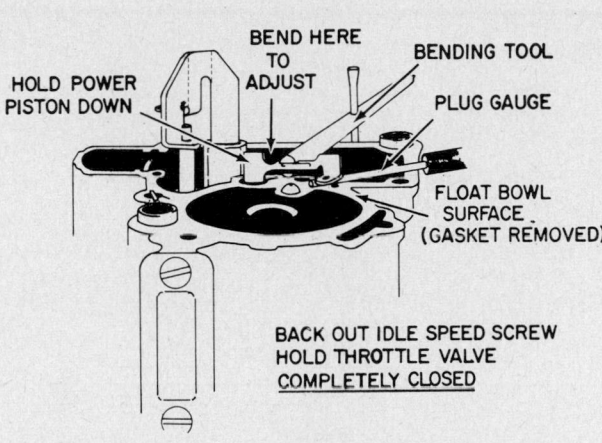

Metering Rod Adjustment
((C) Pontiac Division, GM Corp.)

- HOLD POWER PISTON DOWN
- BEND HERE TO ADJUST
- BENDING TOOL
- PLUG GAUGE
- FLOAT BOWL SURFACE (GASKET REMOVED)
- BACK OUT IDLE SPEED SCREW HOLD THROTTLE VALVE COMPLETELY CLOSED

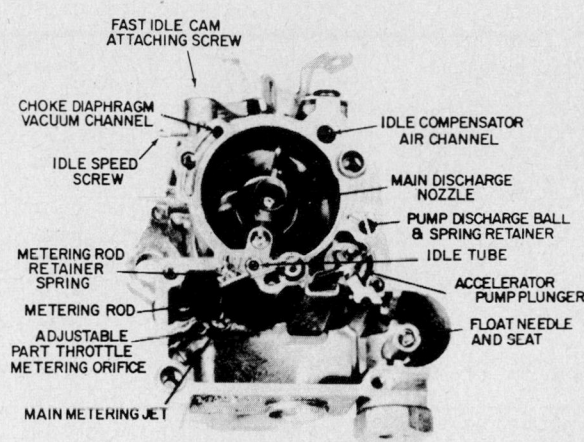

Float Bowl Assembly
((C) Pontiac Division, GM Corp.)

- FAST IDLE CAM ATTACHING SCREW
- CHOKE DIAPHRAGM VACUUM CHANNEL
- IDLE SPEED SCREW
- IDLE COMPENSATOR AIR CHANNEL
- MAIN DISCHARGE NOZZLE
- PUMP DISCHARGE BALL & SPRING RETAINER
- IDLE TUBE
- ACCELERATOR PUMP PLUNGER
- FLOAT NEEDLE AND SEAT
- METERING ROD RETAINER SPRING
- METERING ROD
- ADJUSTABLE PART THROTTLE METERING ORIFICE
- MAIN METERING JET

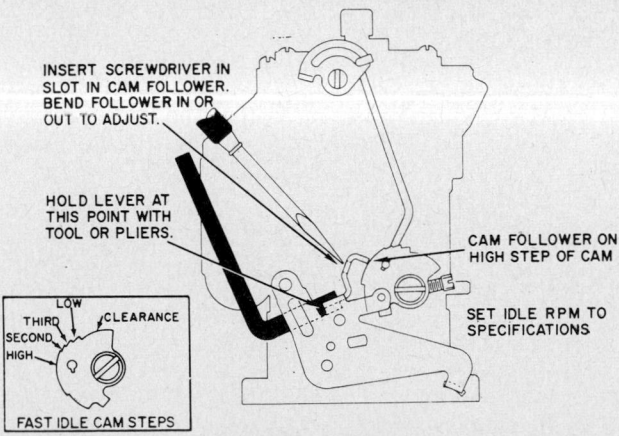

Fast Idle Adjustment
((C) Pontiac Division, GM Corp.)

- INSERT SCREWDRIVER IN SLOT IN CAM FOLLOWER. BEND FOLLOWER IN OR OUT TO ADJUST.
- HOLD LEVER AT THIS POINT WITH TOOL OR PLIERS.
- CAM FOLLOWER ON HIGH STEP OF CAM
- SET IDLE RPM TO SPECIFICATIONS
- LOW
- THIRD
- SECOND
- HIGH
- CLEARANCE
- FAST IDLE CAM STEPS

SINGLE BARREL MV

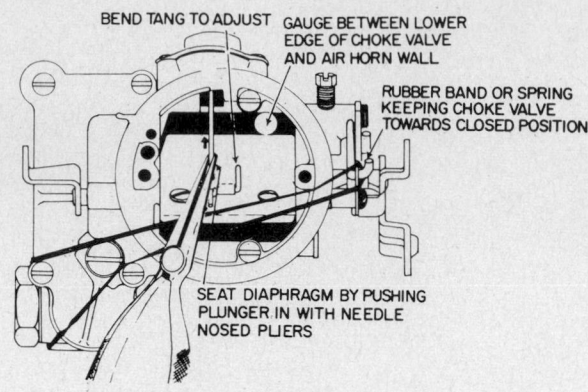

Vacuum Break Setting
(© Pontiac Division, GM Corp.)

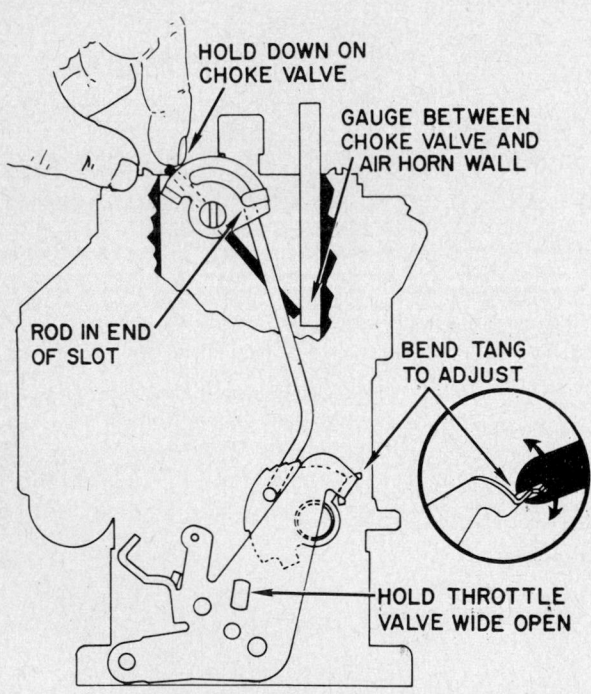

Unloader Adjustment
(© Pontiac Division, GM Corp.)

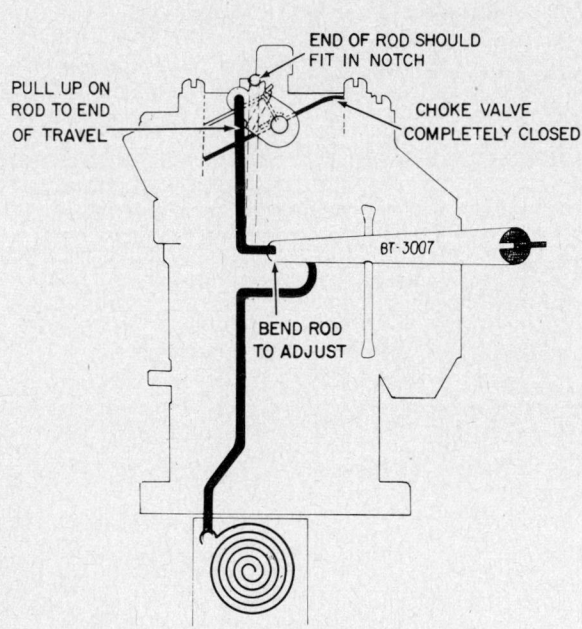

Choke Coil Rod Adjustment
(© Pontiac Division, GM Corp.)

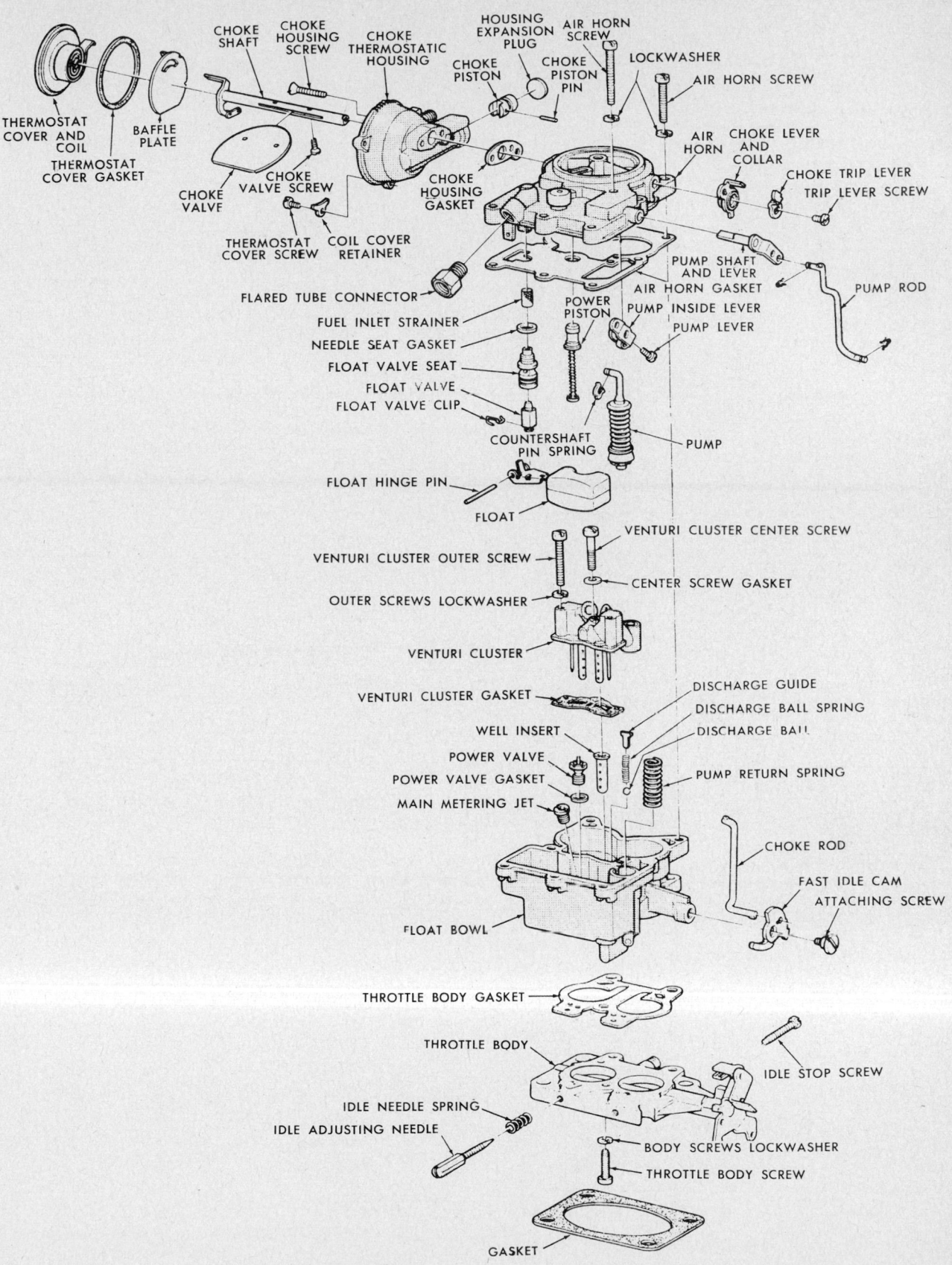

THERMOSTAT COVER AND COIL

THERMOSTAT COVER GASKET

BAFFLE PLATE

CHOKE SHAFT

CHOKE HOUSING SCREW

CHOKE THERMOSTATIC HOUSING

HOUSING EXPANSION PLUG

AIR HORN SCREW

CHOKE PISTON

CHOKE PISTON PIN

LOCKWASHER

AIR HORN SCREW

AIR HORN

CHOKE LEVER AND COLLAR

CHOKE TRIP LEVER

TRIP LEVER SCREW

CHOKE VALVE

CHOKE VALVE SCREW

THERMOSTAT COVER SCREW

COIL COVER RETAINER

CHOKE HOUSING GASKET

FLARED TUBE CONNECTOR

FUEL INLET STRAINER

NEEDLE SEAT GASKET

FLOAT VALVE SEAT

FLOAT VALVE

FLOAT VALVE CLIP

COUNTERSHAFT PIN SPRING

POWER PISTON

PUMP SHAFT AND LEVER

AIR HORN GASKET

PUMP INSIDE LEVER

PUMP LEVER

PUMP ROD

PUMP

FLOAT HINGE PIN

FLOAT

VENTURI CLUSTER CENTER SCREW

VENTURI CLUSTER OUTER SCREW

OUTER SCREWS LOCKWASHER

CENTER SCREW GASKET

VENTURI CLUSTER

VENTURI CLUSTER GASKET

WELL INSERT

POWER VALVE

POWER VALVE GASKET

MAIN METERING JET

DISCHARGE GUIDE

DISCHARGE BALL SPRING

DISCHARGE BALL

PUMP RETURN SPRING

CHOKE ROD

FAST IDLE CAM

ATTACHING SCREW

FLOAT BOWL

THROTTLE BODY GASKET

THROTTLE BODY

IDLE STOP SCREW

IDLE NEEDLE SPRING

IDLE ADJUSTING NEEDLE

BODY SCREWS LOCKWASHER

THROTTLE BODY SCREW

GASKET

Rochester 2GC two-barrel (© Buick Div., G.M. Corp.)

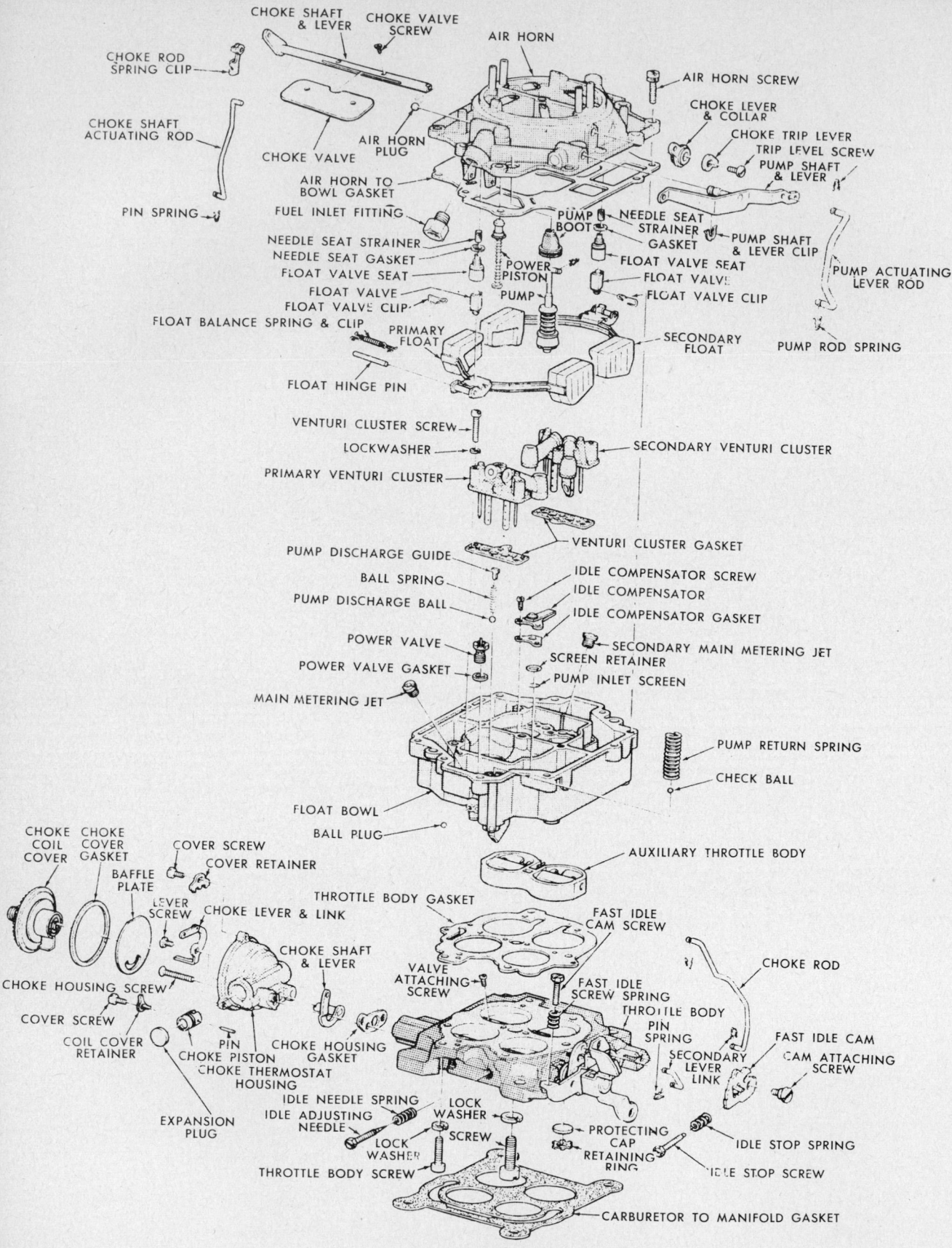

CHOKE SHAFT & LEVER
CHOKE VALVE SCREW
AIR HORN
AIR HORN SCREW
CHOKE ROD SPRING CLIP
CHOKE LEVER & COLLAR
CHOKE TRIP LEVER
TRIP LEVEL SCREW
PUMP SHAFT & LEVER
CHOKE SHAFT ACTUATING ROD
AIR HORN PLUG
CHOKE VALVE
AIR HORN TO BOWL GASKET
FUEL INLET FITTING
PIN SPRING
PUMP BOOT
NEEDLE SEAT STRAINER GASKET
PUMP SHAFT & LEVER CLIP
NEEDLE SEAT STRAINER
NEEDLE SEAT GASKET
FLOAT VALVE SEAT
FLOAT VALVE
FLOAT VALVE CLIP
POWER PISTON
FLOAT VALVE SEAT
PUMP
FLOAT VALVE
FLOAT VALVE CLIP
PUMP ACTUATING LEVER ROD
FLOAT BALANCE SPRING & CLIP
PRIMARY FLOAT
SECONDARY FLOAT
PUMP ROD SPRING
FLOAT HINGE PIN
VENTURI CLUSTER SCREW
SECONDARY VENTURI CLUSTER
LOCKWASHER
PRIMARY VENTURI CLUSTER
VENTURI CLUSTER GASKET
PUMP DISCHARGE GUIDE
IDLE COMPENSATOR SCREW
BALL SPRING
IDLE COMPENSATOR
PUMP DISCHARGE BALL
IDLE COMPENSATOR GASKET
POWER VALVE
SECONDARY MAIN METERING JET
POWER VALVE GASKET
SCREEN RETAINER
PUMP INLET SCREEN
MAIN METERING JET
PUMP RETURN SPRING
CHECK BALL
FLOAT BOWL
BALL PLUG
AUXILIARY THROTTLE BODY
CHOKE COIL COVER
CHOKE COVER GASKET
COVER SCREW
COVER RETAINER
BAFFLE PLATE
LEVER SCREW
CHOKE LEVER & LINK
THROTTLE BODY GASKET
FAST IDLE CAM SCREW
CHOKE SHAFT & LEVER
VALVE ATTACHING SCREW
FAST IDLE SCREW SPRING
CHOKE ROD
CHOKE HOUSING SCREW
THROTTLE BODY PIN SPRING
COVER SCREW
PIN
CHOKE HOUSING GASKET
FAST IDLE CAM
COIL COVER RETAINER
CHOKE PISTON
SECONDARY LEVER LINK
CAM ATTACHING SCREW
CHOKE THERMOSTAT HOUSING
IDLE NEEDLE SPRING
EXPANSION PLUG
IDLE ADJUSTING NEEDLE
LOCK WASHER
PROTECTING CAP RETAINING RING
IDLE STOP SPRING
LOCK WASHER
SCREW
IDLE STOP SCREW
THROTTLE BODY SCREW
CARBURETOR TO MANIFOLD GASKET

Rochester 4GC four-barrel (© Buick Div., G.M. Corp.)

FOUR BARREL QUADRAJET

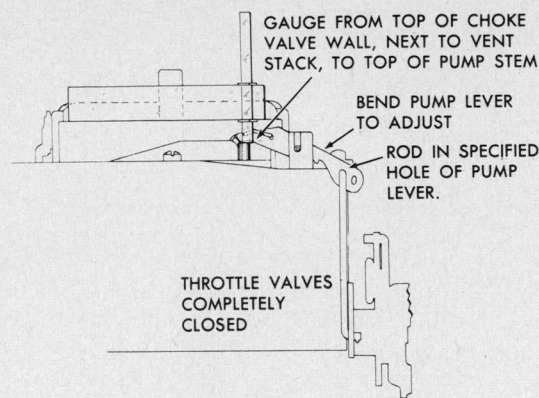

GAUGE FROM TOP OF CHOKE VALVE WALL, NEXT TO VENT STACK, TO TOP OF PUMP STEM

BEND PUMP LEVER TO ADJUST

ROD IN SPECIFIED HOLE OF PUMP LEVER.

THROTTLE VALVES COMPLETELY CLOSED

Pump rod adjustment

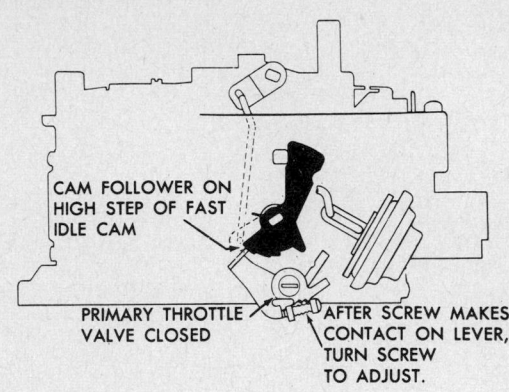

CAM FOLLOWER ON HIGH STEP OF FAST IDLE CAM

PRIMARY THROTTLE VALVE CLOSED

AFTER SCREW MAKES CONTACT ON LEVER, TURN SCREW TO ADJUST.

Fast idle adjustment

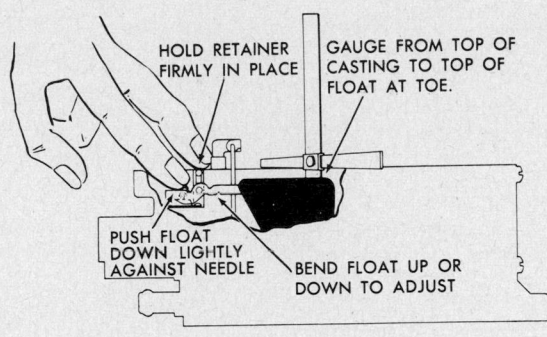

HOLD RETAINER FIRMLY IN PLACE

GAUGE FROM TOP OF CASTING TO TOP OF FLOAT AT TOE.

PUSH FLOAT DOWN LIGHTLY AGAINST NEEDLE

BEND FLOAT UP OR DOWN TO ADJUST

Float level adjustment

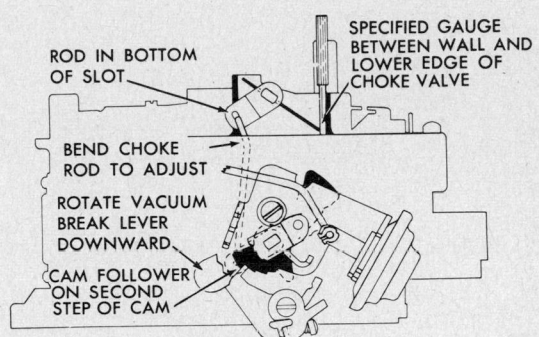

ROD IN BOTTOM OF SLOT

SPECIFIED GAUGE BETWEEN WALL AND LOWER EDGE OF CHOKE VALVE

BEND CHOKE ROD TO ADJUST

ROTATE VACUUM BREAK LEVER DOWNWARD.

CAM FOLLOWER ON SECOND STEP OF CAM

Choke rod adjustment

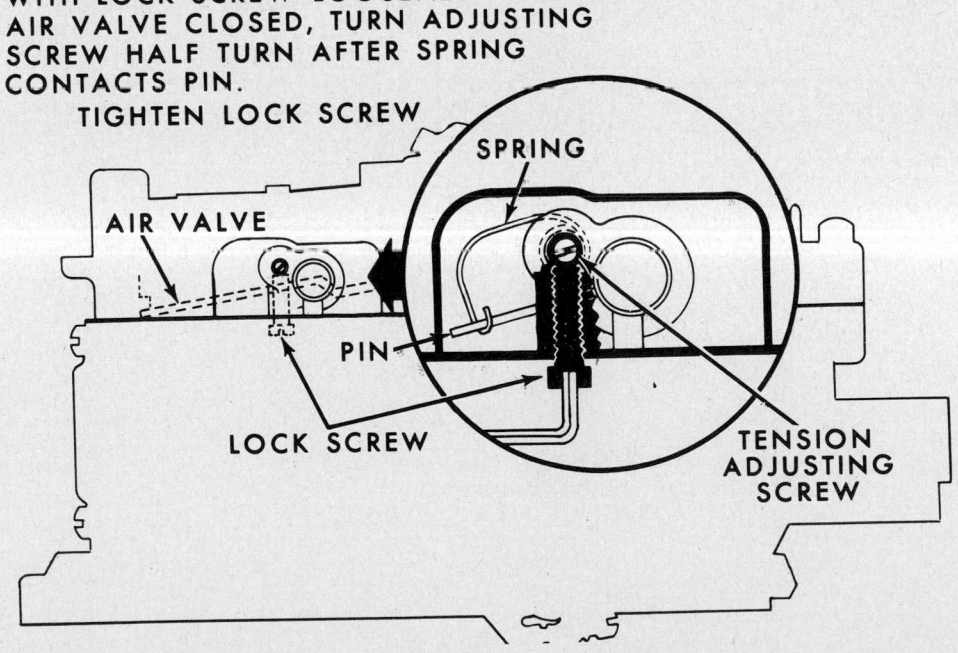

WITH LOCK SCREW LOOSENED AND WITH AIR VALVE CLOSED, TURN ADJUSTING SCREW HALF TURN AFTER SPRING CONTACTS PIN. TIGHTEN LOCK SCREW

SPRING

AIR VALVE

PIN

LOCK SCREW

TENSION ADJUSTING SCREW

Air Valve Spring Setting (© Pontiac Division, GM Corp.)

FOUR BARREL QUADRAJET

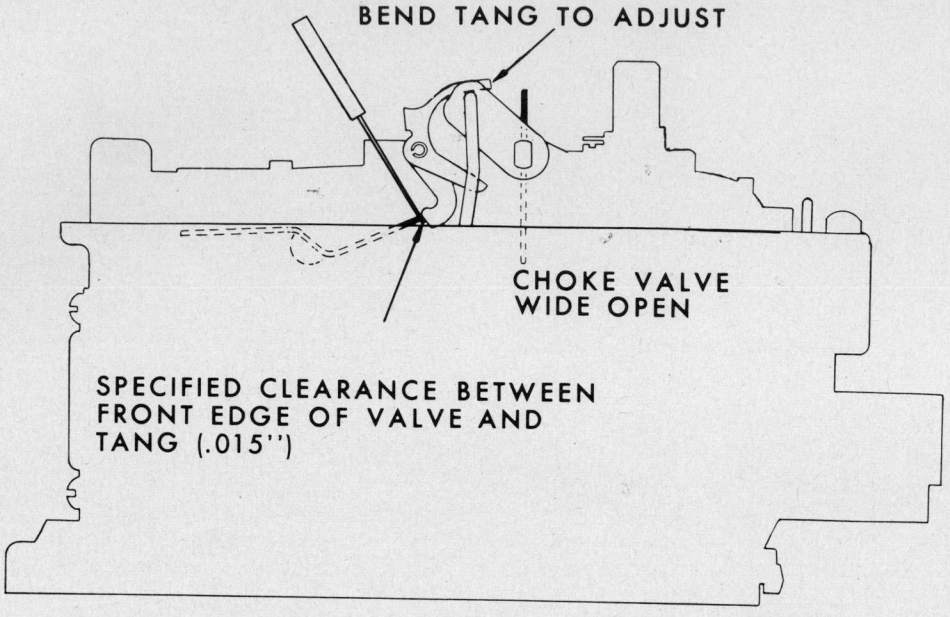

BEND TANG TO ADJUST

CHOKE VALVE
WIDE OPEN

SPECIFIED CLEARANCE BETWEEN
FRONT EDGE OF VALVE AND
TANG (.015'')

Air Valve Lockout Adjustment (© Pontiac Division, GM Corp.)

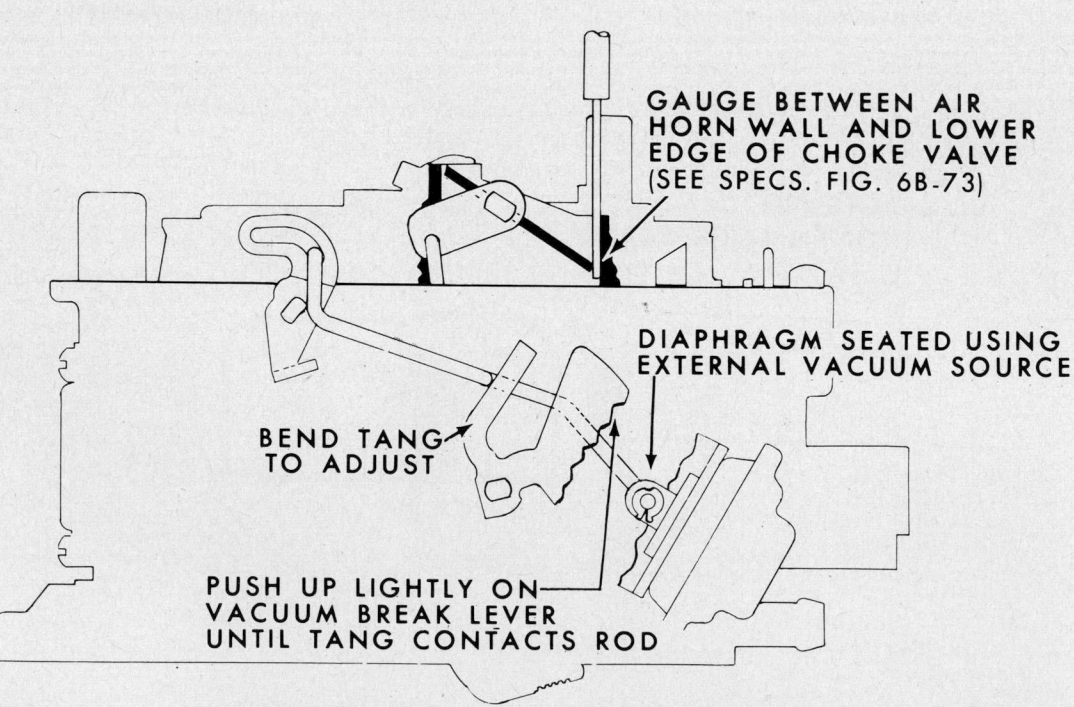

GAUGE BETWEEN AIR
HORN WALL AND LOWER
EDGE OF CHOKE VALVE
(SEE SPECS. FIG. 6B-73)

DIAPHRAGM SEATED USING
EXTERNAL VACUUM SOURCE

BEND TANG
TO ADJUST

PUSH UP LIGHTLY ON
VACUUM BREAK LEVER
UNTIL TANG CONTACTS ROD

Vacuum Break Adjustment (© Pontiac Division, GM Corp.)

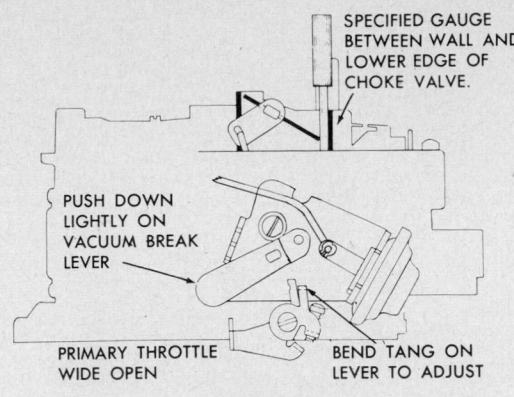

Unloader adjustment

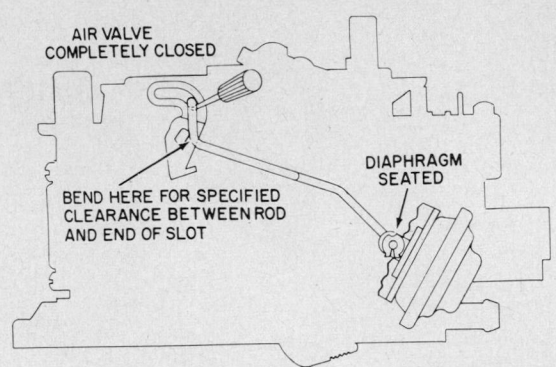

Air valve dashpot adjustment

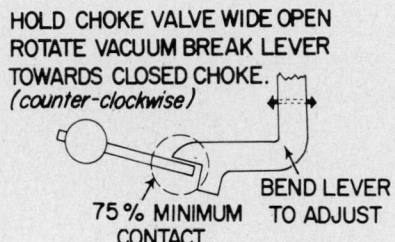

HOLD CHOKE VALVE WIDE OPEN ROTATE VACUUM BREAK LEVER TOWARDS CLOSED CHOKE. (counter-clockwise)

75% MINIMUM CONTACT

BEND LEVER TO ADJUST

SECONDARY LOCKOUT LEVER ADJUSTMENT

①

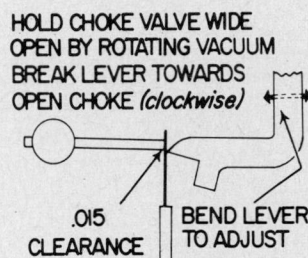

HOLD CHOKE VALVE WIDE OPEN BY ROTATING VACUUM BREAK LEVER TOWARDS OPEN CHOKE (clockwise)

.015 CLEARANCE

BEND LEVER TO ADJUST

SECONDARY LOCKOUT OPENING CLEARANCE

②

Secondary lockout adjustment

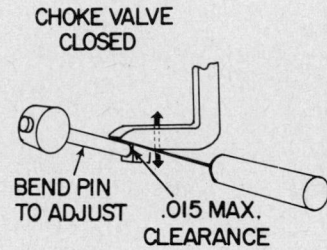

CHOKE VALVE CLOSED

BEND PIN TO ADJUST

.015 MAX. CLEARANCE

SECONDARY LOCKOUT LEVER SIDE CLEARANCE

③

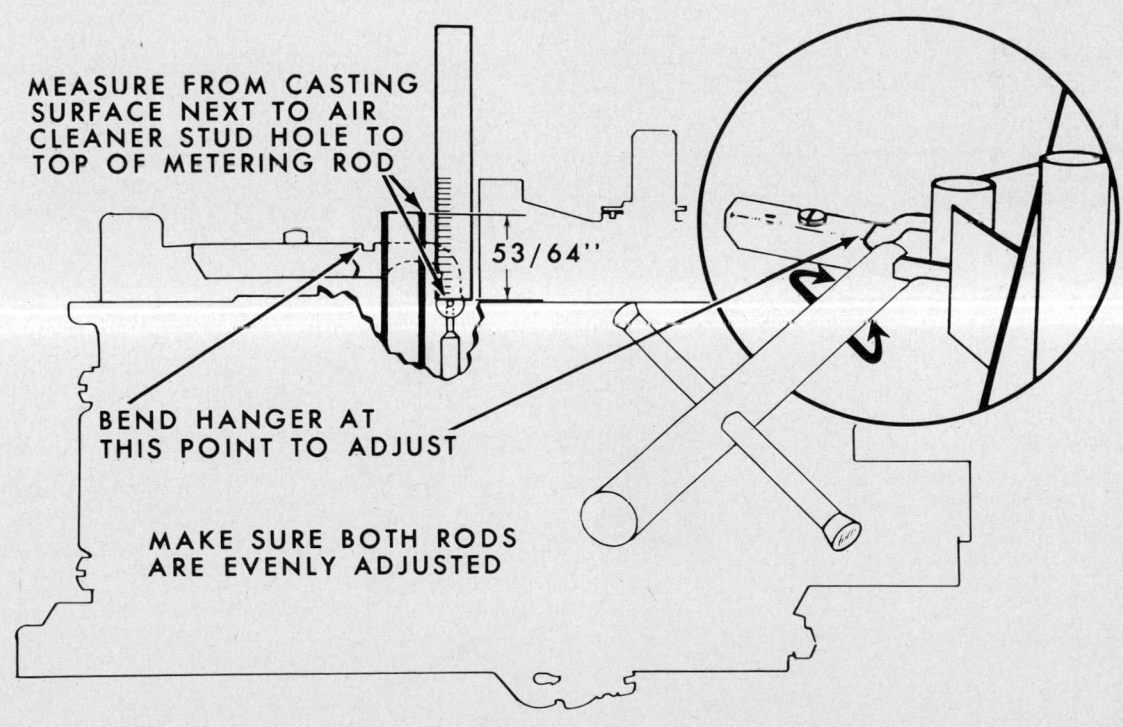

MEASURE FROM CASTING SURFACE NEXT TO AIR CLEANER STUD HOLE TO TOP OF METERING ROD

53/64"

BEND HANGER AT THIS POINT TO ADJUST

MAKE SURE BOTH RODS ARE EVENLY ADJUSTED

Secondary Metering Rod Adjustment (© Pontiac Division, GM Corp.)

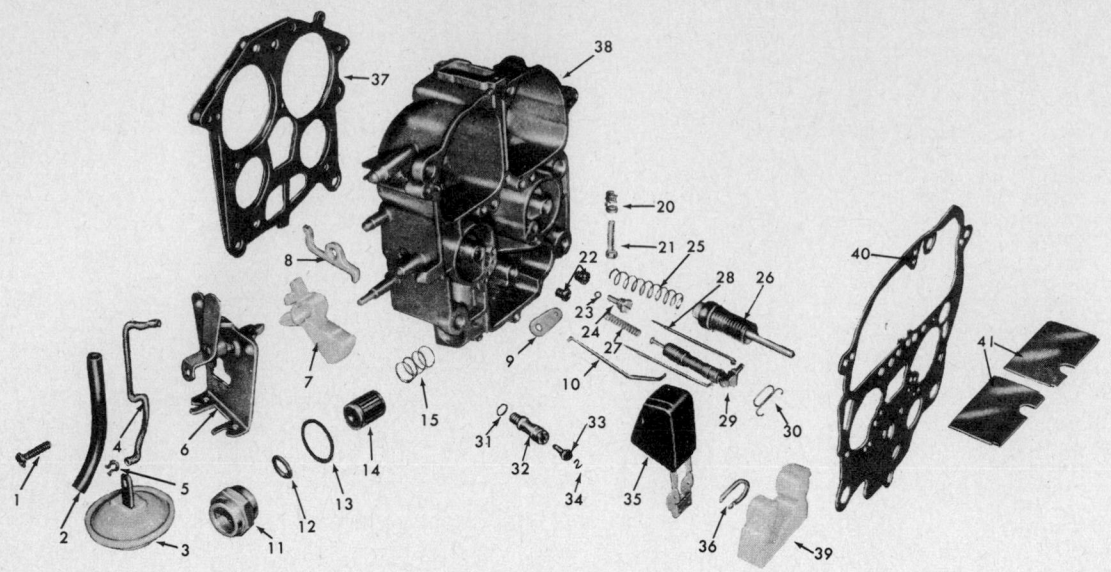

Exploded view—4MV Quadrajet float bowl

1 Screw—choke control
2 Hose—vacuum break
3 Vacuum break
4 Link—vacuum break
5 Clip—Vacuum break rod
6 Bracket assembly—
      choke control
7 Cam—fast idle
8 Lever—secondary lock out
9 Lever—choke intermediate
10 Rod—choke
11 Nut—fuel inlet
12 Gasket—fuel filter
13 Gasket—fuel inlet nut

14 Filter—fuel inlet
15 Spring—fuel filter
20 Spring—idle speed screw
21 Screw—idle speed
22 Jet—primary
23 Ball—pump discharge
24 Retainer—pump discharge
      ball
25 Spring—pump return
26 Pump assembly
27 Spring—power piston
28 Metering rod—primary
29 Power piston assembly—
      primary

30 Spring—metering rod primary
31 Gasket—float needle seat
32 Seat—float needle
33 Needle—float
34 Pull clip—float needle
35 Float assembly
36 Hinge pin—float assembly
37 Gasket—throttle body
38 Float bowl assembly
39 Insert—float bowl
40 Gasket—air horn
41 Baffle—float bowl

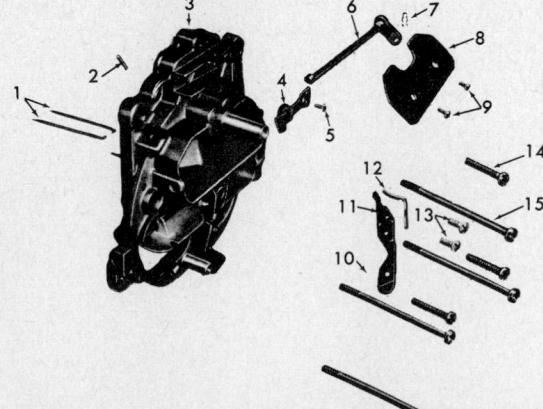

1 Metering rod—secondary
2 Roll pin—pump lever
3 Air horn assembly
4 Idle vent valve
5 Screw—idle vent valve
6 Choke shaft and lever
      assembly
7 Clip—choke rod
8 Choke valve

9 Screw—choke valve
10 Clip—pump rod
11 Lever—pump actuating
12 Lever—idle vent valve
13 Screw—air horn
14 (Counter sunk)
      screw—air horn (short)
15 Screw—air horn (long)

Exploded view—4MV Quadrajet air horn

Stromberg Carburetors

YEAR	MODEL OR TYPE	FLOAT LEVEL		Bowl Vent Drop (In.)	Pump Travel Setting (In.)	CHOKE SETTING		Secondary Lockout Adj.	Throttle Bore Diam.		Venturi Diam.	
		Primary (In.)	Secondary (In.)			Unloader (In.)	Housing		Prim.	Sec.	Prim.	Sec.
Chrysler Corp.												
1965	WW3—248, 49, 50, 51	7/32	...	5/64	...	5/16	INDEX	...	1 7/16	...	1 1/8	...
1965	WWC3—254	5/32	...	1/16 - 3/32	11/32	15/64	1-RICH	...	1 9/16	...	1 5/16	...
1965	WWC3—255	5/32	...	1/16 - 3/32	7/16	15/64	1-RICH	...	1 9/16	...	1 5/16	...
1966	WW3—258, 259	7/32	...	.060	...	5/16	2-RICH	...	1 7/16	...	1 3/16	...
1966	WW3—260, 261	7/32	...	.050	...	5/16	INDEX	...	1 7/16	...	1 1/8	...
1966	WWC3—262	5/32	...	.040	7/16	15/64	2-RICH	...	1 9/16	...	1 5/16	...
1966	WWC3—263	5/32	...	.020	7/16	15/64	INDEX	...	1 9/16	...	1 5/16	...
1967	WW3	7/32	...	.060	...	5/16	2-RICH	...	1 7/16	...	1 1/8	...
1967	WW3	7/32	...	.050	...	5/16	INDEX	...	1 7/16	...	1 1/8	...
1967	WWC3	5/32	...	.040	7/16	15/64	2-RICH	...	1 9/16	...	1 1/8	...

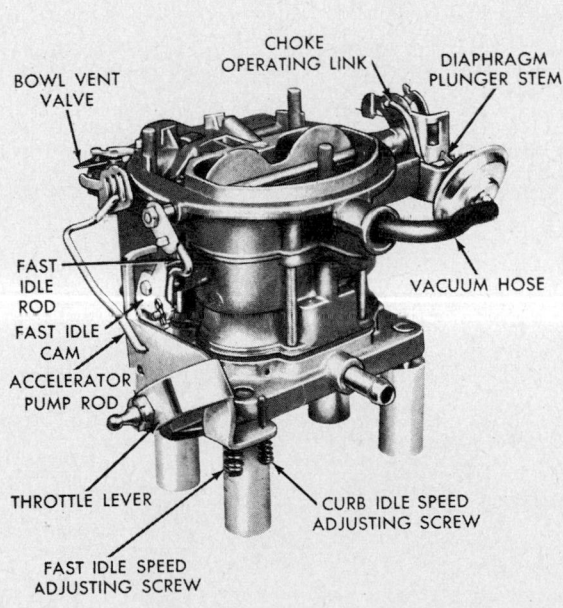

WWC Carburetor, Left Side
(© Plymouth Division, Chrysler Corp.)

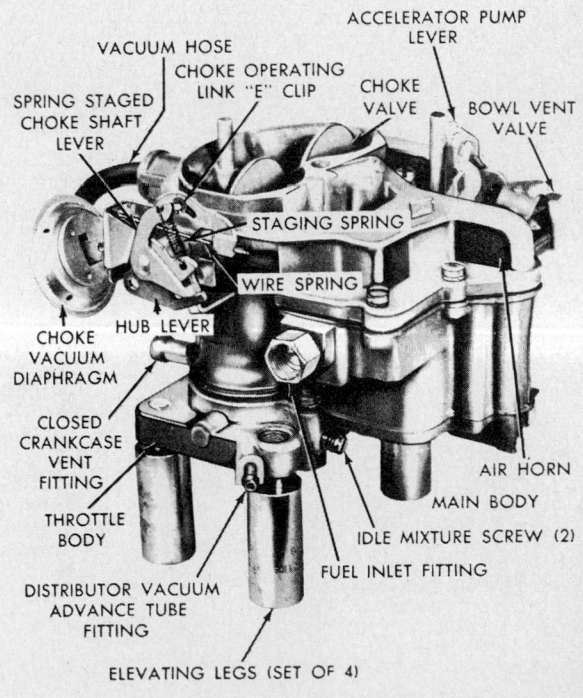

WWC Carburetor, Right Side
(© Plymouth Division, Chrysler Corp.)

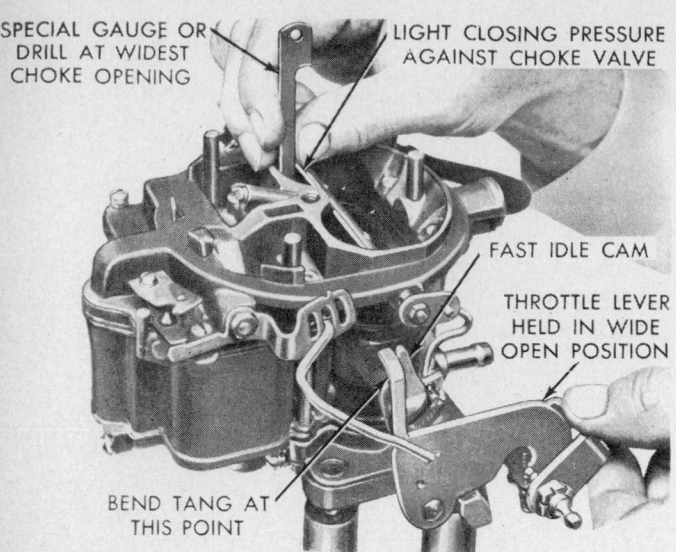

SPECIAL GAUGE OR
DRILL AT WIDEST
CHOKE OPENING

LIGHT CLOSING PRESSURE
AGAINST CHOKE VALVE

FAST IDLE CAM

THROTTLE LEVER
HELD IN WIDE
OPEN POSITION

BEND TANG AT
THIS POINT

Unloader Adjustment
(© Plymouth Division, Chrysler Corp.)

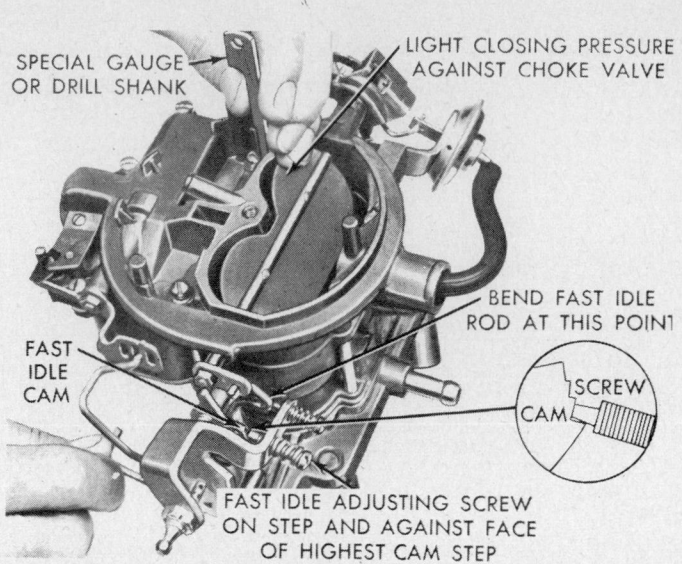

SPECIAL GAUGE
OR DRILL SHANK

LIGHT CLOSING PRESSURE
AGAINST CHOKE VALVE

FAST
IDLE
CAM

BEND FAST IDLE
ROD AT THIS POINT

SCREW
CAM

FAST IDLE ADJUSTING SCREW
ON STEP AND AGAINST FACE
OF HIGHEST CAM STEP

Fast Idle Cam Setting
(© Plymouth Division, Chrysler Corp.)

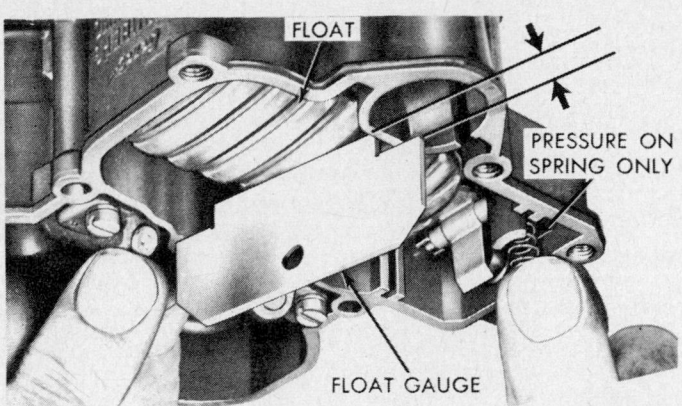

FLOAT

PRESSURE ON
SPRING ONLY

FLOAT GAUGE

Float Setting
(© Plymouth Division, Chrysler Corp.)

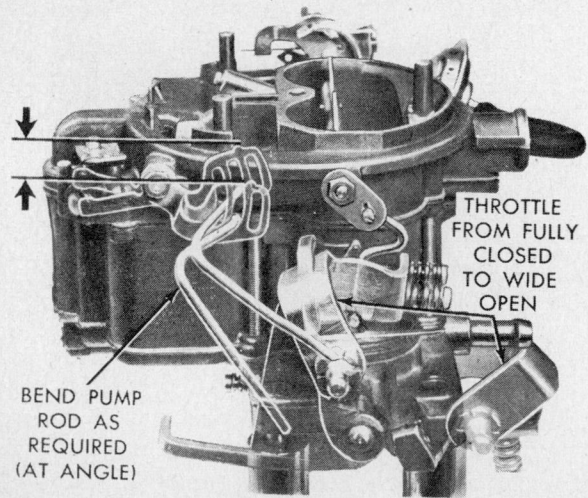

THROTTLE
FROM FULLY
CLOSED
TO WIDE
OPEN

BEND PUMP
ROD AS
REQUIRED
(AT ANGLE)

Pump Travel Setting
(© Plymouth Division, Chrysler Corp.)

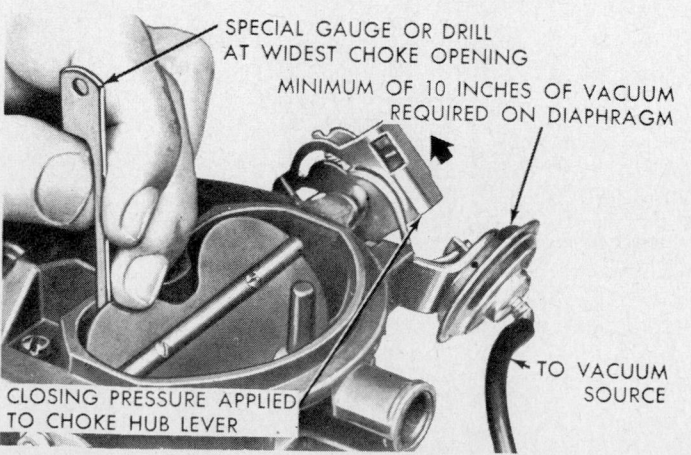

SPECIAL GAUGE OR DRILL
AT WIDEST CHOKE OPENING

MINIMUM OF 10 INCHES OF VACUUM
REQUIRED ON DIAPHRAGM

TO VACUUM
SOURCE

CLOSING PRESSURE APPLIED
TO CHOKE HUB LEVER

Vacuum Kick Adjustment
(© Plymouth Division, Chrysler Corp.)

Exhaust Emission Control Systems

Index

Numbers in columns refer to section numbers in text.

Manufacturer	1965	1966	1967	1968	1969	1970	1971
American Motors Corporation	3,4,5	3,4,5	3,4,5	4,5	4,5	4,5	4,5
Chrysler Corporation	3,4	3,4,6	4,6	4,6	4,6	4,6	4,6
Ford Motor Company	3,4	3,4,7	4,7	4,7	4,7	4,7	4,7
General Motors Corporation	3,4	3,4,8	3,4,8	4,8	4,8	4,8	4,8

Section Page Numbers

Exhaust Emission Systems

Emission Control Systems Diagnosis Guide

In the past few years, development of exhaust emission controls has been stimulated by a growing federal and public concern about air pollution. Regulations are currently in effect prescribing the maximum allowable emission of unburned hydrocarbons (HC) and poisonous carbon monoxide (CO) in engine exhaust. Emissions from engine crankcase and fuel supply are also restricted. In future years, further regulations will be enforced concerning emission of oxides of nitrogen (NO_x). Emission of NO_x is currently regulated in California.

To comply with government regulations concerning vehicle exhaust, many engine alterations had to be made. All of these changes are intended to effect more complete burning of the fuel. The result should be a substantial reduction in unburned hydrocarbons and other noxious fumes in terminal exhaust. This is the prime reason for modification.

To provide best vehicle operation with lowest emission of harmful by-products, the car manufacturer's specifications and maintenance recommendations must be followed to the letter.

To ensure the high state of control needed to minimize terminal exhaust emissions and still preserve safe and satisfactory performance levels, the following engine adjustment and control factors must be maintained:
A. Engine idle speed.
B. Ignition timing.
C. Engine idle air-fuel ratio.
D. Vacuum advance control valve (where used).
E. Air injector pump and circuit (where that type system is used).

Because this information is both vital and relative to engine and engine application rather than to engine alone, pertinent tune up data will be found posted in a conspicuous place in the engine compartment of all American built passenger cars beginning with 1968.

Many service procedures, tests, and adjustments have to be changed from those of previous years, particularly in the areas of fuel induction and ignition. To achieve the required results, the fuel-air ratio must not be overly rich and the engine must be kept in good operating condition.

Symptoms—Rough Idle

Fuel System
1. Leak in vacuum system (lines, connections, diaphragms, etc.).
2. Engine idle too low.
3. Idle fuel mixture incorrect.
4. Air leaks at manifold, carburetor, etc.
5. Power valve leaking fuel.
6. Idle fuel system air bleeds or fuel passages restricted.
7. Secondary throttle not closing (4-V carburetor).
8. Float setting incorrect.
9. Hot and cold air intake system stuck in Heat On position.

Ignition System
1. Defective or poorly adjusted points.
2. Poorly functioning spark plugs.
3. Incorrect ignition timing.
4. Insufficient secondary voltage at plug wires.

Engine
1. Leak in vacuum system (lines, connections, diaphragms, etc.).
2. Air leaks at manifold, carburetor, etc.
3. Poor compression (head gasket, exhaust or intake valve leaks, failure of rings, cracked or broken piston, etc.).
4. Inoperative crankcase ventilator (PCV) valve, or restricted tubing.
5. Improperly adjusted valve tappets.
6. Worn camshaft lobes.
7. Incorrect valve timing.

Overheating at Idle
With engine operating, check warning light, or temperature gauge. Trouble could develop in the distributor vacuum control valve (temperature sensing valve).

Engine Stalls

Fuel System
1. Idle speed too low.
2. Idle mixture out of adjustment.
3. Carburetor fast idle too low.
4. Choke out of calibration or adjustment.
5. Choke mechanism binding.
6. Float level too high.
7. Interference with fuel flow.
8. Bad fuel pump.

9. Obstructed fuel lines or tank vent.
10. Carburetor icing.
11. Vapor lock.
12. Inoperative carburetor dashpot.

Engine Noises
Thermactor Pump
The thermactor pump, like any air pump, may produce a detectable sound. This noise should not, however, be of a level audible to anyone within the passenger compartment.

A new air pump, until broken in, may produce a slight squealing or chirping sound.

If pump noise is objectionable, check the following:
1. Drive belt alignment and tension.
2. Loose mounting.
3. Hoses disconnected or leaking.
4. Interference of hoses and body.
5. Defective centrifugal filter fan.
6. Defective relief valve.
7. Improper pressure-setting plug, broken spring, or plug missing. If, after checking the above noise factors, the trouble still persists, replace or repair the pump.

Ignition
1. Ignition, initial timing, too far advanced.
2. Poor engine mounting.
3. Leaking cylinder head gasket.
4. Crankcase ventilator circuit inoperative (stuck open or closed).
5. Poor compression, valves, tappet clearance, or piston and ring assemblies.
6. Worn camshaft lobes.
7. Incorrect valve timing.

Exhaust System
1. Air by-pass valve vacuum line collapsed, plugged, disconnected or leaking, causing backfire.
2. Malfunctioning air by-pass valve, causing backfire.
3. Malfunctioning distributor vacuum advance control valve, causing backfire.
4. Exhaust system leak.

General

The following systems are used to limit vehicular air pollution. The many designs range from a simple road draft tube, to multiple and complicated gas emission types, some of which include special ignition and induction systems. The breathing devices reduce crankcase oil contamination, engine sludging, and wear. The prime purpose of the more complex designs is to reduce the discharge of poisonous unburned hydrocarbons into the air we breathe.

No matter what the name, how simple or involved the system, they all need attention to a varying degree, depending upon design and the work they perform.

Section 1
Road Draft Tube

The only service required for this system is a periodic cleaning of crankcase air intake filter and road draft tube.

The breathing filter should be thoroughly cleaned with a solvent, then saturated with light oil and blown clean at 6,000 mile intervals (or less, if conditions warrant it).

The road draft tube requires less frequent attention. Driving and engine conditions determine the service intervals to prevent sludge formations in the tube or oil separator.

If there is any evidence of crankcase pressure, (leaking seals, engine sludging, etc.) the tube should be checked as a possible source of trouble. This is always a good precaution on all engine reconditioning jobs.

Type 1 Tests

Symptoms

Symptoms of failure of the Type 1 system are heavy engine sludging, excessive oil filter tube smoking, poor rocker arm and tappet lubrication, fouled spark plugs, main bearing and engine seals leaking, etc.

Test

A simple and tentative test of the ventilating system may be made by the following:

1. Make sure that the oil filter cap and filter is clean and clear of obstruction.
2. Admit small quantities of compressed air into the oil filler tube, while noting the ability of the draft tube to exhaust this air. The engine should be at operating temperature for this test.

Section 2
Air Cleaner Type

Air cleaner type crankcase ventilating systems do not use a control valve. Air entering the carburetor, through the air cleaner, picks up crankcase gases by way of an emission tube. Emission flow is controlled by the amount of air allowed to enter the crankcase via the crankcase breather and cap. The breather cap usually contains a filter.

Service to this type emission sys-

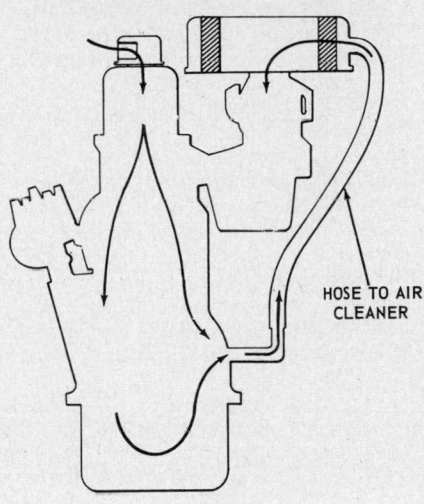

HOSE TO AIR CLEANER

Air cleaner system

tem should focus upon the two points of filtration: the crankcase air inlet, and the carburetor air cleaner.

Service intervals should not exceed 4,000 miles.

Type 2 Tests

Symptoms

Symptoms of failure of the Type 2 system are the same as with Type 1.

Test

1. Make sure that the oil filler cap and cap filter are clean.
2. Clean or replace the carburetor air cleaner element.
3. Bring engine to operating temperature.
4. With the engine not running, blow small quantities of compressed air into the oil filler Note the ability of the crankcase-to-carburetor air cleaner tube to exhaust these oil fumes and air. A clean system will permit free flow of air.

Section 3
Flow Control (PCV) Valve

Outside air entering the engine via the breather cap passes through the crankcase and is admitted, along with poisonous and otherwise harmful by-pass gases, to the intake manifold for combustion in the engine. Because these gases (air and unburned hydrocarbons) are admitted to the induction system on the engine side of the carburetor throttle plate, this flow must be controlled. A valve (many are spring loaded) regulates the flow. During idle intake manifold vacuum is high. The high vacuum overcomes plunger weight (or valve spring tension) and seats the plunger in the valve. With the plunger seated, all of the ventilating air passes through a calibrated orifice in the valve plunger. This results in minimum crankcase ventilation.

As engine speed increases, and manifold vacuum decreases, the

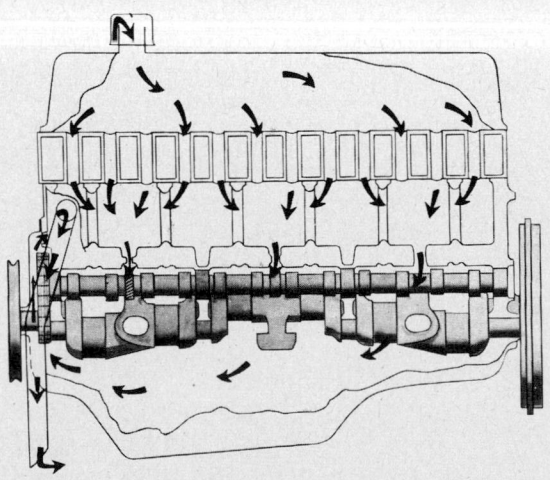

Road draft crankcase ventilation

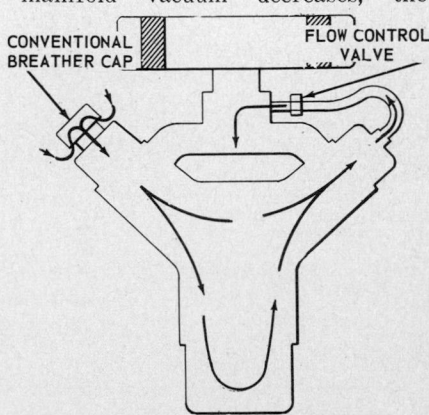

CONVENTIONAL BREATHER CAP

FLOW CONTROL VALVE

Flow control valve system

plunger weight (or valve spring) unseats the control valve plunger. This increases crankcase air flow and results in maximum ventilation.

Service to this unit is confined to the air breather inlet and the regulator valve. In some cases the valve assembly does not come apart. A faulty valve must be repaired or replaced. Service periods on this type of system depend mainly upon driving and engine conditions; however, service intervals should not exceed 6,000 miles.

Type 3 Tests

Symptoms

Because Type 3 enters the induction system on the engine side of the carburetor throttle plate, fuel-air ratio is involved. A plugged or obstructed ventilating system reveals itself in the same manner as Types 1 and 2, sludging, etc.

An open, or poorly seated, regulator valve upsets the carburetor fuel-air mixture. Therefore, excess crankcase fumes entering the intake manifold at idle speed cause an uneven idle and stalling. The degree of imbalance depends upon the amount of crankcase fumes allowed to leak past the poorly seated regulator valve.

Gauge Test

There are various devices available for testing this equipment, mainly by reading positive or negative crankcase pressures.

Alternate Test

Failure of the Type 3 system falls into two general categories: the system is obstructed (reduced, or no crankcase ventilation) or, there is too much ventilation (regulator valve not seated at engine idle).

The first condition, (not enough ventilation) builds up crankcase pressure and results in sludging and other failures peculiar to Types-1 and 2. An obstructed condition may

be detected in the system by observing its ability to pass compressed air and crankcase fumes through the system, (including the regulator valve).

The second condition, too much ventilation, (regulator valve not seating at idle) usually manifests itself in the form of rough engine idle and stalling. This situation is quite common. It may be very misleading because the fuel-air ratio is unbalanced, and resembles a case of intake manifold leak, or carburetor trouble.

To test the second condition:

1. Bring engine to operating temperature.
2. Hook up a tachometer to the idling engine and record the rpm.
3. Disconnect the regulator valve from the line to the intake manifold.
4. Make a plug (see note below) with a metered hole of the same size as that of the disconnected regulator valve. Then insert the plug in the end of the disconnected line to the intake manifold.
5. Compare engine rpm with that which was recorded with the regulator valve in place. Any difference (±20 rpm) indicates a poorly seated regulator valve.

NOTE: make a tapered plug of hard rubber, plastic, hard wood, metal, etc., that will fit into the PCV hose end (or connection) to the intake manifold. Drill a hole, lengthwise, through the tapered plug, the same size as the hole in the end of the regulator valve plunger.

There are various orifice sizes used, depending upon the cubic inch displacement of the engine involved.

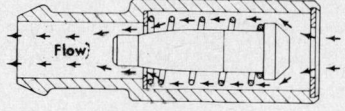

PCV valve (typical)

The following is a general engine size-to-valve plunger orifice chart.

Engine size, cu. in.	Orifice size	Approximate
90-140	.056-.075 in.	1/16 in.
141-200	.074-.088 in.	5/64 in.
201-275	.087-.099 in.	3/32 in.
276-350	.098-.112 in.	7/64 in.
351- up	.111-.125 in.	1/8 in.

When properly inserted, this tool will admit the same amount of air into the induction system as the standard equipment regulator valve, in good operating condition. Five test plugs (of various orifice sizes) are enough to test all popular American made passenger car engines for regulator valve condition at engine idle.

Section 4
Fully Closed System

Under high manifold vacuum conditions, such as idle or deceleration, this system breathes filtered air through a tube running from the carburetor air cleaner to the crankcase (a closed cap is used on oil filler tube). The emission side of the system is of the flow control valve type or a variation thereof. A flame arrestor may be incorporated into the inlet side of the system. Under low manifold vacuum conditions, such as heavy acceleration, the flow reverses and crankcase vapors are drawn through the air cleaner as in Type 2. This is a fully closed ventilating system, so don't forget, when checking engine oil, to replace the dip stick all the way, to completely seal the dip stick opening.

Service to the fully closed system should not exceed 6,000 mile intervals.

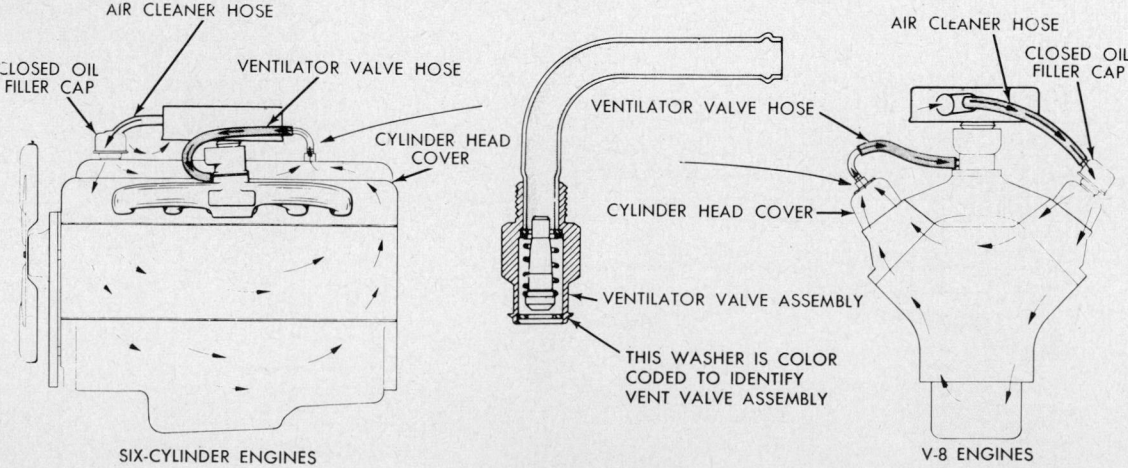

SIX-CYLINDER ENGINES   V-8 ENGINES

Fully closed ventilation system
(© Chrysler Corp.)

Type 4 Tests

Symptoms

This system is fully closed and depends upon the carburetor air cleaner for crankcase inlet breathing. While the engine is idling, or at low throttle operation, system failures are potentially the same as Type 3. However, at part throttle or high speed operation, any restriction of air flow into the system (dirty air cleaner or flame trap) may cause negative crankcase pressures. This condition may tend to cause premature oil failure and sludging.

Test

Make test of the ventilating circuit hose as with Type 3, alternate method. The flame trap must be considered in testing this system as it also can become clogged.

Section 5
American Motors Systems

Through 1970

There are two systems used: Engine-Mod and Air-Guard.

The 199 and 232 six cylinder engines, with either manual or automatic transmission, use the Engine-Mod system.

The 290, 304, 343, 360, and 390 V8 engines with automatic transmission use the Engine-Mod system.

The 290, 304, 343, 360, and 390 V8 engines, with manual transmission, use the Air Guard system.

In 1970 only, a deceleration valve was used on 199, 232, and 390 engines with manual transmission. The function of this valve is to provide full distributor vacuum advance on deceleration.

The Engine Mod System Incorporates the Following:

199-232

1. Low-quench combustion chambers.
2. Emission-calibrated distributor and modified carburetor.
3. Closed positive crankcase ventilation system.

*290-304-343-360-390
Automatic Transmission*

1. Emission-calibrated distributor and modified carburetor.
2. Thermostatic control on air cleaner.
3. Closed positive crankcase ventilation system.

The Air-Guard System Incorporates the Following:

*290-304-343-360-390
Manual Transmission*

1. Air-Guard air pump system.
2. Emission-calibrated distributor and carburetor.
3. Thermostatically-controlled carburetor air-cleaner (four-barrel only).
4. Closed positive crankcase ventilation system.

1971-72

There are two systems used: Air-Guard and Transmission Controlled Spark (TCS).

The Air-Guard air pump system, which injects air at the exhaust ports, is on all V8 engines with manual transmission.

TCS is on all cars sold in California and on all 304 V8 engines with automatic transmission. The primary function of TCS is to reduce the emission of oxides of nitrogen. The system incorporates a temperature override switch, a solenoid vacuum valve, and

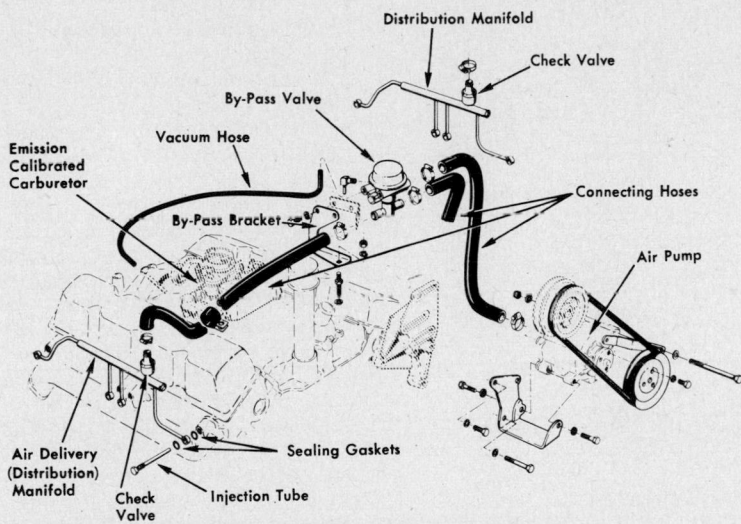

Air-Guard system (©American Motors Corp.)

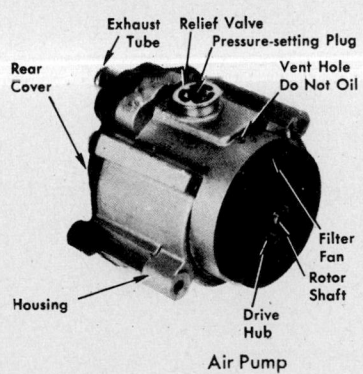

Air Pump

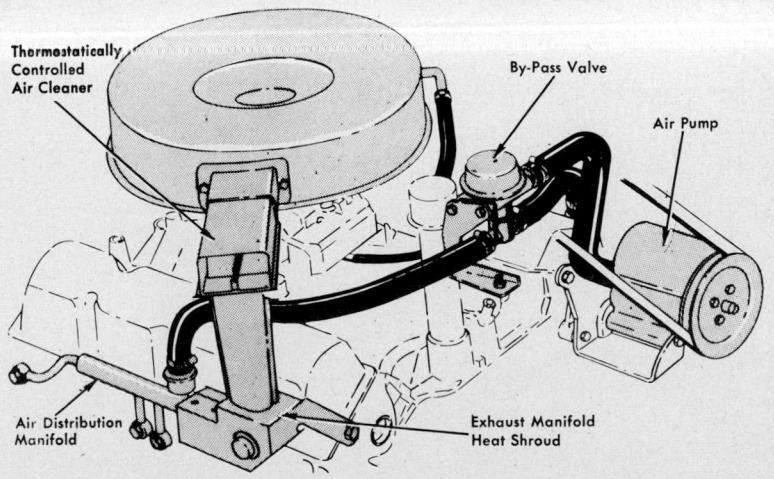

Thermostatically controlled carburetor intake with Air-Guard system
(© American Motors Corp.)

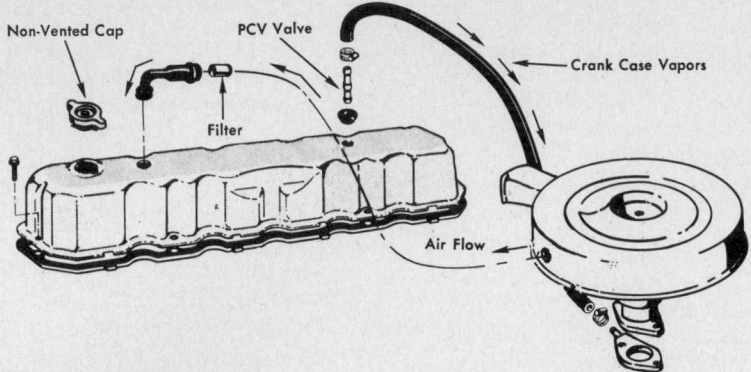

Crankcase ventilation system—six cylinder engines (© American Motors Corp.)

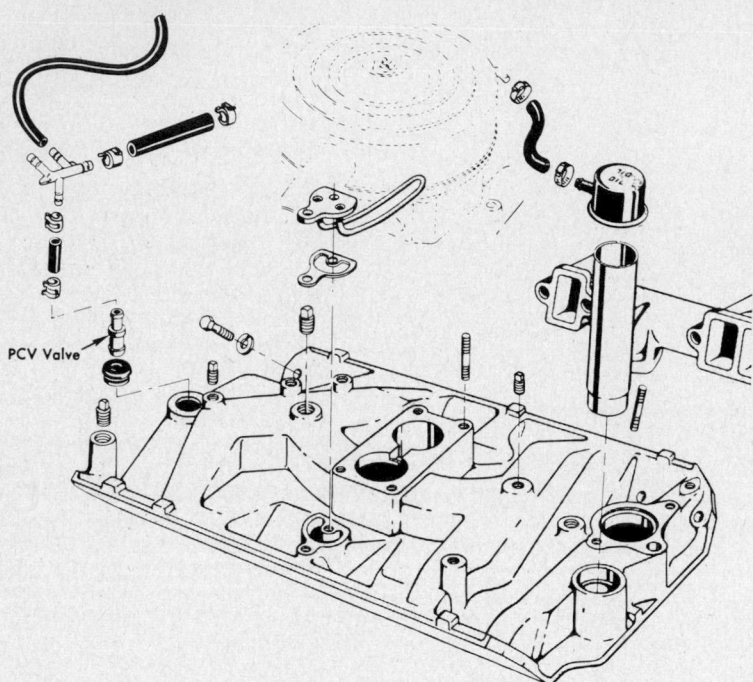

Crankcase ventilation system—V8 engines (© American Motors Corp.)

a solenoid control switch. The temperature override switch, at the front upper crossmember, allows full vacuum advance for easier starting and drive-away when the air temperature is below 63°F. The solenoid control switch, at the transmission, energizes the solenoid vacuum valve in the lower gears (manual) or under 30 mph (automatic). When the solenoid vacuum valve is energized, it vents the distributor vacuum line to the atmosphere, resulting in no vacuum advance. Vacuum advance is provided only in high gear (or above 30 mph) when the temperature is above 63°F.

As in past years, all engines have a closed positive crankcase ventilation system.

Vapor Emission Control System

All 1970 vehicles sold in California, and all 1971 and later vehicles, have a vapor emission control system incorporating the following:

1. Fuel expansion tank.
2. Closed fuel tank vent system.
3. Fuel tank check valve.
4. Pressure and vacuum relief filler cap.

The fuel tank contains an expansion tank to provide an air displacement area for fuel expansion, thus preventing fuel overflow. A special fuel tank, which requires no expansion tank, is used on the Gremlin. The fuel tank vent system routes fuel vapors from the tank into the crankcase ventilation system at the engine valve cover. On 1971 V8 engines with automatic transmission, a vapor storage canister is installed in the vent line, under the hood. The check valve prevents the flow of liquid fuel to the crankcase ventilation system or storage canister through the fuel tank vent system. The check

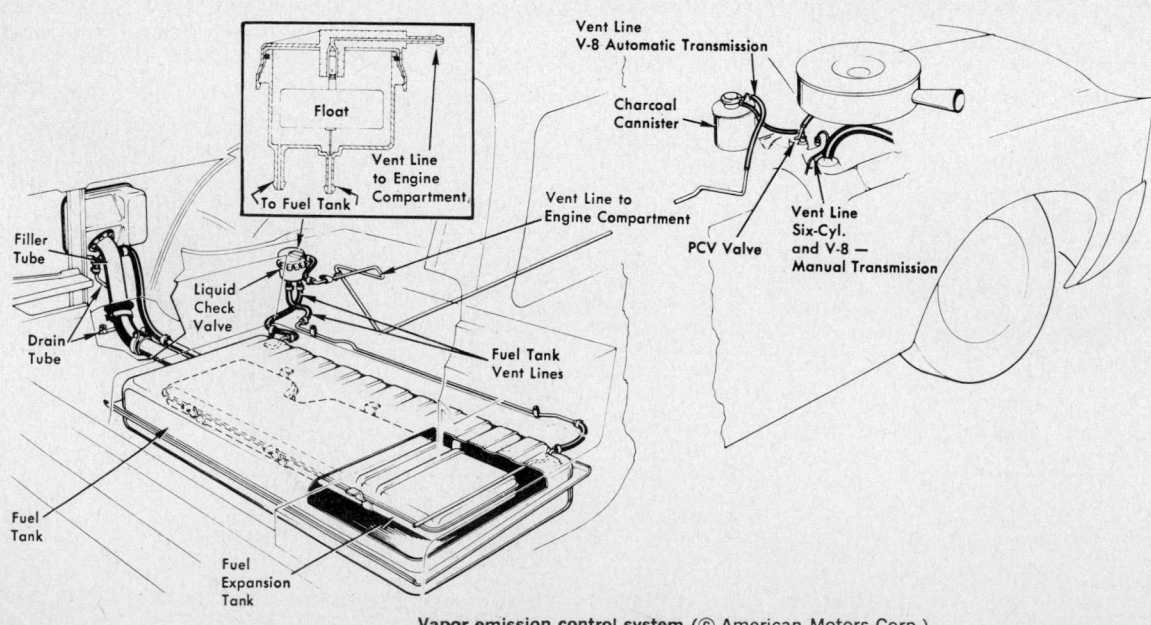

Vapor emission control system (© American Motors Corp.)

valve is not used on the Gremlin. The filler cap has a two way relief valve which is normally closed. The valve is opened by an internal pressure differential of ½-1 PSI, caused by heat expansion, or by external pressure differential, caused by fuel usage.

Services

Required Each 12,000 Miles

Engine oil filler cap (filter type)—clean

Heat valve (exhaust manifold)—inspect and lubricate

Drive belts (condition and tension)—inspect and correct

Carburetor air cleaner element—clean every 12,000 miles; replace every 24,000 miles

PCV valve—replace

PCV filter (6 cylinder)—clean

Carburetor—inspect and adjust choke, adjust idle speed and mixture to specifications

Spark plugs—inspect, clean and re-gap (replace if required)

Ignition points, coil and spark plug wires—inspect (replace if required)

Distributor cam lubricator—rotate at 12-36-60,000 miles; replace at 24-48-72,000 miles

Ignition timing—check and set to specifications.

Deceleration vacuum advance valve—check and set to specifications

Distributor vacuum advances—check

Air-guard hose connections (V-8 manual transmission)—inspect

Fuel tank vapor emission control system—inspect liquid check valve and hose connections, replace charcoal canister inlet filter.

Section 6
Chrysler System

The CAP, Cleaner Air Package, system is designed to constantly maintain carburetion and ignition timing at the best settings for performance and combustion under all driving requirements and conditions. These adjustments, if maintained, will keep the engine at a good performance level and within the exhaust requirements of federal law.

In the past, normal engines have had comparatively low exhaust emissions at cruise and acceleration attitudes. Excessive emissions occur during deceleration and low speed operation. Therefore, the CAP system concentrates on reduction of emissions in the idle and deceleration ranges.

The CAP system uses a carburetor and distributor which have been redesigned, and a vacuum advance control valve on cars with manual transmissions.

The carburetor is calibrated to provide leaner mixtures at idle and at low speed. The distributor is designed to give retarded timing at idle. The vacuum advance control valve, in conjunction with the distributor, provides advanced timing during deceleration.

A number of changes have been made that reshape the intake manifold and combustion chamber for more even mixture distribution and better combustion.

CAP idle timing, for all engines, is retarded. Exhaust emission is reduced at idle by using leaner air-fuel mixtures, increased engine speed, and retarded ignition timing. The increased air flow at this idle condition is similar to the distribution and combustion conditions of cruise.

The system operates with late timing during idle, and with conventional spark advance during acceleration and cruise.

The vacuum advance control valve provides additional spark advance during deceleration.

Engine applications involving manual shift transmissions require slightly different handling. They need earlier ignition of the fuel mixture to accomplish efficient combustion and to more completely consume residual fuels.

The vacuum advance control valve is connected by hoses to the carburetor, the intake manifold, and to the distributor vacuum chamber. Carburetor vacuum and manifold vacuum act on the vacuum advance control valve. From these two signals, the vacuum advance control valve senses engine speed and load conditions, and relays a vacuum command to the distributor to modify spark timing when necessary.

Initial, or basic, timing may be retarded as much as 15° from conventional timing. The vacuum advance control valve does not affect timing at idle because the distributor vacuum chamber receives the same vacuum signal as in the conventional system, namely, carburetor vacuum. This is not strong enough to overcome the distributor vacuum diaphragm spring.

Manifold vacuum acts on the vacuum control valve diaphragm. However, it is not strong enough to overcome the vacuum control spring. The spring holds the vacuum control valve closed to manifold vacuum and open to low carburetor vacuum.

Under acceleration and during normal cruise, the throttle is opened and the increased air flow through the carburetor throat creates carburetor vacuum much greater than under closed throttle conditions.

Manifold vacuum is not enough to overcome the vacuum advance control valve spring. However, the stronger carburetor vacuum overcomes the distributor vacuum diaphragm spring, advancing spark timing.

The conventional system (without exhaust emission control) permits greatest objectionable emissions during deceleration. Carburetor vacuum is too weak to overcome the distributor vacuum advance diaphragm spring.

Manifold vacuum is at its strongest during deceleration. Therefore, the CAP system, when equipped with a vacuum advance control valve, uses manifold vacuum instead of carburetor vacuum to control spark timing. To summarize: during deceleration, manifold vacuum is strong enough to overcome the vacuum advance control valve spring and the distributor vacuum diaphragm spring, moving the spark timing to maximum advance.

1970 thru 1972 Models

The CAP system has been improved to CAS, Cleaner Air System. This system utilizes:

1. Heated air intake system.
2. Modified carburetor.
3. Lower compression ratio.
4. Solenoid retarded distributor.

The heated air system is used on all engines except 340, 426 Hemi, 440 Six-Pack, and those with the fresh air scoop option. When air tempera-

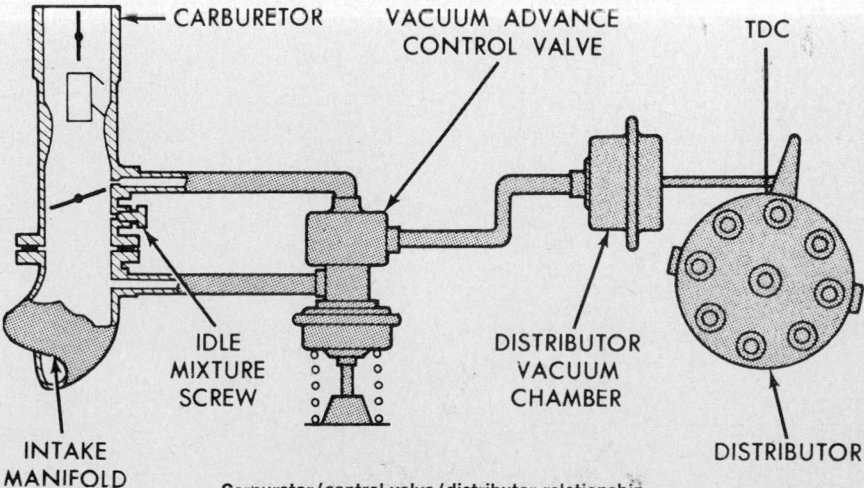

Carburetor/control valve/distributor relationship

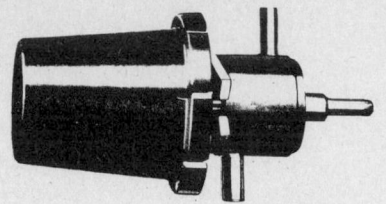

Vacuum advance control valve

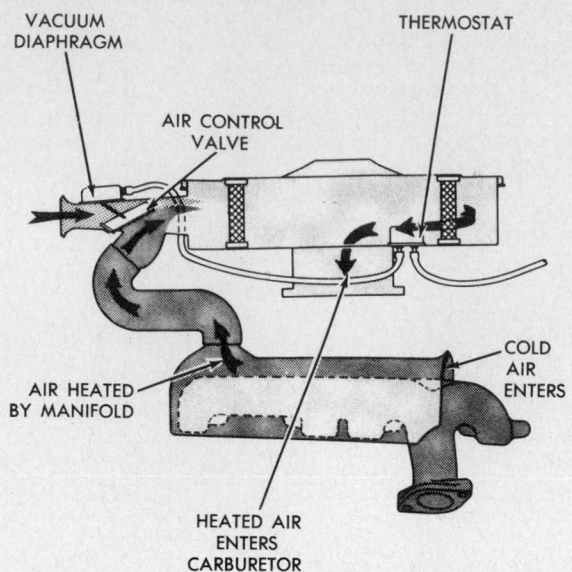

Heated air intake system
(© Chrysler Corp.)

ture is below 10° F, intake air flows through a manifold heat stove into the air cleaner. When air temperature is between 10 and 100°F, intake air is a mixture of heated and unheated air. The volume of heated and unheated air is regulated by a thermostat, a vacuum diaphragm, and an air control valve in the air cleaner housing. The thermostat regulates the air control valve opening. Under conditions of greatly reduced vacuum, such as a sudden burst of acceleration, the vacuum diaphragm overrides the thermostat to open the air control valve fully to unheated air.

Carburetors have leaner mixtures and external idle mixture limiting devices. The automatic choke has been redesigned to release more quickly on engine warmup. An electrical solenoid throttle stop is used on 340, 440, 440 Six-Pack, and 426 Hemi engines. These engines use high idle speeds to achieve acceptable emission levels. The solenoid throttle stop de-energizes when the ignition is switched off, allowing the throttle blades to close more completely. This prevents running on.

318, 383, and 440 (except 440 Six-Pack) engines have lower compression ratios to reduce hydrocarbon emissions.

All 383 and 440 (except 1970 440 Six-Pack) engines have a solenoid in the distributor advance mechanism to retard ignition timing when the throttle is closed. This system is inactivated during cold starting. Timing must be set at closed throttle to give full retard.

All 1970 vehicles sold in California and all 1971 and later vehicles have an evaporation control system to reduce evaporation losses from the fuel system. The system has an expansion tank in the main fuel tank. This prevents spillage due to expansion of warm fuel. A special filler cap with a two way relief valve is used. An internal pressure differential, caused by thermal expansion, opens the valve, as does an external pressure differential, caused by fuel usage. Fuel vapors from the carburetor and fuel tank are routed to the crankcase ventilation system. A separator is installed to prevent liquid fuel from entering the crankcase ventilation system.

NO_x System

All 1971 vehicles sold in California have a NO_x system to control emission of oxides of nitrogen. Engines with this system all have a special camshaft and a 185°F thermostat.

CARBURETOR
- IMPROVED DISTRIBUTION
- LEANER MIXTURES
- FASTER ACTING CHOKE
- EXTERNAL IDLE MIXTURE LIMITER
- SOLENOID THROTTLE STOP

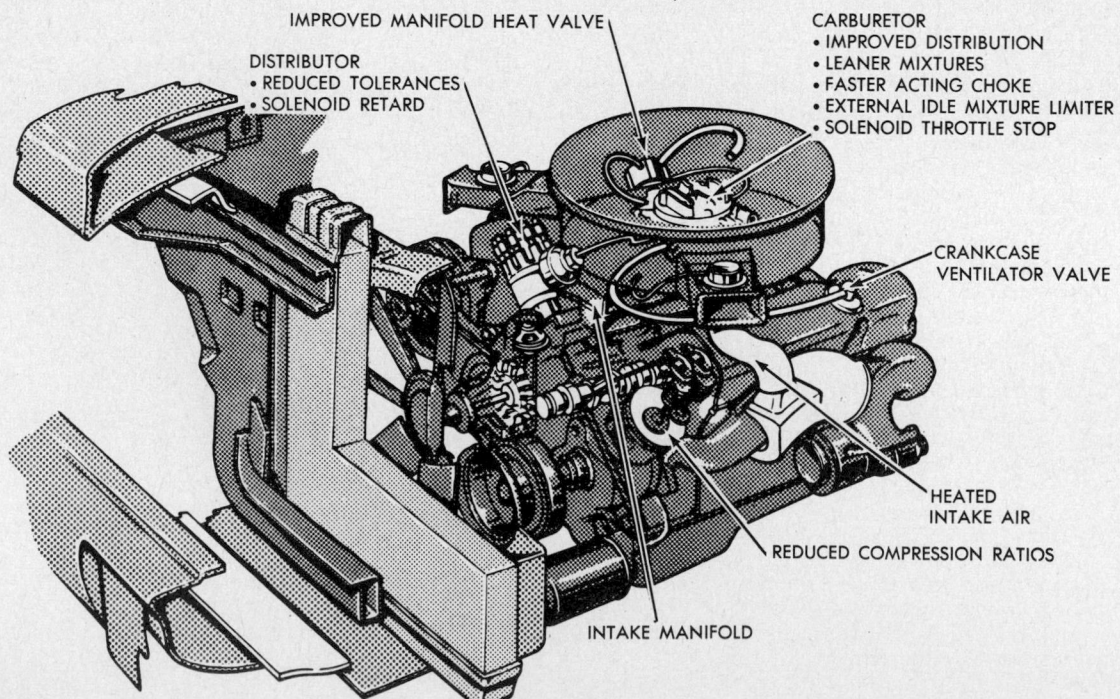

Cleaner air system features (© Chrysler Corp.)

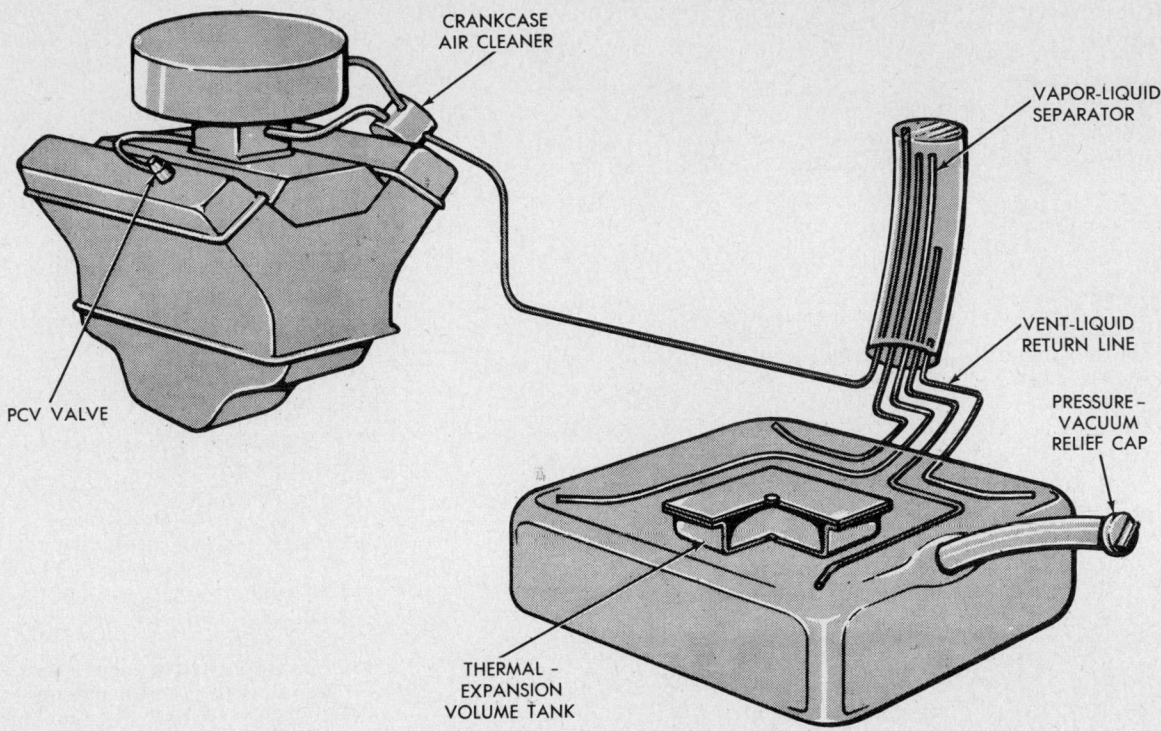

CRANKCASE
AIR CLEANER

VAPOR-LIQUID
SEPARATOR

VENT-LIQUID
RETURN LINE

PRESSURE -
VACUUM
RELIEF CAP

PCV VALVE

THERMAL -
EXPANSION
VOLUME TANK

Evaporation control system (© Chrysler Corp.)

Manual Transmission

The manual transmission NO_x system uses a transmission switch, a thermal switch, and a solenoid vacuum valve. The transmission switch is screwed into the transmission housing and is closed, except in high gear. The thermal switch, mounted on the firewall, is open whenever the ambient temperature is above 70°F. With the transmission is any gear except high and the temperature above 70°, the solenoid vacuum valve is energized. This shuts off the distributor vacuum advance line preventing vacuum advance. Below 70°, the vacuum advance functions normally.

To test the system:

1. Be sure that ambient temperature is well above 70°F.
2. Switch ignition to Run. Shift into neutral.
3. Disconnect wire from B+ connector of ballast resistor while holding solenoid vacuum valve. The valve solenoid should be felt to de-energize.
4. Reconnect the wire. The valve solenoid should be felt to energize.
5. Shift into high. Repeat Steps 3 and 4. The system should be inoperative.
6. To test the solenoid vacuum valve, remove the connector on the valve. Connect the piggyback connector on the ballast resistor

to one of the solenoid vacuum valve terminals. Ground the other terminal. The solenoid should energize with the ignition switch in the Run position.

To test the thermal switch, disconnect and replace it with a length of wire. The solenoid should energize.

To test the transmission switch, turn the ignition switch to Run and shift into neutral. Remove and ground the wire from the transmission switch. The solenoid should energize. Switch installation torque must be 180 in. lbs.

Automatic Transmission

The NO_x system for automatic

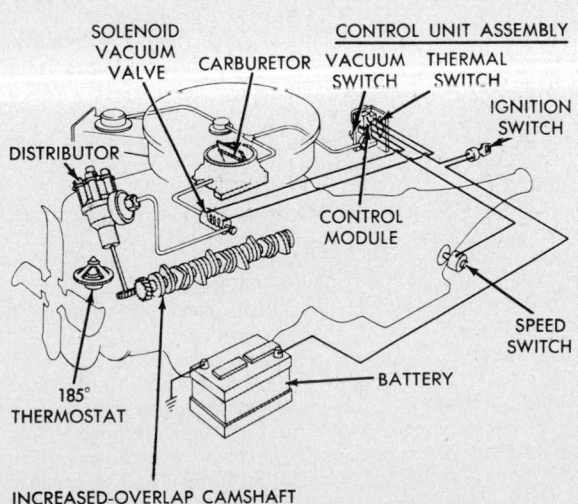

SOLENOID
VACUUM
VALVE

CARBURETOR

CONTROL UNIT ASSEMBLY

VACUUM
SWITCH

THERMAL
SWITCH

IGNITION
SWITCH

DISTRIBUTOR

CONTROL
MODULE

SPEED
SWITCH

185°
THERMOSTAT

BATTERY

INCREASED-OVERLAP CAMSHAFT

NO_x system—automatic transmission (© Chrsyler Corp.)

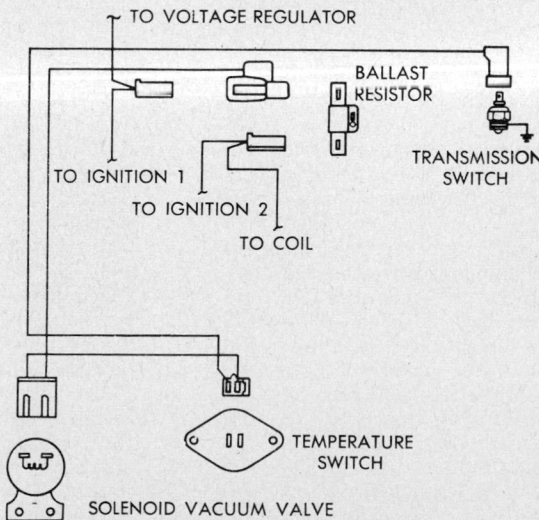

TO VOLTAGE REGULATOR

BALLAST
RESISTOR

TRANSMISSION
SWITCH

TO IGNITION 1

TO IGNITION 2

TO COIL

TEMPERATURE
SWITCH

SOLENOID VACUUM VALVE

**NO_x system schematic manual transmission
(© Chrsyler Corp.)**

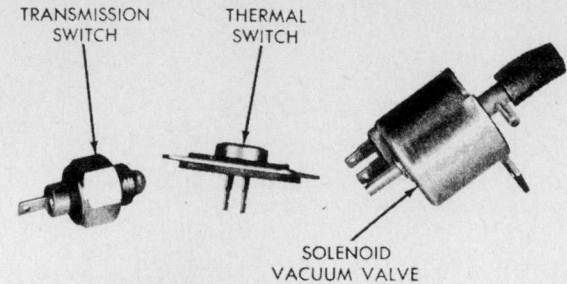

**NOₓ system components—
manual transmission**
(© Chrysler Corp.)

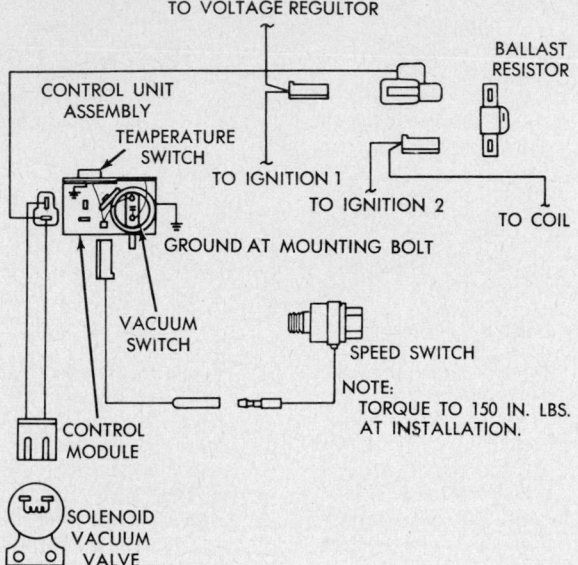

**NOₓ system schematic—
automatic transmission**
(© Chrysler Corp.)

transmission is more complex than the manual transmission system. It prevents vacuum advance when the ambient temperature is above 70°F, speed is below 30 mph, or the car is accelerating. The solenoid vacuum valve is interchangeable with that used in the manual transmission system. The speed switch senses vehicle speed and is driven by the speedometer cable. The control unit is mounted on the firewall. It contains a control module, thermal switch, and a vacuum switch. The control unit senses ambient temperature and manifold vacuum. 383 two-barrel engines without air conditioning also have a coolant temperature operated vacuum valve. The valve is threaded into the engine water jacket. It allows full vacuum advance whenever the engine exceeds normal temperature.

To test the system:
1. Warm the engine to normal operating temperature. Be sure the ambient temperature is well above 70°F.
2. T-connect a vacuum gauge between the distributor and the so-

lenoid vacuum valve.
3. Raise the car on a lift, with the wheels hanging free.
4. Disconnect the vacuum line at the vacuum switch on the control unit.
5. Start the engine and run at a speed above 850 rpm. Vacuum gauge should read zero.
6. Disconnect the wire from the control unit. The vacuum gauge should read normal advance unit operating vacuum. Reconnect the wire. The gauge should drop to zero.
7. Unplug and reconnect the vacuum line to the vacuum switch. Disconnect the wire from the control unit to the speed switch. The gauge should read normal advance unit operating vacuum.
8. Place transmission in Drive. Sharp acceleration should cause the gauge reading to drop sharply to zero. Do not exceed 40 mph.
9. Accelerate above 30 mph. The gauge should read normal vacuum advance unit operating vac-

uum.
10. If solenoid valve did not operate during the tests, replace control unit.

CAP, CAS Services

To ensure that exhaust emissions are maintained within the limits of legislation without objectionable effects on performance, engine inspection is recommended at intervals not to exceed 12 months.

The following engine checks should be made at these periods:
1. Check spark plugs.
   A. Clean/renew and gap as necessary.
   B. Be sure they are of the proper heat range.
   C. Torque to 30 ft. lbs.
2. Check distributor breaker points.
   A. Replace if necessary and adjust to recommended dwell or gap.
   B. Clean and lubricate cam and wick.
   C. Apply five to ten drops of light engine oil to the oil cup.
3. Check ignition system operation.
   A. Connect one end of test probe to a good ground.
   B. Disconnect secondary ignition cable at spark plug end.
   C. Insulate secondary cable end from ground.
   D. With engine idling, move test probe along entire length of cable. If cable insulation is breaking down, there will be a spark jump to the probe.
   E. The secondary (coil to distributor cap cable) should be checked the same way.
   F. Be sure one spark plug cable is disconnected, (to create greater resistance). Then, run probe along the length of the coil secondary cable. Cracked or otherwise poor insulation should be obvious by a spark jump at the point of probe. Bad cables should be replaced.
4. Resistance of secondary cables should also be checked. Use an ohmmeter for this purpose.
   A. Remove cable from spark plug and install adapter between cable and spark plug.
   B. Remove cap from distributor, (secondary cables attached).
   C. Connect ohmmeter between plug adapter and the corresponding electrode inside the cap.
   D. Read the ohmmeter. If resistance is more than 30,000 ohms, remove cable from cap and check cable resistance only.
   E. If resistance is still more than 30,000 ohms, replace cable. If resistance is much less than 30,000 ohms, clean cap wire towers or renew the cap.

5. Inspect ignition coil for indications of oil leakage. Any indication of oil leakage justifies replacing the coil.

6. Test battery with a hydrometer. Specific gravity should be 1.220 or more, with temperature corrections. Add mineral-free water if required, to bring fluid up to correct level.
   A. Clean battery posts and cable terminals.
   B. After tightening the cable post clamps, coat battery posts and clamps with light grease.
   C. Reseal any breaks around the posts with rubber cement to retard corrosion.

7. The carburetor choke shaft should be serviced with carburetor cleaner to prevent sticking from gum deposits. Be sure the choke operates freely.

8. To satisfy normal driving conditions, the carburetor air cleaner should be inspected and cleaned every 6 months. Replace it every 2 years.
   If equipped with an oil bath cleaner, the oil level should be checked every 6 months, and should be thoroughly cleaned and refilled once a year.

9. Inspect, and if necessary, free the manifold heat control valve with manifold heat control valve solvent. Apply solvent and work the shaft only when the unit is cold.

10. A very critical and much neglected item of engine performance is the crankcase emission control (PCV) valve.
    The crankcase emission control valve depends entirely upon the fine balance of spring pressure opposed to manifold vacuum. This balance can very easily be upset by small deposits of varnish or sludge. A closed valve induces crankcase pressure and engine sludge. A poorly seated (open) valve upsets engine idle and results in poor low speed operation.
    Inspect and service the closed crankcase ventilating system every 6 months and replace the control valve every 12 months.
    A. A tentative check of PCV valve operation is to idle the engine.
    B. Disconnect the ventilator valve assembly from the rocker cover. You should be able to hear the valve plunger, when shaking the valve.
    C. If the valve is open, a hissing sound will be heard from the valve opening and vacuum can be felt with the finger.
    D. If the valve is closed, or the line is obstructed anywhere between the valve and the intake manifold, crankcase pressure will develop. Check for plugging of the hose, freedom of the connection at the carburetor base or a valve stuck closed. Free vacuum passages. Replace the PCV valve if necessary.
    E. Another approach is through the use of a tachometer hook-up while pinching the PCV hose. If pinching the hose has no effect on engine idle rpm, the system is plugged or the PCV valve is not opening.
    If pinching the hose smooths out the idle, the PCV valve is not seating.

11. Adjust idle rpm to specifications.

12. Check ignition timing.
    Set ignition basic timing to specifications.
    On 1970-71 models, check distributor solenoid for proper operation by disconnecting wire at carburetor. Timing should advance 5½ degrees and engine speed should increase.

13. Adjust air-fuel ratio. Refer to Car Section for details.

14. To check setting of distributor vacuum control valve:
    A. Warm up engine.
    B. Connect a tachometer.
    C. Connect a vacuum gauge into the distributor vacuum line. Use a T-fitting with the same inside diameter as the line.
    D. If the carburetor is equipped with a dashpot, adjust so that it does not contact the throttle lever at idle speed.
    E. Disconnect and plug the hose that connects the distributor vacuum control valve to the intake manifold.
    F. Remove the distributor vacuum hose at the distributor and plug the hose. Distributor vacuum must be 0-6 in. Hg. with the engine idling. If reading is higher than 6 in. Hg., recheck idle speed, timing, and air/fuel ratio.

15. To check operation of distributor vacuum control valve:
    A. Remove vacuum connection plugs and reconnect vacuum hoses.
    B. Remove the distributor vacuum valve cover.
    C. Run engine speed up to 2,000 rpm and hold for about 5 seconds.
    D. Release the throttle. Distributor vacuum should increase to about 15 in. Hg. for a minimum of 1 second, distributor vacuum must then fall below 6 in. Hg. within 3 seconds after throttle is released.

16. To adjust vacuum control valve. If it requires less than 1 second or more than 3 seconds to obtain the correct vacuum reading:
    A. Turn the adjusting screw counterclockwise to increase the time distributor vacuum remains above 6 in. Hg., or clockwise to decrease the time distributor vacuum remains above 6 in. Hg. One turn of the adjusting screw changes the valve setting about ½ in. Hg. If the valve cannot be adjusted to specifications, it must be replaced.
    B. Install vacuum control valve cover and reset carburetor dashpot.

17. A carburetor dashpot is a device used to slow down the closing of the throttle when the accelerator pedal is suddenly released. The purpose of the dashpot is to prevent engine stalling. To adjust the dashpot:
    A. With engine idling at recommended rpm and air/fuel mixture properly adjusted, connect a tachometer to the engine.
    B. Position throttle lever so that the actuating tab on the lever contacts the stem of the dashpot, but does not depress it.
    C. If adjustment is necessary, loosen the locknut that holds the dashpot to the bracket. Rotate the unit to obtain the desired setting. Tighten the locknut.
    D. Recheck distributor vacuum control valve.
    E. If distributor vacuum does not fall below 6 in. Hg. within 4 seconds after throttle has been released, readjust or replace dashpot.

18. Road test the car, noting performance in all driving ranges. All adjustments should be in the interest of better performance and economy. However, any changes must comply with specifications and legislation.

Caution If contrary or confusing tune-up data is encountered, refer to the decal containing information pertinent to the specific engine - vehicle application. This decal is posted in a conspicuous location in the engine compartment of each vehicle, beginning with 1968 production.

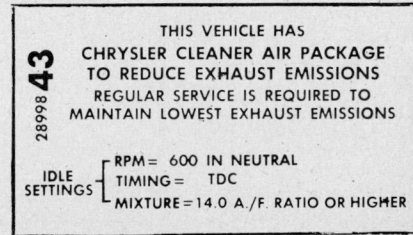

Data plate

Section 7
Ford System

The Ford Motor Company employs two methods of exhaust emission control, the IMCO (improved combustion) and the Thermactor (air injection) types. Both of these types are used extensively throughout their family of engines. The Thermactor type can be readily identified by the belt driven air pump.

The IMCO system produces an acceptable level of emissions by use of carburetor and distributor modifications; no air pump is necessary.

With this system, the exhaust gas emissions are reduced in the combustion system rather than by burning them in the exhaust manifolds.

The Thermactor method of exhaust emission control injects fresh air into the hot exhaust stream through the engine exhaust ports. At this point, the fresh air mixes with the hot exhaust gases, extending the burning period of these gases. This induced burning lowers the hydrocarbon and carbon monoxide content of exhaust by converting some of it into harmless carbon dioxide and water.

The Thermactor system consists of the following major parts:
1. Air supply pump.
2. Air by-pass valve.
3. Check valves.
4. Internal or external air manifold/s.
5. Air supply tubes (external air manifolds only).

Air for the Thermactor system is cleaned by a centrifugal filter fan mounted on the air pump driveshaft.

An element-type air cleaner is not required. A pressure relief valve is installed in the pump housing to prevent air pump outlet pressure from becoming excessive. The pressure setting of the relief valve is controlled by a replaceable plastic plug. Air pump bearings are sealed and lubricated with a lifetime lubricant. Rotor vane and bearing clearances are established during initial assembly. No adjustments are required.

Air supply from the pump is controlled by the air bypass valve. During engine deceleration, the air bypass valve opens and air delivery to the cylinder head ports is momentarily diverted to the atmosphere.

A check valve is incorporated in the air inlet side of the air manifold/s to prevent exhaust backflow into the air pump and air bypass valve during the air bypass cycle. This valve also operates in the case of drive belt or pump failure.

Pertinent tune-up data such as engine idle speed, ignition timing, engine idle air/fuel ratio, etc. will be found posted on a decal, in a conspicuous location in the engine compartment of all cars beginning with 1968.

The car manufacturer installs the necessary equipment to control vehicle air pollutants; it is the responsibility of the owner to see that this equipment remains effective by maintaining it to the manufacturers' recommendations. Even a clogged air cleaner may not seem important to the unknowing car owner, but it is most detrimental to proper performance, fuel economy, and emission control.

Crankcase Ventilation System

Crankcase ventilation systems are covered earlier in this Unit Repair Section and must be maintained in good repair to complement either the IMCO or Thermactor system of exhaust emission control.

Ventilation System Test

1. Replace the crankcase ventilator regulator valve with a known good valve of identical design.
2. Start the engine and compare idle conditions with the prior idle conditions. If engine idle is satisfactory (with new valve installed) trouble exists in the old valve and it should be replaced.
3. If loping or rough idle still persists with the good regulator valve in place, the trouble is elsewhere. Check crankcase ventilator system for restriction at the intake manifold or carburetor spacer.
4. If the system is not restricted, explore further the aspects of tune-up and the various elements of exhaust emission control.

Thermactor Diagnosis and Tests

Prior to performing any extensive tests of the Thermactor system:
1. Be sure that a problem exists.
2. Determine that the engine, as a basic unit, is functioning properly by performing the following:
   disconnect the air bypass valve vacuum sensing line at the intake manifold. Plug the manifold connection to prevent leakage.
3. Normal engine diagnosis procedures can then be performed.

Air Pump Test

1. To test the air supply pump, a test gauge adapter must be made. Make the adapter as follows:
   A. Obtain a ½ in. pipe T.
   B. A 2 in. length of ½ in. galvanized pipe, threaded at one end only.
   C. A ½ in. pipe plug.
   D. A ½ in. reducer bushing or suitable gauge adapter.
   E. Apply sealer to the threads of the 2 in. length of pipe and screw it into one end of the T.
   F. Apply sealer to the pipe plug and install it into the other end of the T.
   G. Apply sealer to the threads of the ½ in. reducer bushing or adapter for the pressure gauge and install it in the side opening of the T.
   H. Drill an 11/32 in. (0.3437) diameter hole through the

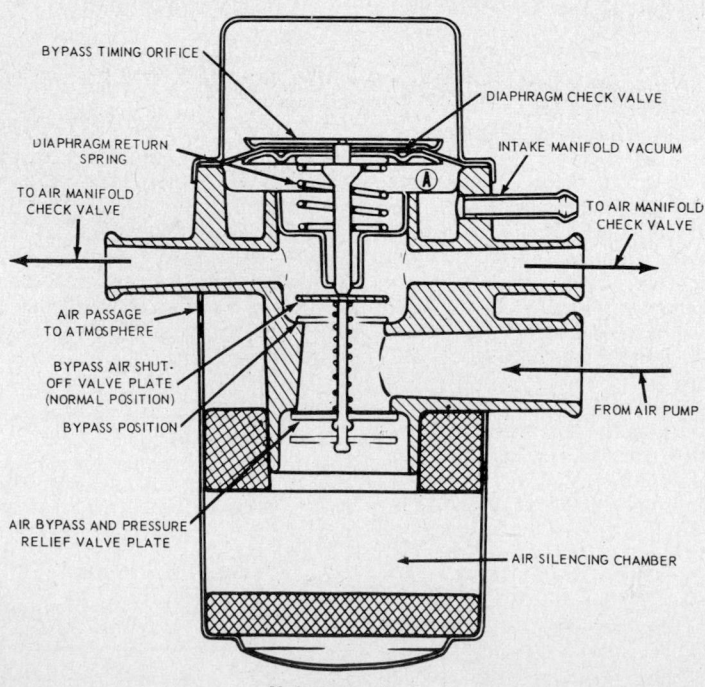

BYPASS TIMING ORIFICE

DIAPHRAGM CHECK VALVE

DIAPHRAGM RETURN SPRING

INTAKE MANIFOLD VACUUM

TO AIR MANIFOLD CHECK VALVE

TO AIR MANIFOLD CHECK VALVE

AIR PASSAGE TO ATMOSPHERE

BYPASS AIR SHUT-OFF VALVE PLATE (NORMAL POSITION)

BYPASS POSITION

FROM AIR PUMP

AIR BYPASS AND PRESSURE RELIEF VALVE PLATE

AIR SILENCING CHAMBER

Air bypass valve

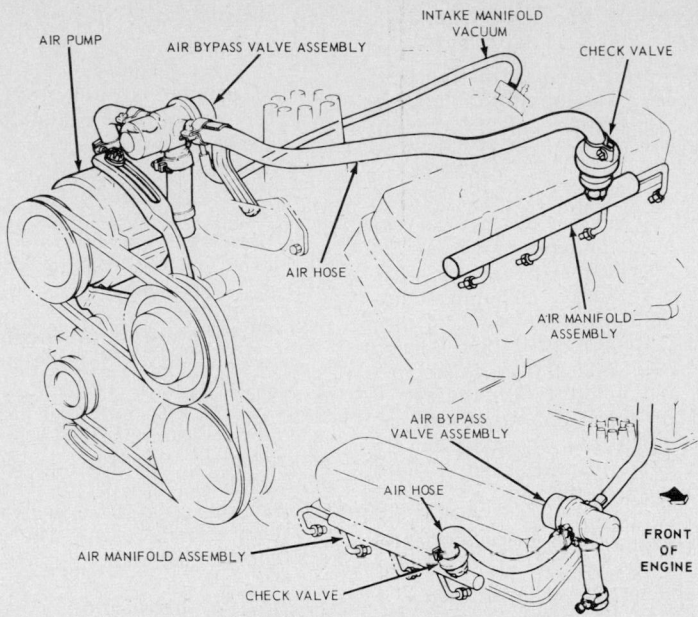

Thermactor installation—V8

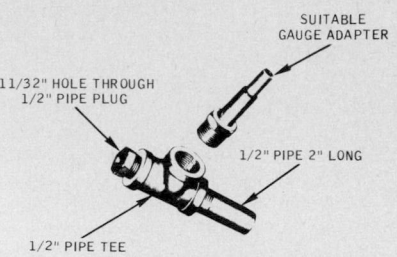

Air supply pump test gauge adapter

center of the pipe plug. Clean out the chips.

I. Install a standard fuel pump or other suitable testing gauge into the side opening of the T. The gauge must be graduated in $\frac{1}{4}$ psi increments.

2. Bring engine to operating temperature.

3. Inspect all hoses and connections for leaks. Correct if necessary.

4. Check air pump belt tension; adjust if necessary.

5. Disconnect air supply hose/s at air manifold check valve/s. If there are two valves, block off one hose with a tapered plug; secure plug with a clamp to prevent blowout.

6. Insert open pipe end of test gauge adapter in other air supply hose. Clamp hose to adapter to prevent blowout.

7. Position adapter and test gauge so that air discharge from the drilled hole in the adapter will cause no trouble.

8. Connect tachometer to engine.

9. Start engine and slowly accelerate to 1,500 rpm. Air pressure registered on the gauge should be greater than 1 psi.

10. If air pressure does not meet or exceed above pressures disconnect and plug air supply hose

at the bypass valve. Clamp the plug in place and repeat the pressure test.

11. If air pump pressure still does not meet minimum requirements, install a new air pump and repeat the pump test.

12. Replace the air pump if necessary.

Check Valve Test

This test can be performed at the same time as the air pump test.

1. Run engine until it reaches operating temperature.

2. Inspect all hoses and connections. Correct any existing leaks before testing check valve operation.

3. Disconnect air supply hose/s at the check valve/s.

4. Note the position of the valve plate inside the valve body. It should be lightly positioned against the valve seat, away from the air manifold.

5. Insert a probe into the hose connection on the check valve and depress the valve plate. It should freely return to its original position against the valve seat when released.

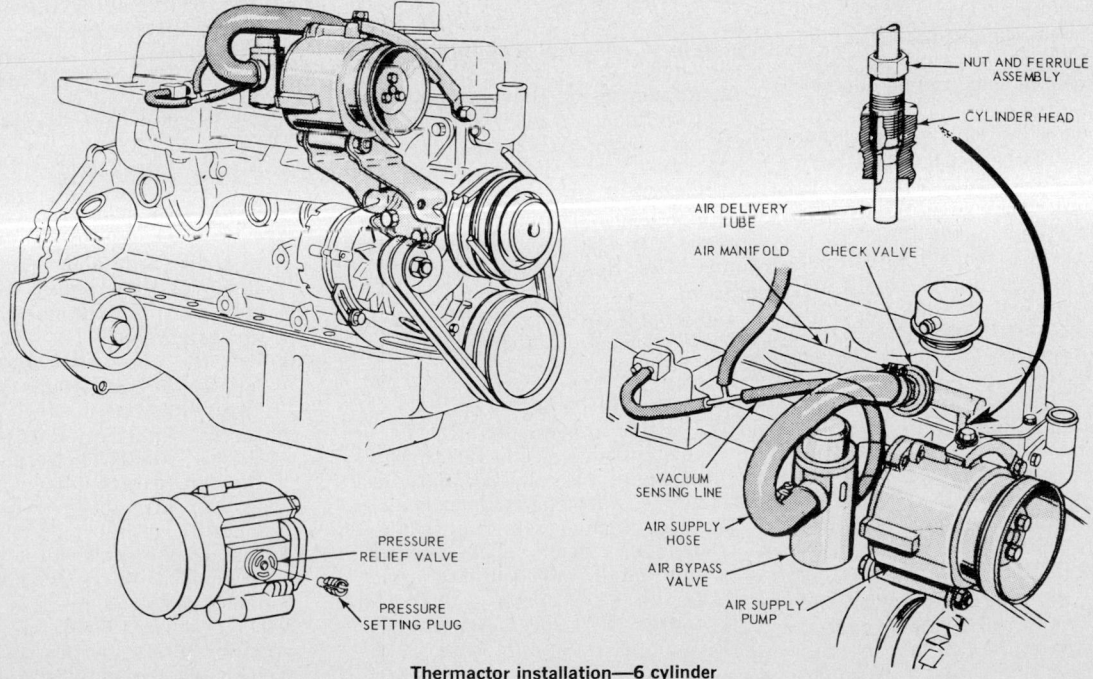

Thermactor installation—6 cylinder

If there are two check valves, check both valves for freedom of operation.

6. With hose/s disconnected, start the engine. Slowly accelerate to 1,500 rpm and watch for exhaust leaks at the check valve/s. There should be none. The valve may flutter or vibrate at idle. This is normal, due to exhaust pulsations in the manifold.

7. If check valve/s does not meet recommended conditions (Steps 4, 5, and 6), replace.

Air Bypass Valve Tests

1. Remove hose that connects air bypass valve to air manifold check valve at the bypass valve side.

2. With transmission in neutral and parking brake on, start engine and operate at normal idle speed. Be sure air is flowing from the air bypass valve hose connection. Air pressure should be noted, as this is the normal delivery flow to the air manifold/s.

3. Momentarily (for about 5 seconds) pinch the vacuum hose to the bypass valve. This duplicates the air bypass cycle.

4. Release the pinched vacuum hose. Air flow through the air bypass valve should diminish or stop for a short period. The length of time required to resume normal flow cannot be established. Variables in engine vacuum and the length of time the vacuum line is pinched off are determining factors.

5. Check the by-pass valve for diaphragm leakage by performing the following check:
   A. Remove the vacuum supply hose to the air bypass valve at the bypass valve connection.
   B. Insert a T-fitting into the vacuum supply hose.
   C. Connect a vacuum gauge to one of the remaining hose connections on the T.
   D. Connect a short length of hose (about 3 in.) to the remaining connection.
   E. Insert a suitable plug in the open end of the short length of hose.
   F. Start engine and note the vacuum gauge reading.
   G. Remove the plug from the short length of hose and connect the hose to the air bypass valve vacuum connection.
   H. Note the vacuum gauge reading. If the indicated reading does not correspond with the previous reading after about 1 minute, replace air bypass valve.

Replacement or Adjustment of Belt

1. Loosen air pump adjusting bolt. Loosen air pump-to-mounting bracket bolt and push air pump toward cylinder block. Remove the belt.

2. Install a new drive belt. With a suitable bar, pry against the rear cover of the air pump to obtain the specified belt tension.

3. Then, retighten the pump mounting bolts.

NOTE: always use a belt tension gauge (T63L-8620-A) to check belt tension, and follow tool manufacturers' instructions and specifications. Any belt that has operated for 10 minutes can be considered a used belt. Adjust accordingly.

Air Bypass Valve Replacement

1. Disconnect air and vacuum hoses at the air bypass valve body.

2. Position the air by-pass valve, and connect the respective hoses.

Check Valve Replacement

1. Disconnect air supply hose at the valve. (Use a 1¼ in. crowfoot wrench, the valve has a standard, right-hand pipe thread).

2. Clean the threads on the air manifold adapter (air supply tube on 289 or 302 V8 engine) with a wire brush. Do not blow compressed air through the check valve in either direction.

3. Install check valve and tighten.

4. Connect air supply hose.

Air Manifold (Except 289, 302, and 460 V8)

Removal

1. Disconnect air supply hose at check valve, position the hose out of the way and remove the valve.

2. Loosen all of the air manifold-to-cylinder head tube coupling nuts (compression fittings).

Cleaning and Inspection

Inspect air manifold for damaged threads and fittings and for leaking connections. Repair or replace as required.

Clean manifold and associated parts with kerosene. Do not dry with compressed air.

Installation

1. Position the air manifold/s on the cylinder head. Be sure all of the tube coupling nuts are aligned with the cylinder head.

2. Screw each coupling nut into the cylinder head, 1-2 threads. Tighten the tube coupling nuts.

3. Install the check valve and torque it to specifications.

4. Connect air supply hose to the check valve.

Air Supply Tube (289 V8)

Removal

1. Disconnect air supply hose at the check valve and position hose out of the way.

2. Remove check valve.

3. Remove air supply tube bolt and seal washer.

4. Carefully remove air supply tube and seal washer from the cylinder head.

Cleaning and Inspection

Inspect air supply tube for evidence of leaking threads or seal surfaces. Examine the attaching bolt head, seal washers and supply tube surface for leaks. Inspect the attaching bolt and cylinder head threads for damage.

Clean air supply tube, seal washers and bolt with kerosene. Do not dry with compressed air.

Installation

1. Install seal washer and air supply tube on cylinder head. Be sure it is positioned in the same manner as before removal.

2. Install seal washer and mounting bolt. Torque to specifications.

3. Install check valve; torque to specifications.

4. Connect air supply hose to the check valve.

Air Nozzle Replacement (Except 289, 302, and 460 V8)

Normally, air nozzles should be replaced during cylinder head reconditioning. A nozzle may be replaced, however, without removing the cylinder head, by removing the air manifold and using a hooked tool.

Clean nozzles with kerosene and a stiff bristle brush. Inspect air nozzles for eroded tips.

Air Pump Filter Fan Replacement

1. Loosen air pump as described in earlier procedures.

2. Remove drive pulley attaching bolts and pull the pulley off the air pump shaft.

3. Pry the outer disc loose, then remove the centrifugal filter fan. Care must be used to prevent foreign matter from entering the air intake hole, especially if the fan breaks during removal. Do not attempt to remove the metal drive hub.

4. Install the new filter fan by drawing it into position with the pulley bolts.

NOTE: some 1966-67 air pumps have air filters with replaceable non-cleanable elements.

Air Pump

Removal

1. Disconnect air outlet hose at the air pump.
2. Loosen pump belt tension adjuster.
3. Disengage drive belt.
4. Remove mounting bolt and air pump.

Installation

1. Position air pump on the mounting bracket and install the mounting bolt.

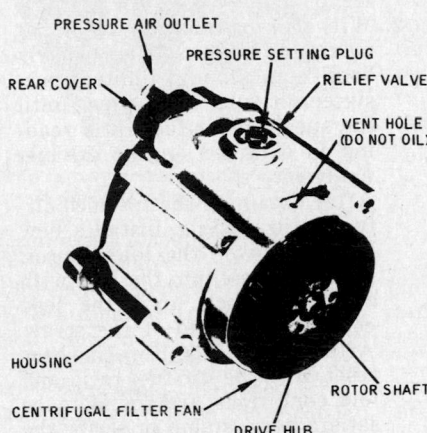

PRESSURE AIR OUTLET
PRESSURE SETTING PLUG
REAR COVER
RELIEF VALVE
VENT HOLE (DO NOT OIL)
HOUSING
ROTOR SHAFT
CENTRIFUGAL FILTER FAN
DRIVE HUB

Thermactor air pump

2. Place drive belt in pulleys and attach the adjusting arm to the air pump.
3. Adjust drive belt tension to specifications and tighten adjusting arm and mounting bolts.
4. Connect air outlet hose to the air pump.

Air Pump Relief Valve

Replacement

Do not disassemble the air pump on the car to replace relief valve, but remove the pump from the engine.

1. Position tool T66L-9A486-D on the air pump and remove the relief valve with the aid of a slide hammer (T59L-100-B).
2. Position relief valve on the pump housing and hold tool T66L-9A486-B in position.
3. Use a hammer to lightly tap the tool until the relief valve is seated.

Relief Valve Pressure-Setting Plug Replacement

1. Compress locking tabs inward (together) and remove the plastic pressure-setting plug.
2. Before installing the new plug, be sure that the plug is the correct one. The plugs are color-coded.
3. Insert the plug in the relief valve hole and push in until it snaps into place.

Fuel System

Hot and Cold Air Intake

All, except some high performance and police interceptor engines use a hot and cold intake system which regulates the temperature of carburetor intake air. This system improves engine performance during warm-up. It reduces the tendency of the carburetor to ice before reaching normal operating temperature.

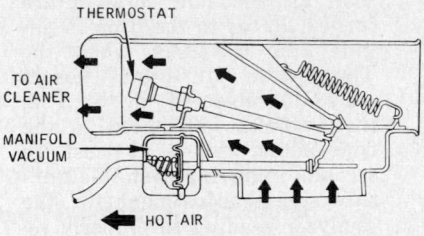

THERMOSTAT
TO AIR CLEANER
MANIFOLD VACUUM
HOT AIR

Duct and valve assembly in heat-on position—warm-up

The temperature of carburetor intake air is controlled by a valve plate and a vacuum override built into a duct attached to the air cleaner. The exhaust manifold shroud tube is attached to a shroud over the exhaust manifold, which is used as a heat source. The duct has an opening at the outer end to permit entry of cooler air from the engine compartment. A thermostatic bulb within the duct and the vacuum override motor attached to the duct and connected to the thermostat lever provides the means to balance the air temperature for various engine operating conditions.

During warm-up, the thermostat is in the retracted position. The valve plate is held in the heat-on position (up) by the valve plate spring, shutting off the air from the engine compartment. All air is then drawn from the shroud around the exhaust manifold.

During cold acceleration, additional intake air is provided by the vacuum motor control. Decrease in intake manifold vacuum during acceleration permits the vacuum motor to override the thermostat control. This opens the system to both engine compartment air and heated air from the exhaust manifold shroud.

On some 1971 models, this system has been simplified by deletion of the vacuum control. The thermostat cannot be overridden.

As the temperature of the air passing the thermostatic bulb increases, the thermostat starts to expand and forces the valve plate down. This allows cooler air from the engine compartment to enter the air cleaner. When the air reaches maximum temperature, the valve plate will be in heat-off position (down) so that only engine compartment air is being used.

All ram air intake models are equipped with a similar duct and valve assembly. It operates in the same manner as on other engines, except that the vacuum override is not used. Instead, a vacuum motor is installed in the air cleaner. When manifold vacuum is low, during engine loading or high-speed operation, a spring in the vacuum motor opens the valve plate in the air cleaner. This provides the optimum air supply for greater volumetric efficiency needed for full-power operation.

Carburetor Adjustments

Since 1968 the carburetors on all Ford Motor Company cars are equipped with idle fuel mixture adjustment limiters. These limiters control the maximum idle fuel richness and help prevent unqualified persons from making overly rich idle adjustments. There are two kinds of idle limiters: external and internal.

The external-type plastic idle limiter cap is installed on the head of the idle fuel mixture adjusting screw/s.

Any adjustment made on carburetors having this type of limiter must be within the range of the idle adjusting limiter.

A satisfactory idle should be obtainable within the range of the idle adjusting limiters, if all other engine systems are operating within specifications.

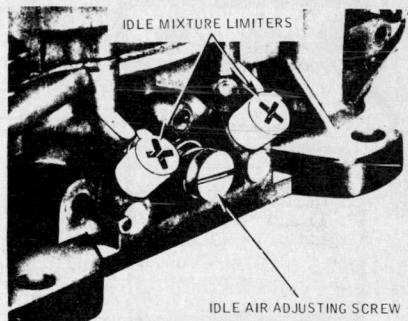

IDLE MIXTURE LIMITERS
IDLE AIR ADJUSTING SCREW

Idle air adjusting screw and mixture limiters (Carter 4-V)

The internal needle-type limiter is located in the idle channel and is not externally visible. It is capped by a lead seal. The limiter is installed and sealed during manufacture.

Refer to the Car Section for carburetor adjustment procedures.

Additional Idle Speed and Mixture Procedures

If a satisfactory idle is not obtained by normal adjustment procedures, additional checks may be necessary.

1. Check the following items and, if necessary, correct.
   A. Vacuum leaks.
   B. Ignition system wiring.
   C. Spark plugs.
   D. Distributor point condition and dwell.
   E. Initial ignition timing.
2. If idle condition is not satisfac-

Engine Tune-Up

Engine tune-up is a procedure performed to restore engine performance, deteriorated due to normal wear and loss of adjustment. The three major areas considered in a routine tune-up are compression, ignition, and carburetion, although valve adjustment may be included.

A tune-up is performed in three steps: *analysis*, in which it is determined whether normal wear is responsible for performance loss, and which parts require replacement or service; *parts replacement or service*; and *adjustment*, in which engine adjustments are returned to original specifications. Since the advent of emission control equipment, precision adjustment has become increasingly critical, in order to maintain pollutant emission levels.

Analysis

The procedures below are used to indicate where adjustments, parts service or replacement are necessary within the realm of a normal tune-up. If, following these tests, all systems appear to be functioning properly, proceed to the Troubleshooting Section for further diagnosis.

—Remove all spark plugs, noting the cylinder in which they were installed. Remove the air cleaner, and position the throttle and choke in the full open position. Disconnect the coil high tension lead from the coil and the distributor cap. Insert a compression gauge into the spark plug port of each cylinder, in succession, and crank the engine with

Maxi. Press. Lbs. Sq. In.	Min. Press. Lbs. Sq. In.	Max. Press. Lbs. Sq. In.	Min. Press. Lbs. Sq. In.
134	101	188	141
136	102	190	142
138	104	192	144
140	105	194	145
142	107	196	147
146	110	198	148
148	111	200	150
150	113	202	151
152	114	204	153
154	115	206	154
156	117	208	156
158	118	210	157
160	120	212	158
162	121	214	160
164	123	216	162
166	124	218	163
168	126	220	165
170	127	222	166
172	129	224	168
174	131	226	169
176	132	228	171
178	133	230	172
180	135	232	174
182	136	234	175
184	138	236	177
186	140	238	178

Compression pressure limits
© Buick Div. G.M. Corp.

the starter to obtain the highest possible reading. Record the readings, and compare the highest to the lowest on the compression pressure limit chart. If the difference exceeds the limits on the chart, or if all readings are excessively low, proceed to a wet compression check (see Troubleshooting Section).

—Evaluate the spark plugs according to the spark plug chart in the Troubleshooting Section, and proceed as indicated in the chart.

—Remove the distributor cap, and inspect it inside and out for cracks and/or carbon tracks, and inside for excessive wear or burning of the rotor contacts. If any of these faults are evident, the cap must be replaced.

—Check the breaker points for burning, pitting or wear, and the contact heel resting on the distributor cam for excessive wear. If defects are noted, replace the entire breaker point set.

—Remove and inspect the rotor. If the contacts are burned or worn, or if the rotor is excessively loose on the distributor shaft (where applicable), the rotor must be replaced.

—Inspect the spark plug leads and the coil high tension lead for cracks or brittleness. If any of the wires appear defective, the entire set should be replaced.

—Check the air filter to ensure that it is functioning properly.

Parts Replacement and Service

The determination of whether to replace or service parts is at the mechanic's discretion; however, it is suggested that any parts in questionable condition be replaced rather than reused.

—Clean and regap, or replace, the spark plugs as needed. Lightly coat the threads with engine oil and install the plugs. CAUTION: *Do not over-torque taper-seat spark plugs, or plugs being installed in aluminum cylinder heads.*

SPARK PLUG TORQUE

Thread size	Cast-Iron Heads	Aluminum Heads
10 mm.	14	11
14 mm.	·30	27
18 mm.	34*	32
⅞ in.—18	37	35

* 17 ft. lbs. for tapered plugs using no gaskets.

—If the distributor cap is to be reused, clean the inside with a dry rag, and remove corrosion from the rotor contact points with fine emery cloth. Remove the spark plug wires one by one, and clean the wire ends and the inside of the towers. If the boots are loose, they should be replaced.

If the cap is to be replaced, transfer the wires one by one, cleaning the wire ends and replacing the boots if necessary.

—If the original points are to remain in service, clean them lightly with emery cloth, lubricate the contact heel with grease specifically designed for this purpose. Rotate the crankshaft until the heel rests on a high point of the distributor cam, and adjust the point gap to specifications.

When replacing the points, remove the original points and condenser, and wipe out the inside of the distributor housing with a clean, dry rag. Lightly lubricate the contact heel and pivot point, and install the points and condenser. Rotate the crankshaft until the heel rests on a high point of the distributor cam, and adjust the point gap to specifications. NOTE: *Always replace the condenser when changing the points.*

—If the rotor is to be reused, clean the contacts with solvent. Do not alter the spring tension of the rotor center contact. Install the rotor and the distributor cap.

—Replace the coil high tension lead and/or the spark plug leads as necessary.

—Clean the carburetor using a spray solvent (e.g., Gumout Spray). Remove the varnish from the throttle bores, and clean the linkage. Disconnect and plug the fuel line, and run the engine until it runs out of fuel. Partially fill the float chamber with solvent, and reconnect the fuel line. In extreme cases, the jets can be pressure flushed by inserting a rubber plug into the float vent, running the spray nozzle through it, and spraying the solvent until it squirts out of the venturi fuel dump.

—Clean and tighten all wiring connections in the primary electrical circuit.

Additional Services

The following services *should* be performed in conjunction with a routine tune-up to ensure efficient performance.

—Inspect the battery and fill to the proper level with distilled water. Remove the cable clamps, clean clamps and posts thoroughly, coat the posts lightly with petroleum jelly, reinstall and tighten.

—Inspect all belts, replace and/or adjust as necessary.

—Test the PCV valve (if so equipped), and clean or replace as indicated. Clean all crankcase ventilation hoses, or replace if cracked or hardened.

—Adjust the valves (if necessary) to manufacturer's specifications.

Adjustments

—Connect a dwell-tachometer between the distributor primary lead and ground. Remove the distributor cap and rotor (unless equipped with Delco externally adjustable distributor). With the ignition off, crank the engine with a remote starter switch and measure the point dwell angle. Adjust the dwell angle to specifications. NOTE: *Increasing the gap decreases the dwell angle and vice-versa.* Install the rotor and distributor cap.

—Connect a timing light according to the manufacturer's specifications. Identify the proper timing marks with chalk or paint. NOTE: *Luminescent (day-glo) paint is excellent for this purpose.* Start the engine, and run it until it reaches operating temperature. Disconnect and plug any distributor vacuum lines, and adjust idle to the speed required to adjust timing, according to specifications. Loosen the distributor clamp and adjust timing to specifications by rotating the distributor in the engine. NOTE: *To advance timing, rotate distributor opposite normal direction of rotor rotation, and vice-versa.*

—Synchronize the throttles and mixture of multiple carburetors (if so equipped) according to procedures given in the individual car sections.

—Adjust the idle speed, mixture, and idle quality, as specified in the individual car sections. If adjustment of carburetors equipped with idle limiter caps is found to be impossible, the caps may be removed by inserting a sheet metal screw into the cap, and tightening until the cap slides off. Final idle adjustments should be made with the air cleaner installed. CAUTION: *Due to strict emission control requirements on 1969 and later models, special test equipment (CO meter, SUN Tester) may be necessary to properly adjust idle mixture to specifications.*

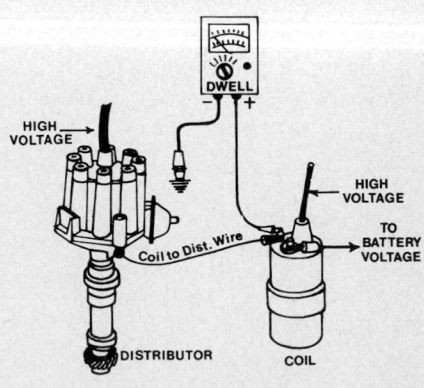

Dwell meter hook-up

Trouble-shooting

The following section is designed to aid in the rapid diagnosis of engine problems. The systematic format is used to diagnose problems ranging from engine starting difficulties to the need for engine overhaul. It is assumed that the user is equipped with basic hand tools and test equipment (tach-dwell meter, timing light, voltmeter, and ohmmeter).

Troubleshooting is divided into two sections. The first, *General Diagnosis*, is used to locate the problem area. In the second, *Specific Diagnosis*, the problem is systematically evaluated.

General Diagnosis

PROBLEM: *Symptom*	Begin diagnosis at Section Two, Number ———
Engine won't start:	
Starter doesn't turn	1.1, 2.1
Starter turns, engine doesn't	2.1
Starter turns engine very slowly	1.1, 2.4
Starter turns engine normally	3.1, 4.1
Starter turns engine very quickly	6.1
Engine fires intermittently	4.1
Engine fires consistently	5.1, 6.1
Engine runs poorly:	
Hard starting	3.1, 4.1, 5.1, 8.1
Rough idle	4.1, 5.1, 8.1
Stalling	3.1, 4.1, 5.1, 8.1
Engine dies at high speeds	4.1, 5.1
Hesitation (on acceleration from standing stop)	5.1, 8.1
Poor pickup	4.1, 5.1, 8.1
Lack of power	3.1, 4.1, 5.1, 8.1
Backfire through the carburetor	4.1, 8.1, 9.1
Backfire through the exhaust	4.1, 8.1, 9.1
Blue exhaust gases	6.1, 7.1
Black exhaust gases	5.1
Running on (after the ignition is shut off)	3.1, 8.1
Susceptible to moisture	4.1
Engine misfires under load	4.1, 7.1, 8.4, 9.1
Engine misfires at speed	4.1, 8.4
Engine misfires at idle	3.1, 4.1, 5.1, 7.1, 8.4

PROBLEM: *Symptom*	Probable Cause
Engine noises: ①	
Metallic grind while starting	Starter drive not engaging completely
Constant grind or rumble	*Starter drive not releasing, worn main bearings
Constant knock	Worn connecting rod bearings
Knock under load	Fuel octane too low, worn connecting rod bearings
Double knock	Loose piston pin
Metallic tap	*Collapsed or sticky valve lifter, excessive valve clearance, excessive end play in a rotating shaft
Scrape	*Fan belt contacting a stationary surface
Tick while starting	S.U. electric fuel pump (normal), starter brushes
Constant tick	*Generator brushes, shreaded fan belt
Squeal	*Improperly tensioned fan belt
Hiss or roar	*Steam escaping through a leak in the cooling system or the radiator overflow vent
Whistle	*Vacuum leak
Wheeze	Loose or cracked spark plug

①—It is extremely difficult to evaluate vehicle noises. While the above are general definitions of engine noises, those starred (*) should be considered as possibly originating elsewhere in the car. To aid diagnosis, the following list considers other potential sources of these sounds.

Metallic grind:
Throwout bearing; transmission gears, bearings, or synchronizers; differential bearings, gears; something metallic in contact with brake drum or disc.

Metallic tap:
U-joints; fan-to-radiator (or shroud) contact.

Scrape:
Brake shoe or pad dragging; tire to body contact; suspension contacting undercarriage or exhaust; something non-metallic contacting brake shoe or drum.

Tick:
Transmission gears; differential gears; lack of radio suppression; resonant vibration of body panels; windshield wiper motor or transmission; heater motor and blower.

Squeal:
Brake shoe or pad not fully releasing; tires (excessive wear, uneven wear, improper inflation); front or rear wheel alignment (most commonly due to improper toe-in).

Hiss or whistle:
Wind leaks (body or window); heater motor and blower fan.

Roar:
Wheel bearings; wind leaks (body and window).

Specific Diagnosis

This section is arranged so that following each test, instructions are given to proceed to another, until a problem is diagnosed.

INDEX

Group		Topic
1	*	Battery
2	*	Cranking system
3	*	Primary electrical system
4	*	Secondary electrical system
5	*	Fuel system
6	*	Engine compression
7	**	Engine vacuum
8	**	Secondary electrical system
9	**	Valve train
10	**	Exhaust system
11	**	Cooling system
12	**	Engine lubrication

*—The engine need not be running.
**—The engine must be running.

SAMPLE SECTION

Test and Procedure	Results and Indications	Proceed to
4.1—Check for spark: Hold each spark plug wire approximately ¼″ from ground with gloves or a heavy, dry rag. Crank the engine and observe the spark.	If no spark is evident:	4.2
	If spark is good in some cases:	4.3
	If spark is good in all cases:	4.6

DIAGNOSIS

Test and Procedure	Results and Indications	Proceed to
1.1—Inspect the battery visually for case condition (corrosion, cracks) and water level.	If case is cracked, replace battery:	1.4
	If the case is intact, remove corrosion with a solution of baking soda and water (CAUTION: *do not get the solution into the battery*), and fill with water:	1.2
1.2—Check the battery cable connections: Insert a screwdriver between the battery post and the cable clamp. Turn the headlights on high beam, and observe them as the screwdriver is gently twisted to ensure good metal to metal contact.	If the lights brighten, remove and clean the clamp and post; coat the post with petroleum jelly, install and tighten the clamp:	1.4
	If no improvement is noted:	1.3

Testing battery cable connections using a screwdriver

1.3—Test the state of charge of the battery using an individual cell tester or hydrometer.

Spec. Grav. Reading	Charged Condition
1.260-1.280	Fully Charged
1.230-1.250	Three Quarter Charged
1.200-1.220	One Half Charged
1.170-1.190	One Quarter Charged
1.140-1.160	Just About Flat
1.110-1.130	All The Way Down

State of battery charge

Electrolyte temperature (°F) / Specific gravity correction

+120	+.016
	+.012
+100	+.008 — ADD to reading
	+.004
+80	no correction
	—.004
+60	—.008
	—.012
+40	—.016
	—.020
+20	—.024 — SUBTRACT from reading
	—.028
0	—.032
	—.036
—20	—.040

The effect of temperature on the specific gravity of battery electrolyte

If indicated, charge the battery. NOTE: *If no obvious reason exists for the low state of charge (i.e., battery age, prolonged storage), the charging system should be tested:* — 1.4

Test and Procedure	*Results and Indications*	*Proceed to*
1.4—Visually inspect battery cables for cracking, bad connection to ground, or bad connection to starter.	If necessary, tighten connections or replace the cables:	2.1

Tests in Group 2 are performed with coil high tension lead disconnected to prevent accidental starting.

2.1—Test the starter motor and solenoid: Connect a jumper from the battery post of the solenoid (or relay) to the starter post of the solenoid (or relay).	If starter turns the engine normally:	2.2
	If the starter buzzes, or turns the engine very slowly:	2.4
	If no response, replace the solenoid (or relay).	3.1
	If the starter turns, but the engine doesn't, ensure that the flywheel ring gear is intact. If the gear is undamaged, replace the starter drive.	3.1
2.2—Determine whether ignition override switches are functioning properly (clutch start switch, neutral safety switch), by connecting a jumper across the switch(es), and turning the ignition switch to "start".	If starter operates, adjust or replace switch:	3.1
	If the starter doesn't operate:	2.3
2.3—Check the ignition switch "start" position: Connect a 12V test lamp between the starter post of the solenoid (or relay) and ground. Turn the ignition switch to the "start" position, and jiggle the key.	If the lamp doesn't light when the switch is turned, check the ignition switch for loose connections, cracked insulation, or broken wires. Repair or replace as necessary:	3.1
	If the lamp flickers when the key is jiggled, replace the ignition switch.	3.3

Checking the ignition switch "start" position

2.4—Remove and bench test the starter, according to specifications in the car section.	If the starter does not meet specifications, repair or replace as needed:	3.1
	If the starter is operating properly:	2.5
2.5—Determine whether the engine can turn freely: Remove the spark plugs, and check for water in the cylinders. Check for water on the dipstick, or oil in the radiator. Attempt to turn the engine using an 18″ flex drive and socket on the crankshaft pulley nut or bolt.	If the engine will turn freely only with the spark plugs out, and hydrostatic lock (water in the cylinders) is ruled out, check valve timing:	9.2
	If engine will not turn freely, and it is known that the clutch and transmission are free, the engine must be disassembled for further evaluation:	Next Chapter

Tests and Procedures	Results and Indications	Proceed to
3.1—Check the ignition switch "on" position: Connect a jumper wire between the distributor side of the coil and ground, and a 12V test lamp between the switch side of the coil and ground. Remove the high tension lead from the coil. Turn the ignition switch on and jiggle the key.	If the lamp lights:	3.2
	If the lamp flickers when the key is jiggled, replace the ignition switch:	3.3
	If the lamp doesn't light, check for loose or open connections. If none are found, remove the ignition switch and check for continuity. If the switch is faulty, replace it:	3.3

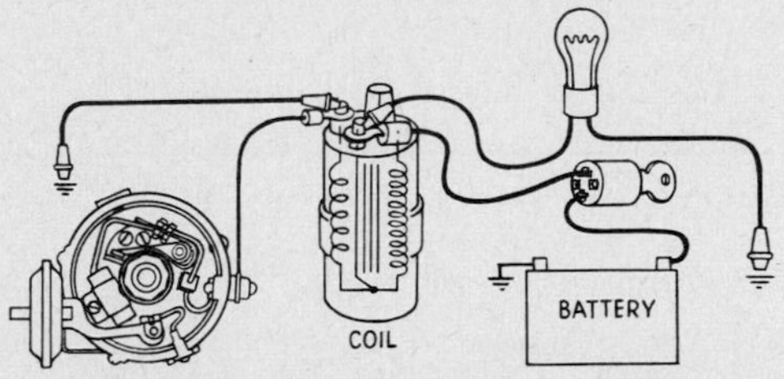

Checking the ignition switch "on" position

3.2—Check the ballast resistor or resistance wire for an open circuit, using an ohmmeter.	Replace the resistor or the resistance wire if the resistance is zero.	3.3
3.3—Visually inspect the breaker points for burning, pitting, or excessive wear. Gray coloring of the point contact surfaces is normal. Rotate the crankshaft until the contact heel rests on a high point of the distributor cam, and adjust the point gap to specifications.	If the breaker points are intact, clean the contact surfaces with fine emery cloth, and adjust the point gap to specifications. If pitted or worn, replace the points and condenser, and adjust the gap to specifications: NOTE: *Always lubricate the distributor cam according to manufacturer's recommendations when servicing the breaker points.*	3.4
3.4—Connect a dwell meter between the distributor primary lead and ground. Crank the engine and observe the point dwell angle.	If necessary, adjust the point dwell angle: NOTE: *Increasing the point gap decreases the dwell angle, and vice-versa.*	3.6
	If dwell meter shows little or no reading:	3.5

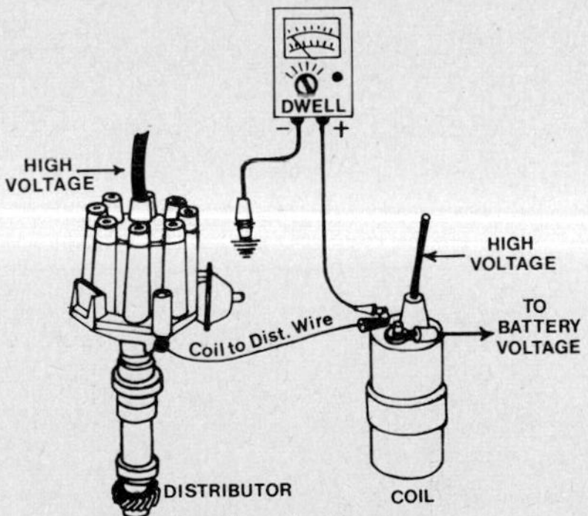

Dwell meter hook-up

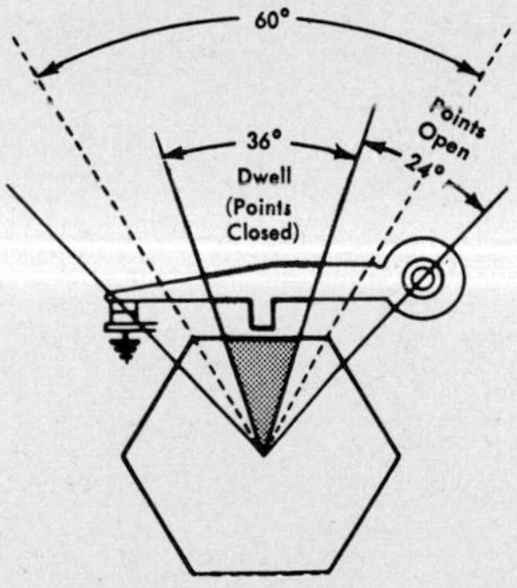

Dwell angle

| 3.5—Check the condenser for short: Connect an ohmmeter across the condenser body and the pigtail lead. | If any reading other than infinite resistance is noted, replace the condenser: | 3.6 |

Checking the condenser for short

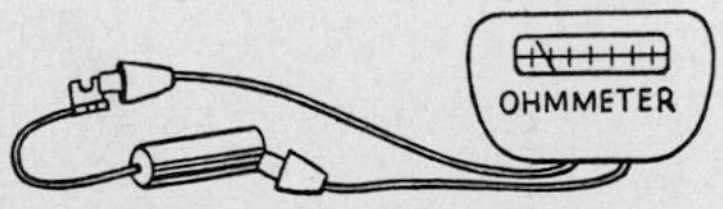

Test and Procedure	Results and Indications	Proceed to
3.6—Test the coil primary resistance: Connect an ohmmeter across the coil primary terminals, and read the resistance on the low scale. Note whether an external ballast resistor or resistance wire is utilized.	Coils utilizing ballast resistors or resistance wires should have approximately 1.0Ω resistance; coils with internal resistors should have approximately 4.0Ω resistance. If values far from the above are noted, replace the coil:	4.1

Testing the coil primary resistance

Test and Procedure	Results and Indications	Proceed to
4.1—Check for spark: Hold each spark plug wire approximately $\frac{1}{4}''$ from ground with gloves or a heavy, dry rag. Crank the engine, and observe the spark.	If no spark is evident:	4.2
	If spark is good in some cylinders:	4.3
	If spark is good in all cylinders:	4.6
4.2—Check for spark at the coil high tension lead: Remove the coil high tension lead from the distributor and position it approximately $\frac{1}{4}''$ from ground. Crank the engine and observe spark. CAUTION: *This test should not be performed on cars equipped with transistorized ignition.*	If the spark is good and consistent:	4.3
	If the spark is good but intermittent, test the primary electrical system starting at 3.3:	3.3
	If the spark is weak or non-existent, replace the coil high tension lead, clean and tighten all connections and retest. If no improvement is noted:	4.4
4.3—Visually inspect the distributor cap and rotor for burned or corroded contacts, cracks, carbon tracks, or moisture. Also check the fit of the rotor on the distributor shaft (where applicable).	If moisture is present, dry thoroughly, and retest per 4.1:	4.1
	If burned or excessively corroded contacts, cracks, or carbon tracks are noted, replace the defective part(s) and retest per 4.1:	4.1
	If the rotor and cap appear intact, or are only slightly corroded, clean the contacts thoroughly (including the cap towers and spark plug wire ends) and retest per 4.1:	
	If the spark is good in all cases:	4.6
	If the spark is poor in all cases:	4.5
4.4—Check the coil secondary resistance: Connect an ohmmeter across the distributor side of the coil and the coil tower. Read the resistance on the high scale of the ohmmeter.	The resistance of a satisfactory coil should be between $4K\Omega$ and $10K\Omega$. If the resistance is considerably higher (i.e., $40K\Omega$) replace the coil, and retest per 4.1: NOTE: *This does not apply to high performance coils.*	4.1

Testing the coil secondary resistance

Test and Procedure	Results and Indications	Proceed to
4.5—Visually inspect the spark plug wires for cracking or brittleness. Ensure that no two wires are positioned so as to cause induction firing (adjacent and parallel). Remove each wire, one by one, and check resistance with an ohmmeter.	Replace any cracked or brittle wires. If any of the wires are defective, replace the entire set. Replace any wires with excessive resistance (over 8000Ω per foot for suppression wire), and separate any wires that might cause induction firing.	4.6
4.6—Remove the spark plugs, noting the cylinders from which they were removed, and evaluate according to the chart below.	See below.	See below.

	Condition	Cause	Remedy	Proceed to
	Electrodes eroded, light brown deposits.	Normal wear. Normal wear is indicated by approximately .001″ wear per 1000 miles.	Clean and regap the spark plug if wear is not excessive: Replace the spark plug if excessively worn:	4.7
	Carbon fouling (black, dry, fluffy deposits).	If present on one or two plugs: Faulty high tension lead(s). Burnt or sticking valve(s).	Test the high tension leads: Check the valve train: (Clean and regap the plugs in either case.)	4.5 9.1
		If present on most or all plugs: Overly rich fuel mixture, due to restricted air filter, improper carburetor adjustment, improper choke or heat riser adjustment or operation.	Check the fuel system:	5.1
	Oil fouling (wet black deposits)	Worn engine components. NOTE: *Oil fouling may occur in new or recently rebuilt engines until broken in.*	Check engine vacuum and compression:	6.1
	Lead fouling (gray, black, tan, or yellow deposits, which appear glazed or cinder-like).	Combustion by-products.	Clean and regap the plugs: (Use plugs of a different heat range if the problem recurs.)	4.7

	Condition	Cause	Remedy	Proceed to
	Gap bridging (deposits lodged between the electrodes).	Incomplete combustion, or transfer of deposits from the combustion chamber.	Replace the spark plugs:	4.7
	Overheating (burnt electrodes, and extremely white insulator with small black spots).	Ignition timing advanced too far.	Adjust timing to specifications:	8.2
		Overly lean fuel mixture.	Check the fuel system:	5.1
		Spark plugs not seated properly.	Clean spark plug seat and install a new gasket washer: (Replace the spark plugs in all cases.)	4.7
	Fused spot deposits on the insulator.	Combustion chamber blow-by.	Clean and regap the spark plugs:	4.7
	Pre-ignition (melted or severely burned electrodes, blistered or cracked insulators, or metallic deposits on the insulator).	Incorrect spark plug heat range.	Replace with plugs of the proper heat range:	4.7
		Ignition timing advanced too far.	Adjust timing to specifications:	8.2
		Spark plugs not being cooled efficiently.	Clean the spark plug seat, and check the cooling system:	11.1
		Fuel mixture too lean.	Check the fuel system:	5.1
		Poor compression.	Check compression:	6.1
		Fuel grade too low.	Use higher octane fuel:	4.7

Test and Procedure		Results and Indications	Proceed to
4.7—Determine the static ignition timing: Using the flywheel or crankshaft pulley timing marks as a guide, locate top dead center on the *compression* stroke of the No. 1 cylinder. Remove the distributor cap.		Adjust the distributor so that the rotor points toward the No. 1 tower in the distributor cap, and the points are just opening:	4.8
4.8—Check coil polarity: Connect a voltmeter negative lead to the coil high tension lead, and the positive lead to ground (NOTE: *reverse the hook-up for positive ground cars*). Crank the engine momentarily.	**Checking coil polarity**	If the voltmeter reads up-scale, the polarity is correct:	5.1
		If the voltmeter reads down-scale, reverse the coil polarity (switch the primary leads):	5.1

Test and Procedure	Results and Indications	Proceed to
5.1—Determine that the air filter is functioning efficiently: Hold paper elements up to a strong light, and attempt to see light through the filter.	Clean permanent air filters in gasoline (or manufacturer's recommendation), and allow to dry. Replace paper elements through which light cannot be seen:	5.2
5.2—Determine whether a flooding condition exists: Flooding is identified by a strong gasoline odor, and excessive gasoline present in the throttle bore(s) of the carburetor.	If flooding is not evident: If flooding is evident, permit the gasoline to dry for a few moments and restart. If flooding doesn't recur: If flooding is persistant:	5.3 5.6 5.5
5.3—Check that fuel is reaching the carburetor: Detach the fuel line at the carburetor inlet. Hold the end of the line in a cup (not styrofoam), and crank the engine.	If fuel flows smoothly: If fuel doesn't flow (NOTE: *Make sure that there is fuel in the tank*), or flows erratically:	5.6 5.4
5.4—Test the fuel pump: Disconnect all fuel lines from the fuel pump. Hold a finger over the input fitting, crank the engine (with electric pump, turn the ignition or pump on), and feel for suction.	If suction is evident, blow out the fuel line to the tank with low pressure compressed air until bubbling is heard from the fuel filler neck. Also blow out the carburetor fuel line (both ends disconnected): If no suction is evident, replace or repair the fuel pump: NOTE: *Repeated oil fouling of the spark plugs, or a no-start condition, could be the result of a ruptured vacuum booster pump diaphragm, through which oil or gasoline is being drawn into the intake manifold (where applicable).*	5.6 5.6
5.5—Check the needle and seat: Tap the carburetor in the area of the needle and seat.	If flooding stops, a gasoline additive (e.g., Gumout) will often cure the problem: If flooding continues, check the fuel pump for excessive pressure at the carburetor (according to specifications). If the pressure is normal, the needle and seat must be removed and checked, and/or the float level adjusted:	5.6 5.6
5.6—Test the accelerator pump by looking into the throttle bores while operating the throttle.	If the accelerator pump appears to be operating normally: If the accelerator pump is not operating, the pump must be reconditioned. Where possible, service the pump with the carburetor(s) installed on the engine. If necessary, remove the carburetor. Prior to removal:	5.7 5.7
5.7—Determine whether the carburetor main fuel system is functioning: Spray a commercial starting fluid into the carburetor while attempting to start the engine.	If the engine starts, runs for a few seconds, and dies: If the engine doesn't start:	5.8 6.1

Test and Procedures	Results and Indications	Proceed to
5.8—Uncommon fuel system malfunctions: See below:	If the problem is solved: If the problem remains, remove and recondition the carburetor.	6.1

Condition	Indication	Test	Usual Weather Conditions	Remedy
Vapor lock	Car will not restart shortly after running.	Cool the components of the fuel system until the engine starts.	Hot to very hot	Ensure that the exhaust manifold heat control valve is operating. Check with the vehicle manufacturer for the recommended solution to vapor lock on the model in question.
Carburetor icing	Car will not idle, stalls at low speeds.	Visually inspect the throttle plate area of the throttle bores for frost.	High humidity, 32-40° F.	Ensure that the exhaust manifold heat control valve is operating, and that the intake manifold heat riser is not blocked.
Water in the fuel	Engine sputters and stalls; may not start.	Pump a small amount of fuel into a glass jar. Allow to stand, and inspect for droplets or a layer of water.	High humidity, extreme temperature changes.	For droplets, use one or two cans of commercial gas dryer (Dry Gas) For a layer of water, the tank must be drained, and the fuel lines blown out with compressed air.

Test and Procedure	Results and Indications	Proceed to
6.1—Test engine compression: Remove all spark plugs. Insert a compression gauge into a spark plug port, crank the engine to obtain the maximum reading, and record.	If compression is within limits on all cylinders:	7.1
	If gauge reading is extremely low on all cylinders:	6.2
	If gauge reading is low on one or two cylinders:	6.2
	(If gauge readings are identical and low on two or more adjacent cylinders, the head gasket must be replaced.)	

Testing compression
(© Chevrolet Div. G.M. Corp.)

Maxi. Press. Lbs. Sq. In.	Min. Press. Lbs. Sq. In.	Maxi. Press. Lbs. Sq. In.	Min. Press. Lbs. Sq. In.	Max. Press. Lbs. Sq. In.	Min. Press. Lbs. Sq. In.	Max. Press. Lbs. Sq. In.	Min. Press. Lbs. Sq. In.
134	101	162	121	188	141	214	160
136	102	164	123	190	142	216	162
138	104	166	124	192	144	218	163
140	105	168	126	194	145	220	165
142	107	170	127	196	147	222	166
146	110	172	129	198	148	224	168
148	111	174	131	200	150	226	169
150	113	176	132	202	151	228	171
152	114	178	133	204	153	230	172
154	115	180	135	206	154	232	174
156	117	182	136	208	156	234	175
158	118	184	138	210	157	236	177
160	120	186	140	212	158	238	178

Compression pressure limits
(© Buick Div. G.M. Corp.)

Test and Procedure	Results and Indications	Proceed to
6.2—Test engine compression (wet): Squirt approximately 30 cc. of engine oil into each cylinder, and retest per 6.1.	If the readings improve, worn or cracked rings or broken pistons are indicated:	Next Chapter
	If the readings do not improve, burned or excessively carboned valves or a jumped timing chain are indicated:	7.1
	NOTE: *A jumped timing chain is often indicated by difficult cranking.*	
7.1—Perform a vacuum check of the engine: Attach a vacuum gauge to the intake manifold beyond the throttle plate. Start the engine, and observe the action of the needle over the range of engine speeds.	See below.	See below

	Reading	Indications	Proceed to
	Steady, from 17-22 in. Hg.	Normal.	8.1
	Low and steady.	Late ignition or valve timing, or low compression:	6.1
	Very low	Vacuum leak:	7.2
	Needle fluctuates as engine speed increases.	Ignition miss, blown cylinder head gasket, leaking valve or weak valve spring:	6.1, 8.3
	Gradual drop in reading at idle.	Excessive back pressure in the exhaust system:	10.1
	Intermittent fluctuation at idle.	Ignition miss, sticking valve:	8.3, 9.1
	Drifting needle.	Improper idle mixture adjustment, carburetors not synchronized (where applicable), or minor intake leak. Synchronize the carburetors, adjust the idle, and retest. If the condition persists:	7.2
	High and steady.	Early ignition timing:	8.2

Test and Procedure	*Results and Indications*	*Proceed to*
7.2—Attach a vacuum gauge per 7.1, and test for an intake manifold leak. Squirt a small amount of oil around the intake manifold gaskets, carburetor gaskets, plugs and fittings. Observe the action of the vacuum gauge.	If the reading improves, replace the indicated gasket, or seal the indicated fitting or plug:	8.1
	If the reading remains low:	7.3
7.3—Test all vacuum hoses and accessories for leaks as described in 7.2. Also check the carburetor body (dashpots, automatic choke mechanism, throttle shafts) for leaks in the same manner.	If the reading improves, service or replace the offending part(s):	8.1
	If the reading remains low:	6.1
8.1—Check the point dwell angle: Connect a dwell meter between the distributor primary wire and ground. Start the engine, and observe the dwell angle from idle to 3000 rpm.	If necessary, adjust the dwell angle. NOTE: *Increasing the point gap reduces the dwell angle and vice-versa.* If the dwell angle moves outside specifications as engine speed increases, the distributor should be removed and checked for cam accuracy, shaft end-play and concentricity, bushing wear, and adequate point arm tension (NOTE: *Most of these items may be checked with the distributor installed in the engine, using an oscilloscope*):	8.2
8.2—Connect a timing light (per manufacturer's recommendation) and check the dynamic ignition timing. Disconnect and plug the vacuum hose(s) to the distributor if specified, start the engine, and observe the timing marks at the specified engine speed.	If the timing is not correct, adjust to specifications by rotating the distributor in the engine: (Advance timing by rotating distributor opposite normal direction of rotor rotation, retard timing by rotating distributor in same direction as rotor rotation.)	8.3
8.3—Check the operation of the distributor advance mechanism(s): To test the mechanical advance, disconnect all but the mechanical advance, and observe the timing marks with a timing light as the engine speed is increased from idle. If the mark moves smoothly, without hesitation, it may be assumed that the mechanical advance is functioning properly. To test vacuum advance and/or retard systems, alternately crimp and release the vacuum line, and observe the timing mark for movement. If movement is noted, the system is operating.	If the systems are functioning:	8.4
	If the systems are not functioning, remove the distributor, and test on a distributor tester:	8.4
8.4—Locate an ignition miss: With the engine running, remove each spark plug wire, one by one, until one is found that doesn't cause the engine to roughen and slow down.	When the missing cylinder is identified:	4.1

Test and Procedure	Results and Indications	Proceed to
9.1—Evaluate the valve train: Remove the valve cover, and ensure that the valves are adjusted to specifications. A mechanic's stethoscope may be used to aid in the diagnosis of the valve train. By pushing the probe on or near push rods or rockers, valve noise often can be isolated. A timing light also may be used to diagnose valve problems. Connect the light according to manufacturer's recommendations, and start the engine. Vary the firing moment of the light by increasing the engine speed (and therefore the ignition advance), and moving the trigger from cylinder to cylinder. Observe the movement of each valve.	See below	See below

Observation	Probable Cause	Remedy	Proceed to
Metallic tap heard through the stethoscope.	Sticking hydraulic lifter or excessive valve clearance.	Adjust valve. If tap persists, remove and replace the lifter:	10.1
Metallic tap through the stethoscope, able to push the rocker arm (lifter side) down by hand.	Collapsed valve lifter.	Remove and replace the lifter:	10.1
Erratic, irregular motion of the valve stem.*	Sticking valve, burned valve.	Recondition the valve and/or valve guide:	Next Chapter
Eccentric motion of the pushrod at the rocker arm.*	Bent pushrod.	Replace the pushrod:	10.1
Valve retainer bounces as the valve closes.*	Weak valve spring or damper.	Remove and test the spring and damper. Replace if necessary:	10.1

*—When observed with a timing light.

Test and Procedure	Results and Indications	Proceed to
9.2—Check the valve timing: Locate top dead center of the No. 1 piston, and install a degree wheel or tape on the crankshaft pulley or damper with zero corresponding to an index mark on the engine. Rotate the crankshaft in its direction of rotation, and observe the opening of the No. 1 cylinder intake valve. The opening should correspond with the correct mark on the degree wheel according to specifications.	If the timing is not correct, the timing cover must be removed for further investigation:	—

Test and Procedure	Results and Indications	Proceed to
10.1—Determine whether the exhaust manifold heat control valve is operating: Operate the valve by hand to determine whether it is free to move. If the valve is free, run the engine to operating temperature and observe the action of the valve, to ensure that it is opening.	If the valve sticks, spray it with a suitable solvent, open and close the valve to free it, and retest. If the valve functions properly: If the valve does not free, or does not operate, replace the valve:	10.2 10.2
10.2—Ensure that there are no exhaust restrictions: Visually inspect the exhaust system for kinks, dents, or crushing. Also note that gasses are flowing freely from the tailpipe at all engine speeds, indicating no restriction in the muffler or resonator.	Replace any damaged portion of the system:	11.1
11.1—Visually inspect the fan belt for glazing, cracks, and fraying, and replace if necessary. Tighten the belt so that the longest span has approximately ½″ play at its midpoint under thumb pressure.	Replace or tighten the fan belt as necessary:	11.2

Checking the fan belt tension
(© Nissan Motor Co. Ltd.)

Test and Procedure	Results and Indications	Proceed to
11.2—Check the fluid level of the cooling system.	If full or slightly low, fill as necessary: If extremely low:	11.5 11.3
11.3—Visually inspect the external portions of the cooling system (radiator, radiator hoses, thermostat elbow, water pump seals, heater hoses, etc.) for leaks. If none are found, pressurize the cooling system to 14-15 psi.	If cooling system holds the pressure: If cooling system loses pressure rapidly, re-inspect external parts of the system for leaks under pressure. If none are found, check dipstick for coolant in crankcase. If no coolant is present, but pressure loss continues: If coolant is evident in crankcase, remove cylinder head(s), and check gasket(s). If gaskets are intact, block and cylinder head(s) should be checked for cracks or holes. If the gasket(s) is blown, replace, and purge the crankcase of coolant: NOTE: *Occasionally, due to atmospheric and driving conditions, condensation of water can occur in the crankcase. This causes the oil to appear milky white. To remedy, run the engine until hot, and change the oil and oil filter.*	11.5 11.4 12.6

Test and Procedure	Results and Indication	Proceed to
11.4—Check for combustion leaks into the cooling system: Pressurize the cooling system as above. Start the engine, and observe the pressure gauge. If the needle fluctuates, remove each spark plug wire, one by one, noting which cylinder(s) reduce or eliminate the fluctuation. **Radiator pressure tester** (© American Motors Corp.)	Cylinders which reduce or eliminate the fluctuation, when the spark plug wire is removed, are leaking into the cooling system. Replace the head gasket on the affected cylinder bank(s).	11.5
11.5—Check the radiator pressure cap: Attach a radiator pressure tester to the radiator cap (wet the seal prior to installation). Quickly pump up the pressure, noting the point at which the cap releases. **Testing the radiator pressure cap** (© American Motors Corp.)	If the cap releases within ± 1 psi of the specified rating, it is operating properly: If the cap releases at more than ± 1 psi of the specified rating, it should be replaced:	11.6 11.6
11.6—Test the thermostat: Start the engine cold, remove the radiator cap, and insert a thermometer into the radiator. Allow the engine to idle. After a short while, there will be a sudden, rapid increase in coolant temperature. The temperature at which this sharp rise stops is the thermostat opening temperature.	If the thermostat opens at or about the specified temperature: If the temperature doesn't increase: (If the temperature increases slowly and gradually, replace the thermostat.)	11.7 11.7
11.7—Check the water pump: Remove the thermostat elbow and the thermostat, disconnect the coil high tension lead (to prevent starting), and crank the engine momentarily.	If coolant flows, replace the thermostat and retest per 11.6: If coolant doesn't flow, reverse flush the cooling system to alleviate any blockage that might exist. If system is not blocked, and coolant will not flow, recondition the water pump.	11.6 —
12.1—Check the oil pressure gauge or warning light: If the gauge shows low pressure, or the light is on, for no obvious reason, remove the oil pressure sender. Install an accurate oil pressure gauge and run the engine momentarily.	If oil pressure builds normally, run engine for a few moments to determine that it is functioning normally, and replace the sender. If the pressure remains low: If the pressure surges: If the oil pressure is zero:	— 12.2 12.3 12.3

Test and Procedure	Results and Indications	Proceed to
12.2—Visually inspect the oil: If the oil is watery or very thin, milky, or foamy, replace the oil and oil filter.	If the oil is normal:	12.3
	If after replacing oil the pressure remains low:	12.3
	If after replacing oil the pressure becomes normal:	—
12.3—Inspect the oil pressure relief valve and spring, to ensure that it is not sticking or stuck. Remove and thoroughly clean the valve, spring, and the valve body.	If the oil pressure improves:	—
	If no improvement is noted:	12.4

Oil pressure relief valve
(© British Leyland Motors)

Test and Procedure	Results and Indications	Proceed to
12.4—Check to ensure that the oil pump is not cavitating (sucking air instead of oil): See that the crankcase is neither over nor underfull, and that the pickup in the sump is in the proper position and free from sludge.	Fill or drain the crankcase to the proper capacity, and clean the pickup screen in solvent if necessary. If no improvement is noted:	12.5
12.5—Inspect the oil pump drive and the oil pump:	If the pump drive or the oil pump appear to be defective, service as necessary and retest per 12.1:	12.1
	If the pump drive and pump appear to be operating normally, the engine should be disassembled to determine where blockage exists:	Next Chapter
12.6—Purge the engine of ethylene glycol coolant: Completely drain the crankcase and the oil filter. Obtain a commercial butyl cellosolve base solvent, designated for this purpose, and follow the instructions precisely. Following this, install a new oil filter and refill the crankcase with the proper weight oil. The next oil and filter change should follow shortly thereafter (1000 miles).		

This chapter describes, in detail, the procedures involved in rebuilding a typical engine. The procedures specifically refer to an inline engine, however, they are basically identical to those used in rebuilding engines of nearly all design and configurations. Procedures for servicing atypical engines (i.e., horizontally opposed) are described in the individual car sections, although in most cases, cylinder head reconditioning procedures described in this chapter will apply.

The chapter is divided into two sections. The first, Cylinder Head Reconditioning, assumes that the cylinder head is removed from the engine, all manifolds are removed, and the cylinder head is on a workbench. The camshaft should be removed from overhead cam cylinder heads. The second section, Cylinder Block Reconditioning, covers the block, pistons, connecting rods and crankshaft. It is assumed that the engine is mounted on a work stand, and the cylinder head and all accessories are removed.

Procedures are identified as follows:

Unmarked—Basic procedures that must be performed in order to successfully complete the rebuilding process.

Starred (*)—Procedures that should be performed to ensure maximum performance and engine life.

Double starred (**)—Procedures that may be performed to increase engine performance and reliability. These procedures are usually reserved for extremely heavy-duty or competition usage.

In many cases, a choice of methods is also provided. Methods are identified in the same manner as procedures. The choice of method for a procedure is at the discretion of the user.

The tools required for the basic rebuilding procedure should, with minor exceptions, be those

TORQUE (ft. lbs.)*

U.S.

Bolt Diameter (inches)	Bolt Grade (SAE)				Wrench Size (inches)	
	1 and 2	5	6	8	Bolt	Nut
1/4	5	7	10	10.5	3/8	7/16
5/16	9	14	19	22	1/2	9/16
3/8	15	25	34	37	9/16	5/8
7/16	24	40	55	60	5/8	3/4
1/2	37	60	85	92	3/4	13/16
9/16	53	88	120	132	7/8	7/8
5/8	74	120	167	180	15/16	1
3/4	120	200	280	296	1-1/8	1-1/8
7/8	190	302	440	473	1-5/16	1-5/16
1	282	466	660	714	1-1/2	1-1/2

Metric

Bolt Diameter (mm)	Bolt Grade				Wrench Size (mm)
	5D	8G	10K	12K	Bolt and Nut
6	5	6	8	10	10
8	10	16	22	27	14
10	19	31	40	49	17
12	34	54	70	86	19
14	55	89	117	137	22
16	83	132	175	208	24
18	111	182	236	283	27
22	182	284	394	464	32
24	261	419	570	689	36

*—Torque values are for lightly oiled bolts. CAUTION: Bolts threaded into aluminum require much less torque.

General Torque Specifications

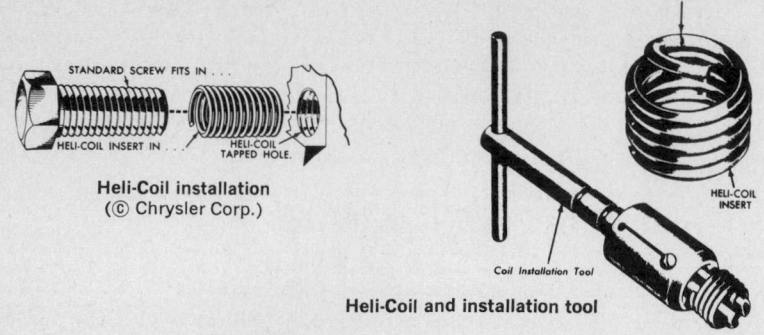

Heli-Coil installation
(© Chrysler Corp.)

Heli-Coil and installation tool

Heli-Coil Insert		Insert Length (In.)	Drill	Tap	Insert. Tool	Extract-ing Tool
Thread Size	Part No.		Size	Part No.	Part No.	Part No.
1/2 -20	1185-4	3/8	17/64(.266)	4 CPB	528-4N	1227-6
5/16-18	1185-5	15/32	Q(.332)	5 CPB	528-5N	1227-6
3/8 -16	1185-6	9/16	X(.397)	6 CPB	528-6N	1227-6
7/16-14	1185-7	21/32	29/64(.453)	7 CPB	528-7N	1227-16
1/2 -13	1185-8	3/4	33/64(.516)	8 CPB	528-8N	1227-16

Heli-Coil Specifications

included in a mechanic's tool kit. An accurate torque wrench, and a dial indicator (reading in thousandths) mounted on a universal base should be available. Bolts and nuts with no torque specification should be tightened according to size (see chart). Special tools, where required, all are readily available from the major tool suppliers (i.e., Craftsman, Snap-On, K-D). The services of a competent automotive machine shop must also be readily available.

When assembling the engine, any parts that will be in frictional contact must be pre-lubricated, to provide protection on initial start-up. Vortex Pre-Lube, STP, or any product specifically formulated for this purpose may be used. NOTE: *Do not use engine oil.* Where semi-permanent (locked but removable) installation of bolts or nuts is desired, threads should be cleaned and coated with Loctite. Studs may be permanently installed using Loctite Stud and Bearing Mount.

Aluminum has become increasingly popular for use in engines, due to its low weight and excellent heat transfer characteristics. The following precautions

must be observed when handling aluminum engine parts:
—Never hot-tank aluminum parts.
—Remove all aluminum parts (identification tags, etc.) from engine parts before hot-tanking (otherwise they will be removed during the process).
—Always coat threads lightly with engine oil or anti-seize compounds before installation, to prevent seizure.
—Never over-torque bolts or spark plugs in aluminum threads. Should stripping occur, threads can be restored according to the following procedure, using Heli-Coil thread inserts:

Tap drill the hole with the stripped threads to the specified size (see chart). Using the specified tap (NOTE: *Heli-Coil tap sizes refer to the size thread being replaced, rather than the actual tap size*), tap the hole for the Heli-Coil. Place the insert on the proper installation tool (see chart). Apply pressure on the insert while winding it clockwise into the hole, until the top of the insert is one turn below the surface. Remove the installation tool, and break the installation tang from the bottom of the in-

sert by moving it up and down. If the Heli-Coil must be removed, tap the removal tool firmly into the hole, so that it engages the top thread, and turn the tool counter-clockwise to extract the insert.

Snapped bolts or studs may be removed, using a stud extractor (unthreaded) or Vise-Grip pliers (threaded). Penetrating oil (e.g., Liquid Wrench) will often aid in breaking frozen threads. In cases where the stud or bolt is flush with, or below the surface, proceed as follows:

Drill a hole in the broken stud or bolt, approximately ½ its diameter. Select a screw extractor (e.g., Easy-Out) of the proper size, and tap it into the stud or bolt. Turn the extractor counter-clockwise to remove the stud or bolt.

Magnaflux and Zyglo are inspection techniques used to locate material flaws, such as stress cracks. Magnafluxing coats the part with fine magnetic particles, and subjects the part to a magnetic field. Cracks cause breaks

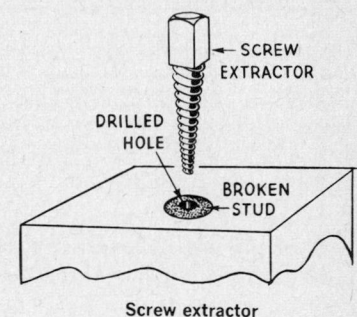

Screw extractor

in the magnetic field, which are outlined by the particles. Since Magnaflux is a magnetic process, it is applicable only to ferrous materials. The Zyglo process coats the material with a fluorescent dye penetrant, and then subjects it to blacklight inspection, under which cracks glow bright-

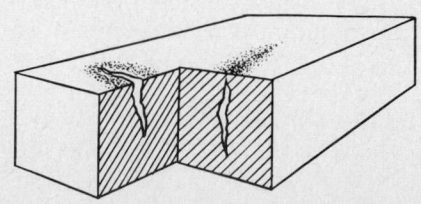

Magnaflux indication of cracks

ly. Parts made of any material may be tested using Zyglo. While Magnaflux and Zyglo are excellent for general inspection, and locating hidden defects, specific checks of suspected cracks may be made at lower cost and more readily using spot check dye. The dye is sprayed onto the suspected area, wiped off, and the area is then sprayed with a developer. Cracks then will show up bright-ly. Spot check dyes will only indicate surface cracks; therefore, structural cracks below the surface may escape detection. When questionable, the part should be tested using Magnaflux or Zyglo.

CYLINDER HEAD RECONDITIONING

Procedure	*Method*
Identify the valves:  **Valve identification** (© SAAB)	Invert the cylinder head, and number the valve faces front to rear, using a permanent felt-tip marker.
Remove the rocker arms:	Remove the rocker arms with shaft(s) or balls and nuts. Wire the sets of rockers, balls and nuts together, and identify according to the corresponding valve.
Remove the valves and springs:	Using an appropriate valve spring compressor (depending on the configuration of the cylinder head), compress the valve springs. Lift out the keepers with needlenose pliers, release the compressor, and remove the valve, spring, and spring retainer.
Check the valve stem-to-guide clearance:  **Checking the valve stem-to-guide clearance** (© American Motors Corp.)	Clean the valve stem with lacquer thinner or a similar solvent to remove all gum and varnish. Clean the valve guides using solvent and an expanding wire-type valve guide cleaner. Mount a dial indicator so that the stem is at 90° to the valve stem, as close to the valve guide as possible. Move the valve off its seat, and measure the valve guide-to-stem clearance by moving the stem back and forth to actuate the dial indicator. Measure the valve stems using a micrometer, and compare to specifications, to determine whether stem or guide wear is responsible for excessive clearance.
De-carbon the cylinder head and valves: 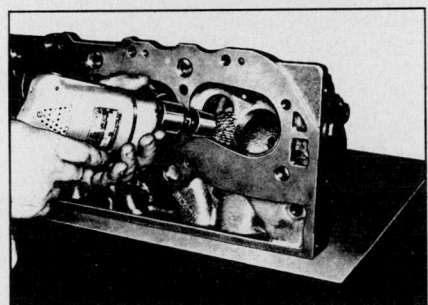 **Removing carbon from the cylinder head** (© Chevrolet Div. G.M. Corp.)	Chip carbon away from the valve heads, combustion chambers, and ports, using a chisel made of hardwood. Remove the remaining deposits with a stiff wire brush. NOTE: *Ensure that the deposits are actually removed, rather than burnished.*

Procedure	Method
Hot-tank the cylinder head:	Have the cylinder head hot-tanked to remove grease, corrosion, and scale from the water passages. NOTE: *In the case of overhead cam cylinder heads, consult the operator to determine whether the camshaft bearings will be damaged by the caustic solution.*
Degrease the remaining cylinder head parts:	Using solvent (i.e., Gunk), clean the rockers, rocker shaft(s) (where applicable), rocker balls and nuts, springs, spring retainers, and keepers. Do not remove the protective coating from the springs.

Check the cylinder head for warpage:

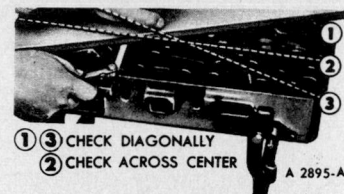

① ③ CHECK DIAGONALLY
② CHECK ACROSS CENTER   A 2895-A

**Checking the cylinder head
for warpage**
(© Ford Motor Co.)

Place a straight-edge across the gasket surface of the cylinder head. Using feeler gauges, determine the clearance at the center of the straight-edge. Measure across both diagonals, along the longitudinal centerline, and across the cylinder head at several points. If warpage exceeds .003″ in a 6″ span, or .006″ over the total length, the cylinder head must be resurfaced. NOTE: *If warpage exceeds the manufacturers maximum tolerance for material removal, the cylinder head must be replaced.* When milling the cylinder heads of V-type engines, the intake manifold mounting position is altered, and must be corrected by milling the manifold flange a proportionate amount.

** Porting and gasket matching:

**Marking the cylinder head for
gasket matching**
(© Petersen Publishing Co.)

**Port configuration before and after
gasket matching**
(© Petersen Publishing Co.)

** Coat the manifold flanges of the cylinder head with Prussian blue dye. Glue intake and exhaust gaskets to the cylinder head in their installed position using rubber cement and scribe the outline of the ports on the manifold flanges. Remove the gaskets. Using a small cutter in a hand-held power tool (i.e., Dremel Moto-Tool), gradually taper the walls of the port out to the scribed outline of the gasket. Further enlargement of the ports should include the removal of sharp edges and radiusing of sharp corners. Do not alter the valve guides. NOTE: *The most efficient port configuration is determined only by extensive testing. Therefore, it is best to consult someone experienced with the head in question to determine the optimum alterations.*

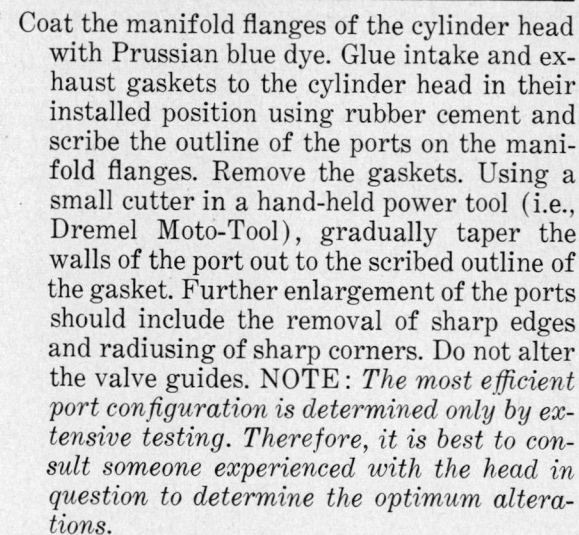

Procedure	*Method*
** Polish the ports:	** Using a grinding stone with the above mentioned tool, polish the walls of the intake and exhaust ports, and combustion chamber. Use progressively finer stones until all surface imperfections are removed. NOTE: *Through testing, it has been determined that a smooth surface is more effective than a mirror polished surface in intake ports, and vice-versa in exhaust ports.*

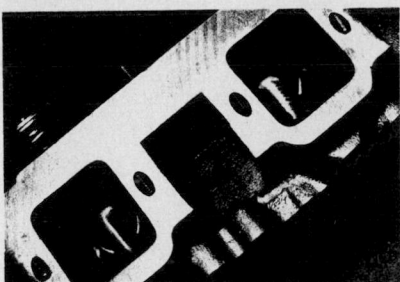

Relieved and polished ports
(© Petersen Publishing Co.)

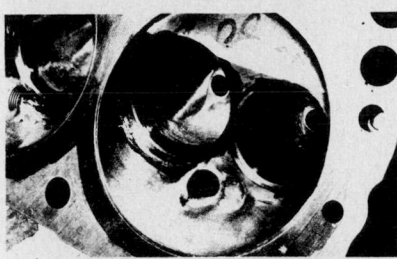

Polished combustion chamber
(© Petersen Publishing Co.)

* Knurling the valve guides:	* Valve guides which are not excessively worn or distorted may, in some cases, be knurled rather than replaced. Knurling is a process in which metal is displaced and raised, thereby reducing clearance. Knurling also provides excellent oil control. The possibility of knurling rather than replacing valve guides should be discussed with a machinist.

Cut-away view of a knurled valve guide
(© Petersen Publishing Co.)

Replacing the valve guides: NOTE: *Valve guides should only be replaced if damaged or if an oversize valve stem is not available.*	Depending on the type of cylinder head, valve guides may be pressed, hammered, or shrunk in. In cases where the guides are shrunk into the head, replacement should be left to an equipped machine shop. In other cases, the guides are replaced as follows: Press or tap the valve guides out of the head using a stepped drift (see illustration). Determine the height above the boss that the guide must extend, and obtain a stack of washers, their I.D. similar to the guide's O.D., of that height. Place the stack of washers on the guide, and insert the guide into the boss. NOTE: *Valve guides are often tapered or beveled for installation.* Using the stepped installation tool (see illustration), press or tap the guides into position. Ream the guides according to the size of the valve stem.

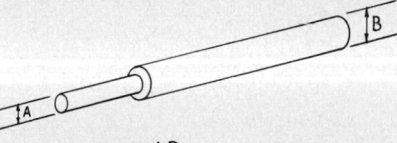

A-VALVE GUIDE I.D.
B-SLIGHTLY SMALLER THAN VALVE GUIDE O.D.

Valve guide removal tool

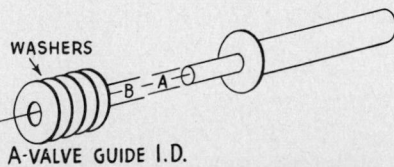

WASHERS

A-VALVE GUIDE I.D.
B-LARGER THAN THE VALVE GUIDE O.D.

Valve guide installation tool (with washers used during installation)

Procedure	Method
Replacing valve seat inserts:	Replacement of valve seat inserts which are worn beyond resurfacing or broken, if feasible, must be done by a machine shop.
Resurfacing (grinding) the valve face: 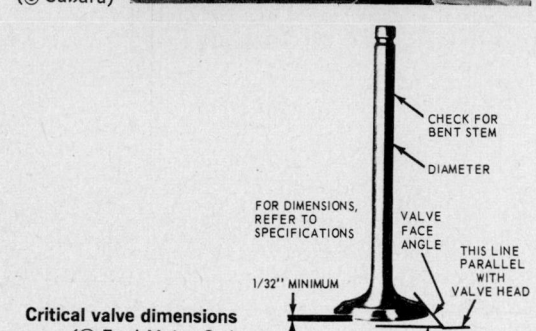 **Grinding a valve** *(© Subaru)*  **Critical valve dimensions** *(© Ford Motor Co.)*	Using a valve grinder, resurface the valves according to specifications. CAUTION: *Valve face angle is not always identical to valve seat angle.* A minimum margin of 1/32″ should remain after grinding the valve. The valve stem tip should also be squared and resurfaced, by placing the stem in the V-block of the grinder, and turning it while pressing lightly against the grinding wheel.
Resurfacing the valve seats using reamers: 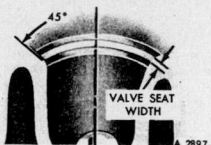 **Reaming the valve seat** *(© S.p.A. Fiat)* **Valve seat width and centering** *(© Ford Motor Co.)*	Select a reamer of the correct seat angle, slightly larger than the diameter of the valve seat, and assemble it with a pilot of the correct size. Install the pilot into the valve guide, and using steady pressure, turn the reamer clockwise. CAUTION: *Do not turn the reamer counter-clockwise.* Remove only as much material as necessary to clean the seat. Check the concentricity of the seat (see below). If the dye method is not used, coat the valve face with Prussian blue dye, install and rotate it on the valve seat. Using the dye marked area as a centering guide, center and narrow the valve seat to specifications with correction cutters. NOTE: *When no specifications are available, minimum seat width for exhaust valves should be 5/64″, intake valves 1/16″.* After making correction cuts, check the position of the valve seat on the valve face using Prussian blue dye.
* Resurfacing the valve seats using a grinder:  **Grinding a valve seat** *(© Subaru)*	Select a pilot of the correct size, and a coarse stone of the correct seat angle. Lubricate the pilot if necessary, and install the tool in the valve guide. Move the stone on and off the seat at approximately two cycles per second, until all flaws are removed from the seat. Install a fine stone, and finish the seat. Center and narrow the seat using correction stones, as described above.

Procedure	Method
Checking the valve seat concentricity: 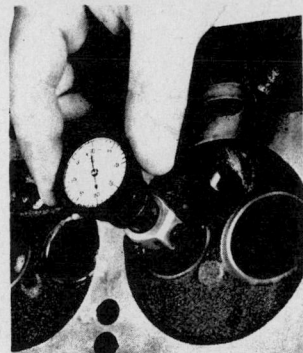 **Checking the valve seat concentricity using a dial gauge** (© American Motors Corp.)	Coat the valve face with Prussian blue dye, install the valve, and rotate it on the valve seat. If the entire seat becomes coated, and the valve is known to be concentric, the seat is concentric.
	* Install the dial gauge pilot into the guide, and rest the arm on the valve seat. Zero the gauge, and rotate the arm around the seat. Run-out should not exceed .002″.
* Lapping the valves: NOTE: *Valve lapping is done to ensure efficient sealing of resurfaced valves and seats. Valve lapping alone is not recommended for use as a resurfacing procedure.*  **Hand lapping the valves** 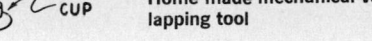 HAND DRILL — ROD — SUCTION CUP — **Home made mechanical valve lapping tool**	* Invert the cylinder head, lightly lubricate the valve stems, and install the valves in the head as numbered. Coat valve seats with fine grinding compound, and attach the lapping tool suction cup to a valve head (NOTE: *Moisten the suction cup*). Rotate the tool between the palms, changing position and lifting the tool often to prevent grooving. Lap the valve until a smooth, polished seat is evident. Remove the valve and tool, and rinse away all traces of grinding compound.
	** Fasten a suction cup to a piece of drill rod, and mount the rod in a hand drill. Proceed as above, using the hand drill as a lapping tool. CAUTION: *Due to the higher speeds involved when using the hand drill, care must be exercised to avoid grooving the seat.* Lift the tool and change direction of rotation often.
Check the valve springs: 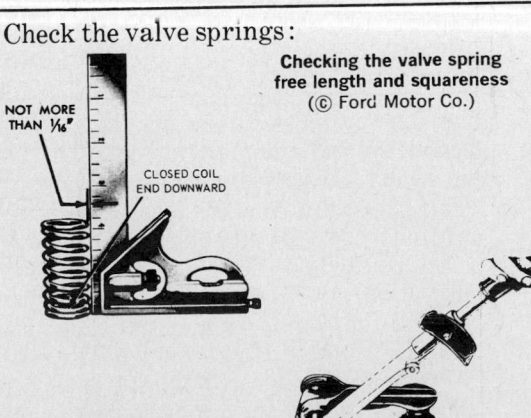 **Checking the valve spring free length and squareness** (© Ford Motor Co.) NOT MORE THAN 1/16″ — CLOSED COIL END DOWNWARD — **Checking the valve spring tension** (© Chrysler Corp.)	Place the spring on a flat surface next to a square. Measure the height of the spring, and rotate it against the edge of the square to measure distortion. If spring height varies (by comparison) by more than 1/16″ or if distortion exceeds 1/16″, replace the spring.
	** In addition to evaluating the spring as above, test the spring pressure at the installed and compressed (installed height minus valve lift) height using a valve spring tester. Springs used on small displacement engines (up to 3 liters) should be ± 1 lb. of all other springs in either position. A tolerance of ± 5 lbs. is permissible on larger engines.

Procedure	Method

* Install valve stem seals:

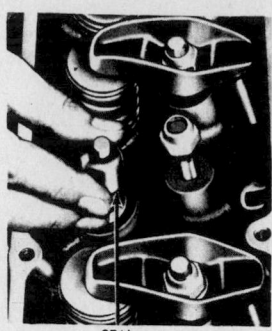

**Valve stem seal
installation**
(© Ford Motor Co.)

SEAL

* Due to the pressure differential that exists at the ends of the intake valve guides (atmospheric pressure above, manifold vacuum below), oil is drawn through the valve guides into the intake port. This has been alleviated somewhat since the addition of positive crankcase ventilation, which lowers the pressure above the guides. Several types of valve stem seals are available to reduce blow-by. Certain seals simply slip over the stem and guide boss, while others require that the boss be machined. Recently, Teflon guide seals have become popular. Consult a parts supplier or machinist concerning availability and suggested usages. NOTE: *When installing seals, ensure that a small amount of oil is able to pass the seal to lubricate the valve guides; otherwise, excessive wear may result.*

Install the valves:

Lubricate the valve stems, and install the valves in the cylinder head as numbered. Lubricate and position the seals (if used, see above) and the valve springs. Install the spring retainers, compress the springs, and insert the keys using needlenose pliers or a tool designed for this purpose. NOTE: *Retain the keys with wheel bearing grease during installation.*

Checking valve spring installed height:

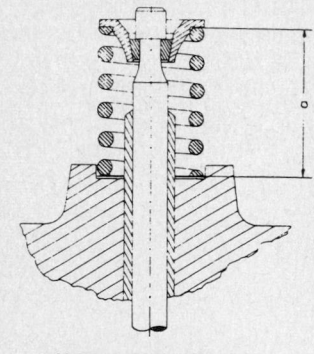

**Valve spring installed
height dimension**
(© Porsche)

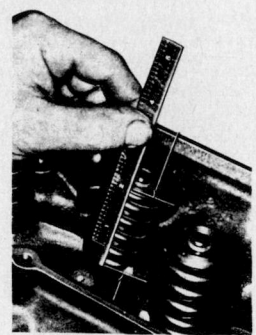

**Measuring valve spring
installed height**
(© Petersen Publishing Co.)

Measure the distance between the spring pad and the lower edge of the spring retainer, and compare to specifications. If the installed height is incorrect, add shim washers between the spring pad and the spring. CAUTION: *Use only washers designed for this purpose.*

** CC'ing the combustion chambers:

** Invert the cylinder head and place a bead of sealer around a combustion chamber. Install an apparatus designed for this purpose (burette mounted on a clear plate; see illustration) over the combustion chamber, and fill with the specified fluid to an even mark on the burette. Record the burette reading, and fill the combustion chamber with fluid. (NOTE: *A hole drilled in the plate will permit air to escape*). Subtract the burette reading, with the combustion chamber filled, from the previous reading, to determine combustion chamber volume in cc's. Duplicate this procedure in all combustion

Procedure	*Method*

CC'ing the combustion chamber
(© Petersen Publishing Co.)

chambers on the cylinder head, and compare the readings. The volume of all combustion chambers should be made equal to that of the largest. Combustion chamber volume may be increased in two ways. When only a small change is required (usually), a small cutter or coarse stone may be used to remove material from the combustion chamber. NOTE: *Check volume frequently.* Remove material over a wide area, so as not to change the configuration of the combustion chamber. When a larger change is required, the valve seat may be sunk (lowered into the head). NOTE: *When altering valve seat, remember to compensate for the change in spring installed height.*

Inspect the rocker arms, balls, studs, and nuts (where applicable):

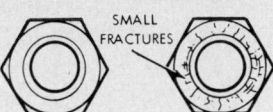

SMALL FRACTURES

Stress cracks in rocker nuts
(© Ford Motor Co.)

Visually inspect the rocker arms, balls, studs, and nuts for cracks, galling, burning, scoring, or wear. If all parts are intact, liberally lubricate the rocker arms and balls, and install them on the cylinder head. If wear is noted on a rocker arm at the point of valve contact, grind it smooth and square, removing as little material as possible. Replace the rocker arm if excessively worn. If a rocker stud shows signs of wear, it must be replaced (see below). If a rocker nut shows stress cracks, replace it. If an exhaust ball is galled or burned, substitute the intake ball from the same cylinder (if it is intact), and install a new intake ball. NOTE: *Avoid using new rocker balls on exhaust valves.*

Replacing rocker studs:

Reaming the stud bore for oversize rocker studs
(© Buick Div. G.M. Corp.)

FLAT WASHERS

AS STUD BEGINS TO PULL UP, IT WILL BE NECESSARY TO REMOVE THE NUT AND ADD MORE WASHERS.

Extracting a pressed in rocker stud
(© Buick Div. G.M. Corp.)

In order to remove a threaded stud, lock two nuts on the stud, and unscrew the stud using the lower nut. Coat the lower threads of the new stud with Loctite, and install.

Two alternative methods are available for replacing pressed in studs. Remove the damaged stud using a stack of washers and a nut (see illustration). In the first, the boss is reamed .005-.006″ oversize, and an oversize stud pressed in. Control the stud extension over the boss using washers, in the same manner as valve guides. Before installing the stud, coat it with white lead and grease. To retain the stud more positively, drill a hole through the stud and boss, and install a roll pin. In the second method, the boss is tapped, and a threaded stud installed. Retain the stud using Loctite Stud and Bearing Mount.

Procedure	Method
Inspect the rocker shaft(s) and rocker arms (where applicable):  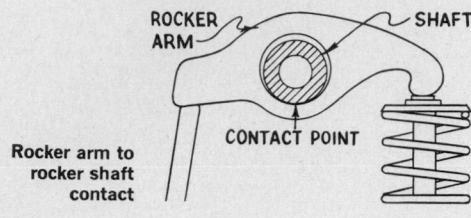 **Disassembled rocker shaft parts arranged for inspection** (© American Motors Corp.) ROCKER ARM — SHAFT CONTACT POINT **Rocker arm to rocker shaft contact**	Remove rocker arms, springs and washers from rocker shaft. NOTE: *Lay out parts in the order they are removed.* Inspect rocker arms for pitting or wear on the valve contact point, or excessive bushing wear. Bushings need only be replaced if wear is excessive, because the rocker arm normally contacts the shaft at one point only. Grind the valve contact point of rocker arm smooth if necessary, removing as little material as possible. If excessive material must be removed to smooth and square the arm, it should be replaced. Clean out all oil holes and passages in rocker shaft. If shaft is grooved or worn, replace it. Lubricate and assemble the rocker shaft.
Inspect the camshaft bushings and the camshaft (overhead cam engines):	See next section.
Inspect the pushrods:	Remove the pushrods, and, if hollow, clean out the oil passages using fine wire. Roll each pushrod over a piece of clean glass. If a distinct clicking sound is heard as the pushrod rolls, the rod is bent, and must be replaced.
	* The length of all pushrods must be equal. Measure the length of the pushrods, compare to specifications, and replace as necessary.
Inspect the valve lifters: 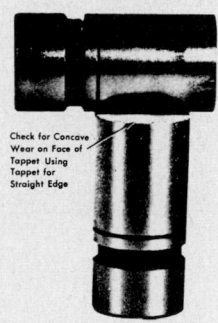 Check for Concave Wear on Face of Tappet Using Tappet for Straight Edge **Checking the lifter face** (© American Motors Corp.)	Remove lifters from their bores, and remove gum and varnish, using solvent. Clean walls of lifter bores. Check lifters for concave wear as illustrated. If face is worn concave, replace lifter, and carefully inspect the camshaft. Lightly lubricate lifter and insert it into its bore. If play is excessive, an oversize lifter must be installed (where possible). Consult a machinist concerning feasibility. If play is satisfactory, remove, lubricate, and reinstall the lifter.
* Testing hydraulic lifter leak down: 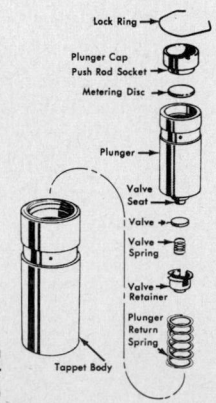 Lock Ring Plunger Cap Push Rod Socket Metering Disc Plunger Valve Seat Valve Valve Spring Valve Retainer Plunger Return Spring Tappet Body **Exploded view of a typical hydraulic lifter** (© American Motors Corp.)	Submerge lifter in a container of kerosene. Chuck a used pushrod or its equivalent into a drill press. Position container of kerosene so pushrod acts on the lifter plunger. Pump lifter with the drill press, until resistance increases. Pump several more times to bleed any air out of lifter. Apply very firm, constant pressure to the lifter, and observe rate at which fluid bleeds out of lifter. If the fluid bleeds very quickly (less than 15 seconds), lifter is defective. If the time exceeds 60 seconds, lifter is sticking. In either case, recondition or replace lifter. If lifter is operating properly (leak down time 15-60 seconds), lubricate and install it.

CYLINDER BLOCK RECONDITIONING

Procedure	Method

Checking the main bearing clearance:

Plastigage installed on main bearing journal
(© Chevrolet Div. G.M. Corp.)

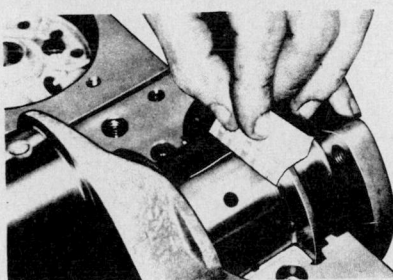

Measuring Plastigage to determine main bearing clearance
(© Chevrolet Div. G.M. Corp.)

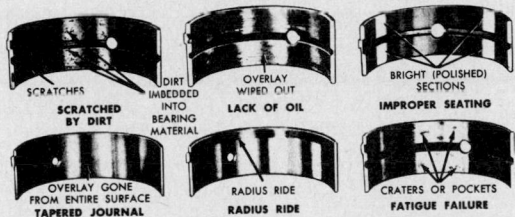

Causes of bearing failure
(© Ford Motor Co.)

Invert engine, and remove cap from the bearing to be checked. Using a clean, dry rag, thoroughly clean all oil from crankshaft journal and bearing insert. NOTE: *Plastigage is soluble in oil; therefore, oil on the journal or bearing could result in erroneous readings.* Place a piece of Plastigage along the full length of journal, reinstall cap, and torque to specifications. Remove bearing cap, and determine bearing clearance by comparing width of Plastigage to the scale on Plastigage envelope. Journal taper is determined by comparing width of the Plastigage strip near its ends. Rotate crankshaft 90° and retest, to determine journal eccentricity. NOTE: *Do not rotate crankshaft with Plastigage installed.* If bearing insert and journal appear intact, and are within tolerances, no further main bearing service is required. If bearing or journal appear defective, cause of failure should be determined before replacement.

* Remove crankshaft from block (see below). Measure the main bearing journals at each end twice (90° apart) using a micrometer, to determine diameter, journal taper and eccentricity. If journals are within tolerances, reinstall bearing caps at their specified torque. Using a telescope gauge and micrometer, measure bearing I.D. parallel to piston axis and at 30° on each side of piston axis. Subtract journal O.D. from bearing I.D. to determine oil clearance. If crankshaft journals appear defective, or do not meet tolerances, there is no need to measure bearings; for the crankshaft will require grinding and/or undersize bearings will be required. If bearing appears defective, cause for failure should be determined prior to replacement.

Checking the connecting rod bearing clearance:

Plastigage installed on connecting rod bearing journal
(© Chevrolet Div. G.M. Corp.)

Connecting rod bearing clearance is checked in the same manner as main bearing clearance, using Plastigage. Before removing the crankshaft, connecting rod side clearance also should be measured and recorded.

* Checking connecting rod bearing clearance, using a micrometer, is identical to checking main bearing clearance. If no other service

Procedure	*Method*

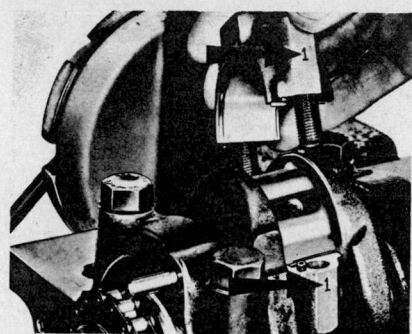

**Measuring Plastigage to determine
connecting rod bearing clearance**
(© Chevrolet Div. G.M. Corp.)

is required, the piston and rod assemblies need not be removed.

Removing the crankshaft:

Using a punch, mark the corresponding main bearing caps and saddles according to position (i.e., one punch on the front main cap and saddle, two on the second, three on the third, etc.). Using number stamps, identify the corresponding connecting rods and caps, according to cylinder (if no numbers are present). Remove the main and connecting rod caps, and place sleeves of plastic tubing over the connecting rod bolts, to protect the journals as the crankshaft is removed. Lift the crankshaft out of the block.

Connecting rod matching marks
(© Ford Motor Co.)

Remove the ridge from the top of the cylinder:

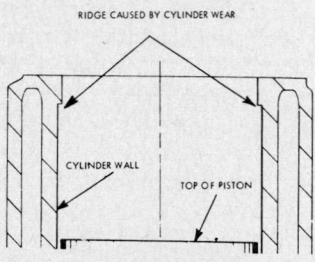

RIDGE CAUSED BY CYLINDER WEAR

CYLINDER WALL

TOP OF PISTON

Cylinder bore ridge
(© Pontiac Div. G.M. Corp.)

In order to facilitate removal of the piston and connecting rod, the ridge at the top of the cylinder (unworn area; see illustration) must be removed. Place the piston at the bottom of the bore, and cover it with a rag. Cut the ridge away using a ridge reamer, exercising extreme care to avoid cutting too deeply. Remove the rag, and remove cuttings that remain on the piston. CAUTION: *If the ridge is not removed, and new rings are installed, damage to rings will result.*

Removing the piston and connecting rod:

Removing the piston
(© SAAB)

Invert the engine, and push the pistons and connecting rods out of the cylinders. If necessary, tap the connecting rod boss with a wooden hammer handle, to force the piston out. CAUTION: *Do not attempt to force the piston past the cylinder ridge (see above).*

Procedure	Method
Service the crankshaft:	Ensure that all oil holes and passages in the crankshaft are open and free of sludge. If necessary, have the crankshaft ground to the largest possible undersize.
	** Have the crankshaft Magnafluxed, to locate stress cracks. Consult a machinist concerning additional service procedures, such as surface hardening (e.g., nitriding, Tuftriding) to improve wear characteristics, cross drilling and chamfering the oil holes to improve lubrication, and balancing.
Removing freeze plugs:	Drill a hole in the center of the freeze plugs, and pry them out using a screwdriver or drift.
Remove the oil gallery plugs:	Threaded plugs should be removed using an appropriate (usually square) wrench. To remove soft, pressed in plugs, drill a hole in the plug, and thread in a sheet metal screw. Pull the plug out by the screw using pliers.
Hot-tank the block:	Have the block hot-tanked to remove grease, corrosion, and scale from the water jackets. NOTE: *Consult the operator to determine whether the camshaft bearings will be damaged during the hot-tank process.*
Check the block for cracks:	Visually inspect the block for cracks or chips. The most common locations are as follows: Adjacent to freeze plugs. Between the cylinders and water jackets. Adjacent to the main bearing saddles. At the extreme bottom of the cylinders. Check only suspected cracks using spot check dye (see introduction). If a crack is located, consult a machinist concerning possible repairs.
	** Magnaflux the block to locate hidden cracks. If cracks are located, consult a machinist about feasibility of repair.
Install the oil gallery plugs and freeze plugs:	Coat freeze plugs with sealer and tap into position using a piece of pipe, slightly smaller than the plug, as a driver. To ensure retention, stake the edges of the plugs. Coat threaded oil gallery plugs with sealer and install. Drive replacement soft plugs into block using a large drift as a driver.
	* Rather than reinstalling lead plugs, drill and tap the holes, and install threaded plugs.

Procedure	*Method*

Check the bore diameter and surface:

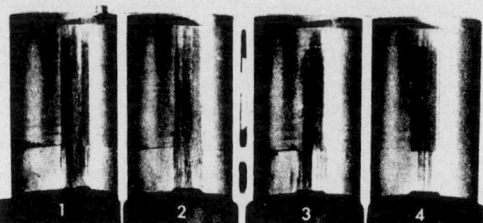

1, 2, 3 Piston skirt seizure resulted in this pattern. Engine must be rebored

4. Piston skirt and oil ring seizure caused this damage. Engine must be rebored

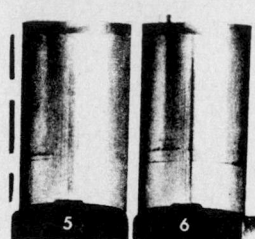
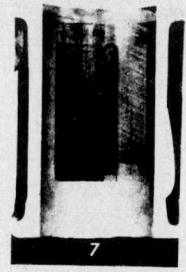

5, 6 Score marks caused by a split piston skirt. Damage is not serious enough to warrant reboring

7. Ring seized longitudinally, causing a score mark 1 3/16" wide, on the land side of the piston groove. The honing pattern is destroyed and the cylinder must be rebored

8. Result of oil ring seizure. Engine must be rebored

9. Oil ring seizure here was not serious enough to warrant reboring. The honing marks are still visible

Cylinder wall damage
(© Daimler-Benz A.G.)

Visually inspect the cylinder bores for roughness, scoring, or scuffing. If evident, the cylinder bore must be bored or honed oversize to eliminate imperfections, and the smallest possible oversize piston used. The new pistons should be given to the machinist with the block, so that the cylinders can be bored or honed exactly to the piston size (plus clearance). If no flaws are evident, measure the bore diameter using a telescope gauge and micrometer, or dial gauge, parallel and perpendicular to the engine centerline, at the top (below the ridge) and bottom of the bore. Subtract the bottom measurements from the top to determine taper, and the parallel to the centerline measurements from the perpendicular measurements to determine eccentricity. If the measurements are not within specifications, the cylinder must be bored or honed, and an oversize piston installed. If the measurements are within specifications the cylinder may be used as is, with only finish honing (see below). NOTE: *Prior to submitting the block for boring, perform the following operation(s).*

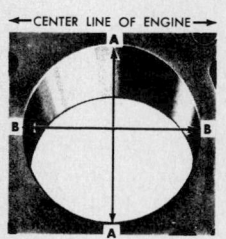
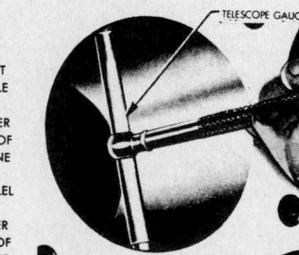
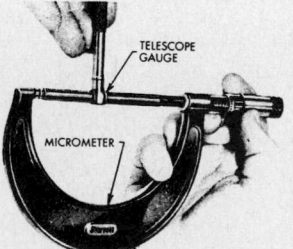

Cylinder bore measuring positions
(© Ford Motor Co.)

Measuring the cylinder bore with a telescope gauge
(© Buick Div. G.M. Corp.)

Determining the cylinder bore by measuring the telescope gauge with a micrometer
(© Buick Div. G.M. Corp.)

Measuring the cylinder bore with a dial gauge
(© Chevrolet Div. G.M. Corp.)

Procedure	Method
Check the block deck for warpage:	Using a straightedge and feeler gauges, check the block deck for warpage in the same manner that the cylinder head is checked (see Cylinder Head Reconditioning). If warpage exceeds specifications, have the deck resurfaced. NOTE: *In certain cases a specification for total material removal (Cylinder head and block deck) is provided. This specification must not be exceeded.*
* Check the deck height:	The deck height is the distance from the crankshaft centerline to the block deck. To measure, invert the engine, and install the crankshaft, retaining it with the center main cap. Measure the distance from the crankshaft journal to the block deck, parallel to the cylinder centerline. Measure the diameter of the end (front and rear) main journals, parallel to the centerline of the cylinders, divide the diameter in half, and subtract it from the previous measurement. The results of the front and rear measurements should be identical. If the difference exceeds .005″, the deck height should be corrected. NOTE: *Block deck height and warpage should be corrected concurrently.*
Check the cylinder block bearing alignment: 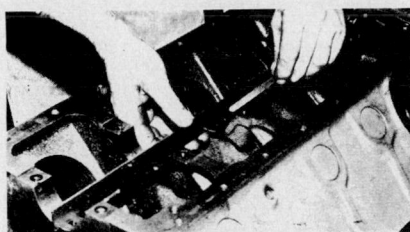 **Checking main bearing saddle alignment** (© Petersen Publishing Co.)	Remove the upper bearing inserts. Place a straightedge in the bearing saddles along the centerline of the crankshaft. If clearance exists between the straightedge and the center saddle, the block must be align-bored.
Clean and inspect the pistons and connecting rods: 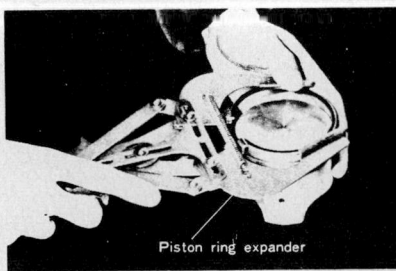 Piston ring expander **Removing the piston rings** (© Subaru)	Using a ring expander, remove the rings from the piston. Remove the retaining rings (if so equipped) and remove piston pin. NOTE: *If the piston pin must be pressed out, determine the proper method and use the proper tools; otherwise the piston will distort.* Clean the ring grooves using an appropriate tool, exercising care to avoid cutting too deeply. Thoroughly clean all carbon and varnish from the piston with solvent. CAUTION: *Do not use a wire brush or caustic solvent on pistons.* Inspect the pistons for scuffing, scoring, cracks, pitting, or excessive ring groove wear. If wear is evident, the piston must be replaced. Check the connecting rod length by measuring the rod from the inside of the large end to the inside of the small end using calipers (see

Procedure	*Method*

Cleaning the piston ring grooves
(ⓒ Ford Motor Co.)

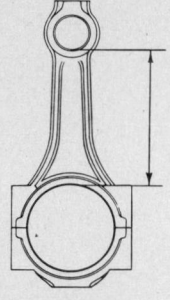

Connecting rod
length checking
dimension

illustration). All connecting rods should be equal length. Replace any rod that differs from the others in the engine.

* Have the connecting rod alignment checked in an alignment fixture by a machinist. Replace any twisted or bent rods.

* Magnaflux the connecting rods to locate stress cracks. If cracks are found, replace the connecting rod.

Fit the pistons to the cylinders:

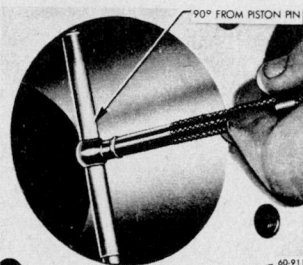

Measuring the cylinder
with a telescope gauge
for piston fitting
(ⓒ Buick Div.
G.M. Corp.)

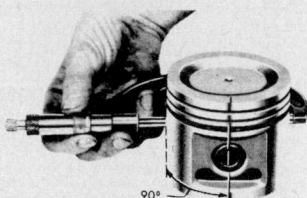

Measuring the piston
for fitting
(ⓒ Buick Div.
G.M. Corp.)

Using a telescope gauge and micrometer, or a dial gauge, measure the cylinder bore diameter perpendicular to the piston pin, 2½″ below the deck. Measure the piston perpendicular to its pin on the skirt. The difference between the two measurements is the piston clearance. If the clearance is within specifications or slightly below (after boring or honing), finish honing is all that is required. If the clearance is excessive, try to obtain a slightly larger piston to bring clearance within specifications. Where this is not possible, obtain the first oversize piston, and hone (or if necessary, bore) the cylinder to size.

Assemble the pistons and connecting rods:

Installing piston pin lock rings
(ⓒ Nissan Motor Co., Ltd.)

Inspect piston pin, connecting rod small end bushing, and piston bore for galling, scoring, or excessive wear. If evident, replace defective part(s). Measure the I.D. of the piston boss and connecting rod small end, and the O.D. of the piston pin. If within specifications, assemble piston pin and rod. CAUTION: *If piston pin must be pressed in, determine the proper method and use the proper tools; otherwise the piston will distort.* Install the lock rings; ensure that they seat properly. If the parts are not within specifications, determine the service method for the type of engine. In some cases, piston and pin are serviced as an assembly when either is defective. Others specify reaming the piston and connecting rods for an oversize pin. If the connecting rod bushing is worn, it may in many cases be replaced. Reaming the piston and replacing the rod bushing are machine shop operations.

Procedure	Method

Clean and inspect the camshaft:

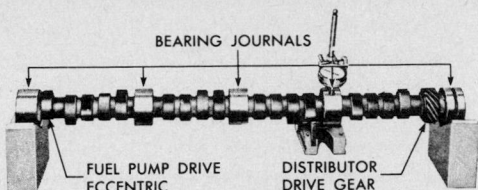

BEARING JOURNALS

FUEL PUMP DRIVE ECCENTRIC · DISTRIBUTOR DRIVE GEAR

Checking the camshaft for straightness
(© Chevrolet Motor Div. G.M. Corp.)

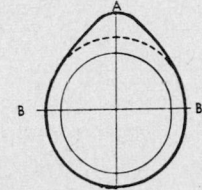

Camshaft lobe measurement
(© Ford Motor Co.)

Degrease the camshaft, using solvent, and clean out all oil holes. Visually inspect cam lobes and bearing journals for excessive wear. If a lobe is questionable, check all lobes as indicated below. If a journal or lobe is worn, the camshaft must be reground or replaced. NOTE: *If a journal is worn, there is a good chance that the bushings are worn.* If lobes and journals appear intact, place the front and rear journals in V-blocks, and rest a dial indicator on the center journal. Rotate the camshaft to check straightness. If deviation exceeds .001″, replace the camshaft.

* Check the camshaft lobes with a micrometer, by measuring the lobes from the nose to base and again at 90° (see illustration). The lift is determined by subtracting the second measurement from the first. If all exhaust lobes and all intake lobes are not identical, the camshaft must be reground or replaced.

Replace the camshaft bearings:

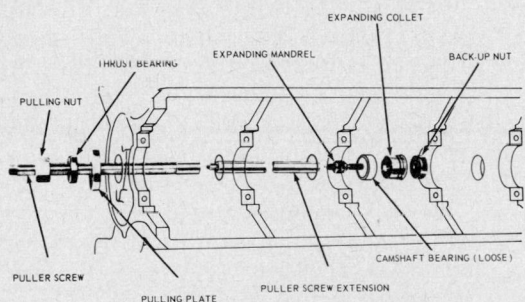

Camshaft removal and installation tool (typical)
(© Ford Motor Co.)

If excessive wear is indicated, or if the engine is being completely rebuilt, camshaft bearings should be replaced as follows: Drive the camshaft rear plug from the block. Assemble the removal puller with its shoulder on the bearing to be removed. Gradually tighten the puller nut until bearing is removed. Remove remaining bearings, leaving the front and rear for last. To remove front and rear bearings, reverse position of the tool, so as to pull the bearings in toward the center of the block. Leave the tool in this position, pilot the new front and rear bearings on the installer, and pull them into position. Return the tool to its original position and pull remaining bearings into position. NOTE: *Ensure that oil holes align when installing bearings.* Replace camshaft rear plug, and stake it into position to aid retention.

Finish hone the cylinders:

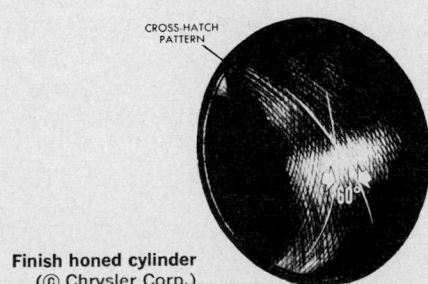

CROSS-HATCH PATTERN

Finish honed cylinder
(© Chrysler Corp.)

Chuck a flexible drive hone into a power drill, and insert it into the cylinder. Start the hone, and move it up and down in the cylinder at a rate which will produce approximately a 60° cross-hatch pattern (see illustration). NOTE: *Do not extend the hone below the cylinder bore.* After developing the pattern, remove the hone and recheck piston fit. Wash the cylinders with a detergent and water solution to remove abrasive dust, dry, and wipe several times with a rag soaked in engine oil.

Procedure	*Method*
Check piston ring end-gap:	Compress the piston rings to be used in a cylinder, one at a time, into that cylinder, and press them approximately 1″ below the deck with an inverted piston. Using feeler gauges, measure the ring end-gap, and compare to specifications. Pull the ring out of the cylinder and file the ends with a fine file to obtain proper clearance. CAUTION: *If inadequate ring end-gap is utilized, ring breakage will result.*

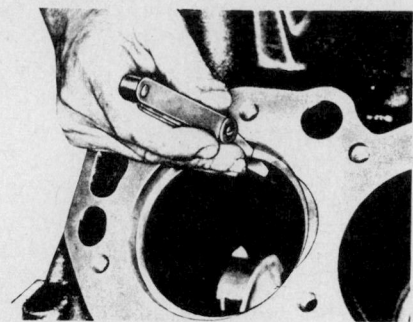

Checking ring end-gap
(© Chevrolet Motor Div. G.M. Corp.)

Install the piston rings:	Inspect the ring grooves in the piston for excessive wear or taper. If necessary, recut the groove(s) for use with an overwidth ring or a standard ring and spacer. If the groove is worn uniformly, overwidth rings, or standard rings and spacers may be installed without recutting. Roll the outside of the ring around the groove to check for burrs or deposits. If any are found, remove with a fine file. Hold the ring in the groove, and measure side clearance. If necessary, correct as indicated above. NOTE: *Always install any additional spacers above the piston ring.* The ring groove must be deep enough to allow the ring to seat below the lands (see illustration). In many cases, a "go-no-go" depth gauge will be provided with the piston rings. Shallow grooves may be corrected by recutting, while deep grooves require some type of filler or expander behind the piston. Consult the piston ring supplier concerning the suggested method. Install the rings on the piston, lowest ring first, using a ring expander. NOTE: *Position the ring markings as specified by the manufacturer (see car section).*

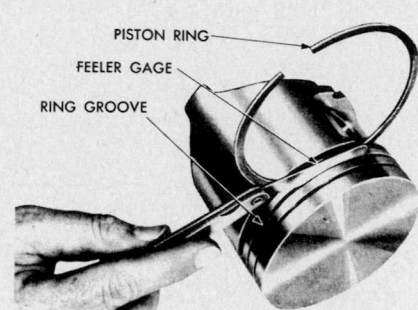

PISTON RING
FEELER GAGE
RING GROOVE

Checking ring side clearance
(© Chrysler Corp.)

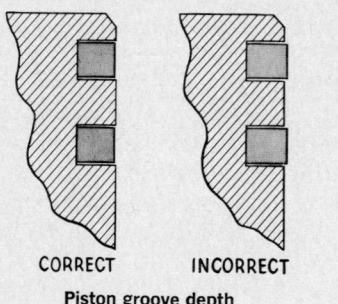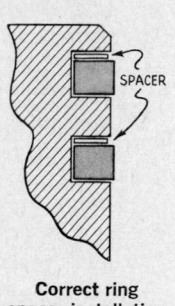

SPACER

CORRECT   INCORRECT   Correct ring
Piston groove depth   **spacer installation**

Install the camshaft:	Liberally lubricate the camshaft lobes and journals, and slide the camshaft into the block. CAUTION: *Exercise extreme care to avoid damaging the bearings when inserting the camshaft.* Install and tighten the camshaft thrust plate retaining bolts.

Check camshaft end-play:	Using feeler gauges, determine whether the clearance between the camshaft boss (or gear) and backing plate is within specifications. Install shims behind the thrust plate, or reposition the camshaft gear (see car section), and retest end-play.

Checking camshaft end-play with a feeler gauge
(© Ford Motor Co.)

Procedure	Method

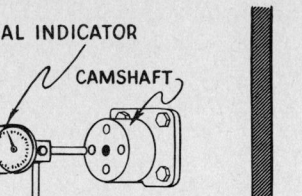

DIAL INDICATOR
CAMSHAFT

Checking camshaft end-play with a dial indicator

* Mount a dial indicator stand so that the stem of the dial indicator rests on the nose of the camshaft, parallel to the camshaft axis. Push the camshaft as far in as possible and zero the gauge. Move the camshaft outward to determine the amount of camshaft end-play. If the end-play is not within tolerance, install shims behind the thrust plate, or reposition the camshaft gear (see car section), and retest.

Install the rear main seal (where applicable):

Seating the rear main seal
(© Buick Div. G.M. Corp.)

Position the block with the bearing saddles facing upward. Lay the rear main seal in its groove and press it lightly into its seat. Place a piece of pipe the same diameter as the crankshaft journal into the saddle, and firmly seat the seal. Hold the pipe in position, and trim the ends of the seal flush if required.

Install the crankshaft:

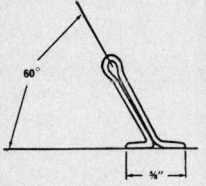

60°   ⅝"

Home made bearing roll-out pin
(© Pontiac Div. G.M. Corp.)

INSTALLING BEARING SHELL
REMOVING BEARING SHELL
60-141

Removal and installation of upper bearing insert using a roll-out pin
(© Buick Div. G.M. Corp.)

Thoroughly clean the main bearing saddles and caps. Place the upper halves of the bearing inserts on the saddles and press into position. NOTE: *Ensure that the oil holes align.* Press the corresponding bearing inserts into the main bearing caps. Lubricate the upper main bearings, and lay the crankshaft in position. Place a strip of Plastigage on each of the crankshaft journals, install the main caps, and torque to specifications. Remove the main caps, and compare the Plastigage to the scale on the Plastigage envelope. If clearances are within tolerances, remove the Plastigage, turn the crankshaft 90°, wipe off all oil and retest. If all clearances are correct, remove all Plastigage, thoroughly

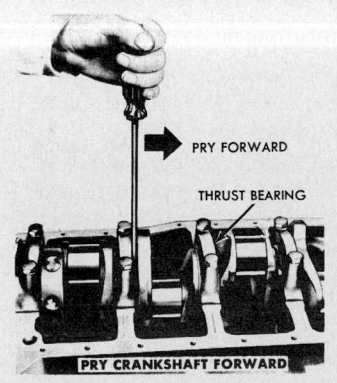

PRY FORWARD
THRUST BEARING
PRY CRANKSHAFT FORWARD

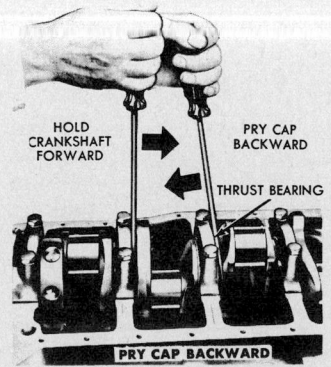

HOLD CRANKSHAFT FORWARD
PRY CAP BACKWARD
THRUST BEARING
PRY CAP BACKWARD

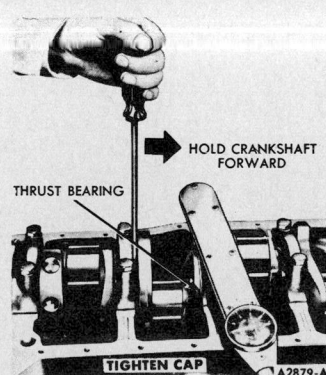

PRY CAP BACKWARD
HOLD CRANKSHAFT FORWARD
THRUST BEARING
TIGHTEN CAP   A2879-A

Aligning the thrust bearing
(© Ford Motor Co.)

Procedure	Method
	lubricate the main caps and bearing journals, and install the main caps. If clearances are not within tolerance, the upper bearing inserts may be removed, without removing the crankshaft, using a bearing roll out pin (see illustration). Roll in a bearing that will provide proper clearance, and retest. Torque all main caps, excluding the thrust bearing cap, to specifications. Tighten the thrust bearing cap finger tight. To properly align the thrust bearing, pry the crankshaft the extent of its axial travel several times, the last movement held toward the front of the engine, and torque the thrust bearing cap to specifications. Determine the crankshaft end-play (see below), and bring within tolerance with thrust washers.

Procedure	Method
Measure crankshaft end-play:  **Checking crankshaft end-play with a dial indicator** (© Ford Motor Co.) A 2908-A 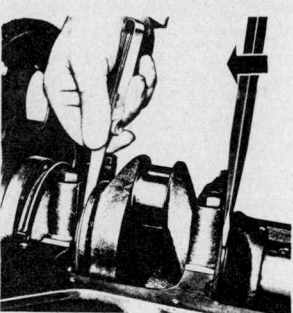 **Checking crankshaft end-play with a feeler gauge** (© Chevrolet Div. (G.M. Corp.)	Mount a dial indicator stand on the front of the block, with the dial indicator stem resting on the nose of the crankshaft, parallel to the crankshaft axis. Pry the crankshaft the extent of its travel rearward, and zero the indicator. Pry the crankshaft forward and record crankshaft end-play. NOTE: *Crankshaft end-play also may be measured at the thrust bearing, using feeler gauges* (see illustration).

Procedure	Method
Install the pistons:	Press the upper connecting rod bearing halves into the connecting rods, and the lower halves into the connecting rod caps. Position the piston ring gaps according to specifications (see car section), and lubricate the pistons. Install a ring compresser on a piston, and press two long (8″) pieces of plastic tubing over the rod bolts. Using the plastic tubes as a guide, press the pistons into the bores and onto the crankshaft with a wooden hammer handle. After seating the rod on the crankshaft journal, remove the tubes and install the cap finger tight. Install the remaining pistons in the same man-

Procedure	Method

**Tubing used as guide when installing
a piston**
(© Oldsmobile Div. G.M. Corp.)

ner. Invert the engine and check the bearing clearance at two points (90° apart) on each journal with Plastigage. NOTE: *Do not turn the crankshaft with Plastigage installed.* If clearance is within tolerances, remove *all* Plastigage, thoroughly lubricate the journals, and torque the rod caps to specifications. If clearance is not within specifications, install different thickness bearing inserts and recheck. CAUTION: *Never shim or file the connecting rods or caps.* Always install plastic tube sleeves over the rod bolts when the caps are not installed, to protect the crankshaft journals.

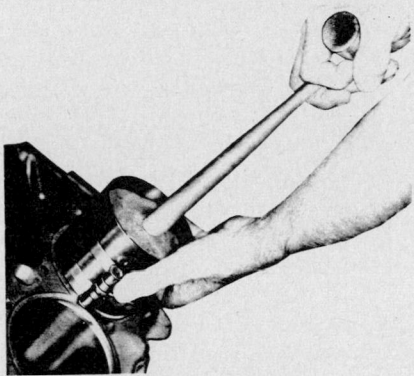

Installing a piston
(© Chevrolet Div. G.M. Corp.)

Check connecting rod side clearance:

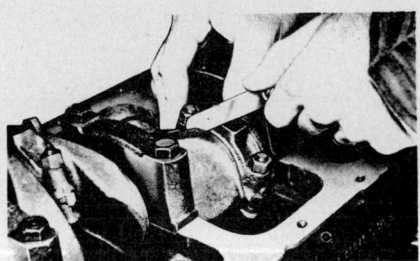

Checking connecting rod side clearance
(© Chevrolet Div. G.M. Corp.)

Determine the clearance between the sides of the connecting rods and the crankshaft, using feeler gauges. If clearance is below the minimum tolerance, the rod may be machined to provide adequate clearance. If clearance is excessive, substitute an unworn rod, and recheck. If clearance is still outside specifications, the crankshaft must be welded and reground, or replaced.

Inspect the timing chain:

Visually inspect the timing chain for broken or loose links, and replace the chain if any are found. If the chain will flex sideways, it must be replaced. Install the timing chain as specified in the car section. NOTE: *If the original timing chain is to be reused, install it in its original position.*

Procedure	*Method*
Check timing gear backlash and runout:  **Checking camshaft gear backlash** (© Chevrolet Div. G.M. Corp.)  **Checking camshaft gear runout** (© Chevrolet Div. G.M. Corp.)	Mount a dial indicator with its stem resting on a tooth of the camshaft gear (as illustrated). Rotate the gear until all slack is removed, and zero the indicator. Rotate the gear in the opposite direction until slack is removed, and record gear backlash. Mount the indicator with its stem resting on the edge of the camshaft gear, parallel to the axis of the camshaft. Zero the indicator, and turn the camshaft gear one full turn, recording the runout. If either backlash or runout exceed specifications, replace the worn gear(s).

Completing the Rebuilding Process

Following the above procedures, complete the rebuilding process as follows:

Fill the oil pump with oil, to prevent cavitating (sucking air) on initial engine start up. Install the oil pump and the pickup tube on the engine. Coat the oil pan gasket as necessary, and install the gasket and the oil pan. Mount the flywheel and the crankshaft vibrational damper or pulley on the crankshaft. NOTE: *Always use new bolts when installing the flywheel.* Inspect the clutch shaft pilot bushing in the crankshaft. If the bushing is excessively worn, remove it with an expanding puller and a slide hammer, and tap a new bushing into place.

Position the engine, cylinder head side up. Lubricate the lifters, and install them into their bores. Install the cylinder head, and torque it as specified in the car section. Insert the pushrods (where applicable), and install the rocker shaft(s) (if so equipped) or position the rocker arms on the pushrods. If solid lifters are utilized, adjust the valves to the "cold" specifications. If hydraulic lifters are used, torque the adjusting nut to 20 ft. lbs.

Mount the intake and exhaust manifolds, the carburetor(s), the distributor and spark plugs. Adjust the point gap and the static ignition timing. Mount all accessories and install the engine in the car. Fill the radiator with coolant, and the crankcase with high quality engine oil.

Break-in Procedure

Start the engine, and allow it to run at low speed for a few minutes, while checking for leaks. Stop the engine, check the oil level, and fill as necessary. Restart the engine, and fill the cooling system to capacity. Check the point dwell angle and adjust the ignition timing and the valves. Run the engine at low to medium speed (800-2500 rpm) for approximately ½ hour, and re-torque the cylinder head bolts. Road test the car, and check again for leaks.

Follow the manufacturer's recommended engine break-in procedure and maintenance schedule for new engines.

Anti-Theft Systems

Preface

Due to the increasing rate of auto theft, automotive anti-theft systems have recently come into general use. Installation of these devices by automobile manufacturers began in 1968, with the installation of key warning buzzers. This buzzer sounds whenever the key is in the ignition switch with the driver's door open. In 1969, the first steering column-transmission locks were installed. Prior to removing the ignition key from the lock, the driver must place the transmission in reverse (manual) or Park (automatic). Upon removal of the key, the steering column and the transmission linkage lock. This device is standard equipment on all 1970 and later model cars.

Aftermarket installations of anti-theft systems, on earlier model cars, or in addition to the above mentioned original equipment systems are becoming increasingly widespread. This section describes the various types of anti-theft devices that are presently commercially available, or readily fabricated.

Two basic types of systems will be considered. Type A are devices which mechanically or electrically inhibit movement of the car. Type B are warning systems (burglar alarms), which deter theft or tampering. In many cases, a system which performs both functions may be devised by combining or modifying the above.

Type A

Mechanical Systems

The most common systems available inhibit the movement of the brake pedal and/or the steering wheel. Of these, the most prevalent (best known by its trade name—Krooklok®) is a locking, telescoping steel bar, with a hook at each end. In use, one hook is positioned around a steering wheel spoke, and the other around the brake pedal arm. The steel shaft is then telescoped down, and locked into position, preventing movement of the brake pedal and limiting steering wheel movement. A similar system utilizes a long steel bar, which hooks and locks onto the steering wheel, and prevents it from turning

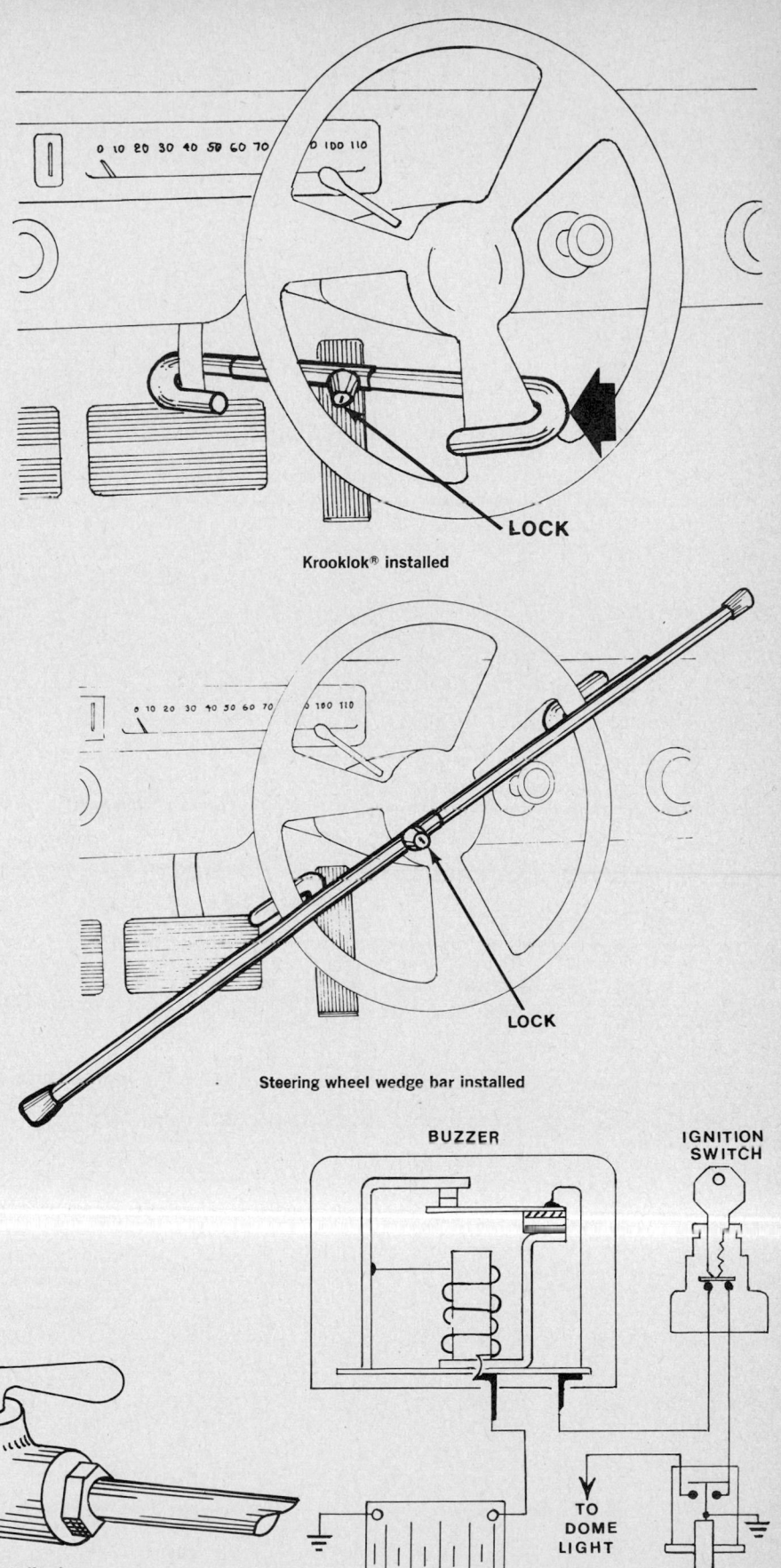

Krooklok® installed

Steering wheel wedge bar installed

Typical fuel shutoff valve

Typical key warning buzzer circuit

REMOVE

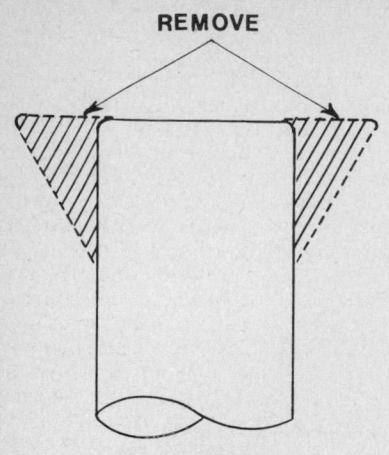

Altered door lock button

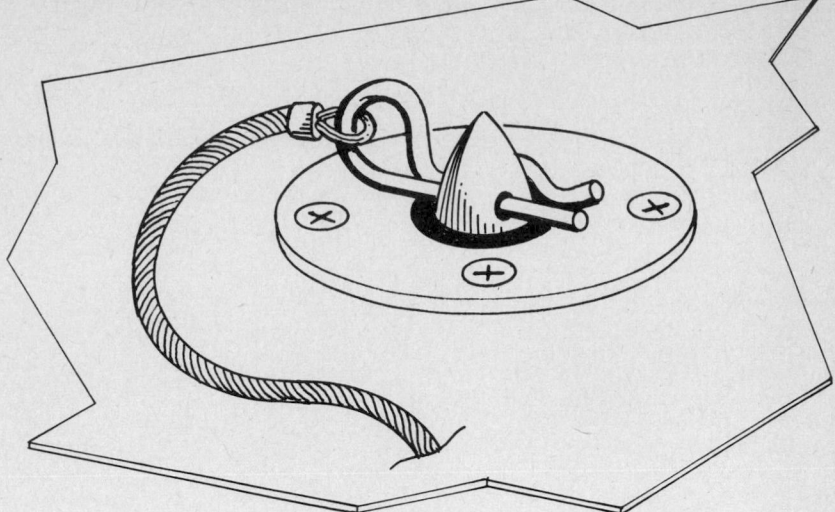

Standard hood pin

LOCK

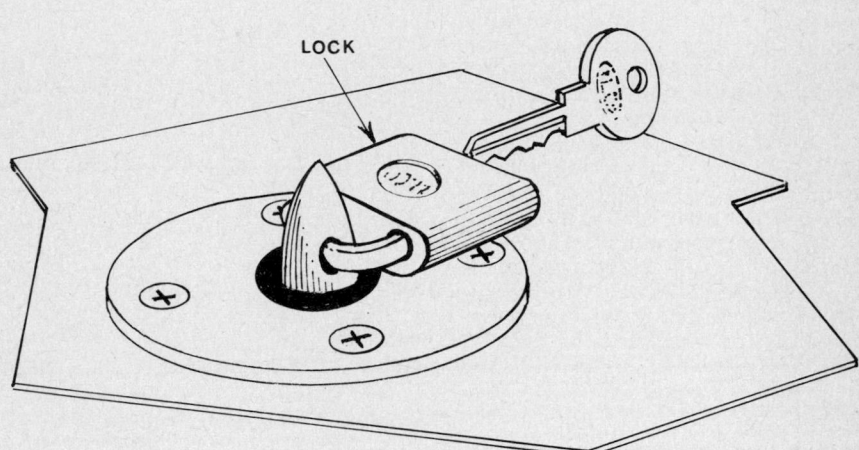

Locking hood pin

LOCK

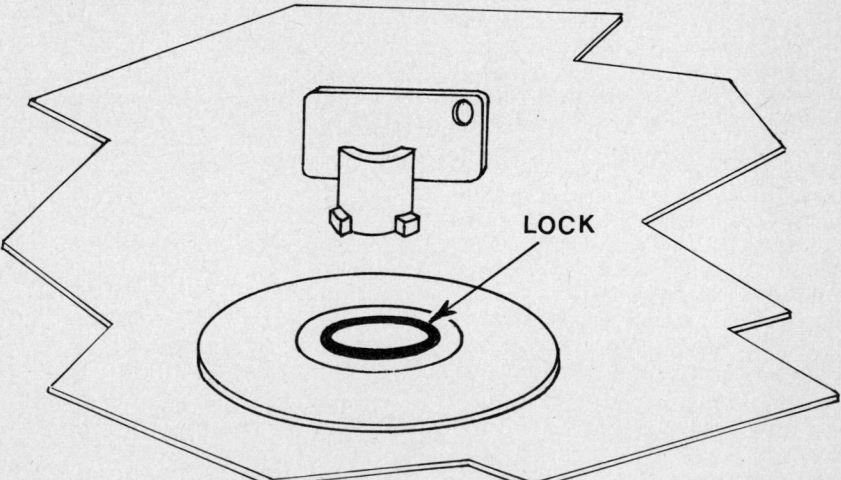

Flush-mount locking hood pin

beyond a certain point by wedging against interior components.

Both of the above devices have the added advantage of being visible from outside the car, to act as a visual deterrent. The disadvantage of these devices is that they are somewhat awkward, and must be removed and installed each time that the car is used.

Another method of limiting the movement of a vehicle is the installation of a fuel shut-off valve in the fuel line, in an inconspicuous place. However, this method is not recommended, as the engine will run until the fuel supply in the float bowl is exhausted, permitting the car to be moved.

Many types of lock mechanisms are available, or may be devised to improve vehicle security. The simplest are lock buttons which cannot be pulled up from outside the car. In many cases, these may be made from the original lock buttons, by removing the raised lip at the top of the button. In cases where the door locks are released by the inside door handles, the lock button may be positioned so that it is flush with the door when the door is locked. It is also advisable (where applicable) to position the door handles so that they cannot be moved from outside the car.

Hood lock mechanisms are available in two basic types—those which are visible when installed, and those that are not. Visible locks (e.g., locking hood pins, flush mount locks) not only deter opening the engine compartment, but act as a visual deterrent. Hidden mechanisms usually consist of a cable actuated release for the hood latch replacing the exterior latch release, or a secondary latch mechanism. Hood locks have the advantage of protecting the engine compartment from theft in addition to protecting the entire vehicle. Their disadvantage lies in the fact that the hood need not be open to start the engine in many cases; therefore, it is advisable to use hood locks in combination with other anti-theft devices.

Electrical Systems

The most effective, and simplest electrical anti-theft device is an ignition ground switch, which will prevent the engine from being started. A single pole single throw switch is wired between the distributor primary lead and ground, and mounted inconspicuously in the interior (e.g., in the glove box, under the dash-

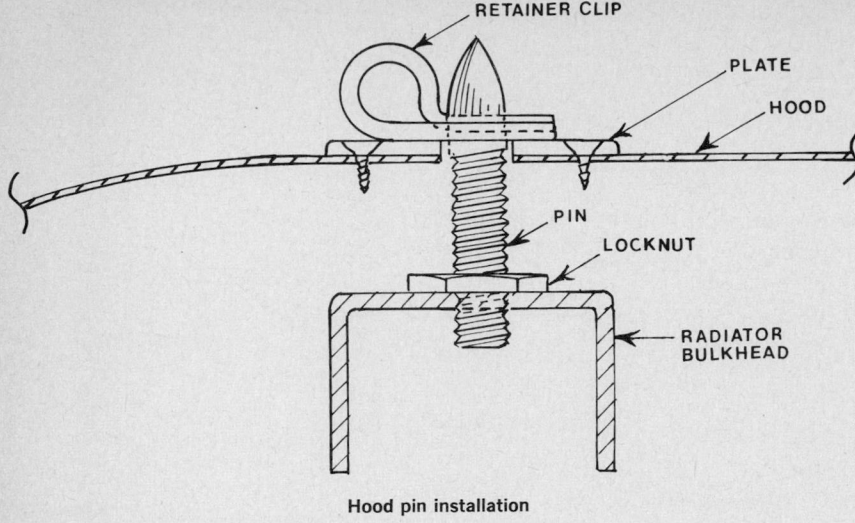

Hood pin installation

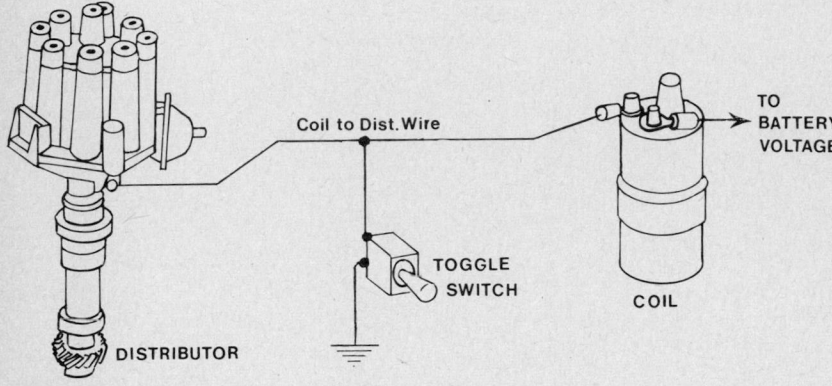

Ignition ground switch

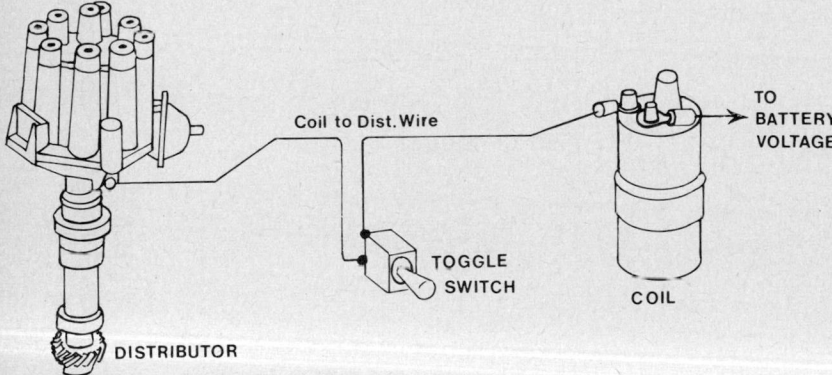

Ignition circuit breaker switch

board, etc.). When the switch is open, the ignition will function normally. When the switch is closed, the ignition is grounded, and the engine will not run.

An alternate method includes a switch in the distributor primary wire (see illustration). In this case, the system will function only when the switch is closed.

Solenoid actuated hood latches or fuel shut off valves, controlled by interior mounted switches are effective and easy to conceal; however, each has the disadvantages of the mechanical version of the same device.

Type B

Warning systems can be broken down into three basic components: the trigger, trigger control, and alarm. Each will be considered separately.

Trigger Mechanisms

The trigger mechanism is the device used to actuate the alarm. In most cases, the trigger consists of a switch, or switches, and a drop relay. A drop relay is a relay that once activated will not recycle until reset manually; therefore, the alarm will not stop functioning even if the trigger switch is deactivated.

Motion sensitive switches (e.g., mercury switches, pendulum switches, reed vibrator switches) are excellent means of detecting tampering. The switch may be mounted anywhere in the car, and its sensitivity may be adjusted to the desired level. The disadvantage of a motion sensitive switch is the accuracy with which it must be adjusted. The switch must respond to the opening of a door, the hood or trunk, but not to parking on an incline, being bumped by a pedestrian, or traffic passing by. Once the proper sensitivity is determined, it is a good idea to include a timer in the trigger circuit, to shut the alarm off after a certain period of time if it is accidentally triggered when the car is disturbed.

Pushbutton switches (i.e., interior lighting door jamb switches), mounted on all doors and the hood and trunk, may also be used to trigger an alarm. These spring loaded, normally closed switches may be positioned adjacent to the existing switches on the door jambs, and on the hood and trunk latch plates. A combination system of motion sensitive and pushbutton switches will provide excellent protection. Mercury switches used to activate hood and trunk lights may be used as triggers, in lieu of pushbutton switches, on the hood and trunk.

Trigger Control Switches

The trigger control switch acts as an ON-OFF switch for the alarm system. It must be arranged in such a manner that the owner may enter the vehicle without triggering the alarm, but that a thief will be unable to detect or disarm.

The simplest control switch is a toggle switch mounted outside the car in an inconspicuous place. (e.g., under the rocker panel, inside a fender well). For this usage, the switch and the wiring must be weatherproofed.

The most popular type of control switch is the locking type which may be mounted anywhere on the outside of the car. These switches use cylindrical "pickproof" locks, and provide excellent protection, in addition to acting as a visual deterrent.

Alarms

An alarm may be devised as an integral part of the existing vehicle electrical system, using the horn. In order to connect this system, proceed as follows: Locate the terminal on the horn relay, that when bridged to ground, will sound the horn. Connect one lead from the ON-OFF switch to this terminal. Connect the other lead from the ON-OFF switch to a terminal of pulsating (flasher type) switch, and connect the open terminal of the pulsating switch to the trigger mechanisms. Firmly ground the trigger mechanisms.

Non-integral, self contained alarm systems may be wired to the accessory position in the fuse box. Sirens or other devices (i.e., bells, buzzers) must be loud enough to attract attention at a reasonable distance, and should be positioned in the car to take maximum advantage of their capabilities (e.g., behind the front grill). A drop relay and/or a timer (e.g., Dodge No. 2889565) should be included in the circuit. The drop relay will keep the alarm activated, even after the trigger(s) is deactivated, until all current is removed from the alarm circuit. The timer is used to deactivate the alarm a certain period of time after the trigger is deactivated, to prevent the alarm running down the battery or disturbing the peace after accidental triggering.

In addition to, or in lieu of the above, it is suggested that a "Protected by Alarm" sticker be mounted on the window. This will act as an excellent visual deterrent to theft, and costs little or nothing. These stickers may be obtained from many burglar alarm manufacturers.

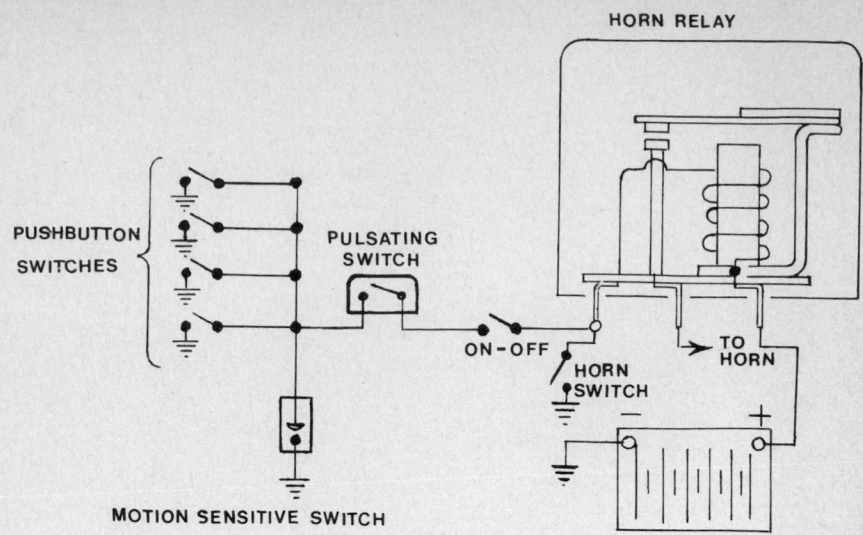

Integral alarm circuit schematic

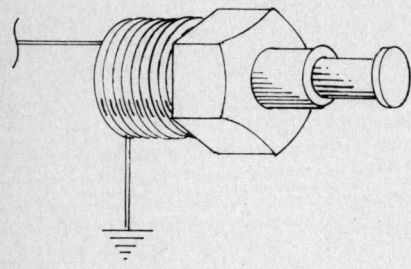

Pushbutton switch

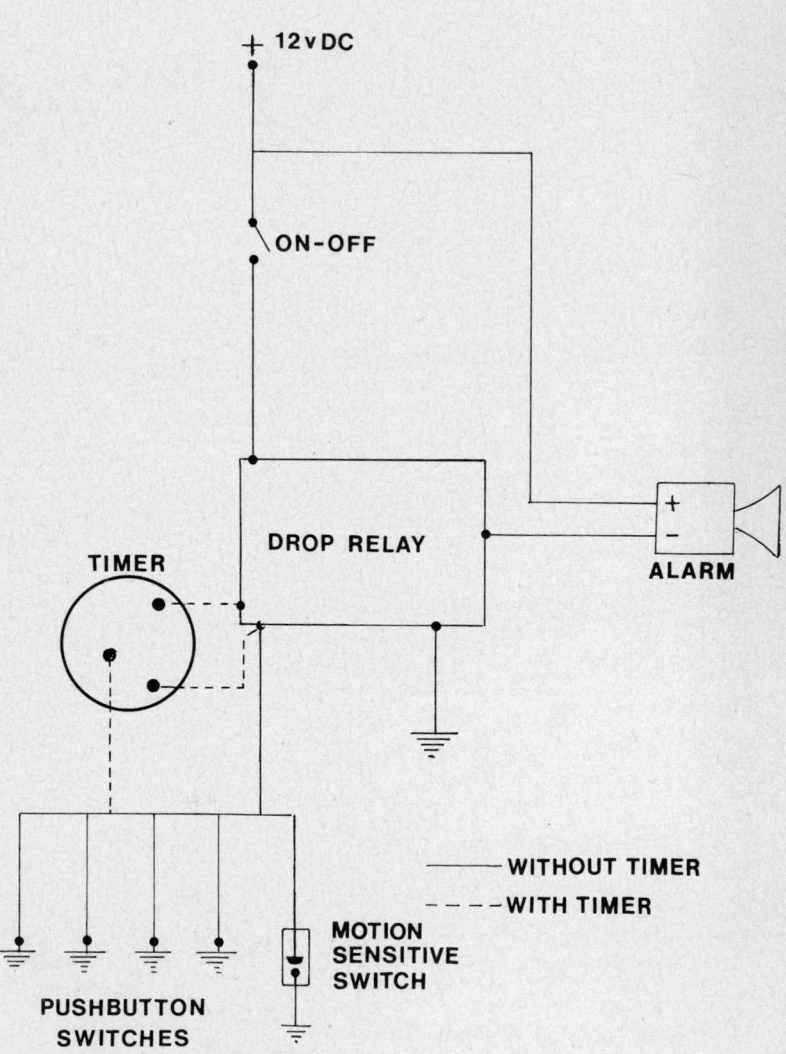

Self contained alarm system schematic

PUSHING OR TOWING CARS WITH AUTOMATIC TRANSMISSIONS

There are two reasons to push or tow a disabled car. One is to supplement the regular electrical starting system of engine cranking. The other reason is to get the crippled car to some other location. In either case care must be used to avoid damage to the transmissions of vehicles equipped with automatic units.

If it becomes necessary to push or tow a vehicle so equipped, the following chart should be used for reference.

For positive transmission-to-car identification, refer to Automatic Transmission Identification chart.

Transmission	Pushing	Towing	
		Maximum Speed	Maximum Distance (Miles)
Flash-o-Matic 1965	Shift into "D1" at 30 mph	15	15
Flash-o-Matic, Shift Command 1966–71	Will not start by pushing	35	50
Torque-Command	Will not start by pushing	30	①
Torqueflite 1965	Shift into "L" at 15 mph	30	①
1966–72	Will not start by pushing	30	①
Ford FMX/MX	Will not start by pushing	30	15
Ford C4	Will not start by pushing	30	15
Ford C6	Will not start by pushing	30	15
Ford C4S	Will not start by pushing	30	15
Powerglide	Will not start by pushing	35	50
Torque Drive	Will not start by pushing	35	50
Dual Coupling 4-speed	Will not start by pushing	35	50
Roto Hydramatic	Will not start by pushing	35	50
G.M. Type 300	Will not start by pushing	35	50
G.M. Type 350	Will not start by pushing	35	50
G.M. Type 400	Will not start by pushing	35	50

① —Do not tow extended distances without disconnecting driveshaft or raising rear wheels.

MECHANICS' DATA

Tap Drill Sizes

Screw & Tap Size	National Coarse or U.S.S. Threads Per Inch	Use Drill Number
No. 5	40	39
No. 6	32	36
No. 8	32	29
No. 10	24	25
No. 12	24	17
1/4	20	8
5/16	18	F
3/8	16	5/16
7/16	14	U
1/2	13	27/64
9/16	12	31/64
5/8	11	17/32
3/4	10	21/32
7/8	9	49/64
1	8	7/8
1 1/8	7	63/64
1 1/4	7	1 7/64
1 1/2	6	1 11/32

Screw & Tap Size	National Fine or S.A.E. Threads Per Inch	Use Drill Number
No. 5	44	37
No. 6	40	33
No. 8	36	29
No. 10	32	21
No. 12	28	15
1/4	28	3
5/16	24	1
3/8	24	Q
7/16	20	W
1/2	20	29/64
9/16	18	33/64
5/8	18	37/64
3/4	16	11/16
7/8	14	13/16
1 1/8	12	1 3/64
1 1/4	12	1 11/64
1 1/2	12	1 27/64

Decimal Equivalent Size of the Number Drills

Drill No.	Decimal Equivalent	Drill No.	Decimal Equivalent	Drill No.	Decimal Equivalent
80	.0135	53	.0595	26	.1470
79	.0145	52	.0635	25	.1495
78	.0160	51	.0670	24	.1520
77	.0180	50	.0700	23	.1540
76	.0200	49	.0730	22	.1570
75	.0210	48	.0760	21	.1590
74	.0225	47	.0785	20	.1610
73	.0240	46	.0810	19	.1660
72	.0250	45	.0820	18	.1695
71	.0260	44	.0860	17	.1730
70	.0280	43	.0890	16	.1770
69	.0292	42	.0935	15	.1800
68	.0310	41	.0960	14	.1820
67	.0320	40	.0980	13	.1850
66	.0330	39	.0995	12	.1890
65	.0350	38	.1015	11	.1910
64	.0360	37	.1040	10	.1935
63	.0370	36	.1065	9	.1960
62	.0380	35	.1100	8	.1990
61	.0390	34	.1110	7	.2010
60	.0400	33	.1130	6	.2040
59	.0410	32	.1160	5	.2055
58	.0420	31	.1200	4	.2090
57	.0430	30	.1285	3	.2130
56	.0465	29	.1360	2	.2210
55	.0520	28	.1405	1	.2280
54	.0550	27	.1440		

Decimal Equivalent Size of the Letter Drills

Letter Drill	Decimal Equivalent	Letter Drill	Decimal Equivalent	Letter Drill	Decimal Equivalent
A	.234	J	.277	S	.348
B	.238	K	.281	T	.358
C	.242	L	.290	U	.368
D	.246	M	.295	V	.377
E	.250	N	.302	W	.386
F	.257	O	.316	X	.397
G	.261	P	.323	Y	.404
H	.266	Q	.332	Z	.413
I	.272	R	.339		

Decimal Equivalents of the Common Fractions

1/64 = .0156	21/64 = .3281	43/64 = .6719
1/32 = .0313	11/32 = .3438	11/16 = .6875
3/64 = .0469	23/64 = .3594	45/64 = .7031
1/16 = .0625	3/8 = .3750	23/32 = .7188
5/64 = .0781	25/64 = .3906	47/64 = .7344
3/32 = .0938	13/32 = .4063	3/4 = .7500
7/64 = .1094	27/64 = .4219	49/64 = .7656
1/8 = .1250	7/16 = .4375	25/32 = .7813
9/64 = .1406	29/64 = .4531	51/64 = .7969
5/32 = .1563	15/32 = .4688	13/16 = .8125
11/64 = .1719	31/64 = .4844	53/64 = .8281
3/16 = .1875	1/2 = .5000	27/32 = .8438
13/64 = .2031	33/64 = .5156	55/64 = .8594
7/32 = .2188	17/32 = .5313	7/8 = .8750
15/64 = .2344	35/64 = .5469	57/64 = .8906
1/4 = .2500	9/16 = .5625	29/32 = .9063
17/64 = .2656	37/64 = .5781	59/64 = .9219
9/32 = .2813	19/32 = .5938	15/16 = .9375
19/64 = .2969	39/64 = .6094	61/64 = .9531
5/16 = .3125	5/8 = .6250	31/32 = .9688
	41/64 = .6406	63/64 = .9844
	21/32 = .6563	